Standards of Admission

The major criterion for determining who will be included in *Who's Who of American Women* is the extent of a woman's reference value. Such reference interest is judged on either of two factors: 1) the position of responsibility held, or 2) the level of achievement attained by the individual.

Admission based on the factor of position includes the following examples:

High-level federal officials

Specified elected and appointed state officials

Mayors of major cities

Principal officers of selected businesses

Outstanding educators from major universities and colleges

Principal figures of cultural and artistic institutions

Heads of major women's organizations

Recipients of major awards and honors

Members of selected honorary organizations

Other women chosen because of incumbency or membership

Admission for individual achievement is based on objective qualitative criteria. To be selected, a woman must have attained conspicuous achievement. The biographee may scarcely be known in the local community but may be recognized in some field of endeavor for noteworthy accomplishment.

Board of Advisors

Marquis Who's Who gratefully acknowledges the following distinguished individuals who have made themselves available for review, evaluation, and general comment with regard to the publication of the seventeenth edition of *Who's Who of American Women*. The advisors have enhanced the reference value of this edition by the nomination of outstanding individuals for inclusion. However, the Board of Advisors, either collectively or individually, is in no way responsible for the final selection of names appearing in this volume, nor does the Board of Advisors bear responsibility for the accuracy or comprehensiveness of the biographical information or other material contained herein.

Preface

In 1958, Marquis Who's Who published the first edition of Who's Who of American Women. Since that time there has been an increasing interest in and need for the biographical data of successful American women.

Many of the biographees in that premier edition were volunteer workers involved in civic, religious, and club activities. This, the seventeenth edition, features biographees in a wide range of endeavors and varying levels of responsibility.

The Marquis researchers have drawn on a wide range of contemporary sources: newspapers, periodicals, professional associations, and other information inherent in the preparation of the more than 30,000 sketches found in this edition. The result has been coverage of personal and professional biographical facts concerning women in virtually every important field of endeavor.

Listed in this volume are outstanding women involved in the performing arts, all areas of government, with increasing prominence in the political arena, and many sectors of business, with an ever-growing number of women entrepreneurs establishing and running businesses of their own.

In most cases, biographees have furnished their own data, thus assuring a high degree of accuracy. Where individuals of great reference interest failed to supply information, data was compiled by Marquis staff members through careful, independent research. These sketches are denoted by an asterisk. As in previous editions, biographees were given the opportunity to review prepublication proofs of their sketches to ensure accuracy.

Selection of a name for inclusion in *Who's Who of American Women* is based on one fundamental principle: reference value. Some women are eligible for listing because of position, while others have distinguished themselves by noteworthy achievements in their fields. Many listees qualify by virtue of both position and accomplishment.

As part of the editorial evaluation process that resulted in the ultimate selection of names for this directory, wealth, social position and a person's desire to be listed were not considered sufficient reasons for inclusion—rather, it was the person's achievements that governed her selection.

Marquis Who's Who editors and researchers have exercised diligent care in the preparation of each biographical sketch. However, despite all precautions, errors do occur. Users of this directory are invited to draw to the attention of the publisher any errors found so that corrections may be made in a subsequent edition.

The seventeenth edition of *Who's Who of American Women* continues the tradition of excellence established in 1899 with the publication of the first edition of *Who's Who in America*. The essence of that tradition is the continuing effort at Marquis Who's Who to produce reference works that are responsive to the needs of their users.

Table of Contents

Sandra S. Barnes—President
Sallie A. Lambert—Senior Product Manager
William H. Hamblin—Director of Production
Jill F. Lazar—Product Manager
Gloria A. Becker—Technical Development Manager
Julia C. DeGraf—Operations Manager
Frederick M. Marks—Manager, Biographical Research
Mary T. Swistara—Editorial Supervisor
Jean S. Donnelly—Researcher/Librarian

James J. Pfister—Information Services Group Vice President, Macmillan, Inc.
Dean A. Davis—Vice President Operations, Information Services Group
Paul E. Rose—President, National Register Publishing Co.

WHO'S WHO OF AMERICAN WOMEN is a registered trademark of
Macmillan Information Company, Inc.

Library of Congress Catalog Card Number 58-13264
International Standard Book Number 0–8379–0417-X
Product Code Number 030587

Distributed in Asia by
United Publishers Services Ltd.
Kenkyu-Sha Bldg.
9, Kanda Surugadai 2-Chome
Chiyoda-Ku, Tokyo, Japan

Who's Who
of American Women ®

17th edition
1991-1992

MARQUIS
Who's Who

Macmillan Directory Division
3002 Glenview Road
Wilmette, Illinois 60091 U.S.A.

Key to Information

[1] **CHAMBERS, ELIZABETH BATES,** [2] lawyer; [3] b. Mitchell, S.D., July 19, 1940; [4] d. Oscar William and Judith (Strait) Bates; [5] m. Richard T. Chambers, Dec. 11, 1967; [6] children: Christopher Dwight, Mary Beth. [7] BA, U. Okla., 1962, MA, 1967; JD, Rice U., 1970. [8] Bar: Tex. 1970, S.D. 1973, U.S. Dist. Ct. S.D. 1982, U.S. Supreme Ct. 1982. [9] Assoc. Newman, Calvin & Swain, Houston, 1967-73, ptnr., 1973-74; ptnr. Hadley, Ellis, Chambers & Gonzalez, Amarillo, Tex., 1974-78; sole practice, Rapid City, S.D., 1978-82; ptnr. Chambers & Costner, Rapid City, 1982-85, sr. ptnr., 1985—; [10] lectr. Black Hills State Coll., Spearfish, S.D., 1987; mem. Gov.'s Task Force on Constl. Revision, Pierre, S.D., 1988—; bd. dirs. Custer Nat. Bank. [11] Contbr. articles to profl. jours. [12] Trustee The Grove Sch., Rapid City, 1982—; active Pennington County United Way. [13] Served with WAC, 1962-63. [14] Named Outstanding Woman of Yr., Amarillo C. of C., 1975; Lincoln Found. grantee, 1980. [15] Mem. ABA, S.D. Bar Assn., S.D. Assn. Def. Counsel, Pennington County Bar Assn., World Wildlife Fedn., Rushmore Hills Country Club, Noontime (Rapid City) Club, Order Eastern Star. [16] Democrat. [17] Lutheran. [18] Home: 5237 Woodbine Way Rapid City SD 57702 [19] Office: Chambers & Costner 964 N Omaha St Rapid City SD 57701

KEY

[1] Name
[2] Occupation
[3] Vital statistics
[4] Parents
[5] Marriage
[6] Children
[7] Education
[8] Professional certifications
[9] Career
[10] Career Related
[11] Writings and creative works
[12] Civic and political activities
[13] Military
[14] Awards and fellowships
[15] Professional and association memberships, Clubs and Lodges
[16] Political affiliation
[17] Religion
[18] Home Address
[19] Office Address

Table of Abbreviations

The following abbreviations and symbols are frequently used in this book

*An asterisk following a sketch indicates that it was researched by the Marquis Who's Who editorial staff and has not been verified by the biographee.

AA, A.A. Associate in Arts, Associate of Arts
AAAL American Academy of Arts and Letters
AAAS American Association for the Advancement of Science
AACD American Association for Counseling and Development
AACN American Association of Critical Care Nurses
AAHA American Academy of Health Administrators
AAHP American Association of Hospital Planners
AAHPER Alliance for Health, Physical Education and Recreation
AASL American Association of School Librarians
AASPA American Association of School Personnel Administrators
AAU Amateur Athletic Union
AAUP American Association of University Professors
AAUW American Association of University Women
AB, A.B. Arts, Bachelor of
AB Alberta
ABA American Bar Association
ABC American Broadcasting Company
AC Air Corps
acad. academy, academic
acct. accountant
acctg. accounting
ACDA Arms Control and Disarmament Agency
ACHA American College of Hospital Administrators
ACLS Advanced Cardiac Life Support
ACLU American Civil Liberties Union
ACP American College of Physicians
ACS American College of Surgeons
ADA American Dental Association
a.d.c. aide-de-camp
adj. adjunct, adjutant
adj. gen. adjutant general
adm. admiral
adminstr. administrator
adminstrn. administration
adminstrv. administrative
ADN Associate's Degree in Nursing
ADP Automatic Data Processing
adv. advocate, advisory
advt. advertising
AE, A.E. Agricultural Engineer
A.E. and P. Ambassador Extraordinary and Plenipotentiary
AEC Atomic Energy Commission

aero. aeronautical, aeronautic
aerodyn. aerodynamic
AFB Air Force Base
AFL-CIO American Federation of Labor and Congress of Industrial Organizations
AFTRA American Federation of TV and Radio Artists
AFSCME American Federation of State, County and Municipal Employees
agr. agriculture
agrl. agricultural
agt. agent
AGVA American Guild of Variety Artists
agy. agency
A&I Agricultural and Industrial
AIA American Institute of Architects
AIAA American Institute of Aeronautics and Astronautics
AICPA American Institute of Certified Public Accountants
AID Agency for International Development
AIDS Acquired Immune Deficiency Syndrome
AIEE American Institute of Electrical Engineers
AIM American Institute of Management
AIME American Institute of Mining, Metallurgy, and Petroleum Engineers
AK Alaska
AL Alabama
ALA American Library Association
Ala. Alabama
alt. alternate
Alta. Alberta
A&M Agricultural and Mechanical
AM, A.M. Arts, Master of
Am. American, America
AMA American Medical Association
amb. ambassador
A.M.E. African Methodist Episcopal
Amtrak National Railroad Passenger Corporation
AMVETS American Veterans of World War II, Korea, Vietnam
ANA American Nurses Association
anat. anatomical
ann. annual
ANTA American National Theatre and Academy
anthrop. anthropological
AP Associated Press
APA American Psychological Association
APGA American Personnel Guidance Association
APHA American Public Health Association
APO Army Post Office
apptd. appointed
Apr. April
apt. apartment

AR Arkansas
ARC American Red Cross
archeol. archeological
archtl. architectural
Ariz. Arizona
Ark. Arkansas
ArtsD, ArtsD. Arts, Doctor of
arty. artillery
AS American Samoa
AS Associate in Science, Associate of Applied Science
ASCAP American Society of Composers, Authors and Publishers
ASCD Association for Supervision and Curriculum Development
ASCE American Society of Civil Engineers
ASHRAE American Society of Heating, Refrigeration, and Air Conditioning Engineers
ASME American Society of Mechanical Engineers
ASNSA American Society for Nursing Service Administrators
ASPA American Society for Public Administration
ASPCA American Society for the Prevention of Cruelty to Animals
assn. association
assoc. associate
asst. assistant
ASTD American Society for Training and Development
ASTM American Society for Testing and Materials
astron. astronomical
astrophys. astrophysical
ATSC Air Technical Service Command
AT&T American Telephone & Telegraph Company
atty. attorney
Aug. August
AUS Army of the United States
aux. auxiliary
Ave. Avenue
AVMA American Veterinary Medical Association
AZ Arizona

B. Bachelor
b. born
BA, B.A. Bachelor of Arts
BAgr, B.Agr. Bachelor of Agriculture
Balt. Baltimore
Bapt. Baptist
BArch, B.Arch. Bachelor of Architecture
BAS, B.A.S. Bachelor of Agricultural Science
BBA, B.B.A. Bachelor of Business Administration

BBC British Broadcasting Corporation
BC, B.C. British Columbia
BCE, B.C.E. Bachelor of Civil Engineering
BChir, B.Chir. Bachelor of Surgery
BCL, B.C.L. Bachelor of Civil Law
BCLS Basic Cardiac Life Support
BCS, B.C.S. Bachelor of Commercial
   Science
BD, B.D. Bachelor of Divinity
bd. board
BE, B.E. Bachelor of Education
BEE, B.E.E. Bachelor of Electrical
   Engineering
BFA, B.F.A. Bachelor of Fine Arts
bibl. biblical
bibliog. bibliographical
biog. biographical
biol. biological
BJ, B.J. Bachelor of Journalism
Bklyn. Brooklyn
BL, B.L. Bachelor of Letters
bldg. building
BLS, B.L.S. Bachelor of Library Science
BLS Basic Life Support
Blvd. Boulevard
BMW Bavarian Motor Works (Bayerische
   Motoren Werke)
bn. battalion
B.& O.R.R. Baltimore & Ohio Railroad
bot. botanical
BPE, B.P.E. Bachelor of Physical
   Education
BPhil, B.Phil. Bachelor of Philosophy
br. branch
BRE, B.R.E. Bachelor of Religious
   Education
brig. gen. brigadier general
Brit. British, Brittanica
Bros. Brothers
BS, B.S. Bachelor of Science
BSA, B.S.A. Bachelor of Agricultural
   Science
BSBA Bachelor of Science in Business
   Administration
BSChemE Bachelor of Science in Chemical
   Engineering
BSD, B.S.D. Bachelor of Didactic Science
BSN Bachelor of Science in Nursing
BST, B.S.T. Bachelor of Sacred Theology
BTh, B.Th. Bachelor of Theology
bull. bulletin
bur. bureau
bus. business
B.W.I. British West Indies

CA California
CAA Civil Aeronautics Administration
CAB Civil Aeronautics Board
CAD-CAM Computer Aided Design-
   Computer Aided Model
Calif. California
C.Am. Central America
Can. Canada, Canadian
CAP Civil Air Patrol
capt. captain
CARE Cooperative American Relief
   Everywhere
Cath. Catholic

cav. cavalry
CBC Canadian Broadcasting Company
CBI China, Burma, India Theatre of
   Operations
CBS Columbia Broadcasting Company
CCC Commodity Credit Corporation
CCNY City College of New York
CCU Cardiac Care Unit
CD Civil Defense
CE, C.E. Corps of Engineers, Civil
   Engineer
cen. central
CEN Certified Emergency Nurse
CENTO Central Treaty Organization
CERN European Organization of
   Nuclear Research
cert. certificate, certification, certified
CETA Comprehensive Employment
   Training Act
CFL Canadian Football League
ch. church
ChD, Ch.D. Doctor of Chemistry
chem. chemical
ChemE, Chem.E. Chemical Engineer
Chgo. Chicago
chirurg. chirurgical
chmn. chairman
chpt. chapter
CIA Central Intelligence Agency
Cin. Cincinnati
cir. circuit
Cleve. Cleveland
climatol. climatological
clin. clinical
clk. clerk
C.L.U. Chartered Life Underwriter
CM, C.M. Master in Surgery
CM Northern Mariana Islands
CMA Certified Medical Assistant
CNA Certified Nurse's Aide
CNOR Certified Nurse (Operating Room)
C.&N.W.Ry. Chicago & North Western
   Railway
CO Colorado
Co. Company
COF Catholic Order of Foresters
C. of C. Chamber of Commerce
col. colonel
coll. college
Colo. Colorado
com. committee
comd. commanded
comdg. commanding
comdr. commander
comdt. commandant
commd. commissioned
comml. commercial
commn. commission
commr. commissioner
compt. comptroller
condr. conductor
Conf. Conference
Congl. Congregational, Congressional
Conglist. Congregationalist
Conn. Connecticut
cons. consultant, consulting
consol. consolidated
constl. constitutional
constn. constitution

constrn. construction
contbd. contributed
contbg. contributing
contbn. contribution
contbr. contributor
contr. controller
Conv. Convention
coop. cooperative
coord. coordinator
CORDS Civil Operations and
   Revolutionary Development Support
CORE Congress of Racial Equality
corp. corporation, corporate
corr. correspondent, corresponding,
   correspondence
C.&O.Ry. Chesapeake & Ohio Railway
coun. council
C.P.A. Certified Public Accountant
C.P.C.U. Chartered Property and Casualty
   Underwriter
CPH, C.P.H. Certificate of Public Health
cpl. corporal
C.P.R. Cardio-Pulmonary Resuscitation
C.P.Ry. Canadian Pacific Railway
CRT Cathode Ray Terminal
C.S. Christian Science
CSB, C.S.B. Bachelor of Christian Science
C.S.C. Civil Service Commission
CT Connecticut
ct. court
ctr. center
CWS Chemical Warfare Service
C.Z. Canal Zone

D. Doctor
d. daughter
DAgr, D.Agr. Doctor of Agriculture
DAR Daughters of the American Revolution
dau. daughter
DAV Disabled American Veterans
DC, D.C. District of Columbia
DCL, D.C.L. Doctor of Civil Law
DCS, D.C.S. Doctor of Commercial Science
DD, D.D. Doctor of Divinity
DDS, D.D.S. Doctor of Dental Surgery
DE Delaware
Dec. December
dec. deceased
def. defense
Del. Delaware
del. delegate, delegation
Dem. Democrat, Democratic
DEng, D.Eng. Doctor of Engineering
denom. denomination, denominational
dep. deputy
dept. department
dermatol. dermatological
desc. descendant
devel. development, developmental
DFA, D.F.A. Doctor of Fine Arts
D.F.C. Distinguished Flying Cross
DHL, D.H.L. Doctor of Hebrew Literature
dir. director
dist. district
distbg. distributing
distbn. distribution
distbr. distributor
disting. distinguished
div. division, divinity, divorce

DLitt, D.Litt. Doctor of Literature
DMD, D.M.D. Doctor of Medical Dentistry
DMS, D.M.S. Doctor of Medical Science
DO, D.O. Doctor of Osteopathy
DON Director of Nursing
DPH, D.P.H. Diploma in Public Health
DPhil, D.Phil. Doctor of Philosophy
D.R. Daughters of the Revolution
Dr. Drive, Doctor
DRE, D.R.E. Doctor of Religious Education
DrPH, Dr.P.H. Doctor of Public Health,
    Doctor of Public Hygiene
D.S.C. Distinguished Service Cross
DSc, D.Sc. Doctor of Science
D.S.M. Distinguished Service Medal
DST, D.S.T. Doctor of Sacred Theology
DTM, D.T.M. Doctor of Tropical Medicine
DVM, D.V.M. Doctor of Veterinary
    Medicine
DVS, D.V.S. Doctor of Veterinary Surgery

E, E. East
ea. eastern
E. and P. Extraordinary and
    Plenipotentiary
Eccles. Ecclesiastical
ecol. ecological
econ. economic
ECOSOC Economic and Social Council (of
    the UN)
ED, E.D. Doctor of Engineering
ed. educated
EdB, Ed.B. Bachelor of Education
EdD, Ed.D. Doctor of Education
edit. edition
EdM, Ed.M. Master of Education
edn. education
ednl. educational
EDP Electronic Data Processing
EdS, Ed.S. Specialist in Education
EE, E.E. Electrical Engineer
E.E. and M.P. Envoy Extraordinary and
    Minister Plenipotentiary
EEC European Economic Community
EEG Electroencephalogram
EEO Equal Employment Opportunity
EEOC Equal Employment Opportunity
    Commission
E.Ger. German Democratic Republic
EKG Electrocardiogram
elec. electrical
electrochem. electrochemical
electrophys. electrophysical
elem. elementary
EM, E.M. Engineer of Mines
EMT Emergency Medical Technician
ency. encyclopedia
Eng. England
engr. engineer
engring. engineering
entomol. entomological
environ. environmental
EPA Environmental Protection Agency
epidemiol. epidemiological
Episc. Episcopalian
ERA Equal Rights Amendment
ERDA Energy Research and Development
    Administration
ESEA Elementary and Secondary Education
    Act

ESL English as Second Language
ESPN Entertainment and Sports
    Programming Network
ESSA Environmental Science Services
    Administration
ethnol. ethnological
ETO European Theatre of Operations
Evang. Evangelical
exam. examination, examining
Exch. Exchange
exec. executive
exhbn. exhibition
expdn. expedition
expn. exposition
expt. experiment
exptl. experimental
Expwy. Expressway

F.A. Field Artillery
FAA Federal Aviation Administration
FAO Food and Agriculture Organization (of
    the UN)
FBI Federal Bureau of Investigation
FCA Farm Credit Administration
FCC Federal Communications Commission
FCDA Federal Civil Defense
    Administration
FDA Food and Drug Administration
FDIA Federal Deposit Insurance
    Administration
FDIC Federal Deposit Insurance
    Corporation
FE, F.E. Forest Engineer
FEA Federal Energy Administration
Feb. February
fed. federal
fedn. federation
FERC Federal Energy Regulatory
    Commission
fgn. foreign
FHA Federal Housing Administration
fin. financial, finance
FL Florida
Fl. Floor
Fla. Florida
FMC Federal Maritime Commission
FNP Family Nurse Practitioner
FOA Foreign Operations Administration
found. foundation
FPC Federal Power Commission
FPO Fleet Post Office
frat. fraternity
FRS Federal Reserve System
Frwy. Freeway
FSA Federal Security Agency
Ft. Fort
FTC Federal Trade Commission

G-1 (or other number) Division of General
    Staff
GA, Ga. Georgia
GAO General Accounting Office
gastroent. gastroenterological
GATE Gifted and Talented Educators
GATT General Agreement of Tariff and
    Trades
GE General Electric Company
gen. general
geneal. genealogical

geod. geodetic
geog. geographic, geographical
geol. geological
geophys. geophysical
gerontol. gerontological
G.H.Q. General Headquarters
GM General Motors Corporation
GMAC General Motors Acceptance
    Corporation
G.N.Ry. Great Northern Railway
gov. governor
govt. government
govtl. governmental
GPO Government Printing Office
grad. graduate, graduated
GSA General Services Administration
Gt. Great
GTE General Telephone and Electric
    Company
GU Guam
gynecol. gynecological

HBO Home Box Office
hdqrs. headquarters
HEW Department of Health, Education
    and Welfare
HHD, H.H.D. Doctor of Humanities
HHFA Housing and Home Finance
    Agency
HHS Department of Health and Human
    Services
HI Hawaii
hist. historical, historic
HM, H.M. Master of Humanics
HMO Health Maintenance Organization
homeo. homeopathic
hon. honorary, honorable
Ho. of Dels. House of Delegates
Ho. of Reps. House of Representatives
hort. horticultural
hosp. hospital
HUD Department of Housing and Urban
    Development
Hwy. Highway
hydrog. hydrographic

IA Iowa
IAEA International Atomic Energy Agency
IBM International Business Machines
    Corporation
IBRD International Bank forReconstruction
    and Development
ICA International Cooperation
    Administration
ICC Interstate Commerce Commission
ICCE International Council for Computers
    in Education
ICU Intensive Care Unit
ID Idaho
IEEE Institute of Electrical and
    Electronics Engineers
IFC International Finance Corporation
IGY International Geophysical Year
IL Illinois
Ill. Illinois
illus. illustrated
ILO International Labor Organization
IMF International Monetary Fund
IN Indiana

Inc. Incorporated
Ind. Indiana
ind. independent
Indpls. Indianapolis
indsl. industrial
inf. infantry
info. information
ins. insurance
insp. inspector
insp. gen. inspector general
inst. institute
instl. institutional
instn. institution
instr. instructor
instrn. instruction
internat. international
intro. introduction
IRE Institute of Radio Engineers
IRS Internal Revenue Service
ITT International Telephone &
   Telegraph Corporation

JAG Judge Advocate General
JAGC Judge Advocate General Corps
Jan. January
Jaycees Junior Chamber of Commerce
JB, J.B. Jurum Baccalaureus
JCB, J.C.B. Juris Canoni Baccalaureus
JCD, J.C.D. Juris Canonici Doctor, Juris
   Civilis Doctor
JCL, J.C.L. Juris Canonici Licentiatus
JD, J.D. Juris Doctor
jg. junior grade
jour. journal
jr. junior
JSD, J.S.D. Juris Scientiae Doctor
JUD, J.U.D. Juris Utriusque Doctor
jud. judicial

Kans. Kansas
K.C. Knights of Columbus
K.P. Knights of Pythias
KS Kansas
K.T. Knight Templar
KY, Ky. Kentucky

LA, La. Loiusiana
L.A. Los Angeles
lab. laboratory
lang. language
laryngol. laryngological
LB Labrador
LDS Church Church of Jesus Christ of
   Latter Day Saints
lectr. lecturer
legis. legislation, legislative
LHD, L.H.D. Doctor of Humane Letters
L.I. Long Island
libr. librarian, library
lic. licensed, license
L.I.R.R. Long Island Railroad
lit. literature
LittB, Litt.B. Bachelor of Letters
LittD, Litt.D. Doctor of Letters
LLB, LL.B. Bachelor of Laws
LLD, L.L.D. Doctor of Laws
LLM, L.L.M. Master of Laws
Ln. Lane
L.&N.R.R. Louisville & Nashville Railroad
LPGA Ladies Professional Golf Association

LS, L.S. Library Science (in degree)
lt. lieutenant
Ltd. Limited
Luth. Lutheran
LWV League of Women Voters

M. Master
m. married
MA, M.A. Master of Arts
MA Massachusetts
MADD Mothers Against Drunk Driving
mag. magazine
MAgr, M.Agr. Master of Agriculture
maj. major
Man. Manitoba
Mar. March
MArch, M.Arch. Master in Architecture
Mass. Massachusetts
math. mathematics, mathematical
MATS Military Air Transport Service
MB, M.B. Bachelor of Medicine
MB Manitoba
MBA, M.B.A. Master of Business
   Administration
MBS Mutual Broadcasting System
M.C. Medical Corps
MCE, M.C.E. Master of Civil Engineering
mcht. merchant
mcpl. municipal
MCS, M.C.S. Master of Commercial
   Science
MD, M.D. Doctor of Medicine
MD, Md. Maryland
MDiv Master of Divinity
MDip, M.Dip. Master in Diplomacy
mdse. merchandise
MDV, M.D.V. Doctor of Veterinary
   Medicine
ME, M.E. Mechanical Engineer
ME Maine
M.E.Ch. Methodist Episcopal Church
mech. mechanical
MEd., M.Ed. Master of Education
med. medical
MEE, M.E.E. Master of Electrical
   Engineering
mem. member
meml. memorial
merc. mercantile
met. metropolitan
metall. metallurgical
MetE, Met.E. Metallurgical Engineer
meteorol. meteorological
Meth. Methodist
Mex. Mexico
MF, M.F. Master of Forestry
MFA, M.F.A. Master of Fine Arts
mfg. manufacturing
mfr. manufacturer
mgmt. management
mgr. manager
MHA, M.H.A. Master of Hospital
   Administration
M.I. Military Intelligence
MI Michigan
Mich. Michigan
micros. microscopic, microscopical
mid. middle
mil. military

Milw. Milwaukee
Min. Minister
mineral. mineralogical
Minn. Minnesota
MIS Management Information Systems
Miss. Mississippi
MIT Massachusetts Institute of Technology
mktg. marketing
ML, M.L. Master of Laws
MLA Modern Language Association
M.L.D. Magister Legnum Diplomatic
MLitt, M.Litt. Master of Literature
MLS, M.L.S. Master of Library Science
MME, M.M.E. Master of Mechanical
   Engineering
MN Minnesota
mng. managing
MO, Mo. Missouri
moblzn. mobilization
Mont. Montana
MP Northern Mariana Islands
M.P. Member of Parliament
MPA Master of Public Administration
MPE, M.P.E. Master of Physical Education
MPH, M.P.H. Master of Public Health
MPhil, M.Phil. Master of Philosophy
MPL, M.P.L. Master of Patent Law
Mpls. Minneapolis
MRE, M.R.E. Master of Religious
   Education
MS, M.S. Master of Science
MS, Ms. Mississippi
MSc, M.Sc. Master of Science
MSChemE Master of Science in Chemical
   Engineering
MSF, M.S.F. Master of Science of Forestry
MST, M.S.T. Master of Sacred Theology
MSW, M.S.W. Master of Social Work
MT Montana
Mt. Mount
MTO Mediterranean Theatre of Operation
MTV Music Television
mus. museum, musical
MusB, Mus.B. Bachelor of Music
MusD, Mus.D. Doctor of Music
MusM, Mus.M. Master of Music
mut. mutual
mycol. mycological

N. North
NAACOG Nurses Association of the
   American Association of Ob-Gyn
NAACP National Association for the
   Advancement of Colored People
NACA National Advisory Committee for
   Aeronautics
NACU National Association of Colleges
   and Universities
NAD National Academy of Design
NAE National Academy of Engineering,
   National Association of Educators
NAESP National Association of Elementary
   School Principals
NAFE National Association of Female
   Executives
N.Am. North America
NAM National Association of
   Manufacturers
NAMH National Association for Mental
   Health

NAPA National Association of Performing Artists
NARAS National Academy of Recording Arts and Sciences
NAREB National Association of Real Estate Boards
NARS National Archives and Record Service
NAS National Academy of Sciences
NASA National Aeronautics and Space Administration
NASP National Association of School Psychologists
NASW National Association of Social Workers
nat. national
NATAS National Academy of Television Arts and Sciences
NATO North Atlantic Treaty Organization
NATOUSA North African Theatre of Operations
nav. navigation
NB, N.B. New Brunswick
NBA National Basketball Association
NBC National Broadcasting Company
NC, N.C. North Carolina
NCAA National College Athletic Association
NCCJ National Conference of Christians and Jews
ND, N.D. North Dakota
NDEA National Defense Education Act
NE Nebraska
NE, N.E. Northeast
NEA National Education Association
Nebr. Nebraska
NEH National Endowment for Humanities
neurol. neurological
Nev. Nevada
NF Newfoundland
NFL National Football League
Nfld. Newfoundland
NG National Guard
NH, N.H. New Hampshire
NHL National Hockey League
NIH National Institutes of Health
NIMH National Institute of Mental Health
NJ, N.J. New Jersey
NLRB National Labor Relations Board
NM New Mexico
N.Mex. New Mexico
No. Northern
NOAA National Oceanographic and Atmospheric Administration
NORAD North America Air Defense
Nov. November
NOW National Organization for Women
N.P.Ry. Northern Pacific Railway
nr. near
NRA National Rifle Association
NRC National Research Council
NS, N.S. Nova Scotia
NSC National Security Council
NSF National Science Foundation
NSTA National Science Teachers Association
NSW New South Wales
N.T. New Testament
NT Northwest Territories

numis. numismatic
NV Nevada
NW, N.W. Northwest
N.W.T. Northwest Territories
NY, N.Y. New York
N.Y.C. New York City
NYU New York University
N.Z. New Zealand

OAS Organization of American States
ob-gyn obstetrics-gynecology
obs. observatory
obstet. obstetrical
Oct. October
OD, O.D. Doctor of Optometry
OECD Organization of European Cooperation and Development
OEEC Organization of European Economic Cooperation
OEO Office of Economic Opportunity
ofcl. official
OH Ohio
OK Oklahoma
Okla. Oklahoma
ON Ontario
Ont. Ontario
oper. operating
ophthal. ophthalmological
ops. operations
OR Oregon
orch. orchestra
Oreg. Oregon
orgn. organization
ornithol. ornithological
OSHA Occupational Safety and Health Administration
OSRD Office of Scientific Research and Development
OSS Office of Strategic Services
osteo. osteopathic
otol. otological
otolaryn. otolaryngological

PA, Pa. Pennsylvania
P.A. Professional Association
paleontol. paleontological
path. pathological
PBS Public Broadcasting System
P.C. Professional Corporation
PE Prince Edward Island
P.E.I. Prince Edward Island
PEN Poets, Playwrights, Editors, Essayists and Novelists (international association)
penol. penological
P.E.O. women's organization (full name not disclosed)
pers. personnel
pfc. private first class
PGA Professional Golfers' Association of America
PHA Public Housing Administration
pharm. pharmaceutical
PharmD, Pharm.D. Doctor of Pharmacy
PharmM, Pharm.M. Master of Pharmacy
PhB, Ph.B. Bachelor of Philosophy
PhD, Ph.D. Doctor of Philosophy
PhDChemE Doctor of Science in Chemical Engineering
PhM, Ph.M. Master of Philosophy

Phila. Philadelphia
philharm. philharmonic
philol. philological
philos. philosophical
photog. photographic
phys. physical
physiol. physiological
Pitts. Pittsburgh
Pk. Park
Pkwy. Parkway
Pl. Place
Pla. Plaza
P.&L.E.R.R. Pittsburgh & Lake Erie Railroad
PNP Pediatric Nurse Practitioner
P.O. Post Office
PO Box Post Office Box
polit. political
poly. polytechnic, polytechnical
PQ Province of Quebec
PR, P.R. Puerto Rico
prep. preparatory
pres. president
Presbyn. Presbyterian
presdl. presidential
prin. principal
proc. proceedings
prod. produced (play production)
prodn. production
prof. professor
profl. professional
prog. progressive
propr. proprietor
pros. atty. prosecuting attorney
pro tem pro tempore
PSRO Professional Services Review Organization
psychiat. psychiatric
psychol. psychological
PTA Parent-Teachers Association
ptnr. partner
PTO Pacific Theatre of Operations, Parent Teacher Organization
pub. publisher, publishing, published
pub. public
publ. publication
pvt. private

quar. quarterly
qm. quartermaster
Q.M.C. Quartermaster Corps
Que. Quebec

radiol. radiological
RAF Royal Air Force
RCA Radio Corporation of America
RCAF Royal Canadian Air Force
RD Rural Delivery
Rd. Road
R&D Research & Development
REA Rural Electrification Administration
rec. recording
ref. reformed
regt. regiment
regtl. regimental
rehab. rehabilitation
rels. relations
Rep. Republican
rep. representative

Res. Reserve
ret. retired
Rev. Reverend
rev. review, revised
RFC Reconstruction Finance Corporation
RFD Rural Free Delivery
rhinol. rhinological
RI, R.I. Rhode Island
RISD Rhode Island School of Design
Rm. Room
RN, R.N. Registered Nurse
roentgenol. roentgenological
ROTC Reserve Officers Training Corps
RR Rural Route
R.R. Railroad
rsch. research
Rte. Route
Ry. Railway

S. South
s. son
SAC Strategic Air Command
SAG Screen Actors Guild
SALT Strategic Arms Limitation Talks
S.Am. South America
san. sanitary
SAR Sons of the American Revolution
Sask. Saskatchewan
savs. savings
SB, S.B. Bachelor of Science
SBA Small Business Administration
SC, S.C. South Carolina
SCAP Supreme Command Allies Pacific
ScB, Sc.B. Bachelor of Science
SCD, S.C.D. Doctor of Commercial Science
ScD, Sc.D. Doctor of Science
sch. school
sci. science, scientific
SCLC Southern Christian Leadership
    Conference
SCV Sons of Confederate Veterans
SD, S.D. South Dakota
SE, S.E. Southeast
SEATO Southeast Asia Treaty Organization
SEC Securities and Exchange Commission
sec. secretary
sect. section
seismol. seismological
sem. seminary
Sept. September
s.g. senior grade
sgt. sergeant
SHAEF Supreme Headquarters Allied
    Expeditionary Forces
SHAPE Supreme Headquarters Allied
    Powers in Europe
S.I. Staten Island
S.J. Society of Jesus (Jesuit)
SJD Scientiae Juridicae Doctor
SK Saskatchewan
SM, S.M. Master of Science
SNP Society of Nursing Professionals
So. Southern
soc. society
sociol. sociological
S.P. Co. Southern Pacific Company
spl. special
splty. specialty
Sq. Square

S.R. Sons of the Revolution
sr. senior
SS Steamship
SSS Selective Service System
St. Saint, Street
sta. station
stats. statistics
statis. statistical
STB, S.T.B. Bachelor of Sacred Theology
stblzn. stabilization
STD, S.T.D. Doctor of Sacred Theology
Ste. Suite
subs. subsidiary
SUNY State University of New York
supr. supervisor
supt. superintendent
surg. surgical
svc. service
SW, S.W. Southwest

TAPPI Technical Association of the Pulp
    and Paper Industry
Tb. Tuberculosis
tchr. teacher
tech. technical, technology
technol. technological
Tel. & Tel. Telephone & Telegraph
temp. temporary
Tenn. Tennessee
Ter. Territory
Terr. Terrace
Tex. Texas
ThD, Th.D. Doctor of Theology
theol. theological
ThM, Th.M. Master of Theology
TN Tennessee
tng. training
topog. topographical
trans. transaction, transferred
transl. translation, translated
transp. transportation
treas. treasurer
TT Trust Territory
TV television
TVA Tennessee Valley Authority
TWA Trans World Airlines
twp. township
TX Texas
typog. typographical

U. University
UAW United Auto Workers
UCLA University of California at Los
    Angeles
UDC United Daughters of the Confederacy
U.K. United Kingdom
UN United Nations
UNESCO United Nations Educational,
    Scientific and Cultural Organization
UNICEF United Nations International
    Children's Emergency Fund
univ. university
UNRRA United Nations Relief and
    Rehabilitation Administration
UPI United Press International
U.P.R.R. United Pacific Railroad
urol. urological
U.S. United States
U.S.A. United States of America

USAAF United States Army Air Force
USAF United States Air Force
USAFR United States Air Force Reserve
USAR United States Army Reserve
USCG United States Coast Guard
USCGR United States Coast Guard Reserve
USES United States Employment Service
USIA United States Information Agency
USMC United States Marine Corps
USMCR United States Marine Corps
    Reserve
USN United States Navy
USNG United States National Guard
USNR United States Naval Reserve
USO United Service Organizations
USPHS United States Public Health Service
USS United States Ship
USSR Union of the Soviet Socialist
    Republics
USTA United States Tennis Association
USV United States Volunteers
UT Utah

VA Veterans Administration
VA, Va. Virginia
vet. veteran, veterinary
VFW Veterans of Foreign Wars
VI, V.I. Virgin Islands
vice pres. vice president
vis. visiting
VISTA Volunteers in Service to America
VITA Volunteers in Technical Service
vocat. vocational
vol. volunteer, volume
v.p. vice president
vs. versus
VT, Vt. Vermont

W, W. West
WA Washington (state)
WAC Women's Army Corps
Wash. Washington (state)
WAVES Women's Reserve, US Naval
    Reserve
WCTU Women's Christian Temperance
    Union
we. western
W. Ger. Germany, Federal Republic of
WHO World Health Organization
WI Wisconsin
W.I. West Indies
Wis. Wisconsin
WSB Wage Stabilization Board
WV West Virginia
W.Va. West Virginia
WY Wyoming
Wyo. Wyoming

YK Yukon Territory
YMCA Young Men's Christian Association
YMHA Young Men's Hebrew Association
YM & YWHA Young Men's and Young
    Women's Hebrew Association
yr. year
YT, Y.T. Yukon Territory
YWCA Young Women's Christian
    Association

zool. zoological

Alphabetical Practices

Names are arranged alphabetically according to the surnames, and under identical surnames according to the first given name. If both surname and first given name are identical, names are arranged alphabetically according to the second given name. Where full names are identical, they are arranged in order of age—with the elder listed first.

Surnames beginning with De, Des, Du, however capitalized or spaced, are recorded with the prefix preceding the surname and arranged alphabetically under the letter D.

Surnames beginning with Mac and Mc are arranged alphabetically under M.

Surnames beginning with Saint or St. appear after names that begin Sains, and are arranged according to the second part of the name, e.g. St. Clair before Saint Dennis.

Surnames beginning with Van, Von or von are arranged alphabetically under letter V.

Compound hyphenated surnames are arranged according to the first member of the compound. Compound unhyphenated surnames are treated as hyphenated names.

Parentheses used in connection with a name indicate which part of the full name is usually deleted in common usage. Hence Abbott, W(illiam) Lewis indicates that the usual form of the given name is W. Lewis. In such a case, the parentheses are ignored in alphabetizing. However, if the name is recorded Abbott, (William) Lewis, signifying that the entire name William is not commonly used, the alphabetizing would be arranged as though the name were Abbott, Lewis.

Who's Who of American Women

AARON, CHLOE WELLINGHAM, former television executive; b. Santa Monica, Calif., Oct. 9, 1938; d. John Rufus and Grace (Lloyd) Wellingham; m. David Laurence Aaron, Aug. 11, 1962; 1 child, Timothy Wellingham. BA, Occidental Coll., 1961; MA, George Washington U., 1966; HHD (hon.), Occidental Coll., 1987. Freelance journalist, 1965-70; dir. pub. media program Nat. Endowment for Arts, Washington, 1970-76; sr. v.p. programming Pub. Broadcasting Service, Washington, 1976-81; pres. Chloe Aaron Assocs., 1981-87; dir. cultural and children's programs KQED-TV, San Francisco, 1987-89; v.p. WNYC-TV, N.Y.C., 1989—. Producer: TV film The Soldier's Tale, PBS (Emmy award 1984), 1984; exec. producer TV film Dead Pan Alley (Emmy award 1989). Mem. trustee com. on film Mus. Modern Art, N.Y.C.; mem. bd. pub. devel. Corp. of N.Y.C., Ctr. Visual History, Nancy Hanks Ctr., Am. Jazz Orchestra. Recipient Alumni Seal award Occidental Coll., 1983.

AARON, SHIRLEY MAE, tax consultant; b. Covington, La., Feb. 28, 1935; d. Morgan and Pearl (Jenkins) King; m. Richard L. King, Feb. 16, 1952 (div. Feb. 1965); children: Deborah, Richard, Roberta, Keely; m. Michael A. Aaron, Nov. 27, 1976 (dec. July 1987). Adminstrv. asst. South Central Bell, Covington, La., 1954-62; acct. Brown & Root, Inc., Houston, 1962-75; timekeeper Alyeska Pipeline Co., Fairbanks, Alaska, 1975-77; adminstrv. asst. Boeing Co., Seattle, 1979—; pres. Aaron Enterprises, Seattle, 1977—. Bd. dirs. Burien 146 Homeowners Assn., Seattle, 1979—, pres., 1980-83. Mem. NAFE. Avocation: singing. Home: 212 SW 146th St CD104 Seattle WA 98166

AARONSON, BRENDA CARYL, educator; b. Pittsfield, Mass., Nov. 13, 1938; d. Jacob Solon and Sally (Golden) A. BMus, U. N.C., 1960; MA, NYU, 1967, sch. adminstr. supr. cert., 1979, sch. dist. adminstr. cert., 1980, PhD, 1979. Asst. to coordinator and film prodn. NYU Med. Ctr., N.Y.C., 1961-62; music libr. NYU, N.Y.C., 1963-65; asst. to advt. and prodn. mgr. Mills Music, Inc., N.Y.C., 1962-63; music educator Union Free Sch. Dist. No. 10, Commack, N.Y., 1965-66; music educator, acting chmn. George Washington High Sch., Bd. Edn. City N.Y., 1966-71; music educator, asst. chmn. Adlai E. Stevenson High Sch., 1971-78; music educator, dean students Martin L. King Jr. High Sch., 1978—; examining asst. Bd. Exams Bd. Edn. City N.Y., 1986—; juror Am. Film Festival, 1961-63. Composer mus. comedy: Extension H., 1959, secular and sacred works, 1962—; author children's texts and musicol. articles, 1964—; conductor, 1960—. Lectr. State of Israel Bonds, N.Y.C., 1980—; bd. dirs. new leadership div. United Jewish Appeal, 1980-82; pres. Aviv chpt. B'nai B'rith Women, N.Y.C., 1983-85; v.p. exec. offices Gotham unit B'nai B'rith, N.Y.C., 1979-82; v.p. Golda Meier group Hadassah, N.Y.C., 1980-82; mem. internat. com. Anti-Defamation League of B'nai B'rith, 1983—. Recipient Outstanding Svc. and Bull. awards B'nai B'rith Women, 1979-86, Outstanding Svc. awards Hadassah, 1980-82, Israel Leadership award State of Israel Bonds, 1982; orchestral conducting scholar Tanglewood, 1959, 60. Mem. Nat. Band Assn., Nat. Sch. Orch. Assn., N.Y. State Sch. Music Assn., A.D.L. (mem. internat. affairs com.). Democrat. Jewish. Home: 170 West End Ave New York NY 10023

ABAD, ROSARIO DALIDA, elementary educator; b. Ilocos Norte, Philippines, Apr. 23, 1936; came to U.S., 1966; d. Primitivo Agoo and Adelaida (Cacal) Dalida; m. Domingo Abad, June 8, 1969; children: Eric, Jon, Jenny. Grad., Philippine Normal Coll., 1954; BA in Edn., Far Eastern U., Manila, 1961; MA in Edn., Far Eastern U., 1966. Educator Rizal Pub. Schs., Philippines, 1955-58, Manila Pub. Schs., 1958-66; instr. Mindoro Coll., Philippines, 1964-66; tchr. Sudbury (Ont., Can.) Schs., 1966-67, St. Bernard (La.) Schs., 1967-68, Jefferson Parish (La.) Schs., 1968-73, New Orleans Sch. Bd., 1973—. Contbr. articles to profl. jours.; free-lance writer. V.p. Philippine-Am. Sports Assn. New Orleans, 1987—, Kapit-Bahay Assn., 1984—. Recipient Recognition award Kapit-Bahay Assn., 1984. Mem. Internat. Reading Assn., NAFE, Am. Fedn. Tchrs., United Tchrs. New Orleans, Philippine-Am. Women's Assn. La. (v.p. 1985-87, pres. 1988—, Recognition award 1986). Democrat. Roman Catholic. Home: 2612 Mercedes Blvd New Orleans LA 70114

ABAJIAN, WENDY ELISSE, instructional design specialist, multi-media producer; b. Selma, Calif., Mar. 16, 1955; d. Mesik Nishon and Blanche Peggy (Emerzian) A. AA, Kings River Community Coll., 1975; BA, Calif. State U., Fresno, 1978; MS, U. So. Calif., 1981, EdD, 1986. Instr., tchr. various sch. dists., Burbank and Fresno, Calif., 1981-82; free-lance writer various corps., Los Angeles area, 1984-86; pres., ind. producer Abhawk Prodns., Inc., Long Beach, Calif., 1986—; cons. multi-media projects. Contbr. articles to profl. jours. Active Rep. Nat. Com., Washington, 1983—, Statue of Liberty Ellis Island Found., 1984—, Women Appointees Coun., Sacramento, 1988, Burbank Ctr. for Retarded; gubernatorial appointee to adv. bd. Lanterman State Hosp., 1986—, gubernatorial appointee to bd. dirs. Protection and Advocacy, Inc., 1990—. Mem. NAFE, Ednl. Grad. Orgn., Am. Film Inst., Farm Bur. Fedn. Armenian Apostolic. Office: Abhawk Prodns Inc PO Box 8654 Long Beach CA 90808-0654

ABARA, CANDACE DEVOOGHT, marriage and family therapist; b. Chgo., July 1, 1950; d. Donald G. and Leola C. (Olson) Stroh; m. David Howe, May 3, 1969; children: Jamie Howe, Bret DeVooght; m. David Abara, July 17, 1988. AA in Sociol., Chabot Coll., 1976; BA in Psychology, Calif. State U., Hayward, 1978; MS in Clin. Counseling, Calif. State U., 1982. Lic. marriage and family therapist, Calif. Intern counselor Emergency Shelter Program, inc., Hayward, 1978-81; adminstrv. liaison to fed. corrections Bu. of Prisons, Pleasanton, 1978-79; intern counselor Aliso House, Hayward, 1979-80; outpatient counselor Project Eden Inc., Hayward, 1980-84; psychiatric assessment counselor Highland Gen. Hosp., Oakland, Calif., 1984; pvt. practice San Leandro, Calif., 1986—; instr. Chabot Coll., 1988—. Author: Counseling the Battered Woman, 1982. Youth and family counselor YWCA, Alameda County Juvenile Probation, San Lorenzo, 1984—; mem. sch. attendance rev. bd. San Lorenzo Unified Sch. Dist.; mem. disciplinary hearing com. Hayward Unified Sch. Dist.; vice-chair Coalition of Alameda County Status Offenders Svcs., Calif. Child, Youth and Family Coalition. Mem. Calif. Assn. Marriage Family Therapists. Democrat. Lutheran. Office: 680 Bancroft Ave Ste 201 San Leandro CA 94577

ABARBANEL, JUDITH EDNA, marketing executive; b. N.Y.C., Jan. 26, 1956; d. Albert Brandt and Dorothy Irene (Fennell) A.; m. Christopher George Lucas, June 17, 1984. BA, UCLA, 1977; MBA, MA, Ohio State U., 1980. Accredited pub. relations profl., 1988. Sales mgr. Columbus Magic, Ohio, 1979; account mgr. Mktg. Centre, St. Petersburg, Fla., 1980-82; asst. mktg. dir. MBI, Inc., Golden, Colo., 1983; dir. mktg. Colo. Outward Bound. Sch., Denver, 1983—; owner A Sporting Proposition, Boulder, Colo., 1984—. Adv. bd. Learning Unltd. Mem. Denver Advt. Fedn., Pub. Relations Soc. Am. Avocations: mountain biking, race organizing, teaching. Office: Colo Outward Bound Sch 945 Pennsylvania St Denver CO 80203

ABARBANELL, GAYOLA HAVENS, financial advisor, consultant; b. Chgo., Oct. 21, 1939; d. Leonard Milton and Lillian Love (Leviten) Havens; m. Burton J. Abarbanell, June 1, 1965 (div. 1972); children: Jeffrey J. and Dena Reddick. Student, UCLA, 1975; student, San Joaquin Coll. Law, 1976-77. Cert. fin. planner; lic. real estate rep., Calif.; lic. life ins. broker, Cliaf., Wash., Nev., N.Y., Ill.; lic. securities broker. Postal clk. Van Nuys, Calif., 1966-69; regional mgr. Niagara Cyclo Massage, Fresno, Calif., 1969-72; owner, mgr. AD Enterprises, Fresno, Calif., 1970-72; agt., field supr. Equitable of Iowa, Fresno, Calif., 1972-73; rep. Ciba Pharms., Fresno, Calif., 1973-75; owner, operator Creativity Unltd., Fresno, Calif., 1975-76; registered fin. advisor Univ. Securities Corp., Los Angeles, Calif., 1976-83, Fin. Network Investment Corp., Los Angeles, Calif., 1983—; lectr. seminars for civic orgns.; mem. adv. bd. Fin. Network, Torrance, Calif., 1985-88. Co-author: Guidelines to Feminist Consciousness Raising, 1985. Mem. bus. adv. bd. of 2d careers. Recipient award Women in Ins., 1972. Mem. Bus. and Profl. Assn. L.A., Internat. Assn. Fin. Planners, Inst. Cert. Fin. Planners, So. Calif. Socially Responsible Investment Profls., ACLU, NOW (nat. consciousness raising coord. 1975-76), So. Calif. Women for Understanding, Gay Acad. Union, Nat. Gay Task Force, Culver City C. of C., Internat. Assn. Fin. Planners, Social Investment Forum, Rotary (founding mem. L.A. Westside Sunrise chpt.). Democrat. Jewish. Home: 5625 Green Valley Cir #103 Culver City CA 90230 Office: 9724 Washington Blvd #203 Culver City CA 90232-2722

ABBAS, ELIZABETH KEUTGEN, market research executive; b. Passaic, N.J., June 10, 1947; d. David Charles and Phyllis Marion (Parry) Keutgen; m. Daniel C. Abbas, July 5, 1969; children: Erika Diane, Geoffrey David. BA, Central Coll., Pella, Iowa, 1969; MS, U. Ill., 1974, PhD, 1980. Rsch. asst. U. Ill., Urbana, 1969-70, 75-77, tchr. asst., 1970-71, 74-75; tchr. comml. foods Warren (Mich.) Cen. Schs., 1972-73; project mgr. Gordon S. Black Corp., Rochester, N.Y., 1980-85, sr. project mgr., 1985-87, v.p. rsch., 1987—; mem. Mktg. Task Force Give 5 Campaign from ind. sector, Washington, 1989. Vol. blood dr. ARC, Webster, N.Y., 1978—; v.p. bd. dirs. Rochester Christian Sch., 1986-88, pres., 1988-89. EPDA fellow Bur. Vocat. Edn., Dept. Edn., 1976-77. Mem. Am. Mktg. Assn., Am. Home Econs. Assn. (treas., higher edn. chair local chpt.), Am. Coun. Consumer Interests, Rochester C. of C. (women's coun.), Rochester Women's Network (sec. bd. dirs. 1984—, v.p. spl. programs), Omicron Nu, Phi Delta Kappa. Presbyterian. Office: Gordon S Black Corp 1661 Penfield Dr Rochester NY 14625

ABBOTT, BARBARA DIANE, foundation executive; b. Charlottesville, Va., Oct. 28, 1959; d. Herbert Davis Jr. and Edna Mae (Lutomski) A. BA, Coll. William and Mary, 1982; postgrad., Am. U., 1990. Tour guide Monticello, home of Thomas Jefferson, Charlottesville, 1979-82; adminstrv. asst. Ctr. Strategic and Internat. Studies, Washington, 1982-83; asst. to pres. Jamestown Found., Washington, 1983-85, v.p., 1985-87, exec. v.p., 1987—. Mem. NAFE, Nat. Fedn. Rep. Women, Chi Omega. Presbyterian. Office: Jamestown Found 1528 18th St NW Washington DC 20036

ABBOTT, BETTY JANE, biologist, cancer researcher; b. Roanoke, Va., Oct. 13, 1931; d. Richard William and Delena Jane (Huffman) A. BS, Radford U., 1952; MS, Va. Poly. Inst. and State U., 1955, postgrad., 1957-59. Cert. tchr., Va. Tchr. Henry County Schs., Martinsville, Va., 1952-53, Roanoke County Schs., 1953-57; grad. instr. zoology Va. Poly. Inst. and State U., Blacksburg, 1957-59; biologist USDA Agrl. Rsch. Svc., Blacksburg, 1959-60; biologist Nat. Cancer Inst. NIH, Bethesda, Md., 1960—. Contbr. to numerous sci. publs. Mem. Am. Assn. Cancer Rsch., N.Y. Acad. Scis., Sigma Sigma Sigma, Chi Beta Phi. Mem. Disciples of Christ Church. Home: 8008 Fieldstone Dr Frederick MD 21702-2916 Office: Nat Cancer Inst Bldg 1021 Frederick Cancer R&D Ctr Frederick MD 21702

ABBOTT, FRANCES ELIZABETH DOWDLE, journalist, civic worker; b. Rome, Ga., Mar. 21, 1924; d. John Wesley and Lucille Elizabeth (Field) Dowdle; m. Jackson Miles Abbott, May, 16, 1948; children: Medora Frances, David Field, Elizabeth Stockton, Robert Jackson. Student, Draughon's Bus. Coll., Columbia, S.C.. Feature writer Mt. Vernon corr. Alexandria Gazette, Va., 1967-75; libr., rsch. assoc. Gadsby's Tavern Mus., Alexandria, 1977—. Chmn. ann. George Washington Birthnight Ball, Mt. Vernon, 1974-82; sec. George Washington 250th Birthday Celebration Commn., 1979-82; chmn. publicity Waynewood Woman's Club, Waynewood Citizens Assn.; treas. Mt. Vernon Citizens Assn., 1967-82; dist. chmn. Mt. Vernon March of Dimes, 1960-62; sec. Waynewood Sch. PTA, 1962-64; tchr. 1st aid Girl Scouts U.S., 1964-65; den mother Cub Scouts, 1966; registrar DAR, 1968-77; chmn. publicity Mt. Vernon Women's Rep. Club, 1955; mem. steering com. Neighborhood Friends of Hist. Mt. Vernon, 1988—. Named Mrs. Waynewood by Community Vote, 1969. Mem. Audubon Naturalist Soc., Nat. Trust Hist. Preservation. Episcopalian. Home: 8501 Doter Dr Alexandria VA 22308 Office: 134 N Royal St Alexandria VA 22314

ABBOTT, MARY ELAINE, photographer, lecturer, researcher; b. LaGrange, Ill., Apr. 23, 1922; d. Vergil and Goldie (Wright) Schwarzkopf; m. Harry Edward Abbott, Oct. 8, 1949; children: John Edward, Jane Ann. BA in English, Psychology, Iowa U., 1944. With child welfare dept. Montgomery County Children's Home, Dayton, Ohio, 1944-47, Mich. Children's Inst., Ann Arbor, 1947-49; photographer, lectr., researcher, 1978—; researcher; lectr. Documentary photography for regional history books, mags., calendars and brochures; commd. Taft Sculpture, Sculputre Jackson County; artistic dir. James Agee's Knoxville Summer 1915 with Jackson Symphony Orch.; Claire Allen architecture, Mich. Dance Assn.; hist. dist. commn. advisor Dance for the Handicapped, Savs. and Loan "40 Doors", Amitech, Jackson Alliance of Businessmen; hung in various exhbns. and juried shows photographer for Ella Sharp Mus., Jackson Symphony Orch., Carnegie Libr., St. Paul's Episcopal Ch., Queens Cath. Ch. Mem. Jr. League, Jackson Chorale, St. Paul's Episcopal Ch., Log Cabin Soc. Mich.; advisor Jackson Hist. Dist. Commn. Laredo Taft scholar. Mem. Internat. Platform Assn., Nat. Mus. of Women in the Arts, Kappa Alpha Theta. Republican. Episcopalian. Home and Office: 721 Oakridge Dr Jackson MI 49203

ABBOTT, MELANIE BETH, law educator; b. New Haven, Aug. 21, 1951; d. John Wilbur and Virginia Ruth (Towns) Abbott. BA in Theatre, Bates Col!., Lewiston, Maine, 1973; MS in Television, Syracuse U., 1978; JD, U. Bridgeport, Conn., 1984. Residence hall dir. U. R.I., Kingston, 1978-79; complex dir. We. Ill. U., Macomb, 1979-81; law clk. U.S. Ct. Appeals, 2nd Cir., New Britain, Conn., 1984-85; assoc. Cadwalader, Wickersham & Taft, Washington, 1985-87, Day, Berry & Howard, Hartford, Conn., 1987-89; asst. prof. law U. Bridgeport Law Sch., 1989—. Adv. bd. U. Bridgeport Law Sch., 1987—; voter registration vol. 3rd Congl. Dist. Dem. campaign, New Haven, 1988; vol. issues com. 3d Congl. Dist. Dem. Campaign, New Haven, 1990. Mem. ABA, Conn. Bar Assn., Conn. Coalition for the Homeless, Conn. Civil Liberties Union. Democrat. Office: U Bridgeport Sch Law 303 University Ave Bridgeport CT 06601

ABBOTT, MURIEL MACPHERSON, psychometrician; b. Montclair, N.J.; d. Graham and Muriel Margaret (Burleigh) Macpherson; B.A., Brown U.; M.A., Newark State Coll., 1961; Ph.D. (NDEA fellow), Columbia U., 1968; m. Charles F. Abbott (div.). Adj. prof. Tchrs. Coll., Columbia U., 1965-75; asst. dir. spl. projects Harcourt Brace Jovanovich Inc. (Psychol. Corp.), N.Y.C., 1965-76, asst. dir. profl. exams., 1976-78; dir. test devel. N.Y.C. Bd. Edn., 1978—; summer fellow in measurement Ednl. Testing Service, 1963. Mem. bd. mgrs. Vanderbilt YMCA, N.Y.C., 1977—, named Woman of Yr., 1982. Mem. Am. Psychol. Assn., Am. Ednl. Research Assn., Nat. Council Measurement in Edn., Nat. Assn. Test Dirs., Brown U. Alumni Assn., Columbia U. Alumni Assn., Sigma Xi. Clubs: Brown U., New Eng. Soc. Contbr. articles to profl. jours. Home: 249 E 48th New York NY 10017 Office: 110 Livingston Brooklyn NY 11201

ABBOTT, ROSALIE BOUCHER, nurse; b. Nashua, N.H., July 29, 1947; d. Laurent Urbain and Clemence Marie (Levesque) Boucher; m. Ronald Marvin Hart, Dec. 31, 1946 (div. 1972); 1 child, Braj Erik; m. John William Abbott; children: Bianca Jane-Marie, Charla-John. Diploma, Catherine Laboure Sch. Nursing, Boston, 1968; BA, Goddard Coll., 1978. RN, Fla., Mass., Pa., Colo. Charge nurse Cambridge (Mass.) City Hosp., 1968-69; o.r. nurse Providence Hosp., Washington, 1969; staff nurse Mercy Hosp., Miami, Fla., 1969; pvt. duty staff Mass. Gen. Hosp., 1972-78; nurse Med. Personnel Pool, Colorado Springs, 1979-80; home health nurse Guardian Healthcare, Naples, Fla., 1986—, Healthcare Personnel, Naples, 1987—; coord. nurses registry Morning Star Nursing Service, Naples, 1988-89; nurse Naples Community Hosp., 1989—; tng. aides, orderlies Cambridge (Mass.) City Hosp., 1969; health cons. div. psychiatry, Mass. Gen. Hosp., Boston, 1972; inst. water safety Jewish Community Ctr., Pitts. Author numerous poems. Safety instr. YWCA, Portland, Maine, 1972-74; chief polit. aide Sen. Joseph Brennan, Portland, 1974; nurse, guidance counselor Camp Susan Curtis, Greenfield, Maine, 1975; coord. Good Day Natural Food Market, Portland, 1973; assoc. bd. mem. Shelter for Abused Women Collier County, Naples, 1989; mem. Scholar Bowl; vol. Fla. Regional Writing Contest. Recipient cert. of merit Poetry Soc. N.H., 1965; named Jr. Great Books Vol. Sunday Sch. Tchr. Unity of Naples, 1990. Mem. AAUW (shelter liaison 1989), Fla. Bd. Realtors, Creative Writing Club (chmn. 1988—). Republican. Home: 1376 11th St N Naples FL 33942

ABBOTT, SHELLEY (ABOUDÉ), writer, business consultant; b. Glens Falls, N.Y., Aug. 10, 1954; d. Samuel and Betty Emma (Rock) Abbott; children: Timothy Abbott, Samantha Abbott. Grad. high sch., Glens Falls. Editor, mgr. TV Data Inc., Glens Falls, 1974-76; computer data entry Off Track Betting, Schenectady, N.Y., 1976-77; columnist United Media Syndicate, N.Y.C., 1974-86, UPI, N.Y.C., 1975—; owner, pres. The Enterprise, Glens Falls, 1974—; lectr. schs. and orgns., N.Y., 1980—; advt. cons. to bus., N.Y., 1984—; cons. Psychic Research Library, Lake George, N.Y., 1985-87, various bus. orgns. Contbr.: (cartoons) Harness Horseman Internat., 1978-81, There Ought To Be a Law, 1980-85; columnist Off Track Betting Newsletter, 1978—; writer short stories, also articles for newspapers and mags.; hostess numerous city homeshows, N.Y., 1985. Mem. Cornell U. Feline Health Ctr. Mem. NAFE, N.Y. State Mus. Assn., Smithsonian Assocs., Assn. for Retarded Children, New Eng. Anti-Vivesect. Soc., Nat. Humane League, State Humane League, Greenpeace. Democrat. Roman Catholic. Avocations: breeding Siamese cats, international travel. Office: The Enterprise PO Box 905 Glens Falls NY 12801

ABBOTT, SUSAN ALICIA, teacher; b. Easton, Pa., July 8, 1947; d. Solomon and Edith Mae (Cooper) Bergstein; m. William Walter Wood, Aug. 28, 1971 (div. Mar. 1975); m. Karl Richard Abbott, Feb. 19, 1977; 1 child, Tracie Ellen. BA in Psychology, Pa. State U., 1969; MS in Edn., Nazareth Coll. of Rochester, N.Y., 1976. Cert. nursery and spl. edn. tchr., N.Y. Tchr. Penn Yan (N.Y.) Cen. Schs., 1970; learning disabilities tchr. Wayne-Finger Lakes Bd. Coop. Schs., Stanley, N.Y., 1970-79; spl. edn. tchr. Victor (N.Y.) Cen. Schs., 1979—; tchr. rep. com. on the handicapped Com. of Spl. Edn., Victor, 1987—; dist. coord. spl. edn. program Victor Cen. Schs., 1987—. Mem. Sta. WXXI Pub. TV, Rochester, 1978—; leader Girl Scouts U.S., Fairport, N.Y., 1987-88, 88—; chairperson publicity program Seneca Zool. Soc., Rochester, 1974-77, bd. dirs., 1975-78. Mem. Monroe County Learning Disabilities Assn., N.Y. State Assn. Learning Disabilities, Internat. Assn. Children and Adults with Learning Disabilities, Victor Tchrs. Assn., N.Y. State United Tchrs, Psi Chi. Democrat. Home: 58 Alina St Fairport NY 14450 Office: Victor Cen Schs 953 High St Victor NY 14564

ABDELLAH, FAYE GLENN, retired public health service executive; b. N.Y.C., Mar. 13, 1919; d. H.B. and Margaret (Glenn) A. BS in Teaching, Columbia U., 1945, MA in Teaching, 1947, EdD, 1955; LLD (hon.), Case Western Res. U., 1967, Rutgers U., 1973; DSc (hon.), U. Akron, 1978, Cath. U. Am., 1981, Monmouth Coll., 1982, Ea. Mich U., 1987, U. Bridgeport, 1987, Georgetown U., 1989; D Pub. Svc. (hon.), Am. U., 1987; LHD (hon.), Georgetown U., 1989. RN. Commd. officer USPHS, Rockville, Md., 1949, advanced through grades to rear adm., 1970, asst. surgeon gen., chief nurse officer, 1970-87, dep. surgeon gen., 1981-89, chief nursing edn. br., div. nursing, 1949-59; chief research grants br. Bur. Health Manpower Edn., NIH, HEW, Rockville, 1959-69; dir. Office Research Tng. Nat. Ctr. for Health Services Research and Devel., Health Services Mental Health Adminstrn., Rockville, 1969; acting dep. dir. Nat. Ctr. for Health Services Research and Devel., Rockville, 1971, Bur. Health Services Research and Evaluation, Health Resources Adminstrn., Rockville, 1973; dir. Office Long-Term Care, Office Asst. Sec. for Health, HEW, Rockville, 1973-80. Author: Effect of Nurse Staffing on Satisfactions with Nursing Care, 1959, Patient Centered Approaches to Nursing, 1960, Better Patient Care Through Nursing Research, 1965, 2d edit., 1979, 3d edit., 1986, Intensive Care, Concepts and Practices for Clinical Nurse Specialists, 1969, New Directions in Patient Centered Nursing, 1972; Contbr. articles to profl. jours. Recipient Mary Adelaide Nutting award, 1983, hon. recognition Am. Nurses Assn., 1986, Outstanding Leadership award U. Pa., 1987, 88, Disting. Svc. award, 1973, 89, Surgeon Gen.'s medal and medallion, 1989, Allied-Signal Achievement award in aging, 1989. Fellow Am. Acad. Nursing (charter, past v.p., pres.); mem. Am. Psychol. Assn., AAAS, Assn. Mil. Surgeons U.S., Sigma Theta Tau (Disting. Rsch. Fellow award 1989), Phi Lambda Theta. Home: 3713 Chanel Rd Annandale VA 22003

ABDERHOLDEN, SUSAN, association executive; b. Chgo., Sept. 10, 1954; d. Edward Robert and Dolores Janet (Raila) A.; m. Lee Joseph Keller, Oct. 25, 1980; children: Ona Abderholden Keller, Eva Abderholden Keller. BA, Macalester Coll., St. Paul, 1976; MPH, U. Minn., 1980. Planner Minn. Dept. Health, Mpls., 1980-81; dir. pub. affairs Assn. Retarded Citizens Minn., Mpls., 1981-83, assoc. dir., 1983-87, exec. dir., 1987—; mem. Gov.'s Interagy. Coun., St. Paul, 1987—; mem. Commrs. Adv. Com. on Developmental Disabilities, St. Paul, 1983—. Pres. Twin Cities NOW, MPls., 1979-81; chairperson 61st Dist. Dem. Farm Labor, Mpls., 1985-90. Named Outstanding Prof. Nat. Coun. Execs. of Assn. for Retarded Citizens, 1989. Mem. Assn. Persons with Severe Handicaps, Nat. Women's Polit. Caucus, Advocating Change Together, Am. Asns. Mental Retardation, Citizens League. Democrat. Roman Catholic. Home: 3444 46th Ave S Minneapolis MN 55406 Office: Assn Retarded Citizens Minn 3225 Lyndale Ave S Minneapolis MN 55408

ABDO, BEVERLY VIRGINIA, public relations professional; b. Mexico City, Oct. 5, 1954; came to U.S., 1983; d. Albert Richard and Joanne (Pardue) A.; m. Richard Collazo, Nov. 19, 1983 (div. 1990); 1 child, Adrienne Elena. BA in Simultaneous Translation, Nat. Autonomous U. Mex., 1976. Account exec. Arouesty and Assocs., Mexico City, 1976-78; account exec. J. Walter Thompson, Mexico City, 1978-80, dir., 1981-83; account supr. Garcia Patto and Assocs., Mexico City, 1980; sr. account exec. N.W. Ayer-Ayer Pub. Rels., N.Y.C., 1984-85; community rels. mgr. 7Up-RC Bottling Co. (div. Westinghouse), L.A., 1987-89; account supr. GCI Group, L.A., 1989—. Bd. dirs. UCLA Mex. Arts series, 1988-90; steering com. YWCA, L.A., 1989; adv. com. L.A. County Mus. Arts, 1990. Recipient Silver Anvil award Pub. Rels. Soc. Am., 1985. Mem. LWV (chair pub. rels. com. 1990).

ABDOO, ANGELA FONTANA, small business owner; b. Bklyn., June 24, 1941; d. Louis and Mary (Acciarito) Fontana; m. Charles David Abdoo, Jan.

17, 1979 (div. 1984). Student, Bklyn. Coll., 1960-62. Adminstrv. asst. North Am. Rockwell, Anaheim, Calif., 1965-67; psychiat. technician Fairview State Hosp., Costa Mesa, Calif., 1967-68; typographer Wells Graphics, Bklyn., 1978-80, Down to Bus. Advt., Bklyn., 1980-82; owner Taurus Typesetters, Bklyn., 1982—. Recipient 1st Place award Columbia Scholastic Press Assn., N.Y.C., 1986, 87. Republican. Roman Catholic. Office: Taurus Typesetters 5005 Ave M Brooklyn NY 11234

ABEL, FLORENCE CATHERINE HARRIS, social worker; b. Phila., Dec. 28, 1941; d. Wilber Fiske and Melda Elizabeth (Beitzel) Harris; m. David Lynn Abel, Jan. 22, 1983. B.S., High Point (N.C.) Coll., 1963; M.S.W., U. Md., 1972. Diplomate in Clin. Social Work. Social work asst. Calvert County (Md.) Dept. Social Services, Prince Frederick, 1964-69; social work asst. Prince George's County (Md.) Dept. Social Service, Hyattsville, 1969-71; social worker Md. Children's Aid and Family Service, Towson, Md., 1972-80, Crownsville (Md.) Hosp. Center, 1980-86; field instr. U. Md. Sch. Social Work, 1985-86; chairperson Social Work Peer Rev. Com., 1982-83; cons. Contact Balt., 1974-79; counselor Family Life Center, Columbia, Md., 1974-80; mem. citizens adv. council N.W. Mental Health Balt. County, 1977-78. sec. bd. dirs. Christian Counseling Assocs., Columbia, 1978—, family therapist, 1980—; mem. Faith at Work Team, Columbia, 1973-75, Calvert County Commn. on Aging, 1967-68, Evang. Women's Caucus, Washington, 1976—, N.W. Coalition Social Agys., Balt. County, 1978; Author: The Beitzel Family a History of hte Descendants of John George Beitzel, 1986. cons. Nursing Home Ministry Evang. Presbyn. Ch., Annapolis, Md., 1978. Vice pres., treas. bd. dirs. Wheaton Animal Hosp., Inc., Kensington, Md. Lic. cert. social worker, Md. Mem. Nat. Assn. Social Workers, Register Clin. Social Workers, Assn. Certified Social Workers, Md. Conf. Social Concern, Christian Assocs. for Psychol. Studies. Democrat. Presbyterian. Home: 120 Hedgewood Dr Greenbelt MD 20770 Office: Stevens Forest Profl Bldg 9630 Santiago Rd Suite 101 Columbia MD 21045

ABELES, FRANCINE, mathematics and computer science educator; children: Edward, Jennifer, Evelyn. MS in Computer Sci., Stevens Inst., Hoboken, N.J., 1986. Prof. math. and computer sci. Kean Coll. N.J. (formerly Newark State Coll.), Union. Editor: The Mathematical Pamphlets of Lewis Carroll, 1990. Mem. Am. Math. Soc., Math. Assn. Am., Assn. Computing Machinery, Can. Soc. History and Philosophy of Math., Lewis Carroll Found. (bd. dirs. 1989—), Lewis Carroll Soc. (treas. 1989—), Phi Beta Kappa, Phi Kappa Phi. Office: Dept Math/Computer Sci Kean Coll NJ Union NJ 07083

ABELL, MILLICENT DEMMIN, university library administrator; b. Wichita, Kans., Feb. 15, 1934; d. Frederic Albert and Euphemia Millicent (Brown) Demmin; m. Julian Leo Abell, June 16, 1962; 1 son, Frederic Julian. B.A. in Psychology, Colo. Coll., 1956; M.A. in Personnel, Columbia U., 1958; M.L.S., SUNY, Albany, 1965; M.A. in Polit. Sci. U. Colo., 1969. Reference librarian U.S. Mil. Acad., West Point, N.Y., 1964-65, Penrose Public Library, Colorado Springs, Colo., 1966-68; asst. librarian Bus. Adminstrn. Library, U. Wash., Seattle, 1969-71; asst. dir. libraries U. Wash., 1971-73; assoc. dir. univ. libraries SUNY, Buffalo, 1973-76; univ. librarian U. Calif., San Diego, 1977-85, Yale U., 1985—; bd. dirs. Center for Research Libraries, 1979-86, chmn., 1984-85; bd. govs. Research Libraries Group, 1985—, mem. exec. com., 1986—. Mem. editorial bd.: Jour. Acad. Librarianship, 1974-76; assoc. editor: Library Research, 1978-82; contbr. articles to profl. jours. Mem. Assn. Coll. and Research Libraries (dir. 1976-78, 79-86, pres. 1980-81), Assn. Research Libraries (dir. 1979-83, pres. 1981-82), ALA (council 1983-86). Office: Yale U Sterling Meml Libr 120 High St PO Box 1603A Yale Sta New Haven CT 06520

ABELLA, MARISELA CARLOTA, business executive; b. Havana, Cuba, Feb. 5, 1943; d. Carlos and Angela (Acosta) Abella; m. Alberto Herrera Nogueira, Apr. 6, 1968 (div. Apr. 1986); 1 child, Carlos Alberto Herrera Abella. Asst. to v.p. and gen. mgr. bonding dept. Manuel San Juan (P.R.) Co. Inc., 1962-64; asst. corp. sec. and exec. sec. to pres. and stockholder Interstate Gen. Corp., Hato Rey, P.R., 1964-72, corp. sec. and pvt. sec. to corp. pres., 1972-79; sec.-treas., dir. A. H. Enterprises Inc., Caparra Heights, P.R., 1979-86; v.p., sec., bd. dirs. El Viajero Inc.; bd. dirs. A. H. Enterprises Inc., San Juan; pres. Marisela Abella Mktg. and Selling Promotional Items and Ideas, Caparra Heights, 1986—. Roman Catholic. Clubs: Caribe Hilton Swimming and Tennis, Barry U. Alumnae Assn. Home: 909 Borinquen Towers 2 Caparra Heights PR 00920 Office: PO Box 10510 Caparra Heights PR 00922

ABERCROMBIE, VIRGINIA TOWNSEND, writer; b. Houston, Dec. 24, 1927; d. F. Lee and Yvonne (Burghard) Townsend; m. John B. Abercrombie, Apr. 1, 1950; children: Virginia Lee, John B. Jr., Gilchreas T. BA, U. Tex., 1950. Founder Brown Rabbit Press, Houston, 1979—. Poetry published in Mississippi Arts and Letter, Poem, Roanoke Rev., Sam Houston Lit. Rev., Bluegrass Lit. Rev., Pudding, Midway Rev. 5, Rising Star, Madison Rev., others; co-author: Catering in Houston, 1977, Places to Take a Crowd in Houston, 1979, Catering to Houston, 1981, Party File, 1986; co-editor: (poem anthology) Christmas in Texas, 1979. Social dir. women's aux. Houston Bar Assn., 1975-76, pres., 1976-77; mem. juried Reading, 1988, S.W. Literary Coun., 1989. Recipient Honorable Mention Houston Poetry Festival, 1988. Clubs: Houston Country, Jr. League (puppet chmn.). Avocations: painting, sculpture. Home: 3 Smithdale Ct Houston TX 77024

ABERNATHY, BARBARA EUBANKS, counselor; b. Mobile, Ala., Aug. 28, 1963; d. Hardy Millard and Sarah Louise (Pate) Eubanks; m. James Abernathy Jr., Dec. 15, 1984. BS, Northwestern U., 1984; MS, U. South Ala., 1986. Mental health worker 11 Charter Southland Hosp., Mobile, 1985-86; counselor Indian River Community Mental Health, Ft. Pierce, Fla., 1986-87; family counselor Youth Svc. Bur., Palm Beach County, Fla., 1987—; behavior mgmt. cons. Okeechobee (Fla.) Sch. System, 1987; cons. Palm Beach County Sch. Bd., 1989—; instr. Palm Beach Community Coll., 1990—. Counselor Rape Crisis Ctr., Mobile, 1985-86, Contact Mobile, 1985-86; troop leader Girl Scouts of Chgo., 1982-84. Named one of Outstanding Young Women of Am., 1987. Mem. Am. Psychol. Assn., Am. Assn. Counseling and Devel., Kappa Delta Pi. Office: Palm Beach County Youth Svc Bur 4210 Australian Ave West Palm Beach FL 33407

ABERNATHY, VICKI MARIE, nurse; b. L.A., Feb. 14, 1949; d. James David and Margaret Helen (Quider) Abernathy; m. Dirk Klaus Ernst Wiese, Aug. 14, 1968 (div. 1973); 1 child, Zoë Erde; m. Gary Yoshiaki Handa, Nov. 15, 1985 (div. 1989). Student, U. Calif., Riverside, 1966-67, L.A. City Coll., 1968-69; AA in Nursing, Riverside City Coll., 1971-74. RN, Calif. Staff nurse Riverside County Hosp., 1974, Oceanside (Calif.) Community Hosp., 1974-76; with Scripps Hosp., Encinitas, Calif., 1976—; unit coord. Surgery Ctr. Scripps Hosp., Encinitas, 1981—. Mem. Calif. Nurses Assn., ACLU, Christic Inst., San Diego Zool. Soc. Parents Assn. Democrat.

ABERNETHY, VIRGINIA DEANE, population and environment educator; b. Havana, Cuba, Oct. 4, 1934; d. Bernard Charles and Helen Adele (Arnold) Deane; m. John Benjamin Kendrick II, 1955 (div.); children: Hugh C., Jack B. III, Helen D. Kendrick Campbell, Diana C.; m. C. Gregory Smith, Jr., Dec. 24, 1980. BA, Wellesley (Mass.) Coll., 1955; MA, PhD, Harvard U., 1970; MBA, Vanderbilt U., 1981. Rsch. assoc. Harvard Med. Sch., Boston, 1971-72, assoc. in psychiatry anthropology, 1972-75; asst. prof. Vanderbilt Med. Sch., Nashville, 1975-76, assoc. prof., 1976-80, prof. psychiatry anthropology, 1980—; dir. studies in population and family Harvard Med. Sch., 1972-75, dir. med. ethics symposium Vanderbilt Med. Sch., Nashville, 1979, dir. health care resources symposium, 1984; fellow Vanderbilt Inst. for Pub. Policy Studies, Nashville, 1985—. Editor-in-chief Population & Environment, 1988; author: Population Pressure and Cultural Adjustment, 1979; editor, author Frontiers in Medical Ethics, 1980; contbr. articles to books and profl. jours. Bd. dirs. Carrying Capacity Network, Washington, 1989—, Fossil Fuels Policy Action Inst., Fredericksburg, Va., 1989—, Population-Environ. Balance, Washington, 1988—; adv. bd., chair Murphy Sch. for Pregnant Teenagers, Nashville, 1976-79. Fellow Am. Anthropology Assn.; m. AAAS, Sigma Xi (exec. com. 1986). Republican. Home: 6501 Grayson Ct Nashville TN 37205 Office: Vanderbilt Med Sch Dept Psychiatry Nashville TN 37232

ABITANTA, JANE N., bank executive; b. Summit, N.J.. BA in Econs. and Polit. Sci., U. Del., 1980; MBA in Fin. and Investment Mgmt., Fordham U., 1985. Intern to Sen. Joseph R. Biden Jr. U.S. Senate, Wilmington, Del., 1979-80; rsch. asst. to pres. Bus. Environ. Risk Info., Ltd., Long Beach, Calif., 1976-80; investment officer Citicorp Investment Mgmt., Inc., N.Y.C., 1981-86; v.p. Bessemer Trust Co., N.A., N.Y.C., 1986-88, Swiss Bank Corp., N.Y.C., 1988—. Del. Emerging Leaders program Am. Ctr. for Internat. Leadership US-USSR, Dallas, 1989, mem. banking and fin. commn., summit conf., Moscow, 1990; dir. Fgn. Policy Assn. Profls. Group, 1987. Mem. Assn. Investment Mgmt. Sales Execs., Fin. Women's Assn. N.Y. Office: Swiss Bank Corp 608 Fifth Ave New York NY 10020

ABLES, JO ANGELA, lawyer; b. Ada, Okla., Jan. 23, 1950; d. A.J. and George Ann (McKoy) A.; B.A., East Central U., Ada, 1972; J.D., Oklahoma City U., 1975. Bar: Okla. 1976, U.S. Dist. Ct. (no. dist.) Okla. 1976, U.S. Ct. Appeals (10th cir.) 1978, U.S. Dist. Ct. (we. dist.) Okla. 1982, U.S. Supreme Ct. 1984. Mem. staff Carl Albert, Speaker of Ho. of Reps., Washington, 1968-70; administrv. asst. to atty. gen. State of Okla., Oklahoma City, 1972-75, asst. atty. gen., 1976-78; asst. gen. counsel Okla. Ins. Commn., Oklahoma City, 1978-79, asst. ins. Commr., 1979-80, dep. ins. commr., 1980-84; mem. firm Kerr, Irvine & Rhodes, 1985—; arbitrator U.S. Dist. Ct. (we. dist.) Okla. Chmn. credentials com. Democratic Party, Oklahoma City, 1980; trustee East Central U. Found., Ada, 1982—. Recipient Outstanding Alumna award East Central U., 1983. Mem. Okla. Bar Assn. (sch. com. 1983—), East Central U. Alumni Assn. (pres. 1982), Chi Omega. Methodist. Office: Kerr Irvine & Rhodes 600 Bank of Okla Pla Oklahoma City OK 73102*

ABNEY, BOBBIE JEAN, financial administrator; b. Ft. Worth, Jan. 3, 1933; d. Joe M. and Minnie M. (Mead) Williams; m. Louis E. Castell, Feb. 24, 1951 (div. 1963); children: Teresa Castell Little, Louis E. Jr.; m. Paul M. Abney, Oct. 9, 1964. Student, Victoria Jr. Coll., 1950-52, Durham Bus. Coll., 1963-64, LaSalle Coll., 1968-70. Acct. Sage Investments, Corpus Christi, Tex., 1970-71; comptroller Barshop Hotel, Inc., Houston, 1971-78; fin. mgr. Charter Oil Co., Livingston, Tex., 1978-84; br. mgr. Security Fin. Corp. Tex., Livingston, 1985—. Active Girl Scouts U.S., Livingston, 1986—, Livingston Parent-Tchr. Orgn., 1986—. Mem. NAFE, Bus. and Profl. Women's Club (treas. 1986-88, v.p. 1989-90, Woman of Yr. award 1987), Am. Legion Aux. Democrat. Mem. Ch. of Christ. Home: PO Box 1359 Livingston TX 77351 Office: Security Fin Corp 613 N Washington St Livingston TX 77351

ABORN, CARLENE MELLO, media specialist, consultant; b. Fall River, Mass., Jan. 2, 1932; d. Joseph Richard and Henrietta (Aragao) Mello; m. Dale Humphrey Aborn, Aug. 1, 1953; children: Roni, Scott, Keith. BA in Edn., Avila Coll., Kansas City, Mo., 1964; MA, U. South Fla., 1969. Tchr. Mo. Sch. Bd., Lee's Summit, 1964-69; media specialist Pinellas County Sch. Bd., Clearwater, Fla., 1970-78; media dir. Sch. Bd. Pinellas County, Clearwater, 1980—; Washington corr. Nat. Opinion Mag., San Jose, Calif., 1977-80; cons. Wollensak div. 3M, St. Paul, 1978-81; cons. Fla. Dept. Edn., Tallahassee, 1975-78, Griffin (Ga.) County Sch. Bd., 1987. Editor: Fla. Media Quar., 1978-80; contbr. articles to ednl. jours. and mag. Vol. ARC, Pinellas County, Fla., 1984. Recipient John Cotton Dana P.R. award ALA and H.W. Wilson Co., 1975, 85; named Outstanding Educator Pinellas County, Fla., 1976, 86. Mem. ALA (John Cotton Dana award 1975, 85), Fla. Assn. Media Educators (publs. bd. 1969—), Pinellas County Tchr.'s Assn., Pinellas County Assn. Library Media Educators, Assn. Ednl. Communication Tech. Home: 9425 Blind Pass Rd #908 Saint Petersburg Beach FL 33706 Office: Osceola High Sch 9751 98th St Seminole FL 34647

ABRAHAM, GAIL DEANA, municipal finance administrator; b. Havre De Grace, Md., May 7, 1945; d. David and Jean Sylvia (Kalata) Newman; m. Alfredo G. Abraham, Apr. 28, 1972 (div. 1978); m. Robert Maurice Lange, May 15, 1984. AS, Eastern Coll., 1967; BSBA, U. Balt., 1969; MS in Health Care Mgmt., Fla. Internat. U., 1975. Adminstrv. asst. Palmetto Gen. Hosp., Hialeah, Fla., 1976-77, Biscayne Med. Ctr., North Miami Beach, Fla., 1977-78; cons. Automated Packing and Crating, Hialeah, 1978-79; fin. mgr. Up Front, Inc., Coconut Grove, Fla., 1979-81; internal auditor City of Miami Beach, 1981-82, acct. II, 1982-83, asst. to fin. dir., 1983-84; fin. cons. Brandon, Conn., 1984-86; fin. dir. Town of Plainville, Conn., 1986-87, City of West Melbourne, Fla., 1987—; program chmn. Brevard County (Fla.) Mcpl. Fin. Officers, 1987—; rep. Brevard County League of Cities, 1987—; rev. com. G.F.O.A. Disting. Budget Award Program, 1989. Adv. bd. Dade County Sch.-Drug Prevention Program, 1981; com. mem. Audubon Elem. PTO, Merritt Island, Fla., 1989. Mem. Fla. Govt. Fin. Officers Assn., Govt. Fin. Officers Assn. U.S. and Can. (cert. achievement in fin. reporting 1987). Republican. Jewish. Home: 1705 Porpoise St Merritt Island FL 32952 Office: City of West Melbourne 2285 Minton Rd West Melbourne FL 32904

ABRAHAM, IRENE, biologist; b. Chgo., Dec. 12, 1946; d. Isadore and Ruth (Terry) A.; m. W. Wayne Franklin, 1973 (div. 1975); m. Gabriel Vogeli, May 26, 1976; children: Greta, Noah. BS, U. Ill., 1968; PhD, U. N.C., 1973. Asst. prof. Emory U., Atlanta, 1975-76; postdoctoral fellow U. Berne, Switzerland, 1976-78; rsch. biologist NIH, Bethesda, Md., 1979-84, sr. staff fellow, 1984; rsch. scientist The Upjohn Co., Kalamazoo, 1984—; postdoctoral fellow Yale U., New Haven, Conn., 1973-75. Author: (with others) DNA-Mediated Gene Transfer in Mammalian Cells, 1985; contbr. articles to profl. jours. Fellow NSF, 1968-72, NIH 1973-75. Mem. AAAS, Am. Soc. Cell Biology, Soc. Neurosci., Sigma Xi. Office: The Upjohn Co 301 Henrietta St Kalamazoo MI 49001

ABRAHAMSON, SHIRLEY SCHLANGER, state supreme court justice; b. N.Y.C., Dec. 17, 1933; d. Leo and Ceil (Sauerteig) Schlanger; m. Seymour Abrahamson, Aug. 26, 1953; 1 son, Daniel Nathan. AB, NYU, 1953; JD, Ind. U., 1956; SJD, U. Wis., 1962. Bar: Ind. 1956, N.Y. 1961, Wis. 1962. Asst. dir. Legis. Drafting Research Fund, Columbia U. Law Sch., 1957-60; since practiced in Madison, Wis., 1960-76; mem. firm LaFollette, Sinykin, Anderson & Abrahamson, 1962-76; justice Supreme Ct. Wis., Madison, 1976—; prof. U. Wis. Sch. Law, 1966—, currently on leave; Mem. Wis. Bd. Bar Commrs.; mem. adv. bd. Nat. Inst. Justice, U.S. Dept. Justice, 1980-82; mem. Mayor's Adv. Com., Madison, 1968-70, Gov.'s Study Com. on Jud. Orgn., 1970-72; bd. visitors Ind. U. Sch. Law, 1972—, U. Miami Sch. Law, 1982—, U. Chgo. Law Sch., 1988—, Brigham Young U. Sch. Law, 1986-88, Northwestern U. Law Sch., 1989—; bd. dirs. LWV, Madison, 1963-65. Editor: Constitutions of the United States (National and State) 2 vols, 1962. Mem. study group program of rsch., mental health and the law John D. and Catherine T. MacArthur Found., 1988—; mem. coun. fund for rsch. on dispute resolution Ford Found., 1987—; bd. dirs. Wis. Civil Liberties Union, 1968-72, chmn. Capital Area chpt., 1969. Mem. ABA (council, sect. of legal edn. and admissions to the bar 1976-86, mem. commn. on undergrad. edn. in law and the humanities 1978-79), Wis. Bar Assn., Dane County Bar Assn., 7th Cir. Bar Assn., Nat. Assn. Women Judges, Am. Law Inst. (coun. 1985—), Order of Coif, Phi Beta Kappa. Home: 2012 Waunona Way Madison WI 53713 Office: Wis Supreme Ct PO Box 1688 Madison WI 53701

ABRAM, ARLENE N., language educator; b. Pitts., Dec. 31, 1942; d. Attilio F. and Vera (Furlan) Natolino; m. George C. Abram, July 6, 1968; children: Michelle, Michael. BA, Duquesne U., 1964, MEd, 1987. French and Spanish tchr. Woodland Hills Sch., Pitts., 1980-90; tchr. Community Coll., Pitts., 1983-88. Allegheny Bus. grantee, 1983, 85, 87, 90. Mem. Pa. State Educators Assn.

ABRAM, MARIAN CHRISTINE, lawyer; b. Avon Lake, Ohio, May 22, 1958; d. Joseph Andrew and Albina Marie (Zadnik) A. BS magna cum laude, Case Western Res. U., 1980, MSSA, 1983, JD, 1983. Bar: Ohio 1983, U.S. Dist. Ct. (no. dist.) Ohio 1984, U.S. Ct. Appeals (6th cir.) 1984. Assoc. Walter, Haverfield, Buescher and Chockley, Cleve., 1983—. Mem. ABA, Ohio Bar Assn., Cleve. Bar Assn., Am. Mut. Lodge Assn., Slovenian Lodge No. 20. Office: Walter Haverfield Boescher & Chockley 1215 Terminal Tower Cleveland OH 44113

ABRAM, PRUDENCE BEATTY, federal judge; b. Kingston, R.I., Nov. 19, 1942; d. Kenneth Orion and Mary Catharine (Carter) Beatty; m. Sam Laud Abram, Dec. 21, 1968; 1 dau., Andrea Beatty. B.A., U. Mich., 1964, J.D. cum laude, 1968. Bar: Mich. 1969, N.Y. 1971, U.S. Dist. Ct. for so. dist. N.Y. 1972, U.S. Dist. Ct. for eastern dist. N.Y. 1972, U.S. Ct. Appeals for 2d circuit 1972, U.S. Supreme Ct. 1979. Assoc. firm Breed Abbott & Morgan, N.Y.C., 1970-72, Weil Gotshal & Manges, N.Y.C., 1972-78, Krause, Hirsch & Gross, N.Y.C., 1978-79; ptnr. firm Stroock & Stroock & Lavan, N.Y.C., 1980-82; judge U.S. Bankruptcy Ct. for So. Dist. N.Y., N.Y.C., 1982—. Mem. ABA. Office: US Bankruptcy Ct US Custom House 6th Fl One Bowling Green New York NY 10004-1408

ABRAMOWITZ, ANN JACOFF, clinical psychologist; b. Bklyn., Aug. 27, 1948; d. Hyman and Florence (Schachnowitz) Jacoff; m. Alan Ira Abramowitz, Aug. 24, 1969; children: Seth, Jeremy. BA, U. Rochester, 1970; MA, U. Oreg., 1974, SUNY, Stony Brook, 1985; PhD, SUNY, Stony Brook, 1988. Lic. psychologist, Ga.; cert. tchr., Calif., Va. Child therapist Peninsula Children's Ctr., Palo Alto, Calif., 1970-73; tchr. San Jose (Calif.) Unified Sch. Dist., 1974-76; program coord. Norge Early Edn. and Devel. Ctr. Williamsburg (Va.) James City County Schs., 1976-78, coord. spl. edn., 1978-81; coord., programs for emotionally disturbed Hampton (Va.) City Schs., 1981-82; psychology intern Emory U. Sch. Medicine, Atlanta, 1987-88, clin. psychologist and asst. prof., 1988—; cons. various sch. dists., Ga., 1989—; dir. summer day treatment program Egleston Hosp., Atlanta, 1988—. Contbr. articles to profl. jours. Mem. James City County Dem. Com., Va., 1980-82; bd. dirs. Coun. for Children's Svcs., Williamsburg, 1979-82. Grad. fellowship U. Oreg., 1973-74, NIMH, 1982-83, SUNY, 1983-87. Mem. Am. Psychol. Assn., Ga. Assn. for Behavior Analysis (sec. 1989—), Ga. Psychol. Assn., Assn. for Advancement of Behavior Therapy, Phi Delta Kappa (v.p. 1979-80). Office: Emory Clinic Psychiat Sect 1365 Clifton Rd NE Atlanta GA 30322

ABRAMS, ANNE, publicist; b. Bklyn., May 11, 1953; d. Sidney and B. Hilda (Langweber) A. BA, SUNY-Fredonia, 1974; MA, U. Kans., 1976. Program coordinator Hashinger Arts Ctr., Lawrence, Kans., 1974-77; artistic/mng. dir. Crown Uptown Theatre, Wichita, Kans., 1977-79; dir. student activities Dickinson Coll., Carlisle, Pa., 1979-80; asst. gen. mgr. Am. Theatre Prodns., N.Y.C., 1980-81; account exec., publicist Fred Nathan Co., N.Y.C., 1981-88; dir., founder Women's Resource Ctr., Carlisle, 1979-80; theatrical cons. and dir. Com. mem. Women in Bus. Against Cancer, Am. Cancer Soc., N.Y.C., 1983; bd. dirs. AIDS Resource Ctr., N.Y.C., 1986-87; ptnr. Browne-Abrams Pub. Relations, 1988—. Democrat. Avocations: cooking, antiques, swimming, writing.

ABRAMS, BARBARA ESMÉ KESSLER, clinical psychologist; b. N.Y.C., Mar. 1, 1927; d. Harry Kessler and Augusta E. Kessler (Rosenzweig) Weil; m. Emanuel J. Abrams, June 17, 1948; children: Zoe Beth Abrams Alley, Katy Lise Abrams Schmidt. BA cum laude, Radcliffe Coll., 1948; EdM, Harvard U., 1954. Lic. psychologist, Mass.; lic. sch. guidance counselor, Mass. Psychologist New Eng. Med. Ctr., Boston, 1950-53, Newton (Mass.) Pub. Schs., 1952-56; staff psychologist Metrowest Youth Guidance Ctr., Framingham, Mass., 1965—; pvt. cons. local sch. systems, Wayland, Hudson, Natick, Sherborn, Mass., 1970-88. Mem. League of Women Voters, Voice of Women, Natick Fair Housing, Common Cause. Mem. Mass. Psychol. Assn., Mass. Nurses Assn., NOW, Mass. Audobon Soc., Greenpeace. Home: 68 Harwood Rd Natick MA 01760 Office: Metrowest Youth Guidance 88 Lincoln St Framingham MA 01701

ABRAMS, CHERYL, nursing administrator; b. Morganfield, Ky., Aug. 28, 1955; d. Harrison and Agnes (Cooke) Horton; m. Randel S. Abrams, May 28, 1988; children: Ron, Samuel. MS in Nursing, Greenville (S.C.) Tech., 1982. Cert. med.-surgical nurse. Staff nurse pediatrics Bapt. Med. Ctr., Jacksonville, Fla.; staff nurse Wooduff Children's Hosp., Jacksonville, Riverside Hosp., Jacksonville, Fla.; head nurse nephrology, gastroenterology St. Francis Hosp., Greenville, S.C. Author: Fluids and Electrolytes. Bd. dirs. Kidney Found.; mem. Nat. Wildlife Fedn. Mem. SGA, ACOA, SEWE, Impaired Nurse Program, Physicians' Wifes' Aux., Sierra Club, Ducks Unltd. Republican. Pentecostal.

ABRAMS, DIANE KOBISHER, computer software sales executive, consultant; b. Bklyn., May 14, 1954; d. Richard and Rosalyn (Gursky) Kobisher; m. Gary Howard Abrams, Mar. 4, 1978; 1 child, Rory Matthew Charles. BBA, Bernard M. Baruch Coll., 1976. Exec. treas. Gary Stevens Designs, Inc., Bklyn., 1976-79; asst. buyer, buyer, mgr. Gimbel Bros. Dept. Store, N.Y.C., 1976-80; nat. sales mgr. Baby Care, Inc., N.Y.C., 1980-82; exec. saleswoman, regional mgr. Sales & Mktg. Resources, Inc., N.Y.C., 1982-84; exec. sales mgr. I.S. Furniture Rental, Inc., N.Y.C., 1984-86; exec. saleswoman Silton Apparel Mgmt. Systems, N.Y.C., 1986—; exec. sales mgr. Cressida Assocs., Inc., Haworth, N.J., 1988-89; sales exec. Resource Data Systems, Inc., N.Y.C., 1989—. Office: Resource Data Systems Inc 145 Hudson St New York NY 10013

ABRAMS, LORI, occupational health and safety specialist; b. Doylestown, Pa., Mar. 22, 1959; d. Charles Robert and Anne (Mask) A. BA in Biochemistry, Princeton U., 1981; MPhil, Yale U., 1983; postgrad., U. Mich., 1990—. Occupational health researcher Pub. Citizen Health Rsch. Group, Washington, 1983-87; occupational health and safety specialist Food & Allied Svc. Trades Dept., AFL-CIO, Washington, 1987-88, Am. Fedn. State, County and Mcpl. Employees, Washington, 1988-90. Vol. Project Northstar tutoring project, 1989—, Washington Free Clinic, 1987—. NIH grantee, 1981; Occupational Health Prog. fellow, U. Mass., 1986. Mem. Am. Pub. Health Assn., Princeton Alumni Assn. (schs. com.). Democrat.

ABRAMS, OUIDA THOMPSON, accountant; b. Meridian, Miss., Oct. 16, 1946; d. Edwin Isaac and Mildred Irene (Roebuck) Thompson; (div.); children: Lisa Renee Stephens, Amanda Joy Abrams. AA, Meridian (Miss.) Jr. Coll., 1967; BS, Miss. State U., 1982, MBA, 1989. Staff writer The Meridian (Miss.) Star, 1964; interior decorator Sears, Meridian, 1967-69; tchr. Miss. Action for Progress (Head Start), Meridian, 1970; office mgr., auditor M.H. Fishman Co., N.Y.C., Meridian, 1971-75; acct. Am. Can Co., Bellamy, Ala., 1982-88, Mitchell Distbg. Co., Inc., Meridian, 1989—; counselor, acct. Navy Relief Soc., Willow Grove, Pa., 1979-80; cons. First Bapt. Ch., C. of C., Meridian, 1988-89. Troop leader Girl Scouts U.S., Meridale coun., Meridian, Miss., 1974-75, 85-90, troop organizer, 1987-89; treas. Lauderdale County Humane Soc., 1988-89; founder Single Parents Action Alliance, Meridian, 1988-89; treas. Officers' Wives Club, Warminster, Pa., 1979-80. Recipient Spl. Achievment in Acctg. award, Nat. Assn. Accts., 1978; scholarship, Clairol Found., 1981, Avon Found., 1988. Republican. Southern Baptist. Home: 2812 Grandview Ave Meridian MS 39301 Office: Mitchell Distbg Co #2 49th Ave Meridian MS 39304

ABRAMS, ROBERTA BUSKY, nurse, hospital administrator; b. Bklyn., Feb. 16, 1937; d. Albert H. and Gladys Busky; m. Robert L. Abrams, June 28, 1959 (div. 1977); children: Susan Abrams Federman, David B. BSN, U. Rochester, 1959; MA, Fairfield U., 1977. Asst. head nurse Jewish Hosp., Bklyn., 1959-60; instr. medicine/surgery Bklyn. Hosp., 1960-62, U. Rochester, N.Y., 1963-64; instr. ob-gyn Malden (Mass.) Hosp. Sch. Nursing, 1965-66; instr. prospective parents ARC, San Rafael, Calif., 1968-69; instr. ob-gyn SUNY, Farmingdale, 1970-71; instr. maternal/child health Stamford (Conn.) Hosp., 1971-75; clinician maternal/child health Lawrence Hosp., Bronxville, N.Y., 1975-78; asst. prof. nursing Ohio Wesleyan U., Delaware, 1981-84; dir. Elizabeth Blackwell Hosp. at Riverside Meth., Columbus, Ohio, 1978-86; dir. nursing Henry Ford Hosp., Detroit, 1986-87, assoc. adminstr. nursing, 1988—; cons. maternal/child nursing currents Ross Labs., 1984-88; lectr. in field. Contbr. articles to profl. jours. Mem. Nurses Assn., Am. Coll. Obstreticians and Gynecologists (vice-chmn. Ohio chpt. 1984-87), Am. Soc. Psychoprophylaxis, Greater Detroit Orgn. Nurse Execs., LWV, Sigma Theta Tau. Home: 32478 Dunford Farmington Hills MI 48018 Office: Henry Ford Hosp 2799 W Grand Blvd Detroit MI 48202

ABRAMS, RUTH IDA, state justice; b. Boston, Dec. 26, 1930; d. Samuel and Matilda A. BA, Radcliffe Coll., 1953; LLB, Harvard U., 1956; hon. degree, Mt. Holyoke Coll., 1977, Suffolk U., 1977, New Eng. Sch. Law, 1978. Bar: Mass. 1957. Ptnr. Abrams Abrams & Abrams, Boston, 1957-60; asst. dist. atty. Middlesex County, Mass., 1961-69; asst. atty. gen. Mass., chief appellate sect. criminal div., 1969-71; spl. counsel Supreme Jud. Ct. Mass., 1971-72; assoc. justice Superior Ct. Commonwealth of Mass., 1972-77, Supreme Jud. Ct. Mass., Boston, 1977—; mem. Gov.'s Commn. on Child Abuse, 1970-71, Mass. Law Revision Commn. Proposed Criminal Code for Mass., 1969-71; trustee Radcliffe Coll., from 1981. Editor: Handbook for Law Enforcement Officers, 1969-71. Recipient Radcliffe Coll. Achievement award, 1976, Radcliffe Grad. Soc. medal, 1977. Mem. ABA (com. on proposed fed. code from 1977), Mass. Bar Assn., Am. Law Inst., Am.

Judicature Soc. (dir. 1978), Am. Judges Assn., Mass. Assn. Women Lawyers. Office: Supreme Ct 1412 New Courthouse Boston MA 02108*

ABRAMSON, ROBERTA B., lawyer; b. Newark, NJ, Mar. 9, 1937; d. Saul and Pearl (Barnett) B.; m. Burt S. Abramson, June 14, 1959; children: Beth, Risa, Maria. BS, Upsal Coll., 1957; JD, Rutgers U., 1981. Pvt. practice law Bridgewater, 1982-89. Author: Blue Donkey (English, Spanish) 1959. Mem. N.J. State Bar Assn., Phi Beta Kappa. Republican. Jewish.

ABRAMSON, ROCHELLE SUSAN, violinist; b. Detroit, Jan. 1, 1953; d. Seymour I. and Mayme (Tureck) A.; B.Mus., U. Mich., 1973; M.Mus., Juilliard Sch. Music, 1975, Profl. Studies degree, 1976. Founding mem. Trio N.Y., 1975-78, Muse-Arts Ensemble, Los Angeles, 1978—; 1st violin N.Y.C. Ballet Orch., 1976-78; 1st violin Los Angeles Philharmonic Orch., 1978—; founding mem. Trio Candide, 1984—. Recipient awards Artists Internat. Young Musicians Auditions, 1977, Nat. Fedn. Music Clubs Biennial String Competition, 1973, Stillman-Kelly String Competition, 1968, Nat. Arts Club, 1976, Palm Beach Flagler-Matthews Competition, 1974, Charleston Symphony Competition, 1976, Kingsport Symphony Competition, 1975, Talman Prize, Soc. Am. Musicians, 1975, Young Artist award Music Study Club Detroit, 1978. Home: 1231 N Ogden Dr Los Angeles CA 90046-4726 Office: care Los Angeles Philharm 135 N Grand Ave Los Angeles CA 90012

ABRAMS SACKS, JULIE BARNETT, management consultant; b. L.A., Dec. 5, 1960; d. Norman Abrams and Lois Barnett; m. David Bevier Sacks, June 25, 1989. BA, Oberlin Coll., 1982; MA in Internat. Studies, U. Pa., 1989, MBA, 1989. English lang. program rep. Time-Life Ednl. Systems, Tokyo, 1982; mgmt. cons. Baia Azul, Bahia, Brazil, 1983; employment counselor/job developer Howard Area Community Ctr., Chgo., 1983-84; mgr. for mktg. and devel. Women's World Banking, N.Y.C., 1985-87; fin. analyst Xerox do Brasil, Rio de Janeiro, 1988; mgmt. cons. strategic mgmt. svcs. Coopers & Lybrand, N.Y.C., 1989—; cons. Phila. Export Network, 1988-89. Fundraiser Wharton Summer Vol. Project, Phila., 1989. Lauder Inst. fellow U. Pa., 1987-89, Selected Professions fellow AAUW, 1988-89. Office: Coopers & Lybrand Strategic Mgmt Svcs 1251 Ave of the Americas New York NY 10020

ABREU, JUDITH ANN, broadcasting company executive; b. Franklin, Pa.; d. Dorothy Mozelle (Cast) Snyder; m. Ralph Francis Abreu, Nov. 16, 1974 (dec. 1980); children: Jennifer, Jessica. BA, U. Tex., 1966, MA, 1967; postgrad. NYU, 1978. Systems engr. IBM, Poughkeepsie, N.Y., 1968-70; sr. programmer Morgan Guaranty Co., N.Y.C., 1970-72; mgr. systems CBS, N.Y.C., 1972-76, dir. mgmt. info. systems edn., 1976-79, dir. systems assurance, 1979-83, dir. advanced office systems, 1983-89, sr. dir. office stsems, 1989—; cons. Vol. Urban Cons. group, N.Y.C., 1979—; bd. dirs. Berkeley Enterprises, Computers and People. Instr. English, Internat. Club, N.Y.C., 1970-74; speaker Open Doors, N.Y.C. Pub. Schs., 1981—; bd. dirs. Berkeley Enterprises; leader Hudson County coun. Girl Scouts U.S.A., 1985. Recipient Outstanding Community award Am. Biographical Inst., 1975. Mem. Office Info. Systems Forum (pres. 1983-84), Office Products Exch. Network (communications officer 1986-87, treas. 1988-89, pres. 1989-90), Assn. for Women in Computing, Office Products Exchange Network (treas. 1988—), U. Tex. Alumni Assn., Phi Mu (pres. 1978-80). Club: 500 (N.Y.C.). Home: 1004 Palisade Ave Union City NJ 07087 Office: CBS Inc 51 W 52d St New York NY 10019

ABREU, SUE HUDSON, physician, army officer; b. Indpls., May 24, 1956; d. M.B. Hudson and Wilma Hudson (Jones) Black; m. Michael H. Abreu, Dec. 24, 1979. B.S. in Engring., Purdue U., 1978; M.D., Uniformed Services U., 1982. Grad. U.S. Army Command & Gen. Staff Coll, 1988, Armed Forces Staff Coll., 1990. Commd. 2d lt. U.S. Army, 1978, advanced to maj., 1988; intern Walter Reed Army Med. Ctr., Washington, 1982-83, resident in diagnostic radiology, 1983-85, fellow in nuclear medicine, 1985-87, staff nuclear medicine physician, 1987-88, med. research fellow, 1988-89; dep. dir. U.S. Army Med. Rsch. Unit, Ft. Bragg, N.C., 1990—. Mem. Soc. Nuclear Medicine, Am. Coll. Nuclear Physicians, Soc. Women Engrs., Tau Beta Pi, Omicron Delta Kappa, Phi Kappa Phi. Avocations: calligraphy, sports. Home: 2055 Saddlebred Ln Raeford NC 28376 Office: Box 118 USAMEDDAC Fort Bragg NC 28307-5000

ABSHIER, SHIRLEY ANN, geologist; b. Vernon Center, N.Y., Oct. 19, 1936; d. Harry E. and Anna (Cuomo) Sauerhafer; BS, U. Tex., El Paso, 1969; m. Jon F. Abshier, Nov. 5, 1964; children: Debrah, Gerald, Thomas, Patricia. Social services welfare caseworker N.Mex. Health and Social Service Dept., Grants, 1969-72; petroleum geologist Mobil Oil Corp., Denver, 1973-80, editor Mobil Denver E & P Newspaper, 1979-80, mem. speakers' bur., 1979-80; sr. geologist Sunmark Oil Co., Denver, 1980-81; dist. geologist Trans-Tex. Energy, Inc., 1981-82; geol. cons., 1982-86; v.p. A-W Systems, Ltd., 1986—; pres., cons., indsl. hygienist Abshier & Assocs., 1986—; environ. specialist Mo. Dept. of Natural Resource, Dept. of Environ. Qualtiy, 1988—. Chmn., N.Mex. Crippled Childrens Assn., 1970-72; charter mem. Grants Boys Ranch, 1970-72; mem. N.Mex. Gov.'s Com. on Mental Health, 1970-72; Jefferson County rep. to Republican County Conv., 1976—. Mem. Am. Assn. Petroleum Geologists, Rocky Mountain Assn. Geologists, Profl. Geologist, Clear Creek County Mining and Metals Assn. Republican. Episcopalian. Editor: RMAG Guidebook, 1979; editor Mobil Messenger, 1979. Home and Office: 524 NE Malibu Dr Lee's Summit MO 64064

ABT, SYLVIA HEDY, dentist; b. Chgo., Oct. 7, 1957; d. Wendel Peter and Hedi Lucie (Wieder) A. Student, Loyola U., Chgo., 1975-77; cert. dental hygiene, Loyola U., Maywood, Ill., 1979, DDS, 1983. Registered dental hygienist. Dental asst. Office Dr. Baran and Dr. O'Neill, DDS, Chgo., 1977-78; dental hygienist Drs. Spiro, Sudakoff, Kadens, Weidman, DDS, Skokie, Ill., 1979-83, Dr. Laudando, DiFranco, Rosemont, Ill., 1980-83; gen. practice dentistry Chgo., 1983—. Vol. Community Health Rotations, VA Hosps., grammar schs., convalescent ctrs., mental health ctrs., Maywood, Ill. and Chgo., 1978-82. Recipient 1st Pl. award St. Apollonia Art Show Loyola U., 1982. Mem. ADA, Ill. Dental Soc., Chgo. Dental Soc., Loyola Dental Alumni Assn. (golf outing registration chmn. 1987, awards in golf and tennis 1987), Ill. Dentists 99th Club (legis. interest com.), Psi Omega (historian, editor Kappa chpt.). Office: 6509 W Higgins Chicago IL 60656

ABTS, GWYNETH HARTMANN, dietitian; b. Union, Ill., Oct. 31, 1923; d. William John and Olga Anna (Krause) Hartmann; m. Rufus Heath Jr., Apr. 6, 1942 (div. Dec. 1945); m. Harold Henry Abts, Feb. 14, 1948; children: Leigh, Michael, Patricia. BS, U. Ill., 1945; postgrad., U. Oreg., 1945-46, U. Ill., Elgin, 1957, No. Ill. U., 1966, 74, 82, 87. Registered dietitian. Clin. dietitian St. Joseph Hosp., Elgin, 1947; asst. dietitian French Hosp., San Francisco, 1948-50, Elgin State Hosp., 1950-58; dietary cons. Ill. Youth Commn., Springfield, 1958-70; food adminstr. Ill. Dept. of Corrections, Springfield, 1970-85; mem. Food and Nutrition Cou. on Govt. Commodities, Springfield, 1980-85; bd. dirs. Ill. Nutrition Assn., Urbana, 1983. Pres. PTO, Geneva, 1972. McHenry County Home Econ. scholar U. Ill., 1941-45. Mem. Am. Dietetic Assn. (citizens ambassador program to Australia and New Zealand), Fox Valley Home Economists, West Suburban Dietetic Assn., AAUW. Lutheran. Home: 1505 Dunstan Rd Geneva IL 60134

ABULS, LARISSA KLAVINS, management recruiter; b. Chgo., Oct. 4, 1962; d. Laimons and Kristine (Kaupas) Klavins; m. Peteris Roberts Abuls, Aug. 15, 1987. BS, Northwestern U., 1984. Asst. to the vice chancellor U. Ill., Chgo., 1985-87; account exec. Terri D. Ltd., Chgo., 1987-88, Group Travel Dirs., Inc., Chgo., 1988-89; Cook Assoc., 1989—; cons. U. Ill., Chgo., 1987—. Republican. Lutheran. Home: 5544 W Berteau Ave Chicago IL 60641

ACCORDINO, MARGARET SPILLANE, financial institution risk manager; b. Staten Island, N.Y., July 18, 1948; d. Joseph Bernard and Mary Catherine (Minogue) S.; m. Thomas Patrick Accordino, Aug. 7, 1971; 1 child, Mary Margaret. BA, Lemoyne Coll., 1970; grad., Richmond Coll., 1970. Rater Thos F. Street & Sons, Rochester, N.Y., 1976-78; ins. analyst Morgan Guaranty Trust Co., N.Y.C., 1978-80; risk mgr. Bank Hapoalim, N.Y.C., 1980-88; asst. v.p., dir. risk mgmt. Am. Express Bank Ltd., N.Y.C., 1988—; seminar leader Risk Ins. Mgmt. Soc., N.Y.C., 1986-87, Ins. Edn. Council of N.Y., 1989. Mem. Risk Ins. Mgmt. Soc. (pres. N.Y.C. chpt. 1989--), Ins. Edn. Coun. of N.Y. (sec. 1988-89). Democrat. Roman Catholic. Home: 219 Davis Ave Staten Island NY 10310 Office: Am Express Bank Ltd AmexTower World Fin Ctr New York NY 10285

ACCURSO, CATHERINE JOSEPHINE, asset manager; b. Kansas City, Mo., Jan. 3, 1955; d. Anthony Carl and Josephine Blaze (Mancuso) A.; m. Kenneth E. Deffenbaugh. Assoc. Liberal Arts, Penn Valley Community Coll., Kansas City, 1975; BFA, U. Kans., 1980. Sales Macy's Dept. Store, Kansas City, 1972-82; dept. mgr. Macy's Dept. Store, 1982, dir. bridal registry, 1982-85; asset mgr. Exec. Hills, Inc., Kansas City, 1985—. Mem. Kansas City Comets Connection (bd. dirs. 1984-87), Nat. Assn. Interior Designers. Home: 4014 Marshall Dr Independence MO 64055 Office: Exec Hills Inc 120 W 12th St Kansas City MO 64105

ACHBAR, FRANCINE, television producer, broadcasting executive; b. Ottawa, Ont., Can., Aug. 24, 1946; came to U.S. 1963; d. Benjamin and Marjorie Ruth (Sinclair) A.; m. Kenneth Schwarz, Aug. 30, 1970 (div. 1978); m. William B. Coughlin, June 5, 1983; children: Jessica Achbar Coughlin, Amy Achbar Coughlin. BS, Boston U., 1967. Reporter Fairchild Publs., Boston, 1967-68, Boston Herald Traveler, 1968-71; news producer Sta. WNAC-TV, Boston, 1972-76; assoc. producer Sta. WBZ-TV, Boston, 1971-72, exec. producer news, 1977, producer documentary programming, 1978-83, exec. producer programming, asst. program mgr., 1983—; nat. exec. producer Group W Broadcasting, Boston, 1988—; gov. NATAS, Boston, 1984-88. Co-developer nat. pub. svc. TV campaigns including For Kids' Sake, 1984 (George Foster Peabody award 1985), Time to Care, 1988. Recipient Emmy award NATAS, 1983, 84, 85, Iris award Nat. Assn. TV Program Execs., 1985-86, Dupont Columbia award Columbia U., 1984, Gabriel award Nat. Cath. Assn. for Broadcast, 1986, 88. Office: Sta WBZ-TV 1170 Soldiers Field Rd Boston MA 02134

ACITELLI, LINDA KATHERINE, research psychologist; b. Detroit, Mar. 30, 1951; d. Peter Hugo and Ruth Evangeline (Gamache) A.; m. James Edward Smolen, June 24, 1988. BA, Hillsdale (Mich.) Coll., 1973; MA, U. Mich., 1974, 84, PhD, 1986. Asst. dir. instnl. rsch., lectr. psychology Hillsdale Coll., 1974-75, instr., 1981-82; instr. psychology and edn. Concordia Coll., Ann Arbor, Mich., 1975-80; postdoctoral fellow, mem. adj. faculty dept. psychology U. Conn., Storrs, 1986-87; program coord. Ctr. for Rsch. on Learning and Teaching, U. Mich., Ann Arbor, 1987-89, rsch. fellow Sch. Social Work,, 1989—. Ad hoc reviewer Jour. Personality and Social Psychology, 1985—, Jour. Social and Personal Relationships, 1985—; contbr. articles and book revs. to profl. jours., chpts. to books. Actor Ann Arbor Civic Theatre, 1978; vol. Child Care Referral Svcs., Washtenaw County, Mich., 1981. Fellow U. Mich., 1973-74, block grantee, 1982, 86, Horace H. Rackham grantee, 1985-86. Mem. APA, Am. Psychol. Soc., Internat. Network on Personal Relationships. Home: 679 Watersedge Dr Ann Arbor MI 48105 Office: U Mich Sch Social Work 1065 Frieze Bldg Ann Arbor MI 48109-1285

ACKER, VIRGINIA MARGARET, nursing educator; b. Madison, Wis., Aug. 11, 1946; d. Paul Peter and Lucille (Klein) A. Diploma in Nursing, St. Mary's Med. Ctr., Madison, 1972; BS in Nursing, Incarnate Work Coll., San Antonio, 1976; MS in Health Professions, S.W. Tex. State U., 1980. RN, Wis., Tex.; NHA, Wis. Staff nurse St. Mary's Hosp., Milw., 1972-73, Kenosha Meml. Hosp., Wis., 1973-74, S.W. Tex. Meth. Hosp., San Antonio, 1974-75, Met. Gen. Hosp., San Antonio, 1975-76; instr. Bapt. Meml. Hosp. System Sch. Nursing, San Antonio, 1976-83; dir. nursing Meml. Hosp., Gonzales, Tex., 1983-84; instr., dir. nursing Victoria Coll., Cuero, Tex., 1984-86; dir. nursing Rocky Knoll Health Care Facility, Plymouth, Wis., 1986-87, Unicare Health Facilities, Milw., 1987-88; coord. nursing edn. St. Nicholas Hosp., Sheboygan, Wis., 1989—. Mem. NAFE, AAUW, Wishet. Roman Catholic. Avocations: cross-stiching, reading, camping, fishing. Home: Rte 1 Lot 68 Plymouth WI 53073 Office: St Nicholas Hosp Sheboygan WI 53081

ACKERLY, WENDY SAUNDERS, engineer; b. Chgo., July 23, 1960; d. Robert S. Jr. and Linda (Loucks) A. BS in Atmospheric Sci., U. Calif., Davis, 1982. Programmer U. Calif, Davis, 1982-83; cons. software Tesco, Sacramento, 1983; software engr. Bently Nev. Corp., Minden, Nev., 1984-85; mgr. computer scis. Jensen Electric Co., Reno, 1985-86; software engr. Jensen Electric Co., Cameron Park, Calif., 1986-89; sr. engr. Aerojet Propulsion Div., Sacramento, 1989—. Mem. Am. Meteorol. Soc. Republican. Office: Aerojet Propulsion Div PO Box 13222 Sacramento CA 95813

ACKERMAN, DIANA FELICIA, philosophy educator, writer; b. Bklyn., June 23, 1947; d. Arthur and Zelda (Sondack) A. AB summa cum laude, Cornell U., 1968; PhD, U. Mich., 1976. Asst. prof. philosophy Brown U., Providence, 1974-79, assoc. prof., 1979—; vis. asst. prof. philosophy UCLA, 1976; vis. hon. lectr. in logic and metaphysics U. St. Andrews, Scotland, 1983; sr. Fulbright lectr. Hebrew U., 1985; fellow Ctr. for Advanced Study in the Behavioral Scis.; recipient O. Henry award for short story published in Prize Stories, 1990. Mem. ACLU, Am. Philos. Assn., NAACP. Contbr. articles, short stories in various mags. Office: Brown U Dept Philosophy Providence RI 02912

ACKERMAN, JACQUELINE KAY, assistant principal; b. Wisconsin Rapids, Wis., May 12, 1943; d. Jack Vernon and Elizabeth Josephine (Johnson) A. BS, Wis. State U., 1966; MS, U. Wis., 1968, PhD, 1971, MS in Curriculum, 1980, MS in Sch. Adminstrn., 1982. Cert. secondary tchr. Tchr., student tchr. supt. Manitowoc County (Wis.) Tchr.'s Coll., 1970-71; tchr., chair Dept. Edn. and Psychology Lakeland Coll., Sheboygan, Wis., 1971-76; tchr., dean students Menominee Indian High Sch., Keshena, Wis., 1976-81; asst. prin. Shawano (Wis.) High Sch., 1981-86, Bay Port High Sch., Green Bay, Wis., 1986—; coordinator, JOM Summer High Sch., Keshena, 1977-80; cons. CESA #3, Gillette, Wis., 1980-81; presenter, author Wis. Dept. Pub. Instruction AODA Programs and Pamphlet, 1983-86, presenter Sch.-Human Service Liaison, 1985-86. Contbr. articles to sci. jours. Musician Shawano Mcpl. Band, 1982-86; bd. dirs. Positive Youth Devel., Shawano, 1983-86. Mem. Assn. Curriculum and Supervision, Nat. Assn. Biology Tchrs., Wis. Entomol. Soc., Assn. Wis. Sch. Adminstrs. (asst. prin. commn. 1981-83, 87—), Nat. Assn. Secondary Sch. Prins. (regional dir. 1983-84), LWV (v.p. 1985-86), Bus. and Profl. Women, Howard-Suamico Bus. and Profl. Assn., Howard-Suamico Lioness Assn. (sec. 1988—). Methodist. Office: Bay Port High Sch 1217 Cardinal Ln Green Bay WI 54303

ACKERMAN, JOLENE KAY, education administrator; b. La Junta, Colo., Dec. 11, 1952; d. Howard Melvin and Eunice Jolene (Onorati); m. Larry Holbrook, Mar. 13, 1972, (div. 1975); m. Dr. David Michael, Mar. 13, 1980; children: Abraham, Colin. BS,BA, Metropolitan State, Denver, 1974; AS, Community Coll. of Denver, 1981. State dir. Colo./Wyo. Green Thumb, Inc., Colo. and Wyo., 1977-80; chiropractic asst. Dr. David M. Ackerman, DC, Denver, 1980-88, office mgr., 1980-88; acct. cons. The Cornflower, About Saving Heat, Denver; tchr. Community Coll., Denver; subs. tchr. Jefferson & Denver County Pub. Schs., Denver; receptionist Ft. Lyon Veterans Adminstra. Hosp.; clk. typist Nat. Farmers Union Ins., Met. State Coll., So. Colo. State Coll., Denver; chiropractic asst., bus. adminstr. Dr. David M. Ackerman, Denver, 1990—; bd. dir. Community Coll. of Denver, 1981—; ind. contractor grant proposals and bus. orgn. restructuring. Author: Teaching Typing to the Handicapped Student, 1975; co-author: Accounting, 1975. Pub. rels. officer Bus. and Profl. Women, Denver, 1977, sec., 1978; pres. Applewood Food Coop., Golden, 1989; bd. dirs. Foothills Acad., 1988-90; com. sec. pack 540 Boy Scouts Am.; docent Denver Mus. Natural History, 1987—. Recipient Scholastic Scholarship Met. State Coll. Bus. Dept., Denver, 1973. Democrat. Roman Catholic. Home: 14280 Foothill Ln Golden CO 80401 Office: Dr David M Ackerman DC 601 Broadway Ste 317 Denver CO 80209

ACKERMAN, LOUISE MAGAW, writer, civic worker; b. Topeka, July 9, 1904; d. William Glenn and Anna Mary (Shaler) Magaw; BS, Kans. State U., 1926; MA, U. Nebr., 1942; m. Grant Albert Ackerman, Dec. 27, 1926; children—Edward Shaler, Anita Louise. Free lance writer, 1930—. Mem. Nat. Soc. Daus. Colonial Wars (nat. pres. 1977-80), Daus. Am. Colonists (regent Nebr. 1970-72), DAR (past v.p. gen.), Americans of Armorial Ancestry (sec. 1976-82), Nat. Huguenot Soc. (2d v.p. 1977-81), Nebr. Writers Guild (past sec.-treas.), Nat. League Am. Pen Women, Colonial Lords in Am., Nat. Gavel Soc., Soc. Descs. of Founders of Hartford, Conn., Phi Kappa Phi. Republican. Club: Nat. Writers. Lodge: Order Eastern Star. Home: Eastmont Towers III Apt 428 6335 O St Lincoln NE 68510

ACKERMAN, MONA RIKLIS, philanthropist; b. Tel-Aviv, Israel, May 22, 1946; d. Meshulam and Judith (Stern) Riklis; m. Irwin Ackerman, Dec. 18, 1966 (div. 1977); children: Ari, Gila. BA, NYU, 1968; MA, Yeshiva U., 1984, PhD, 1987. Story editor Frank Yablans Prodns., N.Y.C., 1975-77; editor Dell Pub., N.Y.C., 1978-79; sr. editor Jove Books, N.Y.C., 1979-80; dir. Rapid Am. Corp., N.Y.C., 1976—, Riklis Family Corp., 1980—; pres. Riklis Family Found., N.Y.C., 1981—, McCrory Corp., 1987—; ly Found., N.Y.C., 1981—; assoc. Yale Child Study Ctr., 1987—. Bd. govs. United Jewish Appeal of Greater N.Y., 1984-86; bd. dirs. United Jewish Appeal-Fedn. Jewish Philanthropies, 1986—, Bd. Jewish Edn., N.Y.C., 1983-84, Am. Friends of Rechov Sumsum, 1984—, Hayeled Found., 1987—, Am. Friends of Israel Mus., 1987—; internat. bd. govs. Weizmann Inst. of Sci., 1985—, Tel Aviv Mus., 1987; mem. exec. com. Nat. Jewish Coalition, 1987—; mem. painting and sculpture com. Mus. Modern Art, 1985-88, drawings com., 1988—; mem. Rockefeller U. Coun., 1986—, mem. Com. for Yr. 2000, NYU, 1986—, overseer faculty arts and scis., 1987—; commr. Commn. on Jewish Edn. in N.Am., 1988—; vis. com. Costume Inst., Met. Mus., 1988—. Mem. Nat. Coun. on Aging (intergenerational program com. 1988), Am. Psychol. Assn. (assoc. 1986—), N.Y. State Psychol. Assn. (assoc. 1986—) Office: Riklis Family Found 595 Madison Ave New York NY 10022

ACKERMAN, SANDRA J., science writer, editor; b. Plainfield, N.J., Aug. 16, 1957; d. Bernard and Nancy (Bernstein) A. BA, Yale U., 1979. Mng. editor Am. Scientist, New Haven, 1985-90. Contbr. articles to profl. jours.

ACKERSON, LYNN M., researcher; b. Feb. 19, 1957. BS in Math., U. Puget Sound, 1979; MS in Biomed. Engring., Case Western Res. U., 1983; PhD in Biometrics, U. Colo., 1988. Biomed. engr. VA Med. Ctr., Cleve., 1982-85; data mgr. Nat. Ctr. Am. Indian and Alaska Native Mental Health Rsch., U. Colo., Denver, 1986-88, rsch. assoc., 1989—, profl. rsch. asst. dept. biometrics, 1989—. U. Colo. Health Scis. Ctr. fellow, 1986-87. Mem. Am. Statis. Assn., Biometric Soc., Mathematical Assn. Am., Phi Kappa Phi. Office: U Colo Dept Biometrics 4200 E Ninth Denver CO 80262

ACKLES, JANICE VOGEL, fundraising executive, writer; b. Pasadena, Calif.; d. Roy George August and Genevieve Irene (Hunter) Vogel; m. David Thomas Ackles, Dec. 9, 1972; 1 child, George Arthur Vogel. BA in Art History, Calif. State U., L.A.; postgrad., U. So. Calif. Free-lance writer, 1972—; asst. editor Am. Jour. Physiology, L.A., 1980-84; dir. devel. rsch. World Vision, Monrovia, 1985-88, Children's Hosp., L.A., 1988—. Contbr. articles to nat. mags. and newspapers. Vol. researcher L.A. County Mus. Art, 1973-75; mem. Assistance League So. Calif., L.A., East African Wildlife Soc., Mus. Contemporary Art, L.A., Greater L.A. Zoo Assn., Natural History Mus. Mem. NAFE, Am. Prospect Rsch. Assn., Nat. Soc. Fund Raising Execs. (bd. dirs.), Nat. Assn. Hosp. Devel., Ind. Writers So. Calif., Calif. Press Women, Inc. (bd. dirs.). Democrat.

ACORD-SKELTON, BARBARA BURROWS, counselor; b. L.A., Dec. 26, 1928; d. Harry and Sophia (Dittman) Burrows; m. Benjamin Raddatz, June 11, 1949 (div. Dec. 1970); children: Randolph, Marjorie, Thomas, Deborah; m. William A. Acord, Feb. 26, 1974 (dec.); m. Gerah Skelton, 1989. AA, Riverside City Coll., 1956; BA, Calif. State U., San Bernardino, 1970; MA, Pacific Oaks Coll., 1974; postgrad., Claremont Coll., 1976-81. Cert. marriage, family, child counselor, Calif., 1974. Dir. pvt. Nursery Sch. and High Sch., Riverside, Calif., 1964-66; career devel., coordinator Riverside County Head Start and Corono Norco Sch. Dist., Riverside, 1966-72; instr. Chaffey Community Coll., Alta Loma, Calif., 1971-82; class room coordinator, family counselor Casa Colina Hosp., Pomona, Calif., 1973-79; counselor LaVerne (Calif.) Ctr. for Edn. Counseling, 1976-82; social worker III San Andreas Regional Ctr., Salinas, Calif., 1984-87; pvt. practice family and individual counseling Medford, 1987—; cons. Pomona U. Sch. Dist., Calif., 1973-80, San Gabriel Valley Regional Ctr., Covina, Calif., 1976-82, Nat. Council Alcoholism, Covina, 1980-82; instr. U. LaVerne, 1976-82. Author: On Learning and Growing, 1974; co-author: Parent Advocacy Training, 1977, Creative Competency, 1978. Vol. Day Springs Hospice, Medford, 1987—; bd. dirs. Gold Coast Arab Horse Assn., Santa Clara County, Calif., 1983-85. Riverside County Headstart scholar, 1967, Ednl. Profl. Devel. Act scholar, 1971-74. Mem. Am. Assn. Marriage and Family Therapists, Calif. Assn. Marriage and Family Therapists. Democrat. Presbyterian. Clubs: Arab Horse Assn. (So. Oreg.), (bd. dirs. 1988, pres. 1989), Region III Arab Horse Assn. (bd. mem. 1983-85). Home: 4373 Tami Ln Central Point OR 97502

ACREE, ELAINE STRONG, software engineer; b. Montgomery, Ala., Oct. 7, 1954; d. Quentin Roosevelt Strong and Sarah Doris (Brett) McCurdy; m. Allen Troy Acree Jr., Sept. 4, 1977. BS in Indsl. Engring., U. Ala., 1976; MS in Info. and Computer Sci., Ga. Inst. Tech., 1978; PhD in Indsl. Engring., Tex. Tech U., 1983. Engr. in Tng., Ala. Rsch. scientist Ga. Tech. Rsch. Inst., Atlanta, 1978-80; software design engr. Tex. Instruments, Lubbock, 1980-83; assoc. prin. engr. Harris Corp., Melbourne, Fla., 1983-85; sr. systems cons. Intergraph Corp., Huntsville, Ala., 1985—. Mem. Assn. for Computing Machinery, IEEE, Inst. Indsl. Engrs., Ops. Rsch. Soc. Am., Tau Beta Pi, Alpha Pi Mu. Methodist. Home: 97 Hartington Dr Madison AL 35758 Office: Integraph Corp One Madison Industrial Pk Huntsville AL 35807-4201

ACZEL, SUSAN KENDE, mathematician; b. Budapest, Hungary, June 22, 1927; d. Lajos and Iren Kende; came to Can., 1965, naturalized, 1972; m. Janos D. Aczel, Dec. 14, 1946; children—Catherina Aczel Boivie Julie Aczel More. BS, U. Budapest, 1948; MS, U. Szeged, 1950. Teaching asst. U. Szeged, 1949-50; asst. prof. Tech. U. Miskolc, 1950-52; head cultural dept. City of Debrecen, 1953-55; research assoc. U. Waterloo, Ont., Can., 1965-71. Author bibliographies on math. books in Hungary and on works on functional equations, 1964—. Home: 97 McCarron Crescent, Waterloo, ON Canada N2L 5M9

ADACHI, AGNES MAGDALENE, association executive; b. Budapest, Hungary, Oct. 26, 1918; came to U.S., 1951; d. Arnold and Lenke Magdalene (Lowenger) Manton; m. Masazumi Adachi, Apr. 27, 1960; children: Taro John, Jiro Paul. Diploma, Montessori Sch., Rome. Asst. to Raoul Wallenberg Swedish Red Cross, Budapest, 1944-45; lectr. Swedish Inst., Stockholm, 1945-46; chmn., lectr. Greater N.Y. Wallenberg Comm., N.Y.C., 1983—. Author: Child of the Winds: My Mission with Raoul Wallenberg, 1989. Recipient Humanitarian award Mammouth chpt. Brandeis Univ. Nat. Women's Com., 1987, Brotherhood award Phila. County coun. J.W.V. of U.S.A., 1987. Mem. Soroptomists. Home: 6902 Dartmouth St Forest Hills NY 11375 Office: Queensborough Community Col Holocaust and Rsch Ctr Bayside NY 11364

ADAIR, YVONNE, corporate administrator; b. Teaneck, N.J., Apr. 22, 1946; d. June Adair; children: Hal, Traci. Corp. treas., cheif fin. officer AAC Assocs., Inc., Vienna, Va. Mem. NAFE, NOW, Inter Account Soc., Nat. Contracts Mgmt. Assn., Va. Assn. Female Execs. Home: 5838 Fitzhugh St Burke VA 22015

ADAMCHEK, JANICE LYNN, personnel director; b. Seattle, Sept. 11, 1949; d. Vernon Wayne and Hazel Kathleen (Butcher) Beranek; m. Stacy Richard Mattox, July 8, 1967 (div. Oc. 1972); 1 child, Michael Sean; m. Thomas Bruce Adamchek, Aug. 4, 1979. Student, Montgomery Coll. and U. Md., 1971-78. Adminstrv. aide Dept. Transpn. Montgomery County, Silver Spring, Md., 1967-74; adminstrv. aide to asst. Community Service Ctr. Program Montgomery County, Silver Spring, 1974-79; various positions John Brown Engrs. & Constructors Inc. Trafalgar House Co., Stamford, Conn., 1979—; mgr. personnel John Brown Engrs. & Constructors Inc. Trafalgar House Co., Stamford, 1983—; rep. Coll. Placement Council, Bethlehem, Pa., 1982—. Active United Way, Silver Spring and Stamford 1968—. Mem. Nat. Constructors Assn. (employee relations com. 1982-85), Engring. Assocs. (exec. com. 1986-87). Home: 5 Boulder Ct Norwalk CT 06854 Office: John Brown E&C Inc 333 Ludlow St PO Box 1432 Stamford CT 06904

ADAMO, MARILYN H(ANK), information specialist; b. Queens, N.Y., July 20, 1953; d. Vincent J. and Evelyn F. (Ingerling) Hank; m. Ernest J. Adamo, June 21, 1975. BA, CUNY, 1975; MS, Pratt Inst., 1978. Reference librarian Citibank N.A., N.Y.C., 1973-81; asst. dir. library svcs. Cravath, Swaine and Moore, N.Y.C., 1981-87; v.p., mgr. info. ctr. Oppenheimer and Co. Inc., N.Y.C., 1987—. Mem. Law Libr. Assn. Greater N.Y., Spl. Libr. Assn., Am. Assn. Law Libr. Office: Oppenheimer & Co Inc World Financial Ctr New York NY 10281

ADAMOVICH, SHIRLEY GRAY, librarian, state official; b. Pepperell, Mass., May 8, 1927; d. Willard Ellsworth and Carrie (Shattuck) Gray; m. Frank Walter Adamovich, Aug. 31, 1960; children: Carrie Rose, Elizabeth Maude. B.A., U. N.H., 1954; M.S., Simmons Coll., Boston, 1955. Cons. Vt. State Libr ., Montpelier, 1955-58; head cataloger Bentley Coll., Waltham, Mass., 1958-60; tchr. U. N.H. System, Durham, 1965-79; asst. state librarian N.H. State Libr., Concord, 1979-81; state librarian N.H. State Library, Concord, 1981-85; commr. N.H. Dept. Cultural Resources, Concord, 1985—. Editor: A Reader in Library Technology, 1975, The Road Taken, 1989. Served in USAF, 1949-53. Mem. New Eng. Libr. Assn., N.H. Libr. Assn., N.H. Libr. Trustees Assn., N.H. Ednl. Media Assn. Office: NH State Libr 20 Park St Concord NH 03301

ADAMS, ALICE, writer; b. Fredericksburg, Va., Aug. 14, 1926; d. Nicholson Barney and Agatha Erskine (Boyd) A.; 1 son, Peter Adams Linenthal. A.B., Radcliffe Coll., 1946. Author: (novels) Careless Love, 1966, Families and Surviviors, 1975, Listening to Billie, 1978, Rich Rewards, 1980, Superior Women, 1984, Second Chances, 1988; (short story collections) Beautiful Girl, 1979, To See You Again, 1982, Return Trips, 1985, After You've Gone, 1989; contbr. short stories to New Yorker mag., others. Recipient Best Am. Short Stories award, 1976, O. Henry awards, 1971-82, 84-90; grantee Nat. Endowment for Arts, 1976; Guggenheim fellow, 1978-79. Mem. PEN. Democratic Socialist. Office: care Press Relations Alfred A Knopf Inc 201 E 50th St New York NY 10022

ADAMS, ALICE PATRICIA, sculptor; b. N.Y.C., Nov. 16, 1930; d. Charles P. and Loretto G. (Tobin) A.; m. William D. Gordy, Feb. 7, 1969; 1 dau., Katherine Adams Gordy. Student, Adelphi Coll., 1948-50; BFA, Columbia U., 1953; postgrad. (French Govt. fellow), 1953-54; postgrad. Fulbright Travel grantee, L'Ecole Nat d'Art Decoratif, Aubusson, France, 1953-54. Lectr. Manhattanville Coll., Purchase, N.Y., 1960-79; instr. sculpture Sch. Visual Arts, 1980-87. One-woman shows, N.Y.C., 1972, 74, 75, Hal Bromm Gallery, N.Y.C., 1979, 80, group shows include, Whitney Museum Am. Art, N.Y.C., 1971, 73, Indpls. Mus. Art, 1974, Nassau County Mus. Fine Arts, Roslyn, N.Y., 1977, Wave Hill, Riverdale, N.Y., 1979, Mus. Modern Art, N.Y.C., 1984; represented in permanent collections, Weatherspoon Gallery U. N.C., Greensboro, U. Nebr., Everson Mus., Syracuse, N.Y., Haags Gemetemuseum, The Hague, Netherlands; pub. commissions include Crosby Gardens, Toledo, Ohio, Design Team Seattle Transit Project, Workers' Place Park, Lawrence, Mass., Port Authority of N.Y. and N.J. Creative Artists Pub. Service grantee, 1973-74, 76-77; Nat. Endowment for Arts Artists grantee, 1978-79; Guggenheim fellow, 1981-82. Home: 3370 Ft Independence St Bronx NY 10463

ADAMS, ANN ELIZABETH, public relations executive; b. Guthrie, Okla., Jan. 29, 1948; d. Jack P. and Billie E. (May) A. BA in Journalism, U. Okla., 1970, MA, 1971; JD, Oklahoma City U., 1984. Lic. atty. Supr. teleshopper advt. KOCO-TV, Oklahoma City, 1971-72; pub. info. officer Met. Libr. System, Oklahoma City, 1972-78; editor, writer Kerr-McGee Corp., Oklahoma City, 1978-79, assoc. editor, 1979-81, mgr. publs., 1981-84, mgr. corp. communications, 1984-88; asst. to chancellor Okla. State Regents for Higher Edn., Oklahoma City, 1988-90; dir. pub. rels. div. Jordan Assocs. Advt./Communications, Oklahoma City, 1990—. Mem. Myriad Gardens Conservatory, Oklahoma City, 1986—; pres. Friends of Met. Libr. System, Oklahoma City, 1990-92; div. chmn. United Way Greater Oklahoma City, 1989—. Recipient Paragon award Leadership Oklahoma City, 1986, Addy award Am. Advt. Fedn., 1984. Mem. Women in Communications, Inc. (pres. Oklahoma City chpt. 1987-88, nat. progress of women in communication com. 1989-90), Pub. Rels. Soc. Am., ABA, Okla. Bar Assn., Friends and Alumni of U. Okla. Sch. Journalism and Mass Communication (pres. 1989-90), Leadership Oklahoma City Alumni Assn. Episcopalian. Home: 2808 NW 66th St Oklahoma City OK 73116 Office: Jordan Assocs 1000 W Wilshire Oklahoma City OK 73118

ADAMS, AUDREY LEE, physician, anesthesiologist, educator; b. Sioux Falls, S.D., Mar. 27, 1952; d. James Robert and Louise (Lewis) A.; m. Edward Lee Schumann, Dec. 9, 1983. BS in Medicine, U. S.D., 1975; MD, Northwestern U., 1976. Diplomate Am. Bd. Anesthesiology; cert. spl. competence in critical care medicine ABA. Intern Northwestern-McGraw Med. Ctr., Chgo., 1977, resident in anesthesiology, 1978-79, fellow, 1980; asst. prof. anesthesiology Pritzker Sch. Medicine, U. Chgo., 1981-82; asst. prof. U. Calif., Irvine, 1982-85, assoc. prof., 1986—; dir. surg. intensive care, Long Beach VA Med. Ctr., Calif., 1982-85. Named Outstanding Tchr., U. Chgo. Med. House Officers, 1982. Mem. Am. Soc. Anesthesiology, Soc. Critical Care Medicine, Internat. Anesthesia Research Soc., Am. Med. Women's Assn. Office: U Calif Coll of Medicine Dept Anesthesiology Irvine CA 92717*

ADAMS, BARBARA HELEN, English language educator, poet, writer; b. N.Y.C., Mar. 23, 1932; d. David S. Block and Helen (Taxter) Block Tyler; m. Elwood Adams, June 6, 1952; children—Steven, Amy, Anne, Samuel. BS, SUNY-New Paltz, 1962, MA, 1970; PhD, NYU, 1981. Adj. instr. Orange County Community Coll., Middletown, N.Y., 1970-77; grad. asst. NYU, N.Y.C., 1974-77; adj. lectr. SUNY-Albany, 1977-81; instr. Mt. St.Mary Coll., Newburgh, N.Y., 1980-81; asst. prof. SUNY-Cobleskill, 1981-83; adj. assoc. prof. Pace U., N.Y.C., 1983-84, assoc. prof. English, 1984—, dir. bus. communications, 1984—; poet in residence Cape Cod Writers' Conf., 1988. Author: Double Solitaire, 1982, The Enemy Self: The Poetry & Criticism of Laura Riding, 1989, The Enemy Self: Poetry and Criticism of Laura Riding, 1990; (poems) Hapax Legomena, 1990; contbr. poems, stories, articles to various mags. and jours. Recipient 1st prize for poetry NYU and Acad. Am. Poets, 1975; Penfield fellow NYU, 1977. Mem. MLA, Assn. Bus. Communication, Poets and Writers. Home: 57 Coach Ln Newburgh NY 12550 Office: Pace U Pace Plaza New York NY 10038

ADAMS, BEEJAY (MEREDITH ELISABETH JANE J. ADAMS), sales executive; b. Jefferson Banks, Mo., June 9, 1920; d. Alden Humphrey and Louise Marion (Banta) Seabury; m. Merlin Francis Adams, July 10, 1948 (dec. 1977); children: S(tephen) Kent, Mark Francis. AB, Bradley U., 1942. Svc. editor Peoria (Ill.) Jour. Star, 1942-46; women's program dir. Sta. WEEK-AM, Peoria, 1946-47; on air personality Sta. KSD-AM, St. Louis, 1948; lectr. Sch. Assembly Svc., Chgo., 1948-49; pres. M.F. Adams, Inc., Quincy, Ill., 1977-85; commodities broker Quincy, 1985-87; pres. MarKent, Inc., Quincy, 1975—; sec., treas. Miss. Belle Distbn. Co., Inc., Quincy, 1976—, v.p., treas., 1979—. Active Quincy Svc. League, 1949-57, local polit. campaigns, co-chmn. local presdl. campaigns, 1952-77; founder, past pres. Quincy Jr. Theatre, 1953-78; charter mem. Quincy Community Theatre; co-chmn. coll. fund drive Quincy Coll., 1988, chmn. 1989. Mem. Quincy C. of C., Adams City Red CrossBd., Sales and Mktg. Execs. Club, Quincy Art Club, Atlantis Study Club, Quincy Country Club, Phi Beta Phi. Episcopalian. Home: 2303 Jersey St Quincy IL 62301 Office: Miss Belle Distbn Co Inc PO Box 768 Quincy IL 62306

ADAMS, BETTY VIRGINIA, petroleum products company executive; b. Butler, Ga., Jan. 6, 1925; d. William Burton and Martha William (Duckworth) A. B.A., Va. Intermont Coll., 1944, U. N.C., 1946. Chmn., chief exec. officer Fuel Oil & Equipment Co., Inc., Roanoke, Va., 1949—. Roanoke Country Club, Yacht and Country Club (Stuart, Fla.), Amb. Club (Stuart). Office: PO Box 12626 Roanoke VA 24027

ADAMS, BEVERLY JOSEPHINE, data processing specialist; b. Kansas City, Kans., Nov. 29, 1951; d. Cecil and Eula Laverne (Lynch) Brown; m. Theodore Lavern Adams, Sept. 20, 1969; children: Theodore Lavern Jr., Terry Levar. AA in Data Processing, Kansas City Kans. Community Coll., 1980; BS in Mgmt. and Computers, Park Coll., Parkville, Mo., 1986; postgrad., Rockhurst Coll. Sr. data processor AT&T Communications, Kansas City, Mo., 1984-86, computer programmer, 1987—; lectr. in field. Editor: (newspaper) Courier, 1969, (newsletter) Kansas City Link, 1987. Cons. Youth of Am., Kansas City, 1983; mem. Kansas City Chiefs Football, 1968-72, Coalition Labor Union Women, Washington, 1984, AFL-CIO City Labor Council, Kansas City, 1984; dir. ch. adult and youth choir, Kansas City, 1982—. Recipient Outstanding Community Services award AT&T Techs., 1984; named one of Outstanding Young Women of Am., 1981. Mem. NAFE, Alliance AT&T Employees (chairperson 1987, treas. 1988-89), Profl. Women's Fedn., Young People's Willing Workers, Alpha Kappa Alpha, Gamma Mu Gamma (program chmn. 1985). Republican. Penacostal. Clubs: Wecomo (Services award 1983), Young Adults Action (bd. dirs., Leadership award 1980), YWCA (Kansas City). Home: 2635 N 22d St Kansas City KS 66104 Office: AT&T Communications 2121 E 63d St Kansas City MO 64130

ADAMS, CAROL ANN JACOBS, artist, art educator; b. Manhattan, Kans., Jan. 10, 1946; d. Stanley Bernard and Mildred Cecil (Mayer) Jacobs; m. Jon Leslie Adams, Feb. 28, 1968 (div. 1976). BFA, Bowling Green State U., 1967; postgrad., U. Syracuse, 1968; MA in Art Edn., Case Western Res. U., 1970; MFA, Kent State U., 1975. Drawing/design instr. U. Akron, Akron, Ohio, 1970-80; fiber dept. head, design instr. U. Akron, 1973-80; fiber dept. head, art instr. Cleve. State U., 1978-80, fiber dept. head, 1983-85; fiber instr. Cleve. Inst. Art, 1986; art cons. CARE, Haiti, 1986; cons. Akron/Summit County Libr., Norton br., 1988;. Exhibited in group shows at Cleve. Mus. Art, 1974, 82, 85-86, 88, Paragon Gallery, Akron, 1987, Edinboro U., 1990, Mansfield Art Ctr., Mansfield, Ohio, 1986; 2 person show Wasmer Gallery, Cleve., 1984, Cuyahoga Community Coll., Vitreous Enamels, San Diego, 1983; commd. by mayor of Cleve. for gift to mayor of Volgograd, USSR; over 30 wallscapes commd. for bldgs. Rochester (N.Y.) Pub. Library, 1973, Menorah Park Home for Aged, Beechwood, Ohio, 1980, Dalad Group Corp. Hdqrs., Independence, Ohio, 1983, others including bldgs. in Washington, Akron, Cleve., Fla., N.C.; work in backstrap and frame looms, enamels, enameling, others. Mem. Big Sisters, Akron, Ohio, 184—, Akron Art Mus., Cleve. Mus. Art; lectr. workshop Nat. Enamels Conv., Covington, Ky., 1989, Women's Art Caucus, 1989, Edinboro U., 1990. Recipient second award 9th Annual Juried Show Baycrafters, Bay Village, Ohio, 1970, second prize All-Ohio Show Canton Art Inst., Canton, Ohio, 1974, Thompson Enamel award Wichita (Kans.) Art Assn., 1985. Mem. Women's Art Caucus, Textile Art Alliance, NOVA, Nat. Enamelist Guild, Hand Weavers Guild Am., Ohio Designer Craftsmen. Democrat. Lutheran. Home and Office: 2355 Main St Peninsula OH 44264

ADAMS, CAROLINE JEANETTE H., sales executive; b. Dallas, June 15, 1951; d. Bill Gene and Anita N. (Murrah) Hickey. BFA, So. Meth. U., 1973. Media buyer Jim Leslie & Assocs., Dallas, 1973; continuity dir. Sta. KZEW-FM, Dallas, 1973-75; adminstrv. asst. Neiman-Marcus Co., Dallas, 1975-77; exec. sec. Harris Data Communications, Dallas, 1978-80; mgr. classified sales ADWEEK/Southwest mag., Dallas, 1980—. Editor, writer Dallas Advt. League newsletter, 1987-89. Methodist. Avocations: travel, antiques, collecting soundtrack and rare record albums, restoring classic automobiles. Office: ADWEEK 2909 Cole Ave #220 Dallas TX 75204

ADAMS, CYNTHIA D., health sciences educator; b. Detroit, Sept. 10, 1946; d. Walter Norbert Tokarz and Eugenia W. (Czastkiewicz) Tokarz; m. Charles Richard Adams, Feb. 18, 1978; children—Erik, Jessica, Kerensa. B.S., Wayne State U., 1968, Ed.D., 1973; M.A., Eastern Mich. U., 1970. Instr., Wayne State U., Detroit, 1970-71; chief technologist, ednl. coordinator Detroit Macomb Hosp. Assn., 1971-74; dir., asst. prof. health adminstrn. program Mercy Coll., Detroit, 1974-76; assoc. prof., chmn. dept. med. tech. Univ. of Health Scis., Chgo. Med. Sch., North Chicago, Ill., 1976-80, prof., dean, 1980—; dir. workshops Profl. Seminars Cons., N.Y.C., 1985—. Contbr. articles to profl. jours. Mem. adv. bd. Coll. Lake County, Grayslake, Ill., 1979-84; sci. fair judge Ill. Jr. Acad. Sci., 1980—; adv. bd. Lake County Urban League, Waukegan, Ill., 1980—; yearbook advisor Lake Bluff Jr. High Sch., Ill., 1983—; adv. bd. Lake County YWCA, Waukegan, 1984—. Recipient Cert. of Achievement for Outstanding Women in Edn., YWCA, Lake County, 1983, 84. Mem. Am. Assn. Allied Health Professionals, Am. Soc. Med. Technologists (cert. Omicron Sigma award 1980), Am. Soc. Clin. Pathologists (dir. workshops 1976—), Am. Soc. Allied Health Profls. (chmn. women's interest sect. 1984—), Am. Midwest Assn. Allied Health Deans, Ill. Med. Technology Assn. (chmn. sci. assembly 1979-80), Chgo. Soc. Med. Technologists (co-chmn. by-laws com. 1984-85, bd. dirs., 1984—). Home: 340 E Scranton Ave Lake Bluff IL 60044 Office: The Univ of Health Scis Sch of Related Health Scis North Chicago IL 60064

ADAMS, FAYE LITSEY, educator; b. Owensboro, Ky., Oct. 16, 1945; d. Tom and Ada Belle (Justus) Litsey; m. Carroll Haydon Adams, Apr. 9, 1971. BS in Edn., We. Ky. U., 1967; MRE, So. Baptist Theol. Sem., Louisville, 1974. Cert. life provisional tchr., Ky. Tchr., librarian Ricks Inst., Monrovia, Liberia, West Africa, 1967-69; tchr. Sutherland, 1969-71; tchr. remedial reading Howard Elem. Sch., Ocala, Fla., 1971-72; 4 and 5 yr. old coord. Clifton Heights Day Care Ctr., Louisville, 1972-74; house parent So. Bapt. Mission, Liberia, 1974-77; tchr. Seven Hills Elem. Sch., Owensboro, 1977-78, Newton Parrish Elem. Sch., Owensboro, 1978-81, Seven Hills Elem. Sch., Owensboro, 1986—; instr. Owensboro Jr. Coll. Bus., 1981-83; tchr. kindergarten Cravens Elem. Sch., Owensboro, 1983-84, Foust Elem. Sch., Owensboro, 1984-86; designer, ptnr. Colletiques by Faye-Carroll, Owensboro,. Contbr. articles to profl. jours. Recipient Daviess, McLean Bapt. Assn. scolar, 1964. Mem. NEA, Ky. Edn. Assn. (rally person 1988), Owensboro Edn. Assn., Internat. Reading Assn. (bldg. rep. 1985—), AAUW, Fonz (Washington). Democrat. Home: 1715 Prince Ave Owensboro KY 42303

ADAMS, FRANCES GRANT, II, lawyer; b. Wheeling, W.Va., Nov. 30, 1955; d. Jack Richard and Frances Irene (Grant) A. BA, W.Va. U., 1976, JD, 1979; MA, Webster U., 1983. Bar: W.Va. 1979, U.S. Dist. Ct. (so. dist.) W.Va. 1979, U.S. Ct. Mil. Appeals 1979, U.S. Supreme Ct. 1988, D.C. 1989. Asst. staff judge advocate armament div. USAF, Eglin AFB, Fla., 1979-82; dep. staff judge advocate USAF, Keflavik, Iceland, 1982-83; staff judge advocate 71st Air Base Group USAF, Vance AFB, Okla., 1984-86; chief gen. torts sect. claims and tort litigation staff hdqrs. USAF, Washington, 1986-88; chief mgmt. and analysis br. claims and tort litigation staff HQ USAF, Washington, 1988—. Mem. Fed. Bar Assn. (program chmn. Pentagon chpt. 1989-90), DAR (W.Va. procedures manual chmn. 1989—), Annandale Lions (sec. 1990—).

ADAMS, GUNILLA MARIE, corporate executive; b. Stockholm, Sweden, Nov. 2, 1960; came to U.S., 1980; d. Hans Gustaf Martin and Britta Johanna (Wiklund) Wranne; m. David Kenneth Adams, Feb. 13, 1981 (div. Apr. 1984). Student, Ostra Real Coll., Stockholm, 1979. Nat. promotions dir. Radar Records, N.Y.C., 1983, Easystreet Records, N.Y.C., 1983-84; regional promotion and mktg. dir. Sunshine Record Distbrs., N.Y.C., 1984-85; gen. mgr. Pro Motion, L.A., 1985-89. Lutheran.

ADAMS, HAZEL GREENLEE REDFEARN (MRS. PAYTON F. ADAMS, II), educator; b. Monroe, N.C., Nov. 12, 1905; d. Ephraim Eugene and Rebecca (Laney) Redfearn; student Radford Coll., 1924; A.B., U. Ky., 1940, M.A., 1953; postgrad. U. Nebr., 1955; m. Payton F. Adams II, July 11, 1928; children: Payton F. III, Juliette Greenlee (Mrs. J. B. Hawk). Elementary tchr. Larchmont Sch., Norfolk, Va., 1924-28, Winchester City Schs. (Ky.), 1943-53; supr. Clark County Schs. (Ky.), 1953-61; supr. student tchrs. Ky. Wesleyan Coll., 1945-48; instr. Wesleyan Coll., Macon, Ga., 1960; asst. and assoc. prof. edn. Dakota Wesleyan U., Mitchell, S.D., 1961-69; assoc. prof. early childhood edn. Pfeiffer Coll., Misenheimer, N.C., 1969—, supr. student tchrs., 1969-73. Chmn., Clark County Community Coun., 1950-52, Clark County Recreation Bd., 1955-60; supr. Teen-Town Winchester, 1954-60; mem. adv. coun. Southeastern Christian Coll., Winchester, Ky., 1973-79; aide Clark County Hosp. Aux. 1980-88. Grad. studies scholar Gatz U., 1965. Mem. AAUW, AAUP, NEA, S.D. Edn. Assn., DAR (treas. chpt. 1975-80), Assn. Supervision Curriculum Devel., Assn. for Childhood Edn., Assn. Childhood Edn. Internat. (adviser Pfeiffer Coll. chpt. 1972-73), N.C. Assn. Supervisory Educators. Mitchell Bus. and Profl. Women Club, Albemarle Bus. and Profl. Women (pres. 1972-73), Ky. Hist. Soc., Nat. Trust Hist. Preservation, Phi Kappa Phi (pres. 1964-66), Delta Kappa Gamma (pres. 1964-66), Pi Gamma Mu. Methodist. Clubs: Irvine (Ky.) Garden, Daniel Boone Music, Christian Women's, Order Eastern Star. Home and Office: 136 College St Winchester KY 40391

ADAMS, HELENE CLAY, advertising executive; b. China Lake, Calif., Apr. 8, 1961; d. Henry George and Dena (Layos) Clay; m. Christopher James Adams, May 31, 1986. AA, Johnson & Wales, Providence, R.I.; BA, Emerson Coll. Pub. relations mgr. Riverside Amusement Park, Agawam, Mass., 1983-85; media specialist Schneider & Assooc., Boston, 1985-87; account exec. Harland, Tine & White, HArtford, Conn., 1987-88; dir. of pub. relations Perreault & Tompkins, Springfield, Mass., 1988—. Campaign mem. Mayor Mary Hurley, Springfield, 1989. Recipient Merit award Western Mass Ad Club, 1989. Mem. Pub. Relations Soc. of Am., Women's C. of C. Republican. Greek Orthodox. Office: 188 Maple St Springfield MA 01105

ADAMS, JEAN RUTH, entomologist; b. Edgewater Park, N.J., Aug. 17, 1928; d. Herbert Raymond and Gertrude Gladys (Budd) A. BS, Rutgers U., 1950, PhD (Trubeck fellow), 1962. Registered profl. entomologist. Lab. technician Rohm & Haas Co., Bristol, Pa., 1951-57; postdoctoral fellow U. Pa., Phila., 1961-62; rsch. entomologist U.S. Dept. Agr., Agr. Rsch. Ctr., Beltville, Md., 1962-89; cons. insect pathology, electron microscopy, 1958—. Mem. nominating com. D.C. Bapt. Conv., 1977-79, dir. Acteens, Mission Youth Orgn., D.C. Bapt. Conv., 1972-87, 88—, Sunday sch. tchr. 1st Bapt. Ch., Hyattsville, Md., 1962-89, chmn. Christian edn. bd., 1973-74, mem. nominating com., 1974-77, mem. bd. missions, 1977-80, ch. treas., 1973-74, mem. choir, 1979-89, diaconate, 1980-86, vice chmn., 1981-82, chmn., 1982-84, trustee Bapt. Home, 1982-83, sec., 1985—; editorial bd. Jour. of Invertebrate Pathology, 1986-89. Mem. Am. Registered Profl. Entomologists (bd. dirs. Chesapeake chpt. 1989—), Electron Microscopy Soc. Am. (chmn. sci. exhibits ann. meeting 1982), Entomol. Soc. Am., Am. Soc. for Cell Biology, Soc. for Invertebrate Pathology (sec. 1982-84), Washington Soc. for Electron Microscopy (coun. 1976-83, sec.-treas. 1976-78, 80-82), Washington Entomol. Soc., Md. Entomol. Soc., Sigma Xi, Sigma Delta Epsilon. Contbr. articles to profl. jours. Home: 6004 41st Ave Hyattsville MD 20782 Office: US Dept Agr Agr Rsch Ctr W Insect Pathology Lab Bldg 011A Room 214 Beltsville MD 20705

ADAMS, JEANETTE, chemistry educator; b. Dallas, Aug. 4, 1955; d. James Edward and Vivian (Lindsey) A. BS, Tex. A&M U., 1976, PhD, 1983. Postdoctoral assoc. medicinal chemistry Northeastern U., Boston, 1983-85; postdoctoral assoc. midwest ctr., mass spectrometry U. Nebr., Lincoln, 1985-87; asst. prof. dept. chemistry Emory U., Atlanta, 1987—. Contbr. articles to profl. jours. Vice-pres. Nat. Audubon, Lincoln, Nebr., 1986-87; judge sci. day Spelman Coll., Atlanta, 1990, Greater Atlanta Regional Sci. Fair, 1988. NASA-Am. Soc. Elec. Engrs. Summer Rsch. fellow, 1979; named Notable Women of Tex., 1984. Mem. Am. Chem. Soc. (councilor Ga. sect. 1990—), Am. Soc. for Mass Spectrometry, N.Y. Acad. Scis., Phi Lambda Upsilon (Sharon Dabney award 1983), Tri Beta, Sigma Xi (v.p. Emory U. chpt. 1988-89, pres. Emory U. chpt. 1989-90). Office: Emory U Dept Chemistry 1515 Pierce Dr Atlanta GA 30322

ADAMS, JOYCE MARILYN, elementary school principal; b. Longview, Wash., July 18, 1934; d. Edward Harry Clark and Reva Dolly (Irish) Lillie; m. Ray S. Adams, Oct. 11, 1953 (div. Apr. 1980); children: Mark S., Gary S., Laura J. BA, Sonoma State U., Rohnert Pk., Calif., 1972; MSEd, Purdue U., 1981, PhD, 1983. Cert. elem. tchr., Calif., sch. adminstr. Teller Bank Am., Napa, Calif., 1965-66; sec. Napa Community Coll., 1966-70; substitute tchr. Plumas and Lassen Sch. Dists., Calif., 1972-73; spl. edn. tchr. Plumas Unified Sch. Dist., Quincy, Calif., 1973-80; asst. prof. spl. edn. No. State Coll., Aberdeen, S.D., 1983-85; prin. Churchill County Sch. Dist., Fallon, Nev., 1985—; grad. asst. Purdue U., 1980-83; cons. S.D. Sch. Visually Handicapped, Aberdeen, 1984, Easter Seals, 1984-85, Lahontan Valley Literacy Orgn., Fallon, 1987-89, bd. dirs., 1989—; adj. prof. We. Nev. Community Coll., Fallon; speaker various profl. groups. Contbr. articles to profl. jours. Pres. Northside PTO, Fallon, 1988-89. Recipient re-entry grant Philanthropic Edn. Orgn., 1981. Mem. AAUW (sec. Chester, Calif. chpt. 1975-76, pres. 1976-78, Project Renew grant 1981), Assn. Supervision and Curriculum Devel., Am. Assn. Sch. Adminstrs., Nat. Assn. Elem. Sch. Prins., Nev. Assn. Sch. Adminstrs., Soroptimists (sec. Fallon chpt. 1987-88), Phi Delta Kappa. Democrat. Methodist. Office: Northside Elem Sch 340 Venturacci Ln Fallon NV 89406

ADAMS, KATHLEEN MARGARET, principal; b. Providence, Aug. 9, 1952; d. Chester E. and Marie R. (Hannon) A. BA, Mt. St. Joseph Coll., 1974; MEd, Providence Coll., 1984. Cert. elem. sch. tchr., R.I., cert. in religion in the Diocese of Providence, 1987; notary public, 1988. Elem. tchr. St. Brendan Sch., East Providence, R.I., 1974-78; jr. high sch. tchr. St. Rose of Lima Sch., Warwick, R.I., 1981-85; asst. prin. St. Kevin Sch., Warwick, 1985-86; prin. Cranston-Johnston Cath. Region, Cranston, R.I., 1986—; park ranger Dept. of Environ. Mgmt., Narragansett, R.I., 1984-85. Apptd. to Ad Hoc com. Diocese Providence For Parish Tax Assessment Program; apptd. to accreditation com. St. Mary's Acad., Bayview; chmn. subcom. edn. before Pres. Bush and U.S. Senate. Named Outstanding Coll. Athlete Am., 1974. Mem. ASCD, Nat. Cath. Ednl. Assn. (mem. exec. com. of dept. elem. schs. N.E. chpt. 1990—), Internat. Reading Assn., Delta Kappa Gamma. Roman Catholic. Home: 50 Deacon Ave Warwick RI 02886-5104 Office: Cranston-Johnston Cath Region 43 Poplar Dr Cranston RI 02920-5788

ADAMS, KAYE HALL, mortgage banker; b. DeKalb, Tex., Sept. 26, 1943; d. J. Roscoe and Minnie Rebecca (Shafer) Hall; m. Carl E. Adams, Oct. 8, 1960; children: Brentley Dean, Rebecca Adams Davidson. Lic. real estate broker, Tex. Owner, mgr. Sq. One Real Estate, Bonham, Tex., 1980-85; v.p. Supreme Mortgage Inc., Sherman, Tex., 1985-86; owner, mgr. Adams First Fin., Inc. (formerly Adams Fin. Resources), Sherman, 1986—; mem. Pvt. Industry Coun., Denison, Tex., 1981—; pres. Texoma Housing Fin. Corp., Denison, 1981—; chmn. Bid Procurement Rsch. Com., Sherman, 1987. Mem. real estate adv. bd. Grayson County Coll. Mem. Nat. Assn. Realtors, Tex. Assn. Realtors, Grayson County Bd. Realtors (affiliate), Dallas Assn. Profl. Mortgage Women, Sherman C. of C. Republican. Mem. Ch. of Christ. Office: Adams First Fin Inc 714 N Travis St Sherman TX 75090

ADAMS, LAURA LEE, health care administrator; b. Greeley, Colo., June 2, 1956; d. Stanley Eugene Christman and Bonnie Jean (Jackman) New; m. Mark Collin Adams, Nov. 7, 1987; children: Anthony Collin, Lindsay Dawn, Nicholas Brigham. BS, U. No. Colo., 1978; MS, U. Colo., 1984. RN, Colo. Dir. nursing Meml. Hosp., Greeley, 1979-84; adminstrv. asst. to v.p. nursing Luth. Med. Ctr., Denver, 1984-85; asst. adminstr. Chalmette (La.) Gen. Hosp., 1985-87; v.p. patient services Parkview Episc. Med. Ctr., Pueblo, Colo., 1987-90; v.p. healthcare programs Exec. Learning, Inc., Nashville, Tenn., 1990—; nat. speaker and lectr. in field; adj. prof. U. So. Colo., U. Colo., 1989—. Vocat. adv. bd. Pueblo Community Coll., 1987-90, pres. adv. bd., 1989; nursing adv. bd., 1987-90, U. So. Colo., 1987-90, v.p. adv. bd.; quality assurance bd. Sangre de Cristo Hospice, Pueblo, 1988-90. Named Leadership Pueblo inductee, 1988, Leadership Pueblo alumni, 1989. Named one of New Orleans Great 100 Nurses New Orleans Dist. Nurses Assn., 1986; recognized for outstanding community service VFW, Chalmette, 1986. Mem. Am. Orgn. Nurse Execs., Colo. Soc. for Nurse Execs. (dist. dir. 1982-84, bd. dirs. 1982-84), Sigma Theta Tau. Democrat. Home: 7823 Leaf Point Ct Houston TX 77095 Office: Exec Learning Inc 7101 Executive Center Dr Ste 235 Brentwood TN 37027

ADAMS, MARGARET ANN, hospital executive; b. Praise, Ky., Aug. 25, 1935; d. John Milburn and Minnie Mae (Crawford) Hicks; m. Homer A. Adams, Oct. 27, 1956; children: Daphney Lynn, Mark Owen, Sammy A. BS, Pikeville Coll., 1963. Cert. med. technologist Am. Soc. Clin. Pathology. Staff technologist Huntsville (Ala.) Hosp., 1963-64, supr. blood bank, 1964-65, asst. chief technologist, 1965-69, chief technologist, 1969-80, adminstrv. dir. lab. svcs., 1980—. Mem. Ala. State Soc. for Med. Tech. (pres. 1986-87, Mem. of Yr. 1988), Ala. Lab Mgrs. Orgn., Clin. Lab Mgrs. Assn. (chpt. network com. 1987-89), Acad. Med. Arts and Scis., Omicron Sigma. Republican. Presbyterian. Office: Huntsville Hosp 101 Sivley Rd Huntsville AL 35801

ADAMS, MARGARET DIANE, association director; b. St. Paul, Oct. 31, 1937; d. William Frank and Margaret Mary (O'Donnell) Rudolph; BA, Met. State U., 1976; m. Ronald Earl Adams, Feb. 25, 1976; children: Margaret, Michelle and Mark (triplets); children by previous marriage: Roberta, Barbara, William, John, Dana. Bookkeeper, Universal CIT Credit Corp., 1956-59; clk. U. Minn., 1963-65; sec. Granville House, St. Paul, 1965-67, adminstrv. asst., 1967-72; adminstrv. asst. Assn. of Halfway House Alcoholism Programs of N.Am., Inc., St. Paul, 1972, project coord., 1973-74, project dir., 1974-78, acting dir., 1978-79, exec. dir., 1979-81; pres. Adams Enterprises, 1981-82; owner Adams Taxi, 1981-85; community faculty mem. Met. State U., 10986—. Asst. chem. dependency counseling program, Conceptual Counseling, St. Paul, 1984-87; vol. counselor Whole Life Ctr., St. Paul, 1987-88; mem. team ministry Shakopee Prison for Women, Minn., 1985-89; program dir. Sarah Family Programs (ministry for women and children), St. Paul, 1987—; cons. Nat. Center for Alcohol Edn.; lectr., adviser Lakewood Community Coll. Mem. NAFE (network dir. 1979-81), Nat. Assn. Alcoholism Counselors, Minn. Assn. Alcoholism Counselors, Ind. Assn. Alcoholism and Drug Abuse Counselors (cert. alcoholism and drug counselor), Nat. Coalition for Adequate Alcoholism Programs, N. Am. Indian Women's Council on Chem. Dependency. Author: Women: On Women in Recovery, 1976; mem. editorial bd. Do It Now Found., 1978-79. Office: Sarah Family Programs 919 W Armstrong Saint Paul MN 55102

ADAMS, MARGERY JANE, nursing administration; b. Confluence, Pa., Aug. 22, 1932; d. Dwight Moody and Gladys Marie (Rodgers) Funk; m. Thornton Dixon Adams, Oct. 7, 1954; children: Tad, Rodger, Neil. BSN, Johns Hopkins U., 1955; M. Nursing, Emory U., 1969. Cert. nursing adminstrn. Nursing instr. Gardner Webb Coll., Boiling Springs, N.C., 1967-72; dir. nursing Catawba Meml. Hosp., Hickory, N.C., 1972-83; v.p. patient svcs. Catawba Meml. Hosp., 1983—; mem. Catawba County Bd. Health, 1982—, N.C. Bd. Examiners of Practicing Psychologists, 1988—. Participant Roosevelt Ctr. for Am. Policy Study-Citizens Assembly, Hickory, N.C., 1988-89. Mem. Am. Orgn. Nursing Execs., Nat. League for Nursing, N.C. Nurses Assn., Sigma Theta Tau. Republican. Methodist. Home: 2548 Eagle Dr Conover NC 28613 Office: Catawba Meml Hosp 810 Fairgrove Church Rd Hickory NC 28602

ADAMS, MAUREEN KAY, consultant; b. Beaver Falls, Pa., May 2, 1948; d. John Franklin Freshwater and Zelda Elizabeth (Simmons) Shuman; m. James Robert Adams, Sept., 1972 (div. May 1974). AA with honors, Edison Community Coll., Ft. Myers, Fla., 1975; BA magna cum laude, Fla. State U., 1977. Regional leasing coord. Gen. Motors Acceptance Corp., Atlanta, 1979-87; area sales mgr. Marine Midland Automobie Fin. Co., Boca Raton, Fla., 1987-89; pres. Leasing Concepts, Roswell, Ga., 1988—. Mem. Nat. Vehicle Leasing Assn. (bd. dirs. 1988—), Ga. Auto Dealers Assn., C. of C. Office: Leasing Concepts 150 Creekmont Ct Roswell GA 30076

ADAMS, ROSE ANN, social service administrator; b. McHenry, Ill., Apr. 4, 1952; d. Clemens Jacob and Marguerite Elizabeth (Freund) A. BS in Edn., Ill. State U., 1974; MEd, U. Ark., 1979. Cert. secondary sch. tchr., Ark., Ill. Supt., exec. dir. Clinton County Children's Services, Wilmington, Ohio, 1979-81; dir. ednl. and adult services Bost Human Devel. Services, Ft. Smith, Ark., 1981-87; adminstrv. officer Cen. Ark. Devel. Coun., Benton, 1987; adminstrv. officer, interim Head Start dir., dir. resource devel. Community Orgn. Poverty Elimination Pulaski, Lonoke Counties, Little Rock, Ark., 1987—; adj. staff Ark. Single Parent Scholarship Fund. Active Welfare Adv. Bd., Clinton County, 1979-81, Home Econs. Ext. Services Adv. Com., 1979-81, adv. bd. U. Ark Women's Ctr., 1979; coord. White House Conf. on Families, 1980; mem. Task Force Child Abuse, 1985; bd. trustees Multiple Sclerosis Soc., Ark. Named one of Outstanding Young Women Am., 1982. Mem. Am. Bus. Women's Assn. Home: 5 Royal Ct Little Rock AR 72211 Office: COPE 3518 W Roosevelt Rd Little Rock AR 72204

ADAMS, SARAH VIRGINIA, family counselor; b. San Francisco, Oct. 23, 1955; d. Marco Tulio and Helen (Jorge) Zea; m. Glenn Richard Adams, Mar 22, 1980; children: Mark Vincent, Elena Giselle, Johnathan Richard. BA, Calif. State U., Long Beach, 1978, MS, 1980. Lic. marriage, family, child counseling. Tutor math. and sci. Montebello, Calif., 1979-82; behavioral specialist Cross Cultural Psychol. Corp., L.A., 1979-80; psychol. asst. Legal Psychology, L.A., 1980-82, Eisner Psychol. Assocs., L.A., 1982-83; assoc. dir. Legal Psychodiagnosis and Forensic Psychology, L.A., 1982-83; adminstrv. dir. Diagnostic Clinic, Calif., 1983-85; dir. Diagnostic Clinic of West Covina, Calif., 1985-87; owner Adams Family Counseling Inc., Calif., 1987—; tchr. piano, Montebello, 1973-84; ins. agent Am. Mut. Life Ins., Des Moines, 1982-84. Fellow Am. Assn. Marriage and Family Therapists; mem. NAFE, Am. Assn. for Marriage and Family Therapy, Calif. Assn. Marriage and Family Therapists, Calif. State Psychol. Assn., Calif. Soc. Indsl. Medicine and Surgery, Psi Chi, Pi Delta Phi. Republican. Roman Catholic. Office: Adams Family Counseling Inc 260 S Glendora #101 West Covina CA 91790

ADAMS, VICTORIA ELEANOR, realty company executive; b. San Francisco, Feb. 8, 1941; d. George Mulford and Sarah Louise (Dearborn) A.; m. Gene M. Richardson, 1965 (div. 1972); 1 child, Raymond; m. Franklin Carlisle Boosman, May 13, 1972 (div. 1990); 1 child, Eric. AA, Palomar Coll., 1976; BBA summa cum laude, Nat. U., 1978. Sales adminstr. Evergreen Internat. Airlines, McMinnville, Oreg., 1983; corp. adminstr. N.N. Jaeschke, Inc., San Diego, 1984—; adminstrv. mgr. Tomlinson Agy., Inc., Spokane, Wash., 1980-86; v.p. Champion Realty Inc., Spokane, 1987—; pub. dir. Champion Pubs., 1987—; bd. dirs. Feline Enterprises, Spokane. Editor: Bravura, 1976; (text) Science Among Us, 1965; designer Astrology game, 1974. Contbr. articles to profl. jours. Solicitor, Am. Heart Assn., 1985. Recipient Cert. Real Estate Sales Achievment, 1978, 1982, 85, 86, 88, 89; Cert. Outstanding Contbn. to Real Estate Edn., 1980. Mem. NAFE, AAUW, Internat. Platform Assn., Adminstrv. Mgmt. Soc. (publicity com. 1980), Exec. Womens Network, Nat. Assn. Realtors, Snohomish County Bd. Realtors (edn. coms. 1988—). Avocations: writing, ednl. rsch., fishing, camping, traveling. Home: 223 105th St SE Everett WA 98208 Office: 19417 36th Ave W Ste B Lynnwood WA 98036

ADAMS, VIRGINIA MARIE, automobile club official; b. Dayton, Ohio, June 21, 1929; d. Frank Ellis and Catherine Hattie (Wallace) Zehring; m. Gene Paul Lowery, June 19, 1948 (dec. Sept. 1957); 1 child, Steven L.; m. Charles A. Adams, Dec. 9, 1960; children: Susan, Steven E. Grad. high sch., Vandalia, Ohio. Cert. tour profl. Motel mgr. Travelodge, Dayton, 1961-69; tour operator Miami Valley Auto Club, Dayton, 1969—; ptnr. U. Dayton Rentals, Dayton, 1968—; sec., treas. Nat. Tour Found., Atlanta, 1985. Bd. dirs. Kettering C. of C., 1976. Recipient spl. achievement award Amtrak, 1981, Golden Spike awards, 1975-81. Mem. NAFE (bd. dirs. 1988—, pres. 1988—), AFE (bd. dirs. 1987—), Miami Valley Mil. Affairs Assn., Nat. Tour Assn. (speaker, cons.), Nat. Assn. R.R. Passengers. Home: 2567 Evelyn Dr Dayton OH 45409 Office: Miami Valley Auto Club 4041 Marshall Rd Kettering OH 45429

ADAMS-ENDER, CLARA LEACH, nurse; b. Willow Springs, N.C., July 11, 1939; d. Otha and Caretha (Sapp) Leach; m. F. Heinz Ender; 1 child, Sven Ingo. BS, N.C. Agrl. and Tech. State U., 1961; MS, U. Minn., 1969; M in Mil. Art and Sci., Command and Gen. Staff Coll., 1976; Diploma Internat. in Mgmt. Relations and Leadership, U.S. Army War Coll., 1982. Reg. nurse. Commd. 2d lt. U.S. Army, 1961, advanced through grade to brigadier gen.; staff nurse intensive care Walson Army Hosp., Ft. Dix, N.J., 1961-63; staff nurse surg. intensive care 121st Evacuation Hosp., Seoul, Korea, 1963-64; nurse instr. U.S. Army Med. Tng. Ctr., Ft. Sam Houston, Tex., 1965-67; asst. prof. U. Md. Sch. Nursing, Balt., 1969-74; asst. chief nurse Kimbrough Army Hosp., Ft. Meade, Md., 1974-75; nurse inspector gen. Hdqrs. Health Services Command, Ft. Sam Houston, 1976-78; chief nurse 97th Gen. Hosp. Frankfurt (Fed. Republic of Germany) Army Med. Ctr., 1978-81, U.S. Army Recruiting Command, Ft. Sheridan, Ill., 1981-84, Walter Reed Army Med. Ctr., Washington, 1984-87; chief army nurse corps staff Surgeon Gen. of the Army, Falls Church, 1987—; vis. com. Care-Western Res. U., Cleve., 1984—; cons. Children's TV Workshop, N.Y.C., 1971-73, 7th Med. Command Europe, Heidelberg, Germany, 1978-81, Chief Army Nurse Corps, Washington, 1972-75. Contbr. articles to profl. jours. V.p. Rocks, Inc., Washington, 1987—; bd. dirs. Boy Scout of Am., Lake Forest, Ill, 1983-84. Recipient Presdl. Sports award, 1980, Legion of Merit award U.S. Army, 1987. Mem. Am. Nurses Assn. (mem. com. 1984—), Nat. League for Nursing (lectr. 1973—), U.S. Army Med. Dept. (Profl. Designator award 1985), NAACP, Am. Orgn. Nurse Execs., Chi Eta Phi (sec., Outstanding Com. Mem. award 1987), U.S. Army War Coll. Alumni Assn. Roman Catholic. Clubs: Walter Reed Officers Wives (chair ways and means com. 1985-86), Washington Area 500. Home: 2003 Gatewood Pl Silver Spring MD 20903 Office: HQ DA (DASG-CN) 5111 Leesburg Pike Falls Church VA 22041-3528*

ADAMSON, DOROTHY MARIE, retired librarian; b. Brookville, Pa., Dec. 18, 1920; d. Howard James and Alice (May) Shaffer; m. George McClelland Adamson, June 30, 1950; children: Elin Havrilla, Alison Reasinger, George M. Adamson Jr. BS in Edn., Clarion U., 1942, postgrad., 1970-71. Jr. high libr. DuBois (Pa.) City Schs., 1942-46, Erie (Pa.) Sch. Dist., 1946-50; elem. libr. Punxsutawney (Pa.) Area Schs., 1963-87; advisor div. librs. Pa. Dept. Edn., Harrisburg, early 1970's. Editor Punxsutawney Area Schs. libr. program 1970s. Mem. AAUW (1st v.p., pres., legis. chmn.), Pi Gamma Mu. Republican. Home: 473 Treasure Lake Du Bois PA 15801

ADAMSON, JANE N., elementary school educator; b. Amarillo, Tex., Feb. 5, 1931; d. Carl W. and Lydie O. (Martin) Ray; 1 child, Dave R. Student, Amarillo Coll., Richland Coll. Univ. Dallas, North Tex. State U.; BS, West Tex. State U., Canyon, 1953; MEd, East Tex. State U., Commerce, 1975. Cert. elem. tchr., Tex.; lic. real estate salesman. Tchr. Dallas Ind. Sch. Dist. Mem. Navy League U.S., N.Y. Acad. Scis., Classroom Tchrs. Dallas, Alpha Chi. Home: PO Box 140783 Dallas TX 75214

ADAMSON, MARY ANNE, geographer, systems engineer; b. Berkeley, Calif., June 25, 1954; d. Arthur Frank and Frances Isobel (Key) A.; m. Richard John Harrington, Sept. 20, 1974. BA with highest honors and great distinction U. Calif., Berkeley, 1975, MA, 1976, postgrad., 1976-78. Cert. tchr. earth scis., Calif.; cert. cave rescue ops. and mgmt., Calif.; lic. emergency med. technician, Contra Costa (Calif.) County, 1983. Teaching asst. dept. geography U. Calif., Berkeley, 1976; geographer, environ. and fgn. area analyst Lawrence Livermore Nat. Lab., Livermore, Calif., 1978-83, cons., 1983-89; systems engr. ESL, Sunnyvale, Calif., 1986—. Contbr. articles to profl. jours. Staff mem. ARC/Am. Trauma Soc/Sierra Club Urgent Care and Mountain Medicine seminars, 1983—. Asst. editor Vulcan's Voice, 1982. Mem. Assn. Am. Geographers, Assn. Pacific Coast Geographers, Nat. Speleol. Soc. (geology, geography sects., sec., editor newsletter Diablo Grotto chpt. 1982-86), Sierra Club (life), Nature Conservancy (life), U. Calif. Alumnae Assn., Phi Beta Kappa. Home: 4603 Lakewood St Pleasanton CA 94588 Office: ESL Inc 495 Java Dr Sunnyvale CA 94088

ADAMS-ROBERTS, IROSE FERNELLA, nurse; b. Potters, St. Johns, Antigua, Sept. 10, 1945; d. George Alexander and Mary Magnalene (Jacobs) Adams; m. Virgil Roberts Sr., May 10, 1969 (div.); 1 child Virgil Jr. Student, Essex County Coll., Newark, 1985, Cranford Coll. Lic. practical nurse. LPN East Orange VA Med. Ctr. Author: Faith, Hope and Love, 1985. Mem. Am. Songwriter's Club. Home: 206 Amherst St East Orange NJ 07018

ADAMS-SLONE, RITA DIANE, physician; b. Portsmouth, Ohio, Apr. 29, 1949; d. Roy Harrison and Sally Ann (Chinn) Adams; m. Roy Henderson Slone, May 29, 1966; children: Duke Edward, Stacy Diane. AS, Ohio U., 1974, BA, 1979, DO, 1984. Lic. physician, Ohio, Ky. Staff nurse Pike County Community Hosp., Waverly, Ohio, 1974; continuing care nurse Scioto Meml. Hosp., Portsmouth, 1975-76, ICU nurse, 1976-77; nurse Scioto County Health Dept., Portsmouth, 1977; physician Adams Clinic, Minford, Ohio, 1985-86; family practice medicine Portsmouth, 1986—; med. dir. U.S. Health Facilities, Jackson, Ohio, 1988—. Mem. Ky. Hist. Soc.; bd. dirs. Am. Heart Assn., Ohio. Mem. Am. Osteopathic Assn., Portsmouth Acad. Family Physicians, NAFE, Ducks Unltd., Nat. Ruffed Grouse Soc., NRA, United Meth. Women, Circle of Faith, Century Club. Republican. Home: 10352 Rt 139 Jackson OH 45640 Office: US Health So Ohio Med Office Bldg 336 E Main St Jackson OH 45640

ADAWI, NADIA SHARON, electrical engineer; b. Princeton, N.J., Aug. 29, 1958; d. Ibrahim Hussein and Gerda (Obert) Adawi; m. Patrick John Loll, June 18, 1983. BSEE, U. Mo., 1980; postgrad., George Washington U., 1980-82. Electronics engr. FCC, Washington, 1980-81; cons. engr. Becker, Gurman, Lukas et al, Washington, 1981-82; dir. engring. Maxcell Telecom Plus, Washington, 1982-84, Lunayach Communications, Washington, 1984-86; dir. tech. support Cellular Radio Corp., Herndon, Va., 1986-87; dir. engring. Vision Systems Inc., Arlington, Va., 1987-89; asst. dir. radio planning and new tech. Ameritech Mobile Communications, Schaumburg, Ill., 1989—; engring. cons. Mobile Radio Systems, Inc., Washington, 1986-89. Mem. IEEE, Soc. for Study of Amphibians and Reptiles, NOW. Democrat. Home: 118 S Wesley Ave Oak Park IL 60302

ADDELSON, KATHRYN PYNE, philosophy educator, writer; b. Providence, Apr. 22, 1932; d. Joseph Abraham and Catherine (Newton) Etchells; m. Terence Parsons, June 10, 1967 (div.); children: Catherine Casey Pyne, Shawn Pyne; m. 2d Richard Ullman Addelson, Oct. 31, 1980. A.B., Ind. U., 1961; Ph.D., Stanford U., 1968. Lectr. Bryn Mawr Coll., (Pa.), 1965-66, CCNY, N.Y.C., 1966-67; asst. prof. philosophy U. Ill., Chgo., 1967-72; prof. philosophy Smith Coll., Northampton, Mass., 1972—; assoc. editor Feminist Studies. Contbr. writings to anthologies and jours. Nat. Endowment for Humanities grantee, 1978-79. Nat. Endowment for Humanities fellow, 1978-79. Mem. Soc. for Women in Philosophy (exec. sec. Eastern div.). Office: Smith College Northampton MA 01060*

ADDIS, KAREN K., editor; b. Vienna, Austria, Jan. 26, 1964; d. Raymond Frank and Alva Nell (Wells) Kemery; m. Scott R. Addis, Oct. 15, 1988. Student journalism, pub. rels., U. Md., 1985. Pub. rels. coord. Nat. Assn. Hearing and Speech Action, Rockville, Md.; editor Am. Soc. Indsl. Security, Arlington, Va. Contbr. articles to publs. block capt. Calverton Citizens Assn., 1990—. Mem. Pub. Rels. Soc. Am. (ch. woman newsletter com. 1990—, mem. task force on drug abuse 1988, mem. task force on illiteracy 1988). Republican. Office: Am Soc Indsl Security 1655 N Fort Myer Dr Ste 1200 Arlington VA 22209

ADDIS, SARA ALLEN, franchise executive; b. El Paso, Tex., May 15, 1930; d. Waldo Rufus and Cordelia Dean (Kerr) Allen; m. Bobby Joe Addis, June 5, 1949; children: Craig Dell, Alan Blake, Neil Clark, Sara Kathleen. Sec. to adminstr. Southwestern Gen. Hosp., El Paso, 1948-49; sec. to dir. of personnel U. Tex., El Paso, 1964-65; pres., founder Sara Care Franchise Corp., El Paso, 1978—; chmn. bd. Sara Care Inc., 1988—. Named Small Bus. Person of Yr., Small Bus. Adminstrn., 1986, 87. Mem. Internat. Franchise Assn., Nat. Fedn. Ind. Businesses, Presidents Assn. Am. Mgmt. Assn., El Paso Better Bus. Bur., El Paso C. of C., Assn. Pioneer Women. (Entrepreneur of Yr.), Bus. and Profl. Women El Paso (Small Bus. Person of Yr. 1983, 85, 86, 87), Exec. Forum, Profl. Women's Network U. Tex. El Paso. Republican. Club: Lower Valley Women's. Lodge: Order Eastern Star. Avocations: oil painting, music, travel. Home: 8417 Parkland St El Paso TX 79925 Office: Sara Care Franchise Corp 1612 Lee Trevino Ste A El Paso TX 79936

ADDISON, MARY JANE, civic worker; b. Beaumont, Tex.; d. Henry Davis and Corinne (Carter) Pond; m. Eugene Morse Addison, Mar. 10, 1946; children: Eugene Morse, Paul Davis. RN, Jefferson Davis Sch. Nursing, 1945; student, U. Houston. Mem. choir First Bapt. Ch.; den mother Cub Scouts, 6 years, recipient Den Mothers award, 1961; pres. Huntsville (Tex.) PTA, 1955-56, v.p. dist. bd., 1956-57, state life mem. PTA, 1967; pres. Women's Missionary Union, First Bapt. Ch., 1965-68, also Sunday Sch. tchr.; chmn. heritage com. Mayor's Bicentennial Com., 1974-76; chmn. city beautification com. Tex. Sesquicentennial Celebration, 1982-86; pres. Woman's Forum, Tex. Fedn. Womens Clubs, 1972-74, 80-81, named Woman of Year, 1974; charter and life mem. Hosp. Aux., pres., 1971-72; pres. Walker County Cancer Soc., 1983-84; bd. dirs. Cultural Arts Ctr., 71-72; chmn. bd. dirs. Sam Houston Meml. Mus. 1983-87; bd. dirs. Walker County Hist. Commn.; mem., dir., sponsor Community Choir; mem. mayors com. Bicentennial of the Constn. of U.S. Celebration, 1987—. Decorated Grand Peiory of Am. Order St. John of Jerusalem, dame Knights Hospitaller; recipient Cert. of Commendation, Heritage Com., 1980, 81. Mem. Daus. Republic of Tex. (pres. Houston chpt. 1970-75, 79-81, registrar 1975—, state rec. sec. gen. 1973-75, state 1st v.p. gen. 1975-77, pres. gen. 1977-79 library bd. 1981-83, Alamo bd. 1983-85, 87-89), DAR (regent Mary Martin Elmore Scott chpt. 1972-74, 82-86), Daus. Am. Colonists (regent Capt. John Utie chpt., state corr. sec. 1977-79, state rec. sec. 1983-85, state 1st vice regent 1985-87, regent 1987-89), UDC (dist. rec. sec. 1974-76, dist. chmn. 1981-83, state div. historian 1984-86, pres. chpt. 1983-85, 88—), Colonial Dames Am., Dames of Ct. of Honor, Tex. Hist. Found. (chpt. regent 1987-89, dir., cert. of commendation 1980, 81, mem. state heritage com.), Walker County Geneal. Soc., San Jacinto Mus. History Assn., Washing-on-the-Brazos State Park Assn., Lone Star Drama Hist. Assn. (state adv. bd.), Am., Tex. (pres. 38th Dist. 1977-83) nurses assns., AMA, Tri-County (past pres.) med. auxs., Tex. Acad. Family Physicians (charter; state parliamentarian 1983-84), Beautify Tex. Council, Nat. Soc. Magna Charta Dames (state sec. 1988—), Daus. War of 1812, Colonial Dames of XVII Century (organizing regent 1988—). Clubs: Garden (past pres. chmn. city beautification com.), Univ. Women Sam Houston State U. (charter).

ADDY, JO ALISON PHEARS, economist; b. Ger., May 2, 1951; d. William and Paula (Lee) Phears; m. Tralance Obuama Addy, May 25, 1979; children: Mantse, Miishe, Dwetri, Naakai. BA, Smith Coll., 1973; MBA, Adelphi U., 1975; postgrad., Stanford U., 1975-78. Economic analyst Morgan Guaranty, N.Y.C., 1973-75; econ. cons. Nat. Planning Assn., Washington, 1976; economist Rand Corp., 1978; economist World Bank, Washington, 1979-80; asst. v.p., internat. economist Crocker Bank, San Francisco, 1980-85; asst. v.p., economist, money markets 1st RepublicBank, Dallas, 1985-87, prin. SEGI Internat., Dallas, 1987—; lectr. in field. Bd. dirs. Shakespeare Festival of Dallas. NSF fellow, 1976-79. Mem. Am. Econ. Assn., Dallas Economist Club, Dallas Women's Found. Home: 1904 Rockcliff Ct Arlington TX 76012

ADELEKAN, PATRICIA ANN, youth association executive; b. Columbus, Ohio, Mar. 13, 1942; d. Arthur H. and Betty Jane Isbell; children: Adebola, Adetokunbo, Aderemi, Adegboyega. BA, Ohio State U., 1966; MA, U. San Francisco, 1975; PhD, U. Ibadan, 1983. Cert. coll. adminstr., secondary tchr. Tchr. various schs., Hartford, Conn. and Oakland, Calif., 1968-75; v.p. Lagos State Coll. Edn., Nigeria, 1976-80; dept. head Ogun State Poly. U., Nigeria, 1980-84; rsch. specialist Sacramento City (Calif.) Unified Sch. Dist., 1985-87; lectr. Sierra Coll., Rocklin, Calif., 1988-89; pres. Youth-on-the-Move, Inc., Sacramento, 1986—; cons. Gifted and Talented Edn., Sacramento, 1985-86; columnist Sacramento Observer, 1987—. Editor numerous articles; contbr. articles to profl. jours.; pubr./editor Youth on the News, mo. newspaper, 1989—. V.p. YWCA, Sacramento, 1988-89; commr. County Children's Commn., Sacremento, 1989—; mem. Leadership Sacramento, 1988-89. Recipient Cert. of Recognition award, assemblyman Norman Waters, 1981, Proclamation award, City of Sacramento Mayor, 1989, Plaque of Achievement award, 1989, Love and Help Children award. Mem. Calif. Tchr.'s Assn., Nat. Assn. French Tchrs., Nat. Mensa Soc., AAUW (chair edn. com.), NAFE, Phi Delta Kappa. Home: 7436 Henrietta Dr Sacramento CA 95822

ADELIS, NANCY C., human resources executive; b. N.Y.C., Nov. 3, 1953; d. BS magna cum laude, NYU, 1975, MA summa cum laude, 1976. Cert. Inst. Personality Ability Testing, Performax Instrument. Chair dept. fgn. lang. B. Kearney H.S., 1980-85; assoc. mgr. mgmt., exec. devel. Office Pers. Mgmt., N.Y.C., 1985-87; adminstr. Orgn. Devel. and Tng. RCA Corp., Princeton, N.J., 1987-89; sr. cons. Hoffmann-La Roche Inc., Nutley, N.J., 1989—; dir. human resources Pa. Cons. Group, Princeton. Author, contbr. corp. devel. manuals and guides. Mem. PMA task force on adv. of Sci. and Math, N.J. Gov.'s task force-Civil Svc. Reform. Mem. Soc. Human Resources Mgmt., Orgn. Devel. Network, Am. Soc. Tng. and Devel., Raritan Bay U.S. Power Squadron. Office: 279 Princeton Rd Hightstown NJ 08520

ADELMANN, PENELOPE OWENS, financial analyst; b. Bklyn.; d. Philip Cromwell and Virginia (Raebeck) Owens; m. Richard Lewis Adelmann, Sept. 11, 1965. BA, Swarthmore Coll., 1966; MBA, NYU, 1981. Chartered fin. analyst. Rating analyst Standard & Poor's, N.Y.C., 1979-81, rating specialist, 1981; asst. v.p. Bankers Trust, N.Y.C., 1981-83, v.p., 1983; v.p. AG Becker Paribas, N.Y.C., 1983-84; v.p./mgr Dean Witter, N.Y.C., 1984-87; v.p. mgr. Nomura Securities Internat., N.Y.C., 1987—. Fin. trustee Scarsdale Congregational Ch., 1989—. Mem. Fixed Income Analysts Soc. Inc. (program chmn., pres. 1984-85), N.Y. Soc. Security Analysts (membership com. 1985—, bd. dirs., membership chair 1989—). Republican. Congregationalist. Office: Nomura Securities Internat 180 Maiden Ln New York NY 10038

ADELSMAN, (HARRIETTE) JEAN, newspaper editor; b. Indpls., Oct. 21, 1944; d. Joe and Beatrice Irene (Samuel) A. BS in Journalism, Northwestern U., 1966, MS in Journalism, 1967. Copy editor Chgo. Sun-Times, 1967-75, editor fin. news, 1975-77, entertainment editor, 1977-80, asst. mng. editor features, from 1980; now mng. editor Daily Breeze, Torrance, Calif. Office: Daily Breeze 5215 Torrance Blvd Torrance CA 90509*

ADEWUSI, OLUKEMI IYABODE, biology educator; b. Ede, Oyo, Nigeria, Nov. 13, 1956; came to U.S., 1978; d. Bejamin Aderinto and Esther Eboade (Adedeji) A.; m. Henry Keke Efevbera, Aug. 16, 1986; 1 child, Yvette Oluseyi Efevbera. BSc, East Tex. Bapt. U., Marshall, 1980; MSc, Stephen F. Austin State U., Nacogdoches, Tex., 1982; PhD, North Tex. State U., Denton, 1986. Lab. asst. East Tex. Bapt. U., Marshall, 1979-80; teaching asst. Stephen F. Austin State U., Nacogdoches, 1980-82; rsch. asst. North Tex. State U., Denton, 1982-83, teaching asst., 1983-86; vis. asst. prof. Va. Commonwealth U., Richmond, 1986-87; asst. prof. biology Ferris State U., Big Rapids, Mich.; cons. McGraw Hill Pub. Co., San Francisco, 1989—, William C. Brown Pubs., Dubuque, Iowa, 1990—; biology coord. Health Careers Opportunity Program, Big Rapids, Mich., 1988—; coord. Gen. Biology Lab., Big Rapids, 1988—. Contbr. articles to profl. jours. Facilitator Newaygo County Explorations in Math., Muskegon, Mich., 1990. North Tex. State U. honor student fellow, Denton, 1985-86; Ferris State U. rsch. grantee, Big Rapids, 1990. Mem. Am. Soc. Parasitologists, Tex. Soc. Electron Microscopy, Sigma Xi, Beta Beta Beta. Baptist. Office: Ferris State U Big Rapids MI 49307

ADEYEYE, CHRISTIANAH MOJISOLA, pharmacist educator; b. Ifewara, Liesa, Nigeria, May 29, 1951; came to U.S., 1982; d. Peter Awoyemi and AbigailOminure (Obilade) Akinsanya; m. Adebisi Olushola Adeyeye, June 25, 1977; children: Tobi, Ibukun, Temi. BS, U. Nigeria, Nsukka, Anambra, 1976; MS, U. Ga., 1985, PhD, 1988. Pharmacist U. Coll. Hosp., Ibadan, Nigeria, 1976-79, Bapt. Med. Ctr., Ogbomoso, Nigeria, 1979-80; asst. prof. Sch. Pharmacy U. P.R., San Juan, 1988-89, Duquesne U., Pitts., 1989—. Mem. AAUP, AAUW (award 1983), Am. Pharm. Assn., Am. Assn. Pharm. Scientists, Am. Assn. Coll. Pharmacy, Rho Chi. Office: Duquesne U Sch Pharmacy Pittsburgh PA 15282

ADIE, NORA SUSAN, environmental educations specialist, film maker; b. Cobbleskill, NY, Feb. 4, 1953; d. William Montford and Astrid Louise (Dahlin) Adie; m. Bradley Wayne Stahl; Leith Bjorn Adie-Stahl. AAS, The Finger Lakes Community Col, Canandaigua, NY, 1974; BS, Cornell U., Ithaca, NY, 1982. Recreation dir. Finger Lakes Commn. N.Y. State Pks., Trumansburg, 1978; outdoor recreation asst. U.S. Fish and Wildlife Svc., Seneca Falls, N.Y., 1981-85; exec. dir. producer Nature Episodes, Locke, NY, 1985--; dir. rsch., devel. and film prod. Nature Episodes, 1981—; self employed environmental edn. cons., Seneca Falls 1980--. Author: Dimensions, 1973-74, Grapevine Press, 1973-75. Bd. mem. Town Fayette Planning bd., 1985-88. Names Conservation Educator of the Yr. N.Y. State Conservation Coun., 1986, 87. Mem. Seneca Falls Area br. AAUW (v.p. 1985--), N.Y.S. Outdoor Edn. Assn. Office: Nature Episodes 1218 Auburn Rd Locke NY 13092

ADILETTA, DEBRA JEAN OLSON, business analyst consultant; b. Gloucester, Mass., Oct. 1, 1959; d. Melvin Porter Jr. and Ruth Margaret (Dahlmer) Olson; m. Mark Anthony Adiletta, Aug. 25, 1984; 1 child, Christopher Michael. BA, Coll. of Holy Cross, Worcester, Mass., 1981; MBA, U. Rochester, 1986. Systems analyst Eastman Kodak Co., Rochester, N.Y., 1981-85, infosystems specialist, 1985-86, personal computer area mgr., 1986-87, bus. analyst cons., 1987—. seminar instr., Rochester, 1987. Fin. advisor Sts. Peter and Paul Ch., Rochester, 1985-86; div. chairperson United Way, Rochester, 1987. Mem. Assn. Systems Mgmt., Holy Cross Alumni Assn. (class agt. 1981—, sec. 1983-84, treas. 1984-88, v.p. 1988—). Office: Eastman Kodak Co 343 State St Rochester NY 14650

ADIN, NANCY EDITH, chemistry educator; b. Englewood, N.J., Sept. 12, 1938; d. Joseph George and Sara (Meyers) Gershman; m. Bernard Adin, Mar. 20, 1966 (div. 1979); 1 child, Scott Kenneth. BA in Chemistry, Syracuse U., 1960; MS in Chemistry, U. R.I., Kingston, 1962; PhD in

Organic Chemistry, Rutgers U., 1966. Rsch. chemist City of Hope, Duarte, Calif., 1966-67, Bell & Howell Rsch. Lab., Pasadena, Calif., 1967-68, Med. Diagnostics Operation/Xerox, Pasadena, 1968-70; documentation chemist Lee Pharms., South El Monte, Calif., 1974-75; sr. scientist Global Geochemisty Corp., Canoga Park, Calif., 1979-81; assoc. prof. chemistry Calif. State U., Long Beach, 1979-84, Fullerton, 1984—, L.A., 1974—; tech. advisor Casmalia Community Adv. Com., Santa Maria, Calif., 1987-89. Contbr. articles to profl. jours. Mem. West Covina (Calif.) Transition Waste Mgmt. Commn., 1984-86; mem. Coalition of West Covina Homeowners' Assns., 1985—. Mem. Am. Chem. Soc., Air and Waste Mgmt. Assn., Union Concerned Scientists, Citizen's Clearinghouse for Hazardous Waste. Democrat. Home: 2633 Maureen St West Covina CA 91792

ADKINS, BETTY A., state legislator; b. Mpls., June 4, 1934; d. John Edward and Barbara (Graff) Whalen; m. Wally Adkins, 1956; children—Patrick, Susan, Michael, Kathleen, Caroline, Nancy. Student North Hennepin Community Coll.; student U. Minn., 1952-53. Formerly dep. clk. Otsego Twp., vice chmn. Wright County Bd. Adjustment, Minn.; mem. Minn. Senate, St. Paul, 1982—. Formerly chmn. Wright County Democratic-Farmer-Labor Party. Home: 1655 Kadler Ave N E Saint Michael MN 55376-9370 Office: State Capitol Saint Paul MN 55155 Other: 550 Central Ave E Saint Michael MN 55376*

ADKINS, ROSANNE BROWN, speech-language pathologist; b. Norfolk, Va., Jan. 10, 1944; d. Melvin Dillard and Mattye Marie (Cox) Brown; BS, U. Ga., 1968, MEd, 1971; m. Steve Bunker, Aug. 24, 1962 (div.); children: Steve , Amy Bunker Hurtado; m. Jon Adkins, May 27, 1988. Speech pathologist Barrow County Schs., Winder, Ga., 1968-69, Madison County Schs., Danielsville, Ga., 1969-70, Hall County Schs., Gainesville, Ga., 1971-72, Hope Haven Sch. for Retarded Children, Athens, Ga., 1972-73, Buford (Ga.) City Schs., 1973-75, Duval County Bd. Pub. Instrn., Jacksonville, Fla., 1975-79, Orange County Pub. Schs., Orlando, Fla., 1979—. Sallie Maude Jones scholar, U. Ga., 1966-68; USPHS grad. fellow, 1970-71. Mem. Am. Speech-Lang.-Hearing Assn. (cert. of clin. competence), Fla. Lang. Speech and Hearing Assn. Delta Zeta, Zeta Phi Eta, Kappa Delta Pi, Phi Kappa Phi. Mem. Disciples of Christ. Clubs: Order Amaranth (past Royal Matron), Ladies of the Elks. Editor, Speakeasy, Speech and Language Newsletter, 1982-90. Home: 606 David St Winter Springs FL 32708 Office: Orange County Sch System 434 N Tampa Ave Orlando FL 32801

ADKINS, TERRI LYNN, sales executive; b. Flint, Mich., Jan. 28, 1957; d. Vernon Adkins and Sandra Kay (Woods) Des Jardin. BA, Mich. State U., 1981. Dist. sales mgr. Chevrolet Motor Div., Mansfield, Ohio, 1983-85; met. dist. mgr. Chevrolet Motor Div., Akron and Canton, Ohio, 1986-87; mgr. dealer network planning Chevrolet Motor Div. Chevrolet Mktg. Ctr., Pitts., 1988-89; area mgr. sales Chevrolet Motor div. Chevrolet Mktg. Ctr., Warren, Mich., 1989—. Mem. NAFE, Smithsonian Assocs. Democrat. Office: Chevrolet Mktg Ctr 30007 Van Dyke Ave Warren MI 48098

ADKINS-REGAN, ELIZABETH KOCHER, biological psychology educator; b. Washington, July 12, 1945; d. Charles Peter and Dorothy Esther (Clay) Kocher; m. David Adkins, 1971 (div. 1973); m. Dennis Thomas Regan, 1980. BS, U. Md., 1967; PhD, U. Pa., 1971. Rsch. assoc. Bucknell U., Lewisburg, Pa., 1971-72, asst. prof., 1972-74; asst. prof. SUNY, Cortland, 1974-75; asst. prof. psychology/neurobiology and behavior Cornell U., Ithaca, N.Y., 1975-81, assoc. prof., 1981-88, prof., 1988—. Assoc. editor Hormones and Behavior, 1986—; contbr. articles and book revs. to profl. jours., chpts. to books. Recipient sr. award NSF, 1986; Woodrow Wilson Found. hon. fellow, 1967, NSF grad. fellow, 1967-71, Fulbright scholar, 1986. Fellow AAAS; mem. Animal Behavior Soc., Soc. Neurosci., Am. Psychol. Soc., Internat. Soc. Psychoneuroendocrinology, Phi Beta Kappa. Office: Cornell U Uris Hall Ithaca NY 14853-7601

ADLER, JANE EVE, internationally syndicated columnist, cartoonist and illustrator; b. Providence, Oct. 8, 1944; d. Frank Kozlov and Ruth Cohen; m. Edwin I. Adler, Feb. 19, 1961; children: Lindsay, Steven. B.A., U. R.I., 1971. Art dir. Trinity Sq. Theatre, 1971-72; T.V. talk show hostess, writer, artistic dir. original plays PBS 1971-72; weekly columnist/illustrator Boston Herald, Providence Journal, National Observer, 1972-77; Whitegate Features Syndicate syndicated columnist/illustrator, 1977-88; tchr., lectr., TV and radio guest in horticulture and writing. Author monthly nat. mag. columns; writer of books on children, 1982—; columnist for Boston Herald on child healthcare, 1984—; travel writer for Whitegate News Syndicate, 1987—. Participant in numerous one woman and group art shows, 1965—. Organizer of free painting course for women at U. R.I.; active in numerous charity and cultural activities. Recipient awards for writing from various groups such as R.I. Fed. Garden Clubs. Mem. R.I. Horticulture Soc. (organizer), Garden Writers of Am., N.Y. Art Dirs. Club, Childhood and Adult Devel. Resources Inst. (founder, bd. dirs.) Jewish. Lodges: Masons, B'nai Brith. Office: 71 Faunce Dr Providence RI 02906

ADLER, LEONORE LOEB, psychologist; b. Karlsruhe, Germany, May 2, 1921; d. Leo and Elsie (Laemle) Loeb; m. Helmut E. Adler, May 22, 1943; children: Barry Peter, Beverly Sharmaine, Evelyn Renée. B.A. cum laude, Queens Coll., CUNY, 1968; Ph.D., Adelphi U., 1972. Rsch. asst. Am. Mus. Natural History, N.Y.C., 1956-84; adj. asst. prof. psychology Coll. S.I., CUNY, 1974-80; rsch. assoc. Mystic Marinelife Aquarium (Conn.), 1976-85; assoc. prof. dept. psychology, dir. Inst. for Cross-Cultural and Cross-Ethnic Studies, Molloy Coll., Rockville Centre, N.Y., 1980—; chmn. internat. and nat. confs. Author book chpts.; translator: This is the Dachshund, 1966, 2d rev. edit., 1975; mem. editorial bd Internat. Jour. of Group Tensions, 1985—; co-editor: Comparative Psychology at Issue, 1973, Language, Sex and Gender: Does "la Différence" Make a Difference, 1979; editor: Issues in Cross-Cultural Research, 1977; Cross-Cultural Research at Issue, 1982; Cross-Cultural Research in Human Development: Life-Span Perspectives, 1989; contbr. articles and chpts. to handbooks, profl. jours. and encys. Mem. to gov.'s com. on women N.Y. State Women's Com., 1977. Recipient Disting. Contbr. of the Decade award Internat. Orgn. for the Study of Group Tensions, 1981, Wilhelm Wundt award, 1989. Fellow N.Y. Acad. Scis. Am. Psychol. Assn. (network of reps. of com. on women in psychology 1982-87); mem. Eastern Psychol. Assn. (bd. dirs. 1985-86, 87-90), N.Y. State Psychol. Assn. (pres. div. social psychology 1978-79, 80-82, 84-85, 90-91; pres. div. acad. psychology 1982-83, 88-89; mem. coun. reps. 1981-84, 86-87; chmn. com. women's issues 1982-84. Plaque for outstanding achievement from women's com. 1984, medallion from social div. 1984, Kurt Lewin award 1985), Internat. Assn. Cross-Cultural Psychology, Soc. Cross-Cultural Rsch., Internat. Orgn. Study Group Tensions (mng. editor Internat. Jour. Group Tensions, 1978-84, assoc. editor 1984-85, mem. editorial bd. 1985—), Animal Behavior Soc., Internat. Soc. Comparative Psychology, Assn. Women in Sci., Soc. Advancement Social Psychology, Internat. Coun. Psychologists (treas. 1983-85), Cheiron, the Internat. Soc. for History of Behavioral and Social Scis., Queens County Psychol. Assn. (pres.-elect 1985-87, pres. 1987-88), Psi Chi (faculty adviser Molloy Coll., 1980—), Alpha Sigma Lambda, Psi Chi, Zeta Epsilon Gamma. Jewish. Home: 162-14 86th Ave Jamaica NY 11432 Office: Molloy Coll Inst Cross Cultural and Cross Ethnic Studies 1000 Hempstead Ave Rockville Centre NY 11570

ADLER, SHARON SWETZ, health administrator; b. Rockville Ctr., N.Y., Nov. 10, 1960; d. Charles Frank and Patricia Marie (Finn) Swetz; m. Ralph William Adler II, Sept. 19, 1987. BA, Colgate U., 1982; M in Healthcare Adminstrn, Duke U., 1984. Administrv. resident Putnam Meml. Hosp., Bennington, Vt., 1984-86; asst. v.p. S.W. Vt. Med. Ctr., Bennington, 1986, v.p., 1986—. Mem. editorial bd. Materiel Mgmt. Quar., 1989—. Bd. dirs. United Way, Bennington, 1986—, campaign chmn., 1987, v.p., 1989, pres., 1990. Mem. Am. Coll. Healthcare Execs. (nominee), Colgate U. Alumni Assn. (bd. dirs. 1987-90, exec. com. 1989-90), Rotary (chmn. projects com. Bennington 1987—). Roman Catholic. Home: RR 1 Box 37 North Bennington VT 05257 Office: Southwestern Vt Med Ctr 100 Hospital Dr Bennington VT 05201

ADMIRE, SHARMAN LYNNE, educational publishing consultant; b. Houston, Aug. 12, 1952; d. Robert Eugene and Evelyn (McEuen) Wainscott; m. Mark Alan Admire, Feb. 18, 1983. B, Tex. Tech. U., Lubbock, 1975, MEd, 1981. Cert. Tchr. Tchr. Lubbock (Tex.) Pub. Sch., 1976-83, Austin Pub. Schs., 1983-86; cons. HBJ Pub., Dallas, 1986--. Author: St. David's Messenger, 1985, 1987. Vol. Austin Women's Resource Ctr., 1986, mem. St. David Episcopal Ch., Austin, 1983--. Mem. Tex. Assn. of Pub., Capital Area Reading Council, Cen. Tex. Council of Tchrs of English, Assn. of Language Arts Supr., Young Marrieds,. Office: HBJ Pub PO Box 612267 Dallas TX 75261-2267

ADOFF, MRS. ARNOLD See HAMILTON, VIRGINIA

ADOLPH, MARY ROSENQUIST, financial executive; b. Springfield, Mass., Oct. 7, 1949; d. Jesse Woodson and Doris May (Marquette) Rosenquist; m. Earl Anthony Soares, Mar. 18, 1972 (div. 1982); m. Joseph Edward Adolph, Oct. 3, 1986. Student San Domenico Sch., 1966-68, Dominican Coll., San Rafael, 1967-69, Calif., San Francisco Conservatory of Music, 1968-70; A.A., Coll. of Marin, 1969. Asst. v.p. Western Travelers Life Ins. Co./Putnam Fin. Services, San Rafael, 1970-80; v.p. Unimarc, Ltd., Novato, Calif., 1980-83; v.p. mktg. Western States Monetary Planning Services, Inc., Newhall, Calif., 1983-88; asst. to pres. Fed. Inventory Wholesale, Inc., 1988—; with RENET Fin.-Newhall/E.W. Richardson & Assocs. Mem. exec. com. San Marin Valley Homeowners Assn., 1979-81. Mem. Internat. Assn. Fin. Planners, Life Underwriters Assn. Democrat. Roman Catholic. Home: 14710 Burbank Blvd #102 Van Nuys CA 91411 Office: RENET Fin-Newhall/E W Richardson & Assocs 24325 Arcadia St Newhall CA 91321

ADREON, BEATRICE MARIE RICE, pharmacist; b. Huntington, W.Va., July 23, 1929; d. Lloyd Emerson and Beatrice (Odell) Rice; student Mary Washington Coll., 1947-49; B.S. in Pharmacy, Med. Coll. Va., 1952; M.A. in Spl. Studies and Women's Studies, George Washington U., 1976; m. Harry Barnes Adreon, Jr., Dec. 27, 1952. Summer vol. worker pharmacies De Paul Hosp., Norfolk, Va., 1949, U.S. Marine Hosp., Norfolk, 1950; pharmacist Washington Clinic, 1954-71; counselor George Washington U., 1976-77, cons. gerontology health scis. dept., 1977—; cons. medicine control traffic patterns nursing homes Cross & Adreon, Washington, 1962-87; founder, pres. Pharmacy Counseling Services, Inc., 1978—; with Harry Adreon, Architect, 1989—. Instr. advanced first aid ARC, 1952—, civil def. instr., 1952—; vol. Spanish Edn. Devel. Center, Washington, 1972; mem. Arlington (Va.) Community Services Bd., 1980-83; chmn. com. substance abuse. Recipient Arnold and Marie Schwartz award in pharmacy, 1980. Mem. Acad. Pharmacy Practice, Am. Pharm. Assn., Va. Pharm. Assn., Potomac Pharmacists Assn., AAAS, Am. Inst. History of Pharmacy, Nat. Council Patient Info. and Edn. (task force pub. info.), Panhellenic Assn., Kappa Epsilon. Episcopalian (mem. bishop's com. neighborhood services 1967-69, chmn. services for aged div. 1967-69). Contbr. articles in field to profl. jours. Home: 4524 N 19th Rd Arlington VA 22207 Office: Pharmacy Counseling Svcs Inc 950 N Glebe Rd #140 Arlington VA 22203

ADRI (ADRIENNE STECKLING), fashion designer; b. St. Joseph, Mo.. Ed., Sch. Fine Arts, Washington U., St. Louis, Parson Sch. Design. With B.H. Wragge; owner, pres. Adri Clotheslab Inc., N.Y.C., 1983—; with Claire McCardell in 2-person showing, Innovative Contemporary Fashion, Smithsonian Instn., Washington, 1971. Recipient Coty award, 1982. Office: Adri 143 W 20th New York NY 10011*

ADRIANOPOLI, BARBARA CATHERINE, librarian; b. Ft. Dodge, Iowa, Jan. 27, 1943; d. Daniel Joseph and Mary Dolores (Coleman) Hogan; m. Carl David Adrianopoli, June 28, 1968; children—Carlin, Laurie. B.S., Mundeline Coll., 1966; M.L.S., Rosary Coll., 1975. Tchr., Father Bertrand High Sch., Memphis, 1966-68; caseworker Dept. Pub. Aid Chgo., 1968; tchr. North Chicago Jr. High Sch. (Ill.), 1968-70, Austin Middle Sch., Chgo., 1970-73; librarian Barrington Pub. Library (Ill.), 1976-79, Schaumburg Twp. Pub. Library (Ill.), 1979—; adv. com. N. Suburban/Suburban Library Systems, LaGrange, Ill., 1981-84 . Contbr. articles to jours. Mem. Com. Schaumburg Twp. Disabled, 1981—; pres. Lakeview Pub. Sch. PTA, Hoffman Estates, Ill., 1983-84; historian Village of Hoffman Estates, 1986—; mem. Sch. Dist. 54-Citizens Adv. Com., Schaumburg, 1983-86, Hoffman Estates Sister Cities, 1988-90, Hoffman Estates Hist. Sites Com., 1988—; advisor Boy Scout Am. handicapped badge, Schaumburg Twp., 1981—; co-chair Dist. 54 study group on low achievers, 1988-89, Hoffman Estates rep. Nat. Orgn. on Disability, 1990—,; bd. dirs. Children's Mus. and Imaginasium, 1990—. Mem. ALA, Ill. Library Assn., Library Assn. No. Ill. (v.p. 1981-84), NOW, Polit. Majority, Common Cause. Democrat. Roman Catholic. Home: 1105 Kingsdale Rd Hoffman Estates IL 60194 Office: Schaumburg Twp Pub Libr 21 W Library Ln Schaumburg IL 60194

ADUBATO, SUSAN ANN, psychologist, infant, toddler, parent program director; b. Newark, Aug. 20, 1954; d. Michael C. and Angela Antonia (DiFino) Adubato. MA in Psychology, U. Nebr., 1978; PhD in Psychology, No. Ill. U., 1984. Lic. psychologist, N.J.; cert. for assessment of newborns, cert. in interdisciplinary studies. Teaching asst. No. Ill. U., DeKalb, 1980-82; intern, rsch. assoc. U. Nebr. MCRI, Omaha, 1982-84; rsch. assoc. Boy's Town Inst., Omaha, 1983-84; clinician-infant toddler parent program Community Mental Health Ctr., U. Medicine and Dentistry N.J., Newark, 1984-86, coord. infant toddler parent program, 1986-89, dir. infant toddler parent program, 1989—; cons. for various social svc. agencies, N.J., 1984—, pvt. practice, child psychologist, 1984; co-founder, v.p. Baby CAMS Video Prodn. Co., N.J., 1985—; co-founder; pres. N.J. Assn. for Infant Mental Health; adv. com. Teen Progress, 1988—, Teen Power House, 1988—, N.J. Adoption Adv. Com., 1987—, infant specialist program Rutgers U., 1986—. Author, scriptwriter, producer (videos) The Little Babies That Could, 1986, The Little Premies That Could, 1989; contbr. articles to profl. jours. Grantee Putgers Health Care Grant, N.J., 1989. Mem. Am. Psychol. Assn., Nat. Ctr. for Clin. Infant Programs, Soc. for PediatricPsychology, Child Clin. Psychology, Assn. for Orthopscyhology, ParentCare Inc., Soc. for Rsch. in Child Devel., Nat. Black Child Devel. Inst., Assn. for the Care of Children, Assn. for Children IN N.J., Essex County Network/N.J. Network for Adolescent Programs, Essex County Network on AIDS. Office: U Medicine and Dentistry NJ Community Mental Health Ctr 65 Bergen St Rm 701 Newark NJ 07107-3001

AEHLERT, BARBARA JUNE, health services executive; b. San Antonio, June 17, 1956; d. Bobby Ray and Ronella Su (Light) Mahoney; m. Dean A. Aehlert, Sept. 6, 1980; children: Andrea, Sherri. AA in Nursing, Glendale (Ariz.) Community Coll., 1976; student, Thomas Edison State Coll., Trenton, N.J. Cert. ACLS instr. and affiliate faculty, BLS instr., PHTLS instr., emergency med. tng./paramedic instr., ATLS course coord. Gen. mgr. Hosp. Ambulance Svc., Phoenix; coord. patient transport, critical care RN Samaritan Health Svcs., Phoenix, mgr. clin. programs. Author: Park Medic Core Curriculum-National Park Service, Basic Dysrhythmia Recognition-Student Handbook, ACLS Study Guide. Recipient hon. award of merit Paramedic Program Glendale Fire Dept., 1987, 88, MMesa Fire Dept., 1989. Mem. ASTM, Emergency Nurses Assn. Republican. Home: 6409 W Turquoise Ave Glendale AZ 85302 Office: Samaritan Health Svcs EMS 1441 N 12th St Phoenix AZ 85006

AERY, SHAILA ROSALIE, state educational administrator; b. Tulsa, Dec. 4, 1938; d. Silas Cleveland and Billie (Brewer) A. B.S., U. Okla., 1964; M.S., Okla. State U., 1972, Ed.D., 1975. Spl. asst., chancellor Okla. Regents for Higher Edn., Oklahoma City, 1977; spl. asst., chancellor U. Mo., Columbia, 1978-80, asst. provost acad. affairs, 1980-81; dep. commr. higher edn. State of Mo., Jefferson City, 1981, commr., 1982-89; sec. higher edn., Md., 1989—; dir. Mo. Higher Edn. Loan Authority, St. Louis, 1982—; commr. Edn. Commn. of the States, Denver, 1983—; mem. exec. bd. State Higher Edn. Offices, Denver, 1983—, So. Regionals Edn. Bd. Contbr. articles to profl. jours. Mem. AAUW. Democrat. Episcopalian. Office: Md Higher Edn Commn 16 Francis St Annapolis MD 21401

AFRIDI, PARVEEN NIAZ, psychiatrist; b. Farrukhabad, India, June 20, 1944; came to U.S., 1972; d. Niaz Mohammed and Zakia Sultana Khan-Afridi; M.D. (Merit scholar), S.M.S. Med. Coll., Japiur, India, 1968; m. Mohammed Kalimi, Apr. 26, 1970 (div. Nov. 1975); 1 son, Omar. Rotating intern S.M.S. Med. Coll. Hosp., Jaipur, 1968-69; attending med. officer dept. ob-gyn, Kota and Meerut, India, 1969-72; postdoctoral research Inst. Cancer Research, Columbia U., N.Y.C., 1972-73; resident in psychiatry N.Y. U.-Bellevue Med. Center, N.Y.C., 1974-77; attending psychiatrist Manhattan Psychiat. Center, N.Y.C., 1977-80; clin. instr. psychiatry Albert Einstein Med. Center, N.Y.C. and attending psychiatrist Jacobi Hosp., 1980-81; clin. instr. psychiatry Downstate Med. Center, N.Y.C. and sr. attending psychiatrist Kings County Hosp., N.Y.C., 1981-83, clin. asst. prof SUNY-Health Sci. Ctr., Bklyn., 1983—, sr. attending psychiatrist Kings County Hosp., 1983—. Vol. Heart and Hand for Handicapped. Named one of best psychiat. residents Manhattan Psychiat. Center, 1974-75; recipient Physicians Recognition award AMA, 1977, 83. Mem. Am. Psychiat. Assn., Menninger Found., N.Y. Acad. Scis., Am. Psychiatrists from India (life), N.Y. U.-Bellevue Psychiat. Soc., Assn. Indians in Am., Assn. Asian and Indian Women in Am. Home: Grammercy Spire 142 E 16th St New York NY 10003 Office: 451 Clarkson Ave Brooklyn NY 11203

AFTALION, BELINDE, pathologist; b. Vienna, Austria, Nov. 6, 1921; came to U.S. 1958; d. Joseph and Anny (Hinl)A. MD, U. Madrid, Spain, 1951. Diplomate Am. Bd. Pathology; lic. physician, N.Y. Intern N.Y. Informary, N.Y.C., 1953-59; resident in pathology L.I. Jewish Med. Ctr., 1960-64; fellow in pathology Columbia Presbyn. Hosp., N.Y.C., 1964-65; asst. pathologist Lenox Hill Hosp., 1965-66; staff pathologist L.I. Jewish Med. Ctr., 1966-88; asst. pathologist St. John's Episcopal Hosp., Smithtown, N.Y., 1988—. Office: Saint Johns Episcopal Hosp Route 25A Smithtown NY 11787

AGARD, EMMA ESTORNEL, psychotherapist; b. Bronx, N.Y.. BA, Queens Coll.; MSW, Fordham U., 1962; cert. in Psychoanalytic Psychotherapy, Tng. Inst. for Mental Health, 1979; cert. in Child and Adolescent Psychotherapy, Postgrad. Ctr. for Mental Health, 1982. Supr. social work Foster Care Div., N.Y.C., 1968-72; asst. dir. Henry St. Settlement Urban Family Ctr., N.Y.C., 1972-74; supr. Tng. Inst. for Mental Health, N.Y.C., 1974—; pvt. practice psychotherapist N.Y.C., 1974—; lectr. social work Columbia U., N.Y.C., 1977-80; adj. asst. prof. NYU, 1978-80; field instr. N.Y.C. Housing Authority, 1974-80; dist. dir., cons. Am. Consultation Ctrs., Bklyn. and N.Y.C., 1985—. Mem. Albemarle-Kenmore Neighborhood Assn., Bklyn., 1974—. Fellow N.Y. State Soc. Clin. Social Work Psychotherapists (pres. Bklyn. chpt. 1988—); mem. Profl. Soc. of Tng. Inst. for Mental Health (sec.), Nat. Assn. Social Workers (diplomate), Acad. Cert. Social Workers, Nat. Coalition 100 Black Women, Delta Sigma Theta. Address: 221 E 21st St Brooklyn NY 11226

AGARWAL, CONSTANCE SNYDER, elementary school teacher; b. York, Pa., Mar. 14, 1943; d. James Kenneth and Marion Elizabeth (Anders) Snyder; m. Dwarika Prasad Agarwal, Nov. 17, 1973; children: Meena Elizabeth, David James. AB magna cum laude, Radcliffe Coll., 1965; AM, The Johns Hopkins U., 1968. Tchr. York Country Day Sch., 1969, The Friends Select Sch., Phila., 1969-70. Republican. Home: 13 Stonehedge Attleboro MA 02703

AGEE, NELLE HULME, art history educator; b. Memphis, May 22, 1940; d. John Eulice and Nelle (Ray) Hulme; m. Bob R. Agee, June 7, 1958; children: Denise, Robyn. Student Memphis State U., 1971-72, postgrad., 1978; BA, Union U., Jackson, Tenn., 1978; postgrad. Jackson State U., 1978, Seminole Okla. Coll., 1982, Okla. Bapt. U., 1984; MEd Cen. State U., Edmond, Okla., 1989. Cert. tchr. art, history, Ky., Tenn., Okla. Offices services supr. So. Bapt. Theol. Sem., Louisville, 1961-64; kindergarten tchr. Shively Heights Bapt. Ch., Louisville, 1965-70; editorial asst. Little Publs., agrl. mags., Memphis, 1973-75; tchr. art Humboldt High Sch., Tenn., 1978-82; vis. artist-in-schs. Tenn. Arts Commn., Nashville, 1978, 81, 82; adj. prof. art history Seminole Coll., Okla., 1985-86, 87, 89; instr. art Okla. Baptist U., 1989, asst. prof. art and edn., 1989—; frequent speaker art orgns., ch. groups; tchr. art workshops Humboldt City Sch. system; tchr. Cultural Arts Day Camp, Jackson, Tenn., 1982; nat. pres. ministers' wives conf. So. Bapt. Conv., 1987-88; vol. Mabee-Gerrer Mus., Shawnee. Exhibited art in various shows. Active Salvation Army Aux., Shawnee; v.p. Union U. Woman's Club, 1976-77, pres., 1978. Recipient Disting. Classroom Tchr. award Tenn. Edn. Assn., 1982. Mem. Univ. Alliance, Okla Bapt. U., Alpha Delta Kappa. Democrat. Baptist. Avocations: stained glass, pottery making, travel. Home: 616 University Pkwy Shawnee OK 74801

AGGER, CAROLYN E., lawyer; b. N.Y.C., May 27, 1909. A.B., Barnard Coll., 1931; M.A., U. Wis., 1932; LL.B. cum laude, Yale U., 1938. Bar: D.C. 1938, U.S. Tax Ct. 1943, U.S. Supreme Ct. 1950, U.S. Ct. Claims 1956, U.S. Ct. Appeals (6th cir.) 1958. Atty., NLRB, 1938-39; atty. tax div. U.S. Dept. Justice, Washington, 1939-43; now ptnr. Arnold & Porter, Washington. Mem. Order of Coif. Office: Arnold & Porter Thurman Arnold Bldg 1200 New Hampshire Ave NW Washington DC 20036

AGINS, CAROL RUTH, computer professional; b. N.Y.C., June 4, 1947; d. Emanuel and Selma (Blumenfeld) Bergman; m. Richard C. Agins, Sept. 27, 1970; 1 child, Suzanne. BA, NYU, 1968; MS, U. Pa., 1969. Systems analyst Shell Oil Co., N.Y.C., 1969-70; mgr. Fed. Res. Bank, N.Y.C., 1970-81; dir. info. svcs. The Rockefeller Group, N.Y.C., 1981-89; chief info. officer FCB/Leber Katz Ptnrs., N.Y.C., 1989—. Mem. Soc. Info. Mgmt., Assn. Computer Users in Advt. Office: FCB Leber Katz Ptnrs 767 5th Ave New York NY 10153

AGNELLO, HIGHLAND MARY, systems analyst; b. Rochester, N.Y., Aug. 17, 1964; d. Charles Richard and Marie (Caponetti) A. BA in Maths. summa cum laude, Geneseo (N.Y.) State U., 1986; MS in Computer Sci., Rochester Inst. Tech., 1990. Cert. tchr., N.Y. Tchr. maths. Lowville (N.Y.) Acad., 1986-87; grad. intern Eastman Kodak Co., Rochester, 1988-89, systems analyst, 1989—. Mem. young adult planning team Blessed Sacrement Ch., 1990—. N.Y. State scholar, 1985. Mem. Novell Internat., Western N.Y. Clipper Users Group. Roman Catholic. Home: 142 Greystone Ln Apt 13 Rochester NY 14618 Office: Eastman Kodak Co 343 State St Rochester NY 14650-1220

AGNEW, MIRIAM NELWYN, educator; b. Henderson, Ky., Oct. 4, 1901; d. William Walter and Lila Rene (Cooper) A. AB, Oxford (Ohio) Coll. for Women, 1924; MA, U. Denver, 1937; postgrad., U. Ky., 1926, U. Chgo., 1928. Tchr. English English Barret Manual Tng. High Sch., Henderson, 1924-25, Chanute (Kans.) High Sch., 1925-27, Ashland (Ky.) High Sch., 1927-44, Bosse High Sch., Evansville, Ind., 1944-67; head English dept. Ashland High Sch., 1940-44. Sunday sch. tchr. First United Meth. Ch., Henderson, 1944-67, 72—. Mem. Evansville Ret. Tchr. Orgn., Ind. State Tchr. Assn., NEA, AAUW. Democrat. Home: 900 S Main St Henderson KY 42420

AGRESS, LYNNE JOY, small business owner; b. Trenton, N.J., Dec. 14, 1941; d. Morris M. and Dorothy (Cobin) A. AB, Douglass Coll., New Brunswick, N.J., 1963; PhD, U. Mass., 1975. Teaching asst. U. Mass., Amherst, 1970-75; freelance writer, editor, 1979—; asst. prof. Goucher Coll., Towson, Md., 1977-78; instr. U. Md., Balt., 1980-82, Johns Hopkins U., Balt., 1980-87, Notre Dame Coll., Balt., 1986-87; pres. Bus. Writing At Its Best, Inc., Balt., 1981—; chairperson edn. com. Engring. Soc. Balt., 1989-90. Author: The Feminine Irony, 1978; contbr. articles to popular jours. Deacon 2d Presbyn. Ch., Balt., 1986—, mem. adult edn. com., 1980—; vol., fundraiser Balt. Symphony Orchestra, 1989. NEH grantee, 1978; recipient Disting. Svc. award Nat. League Am. Pen Women, 1984, 86. Mem. Greater Balt. Com. (various subcoms. 1982—), MLA, Rutgers/Douglass Alumni Club Md. (v.p. 1988—), Balt. Women's Forum (pres. 1981—). Democrat. Home and Office: 20 Alanbrooke Ct Towson MD 21204

AGRESTI, VIRGINIA MARY, limousine service owner; b. Schenectady, N.Y., Mar. 14, 1932; d. Adam Felix and Clara (Turilli) Beneduce; m. Nicholas Agresti, May 14, 1955; children: Claudia, David, John. Grad. high sch., Cranston, R.I., 1948. Bank teller, auditor Union Trust Co., Providence, 1948-56; office mgr., acct. Mobil Oil Co. Tng. Ctr., Warwick, R.I., 1965-67; officer mgr., acct. Palmer Plymouth Inc., Warwick, 1967-70, Jake Kaplan's Ltd., Providence, 1970-77; owner, cons. Wedding's Ltd., Warwick, 1977—, Alexis Limousine Svc., Warwick, 1979—; notary pub. State of R.I., 1977—; piano tchr. Treas., mem. exec. bd. Pawtuxet Village Assn., Warwick/Cranston, R.I., 1987—; mem. exec. bd. Gaspee Day Com., Warwick/Cranston, 1974-79, treas., 1976-79, mem., 1973—; sponsor City Nights Theater, 1988. Recipient Outstanding Dealer award Carlson Craft, 1987-89, Outstanding Dealer award Celebration, 1987-89, Wedding Specialist award Coronet, Providence, 1988. Mem. Friends of Blithewold, Am. MENSA, R.I. MENSA, R.I. Honor Soc., Warwick Consortium for the Arts. Home: 79 Roosevelt St Warwick RI 02888 Office: Weddings Ltd Alexis Limo Svc 1379 Roosevelt St Warwick RI 02888

AGUILAR, CAROLYN DEXTER, hospital administrator, nurse; b. Knoxville, Tenn., Apr. 4, 1948; d. Harold Sr. and Cora (Nichols) Dexter; m. Walter Alexander Aguilar, Dec. 22, 1976; children: Peter Alexander, Eric Michael. BS in Nursing, U. Tenn., 1975, MS in Nursing, 1981. RN, Tenn. Caseworker Salvation Army, Knoxville, 1966-67; risk analyst Travelers Ins. Co., Hartford, Conn., 1967-72; receptionist emergency rm. East Tenn. Bapt. Hosp., Knoxville, 1973-75, critical care nurse, 1975-80, supr. nursing, 1980-84, asst. v.p., 1984-89; dir. nursing U. Tenn. Med. Ctr., Knoxville, 1989—. Bandmaster Salvation Army, Knoxville, 1965-68. Grantee The Fred Roddy Found., U. Tenn., Knoxville, 1966-67. Mem. Am. Orgn. Nurse Execs., Tenn. Orgn. Nurse Execs., Sigma Theta Tau, Phi Kappa Phi. Unitarian. Home: 128 Larry Dr Knoxville TN 37920 Office: U Tenn Med Ctr 1924 Alcoa Hwy Knoxville TN 37920

AGUILAR, INGRID MARIA, agricultural products executive; b. Barranquilla, Colombia, Feb. 8, 1958; came to U.S., 1982; d. Francisco and Magdalena (Suarez) Pernett; m. Francisco L. Aguilar, Nov. 9, 1984; 1 child, Barbara I. Student, Sacred Heart U., Bridgeport, Conn., Univ. Internat. de Santander, Barranquilla; PhD, St. Mary Coll., Bogota, Colombia, Coast U., Barranquilla. With credit loan dept. 1st Nat. City Bank, Barranquilla; with ops. dept. Banco Colombo Am., Barranquilla; with internat. commerce dept. Lloys Internat. Bank, Bogota; mgr. Always Fresh Produce, Bridgeport. Mem. NAFE, Delta Epsilon Sigma (Delta Gamma chpt.). Republican. Roman Catholic. Office: Always Fresh Produce 2036 Main St Bridgeport CT 06604

AGUILAR, ISABEL (CHAVELA AGUILAR), counselor, university official; b. Calexico, Calif., Nov. 5, 1936; d. Silbestre Macias and Petra (Soria) Badajós; m. Ruben Aguilar, Apr. 7, 1956; children: Ruben Anthony, John Xavier. AA, Imperial Valley Coll.; BA, San Diego State U., MS. Cert. community coll. counselor, adminstr., instr., personnel worker, Calif. Med. clinic mgr. M.P. Ajalat Clinic, Calexico, 1961-72; admissions and records officer San Diego State U.-Imperial Valley Campus, Calexico, 1972-77, admissions officer, 1977-80, admissions counselor and vet., 1980-83, outreach coordinator, counselor, alumni dir., scholarship coordinator,campus staff senator disabled students services, student info. coordinator, student life advisor, new student orientation coordinator, supr. high schs., student counselors, student's info., San Diego campus, outreach coordinator for local area, chmn., coordinator ann. Women's Non-traditional Conf. for High Sch. Women, 11 years., 13 yrs.; campus test coord., 1977—; campus liaison Imperial Valley Coll., Imperial, Calif., 1980—; advisor Past Assoc. Student Coun.; dir. student intern program Calif. State U. Chmn. City Beautification Com., Calexico, 1980—; chmn. Affirmative Action Adv. Cons. to Bd. of Suprs., El Centro, 1983—. Recipient San Diego State U. Annual Alumna award, 1980; Delta Kappa Gamma scholar, 1978. Mem. Advocated for Women in Academia, Imperial Valley Guidance Assn. (sec. 1985-86), Raza Advocates for Calif. Higher Edn., Western Assn. of Ednl. Opportunty Personnel. Democrat. Roman Catholic. Lodge: Soroptimists (pres. Calexico club 1983-84, v.p. 1982-83, sec. 1984-85, publicity mgr. 1981-82, alternate del. 1985-86). Home: 814 Rockwood Ave Calexico CA 92231 Office: San Diego State U Imperial Valley 720 Heber Ave Calexico CA 92231

AGUILERA-JONES, LINDA IRMA, real estate executive; b. San Diego, Jan. 15, 1955; d. Donald Stansfield Jones Sr. and Helen Clare (Choquette) Bachman; m. Pablo Manuel Aguilera. BBA, U. No. Fla., 1981. Mgmt. analyst asst. IRS, Jacksonville, Fla., 1979-81; real estate salesperson Berkshire Assocs., Delray Beach, Fla., 1981-84; pvt. practice Pompano, Fla., 1984-85; pres. Prestige Appraisal Service, Inc., Miami, 1985—. Recipient Nat. Pub. Relations award Am. Land Devel. Assn./Nat. Timesharing Coun., 1983. Mem. Miami Bd. Realtors, Greater Miami C. of C., Nat. Assn. Master Appraisers (v.p. 1987—), Nat. Residential Appraisers Inst., Fla. Assn. State Cert. Real Estate Appraisers, Inc. Republican. Office: Prestige Appraisal Svc Inc 3314 Virginia St Coconut Grove FL 33133

AHEARN, JO ANN, construction executive, consultant, accountant; b. Hartford, Conn., Dec. 1, 1948; d. William Joseph and Elizabeth (Riccio) Donahue; m. James A. Ahearn, Aug. 19, 1970 (div. 1977); 1 child, Joseph William. Student, Manchester (Conn.) Coll., 1981-83, U. Conn., 1983-86, U. Conn., 1987. Model Miss Madelaines Modeling Sch., Hartford, 1963-69; freelance bookkeeper Conn., 1969—; chief flight dispatcher C&R ConnAir, Inc., Hartford, 1974-78; asst. to pres., office mgr. air cargo B&H Airways, Inc., Windsor Locks, Conn., 1978-82; air charter svc. mgr. Cross Country Aviation Svcs., Inc., Westfield, Mass., 1982-85; asst. to pres., head acctg. dept. Cross Country Aviation, Inc., Hartford, 1982-85; from adminstrv. asst. to office mgr. Merit Constrn., Inc., Glastonbury, Conn., 1985-89; owner Ahearn Acctg. Svcs., Manchester, 1985—; asst. to pres. Samuel McClendon Bldgs., West Hartford, 1989—; freelance adminstr., acct., Manchester, 1985—; acct., cons., bookkeeper Ahearn Acctg., Manchester, 1985—; acct., bookkeeper Ahearrn Acctg. and Bookkeeping Svcs., Manchester, 1985—. Contbr. Greater Hartford Arts, 1983; tutor to poor and uneducated, Manchester, 1983—; vol. Spl. Olympics, Conn., 1988-89; coord. local elections, Bristol, Conn., 1989—. Mem. NAFE, Am. Inst. Profl. Bookkeepers, Conn. Bus. and Industry Assn., Greater Hartford Bd. Realtors, Conn. Arts and Crafts Guild. Roman Catholic. Office: Samuel McClendon Bldgs PO Box 148 West Hartford CT 06107

AHEARN, JOANNE THERESA, writer; b. N.Y.C., Jan. 4, 1957; d. William Joseph and Mary Theresa (Quinn) A.; m. Scott Wells Browing, July 18, 1981. BA, Washington Coll., Chestertown, Md., 1979; MA, Boston U., 1981; postgrad., U. Pa., 1980-83; MA, Stanford U., 1985. Advt. editor N.Y. Law Jour., 1979; teaching fellow U. Pa., Phila., 1980-83, cons. film programming, 1982-83, acad. adminstr., 1983-84, staff writer, 1987—; commodities asst. McKeany Flavell Co., Oakland, Calif., 1984-86; faculty fellow St. Joseph U., 1986-87. Mem. Univ. Film and Video Assn., Am. Film Inst., Stanford U. Alumni Assn. Democrat. Home: 4161 Tower St Philadelphia PA 19127 Office: U Pa 309 A Coll Hall Philadelphia PA 19104

AHEARN, PATRICIA JEAN, lawyer; b. Amarillo, Tex., Sept. 8, 1936; d. Robert Howard and Lottie Mae (Hillin) Bridges; m. Joseph R. Ahearn, Sept. 26, 1955 (div. 1968); children: Joseph Robert Jr., David Christopher, Steven Paul. BA with honors, West Tex. State U., Canyon, 1972; JD with honors, U. Tex., Austin, 1983. Bar: Tex. 1983. Tchr. Amarillo Ind. Sch. Dist., 1972-76; dep. clk. U.S. Dist. Ct., Amarillo, 1976-80; law clk. Tex. Ct. Appeals (7th cir.), Amarillo, 1983-84; pvt. practice Amarillo, 1984-86; lawyer Tex. Edn. Agy., Austin, 1986-89, Tex. Assn. Sch. Bds., Austin, 1989—; Speaker in field of edn. for handicapped children; cons. to sch. dists. Contbr. articles on laws for handicapped to various publs. Mem. Tex. Bar Assn. Home: 9435 Singing Quail St Austin TX 78758 Office: Tex Assn Sch Bds PO Box 400 Austin TX 78747

AHERN, MARGARET ANN, nun, nurse, educator; b. Manchester, N.H., Nov. 23, 1931; d. Timothy Joseph and Helen Bridget (Kearns) Ahern; R.N., Sacred Heart Hosp. Sch. Nursing, 1952; BS in Nursing, Mt. St. Mary Coll., 1957; MS in Nursing, Cath. U. Am., 1965. Entered Sisters of Mercy, Roman Cath. Ch., 1953; staff nurse Sacred Heart Hosp., Manchester, 1954-57, operating room supr., 1957-62, med.-surg. nursing instr., 1962-66, dir. Sch. Nursing, 1966-75; dir. Sch. Nursing, Cath. Med. Center, Manchester, N.H., 1975-79, dir. dept. edn. and mem. sr. mgmt., 1979-87; pres. Cath. Med. Ctr Networks, Inc., 1987—. Chmn. bd. dirs. Health Edn. Consortium, 1977-89; bd. dirs. Vis. Nurse Assn., 1981-87; adv. bd. Hesser Coll., 1980—, N.H. Voc-Tech. Coll., 1979-87; mem. United Health Systems Agy., 1977-83; mem. adv. council on continuing edn. St. Anselm Coll., 1978-89; mem. gen. chpt. Sisters of Mercy, 1968-70, 79-81, chmn. fin. bd., 1981-86, chmn. Bd. Conciliation and Arbitration, 1982-87. Recipient Distinguished Women Leaders award YWCA, 1986. Mem. Am. Nurses Assn., N.H. Nurses Assn., Nat. League for Nursing, New Eng. Cath. Hosp. Assn., N.H. Heart Assn., Sigma Theta Tau (Disting. Leaders award 1989). Democrat. Roman Catholic. Contbr. articles to profl. jours. Home: 647 Canal St Manchester NH 03104 Office: Cath Med Ctr Network 228 Maple St Manchester NH 03103

AHNEMAN, PATRICIA MAE, JR., pilot; b. Parkersburg, W.Va., Oct. 29, 1951; d. Theodore John and Patricia Mae (Godman) A. Student, Wagner Coll., 1969-73, Embry-Riddle U., 1987—. Cert. airline transport pilot CW46, comml. pilot, flight instr., ground instr., aircraft dispatcher, flight engr.-turbojet. Standardbred trainer Saddle Rock Stables, Westbury, N.Y., 1975-78; flight instr., flight sch. mgr. D.R. Aviation, Inc., Ft. Lauderdale, Fla., 1978-80; co-pilot CW.46, DC 3,4,6, CV 240, 440 Am. Flyers Co., Inc., Ft. Lauderdale, 1978-85; capt. CW.46, office mgr. Miami (Fla.) Air Lease, Inc., 1985-86; FAA liaison Millon Air, Inc., Miami, 1986-87; capt. CW.46 Am. Flyers Co., Inc., Miami, 1987; co-pilot ATR 42 Pam Am. Express, West Berlin, Fed. Republic of Germany, 1987; capt. CW. 46, check airman dir. of ops. Evans Aviation Inc., Kodiak and Cordova, Alaska, Miami, 1988-90. Vol. Sr. Citizens Assisting, Coconut Grove, Fla., 1985—. Recipient Vol. Service award Am. Cancer Soc., 1968, 69, Vol. Service award St. Brigid's Ch., Westbury, N.Y., 1975, 76; named Outstanding Vol. Southside Hosp., Bay Shore, N.Y., 1966-70, Outstanding Vol. March of Dimes, Westbury, 1974. Mem. Aircraft Owners and Pilots Assn., Nat. Assn. Female Execs., Alpha Eta Phi. Republican. Methodist. Home and Office: PO Box 330089 Coconut Grove FL 33233

AHRENS, KATHLEEN KAY, infosystems specialist; b. Pratt, Kans., Oct. 8, 1951; d. Robert Winfred and Mildred Henrietta (Koch) A. BS, Emporia State U., 1973; AA, Washburn U., 1984. Tchr., coach Peabody (Kans.) High Sch., 1973-75, Shawnee Heights High Sch., Tecumseh, Kans., 1975-84; programmer Excel Corp., Wichita, Kans., 1984-85, analyst, mem. standards com., 1985-88, mem. fitness and activity com., 1985—, chmn. standards com., 1987-88, coord. quality assurance, 1988-89, product mgr. acctg. systems, 1988—, project leader yields, quality and tng. systems, 1990—. Coach Wichita West YMCA Volleyball Clinic. Named Area Coach of Yr. Topeka Volleyball Coaches Assn., 1978. Mem. Wichita IBM System 34-36-38 Users Group, U.S. Tennis Assn., Sedgwick County Zool. Soc. Home: 421 Burns St Valley Center KS 67147 Office: Excel Corp 151 N Main St Wichita KS 67202

AHRENS, MARY ANN PAINOVICH, small business owner; b. Des Moines, Oct. 9, 1942; M. Duane Keith Ahrens, June 11, 1966; children: Angela Ann, Alycia Ann. Student, Am. Inst. Bus., 1966-67; BA in Bus. Mgmt. with honors, U. Northern Iowa, 1979. Sec., supr., tour guide Iowa State Edn. Assn., Des Moines, 1960-66; sec. Fairall & Co. Advt. and Pub. Relations, Des Moines, 1966-67; legal sec. Frundt & Hibbs, Blue Earth, Minn., 1967-69; sec., supr. Western State Coll., Gunnison, Colo., 1970-71; sales coord. Henke Mfg., Waverly, Iowa, 1981-82; pres., trainer Ahrens & Affiliates, Waverly, 1982—. Co-author: (with others) (tng. manual) VOLT Training Manual Level 1, 1985, Iowa AAUW Branch Action Team Training, 1986; contbr. articles to Iowa U. Woman publ. Pres. Wartburg Coll. Community Symphony, Inc., Waverly; chmn. adv. bd. City of Waverly Airport, 1987—; vice chmn. Bremer County Dems.; bd. dirs. Iowa Leadership Communication Coun., 1990—. Mem. AAUW (pres. Waverly br. 1983-84, many other offices including selection to nat. VOLT Training Team 1985-88, proj. dir. Voices for Choices 1990—, Iowa reproductive rights, ednl. tng. project, 1990—, tng. and devel. coord. Iowa bd. 1987—), Am. Soc. Tng. and Devel., Waverly C. of C. (co-chair Project: LEAD, bd. dirs.), Iowa Fedn. of Women's Clubs (local pres. 1974-76, 1980-82, Bremer County pres. 1982-84, dir. 3d dist. 1978-80, chair state leadership div. 1980-84). Office: 222 5th Ave NW Waverly IA 50677

AHUJA, MANJU, programmer, analyst, instructor; b. Indore, India, Sept. 12, 1961; came to U.S., 1982; d. Kanaiyalal and Gauri (Kakrani) A. BS, Indore U., 1982; MBA, Pace U., 1985. Prodn. mgr. Superflex Rubbers, Indore, 1979-82; rsch. asst. Pace U., N.Y.C., 1982-84; computer cons. Earthouse, Inc., East Millstone, N.J., 1985; programmer, analyst Raritan Valley Community Coll., Somerville, N.J., 1985—; vis. prof. of MIS No. Ter. U., Australia, 1990—. Contbr. articles to profl. jours. Vol. worker Manavi, N.J., 1985—; social worker Social Svc. Orgn. of India, 1979-80. Pace U. scholar, 1982-84. Home: 32 Mountain View Rd Warren NJ 07060 Office: Raritan Valley Coll PO Box 3300 Somerville NJ 08876

AIELLO, BARBARA, educational company executive, puppeteer; b. Pitts., Nov. 6, 1947; d. Antonio and Helen Ruth (Kaupiek) A.; m. Richard Laurie Dolph, June 8, 1985; 1 child, Rosanna Forrest. BS in Edn., Indiana U. of Pa., 1968; MA in Edn., George Washington U., 1971; postgrad., Harvard U., 1974-75. spl. edn. tchr. pub. schs., Washington, 1969-74; editor Teaching Exceptional Children, Council for Exceptional Children, Reston, Va., 1975-77; edn. cons. Learning mag., Palo Alto, Calif., 1977-78; pres., founder, script writer The Kids On The Block, Inc., Columbia, Md., 1978—; co-author Kids on the Block Children's Book Series, 1989—; mem. adv. bd. Inst. for Mental Health Initiatives, Washington, 1985-88, Ctr. for Children of Div., Washington, 1986-88. Corr. N.Y. Times, 1974-85. Recipient On Behalf of Youth award Camp Fire, Inc., 1980, Instr. Mag. award for The Invisible Children article, 1980, Outstanding Achievement award Epilepsy Found. Am., 1982, Outstanding Pub. Service award Easter Seal Soc., 1984, Margaret Pope Hovey award People-To-People Com., 1984, Disting. Service award Pres.'s Com. on Employment Handicapped, 1985, Washingtonian of Yr., 1989, Surgeon Gen.'s Medalion for Outstanding Svc. Pub. Health, 1989. Mem. Council for Exceptional Children, Nat. Assn. Female Execs. Avocations: cross country skiing, running, reading biographies, cycling. Office: The Kids On the Block Inc 9385-C Gerwig Ln Columbia MD 21046

AIELLO-CONTESSA, ANGELA M., physician; b. N.Y.C., Apr. 28, 1954; d. Salvatore Michael and Margaret Theresa (Torna) Aiello; m. Benjamin John Contessa, Nov. 18, 1984; children: Marjorie Leigh Contessa, Benjamin Salvatore Contessa. BA, Barnard Coll., 1976; Medico Cirujano, Universidad Del Noreste, Tampico, Mex., 1980; MD, Universidad CETEC, Santo Domingo, Dominican Republic, 1981. Resident in pediatrics Winthrop U. Hosp., Mineola, N.Y., 1982-84, chief resident in pediatrics, 1984-85; fellow in neurology Nassau County Med. Ctr., East Meadow, N.Y., 1985; fellow in ambulatory pediatrics Mercy Hosp., Rockville Centre, N.Y., 1989, pediatric house physician, 1990—. Contbr. articles to profl.jours. Mem. Am. Acad. Pediatrics, AMA, Am. Med. Women's Assn. Republican. Roman Catholic. Home: 200 Wyngate Dr Massapequa NY 11758 Office: Mercy Hosp 1000 N Village Ave Rockville Centre NY 11570

AIGEN, BETSY PAULA, psychotherapist; b. N.Y.C., Sept. 13, 1938; d. Abraham H. and Gertrude (Rosenblum) Wasserman; m. Ronald Aigen, Dec. 7, 1957 (div. Jan. 1979); m. Isadore Schumukler, June 20, 1982; 1 child, Jennifer Loren. BA, New Sch. Social Research, 1971; MA, Columbia U., 1972; D of Psychology, Rutgers U., 1980. Group co-leader, asst. psychotherapist Inst. Rational Psychotherapy, N.Y.C., 1967-72; asst. course instr. Columbia U., N.Y.C., 1971-72; psychotherapist Mt. Carmel Guild, Englewood, N.J., 1980-82, SELF Edn. Learning and Feeling, N.Y.C., 1982—; founder, dir. Surrogate Mother Program, N.Y.C., 1985—; cons. Police Chief Tng. Community Workshops Assn., N.Y.C., 1973-74, Richmond Fellowship Mental Health Halfway Houses, Eng. and U.S., 1970-75. Contbr. articles to profl. jours. Chmn. Tenants Com., N.Y.C., 1975-85; active Profl. Theatre, 1956-67. Mem. Nat. Orgn. Women, RESOLVE, Adoptive Parents Com., Am. Psychol. Assn., N.Y. St. Psychol. Assn., N.J. St. Psychol. Assn., N.Y. Assn. Feminist Therapists. (co-founder, charter), Am. Orgn. Surrogate Parenting Practitioners (founder, charter). Democrat. Jewish. Home: 220 W 93rd Ste 1A New York NY 10025 Office: Surrogate Mother Program 640 W End Ave Ste 3D New York NY 10024

AIKEN, LINDA HARMAN, nurse, sociologist; b. Roanoke, Va., July 29, 1943; d. William Jordan and Betty Philips (Warner) Harman; married; children: June Elizabeth, Alan James. B.S. in Nursing, U. Fla., 1964, M.Nursing, 1966; Ph.D. in Sociology, U. Tex., 1973. Nurse Med. Ctr. U. Fla., Gainesville, 1964-65, instr. coll. nursing, 1966-67; instr. sch. of nursing U. Mo., Columbia, 1967-70, clin. nurse specialist sch. of nursing, 1967-70; program officer Robert Wood Johnson Found., Princeton, N.J., 1974-76, dir. rsch., 1976-79, asst. v.p., 1979-81, v.p., 1981-87; trustee prof. nursing and sociology, assoc. dir. for nursing affairs Leonard Davis Inst. Health Econs., U. Pa., Phila., 1988—; mem. task force on long-term health care policies U.S. Dept. Health and Human Services, 1986-87, Sec's. Commn. on Nursing, 1988; mem. panel on quality med. care for consumers Office Tech. Assessment, 1986-88. Assoc. editor: Jour. Health and Social Behavior, 1979-81, Transaction Soc., 1985—; mem. editorial bd.: Evaluation Quar., 1979-80, Med. Care, 1983—; author: Health Policy and Nursing Practice, 1981, Nursing in the 1980's, 1982, Applications of Social Science to Clinical Medicine and Health Policy, 1986, Evaluation Studies Rev. Ann., 1985; contbr. articles to profl. jours. Mem. Adv. Council Social Security, 1982-83. Recipient Joint Secretarial commendation U.S. Dept. Health and Human Services and HUD, 1987; NIH Nurse Scientist fellow, 1970-73. Mem. Inst. Medicine, Nat. Acad. Scis., Am. Acad. Nursing (pres. 1979-80), Am. Sociol. Assn. (chair med. sociology sect. 1983-84), Council Nurse Researchers, Am. Nurses Assn. (Jessie M. Scott award 1984), Sigma Theta Tau, Phi Kappa Phi. Home: 242 Prospect Ave Princeton NJ 08540 Office: U Pa 420 Service Dr Philadelphia PA 19104-6096

AIKENS, MARTHA BRUNETTE, national park service administrator, consultant, educator; b. Jayess, Miss., Aug. 23, 1949; d. Walter and Elnora La Doris (Bridges) A. B.S. in Social Sci., Alcorn State U., 1971; postgrad. George Williams Coll., 1974, Fla. Internat. U., 1977, George Washington U., 1979, Pa. State U., 1979, U. So. Calif.-D.C. Ext., 1980. Social worker Pearl River County Devel. Corp., Picayune, Miss., 1971-72; environ. ednl. specialist Nat. Park Service, Homestead, Fla., 1973-76, environ. ednl. coordinator, 1976-78, communications specialist, 1976-78, park mgr., Bklyn., 1978-79, St. Augustine, Fla., 1979-83, Washington, 1983-88; instr., cons. Coll. African Wildlife Mgmt., Tanzania, Africa, 1980, Fed. Law Enforcement Tng. Ctr., Glynco, Ga., 1983—, Office of Internat. Affairs, Nat. Park Service, Washington, 1980—, Stephen T. Mather Employee Devel. Ctr., Harpers Ferry, W.Va., 1977—, supt., 1988—. Author tchrs. guides on Everglades Nat. Park, 1973-76, park brochure, 1977. Contbr. chpts. to books. Mem. Strategic Planning Task Force, Atlanta, 1981-83, Southeast Regional Equal Opportunity Commn., Atlanta, 1982-83, Dept. Interior's Partnership in Edn. Commn., Washington, 1983—, Fed. Interagy. Commn. on Edn., Washington, 1983—, Nat. Park Service Employee Relations Task Force, Washington, 1983—, mem. 21st Century Task Force, 1988—.

AIKMAN, ELFLORA ANNA, senior citizens center administrator; b. Marion, Ill., July 21, 1929; d. John Frederick and Elsa Flora (Weber) Kaeser; m. Samuel Vick Aikman, Dec. 24, 1949; children: Vicki Ann Aikman Kaeser, Vance J., Valerie Sue Aikman Moore, Samuel Vick III. Student, So. Ill. U., 1949, John A. Logan Coll., 1970, 80, 87; cert. food handler, John A. Logan Coll., 1984. Numerous positions, 1947-67; sec. Color-Craft Products, Detroit, 1967-69; admitting clk. Marion Meml. Hosp., 1969-70, appointed to task force, 1989—; co-owner, office mgr., decorating cons. House of Color, Marion, 1970-79; sec., bookkeeper, receptionist Mitchell-Hughes Funeral Home, Marion, 1979-80; receptionist Meredith Funeral Home, Marion, 1980—; exec. dir. Marion Sr. Citizens Ctr., 1981—; columnist Marion Daily Republican, 1984—; columnist, contbr. Sr. World, 1987—; producer program Sta. WGGH, 1989—. Editor monthly newsletter The Yodler, 1984—; co-designer, decorator Meredith Funeral Home; decorator Marion Meml. Hosp. Chapel, 1971, 77; columnist, contbr. newspaper Old Friends, 1989—. Organist, jr. choir dir. St. Clair, Mo., 1958-63; organist, jr. choir organizer, sr. choir organizer Trinity Episcopal Ch., Mt. Vernon, Ill., 1964-67; choir mem. United Ch. Christ, Plymouth, Mich., 1967-69; organist Myers Funeral Home, Mt. Vernon, 1964-67; com. mem. Girl Scouts Am., Mt. Vernon, 1964-67, PTA, St. Clair, Mo., 1960-63; pack officer Boy Scouts Am., Mt. Vernon, 1964-67; home rm. mother, St. Clair, Mo., Mt. Vernon, 1958-67; chmn. Vols. to Arts, Mt. Vernon, Ill., 1966-67; library asst. Plymouth (Mich.) Mid. Sch., 1968-69; com. mem. Williamson County (Ill.) Sesquicentennial Celebration, 1989; mem. Marion Meml. Hosp. Aux., 1980—, Hearts Helping Heart, Marion, 1987—; asst. organist and choir mem., Sunday sch. tchr. Zion United Ch. of Christ, Marion, mem. numerous other ch. coms.; mem. So. Ill. Easter Seal Soc., 1987. Recipient Svc. Plaque Marion Recreation Dept. Bd., 1983. Mem. Marion C. of C. (com. 1988), Beta Sigma Phi. Home: 516 S Market St Marion IL 62959 Office: Marion Sr Citizens Ctr 507 W Main St Marion IL 61959

AILLONI-CHARAS, MIRIAM CLARA, interior designer; b. Veere, The Netherlands, July 31, 1935; came to U.S., 1958; d. Maurits and Elzina (De Groot) Taytelbaum; m. Dan Ailloni-Charas, Oct. 8, 1957; children: Ethan Benjamin, Orrin, Adam. Degree in Interiors, Pratt Inst., 1962; BSc, SUNY, Albany, 1978. Interior designer S.J. Miller Assocs., N.Y.C., 1960-63; interior design cons. Rye Brook, N.Y., 1963-88, 90—; exec. v.p. Contract 2000 Inc., Port Chester, N.Y., 1988-90. Treas. Temple Guild, Congregation Emanu-El, Rye, N.Y., 1979-88, co-chair, 1988—, trustee, 1986—. Recipient Cert. of Merit, U.S. Jaycees, 1962, March of Dimes, 1988. Mem. Am. Soc. Interior Designers, Allied Bd. Trade, Westchester Assn. Women Bus. Owners (bd. dirs. 1988—), Nat. Trust for Hist. Preservation, Westchester County C. of C. (area devel. coun. 1988—). Office: 23 Woodland Dr Rye Brook NY 10573

AIMÉE, JOYCE, entertainment company executive; b. Bklyn., May 4, 1930; d. David Joseph and Jessica (Ganz) Geronimus; m. Harold L. Epstein, Oct. 16, 1949 (div. 1962); 1 child, Matthew Bruce Epstein; m William McPeck Titchnell, Nov. 2, 1966; 1 child, David Langland Titchnell. Grad. high sch., N.Y.C. Child performer ABC Network, N.Y.C., 1938-44; musician, singer various nightclubs, hotels, Las Vegas, Nev. and N.Y., 1945-57; film actress Fla., Calif., Europe, S.Am., and Reno, Nev., 1945-57; sub-agent George B. Hunt and Assocs., Los Angeles, 1957-62; pres., owner Aimee Entertainment Assn., Los Angeles, 1962—; founder, exec. dir. Americana Dance Theater, Inc., Van Nuys, Calif., 1972—. Producer documentary film De Mille Dynasty, 1985, as exhbn., 1986 (Angel award 1987), TV documentary Americana at Penny Lane, 1988 (Gold Angel award 1989). Dir. Cultural Found., Woodland Hills, Calif., 1979—; pres. San Fernando Valley Arts Council, Woodland Hills, 1978—; commr. Los Angeles County Music and Performing Arts, 1987—. Named Leading Accordionist of Yr. World Accordion Review, London, 1956, 57, 58, 59; N.Y.C. Mus. Mod. Art scholar. Mem. Am. Fed. Musicians, Screen Actors Guild, AFTRA, Writers Guild Am., Am. Guild Mus. Artists. Republican. Clubs: Child Help USA (Los Angeles, v.p. 1972-78), San Fernando Cultural Valley Soc. (v.p. 1974-76). Office: Aimee Entertainment Assn 13743 Victory Blvd Van Nuys CA 91401

AIRHART, JUDITH MOSS, nurse, educator; b. Parkersburg, W.Va., Nov. 6, 1947; d. John Milton and Virginia (Weese) Moss; m. William Francis Airhart, Nov. 9, 1966; children: William Chester, John Patrick. Assoc. degree in nursing, Parkersburg Community Coll., 1978; student, Glenville State Coll., 1980, Marshall U., 1986-89. RN, W.Va.; lic. vocat. tchr., W.Va. Svc. rep. C&P Telephone Co., Parkersburg, 1965-74; staff nurse St. Joseph's Hosp., Parkersburg, 1978—; office nurse Dr. Carl Nichols, Parkersburg, 1984-86; tchr. practical nursing Wood County Bd. Edn., Parkersburg, 1986—; mem. adv. com. Head Start, Parkersburg, 1988—, PCC Nursing, Parkersburg, 1989. Mem. Nat. Diabetic Assn., U.S. Perinatal Assn., K.C. Aux. Democrat. Roman Catholic. Home: 5504 12th Ave Vienna WV 26105 Office: Wood County Vocat Sch 15ll Blizzard Dr Parkersburg WV 26101

AITA, CAROLYN RUBIN, physicist; b. Bklyn., Sept. 7, 1943; d. Kopel and Anne (Lassman) Rubin; m. Michael Aita, Aug. 26, 1965; 1 child, Anna Gabrielle. BA in Art and Art History, Bklyn. Coll., 1966; BS in Physics, Utica Coll., N.Y., 1970; MS in Physics, Queens Coll., Flushing, N.Y., 1974; PhD in Materials Sci., Northwestern U., Evanston, Ill., 1977. Sr. scientist U.S. Gypsum Co., Des Plaines, Ill., 1977-78, Gould Inc., Rolling Meadows, Ill., 1978-81; asst. prof. U. Wis., Milw., 1981-84; assoc. prof. U. Wis., 1984-88, prof., 1988, Wis. Disting. prof. material scis., 1988—; v.p. AKA, Inc., Shorewood, Wis., 1989—. Contbr. articles to profl. jours. Home: 4067 N Farwell Ave Shorewood WI 53211 Office: U Wis Materials Sci Dept 3200 N Cramer Milwaukee WI 53201

AITA, MARY MAJELLA, telephone company administrator; b. Malden, Mo., Apr. 16, 1958; d. George Bernard and Laura Virginia (Meyer) Lampe; m. Anthony Joseph Aita, Apr. 24, 1982; children: Emilio Joseph, Mary Carmela, Laura Regina, George Maurice. AA in Liberal Arts, Meramec Community Coll., Kirkwood, Mo., 1982; acctg. cert., St. Louis U., 1989, BA in Orgn. Adminstrn., 1990. Typesetter, copy writer Malden Press-Merit, 1976-78; mgmt. asst. Comfort Printing, St. Louis, 1978-79; clerical support Southwestern Bell, St. Louis, 1979-85, mgr. cost studies, 1985-86, mgr. tariff support, 1986-89, mgr. fin., 1989—. Mem. Alpha Sigma Lambda (sec. 1988-89). Democrat. Roman Catholic. Office: Southwestern Bell One Bell Ctr 31-N-9 Saint Louis MO 63101

AITCHISON, BEATRICE, transportation economist; b. Portland, Oreg., July 18, 1908; d. Clyde Bruce and Bertha (Williams) Aitchison; AB, Goucher Coll., 1928, ScD (hon.), 1979; AM, Johns Hopkins, 1931; PhD in Math., 1933; MA with honors in Econs., U. Oreg., 1937. Asso. prof. math. U. Richmond, 1933-34; lectr. statistics Am. U., 1934-44; instr. econs. U. Oreg., 1939-41; jr. statistician advancing to sr. statistician ICC, 1938-48, prin. transport economist, 1948-51; dir. transport econs. div. Office Transp., Dept. Commerce, 1951-53; dir. transp. research Post Office Dept., Washington,

1953-58, dir. transp. research and statistics, 1958-67, dir. transp. rates and econs., 1967-71; transp. cons., 1971—. Cons. Traffic Analysis and Forecasting Office Def. Transp., 1942-45; cons. mil. traffic. service U.S. Dept. Def., 1950-53. Recipient Alumnae Achievement citation Goucher Coll., 1954; First Ann. Fed. Woman's award, 1961, Career Service award Nat. Civil Service League, 1970. Fellow Am. Statis. Assn., AAAS; mem. Am. Econ. Assn., Am. Soc. Trans and Logistics, Phi Beta Kappa, Sigma Xi, Pi Lambda Theta, Phi Delta Gamma. Episcopalian. Contbr. to numerous govt. publs.

AITKEN, DIANE LEGNER, pediatric physical therapist; b. Sandwich, Ill., Oct. 25, 1938; d. Armand Arthur and Lucille Irene (Kilgore) Legner; m. John Mattox, June 5, 1960 (div. 1976); children: Gretchen, John, Paul. BS in Phys. Therapy, U. Colo., 1960. Pediatric phys. therapist Denver Children's Hosp., 1960-62, 76-78, Easter Seal Soc., Chgo., 1963-66, U. Nebr., Omaha, 1969-71, U. Wash., Seattle, 1972-73, Sparc Child Devel. Ctr., Mt. Vernon, Wash., 1974-75, John F. Kennedy Child Devel. Ctr., Denver, 1978-81; pvt. practice Denver, 1981—. Bd. dirs. Mile High Downs Assn., 1980-89, Anchor Ctr. for Blind Children, 1983—. Mem. Am. Phys. Therapy Assn., Sensory Internat. Home: 82 Rose Hip Ln Evergreen CO 80439 Office: 1291 S Pennsylvania Denver CO 80210

AITKEN, MOLLY BENNETT, foundation administrator; b. Hollywood, Calif., July 25, 1944; d. Mervyn Dreux Bennett and Valré (Czech) Vasilas; m. Alvin M. Marks, Aug. 25, 1965 (div. 1976); children: Bridget Grace, Sean Christopher, Frederick Peter, Jacqueline Lee; m. Gerard James Aitken III, Dec. 26, 1977 (dec.); children: Gerard James IV, Mary Hannah. BA, Nev. So. U., 1962; MA, NYU, 1968. Hostess, singer Rounders Club Show, Sta. KLAS-TV, Las Vegas, Nev., 1962-63; actress, singer Ed Sullivan Show, Copacabana, Joe Franklin Show, 1962-65; fundraiser U.S. Equestrian Team, 1972-76; spl. asst. to pres. Marks Polarized Corp., N.Y.C., 1965-82; mgr. horse show Assn. for the Help of Retarded Children, 1973-74; mgr. Century Horse Show, N.Y.C., 1974-75; pres. World Energy Found., N.Y.C, 1982—; chmn. bd. Phototherm, Inc., Amherst, N.H. Contbg. editor North Shore Club Life mag., 1971-75, Horsemen's Yankee Peddler Mag., 1970-78; contbr. numerous articles on horses to jours. Pres. United Cerebral Palsy Aux., Long Island, N.Y., 1970-74; founder Riding for the Handicapped, Long Island, 1972; campaign organizer Edward M. Kennedy for Pres., Athol, Mass., 1979-80; chmn. Salute to Spring Ball, Vis. Nurse Svc. N.Y. Benefit, 1989; mem. com. Octoberfest Fundraiser, 1990; del. Internat. Bus. and Arts Congress, Azerbaijan, USSR, 1990. Recipient Disting. Service award United Cerebral Palsy, 1973, numerous horsemanship awards; recieved papal blessing Pope Paul VI, 1964; U.S. flag flown in honor of Mr. and Mrs. Aitken over the Capitol, Washington, 1985. Mem. Am. Horse Shows Assn. (life), N.E. Right to Life Assn., Screen Actors Gulid, Am. Guild of Variety Artists, Vis. Nurse Assn. (chmn. fund raising and benefits 1988-89). Roman Catholic. Home: Green Gables Farm Athol MA 01331 Office: World Energy Found 1270 5th Ave Ste 3B New York NY 10029

AIUTO, BEVERLY BRADLEY, seminarian; b. Battle Creek, Mich., Apr. 19, 1938; d. Raymond L. and Elizabeth (Bradley) Bundy; m. Willard Chichester, June 29, 1958 (div. 1976); children: Richard L., Ronald L., Catherine C.; m. Russell Aiuto, Jan. 3, 1981. BBA, West Mich. U., 1983; postgrad., Va. Theol. Seminary. Organist, choirmaster Ch. of the Resurrection, Battle Creek, 1973-80; seminarian Grace Episc. Ch., Silver Spring, Md., 1989—. Composer 5 hymns. Democrat. Episcopalian. Home: 624 N Ripley St Alexandria VA 22304 Office: Grace Episcopal Ch 1607 Grace Church Rd Silver Spring MD 20910

AJZENBERG-SELOVE, FAY, educator, physicist; b. Berlin, Germany, Feb. 13, 1926; came to U.S., 1940, naturalized, 1946; d. Mojzesz A. and Olga (Naiditch) A.; m. Walter Selove, Dec. 18, 1955. BS in Engring., U. Mich., 1946; MS, U. Wis., 1949, PhD, 1952. Research fellow Calif. Inst. Tech., 1952, 54; lectr. Smith Coll., 1952-53; cons., fellow Mass. Inst. Tech., 1952-53; from asst. prof. to asso. prof. Boston U., 1953-57; mem. faculty Haverford Coll., 1957-70, prof. physics, 1962-70, acting chmn. dept. physics, 1967-69; research prof. U. Pa., 1970-73, prof. physics, 1973—, assoc. chmn., 1989—; vis. asst. prof. Columbia, summer 1955, Nat. U. Mexico, summer 1955; lectr. U. Pa., 1957; cons. in field, 1962-63; vis. asso. Calif. Inst. Tech., 1973-74; Exec. sec. com. physics faculties in colls. Am. Inst. Physics, 1962-65, mem. adv. com. manpower, 1963-68, adv. com. vis. scientists program, 1963-67; commr. Commn. on Coll. Physics, 1968-71; exec. sec. ad hoc panel on nuclear data compilations Nat. Acad. Scis.-NRC, 1971-75; mem. Commn. on Nuclear Physics, Internat. Union Pure and Applied Physics, 1972-78, chmn. 1978-81; mem. U.S. del. low energy nuclear physics to USSR, AEC, 1966; mem. Distinguished Faculty Awards Commn. Commonwealth of Pa., 1976; mem. nuclear sci. adv. com. Dept Energy-NSF, 1977-80; mem. numerical data adv. bd., assembly math. and phys. scis. NRC, 1977-79. Editor: Nuclear Spectroscopy, vol. A and B, 1960; bd. editors: Phys. Rev. C, 1981-83. Smith-Mundt fellow, 1955; Guggenheim fellow, 1965-66. Fellow Am. Phys. Soc. (chmn. div. nuclear physics 1973-74), AAAS (governing council 1974-80, com. on council affairs 1977, 78); mem. Am. Inst. Physics (com. on public edn. and info. 1980-83), AAUP, NRC (phys. scis. panel, associateship program 1988—), Phi Beta Kappa, Sigma XI (nat. lectr. 1973-74). Home: 118 Cherry Ln Wynnewood PA 19096 Office: U Pa Philadelphia PA 19104-6396

AKACICH, RICHELLE DEE, elementary educator; b. Laramie, Wyo., Oct. 8, 1958; d. Richard Lon Gaskell and Delores Joyce (Woods) Colley; m. Randal C. Akacich, June 27, 1981 (div.); 1 child, Ashley Christine. BA in Edn., Linfield Coll., 1982, postgrad., 1988—. Tchr. cert., Oreg., Wash. Classroom tchr. Ewing Young Elem. Sch., Newberg, Oreg., 1983-85, team tchr., 1986-89; 1st grade tchr. Tapteal Elem. Sch., West Richland, Wash., 1989-90; asst. program tchr. chpt. 1 learning Jason Lee Elem. Sch., Richland, 1990—; presentor Oreg. Writing Festival, Eugene, 1989, Oreg. Council Tchrs. English Fall Conf., Portland, 1988. Author: Share A Book/Make A Book, 1989; presentor Oreg. Writing Festival, Portland, 1990. Mem. Doris Day's Animal League, 1989. Participant Oreg. Writing Project, Newberg Sch. Dist., 1988. Mem. Nat. Writing Project, Nat. Council Tchrs. English. Republican.

AKE, MARY KATHERINE, librarian; b. East Chicago, Ind., Mar. 2, 1930; d. William Henry and Elsbeth Marguerite (Lenehan) W.; m. John W. Ake, May 22, 1955 (div. May 1981); children: J. David, Katherine Mary. BA, Youngstown State U., 1952; MS, Carnegie Mellon U., 1953. Cert. tchr. Libr. Pub. Library Youngstown And Mahoning County, Ohio, 1953-55; libr., media specialist Littleton (Colo.) Pub. Schs., 1974—. Author: (with others) Touchstones, 1985, Writers for Children, 1987. Founder Friends of the Library/Mus., 1964; served on numerous county, city, recreational, Littleton, sch. coms., 1962-75. Mem. Am. Assn. Sch. Librs., Children's Lit. Assn. (bd. dirs. 1979-83), Colo. Ednl. Media Assn., AAUW (founder local chpt. 1963), Dr. Watson's Neglected Patients Club (co-founder, chief surgeon 1988-89). Republican. Presbyterian. Home: 1351 Northcrest Dr Highlands Ranch CO 80126 Office: Walt Whitman Elem Sch 6557 S Acoma Littleton CO 80120

AKERKAR, SHOBHA ANAND, medical researcher, scientist; b. Sawantwadi, India, Mar. 19, 1941; came to U.S., 1969; d. Nikantha D. and Usha (Manganka) Dalvi; m. Anand Akerkar, Nov. 8, 1965; children: Geetanjali, Sanket. BS, U. Bombay, 1962, MS, 1966. Cert. biol. researcher. Instr. in chemistry Parle Coll., Bombay; rsch. scientist Am. Health Found., Valhalla, N.Y. pres. Maharshtra Madal, N.Y., 1975-78. Mem. Am. Assn. Clin. Chemistry. Home: PO Box 91 Pomona NY 10970

AKERS, CATHAYANNE MARIE, manufacturing executive, chemist; b. San Jose, Calif., Aug. 13, 1952; d. Charles Marshall Sr. and Georgia Irene (Miller) A.; m. James Floyd Dorris, Jan. 4, 1969 (dec. Nov. 1974); 1 child, Cindy Lee Anne Dorris. Diploma in gen. edn., Clackamas Community Coll.; AAS, Lower Columbia Coll., 1977; student, Monroe County (Mich.) Community Coll., 1986, U. Toledo, 1987—. Inventory clk., receptionist Hood River County Abundant Food Stores, Dalles, Oreg., 1970; guard Lawrence Security, Portland, Oreg., 1971-72; store detective Lipman & Wolfe, Portland, Oreg., 1972-74; exptl. technician I Weyerhaeuser Paper Co., Longview, Wash., 1977-79; water shed technician Wash. State Dept. Agri., Kelso, 1979; chemist Indsl. Chems. div. Am. Cyanamid Co., Longview, 1979-82; lab. technician City of Monroe (Mich.) Wastewater Treatment Plant, 1984-85; electrician apprentice Geal Electric, Monroe, 1985; product engr. intern Monroe Auto Equipment Div. of Tenneco Automatic, 1986; pres., chief exec. officer Gap Plumbing, Inc., Monroe, 1987—, bd. dirs.; lab. analyst Lower Columbia Coll., 1976; plumber's apprentice Plumbers, Pipe Fitters and Refrigeration Joint Apprenticeship and Tng. Com., Tacoma, 1982-84. Participant Hands Across Am., Toledo, 1986; team leader March of Dimes-Walk Am., Monroe, 1988. Pell grantee U. Toledo, 1987-88. Mem. Soc. Women Engrs. (student), VFW Aux., Nat. Safety Council (defensive driving campaign 1977). Democrat. Roman Catholic. Home: 3893 N Custer 237 White Oak Ct Monroe MI 48161 Office: Gap Plumbing Inc 121 N Roessler St Monroe MI 48161

AKIN, NYLA MAUDEAN, genealogical researcher; b. Tecumseh, Nebr., May 11, 1945; d. Loran Elston and Ellyn Lennorah Bartholomew (Lawrence) B.; m. Ray Lee, June 25, 1977; children: Nyla M., Edward Lee. BSBA, Peru State Coll., 1973; MBA, U. Wyoming, Laramie, 1974. Author: Lawrence Bartholomew-Family History 1822--. Recipient Honorary Citizen State Fla. Gov. Rubin Askew Miami. Fla. 1973. Mem. Circle R., F. Bla. Republican. Roman Catholic. Home: 2252 W Drake St Bolivar MO 65613

AKST, BARBARA BLATTNER, human resources development company executive; b. Chgo., Mar. 9, 1955; d. Alexander J. and Bernadine (Strumski) Blattner; m. George Akst; children: Jason, Jennifer. BS in Psychology, U. Ill., 1975; MA in Ednl. Adminstrn., N.Mex. State U., 1976. Jr. coll. teaching credential, Calif. Mgr. vocat. rehab. and spl. projects program Human Svcs., Inc., San Bernardino, Calif., 1976-77; coord. drug abuse prevention San Bernardino County Dept. Mental Health, San Bernardino, 1977-79; coord. substance abuse prevention Fairfax County Pub. Schs., Fairfax, Va., 1979-80, coord. spl. projects, 1981-82; v.p. Performance Inst. Washington, Fairfax, 1982-83; pres. Tng. Unltd., Fairfax, 1983—; condr. workshops, cons. Nat. Inst. on Drug Abuse, Health and Human Svcs. Agy., Ctr. for Naval Analyses, U.S. Dept. Edn., also state depts. edn. and health and human svcs., also others. Active Muscular Dystrophy Assn., Girl Scouts U.S.A., March of Dimes, also others. Mem. Am. Soc. for Tng. and Devel. (membership com., program devel. com.),Assn. part-Time Profls. (v.p., bd. dirs.). Home and Office: 8211 Woodland Ave Annandale VA 22003

AKUNA, JANIS CINDY, financial analyst; b. Honolulu, Aug. 3, 1950; d. Paul and Winifred (Low) A.; m. Andrew D. Friedlander. BS, U. Calif., Davis, 1972. Assoc. v.p. Dean Witter Reynolds, Honolulu, 1978-83; v.p., prin. Cadinha and Co., Inc., Honolulu, 1983—. Sec. YWCA, Oahu, Hawaii, 1986-87, treas., 1982-85. Mem. Am. Soc. Women Accts. (bd. dirs. 1986-87, co-chmn. spring conf. 1989-90), Hawaii Women Lawyers Found. (bd. dirs. 1986-87, budget and fin. com. 1987—), Fin. Analyst Fedn., LIPS Investment Club (pres. 1986-87), Pilot Club (pres. 1988-89). Office: Cadinha and Co Inc 900 Fort St Ste 1240 Honolulu HI 96813

ALAFOUZO, ANTONIA, marketing professional; b. Cairo, Egypt, Oct. 13, 1952; came to U.S., 1982; d. Pano Antony and Agni-Maria (Ranos) A.; m. Thomas D'Ambola, Jr., May 29, 1988. BSC in Econs., Brunel U., London, 1975; Diploma in Econs. and Politics, Oxford (Eng.) U., 1977, M of Philosophy, PhD, 1980. Staff reporter The Economist, London, 1973-75, contbg. writer, 1975-82; communications exec. Rubenstein, Wolfson Co., N.Y.C., 1982-87; founder, pres. Markcom Ltd., N.Y.C., 1987—; contbg. writer Fin. Report, London, 1975-82; cons. writer Fin. Times, London, 1980-82; cons. communications and econs. World Gold Council, N.Y.C., 1982—. Contbr. reports to fin. publs. Mem. Inst. Journalism, Internat. Precious Metals Inst., Oxford Union Soc.

ALAKSZAY, ELIZABETH MARIA, chemical engineer, manufacturing company executive; b. Phila., Nov. 30, 1963; d. Miklos and Eva (Molnar) Alakszay. BS in Chem. Engring., Pa. State U., 1985; MS in Chem. Engring. and Process Control, Villanova U., 1989. Cert. in indsl. computer control, database programming, indsl. electronics. Demonstrator specialist Franklin Inst., Phila., 1985-86; chem. engr., chemist Polyscis. Inc., Warminster, Pa., 1986-87; grad. asst. Villanova (Pa.) U., 1987; product mgr. Betz Equipment Systems, Horsham, Pa., 1988—; sci. educator Bucks County Community Coll., Newton, Pa., 1990. Author sales bulls. and articles. Organizer MCBO Women's Support Group, Phila., 1985. Mem. Nat. Assn. for Female Execs., Chesapeake Bay Found., Pa. State U. Alumni Assn., Tau Beta Pi, Phi Lambda Upsilon. Roman Catholic. Home: 768 Penn Ave Ardsley PA 19038-1725 Office: Betz Equipment Systems 200 Precision Dr Horsham PA 19044

ALATALO, FRANCES E., retired psychologist; b. South Range, Mich., Sept. 20, 1917; d. Herman and Jenni (Niemi) A. BA, Wayne State U., 1949, MA, 1959. Social worker, supr. Detroit Welfare Dept., 1949-59; psychologist Pontiac (Mich.) State Hosp., 1959-71, Newberry (Mich.) Regional Mental Health Ctr., 1971-81; ret., 1981. Contbr. poetry to various publs. With WAC, U.S. Army, 1943-46. Mem. APA (assoc.), Assn. for Humanistic Psychology, Assn. for Transpersonal Psychology, Mich. Psychol. Assn., Mich. Assn. Profl. Psychologists, Psychologists for Social Responsibility, Inst. Noetic Scis., Planetary Soc., Nature Conservancy, Audubon Soc., Wilderness Soc., Sierra Club.

ALAUPOVIC, ALEXANDRA VRBANIC, artist, educator; b. Slatina, Yugoslavia, Dec. 21, 1921; d. Joseph and Elizabeta (Papp) Vrbanic; student Bus. Sch., Zagreb, Yugoslavia, 1940-41, Acad. Visual Arts, Zagreb, Yugoslavia, 1944-48; postgrad. Acad. Visual Arts, Prague, Czechoslovakia, 1949, Art Sch., U. Ill., 1959-60; MFA, U. Okla., 1966; m. Peter Alaupovic, Mar. 22, 1947; children—Betsy, H. Clark Hyde. Came to U.S., 1958. Sec., Arko Liquer & Yeast Factory and Distillery, Zagreb, 1941-44; instr. U. Okla., Norman, 1964-66; instr. three dimensional design sculpture Oklahoma City U., 1969-77, Okla. Sci. Found., Oklahoma City, 1969-75; one-woman shows at Okla. Art Ctr., Oklahoma City, U. Okla. Mus. Art, Norman, La Mandragore Internat. Galerie d'Art, Paris, 1984; exhibited art in group shows retrospective 50 yrs. Struggle, Growth and Whimsy, 1987-88, Okla. Art Ctr., Springfield (Mo.) Art Mus., Okla. U. Mus., Norman, 7th Ann. Temple Emanuel Brotherhood Arts Festival, Dallas, Salon des Nation, Paris, 1983; represented in permanent collections Okla. U. Art Mus., Okla. State Art Collection, Okla. Art Ctr., Mercy Health Ctr. Recipient Jacobson award U. Okla., 1964; hon. mention in sculpture Philbrook Art Ctr., Tulsa, 1967; 1st sculpture award Philbrook Art Ctr., Tulsa, 1970; biography included in Virginia Watson Jones' Contemporary American Women Sculptors, 1986. Mem. Internat. Sculpture Center. Home and Office: 11908 N Bryant St Oklahoma City OK 73131

ALBANESE, ELLEN LOUISE, newspaper editor; b. Cohasset, Mass., Sept. 17, 1949; d. Francis Joseph and Louise (Whittredge) A.; m. William P. Landers, Oct. 23, 1971; children: Abby Jean, Tracy Ellen. Cert., Sorbonne U., Paris, 1970; BA in Sociology and French, Tufts U., 1971; MS in Pub. Rels., Boston U., 1975. Editor MIT Press, Cambridge, 1971-73; publicity dir. Cahners Books, Boston, 1973-75; pub. rels. dir. Ea. Mass. and R.I. dists. Weight Watchers, Attleboro, Mass., 1976-78; editor The Country GAZETTE, Franklin, Mass., 1980—. Publicity chair Women's Success Network, Franklin, 1986-88; leader Girl Scouts U.S.A., Franklin, 1988-89; mem. community coun. Dean Jr. Coll., Franklin, 1989—. Recipient 1st pl. column writing award N.Eng. Press Assn., Boston, 1987. Mem. Internat. Soc. Weekly Newspaper Editors (bd. dirs., Golden Dozen award 1986, Golden Quill award 1987), Mass. Press Assn. (treas. 1986—, pres. 1989), Phi Beta Kappa. Office: The Country GAZETTE PO Box 612 Franklin MA 02038

ALBAUM, JEAN STIRLING, psychologist, lecturer; b. Beijing, China, Jan. 11, 1932; came to U.S., 1936; d. Richard Henry and Emma Bowyer (Lueders) Ritter; m. B. Taylor Stirling, Aug. 15, 1953 (div. 1965); 1 child, Christopher Taylor Stirling; m. Joseph H. Albaum; stepchildren: Thomas Gary, Lauren Jean. BA, Beloit (Wis.) Coll., 1953; MS, Danbury (Conn.) State U., 1964, U. La Verne, Calif., 1983; PhD, Claremont (Calif.) Grad. Sch., 1985. Lic. ednl. psychologist, Calif. Spl. edn. psychologist Charter Oak (Calif.) Sch. Dist., 1966-80; psychologist, coord. elem. counseling Claremont Sch. Dist., 1980—; pvt. practice ednl. psychologist Encino, Calif., 1987—; clin. supr. Marriage, Family and Child Counselor Interns, Claremont, 1987—; part-time lectr. U. La Verne, 1988—; oral commr. Bd. Behavioral Sci. Examiners, Sacramento, 1989—. Contbr. articles to profl. jours. Hostess L.A. World Affairs Coun., 1980—; pres. Woodley Homeowner's Assn., Encino, 1986-89. Durfee Found. grantee, 1986. Mem. Am. Psychol. Assn., Calif. Assn. Marriage, Family and Child Therapists, Calif. Assn. Lic. Ednl. Psychologists. Office: Edn Ctr 2080 N Mountain Ave Claremont CA 91711

ALBERGA, ALTA WHEAT, artist; b. Ala.; d. James Richard and Leila Savannah (Sullivan) Wheat; B.A., M.A., Wichita State U., 1954; B.F.A., Washington U., St. Louis, 1961; M.F.A., U. Ill., 1964; m. Alvyn Clyde Alberga, Dec. 3, 1930. Mem. faculty Wichita (Kans.) State U., 1955-56, Webster Coll., St. Louis, 1962, Presbyn. Coll., Clinton, S.C., 1969-74; pvt. art tchr., Greenville, S.C., 1974—; substitute tchr. Greenville County Schs.; tchr. painting Tempo Gallery Sch., Greenville, 1974—, Greenville County Mus. Sch., 1975—, Tryon (N.C.) Fine Arts Ctr., 1986; one-woman shows include Greenville County Mus., 1979, Greenville Artists Guild Gallery, 1979, 83, Wichita State U., 1954, St. Louis Artists Guild, 1956, N.C. State U., 1965, Met. Arts Council, Greenville, 1980, 83, 85; exhibited in group shows at Pickens County Mus., 1979, 88-89, Inter/Art 81, Washington 1981, Greenville Artists Guild, 1982, 88, Art/7, Washington, 1983, N.C. Univ., Charlotte, 1989, Furman U. Women's Show, 1989; represented in permanent collections S.C. State Mus., Columbia, 1989; represented in pvt. collections; bd. dirs. Greenville Artists Guild, 1977-79, pres., 1985; bd. dirs. Guild Gallery, 1978, Guild Greenville Symphony, 1989-90. Recipient Richard K. Weil award St. Louis Mus., 1957; Purchase prize S.C. Arts Commn., 1972; Merritt award Greenville Mus., 1986, Pickens County Mus., 1987, 88. Mem. Artists Equity (pres. St. Louis chpt. 1962), Internat. Platform Assn. (life), Art Students League, Guild Greenville Artists (pres. 1984-85), S.C. Artists Guild, Southeastern Council Printmakers, Greenville Symphony Guild, Kappa Pi, Kappa Delta Pi. Democrat. Home: 11 Overton Dr Greenville SC 29609

ALBERS, JO-ANN HUFF, journalism educator; b. Cain's Store, Ky., Jan. 3, 1938; d. Vertreese Henry and Olowene (Brown) Huff; m. Henry Hall Albers; children: Stephen G., H. William. BA, Miami U., Oxford, Ohio, 1959; MEd, Xavier U., Cin., 1962. Specialist tech. info. GE, Evendale, Ohio, 1959; supr. traffic Sta. WCPO subs. Scripps Howard, Cin., 1959-60; editing, writing positions The Cin. Enquirer, 1960-81; pub., editor Sturgis (Mich.) Jour., 1981-82, Pub. Opinion, Chambersburg, Pa., 1982-86; gen. news exec. Gannett. Co. Inc., Arlington, Va., 1986-87; head journalism dept. Western Ky. U., Bowling Green, 1987—. Recipient Noel Ross Strader award Coll. Media Advisers, 1988, Bingham Freedom of Info. award Ky. Press Assn., 1989; Poynter teaching fellow, 1988. Mem. Women in Communications Inc. (pres. 1974-75, rep. to Accrediting Coun. on Edn. in Journalism/Mass Communication, 1980, 90—, Nat. Headliner award 1979), Assn. Schs. Journalism and Mass Communication (exec. com. 1989—), Kiwanis. Mem. Church of Christ. Office: Western Ky U Gordon Wilson Hall Bowling Green KY 42101

ALBERT, HELEN MARY, marketing executive; b. Bklyn., Sept. 12, 1953; d. Ambros and Theresa M. (Schreiner) A. BA magna cum laude, Fordham U., 1975; MA, NYU, 1977; postgrad., Columbia U., 1977-78. Sr. copywriter Oxford U. Press, N.Y.C., 1978-79; mktg. mgr. Walter de Gruyter Inc., Hawthorne, N.Y., 1979-82; dir. mktg. M.E. Sharpe Inc., Armonk, N.Y., 1982—. Cons. Westchester County 4-H, White Plains, N.Y., 1988. Mem. Assn. for Scholarly Pub., Mid-Hudson Gem and Mineral Soc. Office: ME Sharpe Inc 80 Business Park Dr Armonk NY 10504

ALBERT, KATHY SWIFT, publication designer, design consultant; b. Lubbock, Tex., Apr. 15, 1961; d. Carroll Eugene and Virginia (Ray) Swift; m. Steven Frank Albert, July 2, 1988; 1 child, Erika Rae. BA in Advt., Tex. Tech. U., Lubbock, 1988. Prodn. systems operator Chgo. Tribune, 1985-87; prodn. editor Hunter Pub., Des Plaines, Ill., 1987-88; designer K.S.A. Communications, Oak Park, Ill., 1988—; desktop pub. cons. Sherman Wolf Advt., Chgo., 1988—; publ. designer freelance profls., Chgo., 1987—. Coach Oak Park (Ill.) River Forest Cheer Squads, 1989—. Mem. Women in Communications, Tex. Tech. Ex Students Assn., Oak Park Newcomers Club (newsletter editor 1990), Zeta Tau Alpha Alumnae (membership com.). Democrat. Methodist. Home and Office: 850 Fair Oaks Oak Park IL 60302

ALBERT, MARY DAY, laboratory administrator; b. Manchester, N.H., Mar. 2, 1926; d. Charles Howard and Sadie Bent (Forbes) Day; m. Richmond G. Albert, July 30, 1955 (div. June 1968); children: Eric, Ross. BS, U. N.H., 1948; MA, Bryn Mawr Coll., 1950; PhD, Brown U., 1955. Rsch. assoc. Harvard U., Boston, 1955-61; asst. prof. Northeastern U., Boston, 1961-62, Wellesley (Mass.) Coll., 1963-64, Newton (Mass.) Coll., 1964-75; dir. biol. labs. Boston U., Chestnut Hill, Mass., 1975—. Contbr. articles to profl. jours. Chmn. Handicapped Com., Newton, 1965-68. Mem. Assn. Biol. Lab. Edn., AAAS. Home: 56 Chapin Rd Newton Center MA 02159 Office: Boston Coll Biology Dept Chestnut Hill MA 02167

ALBERTS, MARY ELIZABETH, director non-profit organization; b. Houston, May 8, 1957; d. Jesse Alfred and Patricia Janice (Davis) A.; children: Serena Christine, Meredith Renee; m. Mark Alan Sendt, Mar. 17, 1984. AA, Victoria Coll., 1982; BA, U. Tex., 1985. Salesperson S&Q Clothiers, Victoria, Tex., 1973-74; asst. dir. YMCA Day Camp, Victoria, Tex., 1979-83; instr. Tinka's Dance and Gymnastics, Austin, Tex., 1983-85; aide Forest Trail Elem., Austin, 1985-86; dir. Kindercare Learning Ctr., Austin, 1986-87; mgr., assoc. dir. Houston READ Commn., 1987—. Author poetry. Vol. Teens Aid the Retarded, Victoria, 1970, March of Dimes, Victoria, 1970-72, Spl. Olympics, Victoria, 1978-82, Muscular Dystrophy, Austin, 1985-86. Mem. Houston Assn. Vol. Adminstrs. (bd. dirs., edn. chmn. 1990-91), NAFE. Home: 4234 "E" St Houston TX 77072 Office: Houston READ Commn 600 Travis Ste 3770 Houston TX 77002

ALBERTSON, SUSAN L., retired federal government official; b. Washington, Dec. 3, 1929; d. J. Mark and Alice (Myers) A. BS, Purdue U., 1952; postgrad. in internat. rels., George Washington U., 1955-57. Numerous profl. positions CIA, Washingtn, 1952-88; ret., 1988. Republican.

ALBIN, MAJORIE ANN, banker; b. Tuscola, Ill., Aug. 8, 1930; d. George David and Mae L. (Perry) Martin; m. John S. Albin, Sept. 10, 1949; children: Perry S., Martin L., David A. Student Ea. Ill. U., 1948, 49, Wharton Sch., U. Ill.Tax acct. Longview, Ill., 1963—; v.p., chief exec. officer Longview State Bank, 1978—, also dir.; v.p. State Bank of Chrisman, 1st Nat. Bank Ogden, Royal Br. Bank; dir. Newman Manor, Inc., Plant Pals, Inc., Longview Capitol Corp., Albi Pork Farm, Inc. Commr. Nat. Commn. on Agrl. Policy and Rural Devel.; chairwoman Ill. Farm Devel. Authority; mem. Rural Ill. Task Force; bd. dirs. Jarman Hosp., Tuscola, Continental Manor Nursing Home, Newman, Ill. Office: Longview State Bank Box 37 Longview IL 61852

ALBINO, PAMELA E., computer systems consultant; b. Waterbury, Conn., Mar. 4, 1963; d. Allan R. and Gloria M. (Champagne) A. BA in Math. and Computer Sci., Boston Coll., 1985. Systems cons., mgr. Andersen Consulting, Boston, 1985—. Mem. NAFE, Am. Prodn. and Inventory Control Soc. (cert. in prodn. inventory control). Office: Andersen Consulting Co 1 International Pl Boston MA 02146

ALBRECHT, GEORGENE LEE, science writer, graphic illustrator, editor; b. Pitts., Oct. 13, 1941; d. Harvey Howard and Effie Caroline (Ishman) Hetrick; m. Lawrence John Albrecht, Aug. 24, 1963; children—Brian James, Christopher Alan. Student in graphic art Inst. Pitts., 1959-61. Illustrator BK&T Advt., Pitts., 1961-63; free-lance artist, 1970-80; hort. columnist Gesneriad Saintpaulia News, Greenwood, Ind., 1981-88, contbg. editor, illustrator, 1981-88, assoc. editor, Greenwood, Ind., 1985-88; docent Phipps Conservatory, Pitts. Columnist: African Violet Mag., 1990—. Cons., mem. Pitts. Civic Garden Ctr., 1984. Recipient Best in Show award Gesneriad Soc. Internat. Show, Indpls., 1983, Louisville, 1984, French Lick, Ind., 1985, Springfield, Ohio, 1986, King, Prince of Show Pitts. Rose Soc., 1987, Best Amateur Dahlia award, Pitts. Dahlia Soc., 1988. Mem. Am. Orchid Soc. (highly commended cert. 1986), Orchid Soc. Western Pa. (dir. 1983-84), Pitts. Guild of Flower Arrangers, African Violet Soc. Am. Democrat. Home: 101 Oak Heights Dr Oakdale PA 15071

ALBRECHT, JANE KATHERINE, lawyer; b. St. Louis, Aug. 31, 1952; d. Edgar Samuel and Geraldine (Hendricks) A. BS magna cum laude, Regis Coll., 1974; JD, Georgetown U., 1980. Bar: D.C. 1980, U.S. Ct. Appeals (fed. cir.) 1981, U.S. Ct. Internat. Trade 1981, U.S. Dist. Ct. D.C. 1982, U.S. Ct. Appeals (D.C. cir.) 1987, U.S. Supreme Ct. Tax auditor IRS, St. Louis, 1975-77; law clk. Solicitor's Office, Gen. Legal Svcs., Dept. Interior, Washington, 1979; rsch. asst. Georgetown U. Law Ctr., Washington, 1978-80; atty. Office Gen. Counsel, U.S. Internat. Trade Commn., Washington, 1980-84; assoc. Verner, Lippert, Bernhard & McPherson, Washington, 1984-85, Dewey, Ballantine, Bushby, Palmer and Wood, 1985-87; internat. trade counsel Schoen & Pflueger, Brussels, 1987-88; of counsel LeBoeuf, Lamb, Leiby & MacRae, 1989—, Brussels. Mem. Internat. Bar Assn., Women in Govtl. Rels., European Trade Law Assn., Am. Club of Brussels (speaker 1989). Office: Le Boeuf Lamb Leiby & MacRae, 30 Sq De Meeus, B-2, Brussels 1040, Belgium

ALBRIGHT, BARBARA JOY, magazine editor; b. Fremont, Neb., July 2, 1955; d. Arthur William and Ruth Ann (Walther) A. BS in Food and Nutrition cum laude, U. Nebr., 1977; MS in Nutrition Communications, Boston U., 1980. Registered dietitian. Dietetic intern San Diego VA Hosp., 1977-78; clin. dietitian Independence (Mo.) Hosp., 1978-79; nutritionist Mktg. Sci. Inst., Cambridge, Mass., 1980; asst. food editor Redbook mag., N.Y.C., 1980-81; free-lance writer, home economist N.Y.C., 1981-82; assoc. food editor Woman's World mag., Englewood, N.J., 1982-83; home economist, dietitian Dudley Anderson Yutzy Pub. Rels., N.Y.C., 1983-85; from food editor to editor-in-chief Chocolatier mag., N.Y.C., 1985—. Co-author: Mostly Muffins, 1984, Simply Scones, 1988, Wild About Brownies, 1985; contbr. articles to Los Angeles Times Syndicate, Country Living, other mags. Named Master U. Nebr., 1986, Outstanding Young Alumnus U. Nebr., 1988. Mem. Am. Dietetic Assn., Soc. for Am. Cuisine, Home Economists in Bus. (editor newsletter 1986), N.Y. Women's Culinary Alliance (contbg. editor newsletter 1985-87), Conn. Women's Culinary Alliance (bd. mem. 1989-90), N.Y. Soc. for Nebr. (bd. dirs.), Chi Omega (sec.-treas. 1976-77). Republican. Lutheran. Home: 885 Post Rd #2B Darien CT 06820 Office: Chocolatier Mag 45 W 34th St Ste 500 New York NY 10001

ALBRIGHT, BARBARA LYNN, sales representative; b. Coatesville, Pa., Nov. 16, 1949; d. Robert Earl and Marion Louise (Henck) Williams; children: Robert Lawrence Gill, Sean Michael Gill, Jennifer Lynn Gill. Diploma, Goldey Beacom Jr. Coll., Wilmington, Del., 1968. Unit organizer Princess House Products, North Dighton, Mass., 1977-87; account exec. Allied Surg. Supply, Lancaster, Pa., 1987-89; sales rep. Optical Apparatus, Ardmore, Pa., 1989—. Home: 1983 W Strasburg Rd Coatesville PA 19320 Office: Optical Apparatus 136 Coulter Ave Ardmore PA 19003

ALBRIGHT, LOVELIA FRIED, art importing executive; b. N.Y.C., Dec. 13, 1934; d. George and Hilda (Lazanov) Fried; m. Lee Albright, Nov. 30, 1958; children: Gregre Scott, Glenn Keith, Todd Cameron. Student, Bennington Coll., 1952-55, Grad. Sch. Internat. Studies, Geneva, 1955-56. Publicist Doubleday & Co., N.Y.C., 1960-63; owner Foley & Robinson, Inc., N.Y.C., 1988—; pres., owner Lovelia Enterprises, Inc., N.Y.C., 1972—, Foley & Robinson, Inc., N.Y.C., 1988—; owner Foley & Robinson, Inc., N.Y.C., 1988—. Monthly columnist home furnishings N.Y. Antique Guide, 1972. Office: Foley & Robinson Inc 56 W 22nd St New York NY 10010

ALBRIGHT, MADELEINE, political scientist; b. Prague, Czechoslovakia, May 15, 1937; d. Josef and Anna (Speeglova) Korbel; m. Joseph Medill Patterson Albright, June 11, 1959 (div. 1983); children: Anne Korbel, Alice Patterson, Katharine Medill. B.A. with honors, Wellesley Coll., 1959; M.A., Columbia U., 1968; cert., Russian Inst., 1968, Ph.D., 1976. Washington coord. Maine for Muskie, 1975-76; chief legis. asst. to U.S. Senator Muskie, 1976-78; mem. staff NSC, 1978-81; fellow Woodrow Wilson Internat. Ctr. for Scholars, Washington, 1981-82; Donner prof. internat. affairs, dir. women in fgn. service Sch. Fgn. Service Georgetown U., 1982—, sr. fellow in Soviet and Eastern European Affairs Ctr. for Strategic and Internat. Studies,, 1981; fgn. policy coord. Mondale for Pres. campaign, 1984, to Geraldine A. Ferraro, 1984; vice chmn. Nat. Dem. Inst. for Internat. Affairs, Washington, 1984—. Author: Poland: The Role of the Press in Political Change, 1983; contbr. articles to profl. jours., chpts. to books. Bd. dirs. Beauvoir Sch., Washington, 1968-76, chmn., 1978-83; trustee Black Student Fund, 1969-78, 82—, Democratic Forum, 1976-78, Williams Coll., 1978-82, Wellesley Coll., 1983-89; mem. exec. com. D.C. Citizens for Better Pub. Edn., 1975-76; bd. dirs. Washington Urban League, 1982-84, Atlantic Council, 1984—, Ctr. for Nat. Policy, 1985—, Chatham House Fedn., 1986-88; sr. fgn. policy advisor Dukakis for Pres. Campaign, 1988. Mem. Council Fgn. Relations, Am. Polit. Sci. Assn., Czeckoslovak Soc. Arts and Scis. Am., Atlantic Council U.S. (dir.), Am. Assn. for Advancement Slavic Studies. Office: Georgetown U Sch Fgn Svc Washington DC 20007

ALBRIGHT, MAUREEN TERESE, personnel manager; b. Chgo., Jan. 21, 1961; d. Robert Emmet and Margaret Rose (Gaffney) O'Malley; m. Randy Albright, Aug. 6, 1983; 1 child, Ryan. BA, Nat. Coll. Edn., 1986. Sec. Am. Nuclear Soc., La Grange, Ill., 1980-86; personnel, office mgr. Am. Nuclear Soc., La Grange, 1986—. Mem. NAFE, Council Engring. & Sci. Soc. Execs., Am. Mgmt. Soc. Democrat. Roman Catholic. Home: 2220 Green Valley Rd Darien IL 60559 Office: Am Nuclear Soc 555 N Kensington Ave La Grange Park IL 60525

ALBRIGHT, NANCY ELIZABETH, recruiter; b. Pitts., May 3, 1938; d. William David and Eleanor Virginia (Adams) Lamb; m. Edward G. Albright Jr.; 1 child, Mark. BA in Speech, Denison U., 1961. Life ins. salesperson Insurance Broker, Pitts., 1961-77; sales rep. Wholesale Arts, Atlanta, 1977-82; pres. Wholesale Art Unlimited, Richmond, Va., 1982-84; acct. exec. NRI Capital, Richmond, 1984-86; nat. recruiter Progressive, Richmond, 1986—. V.p. East Marietta (Ga.) Newcomers, 1980, pres., 1981; resp. United Way, Harrisburg, 1977; mem. adv. bd. Goodwill Industries. Mem. NAFE, Goodwill Industries (bd. dirs.). Republican. Presbyterian. Office: Progressive 4461 Cox Rd Ste 300 Glen Allen VA 23060

ALBRIGHT, PHYLLISTEAN HARDRICK, accountant; b. Lake Cormorant, Miss., Apr. 20, 1956; d. Nathan and Minnie Mae (Guest) Hardrick; m. Samuel L. Albright, Nov. 22, 1980; 1 child, Darrell LaShawn. AS, Draughon Jr. Coll., 1986. Supr., word processor Touche Ross & Co., Memphis, 1979-84; acct., office mgr. Banks, Finley, White & Co., Memphis, 1984—; instr. Jr. Achievement Memphis, 1987-88. Mem. NAFE, Nat. Assn. Black Accts. (sec. 1984-85). Democratic. Baptist.

ALBRIGHT-SAAD, MICHELLE LOUISE, real estate executive; b. Nome, Alaska, Dec. 28, 1961; d. Wayne Paul and Elizabeth Louise (Cavota) Albright. BA, The Catholic U. Am., 1984; MBA, George Washington U., 1988. Real estate appraisers U.S. Dept. Interior, Washington, 1985-86, Urquhart & Assocs., Kensington, Md., 1986-88, Coldwell Banker, Washington, 1988—. Am. Ind. Am. scholar U.S. Dept. Edn., Washington, 1985. Mem. Am. Indian Soc. Republican. Roman Catholic. Home: 13701-13 Modrad Way Silver Spring MD 20904 Office: Coldwell Banker 1001 Pennsylvania Ave #200 Washington DC 20895

ALCANTARA-MEDEL, FLORDELIZA, business educator; b. Manila, Mar. 8, 1944; came to U.S., 1969; d. Arsenio Alcantara and Belen (Robles) Castro; m. Francis I. Medel, Dec. 18, 1980; children: Arthur, Marlyze, Sandra, John Ivy, Arsenio III, Tiara, Judy. BA in Polit. Sci., U. Phillipines, Manila, 1965; MPA, Phillipine Women's U., Manila, 1968; MA in Bus., Columbia U., 1971. Cert. tchr. bus. subjects, N.J. Prof. various univs., Manila, 1967-69; chmn. bus. dept. Washington Bus. Sch., N.Y.C., 1978-80; instr. Comml. Programming Unltd., N.Y.C., 1984-87; mgr. Jersey City Minority Bus. Devel. Ctr., 1988-89; dean bus. dept. Market Tng. Inst. Bus. Sch., Newark, 1989-90; cons. bus. Alcantara Enterprises Inc., Jersey City, 1980—; prof. Hudson County Community Coll., Jersey City, 1987—; instr. N.Y. Inst. Bus. Tech., N.Y.C., 1990—; adj. prof. Montclair (N.J.) State Coll., 1981, Jersey City State Coll., 1983; lectr. Ramapo State Coll., N.J., 1986, ethnic cons. ctr. study pluralism. Chmn./producer Filipino Hour cable TV program, Jersey City, 1988—; guest columnist Filipino Reporter, 1980—. Trustee Jersey City Bd. Edn., 1986-89; pres., founder Asian Am. Civic Assn. Inc., Jersey City, 1989—; co-chairperson Asian Pacific Caucus, Dem. Nat. Com., N.J., 1984; chairperson Philippine Human Svc. Ctr., Jersey City, Philippine Earthquake Fund, Jersey City; pres. women's soc. Christ United Meth. Ch. Recipient Outstanding Young Educator award Philam N.J. Jaycees, 1978, Outstanding Svc. award Congress of Filipino-Am. Citizens, 1979, Filippino Club Internat., 1990 Channel 51 Pub. Access Cable TV, 1989; named Woman of Achievement Jersey Jour., 1985. Mem. Phillippins Businesswomen's Assn. (pres., founder 1980—), United Filipino Am. Assn. (bd. dirs. 1986—), Iloilo Soc. Am. (bd. dirs. 1980-89), Peace Coun., Phi Delta Kappa, Delta Pi Epsilon. Democrat. Office: Alcantara Enterprises Inc 344 Grove PO Box 217 Jersey City NJ 07302

AL-CHALABI, MARGERY LEE, economic development services company executive; b. Tarentum, Pa., Oct. 20, 1939; d. Stephen and Margaretta E. (Wuerfel) Pupach; m. Suhail al-Chalabi, Mar. 9, 1965. BArch, Carnegie-Mellon U., 1961; MSc, Athens Technol. Inst., 1965. Architect, planner Doxiadis Assocs., Athens, Greece, 1962-65; regional planner HUD, Chgo., 1965-67; sr. planner Dept. Urban Renewal, Chgo., 1967-70; ind. planning cons., Chgo., 1970-74; sr. planner Bauer Engring., Chgo., 1971-74; v.p. Real Estate Rsch. Corp., 1974-81; mng. dir. real estate Laventhol & Horwath, Chgo., 1981-82; dir. dept. city devel. Mayor's Office City of Chgo., 1982-83; pres. al-Chalabi Group Ltd., Chgo., 1983—. Author numerous plans on urban and econ. devel. Recipient numerous restoration awards Landmarks Preservation Coun. Ill. and Theater Hist. Soc., 1985-87. Mem. Urban Land Inst., World Soc. Ekistics, Landmarks Preservation Coun. Ill., Nat. Trust Hist. Preservation, Lambda Alpha. Home: 546B Wilson Blvd Beverly Shores IN 46301 Office: al-Chalabi Group Ltd 330 W Diversey Pkwy #1403 Chicago IL 60657

ALCON, SONJA LEE DE BEY RYAN, medical social worker; b. Orange City, Iowa, Aug. 2, 1937; d. Albert Lee Gerard and Clarice Victoria (Brown) deBey; m. Richard J. Gebhardt, June 6, 1959; children: Russell, Cheryl, KurtGebhart Ryan; m. George W. Ryan, Dec. 28, 1968; 1 dau., Alanna (dec.); m. David E. Alcon, July 20, 1985. C BA, Western Md. Coll., 1959; MSW, U. Md., 1973. Caseworker, Springfield State Hosp., Sykesville, Md., 1959-61; dir. social work dept. Hanover (Pa.) Gen. Hosp., 1966—; clin. assoc. prof. sch. social work and social planning U. Md., 1987—; cons. Golden Age Nursing Home, Hanover, 1973-76, Carlisle (Pa.) Hosp., 1974-78, Hanover Vis. Nurse Assn., 1977-83; chmn. profl. adv. com. Vis. Nurse Assn. of Hanover and Spring Grove, Inc., 1986-89; mem. social work adv. coun. Western Md. Coll., 1979, 80. Bd. dirs. Hospice of York, 1980-82, Hanover chpt. ARC, 1976-79, Adams-Hanover Mental Health, 1973-76; pres. Human Svcs. Orgn., 1980, v.p., 1985-86; mem. adv. coun. Hanover Hospice, 1982-85; treas. Hanover Community Progress Com., 1976-80; mem. Adams-Hanover Sheltered Workshop Com., 1968-70; bd. dirs. Hanover Community Players, 1974-77, sec., 1982; organizer local chpt. Make Today Count and Preemie Parent Support Group, 1979; initiator Children's Cardiac Fund, 1979; mem. Hanover Oratorio Soc., 1964-85; active YWCA, 1979-84; co-organizer Adams-Hanover chpt. Compassionate Friends, 1983; mem. vestry All Saints Episcopal Ch., 1973-74, 76-79, 83-86, vestry sec., 1975, diocesan del. Central Pa., 1978, 80-86, mem. altar guild, 1968-86, treas. ch. women, 1979-83; vol. Hanover Gen. Hosp. Aux.; vol., facilitator I Can Cope program Am. Cancer Soc.; mem. adv. coun. Parents Anonymous. Recipient York Daily Record Exceptional Citizen award, 1979, Spl. Recognition cert. Col. Richard McAllister chpt. DAR, 1980; finalist YWCA Salute to Women, 1986, 87. Mem. Nat. Assn. Social Workers, Acad. Cert. Social Workers, Am. Hosp. Assn. Soc. Hosp. Social Work Dirs., Cen. Pa. Hosp. Social Workers (treas. 1981-85, v.p. 1987, pres. 1988), Hosp. Assn. of Pa. Soc. for Hosp. Social Work Dirs., U. Md. Alumni Assn. (bd. dirs. 1983), Order Eastern Star (worthy matron 1985-86), Order of Amaranth (worthy patron 1988-89), White Shrine, Commandery Ladies Aux. (1988-90), Elks Aux. (v.p. local club 1986-88). Home: RD #3 3305-M Tamarind Dr Spring Grove PA 17362 Office: Hanover Gen Hosp 300 Highland Ave Hanover PA 17331

ALCOTT, AMY STRUM, professional golfer; b. Kansas City, Mo., Feb. 22, 1956; d. Eugene Yale and Leatrice (Strum) A. Profl. golfer Ladies Profl. Golf Assn., 1975—; dir. Women's Golf Devel. Elizabeth Arden, Inc.; asst. golf coach UCLA Women's Golf Team; host Amy Alcott Golf Classic for Multiple Sclerosis Soc., 1980—; dir. Youth Golf Devel., Sunkist; winner U.S. Golf Assn. Jr. Girl's Title, 1973; winner 30 profl. titles including Can. Open-Peter Jackson Classic, 1979, Women's U.S. Open, 1980, Nabisco-Dinah Shore Invitational, 1980, 88, Tucson Open, 1985, Moss Creek Invitational, 1985, World Championship of Women's Golf, 1985, Mazda Champions, 1986, Mazda Hall of Fame Championship, LPGA Nat. Pro-Am., 1986-88. Named Rookie of Year Ladies Profl. Golf Assn., 1975, Player of Yr. Ladies Profl. Golf Assn., 1980; Player of Year Golf mag., 1980; Jewish Athlete of Year, 1980; Calif. Golf Writers Hall of Fame, 1987; recipient Seagrams Seven Crown of Sports award, 1980, Vare Trophy, 1980, Ladies Pro Golf Assn. Founders Cup award, 1986. Office: Ladies Profl Golf Assn 2570 Volusia Ave #B Daytona Beach FL 32114-1113 also: LPGA PO Box 956 Pacific Palisades CA 90272*

ALCOZER, ROMALDA FRANCESCA, health system administrator; b. Belton, Tex., July 19, 1950; d. Manuel and Romalda (Gonzales) Vallez; m. Jan D. Rumberger, Dec. 19, 1970 (div. Sept. 1977). BS in Nursing, U. Mary Hardin-Baylor, 1972; MS in Nursing, Pa. State U., 1981. Charge nurse Santa Fe Meml. Hosp., Temple, Tex., 1972; staff nurse VA Ctr., Temple, Tex., 1972-73, head nurse, 1980-81; staff nurse Pitts., 1981; head nurse Phila., 1981-83; pub. health nurse Pa. Dept. Health, Harrisburg, 1973-78; grad. asst. Pa. State U., University Park, 1979; dir. Scott & White Meml. Hosp., Temple, 1983-85, Holy Cross Hosp. Home Health, Austin, 1985-87; project coord. Daus. of Charity Nat. Home Health System, Austin, 1987-89; quality assurance coord. Daus. of Charity Health Svcs. of Austin, 1989—; cons. Joint Commn. on Accreditation of Healthcare Corps., 1988—. Candidate Miss Hope Am. Cancer Soc., Harrisburg, 1977. Capt. Nurse Corps, USAR, 1987—. U. Mary Hardin-Baylor scholar, 1969. Mem. Am. Nurses Assn. (cert. med.-surg. nurse), Tex. Nurses Assn. (recording sec. 1987-88), Am. Diabetes Assn., Oncology Soc., Hispanic C. of C., Zachary Scott Theatre (vo. 1985—). Democrat. Roman Catholic. Home: 2611 Bee Cave Rd #115 Austin TX 78746 Office: Daus of Charity Health Svcs Home Care Adminstrn 3724 Jefferson St Ste 210 Austin TX 78731

ALDAVE, BARBARA BADER, law educator, lawyer; b. Tacoma, Dec. 28, 1938; d. Fred A. and Patricia W. (Burns) Bader; m. Ralph Theodore Aldave, Apr. 2, 1966; children—Anna Marie, Anthony John. B.S., Stanford U., 1960; J.D., U. Calif.-Berkeley, 1966. Bar: Oreg. 1966, Tex. 1982. Assoc. law firm Eugene, Oreg., 1967-70; asst. prof. U. Oreg., 1970-73; vis. prof. U. Calif., Berkeley, 1973-74; from vis. prof. to prof. U. Tex., Austin, 1974-89, co-holder James R. Dougherty chair for faculty excellence, 1981-82, Piper prof., 1982, Joe A. Worsham centennial prof., 1984-89, Liddell, Sapp, Zivley, Hill and LaBoon prof. banking financial and comml. law, 1989; dean sch. law St. Mary's U., San Antonio, 1989—; vis. prof. Northeastern U., 1985-88. Pres. NETWORK, 1985-89; bd. dirs. Women's Advocacy Project, Greater Tex. Legal Found., San Antonio Community Law Ctr. Recipient Teaching Excellence award U. Tex. Student Bar Assn., 1976, appreciation awards Thurgood Marshall Legal Soc. of U. Tex., 1979, 81, 85, 87, Teaching Excellence award Chicano Law Students Assn. of U. Tex., 1984, Hermine Tobolowsky award Women's Law Caucus of U. Tex., 1985, ethics award Kugle, Stewart, Dent & Frederick, 1988, Leadership award Women's Law Assn. St. Mary's U., 1989, Ann. Inspirational award Women's Advocacy Project, 1989. Mem. ABA (com. on corp. laws sect. corp., banking and bus. law 1982-88), Bexar County Women's Bar Assn., San Antonio Bar Assn., William S. Sessions Am. Inn of Ct., World Affairs Coun. San Antonio, Supreme Ct. Hist. Soc., Order of Coif, Stanford Alumni Assn., Stanford Club, Phi Delta Phi, Iota Sigma Pi, Omicron Delta Kappa. Roman Catholic. Home: 323 W Woodlawn San Antonio TX 78212 Office: St Mary's U 1 Camino Santa Maria San Antonio TX 78228

ALDEA, PATRICIA, architect; b. Bucharest, Romania, Mar. 18, 1947; came to U.S., 1976; d. Dan Jasmin Negreanu and Sonia (Friedgant) Philipp-Negreanu; m. Val O. Aldea, Feb. 17, 1971; 1 child, Donna-Dana. MArch, Ion Mincu, Bucharest, 1970. Registered architect, N.Y. Architect, project. mgr. The Landmark Preservation Inst., Bucharest, 1971-76; architect Edward Durell Stone Assn., N.Y.C., 1977-79; assoc. architect, project mgr. Alan Lapidus P.C., N.Y.C., 1980—. Columnist Contemporanul art jour., 1969-73. Hist. landmarks study fellow Internationes Fed. Republic of Germany, 1974. Office: Alan Lapidus PC 2112 Broadway New York NY 11023

ALDER, GAIL CECELIA, medical record administrator; b. Grosse Pointe Farms, Mich., Sept. 9, 1944; d. John Joseph and Lydia Marie (Doom) A. BS, Mercy Coll., Detroit, 1966; MA, Cen. Mich. U., 1984. Registered record adminstr., 1966. Asst. dir. med. records Mt. Carmel Mercy Hosp., Detroit, 1966-71; dir. med. record svs. Providence Hosp., Southfield, Mich., 1971-88; pres. Alder Assocs., Inc., Farmington Hills, Mich., 1988—; cons. Georgian N.W. Extended Care Facility, Detroit, 1969-72, McNamara Hosp., Warren, Mich., 1973-75; cons. to med. record profession, 1969—; instr. directed practice Mercy Coll., 1971-88; instr. directed practice Schoolcraft Community Coll., Livonia, Mich., 1971-88, mem. adv. bd., 1973—; assoc. prof. Oakland Community Coll., Farmington Hills, 1975-76; guest lectr. Wayne State U. Sch. Pharmacy, Detroit, 1980. Mem. Oakland County Comprehensive Health Planning Coun., 1977-83; mem. adv. com. Mich. Cancer Found., 1978-88; chmn. Oakland Health Edn. Program, Rochester, Mich., 1980-81. Mem. Am. Med. Record Assn., Mich. Med. Record Assn. (pres. 1985-86, bd. dirs. 1986-87), Southeastern Mich. Med. Record Assn. (pres. 1977-78, bd. dirs. 1978-79), NAFE. Republican. Roman Catholic. Office: 35526 Grand River Ave Ste 350 Farmington Hills MI 48335

ALDERMAN, MINNIS AMELIA, psychologist, educator, small business owner; b. Douglas, Ga., Oct. 14, 1928; d. Louis Cleveland Sr. and Minnis Amelia (Wooten) A. AB in Music, Speech and Drama, Ga. State Coll., Milledgeville, 1949; MA in Supervision and Counseling Psychology, Murray State U., 1960; postgrad. Columbia Pacific U., 1987—. Tchr. music Lake County Sch. Dist., Umatilla, Fla., 1949-50; instr. vocal and instrumental music, dir. band, orch. and choral Fulton County Sch. Dist., Atlanta, 1950-54; instr. English, speech, debate, vocal and instrumental music, dir. drama, band, choral and orch. Elko County Sch. Dist., Wells, Nev., 1954-59; tchr. English and social studies Christian County Sch. Dist., Hopkinsville, Ky., 1960; instr. psychology, guidance counselor Murray (Ky.) State U., 1961-63, U. Nev., Reno, 1963-67; owner Minisizer Exercising Salon, Ely, Nev., 1969-71, Knit Knook, Ely, 1969—, Minimimeo, Ely, 1969—, Gift Gamut, Ely, 1977—; prof. dept. fine arts Wassuk Coll., Ely, 1986—, assoc. dean, 1986-87, dean, 1987—; counselor White Pine County Sch. Dist., Ely, 1960-68; dir. Child and Family Ctr., Ely Indian Colony, 1988—; supr. testing Ednl. Testing Svc., Princeton, N.J., 1960-68, Am. Coll. Testing Program, Iowa, 1960-68, U. Nev., Reno, 1960-68; chmn. bd. White Pine Sch. Dist. Employees Fed. Credit Union, Ely, 1961-69; psychologist mental hygiene div. Nev. Pers., Ely, 1969-75, dept. employment security, 1975-80; sec.-treas. bd. dirs. Gt. Basin Enterprises, Ely, 1969-71; pvt. instr. piano, violin, voice and organ, Ely, 1981—; bd. dir. band Sacred Heart Sch., Ely, 1982—. Author various news articles, feature stories, pamphlets, handbooks and grants in field. Pres. White Pine County Mental Health Assn., 1960-63, 78—; mem. Gov.'s Mental Health State Commn., 1963-65; bd. dirs. White Pine County Sch. Employees Fed. Credit Union, 1961-68, pres., 1963-68; 2d v.p. White Pine Community Concert Assn., 1965-67, pres., 1967, 85—, treas., 1975-79, dr. chmn., 1981-85; chmn. of bd., 1984; bd. dirs. White Pine chpt. ARC, 1978-82; mem. Nev. Hwy. Safety Leaders Bd., 1979-82; mem. Gov.'s Commn. on Status Women, 1968-74; sec.-treas. White Pine Rehab. Tng. Ctr. for Retarded Persons, 1973-75; mem. Gov.'s Commn. on Hwy. Safety, 1979-81; dir. Ret. Sr. Vol. Program, 1973-74; vice chmn. Gt. Basin Health Coun., 1973-75, Home Extension Adv. Bd., 1977-80; sec.-treas. Great Basin chpt. Nev. Employees Assn.; bd. dirs. United Way, 1970-76; vice chmn. White Pine Coun. on Alcoholism and Drug Abuse, 1975-76, chmn., 1976-77; grants author 3 yrs. Indian Child Welfare Act, originator Community Tng. Ctr. for Retarded People, 1972, Ret. Sr. Vol. Program, 1974, Nutrition Program for Sr. Citizens, 1974, Sr. Citizens Ctr., 1974, Home Repairs for Sr. Citizens, 1974, Sr. Citizens Home Assistance Program, 1977, Creative Crafters Assns., 1976, Inst. Current World Affairs, 1989—; bd. dirs. Sacred Heart Parochial Sch., 1982—, dir. band, 1982—; candidate for diaconal ministry, 1982—. Precinct reporter ABC News 1966. Fellow Am. Coll. Musicians, Nat. Guild Piano Tchrs.; mem. NEA (life), Nat. Fedn. Ind. Bus. (dist. chair 1971-85, nat. guardian coun. 1985—, state guardian coun. 1987—), AAUW (pres. Wells br. 1957-58, pres. White Pine br. 1965-66, 86-87, bd. dirs. 1965-87, rep. edn. 1965-67, implementation chair 1967-69, area advisor 1969-73), Nat. Fedn. Bus. and Profl. Women (1st v.p. Ely chpt. 1965-66, pres. Ely chpt. 1966-68, 74-76, 85—, bd. dirs. Nev. chpt. 1966—, 1st v.p. Nev. chpt. 1970-71, pres. Nev. chpt. 1972-73, nat. bd. dirs. 1972-73), Mensa (supr. testing 1965—), Delta Kappa Gamma (chpt. pres. 1968-72, state bd. 1967—, chpt. parliamentarian 1974-78, state 1st v.p. 1967-69, state pres. 1969-71, nat. bd. 1969-71, state parliamentarian 1971-73), White Pine Knife and Fork Club (1st v.p. 1969-70, pres. 1970-71, bd. dirs. 1979—). Home: 945 Ave H PO Box 457 East Ely NV 89315 Office: 16 Shoshone Circle Ely NV 89301

ALDERSON, KAREN ANN, librarian; b. Caledonia, Minn., Aug. 2, 1947; d. Merle Richard and Zelda Edna (Gray) A. BA, Upper Iowa U., 1968; MA, U. Denver, 1979. Lic. pvt. investigator. Libr. North Linn Community Sch. Dist., Coggon, Iowa, 1968-79; cataloger, acquisitions libr. Coll. of St. Mary, Omaha, 1982; tech. svcs., information libr. Mason City (Iowa) Pub. Libr., 1982-86; free-lance libr. Marion, Iowa, 1986—. Indexer: After Hours Manual for Information and Referral, 1987. Vol. United Way Information and Referral, East Cen. Iowa, Cedar Rapids, 1987—. Named Find-A-Fellow Campaign winner AAUW Ednl. Found., 1988, 89. Mem. ALA, NEA (various local chpt. offices), Cedar Rapids Area C. of C., Profl. Women's Network, AAUW (branch newsletter editor, 1985-86, 88-90), Iowa Libr. Assn., Alpha Delta Kappa (various local chpt. offices). Office: 1164 44th St Ste 2 Marion IA 52302

ALDERSON, MARGARET NORTHROP, arts administrator, educator, artist; b. Washington, Nov. 28, 1936; d. Vernon D. and Margaret (Lloyd) Northrop; m. Donald Marr Alderson, Jr., June 4, 1955; children— Donald Marr III, Barbara Lynn Hennesy, Brian, Graham. Student George Washington U., 1954-55; A.A., Monterey Peninsula Jr. Coll., 1962. Staff, tchr. Galerie Jaclande, Springfield, Va. 1972-73; artist/tchr. Studio 7, Torpedo Factory Art Ctr., Alexandria, 1974—, dir. ctr., 1979-85; tchr. Fairfax County Recreation, 1972-73, Art League Schs., Alexandria, 1978—, ann. Feb. workshop, Accapulco, Mex., Eng., 1989, English Printing Workshop, 1989, 90; cons. in field; project supr. City of Alexandria for Torpedo Factory Art Ctr., 1978-83; ptnr. Soho Hubris Art Gallery (N.Y.), 1977-78; one woman shows at Way Up Gallery, Livermore, Calif., 1971, Lynchburg Coll. (Va.), 1978, Farm House Gallery, Rehobeth, Del., 1979, Art League Gallery, Alexandria, Va., 1980, 86, Lyceum Mus., Alexandria, 1987, Alexandria Mus., 1987-88, William Ris Gallery, Stone Harbor, N.J., 1988; exhibited in group shows at Art League Gallery, Alexandria, 1972—, Lynchburg (Va.) Coll., 1978, Montgomery (Ala.) Mus., 1980, Art Barn, 1989, Moscow-Washington Art Exch. Exhibit Internat., Moscow, 1990; represented in permanent collections Phillip Morse Collection, United Va. Bank, CSX Corp., Fannie Mae Corp., Accacia Fin. Group, Office U.S. Atty. Gen., Office of Ins. Gen. EPA, Aerospace Corp. Festival chmn. City Festival Cultural Arts, Livermore, Calif., 1971; bd. dirs., Cultural Alliance Greater Washington, 1982—; bd. dirs. Torpedo Factory Art Ctr., 1978—; mem. Partners for Liveable Places, 1979—. Recipient Md. found. award Balt. watercolor regional annual, 1989, Elgie and David Ject Kay award Audubon Artists annual, 1989, 1st Place Awards in Watercolor, Art League, 1975, 76, 77, 82, 84-85, also numerous purchase awards, Jane Morton Norman award Ky. Nat. Watercolor Show, 1986, Adrirondack Nat. Watercolor Show, 1987, 3d award Catherine Lorillard Show, N.Y.C., 1987, Albert Ehringer award, 1989; travel show include Chrysler Mus. Biennial, 1988, Audubon Artists Nat. Show, 1989 (Elsie & Davis Ject Key award 1989), Balt. Regional Watercolor Annual, 1989 (Md. Found. award 1989). Mem. Fed. Nat. Mortgage Assn., Va. Watercolor Soc. (pres. 1982, 1st place awards ann. exhibit 1980, 82, excellence award 1989), Potomac Valley Watercolorists (pres. 1978), Torpedo Factory Artists Assn. (pres. 1977-78), Springfield Art Guild (pres. 1977), Artists Equity, Am. Council on Arts, Am. Watercolor Soc., Am. Council of Univ. and Community Arts Ctrs., Nat. League Am. PEN Women, Am. Profl. Artist's League, Am. Mgmt. Assn., Nat. Hist. Trust. Republican. Home: 2204 Windsor Rd Alexandria VA 22307 Studio: Studio 7 Torpedo Factory Art Ctr 105 N Union St Alexandria VA 22314

ALDERSON, MARTHA J., editor; b. Clifton Forge, Va., May 20, 1942; d. Granville Smith and Lillian May (Mann) A. BA, W. Va. Wesleyan Coll., Buckhannon, 1964; MAT, Colo. Coll., 1971. Eng. tchr. Red Creek Cen. Sch., N.Y., 1964-65; sales correspondent McGraw-Hill Book Co., N.Y.C., 1965-66; ednl. cons., McGraw Hill Book Co., N.Y.C., 1966-70, product mgr., 1970-71; textbook editor McGraw-Hill Book Co., Manchester, Mo., 1972-89; freelance writer, editor Kirkwood, Mo., 1989-90; editorial dir. Ligature, Inc., Clayton, MO., 1990—. Co-author: Mystery Novels Criticism,

And Then THere Were Nine 1985, Cops and Constables 1986; Author: Essay on Mystery Novels, Mystery Readers of Am. Mag. 1987, Comic Crime 1987. Mem. League of Women Voters, St. Louis 1988--, Am. Civil Liberties Union, St. Louis 1988--. Recipient Cert. Leadership award YWCA St. Louis 1987. Mem. Women's Commerce Assn., Popular Culture Assn., St. Louis Writers Guild. Democrat. Home: 631 McKinley Ave Kirkwood MO 63122

ALDERTON, SUSAN EDITH, treasurer; b. Malmesbury, Wiltshire, Eng., Mar. 23, 1952; d. Ronald Hubert and Edith (Charnley) Alderton; m. Stephen Andrew Crane, Nov. 3, 1984. BA in Econs. and Stats., U. of Exeter, Exeter, Devon, England, 1973; MBA in Fin., NYU, 1986. Rsch. asst. H.P. Drewry Ltd., London, 1973-76; asst. dir. Bankers Trust Internat., London, 1976-78; asst. treas. Bankers Trust Co., N.Y.C., 1978-81, Avco Corp., Greenwich, Conn., 1981-86; asst. treas. NL Industries, Inc., N.Y.C., 1986-87, v.p., treas., 1987—; v.p., treas. Baroid Corp., N.Y.C., 1988—; bd. dirs. Titanium Metals Corp. Mem. Nat. Assn. Corp. Treas., Soc. of Internat. Treas. Office: NL Industries Inc 445 Park Ave New York NY 10022

ALDO-BENSON, MARLENE ANN, professor medicine, researcher, physician; b. Bridgeport, Conn., July 31, 1939; d. Edward Robert and Geraldine Rachel (Noce) Aldo; m. Merrill Douglas Benson, June 26, 1965; children: Merrill Douglas Jr., Kara Jean, Marshall David, Jeffrey Dana. BA, U. Vt., 1962, MD, 1965. Diplomate Am. Bd. Internal Medicine. Intern, then resident Columbia U. Bellevue Hosp., N.Y.C., 1965-67; resident, fellow Boston U., 1967-69; dir. outpatient dept. Prince George's County Hosp., Cheverly, Md., 1970-71; fellow immunology Tuft's New Eng. Med. Ctr., Boston, 1971-73, instr. medicine, 1973-76; asst. prof. medicine Sch. Medicine Ind. U., Indpls., 1976-79, assoc. prof. medicine, 1979-84, prof. med. microbiology and immunology, 1984—; mem. study sect. NIH, Washington, 1986, 89—; ad hoc reviewer merit rev. bd. VA, Washington, 1981—; staff physician U. Hosp. & Wishard Meml. Hosp., Indpls., 1976—; dir. rsch. multipurpose arthritis ctr. Ind. U., Indpls., 1978—. Contbr. numerous articles to profl. jours. Bd. dirs. Indpls. chpt. Arthritis Found., 1978-83, Ind. Lupus Found., Indpls., 1984—. NIH grantee, 1978, 84, Nat. Inst. Alcohol Abuse and Alcoholism grantee 1987, 88, 89. Fellow ACP; mem. Cen. Rheumatic Assn. (pres. 1983-84), Am. Assn. Immunologists, Am. Fedn. Clin. Rsch. (program com. 1983), Cen. Soc. Clin. Rsch., Am. Coll. Reheumatology. Roman Catholic. Office: Ind U Sch Medicine 541 Clinical Dr Indianapolis IN 46202

ALDREDGE, THEONI VACHLIOTIS, costume designer; b. Athens, Greece, Aug. 22, 1932; d. Gen. Athanasios and Meropi (Gregoriades) Vachliotis; m. Thomas E. Aldredge, Dec. 10, 1953. Student, Am. Sch., Athens, 1949-53, Goodman Theatre, Chgo.; LHD, De Paul U., 1985. Mem. design staff Goodman Theatre, 1951-53; head designer N.Y. Shakespeare Festival, 1962—. Designer numerous Broadway and off Broadway shows, ballet, opera, TV spls.; films include Girl of the Night, You're a Big Boy Now, No Way To Treat a Lady, Uptight, Last Summer, I Never Sang for My Father, Promise at Dawn, The Great Gatsby (Brit. Motion Picture Acad. award 1976), Network, The Cheap Detective, The Fury, The Eyes of Laura Mars (Acad. Sci. Fiction Films award), The Champ, Semi-Tough, The Rose, Monsignor, Annie, Ghostbusters, Moonstruck, We're No Angels, Stanley and Iris; Broadway shows include A Chorus Line (Theatre World award 1976), Annie (Tony award 1977), Barnum (Tony award 1979), Dream Girls, Woman of the Year, Onward Victoria, La Cage Aux Folles (Tony award 1984), 42nd Street, A Little Family Business, Merlin, Private Lives, The Corn Is Green, The Rink, Blithe Spirit, Chess, Gypsy (1989 revival). Recipient Obie award for Disting. Svc. to Off-Broadway Theatre Village Notice, Maharam award for Peer Gynt, N.Y.C. Liberty medal, 1986, numerous Drama Desk and Critic awards; inducted into Theatre Hall of Fame. Mem. United Scenic Artists, Costume Designers Guild, Acad. Motion Picture Arts Scis. (Oscar award Great Gatsby 1975). Office: 35 W 90th St New York NY 10024

ALDRICH, ANN, federal judge; b. Providence, June 28, 1927; d. Allie C. and Ethel M. (Carrier) A.; m. Chester Aldrich, 1960 (dec.); children: Martin, William; children by previous marriage: James, Allen; m. John H. McAllister III. BA cum laude, Columbia U., 1948; LLB cum laude, NYU, 1950, LLM, 1964, JSD, 1967. Bar: D.C. bar, N.Y. bar 1952, Conn. bar 1966, Ohio bar 1973, Supreme Ct. bar 1956. Research asst. to mem. faculty N.Y. U. Sch. Law; asso. firm Samuel Nakasian, Washington, 1952-53; mem. gen. counsel's staff FCC, Washington, 1953-60; U.S. del. to Internat. Radio Conf., Geneva, 1959; practice law Darien, Conn.; asso. prof. law Cleve. State U., 1968-71, prof., 1971-80; judge U.S. Dist. Ct. (no. dist.) Ohio, 1980—; bd. govs. Citizens' Communications Center, Inc., Washington; mem. litigation com.; guest lectr. Calif. Inst. Tech., Pasadena, summer 1971. Mem. Fed. Bar Assn., Nat. Assn. of Women Judges, Fed. Communications Bar Assn., Fed. Judge Assn. Episcopalian. Office: US Dist Ct 210 US Courthouse 201 Superior Ave Cleveland OH 44114*

ALDRICH, JANET ALICE, museum fund raising consultant; b. Billings, Mont., May 3, 1960; d. John Parker and Alice Mae (Humphrey) A. BA in Art and Art History, Ea. Mont. Coll., 1982. Devel. officer Yellowstone Art Ctr., Billings, 1984-88; resident campaign dir. Charles H. Bentz Assocs., Westfield, N.J., 1988—. Mem. Nat. Soc. Fund Raising Execs. (pres. Mont. chpt. 1987-88), Am. Assn. Mus. (pub. rels. com.). Office: Charles H Bentz Assoc 423 South Ave W Westfield NJ 07090

ALDRICH, KAREN BAILEY, architect; b. Lewiston, Maine, Oct. 20, 1959; d. Bernard Barton and Ruth Beverly (Hall) Bailey; m. Dean Freemont Aldrich, Oct. 27, 1984. BFA, R.I. Sch. Design, Providence, 1982, BArch, 1983. Intern architect Swaney & Vogt Architects, Nashville, 1978-85; project coord. Gresham, Smith & Ptnrs., Nashville, 1985-89; project mgr. Gresham, Smith & Ptnrs., Jacksonville, Fla., 1989—; pres. Almost Architects, Nashville, 1986. Mem. AIA (dir., exec. bd. Middle Tenn. chpt. 1986-88, pub. affairs chair 1987-88). Roman Catholic. Home: 10263 Whispering Forest Dr Apt 815 Jacksonville FL 32257 Office: Gresham Smith & Ptnrs 1660 Prudential Dr duPont Center Dr Ste 201 Jacksonville FL 32207

ALDRICH, LYNNE MERRILL, university administrator; b. Detroit, July 23, 1946; d. Claude E. and Irene (Suzanne) (Keil) Gardner; AB in Polit. Sci., W. Va. U., 1969; postgrad., Wayne State U. Asst., then acting area mgr. Fotomat Corp., Detroit, 1969-70; acad. svc. officer dept. biol. scis. Wayne State U., 1970-83; exec. asst. to sr. v.p. univ. rels. Wayne State U., 1983-86, exec. asst. to pres., 1986—. Bd. dirs., sec. LaSalle Townhouse Coop. Assn., 1978-82. Recipient Humanitarian award Wayne State U., 1980, 81, bd. govs. Recognition Award Wayne State U., 1982. Mem. NAFE, Nat. Soc. Fund-Raising Execs., Mich. Advancement Coun., Coun. for Advancement and Support Edn., AAUW (dir. Mich. div. bd., pres. Detroit 1986-90), Leadership Detroit VI, Wayne State U. Club, Women's Econ. Club, Nat. Soc. Fund Raising Execs. Office: Wayne State U Office of Pres Detroit MI 48202

ALDRICH, NANCY ARMSTRONG, psychotherapist; b. Taylorville, Ill., Oct. 4, 1925; d. Guy L. and Alice Irene (Hicks) Armstrong; m. Paul Harwood Aldrich, Sept. 30, 1949; children: Gregory Paul, Mark Douglas, Alice Ann Aldrich White, Ruth Lynne. AB with highest honors, U. Ill., 1947, BS in Chemistry, 1948, MS in Chemistry, 1949; MSS, Bryn Mawr Coll., 1986. Lic. clin. social worker, Del., Pa. Parole bd. mem. State of Del., Dover, 1970-74; instr. continuing edn. U. Del., Newark, 1976-78, program specialist, 1978-83; v.p. Aldrich Assocs. Inc., Landenberg, Pa., 1983—, psychotherapist, 1987—; psychotherapist Family Community Service Del. County, Media, Pa., 1986, Tressler Ctr. for Human Growth, Wilmington, Del., 1987—; clin. affiliate Personal Performance Cons., 1990—; coordinator human resources devel. program Tressler Ctr. for human Devel., 1983-84. Pres. YWCA New Castle County, Wilmington, 1974-76; mem. Statewide Health Coordinating Council, Del., 1978-79; bd. dirs., com. mem. United Way Del., Wilmington, 1975-84. Mem. AAUW (pres. Wilmington br. 1968-70, mem. nat. resolutions com. 1971-72, Fellowship award named in her honor 1970), NASW, Lic. Clin. Social Workers Soc. Del. (co-chair 1990—), Assn. for Humanistic Psychology, Del. Gerontol., Phi Beta Kappa, Phi Kappa Phi, Iota Sigma Pi. Unitarian. Home and Office: 625 Chambers Rock Rd Landenberg PA 19350

ALDRICH, NANCY WELZ, airline pilot; b. Houston, Dec. 9, 1939; d. Robert Wesley and Vivian Beulah (Attaway) Welz; children: Christopher Robin Alexandre, Dawn Venise Alexandre Meyer. Instr. flight Ellsworth Aviation, Longmont, Colo., 1978-80; instr. ground King Accelerated Ground Schs., San Diego, 1980-82; contract pilot Denver, 1982-83; tng. prog. developer United Airlines, Denver, 1983-84, flight ops. instr., 1984-85, airline pilot, 1985—; aviation cons. AvCon., Inc., Broomfield, Colo., 1982-88; accident prevention counselor FAA, Denver, 1981—; safety chmn. Colo. Ninety Nines, Inc., Denver, 1982—. Author: Flying--For Nervous Birds, 1987, various study guides; lectr. Flight Without Fear, 1982—; contbr. articles to profl. jours. Mem. Aircraft Owners and Pilots Assn., Internat. Ninety Nines. Republican. Episcopalian.

ALDRICH, PATRICIA ANNE RICHARDSON, magazine editor; b. St. Paul, Apr. 6, 1926; d. James Calvin and Anna Catherine (Eskra) Richardson; m. Edwin Chauncey Aldrich, July 31, 1948; 1 son, Mason Calvin. Student, Stout Inst., 1944-45; B.S. in Journalism; scholar, Northwestern U., 1948. Editor Child's World News, The Child's World, Inc., Chgo., 1952-57; asso. editor Home Life mag. Advt. Div., Inc., Chgo., 1957-71; editor Home Life mag. Advt. Div., Inc., 1971—; pres. Aldrich Enterprises, Inc., Chgo. Mem. steering com., publicity chmn. Evanston Urban League, 1961-64. Democrat.

ALDRIDGE, ROSEMARY ROBINSON, hazardous waste company official; b. Brookhaven, Miss., Apr. 6, 1962; d. James Fletcher and Carolyn (Johnson) Robinson; m. Jeffrey Doyle Aldridge, Aug. 18, 1986. BEng in Civil and Environ. Engring., Vanderbilt U., 1985. Project engr. Cross/Tessitore & Assocs., P.A., Orlando, Fla., 1985-86, Engring.-Sci., Inc., San Diego, 1986-87; environ. engr. Chem. Processors, Inc., Seattle, 1987-88, process engr., 1988-89, project mgr., 1989—. Contbr. chpts. to Standard Handbook for Hazardous Waste Treatment and Disposal, 1988. Home: 5786 E Collins Rd Port Orchard WA 98366 Office: Chempro 2203 Airport Way S Ste 400 Seattle WA 98134

ALEANDRI, EMELISE FRANCESCA, producer, television personality, actress; b. Riva del Garda, Italy; d. John Baptist and Elodia (Lutterotti) A. AB in French, Coll. of New Rochelle, N.Y., 1965; MA in Theater, Hunter Coll., N.Y.C., 1975; MPhil in Theater, CUNY, 1976, PhD in Theater, 1983. Drama instr. N.Y.C. Tech. Coll., Bklyn., 1971-84, Borough of Manhattan City Coll., N.Y.C., 1973-74, Bennington Coll., 1975, Hunter Coll., NYU, N.Y.C., 1977-78; dir. Ctr. Italian-Am. Studies, Bklyn. Coll., 1984-87; producer Italics Mag. Show CUNY-TV, N.Y.C., 1987—. Author: Italian-American Theatre, 1983; translator various plays from Italian to English; contbr. articles to profl. jours. Recipient N.Y. State Hist. award; NEA grantee Bklyn. Coll. Mem. AGVA, AFTRA, Actor's Equity Assn., Screen Actor's Guild, Dramatists Guild, Soc. Stage Dirs. and Choreographers.

ALEMAN, MINDY ROBIN, advertising and public relations executive, freelance writer; b. N.Y.C., Nov. 23, 1950; d. Lionel and Jocelyn (Cohen) Luskin; m. Gary Aleman, Aug. 27, 1983. BA, U. Akron, 1972, MA, 1975. Instr. speech U. Akron, 1973-83; car salesperson Dave Towell Cadillac, Akron, 1977-79, mgr. fin. and ins., 1979; account exec., pub. rels. dir. Loos, Edwards & Sexauer, Akron, 1980-82; mktg. svcs. coord. Century Products, Stow, Ohio, 1982-83; mgr. advt., pub. rels. Century Products, Gerber Furniture Group, Stow, 1983-86, Macedonia, Ohio, 1986-89; dir. rsch. and promotion Akron Beacon Jour., 1989—. Playwright Danny's Choice, 1972. Mem. Am. Mktg. Assn., Pub. Rels. Soc. Am. (accredited), Akron Advt. Club (various awards 1983-88), Akron Women's Network. Office: Akron Beacon Jour Rsch and Promotion Dept 44 E Exchange St PO Box 640 Akron OH 44309-0640

ALESCHUS, JUSTINE LAWRENCE, real estate broker; b. New Brunswick, N.J., Aug. 13, 1925; d. Walter and Mildred Lawrence; student Rutgers U.; m. John Aleschus, Jan. 23, 1949; children: Verdene Jan, Janine Kimberley, Joanna Lauren. Dept. sec. Am. Baptist Home Mission Soc., N.Y.C., 1947-49; claims examiner Republic Ins. Co., Dallas, 1950-52; broker Damon Homes, L.I., 1960-72; exclusive broker estate of Kenneth H. Leeds, L.I., 1980-90; pres. Justine Aleschus Real Estate. Past-pres. Nassau-Suffolk Coun. of Hosp. Aux., 1981-82; hon. mem. aux. of St. John's Episcopal Hosp., Smithtown, N.Y., past pres., hosp. adv. bd.; pres. L.I. Coalition for Sensible Growth, Inc.; mem. exec. bd. dirs. Suffolk County coun. Boy Scouts Am.; mem. adv. bd. Suffolk County coun. Girl Scouts U.S. Mem. Suffolk County Real Estate Bd. (past pres.), L.I. Builders Inst. (bd. dirs.), L.I. Mid-Suffolk Businessmen's Assn. (pres.), Eastern L.I. Execs. (v.p., sponsor-trustee), Smithtown Bus. and Profl. Women's Network, L.I. Assn., JEI Com., Hauppauge Indsl. Assn. Advancement Commerce & Industry. Republican. Lutheran. Club: Sky Island (gov.). Office: 300 Hawkins Ave Lake Ronkonkoma NY 11779

ALESSIO, DEBRA ANN, sales executive; b. Paterson, N.J., Nov. 18, 1957; d. Robert Carl and Lucy (Derrico) Angele; m. Steven Paul Alessio, Aug. 14, 1976 (div.); m. Lawrence Robert Levine, June 17, 1985; children: Jason Steven, stepchildren: Evan Karin, Dayna. Student, William Paterson Coll., Wayne, N.J., 1975-76. Sales rep. Broadway Bank, Paterson, N.J., 1974-76; import, export mgr. Jet Aer Corp., Paterson, N.J., 1979-82; asst. sales mgr. Am. Clearwater Corp., Paterson, N.J., 1982-84, v.p. sales; v.p. Makers Choice Corp., Paterson, N.J., 1986-87; pres. Unique Apparel Corp., N.J., 1987--; cons. Mini Productions, Allentown , Pa., 1982--, pres. Pasoaic County Adv. Council, Wayne, N.J., 1986-87, mem. 1987--. Ward leader Gov. Kean reelection, Paterson, N.J., 1985; co-chairperson N.J. State Assembly Election, Paterson, 1986, Passaic County Freeholder Election, Paterson, 1987; mem. Hillcrest Civic Com., Paterson, 1985-86.

ALEXANDER, BARBARA LEAH SHAPIRO, clinical social worker; b. St. Louis, May 6, 1943; d. Harold Albert and Dorothy Miriam (Leifer) Shapiro; m. Richard E. Alexander. B in Music Edn., Washington U., St. Louis, 1964; postgrad., U. Ill., 1964-66; MSW, Smith Coll., 1970; postgrad., Inst. Psychoanalysis, Chgo., 1971-73, grad., child therapy program, 1976-80; cert. therapist Sex Dysfunction Clinic, Loyola U., Chgo., 1975. Diplomate in Clin. Social Work. Research asst., NIMH grantee Smith Coll., 1968-70; probation officer Juvenile Ct. Cook County, Chgo., 1966-68, 70; therapist Madden Mental Health Center, Hines, Ill., 1970-72; supr., therapist, field instr. U. Chgo., U. Ill. Grad. Schs. Social Work, also Pritzker Children's Hosp., Chgo., 1972—; therapist, cons., also pvt. practice, 1973—; instr. tng. and advanced tng. Effectiveness Tng. Assocs., Chgo., 1974; instr. psychology Northeastern U., Chgo., 1975; intern Divorce Conciliation Service, Circuit Ct. Cook County, 1976-77. Contbr. articles to profl. jours. Bd. dirs., Grant Park Concerts Soc.; Cathedral Counseling; sec. Art Resources in Teaching. Recipient Sterling Achievement award Mu Phi Epsilon, 1964. Mem. Acad. Cert. Social Workers (cert.), Nat. Assn. Social Workers (sec. 1987—), Nat. Fed. Soc. for Clin. Social Work, Ill. Soc. Clin. Social Work (pres. 1986-90, bd. dirs., chmn. services to mems. com., dir. pvt. practitioners' referral service), Am. Assn. Marriage and Family Therapy, Assn. Child Psychotherapists, Am. Assn. Sex Educators and Counselors, Amateur Chamber Music Players Assn., Jewish Geneal. Soc., Smith Coll. Alumni Assn. (bd. dirs.). Democrat. Home: 179 E Lake Shore Dr Chicago IL 60611 Office: 919 N Michigan Ave #3012 Chicago IL 60611

ALEXANDER, BARBARA TOLL, investment banker; b. Little Rock, Dec. 18, 1948; d. Lawrence Jesser and Geraldine Best (Proctor) Toll; m. Lawrence Allen Alexander, Jan. 25, 1969 (div. 1980); m. Thomas Beveridge Stiles, II, Mar. 7, 1981; stepchildren: Thomas B. Stiles III, Jonathan E. Stiles. BS, U. Ark., 1969, MS, 1970. Asst. v.p. Wachovia Bank & Trust Co., Winston-Salem, N.C., 1972-76; security analyst Investors Diversified Services, Mpls., 1976-78; 1st v.p. Smith Barney Inc., N.Y.C., 1978-84; v.p. Salomon Bros., N.Y.C., 1984-86, dir., 1986, mng. dir., 1987; mem. exec. com. policy adv. bd. Joint Ctr. for Housing Studies of Harvard U.; mem. N.Y. adv. bd. Enterprise Found. Named No. 1 housing analyst in U.S., Instl. Investor, 1983, 86, 87. Mem. Inst. Chartered Fin. Analysts, Fin. Analysts Fedn., N.Y. Soc. Security Analysts, Constrn. and Bldg. Materials Analysts Group (pres. 1984-85), Acad. Women Achievers. Presbyterian. Home: 18 Tuttle Ave Spring Lake NJ 07762 Office: Salomon Bros Inc 1 New York Pla New York NY 10004

ALEXANDER, BEVERLY MOORE, mechanical engineer; b. Portsmouth, Va., Apr. 11, 1947; d. Julian Morgan and Ezefferlee (Griffin) Moore; m. Ronald Lee Rutherford, Dec. 21, 1969 (div. Dec. 1977); m. Larry Ray Alexander, Mar. 4, 1978. BS, Aero. Engring., Va. Poly. Inst. and State U., 1969; postgrad., U. New Orleans. Registered profl. engr., La. Assoc. engr. McDonnell Douglas Corp., St. Louis, 1969-74; design engr. Bell Aerospace Textron, New Orleans, 1974-81; supr. systems integration, New Orleans, 1981-83, chief interface activities, 1983-84; chief engr. Bell Aerospace Textron, New Orleans, 1984-85, dir. engring. planning and control, 1985-86, chief engr. engring. svcs., 1986-88, asst. chief engr., supr. of shipbuilding USN, New Orleans, 1988—. Mem. La. Engring. Soc., NAFE, ASNE, SNAME. Republican. Episcopalian. Office: SUPSHIP C201 Naval Support Activity New Orleans LA 70142

ALEXANDER, DIANE MARIE, telemarketing and sales executive; b. Clinton, Okla., Aug. 31, 1945; d. Edwin Michael Jr. and Gloria Louise (McCray) Drass; m. Larry Edward Allen, Dec. 18, 1965 (div. Aug. 1972); children: Larry Dean, Lynn Edward; m. Nicol Brandon Alexander, June 28, 1980 (div. Jan. 1988); children: Danielle Nicole, Derek Brandon. Student, Lindenwood Coll., 1963-64, Abilene Christian Coll., 1964-65. Cert. neurolinguistic programming practitioner, 1989, cert. customer svc. exec. Telesales rep. GTE Corp., Irving, Tex., 1974-77, dist. telesales mgr., 1977-78; v.p. Brandon and Assocs., Inc., Grand Prairie, Tex., 1980-81; v.p. TeleMktg. Enterprises, Inc., Grand Prairie, 1982-88, pres., owner, 1988—; v.p. mktg. Barakel Corp., Arlington, Tex., 1981-82; lectr. in field; cons., tchr. Internat. Aviation and Travel Acad./Frontier Airlines, Arlington, Tex., 1983-84. Author: Advanced Communications Technology, 1980, Telemarketing Series, 1982-87, Professional TeleAppointments, 1985; contbr. articles to profl. jours. Jr. Achievement scholar Lindenwood Coll., 1963. Mem. Am. Soc. Tng. and Devel., Internat. Customer Svc. Assn. (conv. speaker Nashville chpt. 1989). Republican. Episcopalian.

ALEXANDER, EDNA M. DEVEAUX, elementary educator; d. Richard and Eva (Musgrove) DeVeaux. BBA, Fla. A & M U., 1943; BS in Elem. Edn., Fla. A&M U., 1948; MS in Supervision and Adminstrn., U. Pa., 1954; cert., U. Madrid, 1961; postgrad., Dade Jr. Coll., U. Miami. Sec. Dunbar Elem. Sch., 1943-46, tchr., 194-55; tchr. Orchard Villa Elem., 1959-66; prin. A. L. Lewis Elem. Sch., 1955-57; reading specialist North Cen. Dist., 1966-69; tchr. L. C. Evans Elem. Sch., 1969-71; first black woman newscaster in Miami, Sta. WBAY, 1948. V.p. Fla. Council on Human Relations Dade County, Coun. for Internat. Visitors Greater Miami; past pres. Episcopal Churchwomen of Christ Ch., Miami; bd. dirs. YWCA; vice chmn. Community Action Agy. Dade County; chmn. Dade County Minimum Housing Appeals Bd.; active Vol. Unltd. Project Nat. Coun. Negro Women; sponsor Am. Jr. Red Cross, Girl Scouts U.S.; trustee Fla. Internat. U. Found., 1974-79. Mem. AAUW (life, Edna m. DeVeaux Alexander fellowship named in her honor Miami br.), NEA (life), LWV, Fla. Edn. Assn., Classroom Tchrs. Assn., Dade County Edn. Assn. (chmn. pub. relations com.), Dade County Reading Assn., Assn. for Childhood Edn., Internat. Reading Tchr. Assn., U. Pa. Alumni Assn., Alpha Kappa Alpha. Home: 805 Blue Gill Rd PO Box 26063 Jacksonville FL 32218

ALEXANDER, ELAINE HARRIETT, communications company executive; b. Phila., Oct. 18, 1949; d. Gregory Peter and Cleopatra (Coste) A. AB, Hood Coll., Frederick, Md., 1971; Cert. in Secondary Edn., Villanova (Pa.) U., 1975; MBA, Temple U., 1985. Cert. purchasing mgr. Purchasing agt. Cen. Pa. Nat. Bank div. Meridian Bancorp, Phila., 1976-79; sr. buyer electronics space systems div. Gen. Electric Corp., Valley Forge, Pa., 1979-85; mgr. purchasing govt. systems div. RCA Corp., Camden, N.J., 1985-86; asst. mgr. contracts Bell of Pa. and the Diamond State Telephone Cos., Phila., 1987-88; corp. contract mgr. No. Telecom, Inc., Nashville, 1988-89; contracts and systems specialist Ericsson GE Mobile Communications Inc., Lynchburg, Va., 1989—; guest lectr. exec.-in-residence program Hood Coll., 1982. Grant proposal reviewer Consortium for Advancement of Pvt. Higher Edn., Washington, 1985-86; trustee Hood Coll., 1983-89. Mem. Purchasing Mgmt. Assn. Phila. (pub. relations com. 1979-87), Hood Coll. Alumni Assn. Phila. (v.p., pres. 1980-82), Phila. Jaycees (bd. dirs. 1978-79, v.p. 1979-80). Republican. Eastern Orthodox. club: Hellenic Univ. of Phila. (bd. dirs. 1974-75). Home: Peters Ln Forest VA 24551 Office: Ericsson GE Mobile Communications Inc Mountain View Rd Lynchburg VA 24502

ALEXANDER, ELLIN DRIBBER, financial marketing company executive; b. Albany, N.Y., July 20, 1955; d. Irving S. and Helen (Meyer) Dribben; m. Richard D. Alexander, May 18, 1984; children: Evan R., Elisabeth D., Hannah Claire. BA, St. Lawrence U., 1977; postgrad., Boston U., 1978—. Asst. dir. devel. Northeastern Assn of the Blind, Albany, 1979-80; mktg. rep. Newkirk, Albany, 1980-85, asst. v.p., 1985—, mgr. trust info. and communication systems, 1990—; bd. dirs. Albany Dist. Postal Customer Coun. Fundraiser Am. Cancer Soc., Albany, 1988—; bd. dirs. Arbor House, Albany, 1980-88, ARC, Albany chpt. Mem. N.Y. State Realtors Assn., Albany County Bd. Realtors, Jr. League Albany (bd. dirs. 1980-81, 83, 86, 88, 90—), Phi Beta Kappa, Omega Delta Kappa. Roman Catholic. Office: Newkirk 15 Corporate Circle Albany NY 12203

ALEXANDER, ETHEL SKYLES, state legislator; b. Chgo., Jan. 16, 1925. Ed., Chgo. Loop Jr. Coll. Mem. Ill. Ho. of Reps., 1979-87, Ill. Senate, 1987—. Democrat. Home: 610 E 61st St Chicago IL 60637 Office: Ill State Senate 103C Crystal Bldg Springfield IL 62706*

ALEXANDER, JANE, actress; b. Boston, Oct. 28, 1939; d. Thomas Bartlett and Ruth (Pearson) Quigley; m. Robert Alexander, July 23, 1962 (div. 1969); 1 child, Jason; m. Edwin Sherin, Mar. 29, 1975. Student, Sarah Lawrence Coll., 1957-59, U. Edinburgh, 1959-60. Ind. TV, film and theatrical actress, 1962—. Author: (with Greta Jacobs) The Bluefish Cookbook, 4 edits., 1979-90; translator: (with Sam Engelstad) The Master Builder (Henrik Ibsen), 1978; appeared in prodns.: Charles Playhouse Boston, 1964-65, Arena Stage, Washington, 1965-68, 70—, Am. Shakespeare Festival; plays include Major Barbara, Mourning Becomes Electra, Merry Wives of Windsor, Stratford, Conn., summers 1971-72; Broadway prodns. include The Great White Hope, 1968-69 (Tony award 1969, Drama Desk award, Theatre World award), 6 Rms Riv Vu, 1972-73 (Tony nomination), Find Your Way Home, 1974 (Tony nomination), Hamlet, 1975, The Heiress, 1976, First Monday in October, 1978 (Tony nomination), Goodbye Fidel, 1980, Monday After the Miracle, 1982, Night of the Iguana, 1988; also appeared in plays The Time of Your Life, Present Laughter, 1975, The Master Builder, 1977, Losing Time, 1980, Antony and Cleopatra, 1981, Hedda Gabler, 1981, Old Times, 1984, Approaching Zanzibar, 1989, Mystery of the Rose Bouquet, 1989, Shadowlands, 1990; appeared in films The Great White Hope, 1970 (Acad. award nomination), A Gunfight, 1970, The New Centurions, 1972, All the President's Men, 1976 (Acad. award nomination), The Betsy, 1978, Kramer vs. Kramer, 1979 (Acad. award nomination), Brubaker, 1980, Night Crossing, 1981, Testament, 1983 (Acad. award nomination), City Heat, 1984, Sweet Country, 1986, Square Dance, 1987, Glory, 1989; appeared in TV films: Welcome Home Johny Bristol, 1971, Miracle on 34th Street, 1973, Death Be Not Proud, 1974, This Was The West That Was, 1974, Eleanor and Franklin, (Emmy nomination) 1976, Eleanor and Franklin: The White House Years (Emmy nomination), 1977 (TV Critics Circle award), Lovey, 1977, A Question of Love, 1978, Playing For Time, 1980 (Emmy award 1980), Calamity Jane: The Diary of a Frontier Woman, 1981, Dear Liar, 1981, Kennedy's Children, 1981, In the Custody of Strangers, 1982, When She Says No, 1983, Mountain View, 1989, Daughter of the Streets, 1990; appeared in TV spls. A Circle of Children, 1977, Blood and Orchids, 1986, Calamity Jane, 1984 (Emmy nomination), Malice in Wonderland, 1985 (Emmy nomination), In Love and War, 1987, Open Admissions, 1988, A Friendship in Vienna, 1988. Recipient Achievement in Dramatic Arts award St. Botolph Club, 1979, Israel Cultural award, 1982, Western Heritage Wrangler award, 1985, Helen Caldicott Leadership award, 1984, Living Legacy award Women's Internat. Ctr., San Diego, 1988. Mem. Women's Action for Nuclear Disarmament (bd. dirs. 1981-88), Wildlife Conservation Internat. (bd. dirs. 1984—), Film Forum (bd. dirs. 1985-90), Nat. Stroke Assn. (bd. dirs. 1985—). Office: care William Morris Agy 1350 Ave of the Americas New York NY 10019

ALEXANDER, JOYCE MARY, illustrator; b. Pepin, Wis., Mar. 31, 1927; d. Colonel and Martha (Varnum) Yochem; m. Don Tocher, June 27, 1955 (div. 1962); m. Dorsey Potter Alexander, Nov. 1, 1963. Student, Coll. Arts and Crafts, 1946, Acad. of Art, 1961-62. Co-founder, owner Turtle's Quill Scriptorium Publishers, Berkeley, Calif., 1963—. Author: Thaddeus, 1972, Happy Bird Day, 1980; illustrator numerous books including: Soil and Plant Analysis, A Practical Guide for the Home Gardner, 1963, California Farm and Ranch Law, 1967, Chinatown, A Legend of Old Cannery Row, 1968, The Sea: Excerpts from Herman Melville, 1970, Of Mice, 1970, David: Psalm

Twenty-Four, 1970, Shakespeare: Selected Sonnets, 1974, The Blue-Jay Yarn, 1975, Psalm One Hundred Four, 1978, Messiah: Choruses from Handel's Messiah, 1985, A Flurry of Angels, Angels in Literature, 1986, Eleven Poems by Emily Dickinson, A Packet of Rhymes, 1989; work represented in permanent collections Hunt Botan. Libr. at Carnegie-Mellon U. Republican. Office: Turtle's Quill Scriptorium PO Box 643 Mendocino CA 95460

ALEXANDER, JUDITH ANN, bank consultant; b. Fort Sill, Okla., Oct. 14, 1940; d. James Buchanan and Gerry Lee (Gibbs) Permenter; m. Robert Miles Turner, Oct. 28, 1962 (div. 1972); m. Clarence Withers Alexander, Dec. 19, 1975 (div. Jan. 1987). Student, U. Okla., 1958-59; B.A. in English, U. Tulsa, 1962; M.B.A., U. Okla., 1969; postgrad., U. St. Thomas, 1975-78. Asst. cashier So. Nat. Bank of Houston, 1971-73, asst. controller, 1973-74, asst. v.p. and asst. controller, 1974, v.p., controller, 1974-77, sr. v.p., controller, 1977-79; cons., 1979—. Mem. NOW, Nat. Audubon Soc., Beta Gamma Sigma, Gamma Phi Beta. Republican. Office: 4144 Greystone Way #607 Sugar Land TX 77479

ALEXANDER, LINDA DIANE (LINDA DIANE GRAHAM), lawyer, educator; b. Winchester, Va., May 10, 1953; d. Kenneth A. and Edna Frances (Whitlow) Graham; m. Patrick B. Alexander, May 8, 1975. B.A. in Govt., George Mason U., 1975, B.A. in Philosophy, 1975; J.D., U. Okla., 1978. Bar: Okla. 1978, U.S. Dist. Ct. (we. dist., ea. dist.) Okla. 1979, U.S. Ct. Claims 1980, U.S. Ct. Appeals (10th cir.) 1980, U.S. Ct. Appeals (8th cir.) 1984, U.S. Ct. Appeals (5th cir.) 1987, U.S. Supreme Ct. 1989. Legal intern Foliart, Mills & Niemeyer, Oklahoma City, 1976-79, assoc., 1979-81; sole practice law, Oklahoma City, 1981-84; ptnr. firm Niemeyer, Noland & Alexander, Oklahoma City, 1984—; prof. Sch. Law, Oklahoma City U., 1981-83. Mem. Okla. Bar Assn., Oklahoma County Bar Assn., Assn. Trial Lawyers Am. Democrat. Mem. Ch. of Christ. Office: Niemeyer Noland & Alexander 300 N Walker St Oklahoma City OK 73102

ALEXANDER, LYNN See MARGULIS, LYNN

ALEXANDER, LYNNE, computer specialist, consultant; b. Rochester, N.Y., Oct. 17, 1958; d. Julian and Virginia (Deisher) A.; m. William Ehrat Van Arsdale, May 9, 1987; children: Scott Alexander VanArsdale, Lisa Alexander VanArsdale. BS, Cornell U., 1980; MS, N.C. State U., 1984; postgrad., Rice U. Assoc. scientist Lockheed Emsco, Houston, 1982-84; computer programmer Baylor Coll. Medicine, 1984-85; support mgr. Integrated Solutions, Inc., San Jose, Calif., 1985-86; MTS MITRE, Houston, 1986; tech. support engr. Sun Microsystems, Houston, 1986-88; workstation product project mgr. Positron Corp., Houston, 1989-90; sole propr. Interfaces Xcetera, Houston, 1990—. Contbr. articles to profl. jours. Recipient Citizenship award Kiwanis. Mem. IEEE, ACM, NAFE, Sun User Group (pres. local chpt.). Home: 6528 Sewanee Houston TX 77005

ALEXANDER, MADELYN M., travel educator; b. Cloquet, Minn., Aug. 25, 1953; d. Arnold T. and Esther Margie (Borg) Erickson. Student, U. Minn., Duluth, 1971; diploma, A.C.T. Travel Sch., Pompano Beach, Fla., 1986. Ticket agt. Third Century Tours, Miami, Fla.; customer svc. rep. SystemOne, Miami; travel educator A.C.T. Travel Sch., Pompano Beach. Mem. NAFE. Home: 5897 N Dixie Apt 48 Fort Lauderdale FL 33334

ALEXANDER, MARY E., lawyer; b. Chgo., Nov. 16, 1947; d. Theron and Marie (Bailey) A.; m. Lyman Saunders Faulkner, Jr., Dec. 1, 1984; 1 child, Michelle. BA, U. Iowa, 1969; MPH, U. Calif.-Berkeley, 1975; JD, U. Santa Clara, 1982. Bar: Calif. 1982, U.S. Dist. Ct. (no. dist.) Calif., U.S. ct. Appeals (9th cir.) 1982. Researcher, U. Cin., 1969-74; dept. dir., sr. environ. health scientist Stanford Rsch. Inst., Menlo Park, Calif., 1975-80; cons. Alexander Assocs., Ambler, Pa., 1980-82; assoc. Caputo, Liccardo Rossi Sturges & McNeil, San Jose, Calif., 1982-84; assoc. Cartwright, Slobodin, Bokelman, et al, San Francisco, 1984-88, ptnr., 1988—. Com. mem. Cancer Soc., San Jose, 1983; elder Valley Presbyn. Ch., Portola Valley, 1987—; active Am. Heart Assn., Santa Clara County. Nat. Inst. Occpational Safeyt and Health scholar U. Calif., Berkeley, 1975. Mem. Am. Trial Lawyers Assn., Calif. Trial Lawyers Assn. (PAC bd. 1989—), San Francisco Trial Lawyers Assn., Am. Indsl. Hygiene Assn. (bd. dirs. 1979-81, treas. 1977-79), Nat. Assn. Advancement of Sci., Santa Clara Trial Lawyers Assn. (bd. dirs. 1983-84). Democrat. Office: Cartwrith Slobodin Bokelman et al 101 California 26th Fl San Francisco CA 94111

ALEXANDER, MARY LOUISE, financial planner; b. St. Cloud, Minn., Mar. 5, 1950; d. Thomas E. and Jean E. (Wichman) A.; B.F.A., Stephens Coll., 1972. Registered health underwriter; registered rep. Riding dir. Hidden Valley Farms, Newton, N.J., 1974, El Dorado Ranch, Westtown, N.Y., 1974; riding instr. Frances Reker Sch. of Horsemanship, Rockford, Minn., 1975; instr. Area Learning Center, Dist. 742, St. Cloud, 1976, asst. dean of boys, 1976; sales rep. N.W. Nat. Life Ins. Co., St. Cloud, 1977-78; prin. Mary Alexander Ins. Agy., Cold Spring, Minn., 1978-87; mgr. fin. planning dept., Garnsey Bros., Inc., Sanford, Maine, 1988; pres. M. Alexander & Assocs., Contempory Ins. Concepts, Maxi-Mktg. Inc., 1980—; owner, mgr. Bay Hill Farm. Mem. Nat. Assn. Health Underwriters, Minn. Assn. Health Underwriters, Nat. Fedn. Ind. Bus. Owners, Greater Twin Cities Chow Chow Club, Am. Quarter Horse Assn., Maine Quarter Horse Assn. Lutheran. Home: Chadbourne Ridge Rd Rural Rt F02 PO Box 322 West Buxton ME 04093 Office: M Alexander & Assocs Chadbourne Ridge Rd West Buxton ME 04093

ALEXANDER, MARY LOUISE, biology educator; b. Ennis, Tex., Jan. 15, 1926; d. Emmett F. and Florence (Hill) Alexander. B.A., U. Tex., 1947, M.A., 1949, Ph.D., 1951. Instr., rsch. asst. Genetics Found., U. Tex., 1944-51; postdoctoral fellow biology div. AEC, Oak Ridge, 1951-52; postdoctoral rsch. fellow U. Tex., 1952-55; rsch. assoc. U. Tex.-M.D. Anderson Hosp. and Tumor Inst., Houston, 1956-58, asst. biologist, 1959-62; rsch. scientist Genetics Found. U. Tex., Austin, 1962-67; rsch. cons. Brookhaven Nat. Lab., Upton, N.Y., 1955; rsch. participant Oak Ridge Inst. Nuclear Studies, 1951-77; assoc. prof. biology S.W. Tex. State U., San Marcos, 1966-69, prof., 1970—; mem. People to People's Human Genetics Delegation, People's Republic of China, 1987. Nat. Cancer Inst. fellow Inst. Animal Genetics, Edinburgh, Scotland, 1960-61. Mem. Genetics Soc. Am., Radiation Rsch. Soc., Am. Soc. Human Genetics, Sigma Xi, Gamma Phi Beta, Phi Sigma, Alpha Epsilon Delta. Home: Hunter's Glen Rte 2 Box 119 San Marcos TX 78666

ALEXANDER, MOLLY MARY BUSHONG, archaeologist; b. Chgo., Aug. 9, 1958; d. Harry Whitford and Mary Barbara (Anderson) A.; m. David Joseph Fliehr, Sept. 5, 1982. BA in Anthropology, Washington U., 1980; MA in Archaeology, UCLA, 1982, PhD in Archaeology, 1988. Teaching asst. Washington U., St. Louis, 1979; tchr. supr. Tel Michal Excavations, Israel, 1978-80; rsch. assoc. L.A. County Mus. Art, 1982, FS Wight Art Gallery, UCLA, 1981-83; student mgr. Acad. Pub. Svc., UCLA, 1983-87; rsch. assoc. L.A. County Mus. Art, 1988; archaeologist, cons. Archeol. Assocs., Inc., L.A., 1989—; pres. Archeol. Soc. UCLA, 1984-86; student rep. Grad. Student Coun., UCLA, 1984-86. Asst. scoutmaster Boy Scouts Am. Troop 42, L.A., 1981-88; advisor Explorer Post 42, L.A., 1982-86; vol. Internat. Med. Corps, L.A., 1984—, Citizens for Sheltered Animal, L.A., 1989—. Recipient Andrew W. Mellon Fellowship Conservation Ctr., 1988, Friends of Archaeology Scholarship UCLA, 1986, Washington U. Scholarships, 1978, 79; grantee UCLA Rsch., 1985, 86. Mem. Soc. Profl. Archaeologists, Soc. Calif. Archaeology, Archaeol. Inst. Am., Am. Anthrop. Assn., The Tree Ring Soc., Friends of Archaeology UCLA, Coun. for Brit. Archaeology, Santa Clara Valley Hist. Soc. Home: 22905 W Banyan Pl #227 Santa Clarita CA 91350

ALEXANDER, PATRICIA DARCY, marketing executive; b. Rochester, N.Y., Feb. 6, 1955; d. George Robert and Martha (Harbrecht) Darcy; m. David Todd Alexander, May 23, 1982; 1 child, Colin Darcy. BA in English, Wellesley Coll., 1977. Sales rep. John Wiley & Sons Pub., N.Y.C., 1977-78; store mgr. This End Up Furniture, N.Y.C., 1978-79; asst. media planner Compton Advt., N.Y.C., 1979-81; media planner Doyle, Dane, Bernbach, N.Y.C., 1981-82; mktg. dir. Health Care Mktg. Group, Bala Cynwyd, Pa., 1982-83; advt. dir. Chestnut Hill Mktg. Group, Phila., 1983-85; exec. dir. Chestnut Hill Devel. Group-Mktg. Group-Parking Found., Phila., 1985—. Bd. dirs. Interim House, Phila. Mem. Am. Mgmt. Assn., Nat. Assn. Female Execs. Office: Chestnut Hill Devel Group 610 Wadsworth Ave Philadelphia PA 19119

ALEXANDER, PATRICIA ROSS, administrative assistant; b. Blue Ridge, Ga., May 19, 1955; d. Ernest B. and Sara P. (Williams) Ross; m. Robert W. Alexander Jr., June 24, 1978; 1 child, Sarah E. AA, Young Harris (Ga.) Coll., 1975; BA, North Ga. Coll., 1978, postgrad.; postgrad., Emory U. Fiber artist Morganton, Ga.; clk., postmaster relief U.S. Postal Svc., Mineral Bluff, Ga., 1987—; adminstrv. asst. Indsl. Strength Art, Morganton. Contbr. articles to publs. Recipient artist initiated grant Ga. Coun. for Arts, 1984, NSF grant. Mem. NAPUS, So. Highlands Handicraft Guild, Ga. Mountain Crafts (bd. dirs. 1981—), Copper Basin/Fannin C. of C., Blue Ridge Mountains Arts Assn. (v.p. 1979-80, coord. 1980-81), Basket Weavers Guild of Ga. Baptist. Home: PO Box 599 Morganton GA 30560 Office: U S Postal Svc Mineral Bluff GA 30559-9998

ALEXANDER, RENEE RAFAELA, biochemistry educator; b. Leipzig, Saxony, German Dem. Republic, Jan. 23, 1932; d. Leo M. and Miriam (Koenig) Wulf; m. Martin Alexander, Aug. 26, 1951; children: Miriam Alexander Hureirtz, Stanley W. BS, U. Wis., 1954, MS, 1955; PhD, Cornell U., 1958. Rsch. asst. U. Wis., Madison, 1954-55; rsch. asst. Cornell U., Ithaca, N.Y., 1955-58, rsch. assoc., 1961-70, lectr., 1971-82, sr. lectr., 1982—; acad. advisor Cornell U., Ithaca. Author: (textbook) Biochemical Methods, 1985; contbr. several rsch. articles in molecular biology to profl. jours. Mem. Am. Soc. Microbiology, Sigma Xi. Office: Cornell U Dept Biochemistry 312 Wing Hall Ithaca NY 14853

ALEXANDER, SHANA, journalist, author, lecturer; b. N.Y.C., Oct. 6, 1925; d. Milton and Cecelia (Rubenstein) Ager; m. Stephen Alexander, 1951 (div.); 1 dau., Katherine (dec.). BA, Vassar Coll., 1945. With PM, 1944-46, Harper's Bazaar, 1946-47; with Flair, 1950; reporter Life mag., 1951-61, staff writer, 1961-64; writer twice monthly column The Feminine Eye, 1964-69; editor McCall's mag., N.Y.C., 1969-71; v.p. Norton Simon Communications, Inc., 1971-72; radio and TV commentator Spectrum CBS News, 1971-72; columnist, contbg. editor Newsweek, 1972-75; commentator CBS 60 Minutes, 1975-79; Bd. dirs. Am. Film Inst. Author: The Feminine Eye, 1970, Shana Alexander's State-by-State Guide to Women's Legal Rights, 1975, Talking Woman, 1976, Anyone's Daughter, 1979, Nutcracker: Money, Madness, Murder—A Family Album, 1985, Very Much a Lady: The Untold Story of Jean Harris and Dr. Herman Tarnower, 1983, Dangerous Games: The Pizza Connection Trial, 1988, When She Was Good: The Story of Bess, Nancy, Hortense and Sukhreet, 1989. Recipient Sigma Delta Chi and U. So. Calif. Nat. Journalism award, 1965, Los Angeles Times Woman of Year award, 1967, Golden Pen award Am. Newspaper Womens Club, 1969, Front Page award Newswomen's Club N.Y., 1973, Matrix award N.Y. Women in Communications, 1973-74, Spirit of Achievement award Albert Einstein Coll. Med., 1976; Creative Arts award Nat. Women's div. Am. Jewish Congress. Office: care Joy Harris Lantz 888 7th Ave New York NY 10106*

ALEXANDER, SHERRY A., communications executive; b. Milw., Aug. 4, 1943; d. Paul Frederick and Mildred Ruth (Hansen) Buell; m. Frank D.W. Alexander, June 25, 1960; children: Paul, Peter, Philip. BS, U. Wis., Milw., 1964; grad. in computer programming, Computer Inst., Milw., 1971. Systems analyst McAuto, L.A., Xerox Computer Svcs., L.A.; supr. systems, programming EECO Inc., Santa Ana; MIS dir. AMFAC, L.A.; exec. dir. strategic planning for Internat. Tel. & Tel. Corp. Computer Hardware, Software, Telecommunications Office Automation, L.A. Mem. MENSA, NAFE, Women in Mgmt. Home: 1617 Carlson Ln Redondo Beach CA 90278

ALEXANDER, STACY ANN, mutual fund professional; b. Richmond, Va., Oct. 13, 1959; d. Alexander and Katherine (Poppas) A. BBA, Coll. William and Mary, 1982. Account exec. FCA Asset Mgmt., Boston, 1982-84; account exec., mgr. sales Citibank, N.A., N.Y.C., 1984-86; v.p. Dreyfus Svc. Corp., N.Y.C., 1986—. Mem. Delta Delta Delta (pres. N.Y.C. chpt. 1986). Home: 1812 Second Ave Apt 3FN New York NY 10128 Office: Dreyfus Svc Corp 200 Park Ave 8th Flr New York NY 10166

ALEXANDER, VERA, marine science institute director, dean; b. Budapest, Hungary, Oct. 26, 1932; came to U.S., 1950; d. Paul and Irene Alexander; divorced; children: Graham Alexander Dugdale, Elizabeth Dugdale Jackson. BA in Zoology, U. Wis., 1955, MS in Zoology, 1962; PhD in Marine Sci., U. Alaska, 1965. From asst. prof. to assoc. prof. marine sci. U. Alaska, Fairbanks, 1965-74, prof., 1974—, dean Coll. Environ. Scis., 1977-78, 80-81, dir. Inst. Marine Sci., 1979—, acting dean Sch. Fisheries and Ocean Scis., 1987-89, dean, 1989—; mem. adv. com. Office of Health and Environ. Rsch. Dept. Energy, Washington, 1987—; vice chmn. Arctic Ocean Scis. Bd., 1988-89. Editor: (W.L. Rey) Marine Biological Systems of the Far North. Sec. Fairbanks Light Opera Theatre Bd., 1987-88; chairwoman Rhodes Scholar Selection Com., Ak., 1986—. Research grantee U. Alaska. Fellow AAAS, Arctic Inst. N.Am.; mem. Am. Soc. Limnology and Oceanography, Explorer's Club (sec., treas. local chpt. 1987-89, pres. 1990—), Rotary. Office: PO Box 80650 Fairbanks AK 99708 also: U Alaska Inst Marine Sci Fairbanks AK 99775

ALEXANDER, WILMA JEAN, business education educator, records management/information processing consultant; b. Columbus, Kans., May 25, 1938; d. Glen Burton and Wilma Mae (Jenner) Heavin; m. Leslie Wayne Alexander, Dec. 20, 1958; 1 child, Glenella Jean. BS, Pittsburg State U., 1959, MS, 1967; EdD, Okla. State U., 1973. Tchr. English, Baxter Springs High Sch., Kans., 1959-61; tchr. bus., English, Pineville High Sch., Mo., 1961-63, Netawaka High Sch., Kans., 1963-64; tchr. bus. Hillsboro High Sch., Mo., 1964-68; faculty Ill. State U., Normal, 1970—, prof. bus. edn., 1978—, chmn. dept. bus. edn. and adminstrv. svcs., 1983—; project dir. Dept. Adult Vocat. and Tech. Edn., Ill. State Bd. Edn., Springfield, 1975-83; cons. Pekin Ins. Co., Ill., 1984-87. Author: (workbook, study guide) Introduction to Business, 1976, 79; Advanced Office Systems, 1986. Editor: Business Education into the Eighties, 1980-84, Nat. Assn. Bus. Tchr. Edn. Rev. and Bulletin, 1989—. Mem. Assn. Records Mgrs. and Adminstrs. (pres. 1976-79), Office Systems Rsch. Assn., Nat. Bus. Edn. Assn., Nat. Assn. Tchr. Educators Bus. Edn. (1990—), Ill. Bus. Edn. Assn. (bd. dirs.), Data Processing Mgmt. Assn. Avocation: piano, reading, boating. Home: Rte 1 Box 109 Towanda IL 61776 Office: Ill State U Dept Bus Edn and Adminstrv Svcs 327 Williams Hall Normal IL 61761

ALEXANDRE, JUDITH LEE, social services administrator; b. N.Y.C., Dec. 14, 1944; d. Jerome Jacob and Dorothy Dale (Locks) A. BA, U. Calif., Santa Barbara, 1966; MSW, U. Denver, 1970; PhD, U.S. Internat. U., 1983. Lic. clin. social worker, Calif.; diplomate clin. social work. Social worker II Aid to Families with Dependent Children, Ventura, Calif., 1968-70; social worker IV Protective Services and Intake, Ventura, 1970-72; social worker dir. New Life Homes, Ventura, 1972-79; supr. Foster Care Placement, Ventura, 1973-74; counselor Bible Fellowship Ch., Ventura, 1976-80; asst. prof. sociology Westmont Coll., Ventura, 1976-83, assoc. prof. sociology, 1983—; coordinator counseling and outreach Bible Fellowship Ch. Counseling Ctr., Ventura, 1980-86, dir., 1980—; instr. Calif. Luth. Coll. Grad. Program Clin. Psychology, Thousand Oaks, 1988—; instr. grad. sch. marriage and family counseling Azusa Pacific U., 1982—, human services Ventura Coll., 1974-77; social work supr. II Protective Services Placement, 1974-76; liaison Foster Parents Assn., 1973-76; cons. Coalition Agy. Household Violence, Ventura, 1985—, pub. health dept. Ventura Adolescent Parent Program, 1986—; bd. dirs. Child Abuse and Neglect, Ventura, 1985—, mem. program com. 1985-86, v.p., pres. elect, 1987-88, pres. 1988—; lectr. confs. and sems.; dir. Christian Therapy Program Vista Del Mar Hosp., Ventura, 1989-90. Contbr. articles to profl. jours. and mags. Bd. trustees Ventura (Calif.) Unified Sch. Dist., 1986—; tchr., active leader Sunday sch. Bible Fellowship Ch., Ventura, 1970—; mem. allocations panel United Way; group leader inpatient Vista Del Mar, 1986—; bd. dirs. Rancho del Rey Christian Confraternity, 1990, Ventural Unified Sch. Dist. Ednl. Found.; mem. Eastminster Presbyn. Ch., Sunday sch. tchr. Women's Ministry Team, 1990. Mem. Nat. Assn. Social Workers, Nat. Assn. Social Workers Referral Service (v.p. 1986-87), Bus. and Profl. Women (chmn. spl. program 1984, Channel Island Woman of Yr. award 1986 1st v.p. 1987-88), Nat. Assn. Christian Social Workers (so. Calif. chpt.), Nat. Council on Social Work Edn., Am. Humane Soc. (children's div.). Democrat. Office: Bible Fellowship Ch Counseling Ctr 2021 Sperry Ave #9 Ventura CA 93003

ALFONSO, ROSANNE BRUNELLO, sales executive; b. Cleve., Aug. 26, 1960; d. Carl Carmello and Vivan Lucille (Caranna) B.; married, 1990. Student, U. Cin., 1978-81, Cleve. State U., 1981-82. Indsl. sales engr. Alta Machine Tool, Denver, 1982; mem. sales./purchases Ford Tool & Machine, Denver, 1982-84; sales/ptnr. Mountain Rep. Enterprises, Denver, 1984-86; pres., owner Mountain Rep. Ariz., Phoenix, 1986—; pres., sales mgr. Mountain Rep. Oreg., Portland, 1990—; sec. Computer & Automated Systems Assoc., 1987, vice chmn., 1988, chmn., 1989. Active mem. Rep. Party, 1985—. Mem. NAFE, Soc. Mfg. Engrs. (pres. award 1988), Computer Automated Assn. (sec. 1987, vice chmn. 1988 chmn. 1989), Italian Cultural Soc., Tempe C. of C., Vocat. Ednl. Club Am. (mem. exec. bd., pres. 1987—). Roman Catholic. Office: Mountain Rep Oreg 312 N Hayden Bay Dr Portland OR 97217

ALFORD, JOAN FRANZ, entrepreneur; b. St. Louis, Sept. 16, 1940; d. Henry Reisch and Florence Mary (Shaughnessy) Franz; m. Charles Hebert Alford, Dec. 28, 1978; stepchildren: Terry, David, Paul. BS, St. Louis U., 1962; postgrad. Consortium of State U., Calif., 1975-77; MBA, Pepperdine U., 1987, postgrad., Fielding Inst. Head user svcs. Lawrence Berkeley Lab., Calif., 1977-78, head software support and devel. Computer Ctr., 1978-82, dep. head, 1980-81; regional site analyst mgr. Cray Rsch., Inc., Pleasanton, Calif., 1982-83; owner, pres. Innovative Leadership, Oakland, Calif., 1983—. Contbr. articles to profl. jours. Bd. dirs., sec. Vol. Ctrs. of Alameda, Oakland, 1985, bd. dirs., 1984—; campaign mem. Marge Gibson for County Supr., Oakland, 1984; mem. Oakland Piedmont Rep. Orgn., Alameda County Apt. Owners Assn., 1982. Mem. Assn. Computing Machinery, Spl. Interest Group on Computer Pers. Rsch. (past chmn.), Internat. Platform Assn., Small Owners for Fair Treatment. Republican. Clubs: Claremont Pool and Tennis, Lakeview, San Francisco Opera Guild. Avocations: swimming, skiing, opera, horseback riding, gardening. Home: 2605 Beaconsfield Pl Oakland CA 94611 Office: Innovative Leadership 2605 Beaconsfield Pl Oakland CA 94611

ALI, KAREN SANI, lawyer; b. Hampton, Va., Oct. 7, 1956; d. John Arthur and Ruth Lenore (Fultz) A. AB magna cum laude, Princeton U., 1978; JD, U. Mich., 1981. Bar: Va. 1982, N.Y. 1983. Atty.-adviser Office of Hearings and Appeals, Dept. Energy, Washington, 1981-87; asst. gen. counsel Technology Applications, Inc., Alexandria, Va., 1987-90, gen. counsel, 1990—. Tutor, Community Club, Washington, 1983—. Mem. ABA, Women's Legal Def. Fund, Assn. Black Princeton Alumni (bd. dirs. 1988—), Women's Bar Assn. D.C., Coalition One Hundred Black Women of D.C. Democrat. Roman Catholic. Office: Tech Applications Inc 6101 Stevenson Ave Alexandria VA 22304

ALI, PATTY MARIE, computer consultant, systems analyst; b. Sacramento, Nov. 17, 1963; d. Walter Robert and Diane Gene (Garcia) Patten; m. Ajom Hassan Ali, Jan. 14, 1987. Systems analyst Data Automation-USAF, Vandenberg AFB, Calif., 1984-86; database mgr. Data Automation-USAF, Comiso, Italy, 1986; computer dir. Small Computer Tech. Ctr.-USAF, Comiso, 1986-87; micro-systems specialist Cosumnes River Coll., Sacramento, 1988; instr. Canterbury Career Schs., Roseville, Calif., 1988-89; systems analyst Harmon Pub., Hartz Mountain Corp., Carmichael, Calif., 1989-90; rsch. analyst McGuire Properties, Fair Oaks, Calif., 1990—; computer cons. Sacramento, 1990; computer cons. Friendship Sports Internat., 1987-89; computer cons. graphic design Prism, Pub. Relations, 1989—. Vol., coordinator March of Dimes Bid for Bachelors, Sacramento, 1988-89; sponsor Big Bros./Big Sisters, Vandenberg AFB, 1984-86. With USAF, 1984-87.

ALI, PERVEEN KHAN, engineering company executive; b. Karachi, Pakistan, Jan. 1, 1959; came to U.S., 1972; d. Riaz Ahmed and Jamila (Begum) Khan; m. Ahmed Ali, Sept. 24, 1982; children: Subhan Mustafa, Kamran Ahmed, Sanna Jamila. B.S., U. Southwestern La., 1977. Programmer analyst Ohio Nat. Life Ins., Cin., 1977-79; programmer analyst AT & T Communications, Cin., 1979-82, system analyst, Los Angeles, 1982-86; v.p. Geo-Etka, Inc., Orange, Calif., 1985—. Republican. Moslem. Avocations: reading, travel, music. Home: 3640 E Roundtree Ct Orange CA 92667 Office: Geo-Etka Inc 739 N Main St Orange CA 92668

ALICE, MARY (MARY ALICE SMITH), actress; b. Indianola, Miss., Dec. 3, 1941; d. Sam and Ozelar (Jurnakin) Smith. BE, Chgo. State U.; studied with Lloyd Richards, Negro Ensemble Co., N.Y.C. Sch. tchr. Chgo. Theater debut Purlie Victorious, Chgo.; off-Broadway debut Trials of Jero, Greenwich Mews Theatre, 1967; Broadway debut No Place to Be Somebody, Morosco Theatre, 1971; other N.Y.C. appearances include The Strong Bread, 1967, The Duplex, 1972, Miss Julie, 1973, House Party, 1973, Black Sunlight, 1974, Terraces, 1974, Heaven and Hell's Agreement, 1974, In the Deepest Part of Sleep, 1974, Cockfight, 1977, Nongogo, 1978 (Obie award Village Voice 1979), Julius Caesar, N.Y. Shakespeare Festival, 1979 (Obie award Village Voice 1979), Player #9, Spell #7, N.Y. Shakespeare Festival, 1979, Zooman and the Sign, 1980, Glasshouse, 1984, Take Me Along, 1984, Fences, Goodman Theatre, Chgo., 1985, 46th St. Theatre, N.Y.C., 1987 (Antoinette Perry award for best featured actress in a play, Drama Desk award 1987); other theater appearances include Open Admissions, Long Wharf Theatre, New Haven, 1982, A Raisin in the Sun, Yale Repertory Theatre, 1984; film debut The Education of Sonny Carson, 1974; other film appearances include Sparkle, 1976, Teachers, 1984; appeared in TV films The Sty of the Blind Pig, 1974, Just an Old Sweet Song, 1976, This Man Stands Alone, 1979. Mem. AFTRA, SAG, Actors' Equity Assn. *

ALICH, AGNES AMELIA, chemistry educator, researcher; b. Loman, Minn., June 10, 1932; d. John James and Delvina Rosalie (St. Lawrence) A. BS, Marquette U., 1960, MS, 1961; PhD, Northwestern U., 1971. Instr. sci. Duluth (Minn.) Cathedral High Sch., 1954-57; instr. chemistry Coll. St. Scholastica, Duluth, 1961-64, asst. prof., 1971-74, assoc. prof, 1974-79, chair chemistry dept., 1976—, prof., 1979—; chair sci. div. Gerard High Sch., Phoenix, 1964-67. Contbr. articles to profl. jours. Mem. symphony chorus, Duluth, 1967—. Grantee NSF, 1976, 81, Miller Dwan Med. Found., 1978-80, Duluth Clinic Edn. and Research Found., 1981-83, 3M Co., 1985-90; Mem. IUPAC, Am. Chem. Soc. (chmn. Lake Superior Sect. 1977-79), Chem. Soc. London, Internat. Union Pure and Applied Chemistry, Sigma Xi, Iota Sigma Pi. Democrat. Home and Office: 1200 Kenwood St Duluth MN 55811

ALIM, MARILYN PRYCE, academic administrator; b. L.A., Oct. 10, 1941; d. Edward Lyons and Woodia (Smith) Pryce; m. Skunder Boghossian (div. 1970); children: Aida, Edward; m. Khalil Abdel Alim; children: Camille, Melanie, Khalilah. Student, Sorbonne U., Paris, 1961; BA, Spelman Coll., 1963; postgrad., L'ecole du Cinema Francais, Paris, 1964. Pub. relations officer Ethiopian Tourist Orgn., Addis Ababa, 1966-68; dir. pub. relations Spelman Coll., Atlanta, 1968-69; internal programs adminstr. Tuskegee (Ala.) U., 1984—; founder, dir. A.M. Players, Washington, 1979-82; cons. Montgomery (Ala.) Media, 1986-88; cross-cultural coord. Cen. Am. Peace Scholarship, Tuskegee U., 1986-89. Producer: (videos) French for Francophones, 1983; writer, producer (musical) Oh, Freedom!, 1980; producer: (TV series) The African Connection, 1989, (documentaries) Cen. Am. Peace Scholarship at Tuskegee, 1986. Vol. French instr. Clara Muhammad Sch., Washington, 1979-82. Named Merrill scholar, Spelman Coll., Atlanta, 1961-67. Mem. Nat. Assn. Student Affairs, Am. Film Soc. Democrat. Home: 1508 Logan St Tuskegee AL 36088 Office: Office Internat Program Tuskegee U 219 Kresge Ctr Tuskegee AL 36088

ALLAN, YVONNE LETICIA, medical illustrator, computer graphics designer; b. Buenos Aires, Argentina, Sept. 14, 1927; came to U.S., 1949; d. Miguel Angel Marino and Maria Dominica (Baumgartner) de Marino; m. Laurence Ralph Allan, May 8, 1948; children: Richard Keneth, Edwin Hobbs, Mary Elizabeth. Art teaching degree, Sch. Fine Arts Manuel Belgrano, Buenos Aires, 1945; postgrad., Coll. Fine Arts, Buenos Aires, 1945-49; BFA, U. Cen. Fla., 1976, postgrad. in Biology, 1985-86. Archtl. model maker James A. Britton AIA, Greenfield, Mass., 1950-55; biology illustrator U. Cen. Fla., Orlando, 1974-76; free lance artist, medical illustrator Yvonne L. Allan Studios, Winter Park, Fla., 1976—. Illustrator: Mitral Valve Reconstruction, 1987, (posters) New Method of Ear Cropping, 1977, Light Reflection in Eye, 1978, Chinese Exercises, black and white ink drawings, 1985, Chiropractic Educational Charts, 1984-85, The Human Heart, 1986, Ten Consecutive Cases of Mitral Valve Repair, 1986-87, Transseptal

Technique, a Workbook, 1988-89, Debriment of Annular Abscesses of the Heart and Repair, 1989, Aneurysms of the Aorta, 1990. Active Parents of Hard of Hearing Children, Orlando, 1962—; coord. Parent to Parent Program Seminole County Ct. House, 1982-84, group facilitator, 1984-86; counselor, trainer Cen. Fla. Helpline, Winter Pk., 1987—. Mem. Nat. League Am. Pen Women (past sec.), Assn. Med. Illustrators. Republican. Baptist.

ALLANACH, ELAINE JACQUELINE, nurse, army officer; b. San Jose, Calif., Mar. 26, 1954; d. William Burt and Edith Gwendolyn (Schindler) Moreland; m. Bruce Carlton Allanach, Oct. 8, 1976, (div. Oct. 1989); stepchildren: Dawn Louise, Christopher Bruce, Jeffrey Scott, Sean Michael. BS in Nursing, U.Md., 1976; MS in Nursing, Med. Coll. Ga., 1988; postgrad., Calif. Inst. Integral Studies. RN, Ga., Md., Calif. Commd. 2d lt. Nurse Corps, U.S. Army, 1972, advanced through grades to maj., 1986; staff nurse gen. medicine-oncology Walter Reed Army Med. Ctr., Washington, 1976-78, team leader gen. medicine-oncology, 1978-79, head nurse med. splty. ward, 1979-80; asst. head nurse gynecol. oncology unit Tripler Army Med. Ctr., Honolulu, 1980-81, head nurse med. splty. clinic, 1981-83; staff nurse orthopedics Eisenhower Army Med. Center, Ft. Gordon, Ga., 1983-84, patient edn. coord., 1984-85, head nurse recovery room, 1985-86; head nurse oncology/neurology unit Letterman Army Med. Ctr., Presidio of San Francisco, 1988-89, clin. nurse psychiat. unit, 1989-90, chief nursing adminstrn. E/N, Letterman Army Med. Ctr. Presidio of San Francisco, 1990—; lectr. in field. Contbr. articles to nursing, mil., and med. publs. Mem. pub. edn. com. Am. Cancer Soc., Honolulu, 1982. Decorated Meritorious Service medal; recipient Humanitarian Svc. medal, 1990. Mem. Am. Diabetes Assn., Am. Assn. Diabetic Educators, Grad. Student Nurses Assn. (sec. 1986-87), Am. Nurses Assn., Mensa, Sigma Theta Tau. Avocations: bible studies, jogging, movies, breeding chow-chows. Home: 1933 Ellis St San Francisco CA 94115 Office: The Presidio Letterman Army Med Ctr Dept Nursing San Francisco CA 94129

ALLANSMITH, MATHEA REUTER, ophthalmologist; b. Santa Barbara, Calif., May 31, 1930; d. Harry and Mary (Benthall) Reuter; children: Lynn, Lauren, Kathryn, Carolyn, Andrew, Jennifer. MD, U. Calif., San Francisco, 1955. Diplomate Am. Bd. Pediatrics, Am. Bd. Ophthalmology. Intern San Francisco Hosp., 1955-56; resident in ophthalmology Stanford Hosp., San Francisco, 1957; resident in pediatrics Stanford Hosp., 1958-59, U. Calif. Hosp., San Francisco, 1957-58; fellow in pediatric allergy U. Calif. Hosp., 1959-60; postdoctoral fellow in immunology dept. med. microbiology Stanford U., 1960-63, resident in ophthalmology, 1969-72, research asso. depts. med. microbiology, surgery and ophthalmology, 1963-67, acting asst. prof. surgery and ophthalmology, 1967-68, asst. prof., 1968-74; head Stanford Eye Bank, 1970-75; assoc. prof. ophthalmology Harvard Med. Sch., 1975—; inst. sr. scientist Eye Research Inst., 1975—; Researcher in immunology of the eye, diseases of the external eye. Mem. editorial bd. Am. Jour. Ophthalmology, 1973-87, Ophthalmology, 1979—. Fellow Am. Acad. Allergy; mem. Am. Assn. Immunology, Assn. Research in Vision and Ophthalmology, Phi Beta Kappa, Sigma Xi. Office: 20 Staniford St Boston MA 02114

ALLARD, BRENDA JO, nurse; b. Dayton, Ohio, Sept. 28, 1954; d. Virgil Al and Shirley Ann (Nies) Greider; children: Matthew, Angela. ADN, Sinclair Community Coll., Dayton, 1976. Charge nurse Good Samaritan Hosp., Dayton, 1976-81, 89, staff nurse, 1981-87, relief charge nurse, 1987-89, 1989—, staff nurse labor, delivery, recovery, post operation unit; childbirth educator Good Samaritan Hosp., 1981—. Author video tapes and instrn. booklet Complications of Pregnancy, 1986. Mem. Internat. Assn. Childbirth Educators, Nat. Assn. Ob-Gyn. (cert.). Home: 3957 W National Rd Clayton OH 45415 Office: Good Samaritan Hosp 2222 Philadelphia Dr Dayton OH 45405

ALLARD, JEAN, lawyer; b. Trenton, Mo., Dec. 16, 1924; d. Ben J. and Marion (Watson) McGuire; 1 son, John Preston. AB, Culver-Stockton Coll., 1945, LLD (hon.), 1977; AM, Washington U., St. Louis, 1947; JD, U. Chgo., 1953; LLD (hon.), Elmhurst Coll., 1979. Bar: Ill. 1953, Ohio 1959. Dept. counselor, psychology dept. U. Chgo., 1948-51, research asso. Law Sch., 1953-58, asst. dean, 1956-58; asso. firm Fuller, Harrington, Seney & Henry, Toledo, 1958-59, Lord, Bissell & Brook, Chgo., 1959-62; sec., gen. counsel Maremont Corp., Chgo., 1962-72; v.p. for bus. and finance U. Chgo., 1972-75; ptnr. firm Sonnenschein Nath & Rosenthal, Chgo., 1976—; bd. dirs. Commonwealth Edison Co., La Salle Nat. Bank, Axel Johnson Inc., USF&G Corp. Trustee Culver-Stockton Coll., 1976—; bd. dirs. Chgo. Sch. Fin. Authority, 1980-90. Mem. ABA, Chgo. Bar Assn., Am. Law Inst., Chicagoland Enterprise Ctr. (chair), Leadership Gr. Chgo. (dir.), Latino Inst. (dir.). Clubs: Economic, Commercial, Law, Chicago. Home: 5844 Stony Island Ave Chicago IL 60637 Office: Sonnenschein Nath & Rosenthal 8000 Sears Tower Chicago IL 60606

ALLARD, MARVEL JUNE, psychology educator; b. Detroit; d. Adrian Clarence and Marvel Claudia (Tremper) A.; m. James Donald Widmayer, Mar. 22, 1970 (div. Mar. 22, 1982). AB, Mich. State U., MA, PhD. Rsch. assoc. Mich. State U., East Lansing, 1965-66; project dir., rsch. scientist Am. U., Washington, 1966-67; sr. staff Ops. Rsch., Inc., Silver Spring, Md., 1967-70; rsch. cons., 1970—; prof. psychology Worcester (Mass.) State Coll., 1973—; cons. Leasco Systems, Yankelovich Co., Middlesex county, others. Contbr. rsch. articles to profl. jours. Mem. Pakachoag Hill Community Assn., Auburn, Mass. NSF fellow Mich. State U., 1959-64, Nat. fellow Assn. Am. Colls., 1985; scholar Mich. State U. and pvt. orgns., 1954-58, Phi Kappa Phi scholar Mich. State U.. Mem. Am. Psychol. Assn. (site visitor). Home: 24 Curtis St Auburn MA 01501 Office: Worcester State Coll 486 Chandler St Worcester MA 01602

ALLBRIGHT, KARAN ELIZABETH, psychologist, consultant; b. Oklahoma City, Okla., Jan. 28, 1948; d. Jack Gahnal and Irma Lolene (Keesee) A. BA, Oklahoma City U., 1970, MAT, 1972; PhD, U. So. Miss., 1981. Cert. sch. psychologist, psychometrist; lic. psychologist, Okla., Ark. Psychol. technician Donald J. Bertoch, Ph.D., Oklahoma City, 1973-76; asst. adminstr. Parents' Assistance Ctr., Oklahoma City, 1976-77; psychology intern Burwell Psycho-ednl. Ctr., Carrollton, Ga., 1980-81; staff psychologist Griffin Area Psychoednl. Ctr., Ga., 1981-85; clinic dir. Sequoyah County Guidance Clinic, Sallisaw, Okla., 1985-88; psychologist Baker Psychiatric Clinic, Ft. Smith, Ark., 1988-90; cons. Harbor View Mercy Hosp., 1988-90; pvt. practice, Oklahoma City, 1990—; lectr. various orgns.; bd. dir. workshops. Mem. Task Force to Prevent Child Abuse, Fayette County, Ga., 1984-85, Task Force on Family Violence, Spalding County, Ga., 1983-85; cons. Family Alliance (Parents Anonymous) Sequoyah County, Okla., 1985-88. Named Outstanding Young Women in Am., 1980. Mem. Am. Psychol. Assn., Southeastern Psychol. Assn., Nat. Assn. Sch. Psychologists (cert. sch. psychologist), Okla. Psychol. Assn., Ark. Psychol. Assn., Nat. Assn. Health Svc. Profiders in Psychology, Zonta, Psi Chi, Delta Zeta (chpt. dir. 1970-72). Democrat. Presbyterian. Home: 3941 NW 44th St Oklahoma City OK 73112 Office: Baker Psychiat Clinic 3941 NW 44th St Oklahoma City OK 73112

ALLDREDGE, ALICE LOUISE, biology educator; b. Denver, Feb. 1, 1949. BA in Biology, Carleton Coll., 1971; PhD in Ecology, U. Calif., Davis, 1975. NATO postdoctoral fellow Australian Inst. Marine Sci., Townsville, Queensland, 1975-76; asst. prof. biology U. Calif., Santa Barbara, 1976-82, assoc. prof., 1982-86, prof., 1986—. Author: Tunicata: Yearbook of Science and Technology, 1979; contbr. articles to profl. jours. NSF grad. fellow., 1971-74. Mem. Phi Beta Kappa, Sigma Xi. Office: U Calif Dept Biol Scis Santa Barbara CA 93106

ALLEMAN, AURELIA RUSHTON (LEA ALLEMAN), business executive; b. Fortville, Ind., Sept. 30, 1928; d. Frank M. and Mary M. (Davis) Rushton; m. Zachary T. Bunch, June 5, 1950; children—Zachary Taylor, Tanja Flame, Freeman Enmeier, Olivia Cutcher; m. Ralph J. Alleman, May 7, 1973; children: Stephanie Miller, Bruce, Mark. Student Fortville, Ind. pub. schs. Owner, pres. Be Wise, Inc., Indpls., 1956-62, Miracles Happen, Inc., 1963-67, 20th Century Computer Matching, 1965-73; v.p. Dip-Er-Do Plane Co., Fort Lee, N.J., 1976-77; adminstr. Mgmt. Cleaning Controls, Inc., Chgo., 1981-84; 1st v.p. Am. Indsl. Cleaning Co., Inc., Chgo., 1986—; dir. ASQ Clubs; chmn. Lee Parker Enterprises, Inc. Mem. LVW, Am. Bus. Women (ednl. com. mem., 1973-74). Author: How to Happily Kiss the Singles Scene Goodbye, 1979. Home: 5100 North Marine Dr Chicago IL 60640 Office: Berman Sales Co Inc 1728 S Michigan Ave Chicago IL 60616 also: Am Indsl Cleaning Co Inc 1730 W Belmont Ave Chicago IL 60657

ALLEN, ADRIENNE LYNN, creative director; b. Chattanooga, Oct. 16, 1950; d. Roscoe Bryant and Helen Earlene (Hamilton) A. BFA, So. Meth. U., 1972. Mech. artist Taylor Pub. Co., Dallas, 1972; designer Image Plus Design Studio, Dallas, 1972-73, Bob Knight & Assocs., Dallas, 1973-74; asst. art dir. Comml. Prodns., Inc., Dallas, 1974-76; co-owner, art dir. And Assocs., Inc., Dallas, 1976-77; proprietor, creative dir. Adrienne Allen and Assocs., Dallas, 1977—; creative cons. March of Dimes Gourmet Gala, Dallas, 1986—, Dallas Epilepsy Assn., 1986—, The CoCo Awards, Dallas, 1986—, Treescape Dallas, 1984-85. Designer various advt. campaigns, 1981—. Pub. Awareness Service award Dallas Epilepsy Assn., 1987. Mem. Alpha Delta Pi (v.p. 1970-71). Republican. Home: 9706 Summerwood Circle Dallas TX 75243 Office: Adrienne Allen and Assocs 10670 N Central Expwy Ste 450 Dallas TX 75231

ALLEN, ALICE CATHERINE TOWSLEY, public relations professional, writer, consultant; b. N.Y.C., July 26, 1924; d. George Everett and Alice Sophia (Kunkeli) Goldsmith; m. Harold Dulmage Towsley, Jan. 4, 1940 (div. 1942); m. Charles Kissam Allen, Jan. 20, 1973. Student, U. Hawaii, 1941-42. Writer Honolulu Advertiser, 1942-47; advt. mgr. Paterson Morning Call, Paterson, N.J., 1949-52; publ. cons. N.Y. (N.Y.C.) Herald Tribune, 1953; assoc. editor Mayfair, Travel, Fashion mags., N.Y.C., 1953-54; pub. editor Assoc. Jr. Leagues, Inc., N.Y.C., 1954-59; editor, asst. pub. Doctor's Wife mag., N.Y.C., 1959-65; pub. relations dir., editor Am. Field Svc. Internat., N.Y.C., 1967-72; free-lance writer, pub. cons. N.Y.C., 1973—. Recipient award for outstanding copy promotion Blood Bank Hawaii, 1944, Golden Poet award World of Poetry, 1989. Mem. Overseas Press Club Am., ASCAP. Republican. Home and Office: 325 E 41st St New York NY 10017

ALLEN, ANITA LOUISE, primary school educator; b. Chattanooga, May 1, 1964; d. Ralph Lloyd and Linda Lou (Hodge) Sims; m. Kenneth Doyle Allen, May 27, 1983; 1 child, Jacqueline. Bachelors in Religious Edn., Internat. Bible Inst., Orlando, Fla., 1985. Sales rep. Pizitz Dept. Stores, Birmingham, Ala., 1983-84; tchr. Roosevelt (N.J.) Nursery Sch., 1988—. Coord. N.J. Girls Club, Ch. of God, Freehold, 1988-90, mem. State Ladies Ministries Bd., 1988-90; mem. PTA, Roosevelt, 1988-90; vol. Am. Red Cross, N.J., 1989. Mem. NAFE. Republican. Home: 7075 Zlotkin Circle Freehold NJ 07728

ALLEN, ANNA JEAN, chiropractor; b. Henderson, Ky., Apr. 6, 1955; d. Harold D. and Aiko (Nakashima) A. AS, U. Ky., 1973, BS, 1976; Dr.Chiropractic, Palmer U., 1980; postgrad. Pan Am. U., 1981, San Antonio Coll., 1983. Health instr. Nautilus, Davenport, Iowa, 1978-80; dir. chiropractic, Harlington, Tex., 1980-81, Handley Chiropractic, San Antonio, 1982-83, NE Chiropractic Ctr., El Paso, Tex., 1983-84, Viscount Chiropractic, El Paso, 1984—. Bd. dirs. White Harvest Ministries. Mem. NAFE, Am. Bus. Woman's Assn., Nat. Fedn. Ind. Bus., Chiropractic Orthopedist Assn., Christian Chiropractice Assn., Found. for Chiropractic Rsch., Found. for Chiropractic Rsch., Tex. Palmer Alumni Assn., Palmer Alumni Assn., Am. Chiropractic Assn., Tex. Chiropractic Assn. Avocations: scuba diving, weight lifting, running, bicycling, painting. Office: Viscount Chiropractic Health Ctr 8838 Viscount Ste 0 El Paso TX 79925

ALLEN, BARBARA ANN, musician, educator; b. Abilene, Tex., Apr. 18, 1956; d. Ira James Jr. and Doris Mae (Reid) A. MusB with spl. honors, U. Tex., 1979; MusM, So. Meth. U., 1984. Cert. elem. and secondary tchr., Tex. Orch. instr., condr. Richardson (Tex.) Ind. Sch. Dist., 1979-81; violinist, violist Ft. Worth Symphony Orch., 1979-81; condr. U. Tex. Summer String Inst., Dallas, 1980, 81; violinist, violist AIMS Symphony Orch., Graz, Austria, 1980—; violinist Innsbruck (Austria) Symphony and Opera Orch., 1981-82, Münchner Instrumental Ensemble, Munich, 1981-82; faculty, dir. Am. Inst. of Mus. Studies, Graz, 1982—; violinist So. Meth. U. Opera and Symphony Orchs., Chamber orch., Dallas, 1982-84, Dallas Ballet and Opera Orchs., 1984—; 2d violinist Eger Artist-In-Residence String Quartet, Graz, 1983—; rec. artist Profl. Rec. Studios, Dallas, 1984—; 1st violinist Lone Star String Quartet, Dallas, 1985—; instr. violin and Viola Arapaho Music Studios, Dallas, 1985-88; founder Studio of Barbara Allen-Violin and Viola, 1988—, B. Allen Enterprises, Musical Entertainment Booking, 1990—. Author: Auditioning in Europe for the Instrumentalist-A Guide to Professionalism in Music, 1987. Meadows Found. scholar So. Meth. Univ., 1982-84. Mem. Am. Fedn. Musicians. Methodist. Home and Office: 607 W Rochelle Apt 1087 Irving TX 75062

ALLEN, BEATRICE, piano educator; b. N.Y.C., June 30, 1917; d. Samuel and Rose (Krell) Hyman; m. Eugene Murray Allen, Jan. 23, 1937; children: Marlene Allen Galzin, Julian Lewis. Student NYU, 1933-36; diploma (scholar), Inst. Musical Arts, N.Y.C., 1939, postgrad. (scholar), 1939-40; diploma (fellow, letter commendation), Juilliard Grad. Sch., N.Y.C., 1943; BA magna cum laude Cedar Crest Coll., 1980. Mem. faculty prep. div. Juilliard Sch. Music, 1957-69, Moravian Coll., 1967-68, Northampton County Area Community Coll., 1968-70, Manhattan Sch. Music, 1969—; mem. founding faculty Community Music Sch., Allentown, Pa., 1982—; artist-in-residence, condr. Tchrs. Workshop, Antioch Coll., Yellow Springs, Ohio, 1966; Bach lectr., recitals various univs.; concert appearances Town Hall, N.Y.C., Chautauqua, N.Y., others. Winner N.J. Artists contest, 1936. Mem. Music Tchrs. Nat. Assn. (program chmn. Lehigh Valley chpt. 1981-82), Pa. Music Tchrs. Assn. Address: 2100 Main St Bethlehem PA 18017

ALLEN, BETTY JEANNE, psychologist, writer; b. Newark, NJ, Apr. 23, 1929; d. John Stanley and Hazel Frances (Porter) A. BS, Trenton State Coll., 1951; MA, Tchrs. Coll. Columbia U., 1952; PhD, U. Md., 1970. Lic. psychologist, N.J. Tchr. Army Dependent Schs., Hanau, Fed. Republic Germany, 1954-55, Fair Lawn (N.J.) Pub. Schs., 1952-59; sch. psychologist Ridgewood (N.J.) Pub. Schs., 1959-84; cons., psychologist The Forum Sch., Waldwick, N.J., 1984—; pvt. practice Paramus, N.J., 1984—; adj. instr. Fairleigh Dickenson U., Rutherford, N.J., 1970-80; psychologist, musician, Ridgewood YMCA, 1988—. Author: Mother, Can You Hear Me?, 1983. Grant Found. fellow, 1967-69. Mem. Am. Psychol. Assn., N.J. Psychol. Assn., Adoption Crossroads. Home: 85 Paramus Rd Paramus NJ 07652

ALLEN, BETTY REA, mathematics educator; b. Memphis, Oct. 5, 1937; d. Felix Judson and Eva Katheryn (Rea) A. BS, Ouachita Bapt. Coll., 1959; MA, George Peabody Coll., 1960; MS, Tex. Woman's U., 1968; student, La. State U., 1961. Math. tchr. Benton (Ark.) Pub. Schs., 1960-61, Charleston (Mo.) Pub. Schs., 1961-64, Hughes (Ark.) Pub. Schs., 1964—; sponsor Mu Alpha Theta, Hughes, 1976—, student coun., Hughes, 1967—; cons. Algebra curriculum Ark. Dept. Edn., Little Rock, 1984. Contbr. articles to profl. jours. Mem. PTA (life, pres. 1981-82, v.p. 1971-72, 80-81); treas. Hughes 1st Bapt. Ch. Recipient Presdl. award NSF, 1987, Tandy Tech. scholars Outstanding Tchr. award, 1990, Educator Recognition award Ark. Gov.'s Sch., 1990; named Outstanding Tchr. of Yr. Ark. Power & Light, 1987; Kodak and NEA grantee, 1983, Ark. Scottish Rite grantee, 1966, 67, Southwestern Bell grantee, 1989. Mem. AAUW, NEA, Hughes Edn. Assn. (pres. 1980-81), Math. Assn. Am., Nat. Coun. Tchrs. Math., Ark. Coun. Tchrs. Math. (exec. com. 1981-85, grantee 1986), Nat. Assn. Student Activity Advs., Ark. for Gifted and Talented Edn., Delta Kappa Gamma (sec. 1970), MENSA. Home: PO Box 423 Hughes AR 72348 Office: Hughes High Sch PO Box 9 Hughes AR 72348

ALLEN, CHRISTINA MARIE, marketing professional; b. Seattle, May 7, 1964; d. Ethan and Stephanie Jane (York) A. BABA, Wash. State U., 1987. Sales rep. Russell Stover Candies, Kansas City, Mo., 1987-88, market devel. mgr., 1988, dist. mgr., 1988-89; mktg. rep. Polaroid Corp., Cambridge, Mass., 1989—. Mem. NAFE. Roman Catholic. Office: Polaroid 3232 W MacArthur Blvd Santa Ana CA 92799

ALLEN, CHRISTINA RUTH, savings and loan executive; b. Decatur, Ill., July 2, 1961; d. Townsend Alphonsus and Rose Ellen (Haiducek) Tully; m. Bradley Thomas Allen, June 13, 1981. Student, Ill. State U., 1979-80, Harper Coll., Palatine, Ill., 1986-87. Cashier Mike's Mkt., Bloomington, Ill., 1978-80; teller McLean County Bank, Bloomington, 1980-82, teller supr., 1982-84, head drive-up teller supr.; savings counselor Ben Franklin Savings, Skokie, Ill., 1984-85, Home/Savs. of Am. F.A., Palos Heights, Ill., 1985-86; savings specialist Home/Savs. of Am., Palos Heights, 1986-87; ops. officer Home/Savs. of Am., Skokie, Ill., 1987-88; br. mgr. Home/Savs. of Am., Des Plaines, Ill., 1988—. Recipient Excellence in Art award Cen. Cath. High Sch., 1977, Honor Roll award, 1975-79. Republican. Roman Catholic. Office: Home/Savs of Am FA 1300 Oakton St Des Plaines IL 60018

ALLEN, DEBRA JANIECE, pharmacist; b. Hanford, Calif., June 22, 1953; d. Keith Eugene and Patricia Marie (Falchi) Howe; m. John Alan Allen, July 24, 1976; children: Sean Adrian, Tonya Danielle. Student, West Hills Jr. Coll., Coalinga, Calif., 1969-72; D of Pharmacy, U. of the Pacific, 1972-76. Registered pharmacist, Calif. Pharmacy clk. Svc. Pharmacy, Inc., Coalinga, 1972-73; hosp. pharmacy intern Dameron Hosp., Stockton, Calif., 1974-76; mgr. Kernville (Calif.) Rexall Drug, 1976-78; staff pharmacist Tulare (Calif.) County Gen. Hosp., 1978-80; founder full-time svc., designer floor plans, dir. pharmacy Corcoran (Calif.) Dist. Hosp., 1980-83; staff pharmacist Hillman Health Ctr.-Tulare County Health Svcs., Tulare, 1984-86, Pharmacy Corp. Am. (formerly Rush Pharmacy), Fresno, Calif., 1987—. Vol. Election Com. Tulare County, 1980, Petition Com. for the Prevention of Hosp. Closure, Tulare, 1980. Mem. Calif. Pharmacy Assn., The Video Club Am., Lambda Kappa Sigma. Home: 5240 N Vernal Ave Fresno CA 93722 Office: Pharmacy Corp Am 4191 W Swift Ave Ste 101 Fresno CA 93722

ALLEN, ELIZABETH MARESCA, marketing executive; b. Red Bank, N.J., Jan. 4, 1958; d. Paul William Michael and Roberta Gertrude (Abbes) Maresca. Student, Brookdale Community Coll., 1976-77; A Bus. Adminstrn., Tidewater Community Coll., 1988. Systems analyst Methods Research Corp., Farmingdale, N.J., 1977-79; div. mgr. Abacus Services, Inc., Virginia Beach, Va., 1979—. V.p. Charlestowne Civic League, Virginia Beach, 1983-84; bd. dirs. Arthritus Found., Norfolk, Va., 1986—; advisor Commonwealth Coll., Norfolk, 1984—; chairperson publicity Job Fair Women's Network of Hampton Rds., 1989. Mem. Women's Network of Hampton Rds. (publicity chairperson 1988—), Hampton Roads C. of C. (com. chair 1985, 88), Williamsburg Area C. of C. (exhibit chair 1987). Republican. Roman Catholic. Office: Abacus Svcs Inc 5620 Virginia Beach Blvd Virginia Beach VA 23462

ALLEN, ELLEN LOUISE, health services executive; b. Woodburn, Iowa, Dec. 26, 1939; d. Glenn Walker and Geraldine Jeannette (Charles) A. Diploma, St. Luke's Hosp. Sch. Nursing, Denver, 1961; BS, U. Colo., 1967; MS, Calif. State U., Chico, 1986. RN, Colo., Calif. Staff nurse St. Luke's Hosp., Denver, 1961-62; staff nurse Rangely (Colo.) Dist. Hosp., 1962-63, dir. nursing, 1963-65; head nurse Mt. Zion Hosp., San Francisco, 1967-69; clin. supr. area coord. Vis. Nurse Assn., San Francisco, 1969-78; dir. patient care Community Health Svcs., Chico, 1978-79; faculty Calif. State U., Chico, 1980-81; supr. Vis. Nurse Assn., Santa Cruz, Calif., 1981-83; v.p. and chief operating officer Vis. Nurse Assn. Home Health Care, Inc., San Jose, Calif., 1983—. Com. chairperson AIDS Svc. Provider Network, San Jose, 1988-89. Mem. Am. Pub. Health Assn., Am. Soc. on Aging, Calif. Assn. Health Svcs. at Home (co-chmn. licensing com. 1989-90, bd. dirs. 1990—), No. Calif. Coalition of Vis. Nurse Assns. (pres. 1986, 88), Sigma Theta Tau. Democrat. Presbyterian. Office: Vis Nurse Assn Home Health Care Inc 2025 Gateway Pl Ste 270 San Jose CA 95110

ALLEN, FRANCES ELIZABETH, computer scientist; b. Peru, N.Y., Aug. 4, 1932; d. John Abram and Ruth Genevieve (Downs) A. B.S., State U. N.Y., Albany, 1954; M.A., U. Mich., 1957. Research computer scientist IBM Research Lab., Yorktown Heights, N.Y., 1957—; adj. assoc. prof. N.Y. U., 1970-72; mem. computer sci. adv. bd. NSF, 1972-75, cons., 1975-78; lectr. Chinese Acad. Scis., 1973, 77; IEEE disting. visitor, 1973-74; cons. prof. Stanford U., 1977-78; chancellor's disting. vis. lectr., U. Calif., Berkeley, 1988-89. IBM Corp. fellow, 1989. IBM fellow; mem. Assn. Computing Machinery (nat. lectr. 1972-73), Programming Systems and Langs. (Paper award 1976), Nat. Acad. Engring. (elected 1987). Home: Finney Farm Croton-on-Hudson NY 10520 Office: IBM Corp PO Box 704 Yorktown Heights NY 10598

ALLEN, FRANCES MICHAEL, publisher; b. Charlotte, N.C., Apr. 7, 1939; d. Thomas Wilcox and Lola Frances (Horne) A.; m. Joseph Taylor Lisenbee, Feb. 24, 1955 (div. 1957); 1 child, Leslie Autice. Abilene (Tex.) Christian Coll., 1954-56, Chico (Calif.) State U., 1957-59. Art dir. B&E Publs., L.A., 1963-65; editor B&E Publs., 1969-70; art dir. Tiburon Corp., Chgo., 1970-75; founder, editor Boxers, Internat., L.A., 1970-76; editor The Hound's Tale, 1974, Saints, Incorp., 1974-76; founder, editor Setters, Incorp., Costa Mesa, Calif., 1975-85; founder, owner Michael Enterprises, Midway City, Calif., 1976—; editor Am. Cocker Rev., Midway City, 1980-81; editor, publisher, ptnr. Am. Cocker Mag., 1981—. Author: The American Cocker Book, 1989; illustrator: The First Five Years, 1970, The Aftercare of the Ear, 1975, The Shenn Simplicity Collection, 1976, The Miniature Pinscher, 1967; prin. works include mag. and book covers for USA, most widely published show dog artist world wide, past 15 yrs. Recipient Dog World Award Top Producer, 5 times, 1966-88, numerous 1st awards in art fairs. Mem. Dog Writers Assn. Am. Republican. Mem. Ch. of Christ. Home and Office: 14531 Jefferson St Midway City CA 92655

ALLEN, GINA, author; b. Trenton, Nebr.; d. R.V. and Osa (Hanel) Hunkins; 1 dau., Ginita Allen Wall. B.A., Northwestern U., 1940. Exec. sec. Youth Commn. 3d Jud. Dist., N.Mex., 1955-60; mem. bd. Golden Gate chpt. NOW, 1970—; pres. Humanist Assn. San Francisco, 1976-85; sec. Am. Humanist Assn., 1973-77, v.p., 1979-83, sr. humanist counselor, 1972—, founding chmn. feminist caucus, 1977-86, chmn. div. humanist counseling, 1982-86, exec. coun.div. Humanist Counseling, 1987—. Author: Prairie Children, 1941, On the Oregon Trail, 1942, Rustics for Keeps, 1948, (with R.V. Hunkins) Tepee Days, 1941, Trapper Days, 1942, Sod-House Days, 1945, The Forbidden Man, 1961 (Anisfield-Wolf award 1962), Gold!, 1964, Gold Is, 1969, Intimacy, 1971; also short stories, articles in popular mags.; editorial bd. Humanist mag., 1983—. Chairwoman N.Mex. Democratic Central Com., 1956-59. Named to Humanist Counselors AHA Hall of Fame, 1989. Mem. Authors Guild, Internat. Assn. Humanist Educators, Counselors and Leaders (bd. dirs. 1988—). Unitarian.

ALLEN, JERI, small business owner; b. Concord, Calif., June 22, 1947; d. Earl O. and Joanna (Lewis) Conrad; m. Michael William Allen, Mar. 15, 1969; children: Christopher Lee, Tyson Matthew. Degree in cosmetology, Diablo Beauty Coll., Concord, Calif., 1979. Cert. dermalogist. Owner, operator beauty salon The Cutting Rm., Danville, Calif., 1990—; founder, pub. Money-Go-Round Simplified Bookkeeping Systems, 1985—. Patentee in field. Active Kids Are It Program, Contra Costa County, Calif., Calif. Rep. Assembly Contra Costa County. Office: The Cutting Rm 206 E Linda Mesa Danville CA 94526

ALLEN, JESSIE LEE, nurse; b. Clarke County, Miss., Mar. 8, 1923; d. Roosevelt and Margie (Collins) Harper; m. Lawrence Allen, Oct. 26, 1974; 1 child, Renard Williams. GED, Emily Griffith Opportunity Sch., Denver, 1963; AAS in Mental Retardation Tech., Angelina Jr. Coll., 1972; Lic. Practical Nurse, Meridian Jr. Coll., 1976. Attendant, then head attendant and relief attendant supr. Ridge State Home and Tng. Sch., Denver, 1962-66; attendant, then attendant supr. I Tex. Rsch. Inst. of Mental Scis., Houston, 1968-70; therapist asst. Lufkin (Tex.) State Sch., 1970-72; nurse Watkins Meml. Hosp., Quitman, Miss., 1976-77, staff nurse, 1981-88, ret., 1988 ; nurse Archusa Convalescent Ctr., 1977—. Baptist. Home: Rte 3 Box 176A Vossburg MS 39366

ALLEN, JOAN, actress; b. Rochelle, Ill., Aug. 20, 1956. Student, Ea. Ill. U., Western Ill. U. Founding mem. Steppenwolf Theatre Co., Chgo.; theater appearances include (debut) And A Nightingale Sang, N.Y.C. (Clarence Derwent award, Drama Desk award, Outer Critics Circle award 1984), Steppenwolf Theatre Co., also Boston, 1983, The Marriage of Bette and Boo, N.Y. Shakespeare Festival, 1986, Burn This! (Tony awrd 1988) Mark Taper Forum, L.A., also N.Y.C., 1987, The Heidi Chronicles, N.Y.C., 1988, 89; film appearances include Compromising Positions, 1985, Fat Guy Goes Nutzoid!!, 1986, Peggy Sue Got Married, 1986, Tucker: The Man and His Dream, 1988; TV appearances include miniseries Evergreen, 1985, All My Sons, Am. Playhouse, PBS, 1987, Robert Frost, Voices and Visions, PBS, 1988, TV film The Room Upstairs, 1987. Office: care Internat Creative Mgmt 40 W 57th St New York NY 10019*

ALLEN, JOYCE SMITH, medical librarian; b. Englewood, N.J., Aug. 1, 1939; d. Harold Willard and Mary Elizabeth Smith; m. Jim Frank Allen, Mar. 1974 (div. 1984); 1 child, Shani Jamilla. BA, Howard U., 1961; MLS, Atlanta U., 1966; cert. in advanced studies, U. Ill., 1974. Reference librarian Howard U., Washington, 1966-73; mgr. library Meth. Hosp. Ind., Indpls., 1977—; instr. Ind. Vocat. Tech. Coll., 1979, 85, Med. Library Assn., 1982—, Martin Ctr. Coll., Indpls., 1983-84. Author career materials. Vol. Indpls. Police Dept. Library, 1977, Children's Mus., Indpls., 1987-88. Recipient Minority Bus. and Profl. Achiever award Ctr. for Leadership Devel., Indpls., 1981, Central Ind. Area Libr. Svcs. Authority cert. of Excellence, 1990. Mem. ALA, Internat. Tng. in Communication, Med. Libr. Assn., Coun. on Libr. Technicians, Spl. Librs. Assn. Democrat. Home: 3815 N Bolton Ave Indianapolis IN 46226 Office: Meth Hosp Ind 1701 N Senate Blvd Indianapolis IN 46202

ALLEN, JUDITH RUTH, middle and elementary school educator; b. Potsdam, N.Y., July 8, 1943; d. Gordon Harold and Ruth Elizabeth (Smith) A. BS, SUNY, Potsdam, Potsdam, 1966; MA in History, Political, Coll. of St. Rose, Albany, 1974. Tchr. Tchr. So. Colonie Central Schs., Albany, N.Y., 1966—; del. N.Y. State United Tchrs., Albany, 1971—, Am. Fedn. of Tchrs., Wash., 1974, 1975, 1980, 1984, Nat. Edn. Assn., Wash., 1974-75; sec. So. Colonie Tchrs. Assn., 1971-75; local site coord. Ednl. Rsch. and Dissemination Program, 1989—. Author: Geography Curriculum Guide, 1978, Computer Curriculum Guide, 1983, Elementary School—The Forgotten Corner, 1990; contbr. Vibrations, 1989—. Lobbyist N.Y. State United Tchrs., Albany, 1977—, Chairperson S. Colonie Tchrs. Polit. Action, Albany, 1979-87. Nominated Tchr. of the Year S. Colonie Bd. of Edn., Albany, 1983. Mem. Nat. Coun. Tchrs. Math., Assn. for Supervision and Curriculum Devel., Internat. Assn. for Study Cooperation in Edn., So. Colonie Tchrs. Assn., N.Y. State United Tchrs., Am. Fedn. of Tchrs., N.Y. State P.T.A., Schola Cantorum, Ancient Order of Hibernians. Democrat. Roman Catholic. Home: 109 Beverwyck Dr Apt 10 Guilderland NY 12084 Office: South Colonie Cen Schs 329 Sand Creek Rd Albany NY 12205

ALLEN, JULIA H., software executive; b. Pitts., July 2, 1951; d. William K. and Beata (Hawkins) Allen; m. George R. Brown, Mar. 1, 1975 (div. 1985); 1 child, Michael A. BS in Computer Sci., U. Mich., 1972; MS in Elec. Engring., U. So. Calif., 1976. Programmer, software mgr. TRW Def. Sys. Group, Redondo Beach, Calif., 1973-82; software mgr. Transaction Tech., Inc., Santa Monica, Calif., 1982; v.p., software mgr. Sci. Applications Internat. Corp., Torrance, Calif., 1983-89, v.p., 1989—. Bd. dirs. Housing Adv. and Appeals Bd., City of Redondo Beach, 1982-86; mem. sch. site coun. Pennekamp Elem. Sch., 1989. Mem. Women in Mgmt., ACM, IEEE, Am. Assn. Artificial Intelligence, NAFE. Republican. Office: Sci Applications Intern 21151 Western Ave Torrance CA 90501

ALLEN, KAREN ALFSTAD, management consultant; b. Wichita, Kans., Nov. 21, 1942; d. Harold Daniel and Myrtle (Creach) Keefer; m. Richard, Dec. 16, 1962, (div. 1976). AS, Oreg. Inst. of Tech., L.A., 1964; AA, Pasadena City, 1973; BS,, Calif. State U., Pasadena City, 1974. Administra. asst. Transamerica, Los Angeles, 1974-75; v.p. Calif. Fed., Los Angeles, 1975-86; mgmt. cons. Coopers & Lybrand, Los Angeles, 1986--. Bd. dir. Political Action Com. Calif. Fed., Los Angeles, 1984-86; Vol. Youth Motivation Task Force, Los Angeles, 1982-86. Recipient Honors Calif. State U., Los Angeles, 1974. Mem. Internat. Facility Mgmt., So. Calif. Emergency Assn., NAFE, NOW, U. Club of Los Angeles. Democrat. Home: 164 W Magna Vista Arcadia CA 91006 Office: Coopers & Lybrand 1000 W 6th St Los Angeles CA 90017

ALLEN, KELLIE JEANNE, financial analyst; b. Miami, Fla., Aug. 16, 1963; d. James Hampton and Elizabeth Anne (Smith) A. BA Pub. Policy Study, Duke U., 1985. With sales United Consumers Club, Vienna, Va., 1985-86; adminstrv. asst. Electronic Industries Assn., Washington, 1986-87; fin. analyst Rockwell Internat., Downey, Calif., 1987-89, McDonnell Douglas Corp., Long Beach, Calif., 1989—. Mem. NAFE. Republican. Mem. United Church of Christ. Home: 216 Grand Ave #202 Long Beach CA 90803 Office: McDonnell Douglas Corp 3855 Lakewood Blvd M/C 800-80 Long Beach CA 90846

ALLEN, LEATRICE DELORICE, psychologist; b. Chgo., July 15, 1948; d. Burt and Mildred Floy (Taylor) Hawkins; m. Allen Moore, Jr., July 30, 1965 (div. Oct. 1975); children—Chandra, Valarie, Allen; m. Armstead Allen, May 11, 1978. A.A. in Bus. Edn., Olive Harvey Coll., Chgo., 1975; B.A. in Psychology cum laude, Chgo. State U., 1977; M.Clin. Psychology, Roosevelt U., 1980. Clk., U.S. Post Office, Chgo., 1967-72; clin. therapist Bobby Wright Mental Health Ctr., Chgo., 1979-80; clin. therapist Community Mental Health Council, Chgo., 1980-83, assoc. dir., 1983—; cons. Edgewater Mental Health, Chgo., 1984—, Project Pride, Chgo., 1985—; victim services coordinator Community Mental Health Council, Chgo., 1986-87; mgr. youth family services Mile Square Health Ctr., Chgo., 1987-88; coord. Evang. Health Systems, Oakbrook, Ill., 1988—. Scholar Chgo. State U., 1976, Roosevelt U., 1978; fellow Menninger Found., 1985. Mem. Nat. Orgn. for Victim Assistance, Ill. Coalition Against Sexual Assault (del. 1985—), Soc. Traumatic Stress Studies (treatment innovations task force), Chgo. Sexual Assault Svcs. Network (vice-chair, bd. dirs.). Avocations: aerobics; reading; theatre; dining.

ALLEN, LEILANI ELEANOR, data processing executive; b. Rudesheim, Rhein, Fed. Republic Germany, Nov. 27, 1949; d. John Kaleiapu and Ilse Eva (Ritter) A. BA, San Francisco State U., 1971, MA, 1973; PhD, U. Conn., 1978. Sr. analyst VISA, U.S.A., San Mateo, Calif., 1978-81; asst. gen. mgr. Inst. for Info. Mgmt., Sunnyvale, Calif., 1981-85; pres. Knowledge Consortium, Oakland, Calif., 1985-87; sr. cons. Amdahl Corp., Sunnyvale, 1987-88; v.p. Aon Corp., Chgo., 1988—; chmn. No Cal Computer Measurement Group, San Francisco, 1982-84. Co-author: Management Handbook of Info Center and End User Computer, 1987, Strategic Planning for Info Systems, 1987 (survey); editor: Executive Perspectives on Info Systems, 1985; contbr. articles to profl. jours. Mem. Mensa, NAFE, Computer Measurement Group. Office: Aon Corp 123 N Wacker Chicago IL 60606

ALLEN, LOUISE, writer, educator; b. Alliance, Ohio, Sept. 21, 1910; d. Earl Wayne and Ella Celesta (Goodall) Allerton; m. Benjamin Yukl, June 27, 1936; children: Katherine Anne Yukl Johnston, Kenneth Allen, Richard Lee, Margaret Louise Yukl Border. Student, Cleve. Coll. Western Res. U., 1963, Lakeland Community Coll., 1981-84. Co-founder Sch. Writing, Cleve., 1961-62; founder, dir. Allen Writers' Agy., Wickliffe, Ohio, 1963-84; editorial assoc. criticism service Writer's Digest mag., 1967-69; instr. Cuyahoga Community Coll., 1965-81, Lakeland Community Coll., Mentor, Ohio, 1973-81, Scottsdale Community Coll., 1984-88; writer. Author: (poems) Confetti, 1987; contbr. articles to mags. Mem. Mensa, Assn. Mundial de Mujures Periodistas y Escritoras, Women in Communications, Nat. League Am. Pen Women, DAR Shore Writers Club (founder), Euclid Three Arts Club, Women's City Club (Cleve.). Republican. Congregationalist. Address: 2609 W Southern #11 Tempe AZ 85282

ALLEN, LOUISE CRAWFORD, journalism educator; b. Childress, Tex., Dec. 28, 1903; d. John McHenry and Daisy Margaret (Alexander) Crawford; m. James George Allen, June 30, 1928; 1 child, James Crawford. BA, So. Meth. U., 1924; MA, U. Mo., 1940. Stenographer Crawford & Crawford, Childress, 1920-24; from stenographer to prof. journalism Tex. Tech. U., Lubbock, 1928-63, assoc. prof. emeritus, 1964. Co-author: Radio and Television Continuity Writing, 1952, 1st 62 Years History Methodist Hospital, Lubbock; columnist for weekly newspapers, 1945-63; contbr. numerous articles to newspapers and mags. Active community planning coun.; tchr. St. John's United Meth. Ch.; pres. Meth. Aux., 1967-68. Named Woman of Yr. Altrusa, 1956; recipient Disting. Svc. award Southwest Journalism Congress, 1965, Pathfinder award Lubbock Com. for Women, 1985. Mem. Lubbock Women's Club (life, pres. 1949-50), AAUW (pres. Lubbock br.), Jr. 20th Century Study Club (past pres.), Univ. Women's Club (pres. 1959-60), Sigma Phi, Sigma Kappa Alumnae (past pres.). Democrat. Home: 3110 21st St Lubbock TX 79410

ALLEN, LUNELLE SPENCER, nurse; b. Cherokee County, S.C., Oct. 3, 1931; d. William E. and Nancy Anna (Wilson) Spencer; m. Karl H. Zerbst, Oct. 16, 1955 (div. Feb. 1970); children: Karl H. Zerbst Jr., Chris Anthony Zerbst; m. Raymond D. Allen, Jan. 23, 1973. Diploma in Nursing, Columbia (S.C.) Hosp. Sch. Nursing, 1952. RN, S.C. Staff nurse Columbia Hosp., 1952-54; staff nurse Roper Hosp., Charleston, S.C., 1955, supr. obgyn, 1955-62; staff nurse Westvaco Corp., Charleston, 1962-77, head nurse, 1977—. Vol. Multiple Sclerosis Soc., Am. Cancer Soc., Crippled Children Soc., March of Dimes; mem. North Charleston Election Commn., 1983-89. Mem. S.C. Occupational Health Nurses Assn. (numerous coms. 1963—), Omar 500's Pit Crew. Lutheran. Clubs: Antique Auto of Am., Coastal Carolina (Charleston) (sec.). Lodges: Milcah Temple, Daus. of the Nile. Home: 7631 Hillandale Rd North Charleston SC 29420 Office: Westvaco Corp PO Box 2941105 North Charleston SC 29411-2905

ALLEN, MARIA GEORGINA QUEVEDO, social worker; b. Camaguey, Cuba, Oct. 30; came to U.S. 1961, naturalized, 1970; d. Pedro Manuel and Dolores (Peralta) Quevedo; m. Wilfredo O. Allen, Sept. 8, 1950; children: Wilfredo, Jorge A. Doctora en Leyes, U. La. Habana, Cuba, 1943; MSW, Fla. State U., 1969. Social worker Cuban refugee program Fla. State Dept. Welfare, 1962-67; caseworker Health and Rehab. Services, 1969-71; supr. social services U. Miami Comprehensive Health Care Program, 1971-74; social worker, supr. evaluation unit Goodwill Industries, Miami, 1974-79; regional social services supr. dept. youth and family devel. Met. Dade County Fla., 1974—; asst. prof., field instr. Barry Coll., 1974—. Recipient Miami City Commn. for Vol. Services in Child Day Care award, 1977. Mem. Nat. Assn. Social Workers, Coalition for Spanish Am. Women.Acad. Cert. Social Workers, Cuban Bar in Exile, Fla. State U. Alumni Assn. Roman Catholic. Club: Cuban Women's. Office: 11025 SW 84th St Miami FL 33173

ALLEN, MARILYN MYERS POOL, theater director, video producer; b. Fresno, Calif., Nov. 2, 1934; d. Laurence B. and Asa (Griggs) Myers; B.A., Stanford U., 1955, postgrad., 1955-56; postgrad. U. Tex., 1957-60, W. Tex. State U. summers 1962, 63; m. Joseph Harold Pool, Dec. 28, 1955; children—Pamela Elizabeth, Victoria Anne, Catherine Marcia; m. Neal R. Allen, Apr. 1982. Pvt. tchr. drama, speech, acting, directing, speech correction, Amarillo, Tex., 1960-82, Midland, Tex., 1982—; free-lance radio and TV actress; asst. mng. dir. Amarillo Little Theatre, 1964-66, mng. dir., 1966-68; mng. dir. Horsehoe Players, touring profl. theater, 1969-73; actress, multimedia prodn. Palo Duro Canyon, 1971; dir. touring children's theatre, 1978-79 guest actress in Medea, Amarillo Coll., 1981; guest reciter Midland-Odessa Symphony, 1984. Pres. Tex. Non-Profit Theatres, 1972-74, 75-77, bd. dirs., 1988—; 1st v.p. High Plains Center for Performing Arts, 1969-73; adv. mem. dept. fine arts Amarillo Coll., 1980-82. Adv. mem. Tex. Constnl. Revision Commn., 1973-75; mem. adv. council U. Tex. Coll. Fine Arts, 1969-72; community adv. com. for women Amarillo Coll., 1975-79; conv. program com. Am. Theatre Assn., 1978, program participant 1978-80, bd. dirs., 1980-83; bd. dirs. Amarillo Found. Health and Sci. Edn., 1976-82, program v.p., 1979-81; bd. dirs. Domestic Violence Council, 1979-82, March of Dimes, 1979-81, Tex. Panhandle Heritage Found., 1964-82, Friends of Fine Arts, W. Tex. State U., 1980-82, Amarillo Pub. Library, 1980-82, Amarillo Symphony, 1981-82; publicity chmn. Midland Community Theatre, 1984-87 , bd. govs., 1986—, sec., 1987-88, v.p., 1988—. Recipient cert. of appreciation Woman of Year, Amarillo Bus. and Profl. Women's Club, 1966; Best Actress award for Hedda Gabler role Amarillo Little Theatre 1965, Best Dir. award for Rashomon, 1967, 1st Pl. award for video special Tex. Press Conf., 1988, 1st Pl. award for news Tex. Press Conf., 1989; named Woman of Yr., Beta Sigma Pi, 1980, Broadcaster of the Yr., Rocky Mountain Press Conf., 1988; Travel fellow AAUW, 1973, 78. Mem. Am. Community Theatre Assn. (dir. 1969-72, 82-84, v.p. planning and devel. 1985-87), S.W. Theatre Conf. (dir. 1973-76, 82-84, exec. com. 1982-84), Tex. Theatre Council (dir. 1974-81, exec. com., pres. 1975-76), AAUW (br. pres. 1973-75, state chmn. cultural interests 1975-77, 86-88, state bd. dirs. 1984-88, program v.p. Midland 1988—), ECW (program v.p. Midland 1989—), DAR, (chpt. chaplain 1971-75, historian 1975-77), C. of C. (fine arts council), U.S. Judo Assn., Symphony Guild, Amarillo Art Assn., Midland Symphony Guild (arrangements chmn. 1983-84), Act IX, Amarillo Law Wives Club (pres. 1976-77), Hamhocks (v.p. 1985-86). Episcopalian.

ALLEN, MARY CATHERINE MITCHELL (MRS. WALTON ALBERT ALLEN), educator; b. Iva, S.C.; d. George Francis and Cinderella (Harris) Mitchell; A.A., Anderson Jr. Coll., 1946; B.S. in Edn., Central State Coll., Edmond, Okla., 1962; M.Ed., U. Ga., 1968; Ed.S., Atlanta U., 1974; m. Walton Albert Allen, Apr. 15, 1949; children—Susan Marie, Joel Walton, Barbara Ann. Tchr., prin. Anderson County (S.C.) Schs., 1946-52; tchr. East Clayton Sch., College Park, Ga., 1964-66, guidance counselor, 1966—. Active Girl Scouts U.S.A., 1946-68; bd. dirs. Cherokee Estates, Inc. Mem. NEA, Ga., Clayton County (public relations com. com. 1967-68, chmn. profl. devel. com. 1975-78, mem. exec. bd. 1987—) edn. assns., AAUW, Am. (state coordinator elem. counselors), Ga. personnel and guidance assns., Ga. Assn. Sch. Counselors, Alpha Delta Kappa (chpt. treas. 1970-72, dist. chaplain 1972—, chpt. pres. 1974-76), Kappa Delta Pi. Home: 2765 Jerome Rd College Park GA 30349 Office: 2750 Ellenwood Rd Ellenwood GA 30049

ALLEN, MARY KATHRYN, logistics company executive; b. Bellefontaine, Ohio, Dec. 16, 1953; d. John Gilbert and Mary Elizabeth (Wright) Purcell; m. Stephen Gilbert Allen, June 27, 1976; children: Kevin Douglas, John Patrick, Stephanie Kathryn. BS, Ohio State U., Columbus, 1976, MA, 1986, PhD, 1986; MS, Air Force Inst. Tech., 1980. Commd. 2d lt. USAF, 1976, advance through grades to maj., ret., 1988; chief material mgmt. 301st Supply Squadron, USAF, Rickenbacker AFB, Ohio, 1976-79; lead program mgr. Modular Automatic Test Equipment Systems Program Office, Wright Patterson AFB, Ohio, 1980-83; dir. artificial intelligence program Air Force Logistics Command, Wright Patterson AFB, 1986-88; pres., chief exec. officer Intellogistics, Inc., Columbus, 1988—; mem. Addison-Wesley Tech. Tng. Adv. Bd., 1986—. Author: The Development of an AI System for Inventory, 1986; co-author: Putting Expert Systems To Work in Logistics, 1990; mem. editorial rev. bd. High Tech. Mktg. Rev., 1986-88, Logistics Mgmt. Jour. Internat., 1986-88; mem. editorial bd. Expert Systems, Planning and Implementation; contbr. articles to profl. jours. Recipient Def. Logistics Mgmt. Excellence award Am. Def. Preparedness Assn., 1982, Profl. Achievement award Traffic Mgmt. Mag., 1987, Outstanding Program Mgr. award AF Assn., 1987, Slattery Tech. award Nat. Security Indsl. Assn., 1988. Mem. IEEE, AAAS, Internat. Assn. Knowledge Engrs., Soc. Logistics Engrs.(mng. editor 1988—, Best Tech. Paper award 1987), Am. Assn. Aritifical Intelligence, Decision Scis. Inst., Coun. Logistics Mgmt. (Kearney rsch. award 1985), Inst. Mgmt. Scis., Air Force Assn., Ohio State U. Alumni Assn., Phi Kappa Phi, Beta Gamma Sigma, Sigma Iota Epsilon, Alpha Iota Delta, Alpha Lambda Delta, Mirrors, Chimes, Mortarboard. Roman Catholic. Office: Intellogistics Inc 3620 N High St Columbus OH 43214

ALLEN, MARYON PITTMAN, former senator, journalist, lecturer, interior and clothing designer; b. Meridian, Miss., Nov. 30, 1925; d. John D. and Tellie (Chism) Pittman; m. Joshua Sanford Mullins, Jr., Oct. 17, 1946 (div. Jan. 1959); children: Joshua Sanford III, John Pittman, Maryon Foster; m. James Browning Allen, Aug. 7, 1964 (dec. June 1978). Student, U. Ala., 1944-47, Internat. Inst. Interior Design, 1970. Office mgr. for Dr. Alston Callahan, Birmingham, Ala., 1959-60; bus. mgr. psychiat. clinic U. Ala. Med. Center, Birmingham, 1960-61; life underwriter Protective Life Ins. Co., Birmingham, 1961-62; women's editor Sun Newspapers, Birmingham, 1962-64; v.p., ptnr. Pittman family cos., J.D. Pittman Partnership Co., J.D. Pittman Tractor Co., Emerald Valley Corp., Mountain Lake Farms, Inc., Birmingham; mem. U.S. Senate (succeeding late husband James B. Allen), 1978; dir. pub. rels. and advt. C.G. Sloan & Co. Auction House, Washington, 1981; feature writer Birmingham News, 1964; writer syndicated column Reflections of a News Hen, Washington, 1969-78; feature writer, columnist Maryon Allen's Washington, Washington Post, 1979-81; owner The Maryon Allen Co. Cliff House (Restoration/Design). Mem. Ladies of U.S. Senate unit ARC, Former Mems. of Congress, Ala. Hist. Commn., Blair House Fine Arts Commn.; charter mem. Birmingham Com. of 100 for Women; trustee Children's Fresh Air Farm; trustee, elder Ind. Presbyn. Ch., Birmingham; Democratic Presdl. elector, Ala., 1968. Recipient 1st place award for best original column Ala. Press Assn., 1962, 63, also various press state and nat. awards for typography, fashion writing, food pages, also several awards during Senate service; sponsor, U.S. Navy Nuclear submarine, U.S.S. Birmingham, S.S.N. 695, launched Newport News, Va., 1977, commissioned 1978. Mem. Nat. Press Club, 1925 F Street Club, 91st Congress Club, Congl. Club, Birmingham Country Club. Home: Cliff House 3215 Cliff Rd Birmingham AL 35205

ALLEN, MICHELLE JOANNE, newspaper advertising director; b. Dearborn, Mich., Aug. 29, 1960; d. Edward Norman Durocher and Norma Fannie (Wheatley) Burdett; m. Brian Henry Allen, Oct. 5, 1984 (div. Dec. 1989); 1 child, Paul James. Grad. high sch., Dearborn. Office clk., switchboard operator Dearborn Press and Guide, 1978, coordinator retail sales, 1978-81, asst. dir. advt., 1981-82, dir. advt., 1982—. Designer advt. section Fairlane Town Ctr., 1983. Mem. Dearborn C. of C. (co-chmn. women's div.). Home: 4900 Ternes Dearborn MI 48126 Office: Dearborn Press and Guide 15340 Michigan Ave Dearborn MI 48126

ALLEN, OLIVE MARIE, health facility administrator; b. Frankfort, Ky., May 11, 1949; d. Robert and Beulah F. (Simmons) A. BA in Psychology, U. Ky., 1989. Dir. of ops. Hillhaven Corp., Louisville, Ky., 1984—; mem. Gov.'s Consumer Adv. Com. Mem. Am. Coll. Health Care Adminstrs. (treas. Ky. chpt.). Home: PO Box 8132 Lexington KY 40533 Office: Hillhaven Corp 301 N Hurstbourne Ln Ste 225 Louisville KY 40222

ALLEN, PATRICIA J., library director, professor; b. McLean County, Ky., Nov. 10, 1941; d. Richard Louis and Helen (Hancock) Jones; m. Jerry M. Mize, Mar. 19, 1960 (div. 1978); children: Martin P., Elizabeth M. Atherton; m. Lawrence A. Allen, Nov. 24, 1983 (div. 1985). Student, Murray (Ky.) State U., 1959-60; BA, Ky. Wesleyan Coll., 1962; MA, Western Ky. U., 1974; MLS, U. Ky., 1982; postgrad., U. N.C., 1983-84. Librarian pub. elem. schs. Daviess County, Ky., 1963-70; media specialist pub. elem., mid. and high schs. McLean County, Ky., 1970-78; head pub. svcs., assoc. prof. library sci. Ky. Wesleyan Coll., Owensboro, 1978-83; asst. dir. Evansville (Ind.) Vanderburgh County Pub. Library, 1985-89; dir. Carmel (Ind.) Clay Pub. Library, 1989—; mem. adj. faculty Western Ky. U., Bowling Green, 1977-78, Ind. U., Bloomington, 1988; workshop presenter Nursing Home Activities Dirs. Assn., Owensboro, Ky., 1981; cons. Ky. Dept. for Libraries and Archives, Frankfort, 1982, Purchase (Ky.) Regional Library System, Murray, 1983, Henderson (Ky.) Community Coll. Library, 1988. Editor: handbook Emergency Handbook, 1987, Circulation Policies and Procedures, 1988; contbr. articles to profl. jours. Pres. Ret. Sr. Vol. Program Adv. Coun., Evansville, 1986-88; bd. dirs. Evansville Goodwill Industries, 1987-89. Caroline M. Hewins scholar U. Ky., 1982, Margaret Ellen Kalp scholar U. N.C., 1983-84. Mem. Am. Library Assn., Assn. Coll. and Rsch. Libraries, Friends of Ind. Libraries (sec. 1989—), Ind. Library Assn., Ky. Library Assn., Pub. Library Assn., Library Adminstrs. and Mgrs. Assn., P.E.O., Ohio Valley Scribes, Altrusa Club (bd. dirs. Evansville chpt. 1988), Tales and Scales (pres. Evansville chpt. 1986), Beta Phi Mu. Democrat. Baptist. Office: Carmel Clay Pub Libr 515 E Main St Carmel IN 46032

ALLEN, PATRICIA JEAN, graphic designer; b. Jersey City; d. Joel Morris and Blanche Jeanne (de la Villebeuvre) A. B.F.A., Beaver Coll. Display artist Hahne's, Newark; v.p., assoc. design dir. Doremus & Co., N.Y.C.; judge DESI awards Graphic Design USA, N.Y.C., Art Dirs. Club Phila., PIMNY, N.Y.C. Recipient awards for design excellence Art Dirs. Club N.Y., Type Dirs. Club, Am. Inst. Graphic Arts, Mead Library Ideas, Andy Awards, Art Dirs. Club N.J., Art Dirs. Club Chgo. Mem Soc. Illustrators (assoc.) Home: 267 Laurel Ave Kearny NJ 07032 Office: Doremus & Co 120 Broadway New York NY 10271*

ALLEN, PAULA GINA, collection representative; b. Waterbury, Conn., Jan. 18, 1953; d. Michael Ronald and Pauline Lorraine (Vincenti) Galuppo; m. Louis Carl Sambataro, Nov. 24, 1972 (div. 1978); m. Ronnie E. Allen, June 6, 1982. Grad., High Sch. Teller Hollywood (Fla.) Federal Bank, 1971-74; receptionist Dr. Robert F. Litterio, Miramar, Fla., 1975-76; teller City Nat. Bank, Miami, Fla., 1976-77; receptionist Dr. Karl Morganstein, Hollywood, Fla., 1977-79; adminstrv. clk. So. Bell, Ft. Lauderdale, Fla., 1979-88; collection rep. So. Bell, Pompano Beach, Fla., 1988—. Fundraiser, Jr. Achievement, Ft. Lauderdale, 1988. Democrat. Roman Catholic. Office: So Bell 6451 N Federal Hwy Fort Lauderdale FL 33308

ALLEN, PAULINE VIRGINIA, accountant; b. Guntown, Miss., Feb. 7, 1909; d. Henry James and Madia Jane (Kennedy) A.; student Southwestern U., Memphis, 1927-29, 32-33, U. Miss., 1933-34; A.B., Duke U., 1935. Math. tchr. high sch., Pleasant Grove, Miss., 1936-37; clk. ins. agy., Tunica, Miss., 1940-48; bookkeeper, Tunica, 1952-56; accountant Tunica County Hosp., 1956—. Mem. Hosp. Fin. Mgrs. Assn. Democrat. Methodist. Club: Order Eastern Star. Home: Box 96 Tunica MS 38676

ALLEN, RANDY LEE, management consulting executive; b. Ithaca, N.Y., June 24, 1946; d. Richard Hallstead and Mary Elizabeth (Howe) Hallstead Baker; m. John James Meehan, Apr. 24, 1983 (div. Aug. 1987); 1 child, Scott Hallstead. BA in Physics, Cornell U., 1968; postgrad., Syracuse U., 1968, Seattle U., 1973-74. Cert. mgmt. cons., cert. systems profl. Programmer IBM, Endicott, N.Y., 1968-69; product and industry mgr. Boeing Computer Svc., Seattle, 1968-69; dir. mktg. Androcor subs. Boeing Computer, Calumet City, Ill., 1974-76; ptnr. Touche Ross & Co., Newark, 1976—; ptnr.-in-charge Mgmt. cons. Trade Office, Newark, 1988—; prin. Deloitte & Touche, N.Y.C., 1989—; trustee N.J. Inst. Tech., Newark, 1984-87, bd. of overseers N.J. Inst. Tech., 1988—. mem. adv. bd. computer info. scis. dept. Author: OCR-A Cost/Benefit Guide; Pos Trends in the '80's; Bottom Line Issues in Retailing; Pos Current Trends and Beyond, 1987; also articles. Regional fund raiser Cornell U., 1983-84, 87-88, mem. Cornell Coun., 1989—; chmn. long range plan United Meth. Ch. Bishop Janes, Basking Ridge, N.J., 1983; bd. dirs. Chamber Music Am., 1989—; mem. Pres.'s Coun. Cornell Women, 1989—. Recipient Acad. Women Achievers award YWCA, 1984. Mem. Inst. Mgmt. Cons. (nominating com.), Am. Mgmt. Assn., Am. Arbitration Assn., Exec. Women N.J. (pres. 1979-81, dir. 1981-85), Cornell Club, Basking Ridge Golf Club, Cornell Alumni Ambs. Office: Deloitte & Touche 1633 Broadway New York NY 10019

ALLEN, RAYE VIRGINIA, cultural historian; b. Temple, Tex., May 27, 1929; d. Irvin and Vivian (Arnold) McCreary; m. Henry Kiper Allen, June 9, 1951; children: Henry Kiper, Irvin McCreary, Rave Virginia. BA, U. Tex.-Austin, 1951, MA in Am. Civilization, 1975, PhD candidate. Mem. Am. Folklife Ctr. in Library of Congress, Washington, 1976-84, chmn., 1978-79; trustee, Future Homemakers of Am. Found., 1983—; bd. dirs. Future Homemakers Am., 1978-85; trustee U.S.-N.Z. Arts Found.; bd. dirs. coord. com. Restoration of Ellis Island; bd. dirs. Centennial Commn. of U. Tex.-Austin and chmn. continuing edn. com., 1981-84, bd. visitors U. Tex. astronomy dept. and McDonald Obs., 1984—; bd. dirs. 500 Yrs. of Am. Clothing; adv. council Inst. Texan Cultures; mem. Am. Revolution Bicentennial Commn. of Tex., 1971-75; co-founder, 1st pres. Cultural Activities Ctr. of Temple, Tex., 1957-59; bd. dirs. Tex. State Soc. of Washington, 1980-83, Tex. Cultural Alliance, Inst. Humanities, Salado, Tex., Tex. Folklife Resources. Recipient Outstanding Citizen of Temple award, 1973; Raye Virginia Allen State Pres. scholarship established in her honor Future Homemakers Am., 1986. Mem. Am. News Women's Club, Tex. Breakfast Club of D.C. (bd. dirs. 1989). Episcopalian. Home: 1513 30 St NW Washington DC 20007 also: Green Oaks Farm #19 Hartrick Bluff Rd Temple TX 76502

ALLEN, SALLY LYMAN, biologist; b. N.Y.C., Aug. 3, 1926; d. Alexander Victor and Dorothy (Rogers) Lyman; 1 dau., Susan L. AB, Vassar Coll., 1946, PhD (John M. Prather fellow), PhD (USPHS fellow), U. Chgo., 1954. Research assoc. dept. zoology U. Mich., Ann Arbor, 1955-73, assoc. prof. botany, 1967-71, prof., 1971-75, prof. zoology, 1973-75, prof. biol. scis., 1975—, assoc. dean Coll. Lit., Sci. and the Arts, 1988—; chmn. dept. cellular and molecular biology, div. biol. scis., 1975-77; vis. prof. genetics Ind. U., 1967; cons. Am. Type Culture Collection, 1975—. Mem. editorial bd. Jour. of Protozoology, 1974-76, Developmental Genetics, 1990—; assoc. editor: Genetics, 1973—; contbr. articles to profl. jours. Fellow AAAS; mem. Am. Inst. Biol. Sci., Genetics Soc. Am., Soc. Protozoologists, Am. Naturalists Soc. (v.p. 1978), Am. Soc. for Cell Biology (mem. council 1973-75), Phi Beta Kappa, Sigma Xi, Golden Key (hon.). Office: U Mich Dept Biology Ann Arbor MI 48109

ALLEN, SALLY VANCE, oil company executive; b. Boston, Feb. 3, 1940; d. Henry Thomas and Laurie (Burnaby) V.; m. James W. Allen, May 30, 1964 (div. Nov. 1989); children: James Vance, Craig Wentworth. BA magna cum laude, Smith Coll., 1962; MA in African History, UCLA, 1963; MBA, U. Denver, 1979. Various positions Edn. Commn. of the States, Denver, 1967-81; v.p. adminstrn. govtl. affairs The Gary-Williams Co., Denver, 1981—; co-owner, v.p., bd. dirs. Allen Capital Corp., Denver, 1978—; bd.

dirs. United Bank of Cherry Creek, United Bank of Monoco. Bd. trustees Colo. Sch. of Mines, 1985—, Colo. Sch. of Mines Found., 1986—, chmn.; bd. trustees Colo. Outward Bound Sch., 1977—, Graland Country Day Sch., 1981-83, chmn. 1978-81, 85-89; bd. trustees Denver Boys Clubs, 1983-86, The Shipley Sch., 1976-79; bd. dirs. Pub. Edn. Coalition, 1984-87; Colo. Women's Forum, 1981-82. Woodrow Wilson fellow. Mem. Nat. Petroleum Refiners Assn. (indsl. relations com.), Leadership Denver Assn, Women's Forum, Phi Beta Kappa. Office: Gary Williams Co Ste 5300 370 17th St Rep Plaza Bldg Denver CO 80202

ALLEN, SARAH FRANCES, construction executive; b. Tampa, Fla., Sept. 2, 1943; d. Ralph Walter and Allie Rebecca (Stafford) Overman; student U. South Fla., 1962, BS, U. of the State of N.Y.; postgrad. George Mason U.; children: William Kennon, Heather. Founder, pres. Sarah Allen Homes, Inc., 1974—. With Peace Corps, Jamaica. Bd. dirs. Asolo Theater. Mem. Fla. Bd. Realtors, Sarasota-Manatee Contractors Assn., Nat. Assn. Home Builders, Fla. Assn. Home Builders, Sarasota Bd. Realtors, Fla. Bd. Realtors, DAR. Republican. Episcopalian. Home and Office: 5053 Ocean Blvd Ste 98 Sarasota FL 34242

ALLEN, SHARON AMERINE, educational administrator; b. Alexandria, La., Apr. 22, 1942; B.A. in Speech Therapy, Northwestern State U., Natchitoches, La., 1965, M.A. in Speech Pathology, 1968; children—Lisa, Brooke. Speech therapist public schs., La., 1965-73; speech and hearing cons. Nicholls State U., Thibodaux, La., 1973-78; prin. TARC Houma, La., 1978-87, exec. dir. 1987—. Cert. tchr., La. Mem. Am. Speech, Lang. and Hearing Assn. (cert.), La. Speech and Hearing Assn., Am. Assn. Mental Deficiency, LAC Parents Anonymous. Home: 202 Lynwood Houma LA 70360 Office: 1 McCord Rd Houma LA 70360

ALLEN, SHEILA HILL, nursing executive, counselor, consultant; b. Imperial, Nebr., Sept. 28, 1935; d. Roger William and Lois Marion (Clayton) Hill; children—Lee-Ann Hill, Todd Everett, Andrew James. R.N., St. Lukes Sch. Nursing, 1958; B.S., U. Denver, 1959. Asst. head nurse St. Lukes Hosp., Denver, 1959-62; dir. nursing Ridge Vista Mental Health, San Jose, Calif., 1973-75; primary care nurse O'Connor Hosp., 1981; dir. nursing svcs. Westwood Mental Health Facility, Fremont, Calif., 1975-89, Clem. Dependency Inst. No. Calif., Campbell, 1989—. Bd. dirs., sec. Health Acctg. Svcs., Calif., 1984—; co-founder, co-owner Health Acctg. Svcs., Fremont, 1984—; co-owner Westwood Mental Health, 1984—. Contbr. articles to profl jours. Mem. Am. Nurses Assn., Calif. Assn. Health Facilities, Mental Health Com. on Dual Diagnosis, Nat. Consortium Chem. Dependency Nurses, Calif. Assn. Nurses in Substance Abuse, Brookridge Inst. Serving Addiction and Consciousness Profls., San Francisco Acad. Hypnosis, Hazelden Alumni Assn., Delta Gamma, Sigma Theta Tau, Alpha Sigma Chi. Home: 6513 Trinidad Ct San Jose CA 95120 Office: 3333 S Bascom Ave Campbell CA 95008

ALLEN, SUSAN PHILLIPS, corporate professional; b. Fontana, Calif., Apr. 26, 1963; d. Loren C. and Nanette G. Phillips; m. William S. Allen, Nov. 6, 1962. BA cum laude, U. S.C., Los Angeles, 1985; MA, U. S.C., 1987. Hostess U. S.C. U. Events, Los Angeles, 1984-85; researcher Loren Phillips & Assoc. Inc., Duarte, Calif., 1985-86, office mgr., sec. corp., 1986—. Mem. Delta Delta Delta. Republican. Episcopalian. Office: Loren Phillips and Assn Inc 1740 E Huntington Dr #206 Duarte CA 91010

ALLEN, THERESA OHOTNICKY, neurobiologist, consultant; b. Torrington, Conn., Apr. 27, 1948; d. Frank Richard and Helen Theresa (Drozdenko) Ohotnicky; m. Thomas Atherton Allen, Aug. 12, 1972; children: Melanie Atherton, Abigail Baldwin. BA, U. Conn., 1970; MS, Villanova U., 1975; PhD, Duke U., 1978; cert. in bus. adminstrn., U. Pa., 1983. Rsch. assoc. U. Pa., Phila., 1981-83; sci. dir. Drexel U., Phila., 1983-84; cons. on neurobiology to sci.-oriented cos., 1984—. Contbr. articles to profl. jours., also chpts. to books. Bd. dirs. Gladwyne (Pa.) Libr. League, 1986—, Athena Inst. for Women's Wellness, Haverford, Pa., 1989—; trustee Gladwyne Libr., 1988—; com. chmn. Jr. League Phila., 1989-90. Fellow Inst. Neurol. Scis., U. Pa., 1978-80, NIH, 1980-81. Mem. Phila. Skating Club, Humane Soc., Phi Beta Kappa. Episcopalian. Home and Office: 728 Dodds Ln Gladwyne PA 19035

ALLEN, VICKY, software support and training specialist; b. Springfield, Pa., May 27, 1957; d. James Joseph and Ann Marie (Cifone) Cattafesta; m. James Francis DeLeone, Aug. 11, 1979 (div. 1982); m. Dennis Ronald Allen, June 30, 1990. BBA in Computer Sci., Temple U., 1979. Quality assurance Burroughs Corp., Downingtown, Pa., 1977, software QA, 1978, program systems analyst, 1979-81; program analyst Crocker Internal Systems, San Jose, Calif., 1981-83; systems analyst Avantek, Inc., Santa Clara, Calif., 1983-84; tech. support speclist Micro Focus, Palo Alto, Calif., 1984—; programmer cons. Fin. Group, Palo Alto, 1985-86. Active Sierra Club. Mem. Phi Sigma Sigma (sec. 1978-79). Democrat. Roman Catholic. Office: Micro Focus 2465 E Bayshore Rd Ste 400 Palo Alto CA 94303

ALLEN, VIRGINIA ANN, military officer; b. Phoenixville, Pa., Sept. 29, 1953; d. Eugene Womack and Claire Ruth (Reno) A.; m. Timothy Jackson Northcut, June 1, 1985. B in Music Edn., Catholic U., 1976, MusM, 1977. Commd. 2d lt. U.S. Army, 1977, advanced through grades to maj., 1989; adminstrv. officer U.S. Army Element, Sch. of Music, Norfolk, 1978, student company cmdr., 1978-79, tng. officer, 1979; cmdr. and conductor U.S. Army Forces Command Band, Ft. McPherson, Ga., 1979-82; pub. relations officer U.S. Army Field Band, Ft. Meade, Md., 1982-84, assoc. conductor, 1982-85; pub. affairs officer Dept. of Army, The Pentagon, Washington, 1985-86; staff band officer U.S. Forces Command, Ft. McPherson, 1986-88; exec. officer, assoc. condr. U.S. Mil. Acad. Band, West Point, N.Y., 1988—. Mem. Women Band Dirs. Nat. Assn., Nat. Band Assn., Nat. Assn. Female Execs., Assn. of U.S. Army. Office: US Mil Acad Band West Point NY 10996

ALLEN, VIVIEN GORE, agronomist, researcher; b. Nashville, Mar. 31, 1940; d. Lacy Lawton and Sara Azilee (Parks) Gore; m. Harry Evans Allen Jr., Aug. 14, 1962; children: Harry Evans III, Warren Lawton, Stephen Henry. BS, U. Tenn., 1962; MS, La. State U., Baton Rouge, 1973, PhD, 1979. Owner, mgr. Forage Beef Cattle Farm, Huntland, Tenn., 1970—; rsch. asst. La. State U., Baton Rouge, 1978-79, postdoctoral fellow, 1980; asst. prof. agronomy Va. Polytech. Inst. & State U., Blacksburg, 1980-86, assoc. prof. agronomy, 1986—; supt. Va. Agr. Exptl. Sta., Middleburg, 1984-88. Mem. Am. Forage and Grassland Coun. (v.p. 1989—), Am. Soc. Agronomy, Am. Soc. Animal Sci., Soc. for Range Mgmt., Coll. Agr. and Life Sci. Faculty Assn. (pres. 1989—), Gamma Sigma Delta (pres. 1990—), Sigma Xi. Episcopalian. Office: Va Poly Inst & State U Dept Crop & Environ Scis Blacksburg VA 24061-0404

ALLENDER, JULIE ANN, psychologist; b. Elmhurst, Ill., Feb. 27, 1950; d. Frank and Edith (Gluklick) A.; m. Louis Zivic, May 18, 1980; 1 child, Jonathan Ephriam Allender-Zivic. BS in Psychology, U. Ill., 1973; MEd in Psychoednl. Processes, Temple U., 1974, EdD in Psychoednl. Processes, 1978. Lic. psychologist, Pa., Mass.; cert. sch. psychologist, Pa. Asst. prin. Beth Or Congregation Religious Sch., Spring House, Pa., 1977-78; dir. Homebased Businesswomen's Network, Lebanon, Pa., 1983-88; pvt. practice psychologist Lebanon, 1980—; former adj. faculty Community Coll. Phila., Temple U., Phila., Phila. Coll. Textile & Scis., Thomas Jefferson U. Med. Sch., Phila., Wheelock Coll., Boston, Pa. State U., Hershey, Reading; cons. med. staff Good Samaritan Hosp.; pvt. practice therapy, consultation and testing Pa. Coll. Optometry, Phila., Headstart, Chgo., Peabody (Mass.) Pub. Schs., Lynn (Mass.) Hist. Soc., Mich. Edn. Assn., Lansing, Dept. Agr. Extension Program, Lebanon, Pa., Lebanon Valley Coll., Annville, Pa., other orgns. Contbr. articles to profl. jours. and newspapers; participant media programs Sta. WRKO, Boston, 1983, Sta. WVLV, Lebanon, 1983-84, Sta. WAHT, Lebanon, 1988-90. Active Potential Reentry Opportunities in Bus. and Edn., 1986—, Hombased Businesswomen's Network of the Lebanon Valley, 1983-88, women in bus. com. Lebanon C. of C., 1985-87; bd. dirs. Assn. for Humanistic Edn., 1983-87; women's pavilion adv. bd. Lebanon Valley Gen. Hosp., 1986—. Mem. Am. Psychol. Assn., Pa. Psychol. Assn., Am. Soc. for Tng. and Devel., Orthopsychiatric Assn., Assn. for Humanistic Psychology. Jewish. Office: 19 Berwyn Park Lebanon PA 17042

ALLENDER, NANCY G., commercial print broker, turnaround specialist; b. Eugene, Oreg., May 30, 1957; d. Marvin Loren and Leslie Marie (Ramsey) A. BS in Adminstrn., Oreg. State U., 1979; postgrad., Ariz. State U., 1979, Rockhurst U., Kansas City, Mo., 1983. Asst. gen. mgr./player-coach Dallas Diamonds, Women's Basketball League, 1979-80; circulation asst. Dallas Cowboys, NFL, 1979-82; season ticket mgr., asst. mktg. dir. Kansas City (Mo.) Kings, NBA, 1982-84; sales mgr. Northwest Web, Eugene, Oreg., 1984—; pres., owner NGA & Assocs., Portland, Oreg.; asst. coach Women's Pro-Am Summer League, Garland, Tex., 1979-80; basketball coach NBA Summer/Winter Youth Prog., Kansas City, 1982-83. Big sister Y-Round Table Big Bro./Sister, Corvallis, 1975-79; track ofcl. Spl. Olympics, Tempe, Ariz., 1979; bd. vols. Scottish Rite Hosp. for Crippled Children, Dallas, 1981; coordinator Autistic Soc. for Children, Dallas, 1979-82. Recipient Tex. Disting. Svcs. award, State of Tex., 1981. Mem. NAFE, NOW, Nat. Abortion Rights Action League, Oreg. State U. Alumni Assn., Kappa Alpha Theta (Panehllenic del.), Sigma Chi, Delta Chi. Republican. Office: NGA & Associates 4954 SW Galen St Lake Oswego OR 97035

ALLEN-MORANO, SUSAN ELIZABETH, business owner; b. Aiken, S.C., Jan. 26, 1947; d. Dwight Farley and Lillian (Lambert) Allen; m. James Rocco Morano, Dec. 20, 1983; children: Keena Isabel, James Rocco II. BS, Coker Coll., 1969; postgrad., Clemson U., 1974-75. Tchr. numerous schs. S.C., Ga., 1969-78; sec. Ingredient Tech., Woodbridge, N.J., 1980-82; asst. to mgr. Atari Repair/Svc. Ctr., Somerset, N.J., 1982-85; owner Suzanne's Specialties, Somerset, 1985—. Mem. NAFE, Assn. Women in Natural Foods, N.J. Assn. Women Bus. Owners, Nat. Assn. Women Bus. Owners. Episcopalian. Office: Suzannes Specialties PO Box 5164 Somerset NJ 08875

ALLENSON, ALEXANDRA CHRYSSOMALLIS, accountant; b. Kalamata, Greece, July 8, 1956; came to U.S., 1975; d. Sotirios and Triantafili (Kaliani) Chryssomallis; m. Richard D. Allenson, May 14, 1983. AA in Data Processing, Cuyahoga Community Coll., 1982; BS in Acctg., Dyke Coll., 1984. CPA, Ohio. Staff acct. McQuilkin, Vine, Barber & Co. CPAs, Lakewood, Ohio, 1984-88; chief fin. officer West Side Inst. Tech., Inc., Cleve., 1988—. Pres. Zonta Internat., S.W. Cuyahoga County, 1986—. Mem. Nat. Assn. Acct. (bd. dirs., treas. Cleve. chpt. 1986), Am. Inst. CPAs, Ohio Soc. Cert. Pub. Accts. Greek Orthodox. Home: 15406 Lakewood Heights Blvd Lakewood OH 44107 Office: West Side Inst Tech 9801 Walford Ave Cleveland OH 44102

ALLENSWORTH, DOROTHY ALICE, non-profit organization administrator; b. Willoughby, Ohio, Aug. 12, 1907; d. William and Effie Alice (Minthorn) Etzensperger; m. Carl Allensworth, Jan. 12, 1944; children: Stephen Edward, Robert Minthorn. BA, Smith Coll., Northampton, Mass., 1929; MA, Western Res. U., 1935. Various positions, 1935-41; program dir. Cleve. Festival of Freedom, 1939-41; costume designer Shrine Circus, Cleve., 1941, 49th St. Circus, Rockefeller Ctr., N.Y.C., 1942, Shubert Costume Co., N.Y.C., 1942-44; co-producer Cedarhurst (N.Y.C) Summer Theatre, 1943; costumer Chgo. Ice Circus, 1944; dir. neighborhood youth corps Westchester Community Opportunity Program, U.S. Dept. Labor, Westchester County, N.Y., 1965-68; founder, exec. dir. Coll. Careers Fund of Westchester, Westchester County, 1967—. Co-author: The Complete Play Production Handbook, 1973; co-author (play) Interurban, 1947-48. Pres. Rye Neck Sch. Dist. Community Coun., Mamaroneck, N.Y., 1953-57; mem., co-founder recreation coun. Village of Mamaroneck, 1957-59, chmn. recreation commn., 1960-65; co-founder Village Fours pre-school program for 4-yr. olds. Recipient Award for Improving Human Rels., B'nai B'rith Tri-Town chpt., Larchmont, Mamaroneck, Harrison, N.Y., 1967, Woman of Achievement award Westchester County, 1975, Jesse Hill Meml. award Ionic 108 lodge Prince Hall Masons, Westchester County, 1977, Onward and Upward award New Rochelle (N.Y.) Urban League, 1978, Humanitarian award United Bapt. Deacon's Union and Deaconess' Aux., Westchester County, 1979, Disting. Alumna medal Smith Coll., 1980, citation Gov. of N.Y., 1989. Mem. Westchester Coun. on Crime and Delinquency (bd. dirs.), Westchester Coalition for Legal Abortion (bd. dirs.), Westchester Alliance for Juvenile and Criminal Justice (Marjorie Johnson Margolis award 1985). Home: 220 S Barry Ave Mamaroneck NY 10543

ALLENTUCK, MARCIA EPSTEIN, English language and art history educator; b. Manhattan, N.Y., June 8, 1928; m. 1949; 1 child. B.A., NYU, 1948; Ph.D., Columbia U., N.Y.C., 1964. Lectr. English Columbia U., 1955-57, Hunter Coll., 1957; from lectr. to prof. English, CCNY, 1959—; prof. history of art Grad. Ctr. CUNY, 1974—, prof. emerita, 1988. Author: The Works of Henry Needler, 1961; Henry Fuseli; The Artist as Critic and Man of Letters, 1964; Isaac Bashevis Singer, 1969; John Graham's System and Dialectics of Art, 1971; contbr. articles to profl. jours. Morrison fellow AAUW, 1958-59, Howard fellow Brown U., 1966-67, Huntington Libr. fellow, 1968, 77; fellow Nat. Translation Ctr. U. Tex., 1968-69, Chapelbrook Found., 1970-71, Dumbarton Oaks Harvard U., 1972-73; sr. fellow NEH, 1973-74; vis. fellow Wolfson Coll. Oxford U., 1974—, fellow Brit. Acad. Newberry Libr., 1980, Murray rsch. fellow Radcliffe Coll., Harvard U., 1982, fellow Inst. Advanced Study in the Humanities, Edinburgh U. (Scotland), 1984; Am. Philos. Soc. grantee, 1966-67; Rsch. fellow Swann Found., 1989—. Fellow Royal Soc. Arts London; mem. Brit. Soc. Archtl. Historians, MLA (del. assembly 1989—), Milton Soc. Am., Augustan Reprint Soc., Soc. Archtl. Historians, Coll. Art Assn., Phi Beta Kappa. Home: 5 W 86th St Apt 12B New York NY 10024

ALLER, MARGO FRIEDEL, astronomer; b. Springfield, Ill., Aug. 27, 1938; d. Jules and Claire (Cornick) Friedel; m. Hugh Duncan Aller, Aug. 17, 1964; 1 child, Monique Christine. BA, Vassar Coll., 1960; postgrad., Harvard U., 1961-62; MS, U. Mich., 1964, PhD, 1969. Mathematician programmer Smithsonian Astrophys. Obs., Cambridge, Mass., 1960-62; rsch. assoc. U. Mich., Ann Arbor, 1970-76, assoc. rsch. scientist, 1976-85, rsch. scientist, 1985—; mem. users' com. Nat. Radio Astronomy Observatory, 1984-86. Mem. Am. Astron. Soc., Internat. Astron. Union, Sigma Xi. Office: U Mich Dept Astronomy 817 Dennison Bldg Ann Arbor MI 48109-1090

ALLERS, MARLENE ELAINE, law office business manager; b. Crosby, Minn., Dec. 29, 1931; d. Robert Prudent and Tressa Ida May (Hiller) Huard; m. Herbert Dodge Allers, Aug. 29, 1950 (dec. Aug. 1977); children—Melanie Lynn, Geoffrey Brian. B.S. in Math., U. Minn.-Mpls., 1966, B.A. in Acctg., 1968, M.B.A. in Personnel and Fin. Mgmt., 1972. Bus. mgr., Earl Clinic, St. Paul, 1959-68, Lindquist & Vennum, Mpls., 1968-79, Stacker, Ravich & Simon, Mpls., 1979-82, Wagner, Johston & Falconer, Ltd., Mpls., 1983—; lectr. Inst. of Continuing Legal Edn., Mpls., 1977. Recipient Outstanding Achievement award in Bus. Young Women's Christian Assn., Mpls., 1978. Mem. Minn. Legal Adminstrs. Assn., Mensa. Avocations: bridge; reading. Home: 608 Queen Ave S Minneapolis MN 55405

ALLEY, NANCY PATRICIA, software engineer, consultant, corporate executive; b. Balt., July 7, 1957; d. Albin Warner and Dorothy Elizabeth (Schaeffer) Anderson; m. Ronald Dean Alley, Apr. 24, 1982. BS in Music Edn., Frostburg (Md.) State U., 1980; MS in Computer Sci., Bowie (Md.) State U., 1988. Software engr. Gould Inc./Martin Marietta, Inc., Glen Burnie, Md., 1984-89; software specialist Digital Equipment Corp., Landover, Md., 1989—; cons., pres. Optex Engr. Cons., Inc., Hanover, Md., 1984—. Radio officer Anne Arundel County Govt., Crownsville, 1989—. Recipient Eagles' Achievement award, 1990. Mem. IEEE, Amateur Radio Relay League (emergency coord. Newington, Conn. chpt. 1989—), Digital Equipment Corp. Users Group, Md. Mobileers Amateur Radio Club (sec. 1988-89), Anne Arundel Radio Club, Ft. Meade Radio Club, Delta Omicron (treas. 1978-79). Democrat. Lutheran. Home: 7506 Sandalwood Ct Hanover MD 21076-1535 Office: Digital Equipment Corp DC0/913 Landover MD 20784

ALLEY, PATRICIA MERRYMAN, bank executive; b. Lake Worth, Fla., May 22, 1943; d. Preston Eugene and Rachel (Gunter) Merryman; m. Robert L. Alley, Aug. 18, 1961; children: Katherine, Robert Jr., Patrick. Student, Indian River Community Coll., Fort Pierce, Fla. Mortgage sec.-teller First Fed. Savs. and Loan, Fort Pierce, 1969-75; mgmt. trainee Sun Bank of St. Lucie County, Fort Pierce, 1976-82; v.p., first lady rep. Riverside Nat. Bank, Fort Pierce, 1982—. Pres. Treasure Coast Crime Stoppers; active St. Lucie County Rep. Exec. Com.; trustee St. Lucie Community Theatre, treas.; Christmas Kids in July dance com. WIRA-FM. Mem. Ft. Pierce/St. Lucie County C. of C. (v.p.), Safespace St. Lucie County (bd. dirs.), CItrus Adminstrv. Com., Beta Sigma Phi. Home: 226 E Euclid St Fort Pierce FL 34946

ALLEYNE, BARBARA CHRISTINA, retail executive; b. Bridgetown, Barbados, Oct. 24, 1936; d. Percival and Chriscilda (Mullin) Bennett; 1 child, Eric. AA, Elizabeth Seton Coll., Yonkers, N.Y., 1978; BA in English, Marymount Coll., Tarrytown, 1981. With Community Svc. Soc., N.Y.C., 1962-64; exec. sec. YMCA of Greater N.Y., N.Y.C., 1964-72; adminstrv. asst. Ford Found., N.Y.C., 1972-86, Texaco Inc., White Plains, N.Y., 1975-86; contbns. asst. Texaco Philanthropic Found. of Texaco Inc., White Plains, 1987—; pres., owner Flick City, Inc., White Plains, 1986—; pres. The Texaco Forum, 1989. Vol. YMCA Greater N.Y.; founder, bd. dirs. Greenburgh 4-H Club, N.Y., 1978-80. Recipient Outstanding Svc. award YMCA Greater N.Y., 1970. Mem. Eta Phi Beta. Home: 24 Manitou Trail White Plains NY 10603

ALLF, NANCY LEE, lawyer; b. Hackensack, N.J., Feb. 1, 1957; d. George William and Juanita (Ballard) A.; m. John McNeill Jr., May 14, 1988 (div. Aug. 1990). BA, Transylvania U., 1979; JD, No. Ky. U., 1982. Bar: Nev. 1983, U.S. Dist. Ct. Nev. 1983, U.S. Ct. Appeals (9th cir.) 1984. Assoc. John C. Whelton Chtd., Las Vegas, Nev., 1982-84, John Peter Lee Ltd., Las Vegas, 1984—; instr. Clark County Community Coll., Las Vegas, 1985—. Bd. dirs. Planned Parenthood So. Nev., Las Vegas, 1986—. Mem. Clark County Bar Assn., Nev. Bar Assn., Nev. Assn. Trial Lawyers, So. Nev. Assn. of Women Attys. (v.p. 1989, polit. action com.), ABA, Assn. Trial Lawyers Am., Phi Alpha Delta. Democrat. Club: A.W.W. Home: 9737 Fern Canyon Ave Las Vegas NV 89117 Office: John Peter Lee Ltd 300 S Fourth St #1500 Las Vegas NV 89101

ALLIES, DONNA MARIE KITUN, public health nurse; b. N.Y.C., June 6, 1946; d. Michael and Mary (Bonner) Kitun; m. Mitchell Reed Allies, June 26, 1971; children: Cynthia Jennifer, Karen Elizabeth. BSN, NYU, 1968; MSN, UCLA, 1973. RN, Calif. Staff nurse L.A. County U. So. Calif. Med. Ctr., 1968-69, asst. head nurse L.A. County, 1969-71, mem. nursing faculty L.A. County, 1971-73; pvt. practice L.A. and San Jose, Calif., 1969-76; nursing cons. Foothill-Deanza Community Coll. Dist., Los Altos, Calif., 1975, instr. in nursing, 1975-76; pub. health nurse Santa Clara County Dept. Health, San Jose, 1976—; coord. sr. medication edn. program Santa Clara County Dept. Health, Sunnyvale, Calif., 1987—; owner Allies Assocs., San Jose, 1987—; conf. orgn. speaker Stanford (Calif.) Geriatric Edn. Ctr./Calif. Medication Edn. Coalition, 1989; bd. dirs., sec. Calif. Medication Edn. Coalition, San Francisco. Vol. tchr. Lyceum of Santa Clara Valley, San Jose, 1980—. Mem. ANA (del. 1977-78), AAUW (bd. dirs. 1986-89), Am. Pub. Health Assn., Calif. Pub. Health Assn., Calif. Nurses Assn., Calif. Medication Edn. Coalition (bd. dirs.), San Jose Assn. Univ. Women, Hypertension Coun. of Bay Area. Mem. Christian Reformed Ch. Home: 6428 Mojave Dr San Jose CA 95120-5306 Office: Santa Clara County Nursing 660 S Fairoaks Ave Sunnyvale CA 94086

ALLINGTON, GLORIA JEAN HAM, educational administrator; b. Northwood, N.D., May 21, 1945; d. John Henry Ham and Selma Tina (Haabak) Thorson; m. Gary Francis Allington, June 6, 1966 (div. May 1986). Student, U. N.D., 1963-66; ADN, Miami Dade Community Coll., 1968; BCS, U. Miami, 1976, MS in Edn., 1987. RN, Fla.; cert. meeting profl. Staff nurse Jackson Meml. Hosp., Miami, Fla., 1969-71, asst. head nurse, 1971-73; nurse educator U. Miami Sch. Medicine, 1973-75, adminstrv. asst., 1975-81, asst. dir. div. continuing med. edn., 1981, dir. div. continuing med. edn., 1981—. Contbr. articles to profl. jours. Exec. bd. dirs. Project Newborn, Miami, 1977-86; bd. dirs. Ronald McDonald House of So. Fla., Miami, 1977-82; mem. Zool. Soc. of South Fla., Miami, 1986—. Recipient James W. Colbert, Jr., M.D. award, Health Edn. Media Assn., 1977. Mem. Soc. Med. Coll. Dirs. of Continuing Med. Edn., Alliance for Continuing Med. Edn., Meeting Planners Internat. (internat. dir. 1986-88). Democrat. Roman Catholic. Office: U Miami Sch Medicine PO Box 016960 D23-3 Miami FL 33101

ALLISON, ANNE ELIZABETH, marketing consultant; b. Detroit, Mich., June 14, 1954; d. Douglas Futcher and Alice Margaret (Sellman) Allison. BA in Journalism, U. Ga., 1976; M of Internat. Mgmt., Am. Grad. Sch. Internat. Mgmt., Glendale, Ariz., 1978. Account exec. advt. firms, N.Y.C., 1979-84; product mgr. RJR Nabisco, Parsippany, N.J., 1984-85; founder, mng. dir. Allison Cons., N.Y.C. and Chgo., 1985—; adj. instr. Baruch College, N.Y.C., 1980-89, U. Ill., Chgo., 1990—; pub., dir. Great Dimensions Newsletter, N.Y.C., 1987—; pub. Maxima mag., N.Y.C., 1987-88. Mem. Jr. League of Chgo., 1977—; judge Gold Key awards, Incentive Mfrs. Rep. Assn., Chgo., 1990. Mem. Multiple Sclerosis City Soc., Am. Women's Econ. Devel., West Side Tennis Club. Republican. Presbyterian.

ALLISON, BONNIE J., state legislator; m. Ron Allison. State rep. State of Colo., from 1987, now state senator from dist. 21. Republican. *

ALLISON, JANE SHAWVER, medical school administrator, management consultant; b. San Angelo, Tex., Dec. 29, 1938; d. Floyd McKinzie and Bertha J. (Hicks) Shawver; m. Cecil Wayne Allison, June 22, 1957; children: Jana Lea, David Wayne, Don McKinzie. Student U. Denver, 1954, Northwestern U., 1955, Tex. Tech. U., 1956-57, Midwestern U., Wichita Falls, Tex., 1958. Continuity writer, Sta. KFDX-TV, Wichita Falls, Tex., 1957-58; sec. Wichita Falls Symphony, Tex., 1968-70; adminstrv. asst. Coll. of Bus. Tex. Tech U., Lubbock, 1971-74, coord. programs dept. family medicine Tex. Tech. U. Health Sci. Ctr., 1974-77, adminstr. dept. family medicine, 1978-87, clin. adminstrv. dir. dept. family medicine, 1987—; cons. Family Practice Residency, Amarillo, Tex., 1984, Temple, Tex., 1984-85. Bd. dirs. Lubbock Symphony Orch., Inc., 1976—, mem. nominating com., 1986, exec. com., 1987-88, v.p. 1988-89; bd. dirs. Helen A. Hodges Charitable Trust, Lubbock, 1983—; mem. Tex. Tech U. Coll. Bus. Adminstrn. Lubbock Council, 1988—. Recipient Superior Achievement award Tex. Tech U. Health Scis. Ctr., 1987, HSC award of Excellence Tex. Tech. U. Health Scis. Ctr., 1987; honoree 75th Birthday Celebration, Caprock Council Girl Scouts U.S. Mem. Med. Group Mgmt. Assn., Acad. Practice Assembly, Assn. Family Practice Adminstrs. (bd. dirs. 1985, 87, 88, charter pres. 1984, chmn. steering com. 1983). Mem. Disciples of Christ. Club: Soroptimist Internat. (pres. 1986-87, regional parlimentarian, 1986-88, regional laws and resolutions chmn. 1988-90.). Office: Tex Tech U Health Sci Ctr Dept Family Medicine Lubbock TX 79430

ALLISON, KAREN ANNE, special programs director; b. Detroit, June 6, 1958; d. William C. and Stephanie (Powch) Morris; m. David H. Allison. BA in Psychology, Calif. State U., Fullerton, 1981, MA in Psychology, 1983. Project analyst CompCare, Irvine, Calif., 1982-86; mkt. rsch. analyst Glenbeigh, Inc., Jupiter, Fla., 1986-87; dir. mktg. RehabCare Corp., Chesterfield, Mo., 1987-90; dir. spl. programs ARA Living Ctrs., Houston, 1990—. Mem. NAFE, Phi Kappa Phi. Office: ARA Living Ctrs 15415 Katy Frwy Ste 800 Houston TX 77042

ALLISON, LOYETTE E., construction company executive; b. Delano, Calif., July 7, 1946; d. Dempsey Willard and Billie Wanda (Fink) Bogard; m. Robert Lee, Nov. 30, 1963; children—Cindy Kay, Ann Rena. Student Pima Coll., 1979, U. Denver, 1983. Sales mgr. K-Mart, Tucson, 1975-78; clk.-typist Fairfield Green Valley, Ariz., 1978-81; purchasing agt. Tobin Homes, Tucson, 1981-83; constrn. mgr. Fairfield La Cholla Hills, Tucson, 1983-86; v.p. ops. Fairfield Sunrise, 1986—. Notary public State of Ariz; civic leader on behalf of women and community. Recipient Disting. Leadership award. Mem. Nat. Assn. Female Execs., Am. Bus. Inst. (2000 notable women, Disting. Service award). Baptist. Avocations: stock car racing; aerobics, modern dance. Home: 2151 W Felicia Pl Tucson AZ 85741 Office: Fairfield La Cholla Hills 8700 N La Cholla Blvd Tucson AZ 85741

ALLISON, MELISSA LYNN, lawyer; b. Hagerstown, Md., Mar. 13, 1961. BA magna cum laude, Duke U., Durham, N.C., 1983; JD cum laude, U. Pa. Law Sch., 1988. Legal asst. Venable Baltjer and Howard, Balt., 1984-85; law clerk Piper & Marbury, Balt., 1986, Shapiro & Olander, Balt., 1987, Bazelon, Less & Frice, Phila., 1987-88; attorney Shapiro and Olander, 1988--; vol. Phila. Vol. Lawyers for the Arts, 1987-88; mem. atty. Md. Lawyers for the Arts, Balt., 1989. Contbr. article to profl. jours., 1989. Recipient

Samuel Gerstley Award U. Pa. Law Sch., Phila. 1988. Mem. Md. State Bar Assn., Bar Assn. Balt. City, Duke Club Balt.

ALLISON, PAMELA SUSAN, nurse; b. Chattanooga, Nov. 21, 1950; d. William Kenneth Jones and Helen Katie (Garner) Jones Allison; adopted d. William B. Allison; m. Larry Wayne Thomas, July 6, 1968 (div. Mar. 1981); 1 child, William Forrest; m. Michael Sean O'Flaherty, Oct. 1, 1983. Cert. critical care RN Nursing Baptist Coll. at Charleston, 1978; MSW, Med. U. S.C., 1990. RN, S.C. Cardiothoracic clinician surg. ICU, Med. U. S.C., Charleston, 1978-82; nurse intensive care and cardiac care Trident Regional Med. Ctr., Charleston, 1982-85; instr. advanced cardiac life support Am. Heart Assn., Charleston, 1983—; clin. applications specialist, cons., Baxter-Am. Edwards Critical Care Div., 1987—; cons. Area Health Edn. Consortium, Walterboro, S.C., 1983—. Mem. Am. Assn. Critical Care Nurses. Home: 2430 Pristine View Charleston SC 29407

ALLISON, STACY MARIE, construction executive, speaker; b. Pocatello, Idaho, Oct. 18, 1958; d. James Lawrence and Carole Jean A. Student, Oregon State U., 1976-78. Owner Austin Enterprises, Springdale, Utah, 1982-86, Stacy Allison, Gen. Contracting, Portland, Oreg., 1986-88; speaker Portland, 1988—. Contbr. articles to Am. Alpine Jour. Mem. Bus. & Prof. Women (hon. 1989), Adventures Club. First Am. woman to climb Mt. Everest, 1988. Home and Office: 7431 N Foss Portland OR 97203

ALLISON, SUSAN KATHERINE, buyer; b. Hollywood, Calif., June 10, 1955; d. Carroll Wood and Barbara Lee (Pierce) A. AA in Liberal Arts, Glendale Coll., 1987; BA, Calif. State U., L.A., 1989. Dept. supr. Wal Mart, Hot Springs, Ark., 1972-73; personal asst. Elizabeth King and Assocs., Hot Springs, 1972-73; customer service rep. GAF Photo Service, Los Angeles, 1974-75; purchasing asst. Joy Mfg. Co., Los Angeles, 1975-78; buyer ops. dept. CBS TV Network, Los Angeles, 1978-84; contract negotiator Los Angeles Olympic Orgn. Commn., 1984-85; cons. in materials mgmt. Glendale, Calif., 1985—; promotional news radio hostess Sta. KNX-CBS Inc., Los Angeles, 1985-89. Editor Torchlight newspaper, 1972, Historical Tour guide book, 1986. Mem. Glendale Hist. Soc., 1986-88; cons. Women's Council Verdugo Hills Hosp., Glendale, 1985-86. Mem. Olympic Alumni Assn., Los Angeles Women's Entertainment League, Los Angeles Advt. Softball League, Nat. Trust Hist. Preservation, Alpha Gamma Sigma. Republican. Episcopalian. Office: PO Box 9013 Glendale CA 91206

ALLMAND, LINDA F(AITH), library director; b. Port Arthur, Tex., Jan. 31, 1937; d. Clifton James and Jewel Etoile (Smith) A. B.A., North Tex. State U., 1960; M.A., U. Denver, 1962. Clerical asst. Gates Meml. Library, 1953-55; library asst. Houston Pub. Library, 1955-58; children's librarian Denver Pub. Library, 1960-63; children's coordinator Anaheim Pub. Library, Calif., 1963-65; br. mgr. Dallas Pub. Library, 1965-71; instr. North Tex. State U., Denton, 1967—; chief br. services Dallas Pub. Library, 1971-81; dir. Ft. Worth Pub. Library, 1981—; instr. Dallas County Community Coll., 1981; bldg. cons. Jacksonville Pub. Library, Tex., 1976-79, Haltom City Pub. Library, 1983-85, Carrollton Pub. Library, 1979-81, Hurst Pub. Library, 1977-78, Dallas Pub. Library, 1974-80. Author: 1981-2000, Ft. Worth Public Library—Facilities and Long-Range Planning Study, 1982; contbr. chpts. to books, articles to profl. jours. Bd. dirs. City of Dallas Credit Union, 1973-81; com. chmn. Goals for Dallas, 1967-69; mem. Forum Ft. Worth, 1983; bd. dirs. Sr. Citizen's Centers, Inc., 1982. Pilot Club of Port Arthur scholar, 1954; Library Binding Inst. scholar, 1958; recipient Disting. Alumnus award North Tex. State U., 1983, Leadership Ft. Worth, 1982-83; named Tarrant County Newsmaker of Yr., 1984, Outstanding leader, Ft. Worth Star Telegram, 1989, Outstanding Woman of Yr., Mayor's Commn. on Status of Women, 1989. Mem. ALA, Tex. Library Assn. (pres. pub. library div. 1980-81, chmn. planning com. 1982-84, Librarian of Yr. award 1985; pres.-elect 1985-86, pres. 1986-87), Tarrant Regional Librarians Assn., Am. Mgmt. Assn., Dallas County Librarians Assn. (pres. 1968-69), Freedom to Read Found., Rotary Club (Ft. Worth). Home: 701 Timberview Ct N Fort Worth TX 76112 Office: Fort Worth Pub Libr 300 Taylor St Fort Worth TX 76102-7309

ALLMON, SANDRA RAE, electronics executive; b. Lawrence, Kans., Dec. 27, 1942; d. Theodore Roosevelt and Thelma Jane (Willis) A. AA, Pitts. (Kans.) State U., 1968, Ottawa (Kans.) U., 1986; BS, Saint Mary Coll., Leavenworth, Kans., 1987; postgrad., Avila U., 1989—. Inspector AT&T Microelectronics, Lees Summit, Mo., 1966-78, supr., 1979—, sec., 1988—; order filler Sears Roebuck and Co., Kans. City, Mo., 1976-78; dept. coord. Evangelistic Ctr., Kans. City, Kans., 1980—, tchr., 1988—; tutor Saint Mary Coll., 1987—; speaker Rosedale Middle Sch., Kans. City, Kans., 1989. Author: Issues Involving Singles, 1985—. Aid United Negro Coll. Fund, Kans. City, Kans., 1987; vol. Bethany Hosp., Kans. City, Kans., 1975; coord. Kans. East Women's Dept., 2988; missionary Evangelistic Ctr. Ch., 1986—. Recognized for outstanding leadership Kans. East Women's Dept., 1988-89. Mem. Black Telecommunications Workers, Am. Mgmt. Assn., Single Adult Group (coord. 1987—). Home: 6660 Cleveland Kansas City KS 66104

ALLMOND, FRANCES IRENE, company associate; b. Wilmington, Del., Aug. 29, 1931; d. Francis John and Helen Mary (Kanicki) Oliphant; m. Charles Musgrove Allmond III, May 2, 1953; children: Bayard Wheeler III, Sarah Oliphant Allmond Long. BS, U. Del., 1953; travel agt. cert., Del. Tech. and Community Coll., 1987. Technician E.I. duPont de Nemours & Co., Wilmington, 1953-56; substitute tchr. pub. schs. State of Del., Wilmington, 1971-77; tour guide Hist. Soc. Del., Wilmington, 1977-88, Nemours Mansion, A.I. duPont Inst., Wilmington, 1977-88; with coordinating/decorating studio J.C. Penney Co., Wilmington, 1988-89; customer svc. rep. Barry Cos., Wilmington, 1989; adminstrv. asst. ICI Americas, Inc., Wilmington, Del., 1989—. Editor: First State, First Lady's Recipe Book, 1975, Grand Recipes, 1983. Active Hist. Soc. Del., Del. Art Mus., Rehoboth Art League, Mt. Pleasant Sch. Dist. PTA, 1965-76, Grace Episc. Ch., Wilmington, 1950—; vol. docent Winterthur Mus. and Gardens, 1964-76; bd. dirs. Wilmington Flower Market, Inc., 1972-78, 80-81, chmn. bd., 1974; bd. dirs. Del. Arthritis Found., 1983-86, sec., 1984-86; trustee Lombardy Hall Found., 1986—; pres. Grand Opera House Guild, 1979-81; bd. dirs. Grand Opera House, 1979-81; v.p. Del. Revolutionary War Forum, 1975-77; governing bd. Friends Performing Arts, 1980-89, sec., 1987-89; mem. Libr. Assocs., 1955—, v.p., bd. dirs., 1985—, bishop's diocesan coun., 1987-90, lic. lay reader, 1983—; sr. warden vestry, 1983-85, trustee endowment fund, 1985-89. Mem. AAUW (scholarship com. 1965-67), U. Del. Alumni Assn. (class rep. 1953—, bd. dirs. 1983-85), DAR, U. Del. Human Resources Alumni Assn. (scholarship com. 1981), U. Del. Libr. Assocs. (bd. dirs. 1985—, v.p. 1986—). Democrat. Home: 104 Rowland Park Blvd Wilmington DE 19803

ALLOWAY, ANNE MAUREEN SCHUBERT, industrial waste administrator; b. Martinez, Calif., Mar. 19, 1954; d. James Benjamin and Mariel Ann (Phillips) Schubert; divorced; children: Joseph Benjamin, Odinn Glenn, Aaron Dean. AS in Life Sci., Allan Hancock Coll., 1982, AA in Liberal Arts, 1982. Cert. indsl. waste insp., 1984. Indsl. waste insp. City of Santa Maria (Calif.), 1984-86; mgr. indsl. pretreatment program, collection systems Simi Valley (Calif.) County Sanitation Dist., 1986-88, state pub. edn. com., indsl. hazardous waste com. Chair City Simi Valley Hazardous Materials Mgmt. Task Force; sec., chmn. Tri Counties Voluntary Cert. Com, State Voluntary Cert. Com., Tri Counties Pub. Edn.; indsl./hazardous waste com., pub. edn. com. Calif. Water Pollution Control Assn., sect. chmn. edn., 1986-89, Water Pollution Control Fedn. Mem. Ventura County Hazardous Waste Mgmt. (adv. com. bd. supr.), Hazardous Waste Assn. Calif., Hazardous Materials Control Rsch. Inst. Recipient Merit award Industrial Waste Inspection Tech., 1986, Disting. Leadership award, 1987. Mem. Coast and Valley Health Club, Keepers of the Flame. Republican. Roman Catholic. Home: 1807 Gaviota St Simi Valley CA 93065 Office: Simi Valley County Sanitation Dist 500 W Los Angeles Ave Simi Valley CA 93065

ALLPHIN, HELEN LOUISE, accountant; b. Winfield, Tenn., Dec. 13, 1946; d. Elmon L. and Kathleen (Posey) Stephens; m. John W. Allphin, Feb. 12, 1965; children: Stephen W., Brian L. Student, Richland Coll., Dallas. Sr. acctg. clk. Varo, Inc., Garland, Tex., 1972-74, 76; with acctg. dept. Accelerated Christian Edn., Lewisville, Tex., 1978-80; acctg. asst. Delta Chems., Dallas, 1980-85; bus. mgr. White Rock Radiology Assn., Dallas, 1985—. Mem. NAFE, Radiologists' Bus. Mgrs. Assn. Home: 2509 Sam Houston Dr Garland TX 75044 Office: PO Box 180065 Dallas TX 75218

ALLRED, RITA REED, artist; b. Davenport, Iowa, Apr. 12, 1935; d. Edward Platt and Delia Marie (Quinn) Reed; m. Glenn Charles Scott, June 9, 1956 (div. Nov. 1977); children: Sheryl Marie, Laura Ann; m. Robert Yates Allred, Dec. 9, 1977. Student Marycrest Coll., Davenport, 1953-56; BS in Art Edn., Drake U., 1958. Art tchr. Fayetteville City Schs., N.C., 1961-64, Charlotte-Mecklenburg Schs., N.C., 1967-71; cons., project dir. PCA Internat., Matthews, N.C., 1981; artist, art cons. Rita Reed Allred & Assocs., Charlotte, 1972—, dir. workshops, 1976—; civilian artist USCG, 1981—; instr. portrait painting Cen. Piedmont Community Coll., 1986—; painter in oils; recent commns. include paintings for U.S. Army, USCG, portraits for ABCO Industries, U.S. Naval Inst. Service Head Portrait Series; pres. Willow Reed Studios, 1986—. Bd. dirs. Internat. House, Charlotte, 1985-86; mem. Sister Cities Com., Charlotte, 1984-85, NASA Art Team. Recipient George Gray award USCG, 1983. Democrat. Mem. Internat. Platform Assn., Cedarwood Country Club. Avocation: golf. Home and Studio: 7217 Quail Meadow Ln Charlotte NC 28210 Office: Willow Reed Studios 10811 Pineville Rd Pineville NC 28134

ALLSUP, JUDITH ANN, auditor; b. Pueblo, Colo., Apr. 9, 1959; d. Richard W. and Patricia A. (Whitmore) A. BA in Acctg. summa cum laude, Ft. Lewis Coll., 1981. CPA, Colo. From staff auditor to sr. auditor Grant Thornton (formerly Fox & Co.), Colorado Springs, Colo., 1981-84; audit mgr. Affiliated Bankshares Colo., Greeley, 1984—. Mem. AICPA, NAFE, Colo. Soc. CPAs (vol. mem. career edn. com. 1987-89, Gold Key Acctg. award 1981). Home: 1412 7th St Greeley CO 80631

ALLTOP, JANE ELIZABETH, software engineer; b. Ridgecrest, Calif., May 4, 1963; d. William O'Bannon Alltop and Helen (Seidensticker) Tubbs. BS, U. Calif., Santa Barbara, 1985. Software engr., systems engr. Hughes Aircraft Co., Rancho Santa Margarita, Calif., 1985—. Democrat. Presbyterian. Home: 521 San Nicholas Ct Laguna Beach CA 92651 Office: Hughes Aircraft 29947 Avenida las Banderas Rancho Santa Margarita CA 92688

ALMAN, EMILY ARNOW, sociologist, lawyer; b. N.Y.C., Jan. 20, 1922; d. Joseph Michael and Cecilia (Greenstone) Arnow; B.A., Hunter Coll., 1948; Ph.D., New Sch. for Social Research, 1963; J.D., Rutgers U., Newark, 1977; m. David Alman, Aug. 1, 1940; children—Michelle Alman Harrison, Jennifer Alman Michaels. Probation officer, N.Y.C., 1945-48; assoc. prof. sociology Douglass Coll. Rutgers U., Newark, 1960-86, prof. emeritus, 1986—; admitted to N.J. bar, 1978; individual practice law, Highland Park, N.J., 1978—. Candidate for mayor, City of East Brunswick, 1972; chmn. Concerned Citizens of East Brunswick, 1970-78; pres. bd. trustees Concerned Citizens Environ. Fund., East Brunswick, 1977-78. Mem. Am., N.J. Middlesex County bar assns., Am. Sociol. Assn., Assn. Fed. Bar State of N.J., Assn. Trial Lawyers Am., Trial Lawyers Assn. Middlesex County, Law and Soc. Assn., Am. Judicature Soc., Nat. Assn. Women Lawyers, N.J. Assn. Women Lawyers, ACLU, AAUP, Women Helping Women. Author: Ride The Long Night, 1963; screenplay, The Ninety-First Day, 1963. Home: 611 S Park Ave Highland Park NJ 08904

ALMEIDA, VICTORIA MARTIN, lawyer; b. Pawtucket, R.I., Oct. 9, 1951; d. Antonio Sanches And Lillian (Martin) A. BA, Salve Regina Coll., Newport, R.I., 1973; JD, Suffolk U., 1976. Bar: Mass. 1976, R.I. 1976, U.S. Dist. Ct. R.I. 1976, U.S. Ct. Appeals (1st cir.) Mass. 1984, U.S. Supreme Ct. 1987. Law clk. to sr. assoc. justice R.I. Supreme Ct., Providence, 1976; asst. legal counsel to gov. Gov.'s Office, Providence, 1977-82; assoc. Gunning, LaFazia & Gnys, Inc., Providence, 1980-87, Adler Pollock & Sheehan, Inc., Providence, 1987—; mem. R.I. Parole Bd., Providence, 1984—. Chairperson bd. trustees R.I. chpt. Nat. Multiple Sclerosis Soc., Cranston, 1989—; mem. corp. Roger Williams Coll., Bristol, R.I., 1977—; mem. devel. com. St. Mary Acad.-Bay View, East Providence, R.I., 1988—; mem. retirement fund for religious Roman Catholic Diocese of Providence, 1988—. Named Woman of Yr., Prince Henry Club, 1977; recipient Disting. Alumna award St. Mary Acad.-Bay View, 1982, appreciation award Am. Cancer Soc., 1979. Mem. R.I. Bar Assn. (legal assts com., young lawyers clerkship com. 1985—), Am. Arbitration Assn. (panel of arbitrators 1984—). Democrat. Office: Adler Pollock & Sheehan Inc 2300 Hosp Trust Tower Providence RI 02903

ALMLIE, LINDA LEE, real estate broker; b. Clinton, Iowa, Dec. 7, 1945; d. Laurence Edward and Virginia (Michael) Olds; m. Joseph Kirk Williams Jr., May 16, 1964 (div. Oct. 1972); children: Virginia Michelle, Dawn Christina; m. Michael Kent Almlie, Apr. 4, 1975. AA in Real Estate with honors, Butte Coll., 1978. Unit sec., engr. Boeing Corp., 1964-68; acctg. sec. Columbia Records, Santa Maria, Calif., 1969-73; purchasing sec. Multi-unit Corp., Ontario, Calif., 1973-74; legal sec. Colo. State's Attys. Office, Boulder, 1974-77, Colo. Attys. Office, Chico, 1978-89; owner, real estate broker Linda Almlie Realtor, Chico, 1989—. Leader, lectr. Weight Watchers Internat., Chico, 1988-89; chmn. Easter Seals Soc., Chico, 1978-79; ambassador Chico C. ofC., 1980. Republican. Episcopalian. Office: 1458 Esplanade Ste 3 Chico CA 95926

ALMOND, JOAN, chemistry educator; b. Bklyn., May 19, 1934; d. Harry Christian Nintzel and Helen Pauline (Diviak) Levesen; m. Randall Leroy Field Sr., Nov. 15, 1952 (div. Feb. 1972); children: Randall Leroy Jr., Roland, Gary, Brian, Lorraine, Thomas; m. Bransford Wayne Almond, Dec. 9, 1986. Grad. high sch., Bklyn. Sec. Fulton Savs. Bank, Bklyn., 1952-53; mgr. reprodn. Air Pre-heater Corp., Wellsville, N.Y., 1958; chemistry technician fibers div. Allied Chem., Hopewell, Va., 1963-76; chemistry technician Va. Power Co.-North Anna Power Sta., Mineral, 1976-86, assoc. instr., 1987—. Recipient Cert. Achievement Nat. Acad. for Nuclear Tng., 1988. Mem. Women of Moose (chair Moosehart Hopewell com. chpt. 1971). Roman Catholic. Office: Va Power Co-North Anna Power Sta Box 402 Mineral VA 23114

ALMORE, MARY G., social psychology educator; b. Pitts., Sept. 23, 1932; d. George Peter and Virginia (Thompson) A.; m. Richard Sexton, Oct. 1952 (div. 1955). BS cum laude, Fla. State U., 1955, MS, 1956; MS, Fla. State U., 1958; PhD, Tex. Christian U., 1971. Lic. sch. counselor, Tex. Instr. social scis. Jacksonville (Fla.) U., 1957-59; asst. probation officer Dallas County Juvenile Dept., Dallas, 1960-63; home-sch. coord. Dallas Ind. Sch. Dist., 1963-65; asst. prof., then assoc. prof. psychology Tex. Wesleyan U., Ft. Worth, 1965-73; assoc. prof. urban studies Inst. Urban Studies/U. Tex., Arlington, 1973-86, dir. criminal justice programs, 1974-77; assoc. prof. social psychology U. Tex., Arlington, 1986—, grad. adviser criminal justice program, 1989—; casework coord. Dallas County Inter-Agy. Project, 1963-65; cons. Ft. Worht Human Rels. Commn., 1970-73, chair, 1972-73; cons. teen jury project Human Resources Ctr./United Way Tarrant County, Arlington, 1985-86; rsch. adv. com. Fed. Correctional Instn., Ft. Worth, 1985-87. Contbr. to profl. publs. Mem. subcom. Goals for East Ft. Worth, 1989-90. Fellow Am. Orthopsychiat. Assn.; mem. Am. Psychol. Assn., Am. Soc. Criminology, Assn. for Advancement of Psychology, Law and Soc. Assn., Hastings Ctr., Inst. Criminal Justice Ethics, Phi Kappa Phi, Psi Chi. Office: U Tex Arlington PO Box19599 Arlington TX 76019-0599

ALMY, MARION MARABLE, archaeologist; b. Sarasota, Fla., Dec. 5, 1946; d. Marshall Edward and Ethel Virginia (Yentner) Marable; m. Richard Ernest Almy, June 22, 1968; children: Maranda Marable Almy, Rachael Elaine Almy. BA in Anthropology, Fla. State U., 1968; postgrad., U. Mo., 1969-71; MA in Anthropology, U. South Fla., 1976. Cert. in field archaeology Soc. Profl. Archaeologists. Archaeologist, cultural resource survey coord. Little Salt Spring Rsch. Facility, North Port, Fla., 1974-75; sr. site archaeologist Fla. Dept. of State, 1975-76; pres. Archaeological Consultants, Inc., Sarasota, Fla., 1976—; instr. archaeology Manatee Community Coll., Manatee and Sarasota Counties, Fla., 1987—; mem. Fla. Hist. Preservation Adv. Coun., 1987—, chmn., 1989-90. Contbr. articles to Fla. Anthropologist, 1976-89; co-author pamphlet on archeol. laws in Fla., 1989. Vice chmn. City of Sarasota Planning Bd., 1990; chmn. Sarasota County Hist. Commn., 1988-90; supr. Sarasota Soil and Water Conservation Dist., 1987—; sustainer Jr. League Sarasota, 1989—; mem. citizens adv. com. Sarasota Bay Project, Nat. Estuary Program, 1989—, LWV, Sarasota, 1990—; bd. dirs. South Fla. Mus., Brandenton, 1989—. Project RENEW grantee Sarasota br. AAUW, 1975. Mem. Fla. Women's Alliance, Fla. Anthrop. Soc. (pres. 1982-83, Outstanding Svc. 1988), Fla. Trust for Hist. Preservation, Fla. Archaeological Coun. (pres. 1990-92), Time Sifters Archaeological Soc. (bd. dirs. 1988-91), Altrusa Club Sarasota.

ALPERIN, GOLDIE GREEN, consulting librarian, lawyer; b. Des Moines, Aug. 16, 1905; d. Morris and Bessie (Miliwer) Green; LL.B., Drake U., 1927; m. Moses Alperin, Dec. 25, 1930 (dec. 1950); children—Herschel Burton, Judith Miriam. Admitted to Iowa bar, 1927, U.S. Supreme Ct. bar, 1959; practice in Des Moines, 1927-30; law librarian Chgo. Bar. Assn., 1951-63; dir. Def. Information Office, Chgo., 1963-65; librarian book selections Northwestern U. Law Sch. Library, 1966-72; ret., 1972. Named one of 20 rep. U.S. women lawyers of various phases practice Women's Adjustment Bd., London, Eng., 1957; One of Outstanding Women of Am. Bicentennial, Austin (Tex.) Bicentennial Com., 1976; cert. religious sch. tchr. Bd. Jewish Edn., Chgo., 1951. Mem. Am. (sec. 1960-65), Chgo. (past exec. bd., editor 1958-59) assns. law libraries, Nat. Assn. Women Lawyers (regional) dir. 1960-64). Jewish religion. Asst. editor Women Lawyers Jour., 1961-67, exec. bd., 1961-67. Home: 3100 Lake Shore Dr #1512 Chicago IL 60657

ALPER KRAMER, LORRAINE, advertising executive; b. N.Y.C., Feb. 15, 1949; d. Sidney M. Alper and Evelyn Roslyn (Bercowitz) Opat; m. Bruce Kramer, May 7, 1979; children: Casey, Jeremy, Samantha. BA, Hofstra U., 1970. Adminstrv. asst. Kenyon & Eckhardt, N.Y.C., 1970-71; asst. to pres. Storck & Fitzgerald, N.Y.C., 1971-72; mgr. advt. Kayser-Roth, N.Y.C., 1972-74; mgr. print prodn. The Advt. Agy., L.A., 1974-76, D'Arcy MacManius Masius, L.A., 1976-81; v.p., dir. print prodn. and traffic BBDO, L.A., 1981-90, sr. v.p., creative svcs. dir., 1990—. Mem. Advt. Prodn. Assn. So. Calif. Democrat. Jewish. Office: BBDO West 10960 Wilshire Blvd Los Angeles CA 90024

ALPERN, LINDA LEE WEVODAU, health agency administrator; b. Harrisburg, Pa., July 16, 1949; d. William Irvin Wevodau and Maretia Christine (Mills) Staley; m. Neil Stephen Alpern, Apr. 12, 1985; 1 child, Philip Wevodau. BS in Edn., Shippensburg (Pa.) U., 1971. Unit program coord. Pa. Div. Am. Cancer Soc., Harrisburg, 1973-75, unit exec. dir., 1975-76, div. svc. dir., 1976-81; div. med. affairs dir. Pa. Div. Am. Cancer Soc., Hershey, 1981-83; div. crusade dir. Md. Div. Am. Cancer Soc., Balt., 1983-87, div. v.p. for field ops., 1988, div. dep., exec. v.p. ops., 1988—. Mem. AAUW (publicity chair 1983). Democrat. Methodist. Home: 4108 Colonial Rd Baltimore MD 21208

ALPERN, MILDRED, history educator, consultant; b. Boston, Sept. 10, 1931; d. Samuel and Mary (Poncewicz) Rosoff; m. Hale Nissen Alpern, Aug. 27, 1954; children—Merry, Spenser. BA, Boston U., 1953; MA summa cum laude, Columbia U., 1966. Cert. tchr. social studies. Tchr. history Spring Valley (N.Y.) Sr. High Sch., 1966—; adj. instr. Rockland Community Coll., Suffern, N.Y., 1973-76; instr. Manhattan Coll., Riverdale, N.Y., summers 1983, 84, 85, 87, LaSalle Coll, summer 1988, Columbia U. Tchrs. Coll., 1988; mem. advanced placement European history test devel. com., Coll. Bd. 1979-82, chmn. 1982-86, mem. Coll. Bd. history and social scis. adv. com., 1983-85, chmn., 1985-88, chmn. acad. adv. coun., 1987-89; master tchr. summer inst. Sarah Lawrence Coll., Bronxville, N.Y., 1984; mem. faculty Coll. Bd. Project Equality Inst., 1986, 87. Co-editor (history column) Am. Hist. Assn. Perspectives, 1982-88; co-author (teaching guide) Household and Kin, 1981; contbr. articles to profl. publs. Recipient award for contbns. in edn. Rockland County Women's Network, 1984; Finalist N.Y. State Tchr. of Yr., 1988; Fulbright Commn. study grantee, Italy, 1980, NEH grantee Tufts U., 1983. Mem. Orgn. Am. Historians (chmn. teaching div. 1982-83), Am. Hist. Assn. (teaching div.), Phi Beta Kappa, Pi Gamma Mu. Democrat. Home: 13 Cragmere Rd Suffern NY 10901 Office: Spring Valley Sr High Sch Rt 59 Spring Valley NY 10977

ALQUILAR, MARIA, artist; b. Bklyn., May 25, 1938; d. Samuel and Bessie (Aronson) A.; m. Frank Taffet, June 1959 (dec. Nov. 1973); children: Gilda, Francine, Paul. AB, Hunter Coll., 1959; postgrad., Calif. State U., Sacramento, 1965. Case worker Dept. Social Welfare State of Calif., 1960; elem. and univ. tchr. State of Calif., Sacramento, 1962-70; owner, dir. Jennifer Pauls Gallery, Sacramento, 1973-87. Exhibited in shows at Renwick Gallery, Smithsonian Inst., Washington, 1982, Downey (Calif.) Mus., 1982, 83, 87, Richmond (Calif.) Art Ctr., 1985, Las Vegas Mus., 1984, 85, Monterey (Calif.) Peninsula Mus. Art, 1987, Palo Alto (Calif.) Cultural Ctr., 1989, Art Corridor, Menlo Park, Calif., 1988, othrs; represented in collections at Nat. Gallery Art, Washington, Chase Manhattan Bank, N.Y.C., San Francisco Arts Commn., Sacramento Met. Arts Commn., Kohler (Wis.) Co., Downey Mus. Recipient numerous awards and commns., including art for Water and Sewer Adminstrn. Bldg., Sacramento, 1985, U.S.A. Gen. Svc. Adminstrn., Art-in-Arch, Port of Entry, San Luis, Arz., San Jose Internat. Airport, 1990, Ariz. State U., Tempe, 1990. Home and Studio: 703 Darwin St Santa Cruz CA 95062

ALSCHER, RUTH GRENE, plant physiology educator; b. Chgo., July 17, 1943; d. William David and Marjorie (Glicksman) Grene; m. Lee W. Herman, Nov. 29, 1979 (div. Aug. 1984); children: Nicholas, Lucy. BA, Trinity Coll., 1965; MA, Washington U., 1968; PhD, U. Calif., Davis, 1972. Rsch. assoc. Boyce Thompson Inst., Ithaca, N.Y., 1979-88; adj. asst. prof. Cornell U., Ithaca, 1985-88; rsch. assoc. N.Y. State Agrl. Exptl. Sta., Geneva, N.Y., 1977-79; assoc. prof. plant physiology Va. Tech., Blacksburg, 1988—. Editor: Stress Responses in Plants, 1990; contbr. articles to profl. jours. Governing bd. Women's Network, Va. Tech., 1990; v.p. Cornell U. chpt. Women in Sci., 1984-85; v.p. for programs AAUW, Ithaca, 1983-84. Recipient Nat. Rsch. Svc. award NIH, 1972, 75; NSF grantee Cornell U., 1985-87, grantee U.S.Forest Svc., Va. Tech., 1985—. Mem. Am. Soc. Plant Physiologists, AAAS. Jewish. Office: Va Tech Plant Pathology Physiology Blacksburg VA 24061

ALSTON, BETTYE JO, clergywoman, nurse; b. Memphis, Dec. 17, 1938; d. Thomas L. and Bettie Marie (Golden) Harris; m. Neasbie Alston, Nov. 29, 1980; children: Donna, Robin, Bernetta, Lissa, Karen, Nataline, Rebecca, Neasbie Jr. AA, Memphis State U., 1969; MDiv cum laude, Memphis Theol. Sem., 1984; D Ministry, St. Paul Sch. Theology, Kansas City, Mo., 1986; PhD in Counseling Psychology, Emmanuel Bapt. U., 1990. RN, Tenn. Nursing supr. John Gaston Hosp., Memphis, 1969-78; nurse recruiter W.F. Bowld Hosp., U. Tenn. Coll. Health Scis., Memphis, 1978-81; dir. nursing Collins Chapel Health Care Ctr., Memphis, 1981-82; asst. adminstr. North Memphis Home Health Agy., 1982-84; pastor Brown Chapel A.M.E. Ch., Memphis, 1977-88; pastor, founder New Beginning Ch., Memphis, 1988—; staff adviser, counselor Regional Med. Ctr., Memphis, 1987-89; dir. nursing spl. svcs. Regional Med. Ctr., 1989—; with West Tenn. Audit Conf., Memphis, 1974-78. Author poetry and devotionals. Mem. Leadership Memphis, 1990-91. Named Outstanding Pastor Memphis A.M.E. Ch., 1982, Disting. African Am. Alumnae, Memphis Theol. Sem., 1990. Mem. Tenn. Nurses Assn., Exec. Female, Interdenominational Women Ministerial Alliance (pres. 1989—), Alston Family Evangelistic Assn. (v.p., exec. dir. 1981—), Nat. Coun. Negro Women, Ch. Women United, Toastmasters. Democrat. Office: Regional Med Ctr 877 Jefferson Memphis TN 38103

ALSTON, CHERYL ANN, small business owner; b. Joliet, Ill., June 24, 1946; d. Frank O. and Ruth M. (Barger) Anderson; 1 child, Jennifer L. BS in Psychology, U. Ill., 1970; MA in Psychology, U. No. Colo., 1984; postgrad., Calif. Poly. Inst. Dir. fin. aid, instr. Orange Coast Community Coll., Costa Mesa, Calif., 1974-76; dir. fin. aid Arapahoe Community Coll., Littleton, Colo., 1980-85; cons. Nat. Assn. Student Fin. Aid Adminstrs., Washington, 1985-86; chief exec. officer, pres. Alston Coll. Cons. Svcs., Inc., Fairfax, Va., 1986—; chief exec. officer FREES, Inc. Mem. NAFE, NOW, Nat. Fedn. Ind. Businesses, Nat. Soc. Pub. Accts., Accts. Soc. Va., Nat. Soc. Noetic Scis., Better Bus. Bur., C. of C., Kiwanis (treas. 1987). Democrat. Mem. Unity Ch. Office: Alston Coll Cons Svcs Inc 10501 Braddock Rd Ste 203 Fairfax VA 22032

ALSTON, DORIS FAYE, secondary school educator; b. Marlin, Tex., Jan. 12, 1934; d. Clifton George and Ella Mae (Kenny) Jennings; married, 1955; children: Michael, Angelica, Michele, Melora Anne. BS, Prairie View U., 1955. Tchr. USAF GED Program, Munich, Germany, 1957-59, Rhine Main AFB, Germany, 1959-60; tchr. Washington Pub. Sch., 1961-69, Northern Burlington Regional Sch., Columbus, N.J., 1969—. Mem. Nat. Edn. Assn. State and Local Affiliates. Democrat. Office: Northern Burlington Sch Georgetown Mansfield Rd Columbus NJ 08060

ALSTON, FRANCINE ANN-CATHERINE, infosystems company executive; b. Ely, Minn., Dec. 23, 1962; d. Gregory Joseph and Julie Kathryn

(Fink) K. AA, Mesabi Community Coll., 1983; BS, Mankato State U., 1985. Acct. computer sci. Electronic Data Systems Corp., Dallas, 1985-87; systems engr. Electronic Data Systems Corp., Sarasota, Fla., 1987-89; systems engr. supr. Electronic Data Systems Corp., Plano, Tex., 1989—. Mem. Inst. Cert. Mgmt. Accts., Nat. Assn. Female Execs.

ALSTON, JOANIE DELORIS, nursing administrator; b. Franklin County, N.C., Jan. 18, 1955; d. John Ned and Beulah Mae (Evans) A.; 1 child, Sheena Antoinette. Diploma in nursing, Phila. Gen. Hosp., 1977; BS, La Salle U., Phila., 1989; postgrad., Phila. Coll. Textiles and Scis., 1989—. RN, Pa., N.C. Asst. dir. nursing Care Pavillion, Phila., 1982-83; dir. nursing South Care Nursing Ctr., Phila., 1982-83, Willow Crest Bamberger, Phila., 1988; supr. Bayada Nurses Inc., Phila., 1983-89; dir. nursing Tucker House, Phila., 1989—; mktg. researcher Quest Enterprises, Broomall, Pa., 1985—; community health nurse Caring/Home Cross, Phila., 1988—; clin. coord. Orchid Health Care, Phila., 1988-89; nurse auditor Nurse Auditors Inc., Atlanta, 1989—; disaster nurse ARC, Phila., 1984, nurse, 1985. Nurse Nat. Multiple Sclerosis Soc., Phila., 1977. Recipient letter of commendation from majority whip Pa. Senate, 1987, letter of appreciation Supt. Police, Upper Darby, Pa., 1988, svc. award Mayor of Upper Darby, 1988, Humanitarian award Optimist Club, Upper Darby, 1988. Mem. Am. Nurses Assn. (cert. gerontol. nurse), Pa. Nurses Assn., Delaware County Nurses Assn., Alumni Assn. Phila. Gen. Hosp. Sch. Nursing, Sigma Theta Tau, Chi Eta Phi, Omicron Xi Epsilon. Democrat. Baptist. Home: 201 Powell Ln Upper Darby PA 19082 Office: Tucker House 1001 Wallace St Philadelphia PA 19123

ALSTON, JOANN, marketing professional; b. Jersey City, Feb. 12, 1950; d. Mowdell Alston and Daisy (Bell) McKinney; 1 child, LaQuesha. BS, Jersey City State Coll., 1985. Testing asst. Nielsen Mktg. Rsch., N.Y.C., 1969-75, jr. analyst, 1975-80, sr. analyst, 1980-87, account coordinator, 1987-88, group account coordinator, 1988—. Health fair coordinator Monumental Bapt. Ch., Jersey City, 1988-89, trustee, 1989—, pres. nurses unit, 1979. Recognized for Outstanding Community Service Garnette's Northwest Dist., 1986, Outstanding Service Tinyville Lrng. Ctr., 1985; recipient Cert. Appreciation Monumental Bapt. Ch., 1988. Mem. N.J. State Fedn. Colored Womens Clubs (chmn. adv. bd. urban women's ctr. 1987—, v.p. 1987-89, pres. 1989—), Love, Hope and Charity Club (pres. 1985-87), Northeast Dist. Club (treas. 1987—). Home: 304 Arlington Ave Jersey City NJ 07304 Office: NJ State Fedn Colored Womens Clubs 40 Fowler St Trenton NJ 08618

ALSTON, LEILA JOYCE, hospital administrator; b. Malvern, Ark., Feb. 22, 1956; d. Arthur Harmon and Ouida Beth (Williams) Bean; m. Philip Ray Alston, June 4, 1982; children: Sean Philip, Jana Katherine. BS, Ark. Tech. U., 1977; MS, U. Ark., 1982. Asst. coord. St. Mary's Hosp., Russellville, Ark., 1976-77; dir. Ark. Children's Hosp., Little Rock, 1977-81; adminstrv. resident Bapt. Med. System, Little Rock, 1983; adminstrv. asst. Bapt. Med. Ctr., Little Rock, 1983, v.p., 1984—. Mem. Am. Coll. Healthcare Execs., Health Execs. Forum, Jr. League North Little Rock, Pulaski County Med. Soc. Aux. (asst. treas. 1988-89, treas. 1989—). Office: Bapt Med Ctr 9601 I630 Exit 7 Little Rock AR 72105

ALSTON, LELA, state senator; b. Phoenix, June 26, 1942; d. Virgil Lee and Frances Mae Koonse Mulkey; B.S., U. Ariz., 1967; M.S., Ariz. State U., 1971; children—Brenda Susan, Charles William. Tchr. high sch., 1968—; mem. Ariz. State Senate, 1977—. Named Disting. Citizen, U. Ariz. Alumni Assn., 1978. Mem. NEA, Ariz. Edn. Assn., Am. Home Econs. Assn., Ariz. Home Econs. Assn., Am. Vocat. Assn. Methodist. Office: State Senate State Capitol Phoenix AZ 85007

ALT, DOTTIE KAY HINKLE, real estate broker and business consultant; b. Harrisburg, W.Va., Aug. 15, 1943; d. Daniel Carl and Leafy Ethel (Pitsenbarger) Hinkle; m. Lowell Everett Alt Jr., May 26, 1966; children: Sally Kay, Gregory Lowell. BA in History, W.Va. U., 1965; MS in Recreation/Leisure, U. Utah, 1987. Owner Dottie K. Alt Co., Salt Lake City, 1987--; owner Pitsenbarger Real Estate Co., Petersburg, W.Va., 1989—; sr. arbitrator Salt Lake City Better Bus. Bur., 1987—. Author: Joy of Pre-Retirement Planning, 1985. Mem. Phi Alpha Theta, Kappa Delta Pi, Beta Sigma, Gamma Phi Beta. Republican. Lutheran. Home and Office: 4084 Emma Circle Salt Lake City UT 84124

ALT, JANE EILEEN STONER, hospital executive; b. Salt Lake City, Oct. 20, 1956; d. Donald Lawrence and Alice Marie (Zeyen) Stoner; m. Gary J. Alt, Oct. 12, 1985. BS in Bus. Administrn., Calif. State U., 1982. With Chico Med. Group, Calif., 1974-76, Robert S. Johnson, MD, Chico, Calif., 1977; with N.T. Enloe Meml. Hosp., Chico, 1979-80, bus. office sec., 1980-81, collection clk./dept. sec., 1981-83, with telecommunications, 1983—. Mem. Nat. Notary Assn., Nat. Assn. Female Execs. Lodge: Soroptimist (pres. 1988—). Home: 153 Worthy Ave Oroville CA 95965 Office: N T Enloe Meml Hosp W 5th Ave and the Esplanade Chico CA 95926

ALTA, LINA MARIA, lawyer; b. Boston, Jan. 30, 1961; d. Leon E. Alta and Milda M. (Gedmintas) Scott. BA, U. Calif., Santa Barbara, 1983; JD, U. Calif., San Francisco, 1987. Bar: Calif., 1987. Assoc. Sheppard, Kaufman, England & Logan, San Francisco, 1988-90, Haas & Najarian, San Francisco, 1990—. Mem. ABA (Client Counseling award 1986), Bar Assn. San Francisco (pro bono immigration lawyer 1989). Office: Haas & Najarian 456 Montgomery St San Francisco CA 94104

ALTEMUS, LINDA, controller; b. Washington, May 26, 1951; d. Donald N. and Frances W. (Maier) Rogers; m. Robert H. Altemus Jr., July 2, 1968; 1 child, Dawn M. BS cum laude, Villanova U., 1982, MBA, 1987. Cost acctg. supr. Burroughs Corp., Paoli, Pa.; asst. corp. controller Johnson Matthey, West Chester, Pa., div. controller. Mem. NAFE, Villanova MBA Alumni Assn. (treas.). Home: 934 Aronimink Dr Malvern PA 19355 Office: 1401 King Rd West Chester PA 19380

ALTENHAUS, AMY LOUISE, clinical psychologist; b. N.Y.C., July 7, 1950; d. Julian LeRoi and Corrinne (Batlin) A.; m. Stephen J. Potter, Oct. 17, 1982 (div. Feb. 1989), 1 child, Sarah Rose; m. Ralph Paul Mavis, Nov. 19, 1989. BA in Psychology with honors, U. Wis., 1972; MS in Clin. Psychology, Rutgers U., 1977, PhD in Clin. Psychology, 1978. Lic. clin. psychologist; Diplomate in Behavioral Medicine. Psychology intern Family Svc. & Child Guardian Ctr., Orange, N.J., 1975-76; supervising psychologist Rutgers Coll. Counseling Ctr., New Brunswick, N.J., 1976-80; dir. pregnant adolescent program Jersey Shore Med. Ctr., Neptune, N.J., 1980-84; chief psychologist Jersey Shore Med. Ctr., Neptune, 1981-84; field supr. GSAPP Rutgers U., New Brunswick, 1978—; pvt. practice Freehold, N.J., 1978—; cons. Ctr. State Med. Ctr., Freehold, 1981—, Am. Cancer Soc., Wall, N.J., 1970—. Editor: Behavioral Medicine Abstracts, 1985-88. Mem. Am. Psychol. Assn., N.J. Psychol. Assn. (task force on impaired psychologists, 1986-89), Soc. Behavioral Medicine. Office: 80 E Main St Freehold NJ 07728

ALTER, ELEANOR BREITEL, lawyer; b. N.Y.C., Nov. 10, 1938; d. Charles David and Jeanne (Hollander) Breitel; children: Richard B. Zabel, David B. Zabel. B.A. with honors, U. Mich., 1960; postgrad., Harvard U., 1960-61; LL.B., Columbia U., 1964. Bar: N.Y. 1965. Atty., office of gen. counsel, ins. dept. State of N.Y., 1964-66; assoc. Miller & Carlson, N.Y.C., 1966-68, Marshall, Bratter, Greene, Allison & Tucker, N.Y.C., 1968-74; mem. firm Marshall, Bratter, Greene, Allison & Tucker, 1974-82, Rosenman & Colin, 1982—; fellow U. Chgo. Law Sch., 1988; adj. prof. law NYU Sch Law, 1983-87; vis. prof. law U. Chgo., 1990; lectr. in field. Editorial bd.: N.Y. Law Jour. Contbr. articles to profl. jours. Trustee Clients' Security Fund State of N.Y., 1983—, chmn., 1985—; bd. visitors U. Chgo. Law Sch., 1984-87. Mem. Am. Law Inst., Am. Bar Assn., N.Y. State Bar Assn., Assn. of Bar of City of N.Y. (library com. 1978-80, com. on matrimonial law 1977-81, 87-88, judiciary com. 1981-84, Exec. com. 1988—), Am. Acad. Matrimonial Lawyers. Office: Rosenman & Colin 575 Madison Ave New York NY 10022

ALTER, ELEANOR REED, retired secondary education teacher; b. Montgomery, Ala., May 4, 1908; d. Prentiss Bishop and Eleanor Frey (Cochran) Reed; m. Nicholas Mark Alter, Apr. 11, 1932 (dec. 1970); children: Eleanor Haas, Katharine Cree (dec. 1987), Nicholas Albert, Ernest Henry. AB, Smith Coll., Northampton, Mass., 1930; MA, Syracuse U., 1961; postgrad., SUNY, Plattsburgh, N.Y., 1960, Syracuse U., 1961. cert. secondary English and French tchr., N.Y. and Mass., 1961. Tchr. secondary English Fulton (N.Y.) High Sch., 1959-61; chmn. of English City of Fulton, 1961; tchr. secondary English and French Uxbridge (Mass.) High Sch., 1961-63; tchr. secondary English King Philip Regional Sch., Wrentham, Mass., 1963-87; ednl. cons. Pegasus Projects, Slatersville, R.I., 1987; asst. editor The Beechwood Tree at Scarborough (N.Y.) Sch., 1926-; leader creative writing group Woonsocket (R.I.) Fine Arts Society, 1966-71. editor, author (booklet) Ashes and Sparks I, 1945, Ashes and Sparks II, 1947, (book) Gateways, 1967, Years of Conflict - D.A.R., 1973, (play) An Evening with Le Cèrcle Francais, 1962, (pageant) Upon This Bank, 1965, numerous poems. Mem. Jersey City Symphony Soc.; pres. women's aux. St. Paul's Ch. in Bergen, Jersey City, 1947; bd. dirs. Internat. Inst., Jersey City Mus. Assn. Recipient poetry awards; grantee Milford (Mass.) Arts Lottery. Mem. AAUW (leader creative writing group 1966-71), Nat. Coun. Tchrs. English, Delta Kappa Gamma Society Internat., Coll. Club Jersey City, Monday Afternoon Club, Smith Coll. Alumnae Assn.

ALTER, LYNNE, comptroller; b. Miami Beach, Fla., Dec. 24, 1953; d. Irwin Stanley Alter and Barbara (Messinger) Gottfried; 1 child, Jessica Reneé. Cert. emergency med. technician, Miami-Dade Coll., 1981. Exec. asst. Ecol. Devel. Corp., Miami, Fla., 1972-73; asst. coordinator outreach program Miami-Dade Coll., 1973-74; editor music book Columbia Pictures Publs., Miami, 1974-75; corp. sec., comptroller MAC Parking, Inc., Miami, 1978-81; emergency med. technician Randle-Ea. Ambulance, Miami, 1980-81; comptroller Bay Rag & Grading, Inc., Miami, 1981—. Guardian ad litem Guardian Ad Litem Program, Miami, 1983—. Mem. Nat. Assn. for Female Execs. Democrat. Office: Bay Rag & Grading Inc 6250 NW 35 Ave Miami FL 33147

ALTER, SHIRLEY JACOBS, jewelry store owner; b. Beaumont, Tex., June 23, 1929; d. Morris Louis and Helen (Dow) Jacobs; m. Nelson Tobias Alter, June 12, 1949; children: Dennis, Keith, Brian, Wendy. Student, U. Tex., Austin, 1950. Owner Gem Jewelry Co., Beaumont, 1950—. Pres. Nat. Coun. Jewish Women, Beaumont, 1965, 66, Sisterhood of Temple Emmanuel, Beaumont, 1967, 68, Buckner Bapt. Benevolence Aux., Beaumont, 1970-72; founder Beaumont Reach to Recovery, 1973; active Art Mus. S.E. Tex., Beaumont Heritage Soc.; adv. bd. Bapt. Hosp., 1989—; bd. dirs. Tyrrell Hist. Libr. Assn.; mem. Beaumont Music Commn. Bd., 1990. Democrat. Jewish. Office: Gem Jewelry Co 795 N 11th St Beaumont TX 77702

ALTHAUS, BARBARA DONALSON, realtor, insurance underwriter; b. Fort Worth, Mar. 20, 1937; d. Thomas Kyle and Lucille (Martin) Donalson; student U. Tex., 1955-57; m. Dudley Nolin Althaus, Dec. 25, 1969. Legal exec. sec. firm McCully & Christensen, Houston, 1959-64; office mgr. H.A. Bornefeld, Jr., Houston, 1964-69; owner Althaus Acres Furniture, Fredericksburg, Tex., 1979-84, sec./treas. Althaus Acres Realtors and Auctioneers, Inc., 1969—. Chmn. Damenfest, 1977; Tex. Auctioneers Assn. Aux. (pres. 1977, 1981-84). Mem. Nat. Auctioneers Assn. Aux., (bd. dirs. 1983-86), DAR (organizing regent 1974-76, state chmn. jr. Am. citizens 1976-79, registrar 1980-82, state parliamentarian 1985-88), Daus. Am. Colonists (state chmn. colonial heritage 1981-83), vice regent 1983-86), Fredericksburg C. of C. (amb. 1980-84), Magna Charta Dames, Daus. of Republic Tex. (pres. 1987-89, 89—), Alpha Phi. Democrat. Methodist. Home: Althaus Ranch Fredericksburg TX 78624 Office: 501 W Main PO Box 312 Fredericksburg TX 78624

ALTHOUSE, FRANCES YVONNE SEAY, administrative services manager; b. Fredericksburg, Va., Dec. 2, 1965; d. Horace Baker and Edith Pauline (Curtis) Seay; m. Mark David Althouse, Mar. 8, 1986. Student, Germania Community Coll., Culpeper, Va., 1984-85, George Mason U., 1985-86. Hostess, cashier, cook McDonald's, Fredericksburg, 1981-85; asst. mgr. Pizza Hut, Fredericksburg, 1984-85; office mgr. Picture Perfect Studio, Springfield, Va., 1985-86, Wood, Stear & LeDoux, Inc. Air Cleaning Tech., Springfield, 1986—. Mem. NAFE, Devil's Reach Sport and Health Club. Republican. Baptist. Office: Wood Stear LeDoux Inc 6715 A Electronic Dr Springfield VA 22151

ALTMAN, ADELE ROSENHAIN, radiologist; b. Tel Aviv, Israel, June 4, 1924; came to U.S., 1933, naturalized, 1939; d. Bruno and Salla (Silberzweig) Rosenhain; m. Emmett Altman, Sept. 3, 1944; children: Brian R., Alan L., Karen D. Diplomate Am. Bd. Radiology. Intern Queens Gen. Hosp., N.Y.C., 1949-51; resident Hosp. for Joint Diseases, N.Y.C., 1951-52, Roosevelt Hosp., N.Y.C., 1955-57; clin. instr. radiology Downstate Med. Ctr., SUNY, Bklyn., 1957-61; asst. prof. radiology N.Y. Med. Coll., N.Y.C., 1961-65, assoc. prof., 1965-68; assoc. prof. radiology U. Okla. Health Sci. Ctr., Oklahoma City, 1968-78; assoc. prof. dept. radiology U. N.Mex. Sch. Medicine, Albuquerque, 1978-85. Author: Radiology of the Respiratory System: A Basic Review, 1978; contbr. articles to profl. jours. Fellow Am. Coll. Angiology, N.Y. Acad. Medicine; mem. Am. Coll. Radiology, Am. Roentgen Ray Soc., Assn. Univ. Radiologists, Radiol. Soc. N.Am., B'nai B'rith Anti-Defamation League (bd. dirs. N.Mex. state bd.), Hadassah Club.

ALTMAN, ELLEN, librarian, educator; b. Pitts., Jan. 1, 1936; d. William and Catherine (Wall) Conley. A.B., Duquesne U., 1957; M.L.S., Rutgers U., 1965, Ph.D., 1971. Instr., asst research prof. Rutgers U., 1965-67, 70-72; asst. prof. U. Ky., 1972-73, U. Toronto, 1974-76; assoc. prof. Ind. U., 1976-79; prof. Grad. Library Sch., U. Ariz., Tucson, 1979—; cons. various research orgns., state libraries. Active Exec. Women's Council So. Ariz., 1980—. Author: Performance Measures in Pub. Libraries, 1973, A Data Gathering and Instructional Manual for Performance Measures in Public Libraries, 1976, Local Public Library Administration, 1980. Fulbright-Hayes sr. lectr., 1978. Mem. ALA, AAUP, Am. Mgmt. Assn. Office: 1515 E 1st St Tucson AZ 85721

ALTMAN, JANE CALLAHAN, investment executive; b. Detroit, Feb. 23, 1949; d. Earl J. and Madeline Katherine (Freihaut) Callahan; m. Craig Randall Altman, Sept. 19, 1970 (div. June 1981); children: Christopher Randall, Elisabeth Anne. BA, Albion Coll., 1970; postgrad., Aquinas Coll., Grand Rapids, 1989--. Asst. mgr. Nat. Bank of Detroit, 1971-75; program coord. Muskegon (Mich.) Community Coll., 1978-79; services coord. Muskegon (Mich.) County Community Mental Health, 1979-81; supr. engrng. services Teledyne Continental Motors, Muskegon, MIch.; v.p. investment PaineWebber Inc., Muskegon, Mich., 1982--. Dir. Muskegon Econ. Growth Alliance, 1987--, Every Woman's Place, Muskegon, 1979-86, mem. Comm. on Growth and Devel. Episcopal Diocese of Western Mich., 1985-88, Consumers Power Citizen Adv. Panel, Muskegon, 1983-84. Mem. Zonta Internat. Office: PaineWebber Inc 1060 W Norton Ave PO Box 95 Muskegon MI 49443

ALTMAN, JANICE MARY, religious organization administrator, educator; b. Columbus, Ohio, Apr. 13, 1938; d. Norman John and Nettie Mae (Sullivan) A. BA, Ohio Dominican Coll., 1962; MEd, Marygrove Coll., 1969; ThM, Trinity Coll., 1978; EdD, George Washington U., 1985. Tchr. St. Andrew Sch., Flushing, N.Y., 1969-72, St. Thomas Sch., Zanesville, Ohio, 1972-74; dir. Holy Family & St. Aloysius, Columbus, 1974-76; chaplain intern Children's Hosp. Nat. Med. Ctr., Washington, 1977-80; intern Pastoral Counseling Ctr., Washington, 1979-81; dir. Pastoral Counseling Ctr., Suitland, Md., 1981-88; pres., counselor Alta-Vista Pastoral Counseling Ctr., Inc., Bowie, Md., 1988—; supr. Prince George Pastoral Counseling Ctr., Lanham, Md., 1987—; adj. faculty mem. Howard U. Sch. Divinity, Washington, 1988—. Author: Library of Congress, 1986. Fellow Am. Assn. Pastoral Counselors (chair 1983-87), Md. Mental Health Counselors (pres. elect 1989-90, pres. 1990—), Greater Bowie C. of C. (women in bus. com. 1989—), Prince George C. of C. (edn. com. Lanham chpt. 1989—). Democrat. Roman Catholic. Office: Alta Vista Pastoral Ctr PO Box 876 Bowie MD 20715

ALTMAN, RUTH B., musician, writer; b. Boston, Mass., Jan. 23, 1933; d. Harry and Jean Zelda (Berman) Zide; m. Donald H. Altman, Apr. 15, 1951 (div. 1972); children: Nolan R., Mona B., Sanford D. BS, Fla. Internat. U., 1975, MS, 1980. Childhood concert pianist, presently pianist-singer; author verse and fiction. Mem. Mensa (bd. dirs. 1970), Intertel. Democrat. Jewish.

ALTMANN, ESTHER NESBIN, dean, consultant; b. Denver, Aug. 5, 1910; d. Oscar Anton and Helen (Schmandt) Winter; m. Anthony Nesbin, Sept. 21, 1946 (dec. Sept. 1957); m. John Charles Maxwell Altmann, Aug. 5, 1978. BA, U. Buffalo, 1931, cert. in libr. scis., 1932. With Palomar Coll., San Marcos, Calif., 1947-77, asst. dean, 1970-73, dean, 1973-77, dean emeritus libr. svcs., 1977—; cons. Palo Verdes Jr. Coll. Libr., Blythe, Calif., 1957, Monterey (Calif.) Jr. Coll. Libr., 1958; instr. in flower arranging Palomar Coll., 1965; cons. Camp Pendleton (Calif.) Law Libr., 1964. Author: Shaker Literature in the Governors Library, 1940, rev. edit., 1958. Sustaining mem. Rep. Nat. Com., Washington, 1990—; charter mem. Citizens Against Govt. Waste, Washington, 1990—. Recipient Outstanding Svc. award Escondido C. of C., 1965. Mem. Friends of Palomar Libr. Home: 21430 Questhaven Rd Escondido CA 92029

ALTMILLER, JEANNE ELIZABETH, automotive executive; b. Toledo, Ohio, Jan. 19, 1960; d. Richard Martin and Elizabeth Marcella (Graham) Huffman; m. William Samuel Altmiller, June 6, 1982; children: William Richard Glenn, Daniel James Paul. BS in Bus., Ohio State U., 1982. Market researcher Toledo Scale, Columbus, Ohio, 1980-82; market analyst Caterpillar Tractor Co., Peoria, Ill., 1982-84; dist. mgr. Am. Honda Motor Co., Troy, Ohio, 1984-89, sr. dist. mgr., 1989—; cons. Toledo Scale, Columbus, 1980-82. Young group leader Awana, Peoria, Ill., 1984; advisor Jr. Achievement, Peoria, 1983-84; leader Koinonia, Columbus, Ind., 1989. Mem. Jr. Achievement Alumni Assn., Pi Sigma Epsilon (pres. 1980-81), Alpha Gamma Delta (ritual chmn. 1980). Republican.

ALTOBELLO, MILDRED FRANCES, realtor; b. West Palm Beach, Fla., Mar. 3, 1953; d. Francis Anthony and Ethel Hamner (Martin) A. BA, U. Ala., 1975; MBA, Samford U., 1977. Ter. mgr. Burroughs Corp., Miami, Fla., 1978-80; mgmt. trainee Coral Gables Fed. Savs. and Loan (Fla.), 1981; realtor-assoc. Keyes Co., Coral Gables, 1981-88; mem. Keyes Million Dollar Sales Club, Keyes Inner Circle, 1986; active Coral Gables Bd. of Realtors (realtor-lawyer com. 1985—, communications com. 1985-88, realtors polit. action com. 1987—, govtl. affairs com. 1988—), Civic Opera of Palm Beaches, 1969—; chmn. liturgical com. U. of Ala., Tuscaloosa, 1973. Recipient Spl. award for Outstanding Dedication and Successful Achievement in the RPAC Goal, 1988. Mem. Soc. Profl. Journalists, Women in Communications, Inc., Sunset Jaycees, Coral Gables C. of C. Democrat. Roman Catholic.

ALTON, ANN LESLIE, judge, lawyer, educator; b. Pipestone, Minn., Sept. 10, 1945; d. Howard Robert, Jr. and Camilla Ann (DeMong) A.; m. Gerald Russell Freeman Sr.; children: Matthew Alton Freeman (dec.), Brady Michael Alton Freeman. BA Smith Coll., 1967; JD U. Minn., 1970. Bar: Minn. 1970, U.S. Dist. Ct. Minn. 1972, U.S. Supreme Ct. 1981. Gen. jurisdiction state trial ct. judge Dist. Ct., 4th Jud. Dist., Hennepin County, Minn., 1989—; asst. county atty. Hennepin County, Mpls., 1970-89, felony prosecutor, criminal div., 1970-75, acting chief citizen protection div., 1975-76, chief citizen protection/econ. crime div., 1976-79, chief econ. crime unit, 1979-85, sr. atty. civil div. handling labor and employment law, 1985-89 ; instr. Hamline U. Law Sch., St. Paul, 1973-76; adj. prof. law William Mitchell Coll. Law, St. Paul, 1977—; adj. prof. U. Minn. Law Sch., 1978-82; lectr. in field, 1970—; sr. faculty Minn. Advocacy Inst., 1988—; bd. dirs. Pan-O-Gold Realty Co., 1986-89, Alton Realty Co., 1986-89. Vice-chmn. bd. dirs. Minn. Program on Victims of Sexual Assault, 1974-76; bd. dirs. Physician's Health Plan, Health Maintenance Orgn., 1976-80, exec. com. 1977-80; mem. legal drug abuse subcom. Gov. Minn. Adv. Com. Drug Abuse, 1972-74; bd. visitors U. Minn. Law Sch., 1979-85; mem. child abuse project coordinating com. Hennepin County Med. Soc., 1982-83, chmn. corp., labor, ins. subcom. 1982. Mem. ABA (jud. adminstrn. div.), Minn. Bar Assn. (criminal law, labor and employment law, civil litigation sects.), Hennepin County Bar Assn. (ethics com. 1973-76, criminal law com. 1973—, vice chmn. 1979-80, 83-84, unauthorized practice law com. 1977-78, individual rights and responsibilities com. 1977-78, labor and employment law com. 1985—, civil litigation com. 1985—), Nat. Dist. Attys. Assn. (unit chief econ. crime project 1975-83), Nat. Assn. Women Judges, Minn. County Attys. Assn., Minn. Dist. Judges Assn., Minn. Women Lawyers, U. Minn. Law Sch. Alumni Assn. (bd. dirs. 1979-85). Author articles, pamphlet, manual. Home: 2105 Xanthus Ln Plymouth MN 55447 Office: 1251-C Hennepin County Govt Ctr Minneapolis MN 55487

ALTON, MARGARET ANN, healthcare executive; b. Joplin, Mo., Aug. 8, 1943; d. Charles John and Barbara Jane (Byrne) Hassel; m. William Lewis Alton, Mar. 31, 1943; 1 child, Jennifer. Diploma, St. Mary's Sch. Nursing, Milw., 1965; BS in Health Svcs., No. Ariz. U., 1979, MEd in Human Behavior, 1982. RN, Ariz., Wis. Asst. head nurse Trinity Luth. Hosp., Ashland, Wis., 1965-66; nursing supr. Camelback Hosp., Phoenix, 1966-71; nursing adminstr. Camelback Hosp., 1978-80; emergency room supr. Phoenix Gen. Hosp., 1971-72; psychiatric nursing adminstr. Ariz. State Hosp., Phoenix, 1972-76, asst. adminstr., 1976-78; asst. adminstr. St. Luke's Behavioral Health Ctr., Phoenix, 1980-87, v.p., 1987—; cons. in field. Mem. Am. Orgn. Nurse Execs., Ariz. Orgn. Nurse Execs. Republican. Lutheran. Office: St Luke's Health Ctr 1800 E Van Buren Phoenix AZ 85006

ALTROCCHI, SALLY ARCHER, television sales executive; b. Bethesda, Md., Sept. 4, 1960; d. Paul Hemenway and Pencie (McBride) A. BA, Stanford U., 1982. Sales asst. Sta. KOFY TV 20 (IND), San Francisco, 1982-84; media asst. Macy's Broadcast Advt., San Francisco, 1984-85; media buyer Western Internat. Media Corp., San Francisco, 1985-88; media cons. Sta. KSBW TV 8 (NBC), Salinas-Monterey, Calif., 1988-89, nat. sales mgr., 1989—; student TV Prodn. Workshop, Stanford U., Palo Alto, Calif., 1981; internship com. Bay Area Soc. for TV, Advt. and Radio, San Francisco, 1984-88; media planning class Media Dirs. Coun., San Francisco, 1986; participant broadcast sales seminar Gillett Group, Inc., Virginia Beach, Va., 1988. Chair AIDS Peer Edn., Monterey Bay area, 1989—; mem. Jr. League, San Francisco. Mem. Ad Club Monterey Bay (pres. 1988—), Jr. League (Monterey, com. chair 1988—). Home: 744 Doud Ave Monterey CA 93940 Office: Sta KSBW TV 238 John St Salinas CA 93901

ALTSCHUL, BJ, public relations counselor; b. Norfolk, Va., Jan. 28, 1948; d. Lemuel and Sylva (Behr) A. Student, Goucher Coll., 1965-67; BA, U. South Fla., 1970, postgrad., 1980-84. Reporter St. Petersburg Times, Fla., 1973-74; dir. pub. rels. Valkyrie Press, Inc., St. Petersburg, 1974-77; founding editor Bay Life, Clearwater, Fla., 1977-79, Tampa Bay Monthly, Clearwater, 1977-79; mng. editor Fla. Tourist News, Tampa and Orlando, 1981; founder Capital Communications of Tampa, 1981, since owner, prin., name changed to b j Altschul & Assocs., 1985; mgr. editorial and info. svcs. Va. Port Authority, Norfolk, 1985-88; dir. pub. rels. Va. Dept. Agr. and Consumer Svcs., Richmond, 1988—; adj. faculty Old Dominion U., Norfolk, 1986—. Author: Cracker Cookin' & Other Favorites, 1984; editor: The Underground Gourmet, 1983; contbg. author: Virginia: A Commonwealth Comes of Age, 1988. Bd. dirs. Pinellas County Big Bros.-Big Sisters, 1980-82, Fla. Folklore Soc., 1984-85. Grant rev. panelist Fla. Fine Arts Coun., 1981. Mem. Fla. Motion Picture and TV Assn. (treas. 1976-78), Fla. Freelance Writers Assn., Hampton Rds. C. of C. (co-chmn. pub. rels. Internat. Azalea Festival 1986, chmn. publs. 1987), Va. Conf. on World Trade (chmn. pub. relations com.), Downtown Norfolk Devel. Corp. (chmn. urban living com.), Mensa, Pub. Relations Soc. Am. (chmn. Mid-Atlantic Dist. 1988, chmn. govt. sect. 1989, bd. dirs. accreditation chmn. Hampton Rds. chpt. 1985-88). Avocations: sailing, classical music, folk music, jazz. Home: Pub Rels Counsel 2226 Rockwater Terr Richmond VA 23233 Office: Va Dept of Agr and Consumer Svcs PO Box 1163 Richmond VA 23209

ALVARADO, CAROLINE R., computer company executive; b. Chgo., July 28, 1954; d. Senon Alvarado and Patricia (Garza) Huerta; m. Richard Jimenez, June 15, 1971 (div. Apr. 1981); children: Hector, Richard Jr. Computer ednl. dir. Valentine unit Boys & Girls Club Chgo., 1985-89; v.p., founder Computeledge, Inc., Chgo., 1986—; computer instr. Little People Nursery Sch., Chgo., 1988—; utility program writer Osco Drugs Inc., Oakbrook, Ill., 1988—; computer program coord. McKinley Park Dist., Chgo., 1988—. Recipient spl. award Boys Club Am., 1987. Mem. Nat. Assn. for Female Execs. Inc. Home and Office: Computeledge Inc 2305 W 47th St Chicago IL 60609

ALVARADO, YOLANDA HERNANDEZ, journalist, editor, minority outreach consultant; b. Galveston, Tex., Sept. 27, 1943; d. Raymond G. Hernandez and Maria Luisa (Garcia) Hernandez Vera; div.; children: Rosario Alvrado, Yul Alvarado, Joseph Omar Alvarado. BA, Spring Arbor Coll., 1988. Editor, asst. mgr. El Renacimiento, Lansing, Mich., 1972-74; gen. assignment reporter Lansing State Jour., 1974-80, chief edn. writer, 1980-86, city hall reporter, 1986-87, copy editor, 1987—; Hispanic mentor Lansing Sch. Dist., 1989—; minority media cons. to schs., colls. and community groups, 1974—. Coordinator, editor: (booklet) Mental Illness: A Family Resource Guide, 1988. Coordinator Midwest Hispanic Unity Conf., Mich. State U., 1990; founder, coordinator Hispanic Women in the Network, 1988—; del. U.S.-Soviet Women's Summit, N.Y.C. and Washington, 1990; alumna Nat. Hispanic Leadership Inst., 1989; mem. minority steering com. Nat. Alliance for Mentally Ill, 1989—. Recipient Disting. Svc. award Nat. Newspaper Guild, 1986; Sondra Berlin award for civil rights State Handicapped Assn. Pub. Employees, 1989; Diana award in communications YWCA, 1985; named one of Am.'s Top 100 Hispanic Women in Communications, Hispanic U.S.A. mag., 1987. Mem. Nat. Assn. Hispanic Journalists, Women in Communications Inc., Newspaper Guild Local 24 (past sec., v.p., pres.). Home: 16400 Upton Rd Lot 254 East Lansing MI 48823

ALVAREZ, FRANCIA, video production company executive, consultant; b. N.Y.C., Aug. 12, 1949; d. Francis Alvarez and Marya Brent. AAS, Fashion Inst. Tech., N.Y.C., 1969; BA in Sociology, SUNY, Purchase, 1973. Asst. photographer George Nicholls Studio, London, 1970; asst. dir. Sta. WPBT-TV, North Miami, Fla., 1976-78; prodn. asst. Sta. WNET-TV, N.Y.C., 1978-79; asst. dir. broadcast graphics ABC News, Sports and Entertainment div. Capital Cities/ABC, N.Y.C., 1979-87; pres. Nat. Image Assocs., Inc., Old Greenwich, Conn., 1987—, River Wood Prodns., Inc., Old Greenwich, 1989—. Recipient Emmy award as asst. dir. 1984 Summer Olympics. Mem. Dirs. Guild Am. Office: Nat Image Assocs 13 Arcadia Rd Old Greenwich CT 06870

ALVAREZ, MARIA CECILIA, social services administrator; b. Guayaquil, Ecuador, Nov. 23, 1952; came to U.S., 1958; d. Louis B. and Maria Teresa (Malnati) A. BA in Psychology, U. Tex., San Antonio, 1976; MA in Clin. Psychology, St. Mary's U., San Antonio, 1978. Psychol. assoc. Goodwill Industries, San Antonio, 1981-83; handicap/mental health coord. Parent Child Inc., Head Start, San Antonio, 1983; caseworker III therapist Bexar County Mental Health Mental Retardation Childrens Unit, San Antonio; instr. in psychology Alamo Community Coll. Dist., San Antonio; workshop presenter; part-time counselor Edgewood Sch. Dist., 1980-81; part-time psychologist SWNPI, 1980-81. Vol. counselor San Antonio Free Clinic, 1978-81. Mem. Tex. Psychol. Assn., Tex. Bd. Profl. Examiners Psychologists. Roman Catholic. Home: 221 Flintstone Universal City TX 78148 Office: Bexar County MHMR Childrens Unit 1028 S Alamo San Antonio TX 78210

ALVAREZ, MERCEDES, advertising executive; b. Havana, Cuba; d. José Manuel and Teresita (Rionda) A. BBA, U. Miami, 1963; postgrad., Manhattanville Coll., Purchase, N.Y., 1964. Sr. rsch. analyst J. Walter Thompson, N.Y.C., 1966-78; v.p. rsch. dir. Isidore, Lefkowitz & Elgort, N.Y.C., 1978-79, Bozell & Jacobs, N.Y.C., 1979-85; v.p. assoc. rsch. dir. BBDO, N.Y.C., 1985—; sec., treas. Rsch. Dirs. Coun., 1979-80, Communications Rsch. Coun., 1988-89, pres., 1989—. Mem. Am. Mktg. Assn. (Effie Judge, 1978-85). Office: BBDO NY 1285 Ave of the Americas New York NY 10019

ALVERIO-GIROT, CARMEN ENID, occupational therapist; b. San Lorenzo, P.R., Sept. 13, 1960; d. Emilio and Carmen (Laureano) Alverio; m. Jose Manuel Girot, Oct. 17; 1 child, Jonathan Rene. BS in Occupational Therapy magna cum laude, U. P.R., 1982. Registered occupational therapist. Staff occupational therapist Nuestra Senora de Los Angeles Hosp., Rio Piedras, P.R., 1982, Brooke Army Med. Ctr., San Antonio, 1982-84; occupational therapist, asst. health care adminstr. U.S. Army Health Clinic, San Juan, P.R., 1984-85; occupational therapist, clin. supr. Letterman Army Med. Ctr., San Francisco, 1986; occupational therapist advisor USA Humanitarian Med. Team, El Salvador, Cen. Am., 1986-87; occupational therapist, asst. chief Martin Army Community Hosp., Columbus, Ga., 1987-88. Contbr. articles to profl. jours. Vol. Am. Muscular Dystrophy Summer Camp, P.R., 1979, 2d Ann. Internat. Amputee Soccer Tournament, Seattle, 1987, Santa's Castle Non-Profit Toy Orgn., Ft. Benning, Ga.; mem. registration com. Army Med. Dept. Biathon Race, Ft. Benning, 1987; mem. asst. rescue team Earthquake Nat. Disaster, El Salvador, 1987. Mem. Am. Occupational Therapists Assn., Tex. Occupational Therapists Assn., P.R. Occupational Therapists Assn., Officers Club. Home: 3912 Ashmore Dr Columbus GA 31909 Office: Comml Mail Agy Martin Army Community Hosp Fort Benning GA 31905

ALVERIO-NIEVES, CARMEN SOCORRO, Spanish educator; b. San Lorenzo, P.R., Jan. 11, 1958; d. Alfonso Alverio and Lucia Nieves. BA magna cum laude, U. P.R., 1980, MS in Speech and Language Pathology, 1982; MA in Spanish, Rutgers U., 1985, postgrad. Cert. clin. pathologist. Pvt. practice and speech/language pathologist Home-Care Instns., Rio Piedras, P.R., 1982-83; teaching asst. U. Mass., Amherst, 1983-84, Rutgers U., New Brunswick, N.J., 1984-88; instr. Rutgers U., 1988-89; asst. prof. Spanish Montclair (N.J.) State Coll., 1989—. Scholar, Angel Ramos Found., 1980-82, Nat. Hispanic Fund, 1988; Louis Bevier fellow, 1988-89. Mem. Modern Language Assn., AAUP, Rutgers U. Grad Student Assn. (rep. 1987-88).

ALVES, DOROTHY LOUISE, tax preparer, business management consultant; b. Harlingen, Tex., Dec. 10, 1929; d. Robert Leonard Walker and Frances Louise (Byrn) Witte; m. Milton Clarence Alves, Sept. 20, 1958 (dec. Nov. 1986); children: Donald Estes, Deborah Alves, William Alves. Grad. high sch., San Antonio. Enrolled agt. IRS. Profl. actress, singer, 1947-57; pres. Alves Co., San Antonio, 1960—; adminstr. Woodlawn Hills Nursing Home, Inc., San Antonio, 1964-79; cons. non-profit orgns., Christian ministries, San Antonio, 1975—, Bexar County Detention Ministries, San Antonio, 1985—; speaker on taxes and corp. tax planning. Mem. Nat. Assn. Enrolled Agts., Nat. Assn. Profl. Advisors, San Antonio Women's C. of C., Northside C. of C. Republican. Lutheran. Office: 7300 Blanco Ste 403 San Antonio TX 78216

ALVEY, DORIS MAY GIORDANO, hypnotherapist, nurse; b. N.Y.C., Nov. 1, 1945; d. Dominic Louis Giordono and Agnes (Victoria) Johnson; m. Lorenzo Marcello Margini, June 5, 1974 (div. 75); m. Clifford Charles Alvey, Apr. 11, 1981. RN, Queens Gen. Hosp. Sch. Nursing, 1966; BA in Psychology, Marymount Manhattan Coll., 1973; MS, CUNY, 1978; PhD in Hypnotherapy, Am. Inst. Hypnotherapy, Santa Ana, Calif., 1985. Cert. hypnotherapist, psychiatric, mental health nurse. Nurse in charge Phoenix House Therapeutic Ctr., N.Y.C., 1968-70; research coordinator N.Y. Med. Coll., N.Y.C., 1971-74; pvt. practice psychotherapy N.Y.C., 1974-84; research coordinator UCLA Harbor Gen. Hosp., Torrance, Calif., 1985-86; dir., owner South Ctr. for Hypnosis and Health Edn., Costa Mesa, Calif., 1984—; psychiatric, alcohol cons. Comp Care, Tustin, Calif., 1984-85; home care cons. Med. Home Coll., L.A., 1986; psychiatric nursing supr. Coll., Cerritos, Calif., 1986—; instr. Golden West Coll., Calif., 1988; instr. Golden West Coll., 1988-89. Watercolor painter exhibited in group show's including Madison Sq. Garden Art Show, 1981. Cert. rev. hearing officer Orange County, Calif., 1989—. Named THerapist Who Cares Bayview Manor Home for Adults, Bklyn., 1980. Mem. Calif. Council Hypnotherapy, Holistic Nurses Assn., Costa Mesa C. of C, Biofeedback Soc. of Am. (cert. biofeedback therapist 1988). Episcopalian. Club: GLAZA (Los Angeles). Home: 357 Grenoble Ln Costa Mesa CA 92627 Office: South Coast Ctr of Hypnosis and Health End 1530 W Baker St Costa Mesa CA 92626

ALVINE, CAROL CHRISTINE, fire investigator, expert witness; b. Paterson, N.J., June 3, 1942; d. Ralph James and Rosemarie (Imperato) Imbimbo; m. William Alvine Sr., Apr. 19, 1978. Student, Rutgers U., 1960-62, 76, Villa Nova U., 1979. Lic. fire investigator, pvt. investigator, Fla. Office mgr. Durabilt Homes Corp., Clifton, N.J., 1960-64, Interstate Properties, Clifton, 1968-72; acct. exec. Riedl & Freede Inc., Clifton, 1964-68; spl. asst. corp. v.p. mfg. Gen. Instrument Corp., N.Y.C., 1972-74; corp. v.p. ops. William Alvine Assocs., Inc., Casselberry, Fla., 1974—. Editor, contbr. Fireye Newsletter, 1974—; contbr. to LabVoice, Fire News, Digest; contbr. Arson Investigation Mini guides 1-5, 1985. Fundraiser Alzheimer Resource Ctr., Winter Park, Fla., 1987, 88—; mem. Maitland (Fla.) Audubon Soc., World Wildlife Fund, Greenpeace, Nat. Audubon Soc., Smithsonian. Mem. Internat. Assn. Arson Investigators, Edn. Sect. Nat. Fire Protection Assn., Maitland Woman's Club (pres. 1986, fund raiser 1979—), Cen. Fla. Women's League. Office: William Alvine Assocs Inc 130 N Cypress Way Casselberry FL 32708

ALVORD, SUSAN B., myotherapist; b. Cambridge, Ohio, Jan. 14, 1942; d. Vincent Horace and Helen Lee (Thompson) Bell; m. Frederick Reed Alvord III, Dec. 16, 1967 (div. 1980). BA, Grove City Coll., 1963; MA, Pa. State U., 1965; cert., Acad. for Myotherapy and Exercise Therapy, Lenox, Mass., 1984. Instr. Spanish and French U. Pitts., Johnstown, 1967-68, Alliance Coll., Cambridge Springs, Pa., 1968-71; instr./supr. Ron Hamilton Ski Sch., Findley Lake, N.Y., 1971-79; co-owner Ron Hamilton Rentals, Findley Lake, 1979-81; developer's asst. White Pines Condominiums, Lenox, 1984-86; staff myotherapist Myo, Inc., Chgo., 1986-87; owner Myofascial Pain Control Clinic, Chgo., 1988—; instr. Truman Coll., Chgo., 1988-89. Past Dem. ward worker, Chgo.; past telethon participant Chgo. Lyric Opera. Mem. Nat. Assn. Trigger Point Myotherapists (chairperson pub. relations com. 1988-89, chairperson continuing edn. com. 1989—), Midwest Pain Soc., Nat. Dance Exercise Instrs. Assn., Lakeview C. of C. Democrat. Home: 4738 N Magnolia Chicago IL 60640 Office: Myofascial Pain Control Cln 3354 N Paulina Chicago IL 60657

ALWINE, JANET DARLENE, corporate executive; b. Covington, Va., Jan. 30, 1952; d. Bennie Hilston and Edna Darlene (Phillips) Burkholder; m. David Lynn Snyder, Sr., Jan. 31, 1970 (div. 1975); 1 child, David Lynn, Jr.; m. Thomas Samuel Alwine, June 7, 1986. Student, Dabney S. Lancaster Community Coll., Clifton Forge, Va., 1973-77. Owner, operator The Hair Sta., Covington, 1974-77; with Alleghany/Covington Dept. Social Services, 1977-81; adminstr. Tanglewood Manor Home for Adults, Covington, 1981-86; bus. mgr. Country Comfort Chimney Services, Inc., York, Pa., 1987-88; steward Covington (Va.) Moose Lodge, 1988—. Mem. NAFE, Beta Sigma Phi (pres. 1981-82, treas. 1984-85). Methodist. Lodge: Women of the Moose. Home: 528 Parkin Dr Covington VA 24426

AMACHER, JOAN MARSH, corporation executive; b. Macon County, Ill., Dec. 27, 1926; d. Charles and Vilena Glenn (Augustus) Marsh; m. Charles L. Amacher, Dec. 22, 1950; children: Vern David, Bill Marsh, Carol Jo Beck. BS in Elem. Edn., U. Ill., 1953, EdM, 1968. Elem. tchr. Elem. Schs. Ill., various schs., 1945-70; risk mgr. Burnham Hosp., Champaign, Ill., 1979-88; pres. S & A Bldg. Specialties, Inc., Champaign, 1989--. Placement chairperson Champaign Urbana Jr. League, 1969, moderator, Univ. Place Christian Ch., Champaign, 1973. mem. Am. Soc. Safety Engrs., Champaign Jr. Woman's Club, Fed. Woman's Club Am. Democrat.

AMADIO, BARI ANN, metal fabrication executive; b. Phila., Mar. 26, 1949; d. Fred Deutscher and Celena (Lusky) Garber; m. Peter Colby Amadio, June 24, 1973; children: P. Grant, Jamie Blair. BA in Psychology, U. Miami, 1970; diploma in Nursing, Thomas Jefferson U., 1973, Johnston-Willis Sch. Nursing, 1974; BS in Nursing, Northeastern U., 1977; MS in Nursing, Boston U., 1978; JD, U. Bridgeport, 1983. Faculty Johnston-Willis Sch. Nursing, Richmond, Va., 1974-75; staff, charge nurse Mass. Gen. Hosp., Boston, 1975-78; faculty New Eng. Deaconess, Boston, 1978-80, Lankenau Hosp. Sch. of Nursing, Phila., 1980-81; pres. Original Metals, Inc., Phila., 1985—, also bd. dirs.; owner Silver Carousel Antiques, Rochester, Minn. Treas. Women's Assn. Minn. Orch., Rochester, 1986-87, pres. 1987-89, life advisor, 1989—, newsnotes editor, 1985-87, mem. mayor's coms. All Am. City Award Com., Rochester, 1984-88, Mayor's coms. Entertainment League, Rochester, 1987-88; bd. dirs. Rochester Civic League, 1988—, pres.-elect, 1990—; pres. Rochester Friends of the Mpls. Inst. Arts, 1989-90; pres. Folwell PTA, 1990—; state liaison GATEway, 1990—. Mem. Am. Soc. Law and Medicine, Zumbro Valley Med. Soc. Aux. (Rochester, fin. chmn. 1986-90, treas. 1988-90), NAFE, Nat. Assn. Food Equipment Mfrs., Friends of Mayowood, Phi Alpha Delta, Sigma Theta Tau.

AMAKER, ALIT LEIGH, director public affairs; b. Boston, June 30, 1965; m. Edward Charles Amaker, Nov. 22, 1987. BA magna cum laude, SUNY, Geneseo, 1989. Communications aide BOCES, Rochester, N.Y., 1986-88; pub. affairs dir. Sta. WPXY, Rochester, 1988—. Fellow Women in Communications, Inc., Am. Women in Radio and TV (coord. job program), Rochester Broadcasters Assn. Office: Sta WPXY 55 St Paul St Rochester NY 14604

AMANDOLIA, CYNTHIA LORENE, telephone company executive; b. Atlanta, Feb. 1, 1963; d. John Albert and Eleanor Lorene (Henry) A. BBA, Kennesaw State U., 1985. Reports clk. AT&T, Atanta, 1985, communication cons., 1986—. Pres. Single Adult Ministry, tchr. Sunday sch., coord. Family Tng. Hour local ch.; vol. Spl. Olympics, Woodruff Arts Ctr.; fund raiser Henrietta Egleston Hosp.

AMANN, CYNTHIA CLAIR, art gallery executive, speaker; b. Lakeland, Fla., Feb. 21, 1948; d. Robert M. and Bettye Clair (MacCranie) Kyrzakos; m. Robert Foster Clough, July 22, 1966 (div. Apr. 1973); children: Kacyn A., Kinna M.; m. John Robert Amann, Jr., June 19, 1982. Grad. high sch., West Palm Beach, Fla. TV comml. actress and fashion model Fla., 1983—; owner, mgr. Amann Gallery, Inc., Palm Beach, Fla., 1983—; profl. speaker Speaker's Connection, Sarasota, Fla., 1986—; guest numerous TV and radio shows including Regis Philbin Show, Today in Chgo., Afternoon Show, San Francisco.; condr. seminars; judge beauty pageants throughout U.S. Active numerous civic orgns. including Muscular Dystrophy Assn., Am. Cancer Soc., Leukemia Soc. Am., Am. Finnish Children's Found., Abused Children's Emergency Shelter, Honolulu; mem. budget and allocation com. United Way, West Palm Beach, 1988; bd. dirs. YWCA, West Palm Beach, 1988—, mem. membership and nominating com., 1989—; mem. adv. panel Planned Parenthood, West Palm Beach, 1988—. Winner Mrs. America Pageant, 1986; recipient resolution Fla. Ho. of Reps., 1986, keys to numerous cities. Mem. AFTRA, Internat. Platform Assn. Home: 5200 N Dixie Hwy West Palm Beach FL 33407

AMANTEA, REBECCA ANNE, corporate executive; b. Alhambra, Calif., July 31, 1955; d. Walter P. and Anna F. (Hunt) Acosta; children: Adam, Christopher. AA, Mesa Coll., San Diego, 1979. Exec. sec. Macom/Linkabit, San Diego, 1973-80; support svcs. mgr. Arete, San Diego, 1981-82; v.p. Hdqrs. Cos., San Diego, L.A., 1982—. Home: 4370 La Jolla Village Dr San Diego CA 92122

AMARA, LUCINE, opera and concert singer; b. Hartford, Conn., Mar. 1, 1927; d. George and Adrine (Kazanjian) Armaganian; married, Jan. 7, 1961 (div. June 1964). Student, Music Acad. of West, 1947, U. So. Calif., 1949-50. Appeared at Hollywood Bowl, 1948, soloist, San Francisco Symphony, 1949-50; career includes over 1000 operatic performances; with Met. Opera, N.Y.C., from 1950, sang 800 performances, 9 new prodns., 5 opening nights, 45 radio broadcasts, 4 telecasts including appeared on Met. Opera: In Performance, 1982, 83, 84; recorded Pagliacci, 1951, 60; singer with New Orleans, Hartford, Pitts., Central City operas, 1952-54, appeared Glyndebourne Opera, 1954, 55, 57, 58, Edinburgh Festival, 1954, singer, Aida, Terme Di Caracalla, Rome, 1954, also Stockholm Opera, N.Y. Philharm., St. Louis Civic Light Opera, 1955-56; has appeared in leading or title roles in several operas including: Tosca, Aida, Amelia in Un Ballo in Maschera, Turandot, Riverside Opera Assn., 1986, others; appeared with St. Petersburg (Fla.) Opera, Venezuela Philharm. Orch., 1988; opera and concert tour, Russia, 1965, Manila, 1968, Paris, Mex., 1966, Hong Kong and China, 1983, Yugoslavia, 1988; rec. artist, Columbia, RCA, Victor, Angel records, Met. Opera Record Club; albums include: Beethoven's Symphony No. 9, Leon Cavallo, I Pagliacci, La Bohème, Verdi's Requiem. Recipient 1st prize Atwater-Kent Radio Auditions, 1948. Mem. Sigma Alpha Iota. Office: Met Opera New York NY 10023

AMATO, CAMILLE JEAN, manufacturing executive; b. N.Y.C., Aug. 6, 1942; d. William and Mary Carmela (Lombardi) Tuorto; m. Thomas Amato, June 1, 1963; children—Dawn, Thomas. Assoc. Sci., SUNY-Albany, 1981, B.S., 1983; B.S., Empire State Coll., 1983, M. Bus. and Policy, 1986. Lic. realtor, notary, N.Y. Controller, owner Island Marine Inc., Bellmore, N.Y., 1977—; account mgr. L.I. Luth. Assn., Brookville, N.Y., 1983-84, Borden Inc. Chem., Glen Cove, N.Y., 1984-85; real estate agt. N. of 25A R.E. Inc., Locust Valley, N.Y., 1986—; owner, v.p. Penn Yan (N.Y.) Marine Mfg. Inc., 1986—; pres., owner Camille Properties, Inc., Penn Yan, 1986—; cons. various areas. Cons. sub-com. edn. and safety N.Y. State Senate, 1976-77. Mem. Nat. Assn. Female Execs., L.I. Bd. Realtors. Roman Catholic. Avocation: classical piano. Home: Woodstock Manor Muttontown Oyster Bay NY 11771

AMATO, CHRISTINE COFFIN, advertising executive; b. Boston, June 5, 1951; d. A. Russell Jr. and Sylvia (Fry) Coffin; m. Douglas Armstrong, June 2, 1973 (div. Sept. 1983); m. Robert Amato, May 5, 1989. Student, Boston Mus. Sch., 1974; BFA, Mass. Coll. Art, 1975. Asst. art dir. Gregory Fossella Assocs., Boston, 1974-75, Kenyon & Ekhardt Advt., Boston, 1975-76; art dir. Harold Cabot Advt., Boston, 1976-79; v.p., sr. art dir. Ogilvy & Mather Advt., N.Y.C., 1979-86; v.p., sr. art dir., group head Lord, Geller, Federico, Einstein Inc., N.Y.C., 1986—; mem. adv. bd. Design Rsch. unit Mass. Coll. Art, Boston, 1975—. Mem. Vol. Svcs. Children, N.Y.C., 1983—. Recipient Andy award, 1983, 88, Clio award, 1983, One Show award Internat. Advt. Festival N.Y., 1984, 89. Democat. Home: 200 E 72d St New York NY 10021 Office: Lord Geller Federico Einstein Inc 655 Madison Ave New York NY 10021

AMATO, PAULA ANN, accountant; b. Manchester, N.H., Sept. 15, 1962; d. Richard J. and Marlene A. (Remillard) McInnis; m. Joseph A. Amato Jr., Sept. 29, 1984; 1 child, Meghan R. BS, N.H. Coll., 1984, postgrad., 1984—. Acct. Erin Food Services, Manchester, 1984-85; supervisory acct. AI Network Corp., Manchester, 1985-89, N.H. Ins. Co., Manchester, 1989—. Mem. acad. planning and rev. bd. Hesser Coll., 1988—. Fellow Nat. Assn. Female Execs.; mem. Nat. Assn. Accts. (bd. dirs. 1984—), Nat. Assn. Exec. Females. Home: 44 Gold St Manchester NH 03103 Office: NH Ins Co 1750 Elm St Manchester NH 03107

AMATO, ROSEMARIE HELEN, design company executive, educator; b. Cleve., July 20, 1950; d. August Martin and Helen (Kovanes) A.; m. Richard Adam Damiani, July 3, 1978. BS, Ohio State U., 1972; MS, Cleve. State U., 1978. Educator Lorain (Ohio) City Schs., 1972-74, Cuyahoga Heights Local Schs., Cleve., 1974-81; pres., owner Western Reserve Design Studio, Inc., Cleve., 1980—. Advisor Sohio Riverfest for City of Cleve., Cleveland Flats, 1986, Community Design for Cleveland Flats, 1985-86; community rep. Woman Space, Cleve., 1984-85. Named Outstanding Sr. Woman Leader, Ohio State U., 1972, Outstanding Pace Setter Greater Cleve. Enterprising Women, Directory of Enterprising Women of Greater Cleve., 1985. Mem. Am. Soc. Interior Designers, Greater Cleve. Growth Assn., Cleve. Bus. and Profl. Women's Club (2nd v.p. 1983-86, 1st v.p. 1986-87), Woman Bus. Owners Assn.(mem. at large rep. to bd. dirs. 1986-87, mem. chmn. 1986-87, facilities chmn. 1987-89, sec. 1989), Order Sons of Italy in Am. (local trustee 1981-85, local fin. sec. 1985-87, state scholarship chmn. 1982, 83, 86, Italian awareness in USA state chmn., 1985, orator 1989—), Flats Oxbow Assn. (sec. 1985-86), Cleve. Women's City Club, Westlake C. of C., Alpha Delta Kappa (corresponding sec. 1983-85). Republican. Roman Catholic. Home: 1900 Grove Ct Cleveland OH 44113 Office: Western Res Design Studio 23902 Detroit Rd Westlake OH 44145

AMAZON, ELIZABETH GANNON, retired educator, civic worker; b. Cambridge, N.Y., Sept. 29, 1912; d. John Joseph and Mary Camilla (McGowan) Gannon; m. Maurice D. Amazon (dec. May 1967); children: Mary Alyce, David, Maureen, Sheila, Dana, Jennifer, Rosemary. BS in Edn., SUNY, Albany, 1041; grad., SUNY, Oneonta; postgrad., Skidmore Coll. Elem. tchr. pub. schs., Cambridge, 1932-34, Easton, N.Y., 1936-41; tchr. English, John Bigsbee Jr. High Sch., Schenectady, 1941-46; elem. tchr. pub. schs., Nott Terrace, N.Y., 1959-60, Schenectady, 1941-46, South Colonie, N.Y., 1961-81; ret., 1981. Voluntee Schenectady Mus.; active Sunnyview Aux., Glendale Home Aux., St. Clare's Aux.; intake worker Inner City Ministry; mem. Friends of Libr., Lady of Fatime Sr. Citizen Group, St. Helen's Sr. Citizen Group; v.p. Youth over Fifty, Eastern Parkway Meth. Ch.; active SICM, numerous other orgns. Mem. AAUW, Am. Assn. Ret. Persons (past sec., v.p., chmn.), Cath. Daus. Am., Ea. Zone Ret. Tchrs. Assn., Schenectady County Ret. Tchrs. Assn., SUNY-Oneonta Alumni Assn. (past unit pres.), Schenectady Women's Club, Schenectady Hist. Soc. (past bd. dirs.), Niskayuna Garden Club (v.p.. bd. dirs., com. mem.). Democrat. Home: 1160 Keyes Ave Schenectady NY 12309

AMBROSE, AMY CHRISTINE, business executive; b. Naperville, Ill., June 23, 1963; d. Roger Edward and Natalie Bertha (Schmidt) A. BA in Econs., Gordon Coll., 1985. Cons. Essex County News, Beverly, Mass., 1984-85; sales rep. Hastings Group, Swampscott, Mass., 1985-86, Ira Olds Toyota, Danvers, Mass., 1986-87; sales mgr. New Eng. area Sunflex Co. Inc., Novato, Calif., 1987-88; pres. Ambrose Industries, Lynnfield, Mass., 1988—; sr. ins. agt. Amex Life Assurance Co., Burlington, Mass., 1989—. Mem. North Shore Women in Bus., North Shore C. of C. Republican. Congregationalist. Home and Office: 6l7 Broadway Lynnfield MA 01940

AMBROZIAK, SHIRLEY ANN, communication specialist; b. Saginaw, Mich., July 8, 1953; d. John Joseph and Stella Mary (Wasik) A.; B.A. with honors, Mich. State U., 1975; M.A. (grantee), Purdue U., 1977. Speech instr. Purdue U., West Lafayette, Ind., 1975-77, Hammond, Ind., 1977-78; journalism instr. West Side High Sch., Gary, Ind., 1977-78; dir. communications, asst. dir. Northwestern U. Transp. Center, Evanston, Ill., 1978-83; account exec. Arthur Andersen & Co., St. Charles, Ill., 1983-85, mktg. officer The Old Second Nat. Bank, Aurora, Ill., 1985—; speech instr. Northeastern Ill. U., 1979-80. Bd. dirs. Cook County Am. Cancer Soc., 1977-79; chmn. Gov's. Commn. on Higher Edn. Student Adv. Com., East Lansing, Mich., 1973-75. Mem. Women's Transp. Assn. (chmn. seminar and Chgo. program 1980-81). Internat. Assn. Bus. Communications, Women in Communications (co-chmn. job placement 1980-82), Transp. Research Forum, Speech Communication Assn. Am., Purdue Alumni Assn. Author: Organizational Communication, 1974; Human Communications, 1975; (with L. Stewart) The Relationship Between Adherence to Traditional Sex Roles and Communication Apprehension, 1976; (with Leon N. Moses) Corporate Planning under Deregulation: The Case of the Airline, 1980; (with Robert P. Neuschel) Managing Effectively under Deregulation, 1981; contbr. articles to profl. jours. and newspapers. Home: 2149 Pepper Valley Dr #14 Geneva IL 60134 Office: Old Second Nat Bank 37 S River St Aurora IL 60507

AMCHER, JEANNIE WEBB, data processing executive; b. Greenwood, S.C., Sept. 29, 1953; d. Frank and Ruby (Adams) Webb; m. Ernest Wayne O'Dell, Dec. 24, 1971 (div. May 1987); 1 child, Reggie; m. F. Cary Amcher, Sept. 2, 1990. BS in Bus., Limestone Coll., 1982. Clk. Riegel Textile Co., Ware Shoals, S.C., 1972-82; programmer trainee Riegel Textile Co., Greenville, S.C., 1982-83, programmer, 1983-84; human resource asst. Fries Textile Co., Galax, Va., 1983; programmer I Fluor-Daniel Co., Greenville, 1984-86, programmer II, 1986-88; programmer, analyst Am. Equipment Co., Greenville, 1987-88, supr. data processing, 1988-89, mgr. info. systems, 1989—. Republican. Baptist. Home: 19 Lee East Ct Taylors SC 29687 Office: Am Equipment Co 2106 Anderson Rd Greenville SC 29611

AMEEN, CHRISTINE APPLIN, human services administrator; b. Iron River, Mich., Mar. 20, 1953; d. J. Benjamin and Betty J. (Pierce) A.; m. David John Ameen, Sept. 10, 1977. BS in Social Sci., Mich. Tech. U., 1975; EdS in Adminstrn., No. Mich. U., 1979; EdD in Ednl. Leadership, Western Mich. U., 1983. Rsch. asst. Mich. Tech. U., Houghton, 1973-75; coord. edn. computer lab Portage Twp. Schs., Houghton, 1975-76; coord. planning and evaluation Marquette-Alger (Mich.) Intermediate Schs., 1977-79; spl. program evaluator Jackson (Mich.) Pub. Schs., 1979-81; evaluation specialist Ann Arbor (Mich.) Pub. Schs., 1981-84; dir. planning and evaluation Starr Commonwealth Schs., Albion, Mich., 1984—; pres. Info. Systems, Ann Arbor, 1988—; fellow Edn. Policy Fellowship-Inst. for Ednl. Leadership, Lansing, Mich., 1983-84. Contbr. articles to profl. jours. Vol. Community Health Ctr. of Br. County, Coldwater, Mich., 1984-89, Coldwater Pub. Schs., 1986-87. Mem. Nat. Assn. Homes for Children, Am. Evaluation Assn., Am. Edn. Rsch. Assn. Office: Starr Commonwealth Schs 13725 Starr Commonwealth Rd Albion MI 49224

AMEEN, JUNE DELIA, marketing professional, occupational health nurse; b. Lowell, Mass., June 3, 1955; d. Emil J. and Shirley (Barnaby) A. AS in Med. Assisting, Middlesex Community Coll., 1975; BSN, Boston Coll., 1984. RN, Mass. Med. asst. Family Planning of Merrimac Valley, Lowell, 1975-

79; occupational health nurse New Eng. Nuclear/DuPont, Boston, 1979-84; nurse USCI/div BARD, Billenica, Mass., 1984-86; sales and mktg. rep. Leonard Morse Occupational Health Svcs., Inc., Natick, Mass., 1986-88, dir. mktg. div., 1988-89; v.p. sales and mktg. Omni Health Systems, Inc., Natick, 1989—. Mem. Am. Assn. Occupational Health Nurses (program com.), Sigma Theta Tau, Alpha Sigma Nu. Home: 7 Washington St North Chelmsford MA 01863 Office: Omni Health Systems Inc 6 Union St Natick MA 01760

AMENDE, LYNN MERIDITH, health science association administrator; b. Copaigue, N.Y., June 24, 1959; d. Kurt F. and Louise Amende; m. Edward M. Bird, May 16, 1981. BS, William and Mary, 1972; MS, U. Md., 1976, PhD, 1979. Postdoctoral researcher Nat. Inst. Neurological Communicative Disorders & Stroke NIH, Bethesda, Md., 1979-81; postdoctoral researcher biochemistry dept. Armed Forces Radiobiology Rsch. Inst., Bethesda, 1981-83; sr. staff felloe Nat. Inst. Diabetes and Digestive and Kidney Diseases NIH, Bethesda, 1983-87; program officer internat. fellowship program Fogarty Internat. Ctr. NIH, Bethesda, 1987-89; exec. sec. rev. br. div. extramural affairs Nat. Heart, Lung and Blood Inst. NIH, Bethesda, 1989—; vis. lectr. zoology dept. U. Md., College Park, 1979. Contbr. articles and abstracts to profl. jours. Mem., bd. dirs. Woodstream Village Homeowners Assn., 1983-86, pres., 1984-85; mem., pres., bd. dirs. Autumn Woods Homeowners Assn., 1987—. Postdoctoral fellow Nat. Rsch. Coun. NAS, 1981-83, NIH, 1979-81. Mem. AAAS, Am. Soc. for Cell Biology, Biophysics Soc., Chesapeake Soc. for Electron Microscopy (coun. mem.), Sigma Xi. Office: NHLBI NIH Westwood Bldg Rm 648 Bethesda MD 20892

AMENDT, MARILYN JOAN, personnel director; b. Marshalltown, Iowa, June 21, 1928; d. Floyd Wilford and Helen Mary (Scheid) Peterson; m. Virgil E. Amendt, Sept. 4, 1949 (div. Aug. 1971); children: Gregory F., Scott R., Brad A. AA, Stephens Coll., Columbia, Mo., 1948; postgrad., U. Mich., 1978, U. Wis., Superior, 1980-83. Cert. personnel mgr. Office mgr. S&O Products, Inc., Marshalltown, Iowa, 1961-71; life underwriter Lincoln Liberty Life Ins. Co., Marshalltown, Iowa, 1971-72; retail store mgr. Amy's Fashions, Marshalltown, Iowa, 1972-74, Maurices, Inc., Marshalltown, Iowa, 1974-76; corp. personnel dir. Maurices, Inc., Duluth, Minn., 1976-84; sr. v.p., dir. human resources Ohrbach's, Inc., N.Y.C., 1984-87; dir. personnel adminstrn. AMCENA Corp., N.Y.C., 1987—; lectr. U. Wis, Superior, 1981-82, U. Minn., Duluth, 1981-82. Founder, pres., bd. dirs. Mid-Iowa Sheltered Workshop, Marshalltown, 1968-76; mem. Hostess com., Duluth (Minn.) Day Luncheon, 1983; keynote speaker, Am. Bus. Women's Day, Mpls, Duluth, 1984, 85, 86. Mem. Am. Bus. Women's Assn. (dist. v.p. 1982, nat. v.p. 1983, nat. pres. 1984, woman of the yr. 1978), Am. Soc. Exec. and Profl. Women. Home: 121 Brush Hollow Crescent Rye Brook NY 10573

AMENTA, CAROLINE, travel agency executive; b. Tarrytown, N.Y., Sept. 30, 1928; d. Carmelo John and Rosaria (Cavalieri) Malandrino; m. Sebastian Amenta, Dec. 27, 1952; children—Paul, John, Frank. Student Wood Bus. Sch., N.Y.C., 1946-47. Office sec. Westinghouse Internat., N.Y.C., 1947-49, Polychrome Co. Inc., Yonkers, N.Y., 1949-52, N.Y. State Regional Health Office, White Plains, 1952-55; travel cons. McGregor Travel, White Plains, 1967-70; pres. ATC Travel, Inc., Tarrytown, 1970—; sec. PJF Properties Ltd., Tarrytown, 1984—. Fellow Profl. Bus. Women (v.p. 1983-85). Roman Catholic. Avocations: swimming, reading, travel. Office: ATC Travel Inc 239 N Broadway Suite 3 North Tarrytown NY 10591

AMERINE, ANNE FOLLETTE, aerospace engineer; b. San Francisco, Sept. 27, 1950; d. William T. and Wilma (Carlson) F.; m. Jorge Armando Verdi D'Eguia, July 4, 1970 (div.); m. Donald Amerine, Dec. 18, 1983. AA, Coll. Marin, 1977; BA in Math. with honors, Mills Coll., 1979; MS in System Mgmt. U. So. Calif., 1990. Sr. computer operator Bank of Am. Internat. Services, San Francisco, 1972-74; mathematician Pacific Missile Test Ctr., Pt. Mugu, Calif., 1979-80; engr. Grumman Aerospace Corp., Pt. Mugu, 1979-83; engr. Litton Guidance and Control Systems, 1984-86, product support and assurance dept. project mgr., 1986—. Chmn. Marina West Neighborhood Council, 1982-84; mem. NOW; chmn. subcom. Ventura County Community Coll. Dist. Citizen's Adv. Com. on Status of Women, 1983-84. Aurelia Henry Reinhart scholar, 1978-79; recipient Project Sterling award Grumman Aerospace Corp., 1982. Mem. Nat. Assn. Female Execs., Soc. Women Engrs. (chmn. career guidance com. and speaker Ventura County sect.), Litton Women's Enhancement Orgn. (founder, v.p. and chmn. info. and edn. com. 1985-86, editor newsletter 1986-87), Mills Coll. Alumni, Litton Mgmt. Club (sec. 1990), Alpha Gamma Sigma (life). Office: Litton Guidance & Control Systems 5500 Canoga Ave MS 80 Woodland Hills CA 91367-6698

AMERNICK, ANN SILVERBERG, pastry chef, author; b. Balt., Sept. 15, 1943; d. Morris Martin and Helen (Kravetz) Silverberg; children: Jay Ira, Daniel Philip. BS in Elem. Edn., U. Md., 1964. Pastry chef Big Cheese Restaurant, Washington, 1976-78, Palais des Friandises, Rockville, Md., 1979-80, Elysee Boulangerie-Place Vendome, Washington, 1981-82, Jean Louis at Watergate, Washington, 1982-84, Chanterelle Caterers, Washington, 1984-87; garde manger, pastry chef Le Pavilion Restaurant, Washington, 1979; asst. pastry chef The White House, Washington, 1980-81; pvt. splty. pastry work, cons., Washington, 1987—. Co-author: Soufflés, 1989. Recipient bronze medal East South Regional Restaurant Expn.-Salon Culinary Arts, 1980, lst prize and best piece of show award, 1981, 82. Mem. Les Dames d'Escoffier (charter). Home and Office: 4201 Cathedral Ave NW Apt 222W Washington DC 20016

AMES, BARBARA FRANCES, pharmaceutical company media executive; b. Bklyn., Jan. 26, 1936; d. George and Selma C. (Ruderman) Levine; m. Jonathan Ames, Oct. 14, 1956 (div. 1964). Student, Hunter Coll., 1953-55. Computer liaison Young & Rubicam, N.Y.C., 1958-66; supr. media and planning Young & Rubicam Inc., N.Y.C., 1969-73, sr. v.p., mgr. communications svcs., 1974-87; coord. spot broadcast Ted Bates Advt. Agy., N.Y.C., 1966; mgr. office Advt. Info. Services, N.Y.C., 1966-67; media mgr. corp. advt. group Johnson & Johnson, New Brunswick, N.J., 1989—; bd. dirs. Advt. Info. Svcs. Trustee Homesharing of Somerset County. Office: Johnson & Johnson 501 George St New Brunswick NJ 08933

AMES, DAMARIS, publishing executive; b. Cin., Jan. 31, 1944; d. Van Meter and Betty (Breneman) A. BA, Radcliffe Coll., 1965; MA, Harvard U., 1967. Editing asst. coll. div. Houghton Mifflin Co., Boston, 1969-71, editing mgr. coll. div., 1971-76, sr. editing mgr. coll. div., 1976-77, editing dir. coll. div., 1977-78, corp. analyst for chief exec. officer, 1978-81, communications dir., 1981-86, v.p., dir. pub. and communications, 1986, v.p., pub., 1986-87, sr. v.p., pub., 1987-88, exec. v.p., pub., 1988—, also bd. dirs. Office: Houghton Mifflin Co 1 Beacon St Boston MA 02108

AMES, KATHLEEN MARIE, health facilities administrator; b. Pitts., July 14, 1966; d. Ronald William and Judith Barbara (Deustch) Matthews. BS in Mktg. and Mgmt., Va. Polytechnic Inst., 1984. Sales rep. The Limited, Raleigh, N.C., 1988—; profl. rels. coord. Carolina Physician's Health Plan, Inc., Raleigh, 1989—. Active Vols. Under 30, Raleigh, 1989—. Mem. NAFE, Delta Sigma Pi. Republican. Roman Catholic. Office: Carolina Physicians Health Plan Inc 4020 Westchase Blvd Ste 450 Raleigh NC 27607

AMES, LOUISE BATES, child psychologist; b. Portland, Maine, Oct. 29, 1908; d. Samuel Lewis and Annie Earle (Leach) Bates; m. Smith Whittier Ames, May 22, 1930 (div. 1937); 1 child, Joan Ames Chase. A.B., U. Maine, 1930, M.A., 1933, Sc.D., 1957; Ph.D., Yale U., 1936; D.Sc., Wheaton Coll., 1967. Cert. psychologist, Conn. Research sec., personal asst. to Dr. Gesell Yale Clinc Child Devel., Yale Med. Sch., 1933-36, instr., 1940-44, asst. prof., 1944-50; curator Yale Films of Child Devel., 1944-50; co-founder Gesell Inst. Child Devel., dir. research, sec.-treas., 1950-65, asso. dir., chief psychologist, 1968, co-dir., 1971-77, acting dir., 1978, assoc. dir., 1978—. Author: daily syndicated newspaper column Parents Ask; weekly TV broadcast on child behavior, WBZ, Boston, 1952-55; author 32 books, including: (with Arnold Gesell and others) The Gesell Institute's Child from One to Six; editorial bd. Jour. Learning Disabilities, Jour. Genetic Psychology. Mem. Conn. Psychol. Soc., Am. Psychol. Assn., Soc. Research Child Devel., Internat. Council Psychologists (dir. 1945-47), Soc. Projective Techniques (pres. 1970), Sigma Xi. Home: 283 Edwards St New Haven CT 06511 Office: Gesell Inst Child Devel 310 Prospect St New Haven CT 06511

AMES, SANDRA PATIENCE, sales executive; b. Quincy, Calif., May 23, 1947; d. Bruce Ray Richards and Margaret Elizabeth (Steiner) Richards Johnson; m. Martin P.M. Bettenhausen, Dec. 10, 1965 (div. 1972); m. Thomas William Ames, Nov. 28, 1975. Student Yuba City Jr. Coll., 1965-66. Sales corr. Nat. Can Corp. (now known as Am. Nat. Can Co.), Seattle, 1974-76, Lehigh Valley, Pa., 1976-79, nat. account sales corr., Chgo., 1979-81, dist. sales office mgr., 1981-82, sales analyst I, Oakbrook, Ill., 1982-84, regional sales office mgr., 1984-86; mgr. regional sales office, Oakbrook, 1987-89; mgr. cen. sales adminstrn., Chgo., 1989—. Mem. Nat. Assn. Female Execs. Republican. Office: Am Nat Can Co 8770 W Bryn Mawr Ave Chicago IL 60631-3542

AMEY, RAE, television and video developer, producer; b. Shreveport, La., Sept. 26, 1947; d. Bruce Harold and Genevieve (Amey) Gentry; m. John E. Scarborough, Dec. 18, 1971 (div. Nov. 1979). Student, La. State U., 1968-70, U. Houston, 1972-74; BA in Liberal Arts, Antioch U., 1985; grad., U. So. Calif., 1988—. Free-lance photographer various locations, Calif., 1973—; adminstrn. coordinator Y.E.S. Inc., Sta. KCET-TV, L.A., 1980-83; free-lance ednl. TV writer, cons. L.A., 1983-84; asst. to pres. prodn. So. Calif. Consortium, Cypress, 1984, project mgr., dir. devel., project dir. The Human Condition, 1985-87; prin. Video Nexus, San Pedro, Calif., 1987—; dir. devel. Cal-SPAN: The California Channel, 1990—; dir. devel. Cal-SPAN: The Calif. Channel, 1990—. Editor TV guide book, 1985; photography exhbns. include: Contemporary Art Mus., Houston, 1973, Galveston (Tex.) Arts Ctr., 1975, Cameravision Gallery, L.A.,1980, Aloft, Pasadena, 1989. Co-founder Harbor Arts Alliance. Ellen Torgenson Shaw scholar Annenberg Sch. Communications, U. So. Calif., 1989. Mem. Women in Communications (bd. dirs., v.p. campus svcs. 1987-88, exec. v.p. 1988-89, bd. dirs. scholarship and edn. fund L.A. chpt.), Harbor Arts Alliance (co-founder). Democrat. Home: 703 W 28th St San Pedro CA 90731 Office: Video Nexus 703 W 28th St San Pedro CA 90731

AMGOTT, MADELINE, television producer, media consultant; b. N.Y.C., Aug. 31, 1931; d. Samuel and Rose (Kanter) Barotz; m. David Karr, Sept. 5, 1952 (div. 1956); children: Andrew, Katharine Karr-Kaitin; m. Milton Amgott, Dec. 15, 1962; 1 child, Seth; 1 stepchild, Margo. BA cum laude, Bklyn. Coll., 1952. Feature coordinator CBS News, N.Y.C.; producer WNBC-TV Not for Women Only, CBS News 60 Minutes, Morning Show, 30 Minutes, Bill Moyers' Constitution Hours, Phil Donahue spl. documentary The Human Animal, Good Housekeeping A Better Way, Today Show; now producer CNBC Home and Family Hour; cons. Times Mirror, N.Y.C., King Features Entertainment, IBM; bd. dirs. Am. Jour. Nursing Pub. Co., N.Y.C. Co-author: Teenage Gangs, 1957. Mem. West Pride, W. 86th St. Tenants Assn.; co-founder 168 W 68th St Tenants Assn.; mem. N.Y.C. Bicentennial Commn., 1987-89. Recipeint Emmy Nat. Acad. TV Arts, 1981, 82, 83; Ohio State award, 1976. 78; Peabody award, 1976; Matrix award, 1976, award Greater Miami Film Festival, Internat. Film Festival of N.Y., others. Mem. Women's Forum (v.p. 1982), Women in Communications, Inc. (N.Y. pres. 1984), Newswomen of N.Y. Home: 168 W 86th St New York NY 10024 Office: CBNC 2200 Fletcher Ave Fort Lee NJ 07024

AMICARELLI, DEBRA LEE, financial services professional; b. L.I., N.Y., Nov. 18, 1957; d. Leo M. and Agnes M. (Miceli) Stahley; m. Gene A. Amicarelli, Mar. 7, 1981; children: Andrew, Kristen. BS in Acctg. cum laude, C.W. Post Ctr., Greenvale, N.Y., 1979. Acctg. mgr. EBS, Maitland, Fla.; asst. corp. controller Am. Pioneer, Orlando, Fla.; account rep. Associated Planners Group, Winter Park, Fla. Mem. Nat. Assn. Life Underwriters. Home: 1114 Black Acre Ct N Winter Springs FL 32708

AMIN, JAMILLAH MAARIJ (JOYCE MARIE JOSEPH), real estate agent, food technologist; b. Lake Charles, La., Jan. 11, 1947; d. Anthony Armo and Edna (LeMelle) Joseph; m. Yusuf D. Amin Sr., Aug. 31, 1968 (div. Dec. 1981); children: Laval Vallare, Yusuf, Ishmael, Harun, Caliph; m. Guy R. Grant, July 27, 1985. Student San Jose City Coll., 1965-67, San Jose State Coll., 1967-68, Calif. Poly. Inst., 1970-71; AA, Yuba Coll., 1970; BS, Calif. State U.-Fresno, 1973. Quality control technician Adolph Coors Co., Golden, Colo., 1979, food technologist, 1979-80; asst. mgr. food service Am. River Coll., Sacramento, 1982-83; food service mgr. U. Calif., Davis, 1983-84; pub. service dir. KMFO Broadcasting, Aptos, Calif., 1984-85; real estate agt. Cornish and Carey Realtors, Hollister, Calif., 1985-87; agt., property mgr. IFS Inc., Hollister, 1987-88; owner, broker Newcomer Real Estate, Hollister, 1988—. Vice-chmn. planning commn. City of Hollister, 1989—. Recipient Outstanding Service award Sabin Sch., 1977; Outstanding Service award Gold Oak Sch., 1981. Mem. Inst. Food Technologists, San Benito County Bd. Realtors (sec. 1988). Republican. Avocations: writing poetry; gardening; hiking. Home: 1481 Versailles Dr Hollister CA 95023 Office: Newcomer Real Estate 344 5th St Hollister CA 95023

AMMEN, HELEN JOANNE, fund raiser, consultant; b. Greensboro, N.C., Feb. 10, 1944; d. Russell Marcus and Clara Katherine (Kessler) A. Student, Kernersville Wesleyan Coll., 1965-67, High Point Coll., 1987. Sec. The White House, Washington, 1972-77; asst. to former pres. Gerald R. Ford Transition Office, Washington, 1977; staff asst. U.S. Dept. Energy, Washington, 1978-79; dir. spl. projects Rep. Nat. Com. Nat. Fedn. Rep. Women, Washington, 1979; dir. library Rep. Nat. Com., Washington, 1979-81; dir. White House Library & Research Ctr., Washington, 1981-84; dir. found. relations Bowman Gray Sch. Med. Wake Forest U. and N.C. Bapt. Hosp., Winston-Salem, N.C., 1984—. Bd. dirs. YWCA, Winston-Salem, 1989—, mem. finance com., 1988—, resource devel. com., 1989—. Mem. Nat. Soc. Fund Raising Execs., Nat. Assn. Hosp. Devel., Coun. Advancement and Support Edn., Assn. Acad. Health Ctrs. (govt. rels. reps. 1987—), Assn. Acad. Med. Ctrs. (group on pub. affairs), So. Found. and Corp. Rels. Officers, Triad Fund Raising Execs. Coun. Republican. Presbyterian. Home: 1837 Stonewood Dr Winston-Salem NC 27103 Office: Bowman Gray Sch Medicine 300 S Hawthorne Rd Winston-Salem NC 27103

AMMON, CAROLINE LINDA, occupational therapist; b. Bklyn., Sept. 21, 1965; d. Richard Frank Ammon and Inga Norrberg. BS, NYU, 1987. Registered and lic. occupational therapist. Intern in occupational therapy Ridgewood (N.Y.) Continuing Treatment Ctr., 1987--; therapist St. Francis Hosp. Med. Ctr., Hartford, Conn., 1987, Am. Occupational Therapy Assn., Rockville, Md., 1987, Mt. Sinai Hosp., Hartford, 1988--; Conn. Therapies, Newington; sign language instr. various N.Y. and Conn., 1979--. Contbr. articles to newspapers. Puppeteer Kids on the Block, Assn. Retarded Citizens, Hartford, 1988--; campaigner for re-election of Senator Lowell Weicker, Conn., 1988. Mem. Parish Mission Div. Our Saviors Luth. Ch., Am. Occupational Therapy Assn., Conn. Occupational Therapy Assn. (chairperson Coun. on Govt. Affairs, 1988), Assn. for Advancement of Rehab. Tech., Sierra Club. Lutheran. Home: 81 Crystal St Wethersfield CT 06109

AMNEUS, D. A., English language educator; b. Beverly, Mass., Oct. 15, 1919; d. Nils A. and Harriet S. (Anchersen) Amneus; divorced; children: Paul, Pamela. AB, U. Calif. Berkeley, 1941; MA, U. So. Calif., 1947, PhD, 1953. From asst. prof. to prof. Calif. State U., L.A., 1950—, prof. emeritus; pub. Primrose Press, Alhambra, Calif. Author: Back to Patriarchy, 1979, The Mystery of MacBeth, 1983, The Three Othellos, 1986, The Garbage Generation, 1990; contbr. articles to profl. jours. Mem. NOW. Republican. Home: 2131 S Primrose Ave Alhambra CA 91803 Office: Calif State U English Dept 5151 State University Dr Los Angeles CA 90032

AMOROSO, MARIE DOROTHY, retired EEG technologist; b. Phila., Jan. 16, 1924; d. Salvatore and Clorinda (Gaudio) A. Med. Lab. Tech., Hahnemann Hosp., Phila., 1943; postgrad., Temple U., Phila., 1945-48, U. Pa., Phila., 1947-48, 1950. Registered EEG Technologist; cert. registered EEG Technologist. EEG technician Hahnemann Med. Coll., Phila., 1943-53, Phila. Gen. Hosp., 1953-62; histology technician Temple Med. Coll. Temple U., Phila., 1962-63; allergy technician Harry Rogers, M.D., Phila., 1963; EEG technologist Haverford (Pa.) State Hosp., 1963-85, Irvin M. Gerson, MD, Haverford, 1985-88; EEG technologist to pvt. physician Haverford State Hosp., 1985-88; ret., 1988; instr. EEG Osteopathic Med. Ctr. Sch. Allied Health, Phila., 1978-85. Editor: The Eastern Breeze, 1977-79; contbr. articles to profl. jours.; patentee in field. Mem. Am. Soc. Electroneurodiagnostic Technologists, Inc., Clin. EEG Technicians Technologists Soc., The Western Soc. Electrodiagnostic Technologists, So. Soc. EEG Technicians, Inc., Ea. Soc. EEG and Neurodiagnostic Technicians (sec. 1977-79), Phila. Regional EEG Technician's Assn. (exec. bd. 1967, sec. 1969), Electro-Physiological Technologists Assn. Gt. Britain (subcriber mem.), Ea. Assn. Electroencephalographers (subscriber mem.). Home: 477 Brookfield Rd Drexel Hill PA 19026

AMOS, BETTY ANN, elementary school educator; b. Lindsborg, Kans., Apr. 17, 1948; d. Hubert Edward and Marlys Edith (Spongberg) Mattingly; m. Bruce Jay Amos, Aug. 11, 1979; children: Darin Jay, Kara Joy, Megan Jill. BS in Spl. Edn., U. Kans., 1970; MS in Gifted Edn., Kans. State U., 1979; cert. for adminstrn., Ft. Hays State U., 1988. Cert. tchr., elem. adminstr., spl. educator, Kans. Spl. edn. tchr. Grand Island (Nebr.) Pub. Schs., Grand Island, Nebr., 1970-72, Hoxie Pub. Schs., Hoxie, Kans., 1972-74; elem. tchr. Hoxie Pub. Schs., 1974-78; gifted facilitator Colby Pub. Schs., Colby, Kans., 1978-80; elem. tchr. Colby Pub. Schs., 1980-85, kindergarten tchr., 1985—; dir. pre-vocat. program Grand Island Pub. Schs., summer 1971; migrant tchr. Hoxie Pub. Schs., summers 1973-76; kid coll. dir. Colby Pub. Schs., summers 1979-81; workshop presenter Kans.-NEA, Topeka, 1978—. Contbr. poems to mags. Pianist Trinity Luth. Ch., Colby, 1978—. Named Kans. State Tchr. of Yr., State of Kans., 1984. Mem. Colby Tchrs. Assn. (pres. 1988-89), Kans. Tchrs. of Yr. (treas. 1986—), Assn. for Supervision & Curriculum, NEA, Kans.-NEA, AAUW, Phi Delta Kappa, Delta Kappa Gamma (pres. Gamma Alpha chpt. 1988-90). Republican. Home: 775 W 5th Colby KS 67701

AMOS, JOAN MARIE, insurance agency executive; b. Leominster, Mass., Nov. 22, 1935; d. Louis Adelard and Cecelia Irene (Lamoreux) LaBelle; m. Charles Clinton Amos, Feb. 2, 1962; 1 child, Jonathan Ashley. Cert. in Acctg., LaSalle U., Chgo., 1968; charter property and casualty underwriting courses Boston U., 1968-69. Sec., treas. Henry Leblanc Inc., Fitchburg, Mass., 1969-74, Marsolais Ins. Agy., Ayer, Mass., 1970-74, Aanco Underwriters, Inc., St. Petersburg, Fla., 1973—, Countryside Insurors, Inc., Tarpon Springs, Fla., 1982-85; pres. Ins. Premium Acceptance Corp., St. Petersburg, 1986—; pres. Gulfport Mini-Warehouse, Inc., Fla., 1986—. owner, operator Jomar Charter & Properties, St. Petersburg, 1973—. Bd. dirs. Fla. Orch., St. Petersburg, 1981-83, bd. govs., 1984-87; fund raising chmn. Pinellas Assn. for Retarded Children, St. Petersburg, 1982; life mem. Arthritis Found., Family Services. Am. Nat. Novice Ladies Figure Skating Champion, Roller Skating Rink Operators Assn. Am., 1953. Mem. Nat. Assn. Ins. Women, Ins. Women of St. Petersburg, Nat. Assn. Ins. Agts., Am. Cancer Soc. (life), Arthritis Found. (Sword of Hope chpt.), Nat. Notary Assn., Nat. Assn. Female Execs. Roman Catholic. Clubs: Cross of Lorraine Soc., Infinity, Boley's Angels. Home: 300 Rafael Blvd NE Saint Petersburg FL 33704 Office: Aanco Underwriters Inc 10033 9th St Saint Petersburg FL 33716

AMSTER, LINDA EVELYN, newspaper executive, consultant; b. N.Y.C., May 21, 1938; d. Abraham and Belle Shirley (Levine) Meyerson; m. Robert L. Amster, Feb. 18, 1961 (dec. Feb. 1974). B.A., U. Mich., 1960; M.L.S., Columbia U., 1968. Tchr. English Stamford High Sch., Conn., 1961-63; research librarian The Detroit News, 1965-67; research librarian The N.Y. Times, N.Y.C., 1967-69, supr. news research, 1969-74, news research mgr., 1974—; bd. dirs. Council for Career Planning, N.Y.C., 1982—. Contbr. articles to books, N.Y. Times and other publs. Mem. Spl. libraries Assn. Club: Coffee House. Home: 336 Central Park W New York NY 10025 Office: The NY Times 229 W 43d St New York NY 10036

AMTOFT-NIELSEN, JOAN THERESA, physician, educator, researcher; b. Reading, Pa., Jan. 31, 1940; children: Andre Christian, Nikolaj Johan, Anja. BS, Kutztown (Pa.) State U., 1960; MD, Ansalt U. Munchen, Fed. Republic Germany, 1965; DC, Nat. Coll., 1968; MD, U. Copenhagen, 1978; postgrad., Harvard U., 1989-90. Regional dir. Pa. Acad. Sci., Reading, 1961; intern Cook County Hosp., Chgo., 1966-68; clin. instr. U. Copenhagen, 1975-80; proctor N.C. Coalition Health, Durham, 1985-87; founder, cons. Triangle PMS Ctr., Cary, N.C., 1987—, also bd. dirs. Contbr. articles to profl. jours. Bd. dirs. shelter St. Francis Ho., Chapel Hill, N.C., 1989—; bd. dirs., grant coordinator N.C. Coalition Chs., Raleigh; v.p. Danish Red Cross, 1975-80; cons. physician Handicapped Encounter in Christ, Raleigh, 1984-87. NSF grantee, 1961; recipient award Sardoni Found., 1964, Walter Morris Found., 1957, Community Svc. award K.C., 1989. Mem. Am. Acad. Holistic Physicians, European Acad. Preventative Medicine, AAUW (v.p. Raleigh chpt. 1987—), NAFE, Scandinavian Club. Republican. Roman Catholic. Home: 218 Rosebrook Dr Cary NC 27513

AMYOTTE, SHERRY JO, environmental and medical piping consultant; b. Grand Rapids, Mich., Jan. 22, 1956; d. George Alex and Joan Pauline (Harrison) A. BA in Biology, U. N.C., Charlotte, 1985. Lab. tech. U. N.C., Charlotte, 1983-85, research tech., 1985-88; quality control tech. Unocal Chems.-Mallard Creek, Charlotte, 1986-89; envirom. and med. piping cons. Gas Monitoring Inc., Cary, N.C., 1989—. Contbr. articles to profl. jours. Mem. Am. Soc. Zoologists, N.C. Acad. Sci., Wilderness Soc. Democrat. Methodist. Club: Piedmont Adventure (Concord, N.C.). Lodge: Order Eastern Star. Home: 798 Davis St Concord NC 28025 Office: Gas Monitoring Inc 1140 Kildare Farm Rd Cary NC 27512-1285

ANABLE, ANNE CURRIER STEINERT, journalist; b. Boston, Feb. 18; d. Robert Shuman and Lucy Pettingill (Currier) Steinert; m. Anthony Anable, Jr., 1962 (div. 1965); m. Robert C. Henriques, 1973 (div. 1980). Grad. West Hill Jr. Coll., Boston, 1951. Reporter women's pages N.Y. Jour. Am., N.Y.C., 1961-66, World Jour. Tribune, N.Y.C., 1966-67; fashion editor Cleve. Plain Dealer, 1967-73; fashion and beauty editor New Woman mag., Ft. Lauderdale, Fla., 1973-75, 78-79; contbg. editor Conn. sect. N.Y. Times, 1977-81; beauty editor L'Officiel/USA, 1979, New Woman mag., 1982; fashion editor Am. Salon, 1984-87; contbg. editor Playbill, N.Y.C., 1985—, Harris Publs., 1987-89, Four Season Hotels Mag. 1989—. Recipient Fashion Reporting award N.Y., 1970. Mem. Soc. Profl. Journalists, Fashion Group, Fashion's Inner Circle, Editorial Free Lancers Assn. Home and Office: 7 Flower Hill Pl Port Washington NY 11050

ANAGNOST, CATHERINE COOK, lawyer; b. Tegea, Greece, Feb. 10, 1919; (parents Am. citizens); d. Peter and Athena (Reppas) Cook; m. Themis Anagnost, Aug. 15, 1942; children: Maria, Alexander, James. Diploma in commerce, Northwestern U., 1942; student, Loyola U., Chgo., 1942, U. Ill., 1943, U. Chgo., 1944. Bar: Ill. 1948, U.S. Supreme Ct. 1960; CPA, Ill. Acct., 1942-48; intern Themis Anagnost, Chgo., 1944-48; ptnr. Anagnost & Anagnost, Chgo., 1948—. Bd. dirs., v.p. Beverly Fame Found., Godfrey, Ill., 1963-73; dir. women's adv. coun. N.Y. World's Fair, 1964-65; chairperson Founders' Day program Northwestern U., 1966; alt. del. Rep. Nat. Conv., 1964; mem. United Rep. Fund Ill.; jud. candidate Chgo. Mcpl. Ct., 1960, 62, Cook County Cir. Ct., 1964, 74, 76, Ill. Supreme Ct., 1980. Recipient merit award Northwestern U., 1964. Mem. ABA (ho. of dels. 1965-67), Ill. Bar Assn., Chgo. Bar Assn., West Suburban Bar Assn. (pres. 1958-59), Hellenic Bar Assn. (pres. 1955), Internat. Assn. Women Lawyers, Nat. Assn. Women Lawyers (pres. 1963-64), Am. Assn. Atty.-CPA's, Assn. Trial Lawyers Am., Ill. Trial Lawyers Assn., Am. Judicature Soc., Northwestern U. Alumni Assn., Internat. House Assn. (past pres. Chgo.), Execs. Club, Greek Women's U. Club, Order Ea. Star, White Shrine, Phi Gamma Nu. Home: 2345 N Oak Park Ave Chicago IL 60635 Office: 30 N La Salle St Chicago IL 60602

ANAGNOST, MARIA ATHENA, surgeon; b. Chgo., Oct. 21, 1943; d. Themis John and Catherine (Cook) A.; BA, Northwestern U., 1965; MD, U. Ill., 1973. Resident in surgery U. Chgo. Hosps. and Clinics, 1973-74; gen. surgery resident Michael Reese Med. Center, Chgo., 1975-79, chief resident, 1979-80; pvt. practice surgery; surg. staff Oak Park (Ill.) Hosp., Westlake Community Hosp., Melrose Park, Ill., Gottlieb Meml. Hosp., Melrose Park, Good Samaritan Hosp., Downers Grove, Ill., Ravenswood Hosp., Chgo.; chmn. dept. surgery Loretto Hosp., Chgo. Diplomate Nat. Bd. Med. Examiners, 1974; cert. Am. Bd. Surgery. Recipient Physicians' Recognition award AMA. Fellow ACS, Internat. Coll. Surgeons (vice regent), Am. Soc. Abdominal Surgeons; mem. AMA, Ill. Med. Soc., Chgo. Med. Soc., InterAm. Coll. Physicians and Surgeons, Hellenic Med. Soc., U. Ill. alumni Assn., Northwestern U. Alumni Assn. Contbr. articles to profl. jours. Office: 1545 Clinton Pl River Forest IL 60305 also: 3825 Highland Ave Downers Grove IL 60515 also: 30 N LaSalle St Chicago IL 60602

ANAGNOSTE, VIVIAN GABRIELA, pathologist; b. Risnov, Romania, Mar. 16, 1929; came to U.S., 1973; d. Carlo and Jenny (Zuckman) Androniu;

1 child, Nicole. Student, Medico-Pharmaceutic, Bucharest, Romania, 1947-53. Intern Inst. Dr. Cantacuzino, Bucharest, 1952-53; rsch. nutritionist Inst. Hygiene, Bucharest, 1953-57; attendant, clin. lab. Trauma Hosp., Bucharest, 1957-60, I.C. Frimu Hosp., Bucharest, 1960-63; lab dir. Pantelimon Hosp., Bucharest, 1963-71, G. Alexandrescu Hosp., Bucharest, 1971-73; resident in pathology Middlesex Gen. Hosp., New Brunswick, N.J., 1974-77; clin. instr. Raritom Valley Hosp., New Brunswick, 1977-78; lab. dir. Rolling Hills Hosp., Elkins Park, Pa., 1978—. Mem. Coll. Am. Pathologists, Internat. Acad. Pathology, Am. Soc. Clin. Pathologists, Pa. Assn. Clin. Pathologists. Democrat. Christian Orthodox. Home: 1385 Mill Rd Rydal PA 19046 Office: Rolling Hill Hosp 60E Township Line Elkins Park PA 19117

ANANDAM, KAMALA, associate college dean; b. Tiruchi, Madras, India, Apr. 15, 1929; came to U.S., 1967; d. Michael and Sornammal Pakyanathan; m. Ernest J. Anandam, June 3, 1952 (dec. Nov. 1985); children: Nirmala Tashker, Shanthi Preston. BS, U. Madras, 1949, B. Tng., 1959; MS, U. Tenn., 1963, EdD, 1970. Sci. tchr. Jaivabai Girls' High Sch., Coimbatore, India, 1959-61; instr. Sri Avinahsilingham Home Sci. Coll., Coimbatore, 1961-63; prof., head child devel. Sri Avinahsilingham HOme Sci. Coll., Coimbatore, 1963-68; instr. U. Tenn., Knoxville, 1968-72; asst. prof. Maryville (Tenn.) Coll., 1970-72; assoc. prof. Bethune-Cookman Coll., Daytona Beach, Fla., 1972-74; rsch. specialist Miami (Fla.) Dade Community Coll., 1974-77, dir. computer-based edn., 1977-85, assoc. dean ednl technologies, 1985—; IBS cons. scholar IBM/Acad. Info. System, Milford, Conn., 1988—; steering com. mem. EDUCOM/Ednl. Users of Info. Tech., Washington, 1989—; dir. Multi-institutional Project, Miami, Fla., 1990—; adv. mem. Fla. Dept. of edn., Tallahassee, 1989—, Inst. for Acad. Tech., Chapel Hill, N.C., 1989—. Editor: Transforming Teaching with Technology, 1989; co-author books; contbr. articles to profl. jours.; chair EDUCOM com. publ. Software Snapshots: Where Are You in the Picture?, 1989; prin. designer (software) Camelot, 1980. Exxon Edn. Found. grantee Miami-Dade Community Coll., 1978, 80, Univ. Rels. of IBM grantee Miami-Dade Community Coll., 1990. Mem. Am. Ednl. Rsch. Assn., Assn. for the Devel. of Computer-based Instrn., Fla Assn. Community Colls., Omicron Nu, Sigma Xi, Phi Kappa Phi, Pi Lambda Theta. Office: Miami Dade Community Coll 11011 SW 104th St Miami FL 33176

ANASTASI, ANNE (MRS. JOHN PORTER FOLEY, JR.), psychology educator; b. N.Y.C., Dec. 19, 1908; d. Anthony and Theresa (Gaudiosi) A.; m. John Porter Foley, Jr., July 26, 1933. A.B., Barnard Coll., 1928; Ph.D., Columbia U., 1930; Litt.D. (hon.), U. Windsor, Can., 1967; Sc.D. (hon.), Cedar Crest Coll., 1971, La Salle Coll., 1979, Fordham U., 1979; Paed.D. (hon.), Villanova U., 1971. Instr. psychology Barnard Coll., N.Y.C., 1930-39; asst. prof., chmn. dept. Queens Coll., N.Y.C., 1939-46; assoc. prof. psychology Fordham U., N.Y.C., 1947-51; prof. Fordham U., 1951-79, prof. emeritus, 1979—, chmn. dept. psychology, 1968-74; mem. NRC, 1952-55; pres. Am. Psychol. Found., 1965-67. Author: Differential Psychology, 1937, rev. edit., 1949, 58, Psychological Testing, 1954, 6th edit., 1988, Fields of Applied Psychology, 1964, 2d edit., 1979; also articles in field.; editor: Individual Differences, 1965, Testing Problems in Perspective, 1966; Contributions to Differential Psychology, 1982. Recipient award for disting. service to measurement Ednl. Testing Service, 1977, award disting. contbns. to research Am. Ednl. Research Assn., 1983, Gold medal Am. Psychol. Found., 1984, Nat. Medal of Science, 1987. Mem. Am. Psychol. Assn. (rec. sec. 1952-55, pres. div. gen. psychology 1956-57, bd. dirs. 1956-59, 68-70, pres. div. evaluation and measurement 1965-66, pres. 1971-72, Disting. Sci. award 1981, E. L. Thorndike medal div. ednl. psychology 1984), Ea. Psychol. Assn. (pres. 1946-47, dir. 1948-50), Psychonomic Soc., Phi Beta Kappa, Sigma Xi.

ANASTOLE, DOROTHY JEAN, electronics company executive; b. Akron, Ohio, Mar. 26, 1932; d. Leonard L. and Helen (Sagedy) Dice; student De Anza Jr. Coll., Cupertino, Calif., spring 1969; children—Kally, Dennis, Christopher. Various secretarial positions in mfg., 1969-75; office mgr. Sci. Devices Co., Mountain View, Calif., 1975-76; exec. adminstrv. sec. corp. office Cezar Industries, Palo Alto, Calif., 1976-77; office and personnel mgr. AM Bruning Co., Mountain View, 1977-81; dir. employee relations Consol. Micrographics, Mountain View, 1981-83; personnel mgmt. cons., 1983-84; mgr. adminstrn./employee relations Mitsubishi Electronics Am., Inc., Sunnyvale, Calif., 1984—. Bd. dirs. Agnew State Hosp., San Jose, Calif., 1966-72, div. chmn. program mentally retarded, 1966-72, staff tutor, 1966-72. Recipient Service award Agnew State Hosp., 1972. Mem. Am. Soc. Profl. and Exec. Women, Am. Soc. Personnel Adminstrn. Office: Mitsubishi Electronics Am 1050 E Argues Ave Sunnyvale CA 94086

ANAZAGASTY, MARIA LOUISA, marketing professional; b. Bronx, N.Y., Oct. 4, 1950; d. Francisco and Carmen (Vasquez) A.; m. Raul J. Gonzales, Nov. 22, 1969 (div. Oct. 1984); children: Christopher M., Keith L. Student, Mahoney Bus. Sch., N.Y.C.; student in Mktg., Suffolk County Community Coll., Brentwood, N.Y., 1990—. Cash dividend clk. N.Y. Stock Exchange, N.Y.C., 1969-70; head teller, note teller Marine Midland Bank, N.Y.C., 1970-75; customer svc. rep. European Am. Bank, Central Islip, N.Y., 1976-84; telemarketing rep. Chem. Bank., Jericho, N.Y., 1985-86. Asst. den mother Boy Scouts Am., Central Islip, N.Y. Mem. Alpha Beta Gamma, Pi Alpha Sigma.

ANCKER-JOHNSON, BETSY, physicist, automotive company executive; b. St. Louis, Apr. 29, 1927; d. Clinton James and Fern (Lalan) A.; m. Harold Hunt Johnson, Mar. 15, 1958; children: Ruth P. Johnson, David H. Johnson, Paul A. Johnson, Martha H. Johnson. B.A. in Physics with high honors (Pendleton scholar), Wellesley Coll., 1949; Ph.D. magna cum laude, U. Tuebingen, Germany, 1953; D.Sc. (hon.), Poly. Inst. N.Y., 1979, Trinity Coll., 1981, U. So. Calif., 1984, Alverno Coll., 1984; LL.D. (hon.), Bates Coll., 1980. Instr., jr. research physicist U. Calif., 1953-54; physicist Sylvania Microwave Physics Lab., 1956-58; mem. tech. staff RCA Labs., 1958-61; research specialist Boeing Co., 1961-70, exec., 1970-73; asst. sec. commerce for sci. and tech., 1973-77; dir. phys. research Argonne Nat. Lab., Ill., 1977-79; v.p. environ. activities staff Gen. Motors Tech. Center, Warren, Mich., 1979—; affiliate prof. elec. engring. U. Wash., 1964-73; bd. dirs. Gen. Mills, ; mem. Energy Research Adv. Bd. Dept. Energy, U.S Safety Rev. Panel Nat. Sci. Found. Author of 80 sci. papers; patentee in field. Mem. staff Inter-Varsity Christian Fellowship, 1954-56; mem. visiting com. elec. and computer div. MIT, U. Wash.; mem. bd. visitors Oakland U., Dept. Def. Sci. Bd.; mem. adv. bd. Stanford U. Sch. Engring., Fla. State U., Fla. A&M U., Congrl. Caucus for Sci. and Tech.; trustee Wellesley Coll., 1972-77. AAUW fellow, 1950-51; Horton Hollowell fellow, 1951-52; NSF grantee, 1967-72. Fellow Am. Phys. Soc. (councillor-at-large 1973-76), IEEE, AAAS; mem. Nat. Acad. Engring., World Environ. Ctr. (chmn., bd. dirs. 1988—), Air Pollution Control Assn., NSF (U.S. Safety Rev. Panel), Soc. Automotive Engrs. (bd. dirs. 1979-81), Phi Beta Kappa, Sigma Xi. Office: GM Environ Activities Staff 30400 Mound Rd Warren MI 48090-9015

ANCRUM, CHERYL DENISE, dentist; b. Bklyn., Sept. 28, 1958; d. Ida Jackson. BA in Psychology, Harvard U., Cambridge, 1980; DDS, Columbia U., N.Y., 1986, MPH, 1989. Dentist. Credit analyst Hartford Nat. Bank, Conn., 1980-81; statistical coding instr., analyst Aetna Ins. Co., Hartford, Conn., 1981-82; dental asst. Gouverneur Hosp., N.Y., 1983; clk. typist Columbia Presbyn. Med. Ctr., N.Y., 1984-86; gen. practice resident Beth Israel Med. Ctr., N.Y., 1986-87; dental attending Montefiore Med. Ctr., 1987-90; research assoc. dentist North Central Bronx Hosp., 1989-90; dental dir. Manhattan Men's House of Detention, 1989—; dental extern N. Central Bronx. Hosp., 1985-86. Mem. Girl Scouts Am., Bklyn, 1969-73; vol. St. John Episcopal Hosp., Bklyn, 1974-75, Mt. Auburn Hosp., Cambridge, 1978, Harlem Hosp., N.Y.C., 1987-88; health advocate Harvard U., Cambridge, 1977-80; election campaign worker Sutton For Mayor, Bklyn., 1977; mem. Operation PUSH, Hartford, 1981-82, Hartford Black Women Network, 1980-82, Kuumba Singers, Harvard U., 1976-77, New Temple Singers, Cambridge, 1977-80. Recipient Scholarship A Better Chance, 1973-76, scholarship Am. Fund for Dental Health, 1982-84, Clark Found., 1983-86, AAUW, 1985-86; named Outstanding Young Women of Am., 1983; recipient Letter of Commendation Columbia U., N.Y., 1983. Mem. ADA, N.Y. State Dental Soc., Acad. of Gen. Dentistry, Am. Assn. of Pub. Health Dentistry, Am. Profl. Practice Assn. Democrat. A.M.E. Home: 1043 Tulsa St Uniondale NY 11553

ANDERSEN, DORIS EVELYN, real estate broker; b. Christian County, Ky., Oct. 30, 1923; d. William Earl and Blanche Elma (Withers) Johnston; m. Roger Lewis Shirk, July 9, 1944 (div. 1946); 1 child, Vicki Lee Shirk Sanderson; m. DeLaire Andersen, July 6, 1946; children: Craig Bryant, Karen Rae, Kent DeLaire, Chris Jay, Mardi Lynn. Diploma, South Bend Coll. Commerce, 1942; diploma in banking Notre Dame U., 1946; student Ind. U., 1942-44. Tng. dir. First Nat. Bank, Portland, Oreg., 1963-69; assoc. broker Stan Wiley, Inc., Portland, 1969-79; prin. Doris Andersen & Assocs., Portland, 1979—; co-owner ServiceMaster of the Cascades; speaker at seminars; mem. Gov.'s Task Force Coun. on Housing, Salem, Oreg., 1985-86. Contbr. articles to profl. jours. Mem. task force Oreg. Dept. Energy, Salem, 1984-85. Mem. Nat. Assn. Realtors (dir. 1983—, regional v.p. Northwest region 1988), Oreg. Assn. Realtors (dir. 1979—, pres. 1986—), Portland Bd. Realtors (pres. 1982), Women's Council Realtors (local pres. 1977, state pres. 1978, gov. nat. orgn. 1979), Internat. Platform Assn., Internat. Biog. Assn. Avocations: reading, travel. Home and Office: PO Box 1169 Shady Cove OR 97539

ANDERSEN, KAREN LOUISE, publications specialist; b. Dedham, Mass., Mar. 10, 1951; d. Arnold Rustaad and Muriel Agnes (Lund) A. BA in English, U. N.H., 1974. Asst. bus. mgr. computer svcs. div. U. N.H., Durham, 1974-78; documentation supr. Am. Internat. Group Data Ctrs., Manchester, N.H., 1978-80; with Digital Equipment Corp., Merrimack, N.H., 1980—, publs. mgr., 1985-89, sr. publs. mgr., 1989—. Mem. Soc. for Tech. Communications, Intercompany Publs. Mgmt. Forum (organizing com. 1989-90), DAV. Office: Digital Equipment Corp Continental Blvd Merrimack NH 03054

ANDERSEN, MARIANNE SINGER, clinical psychologist; b. Baden nr. Vienna, Austria; came to U.S., 1940, naturalized, 1946; d. Richard L. and Jolanthe (Garda) Singer; 1 son, Richard Esten. BA, CUNY, 1950, MA, 1974; PhD, Fla. Inst. Tech., 1980. Rsch. assoc. Inst. for Rsch. in Hypnosis, N.Y.C., 1974-76, fellow in clin. hypnosis, 1976, dir. seminars, 1978-82, dir. edn., 1982—; psychotherapist specializing in hypnotherapy Morton Prince Ctr. for Hypnotherapy, 1976—, dir. weight control clinic, 1980—, dir. clin. services, 1981-82; dir. adminstrn. Internat. Grad. U., N.Y.C., 1974-77; pvt. practice psychotherapy, 1977—; adminstrv. coordinator Internat. Grad. Sch. Behavior Sci., Fla. Inst. Tech., 1978; co-dir. The Melbourne Group, 1983—; lectr. hypnosis and hypnotherapy to mental and phys. health profls., 1977—. Author: (with Louis Savary) Passages: A Guide for Pilgrims of the Mind, 1972; rsch. on treatment obesity with hypnotherapy; book editor specializing in psychology and psychiatry including W.W. Norton Co., Sterling Pub. Co., E.P. Dutton Co., 1950-71. Fellow Soc. for Clin. and Exptl. Hypnosis; mem. Internat. Soc. for Clin. and Exptl. Hypnosis, Am. Psychol. Assn., Am. Soc. Bariatric Physicians (affiliate), N.Y. Acad. Scis.

ANDERSEN, SHIRLEY ANNE, technical publications manager, consultant; b. Denver, Aug. 10, 1942; d. George Robert and Ruth Laverne (Ekblad) Hill; m. William Dan Andersen, Apr. 2, 1966; children: Erik Dan, Kevin Robert. BA summa cum laude, Friends U., 1964; MA, U. Kans., 1966, MPhil, 1974. Asst. instr. English U. Kans., Lawrence, 1964-66, 68-73; lectr. in English U. Mo., Kansas City, 1966-67; tchr. English Bonner Springs (Kans.) High Sch., 1967-68; instr. English Memphis State U., 1975-80; communications cons. Andersen & Assocs., Memphis, 1975—; sr. tech. writer Fed. Express Corp., Memphis, 1981-86, mgr. air ops. publs., 1986—; mem. adv. council for tech. communications Memphis State U., 1987—. Author, designer software manuals. Pres. Open Door class Asbury United Meth. Ch., Memphis, 1987-89, adult ministries coordinator, 1987-89. Mem. Soc. for Tech. Communication (sr.; mgr. pub. relations 1985-86, pres. 1983-85, program chmn. 1982-83, recorder-newsletter editor 1981-82, asst. to soc. pres. for pub. rels. 1990, judge internat. audiovisual competition 1989; award of distinction 1985, award of excellence 1985, award of achievement 1986, best of show award 1986), NAFE. Home: 2616 Kirby Rd Memphis TN 38119 Office: Fed Express Corp-Publs 3350 MIAC Cove Memphis TN 38118

ANDERSON, AGNES M., counselor, banker, retired; b. Beloit, Wis., May 2, 1900; d. Albert C. and Rose E. (Welter) Anderson; student Am. Inst. Banking, 1920-50, also various coll. and night sch. courses. With Beloit State Bank, 1918-28; with 1st Wis. Nat. Bank of Milw., 1928-65, secretarial asst., 1928-48, mgr. women's dept., 1949-65, asst. cashier, 1951-65; travel counsellor Bay Travel Mart, Inc., Milw., 1971-90; asso. v.p. customer service Univ. Nat. Bank, Milw., 1971-73. Wis. women's chmn. U.S. Savs. Bonds Program, 1953-70. Sec. to bd. dirs. Bishop Haas Social Service Fund, 1958-69. Bd. dirs. Cerebral Palsy of Greater Milw., 1960-70; treas. bd. dirs., mem. exec. com. Eisenhower Meml. Cerebral Palsy Work Tng. Center, Milw., 1970-80. Recipient Eisenhower award U.S. Savs. Bonds Com., 1956, Cerebral Palsy award, 1963. Mem. Am. Inst. Banking (nat. women's com. 1949), Nat. Assn. Bank Women (chmn. Milw. group 1956, chmn. Wis. membership com. 1958), Lalumiere League (publicity chmn. Milw. 1970-72, chmn. auditing com. 1976-80). Roman Catholic (past pres. Altar Soc.). Clubs: Woman's of Wis., Milw. Tiffany (v.p., mem. bd. 1959-73); Quarter Century (1st Wis. Nat. Bank Milw.). Co-author: Stretching the Dollar, Budget Book, 1951, rev. edit., 1961. Home: 4001 N Prospect Ave Milwaukee WI 53211 Office: Bay Travel Mart Inc 517 E Silver Spring Dr Milwaukee WI 53217

ANDERSON, ALLAMAY EUDORIS, health educator, home economist; b. N.Y.C., July 18, 1933; d. John Samuel and Charlotte Jane (Harrigan) Richardson; B.A., Queens Coll., CUNY, 1975; profl. mgmt. cert. Adelphi U., 1978; M.S. in Edn., Fordham U., 1984; m. Edgar Leopold Anderson, Jr., Apr. 14, 1957; 1 son, David Lancelot. Mem. staff sch. food service, dietitian Bd. Edn., N.Y.C., 1968-88; tchr. home and career skills Louis Armstrong Middle Sch., 1988—. profl. devel. cons., N.Y.C., 1978—; ptnr. Masiba Bldg. Corp., Corona, N.Y., 1975-82; adj. lectr. home econs. Queens Coll., 1987; owner AEA Devel. Svc., 1987—. Devel. coord. League for Better Community Life, Inc., 1977—, treas. exec. bd., 1970-76; officer N.Y.C. Community Devel. Agy., 1980-83; mem. adv. council home econs. dept. Queens Coll.; mem. Kwanzaa Adv. Com. (P.R.) Urban Coalition, 1983; vestry mem. youth ministries Grace Episcopalian Ch., 1982-85. Recipient Elmcor Community Svc. award Elmcor Youth and Adult Activities, Inc., 1989. Mem. NAACP, Nat. Soc. Fund Raising Execs., Langston Hughes Library Action Com. (bd. dirs. 1987—, treas. 1989), Queens Coll. Home Econs. Alumni Assn. (v.p., chmn. bylaws com. 1982). Office: 100-13 34th Ave Corona NY 11368

ANDERSON, ANN, state legislator; b. Yakima, Wash., 1952; married Eric Anderson; 1 child, Cori. Former tchr., mem. Wash. State Senate, majority whip. Republican. Republican. Home: PO Box 128 Acme WA 98220 Office: 2718 McLeod Rd Bellingham WA 98225*

ANDERSON, ANNE VICTORIA, registered nurse; b. Kenitra, Morocco, June 5, 1958; came to U.S., 1964; d. William Roy and Myrtle M. (Raberding) A. Diploma, Louise Obici Sch. Nursing, 1979; BSN, U. Md., 1988. Float pool nurse Physicians Meml. Hosp., La Plata, Md., 1980-82; instr. Charles County Community Coll., La Plata, 1981-84; unit supr. Charles County Nursing Home, La Plata, 1979-84; staff nurse Calvert Meml. Hosp., Prince Frederick, Md., 1984-87; RN, agy. nurse Kimberly Nurses, Inc., Balt., 1986-88, Nurses, Inc., Balt., 1986-88; cross country healthcare traveling nurse Boca Raton, Fla., 1988—. Active ARC, Charles County chpt., 1980-87. Mem. Am. Nurses Assn., U. Md. Sch. Nursing Assn., Ambassador's Club, Sigma Theta Tau. Republican. Methodist. Home: 7 Eastern Cir Middletown MD 21769

ANDERSON, ANNELISE GRAEBNER, economist; b. Oklahoma City, Nov. 19, 1938; d. Elmer and Dorothy (Zilisch) Graebner; m. Martin Anderson, Sept. 25, 1965. B.A., Wellesley Coll., 1960; M.A., Columbia U., 1965, Ph.D., 1974. Assoc. editor McKinsey and Co., Inc., 1963-65; researcher Nixon Campaign Staff, 1968-69; project mgr. Dept. Justice, 1970-71; from asst. prof. bus. adminstrn. to assoc. prof. Calif. State U.-Hayward, 1975-80; sr. policy adviser Reagan Presdl. campaign and transition, Washington, 1980; assoc. dir. econs. and govt. Office Mgmt. and Budget, Washington, 1981-83; sr. rsch. fellow Hoover Instn., Stanford U., Calif., 1983—, assoc. dir., 1989—; mem. Nat. Sci. Bd., 1985—; Author: The Business of Organized Crime: A Cosa Nostra Family, 1979, Illegal Aliens and Employer Sanctions: Solving the Wrong Problem, 1986; co-editor: Thinking About America: The United States in the 1990's, 1988; contbr. articles to profl. jours., chpts. to books. Mem. bd. overseers Rand/UCLA Ctr. for Soviet Studies, L.A., 1987—. Mem. Am. Econ. Assn., Western Econ. Assn., Beta Gamma Sigma. Office: Stanford U Hoover Inst Stanford CA 94305-6010

ANDERSON, BARBARA A., sociologist, educator; b. Ames, Iowa, Aug. 10, 1948; d. A.I. and Carolyn Anna (Barnes) Snow; m. Michael P. Anderson, June 14, 1969. AB in Math., U. Chgo., 1970; PhD in Sociology, Princeton U., 1974; MA, Brown U., 1977 . Research assoc. Office Population Research, Princeton U., 1974-76; research assoc. Econ. Growth Ctr., Yale U., 1974-75, asst. prof. sociology, 1975-76; assoc. prof. Brown U., Providence, 1976-84; prof. U. Mich., Ann Arbor, 1984—; vis. mem. Inst. Advanced Study, 1974. Author (with others): Human Fertility in Russia Since the Nineteenth Century, 1979, Internal Migration During the Modernization of Russia in the Late Nineteenth Century, 1980. Ford-Rockefeller grantee, 1975-76, NIH grantee, 1976-77, 82—, NSF grantee, 1980-82; Guggenheim fellow, 1982-83. Mem. Am. Sociol. Assn., Am. Hist. Assn., Assn. Advancement Slavic Studies, Population Assn. Am. (dir. 1983-85), Social Sci. History Assn. Office: Univ Michigan Population Studies Ctr 1225 S University Ave Ann Arbor MI 48104*

ANDERSON, BARBARA LOUISE, metal processing executive; b. Orange, N. J., Dec. 27, 1951; d. Albert Rudolf Bonass and Alice Jane (Clark); m. J. Robert, Jan. 4, 1969; 1 child, Brian Patrick. Student, Middlesex County Coll., 1980. Bilingual adminstra. U. S. Marine Sec., Paris, 1971-75, Establissement de Travaux et Developments, Versailles, 1975-76; bilingual Telex operator Daval Steel Products, N.Y.C., 1976-78, inside sales; mgr. Francosteel Corp., N.Y.C., 1980-85; v.p. Daval Steel Prodn., 1985-87; v.p.-sales Francosteel Corp., N.Y.C., 1987--. Mem. Assn. of Women in the Metal Industries (pres.), Nat. Assn. for Female Execs. Office: Francosteel Corp 345 Hudson Street New York NY 10014

ANDERSON, BEVERLY DAWN, hospital laboratory administrator; b. Marion, Va., Feb. 2, 1958; d. Milton Otho and Lelia Virginia (Jones) A. BS in Microbiology, East Tenn. State U., 1980. Cert. med. technologist, Va. Staff technologist Buchanan Gen. Hosp., Grundy, Va., 1981-85, asst. lab. mgr., 1985-87, lab. mgr., 1987—; lab. cons. Tri-State Clinic, Grundy, 1987—. Mem. NAFE, C.L.M.A, C.A.P. (inspection team), Am. Med. Technologists Assn. (cert.). Republican. Methodist. Home: PO Box 703 Grundy VA 24614 Office: Buchanan Gen Hosp Rte 5 Box 20 Grundy VA 24614

ANDERSON, BRENDA SHORE, systems analyst; b. Hagerstown, Md., Dec. 29, 1958; d. John Lyle and Frances (DeLauder) Shore. BS, Pa. State U., 1979; MBA, U. Tulsa, 1985. Supr. Del. County Branch of Pa. Assn. For the Blind, Chester, Pa., 1980-81; profl. recruiter Lloyd Richards Personnel Svcs., Tulsa, 1981-82; admissions counselor U. Tulsa, 1982-84; human resource planning analyst Pub. Svc. Co. of Okla., Tulsa, 1985-87; systems analyst Am. Airlines, Tulsa, 1987-88; mgr. benefit system Am. Airlines, Dallas, 1988—. Mem. Alliance of Mental Illness, Dallas, 1989. Mem. Human Resource Systems Profls., Am. Airlines Adminstrv. Assn., Nat. Assn. for Female Execs., MENSA, Alpha Sigma Alpha, Pa. State Alumni Assn. Democrat. Lutheran. Home: 14400 Montfort Dr #205 Dallas TX 75240 Office: Am Airlines 4200 American Way Fort Worth TX 76155

ANDERSON, CARLA LEE, psychologist; b. Edgeley, N.D., Nov. 26, 1930; d. Carl Erick and Ruth Johanna (Isaacson) Erickson; m. Wayne Perry Anderson, Dec. 22, 1952; children: Jerilyn, Debra, Rosalyn, Stephanie. BA, Jamestown Coll., 1952; MA, U. Del., 1964; MS, U. Mo., Columbia, 1977; PhD, U. Mo., 1978. Lic. psychologist, Mo. Tchr. Gilby (N.D.) High Sch., 1952-54, Moberly (Mo.) Jr. Coll., 1954-55, Hickman High Sch., Columbia, Mo., 1955-56; counseling intern U. Mo., Columbia, 1975-77; asst. prof. overseas counseling program Ball State U., Fed. Republic of Germany, 1979; psychologist Ctr. for Family & Individual Counseling, Columbia, 1979—. Contbr. articles to profl. jours. Chair, bd. dirs. Unitarian-Universalist Ch., Columbia, 1985-86. Mem. Am. Psychol. Assn., Mo. Psychol. Assn., Mid-Mo. Network Women in Psychology (chair 1984-86), Women's Network C. of C. Home: 1017 Prospect St Columbia MO 65203 Office: Ctr Family & Individual Counseling 110 N 10th St Ste 7 Columbia MO 65201

ANDERSON, CAROL ANN, public relations executive; b. Jefferson City, Mo., Jan. 15, 1961; d. Jim N. and LeEtta C. (Geiger) Dampf; m. Dave E. Anderson, Oct. 26, 1985. BA in Mag. Journalism, U. Mo., 1983. Pub. rels. account exec. Fletcher/Mayo/Assocs. subs. Doyle Dane Bernbach, St. Joseph, Mo., 1984-85; dir. pub. info. Cloud County Community Coll., Concordia, Kans., 1986-87; dir. publs. Office Edn. and Tng. Resources Ind. U., Bloomington, 1988-89; mgr. pub. rels. Jacques Seed Co. subs. of Agrigenetics Co., Prescott, Wis., 1989—. Mem. Women in Communications (v.p. student svcs. Twin Cities chpt. 1990-91), Nat. Agri Mktg. Assn., Am. Agrl. Editors Assn., Agr. Rels. Coun., U. Mo. Alumni Assn. (life). Office: Jacques Seed Co 720 St Croix St Prescott WI 54021

ANDERSON, CAROL JOYCE, data processing supervisor; b. Elizabeth, N.J., Dec. 30, 1935; d. Edmund C. and Shirley S. (Kluin) Schneider; m. Roy S. Anderson, June 21, 1958 (dec. Mar. 1987); children: Patricia E. Magnus, Bruce D. BS in Chemistry, Tufts U., 1957. Chemist Shell Chem. Corp., Union, N.J., 1957-58, Purdue U., W Lafayette, Ind., 1958-61; programmer Colonial Penn., Phila., 1978-80, Acad. Ins., Valley Forge, Pa.; programming group leader Shared Med. Systems, Malvern, Pa., 1980—. Mem. AAUW (Marple Newtown, v.p. 1977, sec., 1975), Friends of Marple Library, Friends of Mattapoisett Library (pres. 1972-73). Office: Shared Med Systems 51 Valley Stream Pkwy Malvern PA 21535-3089

ANDERSON, CAROL JUNE, systems analyst; b. Milw., Dec. 14, 1942; d. George Walter and Juanita June (Albers) A.; m. Frederick C. Haberland, May 4, 1963 (div. Apr. 1973); children: Christina Louise Haberland, Heather Noel Haberland; m. Kenneth James Ryan, Oct. 5, 1984. Student, Ripon Coll., 1962-63, Boston Coll., 1973-74; BA in Applied Behav. Scis., Nat. Coll. Edn., McLean, Va., 1987. Sec. Corning Med., Medfield, Mass., 1972-76, supr. word processing, 1976-77; customer support rep. Itek Graphic Products, Waltham, Mass., 1977-78; sr. market support rep. Micom Data Systems, Inc., Boston, 1978-79, sales rep., 1979-80; supr. word processing Fidelity Data Systems, Inc., Boston, 1981-82; methods analyst Arkwright-Boston Ins. Co., Waltham, 1982-83; gen. mgr. WordSystems, Inc., Washington, 1983-84; sr. analyst ASI Systems Internat., Falls Church, Va., 1984-88; cons. TEM Assocs., Inc., Washington, 1988-89; sr. systems analyst Integrated MicroComputer Systems, Inc., Rockville, Md., 1989—; guest lectr. Johnston-Wales Coll., Providence, 1975; instr. Needham (Mass.) Adult Edn., 1981-83; mem. adv. com. Occupational Career Edn., Needham, 1982-83. Bd. dirs. Needham Theater Group, 1981-83. Mem. Assn. Info. Systems Profls. (bd. dirs. 1981-83), Women in Info. Processing, DAR. Home: 5300 Holmes Run Pkwy #1516 Alexandria VA 22304 Office: Integrated MicroComputer 2 Research Place Rockville MD 20850

ANDERSON, CAROL LYNN, counseling/career planning administrator; b. Cobleskill, N.Y., June 23, 1952; d. Edward Waldmer and Caroline (Burawa) A. BA in Psychology with honors, McGill U., 1974; MA in Psychology, SUNY, New Paltz, 1976. Social welfare examiner Dutchess County Dept. Social Svcs., Poughkeepsie, N.Y., 1977-78; employment interviewer N.Y. State Dept. Labor, Rego Park, 1978-83; employment counselor N.Y. State Dept. Labor, Jamaica, 1983-85; vocat. rehab. counselor N.Y. State Commn. for the Blind and Visually Handicapped, Harlem, 1985—. Mem. Am. Assn. for Counseling and Devel., Nat. Rehab. Counselors Assn., Am. Coll. Personnel Assn., Nat. Employment Counselors Assn., Greenpeace, Clearwater, People for the Ethical Treatment of Animals. Home: 21-61 Steinway St 2A Astoria NY 11105 Office: NYS Commn for the Blind and Visually Handicapped 163 W 125 St Rm 1315 New York NY 10027

ANDERSON, CAROL MCMILLAN, lawyer; b. Malone, Fla., Aug. 7, 1938; d. Fillmore Allen and Ernestine (Dickson) McMillan; m. Philip Sloan Anderson, Oct. 9, 1965; 1 child, Courtney Beth. BS, Fla. Atlantic U., 1969; JD, Cumberland Sch. Law, 1971. Bar: Fla. 1971. Asst. U.S. atty. Office of U.S. Atty., Miami, Fla., 1971-74; ptnr. Anderson & Anderson, Ft. Lauderdale and Stuart, Fla. 1974—; mem. jud. nominating com. 4th dist. Ct. Appeals, 1987—. Mem. Thousand Plus, Mus. Art, Broward Community Found.; bd. dirs. The Light Brigade, 1988-89, Ft. Lauderdale Philharm. Soc., 1988—, Royal Dames Cancer Rsch., 1988—, Hospice Hundred, pres., 1988-

89. Recipient Alumnae Achievement award Katharine Gibbs Sch., Boston, 1973. Mem. ABA, Assn. Trial Lawyers Am., Fla. Acad. Trial Lawyers, Fla. Bar, Broward County Bar Assn., Broward County Women Lawyers (v.p. 1981). Presbyterian. Clubs: 110 Tower, Coral Ridge Yacht, Amb. Home: 29 Rio Vista Dr Stuart FL 34996 Office: Anderson & Anderson PA 1313 S Andrews Ave Fort Lauderdale FL 33316 also: 517 S California Ave Stuart FL 34994

ANDERSON, CAROL PATRICIA, chemistry educator; b. Bluefield, W.Va., May 19, 1946; d. Carroll Curtis and Naomi Bessie (Bowles) A.; m. James Brent Anderson, Sept. 9, 1978. BS, Concord Coll., Athens, W.Va., 1968; PhD, U. Tenn., 1973. Post-doctoral instr. U. Conn., Storrs, 1973-75, asst. prof., 1975-80, assoc. prof., 1980—; cons. USCG Rsch. and Devel., Groton, Conn., 1976—. Contbr. articles to profl. jours. Mem. Am. Chem. Assn., Nat. Sci. Tchrs. Assn., New England Chemistry Tchrs. Assn. Episcopalian. Home: 143 Pequot Ave Mystic CT 06355 Office: U Conn Avery Point Avery Point Groton CT 06340

ANDERSON, CAROLE ANN, nursing educator; b. Chgo., Feb. 21, 1938; d. Robert and Marian (Harrity) Irving; m. Clark Anderson, Feb. 14, 1973; 1 child, Julie. Diploma, St. Francis Hosp., 1958; BS, U. Colo., 1962, MS, 1963, PhD, 1977. Group psychotherapist Dept. Vocat. Rehab., Denver, 1963-72; psychotherapist Prof. Psychiatry and Guidance Clinic, Denver, 1970-71; asst. prof., chmn. nursing sch. U. Colo., Denver, 1971-75; therapist, coordinator The Genessee Mental Health, Rochester, N.Y., 1977-78; assoc. dean U. Rochester, N.Y., 1978-86; dean, prof. coll. of nursing Ohio State U., Columbus, 1986—; lectr. nursing sch. U. Colo., Denver, 1970-71; cons. The Piton Found., Denver, 1977; prin. investigator biomed. research support grant, 1986, clin. research facilitation grant, 1981-82; program dir. profl. nurse traineeship, 1978-86, advanced nurse tng. grant, 1982-85. Author: (with others) Women as Victims, 1986, Violence Toward Women, 1982, Substance Abuse of Women, 1982. Pres., bd. dirs. Health Assn., Rochester, 1984-86; mem. north sub area council Finger Lakes Health Systems Agy., 1983-86, longrange planning com., 1981-82. Am. Acad. Nursing fellow. Mem. Am. Sociological Assn., Am. Nurses Assn., Ohio Nurses Assn., Sigma Theta Tau. Home: 406 W 6th Ave Columbus OH 43201 Office: Ohio State U Coll Nursing 1585 Neil Ave Columbus OH 43210

ANDERSON, CAROLE LEWIS, investment banker; b. East Stroudsburg, Pa., Oct. 7, 1944; d. William A. and Rosamonde (Lewis) A.; m. John Mason Lee Sweet, Apr. 9, 1983; children: John Mason Lee Anderson-Sweet, Dunn Lewis Anderson-Sweet. B.A. in Polit. Sci., Pa State U., 1966; M.B.A. in Fin., NYU, 1976. Securities analyst PaineWebber, Jackson & Curtis, N.Y.C., 1971-73, assoc. v.p., 1973-75, v.p. research, 1975-77; v.p. PaineWebber, Inc., N.Y.C., 1977-82, mng. dir., 1982-85; sr. v.p. corp. devel. Hasbro, Inc., N.Y.C., 1985-87; also dir. Hasbro, Inc., Pawtucket, R.I., 1985-87; mng. dir. MNC Investment Bank, Washington, 1987-88, pres., chief exec. officer, 1988—; bd. dirs. MNC Credit Corp., Master Media Ltd., Forum for Women Dirs., N.Y.C. County com. person Democratic Party, Manhattan, N.Y., 1975-82; chmn. Hasbro Children's Found., 1985-88, mem. exec. com. and trustee, 1988—; mem. N.Y. com. U.S. Commn. on Civil Rights, 1980-84; trustee Mary Baldwin Coll., Staunton, Va., 1987—, Penn State Alumni Council, 1987—. Named to Acad. Women Achievers, YWCA, N.Y.C., 1982; recipient Disting. Alumna award Pa. State U., 1987. Mem. Pa. State U. Alumni Council. Office: MNC Investment Bank 7474 Greenway Center Dr Greenbelt MD 20770

ANDERSON, CAROLYN MARIE, petroleum engineer; b. Casper, Wyo., June 7, 1955; d. Kenneth Ray and Kay Eloise (Hill) Brittain; m. Darryl Dean Anderson, Mar. 12, 1983; children: Brittany Kirsten, Alex Logan. BS in Petroleum Engring., U. Wyo., 1977. Area engr. Phillips Petroleum Co., Casper, Wyo., 1978-86; prodn. engr. Phillips Petroleum Co., Odessa, Tex., 1986-87; gas gathering systems and spl. projects supr. Phillips Petroleum Co., 1987—; leader Engrs. Quality Team, Odessa, 1987—; reg. rep. Phillips' Child/Elder Care Prog., Odessa, 1989—. Fund raiser United Way, Odessa, 1987; participant Leadership Odessa, 1987. Mem. Soc. Profl. Engrs. (past sec.), Gas processors Assn., Tex. Alliance for Minorities in Engring., Toastmasters (v.p.). Home: 6520 Amber Odessa TX 79762 Office: Phillips Petroleum Co 4001 Penbrook Odessa TX 79762

ANDERSON, CATHERINE AGNES, manufacturing executive; b. Crosby, Minn., Nov. 19, 1946; d. Charles Francis and Mary Flora (Middleton); m. Stephen Thomas Anderson, Dec. 5, 1970; children: Amy Lynn, S. Carver. BS, Coll. of St. Scholastica, 1968. Lic. med. technologist. Med. technologist supr. U. Minn. Hosps., Mpls., 1968-72, assoc. scientist, 1972-76; v.p. Med. Graphics Corp., St. Paul, Minn., 1976-81; exec. v.p. Med. Graphics Corp., St. Paul, 1981-86, pres., chief operating officer, 1986-88, chmn., chief exec. officer, 1988—. Patentee high tech. med. equipment. Dir. Am. Lung Assn. of Hennepin County. Named to Men and Women Under 40 Who are Changing Am. Esquire Mag., 1984; recipient 100 award Inc. Mag.,1983, 84. Mem. Am. Coll. Clinical Pathologists (award 1968), Am. Mgmt. Assn. (award 1986), Nat. Sports Ctr. Found. (bd. dirs.). Roman Catholic. Office: Med Graphics Corp 350 Oak Grove Pkwy Saint Paul MN 55127-8599

ANDERSON, CHARLENE MARIE, editor; b. L.A., Sept. 24, 1952; d. Charles Clifford and Irene Marie (Iverson) A. BA, UCLA, 1973, MA, 1975. Mgr. photo dept. The Sea Libr., Santa Monica, Calif., 1976-77; assoc. editor The Cousteau Soc., L.A., 1978-80; dir. publs. The Planetary Soc., Pasadena, Calif., 1980—. Editor The Planetary Report, 1980—; editor, pub. Mars Underground News, 1989—, Bioastronomy News, 1990. Mem. Am. Soc. Mag. Editors, Am. Soc. Assn. Execs., Soc. Nat. Assn. Publs. Democrat. Office: The Planetary Soc 65 N Catalina Ave Pasadena CA 91001

ANDERSON, CHERYL, government affairs adviser; b. Camp Campbell, Ky.; d. Edward Gustav and Virginia Leona (Case) A.; B.A., U. Wash., 1969; m. Richard T. Ney, July 4, 1975; children—Alexander Case, Justin Anderson. Asst. press sec. Senator Warren G. Magnuson, Washington, 1969-71; parliamentarian officer Australian Senate, Canberra, Australia, 1971-72; adminstrv. asst. Richard Ney Assoc., Inc., Washington, 1972-73, account rep., 1973-74, v.p., 1974-89; sec., dir., v.p. Advocacy Internat., Ltd., Washington, 1977-89; dir. Bellhouse Med., Inc., Washington, 1986-87; mgr. Haemonetics Corp., Braintree, Mass., 1987-88; prin. assoc. Advocacy Svcs. Group, Inc., Washington, 1988-89, sr. v.p., sec., 1989—, also bd. dirs. Contbr. articles to profl. jours. Mem. Am. Assn. Med. Instrumentation, Am. Assn. of Blood Banks, Regulatory Affairs Profls. Assn. Home: 5121 Yuma St NW Washington DC 20016 Office: Advocacy Svcs Group Inc 1825 I St NW Ste 400 Washington DC 20006

ANDERSON, CHERYL KAY, sales professional; b. Springfield, Mo., Apr. 4, 1961; d. Frank Donald and Lois Ilene (Winkler) A.; m. Charles Lee Nichols, Sept. 5, 1981 (div. 1986). Receptionist, customer svc. coord., then sec. Datapoint Corp., San Antonio, 1978-82; sec. Lincoln Property Co., San Antonio, 1982-83; comml. leasing agt. Murray Properties Co., San Antonio, 1983-87; sales rep. DeCoty Coffee Co., San Antonio, 1987-89; dir. sales and mktg. Vollmer Products, San Antonio, 1989—. Republican. Baptist. Office: Vollmer Products 4522 Macro San Antonio TX 78218

ANDERSON, CHRISTINE RUTH MINTON, volunteer; b. Pocatello, Idaho, June 19, 1951; d. Albert Edwin and Ruth Ida (Cate) Minton; m. Albert Gordon Anderson, Aug. 25, 1973; children: Robert Axel, Barbara Ruth. BS in Biology, U. Utah, 1973, MS in Biology, 1976. Teaching fellow in biochemistry U. Utah, Salt Lake City, 1976, sci. asst. biology dept., 1976, curatorial aide biology dept., 1977. Troop leader Chesapeake Bay Girl Scout U.S. coun., Del., 1977-79, 89-90; sec. citizens legis. com. Red Clay Consol. Sch. Dist., Del., 1989-90. Recipient 20 Yr. pin Chesapeake Bay Girl Scouts U.S., 1979, 30 Yr. pin, 1990. Mem. Am. Soc. Limnology and Oceanography, Ecol. Soc. Am., AAUW (book group leader Millcreek, Del. chpt. 1986, study group coord. 1987-89, publicity chair 1989—). Republican. Methodist.

ANDERSON, CYNTHIA ANN, systems analyst; b. Indpls., July 1, 1964; d. George Andrew and Sandra Ann (White) A. BA in Computer Sci., Ind. U., 1987. Computer sci. coop. Mead Johnson & Co., Evansville, Ind., 1983-85; computer programmer Ind. Geol. Survey, Bloomington, 1985-86; computer scientist Ind. U., Bloomington, 1986; analyst Ameritech Applied Techs., Indpls., 1987—; cons. Cath. Ctr., Indpls., 1989. Active Big Sisters of Cen. Ind., Indpls., 1987—; asst. den leader Boy Scouts Am., Indpls., 1988—; pres. community coun. Arsenal Tech. High Sch., 1990; mem. Flanner House Guild, 1987—; mem. steering com. True Vine Missionary Bapt. Ch. Youth, 1989—; facilitator Minority Engring. Program Indpls., 1987—, sec. bd. dirs., 1988—. Recipient Optimism award Ind. Bell, 1988.

ANDERSON, CYNTHIA FINKBEINER SJOBERG, speech and language pathologist; b. Hastings, Mich., Dec. 7, 1949; d. Charles Lavern and Lois Mae (Kenyon) Finkbeiner; m. Peter Carl Sjoberg, Sept. 6, 1974 (div. Dec. 1981); 1 child, Hilary Kenyon; m. Donald Anderson, Sept. 16, 1985. BS, Western Mich. U., 1972, MA, 1974. Dir. speech Hackley Hosp., Muskegon, Mich., 1974-75; speech pathologist Grand Haven Pub. Schs., Mich., 1975—; dir. Ambucs Summer Lang. Clinic, Grand Haven, 1984—. Creator summer lang. program. Pres. Kiddie Carousel, Grand Haven, 1983-86; Stephen minister Christ Community Ch., Spring Lake, Mich., 1984—, elder, 1986—; big sister Grand Haven, 1975-80. Named Ambucs Nat. Therapist of Yr., 1985; recipient Excellence in Service award Grand Haven Pub. Schs., 1987. Mem. Am. Speech/Hearing/Lang. Assn. (cert.). Democrat. Home: 2102 Jane Ct Grand Haven MI 49417 Office: Grand Haven Pub Schs 1415 Beechtree Grand Haven MI 49417

ANDERSON, CYNTHIA GAY, sales executive; b. Salt Lake City, Oct. 29, 1945; d. Robert B. and Louise R. (Snow) Swaner; m. Nathan A. Anderson, Oct. 4, 1968 (div. Nov. 1976); children: Tor B., Kristin L. AAS, Weber State Coll., 1977; BS in Behavioral Sci., U. Utah, 1990, postgrad., 1990—. Registered respiratory therapist. Patient care dir. Home Med. Systems, Wheaton, Md., 1983-85; respiratory therapist U. Utah Med. Ctr., Salt Lake City, 1985-86; asst. dir. Cottonwood Hosp., Salt Lake City, 1986-83, therapist, PRN, 1986—; cons. respiratory therapist Glasrock Home Health Care, Salt Lake City, 1986-90, acct. exec., 1990—; treas. Robert B. Swaner Corp., Salt Lake City, 1986—. Vol. Utah Wilderness Assn., Salt Lake City, 1989; speaker Am. Lung Assn., Salt Lake City, 1990; med. vol. Utah Homeless Shelter Clinic, Salt Lake City, 1989; clin. supr. Weber State Coll., Ogden, Utah, 1978-83. Recipient Advanced Cardiac Life Support award Heart Assn., 1983, 89, Advanced Neonatal Life Support award, 1989, 2nd Place Amazon Rally Road Race, 1967. Mem. Utah Soc. for Respiratory Therapy (edn. com. 1986, 87, bd. dirs. 1982-83), Am. Assn. Respiratory Therapy, Utah Profl. Sales Women, Am. Lung Assn. Va., Wasatch Mountain Club (treas. 1990—), Sierra Club Utah, Earth Watch. Democrat. Home: 160 S 700 E Salt Lake City UT 84102

ANDERSON, DAWN RENEE, accountant; b. Washington, June 24, 1962; d. John Alexander and Emilie Barbara (Curtis) A. Bachelors degree, Calif. State U., Sacramento, 1986. Asst. mgr. Thrifty Drugs, Union City, Calif., 1986-87; program dir. San Francisco Senators, Inc., San Francisco, 1987; gen. mgr. Data Source/EquiSystems, Inc., Miami, Fla./Sacramento, 1987-89; asst. controller Haverfield Corp., Miami, 1989-90; dir. acctg. MD Resources, Inc., Miami, 1990—. Mem. NAFE, Calif. State U. Sacramento Alumnus, Alpha Kappa Alpha (historian 1986-87). Democrat. Episcopalian. Home: 8306 Mills Dr #139 Miami FL 33183 Office: MD Resources Inc 7385 Galloway Rd Miami FL 33173

ANDERSON, DEBBIE ANN, hotel executive; b. Jonesboro, Ark., Sept. 19, 1955; d. Ralph Edward Taylor and Lestal Mae (Pulley) Bruntzel; m. William Winfield Anderson, Feb. 12, 1975; children: William Justin, Shawn Patrick, Breanna Chea. Student, Ark. State U., 1973-75; cert., Holiday Inn U., Olive Branch, Miss., 1988. Asst. mgr. Brooks Fashions, Jonesboro, 1979-81; front desk mgr. Best Western Downtown Inn, Jonesboro, 1981-85; exec. sec. Holiday Inn, Jonesboro, 1985-88, guest svc. mgr., 1988—. Cubmaster Shawnee dist. Boy Scouts Am., 1983-86, dist. cub chmn., 1986-87, mem. dist. com., 1987-89; sec. Craighead County Soccer Assn., Jonesboro, 1986-88; team coach Jonesboro Gifted and Talented program, 1987-88. Recipient Shawnee Dist. Award of Merit, Boy Scouts Am., 1986, Shawnee Dist. Com. award, 1987. Mem. Nat. Honor Soc., Beta Club, Mu Alpha Theta. Home: 611 Dogwood Ln Jonesboro AR 72401 Office: Holiday Inn 3006 S Caraway Rd Jonesboro AR 72401

ANDERSON, DELORES FAYE, medical technologist; b. Elkhart, Kans., Mar. 16, 1936; d. Allen A. and Irene E. (Riley) A.; m. Joe H. Manning, June 1, 1959 (div. Feb. 1987). BS, La. Tech. U., 1958; cert., Kans. State U., 1966; postgrad., U. N.Mex., 1965-88. Registered Med. Technologists, Clin. Chemist. Lab. asst. Ruston (La.) Hosp., 1956-58; lab. technologist Willis Knighton Hosp., Shreveport, La., 1958-59; supr. lab. Vets. Hosp., Shreveport, 1959-61; chemistry supr. Vets. Hosp., Albuquerque, 1961-66; lab. mgr. Meml. Hosp., Albuquerque, 1966-69; lab. instr. U. N.Mex. Med. Sch., Albuquerque, 1969-72; chmistry technologist Presbyn. Hosp., Albuquerque, 1972-74, U. Heights Hosp., Albuquerque, 1974-76; program dir. Pima Med. Inst., Albuquerque, 1976—. Mem. Am. Soc. of Clin. Pathologists, Am. Soc. of Med. Technologists, Am. Soc. of Clin. Chemists. Democrat. Baptist. Home: Star Rte Box 151B Corrales NM 87048

ANDERSON, DENICE ANNA, editor; b. Detroit, Nov. 11, 1947; d. Carl Magnus and Geraldine Elizabeth (Willer) A. BA in Journalism, Mich. State U., 1970. Copy editor/reporter The State News, East Lansing, Mich., 1965-70; reporter/copy editor/photographer The Tecumseh (Mich.) Herald, 1966-68; copy editor/entertainment editor The State Jour., Lansing, Mich., 1970-76; freelance writer State Jour./Lansing Mag., 1977-79; freelance corr. Collier's Year Book, N.Y.C., 1977-79; copy editor, proofreader Booz, Allen & Hamilton, N.Y.C., 1980-81, Rogers & Wells, N.Y.C., 1981-83, Advanced Therapeutic Communications, N.Y.C., 1983-84; freelance editor N.Y.C., Santa Fe, 1984—. Contbr. articles to profl. jours. Bd. dirs., sec. March of Dimes, Lansing, 1972-76; vol./writer Polio Info. Ctr., N.Y.C., 1984-88; vol. Vol. Involvement Svcs., Santa Fe, N.M., 1989—. Mem. Editorial Freelancers Assn. Lutheran. Home: Shadowridge Apts Bldg 985 941 Calle Mejia Apt 304 Santa Fe NM 87501

ANDERSON, DONNA SUE WAGNON, preschool educator; b. Atlanta, Apr. 20, 1956; d. Lovic Pierce and Virginia Evelyn (Slaughter) Wagnon; m. Charles Fletcher Anderson, Mar. 22, 1980. BS in Elem. Edn. and Music, Mercer U., 1977. Ednl. dir. Rowland Hills Bapt. Ch., Stone Mountain, Ga., 1977-80; tchr. County Bd. Edn., Decatur, Ga., 1980-81; co-dir. Suzuki Learning Ctr., Atlanta, 1982-86; dir., sec. PREP Co., Inc., Atlanta, 1986—; dir. Cobb PREP Sch., Marietta, 1986—. Mem. East Cobb Civitan (Marietta, Ga.) (community svc. coord. 1987-88). Republican. Baptist. Home: 879 Bird's Mill Marietta GA 30067 Office: Cobb PREP Sch 255 Village Pkwy Marietta GA 30067

ANDERSON, DORIS EHLINGER, lawyer; b. Houston, Dec. 1; d. Joseph Otto and Cornelia Louise (Pagel) Ehlinger; m. Wiley Newton Anderson, Jr., Aug. 26, 1946; children—Wiley Newton III, Joe E. Permanent high sch. tchr.'s cert. U. Houston, 1948; BA, Rice U., 1946; JD, U. Tex., 1950; MLS in Museology U. Okla. Bar: Tex. 1950, U.S. Supreme Ct. Assoc. Ehlinger & Anderson, Houston, 1950-52, ptnr., 1965—; assoc. Price, Guinn, Wheat & Veltmann, Houston, 1952-55, Wheat, Dyche & Thornton, Houston, 1955-65; life mem. Rice Assocs., Houston, 1984—; dir. Houston Bapt. Mus. Am. Architecture and Decorative Arts, 1980—, curator costume, 1980; hist. lectr. Editor, author Houston, City of Destiny, 1980. Contbr. articles to hist. publs. Partliamentarian Harris County Flood Control Task Force, Houston, 1975—; apptd. ambassador Inst. Texan Culture U. Tex., San Antonio; past pres. gen. Descendants of San Jacinto; docent Bayou Bend Mus. Fine Arts, Houston. Recipient best interpretive exhibit award Tex. Hist. Commn., 1983, Outstanding Woman of Yr. award YWCA, Houston, 1983; named adm. Tex. Navy, 1980. Mem. ABA, Assn. Women Attys. Houston, UDC (pres. Jefferson Davis chpt.) Daus. Republic Tex. (parliamentarian gen.), Am. Mus. Soc., Harris County Heritage Soc. (librarian), Kappa Beta Pi. Episcopalian. Home: 5556 Cranbrook Houston TX 77056 Office: Ehlinger & Anderson 5556 Sturbridge Houston TX 77056

ANDERSON, DORRINE ANN PETERSEN (MRS. HAROLD EDWARD ANDERSON), librarian; b. Ishpeming, Mich., Feb. 24, 1923; d. Herbert Nathaniel and Dorothy (Eman) Petersen; B.S. with distinction, No. Mich. U., 1944; postgrad. Northwestern U., summer 1945, U. Wash., summer 1967, U. Mich. Extension, 1958-65; M.S. in L.S., Western Mich. U., 1970; m. Harold Edward Anderson, Aug. 23, 1947; children—Brian Peter, Kent Harold, Bruce Herbert, David (dec.), Timothy Jon. Tchr. English jr. high sch., Eaton Rapids, Mich., 1944-45; tchr. English, speech Arlington Heights (Ill.) High Sch., 1945-48; tchr. English high sch., Nahma, Mich., 1948-49, 54-61, Gladstone, Mich., 1961-62; librarian Gladstone Sch. and Pub. Library, 1962-70; dir. media services Gladstone Area Pub. Schs., 1971-87, Bicentennial coordinator, 1975-76, ret., 1987; mem. planning com. Upper Peninsula Region Library Cooperation, 1982—; rep.-at-large Mich. Citizens for Libraries. Acting dir. Mid-Peninsula Library Fedn., 1965-66; chmn. Region 21 Media Advisory Council, 1972-85; chmn. adv. coun. Regional Ednl. Materials Center 21, 1973-85; regional del. Mich. White House Conf. on Libraries and Info. Services, 1979. Pres., Delta County League Woman Voters, 1970-72; mem. human resources subcom. Upper Peninsula Com. for Area Progress, 1964—; mem. com. for library devel. Upper Peninsula, chmn. Delta County Library Bd., 1967-76; mem. region 17, Polit. Action Team, 1968-70, Upper Peninsula Region of Library Cooperation Coun., 1983-85, 86—; history chmn. Gladstone City Centennial Com., 1982-87. County del. Delta County Democratic Com., 1968; trustee Library of Mich., 1984-89; bd. dirs. Library of Mich. Found., 1985-89. Named Tchr. of Year, Region 17 (Mich.), 1969. Mem. NEA, Mich. Edn. Assn. (pres. region 17 council 1967-68, chmn. Upper Peninsula dels. to rep. assembly 1966-68), ALA, Mich. Library Assn., Internat. Reading Assn., Mich. Assn. Media in Edn. (state Library Week chmn. 1973-74; recipient leadership award 1977, Spl. Services award 1987), Mich. Assn. Sch. Library Suprs., Upper Peninsula Reading Conf. (program chmn. Leadership award planning com. 1981), AAUW, Assn. Ednl. Communications and Tech., Kappa Delta Pi, Phi Epsilon, Beta Phi Mu, Delta Kappa Gamma (recipient citation for seminars in mgmt. for women 1977, v.p., program chmn. Beta Sigma chpt. 1980-82). Home: 1723 Montana Ave Gladstone MI 49837

ANDERSON, EDITH HELEN, academic dean; b. N.J., June 3, 1927. B.S., Manhattanville Coll., 1951; M.A., N.Y. U., 1958, Ph.D., 1963. Staff nurse Halloran VA Hosp., S.I., N.Y., 1948-49; camp nurse Ten Mile River camp Boy Scouts Am., N.Y., 1949; pub. health nurse Vis. Nurse Assn., Elizabeth, N.J., 1950-54, Community Service Soc., N.Y.C., 1954-56; instr. practical nursing program Elizabeth (N.J.) Bd. Edn., 1956-58; teaching fellow grad. program in parent-child nursing N.Y. U., 1958-60, asst. prof., dir. grad. program in parent-child nursing, 1960-64; acting chief nursing sect. Children's Bur., Social and Rehab. Service, HEW, Washington, 1967-68; nursing edn. cons. Nursing Sect. Children's Bur., Welfare Adminstrn., 1964-69; dean Sch. Nursing, Coll. Health Scis. and Social Welfare, U. Hawaii, Honolulu, 1969-76; dean coll. nursing U. Del., Newark, 1976—; cons. P.R. Dept. Health, U. P.R., 1963, V.I. Dept. Health, 1964, Inst. Tech. Interchange East-West Center, U. Hawaii, U. Panama Sch. Nursing, 1986—; tchr./trainer field tng. program Provincial Health Dept., Republic of China, Taiwan, 1969, tchr./trainer Tb control, Ryukya Islands, Inst. Tech. Interchange, East-West Center, Lyndon B. Johnson Tropical Med. Center, Am. Samoa, 1970, 71; mem. med. adv. bd. VA Hosp., Elsmere, Del., 1977-87; bd. dirs. St. Francis Hosp., Wilmington, Del.; mem. Del. State Coordinating Health Council, 1978-84, Health Resource Mgmt. Council, 1988—; project dir. Tri-regional Ednl. Network Demonstration (Regions I, II, III), 1984-89; bd. dirs. St. Francis Hosp., Welmington, Del., 1989—. Author: Commitment to Child Health, 1967, (with others) Maternity Care in the United States: Gains and Gaps, 1966, Current Concepts in Clinical Nursing, Vol. I, 1967, Vol. II, 1969, Vol. III, 1971, Vol. IV, 1973. Mem. allocation com. United Way, 1986—. Fellow Am. Acad. Nursing; mem. Am. Nurses Assn., Hawaii Nurses Assn. (editor mag. 1973-75, chmn. publicity com. 1973-75), Nat. League Nursing (chmn. maternal child nursing sect. So. region 1965, chairperson bd. rev. of accreditation 1980-81), Hawaii League Nursing (1st v.p. 1973), Mid-Atlantic Regional Nursing Assn. (1st governing bd. 1981, v.p. 1982-83), Del. Nurses Assn. (chmn. cabinet nursery edn., bd. dirs. 1984-86), Pi Lambda Theta, Sigma Theta Tau. Home: 1403 Shallcross Ave Hamilton House Apt 502 Wilmington DE 19806 Office: U Del Sch Nursing Newark DE 19716

ANDERSON, EDNA, Canadian legislator; b. St. Catherines, Ont., Can., Sept. 9, 1922; m. Derek A. Anderson, 1958; children: Norman, Elizabeth, Caroline. Student, Royal Conservatory Music, St. Catherines Bus. Coll. Mem. Ho. of Commons Simcoe Ctr., Ottawa, Ont., 1988—; real estate agt.; concert pianist. Bd. dirs. Fed. Progressive Conservative Women's Caucus. Anglican. Office: House of Commons, Parliament Bldgs, Ottawa, ON Canada K1A 0A6*

ANDERSON, EDWYNA, lawyer; b. Tulsa, Feb. 11, 1930; d. Edward Lawrence and Jeanne (Osby) Goodwin; children: Kathie Dones-Carson, Jenni Robertson Dones. BA, Fisk U., 1950; JD, Detroit Coll. Law, 1974; AA degree (hon.), C.S. Mott Community Coll., Flint, Mich., 1980. Bar: Mich. 1974, U.S. Dist. Ct. (ea. dist.) Mich. 1976, Pa. 1989. Mng. editor, v.p. Okla. Eagle Pub. Co., Tulsa, 1951-53; social dir. and counselor Hurley (Mich.) Sch. Nursing, 1956-62; news reporter and feature writer The Flint Jour., 1963-65; asst. pros. attorney Consumer Protection and Econ. Crime Div., 1974-78; chief Consumer Protection and Econ. Crime div. Genesee County Pros. Atty.'s Office, 1978-80; pub. svc. commr. Mich. Pub. Svc. Commn., 1980-88; gen. counsel Duquesne Light Co., Pitts., 1988—. Bd. dirs. ARC Allegheny County chpt., Family Health Coun., Health Rsch. and Svcs. Found.; producer, director, and writer of numerous variety and dramatic productions in community theater; active in community edn. with chs. and orgns. Recipient achievement award ESOM,, Sojourner Truth award Negro Bus. and Profl. Women's Clubs, Flint, 1979, Outstanding contbn. award in law, Outstanding Community Achievement award 1978, Humanitarian award Flint New Human Rels. Commn., 1982, Outstanding Svc. award Concerned Pastors for Social Action, Flint, 1983, award Mich. conf. bd. Women's Missionary Soc., Quinn Chapel African Meth. Episcopal Ch., 1975. Mem. ABA, Mich. Bar Assn., Allegheny County Bar Assn., Pa. Bar Assn., Am. Corp. Counsel Assn., Exec. Women's Coun., Pitts. Urban League, Flint Women's Forum YMCA, Women in State Govt., Nat. Dist. Attys. Assn., Am. Assn. U. Women, Nat. League for Nursing, Mich. League for Nursing, Citizen's Ady. Bd., Flint Bd. Edn., Prosecuting Attys. Assn. of Mich., Genesee County Mental Health Soc., Mich. Heart Assn. (ea. dist.), Vis. Nurse Assn. Home: 1 Trimont Ln #420B Pittsburgh PA 15211 Office: Duquesne Light Co 1 Oxford Ctr 302 Grant St Pittsburgh PA 15279

ANDERSON, ELISABETH MADGE KEHRER, physician, state administrator; b. Aberdeen, S.D.; d. Robert Ewald and Oriole (Johnston) Kehrer; m. Page Morris Anderson, Jan. 6, 1951; children: Bruce Statham, Catherine Mercer, Mary Elisabeth. BA, U. Louisville, 1946, MD, 1949; MPH, U. Hawaii, 1971. Intern Queen's Hosp., Honolulu, 1949-50, resident, 1950-51; physician, dir. research Pacific Inst. Rehab. Medicine, Honolulu, 1960-69; asst. to pres. Hawaii Med. Assn., Honolulu, 1972-75; chief med. health services div. Hawaii Dept. Health, Honolulu, 1980—; mem. Hawaii Cancer Commn., 1984—; mem. adv. bd. Hawaii Cancer Research Ctr., 1986—; mem. staff Queen's Hosp. Contbr. articles to profl. jours. Sec., bd. trustees Hawaii Loa Coll., Kaneohe, 1966-75; mem. exec. bd. Community Scholarship Program, Honolulu, 1966-71; mem. Stanford Biol. Preserve Docent Council (Calif.), 1978—; chmn. bd. Hawaii Nature Ctr., Honolulu, 1983—; past vice chmn., trustee Multiple Sclerosis Found. Hawaii; mem. exec. bd. Health and Community Service Council Hawaii, Jr. League of Honolulu. Mem. Yosemite Nat. History Assn., Am. Coll. Preventive Medicine, Am. Pub. Health Assn., Hawaii Med. Assn., Honolulu County Med. Soc., Sierra Club, Honolulu Acad. Arts, Outdoor Circle, Hawaii Bot. Soc., Punahou Tennis Club, Trail and Mountain Club, Outrigger Canoe Club. Office: Hawaii Dept Health 1250 Punchbowl St Honolulu HI 96813

ANDERSON, ELIZABETH CARMAL (BETTE ANDERSON), librarian, freelance photographer; b. Henagar, Ala., Jan. 20, 1925; d. Buren Martin and Evelyn Vashtie (Keys) Farr; m. G. Kenneth Anderson, Aug. 23, 1947; 1 child, Merrill Clinton. BA in English, Wayne State U., 1946, MA in English, 1955, MLS, 1966. Cert. secondary edn. and library sci tchr., Mich. Copywriter Mich. Bell Tel. Co., Detroit, 1947-52; sch. libr. Bloomfield Hills (Mich.) Schs., 1964-68; libr. coord., media cons. West Bloomfield Schs., 1968-86; sales rep. Banker's Real Estate, West Bloomfield, Mich., 1987; reference libr. Newport Beach (Calif.) Libr., 1988—; instr. adult edn. West Bloomfield Schs., 1975; instr. part-time Oakland Community Coll., Farmington, Mich., 1980. Mem. L.A. County Art Mus., Detroit Mus. of Arts, Laguna (Calif.) Art Mus., Newport Beach Art Mus., Laguna Canyon Conservancy, Laguna Beach, 1988-89; vice chmn. Cable TV Com., Laguna Beach, 1988—; North Laguna Assn. Homeowners Club. U. Mich. grant, 1979. Mem. NEA (v.p. W. Bloomfield chpt. 1985, union rep. 1986—),

AAUW (Orange County official photographer 1988-89), LWV (pub. rels. dir. Orange Coast 1990—). Democrat. Presbyterian. Home: 611 High Dr Laguna Beach CA 92651 Office: Newport Beach Libr 856 San Clemente Dr Newport Beach CA 92644

ANDERSON, ETHEL AVARA, retail executive; b. Meridian, Miss.; d. Thomas Franklin and Annie Ethel (Jones) Avara.; m. Theron Young Anderson, Aug. 2, 1940 (dec. Aug. 1964); 1 child, Brenda Anderson Jackson. Grad. high sch., Meridian. Owner, mgr. Med. and Mchts. Collections, Meridian, 1977—. Mem. exec. bd., sec. United Way of Meridian, 1983-87; mem. exec. bd., dir. Miss. Industries for Developmentally Disabled, Meridian, 1984-87, Lauderdale Assn. Retarded Children, Meridian, 1983-87; mem. exec. bd. Lauderdale County Mental Health, 1990. Mem. Meridian C. of C. (liaison 1985-87), Xi Gamma, Beta Sigma Phi. Methodist. Lodge: Civitan (bd. dirs. Meridian club 1984-87). Home: 3400 20th St Meridian MS 39301 Office: Med and Mchts Collection 906 20th Ave Ste 205 Meridian MS 39301

ANDERSON, EVA KLAUBER, psychologist, educator; b. Bratislava, Czechoslovakia, June 17, 1935; came to U.S., 1949; d. Gustav C. and Magda M. (Graber) Samak; m. Donald Woolfolk (div.); m. William F. Anderson; 1 child, Adam William. AB, Cornell U., 1957; MA, Syracuse U., 1959, PhD, 1965. Lic. psychologist, N.Y., Md. Sch. psychologist Madison County Schs., N.Y., 1959-63; staff psychologist Children's Psychol. Ctr., Syracuse (N.Y.) U., 1963-65, asst. prof. spl. edn., 1965-66; pvt. practice, Syracuse, 1966-75, Salisbury, Md., 1975—; asst. prof. edn. Salisbury State U., 1975—; mem. various coms. Md. Dept. Edn., 1975-83; grant evaluator U.S. Dept. Edn., Washington, 1984—. Bd. dirs. Wicomico Teen Adult Ctr., Salisbury, 1984—; mem. Mental Health Assn., Salisbury, 1987—. Fellow Md. Psychol. Assn.; mem. Am. Psychol. Assn., Coun. for Exceptional Children. Home: 715 Burning Tree Circle Salisbury MD 21801 Office: 313 Lemmon Hill Ln Salisbury MD 21801

ANDERSON, EVALYN RUTH, lawyer, court reporter; b. Belleville, W.Va., Mar. 22, 1931; d. Rufus Otis and Carolyn (Hunt) A. BA, Ohio State U., 1954, MA, 1956; PhD, Bryn Mawr Coll., 1960; JD, U. Puget Sound, 1985. Bar: Wash. 1985, Fla. 1987, W.Va. 1987, U.S. Dist. Ct. (so. dist.) W.Va. 1987. Lectr. U. Nigeria, Nsukka, 1960-62; asst. prof. U. Wis., Milw., 1963-64, Am. U., Cairo, 1965-67; assoc. prof. No. Mich. U., Marquette, 1967-69, Marietta (Ohio) Coll., 1969-75; freelance ct. reporter, 1975-79; ofcl. ct. reporter Walla Walla (Wash.) County, 1979-82; ct. reporter Ace Reporters, Orlando, Fla., 1987-89; atty.Dept. of Ins. State of Fla., Tallahassee, 1989—. Contbr. articles to profl. publs. Vol. ARC, Parkersburg, W.Va., 1973, Marietta, Ohio, 1974-75. Fellow AAUW, Am. Philos. Soc.; mem. ABA. Democrat. Episcopalian. Home: PO Box 1642 Tallahassee FL 32302-1642

ANDERSON, FRANCES SWEM, nuclear medical technologist; b. Grand Rapids, Mich., Nov. 27, 1913; d. Frank Oscar and Carrie (Strang) Swem; m. Clarence A.F. Anderson, Apr. 9, 1934; children: Robert Curtis, Clarelyn Christine (Mrs. Roger L. Schmelling), Stanley Herbert. Student, Muskegon Sch. Bus., 1959-60; cert., Muskegon Community Coll., 1964. Registered nuclear med. technologist Am. Registry Radiol. Technologists. X-ray file clk., film librarian Hackley Hosp., Muskegon, Mich., 1957-59, radioisotope technologist and sec., 1959-65; nuclear med. technologist Butler Meml. Hosp., Muskegon Heights, Mich., 1966-70; nuclear med. technologist Mercy Hosp., Muskegon, 1970-79, ret., 1979. Mem. Muskegon Civic A Capella choir, 1932-39; mem. Mother-Tch. Singers, PTA, Muskegon, 1941-48, treas. 1944-48; with Muskegon Civic Opera Assn., 1950-51, office vol. Alive '88 Crusade, mem. com. for 60th High Sch. class reunion. Soc. Nuclear Medicine Cert. nuclear medicine technologist Soc. Nuclear Medicine; active Forest Park Covenant Ch., mem. choir 1953-79, 83—, choir sec. 1963-69, Sunday sch. tchr. 1954-75, supt. Sunday sch. 1975-78, treas. Sunday sch. 1981-86, chmn. master planning coun., coord. centennial com. to 1981, ch. sec. 1982-84, 87, registrar vacation Bible sch., 1988-89, 90, mem. Sunday Sch. support team; co-chmn. Jackson Hill Old Timers Reunion, 1982, 83, 85. Home: 5757 E Sternberg Rd Fruitport MI 49415

ANDERSON, GEORGIA RAE, radiologic technologist; b. Sharon, Pa., Apr. 22, 1954; d. Robert George and Ruth Marie (Cutler) Abbott; m. James J. Anderson, Feb. 19, 1977; 1 child, Robert Patrick. Diploma in radiologic tech., Southside Hosp. Sch., 1974; student, Kent State Coll., 1988—. Staff technologist Southside Hosp., Youngstown, Ohio, 1974-75, spl. procedures technologist, 1978-80; asst. dir. dept. med. imaging St. Joseph Riverside Hosp., Warren, Ohio, 1980-85, adminstrv. dir. dept. med. imaging, 1985—. Mem. Tri-County Soc. for Radiologic Tech., Ohio Soc. Radiologic Technologists, Am. Soc. Radiologic Technologists. Democrat. Methodist. Office: St Joseph Riverside Hosp 1400 Tod Ave NW Warren OH 44485

ANDERSON, GERALDINE LOUISE, laboratory scientist; b. Mpls., July 7, 1941; d. George M. and Viola Julia-Mary (Abel) Havrilla; m. Henry Clifford Anderson, May 21, 1966; children: Bruce Henry, Julie Lynne. BS, U. Minn., 1963. Med. technologist Swedish Hosp., Mpls., 1963-68; hematology supr. Glenwood Hills Hosp. lab., Golden Valley, Minn., 1968-70; assoc. scientist dept. pediatrics U. Minn. Hosps., Mpls., 1970-74; instr. health occupations and med. lab. asst. Suburban Hennepin County Area Vocat. Tech. Ctr., Brooklyn Park, Minn., 1974-81, St. Paul Tech. Vocat. Inst., 1978-81; rsch. med. technologist Miller Hosp., St. Paul, 1975-78; rsch. assoc. Children's and United Hosps., St. Paul, 1979-88; sr. lab. analyst Cascade Med. Inc., Eden Prairie, Minn., 1989-90; lab. mgr. VA Med. Ctr., Mpls., 1990—; mem. health occupations adv. com. Hennepin Tech. Ctrs., 1975-90, chairperson, 1978-79; mem. hematology slide edn. rev. bd. Am. Soc. Hematology, 1976—; mem. flow cytometry subcom. Nat. Com. for Clin. Lab. Standards, 1988-90; cons. FCM Specialists, 1989—. Mem. rev. bd. Clin. Lab. Sci., 1990—; contbr. articles to profl. jours. Mem. Med. Lab. Tech. Polit. Action Com., 1978—; charter orgns. rep. troop #534 Boy Scouts Am., charter orgns. rep. Viking Coun.; resource person lab. careers Robbinsdale Sch. Dist., Minn., 1970-79; del. Crest View Home Assn., 1981—; mem. sci. and math. subcom. Minn. High Tech. Council, 1983-88. Recipient svc. awards and honors Omicron Sigma. Mem. AAAS, AAUW, NAFE, Nat. Assn. Women Cons., Inc., Minn. Emerging Med. Orgns., Minn. Soc. Med. Tech. (sec. 1969-71), Am. Soc. Profl. and Exec. Women, Am. Soc. Med. Tech. (del. to ann. meetings 1972—, chmn. hematology sci. assembly 1977-79, nomination com. 1979-81, bd. dirs. 1985-88), Twin City Hosp. Assn. (speakers bur. 1968-70), Assn. Women in Sci., World Future Soc., Minn. Med. Tech. Alumni, Am. Soc. Hematology, Soc. Analytical Cytology, Sigma Delta Epsilon (corr. sec. Xi chpt. 1980-82, pres. 1982-84), Alpha Mu Tau. Lutheran. Office: FCM Specialists Minneapolis MN 55427

ANDERSON, IRIS ANITA, retired educator; b. Forks, Wash., Aug. 18, 1930; d. James Adolphus and Alma Elizabeth (Haase) Gilbreath; m. Donald Rene Anderson, 1951; children: Karen Christine, Susan Adele, Gayle Lynne, Brian Dale. BA in Teaching, U. Wash., 1969; MA in English, Seattle U., 1972. Cert. English tchr., adminstr., Calif. Tchr. Issaquah (Wash.) Sr. High Sch., 1969-77, L.A. Sr. High Sch., 1977-79. Nutrition vol. Santa Monica (Calif.) Hosp. Aux., Jules Stein Eye Inst., L.A.; mem. Desert Beautiful, Palm Springs Panhellenic; mem. Rancho Mirage Reps., Desert Four Reps. W-Key activities scholar U. Wash. Mem. NEA, Wash. Speech Assn., AAUW, LWV, Nat. Thespians, Bob Hope Cultural Ctr., Palm Springs Press Women, Coachella Valley Hist. Soc., Palm Desert Women's Club, Calif. Ret. Tchrs. Assn., CPA Wives Club, Desert Celebrities, Rancho Mirage Women's Club. Republican.

ANDERSON, JANE LOUISE BLAIR, librarian, horse breeder, poet; b. Wilkinsburg, Pa., Nov. 6, 1948; d. Francis Preston and Mary Louise (Maxwell) Blair; m. Russell Karl Anderson Jr., Apr. 20, 1973; children: Christina Lynn, Melissa Jane. BS in Edn., Clarion State Coll., 1971; MS in Library Sci., Duquesne U., 1974. Cert. pub. librarian, Pa. Substitute tchr. Wilkinsburg Schs., 1971, tchr. Head Start, 1971; librarian Franklin Regional Schs., Murrysville, Pa., 1971—; breeder quarter horses, Fenelton, Pa., 1978—; owner, operator Fern Valley Farm Boarding Kennels. Contbr. poems to various anthologies. Vol. mem. Rescue 5 Ambulance, Murrysville, 1974-76, Medic I ambulance, 1976-78; sec. Franklin Area REACT, 1976-78; first aid instr. ARC, Murrysville, 1975-80; instr. CPR, Am. Heart Assn., Westmoreland County, 1976-80; vol. worker with deaf, 1978-83; vol. United Cerebral Palsey, Butler, Pa., 1981—. Mem. Westmoreland County Library Assn. (pres.), Pa. Library Assn., Am. Quarter Horse Assn., Pa. Quarter Horse Assn., Butler County C. of C., Am. Boarding Kennel Assn. Home: Fern Valley Farm PO Box 12 Fenelton PA 16034 Office: 3200 School Rd Murrysville PA 15668

ANDERSON, JANELLE MARIE, advertising executive; b. Beloit, Wis., Mar. 28, 1954; d. Lyle Kenneth Anderson and Helen Catherine (Hammer) Hughes; adopted d. Hilary William Hughes. AA, U. Wis., Fond du Lac, 1976; postgrad., Arnie DeLuca Sem., Chgo., 1983, Women's Bus. Inst., Neenah, Wis., 1986. Legal sec. Nugent & Nugent, Attys., Waupun, Wis., 1976-80; salesman Modern Motors, Fond du Lac, 1980-82; clk., technician Old World Stained Glass, Fond du Lac, 1982-83; mgr. classifieds Pub.'s Devel. Svcs. Inc., Fond du Lac, 1983—, account mgr. nat. sales, 1985—; cons. Decra-Led Corp. Am., Portage, Wis., 1985. Named Outstanding Young Woman of Am., 1986. Mem. Milw. Advt. Club, Wis. Advt. Pubs. Assn. (chmn. bd. 1987-88), Milw. Grocery Mfrs. Reps. (bd. dirs. 1988—, treas. 1989), Milw. Food Brokers Assn., Fond du Lac Jaycees (bd. dirs. 1984-85, 88—, chmn. bd. 1987-88, v.p. individual devel. 1985-86, 1st woman pres. 1986-87, Wis. program dir. Outstanding Wisconsinite and Young Adult awards 1987-88, numerous awards). Roman Catholic. Home: 136 E Merrill Ave Fond du Lac WI 54935 Office: Pubs Devel Svcs Inc 101 S Main St Fond du Lac WI 54935

ANDERSON, JANET ALM, librarian; b. Lafayette, Ind., Dec. 20, 1952; d. Charles Henry and Lenore Elaine Alm; m. Jay Allan Anderson, May 21, 1983. BS, Bemidji State U., 1975; MA, Western Ky. U., 1981, MLS, 1982. Cert. elem. tchr., sch. libr. and media specialist. Storyteller, puppeteer North Country Arts Coun., Bemidji, Minn., 1975-76; head children's libr. Bemidji State U., 1976-77; middle sch. libr. Custer County Sch. Dist., Miles City, Mont.; tchr. for gifted & talented Custer County Sch. Dist., Miles City, 1979-80; folklore archivist Western Ky. U., Bowling Green, 1981-83; head children's and young adults' svcs. Bowling Green Pub. Libr., 1983-85; head of serials Utah State U., Logan, 1986—, chmn. adv. bd. Women's Ctr., 1988—; adj. instr. Mont. Community Coll., 1978-80; cons. to various Am. outdoor mus.; speaker Utah Endowment for the Humanities Speaker's Bur., Salt Lake City, 1987—. Author: Old Fred, 1972, A Taste of Kentucky, 1986 (Ky. State Book Fair award), Bounty, 1990, (with others) Advances in Serials Management, Vol. 3, 1989; contbr. to Ency. Am. Popular Beliefs and Superstitions, articles on folklore, librarianship, museology to mags. and periodicals; delivered radio and TV presentations on folklore and librarianship on nat. network and various local stas. Co-founder and past pres. Rosebud chpt. Nat. Audubon Soc., Miles City, Mont., 1978-80; invited author Ky. State Book Fair, 1986. Recipient Exhibit and Program Grant Nat. Endowment for the Arts, Bowling Green, Ky., 1984-85. Mem. Am. Libr. Assn., Utah Libr. Assn., North Am. Serials Interest Group, Mt.-Plains Libr. Assn., Consortium of Utah Women in Higher Edn., Bridgerland Bus. and Profl. Women (bd. dirs., pub. chmn. Logan Utah chpt. 1986—), Ky. Coun. on Archives, Am. Folklore Soc., Utah Folklore Soc., Assn. of Living Hist. Farms and Agr. Mus. Democrat. Lutheran. Home: 1090 S 400 E Providence UT 84332 Office: Merrill Libr Utah State U Logan UT 84322-3000

ANDERSON, JANET KATHLEEN, broadcast executive; b. Mpls., Mar. 1, 1950; d. Arthur and RuthEllen Patricia (McCormick) Andresen; m. Scott Andrew Anderson, June 16, 1973; 1 child, Megan Christina. BA in Theatre Arts, S.W. State U., Marshall, Minn., 1972. Writer, producer Sta. KAAL-TV, Austin, Minn., 1977-85, TV program dir., promotion dir., community rels. mgr., 1985—. Co-founder, bd. dirs. Matchbox Children's Theatre, Austin, 1974—; bd. dirs. Summerset Community Theatre, Austin, 1986—; v.p. bd. dirs. Austin Area Commn. for the Arts, 1989—; mem. Austin Vision 2000 Cultural Enrichment Taskforce; participant Blandin Found. Community Leadership Program. Mem. Nat. Assn. TV Program Execs. Office: KAAL TV-6 1701 10th Pl NE Austin MN 55912

ANDERSON, JANET STETTBACHER, educator; b. Somerville, N.J., Feb. 9, 1936; d. Norman Albert and Bessie Mildred (Woodruff) Stettbacher; m. David Lloyd Anderson, June 8, 1957; children: Heidi Ellen, Laurie Bette, Eric Woodruff, Douglas Scott. BS, Rutgers U., 1957; MA, San Diego State U., 1961. Cert. secondary tchr., Calif.; advanced profl. cert., Md. Tchr. San Diego Unified Sch. Dist., 1958-62; assoc. home economist McCalls's Corp., N.Y.C., 1963-65; tchr. adult edn. Palo Alto (Calif.) Unified Sch. Dist., 1970-74; substitute tchr. Montgomery County Pub. Schs., Rockville, Md., 1974-78, tchr. home econs., 1978—; cons., mgr. dinner theatre Wootton High Sch., Rockville, 1981-90. Officer, pres. Greendell Sch. PTA, Palo Alto, 1972-74; safety chmn. Cold Spring Sch. PTA, Potomac, Md., 1974-76; sec. Cold Spring Civic Assn., 1976. Mem. NEA, Am. Home Econs. Assn., AAUW (officer 1974—, pres. Bethesda-Chevy Chase br. 1984-86, honoree Ednl. Found. 1977), Smithsonian Assocs., Phi Delta Kappa. Home: 12436 Goldfinch Ct Potomac MD 20854 Office: Montgomery County Pub Schs 2100 W Ritchie Pkwy Rockville MD 20850

ANDERSON, JANICE LINN, real estate brokerage professional; b. Paris, Tenn., Sept. 2, 1943; d. Orel Vernon and Rosie Elizabeth (Brockwell) L.; m. David James Anderson, June 11, 1965 (div. Oct. 1973). Entertainer, recording artist 4-Sons Record Co., Paris, Tenn., 1958-73; med. transcriptionist The Paris Clinic, 1965-73; computer operator, asst. to v.p. Medicare Adminstrn./Equitable, Nashville, 1973-74; property mgmt. asst. Dobson & Johnson, Inc., Nashville, 1974-76; dir. leasing and mgmt. Fortune-Nashville Co., 1976-78; real estate brokerage asst. J.G. Martin, Jr./Caudill Properties, Inc., Nashville, 1978—; pvt. practice resume preparation, Nashville, 1982—. Bd. govs. Interant. Biog. Ctr., Cambridge, Eng.; active Girls Scouts U.S., Paris, 1967-69; mem. ARC, Nashville, 1978, Christian Appalachian Project, Lancaster, Ky., 1986; mem. citizen's adv. coun. Am. Inst. Cancer Rsch., Washington, 1985. Mem. NAFE, Bus. and Profl. Womens Club (pres. 1965-73), Profl. Musicians Union, Womens Missionary Union (bd. dirs. Paris chpt. 1970-71), Internat. Platform Assn., Realtors Secs. Assn., Am. Biog. Inst. Inc. (rsch. bd. advisors), Internat. Biographical Centre of Cambridge, Eng. (bd. govs.). Baptist. Home: 812 Elissa Dr Nashville TN 37217 Office: JG Martin Jr 208 3d Ave N 4th Fl Nashville TN 37201

ANDERSON, JEAN JENSEN, homemaker, professional volunteer; b. Hilo, Hawaii, Aug. 13, 1932; d. Joseph E. and Aimee (Bigelow) Jensen; m. Kenneth W. Anderson, Mar. 21, 1953; children: Kenneth W. Jr., Richard Scott, Wendy Lynn. BS, Northwestern U., 1953. Dir. vols. Letot Ctr. div. Dallas County Juvenile Dept., 1978-80. Co-chmn. Ladies Hdqrs. for Nat. Conv., Jr. C. of C., 1959; bd. dirs. PTA, 1960-63, 64, 68, 69; bd. dirs. Civic Ballet Bd., 1968-70; chmn. ann. box supper Camp Fire Girls, 1970, leader, 1969-70; bd. dirs. Lubbock (Tex.) Symphony Orch., 1967-70; pres. Lubbock Symphony Guild, 1967-70; bd. dirs. Lubbock Theatre Centre, 1969-70; chmn. juvenile dept. com. Jr. League, 1973-74; bd. dirs. "Can do It", 1982; bd. dirs., corp. sec. Park Towers, 1986—; sustaining mem. Dallas Mus. Fine Arts. Recipient Meritorious Svc. award Dallas County Commrs. Ct., 1976, Juvenile Justice Adv. award Dallas County, 1987, Leadership and Dedication award Dallas County Mental Health and Mental Retardation Ctr., 1988. Mem. Women's Coun. Dallas County, Dallas Commn. Childern and Youth, Coalition for Juv. Justice (long-range planning task force 1984), Jr. League, Univ. Club, Chi Omega Alumnae Assn. Republican. Methodist. Home: 3310 Fairmount Park Towers Dallas TX 75201

ANDERSON, JEAN LORRAINE, nursing educator; b. Halifax, N.S., Apr. 22, 1945; d. Colin Francis and Elizabeth Florence (MacDonald) Livingstone; m. Alexander Michael Anderson; children: Colin Henry Michael, Sheena Margaret Isabel, Laura Mary Catherine, Sarah Christina Ann. Diploma in Nursing, St. Martha's Hosp. Sch. Nursing, Antigonish, N.S., 1966; BS in Nursing, St. Francis Xavier U., Antigonish, N.S., 1970, MEd, 1988. Nurse, surgery St. Martha's Hosp., Antigonish, N.S., 1966-67; clin. instr. St. Martha's Hosp., Antigonish, 1981—; staff nurse ICU St. Joseph's Hosp., Victoria, B.C., 1967-68, nurse, 1967-68; nurse in charge Ranklin Inlet (N.W.T.) Nsg. Sta., 1970-76; staff nurse, maternity St. Martha's Hosp., Antigonish, 1979-81; nursing instr. St. Martha's Hosp. Sch. of Nursing, Antigonish, Can., 1981—. Roman Catholic. Home: RR 1 Merigomish, Pictou County, NS Canada B0K 1G0

ANDERSON, JEANNIE ELLEN, christian educator; b. Saginaw, Mich., July 25, 1959; d. Roscoe Roy and Dolores Marie (Endstrasser) A. BS, U. Ark., 1983, MS, 1989; MA, Presbyn. Sch. Christian Edn., Richmond, Va., 1991. Tchr. Fayetteville (Ark.) Pub. Sch. System, 1985-86, 89-90, U. Ark., Fayetteville, 1987-88; youth dir. First United Presbyn. Ch., Fayetteville, 1989-90. Mem. AAUW, Assn. Presbyn. Ch. Educators, NAFE, N.W. Ark. Audubon Soc., Scottish Soc. N.W. Ark., Toastmasters, Rep. Women's Club, LWV, Phi Epsilon Omicron. Home: 2312 Lawson St Fayetteville AR 72703

ANDERSON, JOAN WELLIN FREED, communications executive, consultant, freelance journalist; b. Shreveport, La., Aug. 18, 1945; d. Cyril and Rose (Friedman) F.; m. Steven G. Rapfogel, 1966 (div. 1984); children: Lisa L., Robert B.; m. J. Warren Anderson, July 21, 1984. BA in Gen. Studies, Tex. Christian U. Freelance reporter Sta. KERA-TV, Dallas, 1979-80, Fort Worth Star-Telegram, 1980-83, Fort Worth bur. Dallas Morning News, 1980-82; pub. relations coordinator Amon Carter Mus., Fort Worth, 1982; med. writer Tex. Coll. Osteo. Medicine, Fort Worth, 1982-85; freelance writer, 1985-87; producer video programs for pub. access cable channel, Ft. Worth, 1987—; community programming coord. cable TV channel City/Video-45, Ft. Worth, 1988—; co-owner, playwright, actress Catered Theater. Bd. dirs. Am. Cancer Soc., 1982-84, active Cancer Hotline; facilitator for fair housing edn. and info. for Community Housing Resource Bd., Ft. Worth; bd. dirs. Women's Haven of Tarrant County (Tex.) Inc., 1987-88, chmn. community relations com., 1988, Dispute Resolutions Svcs. Tarrant County (bd. dirs., chmn. community rels. 1989—); m. Court Apptd. Spl. Adv. for Foster Children, 1986-88. Mem. Women in Communications, Inc. (past dir.), Internat. Assn. Bus. Communicators, Soc. for Theatrical Artists' Guidance and Enhancement, Sigma Delta Chi. Contbr. articles to popular mags. Office: 1000 Throckmorton St Fort Worth TX 76102

ANDERSON, JOANN MORGAN, counselor; b. Detroit, Dec. 25, 1933; d. Verbon Anthony and Wanda Joan (Hutchison) Morgan; m. Robert Arthur Anderson; children: Carol Sue, Douglas Ross, Paul William. BA, U. Wash., 1957; MA, Fielding Inst., 1977. Self employed counselor Edmonds, Wash., 1976-78; dir. High Point Counseling Svc., Edmonds, 1978-80, Woodway Counseling Assn., Edmonds, 1980-86; mem. clin. staff N.W. Health Assocs., Edmonds, 1986-89, mem. sabbatical staff, 1989-90, mgr. property devel., 1988-90; cons. Edmonds Sch. Dist. 15, 1979-82, Wash. Edn. Assn., 1980, Non-Profit Bds. Dirs., Seattle, 1985-87. Editor, columnist (quarterly newsletter): Living Well, 1987—; author: Basics of Group Psychosynthesis, 1990. Vol. various agencies, 1957-76; pres. Stevens Meml. Hosp. Aux., Edmonds, 1964-65. Mem. Internat. Transactional Analysis Assn. (cert.), Am. Assn. Counseling and Devel., AAUW, Assn. Transpersonal Psychology, Mortar Bd., PEO, Beta Gamma Sigma. Republican. Methodist. Home and Office: 7370 N Meadowdale Rd Edmonds WA 98020

ANDERSON, JOLENE SLOVER, publisher; b. Tulare, Calif.; d. James P. Sr., and Helen B. (Walters) Slover; ed. Victor Valley Coll., Riverside City Coll.; m. Douglas R. Anderson, June 14, 1975; 1 child by previous marriage, Sabrina Jo. Model, Connor Sch. Modeling, Fresno, Calif., 1955-65; actress M. Kosloff Studios, Hollywood, Calif., 1965; nat. sales mgr. Armed Services Publs., 1966-68; pres., dir. Sullivan Publs., Inc., Riverside, Calif., 1970-82; pres., chief exec. officer Heritage House Publs., 1983-84; pres. Jolene S. Anderson Pub. Cons., Inc., 1987—. Co-comdr. March AFB, Riverside Tourists and Conv.; mem. YWCA, City of Riverside Cultural Heritage Bd., Yr. 2000 Com., 1988, Riverside Symphony Bd., 1988, Riverside County Philharm. Bd. Named Woman of Achievement YWCA, 1989, Humanitarian of Yr. Rotary, 1990. Mem. Riverside Downtown Assn., Sun City/Menifee Valley C. of C., Soroptimists (Riverside chpt.). Office: PO Box 7453 Riverside CA 92513

ANDERSON, JULIE ALM, family and emergency medicine physician; b. Quonset Point, R.I., Mar. 15, 1953; d. Kenneth L. and E. Joan (Burgwaldt) Goepel. BA, So. Ill. U., 1976; MD, Rush Med. Coll., 1980. Diplomate Am. Bd. Family Practice. Resident in family medicine U. Md., Balt., 1980-81, 85-87; resident in pathology Loyola U. Med. Ctr., Maywood, Ill., 1984-85; emergency medicine staff Greater Balt. Med. Ctr., 1988—. Contbr. articles to med. jours. Capt. M.C., USAF, 1982-84. Recipient resident tchr. award Soc. Tchrs. Family Medicine, 1987. Mem. Am. Acad. Family Practice, Wilderness Med. Soc., Undersea and Hyperbaric Med. Soc., Washington Map Soc., Am. Recorder Soc. Office: Greater Balt Med Ctr 6701 N Charles St Baltimore MD 21004

ANDERSON, JUNE, soprano; b. Boston. Grad. in French Lit., Yale U., 1974. Met. Opera debut as Gilda in Rigeletto, 1989; other roles have included Queen of the Night in The Magic Flute, N.Y.C. Opera, 1978, title role in Lucia di Lammermoor, Milw. Florentine Opera, 1982, Chgo., 1990, Gulnara in Il Corsaro, San Diego Opera Verdi Festival, 1982, I Puritani, Edmonton Opera, 1982-83, title role Semiramide, Rome Opera, 1982-83 and Met. Opera, 1990, Rosina in The Barber of Seville, Seattle Opera and Teatro Massimo, 1982-83, Cunigande in Candide, 1989; concert and oratorio vocalist Chgo. Pops. Orch., Handel Festival Kennedy Ctr., Denver Symphony, St. Louis Symphony, Cin. Symphony, Maracaibo (Venezuela) Symphony; recs. performer Egitto, Philips Records. Richard Tucker Found. grantee, 1983. Office: care Columbia Artists 165 W 57th St New York NY 10019*

ANDERSON, KAREN, health services consultant; b. La Grande, Oreg., Mar. 10, 1945; d. Moyle Woodruff and Ethel Hill (Cowley) A. Student, U. Wyo., 1963-66, Ariz. State U., 1967-70. From examiner claims to asst. mgr. Aetna Ins., various locations, 1967-87; cons., Huntington Beach, Calif., 1987-89; regional reimbursement mgr. Glasrock Home Health Care, Costa Mesa, 1988-89; owner, mgr. Andstrum Bus. Cons., Huntington Beach, 1989—, Anderson Health Care, Mesa, Ariz., 1990—. Office: Glasrock Home Health Care 19512 Pompano Ste 108 Huntington Beach CA 92648

ANDERSON, KATHERINE DOSTER, library director; b. Mishawaka, Ind., Mar. 21, 1932; d. Howard George and Edith Katherine (Ratts) Doster; m. George Hamilton Anderson, Sept. 13, 1958; children: Howard H., Gordon L. BA, Wellesley Coll., 1953; MS, Palmer Grad. Library Sch., L.I, Greenvale, N.Y., 1972. Actuarial asst. George B. Buck, Cons. Actuary, NYC, 1953-63; library media specialist Herricks Pub. Schools, New Hyde Park, N.Y., 1972-. Contb. articles to sch. newsletter. Bd. Wheatley Scholarship Fund, 1964-68, mem. Budget Adv. Com. Wheatley Bd. Edn., Old Westbury, N.Y., 1968; elder Community Ch., treas. World Svc., 1988, East Williston, N.Y. Mem. Nassau Suffolk Sch. Librarian Assn. Republican.

ANDERSON, KATHRYN BOYD, natural gas company official; b. Austin, Tex., Jan. 28, 1934; d. Frank Leslie and Augusta Ann (Farrow) Boyd; m. Walter Wiley Anderson, Sept. 8, 1956; children: Christopher Walter, Cherie Anne Anderson Castner. BBA in Personnel Mgmt., U. Texx., 1954. Sec. U. Tex., Dallas, 1955-59, Peyton Packing Co., El Paso, Tex., 1963-64; sr. exec. sec. El Paso Natural Gas Co., 1952-86, manpower planning and performance analyst, 1986—. Mem. Am. Soc. Personnel Adminstrn., AAUW, Christian Womens Club. Republican. Baptist. Home: 1530 Common Dr El Paso TX 79936 Office: El Paso Natural Gas Co PO Box 1492 El Paso TX 79978

ANDERSON, KIM COX, sales executive; b. Louisville, Feb. 6, 1958; d. Gilbert Harris Cox and Lyda Marion (Klinglesmith) Lewis; m. Gary Wayne Anderson, June 4, 1977 (div. July 1981). Radiologic technologist St. Vincent Hosp., Indpls., 1980-81, cardiovascular radiologic technologist, 1981-85; sales rep. Elecath, Cin., 1985-86; clin. specialist Advanced Cardiovascular Systems, Austin, Tex., 1986-87; sales rep. Advanced Cardiovascular Systems, Forest Hills, N.Y., 1987—. Mem. Am. Registry of Radiologic Technologist, 1979-88. Republican.

ANDERSON, LAURA LORENZ, communications executive, consultant, engineer; b. Louisville, Feb. 11, 1948; d. Chester R. and Caroline (Dolt) Lorenz; m. Thomas A. Anderson, Aug. 20, 1969; 1 child, Virginia Leigh. BS in Civil Engring., U. Ky., 1971. Registered profl. engr., Ky. Engr. South Cen. Bell, Louisville, 1971-76; mgr. South Cen. Bell, Paducah, Ky., 1976—; v.p. Masters Cons., Inc., Mayfield, Ky., 1988—; pres. LaMare Distbg. Inc., Mayfield, 1989—. Chairperson Sch. and Community Partnerships, Mayfield, 1987—. Mem. AAUW, Paducah-River City Bus. and Profl. Women. Republican. Methodist. Home: Rt 2 Mayfield KY 42066

ANDERSON, LINDA LEA PENNY, social work administrator; b. Big Spring, Tex., Aug. 6, 1943; d. Charlie Nichol and Bonnie Wayne (Tartt) Farrar; m. Lewis R. Anderson, May 20, 1989; 1 child, Larry Lee II. B in Social Work, Tex. Woman's U., 1975, MA in Sociology, 1977; diploma Inst.

for English Speaking Students, Internat. Grad. Sch., U. Stockholm, 1978. Cert. social worker. Coord. human resources Cath. Charities, Fort Worth, 1975-76; program specialist Tex. Dept. Human Resources, Austin, 1977; program specialist/ombudsman Tex. Gov.'s Com. on Aging, Austin, 1978-80; project dir., tng. dir. Ctr. for Pub. Interest, Dallas, 1980-82; dir. social work dept. Presbyn. Hosp., Dallas, 1982-84, Meml. Hosp., Cleburne, Tex., 1984-86; coord. Johnson County Health Dept. Indigent Health Program, Cleburne, 1986-88; pres., chief exec. officer MASH, Inc., 1988—; ptnr., cons. Gormet Basket, Cleburne, 1985-86. Bd. dirs. Johnson County Family Crisis Ctr., Cleburne, 1985-86; allocations com. Johnson County United Way, Cleburne, 1985-86. Samuel E. Ziegler Found. fellow, Dallas, 1976-77. Mem. NAFE, Tex. Soc. Hosp. Social Work Dirs., Am. Bus. Women's Assn., Assn. Ind. Real Estate Owners, Am. Mensa. Democrat. Lutheran. Avocations: real estate investments; refinishing antiques; collecting glassware. Home: 1305 N Wood St Cleburne TX 76031

ANDERSON, LINDA LEE, nurse; b. Alpena, Mich., May 10, 1957; d. Roy James and Celia Jeanette (Swartzinski) A. Assoc., Lake Superior State U., Sault Ste Marie, mich., 1977; BS, Wayne State U., 1980; MS, U. Mich., 1988. Cert. oncology nurse. Staff nurse Alpena Gen. Hosp., 1977-78, U. Mich. Med. Ctr., Ann Arbor, 1980-81, Catherine McAuley Health Ctr., Ann Arbor, 1981-89; case mgr. Harper Hosp., Detroit Med. Ctr., 1989—. Eucharistic minister St. Francis of Assisi Ch., Ann Arbor, 1989. Mem. Oncology Nursing Soc. (sec. Ann Arbor chpt. 1986-88), Ann Arbor Ski Club, Ann Arbor Bicycle Touring Soc. Democrat. Roman Catholic. Home: 21700 Moross Rd Detroit MI 48236 Office: Harper Hosp 3990 John R Detroit MI 48201

ANDERSON, LINDA MARIE, education educator; b. Mpls., May 24, 1949; d. Raymond L. and Lucille Marie (Uelmen) A. BA, U. Minn., 1973, PhD, 1984. Writer Mediacraft, Inc., Mpls., 1981-87; asst. prof. Va. Polytechnic Inst. and State U., Blacksburg, 1987--. Author: A Kind of Wild Justice. Mem. Modern Language Assn., Shakespeare Assn. Am., Internat. Shakespeare Assn., Midwest Modern Language Assn. Office: Va Polytechnic Dep English Williams Hall Blacksburg VA 24061

ANDERSON, LINDA SUE, land use planner; b. Holland, Mich., May 28, 1948; d. Sidney J. Risselada; m. L.E. Anderson, Aug. 16, 1968; children: Erika, Morgan. BS in Planning, Grand Valley State U., Allendale, Mich., 1984; postgrad., Mich. State U., 1984—. Project mgr. City of Walker (Mich.), 1983-84; planner Grand Rapids (Mich.) Transit Authority, 1984-86, Mich. Twp. Svc., Allegan, 1986-87; planning dir. Barry County, Hastings, Mich., 1987-89; sr. planner West Mich. Regional Shoreline Devel. Commn., Muskegon, 1989-90, The WBDC Group, Grand Rapids, 1990—; officer Barry County Futuring Commn., 1987-89; leader workshops, speaker, cons. in field. Presenter ednl. video tapes. Pres. bd. dirs. Greater Holland Area coun. Camp Fire, Inc., 1975-83; bd. dirs. Barry Area United Way, Hastings, 1988-89. Recipient Meml. award Alvin Bentley Found., 1981. Mem. Am. Planning Assn., Mich. Soc. Planning Officials, Exchange Club, Phi Kappa Phi. Democrat. Home: 12892 New Holland St Holland MI 49424 Office: The WBDC Group 50 Monroe Pl Grand Rapids MI 49503

ANDERSON, LISA RENEE, audio-visual artist; b. Woodland, Calif., May 22, 1954. BA, Vassar Coll., 1976. Film intern Children's TV Workshop, N.Y.C., 1976; media buyer Steifel, Raymond Advt., N.Y.C., 1976-79; pub. info. dir. Project Concern Internat., San Diego, Calif., from 1983; now with Laubach Telecommunication Project, San Marcos, Calif.; cons. Bd. of Edn., N.Y.C., Bronx, 1976, Wholistic Living News, San Diego, 1988, Project Concern Internat., San Diego, 1988-89. Director, editor (video spls.) San Diego Televent, 1985, Commitment-The Cornerstone, 1987, PCI For the Children, 1988; editor: (Newsletter) Concern News, 1985-88. Media vol. Exploring Family Sch., San Diego, 1987-88. Recipient photo journalistic trip to Bolivia, Peru, Project Concern, San Diego, 1989. Mem. San Diego Vassar Club. Office: Laubach Communication Project 751 Rancheros Dr Ste 10 San Marcos CA 92069

ANDERSON, LOIS ANN, college official; b. Pitts., Nov. 27, 1937; d. Arthur and Dorothy (Anderson) Constable; m. James R. Anderson, Aug. 19, 1955; children: Starr Ann Anderson Beauchamp, Vicki Lyn. BA in English and Libr., Fla. State U., 1978; MS in Mgmt., Troy State U., 1981. Historian USAF, Torrejon, Spain, 1971-73; info. specialist Hist. Rsch. Ctr., Montgomery, Ala., 1979-83; instr. mgmt. Troy State U., Montgomery, 1981-83; regional adminstr. Cen. Tex. Coll., Washington, 1983-87; dir. human resources devel. Cen. Tex. Coll., Killeen, 1987-90, dean continental campuses, 1990—. Mem. Assn. for Continuing Adult Edn., Nat. Assn. Instns. for Mil. Edn. Svcs., Am. Assn. for Adult and Continuing Edn., Calif. Colls. and Mil. Edn. Assn., NAFE, Lambda Iota Tau. Office: Cen Tex Coll US Hwy 190 Killeen TX 76540

ANDERSON, LORRAINE MARIE, tire company executive; b. Denver; d. John and Lydia (Schreiner) Dreith; m. James Homer Anderson, Oct. 18, 1953; children: Kristi L., Kirk A., Keith M., Karol A. BS in Bus. Adminstrn., Regis Coll., 1984. Sec.-treas., dir. Anderson Tire Svc., Inc., Arvada, Colo., 1973—; ptnr. Anderson & Anderson, Arvada, 1976—. Elected to coun. City of Arvada, 1985, re-elected, 1989—; elected Mayor ProTem, 1989—; bd. dirs. Arvada Fire Dept. Credit Union, 1974-83; mem. S.E. Arvada Neighborhood Devel. Com., 1979. Mem. Mountain States Tire Dealers Assn. (bd. dirs. 1984-85, treas. 1986, pres. 1988), Colo. Women in Municiple Govt. (v.p. 1989). Home: 5645 Dudley St Arvada CO 80002 Office: Anderson Tire Svc Inc 5503 Marshall St Arvada CO 80002

ANDERSON, LOUISE ELEANOR, biochemistry educator; b. Cleve., May 18, 1934; d. Bertil Gotfrid and Lorraine (Dorothy) Ossian) A. AB, Augustana Coll., Rock Island, Ill., 1956; PhD, Cornell U., 1961. Rsch. assoc. Washington U., St. Louis, 1960-62, Dartmouth Med. Sch., Hanover, N.H., 1962-64, 66-67; Kettering Found. internat. fellow Sydney (Australia) U., 1964-65; rsch. asst. prof. U. Tenn., Oak Ridge, 1967-68; asst. prof. biol. scis. U. Ill., Chgo., 1968-70, assoc. prof., 1970-75, prof. biol. scis., 1975—. contbr. numerous articles to profl. jours. Recipient Outstanding Achievement award Augustana Coll., 1979; Katzir-Katchalsky fellow Weizmann Inst., Rehovat, Israel, 1974-75, Fogarty internat. fellow NIH, Lund, Swedn, 1981-82; rsch. grantee USDA, NSF, U.S. Dept. Energy, Israel-U.S. Binat. Mem. AAAS, Am. Soc. Biochemistry and Molecular Biology, Am. Soc. Plant Physiologists. Lutheran. Office: U Ill Chgo Dept Biol Scis Box 4348 Chicago IL 60680

ANDERSON, LOUISE GOINGS, sales executive; b. Utica, Miss., Jan. 20, 1930; d. Thomas Jefferson and Mary Louella (Stubbs) Goings; m. Walter Thomas Anderson, Apr. 17, 1949; children: Stephen, Cynthia, Jeffrey. Student, Dade Coll., Miami, Fla., 1950-52. Owner, operator Little Hitchin Post, Burlington, N.C., 1973-75; owner Mr. & Mrs. Shoppe, Burlington, A Touch of Elegance, Burlington; mgr. Imp Peddler, Richmond, Va., 1980-82; dist. mgr. Eagles Eye, Inc., Phila., 1983—; lectr. in retail and fashion merchandising local colls. Pres. Miami PTA, 1957-60. Mem. NAFE, Ala. Bus. Women's Assn. Republican. Methodist. Home: 1748 Petty Rd Graham NC 27253 Office: 1236 Plaza Dr Burlington NC 27215

ANDERSON, LUCINDA KAY, food products executive; b. Dell Rapids, S.D., Mar. 25, 1941; d. Kenneth Taylor and Elsie Marie (Qualseth) Faris; m. Lauren Stanley Anderson, June 18, 1965 (div. 1975); 1 child, Melissa Kay. BS, U. S.D., 1963; MEd, S.D. State U., 1969, S.D. State U., 1978; cert. spl. edn., S.D. State U., 1971. Tchr. phys. edn. Des Moines Pub. Sch., 1963-65; prof. phys. edn. Augustana Coll., Sioux Falls, S.D., 1970-71; head phys. edn. dept. Huron (S.D.) Coll., 1971-72; social worker, admissions counselor State Hosp. Mentally Retarded, Redfield, S.D., 1972-74; workshop facilitator S.D. State U., Brookings, S.D., 1975-78; career counselor State S.D., Brookings, 1978-80; tchr. phys. edn., spl. edn. Dell Rapids (S.D.) Pub. Schs., 1965-68, 81-84; mgr. restaurant Meadow Creek Country Club, Mission, Tex., 1986-87, mgr., merchandiser pro shop, 1985-89; mgr., supr. TCBY, Harlingen, Tex., 1989—; counselor career workshop S.D. State U., Brookings, 1976-78; cons. for adult severly mentally retarded, Mission, 1985—; developed phys. edn. curriculum for small high schs., S.D., 1962-63; affiliated with TCBY; supr. privately owned bus. Planning commr. County Planning Commn., Sioux Falls, 1979-84; mem. parent adv. bd. Dell Rapids Pub. Schs., 1980-84, adult edn. bd. Dell Rapids Ind. Sch. Dist., 1981-84; instr. swimming ARC, Sioux Falls, 1960-76. Mem. Kappa Delta Phi. Republican. Baptist. Club: Women's Golf (activities chmn. 1978-80, pres. 1981-82). Lodge: Order of Eastern Star. Home: 5005 N 4th McAllen TX 78504 Office: TCBY 712 N Sunshine Strip Harlingen TX 78550

ANDERSON, LUCY MARGARITA, English teacher; b. Laredo, Tex., Sept. 6, 1940; d. Mario Sr. and Margarita (dela Garza) Meza; m. Gilberto J. Martinez, June 1, 1963 (div. Apr. 1980); children: Rick D., Gilbert J. Jr., Lucy Lynn. BA, BS in Edn., Tex. Woman's U., 1961. Cert. tchr., Tex. Tchr. Laredo (Tex.) Ind. Sch. Dist., 1961-70, United Ind. Sch. Dist., Laredo, 1970-79, Laredo Jr. Coll., 1979-80, Northside Ind. Sch. Dist., San Antonio, 1989—. Mem. Mexican Am. Profl. Women's Club, VFW Women's Aux. (chaplain 1989-90), Villade Guadalupe, Elks (treas.). Roman Catholic. Home and Office: 7939 Green Glen San Antonio TX 78255

ANDERSON, MARGARET LAVINIA, history educator; b. Washington, Oct. 18, 1941; d. David and Margaret Lavinia (Anderson) A.; m. Charles Raff, Sept. 12, 1972; 1 dau., Sarah Elizabeth. B.A., Swarthmore Coll., 1963; Ph.D., Brown U., 1971. Asst. prof. history Swarthmore Coll. (Pa.), 1970-77, assoc. prof., 1977-84, prof., 1985—; mem. com. Ednl. Testing Service, Princeton, N.J., 1983-86. Author: Windthorst: A Political Biography, 1981; contbr. articles to profl. jours. Woodrow Wilson Found. fellow, 1963, 66-67; NDEA fellow Brown U., Providence, 1963-66, grantee, 1972; Humboldt Found. fellow, Bonn, W.Ger., 1974; Lang fellow Swarthmore Coll., 1981-82; Flack Faculty award for teaching, Swarthmore Coll., 1985; Mem. Am. Hist. Assn., Cath. Hist. Assn., German Studies Assn., Conf. Group on Cen. European History (bi-ann. prize for best articles 1984). Democrat. Episcopalian. Office: Swarthmore Coll Dept History Swarthmore PA 19081

ANDERSON, MARIAN, contralto; b. Phila., Feb. 27, 1902; d. John Berkeley and Anna Anderson; ed. Phila. pub. schs.; mus. edn. pvt. study in Phila., N.Y. and abroad; hon. degrees 23 Am. ednl. instns., 1 Korean; m. Orpheus H. Fisher, July 24, 1943 (dec.). As child sang in Union Bapt. Ch. choir, Phila.; a fund raised through a church concert enabled her to take singing lessons under an Italian instr.; won 1st prize in competition with 300 others at N.Y. Lewisohn Stadium, 1925; began singing career, 1924; debut in Un Ballo in Maschera, Met. Opera, 1955; has made many concert tours of the U.S. and Europe; one of the leading contraltos in world; appearances in all famous concert halls, stadia, now ret. U.S. del. to UN, 1955, also 13th Gen. Assembly. Recipient Bok Award, 1940, Congl. Medal of Honor, 1977, Nat. Medal of Arts, 1986; awarded Finnish decoration "probenignitate humana", 1940; decorations from Sweden, Philippines, Haiti, Liberia, France, numerous states and cities in U.S.; Yokus Lo medal (Japan). Mem. Alpha Kappa Alpha. Author: My Lord, What a Morning. Office: care ICM Artists Ltd 40 W 57th St New York NY 10019

ANDERSON, MARILYN JUNE, music teacher; b. Aldrich, Mo., July 3, 1935; d. Lafayette and Helen Louise (Cheek) A. BS in Edn., S.W. Mo. State U., Springfield, 1958; MEd, U. Mo., 1966. Vocal, instrumental music Licking (Mo.) High Sch., 1958-62; vocal music, English I Sullivan (Mo.) High Sch., 1962-65; vocal music Willard (Mo.) High Sch., 1965-67, Hillcrest High Sch., Springfield, Mo.; sponsor Future Nurses Am., Licking, Mo., 1958-62; chpt. organizer, sponsor, pvt. piano and voice tchr. Hillcrest Modern Music Masters, 1988—; singer Mid Am. Singers, Springfield, 1969-76. Chmn. of drive, March of Dimes, Licking, Mo., 1961, edn. chmn. Am. Cancer Soc., Tex. County, 1961-62, bible sch. tchr. Ch. of Christ, Springfield, Mo., 1968-71, 1980—. Mem. NEA, Music Educators Nat. Conf., Am. Choral Dirs. Assn., Delta Kappa Gamma, Mo. Music Educators Assn. (dist. vocal v.p. 1986-87). Republican. Office: Hillcrest High Sch 3319 N Grant Springfield MO 65803

ANDERSON, MARTHA ALENE, environmental health and safety executive, academic administrator; b. Monessen, Pa., June 15, 1945; d. Jesse Lee and Helen Frances (Daugherty) Cain; m. James O. Anderson, Sept. 9, 1966; 1 child, Heather Linn. BS in Biology, U. Pa., 1967. Rsch. asst. W.Va. U., Morgantown, 1967-72; tchr. Hokkaido Internat. Sch., Sapporo, Japan, 1972-73; research asst. Pa. State U., 1974-75, Trudeau Inst., 1975-76; research assoc. U. Ariz., Tucson, 1976-80; mgr. chem. waste Dept. Risk Mgmt., U. Ariz., Tucson, 1980-81, asst. dir., 1981-85, dir., 1985-87; dir. environ. health and safety Thomas Jefferson U., Phila., 1987—. Named Woman of Yr., Tucson Bus. and Profl. Women, 1985, Woman on Move, Tucson YWCA, 1985. Mem. Am. Soc. Safety Engrs. (healthcare rep. local region), Am. Indsl. Hygiene Assn., Am. Soc. Hosp. Engrs., Bus. and Profl. Women, Campus Safety Assn., Am. Chem. Soc. (Phila. local emergency planning com.). Avocations: Japanese literature, sewing. Office: Thomas Jefferson U Dept Environ Health and Safety Edison 1620 Philadelphia PA 19107-5233

ANDERSON, MARTHA GAIL, chemical company executive; b. Bakersfield, Calif., Aug. 27, 1951; d. Charles and Jerline (James) Alford; m. Jan Philip Anderson, Oct. 28, 1969; children: Charles Philip, Bryan Christopher. Cert., Cypress Jr. Coll., 1973-74, Mesa Jr. Coll., 1984-85. Owner ACCO Chem. Co., Chula Vista, Calif. Mem. Beta Sigma Phi (v.p. 1979-82).

ANDERSON, MARTHA JEAN, media specialist; b. Greenville, S.C., May 15, 1946; d. Benjamin Mason and Gladys (Harling) A. BS, Appalachian State U., Boone, N.C., 1968; M.Librarianship, Emory U., Atlanta, 1974, D.A.S.L., 1983. Libr. Arlington Schs., Atlanta, 1968-70, Archer Public High Sch., Atlanta, 1970-74; media specialist Woodmont High Sch. Greenville County Sch. Dist., Piedmont, S.C., 1974-76; media specialist Berea High Sch. Greenville County Sch. Dist., Greenville, S.C., 1976-80; media specialist Hillcrest High Sch. Greenville County Sch. Dist., Simpsonville, S.C., 1980—. Recipient Citation award S.C. Occupational Info. Coord. Com., 1988. Mem. NEA, S.C. Assn. Sch. Librs., S.C. Edn. Assn., Greenville County Idn. Assn., Iowa Alpha Delta Kappa (pres. 1982-84, v.p. 1980-82, historian 1978-80, 88-90, sgt. at arms 1990—). Methodist. Home: 537 Harrison Bridge Rd Simpsonville SC 29681 Office: Hillcrest High Sch 3657 Industrial Dr Simpsonville SC 29681

ANDERSON, MARY JANE, newsletter publisher, public relations specialist; b. Richmond, Va., May 27, 1930; d. Francis W. and Margaret G. (Esbrook) A.; B.A. in Journalism, Wayne State U., 1951. Staff writer Skyline mag. and Mich. Motor Carrier, Detroit, 1952-54; reporter Fairchild Publs., Detroit, 1954-57, Home Furnishings Daily/Footwear News, Chgo., 1957-67; food service editor Vend Mag., Billboard Publs., N.Y.C., 1967-72; owner Anderson Publs. (pubs. The Anderson Report, Foods By Mail); prin. MJA Pub. Relations, Chgo., 1979—. Active local Republican campaigns; broadcaster Chgo. Radio Info. Services for blind and print handicapped; vol. Rec. for the Blind, N.Y.C. Named Food Editor of Yr., Nat. Assn. Coll. and Univ. Food Services. Mem. Women in Communications (past pres.), Internat. Food Editorial Council (past v.p.). Office: Anderson Publs 230 N Michigan Suite 1100 Chicago IL 60601

ANDERSON, MARY LEIGH, police investigator; b. Elizabeth, N.J., Apr. 7, 1956; d. Robert James and Ruth Leola (McRitchie) Anderson. BS, Fla. State U., 1978. Cert. law enforcement officer. Sgt. Governors Sq. Mall Security, Tallahassee, 1979-80, chief, 1980-82; investigator Maas Bros. Dept. Store, Tallahassee, 1982-83; sgt. Plantation Security Inc., Tallahassee, 1981-83; dep. marshall U.S. Marshall's Svc., Tallahassee, 1983-84; investigator Tallahassee Police Dept., 1984—. Recipient Liberty and Justice award of merit Nat. Assn. Chiefs of Police, 1986; Fla. Gov.'s Cert. of Appreciation, 1985. Mem. Police Benevolent Assn., Assn. Profl. Police Investigators, Nat. Assn. Female Execs., Am. Fedn. Police, Police Marksman Assn., Fla. Sheriffs Assn. (hon.), Hon. Order Ky. Cols. Democrat. Roman Catholic. Office: Tallahassee Police Dept 234 E 7th Ave Tallahassee FL 32301

ANDERSON, MARY LOU, educator; b. Mt. Pleasant, Iowa, Aug. 29, 1949; d. Carl Marion and Hazel Lucile (Mitchell) A. BS in Edn., Northeast Mo. State U., 1971, MS in Elem. Guidance, 1974. Cert. elem. tchr., Mo. Elem. tchr. Waynesville pub. schs., Mo., 1971-73, Hannibal pub. schs., Mo., 1973-79, Bel Ridge Elem. Sch., St. Louis, 1979-86; counselor Bel Ridge Elem. Sch., 1986-87; counselor Lincoln Elem. Sch., 1987—; ERA cons. ERAm., Washington, 1980-81, NEA, Washington, 1980-82; state conf. workshop leader NEA, 1979-83; co-founder, chmn. Mo. NEA Women's Caucus, 1975-78. Pres. Mo. ERA Coalition, 1980-82; pres. Polit. Action Com. St. Louis Women's Polit. Caucus, 1984-85, endorsement com. chair, 1987; campaign worker Mo. Democratic Orgn., 1982—; supt. goal setting task force Normandy Sch. Dist., 1988-89; mem. Conf. on Edn. Mem. NEA (LEAST discipline cons. 1981—, Lorna Bottger Polit. Action award 1982), ACLU, St. Louis Suburban Tchrs. Assn. (bd. dirs. 1983-87), Normandy Tchrs. Assn. (chmn. pub. rels. com. 1980-81, chmn. profl. rights and responsibilities com. 1981-83, chmn. instrn. and profl. devel. com. 1987-89, negotians com. 1985-89), Mo. Sch. Counselors Assn., St. Louis Suburban Counselors Assn., Confluence (St. Louis chpt.), Phi Delta Kappa. Mem. United Ch. of Christ. Avocations: playing piano, aerobics, reading, plays and movies. Home: 4497 Pershing St Apt 107 Saint Louis MO 63108 Office: Lincoln Elem Sch 6815 Robbins Saint Louis MO 63133

ANDERSON, MARYANN JANE, bookkeeper, accountant; b. Rome, N.Y., June 22, 1935; d. Joseph Paul Jr. and Ann Maryjane (Czebeniak) Simon; m. Andy William Anderson, May 15, 1954 (dec. Dec. 1987); children: Deborah Jane Anderson-Gaiser, Glen William, Mark William. Grad. high sch., Rome. Ordained to ministry Presbyn. Ch., 1988. Clk. Griffiss AFB, Rome, 1953-55; bookkeeper L&M Wholesale, Inc., Rome, 1969-74; with advt. dept. Rome Daily Sentinel, 1974-79; acct. Conde Milking Machine Co., Sherrill, N.Y., 1979-87; bookkeeper Henderson's Office Supply, Oneida, N.Y., 1987-88; pvt. practice bookkeeper, acct. Verona, N.Y., 1988—; treas. Verona Cemetery Assn., 1988—. Leader Cub Scouts, Verona, 1964-69, 4-H, Fulton, N.Y., 1982-83; sec. PTA, Verona, 1974; lay minister Augusta (N.Y.) Presbyn. Ch., 1988—; youth leader Verona Presbyn. Ch., 1975-79, sec., 1989—, deacon, 1974-77, elder, 1988—, clk. of session, 1989—. Recipient Outstanding Woman award Zonta Club of Am., 1981. Mem. Utica Toastmasters (numerous offices 1977—, youth leader 1982-87, Outstanding Area Gov. award 1981, Disting. Toastmaster Internat. award 1982, Disting. Dist. Gov. award 1985), Order of Eastern Star (matron 1974, 78, 89, dist. dep. grand matron 1990), Dem. Club. Home and Office: RD #2 Rte 31 Box 175 Verona NY 13478

ANDERSON, MAUD, retired educator; b. Cooper, Tex., Sept. 9, 1903; d. Charles B. and Alice (Johnson) A. BA, East Tex. State Coll., 1929; MA, So. Meth. U., 1932; postgrad., St Hilda's Coll., Oxford U., 1961, London U., 1961, U. Oslo, 1963, Trinity Coll., Dublin, 1965. Instr. rural schs. Cooper High Sch., Forney High Sch., 1932-35, Highland Park High Sch., Dallas, 1935-72; with So. Meth. U. Reading Clinic, 1958-70; ret.; mem. Writer's Conf., Breadloaf, Vt., World congress Internat. Reading Assn., Copenhagen, 1968, Sydney, Australia, 1970, Vienna, Austria, 1974, Singapore, 1976. Bd. dirs. Northway Christian Ch., Dallas, 1983-86. Mem. AAUW, Dallas Ret. Tchrs. Assn. (active in community svc. tutoring, chmn. 1982-84, 85-88), Altrusa Club, Delta Kappa Gamma (mem. Delta Omicron).

ANDERSON, MEGAN BOTHWELL, cultural exchange consultant, educator; b. Salt Lake City, Sept. 10, 1944; d. Vernon Edward and Elizabeth (Bothwell) A.; m. Marvin L. Friedland, Apr. 1, 1967 (div. 1970); 1 child, Michael. BS, U. Utah, 1966, MS, 1971, postgrad. Rsch. asst. U. Utah, Salt Lake City, 1962-71; environ. geographer Dept. Trans. Environ. Coun. Utah, Salt Lake City, 1971-74; cons. Utah State U. Found, Salt Lake City, 1974; asst. state planning coord. State of Utah, Salt Lake City, 1974-79; pres. M.T. Enterprises and Cons., Salt Lake City, 1979—; cons. Utah Dept. Transp., Salt Lake City, 1986; liaison palentol. dept. U. Utah, 1968-71; mem. sci. and tech. com. State of Utah, 1979; bd. dirs., exec. dir. Sacramento Gold Mining Co., 1988; exec. dir. Geyser Marion Gold Mining Co., Bothwell and Swaner Corp., Bothwell Farms Co., 1988. Author: Utah Resource Information System, 1979, The Multiple Use and Joint Development, 1975. State rep. Fed. Emergency Mgmt. Agy, L.A., Washington 1976; sch. rep. ARC, Logan, 1961. Mem. Utah Sect. Am. Cong. Surveying and Mapping (hospitality chmn. 1974, sec. 1973-74, editor newsletter 1972, speaker 1973, Washington). Episcopalian. Home: 3939 St Francis Circle Salt Lake City UT 84124 Office: MT Enterprises and Cons 3939 St Francis Cir Salt Lake City UT 84124

ANDERSON, MELISSA EVA, small business owner; b. Grayson, Ky., Sept. 24, 1959; d. Thomas John Anderson and Betty Jane (Mauk) Hall. Student, Araphoe Bus. Coll., Denver, 1976-78; BA, Morehead State U., 1979-84. Sales clk. Cases Hardware and Amtiques, Olive Hill, Ky., 1970-72; waitress Los Gringitos, Morehead, Ky., 1975; tele-mktg. opr. Citi-Corp Fin. Svcs., Denver, 1977, chairperson, advisor; model, spokeswoman Ford Agy. NY, N.Y.C., 1979-81; counselor Christian Social Svcs., 1979-81; activities coord. Dept. Corrections, Denver, 1979; pres. ops. Dimensions Unltd. Inc., Denver, 1981—; owner, pres. Dimensions Unltd. Inc., Huntington, W.Va., 1985—; cons. Home Interior Designs, Inc., Denver, 1985-86; sec. Denver County Real Estate Commn., 1987-88; bd. dir. Found. for Human Concerns, Morehead, Ky., 1987-88; cons. Ky. C. of Comml., Glasgow 1988—; founder, pres. Unified Fortress Group, Inc., 1989. Author: Business Ethics 2nd Moral Values, 1987, Life After Death 2 Cultural Explorations, 1987. Spokesperson Nat. Rep. Group, Morehead, 1981; chairperson Tiffany's Gold Charity Soc., Denver 1986; sec. Bus. Devel. Soc., Las Vegas, 1987; charter sponsor NATO Culture Exch. in W.Va., NY, 1989. Mem. NAFE, Dunn V. Bradstree, Incorp., Nat. Assn. Mchts., Encore Gold Purchasing Club, League Human Rights. Office: Dimensions Unltd Inc 946 4th Ave Huntington VA 25701

ANDERSON, MICHAEL LARSEN, human resources administrator; b. Nashville, Feb. 19, 1941; d. Ralph Michael and Vee (Allen) Larsen; m. William J. Anderson, III, June 4, 1958 (div. 1984); children—Alicia Sayle, William Joseph, Ralph Michael Larsen, Mollie Blair. Student, Vanderbilt U., 1958-60, Xavier Coll., 1977-78. Asst. dir. human resources PEDCo. Inc., Cin., 1979-81, human resources dir., 1981-83. pres. Lupus Found. Am., Inc. Nashville area chpt., 1987-89; bd. dirs. Nashville Mental Health Assn., 1968-71; founding bd. dirs. Children's Hosp., Nashville; child advocacy chmn. Jr. League, Huntington, W.Va., 1974-75; child advocacy co-chmn. Jr. League Cin., 1977-78. Appeared on cover of Time mag., July 1965, Town & Country, Oct. 1972. Episcopalian.

ANDERSON, MILADA FILKO, manufacturing company executive; b. Chgo., Nov. 17, 1922; d. John and Anna (Sianta) Filko; m. George Richard Anderson, Aug. 29, 1945 (div. Sept. 1974); children: Mark, Renee, Teri. BS, Northwestern U., 1944, MS in Mgmt., 1979. Tchr. history Evanston (Ill.) Township High Sch., 1946; tchr. social studies Mt. Prospect (Ill.) Jr. High Sch., 1947-48; dir. F&B Mfg. Co., Chgo., 1965—, pres., chmn. bd., 1972—. Mem. Northwestern U. Profl. Womens Assn., Nat. Assn. Investment Clubs, Zeta Tau Alpha. Republican. Lutheran. Office: F&B Mfg Co 5480 Northwest Hwy Chicago IL 60630

ANDERSON, MO IMOZELLE, real estate broker; b. Ames, Okla., May 12, 1937; d. John H. and Audra B. (Wilson) Gregg; m. Richard T. Anderson, Aug. 31, 1957; children: Richard L., Karin L. BS in Edn., U. Okla., 1959. Cert. real estate broker. Tchr. Midwest City (Okla.) Pub. Schs., 1959-60; tchr. Ponca City (Okla.) Pub. Schs., 1960-62, tchr. music, 1965-73; sales assoc. Bob Turner Realtors, Edmond, Okla., 1974-75; broker, owner Century 21 Titan, Realtors, Edmond, 1975-85; dist. v.p. Merrill Lynch Realty, Edmond, 1985—; bd. dirs. Capitol Fin. Assets; mem. Okla. Real Estate Commn., 1987—. Bd. dirs. Heritage Heights Homeowner's Assn., 1976-77, Edmond YMCA, 1978, Gregg Found., 1983—, Community Awarness Found., 1985—, Daily Living Ctr., 1987—, Frances Tuttle Vo-Tech Found., 1987—, Edmond Meml. Hosp., 1988; mem. Mayor's Econ. Devel. Coun., 1984-86; campaign chmn. Dist. 81 House Race, 1986. Named Corp. Woman of Yr. for real estate and constrn. Oklahoma City, 1984; recipient Citation of Achievement Okla. Senate and Ho. of Reps., 1988, Okla. Women in Bus. Advocate of Yr. award U.S. Small Bus. Adminstrn., 1983, 87. Mem. Okla. Assn. Realtors (chmn. bd. svcs. com. 1984, 85, 86, 87), Edmond Bd. Realtors (chmn. Realtor of Yr. com. 1988), Nat. Assn. Realtors, Edmond C. of C. (bd. dirs.), Edmond Women's Club, Edmond Hist. Soc. Republican. Presbyterian. Home: 1717 Walnut Cove Edmond OK 73013

ANDERSON, NANCY, museum director. Dir. Mus. of Arts and Scis., Macon, Ga. Office: Mus Arts & Scis 4182 Forsyth Rd Ste 501 C3 Macon GA 31210

ANDERSON, NINA KAYE, educator; b. Logan, W.Va., May 21, 1953; d. Frank and Christine (Bailey) A. BA, Marshall U., Huntington, W.Va., 1974, MA, 1975. Reading specialist asst. Marshall U., 1953; tchr. Cleve. Pub. Sch. System, 1986; inside sales rep. Rainsoft Corp., Warrensville

Heights, Ohio, 1987. Mem. NAFE, Am. Fedn. Teachers, Nat. Coun. Negro Women, Cleve. Tchrs. Union, Phi Delta Kappa, Eta Zeta (founding chpt.), Alpha Kappa Alpha. Baptist. Home: 4511 Granada Blvd Apt 209 Warrensville Heights OH 44128 Office: Cleve Pub Schs 1380 E Sixth St Cleveland OH 44114

ANDERSON, PAMELA JO, architect; b. Pomona, Calif., June 29, 1955; d. Roger Alan and Pauline Virginia (Harzler) A.; m. Robert Keith Humbert, Oct. 1, 1981 (div. 1985). BArch, U. Ariz., Tucson, 1978. Registered architect. Architect, draftsman, designer Perkins & Will, Chgo., 1978-81; architect Jacobs & Kahan, Chgo., 1981-82; pres. P.J. Anderson Assocs., Inc., Chgo., 1982—. Mem. AIA. Republican. Methodist. Club: Chgo Yacht. Office: P J Anderson Assocs Inc 403 W North Ave Chicago IL 60610

ANDERSON, PATRICIA ALICE, medical assistant, secretary; b. Jersey City, Jan. 15, 1952; d. Richard John and Alice M. (Leinberger) Dayock; m. Jeffrey Mark Anderson, May 26, 1989. BA in Edn., William Paterson Coll., 1973, postgrad., 1973-74; AA in Acctg., Bay de Noc Community Coll., 1989. Tchr. Epiphany Sch., Cliffside Park, N.J., 1973-74, Alexander St. Sch., Newark, 1974-75, Toms River (N.J.) Intermediate Sch., 1975-76; med. asst., sec. Ocean Orthopedics, Toms River, 1976-80; payroll supr. Basic Industries, Baton Rouge, 1980-81; adminstrv. asst. Stone & Webster Engring., St. Francisville, La., 1981-82; med. asst., sec. K. E. Anderson MD PC, Escanaba, Mich., 1981—; mem. N.J. Edn. Assn., Newark, 1973-76; chairperson SHERO Com., Escanaba, 1988. Mem. Bus. and Profl. Women (bd. mem. 1983-90, Niki award 1989), AAUW (bd. mem. 1983-90), Delta County Ambs., Delta County Alliance Against Violence & Abuse. Democrat. Roman Catholic. Home: 1436 Hwy M-35 Bark River MI 49807 Office: Kent E Anderson MD PC Doctors Park Ste 216 Escanaba MI 49829

ANDERSON, PAULA LEE, marketing professional; b. Akron, Ohio, Feb. 27, 1953; d. Fred Wiemer and Lavonne Esther (Eller) A. BS in Communication, Purdue U., 1973, MS in Mgmt., 1980. Sales merchandiser, account rep. The Pillsbury Co., Louisville, Ky., 1973-75; account mgr. The Pillsbury Co., Anderson, Ind., 1975-78; asst. market devel. mgr. S.C. Johnson and Son, Inc., Racine, Wis., 1980-81, assoc. market devel. mgr., 1982; field sales mgr. S.C. Johnson and Son, Inc., Detroit, 1982-84; territory mgr. John O. Butler Co., Ann Arbor, Mich., 1984-85; regional sales mgr. John O. Butler Co., Dallas, 1985-87; sales adminstrn. mgr. John O. Butler Co., Chgo., 1987-89; dir. promotion devel. John D. Butler Co., Chgo., 1990—; adj. prof. U. Wis.-Parkside, Kenosha, 1980. Advisor Jr. Achievement, Racine, 1982; bd. dirs. Krannert Alumni, West Lafayette, Ind., 1981-82. Office: John O Butler Co 4635 W Foster Ave Chicago IL 60630

ANDERSON, RANAKA KAY, financial agency systems programmer; b. Chgo., May 11, 1960; d. Samuel L. and Nora D. (Fowler) A.; 1 child, Justin Dorsay Jones-Anderson. AA, Black Hawk Coll., 1981; BS, Ill. State U., 1982; postgrad., Govs. State U., 1989—. Corp. account rep. ComputerLand, Bloomington, Ill., 1984; vocat. coord. Thornton Community Coll., South Holland, Ill., 1984-85; data processing asst. Govs. State U., University Park, Ill., 1986; counselor adult edn. Evanston High Sch., Evanston, Ill., 1986-88; AGS exec. asst. gen. Coun. on Fin. and Adminstrn., Evanston, 1987-89; systems programmer Gen. Coun. on Fin. and Adminstrn., 1989—; exec. dir. Progressive Black Women's Network, Chgo., 1988—; programming cons., Chgo., 1988—. Fellow Alpha Lambda Delta, Phi Eta Sigma. Democrat. Methodist. Office: Gen Coun on Fin & Adminstrn 1200 Davis St Evanston IL 60201

ANDERSON, ROBBIE JO, information systems specialist; b. Simpsonville, S.C., Nov. 7, 1952; d. George William and Roberta (Harling) Hance; m. Andrew Clifford Phillips, Jan. 3, 1981 (dec. June 1983); 1 child, Donald Hance; m. William Cary Anderson, Sept. 2, 1984; 1 child, Cary Roberta. BA in Psychology with honors, Clemson U., 1974, MEd in Pers. Svcs. and Vocat. Counseling, 1975, Sch. Psychologist Level I, 1978; MBA in Computer Info. Systems with honors, No. Ariz. U., 1984. Acad. tutor Clemson (S.C.) U., 1972-77, psychoednl. evaluator Coll. Edn., 1975-78; spl. edn. tchr. Palmetto Mid. Sch., Williamston, S.C., 1975-77; bookkeeper Pearsall Refrigeration, Inc., Flagstaff, Ariz., 1980; aide computer lab. Coll. Bus. Adminstrn. No. Ariz. U., Flagstaff, 1981-82, grad. asst., 1983, instr. computer info. systems dept., 1982-83, 84, cons., 1984; adinstrv. specialist MIS, U. Ga. Sch. Law, Athens, 1984-87; mgr. MIS dept. facilities planning and mgmt. Clemson (S.C.) U., 1988—; cons. computer info. systems, Greenville, S.C., 1987-88. Co-organizer Hugo Relief, Clemson, 1989; team mother Mauldin (S.C.) Soccer Club, 1989-90. Mem. Assn. for Phys. Plant Adminstrs. (com.), Am. Mgmt. Assn., Spl. Interest Group MPAC Systems (cochmn. 1989-90), Order of Athena, Beta Gamma Sigma, Phi Kappa Phi, Sigma Tau Epsilon. Republican. Office: Clemson U (FMO) Klugh Ave Clemson SC 29634-5901

ANDERSON, ROBERTA JOAN See MITCHELL, JONI

ANDERSON, RONNI (RHONDA REE), small business owner; b. Denver, Aug. 4, 1947; d. Ralph J. and Marian L. (Hampton) Blakley; m. Richard C. Anderson, Nov. 12, 1971; children: Traci, Susan, Mark. Grad. high sch., Denver, 1965. Office mgr. Crosby Constrn. Co., Denver, 1972-75; prin., pres. Two-Fifty Group Plans, Inc., Denver, 1975-81; account exec. Mgmt. Recruiters, Phoenix, 1981-83; pres., prin. Staff One, Inc., Staff Temps, Inc., Phoenix, 1983%. Mem. NAFE, Nat. Assn. Pers. Cons., Ariz. Search Cons. Assn., Ariz. Bus. Alliance (com. mem.). Home: 2828 N 44th St #225 Phoenix AZ 85008

ANDERSON, ROSALIND COOGAN, testing laboratory executive, toxicologist; b. Cleve., July 23, 1937; d. Peter F. and Barbara (Tracy) Coogan; m. Julius H. Anderson, June 29, 1963; children: Gretchen, Katherine, Margaret. BA, Mt. Holyoke Coll., 1959; MA, Yale U., 1963, PhD, 1965. Rsch. assoc. Yale U., New Haven, 1965-67; from asst. prof. to assoc. prof. Duquesne U., Pitts., 1970-76; rsch. assoc. U. Pitts., Phila., 1976-79; head toxicology dept. Arthur D. Little Inc., Mass., 1979-87; pres. Anderson Labs. Inc., Dedham, Mass., 1987—; cons. in field. Lectr. state, fed. and local regulatory agys., 1983—. Mem. ASTM (group chair Phila. chpt. 1988—), Soc. of Toxicology. Office: Anderson Labs Inc 30 River St Dedham MA 02026

ANDERSON, SANDRA WOOD, data processing executive; b. Lugoff, S.C., Mar. 9, 1949; d. Sam Jr. and Eloise (Wood) Wright; m. James Edward Anderson, Sept. 20, 1974 (div. 1985). BS in Bus. Edn., Benedict Coll., Columbia, S.C., 1970; cert. in data processing, Midland Tech. Coll., Columbia, 1983; cert. Electronics, Kershaw County Vocat. Sch., Camden, S.C., 1985. Accounts receivable clk. Rollins, Inc., Atlanta, 1970-72, Watkins Motor Lines, Atlanta, 1972-75; recapping clk. Nat. Linen Service, Columbia, 1976; proof operator S.C. Nat. Bank, Columbia, 1976-77, accounts payable clk., 1977-81, computer operator, scheduler, tape librarian, 1981-86, shift mgr., data processing officer, 1986—. Mem. S.C. Polit. Action Com., Columbia, 1986-87, Roundtop Bapt. Ch., Blythewood, S.C. Mem. Am. Inst. Banking (basic and standard cert., 1978, 81), Greater Columbia Tennis Club, Zeta Phi Beta. Home: 418 Eskie Dixon Rd Elgin SC 29045 Office: SC Nat Bank 1628 Browning Rd Rm 115 Columbia SC 29226

ANDERSON, SHARON ANNE, gas company executive, financial reporting manager; d. DeWayne C. and Edith (Walker) A. BSBA, U. Tulsa, 1977. CPA, Okla. With Okla. Natural Gas Co., Tulsa, 1965—, asst. mgr. corp. responsibility and community affairs, 1979-80, asst. mgr. fin. reporting, 1980-83, mgr. fin. reporting., 1983—. Mem. Skiatook Reservoir Authority, Tulsa, 1980-84. Mem. Am. Inst. CPA's, Okla. Soc. CPA's, LWV (pres. elect Met. Tulsa chpt. 1987—). Democrat. Club: Toastmasters. Office: Okla Natural Gas Co 100 W 5th St Tulsa OK 74103

ANDERSON, SHARON DENISE, county official; b. Pensacola, Fla., July 14, 1953; d. NeRoy and Lois (Wagstaff) A. BA, Eckerd Coll., 1974; MPA, U. West Fla., 1978. English instr. Am. Lang. Ctr., Casablanca, Morocco, 1974-75; teller First Am. Bank, Pensacola, Fla., 1975-77; housing/community devel. planner West Fla. Regional Planning Coun., Pensacola, 1977-79; analyst community devel. project Joint Ctr. for Polit. Studies, Washington, 1979-81; policy analyst D.C. Dept. Pub. Works, Washington, 1982-88; asst. adminstr. Coun. on the Environment, Richmond, Va., 1988-90; asst. to county exec. Prince William County Govt., Prince William, Va., 1990—. Named Outstanding Young Woman, Outstanding Ams., 1987; Fla. Edn. grantee State of Fla., 1976-77. Mem. Internat. City Mgmt. Assn., Alpha Kappa Alpha (chairperson food bank com. Xi Omega chpt. Washington 1986-87). Office: Prince William County Govt 1 County Complex Ct Prince William VA 22192

ANDERSON, SUSAN RENITA, veterinarian; b. Centralia, Wash., Sept. 20, 1958; d. Arnold Andrew and Helen Evelyn (Sibley) A. BS in Vet. Sci., Wash. State U., 1980, DVM, 1983. Assoc. veterinarian Diamond Vet. Hosp., Everett, Wash., 1983-87; co-owner, veterinarian Diamond Vet. Assocs., Everett, 1987—. Mem. Am. Animal Hosp. Assn., Am. Vet. Med. Assn., Snohomish County Vet. Med. Assn. (pres. 1987), ZONTA Internat. Office: Diamond Vet Assocs 3625 Rucker Ave Everett WA 98201

ANDERSON, TAURA LINDA COLLEEN, special education educator; b. Salzburg, Austria, Apr. 25, 1951; came to U.S., 1954; BA in Biology with honors, Sonoma State Coll.; MA in Early Childhood Spl. Edn., San Francisco State U., 1989. Tchr. spl. edn. Santa Clara County Schs., San Jose, Calif., 1979-80, 82, St. Agnes Children's Ctr., White Plains, N.Y., 1980, San Juan Unified Sch. Dist., Sacramento, 1982-83, Santa Clara County, San Jose, 1983—; pvt. practice tax cons., 1983-87; mentor tchr. Santa Clara County Schs., 1988—. Recipient exemplary program award Calif. Dept. Edn., 1987. Mem. Calif. Tchrs. Assn., NOW, Sierra Club.

ANDERSON, TERRY MARLENE, civil engineer; b. Honolulu, Sept. 26, 1954; d. Stanley Dale and Anna Clara (Heigert) A.; m. Jack Willard Steinberg, Feb. 29, 1980 (div. May 1983). Student, U. San Diego, 1971-72, U. Calif., San Diego, 1972-74; BS in Biol. Scis., U. Calif., Davis, 1974, BS in Aquacultural Engrs., 1979. Registered civil engr., Calif., Colo. Project mgr. John Carollo Engrs., Walnut Creek, Calif., 1979-85; assoc. civil engr. Grice Engring. Inc., Salinas, Calif., 1985; self-employed Durango, Colo., 1985-86; BS in Aquacultural Engring. Charpier, Martin & Assocs., Sacramento, Calif., 1986-87; project engr. CWC-HDR, Inc., Cameron Park, Calif., 1987; sr. civil engr. El Dorado County Dept. Transp., Placerville, Calif., 1987—. Vol. Office Emergency Svcs., Sacramento, 1987—. Recipient Resolution of Appreciaiton, City Coun., City of Gonzales, 1983. Mem. Woman's Transp. Seminar, ASCE, El Dorado County Local Engrs. (ethics com. 1988—, chmn. gen. plan rev. com. 1989—). Republican. Office: El Dorado Dept Transp 2441 Headington Rd Placerville CA 95667

ANDERSON, THERESA LEE, account executive; b. Boston, Aug. 23, 1963; d. William Joseph and Lillie (Jordan) Torrence; m. James Allen Anderson, Jr., July 25, 1987; 1 child, Arianna Ashli. BA in Journalism, Rutgers U., 1986. Acct. exec. WHDH-TV Channel 7, Boston, 1986—. Recipient N.Y. Nat. Assn. TV Arts & Sci. award N.Y. Chpt., 1988. Mem. Nat. Assn. TV Arts and Sci., Nat. Assn. Black Journalists (Boston Black Achiever award 1989). Democrat. Baptist. Home: 7 Alcott Way North Andover MA 01845 Office: WHDH-TV 7 Bulfinch Pl Boston MA 02116

ANDERSON, VEDA LEONE, educator, consultant; b. Exeter, Calif., Aug. 29, 1932; d. Raymond Leon and Fern (Hough) Hurst; m. Horace Stanley Dennis, June 13, 1954 (div. 1963); children: Deborah E. Laws, Sharon L. Coble, Jeanette E. Davis; m. Gerald Eugene Anderson, Sept. 25, 1971; adopted children: Keely J. Sheehey, Tina M. Anderson, Gerald E. Anderson II. BS in Edn., N.Mex. State U., 1954, postgrad., 1970—; MA in Edn., Western N.Mex. U., 1969, postgrad., 1970—; postgrad., U. Tex., El Paso, 1968, San Jose State U., 1970. Tchr. Las Cruces (N.Mex.) Pub. Schs., 1954-55, 1958-59, Ft. Smith (Ark.) Pub. Schs., 1957-58, Deming (N.Mex.) Pub. Schs., 1963—; tchr. ednl. TV, Deming; dir. workshops pub. schs., 1968, state conv., 1969, local tchrs., 1975-77, 1980-82. Author: Three Views. Chmn. Rep. Women's Activities, 1980-84; tchr. Bible class Ch. Christ, Deming, 1963—; speaker to ladies groups, Okla., Ark., N.Mex. Mem. Internat. Fedn. Bus. and Profl. Women (Outstanding Educator 1982, Outstanding Young Woman Am. 1969), NEA (sec. Deming chpt., bldg. rep.), N.Mex. Edn. Assn., Beta Sigma Phi (sec.-treas. 1987, pres. v.p.). Office: Meml Sch 1000 S 10th St Deming NM 88031

ANDERSON OLIVO, MARGARET ELLEN, physiologist, educator; b. Omaha, June 17, 1941; d. Clarence Lloyd and Anita Emma (Kruse) Anderson; B.A., Augustana Coll., Sioux Falls, S.D., 1963; Ph.D. (NSF predoctoral fellow), Stanford U., 1967; m. Richard F. Olivo, Sept. 4, 1971. NIH postdoctoral fellow Harvard U., 1968-70; research asso. Lab. of Neurobiology U. P.R., 1970-71; vis. asst. prof. Clark U., 1972; asst. prof. Bennington (Vt.) Coll., spring 1973; asst. prof. Smith Coll., Northampton, Mass., 1973-79, asso. prof. dept. biol. scis., 1979-85, prof., 1985—. NIH research grantee, 1974-86. Mem. Soc. for Neuro-sci., Soc. Gen. Physiologists, Biophys. Soc. Office: Smith Coll Dept Biol Sci Northampton MA 01063

ANDERSON-TIDWELL, MARY ELLEN, risk/insurance coordinator; b. Liberty, S.C., June 25, 1940; d. William Robert and Ruby Irene (Trammell) Murphy; m. Howard Eugene Anderson, Sept. 8, 1956 (div. Jan. 1987); children: Howard Eugene Jr., Sterling Craig; m. Lear Tidwell, July 9, 1989. Student, Polk Community Coll., 1980. Sec. H. Lamar Stewart Ins. Agy, Frostproof, Fla., 1962-64; accounts payable clk. Ben Hill Griffin, Inc., Frostproof, 1964-65; agt. Bullard Ins. Agy., Inc., Lake Wales, Fla., 1966-79; risk/ins. coordinator Coca-Cola Foods, Auburndale, Fla., 1979—; dir. Fla. Girls State, Inc., Orlando, 1988—. City chmn. March of Dimes, Frostproof, 1964; campaign worker Tom Wheeler for Sheriff, Winter Haven, Fla., 1988. Mem. Risk and Ins. Mgmt. Soc., Inc., VFW., Am. Legion, DAV. Democrat. Baptist. Lodge: Polk Bus. Women's Sertoma. Office: Coca-Cola Foods PO Box 247 Auburndale FL 33823

ANDERSSON, BARBRO LINNEA, small business owner; b. Gothenburg, Sweden, May 28, 1933; came to U.S.; d. Hjalmar and Martha (Gustavsson) Roth; children: Pia Lindholm, John Lindholm, Petra Ullberg. Student, Gothenburg Stadsteatern. Dir. sales, mktg., pub. rels., advt. various cos., Sweden; owner, operator Sunmakers Fifth Ave., Inc., N.Y.C. Contbr. articles to profl. jours. Recipient Blue Ribbon Salon Tanning Trends, 1988. Mem. NAFE, Swedish Womens Ednl. Assn., Am. Womens Econ. Devel., Suntanning Assn. for Edn. (cert.). Office: Sunmakers Fifth Ave Inc 560 Fifth Ave New York NY 10026

ANDERSSON, BILLIE VENTURATOS, reading specialist; b. Pitts., Jan. 16, 1947; d. George Steve and Aphrodite (Bon) Venturatos; m. Wolfgang Paul Andersson, July 12, 1969; children: Dita, Lise, Andrea. BA, Newcomb Coll., 1968; MEd in Counseling, La. State U., New Orleans, 1971; MEd in Spl. Edn., U. New Orleans, 1977, PhD, 1981. Biology and math tchr. Orleans Parish Sch. Bd., New Orleans, 1968-70; biology and gen. sci. tchr. Jefferson Parish Sch. Bd., Metairie, La., 1970-74, guidance counselor, 1974-78; reading specialist Trinity Episcopal Sch., New Orleans, 1978—, admissions evaluator, 1981—, gifted and talented tchr., 1982—; Gesell evaluator, 1985—; instr. U. New Orleans, St. Mary's Dominican Coll., Loyola U.; lectr. in field. Editor: Greek Lagniappe, 1980; author: Filo File for Filophiles, 1985. Sunday sch. coord. Greek Orthodox Cathedral, New Orleans, 1984-87, chmn. gourmet booth, 1981—. Mem. Am. Ednl. Rsch. Assn., Am. Psychol. Assn., Internat. Reading Assn., Nat. Assn. for Gifted Children, Phi Delta Kappa, Phi Kappa Phi, Kappa Delta Pi. Greek Orthodox. Office: Trinity Episcopal Sch 2111 Chestnut St New Orleans LA 70130

ANDES, JOAN KEENEN, information processing company executive; b. Clarksburg, W.Va., Apr. 23, 1930; d. Ree Martin and Mary Ruth (Pyle) Groghan; m. William Anderson Keenen, Oct. 15, 1949 (div. 1969); children: Paula Annette Keenen Skelton, William Ree Keenen; 1 foster child, Donald Monroe Dreyer; m. Ralph Paul Andes, Sept. 29, 1976. Pvt. sec. State Capitol, Charleston, W.Va., 1948-49; statis. typist various acctg. offices, Beaumont, Tex., 1949-60; owner Machine Acctg. and Computing, Beaumont, 1960-70, Automated Enterprises Keypunch Sch., 1962-72; pres. Applied Data Processing, Beaumont, 1970-83; owner Applied Info. Processing, Beaumont, 1983—. Active Better Bus. Bur., Beaumont C. of C., Democratic Party, Westgate Youth Group, 1985-88; vol. Mexican mission Ch. of Christ. Mem. Data Processing Mgmt. Assn. (pres. 1972-73, 80, awards chmn. 1985-86), NAFE, Nat. Fedn. Ind. Bus. Republican. Mem. Ch. of Christ. Avocations: counted cross stitch, collecting Coke memorabilia, coin collecting, skiing. Home: 1410 Marshall Pl Beaumont TX 77706 Office: Applied Info Processing 855 IH 10 South Suite 135 Beaumont TX 77701

ANDREA, ELMA WILLIAMS, retail executive; b. Carroll County, Va.; d. Preston and Macy (Goad) Williams; m. Mario I. Andrea, Nov. 29, 1966; AB with spl. honors, George Washington U., 1953; MA in Public Adminstrn., Am. U., 1961. Asst. program dir., asst. dir. ops. WTOP, CBS-Radio and TV, 1947-51; mem. pub. relations staff George Washington U., 1951-52; registrar Washington Sch. for Secs., 1953; exec. sec. Joint Econ. Com. of U.S. Congress, 1956-59; legis. info. specialist NEA, Washington, 1960-84; asst. mgr. Gem Tree Jewelry Store, Bethesda, Md., 1984—. Bd. dirs. Edn. Assocs. Fed. Credit Union, 1973-83, pres., 1975-77; bd. dirs. Met. Area Credit Union Mgmt. Assn., 1977-82, sec., 1977-82; bd. dirs. Kenwood Beach (Md.) Citizens Assn., 1981-84. Recipient Alumni Service award George Washington U., 1970. Mem. AAUW (br. publicity chmn. 1956-59), NEA (life), Columbian Women George Washington U. (pres. 1965-67), George Washington U. Alumni Assn. (dir. 1965-67, 69-70), Edn. Writers Assn., Gemological Inst. Am., Women's Joint Congressional Com. (chmn. 1974-76), Am. News Women's Club, Nat. Dem. Club, Twentieth Century Club, Nat. Woman's PArty, Woman's Nat. Dem. Club, Phi Delta Gamma (chpt. pres. 1973-74, nat. conv. chmn. 1980, nat. treas. 1980-84, nat. pres. 1984-86 , trustee 1980-86, nat. bylaws 1986—), Pi Sigma Alpha. Address: Il Bel Tramonto White Sands MD 20657 Office: Gem Tree 7720 Wisconsin Ave Bethesda MD 20814

ANDREASEN, NANCY COOVER, psychiatrist, educator; d. John A. Sr. and Pauline G. Coover; children: Robin, Susan. BA summa cum laude, U. Nebr., 1958, PhD, 1963; MA, Radcliffe Coll., 1959; MD, U. Iowa, 1970. Instr. English Nebr. Wesleyan Coll., 1960-61, U. Nebr., Lincoln, 1962-63; asst. prof. English U. Iowa, Iowa City, 1963-66; resident U. Iowa, 1970-73; asst. prof. psychiatry U. Iowa, Iowa City, 1973-77, assoc. prof., 1977-81, prof. psychiatry, 1981—, dir. Mental Health Clin. Rsch. Ctr., 1987—; sr. cons. Norwick Pk. Hosp., London, 1983; acad. visitor Maudsley Hosp., London, 1986. Author: The Broken Brain, 1984; editor: Can Schizophrenia be Localized to the Brain?, 1986, Brain Imaging: Applications in Psychiatry, 1988; book forum editor Am. Jour. Psychiatry, 1980—, dep. editor, 1989—. Woodrow Wilson fellow, Fulbright fellow, Oxford U., London, 1960. Mem. Am. Psychiat. Assn. (coun. on rsch.), Am. Coll. Neuropharmacologists (com. advocacy), Am. Acad. Clin. Psychiatrists, Am. Psychopathol. Assn. (pres. 1989-90). Office: U Iowa Coll Medicine Dept Psychiatry 500 Newton Rd Iowa City IA 52242

ANDRECIC, MARGUERITE MARIE, food products manager; b. Sharon, Pa., June 6, 1958; d. Edmond Krothe and Janice Louise (Mathews) Porterfield; m. Joseph Louise Andrecic, Aug. 26, 1978; children: Michael Joseph, Monica Marie. Baker Valu King & Giant Eagle, Liberty, Ohio, 1979-87; bakery mgr. Spicko Sparkles, Newton Falls, Ohio, 1987-89; baker Cornersburg Giant Eagle, Youngstown, Ohio, 1989—. Home: 517 Redondo Youngstown OH 44504

ANDREEN-SALKIN-PENN, AVIVA LOUISE, academic administrator, educator; b. Frankfurt, Fed. Republic Germany, Jan. 6, 1952; d. Robert Benjamin Andreen and Margie Corinne (LaPointe) Marshall; m. Merrill R. Penn, Nov. 8, 1987; children: Robert Morton Salkin and Elizabeth Aliza Penn. BA, NYU, 1975; postgrad., Laser Inst. Am., 1980. Cert. Mobile Laser Operator, N.Y. Tchr. Kibbutz Regavim, D.N. Menasche, Israel, 1975-76; account rep. Traveler's Ins. Co., N.Y.C., 1976; spl. projects coordinator Sapan Engring. Co., N.Y.C., 1976-78; sec., treas. founder J. Sapan Holographic Studios, N.Y.C., 1979; owner, pres. Universal Media Cons., White Plains, N.Y., 1980-84; dir. edn., owner Am. Ctr. for Laser Edn., Yonkers, N.Y., 1984—; lectr. Hudson River Mus., Yonkers, N.Y., 1986-87, producer laser light show, Andrus Planetarium. Curator Holography A New Dimension White Plains Mus. Gallery, Hudson River Mus., Yonkers, Troster Hall Sci. Mem. Laser Inst. Am., N.Y. Acad. Scis., NAFE, Courage to Change Club (White Plains) (chmn. 1987); Rosh Pina of Yonkers. Office: Am Ctr Laser Edn 317 Hawthorne Ave Yonkers NY 10705

ANDREJEWSKI, PAT See BENATAR, PAT

ANDREJZCHICK, MARSHA LORENE, nurse, hospital services director, entrepreneur; b. Greenville, S.C., Oct. 1, 1954; d. Melvin Laverne and Betty Jean (Oakes) Reed; m. Bruce Jonathan Andrejzchick, June 19, 1981. Nursing diploma, MacMaster Sch. of Nursing, Moncton, N.B., Can., 1976; BS, Bob Jones U., 1980. RN, N.B., Can., S.C. Staff nurse Moncton (N.B.) City Hosp., 1976-79, St. Francis Hosp., Greenville, 1979-80; health nurse Pillsbury Bapt. Bible Coll., Owatonna, Minn., 1980-81; income tax cons. pvt. practice, Owatonna and Gaffney, S.C., 1982-88; charge nurse Upstate Carolina Med. Ctr., Gaffney, 1982-87, dir. infection control, 1987-88, dir. quality svcs., 1988-89; image cons. Gaffney, 1989—; clin. cons. Peachtree Ctr., Gaffney, 1987—; seminar trainer nursing dept. Cherokee Vocat. Sch., 7001 Club, Gaffney Sch. Bd. Prin.'s Conf., 1988—; image cons. Beauti Control, Dallas, 1989. Organist Trinity Bapt. Ch., Gaffney, 1982—. Mem. Assn. Profls. in Infection Control, S.C. Assn. RNs, NAFE. Republican. Home and Office: 208 Brook Dr Gaffney SC 29340

ANDREOLI, KATHLEEN GAINOR, nurse, educator, administrator; b. Albany, N.Y., Sept. 22, 1935; d. John Edward and Edmunda Elizabeth (Ringlemann) Gainor; children: Paula Kathleen, Thomas Anthony, Karen Marie. B.S.N., Georgetown U., 1957; M.S.N., Vanderbilt U., 1959; D.S.N., U. Ala., Birmingham, 1979. Staff nurse Albany Hosp. Med. Ctr., 1957; instr. St. Thomas Hosp. Sch. Nursing, Nashville, 1958-59, Georgetown U. Sch. Nursing, 1959-60, Duke U. Sch. Nursing, 1960-61, Bon Secours Hosp. Sch. Nursing, Balt., 1962-64; ednl. coordinator, physician asst. program, instr. coronary care unit nursing inservice edn. Duke U. Med. Ctr., Durham, N.C., 1965-70; ednl. dir. physician asst. program dept. medicine U. Ala. Med. Ctr., Birmingham, 1970-75; clin. assoc. prof. cardiovascular nursing Sch. Nursing U. Ala. Med. Ctr., 1970-77, asst. prof. nursing dept. medicine, 1971, assoc. prof., 1972—, assoc. prof. nursing Sch. Pub. and Allied Health, 1973—; assoc. dir. Family Nurse Practitioner Program, 1976, assoc. prof. community health nursing Grad. Program, 1977-79, assoc. prof. dept. pub. health, 1978-79; prof. nursing, spl. asst. to pres. for ednl. affairs U. Tex. Health Sci. Ctr., Houston, 1979-82, acting dean Sch. Allied Health Scis., 1981; v.p. for ednl. services, interdisciplinary edn., internat. programs U. Tex. Health Sci. Ctr., 1983-87; v.p. nursing affairs Rush-Presbyn.-St. Lukes's Med. Ctr., Dean Rush U. Coll. Nursing, Chgo., 1987—; cons. in field. Author, editor: (with others) Comprehensive Cardiac Care, 1983; editor: Heart and Lung, Jour. of Total Care, 1971; contbr. articles to profl. jours. Mem. adv. bd. Robert Wood Johnson Clin. Nurse Sch. Program; mem. vis. com. Vanderbilt U. Sch. Nursing. Recipient Founder's award N.C. Heart Assn., 1970, Disting. Alumni award Vanderbilt U. Sch. of Nursing, 1984, Leadership Tex. award, 1985. Fellow Am. Acad. Nursing; mem. Inst. Medicine, Am. Nurses Assn., Nat. League Nursing, Am. Assn. Critical Care Nurses, Ala. Heart Assn., Council Family Nurse Practitioners and Clinicians, Am. Heart Assn. Council Cardiovascular Nursing, Sigma Theta Tau, Alpha Eta, Phi Kappa Phi. Roman Catholic. Home: 1212 W Lake Shore Dr Chicago IL 60610 Office: Rush Presbyn-St Luke's Med Ctr 1653 W Congress Pkwy Chicago IL 60612

ANDRES, MARIAN GAIL, educator, business owner, choreographer, dancer; b. San Diego, Sept. 18, 1944; d. Giles Xavier and Rose Annette (Landsberger) Adrian; m. Frederick S. Andres, Apr. 12, 1963 (div. Feb. 1976); 1 child, Michael Adrian Andres. Student, San Jose State U., 1962-64, West Valley Jr. Coll., 1968-70. Dir., owner Marian Andres Dance Studio, San Jose, Calif., 1972-85, Branham Dance Ctr., San Jose, Calif., 1985—; founder, dir. Valley Dance Tchrs., San Jose, 1972-82; reg. dir. Dance Troupe, 1974-77. Designer: (computer program) Dance Sch. Organizer, 1986. Mem. Nat. Assn. Dance and Affiliated Artists (chpt. pres. 1970-72), Dance Educators of Am. (cert. 1981-89). Office: Branham Dance Ctr 1088 Branham Ln San Jose CA 95136

ANDRESS, CHARLOTTE FRANCES, emerita social work executive; b. Birmingham, Ala., Apr. 22, 1910; d. Francis Samuel and Tommie (Daniel) A.; B.S., Birmingham-So. Coll., 1932; A.M. in Social Service Adminstrn., U. Chgo., 1943. Asst. dir. Girl Scouts U.S., Birmingham, 1932-35, exec. dir., Nashville, 1935-41; instr. Loyola U., Chgo., 1942-45; dir. U.S.O., Augusta, Ga., 1945-48; asst. dir. YWCA, Chgo., 1948-50, exec. dir., St. Louis, 1950-53; dir. group work, youth service Fedn. Protestant Welfare Agys., N.Y.C.,

1953-59; exec. dir. Inwood House, N.Y.C., 1959-82, exec. dir. emerita, 1982—. Chmn. adv. bd. Jefferson Park Center, 1959-65; nat. camp com. Camp Fire Girls, 1959-68; bd. dir. Social Work Vocat. Bur., 1961-66, Trail Blazer Camps, 1957-83, chmn. personnel com., 1982-83; mem. Camp Sharparoon com. N.Y.C. Mission Soc., 1960-76, mem. personnel com., 1962-66; active adv. bd. social welfare Meth. Ch., 1958-63; mem. United Meth. Bd. Missions, 1964-72; bd. dir. Bethel Meth. Home, 1965-72, sec. bd., 1966-72; women's com. Japan Internat. Christian U. Found., 1969-88, exec. com., 1983-88; adv. bd. Isabella Thoburn Coll., 1967-75; chmn. nat. com. Wesleyan Service Guild, 1970-72; trustee Christ United Meth. Ch., 1975-84; trustee Martha Mertz Found., 1979—, sec., 1981—, v.p., 1983—; bd. United Meth. City Soc., 1980-86. Named Disting. Alumna Birmingham So. Coll., 1981; recipient Spl. Recognition award Trail Blazer Camp, 1989. Cert. social worker, N.Y. Mem. Nat. Assn. Social Workers (sec. bd. N.Y.C. chpt. 1958-60, chmn. personnel standards and practices 1960-69, 73-74), Acad. Cert. Social Workers, Nat. Conf. on Social Welfare, Bethany Deaconess Soc. (bd. dir. 1971—, sec. 1974-76, pres. 1976—), Internat. Conf. Social Welfare, N.Y. Deaconess Assn. (bd. dir. 1969—, sec. 1971—), Soc. Women Geographers, Gamma Phi Beta. Democrat. Club: Cosmopolitan. Home: 3030 Park Ave Bridgeport CT 06604

ANDREW, CATHERINE BLANSFIELD, sales executive; b. Danbury, Conn., Dec. 13, 1954; d. Henry Nelson and Lorraine (Lombardi) Blansfield. BSN, U. Vt., 1976. Staff nurse Beth Israel Hosp., Boston, 1976-77, charge nurse intensive care unit, 1977-78, nurse clinician, 1978-81; profl. sales rep. Bristol Labs., Warwick, R.I., 1983-84; territory mgr., mgr. sales devel. and tele-sales critical care div. Baxter-Edwards, Irvine, Calif., 1984-89; we. dist. sales mgr. Interpore Internat., Irvine, 1989—. Mem. Humane Soc., Sierra Club, Nature Conservancy, NOW. Democrat. Roman Catholic. Home: 1 Evening Shadow Irvine CA 92715 Office: Interpore Internat 18008 Skypark Circle Irvine CA 92714

ANDREW, JANE HAYES, ballet company executive; b. Phila., Jan. 1, 1947; d. David Powell and Vivian Muriel (Saeger) Hayes; m. Brian David Andrew, June 14, 1977; 1 child, Kevin Hayes. AB, Barnard Coll., 1968, grad., Harvard Arts Administrn. Instit., 1972. Mgr. theater Minor Latham Playhouse, Barnard Coll., N.Y.C., 1970-74; co. mgr. Houston Ballet, 1974-77, Ballet West, Salt Lake City, 1978-83; gen. mgr. Pacific N.W. Ballet, Seattle, 1983-87; organizer non-profit consortium nat. ballet cos. and nat. presenting orgns., 1987; pres., exec. dir. Ballet/America, 1988—; panelist NEA Dance Program Presentors, 1987-88, 88-89, 89-90, Seattle Arts Commn. dance grants, 1989, 90; cons. Ariz. Arts Commn., Phoenix, 1985-86; com. mem. 25th Anniversary of World's Fair, Seattle, 1986-87; panelist NEA Local Programs, 1987. Editor (directory) Philadelphia Cultural Orgns., 1977. Bd. dirs. Good Shepherd Adv. Bd., Seattle, 1985-87. Recipient Dorothy D. Spivack award Barnard Coll., N.Y.C., 1972. Mem. Dance/USA (chmn. Mgrs. Coun. 1986). Home and Office: Ballet/America 807 NW 56th St Seattle WA 98107

ANDREWS, AUDREY ELAINE, educator; b. Englewood, N.J., July 30, 1961; d. Arcilious and Juanita (Riley) Andrews; m. Jeffery Dewayne Bowles, June 28, 1976. BS in Edn., U. Ga.; postgrad., Ga. State U. Tchr. Brazil's Early Learning Ctr., Athens, Ga., 1982-83, Kinder Care, Athens, Ga., 1983-84, Action, Head Start, Athens, 1984-86; social svcs./health asst. Action, Head Start, 1986-87; phys./occupational therapist technician N.E. Ga. RESA, Winterville, 1987-88, case mgr., 1988-90. Mem. Big Bros./Big Sisters., Athens, 1979-81; tutor/counselor Upward Bound Prog., Athens, 1980-82. Mem. NAFE, Preschool Interagency Coun., N.E. Ga. Bus. League, Athens Area Assn. for Young Children (sec. 1981—), Pastor's Aide Club. Baptist. Home: 4059 Lexington Rd Athens GA 30605 Office: Commerce Elem Sch Minish Dr Commerce GA 30529

ANDREWS, BROOKE, small business owner; b. N.Y.C., Nov. 8, 1941; d. Benjamin and E stelle (Rosenberg) Kohrn; m. Arnold L. Schwalb, Aug. 31, 1959, (div. Jan. 1967); m. James D. Newland, Mar. 18, 1967 (div. Jan. 1979); m. Donald Bruce Andrews, June 20, 1981. Student, Prospect Heights, Brklyn., 1959. Artist, copy writer Feffer and Simon, Henry M. Snyder, N.Y.C., 1960-62; layout artist, copy writer Sears, Roebuck and Co., Phoenix, 1965-67; promotion, pub. rels., art dir. Sta. KTAR TV, Phoenix, 1967-75; adminstrv. dir. Plays for Living of Nev., Las Vegas, 1977-78; pub. rels. dir. Theatre Phoenix/Phoenix Little Theatre, 1979-80; ticket dir. Phoenix Symphony Orchestra, 1980-82; publicist, co-founder Child Sexual Abuse Prevention, Phoenix, 1984; writer, editor, mgr. Profl. Writing and Resume Service, Ariz., 1984-85; owner, writer, editor, mgr. A New Beginning: Bus. Communications & Resumes, Mesa, Ariz., 1985—; charter mem. Profl. Bus. Alliance, Mesa, Ariz., 1989, pres. 1990; founder Ariz Resume Council, Mesa, 1989; pres., Project Prevention, Phoenix, Ariz., 1988-90, bd. dirs. Author Tips for Job Seekers, 1987. Vol. MDA Telethons Celebrity Phone Coord., Las Vegas, Nevada, 1976-78, COMPAS, Phoenix, 1980-84, Friends of Channel 8, Tempe Ariz., 1979-81, deputy registar, bd. of elections, Maricopa County, 1988--. Mem. Nat. Fedn. Ind. Bus., Profl. Bus. Alliance, Ariz. Resume Council, Screen Actors Guild, Profl. Assn. Resumé Writers. Republican. Jewish. Office: A New Beginning 777 W Southern Ave #103 Mesa AZ 85210

ANDREWS, CAROLYN FRASER, psychologist; b. Washington, Sept. 28, 1951; d. John Scott and Ella Selina (Fraser) Andrews. BS in Psychology with highest hons., Denison U., 1973; MA in Clin. Psychology, DePaul U., Chgo., 1976; PhD in Clin. Psychology, DePaul U., 1984. Lic. clin. psychologist, Ill. Staff psychologist DePaul U. Mental Health Ctr., Chgo., 1973-75; intern, mental health trainee DePaul U. Mental Health Ctr., 1976-77; clin. psychology intern Chgo.-Read Mental Health Ctr., 1975-76; psychology instr. DePaul U., 1978-79; live-in camp counselor United Charities of Chgo., 1978; psychiatric crisis worker Ravenswood Hosp. Med. Ctr., Chgo., 1980-83; psychologist Michael Reese Hosp. & Med. Ctr., Chgo., 1984-85; clin. psychologist AAP Mental Health Resources, Skokie, Ill., 1986—; lectr. in field. Contbr. to tng. manual: Adolescent Suicide: Prevention, Intervention, and Postvention Plans, 1987. Mem. Am. Psychol. Assn., Ill. Psychol. Assn., Nat. Register of Health Svc. Providers in Psychology, Mortar Bd., Phi Beta Kappa. Office: AAP Mental Health Resources 5360 Fargo Ave Skokie IL 60077

ANDREWS, CECELIA, broadcast executive. Exec. v.p. bus. affairs Network TV div. Paramount TV Group, Hollywood, Calif. Office: Paramount TV Group Network TV Div 5555 Melrose Hollywood CA 90038*

ANDREWS, CHONTA TEANE, utilities company specialist, engineer; b. Columbus, Ga., Dec. 26, 1962; d. Charles Mitchell and Marianne (Shaw) A. BSEE, Ga. Inst. Tech., 1983; MSEE, U. Miami, Fla., 1990. Systems technician AT&T Long Lines, Atlanta, 1982; S.T.E.P. tutor Ga. Inst. Tech., Atlanta, 1981-83; assoc. systems engr. Fla. Power & Light Co., Miami, 1984-86, load rsch. analyst, 1986-88, purchasing and contracts agt., 1988-90, minority bus. coord., 1990—. Vol. McLamore Children's Home Soc., Miami, 1988—. Mem. Nat. Tech. Assn. (region III dir. 1988-89), Family Christian Assn. Am. (mentor Miami chpt. 1986—), IEEE (mem. computer soc.), Fla. Engring. Soc., Ga. Tech. Inst. Alumni Assn., Delta Sigma Theta (corr. sec. 1982-83, 85-87). Democrat. Presbyterian. Home: 13078 SW 88th Ln Miami FL 33186

ANDREWS, GLORIA MAXINE, fundraiser; b. Cleve., Feb. 23, 1927; d. George Charles and Isabel Maxine (Bryden) Sternad; m. J. Melvin Andrews, July 15, 1950; children: Charles Melvin, Scott Michael, Countess Judith De Maleissye Melun. Student, San Miguel de Allende, Mex., 1947, Queen's U., Kingston, Ont., Can., 1948; BFA, Ohio Wesleyan U., 1949. Pres. Lake County (Ohio) Hist. Soc., 1976-80, trustee, 1965-85; trustee Old Mentor (Ohio) Found., 1970's, Lawnfield Civic Com., 1988—, Western Res. Hist. Soc., Cleve., 1980—; hist. guide tour Lantern Ct. Holden Arboretum, Lake County, 1970—, bd. dirs., 1989; pres. adv. com. Lake Erie Coll., Painesville, Ohio, 1980-87, Lakeland Coll. Found.; foreman Lake County Grand Judge, 1969. Recipient Liberty Bell award Lake County Bar Assn., 1980. Republican. Episcopalian. Home and Office: Echo Hill 8188 Garfield Rd Mentor OH 44060

ANDREWS, JEAN, author, artist, educator; b. Kingsville, Tex., Dec. 23, 1923; d. Herbert and Katharine (Smith) Andrews; B.S., U. Tex., 1944; postgrad. So. Meth. U., 1957-58, U. Corpus Christi, 1960-61; M.S., A&I U., 1966; postgrad. Tex. A&M U., 1970-71; Ph.D., North Tex. State U., 1976; m. Robert F. Wasson, May 5, 1944 (div. May 1969); children—Robert F., Jean A. (dec.); m. 2d, C.B. Smith, Mar. 8, 1980. Exhibited in 25 one man shows Tex. Tech U., 1956, Witte Mus., San Antonio, 1965, Bright Shawl Gallery, San Antonio, 1966, Little Theater, Midland, Tex., 1963, Ame./Gallery, N.Y.C., 1964, McNamarra-O'Connor Mus., Victoria, Tex., 1963, 67, A. and I. U., Kingsville, Tex., 1966; finalist Corcoran Biennial, 1965; Dallas; tchr. art Richard King High Sch., Corpus Christi, Tex., 1967-80; Master judge Nat. Council State Garden Clubs; mem. departmental vis. com. botany U. Tex.-Austin; chmn. edn. com. Sci. Adv. Council, U. Tex.-Austin. Bd. dirs. Planned Parenthood, Austin; sponsor Austin Symphony Assn., Laguna Gloria Art Mus.; bd. dirs. Art Mus. of S. Tex., Corpus Christi, 1960-63; co-chmn. Friends of Women's Studies, U. Tex.-Austin; mem. Pres.'s Council N. Tex. State U.; mem. Chancellor's Council U. Tex.; mem. Padre Island Biol. Survey, U.S. Dept. Interior, 1970-76. Jean Andrews Day declared by Mayor Corpus Christi, 1971; endowed Jean Andrews Smith professorships in human nutrition and tropical and econ. botany U. Tex., Austin; Alice G.K. Kleberg grantee, 1969; Caesar Kleberg Wildlife Fedn. grantee; research prin. grant Dallas Fashion Group N. Tex. State U. Mem. Am. Malacol. Union, Tex. Tchrs. Assn., D.A.R., Colonial Dames VII Century, Coastal Bend Shell Club (hon. life), Nat. Pepper Conf., Tex. Pepper Conf., Houston Conchological Assn., Zeta Tau Alpha. Episcopalian. Author: Sea Shells of the Texas Coast, 1971; Shells and Shores of Texas, 1977; Texas Shells: A Field Guide, 1981; Peppers: The Domesticated Capsicums, 1984.

ANDREWS, JULIE, actress, singer; b. Walton-on-Thames, Eng., Oct. 1, 1935; d. Edward C. and Barbara Wells; m. Tony Walton, May 10, 1959 (div.); 1 dau., Emma; m. Blake Edwards, 1969. Studied with pvt. tutors, studied voice with Mme. Stiles-Allen. Debut as singer, Hippodrome, London, 1947; appeared in pantomime Cinderella, London, 1953; appeared: Broadway prodn. The Boy Friend, N.Y.C., 1954, My Fair Lady, 1956-60 (N.Y. Drama Critics award 1956), Camelot, 1960-62; films include Mary Poppins, 1964 (Acad. award for best actress 1964), The Americanization of Emily, 1964, Torn Curtain, 1966, The Sound of Music, 1966, Hawaii, 1966, Thoroughly Modern Millie, 1967, Star!, 1968, Darling Lili, 1970, The Tamarind Seed, 1973, 10, 1979, Little Miss Marker, 1980, S.O.B, 1981, Victor/Victoria, 1982, The Man Who Loved Women, 1983, That's Life!, 1986, Duet For One, 1986, The Laundromat, After the Laughter; TV debut in High Tor, 1956; star TV series The Julie Andrews Hour, 1972-73; also spls.; Author: (as Julie Edwards): Mandy, 1971, The Last of the Really Great Whangdoodles, 1974. Recipient Golden Globe award Hollywood Fgn. Press Assn., 1964, 65; named World Film Favorite (female), 1967. Office: care Greengage Prodns 11777 San Vicente Blvd #501 Los Angeles CA 90049 also: Hanson & Schwam 9200 Sunset Blvd Los Angeles CA 90069*

ANDREWS, MARGERY MAG, educational consultant, business owner; b. New Britain, Conn., Feb. 21, 1932; d. Samuel Eliot and Fannie (Mittau) Mag; m. Norman S. Andrews; children: Barbara Ellen, Karen Judith. Student, My. Holyoke Coll., 1949-51; BS, Boston U., 1951; MA in Teaching, Conn. Wesleyan U., 1971. Founder, owner, dir. Pvt. Sch. & Coll. Guidance Svc., North Haven, Conn., 1973—; participant Nat. Tng. Lab. Group Dynamics Workshop, Bethel, Maine, 1983. Leader Great Books Discussion Group, New Haven, 1962-67; sec. Continium of Care-Mental Health Residential Facilities, New Haven, 1985—. Fellow Ind. Ednl. Counselors Assn., Nat. Assn. Coll. Admissions Counselors, New Eng. Assn. Coll. Admissions Counselors. Home and Office: 1471 Ridge Rd North Haven CT 06423

ANDREWS, MARY ANN, nursing services director; b. Geneva, N.Y., Apr. 3, 1928; d. Joseph John and Catherine (Gillotte) Yannotti; m. Donald R. Andrews Sr., Mar. 28, 1947 (dec. 1989); children: Donald Jr., Michael J., Thomas C., Maryrose Arimoto. AA in Nursing, De Anza Coll., 1975; BA in Health Sci. Adminstrn., St. Mary's Coll., Morega, Calif., 1982; MPA in Health Sci. Adminstrn., U. San Francisco, 1988; Mgmt. Cert., San Jose State U., 1987. RN. Asst. head nurse San Jose (Calif.) Health Ctr., 1975-82; shift supr. San Benito Hosp. Dist., Hollister, Calif., 1982-86, AMI Community Hosp., Santa Cruz, Calif., 1986-88; dir. nursing svcs. Care West Enterprises Inc., Watsonville, Calif., 1988—. Roman Catholic. Home: 93 Plumtree Dr Hollister CA 95023

ANDREWS, MARY ELLA, nursing administrator; b. Johnson, S.C., July 21, 1935; d. John and Sallie (Dozier) A. Diploma in nursing, Newark City Hosp., 1957; BSN, Calif. State U., L.A., 1975, MS in Nursing, 1985. RN, N.J., Calif., Kans., Ind. Staff nurse Newark (N.J.) City Hosp., 1957-58, VA Hosp., East Orange, N.J., 1958-61, Orange (N.J.) Meml. Hosp., 1966-67, VA Hosp., Long Beach, Calif., 1967-69, Orthopedic Hosp., L.A., 1969-73; head nurse, supr. VA Med. Ctr., L.A., 1973-83; asst. chief nurse VA Med. Ctr., Leavenworth, Kans., 1986-88; assoc. chief nurse VA Med. Ctr., Indpls., 1988—. Capt. Nurse Corps, USAF, 1961-66. Mem. ANA (cert. nursing adminstr.), Ind. Nurses Assn. (del. 1989-90), Sigma Theta Tau, Chi Eta Phi. Democrat. Roman Catholic. Home: 3245 Valley Farms Way Indianapolis IN 46214 Office: VA Med Ctr (118) 1481 W 10th St Indianapolis IN 46202

ANDREWS, MARY GIBSON DUFFY, military officer; b. New Bern, N.C., Nov. 1, 1949; d. Richard Nixon and Mary Hazel (Brock) Duffy. BS in Edn., Biology, U. Tenn., 1971; diploma, U.S. Army Command and Gen. Staff Coll., 1986, Defense Info. Sch., 1984. Commd. 2d lt. U.S. Army, 1972, advanced through grades to lt. col., 1984; intelligence staff officer 9th Infantry Div., Ft. Lewis, Wash., 1973-74; recruiter U.S. Army Aviation Ctr., Ft. Rucker, Ala., 1974-75; adm.'s aide and protocol officer Pacific Command, Hawaii, 1976-78; equal opportunity officer Ft. Devens, Mass., 1979-80; sec. recorder Army Discharge Review Bd. Pentagon, Washington, 1982-84; pub. affairs officer Army Pub. Affairs Pentagon, Washington, 1984-85; cmdr. 228th Adj. Gen. Co. (Postal), Frankfurt, Fed. Republic of Germany, 1986-88; asst. adj. HQ V Corps, Frankfurt, Fed. Republic of Germany, 1988-89; pub. affairs officer DOD Pub. Affairs Office, Pentagon, Washington, 1989—. Mem. Frankfurt Singles Ch. Group, 1987—. Mem. Assn. of the U.S. Army, Nat. Assn. Female Execs., Victory Corps Assn., Alpha Chi Omega. Republican. Presbyterian. Office: Pentagon Office of Asst Def Sec Pub Affairs Rm 1E776 Washington DC 20301-1400

ANDREWS, SUSAN DALTON, nurse, educator; b. Mt. Vernon, N.Y., Sept. 25, 1946; d. William Estill and Aimee Doris (Dalton) A. AS, Bronx Community Coll., 1971; BS in Health Sci., Chapman Coll., 1979; postgrad., Santa Clara U., 1981. RN, N.Y., Calif.; instr. credential in nursing Calif. Community Colls. Staff nurse Cornell Med. Ctr. N.Y. Hosp., N.Y.C., 1968-70, Jacobi Hosp. City of N.Y., Bronx, 1971-72, New Rochelle (N.Y.) Hosp. Med. Ctr., 1972-73, ICU Santa Clara Valley Med. Ctr., San Jose, Calif., 1973-75, ICU El Camino Hosp., Mountain View, Calif., 1975-76, ICU Stanford (Calif.) U. Hosp., 1977-78, Kaiser Hosp., Santa Clara, Calif., 1978—; rsch. nurse Ames Rsch. Bionetics Corp., Irvine, Calif., 1980, 81; part-time instr. Mission Coll., Santa Clara, 1982—. Chmn. nursing edn. com. Am. Heart Assn., 1988-89, guest speaker. Mem. Am. Nurses Assn., Am. Assn. Critical Care Nurses (critical care registered nurse). Republican. Home: 5004 Grey Feather Circle San Jose CA 95136

ANDREWS, SUSAN LYNN, insurance agent, marketing specialist; b. L.A., Feb. 1, 1962; d. John Morton Machunka-Andrews and Charmaine Mary (Wells) Andrews Gordon. Student, U. Colo., Boulder, 1980-83. Dir. Gordon Gen. Ins., L.A., 1978-84; mortgage specialist Am. Internat. Group, L.A. and N.Y.C., 1984-86; U.S. agt. confidential program Bayly Martin and Fay, L.A., 1986-87; sr. account exec. Safeguard Health Enterprises, Inc., Anaheim (Calif.), L.A., 1986—; pres. Infinity Ins. Agy., Beverly Hills, Calif., 1987—; cons. The Cons. Group. Vol. City of West Hollywood City Hall, Calif., 1986; mem. Lupus Found., L.A., Multiple Sclerosis Soc. of L.A., AIDS Project, L.A. Mem. Am. Mgmt. Assn., Hispanic Acad. of Media Arts and Scis., Calif. Assn. of Affiliated Agys., Am. Film Inst., Women in Mgmt. (bd. dirs. L.A. chpt.), Art Deco Soc. L.A., NAFE, L.A. Jr. C. of C., Kappa Kappa Gamma.

ANDREWS, SYLVIA JOYCE, health care specialist, actress; b. L.A., Dec. 13, 1959; d. Louis Phillip Jr. and Juanita (Wright) A. BA, UCLA, 1982; postgrad., Calif. State U., Dominquez Hills, 1982-83. Tchrs. asst. L.A. Unified Sch. Dist., 1975-83; admissions rep. Rutledge Coll., L.A., 1984-85; sr. admissions rep. Watterson Coll., L.A., 1985; admission rep. Biplex Corp., L.A., 1986-87, Eduplex Career Ctr., L.A., 1987-88; sr. employment and tng. specialist City of Compton (Calif.), 1988-89; with Watts Health Found. Inc., Compton, 1990—. Appeared in films including Black Pearl, 1987, The Double Date, 1987; TV shows include The Young and the Restless, 1988-90, The Bold and the Beautiful, 1988-90. Participant Young Adult Retreat Program, Compton, 1988-89, Calif. Employment Dept. and U.S. Dept. Labor Dislocated Workers Conf., L.A., 1989; mem., recording sec. Mid-Cities Veteran Employment Com., Compton, 1988-89; on-the-job tng. coord. City of Compton, 1988-89; adminstr. Job Tng. Partnership, Compton, 1988-89. Recipient Gold Seal Bearer, Calif. Scholarship Fedn., 1978, Maidie Norman Rsch. award, UCLA Theater Ars Dept., 1982. Mem. AFTRA, NAFE, Black Women in Theater West, Calif. Girl's State Alumni Found., UCLA Alumni Assn.

ANDREWS, TERRI DEAN, administrative specialist; b. Seville, Spain, Jan. 7, 1963; d. Collis Dean Jr. and Joan Katherine (McClure) A. BA in Communications magna cum laude, Queens Coll., Charlotte, N.C., 1989. Pers. asst. Duke Power Co., Charlotte, 1981-85, pers. specialist, 1985-89; adminstrv. and budget analyst Duke Power Co., 1989—. Tutor elem. sch. children; vol. Springfest and Jazz, Humane Soc., Metrolina Aids Project. Mem. Am. Bus. Women's Assn., Am. Soc. for Tng. and Devel., People and Energy (sec.). Home: 2137 #8 Sharon Rd Charlotte NC 28207 Office: 422 S Church St Charlotte NC 28242-0001

ANDREWS, THEODORA ANNE, librarian; b. Carroll County, Ind., Oct. 14, 1921; d. Harry Floyd and Margaret Grace (Walter) Ulrey; B.S. with distinction, Purdue U., 1953; M.S., U. Ill., 1955; m. Robert William Andrews, July 18, 1940 (div. 1946); 1 son, Martin Harry. Asst. reference librarian Purdue U., West Lafayette, Ind., 1955-56, pharmacy librarian, instr., 1956-60, pharmacy librarian, asst. prof., 1960-65, pharmacy librarian, assoc. prof. library sci., 1965-71, prof. library sci., pharmacy librarian, 1971-79, prof. library sci., pharmacy, nursing and health scis. librarian, 1979—. Mem. Purdue Women's Caucus, 1973—, v.p., 1975-76, pres., 1976-77; mem. Internat. Women's Yr. Regional Planning Com., 1977; del. Ind. Gov.'s Conf. Libraries and Info. Services, 1978. U. Ill. grad. fellow, 1954-55. Mem. Spl. Libraries Assn. (John H. Moriarty award Ind. chpt. 1972), ALA, Med. Library Assn., AAUP, Am. Assn. Colls. Pharmacy, Kappa Delta Pi, Delta Rho Kappa. Baptist. Author: A Bibliography of the Socioeconomic Aspects of Medicine, 1975; A Bibliography of Drug Abuse Including Alcohol and Tobacco, 1977; A Bibliography of Drug Abuse, Supplement 1977-1980, 1981; Bibliography on Herbs, Herbal Remedies and Natural Foods, 1982; Substance Abuse Materials for School Libraries, an Annotated Bibliography, 1985; Guide to the Literature of Pharmacy and the Pharmaceutical Sciences, 1986; sect. editor Advances in Alcohol and Substance Abuse, 1981—; contbr. articles to profl. jours. Office: Purdue U Pharmacy Bldg West Lafayette IN 47907

ANDREWS, VICTORIA LESLIE, professional association administrator; b. Presque Isle, Maine, June 11, 1949; d. Frank LeRoy and Dorothy Irene (Morse) Manzer. BS, U. South Maine, 1971; MS, Syracuse U., 1983. Tchr. Maine, 1971-73, 75-82, Alaska, 1974-75; asst. dir. housing Syracuse (N.Y.) U., 1982-83; mgr. edn. resources Coll. Am. Pathologists, Skokie, Ill., 1984; edn. specialist Nat. PTA, Chgo., 1985-88; tng. specialist Am. Arbitration Assn., Chgo., 1988-90, dir. regional devel., 1990—; freelance writer, communications cons., Chgo., 1989—. Contbr. articles to mags. and newspapers. Mem. Women in Communications, Inc. (v.p., profl. devel., 1989—, program chmn. career conf. 1988-89, Cub's Cup 1989), Indsl. Rels. Rsch. Assn., Alpha Xi Delta. Home: 3950 N Lake Shore Dr #204 Chicago IL 60613 Office: Am Arbitration Assn 205 W Wacker Dr Ste 1100 Chicago IL 60606

ANDREWS-WILKERSON, MIRON ANN, nurse educator; b. Stokes, N.C., Oct. 28, 1942; d. Estee and Goldie Ann (Roberson) A.; m. John Henry Lee Wilkerson, June 9, 1979. BS, So. Ill. U., 1979; BS in Nursing, Incarnate Word, 1987; MA in Mgmt., Webster U., 1987; Cert. for Anesthesia, Wilford Hall Med. Ctr., 1976. Registered nurse, nurse anesthetist. Asst. supr. operating room N.C. Meml. Hosp., Chapel Hill, 1963-64, supr. clin. rsch., 1964-70; asst. supr. USAF Hosp. Luke AFB, Phoenix, 1970-72, USAF Hosp. Weisbaden, Weisbaden, Germany, 1972-74; staff nurse anesthetist David Grant Med. Ctr., Travis AFB, Calif., 1976-79; nurse anesthetist supr. Clark USAF Regional Med. Ctr., Clark AFB, Tex., 1979-82; nurse anesthetist instr. Wilford Hall Med. Ctr., Lackland AFB, Tex., 1983-85; asst. chief nurse USAF Hosp. Mather AFB, Sacramento, 1987-89, dir. ambulatory svcs., 1989—; cons. in field; advisor for 1990 Western network Inst., Berkeley, Calif., 1989-90. Author: For Air Force Use Only, 1982, 88. Speakers bur. supr. Alamo Rape Crisis Ctr., Tex., 1987; food locker supr. St. Brigid's Parish, San Antonio, 1986, supr. day care, 1987; social chmn. Chapel & Hosp., Mather AFB, 1988—. Mem. Am. Assn. Nursing, Tuskee Airmen's Assn., Aerospace Assn. For Flight Nurses, Nat. League Nursing, Am. Assn. Nurse Anesthetists, NAFE, Phi Kappa Phi. Roman Catholic. Home: 9311 Beowulf San Antonio TX 78250

ANDRICK, ANNITA ARLENE, archivist; b. Binghamton, N.Y., Oct. 27, 1949; d. Earnest Edward and Nellie Carolene (Harrison) A. BA, SUNY, 1971; postgrad., Syracuse U., 1976, Cornell U., 1977; MA in Libr. Sci., U. Denver, 1985. From vol. to asst. dir. and archivist DeWitt Hist. Soc. Tompkins County, Inc., Ithaca, N.Y., 1972-80; asst. to curator U. Denver, Penrose Libr., Denver, 1981-86; libr. and archivist Erie County Hist. Soc., Erie, Pa., 1986-90; Mem. steering com. NW Pa. Inter-libr. Coop. (consortium), Erie, Pa., 1988—; vol. asst. to Registrar, Erie Art Mus., 1989—; selected grant reviewer Nat. Endowment for Humanities, Washington, 1979. Recipient grants NY State Hist. Assn. and Farmers Mus., Nat. Trust Hist. Preservation, Washington, U. Denver Grad. Student Assn., State Libr. Pa., Harrisburg. Mem. Pa. Libr. Assn., Soc. Am. Archivists, Mid-Atlantic Regional Archives Conf., Midwest Archives Conf., Am. Assn. Mus. (profl. coms. media & technology), Mus. Computer Network, Erie Yesterday (consortium, sec. 1989—). Home: 254 W 9th St Apt 2 Erie PA 16501

ANDROS, HAZEL LAVERNE (BRISSETTE ANDROS), educator; b. St. Louis, Sept. 25, 1939; d. Louis Albert and Catherine Virginia (Gonzalas) Brissette; divorced; 1 child, Wendy Gay; m. Nicholas James Andros, Nov. 3, 1962; 1 child, James Nicholas II. AA, Rend Lake Coll., 1976; BS, So. Ill. U., 1979, MS, 1981. Office mgr. Tractor Supply Co., Bloomington, Ill., 1969-70; sec. Ill. State U., Normal, 1970-73; office mgr. Wit and Wisdom, Benton, Ill., 1978; intern So. Ill. U., Carbondale, 1978, instr., 1979-80, office mgr., 1980-83; tchr., coord. Benton High Sch., 1984-89; instr. J.A. Logan Coll., Carterville, Ill., 1989—. Sec. Benton Youth Bd., 1984—, Benton Dist. Libr. Bd., 1987—. Mem. Ill. Women Adminstrs., Ill. Bus. Edn. Assn. (affiliate pres. 1987-88), Bus. and Profl. Women's Assn. (pub. rels. com. Benton chpt. 1989—), Am. Vocat. Assn., Ill. Adult Continuing Edn., AAUW (individual liberties com. Benton chpt. 1987—), Iota Lambda Sigma, Phi Delta Kappa. Democrat. Methodist. Home: 532 E Main St Benton IL 62812 Office: JA Logan Coll Carterville IL 62918

ANDRUZZI, ELLEN ADAMSON, nurse, marital and family therapist; b. Colon, Panama, Dec. 15, 1917 (parents Am. citizens); d. Charles and Annie Isabel (Grinder) Adamson; m. Francis Victor Andruzzi, May 28, 1941; children: Barbara F., Francis C., Judith E., Antonette T., John J. BS in Pub. Health Nursing, Cath. U. Am., 1947, MS in Nursing, 1951. Cert. clin. specialist, psychiat. nurse. Pub. health nurse Washington Health Dept., 1942-44; instr. psychiat. nursing St. Elizabeth's Hosp., Washington, 1948-57; dir. nursing Glenn Dale Hosp., Md., 1961-67; chief mental health nurse dept. human resources D.C. Govt., 1967-73; cons. NIMH, HHS, Rockville, Md., 1973-81; marital and family therapist TA Assocs., Camp Springs, Md., 1973—; assoc. GWITA, Rockville, 1975-79; instr. Charles County Community Coll., LaPlata, Md., 1976-78, Prince George Community Coll., Largo, Md., 1973-81; assoc. Ctr. for Study of Human Systems, Chevy Chase, Md., 1976—. Author chpts. in books. Dist. co-capt. Prince Georgians for Glendening, Prince George County, Md., 1985-86; chmn. plan devel. com. So. Md. Health Systems Agy., Clinton, 1984-89, sec. governing body, 1978-80; chmn. Mental Health Adv. Com. Prince George County, Cheverly, Md., 1983-85. Recipient Disting. Nurse award St. Elizabeths Hosp., 1985, Paula Hamburger Vol. award Mental Health Assn. Md., 1985, Recognition of Service award Md. Nurses Assn., 1983. Fellow Am. Acad. Nursing, Am. Orthopsychiat. Assn.; mem. Internat. Transactional Analysis Assn. (clin.),

Am. Nurses Assn., World Fedn. for Mental Health, Am. Assn. for Marriage and Family Therapy (clin.), Nat. Mental Health Assn. (v.p. 1984-87, bd. dirs. 1982-87), Mental Health Assn. Prince George County (pres. 1974-76, 87-88), Sigma Theta Tau (Kappa chpt., Excellence in Nursing award 1984). Democrat. Roman Catholic. Avocations: theatre, ballet, swimming, foreign travel.

ANGALET, GWENDOLINE BAIN, state agency administrator; b. Melrose, Mass., Mar. 6, 1947; d. Clifton Edward and Irma Gwendoline (Fernandes) Bain; m. Steven Alex Angalet, June 5, 1971 (div. May 1980). BS, U. Fla., 1969, M of Agr., 1970. Asst. prof. U. Fla., Gainesville, 1970-73; foster grandparent supr. Alachua County Foster Grandparent Program, Gainesville, 1973-75; supr. of vols. Del. Div. of Community Svcs., Wilmington, 1975-76, program mgr., 1976-79, dep. dir., 1979-86; dir. adminstrn. Del. Dept. Svcs. for Children, Youth and Their Families, Wilmington, 1986—; constrn. project mgr. Dept. Svcs. for Children, Youth and Their Families, 1986-89. Mem. Forest Knoll Civic Assn., 1990—. Named to Outstanding Young Women of Am., 1978, White House Fellow nominee, Del., 1980, People to Watch - 1990, Delaware Today mag., 1989. Mem. Wilmington Women in Bus. (bd. dirs. 1982-85), Phi Kappa Phi. Home: 1 King's Bridge Ct Newark DE 19702 Office: Dept Svcs Children/Families 1825 Faulkland Rd Wilmington DE 19805

ANGEL, MICHELLE ROBIN, product specialist; b. Queens, N.Y., Feb. 2, 1963; d. Victor and Victoria (Bewaggi) A. AAS, Community Coll. of USAF, 1986. Field engr. UNISYS Corp., Irving, Tex., 1986-88; quality assurance mgr. Mitek Systems, Carrollton, Tex., 1988-89, product mgr., 1989—. Vol. Ellis Island Found., Dallas, 1988, Muscular Dystrophy Assn., Dallas, 1990; fundraising coord. March of Dimes Found., Seaford, N.Y., 1980. Sgt. USAF, 1982-86. Mem. Air Force Assn., Non-Commd. Officers Assn., Unix User's Group, NAFE. Office: Mitek Systems 2033 Chennault Dr Carrollton TX 75006

ANGELASTRO, JANE ELLEN, corporate librarian, biochemist; b. N.Y.C., May 14, 1942; d. George Christian and Edna Frances (Byrnes) Schofield; m. Michael Angelo Angelastro, Jan. 21, 1967; children: Terese, Pat George, Karen. BS, Coll. of Mt. St. Vincent, 1964; MLS, L.I. U., 1985. Biochemist Merck Inst., Rahway, N.J., 1964-67; sr. libr. asst. L.I. Univ. Grad. Sch., Sparkill, N.Y., 1981-85; library dir. Halcon Rsch. div. Tex. Ea. Corp., Montvale, N.J., 1985-86; supr. AT&T Tech. Info. Ctr., White Plains, N.Y., 1986—. Sr. librarian St. Anthony Elem. Sch., Nanuet, N.Y., 1974-84; officer various town and ch. youth orgns., Nanuet, 1975-85. Mem. Spl. Librs. Assn., Assn. Computing Machinery, Internat. Network of UNIX Users, Am. Soc. Tng. and Devel. Home: 13 Glen Rose Ct West Nyack NY 10994 Office: AT&T Network Svcs Div 1 N Lexington Ave 18th Fl White Plains NY 10601

ANGELILLO, LORI ANN, military officer; b. Mt. Kisco, N.Y., Dec. 17, 1963; d. Joseph John and Irene Theresa (Moore) A. BS, USAF Acad., 1986. Commd. 1st lt. USAF, 1986; lead systems contract negotiator electronic systems div. USAF, Hanscom AFB, Mass., 1986-90. coord. blood drive ARC, 1986-90. Mem. Nat. Contract Mgmt. Assn., Co. Grade Officers Coun. Republican. Home: 4239 Beach Ridge Rd North Tonawanda NY 14120

ANGELINI, SHERRY LARAINE (SHERRY LARAINE CRUZ), research laboratory administrator; b. Springfield, Mo., Aug. 23, 1945; d. Robert Eugene and Juanita Maxine (Budd) Ballew; m. Lawrence James Cruz (div. 1981); children: Corey Allen, Wade Lawrence, Lundyn Laraine; m. Victor Enrico Angelini, July, 1988. Grad. high sch., San Lorenzo, Calif. Material services analyst Sandia Nat. Labs., Livermore, Calif., 1978-81, alt. nuclear material rep., 1981-83, nuclear material rep., 1983-86, project leader, security, 1986—, mgr. ops. security, 1987—; rep. to Trade Adv. Council for Word Processing, Oakland, Calif., 1979-81; co-owner Angelini's Italian Restaurant, Manteca, Calif., 1988—. Judge Alameda County Vocat. Olympics, Pleasanton, Calif., 1979; speaker Sonoma Sch. Career Day, Livermore, 1978, Healds Bus. Day, Concord, 1981. Mem. NAFE. Office: Sandia Nat Labs PO Box 969 Livermore CA 94550-0096

ANGELL, BETTY RUTH JOHNSON, research psychologist, instructional development consultant; b. Asheville, N.C., Aug. 18, 1943; d. Reuben James and Linnie Ruth (Keith) Johnson; m. David Edward Angell, Oct. 9, 1965 (div. July 1980); children: Laura Elizabeth, Victoria Marie. BS, Duke U., 1965; MA in Teaching, U. N.C., 1971; MS, N.C. State U., 1982. Tchr. Durham (N.C.) City Schs., 1966, Raleigh (N.C.) City Schs., 1966-73, Wake County Pub. Schs., Raleigh, 1979; rsch. asst. Rsch. Triangle Inst., Research Triangle Park, N.C., 1980; engring. rsch. psychologist U.S. Army Safety Ctr., Fort Rucker, Ala., 1982-85; rsch. psychologist U.S. Army Rsch. Inst., Fort Rucker, 1985-90; instrnl. devel. cons. Sch. Medicine U. N.C., Chapel Hill, 1990—. Co-chmn. AWAKE-Family Centered Birth Support Group, Raleigh, 1978; pres. Caesarean Section Support Group, Raleigh, 1977-80. Nat. Inst. Occupational Safety and Health trainee N.C. State U., 1980-82; Sci. Talent Search Hon. scholar Westinghouse Corp., 1961; NSF stipend recipient U. N.C., 1969-71. Mem. Inst. Indsl. Engrs., Assn. for Devel. of Computer-based Instructional Systems, Human Factors Soc., Wiregrass Human Factors Group (membership chmn. 1983-84, treas. 1985-86), Alpha Chi Omega, Alpha Pi Mu. Democrat. Baptist. Home: 1008 Canterbury Rd Raleigh NC 27607-4147 Office: U NC Office Ednl Devel CB #7530 322 MacNair Bldg Chapel Hill NC 27599-7530

ANGELL, KAROL (KAREL), freelance fashion designer; b. Jersey City, Dec. 15, 1950; d. William and Grace Angell. BA, U. La Verne, Calif., 1980. Freelance designer Perry Ellis, DKNY, Olympic, N.Y. Hat, Liz Claiborne, others, throughout U.S., Europe, 1971—; v.p. sales. Olympic, 1988—. Mem. St. Claire's AIDS com. Spellman Found. Recipient designer award Army and Air Force Exch. Svc., 1988. Mem. NAFE, Nat. Law Enforcement Officers Fund Against Drugs. Home: 3717 Springwood Villa Dr Naples FL 33962

ANGELO, MARGARET IDA, stockbroker; b. Elizabeth, N.J., June 21, 1960; d. Ernest James and Margaret P. (Falcetano) A. BA in History, Seton Hall U., 1982. Sr. option prin., asst. v.p., correspondent liaison Richardson Greenshields Securities Inc., N.Y.C., 1984—. Mem. Met. Mus. Art, N.Y.C., 1986—, Mus. of Natural History, N.Y.C., 1986—. Mem. Securities Traders Assn., Phi Alpha Theta. Roman Catholic. Office: Richardson Greenshields 4 World Trade Ctr New York NY 10048

ANGELONE, CATHERINE, federal agency administrator; b. Queens, N.Y., May 24, 1946; d. Dominick Anthony and Italia Marie (Masone) A.; children: Garrett Keith and Eric Joseph Gorton. AAS, Fashion Inst. Tech., 1965; BSW, Adelphi U., 1977; MSW cum laude, 1978. Asst. regional dir. Nassau County Youth Bd., Mineola, N.Y., 1979-81, coordinator community devel., 1983-86; asst. program dir. Nassau County Dept. Mental Health, Mineola, 1981-83; spl. asst. to regional adminstr. U.S. SBA, N.Y.C., 1986—; nat. coord. young entrpreneurs' program U.S. SBA, 1988-89. Vol. various Island Park (N.Y.) youth orgns., 1961—, Office of First Lady Mrs. Nancy Reagan, 1982—; tchr. religion Sacred Heart Ch., 1974-76, 83-84; sec. Island Park Rep. Club, 1984-86; site coord. Am. Bicentennial Presdl. Inaugral Ball, 1989. Mem. Assn. Cert. Social Workers. Roman Catholic. Home: 31 Waterford Rd Island Park NY 11558 Office: US SBA 26 Federal Pla New York NY 10278

ANGOLI, NANCY ELDERKIN, nurse; b. Berwyn, Ill., Sept. 28, 1949; d. Edward Eugene and Rita Frances (Rissert) Elderkin; m. Louis Edmund Angoli, June 26, 1971. Assoc. Degree in Nursing, Grtr Hartford Community Coll., 1985; BS in Nursing, U. Hartford, 1988. Staff nurse Hartford Hosp., 1985-86, Mt. Sinai Hosp., Hartford, 1986-88, Hebrew Home and Hosp., West Hartford, 1988—. Emergency med. technician Granby (Conn.) Ambulance Assn., 1981-85. Mem. ANA (cert. med-surg. NSG 1988), Nightingale Soc., Nat. Gerontol. Nurses Assn., Phi Theta Kappa, Sigma Theta Tau. Home: 90 Higley Rd West Granby CT 06090 Office: Hebrew Home & Hosp 1 Abrahms Blvd West Hartford CT 06117

ANGSTADT, DEBRA JORDAN, marketing professional; b. Washington, Jan. 16, 1960; d. Forrest A. and Gladys (Goodwin) Jordan; m. Curt David Angstadt, June 6, 1981. BBA, Coll. William and Mary, 1982; MBA, U. Richmond, Va., 1985. Mgmt. assoc. Crestar Bank, Richmond, 1982-83, mgr. trust mktg., 1983-87; v.p. Peter Wong & Assocs. Advt., Richmond, 1987-88; dir. mktg. State Edn. Assistance Authority, Va. Edn. Loan Authority, Richmond, 1988—. Exec. producer video: The One Liner Diner, 1990. Bd. dirs. Muirfield Green Homeowners Assn., Midlothian, Va., 1987—. Mem. Va. Assn. Fin. Aid Adminstrs. (com. chair 1989—). Office: SEAA/VELA 1 Franklin Sq 411 E Franklin St Richmond VA 23219

ANGUIANO, LUPE, business executive; b. La Junta, Colo., Mar. 12, 1929; d. José and Rosario (Gonzalez) A. Student, Ventura (Calif.) Jr. Coll., 1948, Victory Noll Jr. Coll., Huntington, Ind., 1949-52, Marymount Coll., Palos Verdes, Calif., 1958-59, Calif. State U., L.A., 1965-67; M.A., Antioch-Putney-Yellow Springs, Ohio, 1978. S.W. regional dir. NAACP Legal Def. and Ednl. Fund, L.A., 1965-69; civil rights specialist HEW, Washington, 1969-73; S.W. regional dir. Nat. Coun. Cath. Bishops, Region X, San Antonio, 1973-77; pres. Nat. Women's Employment and Edn., Inc., San Antonio, 1979—; pres., cons. Lupe Anguiano & Assocs., 1981—; cons. Tex. Dept. Human Resources, Dept. Labor, Women's Bur.; proposal reader U.S. Office Edn.-Women's Equity Act; mem. Tex. Adv. Coun. on Tech.-Vocat. Edn. Calif. del. White House Conf. on Status Mexican-Ams. in U.S., 1967; founding mem. policy coun. Nat. Women's Polit. Caucus, from 1971; Tex. and nat. del. Internat. Women's Year, 1976-77; chmn. Nat. Women's Polit. Caucus Welfare Reform Task Force, from 1977; co-chmn. Nat. Peace Acad. Campaign, 1977-81; founder, bd. dirs. Nat. Chicana Found., Inc., 1971-78; bd. dirs. Calif. Coun. Children and Youth, 1967, Rio Grande Fedn. Chicano Health Ctrs., S.W. Rural States, 1974-76, Women's Lobby, Washington, 1974-77, Rural Am. Women, Washington, from 1978, Small Bus. Coun. Greater San Antonio; mem. Pres.'s Coun. on Pvt. Sector Initiatives, 1983. Recipient Community award Coalition Mexican-Am. Orgns., 1967, Outstanding Svc. award Washington, 1968, Thanksgiving award Boys' Club, 1976, Outstanding Svc. award Tex. Women's Polit. Caucus, 1977, Liberty Bell award San Antonio Young Lawyers, 1981, Vista award for exceptional svc. to end poverty, 1980, Headliner award San Antonio Women in Communications, 1978, Woman of Yr. award Tex. Women's Polit. Caucus, 1978; named Outstanding Woman of Yr., L.A. County, 1972, Woman of the 80s Ms. mag., 1980; Nat. Pres.'s award Nat. Image, Inc., 1981, Wonder Woman Found. award, 1982, Adv. of Yr. San Antonio SBA, 1984; selected Am. 100 Most Important Women, Ladies Home Jour., 1988. Mem. Assn. Female Execs., Pres.'s Assn., Am. Mgmt. Assn. Democrat. Roman Catholic. Author: (with others) U.S. Bilingual Education Act, 1967, Texas A.F.D.C. Employment and Education Act, 1977; manuals Women's Employment and Education Model Program.

ANGUS, CATHERINE LAVERNE, state agency administrator; b. Columbia, S.C., Oct. 31, 1950; d. Eugene Kirk and Evelyn (Gillespie) Smith; m. Carl S. Pederson, Apr. 30, 1972 (div. 1975); m. Howard R. Angus, Aug. 6, 1988. Student, U. S.C., 1967-70. Sec., advt. sales rep. State Newspaper, Columbia, 1972-76; with Orkin Exterminating Co., Inc., 1978-85; br. mgr. Orkin Exterminating Co., Inc., Charleston, S.C., 1981-83, Florence, S.C., 1984-85; outdoor advt. supr. S.C. Dept. Hwys. and Pub. Transp., Charleston, 1985-88; adminstr. outdoor advt. program S.C. Dept. Hwys. and Pub. Transp., Columbia, 1988—. Contbr. articles to profl. publs. Mem. Civitan Club, Harley Owners Group (sec.-treas. 1987). Republican. Episcopalian. Office: SC Dept Hwys and Pub Transp Columbia SC 29202

ANGUS, MARLENE ANN, naval officer; b. Lima, Ohio, Nov. 10, 1947; d. Bernard Anthony and Lucille Susan (Schmenk) Durliat. BA in English, Cen. Mich. U., 1969; MA in Edn. Adminstrn. with honors, San Diego State U., 1986. Vol., English tchr. Peace Corps, Kusaie Island, Micronesia, 1969-71; commd. ensign USN, 1972, advanced through grades to comdr., 1987; prof. English U.S. Naval Acad., Annapolis, Md., 1972-75; pers. officer Chief Naval Ops., Washington, 1975-79; placement officer Naval Mil. Pers. Command, Washington, 1979-81; head support svcs. Dep. Chief Naval Ops., Washington, 1981-83; officer in charge Pers. Support Detachment, San Diego, 1983-85; dep. dir. Officer Candidate Sch., Newport, R.I., 1987-88; dep. dir. for manpower and pers. U.S. Atlantic Command, Norfolk, Va., 1988—. Pres., Women Officers Profl. Assn., San Diego, 1985-86. Recipient Tribute to Women in Industry award, San Diego, 1984; Faculty Rsch. grantee U.S. Naval Acad., 1974; named Honor Alumni, Cen. Mich. U., 1979. Home: 421 W Bute St 304 Norfolk VA 23510 Office: US Atlantic Command Norfolk VA 23511

ANKA, PHYLLIS CATHERINE, womens apparel executive; b. East Templeton, Quebec, Can., Sept. 18, 1933; came to U.S., 1957; d. Patrick Thomas and Ida (Kelly) Ryan; m. John Jacob Anka, May 21, 1953; children: Cynthia, John Randy, Paul, Gregory. AS, U. of Ottawa, Ontario, Can., 1951. Bacteriologist Ontario Laboratories, 1951-53; owner, custom designer Tenafly, N.J., 1965-72; store and dist. mgr. Fabric Tree, Inc., N.Y.C., 1973-75; gen. mgr. Plymouth Shops, Inc., N.Y.C., 1975-82; reg. dir. Motherhood Maternity Shops, Inc., N.Y.C., 1982-85; nat. sales dir. Motherhood Maternity Shops, Inc., Santa Monica, Calif., 1985-88, v.p. sales, mktg., 1988—. Founder Tenafly Soccer League, 1966-72.

ANNESSI, JEAN LUDEMAN, human resources specialist; b. Whitewater, Wis., Feb. 24, 1958; d. Wilfred Arthur and Jean Ruth (Orcutt) Ludeman; m. Michael L. Annessi, Aug. 16, 1980. BA, U. Wis., Whitewater, 1980; MS in Edn., Purdue U., 1985, postgrad., 1987 --. Profl. in human resources. Communications instr. Ind. Vocat. Tech. Coll., Lafayette, 1983-85; tng. specialist Consolidated Industries Corp., Lafayette, 1985-87; employee rels. coord. Lafayette Home Hosp., 1987 --. Project leader Whitewater 4-H, 1977-79; mem. steering com. Salute to Women Award, Lafayette, 1989-90. Recipient Tiffany Award of Excellence Manpower Temporary Svcs., Lafayette, 1985. Mem. NAFE, ASTD, Lafayette Bus. and Profl. Women (Young Career Woman 1988-89, sec. 1989-90, 2d v.p. 1990-91), Tippecanoe Area Pers. Assn. (sec., treas. 1990), Zeta Phi Eta, Phi Eta Sigma. Home: 3005 Union St Apt 3B Lafayette IN 47904-2778

ANNETTA, CATHERINE, museum business manager; b. Stamford, Conn., Dec. 28, 1951; d. Frank and Donata (Sabia) A.; m. Victor C. Burkhart, Sept. 22, 1984. Cert. African Studies, U. Nairobi, Kenya, 1973; BA, We. Conn. U., 1974; Lic., Internat. Sch. Electrology, Albuquerque, 1979. Mgr. DoPaso Silver Corp., Albuquerque, 1975-79; electrologist Oakley Electrology Clin., Albuquerque, 1979-80, Albuquerque Electrology Clin., 1980-84; membership asst. Denver Mus. Nat. History, 1985-87, bus. mgr., 1987—; designer, owner Catherine Anne Designs, Aurora, Colo., 1987-89. Edn. docent Maxwell Mus. Anthropology, 1980-83. Mem. N.Mex. Electrology Assn. (pres. 1983-84, dlegate 1983-84). Office: Denver Mus Natural History 2001 Colorado Blvd Denver CO 80205

ANNS, ARLENE EISERMAN, publishing company executive; b. Pearl River, N.Y.; d. Frederick Joel and Anna (Behnke) E.; student Bergen Jr. Coll., 1946-48; B.S., Utah State U., 1950; postgrad. Traphagen Sch. Design, 1957, N.Y. U., 1958, Hunter Coll., 1959-60. Rsch. and promotion asst. Archtl. Record, N.Y.C., 1952-56; asst. rsch. dir. Esquire Mag., N.Y.C., 1956-62; rsch. mgr. Am. Machinist, publ. McGraw-Hill, Inc., N.Y.C., 1962-67, mktg. svc. mgr., 1967-69, 1969-71, sales mgr., 1976-77, dir. mktg., 1977-78; v.p. mktg. svcs. Morgan-Gramplan, Inc., N.Y.C., 1971-72; mktg. dir. Family Health & Diversion mag., 1972-74; dist. sales mgr. Postgrad. Medicine, 1974-76; advt. sales mgr. Contemporary Ob/Gyn, 1976-78; dir. profl. devel., 1978-80; pub. graduating engr. and dir. mktg. Aerospace & Def. Group, 1980—, McGraw-Hill Aerospace & Def. Group, 1988—. Mem. Am. Mktg. Assn., Pharm. Advt. Club, Advt. Women N.Y., Advt. Club N.Y., Sales Exec. Club, Employment Mgmt. Assn., Am. Soc. Pers. Adminstrs., Coll. Placement Coun., Am. Assn. Energy Edn., Pi Sigma Alpha. Home: 101 Brianwood Ct Lakes Quinton VA 23141

ANNUNZIATA, KIMBERLY J., wholesale distribution executive; b. Akron, Ohio, Aug. 28, 1955; d. Sherman W. and Rochelle J. (Righter) Grant; m. Michael J. Annunziata. BS in Bus. Adminstrn., Miami U., Oxford, Ohio, 1977; MS in Acquisition and Contract Mgmt., Naval Postgrad. Sch., Monterey, Calif., 1985. Cert. profl. contract mgr. Commd. USN, 1977, advanced through grades to lt. comdr.; payroll office dir. Supply Depot USN, Yokosuka, Japan, 1977-78, storage office dir. Supply Depot, 1978-80; squadron supply officer USN, Sigonella, Italy, 1980-82; acctg. dir. US Naval Air Force/Atlantic Fleet, Norfolk, Va., 1982-83, integrated logistics support dir., 1983-84; dir. procurement support div. Navy Aviation Supply Office, Phila., 1986-88; raw materials mgr. BP Chemicals, Cleve., 1988-89; crude oil trader BP Oil Supply Co., Cleve., 1989—. Mem. North Olmsted (Ohio) League for Edn. of the Gifted, 1989—, exec. steering com. United Way, Cleve., 1989. Lt. comdr. UNSR, 1989—. Recipient full scholarship NROTC, Miami U., 1973-77, graduated first in NROTC class, 1977. Mem. Jr. Achievement Nat. Alumni Assn., NAFE, Nat. Contract Mgmt. Assn. (pres. Monterey chpt. 1984-85, Graelman award). Office: BP Oil Supply Co 200 Public Sq 23-F Cleveland OH 44114

ANOKYE, AKUA DUKU, English educator; b. Pontiac, Mich., Feb. 25, 1948; d. Finus Melvin Harris and Helen Marie (Hatchett) Mitchell; 1 child, Yao Nmanu Opare Dinizulu. BA in Speech/Auditory Sci., Mich. State U., 1970; MA in Speech Pathology, Fed. City Coll., Washington, 1972; MA in Linguistics, CUNY, N.Y.C., 1987. Asst. prof. of English No. Va. Community Coll., Alexandria, 1974-79; instr. speech communications LaGuardia CUNY, L.I., 1980-84; adminstrv. asst. Aims of Modzawe, Jamaica, N.Y., 1976—; rsch. asst. grad. sch. CUNY, N.Y.C., 1985-86; lang. arts coord. LaGuardia CUNY, L.I., 1986; instr. of English Queensborough CUNY, Bayside, 1986—; adj. instr. NYU, 1984-86; cons. WRIT Bridge Project, Bayside, 1986-89, Queensborough Pub. Libr., Queens, N.Y., 1986-90. Editor: Strategies for Speaking and Listening, 1983. Storyteller Black Storytelling Festival, Medgar Evers Coll., 1989; vol. tchr. Bosum Dzemawodzi H.S., Jamaica, 1982—. Named Black Faculty Mem. of the Yr., No. Va. Community Coll., 1978; recipient fellowship Georgetown U., 1971-72. Mem. Linguist Soc. Am., Nat. Coun. Tchrs. of Eng. (nat. storytelling com. 1990), Conf. on Coll. Composition and Communication, Tchrs. of English to Speakers of Other Langs., Assn. Black Storytellers, Assn. Black Women in Higher Edn. African Traditional. Home: 115-98 231st St Cambria Heights NY 11411 Office: Queensborough CUNY Bayside NY 11364

ANSARI, MARY BLANCHE, academic librarian; b. Lincoln, Ill., Jan. 15, 1939; m. Nazir Ahmed Ansari, June 4, 1970. AB, U. Ill., 1961, MLS, 1963; MBA, Western Mich. U., 1967. Asst. librarian U. Ill. Commerce Library, Champaign, 1963-64; asst. reference librarian New Orleans Pub. Library, 1964, Gary (Ind.) Pub. Library, 1964-66; with U. Nev.-Reno Library, 1969—, engring., mines, life and health scis. libr., 1981-86, asst. univ. librarian for adminstrv. svcs. and br. libraries, 1988—. Author: Bibliography of Nevada Geology, 1975, Comstock Place Names, 1986 Mines and Mills of the Comstock, 1989, (with others) Nevada Directory of Maps, 1983; contbr. articles to profl. jours. Mem. Geosci. Info. Soc. (treas. 1985-87, v.p., pres. elect 1989—), Western Assn. Map Libraries, Am. Soc. for Engring. Edn. Office: U Nevada-Reno Libr Reno NV 89557-0044

ANSELL, MARYLEE, real estate consultant; b. White Hall, Ill., Mar. 29, 1936; d. Ellsworth and Harriett Virginia (Rhodes) A. BS, Southern Ill. U., 1958. Exec. sec. The May Dept. Stores, St. Louis, 1958-62; sec., treas. Danter Assoc., St. Louis, 1962-68; exec. asst. Shure Mfg. Co., St. Louis, 1968-72; trainee to asst. div. mgr. The Equitable Life Assurance Soc. of the U.S., St. Louis, 1972-83; dir. ops. Linclay Corp., St. Louis, 1983-88; pvt. practice real estate cons. St. Louis, 1988—. Mem. Lambda Alpha Soc. Republican. Presbyterian. Home: 90 Stoneyside Ln Saint Louis MO 63132 Office: 955 Executive Pkwy Ste 110 Saint Louis MO 63141

ANSHAW, CAROL, writer; b. Grosse Pointe Station, Mich., Mar. 22, 1946; d. Henry G. and Virginia (Anshaw) Stanley; m. Charles J. White III, Mar. 15, 1969. BA, Mich. State U., 1968. Author: They Do It All With Mirrors, 1978. Tutor Literacy Council of Chgo., 1989--. Recipient Nat. Book Critics Circle award for disting. criticism, 1990. Mem. Nat. Book Critics Cir., Nat. Writers Council. Democrat. Office: 3959 N Lincoln Rm 595 Chicago IL 60613

ANTAL, KIMBERLY JOAN, English educator; b. Chicopee, Mass., Apr. 10, 1959; d. Francis Richard Antal and Carol Ann (Grimaldi) Nickerson. BS, Boston U., 1981; MEd, U. Maine, 1982. Substitute tchr. Longmeadow (Mass.) High Sch., 1983-84; dir. pub. rels. Yankee Pedlar Inn, Holyoke, Mass., 1984; ind. sales rep. Bisi Sales, Ludlow, Mass., 1984-85; adminstrv. asst. Stearns & Ferrall Realtors, Longmeadow, 1984-86; instr. in adult edn. Town of Longmeadow, 1986-87; claims rep. Hartford Ins. Co., East Longmeadow, Mass., 1986-87; tchr. English Cathedral High Sch., Springfield, Mass., 1987—; tutor in field. Contbr. articles to profl. jours. Sec. St. Mary's Parish Coun., Longmeadow, 1986-88, vice chairperson, 1989-90; vol. Boston U. Alumni Sch. Com., Longmeadow, 1983—, U. Maine Alumni Ambassadors, Longmeadow, 1984—. Horace Smith Fund fellow, 1981; U. Maine scholar, 1982. Democrat. Home: 73 Barrington Rd Longmeadow MA 01106 Office: Cathedral High Sch 260 Surrey Rd Springfield MA 01118

ANTANAITIS, CYNTHIA EMILY, lawyer; b. Bridgeport, Conn., Oct. 16, 1954; d. George Alexander and Stella Marie (Bernius) A. BS magna cum laude, Western Conn. State U., 1976; JD, SUNY, Amherst, 1980. Bar: Conn., 1983, N.Y., 1989; U.S. Dist. Ct. Conn. 1983. Legis. and regulations specialist State of Conn. Dept. of Banking, Hartford, 1981-83, asst. counsel, 1983-86, sr. adminstrv. atty., 1986-88, asst. dir. securities and bus. investments div., 1988—. Mem. ABA, Conn. Bar Assn., N.Am. Securities Administrators Assn., Inc. (legis./regulation com. 1989—, vice-chmn. 1989—, ad hoc com. on arbitration 1988, fin. planners and investment advisers com. 1984-89, legis. com. 1981-84, vice-chmn. 1982-84). Roman Catholic. Office: State of Conn Dept Banking 44 Capitol Ave Hartford CT 06106

ANTHONY, BETTY ARLENE, medical center executive; b. Jacksonville, Fla., July 14, 1926; d. Glessner Earl and Florence Claudine (Smyth) Pratt; m. Yancey Lamar Anthony, II (Baron Von Burg), Sept. 13, 1983. Student Jones Bus. Coll., Jacksonville, 1944, New Orleans Bapt. Theol. Sem., 1952, U. Fla., 1953-54, Tampa U., 1956. Promotion sec. Fla. Bapt. Conv., Jacksonville, 1945-53; sec. First Bapt. Ch., Tampa, 1955-59; sec. to asst. adminstr. Bapt. Med. Ctr., Jacksonville, 1960-65, sec. to exec. dir., 1966-80, corp. sec., 1980—; asst. sec., treas. Bapt. Health, Inc., Jacksonville, 1983—; sec. Bapt. Health Found., Inc., Jacksonville, 1983—; Bapt. Health Properties, Inc., Jacksonville, 1983—, Bapt. Med. Ctr. of Port St., Inc., Jacksonville, 1981—; sec. and treas. Bapt. Med. Ctr. of Ga., Inc., Jacksonville, 1980—; asst. sec. N.E. Fla. Breast Ctr., Inc., Jacksonville, 1984—; sec. Healthcare Mgmt. Services, Inc., Jacksonville, 1980—; asst. sec., treas. So. Bapt. Hosp. of Fla. Inc., Jacksonville, 1985—, CE-TECH of Jacksonville, Inc., 1989; sec.-treas. Southbank Advt. Inc., 1987, Dr.'s Office Network, Inc., 1989; asst. sec. The Pavilion Developer Inc., 1987; asst. sec., treas. Lakewood Apothecary, Inc., 1988—; Dame of Grace Mil. and Hosp. Order St. Lazarus of Jerusalem, 1983. Mem. Fla. Hosp. Exec. Secs. Assn. (dir. 1973-76, pres. 1975-76, program chmn. 1974-75), Am. Soc. Corp. Secs. Avocations: jogging, creative writing, church activities, oil painting/drawing, gardening. Office: Bapt Health Inc 1300 Gulf Life Dr Ste 303 Jacksonville FL 32207

ANTHONY, ELAINE MARGARET, real estate executive; b. Mpls., Apr. 23, 1932; d. Jerome Pius and Adeline (Shea) Clarkin; m. Ronald Carl Anthony, Aug 28, 1954 (div. 1977); children: Richard, Lisa, Laura. Student, U. Minn., 1950-51; AA, Diablo Valley Coll., 1978; postgrad., San Jose (Calif.) State U., 1979, U. Calif., Berkeley, 1983—. Agt., broker Sycamore Realty, Danville, Calif., 1972-75; broker, project sales mgr. Crocker Homes, Dublin, Calif., 1975-80; exec. v.p. BlackHawk Properties, Danville, 1980-82; broker, project sales mgr. Harold W. Smith Co., Walnut Creek, Calif., 1982-86; pres. Elaine Anthony & Assocs., Inc., Oakland, Calif., 1986—. Mem. vol. coun. San Francisco Symphony, 1986. Mem. Bldg. Industry Assn. (Outstanding Sales Person of Yr. No. Calif. chpt. 1983), Nat. Assn. Home Builders, Inst. Residential Mktg., Oakland Bd. Realtors, Commonwealth Club Calif., Women's Athletic Club Alameda County. Republican. Roman Catholic. Home and Office: 1875 Grand View Dr Oakland CA 94618

ANTHONY, JACQUELINE, college administrator; b. Uniontown, Pa., Mar. 21, 1966; d. Michael James and Margaret Marie (Zavislan) A. BS in Bus. and Behavioral Scis., Pa. State U., Erie, 1988. Asst. admissions counselor The Behrend Coll., Pa. State U., Erie, 1988; admissions counselor Capitol Coll., Laurel, Md., 1988-89, coord. of admissions, 1989-90, assoc. dir. devel., 1990—; staff counselor Capitol Coll. student chpt. Soc. Women Engrs., Laurel, 1989—. Mem. AAUW, NAFE, Pa. State U. Alumni Assn.,

Omicron Delta Kappa. Democrat. Roman Catholic. Office: Capitol Coll 11301 Springfield Rd Laurel MD 20708

ANTHONY, KARA LEE, nutritionist; b. Pitts., Aug. 6, 1965; d. James Joseph and Elva Jean (Roach) A. BS, Seton Hill Coll., Greensburg, Pa., 1988. Registered dietitian. Dietetic intern The Uniontown (Pa.) Hosp.; pvt. practice Concerned Nutrition Cons., McMurray, Pa., 1988—. Author: Cookin' with Class. Mem. NAFE, Am. Dietetic Assn., Cons. Nutritionists Am. Dietetic Assn., Sports Medicine and Cardiovascular Nutritionists Am. Dietetic Assn., Women's Bus. Network Pitts., Am. Running and Fitness Assn., Pitts. Dietetics Assn., Pa. Dietetics Assn. Home: 392 Turkeyfoot Rd Venetia PA 15367 Office: 615 E McMurray Rd McMurray PA 15317

ANTHONY, SARA, registered nurse; b. Greenville, Pa., Aug. 7, 1954; d. Dawna (Anthony) Okin. AS, Augusta (Ga.) Coll., 1978; BSN, U. South Fla., 1986. Staff nurse Sarasota (Fla.) Meml. Hosp., 1979-87, charge nurse, 1987-88, clinical instr., 1988—. With U.S. Army, 1972-75. Mem. Fla. Nurses Assn. (sec. 1984-86, treas. 1989—). Home: 2636 Woodgate Sarasota FL 34231

ANTHONY, SHARON ARNOLD, communications executive; b. Langley, Va., Oct. 26, 1965; d. John Wayne And Kathleen (Kuhl) Arnold, m. David Lee Anthony, Aug. 1, 1987. BA, U. Md. Balt. County, 1983, postgrad., 1989—. Admissions counselor U. Md. Balt. County, 1987, asst. to dir. student activities, 1987-88; asst. to dir. planned giving U. Md. Systems Adminstrn., Adelphi, 1988-89; dir. programs and communications The Media Inst., Washington, 1989—. Mem. Women in Communications, Inc., Nat. Assn. of Sci. Writers, U. Md. Balt. County Alumni Assn. (chmn. career devel. com. 1987-90). Democrat. Roman Catholic. Office: The Media Inst 3017 M St NW Washington DC 20007

ANTILLA, SUSAN, journalist; b. New Rochelle, N.Y., May 18, 1954; d. Oscar E. Antilla and Gloria (Jennings) Claudet; m. James Harlan Burdsall, Sept. 26, 1981. BA, Manhattanville Coll., 1976; MA, NYU, 1981. Reporter Dun's Bus. Month, N.Y.C., 1978-81, asst. editor, 1981-82; contbg. editor Working Woman Mag., N.Y.C., 1980-86; stock market reporter USA Today, N.Y.C., 1982-85, bur. mgr., Money bur. chief, columnist, 1986—; fin. bur. chief Balt. Sun, N.Y.C., 1985-86; guest lectr. Marymount Manhattan Coll., 1984, 85; guest lectr. NYU, 1985, adj. prof., 1987—. Contbr. Savvy mag., 1986-88, also articles to other mags. and profl. jours. Cons. Girls Club Am., N.Y.C., 1983. Mem. N.Y. Fin. Writers Assn., N.Y. Women in Communications. Office: USA Today 535 Madison Ave New York NY 10022

ANTIN, ELEANOR, artist; b. N.Y.C., Feb. 27, 1935; d. Sol and Jeanette (Efron) Fineman; m. David Antin, Dec., 1961; 1 son, Blaise. B.A., CCNY, 1958; student, Tamara Daykarhanova Sch. for Stage, N.Y.C., 1954-56. Prof. visual arts U. Calif., San Diego. Artist, producer videotapes Little Match Girl Ballet, 1975, Adventures of a Nurse, 1976, The Nurse and the Hijackers, 1977, The Angel of Mercy, 1980, from the Archives of Modern Art, 1987; (film) Loves of a Ballerina, 1986, The Last Night of Rasputin, 1988; one-woman shows include Mus. Modern Art, N.Y.C., 1973, Whitney Mus. Film and Video Program, N.Y.C., 1978, Long Beach Mus. Art, Calif., 1979, Ronald Feldman Gallery, N.Y.C., 1977, 79, 80, 83, 86; group shows include, São Paulo Biennal, Brazil, 1975, Phila. Mus. Fine Arts, 1978, Hirschhorn Mus., Washington, 1979, 84, Santa Barbara Mus. Art, Calif., 1979; performances include Battle of the Bluffs, 1975-80, The Angel of Mercy, 1977-80, Before the Revolution, 1979, Recollections of My Life with Diaghilev, 1980-86, El Desdichado (The Unlucky One), 1983, Help! I'm in Seattle, 1986, 87, Who Cares About a Ballerina?, 1987, 88; represented in permanent collections, Mus. Modern Art, N.Y.C., Long Beach Mus. Art, San Francisco Mus. Modern Art, Wadsworth Atheneum, Hartford, Conn.; artist performer at Venice Bienale, 1976, Mus. Contemporary Art, Chgo., 1978, Houston, 1978, 80; author: book Being Antinova, 1983. Nat. Endowment for Arts grantee, 1979; recipient Vesta award, Los Angeles, 1985. Office: U Calif at San Diego Visual Arts Dept La Jolla CA 92093

ANTINOZZI, MARY LOU, technical director; b. Red Bank, N.J.; d. Andrew Frank and Mary M. (Saggese) Russo; children: Evamarie Antinozzi Beich, Sonora Antinozzi Foster, Lorraine. Student, Monmouth Coll., 1981, Atlantic Community Coll., 1982, 88. Mechanic Bally's Park Pl. Casino/Hotel, Atlantic City, 1979, shift mgr., 1980-84, asst. mgr., 1984-85, dir. facilities, 1985—. Mem. N.J. Adv. Water Com., Red Bank Dem. Com.; chmn. planning com. Atlantic County Women's Ctr., 1990; mem. steering com. Red Bank Regional High Sch., 1969-73; PTA charter mem. Red Bank Pub. Schs., 1970; mem. bd. elections County of Monmouth, 1970-75. Mem. NAFE, Constrns. Specifications Inst. (v.p. 1988-90, pres.-elect South Jersey chpt. 1990—), Assn. Profl. Energy Mgmt. Office: Park Pl & Boardwalk Atlantic City NJ 08401

ANTMAN, LORI LINETTE, chiropractor; b. Hackensack, N.J., June 25, 1960; d. Frank James and Ninette Dorothee (Mercier) A. BS in Biochemistry, Tex. A&M U., 1982; D. Chiropractic, Tex. Chiropractic Coll., 1986. Diplomate Nat. Bd. Chiropractic. Small bus. office mgr. Seabrook, Tex., 1986; owner Chirpractic Health Ctr., Galveston, Tex., 1987-90; owner/ptnr. A&M Physical Rehab. Ctr., 1990—; clin. staff asst. Tex. Chiropractic Coll., Pasadena, Tex., 1985-86. Sec. Galveston Police Appreciation Com., 1987-88, pres., 1989—; mem. svc. com. Student Y Assn., College Station, Tex., 1978-82. Mem. Am. Chiropractic Assn., Tex. Chiropractic Assn., Tex. Chiropractic Coll. Alumni Assn., Galveston Republican Womans Club, Alpha Phi Omega, Gamma Sigma Delta. Home: 239 Barracuda Hitchcock TX 77563 Office: Chiropractic Health Ctr 4603 Fort Crockett Blvd PO Box 3367 Galveston TX 77552

ANTOINE, FLORENCE SHEILA, writer; b. Balt., Jan. 12, 1941; d. Abraham and Miriam (Gamerman) Schwartz; m. John Eugene Antoine. BA, Goucher Coll., 1962; MA, Johns Hopkins U., 1970. Chemist research, tech. info. specialist Nat. Inst. Health, Bethesda, Md., 1963; med. legal specialist Cone, Owen, Wagner, West Palm Beach, Fla.; real estate agt. Wilcox Galley Homes, North Palm Beach, 1979-80; technical writer JRB, McLean, Va., 1979-80; speech writer Nat. Int. Health, Bethesda, 1980; med. writer Nat. Inst. Health, Bethesda, 1980-. Contbr. chpt. to book, articles to profl. jours. Bd. dirs. Jew Community Ctr., Palm Beach, 1979. Mem. Am. Med. Writers Assn., Nat. Assn. Sci. Writers, Nat. Inst. Health Sci. Writers Guild. Republican. Office: Nat Cancer Inst Bldg 31 Room 10 A-19 Bethesda MD

ANTOINE, GRETA JANE, management; b. Depauville, N.Y., Mar. 5, 1934; d. Joseph Lavina and Flora Alberta (Darou) LaRose; m. Stanley Antoine. Diploma, E. Jordan High Sch., Mich., 1972. Project dir. Title V-E. Jordan (Mich.) Pub. Schs., 1980-89; exec. dir. Anishinabe Inter-Tribal Coun., E. Jordan, 1980-89, Odawa Bear Clan Coun., E. Jordan, 1989—; cons. Mich. Sch. System, 1980-. Councilman, City Council, E. Jordan, 1982-84; bd. dirs. Am. Indian Dem. Mem. Odawa Bear Clan Coun. Home: 402 Williams St PO Box 656 East Jordan MI 49727

ANTON, CATHERINE GAYLE, personnel executive; b. Whitinsville, Mass., Dec. 19, 1945; d. Elmer Fuller and Esther Irene (Newton) Benton; m. Dennis Anthony Anton, Aug. 5, 1972; 1 child, Geoffrey Darrell. AA, Worcester (Mass.) Jr. Coll., 1966; BS, Clark U., 1972. Policy analyst Aetna Ins. Co., Worcester, 1969-72; asst. to sales adminstr. Buxton Co., Agawam, Mass., 1972-73, adminstrv. asst. sales dept., 1973-76, mgr. traffic dept., 1976-77; mgr. advt. spltys. div. Springfield Photo Mount, Holyoke, Mass., 1977-79; adminstrv. asst. sales dept. Glenshaw Glass Co., Pitts., 1979-81; mgr. clerical personnel Mercy Hosp. Health Ctr., Pitts., 1982-83; mgr. compensation and benefits Springfield (Mass.) Instn. for Savs., 1985-86; personnel dir. Carando, Springfield, 1983-85, 86—; bd. dirs. Tchr.-Bus. Com., Springfield, 1985—. Apptd. mem. Springfield Ret. Bd., 1986—, Safety Coun. Western Mass., 1987—; read aloud vol. Springfield Sch. Vols., 1986-87, 88-89, jr. high sch. mentor, 1986-87. Mem. Am. Soc. for Personnel Adminstrs., Personnel Mgmt. Soc., Am. Compensation Assn., Springfield C. of C. Democrat. Methodist. Home: 119 Tallyho Dr Springfield MA 01118 Office: Carando 20 Carando Dr PO Box 491 Springfield MA 01102-0491

ANTON, CHERYL LYNN, sales executive; b. Toledo, Nov. 3, 1953; d. Ralph Herbert and Coletta Marie (Nickerson) Snyder; student U. Toledo, 1971-73; 1 son, John Daniel. With Kroger Co., Toledo, 1972-80, dept. supr. merchandising; sales dir. Growth Unltd., Toledo, 1979-80; owner CJ's Bar, Toledo, 1980-82; sales rep. Armour Food Co., Orlando, Fla., 1983-85; dist. sales mgr. Jones Dairy Farm, 1985-87; regional sales mgr. Southland Corp., 1987—. Mem. Nat. Assn. Female Execs. (network dir. 1979—), Nat. Assn. for Women. Democrat. Home: 6105 Luzon Dr Orlando FL 32809 Office: Southland Corp Fla 1970 Sand Lake Rd Orlando FL 32859

ANTONACCI, LORI (LORETTA MARIE ANTONACCI), marketing executive, consultant; b. Riverton, Ill., Mar. 31, 1947; d. Antonio and Gena Marie A. BA, Bradley U., 1969. Broadcast copywriter Sta. WIRL-TV, Peoria, Ill., 1969; communications specialist Walgreen Co., Chgo., 1970-72; creative supr. Nat. Assn. Realtors, Chgo., 1973; creative dir., producer Steve Sohmer, Inc., N.Y.C., 1974-77; owner, exec. producer Antonacci Prodns., N.Y.C., 1977-79; promotion specialist Ziff-Davis Publs., 1979-80; promotion mgr. Psychology Today, 1980-81; pres. Antonacci & Assocs., N.Y.C., 1982—; adj. prof. Gallatin div. NYU, 1986—. Bd. advisors Wildcare, Inc., Artists Talk on Art, Inc.; founder Artists Talk on Art Panel series, 1974. Recipient Golden Eagle award CINE, 1976; award U.S. Indsl. Film Festival, 1977; CEBA award, 1979; Bronze medal Internat. Film and TV Festival N.Y., 1979. Mem. Advt. Women N.Y. (profl. devel. com. 1983-85, program com. 1986—, chmn. speakers bur. 1988—), Women in Communications, Am. Women in Radio and TV. Address: 15 E 10th St New York NY 10003

ANTONE, KAREN ANN, real estate executive; b. Mpls., Jan. 21, 1947; d. Carl Harry and Mildred Marion (Johnson) Olson. Student U. Minn., 1966-68. Mortgage closer F&M Bank, Mpls., 1968-73; mortgage dept. coordinator Guarantee Title, Inc., Mpls., 1973-74; real estate closer Bermel Smaby Realtors, Mpls., 1974-75; real estate assoc. Edina Realty, Inc., Mpls., 1976—, sales adv. council, 1986-88, chmn. 1987. Active Minn. Real Estate Polit. Action Com., 1982. Mem. Greater Mpls. Area Bd. Realtors, Minn. Assn. Realtors, Nat. Assn. Realtors, Nat. Assn. Female Execs. Avocations: arts; jogging; reading, traveling. Office: Edina Realty Inc 4015 W 65th St Edina MN 55435

ANTONIO, MARLENE JOAN, commission administrator; b. Moose Jaw, Sask., Can., Apr. 24, 1936; d. John Ewan and Ruby Irene (Bagg) Lauder; m. Harry Antonio, Apr. 27, 1957; 1 child, Jolaine Ann. B of Edn., U. Sask., 1956, BS, 1957; M of Edn., U. Calgary, Alta., Can., 1969. Geologist, Texaco Exploration Co., Calgary, 1957-58; tchr. Calgary Bd. Edn., 1966-70, 79-80; instr. Mt. Royal Coll., Calgary, 1970-74, U. Calgary, 1976-78; chmn. Alta. Human Rights Commn., Edmonton, 1979-85, apptd. chmn's. coun., 1989; mem. gov. coun. geol., geophy. Assn. Profl. Engrs., 1986—; mem. Minister's Consultative Com. on Tolerance and Understanding, Alta., 1983-84. Sec.-treas. Calgary Home and Sch. Assn., 1976-78. Recipient Good Servant award Can. Coun. Christians and Jews, 1984. Nat. Coun. Jewish Women scholar, Saskatoon, Sask., 1955-57. Mem. Alta. Tchrs. Assn., Can. Assn. Statuatory Human Rights Agys. (pres. 1984-85), Assn. Profl. Engrs., Geologists and Geophysicists of Alta. (hon. 1986-87, practice rev. bd. 1987—, governing coun.). Office: Assn Profl Engrs, 1500 Scotia Place Tower One, 10060 Jasper Ave, Edmonton, AB Canada T5J4A2

ANTONIOU, LUCY D., internist, nephrologist; b. Rhodes, Greece, Jan. 3, 1929; came to U.S. 1948; d. Matthew and Augustine (Perakis) A. BA, George Washington U., 1958, MD, 1961. Diploamte Am. Bd. Internal Medicine and Nephrology. Intern Jackson Meml.l Hosp., Miami, Fla., 1961-62; med. resident George Washington U. Hosp., Washington, 1963-64; med. resident, nephrology tngs., research assoc. VA Hosp., Washington, 1964-66, 67-69; asst. prof. medicine Loyola U., Maywood, Ill., 1970-71; asst. chief renal hypertension sect. VA Hosp., Hines, Ill., 1970-71; staff physician VA Hosp., Jamaica Plain, Mass., 1971-73; asst. prof. medicine U. Okla. Health Sci. Ctr., Oklahoma City, 1973-74; asst. prof. to assoc. prof. medicine Georgetown U., Washington, 1974—; asst. chief renal sect. VA Hosp., Washington, 1974-80; assoc. chief renal sect. VA Hosp., 1980—; assoc. dir. renal failure care unit VA Hosp., Oklahoma City, 1973-74. Contbr. articles to profl. jours.; assoc. editor Minerva Medica Greca, 1974—. NIH fellow Georgetown U., 1966-67; VA grantee, 1967-69, 74-80. Mem. Internat. Soc. Nephrology, Hellenic Soc. Health Scis., Soc. for Preservation of Greek Heritage, Friends of Cyprus (v.p. 1975-76), Sigma Xi. Republican. Greek Orthodox. Home: Bizaniou 20, Papagou, 15669 Athens Greece Office: VA Med Ctr 50 Irving St NW Washington DC 20815

ANTOSH, NATALIE JEAN, hotel manager; b. Willoughby, Ohio, July 16, 1964; d. Raymond Felix and Betty Edna (Chappie) A.; 1 child from previous marriage, Michael Anthony. AB, Lakeland Community Coll., Mentor, Ohio, 1985. Rm. receptionist Harley Hotels, Willoughby, Ohio, 1983-85; gen. mgr. Skylight Inn, Willoughby, Ohio, 1985-88, Trusthouse Forte Hotels Internat., Cleve., 1988—. Mem. Girl Scouts U.S., Lake County, 1970—. Mem. Cleve. Hotel/Motel Assn., 1989—, Greater Cleve. Bus. Assn., 1989—, Willoughby C. of C., 1985—. Democrat. Roman Catholic. Office: Trusthouse Forte Hotels Travelodge 34600 Maplegrove Rd Willoughby OH 44094

ANTOUN, SISTER M. LAWREACE, college president emerita; b. Meadville, Pa., Dec. 30, 1927; d. George K. and Freda (Habib) A. BS, Villa Maria Coll., 1954; MS, Notre Dame U., 1959, postgrad., 1959. Instr. chemistry Villa Maria Coll., Erie, Pa., 1955-61, asst. prof. chemistry, 1965-66, pres., 1966-88, pres. emerita, 1988—; past mem. Pa. Commn. on Financing of Higher Edn.; mem. exec. com. Commn. Ind. Colls. and Univs.; evaluator Middle States Assn./Commn. Higher Edn.; trustee Middle States Assn.; mem. Erie Conf. on Community Devel.; past chmn. Pa. Postsecondary Planning Commn.; chmn. Coun. Higher Edn.; past mem. adv. com. edn. Pa. Bd. Edn.; bd. dirs. Sisters of St. Joseph. Chairperson Pa. State Bd. of Edn., 1985—; mem. Commonwealth Jud. Coun.; chairperson adv. coun. McMannis Ednl. Trust Fund; past mem. Home Rule Charter Com.; adv. bd. human ecology Cornell U.; bd. incorporators St. Vincent Health Ctr.; bd. dirs. Hamot Med. Ctr., Erie Conf. on Community Devel., chmn. Pa. State Bd. of Higher Edn. Named Disting. Dau. of Pa., 1990. Mem. Am. Assn. Ind. Colls. and Univs., Pa. Assn. Coll. and Univs., Pa. Assn. Ind. Colls. and Univs, Bd. of Human Ecology.

AONA, GRETCHEN MANN, artist, photographer; b. Omaha, June 25, 1933; d. Albert Paul and Gladys Louise (Mann) Andersen; m. Daniel Kaleikoa Aona, Jr., June 16, 1979. AB, San Jose State U., 1951, MA in Art, 1966. Textbook illustrator math. and stats. dept. Stanford U., 1960-63; sci. illustrator Melabs, Mountain View, Calif., 1967; instr. art, crafts, and photography Kapiolani Community Coll., Honolulu, 1967-88, chmn. humanities dept., 1978-79; one-woman shows in photography include: Fantasy Images, Queen Emma Gallery, Honolulu, 1977, Foyer Gallery, Leeward Community Coll., Honolulu, 1980; one-woman shows in watercolor include: Hawaii Med. Svc. Assn., 1989; group exhbns. include: Photo '70, '71, '72, Sixty Yrs. World in Color, Hague, Netherlands, 1973, Honolulu, Art Hawaii One, Honolulu Acad. Art, 1974, 75, Gt. Hawaiian Open Art Exhbn., 1981, Artists of Hawaii, Honolulu Acad. Arts, 1981, Honolulu Printmakers 55th Ann. Exhbn., 1983, 60th Ann. Exhbn., 1988, Windward Artists Easter Art Show, 1984, 85, 88, Hawaii Watercolor Soc. Exhibit, 1985, 86, 89, Image 13 Hawaii, 1987; invitational exhbns. include Koa Gallery, Kapiolani Community Coll., 1987, Florals and Nature Scenes, Ho'omaluhia Bot. Garden, 1987, Aloha Ho'omaluhia, 1988, 89, 90. Represented by Koolau Gallery, Kaneothe, Chocolate Orchid, Kailua-Kona, Hawaii. Recipient Purchase award Honolulu Acad. Art, 1981, Hawaii State Found. Culture and Arts, 1987 (2). Mem. Hawaii Watercolor Soc., Pacific Handcrafters Guild. Democrat. Roman Catholic. Author: Creative Exploration in Crafts, 1976. Home: 45-453 B Mokulele Dr Kaneohe HI 96744

APEL, MYRNA L., entrepreneur; b. Cleve., July 19, 1942; d. Melvin Artnur and Merle Ruth (Hoffman) Rehlender; children: Timothy, Kristen. BS in Edn., Kent State U., MEd in Counseling. Cert. tchr., Ohio; lic. minister, Ohio. Owner, mgr. real estate investments Ind. Counseling Practice, Kent, Ohio; owner, mgr. Real Estate Investments, Kent, Ohio; owner Counseling Ctr., Kent, Ohio, Winning Edge. Founder, pres. Ind. High Sch. Pers. Devel. Mem. OMHA, Ind. High Sch. Pers. Assn., Alpha Omega, Chi Omega, Sigma Epsilon.

APGAR, B. JEAN, research chemist; b. Tyler, Tex., Mar. 4, 1936; d. Albert Edward and Mary Agnes (Linehan) Francis; divorced; children: Katherine, Michael, John. BA, Tex. Woman's U., 1957; MS, Cornell U., 1959, PhD, 1964. Rsch. chemist Agrl. Rsch. Svc., USDA, Ithaca, N.Y., 1959—. Mem. Am. Inst. Nutrition, Am. Soc. Animal Sci. Office: US Plant Soil Nutrition Lab Tower Rd Ithaca NY 14853-0331

APKING, ANNE MARIE, custom training and consulting firm executive; b. Milw., Oct. 28, 1960; d. Eugene Kenneth and Carol Ann (Wisniewski) Backe; m. Theodore David Apking, June 9, 1984. BA, Western Mich. U., 1982, MA, 1983. Instructional technologist Perry Drug Stores, Pontiac, Mich., 1983-84; instructional technologist Creative Universal, Inc., Warren, Mich., 1984-86, project leader, 1986-89; project mgr. Triad Performance Techs., Farmington Hills, Mich., 1989—. Contbr. articles to profl. jours. Mem. Nat. Soc. for Performance and Instrn., Mich. Soc. for Instructional Tech. (v.p. 1988-89, several awards 1986, 87). Office: Triad Performance Techs 30101 Northwestern Hwy Ste 330 Farmington Hills MI 48334

APPEL, MARSHA CEIL, association executive; b. N.Y.C., Dec. 3, 1953; d. Albert and Stella Joy (Glaser) A.; m. Mark D. Marcellus, Sept. 10, 1978; children: Sam, Jill. BA, SUNY, Albany, 1974; MSLS, Syracuse U., 1975. Info. specialist Am. Assn. Advt. Agys., N.Y.C., 1976-79, mgr. member info. svc., 1979-89, v.p., 1989—. Author: Illustration Index IV, 1980, Illustration Index V, 1984, Illustration Index VI, 1988; editor What's New in Advertising and Marketing, 1978-80. Mem. Spl. Librs. Assn. (chmn. advt. and mktg. div. 1982-83). Office: Am Assn Advt Agys 666 3d Ave New York NY 10017

APPEL, NINA S., university dean; b. Prague, Czechoslovakia; d. Leo and Nora (Thein) Schick; m. Alfred Appel Jr., Sept. 1, 1957; children: Karen Oshman, Richard. Student, Cornell U.; JD, Columbia U. Mem. faculty Loyola U. Sch. Law, Chgo., assoc. dean, now dean, 1973—. Jewish. Office: Loyola U Sch Law 1 E Pearson St Chicago IL 60611

APPEL, VIRGINIA BARR, microbiologist, researcher; b. Denver, Oct. 14, 1955; m. Bruce E. Appel. BS in Microbiology, Colo. State U., 1981. Rsch. technician Clin. Labs., Nat. Jewish Ctr., Denver, 1982-84, rsch. technician dept. pediatrics, 1984—. Contbr. articles to sci. jours. Precinct committeewoman Denver Dem. Com., 1987-88. Lutheran. Office: Nat Jewish Ctr 1400 Jackson St Denver CO 80206

APPELBAUM, JUDITH PILPEL, editor, consultant, educator; b. N.Y.C., Sept. 26, 1939; d. Robert Cecil and Harriet Florence (Fleischl) Pilpel; m. Alan Appelbaum, Apr. 16, 1961; children: Lynn Stephanie, Alexander Eric. BA with honors Vassar Coll., 1960. Editor, Harper's Mag., N.Y.C., 1960-74; mng. editor Harper's Weekly, 1974-76; sr. cons. Atlas World Press Rev., 1977; mng. editor Pubs. Weekly, 1978-81; founder Sensible Solutions, Inc., 1979; contbg. editor Publishers Weekly, 1981-82; columnist N.Y. Times Book Rev., 1982-84; mng. dir. Sensible Solutions, Inc., 1984—; assoc. dir. Ctr. for Book Rsch., U. Scranton, 1985-88; book rev. editor Book Research Quar., 1984-86, editor in chief, 1986-88, cons. editor, 1988—; mem. faculty Pub. Inst. of U. Denver, 1981—, CUNY edn. in pub. program, 1982—; editorial adv. Book Industry Study Group Newsletter, 1980-83; mem. stats. com. Book Industry Study Group, 1984—; adv. bd. Coordinating Coun. Lit. Mags., 1980-84, PEN Ctr. USA West, 1988—. Mem. Authors Guild, Women's Media Group, PEN, Com. Small Mag./Press Editors & Pubs. Author: How to Get Happily Published, 1978, 3d edit., 1988; editor: (with Tony Jones and Gwyneth Cravens) The Big Picture: A Wraparound Book, 1976; The Question of Size in the Book Industry Today, 1978; Getting a Line on Backlist, 1979; Paperback Primacy, 1981; Small Publisher Power, 1982. Office: Sensible Solutions Inc 6 E 39th St New York NY 10016

APPELL, GAIL PECK, banker; b. New Britain, Conn., Apr. 26, 1939; d. Bernard Carl and Molla Rena (Nair) Peck; children: Tad, Neal, Kyle, Bruce. BS in Phys. Edn., Tufts Coll., 1961. Lic. life ins. agt., Conn. Br. mgr. Northwest Bank for Savs., Avon, Conn.; sales specialist Burritt Interfin. Bancorp, New Britain, Conn.; sales rep. Mitchell Subaru, Canton, Conn.; ski dir. Ski Sundown, New Hartford, Conn.; phys. edn. Sedgewick Jr. High Sch., West Hartford, Conn. Mem. Profl. Ski Instrs. Assn. Eastern Region (cert.), Ski Sch. Dirs. Rep., Conn. Womens Golf Assn.

APPELL, KATHLEEN MARIE, management consultant; b. Phila., Apr. 20, 1943; d. Joseph F. and Catherine (Laing) Hudson; m. Vincent M. Mandes (div. Apr. 1968); children: Carren Lee, Vincent, Lori. Cert., Phila. Modeling Sch., 1960-61, Horsham Found., 1979-81, Behavioral Acad., 1981, Fashion Acad., 1984. Adminstr. Phila. Modeling and Career Sch., 1965-68; pres. K.M. Appell Enterprises Ltd., Warwick, Pa., 1968-76, 1988—; exec. asst. Horsham Psychiat. Hosp., Ambler, Pa., 1976-84; cons. Horsham Psychiat. Hosp., Ambler, 1976-84; dir. admissions Career Inst., Phila., 1986-87; cons. Resource Spectrum, Ambler, 1979-82, Horsham Mgmt. Corp., Ambler, 1978-84. Contbr. articles to profl. jours. Mem. Rep. Task Force Com., Washington, 1981; mem. Ch. of Bethesda-By-the-Sea Episcopal Ch. Mem. Women's Econ. Devel., Assn. Fashion and Image Cons., Profl. and Exec. Women. Home and Office: 294 Hibiscus Ave #1 Palm Beach FL 33480

APPERSON, JEAN, psychologist; b. Durham, N.C., June 8, 1934; d. James Harry and Dorothy Elizabeth (Johnson) Apperson; m. Calvin Adams Pope, Mar. 23, 1956 (div. 1967); 1 child, Richard Allan. BA, U. S. Fla., 1966; MA, Mich. State U., 1970, PhD, 1973. Teaching asst. Mich. State U., E. Lansing, 1968-69; psychiatric technician St. Lawrence Community Mental Health Ctr., Lansing, Mich., 1968-69; psychology intern St. Lawrence Community Mental Health Ctr., 1969-71, Mich. State U. Counseling Ctr., 1971-73; clin. psychologist U. Mich. Counseling Ctr., Ann Arbor, 1973-81; pvt. practice psychology and psychoanalysis Ann Arbor, 1974—; mem., chmn. Mich. Bd. Psychology, Lansing, 1984—. Contbr. articles to profl. jours.; cons. editor Am. Psychol. Assn. Catalog of Selected Documents, 1975-80. USPHS grantee, 1969-70; NIMH grantee, 1970-71. Mem. Am. Psychol. Assn. (com. on sci. and profl. ethics and conduct 1977-80), Mich. Psychol. Assn. (chmn. women's issues com. 1981-83), Mich. Assn. for Psychoanalytic Psychology (treas. 1982-86), Mich. Psychoanalytic Coun., Assn. for Advancement Psychology, Am. Women in Psychology, Mich. Women Psychologists. Democrat. Unitarian. Home: 7224 Chelsea-Manchester Rd Manchester MI 48158 Office: 555 E Williams St #23E Ann Arbor MI 48104

APPLE, DAINA DRAVNIEKS, management analyst; b. Kuldiga, Latvia, USSR, July 6, 1944; came to U.S., 1951; d. Albins Dravnieks and Alina A. (Bergs) Zelmenis; divorced; 1 child, Almira Moronne; m. Martin A. Apple, Sept. 2, 1986. BS, U. Calif., Berkeley, 1977, MA, 1980. Economist USDA Pacific S.W. Rsch., Berkeley, 1976-85; mgr. regional and use appeals USDA Forest Svc., San Francisco, 1986-88, mgmt. analysis officer, 1988—. Author: Public Involvement In the Forest Service-Methodologies, 1977, Public Involvement-Selected Abstracts for Natural Resources, 1979, The Management of Policy and Direction in the Forest Service, 1982, An Analysis of the Forest Service Human Resource Management Program, 1984, Organization Design-Abstracts for Natural Resources Users, 1985; sect. editor Jour. of Women in Natural Resources. Mem. Am. Forestry Assn., Assn. Women in Sci., Soc. Am. Foresters, Phi Beta Kappa Assocs. (nat. sec. 1985-88, pres. No. Calif. chpt. 1982-84, 1st v.p. 1981), Commonwealth Club Calif., Sigma Xi. Home: PO Box 11274 Berkeley CA 94701 Office: USDA Forest Svc Engring Staff 2245 Morello Ave Pleasant Hill CA 94523

APPLEBY, MARJORY LU, school counselor; b. Pitts., Mar. 16, 1930; d. Robert Phelps and Mabel Elizabeth (Myers) Dean; m. John Malcom Appleby, Mar. 22, 1975; stepchildren: Jarrett, Brian. BS, West Chester State Coll., 1952; MEd, West Chester U., 1970. Cert. music edn. guidance and counseling, Pa. Music supr. Nether Providence Sch. Dist., Rose Valley, Pa., 1952-56; music tchr. West Chester Area Sch. Dist., West Chester, Pa., 1956-58, elem. tchr., 1958-59, elem. substitute tchr., 1959-68; guidance counselor Downingtown Area Sch. Dist., Downingtown, Pa., 1968—. Contbr. article to Jour. of Coll. Admissions, 1986. Mem. Pa. School Counselors Assn. (Sch. Counselor of Yr. 1987-88), Am. Assn. for Counseling & Devel., NEA, Pa. Sch. Educators Assn., Downingtown Area Ednl. Assn. Home: 53 Pond's Edge Dr Downingtown PA 19335 Office: Downingtown Sr High Sch 445 Manor Ave Downingtown PA 19335

APPLEGARTH, VIRGINIA BEVINGTON, financial planning and investment advisor, author; b. Atlanta, Feb. 24, 1953; d. William Francis and Alice Lenore (Vollmer) Applegarth; m. E. Milton Bevington Jr., Jan. 4, 1974 (div. 1987); children: Alden Keene, Elizabeth Rickey. BA cum laude, Vanderbilt U., Nashville, 1974. CLU; chartered fin. cons. Pension analyst Sun Life Can., Atlanta, 1974-77; trust adminstr. Trust Co. Bank, Atlanta, 1977-78; fin. planning cons. Roe, Martin and Nieman, Atlanta, 1978-79; pres. GRAM Group, Winchester, Mass., 1984-87; sr. fin. planner APEX Adv. Svcs., Cambridge, Mass., 1987-88; v.p. APEX Adv. Svcs., Cambridge, 1988-89; ptnr. TFC Fin. Mgmt., Boston, 1989—; mem. adv. bd. fin. planning Boston U.; mem. risk mgmt. task force AICPA, 1989—. Contbg. editor Fin. Planning mag., 1986—; author: How to Protect Your Family with Insurance, 1990. Mem. AICPA (risk mgmt. task force), Boston Bus. Assn. (pres. 1988—), Internat. Assn. Fin. Planning (bd. dirs. Boton chpt. 1987-88, sec. 1988-89), Am. Soc. CLUs and Chartered Fin. Cons., Inst. Cert. Fin. Planners. Democrat. Office: TFC Fin Mgmt 176 Federal St Boston MA 02110

APPLEGATE, MARY SOLLINGER, pediatrician, internist; b. Basel, Switzerland, Apr. 1, 1961; (parents Am. citizens); d. Willard D. and Rosemary (Rongone) Sollinger; m. David Terrence Applegate II, Aug. 9, 1986. BS in Nursing summa cum laude, Creighton U., 1983; MD cum laude, Ohio State U., 1987. Diplomate Nat. Bd. Med. Examiners. Resident in internal medicine Ohio State U., Columbus, 1987; resident in pediatrics Columbus Children's Hosp., Columbus, 1987; clin. instr. dept. internal medicine and dept. pediatrics Ohio State U. Coll. Medicine. Recipient Faculty Teaching award, 1989 and 90, Clin. Competence award, 1987. Mem. AMA, ACP, Am. Acad. Pediatrics, Ohio Med. Assn. (pres. housestaff orgn.), Acad. Medicine Columbus and Franklin County, Columbus Zoo, Alpha Omega Alpha, Alpha Sigma Nu. Home: 1652 Rhoda Ave Columbus OH 43212 Office: Ohio State U Dept Int Med Means Hall 1659 Upham Dr Columbus OH 43210

APPLETON, MYRA, magazine editor, writer; b. Phila., Dec. 21, 1934; d. Joseph and Sylvia (Pouls) Magid; m. John Johnston Appleton, July 29, 1962. B.A., Temple U., 1955. Researcher TV Guide, Phila., 1956-61; assoc. editor Show Bus. Illustrated, Chgo., 1961-62; contbg. editor Show mag., N.Y.C., 1962-64; free-lance writer N.Y.C., 1964-68; sr. editor Cosmopolitan mag., N.Y.C., 1968-88; editor Lear's mag., N.Y.C., 1988—. Author various mag. articles, film scripts. Mem. Womens Media Group. Office: Lear's Mag 655 Madison Ave New York NY 10021

APYAN, ROSEANNE LUCILLE, nurse; b. Kenosha, Wis., Jan. 25, 1949; d. Sarkis and Angel (Hovigimian) A. Diploma, Decatur Meml. Hosp. Sch. Nursing, 1972; BS, Millikin U., 1972; instr.'s credential, Calif. Community Colls., 1977. RN, Calif., Ill. Med./surg. nurse St. Joseph's Med. Ctr., Burbank, Calif., 1972-74, critical care nurse ICU, 1974-78, asst. head nurse ICU, 1978-80, head nurse ICU, 1980-82; vascular nurse specialist Drs. Dulawa, Andros, Harris and Oblath, Burbank, 1982—. Co-contbr. articles to profl. jours., 1984-86. Active health enhancement adv. coun. MidValley YWCA, Van Nuys, Calif., 1985—; vol. L.A. Marathon, 1989. Mem. Am. Assn. Critical Care Nurses (San Fernando Valley, Calif. chpt.), Am. Heart Assn., Soc. for Peripheral Vascular Nurses (nat. bd. trustees 1989—), Single Ski Club (L.A., sec. 1977-78, membership chmn. 1982-83). Republican. Home: 330 N Maple St #G Burbank CA 91505

AQUILINE, JUDITH, fundraiser; b. Pitts., Apr. 28, 1947; d. Daniel and Rose Marie (Stock) A. Grad. high sch., Pitts. Sec. U. Pitts., 1965-69; with UCLA, 1969—; adminstr. Inst. of Geophysics, 1969-80; asst. dir., fundraiser John Wooden Ctr. Campaign, 1980-83; assoc. dir., fundraiser Anderson Grad. Sch. of Mgmt., 1983-85, Ann. Fund & Chancellor's Assocs., 1985-87; dir., fundraiser Orange County Regional Office, 1987—. Bd. dirs. Master Chorale of Orange County, 1988—; vol. com. Irvine Temp. Housing, 1988-89, Children's Hosp. of Orange County, 1988-89. Office: UCLA Regional Office 1001 Dove St Ste 185 Newport Beach CA 92660

ARADILLOS, NANCY GLIME, pension administration consultant; b. West Haven, Conn., May 10, 1962; d. William Warren and Arbelia (Charles) Glime; m. Felix Magno Aradillos, Aug. 11, 1984. BS, U. New Haven, West Haven, 1985, MBA, 1988. Pension adminstr. Wells, Lamoriello & Co., Inc., New Haven, Conn., 1987—. V.P. First Luth. Ch., West Haven, 1988-89. Republican.

ARAMBURU, JENNIFER TRAVERS, retail buyer; b. Ridgewood, N.J., Aug. 1, 1964; d. Michael Kane and Dorothy (Moore) Travers; m. Mark Stephen Aramburu, Aug. 22, 1987. BA, Ithaca Coll., 1986. Exec. trainee Macy's N.Y., N.Y.C., 1986; sales mgr. Macy's N.Y., White Plains, 1986-87; asst. buyer Macy's N.E., N.Y.C., 1987-88; group mgr. Macy's N.E., S.I., 1989-90; jr. denim buyer Macy's N.E., 1990—. Home: 17 Eagles Notch Dr Englewood NJ 07631

ARANAS, MARIA ELENA LIZARES, physician; b. Talisay, Negros, The Philippines, Mar. 22, 1937; came to U.S., 1961; d. Felix A. and Josefina (Kilayko) Lizares; m. Romeo Saavedra Aranas, Aug. 28, 1965; children: Michelle J., Melinda L., Marsha L., Maria Theresa L. AA, U. St. Thomas, Manila, 1955, MD, 1960. Diplomate Am. Bd. Family Practice. Intern St. Francis Hosp., Poughkeepsie, N.Y., 1961-62, resident in pathology, 1962-63; resident in pathology Wyckoff Heights Hosp., Bklyn., 1963-67, asst. pathologist, 1967-69; pvt. practice The Philippines, 1969-73, Spring Valley, Ill., 1975-77; physician Lincoln Devel. Ctr., 1977; with Ill. Dept. MHDD-Zeller Mental Health Ctr., Peoria, 1978—, med. dir., 1986-87, assoc. med. dir., 1987-89, staff physician, 1989—. Mem. Tazewell Med. Soc., Am. Acad. Family Practice, Ill. Acad. Family Practice. Roman Catholic. Home: 607 W Thousand Oaks Dr Peoria IL 61615 Office: Zeller Mental Health Ctr 5407 N University Peoria IL 61614

ARANEO, BARBARA ANN, pathology educator; b. Newark, Oct. 30, 1948; d. Albert Alphonse and Elearnor Ilka (Gairing) A.; m. Robert Lewis Yowell, Dec. 31, 1978; children: Jennifer Lauren, Keith Richard. BA, Elmira Coll., 1970; PhD, U. Rochester, 1976. Instr. Jewish Hosp. of St. Louis, 1978-81, rsch. asst. prof., 1981-82; asst. prof. dept. pathology U. Utah, Salt Lake City, 1982—. Inventor method for enhancing IL-2 prodn. Grantee NIH, 1980, 82, 83, 88, EPA, 1990. Mem. Am. Assn. Pathologists, Am. Assn. Immunologists. Office: U Utah Dept Pathology 50 N Medical Dr Salt Lake City UT 84132

ARANETA, MYRNA ROBERTA HIPOLITO, consultant; b. Manila, June 7, 1949; came to U.S., 1984; d. Artemio and Asuncion A. BA in Psychology, St. Paul Coll., Manila, 1968; MA in Clin. Psychology, U. St. Tomas, Manila, 1973; postgrad., U. Philippines, Dilliman, 1976-78. Tchr. kindergarten St. Paul Coll., Manila, 1968-70; guidance counselor U. St. Tomas, Manila, 1970-71; with guidance dept. Loyola Heights, Quezon City, Philippines, 1975—, guidance counselor Ateneou U.; assoc. cons., with mgmt. devel. services Economic Devel. Found., Makati, Philippines, 1976-78; orgn. devel. tng. mgr. Procter & Gamble, PMC, Manila, 1979-81, mgr. orgn. and employee devel., 1981-84; orgn. devel. cons. Procter & Gamble, PMC, Makati, 1985-87; mgr. human resources devel. Norwich (N.Y.) Eaton Pharms., Inc. subs. Procter & Gamble Co., 1987-88; organization effectiveness cons. internat. pers. div. Procter & Gamble Co., Cin., 1988-89, proj. involvement profl. corp. sales restructure cen. U.S. region, 1989—. Fellow Psychol. Assn. Philippines; mem. Am. Soc. Tng. Devel., orgn. Devel. Network, World Futurist Soc., Nat. Assn. Female Execs. Office: The Procter & Gamble Co 120 W 5th and Race Tower Bldg Ste 801 Cincinnati OH 45202

ARANOW, RUTH LEE HOROWITZ, academic advisor, chemist, researcher; b. Bklyn., Aug. 25, 1929; d. David and Tillie Ethel (Wolf) Horwitz; m. George Aranow, Jr., June 25, 1950; children: David, Eric, Jeanne. BA, Bklyn. Coll., 1951; MA, Johns Hopkins U., 1952, PhD, 1957. Rsch. scientist Rsch. Inst. for Advanced Studies, Balt., 1957-69; rsch. scientist Johns Hopkins U., Balt., 1970, NIH fellow, rsch. scientist, 1973, lectr. chemistry Sch. Continuing Studies, 1976-87, lectr. chemistry Sch. Arts and Scis., 1978-85, sr. acad. advisor, 1987—, fellow-by-courtesy dept. chemistry, 1974—; rsch. advisor Feingold Assn. U.S., Arlington, Va., 1980—. Contbr. rsch. articles to sci. jours. Fulbright grantee, 1951; recipient Martin-Marietta rsch. award, Balt., 1963. Mem. AAAS (finalist congl. fellowship program 1977), Am. Phys. Soc., Sigma Xi. Office: Johns Hopkins U Baltimore MD 21218

ARANT, PATRICIA M., educator; b. Mobile, Ala., Dec. 2, 1930. B.A., Ala. Coll., 1952; A.M., Radcliffe Coll., 1957; Ph.D., Harvard U., 1963. Researcher U.S. Govt., Washington, 1952-56; asst. prof. Russian Vanderbilt U., Nashville, 1963-65; asst. prof., assoc. prof., prof. Slavic langs. and lits. Brown U., Providence, 1965—, chmn. dept., 1989—, assoc. dean Grad. Sch., 1981-88. Author: Russian for Reading, 1981. Grantee Am. Council Learned Socs.-Social Scis. Research Council, 1969, Internat. Research and Exchanges, 1973. Mem. Am. Assn. Tchrs. Slavic and East European Langs., Am. Assn. Advancement Slavic Studies, Am. Folklore Soc. Home: 5 D Squire Ln East Providence RI 02915 Office: Brown U Box E Providence RI 02912

ARCHABAL, NINA MARCHETTI, historical society administrator; b. Long Branch, N.J., Apr. 11, 1940; d. John William and Santina Matilda (Giuffre) Marchetti; m. John William Archabal, Aug. 8, 1964; 1 child, John Fidel. BA in Music History cum laude, Radcliffe Coll., 1962; MAT in Music, Harvard U., 1963; PhD in Music History, U. Minn., 1979. Asst. dir. humanities art mus. U. Minn., Mpls., 1975-77; asst. supr. edn. div. Minn. Hist. Soc., St. Paul, 1977-78, dep. dir. for program mgmt., 1978-86, acting dir., 1986-87, dir., 1987—. Trustee, bd. dirs. Am. Folklife Ctr., 1989—; bd. dirs. N.W. Area Found., 1989—, Libr. Congress; v.p. Friends St. Paul Pub. Libr., 1986—; mem. adv. com. Perrie Jones Libr. Fund, 1978-88. Nat. Def. Edn. Act fellow U. Minn. 1969-72, U. Minn. grad. fellow, 1974-75. Mem. Am. Assn. for State and Local History (sec. 1986-88), Am. Assn. Museums. Office: Minn Hist Soc 690 Cedar St Saint Paul MN 55101

ARCHER, CLAUDETTE CHERYL, computer marketing professional; b. Georgetown, Guyana, Dec. 8, 1951; d. Claude Archer and Mary (Thompson) Lachmansingh; m. Albert William Walthall, Nov. 21, 1971 (div. Sept. 1978); 1 child, Justin Marcus. BA, Mills Coll., 1979; MBA, U. Calif., Berkeley, 1987. Sales devel. engr. Hewlett-Packard, Cupertino, Calif., 1981-83, 3d party mktg. engr., 1983-84; product mgr. Xerox Corp., Fremont, Calif., 1984-87, Computer Assocs., San Jose, Calif., 1987-88; mgr. product mktg. Pyramid Tech., Mountain View, Calif., 1988—. Recipient scholarship Kennedy King Found., 1977; recipient scholarship State of Calif., 1977, fellowship, 1979. Democrat. Roman Catholic. Home: 7977 Sunkist Dr Oakland CA 94605

ARCHER, ELLEN M. (ELLIE), small business owner; b. L.A., Sept. 13, 1946; d. Maurice Sloan and Vera Dell (Bowers) A.; m. Frank W. Dawson (div.); 1 child, Sloan W. BA in Journalism, U. Minn., 1968. Student affairs dir. Clarkson Sch. Nursing, Omaha, 1970-75; dir. dept. tourism Omaha/Douglas County, Nebr., 1979-84; owner, pres. Archer Dawson, Inc., Omaha, 1984—. V.p. local PTA; mem. adv. com. early childhood edn. Met. Community Coll. Mem. Internat. Nanny Assn., Omaha Connections, Zonta Internat. Office: Archer Dawson Nanny Agy 5136 Spaulding St Omaha NE 68104

ARCHER, KATHLEEN FRANCES, ophthalmologist; b. Dallas, Mar. 20, 1955; d. Joyce S. (Smith) Brown. BS cum laude, Ariz. State U., 1976; MD, U. Ariz., 1981. Diplomate Am. Bd. Ophthalmology. Intern St. Mary's Hosp. and Med. Ctr., San Francisco, 1981-82; resident Kresge Eye Inst. Wayne State U., Detroit, 1983-86; fellow U. Toronto, Ontario, Can., 1986-87; pvt. practice Corpus Christi, Tex., 1987—; staff Spohn Hosp., Corpus Christi, 1982-83, staff ophthalmologist, 1987—; staff ophthalmologist Humana Hosp., Corpus Christi, 1988—, Driscoll Children's Hosp., 1988—, Rehab. Hosp. South Tex., 1989—; asst. clin. prof. U. Tex. Health Sci. Ctr., San Antonio, 1987—. Contbr. articles to profl. jours. Fellow Am. Acad. Ophthalmology; mem. AMA, Tex. Med. Assn., Nueces Co. Med. Soc., Am. Soc. Ophthalmic Plastic and Reconstructive Surgeons (cert. 1990). Republican. Office: Archer Ophthalmology 5022 Holly Rd Corpus Christi TX 78411

ARCHER, MARY JANE, state agency administrator; b. Oakland, Calif., Aug. 23, 1949; d. Francis Evert and Doris Marlene (Howard) Wood; m. Bradley Eugene Archer; Nov. 10, 1984. BS in Acctg., Calif. State U., Hayward, 1971, MBA in Acctg., 1977. Auditor Calif. State Controller's Office, Sacramento, 1972-81, supr., 1981-84, asst. div. chief, 1984—. Mem. operation rev. com. United Way. Mem. Calif. Assn. Mgmt. Republican. Office: Calif State Contr's Office Div Tax Adminstrn PO Box 942850 Sacramento CA 94250-5880

ARCHER, MARY JANE, physical therapist; b. Bethany, Mo., June 7, 1950; d. Ralph Edward and Edna Mae (Golliher) A. Student, Northwestern Mo. State U., 1968-71; BS, U. Mo., 1973; MA in Rehab. Adminstrn., So. Ill. U., 1981. Lic. physical therapist. Staff physical therapist St. John's Hosp., Anderson, Ind., 1973—; staff physical therapist Community Hosp., Indpls., 1975-76, edn. coord. physical and occupational therapy, 1976-78; acad. clin. coord., instr. sch. medicine Ind. U., Indpls., 1978-80; acad. clin. coord., asst. prof. U. Indpls., 1980-85; pres., staff Cen. Physical Therapists, Inc., Indpls., 1985—. Mem. Ind. Chpt. Polit. Action Com., Indpls., 1985-87; mem. Ch. at the Crossing. Mem. NAFE, Am. Nursing Care (adv. bd. 1986—), Am. Physical Therapy Assn. (treas. state dist. 1980-82, Ind. chpt. 1987, del. to nat. 1979, 82-87). Home: 8633 El Rico Dr Indianapolis IN 46240 Office: Cen Phys Therapists Inc 11591 Allisonville Rd Fishers IN 46038

ARCHER, TERI LYNN, electrical engineer; b. Cheyenne, Wyo., Nov. 22, 1965; d. Maurice Gustaaf and Maxine Euretta (Mann) Everaert; m. Stephen Thomas Archer, June 18, 1988. BSEE, U. Wyo., 1988; MSEE, U. Calif., Davis, 1990. Rsch. asst. U. Calif., Davis, 1989—. Superior student scholar U. Wyo., 1984-88; fellow NSF, 1988—. Mem. IEEE, Mortar Bd., Tau Beta Pi, Phi Kappa Phi.

ARCHEY, LISA ANN, community development administrator; b. New Castle, Ind., Jan. 8, 1957; d. Donald Coleman and Ethel Marie (Boatright) Archey. BS, Ball State U., 1979, MA, 1980. Sr. planner City of Muncie, Ind., 1980-84; planning cons. Hughes Assocs., South Bend, Ind., 1984-85; program devel. mgr. City of Fort Wayne, Ind., 1985-87; v.p. Bus. Opportunities Systems, Indpls., 1987-89; exec. dir. Westside Community Devel. Corp., Indpls., 1989—; bd. dirs. Ptnrs. for Westside Housing Renewal, Indpls., Ind. Assn. for Community Econ. Devel., Indpls.; fin. adv. member Indpls. Neighborhood Housing Partnership; housing com. member Regional Ctr. Plan 2010. Active Urban League, Indpls., 1987—, United Negro Coll. Fund, Indpls., 1989—; founder Indpls. Coalition for Neighborhood Devel.; bd. dirs. Sickle Cell Anemia Found., 1985-87, Ind. Black Expo, Ft. Wayne, 1986-87; founder Indpls. Coalition for Neighborhood Devel. Mem. Westside Merchants, Nat. Congress for Community Econ. Devel. Office: Westside Community Devel 1635 W Michigan St Indianapolis IN 46222

ARCHIBALD, CLAUDIA JANE, parapsychologist; b. Atlanta, Nov. 14, 1939; d. Claud Bernard and Doris Evelyn (Linch) A. B in Psychology, Georgia State U., 1962; BTh., Emory U., 1964; DD, Stanton Coll., 1969. Pvt. practice psycho-spiritual counselor Atlanta, 1960—; minister Nat. Spiritualist Assn., Atlanta, 1969-72; parapsychologist Ctr. for Life, Atlanta, 1985-86; parapsychologist Inst. of Metaphysical Inquiry, Atlanta, 1980—, also bd. dirs., founder, 1980—. Author: (book) Quantitative Symbolism, 1980; dir. Phoenix Dance Unltd., 1984—; choregrapher (dance) Phoenix Rising, 1985. Vol. Aid Atlanta, 1987—. Recipient City Grant award Bur. Cultural Affairs, Atlanta, 1985, 86. Mem. Am. Psychical Research Assn., Soc. Metaphysicians (corr. Eng. chpt.), Am. Assn. Parapsychology, Nat. Assn. Alcoholism and Drug Abuse Counselors, Ga. Addiction Counselors' Assn., N.Am. Ballet Assn. Home: 2638 Valmar Dr Atlanta GA 30340

ARCHIE, VICTORIA ESTHER, social worker; b. N.Y.C., June 4, 1960; d. James Lee and Marjorie Ann (Booth) A. Student, New York U., 1978-79, Andrews U., 1979-81; BA with honors, L.I. U., 1983. Case worker N.Y.C. Spl. Svcs. for Children, 1986—, supr. I, 1989—; child care mgmt. worker Pam O'Neill, N.Y.C., 1983—; home health care mgmt. Richmond Home Need Services, S.I., 1985-86. Prin. works exhibited at L.I. U. Named Outstanding Young Woman in Am., 1986. Mem. NAFE. Democrat. Seventh Day Adventist. Home: 61-15 98th St #12 E Rego Park NY 11374 Office: NYC Spl Svcs for Children 165-15 Archer Ave Jamaica NY 11433

ARCIERI, SANDY LEE, collector celebrity personal effects, researcher; b. Chgo., July 23, 1955; d. Adam Eugene and Marie Prudence (Worek) Prucznal; m. Dennis James Arcieri, July 22, 1979. BA in Math. Edn., St. Xavier Coll., Chgo., 1977. Tchr. Sts. Peter and Paul Sch., Chgo., 1977-79; collector Jean Harlow personal effects-rsch. on her life, 1971—. Contbg. researcher Life at the Marmont, 1987, Mayer and Thalberg: The Make-Believe Saints, 1988, Deadly Illusions, 1990. Roman Catholic. Home: 9530 Clifton Park Evergreen Park IL 60642

ARCIERO, JEAN MARY, educator; b. Yorkville, N.Y., Mar. 31, 1932; d. Paul and Theresa (Capuana) A. AAS, SUNY, Alfred, 1952; BA, Syracuse U., 1970; MS, SUNY, Cortland, 1976. Med. technologist various rsch./clin. labs., N.Y., 1960-80; guidance counselor USAF Edn. Svcs., 1980-86; tchr. N.Y. Sch. Sys., 1976-86; dir. edn. svcs. USAF Edn. Svcs., South Korea, 1986-88; asst. dir. edn. svcs. USAF Edn. Svcs., Griffiss AFB, N.Y., 1988—; cons. in field. Author: Education Services Information Book, 1987. Active Utica (N.Y.) Symphony League, League Women Voters, Glimmerglass Opera Guild, UN. Mem. Nat. U. Continuing Edn. Assn., AAUW, Am. Assn. for Counseling Devel., Assn. for Continuing Higher Edn., Mil. Edn. and Counselor Assn., Fed. Women's Progs.

ARDEN, SHERRY W., publishing company executive; b. N.Y.C., Oct. 18, 1930; d. Abraham and Rose (Bellak) Waretnick; m. Hal Marc Arden (div. 1974); children: Doren, Cathy; m. George Bellak, Oct. 20, 1979. Student, Columbia U. Publicity dir. Coward-McCann, N.Y.C., 1965-67; producer Allan Foskko Assoc., ABC-TV, N.Y.C., 1967-68; sr. v.p., pub. William Morrow & Co., N.Y.C., 1968-85; pres., pub. William Morrow & Co., 1985-89; owner Sherry W. Arden Lit. Agy., 1990—. Mem. Assn. Am. Pubs. (dir.). Club: Pubs. Lunch.

ARDISON, LINDA GAIL, author, writing consultant; b. Ft. Smith, Ark., Apr. 11, 1940; d. Bill Eugene and Mildred M. (Fry) Tanner; m. Gary Winship Ardison, June 10, 1962; children: Amy Roberts, Elizabeth Winship, Matthew Tanner. AA, Stephens Coll., 1960; postgrad., Middlebury Coll., 1960-61, Bread Loaf Sch. of English, 1960; BA, U. Ark., 1962. Adminstrv. asst. Wachovia Nat. Bank, Winston-Salem, N.C., 1962-63; English tchr. Wiley Jr. High Sch., Winston-Salem, 1963-64; writing cons. York (Pa.) Coll. of Pa., 1984—; vis. poet York Country Day Sch., 1986. Editor Standard lit. mag., 1959-60; asst. editor Keystone News, 1980-82; contbr. articles, poems, plays, short stories to jours. Bd. dirs. York County Med. Soc. Aux., York, 1978-80; mem. Jr. League of York, 1974-75; adult educator Living Word Community Ch., York, 1980—; bd. dirs. Human Life Svcs., York, 1989—. Recipient 3d place for fiction in annual coll. contest The Atlantic Monthly, 1960; Bread Loaf scholar The Atlantic Monthly, 1960. Mem. York County Med. Soc. Aux., Pa. Med. Soc. Aux. Republican. Home: 260 School St York PA 17402 Office: York Coll of Pa Country Club Rd York PA 17403

AREGLADO, NANCY, reading specialist and consultant; b. Boston, Dec. 10, 1946; d. William Vincent and Julia Marie (Dierkes) Hyland; m. Ronald James Areglado, Aug. 24, 1968; children: Kristin Holly, Kimberly Anne, Julie Lynn. BS, Boston State Coll., 1968; MEd, U. Mass., 1982. Tchr. Quincy (Mass.) Pub. Schs., 1968-70; lang. specialist Mass. Migrant Edn. Program, Holyoke, 1981-83; spl. edn. tutor Greenfield (Mass.) Sch. Dept., 1984; tchr. North Adams (Mass.) Pub. Schs., 1986-89, early childhood coord., 1987-89; adj. instr. North Adams State Coll., 1988-89; pvt. practice whole lang. cons. pvt. practice integrated lang. arts con., Mass., 1987—; 1st grade tchr. Village Sch., West Stockbridge, Mass., 1989-90; whole lang. coord. Berkshire Hills Schs., Stockbridge, 1990—; pres. Areglado Assocs., Williamstown, 1982-89. Co-organizer Cambodia Assisstance Dr., Franklin County, Mass., 1979; bd. dirs. Big Bros./Big Sisters Assn., Greenfield, Mass., 1975-85. Recipient Exemplary Svc. award Big Bros./Big Sisters, 1976, Celebrate Literacy award, Berkshire Reading Coun., 1990. Mem. Wole Lang. Tchrs. Assn. (networking chair Berkshires 1987—, mem. Wole Lang. Umbrella 1988—), Nat. Coun. Tchrs. English, Internat. Reading Assn. Democrat. Roman Catholic. Home: 11107 Robert Carter Rd Fairfax Station VA 22039 Office: Reading Ctr Rolling Valley Sch Fairfax County Pub Schs Springfield VA 22039

ARENSON, KAREN WATTEL, journalist; b. Long Beach, N.Y., Jan. 3, 1949; d. Harold Louis and Sara (Gordon) Wattel; m. Gregory Keith Arenson, Sept. 4, 1970; 1 child, Morgan Elizabeth. S.B., MIT, 1970; M.Pub. Policy, Harvard U., 1972. Assoc. dir. Nat. Affiliation of Concerned Bus. Students, Chgo., 1972-73; corr. Bus. Week Mag., 1973-77, editor, 1977-78; reporter N.Y. Times, N.Y.C., 1978-84, asst. fin. editor, 1985-86; editor Sunday Bus. Sect. N.Y. Times, 1987-89, asst. bus. editor, 1989—; mem. vis. com. dept. econs. MIT, 1980-88, dept. nuclear engring., dept. linguistics and philosophy, 1989—, also edn1. counselor; mem. and bd. dirs. MIT Corp., 1989—. Author: The New York Times Guide to Making the New Tax Law Work for You, 1981. Recipient Matrix award Women in Communications, 1982; recipient Journalism award Washington Monthly, 1981. Mem. MIT Alumni Assn. (bd. dirs. 1986-88). Home: 125 W 76th St New York NY 10023 Office: NY Times 229 W 43d St New York NY 10036

ARENTH, LINDA MAGNUSSON, nursing services executive; b. Orange, Calif., Nov. 6, 1932; d. Crosby Winfred and Roberta (Maxey) Magnusson; m. Donald Craig Arenth, Oct. 24, 1964 (div. Sept. 1985); children: Craig Magnus, Sean Lydick. AA, Cottey Coll., Nevada, Mo., 1952; BS, U. So. Calif., L.A., 1955; MS, U. Md., 1974. Staff nurse, asst. head nurse UCLA Med. Ctr., 1955-58, head nurse, 1958-63, supr., 1963-64; staff nurse The Johns Hopkins Hosp., Balt., 1965-66, instr., 1966-67, 71-72, dir. nursing, oncology dept., 1973-87, v.p. for nursing and patient svcs., 1987—; adj. prof. The Johns Hopkins U. Sch. Nursing; cons. adv. com. Pew Charitable Trust grant, 1988-89. Contbr. articles to profl. jours. Bd. dirs. Brown Meml. Day Care Ctr., Balt., 1974-76, Meml. Counseling Ctr., Balt., 1980-82, Health Care for the Homeless Balt., 1989—; profl. edn. com. Am. Cancer Soc., Balt., 1976-87. Rsch. grant Am. Cancer Soc., 1982-84. Mem. Oncology Nursing Soc. (Excellence in Cancer Nursing Adminstrn. award 1988), Am. Orgn. Nurse Execs., Nat. League for Nursing. Republican. Episcopalian. Office: Johns Hopkins Hosp 600 N Wolfe St Baltimore MD 21205

ARESTY, ESTHER BRADFORD, author, scriptwriter; b. Syracuse, N.Y.; d. Jacob and Bertha (Levin) Bradford; m. Jules Aresty, June 24, 1936; children: Robert Joseph, Jane Aresty Silverman. Student DePaul U., 1929-31. Radio commentator Sta.-WJJD, Chgo., 1931-35; advt. mgr. Mandel Bros., Chgo., 1934-36; free-lance radio advt. writer, Chgo., 1936-41; radio scriptwriter Elsa Maxwell Show, Mut. Broadcasting Corp., N.Y.C., 1945-47; free-lance radio scriptwriter, N.Y.C., 1947—. Author: (young adult novels) he Grand Venture, 1963, (as Elaine Arthur) Romance in store, 1963; (cookbook) The Delectable Past, 1964 (Cookbook Guild choice 1964); (etiquette history) The Best Behavior, 1970; (French gastronomy) The Exquisite Table, 1980. Contbr. articles on cookbooks, Careme, Fanny Farmer, Etiquette, Escoffier, Cordon Bleu to Ency. Americana. Bd. dirs. Trenton Community Found., 1960-72, pres., 1962-64; bd. dirs. Mercer County Guidance Ctr., Trenton, 1965-80, McCarter Theatre Assocs., Princeton, N.J., 1972-83. Mem. Authors Guild, PEN, Am. Inst. Wine and food (adv. bd.). Avocations: collecting rare cookbooks, piano, painting, chamber music. Address: 2784 S Ocean Blvd # 303E Palm Beach FL 33430-5531

ARFFA, SHARON MARY, psychologist; b. Buffalo, Nov. 15, 1954; d. Leon and Florence Christine (Kornaszewski) Kuznik; m. Robert Craig Arffa, June 7, 1981; children: Rachel, Lauren, Matthew. BA in Psychology, SUNY, Buffalo, 1976; MS in Psychology, SUNY, Owego, 1980; PhD in Psychology, Ind. U., 1984. Lic. psychologist. Clin. psychology intern Mt. Sinai Hosp., Hartford, Conn., 1978-79; clin. psychologist Children's Hosp., Boston, 1979-82; neuropsychology intern Ind. U. Med. Ctr., Indpls., 1983-84; neuropsychologist River Oaks Psychiat. Hosp., New Orleans, 1984-86, Children's Hosp., Pitts., 1986-87, Allegheny Gen. Hosp., Pitts., 1987—; asst. prof. psychiatry Med. Coll. Pa., Phila., 1988—. Contbr. articles to profl. jours. Dissertation scholar Ind. U., 1984; fellow Ind. U., 1982-84; teaching grantee Mass. Dept. Mental Health, 1981. Mem. Am. Psychol. Asn., Orgn. for Rehab. Through Tng. Jewish. Office: Allegheny Gen Hosp 320 E North St Pittsburgh PA 15212

ARGERSINGER, MARNIE HAYES, retired educator; b. Syracuse, N.Y., June 7, 1922; d. Charles Howard and Amilda Frances (Jarvis) Hayes; m. William John Argersinger, Jr.; children: William John III, Peter Hayes, Ann

Elizabeth. BA, Kans. U., 1950, MA, 1958. Asst. to dir. summer lang. inst. U. Kans., Barcelona, Spain, 1966; asst. to dir. 12th seminar on higher edn. in the Americas U. Kans., Lawrence, 1974. Co-founder Lawrence Coop. Nursery Sch., 1948; city commr. City of Lawrence, 1975-79, mayor, 1977-78; bd. dirs. Lawrence Housing Authority, 1979-82; trustee Lawrence Meml. Hosp., 1982-. Named Woman of Yr. Jaycees, 1979; recipient Substantial Citizen award Kiwanis Club, 1989. Mem. LWV (bd. dirs. 1955-63, bd. dirs. Kans. state unit 1969-71, pres. Lawrence chpt. 1961-63), Douglas County Hist. Soc. (bd. dirs. 1983-89, vice-chmn. 1989), Anthropology Mus. U. Kans. (chairwoman community adv. bd. 1987-89). Democrat.

ARGO, BETTY EARNEST, business owner; b. Jasper, Ala., Nov. 19, 1934; d. Curtis and Ola (Franklin) Sailors; m. John M. Earnest, Mar. 11, 1955 (dec. 1965); children: Brenda Earnest Foshee, Amy Earnest Freeman; m. Murry C. Argo. Student, Auburn (Ala.) U. Freelance ins. agt., 1965-74, 80—, freelance in mktg. and mgmt., 1975-80; owner Argo Ins. Agy., Jasper, 1986—. Mem. Nat. Underwriters Assn., Beta Sigma Phi. Home: 600 3d Ave Jasper AL 35501

ARGUN, FATIMA HATICE, federal government international trade policy analyst and specialist; b. Bursa, Turkey, June 6, 1959. BA in Polit. Sci. and Internat. Studies, U. Tex., 1983; Cert. de Langue Francaise, U. Paris-Sorbonne, 1983; MPA, U. Tex., 1985. Asst. to pub. sector liaison Office of the U.S. Trade Rep., Washington, 1986; freelance writer Internat. Reports, N.Y.C., 1986-87; dir. internat. trade Competitive Enterprise Inst., Washington, 1987-88; campaign liaison George Bush for President and Bush-Quayle '88 campaigns, Washington, 1987-88; coord. transition office contacts Office of the Pres.-Elect, Washington, 1988-89; confidential asst. to the dir. for internat. trade Minority Bus. Devel. Agy., U.S. Dept. Commerce, Washington, 1989—. Co-author: U.S. Trade with Newly Industrializing Countries, 1985, An Evaluation of Traffic Accident Records Systems in Texas and Other States, 1984; editor: Annual Report of Societe Nationale ELF Aquitaine, France, 1984; contbg. editor: Images; co-author proposal for land devel. project to build the World Trade Ctr. in Istanbul, Turkey, for Istanbul Land Devel. Soc. Mem. LWV, Austin, Tex., 1980-81. Mem. Women in Internat. Trade (charter mem., bd. dirs., spl. events chmn. 1987-88), World Affairs Coun. Washington, Fgn. Policy Assn. N.Y., Great Decisions Fgn. Policy Discussion Group, NAFE, Washington Internat. Trade Assn., Tex. State Soc., Am. Friends of Turkey, Les Compagnons (French club), LBJ Sch. Alumni Assn. (v.p. 1989—), Tex. Breakfast Club Washington, Bravo for Washington Opera Soc. Republican. Office: US Dept Commerce 14th & Constitution Ave NW Rm 5053 Washington DC 20230

ARGYILAN, KRISTI ANN, advertising agency executive; b. Aurora, Ill., Oct. 27, 1958; d. James George and Betty Jane (Poss) A. BA in Music, No. Ill. U., 1980. Fund raiser Chgo. City Ballet, 1980-81; media planner Campbell/Mithun-Esty, Chgo., 1981-85; media supr. Foote, Cone & Belding, Chgo., 1985—. Bd. dir. Gratis Chgo., 1989-90, volunteer advt./mktg. profl. svc., Lyric Oepra Chgo., Chgo. Symphony. Roman Catholic. Home: 1555 N Sandburg Terr Chicago IL 60610 Office: Foote Cone & Belding 101 E Erie St Chicago IL 60611

ARIANO, MARJORIE ANN, neurobiologist, educator; b. Tokyo, Feb. 13, 1951; d. Richard A. and Marjorie W. (Farr) A.; m. George J. Rederich, Dec. 21, 1974 (div. 1979). BS, UCLA, 1972, PhD, 1977. Postdoctoral fellow U. So. Calif., L.A., 1977-80; asst. prof. U. Vt., Burlington, 1980-86, assoc. prof., 1986—; vis. scientist Coll. de France, Paris, 1987-88; vis. scientist Coll. de France, Paris, 1987-88; editorial assoc. Health Sci.: Courts and the Law, Georgetown U., Washington, 1989—; adv. mem. NSF, Washington, 1985-87; mem., adv. Nat. Inst. Neurological Disorders and Stroke, Neurol. Scis., Bethesda, Md., 1987—. Contbr. articles to profl. publs. Mem. exec. bd. Am. Heart Assn., Burlington, 1982-87; docent Shelburne (Vt.) Farms, 1989—. Grantee NSF, 1981-90, Nat. Inst. Neurol. Disorders and Stroke, 1983—. Mem. Soc. Neurosci.

ARICO, MARGARET MARY, communications executive; b. Middletown, Conn., June 10, 1952; d. Peter Anthony and Mary Jane (Regan) A. Student, U. Conn., 1970-74. Assoc. dir. publs. U. Hartford, Bloomfield, Conn., 1980-86; dir. advt. and pub. rels. Bronson & Hutensky, Hartford, Conn., 1986-88; dir. communications St. Joseph Coll., West Hartford, Conn., 1988-89, The Ethel Walker Sch., Simsbury, Conn., 1989—; publs. cons. The Am. Lung Assn. of Conn., East Hartford, 1989. Recipient Merit award Conn. Art Dirs. Club, 1985-86. Mem. Advt. Club of Greater Hartford (1st prize 1983), Women in Communications, Inc. (Conn. chpt.). Democrat. Roman Catholic.

ARKUS, JANE CALLOMON, communications agency executive; b. Pitts., Mar. 29, 1929; d. Verner B. and Florence Madeline (Schoenthal) C.; m. Leon A. Arkus, Dec. 9, 1971. BA cum laude, Vassar Coll., 1950. Copywriter, Lando Inc., Pitts., 1951-53, TV-radio dir., 1953-59, v.p., creative dir., 1959-78; v.p., creative dir. Marsteller Inc., Pitts., 1978-81, v.p., sr. creative dir., 1981-85; v.p., sr. creative dir. HCM, Pitts., 1985-86; v.p., sr. creative cons. Burson-Marsteller, Pitts., 1986—; guest lectr. Chatham Coll., Pitts., 1982, Duquesne U., Pitts., 1984, 85; judge advt. creative competitions Radio Club, Dallas, 1983, Phila. Advt. Club, 1984, Hollywood Internat. TV Festival, 1986. Co-author mus. revue Open Season, 1961; author video Pittsburgh, The Livable 1, 1985 (N.Y. Internat. Film & TV Festival award 1986). Trustee Winchester Thurston Sch., Pitts., 1979-85, Pitts. Cultural Trust, 1987—; mem. women's com. Mus. of Art, Carnegie Inst., Pitts., 1969—; bd. dirs. Goodwill Industries of Pitts., 1978-80, Pitts. Council Internat. Visitors, 1967-70, Pitts. Playhouse, 1957-67, Gateway to Music, 1984-89, Friends of Vassar Art Gallery, 1984-90, Pitts. Symphony Assn., 1956—, mem. adv. bd.; mem. Allegheny Conf. Econ. Devel. Com. Task Force on Quality of Life, Pitts., 1983; bd. dirs. City Theatre Co., 1985—. Recipient First Place award Bus./Profl. Advt. Assn., 1980; Addy awards Am. Advt. Fedn., 1977, 78, 79, 80, 87; Telly award, 1977, 79, 81-84, 90; Total Communications Campaign award Nat. Banking Assn. award, 1982; N.Y. Internat. Broadcasting award, 1983;Clio, Am. TV Commls. Festival, 1969; Effie, Am. Mktg. Assn., 1976, Silver medal Internat. Film and TV Festival of N.Y., 1985, Keep Am. Beautiful Communications award, 1985, Pitts. YWCA Tribute to Women Leadership award/communications, 1987; named Advt. Woman of Yr., Pitts. Advt. Club, 1966, Alumna of Yr., Winchester-Thurston Sch. Vassar Coll., 1989. Mem. Women in Communications Inc., Exec. Women's Council of Pitts. Club: Rivers (Pitts.). Avocations: writing light poetry and musical revue lyrics, music, travel. Home: 420 Coventry Rd Pittsburgh PA 15213 Office: Burson-Marsteller 1 Gateway Ctr Pittsburgh PA 15222

ARLEDGE, PATRICIA O'BRIEN, clergywoman; b. Pitts., Oct. 14, 1934; d. Raymond F. and Anna C. (Hoffman) O'Brien; d. James A. Arledge, Mar. 22, 1958 (dec. Nov. 1989); 1 child, Zeta Ann Turner; 1 stepchild, Rosemary Smith. Bible diploma, Gt. Work Sch. Ministry, Monroeville, Pa., 1983; ThB, Internat. Sem., Plymouth, Fla., ThM, MA. Ordained to ministry Bapt. Ch., 1987. Interim pastor, dir. Christian edn. Shiloh Bapt. Ch., Apollo, Pa. Leader Eastmont coun. Girl Scouts U.S.A., 1964, troup organizer, 1965-66; camping leader, 1967, neighborhood chmmn., 1968-74; vol. chaplain Presbyn. U., Eye and Ear and Children's hosps., Pitts., 1983-88; vol. nursing homes and hosps. Mem. Nat. Women's Ministerial Alliance, Pitts. Regional Assn. Internat. Assn. Women Ministers (charter), Chaplains Soc., Church Women United (v.p. Apollo 1989-90), Kiski Valley Union Chs., NAFE, Allegheny Pekingese Kennel Club (pres. 1974-80), Order Ea. Star (matron 1967). Office: Shiloh Bapt Ch 719 N Warren Ave Apollo PA 15613

ARLEN, JENNIFER HALL, law educator; b. Berkeley, Calif., Jan. 7, 1959; d. Michael John and Ann (Warner) A.; m. Robert Lee Hotz, May 21, 1988. BA, Harvard U., 1982; JD, NYU, 1986, postgrad. econ. studies, 1982—. Bar: N.Y. 1987, U.S. Ct. Appeals (11th cir.) 1987. Summer clk. U.S. Dist. Ct. (ea. dist.) N.Y., Bklyn., 1984; summer assoc. Davis Polk & Wardwell, N.Y.C., 1985; law clk. U.S. Cir. Judge, 11th cir., Savannah, Ga., 1986-87; asst. prof. law Emory U. Law Sch., Atlanta, 1987—. Mem. ABA, Ga. Women's Bar Assn., Order of Coif. Democrat. Office: Emory U Sch Law Gambrell Hall Atlanta GA 30022

ARLINGHAUS, SANDRA JUDITH LACH, mathematical geographer, educator; b. Elmira, N.Y., Apr. 18, 1943; d. Donald Frederick and Alma Elizabeth (Satorius) Lach; m. William Charles Arlinghaus, Sept. 3, 1966; 1 child, William Edward. AB in Math., Vassar Coll., 1964; postgrad., U. Chgo., 1964-66, U. Toronto, 1966-67, Wayne State U., 1968-70; MA in Geography, Wayne State U., 1976; PhD in Geography, U. Mich., 1977. Vis. instr. math. U. Ill., Chgo., 1966; vis. asst. prof. geography Ohio State U., Columbus, 1977-78, lectr. math., 1978-79; lectr. math. Loyola U., Chgo., 1979-81, asst. prof. math., 1981-82; lectr. math. and geography U. Mich., Dearborn and Ann Arbor, 1982-83; guest lectr. U. Mich., Ann Arbor, 1990; founding dir. Inst. Mathematical Geography, Ann Arbor, 1985—; cons. U. Mich. Transp. Rsch. Inst., 1985-86, U. Mich. Coll. Arch., 1985-86; math. cons.; producer Ann Arbor Community Access TV, 1988—. Author: Down the Mail Tubes: The Pressured Postal Era, 1853-1984, Essays on Mathematical Geography, 1986, Essays on Mathematical Geography, II, 1987, An Atlas of Steiner Networks, 1989; co-author: Mathematical Geography and Global Art, 1986, Environmental Effects on Bus Durability, 1990; founder, editor jour. Solstice, 1990—; editor monographs; contbr. articles to profl. jours.; founder Image Interactive Atlases, Image Game Series. Bd. dirs., membership chmn. Bromley Homeowners Assn., Ann Arbor, 1989—; bd. dirs. World Jr. Bridge Championships, Ann Arbor, 1990—; artist Math. Awareness Week, Lawrence Tech. U., 1988—. Mem. AAAS, Am. Math. Soc., Math. Assn. Am., Am. Geog. Soc., Assn. Am. Geographers, N.Y. Acad. Scis. Home: 2790 Briarcliff Ann Arbor MI 48105 Office: Inst Mathematical Geography 2790 Briarcliff Ann Arbor MI 48105

ARMAGOST, ELSA GAFVERT, retired computer industry communications consultant; b. Duluth, Minn.; d. Axel Justus and Martina Emelia (Magnuson) Gafvert; m. Byron William Armagost, Dec. 8, 1945; children: David Byron, Laura Martina. Grad. with honors, Duluth Jr. Coll., 1936; BJ, U. Minn., 1938, postgrad. in pub. rels., bus. mgmt. and computer tech., 1965-81; PhD in Computer Communication Cons. Sci. (hon.), Internat. U. Found. Freelance editor, Duluth, 1939-42; procedure editor and analyst U.S. Steel, Duluth, 1942-45; fashion advt. staff Dayton Co., Mpls., 1945-48; systems applications and documentation mgr. Control Data Corp., Mpls., 1969-74, promotion specialist, mktg. editor, 1974-76, corp. staff coord. info. on edn., 1976-78; instr. communications, publ. specialist, 1978-79, communications cons. peripheral products group, 1979-83; industry communications cons., 1983-88, ret., 1988; mem. steering com. U.S. Senatorial Bus. Adv. Bd., 1962-68; mem. U.S. Congrl. Adv. Bd., 1958-62; mem. adv. bd. North Cen. Deming Mgmt. Forum. V.p. Sewickley (Pa.) Valley Hosp. Aux., bd. dirs. Sewickley Valley Mental Health Coun., LWV Pitts.; bd. dirs. publicity Sacred Arts Expo, World Affairs Coun. radio program, Pitts., 1962-68. Recipient Medal of Merit Rep. Presdl. Task Force. Mem. AAUW (1st v.p. Caracas, Venezuela), Women in Communication (bd. dir. job mart), Am. Security Coun. (mem. adv. bd.), Internat. Platform Assn., Friends of Mpls. Inst. Art., Walker Art Inst., Minn. Alumni Assn. (life), Am. Swedish Inst., Marsh Pk. Condominium Assn. (bd. mem.), Toastmasters (Communications award 1984), Internat. Soc. Newspaper Editors, Nat. Profl. Frat., Internat. Bible Study Fellowship, Phi Beta. Home and Office: 9500 Collegeview Rd Bloomington MN 55437

ARMIJO, JACQULYN DORIS, interior designer; b. Gilmer, Tex., July 2, 1938; d. Jack King and Iris Adele (Cook) Smith; children—John, Christy, Mike; m. Chet Wigton. Student North Tex. State Coll., U. N.Mex. Profl. model, 1961-75; sec. State Farm Ins., Albuquerque, 1965-71; life ins. agt. Mountain States, Albuquerque, 1980; owner Interiors by Jacqulyn, Albuquerque, 1961—; cons., lectr. in field. Mem. Alby Little Theatre, Friends of Little Theatre, Symphony Women; fund raiser for Old Town Hist. Com., Arthritis Fund. Mem. Am. Soc. Interior Design (chmn. historic restoration Albuquerque), Internat. Soc. Interior Design, Internat. Platform Assn., Civil War Club (pres. local chpt.) Republican. Roman Catholic. Clubs: Albuquerque Jr. Women's, Los Amapolas Garden. Home and Office: 509 Chamiso Ln NW Albuquerque NM 87107

ARMISTEAD, KATHERINE KELLY (MRS. THOMAS B. ARMISTEAD, III), travel consultant, interior designer, civic worker; b. Pitts., Apr. 14, 1926; d. Joseph Anthony and Katherine Arnold (Manning) Kelly; grad. Finch Jr. Coll., 1946; m. Thomas Boyd Armistead, III, Nov. 29, 1952; children: Katherine Kelly (Mrs. W. Michael Roark), Thomas Boyd IV. Editor news Sta. WOR, N.Y.C., 1946-51; with Dumont TV, 1951-52; editor Social Service Rev., 1956-57; interior designer, L.A., 1963—; travel cons. Gilner Internat. Travels, Beverly Hills, Calif., 1980—. Editorial bd. Previews Mag., 1984-87. Pres. Jrs. Social Svc.,L.A., 1962-64; nat. chpt. chmn. Associated Alumnae of Sacred Heart, 1960-66; pres. La Floristas, 1967-68, L.A. Orphanage Guild, 1969-70; coord.Jr. Mannequin Assisteens, Assistance League So. Calif., 1971-72; pres. docent coun. L.A. County Mus. Art, 1976-77, pres. decorative arts council, 1977-80, chmn. Am. antiques conf., 1979-81, mem. costume coun., mem. past pres.' coun., 1981—, mem. capital gifts campaign com.; bd. dirs. L.A. Orphanage Guild, 1970—; Cert. travel cons. Recipient Eve award Assistance League So. Calif. Mem. Am. Soc. Travel Agts., Inst. Cert. Travel Agts. (cert.). Republican. Roman Catholic. Clubs: Birnam Wood Golf (Santa Barbara, Calif.), Bel Air Garden.

ARMOCIDA, PATRICIA ANNE, health insurance company official; b. Portland, Maine, July 29, 1956; d. Gerald Arthur and Aileen Patricia (Malone) Faneuf; m. William Joseph Armocida, Jun. 21, 1986. BS, Purdue U., 1980; MBA, Boston U., 1983. RN, Mass. Staff nurse New Eng. Med. Ctr., Boston, 1980-81, Mass. Gen. Hosp., Boston, 1981; cons. Deloitte, Haskins & Sells, Boston, 1981, Health Data Inst., Boston, 1981-82; cons. Blue Cross/Blue Shield Assn., Chgo., 1983, asst. to the pres., 1983-85; mgr. health svcs. Blue Cross/Blue Shield Ill., 1985-86, dir. HMO, dir. utilization mgmt., 1987-90; v.p. mktg. Health Mgmt. Strategies, Alexandria, Va., 1990—. Vol. Sr. Citizens Ctr., Chgo., 1987; vol. instr. Handicapped Riders, Chgo., 1986; campaign vol. United Way, Chgo., 1988. Boston U. scholar, 1983; recipient Leadership award YWCA and Blue Cross/Blue Shield, 1988. Mem. Am. Peer Rev. Assn., Am. Care Rev. Assn., Women Employee Benefits Assn. Roman Catholic. Office: Health Mgmt Strategies 1725 Duke St Ste 300 Alexandria VA 22314

ARMS, MARGARET IRENE (PEGGY ARMS), elementary and secondary school educator; b. Chico, Calif., May 27, 1948; d. George Ulric and Emma Irene (Uhl) Roney; m. Thomas Leonard Arms, Apr. 12, 1969; children: Adam Scott, Lani Michelle. Student, Calif. State U., Chico, 1966, 68, U. Madrid, 1967; BA, U. Calif., Davis, 1969. Cert. elem. and sec. tchr., Calif. Tchr. San Juan Unified Sch. Dist., Sacramento, 1970; substitute tchr. El Dorado County, Placerville, Calif., 1970, Potlatch (Idaho) Elem. Sch., 1971; adult art instr. Shibui Fine Arts Sch., Paradise, Calif., 1971-72; tchr. Paradise Unified Sch. Dist., 1972—; coop. tchr. Calif. State U., Chico, 1982-89, instr., 1986-89; tchr. trainer Butte County Schs., Orovile, Calif., 1983-85, Paradise Unified Sch. Dist., 1985-86; program facilitator Accelerated Learning Program, No. Calif., 1983-86, Calif. Curriculum Com., 1985-87, Project WILD, No. Calif., 1985-90, The Calif. Arts Project, No. Calif., 1988-90. Author: (teaching guides) Jogging the Right Hemisphere, 1982, Outdoor Education, 1984, (scripts) Accelerated Learning, 1983, (art curriculum) Art: The Fourth R in Education, 1985, (handbook) Study Skills, 1988. Named Tchr. of Yr. Table Mt. Masonic Lodge, 1982, Tchr. of Yr., Chico Svc. Ctr., 1982. Mem. NEA, Calif. Tchrs. Assn., Calif. Art Educators Assn., Paradise Unified Tchrs. Assn., Jessee Wardlow Reading Coun. Office: Paradise Elem Sch 588 Pearson Rd Paradise CA 95969

ARMSTRONG, ANNE LEGENDRE (MRS. TOBIN ARMSTRONG), former ambassador, corporate director, educator; b. New Orleans, Dec. 27, 1927; d. Armant and Olive (Martindale) Legendre; m. Tobin Armstrong, Apr. 12, 1950; children: John Barclay, Katharine A. Idsal, Sarita A. Hixon, Tobin and James L. (twins). BA in English, Vassar Coll., 1949. Co-chmn. Rep. Nat. Com., 1971-73; del. Rep. Nat. Conv., 1964-84; counsellor to U.S. Pres., 1973-74; U.S. ambassador Gt. Britain, No. Ireland, 1976-77; chmn. adv. bd. Ctr. for Strategic and Internat. Studies (formerly affiliated with Georgetown U.), 1981-87, chmn. bd. trustees, 1987—; chmn. Pres.'s Fgn. Intelligence Adv. Bd., 1981—; commn. on Integrated Long Term Strategy, 1987; mem. Nat. Commn. Pub. Svc., 1988; pres. Nat. Thanksgiving Commn., 1986—; bd. dirs. GM Corp., Halliburton Co., Boise Cascade Corp., Am. Express Co. Bd. regents Smithsonian Instn., 1978—; bd. overseers Hoover Instn., 1978-90; co-chmn. Reagan-Bush Campaign, 1980; pres. Blair House Restoration Fund, 1985—. Recipient Rep. Woman of Yr. award, 1979, Texan of Yr. award, 1981, Presdl. Medal of Freedom award, 1987; named to Tex. Women's Hall Fame, 1986. Mem. English-Speaking Union (chmn. 1978-80), Coun. Fgn. Rels., Tex. Women's Alliance (chmn. 1985-89), Am. Assocs. of Royal Acad. Trust (trustee 1985—), Phi Beta Kappa. Clubs: Econ., N.Y; F St. (Washington).

ARMSTRONG, CLARA JULIA EVERSHED (MRS. ROLLIN S. ARMSTRONG), retired college administrator; b. Murray, Utah, Aug. 25, 1911; d. Elmer B. and Lenora K. (Tripp) Evershed; m. Rollin S. Armstrong, Sept. 29, 1956 (dec. Sept. 1974); foster children: Maxwell Rollin, Ruth Elizabeth, Robert Neil, Philip Samuel. Student, Henager Bus. Coll., 1936-37. Office mgr., credit mgr. D.N. & E. Walter & Co., Salt Lake City, 1937-48; with Latter Day Saints Bus. Coll., Salt Lake City, 1948-77, sec., 1948-52, fgn. student adviser, 1952-55, vet. coord., 1952-55, rehab. counselor, 1952-55, registar, 1955-62, sec.-treas., 1962-76; vol. worker, 1976-80. Mem. Ch. of Jesus Christ of Latter-day Saints (pres. Ward Mut. Improvement Assn. 1941-45). Home: 475 East 900 South Box 27 Salt Lake City UT 84111 Office: 411 E South Temple Salt Lake City UT 84111

ARMSTRONG, DARLENE L., educator; b. Skowhegan, Maine, June 20, 1949; d. Henry Bernard and Erma Lillian (Morrill) Dillingham; m. Robert W. Armstrong, June 5, 1971; 1 child, Jennifer Gail. BS cum laude, Eastern Nazarene Coll., 1971. Tchr. grades 2 and 3 St. Paul's Epsicopal. Parish Day Sch., Kansas City, Mo., 1971-73; tchr. grade 2 Ridgedale Local Sch. Dist., Marion, Ohio, 1973-76; tchr. grade 6 Sch. Dist. 54, Skowhegan, 1984-85; tchr. 1st grade Sch. Dist. 49, Fairfield, Maine, 1985—. Mem. Christian Edn. Bd., 1990—; ch. bd. dirs., pres. Nazarene Youth Internat., 1990—. Named Workder of Yr. Ch. of Nazarene, 1988. Mem. NEA, Maine Tchrs. Assn., Ohio Tchrs. Assn. (elem rep. exec. bd.), Ridgedale Tchrs. Assn., SAD #49 Tchr's. Assn. (rep. staff devel. team bldg.), Phi Delta Lambda. Democrat. Office: Benton Elem Sch Fairfield ME

ARMSTRONG, DEANNA FRANCES, engineer; b. Winchester, Va., July 14, 1962; d. Gerald Francis and Reta Marie (Wyatt) A. AS in Mech. Engring. Tech., W.Va. Inst. Tech., 1982, AS in Elec. Engring. Tech. cum laude, 1983, BS in Electronics Engring. Tech. cum laude, 1984. Student engring. asst. Monongahela Power Co., Elkins, W.Va., summers 1980-83; machine shop lab. asst. W.Va. Inst. Tech., Montgomery, 1982-83, acad. asst., 1983-84; engring. technician Monongahela Power Co., Elkins, 1984—; competition judge Vocat. & Indsl. Club of Am., Elkins, 1985—. Mem. Elkins Jr. C. of C., Alpha Chi Nat. Honor Soc. Republican. Home: 508 Center St Elkins WV 26241 Office: Monongahela Power Co US Rte 215 & 250 Elkins WV 26241

ARMSTRONG, DENISE GRACE, association executive. Diploma, Briarcliffe Secretarial Sch., L.I., N.Y., 1974. Sec. Klar, Klar & Tifford, law office, East Meadow, N.Y., 1974-76; exec. sec. Nassau Acad. Medicine and Nassau County Med. Soc., Garden City, N.Y., 1976-80; adminstr. Suffolk County Dental Soc., Hauppauge, N.Y., 1980-87, exec. dir., 1988-89; dir. mktg. svcs. Med. Soc. of State of N.Y., 1989—. Mem. NAFE, Am. Soc. Assn. Execs., Am. Assn. Med. Soc. Execs. Office: 420 Lakeville Rd Lake Success NY 11042

ARMSTRONG, JANE BOTSFORD, sculptor; b. Buffalo; d. Samuel Booth and Edith (Pursel) Botsford; m. Robert Thexton Armstrong, July 3, 1960. Student, Middlebury Coll., 1939-40, Pratt Inst., 1940-41, Art Students' League, 1962-64. One-man shows Frank Rehn Gallery, N.Y.C., 1971, 73, 75, 77, Columbus (Ohio) Gallery Fine Arts, 1972, Columbia (S.C.) Mus. Art, 1975, New Britain (Conn.) Mus. Am. Art, 1972, Johnson Gallery, Middlebury Coll., 1973, Mary Duke Biddle Gallery for Blind N.C. Mus. Art, 1974, J.B. Speed Art Mus., Louisville, 1975, Buffalo State U., 1975, Marjorie Parr Gallery, London, 1976, Ark. Art Center, 1977, Dallas Mus. Fine Art, 1978, Wichita (Kans.) Art Mus., 1978, 82, Wadsworth Atheneum, 1979, Harmon Gallery, 1979, 81, Washington County (Md.) Mus. Fine Arts, Hagerstown, 1979, Chautauqua (N.Y.) Nat. Exhbn. Am. Art, 1980, Southeastern Center Contemporary Art, Winston-Salem, N.C., 1980, Rollins Coll., Winter Park, Fla., 1981, The Sculpture Center, N.Y.C., 1981, Sid Deutsch Gallery, N.Y.C., 1983, Boca Raton Mus. (Fla.), 1983, Burchfield Ctr., Buffalo, 1985, Glass Art Gallery, Toronto, 1985, Schiller-Wapner Galleries, N.Y.C., 1987, St. Gaudens Gallery, St. Gaudens Nat. Hist. Site, 1988, Middlebury Coll., Vt., 1988, Grand Cen. Art Galleries, N.Y.C., 1989; exhibited in USIA group exhbn., Europe, 1975-76, Artists of Am., Denver, 1981, 82, 83, 84, 85, 86, 87; represented in numerous acad., indsl., pub. and pvt. collections. Recipient Pauline Law prize Allied Artists Am., 1969, 70, Porton award, 1981, Gold medal, 1976, Ralph Fabri medal of honor, 1978, Chaim Gross Found. award, 1980, Helen Apen Oehler Meml. award, 1988, cert. merit NAD, 1973, Council Am. Artists' Socs. prize Nat. Sculpture Soc., 1973, Helen Apen Oehler Meml. award, 1988. Fellow Nat. Sculpture Soc. (Bronze medal 1976, 88, Tallix Foundry award 1985, Percival Dietsch prize 1986); mem. Nat. Arts Club (Gold medal 1968, 69, 71, Best in Show 1973, Edith W. MacGuire award 1975, Plaque of Honor 1977, Alexander Saltzman award 1983, Exhbn. Com. award 1990), Audubon Artists (Medal of Honor 1972), Sculptors Guild, Allied Artists Am., Nat. Assn. Women Artists (Charles N. Whinston Meml. prize 1973, Anonymous Meml. prize 1979, Elizabeth S. Blake prize 1980, Amelia Peabody award 1986). Home and Studio: Dorset Hill Rd Rural Rt Box 684 East Dorset VT 05253

ARMSTRONG, JOANNA, educator; b. Vienna, Austria, Feb. 3, 1915; came to U.S., 1946; m. David B. Armstrong, Mar. 12, 1946. Diploma, Kindergarten Tchr. State Coll., Vienna, 1933, Sorbonne, 1935; MA, U. Utah, 1951; EdD, U. Houston, 1959. Caseworker, interpreter Czech Refugee Trust Fund, London, 1939-41; tchr. French Gt. Missenden, Bucks, 1941-43; sec., interpreter U.S. Army, England and France, 1943-46; instr. Coll. William and Mary, Williamsburg, Va., 1951-55, U. St. Thomas, Houston, 1957-59; chmn. langs. sect. South Tex. Coll., Houston, 1961-62; assoc. prof. fgn. langs. Tex. So. U., Houston, 1962-68, dir. NDEA Inst., 1964, 65; assoc. prof. sch. edn. tng. headstart tchrs. U. Tex., El Paso, 1968-71; cons. office Child Devel. HEW, Kansas City, Mo., 1973; cons. Tex. Edn. Agy., Austin, 1965; sec. U.S. Forest Svc., Ely, Nev., 1948. Contbr. articles to profl. publs. Vol. Long Beach (Calif.) Symphony, 1978-80, Long Beach Opera, 1982-89, Long Beach Cambodian Svcs., 1989-90, United Cambodian Assn., Long Beach, 1989—. Decorated chevalier Ordre des Palmes Academiques; recipient award Head Start, 1971, President's plaque Alliance Francaise El Paso, 1971. Mem. Long Beach Women's Music Club (program chmn. 1986-88, mem. choral sect. 1989-90, 1st v.p. 1990—), U.S.-China People Friendship Assn. (sec. 1987—). Home: 120 Alamitos Ave #34 Long Beach CA 90802

ARMSTRONG, JOANNE MARIE, clinical psychologist, family mediator; b. Cooperstown, N.Y., Nov. 26, 1956; d. William John and Joan Alice (Larsen) A.; m. Brian Joseph Yore, July 31, 1983; 1 child, Mackensie A. BA, Trinity U., San Antonio, 1978; MA, U. Louisville, 1982, PhD, 1987. Lic. psychologist, Wis. Mgmt. trainee, adminstrv. asst. Gentec Hosp. Supply Co., San Antonio, 1978-79; rsch. asst. U. Louisville, 1980-81; therapist I, Seven Counties Svcs., Louisville, 1981-82; mental health profl. Head Start, Louisville, 1982-83; dir. Kaufman County Outreach Clinic, Tex. Dept. Mental Health-Mental Retardation, Terrell, 1984-85; clin. psychologist Nicolet Clinic/La Salle Clinic, S.C., Menasha, Wis., 1987-89; pvt. practice, Neenah, 1989—; cons. Wellness Counseling Ctr., Appleton, Wis., 1989—, Fox Valley Hosp., Green Bay, Wis., 1990—. Mem. bd. Birthing Network, Neenah, 1988—; mem. Citizens for Better Environment, Neenah, 1989—. Rsch. fellow U. Louisville, 1985-86. Mem. Am. Psychol. Assn., Nat. Register Health Svc. Providers in Psychology, Wis. Psychol. Assn., Fox Valley Psychol. Assn. (founding), Acad. Family Mediators (cert., assoc.). Episcopalian. Office: 307 S Commercial St Ste 202 Neenah WI 54956

ARMSTRONG, MARIAN LOUISE, educator; b. Bedford, Ind., June 24, 1929; d. John Frank and Maude C. (Pafford) A. BS in Edn., Ind. U., 1952, MA in Libr. Sci., 1958. Libr. Edison Sch., Gary, Ind., 1952-56, Paris Am. Sch., 1956-57; libr., instr. Ind. U., Bloomington, 1958-69, prof., 1969—. Pres. Monroe County Pub. Libr., Bloomington, 1989. Mem. ALA, Ind. Libr. Assn., Ind. Library Trustees Assn. Office: Ind Univ Sch Libr and Info Sci Bloomington IN 47405

ARMSTRONG, NANCY L., soprano, voice coach; b. New Rochelle, Aug. 30, 1948; d. Robert Clapp and Beulah Olivette (Harris) A. BS in Music Edn., U. Vt., 1970; MusM, Smith Coll., 1972. Purcell Prima Donna of Our Day soprano soloist on internat. tour Boston Camerata, 1977-85; appears in Boston with Handel and Haydn Soc., Banchetto Musicale, Boston Cecilia, Pro Arte Orch., Boston Mus. Trio, Boston Viol Consort, Philharmonia

Baroque San Francisco, Concert Toyal, N.Y.C. Soloist A Midsummer Night's Dream, Am. Repertory Theatre; Paris debut as Belinda in Dido and Aeneas; interpreter 13 Handel oratorio and operatic heroines; singer prin. roles Coronatin of Poppea, Am. premier Zoroastre; rec. artist Erato, Harmonia Mundi, Nonesuch, Ventadore. Democrat. Episcopalian. Home: 4 Mason Ct Charlestown MA 02129 Office: care R Steven Gordon 1575 Woodbridge Lakes Cir West Palm Beach FL 33415

ARMSTRONG, PAMELA ANN, academic administrator; b. Opelousas, La., Dec. 21, 1948; d. David Albert and Margaret Ouida (Culley) A. BA, U. Iowa, 1970; postgrad., DeCordova Mus. Sch., 1977-78; MEd, Bridgewater State Coll., 1990; grad. with honors Nat. Ctr. Paralegal Tng., 1986. Promotion mgr. Witt-Armstrong Equipment Co., Hopkinton, Mass., 1970-78; dept. head data processing interphase dept. Tropicana Products, Inc., Bradenton, 1979-80; mgr. Burdine's, Sarasota, Fla., 1980-85; asst. dir. continuing edn. Lasell Jr. Coll., Newton, Mass., 1986, dir. continuing edn., 1986—. Mem. Jr. League, U. Iowa Alumni Assn., Ringling Mus. Assn.

ARMSTRONG, PAMELA GAYLE, psychologist; b. Tulsa, Sept. 17, 1945; d. Bernard Charles and Julia Helen (Spillman) A.; m. John D. Wills, Aug. 10, 1968 (div. Oct. 1980); 1 child, Megan Armstrong. AB in Psychology, George Washington U., 1967; MEd, Advanced Grad. Specialist in Counseling, U. Md., 1970, PhD in Counseling, 1981. Cert. rehab. counselor. Dir. out-patient rehab., supervisory rehab. therapist Psychiat. Inst., Washington, 1970-76; regional child devel. coord. Tenn. Office Child Devel., Jackson, 1978-79; intern psychologist Prince George's County Directorate of Mental Health, Cheverly, Md., 1981-82, psychologist and vocat. coord., 1982-88; psychologist Anne Arundel County Dept. Mental Health, Annapolis, Md., 1988—; pvt. practice psychology and rehab. cons, 1986—; mem. mental health adv. com. Rehab. Services Adminstrn. grantee, 1968-70. Mem. Am. Psychol. Assn., Md. Psychol. Assn., Alliance for the Mentally Ill of Md. Home: 5553 Eaglebeak Row Columbia MD 21045 Office: Anne Arundel County Dept Mental Health 3 Harry S Truman Pkwy Annapolis MD 21401

ARMSTRONG, SUE, owner, operator; b. Raton, N.M., Nov. 11, 1942; d. Slavo Louis and Rebecca Veronica (Bigley) Starkovich; 1 child, Laureen Susan. Student, U. N.M., 1975, U. N.M., 1978; BS BA sum cum laude, U. Albuquerque, 1980. Media dir. Bank Securities, Inc., Albuquerque, N.M., 1972-74; office mgr. Great Western Cities, Albuquerque, 1974-75; asst. sec. treas. W. C. Kruger & Assoc. Architects, Albuquerque, 1976-81; office mgr. Precision Drafting Corp., Santa Clara, Calif., 1981; sec. treas., bd. dirs. W. C. Kruger & Assoc. Architects, Albuquerque, 1984-87; sec. treas. bd. dirs. K-Co., Inc. Bus. Mgrs., Albuquerque, 1985-87; bus. mgr. Bridgers & Paxton Engrs., Albuquerque, 1987-88; owner, mgr. Temp. Assoc. Inc., Albuquerque, 1988--; bd. dirs. Armstron Rodgers Bus. Mgrs. Chairperson, Maxie Anderson Small Bus. Award Com.; bd. mem. N.M. Advt. Mem. Assn. Commerce & Industry (chmn. small bus. com.), Project I (bd. dirs., exec. com.), C. of C. Republican. Home: 6128 Katson NE Albuquerque NM 87109 Office: Temp Assoc Inc 4300 San Mateo NE B-265 Albuquerque NM 87110

ARMSTRONG, SYNETTA SILVERSTEIN ANDERSON, communications professional; b. St. Louis, June 7, 1953; d. Clarence and Florine (Jackson) Anderson; children—Ebony C., Charles R. B.S., Northwestern U., 1975. Producer, host Sta. KPLR-TV, St. Louis, 1975-77; promotion dir., account exec. Belleville (Ill.) News-Democrat, 1977-79; communications coordinator Brown Group, Inc., St. Louis, 1979-80, communications mgr., 1980-85; staff mgr. pub. relations Southwestern Bell Publs., St. Louis, 1985—; producer video program 60-minutes/month, Brown Group-United Way (Emmy nomination), 1982; copywriter Jan Matzlinger-Yes I Can (Flair nomination), 1983. Recipient 1st place award Editor's Communication Competition, 1982, 83. Mem. Internat. Assn. Bus. Communicators. Office: Southwestern Bell Publs Inc 12800 Publications Dr Saint Louis MO 63131

ARMSTRONG, VIOLA GIBSON, retired social worker and educator, consultant; b. Peak's, Va., Feb. 7, 1910; d. Silas Parker and Carrie Augusta (Beauregard) Gibson; m. Earl Hampstead Armstrong, Nov. 24, 1934 (dec. May 1979); 1 child, Earl Hampstead Jr. Cert. in social work, Coll. William and Mary, 1938; BS in Edn., U. Va., 1955, MA in Edn., 1969. Cert. tchr., reading specialist, social worker, postgrad. profl. tchr., Va. Primary tchr. Charlottesville (Va.) Pub. Schs., 1936-39; psychiat. social worker U. Va. Hosp., Charlottesville, 1936-39; caseworker Juvenile Ct., Charlottesville, 1939-45; tchr. reading, spl. cons. Charlottesville Pub. Schs., 1956-67, reading specialist, 1970-72; social worker cons. to parents, Charlottesville, 1936-72; lectr. schs. and other agys., Charlottesville, 1936-72. Crafts leader primary dept. Charlottesville Pub. Schs., 1936-39; leader Cub Scouts Am., Charlottesville, 1939-45, Coun. Social Agys., Charlottesville, 1939-50; asst. to coach Little League Baseball, Charlottesville, 1939-45; mem. exec. com. Neighborhood Assn., 1985—. Mem. AAUW, Charlottesville-Albemarle Ret. Tchrs. Assn., Book Club (reviewer 1970—). Republican.

ARMSTRONG-POPPELBAUM, SYLVIA FINCH, personnel executive; b. Jamestown, N.Y., Sept. 28, 1939; d. Charles Leslie and Josephine Van Vliet (Phillips) Finch; m. Thomas L. Poppelbaum, June 16, 1979; children by previous marriage: Ronald C. Armstrong, Andrew D. Armstrong. AB cum laude, Syracuse U., 1961, MBA, 1987. Tchr. secondary social studies, Williamsville, N.Y., 1961-64; dir. Oneida County Youth Bur., Utica, N.Y., 1976-77; asst. for contract mgmt. Oneida County CETA Program, Utica, 1977-79; exec. dir. Planned Parenthood of the Mohawk Valley, Utica, 1979-85; mgr. personnel Jay-K Ind. Lumber Corp., New Hartford, N.Y., 1985—. Vice chair internal planning and allocations com. United Way of Greater Utica. Mem. Cen. N.Y. Personnel Mgrs. Assn. (legis. chair), Utica Met. Bus. and Profl. Women (2d v.p.), Mohawk Valley Bus. and Indsl. Health Care Coalition. Home: 30 Hamilton Pl Clinton NY 13323 Office: Jay-K Ind Lumber Corp Seneca Twp New Hartford NY 13413

ARNDT, CARMEN GLORIA, educator; b. N.Y.C., Mar. 29, 1942; d. Charles Joseph and Pura María (Rios) A. BA in Spanish, Pace U., 1968; MA in Spanish, NYU, 1970; profl. diploma, Fordham U., 1975. Lic. asst. prin. Simultaneous translator UN, N.Y.C., 1968; instr. Marymount Manhattan Coll., N.Y.C., 1968-70; tchr. Bd. Edn., N.Y.C., 1970—, dir. Bilingual Comprehensive High Sch., 1975-78; chairperson sch. based mgmt./shared decision com. L.D. Brandeis High Sch., N.Y.C., 1990—; chairperson restructuring com. Bd. Edn., N.Y.C., 1990—; bd. dirs. First N.Y.C. Comprehensive Bilingual Program, 1975-79; adj. faculty Fordham U., N.Y.C., 1972-75, City Coll., N.Y.C., 1985—. Author: Conversational Spanish, 1975, Native Language Art K-8, 1975; contbr. articles to profl. jours. Electioneer, Dem. Party, N.Y.C. Mem. P.R. Edn. Assn. (chairperson-mentor 1988, del.), United Fedn. Tchr. (del. 1985-88), State Assn. Bilingual Edn., Am. Assn. Tchrs. of Spanish and Portuguese, Assn. Suprs. Curriculum Devel., Phi Beta Kappa. Roman Catholic. Home: 50 W 97th St 3G New York NY 10025 Office: 145 W 84th St New York NY 10024

ARNDT, DIANNE JOY, artist, photographer; b. Springfield, Mass., Dec. 20, 1939; d. Samuel Vincent and Carrie Lillian Annino. Student, Art Students League, 1965-71; BFA with honors in Painting, Pratt Inst., 1974; postgrad., Columbia U., 1979-80, 86; MFA, Hunter Coll., 1981; m. Joseph Vincent Bower, June 16, 1979; 1 child by previous marriage, Christabelle Nita Arndt. Photojournalist, photo cons. to mags. and bus., N.Y.C., 1978—; artist, filmmaker, 1962—; recent exhbns. include Am. Cultural Ctr., U.S., New Delhi and Bombay, 1987, Bathurst Arms Installation, Eng., 1987, Camden Arts, London, 1987, Nat. Inst. of Archtl. Edn., 1988, Phillip Morris Traveling Photo Exhibit, 1988, Centennial Libr. Gallery, Isca Graphics, Edmonton, Alta., Can., 1988, Nat. Inst. Archtl. Edn., 1988, N.Y. Sci. & Tech. Gallery, N.Y., USSR, 1989, Mercer Gallery, 1989, Circolo Pickwick, Alessandria, Italy, 1989, Clocktower Gallery, N.Y., 1989, Alijira Gallery, Newark, 1990, Food Stamp Gallery, 1990, Phila. Art Aliance Exhibit, 1990, P.S.I. & Blum Helman Gallery, 1989-90. Mem. Am. Soc. Mag. Photographers, Artists Talk on Art, Profl. Women Photographers, West Side Arts Coalition, The Nat. Mus. of Women in the Arts.

ARNDT, JOAN MARIE, librarian, educator; b. Stillwater, Minn., Sept. 7, 1945; d. Harriet Joan (Richert) A. BA, Coll. of St. Catherine, St. Paul, 1967; MA, U. Minn., 1970, degree in media specialty, 1973. Cert. librarian, elem. educator. Media generalist, librarian Roseville (Minn.) Area Schs., 1967—; instr. continuing edn. Hamline U., St. Paul, 1981—; guest lectr. U. Wis., Eau Claire, 1985, Upper Mississippi Media Conf., 1988; book reviewer U. Minn., Mpls., 1988—, Five Owls, Mpls., 1988—; guest lectr. Coll. of St. Thomas, St. Paul. Program chairperson Norwegian Explorers subs. Sherlock Holmes Club. Mem. Minn. Edn. Media Orgn., Minn. Reading Assn., Am. Fed. Tchrs., Minn. Fedn. Tchrs, Friends of Ramsey County Library. Lutheran. Home: 5730 Donegal Dr Shoreview MN 55126 Office: Cen Park Media Ctr 535 W County Rd B2 Roseville MN 55113

ARNDT, MARY ELLEN, manufacturers' representative; b. Henderson, N.C., Mar. 1, 1943; d. Horace Woodrow and Mary Livingston (Harris) Robertson; m. John H. Bowen, Mar. 10, 1960 (div. July 1976); children: John Walter, Ellen Anne (dec.); m. Michael William Arndt, Mar. 22, 1986. AA, U. Md., 1964; BA, U. N.C., Wilmington, 1982. Head bookkeeper ins. dept. N.C. Nat. Bank, Henderson, 1964-66; head bookkeeper Frazier Bros. Grocery, Henderson, 1966-76; interior designer Interiors Unltd., Inc., Wilmington, N.C., 1978-82; mfrs.'s rep. Spandorfer-Zimmerman, Inc., Atlanta, 1982-84; owner, mgr. Ellen Arndt, Inc., Charlotte, N.C., 1984—; exec. v.p. Arndt Sales Assocs., Milw. and Charlotte, 1984—; sales mgr. N.Y. div. Success Motivation Inst., Inc., N.Y.C., 1990—; cons. Inndesign, Charlotte, 1984-86. Contbr. articles to profl. jours. Home life chmn. Henderson Jr. Woman's Club, 1966-78; adult leader 4-H Club, Henderson, 1964-70; vol. ARC, Charlotte, 1985-89, Big Sisters, Charlotte, 1985-89, Students Against Drunk Driving, Charlotte and Milw., 1986—. Recipient award Daily Express, 1987, 88. Mem. N.C. Toys, Gifts and Housewares Assn. (bd. dirs. 1986-89), Bus. and Profl. Women's Club (New Bus. Woman of Yr. award 1988), Friends and Alumni U. N.C.-Wilmington 1988), Phi Beta Kappa. Democrat. Lutheran. Home: 69-44 Juniper Blvd S New York NY 11379 Office: SMI 74-10 69th Rd New York NY 11379

ARNDT, NANCY YVONNE, clinical psychologist; b. Rice Lake, Wis., May 2, 1938; d. Guy and Gena (Solie) Olson; m. Gerald Milton Arndt, June 28, 1958; children: Catherine Elizabeth, Leslie Michelle. BA in Psychology and Sociology, U. Wis., Eau Claire, 1962; MA in Sociology, U. Bridgeport, 1972, MA in Counseling, 1974; PhD in Clin. Psychology, The Fielding Inst., Santa Barbara, Calif., 1981. Lic. clin. psychologist; cert. marriage and family therapist. Psychiat. social worker No. Wis. Colony and Tng. Sch., Chippewa Falls, 1962-64; activities therapist U. Rochester (N.Y.) Med. Ctr., 1966-70; sch. social worker City of Bridgeport (Conn.), 1970-75; family therapist Monroe (Conn.) Family Counseling Agy., 1975-77; prof. Sacred Heart U., Fairfield, Conn., 1977-89, U. Bridgeport, 1976—; pvt. practice Westport, Conn., 1976—; cons. psychologist New Eng. synod Luth Ch. in Am., 1980—; human rels. cons. Ridge Consultants, Cazenovia, N.Y., 1976-87; practicum supr. U. Bridgeport, 1976—. Contbr. articles to profl. jours. Bd. dirs. Drug/Alcohol Coun., Bridgeport, 1988; lectr. Conn. Commn. on Aging, Stamford, 1989; vol. Greater Bridgeport Mental Health Ctr., 1977-79, abused women's project YWCA, Bridgeport, 1977-81; lectr., cons. Divorce Program, Stamford, 1987—. Recipient Disting. Alumni award U. Wis., Eau Claire, 1989; scholar Northland Coll., 1956. Fellow Am. Orthopsychiat. Assn.; mem. Am. Psychol. Assn. (full), Am. assn. for Marriage & Family Therapy (clin., approved supr. 1984), Conn. Assn. Marriage & Family Therapy, Conn. Psychol. Assn. Lutheran. Home: 39 Bulkley Ave N Westport CT 06880 Office: 26 Imperial Ave Westport CT 06880

ARNESEN, DEBORAH ARNIE, state legislator; b. Bklyn., Oct. 1, 1953; d. Robert and Teresa (Perna) Arnesen; m. Thomas H. Trunzo Jr., Feb. 6, 1982; children: Melissa Arnesen-Trunzo, Kirsten Arnesen-Trunzo. BA, St. Olaf Coll., 1975; JD, Vermont Law Sch., 1981. Program dir. Listen Inc., Lebanon, N.H., 1981-84; real estate devel. TCG Devel. Group, Lebanon, 1986—; mem. N.H. State Legislature, Concord, 1984—; radio talk show host Sta. WNHV, White River Junction, Vt., 1988—; vis. scientist occupational health and safety Harvard Sch. Pub. Health, 1989-90. Del. N.H. Constl. Convention, Concord, 1984; 1st v.p. Tri-County Community Action Program, bd. dirs., 1986—. Mem. Planned Parenthood of No. New Eng. (mem. coms. 1985-86), N.E. Network of Progressive Elected Officials (exec. com. 1988—), N.H. Sierra Club (exec. com. 1990—). Democrat. Home: RR 1 Box 42 Orford NH 03777 Home: NH State Legislature Concord NH 03301

ARNESON, DORA WILLIAMS, health science research administrator; b. Fayetteville, Ark., Aug. 4, 1947; d. Harry Wilson and Hazel Marie (Keck) Williams; m. Richard Michael Arneson, Mar. 15, 1973 (div. Apr. 1982). BA in Chemistry, U. Mo., 1967, PhD, 1972. Cert. by Am. Bd. Clin. Chemistry. Instr. biochemistry dept. U. Tenn. Med. Ctr., Memphis, 1972-76; assoc. dir. Inborn Errors of Metabolism Lab., Memphis, 1977-83; sr. program mgr. Midwest Rsch. Inst., Kansas City, Mo., 1984—; mem. genetics screening subcom. Tenn. Dept. Pub. Health, Nashville, 1982-83. Contbr. articles to profl. publs. Bd. dirs. Nat. Alliance-Ptnrs. of the Americas, Tenn., 1981-83; mem. instl. rev. bd. Meth. Hosp., Memphis, 1982-83. Mem. Am. Chem. Soc., Am. Assn. Clin. Chemistry, Soc. for Inherited Metabolic Disorders, Eggs and Issues Club. Office: Midwest Rsch Inst 425 Volker Blvd Kansas City MO 64110

ARNETT, JANICE E., educator; b. Kenton, Ohio, May 15, 1942; d. Lewis S. and Lucille M. (Oates) A. BS in Edn., Bowling Green State U., 1964; 1964. Tchr. Pinelas County, St. Petersburg, Fla., 1964-65, Fairview Pk., Ohio, 1965-70; social sci. sch. cons. Ednl. Research Council, Cleve., 1970-71; tchr. Fairview Pk., 1971—. Mem. Ohio Edn. Assn., NEA, Fairview Pk. Edn. Assn., Internat. Reading Assn., Westshore Reading Assn., Kappa Delta Alumnae Assn., Rocky River Meth. Ch., Kappa Delta Found. (chmn. 1989—). Home: 3703 Glenbar Ct Fairview Park OH 44126

ARNEY, KARLA JEAN, administrative assistant; b. Charleston, W.Va., Sept. 11, 1960; d. Jack Allen and Delores Jean (Robinson) Stone; m. Eddie Dean Arney, Aug. 15, 1981; children: Bradley Elliott, Dustin Edward; 1 stepchild, Brandon Edric Arney. Student, Belmont Coll., 1979-81. Teller 1st Am. Bank, Nashville, 1978-80; mgr. McDonald's Corp., Nashville, 1980-81; computer coord., patient account rep. Urology Assocs., Nashville, 1981-90; adminstrv. asst. Diagnostic Radiology, Nashville, 1990—. Author poetry. Mem. Sudden Infant Death Syndrome Parent Support Group. Republican. Home: 6401 Frisco Ave Nashville TN 37209 Office: Urology Assocs 2011 Church St #600 Nashville TN 37203

ARNOLD, BARBARA EILEEN, state legislator; b. N. Adams, Mass., Aug. 3, 1927; d. Lester Flemming and Sarah (Van Hagen) Smith; m. William E. Arnold, Dec. 5, 1946; children: Wynn, Jeffrey, Gayle, Christopher. B.A. in Psychology, U. Mass.; postgrad. Keene State Coll. Spl. Edn. Clinic tchr. Keene State Coll., N.H., 1964-67; spl. edn. tchr. Easter Seal Rehab. Ctr., Manchester, N.H., 1967-74; state legislator N.H., 1982-88, now Republican floor leader Ho. of Reps., 1989—; mem. N.H. Coun. Vocat. Tech. Edn., 1986—; mem. Ways and Means com., State and Fed. Rels. commn.; chmn. Manchester Rep. Del.; Del. Bd. dirs. ARC, 1975—, chmn. bd. dirs., 1977-80; Manchester campaign chmn. Warren Rudman for U.S. Senate, 1980, 86; mem. adv. bd. Greater Manchester Federated Women's Club; mem. vestry, registered lay leader, mem. diocesan commns., del. gen. conv. Episcopal Ch.; mem. com. for children, families, social svcs. on the Nat. Conf. of State Legislatures; state adv. com. Vocat. Child Care Programs. Recipient Norris Colton Republican of Yr. award, 1989. Mem. Kappa Kappa Gamma. Address: 374 Pickering St Manchester NH 03104

ARNOLD, CAROLE ANNE WALCUTT, nurse; b. Paris, Ky., Apr. 29, 1954; d. Hardin Owsley and Cecele Christine (Smith) Walcutt; m. Richard Wood Arnold, Feb. 22, 1976; children: Richard Wood Jr., John Walcutt. A. in Nursing, Midway Coll., 1975; student in Psychology, St. Joseph's Coll., 1985—. Staff nurse, evening supr. U. Ky. Med. Ctr., Lexington, 1976-77; office mgr. Arnold, M.D., Cynthiana, Ky., 1977—; obstetric nurse Humana Corp., Lexington, 1983—. Dir. Woman's Missionary Union, 1982-87, Cynthiana Bapt. Ch., 1982-89, tchr. Sunday sch., 1978-89, mem. choir, 1978-87; mem. Harrison County Fine Arts Council, 1980-85; mem. Ky. Heritage Woman's Mus., Inc. Recipient Woman of Achievement award YMCA, 1982; named to hon. order Ky. Cols., 1986-87; fellow U. Ky. Mem. Midway Coll. Alumni Assn. (named Miss Midway Coll. 1975, Disting. Alumnae award, 1989), Ky. Nurse's Assn., Am. Nurse's Assn., Ky. Hist. Soc., Blue Grass Trust, The Hereditary Register of the U.S., Daus. of 1812 (rec. sec. River Rasen chpt. 1989—), Phi Theta Kappa. Democrat. Clubs: DAR (def. chmn. 1979-81, Good Citizenship award 1975, 1st alt. nat. conv. 1980, Ky. State Page 1987-89, Nat. Congl. Page 1987-89, Nat. Personal Page to Pres. Gen., 1990, nat. vice-chair east cen. div. pages, state program chmn. 1987—, sch. chmn. 1987—, nat. page 1988-89, nat. choir 1987-89, nat. del. 1988, corr. sec. 1989—, Ky. outstanding jr. mem.), Harrison County Women's Club (fine arts chmn. 1978-80, 1st v.p. 1981-83), Colonial Dames (mem. 17th century Sarah Morgan Boone chpt., state nat. def. chair., chaplain, state page 1988, nat. congl. page 1989), chmn. membership com. 1988—), Family of Bruce Soc. in Am., Owsley Family Soc. of Am. (recipient merit award 1987), Sovereign Colonial Soc., Ams. Royal Descent, Harrison Hosp. Aux. (pres. 1979-80). Home: 116 Culpepper Dr Cynthiana KY 41031 Office: 300 E Pleasant St Cynthiana KY 41031

ARNOLD, CHRISTINE ANNETTE, electrical engineer; b. Ann Arbor, Mich., Aug. 11, 1966; d. George William and Patricia Ann (Wisnieski) Gatecliff; m. Curtis John Arnold, Apr. 15, 1989. BSEE, U. Mich., 1988. Quality analyst Ford Motor Co., Saline, Mich., 1988-89; product engr. Kelsey Hayes Co., Romulus, Mich., 1989—. Mem. NAFE, Soc. Automotive Engrs., Alpha Xi Delta (pledge advisor U. Mich. chpt. 1990). Office: Kelsey-Hayes Co 38481 Huron River Dr Romulus MI 48174

ARNOLD, CYNTHIA JEAN, nurse; b. Burlington, Iowa, Feb. 3, 1942; d. George Kenneth and Velma Ruth (Duttweiler) Brun; m. Robert Edward Arnold, Aug. 8, 1964; children: Allison Suzanne, Eric Christopher. BS in Nursing, U. Mo., 1964; M in Adult Psychiat. Mental Health Nursing, U. Kans., 1981. Psychiat. staff nurse U. Mo. Med. Ctr., Columbia, 1964-65; instr. in nursing Research Hosp. Sch. Nursing, Kansas City, Mo., 1965-68, part-time staff nurse, 1968-69; instr. in nursing Johnson County Community Coll., Overland Park, Kans., 1974-77; clin. nurse specialist Research Mental Health Services, Kansas City, 1979-90, Wyandot Mental Health Ctr., 1990—; adj. instr. U. Kansas Sch. Nursing, Kansas City, 1984—. Del. People to People Nurse Profl Del. to Europe, 1988; sec. troop mother's club Boy Scouts Am., Kansas City, Mo., 1986-88; chaplain PEO Sisterhood, Lee's Summit, Mo., 1984-86, v.p., 1988-89, pres., 1990—; rec. sec. Kansas City PEO Reciprocity Group, 1990—. Recipient Rae Lyon Meml. award Rsch. Mental Health Services, 1984, Disting. Nursing Leadership award, 1989. Mem. Am. Nurses Assn. (cert. 1982), Nat. League Nursing, Jackson County Osteopathic Assn. (sec. 1980-82), Sigma Theta Tau. Home: 4332 E 110th St Kansas City MO 64137

ARNOLD, DOROTHY CAVANEE, educator; b. Frederick, Md., Oct. 24, 1922; d. George William and Charlotte Virginia (Smith) Trout; m. Kenneth L. Cavenee, Mar. 9, 1945 (div. 1951); children: Kim L., George C.; m. Kenneth A. Arnold, Dec. 4, 1982. BS, Towson Coll., 1943; ME, Western Md. Coll., 1969. Elem. sch. tchr. Frederick County Bd. Edn., 1943-45, 51-68, elem. math. supr., 1968-77, area II supr., 1977-80; tchr. pvt. sch. Banner Sch., Frederick, 1982-85, 88—. Dir. Bapt. Ch., Frederick, 1980-83, 84-87, treas., 1987—, Sun. Sch. dir., deacon; treas. Homewood Aux., Frederick, 1984-90. Mem. AAUW (past pres.), Hon. Tchrs. Soc. (treas. 1978—), Md. Assn. Supervision and Curriculum Devel. (state pres. 1975-77), Rose Hill Garden Club (treas.), Beta Sigma Phi (past pres.), Alpha Beta (state pres. 1977-79, Golden Anniversary chmn. 1983-87). Democrat. Home: 640 Grant Pl Frederick MD 21701

ARNOLD, JANET NINA, health care consultant; b. Poughkeepsie, N.Y., Apr. 23, 1933; d. Paul Dudley and Pauline Katherine (Board) Bartram; A.B., Vassar Coll., 1955; postgrad. Sch. Med. Tech., Albany Med. Center, 1955-56; M.S., Vassar Coll., 1963; M.H.S.M., Webster Coll., 1981; m. Robert William Arnold, Dec. 19, 1954; children—Paul Dudley, Janet Elizabeth. Research asst., med. technologist H. Aird Boswell, M.D., Troy, N.Y., 1956-59; teaching supr., adminstrv. cons. Vassar Bros. Hosp., Poughkeepsie, N.Y., 1959-69; adv. to med. lab., lectr. med. mycology Vassar Coll., Poughkeepsie, 1961-66; asst. lab. mgr. Boulder (Colo.) Meml. Hosp., 1975-80; cons. hosp. planning Mercy Med. Center, Denver, 1981-82; lab. dir. Valley View Hosp. and Med. Ctr., Thornton, Colo., 1982-85; cons. health care mgmt. Humana, 1982-85, MRI, 1985—, ptnr., 1988; acad./adminstrv. cons. U. Guam, Vassar Coll., Boulder Community Hosp., others. Sec., bd. dirs. Sanitas Fed. Credit Union, 1977-78, pres., 1979-82; teaching fellow Vassar Coll., 1961-63, fund chmn., 1989—. NSF research fellow, 1960-62. Mem. Am. Acad. Microbiology, Soc. for Gen. Microbiology, Am. Soc. Med. Technologists, Colo. Public Health Assn., Med. Mycological Soc. of the Ams. Republican. Episcopalian. Asso. editor Am. Jour. Med. Tech., 1980-88; contbr. articles to profl. jours. Home: 4195 Chippewa Dr Boulder CO 80303

ARNOLD, JEAN ANN, health science facility administrator; b. Coronado, Calif., Nov. 17, 1948; d. Scott Crittenden Daubin and Barbara Jean (Spooner) Annowada; m. Lonnie Lea Arnold, July 14, 1973; children: Danielle Louise, Casey Jean. Student, Santa Barbara City Coll., Calif., 1966-67, U. Wyo., Laramie, 1968-69. Registered Technol., LIc. Technol., Calif., Wash. Staff technol. x-ray Mt. Auburn Hosp., Cambridge, Mass., 1971-72, Victor Valley Hosp., Victorville, Calif., 1972-74, Fairfield Hosp., Calif., 1974-76; chief technol. Oakridge Med. Group, Roseville, Calif., 1976-78; staff technol. radiation therapy U. Cancer Ctr., U. Hosp., Seattle, 1979-84; staff technol. Providence Med. Ctr., Seattle, 1984; relief technol. UCSD Med. Ctr., San Diego, 1984-85; staff technol. Scripps Meml. Hosp., LaJolla, Calif., 1984-87, dir. radiation oncology, 1987—. Producer Video, Occpl. Radiation Safety 1988. Fund Raising Eastside Christian Sch., Bellevue Wash. 1980. Mem. Soc. for Radiation Oncology Adminstrs., Calif. Soc. Radiologic Technologists, Am. Soc. Radiologic Technologists, Am. Registry Radiologic Technologists (job analysis adv. com., item writer Therapy Technology). Republican. Baptist. Office: Scripps Meml Hosp 9888 Genesee Ave La Jolla CA 92038

ARNOLD, JEANNE GOSSELIN, communications executive; b. Rutland, Vt., Dec. 19, 1917; d. Eugene Arthur and Eleanor (Ranberg) Gosselin; children: Eugene Van Rensselaer Arnold, Linda Krull Beattie. Student, SUNY, Albany, 1935-38, 45-47, Russell Sage Coll., 1964-65. Reporter, women's editor, columnist, feature writer Albany Times Union, N.Y., 1945-79; dir. Media Svcs. Unltd., Westerlo, N.Y., 1979—. Author: (poetry) The Flesh Recalls, 1956, Ballad of Witches Hill, 1988; (biography) A Man of Faith, 1983; (children's book) Little Cloud That Couldn't, 1990; contbr.: Things that Go Bump in the Night, by Louis C. Jones, 1959. Chmn. Westerlo Planning Bd., 1978-86. Recipient ann. Journalism award N.Y. State Bar Assn., 1975, Outstanding Woman award Coll. St. Rose, Albany, 1976, Albany YMCA, 1977. Mem. The Newspaper Guild. Roman Catholic. Home: Box 265 Rte 1 Westerlo NY 12193

ARNOLD, JOAN DEAN, publisher; b. Marshall, Mo., Jan. 12, 1944; d. Alfred Douglas and Imogene Devonia (Simmons) Kidd; m. John Gerald Arnold (div.); children: John Douglas, Christopher Alan. Owner, mgr. Harbor Shopping Ctr., Harbor Landing, Mile Sq. Plaza and Garfield Plaza, Huntington Beach, Calif., 1975-83; designer, owner The Dream Factory, Huntington, 1974—; founder, owner Huntington Pacific Thrift and Loan, 1982—; owner, pub. Sandwich Island Pub Co. Ltd., Lahaina, Hawaii, 1984-89; pub. The Best of Maui, 1989—; developer, owner Double Gemini Corp., Huntington, 1978-83; chairwoman Sandwich Islands Pub. Co., Ltd., 1984—. Mem. archtl. com. Orangewood Home for Battered Children, Orange, Calif., 1980; dist. chmn. Maui County Reps.; bd. dirs. W. Maui Youth Ctr., Lahania, Lahania Salvation Army. Mem. Hawaii Pub. Assn., Small Mag. Pub. Assn., Hawaii Visitors Assn., Maui C. of C. (bd. dirs.), Hotel Assn. Hawaii, Soroptimists (bd. dirs.). Home: 31 Kai Pali Pl Lahaina HI 96761 Office: 505 Front St Ste 213 Lahaina HI 96761

ARNOLD, JOANNE EASLEY, journalism educator, university official; b. Hutchinson, Kans., June 18, 1930; d. Orland Royce and Bernice Anna (Daugherty) Easley; B.A., U. Colo., 1952, M.A., 1965, Ph.D., 1971; m. Sanders Gibson Arnold, June 7, 1952 (div. 1983); 1 son, Sanders Gibson. Reporter, mem. editorial staff Boulder (Colo.) Daily Camera, 1955-56; tchr. journalism, speech and English, Boulder High Sch., 1956-71, dir. publs., 1958-69, chmn. dept. English, 1967-69; asst. dir. Nat. Center for Higher Edn. Mgmt. Systems, Western Interstate Commn. for Higher Edn., Boulder, 1971-74; asso. prof. journalism U. Colo., Boulder, 1974—, asso. dean Sch. Journalism, 1974-75, 82—, asso. vice chancellor for acad. affairs, 1975-80; adviser Elem. and Secondary Edn. Act, Title III, Colo., 1972-75; cons. Bur. Communications, U. Colo., 1970-71; cons. elementary and secondary edn., organizational communication, lectr.; mem. Western Interstate Commn. for Higher Edn., 1975-84. . Commr., vice chmn. Boulder Public Libraries, 1973-76; mem. com. on fiscal policy City of Boulder, 1972-73; mem. Boulder

Valley Sch. Dist. Re-2 Bd. Edn., 1975-79; mem. nat. adv. council Girl Scouts Am., 1977-84; trustee Boulder Library Found., 1974-76, Boulder Meml. Hosp. Newspaper Fund fellow Wall St. Jour., 1961; named Nat. Woman of Achievement, Women in Communication Inc., 1987, Nat. Fedn. Press Women, 1979. Mem. Nat. Soc. for the Study of Communication, Speech Assn. Am., Kappa Tau Alpha, Theta Sigma Phi, Alpha Delta Kappa, Phi Kappa Delta, Pi Beta Phi. Club: U. Colo. Alumni (dir. 1954) (Boulder). Editor: Higher Edn. Mgmt., 1971-74. Contbr. articles to profl. jours. Home: 815 Park Ln Boulder CO 80302

ARNOLD, KATHLEEN SPELTS, regent; b. Miami, Fla., Oct. 25, 1941; d. John Keith and Mary Fay (Webber) Shay; m. Harold G. Arnold, Jan. 31, 1982; children by previous marriage: Melinda Kathleen, Meghan Shay, Richard John. BA, U. Colo., 1963. Tchr., Bear Creek High Sch., Jefferson County, Colo., 1963-64, 65-67; asst. prodn. control mgr. Fordwerke, Cologne, Fed. Republic Germany, 1964-65; state rep. Colo. Gen. Assembly, Denver, 1978-83, state senator, 1983-86, chmn. judiciary com., 1980-83, state affairs com., 1985-86; del. Nat. Conf. State Legislatures, 1980-83; candidate for Lt. Gov., 1986; regent U. Colo., 1989—. Bd. dirs. U. Colo. Alumni Bd., Denver, 1987—, United Bank, 1988—; chmn. Chatfield YMCA Fund Drive, Colo. Council of Chs.; mem. curriculum council Jefferson County Schs.; sec. Littleton Fire Bd.; bd. trustees Ind. Inst. Mem. South Jeffeo-Kalewood C. of C. Republican. Presbyterian. Office: 6436 W Frost Dr Littleton CO 80123

ARNOLD, KERTTU HAVOLA, artist, educator; b. Finland, Apr. 10, 1938; came to U.S., 1948; d. Antero and Annikki (Joensuu) Havola; m. Philip Noble Arnold, Apr. 12, 1961; children: Philip Andrew, Kimberley Ann Arnold Werthmann. BA, Coll. William & Mary, 1960; MA in Edn. Adminstrn., George Mason U., 1981. Cert. tchr., Va. Tchr. art 20th Century Gallery, Williamsburg, Va., 1960-61, Recreation Dept. Bowie, Md., 1967-68, Recreation Dept. Fairfax County, Va., 1967-72; sales rep. Pan Am. Airlines, Washington, 1961-63; tchr. art YMCA, Prince Georges County, Md., 1967-68; art program specialist, lead program coord. Fairfax County Pub. Schs., Fairfax, Va., 1978-87, tchr. art/photography, 1982—; artist-owner Art Studio Clifton, Va., 1987-89; cons. in field. Exhibited in group shows at City of Bowie Art Festival, 1968, Vienna Art Soc., Hollyhocks, Va. Beach Boardwalk Art Show, 1977-78 (hon. mention). Judge art exhbn. Womens's Club Fairfax County, Va., 1986-89, Fairfax County Parks and Recreation, Burke Lake Park, 1985. Grantee AAUW, 1980, Va. Found. Humanities, 1983-84. Mem. AAUW (Farifax City br., charter, past pres.), Nat. Art Edn. Assn., Va. Art Edn. Assn., Fairfax Edn. Assn., Fairfax City Art league, Vienna Photography Soc., Finlandia Found. (past sec. nat. capital br.), Chi Omega. Republican. Lutheran. Home: 5340 Balck Oak Dr Fairfax VA 22032

ARNOLD, LESLIE BISGER, liaison program manager; b. Cheyanne, Wyo., Aug. 26, 1956; d. Fred Bennett and Natalie Sylvia (Cohen) B.; m. Kevin Durkin Arnold, July 6, 1980. BS in Spl. Edn. (cum laude), Old Dominion U., 1978, MS in Edn. (cum laude), 1984. Cert. spl. educator, emotionally disturbed, mentally retarded, presch. handicapped, severly and profoundly handicapped. Tchr. multiple handicapped Va. Beach (Va.) Pub. Schs., 1978-81; tchr. autistic Southeastern Coop. Ednl. Programs, Norfolk, Va., 1981-82; tchr. emotionally disturbed/mentally retarded Norfolk Pub. Schs., 1983-86, tchr. specialist, 1986-89, ednl. diagnostician, 1989-90, liaison program mgr., 1990—; mental health worker Tidewater Psychiat. Inst., Va. Beach, 1985-86; curriculum coord. CHANCE program Old Dominion U., Norfolk, 1986—; speaker in field. Recipient Sch. Bell award Norfolk Pub. Sch. Bd., 1989. Mem. Tidewater Soc. for Autistic Children (pres. 1980-82), Coun. for Exceptional Children, PTA, Autism Soc. Am., NEA, Nat. Alliance for Mentally Ill, Assn. Retarded Citizens. Home: 1884 Wolfsnare Rd Virginia Beach VA 23454

ARNOLD, MARY BERTUCIO, pediatric endocrinologist; b. Fitchburg, Mass., Sept. 29, 1924; d. George and Louise (Byrolly) Bertucio; AB, Vassar Coll., 1945; MD cum laude, U. Vt., 1950; MA, Brown U., 1974; m. John Hampton Arnold, July 28, 1956 (dec. Apr. 1972); children—John, Mark, Matthew. Intern, resident Hartford (Conn.) Hosp., 1950-52; asst./sr. pediatric resident Babies' Hosp., Columbia-Presbyn. Med. Center, N.Y.C., 1952-54; pediatric endocrinology research fellow Mass. Gen. Hosp., Boston, 1954-57; asst. in pediatrics Harvard U. Sch. Medicine, Boston, 1955-57; instr. pediatrics/asst. prof. U. N.C. Sch. Medicine, Chapel Hill, 1959-65; lectr. med. sci./assoc. prof. pediatrics Brown U., Providence, 1966-74, assoc. prof., 1974—; chmn. dept. pediatrics, dir. pediatric endocrinology Roger Williams Gen. Hosp., Providence, 1971—. Chmn., Heart Health in the Young Com., Am. Heart Assn., R.I. Affiliate, Inc., 1979-82; mem. adv. com. New Eng. Regional Hypothyroidism Screening Program, 1976—; mem. subcom. pediatric planning rev. guidelines Hosp. Assn. R.I., 1976—; mem. program com. R.I. Clin. Diabetes Assn., 1975-80. Recipient Carrbee award U. Vt. Sch. Medicine, 1950, Excellence in Teaching award Brown U., 1978. Mem. Endocrine Soc., Lawson Wilkins Pediatric Endocrine Soc. (founding mem.), Am. Fedn. Clin. Research, AAAS, Am. Med. Women's Assn., Am. Acad. Pediatrics, AMA, New Eng. Pediatric Soc., R.I. Clin. Diabetes Assn. (pres. 1975-77), Sigma Xi. Episcopalian. Contbr. articles to profl. jours. Office: 825 Chalkstone Ave Providence RI 02908

ARNOLD, MARY PAMELA, mental health counselor; b. Ft. Wayne, Ind., Nov. 30, 1949; d. Charles Stanton and Marjorie Ann (Davis) A. Cert. in psycho-trauma tng., Centralia (Ill.) Hosp., 1970; student, Purdue U., 1975-77; BS in Spl. Edn., Ball State U., 1981; postgrad., Nat. Coll. Edn., 1986-89. Counselor child guidance Hoyleton (Ill.) Children's Home, 1970-72; owner, adminstr. Miss Pam's Nursery Sch., Michigan City, Ind., 1973-75; spl. edn. cons. Michigan City Sch. System, 1975-78; instr. Ind. Vocat. Tech. Coll., Indpls., 1979-86; asst. activity dir. Normandy House Nursing Home, Wilmette, Ill., 1986-87; evening adminstr. Normandy Hall Retirement Residence, Evanston, Ill., 1986-87; rsch. adminstr. Jack Tanzman (Assn. of Cert. Social Workers), Evanston, 1987-88; pvt. practice counseling, 1988—; social worker Michigan City (Ind.) Sch. System, 1989—; mgmt. cons. GM, Indpls., 1982-86; cons. counselor Parents Without Ptnrs., Valparaiso, Ind., 1984-85; tng. cons. Houston Corp., Indpls., 1984; founder, coord. Play Therapy for Abused Children, Michigan City, 1977; presenter, organizer Displaced Homemaker Seminar, Muncie, Ind., 1980. Vol. Muscular Dystrophy Telethon, Michigan City, 1985; counselor Battered Women, Muncie, 1979-81. Nat. Coll. Edn. fellow, 1986-89; Parents' Group for Spl. Student scholar, 1978. Mem. AAUW, Nat. Orgn. Human Svc. Edn. (asst. to pres. 1986-87, conf. coord. 1986-87), Women's Club. Mem. Ch. of Christ.

ARNOLD, MILDRED MAXINE BERRY, association executive; b. Pocahontas, Ark., Feb. 5, 1936; d. John Ephriam and Rubye Pearl (Tyler) Berry; m. Jimmie Lee Arnold, July 30, 1955 (div. 1973); children: Janet E. Arnold Brown, Douglas Lee. BS in Edn., U. Tex., El Paso, 1967, MEd, 1971. Cert. tchr., Tex. Tchr. Ysleta Ind. Sch. System, El Paso, 1966-68; program dir. N.E. YMCA, El Paso, 1968-70, mem. youth ct., 1968—; met. program dir. Cen. Br. YMCA, El Paso, 1970-76; exec. dir. Belleville (Ill.) Family YMCA, 1976-80, Met. YMCA Dallas, Grand Prairie, Tex., 1980—; dist. exec. Met. YMCA Dallas, Dallas, 1988-89; bd. dirs. Mid-Am. region YMCA, 1985-88, chair youth devel. com.; participant YMCA of U.S. and U.K. exchange program, London and Cardiff, Wales, 1986. Contbr. articles to profl. jours. Mem. Mayor's Com. on Drug Abuse, El Paso, 1974-76; chmn. Child Care Task Team, 1985-89. Mem. Assn. Profl. Dirs. (pres. 1984-87, Adminstrv. Excellence award Red River chpt. 1985, Oustanding Svc. award 1986), Grand Prairie C. of C., Grand Prairie Women's Club, Bus. and Profl. Women's Club, Soroptimists. Methodist. Home: 1500 Vanderbilt Dr Arlington TX 76014 Office: Grand Prairie YMCA 333 NE 5th St Grand Prairie TX 75050

ARNOLD, NANCY LEE, human service administrator; b. Davenport, Iowa, Sept. 13, 1950; d. Curtis Elwyn and LaVerne Suzzan (Rundle) Romaine; m. Alan Ross Arnold, Jan. 7, 1972; Justin Alan, Kerry Lee. BS in Nursing, Alverno Coll., Milw., 1984; MS in Nursing, U. Wis., 1986; BS, Coll. St. Francis, Joliet, Ill., 1977. Cert. registered rehab. nurse. V.p. Synergy Systems, Inc., Sarasota, Fla.; dir. program svc. and clin. practice Continental Med. Systems, Mechanicsburg, Pa.; dir. nursing Rehab. Hosp. Svc. Corp., Washington; asst. prof. Columbia Coll. Nursing, Milw. Author: Pressure Sores in SCI Population; contbg. author: Rehabilitation Concepts and Practice, 1987, Take the Pressure Off, 1987, Takeing the Pressure Off Decubitus Ulcers, 1987, Easing Pressure Wound Pain, 1988. Mem. Am. Nurses Assn., Assn. Rehab. Nurses, Sigma Theta Tau.

ARNOLD, OLINDA DIAS, insurance agency executive; b. Santa Barbara, Portugal, Aug. 12, 1945; came to U.S., 1967; d. Manuel Machado and Olinda Da Conceicão (Bretao) Dias; m. Henry Stuart Arnold, Nov. 6, 1966; 1 child, Belinda D. AA, Coll. of the Sequoias, 1965. Legal sec. Grimes & Warwick, San Diego, 1972-75; legal asst. Law Offices of John A. Harin, San Diego, 1975-79; v.p., treas. Henry S. Arnold & Co., San Diego, 1979—. Bd. dirs. Azorean Alliance, San Diego, 1979, Spirit of '76, 1983— (1st Worn and Torn award 1986); mem. San Carlos Area Council, San Diego, 1987. Mem. Nat. Notary Assn., NAFE, Internat. Platform Assn. Roman Catholic. Office: 3444 Camino Del Rio #201 San Diego CA 92108

ARNOLD, ROSE MARY, county commissioner; b. Richmond, Minn., Dec. 9, 1935; d. Anton and Marie (Brunner) Brisse; m. Richard H. Arnold, June 18, 1955; children: Tom, Cheryl, Charles, Joseph. Grad. high sch., Cold Spring, Minn. Reporter St. Cloud (Minn.) Daily Times, 1970-78; steno clk. Burlington No., 1980-88; loan clk. Liberty Loan, St. Cloud, 1978-80; commr. County of Stearns, St. Cloud, 1988—; chmn. Stearns County Planning Commn., St. Cloud, 1989; bd. trustees Great River Regional Libr., St. Cloud, 1989; bd. dirs. Tri-Cap, Sauk Rapids, Minn. Mem. Nat. Assn. Counties, Assn. Minn. Counties. Home: 29353 Lindbergh Ln Avon MN 56310 Office: Stearns County Courthouse Saint Cloud MN 56301

ARNOLD, SHEILA, state legislator; b. N.Y.C., Jan. 15, 1929; d. Michael and Eileen (Lynch) Keddy; coll. courses; m. George Longan Arnold, Nov. 12, 1960; 1 son, Peter; 1 son by previous marriage, Michael C. Young; stepchildren: Drew, George Longan, Joe. Mem. Wyo. Ho. of Reps., 1978—, mem. com. on revenue, com. on rules and procedures, mem. govs. coun. on devel. disabilities, mem. govs. com. on health ins.; dir. First Interstate Bank of Laramie. Former mem., sec. Wyo. Land Use Adv. Coms.; past pres. Dem. Women's Club, Laramie; past vice-chmn. Albany County Dem. Cen. Com.; past mem. Dem. State Com.; mem. adv. bd. Wyo. Home Health Care; mem. State Com. on Long Term Health Care, Nat. Conf. State Legislatures Com. on Fiscal Affairs and Oversight Com. Recipient Spl. Recognition award from Developmentally Disabled Citizens of Wyo., 1985. Mem. Laramie Area C. of C. (pres. 1982; Top Hand award 1977), LWV, Internat. Platform Assn., Faculty Women's Club (past pres.), Zonta, Laramie Women's Club, Cowboy Joe Club. Office: Capitol Bldg Cheyenne WY 82002

ARNOLD, SUSAN BIRD, safety education training, consulting and products company executive; b. Reading, Pa., Feb. 28, 1951; d. Frank Edward and Esther (Savidge) Bird; B.A., Mercer U., Macon, Ga., 1972; m. Robert Melvin Arnold, Jr., Mar. 18, 1972; children—Jennifer Michelle, Amelia Michelle, Stephanie Michelle, Elizabeth Michelle. Audio-video technician Internat. Safety Acad., 1971; with Internat. Loss Control Inst., 1974—, mgr. ednl. products div., 1978-82, v.p. adminstrv. services, v.p. press div., Loganville, Ga., 1982-85, exec. dir., gen. mgr., 1985—. Contbr. to Risk Control Rev. Mem. adv. com. Inst. Safety, Health and Rehab. for the Exceptional, 1978-84; bd. dirs. Bluesprings Day Camp for Handicapped. Mem. AVMA Aux. Methodist. Home: PO Box 609 Loganville GA 30249 Office: Internat Loss Control Inst Hwy 78 Loganville GA 30249

ARNOLD, VALERIE DENISE, registered nurse; b. Camden, N.J., Sept. 2, 1956; d. Cornelius Arnold and Carrie Frances (Cephas) Shorter. Student, Fla. A and M U.; AD, Florida Jr. Coll.; postgrad., Widener U., 1988. Nurse West Jersey Hosp., Vourhees, N.J., 1982-83, Medical Personnel Pool, Cherry Hill, N.J., 1983-84, West Jersey Hosp., Vourhees, N.J., 1984--. Supt. Sunday Sch. Mt. Pisgah AME Ch., Haddonfield, N.J., 1985. Home: W Atlantic Ave E 11 Magnolia NJ 08049 Office: West Jersey Hosp Evesham Ave Voorhees NJ 08043

ARNOT, SUSAN EILEEN, publishing executive; b. East Orange, N.J., Aug. 10, 1957; d. Robert B. and Mae (Cockcroft) A. BA, Coll. William and Mary, 1979; postgrad., Cambridge U., 1977; cert., NYU, 1979. Promotion asst. Viking Press/Penguin Books, N.Y.C., 1979-82; mgr. promotion Rizzoli Internat. Publs., N.Y.C., 1982-83; mgr. advt. promotion USA Today, N.Y.C., 1983-85; promotion dir. 50 Plus mag., N.Y.C., 1985-88, In Fashion mag., N.Y.C., 1988-89; mktg. svcs. mgr. TAXI mag., N.Y.C., 1989—; career adv. Coll. William and Mary, 1980—. Writer/editor quar.: (newsletter) 50 Plus Market Update, 1985-88. Vol. cook, fundraiser Cathedral Soup Kitchen, St. John the Divine Cathedral, 1983-85. Recipient Best of N.Y. Addy award for advt., 1986. Mem. Women in Communications Inc. (chpt. publicity com. 1985-86, fin. com. 1986—, spl. events com. 1986—), NOW, Coll. William and Mary Alumni Soc. (chpt. pres. 1986—, exec. bd. 1983-86), AAUW (chpt. corr. sec. 1983-86, chair com. on women's work 1984-86), Mag. Marketers Assn, Mcpl. Art Soc., Advt. Club of N.Y. Methodist. Avocations: travel, music, theater, reading. Home: 230 W 107th St Apt 3J New York NY 10025

ARNSTEIN, SHERRY PHYLLIS, health care executive; b. N.Y.C., Jan. 11, 1930; m. George E. Arnstein, June 26, 1951; BS, UCLA, 1951; MS in Communications, Am. U., 1963; postgrad. in systems dynamics MIT, summer 1976. Washington editor Current mag., 1961-63; staff cons. Pres. Com. on Juvenile Delinquency, 1963-65; spl. asst. to asst. sec. HEW, 1965-67; chief citizen participation advisor Model Cities Adminstrn., HUD, 1967-68; pub. policy cons., Washington, 1968-75; sr. research fellow HHS, Washington, 1975-78; v.p. govt. relations Nat. Health Council, Inc., Washington, 1978-85; exec. dir. Am. Assn. Colls. Osteo. Medicine, 1985—. Author: (with Alexander Christakis) Perspectives on Technology Assessment, 1975; editor: Government Relations Handbook Series, 1979-85, Washington Report Series, 1985. mem. editorial bd. Tech. Assessment Update, 1975-78, The Bureaucrat, 1975-83, Pub. Adminstrn. Rev., 1978-83, Health Mgmt. Quar., 1985; contbr. articles to profl. jours. Bd. dirs. Youth Policy Inst. Mem. Cosmos Club, Capital Hill Club, Nat. Press Club (Washington). Office: Am Assn Colls Osteo Medicine 6110 Executive Blvd Ste 405 Rockville MD 20852

ARNTSON, JUDITH CHRISTINE, nurse; b. Los Angeles, Mar. 5, 1938; d. Lloyd Calvin and Christine Elizabeth (Eisenbach) Sharpe; m. Joseph R. Fernandez, Oct. 6, 1959 (div. June 1985); children: Tina, Marie Beam; m. David Arnold Arntson, May 24, 1986. BSN, Calif. State U., Fullerton, 1976; MSN, Calif. State U., Los Angeles, 1978; cert., Inst. Profl. Massage & Bodywork, 1989. RN, Calif.; cert. trainer mgmt. of assaultive behavior, interaction mgmt. instr.; cert. massage therapist. Staff nurse Los Angeles County/U. So. Calif. Med. Ctr., 1969-71, City of Hope Nat. Med. Ctr., Duarte, Calif., 1971-77; asst. prof. nursing Calif. State U., Fullerton, 1977-78; dir. emergency and referral services Ingleside Hosp., Rosemead, Calif., 1979-84; inservice dir. Ingleside Hosp., Rosemead, 1979-85, dir. edn. dept., 1985-87; dir. nursing Brea (Calif.) Hosp. and Neuropsychiat. Ctr., 1987—; instr. in nursing San Antonio Coll., Walnut, Calif., 1977-78, U. Calif. Irvine Med. Ctr., 1976, Golden West Coll., 1976, Calif. State U., Fullerton, 1979; guest lectr. Lincoln Tng. Ctr., 1984; speaker on AIDS to various orgns. Chair psychiat. inservice com. Inservice and Health Edn. Council of Los Angeles, 1980-81. Mem. Calif. State U. Nursing Alumni Assn. (pres. 1980), San Gabriel Valley Nursing Consortium. Office: Brea Hosp Neuropsychiat Ctr 875 N Brea Blvd Brea CA 92621

ARONNE-AMESTOY, LIDA BEATRIZ, Spanish educator; b. Mendoza, Argentina, Jan. 26, 1940; d. Oswaldo Pascual José and Lida Rosa (Massei) Aronne; m. Ricardo Roberto Amestoy, Apr. 10, 1965 (dec. June 1984); children: Marcelo Daniel, Laura Ariadna; m. Larry Lee Kreis, July 1987. MA in English Lit., U. Cuyo, Argentina, 1963; PhD in Spanish Am. Lit., U. Conn., 1982. Tchr. ESL A. Schweitzer High Sch., Mendoza, 1964-65; prof. English, English lit. Sarmiento U., San Juan, Argentina, 1965-67, U. Cuyo, Mendoza, 1967-75; prof. Spanish-Am. lit. Córdoba (Argentina) Nat. U., 1976-78; teaching asst. Spanish U. Conn., 1980-82; asst. prof. Spanish U. Cin., 1984-85; asst. prof. Spanish Providence (R.I.) Coll., 1982-84, prof. of Spanish, 1985—; vis. prof., Mexico, 1976, 78, 83; lectr. in field, 1974-87; dir. literary workshops, Providence, 1986-87, Hispanic Arts workshops, Providence, 1986—; cons. R.I. State Council on Arts, 1987—. Author: Cortázar: La Novela Mandala, 1972, América en la Encrucijada de Mito y Razón, 1976, Utopía Paraíso e Historia: Inscripciones del mito en G. Márquez, Rulfo y Cortázar, 1986; author (short stories) Camino a Damasco, 1966, (poetry) Póstumo sueño, 1990; editor Hispanic Jour. of Arts and Culture, Providence, 1987. U. Cuyo grantee, 1973-75, grantee R.I. State Coun. on Arts, 1990; U. Conn. fellow, 1980-82, First Whetten fellow, 1981-82. Mem. MLA, New Eng. Ctr. for Latin Am. Studies, Sigma Delta Pi. Methodist. Office: Providence Coll Dept Modern Langs Eaton and River Ave Providence RI 02918

ARONSON, DEBORAH JAN, marketing professional; b. San Mateo, Calif., Apr. 29, 1955; d. Gilbert Stanley and Eleanor Corinne (Janzen) Aronson. B Social Work cum laude, San Diego State U., 1978; MBA, U. San Francisco, 1984. Mgr. mkt. representation Ford Motor Co., Milpitas, Calif., ops. mgr., field sales mgr. Med. social worker Chula Vista Community Hosp., Calif. Bank of Am. grantee. Mem. NAFE, U.S. Pilots Assn., U. San Francisco MBA Alumni Soc., MBA Assn. (past pres.). Home: 480 Oak Grove Dr 203 Santa Clara CA 95035 Office: Ford div Western Region PO Box 9013 Pleasanton CA 94566

ARONSON, ESTHER LEAH, association administrator, psychotherapist; b. Bklyn., Sept. 8, 1941; d. Nathan and Nellie (Borack) A.; m. Joel Allen Bernstein, Sept. 8, 1967 (div. 1978). BA, Bklyn. Coll., 1965; MA, New Sch. for Social Rsch., N.Y.C., 1982; MSW, NYU, 1984, postgrad., 1985—. Lic. social worker, N.Y. Resource cons. N.Y.C. Human Resources Adminstrn., 1965-82; counselor Fordham-Tremont Community Mental Health Ctr., Bronx, 1982-83, South Beach Psychiat. Ctr., Bklyn., 1983-84; social worker Alfred Adler Clinic, N.Y.C., 1984-85; pvt. practice clin. social work psychotherapist N.Y.C., 1986—; program developer Emanu-El Midtown YM-YWHA, N.Y.C., 1987-88, dir. ret. adult div., 1988—; lectr. Am. Mus. Natural History, N.Y.C., 1978. Contbr. articles to profl. jours. Mem. Am. Orthopsychiat. Assn., Inc., N.Y. State Soc. Clin. Social Work Psychotherapists, Inc., Soc. for Pub. Health Edn., NAFE, Phi Delta Kappa, Kappa Delta Pi. Home: 2 Fifth Ave Apt 31 New York NY 10011

ARONSON, REBECCA, clothing designer; b. Lima, Ohio, Oct. 17, 1941; d. Walter Gilbert Everett and Marian Marciel (Evans) Pearce; m. Niels R. Keiper, Dec. 23, 1968 (div. Apr. 1975); m. Douglas Ira Battenberg, May 19, 1979. Student, Bowling Green (Ohio) State U., 1959-61. Pvt. sec. Chem. Abstracts, Columbus, Ohio, 1961-63; flight attendant Am. Airlines, Chgo., Washington, 1963-69; booking agt. Nat. Concert Bur., Lawrence, Kans., 1969-72; owner The Village Jewel, Columbus and Cin., 1972-75; territory rep. Reynolds Metals Co., Columbus, 1973-75; project coord. Holland & Lyons, Inc., Washington, 1976-78; dir. mktg. Mid. States Constrn., Rockville, Md., 1978-79; asst. dir. condominium devel. Charles E. Smith Cos., Arlington, Va., 1980-81; pres., designer Aronson Enterprises, Inc., Washington, 1982—. Dir. Edn. Foundry Meth. Ch., Washington, 1978-81, trustee, 1988, 89, treas., 1989; rep. Real Estate Developers Task Force, Washington, 1981. Mem. Assn. for Rsch. and Enlightenment, NAFE. Club: KIWI's. Home and Office: Aronson Enterprises Inc 4628 Sedgwick St NW Washington DC 20016

ARONSON, VIRGINIA RUTH, music teacher, conductor; b. Glens Falls, N.Y., May 31, 1931; d. Irving Milton and Florence Estelle (Orcutt) Falkenbury; m. Andrew Thomas Murphy, June 12, 1955 (div. 1970); children: Marion Elizabeth, Katherine Annette, Patricia Lynn, Andrew Thomas; m. Chester Samuel Aronson, July 21, 1984. BA, Colby Coll., Waterville, 1953; Music Cert., U. Pacific, Stockton, 1955; MM, Westminster Choir, Princeton, 1977; ORFF cert., Conn. Cen. State Coll., Hartford, 1987. Classroom tchr. Wash. Sch., Stockton, Calif., 1955-56, Bellemeade Sch., Richmond, Va., 1956-57; bookstore mgr. Union Theol. Sem., Richmond, 1958-60; adminstrv. sec. Wash. Cathedral, Wash., 1970-73; product mgr. Mr. Rogers Neighborhood, Princeton, N.J., 1973-74; music tchr. The Hun Sch., 1975-77, Millstone Sch., N.J., 1978-89; pvt. practice music tchr., 1989—; dir. music St. John's Luth. Ch., Morrisville, Pa., 1990—; choral dir. Mercer County Community Coll., Trenton, summers 1981-82; dir. Colbyettes, Waterville, 1952-53; pres. Glee Club Colby Coll., 1952-53. Arranger: Songs of the Rain, 1952, Thank God I'm Old, 1985; composer Early in the Morn, 1940. Soprano Peace Odyssey Chorus, 1988; laborer World Coun. Chs., France, 1952; recreation dir. Am. Friends Svc. Com., Rapid City, 1951; seminar leader World Coun. of Chs., N.Y.C., 1948, Choral dir. Unitarian Ch., Princeton, 1981-90. Mem. Unitarian Universalist Musicians Network (chmn. profl. concerns com.), Am. Orff Schulwerk Assn., Am. Choral Dirs. Assn., Music Edn. Nat. Conf., N.J. Edn. Assn., Princeton Ski Club, Princeton Pro Musica, Westminster Alumni Choir. Democrat. Home: 66 Sycamore Ln Skillman NJ 08858

AROVA, SONIA, ballet educator, administrator; b. Sofia, Bulgaria, June 20, 1928; came to U.S., 1954; d. Albert and Rene (Melamedoff) Errio; m. Thor Sutowski, Mar. 11, 1965. Grad. Fine Arts Sch., Paris, 1940, Eng., 1944. Ballerina Internat. Ballet, London, 1944-47, Rambert Ballet, London, 1947-50, Royal Ballet, London, 1961, Festival Ballet, London, 1951-54, Ballet deChamps-Elysees, Paris, 1950-51, Am. Ballet Theater, N.Y.C., 1956-58; artistic dir. Nat. Ballet, Oslo, 1964-70, Hamburg Ballet, Fed. Republic Germany, 1970-71; co-dir. San Diego Ballet, 1971-75; dir. State of Ala. Ballet, Birmingham, 1981—, instr. Sch. Fine Arts, 1975—. Recipient World Championship of Dance award Ballet Jury, Paris, 1939; decorated knight of First Order, King Olav of Norway, 1971.

AROWESTY, JILL, financial planner; b. Plainview, N.Y.; d. Harold and Elene (Edelman) A.; m. David Jacobs, Mar. 11, 1989. BA summa cum laude, L.I. U., 1986, MA, 1988; postgrad., Coll. for Fin. Planning, 1989. Adminstrv. asst. AMR Planning Svcs., Inc., Plainview, N.Y., 1986, spl. projects coord., 1986-87, dir. fin. planning, 1987-88; mgr. fin. planning Bandfield Assocs., N.Y.C., 1989-90; mgmt. cons., N.Y.C. and Tucson, 1988—. Co-author: The Experts' Guide to Managing and Marketing a Successful Financial Planning Practice, 1988. Recipient Arthur J. Waterman award L.I. U., 1986. Mem. Internat. Assn. for Fin. Planning, Inst. of Cert. Fin. Planners (cert.), Phi Sigma Alpha, Phi Eta, Pi Gamma Mu, Phi Alpha Theta. Home: 4501 E Coronado Dr Tucson AZ 85718

ARP, MARILYN LADEAN, secretary; b. Bakersfield, Calif., Apr. 25, 1940; d. Lonnie Lee and Maggie Melinda (White) Blake; m. Robert Henry Arp, Apr. 25, 1958 (div. Dec. 1982); children: Raymond Lee, Randall Alan, Ronald Paul, Mary Cathlene. AA in Bus., West Hills Coll., 1975. Sec. Shell Oil Co., Coalinga, Calif., summer 1973-75, Coalinga Huron Unified Sch., 1975—. Executed mural for Shell Oil, 1975. Mem. Coalinga Dist. Hosp. (v.p. 1985-86, pres. 1986-88), Calif. Sch. Employee (pres. 1978-80), Coalinga Women's Club (judge 1970-750, Coalinga Art Club (judge 1982-84). Home: 523 E Polk Coalinga CA 93210 Office: Coalinga Huron Unified Sch 657 Sunset Coalinga CA 93210

ARREOLA, MONA JEAN, university administrator; b. Bklyn., Oct. 4, 1940; d. Robert and Marguerite (MacLeod) Gravel; m. Raoul A. Arreola, May 12, 1973; children: Catherine, Barbara, Thomas, Robert. BA, U. Fla., 1961; MS, Fla. State U., 1972, PhD, 1979. Cert. tchr., Fla. Assoc. dir. Memphis Cancer Ctr. U. Tenn.; specialist ednl. curriculum Creativision, Inc., Daytona Beach, Fla.; asst. prof. Memphis State U. Mem. NAFE, Internat. Reading Assn., Am. Assn. Cancer Insts., Mensa, Phi Beta Kappa, Phi Kappa Phi, Phi Delta Kappa.

ARRINGTON, CAROLYN RUTH, education executive; b. Parkersburg, W.Va., May 20, 1942; d. Robert Ray and Grace (Emrick) Dotson; m. Wayne Vernon Arrington; children: Kevin Ray, Kemp Gray, Korey Shay, Wayne, Kimberly. AA, Ohio Valley Coll., 1962; BA, Fairmont State Coll., 1964; MA, W.Va. U., 1966; supr. cert. Marshall U., 1970. Tchr., Greenbrier Bd. Edn., Lewisburg, W.Va., 1964-68; supr. Mason County Bd. Edn., Point Pleasant, W.Va., 1968-70; media specialist Kanawha County Bd. Edn., Charleston, W.Va., 1970-71; asst. state supt. schs., W.Va. Dept. Edn., Charleston, 1971—; cons. in field. Author numerous poems. Developer workshop materials. Bd. dirs. YWCA, Charleston, 1988—. SEA fellow U.S. Dept. Edn., 1984. Recipient Medal of Merit So. Edn. Ohio Valley Coll. Mem. Assn. Ednl. Communications and Tech. (pres. 1979-80; Edgar Dale award 1975, Spl. Service award 1982), W.Va., Ednl. Media Assn. (pres. 1975-76). Office: W Va Dept Edn Rm B 215 1900 Washington St Charleston WV 25305

ARRINGTON, DORIS BANOWSKY, art therapy educator; b. Nacogdoches, Tex., Mar. 20, 1933; d. Aubra Benton and Verda (Crabtree)

Banowsky; m. Robert Newton Arrington, Feb. 2, 1953; children: Robert N. Jr., Thomas Michael, Christian Carl. Student, U. Tex., 1957-58; BS cum laude, U. Houston, 1963; EdD, U. San Francisco, 1986. Registered art therapist; nat. cert. counselor. Art instr., head dept. Houston Independent Sch. Dist., 1963-65; ednl. curator Contemporary Art Mus., Houston, 1965-68; art instr., therapist Burlingame Sch. Dist., 1969-79; assoc. prof., dir. Coll. Notre Dame, Belmont, Calif., 1979—; clin. cons. Youth and Family Assistance, Redwood City, Calif., 1988-89, Cordilleras Mental Health Ctr., San Carlos, 1984-85; ednl. cons. Fla. State U., Tallahassee, 1989; profl. presenterlocal and nat. mental health agencies, 1979—. Columnist Newsletter Art Therapy, 1986—; contbr. articles to Art Therapy Jour., Gerontology Jour.; one-woman shows at exhbns., 1960—. Vol. San Mateo County Mental Health Dept., 1985-88, San Mateo County Gero Psych Program, 1989-90. Faculty study grantee Coll. Notre Dame, 1984. Fellow No. Calif. Art Therapy Assn. (pres. 1979-83), Friends of the Adv. Coun. on Women San Mateo County Bd. Suprs.; mem. Am. Art Therapy Assn. (standards chair 1987-89, bd. dirs. 1989-91, registered art therapist, rsch. grantee 1978), Am. Assn. Marriage and Family Therapists (clin.), Am. Psychol. Assn. (clin.). Office: Coll Notre Dame 1500 Ralston Belmont CA 94002

ARRINGTON, DOROTHY ANITA COLLINS (DOTTY ARRINGTON), retired real estate broker; b. Laurel, Miss., Sept. 9, 1922; d. Jeff clay and Maude Eula (Sudduth) Collins; m. Robert Newton Arrington, Oct. 27, 1956; children: Robert William, Cynthia Ann Arrington Morris. AA, Jones County Jr. Coll., 1941; student, U. Ala., 1942-43. Assoc. realtor Town & Country Village Realtors, Houston, 1970-72, McGuirt & Co., Realtors, Houston, 1974-77, 79-81, Duffy & LaRoe, Realtors, Houston, 1978-79; owner-broker Dotty Arrington, Realtors, Houston, 1972-74; asst. sales mgr. Realmco, Inc., Houston, 1977-78; pres. Dotty Arrington, Inc., Houston, 1981-89, ret., 1989. Vol. Literacy Vols. Am., 1987—. Mem. Tex. Assn. Realtors, Nat. Assn. Realtors, N.W. Houston C. of C., Daus. for the King (Nomads sponsor), Delphians. Republican. Episcopalian.

ARRINGTON, HARRIET ANN, historian; b. Salt Lake City, June 22, 1924; d. Lyman Merrill and Myrtle (Swainston) Horne; m. Frederick C. Sorensen, Dec. 22, 1943 (div. Dec. 1954); m. Gordon B. Moody, July 26, 1958 (div. Aug. 1963); 1 child, Stephen Horne; m. Leonard James Arrington, Nov. 19, 1983; children: Annette Rogers, Frederick Christian Sorensen, Heidi Swinton. BS, U. Utah, 1957. Utah State Bd. Edn., Ga. State Bd. Edn. Med. receptionist Utah Med. Ctr., Salt Lake City, 1948-50; supr. surg. secs. Latter-day Sts. Hosp., Salt Lake City, 1954-58; tchr. Salt Lake City Schs., 1957-58, Glynn County Schs., Brunswick, Ga., 1957-58; from med. sec. to office mgr. Dr. Horne, Salt Lake City, 1962-83; tchr. Carden Sch., Salt Lake City, 1971-72, women's history researcher, 1983—. Author: Heritage of Faith, 1988; contbr. articles to profl. jours. Active Rep. party (chmn., vice chmn. 1956-76); Delta Gamma Mothers Club (del. legis. coun., 1964-68, program chmn., 1968-70, treas. 1970-71). Nominated Pres. (Reagan) Vol. Action award, 1988. Mem. AAUW (Cert. Appreciation 1987), Utah Women Artist's Exhbn. (trustee chmn. 1986-89, state chmn. 1986-88, com. 1982-86, state cultural arts rep. 1984-86), Utah Women's Conf. (chmn. women's art exhibit 1987), Latter Day Saints Women's Relief Soc., Tchr. Cultural Refinement (pres. Twin Falls ward 1951-52), Chi Omega, Xi Alpha (pres. alumni chpt. 1946-47). Mem. LDS Ch. Home and Office: 2236 S 2200 E Salt Lake City UT 84109

ARRINGTON, PAMELA GRAY, college educator; b. Montgomery, Ala., Feb. 28, 1953; d. Willis Everett and Martha (Davenport) Gray; m. Richard Arrington III, Dec. 25, 1976; 1 child, Gray Rachard. BA in Psychology, Spelman Coll., 1974; MA in Counseling, U. Mich., 1975; ArtsD in Human Resource Devel., George Mason U., 1987. Counselor U. Mich., Dearborn, 1975, Talladega (Ala.) Coll., 1976-77, No. Va. Community Coll., Annandale, 1977-80; coord. affirmative action and grants No. Va. Community Coll., 1980-88; assoc. prof. Bowie (Md.) State U., 1988—; cons. Dept. of Def., Pentagon, Washington, 1989—. Vol., bd. dirs. Fairfax-Falls Ch. United Way Fund, Vienna, Va., 1986-89. Mem. Am. Soc. Tng. and Devel., AAUP, Phi Beta Kappa, Pi Lambda Theta, Psi Chi. Home: 1661 Cedar Hollow Way Reston VA 22094 Office: Bowie State U Bowie MD 20715

ARROWSMITH, MARIAN CAMPBELL, educator; b. St. Louis, Nov. 12, 1943; d. William Rankin and Elizabeth (Mitchell) Arrowsmith; m. William Earl Schroyer, July 23, 1983; stepchildren: Carey Jo, Amy Lynn. BS, La. State U., 1961; MEd, Southeastern La. U., 1978. Lic. tchr., La.; cert. practicum supr. Inst. for Reality Therapy. Tchr. 1st grade McDonough #26, Jefferson Parish Sch. Bd., Gretna, La., 1966; 2nd grade tchr. Woodlawn High Sch., Baton Rouge, 1966-67; kindergarten tchr. Univ. Terrace Elem. Sch., Baton Rouge, summer 1967; 1st grade tchr. Westminster Elem. Sch., Baton Rouge, 1967-72, Elm Grove Elem. Sch., Harvey, La., 1972-73; kindergarten tchr. Westminster Elem. Sch., Baton Rouge, summers 1968, 69, 70, 71, Elm Grove Elem. Sch., summer 1973; 1st grade tchr. St. Andrews Episcopal Sch., New Orleans, 1973-74; kindergarten tchr. St. Tammany Parish Sch. Bd., Folsom, La., 1974-77; early childhood specialist St. Tammany Parish Sch. Bd., Covington, La., 1977-87; prin. Woodlake Elementary Sch., 1987—; off-campus coordinating asst. St. Tammany Parish for Dept. Continuing Edn., Southeastern La. U., 1985-87; condr. workshops in field; selected ofcl. pres. Sunbelt Region of Reality Therapists, 1983; regional dir. La. and Miss. Reality Therapists, Sunbelt Bd. of Reality Therapists, 1983. Author: Helping Your Child at Home, 1982-83; Handbook for Early Childhood Tutorial Program, 1983-84. Mem. AAUW, Friends of Audubon Zoo, Vols. of Am., La. Assn. on Children Under Six, So. Assn. on Children Under Six, La. Assn. Sch. Execs., Nat. Assn. Female Execs., Sunbelt Assn. Reality Therapists (regional bd. 1982—, pres. and internat. bd. dirs. 1986—), Internat. Assn. Reality Therapists, Assn. Tchr. Educators, Delta Kappa Gamma (v.p. 1986), Alpha Delta Kappa (v.p.). Democrat. Presbyterian. Club: Basset Hound Club of Greater New Orleans (dir.). Avocations: horticulture, reading, fishing, showing dogs, racquetball. Home: 2327 Livingston St Mandeville LA 70448

ARROW YASKO, AMY, synthetic DNA company executive; b. Irvington, N.J., Feb. 18, 1957; d. David I. and Gloria June (Weinberg) Arrow; m. Edward John Yasko, Jr., Aug. 23, 1986; children: Melissa Frances, Jessica Rose. BS cum laude, Colgate U., 1978; PhD, Union U., 1983. Researcher Strong Meml. Hosp.-Cancer Ctr., Rochester, N.Y., 1983-84, Yale U. Sch. of Medicine, New Haven, 1984-85; lectr., course dir. U. Conn., Stamford, 1985; dir. research and devel. Internat. Biotech Inc., New Haven, 1985-86; exec. v.p., co-founder Biotix Inc., Danbury, Conn., 1986-89; exec. Amber Inc., Ridgefield, Conn., 1989-90; exec., officer Oligos Etc., Inc., Guilford, Conn., 1990—; cons. Arrow Dale Assocs., Ridgefield, Conn., 1985—. Co-author: Methods in Enzymology, 1988; contbr. articles to profl. jours. 1st violinist N.J. Jr. Symphony, 1970-74. Fellow Albany Med. Coll. Trustee Scholarship, Union U., 1978-83; named beauty pageant winner Long Beach Island C. of C., Ocean County, N.J., 1977; grantee in field. Mem. Nat. Assn. Female Execs., AAAS, Am. Chem. Soc., Sigma Xi. Republican.

ARROYO, MARTINA, soprano; b. N.Y.C.; d. Demetrio and Lucille (Washington) A. Studied successively with Marinka Gurevich, Joseph Turnau and Rose Landver; student, Kathryn Long Course Met. Opera.; BA, Hunter Coll. CUNY, 1954, DHL (hon.), 1987. Debut, Carnegie Hall, 1958, leading soprano, Met. Opera, N.Y.C.; in roles including: Tosca; performed opening night Met. season, 1970-71, 71-72, 73-74, performed at La Scala, Milan, Munich Staatsoper, Berlin Deutsche Oper, Rome Opera, Vienna State Opera, Covent Garden, Teatro Colon, Buenos Aires, San Francisco, Chgo., and all maj. opera houses; soloist, N.Y., Vienna, Berlin, Royal (London), Paris philharmonics, San Francisco, Pitts., Phila., Chgo., Cleve. symphonies, Concertgebouw, other maj. orchs.; frequent performer Saratoga, Ravinia, Tanglewood festivals and festivals Vienna, Berlin, Edinburgh, Helsinki; oratorios include Judas Maccabaeus; recorded for Columbia, London, Angel, DGG, Philips, EMI, RCA; vis. prof. La. State U., Baton Rouge. Former mem. Nat. Endowment of Arts, Washington; trustee Carnegie Hall, N.Y.C. Named Outstanding Alumna Hunter Coll., N.Y.C. Office: care Thea Dispeker Inc 59 E 54th St New York NY 10022

ARSENAULT, LEONA MARIE, financial executive; b. Saratoga Springs, N.Y., May 6, 1954; d. Joseph Abel and Elva M. (Gallant) A. Student Seminole Community Coll., 1982-85, Otterbein Coll., 1987—. Asst. to mng. editor Orlando Sentinel, Fla., 1973-78; asst. to gen. mgr. Cardinal Industries, Inc., Sanford, Fla., 1979-81, asst. v.p., 1981-84, v.p. corp. fin., 1984-86, corp v.p. corp. fin., Columbus, Ohio, 1987—. Republican. Roman Catholic. Office: Cardinal Industries 2255 Kimberly Pkwy E Columbus OH 43232

ARTERBURN, KATHERINE GREER, army medical service corps officer; b. Kansas City, Kan., June 22, 1962; d. Robert Leon Peterson and Sue (Suran) Peterson Dallam; m. David Rice Arterburn, June 11, 1988. BA in French, U. Ia., 1985. Commd. 2d lt. U.S. Army, 1986; advanced through grades to capt., 1989; platoon leader 560th Medical Co., Camp Humphreys, Korea, 1986-87; bn. adj. 28th Combat Support Hosp., Ft. Bragg, N.C., 1987-89; brigade adj. 44th Med. Brigade, Ft. Bragg, 1989-90; comdg. officer 187th Med. Brigade, Ft. Sam Houston, Tex., 1990—; participated in Operation Just Cause, Panama, 1989. Decorated Army Commendation medal with two oak leaf clusters, Army Achievement medal with oak leaf cluster. Mem. Assn. U.S. Army, Smithsonian Instn., Internat. Order Job's Daus. (honored queen 1981), U. Ia. Alumni Assn. Republican. Presbyterian.

ARTERS, LINDA BROMLEY, public relations consultant, writer; b. Phila., Dec. 18, 1951; d. Edward Pollard and Rosalyn Irene (Bromley) A. BA, Thiel Coll., 1973. Cert. emergency med. tech., Ariz., N.Mex. Dir. customer rels. Artmann Devel. Corp. Inc., Media, Pa., 1973-74; with S.E. Nat. Bank, Malvern, Pa., 1974-78, coord. pub. rels., 1976-78; pvt. practice pub. rels. consultant Media, 1978-84, Phoenix, 1984-88; mgr. community rels. City of Tempe, Ariz., 1988-; lectr. in field; past mem. pvt. industry coun. County Del (Pa.) Comprehensive Emplyment Tng. Act Program. free lance writer for local, regional and nat. mags. and newspapers. Past. chmn. Emergency Dept. Vols. Chandler Regional Hosp.; past bd. dirs. South Chester County Advanced Life Support, Inc., United Cerebral Palsy of Del County; mem. Phila. Indoor Tennis Corp., 1977-82; mem. Ariz. Humane Soc.; coord., mem. Critical Incident Stress Debriefing Team Phoenix Fire Dept. Mem. Pub. Rels. Soc. Am. (eligibility com. Phoenix chpt., mem. counselors group), U.S. Tennis Writers Assn., Phoenix C. of C. (communications coun.), Tempe C. of C. (past chmn. communications coun.), Cen. Ariz. Mountain Rescue Assn. (chmn. pub. rel., past chmn.). Republican. Presbyterian. : 204 W Vera Lane Tempe AZ 85284 Office: City of Tempe 31 E 5th St Tempe AZ 85284

ARTHUR, BRENDA KAY, financial consultant; b. Charleston, W.Va., May 28, 1951; d. Earl Washington and Martena (Miller) A. BA in Sociology, W.Va. U., 1972; MS in Edn., U. Dayton, 1975. Lic. ins. rep., Calif., Ariz. Field underwriter N.Y. Life Ins. Co., Long Beach, Calif., 1981-85; registered rep. N.Y. Life Securities Corp., Long Beach, Calif., 1984-85; fin. planner CIGNA Individual Fin. Services Corp., Irvine, Calif., 1985-87; registered rep. CIGNA Securities, Irvine, 1985-87; fin. cons., planner MKA Fin. Svcs., Inc., Newport Beach, Calif., 1987—; registered rep. Southmark Securities, 1987; registered broker, dealer Corp. Benefit Securities, Inc., Mission Viejo, Calif., 1988—. Mem. ARC, Santa Ana, Calif. 1982—; mem. Adam Walsh Resource Ctr., Orange County, planned giving com. Named Distinguished West Virginian, gov. W.Va., 1986. Mem. Nat. Assn. Life Underwriters, Orange County Charitable Giving Council, Planned Giving Roundtable Los Angeles, Orange County Planned Giving Com., Internat. Assn. Fin. Planning. Lodge: Zonta Internat. (v.p. 1985-86, bd. dirs. 1986—). Home: 1737 N Oak Knoll Dr Anaheim CA 92807 Office: MKA Fin Svcs Inc 1101 Quail St Newport Beach CA 92660

ARTHUR, JACQUELYN D., manufacturing executive; b. 1949. AB, City U., London, 1972. With Brit. Petroleum, 1967-85, fin. mgr., 1977-82, v.p. fin., 1982-85; treas. Dennison Mfg. Co., Framingham, Mass., 1986-87, v.p., treas., from 1987, now sr. v.p. strategic planning & corp. devel. Office: Dennison Mfg Co 300 Howard St Framingham MA 01701*

ARTHURS, ALBERTA BEAN, foundation executive; b. Framingham, Mass., Dec. 20, 1932; d. Maurice and Eleanor Irene (Levenson) Bean; m. Edward Arthurs, Dec. 20, 1960; children: Lee Michael, Daniel Jacob, Madeleine Hope. B.A., Wellesley Coll., 1954; Ph.D., Bryn Mawr Coll., 1972. Editor Liberty Mut. Ins. Co. Mag., Boston, 1954-56; dir. admissions Eliot-Pearson Sch.-Tufts U., Medford, Mass., 1957-59, instr. English, 1958-62; instr., lectr. Rutgers U., New Brunswick, N.J., 1964-72, asst. prof., 1972-73; dean Radcliffe Coll., Cambridge, Mass., 1973-75, Harvard U., Cambridge, 1975-77; pres., prof. English Chatham Coll., Pitts., 1977-82; dir. arts and humanities Rockefeller Found., N.Y.C., 1982—; bd. dirs. Culbro Corp., Techo-Serve, The Equitable Funds. Bd. dirs. Harbridge House, 1980-82, Salzburg Seminar in Am. Studies, Presbyn.-Univ. Hosp., Pitts, 1979-82, Pitts. Symphony Soc., 1980-82; trustee Dalton Sch., Hotchkiss Sch., 1975-83, Pine Manor Coll., 1976-81, Ellis Sch., 1977-82. Mem. Council on Fgn. Relations. Clubs: Duquesne (Pitts.); Harvard (N.Y.C.); Signet Soc. (Cambridge). Office: The Rockefeller Found 1133 Ave of Americas New York NY 10036

ARTMAN, FLORENCE JEAN, comptroller and salesperson; b. Pittsburgh, Pa., June 19, 1937; d. John and Gertrude (Clingan) Lang; m. James Clyde Artman, Oct. 23, 1959; 1 child, Sarah Jean. Diploma, We. Pa. Hosp. Sch. Nursing. Sec. Artman Parts & Equipment Co., Murrysville, Pa., 1974-80, comptr., 1976-89, salesperson, 1980-89. Democrat. Office: Artman Parts & Equipment Co 350 Rte 66 N Delmont PA 15626

ARVAY, LISA A., psychiatric nurse; b. Peckville, Pa., Oct. 9, 1960; d. Joseph Paul and Ann Theresa (Makowski) A. BSN, U. Pitts., 1983, MBA, 1989. Psychiatric nurse aide We. Psychiatric Inst. & Clinic, Pitts., 1981-83; psychiatric nurse We. Psychiatric Inst. & Clinic, 1983-89; nursing coord., quality assurance St. John's Mercy Health Ctr.; coord., patient care svcs., quality assurance Mercy Psychiat. Inst., Pitts., 1989—. Mem. NAFE, Am. Healthcare Execs., Pa. Nurses Assn. (treas. 1986-87, negotiating team mem. 1987, cons. team 1986-89). Democrat. Home: 508 Atlantic Ave Pittsburgh PA 15221

ARVAY, NANCY JOAN, public relations executive; b. Pitts., Aug. 27, 1952; d. William John and Cornelia (Prince) A. BA in History, Duke U., 1974; postgrad., Columbia U., 1974-75. Polit. and internat. communications specialist U.S. Senate Fgn. Relations Com., Washington, 1975-77; broadcast media relations rep. Am. Petroleum Inst., Washington, 1977-79; broadcast media relations rep. Chevron U.S.A., San Francisco, 1979-82, coordinator electronic news media relations, 1982-85; sr. media relations rep. Chevron Corp., San Francisco, 1985-87; dir. pub. relations Fireman's Fund Corp., Novato, Calif., 1987-89; v.p., ptnr. The Resource Group, San Francisco, 1989—; lectr. Dept. Interior-Park Service, Beckley, W.Va., 1983; chmn. pub. relations Internat. Oil Spill Conf., Washington, 1984-85. Author, coordinator: Research Studies in Business and the Media, 1980-83; contbg. author This Is Public Relations, 1985. Founding mem. San Francisco chpt. Overseas Edn. Group; mem. pub. relations com. World Affairs Council San Francisco. Mem. Pub. Relations Soc., Radio/TV News Dirs. Assn. (assoc.), San Francisco Women in Bus. Office: The Resource Group 555 DeHaro San Francisco CA 94107

ARZOUMANIAN, LINDA LEE, educational administrator; b. Madison, Wis., Apr. 29, 1942; d. James Arthur Luck and Rosemary M. (Peacock) Engstrom; m. Youri Feridoon Arzoumanian, Oct. 7, 1967; children: Stephan, Aaron. BS, Stout State U., Menomonie, Wis., 1964; MEd, Ohio U., Athens, 1969. Cert. tchr. Ariz.; lic. realtor Ariz. Residence hall asst. Ohio U., Athens, 1965-67; quality control supr. Advalloy, Inc., Palo Alto, Calif., 1967; tchr. adult edn. Eau Claire (Wis.) Pub. Sch., 1964-65; patient svc. dietitian Camden Clark Meml. Hosp., Parkersburg, W.Va., 1970; adminstr. pre-sch. Fishkill (N.Y.) Meth. Nursery Sch., 1976-84; substitute tchr. Tucson (Ariz.) Unified Sch. Dist., 1987-88, cons., 1988—; tchr. pre-sch. Tanque Verde Luth. Presch., Tucson, 1988-89; dist. moderator Sch. Community Partnership Coun., Tucson, 1988-90; mem. supts. adv. cabinet Tucson Unified Sch. Dist., 1988-89, mem. curriculum and instrn. coun., 1988-90, presch. adv. com., info. tech. bond review com., sex edn. curriculum adv. com. Mem. Dutchess County Child Devel. Com., Poughkeepsie, N.Y., 1979-81, Pima County Coalition Against Abuse Now; advancement chmn. troop 1968 Boy Scouts Am., Tucson, 1986, com. person troop 104, 1986-89; mem. joint com. on site based decision making TUSD-TEA; bd. dirs. Parent Resources, Inc. Mem. AAUW, ASCD, Assn. Edn. Young Children nat. com.), Tucson Assn. Young Children, Assn. for Children and Adults with Learning Disability, Santa Cruz Art Assn., Welcome Wagon of Tucson (mem. chmn.), Welcome Wagon of Tucson Noreast Alumnae. Home: 8230 E Ridgebrook Dr Tucson AZ 85715

ASA, CHERYL SUZANNE, research biologist; b. Herrin, Ill., Feb. 21, 1945; d. Robert Adron Asa and Dorotha Elnora (Cravens) Asa Armentrout; children: Brett Clavenna, Scott Clavenna. BA, U. Wis., 1976, MS, 1979, PhD, 1981. Rsch. biologist U. Minn., St. Paul, 1981-84; rsch. fellow Rockefeller U./N.Y. Zool. Soc., N.Y.C., 1985-87; field rsch. in ecology U. Minn., Mpls., 1986-88; rsch. biologist St. Louis Zool. Park, 1988—; cons. Sci. Mus. Minn., St. Paul, 1982-84, Equus mag., 1985—. Contbr. articles to profl. jours. Vol., Planned Parenthood, St. Louis, 1989—. NSF fellow, 1977-80; Noyes Found. fellow, 1985-88; grantee Nixon Griffis Fund, 1989-90, Inst. for Museum Svcs., 1989—. Mem. Am. Assn. Zool. Parks and Aquariums (chmn. contraception com. 1989—, chmn. cryopreservation com. 1989—), Am. Soc. Mammalogists, Animal Behavior Soc., Soc. for Conservation Biology, Soc. Study of Fertility, Soc. Study Reprodn. Office: St Louis Zool Pk Forest Pk Saint Louis MO 63110

ASAI-SATO, CAROL YUKI, lawyer; b. Osaka, Japan, Oct. 22, 1951; came to U.S., 1953; d. Michael M. and Sumiko (Kamei) Asai; 1 child, Ryan Makoto Sato. BA cum laude, U. Hawaii, 1972; JD, Willamette Coll. Law, 1975. Bar: Hawaii 1975. Assoc. firm Ashford & Wriston, Honolulu, 1975-79; counsel Bank of New Eng., Boston, 1979-81; assoc. counsel Alexander & Baldwin, Honolulu, 1981-83, sr. counsel, 1984-88; counsel firm Rush, Moore, Craven & Stricklin, Honolulu; bd. dirs. Hawaii Mother's Milk, Inc., 1986—; mem. Med. Claims Conciliation Panel, 1983—. Willamette Coll. Law Bd. Trustees scholar, 1972-73. Mem. ABA, Hawaii Bar Assn., Hawaii Women Lawyers, Phi Beta Kappa, Phi Kappa Phi. Democrat. Office: Rush Moore Craven & Stricklin 745 Fort St 20th Fl Honolulu HI 96813

ASBED, MONA H., university coordinator; b. Huntington, W.Va., Oct. 5, 1935; d. John Alfred and Esta Elma Houston; children: Steven, Jeffrey, Julie. BA, U. Mo., St. Louis, 1977, MEd, 1982. Lic. profl. counselor, Mo. Coord. program alcohol and drug awareness Southern Ill. U., Edwardsville; sr. specialist substance abuse Cigna Health Plan-MCC subs., St. Louis; mgr. program CD treatment for women Normandy Osteopathic Hosp. South, St. Louis; family therapist Deaconess Hosp., St. Louis; pvt. practice. Profl. mem. Nat. Coun. on Alcoholism and Drug Abuse. Mem. Am. Assn. Counseling and Devel., Coalition on Alcoholism and Other Chem. Dependencies (past pres., v.p.), MAAC (bd. dirs.), Chi Sigma Iota. Office: Counseling & Psychol Assocs 141 N Meramec Ste 217 Clayton MO 63105

ASBERRY, BOBBIE JO, educator; b. Mt. Pleasant, Tex., Aug. 21, 1934; d. Lee and Cornelia (Scott) Wilkerson; m. Robert Lee Asberry, July 13, 1957; children: Robbie Earlene, Cassandra Lynn. BS in Elem Edn., North Tex. State U., 1968, MEd, 1973, cert. kindergarten, 1975. Tchr. Dallas Ind. Sch. Dist., 1968-86; educator, owner Asberry Learning Ctr., Dallas, 1986—; textbook com. mem. Dallas, 1976-78; assoc. childhood edn. historian, Dallas, 1972-73; pupil personnel, faculty advisor, talented and gifted co., kindergarten chmn. Dallas Ind. Sch. Dist., 1978-86. Mem. Bus. and Profl. Women., NEA, Tex. State Tchrs. Assn., Nat. Retired Tchrs. Assn., Assn. Supervision and Curriculum Devel. Dmeocrat. Pentecostal. Home: 2519 E Pentagon Pkwy Dallas TX 75241 Office: Asberry Learning Ctr 2805 Arizona St Dallas TX 75216

ASBURY, JO-ELLEN, psychologist; b. Washington, Pa., Aug. 28, 1956; d. John Thornton and Wilhelmina (Jefferson) A.; m. Kevin L. Young, Mar. 14, 1987. BS, Ind. U. Pa., 1978; MS, U. Pitts., 1983, PhD, 1985. Asst. prof. Coll. Wooster (Ohio), 1984-87; rsch. psychologist Army Rsch. Inst., Alexandria, Va., 1987-88; social sci. analyst U.S. GAO, Washington, 1988-90; asst. prof. Bethany (W.Va.) Coll., 1990—; ind. scholar Coll. Wooster, 1987-88. Reviewer Jour. Black Psychology, 1988—. Predoctoral fellow NIMH, 1982; recipient Psychology Dept. Teaching award U. Pitts., 1984. Mem. Am. Psychol. Assn. Home: RD #1 Box E Bethany WV 26032 Office: Bethany Coll Dept of Psychology Bethany WV 26032

ASCH, CHARLOTTE ENDRES, writer; b. Lincoln, Nebr., June 5, 1930; d. Louis M. and Charlotte (Riefenberg) Endres; m. Morton J. Asch, 1 child, Sandra Louise. BS, Hood Coll., Frederick, Md., 1953; postgrad., Iowa State U., Ames, 1953-54; Postgrad., Loyola U., Chgo., 1960-64. Asst. editor AMA, Chgo., 1954-59; assoc. editor Scott, Foresman and Co., Chgo., 1959-66; free lance writer San Antonio Light, 1976-79; asst. editor HSC Mercury U.S. Army Health Svcs. Command, San Antonio, 1982-88; freelance writer San Antonio, 1989—; mem. Armed Forces Pub. Affairs Coun., San Antonio, 1982-88. Contbr. articles to profl. jours. Elected mem. Leon Valley (Tex.) City Coun., 1980-84; mem. VIAtrans Spl. Svcs. adv. com. San Antonio, 1982—, Leon Valley Libr. Bd., 1984-88. Recipient Commander's Award for Civilian Service Dept. Army U.S. Army Health Services Command, 1988, Award Excellence Dept. Army Command Info., 1984, Cert. Achievement Dept. Army, 1985. Mem. AAUW, Women in Communications, Delta Soc. San Antonio Chpt. (sec. 1988). Democrat. Home: 6012 Rue Sophie San Antonio TX 78238

ASCHER-NASH, FRANZI, writer; b. Vienna, Austria, Nov. 28, 1910; came to U.S., 1938, naturalized, 1944; d. Luise Frankl and Leo Ascher. Grad. cum laude, Humanistisches Maedchengymnasium, Vienna, 1928; student Vienna Acad. Music, 1929-31; m. Edgar R. Nash, Nov. 21, 1959. Free-lance short story writer, Vienna, 1934-38; after arrival in U.S., lectr. women's clubs under auspices of N.Y. Herald Tribune; music reviewer Neue Volkszeitung weekly, N.Y.C.; monthly light essay Austro-Am. Tribune; writer radio playlets German-Am. Writers Assn.; host short German lang. radio programs Sta. WBNX; tchr. New Sch. Social Rsch., N.Y.C.: writer annotations for classical records; host radio program The Story of the Art Song, Sta. WFUV-FM; appearances on Spoken Words Program Sta. WNYC; lectr. on the art song; lectr. music CUNY, York (Pa.) Coll., others; contbr. essays and poems to German-Am. Studies mag., Kreis der Freunde mag., Lyrik und Prosa mag., Lyrica Germanica mag., Inspiré, Swiss mag., Schatzkammer; author: (novella) Das Zwoelftonwunder, 1952; (novella) Confession in the Twilight (1st prize The Villager mag.), 1948; (books) Bilderbuch aus der Fremde, 1948, Gedichte eines Lebens, 1976, others; also poetry anthologies pub. in U.S., India, Fed. Republic Germany and Austria; monography on Charlotte von Schiller; contbr. articles Das Judische Echo mag. Founder Leo Ascher Award program Millersville U. Recipient citation Soc. German-Am. Studies, 1973. Mem. Assn. German Lang. Authors in Am., Soc. German-Am. Studies, Literarische Union (Fed. Republic Germany), Tagore Inst. of Creative Writing (India), B'nai B'rith. Home: 118 N George St Millersville PA 17551

ASCHOFF, LORRAINE MARIE, computer information scientist; b. N.Y.C., Feb. 14, 1950; d. Edward William and Marie Louise (Marshall) A.; m. John Morgan Roquemore III, Feb. 23, 1973 (div. June 1976). BA in Art History, U. Fla., 1971; MBA in Fin., NYU, 1984, advanced profl. cert. in computer applications and info. systems, 1988. Sales rep. VIP Fabrics, N.Y.C., 1978-81; asst. to v.p. mktg. RAM Data, N.Y.C., 1981-82; sales agt. Equitable Life Assurance Soc., N.Y.C., 1982; programmer/analyst Drexel Burnham Lambert, N.Y.C., 1984-86, sr. programmer/analyst, 1986-88, project leader, 1988-89, project mgr., asst. v.p., 1989-90; project mgr. retail banking svcs. application architecture Mfrs. Hanover Trust, N.Y.C., 1990—. Clin. assoc. Suicide and Crisis Prevention Ctr., Gainesville, Fla., 1972. Mem. Mensa, L.I. Alumni Assn., Phi Beta Kappa (sec. 1985-87, pres. 1987—), Alpha Lambda Delta. Democrat. Home: 64-85 Saunders St Apt A-8 Rego Park NY 11374 Office: Mfrs Hanover Trust 130 John St New York NY 10038

ASCONE, TERESA PALMER, artist, educator; b. Cortland, N.Y., Nov. 1, 1945; d. Lawrence Henry and Bernice Rosella (Holcomb) Palmer; m. Michael Wayne Ascone, Oct. 15, 1965; 1 child, Michael Palmer. Student, Alaska Meth. U., Alaska Pacific U., U. Alaska. Painter/tchr. Alaska Pacific U., Anchorage, 1989—; pvt. tchr. watercolor Anchorage, to date; owner Alaskan Portfolio, 1981—. Juried shows include Alaska State Fair, 1979-80, Fur Rendezvous Juried Show, 1979, 80, All Alaska Juried Show, 1981, 84, 85, 90, Alaska Watercolor Soc. juried show, 1981, 83, 85, 86, 87, 88, 89, April in Paris juried exhibit at Capt. Cook Hotel, 1982, 83, 84, 87, Featured Artist, 1986, Watercolor Fairbanks, 1989; sponsor Anchorage Fine Arts Mus., 1990, Women Artist of West 1st Ann. Internat. Show, 1990; one women shows include Anchorage Mcpl. Librs., 1980, 82; group shows NBA Heritage Libr., 1986, Alaska Pacific U., 1989, Chitose City Hall, Chitose, Hokkaido, Japan, 1990; represented in pub. collection Alaska Pacific U.; cover artist Arctic Horizons Mag., 1986, Alaska Horizons Mag., 1986; subject of TV spl., 1988. Recipient Vol. of Yr. Caverly Sr. Ctr., 1986, various art show awards to date. Mem. Alaska Watercolor Soc., N.W. Watercolor Soc., Women Artists of West (v.p. 1983).

ASELAGE, SUSAN SEABURY, aircraft company executive; b. Concord, Mass., Nov. 15, 1954; d. Frank and Nancy Cate (Jenney) Seabury II; m. Charles Randall Aselage; 1 child, Cate Seabury. BA, William Smith Coll., Geneva, N.Y., 1976. Paralegal Skaden, Arps, Slate, Meagher & Flom, N.Y.C., 1977-79; corp. analyst Lehman Bros. Kuhn Loeb, N.Y.C., 1979-81; assoc. Wolsey & Co., N.Y.C., 1981-83; v.p., sec. Sabreliner Corp., St. Louis, 1983—; dir. Sabreliner Corp. Republican. Episcopalian. Office: Sabreliner Corp 18118 Chesterfield Airport Saint Louis MO 63005

ASH, ARLENE SANDRA, statistician, public policy researcher; b. Stamford, Conn., May 15, 1946; d. Barney and Rosalyn (Hain) A. BA, Harvard U., 1967; MS, Washington U., St. Louis, 1972; PhD, U. Ill., Chgo., 1977. Instr. math. U.S. Peace Corps, Mindanao, The Philippines, 1967-69; organizer health clinic Chgo. Women's Health Ctr., 1973-76; rsch. instr. Dartmouth Coll., Hanover, N.H., 1976-78; asst. prof. math Boston U., 1978-84; rsch. cons. sch. of medicine, sch. of pub. health Boston U., Boston, 1984-85; adj. asst. rsch. prof. Univ. Hosp., Boston, 1985-90, adj. assoc. rsch. prof., 1990—; cons. Sidney Farber Cancer Inst., Boston, 1978-80, Mass. Tchrs. Assn., Boston, 1984—, Health Care Financing Adminstrn., Balt., 1984—, Mass. Office of Atty. Gen., 1986—; sci. exchange lectr. Applied Math. Vien Toan Hoc Inst., Hanoi, Socialist Republic of Vietnam, 1987. Contbr. articles to profl. jours. Coord. community input for devel., pres. West Fens Elderly Housing Corp., 1985-90; participant Health Care Fin. Adminstrn.'s Adv. Com. on Adjusted Average Per Capita Cost, 1987. Recipient highest citation Health Care Financing Adminstrn., 1988. Mem. Am. Statis. Assn. (pres. Boston chpt. 1982-84), Am. Pub. Health Assn., Am. Women in Math., Fedn. Am. Scientists, Union of Concerned Scientists, Sci. for People, Caucus for Women in Stats. (pres. 1986). Jewish. Home: 73 Hemenway #207 Boston MA 02115 Office: Health Care Rsch 720 Harrison Ave #1102 Boston MA 02118

ASH, MARY KAY WAGNER, cosmetics company executive; b. Hot Wells, Tex., May 12; d. Edward Alexander and Lula Vember (Hastings) Wagner; m. Melville Jerome Ash, Jan. 6, 1966 (dec.); children: Marylyn Theard, Ben Rogers, Richard Rogers. Student, U. Houston, 1942-43. Mgr. Stanley Home Products, Houston, 1939-52; nat. tng. dir. World Gift Co., Dallas, 1952-63; founder, chmn. emeritus Mary Kay Cosmetics, Inc., Dallas, 1963—; speaker to various orgns. Bd. dirs. Wadley Inst. Molecular Medicine; chmn. bldg. fund. Prestonwood Bapt. Ch., Dallas; hon. chmn. Tex. Breast Screening Project, Am. Cancer Soc. Mem. Bus. and Profl. Women's Club. Office: Mary Kay Cosmetics Inc 8787 Stemmons Frwy Dallas TX 75247

ASH, PATRICIA ELEANORE, construction executive; b. Milw., Oct. 21, 1944; d. Otto Fred and Augenia D. (Heck) Beckman; m. Joseph D. Ash, Feb. 1, 1964 (div. 1986); children: Joseph Jr., Weston R. Student, U. Madison, 1976-83. Cert. bldg. inspector. Owner, operator Quality Bakery, Watertown, Wis., 1971-72; code enforcement officer III, bldg. insp. Madison (Wis.) Bldg. Dept., 1974-80; corp. safety dir. J.H. Findorff and Sons, Inc., Madison, 1980-84, E.O. Kraemer and Sons, Inc., Plain, Wis., 1984-88; chief exec. officer Loss Control Svcs., Madison, 1988—. Mem. Assoc. Gen. Contractors (safety com. 1980—), Southwestern Wis. Bldg. Inspectors Assn. Republican. Office: Loss Control Svcs PO Box 217 Poynette WI 53955

ASH, SHARON KAYE, real estate company executive; b. Altus, Ark., July 21, 1943; d. William Clyde and Odus Marie (Drew) Cline; m. J.W. Ash, June 1, 1966 (div. Oct. 1978); 1 child, Brian Edward. B.S., S.W. Mo. State U., 1985; grad. Realtor Inst.; cert. residential specialist. Lic. real estate broker, Mo. Personal lines asst. Squibb Ins., Springfield, Mo., 1967-69; bookkeeper Hood-Rich, Architects and Engrs., Springfield, 1969-89; owner Ash Computer Service, Springfield, 1985—; owner, broker Ash Real Estate, Springfield, 1985—; dir. Multilist Svc. Mem. Mo. Assn. Realtors, Nat. Assn. Realtors, Springfield Area C. of C., Million Dollar Sales Club (life mem.), NAFE. Democrat. Episcopalian. Avocations: golf, boating, reading, collecting clowns, jogging. Home: 4808 S Glenn Springfield MO 65810 Office: Ash Real Estate 1722X S Glenstone Springfield MO 65804

ASHBROOK, BEULAH MAE, career and educational consultant; b. Murray, Ky., Sept. 28, 1934; d. Eneas Hall and Cozette (Glisson) A. BS, Murray State U., 1955; MA, Duke U., 1964; MEd, Memphis State U., 1971; EdD, U. Tenn., 1973. Cert. counselor. Microbiologist VA Hosp., Durham, N.C., 1958-60; anesthesiology rsch. technician Duke U., Durham, 1960-64; registrar and teaching supr. Duke U., Sch. Med. Tech., Durham, 1964-67; coord. grad. program U. Tenn., Memphis, 1967-71; rsch. assoc. AMA, Chgo., 1972-73; dir. edn. Am. Soc. Allied Health Professions, Washington, 1973-79; cons., owner Ashbrook Assocs., Annapolis, Md., 1979-83; div. chair Shelby State Community Coll., Memphis, 1983-86, dept. head, 1986-90; career and ednl. cons. Ashbrook Career and Ednl. Consultancy, Memphis, 1990—; ednl. cons. Dept. Health and Human Svcs., Hyattsville, Md., 1979-80. Pres. Memphis Symphony Guild, 1987-89. Recipient George H. Weiner scholarship, 1951. Mem. Am. Phsycol. Assn., Assn. of Counseling and Devel., Am. Soc. of Allied Health Professions, Mid-South Assn. of Tng. and Devel., Delta Kappa Gamma. Republican. Methodist. Home: 3623 Beechollow Dr Memphis TN 38128 Office: Ashbrook Career and Ednl Consultancy PO Box 40346 Memphis TN 38174-0346

ASHBY, CHRISTI ANN, publisher; b. Memphis, Dec. 20, 1955; d. John Albin and Mary Ann (Hartwell) Williams; m. Robert Davis Ashby, May 14, 1983; children: Nicholas Robert, Kathryn Linda. AA, Seminole Community Coll., Sanford, Fla., 1975; BS, U. Fla., 1977. Info. specialist Alachua County, Gainesville, Fla., 1977-78; asst. buyer Burdines, Miami, Fla., 1978-79, dept. mgr., 1979; flight attendant Air Fla., Miami, 1979-84; pub. rels. officer Brevard County, Titusville, Fla., 1985-86; asst. pub. Patch Communications, Titusville, 1986, pub., 1986, editor, 1986, editor Shutterbug mag., pub. PhotoPro mag., 1986—; group pub. Patch Communications, 1990—. Editor Doors, 1975, Brevard County Ann. Report, 1986. Donor recruiter Cen. Fla. Blood Bank, Orlando, 1983; exec. com. Jess Parrish Hosp. Golf Tournament, Titusville, 1988-90; asst. sec.-treas. Jess Parrish Hosp. Found., 1990—. Mem. Am. Soc. Mag. Editors, Mag. Pubs. Am., Profl. Photographers Am., Fla. Mag. Assn. (bd. dirs. 1990—, conv. chmn.-elect), Fla. Fedn. Women's Club (dist. pub. rels. chmn. 1987), Jr. Woman's Club Titusville (pres. 1988, mem. of Yr. 1987). Democrat. Methodist. Home: 1825 Fig Tree Dr Titusville FL 32780 Office: Patch Communications 5211 S Washington Ave Titusville FL 32780

ASHBY, DENISE STEWART, speech educator; b. Charleston, W.Va., Aug. 15, 1941; d. Dennison Elmer and Marie Juanita (Queripel) Ellis; m. Rudolph Krutzner III, Dec. 6, 1958 (div. 1961); m. Garth Rodney Ashby, Feb. 15, 1976; children: Kevin Krutzner, Kevin Ashby, Lisa Ashby, Scott Ashby. AAsumma cum laude, Diablo Valley Coll., Pleasant Hill, Calif., 1981; BA in Speech summa cum laude, Calif. State U., Hayward, 1982; MA in Speech and Communication summa cum laude, Calif. State U., 1983. Owner Salon 105, Somerville, N.J., 1964-66; pres. Second Hand Rose, New Providence, N.J., 1966-76, The Place to be Beauty Salon, New Providence, 1966-76, The Place to be Boutique, New Providence, 1966-76; mgr. LaTortuga Boutique, 1977-81; instr. Los Positas Coll., Livermore, Calif., 1985—, Diablo Valley Coll., Pleasant Hill, 1982—; pres. Ashby & Assocs., Danville, Calif.; liaison Ctr. for Higher Edn., San Ramon, 1988—. Vice pres. Danville United Presbyn. Women, 1978-79. Recipient Pres.'s award, Calif. State U., 1983. Mem. Speech Communication Assn., AAUW (bd. dirs. 1988—), Pi Lambda Theta, Pi Kappa Delta (pres. 1982). Home: 82 Cumberland Ct Danville CA 94526 Office: Ctr for Higher Edn 1 Annabel Ln San Ramon CA 94596

ASHBY, LINDA SUE, educator, librarian; b. Crellin, Md., Feb. 20, 1946; d. Lee Leggitt and Wava Adelaide (Bittinger) A. BS in Edn., Kent State U., 1968, MEd in Secondary Supervision; postgrad., Malone Coll., Canton, Ohio, Ashland (Ohio) Coll. Permanent teaching cert., ednl. supervisory cert., Ohio. Libr. Warren G. Harding High Sch., Warren, Ohio, 1968; tchr. English, East Canton (Ohio) High Sch., 1968-89, libr., tchr. remedial reading, 1989—; rep. Stark County Educators Polit. Action Coun., Canton, 1983—. Campaign worker various state and local candidates, 1975—; past sec. Stark County UniServ Coun., Canton; mem. Five County UniServ Coun. Mem. NEA, Ohio Edn. Assn. (del.), East Cen. Ohio Edn. Assn. (del.), East Canton Educators Assn. (pres. 1974-76, 78—, chief negotiator 1975—). Republican. Baptist.

ASHBY, NORMA RAE BEATTY, journalist, beauty consultant; b. Mont., Dec. 27, 1935; d. Raymond Wesley Beatty and Ella Mae (Lamb) Beatty Watson Mehmke; m. Shirley Carter Ashby, Sept. 5, 1964; children—Ann, Tony. BA, U. Mont., Missoula, 1957. Reporter, Helena Ind. Record, 1953-56; picture editor Life mag., N.Y.C., 1957-58; picture researcher MD Med. Newsmag., N.Y.C., 1959-61; producer, hostess TV Show Today in Mont., Sta. KRTV, Great Falls, 1962-85; editor Noon News, Sta. KRTV, 1985-88, beauty cons. Mary Kay Cosmetics, Inc., 1988—; freelance journalist, 1988—; producer Great Falls Centennial program, 1984. Author: What Is A Montanan?, 1971, Montana Woman, 1977, Montanans, 1982, scriptwriter: Last Chance Gulch, 1964, Gentle Giants, 1969, Our Latchstring is Out, 1979, Paris Gibson, 1983, Martha, Pioneer Woman, 1984, Great Falls Centennial, 1984, First Ladies of Montana, 1986, Anuka, Montana's Island Home, 1986, North American Indian Days, 1987, Missiles of October, 1987, (co-author) Symbols of Montana, 1989. Co-chmn. Cascade County Bicentennial Com., Great Falls, 1974-76; founder, chmn. C.M. Russell Auction, Great Falls, 1979; bd. dirs. Mont. Physicians Service, Helena, 1980-87; co-chmn. Great Falls Centennial Com., 1982-85; Festivals chmn. Cascade Coounty 89ers, 1987-89; coord. Mont. Statewide BellRinging Project, 1989; chair Mont. Jefferson awards; pres. Cascade County Mental Health Assn., 1980-82; bd. dirs. Cascade County Hist. Soc., 1987—, Mental Health Assn. Mont., also editor. Co-host Children's Miracle Network Telethon, 1989. Recipient TV Program of Yr. award Greater Mont. Found. 1982-88, Communication and Leadership award Mont. Toastmasters Internat., 1983; named Tribune Most Influential Woman in Great Falls, 1984, hon. mem. Blackfeet Tribe Blackfeet Reservation, Browning, Mont., 1981, Mont. TV Broadcaster Yr., 1985. Mem. Women in Communications (founder, pres. Great Falls, Mont. chpt. 1988-90), Great Falls Advt. Fedn. (dir., Silver medal 1980), AWRT (founder, pres. Mt. Big Sky chpt. 1967, recipient cert. of commendation 1982). Club: PEO, Broadcast Pioneers.

ASHBY, ROSEMARY GILLESPY, college president; b. Farnham, Surrey, Eng., May 16, 1940; came to U.S. 1967; d. Robert Dymock and Margaret Lois (Gillespy) Watson; m. John Hallam Ashby, June 17, 1967. B.A., U. Capetown, S. Africa, 1960; B.A., Cambridge U., 1963, M.A., 1967, M.Litt., 1972. Head resident Radcliffe Coll., Cambridge, Mass., 1968-70, asst. dir. career planning, 1969-70; dir. residence, instr. French Pine Manor Coll., Chestnut Hill, Mass., 1970-71, dean students, 1971-75, acting pres., 1975-76, pres., 1976—; pvt. tutor Sao Paulo, Brazil, 1963-65; teaching asst. U. Capetown, 1959-60; panelist N.E. Assn. Schs. and Colls., Boston, 1983, Nat. Assn. Ind. Schs., Boston, 1985. Author chpt. in book. Adv. bd. Keimei Fund for Internat. Edn., N.Y.C., 1978—. Nat. Endowment of Humanities fellow, 1984. Mem. Mass. Commn. on Post-secondary Edn., Assn. Am. Colls. (exec. com. 1977-78), Assn. Ind. Colls. and Univs. in Mass. (exec. com. 1977-80, 89—), Women's Coll. Coalition (exec. com. 1985-88), Am. Inst. Fgn. Study (bd. acad. advisors 1986—). Home: 41 Crafts Rd Chestnut Hill MA 02167 Office: Pine Manor Coll 400 Heath St Chestnut Hill MA 02167

ASHDOWN, MARIE MATRANGA (MRS. CECIL SPANTON ASHDOWN, JR.), writer, lecturer; b. Mobile, Ala.; d. Dominic and Ave (Mallon) Matranga; m. Cecil Spanton Ashdown Jr., Feb. 8, 1958; children: Cecil Spanton III, Charles Coster; children by previous marriage: John Stephen Gartman, Vivian Marie Gartman. Student, Maryville Coll. Sacred Heart; student, Springhill Coll. Feature artist, women's program dir. daily program Sta. WALA, WALA-TV, Mobile, 1953-58; v.p., dir. Met. Opera Guild, N.Y.C., 1970-78, opera instr. in-svc. program, 1970-80; opera instr. in-svc. program Marymount Coll., N.Y.C., 1979-85; exec. dir. Musicians Emergency Fund, Inc., N.Y.C., 1985—; cons. No. Ill. U. Coll. of Visual and Performing Arts, 1985—; lectr. in field. Author: Opera Collectables, 1979, contbr. articles to profl. jours. Recipient Extraordinary Service award March of Dimes, 1958, Medal of Appreciation award Harvard Bus. Sch. Club N.Y.C., 1974, Cert. Appreciation, Kiwanis Internat., 1975, Arts Excellence award N.J. State Opera, 1986. Mem. Successful Meetings Directory, Nat. Inst. Social Scis., Com. for U.S.-China Relations. Home: 25 Sutton Pl S Apt 16-K New York NY 10022 Office: Musicians Emergency Fund Inc 820 2d Ave Ste 203 New York NY 10017

ASHE, MAUDE LLEWELLYN, home economics educator; b. Bakersfield, Calif., Feb. 9, 1908; d. Richard Samuel and Marguerite J. (Loudon) A. AB, U. Calif., 1928; MS, Oreg. State U., Corvallis, 1944; postgrad., San Jose (Calif.) State Coll., 1936-38, Stanford U., 1948. Cert. tchr., Calif. Instr. in home econs. Oreg. State U., 1943; assoc. prof. home econs. San Jose State U., 1944-73, emeritus prof. home econs., 1973—. Author: Finding West Country Fair Ancestors, 1939. Mem. Santa Clara County Fair Assn., San Jose, 1968; v.p. Kern Genealogy Soc., Bakersfield, Calif., 1986. Mem. AAUW (sec., chmn. San Jose chpt. 1978), Calif. Ret. Tchr.'s Assn., Calif. Ret. State Employees, Emeritus Faculty Assn., Nat. Trust for Hist. Preservation, Family Assn. of Austin, Calif. Home Econs. Assn. (chmn. com. San Francisco chpt. 1965, state advisor to student clubs No. Calif. area 1966), Imperial Valley Gem and Mineral Soc. (charter), Phi Upsilon Omicron. Democrat. Home: 2601 Centur Dr Bakersfield CA 93306

ASHE, SHARON J., construction executive; b. Bowling Green, Ky., Jan. 3, 1950; d. Archie Milo and Grady Hyland (Hudson) Glenn. AA, Bowling Green Bus. Coll., 1970; BA, U. San Francisco, 1982; student, U. Alaska, 1978. Dir. facilities Arix Corp., San Jose, Calif.; pvt. practice Redwood City, Calif.; dir. Nat. Advance Systems, Santa Clara, Calif.; dir. constrn. Pyramid Techs., Mountainview, Calif., 1990—. Mem. NAFE, Nat. Assn. Women in Construction.

ASHFORD, ANITA RHEA, security officer; b. Port Huron, Mich., Sept. 9, 1950; d. Mandel Douglas and Johnnie Mae (Woodley) A.; children: Durrand A., Kelli Lynn, Torri L. Assoc in Law, SC4 Jr. Coll., Port Huron, 1974; student, P H Jr. Coll., 1989—; grad., Dale Carnegie Sch., 1989. Supr. recreation City of Port Huron, 1968-77; childcare worker St. Clair County Juvenile, Port Huron, 1970-77; cashier Coll. Bookstore, Port Huron, 1970-72; cashier, sales rep. Penny's Dept. Store, Port Huron, Sears & Roebuck Store, Port Huron, 1971-73; sec. Southpark Ministerial alliance, 1976-77; security officer Detroit Edison Co., 1977—; reporter WHLS Radio Station, Port Huron, 1989—; chairperson Shiloh Ch. Scholarship, Port Huron, 1980--; section-head NAACP Nat. Security, Balt., 1980--; sec., bd. dirs. Marwood Manor Nursing Home, Port Huron, 1987--; mem. Criminal Justice Adv., Port Huron, 1988--. Author: Funeral, Victims of Drug Abuse, 1988. Chairperson Community Rels. Bd., Port Huron, 1982-83; sec. Dem. Party, Port Huron, 1983; candidate Port Huron City Coun., 1985-87, elected coun. mem., 1989—; mem. Community Priority Program, Port Huron, 1988—; sec. Crime Awareness Prevention Through Unified Reporting Effort Assn. of Port Huron Police Dept., founding sponsor, 1989; mem. Port Huron Area Sch. Dist. Milliage Adv. Coun., 1988-89; trustee, chair Shiloh Ch., 1989; exec. bd. dirs. Child & Family Svcs., 1989. Mem. NAACP, NAFE, Nat. Coun. Negro Women, SC4 Alumni Assn., Detroit Urban League, Power Club., Profl. Women, Order of Ky. Cols. (hon. col. staff of Gov. Ky. 1989). Baptist. Home: 1433 Coventry Ln Port Huron MI 48060 Office: Detroit Edison Co 4505 King Rd Saint Clair MI 48079

ASHFORD, EVELYN, track and field athlete; M. Ray Washington; 1 child, Rana. Student, UCLA. Track and field athlete, 1976—. Competed in 1976 Olympics; winner 2 Gold medals, 1984 Olympics; recipient Flo Hyman award Women's Sport Found., 1989. Address: 818 Plantation Ln Walnut CA 91789*

ASHFORD, ROSALIND MARY, advertising and marketing executive; b. Worcester, Eng., Oct. 8, 1954; came to U.S, 1978; d. Raymond Henry Joseph and Eileen Mary (Churchill) A. Cert. edn. with distinction, Madeley Coll., Staffordshire, Eng., 1976; BEd with honors, U. Keele, Eng., 1977. Promotional dir. Woodstock (N.Y.) Playhouse, 1979-82; dir. mktg. Bardavon 1869 OPera House, Poughkeepsie, N.Y., 1982-84, Pepsico Summerfare and Performing Arts Ctr. SUNY, Purchase, 1984-85, Hipp Waters, Inc., Greenwich, Conn., 1985-87; pres. Ashford Co., White Plains, N.Y., 1987—; cons. Bronx (N.Y.) Coun. on Arts, 1986—, Schoharie County Arts Coun., Cobleskill, N.Y., 1987—, East End Arts Coun., Riverhead, N.Y., 1987—. Contbr. articles to newspapers. Tutor Literacy Vols. Am., White Plains, 1987—. Mem. Actors Equity Assn., AAUW. Anglican. Office: 5 Harmon St White Plains NY 10606

ASHFORD, SUSAN JANE, educator, consultant; b. Inglewood, Calif., July 25, 1954; d. John Morse and Rose Elizabeth (Erickson) A.; m. James P. Walsh, May 21, 1983;1 child, Alice Elizabeth. BA with honors, San Jose (Calif.) State U., 1977; MS, Northwestern U., Evanston, Ill., 1981, PhD, 1983. Lectr. Grad. Sch. Bus. J.L. Kellogg, Evanston, 1980-83; asst. prof. Amos Tuck Sch. Bus. Adminstrn. Dartmouth Coll., Hanover, N.H., 1983-87, assoc. prof. Amos Tuck Sch. Bus. Adminstrn., 1987—. Contbr. articles to profl. jours. Mem. Acad. of Mgmt., Am. Psychology Assn., Phi Kappa Phi Honor Soc., Beta Gamma Sigma Honor Soc. Office: Dartmouth Coll Amos Tuck Grad Sch Bus Hanover NH 03755

ASHINOFF, SUSAN JANE, menswear manufacturing company executive; b. N.Y.C., Dec. 7, 1949; d. Lawrence Lloyd and Thelma B. (Rubens) A.; m. Robert Beier Mintz, June 18, 1983; 1 child, Geoffrey Harrison. A.A., Dean Jr. Coll., 1969; B.A., Finch Coll., 1971; M.P.A., N.Y.U., 1977. Menswear advt. asst. New Yorker Mag., N.Y.C., 1971-72; assoc. Staub, Warmbold & Assocs., Inc., exec. search co., N.Y.C., 1972-80; exec. v.p. Muhammad Ali Sportswear, Ltd., N.Y.C., 1980-81; pres. Forum Sportswear, Ltd., N.Y.C. and Portsmouth, Va., 1981—; group v.p. Coronet Casuals, Inc., Portsmouth, 1985—, also bd. dirs. Trustee Dean Jr. Coll. Named to Outstanding Young Women Am., U.S. Jaycees, 1980. Mem. Nat. Assn. Men's Sportswear Buyers, Men's Apparel Guild Calif. Club: N.Y.U. Office: 2615 Elmhurst Blvd Portsmouth VA 23701

ASHKIN, ROBERTA ELLEN, lawyer; b. N.Y.C., July 1, 1953; d. Sidney and Beverly Ashkin. BA magna cum laude, Hofstra U., 1975; JD, St. John's U., N.Y.C., 1978. Bar: N.Y., 1979, U.S. Dist. Ct. (ea. and so. dists.), 1980. Program dir. Sta. WVHC-FM, N.Y.C., 1974-75; assoc. editor Matthew Bender, N.Y.C., 1975-79; assoc. Morris & Duffy, N.Y.C., 1979-81, Lipsig, Sullivan & Liapakis, N.Y.C., 1981-84, Julien & Schlesinger, P.C., N.Y.C., 1984-89; pvt. practice N.Y.C., 1989—; adminstrv. law judge N.Y.C. Dept. Transp., 1988—. Chmn. bd. Actor's Classical Troupe, 1987-89. Mem. N.Y. State Bar Assn., Assn. Trial Lawyers Am., N.Y. Trial Lawyers Assn., Phi Beta Kappa.

ASHKINAZE, CAROLE LYNNE, columnist, author; b. N.Y.C., Jan. 20, 1945; d. Harry M. and Rose (Goldstein) A. French lang. cert., U. Rouen, Caen, France, 1964-65; A.B. with honors, St. Lawrence U., Canton, N.Y., 1966; M.S. in Journalism, Columbia U., 1967. Reporter Newsday, Garden City, N.Y., 1967-74; reporter Denver Post, 1974-75; producer Sta. WXIA-TV, Atlanta, 1975-76; columnist Atlanta Constn., 1976-89, mem. editorial bd., 1982-89; host weekly TV talk show, newspaper video edit., 1985-88; instr. Emory U., Atlanta, 1976-90; radio commentator sta. WGST, Atlanta, 1982-86; columnist, mem. editorial bd. Chgo. Sun-Times, 1989—. Editor: Saturday Night, Sunday Morning: Singles & The Church, 1978. Atlanta chmn. Holiday Project, 1984-87; mem. Mayor's Task Force on the Handicapped; grad. Leadership Atlanta, 1983, Leadership Ga., 1986; trustee St. Lawrence U., 1987—; nat. mgr. corp. fundraising The Holiday Project, 1986-88; mem. nat. adv. panel Child Care Action Campaign, 1988—. Recipient George Polk Meml. award L.I. U., 1967, Pub. Svc. award N.Y. State Pubs. Assn., 1967, 70, Pulitzer prize, 1970, Media award for Econ. Understanding, Amos Tuck Sch. Bus. Adminstrn., Dartmouth Coll., 1979, first place for best editorial Ga. Press Assn., 1984, Exceptional Merit Media award Nat. Women's Polit. Caucus, 1989, St. Lawrence U. Alumni Citation; named Woman of Yr., Ga. Women's Polit. Caucus, 1983. Mem. Soc. Profl. Journalists (dir. 1976-84, v.p. 1983-84, chmn. 1st Amendment Congress 1980, chmn. profl. devel. 1983; recipient 1st place award in criticism 1976), Columbia Journalism Alumni Assn. (regional v.p. 1985-87), Nat. Kidney Found. Ga. (bd. dirs. 1985-86, v.p. 1986), Sporting Club (Chgo.). Jewish. Office: Chgo Sun-Times 401 N Wabash Ave Chicago IL 60611

ASHLEY, AMBER KIM, chemical executive; b. Rock Hill, S.C., Mar. 5, 1959; d. William H. and Velma M. (Eaton) A. BS, Winthrop Coll., Rock Hill, 1977-82. From receptionist to asst. office mgr. R-M Industries Inc., Ft. Mill, S.C., 1982-87, purchasing exec., 1987-89, office mgr., personnel dir., 1989—. Mem. Nat. Assn. Female Execs. Baptist. Home: 10232 Rose Meadow Ln Charlotte ND 28226 Office: RM Industries Inc Bank St Ext Fort Mill SC 29715

ASHLEY, DARLENE JOY, psychologist; b. N.Y.C., Oct. 29, 1945; d. George Geiger and Ann Debra (Bernstein) Munzer; m. Joseph Michael O'Brien, Sept. 23, 1974 (div. June 1981); 1 child, Sundara Amber. BA with honors, Antioch Coll., 1966; MA, NYU, 1973; PhD, Calif. Grad. Sch. Family Psychology, San Rafael, 1987. Lic. clin. psychologist, Hawaii, Calif.; Diplomate Am. Bd. Med. Psychotherapists; lic. marriage, family and child counselor, Calif.; cert. Calif. Community Coll. instr., biofeedback therapist. Psychology instr. Coll. of the Redwoods, 1977-82, North Am. Coll., San Rafael, 1980; radio presenter KMPO/KKON, Casper, Ohio/Kealakekua, Hawaii, 1980—; cons., psychol. examiner Hawaii Bd. Edn., Hilo, 1982; psychology lectr. U. Hawaii, Hilo and Honolulu, 1982; predoctoral clin. psychology intern Redwood Ctr., Berkeley, Calif., 1983-85; pvt. practice psychotherapist San Rafael and Berkeley, 1985-87; pvt. practice psychologist Kailua-Kona, Hawaii, 1988—; workshop presenter, 1977—. Author: Voluntary Controls Training Handbook, 1982; author: (cassette) Deep Relaxation, 1983. Proponent House bill pertaining to psychologists, 1988; com. Rep. Virginia Isbell's Fundraiser, Kailua-Kona, 1988—. Recipient rsch. grant NSF, Mus. Natural History, N.Y.C., 1965, NIMH, NYU, 1968-70, fellowship NIMH, 1969, Outstanding Rsch. award Biofeedback Soc. Calif., 1987. Mem. Am. Psychol. Assn., Assn. Applied Psychophysiology and Biofeedback, Hawaii Psychol. Assn., Biofeedback/Behavioral Medicine Soc. of Hawaii, NAFE. Office: 75-5744 Alii Dr Ste 237 Kailua-Kona HI 96740

ASHLEY, DIANA GAYE, comptroller; b. Evanston, Ill., Aug. 10, 1948; d. Richard J. Daley and Patricia (Hoover) Shannon; m. Kent Alexander Story, Aug. 30, 1968 (div. July 1987); children: Dawn Nicole, Suzanne Marie; m. Mark Nathan Ashley, Mar. 11, 1988; 1 child, Ryan Emory Ashley. BA in Edn., Ariz. State U., 1981, MBA, 1984. Fin. mgr. Fortune Pers. Cons., Scottsdale, Ariz., 1985; comptr. S.W. Bus. Industry and Rehab. Assn., Scottsdale, 1986—. Mem. Nat. Rehab. Assn., Assn. MBA Execs., Beta Gamma Sigma, Sigma Iota Epsilon. Democrat. Home: 5915 E Juniper Ave Scottsdale AZ 85254 Office: SW Bus/Industry Rehab Assn 4410 N Saddlebog Trail Scottsdale AZ 85251

ASHLEY, KATHY LITTLEFIELD, county official; b. Woodruff, S.C., Apr. 10, 1945; d. William Edwin and Elsie Dorothy (Campbell) Littlefield; m. William Lowry Ashley, July 25, 1981. BS, Lander Coll., 1967; MS, Winthrop Coll., 1982. Extension home economist Clemson U. Extension, Aiken, S.C., 1967-73; county extension agt. Clemson U. Extension, Spartanburg, S.C., 1974-76, Abbeville, S.C., 1976—; asst. dir., dir. food services Wofford Coll., Spartanburg, 1973-74; cons. George W. Park Seed Co., Greenwood, S.C., 1986-88. Author: (slide set) Country Decorating for City Living, 1986 (Nat. Assn. Extension Home Economists award 1986). Named Outstanding Eggucator S.C. Egg Bd., 1986, 87. Mem. Smocking Arts Guild Am., Am. Home Econs. Assn. (cert.), S.C. Home Econs. Assn. (Best of Show award 1987), S.C. Assn. Extension Home Economists (sec. 1984-86, 1st v.p. 1986-88, pres.-elect. 1988-89, pres. 1989-91, Outstanding Home Economist award 1977, comml. awards 1984-86), Nat. Assn. Extension Home Economists (Disting. Svc. award, Continued Excellence award), Epsilon Sigma Phi. Presbyterian. Home: Rt 2 Box 85 Honea Path SC 29654 Office: Clemson U Extension PO Box 640 Abbeville SC 29620

ASHLEY, MERRILL, ballerina; b. St. Paul; m. Kibbe Fitzpatrick. Student, Sch. Am. Ballet. Joined N.Y.C. Ballet, 1967, prin. dancer, 1977—. Prin. roles in Balanchine's Ballo della Regina and Ballade, Jerome Robbins' Four Chambers Works, Robbins'/Tharp's Brahms/Handel, Peter Martins' Barber Violin Concerto, Violin Concerts and Fearful Symmetries; TV appearances include roles in Ballo della Regina, Emeralds, Four Temperments, Divertiments #15, Bournonville Divertissements, Midsummer Night's Dream for Dance in America (PBS), also appeared on Gala of Stars (PBS), 1980, 82, 84; author Dancing for Balanchine, 1984. Recipient Dance Mag. award, 1987. Office: care NYC Ballet Inc Lincoln Center Pla New York NY 10023

ASHLEY, PAULA CLAIRE, engineer; b. Pasadena, Calif., Oct. 23, 1939; d. Pierre Marcel and Mabel Claire (Brown) Honnell; m. Paul Edward Ashley, Dec. 27, 1962 (div. 1986); children: Steven Lane, Loren Kendell. BA, Vassar Coll., 1961; MS, Ariz. State U., 1979. Mathematician Lawrence Radiation Lab., Livermore, Calif., 1961-64; scientific programmer Goodyear Aerospace, Litchfield Park, Ariz., 1976-80; mem. tech. staff Automatic Electric Labs. GTE, Phoenix, 1980-82; sr. software engr. Digital Equipment Corp., Phoenix, 1982-84; systems software engr. comml. flight systems Sperry, Phoenix, 1984-86; prin. engr. comml. flight systems Honeywell Inc., Phoenix, 1986-88, engrng. sect. head comml. flight systems, 1988—. Mem. IEEE. Methodist. Office: Honeywell Comml Flight Sys PO Box 21111 Phoenix AZ 85036

ASHLEY, ROSALIND MINOR, writer; b. Chgo., Oct. 10, 1923; d. Jack and Frances (Wasser) Minor; m. Charles Ashley, Mar. 1, 1941; children: Stephen David, Richard Arthur. Grad., Moser Bus. Coll., Chgo., 1940; BS in Edn., Northwestern U., 1963; postgrad., Nat. Coll. Edn., 1968. Sec. Platt Luggage, Inc., 1944; Chgo. producer, performer Story Book Ladies WEAW, Evanston, Ill., 1954-55; elem. tchr. Sch. Dist. No. 65, Evanston, 1962-63, Sch. Dist. No. 39, Wilmette, Ill., 1964-70; assoc. editor Scott, Foresman & Co., Inc., Glenview, Ill., 1970-74; weekly humor columnist Citizen, Del Mar Citizen and La Costan, Solana Beach, Calif., 1986-87; freelance writer San Diego edit. L.A. Times and Citizen, 1987—; cons. Carlsbad (Calif.) Unified Sch., 1986-87. Author: Successful Techniques for Teaching Elementary Language Arts, 1970, paperback edit., 1981, Activities for Motivating and Teaching Bright Children, 1973, Simplified Teaching Techniques and Materials for Flexible Group Instruction, 1976, Portfolio of Daily Classroom Activities with Model Lesson Plans, 1979; editor: Language and How to Use It, 1970; contbr. articles to profl. and popular publs. Vol. Recs. for Blind, Chgo.; publicity chmn. Rancho Santa Fe (Calif.) Community Concerts Assn., 1986—; play judge Associated Community Theatres. Recipient grand prize for poetry Sta. KFAC-FM, L.A., 1984. Mem. AAUW, Welcome Wagon Club. Democrat. Jewish. Home: 260 Via Tavira Encinitas CA 92024

ASHLEY, SHARON ANITA, pediatric anesthesiologist; b. Goulds, Fla., Dec. 28, 1948; d. John H. Ashley and Johnnie Mae (Everett) Ashley-Mitchell; m. Clifford K. Sessions, Sept. 1977 (div. 1985); children: Cecili, Nicole, Erika. BA, Lincoln (Pa.) U., 1970; postgrad., Pomona Coll., 1971; MD, Hahnemann Med. Sch., Phila., 1976. Intern pediatrics Martin Luther King Hosp., L.A., 1976-77, resident pediatrics, 1977-78, resident anesthesiology, 1978-80, mem. staff, 1981—. Finalist Nat. Merit award, 1966. Mem. Am. Soc. Anesthesiologists, Calif. Med. Assn., L.A. County Med. Soc., Soc. Regional Anesthesia, Soc. Pediatric Anesthesia. Democrat. Baptist. Office: Martin Luther King Hosp 12021 S Wilmington Ave Los Angeles CA 90057

ASHLEY, SHEILA STARR, educator, translator; b. Wichita, Kans., May 29, 1941; d. Burton Edward and Virginia Lee (Capron) A. BA in Spanish, Wilson Coll., 1964; MS in Edn., U. Pa., 1967; translator cert., U. Madrid, 1979. Cert. secondary fng. lang. tchr., Pa. Fgn. lang. tchr. Radnor (Pa.) High Sch., 1967—, chmn. of dept., 1990—; translator Johnson & Johnson, N.J., 1979—, Midas Muffler, Phila, 1979—. Mem. student assistance team, Students at Risk, 1987—. Recipient grant, Coun. for the Humanities, 1983, Rockefeller Found., 1989. Mem. NEA, Pa. State Edn. Assn., Radnor Tchr.'s Edn. Assn., Pa. State Modern Lang. Assn., Am. Coun. on Teaching Fgn. Langs., Phila. LaCrosse Assn. (dist. referee), Lang. and History Collaborative of Phila. and Delaware Valley. Office: Radnor High Sch 130 King of Prussia Rd Radnor PA 19087

ASHLEY-TINNEY, LORI JEAN, financial planner; b. Port Huron, Mich., Dec. 28, 1960; d. Don Ralph and Barbara Jean (Heston) A.; married. A in Bus. Adminstrn., St. Clair County Community Coll., 1981; BS in Mgmt., Oakland U., 1983. Cert. fin. planner. With sales staff Met. Ins. Co., Bloomfield Hills, Mich., 1983-84; cert. fin. planner Provident Mut. Co., Bloomfield Hills, 1984-89; fin. planner Met. Ins. Co., Sarnia, Ont., Can., 1989—. Mem. Inst. Cert. Fin. Planners, Nat. Assn. Life Underwriters (nat. quality award 1986). Republican. Methodist. Office: Met Ins Co, 1202 Lambton Mall Rd, Sarnia, ON Canada N7S 5A1

ASHTON, BETSY FINLEY, broadcast journalist, author, lecturer; b. Wilkes-Barre, Pa., May 13, 1944; d. Charles Leonard Hancock Jones and Margaretta Betty (Hart) Jones Layton; m. Arthur Benner Ashton, Nov. 5, 1966 (div. 1972); m. Robert Clarke Freed, May 18, 1974 (div. 1981); m. Jacob B. Underhill III, Oct. 17, 1987. BA, Am. U., 1966, postgrad. in fine arts, 1969-71; student in painting, Corcoran Sch. Art, 1968. Tchr. art Fairfax County (Va.) Pub. Schs., 1967-70; reporter, anchor Sta. WWDC, Washington, 1972-73, Sta. WMAL-AM-FM, Washington, 1973-75; corr. Sta. WTTG-TV, Washington, 1975-76, Sta. WJLA-TV, Washington, 1976-82; consumer corr. CBS News and Sta. WCBS-TV, N.Y.C., 1982-86; sr. corr. Today's Bus., 1986-87; personal fin. contbr. CBS Morning Program, 1987, Lifetime Cable TV, 1988—; anchor FNN Money Talk, 1989; bd. dirs. Lowell E. Mellett Fund for a Free and Responsible Press, Washington, 1979-82; courtroom artist numerous trials, Washington, 1978-81. Reporter TV news report Caffeine, 1981 (AAUW award 1982); reporter spot news 6 P.M. News, 1979 (Emmy award); author: Betsy Ashton's Guide to Living on Your Own, 1988. Concert master of ceremonies Beethoven Soc., Washington, 1979-82. Recipient Laurel award Columbia Journalism Rev., 1984, Outstanding Alumna award Am. U., 1985, Outstanding Media award Am. U., 1986, Best Consumer Journalism citation Nat. Press Club, 1983. Mem. Soc. Profl. Journalists (pres. Washington chpt. 1980-81, bd. dirs. N.Y. chpt. 1989—), Alpha Chi Omega (v.p. chpt. 1964-66), Liberty Club N.Y.C. Episcopalian.

ASHTON, DORE, author, educator; b. Newark; d. Ralph N. and Sylvia (Ashton) Shapiro; m. Adja Yunkers, July 8, 1952 (dec. 1983); children—Alexandra Louise, Marina Svietlana; m. Matti Megged, 1985. B.A., U. Wis., 1949; M.A., Harvard, 1950; Ph.D. honoris causa, Moore Coll., 1975, Hamline U., 1982. Asso. editor Art Digest, 1951-54; asso. critic N.Y. Times, 1955-60; lectr. Pratt Inst., 1962-63; head humanities dept. (Sch. Visual Arts), 1965-68; prof. Cooper Union, 1968—; art critic, lectr., dir. exhbns. Bd. dirs. Found. for Edn. in Arts; adv. bd. John Simon Guggenheim Found., Smithsonian Instn.; mem. exec. bd. of P.E.N. Author: Abstract Art Before Columbus, 1957, Poets and the Past, 1959, Philip Guston, 1960, The Unknown Shore, 1962, Rauschenberg's Dante, 1964, Modern American Sculpture, 1968, Richard Lindner, 1969, A Reading of Modern Art, 1970, Pol Bury, 1971; Cultural Guide for New York, 1972; Picasso on Art, 1972, The New York School: A Cultural Reckoning, 1973, A Joseph Cornell Album, 1974, Yes, But, A Critical Biography of Philip Guston, 1976, A Fable of Modern Art, 1980, American Art Since 1945, 1982, About Rothko, 1983, Jacobo Borges, 1984, 20th Century Artists on Art, 1985, Out of the Whirlwind, 1987, Fragonard in the Universe of Painting, 1988; co-author: (with Denise Browne Hare) Rosa Bonheur, A Life and Legend, 1981; co-editor: Redon, Moreau, Bresdin, 1961; N.Y. contbg. editor Studio Internat, 1961-74, Opus Internat, 1968-74, XXième Siècle, 1955-70; assoc. editor Arts, 1974—; contbr. to: Vision and Value series (Gyorgy Kepes), 1966, The New Art Anthology (Gregory Battcock), 1966. Adv. bd. Swann Found., Guggenheim Found., PEN. Recipient Mather award for art criticism Coll. Art Assn., 1963, Art Criticism prize St. Louis Art Mus., 1988; Guggenheim fellow, 1964; Graham fellow, 1963; Ford Found. fellow, 1960; Nat. Endowment for Humanities grantee, 1980. Mem. Internat. Assn. Art Critics, Coll. Art Assn., Phi Beta Kappa. Home: 217 E 11th St New York NY 10003

ASHTON, LILLIAN RUTH, health care professional; b. Millville, N.J., Dec. 21, 1944; d. Morris and Florence (Maffia) Jacobs; m. Robert C. Ashton, July 11, 1964; 1 child, Robert C. Jr. High Sch. Grad., 1963. Adminstr. Southern Intercounty Med. Assn., Vineland, N.J., 1974—; exec. sec. Cumberland County Med. Soc., Vineland, N.J., 1974—; travel cons. A Travel World, Vineland, N.J.; adminstr. Vineland Radiology Magnatic Resonance Imaging, 1989-90; bus. mgr. Diagostic Sonics, Inc., Pitman, N.J., 1990—. Volunteer, Am. Cancer Soc., Vineland. 1988--, Millville Hosp. Auxillary, 1988--. Mem. Nat. Assn. Notary Republics, Nat. Assn. Med. Staff Coord., Med. Group Mgmt. Assn., Am. Assn. Med. Soc. Execs. Republican. Catholic. Home: 3051 N E Ave Vineland NJ 08360

ASHTON, SISTER MARY MADONNA, state health commissioner; b. St. Paul; d. Avon B. and Ruth (Fehring) A. B.A., St. Catherine's Coll., St. Paul, 1944; M.S., St. Louis U., 1946; M.H.A., U. Minn., 1958. Mem. Congregation of Sisters St. Joseph of Carondelet; dir. med. social service dept. St. Joseph's Hosp., St. Paul, 1949-56; dir. out-patient dept. St. Mary's Hosp., Mpls., 1958-59; asst. adminstr. St. Mary's Hosp., 1959-62, adminstr., 1962-68, exec. v.p., 1968-72, pres., 1972-82; commr. health State of Minn., 1983—; dir. Nat. City Bank, Mpls., St. Catherine's Coll., St. Paul; mem. bd. scientific counselors Nat. Cancer Inst. Recipient Sabra Hamilton award Program in Hosp. Adminstrn. U. Minn., 1958; Minn. Health Citizen of Yr. award, 1977, Gaylord Anderson Leadership award, 1988; Bush summer fellow Harvard Sch. Bus., 1976. Fellow Am. Coll. Healthcare Execs.; mem. Nat. Catholic Health Assn. (sec.), Assn. State Territorial health Officers (sec.-treas.). Home: 5101 W 70th St #120 Minneapolis MN 55439 Office: Dept Health State of Minn 717 SE Delaware St Minneapolis MN 55440

ASHWORTH, ELINOR GENE, financial analyst; b. Phoenix, Dec. 12, 1942; d. Arvid Wick and Erma Gene (Grant) Cooper; m. Monroe Alfred Ashworth III, Aug. 1, 1964 (div. Aug. 1977); children: Leslie, Monroe. AA, Del Mar Coll., 1963; BA, U. Houston, 1978, MBA, 1980. Adminstrv. asst. audit dept. Houston Nat. Bank, 1976-78; analyst, portfolio mgr. Investment Advisors, Inc., Houston, 1978—, exec. v.p., 1980—, chief adminstrv. officer, 1985—; dir. research, 1989—; also bd. dirs. Investment Advisors, Inc., Houston. Trustee Sch. Woods., Houston, 1974-77; pres., bd. dirs. New Neighbors League, Houston, 1968-73; mem. Mus. Fine Arts, Houston, 1987—. Fellow Fin. Analyst Fedn. (chartered); mem. NAFE, Houston Soc. Fin. Analysts (treas. 1986-87, v.p. 1987-88, pres. 1988-89, dir. 1989—), Investment Counsel Assn. Am., U. Houston Alumni Assn., Phi Theta Kappa (pres.). Republican. Methodist. Office: Investment Advisors Inc 1100 Louisiana Ste 2600 Houston TX 77002

ASHWORTH, PHYLLIS CORBETT, academic administrator; b. Newport News, Va., Aug. 27, 1952; d. Harry Eugene Jr. and Leah Laverne (Lane) Corbett; m. Thomas Edward Ashworth, Aug. 30, 1980. BA, U. N.C., Greensboro, 1974; MS in Edn., Ind. U., 1976; EdD, Va. Polytech. Inst. and State U., 1989. Assoc. dir. of cont. edn. Wytheville (Va.) Community Coll., 1976-82, asst. dir. instructional svcs., 1982-86, adminstrv. asst. to pres., 1986-89, dir. coll. svcs., 1989—. Mem. Reg. Literacy Coordinating Com., Southwest Va., 1988—; mem. Voter Edn. Coalition, Southwest Va., 1984, Humane Soc. of the U.S., Washington, 1987—; reg. panelist, Va. Commn. for the Arts, Southwest Va., 1979-81, 89—; com. chmn. Chautauqua Festival, Wytheville, 1988-90. Recipient Govs. Award for the Arts, Va. Commn. for the Arts, Richmond, 1985; named Chancellor's Fellow, Va. Community Coll. System/Va. Polytech. Inst. & State U., Richmond/Blacksburg, Va. 1986-87. Mem. AAUW (com. chmn.), Va. Community Coll. Assn., Wytheville C. of C., Inst. Rep. Am. Assn. of Women in Community and Jr. Colls. (mem. state exec. com.), Nat. Identification Program for the Adv. of Women in Higher Edn. Adminstrn., Phi Beta Kappa, Phi Kappa Phi. Democrat. Mem. United Ch. of Christ. Office: Wytheville Community Coll 1000 E Main St Wytheville VA 24382

ASKIN, JACALYN ANN, business manager; b. Somerville, N.J., Apr. 2, 1954; d. Kenneth Norman and Ruth Florence (Wagner) Smith; m. Ronald Gene Askin, Sept. 11, 1976; children: Kenneth David, Amanda Christine. BA in English & Psychology, Lehigh U., 1975; MS in Indsl. Mgmt., Ga. Tech., 1979; MA in Acctg., U. Iowa, 1985. Revenue officer I.R.S., Atlanta, 1974-78; rsch. asst. Ga. Tech., Atlanta, 1978-79; dir. of sponsored rsch. U. Iowa, Coll. of Bus., Iowa City, 1979-84; teaching asst. U. Iowa, Iowa City, 1984-85; fin. svcs. supr. A. Rsch. Tucson, Ariz., 1985-88; bus. mgr. Catalina Foothills Sch. Dist., Tucson, 1988—. Contbr. articles to profl. jours. Bd. mem. Friends of Catalina Foothills Sch. Dist., 1990. Democrat. Office: Catalina Foothills Sch Dist 2101 E River Rd Tucson AZ 85718

ASKINE, RUTH PARSE, educator; b. Stuttgart, Ark., Aug. 27, 1936; d. John Edward and Mattie Lee (Scales) Parse; m. David James Askine, June 16, 1960; children: Rebecca Ellen Askine Brown, John Irvine Askine. BA, Rice U., 1958; MS, U. Houston-Clear Lake, 1981, MA, 1989. Cert. tchr., Tex. Elem. tchr. Bailey Elem. Sch., Pasadena, Tex., 1958-60; elem. tchr. Berkeley County Schs., Martinsburg, W.Va., 1967-69, Laurel (Del.) Middle Sch., 1970-77; elem. tchr. sci. Tex. Mil. Inst., San Antonio, 1977-78; elem. tchr. South Houston Elem., Pasadena, 1978-81, Young Elem., Pasadena, 1981-84; tchr. U.S. history Beverly Hills Intermediate Sch., Pasadena Ind. Sch. Dist., Houston, 1984-90; tchr. world history and econs. South Houston High Sch., 1990—; pres. Southeast Coun. for Social Studies, Tex., 1989-90; coach acad. pentathlon team, grades 7, 8, Beverly Hills Intermediate Sch., Houston, 1988-909; coach acad. decathlon team, grades 11, 12, South Houston High Sch., 1990-91. Editor: Handbook for Teachers in Environmental Science, 1978, Confluent Economics Project, Levels 1-5, 1980. Elder First Presbyn. Ch., Pasadena, 1983-86. Mem. Tex. Coun. for the Social Studies, Nat. Coun. for the Social Studies, Tex. State Hist. Soc., Assn. Tex. Profl. Educators, AAUW (sec. 1982-84), Epsilon Rho (1st v.p. Delta Kappa Gamma chpt. 1986-88, scholarship 1986, 87).

ASKINS, NANCY PAULSEN, training and development professional; b. St. Paul, Nov. 2, 1948; d. Charles A. and Stasia (Sawicki) Paulsen; m. Arthur J. Askins, Apr. 28, 1979. B.S.in Home Econs., U. Cin., 1970; B.S. in Edn., 1971, M.Ed., 1972; postgrad. SUNY-Buffalo, 1974-76, Temple U., 1976, Walden U., 1988—; student C.L.U. program, 1979-81, Inst. Fin. Edn., 1982-85; cert. in mgmt. Am. Mgmt. Assn./Monmouth Coll., 1984; postgrad. Walden U., 1988—. Asst. aquatic supr. Cin. Recreation Commn., 1969-72; student affairs adminstr., mem. faculty U. Cin., 1970-72, Tex. Luth. Coll., 1972-73, SUNY-Geneseo, 1974-76, Temple U., 1976-78; tchr. drug awareness coord. Harlandale Schs., San Antonio, 1973-74; career life ins. agt., fin. planning cons. Phoenix Mut. Life Ins. Co., Phila., 1978-81; registered rep., securities agt. Phoenix Equity Planning Corp., Phila., 1980-81; owner Paulsen-Askins Fin. Services, Somers Point, N.J., 1980-81; mem. women's task force Phoenix Cos., 1980-81; tng. services coord. Collective Fed. Savs. & Loan Assn., Egg Harbor City, N.J., 1981-82, asst. v.p., tng. dir., 1982-84; tng. mgr. Shore Meml. Hosp., 1984-86, dir. ednl. devel., 1986-89, adj. prof. bus. & social scis. Atlantic Community Coll, Mays Landing, N.J., 1986-89; owner Nancy's Exquisite Creations, Somers Point, N.J., 1987-89; dir edn. svcs. Holy Gross Hosp., Ft. Lauderdale, Fla., 1990—; also part-time instr. wellness program; facilitator Assertiveness Tng. Group, Interpersonal Communications Group; owner, cons. Nancy P. Askins, MEd; instr. Inst. Fin. Edn., 1982-85. Agy. chmn. United Way Campaign, Phila., 1979, 80; bd. dirs. South Jersey Regional Theater, 1983-86, chmn., 1983-84; active ann. Muscular Dystrophy Telethon, Phila.; active Girl Scouts U.S., 1956-74, 84—; mem. Parish council, parish enrichment com., 1984-88, cantor St. Joseph Roman Cath. Ch., Somers Point, N.J., 1979-89; bd. dirs. Holly Shores Council Girl Scouts U.S., 1984-85; host fgn. exchange students Am. Scandinavian Student Exchange Program, 1985-97; mem. Somers Point Bd. Edn., 1986. Recipient Brotherhood-Sisterhood Achievers award NCCJ, 1985. Mem. Greater Camden Assn. Life Underwriters (chmn. Life Ins. Week for South Jersey 1978-79, bd. dir. 1979-81, pub. relations chmn. 1979-81, chmn. state edn. 1981), Am. Soc. Tng. and Devel. (treas. S. Jersey chpt., nat. dir. savs. and lending industry group 1983-84, hosps. and healthcare industry group 1984-86, nat. conf. speaker 1984—), AAUW, Am. Hosp. Assn., Am Soc. Health Edn. and Tng., Greater Mainland C. of C. (v.p., treas., membership coord. 1979-89, Pres. award 1983), U. Cin. Alumni of Greater Phila. Area (pres. 1980-89), Club: Alliance/The Women's Network (bd. dir. 1983-84). Democrat. Home: PO Box 63-4429 Margate FL 33063-4429 Office: Holy Cross Hosp Ednl Svcs Dept 4725 N Federal Hwy Fort Lauderdale FL 33308

ASLESON, RUTH ANN, ; b. Mpls., Dec. 10, 1926; d. Leonard William and Henriella (Gangelhoff) Hermann; married June 22, 1951 (div. Dec. 1983); children: Sharon Reilly Caldwell, Heidi Kennelly. BA, U. Minn., St. Paul, 1948; BS, Webber Coll., 1949; Hadley's degree, Hadley Sch., 1979. Active Bascom Palmer Eye Inst., Miami; founder U. Miami; mem. U. Com. 1,000; active support lectue series Nova U., Ft. Lauderdale; fundraiser Light Brigade, Broward Ctr. for the Blind. Recipient Giraffe award, Women's Humanitarian award Broward County Women's Advocacy Majority-Minority Group. Mem. AAUW (past pres. Pompano br.), Nova U. Gold Circle, Shriners, Miami City Ballet. Democrat. Methodist. Home: 1147 Hillsboro Mile Apt 414 Hillsboro Beach FL 33062

ASOMANING, SUSAN ADWOA, bank executive; d. Edwin Jackson Asomaming and Sandra (Feldman) Cohen. BA, Yale U., 1984; MBA, Wharton Sch., 1989. Researcher Ford Found., Nairob, Kenya, 1984; assoc. Planned Parenthood, N.Y., 1985-87, Citibank, Europe, Middle East, Africa, 1988. Chairperson, Internat. Forum Whitney Young Conf., 1988--. Fellow, Lauder Inst. Wharton Sch., Am. MBA Assn., Nat. Black MBA Assn.

ASPINALL, MARA GLICKMAN, marketing professional; b. N.Y.C., Aug. 14; d. Alvin and Betty (Klein) Glickman. BA, Tufts U., 1983; MBA, Harvard U., 1987. Assoc. First Boston Corp., N.Y.C., 1986; cons. Bain & Co., Inc., Boston, 1987-90; dir. mktg. Hale and Dorr, Boston, 1990—. Mem. Assn. Tufts Alumnae (pres. 1988-90), Harvard Bus. Sch. Assn., Tufts Club. Office: Hale and Dorr 60 State St Boston MA 02109

ASPLUND, BRONWYN LORRAINE, state legislator; b. Flint, Mich., Nov. 15, 1947; d. Leonard Earl and Clara Ellen (Bailey) Hawks; m. Roger Louis LaClair, June 1, 1971 (dec.); m. Charles Martin Asplund, Feb. 20, 1982; 1 child, David Alan. BA, Cen. Mich. U., 1969; MA, U. Hawaii, 1970; postgrad., U. Wash., 1982-83; JD, Franklin Pierce Coll., 1989. Tchr. Standish-(Mich.)Sterling Cen. High Sch., 1970-75; asst. prof. Mid Mich. Community Coll., Harrison, 1976-77, Ferris State Coll., Big Rapids, Mich., 1977-82; mem. N.H. Ho. of Reps., Concord, 1986—. Home: 296 Webster Lake Rd West Franklin NH 03235 Office: State House PO Box 39 Franklin NH 03235

ASPLUND, DORIS ELAINE, corporate professional; b. Wilton, N.D., Nov. 8, 1931; d. Walfred and Esther (Johnson) A. Student, Trinity Bible Coll., Chgo., 1951. Sec. N.D. Dept. Pub. Instrn., Bismarck, 1951-52; stenographer, clk. Knife River Coal Mining Co., Bismarck, 1952-55; chief clk. Knife River Coal Mining Co., 1955-78, corp. sec., 1978—, v.p. adminstrn., 1979—. Painter oil and watercolor works (various awards). Republican. Mem. Evang. Free Ch. Office: Knife River Coal Mining Com 1915 N Kavaney Dr Bismarck ND 58501

ASPY, JANE CATHERINE, administrator medical facility, hospital executive; b. Decatur, Ind., Feb. 20, 1935; d. Joseph Cyril and Florence Catherine (Bremerkamp) Laurent; m. Ronald Dean Aspy, Sept. 6, 1958; children: Cary Allen, Steven Dean, Rhonda Jane. Student nursing home adminstrn., Ind. U. and Purdue U., Ft. Wayne, 1972-73. Lic. nursing home adminstr. Adminstr. Decatur Community Care Ctr., 1975-78; exec. sec. Adams County Meml. Hosp., Decatur, 1978-85, asst. exec. dir., 1985—; adminstr. Lakeside Manor div. of Hosp., Decatur, 1988—. Coord. Alive & Well Program, 1984-88; exec. advisor Jr. Achievement Co., 1986-88; chmn. Distributive Edn.-High Sch., 1987-88; implementer Lifeline System, 1989; bd. dirs. High Sch. Vocat. Edn., 1986-87, Student Careers, 1989—. Mem. Am. Coll. Health Care Adminstrs., Am. Assn. Homes for Aging, Ind. Health Care Assn. Democrat. Roman Catholic. Home: 348 Mercer Ave Decatur IN 46733

ASSELIN, ANNA, clinical psychologist; b. Lewiston, Maine, June 11, 1954; d. Dolar and Franca (Esposito) A. BA, U. Maine, 1977; postgrad., U. of South Fla., 1975, Salve Regina Coll., 1976; PhD in Clin. Psychology, Calfi. Sch. Profl. Psychology, 1985. Lic. psychologist, Calif. Psychology intern Tri-County Regional Ctr., Fresno, Calif., 1981-83; psychology intern Santa Barbara County Mental Health Svcs., Santa Maria, Calif., Madera (Calif.) Care Unit, Madera Community Hosp.; psychologist, clin. treatment coord. Atascadero (Calif.) State Hosp., 1985-89; pvt. practice clin. psychologist San Luis Obispo, Calif., 1988—; cons. County Mental Health Ctrs., San Luis Obispo County, Santa Barbara County, 1989-90, Tri-County Regional Ctr., San Luis Obispo, Calif., 1989-90. Author: Behavioral Interventions with Autistic Children, 1985. Mem. Am. Psychol. Assn., San Luis Obispo Psychol. Assn. (treas. 1988-90), San Luis Obispo C. of C., Cen. Coast Jungian Soc. (speaker wide range of topics Jungian analysis, stress mgmt. and spiritual devel.). Office: 1317 B Chorro St San Luis Obispo CA 93401

ASTA, PATRICIA ELLEN, human resources management specialist; b. Port Chester, N.Y., July 5, 1945; d. David Norbert and Rita Julia (West) A.; B.S. magna cum laude in Psychology (scholar), C.W. Post Coll., 1967; M.S. (scholar), U. Bridgeport, 1969; M.S. in Counseling (scholar), U. So. Calif. 1972; postgrad. bus. mgmt. Pace U., 1973—; postgrad. Rutgers U., 1983—. Dir., Pirmasens (Ger.) Nursery Sch., 1969; ednl. adminstr. U.S. VA, Kaiserslautern, Germany, 1970-73; asso. dir. counseling Pace U., Pleasantville, N.Y., 1973-75; dir. counseling, tng. and edn. Wildcat Service Corp., N.Y.C., 1975-76; assoc. dir. N.J. Job Corps, Edison, 1976-78; mktg. account exec. mgmt. devel. program AT&T Long Lines, Parsippany, N.J., 1978-80; asst. v.p. Nat. State Bank, Elizabeth, N.J., 1980-81; mgr. tng. and devel., personal products div. Johnson & Johnson, Inc., Milltown, N.J., 1981-86; dir. human resources planning and devel. Rickel Home Ctrs., South Plainfield, N.J., 1986-87, v.p. tng. and devel. Great Atlantic & Pacific Tea Co., Montvale, N.J., 1987—; instr. psychology, bus., edn. depts. Pace U.; trainer staff devel. ITEL Corp. Cons., group leader YWCA, New Brunswick, 1987—; mem. exec. adv. bd. Cornell U. Food Mgmt. Inst.; mem. Pres's. Commn. on Employment of Handicapped; speaker bus. mgmt. classes, civic, ch. groups. Recipient cash award Planned Parenthood, 1967; scholar N.Y. State Regents, 1963-67, Iona Grad. Sch. Bus. Adminstrn., 1967; cert. life skills educator, guidance counselor, therapist, vocat. rehab. counselor; lic. Realtor, N.J. Mem. Nat. Vocat. Guidance Assn., Assn. Measurement in Edn. and Guidance, Am. Soc. Tng. and Devel. (v.p. programming, pres.-elect., N.J. chpt.), Met. Mental Health Assn. (exec. bd. 1975-78), Am. Assn. Higher Edn., Nat. Assn. Bank Women (chpt. ednl. coordinator), AAUW, Nat. Assn. Women Deans and Counselors, Am. Assn. Group Workers, Assn. Humanistic Psychologists, Nat. Assn. Bus. and Profl. Women, Orgnl. Devel. Network, Human Resources Planning Soc., N.J. Mental Health Assn., Mid-Hudson Affirmative Action Task Force, Mu Alpha Theta, Psi Chi, Sigma Tau Delta, Pi Gamma Mu. Club: Mensa. Author: Test Your Vocational Aptitude, 1976; How to Score High on the PACE Exam, 1978; contbr. articles to profl. jours., papers to confs. Avocations: travel, real estate. Address: 78 Monsey Heights Rd South Monsey NY 10952

ASTARITA, SUSAN GALLAGHER, communications company executive; b. Wilmington, Del., Oct. 6, 1941; d. Hugh Francis and Alice Clara (Pepper) Gallagher; m. Bruce Thomas Astarita, May 24, 1969; 1 child, Alice Catherine. AB in Polit Sci., Randolph-Macon Woman's Coll., 1963; MA in Comparative Govt., Georgetown U., 1973; postgrad. U. So. Calif., 1973-75. Adminstrv. asst. George Washington U., Washington, 1964, Ford Found., Nat. Assn. Edn. Broadcasters, Washington, 1965-66; asst. producer Youth Wants To Know, Theodore Granik Enterprises, Washington, 1966-68; community and public relations dir. Del. Tech. and Community Coll., Georgetown, 1968-72; writer-editor Inst. Indsl. Relations, UCLA, 1975-87; prin. Astarita Communications, Rolling Hills Estates, Calif., 1977—; lectr. Harbor Coll. Bd. dirs. The Assocs. (Palos Verdes Community Arts Assn.), 1977-79, Palos Verdes Symphony, 1978-79; mem. peninsula com. Calif. State U., Dominguez Hills; mem. Palos Verdes Transit Adv. Com.; mem. Episcopal Diocese San Diego, 1988; postulant The Sch. Theology, Claremont, Calif., 1989—. Mem. Women in Communications (dir. L.A. chpt. 1980-83), Torrance C. of C., Community Assn. of Peninsula (multi-cultural affairs com.). Democrat.

ASTILL, NORMA DI LAURO, educator; b. Rochester, N.Y.; d. Nicholas and Virginia (Pilla) Di Lauro; m. Bernard Douglas Astill, Apr. 9, 1955; children: Paul, Alexandra. BA, U. Rochester, 1948. Elem. tchr. Brockport (N.Y.) Cen., 1940-56. Chairperson Greece (N.Y.) Food Shelf, 1978—; bd. dirs. Rochester Phila. League, 1972—. Mem. AAUW (pres. Rochester chpt. 1990-92). Episcopalian. Home: 195 Lyell St Spencerport NY 14559

ASTON, SHEREE JEAN, optometrist, educator; b. Red Bank, N.J., Mar. 13, 1954; d. James Robert Camb and Dolly (Bayne Camb) Zannelli; m. Nick T. Aston, July 21, 1974 (div. May 1979). AAS, CUNY, 1975; BS, OD, Pa. Coll. Optometry, 1980, 82; MA in Social Gerontology, U. Pa., 1986, postgrad., 1986—. Lic. optometrist. Asst. buyer Bambergers, Newark, 1975-76, Mandee Shops, Bergen County, N.J., 1976-77; practitioner Doylestown, Pa., 1982-83; asst. dir. external edn. Pa. Coll. Optometry, Phila., 1983-85, faculty, 1983—, dept. chmn. external clin. program, 1985-89, coord. aging, 1987-89, exec. dir. P&D, 1989—; gerontology cons. Assn. Schs. and Colls. Optometry, Rockville, Md., 1987-89; project dir. Pa. Prevention of Blindness, Harrisburg, 1986-89, Am. Optometric Assn. Short Term Tng., Washington, 1986-87, Pa. Dept. Aging, Harrisburg, 1987-88; optometric gerontologist, NIDRR, Washington, 1987-89; external edn. coord, RSA, Washington,

1984-87; project adminstrv. rsch. assoc., NIHR, Washington, 1985-86; lectr. in field. Contbg. author: Low Vision: Principles and Applications, 1987, Aging and Rehabilitation, 1986; contbr. articles to profl. jours. Campaign chmn. United Way, Southeastern Pa., 1988, vice-chmn. 1987, others. Recipient Achievement award Southeastern Pa. United Way, Phila., 1988, Nat. Outstanding Clin. Educator award U. Houston, 1988, grants Pa. Office of BVS, Harrisburg, 1986, Am. Optometric Assn., Washington, 1986, Pa. Dept. Aging, Harrisburg, Pa., 1987, Adminstrn. on Aging, Washington, 1986, NIHR, Washington, 1985, RSA, Washington, D.C., 1984, Southeastern United Way, Phila., 1986. Fellow Am. Acad. Optometry (communications com. 1989—), Am. Optometric Assn., Nat. Soc. Fund Raising Execs., Pa. Optometric Assn., Phila. County Optometric Soc., Pa. Coll. Optometry (sec. 1984-86), Pa. Coll. Optometry Alumni Assn. (class rep. 1983—), others. Democrat. Lutheran. Home: PO Box 844 Skippack PA 19844 Office: Pa Coll Optometry 1200 W Godfrey Ave Philadelphia PA 19141

ASUNCION, PERLA QUEYQUEP, language and sociology instructor; b. Urdaneta, Luzon, Philippines, Mar. 2, 1936; came to U.S., 1971; d. Eusebio Fabia and Carolina (Goroza) Queyquep; m. Romeo T. Asuncion, May 23, 1985. LittB in Journalism magna cum laude, U. San Tomas, Manila, 1958; MA in English, Sam Houston State U., 1964; postgrad., Purdue U., 1974; postgrad. studies, Sam Houston State U., 1985. Asst. editor Dept. Agr., Natural Resources, Manila, 1958-60; reporter, deskman The Evening News, Manila, 1960-62; grad. teaching fellow English Dept. Sam Houston State U., Huntsville, Tex., 1962-64; language arts tchr. Cy-Fair I. Sch. Dist., Houston, 1964-65; instr. U. San Tomas, Manila, 1966-71, Centro Escolar U., Manila, 1966-68; instr. social sci. San Jacinto Coll., Pasadena, Tex., 1971—; moderator U. Santo Tomas student pubs., Manila, 1966-71; pub. rels. officer, moderator Centro Escolar U., Manila, 1966-68; sponsor Sociology Club, San Jacinto Coll., Pasadena, Tex., 1971—. Editor: Filipino Assn. for Metro Houston Newsletter, 1973-75. Vol. Salvation Army, South Shaver, Pasadena, Tex., 1987—. Recipient 4-yr. scholarship U. San Tomas, Manila, 1954, Delta Kappa Gamma state scholar, Austin, Tex., 1985; named teaching fellow Sam Houston State U. Behavioral and Social Sci. Div., 1962-64, Outstanding Tchr., San Jacinto Cen. Coll. Mem. AAUW, Delta Kappa Gamma, Pi Gamma Mu, Tex. Jr. Coll. Tchrs. Assn. Roman Catholic. Home: 503 E Willow Pasadena TX 77506 Office: San Jacinto Coll 8060 Spencer Hwy Pasadena TX 77505

ASWAD, BETSY (BETSY BECKER), writer; b. Binghamton, N.Y., Feb. 10, 1939; d. George Marrinan and Jane (Sprout) Becker; m. Richard N. Aswad, Sept. 22, 1962; children: Jem, Kristin. B.A.in English with honors, Harpur Coll., Binghamton; M.A., SUNY, Binghamton, 1965, Ph.D. with distinction, 1973. Mem. film editing staff Sta. WNBF-TV, Binghamton, 1957; apprentice So. Tier Playhouse, summers 1957, 58; asst. editor Link Log, 1962-63; from teaching asst. to instr. English SUNY, Binghamton, 1963-74, mem. adj. faculty, 1974-83, fellow Coll.-in-the Woods, 1973. Author: Winds of the Old Days (Edgar Allan Poe spl. award Mystery Writers Am.), 1980, paperback edit., 1983; Family Passions, 1985. Sec., Friends of Binghamton Pub. Libr., 1977-78; vol. Probe, Binghamton Gen. Hosp., 1978-79, Meals on Wheels, 1979-82, St. Mary's Soup Kitchen, 1983—, Binghamton Downtown Forum, 1986—. Mem. Women's Nat. Book Assn. (hon. 1986). Home: 192 Deyo Hill Rd Binghamton NY 13905

ATAMIAN, SUSAN, nurse; b. Cambridge, Mass., Sept. 14, 1950; d. Raymond H. and Alice (Chakerian) A. BA, Simmons Coll., Boston, 1972. RN, Mass. Staff nurse Mass. Gen. Hosp., Boston, 1972-74, pvt. duty nurse, 1975-76, staff nurse, 1976-77, rsch. study nurse, 1977-80, instr. nursing, 1982-84, sr. rsch. study nurse, 1984-87, dir. clin. rsch. nurse group, 1985-90, research study nurse, study coordinator, 1987-88, infection control nurse, 1988-90; infection control nurse clincian Mass. Gen. Hosp., 1990—; rsch. asst. III U. Cinn. Hosp., 1980-81; staff nurse Kimberly Nurses, Orange, Calif., 1982; cons. nutrition and liver diseases, McGaw Labs, Santa Ana, Calif., 1980-81; chmn. faculty dev. library com. Shepard Gill Sch., Boston, 1983-84. Agt. Class of 1972 Simmons Coll., 1972, 86—, mem. com. alumnae fund, 1987-89. Mem. Am. Nurses Assn., Mass. Nurses Assn., Am. Nurses Found. Century Club, Nat. Assn. Rsch. Nurses and Dietitians, Assn. Practitioners of Infection Control, Simmons Coll. Nursing Honor Soc., Simmons Club Boston (bd. dirs. 1988—, pres. 1990—). Armenian Apostolic. Office: Mass Gen Hosp Infection Control Unit Clinics 1 Boston MA 02114

ATHAS, ELAINE JOANNA, educational association executive; b. Chgo.; d. James Leonidas and Joanna (Kanelos) Sikokis; m. Leo James Athas, July 30, 1972; children: James Leo, Jayna Elaine. BS in Edn., Loyola U., Chgo., 1964, MEd in Adminstrn., 1975, EdD in Adminstrn., 1980. Cert. tchr., Ill. Tchr. Union Ridge Sch., Harwood Heights, Ill., 1964-71; spl. asst. State Supt. Edn./Supt. Pub. Instrn., Chgo. and Springfield, 1971-75; dir. community edn. Cook County Ednl. Svc. Region, Chgo., 1975-77; assoc. dir. tchr. corps program Northwestern U., Evanston, Ill., 1977-80; asst. prof. Sch. Edn. Loyola U., Chgo., 1980-88, asst. dean Sch. Edn., 1985-88; devl. officer, rep. ind. sector Nat. PTA, Chgo., 1988—; mem. alumni bd. Loyola U., 1988—. Contbr. articles on fundraising to various pubs. Campaign asst. Dem. gubernatorial race, Ill., 1978. Mem. Am. Assn. Sch. Adminstrs., Loyola U. Sch. Edn. Alumni (chair 1985-88), Phi Delta Kappa. Greek Orthodox. Office: Nat PTA 700 N Rush St Chicago IL 60610

ATHERTON, DENISE LYNN, vocal teacher; b. Trenton, N.J., June 7, 1964; d. David Roger and Ellie Ann (Graybeal) A. BMus, Mansfield U., 1986, tchr. cert., 1986; postgrad., Bowie State U., 1988—. Cert. music tchr. Piano tchr. Music and Arts Inc., Bowie, Md., 1988—; vocal music tchr. Bd. of Edn. P.G. County, Greenbelt, Md., 1987—; leader, counselor Md. Nat. Park and Planning Commn., Greenbelt, summer 1988, asst. dir. spl. populations, presch. camp, summer 1989. Mem. NAFE, MSTA, PGEA. Republican. Home: 14105 Bramble Ln Spt #T4 Laurel MD 20708

ATIGH, STEPHANIE ANNE, lawyer; b. Fresno, Calif., Feb. 19, 1951; d. Hassan Atigh and Yolanda (Imperato) Trask. BA in English, San Jose (Calif.) State U., 1972; JD, Santa Clara (Calif.) U., 1975. Bar: Calif. 1975, Mass. 1982. Staff atty. Legal Aid Soc., San Jose, 1975-80; staff atty. Legal Aid for Cape Cod and Island, Hyannis, Mass., 1980-82, exec. dir., 1982-84; asst. city atty. City of Salinas, Calif., 1984-88, city atty., 1988—. Co-founder Independence House, Hyannis, 1980-84; mem. exec. com. Monterey (Calif.) County Justice 1986. Nat. Endowment Humanities fellow, 1979. Mem. Monterey County Bar Assn. (exec. com. 1989—), Monterey County Women Lawyers (chair elect 1989—), Nat. Lawyers Guild (exec. com. 1987—). Office: City of Salinas 200 Lincoln Ave Salinas CA 93901

ATKINS, CANDI, management consultant, small business owner; b. Chgo., Aug. 19, 1946; d. Norman R. and Catherine Kay (Coughlin) Wolfe; children: James N., Amanda Kate. Assoc. in Edn., Thornton Community Coll., 1968. Chief exec. officer Candi Atkins & Assocs., San Francisco, 1981—; owner, ptnr. Big Wonderful Me, Hinsdale, Ill. and San Francisco, 1986-90; faculty Diablo Valley Community Coll., Pleasant Hill, Calif., 1982-85; nat. trainer Nan McKay & Assocs., San Diego, 1984-87. Author: Shopping For Big Wonderful Me, 1988. Candi Atkins Day named in her honor Mayor of San Francisco, 1984; named to hon. Order Ky. Col. Mem. NAFE, Inst. Real Estate mgmt. (exec. com. San Francisco chpt. 1980-84, instr. 1981—, accredited resident mgr., cert. property mgr., Accredited Resident Mgr. of Yr. 1980), Nat. Speakers Assn. Roman Catholic. Home and Office: 2824 Morro Dr Antioch CA 94509

ATKINS, DEBORAH KAYE, state official; b. Bradenton, Fla., July 2, 1958; d. Ralph and Jewelle Vanessa (Gayle) Jones; m. Larry Bobby Atkins, July 30, 1983. AS with distinction, Monroe Community Coll., Rochester, N.Y., 1986; student, Va. State U., 1976-79, Va. Commonwealth Univ., 1990—; cert. Human Svcs., Monroe Community Coll., 1986. Credit investigator Sears Roebuck & Co., Rochester, N.Y., 1980; customer svc. rep. B. Forman Co., Rochester, 1980-81; youth counselor Brighton Youth Agy., Rochester, 1976-81; staff asst. Makro Inc., Capitol Hts., Md., 1981-82; customer svc. rep. MetroVision Inc., Capitol Hts., 1983-84; teen parent counselor Urban League of Rochester, 1985; job developer YWCA of Rochester, 1985-87; program coord. Urban League of Rochester, 1988; prog. support technician, sr. Dept. Med. Assistance Svcs., Commonwealth of Va., Richmond, 1989—. Mem. Women's Resource Ctr., Richmond, 1989—; heir link The Links Inc., Rochester, 1982—; vol. United Negro Coll. Fund Telethon, Rochester, 1988, N.Y. State Dept. Labor Career & Edn. Expo, 1989, WXXI Auction 21, Rochester, 1989, YMCA of Greater Rochester, 1989; vol. The Arts Coun. Richmond Children's Festival, 1989—, Sci. Mus. Va., Richmond, 1989—, Arts Coun. Richmond 15th Ann. June Jubilee, 1990, Children's Book Festival, 1990, Maymont Found. Flower and Garden Show, 1990, Jr. League Richmond 45th Book and Arthur Dance, 1990, Va. Spl. Olympics, 1990; mem. agy. svc. com. Friends Assn. for Children, 1990—. Named Outstanding Young Women Am., 1988. Mem. Nat. Coun. Negro Women, NAFE, Jr. league of Rochester, Nat. Trust Historic Preservation, Jr. League of Richmond, Jaycees. Democrat. Christian Ch. Address: 9300 Sandy Spring Cir Richmond VA 23229

ATKINS, HANNAH D., state official; m. Charles N. Atkins; 3 children: Edmund, Charles, Valerie. BS, 1943, BLS, 1949; LHD (hon.), Benedict Coll., Columbia, S.C.; MPA, U. Okla., 1989. Okla. state rep. Oklahoma City, 1968-80; commr., U.S. Commn. to UNESCO, 1979-82; asst. dir. Okla. Dept. Human Services, 1983-87; Okla. sec. of state, cabinet sec. human resources Oklahoma City, 1987—; del. to UN Gen. Assembly, 1980; former nat. committeewoman, Dem. Nat. Com.; pres., Okla. chpt., Am. Soc. Public Adminstrn.; bd. dirs., Women Execs. in State Govt., ACLU; former chmn., Okla. Advisory Com., U.S. Commn. on Civil Rights. Mem. NAACP, Urban League, Phi Beta Kappa, Alpha Kappa Alpha. Office: 101 State Capitol Bldg Oklahoma City OK 73105-4897

ATKINS, KAY ROBERTA, association executive; b. Flint, Mich., Aug. 21, 1939; d. Robert Henry and Jessie Mary (Cummings) Bueschen; children—Robert, Karla, James. Student Albion Coll., 1957-60; B.S., Eastern Mich. U., 1963; M.S., Ohio U., 1975. Tchr. Raleigh City Schs., N.C., 1967-69; instr. Ohio U., Athens, 1972-73; trainer Ohio Family Planning Tng. Ctr., Columbus, 1974-80; dir. edn. Planned Parenthood of S.E. Ohio, Athens, 1973-74, asst. dir., 1974-75, exec. dir., 1975—. Mem. Kootaga Area coun. Boy Scouts Am., 1980—; treas. United Campus Ministry, Athens, 1983-87; pub. relations com. chmn. United Appeal of Athens County, 1985—. Mem. NAFE, Am. Pub. Health Assn., Am. Home Econs. Assn., Ohio Citizens Coun., Athens County Community Svcs. Coun. (pres. 1988—), Planned Parenthood Affiliates of Ohio (pres.), Planned Parenthood Great Lakes Region Exec. Dirs. Council, Planned Parenthood Nat. Exec. Dirs. Council, Ohio Family Planning Assn. (v.p. 1986—). Democrat. Presbyterian. Avocations: travel; reading; singing; swimming; walking. Office: Planned Parenthood of SE 396 Richland Ave Athens OH 45701

ATKINS, MICHELLE BLAINE, clinical educator, consultant; b. N.Y.C., Feb. 12, 1953; d. Stanley Murray and Gilda Lee (Grossman) A. BSN, Brockport (N.Y.) Coll., 1974; MS, U. Ariz., 1978. Staff nurse Mt. Sinai Hosp., N.Y.C., 1974-76; sr. nurse Kino Community Hosp., Tucson, Ariz., 1976-79; unit dir. St. Mary's Hosp., Tucson, 1979-83; head nurse New Hanover Meml. Hosp., Wilmington, N.C., 1983-84; staff nurse Cape Fear Meml. Hosp., Wilmington, 1984-85; clinical educator, cons. St. Joseph's Hosp., Phoenix, 1985—. Contbr. articles to profl. jours. Chairwoman community rels. Congressman Udall's Hispanic Coalition for Diabetes. 1st lt. Nurse Corps USAR. Mem. ANA, Am. Assn. Diabetes Educators (cert., pres. 1990), Ariz. Nurses Assn., Am. Diabetes Assn. (5-yr. planning coun. Ariz. chpt. 1988—), Phoenix Nurses Consortium (bd. mem.). Office: Saint Joseph's Hosp 350 W Thomas Rd Phoenix AZ 85013

ATKINS, SALLY ANNE, management consultant; b. Canton, Ohio, Aug. 17, 1959; d. Robert J. Rowlands and Norma I. Atkins; m. Kendall Parker Truesdale, Dec. 20, 1983. BS summa cum laude, Northeastern U., 1984; postgrad., Boston U. From programmer to sr. systems analyst John Hancock Fin. Svcs., Boston, 1984-88, cons., 1988—. Active United Way, 1985-87. Mem. NOW, Boston Computer Soc., Computer Profls. for Social Responsibility, Uniforum, World Future Soc., Sigma Epsilon Rho. Lutheran. Office: PO Box 111 Boston MA 02117

ATKINS-MIKE, DEBORAH DENISE, systems engineer, realtor; b. Norfolk, Va., Oct. 19, 1959; d. William A. and Mophecia (Cook) Brickhouse; m. Peter Oswald Mike, Oct. 24, 1987. BA in Math., U. Va., 1981; postgrad., Johns Hopkins U., 1982-83, Johns Hopkins U., 1990—. Primary systems engr. GTE Govt. Systems Corp., Vienna, Va., 1985-87; computer analyst Info. Systems and Networks Corp., Arlington, Va., 1988—; realtor Mount Vernon Realty, Chevy Chase, Md., 1988; resident assoc. Grumman Corp., McLean, Va., 1988—. Active Smithsonian Pres. Assoc. Program, 1988. Mem. NAFE (bd. dirs. Reston, Va. chpt. 1986), Nat. Assn. Realtors, Md. Assn. Realtors, Montgomery County Bd. Realtors, N.Y. Inst. Photography.

ATKINSON, NANCY JANE, association executive; b. Port Huron, Mich., July 21, 1952; d. Harvey Charles and Lila Marie (Ohs) A. BS in Recreation, Mich. State U., 1973, MA in Recreation, 1976, MA in Agy. Counseling, 1982. Recreation dir. E. Lansing (Mich.) Sch. Dist., 1972-73; recreation asst. VFW Nat. Home, Eaton Rapids, Mich., 1973-74; camp dir. South Bend (Ind.) Girl Scouts, summer 1974; community svc. dir. Lansing (Mich.) Sch. Dist., 1975-76; field dir. Mich. Capitol Girl Scouts, E. Lansing, 1976-79; camping svc. dir. Mich. Capitol Girl Scouts, 1979-83; exec. dir. Golden Valley Girl Scouts, Fresno, Calif., 1983—. Mem. Am. Camping Assn. (bd. dirs. 1980-81), Am. Endurance Assn. Christian Scientist. Home: 10485 E Herndon Clovis CA 93612 Office: Golden Valley Girl Scouts 1486 Tollhouse #101 Clovis CA 93612

ATKINSON, REGINA ELIZABETH, medical social worker; b. New Haven, May 13, 1952; d. Samuel and Virginia Louise Griffin. BA, U. Conn., Storrs, 1974; MSW, Atlanta U., 1978. Social work intern Atlanta Residential Manpower Center, 1976-77, Grady Meml. Hosp., Atlanta, 1977-78; med. social worker, hosp. coordinator USPHS, Atlanta, Palm Beach County (Fla.) Health Dept., West Palm Beach, 1978-81; dir. social services Glades Gen. Hosp., Belle Glade, Fla., 1981—; instr. Palm Beach Jr. Coll.; participant various work shops, task forces. Vice pres. Community Action Council South Bay, 1978-79. Whitney Young fellow, 1977; USPHS scholar, 1977. Mem. NAFE, NAACP, Am. Hosp. Assn., Soc. Hosp. Social Work Dirs., Assn. State and Territorial Pub. Health Social Workers, Nat. Assn. Black Social Workers, Nat. Assn. Social Workers, Fla. Soc. for Hosp. Social Work Dirs., Area Agy. on Aging (adv. coun.), Glades Area Assn. for Retarded Citizens. Home: 525 1/2 SW 10th St Belle Glade FL 33430 Office: 1201 S Main St Belle Glade FL 33430

ATKINSON, SHANNON MARLOW, budget technician, personal computer consultant; b. Dallas, Dec. 12, 1962; d. Ronald Edward and Sarah Catherine (Brecheen) Marlow; m. William David Atkinson. Feb. 24, 1990. BBA in Fin., U. Houston, 1984. Asst. to v.p. Kanaly Trust Co., Houston, 1984-85; benefits adminstr. First Actuarial Corp., Austin, Tex., 1986-88; alternate fiscal officer and bus. mgr. Tex. Bd. Licensure for Nursing Home Adminstrs., Austin, 1988-89; budget technician Travis County Budget and Rsch., Austin, 1989—; personal computer cons., Austin, 1988—. Author booklet and several articles. Vol. tchr. pub. speaking Austin Community Schs., 1987; vol. Ann Richards for Gov. of Tex., 19890-90; vol. helping alcohol-addicted individuals, 1988—. Mem. Nat. Assn. for Female Execs., Toastmasters Internat. (Area Outstanding Toastmaster 1986), Austin Toastmasters (pres. 1986). Home: 2114-A Ann Arbor Ave Austin TX 78704

ATLEE, DEBBIE GAYLE, sales specialist, nurse; b. Oklahoma City, Jan. 8, 1955; d. Harold Phillip and Ella Ruth (Birks) A. BS in Nursing, U. Okla., 1977. Registered nurse, Okla.; cert. diabetes educator. Team leader ob-gyn Bapt. Med. Ctr. of Okla., Oklahoma City, 1977-80, asst. clin. supr. urology, 1980-81, nursing educator, diabetes educator, 1981-84; sales specialist Boehringer Mannheim Diagnostics, Inc., Indpls., 1984—; mem. regional piloting adv. group Nat. Diabetes Adv. Bd., Oklahoma City, 1984-85. Named Outstanding Bus. Woman, Bus. and Profl. Women, Capitol Hill chpt., 1981, Salesperson of Yr., 1987; recipient Outstanding Sales Achievement award, 1985, 87, 89. Mem. Am. Diabetes Assn. (exec. bd. Met. chpt. 1985—, pres. 1987), Am. Assn. Diabetes Educators, Western Okla. Diabetes Educators (pres. 1984, Outstanding Service and Dedication award 1984, chpt. service award 1985, chpt. edn. award 1984), Nat. Bd. Cert. Diabetes Educator, U.S. Power Squadron (bd. dirs. Oklahoma City 1984, 87), U. Okla. Alumni Assn. (life). Republican. Roman Catholic. Avocations: sailing, photography, gardening, music. Home: 649 Woodland Way Oklahoma City OK 73127 Office: Boehringer Mannheim Diagnostics Inc 9115 Hague Rd Indianapolis IN 46250

ATNIP, DEBORAH KAY, researcher, consultant; b. Sherman, Tex., Jan. 30, 1960; d. Murrel Wesley and Carron Ann (Howard) A. BA, Tex. Tech U., 1983, MA, 1988. Interim tng. coord. Stenocall/LRPS, Lubbock, Tex., 1986; teaching asst. in psychology Tex. Tech. U., Lubbock, 1984-86, project dir., 1987, mng. editor, assoc. investigator Med. Sch., 1987-88, asst. dir. lang. lab., 1988-89, dir. lang. lab., 1989-90; info. materials cons. Telephone Pioneer's Mus. Tex.-Southwestern Bell, Dallas, 1988-89; manuscript editor, Lubbock, 1986—. Sec. Episcopal Ch. Women, 1989-90, pres.-elect 1990-91. Mem. NAFE, Human Factors Soc. (assoc.), Internat. Assn. Learning Labs., Tex. Tech. Assn. Advancement Women in Higher Edn., South Central Assn. Learning Labs. (editor quarterly bulletin 1990-91). Republican. Home and Office: 4740 Pecan Meadow Dallas TX 75236

ATON, MARY FREDERICKA LAWHON, librarian; b. Arkansas City, Kans., Oct. 2, 1930; d. Fred Ralph and Ethel Alice (Richardson) Lawhon; m. Harry Bruncho Cordes, Aug. 28, 1951 (div. July 1973); children: Frederick Richard, Michael Steven; m. Bert Benton Aton, Jan. 20, 1979. Postgrad., Ark. City Jr. Coll., 1948-50, Kans. State U., 1950-51; BS in Informational Media, Millersville State Coll., 1965-75; postgrad., Towson U., 1980. Law librarian York (Pa.) County Law Library, 1975-76; elem. librarian Franklin Elem. Sch., York, Pa., 1976-78; asst. librarian Petroleum Reference Group, Washington, 1980-81, Foster Assocs., Washington; substitute tchr. Fairfax County Schs., Springfield, Va., 1982-83; proprietor Antique Shop, Pa., 1983; sales clk. Bloomingdale's, McLean, Va., 1983-84; asst. librarian Dickstein, Shapiro and Morin, Washington, 1984-85; law librarian Prince William County Law Libr., Manassas, Va., 1986—. Fellow mem. Am. Assn. Law Libraries, (So. Eastern chpt.), Law Librarians' Soc. Wash., Practising Attys. Roundtable. Republican. Office: Prince William County Law Libr 9311 Lee Ave Manassas VA 22110

ATTARD, ADELAIDE, gerontologist, educator, county administrator; b. N.Y.C., June 2, 1930; d. Consiglio and Elizabeth (Bonnici) Spitery; children: Ronald, Gary. B.A., Empire State Coll., 1974; post masters cert. in gerontology Adelphi U., 1976; M. Profl. Studies, New Sch. for Social Research, 1978. Asst. dir. sr. citizens unit Nassau County Dept. Recreation, 1966-68, recreation supr., 1968-69; supr. community services Dept. Recreation and Community Activities, Oyster Bay, N.Y., 1970-71; adj. prof. Adelphi U., Garden City, N.Y., 1975-77, New Sch. for Social Rsch. gerontological svcs. adminstrn., N.Y.C., 1979—; commr. Nassau County Dept. Sr. Citizen Affairs, Mineola, N.Y., 1971—; dir. Am. Assn. for Internat. Aging, Washington; chairperson Fed. Council on Aging, Washington, 1981-86; chairperson Committee on Family and Community Support Systems, mem. nat. adv. com. White House Conf. on Aging, Washington, 1981; del. to UN World Assembly on Aging, Vienna, 1982, White House Conf. on Aging, 1971, 81; mem. County Exec.'s Task Force on Status of Women, Mineola, 1977-80, mem. Gov.'s Task Force on Aging, Albany, N.Y., 1977-78; mem. adv. coun. N.Y. State Community Svcs. for Elderly, Albany, 1987. Contbr. articles to profl. jours. Bd. dirs. Welfare Research, Inc., N.Y.C., 1982—, Health and Welfare Council of Nassau County, N.Y., 1981—; mem. Nat. and Regional Tng. and Edn. Task Force Adminstrn. on Aging, Washington, 1971-73; mem. policy/adv. council for Columbia U. Ctr. for Geriatrics and Gerontology Long-Term Care Gerontology Ctr., N.Y.C., 1980—; adv., mem. curriculum com. dept. nursing SUNY, Farmingdale, 1982-83; mem. adv. com. on gerontol. services adminstrn. New Sch. for Social Research, 1976—; mem. Nassau County Criminal Justice Coordinating Council, 1982—; mem. Nassau County Republican Com., 1969—. Named Boss of Yr., Nat. Sec.'s Assn., Long Island chpt., 1971; Recipient Congl. award for Meritorious Service, 1981; Long Island Women Achievers' award 110 Ctr. for Bus. and Profl. Women, 1977, cert. of Leadership, L.I. Assn. Commerce and Industry, 1978; Pacemaker award St. Francis Hosp., 1975, Woman of Yr. award Long Beach Rep. Com., 1986; Cert. of Excellence, New Sch. Social Research, 1978-79, Disting. Contbns. in Field of Pub. Mgmt. award L.I. chpt. Am. Soc. Pub. Adminstrn., 1984. Mem. Nat. Assn. Area Agys. on Aging (bd. dirs. 1976-78), N.Y. State Assn. Area Agys. on Aging (pres. 1976-77), Am. Assn. Retired Persons (assoc. mem.), N.Y. Conf. on Aging. Republican. Office: Nassau County Dept Sr Citizen Affairs 400 County Seat Dr Mineola NY 11501

ATTAWAY, NANCY HILLIARD, health services executive; b. West Memphis, Ark., July 22, 1954; d. Eugene Parker and Juanita (Kellogg) Hilliard; m. Wayne Albert Attaway, Apr. 8, 1989. Accredited record technician, AMA, 1976; student, Manatee Community Coll., Venice, Fla., 1988-89. Supr. rsch. info. Bapt. Hosp., Memphis, 1972-80; with utilization rev. dept. Crittenden Hosp., West Memphis, 1980-81; diagnostic-related grouping coord. Venice Hosp., 1981-84; dir. health info. St. Joseph Hosp., Port Charlotte, Fla., 1984—; owner Attaways's Gift's and Svcs., Venice, 1989—, Ven-Wood Trophies, Inc., Venice, 1990—; cons. Life Enrichment Ctr., Port Charlotte, 1987-89. Author: Poems of Great America, 1989; contbr. recipes to Venice Centennial Cookbook, 1988. Active Fla. Network of Victim Witness Svcs., 1988-89, Nat. Victim Advocacy Ctr., 1988—; campaign worker Earl Moreland for State Atty., Sarasota, Fla., 1988, Pat Bidelman for U.S. Rep., Venice, 1988. Victims of Crime scholar Computerized Monitoring Svc. and State of Fla., 1988, 89. Mem. Am. Med. Record Assn., Nat. Orgn. Victim Assistance, Nat. Assn. Foster Care Reviewers, S.W. Fla. Med. Record Assn., Bus. and Profl. Women Orgn., Greater Venice Jaycees. Republican. Baptist. Home: PO Box 2219 Venice FL 34284 Office: St Joseph Hosp 2500 Harbor Blvd Port Charlotte FL 33952

ATTEBURY, JANICE MARIE, accountant; b. Sterling, Ill., Sept. 8, 1954; d. Carl Edwin and Eileen Marie (Gilley) McDonald; m. Rudy Joe Attebury, July 8, 1972 (div. 1977); 1 child, Nicole Marie. Student, Okaloosa Walton Jr. Coll., Fort Walton Beach, Fla., Sauk Valley Coll., Dixon, Ill., Houston Community Coll.; BSBA in Acctg., Calif. U. for Advanced Studies, 1990. Office mgr. Diamond Jim Enterprises, 1973-74; mgr. data processing dept. Sterling High Sch., 1974-75; bookkeeper 3-G Care Mgmt., Inc., 1977-78, office mgr., 1978-81; staff acct. Jerry T. Paul, CPA, 1982-84; staff acct. Lindgren, Callihan, Van Osdol and Co., Ltd., 1984-85, jr. acct., 1985-89; mgr. Riverside Cemetery, Sterling, 1989-90; pvt. practice A & E Acctg. Svc., 1989—; cons. Buckets and Brooms, Sterling, 1989—, Rock Chiropractic Health Ctr., Rock Falls, Ill., 1989—. Corp. bd. Abiding Word Christian Ctr., Sterling, 1985—, Twin City Crisis Pregnancy Ctr., Sterling, 1988—. Mem. Nat. Assn. Female Execs., Nat. Soc. Pub. Accts., Ind. Accts. Assn. Ill. Republican. Mem. Charismatic Ch. Home and Office: 114 W Kent Ave Broken Arrow OK 74012

ATTEE, JOYCE VALERIE JUNGCLAS, artist; b. Cin., Apr. 4, 1926; d. LeRoy Francis and Clara Marie (Becker) Jungclas; B.A., Rollins Coll., 1948; postgrad. U. Cin., 1952, 54, Art Acad. Cin., 1962-64, Edgecliff Coll., 1967; m. William Robert Attee III, Oct. 25, 1952; children: Robin Wilson, Wendy Ann. One-man shows include Loring Andrews Rattermann Gallery, 1964, Town Club, 1966, 69, 72, 75, 78, 81, 82, 83, 84, 90, Jr. League Office, 1975, Court Gallery, 1969, Bissingers', 1970, 76, Cin. Nature Ctr., 1974, 78, Cin. Country Day Sch., 1974; group shows include Town Club Cin., 1984, Bissinger's, 1984, Cin. Art Mus., 1962, Zoo Arts Festival, 1961, 62, 66, Town Club Cin., 1973-75, 77-79, 80-84, 85, Palm Beach (Fla.) Galleries, 1974, Showcase of Arts, 1976, Ursuline Ctr., 1976, Court Galleries, 1977, Indian Hill Artists, 1957-76, 82, 83, regional and local shows Nat. League Am. Pen Women, 77, 78, also nat. biennial art exhibit, 1970, Nat. Bicentennial Show, Washington, 1976, James H. Barker Gallery, Palm Beach, Fla., 1979, 80, 81, 82, Nantucket, 1982, Cin. Women's Club Show, 1979, Cin. Nature Ctr., 1983, Kimberton (Pa.) Gallery, 1988-89; represented in permanent collections: Bissingers, Cin. Recipient 1st prize in still life or flowers Cin. Womans Art Club, 1965, 69; Marjorie Ewell Meml. award, 1975. Mem. Nat. League Am. Pen Women (past pres. Cin. br., past state art chmn. 1st prize graphics 1975), Women's Art Club Cin. (past v.p.), Jr. League Cin., Jr. League Garden Circle (pres. 1974-75, speaker on flower paintings 1990). Episcopalian. Clubs: Town, University, Indian Hill, Cin. Woman's. Author: Elbey Jay, 1964. Home: 8050 Indian Hill Rd Cincinnati OH 45243

ATTIE, DOTTY, artist; b. Pennsauken, N.J., 1938. One-man shows include A.I.R. Gallery, N.Y.C., 1974, 76, 78, 80, 83, 86, Or Gallery, Osaka, Japan, 1986, PPOW, N.Y.C., 1988, 90, Pitts. Ctr. for Arts, 1989, Greenville County

(S.C.) Mus. Art, 1990, Tyler Galleries, Temple U., Elkins Park, Pa., 1990; group shows include Orion Editions, N.Y.C., 1987, Carlo LaMagna Gallery, N.Y.C., 1987, R.I. Sch. Design, Providence, 1988, Bernice Steinbaum Gallery, N.Y.C., 1989, Hillwood Art Gallery, 1989, Lang & O'Hara, N.Y.C., 1990; contbr. articles to jours. Grantee Creative Artists Pub. Svc., 1973, 76, Nat. Endowment Arts, 1975, 83, Hassamm/Speicher Fund Exhibition Purchase, 1982; Creative Artist fellow for Japan, 1985, Mid-Atlantic States Visual Arts Residency fellow, 1987; recipient Childe Hassam Purchase Exhbn. Purchase Prize, 1981. Home: 334 E 22d St New York NY 10010

ATTWOOD, CYNTHIA LOU, lawyer; b. Chgo., Dec. 12, 1946; d. John Gordon and M. Louise (Crenshaw) A.; B.A., Oakland U., 1969; J.D., U. Minn., 1973. Admitted to D.C. bar, 1973; atty. employment sect. civil rights div. U.S. Dept. Justice, Washington, 1973-74, atty. appellate sect., civil rights div., 1974-79; counsel appellate litigation mine safety and health div. Office of Solicitor, U.S. Dept. Labor, Arlington, Va., 1979-80, dep. assoc. solicitor, 1980-81, assoc. solicitor, 1981-86, assoc. solicitor occupational safety and health, 1986—. Mem. ABA, Women's Legal Def. Fund, Audubon Soc., Women's Bar Assn., D.C. Bar. Office: Room S-4004 Office of Solicitor US Dept Labor 200 Constitution Ave NW Washington DC 20210

ATTWOOD, MADGE LOUISE, real estate broker, educator; b. Watsonville, Calif., Feb. 24, 1928; d. Max Lavern and Stella Sara (Childers) Bellamy; m. George Kenneth Attwood, Aug. 20, 1950 (div. 1968); 1 child, Christopher Adrian. BSN, U. Calif., Berkeley, 1949; MPH, U. Calif., L.A., 1968; PhD in Adult and Continuing Edn., U. Mich., 1975. Tchr. health occupations and edn. L.A. City Schs., 1968-71; state supr. health programs Mich. Dept. Edn., Lansing, 1971-72; asst. prof., chair occupational edn. dept., dir. allied health tchr. edn. U. Mich., Ann Arbor, 1972-78; assoc. prof., chair div. health occupations tchr. edn. U. Ill., Champaign, 1978-87; real estate broker, owner, pres. Attwood-Bellamy Co., Chgo., 1987—. Author, editor: (monograph) Health Care in China, 1980, Women & Productivity, 1982; contbr. articles to profl. jours. Bd. dirs. Mostly Music-Chamber Music in the Home, Chgo., 1979—. Recipient Merit award Am. Vocat. Assn., 1978. Mem. Nat. Assn. Realtors, Chgo. Bd. Realtors, Women's Coun. Realtors, Ind. Broker's Assn., Hyde Park C. of C. Office: Attwood Bellamy Co 5118 S Blackstone Chicago IL 60615

ATWATER, TANYA MARIA, marine geophysicist, educator; b. Los Angeles, Aug. 27, 1942; d. Eugene and Elizabeth Ruth (Ransom) A.; 1 child, Alyosha Molnar. Student, MIT, 1960-63; BA, U. Calif., Berkeley, 1965; PhD, Scripps Inst. Oceanography, 1972. Vis. earthquake researcher U. Chile, 1966; research assoc. Stanford U., 1970-71; asst. prof. Scripps Inst. Oceanography, 1972-73; U.S.-USSR Acad. Scis. exchange scientist, 1973; asst. prof. MIT, 1974-79, assoc. prof., 1979-80, research assoc., 1980-81; prof. dept. geoscis. U. Calif., Santa Barbara, 1980—; chairperson ocean margin drilling Ocean Crust Planning Adv. Com.; mem. public adv. com. on law of sea U.S. Dept. State, 1979-83; Sigma Xi lectr., 1975-76; keynote speaker 1st Iberian-Latin Am. Congress on Frontiers of Geophysics. Sci. cons.: Planet Earth: Continents in Collision (R. Miller), 1983; contbr. articles to profl. jours. Sloan fellow, 1975-77; recipient Newcomb Cleveland prize AAAS, 1980; named Scientist of Yr. World Book Ency., 1980. Fellow Am. Geophys. Union (fellows com. 1980-81, Ewing award subcom. 1980), Geol. Soc. Am. (Penrose Conf. com. 1978-80); mem. AAAS, Assn. Women in Sci, Am. Geol. Inst., Phi Beta Kappa, Eta Kappa Nu. Office: U Calif Dept Geoscis Santa Barbara CA 93106*

ATWELL, CONSTANCE WOODRUFF, health services executive, researcher; b. Jan. 27, 1942. AB with high honors in psychology, Mount Holyoke Coll., 1963; MA, UCLA, 1965, PhD, 1968. Asst. prof. psychology Pitzer Coll., Claremont (Calif.) Grad. Sch., 1967-72, assoc. prof. psychology, 1972-77, prof. psychology, 1977-78; grants assoc. div. of rsch. grants NIH, Bethesda, Md., 1978-79; chief, Office of Clin. Applications of Vision Rsch. Nat. Eye Inst., NIH, Bethesda, 1979—, asst. chief, Strabismus, Amblyopia and Visual Processing Br., 1980-81, chief, Strabismus, Amblyopia and Visual Processing Br., 1981—, dep. assoc. dir. Extramural and Collaborative Programs, 1988—; rsch. proposal reviewer for the Nat. Found. March of Dimes, Nat. Inst. of Disability and Rehab. Rsch., Nat. Soc. to Prevent Blindness, U.S. Dept. Edn., NIH office of Program Planning and Evaluation; various adv. bds., exec. coms. and rsch. projects. Contbr. articles to profl. publs. Reader for Recording for the Blind, 1973-78; trustee Claremont Collegiate Sch., 1975-77; chmn. guidance adv. com. Cabin John Jr. High Sch., 1980-81, exec. com., 1980—, pres. parent tchrs. assn., 1981-82; mem. exec. com. Winston Churchill High Sch. PTA, 1982-85. Recipient Nat. Merit scholarship, 1959-63; named Sara Williston scholar, mary Lyon scholar. Mem. AAAS, Am. Psychol. Assn., Soc. for Neuroscience, Assn. for Women in Sci., Assn. for Rsch. in Vision and Ophthalmology, Women in Eye Rsch., Phi Beta Kappa, Sigma Xi. Office: Nat Eye Inst NIH 9000 Rockville Pike Bldg 31/6A47 Bethesda MD 20892

ATWOOD, DIANA FIELD, business owner, innkeeper; b. Rochester, N.Y., Nov. 3, 1946; d. Edwin Havens and Barbara (Field) A.; m. Kenneth Durant Milne, June 10, 1967 (div. Apr. 1982); m. Howard Samuel Tooker, May 5, 1985. BA, Skidmore Coll., 1968. Owner, innkeeper Old Lyme (Conn.) Inn, 1976—; bd. dirs. Maritime Bank & Trust, Essex, Conn. Trustee Conn. River Mus., Essex, 1976—, pres., 1989—; trustee Lyme Hist. Soc., Old Lyme, 1985-87, Lyme Acad. Fine Arts, Old Lyme, 1982—. Mem. Nat. Restaurant Assn., Conn. Restaurant Assn., Profl. Assn. Innkeepers, Master Chef's Inst. Republican. Presbyterian. Home: 12 Tantammaheag Rd Old Lyme CT 06371 Office: Old Lyme Inn Inc 85 Lyme St PO Box 787 Old Lyme CT 06371

ATWOOD, GENEVIEVE, geologist; b. LaJolla, Calif., May 4, 1946; d. Eugene and Margaret (Fisher) A. B.A., Bryn Mawr Coll., 1968; M.A., Wesleyan U., Middleton, Conn., 1973. Field geologist Lamont Doherty/Honduras, Minas de Oro, 1971-72; staff geologist Nat. Acad. Scis., Washington, 1972-74; mem. Utah Ho. of Reps., 1974-80; sr. geologist Ford Bacon and Davis Utah, Salt Lake City, 1975-81; state geologist, dir. Utah Geol. and Mineral Survey, Salt Lake City, 1981-89; pres., geologist Atwood & Mabey, Inc., Salt Lake City, 1990—; dir. Salt Lake City Water and Sewer Bd., 1978-89, Central Utah Project, Orem, 1981-84, Network Mag., Salt Lake City, 1983-85. Editor: 3 books; contbr. articles to profl. jours. Bd. dirs. U. Utah Hosp., Salt Lake City, 1978-89. Recipient Legislator of Yr. award Utah Assn. Social Workers, 1977, Jim Bridger award Utah State U., 1978, John F. Kennedy fellow Harvard U., 1978. Mem. Geol. Assn. Am., Utah Geol. Assn., Alta Club, Town Club, Republican. Episcopalian.

ATWOOD, LINDA, chemistry educator; b. Rochester, N.Y., Nov. 13, 1946. BA, Bard Coll., 1968; MA, Wesleyan U., 1972, PhD, 1974. Prof. chemistry dept. Calif. Poly. State U., San Luis Obispo, 1974—; speaker various clubs and schs., San Luis Obispo, 1980—. Author: Drugs and Poisons, 1990, Biochemistry, Textbook, Workbook, Study Guide, 1987; editor: Laboratory Exercises for General Chemistry, 1989. Mem. AAAS, Am. Chem. Soc., SLOCHEM, Inc., Sigma Xi. Office: Calif Poly State U Chemistry Dept San Luis Obispo CA 93407

ATWOOD, MARGARET ELEANOR, author; b. Ottawa, Ont., Can., Nov. 18, 1939; d. Carl Edmund and Margaret Dorothy (Killam) A. BA, U. Toronto, 1961; AM, Radcliffe Coll., 1962; postgrad., Harvard U., 1962-63, 65-67; LittD (hon.), Trent U., 1973, Concordia U., 1980, Smith Coll., Northampton, Mass., 1982, U. Toronto, 1983, U. Waterloo, 1985, U. Guelph, 1985, Mt. Holyoke Coll., 1985, Victoria Coll., 1987; LLD (hon.), Queen's U., 1974. Lectr. in English U. B.C., 1964-65, Sir George Williams U., 1967-68, U. Alta., 1969-70; asst. prof. English York U., Toronto, 1971-72; writer-in-residence U. Toronto, 1972-73, U. Ala., Tuscaloosa, 1985; Berg Chair NYU, 1986; writer-in-residence Macquarie U., Australia, 1987, Trinity U., San Antonio, 1989. Author: (poetry) Double Persephone, 1961, The Circle Game, 1967, The Animals in That Country, 1968, The Journals of Susanna Moodie, 1970, Procedures for Underground, 1970, Power Politics, 1973, Poems for Voices, 1970, You Are Happy, 1975, Selected Poems, 1976, (Am. edit., 1978), Two-Headed Poems, 1978, True Stories, 1981, Interlunar, 1984, Selected Poems II, 1986; (novels) The Edible Woman, 1969, (Am. edit.), 1970, Surfacing, 1972, (Am. edit.), 1973, Lady Oracle, 1976, Life Before Man, 1979, Bodily Harm, 1981, Murder in the Dark, 1983, The Handmaid's Tale, 1985, Cat's Eye, 1988 (City Toronto Book award 1989, Coles Book of the Yr. 1989, Can. Booksellers Assn. Author of Yr. 1989, Book of Yr. award Found. for Advancement of Can. Letters, Periodical Marketers Can., 1989, Torgi Talking Book 1989); short stories Dancing Girls, 1977, Bluebeard's Egg, 1983; (juvenile) Up in the Tree, 1978, Anna'a Pet, 1980; (non-fiction) Survival: A Thematic Guide to Canadian Literature, 1972, Second Words: Selected Critical Prose, 1982; author: (TV scripts) The Servant Girl, Can. Broadcasting Co., 1974—, (with Peter Pearson) Heaven On Earth, Can. Broadcasting Co., 1986; editor: (with Shannon Ravenal) The Best American Short Stories 1989, 1989; contbr. poems, short stories, revs. and articles to scholarly jours. Recipient E.J. Pratt medal, 1961, Pres.'s medal U. Western Ont., 1965, YWCA Women of Distinction award, Gov. Gen.'s award, 1966, 1st pl. Centennial Commn. Poetry Competition, 1967, Union Poetry prize Chicago, 1969, Bess Hoskins prize of Poetry Chicago, 1974, City of Toronto Book award, 1977, Can. Booksellers Assn. award, 1977, award for short fiction Periodical Distbr. Can., 1977, St. Lawrence award for Fiction, 1978, Radcliffe Grad. medal, 1980, Molson award, 1981, Internat. Writer's prize Welsh Arts Council, 1982, Book of Yr. award Periodical Distbrs. of Can. and Found. for Advancement Can. Letters, 1983, Los Angeles Times Fiction award, 1986, Gov. Gen.'s Lit. award, 1986, Ida Nudel Humanitarian award, 1986, Toronto Arts award, 1986, Arthur C. Clarke award for Best Sci. Fiction, 1987, shortlisted for Ritz Hemingway prize, Paris, 1987, Commonwealth Lit. Prize regional award, 1987, Silver medal for Best Article of Yr. Council for Advancement and Support of Edn., 1987, Nat. Mag. award 1st prize, 1988, YWCA Women of Distinction award 1988, Centennial medal Harvard U., 1990; Guggenheim fellow, 1981; decorated companion Order of Can., 1981, Order of Ont., 1990; named Woman of Yr. Ms. Mag., 1986, Humanist of Yr., 1987. Fellow Royal Soc. of Can., Am. Acad. Arts and Scis. (fgn. hon. lit. mem. 1988). Office: care Oxford U Press, 70 Wynford Dr, Don Mills, ON Canada M3C 1J9

ATWOOD, MARY SANFORD, author; b. Mt. Pleasant, Mich., Jan. 27, 1935; d. Burton Jay and Lillian Belle (Sampson) Sanford; B.S., U. Miami, 1957; m. John C. Atwood, III, Mar. 23, 1957. Author: A Taste of India, 1969. Mem. San Francisco/N. Peninsula Opera Action, Hillsborough-Burlingame Newcomers, Suicide Prevention and Crisis Center, DeYoung Art Mus., Internat. Hospitality Center, Peninsula Symphony, San Francisco Art Mus., World Affairs Council, Mills Hosp. Assos. Mem. AAUW, Suicide Prevention Aux. Republican. Club: St. Francis Yacht. Office: 40 Knightwood Ln Hillsborough CA 94010

AU, ALICE MAN-JING, biochemist; b. Canton, People's Republic of China; d. Ying-Tak and Yeuk-Suet Au. BS, U. Calif., Riverside, 1972, PhD, 1976. Postdoctoral scholar U. Calif., San Diego, 1976-78; postgrad. researcher U. Calif., San Francisco, 1978-80, research biochemist, 1980-81; pub. health chemist sanitation and radiation lab. Calif. State Dept. Health Svcs., Berkeley, 1981-84, pub. health chemist food and drug lab., 1984-88, environ. biochemist food and drug lab., 1988-89, acting chief food and drug lab., 1989-90, environ. biochemist food and drug lab., 1990—; cons. Sci. Innovations, San Francisco, 1983-89. Contbr. articles to profl. jours. dir. adv. com. Calif. State Dept. Health Services EEO Com., Sacramento, 1986. Fellow NSF, 1972; DAR scholar 1970; Disting. Acad. scholar U. Calif., Riverside, 1972-76. Mem. AAAS, Am. Chem. Soc., N.Y. Acad. Scis., Assn. Official Analytical Chemists, We. Assn. Food and Drug Officials, Phi Beta Kappa.

AUB, DEBORAH THRASHER, book store manager; b. New Haven, June 18, 1953; d. James Parker and Doris Ann (Hurd) Thrasher; m. Thomas Joseph Aub, Oct. 12, 1985. AS, Asheville-Buncombe Tech., 1973. Receiving clk. B. Dalton Bookseller, Vorhees, N.J., 1978-79, asst. store mgr., 1979-80; store mgr. B. Dalton Bookseller, Moorestown, N.J., 1980-84, Lynchburg, Va., 1984—. Mem. Nat. Audobon Soc., Nature Conservancy, Nat. Wildlife Fedn., Lynchburg Hist. Found. Methodist. Office: B Dalton Booksellers Rt 29 and Candlers Mt Lynchburg VA 24502

AUBRY, MICHELE CHRISTINE, archaeologist; b. Oakland, Calif., Aug. 23, 1951; d. Jacques Denis and Irene Rachel (Imhof) A.; m. Harvey Malcolm Shields, Aug. 23, 1985. BA cum laude, Occidental Coll., 1972; postgrad., George Washington U., 1973-74; MA, U. Calif., Riverside, 1977. Archeologist Nat. Pk. Svc., Washington, 1978-86, acting chief archeol. assistance div., 1985-86, spl. asst. to asst. dir. archeology, 1987—; archeol. cons. Calif. State U., Long Beach, 1975; archeol. cons. U. Calif., Riverside, 1975, teaching asst., 1977; instr. U. Va., Falls Church, 1982. Contbr. numerous articles to archeol. jours., numerous fed. govt. procedures and reports. Vice pres. Arlington (Va.) Condominium Homeowners Assn., 1985-86, pres., 1987-88. Recipient performance awards Nat. Park Svc., 1983-90; various grants and fellowships U. Calif., Riverside, 1974-76; archeol. fellow U. Ariz., 1976. Mem. Soc. for Hist. Archaeology, Soc. for Am. Archaeology, Archaeol. Inst. Am., Nat. Trust for Hist. Preservation, Archaeol. Soc. Va., Ephebian Soc., Alpha Kappa Delta. Office: Nat Park Svc PO Box 37127 Washington DC 20013-7127

AUBRY, VICKI A., retail fashion buyer; b. Yonkers, N.Y., Apr. 17, 1953; d. Jules K. and Irma B. (Papas) A. BS, U. R.I., 1975. Buyer Steinbach, White Plains, N.Y., 1979-86, Claire's Boutiques, Wooddale, Ill., 1986-87, TSS Finders Keepers, Bkln., 1987-88; now buyer Smart Step, Worcester, Mass., 1988-90; buyer Harem Shoe Care Thom McAn, Worcester, Mass., 1990—.

AUBUCHON, PENNY AMELIA, small business owner; b. St. Louis, Oct. 21, 1952; d. Roy Fredrick and Virginia Mary (Clem) A. B.S in Psychology and Sociology, SW Bapt. U., 1975. Payroll supr. Four Seasons Country Club, Lake of the Ozarks, Mo., 1977-78; accounts payable analyst Banquet Foods Corp., St. Louis, 1979-81; grain settlement controller truck shipment Far-Mar-Co, St. Louis, 1981; asst. instr. adult program St. Louis Assn. for Retarded Citizens, 1981-83, instr. adult program, 1983-85; checking supr. United Postal Savs. and Loan, St. Louis, 1985-86; ptnr. Computerized Bus. Automation, St. Louis, 1987—. Avocations: tennis, computers, music, needlework.

AUCHY, LYNDA GOHO, financial planning executive; b. Phila., Feb. 10, 1942; d. Walter Lessig Goho and Pearl Matz Morrison; m. Alexander H. Ralston, Aug. 4, 1962 (div. Nov. 1976); children: Pamela Ralston, Alexander H. Ralston III. Assoc. Bus., Drexel U., 1962; BS in Econ. Geography, Westchester (Pa.) State Coll., 1976. Fin. sales rep. Security First Group, Wellesley, Mass., 1978-80, mgr. deferred compensation, 1980-83; investment cons. Shearson Am. Express, Providence, 1983-84; exec. dir. Fin. Planning Assocs., Northampton and South Hadley, Mass., 1983—; resident mgr. Anchor Nat. Fin. Services, South Hadley, 1984-86; fin. planner CIGNA Individual Investors Services, Inc., Springfield, Mass., 1986—. Bd. dirs. The Next Step, Springfield, Mass., 1986, Children's Theater of Mass. Mem. Nat. Assn. Securities Dealers, Real Estate Brokers of Mass. Republican. Office: Cigna Individual Fin Svcs 1380 Chestnut St Springfield MA 01103

AUER, RUTH THOMPSON, school system administrator, retired; b. Buffalo, N.Y., Aug. 9, 1928; d. George Harold and Helen Victoria (Peters) Thompson; m. Richard Basil. BS in Edn., N.Y. State Coll., 1949; MEd in Edn. Adminstrn., SUNY, 1952; EdD, U. Sarasota, 1972. Tchr. Pub. Sch., Buffalo, N.Y., 1949-58; asst. prin. P.S. No.19, Buffalo, 1958-64; princ. P.S. No. 42, Buffalo, 1964-67; prin. Allendale Sch., West Seneca, N.Y., 1967-81; dir. elem. edn. Cen. Office, West Seneca, 1981-82, asst. supr., 1982-85; sales assoc. Metro Blaine Realtors, Hamburg, N.Y., 1986-90, Wieder Realty Inc., Pompano Beach, Fla., 1988—. Mem. AAUW, Pompano Beach C. of C., Delta Kappa Gamma. Home (summer): 5675 Brown Hill Rd Springville NY 14141

AUERBACH, NINA JOAN, English language educator; b. N.Y.C., May 24, 1943. B.A., U. Wis., 1964; M.A., Columbia U., 1967, Ph.D., 1970. Instr. English Cleve. State U., 1968; asst. prof. Calif. State U., Los Angeles, 1970-72; asst. prof. U. Pa., Phila., 1972-77, assoc. prof., 1977-83, prof., 1983—. Author: Communities of Women: An Idea in Fiction, 1978; Woman and the Demon: The Life of A Victorian Myth, 1982; Romantic Imprisonment: Women and Other Glorified Outcasts, 1985, Ellen Terry, Player in Her Time, 1987. Contbr. articles to profl. jours. Ford Found. research fellow, 1975-76; fellow Radcliffe Inst., Cambridge, Mass., 1975-76; Guggenheim fellow, 1979-80. Mem. MLA, Coll. English Assn., Northeast Victorian Soc. Office: Dept English U Pa Philadelphia PA 19174*

AUERBACK, SANDRA JEAN, social worker; b. San Francisco, Feb. 21, 1946; d. Alfred and Molly Loy (Friedman) A. BA, U. Calif., Berkeley, 1967; MSW, Hunter Sch. Social Work, 1972. Diplomate clin. social work. Case aide Spaulding Youth Ctr., Tilton, N.H., 1968-69; case worker Lakeside Sch., Spring Valley, N.Y., 1969-70; clin. social worker Jewish Family Services, Bklyn., 1972-73, Hackensack, N.J., 1973-78; pvt. practice psychotherapy San Francisco, 1978—; dir. intake adult day care Jewish Home for the Aged, San Francisco, 1979—. Bd. dirs. Demarest (N.J.) Little Theater, 1977-78. Mem. Nat. Assn. Social Workers (cert., bd. dirs. Bay Area Referral Service 1983-87, chmn. referral service 1984-87, state practice com. 1987—, regional treas. 1989—, rep. to Calif. Council Psychiatry, Psychology, Social Work and Nursing 1987—, chmn. 1989), Mental Health Assn. San Francisco (trustee 1987—), Am. Group Psychotherapy Assn., Am. Soc. Aging, Spouses of Gays (founder). Home: 1100 Gough St Apt 8C San Francisco CA 94109 Office: 450 Sutter San Francisco CA 94108

AUFDENKAMP, JO ANN, librarian, lawyer; b. Springfield, Ill, Mar. 22, 1926; d. Erwin C. and Johanna (Ostermeier) A.; B.A., MacMurray Coll. for Women, 1945; B.L.S., U. Ill., 1946; postgrad. U. Chgo., 1964-66; J.D., John Marshall Law Sch., 1976. Asst. libr. Commerce Libr. U. Ill., 1946-48; libr. Fed. Res. Bank of Chgo., 1948-80; adminstr. info. services legal dept. Lincoln Nat. Life Ins. Co., Ft. Wayne, Ind., 1980-81; asst. trust officer Central Trust and Savs. Bank, Geneseo, Ill., 1981-83; practice law, 1983-84; cons. Ill. Valley Libr. System, 1984-87, Harvey (Ill.) Pub. Libr., 1987-89; libr. Bus. and Econs. Libr. No. Ill. U., DeKalb, 1989—; with Office Nat. Planning, Liberia, 1963. Mem. Ill. Bar Assn., ALA, Spl. Libraries Assn., Ill. Library Assn. Republican. Lutheran. Home: 311 N 2nd St Apt 2 DeKalb IL 60115 Office: No Ill U Library DeKalb IL 60115

AUFDERHAAR-KING, SUSAN, data processing executive; b. Celina, Ohio, Feb. 14, 1951; d. Norman Robert and Eleanor Belle (Shook) Aufderhaar; married (dec. 1989); 1 child, Laura Michelle. B.G.S., U. Nebr., Omaha, 1978; cert. MIT, 1980; M.B.A., Webster U., 1985. Programmer/systems analyst Dept. Def. USAF, 1969-75; sr. programmer, analyst, mgr. quality assurance Majers Market Rsch., 1978-79; staff mgr. bus. systems Northwestern Bell Tel. Co., Omaha, 1979-82; mgr. area consultative staff AT&T Info. Systems, 1982-83; sr. dir. mktg. Datapoint Corp., 1983-85; sr. exec. data processing cons., mgr. exec. cons. services Boeing Computer Services, Seattle, 1985—; mgr. infosystems NASA, Houston. Mem. Assn. Computing Machinery (past sec.), Data Processing Mgrs. Assn. (exec. bd., sec.), NAFE, Am. Mgmt. Assn., Smithsonian Instn., Cousteau Soc., Women Data Processing, Nat. Honor Soc., Eastern Star. Republican. Mem. United Ch. of Christ. Office: 16026 Manor Square Dr Houston TX 77062

AUGENFELD, LORRAINE P. See STOLOVE, LORRAINE P.

AUGSPURGER, ANN MARIE, in-house publication editor; b. Burlington, Iowa, Feb. 14, 1964; d. Terry Duane Kilbourn and Janet Alma (Edwards) Morrison; m. Randall Scott Augspurger, May 14, 1988. BA, Western Ill. U., 1986. Copywriter OGR Svc. Corp., Springfield, Ill., 1986-87; mng. editor Ill. State Bar Assn., Springfield, 1987-89; editor St. John's Hosp., Springfield, 1989—. Mem. Women in Communications. Methodist. Home: 41 Pinto Dr Springfield IL 62702 Office: St John Hosp Community Rels 800 E Carpenter St Springfield IL 62769

AUGUST, JOAN FRIEDA, management consultant executive; b. Paterson, N.J., Jan. 15, 1948; d. John Anthony and Frieda Marie (Schrieb) August; m. Robert Eugene DeBrecht, July 15, 1978; children: Andrew August, Daniel Robert. B.A., Rutgers U., 1978. Sec., St. Joseph Hosp., Paterson, N.J., 1964-68, Manhattan Shirt Co., 1969-71; recruiter McGraw-Hill, Hightstown, N.J., 1971-74; employment mgr. Bulova Watch Co., Jackson Heights, N.Y., 1974-76; dir. compensation and benefits Revlon, Inc., N.Y.C., 1978-86; v.p. human resources Chase Manhattan Bank, N.Y.C., 1986-87; dir. compensation Avon, N.Y.C., 1987-88; sr. cons. EastBourne Cons. Group, N.Y.C., 1988—. Mem. Am. Soc. Personnel Adminstrn., Am. Compensation Assn., N.Y. Compensation Assn. Office: Eastbourne Cons Group 305 Madison Ave New York NY 10165

AUGUSTIN, SALLY JEAN, healthcare product manufacturing company executive; b. Newton, Mass., Mar. 13, 1959; d. Chester Frederick and Jeannette Esther (Bunnell) A.; m. Dean Robert Samos, June 25, 1983. BA, Wellesley Coll., 1981; MBA, Northwestern U., 1983. Product mgr. Hewlett-Packard Co., Cupertino, Calif., 1983-86; mktg. mgr. Shaw's Candy, Millbrae, Calif., 1986-87; consumer products mgr. McKesson Home Health Care, San Francisco, 1987—. Mem. Am. Mgmt. Assn., Commonwealth Club San Francisco, Wellesley Coll. Class of 1981 (treas. 1986—). Home: 695 John Muir Dr #F316 San Francisco CA 94132 Office: McKesson Home Health Care 1 Post St San Francisco CA 94104

AULER, ANGELA CRUZ, banker; b. Rio de Janeiro, Aug. 21, 1949; came to U.S., 1988; d. Homero and Maria Magdalena (Cruz) A. Diplome superieur, Universite de Nancy, Rio de Janeiro, 1971; BA in Econs., Fed. U., Rio de Janeiro, 1978; student, Loyola U., Chgo., 1982. Cert. tchr. of English, Rio de Janeiro. Tchr. pub. and pvt. schs., Rio de Janeiro, 1968-73; English, Portuguese translator Motor Union Ins. Co., Rio de Janeiro, 1972-73; fgn. trade dept. clk. Banco do Brasil S.A., Rio de Janeiro, 1973-78, dir.'s staff advisor, 1978-85; trainee in internat. banking Banco do Brasil S.A., Chgo., 1982; advisor v.p.'s staff internat. banking Banco do Brasil S.A., Rio de Janeiro, 1985-87; mgr. trainee Banco do Brasil S.A., London, 1988; rep. Banco do Brasil S.A., Chgo., 1988—. Mem. Soc. of Ex-students in Great Britain, Instituto dos Economistas do Rio de Janeiro, Ptnrs. of The Americas, Pan Am. Coun. of Chgo. Roman Catholic. Office: Banco Do Brasil SA 2 N LaSalle Ste 2005 Chicago IL 60602

AULETTA-ANZILOTTI, LORI LYNN, controller; b. Bronx, N.Y., Mar. 8, 1959; d. Nicholas Michael and Rose (Troiano) Auletta; m. Robert Dominick Anzilotti, June 14, 1981; children: Christina Lynn, Paula Ann. BBA in Acctg., Iona Coll., 1981, MBA in Fin., 1986. Acct. S & A Concrete Co., Inc., N.Y.C., 1981-84, controller, 1985—; cons. Glen Island Casino, New Rochelle, N.Y., 1983—. Treas. fund raising N.Y.C. chpt. St. Jude's Childrens Research Hosp., 1985-86, exec. com., 1985-88, dinner com., 1985-88. Republican. Roman Catholic. Home: 1073 Grant Ave Pelham Manor NY 10803

AULT, ETHYL LORITA, educator; b. Bklyn., May 30, 1939; d. Albert Nichols Fadden and Marion Cecil (Corrigan) Snow; (div.); children: Debra Marie, Milinda Lei Jones, Timothy Scott. BS, Ga. State U., MEd, 1976, cert. in spl. edn. 6th yr., 1984. Tchr. spl. edn. Butts County Sch. System, Jackson, Ga., 1972-73; tchr. spl. edn. Rockdale County Sch. System, Conyers, Ga., 1973-75, lead tchr., 1975-77; cons. spl. edn. Newton County Sch. System, Covington, Ga., 1977-79; curriculum specialist spl. edn. La Grange (Ga.) Sch. System, 1979-83, dir. spl. edn., 1983—; instr. La Grange Coll., 1984—; mem. Tchr. Competency Testing Commn., Atlanta, 1988—, Task Force Documentation and Decision Making, Atlanta, 1988—. Contbg. editor: (manual) Mainstream Modification Handbook, 1989. Chairperson Jud. Adv. Panel, LaGrange, 1988—; bd. mem. Crawford Tng. Ctr. Adv. Panel, LaGrange, 1985—; v.p. West Ga. Youth Coun. Bd., LaGrange, 1980—; mem. State Adv. Panel for Spl. Edn. Mem. Coun. Exceptional Children, Ga. Assn. Edn. Leaders, Ga. Assn. Curriculum and Instruction Supervision, Ga. Coun. Adminstrs. Spl. Edn. (v.p. 1988—, pres. elect 1989), La Grange Womens Club (v.p. 1989—), Profl. Assn. Ga. Educators. Democrat. Episcopalian. Home: 441 Gordon Cir La Grange GA 30240 Office: La Grange Bd Edn 201 Main St La Grange GA 32040

AULT, LINDA CAE, educator, learning disabilities specialist; b. Dallas, Aug. 10, 1954; d. Carlos Desmond and Carol Beth (Yarborough) Wier; m. Gary Cecil Ault, Apr. 24, 1976; children: Grant Clayton, Alexis Caetlin. B.S., U. Tex.-Austin, 1975; M.S. with honors U. Tex.-Dallas, 1981. Resource tchr. Richardson Ind. Sch. Dist. (Tex.), 1977—. Active 500, Inc., Dallas, 1982—; vol. Young Republicans, Dallas, 1980, Variety Club Tex. Mem. U. Tex.-Austin Ex-Students Assn., Council for Learning Disabilities, Richardson Assn. Children with Learning Disabilities, Richardson Edn. Assn., Delta Zeta. Baptist. Clubs: Daus. of Nile, Masons.

AUSKAPS, AINA MARIJA, dentist; b. Raiskums, Latvia, Sept. 2, 1921; came to U.S., 1949; d. Karlis and Varvara (Shujev) A. MD, U. Latvia, Riga, Latvia, 1944; DDS, Ludwig Maximilian U., Munich, Germany, 1945; DMD, Harvard, 1955. Dentist U.N.R.A., Bavaria, Germany, 1945-48; escort dentist I.R.O., transport boats, 1949; rsch. asst. Yale U., New Haven, Conn., 1949-52; rsch. fellow, instr. Harvard U., Boston, 1952-60. fellow AAAS, mem. Womans Dental Soc. (pres. 1959-61), Boston, Harvard Dental Alumni (pres. 1980-81), Harvard Alumni, Cambridge, Mass. Lutheran. Home: 104 Perkins St Boston MA 02130

AUSTIN, ADA MARY (MOLLY AUSTIN), health association executive; b. Regina, Sask., Can., July 12, 1926; came to U.S., 1956; d. John Corrie and Dora (Thompson) Hodges; m. David Lee Austin Jr., Sept. 23, 1967 (dec. 1971). Diploma, Royal Victoria Hosp. Sch. Nursing, 1949; student, Mitchell Coll., 1957-60, U. Hawaii, 1974-75. RN, Hawaii, Calif. Supr. dept. ophthalmology Royal Victoria Hosp., Montreal, 1949-52; staff anesthetist John Hopkins Hosp., Balt., 1953-54; mem. supervisory staff Montreal Neurol. Inst., 1955-56; staff anesthetist Hosp. of Am. Samoa, Pago Pago, 1963-65; hosp. adminstr. Molokai Gen. Hosp., Hawaii, 1965-68; instr., trainer RNs State of Hawaii, 1963-71; assoc. dir. profl. edn. San Francisco Heart Assn., 1977-78; assoc. dir. Calif. affiliate Am. Heart Assn., Burlingame, 1978-81, dir. pub. affairs and emergency cardiac care, 1981-89, dir. pub. affairs, 1984—. Recipient Spl. Recognition award, Am. Heart Assn., 1989, Calif. Biomed. Rsch. Assn., 1989. Mem. Soc. Pub. Health Educators (membership chmn. 1975-77), Nat. League Nurses, Calif. League Nurses (editor newsletter Hawaii chpt. 1975-77), Am. Nurses Assn., Calif. Nurses Assn., Am. Assn. Nurse Anesthetists, Am. Assn. Critical Care Nurses, Soc. Heart Assn. Profl. Staff, Am. Pub. Health Assn. (bd. dirs. Calif. div. 1982-84), Bus. and Profl. Women, Soroptimists. Republican. Episcopalian. Home: 2030 Vallejo St San Francisco CA 94123 Office: Calif Affiliate Am Heart Assn 805 Burlway Rd Burlingame CA 94010

AUSTIN, BERIT SYNNOVE, inventory control specialist; b. Oslo, Norway, July 22, 1938; came to U.S., 1957; d. Johan Andreas and Astrid (Bjerke) Irgens; m. William Paul Austin, Dec. 22, 1961 (div. 1978); children: Lisa Christine, Paul Erik, Ivar Jon. AA, Saddleback Coll., 1984, AS, 1988. Accounts payable clk. Dynatech Corp., Santa Ana, Calif., 1976-78; accounts payable acct., jr. buyer/Kardex Brunswick Corp., Costa Mesa, Calif., 1978-81; fin. clk. Fluor Corp., Irvine, Calif., 1981-84; admissions and records specialist, warehouse asst., invnetory control specialist Saddleback Coll., Mission Viejo, Calif., 1984—; owner, cons. Home Prescription, Lake Elsinore, Calif., Mission Viejo, 1984—. Mem. NAFE, Calif. Assn. Sch. Bus. Officials, San Juan Capistrano Hist. Soc., Sierra Country Club, Sons of Norway Fraternal Internat. Soc. (historian 1972, publicity dir. 1973, asst. soc. dir. 1974). Republican. Lutheran. Home: 17679 Bobrick Ave Lake Elsinore CA 92330 Office: Home Prescription PO Box 4013 Mission Viejo CA 92690

AUSTIN, CHAROLETTE PRICE, police officer; b. Verdun, France, Oct. 29, 1958; d. James Walter and Edith Irene (Barnes) Price; m. Willie Franklin Austin, Mar. 26, 1988. Student, Nashville State Tech. Inst., 1976-79, Tenn. Law Enforcement Acad., 1979. Bookeeper Revco Discount Drugs, Inc., Nashville, 1980-88; sgt. Tenn. Capitol Police Dept., Nashville, 1978—. Vol. Tenn. Spl. Olympics, Nashville, 1988, 89. Democrat. Baptist. Home: 1916 Meadow Cliff Nashville TN 37210 Office: Tenn Capitol Police B20 John Sevier Bldg 5th Av Nashville TN 37219

AUSTIN, CHERYL LYNNE, school system administrator; b. Cin., Aug. 24, 1955; d. Raleigh and Jessie (Collins) A. BS in Speech, Northwestern U., Evanston, Ill., 1977. Pub. affairs officer USN, Washington, 1977-84; pres., owner Acorn Administrv. Services, Cin., 1984-86; adminstr. Cin. Pub. Schs., Cin., 1986--; dir. Cin. Sch. Employees Credit Union, 1988--. Treas. Cin. Women's Polit. Caucas, Ohio, 1986—, pres., 1989—; pres. Cin. Chpt. Ohio Rep. Lt. comdr. USNR, 1990—. Recipient Vol. Aiken Sr. High Sch. Cin. 1986, Affirmative Action Task. Mem. Cin. Bus. & Profl. Women's Club (legis chair 1987-89). Republican. Home: 5716 North Way Cincinnati OH 45224

AUSTIN, DOROTHY MAYOVER, accountant, music educator; b. Washington, Mar. 22, 1931; d. James Wallace and Dorothy Mayover (Giles) Cross; m. Willatant Lucas Austin; children: Willatant Darvey, Renita Denise Austin Coffen, Lorenzo Darrell. A in Medicine, Laura Sch., Scranton, Pa., 1983; D in Medicine, Columbia U., Mex., 1985; B in Physician's Asst. Studies, George Washington U., 1988; DD, Christian Ministries, Riva, Md., 1989; D in Evangelistic Style, Min. Music, World Christianship, Fresno, Calif., 1989; B in Arts and Music, Washington Saturday Coll., 1988. CPA, Md. Salesperson Avon, Washington, 1959-61; cashier Hechts Dept. Stores, Va., 1960-62; mgr. High Diary Store, Washington, 1962-65; supr. Dept. Pub. Works Govt., Washington, 1965-87; pres., CPA Accountance and File Clk, Inc., Oxon Hill, Md., 1987—; founder, dir., min. music Jesus Christ Music Internat. Baptist Ch., Oxon Hill, Md.; pres., founder, organizer Exec. Income Tax Svcs., Capitol Heights, Md., 1985—, Capitol Heights Music and Arts, 1989—, Fin. Fund Raising for Coll. Inc., Riva, 1989; instr., mgr. record soloist, piano and voice, Riva, 1989—; instr. elem. schs., Anapolis, Riva, 1989; instr. med. field. Author: (books) Play This is Your Life Dorothy, 1984, Religious Musical Plays, 1985, It's All in the Name of Jesus, 1988, Teaching Hands What Mind Tells It, 1989. Sec. bd. trustees Washington Saturday Coll., 1975, 89; sec. bd. dirs. Assn. Community Edn., Washington Saturday Coll., 1975, 89; mem. Jacki Ruffins Ministries, Washington, 1985, 89; tchrs. aid Glassmanor Elem. Sch., Oxon Hill, 1988; singer Rosebud Jr. Chorus Friendship Bapt. Ch., Washington, 1936-50; dir., singer, organist, organizer jr. and sr. choirs, Chgo., 1955-59; dir. Friendship Gospel and Jr. Choirs, Washington, 1963-80; instr., vol. svc. ARC. Recipient plaque Coun. of Bapt. Chs. and Libr., Washington, 1946, plaques and trophies Petworth Mus. Sch., Washington, 1975-78. Mem. Female Exec. Assn. (pres. 1985-89), NAFE (exec. officer 1988-89), Nat. Theaters of the Arts (cast dir. 1986-88), Movie Critics for TV (sec. 1987-90), Exec. Women's Ministries (pres. 1988-89), Order of Eastern Star. Democrat. Home: 5000 Glass Manor Dr Oxon Hill MD 20745 Office: Exec Income Tax Accountance 381 Yorkshire Ln Riva MD 21140

AUSTIN, EILEEN RITA, civic volunteer; b. Phila., Dec. 15, 1933; d. David and Sophia (Lackier) A.; m. Larry Austin, Dec. 17, 1930; children: Jeffrey, Jamie, Stewart. Student, Temple U., Phila., 1953-54, Levitan Sch. of Bus., 1952-53. Pres. Women's Am. ORT, Plainview, N.Y., 1968-69; youth group leader Dix Hills (N.Y.) Jewish Ctr., 1971-72, adult edn. chairperson, 1972-73, also bd. dirs.; campaign chairperson Women's Div. United Jewish Appeal, Eastern Long Island, N.Y., 1984-86; bd. chairperson Women's Div. United Jewish Appeal, 1986-88. Jewish.

AUSTIN, GRACE BALIUNAS, periodontist, educator; b. Vilnius, Lithuania, May 22, 1940; d. Adolph and Anna Catherine (Savage) Baliunas; B.S., U. Chgo., 1963; D.D.S., Northwestern U., 1967; cert. periodontics N.J. Dental Sch., 1976; m. Nov. 28, 1970. Diplomate Am. Bd. Periodontology. Asst. prof. Northwestern U. Dental Sch., Chgo., 1967-69; sr. clin. scientist Warner Lambert Co., Morris Plains, N.J., 1969-71; clin. asst. prof. periodontics N.J. Dental Sch., Newark, 1971-76; assoc. prof., 1978-83; pvt. practice periodontics, Berkeley Heights, N.J., 1982—; mem. staff Overlook Hosp., Summit, N.J., 1979—. Ill. State scholar, 1959; grantee Coll. Medicine and Dentistry N.J. Found., 1976. Mem. Am. Acad. Periodontology, ADA, N.J. Dental Assn., Am. Assn. Dental Schs., Internat. Assn. Dental Research, N.J. Soc. Periodontists (pres. 1988-90), Psi Omega. Contbr. articles to profl. jours. Home: 15 Dominick Ct Short Hills NJ 07078 Office: 576 Springfield Ave Berkeley Heights NJ 07922

AUSTIN, IRMA CAROLINE, magazine publishing company official; b. Dothan, Ala., Oct. 29, 1941; d. Frank A. and Irma (Rocker) Marshall; m. Joseph H. Austin, May 20, 1972 (dec. Mar. 1975). BA, Trenton State Coll., 1963; MA, Columbia U., 1968. Tchr., Dutch Neck, N.J., 1963-66, El Monte, Calif., 1966-67, West New York, N.J., 1968-79; bus. and personnel mgr. Hal Publs. Inc. (pub. Working Woman and Success! mags.), N.Y.C., 1979-86; group mgr. human resources Working Woman/McCall's Group, N.Y.C., 1987-88; dir. personnel and adminstrv. services Frenkel & Co., Inc., N.Y.C., 1988-89; cons. human resources, 1990—. Bd. govs. Palisades Gen. Hosp., North Bergen, N.J. Mem. Soc. for Human Resource Mgt., The Human Resource Network, Soc. for Human Resource Mgmt., Human Resource Network.

AUSTIN, JOANN CLARK, lawyer; b. Balt., Oct. 15, 1939; d. Thomas Winder Young and Aurie Austin Clark; A.B., Earlham Coll., 1961; M.A.T., Johns Hopkins U., 1965; J.D. with honors, U. Md., 1978; 1 son, Lawan Tarn Petty. Research biologist Nat. Cancer Inst., Bethesda, Md., 1961-63; tchr. Brookline (Mass.) Public Schs., 1965-67; sr. computer programmer Computer Usage Co., Inc., Boston, Los Angeles, 1967-70; bookkeeper, bus. mgr. Koinonia Found., Balt., 1974-76; admitted to Maine bar, 1979; individual practice law, South China, Maine, 1979—; staff atty. Legal Services for the Elderly, Augusta, Maine, 1980-82. Bd. dirs. Sch. of Living, York, Pa., treas., 1975-79; trustee Balt. Monthly Meeting of Friends Homewood, 1976-79, clk. Vassalboro Quar. Meeting, 1981—; bd. dirs. Oak Grove-Coburn Sch., Vassalboro, 1982—; mem. permanent bd. New Eng. Yearly Meeting of Friends; mem. exec. com. Am. Friends Service Com., 1977-78; bd. dirs. Sam Ely Community Land Trust, 1981—; bd. dirs. Maine Women's Lobby, 1981-82; selectman Town of China, 1981—; chmn. China Republican Town Com., 1982-86; mem. exec. com. Kennebec County Extension Service, 1985-87. Mem. ABA, Maine Bar Assn., China Area C. of C. (pres. 1988), Vassalboro Grange, NOW, Natural Resources Council. Address: PO Box 150 Rt 32 N South China ME 04358

AUSTIN, KAREN M. N., accountant; b. East Cleveland, Ohio, Apr. 29, 1955; d. Julius J. and Eleanor T. (Malczewski) Niedermeyer; m. James B. Austin, Oct. 27, 1979; children: Timothy B., Alexandra M. BBA, Cleve. State U., 1978. CPA, Ohio. Mem. staff Welty, Wiechel and Co., Sandusky, Ohio, 1979; sr. staff Watson Rice and Co., Cleve., 1979-80, Mathews, Gallovic, Granito and Co., Mentor, Ohio, 1980-83; pvt. practice acctg. Chesterland, Ohio, 1983—. Contbr. articles on individual and small bus. tax and acctg. to local newspaper. Mem. AICPA, Ohio Soc. CPAs, Chesterland C. of C. Republican.

AUSTIN, LOIS ANN LOEHR, academic administrator; b. Mt. Vernon, Ind., Aug. 15, 1939; d. Charles Alois and Golda (Baldwin) Loehr; m. Clyde W. Render Nov. 21, 1956 (div. May 1983); children: Teresa Greathouse, Kimberly Render, Jeffrey Render, Shawn Render (dec.). BS, U. So. Ind., 1977; MS, Ind. State U., 1983; postgrad., Ind. U.-Purdue U., Indpls., 1987—. Mgr. office Miss. Valley Steel Co., Mt. Carmel, Ill., 1976-78; coord. fin. aid Ind. Vocat. Tech. Coll., Evansville, 1978-85; mgr. fin. aid Ind. Vocat. Tech. Coll., Bloomington, 1985-86; asst. dir. fin. aid Ind. Vocat. Tech. Coll., Indpls., 1986-87, collegewide mgr. fin. aid/vet. affairs, 1987—. Leader 4-H, Mt. Vernon, 1965-69, mem. Posey County (Ind.) coun., 1969; sec. Diocesan Coun., Evansville, 1968; coord. Women in Networking, Evansville, 1985. Mem. Nat. Assn. Student Fin. Aid, Midwest Assn. Student Fin. Aid, Ind. Assn. Student Fin. Aid (sec. 1987—), Ind. Assn. Women Deans, Adminstrs. and Counselors, AAUW, VFW Aux. Democrat. Unitarian Universalist. Club: Homemakers (Posey County). Home: 80 N Ritter St Indianapolis IN 46219 Office: Ind Vocat Tech Coll 1 W 26th St Box 7034 Indianapolis IN 46207-7034

AUSTIN, PAGE INSLEY, lawyer; b. Balt., May 1, 1942; d. John Webb and Sallie Byrd (Massey) Insley; m. William H. Austin, June 10, 1967. BA in Philosophy, Valparaiso U., 1962; MA in Philosophy, Washington U., St. Louis, 1963; postgrad., Yale U., 1963-66; JD, U. Tex., 1977. Bar: Tex. 1977, U.S. Dist. Ct. (so. dist.) Tex. 1978, U.S. Ct. Appeals (10th cir.) 1980, U.S. Ct. Appeals (5th cir.) 1981, U.S. Supreme Ct. 1986. Instr. Yale U., New Haven, 1966-67, U. Houston, 1967-73; assoc. Vinson & Elkins, Houston, 1977-84, ptnr., 1984—; adj. prof. U. Tex., 1986-87. Mem. ABA, Tex. Bar Assn., Houston Bar Assn., Am. Law Inst., Order of Coif, Chancellors. Home: 7510 Prestwick Houston TX 77025 Office: Vinson & Elkins 1001 Fannin 3300 First City Tower Houston TX 77002

AUSTIN, RHEA COCHRAN, librarian, information specialist; b. Dallas, July 6, 1938; d. William Rhea and Dorothy (Shaw) Cochran; m. Richard Stephen Austin, Aug. 21, 1965; children: Patricia Louise. BA, So. Meth. U., 1959, MA, 1961; MS, Cath. U. Am., 1982. Teaching asst. So. Meth. U., Dallas, 1959-60; tchr. Dallas Ind. Sch. Dist., 1960-61, Highland Park Ind. Sch. Dist., Dallas, 1961-64; asst. prof. Centenary Coll. La., Shreveport, 1964-65; adminstrv. aide Overseas Edn. Fund of LWV, Washington, 1969; librarian ISC Inc., Vienna, Va., 1984-85, corp. librarian OAO Corp., Greenbelt, Md., 1985-87. Mem. home econs. adv. com. Arlington County Pub. Schs., 1983—. NDEA grantee, 1961, 62. Mem. ALA, Va. Library Assn., D.C. Library Assn., Phi Beta Kappa, Pi Delta Phi, Alpha Lambda Delta. Episcopalian. Home: 4848 27th St N Arlington VA 22207 Office: Pub Tech Inc 1301 Pennsylvania Ave NW Washington DC 20004

AUSTIN, RHONDA TONI, electrical engineer; b. Goldsboro, N.C., Dec. 26, 1956; d. James Tony and Bobbie Sue (Tollison) A.; m. James Manly Holtzclaw, Feb. 25, 1978 (div. 1988); children: James Tony, Edward Cory. BSEE, Clemson U., 1977. Registered profl. engr., N.C., S.C., Tenn., Va. Jr. engr. So. Bell, Greenville, S.C., 1978-79; asst. engr. J.E. Sirrine, Greenville, 1979-80; jr. electric design engr. Piedmont Olsen Inc., Greenville, 1980-84, sr. electric design engr., 1984-89; electrical dept. mgr. Piedmont Olsen Inc., Raleigh, N.C., 1989—. Named Outstanding Female Engr. Soc. of Women Engrs., 1977; scholarship JE Sirrine, Clemson U., 1974-77. Mem. Nat. Soc. Profl. Engrs., Eta Kappa Nu. Home: 5401 Pine Top Circle Raleigh NC 27612 Office: Piedmont Olsen Inc 2710 Wycliff Rd Ste 200 Raleigh NC 27612

AUSTIN, WENDY PAGE, nurse; b. Balt., Apr. 15, 1961; d. Charles Robert and Dorothy (De Fontes) Page; m. Mark R. Austin, Dec. 11, 1988. BSN, Towson State U., 1983; MS, U. Md., 1987. RN, Md.; cert. oncology nurse. Clin. nurse Johns Hopkins Regional Oncology Ctr., Balt., 1983-84, sr. clin. nurse, 1984-87; nurse mgr. U. Md. Cancer Ctr., Balt., 1987—. Bd. dirs. Am. Cancer Soc., Balt., 1988—. Mem. Oncology Nursing Soc. (Greater Balt. chpt.), Am. Nurses Assn., Md. Nurses Assn., Am. Orgn. Nurse Execs. (affiliate). Republican. Lutheran. Office: U Md Cancer Ctr 22 S Greene St Baltimore MD 21201

AUSTIN-LUCAS, BARBARA ETTA, clergywoman; b. Boston, Nov. 9, 1951; d. Robert James and Etta Lee (Amos) Austin; m. Frederick Aloyisious Lucas, Jr., Dec. 24, 1972; children: Kemba Jarena, Hakim Jabez, Kareem Mandela. BA, Tufts U., Meford, Mass., 1973; MA, Boston U., 1975; MDiv, Colgate Rochester Div. Sch., N.Y., 1982. Ordained elder A.M.E. Ch., 1984. Tchr. Monrovia (Liberia) Coll., 1974; instr. U. Liberia, Monrovia, 1974-75; tchr. Henry Buckner Sch., Cambridge, Mass., 1975-76; substitute tchr. Phila. Pub. Sch., 1977; minister missions and outreach Agape A.M.E. Ch., Buffalo, 1979-82; minister to families Bridge St. A.M.E. Ch., Bklyn., 1982-86, dir., organizer After Sch. Tutorial Ctr., 1983-84; asst. pastor Bridge St. A.M.E. Ch., 1986—; ednl. counselor Bklyn. Coll., CUNY, 1984-86; chmn. bd. trustees Bridge St. Prep. Sch., Bklyn., 1988—; mem. A.M.E. Ch. N.Y. Bd. Christian Edn., N.Y.C., 1983—. Bd. dirs. Bklyn. Hist. Soc., 1990. Recipient Sister Sharing award Agape A.M.E. Ch., Buffalo, 1982, Community Svc. awards Kings County Bus. and Profl. Women, Bklyn., 1988, Men's Caucus for Congressman Edolphus Towns, Bklyn., 1990. Mem. AAUW, Religious Edn. Assn., Key Women of Am. (Ch. Woman of Yr. 1984), Ch. Women United, N.Y. Assn. Black Sch. Educators. Office: Bridge St AME Ch 277 Stuyvesant Ave Brooklyn NY 11221

AUTORINO, ANNE TURNBULL, retired social worker; b. Tampa, Dec. 27, 1914; d. Stockton Graeme and Mary Barney (Walker) Turnbull; m. Frank Berlin Holt, Mar. 27, 1943 (div. 1948); m. Michael Autorino, Mar. 26, 1960; 1 stepchild, Michael. BS in Social Sc., Coll. William and Mary, 1936; MS, Psychiat. Social Work, Columbia U., 1947. Diplomate, Am. Bd. Examiners in Clin. Social Work. Med. social worker social svc. dept. N.Y. Infirmary, N.Y.C., 1948-49; sr. social worker, foster home dept. Edwin Gould Found., N.Y.C., 1949-55; med. social worker, polio epidemic emergency worker Boston City Hosp., 1955-56; dir. social svc. dept. Wyckoff Heights Hosp., Bklyn., 1954-55; social worker N.Y. Sch. for Deaf, White Plains, 1956-58; clin. social worker VA, Newark, 1958-61; sch. social worker Div. Child Guidance, Bd. Edn., Newark, 1961-88; ret., 1988. Mem. Nat. Assn. Social Workers, N.J.Assn. Social Workers, N.J. Assn. Sch. Social Workers, AAUW, Ret. Educators Assn.

AUTREY, PAMELA SANDERS, management educator, consultant; b. Dallas, Oct. 13, 1945; d. Joe Vernon and Lorene Evelyn (Palmer) Sanders; m. Jefferson Wyatt Autrey, Sept. 14, 1968; children: Amber Leigh, Jordan Meredith. BA, U. Tex., 1968, MLS, 1970, PhD, 1983; diploma, European Ctr. Langs. and Civilizations, Lausanne, Switzerland, 1966. Sec. Donaldson, Lufkin & Jenrette, Brussels, 1966; purchasing sec. Owens-Corning Co., Waxahachie, Tex., 1968; reference libr. U. Tex., Austin, 1970-73, rsch. asst., 1980-81, asst. instr., teaching asst., 1982-83, lectr. mgmt., 1987—; info. systems analyst Tex. Dept. Community Affairs, Austin, 1974-77; energy coord., coord. policy rsch. Office of Gov., State of Tex., Austin, 1983-84; owner, pres. Strategic Mgmt. Svcs., Austin, 1984—; cons. Cen. Tex. Health Systems Agy., Austin, 1982-83, Am. Physicians Group, Austin, 1984, Am. Lung Assn. Tex., Austin, 1987-88, S.W. Ednl. Devel. Lab., Austin, 1978-83. Editor newsletter State Agys. Librs. Tex., 1976-77, Extract, 1978-83; contbr. articles to profl. jours. Mem. Leadership Tex., 1985, Bus. Expansion and Retention Steering Com., Austin, 1988—; vice chmn., mem. Austin Econ. Devel. Commn., 1986—; mem. steering com. Austin Enterprise Zone, 1988; scholarship chmn. Austin High Sch. PTA, 1988-89, v.p., 1989—. Recipient Bonham award for bus. rsch. U. Tex., 1982. Mem. Acad. Mgmt., Strategic Mgmt. Assn., Inst. for Mgmt. Scis., Am. Soc. for Info. Sci. (Outstanding Young Info. Profl. award Tex. chpt. 1976), Phi Beta Kappa, Phi Kappa Phi, Pi Sigma Delta, Pi Delta Phi, Beta Phi Mu, Pi Beta Phi (alumnae adv. com. 1988—). Methodist. Home: 3503 Windsor Rd Austin TX 78703 Office: U Tex Mgmt Dept Austin TX 78712

AUTRY, GWYNNE WHEELER, banker, realtor; b. Temple, Tex., Mar. 3, 1933; d. Walter L. and Lois (Chancellor) Wheeler; m. D. Alessio, 1950 (div.); children: Ric, Chris; m. Thomas O. Cardwell, 1962 (dec. 1975); 1 child, Heather; m. King Autry, 1980. AA in French and English, Temple Jr. Coll., 1954; BBA in Mktg., So. Meth. U., 1958. Cert. real estate salesperson, Tex., Colo. Sales mgr., trainer Tecon Corp., Dallas, Denver, 1975-78; savs. and investment officer Dallas Fed. Savings and Loan, 1977-80; v.p. money market ops. Nat. Mortgage Corp. Am., Dallas, 1980-83; sr. v.p. nat. funds and money market ops. dept. Commodore Savs. and Loan, Dallas, 1983—. Mem. Sales and Mktg. Execs. Internat., Nat. Assn. Female Execs., Delta Zeta. Republican. Home: 6611 Harvest Glen Dallas TX 75248 Office: Commodore Savs and Loan 1845 Woodall-Rodgers Frwy Dallas TX 75201

AUW, DOROTHY BABETTE, psychologist, health care administrator; b. Chgo., Mar. 13, 1935; d. John Robert and Elise Anna (Tietz) A. BA, DePaul U., 1956; MA, Loyola U., Chgo., 1965. Psychologist guidance ctr. Loyola U., Chgo., 1956-65; psychologist Cath. Charities Child Mental Health Ctr., Chgo., 1965-78; dir. Cath. Charities Family Counseling Ctr., Chgo., 1978-88, Cath. Charities Holbrook Ctr., Chgo., 1988—. Coun. chairperson St. Nicolai United Ch. of Christ, 1975-76, 84-87; sec. Ill. Conf. United Ch. Christ, 1987-90; bd. dirs. United Ministries Higher Edn., treas., 1986-88, vice chmn., 1988-89, chmn., 1989—. Mem. Am. Psychol. Assn., Am. Orthopsychiat. Assn., Ill. Psychol. Assn. Office: Cath Charities 721 N La Salle Dr Chicago IL 60610

AVERBECK, KAREN MARIE, statistical analyst; b. Covington, Ky., June 25, 1961; d. William Terry and Mary Theresa (Decker) A. Student, Murray (Ky.) State U., 1979-81; BS, U. Ky., 1984; postgrad., U. Cin., 1988—. Coop. rsch. asst. Dow Corning Corp., Carrollton, Ky., 1982; engring. asst. Gen. Electric Co., Cin., 1985-89, tech. analyst, 1989—. Tchr. English as a second lang. Travelr's Aid Internat. Inst., Cin., 1987—; mentor project continued success Aiken High Sch., Cin., 1988—. Mem. Tri-State German-Am. Sch. Soc. Cin. Office: GE Aircraft Engines 1 Neumann Way Cincinnati OH 45215

AVERELL, LOIS HATHAWAY, speech and language pathologist, audiologist; b. Boston, Apr. 8, 1917; d. Merle Leon and Mildred Hathaway (Allen) A.. Diploma, Wheelock Coll., 1941; BS in Edn., Boston U., 1942, EdM, 1953, postgrad., 1963-65. Cert. tchr., Mass.; lic. speech-lang. pathologist, audiologist, Mass. Tchr. kindergarten Dana Hall Schs., Wellesley, Mass., 1942-44; head tchr., pre-sch. program Brimmer and May Sch., Boston, 1944-52; speech therapist United Cerebral Palsy of South Shore, Inc., Quincy, Mass., 1952-53; dir. speech and hearing Meeting St. Sch. Children's Rehab Ctr., Providence, 1953-57; head speech and hearing pathologist Children's Hosp. Med. Ctr., Boston, 1957-63; teaching fellow Boston U., 1963-64; dir. speech, hearing and cleft palate clinic North Shore Children's Hosp. Med. Ctr., Salem, Mass., 1966-76; speech pathologist, audiologist South Shore Mental Health Assn., Quincy, 1977-78; speech-alng. pathologist, audiologist Mayflower House Child Care Ctr., Plymouth, Mass., 1978-85; pvt. practice. Mem. Am. Speech-Lang. and Hearing Assn. (dual cert. clin. competence), Mass. Speech and Hearing Assn., Am. Auditory Soc., Am. Assn. Clin. Counselors (diplomate, sec. 1968-75), Nat. Acad. Counselors and Family Therapists, Internat. Soc. for Augmentative and Alternative Communication, NE Communication Enhancement Group, Pi Lambda Theta, Alpha Sigma Alpha. Republican. Baptist. Club: Women's Garden of Whitman (pres.). Lodge: Zonta (1st v.p. 1975-77 Salem club). Home: 815 Washington St Whitman MA 02382

AVERSA, DOLORES SEJDA, educational administrator; b. Phila., Mar. 26, 1932; d. Martin Benjamin and Mary Elizabeth (Esposito) Sejda; BA, Chestnut Hill Coll., 1953; m. Zefferino A. Aversa, May 3, 1958; children: Dolores Elizabeth, Jeffrey Martin, Linda Maria. Owner, Personal Rep. and Pub. Rels., Phila., 1965-68; ednl. cons. Franklin Sch. Sci. and Arts, Phila., 1968-72; pres., owner, dir. Martin Sch. of Bus., Inc., Phila., 1972—; file reader, cons. for ct. reporting and travel tng. Southwestern Pub. Co., 1990; mem. ednl. planning com. Ravenhill Acad., Phila., 1975-76. Active Phila. Mus. of Art, Phila. Drama Guild. Mem. Nat. Bus. Edn. Assn., Pa. Bus. Edn. Assn., Am. Bus. Law Assn., Pa. Sch. Counselors Assn., Am.-Italy Soc., Am. Soc. Travel Agts., Phila. Hist. Soc., World Affairs Coun. Phila., Hist. Soc. Pa. Mem. ASTA (sch. div.), Chestnut Hill Coll. Alumnae Assn. Roman Catholic. Home: 2111 Locust St Philadelphia PA 19103 Office: 2417 Welsh Rd Philadelphia PA 19114

AVERY, CHRISTINE ANN, pediatrician; b. Bklyn., Mar. 30, 1951; d. Basil Steven and Mary P. Goerner; m. Hernry Jakob Wachtendorf, June 7, 1973; 1 child, Henry James. B.S. summa cum laude, U. Houston, 1972; M.D., U. Tex. Health Sci. Ctr., 1976. Resident in pediatrics U. Tex. Health Sci. Ctr., San Antonio, 1976-79, asst. prof. pediatrics and otorhinolaryngology; dir. Otitis Media Study Ctr., NIH, San Antonio, 1980-87, prof. pediatrics Cornell Med. Ctr., 1987-89; asst. dir. anti-inflammatory/pulmonary clin. rsch. pharm. div. Ciba-Geigy Corp., Summit, N.J., 1989—. Contbr. articles to profl. jours. Recipient Physician Recognition award, 1979, 82, 85. Republican. Roman Catholic. Office: Ciba-Geigy Corp Pharm Div 556 Morris Ave 4089 Devel Summit NJ 07901

AVERY, JULIA MAY, speech pathologist, organizational volunteer; b. Holly, Colo., May 2, 1917; d. Willard Smith and Bertha Eudora (Knuckey) A. AA, Colo. Women's Coll., 1936; BA, U. Colo., 1939; postgrad., UCLA, 1942, U. Calif., 1944; MA in Speech Pathology, U. Colo., 1960. Cert. life tchr. and speech pathologist, Colo. Tchr. 4th-8th grades Mt. Harris (Colo.) Pub. Schs., 1939-41; tchr. 2d grade spl. edn., speech pathology Pueblo (Colo.) Pub. Schs., 1941-77, spl. edn. tchr. physically handicapped, 1946-54; speech pathologist Pueblo, 1954—. Co-author: DiBur Speech Therapy Card Games (32 sets), 1959. Mem. adv. bd. Area Agy. on Aging; active United Way, Retarded Citizens Assn.; bd. dirs. YWCA, also past pres.; past pres. Sr. Polit. Action Network; past pres. Pueblo Coordinating Coun. of Women's Orgns.; pres. Greenhorn Valley Arts Coun., 1989-90; bd. dirs. Pueblo Beautiful Assn., 1989-90, Pueblo Social Svcs., 1989-90, Colo. State Adv. Bd. to Office of Consumer Coun., 1989-90; area v.p. Colo. Sr. Lobby, 1990—. Named Tchr. of Yr., Star Jour., 1971, Chieftain, 1949-50; recipient Community Svc. award Optimists, 1985, 86, 87, numerous others. Mem. AARP (Colo. state legis. com. 1984-88), NEA (life), DAR (past pres. local chpt.), Colo. Gerontol. Soc. (bd. dirs.), United Srs. of Colo. (pres. 1989, lobbyist), Am. Speech and Hearing Assn (past local pres.), Colo. Speech and Hearing Assn., Southeastern Colo. Hist. Soc. (pres. 1989-90), Colo. Archeol. Soc. (past state pres.), League Club Bus. and Profl. Women (pres. 1990), Terr. Daus. Colo. Republican. Episcopalian. Home: 725 W Grant Pueblo CO 81004

AVERY, LEE ANN, accounting administrator; b. Hartford, Conn., Feb. 21, 1957; d. William Kenneth and Anna Beatrice (Kerr) A. AA, Holyoke

(Mass.) Community Coll., 1978; BBA, U. Mass., 1980; postgrad., Fordham U., 1988—. CPA, Conn. Sr. acct. Coopers & Lybrand, Hartford, 1980-83; with fin. mgmt. program The Dexter Corp., Windsor Locks, Conn., 1983-85; mgr. fin. analysis Alpha/Mercer div. The Dexter Corp., Newark, 1985-87; mgr. acctg. research Gen. Pub. Utilities, Parsippany, N.J., 1987-89; dir. fin. Am. Express Travel Related Svcs. Co., 1989-. Trustee, treas. The Master's Sch., Simsbury, Conn., 1982-85; del. People to People Citizen Ambassador Program, Peoples Republic of China, 1986. Arthur H. Carter Found. scholar. Mem. NAFE, Am. Inst. CPA's, N.J. Soc. CPA's. Home: 195 Jacoby St Maplewood NJ 07040

AVERY, MARGARET, make-up artist; b. Lorain, Ohio, July 20, 1951; d. Joseph Raymond and Margaret Mae (Meszes) Nagy; m. Jim Avery; (div. 1981). Makeup artist Cinandre Salon, N.Y.C., 1975-77, freelance mags., commls., video, N.Y.C., 1977-90; singer N.Y.C., 1985-90, Jan Wallmans, Trocadero, Angry Squire, Eighty Eights, Avalon, N.Y.C.; spokesperson Complex 15 (moisturizer) Nat'l 1989, Schering Lab. Media (TV-Radio Press); vol. worker for Diana Vreeland, Met. Mus. of Art, N.Y.C., 1980-83. Makeup work for various mags. including Vogue, Self, Glamour, Mademoiselle, Harper's Bazaar, Elle, Bride's, Cosmopolitan, New Woman, Mirabella, New York, New York Times Mag., German Vogue, French Vogue, Italian Vogue, Harper's Queen; makeup work for various notables including Goldie Hawn, Isabella Rosellini, Brooke Shields, Shari Belafonte, Paulina, Tracy Pollan, Nicolette Sheridan, Donna Dixon, Virginia Madsen, Dustin Hoffman, Victoria Principal, Lori Singer, Twyla Tharpe, Joanna Pacula, Barbara Bush, (photographers) Helmut Newton, Richard Avedon, Irving Penn, Denis Piel, Eric Nonan, Deborah Turbeville, Andrea Blanche, Susan Shacter. Democrat. Roman Catholic. Office: Visages RPS NY Inc Vernon Jolly 560 Broadway Ste 407 New York NY 10012

AVERY, MARY ELLEN, pediatrician, educator; b. Camden, N.J., May 6, 1927; d. William Clarence and Mary (Miller) A. AB, Wheaton Coll., Mass., 1948, DSc, 1974; MD, Johns Hopkins U., 1952; DSc (hon.), Trinity Coll., 1976, U. Mich., 1975, Med. Coll. Pa., 1976, Albany Med. Coll., 1977, Med. Coll., Wis., 1978, Radcliffe Coll., 1978; MA (hon.), Harvard U., 1974; LHD, Emmanuel Coll., 1979, Northeastern U., 1981, Russell Sage Coll., 1983. Intern Johns Hopkins Hosp., 1953-54, resident, 1954-57; research fellow in pediatrics Boston, 1957-59, Balt., 1959-69; assoc. prof. pediatrics Johns Hopkins U., 1964-69; prof., chmn. dept. pediatrics McGill U. Med. Sch., 1969-74; prof. pediatrics Harvard U., 1974—; physician-in-chief Montreal Children's Hosp., 1969-74, Children's Hosp. Med. Center, Boston, 1974-85; mem. council Med. Research Council Can.; mem. study sect. NIH, 1967—. Author: The Lung and Its Disorders in the Newborn Infant, 4th edit., 1981, (with A. Schaffer) Diseases of the Newborn, 1971, 5th edit. (with H.W. Taeusch), 1984; (with G. Litwack) Born Early, 1984; author, editor: (with L. First) Pediatric Medicine, 1989; also articles; mem. editorial bd. Pediatrics, 1965-71, Am. Rev. Respiratory Diseases, 1969-73, Am. Jour. Physiology, 1967-73, Jour. Pediatrics, 1974-84, Medicine, 1985—, Johns Hopkins Med. Jour, 1978-82, Clin. and Investigative Medicine, 1978—, New Eng. Jour. Medicine, 1990—. Trustee Wheaton Coll. (1965-85), Radcliffe Coll., Johns Hopkins U., 1982-88. Recipient Mead Johnson award in pediatric research, 1968, Trudeau medal Am. Thoracic Soc., 1984; Markle scholar in med. scis., 1961-66. Fellow AAAS (dir. 1989—), Internat. Pediatric Assn. (standing com. 1986-89), Am. Acad. Pediatrics, Am. Acad. Arts and Scis., Royal Coll. Physicians and Surgeons Can.; mem. Can. Pediatric Soc., Am. Physiol. Soc., Soc. Pediatric Research (pres. 1972-73), Brit. Pediatric Assn. (hon.), Inst. Medicine (counci. 1987—), Assn. Med. Sch. Dept. Chairmen (1969-85), Am. Pediatric Soc. (pres.-elect 1989), Phi Beta Kappa, Alpha Omega Alpha. Office: 221 Longwood Ave Boston MA 02115

AVERY, SHERRIE L., marketing director; b. Oberlin, Ohio, Feb. 20, 1943; d. Robert Sterling and Betty Jane (Bear) A.; divorced; children: Leslie Anne Cedeno, Robert Cedeno. BA, Baldwin-Wallace Coll., 1965; MA, U. Tenn., 1973. Personnel analyst Citibank, N.A., N.Y.C., 1968-69, media coord. graphics & audio-video svcs., 1969-71, pers. ofcl. asst., 1973-74; account officer Citibank, N.A., 1974-82; v.p. Banco de Bogota, Miami, Fla., 1982-83, M Bank, Miami, 1983-85; dir. mktg. 1st Nat. Bank South Miami, Fla., 1985—. Author: Twiglet: A Bank/School Partnership Making History, 1988; editor, writer newsletter, 1985—; contbr. articles to profl. jours. Bd. dirs. South Miami-Kendall C. of C., 1987-90; adv. bd. South Miami Comml. Devel. Bd., 1989-91; chairperson South Miami Bus. Com., 1985-86; chair person South Miami Econ. Devel. Com. Recipient Marketer of the Yr. award Bank Mktg Assn. Fla. Chpt., 1987-88, Dade Ptnrs. Exemplary award Dade County Sch. Bd., 1988, Ptnrs. in Bus. Edn., Fla. Comm. Edn., 1988, PIE Jour. Nat. Partnerships, Presdl. Bd. Advisors, 1988. Red and Sunset Merchants Assn., Women in Communications, Greater South Dade C. of C., Royal Palm Forum. Office: 1st Nat Bank South Miami 5750 Sunset Dr South Miami FL 33143

AVERY, SUSAN PAULA, public relations executive; b. Queens, N.Y., June 7, 1960; d. Alfred and Dona (Cohen) Lieberman. BS, Hunter Coll., 1986; MS in Journalism, Northwestern U., Evanston, Ill., 1990. Pub. relations asst. Davis-Brent Mktg., N.Y.C., 1982-86; reporter Poughkeepsie (N.Y.) Jour., 1987-88; dir. community edn. S.I. (N.Y.) Mental Health Soc., 1988—. Grantee Hunter Coll. Alumni Assn., 1986. Mem. Nat. Assn. Mental Health Info. Officer. Office: S I Community Television 100 Cable Way Ste #2 Staten Island NY 10303

AVINA-RHODES, NINA ALVARADO, health facility director; b. Alamo, Tex., Nov. 29, 1944; d. Pedro Vasques Avina and Enriqueta Alvarado-Avina; m. James Lamar Rhodes Jr., Feb. 14, 1977; children: James Lamar III, Aaron Abraham, David Isaiah. BS in Bus. Adminstrn., Calif. State U., San Jose, 1973, postgrad., 1973-75; MA, La Salle U., 1988, postgrad., 1988—. Cert. tchr., Ariz.; cert. adult basic educator, Calif.; cert. ESL tchr., Calif. Instr. Ctr. for Employment Tng., Santa Clara, Calif., 1976-80; pres. Avina Bros. Trucking Co., Fresno, Calif., 1982-84; writer grants Quechan Nation Indian Tribe, Yuma, Ariz., 1984-86; exec. dir. Western Ariz. Health & Edn. Ctr., Yuma, Ariz., 1986—. Co-host program Sta. KTEH-TV, San Jose, 1983. Co-facilitator Vietnam Vets. Outreach Ctr., San Jose; bd. dirs. Ctr. for Employment Tng., Yuma, 1984—; mem. Milpitas Unified Sch. Bd., 1981-82. Recipient Humanitarian award VA, 1983, Humanitarian award Vietnamese Community of Santa Clara County, 1983, Citizen of Honor award Vietnam Combat Vets., Ltd., 1983; named Woman of Achievement Santa Clara County Bd. Suprs., 1983. Mem. NAFE, AMVETS (pres. aux. Yuma chpt. 1986—), Nat. Network Hispanic Women. Baha'i. Home: 1740 W 24th Ln Yuma AZ 85364 Office: Western Ariz Health & Edn Ctr 281 W 24th St Suite 136 Yuma AZ 85364

AVINO-BARRACATO, KATHLEEN, construction executive, consultant; b. Bklyn., Nov. 30, 1956; d. Charles and Rosanna (Scarlota) A.; m. Joseph Moran Olague (div. Jan. 1985); m. Joseph Louis Barracato Jr., Aug. 23, 1986. B in Architecture, Pratt Inst., 1978; postgrad., U. Tex., 1984; cert. in constrn. mgmt., NYU, 1985—. Draftsperson Michael Harris Spector and Assocs., Great Neck, N.Y., 1974-78; designer Brodsky & Adler, Architects and Engrs., N.Y.C., 1978-79, Emery Roth and Son, Architects, N.Y.C., 1979; borough design mgr., urban park designer N.Y.C. Dept. of Parks and Recreation, Queens, 1979-81; project mgr. Lawrence D. White, Assocs., Austin, Tex., 1981; pvt. practice cons., educator Austin, 1981-85; drafting dept. head Durham Nixon-Clay Coll., Austin, 1982-84; asst. supt. constrn., constrn. mgr. N.Y.C. Dept. Social Services, 1985-87; project mgr. Racal-Chubb Security Systems, East Rutherford, N.J., 1987-88, Herbert Constrn. Co., N.Y.C., 1988-89; constrn. mgr. York/Hunter, Rutherford, N.J., 1989—. Mem. Nat. Assn. Female Execs. Republican. Roman Catholic. Club: Columbian. Home: 166 67th St Brooklyn NY 11220 Office: York/Hunter 201 Rte 17 N Rutherford NJ 07070

AVRAHAM, REGINA, secondary education educator; b. Ludenscheid, Germany, Aug. 15, 1935; Came to U.S., 1937.; d. Joseph and Feiga (Press) Artman; m. Josef Esa Abraham, Mar. 12, 1962; children: Randi Beth, Jesse Richard. BS, City Coll., N.Y.C., 1955. Elem. tchr. N.Y. Bd. Edn., 1955-63; tchr. N.Y. Bd. Edn., Bklyn., 1963—; sci., health magnet tchr. Bd. Edn., N.Y. 1987—. Author: Our Founding Sisters, 1976, Readings in Life Science, 1986, Readings in Physical Science, 1986, The Downside of Drugs, 1988, Substance Abuse Treatment and Prevention, 1988, Circulation, 1989, Digestion, 1989, Reproduction, 1989; contbg. editor Teacher Ctrs. Concortium, 1989. Woodrow Wilson fellow, 1989; named Tchr. of Yr., Bklyn. Sch. Bd., 1987. Mem. United Fed. Tchrs. Democratic. Home: 2218 Ave P Brooklyn NY 11229

AVRAM, HENRIETTE DAVIDSON, government official, information systems specialist; b. N.Y.C., Oct. 7, 1919; d. Joseph and Rhea (Olsho) Davidson; m. Herbert Mois Avram, Aug. 23, 1941; children: Lloyd, Marcie, Jay. Student, Hunter Coll., N.Y.C., George Washington U.; Sc.D. (hon.), So. Ill. U., 1977. Systems analyst, methods analyst, programmer Nat. Security Agy., 1953-59; systems analyst Am. Rsch. Bur., 1959-61, Datatrol Corp., 1961-65; supervisory info. systems specialist Libr. of Congress, Washington, 1965-67, asst. coord. info. systems, 1967-70, chief MARC Devel. Office, 1970-76, dir. Network Devel. Office, 1976-80, dir. processing systems, network and automation planning, 1980-83, asst. libr. for processing svcs., 1983-89, assoc. libr. Collection Svcs., 1989—, chmn. network adv. com., 1981—; chair subcom. 2 sectional com. Z39 Am. Nat. Standards Inst., 1966-80; chair RECON Working Task Force, 1968-73, Internat. Relations Round Table, 1986-87; chair subcom. 4 working group 1 on character sets Internat. Orgn. for Standardization, 1971-80; lectr. dept. library sci. Cath. U. Am., Washington, 1973—, mem. strategies for 80's com. Sch. Library and Info. Sci., 1980-81; mem. Com. for Coordination of Nat. Bibliog. Control, 1976-79, Linked Systems Project Policy Com., 1985—; mem. steering com. MARC Internat. Network Study, 1975—; bd. visitors Library and Learning Resources Com., 1980—; mem. internat. standards coordinating com. Info. Systems Standards Bd., 1983-86; del. to U.S. nat. com. UNESCO/Gen. Info. Program, 1983—; chair internat. relations com. Nat. Info. Standards Orgn., 1983—. Bd. editors: Jour. Library Automation, 1970-72; contbr. articles to profl. jours. Recipient Superior Service award Library of Congress, 1968, Margaret Mann citation in cataloging and classification, 1971, Fed. Woman's award, 1974, award for achievement in library and info. tech. ALA-Library Info. Tech. Assn., 1980; co-recipient ACRL Acad./Research Librarian of Year award, 1979. Fellow Internat. Fedn. Library Assns. and Instns. (hon. chair working group on content designators 1972-77, mem. program mgmt. com. 1983—, chair profl. bd. 1979-81, mem. exec. bd. 1983-87, 1st v.p. 1985-87, Melvil Dewey award 1981, Licppincott award 1988, Disting. Exec. Svc. award 1990); mem. ALA (bd. dirs., past pres. info. sci. and automation div., John Ames Humphry Forest Press award 1990), Am. Soc. Info. Sci. (spl. interest group on library automation and networks 1965—), Spl. Libraries Assn. (award 1990), Assn. Library and Info. Sci. Edn., Assn. Bibliog. Agys. Britain, Australia, Can. and U.S. (del. 1977—). Home: 1776 Elton Rd Silver Spring MD 20903 Office: Libr of Congress Washington DC 20540

AVRUNIN, CHARLENE PATTISHALL, communications executive; b. Greenville, S.C., Apr. 2, 1946; d. Charles Lauder and Gladys (Harris) Pattishall; m. Mark Avrunin, May 4, 1985; 1 child, Michael Allen Jolly. BA in Visual Arts, Ga. State U., 1973, MA, 1974. Media specialist Ga. State U., Atlanta, 1972-74; owner, dir. Impressions Sch. Photography, Atlanta, 1975-76; head prodn. Valencia Community Coll., Orlando, Fla., 1976-77; dir. media ctr. Kennesaw Coll., Marietta, Ga., 1977-83; mgr. Chrysler Satellite Network, Chrysler Corp., Highland Park, Mich., 1983-85; v.p. Avko Underwriters, Inc., Bloomfield Hills, Mich., 1985-90; cons. Bloomfield Hills, 1985-90; owner, pres. C&M Communications Cons., Inc., Orlando, 1990—; presentor numerous seminars on video prodn., cable TV, and satellite communications, 1980-83. Contbr. articles to profl. jours. Sec. corresponding, ECW-Christchurch Cranbrook, Bloomfield Hills; mem. Orlando/Orange County Conv. Visitors Bur. Mem. NAFE, Internat. Teleconf. Assn., Internat. TV Assn. (past dir., membership com. 1982-83, programming com. 1983-84, cert. appreciation 1981-82, Outstanding Svc. plaque Atlanta chpt. 1982-83), Southeastern Regional Media Leadership Coun. (Ga. del.), 5th Wheel Golf League (handicapper). Methodist. Office: PO Box 2662 Winter Park FL 32790

AWAD, SHAHRZAD H., data processing professional; b. Cairo, Jan. 16, 1952; d. Ali Salah El Din Hamdy and Adele Gamino; m. Hani J. Awad; 1 child, Naimeen. BSBA, Ashland (Ohio) U., 1990; diploma with distinction, Inst. Fin. Edn., Chgo., 1988; AA in Data Processing, North Cen. Tech. Coll., Wooster. Data processing mgr. 1st Fed. Savs. and Loan, Wooster, Ohio. Mem. Inst. Fin. Edn., Ohio Fedn. Rep. Women, Nat. Assn. Banking Women. Home: 937 Marilyn Dr Wooster OH 44691

AXELROD, LEAH JOY, tour company executive; b. Milw., Sept. 7, 1929; d. Harry J. and Helen Janet (Ackerman) Mandelker; m. Leslie Robert Axelrod, Mar. 10, 1951; children: David Jay, Craig Lewis, Harry Besser, Garrick Paul, Bradley Neal, Nell Anne. BS, U. Wis., 1951. Creative drama specialist Highland Park Parks & Recreation Dept., Ill., 1962-82; program specialist Pub. Libr., Highland Park, 1972-82; ednl. cons. Bd. Jewish Edn., Chgo., 1973-80; children's edn. specialist Jewish Community Ctr., Chgo., 1975-82; tour cons. My Kind of Town Tours, Highland Park, 1975-79, pres., 1979—. Editor: Highland Park: All American City, 1976. Co-author: Highland Park By Foot or By Frame, 1980; Highland Park: American Suburb, 1982. Bd. dirs. Midwest Fedn. Temple Sisterhoods, 1975-79, Midwest Zionist Youth Commn.; pres. B'nai Torah Sisterhood, 1982-84; founding mem., v.p. Highland Park Hist. Soc., pres. 1987—; mem. adv. bd. Ill. State Hist. Soc., 1989—; founder, bd. dirs. Chgo. Jewish Hist. Soc.; mem. Highland Park Historic Preservation Commn. Mem. Nat. Assn. Women Bus. Owners (bd. dirs. Chgo. chpt. 1988—), Am. Theatre Assn., Ill. Theatre Assn. (dir. creative dramatics 1977-79), Hadassah Club (Highland Park chpt.). Home: 2100 Linden Ave Highland Park IL 60035 Office: My Kind of Town Tours Inc PO Box 924 Highland Park IL 60035

AXELROD, SUSAN ELLEN, city official; b. N.Y.C., Feb. 14, 1948; d. Louis Sanford and Thelma (Litt) Schuman; m. Howard Leon Axelrod, May 27, 1966; children: Marc Steven, Sara Beth, Jon David. BA, Cleve. State U., 1981, M History, 1982. Teaching asst. Cleve. State U., 1982-83; exec. asst. State Senator Lee I. Fisher, Cleve., 1983-87; dir. Handgun Control Fedn./Ohio, Cleve., 1987-90; dir. Dept. Aging City of Cleve., 1990—; dir. spl. events Lee Fisher for Atty. Gen., Cleve., 1989-90; dir. fundraising Eric Fingerhut for Senate, Cleve., 1989—. Editor, author: (newsletter) The Adv., 1987-90. Chairwoman Adam Walsh Child Resource Ctr., Cleve., 1983-85; exec. me. Dem. Cen. Com., Cuyahoga County, Ohio, 1983—; trustee Handgun Control Fedn. Ohio, 1990—; membership chair Cuyahoga Women's Polit. Caucus, Cleve., 1987-88; treas. Common Cause/Ohio, Columbus, 1988-90. Recipient Letter of Commendation, Ohio Senate, 1984. Mem. World Wildlife Fund, Coun. on Older Persons, Jewish Community Fedn., People for Ethical Treatment Animals. Democrat. Office: Dept of Aging 601 Lakeside Ave Cleveland OH 44118

AXELROD, VALIJA M., vocational education professional; b. Riga, Latvia, Apr. 27, 1944; came to U.S., 1950; d. Konstantins and Eizenija (Leimanis) Miske; m. Arnold M. Axelrod, Apr. 7, 1965; children: Martin Alan, Brian Kenneth. BA, Miami U., Oxford, Ohio, 1965; MS, Wayne State U., 1973; PhD, Ohio State U., 1980; MBA, Wright State U. Project dir., rsch. specialist Nat. Ctr. Rsch. on Vocat. Edn., Columbus, Ohio, 1984-88; program dir. Ctr. on Edn. and Tng. for Employment, Columbus, 1988-89; exec. dir. Internat. Vocat. Edn. and Tng. Assn., Columbus, 1987—; pres., mng. dir. Powell (Ohio) Internat., 1988—. Contbr. to topical publs. Mem. Internat. Vocat. Edn. and Tng. Assn. (sec.), Delta Phi Alpha, Epsilon Pi Tau, Phi Beta Delta, Phi Delta Kappa. Home: 1532 Wren Ln Powell OH 43065 Office: Powell Internat Inc 670-C Enterprise Dr Westerville OH 43081

AYCOCK, PAMELA GAYLE, underwriter; b. Kenansville, N.C., July 22, 1961; d. Herbert Carol and Judith Ann (Thigpen) A. Assoc. Bus. Adminstrn., James Sprunt Community Coll., 1990; student, N.C. State U., 1979-80. Adminstrv. specialist Brown & Root, Inc., Bay City, Tex., 1980-81, Houston, 1981-83; litigation supr. Brown & Root, U.S.A., Houston, 1983-85; underwriting asst. Interstate Casualty Ins., Kinston, N.C., 1985-89; account exec. SIA Group, Jacksonville, N.C., 1989—. Author: East Duplin Boosters Club Athletic Program, 1987, 88. Mem. com. Wallace (N.C.) Area Cancer Fund, 1990. Mem. Ins. Women Onslow County (pres. 1990—), NAFE, DAR (award 1979). Democrat. Baptist. Home: Rt 2 Box 253A Wallace NC 28466

AYDELOTTE, MYRTLE KITCHELL, nursing administrator, educator, consultant; b. Van Meter, Iowa, May 31, 1917; d. John J. and Larava Josephine (Gutshall) Kitchell; m. William O. Aydelotte, June 22, 1956; children—Marie Elizabeth, Jeannette Farley. B.S., U. Minn., 1939, M.A., 1947, Ph.D., 1955; postgrad., Columbia U. Tchrs. Coll., summer 1948. Head nurse Charles T. Miller Hosp., St. Paul, 1939-41; supr. surg. teaching St. Mary's Hosp. Sch. Nursing, Mpls., 1941-42; instr. U. Minn., 1945-49; dir., dean State U. Iowa Coll. Nursing, 1949-57, prof., 1957-62; assoc. chief nurse VA Hosp. Research for Nursing, Iowa City, 1963-64; chief nursing research VA Hosp. Research for Nursing, 1964-65; prof. U. Iowa Coll. Nursing, 1964-77, 84-88; exec. dir. Am. Nurses Assn., 1984-89; dir. nursing U. Iowa Hosps. and Clinics, 1968-76; mem. sci. adv. bd. Center for Health Research, Wayne State U., 1972-76, Inst. Medicine, 1973—; cons. U. Minn., 1970, 82, 90, U. Rochester, 1971, U. Mich., 1970, 73, U. Colo., 1970-71, U. Hawaii, 1972-73, Ariz. State U., 1972, U. Nebr., 1972-73. Contbr. articles to profl. jours.; editorial bd.: Nursing Forum, 1969-72, Jour. Nursing Adminstrn, 1971. Mem., v.p. Iowa City Library Bd., 1961-67; mem. Johnson County Bd. Health, 1967-70; mem. adv. com. on family living courses Iowa City Bd. Edn., 1970-72. Served with Army Nurse Corps, 1942-46. Mem. Am. Nurses Assn., Am. Hosp. Assn., Am. Acad. Nursing, Sigma Theta Tau (research com. 1968-72). Home: 201 N 1st Ave Iowa City IA 52245 also: 149 Oswegatchie Rd Waterford CT 06385

AYER, KRISTIN VANDER MEER, color analyst; b. Natick, Mass., Nov. 25, 1951; d. John William and Jeanne (Dunton) Vander Meer; m. Richard Woodman Ayer II, July 1, 1972; children: Richard III, Matthew, Gregory, Amanda. BS in Bus. Acctg., U. Coll. Northeastern U., Boston, 1979. Cert. color analyst. Comml. casualty underwriter Comml. Union Ins., Boston, 1971-80; v.p. living color div. Ayer Enterprises, Natick, 1981—. Treas. Brown Sch. PTA, Natick, 1987-88. Mem. Sigma Epsilon Rho. Republican.

AYERS, PATRICIA ANN, lawyer; b. Dec. 6, 1958; d. Donald Frances and Marie (Gallagher) A. BS, Hartwick Coll., 1979; JD, Union U., 1984. Bar: N.Y. 1985, D.C. 1988, Colo. 1990. Med. technologist Strong Meml. Hosp., Rochester, N.Y., 1979-80; rsch. and devel. technician Eastman Kodak, Rochester, 1980-81; assoc. Nixon Hargrave Devans & Doyle, Rochester, 1984-86, 87-89; sr. personal law clk. to judge N.Y. State Ct. Appeals, 1986-87; assoc. Davis, Graham & Stubbs, Denver, 1989—. Mem. ABA, N.Y. State Bar Assn., Order of Coif. Republican. Episcopalian. Office: Davis Graham & Stubbs PO Box 185 Denver CO 80201-0185

AYLOUSH, CYNTHIA MARIE, personnel director, corporate treasurer; b. Jackson, Mich., July 2, 1950; d. Leonard Edward and Violet Caroline (Kroeger) Ullrich; m. Abbott Selim Ayloush, June 21, 1980; children: Sasha Christine, Nadia Marie, Ramsey Abbott. AA, Fullerton Coll., 1970; diploma in fashion mdse., Brooks Coll., 1975; BS, Pepperdine U., 1980. Receptionist, Hydraflow, Commerce, Calif., 1968-74, pers. mgr., Cerritos, Calif., 1979—, treas., 1979—, corp. sec., 1985—; with sales dept. Robinson's, Cerritos, Calif., 1974-75, dept. mgr., 1975-79. Mem. Am. Soc. Pers. Adminstrs., Pers. Indsl. Rels. Assn., Mchts. and Mfrs. Assn., Cerritos C. of C. (bd. dir. 1983-89). Republican. Roman Catholic. Clubs: Soroptimist (sec. 1979—), Century, Pepperdine U. Office: Hydraflow 13259 E 166th St Cerritos CA 90701

AYOTTE, ELIZABETH ANN, nurse; b. Waltham, Mass., Oct. 1, 1952; d. Theodore Joseph and Barbara Jean (Richardson) A. BS in Nursing, Fitchburg (Mass.) State Coll., 1974; MS, Boston U., 1985; postgrad., Syracuse (N.Y.) U., 1982. RN, Mass., Conn. Nursing coord. VA Med. Ctr., Syracuse; critical care instr. Salem (Mass.) Hosp.; cardiothoracic nurse Brigham and Women's Hosp., Boston; now cardiovascular clin. specialist Hartford (Conn.) Hosp.; cons. to law firms, patient edn. film cos. Mem. Am. Nurses Assn., Mass. Nurses Assn. (nurse expert witness com.), Am. Assn. Critical Care Nurses, Am. Heart Assn., Sigma Theta Tau. Home: 98 Songbird Ln Farmington CT 06032

AYOUB, CHRISTINE WILLIAMS, mathematics educator; b. Cin., Feb. 7, 1922; d. William Lloyd Garrison and Anne Christine (Sykes) Williams; m. Raymond George Ayoub, July 1, 1950; children: Cynthia Anne, Daphne Nazeera. AB, Bryn Mawr Coll., 1942; AM, Radcliffe Coll., 1943; MA, McGill U., 1944; PhD, Yale U., 1947. Instr. math. Cornell U., Ithaca, N.Y., 1948-51; lectr. math. Pa. State U., University Park, 1952-66, assoc. prof. math, 1966-69, prof. math, 1969-84, prof. emerita, 1984—; vis. prof. U. Warwick (Eng.), 1979-80, King Saud U., Riyadh, Saudi Arabia, 1984-85. NSF fellow, Fed. Republic Germany, 1966-67, Fulbright fellow, Rabat, Morocco, 1988. Mem. Am. Math. Soc., Math. Assn. Am. Home: 120 Ridge Ave State College PA 16803

AYOUB, LINDA MARIE, personnel consultant; b. Washington, July 4, 1964; d. Naim Ishaq and Judy Louise (Booker) A. Lic. real estate, Md. U., 1983. Mktg. sec. Lewis & Silverman, Chevy Chase, Md., 1982-83; adminstrv. asst. to chmn. of bd. Manor Care & Quality Inns, Silver Springs, Md., 1983-85; treasury cash asst. Oxford Devel., Bethesda, Md., 1985; legal adminstrv. sec. Electronic Data Systems, Bethesda, 1985-87; legal sec. Protas & Spivok, Chartered, Rockville, Md., 1987-89; personnel cons., pres. ExecuTemps, Inc., Silver Spring, 1988—. Mem. Redskinette Alumni. Home: 15417 Durant St Colesville MD 20904 Office: ExecuTemps Inc PO Box 4527 Silver Spring MD 20904

AYOUNG, JUDITH M., accountant; b. Trinidad, West Indies, July 21, 1965; came to U.S., 1969; naturalized.; d. Henry Jr. and Beverly (Allum) A. BBA/MBA, Pace U., 1987. CPA, N.Y. Acct. Coopers and Lybrand, N.Y.C.; pres./founder Scholastic Resource Svcs., 5. Blood Capt.for Greater Blood Bank N.Y.; vol. for Spl. Olympics; preparer publicity for community tax aid. Mem. AICPA, NAFE, N.Y. Soc. CPAs, Women's Soc. CPAs, Pace U. Alumni Mentors, CPA Candidates Assn., Sponsors for Ednl. Opportunity, Fin. Execs. Inst.

AYRAULT, EVELYN WEST, psychologist, writer; b. Buffalo, Mar. 3, 1922; d. John and Evelyn (West) A.; BS, Fla. State Coll. for Women, 1945; MA, U. Chgo., 1947. Chief psychologist, asst. prin. Crippled Children's Sch., Jamestown, N.D., 1947-48; psychologist, tchr. spl. edn. dept. Sharon (Pa.) Public Schs., 1948-50; chief psychologist, instr. Med. Coll. Va., Richmond, 1950-52; pvt. practice, psychology N.Y.C., 1952-68; clin. psychologist, Erie, Pa., 1968—; dir. psychol. services United Cerebral Palsy Assn., Miami, Fla., 1952-54, Erie County (Pa.) Crippled Children's Soc., 1968-78; mem. med. staff Great Lakes Rehab. Hosp., Erie, Pa., 1986—. Mem. Am., N.Y. State, Pa. psychol. assns., Council for Exceptional Children, Psi Chi. Author: Take Step, 1963; You Can Raise Your Handicapped Child, 1964; Helping the Handicapped Teenager Mature, 1971; Growing Up Handicapped, 1978; Sex, Love, and the Physically Handicapped, 1981. Home: 10054 W Law Rd North East PA 16428 Office: 104 E 2nd St Erie PA 16507

AYRES, JANICE RUTH, social service executive; b. Idaho Falls, Idaho, Jan. 23, 1930; d. Low Ray and Frances Mae (Salem) Mason; m. Thomas Woodrow Ayres, Nov. 27, 1953 (dec. 1966); 1 child, Thomas Woodrow Jr. MBA, U. So. Calif., 1952, M in Mass Communications, 1953. Asst. mktg. dir. Disneyland, Inc., Anaheim, Calif., 1954-59; gen. mgr. Tamasha Town & Country Club, Anaheim, Calif., 1959-65; dir. mktg. Am. Heart Assn., Santa Ana, Calif., 1966-69; state exec. dir. Nev. Assn. Mental Health, Las Vegas, 1969-71; exec. dir. Clark Co. Easter Seal Treatment Ctr., Las Vegas, 1971-73; mktg. dir., fin devel. officer So. Nev. Drug Abuse Coun., Las Vegas, 1973-74; exec. dir. Nev. Assn. Retarded Citizens, Las Vegas, 1974-75; assoc., cons. Don Luke & Assocs., Phoenix, 1976-77; program dir. Inter-Tribal Coun. Nev., Reno, 1977-79; exec. dir. Ret. Vol. Program, Carson City, Nev., 1979—; conductor workshops in field. Named Woman of Distinction, Soroptimist Club, 91988, Outstanding Dir. of Excellence, Gov. State of Nev., 1989, Outstanding Dir., Vol. Action Ctr., J.C. Penney Co. Mem. AAUW, Nat. Pub. Rels. Soc. Am. (chpt. pres.), Women Radio & TV, Am. Assn. Profl. Fund Raisers, Nev. Fair & Rodeo Assn. (pres.). Home: 1624 Karin Dr Carson City NV 89701 Office: Ret Sr Vol Program 308 N Curry St Ste 209 Carson City NV 89703

AYRES, LINDA L., art historian, curator; b. Berlin, Md., May 25, 1947; d. John Pershing and Hilda Margaret (Smallwood) A.; m. David Emmert Brewster, Apr. 21, 1977. BA, Washington Coll., 1969; MA, Tufts U., 1973. Bicentennial coordinator Fogg Art Mus., Cambridge, Mass., 1974-75, asst. to dir., 1975-76; research asst. Nat. Portrait Gallery, Washington, 1977-78, asst. curator Am. art, 1978-84; acting curator Am. art Nat. Gallery, 1983; curator painting and sculpture Amon Carter Mus., Ft. Worth, 1984-89; assoc. dir. exhbns. and pub. programs Wadsworth Atheneum, Hartford,

Conn., 1989—. Author exhbn. catalogue: Harvard Divided, 1976; Thomas Moran's Watercolors of Yellowstone, 1984; co-author exhbn. catalogue: An American Perspective, 1981; Bellows: Boxing Pictures, 1982, George Bellows: The Artist and His Liethographs (1916-1924), 1988; American Paintings, Watercolors and Drawings from the Collection of Rita and Daniel Fraad, 1985; contbg. author: John Hay Whitney Collection, 1983; co-author: John Singer Sargent, 1986, American Paintings: Selections from the Amon Carter Museum, 1986, American Frontier Life: Early Western Painting and Prints, 1987; contbr. Three Centuries of Am. Painting, 1988. Recipient New Eng. Book award, 1976. Mem. Coll. Art Assn. Democrat. Episcopalian. Office: Wadsworth Atheneum Hartford CT 06103

AZAMA-EDWARDS, GWENDOLYN JOYCE, municipal government official; b. Orange City, Fla., Jan. 7, 1949; d. James William and Willie Belle (Taylor) Frazier; m. Curtis Lee Azama, May 31, 1971 (div. Mar. 1984); children: Curtis Lee Jr., Anthony James; m. Larry Tyran Edwards, Feb. 11, 1989. BA, Stetson U., 1970, MA, 1983. Employment interviewer to supr. employment counseling Fla. State Employment Svcs., Daytona Beach, 1971-80; job svc. mgr. State of Fla., 1980-85; regional mgr. Fla. Dept. Labor, Lakeland, 1985-87; city clk. City of Daytona Beach, 1987-88, city clk., asst. to city mgr., 1988—. Bd. dirs. Volusia-Flagler County United Way, Daytona Beach, 1987—; mem. League of Women Voters, Lakeland, 1986-87, Daytona Beach, 1985, 87.; mem. NAACP. Recipient Disting. Svc. award NAACP, 1984. Mem. Fla. Assn. City Clerks, Regional Coordinating Coun., Fla. Employment Counselors Assn. (past officer, Citation), Excelsior Bus. and Profl. Women's Club (pres. 1981-83)., Assn. Records Mgrs. and Adminstrs., U. Cen. Fla. Adv. Bd., Bethune-Cookman Coll. Bd. of Counselors. Baptist. Home: 1147 Edith Dr Daytona Beach FL 32117

AZCUENAGA, MARY LAURIE, government official; b. Council, Idaho, July 25, 1945. AB, Stanford U., 1967; JD, U. Chgo., 1973. Atty. FTC, Washington, 1973-75, asst. to gen. counsel, 1975-76, staff atty. San Francisco regional office, 1977-80, asst. regional dir., 1980-81, asst. to exec. dir., 1981-82, litigation atty. Office of Gen. Counsel, 1982, asst. gen. counsel for legal counsel, 1983-84, commr., Washington, 1984—. Office: FTC 6th & Pennsylvania Ave NW Rm 526 Washington DC 20580

AZLIN, DENISE ROXANE, financial planning professional; b. Fresno, Calif., Feb. 14, 1962; d. William Roy and Sharon Lee (Barton) Lawson; m. Darrell Lee Azlin, Apr. 28, 1984. BS in Organizational Behavior, U. San Francisco, 1990. Reg. rep., reg. prin., N.Assn. Securities Dealers. Chief operational officer, due diligence officer Calif. Planners Network, Inc., Modesto, Calif., 1984-86; v.p. FTFS, Inc., Oakland, Calif., 1986-87; regional security products specialist The Equitable Fin. Cos., Fresno, 1987—, also market devel. cons.; speaker women's leadership program, local ednl. instns. Contbr. articles to corp. communications publs. Advisor funding com. San Joaquin River Pkwy Conservation Trust, 1990. Mem. Internat. Assn. Fin. Planners (v.p. fin. 1989—), Women at the Heart of Things (v.p.), Venture Club Modesto North (pres.). Lutheran. Office: 550 E Shaw Fresno CA 93710

AZPEITIA, LYNNE MARIE, educator, psychotherapist; b. San Pedro, Calif., Mar. 10, 1951; d. Harlan Raymond and Virginia Grace (Dirocco) a.; m. Christopher Joseph Murphy, Mar. 24, 1979 (div. Sept. 1988); children: Jonathan Christopher, Matthew Joseph. AA, Long Beach City Coll., 1971; BA, U. Calif., Santa Barbara, 1973; MA, Azusa Pacific Coll., 1978. Lic. marriage, family and child counselor, Calif. Grad. prof., clin. supr. and adminstr. Calif. Family Study Ctr., N. Hollywood, Calif., 1979—; pvt. practice psychotherapy N. Hollywood, 1979—; bd. dirs. Va. Satir's Avanta Network, Palo Alto, Calif., 1986-89, Va. Satir Family Camp, Big Sur, Calif., 1979—. Mem. Am. Assn. Marriage and Family Therapy (approved supervisor), Am. Family Therapy Assn. Democrat. Roman Catholic. Office: Calif Family Study Ctr 5433 Laurel Canyon Blvd North Hollywood CA 91607

BAAS, ERA DAWN, hospice professional; b. Biloxi, Miss., Dec. 19, 1956; d. James Michael and Shirley Ann (Scott) B.; m. Robert A. Wiley, Mar. 2, 1974; (div. 1979); children: Christopher Wiley, Jeremey Wiley; m. Samuel Jones Grant, Sept. 3, 1988; 1 chld, Craig Grant. Student, Rochester (Minn.) Vocat. Sch., 1975; AA, Fergus Falls Community Coll., 1982; BS, St. Cloud State U., 1982-84; postgrad., Boca Raton Coll., 1985—. Human svc. technician Rochester State Hosp., 1975-81; dir. social svc. Colonial Palms E., Pompana Beach, Fla., 1984-87; nursing team coord. Hospice by the Sea, Boca Raton, Fla., 1987-89, bereavement coord., 1989—; social svc. cons. Ridge Terr., Lantana, Fla., 1988—. Recipient Magna Cum Laude St. Cloud State U., St. Cloud, 1984. Mem. NOW, Nat. Assn. Social Workers, Social Workers Long Term Care Broward & Palm Beach. Home: 9400 Southampton Pl Boca Raton FL 33434

BAAS, JACQUELYNN, art historian, museum administrator; b. Grand Rapids, Mich., Feb. 14, 1948. BA in History of Art, Mich. State U.; Ph.D. in History of Art, U. Mich. Registrar U. Mich. Mus. Art, Ann Arbor, 1974-78, asst. dir., 1978-82; editor Bull. Museums of Art and Archaeology, U. Mich., 1976-82; chief curator Hood Mus. Art, Dartmouth Coll., Hanover, N.H., 1982-84, dir., 1985-89; dir. Univ. Art Mus., Berkeley, Calif., 1989—. Contbr. articles to jours. and catalogues. NEH fellow, 1972-73; Nat. Endowment Arts fellow, 1973-74, 87-88. Mem. Coll. Art Assn. Am., Print Council Am., Am. Assn. Museums, Assn. Art Mus. Dirs.. Office: Univ Art Mus 2625 Durant Ave Berkeley CA 94720

BABA, MARIETTA LYNN, university official, anthropologist, b. Flint, Mich., Nov. 9, 1949; d. David and Lillian (Joseph) Baba; m. David Smokler, Feb. 14, 1977 (div. 1982); 1 child, Alexia Baba Smokler. BA with highest distinction, Wayne State U., 1971, MA in Anthropology, 1973, PhD in Phys. Anthropology, 1975. Asst. prof. sci. and tech. Wayne State U., Detroit, Mich., 1975-80, assoc. prof. anthropology, 1980-88, prof., 1988—, spl. asst. to pres., 1980-82, econ. devel. officer, 1982-83, asst. provost, 1983-85; assoc. provost, 1985—, dir. Internat. Programs and Interim Assoc. Dean of Grad. Sch., 1988-89, assoc. dean grad. sch., 1989-90, acting chair Dept. Anthropology, 1990—; founder, corp. officer Applied Rsch. Teams Mich., Inc., Detroit, Intelligent Techs., Inc., Detroit; evolution researcher Wayne State U., 1975-82; cons. GM Rsch. Labs., 1988-90, Electronic Data Systems, 1990; lectr. nat. and internat. symposia, profl. confs. Contbr. numerous papers and abstracts to tech. jours; patentee in field. Bd. dirs. City-Univ. Consortium, Detroit, 1980-83; v.p. Neighborhood Svc. Orgn., Detroit, 1980-85; mem. State Rsch. Fund Feasibility Rev. Panel, 1982-90; mem. adv. panel on tech., innovation and U.S. trade U.S. Congl. Office Tech. Assessment, 1990; active Leadership Detroit Class IV, 1982-83; dir. Mich. Tech. Coun. (SE div.), 1984-85. Job Partnership Tng. Act grantee, 1981-90; NSF grantee, 1982, 84-85. Issued letters patent for method to map joint ventures and maps produced thereby. Fellow Am. Anthrop. Assn. (bd. dirs. 1986-88, exec. com. 1986-88, del. to the Internat. Union Anthrop. and Ethnol. Sci. 1990-94), Nat. Assn. Practice Anthropology (pres. 1986-88), Soc. Applied Anthropology, Phi Beta Kappa, Sigma Xi. Office: Wayne State U 1050 Mackenzie Hall Detroit MI 48202

BABB, BARBARA CAROLINE, lawyer; b. Fountain Inn, S.C., Dec. 16, 1933; d. Victor Morgan Jr. and Ida Kate (Morrison) B. Student, Sweet Briar Coll., 1951-53; BA, U. N.C., 1959, postgrad., 1963; cert. in teaching, Furman U., 1964; JD, U. S.C., 1968. Bar: U.S. Dist. Ct. S.C. 1968. Sec. Dan River Mills, Woodside Div., Greenville, S.C., 1954-58, 60-65, indsl. & pub. rel. artist, 1954-70; instr. Greenville Tech. Inst., 1969-70; pvt. practice Fountain Inn, 1973—; cons. Appalachian Regional commn., Greenville, 1970, mem. Chief Justice's Com., Columbia, S.C., 1970-71, co-hostess Nat. Conf. of Chief Justices, 1971. Mem. S.C. Bar Assn. (exec. dir. 1970-71), S.C. State Bar (exec. sec., treas. 1970-73). Presbyterian. Home and Office: 407 S Main St Fountain Inn SC 29644

BABB, MARION STANDAHL, journalist, soprano; b. Mayville, N.D., Dec. 1, 1918; d. Ole R. and MInnie (Johnson) Standahl; m. William James McDougall, Apr. 12, 1946 (div. 1963); children: Lawrence Dennis, Gwen McDougall King; m. Albert Leslie Babb, Aug. 27, 1972. BA summa cum laude, Mayville State Coll., 1938; MA, U. Wash., Seattle, 1970; voice pupil, William Pierce Herman and Coenraad Bos, N.Y.C., Fritz Lehmann, Vienna, Austria, Vittorio Ruffo, Milan, Italy. Exec. asst. Seattle Trust & Savs. Bank, 1963-73; editor Nuclearscope, U. Wash., Seattle, 1973-80, newsletter Am. Nuclear Soc., 1973-80; tchr. elocution, 1960—; free lance writer, 1960—; lectr. on artificial kidney, Japan and Korea, 1973, USSR, 1974; media liaison lectr. tours on radiologic imaging to Norway, Sweden, Denmark, Austria, Germany. Profl. opera singer, dramatic soprano, Europe and N.Y.C., 1946-63; debut at Carnegie Hall, N.Y.C., 1958; appeared first U.S. performance of Edgar, 1956; ch. soloist, Seattle and N.Y., from 1958. Patron Seattle Art Mus., Seattle Opera. Mem. Women in Communications, Nat. Fedn. Press Women, Internat. Am. Bus. Communicators, Wash. Press Women, Wash. Athletic Club (bd. dirs.), Pres.'s Club, Univ. Club of Wash. Home: 3237 Lakewood Ave S Seattle WA 98144

BABB, MARVA TEW, human resources company executive; b. Dunn, N.C., Feb. 11, 1951; d. Marvin Iley and Letty (Coleman) Tew; m. William C. Babb III, Mar. 30, 1985; 1 child, MacKenzie Coleman. Student, Hardbarger Jr. Coll., 1969-70, N.C. State U., 1971-72. Account exec. Emery World Wide, Raleigh, N.C. and Atlanta, 1976-78; nat. accounts exec., internat. dir. sales tng. and adminstrn. Profit/LEP Internat., Atlanta, 1978-84; nat. dir. admissions Edn. Mgmt. Corp., Atlanta, 1984-86; pres. Marva Babb & Assocs., Atlanta, 1986—; cons. in field. Author tng. texts and videos. Home: 5520 Powers Ridge Ct Atlanta GA 30327 Office: MBA Inc PO Box 720351 Atlanta GA 30358

BABBAGE, JOAN DOROTHY, journalist; b. Montclair, N.J., Jan. 10, 1926; d. Laurence Washburn and Dorothy A. (Davenport) Babbage; m. Vernon H. Ellsworth, Mar. 6, 1971. B.A. in English, Mt. Holyoke Coll., 1948; postgrad. Art Students League, New Sch. for Social Research. Publicist Paramount Internat. Films, N.Y.C., 1952-58; reporter Newark News, 1960-67, food editor, 1967-72; feature writer, reporter Star-Ledger, Newark, 1972—. Author: (with others) Past and Present Lives of New Jersey Women, 1990; contbr. bus. articles to New Jersey Business mag., articles to Official Dog mag. Operator rescue orgn. SaintSaver, N.J., N.Y., Pa.; v.p. jr. group Women's Nat. Republican Club, N.Y.C., 1955. Recipient recommendation award N.J. br. Humane Soc. U.S., PICA Club N.J. award, 1980, Community Media award Assn. Retarded Citizens, Morris County Unit, N.J., 1987, Willard H. Allen Agrl. Communications Media award, N.J. Agrl. Soc., 1988, Communicator of Yr. award N.J. Dept. Agriculture, 1990. Appeared on NBC-TV to demonstrate dog tng. Home: Washington Ave Montclair NJ 07042 Office: Star-Ledger Court St Newark NJ 07101

BABCOCK, JACQUELINE EILEEN, management; b. Grand Rapids, Oct. 7, 1948; d. Jay LeRoy and Edna Eileen (Miller) Shook; m. Philip Alan Babcock, Feb. 24, 1967; 1 child, Margaret Anne. AA, Lansing Community Coll., 1970; BA (with honor), Mich St. U., E. Lansing, 1979; MPA, Western Mich. U., Kalamazoo, 1988. Sec. 11 Mich. State Univ., E. Lansing, 1974-77; sec. to chairperson dept. Elem. & Special Edn., E. Lansing, 1977-80; office asst. dean's office Coll. Social Sci., E. Lansing, 1980-81; office supr., dept. med. Mich. State Univ., E. Lansing, 1981-84; specialist, adminstrv. asst. to chairperson Dept. of Counseling, Mich. State Univ., E. Lansing, 1984—. Contbr. articles to profl. jours. Mem. non-acad. women's adv. com. Mich. State U., 1984. Mem. Mich. State U. Bus. Women's Assn. (pres. 1986-87). Office: Mich State U Coll Edn 453 Erickson Hall East Lansing MI 48824

BABCOCK, JANICE BEATRICE, health system specialist; b. Milw., June 2, 1942; d. Delbert Martin and Constance Josephine (Dworschack) B. BS in Med. Tech., Marquette U., 1964; MA in Healthcare Mgmt. and Supervision, Cen. Mich. U., 1975, postgrad. in Edn. in Health Care, 1975—. Registered med. technologist and microbiologist., clin. lab. scientist, epidemiologist; cert. bioanalytical lab. mgr. Intern St. Luke's Hosp., Milw., 1963-64; microbiologist St. Michael's Hosp., Milw., 1964-65; supr. clin. lab. svc. VA Regional Office, Milw., 1965-66; hosp. epidemiologist VA Ctr., Milw., 1966-74, supr. anaerobic microbiology and rsch. lab., 1974-78, adminstrv. officer, chief med. tech., 1978-83, quality assurance coord., 1983-86, asst. to chief of staff profl. svcs., 1986—; rsch. assoc. dept. surgery Med. Coll. Wis.; tchr. in field Marquette U., U. Wis., Med. Coll. Wis. Contbr. numerous articles to profl. jours. Sec. Wis. Svc. League, 1989—. Recipient Wood VA Fed. Woman's award, 1975, Profl. Achievement award Lab. World jour., 1981, Disting. Alumni award Cen. Mich. U., 1986. Fellow Royal Soc. Health, Am. Acad. Med. Adminstrs. (Wis. State Dir. of Yr. award 1989); mem. Internat. Acad. Healthcare Mgmt., Am. Soc. Microbiology, Am. Coll. Healthcare Execs., Am. Soc. Med. Tech. (Nat. Sci. Creativity award 1974, Nat. Microbiology Sci. Achievement award 1978, Mem. of Yr. award 1979, Profl. Achievement Lectureship award 1981, French Lectureship award 1983), Assn. Practitioners in Infection Control, Fed. Execs. Assn., Wis. Hosp. Assn., AAUW, Nat. Geog. Soc., Marquette U. Alumni Assn. (Merit award 1979, Profl. Achievement award 1987), Assn. Marquette U. Women (bd. dirs. 1987—, v.p. 1990—), Holiday Camera Club, Inter Group & Wis. Svc. League, Inter Group, Wis. Svc. League, Alpha Mu Tau (pres. 1984-85), Alpha Delta Theta, Sigma Iota Epision, Alpha Delta Pi (Alumni Honor award 1979). Home: 6839 Blanchard St Wauwatosa WI 53213 Office: VA Med Ctr 5000 W National Ave Milwaukee WI 53295

BABCOCK, MADOLYN EVELYN, chemist; b. Miami, Okla., Dec. 11, 1924; d. Clarence Earl and Gladys Evelyn (Robinson) Youse; m. Edmund Page Babcock, Oct. 8, 1950; children: Catherine, Anne, James, Elizabeth, John, Marcia. AA, Stephens Coll., Columbia Mo., 1944; BS Chemistry, U. Minn., 1947, MS, 1952. rsch. fellow U. Minn., Mpls., 1947-52; chemist Gen. Mills, Mpls., 1952-53. Contbr. articles to profl. jours. Bd. dirs. Loring Nicollet Bethlehem Community Ctr., Mpls. Emma Norton Residence, St. Paul, 1986-89; trustee Hennepin Ave. United Meth. Sch.; curator Stephens Coll., Columbia, Mo. Recipient Alumnae awds. Stephens Coll., Columbia, Mo., 1971, 1978. Mem. Fellow Am. Inst. Chemists; mem. AAUW, ASCAP, Am. Chem. Soc., P.E.O, Sister Hood, Iota Sigma Pi, Sigma Xi, Sigma Alpha Iota (patroness), Kappa Kappa Gamma. Home: 1801 Girard Ave S Minneapolis MN 55403

BABCOCK, NELLIE JO, clinical social worker; b. Bozeman, Mont., Mar. 26, 1951; d. Harold C. and Patricia A. (Alexander) B.; m. Christopher J. Krenk, July 3, 1977; 1 child, Hanna Jo. Student, St. Andrews Presbyn. Coll., 1968-70; BA summa cum laude, U. Minn., 1972, MSW, 1974. Registered clin. social worker, Oreg. Psychiat. social worker Lane County Mental Health, Eugene, Oreg., 1974-75, Benton County Mental Health, Corvallis, Oreg., 1975-77, Clackamas County Mental Health, Marylhurst, Oreg., 1978; pvt. psychotherapist and cons. Lake Oswego, Oreg., 1979—; dir. Family Growth Alternatives, Marylhurst, 1980-84; co-founder, dir. Portland Family Inst., 1983—; NIMH trainee, 1972-74. Mem. Nat. Assn. Social Workers, Acad. Cert. Social Workers, Am. Assn. Marriage and Family Therapists (supr.). Democrat. Office: 425 SW 2nd St Lake Oswego OR 97034

BABETTI, DONNA MARIE, dietitian; b. Carbhondale, Pa., Jan. 26, 1953; d. Armond Isadore and Thomassina (Cinti) Mascelli; m. Michael Anthony Barbetti, Nov. 19, 1976; 1 child, Michael Orlando. BS, Marywood Coll., Scranton, 1975, MS, 1978. Dir. County Long Term Care, Olyphant, Pa., 1975-77; coordinator of nutritional svcs. Allied Services, Scranton, 1977-88; lectr. Marywood Coll., Scranton, 1980-89; cons. Health and Human Services Penn., 1987-89. Author: NE Woman Nutrition and Choices, 1982, Rehab Dietetics A Team Approach, 1983. Bd mem. St. Francis Assisi Kitchen Scranton, 1979-89, Boy Scouts Am. Scranton, 1986-89, Philharmonic League Scranton, 1989; mem. Jr. League of Scranton, 1988-89, Women's Resource Ctr. Recipient Service Recognition St. Francis Assisi Kitchen Scranton, 1982, N.E. Woman award Scranton Times, 1982, Community Svc. award Lackawanna County United Way, 1989. Mem. Am. Dietetic Assn. (recognized Young Dietician of Yr. 1982), Pa. Dietetic Assn., Nepa Dietetic Assn., Maywood Coll. Alumni Assn. Democrat. Roman Catholic. Home: 1760 Sanderson Ave Scranton PA 18509

BABICH, JOANNE MARIE, clinical psychologist; b. Sewickley, Pa., Oct. 9, 1951; d. John and Cookie Joanne B.; B.S. summa cum laude, U. Pitts., 1973; M.A., Ariz. State U., 1976, Ph.D. summa cum laude, 1980; m. Frederick W. Meister, June 12, 1982. Predoctoral intern in community medicine and clin. psychology Baylor Coll. Medicine, Tex. Med. Ctr., Houston, 1977-78; pvt. practice clin. psychology, 1982—; psychologist Am. Biodyne Inc., 1985-87; cons. psychologist The New Found., 1987—, Touchstone Community Behavioral Clinic and Student Ctr., 1988—; bd. dirs. The New Ariz. Family. Mem. Am. Soc. Clin. Hypnosis, Ariz. Psychol. Assn. (liaison Maricopa Psychol. Soc. 1989—, co-editor The Ariz. Psychologist 1988-89), Maricopa Psychol. Soc. (sec. 1984), Am. Psychol. Assn., Phoenix Soc. Clin. Hypnosis, Phi Beta Kappa (sec., v.p. Phoenix chpt. 1985-86). Democrat. Office: 240 W Osborn Rd Ste 217 Phoenix AZ 85006

BABIUCH, JACQUELINE MARIE, company executive; b. Kansas City, Mo., Aug. 17, 1964; d. John George and Claire (Kaszuba) B. BBA, U. Mo., Kansas City, 1989. Sec. Ad-Art Advt., Kansas City, 1981; shop keeper Elson KCI Airport, Kansas City, 1982; salon coord. Hair Care Harmony, Kansas City, 1982—; mgr. Hair Care Harmony, 1988—; customer svc. dir. Consolidated Bus. Sys., Kansas City, 1984-86, promotions coord., 1987—. Active Am. Cancer Soc. Mem. NAFE. Democrat. Roman Catholic. Home: 406 Norton Kansas City MO 64124-2025 Office: Consol Beauty Sys 500 Nichols Rd Kansas City MO 64112

BACCUS, SHIRLEY POHL, county official; b. Mendota, Ill., Mar. 20, 1929; d. Edward Jacob and Laura (Hoelzer) Pohl; m. Markus V. Baccus, Dec. 24, 1947; children: Diane Baccus Horsley, Ramone, Michael, Tonya. AA, Brevard Community Coll., Cocoa, Fla., 1978; student, U. Cen. Fla., 1986—. State cert. supr. elections. Mgr. Linvilla, Melbourne Beach, Fla., 1963-71; supr. elections Brevard County, Titusville, Fla., 1973—. Pres. PTA, Fla., 1964, Holmes Regional Med. Ctr. Aux., Melbourne, 1975. Recipient So. Brevard Woman of Yr. award Brevard Sentinel-Star and Cen. Brevard Panhellenic, 1974, Outstanding Women of Yr. award Brevard Soroptimists, 1977, Good Govt. award Titusville Jaycees, 1983, Fla. Mother of Yr. award Fla. Mother's Inc., 1987. Mem. LWV, Fla. State Assn. of Supr. of Elections (pres. 1984-85), Internat. Assn. Clks. Recorders Election Officals and Treas., Civ-Mil, Profl. Women Network, Space Coast Coun. for Internat. Visitors, Brevard Symphony, Rep. Women of South Beaches, Brevard Art Ctr. and Mus. Office: Supr of Elections PO Box 1119 Titusville FL 32781-1119 Home: 300 Atlantic St Melbourne Beach FL 32951

BACDAYAN, CAROLYN BAKKE, hospital administrator; b. New Haven, Conn., Mar. 1, 1936; d. E. Wight and Mary (Sterling) Bakke; m. Albert S. Bacdayan, Feb. 16, 1934; children: Paul Wight, Karen May. BA, Swarthmore (Pa.) Coll., 1958; MA, Yale U., 1959. Tchr. history Brent Sch., Baquio City, Philippines, 1959-60, Ithaca (N.Y.) Sr. High Sch., 1962-67; dir. W.N.O. Preschs., Lexington, Ky., 1967-70; sr. rsch. assoc. Coll. Medicine, U. Ky., Lexington, 1970-76; sr. adminstrv. staff officer Coll. Medicine, Chandler Med. Ctr., U. Ky., Lexington, 1977-81, asst. prof., 1977—; dir. planning Univ. Ky. Hosp., Lexington, 1981—. Home: 221 Catalpa Rd Lexington KY 40502

BACH, CLAUDIA STEWART, theatrical agent; b. Detroit, Aug. 19, 1956; d. William Raymond and Patricia Louise (Kapellas) Stewart; m. George Joseph Evans, Feb. 6, 1978 (div. Nov. 1987); children: Deanna Lynn, Donald Breck; m. David Sebastian Bach, Aug. 28, 1988; 1 child, Jessica Shiri. Student, Bach Acad. for Performing Arts, Hamilton, Ont., Can., 1980-87. Credit mgr. Nat. Bank Royal Oak, Mich., 1974-75; office mgr. Audio-Alert, Royal Oak, 1975-76; accounts mgr. BBDO, Troy, Mich., 1976-78; with customer and pub. relations dept. Paling Inc., Hamilton, 1978-86; theatrical agt. Blue Ox Talent Agy., Hamilton, 1986-89, Scottsdale, Ariz., 1989—; sales and mktg. mgr., casting dir., cons. Willow Entertainment, Scottsdale, 1989—; personal mgr. D.S.B. Enterprises, Scottsdale, 1988—. Mem. Hamilton and Region Arts Coun., 1987-89. Mem. Jewish Bus. and Profl. Women (subcom. for advancement women 1987-89, bd. dirs. Phoenix 1990-91), Am. Fedn. Musicians, Ariz. Film, Theatre and TV Assn., B'nai B'rith. Republican.

BACH, MURIEL DUNKLEMAN, author, actress; b. Chgo., May 14, 1918; d. Gabriel and Deborah (Warshauer) Dunkleman; m. Joseph Wolfson, June 16, 1940 (div. Apr. 1962); 1 child, Susan; m. Ira J. Bach, Apr. 14, 1963 (dec. Mar. 6, 1985); stepchildren: Caroline Bach Marandos, John Lawrence; m. Josef Diamond, May 18, 1986. Student Carleton Coll., 1935-37; BS, Northwestern U., 1939. Researcher original manuscripts for One-Woman Theatre, also costume designer, writer, set designer; actress TV commls., indsl. films, radio commls.; photog. model; tchr. platform speaking techniques to corp. execs. Active sr. citizens groups, youth groups. Recipient Career Achievement award Chgo. Area Profl. Pan Hellenic Assn., 1971. Mem. Screen Actors Guild, AFTRA, Arts Club, Wash. Athletic Club, Seattle Tennis Club, Rainiers Club, Zeta Phi Eta. Author: (plays) Two Lives, 1958; ... because of Her!, 1963; Madame, Your Influence is Showing, 1969; MS ... Haven't We Met Before?, 1973; Lady, You're Rocking the Boat!, 1976; Freud Never Said It Was Easy, 1978; Of All the Nerve, 1982; vignettes for theatre.

BACHER, ROSALIE WRIDE, educational administrator; b. Los Angeles, May 25, 1925; d. Homer M. and Reine (Rogers) Wride; m. Archie O. Bacher, Jr., Mar. 30, 1963. AB, Occidental Coll., 1947, MA, 1949. Tchr. English, Latin, history David Starr Jordan High Sch., Long Beach, Calif., 1949-55, counselor, 1955-65; counselor Lakewood (Calif.) Sr. High Sch., Long Beach, 1965-66; rsch. asst., counselor Poly. High Sch., Long Beach, 1966-67; counselor, office occupational preparation, vocational guidance sect. Long Beach Unified School Dist., Long Beach, 1967-68; vice prin. Washington Jr. High Sch., Long Beach, 1968-70; asst. prin. Lakewood Sr. High Sch., Long Beach, spring 1970; vice prin. Marshall Jr. High Sch., Long Beach, 1981-87, 1981-87; vice prin. Lindbergh Jr. High Sch., Long Beach, 1987—; counselor Millikan High Sch., Calif., 1988—, Hill Jr. High Sch., Calif., 1988-89; ret. Hill Jr. High Sch., 1989; chmn. vocat. guidance steering com. Long Beach Unified Sch. Dist., 1963—. Mem. Internat. Platform Assn., AAUW, Long Beach Personnel and Guidance Assn. (dir. 1958-60), Long Beach Sch. Counselors Assn. (sec. high sch. segment 1963-64), Phi Beta Kappa, Delta Kappa Gamma (pres. Delta Psi chpt., area dir.; Calif. profl. affairs com. chmn. 1972-74), Phi Delta Gamma (pres. chpt. 1977-78, 87—, nat. chmn. bylaws com. 1980-81, Nat. Conv. Com. 1987-88, nat. nominating com. 1989), Pi Lambda Theta (pres. chpt. 1974-76, v.p. So. Calif. coun. 1974-76), Phi Delta Kappa (sec. Long Beach chpt. 1977-80). Home: 265 Rocky Point Rd Palos Verdes Estates CA 90274 also: 17721 Misty Ln Huntington Beach CA 92649

BACHLEDA, KATHLEEN MARGARET, computer manufacturing administrator; b. Trenton, N.J., Dec. 2, 1948; d. John Joseph and Evelyn Marie (Criss) O'Hare; m. Eugene George Most, Nov. 22, 1969 (div. Nov. 1978); 1 child, Michele; m. George Paul Bachleda, Mar. 1, 1987. Grad., Taylor Bus. Inst., Plainfield, N.J., 1967. Sec., IBM Corp., Princeton, N.J., 1967-73, staff asst., 1973-78, adminstrn. mgr., Indpls., 1978-81, adminstrn. ops. mgr., Southfield, Mich., 1981-88; sr. assoc. program office specialist, 1988-89, sr. pers. program specialist, 1989—. Mem. Nat. Assn. Female Execs. Republican. Roman Catholic. Avocations: writing; reading; swimming; traveling. Home: 5101 Fedora St Troy MI 48098 Office: IBM Corp 200 Galleria Officentre Southfield MI 48086

BACHMAN, CAROL CHRISTINE, trust company executive; b. Buffalo, Jan. 20, 1959; d. Christian George and Joan Marie (Fincel) B. Student, Grad. Inst. Internat. Study, 1979-80; AB, Smith Coll., 1981; grad., New Eng. Sch. Banking, 1987. Trust asst. BayBank Middlesex, Burlington, Mass., 1984-85, sr. trust asst., 1985-87, trust adminstr., 1987, trust officer, 1987-88; estate settlement specialist Bank of Boston, 1988-90, system cons., 1990—. Roman Catholic. Home: 10 Marie Dr Wilmington MA 01887 Office: Bank of Boston 100 Federal St PO Box 1861 Boston MA 02105

BACHMAN, JEAN COLLOM, transportation executive; b. Aspermont, Tex., Jan. 23, 1935; d. Ross Collom and Helen (Watson) Rutherford; m. C.M. Shwadlenak, May 22, 1957 (div. 1963); m. J.E. Bachman, June 24, 1964; children: J. Brent, B. Blake. BSc., North Tex. U., 1953-56; student, Abiline Christian Coll., 1963; cert., Inst. Cert. Travel, Welleseley, Mass., 1984. Tchr. Aspermont high sch., Tex., 1956-58, Knox City high sch., Tex., 1958-63, Spur high sch., Tex., 1963-64, Adult Basic Edn. in Lubbock, Tex., Spur high sch., Tex., 1974-75; travel agy. owner Lubbock Travel Inc., Inc., 1975--, Ask Mr. Foster/Premier Travel, Lubbock, Tex., 1988--. V:. Recipient Valeditory award Peacock High Sch. Mem. Am. Soc. Travel Agts. (past pres. S.W. chpt., nat. dir. 1988—), South Plains Travel Assn., Lubbock C. of C., Lubbock Women's Club, Bus. and Profl. Women's Orgn., Sales Exec. Assn., Transp. Club (Lubbock), Delta Kappa Gamma. Republican. Home: 5408 28th St Lubbock TX 79407

BACHRACH, EVE ELIZABETH, lawyer; b. Oakland, Calif., July 3, 1951; d. Howard Lloyd and Shirley Faye (Lichterman) B. AB cum laude, Boston U., 1972; JD with honors, George Washington U., 1976. Bar: D.C. 1976, U.S. Dist. Ct. D.C. 1976, U.S. Ct. Appeals (D.C. cir.) 1976. Assoc. Stein, Mitchell & Mezines, Washington, 1976-79; assoc. gen. counsel Cosmetic, Toiletry, and Fragrance Assn., Washington, 1979-85; v.p., assoc. gen. counsel, corp. sec. Nonprescription Drug Mfrs. Assn., Washington, 1985—; guest lectr. Am. U., Washington, 1986—, George Washington Nat. Law Ctr., Washington, 1986—, Cath. U. Law Sch., 1988—. Author, Editor: Small Business Resource Manual, 1984. Vol. lawyer Legal Counsel for the Elderly, Washington, 1978—. Mem. ABA (food and drug com., antitrust sect., adminstrv. law sect.), D.C. Bar Assn., Women's Bar Assn. D.C., Fed. Bar Assn. (chmn. food and drug com. 1986-90), Food and Drug Law Inst. (chmn. writing awards com. 1982-88, vice chmn. 1987-89, chmn. 1990, editorial adv. bd. Food Drug Cosmetic Law Jour.). Home: 3225 Grace St NW #213 Washington DC 20007

BACHRACH, NANCY, advertising executive; b. Providence, Jan. 29, 1948; d. David and Maida Horovitz. BA magna cum laude, Conn. Coll. for Women, 1969; MA with honors, Brandeis U., 1973, PhD, 1975. Account mgr. Grey Advt., N.Y.C., 1976-80, sr. v.p. account mgmt., 1985—; assoc. dir. Grey France, Paris, 1980-84. Author: The Irrefutability of Skepticism, 1975. Mem. profl. adv. bd. Nat. Ctr. for Learning Disabilities, N.Y.C., 1986-90. Named One of the 100 Best and Brightest Women, Advertising Age, 1988. Office: Grey Advt Inc 777 3d Ave New York NY 10017

BACIEWICZ, GLORIA JEAN, physician; b. Schenectady, N.Y., July 10, 1952. BA in Biology, U. Rochester, 1974; MD, SUNY, 1978; student, U. Rochester, 1978-82. Cert. in Psychiatry, 1983. Sr. instr. U. Rochester Dept. Psychiatry, 1982-83; clin. team leader Genesee Mental Health Ctr., Rochester, N.Y., 1983-90; staff psychiatrist Bryce Hosp., Tuscaloosa, Ala., 1990—; med. dirs. Genesee Alcohol Treatment Ctr., Rochester, 1986--. Mem. Am. Psychiatric Assn. Office: Bryce Hosp 200 University Blvd Tuscaloosa AL 35401

BACKERS-HOYLE, ANGELA CHERIE, lawyer; b. Inglewood, Calif., Apr. 24, 1958; d. Carl Henry Backers and Ann Spencer Moyer; m. Harold J. Hoyle, Mar. 26, 1988. BA, St Mary's Coll., Morage, Calif., 1980; JD, U. San Francisco, 1983. Deputy dist. atty. Alameda County Dist. Atty., Oakland, Calif., 1983-84; dir. Moreau High Sch. Bd. dirs., Hayward, 1986—. Mem. Community Action Task Force, St. Frances de Sales Ch., Oakland, vol. Homeless Shelter, St. Frances de Sales Ch. Mem. Calif. Narcotics Officers Assn., Calif. Dist. Atty.'s Assn. Democrat. Roman Catholic. Office: Alameda County 1225 Fallon St Rm 900 Oakland CA 94612

BACKMAN, JEAN ADELE, real estate executive; b. N.Y.C., Mar. 3, 1931; d. Seraphin Michael and Helen Elma (Matthews) Millon; m. Frank F. Backman, Sept. 27, 1954; children: Carl Eric, Adam Andrew. BA, Hunter Coll., 1954; degree in real estate mgmt., Am. U., 1980. Sales assoc. Ted Lingo Realty, Potomac, Md., 1970-73; sales mgr. House and Home Real Estate, Potomac, 1973-74; dist. mgr. Panorama Real Estate, Md., 1975-78; v.p., dir. mktg., sales Panorama Real Estate, Tysons Corner, Va., 1978-82; sr. v.p., regional sales mgr. Coldwell Banker Real Estate, Vienna, Va., 1983-88; sr. v.p., regional dir. orgnl. devel. and tng. Coldwell Banker Real Estate, Balt. and Washington, 1988—; cons. Reston Pub. Co., Reston, Va., 1979-82, Panorama Condominiums, Tysons Corner, 1979-82. Mem. Realtors for Pol. Action, Falls Church, Va., 1985, profl. stds. com., 1989. Mem. Am. Mgmt. Assn., Nat. Assn. Realtors, Va. Assn. Realtors, No. Va. Bd. Realtors, Montgomery County Bd. Realtors, Washington Bd. Realtors, Va. C. of C., Potomac C. of C., Grad. Realtors Inst., Cert. Residential Brokerage Mgr. Republican. Presbyterian. Office: Coldwell Banker Residential 1953 Gallows Rd Vienna VA 22182

BACKSTROM-BOUAYAD, CAMILLA PAULINE, market research and development executive; b. Stockholm, Nov. 26, 1960; came to U.S., 1981; d. Adam Erik and Monika (Hultberg) Backstrom; m. Khalid Bouayad, June 15, 1988. Student, Akrahall, Sweden, 1979; Degree in French, L'Etoile, Paris, 1981; BS in Internat. Mktg., U. San Francisco, 1985. Personnel asst. Landor Assocs., San Francisco, 1985-86; project mgr. Monarch Resources, N.Y.C., 1986-88; asst. v.p. Standard Security Life, N.Y.C., 1988—. Mem. Am. Mktg. Assn., Fin. Instns. Ins. Assn., Nat. Assn. Fin. Execs. Home: 643 Garden St Hoboken NJ 07030

BACKUS, ANN SWIFT NEWELL, educational association administrator; b. Worcester, Mass., Sept. 23, 1941; d. C. Bradford and Elizabeth C. (Norlander) Newell; m. Robert A. Backus, June 28, 1964; children: Gillian, Bradford. AB, Mt. Holyoke Coll., 1963. Rsch. asst. Eaton-Peabody Lab., Boston, 1963-65; adminstrv. asst. Kakuri Hosp., Kaduna, Nigeria, 1965-66; biology tchr. Milford High Sch., Milford, N.H., 1967-69; organist, tchr. Manchester, N.H., 1969—; performing arts coord. N.H. State Commn. on Arts, Concord, N.H., 1980-83; acting exec. dir. N.H. State Commn. on Arts, 1982-83; dir. ops. Wolf Orgn., Cmbrdge, Mass., 1983-84; coord. collaborative programs N.H. Coll. & Univ. Coun., Manchester, 1984—; coord. profl. devel. N.H. Coll. & Univ. Coun., 1987—; chmn. bd. dirs. N.H. Coun. for Humanities, Concord, 1976-77; pres. N.H. Coun. for Better Schs., Manchester, 1979-81; pres. Am. Lung Assn. N.H., Manchester, 1987-89, mem. coms. Task Force on HIV/AIDS-NH, 1990—, chmn. edn. subcom. HIV/AIDS-NH, 1990—. Author: Annotated Bibliography, 1988; contbr. articles to profl. jours. Founder Manchester Pro Musica, 1979; vol. coord. Nixon for Gov. N.H., Manchester, 1974; bd. dirs. N.H. Symphony Orch., 1977-80, Manchester Hist. Soc. Grantee Bean Found., Concord, 1985. Mem. Nat. Music Tchrs. Assn., Internat Assn. for Campus Law Enforcement Adminstrs., Am. Coll. Health Assn., Nat. Sci. Tchrs. Assn., Nat. Assn. Coll. & Univ. Bus. Officers. Unitarian-Universalist. Office: NH Coll & Univ Coun 2321 Elm St Manchester NH 03104-2290

BACON, KATHLEEN, secretarial school president; b. Jones, Ga., June 29, 1954; d. Enoch and Beatrice (West) B. BS, Ft. Valley (Ga.) State Coll., 1976; MA, Ohio State U., 1977. Adminstrv. sec. Liquid Carbonic Corp., Atlanta, 1977-79; instr. Massey Bus. Coll., Atlanta, 1979-82, secretarial coord., 1982-83; exec. v.p. Quality Plus, Inc., Atlanta, 1983-87, pres., 1987—; instr. Atlanta Area Tech. Sch., 1980-81; cons., trainer U.S. Office Personnel Mgmt., Atlanta, 1987—. Mem. Nat. Bus. Edn. Assn., So. Bus. Edn. Assn., Atlanta Bus. League (bd. dirs. 1988, Salute to Women award 1984), NAACP, Nat. Coun. Negro Women, Toastmasters, Sigma Gamma Rho (sec. 1987-89). Home: 110 Rill Ct College Park GA 30349 Office: Quality Plus Inc 1655 Peachtree St NE 450 Atlanta GA 30309

BACON, MARTHA BRANTLEY, Small business owner; b. Wrightsville, Ga., Apr. 20, 1938; d. William Riley and Susie Mae (Colston) B.; m. Albert Sidney Bacon, Jr., Aug. 3, 1958; children: Albert Sidney, III, Gregory Riley. BS, Ga. So., Statesboro, 1959; Post Grad., U. Va., Charlottesville, 1978-80, Adrian Hall Interior Design, Savannah, Ga., 1984. Real Estate, Grad. Realtors Inst., Assoc. Broker. Tchr. Chatham Bd. Edn., Savannah, Ga., 1961; co-owner mgr. Two Kentucky Fried Chicken Restaurants, Charlottesville, Va., 1967-80; real estate broker Real Estate III, Charlottesville, Va., 1978-83, Landmark Realty, Statesboro, Ga.; tree farmer Self-Employed, Johnson Co., Ga., 1980-89; mgr., co-owner Restaurant, 1987--; V.P. Bd. Realtors Statesboro Ga. 1985. Vol. U. Va. Hosp. 1980-83, Family Cemetery Ga. 1986-90. Chmn. Jaycettes Gov. Columbus, Ga., 1962 (Named Outstanding Jaycette 1961); vol. First Bapt. Ch. Personnel Com., Charlottesville, 1978. Recipient Outstanding Sales award Real Estate III Co. Charlottesville 1980. Mem. Charlottesville Restaurant Assn., Westchester Garden Club, Ga. Restaurant Assn., Ga. So. Univ. Alumni Bd., Ga. So. Symphony Guild, Ga. So. Univ. Athletic Boosters Club, AAUW, Pilot Club. Baptist. Home: 30 Golf Club Circle Statesboro GA 30458

BACON, PAULA, assistant director of university program; b. Bronx, N.Y, May 14; d. John and Helen (Swensen) Jacobsen; m. George H. Bacon, Apr. 2, 1977; children: Lynn, Randy, Kimberly, Lisa. A in Bus., So. Ill. U., 1967; B in Bus., Pace U., 1980, MS in Teaching, 1989. Exec. sec. SUNY, Purchase, 1967-74; adminstrv. asst. Pace U., Pleasantville, N.Y., 1974-85; acad. counselor Pace U., Pleasantville, 1985-87, asst. dir. student svc. ctr., 1987-90, acting dir. student svc. ctr., 1990—; instr. Norwalk (Conn.) Community Coll., 1981-83, The Berkeley Bus. Sch., White Plains, N.Y., 1984-87; adj. instr. lit. and communication dept., Pace U., Pleasantville, 1989—. Vol. Putnam Community Hosp., Carmel, N.Y., 1976-77; mem. Adminstrv. Coun. and Pace U., Sen., Scholastic Standing Com., Pace U., 1987—. Recipient Recognition award Robert A. Taft Inst. of Govt., 1983. Mem. Bus. and Profl. Women's Assn. (sec., treas. 1976-77), Smithsonian Instn. Office: Pace U Bedford Rd Pleasantville NY 10570 :

BACQUÉ, ANGELA, pharmacist; b. Elizabeth, N.J., Aug. 20, 1957; d. Giuseppe and Lucia (Corsentino) M.; m. Stephen Emile Bacque, June 2, 1990. BS, Rutgers U., 1981; postgrad., Kean Coll., 1987. Registered pharmacist, N.J. Pharmacy technician Holmdel (N.J.) Village Pharmacy, 1977-78, Elmora Pharmacy, Elizabeth, 1978; pharmacy extern Clark (N.J.) Drugs, 1980, Schering Corp., Kenilworth, N.J., 1980, Alexian Bros. Hosp., Elizabeth, 1980; pharmacist Rahway (N.J.) Hosp., 1981—, speaker edn. dept., 1981—, mem. speakers bur. community relations dept., nutritional support com., 1985-87, asst. pharmacy adminstr., 1987—; relief pharmacist Horowitz Pharmacy, Elizabeth, 1981. Performer and asst. dir. various local plays, 1982-86. Mem. N.J. Assn. Hosp. Pharmacists, Am. Pharm. Assn. (political action com. 1981—), Pharmacists Against Drug Abuse (lectr. 1986—), Cranford Dramatic Club (chmn. set painting 1985-87, v.p. prodn. 1988-90), Pi Alpha Alpha. Democrat. Roman Catholic. Home: 513 Maple Ave Linden NJ 07036 Office: Rahway Hosp 865 Stone St Rahway NJ 07065

BADALAMENTI, MARGRET, dentist; b. Bklyn., Oct. 6, 1959; d. Anthony Joseph and Margret (Friedberg) B. DDS, Georgetown U., 1985. Pvt. practice L.I., N.Y., 1986—. Mem. Delta Epsilon Sigma. Home: 38 Celano Ln West Islip NY 11795

BADARACCO, CHERYL KAY, educator, administrator; b. Highland Park, Mich., July 28, 1962; d. Larry Alan and Colene (Kitchen) Gutowsky; m. Dante Eugenio Badaracco, Oct. 21,1989. BA, Cambridge U., Eng., 1984; postgrad., Mich. State U., 1984; AA, Northwood Inst., Midland, Mich., 1982. Bank teller Mich. Nat. Bank, West Bloomfield, Mich., 1982-84; lobbist Liz Robbins Assocs., Washington, summer 1983; nurses asst. Botz Health Care Ctr., Inc., West Bloomfield, winter 1984; pub. health nutritionist Peace Corps, Guatemala, Cen. Am., 1985-87; maternal/child nutrition edn. prog. coordinator CARE, Guatemala, 1987-88; pub. health educator/community Outreach worker Migrant Family Health Svc., Hendersonville, N.C., 1988; pub. health educator/community social worker Indiantown Community Health Ctr., Indiantown, Fla., 1989; health careers prog. coord. Everglades Area Health Edn. Ctr., West Palm Beach, Fla., 1989—; dist. coord. Bd. County Commrs. Martin County, Indiantown, Fla., 1989—. Author ednl.manuals: Comamos Mejor, 1988, Prenatal Care, 1989. Recipient Good Govt. award Fla. State Jaycees, 1990. Mem. Health Educator Assocs. Presbyterian. Roman Catholic. Home: 6416 Riverland Dr Fort Pierce FL 34982

BADDOUR, ANNE BRIDGE, aviatrix; b. Royal Oak, Mich., 1930; d. William George and Esther Rose (Pfiester) Bridge; m. Raymond F. Baddour, Sept. 25, 1954; children: Cynthia Anne, Frederick Raymond, Jean Bridge. Student, Detroit Bus. Sch., 1948-50. Stewardess Eastern Airlines, Boston, 1952-54; instr. aeros. Powers Sch., Boston, 1958; co-pilot, flight attendant Raytheon Co., Bedford, Mass., 1958-63; flight dispatcher, ferry Pilot Comerford Flight Sch., Bedford, 1974-76; adminstrv. asst., ferry pilot Jenney Beachcraft, Bedford, 1976; mgr., pilot Balt. Airways, Inc., Bedford, 1976-77; pilot Lincoln Lab. Flight Test Facility MIT, Lexington, 1977—; aviation cons., corp. pilot Energy Resources, Inc., Cambridge, Mass., 1974-84; holder World Class speed records for single-engine aircraft; Boston to Goose Bay, Labrador, 1985, Boston to Reykjavik, Iceland, 1985, Portland, Maine to Goose Bay, 1985, Portland to Reykjavik, 1985, Goose Bay to Reykjavik, 1985; records for twin-engine aircraft: Sept Isles to Goose Bay, 1988, Mont Joll to Goose Bay, 1988, Presque Isle to Goose Bay, 1988, Millinocket to Goose Bay, 1988, Bedford to Goose Bay, 1988, Goose Bay to Narssassrag, Greenland, 1988, Narssassrag to Klevelevic, Iceland, 1988, Narssassrag to Reykjavik, 1988, Bedford to Narssassrag, 1988, Millinochet to Narssassrag, 1988, Presque Isle to Narssassrag, 1988. Bd. dirs. Cambridge Opera, 1977-79; mem. campaign council Mus. Transp., Boston; mem. coun. assocs. French Libr. in Boston; commr. Commonwealth of Mass., Mass. Aero. Commn., 1979-83; chmn. regional adv. coun. FAA, 1984-88. Winner trophy Phila. Transcontinental Air Race, 1954, New Eng. Air Race, 1957, Clifford B. Harmon trophy Internat. Aviatrix, 1988; recipient Spl. Recognition award Fed. Aviation Administrn., 1990. Mem. Fedn. Aeronautique International, Nat. Aero. Assn., Ninety-Nines (winner New Eng. Safety Trophy 1986), Aero Club New Eng. (v.p., dir. 1978—), Aircraft Owners Pilots Assn., Nat. Pilots Assn., U.S. Sea Plane Pilots Assn., Assn. Women Transcontinental Air Race, Bostonian Soc., English Speaking Union, Friends of Switzerland, French Center Library Club, Belmont Hill Club, St. Botolph Club. Republican. Episcopalian. Home: 96 Fletcher Rd Belmont MA 02178 Office: MIT Draper Flight Test Facility Lincoln Lab PO Box 98 Concord MA 01742

BADERTSCHER, NANCY LEE, news reporter; b. Atlanta, May 12, 1955; d. Albert Fredrick and Rosemary Catherine (Reilly) B. BA, Ga. State U., 1979. News reporter Daily Sun, Warner Robins, Ga., 1976-78, Savannah (Ga.) News-Press, 1980-83, Gwinnett Daily News, Lawrenceville, Ga., 1983—. Pulitzer prize finalist Columbia U. 1989; recipient Sweepstakes award AP, 1989, 1st Place award in investigative reporting, 1989, Nat. Edn. Writers Assn., 1990. Home: 3450 Breckinridge Blvd #1009 Duluth GA 30136 Office: Gwinnett Daily News 200 Hampton Green Duluth GA 30136

BADGER, ALISON MARY, immunologist; b. Croyden, Surrey, England, Nov. 25, 1935; d. Ralph Owen and Rose Elizabeth (Parker) Fletcher; m. Paul Boughten Badger, June 4, 1960 (div. 1968); children: Paul Abbott, John Martin. BS, London U., 1958; PhD, Boston U., 1972, MPH, 1979. Asst. prof. microbiology Boston U. Sch. Medicine, 1974-77, assoc. prof., 1977-79; sr. investigator Smith Kline & French, Phila., 1979-82, asst. dir., 1983—. Office: Smith Kline Beecham 709 Swedeland Rd King of Prussia PA 19406-2799

BADGER, LOIS G., federal government official; b. Malden, Mass., May 17, 1944; d. Herbert Langston Jr. and Mary Eugenia (Bowers) B. BA, William Carey Coll., 1964; postgrad., U. So. Miss., 1964-66. Cert. tchr., N.J. Tchr. Slidell (La.) High Sch., 1965-67; vol. Peace Corps, Columbia, 1967; tchr. Bond Brook (N.J.) High Sch., 1968, High Bridge (N.J.) High Sch., 1969-71; revenue officer IRS, Newark, 1972-74; employee devel. specialist IRS, Newark, Chgo., 1974-79; chief tng. br. IRS, Bklyn., 1979-88, recruitment coord., 1988, quality improvement coord., 1989—. Home: 163B Colon Ave Staten Isalnd NY 10308 Office: IRS 35 Tillary St Brooklyn NY 11201

BADGLEY, MARIE MINOR CURRY, educator, counselor; b. Berlin, Wis., Dec. 18, 1926; d. Morris C. and Elizabeth (Klinkenberg) Minor; m. John C. Curry, Apr., 1944 (div. June 1956); children: Robert W., Patricia A., Warren H.; m. E. Kirk Badgley, Jr., Aug. 14, 1967. AA, Mesa State Coll., 1950; BA, Ariz. State U., 1958, MA, 1962; MA, Wash. Coll., 1967; postgrad., U. Colo., 1973, U. No. Colo., 1974, U. Wyo., 1977-78, U. N.Mex., 1984. Cert. tchr., counselor Colo., N. Mex. Tchr. Firestone Elem. Sch., Colo., 1950-51; mem. labor rels. staff Kennecott Copper Co., Ray, Ariz., 1953-56; tchr. Roosevelt Elem. Sch., Casper, Wyo., 1957-58, Cartwright Dist. Sch., Phoenix, 1958-59, Alhambra Sch. Dist., Phoenix, 1959-66; counselor Coeur d'Alene (Idaho) Sr. High Sch., 1966-67; coord. adult edn. Tucson (Ariz.) Sch. Dist. #1, 1967-70; counselor Marycrest High Sch., Denver, 1970-73, Milliken Mid. Sch., Johnstown, Colo., 1973-75; dean of students, counselor Campbell County Jr. High Sch, Gillette, Wyo., 1975-79; counselor Lincoln Jr. High Sch., Billings, Mont., 1979-82, Woodlin (Colo.) Sch. Dist., 1985-87, J.F. Kennedy Mid. Sch., Gallup, N.Mex., 1987—; bd. dirs. Embark Endeavors Ltd., Gallup, N.Mex.; mem. AFB pers. staff, 1944-46. Contbr. articles to profl. jours. NDEA grantee, 1967. Mem. Am. Personnel and Guidance Assn., NEA. Democrat. Home: 310 Bortot Dr Adobe Pl #21 Gallup NM 87301

BADONNEL, MARIE-CLAUDE HELENE MARQUERITE, laboratory administrator, pathology educator; b. Lons le Saunier, France, July 10, 1939; came to U.S., 1978; d. Paul and Pierrette (Lamblot) Badonnel; div. Diploma in biology, Scientia Sch., Paris, 1963; diploma in biol. sci., U. Geneva, 1970, PhD in Exptl. Pathology, 1975. Chief tech. electron microscope Inst. Morphology, Sch. Medicine, Geneva, 1963-65, rsch. asst., 1965-69; instr. physics and chemistry Sch. for Asst. Pharmacists, Geneva, 1965-67; rsch. asst. dept. pathology U. Geneva, 1969-75; rsch. assoc. dept. pathology McGill U., Montreal, 1975-77; research assoc., instr. dept. pathology U. Mass. Med. Sch., Worcester, 1978-80, asst. prof. pathology, 1980—; HLA coordinator blood bank U. Mass. Med. Ctr., Worcester, 1980-87; assoc. dir. HLA Lab. Blood Bank Univ. Med. Ctr., Worcester, 1987—; expert witness parentage testing in ct. Mass. Cts., 1983—; cons. HLA typing; breast cancer cons. U. Mass. Med. Ctr., 1983—. Mem. Am. Heart Assn., Am. Assn. Pathologists, AAAS, Am. Soc. for Histocompatibility and Immunogenetics, Am. Assn. Blood Banks. Office: U Mass Blood Bank 55 Lake Ave N Worcester MA 01655

BADOVINICH, ROBERTA LYNN, court clerk; b. Gary, Ind., Sept. 4, 1952; d. Merle Russell and Kathryn Dias (Felts) Harris; m. Richard John Badovinich, Aug. 16, 1975 (div. Mar. 1989). Grad. high sch., Griffith, Ind. Dep. clk. U.S. Bankruptcy Ct., Gary, 1970-80; chief dep. clk. U.S. Bankruptcy Ct., 1980—. Mem. Fed. Ct. Clks. Assn., Fed. Bar Assn. (lectr., cert. 1984). Democrat. Roman Catholic. Home: 8507 Johnston St Highland IN 46322 Office: US Bankruptcy Ct 610 Connecticut St Gary IN 46402

BADTKE, SANDRA ANN, alcohol/drug abuse professional; b. Cedarburg, Wis., Jan. 23, 1938; d. Eldred Herman and Rose Mary (Jensterle) B. BS in Edn., U. Wis.-Milw., 1960. Cert. alcohol/drug counselor. Tchr. Appleton, Franklin, Oconomowoc (Wis.) Schs., 1960-67; exec. dir. Cambridge House, Inc., Milw., 1967-79; prodn. mgr. Anderson Graphics, Milw., 1979-80; alcohol/drug abuse counselor DePaul Hosp., Inc., Milw., 1980-89; dir. outpatient clinic DePaul Hosp., Inc., 1989—; programming cons. DePaul Hosp., Inc. Author: videotape Substance Abuse and the Elderly, 1985. Recipient Faye McBeath Found. grant for rsch. in elderly substance abuse, 1982. Mem. NAFE. Home: 1420 E Kensington Blvd Shorewood WI 53211

BAENDER, MARGARET WOODRUFF, free-lance writer; b. Salt Lake City, Apr. 1, 1921; d. Russell Kimball and Margaret Angline (McIntyre) Woodruff; m. Phillip Albers Baender, Aug. 17, 1946 (dec.); children: Kristine Lynn, Charlene Anne, Michael Phillip, Russell Richard. BA, U. Utah, 1944. In clerical, personnel work various firms, San Francisco Bay area, 1970-75; reporter, columnist Valley Pioneer, Danville, Calif., 1975-77; editor Diablo (Calif.) Inferno, 1971-76; author Shifting Sands, 1981, Tail Waggings of Maggie, 1982. Fellow Internat. Biog. Assn.; mem. Nat. Writers Club, AAUW, Soc. Children's Book Writers, Am. Biog. Inst. (life, Raleigh, N.C.), Internat. Women's Writers Guild, Alpha Delta Pi. Republican. Episcopalian. Started a Pen-Pal svc. for children and young adults in Nyazura, Zimbabwe, 1986.

BAER, FRANCES DOROTHEA, real estate executive; b. Belserra, Calif.; m. Benjamin Franklin Baer, Mar. 20, 1942; children: Meridith, Marc Bradley, Bartley B.F. BA, U. So. Calif., 1941, cert. social worker, 1942; student, Hastings Coll. of Law, 1959. Social worker Los Angeles County, 1942-46; real estate broker Iowa, Minn., Calif., Md., Va., 1968—. Past pres. Calif. Council of Coop. Nursery Schs., 1950; founder, chmn. community reorgn. Marin County Citizens Com. Child Guidance Clinic; pres. bd. Marin County PTA; past bd. dirs. LWV, Boy Scouts Am., Camp Fire Girls; pres., founder Nat. Inst. Crime Control; mem. Brooke Press; served Dem. and Rep. groups, Calif. Republican. Unitarian. Club: Early Am. Glass. Home: Box 465 Garrett Park MD 20896 Office: Brooke Press Box 526 Garrett Park MD 20896

BAER, SISTER BARBARA, nun; b. Wichita, Kans., July 18, 1936; d. Howard LeRoy and Geneva (Langford) B. BS, St. Mary of the Plains, Dodge City, Kans., 1964; MA, Marquette U., Milw., 1971, PhD, 1976. Cert. tchr., Kans. Elem. tchr. Cath. Diocese Wichita, 1958-71; asst. prof. St. Mary of the Plains Coll., Dodge City, 1976-80, v.p. acad. affairs, 1980-84; asst. gen. superior Sisters of St. Joseph of Wichita, 1984—, dir. ministry, dir. planning, 1984—, dir. ongoing formation, mem. congl. leadership team, 1984—; mem. fedn. rsch. team Sisters of St. Joseph, 1975-80. Bd. trustees Pratt (Kans.) Regional Med. Ctr., 1982-87, Halstead (Kans.) Hosp., 1984—, The St. Mary Hosp., Manhattan, Kans., 1988—; bd. regents St. Mary of the Plains Coll., Dodge City, 1984—; bd. dirs. CSJ Health System Wichita, Inc., 1984—. Roman Catholic. Home and Office: 3700 E Lincoln Wichita KS 67218

BAERMANN, DONNA LEE ROTH, insurance analyst; b. Carroll, Iowa, Apr. 28, 1939; d. Omer H. and Awanda Lucille (Mathison) Roth; m. Edwin Ralph Baermann, Jr., July 8, 1961; children—Beth, Bryan, Cynthia. B.S., Mt. Mercy Coll., 1973; student Iowa State U.-Ames, 1957-61. Cert. profl. ins. woman; fellow Life Mgmt. Inst. Ins. agt. Lutheran Mut. Ins. Co., Cedar Rapids, Iowa, 1973; home economist Iowa-Ill. Gas & Electric Co., Cedar Rapids, Iowa, 1973-77; supr. premium collection Life Investors Ins. Co., Cedar Rapids, 1978-83, methods-procedures analyst, 1983—, supr. policy service, 1987—; bd. dirs., v.p. Roth Assoc., Roth Farms, Roth Inc., Roth Apts., 1988-89; mem. telecommunications study group com. 1982-83, mem. productivity task force, 1984—. Mem. Nat. Assn. Ins. Women, Nat. Mgmt. Assn. (bd. dirs. Cedar Rapids chpt.), DAR, Chi Omega. Republican. Presbyterian. Home: 361 Willshire Ct NE Cedar Rapids IA 52402 Office: Life Investors Ins Co 4333 Edgewood Rd NE Cedar Rapids IA 52499

BAEZ, JOAN CHANDOS, folksinger; b. S.I., N.Y., Jan. 9, 1941; d. Albert V. and Joan (Bridge) B.; m. David Victor Harris, Mar. 1968 (div. 1973); 1 son, Gabriel Earl. Appeared in coffeehouses, Gate of Horn, Chgo., 1958, Ballad Room, Club 47, 1958-68, Newport (R.I.) Folk Festival, 1959-69, 85, 87, 90, extended tour to colls. and concert halls, 1960's, appeared Town Hall and Carnegie Hall, 1962, 67, 68, U.S. tours, 1970—, concert tours, Japan, 1966, 82, Europe, 1970-73, 80, 83-84, 87-90, Australia, 1985; rec. artist for Vanguard Records, 1960-72, A&M, 1973-76, Portrait Records, 1975-80, Gold Castle Records, 1986-89, (awarded 8 gold albums, 1 gold single), European record albums, 1981, 83; other albums include: Speaking of Dreams, 1989; author: Joan Baez Songbook, 1964, (biography) Daybreak, 1968, (with David Harris) Coming Out, 1971, And A Voice To Sing With, 1987, (songbook) And then I wrote, 1979; extensive TV appearances and speaking tours U.S. and Can. for anti-militarism, 1967-68. Visit to Dem. Republic of Vietnam, 1972; founder, v.p. Inst. for Study Nonviolence (now Resource Ctr. for Nonviolence, Santa Cruz, Calif.), Palo Alto, Calif., 1965; mem. nat. adv. council Amnesty Internat., 1974—; founder, pres. Humanitas/Internat. Human Rights Com., 1979, condr. fact-finding mission to refugee camps, S.E. Asia, Oct. 1979; began refusing payment of war taxes, 1964; arrested for civil disobedience opposing draft, Oct., Dec., 1967. Office: care Diamonds and Rust Prodns PO Box 1026 Menlo Park CA 94026 also: PO Box 818 Menlo Park CA 94026

BAGDAN, GLORIA, interior designer; b. Bronx, N.Y., May 24, 1929; d. Max and Molly (Trufelman) Green; m. Kenneth Bagdan, Nov. 25, 1948 (dec. 1974); children: Meryl Bagdan Robins, Scott, Stacy. Student, CCNY, 1947-49, Inst. Interior Design, 1964, Wharton Sch., 1977. Founder, 1st pres. Bronx Mcpl. Hosp. Aux., 1955-60; interior designer Scarsdale, N.Y., 1964—; v.p., treas. Gold Medal Farms, Bronx, 1974-79; Active in fundraising Grasslands Hosp. Heart Assn.; cons. Mental Health Assn., 1967—; bd. dirs. 20 Sutton Pl. S., N.Y.C.; mem. Rep. Senatorial Inner Circle, Washington. Mem. Internat. Platform Assn., Mcpl. Art Soc. N.Y., Nat. Trust Hist. Preservation, U.S. Congl. Adv. Bd., English Speaking Union Club, Atrium Club, Internat. Club, Beaux Arts Club. Home: 20 Sutton Pl S New York NY 10022

BAGLEY, COLLEEN, marketing executive; b. Mountain Home, Ark., Feb. 18, 1954; d. Roy Louis and Dorothy (Fry) B.; m. William A. Haskin, June 28, 1986. BA cum laude, U. South Fla., 1975. Lic. radio broadcaster, FCC 3d class. TV and radio producer Sta. WUSF-TV-FM, Tampa, Fla., 1974-76; TV announcer Sta. WFLA-TV, Tampa, 1974-76, news reporter, 1976-77, news producer, 1977-79; sr. producer Sta. KSTP-TV, Mpls., 1979-80; exec. producer Sta. WPVI-TV, Phila., 1980-82; v.p. mktg. Grand Traverse Resort, Traverse City, Mich., 1982—; cons., bd. dirs. Enough Seminars, Phila., 1981-82. Contbg. author Strategic Hotel/Motel Marketing (Am. Hotel and Motel Assn. award), 1985. Mem. Traverse City Ski Coun., 1983-88, local host com. Nat. Govs.' Assn., 1986-87, Grad. Leadership, Grand Traverse, 1989. Recipient Mich. Lodging Assn. awards, 1988, 89. Mem. Traverse City Ad Club (awards for advt. excellence 1984-89), Traverse City C. of C. (air service transp. com. 1984-87), Grand Traverse Conv. and Visitors Bur. (mktg. com. 1984—), N.Am. Vasa Cross Country Ski Race Mktg. (chmn. 1987-88), No.

Mich. Golf Coun. (exec. bd. 1986, 88, 89, pres. 1990—). Republican. Home: 3344 Hardwood Traverse City MI 49684 Office: Grand Traverse Resort 6300 US 31 N Grand Traverse Village MI 49610-0404

BAGLEY, CONSTANCE ELIZABETH, lawyer; b. Tucson, Dec. 18, 1952; d. Robert Porter Smith and Joanne Snow-Smith. AB in Polit. Sci. with distinction, with honors, Stanford U., 1974; JD magna cum laude, Harvard U., 1977. Bar: Calif. 1978, N.Y. 1978. Tchg. fellow Harvard U., 1975-77; assoc. Webster & Sheffield, N.Y.C., 1977-78, Heller, Ehrman, White & McAuliffe, San Francisco, 1978-79; assoc. McCutchen, Doyle, Brown & Enersen, San Francisco, 1979-84, ptnr., 1984—; mem. Bur. Nat. Affairs Corp. Practice Series Adv. Bd., 1984—; lectr. bus. law Stanford U. Grad. Sch. Bus., 1988—, bd. dirs. exec. program, 1985-87; lectr., mem. planning com. Calif. Continuing Edn. of the Bar, L.A., San Francisco, 1983, 85-87; lectr. Young Pres.'s Orgn. Internat. Univ. for Pres'., Hong Kong, 1988, So. Area Conf., Silverado, 1988. Author: Mergers, Acquisitions and Tender Offers, 1983, (with others) Proxy Contests, 1983, supplement, 1987; contbg. editor Calif. Bus. Law Reporter, 1983—; also articles. Vestry mem. Trinity Episcopal Ch., San Francisco, 1984-85; vol. Moffit Hosp. U. Calif., San Francisco, 1983-84. Mem. ABA, San Francisco Bar Assn., Am. Soc. Corp. Secs., Phi Beta Kappa. Republican. Clubs: Golden Gateway Tennis, Commonwealth (San Francisco). Office: McCutchen Doyle Brown & Enersen 3 Embarcadero Ctr San Francisco CA 94111

BAGLEY, MARY CAROL, educator, writer, broadcaster; b. St. Louis, Mar. 11, 1958; d. Robert Emmet and Harriet Elaine (Hohreiter) B. BA, U. Mo., St. Louis, 1980; MA, U. Mo., 1982; postgrad., St. Louise U. Feature editor Current Newspaper, Normandy, Mo., 1977-82; mng. editor Watermark Lit. Mag., St. Louis, 1982-85; vis. lectr. So. Ill. U., Edwardsville, 1985—; instr., head. bus. writing St. Louis U., 1985—; news broadcaster Am. Cablevision, Florissant, Ferguson, Mo., 1986—; guest speaker Sta. KMOX-TV, KSDK-TV, St. Louis Writing Festival, St. Louis Community Coll., and others, chancellor's com. Sta. KWMU Radio Adv. Bd., 1980, participant McKendree Writer's Conf., 1986. Author: The Front Row: Missouri's Grand Theaters, 1984, Professional Writing Types, 1990; (with others) The Fabulous Fox Theater, 1985; freelance writer, 1976—; editor: A Guide to St. Louis Theaters, 1984; bd. editors (book), Business Writing Concepts, 1986, Handbook for Professional and Academic Writing, 1988, recipient cert. appreciation, 1986; adv. bd., Business Communications Today, 1986. Co-chmn, Theater Hist. Soc. Conclave, St. Louis, 1984; pres., Ambassador Theater Trust, 1986. Mem. Writer's Guild, Theater Hist. Soc. (nom. bd. dirs. 1986), Am. Assn. U. Instrs., Nat. Council Tchrs. English, U. Mo. English Alumni Assn. (v.p. 1985, senator rep. 1979), St. Louis Numismatic Assn., Mo. Numismatic Assn., Pi Alpha Delta (hon.), Sigma Tau Delta (sponsor). Home: 12539 Falling Leaves Ct Saint Louis MO 63141 Office: Mo Bapt Coll 337 Academic Bldg Saint Louis MO 63141

BAGLIORE, VIRGINIA, poet; b. Bklyn., Mar. 14, 1931; d. James and Josephine (Brunetti) Coglietta; m. James Bagliore, Nov. 8, 1953; children: Rosanne, Lisa. Student NYU, Bklyn. Coll.; student of Kimon Friar. Model, 1952-56; freelance promotional model, 1975-80; poet-tchr. creative poetry workshops, 1975—; condr. workshops Assn. Humanistic Psychology, 1978, 5th Am. Imagery Conf., 1981, Carroll St. Sch., 1981, Public Sch. No. 65, 1981, others; lectr. workshop New Sch., 1982, 85; sponsor, judge High Sch. Poetry Contest, 1977—. pres. Bklyn. Poetry Circle, 1985-87. Editor: (first book of poetry) Oracles of Light, 1986, Strange Gods Before Me; co-editor Eve's Legacy Mag., 1980-82, 86; contbr. poems to various poetry mags.; poems represented in anthologies; exhibited 5 poems at Cork Gallery, Lincoln Ctr., 1981, 84; poems translated into Urdu, Greek and Spanish; essays in The Study and Writing of Poetry; developed communication technique for improving lang. known as the art of self dialogue. Recipient Cert. of Merit, Alan Foss Leukemia Found., 1975, Bill Burke award, 1976, Louise Bogan Meml. award, 1972, Louise Louis award, 1978, Woman of Achievemetn award. Mem. World Poets' Resource Ctr. (Creative Svc. award 1979), Nat. League Am. Pen Women (pres. 1982-86, v.p. letters 1978-82, pres. Bklyn. poetry circle 1982-88, v.p. 1986-90, Disting. Svc. award 1986), Acad. Am. Poets, N.Y. Poetry Forum, Avalon Soc., Eleanor Gaylee Found., Shelley Soc. N.Y. (hon.), Composers, Authors, and Artists Am., Nat. Assn. Poetry Therapy, Bklyn. Poetry Circle (pres. 1986-88). Office: PO Box 244 Ryder Street Station Brooklyn NY 11234

BAHCALL, NETA ASSAF, astrophysicist; b. Israel, Dec. 16, 1942; d. Yehezkel Oscar and Gita (Zilberstein) Assaf; m. John Norris Bahcall, Mar. 21, 1966; children: Ron Assaf, Dan Ophir, Orli Gilat. BS, Hebrew U., Jerusalem, 1963; MS, Weizmann Inst. Sci., Israel, 1965; PhD, Tel Aviv U., 1970. Research fellow Calif. Inst. Tech., 1970-71; mem. staff Princeton U., N.J., 1971-75; research astronomer, 1975-79, sr. research astronomer, 1979-83, chief gen. observer br., from 1983; with Space Telescope Sci. Inst., Balt.; prof. dept. astronomy Princeton (N.J.) U., 1990—. Contbr. articles to profl. jours. Mem. Am. Astron. Soc. Office: Princeton U Dept Astronomy Princeton NJ 08455*

BAHNER, SUE (FLORENCE SUZANNA BAHNER), radio broadcasting executive; b. Phila.; d. William and Florence (Quinlivan) McElwee; m. David S. Bahner; children—Suzanna Elizabeth, Carol Aileen. Grad. Columbia Bus. Coll., 1950. Various exec. sec. positions, 1954-74; office mgr. Sta. WYRD, Syracuse, N.Y., 1974, gen. mgr., 1974-80; gen. mgr. Sta. WWWG-AM, Rochester, N.Y., 1980—; v.p. Brandon Radio, Rochester, 1985—; pres. The Cornerstone Group, 1986—. Active Eastern Hills Bible Ch. Mem. Greater Rochester Assn. Evangelicals (v.p. 1982—), Nat. Religious Broadcasters (pres. ea. chpt. 1984—, bd. dirs. 1983—, sec.) Office: Sta WWWG 1850 S Winton Rd Rochester NY 14618

BAHRAWY, LISA DE SERBINE, German language educator, nurse; b. Hannover, Germany, Mar. 6, 1929; arrived in U.S., 1963; d. Wilhem Georg de Serbine and Luise Anna Sophie Lindemann; m. Ibrahim Bahrawy, May 2, 1953; children: Ramsey Ali, Jens Adly, Dina Birgitta. RN, London, 1953; BA summa cum laude, Tufts U., 1978, MA, 1979; PhD in German, Harvard U., 1987. RN Mass., N.H.; cert. educator Mass., N.H. Nurse King Edward Meml. Hosp., London, 1953-54; health and sci. instr. The Brit. Sch., Port Said, Egypt, 1954-56; nurse Taunton (Mass.) State Hosp., 1963-64, Boston State Hosp., 1964-66, VA Hosp., Bedford, Mass., 1966-67, Danvers (Mass.) State Hosp., 1970-72; lectr. German Tufts U., Medford, Mass., 1978—; freelance translator, author. Author. Active PTA, Bedford, 1967-73, Georgetown, Mass., 1973-77, LWV, Bedford, 1967-73. Mem. MLA, AAUP, Am. Assn. Tchrs. German (life), Women in German, Am. Council on Teaching Fgn. Langs., Goethe Soc., Austro-Am. Soc., Bon Secours and Lawrence Gen. Hosps. Aux. (life), Am. Psychiat. Assn. (founding mem.), Bd. Mental Health, Tufts Club, Harvard Club, Phi Beta Kappa. Lutheran. Home: 281 Main St North Andover MA 01845 Office: Tufts U Medford MA 02155

BAIER, ELLEN P., social services administrator; b. Paterson, N.J., June 25, 1948; d. Philip Marion and Janet Fitzpatrick; m. John J. Baier, Feb. 13, 1965; 1 child, John. Student, Orange County Community Coll., Cornell U. Exec. dir. Port Jervis (N.Y.) Area Sr. Citizens Coun., Rural Sullivan County Housing Opportunities, Inc., Monticello, N.Y.; cons., lectr. and trainer in housing for the elderly, county and community rels. Pres., chmn. bd. dirs. Port Jervis Area Sr. Citizens' Coun., 1983—, chair, 1987-89; bd. ethics Town of Deerpark, 1986—; chair lobby orgn. Rural Agys. Coalition. Republican. Office: Rural Sullivan County Housing 375 Broadway PO Box 1497 Monticello NY 12701

BAIGI, MARLA JEAN, hotel executive; b. Jefferson City, Mo., Sept. 13, 1959; d. Robert Louis and Dorothy Louise (Langkop) Goff; m. John H. Baigi, May 25, 1979; 1 child, Kevin Christopher. BA in Edn., Stephens Coll., 1981; MEd in Counseling and Personnel Services, U. Mo., 1983, EdD in Higher and Adult Edn. and Founds., 1988; EdS in Edn. Adminstrn., N.E. Mo. State U., 1985. Counselor Raleigh Hills Hosp., Jefferson City, 1983, Lincoln U., Jefferson City, 1983-84; bus. advisor Northeast Mo. State U., Kirksville, 1984; advisor career planning and placement U. Mo., Columbia, 1984-85; supr. adminstrv. services, meeting and conf. coordinator Mo. State Dept. Elem. and Secondary Edn., Jefferson City, 1985-88; coord. spl. events Miss. State U., 1988-89; hotel adminstr. Marriott Corp., 1989—; acting dir. alumnae Stephens Coll., 1984; placement coordinator U. Mo. Extension, Columbia, 1984-85. Mem. NAFE, Am. Psychol. Assn., Am. Assn. Counseling & Devel., Mo. Assn.Counseling & Devel., Coun. Advancement & Support Edn., Phi Delta Kappa, Kappa Delta Pi. Republican.

BAILAR, BARBARA ANN, statistician, researcher, professional society executive; b. Monroe, Mich., Nov. 24, 1935; d. Malcolm Laurie and Clara Florence (Parent) Dezendorf; m. John Francis Powell (div. 1966); 1 child, Pamela; m. John Christian Bailar; 1 child, Melissa. BA, SUNY, 1956; MS, Va. Poly. Inst., 1965; PhD, Am. U., 1972. With Bur. of Census, Washington, 1958-88, chief Ctr. Rsch. Measurement Methods, 1973-79, assoc. dir. for statis. standards and methodology, 1979-88; exec. dir. Am. Statis. Assn., Alexandria, Va., 1988—; instr. George Washington U., 1984-85; head dept. math. and stats. USDA Grad. Sch., Washington, 1972-87. Contbr. articles, book chpts. to profl. publs. Pres. bd. dirs. Harbour Sq. Coop., Washington, 1988-89. Recipient Silver medal U.S. Dept. Commerce, 1980. Fellow Am. Statis Assn. (pres. 1987), AAAS (chair sect. stats. 1984-85), Internat. Assn. Survey Statisticians (pres. 1989—), Internat. Statis. Inst. (Pres.'s invited speaker 1983), Cosmos Club. Office: Am Statis Assn 1429 Duke St Alexandria VA 22314-3402

BAILEY, ANNETTE LEE, accountant; b. Suffolk, Va., June 30, 1958; d. Robert Lee and Anne Courtney (Reams) B. BSBA cum laude, Meredith Coll., 1979; postgrad., Va. Commonwealth U., 1980-85. Sales asst. Miller & Rhoads, Richmond, Va., 1975-79; pers. intern Graftek div. Exxon Co., Raleigh, N.C., 1979; sec. Fox-Huber Pers. Inc., Richmond, 1979-80, acctg. clk., 1980-81; bookkeeper Merrill Lynch Pierce Fenner & Smith, Richmond, 1980, lead bookkeeper, 1980; acctg. asst. Crestar Bank (formerly United Va.), Richmond, 1981-83; lease staff acct. Best Products Co. Inc., Richmond, 1983-87, supr. fixed asset acctg., 1987-89; mgr. gen. ledger acctg. Med. Coll. Va. Hosp., Richmond, 1989—. Mem. bell choir First Bapt. Ch., Richmond, 1979—; conv. del. Va. Rep. com., 1985. Shell Oil Co. scholar, 1976. Mem. NAFE, Nat. Assn. Accts., McCormack and Dodge Mid-Atlantic User Group (chmn. 1986-88, treas. 1988-89). Baptist. Office: MCV Sta PO Box 152 MCV Sta Richmond VA 23298

BAILEY, BEVERLY ANN, nurse, educator; b. Russellville, Ky., Oct. 8, 1965; d. Vincent John and Joyce Marie (Noltemeyer) B. AAS in Nursing, Marymount Coll. Va., 1985; BSN, Marymount U., 1987; MSN, Med. Coll. of Va., 1988. Staff nurse Washington Adventist Hosp., Takoma Park, Md., 1986, Arlington (Va.) Hosp., 1986-87; staff nurse II St. Mary's Hosp., Richmond, 1987—; preceptor St. Mary's Hosp., Richmond, 1988—; adj. prof. nursing John Tyler Community Coll., Chester, Va., 1990—. Mem. Nat. Assn. Neonatal Nurses, Va. Nurses Assn., Am. Nurses Assn., Nat. Assn. Ob.-Gyn. and Neonatal Nurses, Sigma Theta Tau. Roman Catholic. Home: 2205 Aspen Pl Richmond VA 23233 Office: St Mary's Hosp 5801 Bremo Rd Richmond VA 23226

BAILEY, DEBORAH MITCHELL, systems analyst; b. Hazlehurst, Miss., Mar. 10, 1964; d. Robert Emmett and Georgia Mae (Smiley) M.; m. Bobby Ray Bailey, Sept. 3, 1986; 1 child, Terrance Mitchell. BS in Computer Sci. cum laude, Jackson State U., 1986. Program vaildator IBM, Austin, Tex., 1985; lab. attendant Xerox Corp., Jackson, Miss., 1986; programmer Miss. Dept. Edn., Jackson, 1986-87; systems analyst Miss. Legis. Budget Office, Jackson, 1987—. Mem. NAFE. Methodist. Home: 1595 W Highland Dr Jackson MS 39204

BAILEY, DEBRA SUE, psychologist, neuropsychologist; b. Ravenna, Ohio, Nov. 16, 1953; d. William Joseph Bailey and Mary Alice (Hayford) Caris. BA, Kent State U., 1979, MA, 1982, PhD, 1987. Lic. psychologist, Conn. Hosse trainer TP Long Arabians, Kent, Ohio, 1974-79; teaching fellow Kent State U., 1982-84; psychology intern Conn. Valley Hosp., Middletown, 1985-86; postdoctoral fellow in clin. neuropsychology VA Med. Ctr., West Haven, Conn., 1986-87; cons. clin. neuropsychology Gaylord Hosp., Wallingford, Conn., 1987-88; psychologist The N.Y. Hosp.-Cornell Med. Coll., White Plains, N.Y., 1988-89; staff psychologist Fairfield Hills Hosp., Newtown, Conn., 1989—; pvt. practice psychologist, Woodbury, Conn., 1990—; rsch. assoc., N.Y. Hosp.-Cornell Med. Coll., White Plains, 1989—. Contbr. articles to profl. jours. Named Can. Nat. Champion English Pleasure, Arabian Can. Nats., Calgary, Can., 1977, one of Can. Nat. Top 10 Western Pleasure champs Arabian Can. Nats., Calgary, 1977, East Coast Champ Western Pleasure, Internat. Arab Horse Assn., Devon, Pa., 1979, 3d in U.S. Nat. Saddle Seat Equitation, Internat. Arabian Horse Assn., Oklahoma City, 1970, Internat. Champ Pinto Pleasure Pony, Internat. Pinto Horse Assn. & Am. Horse Assn., Des Moines, 1969. Mem. Am. Psychol. Assn., Internat. Neuropsychol. Soc., Conn. Psychol. Assn., Conn. Soc. for Psychoanalytic Psychologist. Home: 10 Beechwood Ct Woodbury CT 06798 Office: Fairfield Hills Hosp New Town CT 06470

BAILEY, DEENA TAMARA, health care manager; b. Haifa, Israel, June 13, 1947; came to U.S., 1960; d. Fred Ephraim and Devora (Glaser) Mansbacher; m. Wayne W. Bailey, Apr. 4, 1970 (div. 1977); 1 child, Devora Elyse. BS in Health Sci., U. Redlands, 1989. Mgr. dept. surgery Cedars-Sinai Med. Ctr., L.A., 1980-87; mgr. cardiac catheterization lab. Cedars-Sinai Med. Ctr., 1988—. Mem. Health Care Execs. So. Calif., Women in Health Adminstrn. (coast rep.), Am. Coll. Cardiovascular Adminstrs. (regional dir.), Am. Acad. Med. Adminstrs., Healthcare Forum. Democrat. Jewish. Office: Cedars Sinai Med Ctr 8700 Beverly Blvd Los Angeles CA 90048

BAILEY, ELIZABETH ELLERY, academic dean; b. N.Y.C., Nov. 26, 1938; d. Irving Woodworth and Henrietta Dana (Skinner) Raymond; children: James L., William E. BA magna cum laude, Radcliffe Coll., 1960; MS, Stevens Inst. Tech., 1966; PhD, Princeton U., 1972. Successively sr. tech. aid, assoc. mem. tech. staff, mem. tech. staff, supr. econ. analysis group, rsch. head econs. rsch. dept. Bell Labs., 1960-77; commr. CAB, 1977-83, v.p., 1981-83; dean Grad. Sch. Indsl. Adminstrn. Carnegie-Mellon U., 1983—; dir. Honeywell, Inc., Philip Morris, CSX Corp., Natwest Bancorp., Coll. Retirement Equities Fund; adj. asst., then assoc. prof. econs. NYU, 1973-77. Author: Economic Theory of Regulatory Constraint, 1973; editor: Selected Economics Papers of William J. Baumol, 1976; Deregulating the Airlines, 1985; bd. editors Am. Econ. Rev., 1977-79, Jour. Indsl. Econs., 1977-84. Founding mem., v.p. bd. trustees Harbor Sch. for Children with Learning Disabilities; trustee Princeton U., 1978-82, Presbyn. U. Hosp., 1984—, Brookings Inst., 1988—, Catalyst, 1988—, Am. Assembly Collegiate Schs. of Bus., 1987—; mem. exec. coun. Fedn. Orgns. for Profl. Women, 1980-82; chmn. Com. on Status of Women in Econs. Profession, 1979-82; mem. corp. vis. com. Sloan Sch. Mgmt., MIT, 1982-85; mem. adv. bd. Brookings Inst., 1987—, Ctr. Econ. Policy Rsch., Stanford U., 1983—, MIT econs. dept., 1989—, Princeton econs. dept., 1989—. Recipient Program Design Trainee award Bell Labs; Bell Labs grantee Princeton U., 1972. Mem. Am. Econ. Assn. (exec. com. 1981-83, v.p. 1985), Am. Assn. Collegiate Schs. Bus. (bd. mem. 1987—). Home: 220 Schenley Rd Pittsburgh PA 15217 Office: Carnegie-Mellon U 5000 Forbes Ave Pittsburgh PA 15213

BAILEY, EUNICE DELORES, medical association administrator; b. Stratford, Wis., Feb. 12, 1928; m. Richard Bailey, Apr. 20, 1950; 1 child, Lisa. Student, U. Wis., 1947-49. Pres. Lake View Mgmt. Inc., Lincolnwood, Chgo., Ill., 1980—, Physicians Ctrs. Inc., Oakbrook, Skokie, Chgo., Ill., 1983—. Producer, dir. (Sta. WVVX-FM/Radio, metro vision cable TV) Eunice Bailey Show. Mem. Mayors Vets. Coun., Chgo., 1988—, instr. Jr. Achievement, 1988—, vol. Girl Scouts U.S., 1988—. Mem. Chgo. Assn. of Commerce and Industry, Oak Brook C. of C., Skokie Assn. of Commerce (advt. cons. 1986—), Skokie C. of C. (smoking ordinance mem. 1987—), Atty. Gens. Adv. Coun., Rotary, Zonta, Oak Brook Polo Club. Office: Physicians Ctrs Inc 500 N Michigan Ave Chicago IL 60611

BAILEY, FRANCES ANNE LOCKRIDGE, clinical social worker; b. Graham, Tex., Mar. 10, 1927; d. William E. B. and Annie Maude (Underwood) Lockridge; m. Frank A. Bailey Jr., June 5, 1951 (dec. Jan. 1983); children: Julia Bailey Erskine, Jenny Bailey Stelly, Frank Bradford. BA, La. State U., 1948; M in Social Work, Tulane U., 1951. Lic. social worker. Welfare visitor La. Dept. Pub. Welfare, Baton Rouge, La., 1952-54; children's case worker Children's Service Bureau, Shreveport, La., 1952-54; asst. supr. State Indsl. Sch. for Girls, Ball, La., 1954; gen. therapist Alexandria (La.) Guidance Ctr., 1955-61; clin. social worker Crowley (La.) Mental Health Ctr., 1971-78, chief, adolescent and children's svcs., 1980—; gen. clin. social worker Ozark Reg. Mental Health Ctr., Harrison, Ark., 1978-80; cons. Crowley City Court, 1975-78, Head-Start Program. Mem. local bd. La. Coun. on Child Abuse, 1989. Democrat. Office: Crowley Mental Health Ctr PO Drawer 1403 Crowley LA 70527

BAILEY, JANET LEE, vocational educator; b. Dallas, Oct. 30, 1953; d. Francis Pinkham and Jean Louise (Perry) Hescock; m. Edward Lawrence Bailey, Dec. 20, 1975 (div. June 1983); 1 child, Jennifer Louise. BS, Southern Meth. U., Dallas, 1973-75; postgrad., St. Paul Hosp. Sch. Med. Tech., Dallas, 1975-76, Eastfield Coll., Dallas, 1988, U. N. Tex., Denton, 1987--. Cert. Med. Technologist. Lab. asst. Lake Highland Med. Lab., Dallas, 1974; microbiologist St. Paul Hosp., Dallas, 1975-76; research technologist Wadley Inst. of Molecular Medicine, Dallas, 1976-77; spl. chemistry technologist Doctors Hosp., Dallas; med. technologist Hoskins Pathology Lab., Dallas, 1979-81; serology technologist Nat. Health Lab., 1983-86; health occupation educator Dallas Ind. Sch. Dist., 1986--; post adv. Med. Explorers Post 822, Dallas, 1986--. Campaign worker Rep. Party, Dallas, 1986, phone bank caller Dem. Party, Dallas, 1982, worker Boy Scouts of Am., 1989--, facilitator SantaCops Dallas Police Dept., 1988. Mem. Am. Soc. of Clin. Pathologist, Am. Vocational Assn., Metroplex Educators of Sci. Assn., AAUW, Rep. Women's Club, SMU Alumni Assn. Methodist. Home: 9827 Estacado Dallas TX 75228 Office: Plano E Sr High Sch 3000 Los Rios Blvd Plano TX 75074

BAILEY, JOSELYN ELIZABETH, physician; b. Pine Bluff, Ark.; d. Joseph Alexander and Angeline Elaine (Davis) B.; B.Mus., Manhattanville Coll., 1952; M.Music Edn., Manhattan Sch. Music, 1954; M.D., Howard U., 1971. Straight med. intern Huntington Meml. Hosp., Pasadena, Calif., 1971-72, resident, 1972-74; fell in nephrology Wadsworth VA Hosp., Los Angeles, 1975-77; practice medicine specializing in internal medicine and nephrology, Torrance, Calif.; mem. active staff Torrance Meml., South Bay, Little Company of Mary hosps.; cons. staff Del Amo Hosp.; attending staff Harbor Gen. Hosp.;clin. faculty Dept. Medicine, UCLA; active staff Bay Harbor Hosp., trustee, 1982—. Mem. Renal Physicians Assn., Am. Soc. Internal Medicine, Calif. Soc. Internal Medicine, So. Calif. Pvt. Practice Assn.

BAILEY, JOY HAFNER, university program administrator, psychologist, educator; b. Weehawkin, N.J., Aug. 15, 1928; d. Elmar William and Fern (Williams) Hafner; children: Kerry, Jan, Leslie, Liza, Annie Laurie, Kristin. BA, Austin Coll., 1974; MS, East Tex. State U., 1975, EdD, 1977. Lic. marriage and family therapist, profl. counselor; cert. counselor. Counselor, instr. East Tex. State U., 1976-80; dir. spl. services acad./counseling program Ga. State U., 1980—, asst. prof. devel. studies, counseling and psychol. svcs.; pvt. practice marriage and family therapy. Mem. Am. Psychol. Assn., Am. Assn. Marriage and Family Therapists, Am. Assn. Counseling and Devel., Psi Chi. Office: Ga State U Box 649 Atlanta GA 30303

BAILEY, KRISTEN, legal assistant; b. Davenport, Iowa, Jan. 5, 1952; d. Donald Ray and Alta Llewellyn (Mandler) B. AS, Mo. So. State Coll., 1974; cert. paralegal studies, Rockhurst Coll., 1978. Legal sec. Ralph E. Baird, Lawyer, Joplin, Mo., 1972-75; legal asst. Benny J. Harding, Atty. at Law, Kansas City, Mo., 1976-87, Polsinelli, White, Vardeman & Shalton, Kansas City, 1988—; speaker in field. Vol., Heartland's Sch. Riding, Overland Park, Kans., 1988—. Winner Ark. and Iowa state championships, 3-gaited Pleasure Horse, Am. Saddlebred Pleasure Horse Assn., 1981; named Kansas City Legal Sec. of Yr., 1979. Mem. Kansas City Assn. Legal Assts., Kansas City Legal Secs. Assn. (bd. dirs. 1977-89, pres. 1979-81, life mem.), Friends of the Zoo, Kansas City Mus. Assn., Whole Person Inc., Mid-Am. Saddle Horse Club (sec. 1981-83). Republican. Methodist. Office: Polsinelli White Vardeman & Shalton 4705 Central St Kansas City MO 64112

BAILEY, LINDA ANNE, radiologic technologist; b. Binghamton, N.Y., Nov. 12, 1960; d. Ronald Franklin and Rose Marie (Kelly) B. Cert. radiologic tech., Meml. Hosp. System Sch., Houston, 1982. Radiologic technologist U. Tex. Med. Br., Galveston, 1982-83, St. Mary's Hosp., Galveston, 1983-86, Palm Beach (Fla.) Med. Group, 1986-87, Dr. O'Brien, Riviera Beach, Fla., 1987-89; Magnetic Resonance Imaging technologist MRI of South Broward, Hollywood, Fla., 1989, MRI of Boca Raton (Fla.) Ltd., 1989-90; site mgr. MRI of South Wellington, Fla., 1990—.

BAILEY, LONA M., real estate company executive; b. Soltau, W. Ger., Mar. 29, 1928; came to U.S., 1949; d. August and Carolina (Fleischer) Meyer; m. Edward H. Bailey, Feb. 4, 1949; 1 son, Mark Eric. Ed., W. Ger., 1934-44. Lic. real estate broker, N.J. Salesperson Earl W. Calloway, Inc., Wildwood Crest, N.J., 1968-76, Parson Realty, North Wildwood, N.J., 1976-77; broker-salesperson Bailey & Frankenfield, Wildwood, N.J., 1977-78; pres., owner Bailey & Bailey Realty, Inc., Wildwood, 1978—, Wildwood Crest, 1983—. Recipient Million Dollar Sales award, N.J. Assn. Realtors; Real Estate Showcase Cape May County sales awards, 1977-83. Mem. Nat. Assn. Realtors (cert. residential specialist), Greater Wildwood-Cape May County Bd. Realtors (treas. 1980, 81, 2d v.p. 1982, 1st v.p., pres.-elect 1983, pres. 1984—), N.J. Assn. Realtors (grad. Realtor's Inst. 1977). Republican. Lutheran. Home: 217 Fishing Creek Rd Cape May NJ 08204 Office: Bailey & Bailey Realty Inc 5918 New Jersey Ave Wildwood Crest NJ 08260

BAILEY, MARY, educational specialist; b. Camden, S.C., Feb. 22, 1931; d. William and Isabell Brewington; children: Linda Bailey-Walker, Nathaniel. Degree, Wheaton (Ill). Coll, 1960; DD, Philemon Bapt. Inst., 1973. Notary pub. Office mgr. Star of Hope Bookstore, Paterson, N.J.; moderator ordaining coun. of ministers Interdenominational Minister Coun. Assn., Paterson; mktg. rep. Am. Bible Soc., N.Y.C.; pastor, founder Holy House of Prayer Interdenominational Ch., Inc., Paterson; basic skills instr. N.J. Dept. Corrections, Ringwood. Recipient numerous awards. Mem. NAFE, NAACP, YWCA, Am. Soc. Notaries, Nat. Coun. Negro Women, Paterson Clergy Assn., Interdenominational Ministers Fellowship, Christian Edn. Fellowship of ETTA, Clergymens Coun. Human Relationships, Evang. Tchr. Tng. Assn.

BAILEY, MARY BEATRICE, nursing information systems director; b. Pitts., Dec. 24, 1933; d. Harry Chantler and Beatrice Iseli (Koenig) B. Diploma in Nursing, Allegheny Gen. Hosp., Pitts., 1956; BSNE, Chatham Coll., Pitts., 1956; MSN, Duke U., Durham, 1967. Cert. nursing adminstr. Staff nurse, head nurse, nursing supr. Allegheny Gen. Hosp., Pittsburgh, 1956-60; nursing instr. pediatrics Duke U. Sch. Nursing, Durham, N.C., 1960-61; nursing instr. med. surg Rex Hosp. Sch. Nursing, Raleigh, N.C., 1962-63; nursing supr. Rex Hosp., Raleigh, 1964-71, patient care coord., 1972-86, clin. dir., 1987, dir. nursing info. system, 1987-90. Author: The Role of the Mother with her Hospitalized Child, 1966. Vol. RN open door clinic, Raleigh, 1987-88; mem. N.C. United for Equal Rights Amendment, Raleigh, N.C. Coalition for Choice. Mem. NOW, N.C. Coun. Women's Orgns., N.C. League for Nursing, N.C. Nurses Assn. (treas. 1977-79). Democrat. Episcopalian. Home: 311 Furches St Raleigh NC 27607 Office: Rex Hosp 4420 Lake Boone Trail Raleigh NC 27607

BAILEY, MOREEN DELORIS, radio broadcast journalist; b. Bellas Gate, St. Catherine, Jamaica, Oct. 19, 1957; came to U.S., 1972; d. Cecil John and Brenetta Bailey. BA, Ohio State U., 1979; MS, Case Western Res. U., 1989. Salesperson Lazarus Dept. Stores, Columbus, Ohio, 1978-81; news reporter, anchor Sta. WJMO, Cleve., 1981—; pub. affairs dir., 1983—, news dir., 1984—. Mentor Career Beginnings Program Case Western Res. U., 1988-89; mem. com. Black Archives Project, Cleve., 1988, 89; trustee Harambee: Svcs. to Black Families, 1989—; mem. adv. com. Friendly Town/Innercity Renewal Soc., 1989—. Recipient Outstanding Pub. Svc. award Career Women's Civic Club, Cleve., 1984; named one of Outstanding Young Women Am., 1985, 86. Mem. Greater Cleve. Radio News Dirs. Assn. (charter 1989), Radio/TV News Dirs. Assn., Press. Club Cleve., Alpha Kappa Alpha. Home: 10844 Ashbury Ave Cleveland OH 44106 Office: Sta WJMO Radio 11821 Euclid Ave Cleveland OH 44106

BAILEY, PATRICIA PRICE, lawyer, former government official; m. Douglas L. Bailey; 2 children. BA in History cum laude, Lindenwood Colls.; MA in Internat. Affairs, Tufts U.; JD summa cum laude, Am. U. Bar: U.S. Ct. Appeals (D.C. cir.), U.S. Ct. Appeals (8th cir.), U.S. Supreme Ct. Exec. asst. Bur. for Latin Am., then asst. to dep. coordinator Alliance for Progress, AID, 1961-66; advisor fgn. affairs Rep. F. Bradford Morse, 1967-68; with Office of Counsel to Pres. in White House; spl. asst. to asst. atty. gen. U.S. Dept. Justice, 1977-79; exec. legal asst. to gen. counsel U.S.

Merit systems Protection Bd., 1979; commr. FTC, Washington, 1979-88; ptnr., Squire, Sanders & Dempsey, Washington, 1989—. Office: Squire Sanders & Dempsey 1201 Pennsylvania Ave NW Washington DC 20044*

BAILEY, SUSAN CAROL, savings and loan executive; b. Muskogee, Okla., Apr. 10, 1954; d. William E. and Lula M. (Holloway) Green; m. Wayne M. Bailey, Aug. 6, 1976; 1 child, Nathan W. BS in Fin., So. Ill. U., 1982, MBA, 1983. Tech. asst. ops. Marsh Stencil Machine Co., Belleville, Ill., 1973-85; loan officer Delmar Fin. Co., Belleville, 1985-86; asst. v.p., asst. br. mgr. Fidelity Fed. Savs. and Loan Assn., Fairview Heights, Ill., 1986; asst. v.p., br. mgr. Fidelity Fed. Savs. and Loan Assn., Belleville, 1986-87, v.p., br. mgr., 1987-89, v.p., br. mgr., Metro E. Deposit Acquisition & Fin. Svcs. officer, 1989—; fin. cons., Caseyville, Ill., 1985-86. Mem. Belleville Welcome Wagon (treas.); mem. allocations bd. United Way Greater St. Louis. Mem. St. Louis Fedn. Socs. for Coating Tech. (exec. com. 1980-85, chmn. edn. com. 1983-84), Belleville Bd. Realtors, Edwardsville-Collinsville Bd. Realtors, Women's Coun. of Realtors, Homebuilders Assn., Belleville Econ. Progress, Belleville Postal Coun. (bd. dirs.), So. Ill. Network of Women (alliance rep.), Fin. Women Internat., Fairview Heights C. of C., Rotary. Home: 710 Belleville Rd Caseyville IL 62232 Office: Fidelity Fed Savs and Loan Assn 5720 N Belt W Belleville IL 62223

BAILEY, TANIA, education director, consultant; b. Phila., May 10, 1927; d. Henry Richardson and Dorothy (Saylor) Hallowell; m. Omar Bailey, Sept. 17, 1949; children: Bertinia H., Jeffrey, Jonathan. BA in Econs. and Sociology, Mt. Holyoke Coll., 1949; MEd, Temple U., 1969; EdD, Nova U., 1988. Cert. reading specialist, Pa.; cert. nat. counselor. Social case worker Soc. to Protect Children from Cruelty, Phila., 1949-52; reading tutor, sub. tchr. Phila. school dist., 1963-65; tchr., tutor Tredyffrin/Easttwon Sch. Dist., Berwyn, Pa., 1965-67; ednl. cons. Tarleton Sch., Devon, Pa., 1968-75; reading specialist, dir. Chester County Intermediate Unit, West Chester, Pa., 1975-79; faculty field supr. Cabrini Coll., Radnor, Pa., 1977-81; dir. counseling ctr. Harcum Jr. Coll., Bryn Mawr, Pa., 1980—, dir. ACT 101 program, 1984-87, asst. dean student affairs, 1987—, dir. talent devel. program, 1990—; ednl. cons. various schs., Berwyn, West Chester, 1967—. Active Jr. League of Phila., 1945—. Mem. Counseling Assn. Greater Phila. (pres., Counseling Practitioners award 1983), Am. Assn. for Counseling and Devel., Nat. Assn. for Devel. Edn., Pa. Coll. Personnel Assn., ACT 101 (bd. dirs. ea. region). Home: 670 Heatherton Ln West Chester PA 19380 Office: Harcum Jr Coll Montgomery and Morris Aves Bryn Mawr PA 19010

BAILLIE, MARY HELEN, accounting executive; b. Clio, S.C., Aug. 18, 1926; d. Paul Clydus and Laurie (Easterling) Orr; grad. Carolina Bus. Coll., 1946; children—William Sinclair, Carol Anderson. Controller, George I. Clarke, Inc., Atlanta, 1953-57, DuBose Reed Constrn. Co./W. Carroll DuBose, Inc., Ft. Lauderdale, Fla., 1970-74; asst. controller H.B. Fuller Co., Ft. Lauderdale, 1975-76; owner M.H. Baillie & Assocs., Inc., Ft. Lauderdale, 1977—. Mem. Leadership Broward Alumni, 1985—, Ft. Lauderdale Sign Adv. Bd., 1983—, Broward County Commn. on Status of Women, 1985—; bd. dirs., treas. Women in Distress, 1984—. Mem. Nat. Accts. Assn. (dir. 1977-79, dir. spl. activities 1979—), Fla. Accts. Assn. (dir. 1977-79, sec. 1977-79), Ft. Lauderdale C. of C. (dir. 1979—), Internat. Assn. Fin. Planners. Republican. Clubs: Women's Execs. (dir. 1978-80, treas. 1978-80), Ft. Lauderdale Country. Home: 3471 NE 17th Terr Fort Lauderdale FL 33334 Office: MH Baillie & Assocs Inc 746 NE Third Ave Fort Lauderdale FL 33304

BAILLIE, PRISCILLA WOODS, aquatic ecologist; b. Buffalo, N.Y., Jan. 18, 1935; d. George Bryant and Doris (McKay) Woods; m. David Gemmell Baillie, Aug. 23, 1956. Student, Smith Coll., 1953-55; BS, U. Hartford, 1974; MS in Zoology, U. Conn., 1978, PhD in Botany, 1983. Prin., investigator Marine and Freshwater Rsch. Svc., Guilford, Conn., 1983—; vis. prof. U. Conn., Stamford, 1984, Fairfield (Conn.) U., 1984; adj. faculty Middlesex Community Coll., Middletown, Conn., 1985-86; bd. dirs. Little Harbor Lab., Guilford. Contbr. articles to profl. jours. Woman's Seamen's Friend Soc. grantee, 1979-83. Mem. New England Estuarine Rsch. Soc., Aquatic Plant Mgmt. Soc., Soc. Wetland Scientists, Phycological Soc., Sigma Xi. Office: Marine and Freshwater Rsch 276 State St Guilford CT 06437

BAILYN, LOTTE, psychology educator; b. Vienna, Austria, July 17, 1930; came to U.S., 1937; d. Paul Felix Lazarsfeld and Marie (Jahoda) Albu; m. Bernard Bailyn, June 18, 1952; children: Charles, John. BA in Math. with high honors, Swarthmore Coll., 1951; MA in Social Psychology, Radcliffe Coll.-Harvard U., 1953, PhD in Social Psychology, 1956. Rsch. assoc. Grad. Sch. Edn., Harvard U., Cambridge, Mass., 1956-57, rsch. assoc. dept. social rels., 1958-64, lectr., 1963-67; instr. dept. econs. and social sci. MIT, Cambridge, 1957-58, rsch. assoc. Sloan Sch. Mgmt., 1969-70, lectr., 1970-71, sr. lectr., 1971-72, assoc. prof. orgnl. psychology and mgmt., 1972-80, prof., 1980—; trustee Cambridge Savs. Bank; mem. adv. coun. Suffolk U. Mgmt. Sch., Boston, 1983-86; mem. sr. coun. Leadership Devel. Inst., Rutgers U., 1986-89; panel mem. NAS, NRC, Washington, 1988-90; mem. task force in career devel. and maintenance IEEE, Washington, 1982—; vis. scholar Imperial Coll. Sci. and Tech., London, 1982, New Hall, Cambridge (Eng.) U., 1986-87; scholar-in-residence Rockefeller Found. Study and Conf. Ctr., Bellagio, Italy, 1983; vis. univ. fellow U. Auckland, N.Z., 1984. Author: Mass Media and Children, 1959, Living with Technology, 1980; co-author: Working with Careers, 1984; editor: (monograph) The Uses of Television, 1962; mem. editorial bd. Jour. Orgnl. Behavior, Human Resource Mgmt., Jour. Engring. and Tech. Mgmt.; contbr. articles to profl. jours., chpts. to books. Trustee Radcliffe Coll., 1970-77. Fellow Am. Psychol. Assn.; mem. Acad. Mgmt., Am. Sociol. Assn. Home: 170 Clifton St Belmont MA 02178 Office: MIT Sloan Sch Mgmt 50 Memorial Dr Cambridge MA 02139

BAIMAN, GAIL, real estate broker; b. Bklyn., June 4, 1938; d. Joseph and Anita (Devon) Yalow; m. James F. Becker, Oct. 1970 (div. 1978); children: Steven, Susan, Barbara. Student Bklyn. Coll., 1955-57. Lic. real estate broker, N.Y., Pa., Fla. Personnel-pub. relations dir. I.M.C., Inc., N.Y.C., 1970-72; pres., broker Gayle Baiman Assocs., Inc., N.Y.C., 1972-74; v.p., broker Tuit Mktg. Corp., Mt. Pocono, Pa., 1974-83; pres., broker Ind. Timeshare Sales, Inc., St. Petersburg, Orlando and Ft. Lauderdale, Fla., 1983—; Mem. Am. Resort Real Estate Developers Assn, Chairman's League, Better Bus. Arbitrator Assn., Internat. Resale Brokers Assn. (co-founder), Am. Resort and Residential Developers Assn., Chmns. League, Better Bus. Bur. Arbitrators Assn. Office: Ind Timeshare Sales Inc 5680 66th St N St Petersburg FL 33709

BAIN, LINDA VALERIE, executive development consultant; b. N.Y.C., Feb. 14, 1947; d. Carlton Louis and Helen V. (Boyd) B.; m. Samuel Green, Mar. 21, 1986. BA, CCNY, 1975. Exec. sec. N.Y.C. Dept. Social Services, 1966-70; program assoc. N.Y. State Dept. Mental Hygiene, N.Y.C., 1970-71, Nat. Council Negro Women, N.Y.C., 1973-79; sr. cons. Donchian Mgmt. Services, N.Y.C., 1980-85; pres., devel. cons. Bain Assocs., Inc., N.Y.C., 1985—; cons. Bristol Myers-Squibb Co. Sec., bd. dirs. Friends of Alvin Ailey; chairperson bd. dirs. The Friendly Place, Inc. Recipient Mary McLeod Bethune Recognition award Nat. Council Negro Women, 1974. Mem. NAFE, Am. Soc. Tng. and Devel., Nat. Coun. Negro Women Inc., Corp. Women's Network, Nat. and N.Y. Orgn. Devel. Network, Am. Double Dutch League (bd. dirs.), Manhattan Valley Townhouses Assn. (treas.). Democrat. Office: Bain Assocs Inc PO Box 20789 New York NY 10025-9992

BAINBRIDGE, DONA BARDELLI, international marketing executive; b. Irvington, N.J., Feb. 27, 1953; d. Alfred and Dona Ellen (Self) B.; m. Harry M. Bainbridge, May 23, 1981 (dec.); 1 child, Harry Michael. Certificat de Langue, Sorbonne, U. Paris, 1974; BA, U. Ky., 1975; MA in Internat. Studies, Am. U., 1978; MS in Econ. and Social Planning in Developing Countries , U. London, 1979. Research assoc. Woodrow Wilson Internat. Ctr. for Vis. Scholars, Washington, 1976-77, World Bank, Washington, 1977-79; legis. asst. to Congressman Marc Lincoln Marks, Washington, 1979-80; internat. trade analyst Internat. Trade Adminstrn., U.S. Dept. Commerce, Washington, 1980-82; internat. mgmt. cons. Coopers and Lybrand, 1982-86 ; v.p. Bankers Trust Co., Internat. Pvt. Banking, 1986-88; sr. mktg. dir. internat. services BDO Seidman, N.Y.C., 1988-90; founder, pres. D.H. Bainbridge Assocs., 1990—. Chpt. pres. Am. Friends of London Sch. Econs., 1981-83, nat. bd. dirs., 1982-85. Mem. NAFE, Soc. for Internat. Devel. N.Y. Chpt., Bus. and Profl. Women's Clubs Am. (acad. scholar 1971), Am. Platform Assn., Women's Econ. Devel. Corp., Fin. Women's Assn. N.Y., Kiwanis. Democrat. Lutheran. Office: DH Bainbridge Assocs 9 Marisa Ct Montrose NY 10548

BAINTER, PATRICIA ANN, automotive company executive; b. Lancaster, Ohio, Mar. 16, 1961; d. Oscar Eldon and Sara Rose (Burns) B. BSBA, Ohio State U., 1988. Owner rels. analyst Ford Motor Co., Dearborn, Mich., 1988-89; ind. channel zone mgr. Ford Motor Co., Orlando, Fla., 1989—. Mem. Vols. in Action, Orlando, 1990—. Mem. Young Reps. Cen. Fla., Am. Cancer Soc.-New Directions. Home: 221 Fox Chase Point S Longwood FL 32779 Office: Ford Motor Co PO Box 945500 Maitland FL 32794-5500

BAINTON, DOROTHY FORD, pathology educator, researcher; b. Magnolia, Miss., June 18, 1933; d. Aubrey Ratcliff and Leta (Brumfield) Ford; m. Cedric R. Bainton, Nov. 28, 1959; children: Roland J., Bruce G., James H. BS, Millsaps Coll., 1955; MD, Tulane U. Sch. of Medicine, 1958; MS, U. Calif., San Francisco, 1966. Postdoctoral rsch. fellow U. Calif., San Francisco, 1963-66, postdoctoral rsch. pathologist, 1966-69, asst. prof. pathology, 1969-75, assoc. prof., 1975-81, prof. pathology, 1981—, chair pathology, 1987—. NIH grantee, 1978-94. Mem. Am. Soc. for Cell Biology, AAAS, Am. Soc. of Hematology, Am. Soc. of Histochemists and Cytochemists, Am. Assn. of Pathologists. Democrat. Mem. Soc. of Friends. Office: U Calif Dept Pathology 3d and Parnassus Box 0506HSW-501 San Francisco CA 94143

BAIR, FRIEDA AUGUSTA, poet; b. Bowbells, N.D., Oct. 22, 1904; d. Rinehold Frederick and Bertha Marie (Ruhnke) Migge; m. F. Burke Bair, June 4, 1930 (dec. Sept. 1971); 1 child, Byron Burke. Student nursing, Luth. Hosp., Hampton, Iowa, 1923-24; student, Drake U., Des Moines, 1924-25; BS, U. N.D., 1928. Tchr. English and Latin Donnybrook (N.D.) High Sch., 1928-30; elem. tchr. North Versailles Twp., East McKeesport, Pa., 1944-48; elder First Presbyn. Ch., East Aurora, N.Y., 1952-55, clk., 1964-67, assoc. pres. Women's Assn., 1963-64; pres. Western N.Y. Presbyterial Orgn., Buffalo, 1960-63; v.p., trustee Western N.Y. Presbyterial Nursing Homes, Buffalo, 1956-71, ch. historian, 1963-86; sec. Golden Agers Salvation Army, Tonawanda, N.Y., 1986-90; mem. League of Mercy, Salvation Army, Tonawanda, 1983-90, rep. Coun. of Aging, Erie County, 1987-90, mem., sec., chmn. Youth and Camp Commn., Buffalo, 1974—. Author: Church Directory, 1956, Cracker Barrel Verse, 1973, Feather in the Wind, 1975, Twilight Tapestry, 1977, Weathered Years, 1984; contbr. articles to profl. jours. Vol. U.S. War Bonds and Ration Bd., East McKeesport, Pa., 1945-47; inspector elections, East Aurora, N.Y., 1949-59; pres. PTA, East McKeesport, 1942-43, East Aurora, 1949-50. Recipient award Presbyn. Nat. Hdqrs., East Aurora, 1957, Woman of Yr. award Presbyn. Ch., East Aurora, 1963, Blue Bonnett award Buffalo Salvaiton Army, 1963, Plaque of Appreciation award U. N.D. Found., 1990. Mem. NEA (life, award 1947)., AAUW (chmn. tour of homes), Am. Bell Assn., Order of Eastern Star. Democrat. Home: 1110 Payne Apt 109 North Tonawanda NY 14120

BAIR, MYRNA LYNN, state senator; b. Huntington, W.Va., Oct. 26, 1940; d. Charles Thomas and Velma Elvera (Schoenlein) North; B.S. in Chemistry, U. Cin., 1962; Ph.D., U. Wis., 1968; m. Thomas Irvin Bair, Mar. 12, 1966; children—Thomas Irvin, Catherine Lynn. Asst. prof. chemistry Beaver Coll., Glenside, Pa., 1966-70; instr. chemistry U. Del., 1974-76, asst. prof. edn., 1977-79; asst. dir. pub. info. Del. Energy Office, Wilmington, 1978-79; mem. Del. Senate, 1981—. Contbr. articles to sci. jours. Bd. dirs. Del. Lung Assn.; trustee Wesley Coll.; mem. Nat. Republican Com., Brandywine Region Rep. Women's Club. Recipient Freshman award Chem. Rubber Co., 1959; Du-Pont Co. Teaching award, 1963, Pres.'s award Jr. League, 1988; NSF fellow, 1964-66. Mem. AAUW, LWV, Delawareans for Energy Conservation, Phi Beta Kappa, Iota Sigma Pi, Alpha Lambda Delta. Methodist. Office: Del State Senate Dover DE 19901*

BAIRD, PAMELA JO, banker; b. Blue Earth, Minn., July 18, 1948; d. Dennis and Una Mae (Espeland) Fenske; m. Richard Charles Baird Sr., June 10, 1967; 1 child, Richard. Grad., Winnebago (Minn.) High Sch., 1966. Clk., stenographer Mankato (Minn.) State Coll., 1966-69; legal sec. Krahmer & Krahmer Attys., Fairmont, Minn., 1969-70; buyer, expediter Abex/Aerospace, Oxnard, Calif., 1970-73; sec. Security State Bank, Mankato, 1973-74; sec., supr. Bank of Commerce (name changed to Mid America Bank), Mankato, 1974-77, asst. ops. officer, 1978-85, asst. v.p., 1986-89, v.p., 1990—. Vol. United Way, Mankato, 1986—; active Mankato Leadership, 1987—; bd. dirs. YWCA, 1985—, treas., 1987; mem. adv. bd. Luth. Social Svcs., 1989, RSVP, 1989; bd. dirs. Summit Ctr., 1990—. Mem. Nat. Assn. Bank Women (group pres. 1984-86, chmn. Minn. membership 1986—), Am. Inst. Banking (bd. dirs., pres. Mankato chpt. 1981-86, Minn. bd. dirs. 1986—). Lutheran. Club: Mankato Exchange. Lodge: Zonta. Office: Mid America Bank 2d and Main Box 820 Mankato MN 56001

BAIRSTOW, FRANCES KANEVSKY, labor arbitrator, mediator, educator; b. Racine, Wis., Feb. 19, 1920; d. William and Minnie (DuBow) Kanevsky; student U. Wis., 1937-42; BS, U. Louisville, 1949; student Oxford U. (Eng.), 1953-54; postgrad. McGill U., Montreal, Que., 1958-59; m. Irving P. Kaufman, Nov. 14, 1942 (div. 1949); m. David Steele Bairstow, Dec. 17, 1954; children: Dale Owen, David Anthony. Research economist U.S. Senate Labor-Mgmt. Subcom., Washington, 1950-51; labor edn. specialist U. P.R., San Juan, 1951-52; chief wage data unit WSB, Washington, 1952-53; labor research economist Canadian Pacific Ry. Co., Montreal, 1956-58; asst. dir. indsl. relations centre McGill U., 1960-66, asso. dir., 1966-71, dir., 1971—, lectr., indsl. relations dept. econs., 1960-72, asst. prof. faculty mgmt., 1972-74, assoc. prof. faculty mgmt., 1974-83, prof., 1983—; spl. master Fla. Pub. Employees Relations Commn., 1985—; dep. commr. essential services Province of Que., 1976—; mediator So. Bell Telephone, 1985; cons. on collective bargaining to OECD, Paris, 1979; cons., Nat. Film Bd. of Can., 1965-69; arbitrator Que. Consultative Council Panel of Arbitrators, 1968—, Ministry Labour and Manpower, 1971—, United Airlines, 1989—; mediator Canadian Public Service Staff Relations Bd., 1973—; contbg. columnist Montreal Star, 1971—. Chmn. Nat. Inquiry Commn. Wider-Based Collective Bargaining, 1978. Fulbright fellow, 1953-54. Mem. Canadian Indsl. Relations Research Inst. (exec. bd. 1965-68), Indsl. Relations Research Assn. Am. (mem. exec. bd. 1965-68, chmn. nominating com. 1977), Nat. Acad. Arbitrators (bd. govs. 1977-80, program chmn. 1982-83, v.p. 1986-88, nat. coord. 1987-90), Soc. Profls. in Dispute Resolution (adv. council). Home and Office: 1430 Gulf Blvd #507 Clearwater FL 34630

BAISDEN, ELEANOR MARGUERITE, airline compensation executive, consultant; b. Bklyn., Nov. 7, 1935; d. Vernon McKee and Ethel Mildred (Cockle) Baisden. BA, Hofstra U., 1970. Clk., Trans World Airlines, N.Y.C., 1953-55, sec., 1955-64, compensation analyst, 1964-75, compensation mgr., 1975-85, dir. compensation and orgn. planning, 1985-88, dir. compensation and adminstrn., 1988—. Mem. Airline Personnel Dirs. Conf. (personnel com. 1984-85), Airline Tariff Pub. Co. (personnel com. 1978—), Nat. Fgn. Trade Council (compensation com. 1980-84), Internat. Personnel Assn. (co. rep. 1980-84), Mensa, Alpha Sigma Lambda (Scholar of Yr. 1965-66). Republican. Methodist. Club: Weatherby Lake Yacht (Mo.). Avocations: boating, swimming, piano, travel. Home: 7818 NW Scenic Dr Weatherby Lake MO 64152 Office: Trans World Airlines 11500 Ambassador Dr Kansas City MO 64153

BAIZE, DEBORAH ANN, controller; b. Mansfield, Ohio, Apr. 28, 1963; d. David Lee Iliff and Janice Elaine (Sqrow) Tredway; m. Jeffrey Don Baize, Aug. 30, 1986; 1 child, Lauren Ashley. BS magna cum laude, U. Colo., 1984; MBA, U. Tex., 1986. Acctg. profl. IBM Corp., Boulder, Colo., 1984, San Jose, Calif., 1985; sr. fin. analyst Hughes Communications, L.A., 1986-88; asst. controller Terminal Data Corp., L.A., 1988—. U. Tex. fellow, 1985; U. Tex. scholar, 1986. Mem. Fin. Mgmt. Assn. Nat. Hon. Soc., Colo. Bond Dealer's Assn. (scholarship 1984), MENSA, Phi Kappa Phi, Beta Gamma Sigma, Alpha Delta Pi. Office: Terminal Data Corp 5898 Condor Dr Moorpark CA 93021

BAJWA, LACRETIA YVONNE, computer science executive; b. Sylva, N.C., Feb. 10, 1948; d. William Glenn and Sally Sue (Mincey) Allen; m. Kirti Singh Bajwa, Apr. 8, 1972. BA, So. Ill. U., 1969; MA, Calif. State U., Long Beach, Antioch U., Santa Barbara, Calif. Sr. engr. Martin Marietta Aerospace, Denver, 1978-79; sr. geophysicist Exploration Data Consultants, Lakewood, Colo., 1979-81; mgr. tech. systems Anaconda Minerals Colo., Denver, 1981-84; now dep. dir. CSAT Gen Rsch. Corp., Santa Barbara, 1984-90; pres. Trucking Info. Bur., Inc., Ventura, Calif., 1990—; judge Ventura County Sci. Fair; spl. judge Colo. State Sci. Fair. Contbr. numerous tech. papers and articles to profl. publs.; screenwriter, soundtrack composer for film. Vol. VISTA, 1969-70. Mem. NAFE, Soc. Women Engrs., Assn. Artificial Intelligence, Am. Geophys. Union. Democrat.

BAK, SUNNY, photographer; b. N.Y.C., July 25, 1958; d. Chun Suk and Bie Liang (Kwik) B. AB, CCNY, 1976; postgrad., New Sch. for Social Rsch., N.Y.C., 1982-85, UCLA, 1987. Pres. Sunny Bak Photography, N.Y.C., 1976-83; staff photographer The Hamptons Newspaper Mag., Southampton, N.Y., 1978-84; sec., treas. Sunny Bak Studio, Inc., N.Y.C., 1983-87, pres., 1988—; pres. Sunny Bak Pub. Rels., N.Y.C., 1984-85; dir. pub. rels. H.H. Assocs., N.Y.C. and L.A., 1985-87; dir. west coast ops. KCG Prodns., N.Y.C., 1987-88. Photographer: Vamps, Sirens, Temptresses, 1984-85, 32 covers of Womans World mag., 1985-88, Lic. to Ill, 1987, Pupple, 1988, Detail's mag. cover, 1989. Mem. Advt. Photographer's Am., Assn. Asian Pacific Am. Artists, Asian Pacific Women's Network. Democrat. Buddhist.

BAKAC, ANDREJA, chemist, educator; b. Varazdin, Croatia, Yugoslavia, Feb. 12, 1946; came to U.S., 1976; d. Zora (Bakac) Pekisic. BS in Chemistry, U. Zagreb, Yugoslavia, 1968, MS in Chemistry, 1972, PhD in Chemistry, 1976. Asst. scientist Ames Lab., Iowa State U., 1979-82, assoc. scientist, 1982-84, scientist, 1984—. Reviewer jour. articles, grant proposals; contbr. chpts. to books, articles to profl. jours. Mem. AAAS, Am. Chem. Soc., Ia. Acad. Sci., Sigma Xi. Home: 1432 Breckinridge Ct Ames IA 50010 Office: Ames Lab Iowa State U Ames IA 50011

BAKEMAN, CAROL ANN, administrative services manager, singer; b. San Francisco, Oct. 27, 1934; d. Lars Hartvig and Gwendolyne Beatrice (Zimmer) Bergh; student UCLA, 1954-62; m. Delbert Clifton Bakeman, May 16, 1959; children—Laurie Ann, Deborah Ann. Singer, Roger Wagner Chorale, 1954—, Los Angeles Master Chorale, 1964-86; librarian Hughes Aircraft Co., Culver City, Calif., 1954-61; head econs. library Planning Research Corp., Los Angeles, 1961-63; corporate librarian Econ. Cons., Inc., Los Angeles, 1963-68; head econs. library Daniel, Mann, Johnson & Mendenhall, architects and engrs., Los Angeles, 1969-71, corporate librarian, 1971-77, mgr. info. services, 1978-81, mgr. info. and office services, 1981-83, mgr. adminstrv. services, 1983—. Pres., Creative Library Systems, Los Angeles, 1974-83; library cons. ArchiSystems, div. SUMMA Corp., Los Angeles, 1972-81, Property Rehab. Corp., Bell Gardens, Calif., 1974-75, VTN Corp., Irvine, Calif., 1974, William Pereira & Assos., 1975. Mem. Assistance League, So. Calif., 1956-86, mem. nat. auxilaries com. 1968-72, 75-78, mem. nat. by laws com. 1970-75, mem. asso. bd. dirs., 1966-76. Mem. Am. Guild Musical Artists, AFTRA, Screen Actors Guild, Adminstrv. Mgmt. Soc. (v.p. Los Angeles chpt. 1984-87, pres. 1986-88, internat. conf. chmn. 1988-89, internat. bd. dirs. 1988-90, internat. v.p. mgmt. edn. 1990—), Los Angeles Master Chorale Assn. (bd. dirs. 1978-83), Roger Wagner Choral Inst. (com. planning and devel. 1988—). Office: Daniel Mann Johnson & Mendenhall 3250 Wilshire Blvd Los Angeles CA 90010-1599

BAKER, A. VICKI, interior designer; b. Washington; d. Edwin Marvin and Mary Josephine (Dickhaut) Vaughan; m. Daniel Neil Baker, Aug. 14, 1971. BA, U. Iowa, 1969, MA, 1971; MA, U. Iowa, 1978. Interior designer long range facilities planning dept. U. Calif., Los Alamos (N.Mex.) Nat. Lab., 1979-81, interior designer, 1979-84, project mgr. constrn. project devel., 1981-84, sect. leader design dept., 1984-87; dir. of design Eaton Design Group, McLean, Va., 1987-88; project mgr. interior architecture RTKL Assocs. Inc., Washington, 1988—; dir. environ. enhancement program U. Calif., Los Alamos Nat. Lab., 1985-87, chmn. biennial employee art show, 1985-87. Named Ten Best Interior Design Projects, N.Mex. Bus. Jour., 1986; Tow Grad. scholar U. Iowa, 1975. Mem. NAFE, Internat. Facility Mgmt. Assn., Am. Soc. Interior Designers (affiliate). Avocations: travel, gardening, textile design. Office: RTKL Assocs Inc 1140 Connecticut Ave Washington DC 20036

BAKER, ALTHEA ROSS, lawyer, educator; b. San Francisco, Dec. 24, 1949; d. Vernon and Ethel Ross. BA in Psychology, Pepperdine U., 1970, MA in Clin. Psychology, 1974; JD, Loyola U., L.A., 1984. Bar: Calif. 1984, U.S. Dist. (cen. dist.) Calif. 1985, U.S. Ct. Appeals (9th cir.) 1985; lic. marriage, family and child counselor, Calif. Prof., chmn. dept. L.A. Mission Coll., 1975-89; pvt. practice Santa Monica, Calif., 1985-89; marriage therapist Woodland Hills, Calif., 1976-84; mediator Ctr. Dispute Resolution, Santa Monica, 1987—; atty. Harriet Buhai Family Law Ctr.,L.A., 1988. Mem. Los Angeles County Bar Assn., Women Lawyers L.A., Black Women Lawyers L.A., San Fernando Valley Bar Assn., Women Lawyers San Fernando Valley, San Fernando Valley Marriage and Family Therapists (v.p. 1978), Calif. Fedn. Tchrs. Coll. Guild (exec. bd. local 1521, 1982-89, chief negotiator collective bargaining 1988-89). Democrat. Episcopalian. Home: 1059 Glen Arbor Ave Los Angeles CA 90041 Office: 2953 Lincoln Blvd Santa Monica CA 90405

BAKER, ANITA, singer; b. Toledo, Jan. 26, 1958; m. Walter Bridgeforth, Dec. 24, 1988. Mem. funk band Chapter 8, Detroit, 1978-80; receptionist Quin & Budajh, Detroit, 1980-82; ind. singer, songwriter, 1982—. Rec. artist: (with Chapter 8) I Just Wanna Be Your Girl, 1980, (solo albums) The Songstress, 1983, Rapture, 1986 (Grammy award for best rhythm and blues vocal performance 1987), Giving You the Best That I Got, 1988, Compositions, 1990; songs include No More Tears, Angel, Caught Up in the Rapture, Sweet Love (Grammy award best rhythm and blues song 1987), Same Ol' Love, You Bring Me Joy, Been So Long, No One in the World. Recipient: Grammy award, best rhythm and blues performance, 1990. Office: care Elektra Records 75 Rockefeller Pla New York NY 10019*

BAKER, ANITA DIANE, lawyer; b. Atlanta, Sept. 4, 1955; d. Byron Garnett and Anita (Swanson) B. BA summa cum laude, Oglethorpe U., 1977; JD with distinction, Emory U., 1980. Bar: Ga. 1980. Assoc. Hansell & Post, Atlanta, 1980-88, Kitchens, Kelley, Gaynes, Huprich & Shmerling, 1989—. Mem. ABA (com. on savs. and loan instns.), Atlanta Bar Assn., Ga. Bar Assn., Atlanta Hist. Soc., Pace Acad. Alumni Assn. (bd. dirs.), Order of Coif, Phi Alpha Delta, Phi Alpha Theta, Alpha Chi, Omicron Delta Kappa. Office: Kitchens Kelley Gaynes Huprich & Shmerling 11 Piedmont Ctr Ste 900 Atlanta GA 30305

BAKER, BETTY LOUISE, mathematician, educator; b. Chgo., Oct. 17, 1937; d. Russell James and Lucille Juanita (Timmons) B.: B.E., Chgo. State U., 1961, M.A., 1964; Ph.D., Northwestern U., 1971. Tchr. math. Harper High Sch., Chgo., 1961-70; tchr. math. Hubbard High Sch., Chgo., 1970-85, also chmn. dept.; tchr. Bogan High Sch., 1985—; part-time instr. Moraine Valley Community Coll., 1982-83, 84-86. Cultural arts chmn. Hubbard Parents-Tchrs.-Student Assn., 1974-76, 1st v.p., program chmn., 1977-79, 82-84, pres., 1979-81; organist Hope Lutheran Ch., 1963—. Univ. fellow, 1969-70; cert. tchr. high sch. and elem. grades 3-8 math., Ill. Mem. Nat., Ill. councils tchrs. of math., Math. Assn. Am., Chgo. Tchrs. Union, Nat. Council Parents and Tchrs. (life), Sch. Sci. and Math. Assn., Assn. for Supervision and Curriculum Devel., Am. Guild of Organists, Luth. Collegiate Assn., Kappa Mu Epsilon, Rho Sigma Tau, Mu Alpha Theta (sponsor), Kappa Delta Pi, Pi Lambda Theta, Phi Delta Kappa. Club: Walther League Hiking, Met. Math. Club. of Chgo.. Contbr. articles to profl. jours. Home: 3214 W 85th St Chicago IL 60652 Office: 3939 W 79th St Chicago IL 60652

BAKER, CARRI LYNN, public relations specialist; b. Houston, Sept. 27, 1962; d. William Grosvenor and Toni Rae (Mensing) B. BBA, Tex. A&M U., 1984. Pub. rels. specialist Heard, Goggan, Blair & Williams, San Antonio, 1985—. Pres. Delta Zeta Alumnae Chpt., San Antonio, 1986-88, editor, 1986-89; exec. com. Am. Cancer Soc., San Antonio, 1989—. Recipient Outstanding Newsletter award Delta Zeta Sorority, 1989. Mem. 12th Man Found. (dir. 1989—), San Antonio A&M Club (dir. 1987-88), Women In Communications Inc., World Affairs Coun., Tex. Assn. Sch. Adminstrs., Tex. Assn. Sch. Bus. Officials, Tax Assessor Colletors Assn. Tex. Republican. Methodist. Office: Heard Goggan Blair et al Tower Life Bldg 10th Fl San Antonio TX 78205

BAKER, CHERYL LOUISE, rehabilitation professional; b. Wilmington, Del., Sept. 7, 1948; d. Charles Marion and Marion Elizabeth (Todd) Hunter; m. Clarence Theodore Baker, Oct. 26, 1977 (div. Oct. 1984); 1 child, Jennifer Tioja. AA, Centenary Coll. for Women, 1968; BA, U. Del., 1970, M in Counseling, 1979. Probation officer Family Ct., Wilmington, 1970-71; staffing specialist, trainer Blue Cross/Blue Shield, Wilmington, 1974-81; personnel specialist Howard-Brown Assocs., Wilmington, 1984-85, Magee Rehab. Hosp., Phila., 1985-87; cons. supported employment project Del. Dept. Vocat. Rehab., Wilmington, 1987; rehab. specialist Itracorp, Wilmington, 1988, Hamilton & Jordan, West Chester, Pa., 1988-89, Del. Valley Rehab. Svcs., Wilmington, 1990—. Asst. leader Girl Scout U.S. Troop 201, Newark, Del., 1987—. Mem. Del. Lifelong Learning Network, New Castle County Com. on Employment of People with Disabilities. Mem. Christian Ch. Home: 45 Northfield Rd Newark DE 19713 Office: Del Valley Rehab Svcs 2000 Foulk Rd Ste F Wilmington DE 19810

BAKER, CONNIE L., university program director, educator; b. Oakland, Calif., Dec. 8, 1948; d. Harold Dwight and Lewella Grace (Watson) Smith; m. John Joseph Toth, Sept. 18, 1965 (div. Mar. 1974); 1 child, Juanita; m. Harley Eugene Baker, Apr. 6, 1974; 1 child, Michael. BA, Calif. State U., Stanislaus, 1974; MA, San Jose (Calif.) State U., 1986; postgrad., U. San Francisco, 1989—. Cert. secondary English tchr., Calif. Tchr. secondary English Monte Vista Christian Sch., Watsonville, Calif., 1974-76; social svcs. coord. San Jose City Coll., 1976-78; tchr. secondary English Fremont (Calif.) Christian Sch., 1978-81; tutorial coord. ASPIRE program San Jose State U., 1982-84, dir. ASPIRE program, 1984—. U.S. Dept. Edn. grantee, 1984-87, 87-90, 90—. Mem. Am. Assn. Counseling and Devel., Am. Coll. Personnel Assn., Assn. Handicapped Students in Post-Secondary Edn., Western Assn. Ednl. Opportunity Personnel (bd. dirs. at large 1987-88, coord. No. Calif. chpt. 1988-89), NAFE. Democrat. Office: San Jose State U ASPIRE One Washington Sw WLC-212 San Jose CA 95192

BAKER, DEBORAH WARRINGTON, university administrator; b. Hohenwald, Tenn., Oct. 17, 1949; d. Edward Young and Mattie Nelle (Staggs) W.; divorced; 1 dau., Sarah Elizabeth. B.A., Memphis State U., 1971, postgrad., 1977-78. Asst. editor Holiday Inn Mag. for Travelers, 1971-73, mng. editor, 1973-74; editorial asst. Memphis State U. News Bur., 1975-76; asst. dir. Memphis State U. Office Media Relations, 1976-78; dir. communications and public relations Mid-South Fair, Libertyland, Inc., Memphis, 1978-79; dir. media rels. Memphis State U., 1979—. Bd. dirs. Lowenstein House, 1984-85. Mem. Pub. Rels. Soc. Am., Tenn. Coll. Pub. Rels. Assn. (sec. 1982, bd. dirs. 1986—). Office: Memphis State Univ Adminstrn Bldg Rm 303 Memphis TN 38152

BAKER, ELLEN HARTE, administrator; b. Milton, Mass., Sept. 2, 1944; d. Charles Aloysius Sr. and Edith Ann (Nolan) B. BA, Emmanuel Coll., Boston, 1966; MA, U. Ala., 1968; PhD, U. Wisc., 1969; MBA, Boston Coll., 1980. Asst. acctg. mgr. Gilchrist Co., Boston, 1971-73, controller, 1974-77; from asst. acctg. mgr. to administr. exec. compensation plan Federated Dept. Stores Inc., Cin., 1977-88, adminstrv. exec. benefits, 1989, mgr. retirement plans, 1990—; fin. mgr. St. George Newman Ctr., Cin., 1977—. Roman Catholic. Home: 3022 Euclid Ave Cincinnati OH 45219

BAKER, ELLEN SHULMAN, physician, astronaut; b. Fayetteville, N.C., Apr. 27, 1953; d. Melvin Shulman; m. Kenneth J. Baker; 1 child, Karen Sarah. BA in Geology, SUNY, Buffalo; MD, Cornell U., 1978. Diplomate Am. Bd. Internal Medicine. Resident U. Tex. Health Sci. Ctr., San Antonio; med. officer NASA Lyndon B. Johnson Space Ctr., Houston, 1981-84, astronaut candidate, 1984-85, astronaut, 1985—, mission specialist Shuttle Orbiter Atlantis Flight STS-34, 1989. Address: NASA Johnson Space Ctr Astronaut Office Houston TX 77058*

BAKER, FAITH MERO, educator; b. Pitts., May 9, 1941; d. Vincent G. and Georgetta (Rothwell) Mero; m. Gerald A. Baker, Dec. 22, 1968; children: Jeremy D., Kara L. BA, Carlow Coll., Pitts., 1963; MEd, U. Pitts., 1965, postgrad., 1966-68. Cert. elem. and spl. edn. tchr., Pa. Tchr. sci. Pitts. Pub. Schs., 1963-64, tchr. spl. edn., 1968-87, tchr., primary sci. specialist, 1987—; leader instrnl. team Fulton Acad., Pitts., 1988—; facilitator, tchr. Project Wild and project Aquatic Wild, Project Learning Tree, Pitts., 1988—. Leader Girl Scouts U.S.A., Monroeville, Pa., 1979-86; mem. Supts. Roundtable Gateway Schs., Monroeville, Pa., 1987-89. Mem. Pitts. Fedn. Tchrs. (bldg. steward 1968—), Pa. Bus. and Profl. Women's Assn. (asst. bd. dirs. dist. 3, pres. Monroeville club 1987-88), AAUW, U. Pitts. Alumni Assn. (1st v.p. 1987-88, sec. 1989—), Fedn. Bus. and Profl. Women's Club (dir. elect dist. 3, asst. dir. 1989-90), Delta Kappa Gamma, Alpha Delta Kappa, Phi Delta Gamma (Kappa chpt. sec. 1986-90, pres. 1982-84, regional coord. 1984-86). Democrat. Roman Catholic. Home: 102 Penn Lear Dr Monroeville PA 15146 Office: Fulton Acad Hampton St Pittsburgh PA 15206

BAKER, GWENDOLYN CALVERT, association executive; b. Ann Arbor, Mich., Dec. 31, 1931; m. James; children: JoAnn, Claudia, James Jr. BA, U. Mich., 1964, MA, 1968, PhD, 1972. Tchr. Ann Arbor Pub. Schs., 1964-69; lectr. U. Mich., 1969-70, instr., 1970-72, assoc. prof., 1972-76, dir. affirmative action programs, 1976-78; chief minorities and womens' programs Nat. Inst. Edn., Washington, 1978-84; v.p., dean, graduate and children's programs Bank St. Coll. Edn., N.Y.C., 1981-84; exec. dir. YWCA of U.S.A., N.Y.C., 1984—. Office: YWCA of the USA 726 Broadway New York NY 10003*

BAKER, HELEN DOYLE PEIL, realtor; b. Los Angeles, June 26, 1943; d. James Cyril and Jacqueline (White) Doyle; m. Gary Edward Peil, Aug. 5, 1967 (dec. May 6, 1969); children: Andrea Christine, Kevin Doyle; m. Nathaniel W. Baker, Jr., Jan. 1, 1971 (div. July 23, 1983). AA, Santa Monica Coll., 1963; postgrad., U. Wash., 1963-64. Licensed real estate agent. Sales, mgmt. trainee Saks Fifth Ave., Beverly Hills, Calif., 1958-63; flight attendant Am. Airlines, Los Angeles, 1964-67; realtor, assoc. Stapleton Assocs., Honolulu, 1978-80; realtor Dolman Assocs. Inc., Kailua, Hawaii, 1980-87; loan rep. Honolulu Mortgage Co., Kailua, 1986-87; pres., owner, realtor Helen Baker Properties, Inc., Honolulu, 1987—; pres. Global Listing Svc. Hawaii Inc., 1990—. Dir. Kailua Community Council, 1987—; pres., v.p., sec. Aikahi Community Assn., Kailua, 1980-85; vol. Am. Cancer Soc., Heart Assn. Schs., Kailua, 1971-86. Mem. Nat. Assn. Realtors, Hawaii Assn. Realtors, Honolulu Bd. Realtors, Real Estate Brokerage Council, Realtors Nat. Mktg. Inst., Hist. Hawaii Found., C. of C., Rotary. Office: Helen Baker Properties Inc Seven Waterfront Plaza #507 Honolulu HI 96813

BAKER, HELEN HICKS, medical association administrator; b. Greenup, Ky., Dec. 20, 1950; d. Henry and Thelma (Kaut) Hicks. BA, Berea Coll., 1972; MEd, U. N.C., 1975, PhD, 1978; MBA, U. Ariz., 1982. Rsch. asst. U. N.C. Sch. Medicine, Chapel Hill, 1975-78; evaluation cons. U. Ariz. Sch. Medicine, Tucson, 1978-82; assoc. prof. family medicine, asst. dean Ohio U. Coll. Osteo. Medicine, Athens, 1982-88; assoc. dir. Am. Osteo. Assn., Chgo., 1988—. Mem. Am. Ednl. Rsch. Assn. Office: Am Osteo Assn 142 E Ontario St Chicago IL 60611

BAKER, JAN ELIESE, nurse; b. St. Louis, Mar. 11, 1958; d. Stanley Vernon and Faye Eliese (Farrell) B.; m. John Rogers Kennington, May 4, 1990. Diploma in Nursing, Mo. Bapt. Hosp., St. Louis, 1979; BS, U. Mo., 1982; MS, U. Utah, 1989. RN, Mo., Utah. Charge nurse DePaul Community Hosp., St. Louis, 1979-80; camp nurse Camp Thunderbird, Bemidji, Minn., 1980; charge nurse U. Mo. Hosp., Columbia, 1981-83; traveling nurse various traveling nursing cos. in U.S., 1983-84; charge nurse, acting head nurse Wasatch Canyons Hosp., LDS Hosp., Salt Lake City, 1984-87; charge nurse, clin. nurse U. Utah, Salt Lake City, 1987-89, rsch. nurse, 1989—; co-investigator U. Utah, 1988—. Contbr. articles to numerous nursing jours. Active, co-leader for head injury support group Utah Ind. Living Ctr., Salt Lake City, 1985—; coord. free seminar to pub. U. Utah, 1989. Grantee NIMH, 1987-89. Mem. Sigma Theta Tau (Gamma Rho chpt.). Office: U of Utah Dept Ob/Gyn Rm 2B200 50 N Medical Dr Salt Lake City UT 84132

BAKER, JANE ELAINE, municipal government official; b. Hamilton, Ohio, June 4, 1923; d. Ernst Andrew and Lillian (Schaub) Grimmer; m. Harris William Baker, Mar. 8, 1945; children: Cindi Marie, Bruce William. BS, Purdue U., 1944. Nutritionist Stokely-Van Camp Corp., Indpls., 1944-45, Cornell U., Ithaca, N.Y., 1945-46; dietitian U. Colo., Boulder, 1946; nutritionist Dairy Coun. of Indpls., 1947-48; performer Stas. KGO and KRON-TV, San Francisco, 1949-51, Sta. KNTV, San Jose, Calif., 1952; coun. member City of San Mateo, Calif., 1973—, mayor, 1975-76, 78-80, 82-83, 87-88; mem. Met. Transp. Commn., Oakland, Calif., 1983—. Mem. State Job Tng. Coordinating Coun., Sacramento, 1984—; past pres. League of Calif. Cities, Sacramento, bd. dirs., 1979—; sec. Coyote Mus., 1975; bd. dirs. Nat. League of Cities, 1988-90. Recipient Outstanding Alumnus award family and consumer sci. dept. Purdue U., 1986. Mem. AAUW (pres. San Mateo br. 1979), LWV. Republican. Presbyterian. Home: 1464 Woodberry San Mateo CA 94403 Office: City of San Mateo 330 W 20th Ave San Mateo CA 94403

BAKER, JANET LENZ, educator; b. Newark, Dec. 23, 1943; d. Proctor Bond and Janet Carver (Lenz) B. AA, Marjorie Webster Jr. Coll., Washington, 1963. Tchr. phys. edn., coach, athletic dir. Vail-Deane Sch., Elizabeth, N.J., 1963-69; tchr. phys. edn., coach Princeton (N.J.) Day Sch., 1969-71, athletic dir., 1971—, adminstr., athletic dir., 1988—; coord. N.J. Ind. Sch. Girls Soccer Tournament, 1985—, Mercer County Boys and Girls Tennis Tournament, 1986—. Chmn. property com. Windsor Mill Condominium Assn., East Windsor, N.J., 1985-88, 89—. Mem. AAHPER and Dance, N.J. Assn. Health, Phys. Edn. and Recreation, Nat. Assn. Athletic Dirs., N.J. Inter-Scholastic Athletic Assn. (affiliate), N.J. Assn. Ind. Schs., World Wildlife Fund. Republican. Episcopalian. Home: 723 Wood Mill Dr Cranbury NJ 08512 Office: Princeton Day Sch The Great Rd Princeton NJ 08542

BAKER, JEAN HARVEY, history educator; b. Balt., Feb. 9, 1933; d. F. Barton and Rose (Lindsay) Hopkins Harvey; m. F. Robinson Baker, Sept. 12, 1953; children—Susan Dixon, Robinson Scott, Robert W., Jean Harvey. A.B., Goucher Coll., Towson, Md., 1961; M.A., Johns Hopkins U., Balt., 1965, Ph.D., 1971. Lectr., instr. history Notre Dame Coll., Balt., 1967-69; instr. history Goucher Coll., Balt., 1969, asst. prof. history, 1969-75, assoc. prof. history, 1975-78, prof. history, 1979-82, Elizabeth Todd prof. history, 1981—. Author: The Politics of Continuity, 1973, Ambivalent Americans, 1976, Affairs of Party, 1983 (Berkshire prize in history), Maryland: A History, Mary Todd Lincoln: A Biography, 1986; editor Md. Hist. Mag., 1979. Fellow Am. Coun. Learned Socs., 1976, NEH, 1982; recipient Faculty Teaching prize Goucher Coll., 1979, Willie Lee Rose prize in Southern history, 1989. Mem. Orgn. Am. Historians, Am. Hist. Assn., Berkshire Conf. Women Historians, Phi Beta Kappa. Democrat. Home: 8717 McDonough Rd Baltimore MD 21208 Office: Goucher Coll Towson MD 21204

BAKER, JEAN MARY, cable TV executive; b. Laconia, N.H., July 24, 1944; d. Marshall Dwight and Eugenia Mary (O'Mara) Whedon; m. Frank J. Haley, Feb. 3, 1968 (div. Feb. 1978); children: Kathleen A., Colleen E.; m. Frank J. Baker, July 6, 1985 (dec. Sept. 1986). Grad. high sch., Laconia, N.H.; student, Palm Beach Community Coll., 1988—. Supr. OS & D Willeys Express, Concord, N.H., 1974-80; exec. sec. Perry Cable TV, Riviera Beach, Fla., 1981-84; ops. mgr. Perry Cable TV, Riviera Beach, 1984-86; community devel. mgr. Centel Cable TV of Fla., Palm Beach Gardens, 1986-88, Alelphia Cable Communications, Palm Baech Gardens, Fla., 1988—. Team capt. March of Dimes, Walkamerica, West Palm Beach, Fla., 1987-90, steering com., 1990; adv. bd. Palm Beach Community Coll. Lit. Forum, Palm Beach Gardens, 1988-89; mem. pub. rels. bd. Am. Cancer Soc., 1989. Named Vol. of Yr. No. Palm Beach C. of C., 1989. Mem. Women in Cable (pres. S. Fla. chpt. 1988, bd. dirs. 1989), Home Builders and Contractors Assn. Home: PO Box 873 Jupiter FL 33468 Office: Adelphia Cable Communications 10435 Ironwood Rd Palm Beach Gardens FL 33410

BAKER, JEANETTE SLEDGE, educational administrator; b. Atlanta, June 24, 1947; d. Jesse Alexander and Carolyn (Chapman) Sledge; m. Donald Todd Baker, Sept. 6, 1969. B.Mus., Fla. STate U., 1970; MEd, U. Ariz., 1980, PhD, 1983; student, U. Fla., 1965-67. Asst. admissions and fin. aid officer Columbia U., N.Y.C., 1970-72; degree cert. officer U. Ariz., Tucson, 1972-82, acad. advisor, 1982-84; asst. to v.p. No. Ariz. U., Flagstaff, 1984-87, asst. v.p., 1987-89, assoc. v.p., 1989—. Contbr. to book: At The Crossroads: General Education in Community Colleges, 1983. Chmn. Coconino County Silent Witness Bd., Flagstaff, 1988-89 vice chmn. 1987. Mem. Flagstaff C. of C., Nat. Assn. Female Execs., We. States Govtl. Relations Network. Office: No Ariz U PO Box 4115 Flagstaff AZ 86011-4115

BAKER, JOANNE EVELYN, government official; b. Crucible, Pa., Dec. 1, 1933; d. George Joseph and Anna Leona (Kagle) Cormack; m. Warren Clair Baker, July 7, 1956 (dec. May 1968); m. James Lewis Wilson, June 2, 1970; (div. Sept. 1984); former stepchildren: James Lloyd, John Thomas, Charles Edward, Debra Ruth, Jeff Lee Wilson. Cert. applied music Waynesburg Coll., 1951. Various clerical positions, 1951-66; supr. U.S. Navy, Washington, 1966-71; pres., treas. Little Round Top Farm, Inc., Gettysburg, Pa., 1971-86; logistician U.S. Navy-U.S. Army, 1974-81; insp. Office of Insp. Gen., U.S. Army, Ft. Ritchie, Md., 1981-84; chief supply and svcs. div. Fort Detrick, Frederick, Md., 1985-89, chief plans and resources mgmt. div., 1989-90. Author: Reflections, 1974. Bd. dirs. Adams County Mental Health Assn., Gettysburg, 1982-87. Recipient Sustained Superior Achievement award Dept. Navy, 1975, Dept. of Army 1986; named Outstanding Woman of Yr. Ft. Detrick, 1986. Mem. Internat. Graphoanalysis Soc. (Pa. chpt.), Internat. Platform Assn., Adams County Amateur Radio Soc., World Inst. of Achievement (life). Roman Catholic. Avocations: handwriting analysis, writing children's stories, ceramics, piano, studying self-improvement and psychology. Home: 5605 Shookstown Rd Frederick MD 21702-2704

BAKER, JUSTINE CLARA, mathematics and physics educator, researcher; b. Phila., Oct. 1, 1939; d. Michael Angelo and Justine Catherine (DeFlavia) Boni; m. Harold Jerome Baker, July 23, 1966. A.B., Immaculata Coll., 1963; M.A.T.M., Villanova U., 1970; M.S. in Edn., U. Pa., 1973, Ph.D., 1987. Tchr. math. and sci. pvt. and parochial area schs., Phila. area, 1963-66; tchr. math. Phila. High Schs., 1967-69; tchr. math. and sci. parochial and pvt. and pub. area schs., Phila. and Willingboro, N.J., 1973-80; instr. Goldey Beacom Coll., Wilmington, Del., 1980-84; asst. prof. Del. County Community Coll., Media, Pa., 1984-85; systems engr. RCA Moorestown, N.J., 1985-87; tchr. math. and physics Swarthmore (Pa.) Acad., 1987-88; instr. math. and edn. West Chester (Pa.) U., 1988—; adj. instr. edn. rsch. Cabrini Coll., Radnor, Pa., 1989—. Author: The Computer in the School, 1975; Computers in the Curriculum, 1976; Microcomputers in the Classroom, 1982. Mem. Am. Ednl. Rsch. Assn., Math. Assn. Am., Nat. Coun. Tchrs. Math., Phi Delta Kappa (cert. of recog. 1976, 81, 82, 83, 84, service key 1982). Republican. Roman Catholic. Clubs: Edn. Alumni Assn., U. Pa. Alumnae Assn. Immaculata Coll. Home: 1021 Drexel Ave Drexel Hill PA 19026 Office: West Chester U West Chester PA 19383

BAKER, KATHERINE JUNE, educator; b. Dallas, Feb. 3, 1932; d. Kirk Moses and Katherine Faye (Turner) Sherrill; m. George William Baker, Jan. 30, 1955; children: Kirk Garner, Kathleen Kay. BS, BA, Tex. Women's U., 1953, MEd, 1979; cert. in religious edn., Meadville Theol. U., 1970; postgrad., North Tex. State U., 1987—; DD (hon.), Am. Fellowship Ch., 1981. Cert. elem., secondary tchr., adminstr., Tex. Mgr. prodn. Woolf Bros., Dallas, 1953-55; display mgr. J.M. Dyer and Co., Corsicana, Tex., 1954; advt. artist Fair Dept. Store, Ft. Worth, 1954-56; artist, instr. Dutch Art Gallery, Dallas, 1960-65; dir. religious edn. 1st Unitarian Ch., Dallas, 1967-69; dir. day care, tchr. Richardson (Tex.) Unitarian Ch., 1971-73; dir. camp Tres Rios YWCA, Glen Rose, Tex., 1975-76; dir. program of extended sch. instrn. Hamilton Park Elem. Sch. Richardson Ind. Sch. Dist., 1975-78, tchr. Dover Elem. Sch., 1978-79, tchr. Jess Harben Elem. Sch., 1979—. Contbr. articles to ch. newspaper, 1967-69; exhibited in group show at Tex. Art Assn., 1966; one-woman show Dutch Art Gallery - Northlake Ctr., Dallas, 1965. Advocate day care Unitarian Universalist Women's Fedn., Boston, 1975-76, mem. nominating com., 1976-77. Mem. NEA, Nat. Council Social Studies, Assn. Supervision and Curriculum Devel., Tex. State Tchrs. Assn. (treas. Richardson chpt. 1984-85), Women's Ctr. Dallas, Sokol Athletic Ctr., Smithsonian Assn., Dallas Mus. Assn., Alpha Chi, Delta Phi Delta (pres. 1952-53), Phi Delta Kappa. Democrat. Club: Toastmistresses. Home: 2711 Sherrill Park Dr Richardson TX 75082

BAKER, LILLIAN, author, historian, artist, lecturer; b. Yonkers, N.Y., Dec. 12, 1921; m. Roscoe A. Baker; children: Wanda Georgia, George Riley. Student, El Camino (Calif.) Coll., 1952, UCLA, 1968, 77. Continuity writer Sta. WINS, N.Y.C., 1945-46; columnist, freelance writer, reviewer Gardena (Calif.) Valley News, 1964-76; freelance writer, editor Gardena, 1971—; lectr. in field.; founder/editor Internat. Club for Collectors of Hatpins and Hatpin Holders, monthly newsletter Points, ann. Pictorial Jour., 1977—, conv. and seminar coord., 1979, 82, 84, 87, 90. Author: Collector's Encyclopedia of Hatpins and Hatpin Holders, 1976, second edit. 1988, 100 Years of Collectible Jewelry 1850-1950, 1978, rev. edit., 1986, 88, 89, Art Nouveau and Art Deco Jewelry, 1980, rev. edit. 1985, 87, 88, The Concentration Camp Conspiracy: A Second Pearl Harbor, 1981 (Scholarship Category award of Merit, Conf. of Calif. Hist. Socs. 1983), Hatpins and Hatpin Holders: An Illustrated Value Guide, 1983, rev. edit. 1988, Creative and Collectible Miniatures, 1984, Fifty Years of Collectible Fashion Jewelry: 1925-1975, 1986, rev. edit., 1988, Dishonoring America: The Collective Guilt of American Japanese, 1988, American and Japanese Relocation in World War II: Fact Fiction and Fallacy, 1989, Redress and Reparations Demands by Japanese Americans, 1990; established The Lillian Baker Collection Hoover Archives, 1989; author poetry; contbg. author Vol. VII Time-Life Encyclopedia of Collectibles, 1979; numerous radio and TV appearances. Co-founder Ams. for Hist. Accuracy, 1972, Com. for Equality for All Draftees, 1973; chair S. Bay election campaign S.I. Hayakawa, for U.S. Senator from Calif., 1976; witness U.S. Commn. Wartime Relocation, 1981, U.S. Senate Judiciary Com., 1983, U.S. Ho. Reps. Judiciary Com., 1986, U.S. Ho. Reps. Subcommittee on Appropriations, 1989. Recipient award Freedoms Found., 1971, Ann. award Conf. Calif. Hist. Socs., 1983, monetary award Hoover Instn. Stanford (Calif.) U., 1985, award Pro-Am. Orgn., 1987, Golden Poet award Internat. Poets Soc., 1989. Fellow IBA (life); mem. Nat. League Am. Pen Women, Nat. Writers Club, Soc. Jewelry Historians USA, (charter), Art Students League N.Y. (life), Nat. Historic Soc. (founding), Nat. Trust Historic Preservation (founding), other orgns. Home and Office: 15237 Chanera Ave Gardena CA 90249

BAKER, LINDA ANN, public finance company executive; b. Quonset Point, R.I., Apr. 30, 1949; d. Edward and Ruth Ann (Barker) Rapacz; m. Joel David Baker, Aug. 22, 1970; children: Alexis Ann, Brooke Marie. BA, Gordon Coll., 1970. Legal asst. Pitts, Eubanks, Ross & Rumberger, Orlando, Fla., 1973-74; Dixon, Dixon, Lane & Mitchell, Miami, Fla., 1974-75; legal asst. Armco Steel Corp., Middletown, Ohio, 1975-76, Henkle Schueler Assocs., Lebanon, Ohio, 1976-77, Reynolds & Reynolds, Dayton, Ohio, 1978-79; mktg. rep. Roselius Computer Corp., Edmond, Okla., 1980-83; v.p. Pub. Leasing Corp., Oklahoma City, 1983-85; pres. Capital Fin. Assets, Inc., Edmond, Okla., 1985-89, Baker Capital Corp., Edmond, Okla., 1989—. Mem. exec. com. Presbyterians for Renewal. Mem. Assn. Govt. Leasing and Fin., Edmond Women's Club. Democrat. Office: Baker Capital Corp 905 S Bryant Edmond OK 73034

BAKER, LINDA LESLIE, social services administrator, consultant; b. Eugene, Oregon, Sept. 15, 1948; d. Charles Andrew and Ashley Estelle (Durrett) Marcum; m. Brent Delos Cain, May 28, 1983. BS in Psychology, Ft. Hays (Kans.) State U., 1972, MS in Counseling, 1973; MSW, U. Kans., 1984. Lic. Social Worker. Social worker Dept. Social and Rehab. Svcs., Topeka, 1972-79; foster care program specialist Kans. Children's Svc. League, Topeka, 1979—, dist. dir., 1983-88; dir. programs Kans. Children's Svc. League, 1989; cons. Nat. Directory Foster Care Program and Ednl. Consultant, 1985—; cons., trainer Permanency Planning Resources for Children, 1983—; field instr. U. Kans., 1986—; tech. advisor NASW Communications Network, Inc. Active Kans. Children and Adolescent Svc. System Programs, Topeka, 1985-86, Children's Coalition, Topeka, 1985-86; mem. adv. bd. Family Svc. and Guidance Ctr., Topeka, 1985-86, Family Preservation Project, 1986—, Kans. Foster Care Task Force, 1988—, Kans. Adoption Coalition, 1989; mem. Kans. Com. for Prevention Child Abuse. Mem. NAFE, Nat. Assn. Social Workers, Kans. Assn. Social Workers, Kans. Conf. Social Welfare, Kans. Polit. Action for Candidate Election, Topeka Assn. Human Svc. Agys. (exec. treas. 1983-86, exec. v.p. 1986-87, pres. 1987), Coun. on Children and Families (sec. 1979—), Civitans, Phi Kappa Phi. Democrat. Home: 2649 SW Ashworth Pl Topeka KS 66614 Office: Kans Children's Svc League 2053 Kansas Ave Topeka KS 66605

BAKER, LORI ANN, physical therapist; b. Detroit, July 16, 1957; d. Richard Gary and Mary Barbara (Vail) Griffith; m. Joseph Kurtyka, Nov. 22, 1980 (div. Sept. 1984); m. William Randall Baker, June 24, 1989. BS, U. Mich., 1979; postgrad., Kennesaw Coll., 1986—. Phys. therapist Lansing Sch. Dist., Mich., 1979-81, Mich. Sch. for Blind, 1980-81, Ingham Med. Ctr., 1980-81; pediatric phys. therapist Toledo Hosp., 1981-84, Childrens Ortho Hosp. and Med. Ctr., Seattle, 1984-85; pediatric clin. specialist Kennestone Hosp., Marietta Ga., 1985-89, supr. acute care therapy, 1989—; phys. therapist Am. Home Health Care, 1987—. Mem. Am. Phys. Therapy Assn., Neurodevelopmental Treatment Assn. Avocations: stained glass; furniture refinishing; collection of Oriental art; backpacking; cooking. Home and Office: 2923 Country Ln Kennesaw GA 30144

BAKER, LORI KAY, freelance writer; b. Mesa, Ariz., Apr. 10, 1958; d. Frank Grzesiek and Lois Ellen (Sims) Grzesiek Pence; m. Robert Lee Baker, Sept. 12, 1987; 1 child, Alana Jordan. BA magna cum laude, Ariz. State U., 1985. Newspaper reporter Phoenix Gazette, 1979-81, Tempe (Ariz.) Daily News, 1981; freelance reporter Oreg. Jour., Portland, 1981-82; computer programmer Nike, Inc., Beaverton, Oreg., 1983-84, Motorola, Inc., Phoenix, 1984-85; systems analyst City of Mesa, 1985-87; freelance writer Mesa, 1987—. Author numerous articles. William Randolph Hearst Found. grantee, 1979. Mem. Women in Communications Inc., Ariz. Press Women, Phi Beta Kappa. Office: 945 N Pasadena 96 Mesa AZ 85201

BAKER, LORRAINE, educational administrator; b. Los Angeles, Aug. 20, 1935; d. Herbert McDowell and Izalia Lewena (Fee) Young; m. Rolland A. Baker, March 16, 1965; children: Glenn Alin, Eric Jon; AA, Los Angeles City Coll., 1955; BA, Calif. State U., 1972, MEd, U. LaVerne (Calif.), 1978; cert. sch. mgmt., Center for Ednl. Leadership, 1975-76. Tchr., La Canada (Calif.) Unified Sch. Dist., 1972-76, prin. Paradise Canyon Sch., 1976-79, bldg. adminstr. Foothill Intermediate Sch., 1979-80, dir. curriculum, 1980-84, dir. instructional services, 1984-87; dir. tchr. edn. Azusa (Calif.) Pacific U., 1987-88; cons. sch. dists., 1988—; pres. Confidential, Managerial, Supervisorial Assn., 1985-87. Kettering Found. fellow, 1984, Rockefeller Found. fellow, 1975; recipient Hon. Service award, Calif. Congress Parents and Tchrs., 1967. Mem. Glendale (Calif.) Symphony Women's Aux., chmn. scholarship com., 1988—; mem. San Fernando Valley (Calif.) Assn. for Retarded Persons, 1970—; chmn. BLASST Consortium for categorically funded programs, 1985-87. Mem. Assn. Supervision and Curriculum Devel., AAUW, Assn. Calif. Sch. Adminstrs., Women in Bus. (chmn. Retreat com. 1986—), Altrusa (chmn. community services 1987-88, tutor functionally illiterate 1987—), Phi Delta Kappa. Avocations: travel, profl. pianist.

BAKER, MADELINE RUTH, pharmacist; b. Nassawadox, Va., Sept. 5, 1963; d. Allan Cherricks and Shirley May (Kelley) B. BS in Pharmacy, Ohio No. U., 1986. Registered pharmacist, Del., Md. Pharmacist, asst. mgr. Thrift Drug Co., Millsboro, Del., 1986—; lectr. Am. Lung Assn., Salisbury, Md., 1987—. Mem. choir Wilson United Meth. Ch., Bishopville, Md., 1987. Mem. Am. Pharm. Assn., Am. Lung Assn. Md., Ocean City Health and Racquetball Club (Md.), Alpha Zeta Omega. Republican. Home: Box 129 RFD Bishopville MD 21813 Office: Thrift Drug Co Midsussex Shopping Ctr Millsboro DE 19966

BAKER, MARGARET ANN, chiropractor; b. Birmingham, Ala., Dec. 17, 1955; d. Elijah Edward and Charlsie Mae (Carter) B.; m. William Gene Porter, Dec. 26, 1973 (div. 1977); 1 child, April Michelle. Student, Jefferson State Jr. Coll., Birmingham, Ala., 1974-76, Birmingham So. Coll., 1974-77, Tex. Chiropractic Coll., Pasadena, 1977-78, Life Chiropractic Coll., Marietta, Ga., 1978-80. Cert. Dr. of Chiropractic. Ptnr., staff physician Baker Assn. P.C., Birmingham, Ala., 1980-88; pvt. practice Baker Chiropractic Ctr. P.C., Hoover, Ala., 1988—; dir. intern, extern program, Ala. Bd. Chiropractic Examiners, Robertsdale, 1985-87. Mem. Am. Chiropractic Assn., Fla. Chiropractic Assn., Ala. Chiropractic Assn., Jefferson County Chiropractic Soc., Hoover C. of C., Hoover Jaycees, Sigma Phi Chi. Republican. Roman Catholic. Office: 3100 Lorna Rd Ste 300 Birmingham AL 35216

BAKER, MARIAN GRAY, health facility administrator; b. Youngstown, Ohio, Feb. 5, 1931; d. James Edward and Josie Bell (Alston) Chambers; m. James Melvin Baker, Aug. 2, 1958 (div. 1971). BS, Wash. U., 1958; MA, Wayne State U., 1976. Reg. Occupatinal Therapist. Staff therapist Deaconess Hosp., St. Louis, 1958-63; dir. occupational therapy Pontiac (Mich.) Gen. Hosp., 1963—; cons. Grovecrest Care Center, Clarkston Mich., 1983--. Mem. Cultural Council, Pontiac; bd. dirs. YWCA. Mem. Am. Occupational Therapy Assn., Mich. Occupational Therapy Assn., Black Occupational Therapy Caucus, Nat. Assn. Negro Bus. and Profl. Womens Clubs, Pontiac Club (pres. 1987—), Elks Women Aux., Delta Sigma Theta. Democrat. Baptist. Home: 179 Oneida Pontiac MI 48341

BAKER, MARY JORDAN, educator; b. Chgo. A.B., Stanford U., 1961; M.A., U. Va., 1964; Ph.D. in Romance Lang., Harvard U., 1969. Instr. French, DePauw U., 1964-65; asst. prof. U. Tex.-Austin, 1968-75, assoc. prof. French, 1975-88—; prof. 1988—. Contbr. articles to profl. jours. Recipient Pres. Assocs. Teaching Excellence award 1980, Jean Holloway Excellence in Teaching award, 1987. Mem. MLA, Am. Assn. Tchrs. French, Soc. Study Narrative Literature, Modern Humanities Research Assn. Co-author: Panaché Littéraire, 1978. Address: French Dept Univ Tex Austin TX 78712*

BAKER, NELL WILLIAMS, medical record administrator; b. Bond, Miss., Dec. 29, 1934; d. William Wesley and Lela Elizabeth (DeLancey) Williams; div.; children: Richard Wesley Baker, Brian Christopher Baker. BA in Health Info. Adminstrn., Coll. St. Scholastica, Duluth, Minn., 1987. Dir. med. records Meth. Hosp. Stone County, Wiggins, Miss., 1970—, hosp.-wide quality assurance coord., 1989—. Mem. Am. Med. Records Assn., Am. Bd. Quality Assurance and Utilization Rev., Miss. Med. Record Assn. Roman Catholic. Home: 110 Pump Branch Rd Wiggins MS 39577 Office: Meth Hosp Stone County 1434 E Central Ave Wiggins MS 39577

BAKER, PATRICIA ALICE, printing company executive; b. N.Y.C., Sept. 15, 1940; d. Emil Vincent Lutringer and Alice (Rich) Danser; m. Darrell Dean Baker, Nov. 20, 1964; children: Michael, Pamela. BA, U. Miami, Fla., 1962. Tax preparer H & R Block, St. Petersburg, Fla., 1969-80; tchr. Harvest Temple Christian Sch., Largo, Fla., 1977-79; owner, mgr. Baho Graphics, Largo, 1980—. Pinellas County State Rep. Committeewoman, 1988—; mem. Pinellas County Bd. Adjustments; mem. adv. bd. Seminole Community Sch., 1986-89; mem. adv. bd. Pinellas Voc. Tech. Sch., Graphic Arts div., 1988—; pres. Madeira Beach Elem. Sch. PTO, 1975-77. Mem. Printing Industry Fla., Seminole Rep. Club (past first v.p.), Seminole C. of C. (sec. and dir. 1982-84). Mem. Assembly of God Ch. Home: 11644 Irving St Seminole FL 34642 Office: Baho Graphics 6840 Cross Bayou Dr Largo FL 34647

BAKER, PATRICIA MARIE, computer sales executive; b. N.Y., Apr. 26, 1961; d. William Joseph and Patricia Ann (McHugh) B. Student, La Guardia Community Coll., Long Island City, 1979-80, Queensboro Community Coll., Bayside, N.Y., 1985-86. Lic. Real Estate Agt. Real estate agt. A.B.C. Realty Inc., Ozone Park, N.Y., 1979-1981; mktg. rep. Digital Equipment Corp., N.Y., 1981-85; sales rep. Digital Equipment Corp., Tarrytown, N.Y., 1985--. Mem. N.Y. State Realtors Assn., Long Island Bd. Realtors. Republican. Roman. Catholic. Home: 157-20 101 St Howard Beach NY 11414 Office: Digital Equipment Corp 200 White Plains Rd Tarrytown NY 10591

BAKER, ROBIN ROSE, veterinarian; b. Strawberry, Iowa, Sept. 28, 1959; d. Paul Ludvick and Margarete Mathilda (Dunnwolf) Mills; m. Roger John Baker, Apr. 6, 1960. BS, Iowa State U., 1982, DVM, 1987. Veterinarian Cedar Grove (Wis.) Vet. Svcs., 1987—. Mem. AVMA, Am. Assn. Bovine Practitioners, Nat. Holstein Assn., Wis. Vet. Med. Assn., Iowa Holstein Assn. Republican. Lutheran. Office: Cedar Grove Vet Svcs 23 Hwy RR Cedar Grove WI 53013

BAKER, SHEILA ANN, technical writer; b. Atlantic City, N.J., Oct. 19, 1944; d. Herman and Florence Frances (Richer) B.; m. Loren H. Cohen, Oct. 1963 (div. 1969); 1 child, Dana Hilary Cohen; m. Mark Andrew Nielsen, Oct. 26, 1984. BA, Boston U., 1967, U. Iowa, 1967. Tchr. Lisbon (Iowa) Community Sch., 1967-70; tchr. Lone Tree (Iowa) Community Sch., 1970-71; editor Iowa Geol. Survey, Iowa City, 1984; editor, tech. writer Exxon Prodn. Rsch. Co., Houston, 1985; geol. technician Exxon USA, Denver, 1985-86; tech. writer Ebasco Environ., Denver, 1986-88, mgr. tech. writing group, 1988—. Mem. Soc. for Tech. Communications, Assn. Earth Sci. Editors. Democrat. Home: 8928 W Plymouth Ave Littleton CO 80123 Office: Ebasco Environ 143 Union Blvd Ste 1000 Lakewood CO 80228

BAKER, SUSAN HIMBER, school psychologist; b. N.Y.C., Dec. 28, 1943; d. Louis L. and Charlotte T. (Brenner) Himber; m. William M. Baker, June 8, 1963 (div. 1981); children: Laura A., Robin Baker Howse. BA, Oberlin Coll., 1964; MAT, Duke U., 1965; MEd, Converse Coll., 1982; EdS, U. S.C., 1990. Nationally cert. sch. psychologist. Tchr. Orange County Jr. High Sch., Hillsboro, N.C., 1964-65; ednl. evaluator Behavior Evaluation Ctrs., Spartanburg, S.C., 1977-79; sch. psychologist Spartanburg Sch. Dist. 3, 1979—; co-chmn. Youth Suicide Task Force, 1990. Player, Spartanburg Symphony Orch., 1974—, now pres.; mem. Spartanburg Symphony Guild, 1989—; dir. contemporary choir St. Paul the Apostle Cath. Ch., Spartanburg, 1974—. Mem. Nat. Assn. Sch. Psychologists, S.C. Assn. Sch. Psychologists, Piedmont Assn. Sch. Psychologists (treas. 1989-90), Nat. Assn. Pastoral Musicians. Democrat. Home: 148 Henson St Spartanburg SC 29302 Office: Spartanburg Sch Dist 3 PO Box 267 Glendale SC 29346

BAKER, SUSAN P., public health educator; b. Atlanta, May 31, 1930; d. Charles Laban and Susan (Lowell) Pardee; m. Timothy Danforth Baker, June 23, 1951; children—Timothy D., David C., Susan L. A.B., Cornell U., Ithaca, N.Y., 1951; M.P.H., Johns Hopkins U., Balt., 1968. Rsch. assoc. Office of Chief Med. Examiner, Balt., 1968-81; rsch. assoc. Johns Hopkins Sch. Hygiene and Pub. Health, Balt., 1968-71, asst. prof., 1971-74, assoc. prof., 1974-83, prof. health policy & mgmt., 1983—, joint appointment in environ. health scis., 1975—, joint appointment in pediatrics, 1983—, dir. Injury Prevention Ctr., 1987-88, co-dir., 1988—, acting head div. pub. health, 1988—; vis. prof. U. Minn. Sch. Pub. Health, 1975-87; chmn. nat. rev. panel for nat. accident sampling system Dept. Transp., Washington, 1976-81; vice chmn. com. on trauma research Nat. Research Council, Washington, 1984-85; vis. lectr. in injury prevention Harvard Sch. Pub. Health, 1984-87; John T. Law meml. lectr. U. Calgary, Alta., 1984; cons. and lectr. in field. Author: (monograph) Fatally Injured Drivers, 1970 (Prince Bernhard medal 1974); The Injury Fact Book, 1984. Contbr. chpts. to books, articles to profl. jours. Recipient Charles A. Dana award for pioneering achievements in health, 1989. Mem. Am. Assn. Automotive Medicine (bd. dirs. 1971-76, pres. 1974-75, Award of Merit 1985), Am. Pub. Health Assn. (governing coun. 1975-77, jour. bd. 1983-87), Am. Trauma Soc. (bd. dirs. 1972—, Disting. Achievement award 1981, Stone Lectureship award 1985), Aerospace Med. Assn., Assn. for Surgery of Trauma (hon.), Delta Omega, Phi Beta Kappa. Office: Johns Hopkins U Sch Hygiene & Pub Health 624 N Broadway Baltimore MD 21205

BAKER, TERESA LYNN, supermarket operations company executive; b. Newcomerstown, Ohio, Mar. 17, 1958; d. William Vernon and Barbara Anne (Bordenkircher) Casey; m. Gary Edwin Baker; children: Heather Michelle, Sean Ian. Student, Kent State U., Kent, Ohio, 1976-78, Kent State U., New Phila., Ohio, 1978-79. V.p., dir. adminstrn. Baker's Mgmt. Inc., Newcomerstown, 1978-84, co-owner, 1984—; co-owner, operator supermarkets. Republican. Methodist. Home: 1956 Melbourne Dr Coshocton OH 43812 Office: Bakers Mgmt Inc PO Box 540 Coshocton OH 43812

BAKER, VICTORIA JEAN, communications executive; b. Stockton, Calif., June 10, 1955; d. Roger William and Jane Frances (Hungler) B. BA, U. Del., 1977. Pubs. and confs. dir. Pension Real Estate Assoc., Washington, 1984-87, dir. communications div., 1987-88; corp. v.p. communications Nat. Assn. Real Estate Investment Trusts, Washington, 1988—. Vol. Rep. presdl. campaign, Washington, 1984; vol. tchr. English as a second lang. City of Alexandria, Va., 1988—. Mem. Am. Soc. Assn. Execs., Nat. Assn. Real Estate Editors, Am. Assn. Individual Investors, C. of C. Breakfast Bench. Roman Catholic. Home: 5500 Holmes Run Play #1108 Alexandria VA 22304

BAKER, WINDA LOUISE (WENDY BAKER), social worker; b. Suwannee County, Fla., July 16, 1952; d. Austin Sidney Baker and Jessie Mae (Williams) Baker Jones; B.A. in Theology, Berkshire Christian Coll., 1974. Clk.-typist State of Fla., Tallahassee, 1974-76; cashier Tallahassee-Eastern Theatres, 1975-76; field rep. Commn. Human Relations, 1976-77; asst. to dir. retirement living, sec., receptionist Advent Christian Village, Dowling Park, Fla., 1977-79, admissions counselor, social worker, after 1979, multi-purpose worker, 1980; geriatric care worker Advent Christian Village, Dowling Park, Fla., 1983-85, med. transcriptionist, 1985, advt. sales staff, 1986-87; processor H&R Block, 1987-1988; legal sec., McAlpin, Fla., 1987—. Vol. ARC and Asso. Charities, 1977—; founder Suwannee County Overeaters Anonymous, Live Oak, Fla., 1982; live-in companion for the elderly Serve Care Nursing Svcs. of South Ga., 1988-89. Mem. Suwannee County Mental Assn., Assn. Informed Travelers, Christian Fin. Planning, Inc., Cheeks Sch. Gymnastics Alumni. Republican. Advent Christian. Home: 210 E Brookwood Pl Valdosta GA 31601

BAKER HOLLIDAY, KAREN, hotel executive; b. Hollywood, Calif., Mar. 21, 1948; d. Frank A. Kelly Jr. and Dee A. (McWhorter) Kelly Archer; m. Kenneth J. Holliday, June 21, 1969 (div. Mar. 1978); 1 child, Tiffany Ann; m. Toby Evans Baker, June 8, 1980 (separated Sept. 1984). Student pub. schs., Woodland Hills, Calif. Mgr., Zane Grey Hotel, Avalon, Calif., 1969—, owner, 1975—. Chairperson Vehicle Rev. Bd., Avalon, 1982—; chairperson accomodations com. Avalon C. of C. Republican. Club: Catalina Racquet (sec. 1972-80, pres. 1985-87) (Avalon). Avocations: tennis; swimming; water skiing; needlework. Home: 199 Chimes Tower Rd Avalon CA 90704 Office: Zane Grey Pueblo Hotel PO Box 216 Avalon CA 90704

BAKER KNOLL, CATHERINE, state treasurer; b. Pitts.; d. Nicholas James and Theresa Mary (May) Baker; m. Charles A. Knoll Sr. (dec.); children: Charles A. Jr., Mina B., Albert B., Kim Eric. BS in Edn., Duquesne U., 1952, MS in Edn., 1973. Dir. western Pa. region Safety Adminstrn. Dept. Transp., Pitts., 1971-79; exec. dir. community svc. Dept. of Adminstrn., Allegheny County, Pa., 1980-88; treas. Pa. Treasury Dept., Harrisburg, 1988—; owner, operator pvt. bus. firm, Pitts., 1952-70. Mem. Pa. Dem. State Com., Pa. Fedn. Dem. Women, YMCA Bd., Pitts., Harrisburg, Duquesne U. Alumni Bd., Mom's House, Zontas Inc. Bd. Mem. Nat. Assn. State Treas., Women Execs. in State Gov., Coun. State Gov. (exec. com. ea. region). Roman Catholic. Office: Treasury Dept Fin Bldg Harrisburg PA 17120

BAKER-LIEVANOS, NINA GILLSON, jewelry store executive; b. Boston, Dec. 19, 1950; d. Rev. John Robert and Patricia (Gillson) Baker; m. Jorge Alberto Lievanos, June 6, 1981; children: Jeremy John Baker, Wendy Mara Baker, Raoul Salvador Baker-Lievanos. Student, Mills Coll., 1969-70; grad. course in diamond grading, Gemology Inst. Am., 1983; student in diamondtology designation, Diamond Coun. Am., 1986—. Artist, tchr. Claremont, Calif., 1973-78; escrow officer Bank of Am., Claremont, Calif., 1978-81; retail salesman William Pitt Jewelers, Puente Hills, Montclair, Calif., 1981-83, asst. mgr., 1983; mgr. William Pitt Jewelers, Puente Hills, Santa Maria, Calif., 1983—, corp. sales trainer, 1988—. Artist tapestry hanging Laguna Beach Mus. Art, 1974. Recipient Cert. Merit Art Bank Am., 1968. Mem. NAFE, Internat. Platform Assn., C. of C., Compassion Internat. Republican. Roman Catholic. Office: William Pitt Jewelers 158 Towne Ctr Santa Maria CA 93454

BAKKE, JILL MERIE, academic administrator, writer; b. Point Pleasant, N.J., Sept. 24, 1936; d. Donald Burton Hance and Evelyn Inez (Clayton) Truex; m. Maurice Austin Bakke, May 19, 1956; children: Beth Merie Slivkanch, Donna Lynn Mealy, Maura Ann Maneely, Kara Katrin. BA in English, Coll. of Great Falls, Mont., 1988, BA in Communications, 1988. Legal sec. various cos., 1954-74; instr. Malmstrom (Mont.) AFB, 1981-89; freelance writer Great Falls, 1982—; instr. English Great Falls Vocat. Tech. Inst., 1988-89; adminstr. Pk. Coll. at Malmstrom AFB, 1989—; pres. Great Falls Legal Secs., 1964; bd. dirs. Consumer Credit Counseling, Great Falls. Author: Financial Workbook, 1989; contbr. numerous articles to profl. jours. Designed and conducted Poetry Writing Workshop; vol. Deaconess Nursing Home, Great Fells, 1982; v.p. Community Concert Assn., Great Falls, 1985-86; grant writer Cascade County Convalescent Hosp., Great Falls, 1985; chair publicity com. Cascade County 89ers St. Centennial, Great Falls, 1989. Mem. Women in Communications (bd. dirs., newsletter editor 1988-89), AAUW (scholarship 1984-88). Home: 3417 3d Ave S Great Falls MT 59405

BAKKENSEN, LAURIE JEAN, infosystems specialist, volunteer; b. Portland, Oreg., Mar. 11, 1956; d. Joseph Edward and Gwynn (Calkins) B.; m. James Anthony Odlum, Dec. 17, 1983; children: Nicholas James, John Edward. BS in Sci., Oreg. State U., 1978; MBA, Marquette U., 1982. Supr. Miller Brewing Co., Milw., 1978-80; mgmt. cons. Planmetrics, Inc., Chgo., 1982-84; vol. L.A. Olympic Orgn. Commn., 1984; mgmt. cons. Theo Barry & Assoc., L.A., 1984-85; systems mgr. Hughes Aircraft Co., L.A., 1986—; co-chair Westside Arts Ctr. Collector's Afternoon, Santa Monica, Calif., 1988. Vol. Amateur Athletic Found., L.A., 1986—; mem. Jr. League of L.A., 1985—; bd. dirs. Westside Arts Ctr. Mem. SP Mktg. and Pub. Rels. (cons. L.A. chpt. 1987). Republican. Roman Catholic. Home: 3104 Yale Ave Marina del Rey CA 90292 Office: Hughes Aircraft Co PO Box 92919 SC/S64/C403 Los Angeles CA 90009

BAKLANOFF, JOY DRISKELL, university administrator; b. Jackson, Ala., Apr. 2, 1953; d. Roy Watson and Ella (Kinman) Driskell; m. Eric Nicolas Baklanoff, Dec. 10, 1925. MA in Anthropology, U. Ala., 1981, PhD in Ethnomusicology, 1985. Instr. U. Ala., Tuscaloosa, 1979-80; research asst. Columbia U., N.Y.C., 1980-81; instr. Shelton State Community Coll., Tuscaloosa, 1981-82; dir. arts prog. Miles Coll., Eutaw, Ala., 1982-83; dir. internat. Shelton State Community Coll., Tuscaloosa, 1986-88; folklorist U. Ala. State Mus., Tuscaloosa, 1988—; cons. Ala. Council on Arts, Montgomery, 1987—. Editorial assoc. Council for Research in Music Edn., Urbana, Ill., 1988—; contbr. articles to profl. jours.; project dir. record album, Traditional Ala. Songs, 1989. Bd. dirs. Am. Diabetes Assn., Tuscaloosa, 1988—; sec.-treas. Am. Coll. Heraldry, Tuscaloosa, 1989—. Grantee, Ala. Humanities Found., 1988-89, Nat. Endowment for Arts, 1989, Ala. Council on the Arts, 1987, 88; fellow U. Ala., 1985. Mem. Ala. Folklife Assn. (pres. 1987—), Soc. Ethnomusicology (state officer 1985-86), Creek Indian Nation East of Miss. Arts Coun. (bd. dirs. 1988—), Am. Assn. State and Local History, Tuscaloosa County Preservation Soc., Albert Schweitzer Soc. Internat., Ala. Guatemala Ptnrs., Phi Beta Kappa. Democrat. Eastern Orthodox Ch.

BAKROS, LEE ANN, arts council director; b. Des Moines, June 16, 1963; d. Eugene Marion and Norma Lee (Hove) B. BS in Math., Iowa State U., 1985; MBA, U. Iowa, 1987. Box office mgr. Creede Repertory Theatre, Creede, Colo., 1987; exec. sec. Olsten Svcs., Des Moines, 1987-89; exec. dir. Arts/Recreation Coun., Des Moines, 1989—. Bd. dirs. Children's Performing Arts Theatre, Des Moines, 1989—; vol. Des Moines Playhouse, 1979—. Mem. Am. Mktg. Assn., Women in Communications (v.p. 1990—). Republican. Lutheran. Office: Arts/Recreation Coun 310 Shops Bldg Des Moines IA 50309

BALCOM, GLORIA DARLEEN, marketing consultant; b. Porterville, Calif., July 23, 1939; d. Orel A. and Eunice E. Stadtmiller; A.A., El Camino Coll., 1959; student computer sci. Harbor Coll., 1976-77; m. Orville R. Balcom, July 23, 1971; stepchildren—Cynthia Lou, Steven Raymond. Personnel trainee AiResearch div. Garrett Corp., Los Angeles, 1959-60, sales promotion adminstr., 1960-64; sales rep. Volt Temporary Services, El Segundo, Calif., 1965-69, mgr., Tarzana, Calif., 1969-71; co-owner, co-operator Brown Dog Engring., Lomita, Calif., 1972-77; pres., owner, cons. MicroSly Mktg., Lomita, 1977—. Mem. Ind. Computer Cons. Assn., Am. Soc. Profl. and Exec. Women, Nat. Assn. Female Execs. Club: Torrance Athletic. Home and Office: 24521 Walnut St Lomita CA 90717

BALCOM, JEAN ELIZABETH, small business owner; b. Seattle, Mar. 7, 1915; d. Charles Earle and Artie Brown; m. Richard Eslie Walton, Dec. 14, 1935 (div. 1946); children: Joan Elizabeth Walton Melrose, Richard Eslie Jr.; m. Maurice Connick Balcom, Dec. 5, 1952 (dec. 1979); 1 child, Charles Randall. Student, U. Wash., 1936. Owner Globe Antique Shops, Seattle, 1968-87; ptnr. Globe Antiques Appraisers and Cons., Inc., Seattle, 1984—; owner Globe Antiques, Seattle, 1968—. Bd. dirs. Pike Place Market Found., Seattle, 1982—; mem. decorative arts coun. Seattle Art Mus., 1982-87, mem. Valley Mus. of Art, La Conner, 1987—, Greater Seattle C. of C., 1979-82; bd. dirs. Pacific N.W. Ballet, Seattle, 1983—, Seattle Chamber Music Festival, 1982—; mem. Plestcheeff Inst., Seattle, 1988—; bd. dirs. Making a Difference, Seattle, 1988—. Mem. Am. Soc. Appraisers, Queen Anne Fortnightly Club, Seattle Golf Club. Republican. Episcopalian.

BALDASSANO, CORINNE LESLIE, radio executive; b. N.Y.C., May 16, 1950; d. Nicholas and Olga (Phillips) Baldassano. BA cum laude, Queens Coll., CUNY, 1970; MA in Theatre, Hunter Coll., CUNY, 1975; MBA in Fin., NYU, 1986. Program dir., ops. mgr. Sta. KAUM-FM, Houston, 1977-79; dir. programming Sta. WSAI-FM, Cin., 1979-81; dir. programming ABC Contemporary and FM Radio Networks, N.Y.C., 1981-84; regional mgr. affiliate relations United Stations Radio Networks, N.Y.C., 1985-87; dir. ABC Entertainment Radio Network, N.Y.C., 1987-90, v.p. programming, 1990—; guest lectr. Wharton Sch. Bus., Phila., 1983, St. John's U., N.Y.C., 1983-84; bd. dirs. Country Radio Broadcasters, Inc., Nashville. Alumni mem. Govs. Com. Scholastic Achievement, N.Y.C., 1984-85. Mem. NYU Bus. Forum (bd. dirs. 1988—, v.p., treas. 1990—), Internat. Radio and TV Soc. (planning com., faculty/industry seminar 1986, 87, chmn. Summer Fellowship Program 1988), Women in Communications. Democrat. Roman Catholic. Avocations: travel, exercise, dancing, running, music. Office: ABC Radio Networks 125 West End Ave 7th Fl New York NY 10023

BALDINO, JENNIFER, production editor; b. Phila., June 30, 1969; d. Louis and Jean (Cannavo) B. Student, Temple U., 1987—. Sr. clk. Thomas Jefferson U., Phila., 1987-89; freelance writer Welcomat, Phila., 1986—, prodn. editor, 1989—. Contbr. articles to newspapers. Mem. Women in Communications, Inc. Roman Catholic. Office: Welcomat 1816 Ludlow St Philadelphia PA 19103

BALDISSERI, MARIE ROSANNE, physician; b. Providence, R.I., Oct. 31, 1955; d. Aldo Ferrucco and Margaret Teresa (Cavanaugh) B.; m. Srinivas Murali, Oct. 22, 1986. BS with Honors, Boston Coll., 1977; MS, Wagner Coll., 1978; MD, U. Navarra, Pamplona, Spain, 1982. Resident Interfaith Med. Ctr., Bklyn., 1982-85; fellow in critical care medicine Presbyn.-Univ. Hosp., Pitts., 1985-87, mem. ethics and human rights com., 1986-88; assoc. dir. adult ICU Magee-Women's Hosp., Pitts., 1987—; asst. prof. anesthesiology and critical care medicine U. Pitts. Med. Sch., 1987—; lectr. in field. Vol. tchr. Greater Pitts. Literacy Council, Pitts., 1987. Mem. Am. Coll. of Physicians, Pa. Med. Soc., Soc. Critical Care Medicine. Democrat. Roman Catholic. Office: Magee-Women's Hosp Forbes Ave and Halket St Pittsburgh PA 15213

BALDRIDGE, ANITA CAROL, mental health nurse; b. Antlers, Okla., Nov. 22, 1956; d. J.C. and Oneta E. (Bartlett) Howze; m. Roy D. Baldridge, Mar. 14, 1976; children: Roy, Jason, Whitney. AA in Nursing, NEO A&M U., Miami, Okla., 1983. Mental health nurse Eastern State Hosp., Vinita, Okla., psychiat. nurse IV/nurse officer of day. Active little league sports program, Bethel AME Ch.; den leader Cub Scouts. Mem. Nurses for Nurses (treas. Craig County sect.), ESH Employee Coun. (treas.), OPEA, Kiwanis. Democrat.

BALDRIGE, LETITIA, writer, management training consultant; b. Miami Beach, Fla.; d. Howard Malcolm and Regina (Connell) B.; m. Robert Hollensteiner; children: Clare, Malcolm. BA, Vassar Coll., 1946; postgrad., U. Geneva, 1946-48; D.H.L. (hon.), Creighton U., 1979, Mt. St. Mary's Coll., 1980, Bryant Coll., 1987, Kenyon Coll., 1990. Personal-social sec. to amb. Am. Embassy, Paris, 1948-51; intelligence officer Washington, 1951-53; asst. to amb. Am. Embassy, Rome, 1953-56; dir. pub. rels. Tiffany & Co., 1956-60; social sec. The White House, 1961-63; pres. Letitia Baldrige Enterprises, Chgo., 1964-69; dir. consumer affairs Burlington Industries, 1969-71; pres. Letitia Baldrige Enterprises, Inc., N.Y.C. and Washington, 1972—; bd. dirs. Outlet Co., Fed. Home Loan Bank N.Y., Hartmarx Corp. Author: Roman Candle, 1956, Tiffany Table Settings, 1958, Of Diamonds and Diplomats, 1968, Home, 1972, Juggling, 1976, Amy Vanderbilt's Complete Book of Etiquette, 1978, Amy Vanderbilt's Everyday Etiquette, 1979, Entertainers, 1981, Letitia Baldrige's Complete Guide to Executive Manners, 1985, Letitia Baldrige's Complete Guide to a Great Social Life, 1987, Complete Guide to the New Manners for the '90s, 1990; (novel) Public Affairs Private Relations, 1990; columnist Copley News Syndicate; contbr. to popular mags. Bd. dirs. Woodrow Wilson Found., Inst. Internat. Edn.; trustee Kenyon Coll., Gambier, Ohio. Republican. Office: Letitia Baldrige Enterprises Inc PO Box 32287 Washington DC 20007

BALDWIN, DEBORAH, editor; b. Washington, Nov. 1, 1949; d. William H. and Eleanor Mead (Griesemer) B.; m. Irwin B. Arieff, July 27, 1974; 1 child, Alexis B. BA, U. Pa., 1970; MA, U. Oreg., 1973. Editor Environ. Action, Washington, 1974-80; mng. editor Nat. Consumer Coop. Bank, Washington, 1980-82; contbg. editor Common Cause mag., Washington, 1982-83, assoc. editor, 1984-85, sr. editor, 1985-87, editor, v.p. for publs., 1987—; editorial cons. Nat. Consumers League, 1982, FTC, 1981-83. Contbr. articles to mags. Trustee Nat. Urban League, 1979-82. Office: Common Cause 2030 M St NW Washington DC 20036

BALDWIN, DEBRA JO, education educator; b. Muncie, Ind., Aug. 30, 1956; d. Curtis Ray and Cuba Jean (Matthews) Buchanan; m. Ronald Clyde Baldwin, Feb. 5, 1952; children: Stacie Jo, Chad Curtis. BSc., Ball State U., Muncie, Ind., 1978, MA, 1986. Cert. Physical Edn. and Health Instr., Ind. Physical edn. instr., coach Harrison Wash. Community Schs., Gastron, Ind., 1978--; co-dir. Healthercise Wes-Del high sch., Gastron Ind. 1988--. Mem. Am. ALliance for Health Physical Edn., Recreation and Dance. Republican. Home: RR Box 467B Yorktown IN 47396 Office: Wes Del High Sch Yorktown Gaston Pike Gaston IN 47342

BALDWIN, IRENE S., corporate professional, real estate investor; b. Dodge City, Kans., Sept. 8, 1939; d. Albert A. McMichael and Eleanor L. (Johnson) McMichael McGrath; m. Miles Edward Baldwin, June 30, 1961. BS, Friends U., 1961. Dress designer, Wichita, 1959-61; social worker Sedgwick County, Kans., 1963-65; owner motel chain, Kans., 1965—; comml. and agrl. real estate investor, 1971—; corp. sec.-treas. Baldwin, Inc., Kans., 1970—, fin. advisor, 1970—; pvt. practice fin. cons., Colby, Kans., 1975—; founder, advisor Charitable Found., Kans., 1980—. Fundraiser various charitable orgns., 1982—; child sponsor World Vision, 1982—; pvt. placement of homeless animals, Kans. and Nebr., 1965—. Helped developed 1st artifical front leg for canines, 1985. Mem. Panhandle Humane Soc. Avocations: horseback riding; hiking, travel, sewing, drawing. Home and Office: 2032 S Range Colby KS 67701

BALDWIN, JANICE MURPHY, lawyer; b. Bridgeport, Conn., July 16, 1926; d. William Henry and Josephine Gertrude (McKenna) Murphy; m. Robert Edward Baldwin, July 31, 1954; children: Jean Margaret, Robert William, Richard Edward, Nancy Josephine. AB, U. Conn., 1948; MA, Mt. Holyoke Coll., 1950; postgrad. U. Manchester, Eng., 1950-51; MA, Fletcher Sch., Tufts U., 1952; JD, U. Wis., 1971. Bar: Wis. 1971, U.S. Dist. Ct. (we. dist.) Wis. 1971. Staff atty. Legis. Coun., State of Wis., Madison, 1971-74, 75-78, sr. staff atty., 1979—; atty. adviser HUD, Washington, 1974-75, 78-79. Mem. Dane County Bar Assn. (legis. com. 1980-81), Wis. Bar Assn. (pres. govt. lawyers div. 1985-87, bd. govs. 1985-89, treas. 1987-89), Wis. Women's Network, AAUW, NOW, LWV, Legal Assn. for Women, Wis. Women's Polit. Caucus, U. Wis. Univ. League, Older Women's League (health, legis., marital property, state and local taxation coms.). Home: 125 Nautilus Dr Madison WI 53705 Office: 1 E Main St Ste 401 PO Box 2536 Madison WI 53701-2536

BALDWIN, KIM STACY, psychologist; b. Hammond, Ind., Sept. 29, 1959; d. Roger Leslie and Mary Francess (Hoffman) B. BA, So. Ill. U., 1983, MA, 1985, PhD, 1988. Lic. psychologist, Minn. Intern U. Ill., Champaign, 1987-88; psychologist Interstate Med. Ctr., Red Wing, Minn., 1988—. Bd. dirs. LWV, Red Wing, 1990, rsch. chair, 1990; mem. Regional Child Care Referral Network, Red Wing, 1989-90. Mem. Am. Psychol. Assn., Minn.

Psychol. Assn. Home: 1833 W Seventh St Red Wing MN 55066 Office: Interstate Med Ctr PA Highway 61 W Red Wing MN 55066

BALDWIN, LEONA B. (NONI BALDWIN), insurance agent; b. Portland, Jan. 18, 1934; d. Abram Martilla and Ida (Sophia) Heiskari; m. Walter Lee Baldwin, Jan. 26, 1953; children: Cathy Baldwin-Johnson, Keith Baldwin, Julie Templeton, Amy Baldwin. Student, Clark Jr. Coll., 1952-53. CLU, Chartered Fin. Cons., Life Underwriter Tng. Fellow. Sec. Bill Pottle, CLU, Anchorage, 1972-75; office mgr. Wilson & Baldwin, Anchorage, 1976-79; life ins. agt. N.Y. Life, Anchorage, 1979—. Mem. Rep. Assn. Profl. and Bus. Women, Anchorage, 1985-87. Mem. Nat. Assn. Life Underwriters, Women Life Underwriters Confederation (nat. pres. 1987-88, nat. edn. chmn. 1989-90), So. Alaska Life Underwriters (pres. 1986-87), Anchorage Estate Planning Coun., Am. Bus. Women (pres. 1980-81), Alaska State Life Underwriters (pres. 1987-88, nat. commmitteeman 1990—, Man of Yr. 1987), Anchorage Estate Planning Coun. (treas. 1990—). Lutheran. Office: Baldwin Fin Concepts 2525 Blueberry Rd Ste 107 Anchorage AK 99503

BALDWIN, NANCY CHEN, aerospace executive; b. Taipei, Peoples Republic of China, Apr. 2, 1950; came to U.S., 1965; d. Wong Shi (Chen) Warmkessel; m. Gilbert Douglas Baldwin, Aug. 29, 1987; 1 child, Robert Wright. BA in Oriental Langs., U. Calif., Davis, 1972, BA in Internat. Econs., 1972; MBA, Calif. State U., Sacramento, 1981, MSW, 1984. Fin. analyst U. Calif., Davis, 1971-72; program analyst USAF, Sacramento, 1972-76, logistics program specialist, 1976-82, logistics program mgr., 1982-85, avionics integration mgr., 1985-87; dir. logistics USAF, L.A., 1987-88; integrated logistics support program mgr. Grumman Aerospace Corp., Bethpage, N.Y., 1988—; clin. social worker Family Svc. Agy., Sacramento, 1982-85; mgmt. cons. Shannon & Assocs., Sacramento, 1980-84. Chmn. fundraising Women in Politics, Sacramento, 1980-85; advisor Sr. Citizen Ctr., Davis, 1972-76; v.p. Asian Am. Women's Network, Sacramento, 1981-85; treas. Com. to Elect Brian Smith, Davis, 1977; advisor City Coun. Planning Commn., Davis, 1976. Recipient United Way Community award City of Sacramento, 1986. Mem. Soc. Logistics Engrs., Calif. Scholarship Found., Nat. Assn. Social Workers. Republican. Buddhist.

BALDWIN, VELMA NEVILLE WILSON, personnel consultant; b. Meade, Kans., Aug. 31, 1918; d. Charles Chester and Anna Velma (Neville) Wilson; m. Claude David Baldwin, Jan. 31, 1942 (dec. Nov. 1976). AB, U. Kans., 1940. Placement working students U. Kans., 1940-41; with War Dept., Washington, 1942-45; rsch asst. Dr. A.C. Kinsey, Ind. U., 1946; with Carter Oil Co., Denver, 1948-50; with pers. Bur. Budget, Washington, 1951-55; asst. to dir. pers. Treasury Dept., 1955-59; pers. officer, dir. adminstrn. Office Mgmt. and Budget, 1959-79; cons. in field. Recipient Career Svc. award Nat. Civil Svc. League, 1975. Mem. Am. Soc. Pub. Adminstrn. (past exec. bd.), Soc. Pers. Adminstrn. (exec. bd.), Cosmos Club (Washington), Phi Beta Kappa. Home: 2234 49th St NW Washington DC 20007

BALDWIN, WENDY HARMER, social demographer; b. Phila., Aug. 29, 1945; B.A. magna cum laude, Stetson U., DeLand, Fla., 1967; M.A., U. Ky., Lexington, 1970, Ph.D. (NDEA fellow, spl. grantee Population Council), 1973. Research asst. Colombian Assn. Med. Faculties, Bogatá, 1971; research asst. sociology U. Ky., 1971-72; health scientist adminstr. behavioral scis. br. Center Population Research, Nat. Inst. Child Health and Human Devel., NIH, 1972-79, chief demographic and behavioral scis. br., 1979—. Recipient Merit award NIH, 1978; USPHS Superior Service award, 1985; Carl S. Schultz award population amd family planning sec., Am. Pub. Health and Planning Assn. Mem. Population Assn. Am. (dir. 1978-80, 2d v.p. 1984), Am. Sociol. Assn. (sec. population sect. 1977-80, chmn. 1985), So. Sociol. Assn., Phi Beta Kappa. Author articles in field. Office: NIH/NICHD/CPR/DBSB 6130 Executive Blvd EPN/Rm 611 Bethesda MD 20892

BALENTI, JOYCE G., communications executive; b. Tulsa, Dec. 31, 1951; d. John C. and Joyce M. (Jelf) Edmundson; m. Robert E. Balenti, Mar. 24, 1972; 1 child, Michael A. Student, Tulsa Jr. Coll., U. Tulsa. Sales adminstr Bryan Industries, Tulsa; supr. field engring. Telex Computer Products, Inc., Tulsa; co-owner B and J Printing and Equipment, Tulsa; now mgr. custom engring. Memorex Telex Corp., Tulsa. Mem. corp. challenge com. United Way, 1989. Recipient United Way Quarterback award, 1987. Mem. NAFE. Office: 6422 E 41st St Tulsa OK 74135

BALES, SUSAN MORGAN LEE, physicist; b. San Diego, Mar. 28, 1945; d. William Harding and Caro Lee (Morgan) Lee; m. Nathan Kinney Bales, Dec. 12, 1970 (dec. Aug. 1981). BS, Mary Washington Coll. U. Va., 1967; postgrad. computer sci., U. Md., 1968-70. Physicist Naval Ship R & D Ctr., Bethesda, Md., 1967-78; head ocean environ. group David Taylor Rsch. Ctr., Bethesda, 1978-87; asst. dir. for sci. and tech., sci. advisor to chief of naval ops. Chief Naval Ops. Exec. Panel, Alexandria, Va., 1987—; U.S. participant Naval Armaments Group, NATO, 1978-83, chmn. rsch. study group 1 on full-scale wave measurements, 1984-87. Contbr. over 50 articles to profl. jours. Mem. Joint Bd. on Sci. and Engring. Edn. Washington Met. Area, 1988—; sci. counselor Woodrow Wilson High Sch., 1988—. Recipient Meritorious Civilian Svc. award Dept. Def., 1986, cert. of appreciation Naval Sea Systems Command Assn. Scientists and Engrs., 1981, Sr. Engr. of Yr. award D.C. Coun. Engring. and Archtl. Socs., 1988. Mem. Am. Soc. Naval Engrs. (chmn. jour. 1984-84, mem. nat. coun. 1980-82, 84-86, v.p. 1986-89, cert. of appreciation 1977, Pres.'s award 1983, 87, 89), Soc. Naval Architects and Marine Engrs. (cert. of appreciation Chesapeake sect. 1980), Oceanography Soc. (charter), Am. Geophys. Union, Am. Meteorol. Soc., Marine Tech. Soc., U.S. Naval Inst., Oceanic Soc., Cosmos Club (Washington). Methodist. Home: Stonehaven 11402 Meeting House Rd Myersville MD 21773 Office: Chief Naval Ops Exec Panel 4401 Ford Ave Alexandria VA 22302-0268

BALEWA, ESHE, promotions professional; b. Orlando, Fla., Feb. 28, 1939; d. John and Sarah (Neal) Daniels; m. Daoud Balewa, May 1968; children: Moyfune, Kimberly, Brandi, Jason. AA, Valencia Community Coll., 1965; BA, Glasboro (N.J.) Coll., 1967. Rehab. counselor in applied music therapy State of N.J., Newark; coord. sales promotion MMT Sales, Inc. of Calif., L.A.; promotion and publicity dir. Da-Mon Records Orisa Prodns., L.A.; now pres., chief dir. ESP Presentations-Creative Promotion, Lancaster, Pa. Exec. dir. GMD Home for Displaced/Dependant Children, Lancaster, Pa.; v.p. Lancaster County Foster Parents Assn., 1990—; founder Youth Emancipation Assn. Mem. L.A. Women in Music, Cen. Pa. Assn. Women Execs., Am. Assn. Music Socs. Office: 122 Olde Dorwart St Lancaster PA 17603

BALICK, HELEN SHAFFER, judge; b. Bloomsburg, Pa.; d. Walter W. and Clarissa K. (Bennett) Shaffer; J.D., Dickinson Sch. Law, 1966; m. Bernard Balick, June 29, 1967; Admitted to Pa. bar, 1967, Del. bar, 1969; probate adminstr. Girard Trust Bank, Phila., 1966-68; pvt. practice law, Wilmington, Del., 1969-74; staff atty. Legal Aid Soc. Del., Wilmington, 1969-71; master Family Ct. Del., New Castle County, 1971-74; U.S. bankruptcy judge Dist. of Del., 1974—; U.S. magistrate, Wilmington, 1974-80; guest lectr. Dickinson Sch. Law, 1981-87; lectr. Dickinson Forum, 1982. Pres. bd. trustees Community Legal Aid Soc., Inc., 1972-74; trustee Dickinson Sch. Law; mem. Citizens Adv. Com. Wilmington, 1973-74, Wilmington Bd. Edn., 1974. Mem. ABA, Del. Bar Assn., Fed. Bar Assn., Nat. Conf. Bankruptcy Judges, Nat. Assn. Women Lawyers, Nat. Conf. Spl. Ct. Judges, Del. Alliance Profl. Women (Trailblazer award 1984), Nat. Lawyers Club, Nat. Assn. Women Judges, Wilmington Women in Bus. (bd. dirs. 1980-83), Am. Judges Assn., Am. Bankruptcy Inst., Dickinson Sch. Law Gen. Alumni Assn. (exec. bd. 1977-80, 87—, v.p. 1981-84, pres. 1984-87), Phi Alpha Delta. Office: US Bankruptcy Ct 844 King St Wilmington DE 19801

BALIUNAS, SALLIE LOUISE, astrophysicist; b. N.Y.C., Feb. 23, 1953; d. Joseph Ralph and Eleanor (Druiett) B.; m. Scott Edward Butler, 1977. BS, Villanova U., 1975; PhD, Harvard U., 1980. Astrophysicist Smithsonian Astrophys. Observatory, Cambridge, Mass., 1980—; v.p. mktg. and advt. Keep It Simple Software N.Y., Inc., N.Y.C., 1986—; cons. Hale Obs.', Pasadena, Calif., 1980; chair sci. adv. coun. Mt. Wilson Inst., 1987-; mem. sci. adv. bd. George C. Marshall Inst., 1988-; bd. dirs. Mt. Wilson Inst., Global Network and Automatic Telescopes. Editor: Cool Stars, Stellar Systems and the Sun, 1986; contbr. articles to profl. jours. Recipient Villanova Alumni Medallion award, 1977, Billings award U. Colo., 1979, Newton Lacy Pierce prize, Am. Astron. Soc., 1988, Bok prize, Harvard U., 1988; Harvard U. Jewett fellow, 1974, Harvard U. Pickering fellow, 1974, Amelia Earhart fellow, Zonta Internat., 1977-79, Langley-Abbot fellow, Smithsonian Instn., 1980-84. Mem. Am. Astron. Soc., Internat. Astron. Union, Sigma Xi. Office: Smithsonian Astrophys Obs Ctr for Astrophysics 60 Garden St MS15 Cambridge MA 02138

BALKCOM, CAROL ANN, insurance agent; b. Newport, R.I., June 20, 1952; d. Robert Terrence and Barbara Ruth (Hilton) Hannaway; m. Don E. Phillips, Aug. 26, 1974 (div. 1981); m. Richard Roger Balkcom, Oct. 1981; children: Richard Robert, Geoffrey Adam. BA, R.I. Coll., 1974, MA in Teaching, 1981; Cert. Life Underwriter, Am. Coll., 1984, CHFC, 1986. CLU, ChFC. Tchr. Lincoln (R.I.) Jr. High Sch., 1974-78; sales agt. Met. Life Ins. Co., Pawtucket, R.I., 1978-80; mgr., agt. Phoenix Mut., Providence, 1980—; instr. R.I. Lic. Sch., Providence, 1986—. Mem. R.I. Life Underwriters (bd. dirs. 1981-84, 1st v.p. 1983-84). Office: Phoenix Mut 2 Richmond Sq Providence RI 02906-5151

BALKIN, RUTH GOLDRING, law librarian, consultant; b. Oceanside, N.Y., July 4, 1951; d. John C. and Ethel Ann (Pasternack) Goldring; m. Alan G. Balkin, May 18, 1975. BA, SUNY, Albany, 1973; MA, U. Conn., 1976. Teaching asst. U. Conn., Storrs, 1973-75; sr. libr. clk. Rochester (N.Y.) Pub. Libr., 1978-79; pvt. practice cons. Rochester, 1978-86; ptnr. Balkin Libr. Mgmt. Svcs., Rochester, 1986—; mem. law librs. adv. bd. Callaghan & Co., 1987—. Editor: Off the Shelf, 1985—. Vice pres. Rennes-Rochester Sister Cities Com., 1985—. Mem. Am. Assn. Law Librs., Assn. Law Librs. Upstate N.Y. (membership com. 1987—), Rochester Women's Network, Nat. Assn. Women Bus. Owners, Women Bus. Owners I (coord.), Cercle Francais (coord. Rochester chpt. 1985—). Office: Balkin Libr Mgmt Svcs 295 Hurstbourne Rd Rochester NY 14609

BALKUS-KNIGHT, JOAN CLAIRE, psychologist; b. Lynn, Mass., July 13, 1933; d. Frank William and Mary Adeline (Kane) Balkus; children: Katharine, Frank, Karl, Kelley. BS in Edn., Salem State Coll., 1955, MEd, 1972; MEd, Boston U., 1978; postgrad., U. Mass., 1986. Dir. Four Seasons Kindergarten, Lynn, Mass., 1960-74; special educator Lynn Pub. Sch., 1971-77; dir. Camp Kiwanis Special Needs, Lynn, 1972-86, Ingalls Annex, Lynn, 1977-83; early childhood coord. Lynn Pub. Sch. Special Edn. Dept., 1979-86; sch. psychologist Lynn Pub. Sch., 1986--. Mem. Nat. Assn. Sch. Psychologist, Mass. Sch. Psychologist Assn. Democrat. Roman Catholic. Home: 21 Oakville St Lynn MA 01905 also: 154 Main Rd Islesboro ME 01905 Office: Lynn Pub Sch 42 Franklin St Lynn MA 01902

BALL, ANNE H., writer, editor, public relations consultant; b. Dayton, Ohio, June 7, 1939; d. James Leonard and Frieda Engelke Hitch; B.A., Ohio State U., 1961; m. Alan Odendahl, July 21, 1968 (div. May 1985); children—Laura Jean, Cynthia Leonard; m. Robert L. Ball, June 30, 1985 (dec. May 1987). Reporter, Dayton Jour. Herald, 1961-63, Balt. Sunpapers, 1964-66; pub. relations dir. Md. Inst. Coll. Art, 1966, Balt. Mental Health Assn., 1967-68; free lance writer, pub. relations cons., Washington, 1971—; dir. news bur. Cath. U. Am., Washington, 1976-78; co-owner Ad/Ventures, 1986-87; prin. Anne Ball Promotions, 1988—. Mem. Washington Ind. Writers, Zeta Tau Alpha. Democrat. Unitarian. Home: 14828 Fireside Dr Silver Spring MD 20904

BALL, ELIZABETH PIERCE, graphic designer; b. Greenwich, Conn., Aug. 16, 1959; d. Frank Pennington Jr. and Mary (McEvoy) B. Cert., Art Inst. Boston, 1980. Graphic designer St. George Advt., Colonia, N.J., 1980-81; asst. art dir. IMM, Westport, Conn., 1981-84; graphic designer Tom Fowler Inc., Stamford, Conn., 1984-89; v.p. Tom Fowler Inc., Stamford, 1989—. Recipient Cert. of Design Excellence, Print Mag., 1988, Cert. of Distinction, Creativity '89-Art Direction Mag., Creativity '90-Art Direction Mag., 1989; Merit award N.Y. Art Dir.'s Club, 1988, 89, Merit award Art Dirs. Club Boston, 1985. Mem. Conn. Art Dirs. Club (Award of Excellence 1988, Silver award 1990), Am. Inst. Graphic Arts. Office: 9 Webbs Hill Rd Stamford CT 06903

BALL, FRANCES LOUISE, chemist/electron microscopist; b. Murfreesboro, Tenn., Oct. 6, 1924; d. Macie Doak and Gertrude Louise (Miller) B. BS, Middle Tenn. State U., Murfreesboro, 1945; MS in Chemistry, Vanderbilt U., 1948. Instr. Cen. High Sch., Murfreesboro, 1945-46, Limestone Coll., Gaffney, S.C., 1948-49; chemist O.R. Gaseous Diffusion Plant, Oak Ridge, Tenn., 1949-68; physicist MAN program Oak Ridge Nat. Lab., 1968-75, rsch. assoc., 1975-83, ret., 1983. Mem. Electron Microscopy Soc. Am. (coun. sec. 1975-84). Home: 1128 E Northfield Blvd Murfreesboro TN 37130

BALL, LINDA SUZANNE, editorial director; b. Mpls., Aug. 15, 1951; d. Robert David and Evelyn Leone (Anderson) B. BA, Ill. State U., Normal, 1973; MS in Journalism, U. Ill., 1974. Freelance travel journalist and columnist, 1975—; editor transp. guides div. Dun & Bradstreet, Chgo., 1975-85; editorial dir. retail travel group CMP, Inc., Manhasset, N.Y., 1985—. Author: China: A Moment in Time: Coverage of the pro-democracy movement in China, 1989. Mem. Soc. Am. Travel Writers, Chgo. Travel Women's Club. Office: CMP Publs Inc 600 Community Dr Manhasset NY 11030

BALL, M. ISABEL, chemistry educator, dean; b. Elmendorf, Tex., June 1, 1929; d. Raymond Xavier and Jane Elizabeth (Terrell) B. BA, Our Lady of the Lake U., 1950; MA, U. Tex., 1963, PhD, 1969. Cert. elem., secondary tchr., Tex. Tchr. Sacred Heart Sch., El Reno, Okla., 1952-54; head of chemistry Our Lady of the Lake U., San Antonio, Tex., 1969-80, prof. chemistry, 1974—; dir. sci./math. div. Our Lady of the Lake U., San Antonio, Tex., 1974-80; dean Coll. Arts and Scis. Our Lady of the Lake U., San Antonio, Tex., 1980—; assoc. grad. lectr. St. Mary's U., San Antonio, 1974-80. Contbr. articles to profl. publs.; author ednl. software; reviewer manuscript Jour. Chem. Edn. Tri-chair Biosci. Task Force-Target 90 Com., San Antonio, 1983-85; liaison Tex. Senate Commn. on Bus., Tech. and Edn., Tex., 1983, Sci.-Math.-Engr. Support Network-Tech. Hi-Sch, San Antonio, 1983—. Mem. Am. Chem. Soc. (chair 1963—), Tex. Acad. Sci., Nat. Sci. Tchrs. Assn., Soc. Coll. Sci. Tchrs. Office: Our Lady of Lake U 411 SW 24th St San Antonio TX 78207-4666

BALL, MARIA-ELENA, small business owner; b. Mex., Nov. 24, 1940; Arrived in US, 1954.; d. Manuel and Minerva (Ortiz) Correa; 1 child from previous marriage: Teresa-Jeanenne. Owner Mex. in Alaska Restaurant, Anchorage, 1972—. Active Anchorage Neighbor-to-Neighbor Fund, Anchorage Conv. and Visitors Bur. Mem. Alaske Mfs, Assn. Office: Mexico in Alaska Restaurant 7305 Old Seward Hwy Anchorage AK 99518

BALL, MAVIS MAXINE, retired english teacher; b. Girard, Ill., July 5, 1921; d. Lewis Lloyd and Ruth Sarabell (Funk) B. BA, McKendree Coll., 1944; postgrad., Ill. State U., 1949, U. Ill., 1960. English and physical edn. tchr. Cowden (Ill.) High Sch., 1944-45, Mt. Olive (Ill.) High Sch., 1946-47; english and physical edn. tchr. Litchfield (Ill.) High Sch., 1948-52, english tchr., 1952-84. Contbr. articles to local newspapers. Mem. Woman's Club, Litchfield, 1950—, corr. sec. 1980-84, Woman's Club, Girard, 1988—, St. Francis Hosp. Aux., Litchfield, 1975—, scholarship com., 1980—, Women's Ch. Circle, 1980-90. Mem. AAUW (pres. 1984-88, sec. 1988-90), NEA (life), Ret. Tchrs. Assn. (life), Eastern Star, Delta Kappa Gamma Soc. (sec. 1964-66, pres. 1972-74). Home: RR 2 Box 38 Girard IL 62640

BALL, PATRICIA ANN, physician; b. Lockport, N.Y., Mar. 30, 1941; d. John Joseph and Katherine Elizabeth (Hoffmaster) B.; m. Robert E. Lee, May 18, 1973; children—Heather, Samantha. B.S., U. Mich., 1963; M.D., Wayne State U., 1969. Diplomate Am. Bd. Internal Medicine, Am. Bd. Hematology, Am. Bd. Med. Oncology. Intern, resident Detroit Gen. Hosp., 1969-71; resident Jackson Meml. Hosp., Miami, Fla., 1971-72; fellow Henry Ford Hosp., Detroit, 1972-74; staff physician VA Hosp., Allen Park, Mich., 1974-77; practice medicine specializing in hematology and oncology, Bloomfield Hills, Mich., 1977—; mem. faculty dept. medicine Wayne State U. Sch. Medicine, Detroit, 1974—. Mem. Founders Soc., Detroit Inst. Arts. Mem. ACP, AMA, Mich. State Med. Soc., Oakland County Med. Soc., Alpha Omega Alpha. Avocations: photography; skiing. Office: 2515 Woodward Suite 290 Bloomfield Hills MI 48013

BALL, SHERI BETH, bank trust manager; b. Montebello, Calif., June 12, 1963; d. Chester Bert and Shirley Ann (Winnemore) Dickason; m. William Whyte, Jan. 26, 1980 (div. Dec. 1985); m. Andrew Roy Ball, May 23, 1987. Asst. mgr. Van's Tennis Shoes, Anaheim, Calif., 1978-81; supr. trust securities First Interstate Bank, L.A., 1981-85; corp. trust officer Security Pacific Nat. Bank, L.A., 1985-87; asst. v.p. and mgr. corp. trust ops. Security Pacific Nat. Bank, Glendale, Calif., 1987—; work improvement coord. First Interstate Bank, L.A., 1984-85. Coreographer (sacred dances) Behold the Man, 1987, In His Light, 1988. Mem. Western Stock Transfer Assn., Sacred Dance Guild (treas. 1987-89). Republican. Presbyterian.

BALL, SUSAN KAY, marketing executive; b. Beckley, W.Va., Jan. 30, 1959; d. Willard Mayse and Helen (Trump) Johnson; m. Kenneth L. Ball, July 9, 1988; stepchildren: Soctt, Stephanie. BSBA, Fairmont (W.Va.) State Coll., 1981; postgrad., Wheeling Coll., 1989—. Social worker Children & Family Svc., Wheeling, W.Va., 1981-83; employer rels. rep. W.Va. Dept. Employment Security, Wheeling, 1983-85; mktg. rep. Health Plan, St. Clairsville, Ohio, 1985-88, mktg. mgr., 1988-89, dir. of mktg., 1989—. Mem. Nat. Assn. Female Execs., Ohio Valley Svc. Assn. (treas. 1982-85), St. Clairsville C. of C., New Martinsville C. of C. Republican. Baptist. Home: Rt 1 Box 178B Clarington OH 43915 Office: Health Plan Upper Ohio 52160 National Rd E Saint Clairsville OH 43950

BALL, SUSAN LEE, arts administrator, art historian; b. Altadena, Calif., May 25, 1947; d. Charles Russell and Catherine (Piller) B.; m. Edward Kaufman, Mar. 19, 1983; 1 child, Emily Catherine. BA, Scripps Coll., 1969; MA, U. Calif., Riverside, 1974; M of Philosophy, Yale U., 1976, PhD, 1978; postgrad., U. Chgo., 1983-85. Asst. prof. art history dept. U. Del., Newark, 1978-82; asst. treas. Chase Manhattan Bank, N.Y.C. and Chgo., 1982-85; dir. govt. affairs Art Inst. Chgo., 1985-86; exec. dir. Coll. Art Assn., N.Y.C., 1986—. Author: Ozenfant and Purism, 1982; contbr. articles to art catalogs. Mem. Nat. Humanities Alliance (bd. dirs. 1988—), Nat. Cultural Alliance (bd. dirs. 1989—), Am. Coun. Learned Socs. (exec. com. Conf. Adminstrv. Officers 1989—). Democrat. Office: Coll Art Assn 275 7th Ave 5th Fl New York NY 10001-6708

BALL, SUSAN LUCILLE, occupational therapist, business owner; b. Bloomingdale, N.J., Sept. 30, 1961; d. Schuyler Linton and Zana Thekla (Platz) B. Student, W.Va. Wesleyan Coll., 1979-81; BS, SUNY, Buffalo, 1984. Occupational therapist I Magee Rehab. Hosp., Phila., 1984-87; occupational therapist II Sharp Rehab. Ctr., San Diego, 1987—; occupational therapy cons. Vernon (N.J.) Orthopaedic Sports Medicine, 1984—. Mem. Am. Occupational Therapy Assn., Nat. Spinal Cord Injury Assn., Nat. Wheelchair Officials Assn. Methodist.

BALLANFANT, KATHLEEN GAMBER, newspaper executive, public relations company executive; b. Horton, Kans., July 11, 1945; d. Ralph Hayes and Audrey Lavon (Heryford) G.; children: Andrea, Benjamin. BA, Trinity U., 1967; postgrad. NYU, 1976, Am. Mgmt. Inst., 1977, Belhaven Coll., 1985. Pub. info. dir. Tex. Dept. Community Affairs, Austin, 1972-74; pub. affairs mgr. Cameron Iron Works, Houston, 1975-77, Assoc. Builders and Contractors, Houston, 1982-84; pres. Ballanfant & Assoc., Houston, 1977-82, 84—; pres. Village Life Inc., 1985—; pres., chief exec. officer Village Life Publs.; owner Village Life newspaper, Southwest Life newspaper, Houston Observer/Times newspaper, Village Life Printing & Typesetting, South Post Oak newspaper; mem. adv. council on Construction Edn., Tex. So. U., Houston, 1984—; mem. task force on ednl. excellence Houston Ind. Sch. Dist., 1983—; mem. devel. bd. Inter First Fannin Bank, 1986-88. Author: Something Special-You, 1972, Prevailing Wage History in Houston, 1983; editor newspaper Bellaire Texan, 1981-82, Austin Times, 1971. Vice pres. West Univ. Republic Women's Club, Houston, 1984—; fgn. vis. chmn. Internat. Inst. Edn., Houston, 1980—; docent Houston Zoo, 1982. Named Tex. Woman of Achievement Tex. Womans Hosp., 1986; recipient Apollo IX Medal of Honor Gov. Preston Smith, 1970, Child Abuse Prevention award Gov. Dolph Briscoe, 1974, Tex. Community Newspaper Assn. (pres. 1988—, bd. dirs. 1987—). Mem. Bellaire C. of C. (bd. dirs. 1987—, sec., treas. 1988). Republican. Presbyterian. Lodge: Rotary. Avocations: traveling, racquetball, reading. Office: Village Life Inc 6802 Mapleridge Ste 208 Bellaire TX 77401

BALLANTINE, MORLEY COWLES (MRS. ARTHUR ATWOOD BALLANTINE), newspaper publisher; b. Des Moines, May 21, 1925; d. John and Elizabeth (Bates) Cowles; m. Arthur Atwood Ballantine, July 26, 1947 (dec. 1975); children—Richard, Elizabeth Ballantine Leavitt, William, Helen Ballantine Healy. A.B., Ft. Lewis Coll., 1975; L.H.D. (hon.), Simpson Coll., Indianola, Iowa, 1980. Pub. Durango (Colo.) Herald, 1952—, editor, pub., 1975-83, editor, chmn. bd., 1983—; dir. 1st Nat. Bank, Durango, 1976—, Des Moines Register & Tribune, 1977-85, Cowles Media Co., 1982-86. Mem. Colo. Land Use Commn., 1975-81, Supreme Ct. Nominating Commn., 1984-90; mem. Colo. Forum, 1985—, Blueprint for Colo., 1985—; pres. S.W. Colo. Mental Health Ctr., 1964-65, Four Corners Opera Assn., 1983-86; bd. dirs. Colo. Nat. Hist. Preservation Act, 1968-78; trustee Choate/Rosemary Hall, Wallingford, Conn., 1973-81, Simpson Coll., Indianola, Iowa, 1981—, U. Denver, 1984—, Fountain Valley Sch., Colorado Springs, 1976-89. Recipient 1st place award for editorial writing Nat. Fedn. Press Women, 1955, Outstanding Alumna award Rosemary Hall, Greenwich, Conn., 1969, Outstanding Journalism award U. Colo. Sch. Journalism, 1967, Distinguished Service award Ft. Lewis Coll., Durango, 1970; named to Colo. Community Journalism Hall of Fame, 1987. Mem. Nat. Soc. Colonial Dames, Colo. Press Assn. (bd. dirs. 1978-79), Colo. AP Assn. (chmn. 1966-67), Federated Women's Club Durango. Episcopalian. Club: Mill Reef (Antigua, W.I.) (bd. govs. 1985—). Address: care Herald PO Drawer A Durango CO 81302

BALLANTYNE, DOROTHY DUNNING, museum director, retired educator; b. Aetna, Ind., Mar. 17, 1910; d. Harry Leland and Ella L. (Larson) Dunning; m. Donald Bock Ballantyne (dec. June, 1973); children: Elin Christianson, Dorothy Eastwood, Brianne Lowery, Alexander. Student Ind U. Newspaper editor Hobart Gazette, Ind., 1929-32; clk. Home Owners Loan Fed. Govt., Hammond, Ind., 1932; dep. auditor Lake County, Crown Point, Ind., 1932-36; sub. tchr. Hobart Schs., Ind., 1954-65, spl. edn. tchr., 1965-72; vol. dir. Hobart Hist. Soc. Mus., Ind., 1970—. Contbr. articles to profl. jour. Author pamphlets Hobart Hist. Soc. Mem. adv. com. Hobart Sch. Bd., 1980—, Hobart PTA. Recipient Disting Service award West Hobart Civic Club, 1970; named one of 12 most valuable women in county Trade Winds, Lake County, Ind., 1978. Mem. Ind. Hist. Soc., Hobart Hist. Soc. (pres. 1970-76), Mensa, Hobart Jaycees (Laura Bracken Woman of yr. award 1968), LWV (pres.). Lodge: Order Eastern Star (worthy matron 1938, dist. dep. 1940). Home: 121 S Ash St Hobart IN 46342-4251 Office: Hobart Hist Soc Mus Box 24 Hobart IN 46342

BALLARD, BETTY RUTH WESLEY, retired x-ray equipment co. exec.; b. Birmingham, Ala., Nov. 11, 1924; d. Henry Gaston and Ruth Lorine (Whitfield) Wesley; degree Glenn Tech. Inst., 1942-46; m. Douglas Hayden Ballard, Oct. 24, 1941; 1 son, Douglas Hayden. Mgr., Nbc Restaurant, 1960-68; corp. sec. X-Ray Service and Sales, Inc., 1960-68; pres. Ballard X-Ray Co., Birmingham, Ala., 1968—. Exec. com. Democratic Party; election law commr. State of Ala.; hon. dep. sheriff Shelby County, Ala.; mem. adminstrv. bd. 1st United Methodist Ch., Montevallo, Ala. Mem. Ala. Soc. Radiol. Technologists, Ala. Hosp. Assn., Inst. Hosp. Auxilians, Ala. Cattlemen's Assn., LWV, 20th Spl. Forces Group Aux. Methodist (adminstrv. bd., trustee ch.). Club: The Club Inc. Home: Flying-X-Ranch Route 1 Box 29 Montevallo AL 35115

BALLARD, GLENDA DAY, health management executive; b. Washington, N.C., Feb. 14, 1943; d. Rion Glen and Mary (Mercer) Day; m. Ronald G. French, Dec. 10, 1967 (dec. Jan. 1973); m. Alan G. Ballard, Oct. 5, 1974. Grad. high sch., Washington, 1961. Copywriter Sta. WITN-TV, Washington, 1961-63; dir. dance Fred Astaire Dance Studio, Norfolk, Va., 1963-67; office mgr. Eugene W. Hodgson, MD, Aurora, N.C., 1970-74; staff photographer Surg. Specialists, Norfolk, 1974-77; credit mgr. ZoneAir, Inc., Johnson City, Tenn., 1978-79; owner, pres. Ballard Med. Mgmt., Johnson City, Tenn., 1979—; leader seminars, Va. N.C., Tenn., 1985—. Residential chmn. United Way, Johnson City, 1985; bd. dirs. Am. Cancer Soc. Washington County, Johnson City, 1987. Mem. Am. Mgmt. Soc. (bd. dirs. Johnson City chpt. 1981), Johnson City C. of C. (bd. dirs. 1982-85), Health

Svcs. Coun., Lions. Home: 1551 Colony Park Dr Johnson City TN 37601 Office: Ballard Med Mgmt 817 W Walnut St Stes 10 11 12 Johnson City TN 37601 also: 404 Ashe St Johnson City TN 37601

BALLARD, LINDA BURDICK, correctional educator; b. Worcester, Mass., Oct. 3, 1958; d. Charles Valentine Burdick and Barbara Ann (Livingston) Duff; m. Richard E . Ballard, Jr., Feb. 27, 1982. BS, Frostburg State U., 1980; MA, George Washington U., 1987. Cert. correctional and spl. educator. Educational cons. Environments For Human Services, Falls Church, Va., 1982-84; dir. diagnostic and assessment services Educational Support Systems, Washington DC, 1984-86; intern correctional edn. program Office of Vocat. and Adult Edn., U.S. Dept. Edn., Washington, 1986-87; mem. bd. dirs. Systems for Educational Support, Washington, DC, 1986-. Contbr. articles to profl. jours. Sponsor of students Internat. Language Inst. Washington, 1986—, Euro Ctr., Alexandria, Va., 1989—. Recipient Outstanding Tchr. award, D.C. Dept. Corrections, 1988. Mem. Correctional Edn. Assn., Council for Exceptional Children, Odenton C. of C., Phi Delta Kappa. Republican. Roman Catholic. Office: DC Dept Corrections PO Box 99 Ednl Svc Medium Security Facility Lorton VA 22199

BALLARD, MARQUERITE LOUISA CANDLER, retired hematologist, educator; b. Atlanta, June 14, 1920; d. Asa Warren and Hattie Lee (West) Candler; m. George Speights Ballard, Jr., Feb. 3, 1973. BA, Vassar Coll., 1942; MS, Emory U., 1943, MD, 1948. Woodruff malaria rsch. fellow Emory U., Atlanta, 1943, clin. fellow in hematology, 1952-54, clin. assoc. dept. medicine, 1962—; rotating intern, asst. resident, resident in medicine Md. Gen. Hosp., Balt., 1948-51; examining physician Lockheed Aircraft Corp., Marietta, Ga., 1951-52; commd. lt. USPHS, 1954, advanced through grades to capt., 1963; rsch., tng. and cons. hematologist Ctrs. for Dis. Control, Atlanta, 1954-85; ret., 1985; instr. Emory U., Atlanta, 1954-62; presenter sci. papers and exhibits at nat. and internat. meetings; workshop condr. in field; former mem. med. adv. coun. Ga. chpt. Nat. Hemophilia Found. Author: Atlas of Blood Cell Morphology, 1987; contbr. articles to med. jours. Named Woman of Yr. in the Professions, 1972; recipient Meritorious Svc. medal USPHS, 1977. Fellow Am. Soc. Hematology (emeritus), Internat. Soc. Hematology (emeritus); mem. AAAS (life), AMA, Am. Heart Assn., Ga. Heart Assn., Commd. Officers Assn. USPHS (life), So. Med. Assn. (life), Med. Assn. Ga. (life), Med. Assn. Atlanta (life). Episcopalian. Home: 3092 Argonne Dr NW Atlanta GA 30305

BALLARD, MARY MELINDA, financial communications, public relations firm executive; b. Sikeston, Mo., Apr. 21, 1957; d. Claude M. and Mary (Birnbach) B.; m. Emil Pena, Jan. 1, 1989 (div. July 1990). BA, Monmouth Coll. 1976, MBA, NYU 1980, postgrad. Columbia U. V.p. corp. communications United Brands Co., N.Y.C., 1976-79; v.p. mktg. Oscar de la Renta Ltd., 1979-81; pres., chief exec. officer Ficom Internat., Inc., N.Y.C., 1980—; sr. v.p. Ruder Finn Inc., N.Y.C., 1989—; dir., chief exec. officer MBP Interests Inc., 1989—; bd. dirs. Nat. Coun. Real Estate Investment Fiduciaries; cons. to fgn. govts. and major corps. Contbr. articles to profl. jours. Trustee Ballard Family Found., Children's Aid Soc. Mem. Internat. Assn. Bus. Communicators (Golden Quill 1984), Pub. Relations Soc. Am., Urban Land Inst., Nat. Investor Relations Inst. Roman Catholic. Avocations: collecting oriental art, thoroughbred race horses. Home: 1707 Lake Shore Dr Austin TX 78746

BALLARD-SELL, SUSAN ELIZABETH, landscape architect; b. Buffalo, June 26, 1956; d. Robert L. and Francis (Henson) Ballard. BA cum laude, Beloit Coll., 1979; cert., Harvard U., 1979; MLA, U. Mass., 1985. Owner Mystic (Conn.) Florist, 1980-84; design cons. Town of Amherst, Mass., 1984-85; tchg., research asst. U. Mass., Amherst, 1983-85; landscape dir. Riverside Park, Agawam, Mass., 1983-85; dept. head McCrone, Inc., Annapolis, Md., 1985-88; sr. project mgr. Greenhorne & O'Mara, Greenbelt, Md., 1988; cons. Pvt. Devel. in Critical Area, Md., 1986-88; pub. speaker numerous schs., and assns., 1985-88. Author: Design Review Board Handbook, 1984, Inventory and Assessment Procedures for Pedestrian Trails, 1985. Recipient FL Olmsted award Harvard Sch. Design, 1979; named Rhodes scholar U. Mass., 1983. Mem. Am. Soc. Landscape Architects, Am. Planning Assn. Young Bus. Women Am. (Women of Yr. candidate 1980), Nat. Park and Conservancy Assn., Waugh Alumni Assn. (conf. chmn. 1985-88). Avocations: raquetball, swimming, theatre, art and antique collecting. Home: 830 W Central Ave Davidsonville MD 21035 Office: Greenhorne & O'Mara 9001 Edmonston Rd Greenbelt MD 20770

BALLEW, DORIS EVELYN, accountant, company executive; b. Knox County, Tenn., Sept. 6, 1938; d. James Elmer and Grace Elizabeth (Wright) Dossett; m. George Thomas Reep, Feb. 4, 1955 (div. June 1969); children: Sherrie Lynn Akins, Kimberley Michelle; m. David Woodward Ballew, Oct. 9, 1969 (div. Dec. 1989); 1 child, Melissa Marie. Student, U. P.R., 1957, U. Tenn., 1975-84, Draughon's Coll., 1982, Knoxville Bus. Coll., 1974. CPA, Tenn. Acct. Shoney's Restaurants, Knoxville, Tenn., 1961-64, Tinsley Tire Co., Knoxville, Tenn., 1964-65; chief acct. Kuhlman-Murphy Co., Knoxville, Tenn., 1965-77; v.p., contr., treas. Lawler Wood, Inc. and Wood Properties, Inc., Knoxville, Tenn., 1977—. Mem. Old Smoky Railway Mus. (treas. 1978-83). Mem. Nat. Assn. Accts., Knoxville Jaycettes, AICPA, Tenn. Soc. CPA's, Beta Sigma Phi (pres. 1982-83, 89). Home: 406 Broadview Dr Knoxville TN 37912 Office: 1600 Riverview Tower 900 Gay St Knoxville TN 37902

BALLEW, MARY AUGUSTA, management analyst; b. Danville, Pa., Nov. 25, 1951; d. Robert Malcolm and Mary Augusta (York) Sperry; m. Lawrence E. Allred, Apr. 2, 1947 (div. 1978); 1 child, Lawrence Edward Allred; m. Randy Eugene Ballew, Feb. 18, 1949. Office mgr. U.S. Army Pers. Ctr., New Ulm, Fed. Republic Germany, 1976-78; adminstrv. asst. U.S. Army Staff JAGC, Ansbach, Fed. Republic Germany, 1981-82; sec. to dir. indsl. ops. U.S. Army Mil. Community, Schweinfurt, Fed. Republic Germany, 1982-84; adjutant sec. Silas B. Hays Army Hosp. USA Meddac, Ft. Ord, Calif., 1984-87; mgmt. asst. Silas B. Hays Army Hosp. USA Meddac, Ford Ord, Calif., 1986-87; mgmt. analyst Silas B. Hays Army Hosp. USA Meddac, Ft. Ord, Calif., 1987—. Mem. Am. Soc. Mil. Comptrollers, Ladies Aux., VFW. Home: 295 Reservation Rd Apt 35 Marina CA 93933

BALLEW, NELLIE HESTER, retired secondary school educator; b. Feb. 26, 1914; d. Chester Leon and Ethel (Bell) Crank; 1 child, William Wayne Ballew. BA with high honors, Cen. Meth. Coll., 1936; postgrad., U. Mo., 1938, 40, 42, U. Calif., Berkeley, 1957; MA, San Francisco State U., 1970. Tchr. elem. schs., 1936-38, various high schs., 1938-57; tchr., prin. Avalon (Mo.) Union High Sch., 1938-39; counselor Vallejo (Calif.) Jr. High, 1957-67; counselor Taft (Calif.) Union High Sch., 1967-79, dean, info. officer, 1967-72, attendance officer, info. officer, 1972-74, pub. info. officer, 1974-79; area rep. placement and supervision of fgn. students Ednl. Resource Devel. Trust, L.A., 1981-88; dir. placement of fgn. students World Exch., Putnam Valley, N.Y., 1990—; advisor student activities Taft High Sch., 1968-72; mem. coms. and curriculum development Vallejo Jr. High Sch., Taft High Sch., 1944-79. Life mem. PTA, Kern County Calif. Hist. Soc. Recipient Vol. Cert. of Appreciation, Kern County Pub. Health Dept., 1976, Hilltop Convalescent Hosp., 1990. Mem. Kern County Retired Tchrs., Calif. Retired Tchrs., Nat. Edn. Assn., Am. Contract Bridge Club, 60 plus Club, Soroptimists (life mem., past sec., treas., v.p., pres.), Rebekal Lodge, P.E.O. Sisterhood, Delta Kappa Gamma. Presbyterian. Home: 109 Haggin Bakersfield CA 93309

BALLOU, KATHY DEANNE TAYLOR, marketing executive; b. Peoria, Ill., Sept. 20, 1951; d. Chas S. and Carol A. (McDonough) Guynn; m. Harold N. Taylor Jr. (dec. Nov. 1982); 1 child, Shawn; m. John A. Ballou, June 5, 1987. AA in Bus., Ill. Cen. Coll., Peoria; student in mktg. mgmt., Sangamon State, Springfield. Mgr. sales Credit Bur. Accounts, Inc., Peoria, 1986-87; sales exec. Rsch. Inst. of Am., N.Y.C., 1987—, mem. adv. coun., 1989, pres. bd., 1990; dir. cardiac ctr. Proctor Community Hosp., 1972-81, risk mgmt. coordinator, 1981-83; pres. Cen. Ill. Risk Mgmt., Inc., 1983-86. Chmn. bd. Tri-County Heart Assn., Peoria, 1987-88, pres., 1986-87; div. and regional mgr. Am. Heart Assn. Ill. affiliate, Springfield, 1985-89, mem. speakers bur., risk factor com., 1972-81; bd. dirs. Dept. Rehab. Scvs., 1989—; active ARC hospice tng., Meth. Med. Ctr. Vol. Svcs. Mem. NAFE, Am. Inst. Banking, Peoria Jaycee Women (v.p. 1984), Ill. Jaycee Women (state chaplain, mgr. family life program 1984-85), Morton Jayceettes (pres. 1980). Republican. Home and Office: No Oaks Estates RR 1 Pekin IL 61554

BALLWEBER, HETTIE LOU, archaeologist; b. Pitts., Dec. 27, 1944; d. Nicholas George and Harriett Elizabeth (Tucker) Beresh; m. Walter David Boyce, Aug. 24, 1963 (div. 1984); children: Michael David, Steven Todd; m. William Arterberry Ballweber, Nov. 8, 1986. BA summa cum laude, Calif. U., Pa., 1985; M. Applied Anthropology, U. Md., 1987. Cons. archaeologist Monogahela, Pa., 1980-85; archaeologist archeology div. Md. Geol. Survey, Balt., 1985-86; dir. Md. New Directions, Balt., 1987; cons. Columbia, Md., 1987—; bd. dirs. Alternative Directions, Inc., Balt. Author: First People of Maryland, 1985; contbr. articles to profl. jours. State publicity chmn. Pa. Congress Parents and Tchrs., Harrisburg, Pa., 1981-84, regional v.p., 1984. With USN, 1979-87. Fellow Soc. Applied Anthropology; mem. Mon-Yough Archaeol. Soc. (pres. 1983-84), Westmoreland Archaeol. Soc. (v.p. 1982-83), Coun. Md. Archeology (pres. elect 1985—), Wash. Assn. Profl. Anthropologists, Soc. Hist. Archaeology, Shriners, Order Eastern Star. Home and Office: 8849 Youngsea Pl Columbia MD 21045

BALOG, LINDA MARIE, human resources management executive; b. Detroit, Oct. 22, 1946; d. Steven Alex and Sylvia Marie (Gustafson) B.; m. Robert M. Balthrop, 1968 (div. 1984); 1 child, Amy Louise. BA in Bus., Mich. State U., East Lansing, 1968; MA in Indsl. Counseling, Eastern Mich. U., 1979. Tchr. Livonia (Mich.) Pub. Schs., 1968; indsl. rels. analyst car product devel. Ford Motor Co., Dearborn, Mich., 1970-75, 77-78, suggestion program adminstr. car product devel., 1975-77; salaried personnel rep. transmission and axle engring. Ford Motor Co., Livonia, 1978-79; salaried personnel rep. chassis engring. Ford Motor Co., Dearborn, 1979-80, compensation analyst employee rels. staff, 1980-86; orgn. analyst sales ops. Ford Motor Co., Detroit, 1986-88; employee rels. assoc. sales ops. Ford Motor Co., Dearborn, 1988-90; employee rels. assoc. sales ops., employee tng. and communications Ford Motor Co., Detroit, 1990—. Advisor Explorer Officer Assn., Detroit area coun. Boy Scouts Am., 1984—. Recipient Silver Beaver award Boy Scouts Am., Detroit, 1987. Mem. Internat. Assn. Personnel Women (pres. Detroit 1985, plaque 1985), Phi Gamma Nu. Republican. Roman Catholic. Home: 9072 Becker Ave Allen Park MI 48101

BALPH, MARTHA HATCH, educator; b. Boston, May 27, 1943; d. Robert M. and Helen (Addison) Hatch; m. David F. Balph, June 9, 1972 (dec. Feb. 1990); children: Robert H., David C. BA in Biology, Wellesley Coll., 1965; MS in Zoology, U. Wyo., 1969; PhD in Biology, Utah State U., 1975. Mus. tech., biol. illus. Smithsonian Inst., Washington, 1967-70; rsch. asst. prof. fisheries and wildlife Utah State U., Logan, 1975-80, rsch. assoc. prof., 1980-82, 84—; cons. VTN Corp., Denver, 1974-77. Contbr., illustrator articles to profl. jours. F.M. Chapman grantee 1976, 78, Rsch. grantee Utah State U., 1980-81. Mem. Am. Ornithologists Union (life, elective, Carnes award 1979), Western Bird Banding Assn. (pres. 1979-81), Cooper Ornithol. Soc. (bd. dirs. 1984-87), Wilson Ornithol. Soc., Animal Behavior Soc., Wildlife Soc., Sigma Xi. Home: PO Box 68 Millville UT 84326 Office: Utah State U Dept Fisheries & Wildlife Logan UT 84322-5210

BALTER, FRANCES SUNSTEIN, civic worker; b. Pitts.; d. Elias and Gertrude (Kingsbacher) Sunstein. Student Sarah Lawrence Coll., 1939-41, New Sch. Social Rsch., 1941-43, Bennington Coll., 1941, 42; cert. Harvard Inst. Arts Adminstrn., 1973; m. James Stone Balter, May 15, 1948; children: Katherine (Mrs. Ross Anthony), Julia Frances, Constance (Mrs. Owen Cantor), Daniel Elias; m. Harry Philip Blum, Mar. 1, 1982. Adminstrv. asst., assoc. producer Ednl. Television Sta. WQED-TV, Pitts., 1963-67; producer, mng. dir. Freedom Readers, 1964-67; co-founder, incorporator, sec. bd. dirs. Pitts. Coun. for Arts, 1967-70; cultural cons. Mayor's Office, Dir. of Office of Cultural Affairs, Pitts., 1968; initiator Three Rivers Arts Festival 1960; co-dir. Ohio and Miss. River Valley Art Festival, 1961-62; mem. Pa. Coun. on Arts, 1972-78; co-founder Pioneer Crafts Coun. Mill Run Pa., 1972; exec. dir. Poetry On The Buses, 1974—; bd. dirs. Coun. for Arts MIT, 1985—, Palm Beach Festival, 1987-89. Named Woman of Yr. in Art Post-Gazette, 1969. Mem. Assoc. Councs. on Arts, Nat. Soc. Arts and Letters, Nat. League of Am. PEN Women (assoc. 1990—). Home: 1021 Devonshire Rd Pittsburgh PA 15213

BALTZER, KIMBERLY LENORE, civil engineer, consultant; b. Quincy, Ill., Nov. 10, 1964; d. George Washington and Verna Marie (Goodwin) B. Student engring., N.E. Mo. State U., 1982-84; BS in Engring. Mgmt., U. Mo., Rolla, 1986, MS in Engring. Mgmt., 1988. Cert. engr.-in-tng. Engring. aide Ill. Dept. Transport, Quincy, 1985; tech. engr. Poepping, Stone, Bach & Assocs., Quincy, 1986, 87; civil engr. Torres Cons. Engrs., Kansas City, 1989; asst. city engr. City of Leavenworth, Kans., 1990—. Mem. choir Cen. Bapt. Ch., Quincy, 1981—. Pres.'s hon. scholar N.E. Mo. State U., 1982; named Outstanding Coll. Students of Am. and Disting. Am. High Sch. Students. Mem. Rainbow for Girls (life majority mem., officer 1978-84), Kappa Mu Epsilon. Home: 248 Holiday Terr Lansing KS 66043

BALZAC, AUDREY FLOBELLE ADRIAN, psychologist; b. N.Y.C., May 5, 1928; d. Allen Isaac and Mildred Florence (Brown) Adrian; m. Ralph P. Balzac, Jr., May 3, 1961; children: Stephen Rafael, Elena Adrian, Rebecca Lisa. BA in Psychology with honors, Hunter Coll., 1951; MS with honors, Purdue U., 1952; ABD, Columbia U., 1963. Intern in psychology Howard Rusk Inst., NYU and Bellevue Hosp., N.Y.C., 1956-57; clin. psychologist Westchester Community Mental Health Bd., and Children's Ct., White Plains, N.Y., 1957-63; psychol. cons. div. Vocat. Rehab., N.Y.C., 1957—; pvt. practice, 1963—; research psychologist Psychiat. Inst., Columbia Presbyn. Med. Ctr., N.Y.C., 1955-57; cons. Pound Ridge Elem. Sch., 1975-76. Chairwoman Community Relations bd. Pound Ridge Jewish Community Ctr., 1975-79, treas., 1978-79; mem. Westchester Women's Adv. Bd., 1986-87; candidate Bedford Cen. Sch. Bd., 1987, 88. Fellow Rusk Inst., 1956-57; research grantee Columbia U., 1960—. Fellow AAUW; mem. Am. Psychol. Assn., Eastern Psychol. Assn., N.Y. Soc. Clin. Psychologists, Soc. Psychol. Study of Social Issues, Am. Sociol. Assn., Sigma Xi, Psi Chi (treas. 1951-52). Jewish. Home: Rte 4 Box 267 Pound Ridge NY 10576

BAMBER, MARGARET MARY, journalist; b. Washington, July 6, 1953; d. Richard Camille and Ruth Cutting (Heaton) B. BA, U. Md., 1986. Sec. II Internat. Brotherhood of Elec. Workers, Washington, 1973-79, sec. III, 1979-83, editorial asst., 1983-88, sr. editorial asst., 1988—; writer, editor P & C Wordsmiths, Washington, 1989—. Vol. ARC, Washington, 1980, March of Dimes, 1987; mem. Dem. Congl. Campaign Com., Washington, 1988; contbg. mem. Dem. Nat. Com., 1990; sec. bd. dirs. Rutland Court Owners, Inc., Washington, 1989—. Mem. NAFE, Office and Profl. Employees Internat. Union, Local 2, U. Md. Univ. Coll. Alumni Assn., Nat. Assn. Housing Cooperatives, Phi Kappa Phi, Alpha Sigma Lambda, Touchdown Club (Washington). Roman Catholic. Home: 1725 17th St NW #115 Washington DC 20009 Office: Internat Brotherhood Elec Workers 1125 15th St NW Ste 1001 Washington DC 20005

BAMBERGER, GABRIELLE, public relations executive; b. Berlin, Germany, June 8, 1938; d. Fritz and Kate (Schwabe) B. BA, Oberlin Coll., 1960. Asst. account exec. Philip Lesly Co., N.Y.C., 1961-63, account exec., 1963-68; owner Gabrielle Bamberger Pub. Relations, N.Y.C., 1968—; Editor LBI News Leo Baeck Inst., 1974—, Libr. and Archives News, 1975—. Mem. Am. Women in Radio and TV, Women in Communications, Inc. Home: 215 E 79th St New York NY 10021 Office: 250 W 57th St #1527 New York NY 10019

BAMBERGER, JULIA KATHRYN, social worker; b. Phila., Dec. 23, 1960; d. William Thomas and Julia Kathryn (O'Brien) B. BA in Social Work, Holy Family Coll., Phila., 1983. Cert. social worker. Recreational therapy asst., physical therapy asst. Ashton Hall Nursing Home, Phila., 1979-83; hairdresser asst. St. John Neumann Nursing Home, Phila., 1982-83; recreational therapy asst. Evangelical Manor, Phila., 1983; social worker The Consortium/Southwest Sr. Citizens Ctr., Phila., 1983-90; resource specialist Phila. Corp. for Aging, 1990—. Mem., chairperson Alzheimers Disease and Related Disordrs Assn., Phila., 1983—; vol. Ashton Hall Nursing Home, Phila., 1983-89; V.I.P. blood donor ARC, 1978—; solicitor Cath. Charities Appeal, 1979—; mem. Pro Life Coalition of Southeastern Pa., 1986—; soprano singer guitar Mass. group Maternity Blessed Virgin Mary Roman Cath. Ch., Phila., 1977—, soprano singer, Folk Mass Group, 1979—; vol. Eucharistic Adoration, Our Lady of Fatima Roman Cath. Ch., 1988—. Recipient cert. of appreciation Alzheimers Disease and Related Disorders Assn., 1985, Outstanding Young Women of Am., 1985, 86, 88. Mem. Southeastern Pa. Assn. Sr. Ctr. Pers., Pa. Interagy. Coun. on Aging and Mental Health, Social Svc. Workers Assn. of Nursing Homes, Cath. Adult Singles Assn., Assn. Church Musicians in Phila., Epsilon Nu Cath. Adult Singles Assn., Archbishop Ryan High Sch. for Girls Alumnae Assn. (corr. sec. 1985—), Holy Family Coll. Alumni Assn. (recording sec. 1985-90, cert. of appreciation 1984, 89), Classic Thunderbird Club, Smoke Free Soc, Psi Chi. Democrat. Home: 2016 Tomlinson Rd Philadelphia PA 19116 Office: Phila Corp for Aging 642 N Broad St Philadelphia PA 19130

BANASHEK, MARY-ELLEN, writer, editor; b. Wilkes-Barre, Pa., Dec. 7, 1951; d. Walter Joseph and Irene (Rapchak) B. BA, Emira Coll., 1973. Assoc. features editor Mademoiselle mag., N.Y.C., 1973-79; beauty copywriter Harper's Bazaar mag., N.Y.C., 1979-80; beauty and health editor Self mag., N.Y.C., 1980-81; sr. copy writer Avon Products, Inc., N.Y.C., 1982-83; beauty and health editor McCall's mag., N.Y.C., 1983-85; sr. writer Elle mag., N.Y.C., 1986-87; contbg. editor Woman's Day mag., N.Y.C., 1987-90, New Woman Mag., N.Y.C., 1989—; cons. editor In Fashion mag., N.Y.C., 1988. Mem. Phi Beta Kappa. Office: New Woman Mag 215 Lexington Ave New York NY 10016

BANCROFT, ANNE (MRS. MEL BROOKS), actress; b. N.Y.C., Sept. 17, 1931; d. Michael and Mildred (DiNapoli) Italiano; m. Mel Brooks, 1964; 1 son. Broadway stage appearances include Two for the Seesaw, 1957 (Tony award 1957), The Miracle Worker, 1959-60 (Tony award 1960), Devils, 1977, Golda, 1977-78, Duet for One, 1981; stage appearances include Mystery of the Rose Bouquet, 1989; motion pictures include Treasure of the Golden Condor, 1952, Don't Bother to Knock, 1952, Tonight We Sing, 1953, The Kid from Left Field, 1953, Demetrius and the Gladiators, 1954, Gorilla at Large, 1954, The Raid, 1954, A Life in the Balance, 1954, The Brass Ring, 1954, Naked Street, 1955, New York Confidential, 1955, The Last Frontier, 1955, Girl in the Black Stockings, 1957, Restless Breed, 1957, The Pumpkin Eater, 1964, Seven Women, 1966, Slender Thread, 1966, The Graduate, 1967, Young Winston, 1972, The Prisoner of 2nd Avenue, 1975, The Hindenburg, 1975, Lipstick, 1976, Silent Movie, 1976, The Turning Point, 1977, Fatso, 1979, The Elephant Man, 1980, To Be or Not to Be, 1983, Garbo Talks, 1984, Agnes of God, 1985, 'Night, Mother, 1986, 84 Charing Cross Road (Brit. Acad. award 1987), Torch Song Trilogy, 1988, Bert Rigby You're a Fool, 1989; TV appearances include Kraft Music Hall, Jesus of Nazareth, 1977, Marco Polo, 1982; dir., writer, star: (TV spl.) Annie-The Woman in the Life of Men, 1970 (Emmy award 1970). Recipient Acad. award for performance in The Miracle Worker, 1962. Address: care 20th Century Fox Studios PO Box 900 Beverly Hills CA 90213

BANCROFT, ELIZABETH ABERCROMBIE, publisher, analytical chemist; b. Washington, Mar. 2, 1947; d. John Chandler and Ruth Abercrombie (Robinson) B.; A.B., Harvard U./Radcliffe Coll., 1979; postgrad. in forensic scis. John Jay Coll. Criminal Justice, 1982. Asst. dir. research Bagley Fordyce Research Labs., N.Y.C., 1979-83, dir. research and publs., Washington office, 1984-86; dir. Nat. Intelligence Book Ctr., 1986—; dir. Nat. Intelligence Study Ctr. Mem. Assn. Fgn. Intelligence Officers, Naval Intelligence Profls., Nat. Mil. Intelligence Assn., Nat. Intelligence Study Ctr., Assn. Ofcl. Analytical Chemists, Am. Chem. Soc., Am. Inst. Chemists, N.Y. Acad. Scis., Washington Book Pubs. Assn., Am. Bookseller Assn. Republican. Episcopalian. Clubs: Harvard of N.Y.C., Harvard/Radcliffe of Washington; Chemists of N.Y.; English Speaking Union of N.Y. and Washington. Home: 2737 Devonshire Pl NW Washington DC 20008 Office: Nat Intelligence Book Ctr 1700 K St NW Washington DC 20006

BANCROFT, MARGARET ARMSTRONG, lawyer; b. Mpls., May 9, 1938; d. Wallace David and Mary Elizabeth (Garland) Armstrong; m. Alexander Clerihew Bancroft, Mar. 14, 1964; 1 child, Elizabeth. BA magna cum laude, Radcliffe Coll., 1960; JD cum laude, NYU, 1969. Bar: N.Y. 1971. Reporter Mpls. Star and Tribune, 1960-61, UPI, N.Y. and N.J., 1961-66; assoc. Donovan Leisure Newton & Irvine, Paris, France, 1969-71, N.Y.C., 1971-78, ptnr., 1978-84; ptnr. Finley, Kumble, Wagner, Heine, Underberg, Manley, Myerson & Casey, N.Y.C., 1984-88, Dechert, Price & Rhoads, N.Y.C., 1988—; adj. prof. law NYU. Bd. dirs., exec. com. Vis. Nurse Service N.Y.; pres. Vis. Nurse Svc. Home Care. Mem. ABA (mem. subcom. tender offers and proxy contests 1984—), Assn. of Bar of City of N.Y., N.Y. State Bar Assn. (exec. com. banking, bus. law and corps. sect. 1986-89, com. securities regulation 1984—), Am. Law Inst. Democrat. Office: Dechert Price & Rhoads 477 Madison Ave New York NY 10022

BANDA, MARIANNE, artist; b. San Diego, Dec. 21, 1964; d. David Estrada and Mary Lee (Palacios) B. BA, U. Calif., San Diego, 1988; postgrad. in fine art, U. Calif., Irvine, 1988—. Teaching asst. U. Calif., Irvine, 1988—. U. Calif.-Irvine fellow, 1988-89. Democrat.

BANDER, CAROL JEAN, German and English educator; b. N.Y.C., Jan. 5, 1945; d. Frank Samuel and Susie Ruth (Guttfeld) Heimberg; m. Myron Bander, Aug. 20, 1967. BA, Queens Coll., 1966; MA, U. So. Calif., L.A., 1968, PhD, 1972. Cert. life community coll. credential, life standard secondary creditial. Assoc. faculty Orange Coast Coll., Costa Mesa, Calif., 1974-77, North Orange Community Coll., Fullerton, Calif., 1974-77; prof. of German and English as second lang. Saddleback Coll., Mission Viejo, Calif., 1977—, dept. chair English as a second lang., 1989—. NDEA Title IV fellowship U.S. Govt., 1966-70. Mem. Calif. Assn. of Tchrs. of English to Speakers of Other Langs. (bd. dirs. 1988-90, chpt. chair 1989-90, coord. Orange County chpt. 1988-90), Am. Assn. Tchrs. of German, Tchrs. of English to Speakers of Their Langs., Phi Beta Kappa. Home: 18911 Antioch Dr Irvine CA 92715 Office: Saddleback Coll 2800 Marguerite Pkwy Mission Viejo CA 92692

BANDY, MARY LEA, museum official; b. Evanston, Ill., June 16, 1943; d. DeWitt Clinton and Ruth (Coale) Gibson; m. Gary Bandy, June 3, 1967. B.A., Stanford U., 1965. Asst. editor Harry N. Abrams, Inc., N.Y.C., 1966-73; asso. editor publs. Mus. Modern Art, N.Y.C., 1973-76; asso. coordinator exhbns. Mus. Modern Art, 1976-78, adminstr. dept. film, 1978-80, dir. dept. film, 1980—. Office: Mus Modern Art 11 W 53rd St New York NY 10019

BANE, MADELYN RICHARDSON, librarian, educator; b. Akron, Ohio, May 31, 1942; d. William Monroe and Milderd Elizabeth (Gavin) Richardson; m. Norman A. Prince, June 5, 1965 (div. Nov. 1977); children: Darcy Anne, Norman Daniel; m. William D. Bane, May 29, 1982 (dec. Feb. 1985). BEd, Ohio U., 1965; MS, Radford U., 1985. Libr. Cleve. Pub. Schs., 1965-68, Schenectady (N.Y.) Pub. Schs., 1968-72, St. Louis Sch., Cleveland Heights, Ohio, 1972-74; libr., adminstrv. asst. Roanoke (Va.) Cath. Sch., 1974-86, dir. devel., 1986-88. Mem. Va. Ednl. Media Assn., Internat. Reading Assn., Roanoke Valley Reading Coun. (pres. 1984-85, 87-88), Va. Reading Assn. (bd. dirs. 1984-85, 87-88), Ga. State Reading Coun., Phi Kappa Delta. Democrat. Roman Catholic. Home: 3495 Johnson Ferry Rd Roswell GA 30075

BANE, MARGO EWING, state legislator; b. Wilmington, Del., Nov. 14, 1949. BS, U. Del., 1972. Former tchr.; mem. Del. State Senate, 1986—. Mem. AAUW, LWV, Nat. Fedn. Rep. Women. Republican. Home: 9 Laurel Ct Wilmington DE 19808 Office: Del State Senate Dover DE 19901*

BANERDT, DAWN MARIE, military communications technician; b. Milw., May 1, 1964; d. Barry Michael and Joyce Marie (Marasch) B. Grad. high sch. Enlisted USN, 1982; communications tech. USN, various locations, 1982—. Mem. NAFE. Home: 404 Tayco St Menasha WI 54952 Office: Div 713 Comsublant Norfolk VA 23511

BANFIELD, JOANNE, insurance corporation executive; b. Bronxville, N.Y., Feb. 21, 1954; d. George Alfred and Josephine (Bartolotta) B.; m. Thomas Allen Hanlon, Aug. 6, 1978 (div. July 1985). BA, Iona Coll., 1976. Outpatient registrar United Hosp., Port Chester, N.Y., 1976-78; disability benefits specialist Union Mut. Ins. Co., Elmsford, N.Y., 1978-82; staff asst. to exec. adminstr. Am. Assn. Advt. Agys. Ins. Trust, N.Y.C., 1982-83; sr. claims analyst Gen. Reassurance Corp., Stamford, Conn., 1984-88; mgr. benefits and compensation Life Reassurance Corp. Am., Stamford, 1988-89;

benefits staff asst. Pub. Svc. Electric and Gas Co., Newark, 1990—. Mem. Soc. for Human Resource Mgmt., NAFE. Episcopalian.

BANGASSER, ELIZABETH, truck manufacturer executive; b. Seattle, Sept. 25, 1956; d. Paul E. Sr. and Margaret A. (Sheffield) B. Student, U. Santa Clara, 1974-76; BA, BFA, U. Washington, 1978. With retail sales Eddie Bauer, Bellevue, Wash., 1975-79; with retail sales Farwest Sales & Mktg., Seattle, 1979-80; with Kenworth Truck Co., Kirkland, Wash., 1981—; western region mgr. Kenworth Truck Co., Kirkland, 1989—. Tutor Jobs for Youth, Chgo, 1984-86; helper local soup kitchen, Seattle. Democrat. Roman Catholic. Home: 3251 11th Ave W Seattle WA 98119

BANISTER, JUDITH, demographer, educator; b. Washington, Sept. 10, 1943; d. William Price and Helen Barbara (Myers) B.; m. Kim Woodard, Dec. 17, 1966; children: Adrian Banard, Dawn Banard. B.A. in History, Swarthmore Coll., 1965; Ph.D. in Demography, Stanford U., 1978. Postdoctoral rsch. fellow East-West Population Inst., Honolulu, 1978-80; statistician/demographer U.S. Bur. of Census, Washington, 1980-82, chief China br. Ctr. for Internat. Rsch., 1982—; part-time assoc. prof. George Washington U., Washington, 1981—. Author: China's Changing Population, 1987; contbr. articles to profl. jours. Mem. Population Assn. Am., Internat. Union for Sci. Study of Population. Office: Scuderi Bldg Ctr for Internat Rsch US Bureau Of Census Room 606 Washington DC 20233

BANKER, CYNTHIA ANNE, pediatric dentist; b. San Antonio, Tex., Dec. 4, 1949; d. Benjamin Franklin and Beatrice Francis (Ankerson) B.; m. Brett Hensley Mueller, Jan. 5, 1980; children: Brett, Chelby, Bryan, Christina. BS, Tex. Tech. U., 1971; DDS, U. Tex., San Antonio, 1975, MA, 1979. Dentist at clinic City of San Antonio, 1975-76; dentist on sch. van San Antonio Ind. Sch., 1975-76; instr. UTHSCSA, San Antonio, 1975-80; dentist Dr. Spalton, San Antonio, 1975-76, Dr. E. Dean Harmison, San Antonio, 1976-81; pediatric dental resident UTHSCSA, 1980-82, asst. prof., 1985-87; pvt. practice San Antonio, 1982—. Author: Pediatric Radiographic Interpretation, 1980. Mem. Hermann Sons, Providence High Alumni Soc., Conservation Soc., 1975-86. Recipient Med. Career award AAUW, 1976, Table Clinic award TDA, 1975, 79. Mem. Tex. Acad. Pediatric Dentistry, San Antonio Acad. Pediatric Dentistry (pres.). Roman Catholic. Office: San Pedro North Pediatric Dental 14500 San Pedro San Antonio TX 78232

BANKERT, PAMELA BERYL, lawyer; b. N.Y.C., June 28, 1954; d. Willard Edgar and Patricia (Gale) B.; m. Rupert Brandt, Aug. 10, 1986. Student, Pace Coll., 1972-74, Bklyn. Coll., 1974; BS summa cum laude, Ramapo Coll., 1984; JD, Rutgers U., Newark, 1987. Bar: Mass. 1988. Clk. Joint Indsl. Bd. Elec. Workers, Flushing, N.Y., 1975-76; med. asst. Dr. Arthur S. Liggett, Flushing, 1976-78; animal technician customs dept. Kennedy Airport USDA, Jamaica, N.Y., 1978-79; med. sec. Dr. Constantin D. Papadopoulos, Bklyn., 1979; med. asst., mgr. Dr. Irwin Greenbaum, Kew Gardens, N.Y., 1979-81; office mgr. Michael T. Greenwald, Northvale, N.J., 1982-83; exec. dir. Co. Med. Assn., Northvale, 1983-84; assoc., mng. atty. Lawson & Wayne, Provincetown, Mass., 1987-89; ptnr. Lawson, Weitzen & Bankert, Wellfleet, 1989—; mem. Barnstable County Referral Program and Supplemental Lawyer Referral Program; pro bono Legal Svcs. for Cape and Islands, Hyannis, Mass., 1988—. Exhibited in group show Cape Cod Women's Expo, Hyannis, 1988, 89. Mem. adv. bd. Provincetown Positive-People with AIDS Coalition, 1988-89; trustee, bd. dirs. Provincetown Art Assn. and Mus., 1989; pres., bd. dirs. Independence House, Hyannis, 1988—. Ramapo Coll. President's scholar, 1983. Mem. ABA, Mass. Bar Assn., Barnstable County Bar Assn. Democrat. Office: Lawson Weitzen & Bankert RR2 Rte 6 Wellfleet MA 02667

BANKETT, PAULA R., law librarian; b. Travis AFB, Mar. 26, 1959; d. E.L. and Paulyne P. B. Student, Calif. U., Hayward; AB, Fisk U., Nashville, 1982; postgrad., Calif. State U. Libr. The Port of Oakland, Calif.; now supr. libr., archives The State Bar of Calif., San Francisco. Mem. ARMA Internat., Black Women Lawyers Assn., Nat. Assn. Govt. Archives and Records, No. Calif. Assn. Law Librs., Delta Sigma Theta. Democrat. Methodist. Office: 555 Franklin St San Francisco CA 94102

BANKOWSKI, MARY THERESA, school systems administrator; b. Stamford, Conn., Dec. 5, 1931; d. Michael Andrew and Mary Magdalene (Wozny) Jachimczyk; m. Edward Jerome Bankowski, May 30, 1953; 1 child, Mary Ann. BS cum laude, Mercyhurst Coll., 1953; MS, U. Bridgeport, 1958; cert., Fairfield U., 1965. Bus. tchr. Stamford (Conn.) High Sch., 1953-61; chmn. bus. dept. Rippowam High Sch., Stamford, 1961-82, Westhill High Sch., Stamford, 1982-86; dir. Stamford, Tchrs. Credit Union, 1979-89; mem. Stamford Fed. Tchrs., 1953-86; treas. Conn. Bus. Edn. Assn., 1962-66. Rep. Stamford Bd. Reps., 1953-57; mem. Young Dem. Club Conn., 1955-65, Dem. Women's Club, 1965-75, Holy Name Jesus Lay Bd., 1972-76. Mem. AAUW, So. Fairfield County Ret. Tchrs. Assn. (life). Roman Catholic.

BANKS, ANNIE ASHLEIGH, administrative assistant; b. Fresno, Calif., Apr. 19, 1957; d. Gilbert and Myrtle Simone (Spencer) B. BS, Calif. State U., Fresno, 1980. Customer svc. rep. Citicorp, Berkeley, Calif., 1977-81; with new accounts dept. Bank of Am., Fresno, 1981-82; adminstrv. asst. Jeray Weaver Prodns., Hollywood, Calif., 1982-84; counselor Vols. of Am., L.A., 1984-87; adminstrv. asst. IBM Corp., L.A., 1987-88, Letco Interiors, Riverside, Calif., 1989—; asst. mgr. Anna's Linen, Chgo., 1989—. Mem. NAACP, Jr. League (security), L.A., 1985-86.

BANKS, AUDREY C., educator, administrator; b. Chgo., Jan. 22; d. James and Vuelta (Manuel) Carson; m. Fred Bank, Dec. 4; children: Fred, Michael. Student, Chgo. Tchrs. Coll., Roosevelt U., Chgo.; EdD, Vanderbilt U., 1985. Cert. sch. adminstr., Ill. Staff devel. tch. local elem. sch., reading specialist, cons. tchr., team leader for sch.'s peer leadership program; asst. prin. Chgo. Public Sch. Mem. Citizens Sch. Com., Roseland Heights Community Assn. Mem. Internat. Reading Assn., Assn. for Supervisory and Curriculum Devel., Ill. Reading Assn., Phi Delta Kappa.

BANKS, BETTIE SHEPPARD, psychologist; b. Birmingham, Ala., June 8, 1933; d. Francis Wilkerson and Bettie Pollard (Woodson) Sheppard; B.A., Ga. State U., 1966, M.A., 1968, Ph.D., 1970; m. Frazer Banks, Jr., Mar. 22, 1952; children—Bettie Banks Daley, Lee Frazer III. Clin. asso. Lab. for Psychol. Services, Ga. State U., 1968-70; intern Ga. Mental Health Inst., Atlanta, 1970-71, psychologist, 1971-72, chief psychologist, 1973; pvt. practice, Atlanta, 1972—; adj. assoc. prof. clin. psychology Ga. State U.; mem. peer rev. panel Ga. Med. Care Found., 1980-86, chmn., 1986-88. Diplomate in clin. psychology Am. Bd. Profl. Psychology. Fellow Ga. Psychol. Assn. (chmn. div. E 1980); mem. Am. Acad. Psychotherapists (exec. com. 1980-82, sec. 1982-86), Am. Psychol. Assn., Am. Group Psychotherapy Assn., Atlanta Group Psychotherapy Soc. (exec. com. 1982), Southeastern Psychol. Assn. Episcopalian. Club: Jr. League. Cons. editor Voices, 1978-84. Office: 595 Wimbledon Rd NE Atlanta GA 30324

BANKS, JONI WHEELER, interior designer, small business executive; b. High Point, N.C., Oct. 18, 1957; d. Johnny Franklin Wheeler and Mary Helen (Dunbar) Penninger; m. Benjamin Thorpe Banks, Mar. 16, 1985; children: Benjamin II, John Robert. BFA in Interior Design, East Carolina U., 1980. Owner, designer Creative Interiors, High Point, 1979-80; interiors coordinator Sea Pines Co., Hilton Head, S.C., 1980; mgr., buyer Fines, Savannah, Ga., 1980-81, Hudson Bay Trading Co., Hilton Head, 1981, Andrew Arnold Clothier, Hilton Head, 1981-83; mgr, head designer The Decorators Unlimited, Hilton Head, 1983-86; owner, designer J. Banks Design Group Inc., Hilton Head, 1986—. Mem. Evening of the Arts preview Island Sch. Council, Hilton Head, 1986, Hlton Head Plantation Comml. Archtl. Rev. Bd., 1988. Mem. Am. Soc. Interior Designers, Inst. of Arts (party chmn., designers showcase designer 1985). Baptist. Club: Women's of Hilton Head. Home: 8 Myrtle Bank Ln Hilton Head SC 29929 Office: J Banks Design Group Main St Hilton Head SC 29938

BANKS, LISA JEAN, government official; b. Chelsea, Mass., Dec. 19, 1956; d. Bruce H. and Jean P. (Como) Banks. BS in Bus. Adminstrn., Northeastern U., 1979. Coop trainee IRS, Boston, 1975-79, revenue officer, Reno, 1979-81, spl. agt., Houston, 1981-84, Anchorage, 1984-90, Bedford, Mass., 1990; spl. agt. DVA-OIG Procurement Fraud Task force, Boston, 1990—, fed. womens program mgr., 1980-81. Recipient Superior Performance award IRS, 1981, Spl. Achievement award, 1987, 89, Employee Suggestion award, 1990. Mem. Nat. Assn. Treasury Agts., NAFE, Assn. Fed. Investigators. Democrat. Roman Catholic Office: Dept of VA-OIG 200 Springs Rd Rm 122 Bedford MA 01730

BANKS, MARGARET AMELIA, librarian, author, consultant; b. Quebec City, Que., Can., July 3, 1928; d. Thomas Herbert and Bessey (Collins) B. BA, Bishop's U., Lennoxville, Que., 1949; MA, U. Toronto, 1950, PhD, 1953. Archivist Ont. Archives, Toronto, 1953-61; law librarian U. Western Ont., London, 1961-89, assoc. prof. faculty law, 1974-86, prof., 1986-89, prof. emeritus, 1989—. Mem. Can. Assn. Law Libraries, Am. Inst. Parliamentarians, Nat. Assn. Parliamentarians, Osgoode Soc. Anglican. Author: Edward Blake, Irish Nationalist, 1957, Using a Law Library, 1st edit., 1971, 4th edit., 1985, Law at Western, 1959-84, 1984, The Libraries at Western, 1989. Home and Office: 231 Windsor Ave, Unit 9, London, ON Canada N6C 2A5

BANKS, PAULA A., foundation administrator; b. Chgo., Feb. 4, 1950; d. Ralph D. Robinson and Vivian L. (Tillman) Webb; m. Gary L. Banks, Apr. 22, 1978. BS in Psychology, Loyola U., Chgo., 1971; postgrad., U. Ill., 1976-77. Dir. equal opportunity midwestern ter. Sears, Roebuck and Co., Chgo., 1977-78, staff asst. employment and labor rels., 1978-80; pers. mgr. catalog distbn. ctr. Sears, Roebuck and Co., Elk Grove, Ill., 1980-82; mgr. human resources midwestern ter. Sears, Roebuck and Co., Chgo., 1982-86, mgr. human resources distbn., 1986-88, dir. community affairs and corp. contributions, 1988—; v.p. Sear-Roebuck Found., Chgo., 1988-89, pres., 1989—. Corp. assoc., vol. involvement com., baby boom task force United Way of Am., Alexandria, Va., 1988—; bd. dirs. Midwest Assn. Sickle Cell Anemia, Chgo., 1986—, Chgo. Youth Conservation Corps, 1988-90; mem. corp. adv. com. Found. for Ind. Higher Edn., Stamford, Conn., 1988—, ARC, Washington, 1988—; adv. com. Found. Ctr., N.Y.C., 1989—; mem. contributions coun. Conf. Bd., N.Y.C., 1989—; pub. rels. and devel. Cities in Schs., Chgo., 1989—. Mem. Women in Philanthrophy, Nat. Coun. Negro Women. Home: 2024 Garden Terr Hoffman Estates IL 60195 Office: The Sears-Roebuck Foundation Sears Tower 51st Fl Dept 903 Chicago IL 60684

BANKS-TARR, SHARON ELIZABETH, nurse; b. Pitts., Apr. 5, 1950; d. John C. and Myrtle (Banks) Claughton; m. Paul D. Tarr; 1 child, Jesse. BS in Nursing, U. Pitts., 1974, M in Nursing, 1980. Critical care nurse Presbyn. Univ. Hosp., Pitts., 1974-79, relief supr. critical care div., 1979-80; critical care educator Drs. Med. Ctr., Modesto, Calif., 1980-82; critical care nurse Lavina Hosp., Altadena, Calif., 1982-83; commd. lt. (j.g.) USN, 1983, advanced through grades to lt. comdr., 1990; nurse U.S. Naval Hosp., Chinhae, Korea, 1986-88, Great Lakes, Ill., 1988; med. programs officer and programs recruiter Navy Recruiting Dist., Pitts., 1990—; instr. Gt. Lakes Naval Hosp. Corps Sch., 1988-90; mem. 1st del. infection control practitioners to People's Republic China, 1988. Mem. Assn. Pulmonary Clin. Nurse Specialists, Assn. for Practitoners. Democrat. Office: Navy Recruiting Dist PGH 1000 Liberty Ave Rm 711 Pittsburg PA 15222

BANN, KATHLEEN WINTERS, financial analyst; b. Pitts., Sept. 18, 1957; d. James Albert and Jeanne Audrey (Fritschle) Winters; m. John William Bann, July 3, 1983. BA, U. Pitts., 1979, BS, 1979, M of Business, 1987. Cert. cash mgr. Fin. analyst Gen. Nutrition, Pitts., 1987-88, treasury analyst, 1988-89, sr. fin. analyst, 1989—; grad. asst. Dale Carnegie Sch., Pitts., 1988. Campaign coord. state rep., Pitts., 1986. Selected for Am. Assembly Dialogue, Grad. Sch. of Bus., U. Pitts., 1987. Mem. Pitts. Bus. and Profl. Women's Club (bd. dirs. 1988-90, club chmn. 1988-90), NAFE, Nat. Corp. Cash Mgmt. Assn. Home: 763 Glen Manor Rd Pittsburgh PA 15237 Office: Gen Nutrition Inc 921 Penn Ave Pittsburgh PA 15222

BANNISTER, CANDIDA CLEVE, accountant, consultant; b. Lincoln, Nebr., Mar. 3, 1957; d. Robert Lee and Miwako (Yasaki) Cleve; m. Jerome Bannister II, Nov. 16, 1985. BA, U. Calif., L.A., 1980. Acct. history dept. UCLA, 1984-87, contract and grant acct. dept. civil engring., 1987—. Mem. NAFE. Republican. Office: U Calif Dept Civil Engring 405 Hilgard Ave Los Angeles CA 90024-1593

BANONIS, BARBARA ANN CUCCIOLI, nurse, employee health consultant; b. Bklyn., Oct. 6, 1947; d. Robert and Ann (Amalfitano) Cuccioli; m. Edward Joseph Banonis, Nov. 15, 1969; children: Aaron Joseph, Beth Rose. BS in Nursing, Villanova U., 1969; MS in Nursing, W.Va. U., 1988. RN. Coordinator autistic children's research unit Eastern State Sch. & Hosp., Trevose, Pa., 1969-71; pub. health nurse State of Del., Wilmington, 1972; occupational health cons. Div. of Mental Health, New Castle, Del., 1972-75; faculty nursing Del. Tech. and Community Coll., Newark, 1976-78; cons./writer Freelance Contracts, Newark, 1978; dir. Limen House, Inc., Wilmington, 1979-81; pres., chief exec. officer Banonis Assocs., South Charleston, W.Va., 1982—; founder, chmn. peer impaired nurse program Nurse Care Network, W.Va., 1985—; adj. faculty W.Va. Coll. Grad. Studies, U. Charleston and W.Va. U.; bd. dirs. Steps-Seminars, Tng. & Enlightenment Programs, 1988—. Author (book chpt.) Nursing and Alcohol Related Problems; researcher, contbr. articles to profl. jours. Allocations vol. United Way Kanawha Valley, Charleston, 1984—, allocations panel chmn., 1985, bd. dirs., 1986—; commr. council on family sevices Gov. of Del. Pierre Dupont, Wilmington, 1978; co-founder, bd. dirs. Task Force Women and Chem. Dependency, Wilmington, 1976-83. Mem. ANA, Employee Assistance Profls. Assn., ASTD, Employee Assistance Resource Network (chmn. pub. rels. com. 1984—), Employee Assistance Soc. N.Am., Charleston Women's Forum (pres. 1985-86), Sigma Theta Tau. Home: 2302 Claridge Circle South Charleston WV 25303

BANTEL, LINDA MAE, art museum director; b. King City, Calif., May 30, 1943; d. Clifford Burnett and Helen Vernelle (Mallicotte) Bantel; m. David Hollenberg, June 15, 1980; children—Matthew Bantel Hollenberg. M.A., NYU, 1971. Research cons. N.Y. Hist. Soc., N.Y.C., 1975-76; guest cocurator Art Mus. of South Tex., Corpus Christi, Tex., 1977-79; research assoc. Met. Mus. Art, N.Y.C., 1978-80; curator, now dir. of mus. Pa. Acad. Fine Arts, Phila., 1980—. Co-author: (with James Thomas Flexner) The Face of Liberty: Founders of the U.S., 1975; author: The Alice M. Kaplan Collection, 1980; William Rush, American Sculptor, 1982; (with Marcus Burke) Spain and New Spain: Mexican Colonial Arts in Their European Context, 1979; contbr. to American Paintings in the Metropolitan Museum of Art Vol. II: A Catalogue of Works by Artists Born Between 1816-1845, 1985. Mem. Coll. Art Assn., Am. Assn. Mus., Assn. Art Mus. Dirs. Home: 255 S 44th St Philadelphia PA 19104 Office: Pa Acad Fine Arts Broad & Cherry Sts Philadelphia PA 19102

BANYAI, GERALDLINE L., corporate secretary; b. Phila., Feb. 18, 1940; d. Frank Anthony and Alice (Giballa) LePera; m. Joseph Benjamin Banyai, Apr. 30, 1960. Grad. high sch., Lower Merion, Pa. Various positions Meritor Savs. Bank, Phila., 1958-62, asst. corp. sec., 1962-75, corp. sec., 1975—. Mem. Am. Soc. Corp. Secs., Fin. Woman Internat. (exec. bd. 1989-90). Office: Meritor Savs Bank 1212 Market St Bellmawr PA 19107

BAPTIST, SYLVIA EVELYN, data service company executive, consultant; b. Chgo., Feb. 15, 1944; d. Clarence Walter and Evelyn Alphild (Fagerberg) Bonin; m. Jeremy Eduard Baptist, July 21, 1962; children: Sarah, Margaret, Catherine. Student Mich. State U., 1961-62; B.S., Roosevelt U., 1965. Instr. IBM, Chgo., 1965-66, systems engr., Topeka, Kans., 1966-67; tchr. computer sci. Lawrence High Sch., Kans., 1968; pres. Multiple Data Svcs., Leawood, Kans., 1983—; adminstrv. user liaison Kansas City Sch. Dist., 1987-89, sr. adminstrv. user liaison, 1989—; cons. in field. Alumni Disting. scholar Mich. State U., 1961-62, Internat. Ladies' Garment Workers Union scholar Roosevelt U., 1964-65. V.p. Scandinavian Dancers Kansas City (v.p. 1987-89). Mem. NAFE, Internat. Platform Assn., Vasa (master ceremonies 1986-87, vice chmn. 1988-89, chmn. 1990—). Avocations: cooking, writing. Office: Multiple Data Svcs 3501 W 92d St Leawood KS 66206

BAPTISTE, IDELLA LOU, educator; b. Bellamy, Ala., July 27, 1952; d. Elbert and Arizona (Walker) Sanders; m. Rowan Calworth Baptiste, May 4, 1974; children: Rowan Calworth Jr., Samuel Elbert. B. in Elem. Edn., Northeastern U., 1975; M. Adminstrn./Mgmt., Cambridge Coll., 1984. Tchr. remedial edn. Boston Pub. Schs., 1975; tchr. Boston Pub. Schs., Roxbury, Mass., 1975-76, Charlestown, Mass., 1976-77, Roxbury, Mass., 1977; tchr. Title I elem. Highland Parks Free Sch., Roxbury, 1977-79, Boston Pub. Schs., Roxbury, 1979-80; tchr. Boston Pub. Schs., Dorchester, Mass., 1980-83, Mattapan, Mass., 1983—; computer curriculum Boston Pub. Schs., 1982-83; mem. Dist. 5 Tchr. Ctr., Boston Pub. Schs., 1980-85; cons. Dorchester (Mass.) YMCA Day Camp, Lynell's II I.S. Baptiste Co., Boston, 1989. Co-editor: Middle School Computer Curriculum, 1982-83, Middle School Math & Science, 1980-82. Vol. Little League Inc., Upper Roxbury, North Dorchester. Northeastern U. scholar 1970-75; recipient law cert. Boston U., 1970. Mem. NAFE, NAACP, Boston Tchrs. Union, Ala. Orgn., Order Eastern Star. Democrat. Baptist. Home: 119 Hazelton St Mattapan MA 02126

BAPTISTE, NANCY ELLEN, university program director; b. Hartford, Conn., Aug. 9, 1946; d. Sidney and Constance (Tarlow) Neiditch; m. David Adolphus Baptiste, Sept. 12, 1970; children: François, Gabrielle, Emile. BA, Mt. Holyoke Coll., 1968; MEd, Boston U., 1971; postgrad., N.Mex. State U. Tchr. Alpha Nursery Sch., Las Cruces, N.Mex., 1979-80; co-dir., owner Los Pequenos Presch. for Creative Learning, Las Cruces, 1979-81; coord. Las Cruces Pub. Schs. Tchrs. Ctr., 1981-84; asst./acting dir. Dona Ana Head Start Program, Las Cruces, 1984-85; coord. profl. devel. H.E.L.P. Head Start Programs, Las Cruces, 1987—; instr., coord. Child Devel. Assoc. program N.Mex. State U., Las Cruces, 1983—; cons. Las Cruces Pub. Schs. Tchrs. Ctr., 1988—. Contbr. articles to profl. publs., 1988—. Mem. Senator Bingamon's Presch. Task Force, Albuquerque, 1988; vice chairperson child care resource and referral adv. com. City of Las Cruces, 1988—, mem. adv. com. comprehensive child devel. program, 1989—. Child devel. grantee N.Mex. Dept. Vocat. Edn., 1989. Mem. Nat. Assn. for Edn. of Young Children (membership action grantee 1988, 89), N.Mex. Assn. for Edn. of Young Children, Las Cruces Assn. for Edn. of Young Children (historian), Nat. Assn. for Early Childhood Tchr. Educators, Assn. for Supervision and Curriculum Devel., Assn. for Childhood Edn. Internat., Phi Delta Kappa, Phi Kappa Phi. Democrat. Jewish. Home: 2709 Sim Ave Las Cruces NM 88005

BARAD, JILL ELIKANN, toy company executive; b. N.Y.C., May 23, 1951; d. Lawrence Stanley and Corinne (Schuman) Elikann; m. Thomas Kenneth Barad, Jan., 28, 1979; children: Alexander David, Justin Harris. BA English and Psychology, Queens Coll., 1973. Asst. prod. mgr. mktg. Coty Cosmetics, N.Y.C., 1976-77, prod. mgr. mktg., 1977; account exec. Wells Rich Greene Advt. Agy., Los Angeles, 1978-79; product mgr. mktg. Mattel Toys, Inc., Los Angeles, 1981-82, dir. mktg., 1982-83, v.p. mktg., 1983-85, sr. v.p. mktg., 1985-86, sr. v.p. product devel., from 1986, exec. v.p. product design and devel., exec. v.p. mktg. and worldwide product devel., 1988-89; pres. girls and activity toys div. Mattel Toys, Inc., L.A., 1989-; bd. dirs. Arco Toys. Charter mem. Rainbow Guild/Amie Karen Cancer Fund, Los Angeles, 1983, Los Angeles County Mus., 1985; trustee Queens Coll. Mem. Am. Film Inst. (charter). Office: Mattel Inc 5150 Rosecrans Ave Hawthorne CA 90250

BARAN, CAROLYN JONES, military officer, nurse practitioner; b. Valdosta, Ga., Apr. 26, 1942; d. Charles Brooks and Melba Onee (Dameron) Jones; m. Stephen T. Baran, Apr. 7, 1973. RN, Grady Hosp., Atlanta, 1963; BSN, William Carey Coll., 1982; MA in Human Relations, Webster U., 1984; M in Health Svc. Mgmt., 1986. Cert. nurse practitioner. Commd. 2d lt. USAF, 1969, advanced through grades to col.; clin. nurse various USAF hosps., 1969-86; chief nursing svc. adminstrn. Hdqrs. 14th AF, Dobbins AFB, Ga., 1886-89; nurse practitioner 347th Med. Group, Moody AFB, Ga., 1989—. Decorated Meritorious Svc. medal with 2 oak leaf clusters, Commendation medal with oak leaf cluster; recipient Humanitarian Svc. medal USAF, 1979, numerous others. Mem. Air Force Assn., AAUW, Nat. Assn. Am. Coll. Obstet. and Gynecol. Nursing, Uniformed Svcs. Nurse Practitioner Assn., Am. Nurses Assn., Bus. and Profl. Women's Assn. Home: 1208 Linda Dr Valdosta GA 31602

BARANAUCKAS, CARLA MAY, journalist; b. Niagara Falls, N.Y., Aug. 9, 1955; d. Charles Francis and Molly Ann (Mullen) B. BA cum laude, St. Olaf Coll., Northfield, Minn., 1977. News asst. Mpls. Tribune, 1977-78; reporter Pampa (Tex.) News, 1978; reporter, copy editor Texarkana (Tex.) Gazette, 1978-79, Edwardsville (Ill.) Intelligencer, 1979-81; copy editor Grand Forks (N.D.) Herald, 1981-84, St. Louis Post-Dispatch, 1984-88; sports copy editor The New York Times, 1988—. Participant Coro Found. Women in Leadership, St. Louis, 1987-88, mem. Jr. League of N.Y., 1988—. Mem. Soc. Profl. Journalists, Women in Communications, Women in Leadership Alumnae. Roman Catholic. Home: 124 W 60th St #14J New York NY 10023 Office: The New York Times 229 W 43rd St New York NY 10036

BARANSKI, CHRISTINE, actress; b. May 2, 1952; d. Lucien and Virginia (Mazerowski) B.; m. Matthew Cowles, Oct. 15, 1983. BA, Juilliard Sch., 1974. Plays include 'Tis a Pity She's a Whore, The Real Thing (Antoinette Perry award 1984), Cat on a Hot Tin Roof, She Stoops to Conquer, Angel City, Blithe Spirit, Coming Attractions, The Undefeated Rumba Champ, Otherwise Engaged, A Midsummer Night's Dream (Obie award 1983), Rumors, (Antoinette Perry award 1989); (films) Soup for One, 1981, Crackers, Lovesick, The Adams Chronicles, (TV shows) Playing for Time, Murder Ink, All My Children, Texas, Another World.

BARANSKI, JOAN SULLIVAN, publisher; b. Andover, Mass., Apr. 6, 1933; d. Joseph Charles and Ruth G. (McCormack) Sullivan; m. Kenneth E. Baranski, Apr. 20, 1970. B.S., U. Lowell, Mass., 1955. Tchr. Andover Public Schs., 1955-61; assoc. editor sci. and reading sch. dept. Holt, Rinehart and Winston, N.Y.C., 1961-65; promotion coord. sch. dept. Harcourt Brace Jovanovich, N.Y.C., 1965-74; mgr. div. verifiability and testing Harcourt Brace Jovanovich, 1974-75; editor-in-chief Teacher mag., Macmillan Co., Stamford, Conn., 1975-81; editor-in-chief sch. dept. Harper & Row Pubs., N.Y.C., 1981-84; v.p., editor-in-chief Globe Book Co., Simon and Schuster Edn. Group, 1984-88; pub. Joint Coun. Econ. Edn., N.Y.C., 1989—. Contbg. author: Winston Basic Reading Series, 1963, Little Owl Program, 1964. Home: 250 E 87th St New York NY 10128 Office: 432 Park Ave S New York NY 10016

BARANY, KATE, biophysics educator; b. Bekescsaba, Hungary, Apr. 29, 1929; came to U.S., 1960; m. Michael Barany, Oct. 20, 1949; children: George, Francis. MS in Physics, Math. and Phys. Chemistry, Eotvos U., Budapest, Hungary, 1952; PhD in Phys. Chemistry, Goethe U., Frankfurt, Fed. Republic of Germany, 1959. Rsch. asst. electron microscope lab. Hungarian Acad. Scis., Budapest, 1950-57; rsch. assoc. Max Planck Inst. for Physiology, Heidelberg, Fed. Republic of Germany, 1958-60; rsch. assoc. Inst. Muscle Disease, N.Y.C., 1960-66, asst. mem., 1966-71, assoc. mem., 1971-74; assoc. prof. dept. physiology and biophysics U. Ill., Chgo., 1974-80, prof. dept. physiology and biophysics Coll. of Medicine, 1980—. Contbr. articles to profl. jours. and chpts. to books. Recipient Golden Apple award U. Ill., 1989. Mem. Am. Physiol. Soc., Am. Heart Assn. (coun. on basic sci.), Biophys. Soc. Office: U Ill Dept Physiology and Biophys 835 S Wolcott MC901 Chicago IL 60612

BARATTA, PAMELA AMELIA, television station executive; b. Easton, Pa., Feb. 18, 1960; d. Dennis L. and Louise R. (Coccia) B. BS, Seton Hall U., 1982. Traffic mgr. Sta. WDCA-TV, Washington, 1983-85, account exec., 1985-88; account exec. Sta. WTTG-TV, Washington, 1988-89, Sta. WUSA-TV, Washington, 1989—. Mem. Washington Area Advt. Club (co. chmn. edn. com. 1988-89). Republican. Roman Catholic. Home: 3927 Military Rd NW Washington DC 20015 Office: WUSA TV 4001 Brandywine St NW Washington DC 20016

BARBE, BETTY CATHERINE, financial analyst; b. Chgo., Dec. 24, 1930; d. Norbert Lambert and Helen Weishaar; m. Edward William, Aug. 8, 1953; children: Leonard Walter, Roger Andrew. Student, U. Toledo, 1970, 85. Acct. Gorr Printing, Allstate Ins., Muntz TV, Chgo., 1947-53; hostess Welcome Wagon Internat., Maumee, Ohio, 1965-70; v.p. sec., cost acctg. Craftmaster, Toledo, 1970-72; sec., estimator Grinnell Fire Protection, Toledo, 1972-73; exec. sec., payroll Crow, Inc. Aviation, 1973-77; asst. city clk., payroll City of Perrysburg, 1977-83, tax adminstr., 1983—. Vol. George Bush campaign candidates, 1978—; v.p. bd. Zepf Community Mental Health, Toledo, 1986-87; reader for Sight Ctr.; mem. Women Alive! Coalition, 1987—, Nat. Women's Polit. Caucus, 1987—, MADD, 1987—,

YWCA, Perrysburg Arts Coun. Mem. Nat. Fed. Bus and Profl. Women, Maumee Valley Toastmaster (pres. 1989—), Toledo Opera Soc., Assn. Two Toledos, Maumee C. of C., Samagama Club, Zonta II (treas.), Rotary. Republican. Roman Catholic. Home: 724 W Wayne Maumee OH 43537 Office: City of Perrysburg 201 W Ind Ave Perrysburg OH 43551

BARBEAU, SUSANNE, small business owner, receptionist; b. Chgo., May 27, 1950; d. Martin Harvey Pursian and Eleanor (Lauraine) Turnbeaugh; m. James Hughes Barbeau, Mar. 21, 1971. Owner Just Your Type, Burlington, Ky., 1985—; receptionist Eagle Flooring, Hilliard, Ohio, 1988—. Mem. Hilliard C. of C., Heather Ridge Civic Assn. Republican. Methodist. Home: 4976 Harvest Meadow Rd Hilliard OH 43026

BARBER, JACQUELINE RENEE, pharmacist, educator; b. Rapid City, S.D., May 15, 1956; d. John Wesley and Helena G (Ertl) B. AA, U. Minn., 1976, BS, 1979, BS in Pharmacy, 198l; PharmD, U. Tex., Austin and San Antonio, 1983. Registered pharmacist, Minn., S.C., Tex. Am. Soc. Hosp. Pharmacists fellow U. Minn. Hosp. and Clinic, Mpls., 1983-84, dir. nutrition support pharmacy svc., 1984-87, clin. specialist in nutrition support, 1987—; asst. prof. Coll. Pharmacy, Med. U. S.C., Charleston, 1984-87, asst. prof. Coll. Medicine, 1986-87; clin. asst. prof. Coll. Pharmacy, U. Minn., 1987—; pharmacist VA Med. Ctr., Charleston, 1987, Target Pharmacy No. 220, Eden Prairie, Minn., 1987—; presenter in field; manuscript reviewer Drug Intelligence and Clin. Pharmacy, 1987—. Contbr. articles to profl. jours. Robert Klein band scholar, 1974, St. Stephen's Luth. Ch. scholar, 1974, U. Tex.-Austin scholar, 198l-83. Mem. Am. Soc. Hosp. Pharmacists, Am. Soc. for Parenteral and Enteral Nutrition (com. mem. 1987—), Am. Coll. Clin. Pharmacy, Minn. Soc. Hosp. Pharmacists, Omicron Delta Kappa, Rho Lambda, Kappa Kappa Gamma (coll. chpt. adv. bd. 1988—). Republican. Office: U Minn Hosp and Clinic Harvard St & E River Rd 611 Minneapolis MN 55455

BARBER, KATHRYN LEE, pharmaceutical marketing executive; b. Portland, Maine, Aug. 2, 1962; d. Augustus and Marjorie Kathleen (Jordan) B. Gen. course cert., London Sch. Econs., 1983; BS, Skidmore Coll., 1984; MBA, U. Chgo., 1988. Application specialist Ventrex Labs., Portland, 1985-86; assoc. product mgr. G.D. Searle & Co., Skokie, Ill., 1987-88, Abbott Labs., Abbott Park, Ill., 1988—. Mem. Jr. League Portland, 1985. Mem. Drug Info. Assn., Am. Friends London Sch. Econs. Roman Catholic. Office: Abbott Labs 1 Abbott Park Dr Abbott Park IL 60064

BARBER, KIM MICHELLE, marketing executive; b. Washington D.C., Nov. 19, 1964; d. Edwin Hezekiah and Consuelo June (Washington) Brown; M. James Todd Barber, Jan. 07, 1989. BS, Hampton U., 1985. Asst. dept. mgr. Bloomingdales, N.Y., 1985-86, asst. buyer, 1986; group mgr. Hecht Co., Washington D.C., 1986-88; dir. mktg. Kenneth H. Michael Co., Riverdale, Md.; exec. mgr. pub. relations cons., Trade Internat., Greenbelt, Md., 1987--. Named Outstanding Young Women of Am., 1987. Mem. Women of Wash., Women in Mktg. Advt., Women in Pub. Relations, Nat. Assn. Executive Female, Comml. Real Estate Women. Office: Kenneth H Michael Co 6611 Kenilworth Ave #400 Riverdale MD 20737

BARBER, MARSHA, association executive; b. Peoria, Ill., Dec. 7, 1946; d. Jack R. and Dorothy M. (Zeine) Hursey; m. Thomas L. Barber, June 15, 1968; 1 child, Brett A. BS, So. Ill. U., Carbondale, 1968; postgrad., So. Ill. U., Edwardsville. Mgr. adminstrn. Comtrac Info. Systems, Columbus, Ohio; ctr. mgr. Exec. Ctrs. Northeast Ohio/Hdqrs. Cos., Columbus; now pres. Plus 1 Exec. Stes, Columbus. Chairperson new mem. orientation com. Small Bus. Coun. Mem. Nat. Edn. Assn., Soc. Assn. Execs., C. of C., Sport Car Club of Am., Porche Club of Am. Office: 6457 Reflections Dr Ste 200 Dublin OH 43017

BARBER, MARY PAMELA, elementary school educator; b. Murray, Ky., Mar. 12, 1947; d. John Joseph and Mary Susanna (Metzger) Leader; div.; children: Scott F. Barber, Timothy J. Barber. BS in Elem. Edn., Ind. U., 1973, MS, 1978. Tchr. South Bend (Ind.) Community Sch. Corp., 1973—. Author, sec. newsletter Monthly Maintenance Minutes, 1984—. Grantee South Bend Community Sch. Corp., Ind. State Tchrs. Assn. Mem. Internat. Reading Assn., NEA (v.p. South Bend 1983—, sec. tchrs. negotiating team 1982—, PAC mem. 1984—, legis. chmn. 1984—), Ind. State Tchrs. Assn., PTA. Roman Catholic. Home: 2218 York St Mishawaka IN 46544 Office: Lincoln Sch 1425 E Calvert South Bend IN 46613 also: NEA-South Bend 2015 Western Ave Ste 222 South Bend IN 46629

BARBER, PATRICIA LOUISE, clinical specialist; b. St. Paul, Jan. 11, 1953; d. James Bernard and Margaret Mary (Neagle) B. BSN, U. Minn., 1975; cert. nurse practitioner, U. Ill., 1978. Staff nurse U. Minn., Mpls., 1974-75; transplant coord. U. Ill., Chgo., 1978—; cons. in field, Chgo., 1983—. Editor: Resource Manual for Transplant Coordinators, 1982. Co-chmn. S/A Patient Svcs. Com., 1983—. Mem. N.Am. Transplant Coords. Orgn. (cochmn. 1979—, Honors 1983), Am. Diabetes Assn. (speakers bur. 1982—), Nat. Kidney Found. (bd. dirs. 1983—). Office: U Ill 840 S Wood St #518H Chicago IL 60612

BARBER, SUSAN, marketing executive, corporate secretary; b. Cleve., July 9, 1954; d. Elton Rowland Barber and Virginia (Fairbanks) Neale. Student, Sarah Lawrence Coll., 1972-73; BA in Psychology, Ohio U., 1977, BS in Edn., 1977; MBA in Fin., U. Chgo., 1988. Client svcs. rep. Merrill, Lynch, Pierce, Fenner & Smith, Cleve., 1983-85; asst. to chmn. PC Quote, Inc., Chgo., 1985-88, dir. mktg., 1988—; asst. corp. sec. PC Quote, Inc., Chgo., 1986-88, corp. sec., 1988—. Bd. dirs. 2650 Lakeview Assn., Chgo., 1988—. Mem. U. Chgo. Women's Bus. Group. Office: PC Quote Inc 401 S LaSalle St #1600 Chicago IL 60605

BARBERO, MARY BETH, test engineer; b. Cumberland, Md., Mar. 26, 1965; d. Ricardo Bruce and Mary Susan (Stein) B. BSEE, Va. Poly. Inst., 1987. Test engr. Westinghouse Electric Corp., Balt., 1987—. Mem. Nat. Assn. for Female Execs., IEEE. Home: 1 I Winesap Ct Catonsville MD 21228 Office: Westinghouse Electric Corp Camp Meade Rd Baltimore MD 21203

BARBERO, VICTORIA ANIELSKI, editor; b. Cleve., Nov. 11, 1942; d. Henry Frank and Frances Katherine (Szyznar) Anielski; m. Reinaldo. BS, Kent State U., 1964; MA, Columbia U., 1968. Tchr, English Horace Greeley High Sch., Chappaqua, N.Y., 1968-70; tchr., mentor Bklyn. Coll., 1970-72; tchr. English Haile Selassie I Univ., Addis Ababa, Ethiopia, 1972-74; adminstr. Continuing Edn., Columbia, N.Y., 1975-78; sr. office adminstr., editor Cresap, McCormick & Paget, San Francisco, 1979-83; editor Cresap, San Francisco, 1983--. Author:Freshman Writing, 1973; co-author, Advanced Writing, 1974. Vol. aide St. Luke's Hosp., N.Y., 1968-72; staff mem., bd. dirs. Encampment for Citizenship, 1971-72; chmn. internat. rels. study sect. Mem. Commonwealth Club. Office: Cresap 333 Bush St Ste 1700 San Francisco CA 94104

BARBETTA, MARIA ANN, hospital records administrator, consultant; b. Bristol, Pa., Mar. 20, 1956; d. Eugene Charles and Anna (Strozzieri) B. AA, Bucks County Community Coll., 1976; BS, Coll. Allied Health Professions, Temple U., 1978. Dir. med. records Cumberland Regional Health Plan, Vineland, N.J., 1978; dir. med. record dept. St. Mary Hosp., Langhorne, Pa., 1978—; cons. med. records St. Joseph's Home for Aged, Holland, Pa., 1983—; speaker on med. record topics to various orgns., Langhorne, 1983—. Vol. tchr. Jr. High Sunday Sch. Mem. Am. Med. Record Assn., Pa. Med. Record Assn. (edn. com. 1985-87, project mgr. strategic plan 1987-89), Lehigh Valley Med. Record Assn., Southeastern Pa. Med. Record Assn. (chmn. membership com. 1987-88), NAFE, Hosp. Assn. Pa., Delaware Valley DRG Mgmt. Assn., Southeastern Pa. Assn. of Quality Assurance Profls. Avocations: cross-country skiing, volunteer work, reading, traveling, basket weaving. Home: 4707 Grandview Ave Bensalem PA 19020 Office: St Mary Hosp Langhorne-Newtown Rd Langhorne PA 19047

BARBO, DOROTHY MARIE, obstetrician, gynecologist, educator; b. River Falls, Wis., May 28, 1932; d. George William and Marie Lillian (Stelsel) B. BA, Asbury Coll., 1954; MD, U. Wis., 1958; DSc (hon.), Asbury Coll., 1981. Diplomate Am. Bd. Ob-Gyn. Resident Luth. Hosp. Milw., 1958-62; instr. Sch. Medicine Marquette U., Milw., 1962-66, asst. prof., 1966-67; assoc. prof. Christian Med. Coll. Punjab U., Ludhiana, India, 1968-72; assoc. prof. Med. Coll. Pa., Phila., 1972-87, prof., 1988—; acting dept. chair Christian Med. Coll., Punjab U., 1970; dir. Ctr. for Mature Woman Med. Coll. Pa., 1983; examiner Am. Bd. Ob-Gyn, 1984—; mem Drug Adv. Com. FDA, 1986—; bd. dirs. Ludhiana Christian Med. Coll., N.Y.C., Svc. Master Co. Ltd., Downers Grove, Ill. Co-author: Care of Post Menopausal Patient, 1985editor: Medical Clinics of N.A., vol. 71, 1987; contbr. chpt. to book. Student chpt. sponsor Christian Med. and Dental Soc., Phila., 1973—; tchr., elder Leverington Presbyn. Ch., Phila., 1988; interviewer Reader's Digest Internat. fellowships, Brunswick, Ga., 1982—. Named sr. clin. trainee USPHS, HEW, 1963-65, one of Best Woman Drs. in Am. Harper Bazaar, 1985. Fellow ACS (sec. Phila. chpt. 1990—), AFS, Am. Coll. Ob-Gyn.; mem. Am. Cancer Soc. (bd. dirs. Phila. chpt. 1980-86, vol. 1984), Obstet. Soc. Phila. (pres. 1989-90), Phila. Colposcupy Soc. (founding, pres. 1982-84), Phila. County Med. Soc. (com. chair 1989-90), Alpha Omega Alpha. Office: Med Coll Pa 3300 Henry Ave Philadelphia PA 19129

BARBOUR, ANITA ESTELLE, pharmacist; b. Portsmouth, Ohio, May 27, 1958; d. Thomas and Stacia (Franko) Barbour. BS in Pharmacy, Ohio No. U., 1981. Pharmacist, mgr. Kegley's New Boston Pharmacy, New Boston, Ohio, 1981-84; pharmacist, asst. mgr. Kroger N277 Pharmacy, Portsmouth, Ohio, 1984-87; pharmacist, mgr. Kroger N311 Pharmacy, Wheelersburg, Ohio, 1987—. Mem. So. Ohio AIDS Task Force. Mem. So. Ohio Pharmacists Assn., Women, Inc., Portsmouth Area Jaycess (past v.p.). Greek Orthodox. Office: Kroger Pharmacy 9090 Ohio River Rd Wheelersburg OH 45662

BARBOUR, CHARLENE, management firm executive; b. Smithfield, N.C., Aug. 23, 1949; d. Charles Ray and Charlotte June (Langdon) B.; m. Phil Barbour, Apr. 14, 1968; 1 child, Phillip Shaun. AA in Bus., Hardbarger Jr. Coll., 1968. Adminstrv. asst. N.C. Dept. Human Resources, Raleigh, 1970-80; account exec. Olson Mgmt. Group, Raleigh, 1980-86; pres. Mgmt. Concepts, Inc., Garner, N.C., 1986—. Mem. NAFE, Am. Soc. Assn. Execs., Assn. Execs. N.C., Nat. Fedn. Ind. Bus. Owners, Garner C. of C. (communications chair 1989, bd. dirs., vice chmn. membership and communications 1989—), Meeting Planners Internat. Republican. Baptist. Home: 3500 Amelia Rd Clayton NC 27520 Office: Mgmt Concepts Inc 1002 Vandora Springs Rd Garner NC 27529

BARBOUR, DELTA RAE, trade association executive; b. Independence, Va., Apr. 28, 1937; d. Floyd McKinley an Nannie Ellen (Osborne) Boyer; student Strayer Bus. Coll., 1974-76, Prince Georges County Community Coll., 1976-77. Acct., Structural Clay Products Inst., Washington, 1962-66; office mgr. Joseph T. Hunt, D.D.S., Henderson, N.C., 1966-69, McGaughy, Marshall & McMillan, Washington, 1969-74; comptr. Sugar Assn., Inc., Washington, 1974—, asst. corp. sec., 1974-85, v.p., 1984—, sec.-treas., 1986—; realtor Century 21 J.D. Williams Real Estate, Lanham, Md., 1979-89. Mem. polit. action com. Prince Georges County Real Estate Bd., 1977-78. Mem. Am. Soc. Assn. Execs., Washington Assn. Fin. Mgmt. Democrat. Presbyterian. Home: 2141 P St NW Washington DC 20037 Office: 1101 15th St NW Washington DC 20005

BARBOUR, SUE JENNIFER, entertainer, agent; b. Watford, Herts, Eng., May 29, 1950; came to U.S., 1989; d. Peter Dudley Barbour and Jean (Dooley) Davies; m. Alan Christopher Jacobs, Aug. 13, 1969 (div.); 1 child, Genevieve. Student, Elmhurst Ballet Sch., Camberley, Surrey, Eng., 1960-66. Singer, dancer, actress Barnum London Palladium, 1981-83; guest artiste Barnum Theatre Des Westerns, Berlin, Fed. Republic of Germany, 1983; singer, dancer, artist Barnum, London, 1984-86; stilt dancing, puppeteer Cabaret, London, 1987; stilt dancing, puppeteer Babes in the Woods Babes in the Woods, London (Eng.) Palladium, 1988; stilt dancing, puppeteer U.K. Pavilon Epcot Walt Disney World, Orlando, Fla., 1989—. Actors Ch. Union grantee, 1960-66. Mem. Grand Order Lady Ratlings (door guard 1987). Mem. Ch. of Eng. Office: Walt Disney World Lake Buena Vista Orlando FL 32830

BARBOZA, GLORIA, marketing professional; b. Harlingen, Tex., Mar. 24, 1951; d. Sotero and Aurora (Reyna) B. BA in English and Journalism, Tex. Woman's U., 1974. TV editor Houston Chronicle, 1974-79; dir. pub. info. Sta. KUHT-TV, Houston, 1979-81; pvt. practice freelance writer Houston, 1981-82; coordinator mktg. Spaw-Glass/CAHABA, Houston, 1982—. Mem. Soc. Mktg. Profl. Services, Houston Advt. Fedn., Am. Mgmt. Assn. Democrat. Roman Catholic. Office: Spa-Glass/CAHABA 13430 Northwest Fwy #750 Houston TX 77040

BARCA, KATHLEEN, marketing executive; b. Burbank, Calif., July 26, 1946; d. Frank Allan and Blanch Irene (Griffith) Barnes; m. Gerald Albino Barca, Dec. 8, 1967; children: Patrick Gerald, Stacia Kathleen. Student, Pierce Coll., 1964; B in Bus., Hancock Coll., 1984. Teller Security Pacific Bank, Pasadena, Calif., 1968-69, Bank Am., Santa Maria, Calif., 1972-74; operator Gen. Telephone Co., Santa Maria, Calif., 1974-83, supr. operator, 1983-84; account exec. Sta. KRQK/KLLB Radio, Lompoc, Calif., 1984-85; owner Advt. Unltd., Orcutt, Calif., 1986-88; regional mgr. A.L. Williams Mktg. Co., Los Alamos, Calif., 1988-89; supr. Matol Botanical Internat., 1989—; account exec. Santa Maria Times, 1989—. Author: numerous local TV and radio commercials, print advt. Activist Citizens Against Dumps in Residential Environments, Polit. Action Com., Orcutt and Santa Maria; chmn. Community Action Com., Santa Maria, Workshop EPA, Calif. Div., Dept. Health Svcs. State of Calif.; vice coord. Toughlove, Santa Maria, 1988-89; parent coord., mem. steering com. ASAP and Friends, 1988-89. Mem. NAFE, Womens Network-Santa Maria, Cen. Coast Ad (recipient numerous awards), Santa Maria C. of C. (ambassador representing Santa Maria Times 1990—). Democrat. Home and Office: 509 Shaw St PO Box 676 Los Alamos CA 93440

BARCHIE-MCINTYRE, JANET LOUISE, publishing executive; b. McKeesport, Pa., Mar. 12, 1952; d. Edward Joseph Barchie and Anna Irene (Wilds) Hockenbury; m. William Joseph Mc Intyre, Feb. 29, 1980. Student, St. Louis Inst. Music, 1970, U. of Paris, Paris, France, 1973; BA, Montclair State Coll., 1974. Asst. advt. mgr. Stonhard, Maple Shade, N.J., 1975-78; adminstr. Filtech Automotive Industries, Mt. Laurel, N.J., 1979; lead cage clk. Ziff-Davis Pub. Co., Cherry Hill, N.J., 1979-80; control specialist Ziff-Davis Pub. Co., Mt. Laurel, 1980-82, fulfillment coord., 1982-84, quality control adminstr., 1984-85; programmer, analyst Ziff-Davis Pub. Co., Cherry Hill, N.J., 1985-88, programming mgr., 1988—. Republican. Home: 554 Merchantville Ave Pennsauken NJ 08110 Office: Ziff-Davis Pub 20 Brace Rd Cherry Hill NJ 08034

BARCUS, MARY EVELYN, educator; b. Peru, Ind., Apr. 3, 1938; d. Arthur Gibson and Mildred (Neher) Shull; m. Robert Gene Barcus, Aug. 9, 1959; children: Jennifer Sue, Debra Lynn. BS, Manchester Coll., 1960; MA, Ball State U., 1964. Kindergarten tchr. Miami Elem. Sch., Wabash, Ind., 1960-64; elem. tchr. Crooked Creek Sch., Indpls., 1964-72; preschool tchr. Second Presbyn. Preschool, Indpls., 1980-85, Speedway Coop., Indpls., 1985-86; tchr. asst. St. Monica Cath. Sch., Indpls., 1990; preschool tchr., fun club tchr. Arthur Jordan YMCA, Indpls.; preschool tchr. Indpls. (Ind.) Children's Mus., 1979—; docent sch. tours Children's Mus., Indpls., 1987—; interpreter at Indpls. children's mus.; facilitator Systematic Tng. Effective Parenting, Indpls. Writer: (children's songs) Piggback Songs for Infants and Toddlers, 1985, Piggyback Songs in Praise of God, 1986; editor elem. sch. newspaper; producer (with others) a weekly show for cable TV. Profl. vol., libr. helper in local sch. systems; office helper North Cen. High Sch.; served on PTOs in various capacities; Sunday sch./vacation ch. sch. tchr. Mem. AAUW (charter, sec.), Ind. Assn. Edn. Young Children (state conf. com.), Pi Lambda Theta. Democrat. Mem. Church of Brethren. Home: 2230 Brewster Rd Indianapolis IN 46260

BARDAWIL, ANITA AIKEN, television network professional; b. Winston Salem, N.C., Mar. 13, 1931; d. Bedford Elias and Joanna (Simmons) Aiken; m. I.P. Bardawil; 1 child, Anna Victoria. Student, Fla. So. Coll. and Ch. Adminstrv. asst. Christian Television Network, Clearwater, Fla. Mem. Woman's Soc. Christian Svcs., Smithsonian Assocs.

BARDELL, EUNICE RUTH, pharmaceutical educator; b. Milw., Feb. 8, 1915; d. Eric A. and Alma Helen (Stark) Bonow; m. Ross Bardell, Nov. 23, 1972. BS in Pharmacy, U. Wis., 1938, MS, 1949, PhD, 1952. Registered pharmacist, Wis.; registered microbiologist. Pharmacist ED Schuster & Co., Milw., 1940-42, Kremers Urban Co., Milw., 1942-44; instr., pharmacy U. of Wis., Milw., 1948-51, asst. prof., assoc. prof., 1960-72; prof. U. of Wis., 1972-73; emerita prof. U. Wis., Milw., 1973—; adj. prof. pharmacy, U. of Ky., Lexington, 1982—. Author: The Wisconsin Showglobe, 1984; contbr. articles to profl. jours. Recipient Cert. of Merit, Milw. County Hist. Soc., 1981, Disting. Alumna Award, U. Wis. Pharmacy Alumni Assn., 1989. Fellow Am. Found. Pharm. Edn.; mem. Wis. Pharmacist Assn., Am. Pharm. Assn., Am. Inst. History of Pharmacy, Am. Guild Organists. Methodist.

BARDEN, JANICE KINDLER, personnel company executive; b. Cleve.; d. Norman Allen and Bessie G. (Black) Kindler; m. Hal Barden, Nov. 12, 1944 (dec. Jan. 1985) 1 child, Sheryl Andrea. BBA, Miami U., Oxford, Ohio, 1947; M in Indsl. Psychology, Kent State U., 1948. Asst. dir. admissions Fairleigh Dickinson U., Teaneck, N.J., 1950-53; gen. mgr. Pilots Employment Assocs., Teterboro, N.J., 1953-71; founder, pres. Aviation Pers. Internat., New Orleans, 1971—; commr. jury U.S. Dist. Ct. (ea. dist.) La., New Orleans, 1965—; lectr. in field. Chmn. History of Aviation Collection U. Tex., Dallas, 1980—. Recipient Disting. Alumnus award, Kent State U., 1986, Cuyahoga Falls High Sch., 1988. Mem. Nat. Bus. Aircraft Assn. (chmn. conf. 1975, 85, 87, 90), Flight Safety Found. (chmn. corp. seminar), Profl. Aircraft Maint. Assn., AAUW, Bus. and Profl. Women's Club, Kent State Alumni Assn. (bd. dirs. 1976-82), Psi Chi. Republican. Episcopalian. Lodge: Order of Rainbow (grand coordinator 1973-84). Office: Aviation Pers Internat PO Box 6846 New Orleans LA 70174

BARDSLEY, ELIZABETH SKEATS, state legislator; b. Schenectady, N.Y., Dec. 1, 1931; d. Wilfred F. and Victoria W. (Willard) Skeats; m. William Alexander Bardsley, July 21, 1962; children: Jen W., Christina E., Nils A. Student, U. Del., 1949-51; BS, U. Md., 1953; MA in Adult Edn., U. Chgo., 1962. Asst. 4-H club agt. U. Md. Coop. Extension Svc., Montgomery, Md., 1954-56; program dir., asst. club dir. Army Spl. Svcs., Schofield Barracks, Hawaii, 1956-57; assoc. home demonstration agt. U. Conn. Coop. Extension Svc., Fairfield County, Conn., 1958-61; home demonstration agt. U. N.H. Coop. Extension Svc., Belknap County, N.H., 1962-65; mem. N.H. Ho. of Reps., Concord, 1982—; dir. devel. N.H. Tech. Inst., Concord, 1986-87. Bd. dirs. N.H. Assn. Consrvation Comm., Concord, 1984—, Cent. N.H. Com. Mental Health Svcs., Concord, 1984-86; adv. bd. Early Intervention Svcs., Concord, 1984-86; mem. Andover Conservation Comm., 1970—, Andover Planning Task Force, 1988—, N.H. Rep. Com. Mem. Orgn. Women Legislaters. Republican. Unitarian. Home: Elbo-Edge Rte 1 Box 2250 Andover NH 03216 Office: NH Gen Ct Legis Office Bldg Rm 301 Concord NH 03201

BARDYGUINE, PATRICIA WILDE, ballerina, ballet theatre executive; b. Ottawa, Ont., Can., July 16, 1928; came to U.S., 1943; d. John Herbert and Eileen Lucy (Simpson) White; m. George Bardyguine, Dec. 14, 1953; children: Anya, Youri. Student, Profl. Children's Sch., N.Y.C. Dancer Am. Concert Ballet, N.Y.C., 1943-44, Marquis De Queras Ballet Internat., N.Y.C., 1944-45, Ballet Russe De Monte Carlo, tours nationwide, 1945-49; guest artist Roland Petit Ballet De Paris, 1949; prin. ballerina Met. Ballet, touring throughout Europe, 1950, N.Y.C. Ballet, 1950-65; dir. Harkness House, N.Y.C., 1965-67; ballet mistress Am. Ballet Theater, N.Y.C., 1969-82; artistic dir. Pitts. Ballet Theatre, 1982—; dir. Am. Ballet Theater Sch., 1979-82; dance panelist Nat. Endowment for Arts, N.Y. State Council for the Arts; judge Lausanne Internat. Competition; guest tchr., coach N.Y.C. Ballet, Joffrey Ballet, Dance Theater of Harlem, The Royal Ballet of Stockholm, Internat. Summer Seminar, Cologne, Fed. Republic Germany, Heinz Bosl Found., Munich, St. Moritz, Japan, Australia, Republic South Korea. Soloist six European tours, also tour of Orient; numerous TV appearances; commd. by N.Y. Philharm. to choreograph ballets Festival, 1964, At the Ball, 1965, Viennese Evening, 1966, Petite Suite, 1967. Adminstr. scholar fund Sch. Am. Ballet Group; mem. Nat. Bd. Regional Ballet; Fulbright panelist. Fulbright panelist. Mem. Am. Guild Mus. Artists, AFTRA, Dance/USA (bd. dirs.). Office: Pitts Ballet Theatre 2900 Liberty Ave Pittsburgh PA 15201

BARFIELD, SHIRLEY ROSALIS, banker; b. Apalachicola, Fla., Sept. 6, 1940; d. Charles Manuel and Loretta Frances (Nasto) Rosalis; m. Wendell W. Barfield, Mar. 2, 1962; children—Wendell W. Barfield, Charles Darrin Barfield. AS, Polk Community Coll., Fla., 1981; postgrad. Standard and Advanced Tng., Am. Inst. Banking, Washington, 1983; postgrad. U. Okla. 1985, 87. Dep. clk. CCC Franklin County, Apalachicola, 1959-61; mgmt. trainee Apalachicola St. Bank, Fla., 1961-66; pub. relations staff Peoples Bank, Lakeland, Fla., 1967; br. mgr. Fla. Nat. Bank, Port St. Joe, 1968; fin. officer Sch. Bd., Franklin County, Apalachicola, 1968-70; mgr. comml. loans ops., asst. v.p. Barnett Bank of Polk County, Lakeland, 1970—; instr. Polk Community Coll., Winter Haven, Fla., 1981—. Mem. Nat. Assn. Bank Women (com. 1981—), Nat. Assn. Exec. Women, Am. Inst. Banking. Democrat. Roman Catholic. Clubs: Beta (pres. 1956-59), 4-H (Carabelle, Fla., pres. 1953-59). Avocations: piano, reading history, camping. Home: 1125 Lakewood Rd Lakeland FL 33805 Office: Barnett Bank Polk County 331 S Florida Ave Lakeland FL 33802

BARGAMIAN, NANCY C., actress, writer; b. Tucson, Sept. 29, 1950; d. Sam and Josephine (Chobanian) B. BFA, U. Ariz., 1972; studied at, Drama Studio, London, 1972-73. Programs and statis. asst. Ind. Broadcasting Authority, London, 1972-73; stage mgr. Group 64 Theatre, 1973; actress Ariz. Theatre Co., Tucson, 1973-75; freelance concept writer NBC, Burbank, Calif., 1976; actress Gunsmoke CBS, L.A., 1976; producer The Winner Group, Tujunga, Calif., 1977—. Appeared in films Alice Doesn't Live Here Anymore, Lost Horizon, The Life & Times of Judge Roy Bean; appeared in soap operas General Hospital, The Young and the Restless, Capitol, Speedtrap; author: (screenplay) Death Act, 1989. Mem. Group Repertory Theatre, North Hollywood, Calif., 1988-90, Little Landers Tijunga Hist. Soc., 1988-90. Mem. AFTRA, SAG, Actors Equity Assn., Navy League, MENSA (bd. dirs., exec. com. L.A. chpt. 1988-90).

BARGER, DARLENE J., community relations development executive; b. Fleming, Ky., Sept. 19, 1954; d. Eugene Johnson and Lelia June (Johnson) Johnson; m. Harry W. Farmer Jr., Dec. 18, 1976 (div. 1985) m. John Mark Barger, May 7, 1988. BBA, Eastern Ky U., 1976; MA in Edn., 1979. Tchr. Pensacola (Fla.) Cath. High Sch., 1980-81; sales assoc. Century 21 Barbara Buck Realty, Jacksonville, N.C., 1981-84; owner Lady's in Waiting Maternity Fashions, 1983-85; mgr. Stitches Va., Virginia Beach, 1986; project coord. Hazard (Ky.) Community Coll., 1986-88, coord. community rels., 1988—; state dir. Am. Assn. Women in Community and Jr. Colls., 1989. Active in Dem. Women's Club, Hazard 1986-88. Mem. NAFE, Ky. Women Advs., Nat. Coun. Resource Devel. (tng. program specialist, state dir. 1989, Burton Talmage scholar 1989). Home: RR 3 Box 632 Hazard KY 41701 Office: Hazard Community Coll 1 Community Coll Dr Hazard KY 41701

BARHAM, A. CALUDETTE VAIL, charitable organization administrator; b. Idaho Falls, Idaho, Feb. 18, 1953; d. Charles M. and E. Reola (Sanders) Vail; m. Mark B. Barham, July 9, 1977; children: Samuel, Sarah. BA, Boise State U., 1976. Owner, mgr. La Fondita Mexi. Food Restaurant; area dir. United Way of Ada County, Boise, Idaho; now area dir. Canyon Area United Way, Nampa, Idaho. Mem. Caldwell C. of C., Delta Delta Delta. Pres. Mayor's Com. on Hiring Disabled and Older Workers, 1985, 86, sec., 1985, treas., 1984; mem. Gov.'s Com. on Employment of the Disabled Workers. Mem. Nampa C. of C., Rotary, Delta Delta Delta. Baptist.

BARHAM, PATTE (MRS. HARRIS BOYNE BARHAM), publisher, author, columnist; b. Los Angeles; d. Dr. Frank Barham and Princess Jessica Meskhi Gleboff; student U. So. Calif., U. Ariz.; Litt.D., Trinity So. Bible Coll.; Doctorate, Olympian Internat. Sports Found. and Coll., Olympian Internat. Sports Medicine Coll., Cambridge, Eng., Doctorate of Internat. Arts, Sci. and Cable TV, Munich. War corr., Korea; syndicated columnist; acting sec. of state State of Calif., 1980-81. Life mem. AAU, former v.p. pub. relations; mem. internat. com. So. Calif. Philharmonic; dir. Los Angeles Council on Internat. Visitors; mem. hospitality com. U.S. Olympic Com.; active L.A. Orphanage Guild, Bel-Air Guild Decorated dame Sovereign Order of Alfred the Great, grand cross, patron of honor; compagne de la Couronne d'Epines, Ancien Abbaye-Principaute de San Luigi. Mem. Nat. League Am. Pen Women, English Speaking Union, DAR, Social Service

Aux., Delta Gamma. Clubs: Outrigger Canoe, Waikiki Yacht (Hawaii); Wilshire Country, Ebell, Balboa Bay; Metropolitan (N.Y.C.); Tokyo Corrs.; Round the World; Author: Pin up Poems; Rasputin: The Man Behind the Myth. Address: 100 Fremont Pl Los Angeles CA 90005

BARIL, NANCY ANN, gerontological nurse practitioner, consultant; b. Paterson, N.J., May 10, 1952; d. Kenneth Gerald and Jeanette Elenore (Girodet) Keiser; m. Joel Mark Baril, Apr. 15, 1984; 1 child, Jason Kenneth. AA, Gulf Coast Community Coll., 1976; BS in Nursing, Fla. State U., 1978; M in Nursing, UCLA, 1983. Registered pub. health nurse, Calif.; ANA cert. gerontol. nurse practitioner. Charge nurse, nurse preceptor Cedar Sinai Med. Ctr., L.A., 1979-83; RN Nursing Svcs. Incorp., Sherman Oaks, Calif., 1980-83; nurse practitioner Santa Monica Peer Counseling Ctr., Santa Monica, Calif., 1983; nurse cons., gerontol. nurse practioner Summit Health Ltd., Burbank, Calif., 1983-85; nurse cons. Geriatric Assocs., Granada Hills, Calif., 1983-85; nurse cons., gerontol. nurse practitioner Care Enterprises West, Burbank, 1985-86; patient svcs. coord., gerontol. nurse practitioner ARA Living Ctrs., Glendale, Calif., 1986-87; dir. nursing, gerontol. nurse practitioner Sign of the Dove, Chatsworth, Calif., 1988—, Topanga Terrace, Conoga Park, 1988——. Mem. PTA, Granada Hills, 1985. Mem. Calif. Coalition of Nurse Practioners, Am. Nursing Assn., Calif. Nursing Assn., Gerontol. Soc., Sigma Theta Tau (rec. sec. 1983-85). Democrat. Episcopalian. Avocations: reading, crossword puzzles, gardening, jet-skiing. Home: 16921 Bircher St Granada Hills CA 91344 Office: ARA Living Ctrs 516 Burchett St Suite 102 Glendale CA 91203

BARKEMEIJER DE WIT, JEANNE SANDRA, sales executive; b. Santa Ana, Calif., July 6, 1955; d. Hendrik Pieter and Nelly Maria (Fontijn) Barkemeijer de Wit; m. Stephen Michael St. Onge, Jan. 13, 1981 (div. 1982). Student, Am. Coll. Paramed. Arts Scis., Santa Ana, Calif., 1977-78, Computer Learning Ctr., Anaheim, Calif., 1985-86, Regional Occupational Program, Buena Park, Calif., 1986, Cen. Counties Regional Occupational Program, Santa Ana, 1986-87. Cert. respiratory therapy tech. Freelance graphic artist, tech. illustrator Santa Ana, 1972—; respiratory therapist Good Samaritan Hosp., Anaheim, 1978-79, Tustin (Calif.) Community Hosp., 1979-81, United Western Med. Ctrs., Santa Ana, Anaheim, 1981-86; office mgr., asst. dir. internat. sales, dir. spl. accounts D-Link Systems, Inc., Irvine, Calif., 1986—; graphic artist Santa Ana Unified Schs., 1974. Exhibited in group shows including Torrana Art League, 1970-72, Buzza Gibson Gallery, 1970, various galleries in Japan, Amsterdam, and N.Y., 1970; illustrator: Sexual Positions for Chronic Lung and Cardiac Patients, 1984; author, designer numerous storyboard diskettes, 1988—. Vol. therapist Cancer Assn. Great Am. Smoke-Out, Costa Mesa, 1979-86, Lung Assn. Scamp Camp for Asthmatic Children, Santa Ana, 1985; vol. artist Heart Assn., L.A., 1985; vocalist, guitarist Easter Seal Telethon Orange County, 1978. Recipient Cert. Thanks Heart Assn., 1985. Mem. Nat. Assn. Female Execs., Internat. Graphoanalysis Soc. Democrat. Mem. Christian Ch. Home: 1310 S Douglas Santa Ana CA 92704 Office: D-Link Systems Inc 5 Musick Irvine CA 92718

BARKER, ANNE ELIZABETH LATIMER, retail executive; b. Evanston, Ill., May 11, 1964; d. Kenneth Latimer and Kathleen Campbell; m. Joseph Scott Barker, Oct. 1, 1988. BA in Women's Studies, Vassar Coll., 1986; Cert. in food svc. mgmt., No. Va. Community Coll., Alexandria, 1988. Gen. mgr. Old Town Coffee Tea and Spice, Alexandria, 1988-89; mgr. coffee dept. Hay Day Country Farm Market, Hamden, Conn., 1989-90; gen. mgr. Willoughby Coffee and Tea, New Haven, 1990—. Active in Planned Parenthood, Alexandria, 1988, Homeless Shelter, Alexandria, 1988-89, Epis. Youth Group, Alexandria, 1988-89.

BARKER, BARBARA, real estate professional; b. Pulaski, Tenn., July 18, 1938; d. Dan and Anna (Butler) Ingram; m. Emmet Barker, Nov. 25, 1960; children: Melanie, Lynn, Harvey, Dan. BS, U. Tenn., 1960. Home economist Knoxville (Tenn.) Utilities Bd.; tchr. Arlington High Sch., Arlington Heights, Ill.; pres. Barbara Barker and Assocs., Brownsville, Tenn.; now pres. Deerfield (Ill.) Ptnrs.; also owner, mgr. ReMax Deerfield. Exec. bd., treas. Arden Shore Sch.; deacon Presbyn. Ch. Mem. Nat. Assn. Realtors, Ill. Assn. Realtors, Tenn. Home Econs. Assn. (v.p.). Home: 1050 Meadowbrook Deerfield IL 60015 Office: 757 Deerfield Rd Deerfield IL 60015

BARKER, BARBARA ANN, ophthalmologist; b. Paterson, N.J., Nov. 10, 1943; d. Earle Louis and Dorothy Louise (Williamson) Barker; m. Joel Ira Papernik, July 28, 1972. BA, Connecticut Coll., 1965; BA, Yale U., 1967; MA, Rutgers Med. Sch., 1974; MD, Mt. Sinai Sch. Medicine, 1976. Diplomate Am. Bd. Ophthalmology. Intern, Beth Israel Med. Center, 1977; resident Mt. Sinai Sch. Medicine/Beth Israel Med. Center, 1980, fellow in glaucoma, 1980-81, fellow cornea, refractive surgery, 1981-82, now mem. staff; rsch. technician The Rockefeller U., N.Y.C., 1965-66; tchr. Riverdale Country Sch., N.Y.C., 1967-68; rsch. asst. Sloan Kettering Inst., N.Y.C., 1969-72; assoc. clin. prof. Mt. Sinai Sch. Medicine, N.Y.C., 1982—; pvt. practice medicine specializing in ophthalmology, N.Y.C., 1983—; mem. staff N.Y. Eye and Ear Hosp., Cabrini Hosp. Recipient Resident Paper award Beth Israel Med. Center, 1980; Beth Israel Research grantee, 1983; NSF grantee, 1966. Mem. Internat. Soc. Refractive Keratoplasty, AMA, Am. Med. Women's Assn., Women's Med. Soc. N.Y.C., N.Y. County Med. Assn. (mem. com.), Phi Beta Kappa. Home and Office: 11 E 86th St #18B New York NY 10028

BARKER, BETTY LOU STARR, teacher; b. Stilwell, Okla., Jan. 26, 1929; d. Nathaniel and Ada (Barnett) Starr; m. Bill L. Barker, Apr. 16, 1950; children: Linda Dianne Barker Harrold, William Lee (dec.). BS Edn., Northeastern State U., 1950, MEd, 1962. Tchr. Starr Elem. Sch., Stilwell, Okla., 1947-48; clk. typist Hartford Fire Ins. Co., San Francisco, 1948; tchr. Ward Elem. Sch., Stilwell, Okla., 1950, Bryan Elem. Sch., Washington, 1950-51; typing supr. McDonald Douglas Aircraft, Tulsa, 1951-52; tchr. Adair County Schs., Stilwell, Okla., 1952-57, Stilwell (Okla.) City Schs., 1958-89. Editor: History of Adair County, 1900. Named Outstanding Educator, Stillwell Elem. Sch., Adair County Teacher of Year, Adair County Edn. Assn., Stilwell, Okla., 1977. Mem. AAUW, DAR, NEA, Okla. Edn. Assn. (del.), Stilwell (Okla.) Edn. Assn. (pres. 1984-86), Adair County Ret. Educators Assn., Okla. Ret. Educators Assn., Stilwell (Okla.) C. of C., Adair County Hist. Assn., Goingsnake Heritage Assn., Alpha Delta Kappa (state pres., 1988-90, south cen. regional sec., 1989—). Baptist. Home: Rte 2 Box 298 Stilwell OK 74960

BARKER, C. KELLY ANN MURRI, real estate executive, consultant; b. Pontiac, Mich., Dec. 20, 1951; d. Leonard Godfrey and Mary Irene (O'Donnell) B. BA, Oakland U., 1975. Property cons. Remanco, Inc., Chgo., 1975-77; v.p. Rowell, Inc., Roselle, Ill., 1977-79, RCI Properties, Arlington Heights, Ill., 1979-82; sr. asset mgr. Grubb & Ellis Co., Chgo., 1982-85; pres. Paragon Properties, Northbrook, Ill., 1985-87; pres., chief exec. officer CorporateAdvantage, Palatine, Ill., 1987—; bd. dirs. Mid City Industries, Pontiac, RIS Contractors, Waterford, Mich. Contbr. articles to profl.jours. Mem. Nat. Assn. Realtors, Comml. Women in Real Estate, Inst. Real Estate Mgmt. (chmn. 1987-88). Republican. Roman Catholic. Office: CorporateAdvantage 616 North Ct #100 Palatine IL 60067

BARKER, CELESTE ARLETTE, art museum operations manager; b. Redding, Calif., Apr. 19, 1947; d. Edwin Walter Squires and Rachel (Kinkead) Layton; m. Julius Jeep Chernak, Sept. 13, 1970, (div. 1980); children: Sean Matthew, Bret Allen; m. Jackson Lynn Barker, Oct. 8, 1988. BA in Art, San Francisco State U., 1970; AA in Engring. Tech., Coll. Marin, 1980; MBA in Mgmt., Golden Gate U., 1988. Tchr. art San Rafael (Calif.) Recreation Dept., 1971-75; owner, photographer Julius Chernak Photography, Novato, Calif., 1970-76; draftsman Donald Foster Drafting, San Rafael, 1975-76; surveyor Parks Dept. State Calif., Inverness, 1976; electric draftsman Pacific Gas & Electric, San Rafael, 1976-78, electric engring. estimator, 1978-79; mktg. rep. Pacific Gas & Electric, Santa Rosa, 1980-85; valuation analyst Pacific Gas & Electric, San Francisco, 1985-86, budget analyst, 1986-88, budget system project mgr., 1988-89; fin. asset mgr. Pacific Gas & Electric, Vallejo, Calif., 1989-90; ops. mgr. San Francisco Mus. Modern Art, 1990—. Dir. Mariner Green Townhomes Assn., treas. 1987-88. Mem. AAUW, Pacific Coast Gas Assn., Sierra Club. Home: 10 Piper Ln Fairfax CA 94930

BARKER, CYNTHIA RAECHEL, market research analyst; b. Athens, Ohio, Aug. 22, 1959; d. Edward Martin Penson and AnnaBelle (Wald) D'Augustine; m. Timothy Alric Barker, Aug. 9, 1986; 1 child, Cara Marie. BS in Journalism, Ohio U., 1981; MS, Ind. U., 1985. Mdse. officer Miles Kimball Co., Oshkosh, Wis., 1981-83; assoc. instr. dept. telecommunications Ind. U., Bloomington, 1983-85; product mktg. specialist, mgr. of games CompuServe, Inc., Columbus, Ohio, 1985-88; sr. retail cons. Retail Planning Assocs., Inc., Columbus, 1988-89; market rsch. assoc. ECI Advt. & Mktg., Inc., Tallahassee, Fla., 1989—. Contbr. freelance articles on aging in Am. to profl. jours. Mem. Sta. WFSU-TV, Tallahassee, 1990. Mem. Women in Communications, Inc. (sec.), Reg. Econ. Info. Network, Ohio U. Alumni Assn., Chi Omega Alumni Assn. Office: ECI Advt & Mktg Inc 1311 Executive Center Dr Ellis Bldg Rm 220 Tallahassee FL 32301

BARKER, EVA B., federal agency administrator; b. Charleston, Miss., Feb. 5, 1932; d. Bedford and Eva (Bell) Wray; m. Harold L. Barker, Aug. 25, 1962; children: Vanessa D. Brooks, Carolyn D. Wray, DeVonia Robinson, Celestine Johnson. B Gen Studies, Wayne State U., 1984. Revenue agt., exempt orgns. specialist IRS, Detroit; course developer, instr. IRS, Arlington, Va. With WAC, 1950-51. Mem. NAACP, NTEU, Federally Employed Women (v.p., membership chair), Wayne State U. Alumni Assn.

BARKER, JANE ELLEN, research biologist; b. Bangor, Maine, June 2, 1935; d. David Emmons and Eleanor (Stockman (Herrick) B. BA, U. Maine, 1957; MA, Wellesley Coll., 1959; PhD, U. Wis., 1967. Rsch. asst. Wellesley (Mass.) Coll., 1959-61; staff scientist Inst. Cancer Rsch., Putnam Meml. Hosp., Bennington, Vt., 1969-72; sr. investigator Nat. Heart, Lung and Blood Inst., NIH, Bethesda, Md., 1972-80; postdoctoral fellow Jackson Lab., Bar Harbor, Maine, 1967-69, staff scientist, 1980—. Contbr. numerous articles to profl. jours., chpts. to books. Mem. Am. Soc. Hematology, Am. Soc. Cell Biology, Soc. for Devel. Biology, Sigma Xi. Office: Jackson Lab Bar Harbor ME 04609

BARKER, JUDY, foundation executive; b. Burlington, N.C., Feb. 5, 1941; d. Thelma Ferguson; children: Lesa, Lori. Student, Ohio State U., Franklin U.; HHD, Xavier U., 1986. Administrv. asst. Children's Hosp., Columbus, Ohio, 1963-68, Mount Carmel Hosps., Inc., Columbus, 1969-72; administr. Borden Found., Borden, Inc., Columbus, 1973-75, exec. dir., 1975-83, dir. civic affairs, 1977-79, pres., 1983—, dir. social responsibility, 1979—; pres. Borden Found., 1983—. Bd. dirs. Pub./Pvt. Ventures, Ohio State U. Hosps., Columbus Commn. on Ethics and Values; mem. Sch. Home Econs. adv. bd. Ohio State U.; mem found. ctr. adv. bd. nat. Directory Corporate Giving; active N.Y. Contributions Adv. Group; mem. corp. adv. com. Philanthropic Adv. Svc.; mem., bd. dirs. Coun. Better Bus. Bur. Founds., Greater Columbus Arts Coun.; mem. Afro-Am. adv. bd. Columbus Mus. of Art. Named one of 2000 Notable Ams., 1981-82; recipient award to Women Achievers YWCA, 1982, Community Svc. award United Negro Coll. Fund, 1981. Office: Borden Inc 180 E Broad St Columbus OH 43215

BARKER, KAREN JEAN, real estate broker; b. Boggstown, Ind.; d. James Russell Tillison and Gladys Mae (Lancaster) King; m. Bill Gene Barker, 1961 (dec. 1962); 1 child, Toni Karen Barker; m. Charles Lee Koons, 1971 (dec. 1984). Real estate cert., Fresno City Coll., 1987; student, U. Calif., Davis, 1986; BA, MBA, Western States U., 1985; grad., Realtors Inst. Calif., 1982. Lic. real estate broker, Calif.; cert. internat. appraiser; notary pub., Calif. Telephone operator Ind. Bell Telephone, Indpls., 1954-56; clk., typist Hemphill Noyes & Co., Indpls., 1956-57; tchr. Patricia Stevens Modeling Sch., Indpls., 1957-60; clk., typist RCA, Indpls., 1957-60, City of Fresno, Calif., 1960-61; sr. acctg. clk. Fed. Mktg. Order Grape Crush Adminstrn., Fresno, 1963; clk., typist Calif. Hwy. Patrol, Fresno, 1963-67; radio dispatcher Calif. Dept. Fish and Game, Fresno, 1967-71; real estate agt. various cos., Shaver Lake, Calif., 1974-79; pvt. practice real estate Shaver Lake, 1979—. Mem. Nat. Assn. Realtors, Calif. Assn. Realtors, Fresno Bd. Realtors, Internat. Orgn. of Real Estate Appraisers. Democrat. Prebyn. Home: 41617 Tollhouse Rd Shaver Lake CA 93664 Office: PO Box 313 Shaver Lake CA 93664

BARKER, LAURENN RUSSELL, public relations executive, sculptor, artist; b. Morristown, Tenn., Mar. 17, 1945; d. George Herbert and Claire Hortense (Perkins) Prater; m. Rodney Gibson Russell, Aug 27, 1967 (div.); children: Chelse Fore, Josh Barrett, Micaiah Lael; m. 2d. Paul Edward Barker, Feb. 16, 1981. Grad. cum laude Mt. Vernon Sem., 1963; grad. Inst. Am. Univs., France, 1966; B.A., So. Meth. U., 1967; postgrad. Dallas Art Inst., 1967. Cert. pilot, FAA. Graphic designer Taylor Pub., Dallas, 1968-69; art dir. First Nat. Bank-First Family mag., Dallas, 1969-70; graphic artist Tyler Courier Times (Tex.), 1971-74; dir. pub. rels. Marsco Engring., Tyler, 1974-79; owner R&L Design Studio, Tyler, 1979-81, Artworks/Presentation Plus Creative Agy., Austin, Tex., 1988—; dir. pub. rels. Espey Huston & Assocs., Austin-Houston, 1981-88; design cons. S.W. Hist. Wax Mus., Arlington, Tex., 1979, Tex. Hist. Preservation Park, Austin, 1983, Neuroscis. Inst., Los Angeles, 1983; design cons. William Holden Wildlife Fund, Houston, 1984, cons. pub. rels. Gallery Contemporary Southwestern Art, Dallas, 1983; cons.-art dir. Macintosh User's Monthly mag. Featured artist Tyler Courier Times, 1979, Sta. KLTV-TV, Longview, Tex., 1979, Tex. Hwys. State mag., 1979, Austin mag., 1981. Sta. KTVV-TV, Austin, 1982. Mem. Travis County Susquicentennial Exhibit Com.; bd. dirs. Central Tex. March of Dimes, design cons. benefit, 1984—. Recipient State Rep. award Nat. Cherry Blossom Festival, Washington, 1966; U.S. Rep.-Bal de Petit Lits Blanc, Monte Carlo, Monaco, 1967; Design/Modeling award Neiman Marcus, Dallas, 1967. Mem. Women in Communications, Inc., Tex. Press-women's Assn., Glamour Mag. Orgn. Profl. Women, Austin Comtemporary Visual Arts Assn., Soc. for Mktg. Profl. Svcs., Tex. Pub. Rels. Assn. Democrat. Episcopalian. Home: PO Box 5033 Austin TX 78763

BARKER, LINDA GAIL, communications executive; b. Hawthorne, Nev., Feb. 10, 1948; d. Leroy and Juanita Faye (Stone) B.; m. Gary Louis Lowry, Nov. 25, 1966 (div. Feb. 1974); 1 child, Karen Lynnette. Student, Truckee Meadows Community Coll, Nev., 1973-75. Dep. sheriff Mineral County, Hawthorne, 1970-75; fire controller Nev. Div. Forestry, Reno, 1975-76; communications official Nev. Highway Patrol, Carson City, 1976—; instr. Nev. Highway Patrol, 1979-90. Author, editor, pub. Nev. Law Enforcement Telecommunications Guide, 1980-81, various instrn. manuals. Recipient various arts and crafts show awards, 1964-90. Episcopalian. Office: Nev Hwy Patrol 555 Wright Way Carson NV 89711

BARKER, MARY K., retired nurse; b. Roxana, Ill., Feb. 1, 1921; m. Willard H. Barker, May 26, 1962 (dec. Aug. 1986). BS in Nursing, Washington U., St. Louis, 1952, MS in Nursing, 1956; diploma in nursing, Alton Meml. Hosp. Sch. Nursing, Ill., 1942. Surg. instr., assoc. nursing svc. adminstr. St. Catherine Hosp., East Chicago, Ind.; asst. prof. So. Ill. U., Carbondale; staff nurse, instr., asst. dir. Sch. Nursing Alton Meml. Hosp.; now ret. Lt. col. nurse corps AUS, 1942-56, 72-81. Mem. AAUW, Am. Nurses Assn., NLN, AONE, ROA.

BARKER, SARAH EVANS, judge; b. Mishawaka, Ind., June 10, 1943; d. James McCall and Sarah (Yarbrough) Evans; m. Kenneth R. Barker, Nov. 25, 1972. BS, Ind. U., 1965; JD, Am. U., 1969; Doctor Pub. Svc. (hon.) Butler U., 1984; LLD, U. Indpls., 1987. Bar: Ind., 1969, U.S. Dist. Ct. (so. dist.) Ind., 1970, U.S. Ct. Appeals (7th cir.), 1973, U.S. Supreme Ct., 1978. Legal asst. to senator U.S. Senate, 1969-71; spl. counsel to minority govt. ops. com. permanent investigations subcom., 1971-72; dir. rsch., scheduling and advance Senator Percy Re-election Campaign, 1972; mem. Ind. Hist. Soc.; bd. dirs. Meth. Hosp. Ind., Inc.; mem. Conner Prairie adv. coun.; asst. U.S. atty. So. Dist. Ind., 1972-75, 1st asst. U.S. atty., 1976-77, U.S. atty., 1981-84; judge U.S. Dist. Ct. (so. dist.) Ind., 1984—; assoc., then ptnr. Bose, McKinney & Evans, Indpls., 1977-81; mem. exec. com. Jud. Conf. U.S., standing com. rules of practice and procedure, jud. conf. dist. judge rep.; mem. jud. coun. 7th cir. U.S. Ct. Appeals; bd. advisors, bd. visitors, Ind. U., Bloomington and Indpls. Mem. Conner Prairie Adv. Coun.; bd. dirs. Meth. Hosp. Ind. Recipient Coll. Peck award Wabash Coll., 1989, Touchstone award Girls Club of Greater Indpls, 1989; named Ind. Woman of Yr. Women in Communications, 1986. Mem. ABA, Ind. Bar Assn., Indpls. Bar Assn., Fed. Judges Assn., Nat. Assn. Former U.S. Attys., Econ. Club Indpls., Lawyers Club, Kiwanis. Republican. Methodist. Office: US Dist Ct 210 US Courthouse 46 E Ohio St Indianapolis IN 46204

BARKER, TERESA LYNN, utilities metering supervisor; b. Davenport, Iowa, Nov. 17, 1954; d. Charles Felix and Joan Arlene (VanHoorebeck) Gang; m. Wesley S. Barker, May 24, 1975; children: David, Gregory, Paul. BA in Math., Marycrest Coll., 1975; postgrad., St. Ambrose Coll., 1987—. Operating clk. Iowa-Ill. Gas & Electric Co., Davenport, Iowa, 1976-77; gas network analyst Iowa-Ill. Gas & Electric Co., Davenport, 1980-86, sr. gas network analyst, 1986-88, gas supply analyst, 1988-89, metering supr., 1989—. Allocations United Way of the Quad Cities, Rock Island, Ill., 1986—; v.p. Bd. Edn. Ch. Sch., Davenport, 1987-88; adv. council United Way of the Quad Cities, Rock Island, 1988—. Mem. Nat. Transp. & Exch. Assn. Republican. Roman Catholic. Home: 2922 W 37th St Davenport IA 52806 Office: Iowa-Ill Gas & Electric 2759 5th Ave Rock Island IL 61201

BARKETT, ROSEMARY, state supreme court justice; b. Ciudad Victoria, Tamaulipas, Mex., Aug. 29, 1939; came to U.S., 1946, naturalized, 1958; BS summa cum laude, Spring Hill Coll., 1967; JD, U. Fla., 1970. Bar: Fla., U.S. Dist. Ct. (so. dist.) Fla., U.S. Ct. Appeals (5th cir.), U.S. Supreme Ct. Pvt. practice West Palm Beach, Fla., 1971-79; judge 15th Jud. Cir. Ct., Palm Beach County, Fla., 1979-84, 4th Dist. Ct. Appeal, West Palm Beach, Fla., 1984-85; justice Supreme Ct. Fla., Tallahassee, 1985—; mem. faculty U. Nev., Reno, Fla. Jud. Coll. Mem. editorial bd. The Florida Judges Manual. Mem. vis. com. Miami U. Law Sch.; mem. bd. visitors St. Thomas U. Recipient Woman of Achievement award Palm Beach County Commn. on Status of Women, 1985; named to Fla. Women's Hall of Fame, 1986. Fellow Acad. Matrimonial Lawyers; mem. ABA, Fla. Bar Assn. (family law sect., chairperson ct. stats. and workload com. and study commn. on guardianship law, lectr. on matrimonial media and criminal law continuing legal edn.), Palm Beach County Bar Assn., Am. Acad. Matrimonial Lawyers (award 1984), Fla. Assn. Women Lawyers (Palm Beach chpt.), Nat. Assn. Women Judges, Palm Beach Marine Inst. (former chairperson, bd. trustees), Acad. Fla. Trial lawyers (Achievement award 1988), Assn. Trial Lawyers Am. (Achievement award 1986). Office: Fla Supreme Ct Supreme Ct Bldg Tallahassee FL 32399*

BARKLEY, MIRIAM CORN, director of publications; b. Raleigh, N.C., Aug. 1, 1952; d. Dewey M. and Christine (Roberts) Corn; m. C. Timothy Barkley, Feb. 28, 1987. BA, U. N.C., Greensboro, 1974, MLS, 1977. Tchr. middle sch. Randolph County Schs., Asheboro, N.C., 1974-76; media svcs. coord. Guilford Coll., Greensboro, N.C., 1977-78; instructional design specialist Elon College (N.C.), 1978-81; editor Furniture South mag., High Point, N.C., 1981-82; publs. dir. U. N.C., Greensboro, 1982—. Mem. Coun. for Advancement and Support for Edn., Univ. and Coll. Designer's Assn. Home: 1414 W Lake Dr Greensboro NC 27408 Office: U NC 504 Stirling St Greensboro NC 27412

BARKSDALE, CHANDLEE MURPHY, marketing professional; b. Washington, Jan. 20, 1942; d. Roosevelt McKenzie and Ella Pratt (Williams) Lewis; m. Andrew F. Murphy, Oct. 10, 1964 (div. 1975); children: Heather Kristin, Tara Alexis; m. Toby Z. Barksdale, Mar. 29, 1975. AB, Bryn Mawr Coll., 1963; MBA, U. N.C., 1978; cert., Slavic Inst., U. Ind., 1962. Analyst NSA, Ft. Meade, Md., 1963-65; co-dir. Peruvian/Am. Cultural Inst., Ica, Peru, 1965-67; instr. Inst. Modern Langs., Washington, 1967-69; writer Am. C. of C., Mexico City, 1969-72; pvt. lang. instr. Washington, 1972-73; mgmt. analyst EPA, Research Triangle Park, N.C., 1973-76; mktg. mgr. Control Data Corp., Mpls., 1978-85; area mgr. Tennant Co., Mpls., 1985-87, mgr. internat. mktg., 1987—; bd. dirs. Tennant Co. Found., Minn. Internat. Ctr., Playwright's Ctr. Mem. mktg. com. United Way, Mpls.; chmn. fin. com. A Better Chance, Northfield, Minn., 1984-86. Recipient Leadership award Mpls. YWCA, 1988. Mem. NAFE, Am. Mktg. Assn. (v.p. programming 1990—), Bryn Mawr Coll. Alumnae Assn. (dist. councilor 1984-86, dist. admissions rep. 1988—). Office: Tennant Co 701 N Lilac Dr Minneapolis MN 55422

BARLEY, NENA STEWART, infosystems systems; b. Hammond, Ind., Sept. 27, 1958; d. Wilber Eugene and Mary Alice (Tudor) Stewart; m. Kirk Thomas Barley, June 20, 1981; children: Kirk Patrick, Thomas Marion. BSBA, U. Fla., 1980. Computer programmer U. Fla. Office Instnl. Resources, Gainesville, 1980-81; computer programmer/analyst Fedmart, San Diego, 1981-82; owner, pres. consignment shop DeNovo, Jacksonville, N.C., 1985-86; contract photographer First Foto, Jacksonville, 1988-89; case spotter, ins. adjuster Alex Sill Co., Jacksonville, 1988-89; instr. Pensacola (Fla.) Jr. Coll., 1989—; instr. Coastal Carolina Community Coll., Jacksonville, 1988-89. Mem. Fla. Motion Picture and TV Assn. (membership chair N.W. chpt. 1989-90), Onslow-Lejuene C. of C., Officer's Wives Club (mem. newsletter staff 1988-89). Methodist. Home: 222 Merrill Dr Milton FL 32570

BARNARD, BONNIE MARIE, information systems company executive; b. Ft. Worth, Dec. 14, 1957; d. James Montgomery and Lucille Marie (Rebedoux) B.; m. L. Justin Williams, Oct. 26, 1985 (div. 1988). BS in Health Planning, Pa. State U., 1980; MPH in Disease Control, U. Tex., Houston, 1983; postgrad., U. Tex., Austin, 1983-84. Infection control exec. Med. Ctr. Del Oro Hosp., Houston, 1983; info. svcs. adminstrv. asst. Ham-TMC Libr., Houston, 1983; infection control, insvc. coord. Beltway Community Hosp., Pasadena, Tex., 1983-85; asst. infection control coord. Loyola U. Med. Ctr., Maywood, Ill., 1985-89; project mgr. Surveillance By Objectives Mgmt. Systems, Inc., Irvine, Calif., 1989-90, Community Health Computing, Houston, 1990—; cons., speaker in field. Contbr. chpt. to book: Costing On-Line Services, 1984. Vol. Brookfield (Ill.) Pub. Libr., 1989. Mem. Assn. Practitioners in Infection Control (pres. elect. 1985, 89, Ednl. Advancement award 1985). Democrat. Home: 7490 Brompton #262 Houston TX 77025

BARNARD, ELAINE PATRICIA, actress; b. Bklyn., Oct. 6, 1930; d. George William and Agnes (Farrell) Elliott; m. Ernest Raymond Barnard; 1 child, Bryn Elliott. BA, U. Wash., 1953; MFA, U. Calif., Irvine, 1971. Cert. elem., sec. tchr., Calif. Tchr. LaColima Sch., East Whittier, Calif., 1961-65, Laguna Beach (Calif.) Schs., 1965-79; freelance actress, writer L.A., 1979—; Mem. Actors Ctr.-Theatre Wing, Studio City, Calif., 1988-89, SAG Conservatory. Author: (plays) Long Distance, 1977, Ben, 1975, Glory, 1973 (winner of nat. competition), The Cellar, 1971; current film credits include "Susan", "Welcome Home Roxy Carmichael" and commls. for MacIntosh Computers and Gen. Electric. Mem. Laguna Art Mus., Laguna Greenbelt Assn., Laguna Beach Friends of Libr. Artists residency, Edna Millay Colony, N.Y., 1980, Ossabaw Island Found., Ga., 1979, Wurlitzer Found., N.Mex., 1977, Creekwood Colony, Ala., 1977. Mem. SAG, Women in Theatre, Am. Fedn. Radio and TV Arts, Dramatists Guild, Actors Equity Assn., Internat. Women Writers Guild, Sierra Club, UCLA Film Actors Group. Democrat. Home: 28892 Top of the World Dr Laguna Beach CA 92651

BARNARD, KATHLEEN RAINWATER, educator; b. Wayne City, Ill., Dec. 28, 1927; d. Roy and Nina (Edmison) Rainwater; BS, So. Ill. U., 1949, MS, 1953; postgrad. Ind. U., 1953; PhD, U. Tex., 1959; m. Donald L. Barnard, Aug. 17, 1947 (div. Mar. 1973); children: Kimberly, Jill. Tchr. pub. high sch., Wayne City, Ill., 1946-51; faculty asst., lectr. Vocat. Tech. Inst., So. Ill. U., Carbondale, 1951-53; lectr. bus. edn. Northwestern U., Chgo., 1953-55; chmn. dept. bus. adminstrn. San Antonio Coll., 1955-60; chmn. dept. bus. edn. DePaul U., Chgo., 1960-62; chmn. dept. bus. Loop Coll. (now Harold Washington Coll.), City Colls. Chgo., 1962-67, prof., 1968—, exec. sec., bd. dirs. credit union, 1975-78; cons., evaluator Ill. Program for Gifted Children, State Demonstrator Center, Oak Park (Ill.) Pub. Schs.; cons. First Nat. Bank Chgo., 1974; ednl. cons. Ency. Brit., 1969. Cons. edn. and tng. div. Continental Ill. Nat. Bank & Trust Co., Chgo., 1967, Victor Corp., 1965—; cons. IBM, Inc., summer 1968. Mem. North Central Bus. Edn. Assn., Nat. Bus. Edn. Assn., Chgo. Assn. Commerce and Industry, Delta Kappa Gamma, Pi Omega Pi, Alpha Delta Pi (sponsor), Sigma Phi (sponsor), Delta Pi Epsilon (pres. Alpha Theta chpt. 1958). Contbg. author: College Typewriting, 1960; Business Correspondence, 1962. Home: 920 Courtland Ave Park Ridge IL 60068 Office: 30 E Lake St Chicago IL 60601

BARNARD, KATHRYN ELAINE, nursing educator, researcher; b. Omaha, Apr. 16, 1938; d. Paul and Elsa Elizabeth (Anderson) B. BS in Nursing, U. Nebr., Omaha, 1960; MS in Nursing, Boston U., 1962; PhD, U. Wash., Seattle, 1972; DSc (hon.), U. Nebr., 1990. Acting instr. U. Nebr., Omaha, 1960-61; acting instr. U. Wash., Seattle, 1963-65, asst. prof., 1965-69, prof.

nursing, 1972—, now assoc. dean; bd. dirs. Nat. Ctr. for Clin. Infant Programs, Washington, 1980—. Chmn. rsch. com. Bur. of Community Health Svcs., MCH, 1987-89. Recipient Lucille Petry award Nat. League for Nursing, 1968, Martha Mae Eliot award Am. Assn. Pub. Health, 1983, Professorship award U. Wash., 1985. Fellow Am. Acad. Nursing (bd. dirs. 1980-82); mem. Inst. Medicine; mem. Am. Nurses Assn. (chmn. com. 1980-82, Jessie Scott award 1982, Nurse of Yr. award 1984), Soc. Research in Child Devel. (bd. dirs. 1981-87), Sigma Theta Tau (founders award in research 1987). Democrat. Presbyterian. Home: 11508 Durland Ave NE Seattle WA 98125 Office: U Wash Mailstop WJ-10 Seattle WA 98195

BARNARD, ROSALYN MYNETTE, social worker; b. Columbia, N.C., Jan. 28, 1961; d. Charles Edward and Doris Elizabeth (Collins) Weston; children: Brandon Augustus Young, Nicholas Martin Barnard. BS in Social Work, U.N.C., Greensboro, 1984. Social worker III Hyde County Dept. Social Svcs., Swan Quarter, N.C., 1986—. Recipient Otis T. Nixon scholarship Washington-Roper Dist. Assembly, Roper, N.C., 1981. Mem. N.C. Social Svcs. Assn., NAFE, NAACP, Alpha Phi Omega. Democrat. Mem. Disciples of Christ Ch. Office: Hyde County Dept Social Svc PO Box 220 Swan Quarter NC 27885

BARNARD, SANDRA KAY, librarian; b. Redding, Calif., Mar. 8, 1941; d. Hartley Thompson and Edna Catherine (Enos) B. AA, Shasta Coll., Redding, 1963; AB, Calif. State U., Chico, 1966; MS in LS, U. So. Calif., 1973. Media coord. Bass Elem. Sch., Redding, 1977-78; children's libr. Shasta County Libr., Redding, 1979; reference libr. Shasta Info. Ctr., Redding, 1980; docent libr. Redding Mus. and Art Ctr., 1984-88; reference libr. Calif. State U., Chico, 1988—. Libr. Redding United Meth. Ch., 1975-79. Mem. ALA, Calif. Libr. Assn., AAUW (yearbook editor Redding br. 1976, reader lit. festival 1985-90), Shasta Ladies Encampment Aux. (chief matriarch 1989), Order Ea. Star, Rebekahs (noble grand 1971, 87, Good Fellowship award 1976). Republican. Home: 725 Parkview Ave Redding CA 96001 Office: Calif State U Chico Meriam Libr Chico CA 95929-0295

BARNARD, SHERI, mayor. Mayor, city of Spokane. Office: City of Spokane Office of Mayor W 808 Spokane Falls Blvd Spokane WA 99201*

BARNAT, RHONDA KATZ, bank executive, marketing executive, writer; b. Champaign, Ill., Apr. 24, 1952; d. Harold William and Lee (Pankler) Katz; m. Michael Robert Barnat, Aug. 29, 1976; children: Dara Katz, Jeremy Allan. BA, U. Rochester, 1973; MUP, U. Mich., 1976. Rsch. analyst Washtenaw County Planning, Ann Arbor, Mich., 1973-76; community relations editor U. Mich. Hosp., Ann Arbor, 1976-79; freelance writer Ann Arbor, 1979-89; instr. Washtenaw Community Coll., Ann Arbor, 1984-89; community affairs mgr., acting mktg. mgr. River Bank Am., New Rochelle, N.Y., 1989—. Author feature articles. Vice pres. Chapel Hill Condominium Assn., Ann Arbor, 1980. Mem. Women in Communicatons (co-chmn. Ann Arbor 1980-81). Home: 502 Apple Tree Ln Brewster NY 10509 Office: River Bank Am 145 Huguenot St New Rochelle NY 10801

BARNES, AUDREY BRYANT, librarian; b. Boston, May 27, 1930; d. Frank Sewall Bryant and Juliet Elsie (Krause) Hahn; m. Gene C. Burns, Aug. 8, 1959 (div. Mar. 1960); m. Ralph Heywood Barnes, Oct. 5, 1974; stepchildren: Richard A., Donald H. BS in Libr. Sci., Simmons Coll., 1953. Asst. children's libr. East Br. Libr., Watertown, Mass., 1953-56, asst. br. libr., 1956-59; jr. cataloger Boston U., 1959-61; libr. E.I. DuPont de Nemours & Co., Wilmington, Del., 1961-74, ret., 1974. Mem. town com. Rep. Party, Rockport, Maine, 1987—. Mem. AAUW, Order of Ea. Star (star point 1975-78), Rockport Garden Club. Home: RD 1 Box 316 180 Mistic Ave Rockport ME 04856

BARNES, CATHY LYNN, nurse; b. Council Bluffs, Iowa, Feb. 14, 1952; d. Edward L. and Bonita J. (Townsend) B. BS in Nursing, Alverno Coll., 1983; MS in Nursing, Vanderbilt U., 1988. RN. Staff nurse Meth. Hosp., Omaha, 1973-76, charge nurse, 1976-80, clin. supr., 1980-82; assoc. instr. nursing Meth. Coll. Nursing, Omaha, 1983-86; staff nurse New Eng. Deaconess Hosp., Boston, 1988-90; case mgr. Vis. Nurse Assn. Omaha, 1990—. Named one of Outstanding Young Women of Am. Mem. Am. Nurses' Assn., Oncology Nursing Soc., Am. Holistic Nurses' Assn., Sigma Theta Tau. Roman Catholic. Home: 3119 Pleasant Dr Omaha NE 68147

BARNES, CONSTANCE INGALLS (MRS. RUSSELL C. BARNES), retired librarian; b. Atchison, Kans., July 30, 1903; d. Sheffield and Lucy (Van Hoesen) Ingalls; B.A., U. Kans., 1925; M.A., U. Mich., 1950, M.A. in L.S., 1955; postgrad. Ecole du Louvre, France, 1960, Vergilian Soc., Cumae, Italy, summer 1963; m. Russell C. Barnes, Oct. 1, 1927; children—Lucie-Jeanne (Mrs. Todd Seymour), John J.I. Librarian, Cranbrook Acad. Art, Bloomfield Hills, Mich., 1955-74, 80-81. Mem. LWV, AAUW, Internat. Arthurian Soc., Alliance Francaise, Founders Soc. Detroit Inst. Arts, Kappa Alpha Theta. Club: Village Woman's (Bloomfield Hills). Home: 788 Randall Ct Birmingham MI 48009

BARNES, CORINNE ANN, pediatric nurse, educator; b. Greenock Heights, Pa., July 3, 1928; d. George Julius and Elizabeth Sarah (Smythe) Meerhoff. RN, Allegheny Gen. Hosp., Pitts., 1949; BS in Nursing., U. Pitts., 1960, M of Nuring Edn., 1963, PhD in Nursing, 1974. Pediatric nurse adminstr. Allegheny Gen. Hosp., 1950-58; pediatric nurse specialist Children's Hosp. and U. Pitts., 1966-70; undergrad. tchr. U. Pitts., 1965—, chmn. pediatric dept., 1970-72, program dir. grad. programs in nursing care of children, 1978—, program dir. parent-child nursing grad. program, 1979—, interim dir. doctoral program, 1988—; cons. Co-editor Maternal-Child Nursing Jour., 1978—; mem. editorial bd. Jour. Am. Assn. Child Health, 1981-88. Mem. adv. com. Bright Beginnings; pres. Pitts. Women's Tennis Orgn., 1957; interim dir. Doctoral Program, 1988—; dir. Parent-Child Nursing Grad. Program, 1979—. Recipient Disting. Alumnus award U. Pitts. Sch. Nursing, 1982, 86, Recruitment award Coun. Nurse Researchers, 1982; nursing grantee; named Disting. Dau. of Pa. Gov. of. Pa., 1984. Fellow Am. Acad. Nursing; mem. Am. Nurses Assn., Pa. Nurses Assn., Allegheny Gen. Nurses Alumnae (pres. 1952), U. Pitts. Alumnae Assn., Am. Assn. Pub. Health, Assn. Child Care in Health, Soc. Research in Child Devel., Nat. League Nursing, Council Nurse Researchers, Pitts. Tennis Assn., Fox Chapel Racquet Club, Univ. Faculty Club, Zonta (pres. Pitts. chpt. 1989—, treas.), Sigma Theta Tau. Republican. Methodist. Office: 3500 Victoria Hall Sch Nursing Pittsburgh PA 15261

BARNES, DEBORAH DICKSON, social worker; b. Kinston, N.Y., May 1, 1944; d. Robert Gordon and Ruth Larason (Sherer) Dickson; m. Victor Gerard Barnes, Sept. 26, 1970; children: Jennifer Kay, Sara Gordon. AB, Syracuse U., 1966; MSW with Health Care Specialization, U. Houston, 1984. Cert. social worker, Tex. Field rep. Girl Scouts Am., Westfield, N.J., 1966-67; caseworker ARC, Naval Hosp., Chelsea, Mass., 1967-68; caseworker ARC, Andrews Air Force Base, Md., 1968-69, Cam Rahn Bay, Vietnam, 1969-70, Colorado Springs, Colo., 1971-72; social worker ARC, Redstone Arsenal, Ala., 1987—. Bd. dirs. Women's Newtwork Huntsville, Ala., 1988, 1st v.p., 1989. Recipient Cert. Commendation USAF, 1970, Cert. Appreciation U.S. Army, 1989. Mem. Nat. Assn. Social Workers, ARC (bd.-mem.-at-large, com. chair Houston, cert. appreciation 1987), AAUW, Nat. Assn. for Female Execs.

BARNES, DENIS TAT, sales executive; b. Evanston, Ill., Dec. 8, 1929; d. Charles Birchby and Lela Isabel (Bauerfind) B. BS, Northwestern U. 2d v.p. Commerce Clearing House, Inc., Riverwoods, Ill.; owner, prin. Denis T. Barnes Assocs., Dallas; instr. Brookhaven Coll., Farmers Branch, Tex. Vice pres. adminstrn. Shakespeare Guild, Dallas, 1988-89, treas., 1989-90. Mem. North Dallas C. of C., North Tex. Speakers Assn. Office: 15775 N Hillcrest Ste 508-633 Dallas TX 75248

BARNES, GERMAINE EMMA, employment service executive; b. Cleve., May 16, 1948; d. George Zoltan and Emma (Janosi) Deli; m. Jeffry Alan Barnes, May 26, 1982; 1 child, Justin. BS in Edn., Kent State U., 1971; MA in Counseling and Guidance, Ball State U., 1976. English tchr. Del Rio (Tex.)/San Felipe Consol. High Sch., 1971-72, Woodbridge (England) Am. Sch., 1973-75; mgr. Personnel Pool of Tucson (Ariz.), Inc., 1978-81, 85-86; disability examiner Disability Determination Svc. Dept. Econ. Security, Tucson, 1981-85; prin., pres. New Concepts Employment and Bus. Svcs., Inc., Casa Grande, Ariz., 1986—. Mem. allocations com. United Way, 1988; active Casa Grande Econ. Devel. Found., 1986—; governing bd. Casa Grande Town Hall, 1989, del., 1988, 89. Mem. Casa Grande C. of C. (bus. edn. com. 1986—, chmn. 1988, 89, bd. dirs. 1990), Pinal County Personnel Assn. (sec.-treas. 1987-88, pres. 1990-91), Ariz. Assn. Temporary Svcs. Office: New Concepts Employment 550 N Florence St Casa Grande AZ 85222 also: 955 W Chandler Blvd Ste 12 Chandler AZ 85224

BARNES, HELEN CROSS, banker; b. Portsmouth, Va., Mar. 26, 1945; d. Robert Lee and Frances Phyllis (Motley) Cross; m. L. Gary Barnes, Aug. 10, 1968. BA in Math., Westhampton Coll. of U. Richmond, 1967; spl. courses Am. Inst. Banking, Md. Bankers Sch. of U. Md. Tchr., York County Schs. (Va.), 1967-71; internal cons. Equitable Bank N.A., Balt., 1971-78, project mgr., sec. Equitable Found., Inc., 1978-82, v.p., dir. bank svcs., 1982-89, treas. EquiPAC, 1989—. Bd. dirs. exec. com., v.p. programs, corp. sec. Jr. Achievement Met. Balt., 1982—; mem. exec. bd., employment steering com., info. processing tng. ctr. steering com., asst. sec., treas. Balt. Urban League, Inc., 1985—. Mem. Assn. Internal Mgmt. Cons., Assn. Info. Systems Profls., Office Tech. Mgmt. Assn., Am. Soc. Performance Improvement. Recipient Bronze Leadership award Nat. Bd. Dirs. Jr. Achievement, Inc. Republican. Methodist. Office: MNC Fin Inc 100 S Charles St Baltimore MD 21201

BARNES, ISABEL JANET, microbiology educator, college dean; b. Union City, N.J., Sept. 22, 1936; d. Carl Robert and Isabel Sarah (Cappelletti) B.; m. John D. Bowman, June 15, 1978 (dec. Nov. 1986). BS, Pa. State U., 1958; MS, Cornell U., 1960; PhD, Hahnemann Med. Coll., 1969. Asst. prof. microbiology Hershey Med. Ctr., Pa. State U., 1968-73; asst. prof., then assoc. prof. Sangamon State U., Springfield, Ill., 1973-76; assoc. prof. med. tech. U. Wis., Madison, 1976-85, interim dean Sch. Allied Health Professions, 1981-84; prof. med. tech. Ferris State Univ., Big Rapids, Mich., 1985—, dean Sch. Allied Health, 1985—; trustee Mecosta County Gen. Hosp., bd. dirs. 1988—; bd. dirs. Mich. Hemophilia Found., 1989—. Mem. AAAS, AAUP, Am. Soc. Med. Technologists, Am. Soc. Allied Health Profls. (bd. dirs. 1989-92), Coll. Health Deans (pres. 1988—). Office: Ferris State Univ Sch of Allied Health Big Rapids MI 49307

BARNES, JEAN FREDENBURGH, educator; b. Milw., Aug. 22, 1923; d. James Lynn and Helene (Neumer) Fredenburgh. BSEd, Milw. State Tchrs. Coll., 1945; MEd, Wis. State Coll., 1952; postgrad, U. Wis., Milw. Cert. tchr., Wis. Cons. Dept. Edn., Agana, Guam, 1964-70, master tchr., 1970-88; asst. prof. English U. Guam, Mangilao; propr. The Beehive, Agana, 1976—. Contbr. articles, poems to profl. publs.; profl. actress, singer, storyteller on radio, TV. Treas. Civic Ctr. Found., 1988—. Grantee Johnson Wax Found.; received recognition 19th Guam Legislature. Mem. NEA, Nat. Coun. Tchrs. English, Higher Edn. Coun., Guam Fire Casualty Marine Ins. Assn. (sec. 1988—). Home: 1101 Green Pk Mangilao GU 96923

BARNES, JHANE ELIZABETH, fashion design company executive, designer; b. Balt., Mar. 4, 1954; d. Richard Amos and Muriel Florence (Chase) B.; m. Howard Ralph Feinberg, Dec. 12, 1981 (div.); m. 2d, Katsuhiko Kawasaki, Feb. 12, 1988. A.S., Fashion Inst. Tech., 1975. Pres., designer Jhane Barnes for ME, N.Y.C., 1976-78, Jhane Barnes Inc., N.Y.C., 1978—. Recipient Menswear award Coty Am. Fashion Critics, 1980, Contract Textile award Am. Soc. Interior Designers, 1983, 84, Product Design awards Inst. Bus. Designers and Contract Mag., 1983, 84, 85, 86, 89; named Most Promising Designer Cutty Sark, 1980, Outstanding Designer, 1982; Outstanding Menswear Designer, Council of Fashion Designers Am., 1982. Office: Jhane Barnes Inc 24 W 40th St 14th Fl New York NY 10018*

BARNES, JO ANN, university administrator; b. Marengo, Iowa, June 21, 1935; d. Joseph William and Minnie Ellen (Henderson) B. Clerical positions various cities, 1952-67; sec. med. adminstrn. U. Iowa, Iowa City, 1967-74, office coord. dept. anatomy, 1974-75, editorial assoc., 1975—; mem. staff coun., 1989—, ednl program assoc., 1990—; elected to U. Iowa staff coun., 1989-92, sec., 1990. Mem. Am. Bus. Women's Assn. (Woman of the Yr. 1983). Democrat. Office: The U Iowa Dept of Anatomy BSB Iowa City IA 52242

BARNES, JUDITH ANNE, communications executive; b. Rochester, N.Y., Feb. 28, 1948; d. Robert William and Louise (Marriott) B. BA in English, Russell Sage Coll., 1970; MS in Tech. Communication, Rensselaer Polytechnic Inst., 1971, PhD in Communications, 1984. Asst. dir. admissions Russell Sage Coll., Troy, N.Y., 1971-72; spl. cons. communications The Rensselaerville (N.Y.) Inst., 1973-77; dir. advt. The Mayfair Group Stores, Albany, N.Y., 1977-82; dir., communications Cohoes (N.Y.) Specialty Stores, 1984-86, v.p., mktg., advt., and communications, 1986-89; prin. The Communications Co., 1989—; adj. instr., lectr. various univs. and orgns., 1971—; communications and advt. cons. for numerous bus., health, profl., comml. and civic orgns., 1971—. Author: Understanding Freedom of Speech in America, 1976. Co-founder, v.p. mktg. and programming, bd. dirs. Troy Music Hall Assn., 1979-82; co-founder, bd. dirs. Capitol Chamber Artists, Troy, 1978-81; mem., bd. dirs. Capital Regional Mag., Albany, 1988—, Troy Economic Devel. Commn., 1986-88, Cowan & Label Gourmet Marketplace, Friends of Chamber Music, Troy Chromatic Concerts, Heritage Artists, Cohoes Music Hall, Historic Albany Found., Hudson-Mohawk Urban Cultural Park Commn., Samaritan Hosp. Found., Upper Hudson Planned Parenthood; mem. Russell Sage Coll. Coun.. Mem. Rensselaer Poly. Inst. Alumni Assn. Democrat.

BARNES, JULIA O'TEALA, military career officer, healthcare administrator; b. Henderson, N.C., May 13, 1937; d. Bolton Barnes and Annie (Sims) Harris. Diploma, Hahnemann Hosp. Sch. Nursing, 1957; BS in Nursing, U. Pa., 1972; MA in Health Resources Mgmt., Pepperdine U., 1978. RN, Pa. Commd. ensign USN, 1958, advanced through grades to capt., 1980; nurse operating rm. Hahnemann Hosp., Phila., 1957-58; nurse staff operating rm. Naval Hosp., Oakland Hosp., Calif., 1958-62; supr. operating rm. Naval Hosp., Guam, Mariana Islands, 1963-64, Great Lakes, 1964-66, Phila., 1966-70; clin. supr. Naval Hosp., 1972-74; chief nurse Naval Hosp., Guam, 1975-76; dir. nursing Naval Hosp., Lemoore, Calif., 1976-85; exec. officer Naval Hosp., Camp LeJeune, Calif., 1985-86; comdg. officer Naval Hosp., Great Lakes, 1986-89. Bd. dirs. Urban League, Lake County, Ill., 1980-83, Great Lakes Credit Union, 1986—; mem. Waukegan Symphony Chorus; mem. Great Lakes Credit Union Bd. Dirs. Mem. Nat. Naval Officers Assn. (regional v.p. 1977-79), Rotary. Democrat.

BARNES, KATE MILLER, data processing executive; b. Perry, Iowa, Sept. 30, 1953; d. Virgil A. and Cheryl J. (Luellen) Miller. BA with honors, U. Iowa, 1975; MBA, U. Phoenix, 1983. Assoc. dir. Dept. Adult Corrections, Cedar Rapids, Iowa, 1973-79; product mgr. DELTAK, Inc., Naperville, Ill., 1979-81; v.p. Barnes Assocs. Systems, Inc., Tucson, 1981-88; pres. Kate Barnes & Assocs Inc., Tempe, Ariz., 1988—; founder, chairperson Dept. Adult Corrections Adv., 1987, Bus. Tech. Expo, Tucson, 1985-86. Author: Using Multimate, 1985 (Best Selling Author award 1986), Word Perfect: Expert Techniques, 1989, Word: Expert Techniques, 1989, The First Book of Word Perfect, 1989; contbg. editor, columnist PC Week, 1985-86; contbr. articles to profl. jours. Mem. adv. bd. Kirkwood Community Coll., Cedar Rapids, 1977; mem. Citizens Com. on Alcohol, Cedar Rapids, 1978; sec., treas. Houghton Neighborhood Com., Tucson, 1986. Mem. Data Processing Mgrs. Assn. (chairperson edn. 1986-87), Nat. Assn. Women Bus. Owners, Nat. Assn. for Performance in Instrn. (v.p. publs. 1990). Republican. Office: Kate Barnes & Assocs Inc PO Box 61902 Phoenix AZ 85082

BARNES, LINDA JOYCE, writer; b. Detroit, June 6, 1949; d. Irving and Hilda (Grodman) Appelblatt; m. Richard Allen Barnes, June 7, 1970; 1 child, Samuel Jacob. BFA cum laude, Boston U., 1971. Tchr. theater Chelmsford (Mass.) Pub. Schs., 1971-76; dir. drama Lexington (Mass.) Pub. Schs., 1978; writer, 1979—. Author: Blood Will Have Blood, 1982, Bitter Finish, 1983, Dead Heat, 1984, Cities of the Dead, 1986, A Trouble of Fools, 1987 (Am. Mystery award 1987), The Snake Tattoo, 1989, Coyote, 1990. Recipient Anthony award for short story Boucherçon, 1986. Mem. Mystery Writers Am. (bd. dirs. 1986-89, v.p. New Eng. chpt. 1985), Authors Guild, Pvt. Eye Writers Am., Internat. Crime Writers Assn., Am. Crime Writers Union.

BARNES, LORNA ELAINE, not-for-profit education and training organization administrator; b. Chgo., Jan. 5, 1958; d. Clarence David Harty and Madeline Dorita (Sharpe) Littlejohn; m. Andre Cadaryl Barnes, Aug. 9, 1976 (div. June 1988). Student, Barbizon Coll., 1981, DePaul U., 1983-85. Sec. Goldblatt's Bros., Chgo., 1976-78; collection dept. sec. 1st Nat. Bank of Chgo., 1978-79; legal sec. Mayer, Brown & Platt, 1980-82; placement counselor DePaul U., 1984-85; account exec. Minority Econ. Resources Corp., Des Plaines, Ill., 1985-87; pres., chief exec. officer L. Barnes & Assocs., Inc., Chgo., 1988—; founder, pres. Am.'s Back-To-Basics, Inc., Chgo., 1987—; del. Ill. Dept. Pub. Aid, Springfield, Ill., 1988-89; mentor Chgo. Housing Authority, 1989—; model Chgo. Police Dept., 1987—. Contbr. articles to profl. jours. Mem. Student Edn. Assn., Chgo., 1984, North Shore African-Am. Civic, Chgo., 1987; mem. employment adv. bd. Midwest Women's Ctr., Chgo., 1987; pres. DePaulians Organizing an Employment Renaissance, Chgo., 1984; bd. dirs. Ill. Black United Fund, Chgo., 1988. Recipient Vol. Svc. award Edward G. Gardner, 1987, Image award Being Single Mag., 1987, Fred Hampton Image award William Bill Hampton, 1988, Outstanding Role Model of Yr. award WE CARE, Chgo. Pub. Schs., Dept. Police, 1988-89. Mem. NAFE, Am. Soc. for Tng. and Devel., Chgo. Focus on Edn., Ill. Assn. Black Women Bus. Owners, Southside Literacy Coalition, Cosmopolitan C. of C. (v.p. legis. affairs Chgo. chpt. 1989—), Urban League. Democrat. Episcopalian. Office: Ams Back to Basics Inc 330 S Wells Ste 602 Chicago IL 60606

BARNES, MAGGIE LUE SHIFFLETT (MRS. LAWRENCE BARNES), nurse; b. nr. Spur, Tex., Mar. 29, 1931; d. Howard Eldridge and Sadie Adilene (Dunlap) Shifflett; m. T.C. Fagan, Jan. 1950 (dec. Feb. 1952); 1 child, Lawayne; m. Lawrence Barnes, Sept. 2, 1960. Student, Cogdell Sch. Nursing, 1959-60, Western Tex. Coll., 1972-76; postgrad. Meth. Hosp. Sch. Nursing, Lubbock, Tex., 1975; BSN, W. Tex. State U., 1977. RN, Tex. Fl. nurse D.M. Cogdell Meml. Hosp., Snyder, Tex., 1960-64, medication nurse, 1964-76, asst. evening supr., 1976-78, charge nurse, after 1978, evening nursing supr., 1980; nursing supr. Scurry, Borden, Mitchel, Fisher, Howard Counties, West Cen. Home Health Agy., Snyder, 1980-83; emergency rm. evening supr. Root-Meml. Hosp., 1983-89; dir. of nurses Snyder Oak Core Ctr., 1989—; regional coord. home health svcs. Beverly Enterprises, 1983. Den mother Cub Scouts, Boy Scouts Am., Holliday, Tex., 1960-61; mem. PTA, Snyder, Tex., 1960-69; adv. Sr. Citizens Assn.; mem. Tri-Region Health Systems Agy., 1979—; mem. adv. bd. Scurry County Diabetes Assn., 1982—. Mem. Vocat. Nurses Assn. Tex. (mem. bd. 1963-65, div. pres. 1967-69), Emergency Dept. Nursing Assn. Apostolic Faith Ch. (sec., treas. 1956-58). Home: Rte 1 Box 9B Hermleigh TX 79526

BARNES, MARGARET ANDERSON, business consultant; b. Johnston County, N.C.; m. Benjamin Barnes, Dec. 26, 1959. BS, N.C. Cen. U., 1958; MA, U. Md., 1975; PhD, Columbia Pacific U., 1986. Math. tchr. Tarboro (N.C.) Sch. System, 1959-61; math. statistician Bur. of Census, Suitland, Md., 1962-67, 69-70, Dist. of Columbia govt., 1967-68; cons. Nat. Insts. of Health, Bethesda, Md., 1970-72, chief of data standards, 1972-73; with exec. clearance office HEW, Rockville, Md., 1973-77; founder, pres. MABarnes Cons. Assoc., Lanham, Md., 1978—; commr. State of Md. Accident Fund, Balt., 1979—; mem. adv. bd. Universal Bank, Lanham, 1980-83, Interstate Gen. Corp., St. Charles, Md., 1981-83. Chairwoman Glenwood Park Civic Assn., Lanham, 1967-80. Democrat. Home: PO Box 586 Seabrook MD 20706 Office: MABarnes Con Assocs 9470 Annapolis Rd Ste 224 Lanham MD 20706

BARNES, MARY CATHERINE BANNING, administrative assistant; b. Billings, Mont., Sept. 6, 1954; d. John Albert and Betty Weston (Lea) Banning; m. Belve Lonzo Barnes Jr., Nov. 30, 1974; children: Catherine Nicole, Jaclyn Elizabeth. AA, Northeast La. U., 1973; student, La. State U., Shreveport, 1974, La. Tech. Sch., Barksdale, 1975-76. With La. Disabilities Determinations, 1973—, adminstrv. asst., 1985-87, adminstrv. svcs. asst., 1987-90. Mem. presch. com. Airline Bapt. Ch., Bossier City, 1985-87, dir. children's choir, 1985—, money counter, 1985—. Mem. Nat. Assn. Disability Examiners, La. Assn. Rehab. Sec. (v.p. 1976-77), La. Assn. Disability Examiners. Democrat. Home: 3636 Greenacres Pl #36 Bossier City LA 71111 Office: Disability Determinations 2920 Knight St Ste 232 Shreveport LA 71105

BARNES, PHYLLIS LUNDY, finance and administration manager; b. Pittsburgh, Pa., Apr. 13, 1950; d. Kenneth Murl and Julia Tassy Lundy; m. Peter Roger Breggin, Oct. 13, 1972; 1 child, Benjamin Jay Breggin; m. Robert Foster Barnes, Apr. 28, 1985. Student, Allegheny Coll., Meadville, Pa., 1968-71. Research assoc. Ctr. for the Study of Psychiatry, Bethesda, Md., 1971-82; sales rep. TDX Systems, Mclean, Va., 1982-83; office mgr. Dan Levine & Co., Arlington, Va., 1983; office mgr. Compu-Mark US, Bethesda, fin. adminstrn. mgr., 1987--. Author: Mag. Article, 1982; Co-author: Mag. Article. Home: 4409 Fairfield Dr Bethesda MD 20814 Office: Compu-Mark US 7201 Wisconsin Ave Bethesda MD 20814

BARNES, S. ARLENE, security analyst and business executive; b. Johnstown, Pa., Feb. 23, 1934; d. Robert M. and Edith W. (Harper) B. BA, Hood Coll., 1957; MBA, U. Pa., 1963. Rsch. asst. Pitts. Nat. Bank, 1957-62; security analyst The First Boston Corp., N.Y.C., 1964-89; security analyst, founder Retno Enterprises, N.Y.C., 1989—; bd. dirs. North River Enterprises, Hingham, Mass. Trustee Hood Coll., Frederick, Md., 1986—; patron Met. Opera, N.Y.C. Mem. N.Y. Soc. of Security Analysts, Wall St. Utility Group.

BARNES, SANDRA SUE, publishing company executive; b. Seymour, Ind., Jan. 15, 1943; d. Ray C. and Barbara (Cockerham) Henley; m. Ronald D. Barnes, Sept. 3, 1961; children: Laura, Barrett and Garrett (twins). Student, Ind. State U., 1962-63. Asst. sales mgr. Marquis Who's Who, Indpls., Ind., 1973-79, sales, svc. mgr., 1979-82, mktg. ops. mgr., 1982-84; mktg. mgr. Marquis Who's Who, Chgo., Ill., 1984-86; dir. mktg. Marquis Who's Who, Wilmette, Ill., 1986-87; v.p. mktg. Macmillan Directory Div., Wilmette, Ill., 1987-88; group v.p., prodn. mgr. Marquis Who's Who, Wilmette, Ill., 1988-89, pres., 1989—. Mem. Chgo. Assn. Direct Mktg. Republican. Office: Marquis Who's Who 3004 Glenview Rd Wilmette IL 60091

BARNES, SHARON EURICH, employment and training manager; b. Vancouver, Wash., May 27, 1942; d. Wayne Alexander and Wilma Geraldine (Shaffer) Eurich; m. Charles William Barnes, Aug. 26, 1961; children: Matthew Wayne, Andrew William, Susan Elizabeth. BA, Calif. Bapt. Coll., 1965; M in Liberal Arts, Tex. Christian U., 1988. News bur. dir. Calif. Bapt. Coll., Riverside, Calif., 1970-73; employment interviewer Tex. Employment Commn., Ft. Worth, 1975-77; counselor Fuerza de los Barrios Chicanos, Ft. Worth, 1977-78; employment supr., vol. svcs. coord., affirmative action Tarrant Hosp. Dist., Ft. Worth, 1978-83; employment and tng. mgr. Tex. Christian U., Ft. Worth, 1983—; adv. bd. Goodwill Industries, Ft. Worth, 1983-90. Contbr. articles to profl. jours. Mem. Internat. Sister Cities, Ft. Worth, 1989-90; deacon Univ. Bapt. Ch., Ft. Worth, 1988-90. Mem. AAUW, Coll. and Univ. Personnel Assn., Am. Soc. for Tng. and Devel., Soc. for Human Resource Mgmt., Ft. Worth Personnel Assn. (bd. dirs. 1986-88). Home: 6509 Westrock Fort Worth TX 76133 Office: Tex Christian U PO Box 30797 Fort Worth TX 76129

BARNES, VERA LEWIS, aerospace engineer; b. Phila., Jan. 27, 1936; d. John and Anna Mae (Smith) Lewis; m. George Henry Barnes, May 4, 1972; stepchildren: George Henry, Margaret Morris. BA in Math., Temple U., 1958, MA, 1961. Logic design engr. Sperry Univac Corp., Blue Bell, Pa., 1960-65; sr. logic design engr. Burroughs Corp., Paoli, Pa., 1965-66, mgr. program systems dept., 1968-79; project mgr. Ultronics Systems Corp., Mount Laurel, N.J., 1966-68; program mgr. space systems div. Gen. Electric Corp., King of Prussia, Pa., 1979—. Patentee in field. Recipient Cert. Achievement for Outstanding Contbns. to Gen. Electric, Phila. YWCA Orgn., 1983. Democrat. Baptist.

BARNES-MILLER, DOROTHY LOUISE, purchasing agent; b. Charleston, S.C., Jan. 20, 1945; d. Henry Cole Barnes and Millie Almond (Fudge) Rookard; m. LeeRoy Miller, May 17, 1986; children: Devin, Dawn. Student, Milw. Area Tech. Coll., 1973-75, Marquette U., 1980, 1983. From prodn. inv. control clk. to prodn. inv. mgr., buyer Globe-Union, Centralab, Milw., 1966-83; from pic mgr., purchase mgr. to pic purchasing, payroll mgr. Mepco, Centralab, Milw., 1983-87; purchasing agt. MG Industries, Welding Products, Menomonee Falls, Wisc., 1987—. Youth supr. Youth Choir, Greater Galilee Baptist, 1969-72, v.p. Young Adult Choir, 1970-74, fin. sec., Sr. Choir, 1987, Loving Couples, Mt. Zion Baptist Ch., Milw., 1988--. Mem. Nat. Assn. Purchasing Mgmt., Nat. Assn. Female Execs., Wire Assn. Internat., Centralab Women's Club (treas. 1980-83, pub. chmn. 1983--). Democrat. Office: MG Industries Welding Products N94 W14355 Garwin Mace Dr Menomonee Falls WI 53051

BARNET, ANN BIRNBAUM, pediatrician; b. Chgo., Jan. 18, 1930; d. John Solomon and Rosalie (Friedman) Birnbaum; m. Richard J. Barnet, Apr. 10, 1953; children: Juliana, Beth, Michael. AB, Sarah Lawrence Coll., 1951; MD, Harvard U., 1955. Fellow dept. pediatrics Mass. Gen. Hosp., Boston, 1958-61; clin. dir. Cambridge (Mass.) Child Devel. Clinic, 1958-61; rsch. assoc. Walter Reed Army Inst. Rsch., Washington, 1961-73; asst. prof., now prof. pediatrics and neurology George Washington U., Washington, 1967—; dir. evokes response lab. Children's Nat. Med. Ctr., Washington, 1965—; mem. communicative scis. study sect. NIH, Washington, 1973-77; cons. neurol. devices FDA, 1978-83. Contbr. articles to profl. jours. Founding pres. The Family Pl., Washington, 1981—; bd. dirs. Arts in Action, Washington, 1988—, Life Pathways, Washington, 1989—; active Eighth Day Community Ch. of the Saviour. Grantee NIH, 1964-78, W.T. Grant Found., 1972-76, March of Dimes, 1978-80, Cath. Charities, 1984, D.C. Mayor's Office on Latino Affairs, 1985-86, Children's Def. Fund, 1990, Ctr. to Prevent Childhood Malnutrition, 1990; recipient Rsch. Career Devel. award NIMH, 1970-75. Mem. Am. Acad. Pediatrics (exec. com. D.C. chpt. 1985-87), So. Soc. Pediatric Rsch., Family Resource Coalition. Christian Ecumenical. Home: 1716 Portal Dr NW Washington DC 20012 Office: Children's Nat Med Ctr 111 Michigan Ave Washington DC 20010

BARNETT, ELIZABETH, foreign service officer; b. San Bernardino, Calif., May 26, 1954; d. John E., Sr., and Joan Olga (Connor) B. B.A. summa cum laude, U. Mass., 1976; M.A. (fellow), Yale U., 1978. Fgn. svc. officer Dept. State, Washington, 1979—; civilian observer Multinat. Force and Observers, Sinai, 1984-85; U.S. consul, Budapest, Hungary, 1986-89. Mem. Am. Fgn. Svc. Assn., Secs. Open Forum, Consular Officers Assn., Fgn. Svc. Club, Phi Beta Kappa. Address: care Fgn Svc Lounge US Dept State Washington DC 20520

BARNETT, ELIZABETH HALE, management consultant; b. Nashville, Mar. 17, 1940; d. Robert Baker and Dorothy (McCarthy) Hale; m. Crawford F. Barnett Jr., June 6, 1964; children: Crawford F. III, Robert H. BA, Vanderbilt U., 1962. Receptionist, sec. U.S. Atty. Gen. Robert F. Kennedy, Washington, 1962-64; free-lance cons. Atlanta, 1973-76; pres. E.H. Barnett & Assocs., Atlanta, 1976-83; trustee The Ga. Conservancy, Atlanta, 1978—, chmn. bd. trustees, 1986-88. Contbg. author: A New Agenda, 1982; contbr. articles to profl. jours. Bd. dirs. Jr. League Atlanta, 1973-75; mem. Leadership Atlanta, 1976—; chmn., prs. bd. dirs. Vol. Coms. Art Mus. U.S. and Can., 1976-79; bd. dirs. High Mus. Art, Atlanta, 1977—; chmn. bd. dirs. Met. Atlanta chpt. ARC, 1978-80, hon. bd. dirs., 1980—; chmn. bd. dirs. United Way Met. Atlanta, 1981-84; mem. community adv. com. NW Ga. coun. Girl Scouts U.S., 1979-83; mem. coun. USO, Atlanta, 1981—; mem. bd. sponsors Atlanta Women's Network; apptd. to Ga. Clean and Beautiful Citizens Adv. Com., 1990, Ga. Solid Waste Mgmt. Commn., 1990. Named one of Ten Outstanding Young Women of Am., 1977; honored by Ga. State Legis., Atlanta, 1978. Mem. LWV. Episcopalian. Office: The Ga Conservancy 781 Marietta St NW Ste B100 Atlanta GA 31318

BARNETT, FLORENCE LLOYD-JONES, newspaper executive; b. Madison, Wis., Oct. 9, 1913; d. Richard Lloyd-Jones and Georgia (Hayden) B.; m. Howard Gentry Barnett, Jan. 2, 1943; children—Howard G., Hayden Ann. B.A., U. Wis., Madison, 1935. Dir. The Tulsa Tribune, 1940—, pres., 1982-87, vice chmn., 1988—. Bd. dirs. Gilcrease Mus., Tulsa, 1985—, Philbrook Art Mus., 1989. Recipient Spl. News Media Pub. Edn. award ACLU, 1985. Mem. Kappa Kappa Gamma. Republican. Unitarian. Clubs: Jr. League, So. Hills Country. Office: Tulsa Tribune 315 S Boulder Box 1770 Tulsa OK 74103

BARNETT, JACALYN F., lawyer; b. Bklyn., Jan. 7, 1952; d. Melvin and Bette (Epstein) Fischer; m. Michael H. Barnett, June 29, 1975 (div. 1982); m. Ronald A. Ruden, Dec. 3, 1988. BA, U. Wis., 1974; JD, Bklyn. Law Sch., 1977. Assoc. Robinson, Silverman, Pearce, Aronsohn, Sand & Berman, N.Y.C., 1977-78; assoc. Hahn, Hessan, Margolis & Ryan, N.Y.C., 1978-79; ptnr. Shea & Gould, N.Y.C., 1979—; lectr. to orgns., women groups. Mem. legal task force NOW; mem. Task Force on Marriage, Divorce, Fedn. Jewish Philanthropies, N.Y.C.; bd. dirs., chair assocs. div. Friends of David Yellin Tchrs. Coll.; mem. fundraising com. Children's Mus.; mem. adv. bd. Women's Sport Found. Mem. Am. Jewish Congress Met. Coun. (advisory bd.), NAFE (advisory bd.), Wall St. Network Group. Office: Shea & Gould 1251 Avenue of the Americas New York NY 10020-1193

BARNETT, JANE AYNE, marketing professional; b. Hamilton, Ohio, Sept. 4, 1950; d. Fredrick Robert II and Jewell (Wyatt) Shelton; m. Robert E. Bornstein, June 16, 1990; 1 child, Vanessa Lynn. BA in Communications and English, Bowling Green (Ohio) State U., 1971, MA in Interpersonal and Pub. Communication, 1977. Account exec. Creative Promotions, Cin., 1979-80; dir. market rsch. BCC div. Hillenbrand Industries, Batesville, Ind., 1980-83; dir. mktg. Andrew Jergens Co., Cin., 1983-86; v.p. corp. planning Jergens Co., Cin., 1986—, seminar leader, 1981, chmn. mgmt. info. sci. com., 1986—; speaker on computer software, 1985—. Rep. Educators Polit. Action Com., 1974-75; Dem. precinct capt., Chgo., 1978. Mem. NAFE, Am. Mktg. Assn. (v.p. global mktg.), Electronic Data Interchange Assn. Methodist. Home: 19 Hollow Tree Ct Hamilton OH 45013 Office: Jergens Co Spring Grove Ave Cincinnati OH 45214

BARNETT, LENA SUE, lawyer; b. Washington, Apr. 23, 1959; d. Edward Martin and Vivian Charlotte (Pear) B. AB cum laude, Muhlenberg Coll., 1981; JD, U. Md., Balt., 1984. Bar: Md. 1987, D.C. 1988. Intern Md. Sixth Jud. Cir. Ct., Rockville, 1983; gen. mgr. Edward M. Barnett, DDS & Assoc., Silver Spring, Md., 1984-88, Barnett Enterprises, Silver Spring, 1984-88; assoc. Fink, Weinberger, Fordman, Berman, Lowell & Fensterheim, PC, 1988-90; pvt. practice law Rockville, Md., 1990—. Vjol. coord. State Sen. Denis Re-election Com., Bethesda, Md., 1986; asst. vol. coord. Friends of Connie Morella for Congress Com., 1988; alumni admission ambassador Muhlenberg Coll. Mem. ABA (vice chair real property com., gen. practice sect.), Md. State Bar Assn., Bar Assn. Montgomery County, NAFE, Women's Bar Assn. Md., Bar Assn. D.C., Nat. C. of C. for Women, U. Md. Law Sch. Alumni Assn., Phi Alpha Delta, Phi Alpha Theta, Pi Sigma Alpha.

BARNETT, MARGARET EDWINA, nephrologist, researcher; b. Ft. Benning, Ga., July 28, 1949; d. Eddie Lee and Margaret Thomas (Herndon) B. BS magna cum laude with distinction in Zoology, Ohio State U., 1969; MD, Johns Hopkins U., 1973; PhD in Cellular and Molecular Biology, Case Western Res. U., 1984. Intern, Greater Balt. Med. Ctr., Towson, Md., 1973-74; med. resident Cleve. Clinic Ednl. Found., 1974-75, Univ. Hosps. Cleve., 1975-76; nephrology fellow, 1976-78, med. teaching fellow, 1978-84; nephrology rounding physician Community Dialysis Ctr., Cleve. and Mentor, Ohio, 1978-83; rsch. assoc. Case Western Res. U., Cleve., 1978-79, 83-84; physician emergency medicine Huron Regional Urgent Care Ctrs., Inc., Cleve., 1983-84; preceptor renal correlation conf., Case Western Res. Sch. Medicine, 1980-81, lectr. anatomy and histology 1979-83; asst. prof. medicine/nephrology Milton S. Hershey Med. Ctr. Pa. State U., Hershey, 1984-87; practice medicine specializing in nephrology and hypertension Arnett Clinic, Lafayette, Ind., 1987—; clin. assoc. faculty of Lafayette Ctr. Sch. Medicine Ind. U., 1987—; clin. asst. prof. of medicine, Ind. U. Sch. Medicine, 1989—; lectr. in hypertension, 1988—; spl. guest lectr. hypertension Drug Cos., Ill., Ind., S.D., 1988—. Scholar GM, Leo Yassinoff, Alpha Epsilon Delta, Beanie Drake, Am. Heart Assn., 1977; recipient NIH-Nat. Rsch. Service award, 1979-82; Ohio div. Am. Heart Assn. grantee, 1980-81; Ohio Kidney Found. grantee, 1977-78; Pres.'s Scholarship award, 1967-69; AMA Physician Recognition award, 1984-87. Mem. John Hopkins Med. and Surg. Soc., AMA (physician rsch. evaluation panel 1981-83), Internat. Soc. of Nephrology, Nat. Kidney Found., World Tae Kwon Do Fedn., Seoul, Korea, MENSA, Am. Film Inst., Phi Beta Kappa, Alpha Epsilon Delta, Alpha Kappa Alpha. Democrat. Office: Arnett Clin 1500 Salem St Lafayette IN 47904

BARNETT, MARIE, real estate executive; b. LaGrange, Ga., May 19; d. George and D. (Moore) B.; m. James Stephens Dick, Dec. 19, 1960 (div.); children: Karen Marie Dick Vidal, Sonya Stephens Dick Tafolla. Student, Fla. State U., 1955, U. Ga., 1956-58, Perry Coll., 1959; grad., Century 21 Internat. Mgmt. Acad., 1988. Lic. Calif. Dept. of Real Estate. Staff Mastrose Devel. Co., Palm Beach, Fla., 1962-65; pres., owner Century 21 Calif. Hills, Orange, Calif., 1973-79; real estate exec. F.M. Tarbell, Orange, Calif., 1979-85; pres., owner Century 21 Assocs., Newport Beach, Calif., 1985-88; real estate exec. Century 21 Inland Pacific, Newport Beach, Calif., 1988—. Pres. Jr. Auxiliary, Pass Christian, Miss., 1965; VIP panel Easter Seals, L.A., 1989; active 552 Club, Cancer Unit Hoag Hosp., Newport Beach, 1989, Cen Pac, Washington, 1989. Mem. Nat. Assn. of Realtors (Grad. Realtors Inst.), Calif. Assn. of Realtors (state dir. 1976, 78-79, realtor-assoc. rels. com., publicity com., co-chmn. Pvt. Property Week, 99 Club), East Orange Bd. of Realtors (chmn. spl. activities 1974-75, chmn. real estate fin. 1976, chmn. realtor-assoc. rels. com. 1977, chmn. Pvt. Property Week 1978, Pres.'s award 1978, chmn. Pvt. Property Week Luncheon 1980-81, communications com. 1980-81, 83, Pvt. Property Week com. 1981), Newport Harbor/Costa Mesa Bd. of Realtors (communications com. 1986—, CANTREE reception 1986, multiple listings com. 1987-88, chmn. Ann. Awards and Installation 1987, chmn. Equal Opportunity com. 1988), Corona Del Mar C. of C., Newport Harbor C. of C. Democrat. Office: Century 21 Inland Pacific 2 Corporate Plaza Newport Beach CA 92660

BARNETT, MARILYN, advertising agency executive; b. Detroit, June 10, 1934; d. Henry and Kate (Boesky) Schiff; B.A., Wayne State U., 1953; children: Rhona, Ken. Supr. broadcast prodn. Northgate Advt. Agy., Detroit, 1968-73; founder, part-owner, pres. Mars Advt. Co., Southfield, Mich., 1973—. Named Advt. Woman of Yr., Women's Club of Detroit, 1986, Outstanding Woman in Agy Mgmt., Am. Women in Radio and TV, Inc., 1987, Outstanding Woman in Broadcast, 1980. Mem. AFTRA (dir. 1959-67), Screen Actors Guild, Adcraft. Women's Adcraft. Creator, producer radio and TV programs, 1956-58; nat. spokesperson on TV, 1960-70. Club: Economic (Ad Woman of Yr. 1986). Office: Mars Advt 24209 Northwestern Hwy Southfield MI 48075 also: Mars Advt Co 5919 W 3d St Ste 1A Los Angeles CA 90036

BARNETT, MARY LOUISE, elementary education educator; b. Exeter, Calif., May 1, 1941; d. Raymond Edgar Noble and Nena Lavere (Huckaby) Hope; m. Gary Allen Barnett, Aug. 9, 1969; children: Alice Marie, Virginia Lynn. BA, U. of Pacific, 1963; postgrad., U. Mont., 1979-82, U. Idaho, 1984—. Cert. life elem. tchr., Calif.; standard elem. credential, Idaho; elem. tchr., Mont. Tchr. Colegio Americano de Torreon, Torreon, Coahuila, Mexico, 1962-63, Summer Sch. Primary Grades South San Francisco, 1963-66, Visalia (Calif.) Unified Sch. Dist., 1966-69, Sch. Dist. #1, Missoula, Mont., 1969-73, Fort Shaw-Simms Sch. Dist., Fort Shaw, Mont., 1976-83, Sch. Dist. #25, Pocatello, Idaho, 1983—. Foster mom Ednl. Found. Foreign Students, Pocatello, Idaho, 1986-89; vol. Am. Heart Assn., Am. Cancer Soc., Pocatello, 1986-88, Bannock March of Dimes, Pocatello, 1988, Pocatello Laubach Literacy Tutoring, 1989. Recipient scholarship Mont. Delta Kappa Gamma Edn. Soc., Great Falls, Mont., 1976, Great Falls AAUW, 1980, Great Falls Scottish Rite, 1981, Five Valleys Reading Assn., Missoula, Mont., 1982. Mem. NEA, Nat. Coun. Tchrs. English, Internat. Reading Assn., Assn. Supervision and Curriculum Devel., Assn. Childhood Edn. Internat., Mortar Bd., Alpha Lambda Delta, Delta Kappa Gamma (state fellowship chmn., corr. sec. Pocatello chpt. 1986-88), Moose (musician 1981-82), Order Eastern Star (musician 1984-85), Gamma Phi Beta. Republican. Presbyterian. Home: 956 Encino Pocatello ID 83201 Office: Wilcox Elem 427 Lark Ln Pocatello ID 83201

BARNETT, OLA WILMA, psychology educator; b. L.A., Jan. 26, 1940; d. William and Ruth Carol (Phillips) King; m. Donald Joseph Barnett, Nov. 27, 1941; children: Darlene Ola Blake, Donna Shirley Johnson. B.A., UCLA, 1962, M.A., 1965, Ph.D., 1971. Research asst. UCLA, 1961-67; asst. prof. psychology Calif. State Poly. U., San Luis Obispo, 1967-70; asso. prof. psychology Pepperdine U., Malibu, Calif., 1970-79; prof. psychology Pepperdine U., 1979—; sponsor Camp David Gonzales Tutorial Program, 1974-77; researcher on spouse abuse. Contbr. articles to profl. jours. Recipient Vol. Service award Atascadero State Hosp., 1970; Action grantee, 1972-73, Robert Ellis Simm grantee. Mem. Am. Psychol. Assn., Nat. Council Crime and Delinquency, Am. Psychology-Law Soc., Coalition Against Domestic Violence, Am. Soc. Criminology, Acad. Criminal Justice Scis., Psi Chi. Mem. Ch. of Christ. Home: 24301 Sylvan Glen Rd Calabasas CA 91302 Office: Pepperdine U Social Sci Div Malibu CA 90265

BARNETT, PATRICIA ANN (TRICIA BARNETT), public relations director; b. Culver City, Calif., Jan. 25, 1956; d. Howard Taft and Sarah Beatrice (Ross) Barnett. B in Journalism, U. Tex., 1978. Program specialist Dallas C. of C., 1978-79, communications specialist, 1979-81; mgr. pub. rels. Trailways, Inc., Dallas, 1981-82, dir. pub. rels., 1982-85; sr. account exec. Keller Crescent, 1985-87; dir. communications Office of Pvt. Sector Initiatives, The White House, Washington, 1987-89; dir. pub. affairs United Way Am., Alexandria, Va., 1989—. Mem. Women in Communications (bd. dirs. Dallas chpt. 1981-82, Matrix award 1985), Pub. Rels. Soc. Am. (Silver award 1985, accredited 1986), Internat. Assn. Bus. Communicators (Bronze award 1984), Tex. Pub. Rels. Soc. (Silver Spur award 1985). Republican. Avocations: theater, literature, art. Office: United Way Am 701 N Fairfax St Alexandria VA 22314

BARNETT, ROSALEA, federal agency administrator; b. Hugo, Okla., Apr. 21, 1946; d. L.V. and Floradean (Mills) Boyett; 1 child, Billy. Student, Rose Coll., Midwest City, Okla., Dub Stone Real Estate Acad., Oklahoma City. Lic. real estate broker, Okla. Adminstrv. aid, dir. VA Med. Ctr., Oklahoma City; office adminstr to postmaster U.S. Postal Svc., Oklahoma City; acting postmaster U.S. Postal Svc., Jennings, Okla.; broker, assoc. Heritage Realtors, Tulsa; now postmaster U.S. Postal Svc., Leonard, Okla. Mem. Dial Am. team in support of Spl. Olympics; active Pleasant Valley Home for Abused Girls, Tulsa Boys Home, Feed the Children Orgn. Mem. NAFE, Female Exec. Club, Federally Employed Women, Toastmasters Internat. (best speaker award), C. of C. Mem. Assembly of God. Office: PO Box 9998 Leonard OK 74043-9998

BARNETT, VIRGINIA RICH, dancer, associate artistic director; b. Atlanta, Apr. 16, 1934; d. Richard H. and Virginia (Lazarus) Rich; m. Robert James Barnett, May 6, 1925; children: Robert James Jr., David Michael. Student, CKS High Sch., Atlanta, 1952. Dancer Radio City Music Hall, N.Y.C., 1954, N.Y.C. Ballet, 1955-58; prin. dancer, assoc. dir. The Atlanta Ballet, 1958-69; founder, prin. dancer, assoc. dir. Carl Ratcliff Dance Theatre, Atlanta; tchr. Atlanta Sch. of Ballet, 1985--. Recipient Ga. Gov's. awrd for the arts, 1984.

BARNETT, VIVIAN ENDICOTT, curator; b. Putnam, Conn., July 8, 1944; d. George and Vivian (Wood) Endicott; m. Peter Herbert Barnett, July 1, 1967; children: Sarah, Alexander. A.B. magna cum laude, Vassar Coll., 1965; M.A., NYU, 1971; postgrad., CUNY, 1979-81. Research asst. Solomon R. Guggenheim Mus., N.Y.C., 1973-77, curatorial assoc., 1978-79, assoc. curator, 1980-81, rsch. curator, 1981-82, curator, 1982—. Author: The Guggenheim Museum: Justin K. Thannhauser Collection, 1978, The Guggenheim Museum Collection 1900-1980, Kandinsky Watercolors, 1981, Kandinsky at the Guggenheim, 1983, 100 Works by Modern Masters from the Guggenheim Museum, 1984, Works by Robert Barry, Sol LeWitt, Robert Mangold, Richard Tuttle from the Collection of Dorothy and Herbert Vogel, 1987, Kandinsky and Sweden, 1989, Kandinsky in Major Collections in the West, 1989, also articles; contbr. to Kandinsky in Paris: 1934-44, 1985. John Simon Guggenheim fellow, 1990. Mem. Am. Assn. Museums (curator com.), Internat. Council Museums, Coll. Art Assn. Am. Office: Solomon R Guggenheim Mus 1071 Fifth Ave New York NY 10128

BARNETTE, MARGE C., food service company executive; b. Honolulu, Dec. 15, 1944; d. William Leon Sr. and Margaret Elizabeth Barnette. BA in Acctg., Chaminade U., 1966. Supr. ARA/Slater Food Service, San Francisco, 1966-68; restaurant, catering mgr. Spencecliff Corp., Honolulu, 1968, gen. mgr., 1973-77; clubhouse mgr. Mid-Pacific Country Club, Lanikai, Hawaii, 1977; dir. dining svcs. Tulane U., Dillard U., U. Houston, 1978-79, U. Houston ARA, 1978-79; ops. analyst ARA Svcs., Dallas, 1980; labor rels. mgr. Rockwell Internat. ARA Svcs., L.A., 1981; dist. mgr. ARA Svcs., Phila., 1984-88; pers. dir. ARA Olympic Food Svcs., L.A., 1983-84; ptnr. db Connections-Food Industry Cons., Kirkland, Washington, 1989—; pres., owner MCBA inc., Seattle, 1990—. Roman Catholic. Home: 10278 NE 129th Ln Kirkland WA 98034

BARNETTE, SHARON MILDRED, psychologist; b. Salisbury, N.C., Aug. 20, 1951; d. Elmer Jewel and Mildred (Franklin) B. BA in Psychology and Sociology, Appalachian State U., 1973, MA in Rehab. Psychology, 1974; EdD in Spl. Edn. Adminstrn., U.S.C., 1982. Sch. psychologist High Point (N.C.) Pub. Schs., 1975-78; learning disabilities specialist Cabarrus County Schs., Concord, N.C., 1978-80; rehab. and sch. psychologist, pvt. practice Landis and Concord, N.C., 1982—; pvt. psychologist, Landis, 1977-82. Mem. Am. Psychol. Assn., N.C. Psychol. Assn., N.C. Sch. Psychology Assn., Delta Kappa Gamma Soc. Office: Barnette Ednl/Psychol Svcs 99 Church St NE Concord NC 28025

BARNHART, BEVERLY JEAN, scientist; b. Tiffin, Ohio, July 16, 1954; d. Harold Francis and Catherine Jane (Terry) B. BS in Physics and Math., Heidelberg Coll., 1976; MS in Meteorology, Purdue U., 1979; postgrad., Cath. U., Washington, 1983. Rsch. analyst Analytic Svcs., Inc., Arlington, Va., 1979-81; tech. assistance program mgr. U.S. Nuclear Regulatory Commn., Bethesda, Md., 1981-84; rsch. scientist Sci. Applications Internat. Corp., McLean, Va., 1984-89, Dept. of Def., 1989—. Mem. Conservative Network, Washington, 1987-88, Am. Film Inst.; organizer social and charitable singles parties, Eclat, Washington, 1987-89. Mem. Am. Def. Preparedness Assn., Am. Meteorol. Soc. (bd. dirs. women and minorities com. 1982-87), Desiree Club, Eclectics, Ski Club, Circle and Ave. Club (pres. 1986-89). Republican. Roman Catholic. Home: 1300 Army Navy Dr #507 Arlington VA 22202

BARNHART, DOROTHY KOHRS, social services adminstrator; b. Des Moines, Apr. 27, 1933; d. Oliver John and Lily Mabel (Smith) Kohrs.; m. 1954 (div. 1977); children—Jacqueline, Dwaine, Jr., Kelly; stepchildren—Billie Jo, Jack, Cindy. Student pub. schs., New Virginia; Internat. Acctg. Soc., Chgo.; Bookkeeper Iowa Credit Union League, 1954-69;, Grand Printing Art-O-Type, 1970-72; office mgr. Am. Bus. Forms & Systems, Inc., 1972-76; forms dept. mgr. Action Forms/Action Printers Co., 1976-77; office mgr. Elliott Beechcraft Flying Service, 1977-81; telephone selling rep. Coca Cola Co., 1983-84; adminstrv. asst. Coalition for Family and Children's Service in Iowa, Des Moines, 1985—; developed Wellness Game, 1982-85; pres., owner Wellness Games, Ltd., 1985—; coordinator annual statewide conf. (1987) Chronic Pain Outreach of Central Iowa, Mercy Hosp., 1982-84; Midwest regional dir. Nat. Chronic Pain Outreach, 1985-87 . Mem. Iowa Women's Polit. Caucus; mem. choir Grace United Methodist Ch., disability action com. of Des Moines Area Urban Mission Council. Mem. Nat. Assn. Female Execs., Women's C. of C. of Des Moines. Democrat. Home: 2525 SW 80th Ave Lot 15 Des Moines IA 50321 Office: Coalition Family and Children's Services in Iowa 11 E 5th St Des Moines IA 50309

BARNHART, ELIZABETH ANNE, data processing specialist; b. Daytona Beach, Fla., Oct. 14, 1955; d. David Richards and Elizabeth Frances (Frederick) B. AS in Computer Scis., Daytona Beach Community Coll., 1975. Cert. systems profl., data processor. Computer programmer Melweb Signs, Daytona Beach, Fla., 1976; supr. data processing Bunnell (Fla.) Gen. Hosp., 1976-77; computer programmer, operator Daytona Budweiser, Port Orange, Fla., 1977-80; data processing mgr. City of Port Orange, 1980—; cons. Volusia-Lake-Flagler Pvt. Industry Corp., Daytona Beach, 1984-86. Mem. Data Processing Mgmt. Assn. (exec. v.p. Halifax Area chpt. 1983-84, pres. 1985, bylaws dir. 1986, awards dir. 1987, several awards). Democrat. Roman Catholic. Office: City of Port Orange PO Box 290005 Port Orange FL 32029-0005

BARNHART, JO ANNE B., government official; b. Memphis, Aug. 26, 1950; d. Nelson Alexander and Betty Jane (Fitzpatrick) Bryant; m. David Lee Ross, Feb. 14, 1976 (div. June 1983); m. David Ray Barnhart, May 24, 1986. Student U. Tenn., 1968-70; B.A., U. Del., 1975. Space and time buyer deMartin-Marona & Assocs., Wilmington, Del., 1970-73; adminstrv. asst. Mental Health Assn. Wilmington, 1973-75; dir. SERVE nutrition program Wilmington Sr. Ctr., 1975-77; legis. asst. to Senator William V Roth, Jr., Washington, 1977-81; dep. assoc. commr. Office Family Assistance, HHS, Washington, 1981-83, assoc. commr., 1983-86; Rep. staff dir. U.S. Senate Govt. Affairs Com., 1987-90; asst. sec. family support HHS, Washington, 1990—. Mem. Nat. Assn. Title VII Nutrition Project Dirs. (v.p. 1976). Republican. Methodist. Office: HHS Family Support Adminstrn 370 L'Enfant Promenade SW Washington DC 20447

BARNOFF, SHARON HOLLOWAY, health facility administrator, nurse; b. Lorain, Ohio, Mar. 19, 1952; d. Floyd Elmer and Vivian Florence (Starr) Holloway; m. Fred J. Barnoff Jr., Jan. 2, 1981 (div. 1990); 1 child, Melanie. BSN, St. John Coll., Cleve., 1973; M in Postsecondary Edn., Cleve. State U., 1984. Staff nurse Suburban Community Hosp., Cleve., 1975-78; instr. VA Hosp., Cleve., 1978-80; instr., asst. operating rm. supr. St. Vincent Charity Hosp., Cleve., 1980-84; supr. surgery and day surgery Marymount Hosp., Garfield Heights, Ohio, 1985-89; asst. v.p. perioperative svcs. Lake Hosp. System Inc., Willoughby, Ohio, 1989—; developer continuing edn. program Cleve. State U., 1984. Chmn. operating rm. task adv. coun. Vol. Hosp Assn., 1990—. Mem. Assn. Operating Rm. Nurses, Operating Rm. Mgmt. Peer Group (sec. 1987-88, chmn. 1988-89), VFW Aux., NAFE, Ohio Soc. Nurse Execs., Sigma Theta Tau. Home: 592 E Garfield Rd Aurora OH 44202

BARNS, DORETHA MAE CLAYTON, librarian, orgn. exec.; b. Fairmont, W.Va., Nov. 28, 1917; d. Sylvester Richard and Della Pearl (Morgan) Clayton; m. William Derrick Barns, Sept. 3, 1947. AB, Fairmont State Coll., 1939; MA, W.Va. U., 1940; BS in L.S., Western Res. U., 1947. Tchr., librarian Wetzel County (W.Va.) Schs., 1940-41, Preston County Schs., 1944-46; teaching fellow dept. English, W.Va. U., 1941-43, sec. to dean grad. sch., 1942-44, cataloguer library, 1947-48; dir., Internat. relations chmn. LWV W.Va., 1969-89, 2d v.p., 1981-83, 87-89. Bd. dirs. W.Va. affiliate Council of Internat. Programs, 1975-87. Mem. Women's Internat. League for Peace and Freedom, Kappa Delta Pi, Nu Alpha Phi. Republican. Mem. Soc. Friends. Club: Order Eastern Star. Author: An Outline of the West Virginia Merit System, 1957; West Virginia's Interest in Foreign Trade, 1971; International Services Available to West Virginia Businesses, 1980. Home: 512 Beverly Ave Morgantown WV 26505

BARNUM, ANNA MARIA, educator, lawyer; b. Saco, Maine, Apr. 15, 1943; d. Richard Carl and Mary Margaret (Greeley) Pfeiffer; m. Russell Peck Barnum Jr., July 17, 1965 (div. May 1970); children: Rebecca Ellen, Susannah Mary. AB, Middlebury (Vt.) Coll., 1965; MA, U. Vt., 1969; JD, U. Akron, 1977. Bar: Ohio 1977. Spl. edn. instr. Weeks Sch., Vergennes, Vt., 1965-70; assoc. prof. English U. Akron, Ohio, 1970—; ptnr. Powell and Barnum, Akron, 1978-80; with Glinsek & Higham, Akron, 1980-82; pvt. practice Akron, 1982—. Author (poems) Spindrift, 1982, To Meet the Asking Years, 1984, No Bad Poems, 1987; mem. editorial bd. Ohio Assn. Two Year Colls. Jour., 1977—. Chair legal com. Akron Area Civil Liberties Union, 1978-89; bd. dirs. Ohio Civil Liberties Union, 1980-82, 84-86, sec., 1986-88; participant Poetry in the Schs. Project, Friends of the Libr., Akron, 1988—; bd. dirs. Citizens Against System Abuse, 1989—. Recipient grant Nat. Endowment for Humanties, 1973, NSF, AAAS, 1980; named poetry assoc. Atlantic Ctr. for Arts, Nat. Endowment for Arts, New Smyrna Beach, Fla., 1988. Mem. ACLU, Progress Through Preservation, Akron Women's Poetry Support, Poets League of Greater Cleve., Franklin Club. Democrat. Unitarian. Home: 105 Marvin Ave Akron OH 44302 Office: Univ Akron Akron OH 44325

BAROLINI, HELEN, writer, educator; b. Syracuse, N.Y., Nov. 18, 1925; m. Antonio Barolini, Nov. 8, 1950 (dec.); children: Teodolinda Barolini Caverly, Susanna Barolini Mengacci, Nicoletta. AB magna cum laude, Syracuse U., 1947; MLS, Columbia U., 1959. Lectr. Pace U., Pleasantville, N.Y., 1990—; lectr. Padua, Italy and Westchester Community Coll., Valhalla, N.Y., 1988; writer-in-residence Quarry Farm, Elmira Coll., 1989. Creative works include Festa, 1988, Love in the Middle Ages, 1986, The Dream Book, 1985, Umbertina, 1979; stories in Literary Olympian II, Love Stories by New Women and in numerous jours.; translated seven books from Italian. Recipient Susan Koppelman award Am. Culture Assn., 1987, Am.

Book award 1986, Ams. of Italian Heritage Literary award, 1984, Marina-Velca Journalism prize, Italy, 1970; Nat. Endowment for Arts grantee, 1976; fellow MacDowell Colony, 1974, Yaddo fellow, 1965. Mem. PEN Am. Ctr., Authors Guild of Am., Nat. Women's Studies Assn., MELUS, Nat. Writers Union, Phi Beta Kappa. Home and Office: PO Box 307 Scarborough Manor NY 10510

BARON, JESSICA RUTH, insurance executive; b. Pitts., July 1, 1945; d. Ralph Balber and Marion Betty (Schmidt) Baron; m. Robert Alan Baron, Feb. 16, 1969; children: Jonathan I., Laura Rachel. BA in History, U. Toledo, 1968; MA in Broadcasting, U. Cin., 1978, postgrad. exec. program, 1983. Tchr. Walden Sch., N.Y.C., 1969-70; dir. community svcs. Hebrew Union Coll./Jewish Inst. Religion, Cin., 1978-80; dir. mktg. communications Warner Cable Communications, Inc., Cin., 1980-85; dir. product mgmt. and promotion Community Mutual Blue Cross and Blue Shield, Cin., 1985-87, dir. mktg., group bus. div., 1987-89, dir. small group gen. agy. sales, 1989—. Mem. adv. bd. Halom House; tng. adv. com. United Way campaign, 1989; mem. community bd. Sta. WGUC-FM; office and personnel com. Jewish Fedn. Cin.; trustee Jewish Vocat. Svc., exec. com., co-chair employment adv. coun. Mem. Am. Mktg. Assn., Women in Communications Inc. (speakers bur.), Greater Cin.C. of C., Leadership Cin. Alumni Assn. (bd. dirs. 1989—), Alpha Epsilon Rho. Democrat. Office: Community Mut Blue Cross and Blue Shield 1351 Wm Howard Taft Rd Cincinnati OH 45206

BARON, LAURA ANN, personnel executive; b. Glen Ridge, N.J., Oct. 4, 1962; d. Robert Michael and Joan Katherine (Bollhorst) B. BS in Commerce cum laude, Rider Coll., 1984; postgrad., Pace U., N.Y.C., currently. Intern/compensation analyst Campbell Soup Co., Inc., Camden, N.J., 1984; pers. generalist Vital Signs, Inc., Totowa, N.J., 1984-85; indsl. rels. mgr. Crown Cork and Seal Co., Inc., North Bergen, N.J., 1985-87; dir. pers. Nat. Prescription Adm., Inc., Clifton, N.J., 1987-89, asst. v.p., 1990—; conductor seminars in field. Advisor/recruiter Rider Alumni Vols. for Enrollment, Lawrenceville, N.J., 1985—; participant United Labor Agy., Newark, 1986-87; active ARC. 1989 honoree, Tribute to Women and Mgmt. Mem. NAFE, Internat. Narcotic Inforcement Officers Assn., Nat. Lightning Class Assn., Delta Sigma Pi, Sigma Iota Epsilon, Omicron Delta Epsilon. Roman Catholic. Clubs: Lake Wallenpaupak Yacht, Sunfish Fleet (skipper 1978-87). Office: Nat Prescription Adm Inc 1200 Rte 46 Clifton NJ 07013

BARON, LINDA ANN, cosmetic company executive; b. Flushing, N.Y., Nov. 9, 1943; d. Leonard Michael and Margaret Mary Cotone. Grad. Gardner Sch. Bus., 1968; student George Washington U., 1970. Adminstrv. asst. U.S. Underseas Cable Corp., Washington, 1968-69; analyst programmer Friden div. Singer Co., Washington, 1969, programming mgr., 1970, systems sales exec., 1971; acct. exec. Clinique Labs., Inc., Washington and Balt., 1972, regional mktg. mgr. Md. and Va. markets, 1973-75, regional mktg. dir. Washington and Mid-Atlantic states, 1976-81, regional v.p. Southeast, 1981-86; v.p. South and Mid-Atlantic, Lancome Inc., 1986—; instr. merchandising, 1976—. Vol., ARC Walter Reed and Bethesda Naval Hosp., Washington, 1969-71. Mem. Washington Fashion Group, Nat. Assn. for Female Execs., U.S. Dressage Fedn., Potomac Valley Dressage Assn., Am. Horse Show Assn. Roman Catholic. Home: 9110 Town Gate Ln Bethesda MD 20817

BARON, NAOMI SUSAN, linguistics educator, computer specialist; b. N.Y.C., Sept. 27, 1946; d. Leonard and Ruth Joan (Josephson) B. BA, Brandeis U., 1968; PhD, Stanford U., 1972. Asst. prof. linguistics Brown U., Providence, 1972-79, assoc. prof., 1979-85, assoc. dean, 1981-83; vis. instr. R.I. Sch. Design, 1982-83; vis. Nat. Endowment Humanities chair Emory U., 1983-84; Brown vis. chair Southwestern U., 1985-87; assoc. dean, prof. Langs. and Fgn. Studies Am. U., Washington, 1987—; vis. scholar U. Tex., Austin, 1984-85. Bur. Edn. Handicapped grantee, 1975-84; Nat. Endowment for Humanities grantee, 1979-81; Guggenheim fellow, 1984-85. Mem. Linguistic Soc. Am., Semiotic Soc. Am. (pres. 1986-87), Am. Assn. Computing Machinery. Author: Language Acquisition and Historical Change, 1979; Speech, Writing and Sign, 1981; Computer Languages: A Guide for the Perplexed, 1986. Office: Am Univ Dept Langs & Fgn Studies Gray Hall Washington DC 20016

BARONE, ROSE MARIE PACE, writer, former educator; b. Buffalo, Apr. 26, 1920; d. Dominic and Jennie (Zagara) Pace; m. John Barone, Aug. 23, 1947. BA, U. Buffalo, 1943; MS, U. So. Cal., 1950; cert. advanced study, Fairfield (Conn.) U., 1963. Tchr. Angola (N.Y.) High Sch., 1943-46, Puente (Calif.) High Sch., 1946-47, Jefferson High Sch., Lafayette, Ind., 1947-50; dir. Warren Inst., Bridgeport, Conn., 1951-53; instr. U. Bridgeport, 1953-54; tchr. bus. subjects Bassick High Sch., Bridgeport, 1954-74, Harding High Sch., Bridgeport, 1974-80; instr. Fairfield U., Conn., 1969; freelance writer, 1980—; chair State Poetry Festival, 1987; founder Pet Rescue. Area CCW chair, Community Affairs Commn., 1988-90, sec., 1990—. Pace-Barone Minority scholar Fairfield U.; recipient Playwriting prize Conn. Federated Women's Clubs, 1955, 1st prize for poetry, 1985, Federated Women Conn. State Short Story award, 1987, 88, 90, Citizen award Bridgeport Dental Assn., 1982, State/Town Hero award, 1986; Auerbach Found. scholarship, 1956; also craft and flower awards. Mem. NEA, Am. Assn. Retired People (v.p. 1987-88, pres. 1988-89), Owl (sec. 1987-89, pres. 1989-90, instr. 55 Alive), AAUW (treas. 1957-58, named gift grant 1989), Nat. League Am. Pen Women (Bridgeport historian 1966-84, state historian 1983—, treas. br. 1985-88, state pres. 1986-88, state lit. chair, 1988—, br. membership chair 1990, Nat. Historian award 1976, 88), UN Assn. U.S.A. (pres. Bridgeport, 1964-66, 68-70, chmn. area UN Days, 1960—, pres. Conn. 1971—, state chmn. UNICEF to 1984, area UNICEF Ctr., 1984—, state historian 1984—), Conn. Bus. Tchrs., Bridgeport Edn. Assn. (sec. 1966-68), VFW (aux. 1989), Am. Legion (aux. 1989, contest chair 1990), Fairfield Philatelic Soc. (sec. 1971-78, founder advisor Philatelic Jrs. 1972-80), Fairfield Univ. Women's Club (founder, pres. 1950, 74—, v.p. 1973-74) Southport Woman's Club (garden dept. sec. 1981-85, chmn. 1985-87) (Fairfield), Pi Omega Pi. Home: 1283 Round Hill Rd Fairfield CT 06430

BARONI, KAREN MARIE, crime intelligence analyst; b. Cleve., Apr. 10, 1957; d. Robert Emmett Kildea and Sally (Anable) Walkovik; m. Kevin Matthew Baroni, May 12, 1984. BS, Fla. State U., 1979. Counselor Lantana (Fla.) Work Release Ctr., 1981-82; crime analyst City of Miami (Fla.) Police Dept., 1981—. Mem. Internat. Assn. Law Enforcement Intelligence Analysts (So. Regional chpt., sec. 1987-88, membership chmn. 1988—). Home: 3252 Foxcroft Rd #313 Miramar FL 33025

BARR, GINGER, state legislator; b. Kansas City, Mo., Dec. 4, 1947; d. W.M. and Ann (Armstrong) Barr; m. Edwin P. Carpenter, Jan. 2, 1984. BS, Baker U., Baldwin, Kans., 1969. Cemetery mgmt. Topeka Cemetery, Kans., 1969-76, Graceland/Fairlawn Cemeteries, Decatur, Ill., 1976—. Rep. Kans. State Legislature, 1983-91, vice chmn. fed. and state affairs com., 1987-89, chmn., 1989-91; pres. Crifter Care Co., 1987—; bd. dirs. World Topeka Famous Zoo, 1986—, Humane Soc., Topeka, 1983-87; mem. Jr. League, Topeka, 1985. Mem. Am. Cemetery Assn. (dir. 1980-82), Kans. Cemetery Assn. (pres. 1979-80), Ill. Cemetery Assn. Republican, Humane Soc., Critter Care Co. (pres. 1987). Home: RR 1 Auburn KS 66402

BARR, SARAH LOUISE, writer news and commentary, field producer; b. Wethersfield, Conn., Dec. 14, 1963; d. Allan Ferguson and Ursula (Wolf) B. BA, Temple U., 1986. News writer Sta. WPVI-TV, Phila., 1985-86; writer, producer Sta. KYW-TV, Phila., 1986-88; news reporter, anchor Sta. WHYY-TV, Wilmington, Del., 1988—. Mem. AFTRA, Radio, TV, News Dir. Assn., Women Communications, Nat. Assn. Exec. Women. Democrat. Lutheran. Office: Sta WHYY-TV 625 N Orange St Wilmington DE 19802

BARRAGAN, LINDA DIANE, religious organization administrator; b. Oct. 14, 1950. BA summa cum laude, Bklyn. Coll., 1974. Ordained to ministry Ch. of Scientology, 1980. Pub. rels. dir. Ch. of Scientology N.Y., N.Y.C., 1974-82, pres., 1980-87, dir. spl. affairs, 1982—, corp. dir., 1980-88. Dir. Task Force on Mental Retardation, N.Y. chpt., N.Y.C., 1974-76; vol. Narconon, N.Y.C., 1977; dir. Am. Citizens for Honesty in Govt., N.Y.C. chpt., 1979-82, Nat. Commn. on Law Enforcement and Social Justice, N.Y.C. chpt., 1976-79. Mem. Internat. Assn. Scientologists. Office: Ch of Scientology NY 227 W 46th St New York NY 10036

BARRATT, CYNTHIA LOUISE, pharmaceutical company executive; b. El Paso, Tex., Feb. 13, 1953; d. John Edward and Louise Joy (Lacy) B.; m. Nat G. Adkins, Jr., Oct. 5, 1980. BJ, U. Tex., 1975. Buyer Joske's of Tex., San Antonio, 1975-80, Craigs of Tex., Houston, 1981-83; v.p. sales ops. Akorn, Inc., Abita Springs, La., 1980-86; chief exec. officer, chmn. bd. dirs. NGLC Corp., Richmond, Tex., 1983—; exec. v.p. OCuSoft Inc., Richmond, 1986—, also bd. dirs.; exec. v.p. CynaCon Inc., Richmond, 1986—, also bd. dirs. Mem. NAFE, Rosenberg/Richmond C. of C., DAR, Ft. Bend County Mus. Assn. Office: OcuSoft Inc 930 FM 359 Richmond TX 77469

BARRERA, ELVIRA PUIG, educator, counselor, therapist; b. Alice, Tex., Dec. 11, 1943; d. Carlos Rogers and Delia Rebecca (Puig) B.; 1 child, Dennis Lee Jr. BA, Incarnate Word Coll., 1971; M of Counseling and Guidance, St. Mary's U., San Antonio, 1978; specialist degree in marriage and family therapy, St. Mary's U., 1989. Lic. profl. counselor. Tchr. Edgewood Ind. Sch. Dist., San Antonio, 1965-74, Dallas Ind. Sch. Dist., 1971-72, Northside Ind. Sch. Dist., San Antonio, 1974; ednl. cons. Region 20-Edn. Service Ctr., San Antonio, 1974-79; career edn. coordinator San Antonio Ind. Sch. Dist., 1979-84, counselor, 1984—; cons. Small Bus. Adminstrn., 1981, U.S. Office Edn., Washington, 1981-82, Tex. Edn. Agy., Austin, 1979-80; cons., writer San Antonio Ind. Sch. Dist. and Tex. Edn. Agy., 1985; cons. to various edn. publs. Chairperson career awareness exploring div. Boy Scouts Am., 1982-87. Named Disting. Alumna, Incarnate Word Coll., 1983; recipient Spurgeon award Boy Scouts Am., 1985, Merit award, 1986, Growth award, 1986. Mem. So. Tex. Pers. and Guidance Assn. (bd. dirs. 1981-82), San Antonio Area Women Deans, Adminstrs. and Counselors Assn. (treas. 1984-86), San Antonio Assn. for Marriage and Family Therapy, Incarnate Word Coll. Alumni Assn. (mem. adv. bd. 1990—), San Antonio Rd. Runners, San Antonio Hash House Harriers, Delta Kappa Gamma (2d v.p. 1982-84, 1st v.p. 1986-88), Chi Sigma Iota. Roman Catholic. Home: 5015 Fairford Dr San Antonio TX 78228 Office: San Antonio Ind Sch Dist 141 Lavaca St San Antonio TX 78201

BARRES, CARMEN ISABEL, internal medicine educator; b. Rio Piedras, Puerto Rico, Dec. 3, 1961; d. Agustin Barres and Carmen Freiria. BS, U. Miami, Fla., 1983; MD, Temple U., 1987. Resident Cooper Hosp. Med. Ctr., Camden, N.J., 1987—. Recipient AMA-Burroughs Wellcome Co. Leadership Program award. Mem. Am. Med. Women's Assn., AMA, Breast Cancer Detection Awareness Program, Area Health Edn. Ctr., Am. Med. Student Assn. Home: 2013 Arborwood II Lindenwold NJ 08021 Office: 712 Haddonfield Ave Cherry Hill NJ 08002

BARRETO, KATHLEEN ANNE, technical writing consultant; b. New London, Conn., Sept. 5, 1954; d. Eugene Aloysius and Germaine Marie (Hangley) Coogan; m. Oscar Eduardo Barreto, May 28, 1972 (separated 1980); 1 child, Victoria Anne. AA in Tech. Writing magna cum laude, De Anza Coll., 1988. Banker, 1974-80; tech. recruiter Menlo Svc. Corp., Sunnyvale, Calif., 1980-84; tech. writer Textron-Singer-Dalmo Victor, Belmont and Fremont, Calif., 1984-87; tech. writing cons., Sunnyvale, 1987—, design cons., 1988—; cons. Tech. for Communications Internat., Fremont, 1987—, Ultra Systems, Sunnyvale, 1988. Author, co-producer High-Tech for Ind. Living, PBS-TV, 1988 (Waveform award 1988, Bay Area Cable Excellence award for Best Docudrama 1989); writer, producer, host On the Move, Able Cable TV, 1988—. Mem. Soc. for Tech. Communications, Writer's Connection, Mensa. Libertarian. Roman Catholic.

BARRETT, BEATRICE HELENE, psychologist; b. Cin., Dec. 8, 1928; d. Oscar Slack and Helen (Kaiper) B.; m. Harold Sheffield Van Buren, Oct. 6, 1966 (div. Oct. 1985). BA, U. Ariz., 1950; MA, U. Ky., 1952; PhD, Purdue U., 1957. Lic. psychologist, Mass. Grad. tchg. asst. in psychology U. Ky., Lexington, 1950-52; psychology asst. Longview State Hosp., Cin., 1951, staff psychologist, 1952; staff psychologist Children's Outpatient and Cons. Svcs. Ind. U. Med. Ctr., Indpls., 1954-57, chief psychologist, 1957-59; instr. psychology Ind. U. Med. Sch., Indpls., 1956-60; rsch. assoc. dept. psychiatry Ind. U. Med. Ctr., Indpls., 1959-60; pvt. practice clin. psychology Indpls., 1957-60; research fellow in psychology Sch. of Medicine Harvard U., Boston, 1960-62; lectr. in spl. edn. Grad. Sch. Edn., Boston U., 1962-63; dir. psychol. rsch. Walter E. Fernald State Sch., Belmont, Mass., 1962-69; dir. behavior prosthesis lab. Walter E. Fernald State Sch., Belmont, 1963—; chief psychologist, 1969—; assoc. psychologist Enuice Kennedy Shriver Ctr. for Mental Retardation, Inc., Waltham, Mass., 1982—; instr. Mass. Psychol. Ctr., 1972; lectr. in spl. edn. Lesley Coll. Grad. Sch., 1974-76; adj. assoc. prof. Northeastern U., 1983—; psychology cons. Carter Meml. Hosp., Indpls., 1959-60; mem. exec. com. Boston Behavior Therapy Interest Group, 1973-74. Cons. editor, mem. adv. bds. various profl. jours.; contbr. numerous articles to profl. jours. Mem. Ind. Gov.'s Youth Coun., 1959-61; mem. spl. adv. com. on mental retardation Ind. Dept. Pub. Instrn., 1959-61; mem. task force Mass. Mental Retardation Planning Project, 1965-66; mem. adv. bd. Cambridge Ctr. for Behavioral Studies, 1981-87, trustee, 1987—, chair devel. com., 1987-89; mem. com. on dance edn. Spl. Commn. on Performing Arts, 1976-77; mem. art acquisition com. DeCordova Mus., 1978-80, mem. contemporary arts coun., 1985—; trustee Boston Repertory Ballet, 1977-79; trustee Boston Ballet Co., 1970-76, sec. bd., 1974-75, exec. com., 1974-76. Grantee Nat. Assn. for Retarded Citizens, 1963, NIHM, 1963-76. Fellow Am. Psychol. Assn., Mass. Psychol. Assn., Behavior Therapy and Rsch. Soc. (clin.); mem. Assn. for Mentally Ill Children (human rights com. 1979-81), Am. Acad. on Mental Retardation (v.p. 1969-74, at-large exec. com. 1975-77), Eastern Psychol. Assn., Assn. for Advancement of Behavior Therapy, Assn. Behavior Analysis (jour. adv. bd. 1983-87, chair task force on right to effective edn. 1986—). Club: Stage Harbor Yacht (Chatham, Mass.) (race com. 1984-86). Home: RFD 7 Box 236A Winter St Lincoln MA 01773 Office: Walter E Fernald State Sch Box 9108 Belmont MA 02178-9108

BARRETT, DIANA HERRAN, lecturer in management; b. Mexico City, Mexico, Oct. 8, 1944; d. Raphael Herran and Gioconda (Castro) B; m. Robert J Vila, Oct. 3, 1975; children: Christopher, Monica, Susannah. BA, Sweet Briar, 1966; MS, Boston U., 1969; MBA, Harvard Bus. Sch., 1974, D in Bus. Adminstrn., 1979. Cons. Arthur D. Little Inc., Cambridge, Mass., 1969-72; asst. pres. Brigham & Womens, Boston, 1974; research assoc. Harvard Bus. Sch., Boston, 1974-79; asst. prof. Harvard Sch. Pub. Health, Boston; lectr. mgmt. Harvard Sch. Pub. Health, 1984--, dir. grad. prog. health policy and mgmt., 1984--; bd. dirs. Parents & Childrens Services, Boston, 1976-86; co-founder, prin. Strategic Action Inc., Boston, 1983-88; bd. dirs. Goodwill Meml. Industries, Boston, 1988--. Author: (Book) Multihospital Systems; the Process of Devel., 1980. Mem. Govs. Commn., Boston, 1980-82, Bd. Incorporators New Eng. Bapt., Boston, 1984--. Mem. Am. Pub. Health Assn., Oyster Harbors Club. Roman Catholic. Office: Harvard U 677 Huntington Ave Boston MA 02115

BARRETT, EDYTHE HART, retired educational administrator; b. Cleve., Aug. 24, 1915; d. John Armour and Edith Laurence (Crockett) Hart; m. James Douglas Barrett, Oct. 29, 1938; children: Cristabel Hart, Douglas James. BA, Case Western Res. U., 1974, postgrad., 1990. Editor Clover Farm Stores, Cleve., 1940-42; artist Addressograph-Multigraph Corp., Cleve., 1950-61; exec. sec. to provost Case Western Res. U., Cleve., 1964-69, dir. visitors' office Sch. Medicine, 1969-85; mem. Coun. on World Affairs, Cleve., 1969-86. Editor Clover Farm Stores newsletter, 1940-42. Publs. chair Western Res. Coll. Alumni Assn. Bd., 1982-85; rep. Ch. Women United, Cleve., 1984—; pres. Episcopal Ch. Women's Bd., Christ Ch., Shaker Heights, Ohio, 1988-89; sec. Cleve. East region Diocese of Ohio, 1989—. Mem. AAUW (sec. Cleve. chpt. 1982-86, pres. 1989—, honoree Ednl. Found. 1988), Flower Pot Garden Club (rep. to Garden Club Greater Cleve. 1970—, pres. 1987-88), Sigma Tau Delta, Phi Alpha Theta. Home: 3583 Riedham Rd Shaker Heights OH 44120

BARRETT, ELIZABETH ANN MANHART, nursing educator, psychotherapist, consultant; b. Hume, Ill., July 11, 1934; d. Francis J. and Grace C. (Manhart) Fridy; children: Joseph B., Jeffrey F., Paula G. Brown, Pamela M. Shetler Carpino, Scott D. BS in Nursing summa cum laude, U. Evansville, 1970, MA, 1973, MS in Nursing, 1976; grad. Gestalt Assocs. for Psychotherapy, 1982; PhD in Nursing, NYU, 1983. Instr. nursing U. Evansville, Ind., 1970-73, asst. prof., 1973-76; staff nurse Welborn Bapt. Hosp., Evansville, 1975-76; staff nurse Bellevue Psychiat. Hosp., N.Y.C., 1976-79; clin. tchr. CUNY, 1977-82; asst. prof. Adelphi U., 1979-80; group practice Nurse Healers, 1979-82; pvt. practice psychotherapy, 1980—; nurse researcher Mt. Sinai Med. Ctr., N.Y.C., 1982-86, asst. dir. nursing, 1983-86; assoc. prof. Hunter Coll., N.Y.C., 1986-89, dir. grad. studies, 1989—. Mem. com. Regional Health Planning Council, Evansville, 1974-77. Mem. Am. Nurses Assn. (cert. psychiat.-mental health), Nat. League Nursing, Soc. Advancement in Nursing, Soc. Rogerian Scholars (founder, 1st pres. 1988-90), NOW, Phi Kappa Phi, Sigma Theta Tau (Upsilon chpt. pres. 1986-88), Alpha Tau Delta. Home: 415 E 85th St #9E New York NY 10028 Office: Hunter Coll 425 E 25th St New York NY 10010

BARRETT, ELIZABETH ANNE, public relations specialist; b. Evanston, Ill., Dec. 11, 1961; d. Richard Isaac Barrett and Kaye Louise (Benner) Reardon. BS in Journalism, Tex. Christian U., 1984. Asst. pub. rels. mgr. Southland Corp., Dallas, 1984; with Mary Kay Cosmetics, Dallas, 1984—, creative copywriter, 1987-89, corp. pub. rels. coord., 1989—. Exec. com. and mem. pub. rels. com. Corp. Recycling Coun. of Dallas, 1989-90. Mem. Women in Communications, Inc. (asst. program chair 1989-90), Pub. Rels. Soc. Am. Office: Mary Kay Cosmetics 8787 Stemmons Frwy Dallas TX 75247

BARRETT, HELEN HUNT, corporate professional; b. Paris, Tex., Nov. 2, 1943; d. Leo Charles and Gladys (Stewart) Smith; m. Lawrence B. Hunt, July 29, 1961 (div. 1979); 1 child, Susan; m. Norman Lee Barrett, Sept. 11, 1982; children: Brian, Kevin, Mark. Student, Midwestern State U., Wichita Falls, Tex., 1970-74. Exec. sec. Dept. Def., Wichita Falls, 1969-82; cons. Mary Kay Cosmetics, Wichita Falls, 1977-79; sales dir. Mary Kay Cosmetics, 1979-85; mgr., dir. admissions, cons. Vogue Beauty Coll., Austin and San Antonio, Tex., 1985-86; field mgr. Welcome Wagon, Internat., Austin, 1986-88; account exec. Master Check Corp., Austin, 1988-89, Retriever Payment Systems, Houston, 1989—. Solicitor Wichita Falls chpt. Am. Cancer Fund, 1983; fundraiser Lago Vista (Tex.) Women's Club, 1986. Mem. Am. Bus. Women's Assn. (pres. 1973-74), Austin C. of C., Austin Better Bus. Bur. Democrat. Methodist. Clubs: Lago Vista Country, Lago Vista Women's, Retired Officers Wives. Home: 4018 Outpost Trace Lago Vista TX 78645 Office: Master Check Corp 1301 Capital Tex S Bldg A Ste 304 Austin TX 78746

BARRETT, JESSICA (DONNA ANN NIPERT), psychotherapist; b. Paterson, N.J., July 25, 1952; d. Donald Alfred and Gloria Emma (Lustica) Nipert; m. John David Barrett, Sept. 9, 1977 (div. June 1982); 1 child, Ashley Elizabeth. BA, UCLA, 1975; MA, Azusa Pacific U., 1981. Lic. marriage, family, child counselor; cert. hypnosis, employee asst. profl., Calif. With employee relations Engrs. and Architects Exec. Assn., L.A., 1975-79; practicing psychotherapy Toluca Lake and Burbank, Calif., 1983—; instr., supr. Calif. Family Study Ctr., Burbank, 1986—; psychotherapist Pasadena (Calif.) Outpatient Eating Disorders Program, 1987-88; cons. Texaco Employee Assistance Program, L.A., Studio City, 1985-86, NBC Employee Assistance Program, Burbank, 1986-87; lectr. various groups, Burbank, San Fernando Valley, 1983-87; spl. therapist Am. Psychol. Mgmt. Inc.; assessment and referral liaison Nat. Resource Cons., San Diego, Employee Support Sytems Corp., Orange, Calif. Mem. Employee Assistance Profl. Assn. (bd. dirs. 1983-86), Am. Assn. Marriage and Family Therapists, Stepfamily Assn. Am., Calif. Family Study Ctr. Alumni Assn. (sec.-treas. 1987-88, v.p. programs 1988-89). Democrat. Presbyterian.

BARRETT, JUNE BIVINS, dietitian; b. Lewisburg, Tenn., Sept. 14, 1950; d. Joe Herman and Ruth Virginia (Marsh) B.; m. Howell Slade Barrett Jr., Sept. 7, 1974 (div. 1982); 1 child, Scott. BS in Dietetics, U. Tenn., 1972; MEd in Nutrition & Sci., Ga. State U., 1978. Registered dietitian, Ga., Tenn. Nutritionist Jefferson County Bd. Health, Birmingham, Ala., 1973-74; tng. program adminstr. Ga. Retardation Ctr., Ga. State U., Atlanta, 1974-78; nutritionist, nutrition edn. specialist USDA, Ga. State U., Atlanta, 1978-80; nutrition and food systems specialist Ga. Dept. Edn., Atlanta, 1980-82; asst. coordinator food svc. Clayton County Bd. Edn., Jonesboro, Ga., 1982-87; food svc. dir. Chattanooga (Tenn.) Pub. Schs., 1987—; adj. prof. U. Tenn., Chattanooga, 1987—, Emory U., 1974-78. Mag. USAR, 1979—. Named to Outstanding Young Women Am., 1979, 83. Mem. Am. Dietetic Assn. (del. 1979-86), Atlanta Dietetic Assn. (pres. 1980-82), Ga. Dietetic Assn. (Disting. award 1987), Am. Sch. Food Svc. Assn. Mem. Ch. of Christ. Home: 3909 N Mission Oaks Dr Chattanooga TN 37412

BARRETT, LEE ANN, civic volunteer; b. San Antonio, Aug. 29, 1952; d. Lewis Levi and Helen Elizabeth (Cummings) Barrett. BA in Speech/Drama, Winthrop Coll., Rock Hill, S.C., 1974. Exec. asst. ARC, Carolina LowCountry chpt., North Charleston, S.C., 1989—, dir. pub. rel. and adminstrv. svcs., 1987—; counselor, sponsor Hotline, Charleston, 1988—; guardian ad litem Berkeley and Charleston Counties, 1987—; worker Crisis InterFaith Shelter, Charleston, 1987—; active Charleston Women's Network, 1987—; vol. Red Cross Disaster Team. Mem. Palmetto Dramatic Assn., Nat. Pastoral Musicians, Pax Christi, Pi Delta Epsilon. Democrat. Roman Catholic. Office: ARC Carolina Low Country Ch 5290 Rivers Ave #300 North Charleston SC 29418

BARRETT, LIDA KITTRELL, college dean, mathematician; b. Houston, May 21, 1927; d. Pleasant Williams and Maidel (Baker) Kittrell; m. John Herbert Barrett, June 2, 1950 (dec. Jan. 1969); children: John Kittrell, Maidel Horn, Mary Louise. BA, Rice U., 1946; MA, U. Tex., Austin, 1949; PhD, U. Pa., 1954. Instr. math. U. Conn., Waterbury, 1955-56; vis. appointment U. Wis., Madison, 1959-60; lectr. U. Utah, Salt Lake City, 1956-61; assoc. prof. U. Tenn., Knoxville, 1961-70, prof., 1970-80, head math. dept., 1973-80; assoc. provost No. Ill. U., DeKalb, 1980-87; dean, arts and scis. Miss. State U., Mississippi State, 1987—; ind. math. cons., Knoxville, Tenn., 1964-80. Contbr. articles on topology and math. edn. to profl. jours. Mem. Math. Assn. Am. (pres. 1989-90), Am. Math. Soc., Soc. Indsl. and Applied Math., Nat. Coun. Tchrs. Math., Am. Assn. Higher Edn., Phi Kappa Phi, Sigma Xi. Episcopalian. Home: 107 Shadowood Ln Starkville MS 39759 Office: Miss State U Coll Arts & Scis PO Drawer AS Mississippi State MS 39762

BARRETT, LINDA L., real estate executive; b. Hudson, Mich., Aug. 16, 1948; d. David John and Georgia Elizabeth (Spengler) B.; 1 dau., Toni. Student, Jackson Community Coll., 1970, U. Mich., 1973. Cert. residential brokerage mgr. Sales mgr. Collins Real Estate, Hudson, Mich., 1973-79; owner, broker Homeland Real Estate, Lake Leann, Mich., 1979-82; mng. broker Mid-Mich. Real Estate, Jackson, Mich., 1982-85; exec. v.p. Michael Saunders & Co., Sarasota, Fla., 1986—; mem. adv. bd. Sotheby's Internat. Mem. Internat. Real Estate Fedn., Nat. Mktg. Inst., NAFE, Nat. Assn. Realtors, Fla. Assn. Realtors, Sarasota C. of C., Bradenton C. of C., Com. of 100, 200 Notable Am. Women (profl. standards com. women's coun.). Office: Michael Saunders & Co 1801 Main St Sarasota FL 34236

BARRETT, LORETTA ANNE, publishing executive; b. Mt. Vernon, N.Y., July 1, 1941; d. Edward Vincent and Irene Marie (Wynne) B. Student, Rosemont (Pa.) Coll., 1958-60; BA cum laude, U. Pa., 1962, MAT, 1965. Editor Doubleday & Co. Anchor Press, N.Y.C., 1965-67; editorial dir. Doubleday & Co. Special Projects, N.Y.C., 1967-72; exec. editor, publisher Anchor Press, Doubleday & Co., N.Y.C., 1972-83; exec. editorial v.p. Doubleday & Co., N.Y.C., 1983-90; pres. Loretta Barrett Books, Lit. Agy., 1990—; bd. dirs. Reading is Fundamental, Washington, 1967—, Through the Flower, Santa Fe, N.Mex., 1986—. Adv. Women's Campaign Fund, Washington, 1984—; assoc. trustee Coun. Pa. Women U. Pa., 1989; bd. dirs. Athena Inst., Haverford, Pa., 1987—. Mem. Women in the Media. Democrat. Roman Catholic. Office: Loretta Barrett Books 121 W 27th St Ste 601 New York NY 10001

BARRETT, PATRICIA LOUISE, mathematician, educator; b. Pitts., July 11, 1947; d. Walter James and Helen Louise (Booty) White; m. Jan F. Segovis, Aug. 2, 1970 (dec. Aug. 1984); m. Telford H. Barrett, Jr., Nov. 15, 1985; stepchildren: Joseph Keith and Telford Lee (twins). BS, Valdosta State Coll., 1969, MEd, 1970; EdS, Ga. So. Coll., 1985. Tchr. math. Lowndes High Sch., Valdosta, 1970-83, 86—; math. coord. Lowndes County Schs., Valdosta, 1983-86; instr. math. Valdosta State Coll., 1975—; registrar Ga. Math. Conf., Eatonton, Ga., 1985-89, chmn., 1990. Mem. adult choir 1st Bapt. Ch., 1966—, dir. children III Sunday sch., 1972—, pianist presch. choir, 1988—. Recipient Star Tchr. award Valdosta C. of C., 1976, 82. Mem. NEA, Nat. Coun. Tchrs. Math., Ga. Coun. Tchrs. Math. (dist. chmn. 1981-83, Gladys M. Thompson dist. award 1986), Ga. Assn. Educators,

Lowndes Assn. Educators (treas. 1979-80, pres. 1981-82), AAUW. Home: 114 Fairway Dr Valdosta GA 31602 Office: Lowndes High Sch 1112 St Augustine Rd Valdosta GA 31602

BARRETT, PAULETTE SINGER, public relations executive; b. Paris, Dec. 20, 1937; came to U.S., 1947; d. Andrew M. and Agatha (Kinsbrunner) Singer; m. Laurence I. Barrett, Mar. 9, 1957 (div. 1983); children: Paul Meyer, David Allen, Adam Singer. BA, NYU, 1957; MS in Journalism, Columbia U., 1958. News dir. Yardney Electric Corp., N.Y.C., 1958-61; freelance writer newspapers and pub. relations orgns., N.Y.C. and Washington, 1961-73; assoc. dir. pub. info. Columbia U., N.Y.C., 1973-77; from account exec. to v.p., then sr. v.p. Daniel J. Edelman, Inc. of N.Y., N.Y.C., 1977-80, sr. v.p. and gen. mgr., 1980, exec. v.p., gen. mgr., 1986-88, exec. v.p., dir. corp. affairs div., 1988-89; exec. v.p. Rowland Co., N.Y.C., 1980-82; exec. dir. communications UJA-Fedn. of N.Y., N.Y.C., 1982-86; sr. v.p., mng. dir. Hill and Knowlton, Chgo., 1989—; bd. dirs. Ballet Chgo. Mem. Pub. Rels. Soc. Am. (accredited), Counselors Acad., Women Execs. in Pub. Rels., Women in Communications, Inc., Publicity Club of Chgo. Office: Hill Knowlton Inc 111 E Wacker Dr Chicago IL 60601

BARRETTA, JOLIE ANN, professional athletics coach, author; b. Phila., Aug. 17, 1954; d. Philip Francis and Norma Roberta (Podoszek) B. Student, U. Calif., Long Beach, 1972-76, U. Florence, Italy, 1974-75. Tchr. gymnastics Los Angeles City Sch. Dist., 1973-77, judge, 1976-82; coach, choregrapher Kips Gymnastic Club, Long Beach, Calif., 1976-78, So. Calif. Acrobatics Team, Huntington Beach, Calif., 1979-81, UCLA, 1980-82; pres. West Coast Waves Rhythmic Gymnastics, Rolling Hills Estates, Calif., 1980—; mem. coaching staff U.S. Nat. Rhythmic Gymnastics Team, 1983—; tchr., coach Centro Olimpico Nazionale Italia, Rome, 1984-85; lectr. dane phys. edn. Calif. State U., Dominguez Hills, Carson, 1981-86; French lang. mistress of ceremonies rhythmic gymnastics event U.S. Olympic Games, L.A., 1984; invited observer Inst. Phys. Culture, Bejing, 1985, Bulgarian Gymnastics Fedn., Sophia, 1982-90; meet dir. state and regional championships, Los Angeles County, 1984, 86; internat. lectr. body alignment; pres. Rhythmic Gymnasts Devel. Program, 1984—; developer RIGOR (Rhythmic Gymnastics Outreach) for U.S.A. recreation programs. Author: Body Alignment, 1985; columnist Internat. Gymnast Mag., 1987—. Tour leader Acad. Tours Inc. U.S./Bulgaria Friendship Through Sports Ann. Tour, N.Y. and Bulgaria, 1987. Recipient recognition plaque U.S. Womens Sports Awards Banquet, 1984-89. Mem. U.S. Rhythmic Gymnastics Coaches Assn. (pres. 1984—), U.S. Gymnastics Fedn. (bd. dirs. 1985—, nat. team coach 1984—, mem. del., coach internat. competitions U.S., Mex., Hungary, Bulgaria, Belgium, Can. 1984—, choreographer age group devel. compulsorie div. 1987, staff Olympic Tng. Ctr. 1984—), Inst. Noetic Scis. Republican. Office: West Coast Waves 1250 Bonnie Brae Hermosa Beach CA 90254

BARRETT-CONNOR, ELIZABETH L., healthcare administrator, epidemiologist; b. Evanston, Ill., Apr. 8, 1935; m. James D. Connor. BA, Mt. Holyoke Coll., 1956; MD, Cornell U., 1960. Diplomate Am. Bd. Internal Medicine, Nat. Bd. Med. Examiners. Instr. medicine U. Miami, Fla., 1965-68, asst. prof. medicine, 1968-70; asst. prof. community and family medicine U. Calif., San Diego, 1970-74, assoc. prof. community and family medicine, 1974-81, prof. community and family medicine, 1981—, acting chair dept. community and family medicine, 1981-82, chmn. dept. community and family medicine, 1982—; vis. prof. Royal Soc. Medicine, London, 1989; mem. hosp. infection control com. VA Med. Ctr., San Diego, 1971—. Contbr. articles to profl. jours. NIH grantee, 1970-89, 78-80, Janssen Pharm., 1976-78, Am. Heart Assn. grantee, 1980-81. Mem. Am. Heart Assn. (chmn. budget com. coun. on epidemiology 1987-88, chmn. coun. on epidemiology 1988-89), Am. Pub. Health Assn. (chmn. epidemiology sect. 1989—), Assn. Tchrs. Preventive Medicine (bd. dirs. 1987—). Office: U Calif M-007 La Jolla CA 92093

BARRETTE, SARAH CATHARINE, nurse; b. Elverson, Pa., Dec. 12, 1936; d. Joseph Heber and Barbara Ethel (Ruoss) Seifrit; m. Sylvester Arthur Barrette, Sept. 24, 1955; children: Donald Owen, Barbara Lynn, Bana Lee, Brenda Jo. RN, Montgomery Hosp., Norristown, Pa., 1956; student, U. Minn., 1975. Staff nurse Allen Meml. Hosp., Waterloo, Iowa, 1956-57, Sartori Meml. Hosp., Cedar Falls, 1957-61; nursing supr. Sartori Meml. Hosp., 1961-66, dir. inservice edn., asst. dir. nursing, 1966-71, dir. nursing, 1971-80; dir. nursing Spelman Meml. Hosp., Smithville, Mo., 1980-84; asst. adminstr. Spelman Meml. Hosp., Smithville, 1984-89, Spelman Meml. and Spelman/St. Lukes Hosp., Smithville, 1989—. Mem. Mo. Orgn. Nurse Execs. (pres. 1986-87), Am. Orgn. Nurse Execs., Kansas City Area Hosp. Assn. (nursing com.), Kansas City Area Nursing Adminstrs. Republican. Roman Catholic. Office: Spelman Meml Hosp 601 S 169 Hwy Smithville MO 64089

BARRETT-STAFFORD, SUSAN CHRISTINE, accountant; b. Heidelberg, Federal Republic of Germany, Mar. 31, 1960; d. Franklin Eugene and Eleonore (Vöhringer) Barrett; m. Leslie Joel Stafford, Jan. 9, 1982; children: Nathan Edward, Marie Rochelle. BS in Bus. Acctg., Emporia (Kans.) State U., 1982. CPA, Kans. Accountant Arthur Young and Co., Wichita, Kans., 1982-85, F.B. Kubik and Co., Wichita, 1985-88; acct. Rent-a-Ctr., Wichita, Kans., 1988—. Mem. aux. com. bd. dirs. Child Care Assn. Wichita and Sedgwick County, 1986-87; bd. dirs. Planned Parenthood, Wichita, 1987. Mem. Am. Inst. CPA's, Kans. Soc. CPA's, Inst. Internal Auditors, Nat. Assn. Accts., Nat. Assn. Female Execs., Am. Soc. Women Accts., Phi Kappa Phi, Cardinal Key. Lutheran. Office: Rent-a-Ctr 8200 E Rent-a-Center Dr Wichita KS 67226

BARRETT-WEBER, PATRICIA ANN, director of human resources; b. Cleve., Sept. 20, 1953; d.l Francis Patrick Juanita Mae (Helmkee) Barrett; m. David Kevin Weber, June 21, 1975. Assoc. Bus. Adminstrn., Dyke Coll., Cleve., 1972; BS in Bus. Mgmt., Baldwin Wallace Coll., 1983. Accredited profl. in human resources. Personnel generalist E.I du Pont de Nemours & Co., Cleve., 1971-83; employment counselor Champion Personnel, Cleve., 1985; dept. asst. personnel Stouffer Inn on the Sq., Cleve., 1986-87; dir. personnel Stouffer PineIsle Resort, Atlanta, 1987-88, Stouffer Tower City Pla. Hotel, Cleve., 1988—. Counselor, Battered Women's Shelter, Cleve., 1983-87. Mem. NAFE, Am. Soc. Personnel Assn. Lutheran. Office: Stouffer Tower City Pla 24 Public Sq Cleveland OH 44113

BARRICK, AUGUSTA IRENE, retired educator; b. Tiffin, Ohio, Aug. 14, 1903; d. William Luther and Mary (Elizabeth) B. AB magna cum laude, Heidelberg Coll., Tiffin, Ohio, 1925; MA, Ohio State U., 1937. Cert. secondary speech, English and French tchr. Tchr., basketball coach Newcomerstown (Ohio) High Sch., 1925-26; jr. high sch. tchr. Warren (Ohio) Sch. System, 1926-31, tchr. Warren G. Harding Sr. High Sch., 1931-69. Author: The Power of Effective Speech, 1959, Peaceful Use Atomic Power - Public Utilities Fortnightly, 1969. Life bd. mem. YWCA, Warren, 1977—, Am. Cancer Soc., 1989—; pres. Trumbull County Cancer Soc., 1972-73; elder First Presbyn. Ch., 1969-75, trustee, 1980-88. Recipient Valley Forge Tchrs. Medal, Freedoms Found., 1959, Honor Cert., Freedoms Found., 1971, Excellence in Teaching Plaque, Mayor and Warren Community, 1972; named Warren Woman of Yr., Women's Bus. and Profl. Club, 1971. Mem. AAUW (life), NEA, Trumbull County Ret. Tchrs. Republican. Home: 411 Bonnie Brae NE Warren OH 44483

BARRISKILL, MAUDANNE KIDD, preschool educator; b. Balt., Apr. 2, 1932; d. John Graydon and Maudine (Adams) Kidd; m. Peter Herbert Barriskill, Nov. 30, 1957; children: John, Michael. BA, So. Meth. U., 1954; student early childhood edn., Old Dominion U.; student, Katharine Gibbs Sch., N.Y.C., Juilliard Sch. Music, N.Y.C. Exec. sec., copywriter trainee J. Walter Thompson Advt. Agy., N.Y.C., 1955-59; founder Maude Barry Interior Design, Virginia Beach, 1970-73; founder, dir. English Country Day Sch., Virginia Beach, 1975—; tchr. Ea. Shore Chapel Presch., Virginia Beach, 1970-75, Montessori Child Devel. Ctr., Virginia Beach. Author children's books and workbooks. Tchr. Sunday sch. Home: 4721 Newgate Ct Virginia Beach VA 23455

BARRON, BARBARA MARILYN, fibre artist; b. N.Y.C., June 12, 1937; d. Samuel Leo and Anna Laura (Rosenbaum) Weinstein; m. Donald Jerome Barron, June 21, 1959; children: Nancy Ellen, Ruth Allison, Steven Joel. BA, Hunter Coll., 1958; MA, Columbia U., 1965; cert. Oxford U., Eng., 1972, Royal Sch. Needlework, Eng., 1972. With Suffolk Mus., Dowling Coll., Stony Brook, N.Y., 1971, Old Bethpage Village Restoration, Woodbury Country Club, N.Y., 1975; pres. Knicely Knotted by Barbara Barron, Huntington, N.Y., 1973-79, Interior Design Crafts, Inc., Huntington, 1979-88. Interviews given to Barry Farber, N.Y.C. Radio, Joan May Channel 67, Hauppauge, N.Y. One-woman shows include Pindar Gallery, Soho, N.Y., 1982, Goff Gallery, Orlando, Fla., 1984, Suzanne Brown Gallery, Scottsdale, Ariz., 1984; exhibited in group shows: Art Expo, N.Y., Dallas, Los Angeles, 1982-90, Heckscher Mus., Huntington, 1983, Laura Paul Gallery, Cin.; selected commns. AT&T., Trump Pla., Palm Beach, Burt Reynolds, Australian Film Inst., Price Waterhouse, E.F. Hutton, N.Y.C., Shearson, Lehman Hutton, N.Y.C., Premier House, Bklyn., Penn. Cen., Cin.; featured artist Posner Gallery, Milw. Bd. dirs. Huntington Arts Coun., Kehillath Shalom Synagogue, Cold Spring Harbor, N.Y. Democrat. Jewish. Avocations: gourmet cooking, square dancing, gardening. Home: 5 Larkin St Huntington Station NY 11746 Office: Interior Design Crafts Inc 1943 New York Ave Huntington Station NY 11746

BARRON, ILONA ELEANOR, reading educator, consultant; b. Mass, Mich., Sept. 19, 1929; cert. in elem. teaching No. Mich. U., 1951; B.S. in Elementary Edn., Central Mich. U., Mt. Pleasant, 1961; M.A. in Edn., U. Mich., Ann Arbor, 1966; postgrad. Mich. State U., East Lansing; m. George Barron; 1 child, Fred. Tchr. elem. schs., 1952-67; Title I dir. Saginaw (Mich.) Twp. Community Schs., 1967-68, reading cons., 1971—; elem. intern cons. Mich. State U., 1968-71; elem. reading cons. Saginaw Twp. Pub. Schs., 1972—. Mem. NEA, Mich., Saginaw Twp. Edn. Assns., Saginaw Area Reading Coun. Specialist in reading, methods of teaching developmental reading skills and enrichment. Home: 1681 M-64 Ontonagon MI 49953

BARRON, JANICE MARIE, fire fighter; b. Columbus, Ga., Apr. 30, 1966; d. James Arley and Annie Ruth (Brooks) B. AS in Criminal Sociology, Columbus Coll., 1988, BS in Criminal Justice, 1988; AS in Fire Sci., Chattahoochee Community Coll., Phenix City, Ala., 1990. Position mgmt. clk. U.S. Army Inf. Ctr., Ft. Benning, Ga., 1985; surveyor Quality Controlled Svcs., Columbus, 1985-86; sec. Columbus Coll., 1985-87; crew worker Army and Air Force Exch., Ft. Benning, 1986-87; tech. svc. clk. U.S. Army Inf. Ctr., Ft. Benning, 1987; sec. Kelley Svcs., Inc., Columbus, 1987-88; fire fighter Columbus Consolidated Govt., 1988—. Mem. NAFE, Fire Fighter Assn. (sta. rep. Columbus 1989-90), Columbus Coll. Alumni, Phi Beta Kappa, Gamma beta Phi, Lambda Alpha Epsilon.

BARRON, LAURA ROWE, federal agency administrator; b. Tifton, Ga.; d. Lester Harris and Harriette Elizabeth Rowe; m. John Stelk Barron, Jan. 1983. BS magna cum laude, U. Tenn., 1972, MBA, 1982. Comml. interior designer Chattanooga, Tenn., 1973-77; travel mgr. TVA, Knoxville, 1978-87, project mgr., 1987-90; mgr. orgn. planning and human resource devel. Tenn. Valley Authority, Knoxville, 1990—; instr. U. Tenn., Knoxville, 1987-90; speaker, presenter workshops at travel symposia. Elder Westminster Presbyn. Mem. Nat. Bus. Travel Assn. (v.p.), Am. Bus. Women's Assn. (Woman of Yr.), Nat. Mgmt. Assn., Federally Employed Women (v.p. tng.), Phi Kappa Phi, Omicron Nu, Beta Gamma Sigma. Home: 8316 Hunter Hill Dr Knoxville TN 37923

BARRON, PEGGY PENNISI, management consultant; b. Chgo., Jan. 27, 1958; d. Louis Legendre and Jane Harriet (Peters) Pennisi; m. Stan Barron, May 3, 1986. BS with honors, U. Ill., Chgo., 1979. Data processing mgr. Oasis Aviation, Inc., L.A., 1980-87; pres. Millennium Enterprises, Marina Del Rey, Calif., 1987—. Mem. NAFE, Phi Beta Kappa, Phi Kappa Phi. Home and Office: 3008 Yale Ave Marina del Rey CA 90292

BARRON, ROBERTA, human resources management consultant; b. N.Y.C., May 11, 1940; d. Irv and Roslyn (Engerow) Yellin; m. Harold S. Barron, Nov. 17, 1963; children: Lawrence Ira, Jean Louise. Student, UCLA, 1960-61; BA, Conn. Coll., 1962; MSIR, Loyola U., Chgo., 1987. Corp. pub. dept. staff Time Inc., N.Y.C., 1962-64; pub. relations cons., 1965-87; cons. Exec. Assets, Chgo., 1987-88, Barron Assocs., Inc., Chgo., 1988—. Mem. NAFE, Am. Mgmt. Assn., Nat. Assn. Women Bus. Owners, Am. Soc. Tng. and Devel. (Chgo. chpt.), Women's Athletic Club, Casino Club, Franklin Hills Country Club. Office: Barron Assocs Inc 980 N Michigan Ave Chicago IL 60611

BARRON, SUSAN, clinical psychologist; b. Chgo., May 13, 1940; d. Earl and Trixie (Chernoff) B.; m. Eugene Pratt, Jan. 18, 1975 (div. 1983). BBA, CCNY, 1960, MA, 1963; PhD, CUNY, 1973. Lic. psychologist. Intern psychologist Bellevue Psychiat. Hosp., N.Y.C., 1964-65, psychologist, 1966-67; teaching fellow CUNY, 1965-66; staff psychologist Lighthouse, N.Y. Assn. for the Blind, N.Y.C., 1968-71; sr. clin. psychologist Lighthouse, N.Y Assn. for the Blind, N.Y.C., 1971-74; dir. psychol. counseling svcs. Peninsula Ctr. for the Blind, Palo Alto, Calif., 1974-75; cons. psychologist N.Y. State Commn. for Blind and Visually Handicapped, N.Y.C., 1975-78, 86—; dir. psychol. svcs. Thoms Rehab. Hosp., Asheville, N.C., 1978-79; state coord. psychol. svcs. N.Y. State Office Vocat. Rehab., Albany, 1979-85; founder, dir. Family Support Program ICU N.Y. Infirmary-Beekman Downtown Hosp., N.Y.C., 1982-84; cons. clin. psychologist N.Y. Hosp.-Cornell U. Med. Ctr., 1987—; pvt. practice, 1987—; Mem. Nat. Human Svcs. Adv. Bd.-Retinitis Pigmentosa Found., Balt., 1975-82; cons. Del. State Commn. for Blind, 1975-78, Am. Found. Blind, 1974-82, Calif. Dept. Rehab., 1974-82, Hawaii State Svcs. Blind, 1974-82, Ariz. State Svcs. Blind, 1974-82, Nev. State Svcs. Blind, 1974-82; speaker Nat. Multiple Disabilities Conf., 1982, NAS, 1981; mem. adv. bd. doctoral psychology internship program Rusk Inst. of Rehab. Medicine, NYU Med. Ctr., 1979-84. Contbr. articles to profl. jours. Recipient Leadership award Alumni Assn. CCNY, 1960, 62, Rsch. award Retinal Dystrophy Soc., Australia, 1975. Fellow Am. Orthopsychiat. Assn.; mem. APA, AAAS, Calif. State Psychol. Assn., N.Y. Acad. Sci. Office: NY Hosp Cornell U Med Ctr 515 E 71 St S102 New York NY 10021

BARRY, ANNE ELIZABETH JACKSON, writer; b. Columbus, Ohio, Aug. 28, 1928; d. Paul Sherman and Alice Winnifred (Martin) Jackson; m. James Potvin Barry, Apr. 16, 1966. BS in Edn., Ohio State U., 1950; MS in Libr. Sci., U. So. Calif., L.A., 1955. Libr. Bklyn. Children's Mus., 1950-54; spl. svc. libr. Dept. Army Civilian, Frankfort, West Germany, 1955-57; high sch. libr. Columbus Pub. Schs., 1957-82, U.S. Army, Sagamihari Elem., Tokyo, 1960-62; vol. edn. com. Opera/Columbus, 1984—; vol. corr. sec. Ohio State U., Friends of Hist. Costume and Textiles Collection, Columbus, 1987—. Contbr. articles and book revs. to profl. jours. Columbus Pub. Schs. grantee, 1971; recipient John Cotton Dana Pub. Rels. Spl. award ALA, N.Y.C., 1973. Mem. AAUW, Nat. League Am. Pen Women, Soc. Midland Authors, English Speaking Union, Delta Kappa Gamma. Home: 353 Fairway Blvd Columbus OH 43213

BARRY, BETTY LYNN, counselor, school social worker; b. Memphis, Jan. 6, 1946; d. Varda Fulton Smith and Gladys Idelia (Howard) Reid; m. Brian Linda Barry, Feb. 11, 1972. BS in Sociology, Memphis State U., 1968, MEd in Edn. Adminstrn., 1976, EdD in Counseling, 1984. Cert. sch. social worker, sch. counselor, profl. counselor. With Memphis News Co., 1962-68; probation officer Memphis-Shelby Counties Juvenile Ct., Memphis, 1968-70; substitute tchr. Memphis City Schs., 1970-71, attendance tchr., 1971-77, sch. social worker, 1977-84, guidance counselor, 1984—. Mem. choir Good News Singers, Memphis, 1986-88. Mem. NEA, Memphis Edn. Assn. (faculty rep. 1972-73), Tenn. Edn. Assn., West Tenn. Edn. Assn., West Tenn. Assn. Counseling and Devel., Tenn. Assn. Counseling and Devel., Tenn. Bd. Cert. for Profl. Counselors and Marital and Family Therapists, Phi Kappa Phi, Kappa Delta Pi. Republican. Baptist. Office: Lanier Jr High Sch 817 Brownlee Rd Memphis TN 38116

BARRY, BONNIE B., trade association executive; b. Pocatello, Idaho, July 17, 1940; d. Kyle and Lael Corrine (Smith) Bettilyon; 1 child, Robyn Matthies Randall. Student, Mills Coll., 1958-59; BA, U. Utah, 1962; cert., ITCA, 1976. Spl. svcs. mgr. Sperry Rand Missile Div., Salt Lake City, 1962-64; mgr. travel dept. Utah Motor Club, Salt Lake City, 1965-67; owner Aggie Travel Svc., Davis, Calif., 1968-77, also bd. dirs.; founding ptnr. SECRET Travel Svc., Maui, Hawaii, 1979—; exec. v.p. Assn. Retail Travel Agts., 1979-90; v.p. Bettilyon Investment Co., Salt Lake City, 1990—; tng. dir. ednl. work-study programs for mem. travel agys., U.S. and Can.; mem. faculty U. Calif. Extension, Davis, 1974-77. Mem. Nat. Travel Agts. (adv. bd. to Pan Am. World Airways 1973-77), Assn. Retail Travel Agts. (nat. bd. dirs. 1974-78), Giants Travel Coop. (v.p. Western chpt. 1972-74), Am. Assn. Retail Travel Agts., Soroptomists. Republican. Morman. Home: 644 Rossi Hill Dr Box 1388 Park City UT 84060 Office: Bettilyon Investment Co 2250 S Redwood Rd Salt Lake City VT 84119

BARRY, BRIDGET, public relation consultant; b. Shreveport, La., Oct. 5, 1959; d. Robert and Modean (Lafon) B. BS in Journalism, U. North Tex., Denton, 1983, postgrad., 1990—. Reporter The Lewisville (Tex.) News, 1983-84; editorial svcs. mgr., editor Focus mag. Harris Meth. Ft. Worth, 1984-90; freelance writer Ft. Worth, 1990—. Vol. Ft. Worth Zoo, 1987-90; bd. dirs. Tex. Com. for the Humanities, 1988-91. Mem. Women in Communications (bd. dir. 1988-90, Matrix award 1990), Dallas Press Club (Katie award 1989), Acad. Health Svc. Mktg. (Brillance award 1990), Ft. Worth Ad Club (Addie award 1990). Republican. Home: 5025 Overton Ridge Circle #1728 Fort Worth TX 76132

BARRY, ELIZABETH LOTTES, occupational therapist; b. St. Louis, Sept. 8, 1958; d. Arthur Eberhard and Mary CeCelia (Paynter) Lottes; m. Robert Adrian Barry III, May 19, 1989. BS in Occupational Therapy, Tufts U., 1982; postgrad., Webster U., 1987—. Registered occupational therapist. Occupational therapist St. Mary's Health Ctr., St. Louis, 1982-83; neurological occupational therapist Washington U., St. Louis, 1983-86; dir. occupational therapy Health South, St. Louis, 1986-89; pediatric occupational therapist Ranken-Jordan Children's Reha. Ctr., St. Louis, 1989—; conf. coord. Ranken-Jordan Children's Rehab. Ctr., St. Louis; guest lectr. occupational therapy program Washington U., St. Louis, 1983-86, phys. therapy program, 1984-85; presenter in field. Contbr. articles to profl. jours. Adapted aquatics coord. St. Louis Assn. for Retarded Citizens, 1986-89, St. Louis Soc. for Crippled Children, 1986-88, Camp Wonderland-Mo. Nat. Head Injury Found., St. Louis, 1983; rep./interviewer Tufts U. Alumni Admissions Program, St. Louis, Boston, 1983—. Mem. Am. Occupational Therapy Assn., Mo. Occupational Therapy Assn. (conf. planning com. 1983), Nat. Head Injury Found., Mo. Head Injury Found. Roman Catholic. Home: 304 Parkwood Kirkwood MO 63122 Office: Ranken Jordan Childrens Rehab Ctr 10621 Ladue Rd Saint Louis MO 63141

BARRY, ELLEN M., lawyer, consultant; b. Somerville, Mass., Sept. 20, 1953; d. John H. and Margaret Anne (Hurley) B.; m. Michel Peter Florio. BA, Swarthmore (Pa.) Coll., 1975; JD, NYU, 1978. Bar: Calif. 1978. Legal intern Youth Law Ctr., San Francisco, 1976, Women's Prison Clinic, N.Y.C., 1976-77, San Francisco Neighborhood Legal Assistance, San Francisco, 1977, Ctr. for Constnl. Rights, N.Y.C., 1978; dir., mng. atty. Legal Svc. for Prisoners With Children, San Francisco, 1979—; dir. Ex-Offender Employment Project, San Francisco, 1981-83; trustee Root-Tilder Scholarship Program, N.Y.C., 1978—; bd. dirs. Elizabeth Fry Ctr., San Francisco, Nat. Women and the Law, N.Y.C., Solid Found., Oakland, Calif. Contbr. numerous articles to profl. jours. Bd. dirs. YWCA, San Francisco, 1986-88. Mem. Nat. Lawyers Guild (bd. dirs. San Francisco chpt. 1980-84), Nat. Network on Women in Prison, Round Table on Women in Prision, Calif. Bar Assn. (prisoner's com. 1989—). Office: Legal Svcs Prisoners with Children 1535 Mission St San Francisco CA 94705

BARRY, JANET CECILIA, educator; b. Jersey City, May 12, 1944; d. John Aloysius and Mary Elizabeth (Hart) B.; B.A., Paterson State Coll., 1966; M.A., Georgian Ct. Coll., 1978. Tchr., Paterson (N.J.) Pub. Sch. No. 12, 1966-68; tchr. Walnut St. Elem. Sch., Toms River (N.J.) Regional Sch. System, 1968—; supr. instrn. Cedar Grove Elem. Sch., Toms River Regional Sch. System, 1968—. Recipient N.J. Gov.'s Excellence in Teaching award, 1987. Mem. Nat. Coun. Tchrs. English, NEA, N.J. Edn. Assn., Ocean County Edn. Assn., Toms River Edn. Assn., Assn. for Supervision and Curriculum Devel., N.J. Reading Assn., N.J. Assn. for Supervision and Curriculum Devel., Internat. Reading Assn., Ocean County Reading Coun. (rec. sec., 1st v.p., pres.), Georgian Ct. Coll. Grad. Sch. Alumni Assn. (sec.), N.J. Prins. and Suprs. Assn., Delta Kappa Gamma (chmn. programs, ednl. svcs., communications). Address: 219 Wells Mills Rd Waretown NJ 08758

BARRY, JOAN, clinical researcher; b. N.Y.C., Sept. 17, 1953. BA in Polit. Sci., U. Calif., L.A., 1978. Rsch. assoc. div. cardiology UCLA Med. Ctr., 1980-83; rsch. assoc. cardiovascular div. Brigham and Women's Hosp., Boston, 1983—, assoc. scientist Ischemia Lab., 1987—, co-dir. Ischemia Group, 1989—; rsch. assoc. Harvard Med. Sch., 1987—; cons. Boston U. Sch. Medicine, 1983. Contbr. articles to profl. jours. Mem. Am. Heart Assn. (pub. edn. forum com. 1982-83, cons. com. to enhance cardiac patient family support groups), Calif. Soc. Cardiac Rehab. Home: 101 Princeton Rd Chestnut Hill MA 02167 Office: Brigham and Women's Hosp Cardiovascular Div 75 Francis St Rm LZ-196 Boston MA 02115

BARRY, JOYCE ALICE, dietitian; b. Chgo., Apr. 27, 1932; d. Walter Stephen and Ethel Myrtle (Paetow) Barry; student Iowa State Coll., 1950-52, Loyala U., 1952-58; B.S., Mundelein Coll., 1955; postgrad. Simmons Coll., 1963-64, U. Ga., 1979, Calif. Western U., 1980—. Prodn. supr. Marshall Field & Co., Chgo., 1955-59; dir. food services Women's Ednl. and Indsl. Union, Boston, 1959-62; dir. food services Wellesley Public Schs., Mass., 1962-70; cons. Stokes Food Services, Newton, Mass., 1960-70; regional dietitian Canteen Corp., Chgo., 1970-83; gen. mgr. bus. devel. Plantation-Sysco, Orlando, Fla., 1983-87; dir. product devel. corp. procurement Mariott Internat. Hdqrs., Washington, 1987—; vis. lectr.; restaurant cons. Mem. Nat. Consumer Panel; research adv. council Restaurant Bus. Mag.; career adv. council, Am. Dietetics Assn.; treas. Dietitians in Bus. Mem. Am. Home Econs. Assn., Internat. Fedn. Home Economists, Home Economists in Bus., Am. Dietetics Assn., Soc. Nutrition Edn., Nat. Assn. Female Execs., Roundtable Women in Food Service, Dieticians in Bus. Intentional Platform Assn. Republican. Roman Catholic. Club: La Chaine des Rotisseurs. Home: 175 Heron Bay Circle Lake Mary FL 32746 Office: Marriott World Hdqrs 1 Marriott Dr Washington DC 20058

BARRY, LEI, medical equipment manufacturing executive; b. Fitchburg, Mass., May 27, 1941; d. Leo Isaacson and Irene Helen (Melanson) Isaacson Godbout; m. Delbert M. Berry (div.); children: David M., Susan L.; m. Frank H. Mahan III, June 25, 1976; stepchildren: Jodi L., Sarah C., Amy S., Frank H. IV. Grad. high sch., Waltham, Mass. Advt. salesperson, broadcaster various radio and TV stas., N.C. and Tex., 1961-67; New Eng. sales rep. Hollister, Inc., Chgo., 1967-71, Northeastern sales mgr., 1971-76; v.p., ptnr. Mahan Assocs., Blue Bell, Pa., 1976—; pres. Blue Bell Bio-Med., Inc., 1982—. Mem. Whitpain Twp. Planning commn.; pres., bd. dirs. Interfaith of Ambler; dir. Elder Boehm's United Ch. of Christ, 1978—. Mem. Wissahickon Valley C. of C., Wissahickon Valley Hist. Soc. (past bd. dirs.), Wissahickon Valley Watershed Assn., Health Industry Reps. Assn., NAFE, Bus. Women's Network Phila. Republican. Avocations: tennis, skiing, gourmet cooking. Office: Blue Bell Bio-Med Inc PO Box 455 Blue Bell PA 19422

BARRY, MARILYN WHITE, educator; b. Weymouth, Mass., Sept. 12, 1936; d. Harland Russell and Alice Louise (Dwyer) White; m. Dennis Edward Barry, July 11, 1959; children—Dennis Edward, Christopher Gerard. BS in Edn. Bridgewater State Coll., 1958; Ed.M. in Spl. Edn., Boston U., 1969, Ed.D. in Spl. Edn., 1974. Tchr. Weymouth pub. schs. (Mass.), 1958-60; spl. edn. instr. Boston U., 1972-74; asst. prof. in spl. edn. Bridgewater State Coll., (Mass.), 1974-79, assoc. prof., 1979-83, prof., 1983—, chmn. spl. edn. dept., 1979-87, coordinator dept. grad. programs, 1979-87, adminstr. bilingual spl. edn. training grant, 1983-86, dean grad. sch., 1987—. Co-author human service workers curriculum materials. Boston U. fellow, 1967-74; 3 Disting. Service awards, Bridgewater State Coll., 1980, 82, 85; Bilingual Spl. Edn. grantee, 1980, 83. Mem. Council Exceptional Children (Mass. chpt. founder, past pres.), Mass. Assn. Children With Learning Disabilities (past v.p.), Phi Delta Kappa, Pi Lambda Theta. Democrat. Roman Catholic. Home: 138 Bedford St Lakeville MA 02346 Office: Bridgewater State Coll Grad Sch Conant Sci Bldg Bridgewater MA 02324

BARRY, MARY ALICE, financial executive; b. Quincy, Mass., Dec. 31, 1928; d. Lawrence Joseph and Alice Mary (Blaisdell) B. BS, Emmanuel Coll., 1950; postgrad., N.Y. U. With FBI, Boston, 1950-56, Investment Co. Inst., N.Y.C., 1958-59; With Dreyfus Fund, N.Y.C., 1959-62; corp. sec. The Alliance Fund, Inc., 1965—, Surveyor Fund, Inc., 1966—; asst. v.p. Alliance Capital Mgmt. Corp., N.Y.C., 1985—; corp. sec. Alliance Growth and Income Fund, Inc., 1986—; Alliance Balanced Shares, Inc. Home: 520 E 81st

St Apt 6A New York NY 10028 Office: Alliance Capital Mgmt Corp 1345 Ave of Americas New York NY 10105

BARRY, MARYANNE TRUMP, judge; b. 1937; d. Fred C. and Mary Trump. BA, Mt. Holyoke Coll., 1958; MA, Columbia U., 1962; JD, Hofstra U., 1974. Asst. U.S. Atty., 1974-75, dep. chief appeals div., 1976-77, chief appeals div., 1977-82, exec. asst. U.S. Atty., 1981-82, 1st asst., 1981-83; judge U.S. Dist. Ct., N.J., 1983—. Office: US Dist Ct PO & Courthouse Bldg PO Box 999 Newark NJ 07102*

BARRY, PAMELA JANE, cabinet minister, Canadian provincial legislator; b. Halifax, N.S., Can., July 10, 1944; d. John W. and Constance Baird; m. David G. Barry; children: Patrick, Jonathan, Colin, Ryan, Gregor. Student, Mt. St. Vincent's U., 1961-62, 62-63; BSc cum laude, St. Francis Xavier U., Antigonish, N.S., Can., 1965. Chemistry rsch. asst. U. Alta., Can.; chemist Atlantic Sugar Refinery, St. John, N.S., Can.; mem. Legis. Assembly, St. John, 1987-89; minister Ministry of State for Childhood Svcs., Fredericton, N.B., Can., 1989—; co-chairperson Parents & Early Childhood Edn. Task Force, 1985. Pres. St. John Coop., 1982-84; past pres. St. John Coop. Presch.; dir. Lyalist Days, 1980-84, St. John West Liberal Assn., 1984-87; bd. dirs. St. John United Way, 1985-86; chmn. Red Sheild Appeal, 1990, St. John; past trustee Dist 20 Sch. Bd. Mem. St. Francis Xavier Alumni Assn., Univ. Women's Club. Office: Min of State for, Childhood Svcs, PO Box 5100, King St Carleton Pl, Fredericton, NB Canada E3B 5G8

BARRY, PATRICIA POUND, educator of medicine; b. Winter Haven, Fla., June 13, 1941; d. James Al and Arlene Myrle (Ortmeyer); m. David Marshall Barry, June 15, 1963; 1 child, David John. BS in Chemistry, William & Mary Coll., 1963; MD, U. South Fla., 1975; MPH, Boston U., 1987. Diplomate Am. Bd. Internal Medicine. Rsch. chemist Abbott Labs., North Chicago, Ill., 1963-66; asst. prof. U. South Fla., Tampa, Fla., 1979-84, Boston U., 1984-87; assoc. prof. U. Miami Sch. Medicine, 1987—; resident in internal medicine U. South Fla. Hosps., Tampa, 1975-78; chief resident Tampa Gen. Hosp., 1978-79; attending physician in medicine Jackson Meml. Hosp., Miami VA Hosp., 1987—, Jackson Meml. Hosp. Ambulatory Care Clinic, 1987—. Contbr. numerous articles to profl. jours. Bd. dirs. Women's Survival Ctr., Tampa, 1978-81, pres. 1979-80; vol. physician Judeo-Christian Coalition Clinic, Tampa, 1979-84; adv. com. Easter Seals, 1982-84; med. adv. bd. Fla. Dept. Motor Vehicles, 1983-84; profl. adv. com. Family Svc. of Greater Boston, 1986-87; adv. bd. Medicare Alzheimer's Program, Miami Jewish Home and Hosp., 1989—. Recipient Geriatric Medicine Acad. award NIH, 1981; numerous grants. Fellow Am. Geriatrics Soc. (bd. dirs. 1980—), Am. Coll. Physicians; mem. Am. Pub. Health Assn., Gerontol. Soc. Am., Alpha Omega Alpha. Office: U Miami Sch Medicine PO Box 016960 Miami FL 33101

BARRY, SUSAN BROWN, writer, manufacturer; b. San Antonio, Tex., Sept. 14, 1944; d. Earl A. Jr. and Betty (Galt) Brown; m. Richard Hanley Barry, June 25, 1966 (div. 1973); children: Andrew Earl, Brice Galt. AB, Sweet Briar (Va.) Coll., 1966. Lic. real estate agt. Houston, 1983—; scriptwriter Stas. KUHT-TV, KDOG-TV, KEYT Radio, Houston, 1972-77; originator, adminstr., cons. publ. program Rice U., Houston, 1977-79; liaison book promotion Dell. Publs., Viking Pubs., and others, Houston, 1979-85; pres. Savage Designs, Houston, 1985-88; cons. U. Calif., Santa Barbara, 1985; rare book, manuscript cataloguer, writer Randall House Rare Books. Book critic Houston Post; designer greeting cards Neiman-Marcus Dept. Stores; writer Bicentennial Play, Houston Pub. Schs. (now in Nat. Achives). Mem. Santa Barbara Com. on Fgn. Relations, hospice team; founding coord. Reach to Recovery Program regional Am. Cancer Soc. Mem. Jr. League (numerous coms. and chairmanships), The Asia Soc. (adv. com., fin. chmn. Houston chpt. 1984-85). Republican. Unitarian. Home and Office: PO Box 5789 Santa Barbara CA 93150

BARRY, TERESA TRUPIANO, history educator; b. Marshall, Mich., Jan. 15, 1950; d. Stephen Frank and Ernestine Viola (Lake) Trupiano; m. David Nathan Barry, Oct. 1, 1988. BS in Education, Ea. Mich. U., 1972; MA in History, We. Mich. U., 1985. Tour dir. Marshall (Mich.) Hist. Soc., 1983; intern Charlton Pk. Village & Mus., Hastings, Mich., 1984, edn. curator, 1985-89; instr. Kellogg Community Coll., Battle Creek, Mich., 1987—; lectr. Nazareth Coll., Kalamazoo, 1989—. Contbr. articles to profl. jours. State of Mich. scholar., 1968, Mich. Mus. Assoc., 1983, Fellow Kellogg Found. Field Mus., 1986. Mem. AAUW, Am. Assn. State Local Hist. Socs., Hastings Woman's Club, Barry County Geneal. Soc.

BART, POLLY TURNER, realtor; b. Peterborough, N.H., Feb. 28, 1944; d. Benjamin Franklin and Catherine (James) B.; m. Harry Nelson Pharr II, Oct. 27, 1969 (div. May 1972); 1 child, Greta Rose. BA, Radcliffe Coll., 1965; M in City Planning, U. Calif., Berkeley, 1974, PhD, 1979. Cons. city planning Marshall Kaplan, Gans, & Kahn, San Francisco, 1967; city planner County of Napa, Calif., 1968-69; asst. instr. U. Tex., Austin, 1971-72; cons. Dept. HUD, Washington, 1979-81; asst. prof. U. Md., College Park, 1981-84; real estate salesperson Coldwell Banker Comml. Real Estate Services, Balt., 1984-87; pres. Investment Properties Brokerage, Inc., Balt., 1988—; bd. dirs. assoc. Columbia Forum, Md., 1981-85; contbr. Nat Urban Policy Report to Congress, 1980. Co-editor EDRA, 1981; contbr. Nat. Urban Policy Report to Congress; contbr. articles to profl. jours. Mem. Balt. Symphony Chorus. Fellow Radcliffe Coll., 1962-64, Danforth Found., 1975-79, Ford Found., 1981. Mem. Comml. Real Estate Women (founder, treas. 1987). Home: 629 S Hanover St Baltimore MD 21230 Office: Investment Properties Brokerage Inc 629 S Hanover St Baltimore MD 21230

BARTEL, LAVON LEE, university administrator, food scientist; b. Salem, Oreg., Nov. 12, 1951; d. Harvey C. Bartel and Jeanne Marie (Siddall) Bartel Shelton; m. David George Struck, Sept. 14, 1974. BS with honors, Oreg. State U., 1973, MS, 1975; PhD, U. Wis., 1979. Registered dietitian; cert. home economist. Teaching asst. Oreg. State U., Corvallis, 1973-75; rsch. asst. U. Wis., Madison, 1975-79; asst. prof. Whittier (Calif.) Coll., 1979-82; asst. prof. U. Vt., Burlington, 1982-87, extension specialist Extension Svc., 1987-89, assoc. dean, dir., 1989—; cons. Vt. food industry, 1982-89; bd. dirs. Earth's Best, Middlebury, Vt., 1984-88. Contbr. articles to profl. jours. Mem. Vt. Dietetic Assn. (pres. 1989-90, chair coun. of practice 1987-88), Vt. Home Econs. Assn. (sec.-treas. 1987-89), Inst. Food Technologists, Am. Pub. Health Assn., Assn. Women in Sci., Phi Kappa Phi. Office: UVM-Extension Svc 103 Morrill Hall Burlington VT 05405

BARTEL, TINA SLEMMER, advertising publisher; b. L.A., Aug. 5, 1954; d. Frank Charles and Aldona Charlotte (Anderson) Slemmer; m. John Ervin Bartel (div. May 1975); m. Loren Jay Donnell (div. Dec. 1978); 1 child, Jennoah S. AA in Air Transport, Orange Coast Coll., Costa Mesa, Calif., 1979; Advanced Lang. Degree, Desk Sprach Kolleg, Munich, West Germany, 1985; BS in Law, Western State U., San Diego, 1986. Lic. comml. pilot. Real estate sales and mktg. Mission Viejo (Calif.) Co., 1973-75; sr. mktg. rep. The Hartford Ins. Group, Norwalk, Calif., 1975-77; mktg. exec. Piper Aircraft Dealers, Calif., 1978-85; mng. ptnr. syndications Eastgate Fin. Planners, LaJolla, Calif., 1981-83; v.p. internat. and new bus. Calibre Mktg., Inc., Munich and Newport Beach, Calif., 1985-88, pub. ESP: Directory of Executive Suite Offices div., 1988—. Author various books on religion. Active in Friends of Santa Ana Zoo, Orange County Performing Arts Ctr., Air Safety Found. Republican. Office: Calibre Mktg 3857 Birch St Ste 400 Newport Beach CA 92660

BARTELL, NANCY KRAMER, human resources professional; b. Binghamton, N.Y., Nov. 23, 1941; d. Donald W. and Gladys M. (Dorion) Kramer; m. John R. Bartell, Aug. 19, 1967; children: Kevin, Mary, Patrice. BA, Dunbarton Coll. Holy Cross, Washington, 1963; MSW, Fordham U., 1966. Cert. social worker, N.Y. Field instr. SUNY, Alfred, 1980—; asst. dir. St. James Mercy Hosp., Hornell, N.Y., 1977-86, now dir. hosp. social work, 1986—; bd. dirs. So. Tier Hospice, 1989—. Mem. Steuben County Aging Svcs. Coalition, 1985—. Mem. Nat. Assn. Social Workers, Soc. Hosp. Social Work Dirs. Home: 7 Pearl St Hornell NY 14843 Office: St James Mercy Hosp 411 Canisteo St Hornell NY 14843

BARTELSTONE, RONA SUE, gerontologist; b. Bklyn., Jan. 10, 1951; d. Herbert and Hazel (Mittman) Canarick; m. Alan Joel Markowitz. BS in Social Welfare, SUNY, Buffalo, 1972; MSW, Ind. U., 1974. Licensed Clin. Social Worker, Fla. Diplomate of Social Work. Social worker YM-YWHA of Greater N.Y., 1974-75; dist. supr. N.Y.C. Housing Authority, Bklyn., 1975-77; field instr. Barry U. Sch. Social Work, 1980-81; project dir. United Family & Children's Svcs., 1977-81; faculty Miami Dade Community Coll., 1981-82; adult educator Sch. Bd. Dade County, 1981-82; med. social worker Mederi Home Health Agy., 1979-82; adj. faculty NOVA U., 1982-88; pvt. practice Rona Bartelstone Assocs., Inc., North Miami Beach, Fla., 1981—; cons. and trainer in field. Contbr. articles to various mags. Bd. dirs. Jewish Vocat. Svcs., Miami, 1985—; funding panel Area Agy. on Aging, Miami, 1985-89; mem. Friends of the Family Counseling Svcs., Miami, 1983-88. Recipient Dade County Citizen of the Yr. award, 1982, NASW Social Worker of the Yr. award, 1982-83, Trail Blazer award, 1984, Up & Comers award in health care Price Waterhouse and So. Fla. Bus. Jour., 1990. Mem. Assn. Pvt. Geriatric Care Mgrs. (pres. 1988—), Nat. Assn. Social Workers (treas. 1987-89), Gerontology Soc. Am., Nat. Coun. on Aging, Am. Soc. on Aging. Democrat. Jewish. Home: 5005 Collins Ave #903 Miami Beach FL 33140 Office: Rona Bartelstone Assocs Inc 1380 Miami Gardens Dr #260 North Miami FL 33179

BARTELS WILKINSON, JAMI ELIZABETH, innkeeper, rancher, art consultant, artist; b. Armstrong, Iowa, July 16, 1941; d. Homer Wesley and Dorothy Irene (Bunday) Wilkinson; m. Donald Lee Bartels, June 30, 1974; 1 child by previous marriage, Dina Lyn. Student Drake U., 1959; A.A., Orange Coast Coll., 1971; student Napa Valley Coll., 1980-82. Office mgr., asst. to v.p. Zinsco Elec. Products, Los Angeles, 1963-65; office mgr. Raif Realty Inc., Montebello, Calif., 1965-67; gen. mgr. Chris-Craft West, Inc., Newport Beach, Calif., 1967-69; exec. dir. Orange Coast Coll. Vol. Bur., Costa Mesa, Calif., 1970-72; v.p. Newport Pacific, Inc., Newport Beach, 1972-74; owner Willow House Antiques, El Sobrante, Calif., 1974-80; owner Bartels Ranch & Country Inn, St. Helena, Calif., 1979—; ptnr. Bartels Realtors & Investments, St. Helena, Richmond, Calif., 1974—; dir. Napa Valley Repertory, Calistoga, Calif., 1985—. Chmn. Christian Bookstore Benefit, Grace Episcopal, St. Helena, Calif., 1981; chmn. membership Napa Valley Symphony Assn., St. Helena, 1985; chmn. Hearts for the Arts Benefit, St. Helena, 1986; co-founder, dir., pres. Napa County Arts Council, Yountville, Calif., 1980-84; state/local planner Calif. Arts Council/Napa County Arts Council, Napa, Calif., 1982-83; bd. dirs. Napa Valley Visitors Assn., Napa, 1985—; U.S. Friendship Ambassador to Japan, 1978. Named Saleswoman of Yr., Bayliner Boat Corp., Orcas Island, Wash., 1973-74. Mem. Am. Bed and Breakfast Assn., Wine Country Artists (v.p. 1984), Napa Valley Bed and Breakfast Innkeepers Assn. (v.p. 1984), Bed and Breakfast Innkeepers No. Calif. (dir. 1984-86), Calif. Lodging Industry Assn., Napa County C. of C., St. Helena C. of C. (dir. 1985-86), Epsilon Sigma Alpha. Republican. Lutheran. Club: Orange Coast Coll Law (Costa Mesa, Calif.) (pres. 1969-70). Avocations: art, internat. travel, wine appreciation. Office: 1200 Conn Valley Rd St Helena CA 94574

BARTELT, DORIS ANN, systems specialist; b. Elgin, Ill., June 18, 1955; d. Otto John and Geraldine Joyce (Rydell) B. BBA, U. Wis., Eau Claire, 1977. Systems analyst Wausau (Wis.) Ins. Co., 1977-78, St. Paul Co., 1979-80; cons. Cytrol, Inc., Edina, Minn., 1980-87; mgr. bus. systems United HealthCare, Inc., Mpls., 1987-89; project leader Carlson Cos., Inc., Mpls., 1989—. Office: 12755 State Hwy 55 Plymouth MN 55441

BARTER, BARBARA ANN, medical record administrator; b. Washington, Oct. 2, 1934; d. Ferdinand Eldon and Eleanor B. (Crislip) Hopper; m. H. Wallace Barter, July 31, 1954 (dec. 1957); 1 child, Andy Wallace; m. Francis Byrne, Apr. 30, 1960 (div. 1968); 1 child, Katherine Lynne Byrne Mills. Cert. in practical nursing, U. Fla., 1959; BS, U. Cen. Fla., 1972. Consulting med. records adminstr. various nursing homes, Orlando, Fla., 1969-72; dir. med. records St. Mary's Hosp., West Palm, Fla., 1972-75, North Trident Regional Hosp., Charleston, S.C., 1975-76; cons. med. records B & J Consulting, Greenville, N.C., 1979; dir. med. record dept. Brownsville (Tex.) Med. Ctr., 1976-79; dir. med. record utilization rev. Littlefield (Tex.) Med. Ctr., 1979-80; dir. quality assurance and utilization rev. dept. East Liverpool (Ohio) City Hosp., 1980-85, dir. med. record dept., 1985-87; dir. med. record quality assurance and risk mgmt. depts. Fishermen's Hosp., Marathon, Fla., 1988—; cons. Community Mental Health Ctr., West Palm, 1973-75, Nursing Home, East Liverpool, 1982-87; instr. directed practice Fla. Tech. U., Orlando, 1973-75, Southwest Univ. Tex., San Marcos, 1977-79. TReas. Luth. Ch., Big Pine Key, Fla., 1988-90. Mem. Am. Med. Record Assn., Fla. Med. Record Assn. (del. 1974, bylaws chair 1973), Fla. Soc. Risk Mgrs., Fla. Hosp. Assn., Am. Bd. Quality Assurance/Utilization Rev., Parents Without Ptnrs. (bd. dirs. West Palm unit 1972-75), Bus. and Profl. Women (charter mem. East Liverpool, asst. treas. 1982-87, bd. dirs. Brownsville, Tex. 1977-79). Democrat. Home: PO Box 93 Key Colony Beach FL 33051 Office: Fishermens Hosp 3301 Overseas Hwy Marathon FL 33050

BARTER, RUBY SUNSHINE, real estate professional; b. Omaha; d. Harry and Ruth (Gilman) Kolnick; m. Gerson Barter; children: Bruce, Mark, Sharon Sunshine Silverman, Peggy Sunshine Hittelman, Jeffrey, Randi Sunshine Simon, JoAnne Sunshine Trombley, Ronald Sunshine. BS in Med. Tech., Creighton U.; postgrad., Clarkson Meml. Hosp. Sch. Med. Tech., U. Colo. Sch. Continuing Edn. Cert. Comml.-Investment Mems. Med. technologist Creighton Meml. St. Joseph Hosp.; realtor Nat. Real Estate and Mgmt. Co., Heller-Mark & Co., Walpin & Co., Denver; mem. Mayors Adv. Com. on Denver's War on Poverty; project dir. Denver Citywide Headstart Vols.; mem. adv. com. Dialogue Regis Coll.; mem. exec. com. Anti-Defamation League, Hillel Councils; vol. Nat. Jewish Hosp., Jewish Community Ctr.; mem. exec. bd. Beth Joseph Congregation; active Adult Edn. Council Denver, Internat. House, Dolls for Democracy Lady Denver Pub. Schs. Mem. Nat. Real Estate Commn., Colo. Real Estate Commn., Denver Real Estate Commn. (liaison com.), Bd. Realtors, Real Estate Exchangers, Realtors Nat. Mktg. Inst., Real Estate Securities Syndication Inst. Home: 201 S Dexter St Denver CO 80222 Office: 1550 E 17th Ave Denver CO 80218

BARTHEL, CHERYL ANN, director member services/director marketing; b. Lakewood, Ohio, Sept. 29, 1961; d. David Lee and Rita Arlene (Bihn) Block; m. Michael Ernest Barthel, Sept. 13, 1986. Student, Miami U., Oxford, Ohio, 1979-81; BS/Mktg. summa cum laude, Ohio State U., 1983. Cert. exercise leader, aerobics, Am. Coll. Sports Medicine, Aerobics Fitness Assn. Am. Sales coordinator Holiday Inn, Atlanta, 1983-84; sales rep. NCR Corp., Atlanta, 1984-87; mem. svcs. mgr. Tucker (Ga.) Racquet Fitness Ctr., 1987-89; dir. mem. svcs., dir. mktg. YMCA of Cobb County, Marietta, Ga., 1989—. Mem. Aerobics and Fitness Assn. Am., Excellence in Exercise, Reebok Instr. Alliance, Women's Sports Found., Beta Gamma Sigma. Republican. Roman Catholic. Home: 2743 Elmhurst Blvd Kennesaw GA 30144 Office: YMCA of Cobb County 1055 E Piedmont Marietta GA 30062

BARTHEL, HAZEL PHOEBE, health care executive; b. Young America, Minn., Oct. 13, 1933; d. Clarence William and Phoebe Emilie (Affeldt) Schwich; m. Bruce Owen Barthel, July 14, 1956 (div. Feb. 1985); children: Lisa Ellen, Larry, Scott, Paul. BS in Edn., U. Utah, 1955; MBA, Wayland Bapt. U., 1988. Tchr. Good Shepherd Luth. Sch., Englewood, Calif., 1955-56; coordinator music Grace Luth. Ch., Midland, Tex., 1974-77; edn. coordinator St. Anthony's Hospice, Amarillo, Tex., 1983-85, asst. dir., 1985-86; exec. dir. Hospice of the Plains, Plainview, Tex., 1986-89; pres. Monarch Care Resources, Irving, Tex., 1989-90; program dir. family hospice Irving, 1990—; tchr. Clarendon Jr. Coll., Pampa, Tex., 1987; cons. Hospice of Pampa, 1988-89. Mem. exec. bd. Rep. Women's Club, Midland, Tex., 1968; vol. coordinator St. Anthony's Hospice, Amarillo, 1982-86; bd. dirs. Tex. Hospice Orgn., 1988—, ethics and stds. com., 1987—, treas.,1989—. Mem. Am. Guild of Organists (dean Midland chpt. 1976-77), Petroleum Engr. Wives Club (pres. 1980-81). Home: 1407 Scott Ct Irving TX 75060

BARTHMARE, LYNN BARBARA, health care agency administrator; b. Long Island, N.Y., Feb. 16, 1951; d. William E. and Janice H. (Rowley) Pritchett; m. Dennis A. Barthmare; children: Stefanie, Jaime, Adam. BS in Nursing, Adelphi U., 1979, MA, 1984; AAS, SUNY, Farmingdale, 1971. RN, N.Y. Fin. program analyst Long Island Jewish Med. Ctr.-Hillside Div., New Hyde Park, N.Y., 1984-87, adminstrv. asst., 1987; dir. nursing Aides at Home, Inc., Hicksville, N.Y., 1987-89; now regional dir. Contemporary Home Care Svcs./div. of Medlinc, Inc., Mineola, N.Y., 1989—. Mem. Health Care Providers, Inc. (L.I., N.Y. state chpt.). Mem. NAFE, Delta Tau Alpha, Sigma Theta Tau. Home: 2 Lantern Rd Hicksville NY 11801 Office: 200 Old Country Rd Mineola NY 11501

BARTHOLD, CLEMENTINE B., judge; b. Odessa, Russia, Jan. 11, 1921; came to U.S., 1925; d. Joseph Anton and Magdalene (Richter) Schwan; m. Edward Brendel Barthold, July 5, 1941 (dec.); children—Judith Anne Barthold DeSimone, John Edward; m. Joel L. Stokes, Jr., Feb. 7, 1981. Student Aberdeen Bus. Coll., 1940; B.G.S., Ind. U. Southeast, 1978; J.D., Ind. U.-Indpls., 1980. Bar: Ind. 1980, U.S. Dist. Ct. (so. dist.) Ind., 1980. Sec. and asst. to mgr. Clark County C. of C. (Ind.), 1959-60; chief probation officer Clark Circuit Ct. and Superior Cts., Jeffersonville, 1960-72; research cons. Pub. Action Correctional Effort, Clark and Floyd Counties, 1972-75; instl. parole officer Ind. Women's Prison, Indpls., 1975-80; atty. State of Ind., 1980-83; judge Clark Superior Ct. No. 1, Jeffersonville, 1983—. Active in developing and implementing juvenile delinquency prevention and alternative programs, group counseling for juvenile delinquents and restitution programs. Treas. Ladies Elks Aux., Jeffersonville. Recipient Good Govt. award Jeffersonville Jaycees, 1966, Good Citizenship award, 1967; Wonder Woman award, 1984, Robert J. Kinsey award, 1986, Sagamore of Wabash award, 1986, Outstanding Community Service award Social Concerns League, Jeffersonville, 1966, Disting. Service award, Outstanding Contbn. to Field of Correction award, Women of Achievement award, Jeff BPW Appreciation award, Juvenile Justice award, Disting. Contemporary Women in History award, Disting. Leadership award. Mem. ABA, Ind. Bar Assn., Clark County Bar Assn., Ind. Correctional Assn. (pres. 1971, Disting. Service award 1967, 85), Nat. Assn. Women Judges, Ind. Judges Assn., Nat. and Ind. Juvenile and Family Ct. Judges (task force), Am. Judges Assn., NAACP, Jeff Preservation, Inc., Ind. U. Alumni Assn., Howard Steamboat Mus., LWV, Bus. and Profl. Women's Club. Democrat. Roman Catholic. Home: 948 E 7th St Jeffersonville IN 47130 Office: Clark Superior Ct No 1 500 E Court Ave Jeffersonville IN 47130

BARTHOLOMEW, ALICE JEAN, secondary education educator; b. Redbank, N.J., Dec. 4, 1941; d. Dwight Franklin and Cecilia (Silverman) B.; m. David Meyer Newby, June 30, 1962 (div. 1975); children: Jessica, Ethan. BA in French with honors, U. Calif., 1962; postgrad., Calif. State U., 1978, 85, Dominican Coll., San Rafael, Calif., 1989. Claims authorizer Social Security Adminstrn., San Francisco, 1962-65; freelance writer, editor Fairfax, Calif., 1976-80; owner In Other Words Editorial and Graphic Design, Fairfax, 1980—; tchr. Tamalpais Union High Sch. Dist., San Anselmo, Calif., 1984—; editor newsletter Northbay Women's Network, Corte Madera, Calif., 1983-85; team leader North Bay Internat. Studies Project, Marin, Sonoma, Calif., 1986—; liaison Echanges France Amerique du Nord, Paris, 1987—. Contbr. articles to profl. jours. Rockefeller Found. fellow, 1988. Mem. Am. Assn. Tchrs. of French, Fgn. Lang. Tchrs. Assn. of No. Calif. Democrat. Home: 112 Toyon Dr Fairfax CA 94930 Office: Sir Francis Drake High 1327 Sir Francis Drake Blvd San Anselmo CA 94960

BARTHOLOMEW, ANITA, freelance advertising writer; b. Bay Shore, N.Y., Jan. 14, 1949; d. Guido and Elizabeth (Ornato) Del Giudice m. Frank J. Tomaino, Oct. 5, 1968 (div.); 1 child, Alexander G. Tomaino. Student, SUNY, Purchase, 1981-83, Sch. Visual Arts, N.Y.C., 1984. Copywriter Ventura Assocs., N.Y.C., 1982-83, Equity Advt., N.Y.C., 1983-84, Pace Advt., N.Y.C., 1984-85; prin. Anita Bartholomew Communications, Tarrytown, N.Y., 1985—; freelance copywriter Donnelley Mktg., Holt, Rinehart/CBS Pub., SAS Airlines, The Luce Corp., Westchester Women's News, numerous others. Contbr. articles to profl. jours. Vol. Trans-Species Unlimited. Mem. Am. Soc. for Psychical Research, People for the Ethical Treatment of Animals, Internat. Women's Writing Guild, Mensa.

BARTHOLOMEW, CHERYL GIBBONS, psychotherapy educator; b. Neptune, N.J., Oct. 1, 1943; d. Archer Gibbons and Blondine (Bohler) Reddick; m. Stephen C. Bartholomew, June 10, 1967 (div. 1974); 1 child, Nathan Bartholomew; m. michael F. Emig, June 28, 1987. BA in English and Humanities, Ohio Wesleyan U., Delaware, 1965; MEd in Counseling, Westfield (Mass.) State Coll., 1974; PhD in Counseling, Syracuse (N.Y.) U., 1980. Cert. counselor. Tchr. English Joslin St. Sch., Providence, 1966-67, Cherry Hill (N.J.) Jr. High Sch., 1967-68, Barrington (R.I.) Jr. High Sch., 1968-69, Peck Jr. High Sch., Barrington, 1969-70; editorial asst. Water Pollution Control Fedn., Washington, 1965-66; dir. South County Help Phone, Great Barringotn, Mass., 1970-74; asst. prof. SUNY, Oswego, 1980-83, assoc. prof., 1983-89; assoc. prof. psychotherpy George Mason U., Fairfax, Va., 1989—; pvt. clin. practice counselor, Syracuse, 1977-80, Oswego, 1980-89, Falls Church, 1989—; dir. Community Career Counseling Ctr., SUNY, Oswego, 1986-89. Author: What's Wrong With This Practice, 1989; editor N.Y. State Counseling and Devel., 1986-88; editorial rev. bd. N.Y. Jour. Counseling and Devel., 1987-90, Career Info. Rev. Svc. Career Devel. Quar., 1989—. Dir. VISTA, Great Barrington, Mass., 1971-74. Recipient Merit Teaching award SUNY, Oswego, 1980, 81, 82, Rsch. Stipend, 1985, Svc. Above Self award Rotary Club Internat., Oswego, 1983, 84, 85, 86. Mem. Nat. Assn. Rsch. and Counseling Suprs. (pres. 1984), N.Y. State Assn. Counselors, Educators and Suprs. (pres. 1981-83). Office: George Mason U Robinson I Rm 3315 Fairfax VA 22030

BARTHOLOMEW, LYNN MICHELE, merchandising executive, designer, optician; b. Louisville, June 10, 1949; d. Richard Deitz and Bette Jean (Beisler) B. BS, Ind. U., 1971, postgrad., 1987—. Lic. optician, Ky. Office mgr. James A. Way, MD, Bloomington, Ind., 1972-76; office mgr., apprentice optician William J. Collis, Pub. Svc. Co., Lexington, Ky., 1977-78; pvt. practice Lexington, 1978-79; owner, optician Bourbon County Optical Co., Paris, Ky., 1980; optician Gates, Stockler, Lenz Opticians, Louisville, 1980-84; buyer Precision Lens Crafters, Cin., 1984, gen. merchandising mgr., 1985-87, dir. product devel. U.S. Shoe-Optical divs., 1987-88; v.p. E.D.B. Holdings, Inc., Milford, Ohio, 1988-89; chief exec. officer Seven Hills Eyewear, Inc., Glendale, Ohio, 1989—. Author, editor: Basic Optics for Precision Lens Crafters Associates, 1984. Mem. Young Dems. of Ky., Louisville, 1978-80. Mem. Ky. Opticians Assn., YMCA. Roman Catholic. Clubs: Northlake Athletic (Cin.), Scandinavian Health (Cin.). Office: 30 Brandywine Dr Glendale OH 45246

BARTLE, ANNETTE GRUBER (MRS. THOMAS R. BARTLE), artist, writer, photographer; Came to U.S., 1940; d. Henry and Maria (Harczyk) Gruber; m. Thomas R. Bartle, Dec. 5, 1957; 1 child, Eve Marie. Bacheliere, Sorbonne, Paris, 1940; BA, Elmira Coll., Paris, 1943; student, Ecole des Beaux Arts, Paris, 1940, Art Student League (scholar 1949), 1947-50. One-woman shows include: Midtown Galleries, N.Y.C., 1957, 60, 63, 66, Feingarten, Chgo., 1957, Wickersham Gallery, 1970; exhibited in group shows: AAAL, 1963, Detroit Art Inst., 1958, 62, 65, 67, Pa. Acad., 1959, 60, 66, Butler Art Inst., 1960, 64, 65, Cin. Art Mus., 1960, 62, 67; represented in permanent collections: Am. Internat. Underwriters, Union Carbide, Conn. Mut. Life, Mural Port Authority Heliport, N.Y. Worlds Fair; author: African Enchantment, 1980; contbr. articles and photographs to mags., newspapers, jours. including: N.Y. Times, Christian Sci. Monitor, Phila. Inquirer, Los Angeles Times, Palm Beach Life, Travel Weekly, Diverson, American Way, Senior World, numerous others. Active various community drives. Pan Am. Travelling fellow, 1950; recipient citation for outstanding achievements 90th U.S. Congress, 1968. Mem. Am. Fedn. Arts, Artists Equity, Travel Journalists Guild Ltd. Address: 231 E 76th St New York NY 10021

BARTLE, MARLA JO, computer consultant; b. Roswell, N.Mex., Feb. 4, 1964; d. Richard Charles and JoAnn Marlene (Moore) B. BA, Sonoma State U., 1986. Computer cons. CBS, Sacramento, 1986-87; acctg. asst. Royal Constrn. Co., Sacramento, 1987-88; adminstr. Logan Enterprises, Inc., Rancho Cordova, Calif., 1988—; ind. computer cons., Sacramento, 1987—. Organizer fundraiser for local charities including Cystic Fibrosis Soc., Stanford Kidney Rsch. Found., Sacramento, 1989. Mem. NAFE, Beta Sigma Phi. Home: 8759 LaRinera Dr #197 Sacramento CA 95826

BARTLETT, BONNIE, actress; d. E.E. and Carrie Bartlett; m. William Daniels; 2 children: Michael, Robert. Grad., Northwestern U.; studied with Lee Strasberg, N.Y.C. Appeared in TV series Love of Life, Little House on the Prairie, St. Elsewhere, 1982-88, TV miniseries Ike, 1979, Celebrity, 1984, The Deliberate Stranger, 1986, TV films Murder or Mercy, 1974, The Legend of Lizzie Borden, 1975, Killer on Board, 1977, A Death in Canaan, 1978, A Perfect Match, 1980, A Long Way Home, 1981, Dempsey, 1983,

Malice in Wonderland, 1985, film Twins, 1988. Recipient Emmy award Acad. TV Arts and Scis., 1986, 87. Office: care Harry Gold & Assocs 12725 Ventura Blvd Ste E Studio City CA 91604*

BARTLETT, DIANE SUE, mental health counselor; b. Laconia, N.H., Dec. 6, 1947; d. Fred Elmer and Dorothy Pearl (Wakefield) Davis; m. Josiah Henry Bartlett, Aug. 23, 1980; 1 child by previous marriage, Fred Louis Hacker; 1 step child, Juliet. AA, Plymouth State Coll., 1982; B in Gen. Studies summa cum laude, U. N.H. Sch. for Lifelong Learning, 1984; MEd., Plymouth State Coll., 1988. Police communications specialist Div. Motor Vehicles, Concord, N.H., 1970-76, br. office mgr., 1976-83, coordinator motor vehicles registrations, 1983-84; tax collector City of Dover, N.H., 1984; intern Lakes Region Mental Health Div., Laconia, N.H., 1985; counselor Latchkey Pastoral Counseling, Laconia, 1984-87; family therapist, Children's Best Interest, Laconia, 1988—; psychotherapist Carroll County Mental Health Svcs., Wolfeboro, N.H., 1988—. Mem. Town of Moultonboro Sch. Feasibility Study Commn., 1978; adminstrv. bd. mem., chmn. pastor-parish relations com. United Meth. Ch., Moultonboro, N.H., 1983—, N.H. annual conf., 1986-88, participant N.H. Ann. Conf. on Status and Role of Women, Concord, 1985—. N.H. Charitable Found. grantee, 1985. Avocations: skiing, swimming, reading, writing. Home: PO Box 14 Moultonboro NH 03254

BARTLETT, JANELL ALISON, marketing professional, special events coordinator; b. Lafayette, Ind., Apr. 28, 1965; d. Dale Eugene and Judy Mae (Stover) B. BA in Journalism and Advt., Ball State U., 1987. Spl. events coord. Lakeview Square Assocs., Battle Creek, Mich., 1987—. Named Young Career Woman, Bus. and Profl. Women, U.S.A., 1988. Mem. Women in Communications Inc. (publicity dir. Kalamazoo, Mich. chpt. 1989—), Battle Creek Jaycees (com. chair of various events 1988—0. Methodist. Office: Lakeview Sq Assocs 5775 Beckley Rd Battle Creek MI 49017

BARTLETT, JANETH MARIE, pharmacist; b. Cooperstown, N.Y., Sept. 10, 1946; d. Harold C. and Emily Bush (Walker) B. BS in Pharmacy, Temple U., 1969, MS, 1971; PhD, Rutgers U., 1981. Registered pharmacist. Rsch. assoc. E. R. Squibb and Sons, New Brunswick, N.J., 1970-73, asst. rsch. investor, 1973-81; asst. prof. Purdue U., West Lafayette, Ind., 1981-86; rsch. assoc. Dow Chem., Midland, Mich., 1986—. Contbr. articles to profl. jours. Mem. Soc. Nuclear Medicine, Am. Assn. Advance sci., Reg. Affairs Prof. Soc. Office: Dow Chem Co CR Bioproducts 1701 Bldg Midland MI 48674

BARTLETT, JENNIFER LOSCH, artist; b. Long Beach, Calif., Mar. 14, 1941. B.A., Mills Coll., 1963; B.F.A., Yale U., 1964, M.F.A., 1965; studied with Jack Tworkvov, James Rosenquist, Al Held, Jim Dire. Instr. Sch. Visual Arts, N.Y.C. One-woman shows include Mills Coll., Oakland, Calif., 1963, Reese Paley Gallery, N.Y.C., 1972, Paula Cooper Gallery, N.Y.C., 1974, 76, 77, 79, 81, 82, 83, Saman Gallery, Genoa, Italy, 1974, John Doyle Gallery, Chgo., 1975, Contemporary Art Ctr., Cin., 1976, Dartmouth Coll., 1976, Wadsworth Atheneum, Hartford, Conn., 1977, San Francisco Mus. Modern Art, 1978, U. Calif., Irvine, 1978, Hansen-Fuller Gallery, San Francisco, 1978, Balt. Art Mus., 1978, Margo Leavin Gallery, Los Angeles, 1979, 81, 83, U. Akron, 1979, Carleton Coll., 1979, Heath Gallery, Atlanta, 1979, 83, Galerie Mukai, Tokyo, 1980, Akron Art Inst., 1980, Albright-Knox Art Gallery, Buffalo, 1980, Joslyn Art Mus., Omaha, 1982, Tate Gallery, London, 1982, McIntosh/Drysdale Gallery, Houston, 1982, Gloria Luria Gallery, Bay Harbor Islands, Fla., 1983, Rose Art Mus., Brandeis U., Waltham, Mass., 1984, Long Beach Mus. Art., Calif., 1984, Univ. Art Mus., U. Calif.-Berkeley, 1984, Knight Gallery, Charlotte, N.C., 1985, Cleve. Mus. Art, 1986, Greg Kucera Gallery, Seattle, 1986, Whitechapel Art Gallery, London, 1986; group exbhns. include Mus. Modern Art, N.Y.C., 1971, 81, 83, Whitney Mus. Am. Art, N.Y.C., 1972, 77, 79, 81, 82, 83, Walker Art Ctr., Mpls., 1972, Kunsthaus, Hamburg, Fed. Republic Germany, 1972, Paula Cooper Gallery, N.Y.C., 1973, 74, 76, 77, 78, 81, 83, 84, Corcoran Gallery Art, Washington, 1975, Art Inst. Chgo., 1976, Kunstmuseum, Dusseldorf, Fed. Republic Germany, 1976, Kassel, Fed. Republic Germany, 1977, Contemporary Arts Mus., Houston, 1980, Am. Acad. Arts and Letters, N.Y.C., 1983, Sarah Lawrence Art Gallery, Bronxville, N.Y., 1984, Archer M. Hunting Art Gallery, U. Tex.-Austin, 1984, Hudson River Mus., Yonkers, N.Y., 1984, Tucson Mus. Art, 1984, Leo Castelli Gallery, N.Y.C., 1984, numerous others; represented in permanent collections, Mus. Modern Art, N.Y.C., Met. Mus. Art, N.Y.C., Whitney Mus. Am. Art, N.Y.C., Phila. Mus. Art, Walker Art Ctr., Mpls., Yale U. Art Gallery, New Haven, Art Mus. S.Tex., Corpus Christi, R.I. Sch. Design, Providence, Art Gallery S. Australia, Adelaide, Goucher Coll., Balt., Amerada Hess, Woodbridge, N.J., Dallas Mus. Fine Arts, Richard B. Russell Fed. Bldg. and U.S. Courthouse, Atlanta. Recipient Harris prize Art Inst. Chgo., 1976, 86; recipient Creative Arts award Brandeis U., 1983, award Am. Acad. Arts and Letters, 1983, AIA award, 1986; Creative Artists Public Services fellow, 1974; Lucas vis. lectr. award Carleton Coll., 1979. Office: care Paula Cooper Gallery 155 Wooster St New York NY 10012

BARTLETT, SHIRLEY MAE ANNE, accountant; b. Gladwin, Mich., Mar. 28, 1933; d. Dewey J. and Ruth Elizabeth (Wright) Frye; m. Charles Duane Bartlett, Aug. 16, 1952 (div. Sept. 1982); children: Jeanne, Michelle, John, Yvonne. Student, Mich. State U., 1952-53, Rutgers U., 1972-74. Auditor State of Mich., Lansing, 1951-66; cost acct. Templar Co., South River, N.J., 1968-75; staff acct. Franco Mfg. Co., Metuchen, N.J., 1975-78; controller Thomas Creative Apparel, New London, Ohio, 1978-80; mgr. gen. acctg. Ideal Electric Co., Mansfield, Ohio, 1980-85; staff acct. Logangate Homes, Inc., Girard, Ohio, 1985-88; pvt. practice acctg. Youngstown, 1985—; acct. Universal Devel. Enterprises, Liberty Twp., Ohio, 1987-88; v.p. Lang Industries, Inc., Youngstown, 1984—. Author: (play) Our Bicentennial-A Celebration, 1976. Soloist various orchestras, Mich., Va.; mem. Human Relations Commn., Franklin Township, 1971-77, Friends of Am. Art; treas. Heritage Found., New Brunswick, N.J., 1973-74, New London Proceeds Corp., 1979-83; commr. Huron Park Commn., Ohio, 1979-83; elected Dem. com. mem., N.J., Ohio, 1970-82. Mem. NOW (treas. Youngstown chpt. 1986—), Am. Soc. Women Accts. (bd. dirs. 1986-88, v.p. 1988-89, pres. 1989—), NAFE, Bus. and Profl. Women (v.p. 1980—), Am. Soc. Notaries, Women's Jour. Network, Citizen's League of Greater Youngstown, Internat. Platform Assn., Friends of Am. Art, Youngstown Opera Guild. Democrat. Unitarian. Club: Franklin JFK (treas. 1970-72, v.p. 1973-78), Chataqua Literary, Scientific Circle (pres. 1979—). Home and Office: Bartlett Acctg Svcs 4793 Ardmore Ave Youngstown OH 44505-1101

BARTLEY, MARY LOU RUF, school administrator; b. Orange, N.J., Feb. 10, 1940; d. Julius and Florence (Holland) Ruf; 1 child, Marcia Lyn. AB, Upsala Coll., 1961; MA, Seton Hall U., 1965; EdD, Rutgers U., 1976. Dir. testing, lang. arts coordinator East Orange (N.J.) Sch. Dist., 1968-72; prin. Deane-Porter Sch., Rumson, N.J., 1972-73; supt. Rumson (N.J.) Sch. Dist., 1973-78, River Dell Regional Sch. Dist., Oradell, N.J., 1978—; instr. Upsala Coll., 1967-72, Georgian Ct. Coll., Lakewood, N.J., 1977-78. Fellow Rutgers U., 1971-72. Mem. Am. Assn. Sch. Adminstrs., N.J. Assn. Sch. Adminstrs., N.J. Council Edn. (com. chmn. 1982—), N.J. Tchr. Edn. Roundtable (state pres. 1985-86), Northeast Coalition Ednl. Leaders, Gamma Sigma Sigma, Phi Delta Kappa. Roman Catholic. Home: 506 Linwood Ave Ridgewood NJ 07450 Office: River Dell Regional Schs Adminstrv Offices Pyle St Oradell NJ 07649

BARTLEY, SHIRLEY KAY, writer; b. Indpls., Jan. 15, 1955; d. James Albert Bartley and Grace Wilbur Robey. BS, Emerson Coll., 1977; MA, Ind. U., 1979; PhD, Temple U., 1983. Instr. Indiana U., Bloomington, 1978-79, Temple U., Phila., 1979-81, U. Ala., Huntsville, 1982; researcher Social Issues Resources, Boca Raton, Fla., 1983-84, Nat. Enquirer, Lantana, Fla., 1984; instr. Coll. of Boca Raton, 1984; editor Boca Raton Mag., 1985-87; freelance writer Boca Raton, 1989—; instr. Fla. Atlantic U., Boca Raton, 1990. Republican.

BARTLING, PHYLLIS MCGINNESS, oil company executive; b. Chillicothe, Ohio, Jan. 3, 1927; d. Francis A. McGinness and Gladys A. (Henkelman) Bane; m. Theodore Charles Bartling, Aug. 2, 1946; children—Pamela, Theodore, Eric C. Student, Ohio State U., 1944-47. Bookkeeper, Bartling & Assocs., Bartling Oil Co., Houston 1974-80; sec.-treas., dir. both cos., 1980—. Co-chmn. ticket sales Tulsa Opera, 1956-61; bd. dirs. Tex. Speech and Hearing Ctr., Houston, 1967-70. Republican. Episcopalian. Avocations: tennis; gardening; bicycling; cooking. Home: 11 Inwood Oaks Houston TX 77024 Office: 8550 Katy Freeway Suite 128 Houston TX 77024

BARTOLO, DONNA M., hospital administrator, nurse; b. Springfield, Ill., Mar. 21, 1941; d. Elmer Ralph Bartolomucci and Zoe (Rose) Cavatorta. Diploma in nursing, St. John's Sch. Nursing, Springfield, Ill., 1962; BS, Milliken U., 1976; MS, Sangamon State U., 1978. Pediatric nurse Springfield Clin., 1962-64, physician's asst., 1972-74; gynecol. nurse Watson Clin., Lakeland, Fla., 1964-66; cons. state sch. nurses Office of Edn. State of Ill., Springfield, 1974-78; assoc. dir. operating rm. svcs. Cedars-Sinai Med. Ctr., L.A., 1978-82, co-dir. div. nursing, 1981-82; surg. nurse Emory U. Hosp., Atlanta, 1966-70, asst. dir. of nursing, dir. surg. svcs., 1982—. Mem. editorial bd. Perioperative Nursing Quarterly; contbr. articles to nursing jours. Mem. Org. Nurse Execs., Ga. Assn. Nurse Execs., Assn. Operating Rm. Nurses, Sigma Theta Tau. Home: 6130 Windsor Trace Dr Atlanta GA 30092

BARTON, BARBARA ANN, agriculturist, researcher, educator; b. Erie, Pa., May 20, 1954. BS in Animal Sci. with distinction, Pa. State U., 1976; MS in Dairy Sci., U. Wis., 1978, PhD, 1981. Rsch. asst. U. Wis., Madison, 1976-81; asst. prof. U. Maine, Orono, 1981-88, assoc. prof., 1988—; leader agrl. rsch. projects USDA, 1982—, Maine Dept. Agr., Food and Rural Resources, 1984—, Am. Farm Products, 1983—, Agway, Inc., 1985—, Penobscot County-Soil and Water Conservation Com., 1987—; rep. New Eng. Dairy Coll. Conf., 1982—, chmn., 1987; lectr., conductor seminars in field. Mem. editorial bd. Jour. of Dairy Sci.; contbr. articles to profl. jours. Recipient Presdl. Pub. Service Achievement award, U. Maine, 1985, Faculty and Instructional Devel., 1986; Carl and Florence B. King scholar, Winrock Internat., 1983; Merck Animal Health Edn. grantee, Merck Co. Found., 1986, teaching grantee, 1987. Mem. Am. Dairy Sci. Assn. (Gold scholar 1976, jr. faculty advisor 1986, sr. faculty advisor 1987), Am. Soc. Animal Sci. (jr. faculty advisor 1986, sr. faculty advisor 1987, sec., treas. N.E. chpt. 1986-87, v.p. 1987-88, pres. 1988-89, bd. dirs., mem. various coms.), Am. Forage and Grassland Coun., Coun. Agrl. Sci. Tech., Dairy Shrine, Alpha Zeta, Phi Kappa Phi, Sigma Delta Epsilon, Sigma Xi. Office: U Maine Dept Animal Vet Scis 24A Rogers Hall Orono ME 04469

BARTON, BRIGID ANNE, art history educator; b. Honolulu, June 1, 1943; d. William M. and Ellen (Counsell) Shanahan; m. Douglas H. Barton, Sept. 2, 1968 (div. 1982); children—Gregory, Thomas. B.A., Barnard Coll., Columbia U., 1965; M.A., U. Calif.-Berkeley, 1968, Ph.D., 1976. Instr. Coll. Marin, Kentfield, Calif., 1968-71; asst. prof. art history U. Santa Clara, Calif., 1976-82, assoc. prof. art history, 1982—; chmn. art history dept. U. Santa Clara, 1986-87; dir. De Saisset Mus. U. Santa Clara, Calif., 1979-84. Author: Otto Dix and 'Die neue Sachlichkeit', 1981; German Expressionist Woodcuts: the Rifkind Collection, 1980. NEA grad. fellow, 1967. Mem. Coll. Art Assn., AAUP. Office: U Santa Clara Dept of Art Santa Clara CA 95053*

BARTON, CYNTHIA KATHLEEN, architect; b. Houston, Oct. 16, 1958; d. George Randall and Roxanne Inez (Ritter) Hammond; m. Richard Redman Barton, May 28, 1983; childern: Cory Allen, Robert Randall. BS in Archtl. Studies, U. Ill., 1981, MArch, 1983. Aerospace technician exptl. facilities and equipment NASA Johnson Space Ctr., Houston, 1984-85; architect, project investigator U.S. Army Constrn. Engring. Research Lab., Champaign, Ill., 1985-88. Recipient Official Commendation U.S. Army, 1986, 87. Mem. Fed. Women's Program (div. rep. publicity coordinator 1986-88), Bldg. Thermal Envelope Coordinating Council, AIA (mem. Champaign sect.), Alpha Xi Delta. Home: 259 Lakeshire Dr Lexington SC 29072

BARTON, ELLEN LOUISE, lawyer, educator, consultant; b. Harrisburg, Pa., Jan. 17, 1946; d. George Michael and Irene Catherine (Gregor) Schmeltzer; m. Norman W. Barton, Nov. 28, 1987; children: William Michael, Ian Christopher. A.B. in Psychology, Rosemont Coll., 1972; J.D., U. Cin., 1978. Bar: Ohio 1978, U.S. Dist. Ct. (so. dist.) Ohio 1979, Pa. 1985, U.S. Ct. Appeals (3d cir. 1985), Maryland 1989; C.P.C.U. Occupational analyst Commonwealth of Pa., Harrisburg, 1972-74; ins. adjuster Lloyd Deist, Inc., Cin., 1977-78; asst. editor FC&S Bulls., Nat. Underwriter Co., Cin., 1978-81; assoc. dir. risk mgmt. U. Cin., 1981-84, dir. risk mgmt., 1984-85, dir. risk mgmt. U. Pa., 1985-87; ptnr. Fischer, Klimon, Salman & Harpster, Cin., 1984-85, ptnr. Klimon, Salman, Greve & Harpster, Phila., 1985-89; ptnr. Barton & Salman, Balt., 1990—; pres. Neumann Ins. Co., 1987—; corp. dir. risk mgmt. Franciscan Health System, Chadds Ford, Pa., 1987—; dir., chairperson Alternative Ins. Mgmt. Svcs., Inc., 1989—; dir., v.p. Claims, Consolidated Catholic Casulty Risk Retention Group, Inc., 1987—, Preferred Physicians Ins. Co., 1988—; cons. Don Malecki & Assocs., Fort Thomas, Ky., 1983-85; asst. atty. gen. State of Ohio, Columbus, 1983-85; asst. prof. family medicine U. Cin., 1984-85; legal adviser Children's Internat. Summer Villages, Cin., 1984-85. Editor: Insuring the Lease Exposure, Part II, 1981; contbr. articles to profl jours. Mem. Our Lady of Rosary Sch. Bd., Greenhills, Ohio, 1974-81; v.p. Covered Bridge Civic Assn., Cin., 1979-81, area rep., 1979-82; pres. Nat. Underwriter Co. Fed. Credit Union, Cin., 1980-81. Pa. Higher Edn. Assistance Agy. scholar Rosemont Coll., Phila., 1971-72. Mem. ABA, Ohio Bar Assn., Cin. Bar Assn., Soc. C.P.C.U.s, Am. Soc. Law and Medicine, Nat. Health Lawyers Assn., Am. Soc. Healthcare Risk Mgrs., Risk and Ins. Mgmt. Soc. Republican. Roman Catholic. Office: Neumann Ins Co One MacIntyre Dr Aston PA 19014

BARTON, JACQUELINE K., chemistry educator; b. N.Y.C., May 7, 1952; d. William and Claudine (Gutchen) Kapelman; m. Peter Brendan Dervan, Mar. 3, 1990. AB summa cum laude, Columbia U., 1974, PhD, 1978; postdoctoral, Yale U., 1979-80. Asst. prof. Hunter Coll, N.Y.C., 1980-82; asst. prof. Columbia U., N.Y.C., 1983-85, assoc. prof., 1985-86, prof. chemistry and biology, 1986-89; prof. Calif. Inst. Tech., Pasadena, 1989—; vis. rsch. assoc. dept. biophysics Bell Labs., 1979; mem. chemistry adv. com. NSF, 1985-88, oversight panel Presdl. Young Investigator Program, 1987, Alan T. Waterman com., 1988—; mem. metallobiochemistry study sect. NIH, 1986—, chmn., 1988—. Mem. adv. bds. Accounts Chem. Rsch., 1987—, Chem. And Engring. News, 1988—, Inorgic Chemistry, 1989—, Progress in Inorganic Chemistry, 1989—. NSF Predoctoral fellow, 1975-78, postdoctoral fellow, 1979-80, Alfred P. Sloan fellow Sloan Found., 1984; Camille and Henry Dreyfus tchr.-scholar Dreyfus Found., 1986—; recipient Harold Lamport award N.Y. Acad. Scis., 1984, Alan T. Waterman award, NSF, 1985, Fresenius award, Phi Lambda Upsilon, 1986, Eli Lilly Biochemistry award, 1987, Pure Chemistry award, 1988 Am. Chem. Soc. Mem. Phi Beta Kappa. Office: Calif Inst Tech Div Chemistry 164-30 Pasadena CA 91125

BARTON, JEAN MARIE, psychologist; b. Pitts., Mar. 24, 1945; d. Joseph Paul and Jean Marie (Anderson) Adamchic; m. Robert L. Barton, Jr., Aug. 14, 1965; children: Robert Joseph, Katherine Anne. BS summa cum laude, U. Pitts., 1965; MEd, Boston U., 1969; CAGS, Cath. U. Am., 1985, PhD in Ednl. Psychology, 1988. Cert. sch. psychologist, Md. Tchr./curriculum Wellesley (Mass.) pub. schs., 1965-69; lectr. U. R.I./R.I. Coll., Providence, 1969-72; curriculum specialist/tchr. St. Jane DeChantal Sch., Bethesda, Md., 1977-82; computer prog. dir. St. Jane DeChantol Sch., 1982-84; psychology assoc. Long Assocs., Bethesda, 1988—; psychol. cons. Gifted Unit, Montgomery County pub. schs., Rockville, Md., 1985—; sch. psychologist Archdiocese of Washington (Md.), 1987—; mem. faculty Cath. U. Am., Washington, 1989—; evaluation team mem. Cath. Schs. Studies, Corpus Christi, 1987—; dir. Profl. Devel. Inst., Cath. U. Am., 1985-86; chairperson identification/edn. com. Jacob Javits Grants, Montgomery County pub. schs., 1989—; presenter nat. confs. Contbr. articles to profl. jours. U. Pitts. scholar, 1962-65. Mem. Nat. Assn. Sch. Psychologists, Am. Psychol. Assn., Am. Ednl. Rsch. Assn., Assn. for Supervision and Curriculum Devel., Md. Sch. Psychologist Assn., Coun. for Exceptional Children, Pi Lambda Theta. Home: 5008 Benton Ave Bethesda MD 20814 Office: Cath University of America 216 O'Boyle Hall Washington DC 20064

BARTON, JO ANN, secretary, treasurer; b. Jamestown, N.Y., June 4, 1949; d. Harold Austin and Dorothy (Edick) B.; m. Frank Pulver, Nov. 11, 1969 (div. Apr. 1981); children: Aaron, Nathan. Student, Humboldt Inst. Bus. Sch., 1967-68, Jamestown Community Coll., 1986—. Bookkeeper S&S Oil Co., Auburn, Ind., 1976-86; sec., treas. Barton Tool Inc., Falconer, N.Y., 1986—. Democrat. Roman Catholic. Home: Rt 1 Drybrook Rd Falconer NY 14733 Office: Barton Tool Inc Lyndon Pk Falconer NY 14733

BARTON, MARIE TIDWELL, legal administrator, legal assistant; b. Ala., Oct. 4, 1937; d. Grady Ondell and Bula Faye (Ingram) Tidwell; m. James G. Barton, Oct. 15, 1960; children: Randall Keith, David James. Student, Jefferson State Coll., 1976-78; BA, Samford U., 1983. Legal asst. Sirote, Permutt, et al, Birmingham, Ala., 1980-83; legal adminstr., legal asst. Ragsdale, Beals, Hooper & Seigler, Atlanta, 1983—. Pres. Chalkville Sch. PTA, Birmingham, 1974-75; v.p. Trussville Athletic Club, Birmingham, 1978-79; vol. ARC, Birmingham, 1970-75; bd. dirs. Bapt. Women's Missionary Union, Birmingham, 1969-71. Mem. Am. Assn. Legal Adminstrs., Nat. Assn. Legal Assts. (sec. 1982-83), Ga. Assn. Legal Assts. (continuing legal edn. com.), Ala. Assn. Legal Assts. (sec. 1982083), South Fulton Bar Assn. (com. chmn. 1988, law day co-chmn. 1989), Fayette County Bd. Realtors, Clayton/Henry County Bd. Realtors (real property action com.), Clayton/Fayette Young Realtors, Southside Atlanta Assn. Profl. Mortgage Women (chartering officer, recording sec.), Phi Theta Kappa, Alpha Lambda Delta.

BARTON, META PACKARD, business executive; b. Balt., Dec. 2, 1928; d. Charles Lee and Dorothy (Levering) Packard); m. David W. Barton Jr., July 4, 1951 (div. 1989); children: Blair Lee Barton, Meta Barton Patten, Priscilla Taylor, Emilie Packard. AB, Vassar Coll., 1950; MA, Loyola Coll., Balt., 1977. Bus. rsch. Balt. Assn. Commerce, 1950-51; faculty Bryn Mawr (Md.) Sch., 1952-62; staff psychologist Epoch House, Essex, Md., 1973-81; employee benefits coordinator, profit sharing plan adminstr., treas. Barton-Gillet Co., Balt., 1981-89; pres. Friends Med. Sci. Rsch. Ctr., Balt., 1981—, Namaste, Balt., 1987—. Bd. dirs. Wildlife Preservation Trust, Internat. Mem. Am. Psychol. Assn., Am. Evaluation Assn., Md. Vassar Club (pres.). Office: Friends Med Sci Rsch Ctr Inc 22 Bloomsbury Ave Baltimore MD 21228

BARTON, NELDA ANN LAMBERT, political activist, newspaper, bank and nursing home executive; b. Providence, Ky., May 12, 1929; m. Harold Bryan Barton, May 11, 1951 (dec. Nov. 1977); children: William Grant (dec.), Barbara Lynn, Harold Bryan, Stephen Lambert, Suzanne. Student, Western Ky. U., 1947-49; grad., Norton Meml. Infirmary Sch. Med. Tech., 1950; postgrad., Cumberland Coll., 1978. Lic. nursing home adminstr.; registered med. technician. Pres., chmn. bd. Barton & Assocs. Inc., Corbin, Ky., 1977—, Hazard Nursing Home Inc., Ky., 1977—, Health Systems Inc., Corbin, 1978—, Corbin Nursing Home Inc., 1980—, Williamsburg Nursing Home, Inc., 1978—, Key Distbg. Inc., 1980—, Barbourville Nursing Home Inc., 1981—, The Whitley Whiz Inc., Williamsburg, 1983—; chmn. bd. dirs. Tri-County Nat. Bank., 1985—; pres., chmn. bd. dirs. Harlan Nursing Home, Inc., 1986—, Knott Co. Nursing Home, Inc., 1986—; pres. Tri-County Bancorp, Inc., 1987—; mem. exec. com. Corbin Deposit Bank, 1982-84; bd. dirs. Greensburg (Ky.) Deposit Bank, Williamsburg (Ky.) Nat. Bank, 1989—; chmn. Greene County Bancorp Inc.; mem. nat. adv. coun. SBA, 1990—. Mem. Fed. Coun. on Aging, 1982-87; bd. dirs. Leadership Ky., 1984-88, adv. com., 1987—; v.p. Southeastern Ky. Rehab. Com., 1981—; mem. devel. bd. Cumberland Coll., 1981-85, Fair Housing Task Force, Corbin, 1981-84, Ky. Mansions Preservation Found. Inc., Corbin Community Devel. Com., 1970-83; cub scout den mother, 1965-67; pres. Corbin Cen. Elem. PTA, 1963-65; vice chmn. 9th dist. P.T.A., 1958-59; Rep. nat. committeewoman for Ky., 1968—; vice-chmn. Rep. Nat. Com., 1984—; sec.-treas. Nat. Rep. Inst. Internat. Affairs, 1984-86; active numerous other polit. orgns. Recipient Ky. Woman of Achievement award Ky. Bus. and Profl. Women, 1983, recognition award Joint Rep. Leadership, U.S. Congress, Dwight David Eisenhower award, 1970, John Sherman Cooper Disting. Service award Ky. Young Reps. Fedn., 1987; named Ky. Col., 1968; Nelda Barton Day proclaimed by Mayor of Corbin, 1973; named Ky. Rep. Woman of Yr., Ky. Fedn. Rep. Women, 1969; Western Ky. U. acad. scholar, 1947-49. Mem. Am. Coll. Nursing Home Adminstrs., Ky. Assn. Health Care Facilities (legis. com. 1980—), Ky. Assn. Nursing Home Adminstrs. (bd. dirs., polit. action com. 1979—), Ky. Med. Aux. (chmn. health edn. com. 1975-77), Am. Health Care Assn., Ky. Commn. on Women, Women's Aux. So. Med. Assn. (Ky. counselor), Whitley County Med. Aux. (pres. 1959-60), Aux. Ky. Med. Assn., Ky. Mothers Assn. (parliamentarian 1970—, hon. Mother of Ky. award 1983), Ky. C. of C. (bd. dirs. 1983—, v.p. Region 5 1985—, 1st vice chmn. 1989, chmn. 1990—). Home: 1311 7th St Rd Corbin KY 40701 Office: Health Systems Inc PO Box 1450 Corbin KY 40701

BARTZ, MARY RUSSO, environmental protection specialist; b. St. Louis; d. Mariano and Maria (Bonfiglio) Russo; m. Robert O. Bartz, Sept. 14, 1963. BA summa cum laude, Am. U., 1974; MPA, U. New Orleans, 1977. Community planner Bur. Land Mgmt., New Orleans, 1977-84; supervisory environ. protection specialist Minerals Mgmt. Svc., New Orleans, 1984—. Bd. dirs. Coll. Civic and Pub. Affairs, U. New Orleans, 1977—. Recipient numerous awards Dept. of Interior. Mem. U. New Orleans Alumni Bd., Phi Kappa Phi. Roman Catholic.

BARUCH, MONICA LOBO-FILHO, psychology counselor; b. Rio de Janeiro, Jan. 11, 1954; d. Max and Margot (Hollander) Lobo-Filho; m. Robert Karl Baruch, Dec. 30, 1973 (div. May 1985). BA in Psychology, U. Rochester, 1975; MA in Counseling Edn., U. Mo., Kansas City, 1978. Cert. Nat. Bd. Cert. Counselors. Tchr. curriculum devel. St. Patrick's Sch., Rio de Janeiro, 1974-76; tchr., soccer coach Pembroke Country Day Sch., Kansas City, Mo., 1977-78; tchr., trainer Berlitz Sch. Langs., Kansas City and Washington, 1978-79; counselor, cons. Youth Understanding, Washington, 1979-81; pvt. practice, 1981—; academic faculty counselor Georgetown U., Washington, 1982-89. Co-author: Weight Control: A Guide for Counselors and Therapists, 1987. Named one of Outstanding Young Women in Am., 1981. Mem. Am. Assn. Counseling and Devel., Am. Mental Health Counselors Assn., Multiple Personality Study Group, Md. Mental Health Counselors Assn. (program chmn. 1989).

BARWICK, PAMELA JEAN, laboratory specialist; b. Kinston, N.C., July 4, 1957; d. Robert Leonard and Grace (Colie) B. Student, Lenoir Community Coll., Kinston, 1978, East Carolina U., 1978. Computer operator Roche BioMed. Lab., Kinston, 1981, svc. rep., 1981-84, customer svc. br. rep., 1984-86, customer svc. rep., 1986-87, clin. lab. specialist, 1987—. Mem. NAFE. Democrat. Baptist. Office: Roche BioMed Labs 2902A N Heritage St Kinston NC 28501

BARWICK-SNELL, KATHERINE LANE, sociology educator, home economics consultant; b. Jackson, Miss., Feb. 9, 1955; d. Jim Drane and Doris Eloise (Langford) Barwick; m. Daniel Clair Snell, June 28, 1986; 1 child, James David. BS, Miss. State U., 1977; MS, U. Okla., 1981. Cert. home economist, Okla. Adminstrv. asst. Women's Resource Ctr., Norman, Okla., 1977-78; mgr. Norman Shelter, Inc., 1978-80; tchr. Washington (Okla.) High Sch., 1980-81; instr. home econs. U. Okla., Norman, 1981-83, instr. sociology, 1990—; instr. home econs. U. Sci. and Arts Okla., Chickasha, 1983-90; caterer, tchr. pvt. cooking class, Norman, 1982—. Pres. bd. dirs. Women's Resource Ctr., 1983-85; mem., chmn. Human Rights Commn., Norman, 1983-86. Grantee Okla. Arts Coun., 1988. Mem. Am. Home Econs. Assn., Internat. Home Econs. Fedn., Okla. Home Econs. Assn., Adult Edn. Assn. Democrat. Home: 504 Miller Ave Norman OK 73069 Office: U Okla Dept Sociology Norman OK 73019

BARZ, DIANE, state judge; b. Bozeman, Mont., Aug. 18, 1943; d. John G. and E. Bernice (Johnson) MacDonald; m. Daniel J. Barz, Nov. 28, 1970. Student, U. Heidelberg, Fed. Republic Germany, 1964; BA magna cum laude, Whitworth Coll., 1965; JD, U. Mont., 1968. Bar: Mont. 1968. Law clk., rsch. asst. Mont. Supreme Ct., Mont. Criminal Commn., Helena, 1968-70; dep. atty. County of Yellowstone, Mont., 1970-75, pub. administr., 1974-78; ptnr. Poppler & Barz, Billings, Mont., 1973-79; judge Dist. Ct. Mont., Billings, from 1980; justice Mont. Supreme Ct., Helena, 1989—. Account exec. United Way, Billings, 1973; sec. Yellowstone County Rep. Cen. Com., Billings, 1973-75; bd. dirs. South Cen. Mont. Regional Mental Health Ctr., Billings, Yellowstone County Civic Ctr. Commn., 1975-81, Deaconess Hosp., from 1980, 4-H Mont., Salvation Army, from 1982. Bur. Nat. Affairs scholar U. Mont., 1968. Mem. Mont. Bar Assn., Yellowstone County Bar Assn., Young Lawyers Assn. (v.p., sec. 1970), Am. Judges Assn., Mont. Judges Assn., Nat. Assn. Women Judges, Bus. and Profl. Women's Club (named Mont. Young Career Woman 1970), Jr. League Billings, Billings Jr. C. of C., Phi Delta (named Woman of Yr. 1970). Office: Mont Supreme Ct Supreme Ct Bldg Helena MT 59620*

BARZ, PATRICIA, lawyer; b. Mattoon, Ill., Oct. 18, 1953; d. William E. Barz and Rosemary A. (Easton) Scott; m. Herbert P. Wiedemann, Feb. 12, 1983; children: Sarah Barz Wiedemann, Andrew. BA, Yale U., 1974; JD, U. Va., 1978. Bar: Va. 1979, Conn. 1982, Ohio 1985. Assoc. Hunton & Williams, Richmond, Va., 1978-81, Davis, Graham & Stubbs, Denver, 1981-82; counsel legal dept. Aetna Life and Casualty Co., Hartford, Conn., 1982-84; assoc. Jones, Day, Reavis & Pogue, Cleve., 1984—. Trustee St. Anthony Trust Assn., New Haven, 1983-86; class agt. Yale Alumni Fund, New Haven, 1985-89. Mem. ABA, Ohio Bar Assn., Cleve. Bar Assn., Conn. Bar Assn., Va. Bar Assn., Yale Alumni Assn. (v.p. Cleve. chpt. 1986-88, trustee 1988—). Methodist. Home: 3008 Claremont Rd Shaker Heights OH 44122 Office: Jones Day Reavis & Pogue 901 Lakeside Ave Cleveland OH 44114

BASDEN, BARBARA HOLZ, psychology educator; b. Coeur d'Alene, Idaho, Feb. 10, 1940; d. Albert R. and Carol (Utter) Holz; m.David R. Basden, May 25, 1962; children: Leslie H., Derin E. BA, Coll. Idaho, 1962; PhD, U. Calif., Santa Barbara, 1969. Asst. prof. psychology Calif. State U., Fresno, 1973-78, assoc. prof. psychology, 1978-82, prof. psychology, 1983—. Author: (study guide) Psychology, 1984, 2d edit., 1987, Memory, Memory & Aging, Memory & Hypnosis, 1987-90; contbr. articles to profl. jours. Mem. Psychonomic Soc., Am. Psychol. Assn., Am. Psychol. Soc., Western Psychol. Assn. Office: Calif State U Dept Psychology Fresno CA 93740

BASEL, FRANCES RITA, printing company executive; b. Calumet City, Ill., Mar. 8, 1933; d. Henry Adolph and Genevieve Veronica (Novak) Kaminski; m. Raymond John Basel, Feb. 19, 1955; children: Cynthia, Laura, Mark. Grad. Griffith Sch., Ind., 1950. Sec., Aeroquip/Barco, Barrington, Ill., 1955-62; freelance typist, Barrington, 1962-68; bookkeeper, office mgr. R.A.G. Enterprises, Fox Lake, Ill., 1968-78; corp. officer Classic Printery, Inc., Round Lake, 1978—. Republican. Roman Catholic. Office: Classic Printery Inc 316 Main St Round Lake Park IL 60073

BASHAM-TOOKER, JANET BROOKS, geropsychologist, educator; b. Hampton, Va., Sept. 27, 1919; d. Thomas Westmore and Cora Evelyn Brooks; m. Linwood Cecil Basham (div. 1968); m. Frederick Fitch Tooker. BA cum laude, U. N.C., Greensboro, 1948; MS in Psychology, Calif. State U., L.A., 1981; MA in Human Devel., Pacific Oaks Coll., 1984. Tchr., Calif. Grad. asst. psychology Duke U., Durham, N.C., 1948-49; tchr. Albuquerque City Schs., 1950-51; tchr. L.A. City Schs., 1953-54, counselor, 1981; lectr. L.A., 1988—; docent Las Angelitas del Pueblo, L.A., 1971-74. Author numerous poems. Mem. planning com., women's conf. Commn. on Status of Women, Pasadena, Calif., 1982-85, sr. com. Task Force on Aging, San Marino, Calif., 1986-89, United Way, Arcadia, Calif., 1984-88, Symphony Guild, Fayetteville, 1990; adv. mem. San Gabriel Presbytery Commn. on Aging, 1984-88; mem. grad. studies subcom. Calif. State U., L.A., 1975-78; v.p. San Marino Aux. Meth. Hosp., Arcadia, Calif., 1985-86; docent Duarte Hist. Soc., Calif., 1986-89; moderator sr. adults 1st United Presbyn. Ch., Fayetteville, 1990; facilitator fin. info. program for women AARP, Fayetteville, 1990. Recipient Margaret Noffsinger award Va. Intermont Coll., 1937. Mem. AAUW, Am. Soc. Aging, Mental Health Assn., Older Women's League, Duarte Women's Club, Phi Beta Kappa, Phi Theta Kappa. Republican. Presbyterian.

BASHE, ELINOR DIANE, psychologist; b. N.Y.C., Dec. 25, 1958; d. Burton and Ilka (Gross) Giges; m. Gilbert G. Bashe, Sept. 20, 1981. AB magna cum laude, Brown U., 1980; MA magna cum laude, Tel Aviv (Israel) U., 1985; D in Psychology, Rutgers U., 1989. Clinician Elizabeth (N.J.) Gen. Med. Ctr., 1987-88; intern U. of Medicine and Dentistry of N.J., Piscataway, N.J., 1988-89; clinician UMDNJ, Piscataway, 1989—; vis. lectr. Grad. Sch. Applied and Profl. Psychology, Piscataway, 1989—. Rutgers U. disting. fellow, 1985-88. Mem. Am. Psychol. Assn., N.J. Psychol. Assn., Phi Beta Kappa. Office: UMDNJ/CMHC MCR 671 Hoes Ln Piscataway NJ 08855

BASILE, ABIGAIL JULIA ELLEN HERRON, employment counselor, state official; b. St. Louis, June 15, 1915; d. Charles Arthur and Abigail (Edwards) Herron; student Kansas City Jr. Coll., 1948-50, U. Kans., 1959; B.S. in Bus. Adminstrn., Rockhurst Coll., 1965; M.Ed., U. Mo., 1967; m. Joseph Basile, Aug. 15, 1939. Employment security dep. Mo. Div. Employment Security, Kansas City, 1945-59, youth coordinator, employment counselor, 1959-65, counselor, supr., 1965-81. Mem. Mo. Assn. Social Welfare. Mem. Am. Personnel and Guidance Assn., Nat. Vocat. Guidance Assn., Am. Vocat. Assn., Internat. Assn. Personnel in Employment Security (pres. Mo. 1966-67, internat. sec. 1968), Nat. Rehab. Assn., Nat. Employment Counselors Assn., Urban League, Am. Legion Aux., Personnel Research Forum, Profl. Counselors Assn. Democrat. Catholic. Home: 5316 Paseo Kansas City MO 64110

BASILE, CAROL ANN, nurse; b. Phila., June 21, 1953; d. John Samuel and Josephine Anna (Condello) B.; m. Joseph Samuel Camardo, July 25, 1981 (div. Nov. 4, 1983). RN, Hosp. of Univ. Pa., 1974; BS in Nursing, Skidmore Coll., 1983. Cert. critical care and med.-surg. nurse. Staff nurse Hosp. Univ. Pa., Phila., 1974-77, asst. head nurse, 1977-81; nurse Hosp. U. Pa., Phila., 1981-83, staff nurse level III, 1983-89; nurse, rsch. coord. Hosp. Univ. Pa., Phila., 1989; lectr. in field; cons. in field. Mem. People for the Am. Way, 1986-87, 89—. Mem. Am. Nurses Assn., Pa. Nurses Assn., Am. Assn. Critical Care Nurses, S.E. Pa. Chpt. Am. Assn. Critical Care Nurses. Democrat. Roman Catholic. Home: 2620 S Mole St Philadelphia PA 19145 Office: Hosp of the Univ Pa 3400 Spruce St Philadelphia PA 19104

BASILE, MARY KNIGHT, medical terminology educator; b. Ridley Park, Pa., Feb. 10, 1920; d. Albert Richard and Grace Emma (Riegel) Knight; m. Aurelio Basile, Aug. 24, 1941 (dec. July 1987); children: Joan Luthern, Patricia Miller and David (twins). Cert. in med. records adminstrn., Schenectady County Community Coll., Schenectady, N.Y., 1939; student, Union Coll., 1960-64, Russell Sage Coll., 1960-64; Assoc. in Human Svcs., Schenectady Community Coll., 1983. Mgr. med. records dept. Kingston (N.Y.) Hosp., 1939-41, St. Clare's Hosp., Schenectady, 1952-54, Ellis Hosp., Schenectady, 1964-76; instr. med. terminology Schenectady County Community Coll., Schenectady, 1978—; ret., 1989. Mem. worship commn. Trinity United Meth. Ch., Schenectady, 1988—; past mem. election com. Schenectady Sch. Bd. Mem. Am. Med. Records Assn. (registered med. records adminstr.), N.Y. State Med. Records Assn. (past mem. bylaws com.), Adirondack Med. Records Assn. (past. pres.).

BASILIO, MARY LOUISE, diabetes nurse educator; b. Hazleton, Pa., Oct. 21, 1937; d. Leo Anthony and Mary Catherine (Gentle) DeLucca; m. Anthony Joseph Basilio, Aug. 26, 1967; children: Dianna Marie, Maryann Judith. Student, Hazleton Gen. State Hosp., 1958. Cert. diabetes educator. Staff nurse St. Joseph Hosp., Hazleton, Pa., 1958-61; acting mgr. Columbia Presby. Med. Ctr., N.Y., 1961-65; asst. coord. Polyclinic Med. Ctr., N.Y., 1965-67; mgr. Downstate Med. Ctr., Bklyn., 1967-68; coord. Caledonia Hosp., Bklyn., 1968-70; relief mgr. Veterans Hosp., 1971-72; relief supr. Sheephead Nursing Home, Bklyn., 1973-76; admission nurse Maimonides Med. Ctr., Bklyn., 1978-85; project dir., diabetes program Kingsbay YM-WHA, Bklyn., 1986—; cons. Assoc. YM-YWHA's of Greater N.Y., 1988; lectr. Bklyn. Pub. Libr. System, 1990. Contbr. articles to profl. jours. Mem. Am. Assn. Diabetes Educators, N.Y. Met. Assn. Diabetes Educators, Am. Diabetes Assn. Democrat. Roman Catholic.

BASINGER, CHERYL KATHRYN R., human resources professional; b. Lancaster, Ohio, Aug. 6, 1955; d. John Thomas and Rita Joan (Bader) Ricketts; m. Ned Naden Basinger, July 26, 1980; children: Christopher, Kimberly. BS/MS with honors, Ohio State U., 1977. Mgmt. trainee Landmark, Inc., New Philadelphia, Ohio, 1978-79; personnel specialist Landmark, Inc., Columbus, Ohio, 1979-81; co-owner, mgr. Fairfield Mfg., Inc., Pickerington, Ohio, 1983—; mgr. employment and devel. Countrymark, Inc., Delaware, Ohio, 1981-88; dir. devel. and mktg. Comprehensive Tng. and Devel. Inst., Worthington, Ohio, 1988; pres. Performance Dimensions, Inc., Pickerington, 1989—. Instr. new mem. class, Peace United Meth. Ch., Pickerington, 1982-89, dir. Sunday sch. opening, 1987—. Mem. Am. Soc. Tng. and Devel. (pres. cen. Ohio chpt. 1986, asst. regional dir. 1987-89), Ohio State U. Agr. Alumni Coun. Republican. Office: Performance Dimensions Inc 11325 Pickerington Rd Pickerington OH 43147

BASINGER, KIM, actress; b. Athens, Ga., Dec. 8, 1953; d. Don Basinger; m. Ron Britton, 1980 (div. Feb. 1990). Student, Neighborhood Playhouse, N.Y.C. Model Eileen Ford Agy., N.Y.C., 1972-77; ind. actress, 1977—. Starring role (TV series) Dog and Cat, 1977; TV films include Katie-Portrait of a Centerfold, 1978, The Ghost of Flight 401, 1979, (TV miniseries) From Here to Eternity, 1979; (feature films) Hard Country, 1980, Mother Lode, 1982, Never Say Never Again, 1983, The Man Who Loved Women, 1983, The Natural, 1984, Fool for Love, 1985, 9 1/2 Weeks, 1986, No Mercy, 1987, Blind Date, 1987, My Stepmother is an Alien, 1988, Batman, 1989.

BASKINGER, PATRICIA JOANNE, computer scientist; b. Utica, N.Y., Mar. 20, 1949; d. Benjamin P. and Margaret Theresa (Asselta) Graniero; m. Louis George Baskinger, July 5, 1975; 1 child, Margaret Jennifer. AS, Mohawk Valley Community Coll., 1968; BA, SUNY, Buffalo, 1970; MS, Syracuse U., 1978. Tchr. math. Utica (N.Y.) Catholic Acad., 1970-73; computer scientist Rome (N.Y.) Air Devel. Ctr., 1973-85; program mgr. IIT Rsch. Inst., Rome, 1985-87, section mgr., 1987-89; office mgr. TASC, New Hartford, N.Y., 1989—. Mem. Assn. Computer Machinery, IEEE Computer Soc., Phi Beta Kappa. Office: TASC 555 French Rd New Hartford NY 13413

BASNETT, PATRICIA MORELAND, lawyer; b. Perryton, Tex., Mar. 7, 1953; d. William R. and Donna Jane (Sweigart) Moreland; m. Richard D. Basnett, Dec. 27, 1975. BA, Ill. Wesleyan U., 1975; JD, U. Tulsa, 1979. Bar: Okla. 1979, U.S. Dist. Ct. (no. dist.) Okla. 1980, U.S. Tax Ct. 1979. Atty. Legal Svcs Ea. Okla. Inc., Tulsa, 1978—. Contbr. articles to mag. Advisor City of Broken Arrow (Okla.) Task Force, 1988. Mem. ABA, Okla. Bar Assn., Tulsa County Bar Assn., Tulsa County Young Lawyers (sub-com. chmn.). Democrat. Office: Legal Svcs Ea Okla 115 W 3d Ste 700 Tulsa OK 74103

BASS, ADRIENNE PAULA, legislative assistant, researcher; b. Cleve., May 12, 1951; d. Morris and Rose (Aronovsky) B.; m. Frank Hayman, Sept. 8, 1973 (div. May 1974). BA, UCLA, 1973; MLS, U. So. Calif., L.A., 1974. Mgr., book buyer Case Western Res. U., Cleve., 1974-75; with L.A. Pub. Library, 1975-85, children's librarian, 1980-82, svc. to shut-ins vol. coord., 1982-85; adminstrv. asst. City of L.A. Police Dept., 1985-86; spl. events coord. gen. svcs. City of L.A., 1986-87, legis. asst. to city clk., 1987—; lectr. in field. Assoc. Colony Theater, L.A., 1982-88; mem., tour docent Pasadena Heritage, 1987—. Mem. City Hall Exec. Women, AAUW (various bd. positions Pasadena chpt. 1986-89, pres. 1989—), Jaycees, Sierra Club. Democrat. Jewish. Home: 1266 Sinaloa Ave Pasadena CA 91104 Office: City of LA Office City Clk 200 N Main St Rm 395 Los Angeles CA 90012

BASS, MARY ANNA, dietitian; b. Clanton, Ala., June 1, 1930; d. Crawford Dixon and Gatie Mae (Williams) Owen; m. William Marvin Bass, III, Aug. 8, 1953; children: Charles Edward, William, James Owen. BS, U. Montevallo, 1951; MS, U. Ky., 1956; PhD, Kans. State U., 1972. Registered dietitian. Cons. various nursing homes Lawrence, Kans., 1960-70; instr. U. Nebr., Lincoln, 1960; cons. Standing Rock Reservation, Ft. Yates, S.D., 1970-74; instr. U. Kans., Lawrence, 1960-68; asst. prof. home econs. U. Tenn., Knoxville, 1971-77; dir. Community Food & Nutrition Svcs., Knoxville, 1970—; nutrition cons. Cherokee Tribe, 1974—; asst. prof. dept. anthropology U. Tenn., Knoxville, 1977—; cons. Sertoma Learning Ctr., 1988—. Bd. editors Jur. Nutrition Edn., 1975-79; sr. author: Community Nutrition and Individual Food Behavior, 1979; contbr. articles to profl. jours. 1st lt. U.S. Army, 1951-53. Mem. Am. Dietetic Assn., Soc. Nutrition Edn., AAAS, Am. Anthropol. Assn., Omicron Nu, Sigma Xi, Gamma Sigma Delta. Presbyterian. Home: 8201 Bennington Dr Knoxville TN 37909 Office: Anthropology Dept Univ Tenn Knoxville TN 37916

BASS, MICHELE DIANE, educator; b. L.A., Oct. 20, 1950; d. Alexander Leonard and Ruth (Stein) Britton; m. Jeffrey Mark Bass, Aug. 23, 1981; children: Marshall Brett, Leah Brittany. BA, U. Calif., Irvine, 1972; MA, Sonoma State U., 1975; EdD, U. San Francisco, 1982. Cert. elem. tchr., Calif. Tchr. Mark West Sch. Dist., Santa Rosa, Calif., 1973-75; project dir. Bolinas (Calif.)-Stinson Union Sch. Dist., 1975-80; ednl. specialist Calif. State Dept. Edn., Santa Barbara, 1980-85; dir. Coaching Inst. for Coop. Learning, Santa Barbara, 1987—; faculty spl. edn. depts. Calif. State U., Northridge, 1986—, U. Calif., Santa Barbara, 1988—; cons., Calif., 1985—; program dir. Birth Resource Ctr., Santa Barbara, 1985-87; bd. dirs. Children's Mus., Santa Barbara, 1987—. Vol. Peace Resource Ctr., Santa Barbara, 1988—. Mem. Calif. Assn. for Cooperation in Edn. (bd. dirs., sec. 1989—).

BASS, NANCY AGNES, airport executive; b. Beaver Falls, Pa., Feb. 26, 1937; d. John Joseph and Kathleen Lillian (Retzer) Paff; m. Lee Herbert Bass, Jan. 10, 1959; children: Thomas Andrew, Marilee, Laura Kathleen. Student, Clarion State Coll., 1954-56. Purchasing clk. Orange County Purchasing Dept., Santa Ana, Calif., 1957-60; bookkeeper Cal Gas, Ridgecrest, Calif., 1975-78; interline mgr. C and M Airlines, Inyokern, Calif., 1978-82; mgr. CLC Engring and Surveying, Ridgecrest, Calif.; gen. mgr. Indian Wells Valley Airport Dist., Inyokern, Calif., 1985-89, Ridgecrest (Calif.) Redevel. Agy., 1989-90; chairperson Kern County Aviation Transp. Technical Adv. Com., Bakerfield, Calif., 1989--. Bd. mem. Ridgecrest Bd. of Appeals, 1986-90, dir. High Desert Child Abuse Prevention Council, Ridgecrest, 1985-87, Am. Cancer Soc., Ridgecrest, 1988--, sec. Airport Dist. Formation Com., Ridgecrest, 1983-85; planning commr. City of Ridgecrest, 1990—. Mem. Cal Assn. of Airport Execs., Am. Assn. of Airport Execs., Altrusa. Home: 600 W Coral Ave Ridgecrest CA 93555 Office: IWV Airport Dist PO Box 634 Inyokern Airport Inyokern CA 93527

BASSETT, ALICE COOK, state legislator; b. St. Johnsbury, Vt., May 16, 1925; d. Clayton Earlman and Alberta (Campbell) Fisher; m. Clinton Dana Cook, May 21, 1944 (dec. June 1969); children—Dana, Allison, Polly, Timothy, Cynthia; m. Thomas Day Seymour Bassett, May 12, 1979. A.A., Colby Jr. Coll., 1944; B.S., U. Vt., 1971. Bus. mgr. Royall Tyler Theatre, Burlington, Vt., 1977-79; asst. to editor NE Bibliography, Boston, 1979-81; mem. Vt. Ho. of Reps., Montpelier, 1983—. Author (newspaper column) Memo from Montpelier, 1984-86; editor (legis. newsletter) Legis. Alert, 1984-85. Vice pres. LWV, Burlington, 1981-84; bd. dirs. Am. Friends Service Com., Brattleboro, Vt., 1980-85, ACLU, Montpelier, 1983-88, Howard Mental Health Services, 1985—, Friends of the Statehouse, 1987—; mem. Vt. Childrens' Aid Soc., 1989—. Democrat. Mem. United Ch. of Christ. Office: State Legislature Montpelier VT 05603

BASSETT, TINA, communications executive; b. Detroit; m. Leland Kinsey Bassett; children: Joshua, Robert. Student, U. Mich., 1974, 76-78, 81, Wayne State U., 1979-80. Advt. dir. Greenfield's Restaurant, Mich. and Ohio, 1972-73; dir. advt. and pub. relations Kresco, Inc., Detroit, 1973-74; pub's. rep. The Detroiter mag., 1974-75; pub. relations dir. Detroit Bicentennial Commn., 1975-77; prin. Leland K. Bassett & Assocs., Detroit, 1976-86; intermediate job devel. specialist Detroit Council of the Arts, 1977; project dir. Detroit image campaign Dept. Pub. Info., City of Detroit, 1975, spl. events dir., 1978; dep. dir. Dept. Pub. Info. City of Detroit, 1978-83, dir., 1983-86; pres., prin. Bassett & Bassett, Inc., Detroit, 1986—. Publicity chmn. Under the Stars IV, V, VI, VII, VIII, IX and X, Benefit Balls, Detroit Inst. of Arts Founders Soc., 1983-88, Detroit Inst. of Arts Centennial Ball, 1985, publicity chmn. Mich. Opera Theater, Opera Ball, 1987; program lectr. Wayne County Close-Up Program, 1984; mem. cen. planning com. Am. Assn. Mus.; mem. Founders Soc., Detroit Inst. Arts, North Rosedale Civic Assn.; mem. adv. bd. Detroit Jr. League., 1988—; mem. publicity choice Grand Prix Ball, 1989; co-chair producer Mus. Ball Ctr. for Performing Arts. Mem. Detroit Hist. Soc., Music Hall Assn., Pub. Rels. Soc. Am. (Advt. Woman of the Yr. Detroit chpt. 1989), AIA (pub. dir. 1990—). Club: Economics. Home: 18644 Gainsborough Rd Detroit MI 48223 Office: Bassett & Bassettt Inc 672 Woodbridge St Detroit MI 48226-4302

BASSOFF, EVELYN SILTEN, clinical psychologist, author, educator, speaker; b. N.Y.C., Dec. 25, 1944; d. Hans and Helene (Frank) Silten; m. Bruce David Bassoff, June 13, 1965; children: Leah Jael, Jonathan Lev. BS, CCNY, 1965; MS, CUNY, 1970; MA, U. Colo., 1978, PhD, 1981. Lic. clin. psychologist, Colo. Tchr. N.Y.C. Pub. Schs., 1965-70; art tchr. Fine and Folk Art Mus. Sch., Athens, Ohio, 1973-74; project dir. Whittier Elem. Sch., Boulder, Colo., 1977-78; cons. Boulder Valley Schs., 1977-80; counselor, cons. Employee Assistance Programs, Boulder, 1978-81; pvt. practice in psychology Boulder, 1980—; adj. prof. U. Colo., Boulder, 1981—; speaker on topic of mothers and daughters, 1988—; profl. staff mem. Centennial Peaks Hosp.; adv. bd. Women's Recovery Ctr., Community Hosp. Author: Mothers and Daughters: Loving and Letting Go, 1988; contbr. articles to Counseling Psychologist, Jour. of Marriage and the Family, Jour. of Counseling and Devel., others, 1983—. Mem. Amnesty Internat., Am. Assn. Counseling and Devel., Am. Psychol. Assn. Democrat. Jewish. Office: 1634 Walnut St #221 Boulder CO 80302

BASTEDO, ELEANOR MADAY, real estate executive; b. Passaic, N.J., Feb. 12, 1937; d. Victor Joseph and Helena (Frankovsky) Maday; m. Theodore C. Bastedo, Sept. 2, 1960 (wid.); children: Laura Helen Naumann, Thea Lyn, Darin J. BA, Montclair Coll., 1960; grad., Realtors Inst., Orlando, Fla., 1976. Tchr. Pompton Lakes (N.J.) Bd. Edn., 1960-61, Fair Lawn (N.J.) Bd. Edn., 1961-63; chemist Fisher Sci., Fair Lawn, 1965, Brit. Chloride, Tampa, Fla., 1972; real estate broker Tharin Agy., Inc., Dunedin, Fla., 1973-78; pres. Bastedo & Cressman, Inc., Dunedin, Fla., 1978—; cons. in field; active sales of foreclosed properties and sales of trust properties for large bank. Participant in establishing local adult congregate living facility, Clearwater, Fla., 1981-82. Fellow NSF, 1959; RCA Corp. scholar, 1960. Mem. Cert. Residential Specialists (cert.), Cert. Real Estate Appraisers (cert.), Greater Clearwater Bd. Realtors, West Pasco Bd. Realtors, AAUW (pres. Clearwater chpt. 1981-82), Head Injury Support, Inc. (founding mem. Tampa Bay chpt.), Dunedin C. of C. Republican. Unitarian. Office: 500 Main St Dunedin FL 34698

BASTIAN, DEBORA LAINE, industrial hygenist; b. Sacramento, July 25, 1951; d. George Raymond and Mary Ruth (Montgomery) Sommers; m. Widtsoet Bastian, July 4, 1981 (div. Feb. 1989); children: Nathan, Brady. BS, Utah State U., 1983; MS in Pub. Health, U. Utah, 1986. Indsl. hygienist Hill AFB, Utah, 1984-84, Utah Occupational and Safety Health Adminstrn., Salt Lake City, 1986-87, Power Master, Inc., Salt Lake City, 1987-87; mem. faculty Univ. of Utah, Salt Lake City, 1987-89; cons. Kuselaan & D'Angelo Assocs., Inc., Salt Lake City, 1989—. Mem. Women in Sci. and Math, Salt Lake City, 1989. Mem. Am. Conf. Govt. Indsl. Hygiene, Am. Indsl. Hygiene Assn., Alpha Epsilon Delta., Sierra Club (Salt Lake City). Office: Univ Utah Rocky Mt Ctr for Occupation & Environ Health Bldg 512 Salt Lake City UT 84112

BASTIN, KATHY LOUISE, investment company executive; b. Kingston, Pa., June 23, 1953; d. Harold Peter and Anne Louise (Hurst) A.; m. Donald Arlie Bastin, Aug. 17, 1974; children: Michael, Matthew, Andrew. BS in Bus., U. Colo., 1975; MBA, U. Colo., Colorado Springs, 1981. V.p. Vaughn Mortgage, Colorado Springs, 1976-80, Preferred Savs. & Loan, High Point, N.C., 1981-83; pres. First Mortgage and Investment, Greensboro, N.C., 1983-87, Comml. Mortgage & Investment Co., Greensboro, 1987—. Vol. Mobile Meals, Greensboro, N.C., 1986—; bd. dirs. Goodwill Industries, Greensboro, 1986—. Am. Inst. Real Estate Appraisers, U. Colo., 1974. Mem. Mortgage Bankers Assn., N.C. Real Estate Commn. (broker). Republican. Roman Catholic. Home: 2404 Goldfield Ct Greensboro NC 27405 Office: CMI 5509 W Friendly Ave Greensboro NC 27410

BASTOKY, LINDA RAE, English teacher; b. Cleve., Feb. 5, 1949; d. Irving Benjamin and Esther (Naff) B. BS, Miami U., Oxford, Ohio, 1971. English tchr. Cleve. Pub. Schs., 1971-78, West Geauga Local Schs., Chesterland, Ohio, 1979—. Mem. Nat. Coun. Tchrs. of English, Ohio Coun. Tchrs. of English, West Geauga Edn. Assn., Sigma Delta Tau. Democrat. Jewish. Home: 1156 Worton Blvd Mayfield Heights OH 44124 Office: West Geauga High Sch 13401 Chillicothe Rd Chesterland OH 44026

BASTOW, SUSAN LYNELL, financial company executive; b. Auburn, Maine, Aug. 21, 1959; d. Richard Fredrick and Nancy (Dodge) B. BS, U. Maine, Farmington, 1981. Cert. spl. edn. and elem. tchr., Va. Learning disabilities tchr. Prince William County Schs., Manassas, Va., 1981-84; staff supr. Norrell Temp. Svcs., Washington, 1984-85, office mgr., 1985-86, br. mgr., 1986-87, area mgr., 1987-89; dir. Key Fin. Group, Bethesda, Md., 1989—. Active Mar. of Dimes, Washington, 1984—. Mem. Nat. Assn. Temp. Svcs., Bd. of Trade, Kappa Delta Pi. Republican. Office: Key Fin Group 4600 East West Hwy Bethesda MD 20814

BATCHELDER, ALICE M., federal judge; b. 1944; m. William G. Batchelder III; children: William G. IV, Elisabeth. BA, Ohio Wesleyan U., 1964; JD, Akron U., 1971; LLM, U. Va., 1988. Tchr. Plain Local Sch. Dist., Franklin County, Ohio, 1965-66, Jones Jr. High Sch., 1966-67, Buckeye High Sch., Medina County, 1967-68; assoc. Williams & Batchelder, Medina, Ohio, 1971-83; judge U.S. Bankruptcy Ct., Ohio, 1983-85, U.S. Dist. Ct. (no. dist.) Ohio, Cleve., 1985—. Mem. ABA. Office: US Dist Ct 256 US Courthouse 201 Superior Ave NE Cleveland OH 44114*

BATCHELOR, CELIA TUNSTALL ASHE, elementary educator; b. Greenville, N.C., Feb. 8, 1947; d. John Grange Jr. and Katharine Ruth (Jones) Ashe; m. Roy Thomas Batchelor, Dec. 20, 1966; children: John Ashe, William Thomas. BS, East Carolina U., 1969; MEd, U. Ga., 1975. 5th grade tchr. Cliffdale Elem.-Cumberland County, Fayetteville, N.C., 1969-71; 4th grade tchr. South Harnett Elem., Lillington, N.C., 1971-72; 5th grade tchr. Candler Elem., Gainesville, Ga., 1972-75; 4th and 5th grade tchr. Sylvester Jones Elem., Gainesville, 1975—, tchr. English lang. to speakers of fgn. langs., 1989—; with staff devel. rev. and approval coms. Hall County Bd. Edn., Gainesville, 1978—. Dem. lobbyist for ednl. legis. in Congress, 1977; lobbyist Ga. Gen. Assembly, 1974-87. Mem. AAUW, NEA (originator/organizer Child Find picture and finger printing project 1982, nat. del. 1976-88), Ga. Assn. Educators (bd. dirs. 1976-79, 80-83, 86-89, mem. exec. com. 1977-79), Assn. Classroom Tchrs. (Ga. Tchr. of Yr. 1989), Phi Kappa Phi, Delta Kappa Gamma, Phi Delta Kappa. Home: 1055 Green St Circle Gainesville GA 30501 Office: Jones Elem Sch 6th St Chicopee Gainesville GA 30501

BATE, JUDITH ELLEN, artist; b. Cleve., July 8, 1934; d. Edward Thomas and Eleanor Louise (Hyde) B. BA, Denison U., 1956; postgrad., Cleve. Inst. Art, 1957-59; cert. in Drawing and Painting, Yale U., 1985. Asst. mgr. advt. The Halle Bros. Co., Cleve., 1959-66; owner Businessbait Advt., Shaker Heights, Ohio, 1966-67; asst. mgr. promotions Ft. Lauderdale (Fla.) News, 1967-70; creative ptnr. Mielo/Bate Advt., Inc., Ft. Lauderdale, 1970-71; dir. art Data Graphic Services, Inc., Ft. Lauderdale, 1971-74, Brown/Dau & Assocs., Inc., Ft. Lauderdale, 1974-75; owner Florilore Art Studio, Pompano Beach, Fla., 1975-85; pvt. practice artist Pompano Beach, 1985—; May Show asst. Cleve. Mus. Art, also summer intern. One-woman shows include Royal Trust Banks of Palm Beach, Boca Raton, West Palm Beach, North Palm Beach, Fla., 1982, 83, Glendale Fed. Savs. and Loan, Boca Raton, Fla., 1985, Yale U. Gallery/Art & Architecture Bldg., 1985; juried shows include Beaux Arts Promenade, Ft. Lauderdale, 1979-89 (awards 1979, 83, 86), Boca Raton 8th Ann. Outdoor Art Fest., 1980, Pompano Beach Art-in-the-Sun, 1980 (awards 1981, 85, 86), 1st Ann. Art Olympics, Ft. Lauderdale, 1981, Plantation Art Fest., 1982, 83, 84 (awards 1985, 86), Compass Rose Art Fair, Nag's Head, N.C., 1983, New World Fest. of Arts, Manteo, N.C., 1983, Artists' Showcase V at Bapt. Hosp. Miami, Fla., 1984, Key Biscayne (Fla.) Art Fest., 1986, Glades Plaza Art Show, Boca Raton, 1986, Crocker Ctr., Boca Raton, 1987, Meet Me Downtown show, Boca Raton, 1986, 87, Sunfest, West Palm Beach, 1987; represented in permanent collections Goodyear Tire and Rubber Co., Akron, Ohio, Striker Aluminum Yachts, Ft. Lauderdale, Glendale Fed. Savs. and Loan, Ft. Lauderdale, Greater Pompano Beach C. of C., City of Pompano Beach, Royal T Stables, Los Angeles, The Flaming Pit Restaurant, Pompano Beach, D & L Cable Services, Pompano Beach, Consolidated Precision Corp., Riviera Beach, Fla.; exhibited in group shows at Clippinger Gallery, Ft. Lauderdale, 1984, The Delray Affair, Delray Beach, Fla., 1985; represented in permanent collections Design Ctr. of the Americas, Artco Consultants, Hollywood, Fla., numerous pvt. collectors. vol. art dir. House of Hope Pro-Am. Golf Classics, Ft. Lauderdale, 1979-82, Teenagers Against Drugs, Boca Raton, 1986-87; vol. Comp. Alcoholic Rehab. Programs, West Palm Beach, Fla., 1976-78; mem. exec. com. Gordon MacRae's Fest. of Hope, Ft. Lauderdale, 1985-87. Cranbrook Acad. Art scholar, Bloomfield Hills, Mich., 1959. Mem. Ft.

Lauderdale Mus. Art. Republican. Presbyterian. Club: One-oh-One (Pompano Beach). Home and Studio: 404 State St Amherst MA 01002

BATE, MARILYN ANNE, psychologist; b. Dillonvale, Ohio, May 23, 1939; d. Louis Edward and Veronica (Koval) Dezera; m. Brian Richard Bate, Sept. 7, 1968 (div. Apr. 1976); children: Jennifer, Julia. BSc, Ohio State U., 1961; MA, Case Western Res. U., Cleve., 1965, PhD, 1974. Lic. psychologist. Elem. tchr., sch. psychologist Cleve. City Schs., 1961-67; sch. psychologist, spl. edn. coord. Cleveland Heights (Ohio) U., Heights City Schs., 1967-70; sch. psychologist Mayfield (Ohio) City Schs., 1970-71, Cleve. City Schs., 1971-79, North Olmsted (Ohio) Schs., 1979-82; instr. Cuyahoga Community Coll., Cleve., 1967-82; pvt. practice Cleve., 1967-82; psychologist Dept. Def. Dependent Schs., Aviano, Italy, 1982-86; pvt. practice Columbus, Ohio, 1986—; ct. psychologist Franklin County Ct. Common Pleas, Columbus, 1987—. Mem. adv. bd. Eastpark Elem. Sch., Middleburg Heights, Ohio, 1985; vol. Son of Heaven, Columbus, 1989. Mem. Am. Psychol. Assn., Am. Correctional Assn., Nat. Sch. Psychol. Assn., Ohio Psychol. Assn. (mem. ethics com. 1986—), Cen. Ohio Psychol. Assn. (exec. bd. 1986—, treas. 1990—), European Sch. Psychol. Assn. (treas. 1985), Ohio Sch. Psychol. Assn. (co-chmn. ethics com. 1976-86, spl. svc. award 1987), Cleve. Sch. Psychol. Assn. (pres. 1969-71). Home: 3390 Stonehenge Ct Upper Arlington OH 43221 Office: Franklin County Ct 50 E Mount St Columbus OH 43215 Other: 1857 Northwest Blvd Columbus OH 43212

BATEMAN, IRIS HENDRIX, merchandise coordinator; b. Greer, S.C., Oct. 6, 1940; d. Walter Lee and Rosa Bell (Quinn) Hendrix; m. Robert B. Bateman, May 20, 1961. Diploma in bus., Doughn's Bus. Coll., 1959; cert. in bus., Greenville Tech., 1961. Sec. Springs Industries, Lyman, S.C., 1958-90, from sec. to merch. coord., 1990—. Asst. women's dir. Greer Bapt. Assn. Named Woman of Yr., Am. Bus. Woman, Heritage World. Mem. Am. Bus. Women's Assn. (sec. inner circle 1975, v.p. 1976), NAFE, Greer Jaycettes (sec. 1970, pres. 1971). Home: 13 Cottage Ln Taylors SC 29687 Office: Springs Industries Pacific St Lyman SC 29365

BATEMAN, JUSTINE, actress; b. Feb. 19, 1966; d. Kent and Victoria B. Bateman. Appeared in TV series Family Ties, 1982-88, in TV films Right to Kill, 1985, Can You Feel Me Dancing?, 1986, in film Satisfaction, 1988. Office: care Internat Creative Mgmt 8899 Beverly Blvd Los Angeles CA 90048*

BATEMAN, VEDA MAE, industrial psychologist, management consultant; b. Winnipeg, Manitoba, Can., Aug. 8, 1921; came to U.S., 1930; d. Norman Silver and Veda Moncrieff (Maxwell) B. ME, Vanderbilt U., 1944; BA, U. Tenn., 1951, MA, 1953, PhD, 1959. Cert. indsl. psychologist and cons.; lic. psychologist Tenn. Adminstrv. asst. to pres. Nashville (Tenn.) Bridge Co., 1940-45; program dir. Am. Red Cross, Germany, France, Korea, 1945-47; exec. dir. Children's Home, Knoxville, Tenn., 1947-55; corp. dir. of personnel and loss prevention Millers, Inc., Knoxville, 1955-65; corp. dir. rsch. and devel., safety and systems analyst Allied Stores, Millers Inc., Knoxville, 1965-87; mgmt. cons. Bateman Cons., Knoxville, 1987—. Mem., officer Knox Children's Found., Knoxville, 1955—, Volunteers of Am., Knoxville, 1965—, ARC, Knoxville, 1980-83, Overlook Mental Health Ctr., Knoxville, 1983-87; vol. counselor ACE/SBA, 1988—; vol. tax counselor Tax Counseling for Elderly, 1989-90. Mem. Am. Psychol. Assn., Tenn. Psychol. Assn., Deane Hill Country Club. Methodist. Home and Office: 3608 Blow Dr Knoxville TN 37920

BATES, BARBARA J. NEUNER, municipal official; b. Mt. Vernon, N.Y., Apr. 8, 1927; d. John Joseph William and Elsie May (Flint) Neuner; m. Herman Martin Bates, Jr., Mar. 25, 1950; children: Roberta Jean Bates Jamin, Herman Martin III, Jon Neuner. BA, Barnard Coll., 1947. Confidential clk. to supr. Town of Ossining, N.Y., 1960-63, receiver of taxes, 1971-90; pres. BNB Assocs., Briarcliff Manor, N.Y., 1963-83, Upper Nyack Realty Co., Inc., Briarcliff Manor, 1966-71. V.p. Ossining (N.Y.) Young Rep. Club, 1958; pres. Young Womens Rep. Club Westchester County (N.Y.), 1959-61; regional committeewoman N.Y. State Assn. Young Rep. Clubs, 1960-62; mem. Westchester County Rep. Com., 1963—; mem. Ossining Women's Rep. Club, 1960—, pres., 1984-85; mem. Westchester County Women's Rep. Club, 1957—. Mem. DAR, Jr. League Westchester-on-Hudson, N.Y. State Assn. Tax Receivers and Collectors, Receivers of Taxes Assn. of Westchester County, (legis. liaison, v.p., pres. 1984-85), Hackley Sch. Mothers Assn. (pres. 68), R.I. Hist. Soc., Ossining Hist. Soc., Ossining Bus. and Profl. Women's Club, Am. Soc. Notaries, Westchester County Hist. Soc., Briarcliff-Scarborough Hist. Soc. Congregationalist. Home: 78 Holbrook Ln Briarcliff Manor NY 10510 also: 663 Reynolds Rd Chepachet RI 02814

BATES, BARBARA JEANNE, art reference librarian, writer, lecturer; b. Mpls., May 31; d. Gale Pillsbury and Rhetta Hilyer; m. George Walter Bates, Dec. 12, 1951 (div. 1962); 1 child, Brenda Leigh. Student Beaver Coll., 1947-48; B.A. in Edn., U. Pa., 1950; M.A., Drexel Inst., 1951; Tchrs. Cert., Temple U., 1953. Librarian, Free Library of Phila., 1950-54, reference librarian, 1987—; librarian U.S. Army Overseas Schs., Mannheim, Germany, 1956-61, Lansdown Aldan Sch. Dist., Pa., 1961-71, Kulani Honor Camp, Hilo, Hawaii, 1976; library coordinator Springfield Sch. Dist., Erdenheim, Pa., 1971-82; reference librarian in charge Community Coll. Phila., evenings and weekends 1977-80; pres., producer Betsy Ross Living History Presentations, Valley Forge, Pa., 1982-87 to prepare Am. schs. and communities for celebration of U.S. Constn.; kindergarten tchr. Children's Learning Service, King of Prussia, Pa., 1985-86; co-founder, vice pres., sec. Global Edn. Motivators, Erdenheim, 1980-84. Author, producer, coordinator, actress of video film: Happy Birthday George Washington, 1982 (Freedom Found. award 1982); The Rainbow Experience, 1984. Mem. disaster action team ARC, Phila., 1982—; disaster reservist Fed. Emergency Mgmt. Agy. Eastern Div. , 1984-87; vol. asst. to Archivist Medal of Honor Grove Freedoms Found., Valley Forge, 1980-87, worker for Habitat for Humanity at J. Carter Work Camp, Phila., 1988, cons. to Library and Archival Collection at Valley Forge Hist. Park; literacy tutor for Mayor's Commn. on Literacy for the Prison Literacy Project Project, U.S. div. Books for Youth. Recipient George Washington Honor medal Freedoms Found., 1982; Legion of Merit, Chapel of Four Chaplains, 1982. Mem. NEA (del. conv. 1980, 81), Govs.' Conf. on Libraries and Info. Services (del. 1977), White House Conf. on Libraries and Info. Services, Pa. Library Assn. (Pub. Relations award 1959), World Affairs Council, Japan Study Group II, Valley Forge Hist. Soc., Am. Assn. Mus., U.S. Capitol Hist. Soc., Kappa Delta. Democrat. Mem. and tour guide Washington Meml. Chapel at Valley Forge.

BATES, LANA, marketing consultant; b. Ephraim, Utah; d. Farrin L. and Enola (Johnson) Mangelson; m. Ted Bates, Mar. 24, 1973; children: Sterling, Nelson, Morgan. AA, Snow Coll., 1966; BA, Brigham Young U., 1972. French educator Mesa (Ariz.) High Sch., 1972-73; culinary sch. owner Bates Svc., Ariz. and Kans., 1974-82; newsletter pub. Bates Pub., Wichita, Kans., 1982-84; pres., owner Bates Mktg. Svcs., Wichita, 1982—; lectr., speaker various orgns., cons. bus. and mktg., 1983—. Co-author: The Creative Innovators; contbr. articles to profl. jours. Bd. dirs. Kans. chpt. Am. Diabetes Assn., 1983-84, nat. bd. dirs., 1986-88, Internat. Diabetes Found. Com., Drug-Alcohol Abuse Prevention Ctr., Wichita, 1986—; pres., founder Pathways Inst., 1988—. Named Woman of Yr. Mrs. Kans. Pageant, 1984, Best Vol. of Yr. Kans. Am. Diabetes Assn., 1985; recipient Nat. Logo award, 1985. Mem. Am. Soc. Tng. and Devel., Nat. Speakers Assn. Office: Bates Mktg Svcs 1929 White Oak Wichita KS 67207

BATES, LURA WHEELER, trade association executive; b. Inboden, Ark., Aug. 28, 1932; d. Carl Clifton and Hester Ray (Pace) Wheeler; m. Allen Carl Bates, Sept. 12, 1954; 1 child, Carla Allene. BSBA, U. Ark., 1954. Cert. constrn. assoc. Sec.-bookkeeper, then officer mgr. Assoc. Gen. Contractors Miss., Inc., Jackson, 1958-77, dir. adminstrv. svcs., 1977—, asst. exec. dir., 1980—; adminstr. Miss. Constrn. Found., 1977—; sec. AIA-Assoc. Gen. Contractors Liaisonship Coms., 1977—; sec. Carpenters Joint Apprenticeship Coms., Jackson and Vicksburg, 1977—. Sec. Marshall Elem. Sch. PTA, Jackson, 1962-64, v.p., 1965; sec.-treas. Inter-Club Coun. Jackson, 1963-64; tchr. adult Sunday sch. dept. Hillcrest Bapt. Ch., Jackson, 1975-82; dir. Bapt. Women WMU, 1987—; tchr. adult Sunday sch. dept. 1st Bapt. Ch., Crystal Springs, Miss., 1989—; mem. exec. com. Jackson Christian Bus. and Profl. Women's Coun., 1976-80, sec., 1978-79, pres., 1979-80. Named Outstanding Woman in Constrn. Miss., 1962-63, Outstanding Mem. Nat. Assn. Women in Constrn. Fellow Internat. Platform Assn.; mem. NAFE, Nat. Assn. Women in Constrn. (chpt. pres. 1963-64, 76-77, nat. v.p. 1965-66, 77-78, nat. dir. Region 5, 1967-68, nat. sec. 1970-71, 71-72, pres. 1980-81, coord. cert. constrn. assoc. program 1973-78, 83-84 guardian-contr. Edn. Found. 1981-82, chmn. nat. bylaws com. 1982-83, 85-88, nat. parliamentarian 1983-89), Nat. Assn. Parliamentarians, U. Ark. Alumni Assn. (life), Delta Delta Delta. Editor NAWIC Image, 1968-69, Procedures Manual, 1965-66, Public Relations Handbook, 1967-68, Profl. Edn. Guide, 1972-73, Guidelines & Procedures Handbook, 1987-88; author digests in field. Home: 272 Lee Ave Crystal Springs MS 39059 Office: 2093 Lakeland Dr Jackson MS 39216

BATES, MARIETTE J., organizational development professional; b. N.Y.C., Apr. 30, 1950; d. Andrew Hoyt and Mariette Jane (Graef) B. BS, Empire State Coll., 1989; MA in Philosophy, NYU; cert. Inst. Not-for-Profit Mgmt., Columbia U., 1984. Program dir. One to One Found., N.Y.C.; dir. Resource Ctr. for Developmental Disabilities, N.Y.C.; now v.p. Maidstone Found., N.Y.C.; faculty assoc. Columbia U. Inst. Not-for-Profit Mgmt.; trainer Cornell U. ILR Mgmt. Simulation. Contbr. articles to various publs. Past pres. Clinton Housing Devel. Co., past pres.; mem., bd. dirs. Clinton Com. Dispute Resolution Ctr., Inc.; bd. dirs. Embrace Found., Ctr. for Family Support, RIS, Lakeside Family and Children's Svcs.; vol. mediator Children's Aid Soc. Office: Maidstone Found 1225 Broadway 9th Fl New York NY 10001

BATES, MARION VIRGINIA, retired state official, consultant; b. Iowa City, Aug. 1, 1919; d. William Herbert and Alice Cecil (Wilkinson) B.; m. James Edward Bonham, Nov. 6, 1942 (div. Aug. 1948). BA, U. Iowa, 1941, MA, 1942, postgrad., 1965-66; postgrad., Stanford U., 1968-73. Sr. legal editor Commerce Clearing House, Inc., Chgo., 1944-50; rsch. assoc. U. Mich., Ann Arbor, 1951-52; textbook editor Follett Pub. Co., Chgo., 1958-61; mng. editor Grolier, Inc., N.Y.C., 1961-65; tchr. high sch., Des Moines, 1967-68, Davenport, Iowa, 1968-70; assoc. dir. Wis. Devel. Disabilities Coun., Madison, 1975-90, cons., 1990—. Mem. Iowa Gov.'s Commn. on Handicapped, 1973-75, Wis. Coun. on Continuing Edn., 1978-80, Wis. Coun. on Visually Impaired, 1984-89, Wis. Coun. on Hearing Impaired, 1987-89, Wis. Mental Health Coun., 1986-89, Wis. Gov.'s Planning Commn. for White House Conf. on Handicapped. Recipient Exceptional Performance award Wis. Devel. Disabilities Coun., 1987. Mem. AAUW (bd. dirs. Madison br. 1976—, past co-pres., named grant scholarship 1986), Am. Polit. Sci. Assn., Phi Beta Kappa. Presbyterian. Home: 3205 Churchill Dr Madison WI 53713 Office: Wis Devel Disabilities Coun PO Box 7851 Madison WI 53707-7851

BATES, MARY ELLEN, library director; b. San Mateo, Calif., July 10, 1954. BA in Philosophy, U. Calif., 1976, MLS, 1982. Info. specialist Pillsbury Madison & Sutro, San Francisco, 1979-82; research assoc. FDR on Line, Wash., 1982-83; info. specialist Fed. Judical Ctr., Wash., 1983-84; mgr. corp. library MCL Communications Corp., Wash., 1984—. Mem. Conf. Bd. Info. Services Adv. Council, N.Y., 1988—. Mem. Special Libraries Assn., Am. Soc. Info. Sci., Law Libraries' Soc. Office: MCI Communications Corp 1133 19th St NW Washington DC 20036

BATES, MARY LOUISE, land and cattle company executive; b. Dallas, Oct. 26, 1930; d. John H. and Mary Evelyn (Nichols) Mattison; m. Robert L. Bates, 1947 (div. May 1988); 1 child, Daniel Moore. Student, So. Meth. U., Dallas, 1947, U. Ariz., 1962. V.p. Agro Land & Cattle Co., Tucson, Ariz., 1965-87, pres., 1987—. Mem. Rep. Nat. Com.; bd. dirs. Ariz. Children's Home, Tucson, 1985-87, Planned Parenthood, Santa Barbara; bd. visitors St. Luke's, Tucson, 1986-88; bd. mem., founder. Soc. Prevention Cruelty to Animals, Ariz., 1972. Mem. Tex. Longhorn Breeders Assn., Jr. League Tucson, Skyline Country Club, Mountain Oyster Club. Home: 2820 Cerrado Los Palitos Tucson AZ 85718 Office: Agro Land & Cattle Co Inc 6541 Tanque Verde Tucson AZ 85715

BATES, RHONDA BARBER, financial advisor; b. Augusta, Ga., Feb. 18, 1962; d. Howard Wesley Barber and Thelma Jean (Eller) Brown; m. William Bowers III Bates, May 4, 1985. BBA, Augusta Coll., 1989. Fin. advisor William B. Bates III, M.D., P.C., Augusta, Ga., 1985—; fin. tutor Augusta Coll., 1988—. Mem. Fin. Mgmt. Assn. (named to Nat. Honor Soc.), Children's Med. Ctr. Fundraiser Assn., Ga. Med. Assn. Aux., Faculty Wives Club of Med. Coll. Ga., Phi Kappa Phi. Baptist. Home and Office: 2116 Wrightboro Rd Augusta GA 30904

BATES, RUBY LEE, corporate administrator; b. Marion, La., July 14, 1940; d. Roy and Wordie B. (Boyette) Shelbon; m. Julius Green, Aug. 18, 1963 (div. 1968); 1 child, Dana; m. Charles Bates, June 30, 1976 (dec.). AA, Castlemont Coll., Oakland, 1957; SSA, Heald Coll., Oakland, 1958. Exec. sec. Golden State Ins., Oakland, 1958-66; adminstrv. office mgr. Simmons & Travis, Oakland, 1966-74; adminstrv. asst. Castle & Cooke, San Francisco, 1975-77, office coord., 1977-81, corp. bookkeeper, 1981-85; case adminstr. Kornblum, Kelly & Herlihy, San Francisco, 1986; case adminstr. Kornblum & McBride, San Francisco, 1986—. Editor: Handbook for Temporary Personnel, 1979, Basic Training Manual for Case Administrators, 1988. Vol., Gospel Voices, Oakland, 1971-85. Recipient Svc. award Bible Fellowship Ch., Oakland, 1976. Mem. NAFE, Gamma Phi Delta. Democrat. Baptist. Avocations: Gospel singing, walking, reading. Home: 3822 39th Ave Oakland CA 94619 Office: Kornblum & McBride 445 Bush St 6th Fl San Francisco CA 94108

BATES, SUSAN VIOLA, health care administrator, nurse; b. Columbus, Wis., May 23, 1951; d. Lester Otto and Lois Viola (Rath) Henning; children: Rebecca Sue, Kenneth Ryan; m. Bill D. Bates. BS in Nursing, Olivet Nazarene Coll., Kankakee, Ill., 1973; MS, Govs. State U., Park Forest South, Ill., 1977. RN, Calif., Ind. Nurse's aide Columbus Community Hosp., Wis., 1967-69; nurse aide Riverside Hosp., Kankakee, 1971-73, nurse, 1973; nurse Palos Community Hosp., Ill., 1973-74; instr. St. Joseph Hosp. Sch. of Nursing, Joliet, Ill., 1974-76; project coord. Our Lady of Mercy Hosp., Dyer, Ind., 1976-78, asst. dir. nursing, 1978-80, dir. of spl. svcs., 1980-81; dir. of nursing svcs. Culver Union Hosp., Crawfordsville, Ind., 1981-84, dir. of patient svcs., 1984, asst. adminstr., 1984-86; dir. nursing, asst. adminstr. EPIC-Visalia (Calif.) Community Hosp., 1986—. Mem. Orgn. Nurse Execs., Sigma Theta Tau (Kappa Sigma chpt.). Republican. Nazarene. Office: Visalia Community Hosp 1633 S Court St Visalia CA 93277

BATESON, MARY CATHERINE, anthropology educator; b. N.Y.C., Dec. 8, 1939; d. Gregory and Margaret (Mead) B.; m. J. Barkev Kassarjian, June 4, 1960; 1 child, Sevanne Margaret. BA, Radcliffe Coll., 1960; PhD, Harvard U., 1963. Instr. Arabic Harvard U., 1963-66; asso. prof. anthropology Ateneo de Manila U., 1966-68; sr. research fellow psychology and philosophy Brandeis U., 1968-69; assoc. prof. anthropology Northeastern U., Boston, 1969-71; researcher U. Tehran, 1972-74; vis. prof. Northeastern U., 1974-75; prof. anthropology, dean grad. studies Damavand Coll., 1975-77; prof. anthropology, dean social sci. and humanities U. No. Iran, 1977-79; vis. scholar Harvard U., 1979-80; dean faculty, prof. anthropology Amherst Coll., 1980-87; Clarence Robinson prof. anthropology and English George Mason U., 1987—; pres. Inst. Intercultural Studies, from 1979. Author: Structural Continuity in Poetry: A Linguistic Study of Five Early Arabic Odes, 1970, Our Own Metaphor: A Personal Account of a Conference on Consciousness and Human Adaption, 1972, With a Daughter's Eye: A Memoir of Margaret Mead and Gregory Bateson, 1984, Composing a Life, 1989; co-author: Angels Fear: Towards an Epistemology of the Sacred, 1987, Thinking AIDS, 1988; co-editor: Approaches to Semiotics: Anthropology, Education, Linquistics, Psychiatry and Psychology, 1964. Fellow Ford Found., 1961-63, NSF, 1968-79, Guggenheim Found., 1987-88. Mem. Am. Anthrop. Assn., Soc. Iranian Studies, Lindisfarne Assn., Phi Beta Kappa. Address: 172 Lexington Ave Cambridge MA 02138

BATEY, AMANDA, academic administrator; b. Enid, Okla., Apr. 24, 1950; d. Leonard Maurice and Mary Frances (Stanley) B.; m. Bernard Allen Margolis, Nov. 2, 1973. BA, Miss. State U., 1972; MLS, U. Denver, 1973; cert. aging, U. Mich., 1978. Supplement security income, vol. coord. Area Agy. on Aging 1-B, Southfield, Mich., 1974, info. and referral coord., 1974-76, data rsch., librarian, 1976-77; adminstrv. asst. for extension ctrs., continuing edn. Monroe (Mich.) County Community Coll., 1977-80, adminstrv. asst. for program devel., continuing edn., 1980—; chairperson, womens conf., Monroe County Community Coll., 1981-88. Bd. mem. Monroe Women's Ctr., 1982-88, Meadow Montessori, Monroe, 1985-88; adv. coun. mem. Family Counseling & Shelter Svcs., Monroe, 1987-88. Mem. AAUW (bd. mem.), Monroe County C. of C.

BATH, JOANNE MCMATH, violin teacher; b. Seattle, Dec. 28, 1935; d. Roy Jayne and Anne Catherine (Bergstrand) Mc.; m. Charles Frederick Bath, Aug. 23, 1958; children: Pamela, Patricia, Stephen, Andrea. MusB, Denison U., Granville, Ohio, 1957; MusM, U. Mich., 1959. Reg. tchr. trainer, Suzuki Assn. of the Americas. Violinist Wichita (Kans.) Symphony, 1961-66; violin tchr. Bath Sch. of Music, Greenville, N.C., 1966—, dir., 1966—; dir. Suzuki Violinists of Eastern N.C., 1980—, pres. Greenville Suzuki Assn., Greenville, N.C., 1985—, pres. N.C. Suzuki Assn., 1980—. Contbr. articles to profl. jours. Bd. mem., 1978—, pres. Eastern Carolina Orch. and Chamber Music Assn., Greenville, N.C., 1980—; bd. dirs. Greenville Choral Soc., N.C. Sinfonia, 1990—. Mem. Am. String Tchrs. Assn. (state sec. 1972-74), Music Tchrs. Nat. Assn. (chmn. 1982-84, chmn. state string sect. 1990). Episcopalian. Office: Bath Sch Music 1304 Oakview Dr Greenville NC 27858

BATIGNANI, LAURIE A., cable television producer and director; b. Beverly, Mass., Dec. 11, 1953; d. Jerry Williamson and Janet (Pater) Siciliano; m. Lawrence Batignani, Sept. 30, 1978. Student, Newton Coll., 1971-72; student, Keene State Coll., 1972-73, U. Hartford, 1981. Claims reviewer Phoenix Mut. Life, Hartford, Conn., 1974-75; claims supr. Phoenix Mut. Life, Hartford, 1976-78, client svc. rep., 1979-80; svc. coord. Phoenix Mut. Life, Enfield, Conn., 1981-82; trainer Phoenix Mut. Life, Enfield, 1983, assoc. mgr., 1984-86; reporter, writer Hosp. News Assocs., Greenbush, N.Y., 1986; assoc. producer (internship) Sta. WGBY Channel 57 PBS, Springfield, Mass., 1987; producer, dir. Continental Cablevision of Conn., Enfield, 1988—. Mme. NOW, Washington, 1980—, Citizen's Alliance for a Safe Environment, Conn., 1981-82, Am. Women in Radio & TV, N.Y.C., 1988, Pub. Rels. Soc. Am., N.Y.C., 1987; vol. Cystic Fibrosis Found., Conn., 1965-71, 87-89. Scholar South Windsor Scholarship Assn., Conn., 1971. Mem. Women in Communications (profl.).

BATORSKI, JUDITH ANN, art association administrator; b. Eden, N.Y., Oct. 8, 1949; d. John Michael and Ethel (Owens) B.; m. Michael J. Rocco (div. Oct. 1980); 1 child, Flora. Student retail mgmt., Colo. Springs Coll. Bus., 1981; AS in Fine Arts, Suffolk Community Coll., 1983; BA, SUNY, Stonybrook, 1985, MA, 1987; postgrad., Columbia Coll. Chgo. Film Sch., 1985. Caretaker, asst. mgr. Farmer's Shared Home, Danbury, N.H., 1979-80; cert. educator Assn. for Childbirth at Home, Internat., L.A., 1980; accts. payable clk. Pikes Peak Community Coll., Colorado Springs, Colo., 1981-82; office mgr. Three Village Meals-on-Wheels, Stonybrook, 1984; grad. sec. art dept. SUNY, 1986-87, art gallery intern Fine Arts Ctr., 1987; dir. ops., dir. master classes and free concerts Islip Arts Coun., East Islip, N.Y., 1987-89; auditor N.Y. State Coun. on the Arts, N.Y.C., 1989—; participant Arts in Bus. Mgmt. seminar Citibank/ABC, N.Y.C., 1987, community leaders luncheon Fox Channel 5, N.Y.C., 1987; asst. to dir. "Newsday's" L.I. Summer Arts Festival '89 Community Affairs Dept., 1989, Suffolk County Motion Picture and TV Commn., Hauppauge, N.Y., 1989, Summer Film Festival, 1988-90; cons. N.Y. State Coun. on Arts, 1989-90. Photographs included in Photography Forum's Coll. Photography Annual, 1985. Campaign dir. Food for Poland, Colorado Springs, 1982; organizer Granite State Alliance, Portsmouth, N.H., 1979, Safe 'n' Sound anti-nuclear campaign, Shoreham, N.Y., 1979; grad. rep. Sch. Continuing Edn. SUNY Stonybrook, judicial com. on acad. standing, SUNY Stonybrook, 1986-87; vol. Vietnam Vets. Theatre Ensemble, 1988, New Community Cinema, Huntington, N.Y., 1988; active exec. com. Dowling Coll. Spring Tribute Concert, Oakdale, N.Y., 1989; asst. to dir. Newsday Community Rels. Dept. L.I. Arts 89, 1989; founding mem. L.I. Green Party, Brookhaven Township, 1990—. Mem. Internat. Platform Soc. (invited mem. 1989), Contemporary Hispanic Artists of L.I. (advisor to bd. dirs. Cen. Islip 1988-89). Roman Catholic. Home: 260-6 Waverly Ave Patchogue NY 11772

BATTAGLINI, LINDA JACKSON, strategic planner; b. Bridgeport, Conn., May 18, 1950; d. James Richard and Jean Eleanor (Power) Jackson; m. Richard Anthony Battaglini Jr., May 30, 1971; children: Cara Lillian, Adam Richard. AAS, Broome Community Coll., Binghamton, N.Y., 1969; BA in Maths., SUNY, Binghamton, 1971, MS in Acctg., 1977. Staff acct. Wilson Hosp., Johnson City, N.Y., 1977-78, mgr. gen. acctg., 1978-79, planner, 1979-81; planner United Health Svcs., Binghamton, 1981-84, dir. planning, 1984-86, corp. planner, 1986—; cons. strategic planning Louis N. Picciano Constrn., Endicott, N.Y., 1988, Olsen Advt., Binghamton, 1989. Bd. dirs. Planned Parenthood, Binghamton, 1989—; treas. local polit. campaign, 1985. John A. Hartford Found. N.Y.C. grantee, 1982-83. Mem. Soc. Healthcare Planning and Mktg., Healthcare Fin. Mgmt. Assn.(advanced), The Planning Forum, SUNY Binghamton Alumni Assn. (pres. 1987—, v.p. 1986-87, treas. 1983-85). Office: United Health Svcs Mitchell Ave Binghamton NY 13903

BATTIN, PATRICIA MEYER, librarian; b. Gettysburg, Pa., June 2, 1929; d. Emanuel Albert and Josephine (Lehman) Meyer; m. William Thomas Battin, June 16, 1951 (div. 1975); children—Laura, Joanna, Thomas. B.A., Swarthmore Coll., 1951; M.S. in Libr. Sci., Syracuse U., 1967. Asst. libr. SUNY-Binghamton, 1967-69, asst. dir. for reader svcs., 1969-74; dir. libr. svcs. Columbia U., N.Y.C., 1974-78, v.p., univ. libr., 1978-87; interim pres. Research Libraries Group, Palo Alto, Calif., 1982, also dir., 1974-87; pres. Commn. on Preservation and Access, Washington, 1987—; trustee Coun. on Library Resources, Washington, EDUCOM, Princeton, N.Y., 1982-88, Lehigh U., 1989—. Contbr. articles to profl. jours. Mem. ALA, Assn. Rsch. Librs. (trustee 1982-85), Phi Beta Kappa, Beta Phi Mu. Club: Grolier (N.Y.C). Office: Commn on Preservation & Access 1785 Massachusetts Ave NW Ste 313 Washington DC 20036

BATTLE, BARBARA L. BROWN, federal agency administrator; d. Tom Jr. and Irene Bedford (Atkins) Brown; m. Joe Turner Battle; children: Joe Daryl, Kim Charise. MS, Calif. State U., Dominguez Hills, 1978; AA, Compton (Calif.) Coll., 1976. Cert. tchr., Calif. Commodities, fin. products mgr., chief rev. suspense IRS, Santa Ana, Laguna Niguel, Calif.; now field examination br. chief, rep. of dist. dir. IRS, Carson, Calif. Youth minister Cath. Ch., Lynwood, Calif. Mem. NAFE, Profl. Mgrs. Assn., BUST.

BATTLE, BEVERLY LYNN, health educator; b. Bradenton, Fla., Sept. 29, 1943; d. James Whittle and Helen Frances (Hendry) B. BS, Blue Mountain Coll., 1965; MA, U. Md., 1972, PhD in Health Edn., 1989; postgrad., U. Upsala, Sweden, 1975, N.Y. U., 1975. Elem. resource tchr. Newport News (Va.) Pub. Schs., 1965-67, high sch. tchr., dept. chmn., 1967-69, 71-73; asst. prof. Thomas Nelson Community Coll., Hampton, Va., 1974-80; grad. rsch. asst. U. Md., College Park, 1980-81; assoc. prof. Thomas Nelson Community Coll., Hampton, Va., 1981-88; prof. health edn., dept. chair Thomas Nelson Community Coll., 1989—; Appointee, Gov.'s Commn. on Venereal Disease, Richmond, 1974; cons., Newport News YWCA, 1975-77; cons. in sex edn., 1976-77, 82-84; cons. in stress mgmt., Newport News Pub. Schs., 1976-77. Bd. dirs., YWCA, Newport News, 1975-79, Planned Parenthood Southeast Va., Hampton, 1979—, Va. Lung Assn., 1986—. Mem. Am. Assn. Sex Educators, Counselors and Therapists, Nat. Women's Studies Assn., Va. Assn. Health, Phys. Edn. and Recreation, Va. Community Coll. Assn., NOW, Va. Women's Polit. Caucus,Phi Kappa Phi, Eta Sigma Gamma. Democrat. Episcopalian. Home: 3 Bonnie Ln Newport News VA 23606

BATTLE, EMILY ANNE, mathematics educator; b. Enterprise, Ala., Aug. 23, 1934; d. William Vann and Carolyn Adele (Edwards) Parker; m. Richard Leonard Shoemaker, Aug. 27, 1954 (div. Sept. 1978); children: Steven Vann, Benjamin Edgar, William Richard, Robert Leonard; m. John Mosley Battle, Feb. 3, 1989. BS with honors, Auburn (Ala.) U., 1954, MS, 1955; postgrad., U. Ala., Birmingham, summer 1979. Cert. tchr., Ala. Instr. Okla. State U., Stillwater, 1955-56, U. Minn., Duluth, 1956-57, U. Ala., Birmingham, 1968-79; tchr. Indians Springs Sch., Birmingham, 1979-80, Berney Points Bapt. Sch., Birmingham, 1980-84; product svc. rep. Tex. Instruments, Inc., Birmingham, 1982-83; instr. Samford U., Birmingham, 1984-85, U. Montevallo, Ala., 1985—. Mem. Math. Assn. Am., Ala. Assn. Coll. Tchrs. of Math., Lake Shore Investment Assn., Zeta Tau Alpha, Pi Mu Epsilon, Kappa Mu Epsilon, Phi Kappa Phi. Home: 988 Fox Valley Farms Rd

Maylene AL 35114 Office: U Montevallo Dept of Math #6494 Montevallo AL 35115

BATTLE, KATHLEEN DEANNA, soprano; b. Portsmouth, Ohio; d. Grady and Ollie (Layne) B. MusB, U. Cin., MusM, D of Performing Arts (hon.), 1983; D of Performing Arts (hon.), Westminster Choir Coll., Ohio U.; D of Music (hon.), Xavier U., 1989; DHL, Amherst Coll., 1990. Appeared with Met. Opera, San Francisco Opera, Chgo. Opera, Salzburg Festival, N.Y. Philharm., Boston Symphony, Phila. Orch., Chgo. Symphony, Berlin Philharm., Vienna Staatsoper, Paris Opera, Royal Opera/Covent Garden, others; roles include Semele, Cleopatra in Julius Caesar, Pamina in Magic Flute, Susanna in Marriage of Figaro, Zerlina in Don Giovanni, Blonde in Abduction from the Seraglio, Rosina in Barber of Seville, Adina in Elixir of Love, Norina in Don Pasquale, Sophie in Der Rosenkavalier, Zerbinetta in Ariadne auf Naxos, Zdenka in Arabella. Recipient Grammy awards, 1987, 88. Mem. Delta Omicron. Methodist. Office: care Columbia Artist Mgmt Inc 165 W 57th St New York NY 10019

BATTLE, LUCY TROXELL (MRS. J. A. BATTLE), educator; b. Bridgeport, Ala., June 28, 1916; d. John Price and Emily Florence (Williams) Troxell; student U. Ala., Montevallo, 1934-35; B.S. Fla. So. Coll., 1951; postgrad. U. Fla., 1954, Fla. State U., 1963, Oxford (Eng.) U., 1979, 80, 81; M.A., U. South Fla., 1970; m. Jean Allen Battle, Aug. 25, 1940; 1 dau., Helen Carol. Asst. postmaster, Bridgeport, Ala., 1936-40; asst. dir. personnel office Sebring (Fla.) AFB, 1942-44; tchr. Cleveland Court Sch., Lakeland, Fla., also Forest Hill Sch., Carrollwood Sch., Tampa, Fla., 1949-64; dean of girls Greco Jr. High Sch., Tampa, 1964-68. Bd. dirs. Tampa Oral Sch. for Deaf. Recipient Outstanding Service award Fla. So. Coll. Woman's Club, 1942. Mem. NEA, Am. Childhood Edn. Internat., AAUW, Delta Kappa Gamma, Kappa Delta Pi, Phi Mu. Methodist. Club: Carrollwood Village Golf and Tennis. Author: (with J.A. Battle) The New Idea in Education, 1968. Home and Office: 11011 Carrollwood Dr Tampa FL 33618

BATTLES, MAY FAIRY, educator; b. Ocala, Fla., June 28, 1946; d. Irvin and Fairy (Gallmon) Lee; m. Jerry Leonard Battles Jr., June 23, 1963 (dec. Sept. 1963); children: Jerry, Warren, Daryl. AA, Santa Fe Jr. Coll., Gainesville, Fla., 1970; BA in Elem. Edn., U. Fla., 1972; MS in Adminstrn., Nova U., 1978, EdS, 1985. With Marion County Sch. Bd., Ocala, 1972—, tchr. 2d grade, 1981-83, tchr. chpt. I reading, 1983—; mem. T-Shirt Math. Com., Reddick, Fla., 1985-86, Leadership Team, Reddick, 1983-85; chairperson steering com., Reddick, 1979-81; chairperson Comprehensive Planning Com., Reddick, 1981-82. Mem. NEA, Fla. Reading Assn., Marion Edn. Assn. (chairperson 1986-90, Certs.), Fla. Teaching Profl. Assn. Democrat. Baptist. Home: Rt 2 Box 2670 Williston FL 32696

BATTLES, ROXY EDITH, novelist, consultant, educator; b. Spokane, Wash., Mar. 29, 1921; d. Rosco Jirah and Lucile Zilpha (Jacques) Baker; m. Willis Ralph Dawe Battles, May 2, 1941; children: Margaret Battles Holmes, Ralph, Lara. AA, Bakersfield (Calif.) Coll., 1940; BA, Calif. State U., Long Beach, 1959; MA, Pepperdine U., 1976. Cert. tchr. English, adult basic edn. and elem. edn., Calif. Freelance writer, 1940—; tchr. elem. Torrance (Calif.) Unified Schs., 1959-85; tchr. adult edn. Pepperdine U., Torrance, 1969-79, 76-80; freelance children's author, 1966—; mystery novelist Pinnacle Publs., N.Y.C., 1980; with Tex. A&M U., 1988; author, lectr. in field, Calif.; del. Tchrs. to Japan, 1975. Author: Over the Rickety Fence, 1967, The Terrible Trick or Treat, 1970, 501 Baloons Sail East, 1971, The Terrible Terrier, 1972, One to Teeter-Totter, 1973, 2nd edit., 1975, Eddie Couldn't Find the Elephants, 1974, reprints, 1982, 84, 88, What Does the Rooster Say, Yoshio?, 1978, The Secret of Castle Drai, 1980, The Witch in Room 6, 1987, 2nd edit., 1989 (nominee Garden State and Hoosier awards), The Chemistry of Whispering Caves, 1988. Active So. Calif. Coun. on Lit. for Children and Young People, 1973-80, 87—. Recipient Commendation, UN, 1979; Hoosier award nominee, 1990, Garden State award nominee, 1990. Mem. S.W. Manuscripters (founder), Surfwriters. Home: 560 S Helberta Ave Redondo Beach CA 90277

BATTOCLETTE, AUGUSTA ROSE, teacher; b. Steubenville, Ohio, Mar. 30, 1929; d. August L. and Mary Theresa (Rizzuto) Tortorice; m. James William Battoclette, Feb. 4, 1950; children: Mary Ann Madden, Michael J., Renee J. Young, August L. AA, U. Steubenville, 1950; BS, Kent State U., 1970; cert. of enhancement, Wright State U., 1982. Cert. tchr. hearing impaired and learning disabled. Tchr. hearing impaired Kent (Ohio) City Schs., 1971-72, Dayton (Ohio) City Schs., 1972-76, Richmond (Va.) City Schs., 1976-79; tutor Dayton (Ohio) City Schs., 1980-82; cons. for hearing impaired Clermont County Schs., Batavia, Ohio, 1982-89; team leader curriculum Hearing Impaired Program, Dayton, Ohio, 1972-76, adv. com. Spl. Edn., 1972-76; leader Com. for Lang. Devel., U. Cin., 1974-75; mem. Placement Com. Hearing Impaired Program, Richmond, Va., 1976-79; language cons. Hearing Impaired and Viet Nam refugees, Xenia (Ohio) Schs., 1980-82. Mem. Jr. Mothers Club of Kent, 1957-67; v.p. Svc. Club of Kent, 1961-62, pres., 1962-63. Mem. AAUW (2nd v.p. Cin. br. 1984-88, 1st v.p. 1988-89, Cin. gift for Ednl. Found. in her name), Alexander Graham Bell Assn. of the Deaf.

BAUDY, ROMONA THERESA, healthcare executive; b. New Orleans, Sept. 8, 1947; d. Harold August and Alberta Theresa (Clayton) B.; m. John Stanley Keller (div. 1984); children: John Stanley Jr., Natalie Theresa. BS, Xavier U., 1970, MA, 1985. Tchr. New Orleans Pub. Schs., 1970-79, coordinator, 1982-87; assoc. dir. Mayor's Office on Pvt. Sector Initiatives, New Orleans, 1986-87; exec. dir. United Med. Ctr., New Orleans, 1987—. Bd. dirs. Friends of City Park, New Orleans, 1985—, Met. Hosp. Coun., New Orleans, 1987—; mem. com. Amistaad Rsch., New Orleans, 1987—; chmn. individual giving United Negro Coll. Fund, New Orleans, 1990; role model YWCA. Named to Outstanding Young Women Am., 1983, Achiever Am. Coun. Career Women, 1989; recipient Disting. Health award Chi Delta Mu, 1988. Mem. Nat. Assn. Health Svcs. Execs. (pres. local chpt. 1988—), Am. Mgmt. Assn., New Orleans C. of C. (bd. dirs. 1990—), Lakecomers Club (pres. 1980-83), Sunday Hearts Club. Democrat. Republican. Office: United Med Ctr 3419 St Claude Ave New Orleans LA 70117

BAUER, BARBARA GAE, literary executive; b. Bklyn., Sept. 1, 1958; d. James Vincent and Gaetanina Antoinette (Palumbo) Mangano; m. Clinton Bonaventure Bauer; children: Guy, Lucy. BA, Hunter Coll., 1971; MA, St. John's U., N.Y.C., 1979, PhD, 1979. Pres., founder Barbara Bauer Literary Agy., Matawan, N.J., 1979—. Democrat. Roman Catholic. Home: Barbara Bauer Lit Agy 179 Washington Ave Matawan NJ 07747

BAUER, CAROLINE FELLER, author; m. Peter A. Bauer; 1 child, Hilary A. BA, Sarah Lawrence Coll., 1957; MLS, Columbia U., 1958; PhD, U. Oreg., 1971. Children's and reference libr. N.Y. Pub. Libr., N.Y.C., 1958-62; libr. Hewitt Sch., N.Y.C., 1960-61, Eron Prep. Sch., N.Y.C., 1962-63, Colo. Rocky Mountain Sch., Carbondale, 1963-65; art editor Pacific N.W. Libr. Assn. Quar., 1967-72; producer, instr. Oreg. Edn. Pub. Broadcasting System, 1973-74; assoc. prof. Sch. Librarianship U. Oreg., 1966-79; cons. Ednl. Cons. Assocs., Denver, 1979-81; vis. storyteller N.Y. Pub. Libr., 1962-63; producer/performer Caroline's Corner Sta. KSNO, Aspen, Colo., 1964-66, Caroline: Folktales Around the World, NET affiliate, 1965-66, Caroline's Corner, Oreg. Ednl. Pub. Broadcasting System, 1972-80. Author: Children's Literature, 1973, Storytelling, 1974, Getting It Together With Books, 1974, Caroline's Corner, 1974, What's So Funny? Humor in Children's Literature (cassette), 1977, Handbook for Storytellers, 1977, This Way To Books, 1981, My Mom Travels Alot, 1981, Too Many Books! 1984, Celebrations, 1985, Presenting Reader's Theater, 1987, Rainy Day, Windy Day, Snowy Day, 1988, Halloween, 1989, Take a Poetry Break (video cassette) Creative Storytelling (video cassette), 1979, Presenting Reader's Theater, 1987, Rainy Day, Snowy Day, Windy Day, 1988, Halloween, 1989, others; contbr. articles to profl. jours. Recipient Ersted award for disting. teaching U. Oreg., 1968, Christopher award Jr. Literary Guild award of excellence Chgo. Woman in Pub., 1978, Dorothy McKenzie award for disting. contbn. to children's lit. So. Calif. Coun. on Lit. for Young People, 1986. Mem. ALA (notable books com. 1977-79, chmn. 1980, chmn. Laura Ingalls Wilder com. 1973-75, mem. Newbery-Caldecott com. 1972-78, bd. dirs. children's div. 1987—), Pi Lambda Theta, Beta Phi Mu.

BAUER, CATHERINE MARIE, Benedictine nun, social worker; b. Cin., Aug. 3, 1954; d. John Wendle and Catherine Ann (Krantz) B. AAS, U. Cin., 1979; BA in Social Work, Thomas More Coll., 1984; postgrad., Cath. U. Cashier Parkview Market, Owensville, Ohio, 197-74; ins. agt., office mgr. John Bauer & Assoc., Owensville, 1974-79; vol. coord. Covington (Ky.) Community Ctr., 1979-80, housing cons., 1985-86; child's guidance worker Cath. Social Svc., Latonia, Ky., 1980-81; community organizer Working in Neighborhoods, Cin., 1982-83; community garden coord. No. Ky. Community Ctr., Covington, 1984-85; coord. of payee program Welcome House, Covington, 1986—; mentor Thomas More Coll., Crestview Hills, Ky., 1986—. Local chairperson Benedictine for Peace, Villa Hills, Ky., 1980—; bd. dirs. Parish Kitchen, 1988-90, Diocese Justice and Peace Office, 1986-90; chairperson For an Inclusive Ch., 1988—; coord. Benedictine Assocs. Program, 1990—; mem. Benedictine Vocation Ministry Team, 1990—. Recipient Social Work Student of Yr. No. Ky. Social Workers, 1984, Baron Community Svc. award mental Health Assn. of No. Ky., 1988. Mem. Mental Health Assn. (advocacy com. 1988—). Roman Catholic. Home: 2500 Amsterdam Rd Villa Hills KY 41017 Office: Welcome House No Ky 141 Pike St Covington KY 41011

BAUER, ELIZABETH KELLEY (MRS. FREDERICK WILLIAM BAUER), consulting energy economist; b. Berkeley, Calif., Aug. 7, 1920; d. Leslie Constant and Elizabeth Jeanette (Worley) Kelley; A.B., U. Calif. at Berkeley, 1941, M.A., 1943; Ph.D. (fellow), Columbia U., 1947; m. Frederick William Bauer, July 5, 1944; children: Elizabeth Katherine Bauer Keenan, Frederick Nicholas. Instr. U.S. history and studies Barnard Coll., N.Y.C., 1944-45; lectr. history U. Calif. at Berkeley, 1949-50, 56-57; rsch. asst. Giannini Found., 1946-49, asst. rsch. agrl. economist, 1957-60; exec. sec. Internat. Conf. on Agrl. and Coop. Credit, U. Calif. at Berkeley, 1952-53, exec. sec. South Asia Project, 1955-56; registrar Holy Names Coll., Oakland, Calif., 1971-72; rsch. assoc. Brookings Instn. and Nat. Acad. Pub. Adminstrn., Washington, 1973; fgn. affairs officer Internat. Energy Affairs, Fed. Energy Adminstrn. Washington, 1974-77; fgn. affairs officer Office of Current Reporting, Internat. Affairs, Dept. Energy, Washington, 1977-81; dir. policy analysis and evaluation Nat. Coal Assn., Washington, 1981-83. Mem. Calif. Com. to Revise the Tchrs. Credential, 1961; trustee Grad. Theol. Union, Berkeley, 1972-74; bd. dirs. St. Paul's Towers and Episcopal Homes Found, Oakland, 1971-72. Recipient Superior Achievement award Dept. Energy, 1980; U. Calif. Alumni citation, 1983. Mem. AAUW (Calif. chmn. for higher edn. 1960-62), Internat. Assn. Energy Economists, Prytanean Honor Soc., AAAS, P.E.O., Mortar Bd., Phi Beta Kappa, Pi Lambda Theta, Sigma Kappa Alpha, Phi Alpha Theta, Pi Sigma Alpha. Democrat. Episcopalian. Author: Commentaries on the Constitution, 1790-1860, 1952; (with Murray R. Benedict) Farm Surpluses: U.S Burden or World Asset?, 1960; (with Florence Noyce Wertz) The Graduate Theological Union, 1970. Coauthor, editor: The Role of Foreign Governments in the Energy Industries, 1977. Home: 708 Montclair Dr Santa Rosa CA 95409

BAUER, ILONA, service hospital executive; b. Csot, Veszprem, Hungary, Dec. 31, 1936; d. Janos and Juliana Kadi; m. Julius Bauer, Apr. 13, 1957; children: Thomas, Mary Catherine. Student, Budapest U., 1956, Purdue U., 1981. Bookkeeper Gepallomas, Csot, 1952-53; auditor Beruhazasi Bank, Veszprem, 1954-56; dept. mgr. Schiller Millinery, Michigan City, Ind., 1961-65; with Meml. Hosp., Michigan City, 1967—, buyer med. supplies, 1973-78, materials mgr., 1978—. Mem. Am. Soc. Hosp. Materials Mgmt., Am. Soc. Healthcare Cen. Svc. Personnel, Ind. Hosp. Purchasing Mgmt., Internat. Materials Mgmt. Soc. (cert.). Home: 5654 Vintage Hills Trail La Porte IN 46350 Office: Meml Hosp 5th and Pine Sts Michigan City IN 46360

BAUER, JUDY MARIE, minister; b. South Bend, Ind., Aug. 24, 1947; d. Ernest Camiel and Marjorie Ann (Williams) Derho; m. Gary Dwane Bauer, Apr. 28, 1966; children—Christine Ann, Steven Dwane. Ordained to ministry, 1979. Sec. adminstrv. asst. Bethel Christian Ctr., Riverside, Calif., 1975-79; founder, pres. Kingdom Advancement Ministry, San Diego, 1979-89, trainer, mgr. cons., Calif., Oreg., Washington, Ala., Okla., Idaho and South Africa; founder, co-pastor Bernardo Christian Ctr., San Diego, 1981—; evangelism dir. Bethel Christian Ctr., 1978-81, undershepherd minister, 1975-79, adult tchr., 1973-81; condr. leadership tng. clinics, internat. speaker, lectr. in field. Author syllabus, booklet, tng. material packets. Mem. Internat. Conv. Faith Ministries, Inc. (area bd. dirs. 1983-88).

BAUER, LOIS MARLENE, educator, consultant; b. Kingsley, Iowa, Nov. 25, 1931; d. Henry Carl and Dorathea (Hollmer) B. BA, Northern Iowa U., 1953; MA, Mich. State U., 1965, PhD, 1978, MLIR, 1980. Tchr., curriculum dir. Pub. Sch. System, Charles City, Iowa, 1953-56; program dir. YWCA, St. Joseph, Mich., 1956-63; program dir. III Young Women's Christian Assn., Lansing, Mich., 1965-71; grad. asst. Mich. State U., East Lansing, Mich., 1972-73; asst. to the chmn. Adult./Continuing Edn., Mich. State U., East Lansing, Mich., 1974-77; proj. dir., research assoc. Mich. State U., East Lansing, 1982-83, asst. to dean, 1984-88, asst. prof., program coord., 1988—; cons. Lansing, Mich., 1989—. Contbr. articles to scholarly publs.; author learning aids and programs. Bd. dirs., com. mem. ARC, Girl Scouts U.S.A., YWCA, YMCA, learning impaired, Iowa and Mich., 1953-72. Scholar Mildred Erickson Fellowship, 1976, Mich. Assn. Adult Continuing Edn., 1977, Nat. P.E.O. Continuing Edn., 1976. Mem. Lansing Reg. C. of C., Nat. Ctr. for Higher Edn. Mgmt., Am. Assn. Adult And Continuing Edn., Mich. Assn. Adult and Continuing Edn. (Mem. com. 1985-86; Conf. Com. 1989-90).

BAUER, NANCY ELAINE, marketing executive; b. Alexandria, Va., Sept. 4, 1953; d. Donald Robert and Geraldine (Pisko) B. BA, Glassboro State Coll., 1976, postgrad., 1977-78; postgrad., Rutgers U., 1979. Tchr. Gloucester Twp. Sch. Dist., Blackwood, N.J., 1976-80; group service mgr. Harrah's Holiday Inn Resort, Atlantic City, N.J., 1980-83; tour and travel dir. Resorts Internat. Hotel and Casino, Atlantic City, 1983-84, v.p. bus. devel., 1984-85, sr. v.p., 1987—; v.p. Trump's Castle Hotel and Casino, Atlantic City, 1985-87, Trump Taj Mahal, Atlantic City, 1990—; ednl. cons. Blackwood Ednl. Improvement Ctr., 1978-80; speaker Futures Unltd. at Camden County Coll., Blackwood, 1986-87. Author: (with others) Global Education, 1980; contbr. articles to profl. jours. Vol. learning disabled tchr., Runnemede, N.J., 1979. Grantee Fulbright Found./N.J. Dept. Edn. for "Project Kenya", 1979. Mem. Am. Mktg. Assn., Am. Mgmt. Assn., Am. Bus. Operators Assn., Promotion Mktg. Assn., Atlantic City C. of C. Home: 591 4th St Absecon NJ 08201 Office: Trump's Castle Huron and Brigantine Blvd Atlantic City NJ 08401

BAUGE, CYNTHIA WISE, distributing company executive; b. Ottumwa, Iowa, Sept. 7, 1943; d. Donald Carlyle and Opal Dorthea (Douglas) W.; m. Harry Grant Bauge, May 1, 1965; 1 child, Melissa Anne. Student, Iowa State U., 1962-64, Area XI Community Coll., Ankeny 1974-75. Legal sec. City of Ames, Iowa, 1965-69; acctg. mgr. Vivan Equipment Co., Ames, Iowa, 1969; asst. mgr. Bavarian Motor Lodge, Des Moines, 1969-71; bookkeeper TCP of Iowa, Des Moines, 1971-72, Moffitt Bldg Material co., Des Moines, 1972-73, CS Capital/Mid Am. Growth Corp., West Des Moines, 1973-75; v.p. Grant Sales Inc., Plano, Tex., 1976—. Bd. dirs. Power, Allen, Tex., 1985-88, chmn. bd. dirs., 1986-88; bd. dirs. Cultural Arts Coun. of Plano, 1985-88, treas., 1986-87, v.p. classics, 1985-86; bd. dirs. North Tex. Rehab. Svcs., 1987—; adv. bd. Jr. League of Plano, 1988—; community bd. Physicians for Plano, 1988—; mem. found. bd. Collin County Community Coll. Found., 1989—. Mem. NAFE, Women's Div. C. of C. Plano (treas. 1981-82), Plano C. of C. (budget and fin. com., Athena/Bus. Woman of Yr. award 1986), Beta Sigma Phi. Republican. Lutheran. Avocations: home decorating, gaming. Office: Grant Sales Inc 1701 Capital Ave Plano TX 75074

BAUGH, LYNDA LOUISE, real estate company executive; b. Riverside, Calif., Apr. 15, 1962; d. Perry Dean and Sandra Louise (Macek) B. Student, Belmont Coll., 1980, Phillips Bus. Coll., 1981-82. Owner, pres. Reel Time Recording Co., Houston and Nashville, 1982-84; pvt. practice acctg. Nashville, 1985; real estate agt. About Town, Inc., Nashville, 1986-87, Faxon Homes, Nashville, 1987-89; real estate sales & mktg. Phillips Builders Inc, Nashville, 1989—. Fund raiser Bullshooters, Nashville, 1986—; pres. beautification Percy Priest Woods Homeowners, Nashville, 1987—. Mem. NAFE, Nashville Bd. Realtors (chmn. community svcs. 1988). Roman Catholic. Home: PO Box 201 Brentwood TN 37024-0201

BAUKOL, ELSIE SATA, pediatrician, consultant; b. Portland, Oreg., Oct. 3, 1925; d. Charles Kazuo and Ito (Kojima) Sata; m. John Louis Baukol, July 13, 1955 (dec. 1967); children: Sharon Baukol Callahan, John David. BA, Friends U., Wichita, Kans., 1947; MD, U. Utah, 1954; MPH, U. Calif., Berkeley, 1971. Diplomate, Am. Bd. Pediatrics. Intern Harbor Gen. Hosp., Torrance, Calif., 1954-55; resident in pediatrics U. Utah Hosp., Salt Lake City, 1958-61; pediatric cons. Utah State Dept. Health, Salt Lake City, 1961-70; asst. health officer Contra Costa County Health Dept., Martinez, Calif., 1971-82; chief div. family health Ill. Dept. Pub. Health, Springfield, 1983-88; instr., asst. clin. prof. U. Utah Med. Sch., Salt Lake City, 1961-70; clin. assoc. So. Ill. U. Med. Sch., Carbondale, 1983-88; bd. dirs. Family Counseling and Community Svcs., Walnut Creek, Calif., 1990—. Fellow Am. Acad. Pediatrics, Am. Coll. Preventive Medicine; mem. Am. Pub. Health Assn., Contra Costa County Mental Health Assn. (Dr. Glen Kent Meml. award 1980), Ill. Maternal and Child Health Coalition (Recognition award 1988), Japanese Am. Citizens League (v.p. Diablo Valley chpt. 1990). Home: 145 Pickering Pl Walnut Creek CA 94598

BAUM, ELAINE JOAN EISELE, financial executive; b. Blue Island, Ill., Apr. 12, 1948; d. Herman Adam and Jennie (Miedema) Eisele; m. Kenneth LeRoy Baum Jr., May 15, 1968 (div. 1980); children: Kenneth LeRoy III, David Eisele. AS cum laude, Tidewater Community Coll., 1977; student, Old Dominion U., 1980. Police dispatcher City of Virginia Beach, Va., 1968-70; legal sec. Hofheimer, Nusbaum & McPhaul, Norfolk, Va., 1974; office mgr. N.Am. Lighting Products, Norfolk, 1974-75; credit mgr. Rish Equipment Co., Norfolk, 1978-81; regional credit mgr. Richmond, Va., 1981-83; office adminstr. ARCO-ALSCO, Richmond, Va., 1983; mgr. ops. Vinyl Wholesale Supply, Richmond, 1983-85; v.p. mfg. U.S. Hist. Soc., Richmond, 1985-89; corp. credit mgr. Baker Equipment Engrng. Co., Richmond, 1989—. Active West End Civic Assn., Richmond, 1983—; chmn. pack com. Boy Scouts Am., Richmond, 1983-84; mem. adv. com. Va. Ho. Dels., 1988-89. With U.S. Army, 1966-68. Recipient Assocs. award with distinction Nat. Inst. Credit, 1981. Mem. Nat. Assn. Credit Mgmt. (bd. dirs. 1979-82, cert. achievement 1980), Nat. Utility Contrs. Assn. (co-chmn. budget com. Tidewater chpt. 1980-81), NAFE, DAV. Democrat. Home: 4300 Pine Top Ct Richmond VA 23229

BAUM, JEANNE ANN, lawyer; b. Bklyn., Sept. 24, 1937; d. Joseph and Elizabeth (Bengelsdorf) Masch; m. Stanley Baum, June 29, 1958; children: Richard Arthur, Laura Diane, Carol Lisa. BA, Bklyn. Coll., 1958; postgrad., Temple U., 1967, 69-71; JD, Suffolk U., 1973. Social case worker State Bd. Child Welfare, Camden, N.J., 1959, Camden County Welfare Bd., 1960; lawyer Nat. Labor Rels. Bd., Phila. and Boston, 1973-75; assoc. Blank, Rome, Claus & Comisky, Phila., 1976-78; trial atty. Interstate Commerce Commn., Phila., 1979-82; pvt. practice Phila., 1985—; adj. instr. St. Joseph's U., Phila., 1979. Columnist, Newton (Mass.) Times, 1973. Bd. Govs. Lawyers Alliance for Nuclear Arms Control, Phila., 1983—, sec. exec. bd. 1984-88; bd. dirs. Ctr. in Park for Older Adults, Phila., 1984—, Eagleville (Pa.) Hosp., 1986—, Social Action Com. Reconstrn. Coll., Phila., 1984-85. Recipient Am. Jurisprudence prize, Temple U. Sch. Law, Phila., 1971. Mem. Phila. Bar Assn. Office: 1120 PSFS Bldg 12 S 12th St Philadelphia PA 19107

BAUM, MELISSA LAYTON, advertising executive; b. Provo, Utah, Apr. 25, 1968; d. Walter Clarence Layton and Sherrie Ann (Hansen) Savage; m. Todd Olsen Baum, June 14, 1989. AAS in Bus. Mgmt., AAS in Salesmanship, Utah Valley Community Coll., 1988. With customer retention Cen. Bank, Provo, 1986-88; account exec. R & R Advt., Salt Lake City, 1988—. Mem. Advt. Fedn., Pub. Rels. Soc. Am. Republican. Mormon. Office: R & R Advt 837 E South Temple Salt Lake City UT 84102

BAUM, SARA HOFFMAN, artist, designer. Head designer John Wandmakers, N.Y.C.; bibl. costume designer Congregation Temple Emanuel, N.Y.C. Designer miniature box rooms; bibl. character puppets displayed at Temple Emanuel and featured in Brotherhood mag.; quilts photographed Mus. of City of N.Y. Costume designer Drama Sun. Sch., Congregation Temple Emanuel, N.Y.C. Home: 300 Winston Dr #2115 Cliffside Park NJ 07010

BAUM, SELMA, ustomer relations consultant; b. Bklyn., Jan. 15, 1924; d. Samuel and Tillie (Bayer) Goldman; m. Milton W. Baum, Jan. 19, 1947; children: Victor C., Cynthia Baum-Baicker. Student, NYU New Sch. for Social Rsch. Communications mgr. Sobel & Goldman, Inc., N.Y.C., 1941-48; pub. rels. cons., 1948-65; comparison shopper Gimbels, Valley Stream, N.Y., 1965-67, mgr. comparison shopping office N.Y. div., N.Y.C., 1967-75, dir. consumer affairs East div., 1975-84; dir. corp. customer rels. Saks Fifth Ave., N.Y.C., 1984-89; cons. customer rels., Palm Beach, Fla., 1989—; lectr., writer in field. Arbitrator Met. N.Y. Better Bus. Bur. Mem. NAFE, Am. Mgmt. Assn. (industry panelist), N.Y. & N.J. Retail Mchts. Coun. (v.p.), Women in Communication (award N.Y. chpt. 1984), Nat. Retail Mchts. Assn. (consumer affairs com.), Fashion Group, Am. Coun. on Consumer Interests, Soc. Consumer Affairs Profls. in Bus. (chpt. pres. 1981-82, nat. dir. 1983-86, bd. dir. Found. 1985-89; nat. treas., fin. chmn., v.p. 1986-87, award N.Y. chpt. 1983), Greater N.Y. WINS (regional affairs com.), Direct Mktg. Assn. (customer rels. coun. 1987-88). Home and Office: 3460 S Ocean Blvd Ste 715 Palm Beach FL 33480

BAUMANN, ANGELA LAURIA, obstetrical anesthesiologist, educator; b. Bklyn., Aug. 30, 1945; d. Anthony Paul and Faye Marie (Pascucci) Lauria; m. Donald Peter Baumann; children: Donald Peter Jr., Jennifer Laraine. Grad., St. Vincent's Hosp.-Med. Ctr., N.Y.C., 1966; B.S. summa cum laude, Molloy Coll., 1979; MS, SUNY, Stony Brook, 1981; DO, N.Y. Coll. Osteo. Medicine, 1985. RN, N.Y. Critical care nurse St. Vincent's Hosp and Med. Ctr., 1966-67, St. Francis Hosp., Roslyn, N.Y., 1967-74; resident in internal medicine Coney Island Hosp., Bklyn., 1985-86; resident in anesthesiology Univ. Hosp., SUNY, Stony Brook, 1986-88, fellow in obstet. anesthesiology, 1988-89, asst. prof. anesthesiology, 1989—. Treas. Cath. Youth Orgn., Gt. Neck, N.Y., 1972—; mem. St. Aloysius Choral Soc., Gt. Neck, 1972-79. Mem. Am. Soc. Anesthesiologists, Soc. Obstet. Anesthesiologists and Perinatologists, AMA, Am. Women's Med. Assn. Home: 76 Fairview Ave Great Neck NY 11023 Office: Univ Hosp SUNY Dept Anesthesiology Stony Brook NY 11000

BAUMANN, BARBARA JOHNSON, packaging engineer; b. Binghamton, N.Y., Jan. 21, 1957; d. Thomas Blauvelt and Barbara Ann (Larrabee) J.; m. William S. Baumann. AS in Bus. Adminstrn., Broome Community Coll., 1977; BS in Packaging Sci., Rochester Inst. Tech., 1982. Recreation leader Dept. Parks and Recreation City of Binghamton, 1976-80; packaging engr. Boehringer Ingelheim, Danbury, Conn., 1982-85, purchasing buyer, 1985-86; packaging engr. Westreco/Nestle, New Milford, Conn., 1986-89, sr. packaging engr., 1990—. Mem. Parks and Recreation Commn., Brookfield, Conn., 1984-87; sec. Rollingwood III Condominium Bd., Brookfield, 1986. Named Champion Women's B Div. Speed Skating Amateur Speed Skaters, 1980. Mem. Soc. Packaging and Handling Engrs. (cert.), ASTM (subcom. 1982-87), NAFE. Republican. Episcopalian. Office: Westreco Inc-Nestle 140 Boardman Rd New Milford CT 06776

BAUMANN, JANET ANNE, psychoanalyst, educator; b. Newark, Oct. 1, 1938; d. Clifford Elliott and Gladys (Webber) Lockyer; m. Richard Baumann, Dec. 20, 1962 (div. 1967); 1 child, Roberta. BS in Speech, Northwestern U., 1960; MSW, Jane Addams Grad. Sch. Social Work, 1966; cert. in psychoanalysis and psychotherapy, Postgrad. Ctr. Mental Health, 1974. Psychotherapist Lakeview Uptown Mental Health Ctr., Chgo., 1966-70; pvt. practice psychoanalys N.Y.C., 1971—; supr. Washington Sq. Inst. for Psychotherapy and Mental Health, N.Y.C., 1979-83; supr., sr. staff mem. Ctr. for Study of Anorexia and Bulimia, N.Y.C., 1983—; cons. Nat. Council Alcoholism, N.Y.C., 1970-81, mem. faculty, supr. Postgrad. Ctr. Mental Health, N.Y.C., 1983—. Mem. Postgrad. Psychoanalytic Soc., Am. Group Psychotherapy Assn., Assn. Psychoanalytic Self Psychology, Urban League. Democrat. Roman Catholic. Office: 135 E 50 St Ste 508 New York NY 10022

BAUMANN, LILLIAN ROSE, company official; b. N.Y.C., Jan. 15, 1939; d. Carl Lorenz and Anna Marie (Bund) B. Grad. high sch., Jamaica, N.Y. Sec. Union Carbide Corp., N.Y.C., 1957-58, Colgate-Palmolive Co., N.Y.C., 1958-63, Solar Industries, San Diego, 1963-64; exec. sec. Bristol-Myers Co., N.Y.C., 1964-66, Singer Co., N.Y.C., 1966-67, Ted Bates & Co., N.Y.C., 1967-68, Schenley Industries, N.Y.C., 1968-69; adminstrv. asst. Bairnco

Corp., N.Y.C., 1969—. Roman Catholic. Office: Bairnco Corp 200 Park Ave New York NY 10166

BAUMBACH, ALICE THOMPSON, educator. Student, North Shore Community Coll., 1975; BS in Elem. Edn., U. Colo, 1978; postgrad. in edn., Lesley Coll., 1988. Paraprofl. Boulder Valley Sch. Dist., 1978-79; tchr. Denver Pub. Schs., 1979—. Mem. sch. bldg. and sch. improvement accountabilty coms. Kaiser Family Tchr. Orgn. Recipient Outstanding Citizenship award State of Mass., scholar. Mem. Denver Classrm. Tchr. Assn. Home: 2610 S Gaylord St Denver CO 80210

BAUMBERGER, MARTHA KAIL, mayor; b. Poplar BLUFF, Mo., July 24, 1913; d. George W. and Rose E. (Lambertson) Kail; m. Robert E. Baumberger, Oct. 1938. AB, U. Cincinnati, Cincinnati, 1935. Pres. Internat. Women' Club, Addis Ababa, Ethiopia, 1957-59; founder Internat. Women's Club, Meshed, Iran, 1960-61; mem. Bd. Edn., Evanston, Ill., 1970-78; pres. Bd. Edn., Evanston, 1975-78; exec. dir. Zonta Internat., Chgo., Ill., 1970-78; mem. Beaufort (S.C.) County Council, 1983-87, chmn., 1985-87; mayor Town of Hilton Head Island, Hilton Head, S.C., 1987-89; mem., Nat'l Assn. of Parliamentarians, 1985; bd. mem., Municipal Assn. of S.C., Columbia, 1987-89. V.P., Hilton Head Community Assn., Hilton Head, 1981-82. Recipient: Outstanding Community Service, H.H. Community Assn.; Paul Harris fellow Rotary Internat. Republican. Presbyterian.

BAUMEL, JOAN PATRICIA FRENCH, author, lecturer; b. Winona, Minn.; m. Herbert Baumel, July 11, 1971. BA magna cum laude, Douglass Coll., 1952; postgrad., U. Detroit, 1952-55, Case Western Reserve U., 1960, U. Akron, 1962, U. Notre Dame, 1963, Manhattanville Coll., 1971; MA in French, Rutgers U., 1965; PhD in Modern Langs., Fordham U., 1985. Tchr. French lang. and culture, elem., secondary, and coll. levels various schs. including Mother House of Religious of the Sacred Heart, Kenwoord, Albany, N.Y., Ohio, Mich., 1955-66; tchr. French White Plains (N.Y.) Pub. High Sch., 1966-86; curricula creator Akron (Ohio) Pub. Schs.; dir. Baumel Assocs., Yonkers, N.Y.; lectr. CUNY Grad. Ctr., B'nai B'rith Internat. Mus., Washington, First Unitarian Soc. Westchester, N.Y., Rockland (N.Y.) Ctr. for Holocaust Studies, Unitarian Ch. of All Souls, N.Y.C., Barry U., Miami, Fla., Temple Beth Israel, Port Washington, N.Y. Author: Paul Claudel and the Jews: A Study in Ambivalence; lectr. topics include French Anit-Semitism: The Gallic Road to the Concentration Camp; Klaus Barbie and The Children of Izieu; Americans in Paris: An Explosion of Genius in the 20s. Adv. bd. mem. Mark Brent Dolinsky Meml. Found. Recipient Woodrow Wilson fellowship, 1958-59. Mem. Am. Assn. Tchrs. of French, Am. Coun. on Teaching Fgn. Langs., French Inst./Alliance Française, Alliance Françise of Westchester, Phi Beta Kappa. Office: Baumel Assocs 86 Rosedale Rd Yonkers NY 10710

BAUMEL, JUDITH, poet, educator, professional society administrator; b. Bronx, N.Y., Oct. 9, 1956; d. Abraham and Betty (Fogel) B.; m. David Ghitelman, July 4, 1985; 1 child, Samuel Jacob Ghitelman. BA magna cum laude, Radcliffe Coll., 1977; MA, Johns Hopkins U., 1978. Dir. The Poetry Soc. Am., N.Y.C., 1985-88; asst. prof. English Adelphi U., Garden City, N.Y., 1988—. Author (books of poems) The Weight of Numbers, 1988 (Walt Whitman award 1987). Recipient Lloyd McKim Garrison medal Harvard U., 1977; poetry fellow N.Y. Found. for the Arts, 1987. Mem. Poets and Writers, Nat. Book Critics Circle, Signet Soc. Office: Adelphi U English Dept Garden City NY 11350

BAUMER, BEVERLY BELLE, journalist; b. Hays, Kans., Sept. 23, 1926; d. Charles Arthur and Mayme Mae (Lord) B.; BS, William Allen White Sch. Journalism, U. Kans., 1948. Summer intern reporter Hutchinson (Kans.) News, 1946-47; continuity writer, women's program dir. Sta. KWBW, Hutchinson, 1948-49; dist. editor Salina (Kans.) Jours., 1950-57; commd. writer State of Kans. Centennial Year, 1961; contbg. author: Ford Times, Kansas City Star, Wichita (Kans.) Eagle, Ojibway Publs., Billboard, Modern Jeweler, Floor Covering Weekly, other bus. mags., 1962-69; owner and mgr. apts., Hutchinson, 1970—; broadcaster Reading Radio Room, Sta. KHCC-FM, Hutchinson, 1982—; info. officer, maj. Kans. Wing Hdqrs. CAP, 1969-72; participant People to People Citizen Ambassador program, People's Republic of China, summer 1988. Mem. Republican Presdl. Task Force. Recipient Human Interest Photo award Nat. Press Women, 1956, News Photo award AP, 1952. Mem. Fellows Menninger Found., Suffolk County Hist. Soc., Nat. Fedn. Press Women, Kans. Press Women (Communications Contest award 1986), Am. Soc. Profl. and Exec. Women, Am. Film Inst., Nat. Soc. Magna Charta Dames, Nat. Soc. Daus. Founders and Patriots Am., Nat. Soc. Daus. Am. Colonists, Kans. Soc. Daus. Am. Colonists (organizing regent Dr. Thomas Lord chpt., state chmn. insignia com.), Nat. Soc. Sons and Daus. Pilgrims (elder Kans. br.), D.A.R., Ben Franklin Soc. (nat. adv. bd.), Daus. Colonial Wars, Order Descs. Colonial Physicians and Chirurgiens, Colonial Dames 17th Century (chaplain, charter mem. Henry Woodhouse chpt.), Plantagenet Soc., Internat. Platform Soc., U. Kans. Alumni Assn., Nat. Geneal. Soc. Author book of poems, 1941; editor: A Simple Bedside Book for People Who Are Kinda, Sorta Interested in Genealogy, 1983. Home and Office: 204 Curtis St Hutchinson KS 67502

BAUMGARDNER, BARBARA ANN, publishing consultant; b. Harrisburg, Pa., Nov. 8, 1937; d. Otto Lockhart Borke and Margaretta Mildred (Feigley) Borke Traugh; m. E. Wayne Baumgardner, July 12, 1958; children: Brian Wayne, Bruce Edward. AB, Gettysburg (Pa.) Coll., 1959; MLA, Western Md. Coll., 1976, MEd, 1982. Cert. secondary tchr., Md. Sales promoter Scott, Foresman & Co., Chgo., 1959-60; tchr. Carroll County Pub. Schs., Westminster, Md., 1964-84; cons. McDougall, Littell & Co., Evanston, Ill., 1984—; adj. prof. Western Md. Coll., Westminster, 1975. Mem. Savannah Symphony Women's Guild. Mem. AAUW, Women's Assn. Hilton Head, Hilton Head Art League, Mensa, Fed. Garden Clubs of Md. Republican. Baptist. Home: 9 Man-O-War Hilton Head Island SC 29928

BAUMGARDNER, KANDY DIANE, zoology educator; b. Peoria, Ill., Sept. 16, 1946; d. Joseph Fisher and Patricia Dale (Ullrick) B. BS in Biology, Bradley U., 1968; PhD in Zoology, Utah State U., 1973. Asst. prof. zoology Ea. Ill. U., Charleston, 1973-79, assoc. prof., 1979-84, prof., 1984—; judge proposals NSF, Phoenix, 1977; textbook reviewer John Wiley & Sons, Jones-Bartlett, N.Y.C., Boston, 1981-82, 88, 90. Co-author: Population Biology, 1980, Genetics, 1984. Mem. AAAS, AAUP, Am. Genetic Assn., Sigma Xi, Phi Kappa Phi, Phi Sigma. Office: Ea Ill U Dept Zoology Charleston IL 61920

BAUMGARDNER, KAREN T., management; b. Dallas, July 31, 1953; d. Thomas James and Lola Ruth (Russell) Thornton; m. J.W. Baumgardner Jr. BA, U. Tex., Arlington, 1976. Adminstrv. asst. City of LaPorte, Fire Marshal's, Tex., 1977-78; adminstrv. asst., sec. credit/collections/fin. The Houston Post Co., 1978-83; adminstrv. asst., acct. H&C Communications, Inc., Houston, 1983-85, employee benefits mgr., 1985—; mem. Employers Council Flexible Comp., Wash. 1987-. Precinct Del. Rep. State Convention, San Antonio 1980. Republican. Baptist.

BAUMGARTEN, BARBARA DEE, artist; b. Santa Paula, Calif., Dec. 3, 1955; d. Ralph Ramsey and Donna Lee (Ekdall) Bennett; m. William Paul Baumgarten, June 22, 1977; children: Jessica Helene, Austin Lee. BFA, Calif. Lutheran U., 1977; MA/Theology, Visual Art, Pacific Sch. Religion, Berkeley, Calif., 1986; postgrad., Grad. Theol. Union, Berkeley, 1988—. Seamstress, dressmaking design Calif., 1972—, artist, oils, pen and ink, acrylic, 1972—, illustrator cards, books, 1980—; asst. decorator Bourbonnais Interiors, Morgan Hill, Calif., 1983-85; artist, theologian Calif., 1985—; cons. churches, 1986—. Artist: Quilt "World", 1987 (merit award), numerous paintings, quilts, drawings. Recipient Project Renew Grant, AAUW, 1985; nominee Woman of Achievement in the Arts, League of Friends and San Jose (Calif.) Mercury News, 1987. Mem. AAUW (lectr. 1985-87), Catholic Artists of the 80s (four juried shows 1987-90), Christians in the Visual Arts, Christian Artist Networking. Episcopalian. Home and Office: 1237 Laurel Rd Santa Paula CA 93060

BAUMGARTNER, EILEEN MARY, government official; b. St. Cloud, Minn.; d. Florian H. and Kathleen (Keefe) B.B.A., Coll. St. Catherine, St. Paul, 1964; M.P.A., U. Minn., Mpls., 1970. Tchr., U.S. Peace Corps, Ethiopia, 1964-66; researcher N.Y. Med. Coll., N.Y.C., 1967-68, Minn. State Planning Agy., St. Paul, 1970-73; legis. analyst tax com. Minn. Ho. of Reps., St. Paul, 1973-78; legis. dir. to Congressman Sabo, U.S. Ho. of Reps., Washington, 1979—. Bd. dirs. Alumni Assn., Hubert H. Humphrey Inst. Public Affairs, U. Minn., 1982—. Mem. Am. Soc. Pub. Adminstrn. Democrat. Roman Catholic. Office: 2201 Rayburn House Office Bldg Washington DC 20515

BAUMGARTNER, LEONA, physician; b. Chgo., Aug. 18, 1902; d. William J. and Olga (Leisy) B.; m. Nathaniel M. Elias, 1942 (dec. 1964); m. Alexander D. Langmuir, 1970. AB, U. Kans., 1923, DS, 1925; postgrad., Kaiser Wilhelm Inst., Munich, Fed. Republic Germany, 1928-28; PhD, Yale U., 1932, MD, 1934, LLD (hon.), 1970; DSc (hon.), Women's Coll., 1950, NYU, 1954, Russell Sage Coll., 1955, Smith Coll., 1956, Western Coll. Women, 1960, U. Mass., 1963, U. Mich., 1967, McMurray Coll., 1967, N.Y. Med. Coll., 1968, Clark Coll., 1969; LHD (hon.), Keuka Coll., 1963; LLD (hon.), Skidmore Coll., 1959, Oberlin Coll., 1965. Diplomate Am. Bd. Pediatrics, Am. Bd. Preventive Medicine and Pub. Health. Mem. faculty Colby Community High Sch., Kans., 1923-24; mem. faculty Kans. City Jr. Coll., 1925-26, U. Mont., 1926-28; intern, then asst. resident, asst. in pediatrics N.Y. Hosp. and Cornell Med. Coll., 1934-36; lectr. nursing edn. Columbia U., 1939-42; with N.Y.C. Dept. Health, 1937-62, commr. health, 1954-62; exec. dir. N.Y. Found., 1953-54; assoc. chief U.S. Children's Bur., Fed. Security Agy., 1949-50, cons., 1950-56; mem. faculty Med. Coll., Cornell U., 1939-66, mem. pediatrics and pub. health faculty, 1957-66; vis. lectr. maternal and child health Med. Sch. Pub. Health, Harvard U., 1948-62; vis. prof. social medicine Harvard Med. Sch., Boston, 1966-76; asst. adminstr. Office Tech. Coop. and Research, AID, Dept. State, 1962-65; exec. dir. Med. Care and Edn. Found., Inc., Boston, 1968-72; adviser French Ministry Health, 1945, Indian minister health, 1955; mem. exch. mission to USSR, 1958; lectr. for Tokyo Met. Govt., 1961; mem. nat. adv. counc. Peace Corps, 1961-63. Contbr. med. and sci. articles to profl. jours. Bd. dirs. N.Y. Fund for Children; trustee coun. U. Mass., 1973—; trustee New Sch. Social Rsch., N.Y.C., 1966-74, adv. coun., 1964—. Recipient awards, including Elizabeth Blackwell award Hobart and William Smith Colls., 1961, Samuel J. Crumbine award Kans. Pub. Health Assn., 1961, Wilbur Lucius Cross medal Grad. Sch. Assn. of Yale U., 1970, Pub. Welfare Gold medal Nat. Acad. Scis., 1977, others; univ. fellow Yale U. 1930-31; Sterling fellow Yale U., 1931-32. Mem. Harvey Soc., History Sci. Soc., Am. Assn. History Medicine, Am. Pub. Health Assn. (pres. 1958-59, Albert Lasker award 1954), Am. Acad. Pediatrics, Am. Pediatric Soc., Child Welfare League Am. (bd. dirs.), Nat. Social Welfare Assembly (v.p.), Nat. Conf. Social Work (exec. com.), Nat. Health Council (pres. 1956), Am. Acad. Arts and Scis., N.Y. Acad. Medicine, Inst. Medicine of Nat. Acad. Sci., Mortar Bd., Phi Beta Kappa, Sigma Xi, Pi Beta Phi, Phi Sigma. Home: Abel's Hill Chilmark MA 02535

BAUMHOLTZ, LAURIE ANN, sales executive, business owner; b. N. Royalton, Ohio, Feb. 15, 1961; d. Karl Frantz and Elaine Eleanor (Svonava) B. Cert. graphic arts, Cuyahoga Valley Joint Vocat., 1979; student, Cuyahoga Community Coll., 1979—. Repair ctr. asst. Telco, Inc., Cleve., 1979-82; Seiko dept. head Colmans-Borel, Cleve., 1982-85; sales rep. Colmans-Borel, 1986-88; sales mgr. United Cerebral Palsy, 1987—; owner Citywide Banners, 1988—. Democrat. Methodist.

BAUSCH-DAVENSON, WENDY H., foundation administrator; b. Buffalo, N.Y., May 20, 1943; d. Norman W. Howard and Vesta Elisabeth Gow; m. Marshall Lee Davenson, Aug. 15, 1986 (dec.); children: William H. Bausch, Jeffrey D. Bausch, Wendy E. Bausch. BA, Kent State U., 1965; Masters degree, So. Conn. State U., 1986, Gestalt Cert., 1986. Cert. family life edn., alcohol counselor, grief counselor. Dir. Adolescent Youth Svcs./Arms Acres, Carmel, N.Y.; pvt. practice family therapy Newtown, Conn.; dir. Youth Svcs. in Newtown, Conn.; dir. treatment planning Regional Substance Abuse Project United Way, Bridgeport, Conn. Contbg. author: There is a Solution, Cocaine Addiction, 1988. Assoc. dir. sch. partnership Drugs Don't Work, Hartford, Conn. Mem. Am. Assn. Counseling and Devel., AAMFT, CAMFT, NCFR, CAPP, Suicide State Task Force. Home: 88 Church Hill Rd Sandy Hook CT 06482

BAUSEK, VICTORIA LYNNE, health care consultant; b. Walnut Creek, Calif., Aug. 16, 1955; d. Norman Arthur Karvelis and Marilyn Jean (Derry) Richards; m. Gerald Hubert Bausek, June 10, 1984. Diploma nursing, Samuel Merritt Coll. of Nursing, Oakland, Calif., 1976; BA magna cum laude, Golden Gate U., 1987, postgrad., 1988-. RN Calif. RN Herrick Hosp., Berkeley, Calif., 1976-77, John Muir Hosp., Walnut Creek, Calif., 1977-80; mktg. rep. Exxon Office Systems, Florham Park, N.J., 1980-81; sales rep. Parke-Davis Med. Surg., Greenwood, S.C., 1981-83; sr. sales rep. Johnson & Johnson Orthopaedic, New Brunswick, N.J., 1983-84; bus. cons. San Carlos, Calif., 1985-88; mktg. mgr. Advanced Med. Devices, Los Altos, Calif., 1988—; corp. officer Gerald Bausek A Profl. Corp., San Francisco, 1984—; pres., bd. dirs. San Francisco Med. Soc. Aux., Larkin St. Youth Ctr. Found., San Francisco. Med. health care advocate San Francisco Med. Soc. Aux. Legis. Com. Mem. Nat. Assn. Female Execs., Med. Soc. Aux., Calif. Med. Assn. Aux. (media Chmn.). Democrat. Presbyterian. Home and Office: 282 Club Dr San Carlos CA 94070

BAUTISTA, ANGELA MELINDA, software engineer; b. San Angelo, Tex., July 7, 1964; d. Juan Bautista and Ophelia (Badillo) Perez; m. George Gallegos, Dec. 30, 1989. BBA, Angelo State U., 1986, postgrad., 1988-89. Data sales rep. GTE S.W. Telephone Co., San Angelo, Tex., 1985, network engr., 1985-86, customer svc. engr., 1986-89; software engr. GTE Govt. Systems, Vienna, Va., 1989—. Bd. dirs. Tom Green County Lit. Coun., San Angelo, 1988-89, San Angelo Recreation Bd., 1988-89; coun. mem. Sacred Heart Parish Coun., San Angelo; mem. St. Rita's Choral Group. Mem. AAUW (pres. 1988-89), Def. Communications Tennis Club. Democrat. Roman Catholic. Home: 1712 W Abingdon Dr #202 Alexandria VA 22314

BAUTISTA, CAROL STONEY, electric power industry administrator; b. South El Monte, Calif., Nov. 3, 1949; d. Floyd Oakland and Madge V. (Roberts) Stoney; m. Ben Benito Makahanohano Bautista; children: Patty Kawohikukapulani, Oakland N. Kaululaau. AA, Rio Hondo Coll., 1969; BA, Calif. State U., 1977. Cert. ESL and adult edn. tchr., Calif. Various positions So. Calif. Edison Co., Rosemead, 1972-88, project administr., 1988—; seminar chairperson Women and Minority Bus. Enterprises, Rosemead; adv. L.A. County Office of Emergency Mgmt., assistance to fire victims. Author feminist poetry and short stories; contbr. articles to profl. jours.; cartoonist and letterer newspapers and mags. Activist United Farmworkers Union, 1960's, 70's; local organizer Neighborhood Watch Program, 1982—; guest AM L.A. TV Program, 1988—, Channel 7 News, 1988—; instr. Coalition for Literacy, 1987; counselor Amnesty ESL Program, 1987; bd. dirs., mgr. Bobby Sox Softball, 1979-85; bd. dirs. Hui O'Hana Waialua, 1984—, Team USA Women's Softball, 1985; chair reunion com. Rosemead High Sch., 1986—. Recipient Women in Leadership award Calif. State Senate, Community Svc. award Vietnam Vets. Vols., mgmt. awards YWCA of L.A. Mem. NAFE, NOW, Edison Roundtable (steering com., com. chair). Democrat. Home: 2296 Oldridge Dr Hacienda Heights CA 91745 Office: So Calif Edison Co PO Box 800 Rosemead CA 91745

BAUTZ, LAURA PATRICIA, astronomer; b. Washington, Sept. 3, 1940; d. Charles Kothe and Laura (Stauverman) B. B.A. in Physics, Vanderbilt U., 1961; Ph.D. in Astronomy, U. Wis., Madison, 1967. From instr. to assoc. prof. astronomy Northwestern U., Evanston, Ill., 1965-75; sr. staff assoc. NSF, Washington, 1975-79, dep. dir. physics div., 1979-81, dir. astronomy div., 1982—. Mem. Am. Astron. Soc., AAAS, Internat. Astron. Union, Am. Phys. Soc., Phi Beta Kappa. Home: 1325 18th St NW Apt 506 Washington DC 20036 Office: 1800 G St NW Washington DC 20550

BAVUSO, MARGARET, lawyer; b. N.Y.C., June 10, 1948; d. Joseph B. and Margaret (Sciabbarrassi) B. AA, Queens Borough Community Coll., 1976; BA, Adelphi U., 1979; JD, New Eng. Sch. Law, 1985; postgrad., NYU, 1990—. Bar: N.Y. 1987. Various positions Am. Airlines, various cities, 1967-87; sr. investigator N.Y. Commn. Govt. Integrity, N.Y.C., 1987-88; dep. chief investigator fin. Fulton Fish Market, N.Y.C., 1988—. Adv. Women Against Abuse, Phila., 1987, Fulton Market. Mem. ABA, N.Y. State Bar Assn., N.Y. County Lawyers Assn., Assn. Bar of City of N.Y., N.Y. Women's Bar Assn., Assn. Queens Bar Assn., Queens County Bar Assn., N.Y. Women's Bar Assn., Internat. Assn. Law Enforcement Intelligence Analyst, Nat. Orgn. Italian Am. Women. Office: Fed Adminstr Fulton Fish Market 180 Maiden Ln 20th Fl New York NY 10038

BAXLEY, KATHRYN WISE, social services administrator; b. Little Mountain, S.C., Dec. 15, 1927; d. Burke Miller and Annie (Rast) Wise; m. Daniel Carlyle Baxley, July 18, 1948; children: Carol Lynn Doster, Charles Burke, Ann Baxley Carpenter, Daniel C. Jr. BA, Columbia (S.C.) Coll., 1947. Sec. to chaplain VA Med. Ctr., Columbia, 1947-48; sec. purchasing E.I. duPont Co., Camden, S.C., 1950-51; sec. Baxley Appliance Co., Kershaw, S.C., 1952-54; tchr. Kershaw County Schs., 1954-56; caseworker Dept. Social Services County of Kershaw, Camden, 1961-66, supr., 1966-72, dir., 1972—. Chmn. Camden service unit Salvation Army, 1982-84; pres. dist. S.C. Assn. Conservation Aux., 1979; bd. visitors Columbia Coll., 1988—; mem. adv. council Kershaw County Vocat. Ctr., 1980, Kershaw County Hist. Soc., 1981—. Recipient S.C. Regional Family of Yr. award, 1987, Career Woman of Yr. award Camden Bus. and Profl. Women's Club, 1987. Mem. Am. Pub. Welfare Assn., S.C. Dirs. and Suprs. Assn. (bd. dirs. 1975), Kershaw County Mental Health Assn. (treas. 1972), Kershaw County Interagy. Council (pres. 1975-76), Columbia Coll. Alumnae Club (pres. 1984, 85). Lutheran. Clubs: Camden Dinner (pres. 1987-88), MacDowell Music (pres. 1968). Office: Kershaw County Dept Social Svcs 816 DeKalb St Camden SC 29020

BAXT, BARBARA STEFANIE, bridal industry executive, editor; b. Paterson, N.J., Apr. 10, 1949; d. Sydney Joseph and Rita Lucielle (Seidman) B. BS cum laude, Syracuse U., 1968. Dir. travel industry sales Sonesta Hotels, N.Y.C., 1969-73, Princess Hotels, Hamilton, Bermuda, 1974-76; pres. Hotels Internat., Paterson, 1976-88; founder, sec. Bridal Assoc. N.J., chmn., 1989—. Editor Bride to Be mag., 1985—. Mem. earthquake relief benefit com. ARC. Design patentee mug shirt. Office: Bride to Be Mag PO Box 384 Totowa NJ 07511

BAXTER, BETTY CARPENTER, educational administrator; b. Sherman, Tex., 1937; d. Granville E. and Elizabeth (Caston) Carpenter; m. Cash Baxter; children: Stephen Barrington, Catherine Elaine. AA in Music, Christian Coll., Columbia, Mo., 1957; MusB in Voice and Piano, So. Meth. U., Dallas, 1959; MA in Early Childhood Edn., Tchrs. Coll., Columbia, 1972, MEd, 1979, EdD, 1988. Tchr. Riverside Ch. Day Sch., N.Y.C., 1966-71; headmistress Episcopal Sch., N.Y.C., 1972-87, headmistress emeritus, 1987—; founding head Presbyn. Sch., Houston, 1988—. Author: The Relationship of Early Tested Intelligence on the WPPSI to Later Tested Aptitude on the SAT. Mem. Nat. Assn. Episcopal Schs. (former gov. bd., editor Network publ.), Ind. Schs. Assn. Admissions Greater N.Y. (former exec. bd.), Nat. Assn. for Edn. of Young Children, Houston Area Assn. for Edn. of Young Children, Houston Area Assn. Ind. Schs., Houston Area Assn. Edn. Young Children, Kappa Delta Pi, Delta Kappa Gamma. Republican. Presbyterian. Office: 5300 Main St Houston TX 77004

BAXTER, CARLA LOUISE CHANEY, insurance underwriter; b. Indpls., Nov. 4, 1955; d. Carlton S. and Jennie B. (Yates) Chaney; m. Andrew Louis Baxter, Sept. 20, 1980; 1 child, Andranise Louise. BA in Mktg., Ball State U., 1979. Lic. realtor, Ind.; CPCU. Zoning technician Dept. Met. Devel., Indpls., 1975; dir. mktg. Urban Tng. and Devel. Systems Inc., Indpls., 1979-80; casualty underwriter Wausau Ins. Cos., Indpls., 1980-84; sr. casualty underwriter CNA Ins. Cos., Indpls., 1984-85; nat. accounts underwriter Nationwide Ins. Cos., Columbus, Ohio, 1985-87; sr. casualty underwriter Home Ins. Co., Indpls., 1987-90, Am. States Ins. Cos., 1990—; instr. Profl. Ins. Agts. of Ind. Speaker various chs. and civic groups; dir. choir Trinity Ch., Indpls., 1983—; mem. Consortium African-Am. Christian Women. Statonian scholar, 1975-76; N.G. Gilbert scholar Ball State U., 1978. Mem. Indpls. Assn. Ins. Women, Indpls. Underwriters Assn., Ins. Inst. Am. (cert.), Urban League, Alpha Kappa Alpha (Career Day group leader 1984, scholar 1974-75, 75-76). Methodist. Avocations: skating, racquetball, singing, dancing. Office: Am States Ins Co 500 N Meridian St Indianapolis IN 46204

BAXTER, CAROL CAIRNS, computer scientist; b. Oakland, Calif., Dec. 24, 1940; d. Walter V. and Helen Cairns; m. William F. Baxter, Mar. 27, 1987; 1 child, Bernard Treanor. AB, Stanford U., 1962; MA, U. Calif., Berkeley, 1966, EdD, 1969. Systems engr. Internat. Bus. Machines, Oakland, Calif., 1962-64; rsch. specialist U. Calif., Berkeley, 1969-71; rsch. dir. Ctr. for Advanced Study, Stanford, Calif., 1972-81, 83—; dir. computer rsch. Am. Enterprise Inst., Washington, 1981-83. Office: Ctr for Advanced Study 202 Junipero Serra Blvd Stanford CA 94305

BAXTER, DUBY YVONNE, personnel classification specialist; b. El Campo, Tex., July 21, 1953; d. Ray Eugene and Hazel Evelyn (Roades) Allenson; m. Loran Richard Baxter, April 7, 1979. Student, Alvin Jr. Coll., 1971, Tex. Tech U., 1972; cert. legal sec., Alaska Bus. Coll., 1974; student, Alaska Pacific U., 1981, Anchorage Community Coll., 1981-85, U. Santa Clara, 1982-83; BBA in Mgmt. cum laude, U. Alaska, Anchorage, 1985. Sr. office assoc., legal sec. Municipality of Anchorage, 1975-78; exec. sec. Security Nat. Bank, Anchorage, 1978-80, Alaska Renewable Resources Corp., Anchorage, 1980-82; personnel mgmt. specialist Dept. of Army, Ft. Richardson, Alaska, 1986-87; personnel mgmt., position mgmt. & classification specialist Civilian Personnel Office, Ft. Drum, N.Y., 1987-88; position classification specialist U.S.A. Corps of Engrs., Ft. Drum, N.Y., 1989-90; position mgmt. and classification specialist Civilian Pers. Office, 6th Inf. Div. (L) & USA Garrison, Ft. Richardson, 1990—; by-laws com. mem. spl. emphasis program Fed. Women's Program, Ft. Richardson, 1986-87; instr. Prevention of Sexual Harassment, Ft. Richardson, 1986-87. Contbr. Alaska Repertoire Theater, Anchorage, 1982-87; leader Awana Christian Youth Orgn., Anchorage, 1985-87. Mem. NAFE, Classification and Compensation Soc., U. Alaska Alumni Assn., Bernese Mountain Dog Club. Mem. Brethren Ch.

BAXTER, ELAINE, secretary of state; b. Chgo., Jan. 16, 1933; d. Clarence Arthur and Margaret (Clark) Bland; m. Harry Youngs Baxter, Oct. 2, 1954; children: Katherine, Harry, John. BA, U. Ill., 1954; teaching cert., Iowa Wesleyan Coll., 1970; MS, U. Iowa, 1978. History tchr. Burlington (Iowa) High Sch., 1971-72; mem. Burlington City Coun., 1973-75; sr. liaison officer U.S. Dept. HUD, Washington, 1979-81; state rep. Iowa Ho. Reps., Des Moines, 1982-86; sec. state State of Iowa, Des Moines, 1987—. Nat. cochmn. Dukakis-Bentsen campaign, 1988; del. Dem. Nat. Conv., Atlanta, 1988, mem. at large Dem. Nat. Com.; mem. Exec. Coun. and Voter Registration Commn.; chair State Records Commn., State Ins. Commn., Iowa; internat. del. Nat. Dem. Inst. for Internat. Affairs to Paraguay, 1989; hon. res. chair Iowa chpt. Am. Heart Assn., 1989. Recipient RJR Nabisco Fellowship to Sr. Execs. in State and Local Govt., J.F. Kennedy Sch. Govt., Harvard U., 1988. Mem. Nat. Assn. Secs. State, Women Execs. in State Govt., Women's Equity Action League (bd. dirs.), Am. Soc. of Pub. Adminstrn. (bd. dirs. Iowa chpt.). Home: 1016 N 4th St Burlington IA 52601 Office: State House Des Moines IA 50319

BAXTER, JANET SCHWARTZ, motivational company executive; b. Chgo., Dec. 3, 1947; d. Joseph Robert and Marta Henrietta (Somlo) Schwartz; m. Richard Raymond Baxter, June 30, 1936. BA, U. Calif., Berkeley, 1969. Rsch. asst. Neuropsychiat. Inst. UCLA, 1967; tchr. Spaulding Youth Ctr., Tilton, N.H., 1969-73, Ind. Learning Sch., Corte Madera, Calif., 1974; mgr. office svc. Synanon, Marshall, Calif., 1974-77; tchr. Synanon Sch., Marshall, 1977-80; account exec. Synanon Fin. Mktg. Group, Badger, Calif., 1980-90; sr. mktg. cons. The AdGap Group, Miramonte, Calif., 1990—; cons., corp. motivation, drug rehab., operant psychology. Vol., VISTA, Harlem, N.Y.C., 1967. Mem. Advt. Splty. Inst., Inst. Productivity, Phi Sigma Sigma. Republican. Jewish. Home and Office: The AdGap Group 50300 Hwy 245 Miramonte CA 93641

BAXTER, LORI DEANNE, accountant, management consultant; b. Cartersville, Ga., Jan. 12, 1963; d. William Clifford and Mary Luine (Wilson) Baxter Miller. BA, Wake Forest U., 1985; postgrad., Duke U., 1988—. CPA, N.C. Adminstrv. asst. Coastal Group, Inc., Durham, N.C., 1985-86; cons. Ernst and Whinney, Charlotte, N.C., 1988—. Vol. Charlotte Meml. Hosp., 1989—. Mem. N.C. Assn. CPAs, Am. Coll. Healthcare Execs., Healthcare Fin. Mgmt. Assn., Metrolina. Home: 2101 Hopedale Ave Charlotte NC 28207 Office: Ernst & Whinney 1100 Independence Ctr Charlotte NC 28246

BAXTER, MARY ABIGAIL, marketing consultant; b. Houston, Sept. 24, 1956; d. James Reagan and Edna Marie (Bargar) Connor; m. James Clarence Baxter, Apr. 25, 1981; 1 child, Mia Abigail. BA in Interior Design cum laude, Incarnate Word Coll., 1982. Pres. Abigail Baxter Inc., San Antonio, 1981-89; sales, mktg. prod. developer Materials Mktg. Corp., San Antonio, 1989—; vol. juror Nat. Council For Interior Design Qualification, Houston, 1986—; design cons. Holmgreen Children's Shelter, San Antonio, 1985-86; design coordinator Am. Cancer Soc., SAn Antonio, 1987. Contbr. various articles to mags. Designer San Antonio Symphony Designer Showhouse, 1983, 84, 85. Mem. Am. Soc. Interior Design (award of recognition 1985). Republican. Home: 3219 Oak Leaf San Antonio TX 78209 Office: Materials Mktg Corp 922 Isom San Antonio TX 78216

BAXTER, MILLIE MCLEAN, real estate owner, educator; b. Denver, Mar. 14, 1926; d. Stanley Allan and Jessie (Brown) McL.; m. Glenn A. Hettler, Dec. 28, 1949 (div. Mar. 1969); children: Douglass Kent, Linda Horn, Joni Birdsall; m. Jack Stanley Baxter, Feb. 4, 1977; children: David, Fred. Grad., Dickenson Bus. Sch., 1944; student, U. Colo., 1944-46; grad., McConnell Modeling Sch., 1946, Jones Real Estate Coll., 1971. With sales and mktg. The Arnold Corp., Denver, 1973-84; broker, mgr. Evergreen (Colo.) Properties, 1984-87; broker, owner Century 21, Evergreen, 1987—; ind. mgr. Real Estate Tng. Ctr., Evergreen, 1987—. Mem. Denver Bd. Realtors (Salesperson of Yr. 1978), Denver Brokers Council, Evergreen Bd. Realtors, Jefferson County Bd. Realtors, Sales and Mktg. Council (Salesperson of Yr. 1979, Golden Medallion award 1978, 79, 80, 81, 82, 83). Republican. Office: Century 21 Evergreen 30440 Stage Coach Blvd Evergreen CO 80439

BAXTER, RUTH SACKETT, elementary teacher; b. Syracuse, N.Y., June 18, 1928; d. Walter Lyman and Esther Lucille (Barrett) Sackett; m. Jack Tidd Baxter, June 24, 1950; children: Katharine Baxter Visser, Robert Tidd. BS, Potsdam State Tchrs. Coll., 1950. Tchr. New Hartford (N.Y.) Cen. Sch., 1960-86; bd. dirs. New Hartford Tchr.'s Ctr. Mem. Green Thumb Gardeners, William Proctor Mus., Faxton Hosp. Coun., Utica, N.Y. Mem. AAUW, New Hartford Ret. Tchrs. Assn., Alpha Delta Kappa (treas.), Delta Kappa Gamma (coms.). Home: 25 Lower Woods Rd Utica NY 13501

BAXTER, VICTORIA LYNN, management consultant; b. Andalusia, Ala., Apr. 8, 1948; m. Arthur Pearce Baxter, May 17, 1981; 1 child, Jessica Victoria. BS in Secondary Edn., U. S. Ala., Mobile, 1971; M. of Edn. Media, U. S. Ala., 1972. Rsch. librarian ALZA Corp., Palo Alto, Calif., 1972-74; cons. U. S. Ala., 1974-75; media dir. Tarrant City Schs., Birmingham, Ala., 1975-77; cons. Metro CESA, Atlanta, 1977-78; mgr. ednl. svc. Ala. Power Co., Birmingham, 1978-83; pres. Baxter & Assocs., Birmingham, 1983—; pres. Birmingham Internat. Edn. Film Festival, 1980-83. Bd. dirs. Jr. Women, Ala. Symphony, Birmingham, 1988-89. Named Region 9 Mem. of Yr., Am. Soc. Tng. and Devel., 1983, Pres.'s award, Birmingham Edn. Film Festival, 1983. Mem. Am. Soc. Tng. and Devel., Council of Human Resource Execs., Exec. Women Forum (pres. 1986), Women's Network (bd. dirs.), Breakfast Club (bd. dirs.

BAXTER-BIRNEY, MEREDITH, actress; b. Los Angeles, June 21, 1947; d. Tom and Whitney (Blake) Baxter; m. David Birney, Apr. 10, 1974; children: Ted, Eva, Kate, Peter and Mollie (twins). Student, Interlochen Arts Acad., Mich. Actress (films) including Ben, 1972, Bittersweet Love, 1976, All the President's Men, 1976, (TV movies) The Imposter, 1975, The Night That Panicked America, 1975, Target Risk, 1975, The Stranger Who Looks Like Me, The Rape of Richard Bech, 1985, Kate's Secret, The Long Journey Home, (plays) Guys and Dolls, Talley's Folley, Butterflies are Free, Varieties, She Knows Too Much, 1989, The Kissing Place, 1990; star (TV series) Bridget Loves Bernie, 1971-72, Family, 1976-80, Family Ties, 1982-89; other TV appearances include The Interns, Police Woman, Medical Story, City of Angels, McMillan and Wife, The Streets of San Francisco. Office: care Triad Artists Inc 10100 Santa Monica Blvd 16th Fl Los Angeles CA 90067*

BAY, CATHERINE MARIE, banker; b. Ottumwa, Iowa; d. Stanley Leo and Emily Ella (Newlin) B. BS in Agr., Iowa State U., Ames, 1982. Prog. asst., acting CED Monroe County ASCS, Albia, Iowa, 1967-77; loan svc. officer Peoples Nat. Bank, Albia, 1982-86; cashier, dir. Peoples State Bank, 1987—. Treas. Rathbun Lake Assn., 1988—; mem. compensation bd. County of Monroe, 1988—. Mem. Christian Ch. Home: Rte 5 Albia IA 52531 Office: Peoples State Bank 102 S Main St Albia IA 52531

BAYER, DARRYL LEE, psychologist; b. Cin., Oct. 24, 1944; s. Robert Emerson and Iris Vivian (Krueger) Owens; 1 child, Alicia Vivian. BA in Psychology, San Jose (Calif.) State U., 1976, MA in Research Psychology, 1977; postgrad., U. Maine. Cert. clin. psychologist Ky., Minn.; psychol. examiner, Maine. Teaching asst. San Jose (Calif.) State U., 1976-77; psychol. examiner, dr. clin. tng. Bangor (Maine) Mental Health Inst., 1979-81; instr. U. Ark. Med. Ctr., Little Rock, 1981-82; asst. prof. psychology Bemidji (Minn.) State U., 1982-85; clin. psychologist dept. family practice and community health U. Minn. Med. Ctr., Mpls., 1985-86; clin. psychologist Cumberland River Comprehensive Care Ctr., Harlan, Ky., 1986-87. Contbr. articles to profl. jours.; jour. referee Am. Jour. Hospice Care, 1984—. Fellow U. Maine, 1979-80; grantee Sigma Xi, U. Maine, 1980-81, Bemidjie State U., 1984-85. Mem. Am. Psychol. Assn., Nat. Orgn. Human Svc. Educators. Office: Spoon River Ctr 2323 Windish Dr Galesburg IL 61402-1447

BAYER, MARGRET HELENE JANSSEN, biologist, botanist; b. Hamburg, Fed. Republic Germany, July 8, 1931; came to U.S., 1962; d. Ernst Johann and Hildegard (Sens) J.; m. Manfred Erich Bayer, Aug. 26, 1958; children: Ada-Helen, Thora Ilin. Diploma in Biology, U. Hamburg, Fed. Republic Germany, 1958, D Rer. Nat., 1961, Dr. rer nat. Botany and Plant Physiology, 1976. Educator U. Hamburg, 1958-61, U. Düsseldorf, Fed. Republic Germany, 1959; rsch. assoc. Inst. Cancer Rsch., Phila., 1962-76, sr. rsch. assoc. microbiology, 1977—; vis. prof. biology dept., U. Hamburg, 1975-76; vis. lect. U. Pa., 1979-80. Contbr. articles to profl. jours. NSF and NIH Fed. grantee, 1977—. Fellow Royal Entomol. Soc. London; mem. Am. Soc. Microbiology, Am. Soc. Plant Physiology, Am. Soc. Plant Pathology, German Bot. Soc. Office: Fox Chase Cancer Ctr Inst for Cancer Rsch Philadelphia PA 19111

BAYERS, HAZEL JOYCE, small business consultant; b. Malden, Mass., July 24, 1947; d. Frederick Walter and Bonnie Virginia (Pittman) Hobbs; m. George Nelson Bayers, May 14, 1966 (div. 1981); children: Scott A., Bonnie L. Student, U. Tenn., Nashville, 1976-78. Freight payment cashier Roadway Express, Malden, Mass., 1965-67; adminstrv. asst. Francis Assocs., Cambridge, Mass., 1967-72; legal sec. Levine & Rosenblum, Nashville, 1974-81; office mgr. D.N. Cole, Inc., Richmond, Va., 1982-86; fin. adminstr. R.P. Ingram, Inc., Richmond, 1986-87; asst. bus. office mgr. McGuire Clinic, Inc., Richmond, 1987-88; fin. asst. VA Sml. Bus. Fin. Authority, Richmond, 1988-89; fin. cons. for sml. bus. Richmond, 1989—; chief fin. officer Germ Free, Inc., Doswell, Va., 1989—. Youth coordinator Providence United Meth. Ch., Richmond, 1986—. Mem. NAFE. Democrat. Home: 10303 Brickland Ct Richmond VA 23236

BAYLES, DEBORAH LEIGH, business owner; b. Bethesda, Md., Oct. 22, 1953; d. Herbert Alexander and Dorothy Mildred (Lazenby) Berry; m. Robert Scott Bayles, July 10, 1976 (div. July 6, 1985). BA in English & Art, Calif. State U., Chico, Calif., 1975. Cert. Bus. Communicator; accredited Pub. Rels. Practitioner. Tchr., reading specialist Santa Ana (Calif.) Unified Sch. Dist., 1977-79; sr. product evaluation specialist Raytheon Data Systems, Thousand Oaks, Calif., 1979-81; branch support mgr. Wang Labs., Woodland Hills, Calif., 1981-83; nat. mktg. support mgr. Omnidata, Westlake Village, Calif., 1983-84; mgr. mktg. svcs. Western Data Systems, Woodland Hills, 1984-85; mgr. mktg. communications Computer Scis. Corp/Compufact, Garden Grove, Calif., 1985-88; pres. Value Added Mktg., Irvine, Calif., 1988—. Contbr. numerous articles to profl. jours. Mem. Indsl. League of Orange County, 1989—. Mem. Pub. Rels. Soc. Am., Bus. & Profl. Advt. Assn. Republican. Office: Value Added Mktg 227 Stanford Irvine CA 92715

BAYLES, JANIS RYLO GOLON, oil company executive; b. Cleve., Sept. 18, 1946; d. Francis Andrew and Josephine Elnora (Rylo) Golon; m. William Henry Bayles V, Feb. 16, 1985; children: Andrea Rylo, William Henry VI. BA, Miami U., Oxford, Ohio, 1967; MA, Miami U., 1968; postgrad., Cleve. Inst. Art, 1969, NYU, 1971-72. Producer Station WKYC-TV, Cleve., 1968-69; mgr. promotion Popular Mechanics Mag., N.Y.C., 1970-72; dir. customer service Trans World Airlines, N.Y.C., 1973-75; regional mgr. public relations Trans World Airlines, Phila., 1975-77; mgr. spl. projects corp. communications Trans World Airlines, N.Y.C., 1977-79; sr. specialist media relations Texaco Inc., White Plains, N.Y., 1980-85; regional dir. corp. communications Chevron Corp., N.Y.C., 1985—. Contbr.-photographer to various trade mags., 1975—; photographer profl. jours., 1981-85. Mem. Jr. League City N.Y., 1982-87, Jr. League Fairfield County, Conn., 1987—. Mem. Internat. Assn. Bus. Communicators, Nat. Forensic League (Ohio chpt.), Pub. Relations Soc. Am. (N.Y. chpt. coordinator promotion 1985-86), Assn. Petroleum Writers (assoc.), Young Profls. Group Foreign Policy Assn. Clubs: Nat. Press (assoc.), Sandbar (N.Y.). Office: Chevron Cos 520 Madison Ave New York NY 10022

BAYLES, LIBRADA C., chemist, chemicals executive; b. Havana, Cuba, July 18, 1936; came to U.S., 1961; d. Joseph I. and Maria C. (Fontanilles) Ortega; m. George D. Bayles, June 20, 1988; children: Carlos, Gustavo, Joseph. BS, Havana U., 1957. Lic. in Radioactive Material. Tchr. St. John The Evangelist, Carmichael, Calif.; chemist Campbell Soup Co., Sacramento, Calif.; radiation safety officer CDFA, Sacramento, agrl. chemist II, supr. Recipient Calif. State Employee Safety Commendation, 1989. Mem. NAFE, Am. Chem. Soc., Toastmasters Internat. (sec. 1989). Democrat. Roman Catholic. Office: 3292 Meadowview Rd Sacramento CA 95832

BAYLEY, MOLLY GILBERT, management consultant; b. Spokane, Wash., Nov. 19, 1944; d. Frederick Wolcott and Clare Emily (Whitehouse) G.; m. James Burt, June 29, 1968; 1 child, Christopher Whitehouse. B.A. in French, Wellesley Coll., 1967. Sr. analyst market surveillance Nat. Assn. Securities Dealers, Washington, 1972-74, supr. market surveillance, 1974-76, asst. dir. market surveillance, 1976-78, dir. market surveillance, 1978-79, v.p., 1979-84; exec. dir. Commmodity Futures Trading Commn., Washington, 1984-89; prin. Molly G. Bayley Cons., Washington, 1989—. Contr. articles to profl. jours. Pres. Jr. League of Washington, Inc., 1982-83; bd. dirs. Assn. Jr. Leagues, Inc., 1985-87; bd. dirs. Rec. for the Blind Inc., Washington, 1983—, chmn., 1990—. Recipient of Volumtarism award Jr. League of Washington, 1986. Mem. Exec. Women in Govt. (v.p., bd. dirs.). Episcopalian. Home and Office: M G B Cons 3325 Ordway St NW Washington DC 20016

BAYM, NINA, English educator; b. Princeton, N.J., June 14, 1936; d. Leo and Frances (Levinson) Zippin; m. Gordon Baym, June 1, 1958; children—Nancy, Geoffrey; m. Jack Stillinger, May 21, 1971. B.A., Cornell U., 1957; M.A., Harvard U., 1958, Ph.D., 1963. Asst. U. Calif.-Berkeley, 1962-63; instr. U. Ill., Urbana, 1963-67, asst. prof. English, 1967-69, assoc. prof., 1969-72, prof., 1972—; Jubilee prof. liberal arts and scis. U. Ill., 1989—; dir. Sch. Humanities U. Ill., Urbana, 1976-87, LAS Jubilee prof. English, 1989—; assoc. Ctr. Advanced Studies U. Ill., 1989-90; jubilee prof. English LAS, 1989—. Author: The Shape of Hawthorne's Career, 1976, Woman's Fiction: A Guide to Novels By and About Women in America, 1978, Novels, Readers and Reviewers: Responses to Fiction in Antebellum America, 1984, The Scarlet Letter: A Reading, 1986, Ed Norton Anthology of American Literature; also essays, reviews; mem. editorial bd. Am. Quar., New Eng. Quar., Legacy, A Journal of 19th Century American Women Writers, Jour. Aesthetic Edn., Am. Lit., Tulsa Studies in Women's Lit., Am. Studies., Studies Am. Fiction. Recipient U. Ill. sr. univ. scholar award, 1985; Guggenheim fellow, 1975-76; AAUW hon. fellow, 1975-76; NEH fellow, 1982-83. Mem. Robert Frost Soc. (adv. bd.), Am. Studies Assn. (exec. council 1982-84), MLA (exec. com. 19th century Am. lit. div., chmn. 1984, adv. council Am. lit. sect., chmn. 1984), Orgn. Am. Historians, Am. Lit. Assn. Office: U Ill Dept English 608 S Wright St Urbana IL 61801

BAYMILLER, LYNDA DOERN, social worker; b. Milw., July 6, 1943; d. Ronald Oliver and Marian Elizabeth (Doern) B. B.A., U. Wis., 1965, MSW, 1969; student U. Hawaii, 1962, Mich. State U., 1965. Peace Corps vol., Chile, 1965-67; social worker Luth. Social Svcs. of Wis. and Upper Mich., Milw., 1969-77, contract social worker, 1978-79; dist. supr. Children's Svc. Soc. Wis., Kenosha, 1977-78; social work supr. Sauk County Dept. Human Svcs., Baraboo, Wis., 1979—. Bd. dirs. Zoo Pride, Zool. Soc. Milw. County, 1975-77, Sauk County Mental Health Assn., 1979-84; mem. Harmony chpt. Sweet Adelines, West Allis, Wis., 1970-75, pres. chpt., 1971; pres. bd. dirs. Growing Place Day Care Center, Kenosha, 1977-78; mem. Baraboo (Wis.) Centennial Com., 1982; pres. bd. dirs. Laubach Literary Coun., Baraboo, 1986-88, sec. Sauk County Humane Soc., 1990—. Mem. Nat. Assn. Social Workers, Acad. Cert. Social Workers, Wis. Social Svcs. Assn., AAUW (br. sec. 1982-84), U. Wis. Alumni Assn. (life mem.), Am. Legion Aux., DAR, Mental Health Assn., Nat. Soc. Magna Carta Dames, Eddy Family Assn. (life mem.), Nat. Soc. Ancient and Hon. Arty. Co. of Mass., Morris Pratt Inst., Sauk County Hist. Soc., Internat. Crane Found. (patron), Daus. Colonial Wars, Zool. Soc. Milwaukee County (life), Am. Bus. Women's Assn., Friends of Baraboo Zoo, Alpha Xi Delta. Lodges: Order Eastern Star (grand rep. Miss. in Wis. 1988—), Ladies Aux. of Fraternal Order Eagles. Author: (with Clara Amelia Hess) Now-Won, A Collection of Feeling (poetry and prose), 1973. Home: 332 4th Ave Baraboo WI 53913

BAYNE, ADELE WEHMAN (ADELE WEHMAN), musician, educator; b. Burlington, Iowa, July 17, 1916; d. Edward J. and Ina B. (Hildebrand) W.; m. William H. Bayne Jr., May 29, 1946; children: Edward J., William H. III. MusB, Chicago U., Am. Conservatory Music, 1941. Cello instr. music dept. Northwestern U., Evanston, Ill., 1936-39; faculty Am. Conservatory Music, Chgo., 1937-40; cellist, harpist Chgo. Women's Symphony, 1937-40; cellist Chgo. Civic Orch., 1938-40; harpist NBC Symphony Orch./Toscanini, 1941-46; staff harpist radio stas. including WTIC, Hartford, Conn., WLS, WGN, Chgo., NBC, Blue Network, N.Y.C., 1938-45; harpist So. Symphony, Columbia, S.C., 1943-45, Lucky Strike Hit Parade, N.Y.C., 1944-46; harpist various artists including Helen Hayes, Lorette Taylor, Morton Downey, Frank Sinatra, N.Y., 1944-46, Nat. Symphony, Washington, 1945-52; instr. harp, cello, freelance performer, soloist Washington, 1950—; mem. Nat. Youth Orch., N.Y.C., 1940-41; harpist various orchs. including Paul Whiteman, Leo Reisman, Vaughan Monroe, Hal Saunders, Devron, Spike Jones, Raymond Paige, Radio City, inaugural balls of Presidents Truman, Eisenhower, Kennedy, Nixon, Carter, Reagan; accompanist for Victor Borge, Dinah Shore, Gregor Piatagorski, Laurenz Melchior, Helen Traubel. Harpist Twelfth Night with Helen Hayes, Glass Menagerie with Lorette Taylor; recs. include Gotterdamerung (with NBC Symphony, Helen Traubel); appeared in film Carnegie Hall, 1947. Mem. Des Moines County Historical Assn., Burlington, Iowa, Prince George's Historical Assn., Md., Prince George's Geneological Soc., Md. Recipient 1st Place award State of Iowa Music Competition, 1934, 1st place award Nat. Music Competition, Cleve., 1934; named to Women's Hall of Fame, Prince George's County, Upper Marlboro, Md., 1987. Mem. Am. Fedn. Musicians (life), Chgo. Women's Symphony Assn., Am. Harp Soc., Mu Phi Epsilon (life). Home and Studio: 5709 38th Ave Hyattsville MD 20782

BAYOL, IRENE SLEDGE, information services specialist; b. Franklin County, N.C., Oct. 11, 1933; d. Walter Ernest and Nonie (Parrish) Sledge; m. Charlie Morton Hamlet, Aug. 23, 1950 (div. Mar. 1956, dec. 1981); 1 child, Marcia Jean; m. Jerome Stollenwerch Bayol, Aug. 9, 1958 (div. May 1972, dec. 1980); children: Jerome Jr., Susan Carol, Keenan Jules. Student, Louisburg (N.C.) Jr. Coll., 1952-53, U. Va., 1970, No. Va. Community Coll., 1984, Am. U., 1986-88. Computer equipment analyst USAF, Washington, 1970-73; supr. GSA, Washington, 1973-84; ind. real estate agt. Washington, 1973—; computer equipment specialist GSA Inst. for Info. Tech., Washington, 1984-85; policy officer GSA, Washington, 1985-87, agy. liaison mgr., 1987-89; realtor Shannon & Luchs, Realtors, Alexandria, Va., 1988—. Mem. Profl. Women's Club, Toastmistresses, Travel Club, Investments Club. Episcopalian.

BAYZIK, BARBARA A., nutritionist; b. Hazleton, Pa., Feb. 7, 1948; d. John James and Aldona Lucy (Ankudovich) B. BS, Marywood Coll., 1976; postgrad., Alvernia Coll. Registered dietician, Ohio; cert. sanitarian. Food svc. dir., ARA Svcs. Ft. Sanders-Sevier Med. Ctr., Sevierville, Tenn.; asst. dir. food svcs., ARA Svcs. Marietta (Ohio) Meml. Hosp., dir. Ctr. for Weight and Nutrition, ARA Svcs.; speaker various community orgns.; mem. home econs. adv. bd. local high sch. Columnist on nutrition local paper. Named Woman of Yr. ABWA, 1987, 88. Mem. Am. Dietetic Assn., Mid-Ohio Valley Dietetic Assn. (pres.-elect 1988-89, pres. 1989-90, nominating com. 1990—), Washington County Diabetes Assn. (bd. dir., pres.), Washington County Unit Am. Cancer Soc. (bd. dirs.). Home: 1209 D County House Ln Marietta OH 45750 Office: 401 Matthew St Marietta OH 45750

BAZELA, JEAN ANN, medical technologist; b. Detroit, July 30, 1947; d. Robert Dale and Edna Marie (Mortimer) Chilton; m. Daniel James Bazela, June 1969 (div. 1978); 1 child, Robert Dale. BS, East Mich. U., 1969; cert. internship, Providence Hosp. Sch. Med. Tech., 1969. Cert. Med. Technologist (Am. Soc. of Clin. Pathologists). Rotating technologist Providence Hosp., Southfield, 1969-70; lectr., lab instr. Carnegie Inst., Detroit, 1972-75; sr. clin. lab specialist Roche Biomedical Labs. (predecessor firm Consolidated Biomedical Labs.), Columbus, Ohio, 1976—. Recipient Disting. Alumni award Coll. Allied Health East Mich. U., 1983, Pres.'s Achievement award, 1983, 85, 86, 88. Mem. Am. Assn. Clin. Chemistry (sec. 1983), Mich. Soc. Med. Tech., Detroit Soc. Med. Tech. (pres. 1980-81, 1984-85, 90—), Detroit Yacht Club. Home: 6903 Dandison Blvd West Bloomfield MI 48324

BAZER, ANGIE, hotel executive; b. Decatur, Ill., Jan. 2, 1928; d. Robert J. and Erma (Eskew) Durbin; m. Raymond Schick, June 2, 1951 (div.); m. Harold Bazer, Dec. 31, 1982; children: Raymond, John, Joy, Jean, Denise, Stephen, Theresa. Indsl. mgmt. cert., Solano Jr. Coll., 1965; postgrad., Coll. of Desert, 1979. Cert. indsl. mgr. Chief P.B.X. Riveria Hotel, Palm Springs, Calif., 1970-72; chief P.A.B.X. Canyon Hotel Golf and Racket Club, Palm Springs, 1972-78; asst. controller Ocotillo Lodge, Palm Springs, 1976-80; resident mgr. Golden West Hotel, San Diego, Calif., 1980—. Mem. exec. bd. Girl Scouts U.S., 1963-75. Recipient Cert. of Appreciation Vallejo City Coun., San Diego Sr. Ctr., award for organizing first drill team in U.S. Girl Scouts U.S.; award winning video tape on S.R.O. Housing for Srs., 1988. Mem. Am. Bus. Women's Assn. (pres. and Woman of Yr. 1978), Nat. Assn. Exec. Women, Ctr. City Assn. (San Diego), Palm Springs C. of C. (Cert. of Appreciation). Home: 158 Saturn Palm Springs CA 92264

BAZIE, MARY IDA, social worker; b. Mansfield, Ohio, Jan. 15, 1953; d. Sylvester Frank and Sadie Belle (Benjamin) Petty; m. Jack Archibald Bazie, May 4, 1978; children: Kamau, Keesa Ouidia. BA, Heidelberg Coll., 1970. Lic. social worker, Ohio; cert. chem. dependency counselor, Ohio. Social worker Hough Norwood, Cleve., 1974-77; counselor Community Action against Addiction, Cleve., 1979-80; intake coord. Cleve. Treatment Ctr., 1982-84, vocat. assessment coord., 1984-85, dir. social svcs., 1985—; chairwoman, mem. Women in Treatment, Cleve., 1984—; cons. Ohio Com. on Women, 1985-87; chairwoman Woman's Alliance Recovery Svcs., Cleve., 1986-87; bd. dirs. Health Issues Task Force, Cleve., 1987—. Mem. NAFE. Democrat. Baptist. Office: Cleve Treatment Ctr ll27 Carnegie Ave Cleveland OH 44115

BAZIGIAN, ANITA KIZIRIAN, manufacturing company executive, jewelry designer; b. Worcester, Mass.; d. Serop John and Mary (Pilibosian) Kizirian; m. Paul Bazigian, Aug. 25, 1957; children—Lesley Karen, Craig Michael. Student Worcester Art Mus., 1949-53, Sch. Nursing, Cambridge City Hosp., 1953-54; A.S., Becker Coll., 1956. Clerical positions Blackstone Valley News, Northbridge, Mass., 1953-56; med. asst. Bennett I. Fielding, M.D., Worcester, Mass., 1956-58, Agostine Del Signore, M.D., Worcester, 1958-60; freelance artist, Worcester, 1960-64; tchr. Armenian lang. Lang. Sch., Worcester, 1960-64; tchr. art, sci. Worcester Pub. Schs., 1964-70; tchr. Southwest Ednl. Ctr., Walled Lake, Mich., 1970-75; designer fine jewelry Birmingham Jewelers, Mich., 1975—; pres. ANI Designs div. Birmingham Mfg. Corp., Troy, Mich., 1984-88, Burlingame, Calif., 1988—; designer copyrighted jewelry. Exhibited various jewelry trade shows, N.Y.C., San Francisco, Los Angeles, Dallas. Counselor Girl Scouts U.S.A., Farmington Conn., 1952-53. Mem. Jewelers Bd. Trade, Pacific Jewelers Trade Show, Dallas Jewelers Trade Show, Jewelers of Am. Inc., Internat. Jewelry Show. Republican. Armenian Orthodox. Club: Mr. and Mrs. (Southfield, Mich.). Avocations: piano; boating; tennis; surfing; skiing. Office: ANI Designs PO Box 1039 Millbrae CA 94030

BAZZANO, EDIE See MILLERS, EDIE

BEACH, BARBARA EILEEN, commercial artist, business owner; b. Elmira, N.Y., July 17, 1944; d. Raymond E. and Norma E. (Rounsville) B. Grad., Famous Artist's Sch. Elmira Bus. Inst., 1974, Corning Community Coll., 1986, Elmira Coll., 1987. Comml. artist and illustrator Comml. Press of Elmira; negative and illustration stripper specialist Moore Bus. Forms, Inc., Elmira; art instr. Adult Community Edn. and City of Elmira Sch. Dist.; advt. mgr. Ea. Metal/USA-Sign, Elmira; owner, mgr. Barbara Eileen Comml. Art Studio, Elmira, Barbara Eileen Custom Souvenirs, Elmira. Mark Twain exhbn. Arts in the Park Arnot Art Mus., 1987-89, Octogon Fair Elmira Coll., 1988-89. Exhibit chmn. preservation com. Hist. 1897 Firehouse, 1987-89; fundraiser festival and exhibit com. Near Westside Neighborhood Assn. Recipient Scholastic Art award Rochester, N.Y., 1959, Elmira Coll., 1958, 59. Mem. Bus. and Profl. Women (pub. rels. 1989, v.p. 1990), Elmira Art Club (chmn. 1986—), Finger Lakes Assn. Spl. Projects, Chemung County Hist. Assn. (chmn. Oktoberfest 1988-90, Christmas Festival 1989), Chemung County C. of C. (com. chmn. Bluegrass Festival 1987-88), Zonta. Home: 10-C Eastgate Homes Elmira NY 14902 Office: PO Box 903 Elmira NY 14902

BEACH, LISA ANN, public relations executive; b. Harrisburg, Pa., Sept. 7, 1964; d. Richard Andrew and Shirley Ann (Collotty) Kaminski; m. Kevin Michael Beach. BA in Communications, King's Coll., 1986; MA in Pub. Relations, Glassboro (N.J.) State Coll., 1988. Intern Citizen's Voice Newspaper, Wilkes-Barre, Pa., 1986; grad. asst. Glassboro State Coll., 1986-87; dir. pub. relations Burlington County Bd. Realtors, Cinnaminson, N.J., 1988—. Contbr. articles to profl. publs. Tutor Literacy Vols. Am., Rancocas chpt., N.J., 1988-89, Big Sister, Big Bros./Big Sisters, Willingboro chpt., N.J., 1989, bd. dirs., mem., Burlington County. Recipient scholarship, King's Coll., 1983, Grady Grad. Sch. scholarship, 1986, John E. Kierzkowski scholarship, 1986. Mem. Pub. Relations Soc. Am. (asst. editor for chpt. newsletter 1989). Democrat. Roman Catholic. Office: Burlington Co Bd Realtors 1630 Riverton Rd Cinnaminson NJ 08077

BEACH, MARGARET GASTALDI (MRS. EDWARD WOODBRIDGE BEACH), found. exec., nurse; b. Placerville, Calif., Aug. 10, 1915; d. Giovanni Batista and Josephine (Bisagno) Gastaldi; student Sacramento City Coll., 1934; grad. Mercy Coll. Nursing, 1938; m. Edward Woodbridge Beach, Feb. 15, 1946 (dec. Aug. 1968); children—Laura G. (Mrs. Robert L. Phillips), Edward Woodbridge, Margaret J. In charge urol. dept. Mercy Hosp., Sacramento, 1938-42; tchr. urology to student nurses, 1943-45. Treas., Germana M. Wilson Meml. Scholarship Found., 1967—. Mem. Woman's Aux. AMA, Sacramento County Women Med. Soc., Am. Legion Aux., Italian Cultural Soc. Clubs: Carriage Trade, Women of the Moose, Hon. Guild St. Patrick's Day Mummurs. Home: 6255 14th Ave Sacramento CA 95820

BEADERSTADT, ANDREA ANGLIN, journalism educator; b. Detroit, Feb. 11, 1949; d. Hartley Raymond and Margaret Mary (Ward) Anglin; m. John Henry Beaderstadt, Dec. 22, 1977; children: Matthew Geoffrey, Christopher Erik. BA in Journalism magna cum laude, Wayne State U., 1970; MA in Print Communications, Am. U., Washington, 1971. Legis. asst. Rep. Martha W. Griffiths, Mich., 1971-74; legis. specialist LWV, Washington, 1974-75; legis. asst. Rep. James V. Stanton, Ohio, 1976-77; instr. Ferris State Coll., Big Rapids, Mich., 1977-78; dir. Small World, Inc., Kodiak, Alaska, 1980-81; personnel asst. USCG, Kodiak, 1981-82; copy editor The Anchorage Times, 1982-83; asst. prof. St. Michael's Coll., Winooski, Vt., 1983-89; mem. English dept. SUNY, Plattsburgh, 1989—; reporter The Alaska Fisherman mag., Juneau, 1980. Bd. dirs. Vt. Woman, 1988-90. Research fellow St. Michael's Coll. Ctr. for Advancement of Pvt. Higher Edn., Japan, 1987. Mem. Nat. Fedn. Press Women, Nat. Newspaper Assn., New Eng. Press Assn. (writing coach), New Eng. Newspaper Assn., Vt. Press Assn. (sec. 1984-89), Women in Communication. Lutheran. Home: RD #1 Box 1489E Sheldon VT 05483 Office: SUNY English Dept 216 Champlain Valley Hall Plattsburgh NY 12901

BEAL, SUSAN RUTH, mathematics and computer science educator; b. N.Y.C., Oct. 20, 1940; d. Milton and Sylvia L. (Greenspan) Neuwirth;

children: David, Benjamin. AB, Antioch Coll., 1962; MST, U. Chgo., 1974, PhD, 1983. Statis. programmer U. Ill., Urbana, 1962-65, U. Chgo., 1965-68; tchr. math. New Community Sch., Chgo., 1971-72; tchr. Chgo. Pub. Schs., 1974-75; math. cons. Sch. Dist. 147, Harvey, Ill., 1975-77; assoc. prof. math. and computer sci. St. Xavier Coll., Chgo., 1978-90, prof., 1990—, chmn. dept., 1988—; cons. St. Athanaseus Sch., Evanston, Ill., 1986-88; dir. math. Chgo. Area Pre-Coll. Engring. Program, 1987-88. Author: Teaching with Fraction Stax, 1987, Base Ten Blocks, 1988; co-dir. video tape Thinking about Thinking, 1988. Mem. Nat. Coun. Suprs. Math. (regional dir. 1989—), Rsch. Coun. for Diagnostic and Prescriptive Math. (conf. com. 1987—), Ill. Coun. Tchrs. Math. (co-editor Jour. 1989—), Woman and Math. Edn. (sec. 1989—). Home: 5532 S Shore Dr Chicago IL 60637 Office: St Xavier Coll 3700 W 103d St Chicago IL 60655

BEALE, BARBARA EDWARDS, rehabilitation consultant; b. Roanoke Rapids, N.C., Oct. 17, 1951; d. Bob Claude and Virginia (Allen) Edwards; m. Joseph Thurman Beale, Apr. 22, 1972; children: Douglas Craig, Daniel Edward. AS in Nursing, John Tyler Community Coll., Chester, Va., 1974. Staff nurse to charge nurse ICU Greensville Meml. Hosp., Va., 1974, Southampton County Correctional Ctr., Capron, Va., 1975; pub. health nurse, team leader Southampton County, Franklin City Health Depts., Courtland, Va., 1975-87; staff nurse, charge nurse Catawba (Va.) Geriatric Psychiat. State Hosp., 1987; home health dir. Montgomery Hosp., Blacksburg, Va., 1987; rehab. cons. Am. Internat. Health and Rehab. Svcs., Roanoke, Va., 1987—. Mem. Roanoke Rehab. Assn., Va. Assn. for Rehab. Nurses, Am. Heart Assn. Southern Baptist. Office: AIHRS PO Box 21386 Roanoke VA 24018

BEALE, GEORGIA ROBISON, historian; b. Chgo., Mar. 14, 1905; d. Henry Barton and Dora Belle (Sledd) Robison; m. Howard Kennedy Beale, Jan. 2, 1942; children: Howard Kennedy, Henry Barton Robison, Thomas Wight. AB, U. Chgo., 1926, AM, 1928; PhD, Columbia U., 1938; student Sorbonne and Coll. de France, 1930-34. Reader in history U. Chgo., 1927-29; lectr. Barnard Coll., 1937-38; instr. Bklyn. Coll., 1937-39; asst. prof. Hollins (Va.) Coll., 1939-41, Wellesley Coll., 1941-42, Castleton (Vt.) State Coll., 1968-70; vis. asso. prof. U. Ky., Lexington, 1970-72; professorial lectr. George Washington U., 1983-84. Author: Revelliere-lépeaux, Citizen Director, 1938, 72, Academies to Institut, 1973, Bosc and the Exequatur, 1978; contbg. author Historical Dictionary of the French Revolution, 1985; also articles. Mem. Madison (Wis.) Civic Music Assn. and Madison Symphony Orch. League, 1958—; hon. trustee Culver-Stockton Coll., 1974—. Univ. fellow Columbia U., 1929-30. Mem. AAUW (European fellow 1930-31), Am., So. hist. assns., Soc. French Hist. Studies, Western Soc. French History (hon. mem. exec. council), Am., Brit. socs. 18th century studies, Phi Beta Kappa, Pi Lambda Theta, Phi Alpha Theta, Pi Kappa Delta. Clubs: Reid Hall (Paris); Brit. Univ. Women's (London). Address: The Ridge Orford NH 03777 also: 2816 Columbia Rd Madison WI 53705 also: 110 D St SE Washington DC 20003

BEALE, VIRGINIA DAVIS, educator; b. Columbia, S.C., Oct. 14, 1936; d. John Ashmore and Willie Gertrude (Rodgers) Davis; m. Sterling Edward Beale, Aug. 17, 1958 (div. Mar. 1985); children: John Edward, Charles Sterling. BA, Columbia Coll., 1958, MA, 1983. Tchr. Richland Sch. Dist. 1, Columbia, S.C., 1958-62, 63-64, Dekabe Sch. Dist., Atlanta, 1962-63; tchr. Lexington (S.C.) Sch. Dist. 2, Columbia, 1976-79, 1976-79; tchr. Caughman Road Elem. Sch., Columbia, 1979—; cons. State Adv. Coun., 1985—; evaluator So. Assn. Colls. & Schs., Columbia, 1987—. Pres. PTA Withers, 1975; hearing officer Richland Sch. Dist. 1, 1981; chmn. planning Parent Educator Partnership, Columbia, 1985. Mem. NEA, S.C. Edn. Assn., Richland Edn. Assn., Woman's Club (1st v.p. 1980-81), Garden Club (2nd v.p. 1974-75). Republican. Baptist. Home: 114 Wembley St Columbia SC 29209 Office: Caughman Rd Elem Sch 7725 Caughman Rd Columbia SC 29209

BEALL, INGRID LILLEHEI, lawyer; b. Cedar Falls, Iowa, June 18, 1926; d. Ingebrigt Larsen and Olive (Allison) Lillehei; m. George Brooke Beall, Dec. 21, 1951 (div. 1971). A.B., U. Chgo., 1945, M.A., 1948, J.D., 1956. Bar: Ill. 1956. Assoc. firm McDermott, Will & Emery, Chgo., 1956-58, Baker & McKenzie, Chgo., 1958-61; ptnr. Baker & McKenzie, Chgo., Brussels and Paris, 1961—. Mem. ABA, Ill. Bar Assn., Chgo. Bar Assn., Internat. Fiscal Assn. Home: 175 Delaware St Chicago IL 60611 Office: Baker & McKenzie Prudential Pla Ste 2800 Chicago IL 60601

BEALL, JOANNA MAY, painter; b. Chgo., Aug. 17, 1935; d. Lester Thomas and Dorothy Welles (Miller) B.; student Yale U. Sch. Fine Arts, 1953-57, Art Inst. Chgo., 1957; m. H.C. Westermann, Mar. 31, 1959. One-man shows include: Great Bldg. Crack-Up Gallery, N.Y.C., 1973, James Corcoran Gallery, Los Angeles, 1974, Gallery Rebecca Cooper, Washington, 1975; group shows: Allan Frumkin, Chgo., 1960, 61, Whitney Mus., N.Y.C., 1973, Art Inst. Chgo., 1976, Univ. Galleries, Los Angeles, 1979, Xavier Fourcade, N.Y.C., 1980, 85; vis. artist U. Colo., Boulder, 1979, 84. Mem. Artists Equity Assn., Visual Artists and Galleries Assn. Article The World of Joanna Beall (Melinda Wortz) appeared in Art Week mag., 1974. Home: Box 5028 Brookfield Center CT 06804

BEALS, SHARON KATHLEEN KEY, quality assurance executive; b. Old Tappan, N.J., Apr. 22, 1958; d. Frank Alfred and Phyllis Ann (Arnold) Key; m. Loran Donald Beals, Oct. 15, 1983. BS, Cornell U., 1980. Quality control technician Land O'Frost of Ind., Hammond, 1980-82; on site auditor Arby's Inc., Milw., 1982-84; sr. auditor Arby's Inc., Atlanta, 1984-85, quality assurance mgr., 1985, sr. mgr., 1986-87, dir., quality assurance, 1987-88, group dir., 1989—; lectr. Southeastern Meat Assn., Gainesville, Fla., 1988. Coach, Ga. Spl. Olympics, 1988; key exec. United Way, 1988. Mem. Nat. Restaurant Assn. (chmn. quality assurance exec. study group). Office: Arby's Inc 3495 Piedmont Rd Atlanta GA 30305

BEAM, BEVERLY J., communications company executive; b. Holton, Kans., May 3, 1941; d. Walter Cecil and Edith Elizabeth (Ingels) Schumann; m. Larry Charles Beam, Jan. 19, 1963; children: Jeffrey Charles, Jared Walter. AA, Washburn U., Topeka, 1989, postgrad., 1990—. Cert. profl. sec. Legal sec. Shaw, Hergenreter & Quarnstrom, Topeka, 1960-66; exec. sec. Fleming Cos., Inc., Topeka, 1974-86; corp. sec. Stauffer Communications, Inc., Topeka, 1986—. Precinct committeewoman Dem. Party, Sioux Dist., Soldier Twp., Kans., 1990. Mem. Greater Topeka C. of C. (ambassador 1988—). Lutheran. Office: Stauffer Communications Inc 616 Jefferson Topeka KS 66607

BEAMAN, ANN THOMSON, state government worker; b. Waukon, Iowa, May 10, 1933; d. Andrew and Ruth Augusta (Ludeking) Thompson; m. Robert L. Beaman, June 25, 1955; children: Roderick Lewis, Alerick Robert, Scott Andrew. BA in Journalism, U. Mont., 1955; postgrad., U. South Fla., autumn 1983, 84. Adminstr. TV programming, radio local news, women's program Bozeman (Mont.) Cable TV, 1955-56; with Sta. KBMN-AM, Bozeman, 1955-56; salesperson Sewing Circle Fabrics, St. Petersburg, Fla., 1978-79, Tall Girl Fashions, St. Petersburg, 1979-80; asst. store mgr. Motherhood Maternity, St. Petersburg, 1980-81; office mgr. Accurate Personnel, St. Petersburg, 1981-82; exec. sec. to State Senator Jeanne Malchon, St. Petersburg, 1982—. Den leader coach Boy/Cub Scouts Am., Woodland Hills, Calif., 1967-71; mem. exec. bd. local PTA, Woodland Hills, 1972-74, St. Petersburg, 1976; pres. Welcome Wagon, St. Petersburg, 1977. Mem. Ord. Ea. Star. Democrat. Presbyterian. Home: 4348 43rd St S Saint Petersburg FL 33711 Office: Senator Jeanne Malchon 100 2nd Ave S Ste 904 Saint Petersburg FL 33701

BEAMAN, JANICE ELLEN, nurse; b. Auburn, N.Y., Sept. 23, 1961; d. Jack Edward and Frances Mary (Kenney) Hole; m. Glenn Peter Beaman, June 6, 1981; children: Nathan James, Brandon Taylor. AS, Cayuga County Community Coll., 1981, postgrad. Syracuse U. RN, N.Y. Med.-surg. staff nurse Community Gen. Hosp., Syracuse, N.Y., 1981-84, labor and delivery staff nurse, 1984-88, asst. head nurse, 1988—. Roman Catholic. Avocations: softball; racquetball; tennis; sewing. Home: 4936 Limehill Dr Syracuse NY 13215-1325 Office: Community Gen Hosp Broad Rd Syracuse NY 13215

BEAMAN, MARGARINE GAYNELL, scrap metal broker; b. Feb. 26; d. Margaret Lena Geisweidt; m. Robert W. Beaman; children: Richard Beaman, Ronald Beaman, Lorene Barrera, Jessica Barrera, Vincent Thompson. Student, U. Houston, U. Mich. Pres. Beaman Metal Co., Inc., Austin, 1972—; pres. Beaman Acctg. and Cons., Austin, 1975—. Bd. dirs. Cen. East Austion Community Orgn., Austin Resource for Ind. Living, City of Austin/Travis County Pvt. Industry Coun.; vol. Juveniles in Jail, Women Prisoners, Old Bakery; vol. tax preparer VITA, TCE; founder project for ind. living for blind; fund raiser Austin Crime Stoppers. Recipient Gov.'s Vol. of Yr. award, 1982, Mayor's Meritorious award, 1982; named Outstanding Blind Worker of Tex., 1982; recipient svc. awards Sertoma Club, N.Y. Am. Coun. of Blind, Nat. Community Schs. award; inducted into Tex. Assn. Pvt. Colls. Hall of Fame, Austin Women's Hall of Fame; numerous others. Mem. Tex. Fedn. Bus. and Profl. Women's Clubs, Exec. Women Internat., Zonta Internat., Cert. Consumer Credit Execs., Nat. Assn. Fin. Aid Adminstrs., Austin C. of C., Austin Women's C. of C., Gen. Fedn. Women's Club, Pvt. Industry Coun., Am. Coun. of Blind. Home: 1406 Wilshire Blvd Austin TX 78722 Office: 3409 E 5th St Austin TX 78702

BEAMER-PATTON, JUNE ELIZABETH, dermatologist; b. Martin's Ferry, Ohio, Mar. 9, 1944; d. Ralph Clark and Betty June (Sedgwick) Patton; m. Yancey Brintle, Aug. 20, 1967 (div. Dec. 1986). BS in Chemistry, Marshall U., 1965; MD, Med. Coll. Va., 1969. Diplomate Am. Bd. Dermatology; cert. Nat. Bd. Med. Examiners, Calif.; cert. Colo. Basic Sci., Colo., Utah; cert. X-ray Supr. and Operator, Calif. Intern Med. Coll. Va., Richmond, 1969-70, U. Calif., Irvine, 1970; resident in dermatology Long Beach (Calif.) Veteran's Hosp., 1970-73; with U. Calif. Med. Ctr., Irvine, 1970-82, Healthcare Med. Ctr. Tustin, 1988; pvt. practice Tustin, 1973—; clin. assoc. medicine dermatology, U. Calif., Irvine, 1972, clin. instr. medicine dermatology, 1973, asst. clin. prof. 1976, clin. prof. 1977-82. Contbr. articles profl. jours. Mem. Calvary Ch. Mem. AMA, Am. Med. Women's Assn., Calif. Med. Assn., Pacific Dermatologic Assn., Orange County Med. Assn., Orange County Dermatological Soc., Am. Acad. Dermatology, Am. Coun. Hosp. Staffs, Internat. Acad. Cosmetic Surgery, Cooperative of Am. Physicians, Inc., Am. Soc. Dermatology Surgery, Audio Engring. Soc., Am. Mgmt. Assn., Nat. Assn. Women Bus. Owners, Am. Soc. Profl. and Exec. Women, Tustin C. of C., Wings Club, Alpha Epsilon Delta, Chi Beta Phi, Phi Alpha Theta. Republican. Office: June E Beamer-Patton MD 13372 Newport Ave #A Tustin CA 92680

BEAMGUARD, ELIZABETH PARKS, librarian; b. Fayetteville, Tenn.; d. Joel Dodson and Emma Wenifred (Puckett) Parks; m. Elbert Strode Beamguard; 1 child, Elizabeth Beamguard Swanson. AB in Journalism, U. Tenn., 1931; BS in Library Sci., Emory U., 1944; postgrad., U. Chattanooga; DHL (hon.), Livingston U., 1981. Librarian Hamilton County Sch. System, Chattanooga, 1940-44, Huntsville (Ala.) Madison County Library, 1944-55, U. Ala., Huntsville, 1953-54; field rep. Ala. Pub. Library Service, Montgomery, 1955-60; instr. U. Ala. Library Sch., Tuscaloosa, 1962-66; dir. Ala. Pub. Library Service, Montgomery, 1960-76; library cons. Montgomery, 1975—; chmn. sr. univ. adv. bd. continuing edn. div. Auburn U., Montgomery, 1984—; library cons. Battelle Columbus Labs., Columbus, Ohio, 1975. Contbr.: (poetry) Southern Style, 1984, Contemporaries from Tennessee; contbr. articles to profl. publs. Bd. mem. Friends of Ala. Archives, Montgomery, 1987—, Coun. on Aging, Montgomery, 1985; mem. So. State Work Conf. Adult Edn., 1976—; pres. Zonta Internat., Montgomery chpt., 1975-76; mem. exec. bd. Montgomery Area on Aging, 1986—. Recipient Citation for Service, U.S. Congress, Washington, 1967, Ala. State Legis., Montgomery, 1967. Mem. ALA (John Cotton Dana award 1971), Ala. Libr. Assn. (Exceptional Svc. award 1976), AAUW (pres. Montgomery br. chpt. 1975-79), Nat. Assn. Adult Edn., S.E. Libr. Assn. Home: 3373 Dartmouth Circle Montgomery AL 36111 Office: Auburn U Sr Univ Adv Bd Div Continuing Edn Montgomery AL 36193-0401

BEAMS, MARY ANN, editor; b. Greensburg, Ind., Nov. 13, 1939; d. James Charles and Mary Elizabeth (Link) McLaughlin; m. David Curie Beams, Nov. 7, 1970 (div. 1987); children: Christian Curie, Geoffrey Graham. AB in Journalism, Ind. U., 1961. Reporter Greensburg (Ind.) Daily News, 1958-61; spl. advt. trainee The Chgo. Tribune, 1961-63; copy writer media dir. Shaw-Hagues, Inc., Chgo., 1963-65; copywriter Caldwell-Larkin-Sidener-VanRiper, Indpls., 1965-67; copywriter, media dir. MacGill-Ross, Inc., Indpls., 1967-69; dir. publicity Coll. Div. Bobbs, Merrill Pub., Indpls., 1969-74; audience devel. assoc. Phoenix Symphony Orch., 1984-86; staff asst. Data Network for Human Svcs., Phoenix, 1986-88; editor Ctr. for Bus. Rsch., Ariz. State U., Tempe, Ariz., 1988—; cons. The Poisoned Pen-A-Mystery Bookstore, Scottsdale, Ariz., 1989—; editor Cloud Assocs. Pub., Phoenix, 1987—. Editor: (newsletter) Arizona Business, 1988, Arizona Blue Chip, 1988, Western Blue Chip, 1988, Forum, 1988, Focus, 1988. Pres. Cen. Ariz. Dental Aux., Phoenix, 1980-81; charter mem. Phoenix Symphony Aux., 1982; merit badge counselor Boy Scouts Am. Recipient Award for Publication Excellence Assn. for Univ. Bus. and Econ. Rsch., 1989, Outstanding Advt. Student St. Louis Advt. Club, 1961. Mem. Women in Communications, Inc. (faculty advisor 1989-90), P.E.O. Sisterhood, Phoenix Symphony Friends. Office: Ctr for Bus Rsch NBJ Ariz State U Tempe AZ 85287-4406

BEAN, JOAN NONA, merchant, consultant; b. Chgo., Aug. 9, 1929; d. Joseph John and Otylia Jeanette (Lokanski) Nowicki; m. Alfred E. Brock, Feb., 1950 (div. 1953); m. Harry Raymond Bean, July 22, 1954 (dec. Mar. 1973); children: Harry R. II, Elise Josan, James Nathaniel. Student, N.W. Bus. Coll., 1947, Columbia Coll., 1951, Christine Valmy Sch., 1971. Model Patricia Vance Agy., Chgo., 1944-48, Conover Agy., N.Y.C., 1949-50; model, officer mgr. Daisy's Originals, Miami, Fla., 1950-54; owner Judy Bean, Inc., St. Louis, 1966—; sec. Fashion Group St. Louis, 1978—. Contbr. Affairs mag., 1981—. Active Mo. Botanical Gardens, St. Louis, Friends of St. Louis Art Mus., St. Louis Zoo Friends. Home: 4466 W Pine #18C Saint Louis MO 63108

BEAN, NANCY ANN MORGAN, food service broker; b. Williamstown, Ky., Feb. 9, 1936; d. Dora Bell Morgan and Helen (Dunlap) Strother Morgan; m. Philip Lee Crume, Oct. 26, 1960 (div. 1974); children—Ann Morgan Crume Redmon, Lynn Ellis Bean; m. James Ellis Bean, July 26, 1980. B.S., Eastern Ky. U., 1959; M.Pub.Affairs, Ky. State U., 1976. Nutritionist, Ky. Health Dept., Georgetown, 1966-68; dietary cons. Central Ky. Nursing Home, Lexington, 1968-71; dir. food service Ky. Bur. Corrections, Frankfort, 1971-76; sales rep., account exec. A.J. Seibert, Louisville, also Lexington, Ky., 1976-81; owner, pres. Profl. Food Service, Louisville, 1981—. Mem. Louisville Dietetic Assn., Ky. Dietetic Assn., Am. Dietetic Assn., Ky. Restaurant Assn., Nat. Food Brokers Assn., Am. Sch. Food Service Assn. Democrat. Methodist. Lodge: Order Eastern Star. Avocations: gardening, reading. Home: Route 2 Box 266 Cox's Creek KY 40013 Office: Profl Food Service 1006 Phillips Ln Louisville KY 40213

BEANE, LOIS VELLEDA, county official, bookkeeper; b. Georgetown, Ind., Aug. 2, 1938; d. Henry Condar and Irene (Banet) Dreher; m. Walter Maxwell Beane, Dec. 12, 1958; children: Cynthia, Velleda, David, Jeffrey. Student, Lynchburg (Va.) Bible Coll., 1982. Bookkeeper Spalding Laundry, Louisville, 1957-58; bookkeeper, clk. Naval Supply Ctr., Norfolk, Va., 1963-73; nurse's asst. Andrew S. Rowan Home, Sweet Springs, W.Va., 1975-77; bookkeeper Monroe County Coun. on Aging, Lindside, W.Va., 1977-89, exec. dir., 1989—. Trustee, treas. Nazarene Ch., Peterstown, W.Va., 1989—; Sunday sch. tchr., bd. dirs., quizz pastor, trustee, stewart, treas. Nazarene Ch., Gap Mills, W.Va., 1974-89; treas., sec. Bapt. Ch., Norfolk, 1963-73. Mem. NAFE, Am. Assn. Retired Persons, W.Va. Assn. for Dirs. Home: RR 1 Gap Mills WV 24941 Office: Monroe County Coun on Aging PO Box 149 Lindside WV 24951

BEAR, DINAH, lawyer; b. Lynnwood, Calif., Oct. 22, 1951; d. Henry Louis and Betty Jean (Isenhart) B. BJ, U. Mo., 1974; JD, McGeorge Sch. Law, 1977. Bar: Calif. 1978, D.C. 1981, U.S. Supreme Ct. 1982. Dep. gen. counsel Council on Environ. Quality, Washington, 1981-83, gen. counsel, 1983—. Staff asst. Dems. for Ronald Reagan, Arlington, Va., 1980. Recipient Am. Jurisprudence award Bancroft Whitney Co., 1975. Mem. ABA, D.C. Bar Assn. (environ. energy and natural resource sect. 1986—). Republican. Jewish. Office: Coun Environ Quality 722 Jackson Pl NW Washington DC 20503

BEARD, ANN SOUTHARD, travel company executive, art framing company executive; b. Denver, Jan. 13, 1948; d. William Harvey and Cora Alice Cornelia (Caldwell) Southard; m. Terrill Leon Beard, Dec. 20, 1970 (div. Oct. 1980); 1 son, Jeffery Leon; m. Rainer G. Froehlich, Feb. 12, 1988. B.A., Willamette U., 1970; postgrad U. Calif.-San Diego, 1981-82. Exec. asst. Kidder Peabody & Co., San Francisco, 1970-72; adminstrv. aide Arthur Anderson & Co., Portland, Oreg., 1972-73; owner, mgr. Beard's Frame Shoppes, Inc., Portland, 1973-80; dir. mktg. Multnomah County Fair, Portland, 1979; owner, chief exec. officer Ann Beard Spl. Events, San Diego, 1980-82; pres. Frame Affair, Inc., San Diego, 1982-86, Jack Oil Co., Inc., Greeley, 1982—; co-owner, v.p. Froehlich Internat. Travel, La Jolla, Calif., 1987; v.p. 146 Co., Inc., Greeley, pres., 1970-88; lectr., cons. SBA, San Diego, 1980-85. Mem. Civic Light Opera, Old Globe Theatre; bd. dirs. San Diego Master Chorale, 1981—; mem. citizens adv. bd. Drug Abuse Task Force/Crime Prevention Task Force, San Diego, 1983-87; campaign coord. Bill Mitchell for City Coun., 1985; candidate for Congress; staff aide to dep. mayor, 1987; mem. La Jolla Rep. Women. White House fellow, 1976. Mem. Am. Mktg. Assn., San Diego C. of C., Save Our Heritage Orgn., Charter 100 San Diego, Univ. Club San Diego (mktg., devel. and social dir. 1987-88), Delta Gamma. Office: Froehlich Internat Travel 6671 La Jolla Scenic Dr S La Jolla CA 92037

BEARD, CYNTHIA ALDRIDGE, writer, poet; b. Ft. Campbell, Ky., Mar. 21, 1953; d. Eugene Volney Jr. and Ina Cleo (Watts) Aldridge; m. William Robb Dorris, Sept. 10, 1977 (div. Mar. 1981); m. Charles Wayne Beard, Jan. 29, 1982; children: Jason Aldridge, Matthew Lee. Student, U. Tenn., 1971-73. Various positions Nashville, 1971-80; exec. asst. ops. bldg. Commerce Union Bank, Nashville, 1981-82; salesperson Royce Johns Realty & Auction, Franklin, Tenn., 1983-84; asst. Williamson County War Meml. Libr., Franklin, Tenn., 1988. Contbr. poetry to anthologies. Mem. Am. Assn. Poets, World of Poetry, Sparrowgrass Poetry Forum. Episcopalian.

BEARD, NANCY MARIE, training organization executive; b. Muskegon, Mich., Feb. 18, 1955; d. Harry Orve and Evelyn Irene (Janousek) Pittard;m. James O. Beard, Jr., Feb. 24, 1990. BBA, Western Mich. U., 1977. Mgmt. trainee Wickes Lumber Co., Davison, Mich., 1977-78; mgr. consumer sales Wickes Lumber Co., Petoskey, Mich., 1978-81; with mgmt. devel. dept. Wickes Lumber Co., Saginaw, Mich., 1981-82, elec. buyer, 1982-83; saleswoman Dale Carnegie Inst. No. Mich., Saginaw, 1983-86, sales mgr., 1986-89, inst. mgr., 1989—, instr., 1983—. Vol. Big Bros.-Big Sisters, Saginaw, 1990. Mem. Am. Soc. for Tng. and Devel., Saginaw Area C. of C. (amb. 1990). Office: Dale Carnegie Inst No Mich 3131 Davenport Ave Saginaw MI 48602

BEARDSLEY, ALBERTA, lawyer; b. Allegan, Mich., Mar. 15, 1946; d. Warren Ernest and Clara Helen (Graham) B.; m. Daniel Dusette, Apr. 28, 1972; children: Andre, Brendan. BA, Andrews U., 1968; MA, U. Mich., 1971; JD magna cum laude, U. Pitts., 1979. Atty. Laurel Legal Svcs., Kittanning, Pa.; pvt. practice Kittanning. Mem. Law Rev., U. Pitts. Rackham fellow U. Mich. Mem. Armstrong City Bar Assn. (past pres.), Pa. Bar Assn. Home: 158 Foreman Rd Freeport PA 16229

BEARDSLEY, JEANNE MARGARET, clinical social worker, orchardist; b. Des Moines, Feb. 28, 1940; d. Paul Franklin and Mary Loretta (Hawkins) B.; m. Michael Francis Turner, Aug. 1, 1986; children: Valerie Kae Wagoner, Angela Lynn Boles. BSW, Graceland Coll., Lamoni, Iowa, 1979; MSW, U. Iowa, 1980. Lic. social worker, Iowa; cert. trainer Parents Anonymous; diplomate in clin. social work. Mgmt. forecaster Meredith Corp., Des Moines, 1970-75; program coord. Peer Counseling for Elderly, Ames, Iowa, 1980-86; owner, operator Beardsley's Orchard, Van Wert, Iowa, 1982—; pvt. cons., Des Moines, 1983—; psychotherapist Behavioral Medicine Ctr., Des Moines, 1984—; program dir. Parents United, Ames, 1983-86; co-founder, co-dir. Mid-West Treatment Assocs., Ames, 1983-86; program dir. Adolescent Personal Awareness, Des Moines, 1990—; cons. Youth and Shelter Svcs., Ames, 1984-86; cons. Juvenile Offender's Program, Des Moines, 1990, First Resources, Ottumwa, Iowa, 1990, Childsafe, Ames, 1980. Mem. Decatur County Dem. Com., 1989. Recipient ann. recognition award Childsafe, 1988. Mem. NASW, Acad. Cert. Social Workers, Nat. Registry Health Care Providers in Social Work, Lions. Home: RR 1 Box 63A Van Wert IA 50262 Office: Behavioral Medicine Ctr 2940 Ingersoll Ave Des Moines IA 50314

BEARMAN, TONI CARBO, information scientist; b. Middletown, Conn., Nov. 14, 1942; d. Anthony Joseph and Theresa (Bauer) Carbo; m. David A. Bearman, Nov. 14, 1970; 1 dau., Amanda Carole. AB, Brown U., 1969; MS, Drexel U., 1973, PhD, 1977. Bibliog. asst. Am. Math. Soc., Math. Revs., 1962-63; supr. Brown U. Phys. Scis. Library, Providence, R.I., 1963-66, 67-71; subject specialist U. Wash. Engring. Library, Seattle, 1966-67; teaching and research asst. Drexel U., 1971-74; exec. dir. Nat. Fedn. Abstracting and Indexing Services, Phila., 1974-79; cons. for strategic planning and new product devel. Instn. Elec. Engrs., London, 1979-80; exec. dir. U.S. Nat. Commn. on Libraries and Info. Sci., Washington, 1980-86; dean Sch. Library and Info. Sci. U. Pitts., 1986—; mem. adv. com. U.S. Dept. Commerce, Patent and Trademark Office, 1987—; trustee Engring. Info., Inc., 1985-87; Schwing lectr., La. State U., 1988. Co-editor: Internat. Libr. Rev., 1989—; contbr. articles to profl. jours; mem. editorial bds. profl. jours. Bd. dirs. Greater Pitts. Literacy Coun.; mem. rsch. com. Spl. Libraries Assn. Fask Force; mem. presdl. adv. com. Carnegie Mellon U. Library; mem. Gov.'s Conf. program subcom. Recipient Disting. Alumni award Drexel U. Coll. Info. Studies, 1984. Fellow AAAS (chmn. sect. T nominating com.), Inst. Info. Scientists; mem. ALA (coun. 1988-92), Am. soc. for Info. Sci. (internat. rels. com., dir., chmn. networking com., chmn. 50th ann. conf., Watson Davis award 1983, pres. 1989-90), Pa. Libr. Assn. (adv. bd. Pa. Gov.'s Conf. on libr. and info. svcs.), Nat. Info. Standards Orgn. (bd. dirs. 1987-90). Home: 5600 Northumberland St Pittsburgh PA 15217 Office: U Pitts Sch Libr & Info Sci 135 N Bellefield St Pittsburgh PA 15260

BEARN, MARGARET SLOCUM, lawyer, educator; b. Fanwood, N.J., June 20, 1924; d. Clarence W. and Emma (Elliot) Slocum; m. Alexander G. Bearn, Dec. 20, 1952; children: Helen Bearn Pennoyer, Gordon. BA with honors, Swathmore Coll., 1945; LLB, Yale U., 1948. Bar: N.Y. 1950. Assoc. Grossman & Grossman, N.Y.C., 1948-50, Lewinson, Lewinson & Fieland, 1950-53, 54-55; dir. admissions Lab. Inst. Mdse., N.Y.C., 1953-54; 55-56, dean, 1956-73; asst. prof. N.Y. Law Sch., 1973-76, assoc. prof., 1976-85, asst. dean, 1973-74, assoc. dean, 1974-85, acting dean, spring 1980, dir. joint program with U. Bologna (Italy), 1976-85; assoc. prof. law St. John's U. Sch. Law, Jamaica, N.Y., 1985—, asst. dean, 1986—; mem. N.Y.C. Mayor's Com. Judiciary, 1980, 83. Mem. N.Y.C. Community Bd. 1, 1979-85; sec., bd. dirs. Chambers-Canal Civic Assn., 1977-85. Woodrow Wilson fellow, 1979, 80, 83. Mem. ABA (law schs. insp. teams 1978—, com. on jud. edn. and internat. law 1982-89), Assn. Am. Law Schs. (chmn. sect. on teaching law outside law sch. 1980-81), N.Y. County Lawyers Assn. (chmn. com. on legal edn. and admission to bar 1980-85), U.S. Supreme Ct. Hist. Soc. (com. student chpts.), Internat. Assn. Jurists (v.p. Am. com. 1981-86, treas. 1986—, chmn. 1983 conf.), Am. Law Inst., Scribes (pres. 1983-84, bd. dirs. 1984—). Presbyterian. Office: St John's U Sch Law Grand Central and Utopia Pkwys Jamaica NY 11439

BEARWALD, JEAN HAYNES, company executive; b. San Francisco, Aug. 31, 1924; d. Joseph Robert and Edna Haynes (Goudey) Bearwald; m. William Henry Sherburn, Apr. 12, 1969 (dec. 1970); 1 child by previous marriage, David Richard Cross. BA, Stephens Coll., Columbia, Mo., 1945. Adminstrv. asst. Bearwald & Assocs., Sacramento, 1966-78; acct. Truck Parts Co., Sand City, Calif., 1979-80; pres., chief exec. officer Bearwald & Assocs., Fresno, Calif., 1980-89, Las Vegas, N.Mex., 1989—. Prog. dir. Alcoholics Anonymous, Sacramento, 1980-82. Republican. Episcopalian. Home: Box 200 F- Montezuma Rte Las Vegas NM 87701

BEASLEY, BARBARA STARIN, cosmetics executive; b. Nashville, Dec. 31, 1955; d. Donald Francis and Martha Murry (Bridges) S.; m. Johnny Mark Beasley, Oct. 22, 1983; 1child, John Thomas. BFA, So. Meth. U., 1976. Cert. strategic mktg. mgmt., Harvard Bus. Sch. Producer Bill Stokes Assn., Dallas, 1976-80; Mary Kay Cosmetics, Inc., Dallas, 1980—; sr. v.p. mktg., 1987-89, exec. v.p. sales div., 1990—. Mem. Dallas Women's Found., Leadership Tex., Leadership Tex. Alumni Assn., Dir. Mktg. Assn. Office: Mary Kay Cosmetics Inc 8787 Stemmons Frwy Dallas TX 75247

BEASLEY, BEA CASSANDRA, small business owner; b. Pitts., Dec. 11, 1942; d. Hunter William Beasley and Ethel Lee (Moore) Smith; 1 child, Terrie Lynn Smith. Student, Robert Morris Jr. Coll., Pitts., 1968-70, Calif.

Culinary Acad., San Francisco, 1983-85; profl. chef, 1984. Supr. rate rsch. and analysis sect. Aluminum Co. Am., Pitts., 1962-70; exec. sec. McKinsey and Co., Inc., N.Y.C., 1970-71, personnel coordinator, 1971-73; sec. supr. McKinsey and Co., Inc., N.Y.C., San Francisco, 1973-78; office mgr. PLM, Inc., San Francisco, L.A., 1978-79; office mgr. dept. human resource mgmt. City of Oakland, San Francisco, Calif., 1979-83; ptnr. Incredible Edibles Catering Co., Oakland, 1982-85; chef Chateau St. Jean Winery, Kenwood, Calif., 1985-86; chef, owner Bea Beasley and Co., Santa Rosa, Calif., 1986—; guest chef McCully's Rooftop Restaurant, Bonita Springs, Fla., 1987. Contbr. articles to popular mags. Mem. San Francisco Profl. Food Soc., Sonoma County Wine Library Assn. Democrat. Methodist. Office: 906 Morgan St Santa Rosa CA 95401

BEASLEY, DEBRA KAY, accountant; b. Atlanta, Mar. 8, 1954; d. John Kelly and Dorothy Nell (Locke) B.; m. William Patrick Carey (div. 1986); m. John Randal Kading. AA, Oxford Coll., 1973; BBA, Emory U., Atlanta, 1976; MBA, Kennesaw State, 1989. C.P.A., Cert. Internal Auditor. Fin. intern Comptroller of the Currency, Atlanta, 1973-76, asst. nat. bank examiner, 1976-77; gen. acctg. supr. Great Am. Mgmt., Atlanta, 1977-78, Gulf Western Industries, Nashville, 1978-79; internal auditor Commerce Union Bank, Nashville, 1979-83; gen. acctg. supr. Commerce Union Bank, 1983-85; gen. acctg. mgr. Nat. Bank of Ga., Atlanta, 1985-87; gen. acctg. supr. Hewlett Packard Co., Atlanta, 1987-89, fin. analyst, 1989—. Fellow Ga. Soc. CPAs; mem. Tenn. Soc. CPAs (mem. p.c. adv. com. 1989—), Atlanta Track Club, Ga. Appalachian Trail Club, Sierra Club. Southern Baptist. Home: 695 Codes cove Ct SW Austell GA 30001 Office: Hewlett Packard Co 2015 S Park Pl Atlanta GA 30339

BEASLEY, MARY CATHERINE, home economics educator, administrator, researcher; b. Portersville, Ala., Nov. 29, 1922; d. Albert Otis and Beulah Green (Killian) Reed; m. Percy Wells Beasley, Dec. 15, 1956 (dec. Dec. 1958). BS in Home Econs., Bob Jones U., 1944; MS, Pa. State U., State College, 1954, EdD, 1968. Cert. home economist. Tchr. Geraldine and Collinsville (Ala.) High Sch., 1944-45; vocat. home econs. tchr. Glencoe (Ala.) High Sch., 1945-48; home econs. tchr. Washington County High Sch., Chatom, Ala., 1948-51, Homewood Jr. High Sch., Birmingham, Ala., 1958-60; asst. supr. and subject matter specialist Ala. Dept. Edn., Montgomery, 1951-57; asst. prof. Samford U., Birmingham, 1960-62; instr. U. Ala., Tuscaloosa, 1951, asst. prof. then assoc. prof., 1962-68, dir. continuing edn. in home econs., 1968-84, prof., 1984—. Author: (with others) Human Ecological Studies, 1988. Pres. Joint Legis. Coun. of Ala., Tuscaloosa, 1973-75; dir. On Your Own Program, 1970-80. Recipient Creative Programming award Nat. U. Extension Assn., 1979. Mem. Am. Home Econs. Assn. (chmn. rehab. com. 1973, 75, leader 1986), Southeastern Coun. on Family Rels. (pres. 1956-84, Disting Svc. award 1988), Ala. Home Econs. Assn. (pres. 1961-63, leader 1985), Ala. Coun. on Family Rels. (pres. 1981-83, Disting. Svc. award 1987), Altrusa Club of Tuscaloosa, Inc. (pres. 1988-89), Alpha Delta Kappa (treas. Tuscaloosa chpt. 1973, 75), Phi Upsilon Omicron Nu. Republican. Baptist. Home: 14 Parkwood Tuscaloosa AL 35401

BEASLEY, MAURINE HOFFMAN, journalism educator, historian; b. Sedalia, Mo., Jan. 28, 1936; d. Dimmitt Heard and Maurine (Hieronymous) Hoffman; m. William C. McLaughlin, May 20, 1966 (div. 1969); m. 2d, Henry R. Beasley, Dec. 24, 1970; 1 child, Susan Sook. B.J., B.A. in History, U. Mo., 1958; M.S. in Journalism, Columbia U., 1963; Ph.D. in Am. Civilization, George Washington U., 1974; Cert. in Brit. History, U. Edinburgh, Scotland, 1964. Edn. editor Kansas City (Mo.) Star, 1959-62; staff writer Washington Post, 1963-73; asst. prof. journalism U. Md., College Park, 1975-80, assoc. prof., 1980-86, prof. 1987—. Author: Eleanor Roosevelt and the Media: A Public Quest for Self-Fulfillment, 1987; (with others) Women in Media, 1977, The New Majority, 1988; editor: (with others) Voices of Change: Southern Pulitzer Winners, 1978, One Third of a Nation (hon. mention Washington Monthly Book Award 1982), 1981; editor: White House Press Conferences of Eleanor Roosevelt, 1983; mem. adv. bd. Am. Journalism, 1983—, Jour. of Mass Media Ethics; contbr. articles to acad. jours. Violinist, Montgomery Coll. Symphony Orch., 1975—; pres., Little Falls Swimmings Club, Inc., 1988-89. Gannett Teaching Fellowships Program fellow, 1977; Pulitzer traveling fellow Columbia U., 1963; Eleanor Roosevelt studies grantee Eleanor Roosevelt Inst., 1979-80; named one of nation's outstanding tchrs. of writing and editing Modern Media Inst. and Am. Soc. Newspaper Editors, 1981. Mem. Assn. Edn. in Journalism and Mass Communications (exec. com. 1990—, standing com. on profl. freedom and responsibility 1985, vice chair 1987-89, chair 1990—, sec. history div. 1986-87, vice-head 1987-88, head 1988-89), Am. Journalism Historians Assn. (pres.-elect 1988-89, pres. 1989-90), Am. News Women's Club (bd. govs. 1986-87), Women in Communications (bd. dirs. Washington chpt. 1985-87), Nat. Fedn. Press Women, Soc. Profl. Journalists (chair nat. hist. site com. 1986-87, bd. dirs. Washington chpt. 1988-90, pres. Washington chpt. 1990-91), Phi Beta Kappa, Omicron Delta Kappa. Democrat. Unitarian. Home: 4920 Flint Dr Bethesda MD 20816 Office: U Md Coll Journalism College Park MD 20742

BEATO, MARITZA, psychologist, counselor; b. Havana, Cuba, Oct. 9, 1949; came to U.S., 1967; d. Jorge Julio and Coralia (Zarragoitia) B.; m. Alejandro Martinez, June 24, 1971 (div. Sept. 1978); children: Alex, David. BA, U. Tex., San Antonio, 1976; MA in Psychology with honors, St. Mary's U., San Antonio, 1981. Cons. Edn. Svc. Ctr., San Antonio, 1982-83; primary therapist Raleigh Hills Hosp., San Antonio, 1983-84; mental health counselor United Med. Ctr., Del Rio, Tex., 1984-87; pvt. practice psychol. San Antonio, 1987—. Sec. Rep. Nat. Hispanic Assembly, San Antonio, 1980-81; fin. chmn. LWV, San Antonio, 1980-82; press liaison campaign to elect Maria Rerriozaba to San Antonio city coun., 1980; mem. Rep. Hispanic Women Club, San Antonio, 1989—. Mem. Bexar County Psychol. Assn., Am. Psychol. Assn., Am. Counseling and Guidance Assn., Alliance Française of San Antonio, Mex.-Am. Bus. and Profl. Women's Club, San Antonio Mus. Assn. Republican. Roman Catholic. Home and Office: 111 Chattington Ct San Antonio TX 78213

BEATON-SIMMONS, KAREN, fundraiser; b. Providence, Mar. 9, 1944; d. Allan and Arlene Beaton; m. 1965 (div.); children: Laura, Andrew. BA, U. R.I., 1965; MEd, U. Ga., 1974. Speech pathologist, 1965-79; faculty U. R.I., 1978-79; dir. ann. giving Bryant Coll., Smithfield, R.I., 1979-80, dir. devel., 1980-83; v.p. membership svcs. Greater Providence C. of C., 1983-84; dir. pub. rels. and devel. Jewish Home for the Aged, 1985-87; dir. devel. and pub. rels. St. Anne's Hosp., Fall River, 1987-89; dir. devel. R.I. Philharm. Orch., Providence, 1989; pvt. practice speech pathology, Cranston, R.I., 1979-81. Mem. State Advs. for Gifted Edn., 1980—, pres., 1980-81; mem. nat. adv. coun. Small Bus. Adminstrn., 1983-85; mem. choir, deaconess, chair properties com., 1st Bapt. Ch. in Am. Mem. Nat. Soc. Fundraising Execs. (R.I. chpt. v.p. 1987-88, cert. fundraising exec. 1988), Leadership R.I., Alpha Chi Omega, Kappa Delta Pi. Baptist. Office: RI Philharm Orch 334 Westminster Mall Providence RI 02905

BEATTIE, PAMELA MARIE PASH, bank official; b. Tucson, May 1, 1944; d. Robert Norman and Patricia Wilson (Greenwood) Pash; m. Charles Beattie, July 1964 (div. 1968); 1 child, John Charles. BA, Temple U., 1967. Asst. investment counselor Bank of N.Y., N.Y.C., 1967-73; pension cons. Moneymasters, Inc., San Antonio, 1973-77, GroupPlan Systems, N.Y.C., 1977-79; pension trust officer Chem. Bank, N.Y.C., 1979-81; trust sales officer Bankers Trust Co., N.Y.C., 1981-88; regional dir. Bankers Trust Co. of the Southwest, Houston, 1988—; bd. dirs. Bankers Trust Co. of Southwest, Houston, Southwest Pension Conf., Dallas. Mem. corp. contbns. com. Houston Livestock Show and Rodeo, 1989; bd. dirs. Boston Renaissance Ensemble. Office: Bankers Trust Co SW 3000 Two Houston Ctr Houston TX 77010

BEATTY, CAROLYN ANN, educator; b. Pitts., Apr. 17, 1942; d. Charles Anderson and Manualla Grace (Snyder) Beatty. BA in English, History, U. Houston, 1964; MEd, Houston Bapt. U., 1981; Cert., U. London, U. Liverpool, 1968. Tchr. Johnston Middle Sch., Houston, 1964—; cons. Fed. Land Bank, Houston, 1982; mem. central textbook com. Houston Ind. Sch., 1978, 88; mem. instructional council Johnston Middle Sch., Houston, 1978-86, mem. faculty adv. com., 1976-78, 1980, chmn. English dept., 1972—. Author: (with others) Pre-International Baccalaureate Program Grade 7, 1982-83 (with others) Texas Assessment of Academic Skills, 1989-90. Vol. Meth. Hosp. Service Corps, Mus. Fine Arts, Harris County Heritage Soc., Channel 8 (Pub. TV), Houston Church Coalition Food Pantry; presenter Dist. Insvc., 1978, 84, 90. Named Outstanding Young Educator Houston Ind. Sch. Dist., 1977. Mem. Houston Area Council Tchrs. English (pres. 1976), Tex. Council Tchrs. English (state workshop chmn. 1976), Nat. Council Tchrs. English (bd. dirs. 1975-77), Congress Houston Tchrs., Nat. Assn. Secondary Dept. Chmn., Delta Kappa Gamma (pres. 1978-80), Kappa Delta Pi, Kappa Kappa Iota (historian 1983-85, sec. 1987-89), Beta Sigma Phi (pres. 1968-70, named Girl of Yr. 1970). Club: College Women's (Houston). Office: Johnston Middle Sch 10410 Manhattan St Houston TX 77025

BEATTY, FRANCES, civic worker; b. Chgo., Apr. 17, 1940; d. Pasquale and Rose (Brunetti) Calomeni; m. Robert Alfred Beatty, Aug. 24, 1963; children: Bradford, Roxanna. BA, Northwestern U., 1961; MA, U. Chgo., 1967. Tchr. math. Proviso West High Sch., Hillside, Ill., 1961-66. Mem. Oak Brook Dist. 53 Sch. Bd., 1979-85; mem. women's bd. Field Mus. Natural History, Chgo., 1985—, mem. founder's coun., 1988—; mem. governing bd. Chgo. Symphony, 1985—; mem. women's bd. Ravinia Festival, Highland Park, Ill., 1987—, Northwestern U., Evanston, Ill., 1988—. Mem. Woman's Athletic Club (Chgo., v.p. 1985-87), John Evans Club.

BEATTY, KAREN L., education educator; b. Bethtlehem, Pa., Aug. 19, 1948; d. Charles N. and Jeanne Elizabeth (Klein) B. BA, Bucknell U., Lewisburg, Pa., 1970; MEd., Lehigh U., Bethlehem, Pa., 1973, Ed. D., 1985. Spl. edn. tchr. Wiley House, Bethlehem, Pa., 1970-71; case worker Children's Aid Soc., Bethlehem, Pa., 1971-72; program dir. Wiley House Preschool, Bethlehem, Pa., 1972-75; spl. edn. tchr. Allentown Sch. Dist., Pa., 1975-84, ednl. disgnostician, 1984-86, spl. edn. supr., 1986-88; spl. edn. tchr. Lucia Mar Unified Schs., Arroyo Grande, Calif., 1988—; pres. Assoc. Cons. in Edn., Lehigh Valley, Pa., 1986-87; adj. prof. Lehigh U., 1985-88, Pa. State U., 1985-88. Mem. Coun. for Exceptional Children (pres. 1972-73), Alpha Phi (adminstr. standards 1988—, Ursa Major award 1988). Democrat.

BEATTY, TINA MARIE, bank executive; b. Charlotte, N.C., Dec. 21, 1955; d. Jacob Clyde and Ollie Blandina (Glover) B. BA, Winthrop Coll., 1976; MBA, U. N.C., Charlotte, 1984; cert., The Nat. Ctr. for Paralegal Tng., 1976; postgrad., Winthrop Coll. Legal asst. Whitesides and Robinson, Gastonia, N.C., Garland and Alala, P.A., Gastonia, Kennedy Covington Lobdell and Hickman, Charlotte; documentation policy supr. Corp. Banking Group, First Union Nat. Bank N.C., Charlotte; asst. state dir. Am. Inst. for Paralegal Studies, Inc., Charlotte. Mem. area alumni steering com. Winthrop Coll., Charlotte, 1984. Mem. Nat. Parks and Conservation Assn., Nat. Wildlife Fedn., Smithsonian Assoc., Audubon Soc., Sci. Mus. of Charlotte, Mint Mus. of Art, The Wilderness Soc., N.C. Wildlife Fedn., Phi Kappa Phi, Phi Alpha Theta . Home: 1532-D Rensselaer Pl Charlotte NC 28203

BEAUCHAMP, SISTER LUCILLE MARIE, nursing education administrator, nun; b. Escanaba, Mich., May 4, 1922; Joined Daus. of Charity of St. Vincent de Paul, 1945. RN, St. Joseph Sch. Nursing, Chgo., 1944; BS in Nursing Edn., DePaul U., Chgo., 1952; MS in Nursing, Cath. U. Am., Washington, 1961; postgrad., Marquette U., Milw., 1968-69. Supr. med.-surg. nursing St. Thomas Hosp., Nashville, 1946-50, County Hosp., Mobile, Ala., 1950-55; dir. Sch. Nursing and Nursing Svc., Mobile, 1955-59; dir. Sch. Nursing, nursing svc., coord. St. Mary's Hosp., Milw., 1961-69; dean Sch. Nursing Troy (Ala.) State U., 1969-72; dir. hosp. edn. dept. St. Vincent Hosp., Birmingham, Ala., 1972-76; archivist, communication coord. Mater Dei Provincialate, Evansville, Ind., 1976-87, local superior, 1981-87, Vincentian svc. coord., 1984-87; mission svc. coord. St. Mary's Hosp., Milw., 1987-90—, coord. health care, 1987—; mem. leadership devel. task force Daus. of Charity Nat. Health System, East. Cen., 1989—, mem. spiritual formation study process, 1989—, mem. governance adv. com., 1987—. Chmn. bd. dirs. St. Mary's Hosp., Milw., Port Washington, Wis., 1987—, St. Mary's Med. Ctr., Evansville, 1988, Seton Health Corp. So. Ind., 1988; chmn. bd. dirs. Warrick Hosp., Boonville, Ind., 1978-87, vice chmn. 1988; chmn. bd. trustees Providence Hosp., Southfield, Mich., 1987—, Seton Health Corp. S.E. Mich., Southfield, 1987—; vice chmn. St. Joseph Hosp. and Health Care Ctr., Chgo., 1987-88. Mem. Soc. Am. Archivists, Am. Assn. State and Local History, Midwest Conf. Archivists, Soc. Ind. Archivists, Cath. Hosp. Assn. Wis. (mission support network), Sigma Theta Tau. Roman Catholic. Address: St Mary's Hosp 2323 N Lake Dr Milwaukee WI 53211

BEAUCHEMIN, FRANCINE LAHAIE, Canadian stock exchange executive; b. Quebec City, Que., Can., July 13, 1951; d. Rostand H. and Marcelle (Raymond) Lahaie. BCom, Sir George Williams U., Montreal, Que., 1975. Various positions Montreal Exch., sr. v.p. listings, mem. regulation, 1988—. Office: Montreal Exch, 800 Sq Victoria, PO Box 61, Montreal, PQ Canada H4Z 1A9

BEAUDOIN, CAROL ANN, psychologist; b. Lowell, Mass., Mar. 30, 1949; d. Adrien P. and Rita J. (LeBlanc) B.; B.A. with honors, U. Fla., 1971; M.Ed. in Counseling, Boston U., 1973, Ed.D. in Counseling Psychology, 1979. Psychiat. aide U. Fla.-Shands Teaching Hosp., Gainesville, 1970-71; trainee VA Hosp., Gainesville, 1971-72; attendant Boston State Hosp., 1972, intern, 1973; intern Univ. Hosp., also Counseling Center, Northeastern U., Boston, 1973-74, Dorchester Mental Health Center, also Carney Hosp., 1974-75; staff psychologist Human Resource Inst., Boston, 1974-80, treatment team leader, 1975-80; pvt. practice psychology, Brookline, Mass., 1980—. Mem. Am. Psychol. Assn. Office: 1101 Beacon St Brookline MA 02146

BEAUMONT, MONA, artist; b. Paris, Jan. 1, 1927; d. Jacques Hippolyte and Elsie M. (Didisheim) Marx. m. William G. Beaumont; children: Garrett, Kevin. BA, U. Calif., Berkeley, 1945, MA, 1946; postgrad., Harvard U., Fogg Mus., Cmbridge, Hans Hoffman Studios, N.Y.C., 1946. One-woman shows include Galeria Proteo, Mexico City, Gumps Gallery, San Francisco, Palace of Legion of Honor, San Francisco, L'Armitiere Gallery, Rouen, France, Hoover Gallery, San Francisco, San Francisco Mus. Modern Art, Galeria Van der Voort, San Francisco, William Sawyer Gallery, San Francisco, Palo Alto (Calif.) Cultural Ctr., Galerie Alexandre Monnet, Brussels, Honolulu Acad. Arts; group shows include San Francisco Mus. Modern Art, San Francisco Art Inst., DeYoung Meml. Mus., San Francisco, Grey Found. Tour of Asia, Bell Telephone Invitational, Chgo., Richmond Art Ctr., L.A. County Mus. Art, Galerie Zodiaque, Geneva, Galerie Le Manoir, La Chaux de Fonds, Switzerland, others; represented in permanent collections Oakland (Calif.) Mus. Art, City and County of San Francisco, Hoover Found., San Francisco, Grey Found., Washington, Bulart Found., San Francisco; also numerous pvt. collections. Mem. Soc. for Encouragement of Contemporary Art, Bay Area Graphic Art Coun., San Francisco Art Inst., San Francisco Mus. Modern Art, Capp Street Project, others. Recipient Jack London Sq. Ann. Painting award, Purchase award Grey Found., Ann. awards San Francisco Women Artists (2), Purchase award San Francisco Art Festival, One-man Show award San Francisco Art Festival, included in Printworld Internat., 1982-88, Internat. Art Diary, Am. Artists, N.Y. Art Review, Calif. Art Rev., Art in the San Francisco Bay Area. Address: 1087 Upper Happy Valley Rd Lafayette CA 94549

BEAUPAIN, ELAINE SHAPIRO, psychiatric social worker; b. Boston, Nov. 1, 1949; d. Abraham and Anna Marilyn (Gass) S.; m. Dean A. Beaupain, Feb. 14, 1987; B.A., McGill U. (Montreal, Que., Can.), 1971, M.S.W., 1974. Psychiat. social worker Bangor (Maine) Mental Health Inst., 1974-75; outpatient therapist The Counseling Center, Bangor, 1975-76, The Counseling Center, Millinocket, Maine, 1979-86; asst. core group leader adolescent unit Jackson Brook Inst., Portland, Maine, 1986-87; area dir. Community Health and Counseling Services, 1981-86; pvt. practice social work, 1987—, psychotherapy with individuals, couples and families Millinocket and Bangor, 1987—. Cert. social worker with pvt. practice lic. (CSW/IP) Maine. Mem. Nat. Assn. Social Workers, AAUW, Acad. Cert. Social Workers. Republican. Office: 122 Pine St Bangor ME 04401

BEAUPRE, VICKI LOUISE, social services administrator; b. Charleston, S.C., Mar. 30, 1953; d. Thomas Jonathan Hubbard and Anja Helga Amanda (Koenkyto) Johnson; m. Ronald George Beaupre, Aug. 5, 1972 (div. Feb. 1981); children: Nicole Danielle, Matthew Paul. BA, U. Minn., 1974; MA in Mgmt., Coll. of St. Scholastica, Duluth, Minn., 1990. Lic. social worker, Minn. With St. Louis County Social Svcs., Duluth, 1975—, adminstrv. asst., 1983-89, program adminstr., 1989—; mem. rev. bd. Moose Lake (Minn.) State Hosp., 1984-89. Negotiator Arrowhead Pub. Svc. Union, Duluth, 1988—, mem. exec. bd., 1989-90; historian Duluth Spl. Olympics, 1990—; mem Planned Parenthood. Recipient Cert. of Appreciation, AFSCME, 1983, Commendation, Gov. Rudy Perpich, 1989. Mem. Am. Pub. Welfare Assn., Minn. Social Svc. Assn., Assn. for Retarded Citizens, NOW, NAFE, Nat. Audobon Soc., Smithsonian Assocs. Home: 4901 Colorado St Duluth MN 55804-1607 Office: St Louis County Social Svc Dept 320 W Second St Duluth MN 55802

BEAUSEY, MAUREEN MCARDLE, manufacturing executive; b. Troy, N.Y., June 21, 1951; d. E. Murray and Kathleen (Watt) McArdle; m. Alfred W. Beausey, June 1, 1975. BA in English cum laude, Wagner Coll., 1973; MS in Instructional Tech., Rochester Inst. Tech., 1982. Advt. rep. Capital Newspapers, Albany, N.Y., 1973-75; advt. mgr. Present Co., Rochester, N.Y., 1975; instr. Bryant & Stratton, Rochester, 1976-85, Rochester Inst. Tech., 1982-85; tng. mgr. JAM, Inc., East Rochester, N.Y., 1985; tng. supr. Eastman Kodak Co., Rochester, 1985-88, staff asst., 1988-89, strategic planner, 1989-90, ops. mgr., 1990—; speaker in field. Com. chair Home Sch. Assn., Penfield Cen. Schs., 1990. Mem. Women in Communication (v.p. spl. projects 1990-91), Nat. Soc. Performance and Instrn., Soc. Tech. Communications, Assn. Tng. and Devel. Office: Eastman Kodak Co 343 State St Rochester NY 14650-0711

BEAUSOLEIL, DORIS MAE, housing specialist, government agency official; b. Chelmsford, Mass., Jan. 9, 1932; d. Joseph Honorius and Beatrice Pearl (Smith) B.; student State Tchrs. Coll., Lowell, Mass., 1949-51; BA in Sociology and Psychology, Goddard Coll., Plainfield, Vt., 1954; MA in Human Relations, N.Y. U., 1957. With div. human rights N.Y. State, N.Y.C., 1960-69, housing dir., 1966-68; housing cons. Nat. Com. Against Discrimination in Housing, N.Y.C., 1969-70; housing cons. Edwin Gould Found., N.Y.C., 1970-71; human resources cons. interfaith housing strategy com., housing cons. Fedn. Prot. Welfare Agencies, Inc., N.Y.C., 1971-72; self-employed housing cons., 1972-74; equal opportunity compliance specialist Region II HUD, N.Y.C., 1975—, Fed. women's program coordinator, 1975-79; br. chief Title VI Sect. 109 Compliance div. fair housing and equal opportunity Region II, HUD, N.Y.C., 1979-84; founding mem. N.Y. State HUD Com.; adv. panel Housing Mag., 1979; cons., examiner N.Y. State Civil Service Commn., 1970—. Mem. Nat. Assn. Human Rights Workers (Outstanding Service award 1974), Citizens Housing and Planning Council, Federally Employed Women, Nat. Assn. Housing and Devel. Ofcls., Goddard Coll. Alumni Assn. (sec. 1988-90), Women's City Club N.Y., Rep. Bus. Women's Club (pres. 1985-88, bd. dirs. 1989—). Republican. Unitarian. Home: 392 Central Park W New York NY 10025 Office: 26 Federal Pla Rm 3532 New York NY 10278

BEAUVAIS, LAURA LYNN, management educator, consultant; b. Charleston, S.C., Sept. 12, 1957; d. Warren Joseph Jr. and Carmel Frances (Conlon) B. BS, Coll. of Charleston, 1979; PhD, U. Tenn., 1987. Pers. researcher, cons. Oak Ridge (Tenn.) Nat. Lab., 1981-84; asst. prof. dept. mgmt. U. R.I., Kingston, 1984—; condr. seminars dept. employment security State of R.I., Providence, 1988. Contbr. articles and book revs. to profl. jours. Recipient Woman of Achievement award U. Tenn., 1985. Mem. Am. Psychol. Assn., Acad. Mgmt., Assn. Mgmt., Ea. Acad. Mgmt., New Eng. Psychol. Assn., Sigma Xi, Beta Gamma Sigma, Phi Kappa Phi, Sigma Alpha Psi. Office: U RI Dept Mgmt Kingston RI 02881

BEAVERS, PATSY A., elementary teacher; b. Omaha, Nov. 15, 1937; d. William and Ethelyn Esther (Rowan) Murphy; m. Thomas E. Beavers, June 19, 1959; children: Brian Lee, Amy Lyn. BA Elem. Edn., NW Mo. State U., 1966, postgrad. Tchr. schs., Iowa, 1958—. asst. chmn. Am. Cancer Crusade, Shenandoah, Iowa, 1964-66; bd. dirs. Meals on Wheels, Shenandoah, Iowa. Recipient Am. Citizenship awd., Iowa State Bar Assn., 1956; named Outstanding Young Woman Am., 1966, Young Mother of Year, Young Mother's Club, Shenandoah, Iowa, 1972. Mem. AAUW (treas. 1987-90), Iowa Reading Assn., SW Iowa Reading Assn., Order Eastern Star (chaplain, Esther, electa), Delta Kappa Gamma, Beta Sigma Phi (pres., sec., treas.). Mem. First Christian Ch. Home: 1304 Mitchell Shenandoah IA 51601

BEAVERS, SUSAN JANE, art educator; b. Pittsville, Wis., Nov. 19, 1945; d. Carl Malcolm and Irma Anna (Wolf) Hirsch; m. Philip Joseph Beavers, Aug. 12, 1967. BA, U. Wis., Oshkosh, 1969; MA (hon.), U. Wis., 1989. Art educator Madison Met. Sch. Dist., 1969—. Mem. Nat. Art Edn. Assn., Wis. Art Edn. Assn. Office: Madison Met Sch Dist 545 W Dayton St Madison WI 53703

BECCARI, NANCY HALL HIERS, educator; b. Marietta, Ohio; d. Robert Earl and Bernice (Underwood) Hall; B.A. cum laude, U. Miami, 1958, M.Ed., 1961, postgrad., 1970—; m. Turner M. Hiers, Oct. 29, 1942; m. Armano A. Beccari, Aug. 31, 1974. Tchr. pub. schs., Ga., Fla.; dir. Reading Center, Nova High Sch., Fort Lauderdale, Fla., 1963-73, Lauderdale Reading Clinic, 1965—. Author: Little Pitchers With Big Ears. Mem. Internat. Reading Assn., Am. Ednl. Research Assn., AAUW, Nat. Soc. for Study Edn., Kappa Delta Pi, Alpha Delta Kappa, Kappa Kappa Iota, Epsilon Tau Lambda, Phi Lambda Pi. Clubs: Le Club Internationale, Rolls Royce Owners. Home: 1224 E Las Olas Blvd Fort Lauderdale FL 33301

BECHER, NANCY ANN KLOPP, educator; b. West Reading, Pa., June 18, 1931; d. Russell William and Alice Elizabeth (Deeds) Klopp; m. William Alfred Becher, Nov. 23, 1957; children: Erica Becher Dye, Mark William. BS in Elem. Edn., Kutztown U., 1953; MS in Reading, Hofstra U., 1975, diploma, 1983, EdD in Reading, Lang. and Cognition, 1990. Cert. tchr., sch. adminstr., reading tchr. Tchr. Lindenhurst (N.Y.) Pub. Schs., 1953-54, 1957-58, Wyomissing (Pa.) Pub. Schs., 1954-57, West Islip (N.Y.) Pub. Schs., 1963-65, Amityville (N.Y.) Pub. Schs., 1966-73; specialist reading Intermediate Sch., Bay Shore, N.Y., 1976-83, Jr. Bay Shore Pub. Schs., N.Y., 1983-86; dir. project Summer Sch., Bay Shore, 1979-80; instr. inservice Bay Shore Schs., 1973-80; specialist reading St. Patrick's Sch., Bay Shore, 1986-87; cons. Bay Shore Pub. Schs., 1986-88, ret., 1988; adj. prof. Coll. New Rochelle, 1986-87; adj. instr. SUNY, Westbury, 1988; adj. instr. supr. student tchrs. Hofstra U., 1989—; cons. Spl. Edn. Tng. Ctr., Westbury, 1986-88; instr. Nassau Bd. Coop. Svcs., Plainview, 1980-82; chair adv. bd. NEWSDAY, Melville, 1982—. Author nat. curriculum for Newspaper in Edn.; contbr. articles to profl. jours. Trainer Literacy Vols. Am., Hempstead, N.Y., 1987; co-founder Friends West Islip Libr., 1968—; leader, cons. Girl Scouts U.S., 1966-70. Grantee N.Y. Pub. Found. 1984-86, N.Y. St. Edn. Dept. 1973-74. Mem. N.Y. State Reading Assn. (chair tchrs. spl. interest group 1986—, speaker state conf. 1980-89, chair newspaper edn. 1983-85), Internat. Reading Assn. (editor newspaper 1988, adv. group newspaper in edn.), Suffolk Reading Specialist Coun. (pres. 1982-84), Nat. Coun. Tchrs. English (cons. on commn. for English edn. 1985—), Am. Newspaper Pubs. Assn., Delta Kappa Gamma (hon. soc. women educators). Democrat. Home: 472 Everdell Ave West Islip NY 11795 Office: Hofstra U Curriculum & Teaching Dept Mason Hall Hempstead NY 11550

BECHERER, DEBORAH ZORN, banker; b. Youngstown, Ohio, Feb. 9, 1958; d. Robert L. and Joan M. (Wilkos) Zorn; m. William B. Becherer Jr., May 22, 1983. BS in Bus. Edn. magna cum laude, Youngstown State U., 1980; MBA, Coll. of William and Mary, 1983; cert., Grad. Sch. Banking, Madison, Wis., 1987. Trainee advanced mgmt. Bank One of Ea. Ohio, Youngstown, 1983-84, officer comml. loans, 1984-86, asst. v.p., 1986—. Mem. allocation com. United Way Planning, Youngstown, 1984-86; pres. Lake to River Girl Scout Council, Youngstown, 1987—; liaison bd. dirs. Mahoning County Red Cross, Youngstown, Cen. Christian Day Care Ctr., Youngstown. Mem. Am. Inst. Banking, Nat. Assn. Female Execs., Alumni Assn. Coll. of William and Mary, Delta Zeta Alumni Assn. Republican. Methodist. Home: 7099 Oak Dr Poland OH 44514 Office: Bank One of Ea Ohio 6 Federal Plaza W Youngstown OH 44503

BECK, ANNA NADINE, book store executive; b. Woodlawn, Ill., Dec. 6, 1922; d. Herbert Glenn and Mary (Gerrish) Wood; m. Robert Lee Beck, May 20, 1947; children: Linda Beck Olson, Philip Scott. BS in Edn., Ill. State Normal U., 1945. Tchr. English Lemont (Ill.) High Sch., 1945-46; bookkeeper Faulkner's Ednl. Bookstore, Chgo., 1945-48; clk., bookkeeper, office mgr. Beck's Book Store, Chgo., 1955—; sec.-treas. Beck's Book Store, 1976-89, pres., 1989—. Mem. Gurdjieff Soc. Ill. Democrat. Office: Becks Book Stores Inc 4520 N Broadway Chicago IL 60640

BECK, AUDREY, data management company executive; b. Mpls., July 23, 1954; d. John George and Shirley Hope (Dahley) Neis. Student, Hennepin County Vo-Tech. Coll. Software engr. CPT Corp., Mpls., 1978-85, Datamyte Corp., Minnetonka, Minn., 1985; sr. system support rep. Moore Data Mgmt. Services, Mpls., 1985—; computer contractor, Mpls., 1980—. Avocations: programming, electronics, horses, carpentry. Home: 5601 Judy Ln Brooklyn Center MN 55430 Office: Moore Data Mgmt Services 1660 South Hwy 100 Minneapolis MN 55416

BECK, BRENDA FAYE, communications company executive; b. Grenada, Miss., June 1, 1952; d. Thomas Watson, Jr. and Dorothy Eloise (Clemons) McCaulla; m. Lee Roy Tubbs, Oct. 10, 1971 (div. 1977); m. Charlie Eugene Beck, Apr. 14, 1980; children: Lee Gabriel, Thomas Hugh, Brenda Georgianna, (stepchild) Alethea Dawn. Student, U. Miss., 1978, George Meany Ctr. Labor Studies, 1984, Holmes Community Coll., 1988—. Long distance operator South Central Bell Telephone, Grenada, 1969-83; computer operator South Central Bell Telephone, Houston, 1975-76; asst. chief operator South Central Bell Telephone, Grenada, 1977; TSPS operator AT&T Communications, Grenada, 1980, chmn. quality of worklife, 1987—; directory editor Telephone Pioneers Am., Grenada, 1980-81; editor Union First Class, Communications Workers Am., Grenada, 1984—, job steward, 1985—. Editor: Telephone Pioneers Am. Cookbook, 1981. Fund raiser Am. Cancer Soc., Grenada, 1986, St. Jude Children's Hosp., Memphis, 1987, LeBonheur Children's Hosp., Memphis, 1988. Named Operator of the Year, 1973; recipient first place award Hobby Directory for Telephone Pioneers Am., 1980, first place editorial writing award Communications Workers Am./AFL-CIO, 1984. Mem. Future Pioneers Am., Grenada Exchangites. Republican. Baptist. Home: 815 Mary Ave Grenada MS 38901-4907 Office: AT&T Communications 404 1st St Grenada MS 38901

BECK, CYNTHIA A.S., advertising executive; b. N.Y.C., Oct. 19, 1949; d. Robert Ellis and Marcia Joy (Heatter) Shalen; m. Jack Wofgang Beck, May 20, 1970 (dec. Aug. 1988). BA, Smith Coll., 1969. Copywriter Doyle Dane Bernbach, N.Y.C., 1969-86; creative dir. Young & Rubicam, N.Y.C., 1986—. Office: Young & Rubicam NY 285 Madison Ave New York NY 10017

BECK, DORIS JEAN, microbiology educator; b. Blissfield, Mich.; d. Willard L. and Mary Ann (Fojtik) DeGroff; m. Larry H. Harris, Mar. 21, 1987; children: Bill, Dawn. BS, Bowling Green (Ohio) State U., 1960; MS, Mich. State U., 1971, PhD, 1974. Assoc. prof. microbiology Bowling Green State U., 1974—; rsch. assoc. Yale U. Sch. Medicine, New Haven, 1981; rsch. prof. Oak Ridge (Tenn.) Nat. Lab., U. Tenn., 1989. Recipient Faculty Devel. award NSF, 1981-82, Nat. Rsch. Svc. award NIH, U. Tenn., Oak Ridge Nat. Lab., 1989-90. Office: Bowling Green State U Dept Biol Sci Bowling Green OH 43403

BECK, DOROTHY FAHS, social researcher; b. N.Y.C.; d. Charles Harvey and Sophia (Lyon) Fahs; m. Hubert Park Beck, Aug. 20, 1930 (dec. Jan.); 1 child, Brenda E.F. AB, U. N.C., 1928; MA, U. Chgo., 1932; PhD (Gilder fellow), Columbia U., 1944, postdoctoral study, 1955-56. Am.-German Student Exch. fellow, Fed. Republic Germany, 1928-29. Dir. econ. rsch. ADA, 1929-32; social worker Emergency Relief Adminstrn. N.J., 1933-34, statistician, 1934-35; statistician U.S. Office Edn., 1935-36; assoc. social economist U.S. Cen. Statis. Bd., 1936-38; rsch. supr., author Am. Coll. Dentists, 1940-42; statistician Am. Heart Assn., 1947-53, Cornell U. Med. Coll., 1951-53; asst. prof. biostats. Am. U. Beirut, 1954: bd. dir. rsch. Family Svc. Am., N.Y.C., 1956-81, dir. study counselor attitudes and feelings, 1982-87, evaluation rsch. cons., 1982-87. Co-founder Fahs-Beck Fund for Rsch. and Experimentation. Fellow Am. Sociol. Assn.; mem. Acad. Cert. Social Workers, Am. Assn. Marriage and Family Therapy (affiliate), Nat. Coun. Family Rels., Groves Conf., Am. Statis. Assn., Nat. Assn. Social Workers, Soc. Study Social Problems, Am. Pub. Health Assn., Phi Beta Kappa. Unitarian-Universalist. Author: Patterns in Use of Family Agency Service, 1962, Marriage and the Family Under Challenge, 1976, New Treatment Modalities, 1978, Counselor Characteristics: How They Affect Outcomes, 1988; co-author: Costs of Dental Care Under Specific Clinical Conditions, 1943, Myocardial Infarction, 1954, Clients' Progress within Five Interviews, 1970, How to Conduct a Client Follow-Up Study, 1974, 2d enlarged edit., 1980, Progress on Family Problems, 1973. Home: Crosslands Apt 50 Kennett Square PA 19348

BECK, JOAN WAGNER, journalist; b. Clinton, Iowa, Sept. 5, 1923; d. Roscoe Charles and Mildred (Noel) Wagner; m. Ernest William Beck, Sept. 9, 1945; children—Christopher, Melinda. B.J. cum laude, Northwestern U., 1945, M.S. in Journalism, 1947. Radio script writer O.W.I. Voice of Am., 1945-46; copy writer Marshall Field & Co., 1947-50; feature writer Chgo. Tribune, 1950—, writer syndicated column about young people, 1956-61, syndicated column about children, 1961-72, editor daily features sect., 1972-75, mem. editorial bd., 1975—; syndicated editorial page columnist, 1974—. Author: How to Raise a Brighter Child, 1967, (with Dr. Virginia Apgar) Is My Baby All Right?, 1973, Effective Parenting, 1976, Best Beginnings, 1983. Hon. chmn. Mother's March of Met. Chgo. chpt. Nat. Found. March of Dimes, 1970-75; trustee Ill. Children's Home and Aid Soc., 1971—; mem. Women's Bd. Northwestern U. Recipient AP award for best newspaper feature series award Ill., 1964; best feature, 1966, best columns, 1983, 84; Alumni Merit award Northwestern U., 1965; Alumnae award, 1977; Nat. award of Achievement Alpha Chi Omega, 1966; 1st place award Penney-U. Mo., 1973; UPI Ill. award for editorial writing, 1984; Woodrow Wilson Found. vis. fellow, 1983—. Mem. Chgo. Network, Chgo. Headline Club, Theta Sigma Phi, Alpha Chi Omega. Methodist. Clubs: Northwestern, Lake Forest. Office: Chgo Tribune 435 N Michigan Ave Chicago IL 60611

BECK, MAE LUCILLE, retired chemistry educator, artist; b. Buffalo, Mar. 27, 1936. BS, Mich. State U., 1958; AM, Smith Coll., 1959; PhD, U. Pa., 1962. Prof. chemistry Simmons Coll., Boston, 1962-85; freelance artist Boston Sch., N.H., 1980—. Home and Studio: RFD Marlborough NH 03455

BECK, MARGIT, artist; b. Tokay, Hungary; came to U.S., naturalized, 1938; d. Samuel and Johanna (Blau) B.; m. Sidney Schwartz; children: Joan, John. Student, Art Inst. Oradeamare, Rumania, Art Student League, N.Y.C., 1945-46. Theatrical scenic designer, 1934-36; formerly mem. art faculty Hofstra U.; now adj. asst. prof. art faculty NYU; faculty Empire State Coll., N.Y. State U. Exhibited works in one man shows, Contemporary Arts, N.Y.C., 1955, 58, 59, San Joquin Mus., Stockton, Calif., 1956, Hofstra Coll., L.I., 1958, Mus. Fine Arts, Greenville, S.C., 1959, Babcock Gallery, N.Y.C., 1962, 64, 66, 68, 71, 72, 75, Phila. Art Alliance, 1968, Mansfield (Pa.) State Coll., 1965, Queens Coll., N.Y.C., 1973, Port Washington (N.Y.) Library, 1978; exhibited in group shows, Whitney Mus. Ann., Corcoran Biennial, Art Inst. Chgo. Ann., Pa. Acad. Ann., Allentown (Pa.) Mus. Fine Arts, Lehigh U., Bethlehem, Pa., Bklyn Mus. Internat. W.C. Biennial, NAD Ann., Butler Inst. Ann., U. Nebr. Ann., Springfield (Mass.) Mus., Akron Art Inst., Am. Acad. Arts and Letters, N.Y.C., Am. Soc. Contemporary Artists, Riverside Mus., N.Y.C., Southeby Parke Bernet, N.Y.C., Art U.S.A., Ringling Mus., Davenport (Iowa) Municipal Gallery, São Paulo Mus., N.Y. World's Fair, Am. Fedn. Arts Internat, travelling exhbns. include State Dept. sponsored exhbns., Am. embassies and museums abroad, Am. embassies in Europe; represented in permanent collections, Peabody Mus., Cambridge, Mass., Speed Mus., Louisville, Morse Mus., Rawlins Coll., Hofstra Coll., Hunter Coll., Herbert Lehman Coll., N.Y.C., Miami U., Oxford, Ohio, Norfolk (Va.) Mus., Sheldon Meml. Mus., Lincoln, Nebr., Glichtenstein Mus., Safaad, Israel, Lyman Allen Mus., New London, Conn., Mansfield (Pa.) State Coll., Whitney Mus., Sofia Mus., Bulgaria, others, also many pvt. collections and pub. bldgs. Recipient Gold medal oil Hofstra Coll., 1954; Purchase prize watercolor, 1955; Silver medal, 1956; Gold medal, 1957; Medal of Honor Nat. Assn. Women Artists, 1956; watercolor award, 1957, 63; oil award, 1958, 64; Winsor and Newton oil award, 1959; others; MacDowell Found. Residence fellow, 1957, 59, 60, 75; Walker award oil Audubon Artists, 1965; Medal Honor, 1968, 71; Henry Ward Ranger Fund Purchase awards (3) N.A.D., 1965, 73; Andrew Carnegie award, 1973; Child Hassam award Am. Acad. Arts and Letters, 1968, 69, 72. Mem. Artists Equity Assn. (past mem. exec. bd.), Audubon Artists (v.p. 1968-71, Stephen Hirsch award 1975, annual exhibit award 1981), NAD (full academician, Edwin Palmer award 1975), Coll. Art Assn. Am., Women in Arts. Address: 35 Nightbridge Rd Great Neck NY 11021

BECK, MARILYN MOHR, columnist; b. Chgo., Dec. 17, 1928; d. Max and Rose (Lieberman) Mohr; m. Roger Beck, Jan. 8, 1949 (div. 1974); children: Mark Elliott, Andrea; m. Arthur Levine, Oct. 12, 1980. AA, U. So. Calif., 1950. Freelance writer nat. mags. and newspapers Hollywood, Calif., 1959-63; Hollywood columnist Valley Times and Citizen News, Hollywood, 1963-65; West Coast editor Sterling Mags., Hollywood, 1963-74; freelance entertainment writer Los Angeles Times, 1965-67; Hollywood columnist Bell-McClure Syndicate, 1967-72; chief Bell-McClure Syndicate (West Coast bur.), 1967-72; Hollywood columnist NANA Syndicate, 1967-72; syndicated Hollywood columnist N.Y. Times Spl. Features, 1972-78, N.Y. Times Spl. Features (United Feature Syndicate), 1978-80, United Press abroad, 1978-80, Editors News and Features, Internat., Chgo. Tribune/N.Y. Daily News Syndicate, 1980—; Grapevine columnist TV Guide, 1989—. Creator, host: Marilyn Beck's Hollywood outtakes spls. NBC, 1977, 78; host: Marilyn Beck's Hollywood Hotline, KFI, L.A., 1975-77; Hollywood reporter: Eyewitness News KABC-TV, L.A., 1981; TV program PM Mag., 1983-88; Author: Marilyn Beck's Hollywood, 1973, (novel) Only Make Believe, 1988; columnist Grapevine TV Guide, 1989—. Recipient Citation of Merit Los Angeles City Council, 1973, Press award Pub. Guild Am., 1974, Bronze Halo award So. Calif. Motion Picture Council, 1982. Office: PO Box 11079 Beverly Hills CA 90213

BECKELHEIMER, CHRISTINE ELIZABETH CAMPBELL, nurse; b. Oak Hill, W.Va., Sept. 6, 1916; d. Charles Earl and Macie Avis (Boothe) Campbell; diploma in nursing Somerset Hosp., Somerville, N.J., 1938; B.S. in Nursing Edn., Hunter Coll., 1954; M.A. in Nursing Service Adminstrn., Tchrs. Coll. Columbia U., 1959, profl. diploma, 1961, postgrad, 1961-65; m. Joseph Howard, June 6, 1941 (dec.); 1 dau., Mary Elizabeth; m. 2d, Harry Abrahamsen, Oct. 10, 1943; 1 dau., Cherri Georgette; m. 3d, Robert Ernest Beckelheimer, Jan. 18, 1980. Staff nurse obstetrics Somerset Hosp., 1939; staff nurse Goldwater Meml. Hosp., Welfare Island, N.Y.C., 1939-40, research nurse, 1940-41; staff nurse St. Vincent's Hosp., N.Y.C., 1941-43; lab. asst. Am. Cyanamid Co., Bound Brook, N.J., 1943; charge nurse Paul Kimball Hosp., Lakewood, N.J., 1943-44; staff nurse to head nurse Pinewald Hosp., Bayville, N.J., 1944-46; staff nurse Morrisania City Hosp., Bronx, N.Y., 1946-49, head nurse, 1949-50, clin. instr., 1950-54; instl. insp. Dept. Hosps. City of N.Y., 1954-58; supr. edn. City Hosp., Elmhurst, N.Y., 1958-60, research asst. Fedn. of the Handicapped, 1962-63; research asso. Yeshiva U. Lincoln Hosp., N.Y.C., 1963-64; asst. coordinator exchange grad. nurse program St. Luke's Hosp., N.Y.C., 1964-65, asst. dir. nursing service inservice edn., 1966-67; cons. research and hosp. nursing service Nat. League Nursing, N.Y.C., 1968-70, acting dir. research (cons.), 1970-71; assoc. prof. nursing W.Va. Inst. Tech., 1971-73, chmn. dept. nursing, 1973-75; coordinator patient care Raleigh Gen. Hosp., Beckley, W.Va., 1975-78, dir. hosp. inservice, 1978-79. USPHS Nurse Research fellow, 1961-63; USPHS grantee, 1965-66. Mem. Am., W.Va. Nurses Assns., Tchrs. Coll. Nurses Alumni Assn., Hunter Coll. Alumni Assn., Nurses Alumni Assn. Somerset Hosp., Sci. Fiction Writers of Am., Pi Lambda Theta, Kappa Delta Pi, Am. Legion Aux., DAR, UDC (past pres. W.Va. div.), Fayette County Hist. Soc., Genealogy Soc. Fayette and Raleigh Counties, Fayette County Hist. Landmark Commn., Wittenfort Long Rifles, Mountaineer Flintlock Rifles, Rosicrucian Order. Author: Cristabel Manalacor of Veltakin, 1970; The Cruachan and the Killane, 1970; The Mortal Immortals, 1971; The Golden Olive, 1972; The Bride of Kilkerran, 1972; The Pettus Family of England and Virginia, 1989. Home: 213 Washington Ave Oak Hill WV 25901

BECKER, BETSY See ASWAD, BETSY

BECKER, BETTIE GERALDINE, artist; b. Peoria, Ill., Sept. 22, 1918; d. Harry Seymour and Magdalene Matilda (Hiller) B.; m. Lionel William Wathall, Nov. 10, 1945; children: Heather Lynn (dec.), Jeffrey Lee. BFA cum laude, U. Ill., Urbana, 1940; postgrad. Art Inst. Chgo., 1942-45, Art Student's League, 1946, Ill. Inst. tech., 1948. Dept. artist Liberty Mut. Ins. Co., Chgo., 1941-43; with Palenskie-Young Studio, 1943-46; free lance illustrator N.Y. Times, Chgo. Tribune, Saturday Rev. Lit., 1948-50; co-owner, operator Pangaea Gallery/Studio, Fish Creek, Wis.; pvt. tutor, tchr. studio classes. Exhibited one-man show Crossroads Gallery, Art Inst. Chgo., 1973; exhibited group shows including Critics' Choice show Art Rental Sales Gallery Art Inst. Chgo., 1972, Evanston-North Shore exhbns., 1964, 65, Chgo. Soc. Artists, 1967, 71, Union League, 1967, 72, Women in Art, Appleton (Wis.) Gallery Art, Milw. Art Mus., 1986, Neville Pub. Mus., Green Bay, Wis., 1987, Valperine Gallery, Madison, Wis. 1989, Wis. Arts Gallery, Allouez, 1990; represented in permanent collection Witte Meml. Mus., San Antonio, Miller Art Ctr., Stugeon Bay, Wis.; executed mural (with F. Wiater) Talbot Lab. U. Ill., Urbana, 1940; contbr. articles and illustrations to mags. and newspapers. Active Campfire Girls, Chgo., 1968, 70; art chmn., mem. exec. bd. local PTA, 1959-60; active various art festivals, 1967—. Mem. Chgo. Soc. Artists (rec. sec. 1968-77), Internat. Platform Assn., Accademia d' Europa, Soc. Illustrators, Wis. Arts Coun., N.E. Wis. Arts Coun. (bd. dir.), Alumni Assn. Art Inst. Chgo., Door County Art League. Republican. Mem. Unity Ch. Home: 3992 Juddville Rd Fish Creek WI 54212

BECKER, CAROL ANN, administrative assistant; b. Dayton, Ohio, July 15, 1949; d. David Alvin and Antoinette Rose (Butkus) Knisely; m. Herbert Henry Becker, Apr. 23, 1977; children: Angela Rose, Jennifer Sue, Douglas Edward. Student, Miami Jacobs Coll., 1967-68, Sinclair Community Coll., 1972-73, Wright State U., 1974-76. Sec. Elder-Beerman Corp., Dayton, 1968-80; sec. to city mgr. City of Beavercreek, Ohio, 1982—; clk. of coun. City of Beavercreek, 1982-84; tchr. shorthand, adult edn. program, Beavercreek Bd. Edn., 1986—. Coun. mem.-at-large St. Luke's Cath. Ch., Beavercreek, 1987, 88, 89; mem. Mayor's Communication Com., 1985—; cheerleading coach Beavercreek schs., 1984-89, St. Luke's Grammar Sch., 1987-88. Mem. Profl. Secs. Internat., Internat. Inst. Mcpl. Clks. Home: 1690 Kingsway Dr Beavercreek OH 45385 Office: City of Beavercreek 1368 Research Park Dr Beavercreek OH 45432

BECKER, DONNA MARIE, French instructor; b. Chillicothe, Ohio, June 27, 1942; d. Ranald Milton and Julie Marie (Good) Wolfe; m. Lee Alan Becker, Sept. 15, 1968; children: Brian Eric, Kevin David. student, universities, Quebec, Strasbourg, Japan, 1963-64; BA, Otterbein Coll., 1964; MA, Ohio State U., 1966. French instr. Ohio State U., Columbus, Ohio, 1964-66, Ohio Dominican Coll., Columbus, Ohio, 1966, Ohio Wesleyan U., Delaware, Ohio, 1966-68, U. Md., College Pk., Md., 1968-70, U. Mo., Columbia, Mo., 1970-71, Stephens Coll., Columbia, Mo., 1974, U. Colo., Colorado Springs, Colo., 1980—; Dir. Foreign Lang. Ctr., Colorado Springs, Colo., 1978—. Mem. Colo. Congress Foreign Lang. Tchrs., Am. Translators Assn. Democrat. Home: 927 Ellston St Colorado Springs CO 80907

BECKER, JULIE A. TAYLOR, computer layout manager; b. Toledo, June 27, 1961; d. Leonard Joseph and Mary Rose (Schlachter) Taylor; m. Michael Allen Becker, Nov. 7, 1987. BFA, Bowling Green (Ohio) State U., 1983, M in Home Econs., 1986; cert., Dale Carnegie Inst., 1987. With La-Z-Boy Chair Co., Monroe, Mich. Mem. NAFE, Bus. and Profl. Women's Assn. (chmn. long range planning com. 1987, young careerist chmn. 1988, 89—), Phi Upsilon Omicron. Roman Catholic. Office: La-Z-Boy Chair Co 1284 N Telegraph Rd Monroe MI 48161

BECKER, MAGDALENE NEUENSCHWANDER, educator; b. Beaverdam, Ohio, Sept. 5, 1915; d. Walter and Viola Etta (Gratz) Neuenschwander; m. Homer Gerald Becker, Aug. 18, 1935; 1 child, Rachel Etta. BA, Westminster Coll., New Wilmington, Pa., 1954, MEd in Guidance and Counseling, 1971; postgrad. in English, U. Pitts., 1962-65. Cert. tchr. Tchr. pub. speaking New Castle (Pa.) Sr. High Sch., 1954-61; tchr. advanced English Butler (Pa.) Area Sr. High Sch., 1961-77; with Learning Ctr. Sheldon Jackson Coll., Sitka, Alaska, 1977-79; cataloger, reference librarian Lees Coll., Jackson, Ky., 1979-83; coordinator conf. ctr. Cook Christian Tng. Sch., Tempe, Ariz., 1983-85; tutor Armstrong-Ind. County Intermediate Unit, Indiana, Pa., 1985—; evaluator Mid-Atlantic Sch. Examiners, 1966; examiner Nat. Council Tchrs. of English, 1964-76; tutor Indiana Literacy Council, 1985—, Armstrong/Indiana County, 1985—. Author 12 computer discs of GED programs, 1987-88. Tchr. Sunday Sch., Presbyn. Ch., 1940—, deacon, elder, 1985—; bd. dirs. Group Homes, Indiana, 1986-89. Mem. NEA, Pa. State Edn. Assn., Indiana County Edn. Assn., AAUW (pres. Indiana br. 1988—, exec. v.p. 1986-88). Republican. Home: 951 Lilac St Apt 10 Indiana PA 15701

BECKER, MARY LOUISE, political scientist; b. St. Louis; d. W. R. and Evelyn (Thompson) Becker; div.; children: James, John. BS, Washington U., St. Louis, 1949, MA, 1951; PhD, Radcliffe Coll., 1957; postgrad., U. Karachi (Pakistan), 1953-54. Intelligence rsch. analyst Dept. State, Washington, 1957-59; internat. rels. officer AID, Washington, 1959-64, community rels. officer, 1964-66, sci. rsch. officer, 1966-71, UN rels. officer, 1971—; adviser U.S. dels. 19th, 21st, 23d, 24th, 26th, 28th, 30th, and 32d Governing Coun. sessions UN Devel. Program; adv. U.S. del. 3d prep. com. meeting World Conf. UN Decade for Women; adviser U.S. dels. UNICEF exec. bd. sessions, 1987-89; lectr. internat. rels. civic orgns., student groups, 1954—. Author: Muhammed Iqbal, 1965; contbg. editor: Concise Ency. of Middle East, 1973; contbr. articles to govt. publs. Mem. adv. bd., chmn. student placement Washington Citizenship Seminar, Nat. YMCA-YWCA, Washington, 1961-71. Blewett fellow Washington U., 1951, Resident fellow Radcliff Coll., 1952-56; Fulbright scholar U. Karachi, 1953-54. Mem. AAUW, Am. Polit. Sci. Assn., Soc. Internat. Devel., Assn. Asian Studies, Asia Soc., Am. Soc. Public Adminstrn., Mo. Soc. Washington (sec. 1959-60), Mortar Bd., Chimes, Internat. Club, Harvard Club (Washington), Alpha Lambda Delta, Beta Gamma Sigma, Eta Mu Phi, Pi Sigma Alpha. Presbyterian. Office: Agy for Internat Devel Washington DC 20523

BECKER, OLGA AGATHA, law publisher, lawyer; b. St. Louis, Dec. 13, 1909; d. Frank A. and Agatha (Hartmann) B. Student pre-law, Washington U., St. Louis, 1926-28; LLB, Benton Coll. Law, St. Louis, 1933. Bar: Mo., 1931. Sr. tax editor Prentice-Hall, Inc., N.Y.C., 1942-45; opinions atty. U.S. Dept. Justice Mil. Govt. in Korea, 1947-48; adminstrv. asst. to treas. and chmn. bd. Harcourt, Brace & Co., N.Y.C., 1955-57; sole practice St. Louis, 1962—; pres., treas. Index/Citator System, Inc., St. Louis, 1969—. Author: Becker's Insurance Index/Citator, Poems by Olga. Mem. Mo. Bar Assn., St. Louis Bar Assn., Law Library Assn. St. Louis. Republican.

BECKER, SUSAN KAPLAN, consultant, educator; b. Newark, Jan. 4, 1948; d. Charles and Janet Kaplan; m. William Paul Becker, Mar. 9, 1969 (div. Feb. 1977). BA, U. Pa., 1968, MA, 1969, PhD, 1973, MBA, 1979. Instr. English Bryn Mawr (Pa.) Coll., 1972-74; assoc. editor U. Pa., Phila., 1975, asst. dir., lectr. urban studies, 1975-77; fin. analyst Phila. Nat. Bank, 1979-82; asst. v.p. Chem. Bank, N.Y.C., 1982-84; v.p. Bankers Trust Co., N.Y.C., 1984-85; prin. Becker Cons., N.Y.C., 1985—; clin. assoc. prof. Stern Sch. Bus. N.Y.U., 1990—; cons./evaluator Pa. Humanities Council, Phila., 1977-78. Author: How to Develop Profitable Financial Products for the Institutional Marketplace, 1988; contbr. columns and book revs. to profl. jours. Vol., N.Y. Cares, 1989—. U. Pa. fellow, 1968-72; E.I. DuPont de Nemours fellow, 1979, N.Y. Regents Coll. Teaching fellow, 1968-70. Mem. Assn. for Bus. Communication, Speech Communication Assn., Am. Mktg. Assn. (leadership council N.Y. chpt. 1988—), Mcpl. Art Soc. Democrat. Office: 155 E 29th St 22d Floor New York NY 10016

BECKETT, GRACE, economics educator emerita; b. Smithfield, Ohio, Oct. 7, 1912; d. Roy Martin and Mary (Hammond) Beckett. AB, Oberlin Coll., 1934, AM, 1935; PhD, Ohio State U., 1939. Music supr. Pub. Schs., Kelleys Island, Ohio, 1935-36; grad asst. econs. Ohio State U., 1936-39; assoc. prof. econs. and music Ind. Central Coll., 1939-41: with U. Ill., Champaign-Urbana, 1941—, asst. prof. econs., 1945-51, assoc. prof. econs., 1951-73, assoc. prof. emerita Coll. Commerce and Bus. Adminstrn., 1973—. Author: Reciprocal Trade Agreements Program, 1941, 72; contbr. profl. pubs. Mem. AAAS, Am. Econ. Assn., Music Educators Nat. Conf., Ill. Music Educators Assn., Econ. History Assn., Am. Finance Assn., Am. Hist. Assn., N.Y. Acad. Scis., Midwest Econs. Assn., Md. Geneal. Soc., Ohio Acad. History, Ohio Hist. Soc., Winchester-Frederick County (Va.) Hist. Soc., Ill. Music Tchrs. Assn., Music Tchrs. Nat Assn., Interlochen Alumni Assn. (life), Nat. Band Assn., U. Ill. Alumni Assn. (assoc.), Friends of Art of the Allen Meml. Art Mus. at Oberlin Coll., Nat. Sch. Orch. Assn., Krannert Art Mus. Assos. (U. Ill.), Ohio State U. Alumni Assn., Nat. Honor Soc., Mary Ball Washington Mus. & Libr., Met. Mus. Art (N.Y.C.) (nat. asso.), Oberlin Coll. Alumni Assn., Alpha Lambda Delta (hon.), Phi Beta Kappa, Pi Lambda Theta, Phi Chi Theta (hon.). Methodist. Club: Women's at the University of Ill., Oberlin Coll. Half-Century. Address: PO Box 386 Urbana IL 61801

BECKETT, SUSAN KAY, television executive; b. Webster City, Iowa, June 5, 1948; d. Ed Logan and Doris Darlene (Beckett) Oard; children—Gabrielle, Jessica. B.S., Iowa State U., 1969; J.D., U. Iowa, 1974; LL.M., NYU, 1977. Bar: Iowa 1974, N.Y. 1975, D.C. 1978. Assoc., Dewey, Ballantine, Bushby, Palmer & Wood, N.Y.C., 1974-76; trial atty. U.S. Dept. Justice, Washington, 1977-78; sr. atty. law dept. NBC, Inc., N.Y.C., 1978-80, sr. counsel, 1980-81, v.p. bus. affairs enterprises div., from 1981; v.p. NBC Internat. Ltd., Bermuda, 1982—; dir., asst. sec. Living Music, Inc., N.Y.C., 1979, Spectacular Music, Inc., N.Y.C., 1979—; dir., vice chmn. NBC Enterprises, Inc., N.Y.C., 1980—; v.p. NBC Ednl Enterprises Inc., Del., 1982—. Recipient Am. Jurisprudence award Lawyers Coop Pub. Co., 1973. Mem. N.Y. State Bar Assn., Iowa Bar Assn., D.C. Bar Assn., Order of Coif. Office: NBC 30 Rockefeller Pla New York NY 10112*

BECKEY, SYLVIA LOUISE, lawyer; b. L.A., Feb. 8, 1946; d. Andrew Gabriel and Rita Jane (Mayer) B. BA with spl. honors, U. Tex., 1968, postgrad., 1968-69; JD, Duke U., 1971; MA, Johns Hopkins Sch. Advanced Internat. Studies, 1973-74; LLM, NYU, 1981. Bar: D.C. 1972, N.Y. 1975, U.S. Dist. Ct. (so. and ea. dists.) N.Y. 1975, U.S. Supreme Ct. 1975, U.S. Ct. Appeals (2d cir.) 1980. Legis. atty. Am. law div. Congl. Rsch. Svc., Libr. of Congress, Washington, 1971-74; assoc. Cole & Deitz, N.Y.C., 1975-76, Milberg, Weiss, Bershad & Specthrie, N.Y.C., 1976-78; law. clk. to judge U.S. Dist. Ct. (so. dist.) N.Y., 1979-80; asst. chief div. comml. litigation Office of Corp. Counsel of City of N.Y., 1980-86; spl. master Supreme Ct. State of N.Y./N.Y. County, 1984-86; spl. counsel-enforcement U.S. Securities and Exch. Commn., N.Y.C., 1986-89; atty. Sheft and Sweeney, N.Y.C., 1989—; guest speaker U. Witwatersrand Sch. Law, Johannesburg, Republic of South Africa, 1973; guest researcher Ct. Libr., Nairobi, Kenya, 1973; pro bono Internat. League Human Rights, N.Y.C., 1974-75, 8th ann. Conf. for World Peace Through Law, Abidjan, Ivory Coast, West Africa, 1973. Co-author: Handbook for Drafting Jury Instructions, U.S. Dept. Justice Civil Rights Div., 1970; assoc. editor: The Constitution of the United States of America-Analysis and Interpretation, 1972; author legis. reports on Equal Credit Opportunity Act; referee Am. Bus. Law Jour., 1980-81. Bd. dirs. Chalon Coop. Bldg., Washington, 1972-73; chmn. fine arts com., mem. bd. dirs. St. Bartholomew's Community Club, St. Bartholomew's Episcopal Ch., N.Y.C., 1982-83. Hinds Webbs Fund grantee, 1967. Mem. Women's Bar Assn. City of N.Y., NYU Law Alumni Assn., Duke U. Law Alumni Assn., Fed. Bar Coun., Am. Fgn. Law Assn., Consular Law Soc., Dramatists Guild, Protestant Lawyers Guild, English Speaking Union, Met. Mus. Art, Chelsea Block Assn. and Hist. Soc. Democrat. Home: 235 W 22d St New York NY 10011 Office: Sheft & Sweeney 11 Broadway New York NY 10004

BECKHAM, GAYNELLE MATHEWS, chemistry educator; b. Roanoke, Ala., July 6, 1944; d. H. Gay and Mattie Blanche (Sheppard) Mathews; m. James Eugene Beckham, Jr., July 25, 1970; 1 child, James Eugene III. BA in Chemistry, W. Ga. Coll., 1967, MEd in Sci., 1988. Cert. tchr., Ga. Tchr. chemistry DeKalb County Bd. Edn., Decatur, 1967-69, Carrollton (Ga.) City Bd. of Edn., 1969-72, Arlington Schs. of Greater Atlanta, 1986; instr. chemistry dept. West Ga. Coll., Carrollton, 1987, 89—, W. Ga. Coll., 1989—. Vice pres. Carrollton Garden Club, 1980, pres. 1981; pres. Oak Mountain Acad. Parents Coun., 1984-85, Art Study Club, Carrollton, 1985; chmn. projects, fundraiser Oak Mountain Acad., 1982-83, 85-88, trustee, 1986—. Named Tchr. of the Yr., Ga. Acad. Sci., 1972. Mem. Sunset Hill Country Club (pres. Ladies Tennis Assn.). Baptist. Home: 427 Sunset Blvd Carrollton GA 30117

BECKHAM-BURNETT, SUSAN GAY, exercise physiologist; b. Wichita, Kans., Mar. 27, 1956; d. Rex Larkin and Mary JoAnn (Maddox) Beckham; m. Larry Thomas Burnett, June 20, 1986. BS in Geology cum laude, S.W. Mo. State U., 1980; MS in Health Sci. magna cum laude, Okla. State U., 1984, postgrad. Geologist NEMO Coal, Moberly, Mo., 1980-81, Assoc. Elec. Coop., Springfield, Mo., 1981-82, Jim Winnek, Inc., Tulsa, 1982-84; fitness instr. Tulsa Racquetball Aerobics Club, Tulsa, 1983-85; exercise technician/leader cardiac rehab. Okla. State U. Health Fitness Ctr., Stillwater, 1983-84; exercise technician St. Francis Phys. Performance Ctr., Tulsa, 1985; fitness dir. Okla. Ctr. for Athletes, Oklahoma City, 1985-88; exercise physiologist/cons. Okla. Ctr. for Athletes, 1989—; ptnr. Fitness Inc.

Contbr. articles to profl. jours.; author: (with others) ARC Injury Manual, 1987, Clinical Sports Medicine, 1990. Mem. ARC spl. projects com., 1989—, Gov.'s Coun. on Phys. Fitness & Sports, Okla., 1988—. Mem. Okla. Aerobic Tchrs. Assn. (co-founder, bd. dirs. 1986—), Am. Coll. Sports Medicine. Methodist. Home: 2604 N Grant Bethany OK 73008

BECKMAN, JEAN CATHERINE, chemistry educator; b. Detroit, Sept. 25, 1951; d. Charles Rilling and Elizabeth Jordan (Schabacker) B. AB, Colby Coll., 1973; PhD, Ind. U., 1977. Assoc. instr. Ind. U., Bloomington, 1974-77; rsch. asst. Purdue U., West Lafayette, Ind., 1977-78; asst. prof. U. Evansville (Ind.), 1978-84, assoc. prof., 1984—; chair dept. chemistry U. Evansville, 1989—. Mem. Am. Chem. Soc. (sec. Ind.-Ky. border sect. 1985—). Home: 208 S Taft Ave Evansville IN 47714 Office: U Evansville 1800 Lincoln Ave Evansville IN 47722

BECKMAN, JUDITH, art educator; b. Amityville, N.Y., Mar. 12, 1951; d. Charles Frederick and Helen Marie (Colville) B. Student, U. Miss., 1969-71, George Washington U., 1971, U. Guadalajara, Mex., 1972, City Coll. City U. N.Y., 1978, Columbia U., 1979; BFA, Colo. U., 1973; MFA, Ohio U., 1975. Teaching assoc. Ohio U., Athens, 1974-75; silkscreen artist Chromacomp, Inc., N.Y.C., 1976; vis. artist Coll. Misericordia, Dallas, Pa., 1977; instr. Spanish Am. Inst., N.Y.C., 1978-79; prodn. coordinator Chromacomp, Inc., N.Y.C., 1978; instr. Coll. Misericordia, Dallas, Pa., 1978, Malcolm-King Coll., N.Y.C., 1979-80; bilingual instr. Lincoln Sch., Orange, N.J., 1979-80; teaching assoc. Ohio State U., Columbus, 1980-88; gallery dir. Kenyon Coll., Gambier, Ohio, 1988-89, Franklin U., Columbus, 1989—; mem. curriculum com. dept. art history Ohio State U., Columbus, 1984-85; vis. lectr. Ohio State U., Mansfield, 1988; vis. instr. Oberlin (Ohio) Coll., 1988, Kenyon Coll., 1989; art instr. Columbus Torah Acad., 1989—. Exhibited in group shows at Community Gallery, N.Y.C., 1978, The Massillon (Ohio) Mus., 1978, Western Ill. U., Macomb, Ill., 1979, Springfield Art Mus., 1980, Zaner Gallery, Rochester, N.Y., 1981, Frick Art Mus., Wooster, Ohio, 1983, Spark Gallery, 1984, Ohio State U. Gallery, 1985, El Paso Mus. of Art, 1987, Artreach Gallery, Columbus, 1987, Artreach Gallery, Columbus, 1987, 88, Columbia Coll., Mo., 1988, Columbus Art League, 1988-89, North Coast Coll. Soc., Cleve., 1990; presentations include Case Western Res. U., 1982, Ohio State U., 1984, 85, Newcomb Coll./Tulane U., New Orleans, 1985; contbr. articles to profl. jours. Instr. Rape Prevention Program Ohio State U., 1980—; mem. adv. bd. Thompson Recreation Ctr., Columbus, Ohio, 1986-89. Ohio State U. grantee, 1986; Com. for the Visual Arts, Inc. Exhbn. grantee, 1978, Bklyn. Arts and Culture Assn. grantee, 1979. Mem. Coll. Art Assn., Women's Caucus for Art (pres., co-founder Ohio chpt.), Nat. Women's Studies Assn., Nat. Mus. Women in Arts, Columbus Art League, Artreach Inc., Ohio State U. Grad. Student Assn. (pres. 1983-84), Zeta Tau Alpha, Alpha Lambda Delta. Home: 5635 Thompson Rd Ashville OH 43103

BECKMAN, JUDITH KALB, financial counselor and planner, educator, writer; b. Bklyn., June 27, 1940; d. Harry and Frances (Cohen) Kalb; m. Richard Martin Beckman, Dec. 16, 1961; children: Barry Andrew, David Mark. BA, Hofstra U., 1962; MA, Adelphi U., 1973. cert. fin. planner. Promotion coordination pub. rels. Mandel Sch. for Med. Assts., Hempstead, N.Y., 1973-74; exec. dir. Nassau Easter Seals, Albertson, N.Y., 1974-76; dir. pub. info. Long Beach Meml. Hosp., Albertson, N.Y., 1976-77; account rep. First Investors, Hicksville, N.Y., 1977-78; sales asst., then account exec. Josephthal & Co. Inc., Great Neck, N.Y., 1978-81; v.p., cert. fin. planner Arthur Gould Inc., Great Neck, N.Y., 1981-88; pres. Fin. Solutions (affiliated with Seco West Ltd., Goldner Siegfried Assocs. Inc.), Westbury, N.Y., 1988—; adj. instr. Adelphi U., Garden City N.Y., 1981-83, Molloy Coll., Rockville Ctr., N.Y., 1982-84; lectr. SUNY-Farmingdale, 1984-85; creater, presenter seminars, workshops on fin., investing, 1981—. Fin. columnist The Women's Record, 1985—; writer quar. newspaper The Reporter, 1987. Coord. meat boycott, L.I., 1973; mentor SUNY Old Westbury, 1989—; co-founder, chair L.I. del. High Profile Men and Women, Colonie Hill, Hauppauque, N.Y., 1985; treas. L.I. Alzheimers Found., 1989—; apptd. to Nassau County Women's Adv. Coun. by County Exec., 1990. Recipient citation for leadership Town of Hempstead, N.Y., 1986, 89, L.I. Press Club award Bus. Writer award Press Club, 1987, Mentor award SBA, 1989, Woman of Distinction in Bus. award Women on the Job, 1989, Bus. Leadership citation Nassau County, N.Y., 1989, Supr. award Town of Hempstead, 1989. Mem. Nat. Assn. Women Bus. Owners L.I. (bd. dirs. 1987-89), Women's Econ. Developers of L.I. (bd. dirs. 1985—), Internat. Assn. Fin. Planners (L.I. chpt.), Inst. Cert. Fin. Planners, L.I. Ctr. Bus. and Profl. Women (pres. 1984-86), Advancement Commerce and Industry, Am. Soc. Women Accts. Republican. Jewish. Home: 2084 Beverly Way Merrick NY 11566 Office: Fin Solutions Fin Planning Office 2084 Beverly Way Merrick NY 11566

BECKMAN, PENNY ELIZABETH, nurse; b. Lodi, Calif., Mar. 6, 1949; d. John Henry and Charlyn (Coburn) Lauchland; m. Ronald Myron Beckman, May 31, 1968 (div. 1976); children: John Raymond, Chad Lauchland; m. Donald Linn, Sept. 1, 1978 (div. 1980); m. Donald E. Irvine, Mar. 5, 1982 (div. 1983). Student, Highland Sch. Nursing, Oakland, Calif., 1968; RN, AA with high honors, San Joaquin Delta Coll., Stockton, Calif., 1970; BS in Nursing, Sacramento State U., 1986. RN, Calif. Charge nurse maternity Lodi Community Hosp., 1970-72, charge nurse emergency dept., 1972-76; paramedic nurse coord. San Joaquin County (Calif.), 1976—; emergency nurse St. Joseph Hosp., Stockton, 1978-87; emergency nurse, clin. coord. Dameron Hosp., Stockton, 1987—; relief PM supr. Lodi Community Hosp., 1975-76; instr. advanced cardiac life support LaMaze Am. Soc. Psychoprophylactic Childbirth, 1974-76, 80-81. Vice pres. Tiny Tots Nursery Sch., Lodi, 1972-73; pres. Vinewood Sch. PTA, Lodi, 1986-87; vol. Salvation Army; camp nurse, merit bade instr. Boy Scouts Am., 1983-84; soccer coach, 1985; ; evangelism-explosion trainor Temple Bapt. Ch., Lodi; ; leader Bible study Juvenile Justice Ctr., Stockton and Matthews, Calif., 1989—; docent Lodi Lake Mokelumne River Wilderness Trail, 1988-89; ptnr. Calif. Prisons for Women, Stockton, 1988; vol. Lodi's Ctr. of Hope, Stockton Women's Ctr.; high sch. speaker on dating violence, Stockton, 1988-89. Mem. Calif. Nurses Assn., Emergency Nurses Assn. (legalities and legis. com. 1988-89). Republican. Home: 1022 Downing Lodi CA 95242 Office: Dameron Hosp Acacia St Stockton CA 95200

BECKMANN, MICHELE LILLIAN, secretary; b. Bklyn., Feb. 15, 1957; d. Anton (Tony) and Alice Naomi (Williams) Prudich; m. Robert Westcott Beckmann, Apr. 18, 1981. BA, Ea. Wash. U., 1978. Cert. profl. sec. Lead sec. New Way Homes, Spokane, 1980-81; libr. asst. Spokane Pub. Librs., 1981-82; office asst. Spokane County Assesor's Office, 1982; data processing clk. Aztech-Comstock, Spokane, 1983-84; finishing opr. Hollister-Stier Labs., Spokane, 1984; pvt. sec. Daniel Kallestad, CLU, ChFC, Spokane, 1985; office asst. Wash. State U., Pullman, 1986-87, sec. III, 1987-89, project sec., 1989—. Mem. City of Pullman Fair Housing Commn., 1989—; vice chair Pullman Fair Housing Commn. 1989-90; mem. nominating chair local coun. Camp Fire, Inc., 1989-90; precinct officer Whitman County Dems., Colfax, Wash., 1988-90. Recipient WO-HE-LO medallion Camp Fire Inc., 1975; cert. appreciation Pullman Fair Housing Commn., 1989. Mem. Bus. and Profl. Women (state PAC vice chair 1989-90, state lobby corps com. 1988—), Profl. Secs. Internat. (chair com. 1986-90). Democrat. Home: SW 528 Summer St Pullman WA 99163 Office: Wash State U 706 Johnson Tower Pullman WA 99164-4870

BECKWITH, BARBARA JEAN, journalist; b. Chgo., Dec. 11, 1948; d. Charles Barnes and Elizabeth Ann (Nolan) B. BA in Journalism, Marquette U., 1970. News editor Lake Geneva (Wis.) Regional News, 1972-74; asst. editor St. Anthony Messenger, Cin., 1974-82, mng. editor, 1982—. Mem. Cath. Press Assn. (bd. dirs. 1986—, v.p. 1988-90, pres. 1990-92, best interview 1982, best photo story 1985), Women in Communications, Cin. Editors Assn. Office: St Anthony Messenger 1615 Republic St Cincinnati OH 45210

BECKWITH, CATHERINE S., veterinarian; b. St. Louis, Apr. 8, 1958; d. John P. Sr. and Dolores A. BS in Biology and BA German Lang., U. Ill., 1981, BS in Vet. Medicine with honors, 1984, DVM with honors, 1986. Assoc. vet. Cen. Hosp. for Animals, Carterville, Ill., 1986-87, Coble Animal Hosp., Springfield, Ill., 1987—. Contbr. articles to profl. publications. Fulbright grantee Tech. U., Munich, 1981. Mem. AVMA, Gold Key Nat. Honor Soc., McBrian-Lincoln Douglas Toastmasters, Phi Zeta. Republican. Home: 1347 N Fourth St Springfield IL 62702 Office: Coble Animal Hosp 2828 S MacArthur Springfield IL 62704

BEDASKE, ANGELA MARGARET, banker; b. Buffalo, N.Y., Jan. 20, 1961; d. Chester Jay and Rose Mary (Carriero) B. BS in Fin., Canisius Coll., 1983. Proof machine operator Metroteller Systems, Inc., Buffalo, 1983-84, mgr. proofing dept., 1984-85, mgr. point of banking dept., 1985-86, asst. v.p. settlement ops. dept., 1986—. Active Ladies aux. Brant (N.Y.) Vol. Fire Co. #1, 1977—, Altar and Rosary Soc. Our Lady of Mt. Carmel Ch., Brant, 1977—, organist, choir dir., 1984—. Mem. Am. Inst. Banking, Nat. Assn. Female Execs. Republican. Home: 10083 Brant Angola Rd Angola NY 14006 Office: Metroteller Systems Inc 237 Main St Ste 1200 Buffalo NY 14203

BEDELL, CATHERINE MAY, international consultant, former congresswoman. Mem. U.S. Ho. of Reps. from Wash. State, 1958-70; bd. incorporators Amtrak, Washington, 1970-71; chmn. U.S. Internat. Trade Commn., Washington, 1971-75, 1975-79, 80-81; commr. Internat. Trade Commn., Washington, 1979-80; spl. cons. White House, Pres.' 50 States Project, Washington, 1982-83; dir. Am. Brands, Inc., 1983—. Bd. dirs. Former Mems. of Congress. Home and Office: 514 Sandpiper Palm Desert CA 92260

BEDFORD, MADELEINE ALANN PECKHAM, civic worker; b. Ontario, Calif., Jan. 25, 1910; d. Allen Lewis and Madeleine (Elliott) Peckham; A.B., U. Calif., Berkeley, 1930, M.A., 1937; LL.D. (hon.), Tex. Christian U., 1973; m. Charles Francis Bedford, Dec. 30, 1930; children—Madeleine Alann, Frances Ellen, Charlotte Jean. Supr. tchr. tng. and counseling, in charge testing Univ. High Sch., U. Calif., Berkeley, 1931-38; tchr. English to fgn. born San Leandro (Calif.) Evening Schs., 1931-38; treas. Tarrant County Day Care Assn., 1953-54; pres. Ft. Worth and Tarrant County council Camp Fire Girls, 1961-63, mem. Nat. council, 1968-75, pres. Nat. council, 1965-68, NGO rep. to UN, 1968-69, nat. bd. dirs., 1960-68, bd. dirs. Houston council, 1971-72, mem. congress of Nat. Camp Fire Girls, 1975—; pres. Ft. Worth Lit. Council, 1963-65; v.p. Tarrant County United Fund and Community Council, 1963-66, mem. exec. com. bd. dirs., 1963—; pres. Ft. Worth chpt. Am. Field Service, 1964-66; chmn. budget sub-com. United Fund, 1959-68, chmn. met. div. Tarrant County, 1970; chmn. speakers tours, films div., United Way Tarrant County Campaign, 1973, chmn. planning and research div., 1973-75; v.p. United Way Met. Tarrant County, 1973-75, chmn. community services div., 1985-86; mem. exec. com. United Way Tex., 1979—; sec. Tex. United Community Services, 1968-70, v.p., 1970-73, pres., 1973-75; mem. Mid-Am. Regional Vol. Task group United Way Am., mem. nat. com. agy. support, 1975-80; Tex. state rep. for UNICEF, 1969—, mem. coordinating bd. for U.S. Com. of UN Childrens Fund, 1981—; chmn. Mayor's Council on Youth Opportunity, 1972-73; del. White House Conf. on Children and Youth, 1970; sec. social services adv. com. Tex. Dept. Human Resources, 1975-76, chmn., 1976-77; mem. nat. bd. Nat. Conf. Social Welfare, 1976-80; colleague nat. assembly Nat. Vol. Health and social welfare orgns., 1978-80; bd. dirs. Tarrant County chpt. ARC; bd. dirs. United Cerebral Palsy, pres. Tarrant County Br., 1976-78, mem. nat. corp., 1976—, v.p., Tex., 1977-83, pres., 1983-85; bd. dirs. Tarrant County Community Action Agy., Tarrant County Community Council, Tex. Social Welfare Assn.; trustee Assn. Grad. Edn. and Research, 1971—; trustee Tex. Christian U., also bd. visitors; trustee Tex. Coll. Osteo. Medicine Found., 1980—; mem. adv. council Sch. Social Work, U. Tex., Austin, 1980—; mem. adv. council for fin. assistance Tex. Dept. Human Resources, 1980—; pres. Womens Haven Tarrant County, 1979-81, bd. dirs., 1979-86; mem. exec. com. Community Trust Tarrant County, 1981—; bd. dirs. Family and Individual Services Tarrant County, 1981-87, pres., 1985-87; bd. dirs. Ft. Worth Girls Club, 1979—; mem. nat. bd. dirs. Girls Club Am., 1983-86; bd. dirs. Ft. Worth Acad., 1985—; Fed. Emergency Mgmt. Act, 1985—; pres. bd. dirs. Family Service, 1985—; mem. adv. council for adult basic edn. Ft. Worth Ind. Sch. Dist., 1976—; fellow Forum of Ft. Worth, 1981—; mem. Dallas/Ft. Worth Chaplaincy Bd., 1983—; bd. dirs. Tarrant Area Community of Chs., 1979—, pres., 1984-87. Recipient Gulick award, 1961, Wo-he-lo award, 1968 Camp Fire Girls; award of Excellence for Outstanding Leadership and Service Tarrant County Community Council, 1964, Civic award First Lady Ft. Worth Altrusa, 1966, Hercules award for Outstanding Vol. Leadership in Social Welfare United Way, 1977, award for service to students 1983, Alumni Royal Purple award 1983 (both Tex. Christian U.), award for human service Sertoma, 1983; declared Ecumenist of Yr., Tarrant Area Community of Chs., 1986. Mem. Council World Affairs (pres. 1985-87, v.p. 1987—), Internat. Good Neighbor Council (v.p. 1987-87, pres. 1987—), Ft. Worth Lecture Found., DAR, Mortar Board, Family Service Assn. (bd. dirs.), Phi Beta Kappa (pres. Ft. Worth 1958-59), Alpha Chi Omega, Pi Sigma Alpha. Episcopalian. Clubs: Ft. Worth Woman's (past pres. history sect., Tex. Christian U. Woman's). Home: 7 Westover Rd Fort Worth TX 76107

BEDFORD, VIRGINIA MARY, real estate company officer; b. Rockville Center, N.Y., Oct. 8, 1951; d. Roy Thomas and Mary Elizabeth (Hall) B. AAS, SUNY, Farmingdale, 1978, AAS in Bus., 1984; BS in Acctg., SUNY, Old Westbury, 1987. Lic. real estate sales person, N.Y.; lic. dental hygienist. Book-keeper Ralar Distbrs., Plainview, N.Y., 1971-76, Paragon Enterprises, Melville, N.Y., 1976-82; asst. controller Rana Mgmt., Hempstead, N.Y., 1983; dir. fin. Kreisel Co., Inc., N.Y.C., 1984-87; v.p. fin. ABR Mgmt. Inc., N.Y.C., 1988—; cons. Zennor Corp. Am., N.Y.C., 1988. Mem. Real Estate Bd. N.Y., Anchorage Yacht Club. Office: ABR Mgmt Inc 554 Fifth Ave New York NY 10036

BEDICS, LYNN FAY, nurse; b. Scranton, Pa., May 13, 1947; d. Gerald Joseph and Esther Naomi (Sachse) O'Malley; m. John Joseph Zima, Jr., Aug. 19, 1972 (div. Sept. 1976); m. Francis Joseph Bedics, Jr., Mar. 11, 1989. Grad., St. Luke's Hosp. Sch. Nursing, N.Y.C., 1968; student, U. Pa., 1971-72; BS, Cedar Crest Coll., Allentown, Pa., 1982. RN, Pa.; cert. community health nurse and med. surg. nurse Am. Nurses Assn. Staff nurse emergency room Allentown Gen. Hosp., 1971; part-time charge nurse Phila. VA Hosp., 1971-72; critical care nurse St. John's Hosp., Tulsa, 1972-74, Allentown Osteo. Hosp., 1975-79; head nurse outpatient clinic Dept. Vets. Affairs, Allentown, 1979—; instr.-trainer CPR, Am. Heart Assn., Allentown, 1980-89. Mem. coordinating com. Combined Fed. Campaign, Lehigh Valley, Pa., 1984-86; bd. dirs. YWCA, Allentown, 1986-88, Korea-Vietnam Meml. Com. Inc., Lehigh Valley, 1987—. 1st lt. Nurse Corps, U.S. Army, 1967-70, Vietnam. Decorated Bronze Star medal; recipient Excellence in Nursing award Dept. Vets. Affairs, 1989, VA Adminstr.'s Hands and Heart award Dept. Vets. Affairs Med. Ctr., Wilkes-Barre, Pa., 1989. Mem. Assn. for Ambulatory Care Providers Ea. Pa. (pres. 1989-90), United Women Vets. Pa., VFW, Sigma Theta Tau, Beta Sigma Phi (internat. hon.). Republican. Home: 1118 N 27th St Allentown PA 18104 Office: Dept Vets Affairs Outpatient Clinic 2937 Hamilton Blvd Allentown PA 18103

BEDKE, KATHRYN LYNN, lawyer; b. Kearney, Nebr., Nov. 3, 1951; d. Richard August Tatem and Helen Kathryn (Weitzel) Bedke. B.A. in English and German, Kirkland Coll., 1974; student U. Vienna-Austria, 1972-73; M.T.S. in Religion, Harvard Div. Sch., 1976; J.D., Case Western Res. U., 1979. Bar: N.Y. 1981. Assoc., Demov, Morris, and Hammerling, N.Y.C., 1979-81, White & Case, N.Y.C., 1981—. Pres., Kirkland Coll. Alumnae Assn., 1982-88; mem. Hamilton Coll. Alumni Assn., 1981-84. George F. Baker Trust fellow, 1971-72, 73-74; Rockefeller fellow, 1974-75; Soc. Benchers award, 1979. Mem. Case Western Res. Jour. Internat. Law, 1976-77, Case Western Res. Law Rev., 1977-79. Mem. ABA, N.Y. State Bar Assn., (com. on internat. law 1984—), Nebr. Soc. of N.Y., Inc. (pres. elect 1986-87, pres. 1987-88, legal advisor 1984—). Democrat. Home: 250 W 24th St Apt 1CE New York NY 10011

BEDLIN, DOROTHY ROBERTA, retail executive, consultant; b. Tampa, Fla., Mar. 5, 1951; d. Robert Fredrick and Mary Catherine (Nalley) Kunstman; m. Michael Howard Bedlin, Sept. 1, 1972 (div. Jan. 1977). BA in Sociology, U. South Fla., 1972, student in mktg., 1985—. Exec. sec., adminstrv. asst. Am. Title Ins., Miami, Fla., 1972-76; ops. mgr. K-Mart Corp., Tampa, 1976—, mem. Good News, pub. rels. and employee communication com.; mktg. and mgmt. cons. Carico Internat., Tampa, 1989—. NAFE. Republican. Baptist. Home: 3007 E 148th Ave Lutz FL 33549

BEDNAR, CAROLYN DIANE, dentist; b. Akron, Ohio, Oct. 7, 1953; d. William Adolph and Marilyn Minns (Hadfield) B.; m. Steven Kent Good, Sept. 25, 1982; 1 child, David Steven Good. BA in Chemistry, De Pauw U., 1975; DDS, Ohio State U., 1978. Gen. practice dentistry Columbus, 1978—; mem. staff Southwest Community Health Ctr., Columbus, Ohio, 1979-82. Vol. pub. oral cancer screenings and dental edn., Am. Cancer Soc., Columbus; vol. speaker dentistry Columbus Pub. Schs., 1982-85, 88; vol. fundraiser Multiple Sclerosis Soc., Columbus, 1986-88. Mem. ADA, Ohio Dental Assn., Columbus Dental Assn., Profl. Women's Forum (sec. 1982-84), Ohio State U. Coll. Dentistry Alumni Assn., Alpha Phi. Republican. Home: 8862 Easton Dr Pickerington OH 43147 Office: 1600 Brice Rd Reynoldsburg OH 43068

BEDNAREK, JANA MARIA, biochemist; b. Bratislava, Czechoslovakia, Mar. 8, 1934; came to U.S., 1966, naturalized, 1971; d. Rudolf and Helena (Lastovickova) Kozdera; m. Milan Kraus, June 23, 1957 (div. 1963); m. Milan B. Bednarek, Nov. 27, 1966; 1 child, Paula Helen. M.S., Charles U., 1959; postgrad. NYU, 1966-67; Ph.D., Med. Sch. Va., 1973. Fellow dept. biochemistry Med. Sch. Va., Charlottesville, 1973-75; rsch. assoc. dept. chemistry U. S.C., Columbia, 1975-79; rsch. assoc. dept. biochemistry, Med. Sch. S.C., Charleston, 1979-80; rsch. chemist hematology and oncology svc. Walter Reed Army Med Ctr., Washington, 1981—. Contbr. articles to profl. jours. Mem. N.Y. Acad. Scis., Am. Soc. for Molecular Biochemistry and Molecular Biology, Sigma XI. Democrat. Roman Catholic. Avocations: hiking, skiing, volleyball. Office: Walter Reed Army Med Ctr Dept Hematology Div Medicine Georgia Ave Washington DC 20307-5100

BEDNARZ, SUSAN CLARE, educational administrator; b. Omaha, Aug. 9, 1955; d. Michael Francis and Theresa Ann (Kosuth) B. EdB magna cum laude, U. Nebr., 1977, MS in Elem. Edn., 1982. Tchr. St. Peter and St. Paul Sch., Omaha, 1977-78, Miller Park Pub. Schs., Omaha, 1978-79, St. Bernadette Sch., Bellevue, Nebr., 1979-86, St. Columbkille Sch., Papillion, Nebr., 1986-88, St. Stanislaus Sch., 1988-89; dir. edn. Sylvan Learning Ctr., Omaha, 1989—; advisor Archdiocesan Kindergarten Tchrs., Omaha, 1987—. Mem. AAUW, Nat. Orgn. Edn. Young Children, Delta Kappa Gamma Soc., Young Adult Singles Club. Democrat. Roman Catholic. Home: 4507 S 34th St Omaha NE 68107

BEDSOLE, ANN SMITH, state senator; b. Selma, Ala., Jan. 7, 1930; d. Malcolm White and Sybil (Huey) Smith; m. Massey Palmer Bedsole, 1958; children: Mary Martin Bedsole Riser, John Henry Martin, Margaret Loraine. Student, U. Ala., 1948, U. Denver, 1955-56; LLD (hon.), Mobile Coll., 1984, Huntingdon Coll., 1985. Mem. Ala. Rep. Exec. Com., 1966-74; del. seconded nomination Nixon for Pres. Rep. Nat. Conv., 1972; Rep. Presdl. Elector, 1972; Ala. state senator, chair com. on agr., conservation and forestry, mem. coms. on edn., health, judiciary, mem. joint interim com. on mcpl. govt., mem. com. arts, tourism and cultural resources; mem. Nat. Conf. State Legislatures. V.p. Mobile Child Care Found.; trustee Huntington Coll., Mobile United, Dauphin Way United Meth. Ch., Hist. Blakeley Authority; active Mobile Hist. Devel. Found., Spring Hill Coll., Hist. Mobile Tours, Inc.; mem. Jr. League of Mobile; bd. dirs. Vol. Mobile, Inc. Recipient M.O. Beale Scroll of Merit award Mobile Press Register, 1971-72, award for outstanding contbn. to forestry in Ala. Soc. Am. Foresters, 1986, Legislative Conservationist of Yr. award Ala. Wildlife Fedn., 1987; named 1st Lady of Mobile, 1972. Mem. Ala. Bus. and Profl. Women's Found. (trustee, inducted into Women's Acad. of Honor 1987). Methodist. Office: PO Box 16642 Mobile AL 36616*

BEDSWORTH, O. DIANE, corporate executive; b. Detroit, Nov. 30, 1942; d. William H. and Olive Emily (Ludwig) Goodson; m. Gary J. Bedsworth, Apr. 4, 1964 (div. Feb. 1983); children: Jay William, Pamela Diane. Student, Mich. State U., 196-164. Interior designer Dayton-Hudson Corp., Mpls., 1973-85; pres. Bedsworth Design Internat., Blackhawk, Calif., 1985—; cons. San Souci Hotel, Taipei, Taiwan, 1980—, Hotel Group, Inc., 1982-83. Mktg. dir. Sta. KTCA-TV Pub. Auction, Mpls., 1979-83, chairwoman, 1983, 84. Mem. Am. Soc. Interior Designers (profl.). Republican. Episcopalian. Home: 387 S Eagle Nest Ln Blackhawk CA 94506 Office: Bedsworth Design Internat 4018 Blackhawk Pla Circle Blackhawk CA 94506

BEDWAY, MARIANN LOUISE, small business owner; b. Pottsville, Pa.; d. John Joseph and Mary Ann (Sahadi) B. AA, Pa. State U., Pottsville, 1960. Asst. buyer Woodward and Lothrop, Washington, 1961-67; hostess, guide U.S. Pavilion at Expo '67 U.S. Info. Agy., Montreal, Can., 1967; travel sales rep. Pan Am. Airlines, Washington, 1968-78; pres Internat. Elegance, Washington, 1978—; fashion cons., Washington, 1984—. Mem. NAFE, Am. Women's Econ. Devel., Japan Am. Soc., Assn. Image Cons. Internat. Roman Catholic. Home and Office: PO Box 32272 Washington DC 20007

BEEBE, DIANE MARIE, photographer, designer; b. Maywood, Ill., Mar. 31, 1961; d. Robert Wesley and Catherine Ann (Ewers) B. Degree, Visual Arts Inst. Photo specialist Bambergers, White Marsh, Md., 1979-81; photographer Hollywood Photo Studio, Balt., 1981-84; multi-line ins. agt. Met. Life Ins. Co., Towson, Md., 1984-88, assoc. mgr., 1988-89; photographer Segal Majestic Photography, Balt., 1989-90; designer, salesspecialist Ethan Allen Gallery, 1990—. Mem. Nat. Assn. Life Underwriters, NAFE. Democrat. Roman Catholic. Home: 6507 Brook Ave Baltimore MD 21206

BEECHLER, SYLVIA HART, volunteer; b. Bessemer, Ala., Sept. 20, 1926; d. Harry and Dora (Barr) Hart; divorced; children: Martin Hart, Jeanie Ellen Beechler Curley, Stuart Alan. Student, Beaver Coll., Jenkintown, Pa. Owner, mgr. Hart's Lingerie & Boutique, Cleve., 1953-72; exec. accts. rep. Travel Town, Inc., Cleve., 1983-84; dir. corp. accts. New Dimensions In Travel, Cleve., 1984-85; sales mgr. IVI Travel Inc., Cleve., 1985-87. Trustee N.E. Ohio Am. Heart Assn., 1969—, communications and mktg. com.; chmn. Heart Sunday Cuyahoga County, 1969; trustee Soc. for Crippled Children, 1971—, v.p., 1979-84, chmn. various coms., 1970—; trustee Great Lakes Shakespeare Festival, 1973-80, 2nd v.p., 1973, chmn. opening night gala, 1973; trustee USO, Cleve., 1987-90, co-chmn. Birthday Gala; active Cleve. Health Mus., 1987, Mid Town Corridor, 1984-86; trustee United Cerebral Palsy, Cleve., 1987-89, active various coms., 1987-89; bd. dirs. "Rainbow Guild" Amie Karen Cancer Fund for Children Cedars-Sinai Med. Ctr., L.A., 1989—; chair, mem. of com. Am. Heart Assn. N.W. Div. of Greater L.A., 1989—, Greater L.A. Affiliate. Republican. Jewish. Home: 25704 Emerson Ln Stevenson Ranch CA 91381

BEELER, BARBARA LOUISE, auditor; b. Sterling, Ill., Sept. 24, 1963; d. Horace Walter and June (Norem) B. AA, Cottey Coll., Nevada, Mo., 1984; BBA in Acctg., U. San Diego, 1987. CPA. Auditor trainee Def. Contract and Audit Agy., San Diego, 1987-88; auditor Def. Contract Audit Agy., San Diego, 1988—. Mem. Assn. Govt. Accts., Beta Alpha Psi, Beta Gamma Sigma. Republican. Presbyterian. Office: Gen Dynamics Corp PO Box 85357 San Diego CA 92138

BEEM, JANE ARLYNE, education educator; b. Forest City, Iowa, Aug. 6, 1934; d. Frank Stafford and Elsie Aurora (Anderson) Engels; m. Wendal Wayne Beem, Nov. 29, 1952; children: Gregory Wayne, Timothy Scott, Pamela Jane Gustafson, Angela Lynn Ashmore. BA, Carthage Coll., Kenosha, Wis., 1970; MA, Northwestern U., Evanston, Ill., 1977; postgrad., Nat. Coll. Edn., Evanston, Ill., 1986--. Sec. Zion State Bank, Ill., 1952-54; homemaker, 1954-70; eng. tchr. Warren Township High Sch., Gurnee, Ill., 1970-89; curriculum leader Warren Township high sch., Gurnee, Ill.; cons. Coll. Bd., Evanston, Ill., 1984—. Author: Article, 1984—; poetry, 1989. Mem. Nat. Coun. of Tchrs. English, Ill. Assn. Tchrs. English (conf. speaker 1985, 87, 88, planning com. Northlake div. 1986—), Assn. Supr. and Curriculum Devel. Republican.

BEENE, GERALDINE WALLIS, nursing educator; b. New Orleans, La., Feb. 18, 1931; d. Reginald Wallis and Hilda Marie (Domanque) Gissing; m. Wallace Dee Beene, Dec. 22, 1951; children: William, Lauren. BS, Chapman Coll., 1978; MPH, Calif. State U., Northridge, 1982; postgrad., UCLA, 1983-84. RN. Staff and supr. nurse various hosps., La., Ariz., 1951-73; project dir. Home Health Svcs. Tucson (Ariz.) Dept. Human Community Devel., 1973-75; pub. health nurse educator Kaiser Med. Ctr., L.A., 1976-81;

nursing educator Pacific Coast Coll., L.A., 1981-84; writer pvt. practice, Tucson, Ariz.; pub. rels. assoc. Beene Pub. Rels., Madrid, Spain, 1962-64, vol. English advisor Seijo U., Tokyo, 1965-66. Contbr. articles to profl. jours. Mem. ARC, Tucson, Ariz., Jet Lag Travel Club (coord. 1989-90), Opera League S. Ariz., Tucson (Ariz.) Symphony Womens Assn., Tucson Coun. Internat. Visitors. Named Top rated Home Health Community Nursing Project, Tucson(Ariz.) Dept. Human Community Devel., 1975. Mem. Soc. SW Authors, U. Ariz. Faculty Womens Club, U. So. Calif. Alumni Club., Pi Lambda Theta, Sigma Theta Tau. Home: 4730 E Apple Valley Dr Tucson AZ 85718

BEER, ALICE STEWART (MRS. JACK ENGEMAN), musician, educator; b. Redwood Falls, Minn., Sept. 29, 1912; d. Robert and Isabel (Montgomery) Stewart; m. Jack Engeman, Dec. 14, 1974; children by previous marriage: W. Robert, Jane K. Beer Mosher, Elizabeth S. Beer-Shilling. MusB, Northwestern U., 1934, MusM, 1952; postgrad., Johns Hopkins U., 1954, 60, Mexico City Coll., 1956, U. Md., 1957. Tchr. pub. schs., Lawton, Mich., 1934-39, Battle Creek, Mich., 1949-51; tchr. Balt. Pub. Schs., 1951-53, supr. music, 1953-77; tchr. summer sessions various colls. and univs., 1957-85; adj. faculty Peabody Inst., John's Hopkins U., Balt., 1981-85; cons. Alliance for Arts in Edn., Balt. County Pub. Schs., 1982—, cons. curriculum, 1984—. Author: Teaching Suggestions, Birchard Music Series II and III, 1962, Teaching Music: What, How and Why, 1973, Teaching Music to the Exceptional Child: A Handbook for Mainstreaming, 1980, Teaching Music, 1982, Patriotic Color Sound Filmstrips, 1967-69; contbr. articles to profl. jours. Mem. bd. lady mgrs. Balt. Street Clinic, 1986—. Recipient Director's Recognition award for commitment to music edn. and extraordinary contbn. to art of teaching, 1986; inductee Md. Music Educators Hall of Fame, 1989. Mem. Md. Hist. Soc., Balt. Mus. Art, Balt. Symphony Assn. Mem. Nat. Fedn. Press Women, Md. Fedn. Press Women, Nat. Conf. Music Educators, Md. Music Educators Assn., Pres.'s Club U. Md., Towson U. Club, Women's Club of Johns Hopkins U., Officers and Faculty Club of U.S. Naval Acad., Phi Beta. Democrat. Home: 611 Debaugh Ave Towson MD 21204 Office: Johns Hopkins U Peabody Inst Dept Music Edn Baltimore MD 21202

BEER, JEANETTE MARY AYRES, foreign language educator; b. Wellington, N.Z.; d. Alexander Samuel and Una Doreen (Castle) Scott; m. Colin Gordon Beer; children: Stephen James Colin, Jeremy Michael Alexander. B.A., Victoria U., N.Z., 1954, M.A. 1st class, 1955; B.A. 1st class, Oxford U., Eng., 1958, M.A., 1962; Ph.D. (fellow), Columbia U., 1967. Asst. lectr. French Victoria U., Wellington, 1956; lectrice French and English U. Montpellier, France, 1958-59; instr. French Otago U., Dunedin, N.Z., 1963-64, Barnard Coll., Columbia U., N.Y.C., 1966-68; asst. prof. French Fordham U., Bronx, N.Y., 1968-69, assoc. prof., 1969-76, prof., 1976-80; acting assoc. dean Thomas More Coll., 1972-73, dir. medieval studies, 1972-80; prof. French Purdue U., West Lafayette, Ind., 1980—; head dept. fgn. langs. and lits. Purdue U., 1980-83; mem. nat. bd. cons. NEH, 1977—, asst. dir. div. fellowships and seminars, 1983-84. Author: Villehardouin—Epic Historian, 1968, A Medieval Caesar, 1976, Narrative Conventions of Truth in the Middle Ages, 1981, Medieval Fables: Marie de France, 1981, Master Richard's Bestiary of Love and Response, 1985; editor: Medieval Translators and Their Craft; gen. editor: Teaching Language through Literature, 1971-88; contbr. articles to profl. jours. NEH grantee, 1975, rsch. fellow, 1980; summer fellow Ind. Com. for Humanities, 1985; Am. Philos. Soc. grantee, 1986, Am. Coun. Learned Socs. grantee, 1990. Mem. MLA, Medieval Acad., Internat. Arthurian Soc., Internat. Courtly Lit. Soc., Soc. Rencesvals, Am. Assn. Tchrs. French, Am. Philol. Assn. Anglican. Home: 256 W Hudson Ave Englewood NJ 07631

BEERBOWER, CYNTHIA GIBSON, lawyer; b. Dayton, Ohio, June 25, 1949; d. Charles Augustus and Sara (Rittenhouse) Gibson; m. John Edwin Beerbower, Aug. 28, 1971; 1 child, John Eliot. BA, Mt. Holyoke Coll., 1971; JD, Boston U., 1974; LLB, Cambridge U., Eng., 1976. Bar: N.Y. 1975. Assoc., Cadwalader, Wickersham & Taft, N.Y.C., 1975-76; assoc. Simpson, Thacher & Bartlett, N.Y.C., 1977-81, ptnr., 1981—. Mem. ABA, Assn. Bar City N.Y., N.Y. State Bar Assn. (com. co-chmn. 1987—). Presbyterian. Home: 720 Park Ave New York NY 10021 Office: Simpson Thacher & Bartlett 425 Lexington Ave New York NY 10017*

BEERE, CAROLE ANN, psychology educator; b. Chgo., June 16, 1944; d. Samuel Harry and Lucille Ruth (Wolf) Berger; m. Jeffrey David Austin, Dec. 26, 1964 (div. Sept. 1965); m. Donald Butler Beere, Sept. 1, 1968; children: Jonathan Blake, Jennifer Lee. BA, Mich. State U., 1966, MA, 1968, PhD, 1970. Researcher State of Mich. Dept. Edn., Lansing, 1969-70, rsch. coord., 1970-71; asst. prof. psychology Cen. Mich. U., Mt. Pleasant, 1971-74, assoc. prof. psychology, 1974-84, prof. psychology, 1984—, assoc. dean Sch. Grad. Studies, Office Rsch., 1990—. Author: Women & Women's Issues, 1979, Gender Roles, 1990, Sex & Gender Issues, 1990; cons. editor: Psychology of Women Quarterly, 1981-85. Leader Jr. Great Books, Mt. Pleasant Schs., 1983-87; pres. elem. sch. PTA, Mt. Pleasant, 1983-84; chairperson local day care ctr. bd., Mt. Pleasant, 1977-82; bd. dirs. local swim club, Mt. Pleasant, 1983-86. U.S. Office of Edn. fellow, 1966-69; Rockefeller Found. Rsch. grantee, 1988-89. Mem. Am. Psychol. Assn., Soc. for the Psychol. Study of Social Issues, Sierra. Home: 4472 S Crawford Rd Mount Pleasant MI 48858 Office: Cen Mich U Dept Psychology Mount Pleasant MI 48859

BEERS, CHARLOTTE L., advertising agency executive; b. Beaumont, Tex., July 26, 1935; d. Glen and Frances (Bolt) Rice; m. Donald C. Beers, 1971; 1 dau., Lisa. B.S. in Math. and Physics, Baylor U., Waco, Tex., 1958. Group product mgr. Uncle Ben's Inc., 1959-69; sr. v.p., dir. client services J. Walter Thompson, 1969-79; chief operating officer Tatham-Laird & Kudner, Chgo., from 1979, now mng. ptnr., chmn. and chief exec officer; dir. Federated Dept. Stores, Chgo. Public TV Channel 11. Named Nat. Advt. Woman of Yr. Am. Advt. Fedn., 1975. Mem. Am. Assn. Advt. Agencies (chmn. from 1987), Women's Advt. Club Chgo., Chgo. Network. Republican. Episcopalian. Office: Tatham-Laird & Kudner 980 N Michigan Ave Chicago IL 60611*

BEESON, DOROTHY PATTON, artist; b. Kansas City, Mo., Jan. 10, 1921; d. Wade Keedwell and Adelaide Hord (McBride) P.; m. Donald Russell, Dec. 4, 1943; children: Diane Kay, David RusselSl. BS in Bus. Fin., NW U., Evanston, Ill., 1943. Statistician, sec. U. Colo., Boulder, 1946-49; tchr. Boulder Pub. Schs., 1951-56; tres. Mustard Seed Gallery, Boulder, Colo., 1969-79; artist Self-Employed, Green Valley, Ariz.;, -; Bd. Trustees Boulder Com. Unity Hosp. 1962-71; Organizer, Dir. Boulder Art Assn. 1970; Treas. Mustard Seed Gallery Boulder 1969-79; Bd. Dirs. Sno-Bird Gallery Green Valley 1981-83. Artist Paintings (honorable mention 1988, award of excellence 1988). Sec. Sonora Desert Br. Nat. Assn. Am. Pen Women Green Valley 1988-89. Recipient Vol. ofS the year award Boulder Com. Hosp. 1981, Am. Red Cross 1978. Mem. Nat. Assn. Am. Rec. Sec. Local Br. Pen Women, Ariz. Watercolor Assn. Republican. Methodist.

BEESON, MONTEL EILEEN, human services administrator, gerontologist; b. El Dorado, Ark., Dec. 22, 1939; d. Waymon Willett and Myrtle May (Roach) B. BS in Recreation, Calif. State U., Hayward, 1963; MA in Edn. and Human Devel., Holy Names Coll., Oakland, Calif., 1979. Lic. nursing home adminstr.; cert. community coll. instr.; cert. gerontologist. Dist. exec. Ariz. Cactus-Pine council Girl Scouts U.S.A., Phoenix, 1963-66; dist. exec. San Francisco Bay council Girl Scouts U.S.A., Oakland, 1966-68, bus. mgr., 1968-71; exec. dir. Shabonee council Girl Scouts U.S.A., Moline, Ill., 1971-73, Tongass-Alaska council, Ketchikan, 1973-74, Muir Trail council, Modesto, Calif., 1974-78, Community Adult Day Health Services, Oakland, 1987-88; asst. adminstr. Beulah Home, Inc., Oakland, 1980-86, elder care cons. 1986—; adminstr. Greenhills Retirement Ctr. Millbrae, Calif., 1988—; preceptor Bd. Examiners Nursing Home Adminstrs., Sacramento, 1985. Mem. Am. Coll. Health Care Adminstrs., Am. Soc. on Aging. Avocations: cross-country skiing, history, travel, reading, music. Home: 3393 Kiwanis St Oakland CA 94602

BEFOURE, JEANNINE MARIE, writer, accounting and business consultant; b. N.Y.C., Aug. 6, 1923; d. Thomas James and Frances Marie (Thompson) Nicholson; m. Willard Rockne, Oct., 1940 (div. 1946); children—Rodger Lloyd, Lenore Irene; m. Jean Maure Befoure, Aug. 3, 1974. BS in Communications magna cum laude, Woodbury U., 1979, MBA, 1981. Audit clk. Sears Roebuck, Seattle, 1946-50; supr. materials USN, Guam, 1951-52; pvt. practice accounting Nev., Calif. ans Ariz., 1953-68; chief oper. officer, chief exec. officer Yearound Bus. Svcs., Las Vegas, 1969-73; writer, cons. The JM People, San Gabriel, Calif., 1982—; instr. bus. and indsl. mgmt. Calif. Community Colls., 1979-82; mem. IRS/Tax Practioner Bd., Las Vegas, 1972-73; tutor Lauback Lit. Action, L.A., 1981—; researcher adult edn. methods for bus., 1954—. TV producer Channel 20, El Monte, Calif., TV access producer Channel 3, El Monte, 1987—, researcher mgmt. tng. methods, 1988—; author children's stories and poetry, bus. articles. Trainer Kellogg Found.-United Way, L.A., 1988—. Founding sec. Home-owners of Golden Valley, Ariz., 1961. Mem. NAFE, World Future Soc., Assn. MBA Execs., Greater L.A. Press Club, Phi Gamma Kappa. Republican.

BEGG, KATHLEEN MIKEL, insurance company executive; b. Phoenix. BA in Polit. Sci., Edinboro U., 1977. Casualty supr. Aetna Casualty and Surety Co., Pitts., 1978-87; sr. account exec. Home Ins., Pitts., 1987—. Mem. NAFE, NOW, Greenpeace. Office: Home Ins Co Ten Parkway Ctr 875 Greentree Rd Pittsburgh PA 15220

BEGLEY, KATHLEEN A, writer, publicist; b. Phila., Mar. 28, 1948; d. Thomas and Kathleen (Harvey) B. BA in English, Temple U., 1970; MA in Polit. Sci., Villanova U., 1974. Reporter Del. County Daily Times, 1966-70, Camden (N.J.) Courier Post, 1970-71, Phila. Inquirer, 1971-76, Chgo. Daily News, 1977-78; producer WITF-TV, Hershey, Pa., 1979; pres. Bear Group Inc., Tampa, Fla., 1980-82; writer, editor Seattle Times, 1983-87; prin. The Write Co., Wilmington, Del., 1988—; mktg., communications cons. DuPont Co., Addictions Coalition Del., Recovery Ctr. Del., Del. Drinking Driver Program, Del. Coun. on Gambling Problems, Del. Div. Alcoholism Drub Abuse and Mental Health, Del. Assn. for Children. of Alcoholics, Del. Assn. Alcoholism and Drug Abuse Counselors. Author: Deadline, 1977; contbr. articles to newspapers and mags. Recipient 1st State award for writing Internat. Assn. Bus. Communication, 1990. Mem. Pub. Relations Soc. Am., Del.Media Assn. Home: 1401 Pennsylvania St Apt 1602 Wilmington DE 19806

BEGUIN, NANCY ELLYN, nurse; b. Luana, Iowa, Oct. 16, 1943; d. John and Hellen (Miller) Doerring; (div.); children: E. Allen, J. Erik. Diploma in nursing, Coe Coll., 1963; BS in Health Edn., U. Wis., 1983. RN, Wis., Iowa, Mo., Ill. Staff nurse pvt. medicine Barnes Hosp. Complex, St. Louis, 1966-68; med. and surg. staff nurse Rockford (Ill.) Meml. Hosp., 1965-66; staff nurse ICU Univ. Hosps., Madison, Wis., 1964-65; dir. Wis. nutrition project LaCrosse (Wis.) County Buddy Support, 1983-84; charge nurse Onalaska (Wis.) Care Ctr., 1984; clin. nurse III same day surgery LaCrosse Luth. Hosp., 1985—. Publicity coord. Onalaska High Sch. Show Choir, 1986-87; publicity chmn. LaCrosse Boychoir, 1980-84, choir mgr. 1982-83. Mem. LaCrosse County Med. Aux. (chmn. legis. program com. 1988-89), AAUW, Fauver Hill Study Club. Office: Luth Hosp LaCrosse WI 54601

BEHAR, DIANE SUSAN, marketing professional, consultant; b. N.Y.C., May 17, 1952; d. Solomon and Frieda Marie (Greenberger) B. Spanish language cert., La Universidad Internacional, 1969; BA, Cornell U., 1974; MBA, U. Pa., 1983. Legis. analyst Com. on the Budget U.S. Ho. of Reps., Washington, 1975-77, legis. asst. and speechwriter Office of Congressman Oberstar, 1977-81; account exec. Doyle Dane Advt., N.Y.C., 1983-85; dir. of pub. affairs and speechwriter Mayor's Offfice of Bus. Devel., N.Y.C., 1985-88, dir. of mktg., 1988—; mktg. cons. Clamer Internat., N.Y.C., 1985—, Work Late/Eat Right Gourmet Food Delivery Svcs., N.Y.C., 1985-87; lectr. in field. Contbr. articles to profl. jours. Coun. mem., fundraiser Fresh Air Fund, 1987—; bd. dirs., fundraiser Pentacle Danceworks, 1984—. Nat. Endowment for the Arts fellow, 1983, Dupont fellow, 1981-83, Morgenthau fellow, 1981-83. Mem. Am. Mgmt. Assn., Am. Mktg. Assn., Cornell Club, Musician's Soc. of N.Y. Home: 201 E 69th St Apt 14I New York NY 10021 Office: NYC Office of Bus Devel 17 John St 11 Fl New York NY 10038

BEHLING, DOROTHY CLARA, fashion professional; b. Scotia, N.Y., May 25, 1930; d. Paul Carl and Evelyn Elizabeth (Blinsinger) Bazar. m. William Herman Behling, May 21, 1949; children: Gary Paul, Bruce William, Corrine Elizabeth. Student profl. modeling, Roemary Bischoff Studios, Milw., 1965. Cert. modeling instr., Wis. Payroll mgr. Sears, Roebuck & Co., Schenectady, N.Y., 1947-49; sec., treas. Maple Grove Oil Co., West Allis, Wis., 1957-70; staff instr. Rosemary Bischoff Studios, 1966-81, profl. model, 1966-85; staff model Boston Stores, Milw., 1967-68, Gimbel Stores, Milw., 1968-69; instr. Alyce Stoney Modeling Sch., Milw., 1969-70; free-lance fashion profl. Mequon, Wis., 1985—; cons. Max Factor, 1970; fashion model, cons. Alston Stores, Cedarburg, Wis., 1980—. Treas., PTA, Hales Corners, Wis., 1957-58; leader Hales Corners Boy Scouts Am., 1962-63; chmn. Hales Corners coun. Girl Scouts U.S., 1967-68; mem., coord. Milw. Soc. Models for United Assn. for Retarded Citizens, 1972-76; mem. Ozaukee (Wis.) Humane Soc. Pet Therapy Program, 1986-87. Mem. Bus. and Profl. Women' Assn., River Oaks Assn. (sec. 1976). Republican. Roman Catholic. Club: Christian Women Orgn. Home: 10635 N Ivy Ct Mequon WI 53092 also: 154 Palm Dr Naples FL 33962

BEHM, CYNTHIA JOAN, controller; b. Kaukauna, Wis., July 12, 1962; d. John R. and Joann B. (Faust) Mau; m. Steven L. Behm, Oct. 22, 1988. BA, St. Norbert Coll., DePere, Wis., 1983. Acct. Gillett Broadcasting, Inc., Nashville, Wis., 1984-86; acctg. mgr. Maggie Springer & Assoc., Inc., Appleton, Wis., 1986-87; acctg. and data processing mgr. Berlin (Wis.) Hosp. Assn., 1987-88, controller, 1988—. Mem. Healthcare Fin. Mgmt. Assn., Berlin Hosp. Aux. Republican. Roman Catholic. Home: 1165 W Southpark Ave Oshkosh WI 54904 Office: Berlin Hosp Assn 225 Memorial Dr Berlin WI 54923

BEHMER, ELSIE ANN, advertising agency executive; b. Plainfield, N.J., Sept. 30, 1943; d. John Henry and Elsie M. (Dietz) B. Student, Cedar Crest Coll., Allentown, Pa., 1961-63; BA, U. Bridgeport, 1965; MA, Syracuse U., 1966; MBA, U. Pa., 1978. Reporter Long Branch (N.J.) Daily Record, 1967; assoc. editor McGraw-Hill, N.Y.C., 1968-70; mgr. pub. rels. Paillard Inc., Linden, N.J., 1970-74, Merck & Co. Inc., Rahway, N.J., 1974-77; dir. communications Nat. Ry. Utilization Corp., Phila., 1978-80, McNeil Consumer Products, Ft. Washington, Pa., 1980-89; pres. Glick & Lorwin/RSH&S, N.Y.C., 1989—. Pres., bd. dirs. Alice Paul Centennial Found., 1985—; bd. dirs. Moorefield Owners Assn., Moorestown, N.J., 1981-89, Samaritan Hosp., Moorestown, 1986-89, Interfaith Care Givers, Moorestown, 1986-89. Mem. Pub. Rels. Soc. Am. (Silver Anvil award 1983). Lutheran. Office: Glick & Lorwin/RSH&S 111 5th Ave 7th Fl New York NY 10003

BEHNER, JANICE ROSE, real estate broker; b. Phoenix, May 20, 1938; d. Jefferson Robert and Oveita (Lawrence) Moore; m. Harvey Lee Acridge, June 8, 1956 (div. Dec. 1968); children—Sharma L., Lainee A., Scott Michael; m. 2d, Richard Leo Behner, Oct. 27, 1973. Student Ariz. State U., 1961-62. Lic. real estate broker; cert. residential specialist. and cert. real estate brokerage mgr. Salesman Goebel Realty, Phoenix, 1969-71, Apollo Enterprises, Glendale, Ariz., 1971-73; pres. Metro Realty, Inc., Phoenix, 1974-78; broker Century 21 Metro, Phoenix, 1973-78; co-founder 50 States Real Estate franchise (doing bus. as Behner and Assocs. Realtors), Phoenix, 1978, broker 1978-83 sec., treas., 1978-87, pres. 1987—, dir., 1978—; co-owner Metro Movers, Phoenix; cons. curriculum com. Glendale (Ariz.) Community Coll., 1978—. Mem. Valley Cathedral, Phoenix, 1969—, Phoenix Bd. Realtors Grievance com., 1985-87. Mem. Women's Council Realtors (pres. 1983-84). Republican. Office: Behner and Assocs Realtors 3504 W Peoria Ave Phoenix AZ 85029-4026

BEHNKE, MARYLOU, neonatologist, educator; b. Orlando, Fla., Sept. 1, 1950; d. Ernest Edmund and Elizabeth (Kolb) B. BS in Chemistry, U. Fla., 1972, MD, 1976. Diplomate Am. Bd. Pediatrics, Am. Bd. Neonatology-Perinatology. Intern dept. pediatrics Coll. Medicine, U. Fla., Gainesville, 1976-77, resident, 1977-79, chief resident, 1979-80, fellow in neonatology, 1981-83, asst. prof., 1979-81, 83-89, assoc. prof., 1989—; adj. asst. prof. Coll. Nursing, Gainesville, 1988-89, adj. assoc. prof., 1989—, mem. senate-at-large, 1984—, mem. grad. studies faculty, 1988—; med. dir. neonatology ICU Shands Hosp., Gainsville, 1983-89, neonatal developmental follow-up program, 1989—; presenter at nat. and internat. meetings, 1981—. Mem. editorial bd. Death Studies, 1983—; contbr. articles to med. jours., chpts. to books. NIH grantee, 1984-87. Fellow Am. Acad. Pediatrics; mem. Fla. Med. Assn., Alachua County Med. Soc., Nat. Perinatal Assn., So. Soc. for Pediatric Rsch., Fla. Soc. Neonatal Perinatologists. Republican. Mem. Ch. of Christ. Home: 426 SW 40th St Gainsville FL 32607 Office: J Hillis Miller Health Ctr Dept Pediatrics Box J-296 Gainesville FL 32610

BEHR, MELISSA JOAN, veterinary pathologist; b. Portland, Oreg., July 24, 1954; d. Peter Goodloe and Marjorie Anne (Kline) B.; m. Byron Dale Dieterle, Sept. 17, 1984; 1 child, John. BA, Smith Coll., Northampton, Mass., 1975; DVM, Cornell U., 1979. Diplomate Am. Coll. Vet. Pathologists. Veterinarian Honeoye Falls (N.Y.) Vet. Hosp., 1979-80; instr. anatomy N.Y. State Coll. Vet. Medicine, Cornell U., Ithaca, N.Y., 1980-81, intern pathology, 1981-82; postdoctoral in pathology Inhalation Toxicology Rsch. Inst., Albuquerque, 1982-84; resident pathology U. Calif., Davis, 1984-86; lab. animal veterinarian Los Alamos (N.Mex.) Nat. Lab., 1986—; vet. pathologist N.Mex. Vet. Diagnostic Svcs., Albuquerque, 1986—; cons. Los Alamos (N.Mex.) Nat. Lab., Inc. Div., 1986—. Contbr. articles to profl. jours. Judge N.Mex. Sci. Fair, Socorro, 1988. Nat. Cancer Inst. grantee, 1981. Mem. Am. Vet. Med. Assn., Am. Assn. Bovine Practitioners, Am. Asns. Lab. Animal Sci., Am. Asns. Vet. Lab. Diagnosticians, Sigma Xi. Home and Office: 39 Darby Dr Sandia Park NM 87047

BEHREND, RONA ANN, chemist; b. Phillipsburg, N.J., Apr. 14, 1959; d. Walter and Dorothea (Rinak) B. BS in Chemistry, Cedar Crest Coll., 1981. Rsch. and devel. chem. lab. technician Pfizer, Inc., Easton, Pa., 1982-85; rsch. asst. Resource Recovery Systems, Inc., Easton, 1985-86; electron device processor Eagle Svcs. Corp. for AT&T, Piscataway, N.J., 1986; rsch. and devel. tech. Union Carbide Corp., Somerset, N.J., 1986-88; quality control/quality assurance chemist Union Carbide Corp., Bound Brook, N.J., 1988-89, Seadrift, Tex., 1989—. Recipient Freshman Chemistry Achievement award Chem. Rubber Co., 1978. Mem. Beta Beta Beta (pres. Theta Psi chpt.).

BEHRENDS, CYNTHIA JOAN, trust company accounting; b. Watseka, Ill., Apr. 21, 1961; d. Herman Adolph and Shirley Ione (Colebank) Saathoff; m. Glenn Arthur Behrends, Aug. 8, 1987; children: Jeremy Eden, Brian Eden. AS, Kankakee Community Coll., Kankakee, 1984; student, Ill. State U., 1988. Computer operator Gen. Foods, Kankakee, 1984-86; acctg. coord. Barney's Service & Supply, Gilman, Ill., 1987—; trust adminstr. IAA Trust Co., Bloomington, Ill.; computer programmer Gaines Foods, Kankakee, 1984—. Softball player IAARA Bloomington, Ill., 1988; asst. coach Prairie City Soccer League Normal, Ill., 1989; baseball coach Am. Legion, Bloomington, 1990; active Colene Hoose Elem. Sch. PTO. Mem. Kankakee Community Coll. Alumni Assn. Republic. Lutheran. Office: IAA Trust Co 1701 Towanda Ave Bloomington IL 61701

BEHRENS, BEREL LYN, physician, academic dean; b. New South Wales, Australia, 1940. MB, BS, Sydney (Australia) U., 1964. Cert. pediatrics, allergy and immunology. Intern Roayl Prince Alfred Hosp., Australia, 1964; resident Loma Linda U. Med. Ctr., 1966-68; with Henrietta Egleston Hosp. for Children, 1968-69, T.C. Thompson Children's Hosp., 1969-70; instr. pediatrics Loma Linda U., 1970-72, with dept. pediatrics, 1972—, dean Sch. Medicine, 1986—. Office: Loma Linda U Sch of Medicine Office of the Dean Loma Linda CA 92350

BEHRMANN, JOAN METZNER, newspaper editor; b. N.Y.C.; d. Jerome and Jeannette (Silberman) Metzner; m. Larry Jinks, Oct. 2, 1960 (div. 1970); children: Laura Beth, Daniel Carlton; m. Nicolas Lee Behrmann, Dec. 21, 1972. BA, Queens Coll., 1956; MS, Columbia U., 1958. Reporter Miami (Fla.) Herald, 1960-63; asst. prof. Miami-Dade Community Coll., 1968-72; lifestyle editor Middlesex News, Framingham, Mass., 1973-75; assoc. prof. Boston U., 1975-78; Sunday editor The Saratogian, Saratoga Springs, N.Y., 1978-80; mng. editor, city editor Westchester-Rockland Newspapers, White Plains, N.Y., 1980-82; page one editor USA Today, Arlington, Va., 1982-84, entertainment editor, 1984-87; exec. editor The Desert Sun, Palm Springs, Calif., 1987—. Co-author: Questioning Media Ethics, 1978. Founding mem. Every Woman's Coun., Glens Falls, N.Y., 1978-80; rec. sec., Palm Springs Opera Guild, 1990—. Mem. AP Mging. Editors Assn. (com. chmn. 1989-90), Am. Soc. Newspaper Editors, Women in Communications. Home: 785 High Rd Palm Springs CA 92262 Office: The Desert Sun 750 N Gene Autry Tr Palm Springs CA 92262

BEICKEL, SHARON LYNNE, psychologist; b. Hanford, Calif., Mar. 1, 1943; d. William Wayne and Kathleen (Haun) B.; m. Wilbur Oran Hutton, Aug. 8, 1964 (div. Aug. 1974). BS, Ea. Oreg. State U., 1965; MS, U. Oreg., 1970, PhD, 1977. Lic. psychologist, Oreg., Ariz. With U. Oreg., Eugene, 1966-78, dir. Debusk counseling ctr., 1976-77, intern in psychology, 1977-78; psychologist Ariz. State U., Tempe, 1978-84; pvt. practice Tempe, 1978-84; psychologist Beickel and Assocs., Eugene, 1984—; clin. dir. Aslan House Counseling Ctr., Eugene, 1985-86; cons. Vocat. Rehab., Eugene, 1986—. Mem. Am. Psychol. Assn., Oreg. Psychol. Assn. (chair profl. affairs 1989—), Lane County Psychol. Assn. (sec., treas. 1986-87), Western Psychol. Assn., Ariz. Psychol. Assn., Vocat. Rehab. or Psychology Assn. (con. Eugene chpt. 1986—, chair profl. affairs com. Portland, Oreg. chpt. 1988—, chair practice div. 1987-88, bd. dirs. 1986-87), Zonta. Home: 1678 Orchard St Eugene OR 97403 Office: Beickel & Assocs 1244 Wlanut Ste E Eugene OR 97403

BEIER, B. J., developer, director; b. Ripon, Wis., July 10, 1956; d. Herman Christian and Lucille (Malzhan) Beier; m. Thomas Frederick Wilkes, Oct. 4, 1975 (div. Oct. 1979); m. Randy Lynn Liptow, Apr. 20, 1985 (div. Sert. 1989). Cert. in real estate, Moriane Park Tech. Bookkeeper Fred Wilkes Excavating, Ripon, 1974-88; salesperson Ripon Modular Homes, 1974-88; owner Custom Housing of Distinction, Ripon, 1988—; bd. dirs. Diggers and Contractors Wis. Power & Light Co., Ripon, 1984—. Mem. NAFE, C. of C. (ambassdor com.), Kiwanis. Democrat. Lutheran. Home: RR 2 Ridgeview Estates Ripon WI 54971 Office: Custom Housing Distinction Aspen St Ripon WI 54971

BEIGHTS, NANCY CRAIK, educator; b. Ann Arbor, Mich., Feb. 2, 1951; d. Roy Alton and Grace Ann (Bosker) Craik; m. Stephen Robert Beights, June 7, 1946; children: Andrew Stephen, Eric Richard. BS, U. Mich., 1972; MS, Purdue U., 1976. Tchr. sci./math. S.W. Allen County Schs., Fort Wayne, Ind., 1972-83; tchr. math. Collier County Pub. Schs., Naples, Fla., 1985—; pvt. math tutor; pvt. study skills counsellor. Sun. sch. asst. Marco Luth. Ch., Marco Island, Fla., 1985—. Mem. AAUW (study group coordinator 1984—), Collier County Edn. Assn. Republican. Lutheran. Office: Lely High Sch 324 Lely Blvd Naples FL 33962

BEILBY, MARGARET GLENN, technical writer; b. Bakersfield, Calif., Nov. 5, 1949; d. Reuben Hartsel and Ivy Lorena (Blakemore) Fraley; m. Theodore Lee Beilby, Feb. 26, 1969 (div. 1976); 1 child, Christopher. Student, Coll. of Ozarks, 1967-69; BA, Calif. State U., Bakersfield, 1977, MA, 1980. Sec., regional adminstr. Cincom Systems, San Francisco, 1979-82; tech. writer, project leader Cincom Systems, Irvine, Calif., 1982-83; sr. tech. writer, supr. Peregrine Systems, Inc., Irvine, 1983-85; sr. tech. writer FileNet Corp., Costa Mesa, Calif., 1985—; AIDS educator Women's Am. ORT, Huntington Beach, Calif., 1988, Orange County Bd. Jewish Edn., Calif., 1989-90, United Meth. Women, Shafter, Calif., 1989, United Synagogue Youth, Newport Beach, Calif., 1989, Harbor Bd. Rabbis and Synagogue Profls., Long Beach, Calif., 1990. Author: Chaucer's Women: Free to Be Submissive, 1980, Field Secretary's Handbook and Training Manual, 1981, Logical User View COBOL Programmer's Guide, 1982, Logical Usaer View Pl/I Programmer's Guide, 1982, PNMS II Overview, 1983, Peregrine Four: A New Approach to Applications Development, 1984, and numerous others; composer, lyricist: Remembrance, 1990, Light These Candles, 1988, Ease My Mind, 1987, Gathered Together, 1984, Baby Bear's Lullaby, 1983, Remember Me, 1983, and several others. Foster mother Animal Assistance League, Santa Ana, Calif., 1985-87; chmn. Long Beahc Jewish AIDS Task Force, 1988—; AIDS buddy Laguna Shanti, Laguna Beach, Calif., 1987, massage buddy, 1988—, newsletter editor, 1988-89; AIDS educator Nechama, L.A., 1988—; active AIDS Interfaith Coun., L.A., 1989—, Union Am. Hebrew Congregations Regional AIDS Com., L.A., 1989—, Long Beach AIDS Network, 1988—; AIDS educator, outreach team leader AIDS Walk Long Beach, 1989—; blood donor ARC, Tustin, Calif. Named Vol. of Yr. Temple Israel, 1989; recipient Community Vol. award Laguna Shanti, 1989. Mem. World Union for Progressive Judaism, Assn. Reform Zionists in Am., Nat. Coun. Jewish Women, Royale Touring (editor 1987-88). Democrat.

BEILING-SHEERER, CHRISTINE LYNN, optometrist; b. Pontiac, Mich., May 22, 1963; d. Charles Leroy and Sandra Sue (Cobourn) Beiling; m. Timothy Alan Sheerer, Jan. 14, 1963; 1 child, Elsa Caroline. OD cum laude, Ohio State U. Coll. Optometry, 1987. Pvt. practice Medine (Ohio) Vision Ctr., 1990—. Vol. local elem. schs.; speaker to local groups, 1987-90. Mem. Am. Optometric Assn., Ohio Optometric Assn., Northeast Ohio Vision Assocs., Coll. Optometrists in Vision Devel. Office: Medina Vision Ctr 215 S Court St Medina OH 44256

BEINECKE, CANDACE KRUGMAN, lawyer; b. Paterson, N.J., Nov. 26, 1946; d. Martin and Sylvia (Altshuler) Krugman; m. Frederick W. Beinecke II, Oct. 2, 1976; children: Jacob Sperry, Benjamin Barrett. BA, NYU, 1967; JD, Rutgers U., 1970. Bar: N.Y. 1971. Assoc., then ptnr. Hughes, Hubbard & Reed, N.Y.C., 1970—; bd. dirs. Laporte Inc.; lectr., chmn. Practising Law Inst., N.Y.C. Bd. dirs. Merce Cunningham Found., N.Y.C., Jacob's Pillow Dance Festival, Lee, Mass., Trinity Episcopal Sch. Corp., N.Y.C., Hist. Preservation Projects, Inc. Mem. ABA, N.Y. State Bar Assn., Assn. Bar City N.Y., River Club, Women's Forum. Office: Hughes Hubbard & Reed 33 Battery Park Pla New York NY 10004

BEISEIGEL, SHIRLEY-ANN, psychologist; b. Allentown, Pa., May 27, 1927; d. John Calvin and Dorothy Irene (Bear) Shumberger. C.A.G.S. in Psychology and Counseling, Assumption Coll., 1982; A.B. in Biology, Bucknell U., 1949; M.S. in Rehab. Counseling, Va. Commonwealth U., 1969. Cert. psychol. svcs. supr., Pa.; nat. cert. rehab. counselor; m. Howard Alan Beiseigel, June 18, 1949; children: Robert Alan, Barry John, John Howard. Supervisory guidance counselor Woodrow Wilson Rehab. Ctr., Fishersville, Va., 1963-64; spl. edn. tchr. Lansing (Mich.) Pub. Schs., 1964; asst. home life dir. VFW Nat. Home, Eaton Rapids, Mich., 1964-66; exec. dir. Easter Seal Soc. of Ingham County, Lansing, Mich., 1966; profl. rehab. counselor Woodrow Wilson Rehab. Ctr., Fishersville, 1966-70, supr. counselors evaluation dept., 1970-71; counselor II, N.H. State Prison, Concord, 1971-72; vocat. evaluation coord. Vocat. Devel. Ctr., Manchester, N.H., 1972-77; supr. psychodiagnostic and vocat. evaluation svcs. Good Shepherd Home and Rehab. Hosp., Allentown, Pa., 1977-79, dir. psychol. svcs., 1978—, dir. chronic pain mgmt. program, 1979-88. Mem. N.H. bd. dirs. Pres.'s Com. on Employment of Handicapped, 1975-76. Mem. Am. Psychol. Assn., Pa. Psychol. Assn., Nat. Rehab. Assn., Nat. Rehab. Counseling Assn. (charter), Pa. Rehab. Assn., N.H. Rehab. Assn. (bd. dir. 1973-76), N.H. Rehab. Counseling Assn. (past pres. 1975-76), Va. Rehab. Counseling Assn. (dir. 1967-70), Va. Rehab. Assn. (membership chmn. 1968-69), Phi Mu. Republican. Presbyterian. Club: Order of Eastern Star (matron 1961-62). Home: 438 W Locust Ln Nazareth PA 18064 Office: Fifth and St John Sts Allentown PA 18103

BEISER, HELEN RUTH, psychiatrist; b. Chgo., Nov. 15, 1914; d. Arthur Jean and Agnes Emily (Hamer) B. BSE, U. Ariz., 1935; MS, MD, U. Ill., 1941. Diplomate Am. Bd. Neurology and Psychiatry. Staff psychiatrist Inst. for Juvenile Rsch., Chgo., 1951-53, tng. dir., 1954-57; med. dir. North Shore Mental Health Clinic, Chgo., 1953-54; with Inst. for Psychoanalysis, Chgo., 1954—; tng. and supervising analyst Inst. for Psychoanalysis, Highland Park, 1965—, chair child analysis tng., 1967-77, ret., 1989; freelance cons. Chgo., 1950-89; cons. Barr-Harris Clinic on Parent Loss, Inst. for Psychoanalysis, Chgo., 1975—; cons. psychiatrist Blue Cross/Blue Shield, Chgo., 1984—. Contbr. articles to profl. jours. Pres. bd. West Side Inst. Religion and Medicine, Chgo., 1960-82; hon. bd. dirs. Altenheim German Old Peoples Home, Forest Park, Ill., 1960-82; elder Fourth Presbyn. Ch., Chgo., 1972-89; mem. Med. Disciplinary Bd. of Ill., Chgo. and Springfield, 1979-84. Fellow Am. Psychiat. Assn., Am. Acad. Child and Adolescent Psychiatry (pres. 1983-85), Am. Psychoanalytic Assn.; mem. AMA (del. 1987-88), Ill. Psychiat. Assn. (councilor 1974-76), Chgo. Analytic Soc. (peer review panel 1968-76), Phi Kappa Phi, Alpha Omega Alpha.

BEISPIEL, HARRIETTE JUDITH, personnel assistant; b. N.Y., Nov. 19, 1934; d. David and Clara (Tucker) Greenstein; m. Myron, Sept. 19, 1954; children: Maura, Jay, Amy. BA in Social Sci., Edison State Coll., Trenton, 1985. Adult edn. tchr. Keyport High Sch. Adult Edn., Keyport, N.J., 1976-- ; clk., typist Dept. of Def. Procurement Div., Ft. Monmouth, N.J., 1978-79; procurement clk. Dept. of Defense Procurement, Ft. Monmouth, N.J., 1979-80; sec. Info. Mgmt. div. Dept. Def., Ft. Monmouth, N.J., 1980-82, sec. Avionics div., 1982-83; asst. adminstrv. officer, program mgr. Test Meas Diagn. Equipment, Fort Monmouth, 1983-88; personnel asst. Dept. Def. Personnel & Tng., Ft. Monmouth, 1988—; pres. Federally Employed Women Chpt. 2, Ft. Monmouth, 1988-90. Recipient Community award B'nai B'rith, 1974-77, Letter of Appreciation Col. Lynn, Dep. Comdr., Ft. Monmouth, 1980. Mem. Federally Employed Women Ch 2 (v.p.), Fed. Personnel Assn., Am. Assn. of U. Women, Internat. Personnel Assn. of N.J. Women, Fed. Women's Program, Women's Am. ORT, B'nai B'rith, Bus. & Profl. Women, Nat. Council Jewish Women, Meals on Wheels. Home: 11 Gayle St Middletown NJ 07748 Office: Dept of Def HQ CECOM Pers & Tng Direct Fort Monmouth NJ 07703

BEISSER, JUDITH KAY, city official; b. Sheboygan, Wis., May 31, 1946; d. Frederick Theodore and Edith Hulda (Hoffmann) B.; m. Robert Wesley Nack, Sept. 9, 1967 (div. Dec. 1975); m. Gerald Pollo Peppler, May 15, 1983. Student, U. Chgo., 1964-66; BA, U. Wis., 1968; MA, Loyola U., Chgo., 1981. Cert. pub. housing mgr. Pub. aid caseworker Ill. Dept. Pub. Aid, Springfield, 1969-70; social worker Ill. Dept. Children and Family Svcs., Chgo., 1970-77; juvenile justice specialist Ill. Law Enforcement Commn., Chgo., 1977-80; energy specialist U.S. Dept. Health and Human Svcs., Chgo., 1981-82; sect. 8 program mgr. Chgo. Housing Authority, 1983-88, dep. dir. sect. 8 housing programs, 1988—. Author, editor Lutherans Concerned-Chgo., 1983-86. Vice chmn. St. Gregory of Nyssa Luth. Ch., Chgo., 1980-82, chmn., 1982-84; v.p. Austin Schock Neighborhood Assn., Chgo., 1984-85. Mem. Nat. Assn. Housing and Redevel. Ofcls. Office: Chgo Housing Authority 22 W Madison St Rm 235 Chicago IL 60602

BEISWINGER, VIRGINIA GRAVES, educator; b. Algood, Tenn., July 9, 1928; d. James Wallace and Anna Virginia (Swackhammer) Graves; m. George Lawrence Beiswinger, Dec. 24, 1950; children: Gail Anne Beiswinger Rexon, George William. BS, U. Mo., 1950; MA, Washington U., St. Louis, 1954; postgrad., Immaculata (Pa.) Coll., 1982. Tchr. John Burroughs Sch., Clayton, Mo., 1950, Maplewood (Mo.)-Richmond Heights Schs., 1950-52, St. Louis Pub. Schs., 1952-59, Birmingham (Mich.) Pub. Schs., 1966-67; tchr. chemistry Conestoga Sr. High Sch., Berwyn, Pa., 1967—. mem. adv. bd. Tredyffrin-Easttown Tchrs. Ctr., 1990—. Mem. NEA, ASCD, Pa. Edn. Assn., Pa. Assn. for Supervision and Curriculum Devel., Tredyffrin-Easttown Edn. Assn. Republican. Episcopalian. Home: 29 Oak Knoll Dr Berwyn PA 19312 Office: Conestoga Sr High Sch Conestoga and Irish Rds Berwyn PA 19312

BEITINS, INESE ZINTA, pediatric endocrinologist, educator; b. Riga, Latvia, Oct. 24, 1937; came to U.S., 1962; d. Reinholds and Anna Aina (Jermlilis) B.; children: Marks, Reinis. MD, U. Toronto, 1962. Intern Toronto Western Hosp., 1962-63; resident Hosp. for Sick Children, Toronto, 1963-65, instr. in pediatrics, 1967-68; resident Toronto Gen. Hosp., 1967; fellow in pediatrics Johns Hopkins Hosp., Balt., 1965-66, fellow in pediatric endocrinology, 1968-71; rsch. asst. prof. SUNY, Buffalo, 1972-73; from asst. to assoc. prof. Harvard U., Boston, 1973-83; prof., chief pediatric endocrinology U. Mich., Ann Arbor, 1983—; mem. study sects. NIH, Bethesda, Md., 1976—. Editor: Journal of Clinical Endocrinology and Metabolism, 1982-87; contbr. numerous articles and reviews to profl. jours. Recipient Career Devel. award NIH, 1977-81. Office: U Mich Dept Pediatric Endocrinology 1500 E Medical Ctr Dr Med Profl Bldg D3252 Ann Arbor MI 48109

BEKENSTEIN, SUSAN, health care manager; b. Chgo., Aug. 8, 1952; d. Harry and Carol (Sinsheimer) B. B Social Welfare, U. Ill., 1974, MSW, 1977. Program analyst Champaign County Mental Health Bd., Urbana, Ill., 1977-78; criminal justice specialist Ill. Law Enforcement Commn., Chgo., 1978-81; program coord. Lake County Health Dept., Waukegan, Ill., 1981—; mem. Ill. Family Planning Adv. Coun., Springfield, 1983-87, 89—, alderwoman Urbana City Coun., 1973-77. Alderwoman Urbana City Coun., 1973-77. Mem. Ill. Pub. Health Assn. (sec.-treas. family planning sect. 1989—). Jewish.

BEKES, CAROLYN ETHEL, nephrologist; b. Phila., Sept. 8, 1947; d. Walter Thomas and Ethel (Finger) B. BA, Ea. Coll., 1968; MD, Jefferson Med. Coll., 1972. Intern, resident Cooper Hosp., Camden, N.J., 1972-75; chief med. resident Cooper Hosp., Camden, 1974-75, nephrology fellow, 1975-76; nephrology fellow Hahnemann Hosp., Phila., 1976-77; dir. intensive care unit Cooper Hosp., Camden, N.J., 1977—; assoc. prof. clin. anesthesia & medicine Robert Wood Johnson Med. Sch., Camden, 1986. Contbr. articles to profl. jours. Foster parent for Vietnamese boy and girl, 1983-90. Named fellow Am. Coll. Physicians, 1986, Am. Coll. Critical Care Medicine, 1989. Mem. N.J. Soc. Critical Medicine (pres. 1981-82), Soc. Critical Medicine (chair com. for guidelines 1986—, alt. coun. mem. 1988-90). Office: Cooper Hosp 3 Cooper Pla Ste 312 Camden NJ 08703

BEKHRAD, FERESHTEH, planner developer; b. Tehran, Iran, Nov. 3, 1946; came to U.S., 1970; d. Mozaffar and Robabeh (Farahani) B. BArch, U. Tehran, 1968, M of Archtl. Engring., 1970; MS of Urban Design and Architecture, Washington U., St. Louis, 1973; postgrad., U. Pa., 1979. Project mgr. AZZZ Farman Farmaian Assocs., Tehran, 1964-69; dir. planning and urban design, cons. devel. AFFA, Tehran, 1977-79; project mgr., architect Strivers Assocs. Connie Napur, St. Louis, Hartford, Conn. and P.R., 1970-74; prin. land use planner O.D.A. Office of Devel. Adminstrn., 1974-77; pres., gen. mgr., cons. planning and urban design Dakin Assocs., Tehran, 1976-80; pres. Bekhrad Co., N.Y.C., 1979-81; sr. v.p., gen. mgr. York-Hannover Devel. Inc., N.Y.C., 1981—; ptnr., prin., cons. downtown revitalization Alexander/Bekhard Cons., N.Y.C., 1984—; cons. devel. Bekhrad Co. Major devel. projects include town developments in Tehran, resort devel., Iran, Caspian Sea, St. George's, Bermuda, hist. residential revitalization project, Armstrong Square, Pitts., major downtown revitalization complex, Hannover Square, Raleigh, N.C. Bd. dirs., mem. exec. com. Downtown Raleigh (N.C.) Devel. Corp., 1987. Recipient First Place award Am. Land Devel. Assn., St. George's Resort, Bermuda, 1983, Honorable Mention award, 1983, Sir Walter Raleigh award City of Raleigh, 1984. Mem. AIA (assoc.), Am. Inst. Cert. Planners (cert.), Am. Planning Assn., Inst. Urban Design, Urban Land Inst., Internat. Assn. Corp. Real Estate Execs., Iranian Inst. Planners (founder 1968), Raleigh C. of C. (bd. dirs. 1989), NACORE. Home: 145 E 15th St New York NY 10003 Office: York Hannover Devel Inc 488 Madison Ave New York NY 10022

BELANGER, SANDRA EMILY, librarian; b. Sault Ste Marie, Mich., Jan. 17, 1944; d. Elden John and Florence Grace (Feller) B. BS, U. Wis., Milw., 1966; MSLS, Syracuse U., 1974; MS, San Jose State U., 1979. Tchr. Wells St. Jr. High Sch., Milw., 1966-68; asst. editor The Biol. Bull., Marine Biol. Lab., Woods Hole, Mass., 1968-74; librarian San Jose (Calif.) State U., 1975—. Author: Better Said and Clearly Written, 1989. San Jose State U. rsch. grantee, 1988-89. Mem. ALA (reviewer 1983—), Spl. Librs. Assn. (referee 1986—, assoc. editor bull. San Andreas chpt. 1988), Calif. Media and Libr. Educators Assn. (mng. editor jour. 1979-86). Office: San Jose State U Libr 1 Washington Sq San Jose CA 95192

BELAU, JANE CAROL GULLICKSON, computer products and services company executive; b. Fertile, Minn., Oct. 21, 1934; d. Solon Hubert and Orpha (Love) Gullickson; m. Paul G. Belau, June 22, 1957; children: Steven, Matthew, Nancy Belau Collins. Student, Concordia Coll., Moorhead, Minn., 1952-53; grad., RN, Fairview Hosp. Sch. Nursing, 1956; postgrad., U. Minn. Spl. events dir. Retail Merchants Assn., 1966-71; cons. U.S. HEW, Washington, 1971-77; commr. Minn. State Corrections Authority, Mpls., 1974-75; cons. McKnight Found., Mpls., 1974-78; commr. Minn. State Cable Communications Bd., 1975-78; v.p. state mktg. and govt. affairs Control Data Corp., Mpls., 1978—; cons. in field. Illustrator: Fashiongrams; producer-host cable TV program Community Affairs; contbr. articles to profl. jours. Bd. advisors U. Minn. Grad Sch., 1985—; chmn. nat. adv. council St. John's U., Minn., 1986—; bd. dirs. Minn. Meeting, 1986—, Minn. High Tech Council, 1986—, Minn. Alliance for Sci., 1986—, Minn. Acad. Sci., 1985—; pres. Rochester (Minn.) Area Econ. Devel. Co., 1986—; v.p., bd. dirs. Nat. Luth. Acad., 1985—; founding dir. Vinland Nat. Ctr.; founder Nat. Conf. Developmental Disabilities; chmn. Nat. Developmental Disabilities Adv. Council. Named Bus. and Profl. Woman of Yr., 1974; recipient Outstanding Leadership award Internat. Assn. Women Execs., 1981. Mem. Am. Electronics Assn. (Minn. govtl. chmn.), Women's Econ. Roundtable Minn. (founder, bd. dirs.), U.S. C. of C. (nat. health care com.). Club: Mpls. Decathlon. Home: 433 9th Ave SW Rochester MN 55901 Office: Control Data Corp 8100 34th Ave S Minneapolis MN 55440

BELCHER, ALICE ANN, county official; b. N.Y.C., June 16, 1960; d. Edward Knight and JoAnn (Ederington) B. BA, Colgate U., 1982; MCRP, Rutgers U., 1985, postgrad., 1985-86. Program evaluator N.J. Dept. Human Svcs., Edison, 1984-85; asst. planner Jersey City Dept. of Housing, N.J., 1985; rsch. interviewer Rutgers Ctr. Health Policy, New Brunswick, N.J., 1986; adminstrv. asst. U. Medicine and Dentistry of N.J., Newark, 1986-87; assoc. planner Robert Caitlin and Assocs., Denville, 1987-88; sr. planner Sussex County Planning Dept, Newton, 1989 --. Mem. Wyckoff (N.J.) Mcpl. Band, 1986-90. Mem. Am. Planning Assn., N.J. Chpt. Am. Planning Assn. Democrat. Presbyterian.

BELCHER, JENNIFER MARION, state legislator, management consultant; b. Beckley, W.Va., Jan. 4, 1944; d. Grover Emerson and Virginia Dare (Phillips) Marion. Student, Bethany Coll., 1962-63; program for sr. execs., Harvard U., 1986. Adminstrv. sec. Planning and Community Affairs Agy. State of Wash., 1967-72; spl. asst. Office of Gov., Olympia, Wash., 1973-79; owner, pres. Mgmt. Dynamics, 1980—; mem. Wash. Ho. of Reps., Olympia, 1982—. Bd. dirs. United Way Thurston County, Olympia, 1976—; pres. Wash. State's Women's Polit. Caucus, 1979. Mem. Wash. State Employees Credit Union (bd. dirs. 1976-82), Wash. Bus. anf Profl. Women's Club. Democrat. Home: 323 Maple Park Olympia WA 98501-2360 Office: Wash State Ho Reps 406 House Office Bldg Olympia WA 98504

BELCHER, LA JEUNE, automotive parts company executive; b. Chgo., Nov. 16, 1960; d. Lewis Albert and Dorthy (Brandon) B. BA, Northwestern U., 1982; postgrad., Am. Inst. of Banking, 1983-84. Securities processor Am. Nat. Bank, Chgo., 1983, divisional asst., 1983-84; mgmt. trainee Toyota Motor Distbrs., Carol Stream, Ill., 1984-85, dist. parts mgr., 1985—; rep. to Japan-U.S. Toyota Dealer Meeting, Tokyo, 1985. Mem. NAFE, NAACP, Am. Soc. Profl. and Exec. Women, Am. Mgmt. Assn., Am. Assn. Individual Investors, Northwestern U. Alumni Admissions Coun., Northwestern Club Chgo., Toastmasters (edn. v.p. 1988, advt. v.p. 1989, pres. 1990—), Delta Sigma Theta. Home: 6436 S Green Chicago IL 60621 Office: Toyota Motor Distbrs 500 Kehoe Blvd Carol Stream IL 60187

BELETZ, ELAINE ETHEL, nurse, educator; b. N.Y.C., Jan. 5, 1944; d. Harry and Rose (Friedman) B. RN, Mt. Sinai Hosp., N.Y.C., 1968; BS in Nursing, Fairleigh Dickinson U., 1970; MA, NYU, 1974; MEd, Columbia U., 1978, EdD, 1979. Staff nurse ICU Mt. Sinai Hosp., 1968-70, asst. head nurse, 1970; adminstrv. supervisory relief nurse, 1973-74, 77-78; clin. instr. Roosevelt Hosp. Sch. Nursing, N.Y.C., 1970-73; nurse gerontologist St. Luke's Hosp. Ctr., N.Y.C., 1974; asst. dir. nursing Bklyn. Hosp., N.Y.C., 1975-77; asst. prof. nursing Hunter Coll., CUNY, 1978-81; v.p. nursing Mt. Sinai Hosp., Med. Ctr., Chgo., 1982-83; assoc. prof. nursing Villanova (Pa.) U., 1983—; lectr.; cons. nursing adminstrn., labor relations in health care; mem. task force on block grants. Ill. Dept. Health. Contbr. articles to profl. jours. Recipient Disting. Achievement award Columbia U. Nursing Edn. Alumni Assn., 1989. Fellow Am. Acad. Nursing; mem. Am. Nurses Assn. (bd. dirs. 1982-87, mem. polit. action com. 1982-86), Acad. Polit. Sci., N.Y. State Nurses Assn. (treas. 1977-78, pres.-elect 1978-79, pres. 1979-81, bd. trustees, cert. of appreciation 1981, hon. recognition award 1987), Pa. Nurses Assn., N.Y. Counties Registered Nurses Assn. (nominating com. 1973, dir. 1975-78, Amanda Silvers award 1981), Shershower Benevolent Assn., Nursing Edn. Alumni Assn. (Leadership award 1989), Sigma Theta Tau, Phi Kappa Phi. Jewish. Office: Villanova U Grad Program Coll Nursing Villanova PA 19085

BEL GEDDES, BARBARA, actress; b. N.Y.C., Oct. 31, 1922; d. Norman and Helen Belle (Sneider) Bel G.; m. Carl Schreuer, Jan. 24, 1944 (div. 1951); 1 child, Susan; m. Windsor Lewis, Apr. 15, 1951 (dec.); 1 child, Betsy. Student, Buxton Sch., Putney, Andrebrook. Debut on stage in School for Scandal, Clinton (Conn.) Playhouse, 1939, on Broadway in Out of The Frying Pan, 1940; actress: (Broadway plays) Little Darling, 1942, Nine Girls, 1943, Mrs. January and Mr. X, 1944, Deep Are the Roots, 1945 (Clarence Derwent award), The Moon Is Blue, 1952, The Living Room, 1954, Cat on a Hot Tin Roof, 1955, The Sleeping Prince, 1956, Silent Night, Lonely Night, 1959, Mary, Mary, 1961, The Porcelain Year, 1965, Everything in the Garden, 1967, Finishing Touches, 1973, Ah, Wilderness, 1975; films include The Long Night, 1946, I Remember Mama, 1948, Blood on the Moon, 1948, Caught, 1949, Panic in the Streets, 1950, Fourteen Hours, 1951, Vertigo, 1958, The Five Pennies, 1959, Five Branded Women, 1960, By Love Possessed, 1961, The Todd Killings, 1970, Summertree, 1971; appears regularly as Eleanor Southward Ewing on TV show Dallas, 1978-84, 85—; author, illustrator: (children's books) I Like to Be Me, 1963, So Do I, 1972; designer greeting cards for George Caspari Co. Recipient Theatre World award, 1946. Office: Lorimar Productions 3970 Overland Ave Culver City CA 90230*

BELGRAVE, JOYCE MARY CYNTHIA, nurse; b. San Pedro Poole, Trinidad, West Indies, Apr. 22, 1935; came to U.S., 1967; d. Carl K. Cooper and Gladys Anitha (Montano) Osborne; m. Owen Livingstone Belgrave, Nov. 5, 1960; children: Denise Ynolde, Jared Keith. BA in Health Scis., Jersey City State Coll., 1974, MA in Health Adminstrn., 1975; Assoc. (hon.), Royal Soc. Health, 1960-61. Student staff, charge nurse San Fernando (Trinidad) Gen. Hsop., 1953-59; nurse surveyor nutrition WHO, Trinidad, 1960; pub. health nurse Govt. Trinidad Tobago, 1960-66; staff nurse, asst. head nurse Bklyn. Jewish Hosp., 1967-70; insvc. instr. St. John's Episcopal Hosp., Bklyn., 1971-73; adj. prof. S.I. (N.Y.) Coll., 1973-75; adminstrv. supr. inservice Peninsula Hosp. Ctr., Queens, N.Y., 1975-77; pvt. duty nurse Queens, 1977-81; supervising nurse, exec. dir. Social Concern Community Devel. Corp., Queens, 1981—; cons. inservice edn. Nursing Homes, Queens, 1976-77; cons. Continuing Edn. of Queens Lic. Practical Nurses' Assn., Queens, 1971-73; trustee Health Fund Service Employees, Internat. Union, N.Y.C., 1988—; mem. Q13 Adv. Coun., Queens, 1984; mem. Queens Medicaid Adv. Com., 1985. Pres. Block Assn., Queens, 1985, PTA, Christ Luth. Sch., Rosedale, N.Y., 1984-85. Recipient Founder Svc. award Trinidad and Tobago Nurse Assn. Am., Bklyn., 1981. Mem. Am. Bus. Women Assn. (treas. 1987-88), Home Care Coun. of N.Y.C. Inc. (asst. sec., cert. 1985-86, 89—), Laurelton C. of C. (bylaws com. 1988—, 3d v.p. 1990—), Top Ladies of Distinction Queens (recording sesc. Empire state chpt. 1986—). Democrat. Home: 135-29 Francis Lewis Blvd Laurelton NY 11413 Office: Social Concern Community 226-18 Merrick Blvd Laurelton NY 11413

BELINA, MARIA, import company administrator; b. Mexico, Jan. 23; came to U.S., 1969; d. Manuel and Rosa (Murua) Garcia; m. July 28, 1979; 1 child, Joseph John. B.A. summa cum laude, Tchr.'s Coll., 1965; M.A., Manhattan Coll., 1974; postgrad. in Japanese lang. and history, Japan Sch. Langs., 1965-68. Cert. tchr., N.Y., N.J. Coll. prof. Aoyama Gakuin U., Tokyo, 1967-69; prof. Technologico de Monterrey U., Mexico City, 1980-81; mgr. adminstrn., corp. sec. Sodick, Inc., Saddle Brook, N.J., 1982-85; import mgr. Eiseman Ludmar, N.Y.C., 1985—; counselor, tchr. St. Catherine of Genoa, N.Y.C., 1970-80. Author: Spanish for Japanese, 1968; The Nobody Bird, 1980; translator: Psychology, 1981. Mem. Multiply Handicapped of N.J. Assn. Republican. Roman Catholic. Office: Eiseman Ludmar Co Inc 56 Bethpage Dr Hicksville NY 11801

BELISSARY, KAREN, interior designer; b. Columbia, S.C., May 20, 1959; d. James Charles and Linda Gail (Bouknight) B. BFA in Design, N.Y. Sch. Interior Design, 1989. Pvt. practice interior design, Florence, S.C., 1989—; dir. Pee Dee region Am. Intercultural Exch., Florence, 1989—. Sec. Soc. for Autistic Children, Florence, 1983; v.p. Florence County Dem. Com., 1985; group leader Friends Florence Mus., 1986; bd. dirs. Heart Fund, Florence, 1987, Internat. Women's Club Florence, 1988-89, Florence Area Arts Coun., 1986-87; mem. Friends of Libr., Florence. Named Outstanding Mem., Soc. for Autistic Children, 1983; grantee Young Adult League, 1987. Mem. Am. Soc. Interior Designers. Greek Orthodox. Home: 3719 W Gentry Dr Florence SC 29501 Office: Am Intercultural Exch 804 2d Loop Rd Florence SC 29501

BELIVEAU-JONES, MARGUERITE ANITA, corporate executive; b. Woonsocket, R.I., May 1, 1944; d. Ephrem Alfred and Jeanne Cecile (Thibodeau) B. BS in Sociology and Social Work, Suffolk U., 1971; MBA, Bentley Coll., 1983. Supr. child care departmental adminstrn. Madonna Hall, Marlboro, Mass., 1966-73; dir. pers. devel. Mt. Florence, Peekskill, N.Y., 1973-77; asst. contr., contract mgr. Solomon Carter Fuller Mental Health Ctr. Univ. Hosp., Boston, 1978-82, dir. material mgmt., 1982-84, dir. purchasing, 1984-85; assoc. dir. design and constrn. mgmt. Hosp. of U. Pa., Phila., 1985-88; v.p. support svcs. West Jersey Health System, Camden, 1988—. Mem. Health Care Fin. Mgmt. Assn., Health Care Materials Mgmt. Assn. Roman Catholic. Office: West Jersey Health Systems Corp Offices Mt Ephraim & Atlantic Aves Camden NJ 08104

BELK, AUDREY MARIE WALTERS, hospital executive, nurse; b. Dillon, S.C., Feb. 13, 1938; d. Aubrey Lee and Dollie Marie (Coates) Walters; m. Fred Lewis Short, Dec. 28, 1958 (div. 1968); 1 child, Joel Kevin; m. Amos Belk, May 1, 1970 (div. 1989); children: John Eric, Barbara Diane. Diploma, Presbyn. Hosp. Sch. Nursing, Charlotte, N.C.; student, Queens Coll., Charlotte, 1987—. RN, N.C. Critical care staff nurse Presbyn. Hosp., 1962-68, home health mgr., 1984—; pub. health nurse Mecklenburg County Health Dept., Charlotte, 1968-72; home health nurse Home Health Mecklenburg County, Inc., 1978-84; expert witness Subcom. on Foster Care and Adoption, U.S. Senate, 1977. Dir., writer video Home Health Care: An Alternative, 1983. Commonwealth Fund/Duke Endowment Consortium grantee, 1986; James D. Vail III fellow, 1988-90. Mem. Am. Nurses Assn., N.C. Nurses Assn., Dist. V Nurses Assn. (treas. 1988), N.C. Foster Parent Assn. (organizing charter, past pres. sec.), Pilot Club. Democrat. Baptist. Home: 12100 McCord Rd Huntersville NC 28078 Office: Presbyn Home Care 1710 E 4th St Charlotte NC 28204

BELKIN, JANET EHRENREICH, lawyer; b. N.Y.C., Feb. 17, 1938; d. Irving and Pauline (Hamburger) Ehrenreich; m. Myron D. Belkin, June 29, 1958; children: Lisa Belkin Geld, Gary, Kira. AB, Vassar Coll., 1958; PhD, St. John's U., 1975; JD, Hofstra U., 1978; LLM, NYU, 1983. Bar: N.Y. 1979, U.S. Dist. Ct. (so. dist.) N.Y. 1979. Vice pres., counsel Equitable Life Assurance Soc., N.Y.C., 1978—. Mem. ABA (coun. mem. adminstrv. law sect. 1985-88). Home: 3014 Hewlett Ave Merrick NY 11566 Office: Equitable Life Assurance 787 7th Ave New York NY 10019

BELL, ALBERTA S., newspaper executive; b. Knoxville, Tenn., Sept. 25, 1944; d. Alfred Joshua and Mildred Mae (Jordan) Saffell; m. C. Gordon Bell, Oct. 26, 1985. BS, Tenn. State U., 1966, MS, 1968; DDS, Howard U., 1976. Cert. gen. dentistry. Tchr. Nashville Pub. Sch. Systems; maj. U.S. Army, 1976-86; gen. mgr. The Gardner (Mass.) News; mem. literacy com., work task force com.; coord. Newspaper in Edn. Active Girl Scouts U.S., United Way. Pvt. Industry Coun., Delta Sigma Theta. Home: 309 Central St Gardens MA 01440

BELL, ANITA JAYNE WISE, clinical psychologist; b. Versailles, Ky., Jan. 14, 1961; m. Bruce D. Bell, Oct. 6, 1990. BA, Georgetown (Ky.) Coll., 1983; D Psychology, Wright State U., 1987. Lic. clin. psychologist, Tenn. Clin. psychologist Luton Ctr., Nashville, 1987-90, Clin. Psychology Assocs., Gallatin, Tenn., 1989—; cons. child abuse team Gallatin Dept. Human Svcs., 1990—; cons. staff Hendersonville Hosp., Sumner Meml. Hosp. Mem. Am. Psychol. Assn. (div. clin. psychology, div. psychologists in pvt. practice), Tenn. Psychol. Assn., Nashville Area Psychol. Assn. Office: Clin Psychology Assocs 590 Hartsville Pike Gallatin TN 37066

BELL, ANN, administrative human resources professional; b. DeKalb County, Ala., Jan. 5, 1951; d. Hoyt and Ilaree (Harris) Phillips; m. Raymond C. Bell, Nov. 7, 1981; children: Carrie Cristin, Alena Dane. AA, N.E. State Coll., 1971, AS, 1981; student, Albany State U. Cert. image cons., trainer, supervisory leader. Pharmacy technician Hadden's Pharmacy, Henagar, Ala., 1973-75; adminstrv. asst. Bapt. Med. Ctrs.-DeKalb, Fort Payne, Ala., 1977-82; installment loan clk. First & Mchts. Nat. Bank, Fairfax, Va., 1982; sr. jobsite constrn. asst. So. Calif. Edison, Daggett, 1982-85, Romoland, Calif., 1985-86; adminstrv. asst. R&W Gen. Contractor, San Diego, 1986-87; adminstrv. dir. Phoenix Cos., San Diego, 1987—; corp. officer svc. Benefit Corp. Am. Active Baptist Mission work; disaster relief team Salvations Army, So. Bapt. Assn. Mem. NAFE, Internat. Assn. Concrete Repair

Specialists (officer), Assn. Builders and Contractors (safety com. 1987-88), Summit Orgn. Democrat.

BELL, ARAMINTA HOBBS, interior designer; b. Edenton, N.C., Jan. 28, 1941; d. Guy Cornelius and Mary Davenport (Woodley) Hobbs; m. Willis harvey, Aug. 31, 1963 (div. May 1982); children: Alexander A., David W. BS,HE, U.N.C.G, Greensboro, 1963. Interior designer Claude M. May Inc., Durham, N.C., 1963-71; interior designer, owner Minta Bell Interiors, Durham, 1971-84; prin. Bell Cline Inc., Durham, 1984-88; interior designer, owner Minta Bell Interior Design, Durham. Mem. Friends of the Gallery, No-Car State U., Durham C. of C., Nat. Soc. Daughters of the Am. Revolution, Am. Soc. of Interior Designers. Democrat. Presbyterian. Home: 34 Oak Dr Durham NC 27707

BELL, BARBARA GAIL, nurse; b. Sheridan, Feb. 6, 1938; d. James and Rachel Ella (Sanders) B. BSN, Mont. State Coll., 1960; postgrad., West Valley Coll., Saratoga, Calif., 1975-77, Santa Clara U., 1987--. Cert. Psychiatric and Mental Health Nurse. Staff nurse psychiatry Mont. Deaconess Hosp., Great Falls, 1960-62; staff nurse medicine Billings (Mont.) Deaconess Hosp., 1962-63; staff nurse psychiatry Santa Clara County Hosp., San Jose, Calif., 1963-65; psychiatric nurse Deodor House, San Jose, Calif., 1965-68; staff nurse, dir. nurses Conlee Convalescent Hosp., San Jose, Calif., 1968-70; dir. nurses Statewide Convalescent Hosp., 1970-72; staff nurse, dir. nurses Hillhaven Convalescent Hosp., Mountain View, Calif., 1972-74; dir. nurses Los Altos Sanitarium, Palo Alto, Calif., 1975-79; staff nurse, head nurse Veterans Adminstra. Hosp., Palo Alto, 1979—; self-employed educator, San Jose, Calif., 1974-75. Author: Opinion Column, 1988. Mem. Nat. Nurses Soc. on ŠAddictions . Democrat. Home: 3023 F Kaiser Dr Santa Clara CA 95051

BELL, BRENDA ESTELLE, nurse; b. Aiken, S.C., Feb. 26, 1944; d. Ralph Harold and Frances Helen (Riley) B.; m. David Nesbitt Harvey III, Mar. 29, 1970 (div. 1972). BS in Nursing, Med. Coll. Ga., 1966. R.N., Ga. Staff nurse Talmadge Meml. Hosp., Augusta, Ga., 1966-67, Piedmont Hosp., Atlanta, 1969-70, Houston County Hosp., Warner Robbins, Ga., 1970-71, Univ. Hosp., Augusta, 1971-73; head nurse inpatient clinics Gracewood (Ga.) State Sch. and Hosp., 1967-68; clin. coord. telemetry and surg. units Humana Hosp., Augusta, 1973-75, staff nurse ICU, 1975-86; charge nurse ICU Humana Hosp. Augusta, 1986-90, critical care educator, 1990—; mem. nurse crisis team, Humana Corp., Augusta, 1980—; office nurse to cardiologist, Augusta, 1988—; instr. critical care and basic life support courses. Mem. Am. Assn. Critical Care Nurses, Ga. Nurses Assn., Am. Nurses Assn., Cen. Savannah River Area Chpt. Am. Assn. Critical Care Nurses, Augusta Jr. Woman's Club, Augusta Flute Club, Sierra Club, Nat. Audubon Soc. Republican. Baptist. Office: Humana Hosp Augusta 3651 Wheeler Rd Augusta GA 30910

BELL, CAROL WILLSEY, certified genealogist; b. Jamestown, N.Y., May 31, 1939; d. Alfred Edward and Corinne (Braun) Willsey; m. Ralph R. Bell, May 17, 1958 (div. 1973); children: Leslie Bell Redman, Christopher K. Student, Youngstown State U., 1975-78. Acquisitions clerk Youngstown (Ohio) State U. Libr., 1974-75; genealogist Ohio Hist. Soc., Columbus, 1975, 1979-81; pvt. practice Youngstown, 1975-78, 82-88; receptionist Belmont Park Cemetery, Youngstown, Ohio, 1978-79; investigator Ohio Occupational & Phys. Therapy Bd., Columbus, 1981-82; head, local hist. and genealogy dept. Warren-Trumbull County Pub. Libr., Warren, Ohio, 1988—. Author: Ohio Wills & Estates to 1850, 1981, Ohio Guide to Genealogical Sources, 1988, Columbiana County Ohio Marriages, 1800-1870, 1990. Fellow Ohio Genealogical Soc. (trustee 1973-88, editor The Report); mem. Nat. Genealogical Soc. (Merit award 1982, disting. svc. award 1990), DAR, Colonial Dames of 17th Century, First Families of Ohio. Home: 4649 Yarmouth Ln Youngstown OH 44512

BELL, CAROLYN SHAW, economist, educator; b. Framingham, Mass., June 21, 1920; d. Clarence Edward and Grace (Wellington) Shaw; m. Nelson S. Bell, Aug. 26, 1953; 1 dau. by previous marriage, Tova Maria. AB magna cum laude, Mt. Holyoke Coll., 1941; PhD, London (Eng.) Sch. Econs., 1949; LHD (hon.), Babson Coll., 1983, Denison U., 1988. Economist OPA, 1941-45; research economist London Sch. Econs., 1946-47, Social Sci. Research Council, Harvard, 1950-53; mem. faculty Wellesley Coll., 1950-89, prof. econs., 1962-89, chmn. dept., 1962-65, 79-82, Katharine Coman prof. econs., 1970-89, Katharine Coman prof. econs. emerita, 1989—; pub. mem. Fed. Adv. Coun. on Unemployment Ins., 1974-77, chairwoman, 1975-77; bd. econ. advisors Pub. Interest Econ. Ctr.; bd. overseers Amos Tuck Grad. Sch. Bus. Adminstrn., Dartmouth, 1973-79; mem. econ. policy coun. UN Assn., 1976-85; trustee Joint Coun. Econ. Edn., 1975-83, Tchrs. Ins. and Annuity Assn., 1977-85, UN Assn., 1981—; bd. dirs. Red Acre Farm Hearing Dog Ctr.; mem. NRC Assembly Behavioral and Social Scis., 1977-83. Author: (with W.W. Cochrane) Economics of Consumption, 1956, Consumer Choice in the U.S. Economy, 1967, The Economics of the Ghetto, 1970, (with others) Coping in A Troubled Society, 1974, also articles; radio and TV commentator; mem. bd. editors: Challenge, Jour. Econs. Edn., Jour. Econ. Issues. Mem. AAUP (pres. Wellesley chpt. 1965-66), AAUW (Shirley Farr fellow 1961-62), ACLU, Manhattan Inst. (adv. bd.), Inst. for Socio-Econ. Rsch., Am. Econs. Assn. (chmn. com. on status of women in econs. profession 1972-74, mem. exec. com. 1975-77), Assn. Evolutionary Econs. (bd. dirs. 1973-75), Eastern Econ. Assn. (exec. bd. 1983-85), Hearing Dog Adv. Coun., Boston Econ. Club, Phi Beta Kappa (pres. Eta of Mass. chpt. 1978-80), Delta Soc. Home: 1010 Waltham St Brookhaven Fairfield 8 Lexington MA 02173 Office: Wellesley Coll Wellesley MA 02181

BELL, CYNTHIA SUE, electrical engineer; b. Shawnee, Okla., June 3, 1959; d. Weir Harry and Ethel Jane (Koutnik) B. BSEE, Gonzaga U., 1981; MSEE, Rochester Inst. Tech., 1984. Rsch. sci., physics div. Kodak Rsch. Labs., Rochester, N.Y., 1981-87, sr. rsch. sci. microelectronics tech. div., 1987-88, program leader, microelectronics tech. div., 1988—. Patentee in field. Mem. IEEE, Soc. for Info. Display, Soc. Vertebrate Paleontology, Rochester Browns Backers Club (photographer 1988—), Huggers Ski Club (past winter chmn.), Mensa, Alpha Sigma Nu. Office: Eastman Kodak Rsch Labs 81/400/RL/02015 Rochester NY 14650-2015

BELL, DEBORAH MARIE, management; b. Syracuse, N.Y., Dec. 3, 1955; d. William Samuel and Helen (Kaminski) Spoto; m. Todd Kevin Bell, Aug. 19, 1989. AS in Adm. Justice, Onondaga Comm. Coll., Syracuse, N.Y., 1976; BS in Pub. Justice, SUNY, Oswego, 1978. Sch. social worker City of Syracuse, 1978-79; program dir. Rape Crisis Ctr., Syracuse, 1979-85; case mgr. supr. Charlotte County, Port Charlotte, Fla., 1986-87; family resource specialist Charlotte Mental Health, Port Charlotte, 1987-90; parent involvement/social svcs. coord. Charlotte County Head Start, Punta Gorda, Fla., 1990—; bd. dirs. Exchange Ctr. for Child Abuse Prevention, Port Charlotte, 1987—, Children Action Network, 1987—, Time Out Respite, Pregnancy Care Line. Co-Author: Book, Rape Awareness for Educators 1982, Rape Resource Book. Mem. adv. coun. Health Dept. Indigent Care com., Port Charlotte, 1988, YMCA Youth Enrichment Coun., H.R.S. dist. 8 Abuse Task Force, PreSchool Interagency. Recipient Outstanding Svc. in Field of Child Abuse Prevention award Fla. Com. for Prevention Child Abuse, 1988. Mem. LWV, Nat. Coalition Against Sexual Abuse, Assn. Sexual Abuse Prevention. Republican. Roman Catholic. Office: Charlotte County Headstart 311 E Charlotte Ave Punta Gorda FL 33950

BELL, DOROTHY FRANKLIN, nurse; b. Lynchburg, Va., Jan. 8, 1927; d. Clyde and Janie Julia (Wright) Franklin; m. Henry Ross Bell Jr., Jan. 31, 1948; children: Patricia B. Lea, Carolyn B. Dixon, Timothy R., Thomas E. Grad., Va. Bapt. Hosp. Sch. Nursing, Lynchburg, 1947; real estate assoc., Phillips Bus. Coll., Lynchburg, 1975. Head nurse, supr. Va. Bapt. Hosp., Lynchburg, 1949-62; exec. dir. Florence Crittenton Home, Lynchburg, 1962-75; real estate assoc. Hollandworth-Templeton, Lynchburg, 1975-77; hosp. supr. Cen. Va. Tng. Ctr., Madison Heights, 1977-83; co-owner, bookkeeper, office mgr. Bell's Repair Svc., Lynchburg, 1980—. Vol. United Way, Lynchburg, 1963-80, Community Market, Lynchburg, 1988—; vol. instr. mother and baby care ARC, 1955-75, bloodmobile vol., 1975-80; treas. PTA Boonsboro Sch., Bedford County, 1959-60. Mem. Lynchburg Computer Soc. (newsletter editor, librarian 1986-89), Altrusa Club (pres. 1974-75), Christian Women's Club. Baptist. Home: 1115 Wiggington Rd Lynchburg VA 24502

BELL, EILEEN EBERENZ, stockbroker; b. Wellsboro, Pa., Jan. 31, 1936; d. John Gorden and Marion (Reinwald) Eberenz; m. Paul Hayden Bell, Sept. 6, 1935, children: Candace, Christian, Brian. BA, Syracuse U., 1957. Tech. asst. Bell Telephone Labs., Whippany, N.Y., 1956; systems analyst Gen. Electric, Syracuse, 1957-64, Corning (N.Y.) Glass Works, 1966-70; substitute tchr. Corning Painted Post Schs., 1970-76. Chmn. Prof. Women's Network, Corning, 1983-86; treas. Chemung County SPCA and Humane Soc., Elmira, 1986-87; mem. Women's Ctr., Corning, 1986—, Elmira Kiwanis club, 1989—. Mem. Soc. Women Engrs. Republican. Methodist. Home: RR 2 Box 76 Corning NY 14830 Office: First Albany Corp 100 Baldwin St Elmira NY 14901

BELL, FRANCES LOUISE, medical technologist; b. Milton, Pa., Apr. 28, 1926; d. George Earl and Kathryn Robbins (Fairchild) Reichard; m. Edwin Lewis Bell II, Dec. 27, 1950; children: Ernest Michael, Stephen Thomas, Eric Leslie. BS in Biology cum laude, Bucknell U., 1948; MT, Geisinger Meml. Hosp., 1949. Registered med. technologist. Med. technologist Burlington County Hosp., Mt. Holly, N.J., 1949-50, Robert Packer Hosp., Sayre, Pa., 1950, Carle Hosp./Clinic, Urbana, Ill., 1951-52, St. Joseph Hosp., Reading, Pa., 1972-83. Vol. Crime Watch, City Hall, Reading, 1985—, Am. Heart Assn., Reading, 1956—, Mar. of Dimes, Reading, 1956—, Am. Cancer Soc., Reading, 1956-71, Multiple Sclerosis, Reading, 1956—, Reading Mus. Found., 1985—, Hist. Soc. Berks County, 1989—, corr. sec. women's aux., 1986-90; fin. sec. women's aux. Albright Coll., 1988—; hospitality co-chmn. women's com. Reading Symphony Orch., 1985-90, co-editor yearbook women's com., 1990—; chmn. hospitality Reading-Berks Pub. Librs., 1988—; mem. Friends Reading Mus., Berks County Conservancy. Mem. Woman's Club of Reading (treas. 1986-88), AAUW (assoc. editor bull. 1961-63, cultural interests rep. 1967-68), United Meth. Women, Phi Beta Kappa. Republican. Methodist. Home: 1454 Oak Ln Reading PA 19604

BELL, IRIS ROBERTA, psychiatrist, educator; b. Boston, Dec. 23, 1950; d. John Algernon and Ruth (Goldberg) B. AB in Biology, Harvard U., 1972; PhD in Neurosci., Stanford U., 1977, MD, 1980. Diplomate Am. Bd. Psychiatry and Neurology. Intern in psychiatry U. Calif., San Francisco, 1980-81, resident in psychiatry, 1981-84, adj. asst. prof. dept. psychiatry, 1984-86; instr. psychiatry Harvard U. Med. Sch., Boston, 1987—; psychiatrist-in-charge geriatric inpatient unit McLean Hosp., Belmont, Mass., 1987—. Author: (monograph) Clinical Ecology: A New Medical Approach to Environmental Medicine, 1982; contbr. numerous articles to profl. jours. MIT nat. scholar, 1968. Mem. Am. Psychiat. Assn., AAAS, Soc. Behavioral Medicine. Office: McLean Hosp 115 Mill St Belmont MA 02178

BELL, JEANNE VINER, public relations counselor; b. Los Angeles, Feb. 27, 1923; d. Herman and Mary (Kaufman) Spitzel; m. Melvin A. Viner, Feb. 1, 1942 (dec.); children—Michael, Karen Viner Fawcett; m. 2d, J. Raymond Bell, Dec. 15, 1974 (dec.). Student UCLA, Am. U., George Washington U. Prin. Jeanne Viner Spl. Services, Washington, 1958-61, Jeanne Viner Assocs., Washington, 1961-82; pub. relations counselor, 1982—; dir. Independence Fed. Bank, Washington, Independence Fed. Fin. Corp., Washington. Contbr. articles to profl. jours. Presdl. appointee to adv. council SBA, 1983, Pres.'s Com. on Employment of Handicapped, 1982; mem. nat. adv. bd. Fedn. Am. Immigration Reform, Washington, 1984—; bd. dirs., mem. exec. com. Arthritis Found. of Met. D.C., 1982—; mayoral appointee to D.C. Adv. Com. on Resources and Budget, 1981—, D.C. Pvt. Industries Council, 1983—. Recipient Outstanding Leadership and Achievement award State Bus. and Profl. Women's Clubs, Washington, 1981. Mem. Pub. Relations Soc. Am., Capital Press Women (pres. 1980-82, Woman of Achievement 1982), Am. News Women's Club (bd. govs. 1969-70, pres. 1988—). Club: 1969-70), Nat. Press (Washington). Address: 3506 Winfield Ln Washington DC 20007 also: 9460 Hidden Valley Pl Beverly Hills CA 90210

BELL, KATHERINE VALOIS, owner, operator; b. Stecker, Okla., Sept. 25, 1930; d. Willis D. and Vana L. (Hodges) Stafford; m. James E. Bell, Dec. 12, 1951. Student, Clarendon Jr. Coll., 1951. Operator, cashier Clarendon (Tex.) Telephone Co., 1949-53; owner Fritch (Tex.) Hardware & Appliance, 1973--. Mem. C. of C. Home: 534 Nara Visa Box 297 Fritch TX 79036

BELL, LILAH MAE, retired, registered nurse, civic volunteer; b. Davenport, Iowa, July 16, 1908; d. Edwin Harry and Mabel Grace (Hitchcock) Mergy; m. Walter Samuel Bell, Mar. 1, 1932; children: Jerry Alan, Thomas Lee. RN, St. Luke's Hosp., Davenport, Iowa, 1929. Staff nurse Vis. Nurses, Davenport, 1930-33; fin. sec. Pleasant Valley (Iowa) Sch. Dist., 1949-63. Vol. ARC, Scott County, Iowa, 1938-63, Putnam Mus., Davenport, 1980—, Salvation Army, Davenport, 1983—; founder, adminstr. Homemaker Svc., Scott County, 1963-77; fin. sec. Trinity Luth. Ch., Pleasant Valley, 1977—; reviewer Nat. Homemaker Assn., N.Y.C., 1970-77; bd. dirs. Meals on Wheels, 1965—, C. C. Cook Home for Indigent, 1984—, Pleasant Valley Farm Bur., 1978—. Named Most Admired Woman Quad-City Times, Davenport, 1975, Outstanding Iowan Area on Aging, Scott Countt, Iowa, 1978; recipient Diane Award Epsilong Sigma Alpha Internat., Davenport, 1980, Award for Exceptional Svc. to Humanity Disting. Internat. Acad. Noble Achievement. Mem. Putnam Mus. and Guild (past pres.), Order Ea. Star (Worthy Matron 1943). Home: 5515 Valley Dr Bettendorf IA 52722

BELL, LINDA CRAWFORD, magazine editor; b. Harrisburg, Pa., Jan. 13, 1948; d. Elwood F. and Reba J. (Stakley) Crawford; student Pa. State U., 1965-68; m. Daniel Locke Bell II, July 18, 1970 (div.); children: Daniel Locke III, Ian Spencer; m. John W. Wine, Sept. 19, 1986; 1 child, Hannah Virginia. With Soviet Life Mag., Washington, 1969—, sr. editor, 1976—. Bd. dirs., public relations adv. Emerson Gallery Art, McLean, Va., 1976-89 ; cons. polit. campaign, fgn. lit. style editor. Democrat. Episcopalian.

BELL, MARY CATLETT (COCABELL BELL), artist; b. Weleetka, Okla., Sept. 26, 1924; d. Stanley Boulware and Alma Bertha (Cagle) Catlett; BA in Lang., U. Okla., 1946; m. J. Stewart Bell, Sept. 15, 1951; 1 son, William Catlett. One woman shows at R.S. Barnwell Art Center, Shreveport, La., 1980, Exhibit in Gov.'s Gallery, State Capitol, 1981, Okla. Art Center, 1984, Ada Arts & Heritage Ctr., 1986; exhibited in group shows at 61st ann. exhbn. Allied Artists of Am., N.Y.C., 1974, Watercolor U.S.A., Springfield, Mo., 1975, 150th, 153d exhbns. Nat. Acad. Design, N.Y.C., 1975, 78, Okla. Bicentennial Art Exhbn., 1976, White House, Washington, 1988, Smithsonian Inst., Living Women Living Art, Okla. Art Center, Kerr Conf. Center, others; represented in permanent collections at Okla. Heritage Assn., Oklahoma City, Arts Council Oklahoma City, Omniplex Arts and Scis. Mus., Oklahoma City, White House, Washington, 1988, Smithsonian Inst.; numerous commns. Mem. Okla. Art Center, Okla. Watercolor Assn., Okla. Mus. Art, Jr. League of Oklahoma City, Delta Delta Delta. Republican. Methodist. Address: 2 Colony Ln Oklahoma City OK 73116

BELL, MAXINE TOOLSON, librarian, state legislator; b. Logan, Utah, Aug. 6, 1931; d. John Max and Norma (Watson) Toolson; m. H. Jack Bell, Oct. 26, 1949; children: Randy J. (dec.), Jeff M., Scott Alan (dec.). Assocs. in Libr. Sci., Coll. So. Idaho; CSI, Idaho State U., 1975. Librarian Sch. Dist. 261, Jerome, Idaho, 1975-88; mem. Idaho Ho. of Reps., 1988—. Mem. Am. Nat. Women's Com., 1982—; mem. farm bur. Rep. Western States; mem. Jerome County Rep. Precinct Com., 1980—; mem. Am. Farm Bur. Women's Com., 1982—. Home: 194 S 300 E Jerome ID 83338

BELL, MILDRED BAILEY, law educator; b. Sanford, Fla., June 28, 1928; d. William F. and Frances E. (Williford) Bailey; m. J. Thomas Bell, Jr., Sept. 18, 1948 (div.); children: Tom, Elizabeth, Ansley. AB, U. Ga., 1950, JD cum laude, 1969; LLM in Taxation, N.Y. U., 1977. Bar: Ga. 1969. Law clk. U.S. Dist. Ct. No. Dist. Ga., 1969-70; prof. law Mercer U., Macon, Ga., 1970—; mem. Ga. Com. Constl. Revision, 1978-79; v.p., bd. dirs. Arrowhead Travel, Inc. Mem. ABA, Ga. Bar Assn., Phi Beta Kappa, Phi Kappa Phi. Republican. Episcopalian. Bd. editors Ga. State Bar Jour., 1974-76; contbr. articles to profl. jours., chpts. in books. Home: 516 High Point North Rd Macon GA 31210 Office: Mercer U Sch Law Georgia Ave Macon GA 31207

BELL, PATRICIA JIMERSON, publisher; b. Afton, Okla., Nov. 19, 1931; d. Fred Pattterson and Marguerite Drennan (Allison) Jimerson; m. Donald Ryan Bell, Apr. 5, 1953; children: Margaret Lynne, Jean Allison, David Ryan, Amanda Ann. BS in Edn., U. Okla., 1953, MA in English, 1956. Cert. tchr., Tenn., Minn. Tchr. Tullahoma (Tenn.) City Schs., 1960-66, Eden Prairie (Minn.) Schs., 1970-76; newsletter editor Minn. Solar Energy Assn., Mpls., 1978-87; pres., owner Cat's-paw Press, Eden Prairie, 1986—; co-owner Tessera Pub., Inc., Eden Prairie, 1989—. Author: Roughing It Elegantly, 1987, Paddler's Planner, 1989; editor: Dark Sky, Dark Land, 1989. Mem. Minn. Independent Pub. Assn. (v.p. 1988—). Office: Cat's Paw Press 9561 Woodridge Circle Eden Prairie MN 55347

BELL, PATRICIA LAUDERDALE, government administrator; b. Louisville, July 20, 1930; d. Harry Edward and Mary Theresa (Hayden) Lauderdale; m. Hugh Clay Bell, Jr., Aug. 1, 1953 (dec. Dec. 1974); children—Gordon Edwin, Joanne Marie, Gloria Patricia-Leigh. B.S. in Gen. Edn., Spalding U., Louisville, 1951, postgrad., 1968-69; M.S. in Community Devel., U. Louisville, 1970; postgrad. Fla. State U., Western Ky. State U., 1970-75; Ph.D. in Adult Continuing Extension Edn., Mich. State U., 1979. Continuity writer, announcer, receptionist Sta. WLOU, Louisville, 1952-54; file clk., spl. searcher IRS, Louisville, 1956-65, employment devel. specialist Detroit dist., 1980-83, tng. specialist Data Ctr., 1983—; tchr. St. Bartholomew Sch., Buechel, Ky., 1965-67; tchr. social studies Central High Sch., Louisville Pub. Sch. System, 1967-69; tchr. econs. and sociology Ahrens Nigh Sch., Louisville, 1966-69; supr. social studies Louisville Pub. Sch. System, 1969-70, coordinator Hill Adult Learning Ctr., 1970-73; instr. social sci. Univ. Coll., instr. Office Interdisciplinary Programs, Speed Sci. Sch., asst. dir. profl. devel. U. Louisville, 1973-75, 77-78, dir. Life Planning Ctr., 1978-80; workshop presenter adult and career edn. Chmn. bd. Sacred Heart Model Sch., 1966; mem. Young Artists Promotions, 1969-72; mem. citizens adv. com. Louisville and Jefferson County Air Bd., 1970-72; mem. nominating com. Metro United Way; former mem. adult edn. com. St. Agnes Parish; past mem. bd. dirs. Planned Parenthood, Louisville; former chmn. bd. dirs. Louisville Area Planning Council; mem. women's council Bellarmine Coll.; mem. adv. bd. Creative Employment Project. Recipient Disting. Citizen award Mayor of Louisville, 1980; Black Achiever's award, 1980; Disting. Service award IRS Dist. Office, Detroit, 1981; Service to Edn. award Lewis Coll. Bus., Detroit, 1985. Mem. Am. Soc. for Engring. Edn., Am. Personnel and Guidance Assn., Nat. Assn. Student Personnel Adminstrs., Women in Higher Edn. Adminstrn. (nat. identification program), Ky. Personnel and Guidance Assn., AAUP, Blue Monday Network, Urban League. Democrat. Roman Catholic. Clubs: Friday Niters, Federally Employed Women (Detroit). Avocations: bridge; camping; interior design; promoting unknown artists. Home: 1925 Orleans Detroit MI 48207 Office: IRS Data Center Treasury Dept 1900 John C Lodge Dr Detroit MI 48207

BELL, PEARL THOMAZENA, educator; b. Jamaica, Mar. 25, 1936; came to U.S., 1978; d. Zedekiah Augustus and Clementina (Morris) Morgan; m. Easton Alexander Bell, Apr. 15, 1962; children: Harolde, Easton Jr., Ronald, Omar. BA, U. West Indies, 1973; MS, Adelphi U., 1980; EdM. in Psychol. Counseling, Columbia U., 1988. Cert. counselor, tchr., N.Y. Prin., tchr. West Indies Union Conf. 7th Day Adventist, Mandeville, Jamaica, 1959-66; tchr. Wolmers Prep. Sch., Kingston, Jamaica, 1966-72; edn. officer, trainer of tchrs., program developer Jamaica Ministry Edn., Kingston, 1972-78; coordinator communications studies N.Y.C. Bd. Edn., 1978-80; tchr. Northeastern Acad., N.Y.C., 1980-87, dir. student affairs, guidance, counseling services, 1987—, prin., 1990—; coordinator secondary sch. curriculum Seventh Day Adventists, South Lancaster, Mass., 1984—. Mem. Am. Assn. Counseling Devel., Am. Soc. Counseling Assn., Am. Assn. Curriculum Devel., Assn. Supervision and Curriculum Devel., Nat. Council Tchrs. Eng., Kappa Delta Pi. Adventist. Club: Ladies Fellowship (Corona, N.Y.). Home: 23-29 100 St East Elmhurst NY 11369

BELL, REAVER GARLAND, day care center administrator; b. Forrest City, Ark.; d. William and Bessie (Bragg) Garland; m. William A. Barlowe III, Dec. 22, 1957 (div.); children: Victor A., Simone; m. Thomas Bell, June 12, 1978; 1 child, Jennifer Rae. BS, Roosevelt U., Chgo., 1973, postgrad., 1974; postgrad., Chgo. State U., 1976, Nat. Coll. of Edn., 1989—. Dental nurse Dr. T.H. Herman, DDS, Chgo., 1955-57; bookkeeper Dobson Cleaners & Laundry, Chgo., 1955-58; adminstr. asst. Favor Ruhl & Watson Co., Chgo., 1960-68; legal librarian Seyfarth, Shaw, Fairweather and Geraldson, Chgo., 1968-70; project reviewer Northeastern Ill. Planning Commn., Chgo., 1970-72; organizer, dir. Shiloh Day Care Ctr., Inc., Chgo., 1972-80, Simone's Kiddy Kollege, Inc., Chgo., 1975-80; organizer, adminstr. V & J Day Care Ctr., Chgo., 1980—; chmn. edn. com. Vision for Life, Chgo., 1988—; coun., resource and referral V & J Day Care Ctr., Chgo., 1980—. Chmn. Christian social rels. com. Shiloh Bapt. Ch., Chgo., 1987—; chmn. edn. com. Community Rels. Coun. of Brainerd, Chgo., 1987—; fin. sec. Roseland Hosp. Aux., 1976. Mem. Nat. Black Child Devel. Inst., 90th and Throop Block Club (v.p. 1987—). Democrat. Office: Simone's V&J Day Care Ctr 1 E 113th St Chicago IL 60628

BELL, REGINA JEAN, business owner; b. Lebanon, Mo.; d. Stephen S. and Ida M. (Reaves) B. B.A., Draughens U., 1948; postgrad., Butler U., 1958, Ind.-Purdue U., Indpls., 1968. Prodn. mgr. Howe Mfg. Co., Inc., Indpls., 1958-64; v.p. budgetary control Howe Engring. Co., Inc., Indpls., 1964-67; mgr. material control Nat. Aluminum Div., Indpls., 1968-84; now owner Brown County Letter Shop, Nashville, Ind. Mem. Indpls. Real Estate Assn.

BELL, ROSEANNE, business owner, consultant, real estate associate; b. Newark, June 15, 1946; d. Frank Leonard and Antoinette Delores (DeTulio) Rappa; m. Harold Charles Bell, Nov. 25, 1965 (div. 1978); children: Justin, Adrienne, Bethany; m. Clifford Neil Ribner, Aug. 26, 1979. Student, Latin Am. Inst., N.Y.C., 1964-65; BA, Kean Coll., 1979. Bi-lingual exec. sec. Schering Corp., Bloomfield, N.J., 1965-67, Purolator Products, Inc., Rahway, N.J., 1967-69; interior designer Campbell Assocs., Metuchen, N.J., 1979, Kelleher Design Assocs., Tulsa, 1979-80; owner Bell & Co., Tulsa, 1980—; cons. Greenwood Performance Systems, Tulsa, 1988—; sales assoc. Bethany Real Estate, Tulsa, 1989; mktg. cons. Natale Inst., Houston, 1986-88; pub. rels. advisor Support Ctr., Tulsa, 1988; lectr. Leadership Tulsa 1988, mem. pub. rels. com. 1988-89, edn. com., bd. dirs., 1989—; facilitator Vol. Okla. Conf. 1989; lectr. U. Tulsa 1989. Stage mgr. arts and humanities coun. Mayfest, Tulsa, 1989, performing arts com., 1989—; bd. dirs. Theater Tulsa, 1982-85, chmn. play selection com., 1984-85; facilitator Met. Tulsa Transit Authority, 1989; chair warm-up party FAT, 1989-90. Mem. Bldg. Owners and Mgrs. Assn. (co-chair bldg. awards com. 1986), ASTD (v.p. accomodations com. 1988, bd. dirs. 1988—, v.p. communications com. 1989—), Am. Soc. Interior Design (treas. 1982, pres. networking team Tulsa chpt. 1989-90), Bohemian Soc. Office: Bell & Co 2121 S Columbia #500 Tulsa OK 74114

BELL, SHARON KAYE, small business owner; b. Lincoln, Nebr., Sept. 14, 1943; d. Edwin B. and Evelyn F. (Young) Czachurski; m. James P. Kittrell (div. Sept. 1974); children: Nathan James, Nona Kaye; m. Joseph S. Bell, June 5, 1976; stepchildren: Patricia, Bobbie, Linda. Various positions mgmt., bookkeeping, 1961-71; bookkeeper Internat. Harvester, Chesapeake, Va., 1971-73, Cheat'AH Engring., Santa Ana, Calif., 1973-74, Fre Del Engring., Santa Ana, Calif., 1974-75; bookkeeper/mgr. Tek Sheet Metal Co., Santa Ana, Calif., 1975-79; owner, bookkeeper Bell's Bookkeeping, Huntington Beach, Calif., 1979-86, Fountain Valley, Calif., 1986-88, Laguna Hills, Calif., 1988—. Mem. Nat. Assn. Accts. (bd. dirs. 1985-86, sec. 1986-87, v.p. 1987-90, dir. of manuscripts 1990—), Nat. Notary Assn., NAFE, Wives of Submarine Vets. World War II (v.p. L.A. chpt. 1986-87, treas. 1990—), Nat. Soc. Pub. Accts., Internat. Platform Assn. Republican. Office: Bell's Bookkeeping PO Box 2713 Laguna Hills CA 92654-2713

BELL, SHARON TERESA ECHERD, physical education and health teacher; b. Gastonia, N.C., June 23, 1950; d. Lyman Joe and Ruby Colleen (Hicks) Echerd; m. Rufus Joseph Jr., Oct. 19, 1974; children: Emily Brooke, Lauren Nicole. BS, Mars Hill Coll., 1972. Tchr. Grier Jr. High, Gastonia, N.C., 1972—. Republican. Methodist. Home: 1208 McCorkle Rd Charlotte NC 28214 Office: Grier Jr High 1622 E Garrison Blvd Gastonia NC 28054

BELL, SUSAN JANE, nurse; b. Columbus, Ohio, July 24, 1946; d. Donald Richard Bell and Martha Jane (McDowell) Nichols; m. Robert Earlin Ward, Oct. 24, 1964 (div. 1984); children: Duane Allen Ward, Melissa Jane Ward, Bryan Thomas Ward. Degree in nursing, Columbus Sch. Practical Nursin,

1986; ADRN, Columbus State Community Coll., 1989. RN, Ohio. Nurse's asst. Riverside Meth. Hosp., Columbus, 1970-80, Norworth Convalescent Ctr., Columbus, 1980-86; lic. practical nurse, charge nurse Heartland Thurber Care Ctr., Columbus, 1986-89; staff nurse Am. Nursing Care, Columbus, 1989—; medicare home visitation, staffing and pvt. duty nurse Telemed, Columbus, 1989—; asst. head nurse Northland Terr., Columbus, 1989; supr. Elmington Manor, Columbus, 1989; staff nurse cardiac step down unit Grant Hosp., Columbus, 1989—; pres. Bell Mktg. Distbrs. Reverend Am. Fellowship Ch.; notary pub. State of Ohio. Mem. NAFE, Ohio Practical Nurses' Assn. Democrat. Home: 605 Dennison Apt 3 Columbus OH 43215

BELL, VANESSA REGINA, nurse; b. Detroit, Mar. 29, 1955; d. L. J. Harris and Mary Louise (Respress) Kyser; m. Jasper Bell, Nov. 13, 1984 (div.); children: Tanisha Akira, Kevin ReShaun. AS in Nursing, Troy State U., 1983. Cert. chemotherapist, med./surg. nurse. Nursing asst. Harper Grace Hosp., Detroit, 1975-78, St. Margaret's Hosp., Montgomery, Ala., 1978-80; staffing clk., sec. St. Margaret's Hosp., Montgomery, 1981-82, charge nurse pediatrics, nursery, post-partum, 1983-85, charge nurse med.-surg., orthopedics, otolaryngology, 1985-87, head nurse oncology, surg. unit, 1987-89; nurse mgr. of surgical oncology Humana Corp., Montgomery, 1989—; instr. basic cardiac life support ARC, Montgomery, 1987. Active PTA, Montgomery, 1981—; mem. Cardio-Pulmonary Resuscitation Com., Humana Hosp., Montgomery, St. Margaret's Hosp., 1986—. Mem. NAFE, Troy State U. Alumni Assn. (ways and means com. 1986—, bd. dirs. 1987—), Montgomery Area Mgmt. Assn., Jazzy Ladies Soc. and Savs. Club (pres. 1985-86, sec. 1986-87), Chi Eta Phi (recording sec. Sigma Eta chpt.). Democrat. Baptist. Club: Jazzy Ladies Soc. and Savs. (Montgomery) (pres. 1985-86, sec. 1986-87). Home: 2833 Peabody Rd Montgomery AL 36116

BELLAMY, JEANNE (MRS. JOHN T. BILLS), journalist, banker; b. Bklyn., Nov. 15, 1911; d. Donald Lamont and Ethel Park (Houston) Bellamy; student Barnard Coll., 1928-29; AB, Rollins Coll., 1933; PhD (hon.), Biscayne Coll., 1975; m. John Turner Bills, Jan. 30, 1942. Reporter, Miami (Fla.) Tribune, 1935-37; staff writer Miami Herald, 1937-58; sr. editorial writer, 1958-73; chmn. bd. Sun Bank Midtown, Miami; 1973-77; dir. Sun Bank of Miami, 1977-82; commentator Sta. WGBS, 1962-63; moderator We Want to Know, Sta. WLBW-TV, 1961-63. Mem. Miami-Dade Water and Sewer Authority, 1975-80; mem. governing bd. So. Fla. Water Mgmt. Dist., 1979-83; bd. dirs. Nat. Audubon Soc., 1963-71; trustee Biscayne Coll., 1976-82, Rollins Coll., 1977-80; vestryman St. Stephen's Ch., 1975-78; trustee Fairchild Tropical Garden, Coral Gables, 1961—, pres., 1977-82; bd. dirs. Fla. chpt. Nature Conservancy, 1983-90, WPBT-TV, 1984—. Recipient ann. awards Fla. Bar, 1959, 62; Jose Marti Journalism award, 1966; Thomas Barbour medal for conservation Fairchild Tropical Garden, 1984. Mem. Fla. Soc. Editors (pres. 1962), Hist. Assn. So. Fla., Greater Miami Opera Assn., Vizcayans, Women in Communications, Greater Miami C. of C. (chmn. 1977-78), Soc. Woman Geographers, Kappa Alpha Theta. Episcopalian. Author: Taming the Everglades, 1947; Newspapers of America's Last Frontier, 1952; Communism: What It Means to You, 1961. Avocations: travel, photography, bridge, reading, painting. Home: 2718 Segovia St Coral Gables FL 33134

BELLAMY, MARKITA MOORE, nutritionist; b. Trenton, N.J., Dec. 12, 1958; d. George Azel Jr. and Katherine (Easley) Moore; m. Charles Henry Bellamy Jr., Aug. 1, 1987. BA, Dartmouth Coll., 1980; BS in Pub. Health, U. N.C., 1982, MPH, 1983. Nutritionist I West Midlands health dist. S.C. Dept. Health and Environ. Control, West Columbia, 1984-85; rsch. asst. bieenial survey pub. health nutrition programs U. N.C., Chapel Hill, 1986-89, teaching asst. in maternal child and infant nutrition, 1987, acting nutrition sect. head Clin. Ctr. for Study of Devel. and Learning, 1987-88; outpatient clin. dietitian Richland Meml. Hosp., Columbia, S.C., 1988; nutritionist II high risk channeling programs East Midland Health Dist. S.C. Dept. of Health and Environ. Control, Columbia, 1988; rsch. asst. Carolina Inst. for Rsch. on Infant Pers. U. N.C., Chapel Hill, 1988—; doctoral student rep. dept. nutrition U. N.C., 1985-86, chair of mem. search com. dept. nutrition, 1986-87, speaker health careers acad. advancement program, 1989; mem. adv. bd. Durham (N.C.) County Disabilities Nutrition Edn. Project, 1988—. Mem. NAACP. U. N.C. fellow, Chapel Hill, 1982-83, 86—; USPHS grantee, 1985-86; traineeship Boling Ctr., Child Devel. Ctr., U. Tenn., Memphis, 1989. Mem. N.C. Dietetics Devel. Disabilities Practice Group, Delta Sigma Theta. Home: 1006 Karen Dr PO Box 5023 New Bern NC 28561 Office: U NC Dept Nutrition 315 Pittsboro St CB# 7405 Chapel Hill NC 27599-7405

BELLANTONI, MAUREEN BLANCHFIELD, manufacturing executive; b. Warren, Pa., Mar. 18, 1949; d. John Joseph and Patricia Anne (Southard) Blanchfield; m. Michael Charles Bellantoni, Aug. 12, 1972; children: Mark Christopher, Melissa Catherine. BS in Fin., U. Bridgeport, 1976; MBA, U. Conn., Stamford, 1979. Fin. analyst Dictaphone Corp., Rye, N.Y., 1970-73, Gen. Telephone & Electronics, Stamford, 1973-74, Smith Kline Ultrasonic Products, now Branson, Danbury, Conn., 1974-77; fin. mgr. Gen. Foods, White Plains, N.Y., 1977-80; contr. Branson Ultrasonics Corp. div. Emerson Electric, Danbury, Conn., 1980-88; v.p. fin. Branson Ultrasonics Corp. div. Emerson Electric, Danbury, 1988-90; v.p. fin., chief fin. officer Automatic Switch Co. div. Emerson Electric, Florman Park, N.J., 1990—. Mem. Fin. Execs. Inst., Danbury C. of C. (leadership prog. 1989), Internat. Platform Assn., Beta Gamma Sigma. Home: PO Box 366 Mount Freedom NJ 07970-0366 Office: Automatic Switch Co 50-60 Hanover Rd Florham NJ 07932

BELLE, NANCY KROME, nurse consultant service executive; b. Balt., May 27, 1944; d. Charles and Sarah (Herlich) Krome; m. Dec. 21, 1964 (div. Jan. 1986). BS Nursing, U. Md., 1966. Cert. nurse practitioner Md. Bd. Examiners Nurses. Sr. pub. health nurse Project 501, Balt., 1966-69; from staff nursing to asst. head nurse Sinai Hosp., Balt., 1969-74; co-founder,organizer The Nurse Bank, Balt., 1974-75; oncology nurse Dr. J. Leonard Lichtenfeld et al., Balt., 1975-78; from RN to nurse practitioner Drs. Scher, Muher, Lowen, PA, Balt., 1978-85; dir. nurse consultants Rombro Health Svcs., Balt., 1986—. Co-writer, contbr. (quar. newsletter) Rombro Health Svcs. Protocols. Vol. local and nat. Dem. Party, Balt., 1986; pro-choice activist. Mem. Health Facilities Assn. Md. (pub. rels. com. 1987—, nursing affairs com., assoc. mem., speaker seminar 1988), Nat. Assn. Dirs. Nursing (conv. and legis. coms. chairperson Md. chpt. 1989—, Vol. award 1989), NAFE. Jewish. Office: Rombro Health Svcs 2930 Washington Blvd Baltimore MD 21230

BELLES, ANITA LOUISE, medical service executive, educator; b. San Angelo, Tex., Aug. 30, 1948; d. Curtis Lee and Margaret Louise (Perry) B.; m. John Arvel Willey, July 13, 1969 (div. Aug. 1978); children: Suzan Heather, Kenneth Alan. BA, U. Tex., 1972; MS in Health Care Adminstrn., Trinity U., 1984. Registered emergency med. technician; cert. CPR instr., emergency med. technician tchr., La. Regional emergency med. service tng. coordinator Bur. Emergency Med. Service, Lake Charles, La., 1978-79; exec. dir. Southwest La. Emergency Med. Service Council, Lake Charles, 1979-83; project coordinator Tulane U. Med. Sch., New Orleans, 1982-83; dir. La. Bur. of Emergency Med. Service, Baton Rouge, 1982; pres. Computype, Inc., San Antonio, 1983-86, Emergency Med. and Safety Assocs., La. and Tex., 1982—; dir. family planning Bexar County Hosp. Dist., Tex., 1987; mgmt. engr. Inpatient Support Applications, 1987-88; instr. grad. sch. health care adminstrn. S.W. Tex. State U. Editor A.L.E.R.T., 1980-83, San Antonio Executive News, 1987—, Family Living, 1987-88; feature writer Bright Scrawl, 1985-86; contbr. numerous articles on emergency med. services to profl. jours. Bd. dirs. Thousand Oaks Homeowner's Assn., sec., treas., 1985; active Trinity U. Health Care Alumni Assn., Jr. League San Antonio, The Parenting Ctr., Baton Rouge, 1982-83, Jr. League Lake Charles, 1982, Campfire Council Pub. Relations Com., Lake Charles, 1982; newsletter editor Community Food Co-Op, Newsletter Editor, 1979; vol. Lake Charles Mental Health Ctr., 1974. Recipient Outstanding Service award La. Assn Registered Emergency Med. Technicians, 1983, Southwest La. Assn. Emergency Med. Technicians, 1983; named Community Leader KPLC TV, Lake Charles, 1981, regional winner Assn U. Programs in Health Adminstrn., HHS Sec's. Competitions for Innovations in Health, 1982. Mem. Nat. Assn. Emergency Med. Technicians., Tex. Assn. Emergency Med. Technicians, Am. Coll. Health Care Execs., Am. Assn. Automotive Medicine, Southwest La. Assn. Emergency Med. Technicians (founding mem., v.p. 1979-80, CPR com. chmn. 1980-81, pub. relations com. chmn. 1981-82, bd. dirs. 1980-82), Am. Mgmt. Assn., Nat. Soc. Emergency Med. Service Adminstrs., Nat. Coalition Emergency Med. Services, Am. Composition Assn. Methodist. Office: Bexar County Hosp Dist 4502 Medical Dr San Antonio TX 78284

BELL-HANSON, KAREN SUE, marketing consultant; b. Des Moines, Mar. 17, 1958; d. Max Lee and Ila Jane (Hegwood) Bell; m. Jeffrey Lane Bell-Hanson, July 10, 1982. BA, U. No. Iowa, 1980; MA, Mich. State U., 1982. Account exec. Sampson Communications, Sta. KSKU, Hutchinson, Kans., 1982-83; mktg. coord. Newton (Kans.) Cable TV, TCI Inc., 1983; with customer svc. Cable TV Systems, Inc., Hutchinson, 1983-85; office mgr. Coffeyville (Kans.) Cable TV, 1985-86; kiosk mgr. Hickory Farms Ohio, Houghton, Mich., 1986; office mgr. Aurora Cable TV, Houghton, 1987, Northern Cable TV, Petoskey, Mich., 1988-89; owner Communiqué, Chassell, Mich., 1989—; adj. faculty McNeese State U., Lakes Charles, La., 1988. Mem. Women in Communications (ind.), NAFE. Methodist. Home and Office: Rte 1 Box 152A Chassell MI 49916

BELLIN, ANNE, obstetrician-gynecologist; b. Bklyn., Apr. 11, 1957; d. Eugene and Judith (Shreyver) B.; m. Edward Eugene Shelton, June 30, 1989. BA, SUNY, Purchase, 1979; MD, N.Y. Med.Coll., 1984. Intern Med. Ctr. Del., Wilmington, 1984-85, resident, 1985-88; physician Roswell (Ga.) Women's Ctr., 1988-89, Bellin & Lee Pvt. Corp., Atlanta, 1989—; med. dir. Planned Parenthood, Atlanta, 1990—. Fellow Am. Coll. Ob.-Gyn. (jr.); mem. Atlanta Med. Assn., Am. Assn. Gynecol. Laparoscopists, Am. Med. Women's Assn., Am. Fedn. Clin. Rsch., Ga. Med. Soc. Office: Bellin & Lee PC 3193 Howell Mill Rd Ste 306 Atlanta GA 30327

BELLM, PEGGY A(NN), public relations executive, civic worker, consultant; b. Highland, Ill.; d. Erwin A. and Margaret J. (Knebel) B. BA in Theatre and Mass Communications, So. Ill. U., 1976. Ptnr. Pig Patch U.S.A., Highland, 1977-83; owner Pegalie's Helvetia Haus, Highland, 1977-83; mng. ptnr. Recollections, St. Louis County, Mo., 1982-86; exec. dir. Highland C. of C., 1987—, bd. dirs., 1979-83, 87—, pres., 1981-82; owner Helvetia Trading Co., Highland, 1988—, Center Stage Promotions, Highland, 1988—; pub. speaker; retail cons. Dir./choreographer numerous local and area theatrical prodns.; emcee/coordinator numerous bridal showcases, fashion shows, beauty pageants and festivals, 1979—. Bd. dirs., founding mem. Friends of Theatre and Dance So. Ill. U., Edwardsville, 1979—, mem. Students in Free Enterprise adv. bd., 1987—; mem. Southwestern Ill. Leadership Council Mktg. Com., 1987—; mem. small bus. adv. bd. U. Ill. Extension Bur., 1987—; mem. Highland Econ. Devel. Research Com., 1986-87; chmn. Highland Interim Econ. Devel. Com., 1987—; producer, dir. Highland Summer Theatre, 1986—, exec. bd., directorial advisor, 1981-86; theatrical pageant author/dir. Highland Bicentennial Commn., 1975-76; mem. post prom com. Highland High Sch., 1987—; coordinator Maifest Festival, 1979-83, 86-88; bd. dirs., theatrical pagent chmn. Highland Sesquicentennial Assn., 1984-87; theatrical pageant producer/dir. Highland Sesquicentennial Commn., 1985-87; bd. dirs. Madison County Arts Council, Ill., 1987—, chmn. fin. com., 1988—; bd. dirs. Helvetia Schweizerfest Assn., Highland, 1988—. Mem. Nat. Assn. Female Execs., So. Ill. U. Alumni Assn., Highland Hist. Soc., Ill. Assn. C. of C. Execs., Metro East C. of C. Assn. Club: Internat. Fedn. Bus. and Profl. Women's (Young Career Woman 1979, Dist. Young Career Woman 1980). Office: PO Box 294 Highland IL 62249

BELLMAN, JOAN Y., office manager, educator, business owner; b. Fairfield, Ill., Dec. 7, 1952; d. Harold M. and Pauline (Trailor) Reeder; m. Herschel E. Bellman, Dec. 9, 1970; children: Tammy Ann, James Edward. AS, Vol. State Community Coll., 1984; postgrad., Am. Inst. Bankers, 1987; Austin Peay STate U. Jr. audit staff mem. Duane M. Brown, Springfield, Tenn.; ops. supt. Joint Indsl. Techs., Portland, Tenn.; tchr. Nashville State Tech. Inst.; owner Springfield Bookkeeping Svcs.; speaker Women's Bus. Ownership Conf., Home and Minister's Inst. Copyrights rsch.: bus. devel. home based and home bound. Active Girl Scouts U.S. Gamma Beta Phi. Home: 101 Stratford Ct #903 Gallatin TN 37066

BELLO, CARMELITA ANGELA, social welfare administrator; b. Worcester, Mass., Mar. 6, 1955; d. Angelo Michael and Rosina Elizabeth (Palumbo) B. AA, Worcester Jr. Coll., 1975; BS in Mgmt. and Econs., Worcester State Coll., 1977; MBA, Anna Maria Coll., 1980; cert., Auditor's Inst., Boston, 1988; cert. in mgmt., Clark U. Bank mgr. Freedom Fed. Savs. Bank, Worcester and Holden, Mass., 1978-80; fiscal officer So. Middlesex Opportunity Coun., Framingham, Mass., 1980-85; contract officer Commonwealth of Mass., Fitchburg and Worcester, 1985-88; dir. of adminstrn. North Cen. Human Svcs., Inc., Gardner, Mass., 1988—; cons. Bello Associated, Worcester, 1980-90. Creator computer contract tracking system, 1985; developer automated processes for client tracking, 1988. Treas. Beacon of Hope, Inc., Leominster, Mass., 1989-90; accountant Mount Carmel Ch., Worcester, 1986-88; adv. bd. Worcester Cable Commn., 1989-90; bd. dirs. Welfare Commn., Worcester, 1985; mem. Dem. City Com., Worcester, 1986-90; v.p. Sandy Shores, Garden City, S.C., 1986-90. Mem. Christopher Columbus Realty Trust (mgr. 1986-90), Order of Sons of Italy in Am. (trustee 1988, orator 1989, v.p. 1990), Mass. Mental Health Corp. (mem. fin. com.). Office: North Cen Human Svcs 31 Lake St Gardner MA 01440

BELLO, SHERE CAPPARELLA, sales and marketing executive; b. Norristown, Pa., Sept. 4, 1956; d. Anthony Carmen and Patsy Ann (Robbins) Capparella. BA in Langs., Rosemont (Pa.) Coll., 1978; postgrad. in bus., Ursinus Coll., 1986—. Mem. sales staff Spectrum Communications Corp., Norristown, 1977-79, mgr. sales and mktg., 1986-87, 89—; asst. sales and adminstrv. asst. Tettex Instruments, Inc., Fairview Village, Pa., 1979-83; owner, instr. Shere's World of Dance and Fine Arts, Jeffersonville, Pa., 1982-88; exec. sec. internat. dept. Syntex Dental Products, Inc., Valley Forge, 1984-86; v.p. Captrium Devel. Corp., Exton, Pa., 1987-88; sales cons. Mary Kay Cosmetics, Limerick, Pa., 1988—; sales mgr. Spectrum Communications, 1989—; free-lance tutor langs., Pa. area, 1976-78; free-lance model, a, 1977—; v.p. La Bella Modeling Agy., Collegeville, Pa., 1979-82; choreographer La Bella Sch. Performance, Collegeville, 1979-82; free-lance lang. translator, 1984—. Judge state and nat. pageants Miss Am. Scholarship, Jr. Miss, Nat. Teen and Pre-Teen, All-Am. Talent, Ofcl. Little Miss Am., Little Miss Diamond, Talent Olympics, Talent Unltd., 1979—; producer, choreographer Miss Montgomery County Pageant, Plymouth Meeting, Pa., 1985; co-producer, choreographer Miss Del. Valley Pageant, Horsham, Pa., 1983-84.; Confraternity Christian Doctrine kindergarten tchr. Visitation Parish, 1987-88. Recipient award Internat. Leaders in Achievement, 1989, Community Leaders of Am., 1989. Mem. NAFE, Christian Children's Fund, Humane Soc. U.S., Greenpeace, Doris Day League for Animals, People for the Ethical Treatment of Animals. Republican. Roman Catholic. Home: 2 N Limerick Rd Limerick PA 19468

BELLO-REUSS, ELSA NOEMI, physician, educator; b. Buenos Aires, Argentina, May 1, 1939; came to U.S., 1972; naturalized, 1989; d. Jose F. and Julia M. (Hiriart) Bello; B.S., U. Chile, 1957, M.D., 1964; m. Luis Reuss, Apr. 15, 1965; children: Luis F., Alejandro E. Intern J.J. Aguirre Hosp., Chile, 1963-64; resident in internal medicine U. Chile, Santiago, 1964-66; pvt. practice medicine specializing in nephrology Santiago, 1967-72; Internat. NIH fellow U. N.C., Chapel Hill, 1972-74; vis. asst. prof. physiology U. N.C., Chapel Hill, 1974-75; Louis Welt fellow U. N.C.-Duke U. Med. Ctr., 1975-76; mem. faculty Jewish Hosp. St. Louis, 1976-83, asst. prof. medicine, physiology and biophysics Washington U. Sch. Medicine, St. Louis, 1976-86, assoc. prof. physiology dept. cell biology and physiology, 1986; assoc. prof. medicine U. Tex. Med. Br., Galveston, 1986—. Contbr. articles on nephrology and epithelial electrophysiology to med. and physiology jours., chpt. to nephrology text. Mem. Internat., Am. Socs. Nephrology, Royal Soc. Medicine, Nat. Kidney Found. of S.E. Tex. (med. adv. bd.), Coun. of Women in Nephronology, Tex. Med. Assn., Am. Fedn. Clin. Rsch., Am. Physiology Soc., Am. Heart Assn., Kidney Coun., Soc. Gen. Physiologists, Math. Assn. Am., Gt. Houston and Gulf Coast Nephrology Assn., NIH Gen. Medicine B Study Sect. (mem. 1987—). Office: U Tex Med Br Dept Medicine Nephrology OJS 4 200 Galveston TX 66550

BELLOWS, BAMBI KIM, software dvelopment consultant; b. Evanston, Ill., Feb. 11, 1963; d. Joel J. Bellows and Priscilla S. (Pearl) Rocca. Student, U. Okla., 1978; student, Ill. Inst. Tech., 1979-80, U. Ill., 1981-82. Cons. U.S. Dept. Interior, Lakewood, Colo., 1984; programmer/analyst U. Denver, 1984-86; cons. Chrysler Corp., Detroit, 1986-87; system engr. Datalogics, Chgo., 1987-88; cons. Lorex Pharmaceuticals, Skokie, Ill., 1988—; owner BKB Cons. Co., Chgo., 1988—. Mem. Soc. Women Engrs., NAFE, Decus. Democrat. Office: BKB Consulting Co 525 W Hawthorne Chicago IL 60657

BELLOWS, CAROLE KAMIN, judge; b. Chgo., May 24, 1935; d. Alfred and Sara (Liebenson) Kamin; B.A., U. Ill., 1957; J.D., Northwestern U., 1960; m. Jason E. Bellows, June 28, 1958 (dec. June 1980); children—Marcia, Douglas, Daniel. Admitted to Ill. bar, 1960; law clk. Chief Justice Ill. Ct. of Claims, Chgo., 1962-72; partner Bellows & Bellows, Chgo., 1970-79, Reuben & Proctor (now Isham, Lincoln & Beale), Chgo., from 1979; now judge Ill. Cir. Ct. Cook County. Bd. dirs. Uptown Poverty Law Center, 1982—. Recipient Maurice Weigle award for outstanding service to organized bar, 1970, U. Ill. Mothers Assn. medallion of honor, 1975, Northwestern U. Alumnae award, 1978. Fellow Am. Bar Found. (bd. dirs. 1982-85); mem. Am. Bar Assn. (sec. 1967-73, chmn. sect. individual rights and responsibilities 1975—, mem. ho. of dels. 1975—, com. on bar activities and services 1978—), Ill. Bar Assn. (chmn. Bill of Rights com. 1965-67, bd. govs. 1969-79, mem. assembly 1972-79, chmn. budget com. 1976-77, chmn. legis. com. 1978-79, pres. 1977-78), Chgo. Bar Assn. (chmn. constl. revision com. 1973-74), Am. Law Inst., League Women Voters of Ill., Womens Bar Assn. Ill., Decalogue Soc., Nat. Conf. Bar Presidents (exec. council 1977—), Am. Jewish Com. (bd. dirs. 1985—), Northwestern U. Sch. Law Alumni Assn. (pres. 1982-83). Club: Law (Chgo.). Editor: Your Bill of Rights, 1967, 69. Office: 1602 RJ Daley Ctr Chicago IL 60603*

BELMONT, ELISABETH, lawyer; b. Sanford, Maine, Dec. 19, 1956; d. Ralph Sidney and Patricia (Sanders) B. BA magna cum laude, U. N.H., 1979; JD cum laude, U. Maine, 1983. Bar: Maine, 1984, U.S. Dist. Ct. Maine 1984. Corp. counsel Maine Med. Ctr., Portland, 1982—; speaker on health law topics. Editor: Maine Law Rev., 1983; contbr. articles to legal and med. jours. Bd. dirs. So. Maine Cable Television Consortium, 1983-85, Ram Island Dance, Portland, 1987-89; mem. publicity coord. Portland Mus. Art Women's Guild, 1984-85. Mem. Nat. Health Lawyers Assn., Am. Acad. Hosp. Attys., Am. Soc. Law and Medicine, Phi Beta Kappa, Pi Gamma Mu. Office: Maine Med Ctr 22 Bramhall St Portland ME 04102

BELMONTE, KATHLEEN ANN, real estate executive; b. Boston, June 9, 1961; d. Frank Anthony and Kathleen Ann (Connolly) B. BS cum laude, Salem St. Coll., 1983; real estate sales lic., Am. Real Estate Acad., Waltham, Mass., 1986. Lic. real estate salesperson. Order processor Matrix Internat., Allston, Mass., 1984; dir. leased housing Revere (Mass.) Housing Authority, 1984-88; property mgr. Cooperative Svcs., Inc., Chelsea, Mass., 1988—. Mem. Greater Boston Real Estate Bd., Dante Alighieri Honor Soc. Democrat. Roman Catholic.

BELOFF, FAE CLAIRE, construction executive; b. N.Y.C., Jan. 21, 1937; d. Joseph and Esther (Weschler) Kleinman; m. Stuart Arthur Beloff, July 31, 1966; children: Randy, Howard, Susan, Bari. AA in Merchandising, Bklyn. Coll., 1956. Sales person Macy's, N.Y.C., 1952-54; trainer Gimbel's Dept. Store, N.Y.C., 1955; asst buyer sportswear Grayson Robinson Stores, N.Y.C., 1956-58; buyer ladies sportswear Cato Stores, N.Y.C., 1958-60; buyer accessories Abraham & Strauss Dept. Store, Bklyn., 1962-66; sec. Sheridan & Behm Architects, Arlington, Va., 1972-74; corp. adminstr. Residential Carpentry Corp., Rockville, Md., 1974—; pres. Bari Custom Cabinets, Sarasota, Fla., 1984—, Residential Carpentry of Fla., Sarasota, 1987—; Bd. dirs. Residential Carpentry Corp., Rockville, Md., 1974—, Residential Carpentry of Fla., Rockville, 1983—, Bari Custom Cabinets, Rockville, 1985—. Mem. President's Club U. Md., 1978—; bd. dirs. Jewish Community Ctr. of Greater Washington, 1981— (Russian Resettlement Com., Mem. Com., 1989); chmn. Israel Bonds Women's Div., Washington, 1985. Mem. Nat. Kitchen & Bath Dealers Assn., Board of Trades, Long Boat Key Club. Republican.

BELOVANOFF, OLGA, healthcare facility administrator; b. Buchanan, Sask., Can., July 1, 1932; d. Frederick Alexander and Dora (Konkin) B. Grad. high sch., Kamsack, Sask., Can. From clk. to adminstrv. officer Sask. Health Dept. Cancer Clinic, Saskatoon, 1951-78; bus. mgr. Sask. Cancer Found. Saskatoon Clinic, 1979—. Dir. Sask. Br. Can. Tenpin Fedn., Inc. Mem. Assn. Adminstrv. Assts. Home: 420 3rd Ave N, Saskatoon, SK Canada S7K 2J3 Office: Saskatoon Cancer Ctr, 20 Campus Dr, Saskatoon, SK Canada S7N 4H4

BELSITO, LINDA JO, registered nurse, nutritional consultant; b. Bethpage, N.Y., May 29, 1957; d. Luke Bartholomew and Greta (Anderson) Belsito. AS in Health Edn., Nassau Community Coll., 1977; BS in Nursing, Molloy Coll., 1980; postgrad., Adelphi U., 1986—. RN. Staff nurse North Shore Univ. Hosp., Manhasset, N.Y., 1980-84, asst. head nurse, 1984-86, supr. cen. svc. dept., 1986—. Mem. L.I. Chpt. for Cen. Svc. Personnel (pres.-elect 1990—), Am. Drug Free Powerlifting Assn. (N.Y. state powerlifting champion 1985, 86, nat. powerlifting champion 1990, world powerlifting champion 1990), All Natural Bodybuilding Conf. (4th pl. U.S.A. Natural Bodybuilding 1986). Republican. Roman Catholic. Home: 209 W Nicholai St Hicksville NY 11801 Office: North Shore U Hosp 300 Community Dr Manhasset NY 11030

BELSTERLING, JEAN INNES, retired librarian; b. Phila., Feb. 2, 1928; d. George McNeely Belsterling and Mary Thornton (Innes) Bowman. Grad., Bryn Mawr Hosp. Sch. Nursing, 1948; BA, U. Pa., 1974; MS, Drexel U., 1976. RN, Pa. Nurse Bryn Mawr (Pa.) Hosp., 1948-51; commd. ensign USN, 1951, advanced through grades to lt. comdr., 1961; ret., 1971; med. libr. West Jersey Health System, Voorhees, N.J., 1976-90, ret., 1990; coord. S.W. N.J. Libr. Consortium, 1985-90. Deacon Trinity Presbyn. Ch., Cherry Hill, N.J., 1976-79, trustee, elder, 1984-87; mem. Rep. Nat. Com. Mem. Med. Libr. Assn. (cert. med. libr.), N.J. Health Sci. Libr. Assn. Home: 214 Shady Ln Marlton NJ 08053

BELT, AUDREY EVON, social worker, consultant; b. New Orleans, June 23, 1948. BS, Grambling (La.) State U., 1970; MSW, U. Mich., 1972. Adult probation officer City/County San Francisco Hall of Justice, 1973-74; child welfare worker dept. social svcs. City/County San Francisco, 1974-79; rsch. and planning spcialist City of Ann Arbor (Mich.) Model Cities Interdisciplinary Agy; cons. San Francisco; cons. in field. Grambling State U. scholar, 1966-70, U. Mich. scholar, 1971-72. Mem. ABA, Nat. Assn. Social Workers (edn. task force) Am. Orthopsychiat. Assn., Am. Humane Soc., Child Welfare League Am., Black Am. Polit. Assn. Calif. (legis. com.). Democrat. Roman Catholic. Home and Office: PO Box 5319 San Francisco CA 94101-5319

BELTRANE, SHERYL ANN, dentist; b. Easton, Pa., Sept. 11, 1945; d. John Raymond and Jean Elizabeth (Doyle) B.; m. Richard Herbert Clark, Mar. 4, 1967 (div. July 1972); children: Scot, Heather. AAS, SUNY, Farmingdale, 1965; BS, Hardin Simmons U., 1972; MS, Boston U., 1977; DDS, U. Tex., San Antonio, 1983. Cert. Tex. Bd. Dental Examiners. Dental hygienist Dr. Weinstein, Poughkeepsie, N.Y., 1965, Dr. Larry Nash, Fairfield, Iowa, 1966, Dr. James Conguer, Bladensburg, Md., 1972-74, Dr. Peter Weiss, Needham, Mass., 1974-77; asst. prof., dept. dental hygiene U. Tex., San Antonio, 1977-78; pvt. practice San Antonio, 1983—; dental cons. Head Start, Tex. Migrants, San Antonio, 1977; cons. Health Objectives Year 2000 Work Group. Mem. Tex. Work Force, Health Goals 2000. Fellow Acad. Dentistry Internat.; mem. ADA (Citizen Ambassador to Russia del. 1990, options seminar presenter 1989-90), Tex. Assn. Women Dentists (pres. student chpt. San Antonio 1981-83), Tex. Dental Assn., Am. Assn. Women Dentists (dist. trustee 1983-85, sec. 1985-86, v.p. 1986-87, pres. 1988-89, Outstanding Recruitment award 1983, Cert. Appreciation 1984, 85). Democrat. Roman Catholic. Office: 14845 Nacogdoches #4 San Antonio TX 78247

BELTZNER, GAIL ANN, educator; b. Palmerton, Pa., July 20, 1950; d. Conon Nelson and Lorraine Ann (Carey) Beltzner. BS in Music Edn. summa cum laude, West Chester State U., 1972; postgrad., Kean State Coll., 1972, Temple U., 1972, Westminster Choir Coll., 1972, Lehigh U., 1972. Tchr. music Drexel Hill Jr. High Sch., 1972-73; music specialist Allentown (Pa.) Sch. Dist., 1973—; tchr. Corps Sch. and Community Developmental Lab., 1978-80, Corps Community Resource Festival, 1979-81, Corps Cultural Fair, 1980, 81. Mem. aux. Allentown Art Mus.; mem. womans com. Allentown Symphony; bd. dirs. Allentown Area Ecumenical Food Bank. 2 Rider-Pool Found. Excellence in the classroom grantee, 1988. Decorated dame comdr. Ordre Souverain et Militaire de la Milice du Saint Sepulcre, 1988; recipient Cert. of Appreciation Lehigh Valley Sertoma Club. Mem. NEA, AAUW, Allentown Edn. Assn., Music Educators Nat. Conf., Pa. Music Educators Assn., Pa. State Edn. Assn., Am. Orff-Schulwerk Assn., Soc. Gen. Music, Am. Assn. Music Therapy, Internat. Soc. Music Edn., Assn. Supervision and Curriculum Devel., Choristers Guild, Lenni Lenape Hist. Soc., Allentown Symphony Assn., Allentown 2d Civilian Police Acad., Nat. Sch. Orch. Assn., Lehigh County Hist. Soc., Confederation of Chivalry (life mem. of merit, grand coun. 1988), Ordre Souverain et Militaire de la Milice du Saint Sepulcre (dame comdr. 1988), Maison Internationale Des Intellectuels Akademie, Order of the White Cross Internat. (nobless of humanity), Kappa Delta Pi, Phi Delta Kappa, Alpha Lambda. Republican. Lutheran. Home: PO Box 4427 Allentown PA 18105

BELZER, ELLEN J., management and communications executive, consultant; b. Kansas City, Mo., May 22, 1951; d. Meyer Simmon and Fay (Weinstein) B. Student, U. Okla., 1969-70, U. Ibero-Americana, Mexico City, 1971; BA, Northwestern U., 1973; MPA, U. Mo., Kansas City, 1976. Rsch. asst. dept. polit. sci. Northwestern U., Evanston, Ill., 1970-73; adminstrv. asst. Ctrs. for Regional Progress Midwest Rsch. Inst., Kansas City, 1974; various positions to dir. socioecons. div. Am. Acad. Family Physicians, Kansas City, 1974-86; pres. Belzer Seminars and Cons., Kansas City, 1986—; instr. communication Avila Coll., Kansas City, 1987—; instr. dept. continuing edn. U. Kans., Lawrence, 1989—; speaker on negotiation strategies, conflict resolution techniques, communication skills, 1986—; mediator for hosps., physician groups, state health depts., community health ctrs., also others. Contbr. articles to profl. publs., also monographs. Campaign vol. for local candidate, Kansas City, 1970, 82. Mem. Nat. Rural Health Assn., NAFE. Democrat. Home and Office: 21 W Bannister Rd Kansas City MO 64114

BENACH, SHARON ANN, physician assistant; b. New Orleans, Aug. 28, 1944; d. Wilbur G. and Freda Helen (Klaas) Cherry; m. Richard Benach, Dec. 6, 1969 (div. Oct. 1976); children: Craig, Rachel. Degree, St. Louis U., 1978. Physician asst. VA Hosp., St. Louis, 1982-84, Maricopa County Health Svcs., Phoenix, 1984—. Served with USPHS, 1978-82. Recipient Outstanding Performance award Dept. Health and Human Services. Mem. Mensa. Jewish. Home: PO Box 1272 Mesa AZ 85211

BENAKSAS-SCHWARTZ, ELAINE JULIE, education educator; b. Queens, N.Y., Nov. 12, 1959; d. Prosper and Dory (Saul) Benaksas; m. Michael David Schwartz, Sept. 1, 1985. BS, UCLA, 1982, PhD, 1989. Teaching asst. UCLA, 1982-84, rsch. assoc., 1983-89; asst. rsch. prof. Loma Linda (Calif.) U., 1988—. Co-author (with W.J. Wechter): Progress in Drug Research, Vol. 38, 1990. Recipient DuPont Teacher award, UCLA, 1983, rsch. fellowship NSF, Fullerton, Calif., 1980. Mem. AAAS, Am. Chem. Soc., Alpha Chi Sigma (pres. 1981-82). Office: Loma Linda U LLUMC #1516 Loma Linda CA 92350

BENATAR, PAT (PAT ANDREJEWSKI), rock singer; b. Bklyn., 1953; m. Neil Geraldo; 1 child, Haley. Albums include: In the Heat of the Night, 1979, Crimes of Passion, 1980, Precious Time, 1981, Get Nervous, 1982, Live From Earth, 1983, Tropico, 1984, Seven the Hard Way, 1985, Wide Awake in Dreamland, 1988; popular recs. include Treat Me Right, Hit Me With Your Best Shot, Love is a Battlefield, Hell is for Children. Recipient Grammy award for best female rock vocal performance, 1981, 82, 83, 84. Office: care Tom Ross Creative Artists Agy Inc 9830 Wilshire Blvd Beverly Hills CA 90212-1825 also: care Danny Goldberg Gold Mountain Mgmt 2575 Cahuenga Blvd W #470 Los Angeles CA 90068*

BENAVIDES, JULIE MARIA, banker; b. Hartford, Conn., Nov. 30, 1952; d. Joseph F. and Pauline (Bourret) B. BS in Math. magna cum laude, U. Hartford, 1974; postgrad., U. So. Maine, 1983. Mortgage clk. Windsor (Conn.) Fed. Savs., 1970-74; head teller Consumers Savs. Bank, Worcester, Mass., 1975-81; credit analyst N.E. Bank, Portland, Maine, 1981-84; supr. Eastland Bank, Woonsocket, R.I., 1984-85; loan rev. analyst Conifer Corp., Worcester, 1985-87; loan officer Bank of Boston, Worcester, 1987-88; pvt. banking officer Bank of New Eng., Worcester, 1988--. Bd. dirs. Crisis Intervention Ctr., Worcester; vol. Sta. WCUW-FM. Office: Bank New Eng Worcester MA 01608

BENBERRY, CUESTA RAY, historian; b. Cin., Sept. 8, 1923; d. Walter and Marie (Jones) Ray; m. George Lynn Benberry, Mar. 25, 1951; 1 child, George Valdez Benberry. BA, Stowe Tchrs. Coll., St. Louis, 1945; postgrad., St. Louis U., 1954-56; Cert. Library Sci., Harris-Stowe Coll., St. Louis, 1968; MEd, U. Mo., St. Louis, 1974. Reading specialist St. Louis pub. schs., 1945-85; ind. scholar and lectr. quilt history St. Louis, 1969—; cons. Calif. Afro-Am. Mus., L.A., 1985, Ferrero Films, San Francisco, 1985-86, Williams Coll. Mus. Art, Williamstown, Mass., 1988-89, Met. Mus. Art, N.Y.C., 1990. Rsch. editor Nimble Needle mag., 1972-76; contbr. articles to profl. jours. Established African-Am. Quilt Archive, Vaughn Cultural Ctr., Urban League, St. Louis, 1984. Named to Quilters Hall of Fame, Continental Quilting Congress, Vienna, Va., 1983; First Place in the Arts, African Meth. Episcopal Ch., Tucson, 1989, award for Leadership in the Arts, YWCA, St. Louis, 1989, for contbn. to arts, Sigma Gamma Rho, St. Louis, 1981. Mem. Am. Quilt Study Group (bd. dirs. 1983-86), Elder Craftsmen of N.Y.C. (adv. com. 1990—), Nat. Quilting Assn., Quilters Guild London. AME Ch. Home and Office: 5150 Terry Ave Saint Louis MO 63115

BENBOW, CAMILLA PERSSON, psychology educator, researcher; b. Lund, Sweden, Dec. 3, 1956; came to U.S., 1965, naturalized, 1985; m. Robert Michael Benbow, Jan. 5, 1975; children: Wystan R., Bronwen G., Trefor A., Evan M., A. Lovisa, G. Byron, Lena C. BA in Psychology with honors, Johns Hopkins U., 1977, MA in Psychology, 1978, MS in Edn. of the Gifted, 1980, EdD with distinction in Gifted Edn., 1981. Dir. Study of Mathematically Precocious Youth, Iowa State U., 1986—, Johns Hopkins U., Balt., 1977-79, asst. dir., 1979-81, assoc. dir., 1981-85, co-dir., 1985-86; assoc. research scientist dept. psychology Johns Hopkins U., 1981-86, asst. prof. sociology, part-time 1983-86; assoc. prof. psychology Iowa State U., Ames, 1985—. Contbr. articles to profl. jours.; sr. editor: Academic Precocity: Aspects of Its Development, 1983; editor Intellectually Talented Youth Bull., 1979. Recipient John Curtis Gowan prize Nat. Assn. Gifted Children, 1980, 81; research award Am. Ednl. Research Assn., 1982; Spencer fellow, alt., 1984, 85, 86; research paper award Mensa, 1985, 86, 89; Early Scholar award Nat. Assn. Gifted Children, 1985. Mem. Phi Beta Kappa, Sigma Xi. Office: Iowa State U Dept Psychology Ames IA 50011-3180

BENCINI, SARA HALTIWANGER, concert pianist; b. Winston Salem, N.C., Sept. 2, 1926; d. Robert Sydney and Janie Love (Couch) Haltiwanger; m. Robert Emery Bencini, June 26, 1954; children: Robert Emery, III, Constance Bencini Waller, John McGregor. Mus. B., Salem Coll., 1947; postgrad. grad. Juilliard Sch. Music, 1948-50; M.A., Smith Coll., 1951; D In Mus. Arts, U. N.C., Greensboro, 1989. Head piano dept. Mary Burnham Sch. for Girls, Northampton, Mass., 1949-51; pianist, composer dance and drama dept. Smith Coll., 1951-52; head music dept. Walnut Hill Sch. for Girls, Natick, Mass., 1952-54; pvt. piano tchr., High Point, N.C., 1954-66; concert pianist appearing in Am. and Europe, 1948—; duo-piano performances with PBS-TV, Columbia, S.C., 1967, Winston Salem Symphony, N.C., 1964-68, Ea. Mus. Festival, Greensboro, N.C., 1969. Democrat. Presbyterian.

BENCZE, EVA IVANYOS, mechanical engineer; b. Budapest, Hungary, Mar. 6, 1932; came to U.S., 1956, naturalized, 1977; d. Jozsef and Katalin (Szabo) Ivanyos; m. Joseph Steven Bencze, Aug. 4, 1956; children: Christina, Ingrid, Caroline, Andrew. MS in Mech. Engring., Tech. U. Budapest, 1955. Registered profl. mech. engr., Calif. Mech. designer Lockwood Greene, Inc., N.Y.C., 1968-69, Elster's, Inc., Hollywood, Calif., 1972-74; mech. engr. DMJM, L.A., 1974-75; sr. mech. engr. DMJM/KE, Balt., 1975-82, DMJM/HTC, Houston, 1982-83; sr. mech. engr. DMJM/Metro Rail Transit Cons., L.A., 1983-87, supr. mech. engring., 1985—. Mem. ASHRAE (assoc.), NSPE. Avocations: reading, listening to music. Home: 5326 Townsend Ave Los Angeles CA 90041 Office: DMJM/Metro Rail Transit 548 S Spring St Los Angeles CA 90013

BENCZIK, TERRY ANN, public information officer, writer; b. New Brunswick, N.J., Dec. 24, 1957; d. Bela Steven and Helene Lenka (Bodnar) B. BA in Communications, U. Houston, 1978. Writer, asst. producer Live at 5 Sta. KTRK-TV, Houston, 1978-79; freelance producer documentaries N.J. Network, Newark, 1980; staff writer Nightwatch CBS, N.Y.C., 1982-83, freelance writer CBS Morning News show, 1984-85; sr. writer, program mgr. JC Penney Corp. Communications, N.Y.C., 1985-88; pub. rels. dir. Del-Raritan Coun. Girls Scout U.S. Am., 1989; sr. pub. info. officer Port Authority of N.Y. and N.J., 1990—. Photographer East Brunswick Photo Competition (Photo of Yr. award 1984). Mem. Am.-Hungarian Dem. Club, Middlesex County, N.J., 1988. Named George Kirksey scholar The George Sch., 1975, William Measley scholar U. Houston, 1978; recipient First Place award Bus. TV Mag., 1988. Mem. N.Y. Women in Film, Writers Guild Am. (judge nat. awards 1988), Am. Women in Radio and TV, Internat. TV Assn., Internat. Women's Writing Guild, Raritan Photog. Soc. (v.p. 1982-84), U. Houston Honor Soc. (sr. class rep. 1978). Home: 17 Elmwood Dr Milltown NJ 08850 Office: 1 World Trade Ctr 68S New York NY 10048

BENDA, MARILYN VIRGINIA, small business owner; b. Leroy, Ind., Sept. 21, 1935; d. Charles Edward and Bertha Mae (Hoagland) Poisel; m. Augustine A. Benda, May 19, 1956; children: Michelle Bates, Lisa Brickman. Student, Purdue North Cen. U., 1983-84. Exec. sec. McGill Mfg. Co., Valparaiso, Ind., 1965-72, cost estimator, 1972—; owner, operator Benda's Bridal and Evening, Demotte, Ind., 1985—, Benda's Heritage House, Valparaiso, 1985—; co-owner Women's Resource, Inc., 1989—; pres., treas. Women's Resource, Inc. Mem. Nat. Bridal Services, Nat. Network of Women in Sales (charter mem. Ind. chpt.), Nat. Assn. Female Execs., Nat. Assn. Women Bus. Owners, Sigma Alpha Chi (pres. 1979). Home: 1806 Alice St Valparaiso IN 46383 Office: 606 N Morgan Valparaiso IN 46383

BENDER, BETTY BARBEE, food service professional; b. Lexington, Ky., Apr. 29, 1932; d. Richard Carroll and Sarah Elizabeth (Rodes) Barbee; m. David H. Bender, Dec. 14, 1957; children: Bruce, Carroll. BA in Home Econs., Mont. State U., 1954; MS in Food Service Mgmt., Miami U., Oxford, Ohio, 1980. Adminstrv. dietitan Mass. Gen. Hosp., Boston, 1955-56; asst. chief dietitan Meth. Hosp., Indpls., 1957-61; chief dietitan Community Hosp., Indpls., 1961-63; supervising dietitian Chgo. Area ARA, 1963-67; asst. food service supr. Dayton (Ohio) Bd. Edn., 1969, mgr. food service, 1969—; cons. Nat. Frozen Food Assn., Washington, 1983, Crescent Metal Products Co., Cleve., 1985. Contbr. articles to profl. jours. Recipient 26th Ann. Foodservice Facilities Design award Insts. Mag. for Commissary Design, 1972, Silver and Gold Plate awards Internat. Foodservice Mfrs. Assn.,1985, President's award Ohio Sch. Food Service Assn., 1987; recognized for outstanding contributions to child nutrition programs Ohio Ho. Reps., 1972, 84. Mem. Am. Sch. Food Service Assn. (nat. pres. 1983, chmn. 1978-80 major city sect.), Ohio Sch. Food Service Assn. (pres. 1977), Dayton Sch. Adminstr. Assn., Dayton Sch. Mgmt. Assn., Am. Dietetic Assn. (cert.), Ohio Dietetic Assn., Dayton Dietetic Assn., Soc. Nutrition Edn. (panel 1983). Democrat. Home: 7217 Tarryton Rd Dayton OH 45459 Office: Dayton Bd Edn Food Svc Dept 125 Heid Ave Dayton OH 45404

BENDER, BETTY WION, librarian; b. Mt. Ayer, Iowa, Feb. 26, 1925; d. John F. and Sadie A. (Guess) Wion; m. Robert F. Bender, Aug. 24, 1946. B.S., N.Tex. State U., Denton, 1946; M.A., U. Denver, 1957. Asst. cataloger N. Tex. State U. Library, 1946-49; from cataloger to head acquisitions So. Meth. U., Dallas, 1949-56; reference asst. Ind. State Library, Indpls., 1951-52; librarian Ark. State Coll., 1958-59, Eastern Wash. Hist. Soc., Spokane, 1960-67; reference librarian, then head circulation dept. Spokane (Wash.) Public Library, 1968-73, library dir., 1973-88; vis. instr. U. Denver, summers 1957-60, 63, fall 1959; instr. Whitworth Coll., Spokane, 1962-64; mem. Gov. Wash. Regional Conf. Libraries, 1968, Wash. Statewide Library Devel. Council, 1970-71. Bd. dirs. N.W. Regional Found., 1973-75, Inland Empire Goodwill Industries, 1975-77, Wash. State Library Commn., 1979-87, Future Spokane, 1983—, vice chmn., 1986-87, pres., 1987-88. Recipient YWCA Outstanding Achievement award in Govt., 1985. Mem. ALA (mem. library adminstrn. and mgmt. assn. com. on orgn. 1982-83, chmn. nominating com. 1983-85, v.p./pres.-elect. 1985-86, pres. 1986-87), Pacific N.W. Library Assn. (chmn. circulation div. 1972-75, conv. chmn. 1977), Wash. Library Assn. (v.p./pres.-elect 1975-77, pres. 1977-78), AAUW (pres. Spokane br. 1969-71, rec. sec. Wash. br. 1971-73, fellowship named in honor 1972), Spokane and Inland Empire Librarians (dir. 1967-68), Am. Soc. Pub. Adminstrn. Republican. Lutheran. Club: Zonta (pres. Spokane chpt. 1976-77, dist. conf. treas. 1972). Home: 119 N 6th St Cheney WA 99004

BENDER, DENISE MARGARET, retail liquor manager; b. Pittsburgh, Pa., Mar. 13, 1960; d. Lane Edward and Clarice Anne (Piekos) B. BS, U. Pitts., 1982. Mgr. Hardees, Pitts., Pa., 1976-84, Burger King, Riverhead, N.Y., 1984-86; mgr., v.p. Rocky Pt. Wine and Liquor, Rocky Pt., N.Y., 1985-88; mgr. North Mall Wine and Liquor, Westhampton Bch., N.Y.; pres. Select Vineyards Ltd., Wading, N.Y., 1989--. Mem. Les Amis In Vin, L.I. Connoisseurs of Fine Wine, Suffolk City Retailers Assn., NAFE, Smithsonian Inst. Home: PO Box 233 Shoreham NY 11786 Office: Select Vineyards Ltd 44 Cross Rd Wading River NY 11792

BENDER, DIANE LOUISE WOLF, lawyer; b. Evansville, Ind, Oct. 21, 1955; d. Thomas Joseph and Margaret Gertrude (Horn) Wolf; m. John Frederick Bender, June 15, 1985. BBA with highest honors, U. Notre Dame, 1977, JD cum laude, 1980. Bar: Ind. 1980. Ptnr. Kahn, Dees, Donovan & Kahn, Evansville, Ind., 1980—. Bd. dirs. Vis. Nurses Assn. of Southwestern Ind., Inc., 1983—, United Way of Southwestern Ind., Inc., 1984-89, Health Skills, Inc., Evansville, 1984—, Cath. Press of Evansville, Inc., 1985—. Mem. ABA, AICPA, Ind. Bar Assn., Evansville Bar Assn., Ill. CPA Soc. Home: PO Box 9164 Evansville IN 47724 Office: Kahn Dees Donovan & Kahn PO Box 3646 Evansville IN 47735-3646

BENDER, EILEEN TEPER, university administrator, English educator; b. Madison, Wis., Dec. 1, 1935; d. Samuel and Sonia (Roitblat) T.; m. Harvey Alan Bender, June 16, 1956; children: Leslie, Samuel, Philip. BSJ with distinction, Northwestern U., 1956; PhD in English, U. Notre Dame, 1977. Editor, photographer, adv. mgr., free-lance writer, book reviewer, Chgo., South Bend, Ind., Pasadena, 1956-66; lectr. English lit. and writing Ind. U.-South Bend, 1966-70; asst. instr. Yale U., New Haven, 1973-74; asst. chmn. div. arts and scis. Ind. U., 1978-80; asst. prof. English, U. Notre Dame (Ind.), 1980-84; lectr. English, St. Mary's Coll., Notre Dame, 1984-86; exec. dir. Community Edn. Roundtable, 1985-86, asst. dean faculties, assoc. prof. English Ind. U., South Bend, 1987—, assoc. vice chancellor acad. affairs, 1988—, spl. asst. to chancellor, 1989—, assoc. acad. advisor to the pres., Bloomington, 1988—, assoc. dean faculties, 1988—; cons. Danforth Found., Newcombe Fellowship, Rhodes Scholarship. Vice chmn. exec. com. Ind. Com. for Humanities, 1978-82; pres. St. Joseph County Libr. Bd., 1980-82; trustee South Bend Bd. Schs., 1978-82; advisor Michiana Arts and Scis. Coun., 1980—. Kent fellow, 1968; Danforth Found. fellow, 1968; NEH summer grantee, 1983; Ind. Commn. on Higher Edn. grantee, 1977-78. Mem. Soc. for Values in Higher Edn., MLA, Nat. Conf. Tchrs. English, Ind. Congress on Edn., LWV. Democrat. Jewish. Editor Yarns, 1956-58, Cable Newsletter, 1976-77, Cable Access Guide, 1979; editorial bd. Soundings; artist in residence Ind. U. Press, 1987; contbr. articles to profl. jours. Home: 1512 Belmont Ave South Bend IN 46615 Office: 1700 Mishawaka Ave Box 7111 South Bend IN 46634

BENDER, ELIZABETH MELCHERT, optometrist; b. Appleton, Wis., Nov. 27, 1960; d. Henry William and Adela Fern (Peters) Melchert; m. Edward Walter Bender Jr., May 24, 1987; 1 child, Kathryn. BA, Ripon (Wis.) Coll., 1982; BS, Ill. Coll. Optometry, Chgo., 1983, OD, 1985. Optometrist Broadway Optical, Waupaca, Wis., 1985-86, Pearle Vision Ctr., Oshkosh, Wis., 1986-87, Ophthalmology N.W., Chgo., 1987—. Named one of Outstanding Young Women Am., 1983, 88. Mem. Am. Optometric Assn., Ill. Optometric Assn., North Suburban Optometric Assn. (v.p. 1988—), Tomb and Key, Beta Sigma Kappa. Home: 334D Higgins Rd Park Ridge IL 60068 Office: Ophthalmology NW 7447 W Talcott Ste 503 Chicago IL 60631

BENDER, PHOEBE POWELL, civic worker; b. Albany, N.Y., Sept. 25, 1933; d. Ten Eyck Bronk and Kate Van Antwerp (Easton) Powell; m. Matthew Bender IV, Sept. 6, 1958; children: M. Christian, Jeffrey Powell, Jean Hammond. BS in Edn., Tufts U., 1956. Tchr. Johnstown (N.Y.) High Sch., 1957-58; bd. dirs. Shaker Mus., Ild Chatham, N.Y., Scenic Hudson, Inc., Poughkeepsie, N.Y. Pres. Common Cause N.Y. State, 1974-75, N.Y. State Legis. Forum, 1976-78, Family Planning Advocates N.Y. State, 1978-80, Combined Health Appeal of Capital Dist., 1983-87, Upper Hudson Planned Parenthood, Albany, 1980-82, pres., Shaker Heritage Soc., Albany, 1982-88, bd. dirs., 1982—; pres., Albany Inst. History and Art, 1986—, bd. dirs., 1983—. Mem. Jr. League Albany. Home: 6 Lower Sage Hill Ln Albany NY 12204

BENDER, VIRGINIA BEST, computer educator; b. Rockford, Ill., Feb. 10, 1945; d. Oscar Sheldon and Genevieve (Windle) Best; m. Robert Keith Bender, July 19, 1969; children: Victoria Ruth, Christopher Keith. BS in Chemistry, Math., No. Ill. U., 1967; postgrad., U. of Ill. Coll. of Med., 1967-69; MBA, Loyola U., Chgo., 1973. Nat. cert. data processor. Sr. systems rep. Burroughs Corp., Chgo., 1969-73; systems analyst Marshall Field & Co., Chgo., 1973-74; project leader Fed. Home Loan Bank, Chgo., 1974-76; sr. systems analyst United Air Lines, Elk Grove Village, Ill., 1976-78; supr. Kemper Group, Long Grove, Ill., 1978-82; prof., coord. William Rainey Harper Coll., Palatine, Ill., 1982—; speaker Midwest Computer Conf., DeKalb, Ill., 1988; exch. faculty Maricopa Community Colls., Mesa, Ariz., 1990. Nation chief YMCA mother-dau. group Indian Maidens, Des Plaines, 1982-83. Named Tchr. of the Month Burroughs Corp., Chgo, 1972. Mem. Assn. Inst. Certification Computer Profls. (life), Ill. Assn. of Data Processing Instrs., No. Ill. Computer Soc., Inst. for Cert. for Computer Profls., No. Ill. Alumni Assn. (life). Methodist. Home: 411 W Hackberry Dr Arlington Heights IL 60004 Office: William Rainey Harper Coll 1200 W Algonquin Rd Palatine IL 60067-7398

BENDER, WANDA MARIE, bank executive; b. Ft. Myers, Fla., Nov. 25, 1958; d. Dennis and Barbara Sagstetter; m. Garth A. Bender, Feb. 17, 1989. Student, U. Minn. Mgr. banking systems and end user support Midwest Savs. Assn., F.A., Mpls. Del. N.E. Park Neighborhood Assn., 1989-90. Mem. NAFE, Nat. Honor Soc.

BENDIG, JUDITH JOAN, systems consultant, computer company executive; b. Erie, Pa., Oct. 28, 1955; d. Richard W. and Rhea Agnes (Hain) B. B.S. in Music Edn. magna cum laude, Edinboro State Coll., 1977. Tech. cons. Inco, Inc., Washington, 1982; sr. systems analyst Devel. Sci. Services, Inc., Washington, 1982-85; dir. computer systems ADEENA Corp., Arlington, Va., 1985-86; prin. systems cons. WANG Labs., Inc., Bethesda, Md., 1986—; v.p. F&B Computer Assocs., Bethesda, Md., 1985—. Mem. Arlington Community Band, 1986—. Served to lt. comdr. USNR, 1978—, with USN, 1978-82. Mem. Assn. Computing Machinery, IEEE (assoc.), Naval Res. Assn., Nat. Assn. Female Execs. Republican. Roman Catholic. Home: 2783 Stone Hollow Dr Vienna VA 22180

BENDIXEN, ETHEL TOLENA, author, educator; b. Ward County, N.D.; d. Olaus and Ina (Simonsen) B. BA, U. N.D., 1924; postgrad., Wash. State Coll., 1932, U. Idaho, 1935; MA, Columbia U., 1940. Instr. U. Idaho, Moscow, 1939, 1940, U. Colo., Boulder, 1943, U. Mont., Missoula, 1950; assoc. prof. NYU, N.Y.C., 1940-70; book reviewer Prentice Hall, N.Y.C., 1952. Sr. author: (textbook) Production Typing, 1951, 4th rev. edit., 1975. Republican. Presbyterian. Home: 7450 Olivetas Apt B2a La Jolla CA 92037

BENDT, NORMA JUNE, procurement professional; b. Hawthorne, Nev., July 25, 1955; d. William Boyd and Sally Lou (Ramsey) Worsham; 1 child, Steven Eric II. Student, Coll. Charleston, S.C., 1983-86. Sec. Med. U. S.C., Charleston, 1974-76, staff asst., 1976-82, ops. mgr., 1982-83; procurement officer Coll. of Charleston, 1983-86; purchasing officer Wildlife and Marine Resources Dept., State of S.C., Charleston, 1986—. Mem. NAFE, Sea Island Bus. and Profl. Women's Club (Young Career Women award 1983, treas. 1984—), Nat. Assn. Edn. Buyers, Nat. Inst. Govtl. Purchasing Ofcls., S.C. Assn. Govtl. Purchasing Ofcls. (conf. com. 1985, program com. 1985—, chair, 1988, profl. devel. com. 1986-87, chair, 1986-87, bd. dirs. 1986-88, mem. exec. com. 1988, v.p. 1988, pres. 1989, chair past pres.' coun. 1990, nominating com. 1990), Purchasing Mgmt. Assn. of Carolinas and Va. (program com. 1985, bd. dirs. local chpt. 1986). Republican. Lutheran. Avocations: scuba diving, racquetball, aikido, running. Office: SC Wilflife & Marine Resources PO Box 12559 Charleston SC 29412

BENEDETTO, LORRAINE ANN, computer science professional; b. Newark, Oct. 17, 1949; d. Frank and Hilda May (Holt) Vanna; m. William Robert Benedetto, Sept. 12, 1970; children: Annemarie Lyn, William Francis. BA, Newark State Coll., 1972. Secondary tchr. St. Casimir's Sch., Newark, 1972-73; substitute tchr. various schs., N.J., 1975-86; mgr. Burger King, Hazlet, N.J., 1979-81; computer operator Miller-Wohl Corp., Secaucus, N.J., 1981-83, supr. computer ops., 1983-84, mgr. computer ops., 1984-86; tech. support computer ops. Petrie Stores Corp., Secaucus, 1986—. organizer Local Neighborhood Improvement, Union Beach, N.J., 1977-80. Mem. Nat. Assn. Female Execs. Democrat. Roman Catholic. Home: 100 Beech St North Arlington NJ 07032

BENEDETTO, LYNDA ELIZABETH, staff production specialist; b. N.Y., May 11, 1943; d. Joseph Vincent and Helen (Della Jacova) B. BA in English, Notre Dame Coll., 1963; MA in English, Wagner Coll., 1969. Tchr. English, journalism N.Y.C. Bd. Edn., Staten Island, N.Y., 1963-76; tchr. journalism N.Y.C. Bd. Edn., 1976-77, program dir., 1977-82; adminstr. program control Rockwell Internat. NAAO, El Segundo, Calif., 1982-83; advisor program control Rockwell Internat., El Segundo, 1983-85, mgr. program mgmt. info., 1985-87, mgr. program fin. program control, 1987--, adv. program control, 1987; fin. analyst semiconductor products div. Rockwell Internat., Newport Beach, Calif., 1987-89; staff specialist McDonnell Douglas Corp., Long Beach, Calif., 1989—; adj. lectr. in English CUNY, 1971-73. Photographic editor Notre Dame Coll., 1962-63. Mem. Nat. Mgmt. Assn., United Fed. Tchrs., Am. Inst. Aeronautics and Astronomics, C. of C.

BENEDICT, DEBBIE SWEENEY, employment training executive, computer analyst; b. Newport News, Va., Jan. 10, 1952; d. Richard Cole and Ruth (Warren) Tyler; m. Thomas J. Sweeney Jr., Apr. 30, 1971 (div. Jan. 1987); 1 child, Matthew Richard Sweeney; m. Alan Griswold Benedict III, Sept. 9, 1989. BS in Computer Sci., Franklin Pierce Coll., 1989; Student, U. So. Maine, 1981-84. Adminstrv. asst. U.S. Dept. Army, Aberdeen, Md., 1976-78; engring. technician U.S. Dept. Navy, Portsmouth, N.H., 1984-89, computer programmer/analyst, 1989—; pres. Success Unlimited, Inc. The Learning Ctr., Portsmouth, 1989—; participant Commn. on the Status of Women, State of N.H., 1989-90; speaker for Dept. Edn., Project Second Start--Tradeswomen's Fair, Concord, N.H., 1987, Career Days, local high schs., N.H., 1987-89; presenter seminars on careers and motherhood, 1989, success image workshop for women, 1989. Chairperson EEO com. Portsmouth Naval Shipyard, 1987-89; mem. Portsmouth C. of C., 1989; mem. U.S. Dept. Def. Wage Fixing Authority, Aberdeen, Md., 1978; cert. instr. Aids in the Workplace, ARC, Portsmouth, 1989. Mem. NAFE, Am. Soc. Naval Engrs., Seacoast Women's Network, Internat. Fedn. Profl. & Tech. Engrs. Office: Success Unltd Inc The Learning Ctr 10 Vaughn Mall PO Box 4762 Portsmouth NH 03802-4762

BENEDICT, ELINOR DIVINE, editor; b. Chattanooga, June 4, 1931; d. Thomas McCallie and Mary Hills (Faxon) Divine; m. Samuel Sollie Benedict, Oct. 3, 1953; children: Samuel, Jonathan, Kathleen. BA in English, Duke U., 1953; MA in English, Wright State U., 1977; MFA in Writing, Vt. Coll., 1983. Staff writer Times Publs., Kettering, Ohio, 1968-76; pub. info. cons. Centerville (Ohio) Pub. Schs., 1976; editor Passages N. Literary mag., Escanaba, Mich., 1979—, Passages N. Anthology, Escanaba, Mich., 1990; instr. part-time Bay de Noc Community Coll., Escanaba, 1977-86. Author: short story The Onlooker, 1953 (Mademoiselle Fiction prize 1953); authorpoetry. Sec. bd. dirs. William Bonifas Fine Arts Ctr., Escanaba, 1985-86, v.p., 1986-87; bd. dirs. Concerned Citizens for the Arts in Mich., Detroit, 1986—; mem. Commn. on Art in Pub. Places, Detroits, 1987—; mem. arts project panel Mich. Coun. for the Arts, Detroit, 1987—. Wright State U. fellow, 1976; recipient Creative Artist award Mich. Coun. for the Arts, 1985; Coordinating Coun. Literary Mags. grantee, 1987. Mem. AAUW, Associated Writing Programs, Soc. for Study of Midwestern Lit., Poetry Resource Ctr. Mich. (bd. dirs.). Democrat. Presbyterian. Home: 8627 S Lakeside Dr Rapid River MI 49878

BENEDICT, ELLEN MARING, biology educator; b. Eugene, Oreg., Aug. 28, 1931; d. Charles Lester and Zoe Z. (Patterson) Stephens; m. Benjamin Albert Benedict, June 17, 1951; children: Mark, Earl, Lyle, Alice, Alan. Student, U. Oreg., 1949-51; BS, Portland State Coll., 1965; MS, Portland State U., 1969, PhD, 1978. Instr. Portland State U., 1969-72; ecologist Bur. of Lang Mgmt., Burns, Oreg., 1980; tchr. Malheur Field Sta., 1990—; part-time instr. Malheur Field Stat., Princeton, Oreg., 1974-90; adj. prof. biology Pacific U., Forest Grove, Oreg., 1980-88; scientist Gov.'s Oreg. Natural Heritage Adv. Coun., Salem, 1983-87. Editor North Am. Biospeleology newsletter, 1981-85; author scientific papers in field, 1971-86. Recipient Conservation award Northwest Caving Assn., Nelson Brit Coll., 1980, State Appreciation award Bur. of Land Mgmt., Portland, 1981, Robert K. Potter award Oreg. Wilderness Coalition, 1981. Fellow, Nat. Speleol. Soc. (nat. conv. chmn. 1982); mem. Am. Arachnol. Soc., Nat. Geneal. Soc. (nat. program chmn. Conf. of the States 1991), DAR (state registrar, Oreg., 1988-90, state vice-regent, 1990-92), Geneal. Forum of Oreg., Inc. (v.p. 1987-91), Sigma Xi. Home: 8106 SE Carlton St Portland OR 97206

BENEFIEL-ERTTER, ANNETTE MARIE, travel agent; b. Cheverly, Md., Mar. 26, 1962; d. Harry Benton and Joan Taylor Benefiel; m. Timothy James Ertter, May 14, 1988; children: Amanda Nicole, Benjamin Curtis. BA in History, U. Md., 1987. Travel cons. Empress Travel, Bethesda, Md., 1985-86, Encore Mktg. Internat., Lanham, Md., 1986—. Mem. Internat. Travel Soc. Republican.

BENES, MARCIA ELIZABETH, health association administrator; b. Attleboro, Mass., Dec. 18, 1949; d. Howard Marvin and Hildred Jean (Bagshaw) Reid; m. Miguel M. Benes, Dec. 26, 1970; children: Satyavati Maria, Lucian M. BS, Goddard Coll., 1972; MS, Boston U., 1989. Mem. Conservation Commn., Plainville, Mass., 1979-83, Bd. of Health, Plainville, 1983-89; pres. Mass. Assn. Health Bds., Plainville, 1986-89; exec. dir. Mass. Assn. Health Bds., 1989—; founder, exec. dir. Mass CLEAN, Mansfield, Mass., 1986-90. Author: Private Well Protection Handbook for Local Boards of Health, 1989; editor MAHB Quar., 1989-90. Founder, pres. Natural Resources Trust Plainsville, Inc.; del. Mass. Dem. Conv., Springfield, 1990; pub. mem. Mass. Hazardous Waste Facility Site Safety Coun., Boston, 1986-90. Recipient Cert. of Recognition for Outstanding Citizen Activism on Toxics Issues, Mass. Campaign to Clean Up Hazardous Waste, 1987. Home and Office: 56 Taunton St Plainville MA 02762

BENESI, BETTY-ANN B., controller, business owner; b. Monmouth, N.J., Jan. 13, 1952; d. George Paul and Ruth Virginia (Samuel) Lunday; m. Stephen Vincent Branca, Sept. 16, 1974 (div. Dec. 1980); m. Jack Erwin Benesi, June 12, 1982; 1 child, Maxwell Jack. BA in Art, E. Mont. Coll., 1973; BA in Edn. with honors, U. Mont., 1975. Tchr. West Jr. High Sch., Great Falls, Mont., 1975-76; buyer Dalmo Victor, San Mateo, Calif., 1977-78, Nationa Semi, Santa Clara, Calif., 1978-82, ASMS, Cupertino, Calif., 1982-84, Versatec-Xerox, Santa Clara, 1984-86; supr. repairs Versatec-Xerox, 1986-88; controller, owner Faultline Express, Santa Clara, 1988—. Mem. NEA, Great Falls, 1975-76, Purchasing Mgmt. Assn. of Silicon Valley, Santa Clara, 1985-87; com. chair bd. dirs. Centerspace Dance Found., San Francisco, 1986-88. Mem. Am. Soc. Interior Designers, West Valley Interior Design Club. Democrat. Episcopalian. Office: Faultline Express 2118 Walsh Ave Ste 145 Santa Clara CA 95050

BENGE, CHRISTINE J. H., engineering specialist; b. LaCrosse, Wis., June 12, 1951; d. William Davenport Jr. and Carolyn Ann (Johnson) Heaton; m. Ruthford Dean Benge Jr., Nov. 29, 1975. BA, Ind. U., 1974, MLS, 1975. Info. analyst Ind. U., Bloomington, 1975-77; with Western Electric, Ballwin, Mo., 1977-83, sect. chief of staff, 1978-80, chief data processing sect., 1981-83; with AT&T, Ballwin, 1983—, technician pro rels., staff mgr., 1987-89, engring. mgr. records dept., 1989—; olympics site mgr. AT&T/U. So. Calif., L.A., 1984. Host family YMCA/Colombia Exch. Program, St. Louis, 1986-87; cons. project bus. Jr. Achievement, St. Louis, 1983-84; pres., treas. Overland Unity Ctr., Overland, Mo., 1984-86; mem. fair com. St. Louis Genealogial Soc., 1983-86. Della J. Evans scholar Ind. U., 1970-74. Mem. Profl. Women's Alliance, St. Clair County Genalogical Soc., Jackson County Iowa Genalogical Soc., Lafayette County Genalogy Workshop, NAFE, Phi Beta Kappa, Alpha Lambda Delta. Office: AT&T NFSW 93D300 1111 Woods Mill Rd Ballwin MO 63011

BENGTSON, ESTHER G., state legislator; b. Froid, Mont., Oct. 30, 1927; d. Goodwin and Elizabeth (Jorgensen) Bergh; m. Lawrence E. Bengtson, 1948; children: Kristianne, Monica, Jennifer. BS, Ea. Mont. Coll., 1967. Mem. Mont. Ho. of Reps., 1975-83, Mont. State Senate, 1985—. Mem. Sigma Kappa. Democrat. Lutheran. Office: 8124 Clark Rd Shepherd MT 59079*

BENGTSON, KATHLEEN ANN, weight loss system executive, counselor; b. Anacortes, Wash., June 3, 1949; d. Walter Roy and Gladys Clemance (Norgard) Huttula; m. Carl Edwin Bengtson, Dec. 21, 1975; children: Aaron, Andrew. BS in Art Edn., Oreg. State U., 1971; postgrad., Portland State U., 1976. Substitute art tchr. Portland (Oreg.) Pub. Schs., 1972; art tchr. Lebanon (Oreg.) Jr. High Sch., 1972-75; supr. Lebanon Christian Sch., 1975-76; guitar tchr. Linn Benton Community Coll., Lebanon, 1983; owner and salesperson Direct Response Advt., Lebanon, 1984-85; diet counselor Diet Light Weight Loss System, Lebanon, Albany, Salem,, Corvallis, 1983—; counselor trainer and sales trainer Diet Light Inc., Lebanon, 1985—. Republican. Home: 36287 Blueberry Dr PO Box 629 Lebanon OR 97355 Office: Diet Light Inc 300 Market St Lebanon OR 97355

BENHAM, ISABEL HAMILTON, public policy company executive; b. Buffalo, Aug. 4, 1909; d. Wesley Hamilton and Eva (Thorp) B. AB, Bryn Mawr Coll., 1931. Security analyst R.W. Pressprich & Co., N.Y.C., 1934-68, ptnr., 1965-68; 1st v.p. Shearson, Hammill & Co., N.Y.C., 1968-74; sr. v.p. Shearson Hayden Stone, N.Y.C., 1974-78; pres. Printon, Kane Rsch., Inc., N.Y.C., 1978—; speaker on r.r. industry. Trustee John W. Barriger R.R. Libr. of Merc. Library, St. Louis; qualified expert witness ICC. Mem. Fedn. Fin. Analysts N.Y., Transp. Policy Assocs., Women's Bond Club N.Y. (pres. 1949), Cosmopolitan Club (treas., bd. dirs. 1950-54). Republican. Presbyterian. Home: 45 Sutton Pl S Apt 14-M New York NY 10022 Office: Printon Kane Rsch Inc 509 Madison Ave Ste 802 New York NY 10022

BENITEZ, SHIRLEY ANN, protective services official; b. Lawton, Okla., July 15, 1943; d. William Allen and Zealon Marie (Yarbrough) Sheffield; m. Gary Wallace Brown, Mar. 4, 1966 (div. July 1972); 1 child, Eric Eugene; m. Ramon Bentiez, Nov. 17, 1973; 1 child, Jeremy Daniel. Correction certificate, Lakewood Community Coll., 1981. Sr. fin. worker Hennepin County Welfare, Mpls., 1971-78; rep. service Northwestern Bell Tel., Mpls., 1979-81; counselor correctional State of Minn. Corrections, Shakopee, 1981-84; correctional officer Bur. Corrections Hennepin County, Mpls., 1984—; organizer, leader Community Crime Prevention Block Club, 1978-81; vol. Advocate Women Minn. State Prison, 1981—; case mgr. Hennepin County Misdemeanant Probation, 1981—. Co-author: N.E. Resource Directory, 1976. Mem. Food Shelves Hennepin County 1974-78; leader Cub Scouts Am. 1981-83; bd. dirs. Am. Indian Commn. 1973, Am. Indian Haven 1973-75, group leader, facilator Battered Womens Group 1974-78; family violence adv. East Side Neighborhood Services, Mpls., 1988—. Recipient Dirs. award for Exceptional Contbns. to Vol. Program Hennepin County Ct. and Field Services, 1988. Mem. Nat. Assn. Female Exec., Am. Correction Assn., Minn. Corrections Assn., Triune Ministries (bd. dirs. 1987—). Democrat. Pentecostal. Home: 440 2nd St NE Minneapolis MN 55413

BENJAMIN, ADELAIDE WISDOM, education educator; b. New Orleans, Aug. 23, 1932; d. William Bell and Mary (Freeman) Wisdom; m. Edward Bernard Benjamin Jr., May 11, 1957; children: Edward Wisdom, Mary Dabney, Ann Leith, Stuart Minor. Student, Hollins Coll., 1950-52; BA in English, Newcomb Coll., 1954; JD, Tulane U., 1956; student, Loyola U., New Orleans, 1980-81; grad. extension program Sewanee Theol. Sch., U. South, 1982. Assoc. Wisdom, Stone, Pigman and Benjamin, New Orleans, 1956-58; tchr. ext. courses Sewanee Theol. Sem., 1984—; speaker on school issues various local and nat. groups. Mem. Tulane Law Rev., 1954-56. Pres. bd. New Orleans Symphony, 1984-89; trustee, sec. Mary Freeman Wisdom Charitable Found., 1987—; pres. E&A Charitable Found., New Orleans, 1983—; bd. dirs. RosaMary Charitable Found., New Orleans, 1978—, Loyola Univ., New Orleans, 1989—, La. Mus. Found. Bd., New Orleans, 1989—, Children's Hosp., New Orleans, 1976079, Southeast La. Girl Scouts Coun., New Orleans, 1989—, Louise S. McGehee Sch., New Orleans, 1990—; active Trinity Episc. Ch., New Orleans, sec. parish coun., 1973-75, sec. vestry, 1975-79, leader Trinity Quartet, 1979-84; local YWCA, 1967-75, 76-79, sec. bd. dirs., 1967-68, 1st v.p., 1968-69; trustee Metairie Park Country Day Sch., 1971-79, sec., 1976-79, pres. PTA, 1975-76; mem. Loving Cup selection com. New Orleans Times Picayune, 1985, Bur. Govtl. Rsch.; adv. bd. Pub. Radio Sta. WWNO, 1980—; bd. dirs Parenting Ctr., 1981—, chmn. by-laws com., 1983-84, chmn. pers. com., 1982-83; adv. bd Tulane Summer Lyric Theatre, Tulane U., 1972—, pres. adv. bd., 1977-79. Recipient Weiss Brotherhood award Nat. Conf. Christians and Jews, 1986, Outstanding Philanthropist, Nat. Soc. Fundraising Execs., 1986, Volunteer Activist Award, St. Elizabeth Guild, 1986, Jr. League Sustainer award, 1987, Disting. Alumna award McGehee Sch., 1987, George Washington Honor Medal for Individual Achievement, Freedom Found. at Valley Forge, 1988; named Goodwill Ambassador for Louisiana Gov.'s Commn. Internat. Trade, Industry and Tourism, 1987, Sweet Art, Contemporary Arts Ctr., 1988, Significant Role Model, Young Leadership Council, 1988. Mem. ABA, LWV, La. Bar Assn., New Orleans Bar Assn., Jr. League New Orleans (exec. com. 1971-72, bd. dirs. 1967-72), Ind. Women's Orgn., Com. 21, Am. Symphony Orch. League, Quarante Club (2d v.p. 1978-79), Sybarites Club, Debutante Club, Le Debut des Jeunes Filles Club, New Orleans Town Gardners (pres. 1979-80). Home: 1837 Palmer Ave New Orleans LA 70118 Office: Pl St Charles 201 St Charles Ave New Orleans LA 70170

BENJAMIN, LISA CAROL, marketing executive; b. Salisbury, Md., Dec. 22, 1959; d. Alvin Ira and Harriet (Goodman) B.; m. Robert Lipsher, June 18, 1988. BA in Econs., U. Pa., 1981, MBA in Mktg., Real Estate, 1985. Product analyst Western Devel. Corp., Washington, 1985-86; assoc. RPR Cons., Alexandria, Va., 1986-87; mktg. asst. The Milton Co., McLean, Va., 1986-88; dir. mktg The Milton Co., McLean, 1988—. Mem. Nat. Assn. Home Builders, Mongomery County C. of C., Washington Sales & Mktg. Coun., B'nai B'rith Women, UJA Fedn. Democrat. Jewish. Home: 11158 Cedarwood Dr North Bethesda MD 20852 Office: The Milton Co 1430 Springhill Rd McLean VA 22102

BENJAMIN, ROBBA LEE, publisher; b. Glendale, Calif., Dec. 1, 1947; d. Gilbert Searle Benjamin and Vivian (Durr) Carpenter; m. Keshavan Nair. AB, Occidental Coll., 1969; MBA, Stanford U., 1978. Treas. Kirk Knight & Co., Inc., Menlo Park, Calif., 1970-74; transaction mgr. Itel Corp., San Francisco, 1975-76, 79-80; mgr. sales adminstrn. Shaklee Corp., San Francisco, 1978; founder, exec. v.p. Benjamin/Nair, Inc., San Francisco, 1981-84; exec. v.p., chief adminstrv. officer MeraBank, Phoenix, 1984-88; pres. Trans Western Pub., a U S WEST Co., San Diego, 1988—. Bd. dirs., chmn. Jr. Achievement, Ariz., 1988-89; bd. dirs. Ariz. Clean and Beautiful, 1986-87; mem. adv. bd. Ariz. Theatre Co., 1986-88; mem. Phoenix Symphony Steering Com., 1987, Mayor's Commn. on Excellence in Edn., 1987-88. Mem. Am. Mgmt. Assn., Nat. Assn. Bank Women, Council Fin. Competition, (adv. bd.), Charter 100, Econ. Club Phoenix (bd. dirs. 1985-87). Office: Trans Western Pub a US WEST Co 8328 Clairemont Mesa Blvd San Diego CA 92111

BENJAMIN, SUSAN PIETRZYK, marketing professional; b. Niagara Falls, NY, July 4, 1948; d. Mathew Victor and Stella Julia (Religa) Pietrzyk; m. Gerald C. Benjamin, July 24, 1971. BA, SUNY, 1970, MLS, 1980. Caseworker, sr. caseworker Niagara Co. Dept. of Social Svcs., Niagara Falls, NY, 1970-79; pvt. practice rsch. cons. Cohoes, NY, 1980-85; mktg. and info. mgr. Ryan-Biggs Assocs., P.C., Troy, NY, 1985—, assoc.; sec. Upstate NY chpt. Spl. Librs. Assn., Albany, 1982-83. Editor chpt. bull. upstate N.Y., chpt. N.Y. State Librs. Assn., 1983-85, Modern Steel Constrn. mem. Soc. for Mktg. Profl. Svcs. (historian, Upstate N.Y. chpt. 1990), Assn. of Architectural Librarians, Rensselaer County Regional C. of C. Office: Ryan-Biggs Assocs P C 291 River St Troy NY 12180

BENKO, ELAINE TERRETTA, real estate partner; b. Evansville, Ind., Aug. 17, 1944; d. Trofim Sylvester and Lillian Doris (Gominick) Terretta; m. John E. Benko, Aug. 15, 1965; children: Deborah, Marjorie, Jennifer. BS, Columbia Union Coll., 1989—. Sec. Phys. Therapy Sch., Med. Coll. Va., 1975-79, William Byrd Press, Richmond, Va., 1979-83, Data Base, Richmond, 1983-84; adminstrv. asst. Thalhimers Dept. Stores, Richmond, 1984-88; ptnr. Terretta Investment & Mgmt., Richmond, 1988—, C.O.R.E. Mgmt., Richmond, 1989—. Mem. Am. Soc. Personnel Adminstrs., Assn. Adventist Women, Bryan Park Civic Assn. (dir. 1986-88). Republican. Seventh Day Adventist. Office: CORE Mgmt 2306 Bryan Park Ave Richmond VA 23228

BENKOVITZ, CARMEN MARY, environmental scientist; b. Havana, Cuba, July 6, 1940; came to U.S., 1961; d. Antonio M. and Guillermina M. (Pineiro) Navarrete; m. Stephen J. Benkovitz, Sept. 2, 1962; children: Stephen A., Anthony J., Susan M., Robert F. BS in Chem. Engring., Universidad de Villanueva, Habana, Cuba, 1961; MS in Chem. Engring., Columbia U., 1967; postgrad., NYU, 1982—. Computer programmer, analyst Brookhaven Nat. Lab., Upton, N.Y., 1967-74, sr. environ. sci. assoc., 1974—; mem. task group I Nat. Acid Precipitation Assessment Program, 1981—90. Mem. editoral bd. Environ. Software Jour., 1986—. Mem. Am. Inst. Chem. Engrs., Assn. for Computing Machinery, Air & Waste Mgmt. Assn. Office: Brookhaven Nat Lab Bldg 426 Upton NY 11973

BENLIFER, GINGER ENGEL, clinical psychologist; b. N.Y.C., June 4, 1949; d. Henry William and Edith (Schick) Engel; m. Brian David Benlifer, June 3, 1972; children: Brooke Joanna, Adam Ethan. BA, Conn. Coll., 1970; MS, Yeshiva U., 1973, specialist's cert., 1975, PhD, 1977. Lic. psychologist, N.Y., Conn.; cert. sch. psychologist, N.Y., Conn. Clin. psychologist intern N.Y. Hosp.-Cornell Med. Ctr., White Plains, N.Y., 1973-74; sch. psychologist Stamford (Conn.) Pub. Schs., 1974-79; pvt. practice psychologist New Canaan, Conn., 1979-86, Pound Ridge, N.Y., 1986—; vol. psychotherapist Am. Cancer Soc., White Plains, 1988—. Inventor road sign cover, 1989. Fellow Pub. Health Svc., Columbia U., 1970-71, NIMH, Yeshiva U., 1971-73. Mem. Westchester County Psychol. Assn., Am. Psychol. Assn., Coun. for the Nat. Register Health Svc. Providers in Psychology. Home: RR2 Box 2 Glen Dr South Salem NY 10590 Office: Box 164 Westchester Ave Pound Ridge NY 10576

BENN, SALLY ANN, healthcare executive; b. Augsburg, Germany, July 30, 1956; parents Am. citizens; d. Clair LaVerne and Betty Sue (Hoskins) Seglem; m. Charles Howard Benn, Dec. 1, 1978; children: Candice Elizabeth, Ryan Michael. AAS, Rose State Coll., Midwest City, Okla., 1976-79; BS in Radiologic Tech., U. Okla., 1984, postgrad., 1988—. Registered radiologic technologist. Radiologic technologist Children's Hosp. of Okla., Oklahoma City, 1976-79; instr./supr. radiography Presbyn. Hosp., Oklahoma City, 1980-87, dir. Sch. Radiologic Tech., 1987-89, dir. Women's Ctr., 1989—. Contbr. articles to profl. jours. Mem. Am. Coll. Healthcare Execs. (promotions chmn. 1989—, Achievement award 1990), Women in Communication, Healthcare Execs. Cen. Okla. (Technologist of Yr. 1980), Nat. Assn. Women's Hlth. Profls., Oklahoma City C. of C., Midwest City C. of C., Edmond C. of C. Office: Adminstrn Presbyn Hosp 700 NE 13th St Oklahoma City OK 73104-5070

BENNER, DOROTHY SPURLOCK, teacher; b. Greeley, Colo., Dec. 17, 1938; d. Lloyd Elsworth and Helen Rosalee (Pierce) Spurlock; m. Jerry Lee Benner, June 7, 1959; children: Shey Lee, Craig Lloyd. BA, Colo. State Coll., 1962, MA, 1968; EdS, U. No. Colo., 1978. Cert. tchr. elem. and bus. edn., spl. edn. and sch. psychology. Telephone operator Mountain Bell, Greeley, Colo., 1957; sec. Conn. Mut. Life, Greeley, Colo., 1960-61; substitute tchr. Sch. Dist. 6 and Outlying Dists., Greeley, Colo., 1962-67; tchr. Sch. Dist. 6, Greeley, Colo., 1968—; cons. Right to Read, Weld County, Colo., 1980—; tchr. night sch. Aims Community Coll., 1989—. Mem. Greeley Tchrs. Assn. (mem. negotiating team 1981—, sec. 1985—), Nat. Edn. Assn. (life), Colo. Edn. Assn., Kappa Delta Pi, Delta Kappa Gamma (pres. 1980-81). Republican. Methodist. Home: 1839 26th St Greeley CO 80631

BENNETT, AMANDA ANNE, engineering executive, management consultant; b. Pensacola, Fla., Apr. 2, 1956; d. Sam Kenneth Edward and Mary Anne (Phillips) Williams; m. James Ellis Bennett, June 17, 1979; children: Kathryn Anne, James Ellis Thaddeus. BS in Mech. Engring., U. Fla., Gainesville, 1979. Mech. engr. Tennessee Valley Authority, Chattanooga, 1979-84; pvt. cons. Washington, N.J., 1984-87; dir. research Wellington Mgmt. Group, Phila., 1987-88; exec. engring. v.p. The Bradford Group, Inc., Downingtown, Pa., 1988-89; exec. v.p. rsch. B&W Rsch. Assocs., Indian Harbour Beach, Fla., 1989—. Mem. Nat. Soc. Profl. Engrs., Am. Inst. Plant Engrs., Assn Energy Engrs., Fla. Engring. Soc., Tech. Assn. Pulp and Paper Industry. Republican. Presbyn. Office: B&W Rsch Assocs 208 E Eau Gallie Blvd Ste 74 Indian Harbor Beach FL 32937

BENNETT, AMY SPEAR, nursing educator; b. Albuquerque, June 15, 1949; d. Edward D. and Amy (Clark) Spear; m. Gary W. Bennett, June 1, 1970; children: Amy Lee, Margaret, Katherine. Student, Cornell U., 1969-70; BA, Northwestern State U. of La., 1971, BS in Nursing, 1973; MS in Nursing, U. Pa., 1981; doctoral studies, Widener U., 1988—. Cert. med.-surg. nursing Am. Nurses Assn. Staff nurse Rolling Hill Hosp., Elkins Pk., Pa., 1973-77; nursing instr. Albert Einstein Med. Ctr. Sch. Nursing, Phila., 1977-80, Episcopal Hosp. Sch. Nursing, Phila., 1982—. Brownie leader Girl Scouts, Wyncote, Pa., 1987—. Mem. Am. Nurses Assn., Nat. League for Nursing, AAUW, Sigma Theta Tau. Democrat. Unitarian-Universalist. Home: 7931 Green Ln Wyncote PA 19095 Office: Episcopal Hosp Sch Nursing Front St & Lehigh Ave Philadelphia PA 19125

BENNETT, BARBARA ESTHER, controller; b. Norfolk, Nebr., Nov. 24, 1953. AA, Northeastern Nebr. Community Coll., Norfolk, Nebr., 1973; student, U. Nebr., 1980, U. Colo., Denver, 1985, Harvard U., 1985. Bookkeeper McIntosh, Inc., Norfolk, 1971-77; credit, office mgr. Goodyear Service Stores Inc., Norfolk, 1977-81; pvt. practice acct. Norfolk, 1971-81; base adminstr. Evergreen Helicoptors Inc., Greeley, Colo., 1981-82; pvt. practice acctg. and tax service Denver, 1984—; acctg. supr. asst. controller Saltzgitter Machinery, Inc., Louviers, Colo., Saltzgitter, Fed. Republic Germany., 1982-85; corp. controller Satter, Inc., Denver, 1985—. Phi Theta Kappa, Phi Beta Lambda. Republican. Lutheran. Club: 4H. Home: 963 S Patton Ct PO Box 19070 Denver CO 80219 Office: Satter Distbg Co Inc 4100 Dahlia Denver CO 80207

BENNETT, CAROL ELIZABETH, immunopathologist, researcher; b. Perry, Ga., July 26, 1951; d. William Hearn and Dessie (Rollins) B. BS in Zoology, U. Ga., 1973. Research technician III dept. cell and molecular biology, Med. Coll. Ga., Augusta, 1973-76; research specialist II dept. lab. medicine, Med. U. S.C., Charleston, 1976-81; project coordinator III dept. path. and lab. medicine, Emory U., 1981—; adj. research assoc., Med. U. S.C., 1983—; dir. research adminstrn. and tech. coordination CytRx Corp., Norcross, Ga., 1987—. Contbr. more than 125 articles and abstracts to sci. jours. Chmn. Bloodmobile, Med. U. S.C., 1978-81. Rotary Club scholar, 1969, Regent scholar, 1969-73. Mem. Tissue Culture Assn., Am. Soc. Microbiology, Southeastern Assn. Clin. Microbiologists, Assn. Clin. Scientists (athletic com. 1980-85), AAAS, Ga. Acad. Sci., S.C. Acad. Sci., Sigma Xi (treas. Emory U. chpt. 1984-85). Office: Emory U Dept Path 760 WMB Atlanta GA 30322

BENNETT, CATHERINE CECILIA, educator; b. Seattle, Dec. 28, 1958; d. Stanley H. and Doris H. (Schossow) B. BA in Edn., Pacific Luth. U., 1981. Cert. tchr., Wash. Tchr. Reeves Mid. Sch., Olympia, Wash., 1982—; mus. dir. local theatres, Tacoma annd Olympia, 1979-89. Composer over 40 choral compositions, 1985—. Named Tchr. of Yr., Olympia Edn. Assn., 1990. Mem. Am. Choral Dirs. Assn. (organizing com. regional and nat. jr. high sch. honor choirs Seattle and Louisville 1978, 79, state chmn. jr. high choral standards and repertoire 1988-89), Music Educators Nat. Conf., SW Wash. Music Educators Assn. (sec.-treas. 1988—). Democrat. Lutheran. Home: 7929 Warbler Ct SE Olympia WA 98503 Office: Reeves Mid Sch 2200 N Quince Olympia WA 98506

BENNETT, CATHERINE JUNE, data processing manager, educator, consultant; b. Augusta, Ga., June 19, 1950; d. Robert Stogner and Catherine Sue (Jordan) Robinson; m. Danny Marvin Bennett, Sept. 5, 1971; children: Timothy Jordan, Robert Daniel. BS in Stats., U. Ga., 1971, MA in Bus., 1973. Programmer William M. Shenkel & Assocs., Athens, Ga., 1971-73; systems analyst U. Ga., Athens, 1973-76; product cons. Info. Systems Am., Atlanta, 1976-78, project leader, 1978-80, mgr. product support, 1980-85, hotline mgr., sr. fin. specialist, 1986-88; mem. edn. staff Investment Client Support. Den leader pack #419 Cub Scouts. Mem. Duluth coun. Gwinnett County (Ga.) Swim League. Avocations: bridge, swimming, travel. Home: 3458 Larch Pine Dr Duluth GA 30136 Office: Info Systems Am 500 Northridge Rd Atlanta GA 30350

BENNETT, CELESTINE C. T., librarian; b. Winston-Salem, N.C., Nov. 9, 1932; d. Arthur Loveliest and Mamie (Guerrant) Tutt; B.A., Winston-Salem State U., 1952; M.L.S., Columbia U., 1971, D.L.S., 1983; m. Henry McNeal Bennett, Dec. 28, 1977; children—Richard Bennett, Kathryn Bennett. Librarian, Urban Center, Columbia U., N.Y.C., 1971-73, asst. librarian Whitney M. Young Jr. Meml. Library Social Work, 1973-77, librarian, 1978-83; mem. papers adv. com. Whitney M. Young Jr., 1975-78, chmn., 1979-83; mem. adv. com. Whitney M. Young Jr. Disting. Lecture Series, 1983; mem. Oakland's Commn. on Aging, 1986—. Fellow Brookdale Inst. on Aging and Adult Human Devel., Columbia U., 1983—. Mem. ALA, Calif. Library Assn., Internat. Council Social Welfare, Bay Area Urban League. Home: Lakeside Regency Plaza 1555 Lakeside Dr #22 Oakland CA 94612

BENNETT, CHRISTINE LORA, English educator; b. Summit, N.J., July 25, 1948; d. Carl Emil and Helen Katherine (Rajoppi) Gerber; m. James Martin Bennett, Nov. 25, 1971; children: Stephan, Karin, John-David. BA, Fairleigh Dickinson U., 1970; MA, Kean Coll., 1989; postgrad., U. Md., 1975, U. Heidelberg, Fed. Republic Germany, 1975. Tchr. Elliott St. Sch., Newark, 1970-71, Lake Parsippany (N.J.) Sch., 1971-74; art specialist Big Bend Community Coll., Mannheim, Fed. Republic of Germany, 1975-76; instr. English as a Second Lang. Inlingua Sch. Langs., Summit, N.J., 1980-81, Summit Sch. System, 1986-89, Summit Community Sch., 1989—; adj. faculty Union County Coll., Cranford, N.J., 1989—. Vice chair Young Reps., Summit, 1966-70; mem. Union County Environ. Health Adv. Com., Westfield, N.J., 1971-73. Mem. N.J. Tchrs. English to Speakers of Other Langs.-Bilingual Educators, Inc., Phi Kappa Phi, Kappa Delta Pi. Republican. Presbyterian.

BENNETT, CONNIE SUE, food product executive; b. Richland Center, Wis., Oct. 4, 1955; d. Robert Eugene And Lillian Theresa (Crusan) Cottrill; m. James A. Bennett III,Oct. 22, 1977 (div. Jan. 1989). Grad. high sch., Ithaca, Wis. Owner, chef A Taste Of Heaven Restaurant, Anchorage, 1978-80, Saucy Sisters Catering, Anchorage, 1980-86; pres. Good Taste Inc., Anchorage, 1986—, Sable Properties, 1990—; owner Flamingo Properties, 1989—. Mem. adv. bd. Hugh O'Brian Found., 1987-89. Named Small Bus. Person of Yr. State of Alaska, 1987, U.S. Western Region, 1987. Mem. Alaska St. C. of C., Anchorage C. of C., Internat. Assn. Cooking Profl., Am. Inst. Wine and Food, James Beard Found., Inflight Food Svc. Assn. Office: Good Taste Inc 2000 W Internat Airport #C Anchorage AK 99502

BENNETT, DEBORAH R., employment agency executive; b. Los Angeles, Apr. 8, 1941; d. William H. and Harriet (Hatch) Roome; m. Raymond James Bennett, July 10, 1969; 1 child, Shauna. BS, U. Redlands, 1962. Cert. pers. cons., employment specialist. Exec. sec. L.A. Tchrs. Credit Union, 1965-81; sec.-bookkeeper Ronald Sinclair, CLU, Encino, Calif., 1981-83, Gruenfelder's, Canoga Park, Calif., 1984; self-employed, Granada Hills, Calif., 1983-84; owner, mgr. D.R. Bennett and Assocs., Panorama City, Calif., 1984—. Mem. Nat. Alliance of Homebased Women (v.p. 1983-85), Calif. Assn. Pers. Cons. (v.p. L.A. chpt. 1988), Nat. Assn. Pers. Cons., Granada Hills C. of C. Republican. Christian Scientist. Avocations: reading, sewing. Home: 17306 Trosa St Granada Hills CA 91344 Office: DR Bennett & Assocs 14600 Roscoe Blvd Suite 207 Panorama City CA 91602

BENNETT, ELSIE MARGARET, music school administrator; b. Detroit, Mar. 30, 1919; d. Sy and Ida (Carp) Blum; m. Morton Bennett, June 20, 1937 (dec.); children—Ronald, Kenneth. Cert., Ganapal Conservatory Detroit, 1941; B.Mus. in Theory, Wayne State U., 1945; M.A. in Music Edn., Columbia U., 1946; postgrad. Columbia U., Manhattan Sch. Music. Music studio mgr., tchr. Bennett Music Sch., Bklyn., 1946—, dir. 1946—; music arranger, 1946—; tchr. Schiff Sch. Music, 1972-80, owner, 1972—; tchr.

Robotti Accordion Acad. and Pkwy. Music Sch., 1945-46; owner Margolies Sch. Music, Acad. of Music Sch.; editor Accordion World Mag., 1945-56; works include: Easy Solos for Accordion, 1946; Bass Solo Primer, 1948; Hebrew and Jewish Songs and Dances for Accordion, 1959, Vol. 1, 1951, Vol. 2, 1953; Hanon for Accordion, 1953; Accordion Music in the Home, 1953; Folk Melodies for Accordion, 1954; Five Finger Melodies for Accordion, 1954; First Steps in Scaleland for Accordion, 1956; First Steps in Chordland for Accordion, Vol. 1, 1961, Vol. II, 1961. Mem. Bklyn. Community Council. Mem. Am. Accordionists Assn. (governing bd., pres. 1973-74, plaque, 1962, service to governing bd. award 1942-60, Silver Cup 1974-75), Bklyn. Music Tchrs. Guild (dir., past sec.),, Accordion Tchrs. Guild, L.I. Music Tchrs. Assn.

BENNETT, HELEN DONELE, educator; b. Spartanburg, S.C., Feb. 24, 1948; d. Freddie and Julia Beatrice (Rogers) B. BA, U. S.C., 1969; MEd, Converse Coll., 1977, cert. in adminstr., edn. specialist, 1990. Cert. spl. edn. tchr., psychology, sociology. City planner Model Cities, Inc., Spartanburg, S.C., 1969-70, planning coordinator, 1970-71; tchr., learning disabilities, emotionally handicapped Teszler Learning Adjustment Spartan County Schs., Spartanburg, 1971-87, coordinator Transition Program, 1987—. Active County Bd. Domestic Violence, Spartanburg, 1980-86; exec. committeeman Ward 5 Dems., Spartanburg, 1979—; mem. Spartanburg City Housing Bd. Mem. NEA, NAACP (sec. Spartanburg chpt.), Coun. on Exceptional Children (Spl. Educator of Yr. 1986), S.C. Edn. Assn., Assn. Suprs. and Curriculum Specialists, Spartanburg County Dem. Women's Club (sec.), Sigma Gamma Rho (Basileus-Xi Sigma chpt.). Home: 178 Aden St Spartanburg SC 29303 Office: Spartanburg County Sch Dist #7 Dupree Dr Spartanburg SC 29303

BENNETT, JOANNE B., reading specialist, consultant; b. Pasadena, Calif., Sept. 9, 1931; d. Theodore Parker and Mabel Priscilla (Lloyd) Bennett; m. William George Bennett, Dec. 19, 1953; children: Camille, William, Theodore, Frederick. BA, Occidental Coll., 1953; MEd, U. Ariz., 1971. Tchr. Newport Beach Schs., Corona del Mar, Calif., 1953-54, Calabassas (Ariz.) Sch., 1967-69; title I program mgr. Pima County Schs., Tucson, 1973-79; title I reading tchr. Tucson Unified Sch. Sch., 1977-78; reading coord. Catalina Foothills Sch. Dist., Tucson, 1978—. Author: Training Paraprofessionals, 1976. Chair rummage sale Jr. League of Tucson, 1968-69, v.p., 1970-71; mem. Young Authors State of Ariz., Tucson, 1988-90. Mem. Tucson Area Reading Coun. (pres. 1977-78, liaison), Ariz. State Reading Coun. (pres. Phoenix chpt. 1980-81). Home: 5235 N Valley View Rd Tucson AZ 85718

BENNETT, KATHLEEN MCMANUS, forest products company executive; b. S.I., N.Y., May 11, 1948; d. Leo Giblin and Rosemary Katherine (Keenan) McManus; m. Michael Canville Bennett, May 6, 1972; 3 children. BA, Manhattanville Coll., 1970. Adminstrv. asst. Office Congressional Affairs, U.S. Gen. Services Adminstrn., Washington, 1971-72; rep. Pub. Affairs Analysts, Inc., Washington, 1972-74; dir. legis. affairs Am. Paper Inst., Washington, 1974-77; fed. affairs rep. Crown Zellerbach Corp., Washington, 1977-81; presdl. appointee asst. adminstr. air noise radiation EPA, Washington, 1981-83; dir. regulatory affairs Champion Internat. Corp., Stamford, Conn., 1983-86, dir. environ. planning, 1986-87;, mng. dir. corp. environ. affairs dept., James River Corp., Richmond, Va., 1987—; mem. presdl. appointed Nat. Task Force Acid Precipitation, Washington, 1984—; mem. adv. com. to U.S. trade rep. on negotiations implementing Geneva Trade Agreement, 1978-80; head U.S. delegation 1982 Conv. Acidification Environ., Stockholm. Mem. Air Pollution Control Assn. (chmn. 1978-80), Air Quality Subcom. Prevention Significant Deterioration. Republican. Roman Catholic. Office: James River Corp PO Box 2218 Richmond VA 23217

BENNETT, LOIS, real estate broker; b. N.Y.C., Dec. 23, 1933; d. Richard and Fern (Steinberg) B.; m. Barry Silverstein, June 8, 1958 (div. May 1978); children: Mark Shale, Susan Beth, Thomas Benjamin. BA, Smith Coll., 1955. Cert. residential specialist, broker/salesman, Fla. Counselor Women's Health Ctr., Sarasota, Fla., 1977-78; investment counselor, stockbroker Pvt. Bourse Inc., Sarasota, 1978-79; realtor-assoc. Harrison Properties, Inc., Sarasota, 1984-86; broker/salesman Mt. Vernon Realty Co., Inc., Sarasota, 1986—. Bd. dirs. Planned Parenthood SW Fla., Sarasota, 1978-84, fundraising chmn., 1982-84; bd. dirs. Family Counseling Ctr., Sarasota, 1978-81, 90; mem. exec. com., bd. dirs. Fla. Studio Theatre, Sarasota, 1981-87; bd. dirs. Fla. West Coast Symphony, Sarasota, 1982-88; chmn. spl. events lst ann. Sarasota French Film Festival, 1989, co-chmn. spl. events, 1990; bd. dirs. Asolo Performing Arts Ctr., Sarasota, 1990—; mem. film commn. Com. of 100, Sarasota, 1989-90. Mem. Women's Coun. Realtors, Realtors Inst. (grad.), Sarasota C. of C. Office: Mt Vernon Realty Co Inc 3701 S Osprey Ave Sarasota FL 34239

BENNETT, LYNNE DEE, writer; b. Seattle, Feb. 28, 1953; d. Hale Burroughs and Marge Ruth (Perkins) B.; m. Mark Robert Clark, Apr. 23, 1983; 1 child, Jessica Bennett Clark. BA, U. Nev., 1974; MBA, U. Calif., Berkeley, 1987. Contracts mgr. U.S. Govt., Washington, Italy, Singapore, 1975-85; freelance writer Pleasant Hill, Calif., 1987—. Contbr. articles on bus. and lifestyle subjects to numerous mags. Mem. AAUW (chair communications local br. 1989-90, treas. 1990-91), Mensa.

BENNETT, MAISHA B. HAMILTON, psychological service executive, psychologist; b. Russellville, Ala., Sept. 20, 1948; d. Robert Morgan and Hannah Mae (Johnson) Hamilton; m. Robert Eugene Bennett, Oct. 12, 1974; children: Kinshasa Ayo, Karega Makesi, Ayinde Kofi. BA, Mt. Holyoke Coll., 1970; MA, U. Chgo., 1972, PhD, 1973. Dir. psychiat. clinic Jackson Pk. Hosp., Chgo., 1974-82; dep. commr. Chgo. Dept. Health, 1984-87; pres. Maisha Bennett & Assocs., Chgo., 1982—; mem. minority adv. com. U.S. HHS, Washington, 1980-83; bd. dirs. Ill. Sch. of Profl. Psychology, Chgo., 1983—, Univ. Hosp., Chgo., 1989—. Contbr. articles to books. Mem. fundraising com. Emil Jones for Ho. of Reps., 1987; treas. Tim Wright campaign for Ill. Ho. of Reps., 1987-88; mem health com. Harold Washington for Mayor Campaign, 1983-84, 87-88, Tim Evans for Mayor Campaign, 1988-89. Recipient Community Svc. award Chgo. State U., 1983, Kizzie award, 1984, Black Rose award League Black Women, 1986, Sesquicentennial award Mt. Holyoke Coll., 1987. Mem. Am. Psychol. Assn., Ill. Psychol. Assn. (Outstanding Profl. Psychologist award 1987), Assn. Black Psychologists (sec. 1976-77, pres. 1977-79, Outstanding Psychologist award 1981), Am. Orthopsychiat. Assn., Rotary (various coms.), Renaissance Women Club (various coms.). Office: Bennett & Assocs 343 S Dearborn St #1616 Chicago IL 60604

BENNETT, MARGARET ETHEL BOOKER, psychotherapist; b. Spartanburg, S.C., June 15, 1923; d. Paschal and Ovie (Grey) Booker. BS, N.C. A&T State U., 1944; MSW, U. Mich., 1947; PhD, Wayne State U., 1980. Diplomate Cert. Bd. Social Workers; cert. marriage counselor, cert. social worker, Mich. Caseworker, field instr. Family Svcs. Soc. Met. Detroit, 1947-52; caseworker, field instr., casework supr. Wayne County Cons. Center, 1952-60, Psychiat. Social Svcs., Wayne County Gen. Hosp., 1960-62; psychotherapist, field instr., asst. dir. Wayne County Mental Health Clinic, 1962-76; asst. dir. psychiat. social svc. Wayne County Psychiat. Hosp., 1976-77; dir. med. social svc. Wayne County Gen. Hosp., 1977-78; treatment cons. Project Paradigm, 1978-83; pvt. practice psychotherapy, Detroit, 1965—; psychotherapist, pres. Booker Bennett & Assocs., 1980—; founder Consultation Center of Ecorse, Mich., 1961; instr. Immanuel Luth. Coll., 1944-45; lectr. U. Mich., 1969-76. Bd. dirs. Crossroads, 1980-86; exec. coun. Episcopal Diocese of Mich., 1974-77, 80-83, exec. com. 1982-85, lic. lay reader, 1983—; trustee Bishop Page Found., 1983—; governing bd. Cathedral Ch. of St. Paul, Detroit, 1971-74, 76-77, 79-82, v.p. governing bd., 1977, sub-deacon, 1985—; bd. dirs. Cathedral Terr., 1981-87, U. Mich. Women, 1982-88, v.p., 1988-90, pres., 1990—, Wayne State U. Sch. Social Work Alumni Assn., 1981-86. Lic. Lay reader Episcopal Diocese Mich., 1983—, sub deacon Cathedral Ch. St. Paul, Detroit, Mich., 1985—; trustee bishop Page Found., 1986—. Fellow Am. Orthopsychiat. Assn.; mem. Mich. Assn. Marriage and Family Therapy, Nat. Assn. Equal Opportunity in Higher Edn. (Disting. Alumni award), Am. Assn. Marriage and Family Therapy, Acad. Cert. Social Workers (cert.), Mich. Assn. Clin. Social Worker's Nat. Assn. Social Workers, Nat. Coalition 100 Black Women, Phi Delta Kappa, Alpha Kappa Alpha. Democrat. Episcopalian. Co-author: The Handbook of Psychodynamic Therapy; contbr. articles to profl. jours. Home: 1971 Glynn Ct Detroit MI 48206 Office: 11000 W McNichols Rd Detroit MI 48221

BENNETT, MARSI ANN, marketing professional, industrial engineer; b. San Diego, Mar. 8, 1960; d. Edwin Moody and Helen C. (Buchner) B. BS in Indsl. Engring., Stanford (Calif.) U., 1982; MBA in Mktg., U. Pa., 1988. Systems engr. Xerox (Diablo) Corp., Hayward, Calif., summer 1981; from analyst to systems analyst Procter & Gamble, Cin., 1982-84, sr. systems analyst, 1984-86; intern Hewlett-Packard, San Diego, 1987, product mgr., 1988—. Mem. Jr. League Cin., 1983-88, Jr. League San Diego, 1989—; mem. task force Great Rivers coun. Girls Scouts U.S., Cin., 1984-86. Mem. Inst. Indsl. Engrs. (sr.), Wharton Club San Diego (v.p. 1988—), Stanford U. Alumni Club, Cin. Tennis Club, Kiwanis (pres. Stanford chpt. 1980-81), Alpha Phi (treas. Stanford chpt. 1980-81, rush chmn. 1981-82). Republican. Home: 10885-1 Scripps Ranch Blvd San Diego CA 92131 Office: Hewlett Packard 16399 W Bernardo Dr San Diego CA 92127

BENNETT, MARY See THOMPSON, DIDI CASTLE

BENNETT, MICHELE MARLENE, sales representative; b. Aurora, Ill., Sept. 11, 1964; d. James T. and Marlene F. (Johnson) B.; m. Charles H. Wolter, Apr. 28, 1990. BA in Psychology, Clarke Coll., 1985. Sales support Dun & Bradstreet, Chgo., 1986-87, account exec., 1987-89; account mgr. Sta. CSTV, Chgo., 1989; sales rep. Syntrex Incorp., Chgo., 1990—. Leadership scholar Clarke Coll., 1982-85. Mem. NAFE, Alpha Phi. Home: 1 Wheaton Center 1311 Wheaton IL 60187

BENNETT, PAMELA MCHARDY, production company executive, actress; b. Chgo., Mar. 4, 1947; d. George and Iris McH.; m. Robert K. Bennett, Mar. 19, 1983; 1 child, Melissa Ashley. B.A., Carroll Coll., 1969. TV and radio spokesperson Allied Van Lines, 1978-80; pres. Square One Prodns. Inc., N.Y.C., 1980—, pres. TV Presence, 1986— . Appeared in various stage and TV shows, radio and TV commls., 1969-80. Mem. Judith Harris Selig Found., N.Y.C., 1979—; sec. Widow to Widowed Internat., Inc., N.Y.C., 1986—. Recipient Wis. Broadcasters award, 1967, 68. Mem. Screen Actors Guild, Actors Equity Assn., AFTRA, Nat. Assn. Female Execs., Internat. Exhibitors Assn., Delta Nu Alpha. Republican. Avocations: singing; piano; guitar; jogging; reading. Office: Square One Prodns Inc PO Box 5122 New York NY 10150

BENNETT, PHYLLIS REDMON, human services agency executive; b. Smithville, Tenn., Aug. 1, 1944; d. Henry Clarence and Evelyn Louise (Ours) Redmon; m. Milburn Smith Rodgers, Jr., June 15, 1962 (div. June 1972); 1 child, Milburn Smith III; m. Weyman Herbert Bennett, Dec. 31, 1984; stepchildren: Nancy Lee, Gary Parks, Christian Elliot. Student Tenn. Tech. U., 1963-69. Editorialist Smithville Rev., 1963-65; teller 1st Nat. Bank, Smithville, 1965-68; site mgr. LBJ&C Devel. Corp., Monterey, Tenn., 1969-73; CETA dir. Upper Cumberland Human Resource Agy., Algood, Tenn., 1973-75, transp. dir., 1975-78, exec. dir., 1978—; coun. mem. Tenn. Dept. Human Svcs., Cookeville, 1983—. Pres. Cancer Soc., Smithville, 1968-73; hon. staff mem. Tenn. State Senate, 1985; col.-aide de camp Tenn. Gov.'s Staff, Nashville, 1987. Recipient Nat. Rural Transp. award U.S. Dept. Transp., Kansas City, Kans., 1985, Outstanding Service award Tenn. Assn. of HRA's, 1986, Cert. Appreciation Tenn. Commn. on Aging, 1986. Mem. Tenn. Assn. Human Resource Agys. (state pres. 1985—), Tenn. Assn. Spl. Transp. (dir. 1984—), Bus. and Profl. Women's Club (sec.-treas. 1966-72). Democrat. Baptist. Club: Jaycettes (Smithville) (v.p. 1970, Jaycette of Yr. 1972). Home: Route 6 Box 24 Cookeville TN 38501 Office: Upper Cumberland Human Resource Agy 150 W Church St Algood TN 38501

BENNETT, STEPHANIE MITCHELL, college president; b. Albuquerque, Jan. 19, 1941; d. Claude Stephen and Alma Nelle (Cashion) Mitchell; 1 child, Brendan T. BA, U. N.Mex., 1963, MA, 1966; PhD, U. Iowa, 1973. Instr. Loretto Heights Coll., Denver, 1967-68; asst. prof. Albion (Mich.) Coll., 1968-76; dean Westhampton Coll., U. Richmond, Va., 1976-84; pres. Centenary Coll., Hackettstown, N.J., 1984—; pres. So. Assn. Colls. for Women, 1981-82; state coord. Va. Women Adminstrs. Program, 1983-84; bd. dirs., exec. com. Va. Women's Cultural Hist. Project, Richmond, 1983-84; treas. Ind. Coll. Fund N.J., 1987-89, v.p., 1989-90; bd. dirs. United Jersey Bank N.W. Author filmstrip series Am. Invention and Ingenuity, 1968; contbr. articles and book revs. to profl. jours. Pres. Maymont Vol. Guild, Richmond, 1980-81; mem. Univ. Senate Bd. Higher Edn.; bd. trustees Blair Acad., N.J., 1987—. Ford Found. fellow, 1963-65, Earhart Found. fellow, 1974, NEH summer fellow, 1975, program grantee Xerox, IBM, 1978. Mem. Am. Studies Assn., Assn. for Study Higher Edn., Assn. Ind. Colls. and Univs. of N.J. (treas. 1986—, v.p. 1988—), Nat. Assn. Schs. and Colls. of United Meth. Ch. (bd. dirs. 1987—), Hackettstown Area C. of C. (bd. dirs. 1986-88). Episcopalian. Home: 407 Moore St Hackettstown NJ 07840 Office: Centenary Coll 400 Jefferson St Hackettstown NJ 07840

BENNETT, SUSAN CARROLL, marketing professional; b. Boston, Jan. 16, 1953; d. James Joseph and Mary Helean (Hurley) Carroll; m. David Herschel Bennett, July 31, 1953; 1 child, Matthew James. BS, Okla. State U., 1975. Retail buyer McClurkan's Dept. Stores, Wichita Falls, Tex., 1975-76, Connolly's, Oklahoma City, 1976-79; from dir. acctg. to dir. personnel Tener's Western Outfitters, Oklahoma City, 1979—, mdse. mgr., 1985—. Bd. dirs. Okla. State U., 1977—, Oklahoma City Jr. League, 1984—, Okla. Art Mus., 1982—. Mem. Fashion Group, Am. Mgmt. Assn., Am. Soc. for Personnel Adminstrn., March of Dimes. Republican. Roman Catholic. Home: 1407 Andover Ct Oklahoma City OK 73120

BENNETT-KASTOR, TINA L., linguist; b. La Mesa, Calif., Feb. 8, 1954; d. Clayton Leon and Patricia Jean (Howard) Bennett; m. Frank Sullivan Kastor, Oct. 28, 1979; children: Kristina Rebecca, Patrick Bennett, Liam Sullivan, Mary-Elizabeth. BFA, Calif. Inst. Arts, 1973; MA, U. So. Calif., 1976, PhD, 1978. Teaching asst. linguistics dept. U. So. Calif., 1975-78, research asst., 1975-76; research asso., co-dir. research John Tracy Clinic, Los Angeles, 1977; research cons. R. M. Lencione, U. Calif. Rehab. Center, Los Angeles, 1977; asst. prof. English and linguistics Wichita (Kans.) State U., 1978-87, assoc. prof. 1987—, interm coord. MA in liberal studies program, 1988-89, 90—; humanities cons. Children's Audio Svc., Sta. WUNC radio, Chapel Hill, N.C., 1985—. Faculty Rsch. award Wichita State U., 1979-80, 81-82, 85-86. Mem. AAAS, MLA, Linguistic Soc. Am., Am. Speech-Lang.-Hearing Assn., N.Y. Acad. Scis. Democrat. Episcopalian. Author: Analysing Children's Language, 1988; co-editor: Discourse Across Time and Space, 1976; contbr. articles to profl. publs. Avocations: writing, photography, music. Home: 115 N Fountain Wichita KS 67208 Office: Wichita State U Dept English 1845 N Fairmount Wichita KS 67208

BENO, CANDICE LYNN, chemical company executive; b. New Brunswick, N.J., Mar. 25, 1951; d. Andrew Jule and Claire May (Blanchard) B. BA magna cum laude, U. Conn., 1973, MS in Biochemistry, 1974, postgrad., 1974-75. Grad. asst. U. Conn., 1973-75; lab. technician Linde div. Union Carbide Corp., Keasbey, N.J., 1976-78, sr. lab. technician Linde div., 1978-79; regional tech. supr. Linde div. Union Carbide Corp., South Plainfield, N.J., 1979; asst. staff engr. Linde div. Union Carbide Corp., Springfield, N.J., 1979-82, staff engr. Linde div., 1982-84; tech. bus. cons. Linde div. Union Carbide Corp., Danbury, Conn., 1984-85; staff engr. Linde div. Union Carbide Corp., Somerset, N.J., 1985-87; mgr. Linde div. Union Carbide Corp., Springfield, 1987-89, Danbury, Conn., 1989—; supr. Werner Erhard & Assocs., Edison, N.J., 1984-87; guest seminar leader, 1985—, course mgr., 1984-86. Mem. Compressed Gas Assn. (chmn. 1984—, vice chmn. 1982-88), Am. Soc. Quality Control, Semiconductor Equipment and Material Inst. (co-chmn. 1987—, editor jour. 1982-88, Outstanding Svc. award 1984-89, Leadership award 1988), Mortar Bd., Phi Beta Kappa, Phi Kappa Phi. Democrat. Home: 405 Newark Ave Point Pleasant Beach NJ 08742 Office: Union Carbide Corp Linde Div 39 Old Ridgebury Rd Danbury CT 06817

BENOIT, NANCY LOUISE, state legislator, educator; b. New Haven, Conn., Jan. 25, 1944; d. James Michael and Florence Louise (Bray) Wynne; m. Raymond George Benoit, Aug. 8, 1970; children: Michael, Patrick. BA, Albertus Magnus Coll., 1965; MEd, Wayne State U., 1969. Tchr. St. Vincent de Paul High Sch., Detroit, 1965-69; community organizer Social Progress Action Corp., Woonsocket, R.I., 1969-71; dir. Little Shares Day Care Ctr., Woonsocket, 1971-73; edn. coordinator Northwest Head Start, North Providence, R.I., 1978-84; mem. R.I. Ho. of Reps., 1985—, chair joint legis. commn. on child care, 1985—, mem. adult edn. commn., 1985-88, mem. health, edn. and welfare com., 1986-88, mem. fin. com., 1989—. Mem. bd. mgrs. Woonsocket Family & Child Care Svcs.,, 1973-87; v.p., bd. dirs. Health Svcs., Inc., Woonsocket, 1974-87; founder Women for Women, 1983—; vol. coordinator Vols. in Action, Providence, 1984-86; bd. dirs. R.I. affiliate Literacy Vols. of Am., 1985-88; grant coordinator Community Coll. R.I., Lincoln, 1986-87. Named one of Outstanding Young Women Am., Woonsocket and R.I. Jaycees, 1980; recipient Francesco Cannistra Service award Health Services, Inc., 1986, Outstanding Service award R.I. Day Care Dirs. Assn., 1986. Mem. Common Cause, Sierra Club, Audubon Soc. Democrat. Roman Catholic. Office: RI Gen Assembly Providence RI 02903

BENRUD, AUDREY ELAINE, librarian; b. Mpls., Nov. 17, 1927; d. Edward and Alice Nathalia (Larson) Anderson; m. Charles Harris Benrud, Oct. 1, 1949; children: Edith B. Roberts, Kurt Michael, Erik Charles. BS, S.D. State Coll., 1961; MLS, N.C. Central U., 1987. Cert. tchr., N.C. Tchr. Toronto (S.D.) High Sch., 1961-63, Auntie Oyo's Comprehensive Sch., Lagos, Nigeria, 1963-64, Obalende Secondary Modern Sch., Lagos, 1964-65, Am. Sch. Lagos, 1966-67, Needham B. Broughton High Sch., Raleigh, N.C., 1968-86; tchr., libr. Needham B. Broughton High Sch., Raleigh, 1986-88, libr., 1988—. Nat. Humanities Ctr. grantee, 1984. Mem. AAUW, N.C. Assn. Educators, N.C. Library Assn., Capital Area Libr. Assn., Friends of Scandinavia (historian 1987-88), Vasa. Republican. Lutheran. Home: 929 Warren Ave Cary NC 27511

BENSCHOTER, REBA ANN, psychiatrist, educator; b. Smithland, Iowa, June 14, 1930; d. Glenn F. Patterson; m. Leon G. Benschoter, Sept. 1, 1956; children: Brooke Ann Benschoter Mowitz, Lorraine Ann Benschoter Dunn, Brian, Annmarie. BA in English, Briar Cliff Coll., 1952; MS in Psychology, Iowa State U., 1956; PhD Adult and Continuing Edn., U. Nebr., 1978. Chief com. div. Nebr. Psychiat. Inst., Omaha, 1957-65; dir. biomed. com. U. Nebr. Med. Ctr., Omaha, 1965—, dir. post baccalaureate tng. program, 1970—, assoc. prof. Sch. Allied Health Professions, 1978-80, assoc. prof. dept. psychiatry, Coll. Nursing, 1979—, assoc. dean. Sch. Allied Health Professions, 1985—; cons. Pub. Health Service, Dallas, 1974-76, Nat. Heart, Lung, Blood Inst., Bethesda, Md., 1974—, Stockton (N.J) State Coll., 1978. Contbr. articles to profl. jours.; producer, editor (film) Hands: Psychiat. Occupational Therapy, 1958, Help Wanted: Vocat. Rehab. of the Mentally Ill, 1961, Dr. and the Law Series, 1961, Plan Ahead for Mental Health, 1965 (Cert. Merit Am. Film Festival), How Are You? Nature of Mental Health and Mental Illness, 1966 (Cert. Merit Am. Film Festival), World of the Right Size: Nature of Mental Retardaion, 1968, How to Make a Miracle, 1977; dir., editor 50 tng. films, 1958-68. Mem. Health Scis. Communications Assn. (pres. 1976-77, Golden Raster award 1981), Assn. Biomed. Communications Dirs., Assn. Communications and Ednl. Technology, Med. Library Assn. Roman Catholic. Home: 2528 S 40th St Omaha NE 68105 Office: U Nebr Med Ctr 600 S 42nd St Omaha NE 68198

BENSEL, CAROLYN KIRKBRIDE, psychologist; b. Orange, N.J., Sept. 21, 1941; d. William Everitt and Margaret Mary (McGlynn) B.; A.B. with honors in Psychology, Chestnut Hill Coll., 1963; M.S., U. Mass., 1964, Ph.D. (Univ. fellow), 1967. Teaching asst. U. Mass., Amherst, 1963-64, research asst., 1964-66; human factors psychologist Grumman Aerospace Corp., Bethpage, N.Y., 1967-71; chief human factors group U.S. Army Natick (Mass.) Research, Devel. and Engring. Ctr., 1971—. Lic. psychologist, Mass. Fellow Human Factors Soc.; mem. Am. Psychol. Assn., Human Factors Soc., Ergonomics Soc., Soc. Engring. Psychologists, Internat. Ergonomics Assn., AAAS, Sigma Xi. Editor: Proc. 23d Ann. Meeting of Human Factors Soc., 1979. Office: Sci & Advanced Tech Directorate Army Natick Research Devel Engring Ctr Kansas St Natick MA 01760

BENSIMON, HELEN FRANK, public relations executive; b. Winnipeg, Man., Can., Nov. 22, 1941; d. Heinz Georg and Sabina (Glattenberg) Frank; m. Simon Chalom Bensimon, Aug. 7, 1963. BA, U. Man., 1962; postgrad., Roosevelt U., Chgo., 1970s. Reporter Jersey Jour., Jersey City, 1964-68; writer devel. publs. U. Chgo., 1968-72; dir. pub. affairs Mile Sq. Health Ctr., Inc., Chgo., 1972-74; coord. pub. info. ACS, Chgo., 1974-75; sr. sci. writer, news bur. mgr. Rush-Presbyn.-St. Luke's Med. Ctr., Chgo., 1975-79; dir. communications Voluntary Effort to Contain Health Care Costs, Chgo., 1979-81; dir. info. svcs. Am. Speech, Lang., Hearing Assn., Rockville, Md., 1981-86; dir. pub. rels. Am. Soc. Tng. and Devel., Alexandria, Va., 1986—. Contbr. articles to various publs.; author brochures, ann. reports. Recipient Award of Excellence Soc. Tech. Communications, 1983, 85, Morris Fishbein award Am. Med. Writers Assn., 1978. Mem. Pub. Rels. Soc. Am. Home: 804 Dale Dr Silver Spring MD 20910 Office: Am Soc Tng and Devel 1630 Duke St Box 1443 Alexandria VA 22313

BENSKINA, PRINCESS ORELIA (MARGARITA O. BENSKINA), dancer, singer, musician; b. Colon, Panama, Mar. 16; naturalized U.S. citizen, 1956; d. Jose and Amelia Benskina; 1 child, Pearl Am. Quintyne. diploma in modeling instrn., N.Y. Acad. Theatrical Arts, 1962; grad. N.Y. Sch. Floral Designing, 1971; BA in Interdisciplinary Studies, Queens Coll., 1983. Ordained to ministry Internat. Spiritual Healers Fellowship, 1956. Owner, mgr. retail religious mdse. store, N.Y.C. Has appeared in theatres, night clubs in various cities U.S., including Connie's Inn Broadway Night Club, Broadway Cotton Club, Leon and Eddie's; in Dance with Your Gods, Calling All Stars, Broadway Parade, N.Y.C., after 1935; mem. Afro-Cuban dance team, Orelia and Pete, 1942; toured with Asadata Dofara Dance Opera, Kykunkor, 1947; now appearing with own ensemble; toured Can. with own dance co., Bacanal, 1950; starred in UN program Stars of the West Indies, also TV program Tropical Holiday, CBS; toured with Sam Manning Calypso Concert Co., 1954; personal mgr. for modern jazz group Rouse-Watkins-Les Modes Quintet, 1956, also dance and mus. groups; prod., dir. concerts, N.Y.C., 1959; produced, directed, starred in concert program Princess Orelia's Pot Puree, Town Hall, N.Y.C., 1964; appeared on Ghana radio, 1971-77 . Vol. Bellevue Hosp., N.Y.C. Recipient J.F. Kennedy Libr. for Minorities Heritage award, Am. Honorarium award, 1966, Merit cert. World of Poetry, 1987, Gold Poet award World of Poetry, 1988, Silver Poet award World of Poetry, 1988. Mem. Broadcast Music, Inc., Synanon, Negro Women's Guild, Washington, Council Negro Am. Women (life), Media Women, Temple of the Arts Soc. (life), Sigma Gamma Rho (hon., Community Svc. award 1984). Author: (poetry) No Longer Defeated and Other Poems, 1972; The Inflammable Desire to Rebel, 1973; I Have Loved You Already, 1974; I Thank You, Father, 1976; Library To Whom It May Concern, 1978; In Retrospect, 1987. Contbr. to New Voices in American Poetry, 1972-73. Avocations: music, astrology, dancing, reading, sports. Home: 192-22 100th Ave Hollis NY 11423

BENSON, BETTY JONES, educator; b. Barrow County, Ga., Jan. 11, 1928; d. George C. and Bertha (Mobley) Jones. B.S. in Edn., N. Ga. U., Dahlonega, 1958; M.Ed. in Curriculum and Supervision, U. Ga., Athens, 1968, edn. specialist in Curriculum and Supervision, 1970; m. George T. Benson; children: George Steven, Elizabeth Gayle, James Claud, Robert Benjamin. Tchr. Forsyth County (Ga.) Bd. Edn., Cumming, 1956-66, curriculum dir., 1966—; asst. supt. for instrn. Forsyth County Schs., 1981—. Active Alpine Ctr. for Disturbed Children; chmn. Ga. Lake Lanier Island Authority; mem. N. Ga. Coll. Edn. Adv. Com., Ga. Textbook Com.; adv. Boy Scouts; Sunday sch. tchr. 1st Baptist Ch. Cumming; active Forsyth County Substance Abuse Commn. Mem. NEA, Ga. Assn. Educators (bd. dir.), Nat. Assn. Supervision and Curriculum Devel., Ga. Assn. Supervision and Curriculum Devel. (pres.), Assn. Childhood Edn. Internat., Bus. and Profl. Women's Club, Internat. Platform Assn., Ga. Future Tchrs. Adv. Assn. (pres.), Profl. Assn. Ga. Educators, Ga. Assn. Ednl. Leaders (dir.), HeadStart Dirs. Assn., Forsyth County Hist. Soc. Home: 1235 Dahlonega Hwy Cumming GA 30130 Office: 101 School St Cumming GA 30130

BENSON, DEBRA A., programming director; b. Huntsville, Ala., Oct. 14, 1953; d. Vernon and Betty Lou (Taylor) B. Student, Jacksonville State, Ala., 1971-73, U. Ala., Huntsville, 1975-86. Blind aid Jacksonville State U., Ala., 1971-73; sec. Recreation Dept., Madison, Ala., 1974-77; sales fin. rep. 1st Nat. Bank, Huntsville, 1977-81; asst. program dir. WAAY-TV, Huntsville, Ala., 1981-84, promotion mgr., 1984-88, program dir., 1988—. Bd. Dirs. Crime Stoppers, Huntsville, 1985-90; campaign mgr., Betty Benson, Huntsville, 1984; newsletter editor, Tommy Battle, Huntsville, 1985. Recipient ADDY (gold), Muscle Shoals Ad Club, Florence, Ala., 1985, ADDY (four gold) Greater Huntsville Ad Club, 1986-87. Mem. Stop Child Abuse Now, Viewers for Quality TV, Inc., Nat.Assn. TV Programming Execs. Home: 106 Suffolk Dr Madison AL 35758 Office: WAAY-TV 1000 Monte Sano Blvd Huntsville AL 35801

BENSON, ELAINE K. G., journalist, art gallery owner; b. Phila., Apr. 30, 1924; d. Benjamin P. and Elizabeth (Miller) Klebanoff; m. Warren Goff, July 3, 1943 (div. 1964); children: William M., Virginia L., Neal M., Kimberly Goff Kay; m. Emanuel M. Benson, Dec. 26, 1964 (dec. 1971); m. Joseph F.X. Kaufman, Jan. 21, 1974. BA, U. Pa., 1944; LHD (hon.), L.I. U., 1987, L.I. U., Southampton, 1988. Dir. pub. rels. Phila. Mus. Coll. Art, 1957-62; free lance journalist, 1960—; dir. Elaine Benson Gallery, Bridgehampton, N.Y., 1965—; dir. of community rels. Southampton (N.Y) Hosp., 1968-89; dir. Elaine Benson Gallery, Bridgehampton, N.Y., 1964—; editor The Hampton Mag., Bridgehampton, 1983-84, Dan's Papers, 1989. Author: Coffee and Brazil, 1962. Bd. dirs. Hampton Classic Horse Show, Bridgehampton, 1980—, Save Our World, 1983—, Cultural Ctr. Southampton, 1988-89; mem. Nassau Suffolk Hosp. Pub. Rels. Coun.; cons. Southampton Hosp. Home: PO Box AJ Montauk Hwy Bridgehampton NY 11932

BENSON, KIM DERRICK, communications company executive, writer; b. Salt Lake City, Dec. 3, 1954; d. Lee Richard and Carolyn (Redd) Derrick; m. Gary Ernest Benson, July 3, 1976. Tech. writer Evans & Sutherland Computer Corp., Salt Lake City, 1980-85; owner, pres. Advantage Communications, Phoenix, 1986—; cons. on tech. writing and desktop pub., Phoenix, 1986—. Contbr. articles to mags. Mem. Women in Communications (v.p. mem. and computer svcs. 1989—), NAFE. Office: Advantage Communications 4532 W Aster Dr Glendale AZ 85304

BENSON, LENORE J., association executive; b. Cleve., Aug. 20; d. Charles Robert and Eleanor Margaret (Hauck) B. Student, Wellesley Coll., Mass., 1942-43, U. Minn., Mpls., 1943-44. Fashion coordinator Young-Quinlan, Mpls., 1945-47; fashion promotion dir. Franklin Simon, N.Y.C., 1947-55; merchandising dir. Mademoiselle Mag., N.Y.C., 1955-78; fashion promotion dir. Harper's Bazaar, N.Y.C., 1978-81; merchandising dir. Vogue Mag., N.Y.C., 1981-84; exec. dir. The Fashion Group, N.Y.C., 1984—. Home: 430 E 56th St New York NY 10022 Office: The Fashion Group Internat 9 Rockefeller Pla New York NY 10020

BENSON, LUCY PETERS WILSON, political and diplomatic consultant; b. N.Y.C., Aug. 25, 1927; d. Willard Oliver and Helen (Peters) Wilson; m. Bruce Buzzell Benson, Mar. 30, 1950 (dec. Mar. 1990). B.A., Smith Coll., 1949, M.A., 1955; L.H.D. (hon.), Wheaton Coll., Norton, Mass., 1965; LL.D. (hon.), U. Mass., 1969; L.H.D. (hon.), Bucknell U., 1972; LL.D. (hon.), U. Md., 1972; L.H.D. (hon.), Carleton Coll., 1973; LL.D. (hon.), Amherst Coll., 1974, Clark U., 1975; H.H.D., Springfield Coll., 1981; L.H.D. (hon.), Bates Coll., 1982. Mem. jr. exec. tng. program Bloomingdale's, N.Y.C., 1949-50; asst. dir. pub. rels. Smith Coll., 1950-53; rsch. asst. dept. Am. studies Amherst Coll., 1956-57; pres. Amherst LWV, Mass., 1957-61; pres. Mass. LWV, 1961-65, nat. pres., 1968-74; mem. Gov.'s cabinet and sec. human svcs. Commonwealth of Mass., 1975; mem. spl. commn. on adminstrv. rev. U.S. Ho. of Reps., Washington, 1976-77; under sec. State Security Assistance, Sci. and Tech. U.S. Dept. State, Washington, 1977-80; cons. U.S. Dept. State and SRI Internat., Washington, 1980-81; pres. Benson and Assocs., Amherst and Washington, 1981—; vice chmn. Citizen Network for Fgn. Affairs; trustee N.E. Utilities, 1971-74, 76-77; bd. dirs. Continental Group, Inc., 1974-77, 80-85, Dreyfus Fund, Dreyfus Liquid Assets, Dreyfus Convertible Securities Fund, Dreyfus Third Century Fund, Inc., Grumman Corp., Communications Satellite Corp., Gen. Reins. Corp. Mem. steering com. Urban Coalition, 1968, exec. com., 1970-75, 80-84, co-chmn., 1973-75; mem. Gov. Mass. Spl. Com. Rev. Sunday Closing Laws, 1961; mem. spl. commn. Mass. Legislature to Study Budgetary Powers of Trustees U. Mass., 1961-62; mem. Gov. Mass. Com. Rev. Salaries State Employees, 1963, Mass. Adv. Bd. Higher Ednl. Policy, 1962-65, Mass. Bd. Edn. Adv. Com. Racial Imbalance and Edn., 1964-65, Mass. adv. com. U.S. Commn. Civil Rights, 1964-73; vice chmn. Mass. Adv. Council Edn., 1965-68; mem. Mass. Com. Children and Youth Com. to Study Report by U.S. Children's Bur., Mass. Youth Svc. Div., 1967; mem. pub. adv. com. U.S. Trade Policy, 1968; mem. vis. com. John F. Kennedy Sch. Govt.; mem. Trilateral Commn., Coun. Fgn. Rels. Mem. town meeting, Amherst, 1957-74, finance com., 1960-66; trustee Edn. Devel. Center, Newton, Mass., 1967-72, Nat. Urban League, 1974-77, Smith Coll., 1975-80, Brookings Instn., 1974-77, Alfred P. Sloan Found., 1975-77, 81—, Bur. Social Sci. Rsch., Inc., 1985-87; bd. dirs. Catalyst, 1972—, Internat. Exec. Svc. Corps; former bd. govs. Am. Nat. Red Cross, Common Cause, Women's Action Alliance; bd. govs. Internat. Ctr. on Election Law and Adminstrn., 1985-87; trustee Lafayette Coll., 1985—, vice chmn., 1990—; bd. dirs. Logistics Mgmt. Inst. Recipient Achievement award Bur. Govt. Research, U. Mass., 1963; Distinguished Service award Boston Coll., 1965; Smith Coll. medal, 1969; Distinguished Civic Leadership award Tufts U., 1965; Distinguished Service award Northfield Mount Hermon Sch., 1976; Radcliffe fellow Radcliffe Inst., 1965-66, 66-67. Mem. Nat. Acad. Pub. Adminstrn., ACLU, UN Assn., Urban League, NAACP, Assn. Am. Indian Affairs, East African Wildlife Soc., Jersey Wildlife Preservation Trust Channel Islands, Internat. Inst. Strategic Studies. Home: 46 Sunset Ave Amherst MA 01002 Office: Benson & Assocs 1300 19th St NW Ste 700 Washington DC 20036

BENSON, MICHAELA CHASSER, academic administrator; b. Cleve., June 18, 1948; d. Raymond Francis and Agnes Rita (Horkan) Chasser; m. Philip Drew Benson Sr., May 31, 1975; children: Philip Jr., Bruce Allen, Christopher Michael, Lauren Kelly. BA, U. Dayton, 1970; postgrad., Columbia U., 1978. Student affairs asst. Columbia Univ., N.Y., 1973-79; asst. dir. Grad. Sch. Arts & Sci., N.Y., 1980-84, asst. dean, 1984-87; v.p. P.D. Benson Assocs., Lawrenceville, N.J., 1988--; cons. Trenton Head Start, 1988—; ea. regional chmn. Ednl. Testing Svc., Princeton, NlJ., 1984-85;. Vice pres. Mercer County Women's Polit. Caucus, Eastside Neighborhood Assn. Mem. LWV (bd. dirs., treas.), AAUW. Democrat. Roman Catholic. Home: 12 Stonicker Dr Lawrenceville NJ 08648

BENSON, SUSAN M., health care administrator; b. Springfield, Ohio, Jan. 17, 1957; d. Arthur Stewart and Patricia Ann(Groeber) Fairbanks B.; m. Richard Myrle Benson, June 25, 1982; children: Jessica Ellen, Bradley Allen. BS, U. Ohio, 1979. Therapeutic recreation specialist Children's Med. Ctr., Dallas, 1980-85; asst. program dir. Crossroads Devel. Ctr., Haltom City, Tex., 1983-84; activity dir. Lakewood (Colo.) Nursing Home, 1986-87, Cambridge Health Care Ctr., Lakewood, 1987-89, Ft. Logan Mental Health Ctr., Denver, 1989—. Mem. Nat. Therapeutic Recreation Soc., Nat. Recreation and Parts Assn. Roman Catholic.

BENSUSSEN, ESTELLE ESTHER, writer, illustrator, artist; b. Chgo., July 6, 1926; d. Samuel A. and Sophia (Chubin) Russ; m. Edward M. Bensussen, Dec. 28, 1947; children: Gayle M. Bensussen Carrol, Wendy Bensussen Walls. Student, Chgo. Acad. Fine Arts, 1940-45, Art Inst. Chgo., 1939-43. Copy writer, fashion illustrator Marshall Field & Co., Chgo., 1945; display and fashion coord. The Fair, Chgo., 1946-47; contbg. author, marketplace editor Sew News mag., Seattle, 1984-85; contbr. author Sew-It-Seems mag., Seattle, 1988—; freelance illustrator and copy writer, Chgo., 1942-47. Author, illustrator: Making Patterns from Finished Clothes, 1985, 4 Patterns to Sew a Complete Wardrobe, 1987, Shortcuts to a Perfect Sewing Pattern, 1989, Sew Your Own Fashion Accessories, 1990; fine artist Seattle, 1948-70, Art Week on Pine Street, 1948-68, N.W. Ann., Seattle Art Mus., 1952-70; one man show Woessner Gallery, 1958, 59, 62. Home and Office: 3320 Cascadia Ave S Seattle WA 98144

BENT, JAN BRIGHAM, academic administrator; b. Berkeley, Calif., June 25, 1939; d. Carroll Walter and Elizabeth Anne (Anderson) B.; m. John Walter Strohbehn (div. 1977); children: Jo Anne, Kris, Carolyn; m. Charles Colby Bent. Student, San Diego State Coll., 1957; MA, Dartmouth Coll., Hanover, N.H., 1982. Retail mgr. Omer's and Bob's, Hanover, N.H., 1970-74; co-chair, coach Ford Sayre Racing Team, Hanover, N.H., 1973-74; tennis coach Dartmouth Coll., Hanover, N.H., 1973-75, Hanover (N.H.) High Sch., 1973-75; conf. coordinator Dartmouth Coll. The Amos Tuck Sch. Bus. Adminstrn., Hanover, N.H., 1973-76; research coordinator Dartmouth Coll. Dept. Edn., N.H., 1976-78; exec. dir. Dartmouth Inst., Dartmouth Coll., Hanover, N.H., 1986--; dir. Champion-Tuck awards, Minority Exec. Edn., Amos Tuck Sch., Dartmouth Coll., Hanover, 1978-86; lectr., presenter Nat. Minority Supplier Devel. Coun., Detroit, 1984; cons. Nat. Bus. Coun., Detroit, 1984, Nat Bus. League, Atlanta, 1985, Mt. Holyoke Coll., South Hadley, Mass. Co-author, editor: Aspirations and Attitudes High Sch. Students: A Report of the Options Project, 1977; author: Approximate Shorelines for Lakes Hitchcock and Upham, 1982. Ski instr. Ford Sayre Alpine Racing Program, 1963-76, co-chair, treas., 1973-77, publicity chair LWV, Hanover, 1964-67. Office: Dartmouth Coll Dartmouth Inst Hallgarten Hanover NH 03755

BENTALL, SHIRLEY FRANKLYN, author, lay church leader; b. Regina, Sask., Can., July 28, 1926; d. Frank and Viola Louise (Thom) May; m. Charles Howard Bentall, June 15, 1946; children: Edna Louise, Kathleen Margaret, Joan Elizabeth, Barnard Franklin. BA, McMaster U., Hamilton, Ont., 1946; DD (hon.), McMaster U., 1989. Retreat leader The Bapt. Union Western Can., 1971—; lectr. Bapt. Leadership Tng. Sch., Calgary, Alta., 1975-85; pres. The Bapt. Union of Western Can., 1976-77; pres. Can. Bapt. Fedn., 1985-88, chmn. pub. affairs com., 1989-91; mem. The Bapt. World Alliance Coun., 1985-88, mem. Human Rights Commn., 1985-90; v.p. Christian Ethics Commn., 1990—.. Writer Musings column for The Can. Bapt., 1965-88; author: Buckboard to Brotherhood, 1975, Amusings, 1980, The Charles Bentall Story, 1986, Discovering the Deep Places, 1988. Recipient Merit award The Bapt. Union of Western Can., 1982. Home: 500 Eau Claire Ave SW, Apt H 202, Calgary, AB Canada T2P 3R8

BENTEL, MARIA-LUISE RAMONA AZZARONE (MRS. FREDERICK R. BENTEL), architect; b. N.Y.C., June 15, 1928; d. Louis and Maria-Teresa (Massaro) Azzarone; m. Frederick R. Bentel, Aug. 16, 1952; children: Paul Louis, Peter Andreas, Maria Elisabeth. B.Arch., MIT, 1951; Fulbright scholar, Scuola d'Architettura, Venice, Italy, 1952-53. Registered profl. architect, Conn., N.Y., N.J., Va., Vt. registered profl. planner, N.J. Partner Bentel & Bentel (Architects), Locust Valley, N.Y., 1955—; pres. Testoria Realty Corp., N.Y.C., 1961—; v.p., sec.-treas. Correlated Designs, Inc., Locust Valley, 1961—; partner Cobblestone Enterprises, 1967; founding mem. Locust Valley Bus. Dist. Planning Commn., 1968—; regional vice-chairperson MIT Ednl. Council; adv. mem. MIT Council for the Arts; asso. prof. architecture N.Y. Inst. Tech.; adv. prof. Queensboro Community Coll., Bayside, N.Y., 1971—; mem. APD panel N.Y. State Council for Arts, 1985—. Archtl. works include C.W. Post Coll. L.I. U (N.Y. State Assn. Architects award 1975, Gold Archi award L.I. Assn. Architects 1974), Hempstead Bank, Nassau Centre Office Bldg, (L.I. Assn. Architects award 1972, N.Y. State Assn. Architects award 1975), North Shore Unitarian Sch, Plandome, N.Y. (L.I. Assn. Architects Silver Archi award 1967, N.Y. State Assn. Architects award 1970), Shelter Rock Library, Searingtown, N.Y. (L.I. Assn. Architects award 1970), St. Anthony's Ch, Nanuet, N.Y. (N.Y. State Assn. Architects award 1972), Kinloch Farm, Va, Steinberg Learning Center-Woodmere (N.Y.) Acad, (N.Y. Library Assn. award 1972, L.I. Assn. Architects award 1975), St. Francis de Sales Ch, Bennington, Vt., Neitlich residence, Oyster Bay Cove, N.Y. (L.I. Assn. Architects Silver Archi award 1971, N.Y. Assn. Architects award 1971), Amityville (N.Y.) Pub. Library, (Silver Archi award L.I. Assn. Architects, N.Y. State Assn. Architects award 1973), Jericho (N.Y.) Pub. Library, (N.Y. State Assn. Architects award, Silver Archi award L.I. Assn. Architects 1974), John B. Gambling residence, Lattingtown, N.Y. (Silver Archi award L.I. Assn. Architects 1974), Glen Cove (N.Y.) Boys' Club at Lincoln House, (Silver Archi award L.I. Assn. Architects 1978), Aquatics Component Mitchel Park, Nassau County, N.Y., Salten Hall, N.Y. Inst. Tech (award N.Y. State Assn. Architects 1977), N.Y. Coll. Osteo. Med. at N.Y. Inst. Tech, Old Westbury, Commack Pub. Library, Commack (N.Y. State Assn. Architects award 1977), St. Mary Star of the Sea Ch, Far Rockaway (Queens C. of C. grand prize 1977), Oberlin Residence (N.Y. State Assn. Architects/L.I. Assn. Architects Archi award 1983), St. Hyacinth's Ch. (Archi award 1988) St. Hyacinth's Ch., Glen Head (L.I. Assn. Architects award); contbr. religious architecture chpt. to Time Saver Standards (De Chiara and Callender), 1973. Mem. comml. panel Am. Arbitration Assn.; mem. N.Y. State Council on the Arts Panel; bd. dirs. MIT Alumni Assn., 1984-86; bd. dirs. L.I. Soc. Am. Inst. Architects; chmn. adv. panel on govt. bldg. projects GSA, 1976; chmn. Inst. Internat. Edn.; nat. adv.-selection com. Fulbright-Hays awards, 1976-78, 80, 82; Chairperson Locust Valley Library Adv. Bd., 1973—. Recipient 1st place award for Islip Downtown Urban Renewal Competition, 1976, Design award N.Y. State State Assn. Architects, 1988; named Woman Architect of Year Nassau-Suffolk County, 1976. Fellow AIA (corp. mem., chmn. design com., dir. L.I. chpt.); mem. N.Y. State Assn. Architects (chmn. design awards com.), Nat. Council Archtl. Registration Bds., MIT Alumnae Assn., MIT Alumni L.I. (dir., v.p.). Home: 23 Frost Creek Dr Lattingtown NY 11560 Office: 22 Buckram Rd Locust Valley NY 11560

BENTLEY, ANTOINETTE COZELL, insurance executive, lawyer; b. N.Y.C., Oct. 7, 1937; d. Joseph Richard Cozell and Rose (Lafata Cozell) Vila; children: Robert S., Anne W. BA with distinction, U. Mich., 1960; LLB, U. Va., 1961. Bar: N.Y. 1962, N.J. 1971. Assoc. Sage Gray, Todd & Sims, N.Y.C., 1961-65; of counsel Farrell, Curtis, Carlin & Davidson, Morristown, N.J., 1971-73; asst. sec. Crum and Forster, Basking Ridge, N.J., 1973; v.p., of counsel Crum and Forster, Morristown, 1975-87, sr. v.p., assoc. gen. counsel, 1987—; bd. dirs. Ramapo Bank, Wayne, N.J., Internat. Ins. Co. Mem. policy com. N.J. Future, 1986; trustee Crum and Forster Found., 1979—; vice pres. Mendham Borough (N.J.) Bd. Edn., 1976-79; trustee N.J. Conservation Found., 1981—, pres., 1986-89; trustee Morris Mus., 1982—, St. Peter's Coll., 1982—, Drew U., 1989, Delbarton Sch., 1989. Recipient award Exec. Women of N.J., 1988. Mem. ABA, N.J. Bar Assn., Am. Soc. Corp. Secs. (pres. N.Y. regional group 1987-88, mem. adv. com.), Am. Assn. Corp. Counsel, Women's Econ. Roundtable, LWV, Order of Coif, Chi Omega. Home: Fowler Rd Far Hills NJ 07921 Office: 211 Mt Airy Rd Basking Ridge NJ 07920

BENTLEY, BETH SINGER, poet; b. St. Paul, Oct. 7, 1921; d. Arthur G. and Helen (Blumenfeld) Singer; m. Bentley George Nelson, Oct. 24, 1952; children: Sean David, Julian Margaret. BA, U. Minn., 1943; MA, U. Mich., 1946. Instr. Bellevue (Wash.) Community Coll., 1969-74, Gifted in Humanities, Tacoma (Wash.) Pub. Schs., 1975-79, U. Wash., Seattle, 1980—; founder, dir., N.W. Poets Reading Series, Seattle, Wash., 1960-74. Author: (chpt. book) Field of Snow, 1973, Philosophical Investigations, 1977, The Purely Visible, 1980; (poetry) Phone Calls from the Dead, 1971, Country of Resemblances, 1976; editor: Selected Poems of Hazel Hall, 1980. Mem. Poetry Soc. Am. Home: 8762 25th Pl NE Seattle WA 98115

BENTLEY, CAROL JANE, state legislator; b. Riverside, Calif., Feb. 26, 1945; d. Francis and Florence Irene (Ingberg) Curtis. BS, San Diego State U., 1968. Field rep. Calif. State Senate, San Diego, 1972-76; field rep. Calif. State Assembly, San Diego, 1976-78, adminstrv. asst., 1978-80; adminstrv. asst. Calif. State Senate, San Diego, 1980-88; legislator Calif. State Legislature, San Diego, 1988—. Mem. East County Coun. Aging. Mem. Calif. Women in Government, El Cajon C. of C. Republican. Presbyterian. Office: State Capitol Sacramento CA 95814

BENTLEY, HELEN DELICH (MRS. WILLIAM ROY BENTLEY), congresswoman; b. Ruth, Nev.; d. Michael and Mary (Kovich) Delich; m. William Roy Bentley, June 7, 1959. Student, U. Nev., 1941-42, George Washington U., 1943; BJ, U. Mo., 1944; LLD (hon.), U. Md., 1970, U. Alaska, 1973, U. Mich., 1974; LHD (hon.), Bryant Coll., 1971, U. Portland, 1972, L.I. U., 1976, Goucher Coll., 1979, Villa Julie Coll. Reporter Ely (Nev.) Record, 1940-42; polit. campaign mgr. for late Senator James G. Scrugham, White Pine County, Nev., 1942; bur. mgr. UP, Fort Wayne, Ind., 1944-45; reporter Balt. Sun, 1945-53, maritime editor, 1953-69; chmn. FMC, Washington, 1969-75, Am. Bicentennial Fleet, Inc., 1973-76; pres. Internat. Resources & Devel. Corp., Washington, 1976-85, HDB Internat., Inc., 1977-85; pub. relations adviser Am. Assn. Port Authorities, 1958-62, 64-67; mem. 99th— Congresses from 2d Md. dist., 1985—. TV and film producer world trade and maritime shows, 1950-64; Editor: Ports of Americas, 1961. Bd. dirs., mem. coun. Ch. Home and Hosp.; bd. dirs. United Seamen's Svc., Oceanic Ednl. Found.; mem. coun. Md. Hist. Soc., Villa Julie Coll., Stevenson, Md., Montessori Soc. Cen. Md., Slavic-Am. Nat. Assn.; Rep. nominee for Ho. of Reps., 2d dist. Md., 1980, 82, 84, 86, 88; Md. nat. committeewoman, 1988; chmn. Md. campaign Bush for U.S. Pres., 1988. Recipient numerous honors including awards from AFL-CIO Maritime Port Council Greater N.Y., 1965, Ironworkers and Shipbuilders Council AFL-CIO, 1966, AOTOS award United Seamen's Service, 1971, Man of Yr. award N.Y. Freight Forwarders and Brokers Assn., 1972, Robert L. Hague Post award Am. Legion, 1973, Robert M. Thompson award Navy League U.S., 1973, Jerry Land medal Soc. Naval Architects and Marine Engrs., 1974, George Washington Honor medal Valley Forge Freedoms Found., 1971, 76, Salute To Congress award Propeller Club of U.S., 1987, Freedom award Alliance Metalworking Industries, 1987, Maritime Industry Salute to Congress award, 1987, Dr. John H. Griffin award KC, 1988, Minute Man award Reserve Officers Assn., 1988, Free State award of Excellence AMVETS Dept. Md., 1989, Sr. John H. Griffin award KC, 1989, Minute Man award Res. Officers Assn., 1988, AMVETS award Dept. Md., 1989, Free State award of Excellence, 1989; named GOP Woman of Year, 1972, Ethnic Woman of Yr., Republican Nat. Heritage Council, 1985; 1st non-Briton to address and be honored by U.K. Chamber Shipping, 1973; only woman to trek Northwest Passage on S.S. Manhattan, 1969. Greek Orthodox. Home: 408 Chapelwood Ln Lutherville MD 21093 Office: PO Box 10619 Towson MD 21285

BENTLEY, LISA JANE, retail executive; b. Lansdale, Pa., Mar. 20, 1936; d. Fred Olin and Beulah Sailor (Flagler) Ricker; m. Ronald F. Pepka, May 20, 1956 (div. 1969); 1 child, Ronald Glenn; m. John Lee Bentley, July 30, 1972. Student, Fresno (Calif.) State U., 1949-51; ordained, Living Bible Ctr., Phoenix, 1987. Mgr., owner Arthur Murray, N.Y.C., Phila. and Key West, Fla., 1956-65; interior designer Lisa's Interiors, Phila., 1965-75; exec. cons. Snelling & Snelling, Phila., 1975-78; pres., treas. Bentley Glass and Mirror, Inc., Las Vegas, Nev., 1979—; also chmn. bd. dirs. Bentley Glass and Mirror, Inc., Las Vegas; pres., treas. Bentley Enterprises, Inc., Las Vegas, 1980—, also chmn. bd. dirs.; pres., treas. Bentley Interiors Worldwide, Las Vegas, 1982—; tchr. Higher New Thought Ctr., Las Vegas, 1987—. Pastor, minister, pres., sec. Worldwide Outreach Awareness Ctr., 1987—; founder, chmn. bd. dirs., pres., sec. metaphysical tchr., healer, counselor Nev. Inst. Applied Metaphysics Inc., 1987—; v.p. Mt. Charleston (Nev.) Home Owners Assn., 1987. Mem. Associated Gen. Contractors, Internat. New Thought Alliance, Glazing Contractors Assn. (legis. chmn. 1985, fin. chmn. 1985, membership chmn. 1985).

BENTLEY, NORMA ELIZABETH, English educator; b. Syracuse, N.Y., Sept. 17, 1916; d. Robert Walter and Norma Harriet (Ackerman) B. AB, Harvard U., 1938; AM, Syracuse U., 1940, PhD, 1944, MLS, 1957. Instr. Syracuse (N.Y.) U., 1940-45; asst. prof. Lake Erie Coll., Painesville, Ohio, 1945-47, Earlham Coll., Richmond, Ind., 1947-51; prog. dir. YWCA, Syracuse, 1952-55; asst. librarian Syracuse U., 1955-57; prof. English Cazenovia (N.Y.) Coll., 1957-81, prof. emeritus English, 1981—. Contbr. articles to profl. jours. Pres. YWCA of Onendaga County, Syracuse, 1987-90. Recipient Community Svc. award, NAACP, 1961. Mem. AAUW (pres. 1989—), Pi Lambda Sigma, Beta Phi Mu. Mem. Society of Friends. Address: 124 Rugby Rd Syracuse NY 13206

BENTLEY, SHARON RUTH, banker; b. El Paso, Tex., Sept. 17, 1947; d. Ralph Richard and Ruth Garnet (Logue) Wood; m. Ronald Keith Bentley, June 6, 1975 (div. Feb. 1984); children: Deana Lashel, William Warren; m. Harry Mason McCall, June 12, 1985 (div. 1989). Student Am. Inst. Banking, 1975-80, Jones Real Estate Coll., 1978, El Paso Community Coll., 1976-78, U. Wis., 1989—. Lic. real estate salesman, securities dealer. Cashier, Bank of Ysleta, El Paso, 1969-78; real estate salesman Pan Am. Realty, El Paso, 1979-80; with First City Bancorp. Tex., Inc., 1980—, asst. v.p. First City Nat., El Paso, 1980-83, v.p., cashier First City Bank-East, El Paso, 1983-87, sr. v.p., 1987, v.p. First City Nat. Bank El Paso, 1988-89, sr. v.p., cashier, 1989—. Mem. vocat. adv. com. El Paso Job Corps, 1985-88; vol. fundraiser El Paso Lighthouse for Blind, 1984-85; vol. Amigo Air Show, 1984-85, El Paso Council on Aging, March of Dimes Walkathon, 1989; treas. Eastwood High Class of 1965, El Paso, 1984—; speaker El Paso Opportunity Ctr. for Handicapped, 1986; bd. dirs. El Paso Ctr. For Found. For Child Abuse Prevention, 1989—. Recipient Honor Roll award United Way El Paso County, 1977, Outstanding Achievement awards, 1984, 85; YWCA REACH honoree, El Paso, 1981, 83, 84, named Outstanding Young Woman of America, 1977, 1984. Mem. Fin. Women Internat. formerly Nat. Assn. Bank Women (pres. El Paso 1985-86, local scholarship 1985, state awards and scholarship com. 1987, state conf. co-chmn. 1990), Am. Inst. Banking (bd. govs. 1984-86), El Paso Assn. Personnel Adminstrs., Nat. Assn. for Female Execs., Bank Adminstrn. Inst. (dir. 1984-86).Democrat. Methodist. Club: Vista Hills Exchange (bd. dirs 1988—).Avocations: reading; swimming. Home: 3117 Eads Pl El Paso TX 79935 Office: Fist City Tex-El Paso NA PO Box 1572 320 N Stanton El Paso TX 79948

BENTON, ELIZABETH LAQUETTA, real estate executive, consultant, educator; b. Ozark, Ala., Apr. 1, 1936; d. Horace and Dovie Lee (Gulledge) Pippin; m. Charles Wayne Benton, Dec. 17, 1954; children: Lisa Ann, Charles W. Jr. Diploma Napier Bus. Coll., 1955; student Minot State Coll., 1963-64, U. Md., 1965, 67; grad. Realtors Inst. Cert. residential broker residential specialist. Sec., Aeronca Aircraft Corp., Ft. Rucker, Ala., 1955, Strachan Shipping, Savannah, Ga., 1956, USAF, Savannah, 1956-58; supr. Internal Revenue, Denver, 1959-60; adminstrv. asst. Chrysler Corp., Izmir, Turkey, 1961-63; substitute tchr. Dept. Edn., Honolulu, 1968-71; agt. Naomi Grout Real Estate, Ewa Beach, Hawaii, 1971-77; v.p., ptnr. Benton & Large Realty, Honolulu, 1977; pres., owner Liz Benton, Inc., Aiea, Hawaii, 1977—; dir. Founders Title & Escrow Co., Honolulu, 1983—; resource person, study on agy. Nat. Assn. Real Estate Lic. Law Ofcls., Salt Lake City, 1984, 85; mem. adv. council Hawaii Real Estate Research and Edn. Ctr., 1985—. Contbr. articles to profl. jours. Mem. Small Bus. Council Am., Honolulu, 1977—; mem. Aloha United Way, Honolulu 1974—; bd. dirs. Big Bros., Big Sisters, Honolulu, 1982—; chmn. Easter Seals VIP Panel, Honolulu, 1981—; mem. Realtors Polit. Action Com., Honolulu, 1980—; bd. dirs. Am. Cancer Soc., 1985-86. Recipient Vol. of Yr. award ARC, 1965, Outstanding Service award Dept. of Air Force, 1966, Top Producer award Naomi Grout Real Estate, 1972, 73, 74, 75, 76, Cert. of Excellence award Nat. Research Co., 1980-87. Mem. Hawaii Assn. Realtors (chmn. convention com. 1984, chmn. edn. com. 1979, dir.-at-large 1979, 80, bd. dirs. 1979, chmn. fin. and audit com. 1980, 81, sec. 1981, judge parade of homes 1982, treas. 1982, v.p. 1983, pres. elect 1986, pres. 1987, mem. strategic planning com. 1984, chmn. strategic planning com. 1986, chmn. nominating com. 1986), Honolulu Bd. Realtors (bd. dirs. 1978, chmn. election com. 1979, sec. 1979, chmn. multiple listing service, 1980, 81, pres.-elect 1982, chmn. realtor of yr. selection com. 1983, pres. 1983, chmn. nominating com. 1984, Realtor of Month award June 1981, Realtor of Yr. award 1981, chair strategic planning com. 1986, chair nominating com. 1986, liaison to real estate commn. 1986), Nat. Assn. Realtors (chmn. convention activities subcom. 1984, nat. bd. dirs. 1984-86, prof. standards and arbitration com. 1986, 87, state leadership forum, 1986-87), The Investment Group Realtors, Leeward Regional Group, Realtors Nat. Mktg. Inst. (cert., Hawaii chpt., v.p. 1981, pres. 1982, treas. cert. residential brokers chpt. 1985), C. of C. Office: 98-211 Pali Momi St Suite 411 Aiea HI 96701

BENTON, FAYE LOUISE, child care administrator; b. Mecklenburg Cou, N.C., Feb. 18, 1939; d. Johny Mack and Myrtle Reid (Brown) B.; m. Marshall Durwood Parrish, Nov. 20, 1959 (div. 1966); children: Marty, Tamra, Jeff; m. William A. Soiset, Nov. 24, 1967 (div. 1982); children: Chris, Tiffany. Assoc. Applied Sci., U. N.C., 1959. RN. Staff nurse Moses Cone Hosp., Greensboro, N.C., 1959-60, High Point (N.C.) Meml. Hosp., 1960-61, Presbyn. Hosp., Charlotte, N.C., 1961, 65; office nurse Dr. Kenneth Downs, Charlotte, 1982; intensive care staff nurse Long Beach (Calif.) Meml. Hosp., 1963; intensive care charge nurse Dominquez Valley Hosp., Long Beach, 1964; office nurse Charlotte Youth Clinic, Charlotte, 1965-67; founder, pres., dir. Matthews (N.C.) After Sch. Club, Inc., 1967—. Sunday sch. tchr. Matthews Presbyn. Ch., 1969-72; den mother Matthew Area Boy Scouts Am., 1979, merit badge counselor, 1975-80, pack rep.; mem. human rights com. N.C. Broughton Hosp., 1988, 89; v.p. Alliance for Mentally Ill, Metrolina, Charlotte, 1985, 86, pres. 1989, 90; mem. Meck County SPMI Interagy. Coun., Area SPMI Citizens Adv. Coun. Named Advocate of Yr., N.C. Alliance for Mentally Ill, 1989. Mem. Matthew C. of C., Mental Health Assn. (mem. task force on goals), Apple Club, U.S. Tennis Assn., Ski Bees (Charlotte), Cedar Forest Tennis. Republican. Home: 9820 McClendon Ct Matthews NC 28105 Office: Matthews After Sch Club 1373 W John St Matthews NC 28105

BENTON, GERALDINE ANN, sales executive, tutor; b. Plymouth, N.H., Apr. 25, 1960; d. Alton G. and Geraldine (Holecek) B. BS, Plymouth State Coll., 1984. Cert. bus driver, N.H. Tutor, Math., reading; bus driver Robertson Transit, Campton, N.H.; sales rep. White Mountain Shopper, Lincoln, N.H. Mem. Nat. Head Injury Found., Nat. Arbor Day Found.,

Nat. Audubon Soc., Nat. Wildlife Found. Home: PO Box 25 Campton NH 03223

BENTON, JEAN ELIZABETH, education educator; b. Monticello, N.Y., Feb. 21, 1943; d. Alvin Oscar and Elizabeth Esther (Scriber) B. BA, SUNY, Fredonia, 1964; MS, Syracuse U., 1968; EdD, Columbia U., 1984. Tchr. Monticello (N.Y.) Cen. Schs., 1964-66; reading specialist Ramapo Cen. Schs., Suffern, 1967-70; instr. Sch. for Internat. Tng., Brattleboro, Vt., 1971-72; acad. dir. ind. study programs Expt. in Internat. Living in Mex. and Eng., Brattleboro, 1972-73; dir. ESL courses Inst. Mexicano-Norteamericano, Cordoba, Mex., 1973; dir. Learning Ctr., Cornwall (N.Y.) Cen. Schs., 1974-81; coord. English programs Maktab Sains Majlis Amanah Rakyat, Kuantan, Malaysia, 1985-87; coord. faculty devel. project Shanghai (People's Republic China) Tchrs. U., 1988; prof. edn. SE Mo. State U., Cape Girardeau, 1987—, coord. internat. exchange programs, 1987—; curriculum cons. Majlis Amanah Rakyat Edn. Found., Kuala Lumpur, Malaysia, 1985-87, Shanghai Bur. Higher Edn., 1988—. Mem. Rotary. Office: SE Mo State U One University Pla Cape Girardeau MO 63701

BENTON-BORGHI, BEATRICE HOPE, educational consultant; b. San Antonio, Nov. 7, 1946; d. Donald Francis and Beatrice Hope (Peche) Benton; A.B. in Chemistry, North Adams State Coll., 1968; M.Secondary Edn., Boston U., 1972; m. Peter T. Borghi, Aug. 12, 1980; children—Kathryn Benton Borghi, Sarah Benton Borghi. Tchr. chemistry Cathedral High Sch., Springfield, Mass., 1968-69; tchr. sci. and history Munich (W.Ger.) Am. High Sch., 1969-70; tchr. English, Tokyo, Japan, 1970-71; tchr. chemistry and sci. Marlborough (Mass.) High Sch., 1971-80; project dir., adminstr. ESEA, Marlborough Pub. Schs., 1976-77; project dir., proposal writer Title III, Title IX, U.S. Dept. Edn., 1975-76, 76-77; evaluation team New Eng. Assn. Schs. and Colls., 1974, 78; mem. regional dept. edn. com., 1977-78; ednl. cons., lectr., 1978—. Energy conservation rep. Marlborough's Overall Econ. Devel. Com., 1976; chmn. Marlborough's Energy Conservation Task Force, 1975; dir. Walk for Mankind, 1972; sec. Group Action for Marlborough Environment, 1975-76; bd. dirs. Girls Club, Marlborough, 1979; pres. Sisters, Inc., 1979-83. Mem. Council for Exceptional Children, Nat. Women's Health Network. Home and Office: 2449 Edington Rd Columbus OH 43221

BENTZEN, JANET ROSE, insurance company executive; b. Kirksville, Mo., June 21, 1934; d. C. Downing and Virginia Alice (Cottey) Huffman;; m. William Nelson Kelley, Aug. 23, 1953 (div. 1966); children: Brett Alan, Tracy Alison Zanone; m. William F. Bentzen III, June 29, 1969. Student, Columbia Coll., 1952-53. Med. sec. Dr. Rack Benthall, Alexandria, Va., 1953-56; acctg. clk. Shelter Ins. Co., Columbia, Mo., 1956-60, subrogation clk., 1960-61; vet. asst. Camdenton (Mo.) Vet. Clinic, 1962-66; adminstrv. asst.. Shelter Ins. Companies, Columbia, Mo., 1966-80; claims consumer asst. Shelter Ins. Companies, Mo., 1980--; exec. sec., consumer asst. Shelter Ins. Companies, Columbia, Mo., 1987--; sec. Nat. Assn. of Ins. Women, Columbia, Mo., 1985-86. Parliamentarian Cosmopolitan Internat., 1984, historian, 1987, recording sec., 1981, v.p., 1979, pres., 1980. Democrat. Office: Shelter Ins Cos 1817 W Broadway Columbia MO 65218

BENYA, ROSEMARIE ANN, educator; b. Cleve., May 20, 1942; d. Vincent Francis and Marie Rita (Galb) B. BA, Notre Dame Coll., Cleve., 1964; MA, Middlebury (Vt.) Coll., 1968; PhD, Ohio State U., 1980. Tchr. Cleve. pub. schs., 1964-67; instr. Kent (Ohio) State U., 1968-74; prof. East Cen. U., Ada, Okla., 1980—; organizer First Internat. Conf. on Second/Fgn. Land. Acquisition by Children, Oklahoma City, 1985, prog. chmn. 1986, 88, 89. Compiler book: Children and Languages, Research, Practice and Rationale for the Early Grades, 1988. Mem. Am. Council on Teaching Fgn. Lang., Cen. States Conf. on Teaching Fgn. Lang., Okla. Fgn. Lang. Tchrs. Assn. (pres. 1984-85), Am. Classical League, Am. Assn. Tchrs. of Spanish and Portuguese. Democrat. Roman Catholic. Office: East Cen U Ada OK 74820

BENYEI, CANDACE REED, psychotherapist; b. N.Y.C., Feb. 25, 1946; d. Harlow John and Jacqueline de la Valtaire (Smyth) Reed; m. Curt Christian Benyei, July 1, 1967; children: Tara Elaine, Christian Harlow. BA in Chemistry, Colo. Coll., 1967; MS in Sch. Psychology, So. Conn. State U., 1985; MS in Marriage and Family Therapy, U. Bridgeport, Conn., 1987; PhD in Clin. Psychology, Union Inst., Cin., 1988. Rsch. assoc. Cornell U., Ithaca, N.Y., 1967-68; rsch. asst. Yale-New Haven Hosp., 1968-70, Clairol, Inc., Stamford, Conn., 1970-71; asst. chaplain So. Conn. State U., New Haven, 1984-85; intern Hamden (Conn.) Mental Health Svc., 1985-86; adj. prof. U. Bridgeport, 1988-89; cons. family svcs. unit Danbury (Conn.) Superior Ct., 1990—; mgr., pres. Whimsy Brook Farm, Ltd., Redding, Conn., 1972—; dir. Inst. Human Resources, Redding, 1985—. Author: Called to Be Lonely: A Company of Clowns, 1984; published poetry. Leader Redding Horse Masters 4-H, 1972-75; pres. Fairfield Coop. Extension Coun., 1975-78; horse show mgr. Redding Boys Club, 1978, 79; mem. Redding Bd. Edn., 1978-86; lic. lay reader Episc. Diocese Conn., 1982—, mem. diocesan com. on spiritual direction, 1985—; vestryperson Christ Ch. Episc., Redding, 1983-85; assoc. Order of Holy Cross, 1986—. Winner nat. horse show competitions. Mem. Am. Psychol. Assn., Conn. Psychol. Assn., Am. Assn. Marriage and Family Therapists, Conn. Assn. Marriage and Family Therapists, Nat. Psychology Adv. Assn. (chairperson), Consortium for Diversified Programs in Psychology (bd. dirs.), Am. Quarter Horse Assn. Democrat. Office: Inst Human Resources 29 Giles Hill Rd Redding CT 06896

BENYO, ALISON SHALLCROSS, controller; b. Oklahoma City, Aug. 1, 1961; d. Harry Charles and Ruth Elizabeth (DeHoff) Shallcross. BSBA, U. Fla., 1982; MBA, Brenau Coll., 1986. Rep. customer svc. GTE Sprint Communications (formerly called So. Pacific), Atlanta, 1982, sales rep., 1982-83, coord. bus. svcs., 1983-84, analyst ops., 1984-85, svc. ops. analyst, 1985-86; sr. fin. analyst Macy's of Atlanta, 1985; mgr. planning and analysis US Sprint Communications, Atlant, 1986-87; mgr. revenue and pricing US Sprint Communications, Reston, Va., 1987-88, dir. fin., 1988—. Active on steering com. Lake Anne Elem. Sch./US Sprint Partnership, Reston, 1988-89. Mem. NAFE, U. Fla. Alumni. Republican. Methodist. Home: 12159 Penderview Terr Fairfax VA 22033 Office: US Sprint Communications PO Box 4466 Reston VA 22090

BERBANO, VICTORIA P., marketing specialist, nurse; b. Manila, Aug. 3, 1946; came to U.S., 1970; d. Santiago Ancheta and Angelica (Palad) B. BA in Psychology, U. Santo Tomas, Manila, 1965, BS in Nursing, 1969; MS in Health Care Adminstrn., La Verne (Calif.) U., 1987. RN, Pa., Calif. Pediatric nurse Mercy Cath. Med. Ctr., Phila., 1971-73; pediatric head nurse Tri County Hosp., Springfield, Pa., 1973-75, staff nurse ICU, 1975-77; staff nurse ICU Med. Ctr. La Mirada, Calif., 1977-81, evening supr., 1979-81, asst. dir. nursing, 1981-85, assoc. dir. nursing, 1985-89, program dir., 1988-89; regional mktg. specialist MediQ Care, Inc., Chatsworth, Calif., 1989—. Mem. Orgn. Nurse Execs., Continuity of Care. Roman Catholic. Home: 12318 Picrus St San Diego CA 93129 Office: MediQ Care Inc 20500 Plummer St San Diego CA 91311

BERCEL, DANIELLE SUZANNE, software engineer; b. L.A., Mar. 5, 1951; d. Joseph Irwin Bleeden and Barbara Elaine Simons. BA in Music, Antioch Coll., Yellow Springs, Ohio, 1976. Cons. D.S. Bercel and Assoc., Beverly Hills, Calif., 1983-85; sr. engr. Sun Microsystems, Mountain View, Calif., 1985-88; sr. engr. software The Wollongong Group, Palo Alto, Calif., 1988-89; engr. software design Hewlett Packard, Palo Alto, 1989—. Contbr. articles to profl. jours. Mem. IEEE, Assn. Computing Machinery, Scrug, Interex, Internat. Midi Assn. Office: Hewlett Packard 1501 Page Mill Rd Palo Alto CA 94304

BERCHIN, HOLLY ANN, nurse; b. Canton, Ohio, Dec. 29, 1953; d. Stephen Albert and Helen Marie (McKetta) B. BS in Nursing, Kent State U., 1976; MS in Nursing, Kent State U, 1982. Cert. Specialist in Psychiatric, Mental Health Nursing of Children and Adolescents. Staff RN Children's Hosp., Akron, Ohio, 1976-77; instr. pediatric nursing Mercy Sch. Nursing, Canton, Ohio, 1977-82; screening, follow-up and after care coord. Child and Adolescent Svc. Ctr., Canton, 1982-84; psychiat. clin. nurse specialist Children's Hosp., Akron, 1984—; psychotherapist in pvt. practice Summit County Psychol. Assocs., Akron, 1988-89; adj. faculty Kent State U. Sch. of Nursing, 1990. Active multidisciplinary adv. team to Summit County Children's Svcs. Bd. Mem. Am. Nurses Assn. (bd. dirs. dist. 1982-84), Sigma Theta Tau, Alpha Lambda Delta, Chi Omega. Democrat. Roman Catholic. Home: 5711 Vantage Hill NW Massillon OH 44646 Office: Children's Hosp 281 Locust St Akron OH 44308

BERCOWETZ, BONNIE SHANE, shopping center executive; b. Hartford, Conn., Aug. 17, 1947; d. Irving Isaac and Millie (Fleishman) B.; m. Paul L. Klopp, Apr. 1, 1979. Student, Brandeis U., 1965-68; BA, Boston U., 1970; postgrad., Tufts U., 1971-75. Sect. leader, Am. studies reader Tufts U., Medford, Mass., 1973-75; mgmt. trainee Conn. Packing Co., Inc. (doing bus. as COPACO), Bloomfield, Conn., 1975-82; fin. v.p. COPACO Shopping Ctr., Bloomfield, 1982—; also bd. dirs. —, Bloomfield; mgr. COPACO Liquors, Bloomfield, 1979-80; owner, operator 7-Eleven, New Britain, Conn., 1984-85. Mem. Bloomfield Econ. Devel. Commn., 1985—, Regional Transp. Com., Hartford, 1988—; bd. dirs. Keep Am. Beautiful, Bloomfield, 1988—. Recipient Oliver J. Filley Community Svc. award, 1990; N.J. Hist. Soc. rsch. grantee, 1973, 75. Mem. Internat. Coun. Shopping Ctrs., Bloomfield C. of C. (bd. dirs. 1983-84, 86—, sec. 1989—, v.p. 1990-91). Office: COPACO Shopping Ctr 335 Cottage Grove Rd Bloomfield CT 06002

BERCOWETZ, CYNTHIA SUSAN, newspaper editor, TV scriptwriter; b. Pittsfield, Mass., Jan. 13, 1930; d. Louis and Grace (Minsky) Barnett; m. Herbert Kallman, June 22, 1958 (div.); children: Allan David, Wendy Ann, Allison; m. Herman Samuel Bercowetz, May 7, 1978; stepchildren: Heidi, Barbara, Donald, Debbie. BA, Am. Internat. Coll., Springfield, Mass., 1950; postgrad., Trinity Coll., Hartford, Conn. With Pharm. Mag., N.Y.C., 1950-52; editor Red Book Travelers Ins. Co., Hartford, 1952-60; press and pub. rels. rep. The Hartford Times, 1963-76; editor Editor, Get Help! column Jour. Inquirer, Manchester, Conn., 1978—; producer, writer weekly program Bloomfield (Conn.) Access TV, 1980—; presenter consumer issues various groups and orgns. Fund raiser March of Dimes, West Hartford, Conn., 1982—, Leukemia Found., Hartford, 1986-89. Recipient consumer edn. and consumer work awards Better Bus. Bur. Western Conn.; recipient Women in Leadership award YWCA, 1989. Mem. Internat. Tng. in Communication (toastmistress/pres. Greater Hartford chpt. 1982), Bus. and Profl. Women (Hartford chpt.). Jewish. Home: 22 Oak Ln Bloomfield CT 06002 Office: Jour Inquirer 306 Progress Dr Manchester CT 06040

BERDANIER, CAROLYN DAWSON, foods and nutrition educator, administrator, researcher; b. East Brunswick, N.J., Nov. 14, 1936; d. Frederick H.C. and Mabelle (Virginia McNiven) Dawson; m. Charles Reese Berdanier, Aug. 10, 1957; children: Lynnette, Charles, Robert. BS, Pa. State U., 1958; MS, Rutgers U., 1963, PhD, 1966. Therapeutic dietitian St. Peters Hosp., New Brunswick, N.J., 1960-61; research asst. Rutgers U., 1961-63, grad. research fellow, 1963-66; postdoctoral fellow Rutgers U., 1966-67; research nutritionist Nutrition Inst. U.S. Dept. Agr., Beltsville, Md., 1968-75; asst. prof. nutrition U. Md., College Park, 1970-75; assoc. prof. biochemistry and medicine U. Nebr., Omaha, 1975-77; prof. U. Ga., Athens, 1977—, head dept. foods and nutrition Coll. Home Econs., 1977-88; nutrition study sect., NIH, 1987; mem. review panel in human nutrition U.S. Dept. Agr. Competitive Grants Program, 1978, 79, 81. Recipient Ga. Nutrition Council award for Outstanding Contbns. to Research in Human Nutrition, 1982; Lamar Dodd award for research, 1984; NIH fellow, 1966-67. Fellow Am. Inst. Chemists; mem. N.Y. Acad. Sci., AAAS, Soc. Exptl. Biology and Medicine, Am. Inst. Nutrition, Am. Home Econs. Assn., Endocrine Soc., Am. Soc. Clin. Nutrition, Sigma Xi, Gamma Sigma Delta, Phi Kappa Phi, Sigma Delta Epsilon. Mem. editorial bd. Jour. Nutrition, 1977-81; contbr. articles to profl. jours.

BEREITER, SUSAN ROBERTA, systems engineer; b. Connellsville, Pa., Feb. 8, 1962; d. Robert James and Ann Margaret (Bailey) B. BSEE-Engring.-Pub. Policy, Carnegie-Mellon U., 1983, PhD Engring.-Pub. Policy, 1988. Mem. tech. staff AT&T Bell Labs., Holmdel, N.J., 1988—. Author: Troubleshooting and Human Factors in Automated Manufacturing Systems, 1989; contbr. articles to profl. jours. AAAS mass media sci. and Engring. fellow. Mem. IEEE, Lambda Sigma, Eta Kappa Nu. Roman Catholic. Home: 16 Michael Circle Sandown NH 03873 Office: AT&T Bell Labs Rm 3J310 Crawfords Corner Rd Holmdel NJ 07733

BERENDA, RUTH W., psychotherapist, consultant; b. Kolomya, Poland; came to U.S, 1930; d. Harry L. and Anna (Schwartz) Weinreb; m. Carlton W. Berenda, Dec. 9, 1939 (div. 1946); m. Charles Eugene Carter, Apr. 12, 1959. BS in Edn., CCNY., 1936; MA, Columbia U., 1939; PhD, New Sch. for Social Rsch., 1948; postgrad., U. of Rochester, N.Y., 1941-42. Pvt. practice psychotherapist N.Y.C., 1946—; lectr. in field. Mem. Whitney Mus., Mus. of Modern Art, Guggenheim Mus., Jewish Mus., Jerusalem Mus., Tel Aviv Mus., Friends of the Field Mus. Mem. Internat. Coun., APA, Acad. of Sci., Inst. Erich Fromm Soc. Home and Office: 145 W 55th St New York NY 10019

BERENT, JANET LEE, accounts receivable supervisor; b. Hammond, Ind., Nov. 26, 1960; d. Vern Wright and Barbara Jean (Miller) Huddleston; m. James Francis Berent, Aug. 18, 1984. AA, Coll. DuPage, 1980; BA, Calif. State U., Fullerton, 1983. Customer svc. rep. RCA Svc. Co., Downers Grove, Ill.; credit mgr. USA Today, Downers Grove; credit/collection supv. Multicom, Inc., Downers Grove; accounts receivable supr. Checkers, Simon and Rosner, Chgo.; intern U.S. SBA. Author: Credit/Collection Policy and Procedure Manual, 1988, Monthly Billing and Receivables Newsletter, 1987—. V.p. Camp Fire, DuPage County, Ill., 1977-78, leader, Glen Ellyn, Ill., 1978-79, alumni mem., Chgo., 1990; staff mem. N.E. DuPage Spl. Recreation Day Camp, 1977. Mem. NAFE, Nat. Assn. Credit Mgrs. (adjustment svcs. com. 1990), Toastmasters. Republican. Home: 458 Byrant Ave Glen Ellyn IL 60137 Office: 1 S Wacker Dr Ste 1700 Chicago IL 60606

BERENTSEN, FERN FLORENCE, dietitian; b. Hartland, Wis., Dec. 31, 1927; d. Claude Clarence and Aurelia Catherine (Bong) Smith; m. Richard Albert Berentsen, Sept. 22, 1951; children: Thomas Richard, Craig Thomas. BS in Food, Nutrition, U. Wis., 1950. registered dietitioan, Wis. Dietetic intern Christ Hosp., Cin., 1950-51; cons. dietitian Mercy Hosp., Milw., 1953-57; asst. dietitian Waukesha (Wis.) Meml. Hosp., 1957-62; cons. dietitian River Hills Nursing Home, Pewaukee, Wis., 1962-63; dir.food svc. Community Meml. Hosp., Menomonee Falls, Wis., 1963-78; clin. dietitian Falls Med. Group, Menomonee Falls, 1978-83. Alderman, 9th dist., City of Waukesah, 1983—. Mem. Am. Dietetic Assn., AAUW, Waukesha Toastmistress Club (pres. 1975). Republican. Roman Catholic. Home: 1110 Sweetbriar Dr Waukesha WI 53186

BERESFORD, MARIAN SWEENY, homemaker; b. L.A., Jan. 5, 1939; d. Benjamin Patton and Margaret Mary (Malone) Sweeny; m. Dennis R. Beresford, Apr. 15, 1961; children: Craig Robert, Elizabeth. Student, Mt. San Antonio Coll. Clk. Superior Oil Co., L.A., 1958-63. Mem. Shaker Heights Country Club, Am. Ex-Prisoners of War. Republican. Roman Catholic. Home: 15 Heather Dr Stamford CT 06903

BERG, BARBARA J., clinical psychologist; b. Jamestown, N.D., Sept. 9, 1958; d. Robert Wilson and Dorothy Jean (Tangney) B. BA, U. South Fla., 1980; PhD, U. S.C., 1987. Lic. clin. psychologist, Ky. Treatment and rehab. specialist Fla. Mental Health Inst., Tampa, 1979-80; psychiat. cons. Richland Meml. Hosp., Columbia, S.C., 1981-82; coord. Rsch. Team on Domestic Violence, Columbia, 1982-84; intern U. N.C. Med. Sch., Chapel Hill, 1984-85; cons. N.C. State Counseling Ctr., Raleigh, 1985-86; asst. prof. dept. psychology Western Ill. U., Macomb, 1986-88; postdoctoral fellow dept. behavioral sci. U. Ky. Med. Sch., Lexington, 1988—; instr. U.S.C., Columbia, 1982-84; pres. Western Orgn. for Women, Macomb, 1987-88; contbr. articles to profl. jours. Big sister Big Sisters-Big Bros., Lexington. Mem. NOW, Am. Psychol. Assn., Soc. Behavioral Medicine, Am. Fertility Soc. (rsch. com.), Am. Soc. Psychosomatic Ob-Gyn., Sierra Club, Nat. Abortion Rights Action League, Phi Kappa Phi, Psi Chi. Democrat. Office: Dept Behavioral Sci U Ky Coll Medicine Coll Medicine Office Bldg Lexington KY 40536-0086

BERG, CAROLYN NOURSE, research analyst; b. Des Moines, July 17, 1938; d. Archie B. and Katie Matilda (Taylor) Nourse; divorced; children: Christina Carole, Anna Lorraine. BA in History, U. Idaho, 1971; MBA, Ariz. State U., 1983. Sr. sec. U. Idaho, Moscow, 1972-74; owner, mgr. Something Different, Moscow, 1974-79, Inner Space, Moscow, 1979-81; coord. Moscow Downtown Assn., 1981-82; rsch. asst. Ariz. State U., Tempe, 1982-84; mgr. Door Store, Mesa, Ariz., 1984-86; rsch. analyst O'Neil Assocs., Tempe, 1986-89; faculty rsch. assoc. Ariz. State U., Tempe, 1989—. Home: 11202 S Mandan St Phoenix AZ 85044

BERG, JEAN HORTON LUTZ, writer; b. Clairton, Pa., May 30, 1913; d. Harry Heber and Daisy Belle (Horton) Lutz; m. John Joseph Berg, July 2, 1938; children: Jean Horton, Julie Berg Mulvey, John Joel. B.S. in Edn, U. Pa., 1935, A.M. in Latin, 1937. Tchr. creative writing Wayne, Pa., 1968—; speaker in field of creative writing. Author 50 books for children and young people, 1950—, articles, stories, poems for young people, articles for adults. Former mem. Health and Welfare Bd., Phila.; former chmn. Main Line Parents Council. Recipient U. Pa. Alumni award of merit, 1969; Follett award for beginning-to-read book, 1961; medallion City of Phila.; Friends' Central Sch. Distinguished Alumna award, 1978. Mem. Authors Guild, Authors League, ASCAP, Nat. League of Am. Pen Women, Phila. Childrens Reading Round Table, League Women Voters. Home: 207 Walnut Ave Wayne PA 19087

BERG, JEAN SCHOLL, lawyer; b. LaPorte, Ind., Nov. 21, 1950; d. John David and Winifred Viola (Jourdain) Scholl; m. Raymond Charles Berg, June 13, 1970; 1 child, Raymond Christopher. BA in Social Sci. Edn., Purdue U., 1973; MA in Liberal Studies, Valparaiso U., 1976; JD, Notre Dame U., 1982; postgrad. in internat. law Exeter (Eng.) U., summer 1981. Bar: Ind. 1982, U.S. Dist. Ct. (no. dist.) Ind. 1982. Cert. secondary tchr., Ind., real estate broker, Ind. Tchr. Diocese of Gary, Michigan City, Ind., 1973-79; mng. broker United Realty, LaPorte, Ind., part-time 1974-78; compliance officer, asst. to pres. Lakeshore Bank, Michigan City, 1983-84; EEO counselor U.S. Postal Svc., Gary, Ind., 1984-86, real estate specialist, Kent, Wash., 1986-87, Chgo., 1987-88, realty mgmt. specialist, prin., Washington, 1988—. Notes editor, Jour. of Legislation, 1981-82. Campaign worker re-election Congressman Hiler and Senator Lugar, LaPorte, 1982. Mem. Ind. Bar Assn., AAUW, Am. Quarter Horse Assn. Republican. Roman Catholic. Office: US Postal Svc Facilities Svc Ctr 222 S Riverside Pla Ste 1200 Chicago IL 60606-6155

BERG, KAREN ELEANOR, communication and management development executive; b. Rochester, Minn., Apr. 19, 1943; d. Arthur Joseph and Eleanor (Morton) Nelson; m. Richard Harvey Berg, Aug. 16, 1970; 1 child, Alexander Samuel. Student, U. No. Colo., Greely, 1961-63, Frankfurt (Fed. Republic Germany) Conservatory, 1967-68. V.p. Hill & Knowlton, N.Y., 1969-77; cons. various firms, 1977-83; chief exec. officer Commcore, N.Y., 1985—. Author (book, audio tape) Get to the Point, 1989. Office: Commcore Inc 156 Fifth Ave Ste 701 New York NY 10010

BERG, LINDA LEE, religious association administrator; b. Daggett, Mich., Feb. 20, 1955; d. Arnold August and Violet Anita (Bartels) Berg; m. Peter Jonathan Luton, Dec. 30, 1989. BA, U. Wis., Green Bay, 1977. Spl. activities coordinator Whitney Elem. Sch., Green Bay, 1978; tchr. Eliot (Maine) Elem. Sch., 1979-81; dir. membership Greater Portsmouth (N.H.) C. of C., 1982-85; dir. mktg. Beacon Health, Inc., Greenland, N.H., 1985-87; dir. bldg. programs Unitarian Universalist Assn., Boston, 1987—; speaker Sacred Trusts Conf., Phila., 1988-90. Recipient Achievement award Nat. Assn. Membership Dirs., 1983. Mem. Seacoast Women's Network. Unitarian Universalist.

BERG, LORINE MCCOMIS, educator; b. Ashland, Ky., Mar. 28, 1919; d. Oliver Botner and Emma Elizabeth (Eastham) McComis; m. Leslie Thomas Berg, Apr. 27, 1946; children: James Michael, Leslie Jane. BA in Edn., U. Ky., 1965; MA, Xavier U., 1969. Tchr. 6th dist. Elementary Schs., Covington, Ky., 1965-69; guidance counselor Twenhofel Sr. High Sch., Independence, Ky., 1969-78, Scott High Sch., Independence, 1978-84. Bd. dirs. Mental Health Assn., Covington, Ky, 1970-76, v.p., 1973 (valuable svc. award 1973). Cited by U.S. Navy Recruiting Command for valuable assistance to U.S. Navy, 1981; named Hon. Admissions Counselor U.S. Naval Acad., 1983. Mem. Am. Assn. of Univ. Women, Covington Art Club, Retired Tchrs. Assn., Kappa Delta Pi, Delta Kappa Gamma, Phi Delta Kappa. Democrat. Home: 11 Idaho Ave Fort Mitchell KY 41017

BERG, SISTER MARIE MAJELLA, university president; b. Bklyn., July 7, 1916; d. Peter Gustav and Mary Josephine (McAuliff) B. BA, Marymount Coll., 1938; MA, Fordham U., 1948; DHL (hon.), Georgetown U., 1970, Marymount Manhattan Coll., 1983. Registrar Marymount Sch., N.Y.C., 1943-48; prof. classics, registrar Marymount Coll., N.Y.C., 1949-57; registrar Marymount Coll. of Va., Arlington, 1957-58, Marymount Coll., Tarrytown, N.Y., 1958-60; pres. Marymount U., Arlington, Va., 1960—; pres. Consortium for Continuing Higher Edn. in Va., 1987-88; com. mem. Consortium of Univs. Washington Met. Area, 1987—. Contbr. five biographies to One Hundred Great Thinkers, 1965; editor Otherwords column of N.Va. Sun, Arlington. Bd. dirs. Internat. Hospice, 1984—, HOPE, 1983—, 10th Dist. Congrl. Award Council, No. Va. Recipient commendation Va. Gen. Assembly, Richmond, 1986. Mem. Council of Ind. Colls. (pres. 1986-87), Nat. Assn. Ind. Colls. and Univs., Nat. Assn. of Catholic Colls. and Univs., Arlington C. of C. (bd. dirs. 1978-83). Roman Catholic. Home: 2807 N Glebe Rd Arlington VA 22207 Office: Marymount U Office of Pres 2807 N Glebe Rd Arlington VA 22207-4299

BERG, NAOMI LOUISE, management consultant; b. Washington, Apr. 8, 1951; d. Clifford John and Audrey Ann (Kolowrat) Miller; m. Fredric Robert Berg, June 1, 1969; children: Jesse Leon Philip, Katherine Audrey Fannie. BA cum laude, Columbia U., 1980; MSW, NYU, 1982. Cert. social worker, N.Y. Asst. v.p., cons. Fromkin Van Horn Handley-N.Y., Inc., N.Y.C., 1982-87; prin., cons. N.L. Berg Assocs., Groton, N.Y., 1987—. Bd. dirs. Warren Pl. Assn., Bklyn., 1981-86; bd. dirs., head personnel com. Groton Child Devel. Ctr., 1989—. Mem. ACLU, Amnesty Internat., Planned Parenthood Tompkins County. Office: NL Berg Assocs 183 Cayuga St Groton NY 13073

BERGBAUER, PATRICIA ANNE, communications director; b. Phila., Dec. 27, 1949; d. John Joseph and Anne Mary (Olejnick) B.; m. Aaron Julius Ladman, July 3, 1925; 1 child, Peter John Ladman. BA (english), St. Joseph's U., Phila., 1972; MA, Villanova U., 1975. Asst. mng. editor Cancer Research, Phila., 1972-82; info. officer Princeton U. Physics Lab., Princeton, N.J., 1982-83; editor, writer Nat. Com. Clin. Lab., Villanova, Pa., 1982-84; dir. communications Clin. Lab. Mgmt. Assn., Paoli, Pa.; prog. com. chair, Council Biology Editors Rockville, M.D., 1984-87. Democratic. Roman Catholic. Office: CLMA 195 W Lancaster Ave Paoli PA 19301

BERGEN, CANDICE, actress, photojournalist; b. Beverly Hills, Calif., May 9, 1946; d. Edgar and Frances (Westerman) B.; m. Louis Malle, Sept. 27, 1980; 1 dau., Chloe. Ed., U. Pa. Model during coll. Films include The Group, The Sand Pebbles, The Day the Fish Came Out, Live for Life, The Magus, Soldier Blue, Getting Straight, The Hunting Party, Carnal Knowledge, T.R. Baskin, The Adventurers, 11 Harrowhouse, Bite the Bullet, The Wind and the Lion, The Domino Principle, The End of the World in Our Usual Bed in a Night Full of Rain, Oliver's Story, Starting Over, Rich and Famous, Gandhi, 1982, Stick, 1985; TV series: Murphy Brown, 1988—; TV films Arthur the King, 1985, Murder by Reason of Insanity, 1985, Mayflower Madam, 1987; TV miniseries Hollywood Wives, 1985, Trying Times, Moving Day. Photojournalist credits include articles for Life, Playboy; dramatist: play The Freezer (included in Best Short Plays of 1968). Recipient Emmy awards for lead actress in a comedy series, 1989, 90. Office: care William Morris Agy 151 El Camino Beverly Hills CA 90212*

BERGER, AUDREY MARILYN, psychologist; b. Bklyn., Nov. 2, 1955; d. Alexander and Elaine (Kosloff) B.; m. Steven Davis, May 26, 1951; children: Michelle Caitlin, Rachel Lynn. BA with highest honors, SUNY, Binghamton, 1976; MA, U. Iowa, 1978, PhD, 1981. Lic. clin. psychologist, N.Y. Staff psychologist Rochester (N.Y.) Psychiat. Ctr., 1981-83, Rochester Regional Forensic Unit, 1984-85; dir. Counseling Ctr., Rochester Ints. Tech., 1985-87; pvt. practice, Rochester, 1987—. COntbr. chpt. to Handbook of Family Psychology and Therapy, 1985; contbr. articles to profl. jours. Named one of Outstanding Young Women of Am., 1983. Mem. Am. Psychol. Assn., Genesee Valley Psychol. Assn., Rochester Area Assn. Clin.

Psychologists, Amnesty Internat., Rochester Women's Network, Phi Beta Kappa. Office: 496 White Spring Blvd Rochester NY 14623

BERGER, BARBARA A., health facilty administrator; b. Trenton, N.J., Apr. 10, 1958; d. Louis and Ruth (Schwalbe) Agress; m. Eric M. Berger, Aug. 28, 1983; 1 child, Amanda. BS in Nursing, Ohio State U., 1981; MS in Nursing, U. Pa., 1983. Staff nurse Monmouth Med. Ctr., Long Branch, N.J.; grant coord. MCOSS Nursing Svcs., Red Bank, N.J.; neonatal clin. specialist Thomas Jefferson U. Hosp., Phila.; asst. dir. nursing The Med. Ctr. at Princeton, N.J. Contbr. articles to profl. jours. Mem. NAACOG, Phila. Perinatal Soc., Nat. Perinatal Assn., N.J. Perinatal Assn. (bd. trustees 1990—), Sigma Theta Tau. Home: 108 W Maple Tree Dr Mount Holly NJ 08060

BERGER, BEVERLY JANE, association executive; b. Morristown, N.J., Apr. 28, 1939; m. William R. Bode. BA, U. N.Mex., 1961, MEdSci, 1965, MS, 1967; PhD, U. Calif., Davis, 1971. NIH postdoctoral fellow U. Calif., Berkeley, 1971-73; mathematical biologist Lawrence Livermore (Calif.) Nat. Lab., 1973-75, group leader energy and resource planning, 1975-77; program mgr. chem. storage systems U.S. Dept. Energy, Washington, 1977-79, dir. biomass energy systems div., 1979-86; asst. dir. Office of Sci. and Tech. Policy Exec. Office of Pres., Washington, 1987-89; Washington rep. Fed. Lab. Consortium, 1990—; mem. Panel for Chem. Engring., NRC, Nat. Acad. Sci., Washington, 1986-88; mem. fed. sci. and tech. subcom. Indsl. Rsch. Inst., Washington, 1990—; chmn. Fed. Coord. Coun. on Sci., Engring. and Tech., com. on life scis., 1987-89; mem. Domestic Policy Coun. Working Groups on Health Policy, Agt Orange, and Energy, Environ. and Natural Resources, 1987-89; mem. Fed. Coord. Coun. on Sci., Engring. and Tech. Com. on Earth Scis., Biotech. Sci. Coord. Com., Com. on Interagy. Radiation Rsch. and Policy Coordination, 1987-89, White House delegation on Sci. and Tech. to Japan, 1988. Mem. AAAS, Technology Transfer Soc., Soc. for Risk Analysis, Sigma Xi, Phi Kappa Phi. Office: Fed Lab Consortium 1550 M St NW Washington DC 20005

BERGER, CHRISTINE LEE, insurance company executive; b. Portland, Oreg., Sept. 5, 1956; d. Edmund Henry and Agnes Lee (Nelson) B. BA in Chemistry, Williamette U., 1978; postgrad., U. Hokkaido, Sapporo, Japan, 1973. Cert. ICA designee. Phlebotomist U. Oregon Health Scis. Ctr., Portland; supr. group benefits, sr. analyst group benefits Standard Ins. Co., Portland, dir. claim mgmt. resources. Home: 900 SW 5th Ave Portland OR 97201

BERGER, ELIZABETH ANN, graphic designer; b. Lima, Peru, Sept. 17, 1955; came to U.S., 1959; d. Henry C. and Margaret S. (Benton) B.; m. Howard E. Goldthwaite, Sept. 29, 1978; children: Andrew Thomas, Jonathan Bennett. Student, U. N.C., 1973-75; BFA in Advt. Art and Biology, North Tex. State U., 1977; postgrad., SMU, 1987—. Jr. art dir. KCBN Advt., Dallas, 1977-78; art dir., writer Steve Moi & Assocs., Dallas, 1978-79; art dir. Eisenbeig, Inc., Dallas, 1979-81; creative dir., pres. Betsy Berger Assocs., Inc., Dallas, 1981—; vis. lectr. communication dept. So. Meth. U., 1986; adj. prof. advt. and graphic design North Tex. State U., 1986, Art. Inst. of Dallas, 1986, Brookhaven Community Coll., 1987. Creator, designer Mag. Published work, 1983, 86; creator Print mag., Am. Inst. Graphic Arts Annual, Graphis mag. (Gold Medal N.Y. Art Dirs. Club, 1986), 1986. Communications cons. 500, Inc., Dallas, 1985-86. Mem. Dallas Soc. Visual Communications, Am. Inst. Graphic Artists Internat., 500 Inc. Club: Gourmet Soc.

BERGER, ELLEN, occupational therapist; b. Boston, May 27, 1955; d. David and Ruth (Feldman) B. BS in Occupational Therapy, Tufts U., 1976; MS in Mgmt., Lesley Coll., 1987. Dir. Berkshire Devel. Svcs., Pittsfield, Mass., 1976-78, Valley Infant Devel. Svcs., Springfield, Mass., 1978-88; dir. occupational therapy Weldon Ctr. for Rehab. Mercy Hosp., Springfield, 1988-89; asst. prof. Springfield Coll., 1990—; cons. Continuing Edn. Consortium for Early Intervention, Waltham, Mass., 1988—. Co-author: Guidelines for Occupational Therapy in Early Childhood, 1988. Mem. Coun. for Children, Springfield, 1978—. Fellow Am. Occupational Therapy Assn. (Mass. rep. 1979-89, chair fees com. 1985-89, Svc. award 1989, 90); mem. Mass. Assn. for Occupational Therapists (Cert. of Appreciation 1985—), Mass. Early Intervention Consortium (past pres., cons. 1978-83, Cert. of Appreciation 1987, D'Amico award 1982). Jewish. Home and office: 229 Emerson St Springfield MA 01118 also: Springfield Coll Occupational Therapy Program Springfield MA 01109

BERGER, FRANCINE ELLIS, radio executive, educator; b. Albany, N.Y., July 27, 1949; d. David George and Harriet Sylvia (Bookstein) Ellis; m. Jerome Morris Berger, Oct. 9, 1977. BS in Broadcasting and Film, Boston U., 1971; EdM in Adminstrn., Planning and Social Policy, Harvard U., 1981. Traffic mgr. Sta. WCAS Kaiser Globe Broadcasting, Boston, 1971, Sta. WJIB-FM, 1971; continuity supr. WBZ-AM-Westinghouse, Boston, 1971-75; producer, traffic dir. Sta. WMEX/WITS, Boston, 1975-78; newswriter CBS Radio, Sta. WEEI, Boston, 1980; gen. mgr. Sta. WERS-FM, Emerson Coll., Boston, 1980—, asst. prof. radio dept., 1981—, head radio dept., 1983—. Contbg. editor Cobblestone Pub., Inc. Mem. monitoring com. Brookline Cable Commn. Mem. Nat. Acad. TV Arts and Scis., Kappa Gamma Chi, Alpha Epsilon Rho. Avocations: music, cooking. Office: Sta WERS-FM/ Emerson Coll 126 Beacon St Boston MA 02116

BERGER, KATHLEEN KAMMERER, pharmaceutical district sales manager; b. Evanston, Ill., Apr. 13, 1958; d. Richard Harrison and Doreen Kehoe Kammerer; m. Joseph Edwards Berger Jr., Aug. 9, 1980; 1 child, William Edwards. BS in Nursing, U. Va., 1980. Profl. rep. Rorer Group Inc., Ft. Washington, Pa., 1983-86; sales trainer Rorer Group Inc., Ft. Washington, 1985-86; dist. sales mgr. Whitehall Labs. div. Am. Home Products, N.Y.C., 1986—. Mem. Jr. League. Republican. Presbyn.

BERGER, KAY, public relations executive; b. Pitts., Feb. 18, 1939; d. Alex and Eve (Lando) Singer; m. Ted Stern, Mar. 24, 1984. B.S., UCLA, 1961; M.B.A., Pepperdine U., 1981. Demonstrator Carl Byoir Pub. Relations, Los Angeles, 1960-66; mgr. home econs. Calavo Co., Los Angeles, 1966-69; asst. dir. consumer relations Thermador-Waste King Corp., Los Angeles, 1961-66; exec. v.p. western div. Harshe-Rotman & Druck, Inc. (now Ruder Finn & Rotman), Los Angeles, 1969-80; pres. western region Manning, Selvage & Lee, Inc., Los Angeles, 1980-84; exec. v.p. U.S. regional ops. Manning, Selvage & Lee, Inc., Chgo., 1985-88, exec. v.p. European ops., 1988-90; mng. dir. Cross border Cons., 1990—. Mem. com. 1986 Chgo. Internat. Theatre Festival. Recipient 1st place award Nat. Council Farm Coops., 1967, Los Angeles Advt. Women, 1967, cert. creative excellence U.S. Indsl. Film Fair, 1974. Mem. Home Economists in Bus. (group chmn. Los Angeles chpt. 1968-69), Internat. Assn. Bus. Communicators, Nat. Investor Relations Inst., Pub. Relations Soc. Am. Home and Office: 129 Crown Lodge, 12 Elystan St, London SW3 3PR, England

BERGER, MAUREEN, seminar management executive; b. Leicester, Eng., Mar. 10, 1941; came to U.S., 1962; d. George Frederick and Katherine Irene (Ridgeway) Hill; m. David W. Lucier; children: Deborah, Steven, Donna; m. Richard William Berger, Aug. 10, 1985. Student bus. adminstrn. Leicester U., 1961. Test proctor U.S. Air Force, Phalsbourg, France, 1965-66; asst. adminstr. Oversea Div., Gen. Electric Co., Ramstein, Germany, 1966-67; prodn. mgr. Norman Harwell Assocs., Dallas and Saigon, 1968-7Vietnam, 2; sec. Coopers & Lybrand, Springfield, Mass., 1972-75; owner Latent Image Photography, Springfield, 1975-77; v.p. Tech. Seminars, Inc., Great Neck, N.Y., 1978—. Vol. Jansen Meml. Hospice Program, Tuckahoe, N.Y. Mem. Nat. Assn. Female Execs., NOW, Atomic Indsl. Forum Inc., Assn. Research and Enlightenment. Avocations: golf, racquetball, aerobics, collecting antique bottles and Maxfield Parrish prints. Home: 122 Forest Ave New Rochelle NY 10804 Office: Tech Seminars Inc 305 Northern Blvd Great Neck NY 11021

BERGER, MIRIAM ROSKIN, creative arts therapy director, educator, therapist; b. N.Y.C., Dec. 9, 1934; d. Israel and Florence (Frankel) Roskin; m. Meir Berger, July 16, 1967 (div. June 1981); children: Jonathan Israel. Student, Barnard Coll., 1952-53; BA, Bard Coll., 1956; postgrad., CCNY, 1956-58, NYU, 1981—. Alumni dir. Bard Coll., Annandale-on-Hudson, N.Y., 1958-59; dance therapist Manhattan Psychiatric Ctr., N.Y.C., 1959-60; performer, educator Jean Erdman Theater of Dance, N.Y.C., 1959-62; dir. adult program Hebrew Arts Sch., N.Y.C., 1964-68; faculty Dance Notation Bur., N.Y.C., 1974-75, 77; asst. prof. dance therapy program NYU, 1975—; dir. creative arts therapies Bronx Psychiatric Ctr., N.Y.C., 1970—; leader internat. workshops on arts therapy, Gt. Britain, France, Sweden, Brazil, Italy, Yugoslavia, and Holland. Producer off-Broadway The Coach with the Six Insides, 1962-63; author, producer Non-Verbal Group Process, 1978; contbr. articles to profl. jours. Bd. dirs. Theater Open Eye, 1978-82, v.p. bd. trustees, 1982-89, pres., 1989—. Recipient NYU scholarship, 1981. Mem. Am. Dance Therapy Assn. (founder, bd. dirs. 1967-76, v.p. 1974-76, credential com. 1976-82), Acad. Registered Dance Therapists, Am. Orthopsychiatric Assn. Home: 2 Horizon Rd Fort Lee NJ 07024 Office: Bronx Psychiat Ctr 1500 Waters Pl New York NY 10461 also: NYU 35 W 4th St New York NY 10003

BERGER, NATALIE STELLE, psychologist; b. Pitts., July 25, 1950; children: Colleen, Robyn. BS, U. Pitts., 1971, MEd, 1972, PhD, 1975. Diplomate Am. Bd. Med. Psychotherapists. Substitute tchr. Pitts. Bd. Edn., 1971-72; learning disabilities resource tchr. Westmoreland Intermediate Unit VII, Greensburg, Pa., 1972-73; project evaluater U. Pitts., 1973-74, part time instr., 1975-76; part time instr. Pa. State U., New Kensington, 1975-76; psychologist Allegheny Intermediate Unit III, Pitts., 1976-80; pvt. practice Camp Hill, Pa., 1975—; mem. allied health staff Polyclinic Med. Ctr., med. staff Holy Spirit Hosp. Grantee U. Pitts., 1974-75, Frick Edn. Commn., 1979. Fellow Am. Psychol. Assn., Pa. Psychol. Assn., Harrisburg Area Psychol. Assn. Office: Individual/Family Svcs 115 S Saint Johns Dr Camp Hill PA 17011

BERGER-HOMAN, ANJE, advertising executive; b. Chgo., July 19, 1945; d. Arnold Frederick Berger and Marion Fay (Friedlen) Homan. BS in English and Journalism, U. Mich., 1967, PhD in Clin. Psychology, 1971; MBA, U. Chgo., 1976. Writer Doyle Dane Bernbach, N.Y.C., 1967-69; copy group head Leo Burnett, Chgo., 1969-74; ptnr. Creative Consortium, Chgo., 1974-77; v.p., copy dir. Ogilvy & Mather, Chgo., Houston, N.Y.C., 1978-86; v.p., creative dir. The Saunders Co., Washington, 1987—; guest lectr. U. Md., College Park, 1989-90; adj. prof. Georgetown U., Washington, 1990—. Recipient Clio award, N.Y.C., 1982, Addy award Am. Advt. Assn., N.Y.C., 1988, Gold Maxie award Direct Mail Mktg. Assn., Washington, 1988, 89. Mem. Women in Communications (bd. dirs. 1974-75), Women in Advt., Direct Mail Mktg. Assn., Am. Mktg. Assn., Nat. Coun. Women Bus. Execs., Washington Bd. Trade (bus. devel. com.), Ad Club Washington. Home: 3005 Seven Oaks Pl Falls Church VA 22042 Office: The Saunders Co 2213 M St NW Ste 200 Washington DC 20037

BERGESON, MARIAN, state legislator; m. Garth Bergeson; children: Nancy, Garth Jr., Julie, James. Student UCLA; BA in Edn. Brigham Young U.; postgrad. UCLA. Pres., regional dir. Calif. Sch. Bds. Assn.; officer, dir. Orange County Sch. Bds. Assn.; mem. Newport Beach City Sch. Dist. Bd. Edn., 1964-65; mem. Newport-Mesa Unified Sch. Dist. Bd. Edn., 1965-77; mem. Calif. Assembly, 1978-82, Calif. Senate, 1984—. Past mem. Orange County Juvenile Justice Commn., Riles-Younger Task Force for Prevention of Crime and Violence in the Schs., Com. for Revision State Edn. Code, Joint Com. on Revision Penal Code; mem. Calif. YMCA Model Legislature/ Ct.; mem. bd. advisors Calif. Elected Women's Assn. Edn. and Research; bd. dirs. Sta. KBIG Adv. Bd.; mem. govt. relations com. Orange County Arts Alliance. Recipient Marian Bergeson Community Services award Orange County Sch. Bds. Assn., 1975; Anchor award Newport Harbor C. of C., women's div., 1967; Community Services award AAUW, 1976; Disting. Women's award Irvine Soroptimists, 1981; Disting. Service award Brigham Young U., 1980-81; Woman of Achievement award Newport Harbor Zonta Club, 1981; Silver Medallion, YWCA, 1983; Pub. Service award Calif. Speech-Lang.-Hearing Assn., 1983; named Outstanding Pub. Ofcl., Orange County chpt. Am. Soc. Pub. Adminstrn., 1983, Woman of Yr., Anti Defamation League B'nai B'rith, 1987, So. Dist. Legislator of Yr., Calif. Assn. for Health., 1987. Office: 140 Newport Ctr Dr Ste 120 Newport Beach CA 92660 also: State Capitol #4092 Sacramento CA 95814*

BERGLIN, LINDA, state senator; b. Oakland, Calif., Oct. 19, 1944; d. Freeman and Norma (Lund) Waterman. BFA, Mpls. Coll. Art and Design. Mem. Minn. Ho. of Reps., St. Paul, 1972-80; mem. Minn. Senate, St. Paul, 1980—, chmn. Health and Human Svcs. Com. Mem. Democratic-Farmer-Labor Party. Office: Minn Senate Saint Paul MN 55155

BERGMAN, TRISH, community services specialist, consultant; b. Ft. Worth, Mar. 12, 1953; d. Glenn Marshall and Evelyn Mae (Bowman) B. BA in Pub. Rels., Ottawa (Kans.) U., 1975; MLS, Emporia (Kans.) State U., 1979. Receptionist materials mgmt. dept. St. Francis Hosp., Topeka, 1976-77; reader's advisor fine arts dept. Topeka Pub. Libr., 1977-79, bookmobile libr., 1979-80; libr. I Ft. Worth Pub. Libr., 1980-83, libr. II, 1983-84; community edn. specialist N.E. Community Hosp., Bedford, Tex., 1984-86, dir. community affairs, 1986-88; community svc. coord. Harris Meth. S.W. Hosp., Ft. Worth, 1988—; cons. in field. Job counselor Women's Ctr. for Tarrant County, Tex., 1983, mentor, participant progra, 1986-88; adopt-a-sch. coord. Ft. Worth Ind. Sch. Dist., 1990—; coord. skin cancer screening program Am. Cancer Soc., Ft. Worth, 1990—. Recipient Mary Dunn award N.E. Community Hosp., 1986, Good Neighbor award ARC of Tarrant County, 1988. Mem. Am. Soc. for Hosp. Mktg. and Pub. Rels., S.W. Soc. for Healthcare Mktg., Network for Exec. Women (2d v.p. 1984-85), Women in Communications, Inc. (publicity chairperson 1989-90). Presbyterian. Home: 4405 Pershing Ave Fort Worth TX 76107

BERGMANN, BARBARA ROSE, economics educator; b. N.Y.C., July 20, 1927; d. Martin and Nellie (Wallenstein) Berman; m. Fred H. Bergmann, July 14, 1965; children: Sarah Nellie, David Martin. B.A., Cornell U., 1948; M.A., Radcliffe Coll.-Harvard U., 1955, Ph.D., 1959. Economist U.S. Bur. Labor Stats., N.Y.C., 1949-53; sr. staff ecomomist, cons. Council Econ. Advisors, Washington, 1961-62; mem. sr. staff Brookings Inst., Washington, 1963-65; sr. econ. advisor AID, Washington, 1966-67; assoc. prof. U. Md., College Park, 1965-71, prof. econs., 1971-88; disting. prof. econs. Am. U., Washington, 1988—. Author: (with Chinitz and Hoover) Projection of A Metropolis, 1961, (with George W. Wilson) Impact of Highway Investment on Development, 1966, (with David E. Kaun) Structural Unemployment in the U.S., 1967, (with Robert Bennett) A Microsimulated Transactions Model of the United States Economy, 1985, The Economic Emergence of Women, 1986; mem. bd. editors: Am. Econ. Rev., 1970-73, Challenge, 1978—, Signs, 1978-85; columnist econ. affairs, N.Y. Times, 1981-82, Los Angeles Times, 1983—. Mem. Economists for McGovern, 1977; mem. panel econ. advisors Congl. Budget Office, Washington, 1977-87; mem. price adv. com. U.S. council on Wage and Price Stability, 1979-80. Mem. AAUP (coun. 1980-83, pres. 1990—), Am. Econ. Assn. (v.p. 1976, adv. com. to U.S. Census Bur. 1977-82), Eastern Econ. Assn. (pres. 1974), Phi Beta Kappa. Democrat. Home: 5430 41 Place NW Washington DC 20015 Office: Am U Dept Econs Washington DC 20016

BERGNER, CATHY L., editor; b. Pratt, Kans., Dec. 11, 1951; d. Donald Wayne and W. Jean (King) B.; 1 child, Jon Joseph. Student, Blackstone Sch. Law, 1989; BS, Kans. State U., 1989. Editor Lifestyle sect. The El Dorado (Kans.) Times, The Pratt (Kans.) Tribune, Abilene (Kans.) Reflector Chronicle. With USAF, 1970-73. Recipient Community Svc. award, Individual Journalist award; Fred M. Paris Meml.scholar; incentive grantee AAUW. Mem. Am. Agriculture Movement. Home: 2133 Patricia Pl Manhattan KS 66502

BERGNER, JANE COHEN, lawyer; b. Schenectady, N.Y., Apr. 6, 1943; d. Louis and Selma (Breslaw) Cohen; m. Alfred P. Bergner, May 30, 1968; children: Lauren, Justin. AB, Vassar Coll., 1964; LLB, Columbia U., 1967. Bar: D.C. 1968, U.S. Dist. Ct. D.C. 1968, U.S. Ct. Appeals (D.C. cir.) 1968, U.S. Ct. Claims, 1969, U.S. Ct. Appeals (fed. cir.) 1969, U.S. Tax Ct. 1979. Trial atty. tax div. U.S. Dept. Justice, Washington, 1967-74; assoc. Arnold & Porter, Washington, 1974-76, Rogovin, Huge & Lenzner, Washington, 1976-83; of counsel Arter & Hadden, 1983-86, ptnr. Spriggs & Hollingsworth, 1986-89; ptnr. Feith & Zell, P.C., 1989—. Contbr. articles to profl. jours. Bd. dirs. Jewish Social Svc. Agy., Washington, Jewish Coun. for the Aging; mem. Nat. Women's Com. Brandeis U.; former mem. community adv. bd. WAMU-FM, Washington. Semi-finalist Harlan Fiske Stone Honor Moot Ct. Competition, Columbia U. Law Sch. Mem. Vassar Coll. Class Alumnae (chair spl. gifts. com. 25th reunion), D.C. Bar (chair taxation sect.), Fed. Bar Assn., Women's Bar Assn. D.C., Women's Legal Def. Fund, Nat. Assn. Women Lawyers, Women's Tax Luncheon Group, ABA (sect. taxation, ct. procedure com., regional liason mid-Atlantic, regional liaison meetings), Columbia U. Law Sch. Alumni Assn., Svc. Guild Washington, Vassar Club, Hadassah Club. Home: 5659 Bent Branch Rd Bethesda MD 20816 Office: Feith & Zell PC 2300 M St NW Ste 600 Washington DC 20037

BERGSTROM, BETTY HOWARD, association executive; b. Chgo., Mar. 15, 1931; d. Seward Haise and Agnes Eleanor (Uek) Guinter; BS in Speech, Northwestern U., 1952, postgrad., 1983; postgrad U. Nev., Reno, 1974; m. Robert William Bergstrom, Apr. 21, 1979; children: Bryan Scott, Cheryl Lee, Jeffrey Alan, Mark Robert, Philip Alan. Dir. sales promotion and pub. relations WLS-AM, Chgo., 1952-56; account exec. E.H. Brown Advt. Agy., Chgo., 1956-59; v.p. Richard Crabb Assocs., Chgo., 1959-61; pres., owner Howard Assocs., Calif. and Chgo., 1961-76; v.p. Chgo. Hort. Soc., 1976—. Del., Ill. Constl. Conv., 1969-70, mem. com. legis. reform, 1973-74, cts. and justice com., 1971-74; apptd. mem. Ill. Hist. Library Bd., 1970, Ill. Bd. Edn., 1971-74. AAUW fellowship grant named in her honor; recipient Communicator of Yr. award Women in Communication, 1983. Mem. Nat. Soc. Fund Raising Execs. (cert. fund raising executive, bd. dirs. 1983-90, sec. 1986, v.p. 1990, nat. bd. dirs., 1990—, Pres's. award, 1988), Am. Assn. of Museums, Am. Assn. Bot. Garden and Arboreta, Garden Writers Am., AAUW, Northwestern U. Alumni, U. So. Calif. Alumni Assn., LWV. Mem. editorial bd. Garden mag. Glenview Community Ch., 1977-89; editor Garden Talk, 1976-86; contbr. articles on fund devel., horticulture, edn. advt. and agr. to profl. jours.; editor Ill. AAUW Jour., 1966-67. Office: Chgo Botanic Garden PO Box 400 Glencoe IL 60022

BERGSTROM, HELEN MARIE, hospital administrator; b. Fremont, Nebr., Sept. 7, 1930; d. Charles Opal and Florence Franchesa (Farrari) Bertram; m. George Wallace Bergstrom, Sept. 13, 1953; children: Robert Jay, George Alan. Nursing Diploma, Nebr. Meth. Hosp., Omaha, 1953. RN, Nebr. Staff nurse to supr. Meth. Hosp., Omaha, 1953-66; with Douglas County Hosp., Omaha, 1966—; adminstr. Douglas County Hosp., 1982—. Bd. dirs. Health Occupations Adv. Com., Omaha, 1975-78; ad hoc com. Douglas County Mental Health, 1971. Mem. Nebr. Assn. Homes for Aging (chmn. com. 1984-85), Nat. League Nursing, Omaha Women's C. of C., Nebr. Health Care Assn., Nebr. Nursing Home Assn., Nebr. Nurses Assn. (fin. com. 1973-74), Altrusa Club (bd. dirs. 1975-77, co-chmn. info. com. 1975-76), Nebr. Meth. Hosp. Alumni Assn. (bd. dirs. 1969-73). Republican. Lutheran. Home: 6921 Mormon Bridge Rd Omaha NE 68152 Office: Douglas County Hosp 4102 Woolworth Ave Omaha NE 68105

BERING, CAROL GRETCHEN, library administrator, cataloger; b. Carlsbad, N.Mex., Apr. 3, 1938; d. Karl and Vivian Avis (Brown) Bering; divorced; children: Kurt Alan Grasmick, Amy Christine Grasmick. BA, Colo. Coll., 1960; MA in Librarianship, U. Denver, 1963. Reference libr. Ft. Worth Pub. Libr., 1963-64; catalog libr. Ft. Collins (Colo.) Pub. Libr., 1964-67, libr. program adminstr. for tech. svcs., 1973—. Mem. ALA, Colo. Libr. Assn. (sec. tech. svcs. div. 1986-87), Alpha Phi (Michaelanean award 1982). Home: 2919 Fauborough Ct Fort Collins CO 80525 Office: Ft Collins Pub Libr 201 Peterson St Fort Collins CO 80524

BERK, ANN E., novelist, television executive; b. N.Y.C., Mar. 19; d. Herman Robert and Ruth Fox; BS, Cornell U., 1961; m. Louis Romano; 1 child, Melinda. Dir. broadcast ops., program dir. WNBC-TV, N.Y.C., 1975-77, sta. mgr., 1977-79; sta. mgr. WRC-TV, Washington, 1979-83; v.p. advt., promotion and publicity NBC-TV Stas., N.Y.C., 1983-87. Novelist: Fast Forward, 1983, Laugh Lines, 1989.

BERK, KERRY M., telecommunications industry executive; b. Mt. Holly, N.J., Jan. 25, 1953; d. William H. and Marilyn (Raisner) Mac Cartney; m. Michael Alan Berk, Jan. 3, 1981; children: Kelly Lynn, Karen Ann. BA summa cum laude, Gettysburg Coll., 1975; MS with honors, Drexel U., 1981. Mgmt. asst. pub. rels. dept. Bell of Pa./Bell Atlantic, Phila., 1975-76, account exec. mktg. dept., 1976-78, promotions mgr. mktg. dept., 1978-79, assessor and assessment ctr. leader pers. dept., 1979-80, staff mgr. strategic planning/witness support, 1980-84, staff mgr. sales delivery and regulatory dept., 1984-85, project mgr. tng. and devel., 1985-86, mng. editor employee communications, 1986-87, dir. employee communications, 1987—; cons. pub. rels.; leader seminars and workshops. Officer bd. fellows Gettysburg (Pa.) Coll., 1979-83, bd. trustees, 1984-88, chair student affairs com., 1987-88; exec. bd. PTA Lynnewood Sch. Named Outstanding Young Leader, Gettysburg Coll., 1979, one of mems. Outstanding Com. of Yr., Phila. Jaycees, 1980. Mem. NAFE, Internat. Assn. Bus. Communicators (cert.), Pub. Rels. Soc. Am., Nat. Assn. for Edn. of Young Children, Phi Beta Kappa. Office: Bell of Pa One Parkway Ste 9C Philadelphia PA 19102

BERK, PEGGY FAITH, public and financial relations consultant; b. N.Y.C., Feb. 3, 1951; d. Stanley and Naomi Elaine (Herskowitz) B.; divorced; 1 child, Mason Ben-Yair. Student, NYU, 1968-71, New Sch. for Social Rsch., 1971-73. News editor Herald Newspapers, N.Y.C., 1972-73; mktg. liaison U.S. Dept. Commerce, Tel Aviv, Israel, 1973; mgr. fgn. currency dept. Bank Le'umi BM, Arad, Israel, 1974-75; exec. v.p. Peter Small & Assocs., N.Y.C., 1978-81; prin., pres. Strategic Communications, N.Y.C., 1981—; cons. sr. v.p. The Rowland Co., N.Y.C., 1984-85; prin., pres. BFP Internat. Inc., N.Y.C., 1987—; cons. X-On Software, London, 1989—; cons. Coun. on Fin. Aid to Edn., N.Y., 1979-81, Global Link, Tokyo, 1986—; bd. dirs. New Networking Aquisition Corp., Hartford, Conn., 1988—. Contbr. numerous news articles. Bd. dirs. Child Net, Inc., Mass., 1987—; steering com. Am. Mus. Fin. History, 1989—. Mem. Citiwomen, Women's Am. ORT, U.S. Amateur Snowboard Assn. Office: Strategic Communications 276 Fifth Ave New York NY 10001

BERKA, MARIANNE GUTHRIE, health and physical education educator; b. Queens, N.Y., Dec. 25, 1944; d. Frank Joseph and Mary (DePaul) Guthrie; B.S., Ithaca (N.Y.) Coll., 1966, M.S. (grad. asst.), 1968; doctoral candidate NYU; m. Jerry George Berka, June 1, 1968; children: Katie, Keri. High sch. tchr. Northport High Sch., 1966-67; full prof. health, phys. edn. and recreation Nassau Community Coll., Garden City, N.Y., 1968—. Mem. Assn. Women Phys. Educators N.Y. State (chpt. chmn. 1973-74, chpt. treas. 1980-84), AAHPER, N.Y. State Assn. Health, Phys. Edn. and Recreation (J.B. Nash scholarship com. 1983—), Am. Assn. Sex Educators, Counselors and Therapists (cert. sex educator). Roman Catholic. Home: 90 Bay Way Ave Brightwaters NY 11718 Office: Nassau Community Coll P226 HPER Garden City NY 11530

BERKBIGLER, MARSHA LEE, gold mining company executive; b. Flint, Mich., May 2, 1950; d. Herbert Ules and Rosy Vernell (Grimes) Cornelison; m. Gary Robert Koontz, June 22, 1968 (div. Nov. 1976); children: Deron Robert, Alicia Michelle; m. James Herbert Berkbigler, Dec. 16, 1977. A. in Bus., Reno Bus. Coll., 1979. Hosp. coordinating sec. LaHabra Community Hosp., Calif., 1973-76; sec., office mgr. Sierra Med. Assocs., Reno, 1976-78; claims rep. Equifax, Reno, 1978-79; legal asst. Freeport Export Co., Reno, 1979-85; dir. govt. rels. Freeport-McMoRan Gold Co., Reno, 1985—; cons. Neva. Wilderness Minerals Exploration Coalition, Denver, 1985. Named one of 88 people to watch in 1988, Reno Mag., 1988. Mem. Nev. Rep. Woman's Caucus, Reno, 1986; apptd. Reno Commn. Status of Women, 1985. Mem. Nev. Mining Assn., Nev. Landman's Assn., Assn. Exec. Females, Nev. Coun. Econ. Edn. (exec. com.), Reno Sparks C. of C. (bd. dirs., v.p. community affairs), Concerned Nevadans for Practical Wilderness. Avocations: skiing, golf, travel. Office: 2090 Allen St Reno NV 89509

BERKE, ANITA DIAMANT, literary agent; b. N.Y.C., Jan. 15; d. Sidney J. and Lea (Lyons) Diamant; m. Harold Berke, Dec. 22, 1945 (dec. 1972); 1 child, Allyson. B.S., NYU. Mem. editorial bd. Forum Mag., N.Y.C., McCalls Mag.; reporter Macy Newspapers; literary agt., pres. Anita Diamant Lit. Agy., N.Y.C.; adj. prof. L.I.U. Contbr. articles to profl. jours. Mem. Women in Communications, Inc. (past pres. N.Y. chpt.), Nat. Assn. Newspaper Women, Soc. Author's Reps. Club: Overseas Press (pres. 1981-86). Home: 16 Fanton Hill Rd Weston CT 06883 Office: 310 Madison Ave New York NY 10017

BERKE, JUDIE, publisher, editor; b. Mpls., Apr. 15, 1938; d. Maurice M. and Sue (Supak) Kleyman; student U. Minn., 1956-60, Mpls. Sch. Art, 1945-59. Free lance illustrator and designer, 1959—; pres. Berke-Wood, Inc., N.Y.C., 1971-80, Manhattan Rainbow & Lollipop Co. subs. Berke-Wood, Inc., 1971-80; pres. Get Your Act Together, club act staging, N.Y.C., 1971-80; pres. Coordinator Pubs.,Inc., 1982-87; pres., chief exec. officer, Health Market Communications, 1987—; pres. Pub. and Media Services, Burbank, 1987—; pub., editor Continuing Care Coordinator, Health Watch mags.; pres. Continuing Care Coordinator Convs. and Seminars; cons. to film and ednl. cos.; guest lectr. various colls. and univs. in Calif. and N.Y., 1973—; cons., designer Healthy Lifestyles mag.; writer, illustrator, dir. numerous ednl. filmstrips, 1972—, latest being Focus on Professions, 1974, Focus on the Performing Arts, 1974, Focus on the Creative Arts, 1974, Workstyles, 1976, Wonderworm, 1976, Supernut, 1977; author, illustrator film Fat Black Mack (San Francisco Ednl. Film Festival award, part of permanent collection Mus. Modern Art, N.Y.C.), 1970; designer posters and brochures for various entertainment groups, 1963—; composer numerous songs, latest being Time is Relative, 1976, Love Will Live On in My Mind, 1976, My Blue Walk, 1976, You Make Me a Baby, 1982, Let's Go Around Once More, 1983, Anytime Anyplace Anywhere, 1987, Bittersweet, 1987, Sometimes It Pays, 1987; composer/author off-Broadway musical Street Corner Time, 1978; producer: The Reals Estate TV Shows 1988—; contbr. children's short stories to various publs., also articles. Trustee The Happy Spot Sch., N.Y.C., 1972-75. Mem. Nat. Fedn. Bus. and Profl. Women, Nat. Assn. Female Execs., Am. Acad. Polit. and Social Sci.

BERKE, PAMELA SUE, dentist; b. Rochester, N.Y., July 1, 1959; d. Harry Lee and Betty (Leader) B. BS with honors, U. Fla., 1981; DDS, Emory U., 1985. Lic. dentist, Fla., Ga. Residency in gen. practice Emory U., VA, Atlanta, 1986; assoc. D. Piroli DDS, Jupiter, Fla., 1986-89, J. McDowel DDS, Tequesta, Fla., 1989—, C.D. Lindahl DDS, Tequesta, 1989—. oral cancer examiner Free Health Screening Martin County Hosp., Stuart, 1988. Mem. Am. Assn. of Women Dentists, Phi Kappa Phi, Alpha Omega. Jewish. Home: 1146 11th Ct Jupiter FL 33477

BERKE, YVETTE NANCY, purchasing executive; b. L.A., Aug. 12, 1961; d. Larry and Evelyn (Mandelbaum) B. Student, Merit Coll. Ct. Reporting, Van Nuys, Calif., 1979-84; cert. in purchasing mgmt., Calif. State U., 1990. Pub. rels. rep. Merit Coll. of Ct. Reporting, Van Nuys, 1981-84; office adminstr. tax svcs. div. IDS Fin. Svcs./Am. Express, Glendale, Calif., 1985-86; asst. to pres. Lundberg Survey, Inc., North Hollywood, Calif., 1986-87; litigation office adminstr. Intermed Mgmt. Corp., Glendale, 1987; buyer, minority bus. coord. NBC, Burbank, Calif., 1987-90; purchasing cons. Major Motion Picture and TV Studios, Burbank, 1990—. Bd. adv. L.A. chpt. MADD, 1990; pub. speaker; author-editor Designated Driver News, program coord., Designated Driver Coalition, vol. Crime Prevention Specialist, L.A. Police Dept. Recipient Spl. Vol. Achievement award MADD, 1989, Community Svc. Leader GE, 1988-89, Vol. Svc. award U. Calif., 1984. Mem. Purchasing Mgmt. Assn. of L.A. (profl. devel. com. 1987—), Nat. Assn. of Purchasing Mgrs., Nat. Notary Assn. Home: 13618 Lemay St Van Nuys CA 91401-1114

BERKELEY, BETTY LIFE, educator; b. St. Louis, May 25, 1924; d. James Alfred and Anna Laura (Voltmer) Life; m. Marvin Harold Berkeley, Feb. 7, 1947; children—Kathryn Elizabeth, Barbara Ellen, Brian Harrison, Janet Lynn. A.B., Harris Tchrs. Coll., 1947; M.A. in Ednl. Adminstrn., Washington U., St. Louis, 1951; Ph.D., U. North Tex. , 1980. Tchr. St. Louis pub. schs., 1946-48, Clayton pub. schs., Mo., 1948-49, Lamplighter Pvt. Sch., Dallas, 1964-67; program devel. specialist Richland Coll., Dallas, 1980-84, instr., 1981—; adj. prof. U. North Tex., Denton, 1981—, cons. Sch. Community Services Ctr. for Studies on Aging, 1981—; pres. Retirement Planning Services, Dallas, 1984—. Contbr. articles to profl. jours. Mem. Dallas Commn. on Status of Women, 1975-79; bd. dirs. Dallas Municipal Library, 1979-83; bd. dirs. Council on Adult Ministry Lovers Lane United Meth. Ch., 1982; charter mem. bd. dirs., life mem. Friends of U. North Tex. Libr.; mem. Pres.'s Coun. U. North Tex., mem. vol. mgmt. edn. task force, 1978-82. Mem. AAUW (pres. 1973-75; Outstanding Woman of Tex. 1981). Club: Women's Council of Dallas County (v.p. 1977-79). Avocations: travel, cooking, gardening, needlework. Home and Office: 13958 Hughes Ln Dallas TX 75240

BERKENES, JOYCE MARIE POORE, family counselor; b. Des Moines, Aug. 29, 1953; d. Donald Roy and Thelma Beatrice (Hart) Poore; m. Robert Elliott Berkenes, Jan. 3, 1976; children: Tiffany Noelle, Cory Matthew. BA in Social Work and Biology, Simpson Coll., Indianola, Iowa., 1975. Resident counselor and group home mgr. Chaddock Boys Home, Quincy, Ill., 1976-78; social service dir. North Adams Nursing Home, Mendon, Ill., 1978; home tchr. Head Start, Camp Point, Ill., 1978-79, home tchr. supr./edn. and parent involvement coordinator, 1979-82; family counselor Iowa Children's and Family Services, Des Moines, 1982-85; family counselor and vol. coordinator Luth. Social Services, Des Moines, 1985-89; educator/social worker Parent-Infant Nurturing Ctr., Meth. Med. Ctr., Des Moines, 1989—; mem. Greater Des Moines Child Abuse and Neglect Coun. Bd., Friends of New Parents Bd.; cons. in field, 1975-76. Democrat. Methodist. Home: 2901 NE 80th St Altoona IA 50009 Office: Parent-Infant Nurturing Ctr 1111 9th St Ste 230 Des Moines IA 50314

BERKEY, BARBARA ANN, management consultant; b. Rochester, Ind., Aug. 1, 1943; d. Arthur Frederick and Edith Mae (Scott) Mohn; children: Debra Ann Berkey Metzger, Terri Lynn. A of Bus. Adminstrn., Internat. Bus. Coll., Ft. Wayne, Ind., 1982. Fin. mgr. Western Rubber Co., Goshen, Ind., 1966-87, Goshen Die Cutting, 1987; prin. Berkey and Assocs., Goshen, 1987—; cons. Western Rubber Co., 1987—; chief oper. officer Burnstine's Distbg. Corp. Budget dir. Elkhart (Ind.) United Way, 1984-86, 88-89, 90; emergency room vol. Goshen Gen. Hosp. Aux., 1984—; fundraising chairperson Greencroft Retirement Group, Goshen and Elkhart, 1985. Mem. Bus. Women's Inst. (charter), Nat. Assn. Female Execs. Republican. Baptist. Office: Berkey and Assocs 62231 County Rd 17 Goshen IN 46526

BERKHAN, SHARON LEE, data systems specialist; b. Long Beach, Calif., Dec. 31, 1954; d. Robert Eugene Berkhan and Margaret Adele (Smith) Maloney. BA in Studio Art, U. Calif., Irvine, 1980; cert. in bus. info. systems, Orange Coast Coll., 1984. Word processing mgr. Peat Marwick Mitchell & Co., Newport Beach, Calif., 1980-82; data systems mgr. Orange County Performing Arts Ctr., Costa Mesa, Calif., 1982—; cons. in field. Mem. NAFE, Assn. Systems Mgmt., NOW, ACLU, Sierra Club. Office: Orange County Perf Arts Ctr 600 Town Center Dr Costa Mesa CA 92626

BERKLEY, ERMA VAN METER, retired librarian; b. Thayer, Kans., Nov. 18, 1922; d. George William and Elizabeth (Hamill) Van Meter; m. Donald William Berkley, May 28, 1944 (dec. 1980); children: Ann Elizabeth, James Donald. BA in Bus. Edn. magna cum laude, Western Wash. U., 1964; MLS, U. Wash., 1973. Cert. profl. libr., 1976. Sec., bookkeeper Blue Ribbon Growers, Inc., Yakima, Wash., 1941-44; aircraft communicator CAA, Kodiak, Alaska, 1944-47; libr., sec., tchr. Crescent Consol. Sch., Joyce, Wash., 1965-66; asst. libr., reference libr. Port Angeles (Wash.) High Sch., 1966-68, secretarial tchr., 1968-75, head libr., 1975-86; ret., 1986; bd. dirs. exec. com. Wash. Libr. Network, 1979-81; N.W. rep.-at-large Washington Libr. Media Assn., 1983-84; del. Gov.'s Conf. on Libr. and Info. Svcs., Olympia, 1979; sec. Western Wash. Bus. Edn. Assn., 1973-74. Mem. AAUW (treas. 1966-67, pres. 1982-84, v.p. 1988-90), PEO, Nat. Ret. Tchrs. Assn., Phi Theta Kappa, Beta Phi Mu.

BERKLEY, FLORENCE PFULLMANN, lawyer; b. Seguin, Tex., Apr. 13, 1953; d. Robert Carl and June Pauline (Peters) Pfullmann; m. Richard Warren Berkley, July 2, 1977. MusB with highest honors, U. Tex., 1975, MFA, 1977, JD with high honors, 1986. Bar: Tex. 1987. Assoc. Joseph, Rider & Cameron, P.C., Austin, Tex., 1987-89, Haynes and Boone, Austin, 1989—. Author: Computerized Check Processing and a Bank's Duty to Use Ordinary Care, TEx. Law Rev., 1987; co-author: Borrowers and Buyers: Dealing with Failing and Failed Financial Institutions. Commr. Round Rock (Tex.) Planning and Zoning Commn., 1984-85, 86-87. Mem. ABA, Tex. Bar Assn., Travis County Bar assn., Austin Young Lawyers Assn., Order of Coif. Office: Haynes and Boone 600 Congress Ave Ste 1600 Austin TX 78701

BERKMAN, CLAIRE FLEET, psychologist; b. New Orleans, Dec. 5, 1942; d. Joel and Margaret Grace (Fishler) Fleet; m. Arnold Stephen Berkman, Apr. 27, 1975; children: Janna Samantha, Micah Seth Siegel. BA, Boston U., 1964; MEd, Harvard U., 1966; EdD, Boston U., 1970. Asst. prof. Counseling Ctr., Mich. State U., East Lansing, 1971-75, assoc. prof., 1975-78, assoc. prof. dept. psychiatry, 1975-82, clin. assoc. prof., 1986-87; pvt. clin. practice, 1975—; cons. Cath. Family Social Service, Lansing, 1979-83; mem. adv. bd. Cir. Ct. Family Counseling Program, 1982-88. V.p. Kehillat Israel Synagogue, 1975-76; bd. dirs. Jewish Welfare Fedn., Lansing, 1974-75, 84-87. NDEA fellow, 1968-70. Mem. Am. Psychol. Assn., Mich. Psychol. Assn., Am. Mental Health Assn. of Israel, Mich. Soc. Forensic Psychologists. Office: 4084 Okenos Rd Okemos MI 48864

BERKMAN, JOYCE ELEANOR AVRECH, history educator; b. San Jose, Calif., Nov. 20, 1937; d. Benjamin and Lillian (Yudelowitz) Avrech; m. Leonard Berkman, Sept. 2, 1962; children: Jeremy Saul, Zachary Alexander Toke. BA in History, UCLA, 1958; MA in History, Yale U., 1959, PhD in History, 1967. Instr. Conn. Coll., New London, 1962-63; from instr. to prof. history U. Mass., Amherst, 1965—, founder, policy bd. mem. Women's Studies Dept., 1975—; cons. in field. Author: Feminism on the Frontier, 1980, The Healing Imagination of Beyond South African Colonialism, 1989; contbr. articles to profl. jours. Rep., Amherst Town Meeting, 1973-90; chairperson com. on sex role stereo typing Amherst Sch. System, 1973-80, Wildwood Elem. Sch. Parent Adv. Com., 1980-81. Danforth Teaching fellow, 1975—. Mem. Nat. Women's Studies Assn., Am. Hist. Assn., Northeastern Victorian Studies Assn., Berkshire Conf. Women Historians. Democrat. Home: 66 Cottage St Amherst MA 01002 Office: U Mass 605 Herter Hall Amherst MA 01003

BERKOVITS, ANNETTE ROCHELLE, association administrator, consultant, biologist, educator; b. Kizyl-Kija, Kirgiz Republic, USSR, Sept. 13, 1943; came to U.S., 1959; naturalized, 1964; d. Nachman and Dora (Blaustein) Libeskind; m. David Berkovits; children: Jessica Dawn, Jeremy Haskell. BS in Biology, CUNY, 1965; MS in Adminstrn. and Supervision, Manhattan Coll., 1977. Cert. sch. adminstr., N.Y. Research asst. Sloan Kettering Cancer Research Inst., N.Y.C., 1965-66; sci. tchr. N.Y.C. Bd. Edn., 1966-72; zoology instr. N.Y. Zool. Soc., N.Y.C., 1972-75, coordinator curricula and programs, 1975-77, asst. curator of edn., 1978-80, assoc. curator edn., 1980-82, curator of edn., 1983-88, dir. edn., 1988—; project dir. Wildlife Inquiry through Zoo Edn. program, N.Y. Zool. Soc., 1981—; dir. Animal Kingdom Zoo Camp, N.Y. Zool. Soc., 1977—; project dir., prin. investigator grants program NSF, 1980—; panelist N.Y. State Council on Arts, 1986—; cons., panelist NSF; chairwoman edn. N.Y. Zool. Soc. Author: (with others) Science for the Fun of It, 1988; editor numerous ednl. publs.; speaker in field. Chairwoman Pan-Am. Congress on Conservation of Wildlife Through Edn., Caracas, Venezuela, 1989—. Fellow Am. Assn. Zool. Parks and Aquariums (profl.), Consortium of Aquariums, Univs., and Zoos (bd. dirs.), N.Y.C. Mus. Educators Roundtable (chmn. 1982). Office: NY Zool Soc 185th St & Southern Blvd New York NY 10460

BERKOVITZ, ROSLYN A., counselor; b. N.Y.C., Sept. 27, 1942; d. Herbert Justin and Bernice Mabel (Meirowitz) B. BBA, Adelphi U., 1965; MEd, SUNY, Buffalo, 1968; PhD, Cornell U., 1982. Cert. counselor, N.Y. Jr. acct. J.K. Lasser and Co., N.Y.C., 1965-66; tchr. math. John Adams High Sch., Ozone Park, N.Y., 1966-67; rsch. asst. SUNY, Buffalo, 1967-68; head guidance and counseling Buffalo Acad. Sacred Heart, 1968-69; counselor, chief counselor Buffalo State Coll., 1969—, supr. grad. students, 1971-81; cons. N.Y. State Div. for Youth, Buffalo, 1978. Author: Guide to Graduate Opportunities for Minorities, 1971. Cons. B'nai B'rith, Buffalo, 1977, Project WHEAT, Buffalo, 1977; chmn. Women's Studies By-Laws Com., Buffalo, 1987, Pres. Task Force on Women's Issues, Buffalo, 1987; troop leader Girl Scouts U.S.A., Flushing, N.Y., 1961. Recipient staff award Ednl. Opportunity Prog., 1984, svc. award, SUNY, Buffalo, 1989. Mem. AAUW, Phi Delta Kappa (sec. 1988-89, v.p. 1989-90, pres. 1990-91), Phi Kappa Phi.

BERKOWITZ, EMILY SUE, research administrator; b. N.Y.C., June 9, 1954; d. Herbert and Anne (Korngold) Goldstein; m. Jay A. Berkowitz, June 15, 1975; 1 child, Justin S. BS, Cornell U., 1975; MS with distinction, Hofstra U., 1980. Vocat. evaluator N.Y. Assn. for Blind, The Lighthouse, N.Y.C., 1980-82; rehab. counselor Helen Keller Nat. Ctr., Sands Point, N.Y., 1982-83; placement coord. Human Resources Ctr., Albertson, N.Y., 1985; adj. asst. prof., asst. dir. community svcs. Hofstra U., Hempstead, N.Y., 1986, assoc. dir. grants devel., 1987-89, instr. grantsmanship workshop, 1988, 89; dir. grants and contracts Winthrop-Univ. Hosp., Mineola, N.Y., 1989—. Contbr. chpt. to book. Bd. dirs. Port Washington (N.Y.) Children's Ctr., 1989. Carolyn J. Reiger scholar, 1972, N.Y. Stat Regents scholar, 1972. Mem. Nat. Soc. Fund Raising Execs., Nat. Coun. Univ. Rsch. Adminstrs., Soc. Rsch. Adminstrs., Omicron Nu. Democrat. Jewish. Office: Winthrop-Univ Hosp 259 1st St Mineola NY 11501

BERLACHER, PHYLLIS O'BRIEN, communications consultant; b. Providence, Sept. 8, 1958; d. Thomas Jenkins and Margaret (Cimini) Pons; m. Mark James Berlacher, May 19, 1984. BA in Communications, U. Toledo, 1980; MA in Communications, Bowling Green State U., 1981. Account exec. Sta. WLQR-FM, Toledo, 1982-83; communications specialist Owens-Corning, Toledo, 1983-87; publs. dir. Oakwood Hosp., Dearborn, Mich., 1987-88; prin. Gremel/Berlacher Assoc., West Bloomfield, Mich., 1989; communications cons. TPF&C, Detroit, 1989—; instr. Wayne State U., Detroit, 1988—. Com. mem. Vol. Action Ctr., Toledo, 1983-87. Recipient Crystal award Toledo chpt. Women in Communications, Inc., 1986. Mem. Internat. Assn. Bus. Communicators (Gold Quill award 1987), Am. Soc. Hosp. Mktg. and Pub. Relations. Roman Catholic. Office: TPF&C 200 Renaissance Cen Ste 2700 Detroit MI 48243

BERLAGE, GAI INGHAM, sociologist, educator; b. Washington, Feb. 9, 1943; d. Paul Bowen and Grace (Artz) Ingham; m. Jan Coxe Berlage, Aug. 7, 1965; children: Jan Ingham, Cari Coxe. BA, Smith Coll., 1965; MA, So. Meth. U., 1968; PhD, NYU, 1979. Tchr. math. Piner Jr. High Sch., Sherman, Tex., 1968-69; asst. prof. sociology Iona Coll., New Rochelle, N.Y., 1971-83, assoc. prof., 1983-88, chmn. dept., 1981-90, prof., 1988—; coord. urban studies program, 1984-90, gerontology program, 1985-90. Author: Experience with Sociology: Social Issues in American Society, 1983, Understanding Social Issues: Sociological Fact Finding, 1987, 2d edit., 1990; editorial bd. Jour. Sport and Social Issues; contbr. articles to profl. jours. Commr. Wilton Commn. on Aging and Social Svcs., 1980-88, chmn., 1982-88; co-chmn. Wilton Task Force on Youth Coun., 1988; chmn. Wilton Task Force Com. for Outreach Program, 1981-82, Wilton Task Force on Day Care, 1983-88; mem. Wilton Task Force for Pub. Health Nursing Assn., 1981-82, Wilton Sport Coun., 1985-88; bd. dirs. Wilton Meals on Wheels, 1983-88; fellow N.Am. Faculty Network of Northeastern Univs. Ctr. for Study of Sport in Soc. NSF trainee, 1967-68. Mem. Am. Sociol. Assn., N.Y. State Sociol. Assn., N.Am. Soc. Sociology of Sport, Inst. Sport and Social Analysis, Internat. Com. Sociology of Sport, Wilton Assn. Gifted Edn. (pres. 1980-81), Internat. Soc. of Sport Psychology. Office: Iona Coll Dept Sociology New Rochelle NY 10801

BERLAND, KAREN INA, psychologist; b. N.Y.C., Nov. 14, 1947; d. Max and Lillian (Graf) B. BA in Psychology, SUNY, Buffalo, 1969; MEd in Ednl. Psychology, U. Ill., 1971; D. Psychology, U. Denver, 1984. Cert. sch. psychologist, clin. psychologist. Sch. psychologist City Sch. Dist. Rochester (N.Y.), 1971-73, Denver Pub. Sch., 1973—; psychology intern Vets. Hosp., West Haven, Conn., 1983-84; psychologist Aurora (Colo.) Community Mental Health Ctr., 1985—. Mem. Colo. Soc. Sch. Psychologists (pres. 1986-87, Leadership award 1987), Am. Psychol. Assn., Colo. Psychol. Assn., Colo. Women's Psychologists, Nat. Assn. Sch. Psychologists (western regional dir. and Colo. rep. 1976-83), Assn. for the Advancement of Behavior Therapy. Democrat. Jewish. Home: 1171 Forest St Denver CO 80220

BERLIN, EMILY, lawyer; b. Bethesda, Md., Apr. 29, 1947; d. Eugene A. and Sylvia W. Berlin; m. John T. Schmidt. BA, Barnard Coll., 1968; MA in Art History, Columbia U., 1970, JD, 1973. Legis. asst. U.S. Senator Joseph Biden, Washington, 1973-74; assoc. Shearman & Sterling, N.Y.C., 1974-81, ptnr., 1981—. Home: 50 Sutton Pl S 19H New York NY 10022 Office: Shearman & Sterling 599 Lexington Ave New York NY 10022 also: Shearman & Sterling 599 Lexington Ave at 53rd St New York NY 10022*

BERLIN, LORNA CHUMLEY, artist; b. Wadena, Minn., Oct. 24, 1938; d. Eugene Edgar And Bertha Lenora (Otterstad) Chumley; m. Jacques Arkin Berlin, Dec. 17, 1960; children: John Paul, Amy Kay. BS, Gustavus Adolphus Coll., 1960; M., Iowa State U., 1966. Rsch. assoc. Purdue U., Lafayette, Ind., 1961-63; tech. publs. editor U.S. Naval Hosp., Jacksonville, Fla., 1964-66; cons. Buffalo Tourbine, Inc., Gowanda, N.Y., 1980-86; watercolor tchr. Amherst Cen. Sch. Dist., Amherst, N.Y., 1987-88, Town of Amherst, 1988—; instr. Niagara County Community Coll., Sanborn, N.Y., 1988—; workshop instr. Grand Island (N.Y.) Art Soc., 1987, Art Guild of Silver Lake, N.Y., 1989, Northstar Watercolor Soc., Mpls., 1989. One-Woman show Buscaglia-Castellani Art Gallery, Niagara Falls, N.Y., 1988-89; exhibited in group show 121st Am. Watercolor Show, N.Y.C., 1987, Allentown Art Festival, 1989 (1st and 2d prizes), Rochester (N.Y.) Meml. Art Gallery, 1987-89, Niagara Frontier Nat., 1988 (award), Watercolor West, 1989, Okla. Nat., 1989. Recipient Achievement award Town of Amherst, 1983. Mem. Am. Artists Profl. League, Niagara Frontier Watercolor Soc. (bd. dirs., com. chmn.), Amherst Soc. Artists (past pres.), Buffalo Soc. Artists, Nat. League Penwomen (Bronze medal of honor 1988), AAUW (chmn. membership 1983, past 2d v.p.), Amherst Skating Club (jr. coach ice show). Home and Office: 59 Catherine St Williamsville NY 14221

BERLIN, MEREDITH RISE, editor; b. Bronxville, N.Y., Nov. 22, 1955; d. Marvin and Seena (Goldsmith) Brown; m. Jordan Stuart Berlin, Aug. 13, 1988; 1 child, Gregory Samuel. BS, Emerson Coll., 1976. With circulation-subscription World Bus. Weekly, N.Y.C., 1978-79; feature editor Soap Opera Digest, N.Y.C., 1979-82, editor-in-chief, 1982—; news commentator WCBS-TV, N.Y.C., 1987—; exec. producer Soap Opera Awards NBC-TV, L.A., 1988—; commentator NBC's House Party. Producer, journalist Afternoon TV Show, 1982. Recipient 2 Emmy nominations, 1988, 89; named N.Y. Alumni of Yr. Emerson Coll. Mem. NOW, AFTRA, Am. Soc. Mag. Editors, Internat. Platform Assn., Overseas Press Club. Office: Soap Opera Digest 45 W 25th St New York NY 10010

BERLINCOURT, MARJORIE ALKINS, government official; b. Toronto, Ont., Can., June 2, 1928; came to U.S., 1950, naturalized, 1956; d. Herbert John and Ellen Florence (Barker) Alkins; B.A., U. Toronto, 1950; M.A., Yale U., 1951, Ph.D., 1954; m. Ted Gibbs Berlincourt, Feb. 28, 1953; 1 dau., Leslie Ellen Berlincourt Yale. Editorial dir. Tech. Publs., Rocketdyne, 1956-59; lectr. classics U. So. Calif., 1959-61; assoc. prof. classical history Calif. Luth. Coll., 1961-67, Calif. State U., Northridge, 1967-71; prof. Met. State Coll., Denver, 1971-72; program dir. div. fellowships Nat. Endowment Humanities, for summer seminars and fellowships Washington, 1972-78, dep. dir. div. research programs, 1978-84, dir. div. state programs, 1984—; vis. lectr. Georgetown U., 1972. Recipient Calif. Faculty Research award, 1970; Sterling fellow Yale U., 1950-53. Mem. Am. Assn. Ancient Historians. Episcopalian. Author: De Surprise en Surprise, 1953; Entrez Petits Amis, 1954; Victory as a Coin Type, 1973; contbr. articles to profl. jours. Office: 1100 Pennsylvania Ave NW Washington DC 20506

BERLINER, PATRICIA MARY, psychologist; b. Bklyn., Mar. 14, 1946; d. Monroe and Rose (Schmidt) B. BA, St. Joseph Coll., Bklyn., 1966; MA, NYU, 1974, PhD, 1990. Tchr. parochial schs., Bklyn., Queens, L.I., 1968-73; counselor Bishop Kearney High Sch., Bklyn., 1973-79; dir. religious edn. Our Lady of Guadalupe Parish, Bklyn., 1979-82; counselor Office Counseling Svcs., NYU, 1982-84; psychotherapist Mich. State U., E. Lansing, 1984-85; dir. counseling svc. St. John's Hosp., Elmhurst, N.Y., 1985-89; psychotherapist New Hope Guild Ctr., Howard Beach, N.Y., 1989—; co-founder/dir. Women for a New World, 1980—. Contbr. articles to profl. jours. NYU grad. assistantship, 1982-84. Mem. Am. Psychol. Assn., Sisters of St. Joseph. Roman Catholic. Home: 111-20 115 St South Ozone Park NY 11420 Office: New Hope Guild Center 151-20 88th St Howard Beach NY 11414

BERLINER, RUTH SHIRLEY, real estate company executive; b. N.Y.C., June 20, 1928; d. Irving William and Florence (Tomback) Blum; m. Arthur Ivan Berliner, Sept. 23, 1948; children: Daniel Scott, Michael Robert, Eric Lance. BA, Empire State Coll., Westbury, N.Y., 1974; diploma, Wilsey Sch. Interior Design, Hempstead, N.Y., 1975; MBA, Adelphi U., 1980. Lic. real estate broker, N.Y. Sec. to dir. librs. NYU, N.Y.C., 1948-50; sec. Paragon Mut. Syndicates Inc., N.Y.C., 1958-72; v.p. Paragon Mut. Investors Svcs., N.Y.C., 1972-78; pres. Ruth S. Berliner, Inc., N.Y.C., 1978—; pres. Irmed Corp., 1983-90; cons. E. 59th Street Assocs., N.Y.C., 1962-70, Amrep Corp., N.Y.C., 1968-75, FKBA Assocs., N.Y.C., 1974-78. Vice pres. NYU Dental Sch. Parents Assn., 1974-76; bd. dirs. Hadassah, Hewlett, N.Y., 1978-87; advisor Citizens for Charter Change, N.Y.C., 1987—. Mem. Nat. Assn. Realtors, Real Estate Bd. N.Y. (stores com. 1984-90), Town Club, Inwood Club (N.Y.). Office: 450 7th Ave Rm 1604 New York NY 10001

BERMAN, BARBARA SANDRA, educational administrator; b. N.Y.C., Oct. 15, 1938; d. Nathan and Regina (Pasternak) Kopp; m. Murray Berman, June 27, 1959; children: Adrienne, David. BS, Bklyn. Coll., 1959, MS, 1961; cert., Coll. S.I., 1971; EdD, Rutgers U., 1981. Tchr. N.Y.C. Pub. Schs., 1959-70; project coord., dir. fed. projects Rutgers U., New Brunswick, N.J., 1976-80; math. cons. B & F Ednl. Cons., Inc., S.I., N.Y., 1978—; staff devel. cons. Ednl. Support Systems, Inc., S.I., 1981—; adminstrv. dir. Foresight Sch., S.I., 1985—; dir. Great Beginnings Infant and Toddler Ctr., 1989—; mem. curriculum instrn. task force Nat. Coun. Suprs. Math., 1988—. Co-author: (books) Fractions and Decimals for Junior High School: A Model Integrating Process and Content Skills, 1980, Metric Mini-Course, 1981, Mathematics: Getting in Touch, Books I and II, 1985, Color Tiles, 1986, Mathematics Through Measurement, 1983, Mathematics Institute for the Elementary School Teacher, 1980; revs. for N.Y. State Math. Tchrs. Jour., Arithmetic Tchr.; contbr. articles to profl. jours. Mem. Nat. Coun. Tchrs. Math., Nat. Staff Devel. Coun., N.Y. Acad. Scis., Nat. Coun. Suprs. Math., Assn. Tchrs. Math N.Y., Assn. Supervision and Curriculum Devel., Sch. Sci. and Math. Assn., Early Childhood Edn. Coun., Mensa, Kappa Delta Pi. Home: 512 Valleyview Pl Staten Island NY 10314

BERMAN, HELEN MIRIAM, chemistry educator; b. Chgo., May 19, 1943; d. David and Dorothy (Skupsky) Bernstein; m. Victor Berman (div.); m. Peter Young, Feb. 29, 1976; 1 child, Jason. AB with honors in Chemistry, Barnard Coll., 1964; PhD, U. Pitts., 1967. Asst. mem. Inst. for Cancer Rsch., Phila., 1973-76, assoc. mem., 1976-78, mem., 1978-86, sr. mem., 1986-89; prof. II chemistry Rutgers U., New Brunswick, N.J., 1989—; mem. study sects. NIH, 1973—; mem. panels NSF; mem. ad hoc com. Coun. Gen. Medicine Inst., NIH. Contbr. numerous articles to sci. jours. Cons. Franklin Inst. Sci. Mus., Phila., LWV. NIH rsch. grantee, 1974—. Mem. N.Y. Acad. Scis., Am. Soc. Biochemistry and Molecular Biology, Am. Women in Sci., Am. Crystallographic Assn. (pres. 1988-89), Biophys. Soc., Am. Chem. Soc., Sigma Xi. Jewish. Office: Rutgers U Chemistry Dept PO Box 939 Piscataway NJ 08855

BERMAN, JENIFER M., small business owner; b. Hartford, Conn., Mar. 26, 1940; d. Henry John and Alma Helen (Pritchard) Meyer; m. Richard J. Berman, July 18, 1972; children: Karlene, Frank, James, Paul. Student, U. Conn., 1958-60; postgrad., St. Joseph Coll., Hartford, Conn., 1987--. Librarian Arthur Andersen & Co., Hartford, Conn., 1975-82; office mgr. Ernst & Young, Hartford, Conn., 1982-88; owner UPDATES Library Mgmt., Wethersfield, Conn., 1988—. Author: Poetry, 1980--. Mem. Hartford Women's Network, Assn. Entrepreneurial Women, Spl. Libraries Assn., Am. MENSA Ltd., Capital Region Library Coun., Philharmonica Soc. Club Hartford, First Ch. Choir Club Wethersfield. Office: UPDATES Libr Mgmt Svcs PO Box 9723 Wethersfield CT 06109

BERMAN, LINDA FRAN, lawyer; b. Phila., Feb. 26, 1952; d. Martin and Ruth (Krum) B.; m. Paul M. Perlstein, May 25, 1986; 1 child, Simone E. A.B., Princeton U., 1973; postgrad. U. Pa., 1973-74, 80; J.D., Villanova U., 1978. Bar: Pa. 1978. Asst. dir. grants Villanova U. (Pa.), 1978; dir. grants Wistar Inst., Phila., 1979; asst. dir. Am. Law Inst., Phila., 1980; exec. editor Pa. Law Jour., 1980-82; mem. firm Schwartzman & Hepps, Phila., 1982-84; assoc. Berger & Montague, P.C., 1984-85; asst. city solicitor, City of Phila., 1985-86; supervising atty. Dessen, Moses & Sheinoff, Jenkintown, Pa., 1986-87; sole practice Phila., 1987—. Bd. dirs. Bus. and Profl. Women's Coalition-Fedn. Jewish Agencies, 1982-84; mem. adv. com. Women's Alliance for Job Equity, 1983-85; mem. budget allocation rev. com. United Way, 1982-86; bd. dirs. Women's Resource Ctr., Wayne, Pa., 1986-89, Phila. Vol. Lawyers and the Arts, 1984-87, Women's Agenda, 1989—, Haverford Sch. Mothers' Assn., 1989—. Mem. Pa. Bar Assn., Phila. Bar Assn. (chmn. lawyers and arts com. 1982-84), Princeton U. Alumni Schs. Com., ABA, LWV (bd. dirs. Lower Merion chpt. 1987-88, Noberth chpt. 1988-89), Jr. League, Hadassah, Sigma Delta Chi. Democrat. Jewish. Home: 634 Fariston Dr Wynnewood PA 19096 Office: 525 Swede St Norristown PA 19401

BERMAN, LISA MYRA, psychologist; b. Balt., Jan. 13, 1960; d. Merrill Ian and Roslyn Tamyra (Lazerov) B. BA, Brandeis U., 1981; MA, La. State U., 1984, PhD, 1988. Lic. clin. psychologist, Va. Clin. extern Baton Rouge Psychol. Assn., Baton Rouge, 1983-86; psychology intern George Washington U. Med. Ctr., Washington, 1986-87; psychologist No. Va. Mental Health Inst., Falls Church, 1987-88, Loudoun County Mental Health Ctr., Leesburg, Va., 1987—. Mem. Am. Psychol. Assn., Phi Kappa Phi. Democrat. Jewish.

BERMAN, MARLENE OSCAR, neuropsychologist, educator; b. Phila., Nov. 21, 1939; d. Paul Oscar and Evelyn (Hess) (Oscar) Weizenblut; m. Michael Brack Berman, June 23, 1963 (div. Feb. 1980); 1 son, Jesse Michael. B.A., U.Pa., 1961; M.A., Bryn Mawr Coll., 1964; Ph.D., U. Conn., 1968; postgrad., Harvard U., 1968-70. Research assoc. Boston VA Med. Ctr., 1970-72, clin. investigator, 1973-76, research psychologist, 1976—; assoc. prof. neurology Boston U. Sch. Medicine, 1975-82, prof. neurology and psychiatry, 1982—, dir. Neuropsychology Lab., dept. psychiatry, 1981—; mem. Com. for Protection Human Participants in Rsch., 1988-85, chmn., 1983-85; affiliate prof. psychology Clark U., Worcester, Mass., 1975—; mem. biomed. rsch. initial rev. group Nat. Inst. Alcohol Abuse and Alcoholism, 1987—. Contbr. articles to profl. jours. Coordinator Newton Community Schs. (Mass.), 1978-80. Recipient Research Scientist Devel. awards Nat. Inst. Neurol. and Communicative Disorders and Stroke, 1976-81, Nat. Inst. Alchol Abuse and Alcholism, 1981-86; Clin. Investigator award VA, 1973-76; USPHS and Dept. Health and Human Services grantee, 1964—. Fellow Mass. Psychol. Assn., Am. Psychol. Assn. (sec.-treas. 1981-83) ; mem. Acad. Aphasia, Soc. Neurosci., Internat. Neuropsychol. Soc., Psychonomic Soc., Huntington's Disease Soc. Am., Internat. Council Psychologists, N.Y. Acad. Scis., Eastern Psychol. Assn. Democrat. Jewish. Office: Boston U Lab Neuropsychology Dept Psychiatry M-9 85 E Newton St Boston MA 02118

BERMAN, MIRA, advertising agency executive; b. Danzig, June 1, 1928; d. Max and Riva (Gutman) B.; m. Richard D. Freedman, Jan. 23, 1972. Student, Profl. Children's Sch., Berkshire Music Sch. and Festival, Juilliard Sch. Music, David Mannes Coll. Music, NYU, Columbia U. Chief copywriter Girl Scouts U.S., 1948-50; sr. copywriter Bamberger's, 1950-52; advt. dir., head women fashions Bond Stores, 1952-55; copy dir. Robert Hall, 1955-56; advt. copy dir. Gimbel's, N.Y.C., 1956-57; dir. pub. rels., fashion Snellenburg's, 1957-59; sr. v.p. pub. rels. and advt. Lavenson Bur. Advt., 1959-66; pres. Allerton, Berman & Dean, 1966-76; chairperson, chief exec. officer Gemini Images, Inc., 1976-86, The Bradford Group, 1986—; mem. faculty master's degree program in tourism and travel adminstrn. New Sch. for Social Research, N.Y.C.; Co-chmn. 1st ann. Internat. Symposium Travel and Tourism, Am. Mgmt. Assn.; co-chmn. 1st ann. Marketing Through Retailers Symposium, 1966-67, staff lectr., 1967-70; condr. Modern Bank Practices Seminars; Am. Assn. Advt. Agencies rep. to Nat. Advt. Rev. Bd. Author: Marketing Through Retailers, 1967, also Spanish and Japanese edits; Travel editor: Woman's Life Mag. Exec. dir. Am. Friends of Ezrath Nashim Hosp., Jerusalem Geriatric and Mental Health Ctr., 1986—, The Africa Travel Assn., 1990—, Nat. Coun. of Women U.S.A., 1988-90, Am. Israel Opera Found., 1986-89. Recipient Israel Ministry Tourism award; Fashion Gold medal; Carl V. Cesery award Tile Contractors Assn. Am.; silver award; bronze award; AMITA Sister award; winner Gold medal Internat. Film and TV Festival N.Y., Grand award. Mem. Am. Advt. Fedn. (named one of Ten Top Women in Advt.), Fin. Publicist Assn. Am., The Fashion Group, Pub. Rels. Soc. Am. (bd. govs.), Phila. Pub. Rels. Assn., Am. Soc. Travel Agts., Soc. Advancement Travel for Handicapped, International Tourism Assn., Nat. Coun. Women., Women Execs. Internat. (exec. dir.). Home: 116 Central Park S New York NY 10019 Office: 347 Fifth Ave Ste 610 New York NY 10016

BERMAN, MONA S., playwright, theatrical director and producer; b. Jersey City; d. Edward and Mary (Auster) Solomon; m. Carroll Z. Berman; children—Marcie S. Berman Ries, Laura Jane. B.A., Beaver Coll., postgrad. Columbia U., M.F.A., Boston U. Tchr. English, drama Jersey City High Schs.; actress Mass. Valley Players, Holyoke; owner, dir. The Theatre Sch. and Producing Co., Maplewood, N.J.; chmn. drama edn. YM-MWHA of Met. N.J. Cons., Clark Ctr. for Performing Arts, N.Y.C., 1965-66; instr. South Orange, Maplewood Adult Sch., 1967; artistic dir. Children's Theatre Co. Inc., Maplewood, 1968-70; cons. The Whole Theater Co., 1974—; dir. pub. relations Co. 3 by 2. Playwright: Hello Joe, 1967; That Ring in the Center, 1968; The Big Show, 1970; Interim, 1974; Who Can Belong?, 1979; Sudden Changes, 1985; Actual Malice, 1987; Interim 2, 1988; producer, dir. A Night of Stars; guest theatre reviewer El Paso Herald Post, 1980-82. Active Boston United Fund, 1955-59, chmn. Boston residential area, 1957; bd. dirs. Greater Boston Girl Scouts Am., 1956-58, Tufts Med. Faculty Wives, 1956-58. Mem. Am. Theater Assn., Playwrights Unit 42d St. Theater Ctr. N.Y.C., Dramatists Guild. Address: 454 Prospect Ave #176 West Orange NJ 07052

BERMAN, PAMELA JILL, lawyer; b. Los Angeles, Apr. 2, 1947; d. William MacArthur Robertson and Virginia Lee (Mathews) Winford; m. Ronald Berman, Jan. 10, 1982 (div. Apr. 1986); m. Joseph F. Byrne, Feb. 14, 1989. BA, UCLA, 1969; MSW, U. Hawaii, 1973, JD, 1977. Bar: Hawaii 1977, U.S. Dist. Ct. Hawaii 1977, U.S. Supreme Ct. 1985. Dep. Office of Pub. Defender, Honolulu, 1977-79; ptnr. Wilson & Berman, Honolulu, 1979-82; pvt. practice Honolulu, 1982-90; assoc. Carla Larson, Honolulu, 1988—. bd. dirs. ACLU, Honolulu, 1977-85, Salvation Army, Honolulu, 1979-82, Protection and Advocacy, Honolulu, 1983-84; pres. bd. dirs. Parents' Anonymous, Honolulu, 1985—. Named Pacesetter of the Pacific, Honolulu Star Bull., 1985. Mem. ABA, Assn. Trial Lawyers Am., Hawaii Bar Assn., Nat. Assn. Criminal Def. Lawyers, Honolulu C. of C., Honolulu Club. Democrat. Home: 1028 Iopono Loop Kailua HI 96734 Office: Hawaii Times Bldg Ste 400 928 Nuuanu Ave Honolulu HI 96817

BERMAN, PATRICIA KARATSIS, visual arts specialist; b. San Francisco, Oct. 2, 1953; d. George Emanuel and Hermoine Linda (Foster) Karatsis; m. William Issachar Berman, May 15, 1979; children: Ian, Melissa, Benjamin. BS, Duke U., 1975; MA, NYU, 1977. Dir. Vorpal Gallery, N.Y.C., 1976-83; visual arts coordinator East End Art and Humanities Council, Riverhead, N.Y., 1983—; cons. N.Y. State Council on Arts, N.Y.C., 1985—, Suffolk Assn. Jewish Schs., Huntington, N.Y., 1985; adj. lectr. dept. anthropology Bklyn. Coll., 1976-77, Drew U., 1977. Contbr. articles to East End Arts News; host cable arts show, 1986-87. Trustee Commack Jewish Ctr., N.Y., 1984-86. Home: 22 Daisy Ln Commack NY 11725 Office: East End Art and Humanities Council 133 E Main St Riverhead NY 11901

BERMAN, SHERYL HOPE, insurance; b. Bronx, N.Y., Aug. 27, 1957; d. Hilliard Marvin and Roseann (Meyerowitz) B. Student, U. Fla., 1975-77; BA, Fla. Atlantic U., 1979. Claim rep. State Farm Ins., Miami, 1979-81; procedure training specialist State Farm Ins., Winter Haven, Fla., 1981-83; systms analyst State Farm Ins., Bloomington, Ill., 1983-88; claim supr. State Farm Ins., Langhorne, Pa., 1988-89; claim supt. State Farm Ins., Langhorne, 1989—. Vol. Red Cross, W. Palm Beach, Fla. 1975, Sampson Program, Gainesville, Fla. 1977, Democratic Party, W. Palm Beach, 1979. Jewish. Home: 196 Cambridge Ln Newtown PA 18940 Office: State Farm Ins 600 Oxford Valley Rd Langhorne PA 19047

BERMAN, SIEGRID VISCONTI, interior designer; b. Bremen, Germany, May 22, 1944; came to U.S., 1951, naturalized, 1956; d. Walter L. and Annegrete M. (Wolf) Knapp; self-educated. Designer, Shepard Martin Assocs., N.Y.C., 1968-76; facilities mgr. Unifert, USA, N.Y.C., 1976-78; owner Siegrid Visconti Berman Interiors, N.Y.C., 1978—; dir. interiors DAT Cons., N.Y.C., 1980-83; dir. design Ralph Mancini Assocs., N.Y.C., 1983-85, Karco Davis, Inc.; dir. Ten Park Ave Corp., 1979-81. Bd. dirs. Temple Spiritual Research and Learning, 1981-82; reader Lighthouse for Blind. Colo. State Coll. scholar, 1962. Mem. AFTRA, Screen Actors Guild. Composer songs, illustrator book.

BERMANN, NANCY STEWART, sales executive; b. Chgo., Oct. 26, 1957; d. John Stewart and Carolyn Jean (Kurt) G. BA in Internat. Bus., Carthage Coll., Kenosha, Wis., 1982. Ski instr., race coach Wilmot Mt. (Wis.), Inc., 1979—; leader div. clinic Profl. Ski Instrs. of Am., Milw., 1986-88; asst. dir. Ski Sch., Wilmot Mt., 1980-82; regional mgr. Carrol Corp., Chez Chocolat, Arlington Heights, Ill., 1982-84; area sales mgr. Unitog Bus. Clothing, Kansas City, Mo., 1985—. Mem. Profl. Ski Instrs. of Am., Internat. Ski Instrs. Fedn., Chgo. Met. Ski Coun., NOW, Nat. Assn. Female Execs., Alpha Kappa Psi. Republican. Office: Unitog Bus Clothing 101 W 11th St Kansas City MO 64105

BERNABELA, JOSEPHINE E. WALKER, secretarial services executive; b. Boydton, Va., Feb. 8, 1954; d. Joseph Earl and Mattie (Pulliam) Walker; m. McCarthy Lewis II, Apr. 5, 1975 (div.); 1 child, Khaileah Elizabeth; m. Felix Raymond Bernabela, May 4, 1985. BA, Rutgers U., 1977; postgrad., 1980-82. Legal asst. Rutgers U., 1976-80; paralegal Riker, Danzig, Scheerer & Hyland, P.C., Morristown, N.J., 1981, Shanley & Fisher, P.C., Morristown, 1982-83; instr. secretarial sci. Essex County Tech. Career Ctr., Newark, 1984; pres. Courtscribers/Confidential Typing Service, East Orange, N.J., 1975—. Moderator project alert Dept. Child Guidance, Newark, 1981. Recipient Appreciation award Newark Tchrs.' Caucus, 1979; Grad. and Profl. Edn. grantee, 1981; Coun. on Legal Edn. Opportunity fellow, 1980. Mem. Nat. Assn. Female Execs. (dir.), Nat. Assn. Secretarial Services, Internat. Profl. Typist Network, Nat. Shorthand Reporters Assn., Rutgers Alumni Assn. (Judge F.J. Bloustein scholar). Office: Courtscribers/Confidential Typing Svc PO Box 3276 Brick Church Station East Orange NJ 07019

BERNAL, HARRIET JEAN, real estate salesperson; b. Cin., Sept. 28, 1931; d. Ernest Richard and Amy Lillian (Jeffries) Daniels; m. Gil Bernal, July 9, 1950; children: Gil Jr., Lisa, Nicholas, Colette, Michelle. AA in Theatre Arts, Los Angeles City Coll., 1949-62; student, Kimballs Real Estate Sch., Burbank, Calif., 1974; AA in Humanities, Glendale Coll., 1982; BA in Polit. Sci. Pre-Law, Calif. State U., Los Angeles, 1987. Lic. real estate agt. Dancer, entertainer Greek Theatre, Los Angeles, 1949-50; travel, reservation agt. Iver's Dept. Store, Los Angeles, 1970-73, editor, dept. store news letters, 1972-73; sec. to area supt. and social chmn. Los Angeles Bd. Edn., 1973-74; exec. sec. CBS-TV City, Los Angeles, 1974; real estate salesperson, relocation mgr. Century 21 Realty, Los Angeles, Pasadena, Calif., San Marino, Calif., 1974-86; real estate salesperson Coldwell Banker Residential, Pasadena, Calif., 1986-89, Glendale, Cailf., 1989—. Contbr. articles on sch. sci. ctrs., schs. in Russia, and schs. for the handicapped for local sch. paper, Ann. awards. Pres. San Pascual Elem. Sch. (PTA), Los Angeles, 1969-70, hon. life mem., 1970—; fundraiser various groups to elect Mayor Tom Bradley, Los Angeles; wedding hostess Pasadena Ch. of Angels, Calif., 1980-88, also lic. lay minister. Mem. Glendale Bd. Realtors, Met. Player Guild. Democrat. Episcopalian. Home: 1075 Rutland Ave Los Angeles CA 90042 Office: Coldwell Banker Real Estate 901 W Glendale Blvd Glendale CA 91202

BERNARD, CATHY S., management corporation executive; b. Bronx, N.Y., Nov. 13, 1949; d Burton and Norma (Ebb) B. BBA, George Washington U., 1971, M of Pub. Adminstrn., 1978; MA, U. Miami, 1972. Staff asst. HEW, Washington, 1970-74; evaluation specialist OEO, Washington, 1974; tchr. St. Patrick's Acad., Washington, 1975; asst. prof. No. Va. Community Coll., Woodbridge, 1976; staff dir. Dem. Nat. Conv., N.Y.C., 1976; pres., chief exec. officer CSB Assocs. Mgmt. Corp., Hyattsville, Md., 1977—; mem. Housing Opportunities Commn., Kensington, Md., 1979—, chmn., 1988, vice chair, 1980, 87, chair pro tem, 1986, chair housing honor roll, 1985-88, Moderate Priced Dwelling Unit commn.; mem. exec. coun. Inst. Real Estate Mgmt., Washington, 1982—, cert. property mgr. Mem. adv. coun. Suburban Hosp., Bethesda, Md., 1984-89; bd. dirs. Ivymount Sch. for Handicapped, Potomac, Md., 1986—, Maximum Savs. Bank F.S.B.; bd. dirs. Jewish Coun. on Aging, Jewish Found. for Group Homes, Rockville, Md., 1987-90, treas.; candidate Md. State Legislature, 1986; pres. Community Housing Res. Bd., 1985. Mem. Montgomery County C. of C. (bd. dirs., v.p. housing com. 1981-82), Apt. and Office Bldg. Assn. (bd. dirs.). Office: CSB Assocs Mgmt Corp PO Box 274 Hyattsville MD 20781

BERNARD, LOLA DIANE, social work educator; b. Rockaway Beach, N.Y., Nov. 9, 1928; d. Clark C. and Antoinette (Berger) B. BA, Roosevelt U., 1949; MA, U. Houston, 1952; MSW, Tulane U., 1954; PhD, Bryn Mawr Coll., 1967; DHL (hon.), Tulane U., 1989. Psychometrician counseling and testing dept. Roosevelt U., 1948-49; Rorshach interpreter Dr. Ralph J. Wentworth-Rohr, N.Y.C., 1949-50; psychometrician Dr. J. Sanford Davis Vocational Bur., N.Y.C., 1949-50; psychometrician counseling and testing dept. U. Houston, 1950; psychologist Woman's Fed. Penitentiary, Huntsville, Tex., 1951; social worker M.D. Anderson Hosp. Cancer Research, Houston, 1952; med. social worker Bur. Tb Control, New Orleans, 1954-56; dir. social service dept. Touro Infirmary, New Orleans, 1956-60; instr. Bryn Mawr Coll., 1964-65; field instr. Tulane U., 1958-62, asst. prof., 1965-66, assoc. prof., 1966-69; prof., chmn. dept. social work Fla. State U., 1969-72; acting dean Sch. Social Welfare, 1972-73; dean Sch. Social Work, 1973-78, dir. women's studies, 1978-79; prof. Va. Commonwealth U., 1979-85, dir. doctoral program social policy and social work, 1980-85; interim exec. dir. Council on Social Work Edn., 1985-86; prof. Southern U., New Orleans, 1990—; rsch. cons. U. Alaska, Anchorage, 1988; Belle Spafford chair U. Utah, Salt Lake City, 1988-90; vis. prof. U. Wash., Seattle, 1978, Smith Coll., 1988, 90; chmn. nat. commn. on accreditation Council Social Work Edn., 1972-75; cons. U. Alaska, Anchorage, 1988. Mem. edit. bd. Affilia Women in Social Work, 1984-90; contbr. articles to profl. jours., encys. Mem. manpower study Fla. Bd. Regents, 1971-72; Disaster worker ARC, 1965-69; mem. Leon County (Fla.) Assn. Community Services, 1970-79, Leon County Humane Soc., 1970-79, Tallahassee Urban League, 1970-79; bd. dirs. Home for Incurables, New Orleans, 1966-69, Le Moyne Art Found., Tallahassee, 1970-79; Belle Spafford chair U. Utah, 1988-90. Recipient Outstanding Alumnae award Tulane U. Sch. Social Work, 1977; Nat. Found. Infantile Paralysis grantee, 1952-54; NIMH grantee, 1962-64, 77. Mem. AAUP, Nat. Assn. Social Workers (mem. nat. commn. casework 1967-69), Council Social Work Edn., Nat. Conf. Social Welfare, So. Regional Ednl. Bd., Psi Chi. Office: So U 6400 Press Dr New Orleans LA 70126

BERNARD, MARY ELIZABETH, state legislator; b. Dover, N.H.; d. Arthur P. and Margaret (Donnelly) O'Gorman; m. Albert O. Bernard, June 29, 1935. Grad. Carney Hosp. Sch. Nursing, Boston, 1929; student McIntosh Bus. Coll. R.N., Mass. Mem. N.H. Ho. of Reps., 1967-75, 81-87, 88-89, 5-term mem. regulated revenues com.; historian State of N.H., 1973-74; county clk. County of Strafford (N.H.), 1973-74. Treas. Dem. City Com., Dover, 1965-82; clk. Strafford County Delegation, 1973-74, 81-84; supr. checklists, 1964—. Mem. St. Mary Parish Coun., Dover, 1977-80; trustee Cath. Daus. Am., 1977-90.

BERNARD, NANCY S., archaeologist, educator; b. L.A., Mar. 31, 1934; d. Lionel S. and Helen (Nathan) Stone; m. Allan H. Bernard, July 14, 1957; children: Nicholas William, Matthew Lionel, Jason Paul. BA with distinction, Stanford U., 1955; postgrad., I.A. State Coll., 1958-59; MA equivalent, UCLA, Mus. Cultural History, 1969-74. Rsch. assoc. UCLA Inst. of Archaeology, 1973-74; adj. prof. Fairfield U., 1977-79; dir. Archeol. Assocs. of Greenwich, Greenwich, Conn.; dir. Prehistoric People Project Archeol. Assocs. of Greenwich, Greenwich; adj. prof. U. Bridgeport; faculty mem. UCLA Inst. of Archaeology Project in Manfredonia, Italy, summer 1980; coleader UCLA Inst. of Archaeology Project in Greece, summer 1988; lectr., presenter in field. Author: A Manual of Preshistory, 1985. Trustee Bruce Mus., Greenwich, Conn., 1976-86; conservator N.Y. Pub. Libr. Fellow UCLA Inst. Archaeology; mem. N.Y. Acad. Scis., Oriental Inst., Am. Mus. Natural History, Univ. Pa. Mus. of Archaeology and Anthropology, Smithsonian. Home: 33 Byron Dr Greenwich CT 06830

BERNARD, SHARON ELAINE, lawyer; b. Detroit, Apr. 19, 1943; d. John Robert and Dorothea Cleo (Graves) B.; m. George B. Miller (div.). BSL, JD, U. Ark., 1969. Pres., chief exec. officer Plaza Theater & Miller Enterprises, Helena, Ark., 1961-74; pvt. atty. Helena, 1970-74; various Mich. Nat. Bank, Detroit, 1975-82, v.p., 1982—; bd. chair Children's Trust Fund, Mich., 1982-88; police commr. Detroit. Bd. dirs. Boys Hope, Nat. Com. for Prevention Child Abuse; chmn. Detroit Urban League, 1986-89. Mem. Kappa Beta Pi. Democrat. Roman Catholic. Home: 16160 Chapel Detroit MI 48219 Office: Mich Nat Bank 300 River Pl Ste 6000 Detroit MI 48207

BERNARDEZ, TERESA, psychiatrist; b. Buenos Aires, June 11, 1931; d. Francisco and Dolores (Novoa) B.; 1 child, Diego Bonesatti Bernardez. BA, Liceo No 1, Buenos Aires, 1948; MD, U. Buenos Aires, 1956. Diplomate Am. Bd. Psychiatry. Psychiat. resident Menninger Sch. Psychiatry, Topeka, 1957-60; fellow Menninger Found., Topeka, 1960-62; staff psychiatrist C.F. Menninger M. Hosp., Topeka, 1962-71; prof. psychiatry Dept. Psychiatry Mich. State U., East Lansing, 1971-89; tng. and supervising faculty The Mich. Psychoanalytic Coun., East Lansing, 1989—; pres.-elect Mich. Psychoanalytic Coun. Contbr. articles to profl. jours. Physician's health team Amnesty Internat.; mem. Physician's for Social Responsibility, 1985; cons. Coun. Against Domestic Abuse, 1975-79. Recipient Physician's Recognition award AMA, 1970. Fellow Am. Psychiat. Assn. (chairperson com. on women), Am. Orthopsychiat. Assn., Am. Group Psychotherapy (bd. dirs.), Am. Med. Women's Assn. (First Leadership award 1977); mem. Soc. for Psychosomatic Ob/Gyn., Mich. Soc. for Psychoanalytic Psychology. Office: Mich Psychoanalytic Coun 835 Westlawn East Lansing MI 48823

BERNARDINI, ISA, biochemist; b. Cagliari, Sardinia, Italy, Jan. 1, 1943; came to U.S., 1962; d. Giovanni and Anna Maria (Lastrucci) B.; m. Zmarak Mohandas Shalizi, Dec. 21, 1972; children: Cosma Rohilla, Aryaman Kumarappa. BS magna cum laude, San Diego State U., 1964; MEd in Chemistry, Boston U., 1970. Rsch. asst. in biophysics Children's Cancer Rsch. Found., Boston, 1966-73, Rosenstiel Basic Med. Sci. Rsch. Ctr., Brandeis U., Waltham, Mass., 1974-75; rsch. chemist NIH, Bethesda, Md., 1979—. Contbr. articles to biomed. rsch. jours. Recipient awards NIH, Bethesda, Md., 1984, 86, 88, 89, 90. Office: NIH/NICHD Human Genetics Br 9000 Rockville Pike Bldg 10 Rm 10N313 Bethesda MD 20894

BERNARDINO, MINERVA, retired ambassador; b. Dominican Republic, May 7, 1907; d. Alvaro and Altagracia (Evangelista) B.; widowed. BS, Santo Domingo U., Dominican Republican. Appointed A. E. and P. of Dominican Republic to Netherlands, 1971, Inspector Embassies and Consulates, 1974; signer of UN Charter, San Francisco, 1945, and OEA Charter; active in equal rights clauses inclusion. Founder Nat. Council for Women, Dominican Republic, 1947; mem. sub-com. on status of women, U.N., 1946; served 14 years Inter-Am. Commn. of Women, OAS, 1945-59; co-founder Commn. on Status of Women, UN, 1948; 1st v.p. ECOSOC, 1957, 1st v.p. exec. bd. UNICEF, 1957; Dominican del. Trusteeship Council UN, 1950-54. Recipient Medal Bolivar and San Martin, 1944, Diploma Nat. Council Negro Women, 1950, Cert. Recognition Nat. Conf. Christians and Jews, 1956, Duarte Decoration Govt. Dominican Republic, 1986, Spl. Gold medal Govt. Dominican Republic; named Woman of Ams. United Women Ams., 1948, Outstanding Dir. Causes of Women in Am. Republics UN, 1949, Most Outstanding Feminist of Yr. United Women Am., 1975; decorated Grand Cross of Order Oranje and Nassau by Queen Juliana Netherlands, 1973. Mem. Am. News Women's Club, United Women Ams., Internat. Platform Assn., Nat. Council Women U.S., LWV, Nat. Assn. Female Execs., Nat. Women's Party, Am. Assn. Internat. Law. Home: 1040 Park Ave 8J New York NY 10028

BERNAS, DENISE MARY, social services administrator; b. Ashland, Pa., Aug. 29, 1943; d. Clement Joseph and Agnes Clara (Brzezicki) B. BA, St. Vincent Coll., 1987, postgrad.; phys. therapy tng., Ind. U., 1967-68, St. Francis Hosp., Pitts., 1968. Clk. typsit St. Anne HOme, Greensburg, Pa., 1966-67, nursing asst., 1967-68, phys. therapy aide, 1968, activity dir., 1970-85; with St. Joseph Nursing Care Ctr., Point Charlotte, Fla., 1987—; advisor St. Anne Women's Assn., Greensburg, Pa., 1970-87; cons. Nat. Cert. Coun. for Activity Profls., 1990-93. Author: Death is a Profound Lesson for the Living, 1987. Bd. dirs. Am. Cancer Soc. S.W. Fla., 1988-90. Recipient Supporting Role award St. Joseph Health Care Group, Fla., 1987. Mem. AAUW, Bon Secours St. Joseph Group Found. (bd. dirs.), Nat. Therapeutic Recreation Soc., Nat. Activity Cert. Dir. Profls. Democrat. Roman Catholic. Home: 2450 Harbor Blvd Port Charlotte FL 33952

BERNAS, LILIAN HELEN, therapist; b. Winnipeg, Man., Can., July 28, 1948; d. Stanley and Anelia (Walus) B. BPE, U. Man., 1973; MEd, U. Minn., 1980. Cert. therapist in psychogeriatrics. Activity worker Tache Nursing Home, Winnipeg, 1976-78; therapeutic recreation specialist Concordia Hosp., Winnipeg, 1981-88; gerontology educator Red River Community Coll., Winnipeg, 1983-88; tchr. Algonquin Coll.; gerontology educator Tuxedo Villa Personal Care Home, 1988-89; staff recreologist St. Patrick's Nursing Home, Ottawa, Ont., Can., 1989—. Named to Can. Hosps. Honor Roll Concordia Hosp., Winnipeg, 1986. Mem. Nat. Therapeutic Recreation Orgn., Nat. Remotivation Technique Orgn. (instr. 1982—), Assn. Remotivation Therapists Can. (instr. 1982—), Therapy Dogs Internat. (Pet Therapy Dog of Yr. award 1986), Alzheimer Soc. Can. Mem. New Democratic Party. Roman Catholic. Clubs: Irish Setter Am., Irish Setter Minn. (Mpls.). Home: 2827 Springland Dr, Ottawa, ON Canada K1V 9S7 Office: Extendicare Laurier Manor, 1715 Montreal Rd, Gloucester, ON Canada K1J LN4

BERNAY, BETTI, artist; b. 1926; d. David Michael and Anna Gaynia (Bernay) Woolin; m. J. Bernard Goldfarb, Apr. 19, 1947; children: Manette Deitsch, Karen Lynn. Grad. costume design, Pratt Inst., 1946; student, Nat. Acad. Design, N.Y.C., 1947-49, Art Students League, N.Y.C., 1950-51. Exhibited one man shows at Galerie Raymond Duncan, Paris, France, Salas Municipales, San Sebastian, Spain, Circulo de Bellas Artes, Madrid, Spain, Bacardi Gallery, Miami, Fla., Columbia (S.C.) Mus., Columbus (Ga.) Mus., Galerie Andre Weil, Paris, Galerie Hermitage, Monte Carlo, Monaco, Casino de San Remo, Italy, Galerie de Arte de la Caja de Ahorros de Ronda, Malaga, Spain, Centro Artistico, Granada, Spain, Circulo de la Amistad, Cordoba, Spain, Studio H Gallery, N.Y.C., Walter Wallace Gallery, Palm Beach, Fla., Mus. Bellas Artes, Malaga, Harbor House Gallery, Crystal House Gallery, Internat. Gallery, Jordan Marsh, Fontainebleau Gallery, Miami Beach, Carriage House Gallery, Galerie 99, Pageant Gallery, Carriage House, Miami Beach, Rosenbaum Galleries, Palm Beach; exhibited group shows at Painters and Sculptors Soc., Jersey City Mus., Salon de Invierno, Mus. Malaga, Salon des Beaux Arts, Cannes, France, Guggenheim Gallery, Nat. Acad. Gallery, Salmagundi Club, Lever House, Lord & Taylor Art Gallery, Nat. Arts Gallery, Knickerbocker Artists, N.Y.C., Salon des Artistes Independants, Salon des Artistes Francais, Salon Populiste, Paris, Salon de Otono, Nat. Assn. Painters and Sculptors Spain, Madrid, Phipps Gallery, Palm Beach, Artists Equity, Hollywood (Fla.) Mus., Gault Gallery Cheltenham, Phila., Springfield (Mass.) Mus., Met. Mus. and Art Center, Miami, Fla., Planet Ocean Mus., Charter Club, Trade Fair Ams., Guggenheim Gallery, N.Y.C.; represented in permanent collections including Jockey Club Art Gallery, Miami, Mus. Malaga, Circulo de la Amistad, I.O.S. Found., Geneva, Switzerland, others. Bd. dirs. Men's Opera Guild; mem. adv. bd. Jackson Meml. Hosp. Project Newborn; mem. women's com. Bascon Palmer Eye Inst.; mem. working com. Greater Miami Heart Assn., Am. Heart Assn., Am. Cancer Soc., Alzheimer Grand Notable, 2d Generation Miami Heart Inst., Sunrisers Mentally Retarded, Orchid Ball Com., Newborn Neonatal Intensive Care Unit, U. Miami, Jackson Meml. Hosp. Recipient medal City N.Y., medal Sch. Art Leagues, N.Y.C., Prix de Paris Raymond Duncan, 1958, others. Mem. Nat. Assn. Painters and Sculptors Spain, Nat. Assn. Women Artists, Société des Artistes Français, Société des Artistes Independants, Fedn. Francais des Sociétés d'Art Graphique et Plastique, Artists Equity, Am. Artists Profl. League, Am. Fedn. Art, Nat. Soc. Lit. and Arts, Met. Mus. and Arts Center Miami, Pres.'s Club U. Miami. Clubs: Palm Bay, Jockey, Turnberry, Club of Clubs Internat. Address: 10155 Collins Ave Apt 1705 Bal Harbour FL 33154

BERNAYS, ELIZABETH ANNA, entomologist, zoologist, educator; b. Chinchilla, Queensland, Australia, Dec. 31, 1940; came to U.S., 1983; d. Philip Chisholm and Nylita Elwyn (Morgan) B.; m. Reginald Frederick Chapman. BS, U. Queensland, Brisbane, 1962; MS, U. London, 1967, PhD, 1970. Scientist Antilocust Research Ctr., London, 1970-74; sr. scientist Ctr. for Overseas Pest Control, London, 1974-78; prin. scientist Tropical Devel. and Research Inst., London, 1978-83; prof. entomology, zoology U. Calif., Berkeley, 1983-90; prof. entomology, ecology, evolutionary biology, head dept. U. Ariz., Tucson, 1989—. Editor books and jours.; contbr. sci. papers to profl. jours. Recipient Gold medal Pontifical Acad. Scis., 1986. Fellow Royal Entomol. Soc. London; mem. Am. Soc. Zoologists, Internat. Soc. Chem. Ecology, Entomol. Soc. Am. Office: U Ariz Dept Entomology Tucson AZ 85721

BERNETT, CAROLE MARIE, mathematics educator, statistical consultant; b. Berwyn, Ill., Nov. 19, 1943; d. George F. and Elsie M. (Cepek) Staab; m. Larry R. Bernett, Mar. 6, 1967; children: Roberta, Pam, Becky. BA in Math., DePaul U., 1965, MS in Math., 1971; MS in Ops. Rsch., Ill. Inst. Tech., 1982, PhD, 1988. Tchr. math. Siena High Sch., Chgo., 1965-66, Nazareth Acad., La Grange, Ill., 1966-67; instr. math. Harper Coll., Palatine, Ill., 1968-76, assoc. prof., 1976—; statis. cons. Quaker Oats Co., Barrington, Ill., 1981-83, Nuclear Data Co., Schaumburg, Ill., 1985-87. Sunday sch. supt. St. Matthew Ch., Itasca, Ill., 1972-75; judge, coord. Ill. Jr. Acad. Scis., Chgo., 1979—; group leader 4-H Group Itasca, 1980-84. Mem. Tech. Inst. Managerial Scis., Inst. Indsl. Engrs., Soc. and Inst. Applied Math., Am. Statis. Assn., Inst. Math. Stats., Ill. Math. Tchrs. Community Colls., Pi Mu Epsilon, Sigma Iota Epsilon. Home: 506 E Washington St Itasca IL 60143 Office: Harper Coll 1200 W Algonquin Rd Palatine IL 60067

BERNEY, ISABEL MCPHEE, school supervisior; b. Salt Lake City, Sept. 29, 1941; d. William Miller and Mary Watson (Shields) McPhee; m. Donald Whitney Berney, Dec. 27, 1963 (dec. Mar. 1987); children: Elizabeth McPhee, Adreinne Whitney; m. Morton Nadler, July 2, 1989. BA, Whitman Coll., 1963; M in Librarianship, U. Wash., Seattle, 1967. Tchr. jr. high Walla Walla (Wash.) Pub. Schs., 1963-65, Shoreline Pub. Schs., Seattle, 1966-68; high sch. libr. Northshore Pub. Schs., Bothell, Wash., 1970-71; libr. U. Wyo. Law Libr., Laramie, 1972-73; libr. high sch. Pulaski (Va.) Pub. Schs., 1974, libr. middle sch., 1974-76, media and tech. supr., 1974—; reviewer Booklist, Chgo., 1975-80. Bd. dirs. Va. Civil Liberties Union, Blacksburg, 1974-76; mem. pub. libr. bd. Radford (Va.) City, 1974-82, 87-90, mem. sch. bd., 1983-86. Mem. NEA, Va. Edn. Assn., Va. Ednl. Media Assn., Va. Libr. Assn., Pulaski County Edn. Assn., Delta Kappa Gamma (pres. 1978-80). Democrat. Unitarian. Home: 414 Stonegate Dr Blacksburg VA 24060 Office: Pulaski County Schs 44 Third St NW Pulaski VA 24301

BERNFIELD, AUDREY ANNE, student affairs administrator; b. Chgo., Nov. 3, 1937; d. Samuel William Rivkin and Bernice (Oster) Simon; m. Merton R. Bernfield, Aug. 30, 1959; children: Susan, James, Mark. BA, U. Ill., 1958; MA, Santa Clara (Calif.) U., 1976. Cons. english, econs., history depts. Stanford (Calif.) U., 1979-85, dir. of advt. and career planning Program in Human Biology, 1977-85, dir. of undergraduate advising, Undergraduate Advising Ctr., 1985-89; pvt. practice ednl. cons. Boston, 1989-90; assoc. dir. student affairs Harvard Med. Sch., Boston, 1990—; cons. Stanford U., 1980-82, 89, St. Lawrence U., Canton, N.Y., 1981, Exec. Recruitment Agys., Boston, 1989. Coord. (booklet) The Major Decision, 1983. Mem. pub. affairs com., edn. com. Planned Parenthood, Cambridge, Mass., 1989-90; bd. dirs. Family Planning Alternatives, Cupertino, Calif., 1987-89. Recipient Richard Dodge award Calif. Coll. Personnel Assn., 1980. Mem. Nat. Acad. Advising Assn., Mass. Assn. Women Deans & Adminstrs. Democrat. Home: 25 Brimmer St Boston MA 02108

BERNHARDT, DONNA BETH, educator, physical therapist; b. Trenton, N.J., Oct. 29, 1945; d. John Warren and Edna Elizabeth Bernhardt. BS in Phys. Therapy, Boston U., 1967, EdD in Human Movement, 1990; MS in Phys. Therapy, U. N.C., 1982. Staff phys. therapist South Bay Phys. Therapy, Chula Vista, Calif., 1969-71, Riverside Hosp., Newport News, Va., 1971-72; supr. phys. therapy dept. Children's Hosp. Med. Ctr., Boston, 1972-80; instr. phys. therapy U. N.C., Chapel Hill, 1982-83; clin. asst. prof. Sargent Coll. Boston U., 1983-86, dir. out-patient clinic Sargent Coll., 1986-88, asst. prof. MGH Inst. Health Professions, 1986-89, asst. prof., dir. program in athletic tng. Sargent Coll., 1989—; phys. therapy rep. interspecialty med. adv. bd. Blue Cross/Blue Shield, Boston, 1987—; chair profl. edn. com. Am. Lung Assn., Boston, 1988—, mem. bd. trustees, 1989—. Editor: Recreation for Disabled Child, 1984, Sports Physical Therapy, 1986. Mem. Mass. Pub. Interest Rsch. Group, Boston, 1988-89; mem. Outreach Community Rowing, Boston, 1989—. U. N.C. grantee, 1982, Found. for Phys. Therapy grantee, 1987. Mem. Am. Phys. Therapy Assn., Am. Coll. Sports Medicine, Nat. Athletic Trainer Assn., Green Mountain Club, Phi Lambda Theta. Office: Boston U Sargent Coll University Rd Boston MA 02215

BERNHARDT, KAREN LEE, nuring executive; b. Geneva, N.Y., Apr. 12, 1955; d. Donald Lawrence and Nancy Fay (Dorfer) B. BSN, Roberts Wesleyan Coll., 1977; MBA, U. Rochester, 1987. RN, N.Y. Staff nurse St. Jerome Hosp., Batavia, N.Y., 1977-79; charge nurse surg. fl. St. Jerome Hosp., Batavia, 1979-80; staff nurse ICU Park Ridge Hosp., Rochester, N.Y., 1980-82; clinician I ICU Park Ridge Hosp., Rochester, 1982-83, clinician II Cardiopulmonary, 1983-84, head nurse ICU fl., 1984—. Instr. Am. Heart Assn., Rochester; flautist Greece Community Orch., Rochester. Mem. Am. Mgmt. Assn., Nat. Assn. Female Execs., Am. Assn. of Critical Care Nurses, Nat. League for Nursing. Office: Park Ridge Hosp 1555 Long Pond Rd Rochester NY 14624

BERNHEIM, HEATHER STANCHFIELD PETERSON (MRS. CHARLES BERNHEIM), civic worker; b. Houston; d. Weed and Mylla (Stanchfield) Peterson; student U. Tex., 1938-42; m. Charles A. Bernheim, July 18, 1973. Docent chmn. Harris County Heritage Soc., 1969-70, v.p., after 1970; vol. worker Hermann Hosp., 1968-69; team capt. Mus. Fine Arts Ball, Houston, 1969; maintenance fund drive worker Mus. Fine Arts, 1970, trustee, chmn. costume council, 1986-88; docent Costume Inst., Met. Mus. Art, N.Y.C., 1978, co-chmn. Costume Inst., 1980-81, chmn., 1981-82, mus. guide, 1978—; chmn. Costume Inst. Mus. Fine Arts, Houston, chmn. Grand Gala Ball, 1989; trustee Mus. Fine Arts, Houston; auction chmn. Bluebonnet Ball, Harris County Heritage Soc., 1984; bd. dirs. Planned Parenthood N.Y.C. Mem. N.Y. Jr. League, Kappa Alpha Theta Alumni Assn. Club: Houston. Home: 33 E 70th St Apt 5-E New York NY 10021 Other: 173 Sage Rd Houston TX 77056

BERNINGER, VIRGINIA WISE, psychologist, educator; b. Phila., Oct. 4, 1946; d. Oscar Sharpless and Lucille (Fike) Wise; m. Ronald William Berninger, Aug. 3, 1968. BA in Psychology, Elizabethtown (Pa.) Coll., 1967; MEd in Reading and Lang., U. Pitts., 1970; PhD in Psychology, Johns Hopkins U., 1981. Lic. psychologist, Wash. Educator Phila. Pub. Schs., 1967-68, Pitts. Pub. Schs., 1968, Baldwin-White Hall Pub. Schs., Pitts., 1969-72, Frederick (Md.) Pub. Schs., 1972-75, Balt. Pub. Schs., 1975-76; instr. Med. Sch. Harvard U., Boston, 1981-83; asst. prof. Sch. of Medicine Tufts U., Boston, 1983-86; asst. prof. Sch. of Medicine U. Wash., Seattle, 1986-89, assoc. prof., 1989—; mem. Ctr. for Study of Capable Youth, U. Wash., Seattle, 1989—; cons. in field. Contbr. articles to profl. jours. NIMH fellow, 1978-80; U. Wash. Rsch. grantee, 1987-88, Inst. for Ethnic Studies in the U.S. Rsch. grantee, 1989-90, NIH Rsch. grantee, 1989—. Mem. Am. Psychol. Assn., Am. Ednl. Rsch. Assn., Soc. for Rsch. on Child Devel., Nat. Assn. Sch. Psychologists, AAAS, N.Y. Acad. Sci. Office: U Wash 322J Miller Hall DQ-12 Seattle WA 98195

BERNSTEIN, AIMEE SUSAN, psychotherapist, management consultant, educator; b. N.Y.C., Feb. 27, 1949; d. Walter and Sally (Grossman) B. BA, Hunter Coll., 1969; MEd in Counseling Psychology, Boston U., 1975. Cert. marriage family and child counselor, Calif. Counselor New Perspectives, Larkspur, Calif., 1975-78; cons. Marin Juvenile Probation, Larkspur, 1975-78; founder, dir. Living Arts Sch., Marin County, Calif., 1978-80; div. mgr. Lawrence & Assocs., San Rafael and San Francisco, Calif., 1980-83; founder, pres. Women's Devel. Co., Mill Valley and San Francisco, Calif., 1983—; founder and pres. Aimee Bernstein & Assocs., San Francisco and Ft. Lauderdale, Fla., 1986—; nat. speaker, 1987—. Co-writer Rock 'n' Roll Opera (televised on ABC-TV show Tell It Like It Is, 1969). promoter Women Emerging Internat. Inst., Marin County, 1987. Brown belt, aikido 1972. Mem. Calif. Assn. Marriage Family and Child Counselors, NOW, Women's Exec. Club Ft. Lauderdale. Democrat. Jewish. Home: 1126 S Federal Hwy #326 Fort Lauderdale FL 33316

BERNSTEIN, BARBARA JANE, marketing executive, research analyst; b. Baldwin, Wis., Oct. 23, 1961; d. Edwin Douglas and Gloria Florence (Lutz) B. BBA in Mktg., U. Wis., Oshkosh, 1984. Mgr. Super 8 Motels, Hudson, Wis., 1984-85; dir. mktg. Lancer & Assocs., St. Paul, 1985-88; rsch. analyst Network Resource Moli-D Cos., Eden Prairie, Minn., 1988—. Mem. Downtown Community Devel. Coun., St. Paul, 1987-88. Lutheran. Home: 612 Michaelson N Hudson WI 54016 Office: Moli-D Cos Network Resource 9531 Cabride Ctr W 78th St Eden Prairie MN 55344

BERNSTEIN, CAROL ANN, psychiatrist; b. N.Y.C., Nov. 21, 1947; d. Stanley Herbert and Enid Lucille (Littwin) B. AB, Bryn Mawr Coll., 1969; MA in Teaching, Antioch Grad. Sch., Yellow Springs, Ohio, 1971; MD, Columbia U., 1980. Diplomate Nat. Bd. Med. Examiners. Tchr. Leeds Jr. High Sch., Phila., 1969-70; tenant organizer Community Action Programs Intercity, Chelsea, Mass., 1970-72; social worker St. Joseph's Hosp., Hamilton, Ontario, Can., 1972-74; gyn counselor Ea. Women's Ctr., N.Y.C., 1975-77; intern St. Luke's Hosp., N.Y.C., 1980-81; resident in psychiatry Presbyn. Hosp., N.Y.C., 1981-84; attending psychiatrist Washington Heights Community Service, N.Y.C., 1984-85; asst. dir. med. student edn. in psychiatry Columbia U., N.Y.C., 1985-89; assoc. dir. postgrad. edn. N.Y. State Psychiat. Inst., N.Y.C., 1989—. Exxon scholar, 1975; recipient Cammer Teaching award Psychiat. Inst. Alumni Assn., 1984. Mem. Am. Psychiat. Assn. (coun. N.Y. county dist. br. 1987—, assembly rep. 1989—, med. student edn. com. 1989—), Am. Med. Women's Assn. (Virginia Kneeland Frantz award 1988), Am. Assn. Dirs. Psychiat. Residency Tng., Assn. for Acad. Psychiatry, Am. Pub. Health Assn., Physicians for Social Responsibility. Office: NY State Psychiat Inst 722 W 168 St New York NY 10032 also: 1700 York Ave #1-L New York NY 10128

BERNSTEIN, CARYL SALOMON, lawyer; b. N.Y.C., Dec. 22, 1933; d. Gustav and Rosalind (Aron) Salomon; m. William D. Terry, June 12, 1955 (div. 1967); children: Ellen Deborah, Mark David; m. Robert L. Cole, Jr., Oct. 25, 1970 (div. 1975); m. George K. Bernstein, June 17, 1979. B.A. with honors, Cornell U., 1955; J.D., Georgetown U., 1967. Bar: D.C. 1968, U.S. Dist. Ct. D.C. 1968, U.S. Ct. Appeals (D.C. cir.) 1968, U.S. Supreme Ct. 1971. Atty. Covington & Burling, Washington, 1967-73; staff atty. Overseas Pvt. Investment Corp., Washington, 1973-74, asst. gen. counsel, 1974-77, v.p. for ins., 1977-81; sr. v.p., gen. counsel, sec. Fed. Nat. Mortgage Assn., Washington, 1981-82, exec. v.p., gen. counsel, sec., 1982—; bd. dirs. Citizens Bank of Md., Nat. Housing Conf. Contbr. articles to profl. jours., chpt. to book; mem. bd. editors Georgetown Law Jour., 1966; mem. editorial adv. bd. Housing and Devel. Reporter, 1986-87. Mem. bd. regents Georgetown U., 1986—; bd. dirs. Council for Ct. Excellence, Washington, 1986—. N.Y. Regents scholar, 1951-55. Mem. ABA, Fed. Bar Assn., D.C. Bar Assn., Phi Beta Kappa, Phi Kappa Phi. Office: Fed Nat Mortgage Assn 3900 Wisconsin Ave NW Washington DC 20016

BERNSTEIN, EVA GOULD, retired elementary educator, reading specialist; b. Milw., Nov. 25, 1918; d. Nathan and Lena Fried Gould; m. E. Ace Bernstein (dec.); children: Marcy B. Lichtig, Lynn C. BS in Elem. Edn., State Tchrs. Coll., Milw., 1940; MS in Reading, U. Wis., Milw., 1970. Tchr. S.S. Jr. High, Sheboygan, Wis., 1940-42, Greendale (Wis.) Pub. Sch., 1947-49; reading specialist Milw. Pub. Schs., 1970-79. Docent Milw. Art. Mus., 1986—. Mem. AAUW (coll. women's club, leader, mem. book group 1989—), Nat. Coun. Jewish Women (v.p. pub. affairs 1950-54), Hadassah (v.p. Am. affairs 1951-53), Pi Lambda Theta (v.p. conv. tours chair, v.p. U. Wis.-Milw. chpt. 1976-78). Jewish.

BERNSTEIN, LAUREL, publishing executive; b. N.Y.C., Sept. 24, 1945; m. Arthur G. Bernstein, Nov. 19, 1972; 1 child, Ari. BA in Secondary Edn., Montclair State Coll., 1966; postgrad., Adelphi U., 1969. Cert. secondary sch. tchr., N.J. Tchr. biology Cranford (N.J.) Bd. Edn., 1966-69; copy chief Am. Inst. Physics, N.Y.C., 1969-70, editorial supr., 1971-78, asst. supr., 1978-79; writer Louis DeRochemont Internat. Filmmakers, N.Y.C., 1970-71; prodn. supr. Acad. Press, Inc., N.Y.C., 1981-82; editorial supr. Marcel Dekker, Inc., N.Y.C., 1982-84; mgr. prodn. Elsevier Sci. Pub. Co., N.Y.C., 1984-85; dir. prodn. John Wiley & Sons, Inc., N.Y.C., 1985-88; mgr. electronic pub. Sci. Am. Medicine, N.Y.C., 1989; prodn. mgr. Northeastern Graphic Svcs., Englewood, N.J., 1989-90; sr. mng. editor Standard & Poor's Corp., N.Y.C., 1990—. Contbr. articles to jours. V.p. edn. Hadassah, Teaneck, N.J., 1983; treas. Boy Scouts Am. Pack 55, Teaneck, 1986; active PTA, Bogota, N.J., 1988. Mem. Women in Prodn., Soc. for Scholarly Publs., Fantacy Investment Club (founder, pres. Teaneck chpt. 1983—), Psi Lambda Tau (pres. 1961-62). Democrat. Jewish. Home: 323 Larch Ave Bogota NJ 07603 Office: Standard & Poor's Corp 25 Broadway New York NY 10004

BERNSTEIN, LORI ANN, computer manufacturing company executive; b. N.Y.C., Oct. 5, 1961; d. Richard Harold and Pauline (Thomas) B.; m. Guy Francis Gaudioso, May 20, 1989. BS Mktg.-Computer Info. Systems, Manhattan Coll., 1983. Advt. asst. J. Walter Thompson, N.Y.C., 1980-81; asst. mgr. Macy's, New Rochelle, N.Y., 1981-83; computer programmer, project mgr. Melco Corp., Mt. Vernon, N.Y., 1983-85; computer programmer, market analyst Z.C. Assocs. N.Am., Flushing, N.Y., 1985-87; mktg. mgr. Am. Data Systems Inc., Yonkers, 1987—. Mem. Am. Mktg. Assn. Republican. Roman Catholic. Home: 500 High Point Dr Hartsdale NY 10530 Office: Am Data Systems Inc 4 Executive Pla Yonkers NY 10701

BERNSTEIN, PATRICIA ROBIN, medical technologist; b. Jacksonville, Fla., Sept. 20, 1956; d. Sol and Artelia (Moorman) B. Student, Jacksonville U., 1974-75; BA in Biology, Hofstra U., 1978; MS in Med. Biology, L.I. U., 1988; postgrad., Pa. Coll. Podiatric Medicine, 1989—. Cert. chemistry supr., N.Y., med. technologist in chemistry, hematology and microbiology, Fla., supr. for chemistry, Hematology and microbiology, Fla. Med. technologist St. Clare's Hosp. & Health Ctr., N.Y.C., 1982-89; med. technologist Meml. Sloan-Kettering-Cancer Ctr., N.Y.C., 1984-89; lab. rep. pub. relations com. St. Clare's Hosp. & Health Ctr., N.Y.C., 1983-84; chairperson for Nat. Med. Lab. week, 1984; chemistry chairperson Nat. Med. Lab. week Meml. Sloan Kettering Cancer Ctr., N.Y.C., 1988. Mem. NAFE, Am. Soc. Clin. Pathologists (assoc.), Am. Soc. for Microbiology, Am. Assn. Women Podiatrists, Pa. Podiatric Med. Students Assn., Am. Podiatric Med. Students Assn., Student Nat. Podiatric Med. Assn., Iota Sigma Pi. Home: 2940 Jerusalem Ave Wantagh NY 11793

BERNT HAZZARD, CHARLOTTE IRENE, college administrator; b. Denver, Nov. 9, 1953; d. Harold Eugene Smith and Loretta Marie (Gillham) Schmidt; m. Thomas Joseph Bernt, July 2, 1969 (div. 1989); children: Marcus Thomas, Michele Irene; m. Rodney Ray Hazzard, June 15, 1990. BS in Computer Sci. and Bus. Adminstrn., Kearney (Nebr.) State Coll., 1981, MS in Bus. Adminstrn., 1984. Office mgr. Knapp, Mues, Anderson, et al Law Offices, Kearney, 1981-82; computer programmer Stanal Sound, Ltd., Kearney, 1982; owner, mgr. Computers In Bus., Kearney, 1982-84; instr. Kearney State Coll., 1983-89, head access services Calvin T. Ryan Library, 1984-90, Nebr. State Coll.'s automation dir., 1990—; cons. bus. computers, computer programmer, Kearney, 1987—. Author computer programs. Active Buffalo County Dems., Kearney, 1980—; sec. Kearney Area Baseball Assn., 1986—. Mem. Jr. Mems. Round Table of Nebr. Librarians Assn. (planning com. 1987—), Nebr. Library Assn., Kearney State Coll. Faculty Women, Nat. Assn. for Female Execs. Roman Catholic. Home: 3407 20th Ave Kearney NE 68847 Office: Kearney State Coll Calvin T Ryan Libr Kearney NE 68849

BERO, MARILYN PROCINO, civic worker, corporate professional; b. Auburn, N.Y., Sept. 12, 1937; d. Jack Anthony and Mary Louise (Cefaratti) Procino; B.A. in Elem. Edn., Marywood Coll., 1959; postgrad. Syracuse U., 1961; m. James Donald Bero, Feb. 10, 1962; children: Mark J., Michael A., Matthew R. Tchr. 3d grade Auburn Sch. System, 1959-61. Sec.-treas. Hampton Rd. Constrn. Corp., Seneca Falls, N.Y.; adviser to jury design competition Wesleyan Chapel. Mem. Seneca Falls (N.Y.) Sch. Dist. Bd., 1976-85, v.p., 1978, pres., 1980-83, dir., 1978—; co-chmn. bldg. fund drive Nat. Women's Hall of Fame, Inc., Seneca Falls, 1978-79, pres., 1980-83; bd. dirs. Seneca County Child Care Ctr., 1975-84, pres., 1976-79; bd. dirs. Alpha Day Sch., Seneca Falls, 1972-75, Happiness House, Geneva, N.Y., 1968-72, CAUSE, United Way; bd. dirs. Seneca County United Way, 1986-90; adv. commn. Women's Rights Nat. Hist. Park. Named Rotary Citizen of Yr., 1983. Mem. AAUW, Women's League Seneca Falls (pres. 1978-79). Republican. Roman Catholic. Home: Box 670 2934 Route 89 Seneca Falls NY 13148 Office: Hampton Rd Construction Corp 2934 Rt 89 Seneca Falls NY 13148

BERON, GAIL LASKEY, real estate analyst, consultant, appraiser; b. Detroit, Nov. 13, 1943; d. Charles Jack Laskey and Florence B. (Rosenthal) Eisenberg; divorced; children: Monty Charles, Bryan David. Cert. real estate analyst, Mich. Chief/staff appraiser Ft. Wayne Mortgage Co., Birmingham, Mich., 1973-75; pvt. practice fee appraiser S.C., Iowa, Mich., 1976-80; pres. The Beron Co., Southfield, Mich., 1980—; cons. ptnr. Real Estate Counseling Group Conn., Storrs, 1983—, Real Estate Counseling Group Am., prin., 1984—; lectr. real estate confs. Recipient M. William Donnally award Mortgage Bankers Assn. Am., 1975. Mem. Soc. Real Estate Appraisers (bd. dirs. Detroit chpt. 1980-82, nat. faculty mem. 1983—), Am. Inst. Real Estate Appraisers (bd. dirs. Detroit chpt. 1982-86, nat. faculty mem. 1984—), Nat. Assn. Realtors, Detroit Bd. Realtors, Southfield Bd. Realtors, Women Brokers Assn. (treas. Southfield chpt. 1981-83), Young Mortgage Bankers (bd. dirs. 1974-75). Lodge: B'nai Brith. Home: 7008 Bridge Way West Bloomfield MI 48322 Office: Beron Co 17228 W Hampton Rd Southfield MI 48075

BERRY, ANN ROPER, diplomat; b. Cleve., Nov. 9, 1934; d. Frank Carson and Doris (Decker) Roper; m. Maxwell K. Berry, Feb. 11, 1959; children: Walter F., Helen D. BA, Ohio Wesleyan U., 1956; MEd, U. Md., 1964. Asst. budget and fiscal officer Am. Embassy, Baghdad, Iraq, 1958-59; various teaching positions, Turkey, Zambia and U.S., 1961-75; internat. economist Dept. of State, Washington, 1975-77, asst. chief textiles div., 1977-80; econ. officer Am. Embassy, Athens, Greece, 1980-82; dep. chief textile negotiator U.S. Trade Rep., Washington, 1982-84; mem. NATO Def. Coll., Rome, 1984; counselor for econ. affairs Am. Embassy, Paris, 1985-89; min. econ. affairs Am. Embassy, London, 1989—. Recipient Superior Honor award Dept. of State, 1980. Mem. Phi Beta Kappa. Office: Am Embassy Box 27 FPO New York NY 09509

BERRY, DEBRA L., banker; b. New Rochelle, N.Y., May 31, 1949; d. Carroll M. and Beatrice T. (Tozour) Stone; m. James F. Berry, July 1, 1969. AA, Del. Tech. and Community Coll., 1983; BA, Wilmington Coll., Dover, Del., 1985; postgrad., Wilmington Coll. Cert. fin. planner. Asst. v.p. Wilmington Trust Co., Dover, Del. Treas. Del. Hospice-Cen. Div., 1987—; v.p. Del. Heart Assn., 1989—; vice chmn. adv. coun. Salvation Army, 1990—. Named Outstanding Coll. Grad., 1983, Del. Tech. and Community Coll. Mem. AAUW, Women Bus. Leaders, Soroptimist Internat., Rotary. Home: 139 S State St Dover DE 19901

BERRY, JOYCE T., government administrator; B.A., Howard U., 1969, M.A., 1970; Ph.D., Fordham U., 1976; J.D. Georgetown U., 1983. Edn. program officer AID, U.S. Dept. State, 1970-71; manpower devel. specialist U.S. Dept. Labor, 1971-74; edn. and tng. officer Adminstrn. on Aging, U.S. Dept. Health and Human Services, N.Y.C., 1974-77, assoc. commr. edn. and tng., 1980-83, dep. assoc. commr. program devel., 1983-85, assoc. commr. Adminstrn. on Aging, from 1985, now commr.; adj. prof. New Sch. Social Research, 1976; spl. asst. to asst. sec. for rural devel. U.S. Dept. Agr., 1978-80; guest lectr. Recipient Spl. Achievement award U.S. Dept. Agr., 1979, Outstanding Achievement award, 1979. Mem. Nat. Bar Assn., Assn. Gerontology in Higher Edn., Gerontol. Soc., Nat. Council on Aging, Southeast D.C. Community Orgn., Nat. Ctr. for Black Aged. Office: Dept of Health & Human Svcs Adminstrn on Aging 330 Independence Ave SW Washington DC 20201

BERRY, JULIANNE ELWARD, polymer and colloid chemist, researcher; b. Chgo., Nov. 25, 1946; d. Thomas Stephen and Helen Marie (Siffer) Elward; m. Michael James Berry, Apr. 28, 1967 (div. 1982); children: Michael James II, Jennifer Anne. BS, U. Calif., Berkeley, 1968, MS, 1969; PhD, U. Wis., 1978. Tchr. chemistry Moreau High Sch., Hayward, Calif., 1969-70; rsch. asst. chemistry dept. U. Wis., Madison, 1972-76; chemist Allied Chem. Corp., Morristown, N.J., 1976-78; sr. rsch. chemist Merck, Sharpe & Dohme Rsch. Labs., Rahway, N.J., 1978-80; sr. rsch. chemist Exxon Prodn. Rsch. Co., Houston, 1980-83, rsch. specialist, 1983—. Asst. race dir. Valentine's Day Women's Run, Houston, 1985, 86. Mem. Am. Chem. Soc., Soc. Petroleum Engrs., Clay Minerals Soc., U. Calif. Alumni of Tex. (bd. dirs. 1984-88, pres. 1985-86, 90—), Iota Sigma Pi. Office: Exxon Prodn Rsch Co PO Box 2189 Houston TX 77252

BERRY, MARIE BRAUN, librarian; b. San Antonio, Aug. 15, 1913; d. Alois E. and Pauline Marie (Schattenberg) Braun; m. Clarence Matthew Barry, Feb. 3, 1942 (dec. Apr. 1979); 1 child, Marie Suzette. Student, San Antonio Jr. Coll., 1934-35, Tex. Luth. Coll., 1936, St. Mary's U., San Antonio, 1937-40; BA in Library Sci., Our Lady of the Lake U., 1957. Library asst. San Antonio Pub. Library, 1934-35, reference librarian, 1937-42, head librarian history, gen. reference and social sci. dept., 1954-58, 74—, reference librarian, 1969-73; chmn. People, Places & Events Travelogue, San Antonio, 1965-68; conductor Geneology Workshop, San Antonio, 1987. Mem. Bexar County Hist. Commn., San Antonio, 1974—, San Antonio Conservation Soc., 1956—; mem. rsch. com. San Antonio Bicentennial Commn., 1975-77; pres. San Antonio Hist. Assn, 1976. Recipient Disting. Svc. award Tex. State Hist. Commn. and Hist. Found., 1978, 79. Mem. Librarian's Coun. (chmn. 1958-59), Bexar Library Assn. (Julia Grothaus award 1983), Tex. Library Assn. (archives chmn. Austin chpt. 1978-79), Tex. State Library Assn., Tex. Assn. Pioneers, Staff Assn. San Antonio Pub. Library, AAUW (life). Home: 213 Overhill Dr San Antonio TX 78228 Office: San Antonio Pub Libr 203 S St Marys St San Antonio TX 78205

BERRY, NORMA JEAN, social worker; b. Charleston, W.Va., Jan. 7, 1946; d. Carl E. and Dora Lee (Hamm) Inman; m. Julian, July 5, 1974, (div. 1980); m. Vincent L. Swadis, Sept. 12, 1985. BS, Morris Harvey Coll., 1967; MSW, W.Va. U., 1975. Social Worker. Social worker Fla. State Dept. of Welfare, Crestview, 1968-69; asst. adminstr. Hilltop Home for the Elderly, Charleston, 1970-71; social worker W.Va. Dept. of Welfare, Charleston, 1971-74; social worker VA Hosp., Huntington, W.Va., 1974-82, Temple, Tex., 1982-1990; psychotherapist Minirth-Meier, Tunnell & Wilson Psychiatric Clinic, Belton, Tex., 1990—; cons. VA Hosp., Temple, 1974-82; real estate agt. Bruzzese Realty Co., Huntington, 1980-81; salesperson Mary Kay Cosmetics, Temple, 1983-84. Recipient Outstanding Svc. award DAV, 1981. Republican. Home: 8920 Trail Ridge Dr Temple TX 76502 Office: Minirth-Meier Tunnell & Wilson Clinic 620 N Main St Belton TX 76513

BERRY, SHIRLEY NICHOLS, early childhood education consultant; b. Williamsburg, Mass., July 12, 1930; d. Alfred Spencer and Elizabeth May (Abbott) Nichols; m. William Raymond Berry, Sept. 25, 1954; children: Bonnie Lynn Berry Childs, Paul Nikolas. BS, U. Mass., 1952; MA, Hartford Sem., 1954; postgrad., Black Hills State Coll., 1971-76, No. State Coll., Aberdeen, S.D., 1974-75. Dir. field svcs. No. Ala. Girl Scouts U.S., Huntsville, 1966-67; supervising tchr. Cheyenne River Sioux Head Start, Eagle Butte, S.D., 1972-73, resource tchr., 1973-74; resource tchr., career devel. coord. Standing Rock Sioux Head Start, Ft. Yates, N.D., 1974-77, edn. coord., 1978-79, asst. Head Start dir., 1980, 81-83; day care tchr. Hampshire County Day Care, Northampton, Mass., 1981; ind. early childhood edn. cons. Mobridge, S.D., 1983—; adminstrv. asst. Dakota Assn./Indian United Ch. of Christ Churches, Mobridge, 1983—; presenter workshops in early childhood edn., 1957—; cons. Head Start programs, N.D. and S.D., 1980—, adviser Child Devel. Assoc. program, 1975—. Contbr. articles to church and Head Start newsletters. Mem., officer Ch. Women United, Huntsville, Ala., 1960-67. Mem. AAUW (chair ann. spelling contest Oahe area 1985-90, state historian 1986-88, satellite pres. Gettysburg br. 1988—, charter mem., then pres. Oahe area br.), Nat. Assn. Edn. Young Children, S.D. Assn. Edn. Young Children (mem. Capital Connection). Democrat. Congregationalist. Office: Early Childhood Edn Cons 1214 10th Ave W Mobridge SD 57601-1211

BERRY, VICKIE LEE, architect; b. St. Louis, June 23, 1954; d. John Wesley and Martha Lee (Hughey) Berry; m. Gary Wayne Hazelwood (div.). B in Environ. Design, U. Kans., 1976, BArch, 1977. Lic. architect, Mo., Tex. Architect Southwestern Bell Telephone Co., St. Louis, 1976-77; project architect Southwestern Bell Telephone Co., San Antonio, 1977-78; constrn. budget adminstr. Southwestern Bell Telephone Co., Dallas, 1978-80, project architect, 1980-84; bus. plan writer Southwestern Bell Telephone Co., St. Louis, 1984-86, project architect, master planner, 1986--. Mem. adv. appeals bd. Dallas Electrical Code Examiners. Mem. AIA, Mo. Coun. Architects. Republican. Home: 6343 Waterman Ave Saint Louis MO 63130 Office: Southwestern Bell Tel Co 1 Bell Ctr 32-D-7 Saint Louis MO 63101

BERSCHEID, ELLEN S., psychology educator, author, researcher; b. Colfax, Wis., Oct. 11, 1936; d. Sylvan L. and Alvilde (Running) Saumer; m. Dewey Mathias Berscheid, Nov. 21, 1959. BA, U. Nev., 1959, MA, 1960; PhD, U. Minn., 1965. Market rsch. analyst Pillsbury Co., Mpls., 1960-62;

asst. prof. psychology and mktg. U. Minn., Mpls., 1965-66, asst. prof. psychology, 1967-68, assoc. prof., 1969-71, prof., 1971-88, Regent's prof. psychology, 1988—; mem. NRC Assembly Behavioral and Social Scis., 1973-77. Co-author: Interpersonal Attraction, 1969, 78, Equity: Theory and Research, 1978, Close Relationships, 1983, also numerous articles; mem. numerous editorial bds., past editorships. Recipient Berscheid-Hatfield award for disting. scholarship in interpersonal relationships, Iowa/Internat. Network for Interpersonal Relationships. Fellow Am. Psychol. Assn. (Donald T. Campbell award 1984, editor Contemporary Psychology jour. 1985—), Soc. Personality and Social Psychology (pres. 1985), Soc. for Psychol. Study Social Issues; mem. Internat. Soc. for the Study Personal Relationships (pres. 1990—), Soc. Exptl. Social Psychology (exec. bd. 1971-74, 77-80, 85-89), Cosmos Club (Washington), Gown-in-Town Club. Presbyterian. Home: 506 Grand Hill Saint Paul MN 55102 Office: U Minn Dept Psychology N309 Elliott Hall Minneapolis MN 55455

BERSON, IOLA PORTIA, electronics executive; b. Paris, June 16, 1952; came to U.S., 1974; d. Pierre Auguste and Matilde C. (Cervelle) B. BFA, Yale U., 1977; MS in Computer Sci., MIT, 1979; PhD in Computer Sci., Calif. Tech. U., 1982; lycée honoeur, U. Duvaillier, Port-au-Prince, Haiti, 1986. Curatorial asst. Louvre, Paris, 1973-74; programmer Archicad Corp., Waltham, Mass., 1977-79, Calcomputectronics, Pasadena, Calif., 1979-84; chief exec. officer Computecture Corp., New City, N.Y., 1984—. Author: L'Edifice d'Amour, 1977, La Pitre au Pont, 1984, Computer Designed Living Spaces, 1987. Home: 6 Rollingwood Dr New City NY 10956

BERT, CAROL LOIS, educational aide; b. Bakersfield, Calif., Oct. 15, 1938; d. Edwin Vernon and Shirley Helen (Craig) Phelps; m. John Davison Bert, Sept. 26, 1964; children: Mary Ellen, John Edwin, Craig Eric, Douglas Ethan. BS in Nursing, U. Colo., 1960. Med. surg. nurse U.S. Army, Washington, 1960-62, Ascom City, Korea, 1962-63, San Antonio, 1963, Albuquerque, 1964-65; tchrs. aide Jefferson County Schs., Arvada, Colo., 1979—. Sec. Parent, Tchr., Student Assn. Arvada West High Sch., 1987-88. Club: Colo. Quilting Council (1st v.p. 1988, 89). Avocations: reading, quilting, camping, fishing, tennis. Home: 5844 Oak St Arvada CO 80004 Office: Allendale Elem Sch 5900 Oak St Arvada CO 80004

BERT, CLARA VIRGINIA, home economics educator, administrator; b. Quincy, Fla., Jan. 29, 1929; d. Harold C. and Ella J. (McDavid) B. BS, Fla. State U., 1950, MS, 1963, PhD, 1967. Cert. tchr., Fla.; cert. home economist; cert. pub. mgr. Tchr. Union County High Sch., Lake Butler, Fla., 1950-53, Havana High Sch., Fla., 1953-65; cons. rsch. and devel. Fla. Dept. Edn., Tallahassee, 1967-75, sect. dir. rsch. and devel., 1975-85, program dir. home econs. edn., 1985—; cons. Nat. Ctr. Rsch. in Vocat. Edn., Ohio State U., 1978; field reader U.S. Dept. Edn., 1974-75. Author, editor booklets. U.S. Office Edn. grantee, 1976, 77, 78. Mem. Am. Home Econs. Assn. (state treas. 1969-71), Am. Vocat. Assn., Fla. Vocat. Assn., Fla. Vocat. Home Econs., Fla. Home Econs., Am. Vocat. Edn. Rsch. Assn. (nat. treas. 1970-71), Nat. Coun. Family Rels., Am. Edn!. Rsch. Assn., Fla. State U. Alumni Assn. (bd. dirs. home econs. sect.), Havana Golf and Country Club, Kappa Delta Pi, Omicron Nu (chpt. pres. 1965-66), Delta Kappa Gamma (pres. 1974-76), Sigma Kappa (pres. corp. bd.), Phi Delta Kappa. Office: Fla Dept Edn FEC Tallahassee FL 32399

BERT, ELEANOR LUCILLE, public school system business administrator; b. Fall River, Mass., June 14, 1939; d. Edward Joseph and Eleanor Lucille (Simpkins) Bertolini. BS Marist Coll., 1976; M.B.A., M.H.A., U. Miami, 1977; postgrad. Rider Coll., 1984, SUNY-Albany, 1984, Fordham U., 1986—. Intergovtl. coordinator Ulster Co., Kingston, N.Y., 1977-78; bus. mgr. Stuyvesant Inns, Kingston, 1978-79, Morrisville Sch. Dist., Pa., 1979-82; dir. bus. mgmt. service Bensalem Towns Sch. Dist., Pa., 1982-84; bus. adminstr. Catskill Central Schs., N.Y., 1984-86; asst. supt. for bus. Pine Plains Cen. Sch. Dist., 1986—; presenter workshops in field. Bd. dirs. Ulster County council Girl Scouts U.S.A., 1977-78, Ulster County YWCA, 1977-78, Ulster County CAP, Kingston, 1985—. Mem. Delaware Valley Assn. Sch. Bus. Ofcls. (pres. 1981-82), Assn. Sch. Bus. Ofcls., N.Y. Assn. Sch. Bus. Ofcls., Pa. Assn. Sch. Bus. Ofcls. Home: UPO Box 3234 Kingston NY 12401 Office: Pine Plains Cen Sch Dist Box 86 Pine Plains NY 12567

BERTELLE, JEANNE T., publishing company executive, personnel director; b. Bklyn., Oct. 14, 1947; d. John A. and Florence (Bellitti) B.; m. Silvio Rosato. BA in English, Bklyn. Coll., 1968; postgrad. in Drama, Hunter Coll., 1975-77. Pers. adminstr. Chem. Bank, N.Y.C., 1968-70; employment interviewer L.I. Coll. Hosp., Bklyn., 1970-71; sr. job analyst health svcs. mobility study, Rsch. Found. CUNY, N.Y.C., 1971-76; pers. mgr. Doubleday & Co., N.Y.C., 1976-88; dir. human resources McGraw-Hill Inc., N.Y.C., 1988—; com. mem. Direct Mail Assn., N.Y.C., 1984; cons., editor Health Services Mobility Study, N.Y.C., 1976-77. N.Y. State Regents scholar, 1964-68. Mem. Am. Soc. Personnel Adminstrs., Assn. Am. Publishers (chair industry salary survey 1987—). Roman Catholic. Club: Scott House (Bklyn.) (v.p.). Home: 1104 Hunters Run Dobbs Ferry NY 10522 Office: McGraw-Hill Inc 1221 Ave of the Americas New York NY 10020

BERTELSEN, CYNTHIA DIANE, educator; b. Bowling Green, Ohio, May 30, 1960; d. Raymond N. and Roberta (Alloway) B. BS in Edn., Bowling Green State U., 1982; postgrad., Ohio State U. Tchr. summer sch., back to basics tutoring Westerville, Ohio, 1982-85; tchr. summer sch. Delaware (Ohio) city schs., 1985-88, tchr. primary grades developmentally handicapped, mem. state-wide com. on developmentally handicapped issues, 1984-89; tchr. No. Local Schs., Thornville, Ohio, 1989—; lectr. in field. Bd. trustees Delaware County chpt. Assn. Retarded Citizens, 1989—. Recipient Quality Initiative in Edn. award DARC, 1989; named Spl. Edn. Tchr. of Yr., Delaware City Schs., 1986; Eagles grantee Columbus, Ohio chpt. KC, 1988. Mem. Internat. Reading Assn. (v.p. Delaware County coun. 1990—), Coun. Exceptional Children (pres.-elect mental retardation div. and Columbus chpt. 1990—), Nat. Coun. Tchrs. English, Assn. for Supervision and Curriculum Devel.Cen. Ohio Spl. Edn. Reg. Resource Ctr. (task force mem.), Southeastern Ohio Coun. Tchrs. Eng., Grady Hosp. Guild, Ohio Ea. Star, Phi Delta Kappa.

BERTELSON, AMY DAYLE, psychologist; b. Council Bluffs, Iowa, June 7, 1952; d. Jack Dale and Eloise Marie (Kierscht) B.; m. David Bernell Clark, Sept. 8, 1979. BA, Nebr. Wesleyan U., 1974; MA, Ohio State U, 1976, PhD, 1979. Intern U. Minn., Mpls., 1978-79; fellow Baylor Coll. Medicine, Houston, 1979-80; dir. psychol. svcs. ctr. Washington U., St. Louis, 1980—. Editorial cons. McGraw Hill, 1985—, Macmillan Publs., 1983—; reviewer Jour. Cons. and Clin. Psychology, 1987—; contbr. chpt. in book, articles in refereed profl. jours.; editor Clinical Aspects of Sleep Disorders, 1983; 21 presentations profl. convs., 1974—. Mental health vol. ARC, St. Louis, 1990—. Named Outstanding Young Woman of Am., 1981. Mem. Am. Psychol. Assn., Soc. Psychophysiol. Rsch., Assn. Profl. Sleep Socs., Midwestern Psychol. Assns., Mo. Psychol. Assn. Democrat. Office: Washington U 1 Brookings Dr Saint Louis MO 63130

BERTHOLD, BONNIE MADELINE, day care school administrator, consultant; b. Sellersville, Pa., Nov. 23, 1950; d. Willard Miller and Anna Agnes (Dugard) Berthold. BS in Elem. Edn. cum laude, Kutztown State U., Pa., 1972; MS in Edn. with disting. recognition, Temple U., 1975; Prin.'s cert., U. Pa., 1978. Elem. sch. tchr. Reading Sch. Dist., Pa., 1972-79, summer sch. instr., 1972-79, workshop presenter, 1972-79, curriculum developer, 1974-79, adminstv. inter, 1977-79; owner, adminstr. Wooly Bear Day Care Sch., Lansdale, Pa., 1979—; asst. prof. Montgomery County Community Coll., Blue Bell, Pa., 1985—; cons. in field. Contbr. articles to mags. Recipient Outstanding Tchrs. Am. award Bd. of Advisors, 1975; named Tchr. of Yr. Reading/Berks County C. of C., 1976; George B. Hancher scholar Kutztown State U., 1971. Mem. Montgomery/Bucks Assn. for Edn. of Young Children (pres. 1982-84), Nat. Assn. for Edn. of Young Children, Pa. Assn. for Edn. of Young Children, Pa. Assn. Child Care Adminstrs., Del. Valley Child Care Council (sec.), North Penn C. of C. Republican. Lutheran. Club: Newcomers. Avocations: piano, water sports, reading, constructing and designing learning materials. Home: 106 Holly Dr Lansdale PA 19446 Office: Wooly Bear Day Care Sch 128 S Broad St Lansdale PA 19446

BERTIGER, KAREN LEE, real estate broker and asset manager; b. Louisville, Ky., Aug. 25, 1954; d. Joseph Henry and Phyllis June (Hupp) Dickhaus; m. Paul Robert Kastensmith, June 3, 1978 (div. June 1980); children: Christine, Jennifer; m. Bary Robert Bertiger, Dec. 28, 1985; stepchildren: Karen, Jeff. Student, Miami U., 1972-73, U. Cin., 1973-75, Am. Open U., 1986-88. Pres. Seville Realty and Investment Co., Phoenix, 1983-84; realtor Realty Execs., Scottsdale, Ariz., 1984-89; chief exec. officer Landvest, Ltd., 1989—, Landvest Securities, Ltd., Scottsdale, 1987—; designated broker Landvest Ltd., Scottsdale, 1989—. Leader Ariz. Cactus-Pine Girl Scouts, Phoenix, 1985-86. Mem. Nat. Assn. Realtors (grad. Realtor's Inst. 1986, cert. residential specialist 1989), Scottsdale Bd. Realtors (mem. grievance com., community rels. com. 1989—, local city govt. com. 1988-89, govt. affairs com. 1989—). Republican. Office: Landvest Ltd PO Box 5131 Scottsdale AZ 85261-5131

BERTRAM, AMY ANN, writer; b. Phoenix, July 19, 1960; d. Richard Justin and Wilma Dorothy (Oetken) B.; m. Steven Israel Celniker, Mar. 27, 1982 (div. July 2, 1987). BS in Telecommunications magna cum laude, Ariz. State U., 1981. Adminstrv. asst., jr. publicist Feltheimer/Knofsky Mgmt. Co., Los Angeles, 1981-82; jr. publicist Rogers & Cowan Pub. Relations, Beverly Hills, Calif., 1982-83, account exec. Lippin & Grant Pub. Relations Co., Los Angeles, 1983-86; account supr. Bozell, Jacobs, Kenyon and Eckhardt Entertainment Group, Los Angeles, 1986; dir. publicity domestic TV div. Paramount Pictures Corp., L.A., 1987-89; freelance writer 1989—; guest lectr. UCLA; speaker in field. Chevron USA scholar, 1979-81. Mem. Hollywood Radio and TV Soc., NAFE, Women in Communications Inc., Phi Kappa Phi.

BERTRAM, GWENDOLYN SEIBERT, library automation specialist, librarian; b. St. Clair Shore, Mich., Jan. 4, 1958; d. Jack H. and Margaret C. (Quick) Seibert; m. Fred Bertram III, Aug. 3, 1983. BA, Blackburn Coll., 1980; MLS, U. Mich., 1983. Head librarian Strauss Library, U. Mich., Ann Arbor, 1981-83; reference librarian Champaign (Ill.) Pub. Library, 1983-84; info. broker Info. Finders, Champaign, 1984-85; trainer Nelinet, Inc., Newton, Mass., 1985-87; mktg. rep. Carlyle Systems, Inc., Emeryville, Calif., 1987-88; supr. client svcs. The Faxon Co., Westwood, Mass., 1988-90, sales rep. Medicac Info. Svcs., 1990—. Libr. Presbyn. Ch., Whitinsville, Mass., 1987—, deacon, 1987-90, elder, 1990—. Mem. Am. Library Assn., Library Info and Tech. Assn.

BERTRAND, ANNABEL HODGES, civic worker, artist, calligrapher; b. Birmingham, Ala., Jan. 4, 1915; d. Thomas Edmund and Mae (Crawford) Hodges; m. John Raney Bertrand, Oct. 23, 1942; children: John Thomas, Diana Bertrand Williams, Karen Bertrand Wilson, J'May Bertrand Rivara. BS, Tex. Woman's U., 1935, MA, 1936; postgrad., Columbia U., 1938. Tchr. White Deer (Tex.) Consol. Sch., 1936-37, Tyler (Tex.) Pub. Sch. System, 1938-39; instr. Sam Houston State U., Huntsville, Tex., 1939-42; interim tchr. Portsmouth (N.H.) Pub. Sch., 1943. Bd. dirs. Ga. Coun. for Arts and Humanities, Atlanta, 1979-83, Mental Health Assn. Floyd County, Rome, Ga., 1990; active High Mus. Art, Atlanta, 1979—, Rome Symphony Guild, 1980—, Friends of Rome/Floyd County Libr., 1985—, Christian Personhood Book Discussion Group of First United Meth. Ch., 1980—. Mem. AAUW, Rome Music Lovers Club, United Meth. Women, Coosa Country Club, Nat. Trust for Hist. Preservation (assoc.), Ga. Trust for Hist. Preservation, Sigma Alpha Iota (patroness). Republican. Home: 18 Rosewood Rd Rome GA 30161

BERTRAND, CARIE LYNN, personnel director; b. Painesville, Ohio, July 2, 1964; d. Lyle James and Ruth Geraldine (Krestensen) B. Assoc. in Bus., Coll. Lake County, Grayslake, Ill., 1984; BS in Bus., Barat Coll., 1986. Personnel asst. Leider Cos./Tropical Plant Rentals, Riverwoods, Ill., 1986-88; dir. personnel Leider Hort. Cos., Buffalo Grove, Ill., 1988—. Mem. No. Ill. Indsl. Assn., Ill. C. of C. Home: 22216 W Orchard Ln Antioch IL 60002

BERTRAND, GABRIELLE, Canadian legislator; b. Sweetsburg, Que., Can., May 15, 1923; d. Louis Arthur and Juliette (Bolduc) Giroux; m. Jean-Jacques Bertrand, Oct. 14, 1944; children: Andrée, Jean-François, Suzanne, Pierre, Louise, Philippe, Marie. BSc. Mem. from Brome-Missisquoi Can. Ho. of Commons; former parliamentary sec. to min. of Nat. Health and Welfare, former parliamentary sec. to Minister of Consumer and Corp. Affairs. Pres. Que. div. Red Cross, 1981-83; mem. bd. dirs. Casisse Populaire, Le Centre d'Accueil de Cowansville, Brome-Missisquoi Perkins Hosp., Cie Theatrale des Cantons. Mem. Progressive Conservative Party. Roman Catholic. Address: 769 Principale St, Cowansville, PQ Canada J2K 1J8

BERTRAND, MARY ELLEN, stockbroker, trader; b. N.Y.C., Feb. 16, 1955; d. Charles Arthur Bertrand and Mary (Lynch) Perez; m. Scott Douglas Ballin (div. 1986). BA in Polit. Sci., Mt. Vernon Coll., Washington, 1976. Dir. materials ctr. Gen. Fedn. of Women's Clubs, Washington, 1978-80; broker, asst. to the chmn. Folger Nolan Fleming Douglas, Washington, 1980-85; broker, account exec. Rose & Co., N.Y.C., 1985-86; trader Bear Stearns, N.Y.C., 1986-88; trader, broker Robyns Capital, N.Y.C., 1988-89; trader, v.p. trading Jessop Capital Corp., N.Y.C., 1989—. Roman Catholic.

BERUBE, MARGERY STANWOOD, publishing executive; b. Middleborough, Mass., Nov. 18, 1943; d. John Peter and Dorothy Cole (Stanwood) Wholan; m. Edgar Roger Berube, Sept. 12, 1967. BA in English, Wilkes Coll., 1965. Creative and prodn. mgr., dir. editorial ops. Med. div. Houghton Mifflin Co., Boston, 1978-81, dir. editorial ops. Reference div., 1982-85, v.p., dir. editorial ops. Trade and Reference div., 1986-87, v.p., dir. editorial art prodn. and mfg. services, 1987—. Mem. Bookbuilders (bd. dirs. 1976-80). Office: Houghton Mifflin Co Two Park St Boston MA 02108

BERZINS, ERNA MARIJA, physician; b. Latvia, Nov. 27, 1914; d. Arturs and Anna (Steckenbergs) Meilands; came to U.S., 1951, naturalized, 1956; M.D., Latvian State U., 1940; m. Verners Berzins, Aug. 24, 1935; children—Valdis, Andis. Mem. pediatric faculty Latvian State U., 1940-44; intern Good Samaritan Hosp., Dayton, Ohio, 1951-52; resident in pediatrics Children's Hosp. of Mich., Detroit, 1953-55; practice medicine specialising in pediatrics, Detroit, 1956-60; with ARC, Cleve., 1961-63; physician pediatric outpatient dept. Cleve. Met. Gen. Hosp., 1963-84; asst. prof. emeritus Case-Western Res. U., Cleve. Mem. Am., Ohio med. assns., Acad. Medicine, No. Ohio Pediatric Soc., Am. Women's Med. Assn., Am. Med. Polit. Action Com. Lutheran. Address: 5460 Friar Circle Cleveland OH 44126

BERZON, BETTY, psychotherapist; b. St. Louis, Jan. 18, 1928; d. Irvin and Eva (Zarfas) B. BA in Psychology, UCLA, 1957; MS in Psychology, Calif. State U., San Diego, 1962; PhD in Psychology, Internat. Coll., L.A., 1978. Lic. marriage, family and child counselor, Calif. Rsch. assoc. Western Behavioral Scis. Inst., La Jolla, Calif., 1962-68; dir. group program devel. Human Devel. Inst., Inc. (A Bell & Howell Co.), L.A., 1968-70; dir. rsch., v.p. Kairos, L.A., 1970-72; project dir./program developer Rsch. for Better Schs., Inc., Phila., 1973-76; pvt. practice, tng. cons. L.A., 1970—, pvt. practice, psychotherapy, 1970—; guest lectr. ext. divs. UCLA, U. Calif., Riverside, U. Calif., Irvine, U. Calif., San Diego; tng. cons. in field, rsch. projects in field; bd. dirs. Gay and Lesbian Adolescent Social Svcs., L.A. Editorial bd. Jour. of Humanistic Psychology, 1979-85; author numerous books including Permanent Partners, 1988; editor: New Perspectives on Encounters Group, 1972, Positively Gay, 1979; contbr. articles to profl. jours. Tng. cons. Gay Community Svcs. Ctr., L.A., bd. dirs. 1972-75; tng. cons. Metro. Community Ch., 1971-73; bd. dirs. Whitman-Radclyffe Found., 1976-77, exec. v.p. 1976; bd. suprs. West Hollywood Adv. Coun., L.A. County, 3d dist., 1975-77; gay rights advocate, others. Mem. Assn. Gay Psychologists, Gay Acad. Union (nat. pres. 1977-79). Office: 8901 Melrose Ave Ste 202 West Hollywood CA 90069

BERZON, FAYE CLARK, nursing educator; b. New Britain, Conn., Sept. 26, 1926; d. Bernard Francis and Elizabeth Tillie (Gross) Clark; m. Harry Berzon, June 18, 1961. Diploma Beth Israel Hosp., 1947; B.S.N., Boston U., 1957, M.S.N., 1959; cert. advanced grad. studies, U. Mass., 1987. Staff, head nurse, instr. Beth Israel Hosp., Boston, 1948-58; instr. nursing Simmons Coll., Boston, 1958-62, Cath. Labore Sch. Nursing, Dorchester, Mass., 1962-67; asst. prof. nursing Boston U. Sch. Nursing, 1967-70; div. chmn. human services Massasoit Community Coll., Brockton, Mass., 1973-79, prof. nursing, 1970—, chair nursing dept. 1988—; mem. acad. adv. com. to Mass. Bd. Higher Edn., 1975-76. Author: (with Govoni, Berzon, Fall) Drugs and Nursing Implications, 1965, Nursing Outlook, 1990. Vol., Milton (Mass.) Meals on Wheels, 1978—. Mem. Am. Nurses Assn., Am. Assn. Women in Community and Jr. Colls., Nat. League Nursing (scholar 1963-79, accreditation visitor 1976—), AAUW (v.p. Milton br. 1981-83), Nursing Archives, Nat. Assoc. for Advancement of Assoc. Degree Nursing, Sigma Theta Tau, Delta Kappa Gamma. Jewish. Home: 37 Brandon Rd Milton MA 02186

BESEN, JANE PHYLLIS TRIPTOW, civic worker; b. Chgo., Aug. 6, 1921; d. Richard Herman and Rose (Krips) Triptow; student Northwestern U., 1946-47, East Los Angeles Coll., 1967-68; B.A. in English, Calif. State U., Los Angeles, 1978, postgrad. in English; m. Irving Besen, Mar. 25, 1951 (div. 1978); children—Glenn, Allen. Exec. sec. Chgo. Ordnance Dist., War Dept., 1941-46, Aubrey, Moore & Wallace, Advt. Agy., Chgo., 1946; exec. sec. sales office McGraw-Hill Pub. Co., Chgo., 1947-51; exec. sec. Security Pacific Nat. Bank, Los Angeles, 1978—. Publicity chmn. Am Field Service, 1967-68; sec. Citizens Com for Good Govt., 1961; capt. United Crusade, Monterey Park, Calif., 1967—; publicity chmn. Monterey Park Art Assn., 1966-67, coor. sec., 1968, dir., 1965—, past pres., dir. newsletter, 1970—; chmn. Monterey Park Arts and Culture Com.; dir. in charge Bruggemeyer Library Shows, 1973-74; dep. registrar voters Calif. State U., Los Angeles, 1971-74; 3d v.p. in charge publicity Community Concerts Monterey Park; v.p. United Dem. Club of Monterey Park, 1988—. Recipient Top award Alhambra Open Show, 1972. Mem. Nat. League Am. Pen Women (rec. sec., treas. 1961-65), LWV (sec. Alhambra chpt. 1971-73, pres. chpt. 1973-74, action chmn., publicity chmn. 1977-78, hospitality chmn. 1980—), Residents Assn. Monterey Park. Club: Northwestern U. Alumni So. Calif. (corr. sec. 1979-80). Home: 1540 Arriba Dr Monterey Park CA 91754

BESHAR, CHRISTINE, lawyer; b. Paetzig, Germany, Nov. 6, 1929; came to U.S., 1952, naturalized, 1957; d. Hans and Ruth (vonKleist-Retzow) von Wedemeyer; m. Robert P. Beshar, Dec. 20, 1953; children: Cornelia, Jacqueline, Frederica, Peter. Student, U. Hamburg, 1950-51, U. Tuebingen, 1951-52; B.A., Smith Coll., 1953. Bar: N.Y. 1960, U.S. Supreme Ct. 1971. Assoc. firm Cravath, Swaine & Moore, N.Y.C., 1964-70; partner Cravath, Swaine & Moore, 1971—. Bd. dirs. Catalyst for Women Inc., 1977—; trustee Colgate U., 1978-84, Smith Coll., 1987—. Inst. Internat. Edn. fellow, 1952-53; recipient Disting. Alumnae medal Smith Coll., 1974. Fellow Am. Coll. Probate Counsel, Am. Bar Found. (sec., treas.); mem. Assn. of Bar of City of N.Y. (exec. com. 1973-75, v.p. 1985-86), N.Y. State Bar Assn. (ho. of dels. 1971-80, v.p. 1979-80), N.Y.C. Bar Found. (bd. dirs. 1977—), UN Assn. (bd. dirs. 1975-89), Fgn. Policy Assn. (bd. dirs. 1978-87). Presbyterian. Clubs: Downtown Assn., Cosmopolitan, Gipsy Trail. Home: 120 East End Ave New York NY 10028 Office: Cravath Swaine & Moore 1 Chase Manhattan Pl New York NY 10005 also: Stone House Farm Box 533 Somers NY 10589

BESHEARS, LYDIA JEAN, hospital executive; b. New Orleans, Sept. 21, 1945; d. Milton Eliot and Edna Ruth (Patterson) Landry; m. Earl Dixon Beshears, Jan. 13, 1968; 1 child, Aaron. BA in Govt., U. New Orleans, 1967; postgrad., young execs. program U. N.C., 1986. Personnel analyst civil svc. City of New Orleans, 1967-68; employment interviewer/counsellor N.C. Employment Security Commn., Durham, 1968-70; pers. analyst, asst. dir. U. N.C., Chapel Hill, 1971-80; asst. mgr. pers. Nash Gen. Hosp., Rocky Mount, N.C., 1980-81, mgr. pers., 1981-89; dir. human resources Am. Social Health Assn., Research Triangle Park, N.C., 1989—; cons. VIP Mgmt. Svcs., Durham, 1980. Precinct committeewoman, state and dist. del., Durham County Dem. Com., 1971-74; mem. exec. com. Parkwood Elem. Sch. PTA, Durham, 1974, Parkwood Athletic Assn., 1974. Mem. N.C. Hosp. Pers. Assn. (rep. dist. VI 1986-87), Am. Hosp. Pers. Assn., Rocky Mount Area Pers. Assn. (sec.-treas. 1984, v.p. 1985, pres. 1986), Rocky Mount C. of C. (legis. com. 1985-86), Am. Soc. Pers. Adminstrn., Luncheon Pilot Club Rocky Mount (historian 1985). Methodist.

BESONEN, JOANNE FRANCES, purchasing consultant; b. Somerville, Mass., July 21, 1946; d. Leo Joseph and Rose Marie (Costa) Fava; m. David Eino Besonen, Apr. 21, 1968; children—David M., Mark R., Amy E., Mara R., Matthew P., Rachel M. Student, Regis Coll. Sales team leader Avon Products Inc., Ayer, Mass., 1975-77; br. office clk. Army and Air Force Exchange Service, Ayer, 1976; asst. to sales/service mgr. John E. Cain Co., Ayer, 1976-77; purchasing agt. Scopus Corp., Lowell, Mass., 1978-81; contract buyer Network Personnel, Billerica, Mass., 1983-84; sr. buyer NETCO Automation, Haverhill, Mass., 1984-86; buyer M/A-COM, Inc., Burlington, Mass., 1986-88; ind. purchasing cons., 1988; purchasing agent MAST Microwave, 1988—. Mem. PTO, South Row Sch., Chelmsford, Mass., 1980—. Mem. Nat. Assn. Purchasing Mgmt., Nat. Assn. Female Execs., Purchasing Mgmt. Assn. Boston. Democrat. Roman Catholic. Avocations: cooking, knitting, crocheting, aerobics, biking. Address: 55 Billerica Rd Chelmsford MA 01824

BESSELL, IRIS KAREN, theatre managing director; b. Bklyn., Jan. 5, 1948; d. Jerome J. and Jeanette J. (Sova) Cohen; m. Frank D. Bessell, Dec. 21, 1973; 1 child, Norma Rose. BA, Syracuse U., 1970. Mng. dir. Berkshire Pub. Theatre, Pittsfield, Mass., 1976—. Office: Berkshire Pub Theatre 30 Union St Pittsfield MA 01201

BEST, DIANA RAMSBOTTOM, financial planner; b. Memphis, May 10, 1962; d. William David Ramsbottom and Betty Ann (Moseley) Luce; m. Peter Bennett Best, Aug. 29, 1987. BS, Clemson U., 1984. Cert. fin. planner. Acct. R&B Enterprises, L.A., 1985-87, Calmark Properties, L.A., 1987-88; fin. planner IDS Fin. Svcs., Inc., L.A., 1988—; writer, journalist Brentwood (Calif.) Bla-Bla, 1989. Mem. homeless com. Jr. League L.A., 1987, pub. issues advocate, 1988, com. treas., 1989, asst. treas., 1990; mem. Ocean Park Community Orgn., Santa Monica, Calif., 1989. Mem. Internat. Assn. Fin. Planners, NAFE, Internat. Bd. Cert. Fin. Planners. Republican. Presbyterian. Office: IDS Fin 11835 W Olympic Blvd 900E Los Angeles CA 90064

BEST, ELIZABETH ALLAIRE, lawyer, rancher; b. Louisville, June 12, 1956; d. Francis John and Helene Torrey (McPhail) Allaire; m. Michael Joseph Best, Aug. 30, 1980; children: Matthew, Sydney. BA, Mont. State U., 1978; JD, U. Mont., 1981. Bar: Mont. 1981, U.S. Dist. Ct. Mont. 1981. Law clk. to presiding justice U.S. Dist. Ct. Mont., Great Falls, 1984-85; ptnr. Lynch & Best, Great Falls, 1985-89; prin. Best Law Offices, Great Falls, 1989—. Bd. dirs. Western Found. for Clin. Rsch., Great Falls, 1988—. Capt. U.S. Army, 1981-84. Mem. Mont. Bar Assn., Trial Lawyers Assn. Am., Mont. Trial Lawyers Assn., Am. Quarter Horse Assn., Mont. Reining Horse Assn. Unitarian. Office: Best Law Offices 410 Central Ave Strain Bldg Ste 514 Great Falls MT 59403

BEST, PATRICIA MARIE, office manager, legal secretary; b. Mpls., July 25, 1953; d. Warren Andrew and Margaret Augusta (Nelson) Franke; m. Robert William Best, Apr. 6, 1974 (div. Feb. 1989); children: Jennifer Lynn, Cory William. Student, North Hennepin Community Coll., Brooklyn Park, Minn., 1989—. Sec. Fariview Hosp., Mpls., 1972-74; legal sec. General Mills Corp., Mpls., 1975-80; ind. daycare provider Mpls., 1980-83; legal sec. Curtis Homes, Inc., Mpls., 1983-85; legal sec., adminstrv. asst. Rerat Law Firm, Mpls., 1985-89; office mgr., legal sec. Eckman, Collins, Strandness & Egan, Mpls., 1989—. Mem. NAFE.

BESTDORF, ELLEN BELL, plumbing and heating company executive; b. Columbus, Ohio, Dec. 21, 1915; d. Randolph Murray and Ella Florence (Bell) Ronk; m. Jack Orus Bostdorf, Oct. 9, 1937; 1 child, Wendy Ann Bostdorf Novotny. BA, BSc in Edn., Bowling Green State U., 1936. Co-owner JackBostdorf Plumbing & Heating, Bowling Green, Ohio. Mem. AAUW, Am. Bus. Women's Assn., Friends Wood County Pub. Libr., Bowling Green Woman's Club. Presbyterian. Home: 322 N Grove St Bowling Green OH 43402

BESTEHORN, UTE WILTRUD, librarian; b. Cologne, Fed. Rep. of Germany, Nov. 6, 1930; came to U.S., 1930; d. Henry Hugo and Wiltrud Lucie (Vincentz) B. BA, U. Cin., 1954, BEd, 1955, MEd, 1958; MS in Library Sci., Western Res. U. (now Case-Western Res. U.), 1961. Tchr. Cutter Jr. High Sch., Cin., 1955-57; tchr., supr. library Felicity (Ohio) Franklin Sr. High Sch., 1959-60; librarian sci. dept. Pub. Library Cin. and Hamilton County, 1961-78, librarian info. desk, 1978—; textbook selection com., Felicity-Franklin Sr. High Sch., 1959-60; supr. Health Alcove Sci. Dept. and annual health lectures, Cin. Pub. Library, 1972-77. Book reviewer Library Jour., 1972-77; author and inventor Rainbow 40 marble game, 1971,

Condominium game, 1976; patentee indexed packaging and stacking device, 1973, mobile packaging and stacking device, 1974. Mem. Clifton Town Meeting, 1988—; mem. Bookfest 90 com. Pub. Libr. Cin. and Hamilton County. Recipient Cert. of Merit and Appreciation Pub. Library of Cin., 1986. Mem. Cin. Chpt. Spl. Libraries Assn. (archivist 1963-64, 65-70, editor Queen City Gazette bull. 1964-69), Pub. Library Staff Assn. (exec. bd., activities com. 1965, welfare com. 1966, recipient Golden Book 25 yr. service pin, 1986), Friends of the Library, Greater Cin. Calligraphers Guild (reviewer New Letters pub. 1986—), Delta Phi Alpha (nat. German hon. 1951). Republican. Mem. United Ch. of Christ. Home: 3330 Morrison Ave Cincinnati OH 45220 Office: Pub Libr Cin 800 Vine St Cincinnati OH 45202

BESTER, HESTER, accountant; b. Ventersburg, Orange F., South Africa, Mar. 26, 1945; came to U.S., 1988; d. Willem Adolph and Anna Elizabeth (Landman) Crous; m. Dirk Jacobus A. Bester, May 15, 1965 (div. Apr. 1975); children: Dirk Jacobus Adriaan, Annelize, Carine. B of Commerce, U. South Africa, 1981. CPA. Apprenticeship to sr. auditor Reay Lee, Vernon Lee CPAs, Ladysmith, Natal, South Africa, 1973-80; asst. to group acct. Bayer Pharmaceuticals, Johannesburg, South Africa, 1980-81; sr. tech. Price Waterhouse, Vancouver, Can., 1981-83; acctg. cons. to acct. Homestake Mining Co., Vancouver, 1984-88; acctg. mgr. M.C. Gill Corp., El Monte, Calif., 1988—. Dutch Reformed Ch. Office: MC Gill Corp 4056 Easy St El Monte CA 91731

BESTON, ROSE MARIE, college president; b. South Portland, Maine, Sept. 27, 1937; d. George Louis and Edith Mae (Archibald) Beattie; m. John Bernard Beston, Feb. 1, 1970. B.A., St. Joseph's Coll., 1961; M.A., Boston Coll., 1963; Ph.D., U. Pitts., 1967; Cert. of Advanced Study, Harvard U., 1978. Mem. faculty St. Joseph's Coll., Maine, 1967-70, U. Queensland and Western Australian Inst. Tech., 1970-76, Western Australian Inst. Tech., 1970-76, U. Hawaii, Manoa, 1976-77; assoc. acad. dean Worcester (Maine) State Coll., 1978-80; dean for acad. affairs Castleton (Vt.) State Coll., 1980-84; pres. Nazareth Coll. of Rochester, N.Y., 1984—; bd. dirs. Council of Ind. Colls., Ind. Coll. Fund of N.Y., Nat. Assn. Ind. Colls. and Univs., Commn. Ind. Colls. and Univs. Contbr. articles to profl. jours. Bd. dirs. United Way of Rochester; bd. govs. Genesee Hosp., Rochester. Mem. AAUW, Mediaeval Acad. Am., Assn. Commonwealth Lang. and Literature Studies, Rochester C. of C. (trustee 1985—), Phi Delta Kappa. Clubs: Harvard (N.Y.C.); Oak Hill Country (Rochester); Genesee Valley. Office: Nazareth Coll 4245 East Ave Rochester NY 14610

BESZTERCZEY, LESLEY MARGARET, bank holding company executive; b. Otley, Eng., Mar. 14, 1945; came to U.S., 1979; d. John Geoffrey Jim and Kathleen Mary (Clapham) Scott; m. Akos Csaba Beszterczey, Aug. 17, 1968; children: Sara, Stephen. BE, McGill U., 1966; MS in Acctg., Northeastern U., Boston, 1982. CPA, Mass. Tchr. math. pub. schs., Montreal, Que., Can., 1966-67, 69-73, Hull, Que., 1967-69; mem. audit staff Arthur Young & Co., Boston, 1982, mem. tax staff, 1983-85; corp. tax dir., v.p. Multibank Fin. Corp., Dedham, Mass., 1985—. Mem. AICPA, Mass. Soc. CPAs, Tax Execs. Inst., Delta Kappa Gamma, Beta Gamma Sigma. Home: 47 Pioneer Rd Hingham MA 02043

BETHEL, JEANNE ANITA, drug abuse program administrator; b. Spur, Tex., May 4, 1942; d. Vody Odell and Arlie E. (Bowen) Holly; m. Howard Bethel (div. 1988); children: Tasia Robinson, Ronnie, Howk. BA in Sociology, U.T.P.B., 1987. Cert. social work. Caseworker Dept. Human Svcs., Odessa, Tex., 1984-85, 87-88, Teen Challenge, Odessa, 1989-90; program dir. Clover House, Odessa, 1990—. Vol. Teen Challenge, Odessa, 1989—. Republican. Baptist. Home: 6141 Denis Ln A6 Odessa TX 79762 Office: Clover House 700 N Dixie Odessa TX 79761

BETHUNE, ZINA, actress, dancer, choreographer; b. N.Y., Feb. 17, 1950; d. William Charles and Ivy (Vigder) B.; m. Sean Feeley, Dec. 27, 1975. Grad. high sch., N.Y.C. Artistic dir., choreographer, performer Bethune Theatredanse, L.A., 1980—; head sound technician Paradigm Prodns., N.Y.C., assoc. producer. Actress TV soap opera The Guilding Light, 1956, TV series The Nurses, 1964-67, film Who's That Knocking at My Door, 1969, Nutcracker: Money, Madness, Murder, 1987; dancer Broadway show Most Happy Fella, Nutcracker, N.Y.C., 1957, N.Y.C. Ballet, 1965-69, Royal Danish Symphony, Arhus, Denmark, 1979; singer, actress (stage) Carnival, Chgo., 1967; dancer, singer (stage) Sweet Charity, 1969-70; choreographer (stage) The Trials of Saint Joan, 1986, Mind's Eye-Year 2031, 1988; dance, choreograher (stage, video) The Rose, 1987; dirs., choreographer (video) Cradle of Fire, 1988. Dance tchr. for disabled children Dance Outreach, L.A., 1983—. Recipient 2 citation awards Mayor of N.Y.C., 1965, 69, 2 proclamation awards, 1985, 89, Cece Robinson's Humanitarian award, L.A., 1986. Mem. SAG, AFTRA, Actors Equity Assn. Democrat. Office: Bethune Theatredanse 8033 Sunset Blvd Ste 221 Los Angeles CA 90046

BETROS, JOANNE, government official; b. Gt. Barrington, Mass., May 7, 1959; d. George Edward and Samia (Choueri) B. BA, Bostn Coll., 1981. Cert. tchr., Mass. Office mgr. Creative Gourmets, Ltd., Boston, 1981-89; confidential asst. U.S. Dept. Edn., Washington, 1989—. Fundraiser Fund for Am.'s Future, Boston, 1987, Bush-Quayle Campaign, Boston, 1988. Republican. Roman Catholic. Home: 5601 Derby Ct Apt 201 Alexandria VA 22311 Office: US Dept Edn 555 New Jersey Ave Rm 300M Washington DC 20208

BETROSOFF, PAMELA ANNE, military career officer; b. Detroit, July 15, 1950; d. Theodore Louis and Martha Marie (Nordstrom) Cogut; children: Tessa A., Sean L. BS in Vocat. Indsl. Edn., U. Md., 1976; student, Mich. State U., East Lansing, 1969-71; MS, Troy (Ala.) State U., 1986. Commd. 2d lt. USAF, 1980, advanced through grades to capt., 1984; chief cargo ops., reports and systems div. 22d Air Force, Travis AFB, Calif., 1989-90; chief support div. directorate transp. Hdqrs USAF Res., Robins AFB, Ga., 1990—; lectr. Clifton-Morenci (Ariz.) Rotary Club, 1989. Co-dir. Siddha Yoga Dham of Am., Bitburg, 1976-78; soccer team coord. Am. Youth Assn., RAF Laken Heath, Eng., 1983; troop leader Girl Scouts U.S., RAF Laken Heath, 1982; membership chmn. Boy Scouts Am., RAF Laken Heath, 1983. U. Md. scholar, 1976. Mem. Nat. Def. Transp. Assn., Air Force Assn. (life), Alpha Sigma Lambda.

BETSCH, MADELINE, advertising executive; b. N.Y.C.. Edu. Hunter Coll., N.Y.C., Harvard U. Account exec. Dancer-Fitzgerald-Sample, Inc., N.Y.C., 1963-69; account exec. Knox-Reeves, Mpls., 1970-71; v.p., mktg. dir. Langyn Labs., Potomac, Md., 1971-73; exec. v.p. Campbell Mithun Inc., Mpls., 1973—; dir. client svcs. Campbell-Mithun-Esty (formerly Campbell-Mithun Advertising), Mpls., 1976—, now exec. v.p. Bd. dirs. Girl Scouts Am., 1985, YWCA, 1989—; mem. Womens Econ. Roundtable. Office: Campbell-Mithun-Esty 222 S 9th St Minneapolis MN 55402

BETT, ARLENE MARCY, medical librarian; b. Bklyn., Aug. 28, 1962; d. Arnold Norman and Lila (Mendelsohn) B. BS in Health Scis., SUNY, Cortland, N.Y., 1983; postgrad., CUNY, Queens, N.Y., 1985—. Libr. asst. Mem. Sloan-Kettering Cancer Ctr., N.Y.C., 1983-84; libr. Nat. Multiple Sclerosis Soc., N.Y.C., 1984-86; med. libr. Klemtner Advt., N.Y.C., 1986—. Mem. Med. Libr. Assn., Spl. Libr. Assn. Office: Klemtner Advt 375 Hudson St New York NY 10014

BETTERIDGE, FRANCES CARPENTER, lawyer, mediator; b. Rutherford, N.J., Aug. 25, 1921; d. James Dunton and Emily (Atkinson) Carpenter; m. Albert Edwin Betteridge, Feb. 5, 1949 (div. 1975); children: Anne, Albert Edwin, James, Peter. A.B., Mt. Holyoke Coll., 1942; J.D., N.Y. Law Sch., 1978. Bar: Conn. 1979, Ariz. 1982. Technician in charge blood banks Roosevelt Hosp., N.Y.C. and Mountainside Hosp., Montclair, N.J., 1943-49; substitute tchr. Greenwich High Sch. (Conn.), 1978-79; intern and asst. to labor contracts office Town of Greenwich, 1979-80; vol. referee Pima County Juvenile Ct.,c Tucson, 1981-85, judge Pro Tempore Pima County Justice Cts., 1988—; bd. dirs. Fenster Sch. So. Ariz., Tucson; sole practice immigration law, Tucson, 1982-87; commr. Juvenile Ct., Pima County Superior Ct., Tucson, 1985-87; hearing officer Small Claims Ct., Pima County Justice Cts., Tucson, 1982; mediator Family Crisis Svc., Tucson, 1982-85. Pres. High Sch. PTA, Greenwich, 1970, PTA Council, 1971; mem. Greenwich Bd. Edn., 1971-76, sec., 1973-76; com. chmn. LWV Tucson, 1981, bd. dirs., 1984-85; bd. dirs., sec. Let The Sun Shine Inc., Tucson, 1981—; vol. referee Pima County Superior Ct., 1981-85. Mem. ABA, Conn. Bar Assn., Ariz. Bar Assn., Pima County Bar Assn., Ariz. Women Lawyers Assn., Point o'Woods Club. Republican. Congregationalist. Home and Office: 5320 N Campbell Ave Tucson AZ 85718

BETTIN, JANENE EDNA, real estate broker; b. Schaller, Iowa, Nov. 11, 1943; d. Robert A. and Edna (Harris) Bath; m. Thomas L. Bettin, June 20, 1964; 1 child, Christopher. Student U. No. Iowa, 1961; B.S., Tex. A&I U., 1965. Grad. Realtors Inst.; cert. residential residential brokerage mgr. Tchr. high sch., Corpus Christi, Tex., 1965-70; tchr. Village Acad., Mt. Lebanon, Pa., 1973-76; broker, assoc. Re/Max Metro Properties, Inc., Denver, 1977-86; broker, br. mgr. Perry & Butler, Littleton, Colo., 1986-89; broker Van Schaack Residential Realty, Inc., 1989—; broker, owner Prime Properties, Englewood, Colo., 1989—. Chmn. Blood Bank, South Suburban Bd. Realtors, 1980, chmn. Schs. Com., 1980; pres. South Suburban Bd. Realtors, 1985-86. Bd. dirs., officer Bristol Cove Homeowners Assn., Littleton, Colo., 1983; officer, treas. Arapahoe Youth League-Warriors, 1981. Mem. Realtors Nat. Mktg. Inst., Womens Coun. Realtors (pres. 1982-83), Colo. Assn. Realtors (instr. 1981—, dir. 1984, v.p. 1987), Cert. Residential Specialists (pres. Colo. chpt. 1984), Omega Tau Rho (nat. instr. 1985-86), Cert. Residential Brokerage Mgrs. (instr. 1986—). Republican. Methodist. Club: Mt. Lebanon Newcomers (pres. 1973-74). Home: 7540 S Cove Circle Littleton CO 80122

BETTS, ANN BRANTLY, sales executive; b. Nashville, Apr. 22, 1947; d. Samuel David and Isabel Annie (Livingstone) Brantly; m. Hugh Martin Brown, Apr. 29, 1972 (div. 1977); m. James Michael Betts, Aug. 11, 1984. BS in Edn., Austin Peay State U., 1969. Teller First Tenn. Nat. Bank, Memphis, 1969-70; with Xerox Corp., Memphis, 1970-82; sales exec. Raytheon Data Systems, Dallas, 1982; maj. account sales trainer Panasonic Office Products, Dallas, 1982-84; dealer rep. Ricoh Corp., Austin, 1985-86; sales exec. OCE, Austin, 1986-87; dir. sales tng. and devel. The Hartford, Conn., 1987—. Republican. Presbyterian. Home: 6830 Constitution Ln Charlotte NC 28210 Office: The Hartford Hartford Pla Hartford CT 06115

BETTS, DORIS JUNE WAUGH, author, English language educator; b. Statesville, N.C., June 4, 1932; d. William Elmore and Mary Ellen (Freeze) Waugh; m. Lowry Matthews Betts, July 5, 1952; children: Doris LewEllyn, David Lowry, Erskine Moore II. Student, Woman's Coll., U. N.C., 1950-53, U. N.C., 1954; DLitt (hon.), Greensboro Coll., 1987. Newspaperwoman Statesville Daily Record, 1950-51, Chapel Hill (N.C.) Weekly and News-Leader, 1953-54, Sanford Daily Herald, 1956-57; editorial staff N.C. Democrat, newspaper, 1961-62; editor Sanford (N.C.) News Leader, 1962; lectr. creative writing, English dept. U. N.C., Chapel Hill, 1966—; dir. Freshman-Sophomore English U. N.C., 1972-76, assoc. prof., 1974-78, prof., 1978—, Alumni Disting. prof., 1983—, dir. Fellows program, 1975-76, asst. dean Honors program, 1979-81, chmn. faculty, from 1983; vis. lectr. creative writing Duke U., 1971; staff Ind. U. Summer Writers Conf., 1972, 73; mem. bd. Asso. Writing Programs; mem. lit. panel Nat. Endowment for Arts, 1979-81, chmn., 1981. Author: story collections The Gentle Insurrection, 1954, Beasts of the Southern Wild, 1973; novel Tall Houses in Winter, 1957 (Sir Walter Raleigh award for best fiction by Carolinian 1957), Scarlet Thread (Sir Walter Raleigh award 1965), The Astronomer & Other Stories, 1966, The River to Pickle Beach, 1972, Heading West, 1981; Contbr. stories collections, anthologies.; Editor: Young Writer at Chapel Hill, 1968. Dramatized version of The Ugliest Pilgrim appear as Violet (recipient Acad. Award, Tex. Film Festival award). Mem. N.C. Tercentenary Commn., 1961-62, Sanford City Sch. Bd., 1965-71. Recipient short story prize Mademoiselle mag., booklength fiction prize G. P. Putnam-U. N.C., 1954; N.C. medal for lit., 1975, John Dos Passos award, 1983, medal of merit in short story div. Am. Acad. Arts and Letters, 1989; Guggenheim fellow, 1958-59. Mem. N.C. Writers Assn. Office: U NC Dept English 230 Greenlaw Hall 066A Chapel Hill NC 27514

BETTS, MARY AVIS, marketing professional; b. Euclid, Ohio, Jan. 21, 1959; d. William Patrick and Correan Catherine (Flack) Mulhern; m. Thomas Alan Betts, Nov. 27, 1982. BS in Chem. Engring., Purdue U., 1980. Sales rep. Nalco Chem. Co., Concord, Calif., 1980-82; chem. engr. Marmac Engring., Bakersfield, Calif., 1983; v.p. sales and mktg. biotech. group Monitek Techs., Inc., Hayward, Calif., 1984—. Mem. Am. Inst. Chem. Engrs., Soc. Women Engrs. Office: Monitek Techs Inc 1495 Zephyr Ave Hayward CA 94544

BETTS, SUSAN JEANNETTE, optometrist; b. Seaford, Del., Apr. 10, 1955; d. Arthur Dean and Rosemary Cecila (DiPaula) B. BS, Va. Poly. Inst., 1977, Pa. Coll. Optometry, 1978; OD, Pa. Coll. Optometry, 1981. Lic. optometrist, Del., Md., Pa. Pvt. practice Berwyn Heights, Md., 1981-82, Seaford, 1982—; chmn. regional bd. Second Nat. Bank, Salisbury, Md. Com. woman Sussex County Dem. Com., Georgetown, Del., 1982—; bd. dirs. Del. Music Sch., Milford, 1987—; tchr. Confraternity of Christian Doctrine Our Lady of Lourdes Ch., Seaford, 1982—; active city planning com., Seaford, 1989; mem. environ. com., Seaford, 1990—. Recipient Athena award, 1990. Mem. Am. Optometric Assn., Del. Optometric Assn., Bus. and Profl. Woman's Club, Seaford C. of C. (pres. 1988-90). Roman Catholic. Home: 205 Cedar Ln Seaford DE 19973 Office: 1100 Atlanta Rd Seaford DE 19973

BEU, MARJORIE JANET, music director; b. Elgin, Ill., Nov. 22, 1921; d. Herman Henry and Hattie Belle (Beverly) B. MusB, Am. Conservatory Music, 1949; B Musical Ed, 1949, M in Musical Ed., 1953; advanced cert. No. Ill. U., 1969; DEd, U. Sarasota, 1979. Music tchr. Sch. Dist. 21, Wheeling, Ill., 1961-64; music and fine arts coord., 1964-68, asst. supt. instrn., 1968-79; min. of music United Meth. Ch., Sun City Center, Fla., 1980—; dir. Sun City Ctr. Kings Point Community Chorus, 1984-89; pres. Council Study and Devel. Ednl. Resources, 1971-79. Pres., Wheeling Community Concerts Assn.; dir. Community Chorus; pres. Sun City Center Concert Series. Mem. NEA, Am. Guild Organists and Choir Dirs., Music Educators Nat. Conf., Assn. Supervision and Curriculum Devel., Ill. Edn. Assn., Ill. Council Gifted, No. Ill. Assn. Ednl. Research, Evaluation and Devel. (pres.), Mu Phi Epsilon, Phi Delta Kappa (sec. N.W. Suburban Cook County chpt.), Kappa Delta Pi (pres. also counselor alumni com.). Home: 610 Fort Duquesna Dr Sun City Center FL 33563

BEUERLEIN, SISTER JULIANA, hospital administrator; b. Lawrenceburg, Tenn., June 19, 1921; d. John Adolph and Sophia (Held) B. R.N., St. Joseph's Sch. Nursing, Chgo., 1945; BS in Edn., DePaul U., 1947; MS in Nursing Edn., Marquette U., 1954; postgrad., St. Louis U., 1966-69. Operating room supr. St. Joseph's Hosp., Alton, Ill., 1945-48; dir. sch. of nursing and nursing svc. Providence Hosp., Waco, Tex., 1948-56, St. Joseph's Hosp., Chgo., 1956-62; asst. adminstr. St. Joseph's Hosp., 1962-63; adminstrv. asst. St. Mary's Hosp., Evansville, Ind., 1963-65; adminstr. St. Mary's Hosp., 1965-73, pres. governing bd., 1965-73; adminstr. St. Joseph Hosp., Chgo., 1973-81; pres. governing bd. St. Joseph Hosp., 1973-75; adminstr. St. Thomas Hosp., Nashville, 1981-89, Providence Hosp., Southfield, Mich., 1989—; Mem. governing bd. St. Vincent's Hosp., Indpls., 1969-73; mem. governing bd. St. Mary's Hosp., Milw., 1974-75, chmn., 1978-79; mem. governing bd. Providence Hosp., Southfield, Mich., 1975-78, chmn. governing bd., 1977-78; mem. Chgo. Health Systems Agy., 1976-79; mem. governing bd. DePaul Community Health Ctr., Bridgeton, Mo., 1980—, St. Thomas Hosp., Nashville, Hubbard Hosp., Nashville; pres. governing bd. St Vincent Hosp., Birmingham, Ala.; mem. Am. Hosp. Assn. Commn. on Nursing, 1980—. Mem. bd. dirs. St. Mary's Med. Ctr., Evansville, Ind., Middle Tenn. Med. Ctr., Murfreesboro. Fellow Am. Coll. Hosp. Adminstrs. (com. on elections); mem. Cath., Tenn. Hosp. Assns., Nasville C. of C. (bd. dirs.). Office: Providence Hosp Found 22255 Greenfield Rd Ste 228 Southfield MI 48075

BEUGEN, JOAN BETH, communications company executive; b. Chgo., Mar. 9, 1943; d. Leslie and Janet (Glick) Caplan; B.S. in Speech, Northwestern U., 1965; m. Sheldon Howard Beugen, July 16, 1967. Founder, prin., pres. The Creative Establishment, Inc., Chgo., N.Y.C., San Francisco and Los Angeles, 1969-87, founder, pres. Cresta Communications Inc., Chgo. 1988—; speaker on entrepreneurship for women. Del., White House Conf. on Small Bus., 1979; vice-chmn. Ill. Del. to White House Conf., 1979; trustee Mt. Sinai Hosp. Med. Ctr.; bd. dirs. Chgo. Network; bd. dirs. Chgoland. Enterprise Ctr. Recipient YWCA Leadership award, 1985; named Entrepreneur of Yr., Women in Bus. Mem. Nat. Assn. Women Bus. Owners (pres. Chgo. chpt. 1979), Ill. Women's Agenda, Chgo. Assn. Commerce and Industry, Midwest Soc. Profl. Cons., Chgo. Audio-Visual Producers Assn., Chgo. Film Council, Women in Film, Com. of 200, Nat. Women's Forum, Overseas Edn. Fund Women in Bus. Com. Contbr. articles in field to profl. jours. Office: Cresta Communications Inc 11 W Delaware Pl Chicago IL 60610

BEUTLER, ABIGAIL ELAINE, engineering executive, flight instructor; b. Boston, Apr. 21, 1930; d. Moses and Ida (Levinson) Caplan; children: Arthur David, Kathryn Ruth Beutler Peterson, Michael Ernest. BA, Radcliffe Coll., 1950; MEd, Boston U., 1951; MS, U. Mich., 1960, Stanford U., 1965. Rsch. physicist U. Mich., Ann Arbor, 1961-69; mem. tech. staff Lincoln Lab. MIT, Lexington, Mass., 1969-78; asst. staff engr. Pontiac Motor Co. div. Gen. Motors, Detroit, 1978-82; program mgr. Gen. Electric Co., Syracuse, N.Y., 1982-88; mgr. advanced programs Gen. Electric Co., Utica, N.Y., 1988-90; asst. dept. head MITRE Corp., Bedford, Mass., 1990—; pres. Abby Aero Inc., 1980-90; bd. dirs. Nat. Aviation Purchasing Group, St. Louis. Amelia Earhart fellow Zonta Internat., 1964-65. Mem. Soc. Women Engrs. (sr.), Nat. Assn. Flight Instrs., Aircraft Owners and Pilots Assn. Home: 7 Hammar Rd Nashua NH 03062 Office: MITRE Corp Burlington Rd Bedford MA 01730

BEVEL, CHRISTINE MACDONALD, small business owner; b. L.A., Sept. 27, 1944; m. Gerald MacDonald (dec.) children: Holly, Tobby Scott; m. Norman W. Bevel, Apr. 5, 1980. Student, Sawyer Bus. Coll., 1963; cert., UCLA, 1984; postgrad., Calif. Pacific U., San Diego, 1989—. Cert. tchr. Mgr. Cal Data Svcs., L.A., 1969-74; data control supr. O.R.C., Santa Monica, Calif., 1974-78; systems rep. Pertec Computer Co., L.A., 1978-81; sr. systems analyst Sperry Corp., San Diego, 1981-85; info. ctr. coord. IMED Corp., San Diego, 1985-86; customer supt. mgr. Sungard, 1986-88; ptnr. info. svcs., mgr. CNB Data Svcs., San Diego, 1988—; bd. dirs. seminars Kaleidoscope Presentations, San Diego, 1984-88. Mem. Info. Systems Mgmt. Republican. Home: 6250 Printwood Way San Diego CA 92117 Office: CNB Data Svcs 7710 Balboa Ave Ste 321 San Diego CA 92111

BEVERLAND, WANDA LOU, textile executive, consultant; b. Rising Sun, Ind., Mar. 17, 1941; d. Leslie Lyle and Hazel Marie (Welch) Silvers; m. Jerald Banks Beverland, Mar. 12, 1956; children: Robyn, Hope, Jeri Shaine, Shawn. Grad. high sch., Tampa, Fla. Sec. Beverland Enterprises, Inc., Oldsmar, Fla., 1968—; v.p. Beverland Enterprises, Inc., Oldsmar, 1987—; owner Wanda's Quilts, Oldsmar, 1980—; cons. and purchasing agt. in field. Author: Quilts-A Southern Legacy, 1989, Black American Folk Art Quilts, 1990. Mem. Better Bus. Bur. W. Fla., Inc., Greater Suncoast C. of C., Oldmar C. of C. Republican. Home: PO Box 250 Oldsmar FL 34677

BEVERLEY, JANE TAYLOR, artist; b. Columbus, Ohio, July 22, 1918; d. William Worland and Elsie Mary (Blum) Taylor; m. William Elmer Halley, Aug. 7, 1941 (dec. 1971); 1 Child, Hannah Jane Halley Denbow; m. George Treadgold Beverley, June 17, 1972 (dec. Dec. 1983); 1 stepson, George T. Beverley. BS in Social Adminstrn., Ohio State U., 1939. Statistician Ohio Dept. Pub. Welfare, Columbus, 1939-41; adminstrv. asst. Legis. Digest and Review, Columbus, 1954-71; custody mediator, court investigator Court of Domestic Relations, Columbus, 1971-86; freelance artist Columbus, 1986—; v.p. Ohio Correctional and Court Services 1980-82. Author: Report Ohio Sch. Survey Commission, 1955. Pres. Nat. Women's Party Ohio, 1956-60, Women's State Com. Ohio, 1961-62; bd. dirs. Ohio Sch. Survey Commn., 1953-55, Bexley Movie Bd. of Review. Mem. AAUW, Bexley Art Guild, Bexley Woman's Club (pres. 1989-90), Sigma Alpha Sigma (pres. 1938-39), Ladies Oriental Shrine (class pres. 1983). Republican. Methodist. Home and Office: 177 N Remington Rd Bexley OH 43209

BEVERLY, PATTY LIBBY, escrow officer; b. Glendale, Calif., Mar. 2, 1954; d. Alfred Forrest and Norma Irene (Mathias) Libby; m. Jim Edward Beverly, Jan. 1, 1982. AA, Fullerton Coll., 1978. Mgr. Calif. Escrow, La Habra, 1975-85, Park Escrow, Fullerton, Calif., 1985-88; owner, mgr. Carousel Escrow, Brea, Calif., 1988-90; mgr. Gold Country Escrow, Fullerton, 1990—. Contbr. articles to profl. publs. Mem. Am. Escrow Assn., Calif. Escrow Assn. (bd. dirs. 1987—, exec. com. 1990), Orange County Escrow Assn. (bd. dirs. 1986—, pres. 1989), North Orange County Bd. Realtors, Childhelp USA, Am. Soc. Interior Designers. Office: Gold Country Escrow 444 N State College Blvd Fullerton CA 92631

BEVERSDORF, ANNE ELIZABETH, technology sales and educational marketing consultant, small business owner; b. Houston, Tex., Aug. 14, 1949; d. S. Thomas and Norma (Beeson) B. BA, U. Tex., 1972; MLS, Ind. U., 1974. Founding librarian Social Studies Devel. Ctr. Ind. U., Bloomington, 1975-79, info. specialist Vocat. Edn. Services, 1982-83, info. dissemination specialist Devel. Tng. Ctr., 1983; librarian Agy. for Instructional TV, Bloomington, 1980-82; info. specialist Ind. Clearinghouse for Computer Edn., Indpls., 1983-86; Calif. mktg. rep. Minn. Ednl. Computing Corp., San Marcos, Calif., 1986-88; pres. Beversdorf Assocs. div. Imagmation Learning, Inc., Vista, Calif., 1988—; chief exec. officer Imagmation Learning, Inc., Vista, 1989—; conf. planner Ind. Council for the Social Studies, Bloomington, 1976-79; cons. Procter & Gamble Ednl. Services, Cin., 1981-85, Brazil Office of Tech. Edn., Rio de Janeiro, Porto Alegre, 1986; instr. Ind. U., Indpls., 1986; mem. faculty San Diego State U., 1988—. Editor computer newsletter; contbr. over 30 articles to profl. jours. Mem. Computer Using Educators, Computers and Social Edn., Women in Sales. Home: 1119 Anza Ave Vista CA 92084 Office: Beversdorf Assocs 956 Vale Terrace Dr Suite 204E Vista CA 92084

BEVINGTON, MARIETTE DE CORIOLIS, artist; b. Conway, N.H., Nov. 2, 1925; d. Harold and Therese (deCoriolis) Eastman Mudgett; m. Alistair Bevington, Nov. 2, 1955 (div. 1966); m. R. Leigh Glover, Sept. 15, 1968. Diploma, Cen. Sch. Art and Design, London, 1951-53; MS in Edn., Columbia U., 1973. Display designer The Interchurch Ctr., N.Y.C., 1967-87; lectr. design and techniquesof stained glass at various groups. One-man shows include Nat. Design Ctr., N.Y.C., 1962, annually in N.Y.C. and Westchester Galleries; featured craftsman Hudson River Mus., 1988; represented in corp. collections Readers Digest, R.H. Donnelly, BBDO and many pvt. collections; prin. works include Ch. St. Frances de Sales, Muskegon, Mich., First Presbyn., Franklin Lakes, N.J., Seaview Hosp., S.I., N.Y.; executed mosaic lobby mural Murry Bergtraum Sch., Pearl St., N.Y.C. Recipient award The Tiffany Found., 1962-63. Mem. Soc. N.Am. Goldsmiths, Am. Crafts Coun., Nat. League Am. Pen Women, Inc., Artist Craftsman N.Y. (bd. govs. 1960-66, hon. mention ann. shows), Fla. Soc. Goldsmiths, Hudson River Contemporary Artists (pres. 1975-76). Democrat. Home: 2145 Lemon Ave Englewood FL 34223

BEVIS, PATRICIA ANN, finance and marketing executive; b. Florence, Ala., May 9, 1955; d. G. Joe and Billie (Grisham) B. Ed., U. Ala., 1977, Smith Coll., 1977; cert., U. Paris Sorbonne, 1977. Buyer R.H. Macy's, N.Y.C., 1981-82; bank officer dept. mktg. Citibank, N.Y.C., 1982-83; fin. and mktg. analyst, asst. v.p. Shearson Lehman Hutton Co. (formerly E.F. Hutton Co., Inc.), N.Y.C., 1983-89, v.p., 1989; mgr. equity mktg. Merrill Lynch, N.Y.C., 1989—. Bd. dirs. Mary Anthony/Phoenix Dance Co.; mem. vol. coun. N.Y. Philharm. Symphony; vol. Bellevue Childlife Hosp. Recipient Outstanding Young Alumnae award U. Ala., 1982; named one of Outstanding Young Women Am., 1985. Mem. Panhellenic (rec. sec. 1980), U. Ala. Alumni Assn. (v.p. student affairs, v.p. alumni), N.Y. Jr. League, Fin. Women's Assn., Ptnrship. Analyst Soc. N.Y. (founder), Am. Crafts Mus. (co-chmn. docent com.), Am. Mktg. Assn., Smith Coll. Club (N.Y.C., co-treas., bd. dirs.), Am. Crafts Coun. (docent, com. chmn.), Mu Phi Epsilon, Alpha Delta Pi (pres. 1989-90, holder various offices, Outstanding Alumna). Episcopalian. Office: Merrill Lynch World Fin Ctr New York NY 10281-1203

BEXTERMILLER, THERESA MARIE, architect; b. St. Charles, Mo., Feb. 9, 1960; d. Charles Frederick and Loretta Joan (Unterreiner) B. BArch, Kans. State U., 1983; MFA in Computer Graphics, Pratt Inst., 1990. Intern Intratec Group, Inc., 1989; grad. architect Fleming Corp., St. Louis, 1984-85; project architect, prototype mgr. Casco Corp., St. Louis, 1985-87; architect HBE Corp., St. Louis, 1987-88, Hal A. Dorfman, N.Y.C.,

1988-89; freelance architect N.Y.C., 1989—. Mem. AIA, Assn. for Computing Machinery-Siggraph. Roman Catholic.

BEYER, BARBARA LYNN, aviation consultant; b. Miami, Fla., Feb. 16, 1947; d. Morten Sternoff and Jane (Hartman) B. BA, George Washington U., 1978. Supr. printing office Saudi Arabian Airlines, 1966-67; ops. coord. Modern Air Transport, Miami, Fla., 1968-70; acct. Modern Air Transport, Berlin, 1970-72; rep. Johnson Internat. Airlines, Washington, 1974-75; v.p., bd. dirs. Avmark, Inc., Washington, 1975-89, pres., 1989—; chmn., bd. dirs. Avmark Internat., London, 1985—; mng. dir. Avmark Asia Ltd., Hong Kong, 1988-89, also bd. dirs., chmn. bd. dirs., 1989—; pub. Avmark Aviation Economist, London, 1986—. Mem. Aviation Space Writers (award 1978, internat. bd. dirs. 1986-88), Nat. Bus. Aircraft Assn., Am. C. of C., Fgn. Corr. Club, Aero Club, Internat. Aviation Club. Office: Avmark Inc 1911 N Ft Myer Dr Arlington VA 22209

BEYER, CHARLOTTE BISHOP, investment management marketing executive; b. N.Y.C., Oct. 16, 1947; d. Edward Morton and Charlotte Reid (Handy) Beyer; B.A., Hunter Coll., 1969; m. Warren P. Weitman, Jr., July 28, 1967; children—Catherine Scott, Michael Benjamin. With Bankers Trust Co., N.Y.C., 1970-81, v.p. trust services and securities ops., 1979-81; dir. Can. mktg. Technimetrics, 1981-83; new bus./mktg. trust officer Fidelity Union Bank, Morristown, N.J., 1983-85; v.p. dir. client service and mktg. Wood Struthers and Winthrop Mgmt. Corp. subs. Donaldson Lufkin and Jenrette, N.Y.C., 1985-87, sr. v.p., 1987-89; v.p. Lazard Freres Asset Mgmt., N.Y.C., 1989—. Trustee Westover Sch., Middlebury, Conn., 1987—. Episcopalian.n., 1987—. Episcopalian. Office: Lazard Freres & Co 1 Rockefeller Pla New York NY 10020

BEYER, HEIDI BERYL, legal personnel consultant; b. N.Y.C., Feb. 13, 1964; d. Jacob Norton and Barbara Gail (Friedman) B. Student, Emerson Coll., 1982-83; BA in Organizational Commmunication, Ariz. State U., 1987. Talent agt. Premier Talent, Phoenix, 1985-88; legal search cons. Chosen Few Personnel, L.A., 1988—; casting agt. Film Showcases, Phoenix, 1987-88. Contbr. poetry to Salt River Anthology, 1985, Last Ditch, 1985, Hidalgo Trading Co., 1986. Mem. Mcpl. Elections Com. L.A., 1989-90; talent coord. cystic fibrosis event, Phoenix, 1988. Mem. Women in Communications, Beta Beta Gamma, Phi Kappa Delta (v.p. 1981-82). Democrat. Jewish. Home: 424 Ocean Park 2 Santa Monica CA 90405 Office: Chosen Few Personnel 911 Wilshire Blvd 1880 Los Angeles CA 90017

BEYER, JACQUELYN L., geography educator; b. Mitchell, S.D., July 11, 1924; d. Hayes Rutherford and Olive Grace (Garver) B.; B.A. in Journalism, U. Colo., Boulder, 1944, M.A. in Geography, 1954; Ph.D. in Geography, U. Chgo., 1957. Asst. prof. geography U. Mont., 1957-58, 59-60; vis. lectr. U. Tex., 1958-59; lectr. U. Cape Town (South Africa), 1960-64; asst. prof. Rutgers U., 1964-69; assoc. prof. U. Colo., Colorado Springs, 1970-73, prof., 1973—. Bd. dirs. Social Service Edn. Consortium. Served with AAF, U.S. Army, 1944-48, 52. Water Resources Research Inst. grantee, 1968-69. Mem. Assn. Am. Geographers, Nat. Council Geog. Edn., AAAS, African Studies Assn., Consortium on Peace Research, Edn. and Devel., Western African Studies Assn., Colo. Women Studies Assn., Soc. Woman Geographers. Contbr. chpts., articles to profl. publs. Office: U Colo Dept Geog & Environ Studies Colorado Springs CO 80933

BEYER, KAREN ANN, social worker; b. Cleve.; d. William and Evelyn Haynes; B.A., Ohio State U., 1965; M.S.W., Loyola U., Chgo., 1969; postgrad. Family Inst., Northwestern U., 1979. Diplomate Clin. Social Work; cert. employee assistance profl. With Cuyahoga County Div. Child Welfare, Cleve., 1965, Dallas County Child Welfare Unit, Dallas, 1966; with Luth. Welfare Svcs. Ill., Chgo., 1967-73; pvt. practice psychotherapy, family mediation, Schaumburg, Ill., 1975—; therapist Family Svcs. Assn. Greater Elgin (Ill.), 1973-77, bd. dir. profl. svcs., 1977-83; bd. dirs. HHS Village of Hoffman Estates, Ill., 1983—; fieldwork social work instr. for Loyola U., U. Ill., 1977-85. Bd. dirs. Talkline, 1982-85; mem. mental health adv. bd. Schaumburg Twp. Mem. Am. Assn. Pub. Adminstrs., Nat. Assn. Social Workers, Acad. Cert. Social Workers (clin. and approved supr.), Am. Assn. Marriage and Family Therapy. Unitarian.

BEYER, NORMA WARREN, educator; b. Bklyn., Dec. 1, 1926; d. Norman Hayden and Catherine Mary (Kline) Warren; m. Daniel Joseph Beyer, July 10, 1954; children: Catherine Norma, Daniel Joseph Jr., Peter Norman, Maureen Bernadette. BS, CUNY, Bklyn., 1949; MA in Edn., NYU, 1953. Investigator Nat. Bd. Fire Underwriters, N.Y.C., 1944-48; bridal cons. Best & Co., N.Y.C., 1948-50; tchr. home econs. N.Y.C. Bd. Edn., Bklyn., 1950—; pres. Norma Beyer Home Econs. Cons., East Meadow, N.Y., 1985—. Bd. dirs. Clearmeadow Civic Assn., East Meadow, 1985-88; pres. St. Brigid's Rosary Soc., Westbury, N.Y., 1987—. Recipient St. Pius award Diocese of Rockville Ctr., 1975, Leader's Gold medal Nassau County 4H, 1978. Mem. Am. Home Econs. Assn., N.Y.C. Home Econs. Assn. (historian 1978—), Cath. Tchrs. Assn., Bklyn. Coll., NYU Alumni Assn. Republican. Roman Catholic. Club: Salisbury Republican (Westbury). Home: 251 Clear Meadow Dr East Meadow NY 11554

BEYER, SONYA VON ZITZEWITZ, manufacturing executive; b. Chgo., Oct. 3, 1931; d. Arthur Frank and Sonya Anina (Kear) von Zitzewitz; m. Hal F. Beyer, Jr., Sept. 25, 1953 (dec. Mar. 1988); children: Teryl Ann Beyer Stanger, Hal F. Beyer III. Student, Colo. Coll., 1949-50, Northwestern U., 1950-51. Media dir. George Hartman Agy., Chgo., 1951-53; art dir. Plymouth Indsl. Products, Sheboygan, Wis., 1953-55; credit mgr. Midco Internat., Inc., Chgo., 1979-87, treas., 1984—, chmn. bd., pres., chief exec. officer, 1988—. Leader Girl Scouts U.S., Wilmette, Ill., 1962-70; area sec. Boy Scouts Am., Wilmette, 1966-77; area chmn. New Trier Rep. Orgn., Kenilworth, Ill., 1968—. Home: 1320 Ashland Ave Wilmette IL 60091 Office: Midco Internat Inc 4140 W Victoria St Chicago IL 60646

BEYER, SUZANNE, advertising agency executive; b. N.Y.C., Dec. 28, 1928; d. Harry and Jennie Hillman; student Nassau Community Coll., 1963-65; grad. Conservatory of Musical Art, N.Y.C., 1947; m. Isadore Beyer, Oct. 19, 1947; children—Pamela Claire, Hillary Jay. Singer, tchr. piano, N.Y.C., 1947-66; asst. to v.p. media dir. Robert E. Wilson, Advt., N.Y.C., 1967-72; media planner, media buyer Frank J. Corbett div. BBDO Internat., N.Y.C., 1972-77; media planner, media buyer Lavey/Wolff/Swift div. BBDO Advt., N.Y.C., 1977-80, sr. media planner, 1980-83, media supr., 1983—; soprano Opera Assn. Nassau, 1976—; soprano United Choral Soc., Woodmere, L.I., 1970—, Armand Sodero Chorale, Baldwin, L.I., 1980-86, Rockville Centre Choral Soc, 1986—. Mem. Pharm. Advt. Council, L.I. Advt. Club, Healthcare Bus. Women's Assn. Home: 66 Fonda Rd Rockville Centre NY 11570 Office: 488 Madison Ave New York NY 10022

BEYER-MEARS, ANNETTE, physiologist; b. Madison, Wis., May 26, 1941; d. Karl and Annette (Weiss) Beyer. B.A., Vassar Coll., 1963; M.S., Fairleigh Dickinson U., 1973; Ph.D., Coll. Medicine and Dentistry N.J., 1977. NIH fellow Cornell U. Med. Sch., 1963-65; instr. physiology Springside Sch., Phila., 1967-71; teaching asst. dept. physiology Coll. Medicine & Dentistry N.J., N.J. Med. Sch., 1974-77, NIH fellow dept. ophthalmology, 1978-80; asst. prof. dept. ophthalmology U. Medicine and Dentistry N.J., N.J. Med. Sch., Newark, 1979-85, asst. prof. dept. physiology, 1980-85, assoc. prof. dept. physiology, 1986—, assoc. prof. dept. ophthalmology, 1986—; cons. Alcon Labs. Contbr. articles in field of diabetic lens and kidney therapy to profl. jours. Chmn. admissions No. N.J., Vassar Coll., 1974-79; mem. minister search com. St. Bartholomew Episcopal Ch., N.J., 1978, fund-raising chmn., 1978, 79; del. Episc. Diocesian Conv., 1977, 78; long range planning com. Christ Ch., Ridgewood, N.J., 1985-87. Recipient NIH Nat. Rsch. Svc. award, 1978-80, Found. CMDNJ Rsch. award, 1980; grantee Juvenile Diabetes Found., 1985-87, NIH, NEI grantee, 1980—, Pfizer, Inc. grantee, 1985-87. Mem. Am. Physiol. Soc., N.Y. Acad. Scis., Soc. for Neurosci., Am. Soc. Pharmacology and Exptl. Therapeutics, Assn. for Rsch. Vision & Ophthalmology, Internat. Soc. for Eye Research, AAAS, The Royal Soc. Medicine, Internat. Diabetes Found., Am. Diabetes Assn., Aircraft Owners and Pilots Assn., Civil Air Patrol, Sigma Xi. Office: NJ Med Sch Dept Physiology 185 S Orange Ave Newark NJ 07103

BEYERS, PATRICIA JOAN, public relations executive; b. Pipestone, Minn.; d. Edwin F. Henry and Irene M. Feldman; children: Cheryl, Scott, Brendon, Cynthia. Editor, reporter, photographer Pipestone County Star, 1971-84; market rsch. interviewer, night supr. Quick Test Opinion Ctr., Burnsville, Minn., 1984-85; program mgr. Northfield (Minn.) Arts Guild, 1985; dir. Delaware County Econ. Devel. Commn., Manchester, Iowa, 1986-89, Granite Falls (Minn.) Community Devel., 1989—. Coun. mem. City of Pipestone; creator county tourism coun., 1986; active numerous leadership roles in community orgns. Recipient Minn. Newspaper Assn. award, 1981, Econ. Devel. award City of Manchester, 1987, Gov.'s Community Betterment Good Neighbor award, 1988. Mem. Iowa Profl. Developers, Backbone Area Tourism Coun., Ea. Iowa Tourism Assn., Pvt. Industry Coun., Pipestone C. of C., Mensa, Kiwanis, Toastmasters. Home: 817 7th St Granite Falls MN 56241

BEYERSDORF, MARGUERITE MULLOY, educator; b. Terry, Mont., Apr. 20, 1922; d. John William and Laura Agnes (Mahar) Mulloy; m. Curtis Alexander Beyersdorf, 1950; 1 child, Mary Jo Wright. Kindergarten-Primary Cert., Coll. St. Catherine, St. Paul, 1942; PhB, Marquette U., 1945; postgrad., Gonzaga U., Spokane, Wash., 1957-62, Ea. Wash. State U., 1977-79. Tchr. grade 3 Sacred Heart Sch., Oelwein, Iowa, 1942-43; tchr. grades 1 and 2 Jr. Mil. Acad., Chgo., 1943-45; tchr. history, English Fairfield (Wash.) High Sch., 1945-46; substitute tchr. Riverside High Sch., 1957; tchr. Mead (Wash.) Sch. Dist., 1958-75; owner/mgr. First Ave. Parking Lot, Spokane, Wash., 1975—. Vol. Spokane N.W. Communities Found., 1982—; active United Way of Spokane, 1950%; active ARC, Am. Cancer Soc., Multiple Sclerosis Soc., others; canteen vol. Spokane Blood Bank, 1981—; vol. Miryam's House of Transition, 1989—. Mem. AAUW. Address: 2923 S Howard St Spokane WA 99203-1717

BEZAIRE, HELEN DARLINE, hospital administrator; b. Grass Valley, Calif., Apr. 29, 1937; d. Alfred Edward and Emma (Louise) Reeves; m. Robert Donald Bezaire, Dec. 27, 1958; children: Diane Louise, Roland Edward. AA in Nursing, Pasadena (Calif.) City Coll., 1960; BA, Redlands (Calif.) U., 1975; MS in Healthcare Adminstr, Chapman U., 1984. Instr. staff devel. Huntington Meml. Hosp., Pasadena, 1970-75, inf. cont. practitioner, 1972-75; inf. cont. practitioner Sierra Nevada Meml. Hosp., Grass Valley, 1976-77, asst. dir. nursing svcs., 1977-81, asst. adminstr., dir. nursing svcs., 1981-89, v.p. patient care svcs., 1989—. Mem. adv. bd. Sierra Coll., Rocklin, Calif., 1981—. Recipient Profl. Activity award Soroptomists, 1982. Mem. Soc. Calif. Nurse Adminstrs., Soc. Sierra Women's Healthcare Execs., Soc. Sierra Nurse Adminstrs. (pres. elect. 1989), Calif. Nurses Assn. Republican. Roman Catholic. Home: 10227 Comerate Pl Grass Valley CA 95940 Office: Sierra Nev Meml Hosp 155 Glasson Way Grass Valley CA 95945

BEZIK, CYNTHIA BURNS, director of financial analysis; b. Youngstown, Ohio, Feb. 8, 1953; d. Paul A. and Beverly J. (Sutter) B.; m. Mark H. Bezik, Jan. 22, 1977 (div. May 1981. Assoc. in Applied Bus., Youngstown State U., 1972, BSBA, 1974; MBA, Case Western Reserve U., 1981. Cert. Mgmt. Acct. Sr. acct. Ernst & Whinney, Cleve., 1974-77; internal auditor AM Internat., Cleve., 1978; fin. asst. Pickands Mather & Co., Cleve., 1979-81, mgr. fin. analysis, dir. internal audit, fin. analysis, 1983-86; dir. internal control Cleve. Cliffs Inc., 1986-88, sr. fin. assoc., 1988--. Mem. The Planning Forum, Nat. Assn. Accts., Am. Soc. Women Accts. (Cleve. chpt.), Women's City Club. Office: Cleve Cliffs Inc 1100 Superior Ave Cleveland OH 44116

BHARATI, SAROJA, health facility administrator, educator, researcher; b. Madras, India; came to U.S., 1966; d. Raghuraja and Rajam Bharati. MD, Madras U., 1966. Assoc. dir. Congenital Heart Disease Rsch. and Tng. Ctr. Hektoen Inst., Chgo., 1976-82; chair dept. pathology Deborah Heart and Lung Ctr. Deborah Heart and Lung Ctr., Browns Mill, N.J., 1982-88; dir. Congenital Heart and Conduction System Ctr. Heart Inst. for Children of Christ Hosp. and Med. Ctr., Oak Lawn, Ill., 1988—; prof. pathology Presbyn.-St. Lukes Rush Med. Coll., Chgo. Author: (with others) Cardiac Surgery and the Conduction System, 1983; contbr. numerous articles to profl. jours. Fellow Am. Coll. Cardiology, Am. Coll. Chest Physicians; mem. N.Am. Soc. Pacing and Electrophysiology, Chgo. Med. Soc. (continuing med. edn. com. 1990—). Home: 950 N Michigan Ave #5302 Chicago IL 60611 Office: Congenital Heart and Conduction System Ctr 11745 SW Hwy Palos Heights IL 60463

BHATTACHARYA-CHATTERJEE, MALAYA, cancer research scientist; b. Cooch-Behar, India, Jan. 16, 1946; came to U.S., 1969; d. Nalini Nath and Kanak Prova (Chakravorty) Bhattacharya; m. Sunil Kumar Chatterjee, Oct. 25, 1972; children: Indranil, Sumana. BS, Presidency Coll., Calcutta, 1963; MS, Calcutta U. Coll. Sci., 1965, PhD, 1969. Postdoctoral fellow Roswell Park Cancer Inst., Buffalo, N.Y., 1969-71, cancer rsch. scientist III, 1971-79, cancer rsch. scientist IV, 1979—; asst. rsch. prof. exptl. pathology Grad. Study div. Roswell Park, 1990—; asst. rsch. prof. ob-gyn. SUNY, Buffalo, 1989—. Contbr. chpts. to books, articles to profl. jours. Grantee NIH, 1976-79, NSF, 1980-81, Am. Cancer Soc., 1983-86, Nat. Cancer Inst., 1989—. Mem. Am. Assn. for Cancer Rsch., Fedn. Am. Socs. for Exptl. Biology. Office: Roswell Park Cancer Inst Elm and Carlton Sts Buffalo NY 14263

BIAFORA, ROSANNE, marketing executive; b. Morgantown, W.Va., Apr. 2, 1962; d. Frank A. and Phyllis Sue (Robinson) B. BS in Pub. Relations, U. Fla., 1984; MBA, Nova U., 1988. Pub. relations asst. Shands Hosp., Gainesville, Fla., 1985, pub. relations specialist, 1985-87, coordinator mktg., communications, 1987-88; dir. mktg. Winter Park (Fla.) Pavilion, 1988-89; dir. pub. rels. Glenbeigh Hosp., Orlando, Fla., 1989—. Co-chmn. Am. Heart Assn., Gainesville, 1986, bd. dirs. 1986-88. recipient Best in East award Va. Soc. PRMC, Addy award, Gainesville Advt. Soc., 1986. Mem. Am. Hosp. Assn., Fla. Hosp. Assn., Nat. Assn. Female Execs., Fla. Pub. Relations Exec. Republican. Baptist. Office: Glenbeigh Hosp Orlando 7450 Sand Lake Commons Orlando FL 32819

BIAGGI, CRISTINA SHELLEY, sculptor; b. Lausanne, Switzerland, July 24, 1937; came to U.S., 1948; d. Leo Luciano Biaggi and Virginia Musser (Howard) Redmond; m. Clark Anderson (div. 1964); children: Diana Athena Green, John Clark. Student, Vassar Coll., 1955-57, U. Mexico City, Mexico, 1956, Harvard, 1957; BA in Classics, U. Utah, 1969; MA in Art Edn., NYU, 1975, PhD in Art and Philosophy, 1983. Dir. Spectrum Gallery, Rome, 1961-64; actress various cos., N.Y. and N.J., 1965-69; instr., gallery dir. Rockland Community Coll., Suffern, N.Y., 1972-80; costume and set designer Youth Shakespeare Theater, Palisades, N.Y., 1974-78; instr. art Dominican Coll., Sparkill, N.Y., 1977-80; sculptor Cristina Studios, Palisades, N.Y., 1980—; lectr. Female Imagery in the Works of 20th Century Women Sculptors, Hopper House, Nyack, N.Y., 1977, The Great Goddess, U. Besancon, France, 1986, The Soc. of Women Geographers and Mt. Holyoke Coll., 1990; facilitator conf. Ecofeminism, 1989; presenter papers Malta Archaeology and Fertility Cult Conf., 1985, World Archaeol. Conf., Eng., 1986. One woman shows include Spectrum Gallery, Rome, 1962, Palisades Presbyn. Ch., 1968, Rockland Community Coll., 1980, Rising Phoenix Gallery, Cambridge, Mass., 1984, Soho 20 Art Gallery, N.Y.C., Ariel Gallery, N.Y.C., 1989; exhibited in group shows at Ctr. Internat. d'Art Contemporain, Paris, 1984, Metropolis Gallerie Internat. d'Art, Geneva, 1985, Pleiades Gallery, N.Y.C., 1985-86, La Mandragore Galrie, Paris, 1986, Rockland Ctr. for Arts, 1987, Soho 20, 1988; contbr. articles to archaeol.books. Mem. Women's Ancient Studies Group, Edn. Assocs. NYU, Martial Arts Inst. Am. (black belt 2d dan), People for Ethical Treatment of Animals, Animal Agenda, Soc. Women Geographers (exec. coun.), Seneca Falls Peace Encampment, Nuclear Freeze, Sierra Club, Fund for New Priorities (bd. dirs.). Democrat. Home: 1 Ludlow Ln Palisades NY 10964 Office: Cristina Studios PO Box 208 Palisades NY 10964

BIALOW, LINDA GORDON, educator; b. New Haven, Conn., Sept. 10, 1940; d. Jack J. and Ida (Echter) Gordon; m. Martin R. Bialow, June 23, 1963; children: Elizabeth, Jennifer, David. AB, Radcliffe Coll., 1962; MAT, Harvard U., 1963. Cert. tchr., Fla. Tchr. Ocala (Fla.) High Sch., 1963-65, Shorecrest Sch., St. Petersburg, Fla., 1974-75; rsch. assoc. dept. psychiatry U. Fla., 1965-66; adj. instr. dept. communications St. Petersburg Jr. Coll., Clearwater, Fla., 1983—. Editor: Handbook of Consultation Psychiatry, 1967. Chmn. Clearwater High Sch. Adv. Com., 1980-81. Mem. Nat. Coun. Jewish Women, Woman's Am. ORT. Republican. Office: Saint Petersburg Jr Coll 2465 Drew St Clearwater FL 34625

BIANCHI, LAURIE ANN, advertising and public relations executive; b. Stockton, Calif., Nov. 26, 1964; d. Ermete and Rosetta (Jorio) B. BS in Mktg., San Diego State U., 1986, MBA, 1990. Asst. v.p., mktg. coord. Am. Valley Bank, El Cajon, Calif., 1987—; pres. Promotion Commotion, San Diego, 1988—. Co. chair Unied Way/CHAD, 1987-88. Recipient Coach/Vol. award Spl. Olympics, San Diego, 1988. Mem. NAFE, Nat. Assn. Desktop Pubs., Ad Club San Diego, San Diego State U. Bus. Alumni Assn. (advt. chair 1987-88, pres. 1988-89, pres. award 1988), Sierra Club.

BIANCO, JOAN, lawyer; b. N.Y.C., May 30, 1954; d. Vincent and Mary Patricia (Kiernan) O'Connell. BA, Iona Coll., 1976; MA, Columbia U., 1978, MPhil, 1981, JD, 1986. Bar: N.Y. 1987, U.S. Dist. Ct. (so. and ea. dists.) N.Y. 1987. Instr. Iona Coll., New Rochelle, N.Y., 1977-78; teaching asst. Columbia U., N.Y.C., 1978-80, preceptor, summer 1981; researcher, instr. project on issues of ethics in healthcare Columbia-Presbyn. Med. Ctr., N.Y.C., 1982-83; law clk. women's rights project ACLU, N.Y.C., summer 1984; assoc. Brown & Wood, N.Y.C., 1986—; asst. counsel N.Y. State Jud. Screening Com., N.Y.C., 1989; adminstrv. editor Columbia Human Rights Law Rev., N.Y.C., 1985-86. Mem. ABA, Assn. Bar City N.Y. Office: Brown & Wood One World Trade Ctr New York NY 10048

BIBEL, DEBRA JAN, microbiologist, immunologist; b. San Francisco, Apr. 6, 1945; d. Philip and Bassya (Malzer) B. AB, U. Calif., Berkeley, 1967, PhD, 1972. Research microbiologist Letterman Army Inst. Research, San Francisco, 1972-79; tech. writer Hoefer Sci. Inst., San Francisco, 1979; research assoc. Kaiser Found. Research Inst., San Francisco, 1981-83; product mgr. Tago Inc., Burlingame, Calif., 1983-85; dir. Elie Metchnikoff Meml. Library, Oakland, Calif., 1977—, historian, 1986; research assoc. U. Calif., San Francisco, 1987—; lectr. U. Calif., Berkeley, 1975, Antioch Coll. West, San Francisco, 1975. Author, editor: Milestones in Immunology. A Historical Exploration, 1988; columnist Rummagings Along the Dusty Shelf, 1982—; contbr. articles to profl. jours. Mem. Ali Akbar Coll. Music, San Rafael, Calif.; instr. Berkeley Community Health Project, 1971-75. Served to capt. U.S. Army, 1972-76. Mem. ACLU, Am. Soc. Microbiology (archives com. 1986—), AAAS, Fedn. Am. Scientists, Assn. Women in Sci., No. Calif. Am. Soc. Microbiology, Sierra Club. Buddhist. Home: 230 Orange St #6 Oakland CA 94610 Office: U Calif Dept Dermatology Box 0536 San Francisco CA 94143-0536

BICE, SUE ELLEN, health information services director, consultant, teacher; b. New Berlin, N.Y., Jan. 31, 1952; d. William Harold and Helen Jane (Pritchard) B. AAS, Broome Community Coll., Binghamton, N.Y., 1974; B in Health Svcs. Mgmt. and Med. Record Adminstrn., SUNY, Utica, 1983; MS, SUNY, Binghamton, 1986. Supr. chenango Meml. Hosp., Norwich, N.Y., 1972-73, asst. dir., 1973-75; asst. dir. Crouse Irving Meml. Hosp., Syracuse, N.Y., 1975-76, dir., 1976-86; dir. A.O. Fox Meml. Hosp., Oneonta, N.Y., 1987—; med. records cons. several nursing homes and acute-care hosps., 1973-85; med. records cons. Harrison Ctr. Outpatient Surgery, Syracuse, 1987—; instr. several colls., Utica and Syracuse, 1976—. Mem. Med. Record Assn. N.Y. State (pres. 1983-84, 89-90, Disting. Svc. award 1987), Leatherstocking Med. Record Assn. (pres. 1988-89), Cen. N.Y. Med. Record Assn. (pres. 1981-82), NAFE, Med. Record Assn. Democrat. Office: Aurelia Osborn Fox Hosp 1 Norton Ave Oneonta NY 13820

BICK, KATHERINE LIVINGSTONE, scientist, government official; b. Charlottetown, Can., May 3, 1932; came to U.S., 1954; d. Spurgeon Arthur and Flora Hazel (Murray) Livingstone; m. James Harry Bick, Aug. 20, 1955 (div.); children: James A., Charles L.; m. Ernst Freese, 1986. BS with honors, Acadia U., Can., 1951, MS, 1952; PhD, Brown U., 1957. Research pathologist UCLA Med. Sch., 1959-61; asst. prof. Calif. State U., Northridge, 1961-66; lab. instr. Georgetown U., Washington, 1970-72, asst. prof., 1972-76; dep. dir. neurol. disorder program Nat. Inst. Neurol. and Communicative Disorders and Stroke, NIH, Bethesda, Md., 1976-81, acting dep. dir., 1981-83, dep. dir., 1983-87; dep. dir. extramural research Office of Dir. NIH, 1987-90; sci. liaison Centro Studio Multicentrico Italino Sulla Demenza, Washington, 1990—. Editor: Alzheimer's Disease: Senile Dementia and Related Disorders, 1978, Neurosecretion and Brain Peptides, Implications for Brain Functions and Neurol. Disease, 1981, The Early Story of Alzheimer's Disease, 1987; contbr. articles to profl. jours. Pres. Woman's Club, McLean, Va., 1968-69; bd. dirs. Fairfax County (Va.) YWCA, 1969-70; pres. Emerson Unitarian Ch., 1964-66, Bethesda Place Homeowner's Assn., 1982. Recipient Can. NRC award Acadia U., 1951-52, fellow, 1951-52; Universal Match Found. fellow Brown U., 1956-57; NIH Dir.'s award, 1978; Fed. Exec. Inst. Leadership fellow, 1980; Spl. Achievement award NIH, 1981, 83; Superior Service award USPHS, 1986, Presdl. Rank award meritorious sr. exec., 1989. Mem. AAAS, Am. Neurol. Assn., Am. Acad. Neurology, Am. Soc. Zoologists, Western Soc. Naturalists, Assn. for Research in Nervous and Mental Disease, Internat. Brain Research Orgn., World Fedn. Neurology Research Group on Dementias (exec. sec. Am. region 1984-86, chmn. 1986—). Office: Centro SMID 1775 K St NW Ste 800 Washington DC 20006

BICKET, NANCY BROWN, data processing executive; b. Bloomington, Ill., Nov. 17, 1945; d. Henry R. and Betty Lyn (Weaner) B.; m. Robert Martin Bicket, Mar. 2, 1968; 1 child, Robin Leigh. BA in Biology, Ill. Wesleyan U., 1967. Cert. data processing, Ill. Jr. programmer State Farm Ins., Bloomington, 1967-68, data processing analyst, 1968-72, sr. analyst, 1972-75, mgr. data processing, 1975—. Pres. bd. Cen. Ill. Wesleyan Fund, Bloomington, 1988—; leader Stylistics 4-H Club, Bloomington, 1988-89; pres. Crestwicke Homeowners Assn., Bloomington, 1982. Mem. CPCU, Data Processing Mgmt. Assn. (publs., seminar coms. Twin City chpt. 1968—), Ill. Wesleyan Alumni Coun., Sigma Kappa Alumnae (mag. corr. Bloomington chpt. 1988-89).

BICKFORD, CAROL JEAN, naval officer; b. Madison, Wis., May 3, 1948; d. Melvin C. and Loretta F. (Neumann) B.; m. Troy J. Pierce, Sept. 15, 1974; children: Timothy, Adam. BS in Nursing, U. Wis., Eau Claire, 1971; MS, Rush U., Chgo., 1984; postgrad., U. Md., Balt. Commd. ensign USN, 1971, advanced through grades to comdr., 1986, nurse corps officer, 1971-90; charge tng. coord. composite healthcare system Naval Med. Data Svcs. Ctr., Bethesda, Md., 1989—. Recipient Cert. of Excellence, Hosp. Systems Prog. Office, Washington, 1988. Mem. NAFE, Nat. League for Nursing, Am. Nurses Assn., Phi Kappa Phi, Sigma Theta Tau. Home: 3517 Singers Glen Dr Olney MD 20832

BICKFORD, DRUCILLA, state legislator; b. Lebanon, Maine, Oct. 4, 1925; d. Lester Hancom and Doris Evelyn (Covey) Roberts; m. Everett John Bickford; children: Thomas Lee, Tara Elizabeth, Timothy Roberts, Tad John. AS, Lasell Jr. Coll, 1945. Mem. N.H. Ho. of Reps., Concord, 1980—. Mem. Nat. Soc. DAR (regent Mary Torr chpt. 1976, 78), Frisbie Aux. (pres. Rochester chpt. 1986, 88). Republican. Congregationalist. Home: 5 Birch Dr Rochester NH 03867

BICKFORD, GAIL HOLMGREN, publishing executive; b. N.Y.C., Feb. 14, 1930; d. R. John and Emilie Mary Antonia Doyle (Pope) Holmgren; m. Arthur Fillmore Bickford, Dec. 16, 1951 (div. Jan. 1980); children: Geoffrey, Alison. BA, Wellesley (Mass.) Coll., 1951; MA, U. Pa., 1956, PhD, 1972. Asst. instr. U. Pa., Phila., 1953-58; prof. Cape Cod Community Coll., Hyannis, Mass., 1965-68; owner, operator Freedom (N.H.) Press Assocs., 1979—. Author: Here Is Freedom, 1975, Freedom Crossroads, 1989; editor: Reminiscences of the French War, 1988, Tales of Effingham, 1988; columnist Carroll County Ind., 1988-89; contbr. articles to various mags. Mem. com. Dennis (Mass.) Sch., 1968-76; trustee Freedom Pub. Library, 1985—; sec. Old Home Week Assn., 1988—; recording sec. Freedom Conservation Commn., 1987-89. Democrat. Office: Freedom Press Assocs Box 88 Freedom NH 03836

BICKFORD, SHARON SUE, electrical design engineer; b. Arkansas City, Kans., Mar. 11, 1962; d. Robert Norman and Avis Ann (Johnson) B. BS in Archtl. Engring., Kans. State U., 1985. Elec. engr. Gerling-Thomas-Ward, Austin, Tex., 1985-88; elec. engr. Steve Dunn & Ptnrs., Dallas, 1988-89, Talex, Inc., Engrs., Austin, 1989—. Mem. Nat. Soc. Archtl. Engrs. Office: Talex Inc Engrs 6300 La Calma Ste 150 Austin TX 78752

BICKLING, DOROTHY INEZ, sales executive, psychologist, financial planner; b. Greeley, Colo., Feb. 20, 1939; d. Norman Melvin and Florence Florene (Krebill) B.; children: Andrew Harrison Betts, Spencer Norman Betts. BS, U. Colo., 1961; MA, U. North Colo., 1967; EdD, Auburn (Ala.) U., 1977. Asst. prof. Northeastern U., Boston, 1977-84; pvt. practice psychologist Acton, Mass., 1979—; pvt. practice fin. planner Acton, 1984-86, Bromfield & Bickling, Lexington, Mass., 1986—. Mem. Am. Psychol. Assn. Unitarian. Home: 26 Minot Ave Acton MA 01720

BIDDICK-LIEPINS, DIANE KAY, healthcare administrator; b. Madison, Wis., Nov. 8, 1954; d. Scott Hathaway and Betty Darlene (Womack) Biddick; m. Edgars Liepins, May 29, 1989. BS in Nursing, Wash. State U., Pullman, 1976; M of Mgmt. Info. Systems, West Coast U., 1986. Cert. nursing adminstr. Charge nurse Del Amo Hosp., Torrance, Calif., 1976-78; supr. mental health Kaiser Found. Hosp., L.A., 1978-81; asst. dept adminstr. So. Calif. Permanente Med. Group, L.A., 1981-84, dept. adminstr., 1984-89, adminstrv. asst., 1989—. Sec., bd. dirs. Fair Oaks Homeowners Assn., 1988-89, v.p., 1989—. Mem. Am. Nurses Assn., Phi Kappa Phi, Alpha Chi. Republican. Lutheran. Office: So Calif Permanente Med Group 1505 N Edgemont St Los Angeles CA 90027

BIDDIX, SHARON YVONNE, marketing executive, public relations specialist; b. Asheville, N.C., July 1, 1947; d. Francis Clarence and Virginia Lynn (McLean) Emory; m. Robert Stanley Biddix (div. 1984); children- :Gregory Bruce, April Lynn, Robert Brant, Stanley Brent, Brandy Jean. Student, Asheville Buncombe Tech. Coll., 1972, Mars Hill Coll., 1973, Daytona Beach Community Coll., 1987-88. Sec. shipping and freight Tropical Blosson Honey Co., Edgewater, Fla., 1982-83; focus group coordinator Z. Leatherwood & Assocs., Daytona Beach, Fla., 1984-87; pub. relations and rsch. specialist Einhorn & Lewis, Inc., Daytona Beach, 1983-87; adminstrv. asst., counselor Bethune-Cookman Coll., Daytona Beach, 1987-88; mktg. coordinator Russell & Axon, Inc., Daytona Beach, 1988—. Mem. communications com. ARC, 1985-89; mem. rev. com. United Way of Volusia County, 1985, 87, 89; active Mental Health Assn., Daytona Beach, 1983-89. Recipient awards for civic work. Mem. Excelsior Bus. and Profl. Women's Club (corr. sec. 1987-88), Nat. Assn. for Female Execs., Nat. Assn. for Mktg. Profls., Fla. Pub. Relations Assn. Home: 1094 Wild Holly Dr Port Orange FL 32119 Office: Russell & Axon Inc 1620 Mason Ave Daytona Beach FL 32117

BIDWELL, JACALYN, health care human resources executive; b. Bklyn., July 5, 1946; d. Abraham and Ethel Susan (Winkeeper) Glass; m. Timothy Michael Bidwell, June 30, 1979. BA, CUNY, 1966, MBA, 1978. Tchr., translator Bologna, Italy, 1966-71; asst. dir. pers. New Rochelle (N.Y.) Hosp. Med. Ctr., 1975-76; supr. wage and salary Roosevelt Hosp., N.Y.C., 1976-77; adminstrv. resident St. Clares Hosp., Denville, N.J., 1977, mgr. pers. adminstrn., 1977-78, divisional dir. pers., 1978-84; v.p. human resources St. Clares Riverside Med. Ctr., Denville, N.J., 1984—; De. Mem. N.J. Soc. for Healthcare Human Resources Adminstrs. (officer), Beta Gamma Sigma. Democrat. Office: St Clares Riverside Med Ctr Pocono Rd Denville NJ 07834

BIEGEL, EILEEN MAE, hospital executive; b. Eau Claire, Wis., Nov. 13, 1937; d. Ewald Frederic and Emma Antonia (Conrad) Weggen; student Dist. One Tech. Inst., 1974, also part time, corr. student U. Wis., Madison; grad. mgmt. seminars; student Upper Iowa U., 1984—; m. James O. Biegel, Oct. 6, 1956; children: Jeffrey Alan, John William. Exec. sec. to pres. Broadcaster Services, Inc., Eau Claire, Wis., 1969-74; exec. sec. to exec. v.p. Am. Nat. Bank, Eau Claire, 1975-77; exec. asst. to pres. Luther Hosp., Eau Claire, 1977—, asst. corporate sec., 1984—; mem. exec. staff, 1985—; asst. corp. sec. Luther Health Care Corp., 1984—; mem. secretarial adv. council Dist. One Tech. Sch. 1975—; corp. sec. Northwest Health Ventures, 1988—, bd. dirs. State pres. Future Homemakers Am., 1955; mem. governance com. Wis. Hosp. Assn. Cert. profl. sec., 1980; sec. bd. dirs. Chestnut Properties. Mem. Eau Claire Womens Network (founder, mem. steering com.), Profl. Secs. Internat. (chmn. goals and priorities com., pres. Eau Claire chpt. 1982-83), Wis. Hosp. Assn. Home: 4707 Tower Dr Eau Claire WI 54701 Office: 310 Chestnut St Eau Claire WI 54701

BIEHLE, KAREN JEAN, pharmacist; b. Festus, MO, July 18, 1959; d. Warren Day and Wilma Georgenia (Hedrick) Hargus; m. Scott Joseph Biehle, Aug. 22, 1981; children: Lauren Rachel, Heather Michelle. Student of pre-pharmacy, U. Mo., Columbia, Mo., 1977-79; BS in Pharmacy, U. Mo., Kans. City, Mo., 1982. Reg. Pharmicist. Pharmacy res. U. Iowa Hosp. & Clinics, Iowa City, Iowa, 1982-83; chief pharmacist Patterson Pharmacy, Florssant, Mo., 1983-84; pharmacist Jewish Hosp. of St. Louis, St. Louis, Mo., 1983-86; pharmacy mgr. Foster Infusion Care, St. Louis, Mo., 1986-88; staff pharmacist Cardinal Glennon Children's Hosp., St. Louis, Mo., 1988—; pres. Lauren's Specialty Foods, Inc., St. Louis, Mo., 1988-89; pharmacy mgr. Curaflex Health Svcs., 1989—; Preceptor, St. Louis (Mo.) Coll. of Pharmacy, 1984—. Vol. March of Dimes Walk-a-thon, 1985-90. Recipient Roche Pharmacy Communications Award, Roche Pharmaceuticals, Kans. City, 1982, "I Dare You" Award, 4-H Club, Nevada, Mo., 1976. Mem. Am. Soc. of Hosp. Pharmacists, St. Louis Soc. of Hosp. Pharmacists, Kappa Epsilon, Alpha Delta Pi (St. Louis Alumnae pres. 1989—). Republican. Baptist. Home: 803 Timberfield Ballwin MO 63021

BIELAWSKI, BARBARA A., nurse; b. Chgo., Sept. 22, 1960; d. John F. and Anne (Maodush) B. BSN, Valparaiso U., 1982; MS, U. Ill., Chgo., 1990. Cert. CEN, ACLS, TNCC, MICN. Staff nurse, alt. charge nurse ER Community Hosp., Munster, Ind.; staff nurse ER Parkland Meml. Hosp., Dallas; staff nurse, alt. charge nurse Northwestern Meml. Hosp., Chgo.; quality mgmt. coord. Evanston (Ill.) Hosp. Corp. Mem. ENA, AACN, Ill. Nurses' Assn., Sigma Theta Tau (Alpha Lambda chpt.). Presbyterian. Home: 1157 Johnson Dr Apt 3023 Buffalo Grove IL 60089 Office: Evanston Hosp Corp 2650 Ridge Ave Evanston IL 60201

BIELAWSKI, ELIZABETH ANNE, Native American government administrator; b. Fall River, Mass., Jan. 27, 1950; d. Joseph Paul and Frances Sophie (Wojcik) Czerwonka. Rsch. assoc. R.I. Hosp., Providence, 1972-74; planner, evaluator Bristol County Home Care, Fall River, Mass., 1974-75; exec. dir. Bristol County Home Care, Fall River, 1975-86; v.p. long term care PACE Shared Svcs., Sioux Falls, S.D., 1986-88; exec. dir. Nebr. Assn. Pvt. Resources, Lincoln, 1988-89, Winnebago Tribe of Nebr., Winnebago, 1989—; instr. Bristol Community Coll., Fall River, 1985-86, bus. sch. Coll. of St. Mary's, 1988, Met. Community Coll., 1988-89; adj. prof. bus. and engring. div. Augustana Coll., 1987—. Host (talk show) The Best Times, 1986. Chair chpt. ARC, Fall River, 1978-86, bd. dirs. Sioux Falls chpt., 1986; zone chair United Way, Fall River, 1983-86. Mem. Am. Soc. on Aging, Mass. Assn. Home Care Programs, Inc. (treas. 1975, v.p. 1985), Nat. Coun. on Aging, Nat. Coun. of Sr. Citizens. Democrat. Roman Catholic. Home: RR 1 Box 41F Blair NE 68008 Office: Winnebago Tribe of Nebr PO Box 687 Winnebago NE 68071

BIELEFELDT, CATHERINE C., sales executive; b. Bellwood, Ill.; d. William Anton and Linda (Buchert) B. B.Music in Piano Performance, Chgo. Conservatory Coll.; student El Conservatorio de Mex., Mexico City; postgrad. Northwestern U., CBS Sch. Mgmt., 1980. Dept. mgr. Fair Store, Oak Park, Ill., 1950-62; piano sales cons. Lyon & Healy Co., Oak Park and Oak Brook, Ill., 1963-77; dir. Steinway Hall, dir. nat. sales tng. Steinway & Sons, Long Island City, N.Y., 1978-82; v.p. sales, pub. relations and advt. Hendricks Music Co., Downers Grove, Ill., 1983—; sales seminar instr. Jordan-Kitt's Music, Wells Music, Washington and Denver, 1983-85, Lauzon Music, Ottawa, Can., 1986-89, Meridian Music, Indpls., 1989. Author: The Wonders of the Piano, The Anatomy of the Instrument, 1984; editor The Keynote Newsletter; contbr. articles to profl. jours. Mem. Women in Communications, Inc., Evanston Music Club, Sigma Alpha Iota (past pres. alumnae chpt., recipient numerous awards). Republican. Lutheran. Home: 190 S Wood Dale Rd Apt 1101 Wood Dale IL 60191 Office: Hendricks Music 421 Maple Ave Downers Grove IL 60515

BIENEMA, KRISTINE K., human resources professional, real estate agent; b. Ft. Lauderdale, Fla., Apr. 3, 1962; d. Richard John and Patricia Joyce (Knaack) B. BS, Orlando (Fla.) Coll., 1986. Lic. real estate agt. Pers. adminstr., acct. exec. Temptalent, Orlando; account exec., office mgr. Workers of Orlando; lic. real estate agt. Jim Royer Realty, Dunwoody, Ga. Mem. NAFE, Nat. Assn. Enterpreneurs. Address: 449 Kingspoint Ln Roswell GA 30076

BIERBAUM, JANITH MARIE, artist; b. Evanston, Ill., Jan. 14, 1927; d. Gerald Percy and Lillian (Sullivan) Turnbull; m. J. Armin Bierbaum, Apr. 7, 1948; children: Steve, Todd, Chad, Peter, Mark. BA, Northwestern U., 1948; postgrad., Mpls. Art Inst., 1964, St. Paul Art Inst., 1969-70. Rsch. asst. AMA, Chgo., 1948-49; tchr. Chgo. high schs., 1949-51; freelance artist Larkspur, Colo., 1951—. Exhibited in group shows at Foot Hills Art Ctr., 1985, 86, 87, Palmer Lake (Colo.) Art Assn., 1986-87, 88-89, Gov.'s Mansion, Bismarck, N.D., 1960; oil painting appeared in 1989 Women in Art Nat. calendar pub. by AAUW. Recipient 1st Place Purchase award U. Minn., Mpls., 1966, Coors Classic award Coors Beer, Golden, Colo., 1987. Mem. Colo. Artists Assn., Perry Park Country Club. Republican. Home and Office: 7787 Perry Park Blvd Larkspur CO 80118

BIERCE, CAROL ANNE HOOVER, computer software company executive, consultant; b. Pensacola, Fla., Jan. 30, 1954; d. Ralph Alwin Hoover Jr. and Hazel Floyce (Warren) Roberts; m. Daniel Ambrose Bierce, Oct. 17, 1975; children: Adam Anthony, Joseph Alexander. BA in Math. with highest distinction, U. North Fla., 1975, BAE with highest distinction, 1976, MBA, 1979. Programmer Sav-A-Stop, Inc., Orange Park, Fla., 1975-76; with City of Jacksonville, Fla., 1976-89, sr. application analyst, 1980-82, asst. computer systems officer, dep. tech. dir., 1982-88, tech. dir., 1988-89; project leader water and electric computer services, tech. support; pres. A & J Computer Cons., Inc., Jacksonville, Fla., 1989—. Active Riverside-Avondale Preservation Soc., Fla. Epilepsy Found., Jacksonville Zool. Soc., Jacksonville Mus. Arts and Scis., St. Mark's Women of Ch. Mem. Assn. MBA Execs., NAFE, Phi Theta Kappa, Pi Mu Epsilon. Democrat. Episcopalian. Home: 1624 Cherry St Jacksonville FL 32205 Office: A & J Computer Cons Inc PO Box 37124 Jacksonville FL 32236-7124

BIERI, JACQUELINE ELIZABETH, banker; b. Chgo., Sept. 25, 1962; d. Joseph Bieri and Pauline (Schaffer) Hahn. BBA, Bernard Baruch Coll., 1985; cert., U. Vienna, Austria, 1982. Coll. asst. in pres.'s office Bernard M. Baruch Coll., N.Y.C., 1980-84; jr. acct. Alan D. Rosenberg, CPA, N.Y.C., 1983-85; money market position keeper Dai Ichi Kangyo Bank, Ltd., N.Y.C., 1986; ops. officer, asst. mgr. Citicorp-Investment Bank, N.Y.C., 1986-89; fgn. exchange corp. dealer Hong Kong and Shanghai Banking Corp. Ltd., N.Y.C., 1989—. Religious lectorer Saint Hugh of Lincoln Roman Cath. Ch., Huntington, N.Y., 1989—, Saint Fidelis Roman Cath. Ch., College Point, N.Y., 1982-87, eucharistic min., 1985-87; mem. G.T.E.V. Schlieractaler Stamm-Bavarian Folk Dance Club. Republican. Roman Catholic. Home: 7 Longford St Huntington NY 11743 Office: Hong Kong and Shanghai Bank Corp Ltd 140 Broadway New York NY 10015

BIES, BARBARA AGNES, police officer; b. Chgo., Oct. 29, 1962; d. Alexander Aloyisius and Jean Mary (Balicki) Bies; m. Nicholas James Pappas, Nov. 6, 1988. BA, Loyola U., Chgo., 1985; cert., Am. Inst. Paralegal Studies, 1990. Contract analyst Benefit Trust Life, Chgo., 1985-86; police officer Chgo. Police Dept., 1986—. Mem. Ill. Women in Law Enforcement, Nat. Assn. Female Execs. Office: Chgo Police Dept 6464 N Clark St Chicago IL 60626

BIES, SUSAN SCHMIDT, finance company executive; b. Buffalo, May 5, 1947; d. Louis Howard and Gladys May (Metke) Schmidt; m. John David Bies, Aug. 29, 1970; children: John Matthew, Scott Louis. BS, State U. Coll.-Buffalo, 1967; MA, Northwestern U., 1968, PhD, 1972. Banking structure economist FRS, St. Louis, 1970-72; asst. prof. econs. Wayne State U., Detroit, 1972-77; assoc. prof. Rhodes Coll., Memphis, 1977-80; tactical planning mgr. First Tenn. Nat. Corp., Memphis, 1980-81, dir. corp. devel., 1982-83, treas., 1983-84, sr. v.p., chief fin. officer, 1984-85, exec. v.p., chief fin. officer, 1985—; mem. fin. adv. com. City of Germantown, Tenn., 1978—, also budget com.; mem. investment adv. com. Tenn. Consol. Retirement System, Nashville, 1981-86; instr. MidSouth Sch. Banking, 1985-86; bd. dirs. Memphis Ptnrs. Pres., bd. dirs. North Germantown Homewoners Assn., 1978-83; treas. Germantown Area Soccer Assn., 1985-86; treas. Fury Soccer Club, 1988—; vice chmn. task force Com. on 21st Century, Rhodes Coll., Memphis, 1986-87; mem. exec. adv. bd. Sch. Accountancy Memphis State U.; bd. dirs. Memphis Youth Initiative, 1988; mem. BAI Acctg. and Fin. Commn., 1988—. Fellow Ctr. for Urban Affairs, 1968-69, Fed. Res. Bank Chgo., 1970. Mem. Am. Bankers Assn. (exec. com. 1986-88), Nat. Assn. Bus. Economists, Am. Econ. Assn., Planning Execs. Inst., Fin. Execs. Inst., (bd. dirs. Memphis chpt. 1988—), Planning Forum (Managerial Excellence award Memphis chpt. 1986), Memphis Area C. of C. (bd. dirs. 1988—, tax com. 1988—, chair 1989—), Econ. Club Memphis (bd. dirs. 1986—, vice chmn. 1987-88, chmn. 1988-89), Omicron Delta Epsilon, Lambda Alpha. Episcopalian. Office: 1st Tenn Nat Corp 165 Madison Ave Memphis TN 38103

BIESEL, DIANE JANE, librarian; b. N.Y.C., Feb. 15, 1934; d. Douglas and Runa (Patterson) Stevens; m. Donald W. de Cordova, June 24, 1956 (div. July 1971); m. David Barrie Biesel, Sept. 25, 1982. BS, Trenton State Coll., 1956; MLS, Rutgers U., 1969; MA in Edn., Seton Hall U., 1974, cert. in supervision, 1976. Tchr., librarian Arlington (Va.)) Bd. Edn., 1956-58; media specialist elem. schs., librs. River Edge (N.J.) Bd. Edn., 1958—; lectr., instr. children's lit. Alphonsus Coll., Woodcliff Lake, N.J., 1969-72; field svc. cons. N.J. Dept. Edn., 1969-71; cons. New Books Preview Baker and Taylor Co., 1972-76; adj. prof. Seton Hall U., 1978-79; mem. awards com. Rutgers U. Grad. Sch. Libr. Svc., 1978-79; mem. River Dell Libr.'s Coop., Study Skills and Affirmative Action coms. River Edge Bd. Edn., 1988—. Mem. com. cademically gifted River Edge Bd. Edn., 1977-83, study skills com., 1988—, affirmative action com., 1988—, River Dell Librs. Coop., 1988—; mem. choir All Saint's Ch., Bergenfield, 1971—, vestrywoman, 1980-83, del. Diocesan Conv., 1978—; active Affirmative Action, 1988—. Mem. ALA, Am. Assn. Sch. Librarians (mem. com. instrnl. media 1971-76, affiliate assembly by-laws com. 1977-78, Ednl. Media Assn. N.J. (state chmn. recruitment 1968-69, state chmn. hospitality 1972-73, state chmn. county liaison 1973-74, co-pres. 1977-78), Bergen County Sch. Librs. Assn. (pres. 1966-68), River Edge Tchrs. Assn. (pres. 1964-66), Assn. Ednl. Communications Tech. (nat. nominating com. 1978-79, council 1978-79, steering com. 1979-80, evaluation com. 1979, co-chmn. liaison com. with Am. Assn. Sch. Librarians 1979-83, nat. nominating com. 1980-82, awards com. 1981—), Sch. Media Specialists (program com. 1982-84, bd. dirs. region II 1983-84, pres. 1986, mem. task force on librs. and info. sci., White House, writing com., co-author: Information Power, 1988). Home: 315 Schraalenburgh Rd Haworth NJ 07641-1203 Office: 410 Bogert Rd River Edge NJ 07661

BIESS, BARBARA DZIEDZIC, communications executive; b. Detroit, Mar. 26, 1963; d. Joseph Roman and Emma Lucy (Lewinski) Dziedzic; m. Robert Donald Biess, Oct. 8, 1988. AB with distinction, U. Mich., 1985, BSA with distinction, 1985. Mktg. asst. Park West Galleries, Inc., Southfield, Mich., 1985; market researcher Gen. Motors Corp., Warren, Mich., 1985; staff cons. KPMG Peat Marwick, Detroit, 1986-87, assoc. cons., 1987-87, dir. communications, 1987-90; mgr. communications and mem. svcs. Mich. Assn. CPAs, Farmington Hills, 19906. Pub. rels. com. mem. Founders Jr. Coun., Detroit Inst. of Arts, 1989 . Mem. Internat. Assn. Bus. Communicators (mission statement com. mem. Detroit chpt., profl. devel. com. mem., v.p. membership, bd. dirs.), Women's Econ. Club, U. Mich. Alumni Assn. Roman Catholic. Office: Mich Assn CPAs 28116 Orchard Lake Rd PO Box 9054 Farmington Hills MI 48333

BIEWENER, KELLY ANN See HELFINSTINE, KELLY ANN

BIG, SUSAN NAGY, management consultant; b. Cornwall, N.Y., Mar. 9, 1946; d. Joseph Nagy and Rose Helen (Lakatos) B. Cert. in Hisp. studies, U. Madrid, 1967; BA, SUNY, Potsdam, 1968; MS in Spanish Edn., SUNY, New Paltz, 1971; MBA, Simmons Coll., 1980. Asst. to dir. Potsdam Jr. Year Abroad, Madrid, 1968-69; Spanish instr. Newburgh (N.Y.) Free Acad., 1969-70, Hingham (Mass.) High Sch., 1970-79; cons. Harbridge Ho., Inc., Boston, 1981-84; pres. SNBig & Assocs., Cambridge, Mass., 1984—; pvt. practice Cambridge; English instr. Univ. Mex., Mexico City, 1976; mem. faculty Ctr. for Lifelong Learning Harvard U., Cambridge, 1984-89; speaker Grad. Sch. Mgmt. Simmons Coll., Boston, 1986-89, 90, nat. conf. advisor, 1989—. Active Mid-Cambridge Neighborhood Assn., 1988-89, Mus. Fine Arts, Boston, 1986-89, Mass. Women's Polit. Caucus, Boston, 1987-89, Murphy election com., Boston, 1987. Continental Bank scholar, Chgo., 1979; recipient Big W award Advt. Club of Westchester, 1989. Mem. Am. Soc. Tng. and Devel. (Mass. chpt., dir. auto industry group 1990, nat. conf. speaker auto industry group 1989), World Affairs Coun. (bd. dirs. 1989, 90, mem. corp. recruiting com. 1988—), Boston Computer Soc., Grad Sch. Mgmt. Simmons Coll. Alumnae Assn. Democrat. Methodist. Office: SN Big & Assocs 20A Prescott St #55 Cambridge MA 02138

BIGBACK, BONNIE DEE WOODWARD, educator; b. Great Falls, Mont., Jan. 15, 1950; d. Lee Wiley and Edith Violet (Sloan) W.; m. Robert Bigback Sr., May 7, 1975; children: Jennifer Lee, James Wiley. BS, Mont. State U., 1972; Postgrad., Ea. Mont. Coll., 1986. Cert. elem. edn. adminstr. Tchr. Busby (Mont.) High Sch., 1972-75, tchr. home econs., 1977-79, 87—, disciplinarian, bilingual ESL adminstr., 1986-87; tchr. career edn. Lame Deer (Mont.) Elem. Sch., 1976-77; congregate Housing coord. No. Cheyenne Housing Authority, Lame Deer, 1979-80; tchr. elem. edn. Lame Deer Pub. Sch., 1980-86; instr. home econs. Billings Pub. Schs., 1990—; cons. home econs. No. Cheyenne Tribe, Lame Deer, 1975-89. Editor, contbr. Lame Deer Community Cookbook 1984. Bd. Dirs. Girl Scouts U.S., Lame Deer, 1981-86; dir. Tri-Sch. Field Events Busby Sch., 1988. Appreciation award No. Cheyenne Pub. Health Svc., 1987. Mem. Nat. Wildlife Assn., Nat. Arbor Day Assn., Mont. Edn. Assn., Am. Assn. Retired Persons, Am. Home Econs. Assn., Mont. Nutrition Bd., Pentecostal Ladies Aux., Lame Deer Women's Guild. Home: Box 600 Lame Deer MT 59043

BIGELOW, BEVERLY, security agency executive; b. Providence, R.I., Mar. 28, 1947; d. Antonio Joseph and Josephine (Soccio) Tartaglia Zaccaria; m. Anthony Michael Alviti, Jan. 4, 1969 (div. Feb. 1977); children—Anthony, Kevin, Jason; m. Elwin L. Bigelow, May 14, 1983. Student R.I. Jr. Coll. Bookkeeper, Alan I. Maylor Co., East Providence, R.I., 1979-82, Escom Devel. Corp., Fort Lauderdale, Fla., 1982-85; v.p. Bigelow Security Agy., Inc., Ft. Lauderdale, Fla., 1986—; owner, operator The White House Bed and Breakfast Inn, Tyrone, Pa., Somewhere in Time Gowns & Dresses, Tyrone, 1990—. Bd. dirs. Ravenswood Mgmt. Assn., Fort Lauderdale, 1984-85, 86—, sec., 1984-85, 86—, bookkeeper, 1982—; com. mem. Blair County Rep. Party, 1990—; mem. Nat. Trust for Hist. Preservation, Tyrone Zoning and Hearing Bd. Baptist. Club: Ravenswood Social (Fort Lauderdale) (sec. 1982—). Avocations: sewing, cooking, collecting dresser boxes and antiques, doll making, interior design.

BIGELOW, LYNNE THAYER, registered nurse; b. Rockville Centre, N.Y., May 12, 1942; d. Stanley K. and Bertha (Kerschenbaum) B. Dip., Mass. Gen. Hosp. Sch. of Nursi, 1964; BSN, St. Anselms Coll., 1976; MS, Boston U., 1977. Am. Nurse Assn., Adult Nurse Practitioner, 1980. Adult n.p. homecare coord. Whittier St. Neighborhood Health Ctr., Boston, Mass., 1977-78; sr. nurse practioner Beth Israel Hosp., Boston, Mass., 1978-81; v.p., clinical svcs. Jewish Memorial Hosp., Boston, 1981-89; dir. nursing svcs. Cushing Hosp., Framingham, Mass., 1989—; cons. Prof. Educ. and Practice of Nursing Administr. in Long Term Care, 1985, advisory comm., Primary Care Program, 1985-88. Author: Books. "Geronotology Clinical Role Study" in Jarvis, Linda, Ed., Community Health Nursing: Keeping the Public Healthy, 1981, "Primary Nursing in a Home Care Setting:", Journal of Nursing Adminstration Quarterly, 1981, "The Continuing Care Nurse", Nursing Outlook, 1985. Democrat. Lutheran. Home: 19 Village Rock Ln Natick MA 01760 Office: Cushing Hosp Box 9008 Dudley Rd Framingham MA 01701-9008

BIGELOW, MARGARET ELIZABETH BARR, mycologist educator; b. Elkhorn, Manitoba, Can., Apr. 16, 1923; came to U.S., 1952; d. David Hunter and Mary Irene (Parr) Barr; m. Howard Elson Bigelow, June 9, 1956 (dec.). BA with honors, U. B.C., Vancouver, Can., 1950, MA, 1952; PhD, U. Mich., 1956. Attache d'research U. Montreal (Can.), 1956-57; instr. U. Mass., Amherst, 1957-65, asst. prof., 1965-71, assoc. prof., 1971-76, prof., 1976-89, prof. emeritus, 1989—. Author: Diaporthales in N.A., 1978, Prodromus to Loculo-Iascomycetes, 1987; contbr. articles to profl. jours. With Can. Women's Army Corps, 1942-46. Mem. Mycological Soc. Am. (v.p. to pres. 1980-82, editor 1975-80), Brit. Mycological Soc., Am. Inst. Biol. Sci. (gen. chmn. annual meeting 1986). Home: 9475 Inverness Ave, Sidney, BC Canada V8L 3S1

BIGELOW, MARTHA MITCHELL, historian; b. Talladega Springs, Ala., Sept. 19, 1921; divorced; children—Martha Frances, Carolyn. B.A., Montevallo U., 1943; M.A. (tuition fellow, Julius Rosenwald scholar 1943-44, Cleo Hearson scholar, summer 1944, Ency. Brit. fellow 1944-45), U. Chgo., 1944, Ph.D., 1946. Assoc. prof. history Miss. Coll., Clinton, 1946-48, Memphis State U., 1948-49, U. Miss., 1949-50; assoc. curator manuscripts Mich. Hist. Collections, U. Mich., Ann Arbor, 1954-57; prof. history Miss. Coll., 1957-71, chmn. dept. history and polit. sci., 1964-71; dir. Bur. History, Mich. Dept. State; sec. Mich. Hist. Commn., Mich. Dept. State, also state historic preservation officer, 1971—; coordinator for Mich., Nat. Hist. Publs. and Recs. Commn., 1974—. Contbr. articles prof. publns. Mem. Am. Assn. State and Local History (pres. 1979-81, fellow summers 1958, 59), Orgn. Am. Historians, Nat. Assn. State Archives and Recs. Assn., So. Hist Assn., Mich. Hist. Soc., Miss. Hist. Soc. Home: 223 Cowley St East Lansing MI 48823 Office: Bur History Mich Hist Mus 717 W Allegan Lansing MI 48918

BIGELOW, PAGE ELIZABETH, public policy professional; b. Louisville, Feb. 9, 1948; d. William Simpson and Page Elizabeth (Smith) B. BA, Wells Coll., 1970; postgrad., NYU, 1971-72, Gen. Theol. Sem., 1971-72. Research asst., librarian Nat. Mcpl. League, N.Y.C., 1970-75, research dir. ethics in govt. project, 1975-80, dir. representation project, 1981-84; sr. assoc. Nat. Civic League (formerly Nat. Mcpl. League), N.Y.C., 1983-87; staff cons. state-city commn. on integrity in govt. N.Y., N.Y.C., 1986-87; mem. sr. staff Inst. Pub. Adminstrn., N.Y.C., 1987—. Author: Lobbying Laws in the States: A Comparative Study, 1980, From Norms to Rules, Regulating the Outside Interests of Public Officials, 1989; editor: Forms of Local Representation, 1982. Mem. citizens adv. panel to joint legis. com. on revision and simplification of tax code, N.Y., 1982-86; del. Ednl. Priorities Panel, N.Y.C., 1984—; mem. Citywide Sch. Bd. Elections Com., N.Y.C., 1985—. Mem. Coun. on Govtl. Etics Laws, NAFE, Jr. League (N.Y.C.) (corp. sec. 1986-88, 90, Honored Vol. 1990). Episcopalian. Office: Inst Pub Adminstrn 55 W 44th St New York NY 10036

BIGELOW-LOURIE, ANNE EDWIGE, graphic designer; b. L.A., Mar. 3, 1946; d. Eugene and Laure Mathilde (Ortiz de Zarate) Lourie; m. Charles Andrew Bigelow, 1972 (div. 1974). BA, Reed Coll., 1967; student, San Francisco Art Inst., 1967-69; MA, Portland State U., 1975; AS, Portland Community Coll., 1985. Cert. secondary teacher. Basic skills tchr. Portland, Oreg., 1972-82; freelance graphics Portland, 1967—; computer programmer Consol. Freightways, Portland, 1984-87, systems analyst, 1987—. Illustrator: Time And The White Tigress, 1986 (Western States award 1986), Collected Poems: Mary Barnard, 1979 (Elliston award 1979), Tale of My Tribe, 1989. Recipient 3rd place Exhibits Competition, Dickinson Coll., 1987. Mem. Am. Soc. Bookplate Collectors and Designers, Portland Rowing Club (sec. 1989), Sta. L Rowing Club.

BIGGER, HESTER, health care executive; b. Clay County, Ind., Mar. 6, 1919; d. Heston Griffith and Effa Worth; m. Charles E. Bigger, Nov. 8, 1941 (dec.); children: Charles E., Barbara. RN, Union Hosp. Sch. Nursing, 1940; BS, St. Mary of Woods Coll., Ind., 1975; postgrad., Ind. U., Ind. State U., Terre Haute. Cert. Alcohol/Drug Abuse Counselor. Supr. Union Hosp., Terre Haute; dir. nsg. svc. Mary Sherman Hosp., Sullivan, Ind.; alcohol/drug abuse counselor Hamilton Ctr., Inc., Terre Haute; dir. Parke County Alcohol/Drug Ctr. Prog., Rockville, Ind. Mem. Vigo County Alcohol/Drug Abuse Task Force, Vigo County Mental health Assn., Vigo County Cancer Soc. Named Ind. Counselor of the Yr., 1986, Nat. Counselor of the Yr., 1987, Florence Nightingale award, 1988. Mem. Am. Nurses Assn., Ind. State Nurses Assn. (mem. peer rev. and assistance program for impaired nurses), Nat. Counselors Assn. on Alcohol/Drug Abuse, Ind. Counselors Assn. on Alcohol/Drug Abuse, Ind. Coalition of Alcohol Drug Ct. Programs. Home: 407 S 31st St Terre Haute IN 47803

BIGGS, RITTIE JEAN, county official; b. Martin County, N.C., Jan. 16, 1942; d. Dennis Robert and Marie (Wynn) B. B.S., East Carolina U., 1964, M.S., 1974. Tchr., Edenton City Schs., N.C., 1964-67, Martin County Schs.,

Williamston, N.C., 1967-68; social worker Martin County Dept. Social Services, Williamston, 1968-72, dir., 1972—. Named Outstanding Dir. Social Services in N.C., N.C. Assn. County Commrs., 1979-80. Mem. N.C. Assn. County Dirs. Social Services (pres. 1979-80), N.C. Social Services Assn. Democrat. Baptist. Club: Williamston Bus. and Profl. Women (pres. 1977-78). Avocations: reading, quilting, crocheting, gardening, church work. Office: Martin County Dept of Social Svcs PO Box 809 Williamston NC 27892

BIGGS, TINA CORNELIUS, engineering technician; b. Herrin, Ill., Jan. 24, 1957; d. Merle Leon and Jeanette Maxine (O'Neal) Cornelius; m. Russell Hines Allen, July 1, 1977 (div. Dec. 1, 1981); m. Jeffery Ray Biggs, Sept. 3, 1988. AAS, Rend Lake Coll., 1977; postgrad., So. Ill. U., 1989—. Draftsman Lawrence A. Lipe & Assocs., Benton, Ill., 1977-84, Clarida Engring., Marion, Ill., 1984-85; engring. tech. Lawrence A. Lipe & Assocs., Benton, 1985—; bd. dirs. Rend Lake Coll., Ina, 1980—, Herrin (Ill.) High Sch., 1979—. Mem. NAFE. Democrat. Home: 513 N 7th St Herrin IL 62948 Office: Lawrence A Lipe & Assocs 901 N Duquoin St Benton IL 62812

BIGGY, MARY VIRGINIA, educator emeritus; b. Boston, Oct. 15, 1924; d. John J. and Mary C. (Dwyer) B. B.S., Boston U., 1945, Ed.M., 1946, Ed.D., 1953. Tchr. bus. edn. Needham (Mass.) High Sch., 1944-45; reading cons. Plainville (Conn.) Public Schs., 1946-47; coord. elem. edn. Concord (Mass.) Public Schs., 1947-62; dir. N.E. instrnl. TV project, dir. instrnl. TV Eastern Ednl. Network, Boston, 1962-67; asst. supt., supr. Concord Public Schs. and Concord Carlisle Regional Sch. Dist., 1967-69; prof. edn. U. Lowell, Mass., 1969-89; prof. edn. emerita U. Lowell, 1989—; dean Coll. Edn. U. Lowell, Mass., 1979-89; pres. Designs for Edn., 1969—; cons. Corp. Pub. Broadcasting; mem. Acton Boxborough (Mass.) Regional High Sch. Dist. Sch. Com., 1963-66; chmn. Mass. Bd. Library Commrs., 1973-78; project dir. criteria for funding major initiatives Corp. Pub. Broadcasting, 1981-85. Author: Independence in Spelling, 1966, (with others) Spell Correctly, 1965-86, 5th edit., 1986. Recipient Ida M. Johnston award Boston U., 1981. Mem. NEA (life), Pi Lambda Theta (nat. pres. 1961-65, 83 Disting. Pi Lambda Thetan awards). Democrat. Roman Catholic. Home: 65 Park Ln Concord MA 01742

BIGHAM, WANDA DURRETT, academic administrator; b. Barlow, Ky.; m. William Bigham; children: Jan, Bill, Julie. B of Music Edn., Murray State U., 1956; MusM, Morehead State U., 1971, M of Higher Edn., 1973; EdD, U. Ky., 1978; cert. in ednl. mgmt., Harvard U., 1982; LittD (hon.), Loras Coll., 1990. Tchr. music, English pub. schs., Ky.; dir. Trio Programs Morehead (Ky.) State U., dir. instructional systems, assoc. dean acad. affairs, acting dean grad. and spl. acad. programs; exec. asst. to pres. Emerson Coll., Boston; v.p. devel. and coll. relations Emerson Coll.; pres. Marycrest Coll., Davenport, Iowa, 1986—; Ky. state coord. Am. Council on Edn.'s Nat. Identification Program for Women in Higher Edn., 1981-84; 1st treas. Nat. Council of Ednl. Opportunity Assns., 1981-83, bd. dirs., 1983-85. Contbr. articles to ednl. jours. Bd. dirs. Iowa Student Loan Liquidity Corp., Sta. WQPT-TV, Friendly House, Jr. Achievement; co-chair Quad Cities Vision for the Future, 1987—, metro strategic planning com., pres. CPC Found. Recipient Disting. Alumnus award Murray State U., 1988, Pres.'s award Davenport C. of C., 1988, Linda K. Neuman award Quad Cities Leader Luncheon, 1990; named to Alumni Hall of Fame Morehead State U., 1988; Title III and IV grantee, Morehead State U.; Am. Council on Edn. fellow, 1983-84. Mem. So. Assn. Ednl. Opportunity Program Personnel (v.p. 1979-81, pres. 1983-85), Ky. Assn. of Ednl. Opportunity Program Personnel (pres. 1973-74, 77-78), Sigma Alpha Iota, Kappa Delta Pi, Phi Kappa Phi, Phi Delta Kappa. Office: Marycrest Coll 1607 W 12th St Davenport IA 52804

BIGONGIARI, MARY JULIA, nurse anesthetist; b. Chgo., Oct. 27, 1945; d. Achilles and Victoria (Lucetti) B. BSN, Loyola U., Chgo., 1967; MS, U. Calif., San Francisco, 1972; diploma, Rush Sch. Nurse Anesthesia, Chgo., 1978. Cert. nurse anesthetist. Head nurse VA Lakeside Hosp., Chgo., 1969-71; instr., practitioner Rush U. Coll. Undergrad. Nursing, Chgo., 1974-76; staff anesthetist Rush Presbyn. St. Luke's Hosp., Chgo., 1978-81; faculty, cour dir. Rush Presbyn. St. Luke's Hosp., 1980-81; faculty, clin. coordinator Rush U., Chgo., 1980-81; chief anesthetist St. Anthony Hosp., Chgo., 1981-82, Louise Burg Hosp., Chgo., 1985; staff anesthetist St. Mary Nazareth, Chgo., 1980—; ind. contr. anesthesia svcs. Chgo., 1982—; flight nurse instr. Scott AFB, Ill., 1971—; cons. to Surgeon Gen. on flight nursing, Washington, 1984—; instr. CPR, ARC.; guest lectr. Air Force Flight Nurse Sch., Brooks AFB, Tex., 1984—. First aid nurse Am. Diabetes Assn. Ann. Bike Ride, 1987—, Chgo. ARea Running Assn., 1987—, others. Lt. col. USAF, 1968—. Decorated Air Force Commendation medal. Mem. Am. Assn. Nurse Anesthetists, Am. Heart Assn. Roman Catholic. Home and Office: 237 S Home Ave Oak Park IL 60302-3101

BIHARY, JOYCE, federal judge. BA, Wellesley Coll.; JD, U. Mich. Admitted to bar, 1975. Bankruptcy judge U.S. Dist. Ct., Atlanta. Office: US Dist Ct 1783 US Courthouse 75 Spring St SW Atlanta GA 30303*

BIJLANI, JUDITH ANN, marketing professional; b. Ann Arbor, Mich., Sept. 28, 1949; d. Frederic David Nabeack and Marjorie Jean (Simmons) Alderson; m. Ashok H. Bijlani, June 30, 1976; 1 child, Anjuli A. Student, U. So. Fla., 1967-68, Brevard Coll., 1969, Mich. State U., 1981. Copywriter Noel Schram & Assocs., Seattle, 1971-73; account exec. Reisner Communications, Seattle, 1973-75; dir. advt. and pub. rels. Thrift Village, Inc., Renton, Wash., 1975-76; report coord. Pratt & Whitney Aircraft Co., Palm Beach, Fla., 1976-77; mktg. dir. Federated Stores Realty, Inc., Ft. Lauderdale, Fla., 1978-81, JMB/Federated Realty, Memphis, 1981-88; sr. mktg. dir. JMB Properties Co., Santa Ana, 1988—. Bd. dirs. March of Dimes, 1985-88, United Cerebral Palsy, 1985-88, Hemophilia Found., 1985-88; troop leader Girl Scouts U.S., 1971-89. Recipient Maxi award Internat. Coun. Shopping Ctrs., N.Y.C., 1981, 83, merit award, 1982, 85, 86, 88. Mem. Hotel and Motel Mktg. Execs. Assn., So. Calif. Mktg. Dir.'s Assn. (exec. bd. 1988-89, dir. speakers bur. 1988-89), Orange County C. of C., Santa Ana C. of C. (bd. dirs., chmn.'s circle 1988-90), Internat. Coun. Shopping Ctrs. Democrat. Office: JMB Properties Co MainPlace/Santa Ana 2800 N Main St Santa Ana CA 92701

BILANIUK, LARISSA TETIANA, neuroradiologist educator; b. Potik, Ukraine, USSR, July 15, 1941; came to U.S., 1951; d. Yaroslav and Myroslava (Hryculak) Zubal; m. Oleksa-Myron Bilaniuk, Nov. 14, 1964; children: Larissa Indira, Laada Myroslava. BA, Wayne State U., 1961, MD, 1965. Diplomate Am. Bd. Radiology. Resident in radiology Hosp. of U. Pa., Phila., 1966-70; fellow Fondation Ophtalmologique, Paris, 1972; assoc. in radiology U. Pa. Sch. Medicine, Phila., 1973-74, asst. prof., 1974-79, assoc. prof., 1979-82, prof., 1982—; vis. radiologist Fondation Ophtalmologique, Paris, 1980; reviewer grants rsch. NIH, Washington, 1983-86; st. Göran lectr. Karolinska Inst., Stockholm, 1984; vis. prof. Grosshadern Clinics, U. Munich, 1988; invited lectr. USSR, 1976, 90, People's Republic China, 1977, France, 1980, 82, 89, Japan, 1984, 90, Sweden, 1984, Eng., 1985, The Netherlands, 1985, Italy, 1986, 87, 90, Fed. Republic Germany, 1987, 89. Co-editor 3 radiology books; contbr. over 200 articles on radiology to med. jours. and chpts. to books. Rsch. fellow Cancer Rsch. Ctr., Heidelberg, Fed. Republic Germany, 1967-68. Fellow Am. Coll. Radiology; mem. Radiol. Soc. N.Am., Am. Soc. Neuroradiology, European Soc. Neuroradiology, Soc. Magnetic Resonance in Medicine, Ukrainian Med. Assn. N.Am., Sigma Xi. Ukrainian Catholic. Office: Hosp of U Pa 3400 Spruce St Philadelphia PA 19104

BILES, MARILYN MARTA, painter; b. Wilmington, Del., Oct. 3, 1935; d. Albert Humbert and Anne Marie (DeRogatis) Marta; m. George Ronald Bower, June 30, 1956 (div. May 1970); children: Michele Bower Alvarado, Nancy Bower Guthrie, Randall William. Student Moore Coll. Art, 1953-54, St. Mary's Coll., 1959-61, Mus. Fine Arts, Houston, 1972-74. Art tchr. Contemporary Arts Mus., Houston, 1969-73, 80-81; head art dept. preprimary div. Duchesne Acad., Houston, 1970-72; project coordinator Nan Fisher, Inc., Houston, 1983-84; one-woman shows: 1st Nat. City Bank, Houston, 1980, Christ Ch. Cathedral, 1981-82, Toni Jones Gallery, 1981, U. Houston, 1982, Station Gallery, Greenville, Del., 1984, Boyar Norton & Blair, 1986, Martha Turner Properties, 1986; group shows include: U. Houston, 1977, 79, Nat. Cape Coral Exhbn., Fla., 1979, Toni Jones Gallery, 1979, Assistance League of Houston, 1979, 80, Golden Crescent Gallery, Houston, 1984; coordinator, designer art programs Spring Branch Schs., Houston, 1968-70. Bd. dirs. Spring Branch YWCA, Houston, 1973-74; docent Harris County Heritage Soc., Houston, 1970-72; mem. bd., v.p. Arcs Found., Inc., Houston, 1983; bd. dirs., gala chmn. Houston Grand Opera Guild, 1983-84, governing bd. assn., 1984-85, co-chmn. gala, 1985; founder, pres. Mus. Med. Sci. Assn., Houston, 1986-87; mem. com. Can-Do-It Charity Fundraiser, Peter W. Guenther Art History Scholarship Fund at U. Houston. Mem. Artists Equity (dir. Houston chpt. 1980), Art League Houston, Tex. Fine Arts Assn., Univ. Club Houston, Houston Racquet Club, World Trade Club (v.p. women's assn. 1974-75), Walden Yacht Club, Univ. Club Houston. Republican. Episcopalian. Home: 13022 Wood Harbor Montgomery TX 77356

BILKER, MINDY SUE, laboratory technician; b. Phila., July 16, 1952; d. Stanley Burton and Beatrice (Weiner) Bloom; m. David Alan Bilker, June 20, 1976; 1 child, Stefanie. AAS, Community Coll. of Phila., 1971; cert. in med. lab. tech., Dobbins Tech. Sch., 1972. Med. lab. technician U.S. VA Hosp., Phila., 1978-82; with Social Security Adminstrn., Phila. and Washington, 1983-89; med. lab. technician Nat. Naval Med. Ctr., Bethesda, Md., 1989—. Parent advocate Easter Seal Soc., Phila., 1985-87. Mem. Am. Soc. Med. Tech., Am. Assn. Chem. Chemistry. Democrat. Home: 9912 Foxborough Circle Rockville MD 20850 Office: Nat Naval Med Ctr 8901 Wisconsin Ave Bethesda MD 20814

BILKEY, BEVERLY YVONNE, medical technologist, social services official; b. Madison, Wis., Oct. 14, 1926; d. Rush Hillary and Amalie (Christen) Watson; m. Frederick Williams Bilkey, June 29, 1950 (dec. Dec. 1974); children—Barry W., Frederick D., Lorelei. B.S. in Med. Technology, U. Wis.-Madison, 1948. Lic. medical technologist. Chief technician Levin-Delavan Clinic, Delavan, Wis., 1948-49; asst. supr. Meml. Hosp., Wausau, Wis., 1949-50; supr. Gen. Hosp., Dodgeville, Wis., 1950-74; staff technologist Meml. Hosp. of Iowa County, Wis., 1974-76; supr. Dodgeville Clinic Lab., Wis., 1976-84. Mem. Health Planning Council, Dodgeville, 1978-84; chmn. Iowa County Social Services, Dodgeville, 1980-84, Iowa County Pub. Health Agy., Dodgeville, 1979-84; Iowa County bd. suprs. Fin. Personnel Community Action Agy.; gov.'s appointee Regional Planning Commn., 1980-82; chmn. bd. trustees Dodgeville United Ch. of Christ; candidate for State for Rep., 1980. Mem. Registry Am. Soc. Clin. Pathologists. Republican. Lodges: Rainbow Girls (mother adviser 1960), Order of Eastern Star (worthy matron 1964). Avocations: politics, crafts. Home: 4929 Whitcomb Dr Madison WI 53711

BILL, SHARON LYNN, real estate company official; b. Pottstown, Pa., Aug. 9, 1946; d. Edward and Elizabeth (Core) B. AA, Atlantic Community Coll., 1978; BS in Mktg. Mgmt., Stockton State U., 1978. Asst. mgr. LaConcha Hotel, Atlantic City, N.J., 1969-81; secretary Paxten & Ford Temporary Secretaries, Atlantic City, 1982-84; sales assoc. Grace Knupp Realty, Ventnor, N.J., 1989—. Mem. N.J. Econ. Supporters, Friends Stockton Libr. Mem. NAFE. Republican. Roman Catholic. Home: 605 Pitney Rd Absecon NJ 08201 Office: Grace Knupp Realty 5313 Atlantic Ave Ventnor NJ 08406

BILLAU, ROBIN LOUISE, health science facility administrator; b. Denver, Colo., Sept. 19, 1951; d. Emerson Roy and Catherine Louise (Brewster) Billau; m. Edward E. Adams. BA, Western State Coll., 1973; MS, Colo. State U., 1977. Cert. Indsl. Hygienist;. Life sci., indsl. hygienist Montana Energy Devel. & Research Inst., Butte, Mont., 1977-79; indsl. hygiene supr. Mountain States Energy, Butte, 1979-81; asst. prof. Mont. Coll. Mineral Sci. Tech., Butte, 1981-83; indsl. hygiene supr. EG & G Idaho, Idaho Falls, 1983-85, unit mgr., 1985-87, group mgr., 1987-88; sr. tech. adv. EG&G Idaho, Idaho Falls, 1988-90; cons. environ. mgmt., indsl. hygiene Houghton, Idaho, 1990—. Mem. Am. Indsl. Hygiene Assns., Am. Bd. Indsl. Hygiene Idaho Am. Indstl. Democrat. Home and Office: PO Box 128 Houghton ID 49931

BILLER, PAMELA MANNO, real estate agent; b. Balt., Sept. 22, 1954; d. Frank Angelo and Rose Elizabeth (Confrancesco) Manno; m. Michael Pritzter, Aug. 30 1975 (div. Aug. 1979); m. Michael Jay Biller, Se. 16, 1979; children: Aaron Robert, Melissa Lauren. AA, Catonsville Community Coll., 1974. Settlement officier Real Estate Title Co., Balt., 1974-77; media buyer W.B. Doner and Co. Advt., Balt., 1977-79, account exec., 1979-81, broadcast bus. mgr., 1981-83; pres., owner Little Stars Ltd., Owings Mills, Md., 1987—; with real estate sales Hannah Tabor, Inc., Balt., 1983—; bd. dirs. Child Study Assn. Md., Balt. Mem. Million Dollar Assn. Md. (Bronze Statue 1984, gold pin 1987, life), Greater Balt. Bd. Realtors.

BILLHARZ, CONSTANCE ELLEN CLARK, speech and language pathologist, educational diagnostician; b. Golden City, Mo., July 29, 1921; d. Harley B. and Flossie J. (Mitchell) Clark; m. Roger William Billharz, Jan. 12, 1946; 1 child, Roger Clark. BA, Pace U., 1971; MA, NYU, 1975; MPS, Manhattanville Coll., 1978. Cert. tchr. N.Y. Speech pathologist St. Joseph's Mental Health Clinic, Peekskill, N.Y., 1978-79; speech and lang. pathologist Rye (N.Y.) City Sch. Dist., 1980-82; speech therapist, spl. edn. tchr. Hartsdale Sch., Elmsford, N.Y., 1985-90; pvt. practice ednl. diagnostician North Tarrytown, N.Y., 1979—. Mem. Am. Speech, Lang., and Hearing Assn. (cert.), N.Y. State Speech, Lang., and Hearing Assn., Westchester Assn. for Children with Learning Disabilities, Am. Arbitration Assn. Republican. Home and Office: 467 Munroe Ave North Tarrytown NY 10591-1610

BILLIA, DARLENE A., advertising executive; b. N.Y.C., Nov. 3, 1948; d. Peter and Dorothy (Ziomek) B. AAS in Retail Mktg., N.Y.C. Community Coll., 1968; BBA in Mktg., Pace U., 1971. Research asst. Kendall Co., N.Y.C., 1971-72; research project dir. Needham Harper & Steers (now DDB Needham), N.Y.C., 1972-74; assoc. research dir. Batten, Barton, Durstine & Osborne, N.Y.C., 1974-76; sr. v.p., group dir. D'Arcy Masius Benton & Bowles, N.Y.C., 1976—; loaned exec. Am. Assn. Advt. Agys., Washington, 1979-80. Mem. Am. Mktg. Assn. (asst. treas. 1979, asst. sec. 1982-83, bd. dirs. N.Y. chpt. 1983-84, 86—). Office: D'Arcy Masius Benton 1675 Broadway 909 3rd Ave New York NY 10019

BILLINGS, CYNTHIA ANNE, editor; b. Mexico City, Feb. 9, 1933; d. Raymond Richard and Virginia (Forsyth) B. BA, Wells Coll., Aurora, N.Y., 1954. Advt. sales Time Inc., N.Y.C., 1955-58, edit. research, 1959-60; sr. editor News Front Mag., N.Y.C., 1961-65; assoc. editor The Gallagher Report, N.Y.C., mng. editor, 1968-73; editor The Gallagher Report, 1974-. V.p. Gallagher Found., 1978—. Episcopalian. Office: The Gallagher Report Inc 230 Park Ave New York NY 10017

BILLINGS, PATRICIA ANN COLLINS, nurse; b. San Diego, Jan. 31, 1946; d. Normon Clyde and Mary Asunda (Fantoni) Collins; m. George M. Whitehead, June 12, 1966 (div. Mar. 1975); children: Garrett Grafton Rayne, Sharna Raynel; m. Russell F. Billings II, Aug. 19, 1989. BS in Nursing, Loma Linda (Calif.) U., 1967, MPH, 1971; cert. Pediatric Nurse Practitioner, U Calif, San Diego, 1979. RN, Calif. Pub. health nurse San Bernadino County, Calif., 1967-72, San Diego County, 1974; sch. nurse, pediatric nurse practitioner Vista (Calif.) Unified Sch. Dist., 1974-85; pediatric nurse practitioner Sharp Rees-Stealy Med. Group, San Diego, 1985—. Mem. Pres.'s Council, San Diego, 1984-85. Recipient USPHS scholarship, 1971. Fellow Nat. Assn. Pediatric Nurse Practitioners (cert. chmn. 1987—); mem. San Diego Assn. Pediatric Nurse Practitioners, Mothers Against Drunk Driving. Republican. Office: Sharp Reese Stealey Med Group 7808 El Cajon Blvd La Mesa CA 92041

BILLINGS, PEGGY MARIE, religious organization administrator, teacher,; b. McComb, Miss., Sept. 10, 1928; d. Clement David and Eynes Melissa (Dickerson) B. BS, Millsaps Coll., 1950; MA, Columbia U., 1957; D in Liberal Arts (hon.), Ewha Woman's U., 1986. Clk. Ill. Cen. R.R., McComb, 1947; instr. tennis YWCA, Jackson, Miss., 1950; missionary Republic of Korea, People's Republic of Korea, 1952-63; ch. exec. Global Ministries of the United Meth. Ch., N.Y.C., 1963—; vis. prof. religion and society Chandler Sch. Theology, 1972-73; lectr. in world christianity Yale Divinity Sch., 1989. Author: The Waiting People, In No One's Pocket, Paradox and Promise in Human Rights, Fire Beneath the Frost: Korea. Chairperson N.Am. Coalition for Human Rights in Republic of Korea, 1979-; mem. adv. bd. Ctr. for Internat. Policy, 1984-, Global Edn. Assocs., 1989-; bd. dirs. Ctr. Constitutional Rights, 1979-89. Recipient Human Rights award Korean Christina Scholars Assn. N.Am., Pub. Welfare medal Republic of Korea, 1963, Ball award Methodist Fedn. for Social Action, 1989. Democrat. Methodist. Home: Rt 1 Box 381 Trumansburg NY 14886

BILLINGS, SUZANNE CHUNG-A-ON, epidemiologist; b. Georgetown, Guyana, Jan. 1, 1963; d. Kenneth W. and Shirley (Edwards) Chung-A-On; m. Jeffrey C. Billings, May 4, 1961. BA in Chemistry, Emory U., 1983, MPH, 1987. Researcher chemistry dept. Emory U., Atlanta, 1981, Medcom, Inc., Atlanta, 1984; mgr. Student Ctr. Emory U., Atlanta, 1984-87, library asst. health scis., 1987-88; sr. abstracter Ga. Dept. Human Resources, Office Epidemiology, Atlanta, 1988, data mgmt. coord., 1988-89; project coord. Sergievsky Ctr. Columbia U., N.Y., 1989—. Vol. Grady Meml. Hosp., Atlanta, 1980-81, DeKalb County Health Dept., Atlanta, 1987; mem. exec. com. Pres. Commn. on Status of Minorities, Emory U., Atlanta, 1986-87. Mem. Am. Pub. Health Assn. Home: 542 W 112th St Apt 5M New York NY 10025

BILLINGTON, DEBORAH GAIL, property management executive; b. San Angelo, Tex., Dec. 17, 1949; d. Donald Gene and Verna Ruth (Fleming) Whited; m. Bruce Bennett Billington, Nov. 10, 1968; children: Bruce Ryan, Mitzi Marie. Grad. high sch., Hamilton, Ohio. Property mgr. Walter Carrington Co., Austin, Tex., 1968-71; owner Dog Shop Pet Supply and Grooming, Austin, 1971-73; payroll acct. Glasstron Boat Mfrs., Austin, 1973-74; dir. Kindercare Learning Ctr., Austin, 1972-74; owner Magic Rainbow Daycare and Kindergarten, Austin, 1974-78; gen. mgr. Access Mini Storage Co., Austin, 1979-88; pres. Effective Property Mgmt. Inc., Austin, 1988—. Mem. Tex. Mini Storage Assn. (founder, dir. 1986—, v.p. 1986, 89), Self Storage Assn. (nat. dir. 1988-90, cen. region dir. 1985-88, v.p. 1987, 88, contbr. trade jour. 1984—, top membership recruiter 1983-84), Womens C. of C., N.W. C. of C. Republican. Home: 9708 Vista View Dr Austin TX 78750 Office: 13706 Research Blvd Ste 312 Austin TX 78750

BILLS, MRS. JOHN T. See BELLAMY, JEANNE

BILOTTA, DIANE BRILEY, physician assistant; b. DesMoines, Iowa, Jan. 9, 1953; d. Albert and Martha Jean (Sloan) Briley; m. Dennis Dean Pueschel, Jan. 26, 1973 (div. 1982); children: Aaron, Shaun; m. Anthony Louis Bilotta, Nov. 16, 1985. BS in Health Sci., U. Osteopathic Medince, Des Moines, Iowa, 1983. Cert. physician asst. Physician asst. Dan L. Duberstein, D.O., P.C., Des Moines, 1983-85, Manfred W. Raiser, M.D., P.C., Hinsdale, Ill., 1985—; pres. Park Place of Palos Park (Ill.) Ltd., 1989—. Contbr. articles on gastroenterology to publs. Vol. Am. Heart Assn., Chgo., 1983—, nursing home. Mem. Am. Acad. Physicians Assts., Soc. Gastrointestinal Assts., Nat. Found. Ileitis and Colitis. Republican. Office: Manfred W Raiser MD PC 333 Chestnut Rd Ste 102 Hinsdale IL 60521

BILOW, ALISON LEIGH, advertising professional; b. Plattsburgh, N.Y., Aug. 25, 1960; d. Lester William and Lucy Ellen (Moody) B. BS in Nutrition, Marymount Coll., 1982. Adminstrv. asst. internat. money markets div. The Royal Bank of Can., N.Y.C., 1982-86; with U.S. Lines, 1983-86; account mgr. U.S. Lines, Charleston, S.C., 1983-84; sr. account mgr. U.S. Lines, Charlotte, 1984-86, dist. sales mgr., 1986; dist. sales mgr. Sea Land, Charlotte, 1987; account sales mgr. So. Steam, Inc., N.Y.C., 1987; with directory and tickler advt. sales div. Jour. of Commerce, N.Y.C., 1987-88; S.E. advt. sales mgr. Jour. of Commerce Newspaper, N.Y.C., 1988-90, Atlanta, 1988—. Mem. Charlotte Jaycees, 1985, 86. Presdl. scholar Marymount Coll., 1978-82; recipient Top Dept. Honor award, Graduating Class, 1982, Marymount Coll. Mem. N.C. World Trade Assn. Roman Catholic. Office: Jour of Commerce Newspaper 3121 Maple Dr Ste 110 Atlanta GA 30305

BINDER, AMY FINN, public relations company executive; b. N.Y.C., June 13, 1955; d. David and Laura (Zeisler) Finn; m. Ralph Edward Binder, Aug. 15, 1976; children: Ethan Max, Adam Finn, Rebecca Eve. BA with honors, Brown U., 1977. Freelance photographer N.Y.C., 1977-78; account exec. Newton & Nicolazza, Boston, 1978-79, Agnew, Carter, McCarthy, Boston, 1979-80; dir. pub. relations City of New Rochelle, N.Y., 1980-82; dir. urban communications Ruder-Finn, N.Y.C., 1982-85, v.p., 1985-86, exec. v.p., 1986-87, pres., 1987—; bd. dirs. Castle Art Gallery, New Rochelle. Photographer: Museum without Walls, 1975, The Spirit of Man: Sculpture of Kaare Nygaard, 1975, Knife Life and Bronzes, 1977, St. Louis: Sculpture City, 1988, The Triumph of the American Spirit: Johnstown, Pennsylvania, 1989. Bd. dirs. New Rochelle Community Fund. Democrat. Jewish. Office: Ruder Finn Inc 301 E 57th St New York NY 10022

BINDER, ELIZABETH ANN, nurse; b. St. Louis, Feb. 21, 1957; d. William Carl and Eleanor Olivia (Mueller) B. BSN, St. Louis U., 1983; MSN, U. N.C., 1987. RN, Mo., N.C., Md. Staff nurse St. Mary's Health Ctr., St. Louis, 1978-80, Vis. Nurses Assn., St. Louis, 1980-83, N.C. Meml. Hosp., Chapel Hill, 1983-86; with clin. rsch. dept. U. N.C., Chapel Hill, 1986-88; nurse practitioner Johns Hopkins Hosp., Balt., 1988-89, U. Md., Balt., 1989—; cons. Frontier Adjusters, Balt., 1989—. Bd. dirs. N.C. Kidney Found., Chapel Hill, 1986. Mem. Am. Nurses Assn. (cert. family nurse practitioner), Md. Nurses Assn., Md. Coun. Nurse Practitioners, Sigma Theta Tau. Republican. Lutheran.

BINDER, MILDRED KATHERINE, retired county public welfare agency executive; b. York, Pa., Jan. 5, 1918; d. Jemie Irving and Emma Jane (Billet) Binder. BA magna cum laude in Sociology, Hood Coll., 1940. Sec., mgr. Stock's Appliances, York, 1940-42; caseworker York County Bd. Assistance, Pa. Dept. Public Welfare, 1942-49, 1953-58, supr., 1949-53, 1958-59, exec. dir., 1959-83. Past mem. exec. com. York County Employment and Tng. Com.; past mem. dept. task forces Social Service Delivery to Client Info. System, also mem. ops. rev. bd.; past mem. bd. York County Council Alcoholism, 1959-62, Community Progress Council, 1965-67; co-chmn. Community Dialogue Com., 1968-69; mem. bd. Pre-Paid Health York, Inc., 1979; mem. human services planning coalition United Way, 1978-83, chmn. council agy. execs., 1967-71, 1976-78; past mem. consumer adv. councils Gen. Telephone, Met. Edison; bd. dirs. Literacy Council of York County, 1985-86; mem. York County Human Services Adv. Com., 1983-87; mem. York County Area Agy. on Aging Adv. Com., 1989—. Named Boss of Yr., Am. Bus. Women, 1973; named in commendations Pa. gov., Pa. Ho. of Reps. Mem. Am. Public Welfare Assn., Exec. Dirs. Assn. Pa. (exec. com. 1979-83, sec. 1980-83), AAUW (bd. dirs. York br. 1984—), York County Hist. Soc., York Transp. Club (bd. dirs. 1987—), Coll. of York Club, Hood Coll. Club. Home: 1611 W Market St York PA 17404

BINER, MARGARET LAVIN, communications company executive; b. Worcester, Mass., May 1, 1952; d. Walter Douglas and Ellen M. (Gilligan) Lavin; m. Stanley Biner, Sept. 4, 1983; children: Walter Joseph, Adam Tobias. B.A., Assumption Coll., 1974; M.B.A., Clark U., 1976, postgrad., 1976-77. Asst. mgr. New Eng. Tel. and Tel., Boston, 1978-80; sr. rate analyst Am. Electric Power, Columbus, Ohio, 1980-81; mkt. supr. GTE Satellite Co., Stamford, Conn., 1981-83; dist. mgr. AT&T Communications, Basking Ridge, N.J., 1983—. Solicitor AT&T Polit. Action Com., Basking Ridge, 1985; ritual com. Temple Emanu-El, Westfield, N.J., 1982. Mem. Am. Statis. Assn., Nat. Assn. Bus. Economists, Am. Mktg. Assn. (v.p. programs for N.J. 1985-86). Jewish. Office: AT&T Communications 295 N Maple Ave Basking Ridge NJ 07920

BINFORD, VALORIE YDETTE, municipal government official; b. Macon, Ga., Apr. 7, 1964; d. Charles O'Neal and Mozell (Cornelius) B. BA, Spelman Coll., Atlanta, 1985; MPA, Ga. Coll., Milledgeville, 1988. Legal tech. U.S. Army Corps of Engrs., Savannah, Ga., 1986; academic intern Mayor's office City of Macon, 1988, mgmt. intern Mayor's office, 1988-89, grants specialist Econ. and Community Devel. Dept., 1989—. Author: (play) Dreams of the Present/Voices from the Past, 1986. leader, tutor Sickle Cell Anemia Found., Atlanta, 1984-85; bd. dirs. Macon chpt. United Cerebral Palsy, 1989-90; active Booker T. Washington Community Ctr., Macon, 1990. Ga. Regents scholar Ga. Coll., 1986-88. Mem. NAFE. Democrat. Baptist. Home: 2555 Date Ave Macon GA 31204

BINGHAM, EULA, university official; b. Covington, Ky., July 9, 1929. BS, Eastern Ky. U., MS, 1954; PhD, U. Cin., 1958. Analytical chemist Cin., 1951-52; research assoc., 1958-61; asst. prof. Coll. Medicine, U. Cin., 1961-70, assoc. prof., 1970-77; prof. environ. health Sch. Medicine, U. Cin.,

1981—, v.p., univ. dean for grad. studies and research, 1981-90; asst. sec. for occupational safety and health Dept. Labor, Washington, 1977-81; mem. study sect. safety and occupational health Nat. Inst. Occupational Safety and Health, 1972-76; mem. Food and Drug Adv. Commn., FDA, Environ. Health Adv. Commn.; sci. adv. bd. EPA, 1976; mem. Nat. Air Quality Criteria Adv. Commn., 1975-76; mem. ad hoc Lead in Paint Commn., Nat. Acad. Scis., 1974-75; chmn. standards Adv. Commn. on Coke Oven Emissions, Dept. Labor, 1974-75; mem. Nat. Acad. Scis.-NRC com. on Ground Water Protection, 1985-86, mem. com. on methods for invivo toxicity testing Com. on Life Scis. and Tech., 1984-86; trustee Natural Resources Def. Council, 1983—; dirs. Ohio Hazardous Substance Inst., 1990—. Adv. Commn. on Carcinogens, 1973. Recipient Rockefeller Found. Pub. Service award, 1980, Alice Hamilton award Am. Pub. Health Assn., 1984. Mem. Inst. of Medicine. Office: U Cin Cincinnati OH 45221

BINGHAM, JINSIE SCOTT, broadcast company executive; b. Greencastle, Ind., Dec. 28, 1935; d. Roscoe Gibson and Alpha Edith (Robinson) Scott; m. Frank William Wokoun, Jr. (dec.); children: Douglas Scott, Richard Frank; m. Richard Innes Bingham, June 24, 1964. Student, DePauw U., Greencastle, 1952-53, Northwestern U., 1953, Coe Coll., 1953-54. Exec. sec. Ind. Young Dems., 1958-60; receptionist Ind. House of Reps., Indpls., 1959; saleslady Avon Products, Greencastle, 1961-64; sales mgr. Sta. WJNZ (formerly WXTA), Greencastle, 1969-77, owner, pres., gen. mgr., 1977—; former ptnr. Sta. WVTL, Monticello, Ill., Sta. KBIB, Monette, Ark.; speaker DePauw U. Communications Seminar, 1981, 85; vis. lectr., 1986-89. Com. chair Legis. Awareness Seminar, 1978-86; co-chair Greencastle Gaelic Festival, 1983-84; charter mem. Greencastle 2001, 1985—, Greencastle Civic League, 1984—, Greencastle Merchant's Assn., 1983—, Community Resources Council, 1982—; charter mem., corp. sec. Main St., Greencastle, 1983—, v.p., 1987-88, pres., 1988-89; bd. dirs. Greencastle Vol. Fire Dept., 1986, Greencastle Devel. Ctr., 1988-89, Greencastle Community Child Care Ctr., 1983—; mem. Greencastle Zoning Bd. Appeals, 1984—, v.p., 1985-88, pres., 1988—; announcer Putnam County Fair Parade, 1977—; community host Hoosier Hospitality Days, 1981-84; active Putnam County Com. for Econ. Strength, 1979-83. Named Outstanding Citizen, Greencastle Jaycees, 1981. Mem. Am. Women in Radio and TV (pres. Ind. chpt. 1979-82), Indpls. Network Women in Bus. (charter), Women in Communications, Inc. (bd. dirs. 1983-84, MATRIX co-chair 1984), Am. Legion Aux., Nat. Assn. Broadcasters, Ind. Broadcasters Assn. (v.p. FM 1982), Greencastle Bus. and Profl. Women's Club (pres. 1976-77, 79-80), Indpls. Ad Club, Women's Press Club Ind., Indpls. Press Club, Nat. Fedn. Press Women, Ind. Dem. Editorial Assn. (sec. 1987, v.p. 1988, pres. 1990), Ind. C. of C., Greencastle C. of C. (bd. dirs. 1979-83, pres. 1982), VFW (pres. ladies aux. 1966-68), Milestone Car Soc., Packard Club Ind., Ind. Soc. Pioneers, Daus. of 1812 (pres. Tippecanoe chpt. 1981, state v.p. 1982), DAR, Delta Theta Tau, Sigma Delta Chi, Soc. Profl. Journalist. Mem. Christian Ch. (Disciples of Christ). Club: Windy Hill Country. Lodges: Order Eastern Star, Internat. Order Job's Daus. (life), Women of Moose. Office: Sta WJNZ PO Box 494 Greencastle IN 46135

BINGO-DUGGINS, KAREN LEIKO, personnel specialist; b. Honolulu, Dec. 15, 1942; d. Warren Tsutomu and Shizue (Shiroma) Bingo; m. Michael Oniel Bingo-Duggins, Aug. 18, 1976. Student, Chaminade Coll., 1963-64; BA, U. Hawaii, 1965. Classification trainee Pacific region U.S. Army, Okinawa, Japan, 1967-71, personnel staffing specialist Pacific region, 1971-72; position classification specialist U.S. Army, San Francisco, 1972-74; personnel mgmt. specialist material command U.S. Army, Washington, 1974, mgmt. employee specialist material command, 1974-76, personnel evaluation specialist material command, 1976-78, classification specialist, 1978-80; personnel mgmt. specialist USAF, Washington, 1980-84, chief sr. exec. service mgmt., 1984—. Mem. Internat. Personnel Adminstrn., Minority Women in Govt., Fed. Exec. Inst. alumni Assn. Home: 4327 Stream Bed Way Alexandria VA 22306 Office: Hdqrs USAF/DPCZ Pentagon Rm 4E232 Washington DC 20330-5060

BINION, BEATRICE MARIE See HARRISON, BEATRICE MARIE

BINION, LINDA DIANE, systems technologies researcher; b. Birmingham, Ala., Apr. 21, 1948; d. James Marvin and Sara Meredith (Moore) Binion; m. Norman Willard Holman, June 20, 1981 (div. 1983); m. Paul Anthony DeLorenzo, Aug. 16, 1986. Student, U. Ala.-Tuscaloosa, 1966-67, U. Ala.-Birmingham. Data base adminstr. Carraway Methodist Med. Ctr., Birmingham, Ala., 1970-78; mgr. systems and program Brookwood Health Services Inc., Birmingham, 1979-80; sr. v.p. Innovative Systems Inc., Birmingham, 1980-83; pres. Amitec Inc., Birmingham, 1983-85; dir. research-info. systems technologies Ala. Metal Industries Corp., Birmingham, 1986; pres. AMICO Research Corp., 1986— ; cons. in field. Designer: (software system) Innovative Healthcare Support System, 1980. Guest speaker U. Ala. Sch. Community Allied Health Services, 1986, numerous others. Mem. C. of C. (Birmingham), Mensa, Assn. Systems Mgmt. (past pres.), Internat. Platform Assn. Democrat. Am. Baptist. Office: AMICO Research Corp 1075 S 13th St Suite 250 Birmingham AL 35205

BINKLEY, JANET RAMAGE, editor; b. Prescott, Ariz., Mar. 18, 1930; d. Russell A. and Elva Caroline (Brobst) Ramage; m. Thomas Eden Binkley, Nov. 26, 1953 (div. 1964); 1 child, Christina Kreider Binkley. BA cum laude, Colo. U., 1952; postgrad., U. Munich, 1960-61; MA, Colo. U., 1964; PhD with distinction, U. Kans., 1974. Editor rsch. publs. U. Ill. Press, Urbana, 1953-60; asst. prof. German Stephens Coll., Columbia, Mo., 1963-68; asst. prof. fgn. langs. Emporia Kans. State Tchrs. Coll./U., 1969-74; jours. editor Internat. Reading Assn., Newark, Del., 1975—. Editor Jour. of Reading, 1975—, The Reading Tchr., 1975-89; contbr. articles to profl. jours. Scholar Pepsi Cola Scholarship Bd., 1948, Exchange scholar Deutscher Akademischer Austauschdienst, Bonn, Fed. Republic Germany, 1960. Mem. Soc. for Scholarly Publishing, Edn. Writers Assn., Phi Beta Kappa. Democrat. Unitarian Universalist. Home: 922 Rockmoss Ave Newark DE 19711 Office: Internat Reading Assn 800 Barksdale Rd PO Box 8139 Newark DE 19714

BINKS, REBECCA ANNE, communications executive; b. Oak Park, Ill., July 23, 1955; d. Donald Melvin and Elizabeth June (Lobdell) B.; m. Cary Emmett Donham, June 22, 1980. Student, Goodman Sch. Drama, Chgo., 1973-76; BA in Liberal Arts, Columbia Coll., Chgo., 1983; postgrad., Roosevelt U., 1987—. Freelance lighting designer, theater tech. Chgo., N.Y.C., 1975-80; retail mgr. Coffee and Tea Exch., Chgo., 1981-84; sales assoc. K&S Photographics, Chgo., 1985-87; supr. client services AGS&R Communications, Chgo., 1987-88; mgr. Meeting Express Systems, Chgo., 1988-90; pres. Binks & Assocs. Inc., Chgo., 1990—; tchr. travel photography, Chgo., 1987. Exhibited in group and one-woman shows. Mem. internal communications com. Girl Scouts, Chgo., 1989—. Office: 2311 N Karlov Ave Chicago IL 60639

BINNIE, FRANCES SUE, technical pump engineer; b. Covina, Calif., Sept. 2, 1954; d. Frank William and Rose Marie (Wollery) B.; 1 adopted child. Student, Citrus Coll., 1975-77, Mt. San Antonio Coll., 1979-81, State Tech. Inst. Memphis, 1986—. With Aurora Pump Verti-Line, La Puente, Calif., 1972-86; sr. tech. engr. Aurora Pump Verti-Line, La Puente, 1978-86; application specialist Layne-Bowler Verti-Line, Inc., Memphis, 1986—. Author instrn. manuals. Sports ofcl., Calif. Interscholastic Fedn., 1979-86, Memphis Park Commn., 1986—; instr. Each-One-Teach-One program, Memphis United Way, 1988—. Mem. ASME (sec.-treas. Calif. chpt. 1983-86), Am. Soc. Cert. Engring. Technicians. Office: Layne Bowler Inc 1993 Chelsea Ave Memphis TN 38108

BINSFELD, CONNIE BERUBE, state senator; b. Munising, Mich., Apr. 18, 1924; d. Omer J. and Elsie (Constance) Berube: B.S., Siena Heights Coll., 1945, D.H.L. (hon.), 1977; postgrad. Wayne State U., 1966-67; m. John E. Binsfeld, July 19, 1947; children—John T., Gregory, Susan, Paul, Michael. County commr., Leelanau County, Mich., 1970-74; mem. Mich. Ho. of Reps., 1974-82; mem. Mich. Senate, 1982—, asst. majority leader. Del., Republican Nat. Conv., 1980. Named Mich. Mother of Year, Mich. Mothers Com., 1977; Northwestern Mich. Coll. fellow. Mem. Nat. Council State Legislators, LWV, Siena Heights Coll. Alumnae Assn. Republican. Roman Catholic. Home: 8944 County Rd 675 Maple City MI 49664 Office: Mich Senate Lansing MI 48909*

BIR, MICHELLE MARIE, sales executive; b. Canandaigua, N.Y., June 29, 1965; d. Thomas A. and Carol A. (Genecco) B. BS in Econs., Wells Coll., 1987. Merchandiser Bratt-Foster, Syracuse, N.Y., 1988-89; sales exec. Eastman-Kodak, Cape Girardeau, Mo., 1989—. Mem., starter Make-A-Wish Found., Cape Girardeau, 1989. Mem. Am. Women's Econ. Devel. Assn. Democrat. Roman Catholic. Office: Eastman Kodak 11525 Olde Cabin Rd Saint Louis MO 63141

BIRAM, GERALDINE LOUISE, elementary education educator; b. Bosler, Wyo., May 10, 1923; d. Frank Walther and Jeanette Caroline (Gluesing) Berner; m. George Emery Biram, Nov. 29, 1946; children: Beverly Kay Biram Burban, Barbara Lynn Biram Davis. BA, U. Wyo., 1944; postgrad., Western Wash. Coll. Edn., Bellingham, 1946, Coll. Puget Sound, Tacoma, Wash., 1956, Johns Hopkins U., Balt., 1958-59. Instr. Superior (Wyo.) Pub. Schs., 1944-45, Yakima (Wash.) Pub. Schs., 1945-47, Am. Sch. System, Baumholder, Fed. Republic Germany, 1952-53, Sch. Dist. 400 Pierce County, Lakewood, Wash., 1949-50, 55-57, Balt. County Pub. Schs., Towsen, Md., 1958-60, Albany County Sch. Dist. 1, Laramie, Wyo., 1960-82; vol. tchr. Cherry Creek Schs., Denver, 1989-90. Contbr. articles to profl. jours. and mags. Troop leader Girl Scouts U.S., San Antonio, 1957, Balt., 1958-60, Laramie, 1960-71. Mem. Assn. Vols. Children's Hosp. (pres. Windsor Gardens unit 1986-90), Ladies Aux. to VFW (pres. 1969-70, dist. 6 pres. 1972-73), Order Eastern Star (chaplain 1965, 67, 69, 73-75), Women's Club Windsor Gardens (Denver) (Treas. 1986, 90), Psi Chi, Kappa Delta Pi, Phi Kappa Phi, Delta Kappa Gamma. Home: 9335 E Center St 4A Denver CO 80231

BIRCH, GRACE MORGAN, library administrator, educator; b. N.Y.C., June 3, 1925; d. Milton Melville and Adeline Ellsdale (Springer) Morgan; m. Kenneth Francis Birch, Oct. 26, 1947; children: Shari R., Timothy F. B.A., U. Bridgeport, 1963; M.L.S., Pratt Inst., 1968. With Bridgeport Pub. Library, Conn., 1949-66; asst. town librarian Fairfield Pub. Library, Conn., 1966-69; dir. Trumbull Library System, Conn., 1969—; lectr. Housatonic Community Coll., Bridgeport, 1970—; lectr. self-motivation, 1989—. Judge, Barnum Festival Soc. Bridgeport, 1971-73; mem. Trumbull Multi-Arts Com., Trumbul Prevention Coun. Mem. ALA, New Eng. Library Assn., Conn. Library Assn. (pres. 1972), Southwestern Conn. Library Council (pres. 1975-77), Fairfield Library Adminstrs. Group (pres. 1976-77). Democrat. Episcopalian. Avocations: sketching, dancing, traveling. Home: 175 Brooklawn Ave Bridgeport CT 06604 Office: The Trumbull Libr 33 Quality St Trumbull CT 06611

BIRCHEM, REGINA, cell biologist, educator; b. Sisseton, S.D., Dec. 20, 1938; d. Victor John and Hazel Mary (O'Brien) Birchem; m. Dan I. Bolef, Aug. 29, 1981. BS in Edn., U. N.D., 1964; MEd, U. Ga., 1970, PhD, 1977. Rsch. assoc. U. Ga., Athens, 1977-79, U. Colo., Boulder, 1979-80, Washington U., St. Louis, 1980-81; asst. prof. Fontbonne Coll., St. Louis, 1981-84; vis. asst. prof. U. South, Sewanee, Tenn., 1984; asst. rsch. prof. St. Louis U. Sch. Medicine, 1985-88; assoc. prof. Pa. State U., McKeesport, Pa., 1988-90; assoc. prof., Florence Scott chair in devel. biology Seton Hill Coll., Greensburg, Pa., 1990—; biology cons. Pa. Environ. Network, Yukon. Contbr. numerous articles to profl. jours.; editorial bd.: Haversack: A Franciscan Review, 1987—. Nat. bd. Womens Internat. League for Peace and Freedom, Phila., 1986-90. NSF grantee, 1982, 84, 69-70, NIH grantee, 1979-80, Nat. Def. Edn. Act fellow, 1971-74; recipient Presdl. award for student rsch. Electron Microscope Soc., 1977. Mem. Am. Soc. for Cell Biology, Fedn. Am. Socs. for Experimental Biology, Sigma Xi. Roman Catholic. Office: Seton Hill Coll Greensburg PA 15601

BIRCHFIELD, MARY EVA, retired librarian; b. Sarasota, Fla., Mar. 8, 1909; d. Benjamin Franklin and Mary Charlotte (Farnbach) McCall; m. William Otto Birchfield, Dec. 5, 1933; children—William, Benjamin, Hal, James. B.S. in Physics, Fla. State Coll. for Women, 1929; M.S., Fla. State U., 1961, M.S. in L.S., 1963. Cert. tchr. Tchr., Lafayette County, Mayo, Fla., 1930-61; librarian Fla. State U., Tallahassee, 1963-77, London br., 1973; bibliographer Fla. Constitution Revision Commn., 1977-78. Compiler bibliographies: Consolidated Catalog of League of Nations Publications Offered for Sale, 1976, Complete Reference Guide to United Nations Sales Publications, 1946-1978, 1982. Pres. PTA, Mayo, 1940-42. NSF study awardee, 1958-60. Mem. Phi Kappa Phi, Kappa Delta Pi, Delta Kappa Gamma, Beta Phi Mu. Democrat. Baptist. Home: 125 Westridge Dr Tallahassee FL 32304

BIRD, JACQUELINE FAYE, state agency administrator; b. Jacksonville, N.C., Apr. 30, 1954; d. Harold Edgar and Leah Ferris (Nutting) B. BS in Bus. Edn., Ohio State U., 1977. Programs coord. Ohio Dept. Energy, Columbus, 1978-84; sr. policy analyst energy div. Ohio Dept. Devel., Columbus, 1978-84; liaison officer dept. devel. Ohio Coal Devel. Office, Columbus, 1984-89; dir. dept. devel. Ohio Coal Devel. Office, 1989—; bd. dirs., Iopis Corp., Columbus. Coord. disaster vols., mem. vol. recruitment task force, Columbus chpt. ARC. Mem. Women in Mining (co-founder 1987, pres. Ohio chpt. 1989-90, chmn. nat. pub. rels. 1990—). Methodist. Office: Ohio Coal Devel Office PO Box 1001 SOTII-25 Columbus OH 43266-0101

BIRD, JOANNE LYNNE, automobile agency owner; b. Wheeling, W.Va., July 27, 1954; d. Franklin Byarm and Carrie Christina (Suppes) Kirkland; m. Sherman Lee Bird, Apr. 26, 1955. BS in Edn., Abilene Christian U., 1978. Cert. tchr., Tex., Ohio. Tchr. Valley View Schs., Apple Creek, Ohio, 1980-81, Channelview (Tex.) Ind. Sch. Dist., 1982-84; student svcs. coord. Nat. Edn. Ctr., Houston, 1984-85; substitute tchr. Cypress Fairbanks Ind. Sch. Dist., Houston, 1984-85; pres., owner Euro-Tech Automotive Co., Houston, 1986—. Editor-in-chief newsletter Nat. Edn. Ctr., 1984-85. Vol. Anti-Gay Referendum, Houston, 1985. Mem. Tex. Speech Communication Assn., Tex. Forensic Assn., Am. Forensic Assn., Abilene Christian U. Alumni Assn. Republican. Office: Euro-Tech 5930 J Hwy 6 N Houston TX 77084

BIRD, ROSE ELIZABETH, former state chief justice; b. Tucson, Nov. 2, 1936. B.A. magna cum laude, L.I. U., 1958; J.D., U. Calif., Berkeley, 1965. Bar: Calif. 1966. Clk. to chief justice Nev. Supreme Ct., 1965-66; successively dep. public defender, sr. trial dep., chief appellate div. Santa Clara County (Calif.) Pub. Defenders Office, 1966-74; tchr. Stanford U. Law Sch., 1972-74; sec. Calif. Agr. and Services Agy., also mem. governor's cabinet, 1975-77; chief justice Calif. Supreme Ct., 1977-86; chairperson Calif. Jud. Council, Commn. Jud. Appointments; pres. bd. dirs. Hastings Coll. Law, U. Calif.; bd. councilors U. So. Calif. Law Center, 1975-77; past mem. Western regional selection panel President's Commn. White House Fellowships; bd. assos. San Fernando Valley Youth Found; TV commentator, 1988. Named Most Outstanding Sr. L.I. U., 1958; Ford Found. fellow, 1960. Democrat. Address: PO Box 51376 Palo Alto CA 94306

BIRD-PORTO, PATRICIA ANNE, personnel director; b. N.Y.C., June 16, 1952; d. Jacques Robert and Muriel (Cooper) Bird; m. Joseph Porto, May 5, 1984; 1 child, Jennifer Ashley. BA, U. So. Calif., 1975; cert. in legal assistantship, U. Calif., Irvine, 1987. Cert. in transp. demand mgmt. Orange County Transit Dist., 1988. Mgr. Bullock's Westwood, West L.A., 1976-78; mgr. ops. Lane Bryant, L.A., 1978-79; supr. employment, dir. personnel May Co. Dept. Stores, 1979-81; adminstr. personnel, dir. benefits Zoetrope Studios, Hollywood, Calif., 1981-82; personnel and ops. analyst Auntie Barbara's, Beverly Hills, Calif., 1982-86; dir. personnel Baylylop, Santa Ana, Calif., 1986-88; pres. Creative Personnel Assocs., 1986—. Bd. dirs. Planned Parenthood; co-chair Pro-Wilson '90, 1990. Mem. Personnel Indsl. Relations Assn. Home: 7 Stardust Irvine CA 92715 Office: PO Box 9663 Newport CA 92658-9663

BIRDSALL, JANE ELAINE, financial executive; b. Buffalo, Aug. 26, 1947; d. Roy George and Geraldine J. (Steffan) Fink; m. Arthur Anthony Birdsall, Jan. 28, 1967; children—Robert James, Thomas Michael, William Mathew. B.B.A., Saginaw Valley State Coll., 1982. Cert. fin. planner, fin. cons. Thomson McKinnon Securities, Inc., Midland, 1982-88, fin. cons., 1988—. Mem. Tri City Task Force for Econ. Devel. of Women, Midland, Bay City, Saginaw, Mich., 1984-86; bd. dirs. Bay County YWCA, 1986—. Mem. Am. Bus. Women's Assn. (pres. 1985-86, Woman of Yr. award 1986-87), Bus. & Profl. Women's Assn. (v.p. 1984-86, pres. 1986-87), Inst. Cert. Fin. Planners, Internat. Assn. Fin. Planning, Women's Bus. Alliance Mid. Mich. (v.p. 1986-87, pres. 1988-89), AAUW (women's chmn. 1987—), Diocese of Saginaw Fin. Council (chmn. 1989—). Office: Thomson McKinnon Securities Inc 121 1/2 E Main St Midland MI 48640

BIRDSELL, REGINA SULLIVAN, principal; b. Waterbury, Conn., Sept. 30, 1946; d. John William and Dorothy Ann (Payne) Sullivan; m. William Henry Birdsell, Jr.; 1 child, Scott William. BA in Psychology, Sacred Heart U., 1969; MS in Spl. Edn., So. Conn. State U., 1976, postgrad., 1980. Cert. spl. edn. tchr., Conn. Tchr. Monroe (Conn.) Elem. Sch., 1969-70, Masuk High Sch., Monroe, 1971-73, Hillside Mid. Sch., Naugatuck, Conn., 1973-74, City Hill Mid. Sch., Naugatuck, 1974-76, Naugatuck High Sch., 1977-82; learning disabilities coord. Town of Naugatuck, 1977-82; prin. Central Avenue Sch., Naugatuck, 1982-89, Acad. Elem. Sch., Madison, Conn., 1989—; corporator Naugatuck Savs. Bank. Editor: Prin.'s Forum Jour., 1984—. Edn. advisor Adv. Bd. for Congressman John Rowland, Waterbury; chmn. human resources com. United Way Naugatuck and Beacon Falls, Conn.; mem. Naugatuck Campership Bd. Recipient Computer award Diversified Electronics, 1982, Promising Practice award State of Conn., 1982; named Naugatuck Educator of the Month, Naugatuck Daily News, 1984. Mem. Nat. Assn. Elem. Sch. Prins. (state editor, resolutions com.), Elem. and Mid. Sch. Prins. Assn. (editor fed. rels., Presdl. award 1985-90), Adminstrn. and Supervision Assn. (past pres.), AAUW (past pres.), Jr. League Waterbury, Phi Delta Kappa (v.p. rsch. and program). Roman Catholic. Home: 35 Northridge Rd Naugatuck CT 06770 Office: Acad Elem Sch 4 School St Madison CT 06443

BIRDSEY, ANNA CAMPAS, civil engineer, architect; b. Balt., Nov. 21, 1949; d. William and Katy (Hondros) Campas; m. Tom D. Birdsey, June 3, 1973; children: Thomas William, Scott Stratton. BArch, Rensselaer Polytech. Inst., 1972; BSCE, Union Coll., 1977. Registered profl. engr., architect, N.Y. Staff architect-engr. GE Co., Schenectady, N.Y., 1972-73; architectural designer Fay Evans, P.C., Troy, N.Y., 1974-75, Golub Corp., Schenectady, 1975-77, Einhorn, Yaffee, Prescott, P.C., Albany, N.Y., 1979-80; jr. engr. N.Y. State Office of Gen. Svc., Design and Constrn. Group, Albany, 1980-82, asst. bldg. structural engr., 1982-87, sr. bldg. structural engr., 1987—; bd. dirs. Montessori Sch. of Albany, 1990—. Bd. dirs. Montessori Sch. Albany. Mem. AIA, ASCE, Bethlehem Music Assn., Soc. Women Engrs. (sr.), N.Y. State Assn. Architects, Rensselaer Alumni Assn. (alumni news class corr.). Home: 41 Darroch Rd Delmar NY 12054 Office: Gen Svcs Design & Constrn Group-Mayor Corning 2d Tower Empire State Pla Albany NY 12242

BIRDSONG, ALTA MARIE, volunteer; b. Ft. Worth, July 18, 1934; d. Alton Roy and Artie Marguerite (Bentley) Flowers; m. Kenneth Layne Birdsong, Oct. 18, 1958; children: Suzanne Denise, Jeffrey Layne. BBA in Acctg. magna cum laude, U. North Tex., 1955. Cost engr. Tex. Instruments, Inc., Dallas, 1955-62; self-employed part-time acct. Atlanta, 1972—. Mem. DeKalb County Community Rels. Com., 1981—, chair, 1984-87; mem. Atlanta Regular Commercial Adv. Group, 1981-88, Met. Atlanta United Way, 1985—; chair Sch. Age Childcare Coun., 1987-90, DeKalb North Arts Ctr. Guild. Mem. AAUW (div. pres. 1987-89, pres. elect 1987-89, mem. v.p. 1984-86, recording sec. 1982-84), Ednl. Info. and Referral Svc. Inc. (chmn. 1983-84, treas. 1981-83, 1987—, sec. 1986-87), Atlanta Coun. Camp Fire, Atlanta Alumnae Panhellenic (pres. 1978-79, v.p. 1977-78), Freedoms Found. at Valley Forge (Atlanta chpt. v.p. publicity 1988-89, treas. 1985-87, sec. 1983-85), Nat. Women's Conf., Delta Gamma Alumnae (Atlanta chpt. 1st v.p. 1985-87, treas. 1972-74). Home: 5241 Manhasset Cove Dunwoody GA 30338

BIRDWELL, CAROLYN CAMPBELL, public relations executive; b. Nashville, July 8, 1947; d. Harvell Hite and Martha (Pentecost) Campbell. Exec. sec. RCA Records, Nashville; receptionist WKDA Radio, Nashville; sec. Country Music Assn., Nashville; adminstr. Chet Atkins, Nashville; notary public. V.p. Music City B&PW, 1980-88; chmn. celebrity auction Tenn. Heart Assn., Cerebral Palsey Fundraising, 1987. Mem. nat. Acad. Recording Arts and Sci., Beta Sigma Phi. Democrat. Baptist. Home: 629 American Rd Nashville TN 37209 Office: 4300 Park Ave Washville TN 37209

BIRKEMEIER, SUSAN GAIL, obstetrician, gynecologist; b. Portland, Oreg., May 26, 1947; d. George Renny and Mary Gairns (Thomson) B.; m. Gregory Michael Gosser, Aug. 12, 1990. BS, Oreg. State U., 1969; MD, Oreg. Health Scis. U., Portland, 1973. Intern N.C. Meml. Hosp., Chapel Hill, 1973-74; resident Oreg. Health Scis. U., Portland, 1974-78; pvt. practice Columbia Dist. Hosp., St. Helens, Oreg., 1978-81, Good Samaritan Hosp., Portland, 1981—. Fellow Am. Coll. Ob-Gyn.; mem. oreg. Soc. Ob-Gyn. (sec.-treas. 1985-86), Portland Soc. Ob-Gyn. (sec.-treas. 1989-90), Multnomah County Med. Soc. (bd. trustees 1988-90), City Club, Alpha Lambda Delta. Office: 1130 NW 22d St Ste 360 Portland OR 97210

BIRKENHAUER, CANDACE LUDWIG, mortgage banker; b. Englewood, N.J., July 28, 1947; d. Donald Bond and Ruth Constance (Edwards) Ludwig; m. Edward H. Birkenhauer, Feb. 14, 1985; 1 child, Amanda B. AA, Va. Intermont, Bristol, 1967; BS, Fairleigh Dickinson U., 1971. Lic. realtor. With quality control Thomas J. Lipton, Inc., Englewood Cliffs, N.J., 1967-70; account exec. Young & Rubicam, N.Y.C., 1970-76, Wilson, Haight & Welch, Greenwich, Conn., 1976-77; real estate broker Sterling Thompson, Matawan, N.J., 1977-79; loan officer Lumbermens Mortgage Corp., Union, N.J., 1979-81; project fin. Mortgage Guaranty Ins. Corp., Phila., 1981-84; v.p. Lumbermens Mortgage Corp., Union, 1984—. Mem. Mortgage Bankers Assn. N.J. (gov. 1988—, chmn. task force for uniform condominium and planned unit devel. procedures 1987—, chmn. new products com. 1987-88, affordable housing com. 1990—), MBA Edn. Found. (trustee 1990—), N.J. Mortgage Bankers Assn. Republican. Home: 1108 Aileen Rd Brielle NJ 08730 Office: Lumbermens Mortgage Corp Project Financing Div Toms River NJ 08753

BIRKETT, MARIA GRACE LIGGIERA, portrait artist; b. Glen Cove, N.Y., Jan. 4, 1956; d. John Gerald and Edna Louise (Creeden) Liggero; m. Nigel Eric Birkett, Sept. 2, 1984. Student, U. Perugia, Tuscany, Italy, 1976; BA, McGill U., Montreal, Canada, 1977; MEd, U. Houston, 1982. Asst. program coordinator of USSR acad. exchanges Internat. Research and Exchanges Bd., N.Y.C., 1979-80; ESL tchr. Houston I.S.D. Lamar High Sch., 1982-84; ESL tchr., sports mistress Catholic Intensive Language Ctr., Sydney, Australia, 1984-88; pvt. tutor in foreign languages, 1978-84, multi-language profl., Glen Cove, N.Y. interpreter of foreign languages, Nassau County Court System, Mineola, N.Y. Home: 2100 Huldy #6 Houston TX 77019

BIRKHOFF, DEBORAH LORRAINE, paralegal; b. Roanoke, Va., Feb. 12, 1959; d. Cornelius F. and Anna S.M. (Anderson) B. B.S. in Econs., Radford U., 1981; cert. paralegal George Washington U., 1982. Sec., Radford U., Va., 1980-81; congl. asst. Congressman Robinson, Washington, 1981-83; police officer U.S. Capitol Police, 1983-86, research analyst, 1985-86; legal sec. Woods, Rogers & Hazlegrove, Roanoke, 1986-89; paralegal H. Morgan Griffith, Salem, Va., 1989-90; paralegal, title ins. underwriter Investor Title Agys., 1990—. Active congl. campaigns. Mem. Fraternal Order of Police, Internat. Narcotic Enforcement Officers Assn., Am. Fedn. Police, Roanoke Valley Paralegal Assn., Sigma Sigma Sigma. Republican. Baptist. Office: Investors Title Agys 3959 Electric Rd SW Ste 200 Roanoke VA 24018

BIRKHOLZ, GABRIELLA SONJA, communications executive; b. Chgo., Apr. 11, 1938; d. Frank E. Vosicky and Sonja (Kosner) Becvar. BA in Communications and Bus. Mgmt., Alverno Coll., 1983. Editor, owner Fox Lake (Wis.) Rep., 1962-65, McFarland (Wis.) Community Life and Monona Community Herald, 1966-69; bur. reporter Waukesha (Wis.) Daily Freeman, 1969-71; community rels. staff Waukesha County Tech. Coll., Pewaukee, Wis., 1971-73; pub. rels. specialist JI Case Co., Racine, Wis., 1973-75, corp. publs. editor, 1975-80; v.p., bd. dirs. publs. Image Mgmt., Valley View Ctr., Milw., 1980-82; pres. Communication Concepts, Unltd., Racine, 1983—; guest lectr. Alverno Coll., U. Wis.; adj. faculty U. Wis.-Parkside; bd. dirs. Downtown Racine Corp. Contbr. articles to profl. jours. Bd. dirs., v.p. Big Bros./Big Sisters Racine County; bd. dirs. Racine County coun. Girl Scouts U.S.A.; mem. community adv. bd. Sta. WGTD-FM. Recipient awards Wis. Press Assn., Nat. Fedn. Press Women; named Wis. Woman Entrepreneur of Yr., 1985. Mem. Internat. Assn. Bus. Communicators (accredited mem.; bd.

dirs. 1982-85, various awards), Wis. Women Entrepreneurs, Alverno Alumnae Assn., Sigma Delta Chi. Home: 3045 Chatham St Racine WI 53402 Office: 927 Main St Racine WI 53403

BIRNBAUM, JOAN WELKER, religious foundation executive; b. Oil City, Pa., Apr. 26, 1923; d. George Ernest and Josephine Wilson (Powell) Welker; m. Theodore Birnbaum, Jan. 8, 1949 (div. 1977); children: Lyuba, Margaret Jane, L. Crispin. B.A. in Econs., Wellesley Coll., 1945; postgrad. Northwestern U. Grad. Sch. Bus. Adminstrn., summer 1945, Nat. Planned Giving Inst., 1979, Philanthropy Tax Inst. Jr. acct. Price, Waterhouse and Co., N.Y.C., 1945-50; sec. to asst. treas. Rockefeller Found., N.Y.C., 1950; acct. Rye Youth Coun., N.Y., 1976-84; exec. dir. Mamaroneck/Larchmont LIFE Ctr., N.Y., 1973; assoc. dir. vols. United Hosp., Port Chester, N.Y., 1974; bus. mgr. Burke Rehab. Ctr. Day Hosp., White Plains, N.Y., 1974-78; planned giving officer Save the Children Fedn., Inc., Westport, Conn., 1979-82; exec. dir. N.Y.-Conn. Found. of United Meth. Ch., White Plains, 1982—. Bd. dirs. Rye United Fund, sec., mem. nominating com.; elder, deacon pres. Women's Assn. Rye Presbyterian Ch.; chmn. maj. reunion fund campaign Wellesley Coll. Class, 1980-85, chmn. reunion, 1975, 90, class historian, 1965—, admissions chmn. for Wellesley in Westchester Club; bd. dirs., pres. Planned Parenthood of Eastern Westchester; pres. Rye Family Svc.; telephone listener and source of referral Rye/Larchmont/Mamaroneck Hot Line; treas., exec. com. Rye Youth Coun.; sec., treas., v.p., pres. 15th Twig of United Hosp., also bd. dirs.; past pres. Rye High Sch. Mothers' Guild, chmn. 1st direct solicitation fund drive; bd. dirs. Woman's Club of Rye, pres. jr. sect.; membership chmn., bd. dirs. Midland Sch. of Rye (voted Parent of Yr.). Mem. Nat. Assn. United Meth. Founds. (treas. 1983-87), Planned Giving Group of Greater N.Y. (v.p. 1983-84, pres. 1984-85), Internat. Assn. Fin. Planners, Devel. Assn. of So. Conn. (chmn. program com. 1983-84), Nat. Soc. Fund Raising Execs., Assn. Westchester Devel. Officers. Republican. Presbyterian. Clubs: Wellesley (South Conn.), Wellesley Fairfield Villages. Avocations: silversmithing, handweaving, piano, guitar, Great Books.

BIRNBAUM, SHEILA L., lawyer, educator; b. 1940. B.A., Hunter Coll., 1960, M.A., 1962; LL.B. NYU, 1965. Bar: N.Y. 1965. Legal asst. Superior Ct., N.Y.C., 1965; assoc. Berman & Frost, N.Y.C., 1965-70, ptnr., 1970-72; prof. Fordham U., N.Y.C., 1972-78; prof. NYU, N.Y.C., 1978-86; ptnr. Skadden, Arps, Meagher, Slate & Flom, 1984—; assoc. dean NYU, 1982-84. N.Y.C Bar Assn. (mem. exec. com. 1978—, jud. com. 1977), ABA (chmn. product gen. liability, consumer land coms.), Assn. of Bar of City of N.Y. (exec. com. 1978—, 2d century com. 1984-86), Phi Beta Kappa, Phi Alpha Theta, Alpha Chi Alpha. Author: (with Rheingold) Products Liability, Law, Practice Science, 1974. Office: Skadden Arps Slate Meagher & Flom 919 3d Ave New York NY 10022*

BIRNHAK, SANDRA JEAN, film company executive; b. L.A., Apr. 27, 1945; d. Charles William and Edna Mae (Cante) Reynolds; m. Bruce I. Birnhak, Feb. 4, 1964 (div. 1970); 1 child, Scott Alan; m. David R. Ames, Dec. 22, 1984. Degree in Advanced Film Studies, MIT, 1981-82, Am. Film Inst., 1983. Pres., dir. Subtle-T, Inc., Boston, 1974-77; dir. mktg. RKO Gen. Broadcasting, Boston, 1978-80; vis. lectr. pub. relations Boston Coll., 1980-81; line producer, auditor Cannon Films Internat., N.Y.C., 1983; exec. v.p., chief fin. officer Hartwest, Inc., N.Y.C., 1983-85; chmn., chief exec. officer Showcase Prodns. Internat., N.Y.C., 1985—; bd. dir. Women's Perspective Prodns., Boston, 1981; cons. in field. Producer, dir. Corporate Women, 1980, Balloons, 1981, Father, Son End Holy Coach, 1990; producer Curse of the Starving Class, 1990; assoc. producer Mr. North, 1987; exec. producer Curse of the Starving Class. Vol. Kennedy Meml. Hosp. for Children, Boston, 1980, St. Vincent's Hosp., N.Y.C. Recipient Nat. Disting. Service award March of Dimes, Boston, 1980, Govs. award, Boston, 1979. Mem. NOW, N.Y. Women in Film, Ind. Filmmakers Assoc., Nat. Assn. Broadcasters, Am. Fedn. TV and Radio Artists. Democrat. Unitarian. Home: 145 W 55d St Apt 7-D New York NY 10019

BIRNIE, JANICE DOROTHY, nurse; b. Wawota, Sask., Can., Nov. 21, 1940; d. John and Laura E. (Campbell) B. Diploma in nursing, Saskatoon City Hosp., 1963; student, Charity Hosp., New Orleans, 1975. RN. Staff nurse Western Can., 1963-67; nurse King Edward VIII Hosp., Hamilton, Bermuda, 1967-70, West Jefferson Hosp., New Orleans, 1972-75; freelance nurse anesthetist Oppelousus, La., 1975-78; staff nurse anesthetist Kaprolani Med. Ctr., Honolulu, 1978; staff CRNA Kaisar Hosp., 1978—. Mem. Am. Assn. Nurse Anesthetists, Hawaii Assn. Nurse Anesthetists. Home: 2533 Ala Wai Blvd Apt 604 Honolulu HI 96815

BIRNKRANT, JEANNE ANN, artist, actress, social worker; b. N.Y.C.; d. William Benjamen and Dorothy Leona (Solow) B. BA, Barnard Coll.; MSW, Columbia U.; postgrad., New Sch. Social Research, 1968-70, Arts Students League, 1970-75, Berghoff Acting Studios, 1975-80, 88-89. Chief psychiat. social worker N.Y. Psychoanalytic Inst., 1970-76; children's psychotherapist Bellevue Hosp., N.Y.C., 1976-78; psychotherapist, dir. social work Met. Hosp., N.Y.C., 1978-84; actress various cos.; dir. Park Ave Psychotherapy Ctr., N.Y.C., 1988-89. Prin. sculpture works include (bronze) Strident Man (1st prize South Park Artist Group, N.Y.C. 1984), Winged Bird Fantasy (1st prize Nantucket Contemporary Gallery, Mass., 1985), Screaming Motherland and Child (1st prize 1989), Nat. Contemporary Juries Art Show, 1989, Fifth Ave Contemporary Gallery, N.Y.C., 1989; appeared in movies Turk 182, Cotton Club, Nuts, Radio Days, Ghostbusters, Round Midnight, Prizzi's Honor, Fatal Attraction, Last Exit to Brooklyn, See No Evil, Hear No Evil; appeared in TV shows Superman Anniversary Spl., 1988, Dreamstreet. County Com. woman Village Ind. Dems., N.Y.C.; patron Mus. Modern Art. Nat. Mental Health fellow, Jewish Guild for Blind fellow. Mem. Screen Actors Guild, Actors Equity Assn., Nat. Assn Social Workers (cert.), AFTRA. Home and Office: PO Box 20953 New York NY 10023-1489

BIRON, CHRISTINE ANNE, medical science educator, researcher; b. Woonsocket, R.I., Aug. 8, 1951; d. R. Bernard and Theresa Priscilla (Sauvageau) B. BS, U. Mass., 1973; PhD, U. N.C., 1980. Rsch. technician U. Mass., Amherst, 1973-75; grad. researcher U. N.C., Chapel Hill, 1975-80; postdoctoral fellow Scripps Clinic and Rsch., La Jolla, Calif., 1980; fellow U. Mass. Med. Sch., Worcester, 1981-82, instr., 1983, asst. prof., 1984-87; vis. scientist Karolinska Inst., Stockholm, 1984; asst. prof. Brown U., Providence, R.I., 1988-90, assoc. prof., 1990—. Assoc. editor Jour. Immunology, 1990—; contbr. articles, revs. to sci. jours. Leukemia Soc. Am. fellow, 1981, Spl. fellow, 1983, scholar, 1987. Mem. Am. Assn. Immunologists (co-chmn. symposium 1990), AAAS, Sigma Xi. Office: Brown U Biomed Ctr Box G-B618 Providence RI 02912

BIROS, LORRAINE, mental health counselor; b. Cleve., June 8, 1946; d. John A. and Ann L. (Ferrara) Biros. B.S., Ohio State U., 1967; M.A., Goddard Coll., 1979. Nat. cert. counselor, 1986. Cert. profl. counselor, Md. Tech. editor Am. Psychol. Assn., Washington, 1968-72; prodn. coord.,sr. staff editor John F. Holman & Co., Inc., Washington, 1974-79; mem. core faculty Goddard Coll., 1980-81, cons., 1981-82; feminist counselor in pvt. practice, Frederick and Montgomery Counties, Md., 1979—; mem., bd. dirs. Whitman-Walker Clinic, Inc., Washington, 1979-80; co-founder/coord. Lesbian Resource & Counseling Ctr., Washington, 1978-80, mem. core staff, 1985-88, cons., 1980—; charter mem. D.C. Area Feminist Alliance, 1976-78; mem. core staff Washington Area Women's Ctr., 1976-78. Mem. editorial bd. Women and Therapy: A Feminist Quar., 1986—. Recipient Gene Frey award Whitman-Walker Clinic, 1987. Mem. Am. Assn. Counseling & Devel., Nat. Assn. for Children of Alcoholics, Assn. for Women in Psychology, Himalayan Internat. Inst. Yoga Sci. & Philosophy, Nat. Assn. Lesbian and Gay Alcoholism Profls., Nat. Gay and Lesbian Task Force, Women's Nat. Health Network, Feminist Bus. and Profl. Network, Women Strike for Peace. Democrat. Home: 6212 Mountain Church Rd Burkittsville MD 21718

BIRSCHTEIN, BARBARA ANN, county official; b. Atlantic, N.J., Apr. 22; d. Morris and Helen (Rellis) B. BEd, U. Toledo, 1976. Cert. tchr. Ohio, N.J. Income maintenance technician Atlantic County Div. Welfare, Atlantic City, 1977-78, income maintenance specialist, 1978-80, income maintenance supr. non-pub. assistance food stamps, 1980-85, income maintenance supr. match overissuance/overpayment unit, 1985—. Mem. Am. Pub. Welfare Assn., United Council Welfare Fraud, Welfare Assn. So. N.J., AAUW. Home: 6416 Monmouth Ave Ventnor NJ 08406 Office: Atlantic County Div Welfare 1333 Atlantic Ave Atlantic City NJ 08401

BIRSIC, DOROTHY ANN, management consultant; b. Fullerton, Calif., July 14, 1961; d. Rudolph J. and Bozena (Juricic) B. BA, U. So. Calif., L.A., 1983; MALD, Tufts U., 1990; MBA, Harvard U., 1990. Legis. analyst Legis. Affairs Office The White House, Wash., 1981; guest rels. staff Gen. Alumni Assn. U. So. Calif., 1982-83; media cons. ABC TV News and Sports Olympic Unit, Sarajevo,, Yugoslavia, and L.A., 1984; asst. accounts exec. Manning, Selvage and Lee, L.A., 1984-85; mgmt. cons. Theodore Barry & Assoc., L.A., 1986-88; pres. Globalink, 1989; mgmt. cons. A.T. Kearney, 1990—; mem. Japan Soc. Boston, Mass., 1988—, Fgn. Trade Assn. L.A., 1988—. Vol. Consulting Amnesty Internat. Mass., 1988; ESL Tutor Refugee Ministry Boston, Mass., 1989. Merit fellow Tufts U. Fletcher Sch. Law & Diplomacy, Medford, 1988-89, Japanese-Am. Citizens League fellow, 1989-90. Republican. Roman Catholic.

BIRSNER, ELEANOR PATRICIA, writer; b. Morrisonville, Ill., Apr. 12, 1928; d. William Philip and Helen Dee (Kitchell) Balsley; m. Hubert J. Birsner, Nov. 13, 1948 (div. 1969); children: Jane Ellen Compton, Peggy Lynn Coughlin. BA, U. Ill., Urbana, 1948; MA, Tex. Woman's U., 1957; postgrad., U. Houston. Tchr. McAllen (Tex.) Ind. Sch. Dist., 1953-56, Dickinson (Tex.) Ind. Schs., 1956-59; saleswoman Reagan Audio Visuals, Dickinson, 1959-62; owner, pres. Birsner Ednl. Svcs. Tex., League City, Tex., 1962-70; sr. editor McGraw-Hill Book Co., N.Y.C., 1970-79; writer, cons. Birsner Assocs., Budd Lake, N.J., 1979-86, Data Communications, Parsippany, N.J., 1986-88, Trecom Bus. Systems, Edison, N.J., 1988-89, Budd Lake, N.J., 1989—; cons., seminar speaker Forty Plus of Dallas, 1987-89; seminar speaker Forty Plus of N.Y., N.Y.C., 1982-89, Am. Mgmt. Assn., N.Y.C., 1979-87. Author: Practical Guide to Customer Service Management and Operations, 1982, Job Hunting for the 40 Plus Executive, 1985, 40 Plus Job Hunting Guide, 1987, Selling: Marketing Personified, 1987, others. Lay leader United Meth. Ch., Stanhope, N.J., 1986-89; asst. lay leader Northern N.J. United Meth. Ch. Ann. Conf., Madison, 1988-. Mem. Internat. Customer Svc. Assn. Republican. Home and Office: 40G Village Green Budd Lake NJ 07828

BIRTCHER, WENDY CATHARINE, real estate executive; b. Newport Beach, Calif., Sept. 6, 1962; d. Arthur Belt and Shirley Rae (Garibaldi) B. BA magna cum laude, Sweet Briar (Va.) Coll., 1984. V.p. aquisitions Birtcher Investments, Laguna Niguel, Calif., 1984—. Bd. dirs. S. County Community Clinic, San Juan Capistrano, Calif., 1985—; bd. overseers Sweet Briar Coll., 1984-87. Sweet Briar scholar 1984. Mem. Nat. Assn. Indsl. and Office Parks, Urban Land Inst., Young Execs. Am., Internat. Coun. Shopping Ctrs., C. of C. (bd. dirs. San Juan Capistrano 1987—), Phi Beta Kappa, Pi Gamma Mu. Republican. Roman Catholic. Office: Birtcher Investments 27611 La Paz Rd Laguna Niguel CA 92677

BISCHAK, CYNTHIA D., technical publishing administrator; b. Columbus, Ohio, Apr. 1, 1956; d. Donald Rex, Jr., and Nancy May (Dawson) Barnes; m. Frank William Bischak, Mar. 16, 1977. BS in Botany and Marine Sci., U. Wash., 1981, MPA, 1985. Water quality technician Ohio EPA, Columbus, 1978; exec. sec. Dan A. Carmichael, AIA, Columbus, 1978-79; supr. publs. Vitro Corp., Silverdale, Wash., 1982-85; sr. tech. writer water pollution control dept. Municipality Met. Seattle (Metro), 1985-87, supr. 1987—; bd. dirs. Hood Canal Environ. Council, Seabeck, Wash., 1985-88; chmn. conservation com. Kitsap Audubon, Poulsbo, Wash., 1982-84. Author: Citizen's Guide to Municipal Incorporation in the State of Washington, 1985. Tech. advisor and publicity co-chmn. Silverdale Inc. Com., 1983-85. Mem. Am. Soc. Pub. Adminstrn. (student rep. Evergreen chpt. Council 1984-85, council mem. Evergreen chpt. 1986—), Soc. for Tech. Communication, Council Biology Editors, Western Govtl. Research Assn., Am. Mgmt. Assn. Club; Cityclub (Seattle). Avocations: backpacking, canoeing, scuba diving, gardening, stained glass. Home: 2245 E Crescent Dr Seattle WA 98112 Office: Metro 821 Second Ave MS-201 Seattle WA 98104

BISCHOF, MERRIEM LANOVA, artistic director, choreographer, educator; b. San Diego; d. Samuel James and Eva (Mills) Crowe; m. John Denning Bischof, Aug. 3, 1947. BA, Pacific Western U., 1987, PhD, 1988. Cert. dance instr., Calif. Stars' double MGM, Hollywood, Calif., 1939-40; dancer various Broadway mus., 1940-41; dancer USO revues U.S. Armed Svcs., 1941-43; soloist Ballet Russe de Monte Carlo, N.Y.C., 1944-48; dir. Pacific Dance Theater, San Francisco, 1948—; instr. San Francisco Coll. Music & Theater Arts, 1988—; guest tchr. various colls. Author 27 ballets for jrs. and profls., 1947—. Recipient numerous grants City of San Francisco, 1964-74, Sears Roebuck & Co., 1975-79, Calif. Arts Coun., 1976-80, Walter Johnson Found., 1981; named Baroness Dame Grand Comdr. Order of Star of Karkov (Poland), 1943. Republican. Christian Scientist. Home: 2215 R Market St #163 San Francisco CA 94114 Office: San Francisco Coll Music & Theater Arts 60 Brady St San Francisco CA 94102

BISCHOFF, CAROL LOUISE, scientific publishing company executive; b. Flushing, N.Y.; d. Charles Thomas and Louise Josephine (Knaust) B. BS in Chemistry, Wagner Coll., 1964. Editorial asst. Plenum Pub. Corp., N.Y.C., 1964-66, prodn. editor, 1966-68, jours. editor, 1969-72, asst. mng. editor, 1972-78, mng. editor jours., 1978—, asst. v.p., 1985—. Mem. Assn. Am. Pubs. (jours. com. profl. and scholarly pub. div. 1984-86). Office: Plenum Pub Corp 233 Spring St New York NY 10013-1578

BISCHOFF, JOYCE ARLENE, information systems consultant; b. Chgo., Apr. 1, 1938; d. Carl Henry and Gertrude Alma (Lohn) Winterberg; m. Kenneth B. Bischoff, June 6, 1959; children: Kathryn Ann, James Eric. BS in Math., Ill. Inst. Tech., 1959; cert. computer tech., U. Del., 1979. Programmer, analyst Inst. of Gas Tech., Chgo., 1959-60, U. Ghent, Belgium, 1960-61; database adminstr. Med. Ctr. Del., Wilmington, 1979-84; sr. database analyst ICI Ams., Wilmington, 1984-87; sr. cons. CSC Ptnrs., Malvern, Pa., 1987-90; pvt. practice cons. Hockessin, Del., 1990—; chairperson, founder Del. Valley DB2-SQL/DS Users Group, Phila., 1986—; task force leader DB2 performance task force Guide Internat., Chgo., 1987-90. Contbr. articles to profl. jours. Mem. Assn. for Computing Machinery (Del. Valley chpt. pres. 1986-87, program chair 1985-86), Data Processing Mgmt. Assn. (Wilmington chpt.), Wilmington Women in Bus., Network of Women in Computer Tech., Sigma Kappa (pres. 1958-59). Home: 1007 Benge Rd Hockessin DE 19707 Office: 1007 Benge Rd Hockessin DE 19707

BISCHOFF, WENDY WINONA, pharmacist; b. Denver, Jan. 21, 1960; d. Raymond Charles and Doris Jean (Davis) B. BS in Pharmacy, Ohio State U., 1984. Lic. pharmacist, Ohio. Sec. Firestone Steel Products Co., Akron, Ohio, 1978-79; staff pharmacist Youngfellow Pharmacy, Cuyahoga Falls, Ohio, 1985-88, pharmacist mgr., 1988—; staff pharmacist Children's Hosp. Med. Ctr. of Akron, 1989—. Mem. Summit County Pharm. Assn. (mem. coun. 1989—), Am. Pharm. Assn., Ohio Pharm. Assn. (del. 1988), Ohio State U. Alumni Assn., Ohio State U. Coll. Pharmacy Alumni Assn., Ohio State U. Alumni Club (Summit County chpt.). Office: Youngfellow Pharmacy 2900 State Rd Cuyahoga Falls OH 44223

BISGARD, SHARON KAY, advocate; b. Des Moines, Nov. 9, 1939; d. James Edward and Herma Evelyn (Hudgel) Cummings; m. Gerald Edwin Bisgard, Sept. 9, 1961; children: Jennifer, Kristine, Bradley. BA, Colo. State U., Ft. Collins, 1961; MA, U. Wis., 1979. With State of Wis., Madison, 1975—, asst. for legis. liaison Office of the Sec., 1984-86, supr. client advocacy program Div. Care & Treatment Facility, 1986—. Mem. Dane County (Wis.) Lakes & Watershed Commn., 1988—; pub. mem. bldg. code adcv. rev. bd. State of Wis., Madison, 1985—; elected ofcl. Dane County Bd. Suprs., 1985—; chmn. zoning and natural resources com. County of Dane, 1985—. Home: 1 Julia Circle Madison WI 53705

BISH, KATHERINE KAYE, environmental protection professional; b. San Antonio, Jan. 16, 1958; d. Daniel William and Jeannette Louise (Larson) B. BS in Pub. Health, Loma Linda U., 1980, MPH, 1981. Registered environ. health specialist. Environ. health sanitarian Orange County Health Care Agy., Santa Ana, Calif., 1981-83, hazardous waste specialist, 1983-86, supr. hazardous waste specialist, 1986—. Mem. Delta Omega (life). Republican. Presbyterian.

BISHOP, ALICE JUNE, human resources manager; b. Blytheville, Ark., June 9, 1955; d. Walter Roland Bishop and Wanda June (Berry) Haggard. BS in Vocat. Home Econs., Abilene Christian U., 1976, MS in Mgmt. and Human Rels., 1982. County extension agt. Tex. Agrl. Extension Svc., Childress, 1976-78; cons. electric living West Tex. Utilities Co., Abilene, 1978-81, pers. asst., 1981-84; asst. pers. dir. Hendrick Med. Ctr., Abilene, 1984-85, corp. rels. rep., 1985-87; mgr. human resources Melvin Simon and Assocs., Inc., Bedford, Tex., 1987—. Grad. Leadership Hurst-Euless-Bedford, Tex., 1990. Mem. Internat. Coun. Shopping Ctrs., Am. Soc. Pers. Adminstrn., Hurst-Euless-Bedford C. of C. Office: Melvin Simon & Assocs 2350 W Airport Frwy Ste 310 Bedford TX 76022

BISHOP, BARBARA EVELYN, editor; b. Des Moines, Iowa, Nov. 14, 1940; d. Wendell William and Margaret Evelyn (Sullivan) B. BS (Cum Laude), St. Olaf Coll., 1962; MN, U. Washington, 1965. Registered nurse. Staff nurse Children's Orthopedic Hosp., Seattle, Wash., 1962-63; instr. Central Wash. Deacconess, Wenatchee, Wash., 1964-65; instr. St. Olaf Coll., Northfield, Minn., 1965-67, asst. prof., 1967-69; asst. prof. U. Minn. Sch. of Pub. Health and Pilot City Health Ctr., Northfield, Minn., Dual Appointment Univ of Health and Pilot City Health Ctr., Mpls., Minn., 1969-71; program coord. Div. of Maternal and Child Health Am. Nurses Assn., Mo., 1973-75; originator MCN The Am. Journal of Maternal Child Nursing, N.Y., 1975--; organator MCN Convention, N.Y.C., 1985-90, cons., 1985--; grant reveiwer Nat. Found., Mar. of Dimes, White Plains, 1981-82, perinatal site visit teams, Robert Wood Johnson Found., 1975, Bur. of Maternal and Child Health, Dept. HHS, 1988. Author, Book, Maternity Cycle One Nurse's Reflection, 1979, Readiness Today's Maternal Child Nurse, 1987, contbr. articles to prof. mags. Mem. Health Services Committee Children's Aid Soc., N.Y. 1981-86, Natl. Advisory Committee Health Service and Education Boy's Club of Am., Health Advisory Bd. Committee Family Planning Council, 1989. Mem. Leinhard Sch. of Nursing, (advisory bd. 1985--), Am. Nurses Assn., Natl. Assn. of Female Executives. Presbyterian. Home: 220 Central Pk S 7E New York NY 10019

BISHOP, BARBARA N., librarian, archivist; b. Louisville; d. Bernard Ross and Mayme Nell (Thompson) HIggason; children: Anthony Taylor, Christopher Allan, Sarah Jean. AAS, U. Louisville, 1981, BA, 1981, MA, 1988; MSLS, U. Ky., 1989. Project archivist City of Louisville Archives, 1984; archivist Cabbage Patch Settlement House, Louisville, 1984-85; asst. archivist Ind. U. S.E., New Albany, 1986-88, ref. and archives librarian, 1988-90; dir. libr. svcs.Montgomery Libr. Campbellsville (Ky.) Coll., 1990—; cons. in field. Author: Oakdale: An Early Twenthieth Century Suburb, 1989; author booklet: Love and Hope Throughout the Years: The Cabbage Patch Settlement House, 1985. Pres. Oakdale Neighborhood Assn., Louisville, 1988-89, bd. dirs., 1984-86; mem. 4th & Central Task Force, Louisville, 1986-88, Operation South Louisville, 1986-88. Ky. Humanities Council grantee, 1985-86; Ind. U. Pres. Council on Social Scis. Pub. grantee, 1988. Mem. Soc. Ind. Archivists, Soc. Am. Archivists, Ky. Coun. on Archives, Assn. Records Mgrs. and Adminstrs., Ancient Ky. Hist. Assn., ALA, Ky. Libr. Assn. Office: Campbellsville Coll Montgomery Libr 200 W College St Campbellsville KY 42718

BISHOP, BETTY JOSEPHINE, financial consultant; b. Seattle, Wash., Feb. 27, 1947; d. Arthur Joseph and Julia Teresa (Azzolina) Lovett; children: Deborah, Scott. BS, Wash. State U., 1969; postgrad., Ohio State U., 1983. Tchr. Seattle Sch. Dist., 1973-75; appraiser Pacific First Fed., Tacoma, 1977-78, asst. v.p., mgr., secondary market ops., 1978-82; regional exec. United Guaranty, Westlake Village, Calif., 1982-83; sr. v.p. comml. secondary mktg. FCA Am. Mortgage Corp./ Am. Savs., Santa Monica, Calif., 1983-85; v.p., mgr. secondary market ops. County Savs. Bank, Santa Barbara, Calif., 1985-88; pres., fin. cons. SMC Fin. Svcs., Montecito, Calif., 1988—; mem. conf. subcom., sec. mktg. com. Calif. Savs. and Loan League, L.A., 1985-88; document subcom., sec. mktg. subcom. U.S. Savs. and Loan League, Chgo., 1987-88. Contbr. articles to profl. jours. Fund drive chmn. Easter Seal Soc., Seattle, 1972. Mem. Univ. Club, S.B. Assocs., Conejo Ski Club, Auslich Ski Club, Santa Barbara Ski Club (pres., rep. L.A. coun.). Republican. Roman Catholic. Home and Office: 2696 Sycamore Canyon Rd Montecito CA 93108

BISHOP, BEVERLY PETTERSON, physiologist; b. Corning, N.Y., Oct. 19, 1922; d. Elof B. and Bonnie (Hunderford) Petterson; m. Charles William Bishop, May 2, 1944; 1 child, Geoffrey. BA, Syracuse U., 1944; MA, Rochester U., 1946; PhD, U. Buffalo, 1958. Asst. in physiology Glasgow (Scotland) U., 1956-57; instr. physiology U. Buffalo, 1958-62, asst. prof., 1962-67; assoc. prof. SUNY, Buffalo, 1967-75, prof. of physiology, 1976—. Author: Basic Neurophysiology, 1982; contbr. over 100 papers to profl. jours. Mem. Am. Physiol. Soc. (councillor, chair coms. 1989—), Soc. Neurosci., Am. Thoracic Soc., Am. Congress Rehab., Am. Assn. of Electrodiagnostic Medicine. Home: 508 Getzville Rd Buffalo NY 14226 Office: SUNY Dept Physiology S Campus Buffalo NY 14214

BISHOP, C. DIANE, state agency administrator, educator; b. Elmhurst, Ill., Nov. 23, 1943; d. Louis William and Constance Oleta (Mears) B.; m. Richard Lee Morse, Oct. 20, 1984. BS in Maths., U. Ariz., 1965, MS in Maths., MEd in Secondary Edn., 1972. Lic. secondary educator. Tchr. math. Tucson Unified Sch. Dist., 1966-86, mem. curriculum council, 1985-86, mem. maths. curriculum task teams, 1983-86; state supt. of pub. instrn. State of Ariz., 1987—; assoc. faculty Pima Community Coll., Tucson, 1974-84; adj. lectr. U. Ariz., 1983, 85. Active Ariz. State Bd. Edn., 1984—, chmn. quality edn. commn., 1986-87, chmn. tchr. crt. subcom., 1984—, mem. outcomes based edn. adv. com., 1986-87, liaison bd. dirs. essential skills subcom., 1985-87, gifted edn. com. liaison, 1985—; mem. Ariz. State Bd. Regents, 1987—, mem. com. on preparing for U. Ariz., 1983, mem. high sch. task force, 1984-85; mem. bd. Ariz. State Community Coll., 1987—; mem. Ariz. Joint Legis. Com. on Revenues and Expenditures, 1989, Ariz. Joint Legis. Com. on Goals for Ednl. Excellence, 1987-89. Woodrow Wilson fellow Princeton U., summer 1984; recipient Presdl. Award for Excellence in Teaching of Maths., 1983, Ariz. Citation of Merit, 1984, Maths. Teaching award Nat. Sci. Research Soc., 1984, Distinction in Edn. award Flinn Found., 1986; named Maths. Tchr. of Yr. Ariz. Council of Engring. and Sci. Assns., 1984. Mem. AAUW, NEA, Nat. Coun. Tchrs. Maths., Coun. Chief State Sch. Officers, Ariz. Edn. Assn., Tucson Edn. Assn., Ariz. Assn. Tchrs. Maths., Women Maths. Edn., Math. Assn. Am., NRC (math. scis. edn. bd. 1987—), Ednl. Commn. of the States (steering com.), NSF Sci. & Engring. Edn. (dir. adv. bd.), Nat. Endowment Arts (adv. bd. for arts edn.), Nat. Forum Excellence Edn., Nat. Honors Workshop, Pi Mu Epsilon, Pi Lambda Theta, Phi Delta Kappa. Democrat. Episcopalian. Office: Ariz State Dept Edn 1535 W Jefferson Phoenix AZ 85007

BISHOP, CAROLYN LOUISE, consulting company executive; b. Temple, Pa., Oct. 24, 1946; d. Westley Lynn Albert and Hannah Florence (Hepner) Boyer; children: Tracy, William; m. Kenneth Leroy Bishop, Oct. 20, 1979. Grad. high sch., Oley, Pa. Systems analyst Bechtel Power Corp., San Francisco, 1978-82; cons. Cin. Gas & Electric, 1982-84, Cleve. Electric, Perry, Ohio, 1984-86, Tex. Utilities, Dallas, 1987-89; v.p. K & C Cons. Svcs. Inc., Granbury, Tex., 1986—. Mem. NAFE, Computer Soc. of IEEE. Republican. Home and Office: 117 Aqua Vista Dr Granbury TX 76048

BISHOP, CONNIE BOSSONS, healthcare administrator; b. Atlanta, June 4, 1953; d. Robert R. and C. Virginia (Mato) Bossons; m. Benjamin B. Bishop. BSN, Duke U., 1975; M.Nurisng, U. S.C., 1980; MBA, U. New Haven, 1987. Staff nurse VA Med. Ctr., Durham, N.C., 1975-76; head nurse Alcohol Rehab. Ctr., Butner, N.C., 1976-77; teaching assoc. U. S.C., Columbia, 1978-80; community counselor Newberry Drug/Alcohol. S.C., 1980-81; dir. social svcs. Newberry County Hosp., 1981-82; employee assistance program coord., dir. pers. Nautilus Fitness Ctr., Jacksonville, N.C., 1982-83; asst. adminstr. clin. healthcare svcs. Brynn Marr Hosp., Jacksonville, 1983-85; asst. adminstr. Elmcrest Psychiat. Inst., Portland, Conn., 1985-86; corp. clin. dir. Mediplex Inc., Newton, Mass., 1986-87; nat. trainer RBM Inc., Londonderry, N.H., 1987-89; faculty mem. Salve Regina Coll., 1987-89; edn. and tng. coord. Child & Family Svcs. Newport, R.I., 1989; exec. dir. mental health svc. line Alta Bates-Herrick Hosp., Berkeley, Calif., 1989—; cons. S.C. Com. Role/Status of Women, United Meth. Ch., Columbia, 1978-80, Jacksonville Bd. Realtors, 1982-83. Emergency disaster coord. Middlesex Red Cross (Conn.); active community vol. Named Outstanding Young Woman of Am., 1982. Mem. Nat. Forensic League (Degree of Distinction), Nat. Orgn. for Pub. Speaking and Debate, Nat. Assn. Female Execs., Am. Soc. Profl. Bus. Women, Am. Coll. Healthcare Execs., Sigma Theta Tau. Methodist. Avocations: reading, racquetball, gardening, cooking. Office: Alta Bates-Herrick Hosp 2001 Dwight Way Berkeley CA 94704

BISHOP, DIANE MARIE, corporate professional; b. Toledo, Feb. 5, 1958; d. Stanley William and Mary Louise (Konesni) B. AS in Bus., Michael J. Owens Coll., 1988; BS in Orgnl. Svcs., U. Toledo, 1989. Auditor, processing specialist Lucas County Children Svcs., Toledo, 1979-85; auditor, systems operator City of Rossford, Ohio, 1985-87; sales assoc. The Lion Store, Toledo, 1987; fiscal and quality control asst. Johnson Controls, Inc., Holland, Ohio, 1987; adminstrv. asst. Owens-Illinois, Maumee, Ohio, 1987-88; adminstrv. mgr. Sunnybrook Conf. Ctrs., Inc., Sandusky, Ohio, 1988—. Mem. Internat. Assn. Conf. Ctrs., Nat. Wildlife Fedn., Toledo Zool Soc., Conservation Alliance, Golden Key Nat. Honor Soc., Sierra Club. Roman Catholic. Home: 1104 Fremont Ave Sandusky OH 44870 Office: Sunnybrook Conf Ctr Inc 1104 Fremont Ave Sandusky OH 44870

BISHOP, ELIZA H., public relations executive; b. Crockett, Tex., June 18, 1920; d. William Penn and Carey Ann (LeGory) B. BA, U. Mary Harding Baylor, Belton, Tex., 1941. Cert. med. asst. Editor Crockett (Tex.) Democrat, 1941-45; Houston County corr. Houston Post, Crockett, 1942-78; dep. clk. Houston County Commrs. Ct., Crockett, 1945-47; dep. clk., ct. reporter 3d Jud. Dist. Ct., Crockett, 1947-63; Houston County corr. Houston Chronicle, Crockett, 1957-81; sec. City of Crockett, 1961-63; telegrapher Western Union, 1963-65; med. asst. John L. Dean, MD, 1965-77; owner, mgr. EB Promotions for Everybody, 1978—; mem. pub. rels. com. Am. Museum Assn., Tex., 1985—. Author: Houston County History, 1980, Mini History of Houston County, 1972, 76, 86, 87; author, editor: Houston County Cemeteries, 1977, 78, 87; editor: Historical Markers of Houston County, Texas, 1974. Mem. city coun. City of Crockett, 1985-86; active pub. rels. Girl Scout Movement, 1980—. Recipient Best County Commn. Chmn. award Tex. Hist. Commn., Austin, 1972, 74, 78, Disting. Svc. award Tex. Hist. Commn., Austin, 1981, 82, 83, 84, Hist. Preservation award City of Crockett, 1983-84, Svc. award San Jacinto Coun., Houston, 1987, 88, 89, Tex. Sesquicentennial Excellence award Sesquicentennial Commn., Austin, 1986—, Houston County Svc. award Houston County Commrs. Ct., Crockett, 1989. Mem. Women in Communications Inc., Nat. Fedn. Press Women Inc. (life), Tex. Press Women Inc. (life, historian 1986—, hon. achievement award 1977), Tex. State Hist. Assn. (life.), Tex. Hist. Found. (life), East Tex. Hist. Assn. (life, dir. 1980-86), Hist. Projects of Houston County, Tex. (pres. 1988—). Episcopalian. Home: 629 N 4th St Crockett TX 75835 Office: Hist Projects 303 S 1st St Crockett TX 75835

BISHOP, HEDY MANON, retail management executive; b. Biloxi, Miss., Nov. 9, 1960; d. Lee Roy and Chao-Ying (Liu) B. Student, Weber State Coll., 1984; BS, U. Md., Athens, Greece, 1986. Command ombudsman Naval Security Group Activity, Athens, Greece, 1985-86; asst. mgr. Casual Corner, U.S. Shoe Corp., Lawton, Okla., 1986; assoc. mgr. Casual Corner, U.S. Shoe Corp., 1986-87; store mgr. Casual Corner, U.S. Shoe Corp., Oklahoma City, 1987; area mgr. Your Choice, Charlotte, N.C., 1987-88; dist. mgr. Your Choice, 1988-89, Victorias Secret, Limited Inc., 1989—. Vol. Charlotte Arts & Sci. Coun., 1989. With USN, 1979-83. Mem. Nat. Assn. Female Execs., Nat. Trust Hist. Preservation. Republican. Roman Catholic. Home: 6409 3D Cameron Forest Ln Charlotte NC 28210 Office: Victorias Secret 4400 Sharon Ln Charlotte NC 28210

BISHOP, JOYCE ANN, special programs counselor; b. West Mansfield, Ohio, June 16, 1935; d. Frederic J. and Marjorie Vere (Stephens) Armentrout; m. Belinda Lee, Thomas James. AB, Albion Coll., 1956; MA, Western Mich. U., 1969, postgrad., 1972-87. Cert. social worker. Tchr. phys. edn., health and cheerleading Walled Lake (Mich.) Jr. High Sch., 1956-58; instr. slimnastics adult edn. Milw. Pub. Schs., 1959-65; demonstrator, co. rep. Polaroid Corp., Cambridge, Mass., 1960-81; research asst. fetal electrocardiography Marquette U., Milw., 1962-64; tchr. phys. edn., health and cheerleading Brown Deer (Wis.) High Sch., 1963-65; instr. slimnastics adult edn., instr. volleyball Lakeview High Sch., Battle Creek, Mich., 1966—; dir. student activities, asst. prof. Olivet (Mich.) Coll., 1969-71; transfer counselor spl. programs Kellogg Community Coll., Battle Creek, 1971—; fin. planner Richard M. Groff Assocs., Inc., 1987. Sec. adult bd. Teens, Inc., 1965-68; bd. dirs. Battle Creek Day Care Ctrs., sec., 1984, pres., 1984-86; team capt. United Way Awareness Week, 1984, allocations com. 1985-89; chmn. allocations com. United Way, 1990, United Arts Fund Dr., 1985, chmn., 1986; mem. Battle Creek Leadership Acad. Recipient Master Teaching award Lakeview Schs., 1969, 87. Mem. AAUW, Mich. Assn. Collegiate Registrars and Admissions Officers (pres. 1979-80, historian 1984-87), Am. Assn. Collegiate Registrars and Admissions Officers (mem. com. 1984-87), Am. Personnel and Guidance Assn., Am. Coll. Personnel Assn., Mich. Personnel and Guidance Assn., Mich. Coll. Personnel Assn., Mich. Assn. Women Deans, Adminstrs. and Counselors, Mich. Assn. Coll. Admissions Counselors, Alpha Chi Omega, Beta Beta Beta. Clubs: Battle Creek Road Runners (v.p. 1983-85), Battle Creek Altrusa. Home: 721 Eastfield Dr Battle Creek MI 49015 Office: Kellog Community Coll 450 North Ave Battle Creek MI 49017

BISHOP, KATHRYN ELIZABETH, film company executive, writer; b. Seattle, July 7, 1945; d. Wesley Thomas Bishop and Muriel (Robert) Leisher; m. Randolph Stiles, May 22, 1985; 1 child, Zachary. BA, Wartburg Coll., 1966. Voice over talent Chgo. Bd. Edn. Radio Network, 1960-62; prodn. asst. Sta. CBS-TV, WBBM-TV, Chgo., 1961-63; disk jockey, engr., writer Sta. KWAR-FM, Waverly, Iowa, 1964-65; assoc. producer Bing Crosby Prodns. Inc., Chgo., 1966-69; producer Sedelmaier Films, Chgo., 1969-73; v.p., head prodn. Wakeford/Orloff Inc., L.A., 1977-78; producer Katy Bishop Prodns. Inc., L.A., 1973—; exec. producer The Colman Group Inc., L.A., 1982-87; co-founder, co-owner Rapport Films, Inc., Hollywood, Calif., 1987—. Co-author: (screenplay) Millionaire's Club; screenwriter: Cinnamon Bear. Mem. TV Acad. Arts and Scis., Dirs. Guild Am. Office: Rapport Films Inc 1151 N Las Palmas Los Angeles CA 90038

BISHOP, LOUISE WILLIAMS, state legislator; b. Cairo, Ga., June 27, 1933; d. Elijah and Sarah (Hines) Williams; m. James Alburn Bishop (div.); children: Todd James, Tabb Jody, Tamika Joy, James Alburn Jr. B in Communications and Radio Broadcasting, Am. Found. Dramatic Arts. Ordained min. Baptist Evangelist Ch., 1978. With Sta. WHAT; program host Sta. WDAS; mem. Pa. Ho. of Reps., Harrisburg, 1988—. Recipient numerous awards including Richard Allen award African Meth. Episc.Ch., Community Svc. award Missionary Baptist Pastors Conf., Outstanding Citizen award Phila. Mayor's Coun. on Youth Opportunity. Mem. Pa. Legis. Black Caucus (sec.), NAACP, Nat. Assn. Women Legislators, Nat. Polit. Congress Black Women, Nat. Assn. Women's Clergy, Bapt. Min.'s Conf., Afro-Am. Hist. and Cultural Mus. Democrat. Home: 2460 N 59th St Philadelphia PA 19131 Office: Pa Ho of Reps South Office Bldg Rm 307 Harrisburg PA 17120

BISHOP, MARGARET, retired educator, writer; b. Urbana, Ill., July 4, 1920; d. Charles Maxwell and Prudence Emily (Pratt) McConn; m. Edwin Samuel Bishop, Aug. 22, 1942; children—Peter Boehler, Margaret. B.A., Barnard Coll., N.Y.C., 1943. Reporter, wire editor York Gazette and Daily, York, Pa., 1942-45; remedial reading tutor, Queens, N.Y., 1958-68; in-house writer Appleton-Century-Crofts, N.Y.C., 1964-70, McGraw-Hill, N.Y.C., 1971-74; reading specialist Fortune Soc., N.Y.C., 1976-85. Author: The ABC's and All Their Tricks, 1986, Ode on Reason and Faith, 1981, (workbooks) Phonics with Write and See, 1968, also articles. Exec. sec. NAACP, York, 1943-48; mem. LWV, York, 1946-50, Reading Reform Found., N.Y.C., 1958—; pres. N.Y.C. met. chpt., 1981-85. Mem. Mayor's Profl. Exchange, Adult Basic Edn. Providers. Democrat. Humanist. Avocations: hiking; camping; backpacking.

BISHOP, MARY ROBINSON, educator, administrator; b. Chickasha, Okla., July 9, 1922; d. Scott Vernon and Mary Eugenia (Peery) Robinson; m. Ray Phillip Kawal, Sept. 17, 1944 (div. 1960); children: Ray, Ronald; m. George Bishop (div. 1980). BA, Okla. Coll. for Women, 1943; spl. cert. engring., U. Tex., 1944; cert. in adminstrn., Calif. State U., 1959, MA, 1968. Aero. engr. Curtiss-Wright Aircraft Corp., St. Louis, 1944-45, North Am. Aviation, Inglewood, Calif., 1945-46; tchr. Los Angeles Unified Sch. Dist., 1959-67, tchr. of gifted children, 1968-74, curriculum cons., 1974-76, advisor gifted program, 1976-77, with staff-devel. div., 1977-78; with adminstrn. staff Victoria Ave. Sch., Southgate, Calif., 1978-81, Chatsworth, Calif., 1982-86; with adminstrn. staff Germain St. Sch., Chatsworth; Author and editor: Critical Thinking, 1978. Hon. life mem. PTA, 1986—; chmn. 43d Ch. of Christ Scientist, Woodland Hills, Calif., 1972-85. Mem. Delta Kappa Gamma (pres. 1976-78, internat. rep. 1976). Republican. Home: 17260 Signature Dr Granada Hills CA 91344

BISHOP, RUTH ANN, coloratura soprano, voice educator; b. Homewood, Ill., Feb. 21, 1942; d. George Bernard and Grace Mildred (Hoke) Riddle; m. John Allen Reinhardt, June 9, 1962 (div. 1975); children: Laura, Jonathon; m. Merrill Edward Bishop, Aug. 16, 1975; stepchildren: Mark, Lynn. BS in Music Edn., U. Ill., 1962; M of Music in Voice, Cath. U. Am., 1972; postgrad., U. Md., 1975. Music tchr. Prince Georges County (Md.) Schs., 1963-71, Yamaha Music Co., College Park, Md., 1971-73; voice tchr. Prince Georges Community Coll., Largo, Md., 1972-75, U. Md., College Park, 1975; profl. lectr. voice Chgo. Mus. Coll. Roosevelt U., 1977-82; tchr. voice McHenry Co. Coll., Crystal Lake, Ill., 1978—, Elgin (Ill.) Community Coll., 1981—; pvt. voice tchr. Crystal Lake, 1975—; dir. music Epworth United Meth. Ch., Elgin, 1984-86, Cherub choir 1st Congl. Ch., Crystal Lake, 1986-88; mem. Camerata Singers, Lake Forest, 1988—. soprano soloist, Oratorio-The Psalms of David, 1986, opera, The Light of the Eye, 1985-86, Children's Day at the Opera, Washington, 1972, U.S. Navy Band, The White House, 1969; soloist with Crystal Lake Community Choir and Band, 1987, First Congl. Ch., 1975—, others. Ill. State scholar, 1959. Mem. Nat. Assn. Tchrs. Singing (chpt. recording sec. 1984-86), Sigma Alpha Iota, Pi Kappa Lambda, Kappa Delta. Republican. United Ch. of Christ. Home: 951 Cambridge Ln Crystal Lake IL 60014-7608 Office: Elgin Community Coll Dept Music 1700 Spartan Dr Elgin IL 60123

BISHOP, SUE, management consultant; b. Boston, Apr. 29, 1953; d. Robert J. and Gladys M. (Petitpas) B. BS, Boston U., 1976. Sales and gen. mgr. Digital Mus. Systems, Inc., Boston, 1981-84; ops. mgr. Harvard Student Agy., Harvard U., Cambridge, Mass., 1984-85; retail ops. mgr. Moynihan Lumber, Inc., N. Reading, Mass., 1985-88; Mill ops. mgr. Moynihan Lumber, Inc., N. Reading, 1988-89; ptnr. TIC Bus. Cons., Chelsea, Mass., 1988—. Mem. Nat. Retail Lumberpersons Assn., Am. Mgmt. Assn. Home: 48 Tudor St Chelsea MA 02150 Office: TIC Bus Cons 48 Tudor St Chelsea MA 02150

BISHOP, SUSAN KATHARINE, executive search company executive; b. Palm Beach, Fla., Apr. 3, 1946; d. Warner Bader Bishop and Katharine Sue (White) McLennan; m. Robert Uchitel, Dec. 27, 1973 (div. 1979); 1 child, Rachel. B.A., Briarcliff Coll., 1968; M.B.A., Fordham U., 1985. Actress N.Y.C., 1968-72; producer, hostess Sta. KIMO-TV, Anchorage, 1972-74; dir. programming Visions Pay TV, 1974-79; recruiter Joe Sullivan & Assocs., N.Y.C., 1980-82; prin. Johnson, Smith & Knisely, 1982-88; ptnr. Schmitt Bishop Tolette, N.Y.C., 1989—. Mem. Cable TV Adminstrn. and Mktg. Soc., Women in Cable. Office: Schmitt Bishop Tolette 708 Third Ave New York NY 10017

BISHOP, VIRGINIA WAKEMAN, librarian, humanities educator; b. Portland, Oreg., Dec. 28, 1927; d. Andrew Virgil and Letha Evangeline (Ward) Wakeman; m. Clarence Edmund Bishop, Aug. 23, 1953; children: Jean Marie Bishop Johnson, Marilyn Joyce. BA, Bapt. Missionary Tng. Sch., Chgo., 1949, Linfield Coll., McMinnville, Oreg., 1952; MEd, Linfield Coll., McMinnville, Oreg., 1953; MA in Librarianship, U. Wash., 1968. Ch. worker Univ. Bapt. Ch., Seattle, 1954-56, 59-61, pre-sch. tchr. parent coop presch., 1965-66; libr. N.W. Coll., Kirkland, Wash., 1968-69; undergrad. libr. U. Wash., Seattle, 1970; libr., instr. Seattle Cen. Community Coll., 1970—. Leader Totem council Girl Scouts U.S., 1962-65; pres. Wedgwood Sch. PTA, Seattle, 1964-65; chairperson 46th Dist. Dem. Orgn., Seattle, 1972-73; candidate Wash. State Legislature, Seattle, 1974, 80; mem. LWV. Recipient Golden Acorn award Wedgwood Elem. Sch., 1966. Mem. Wash. Commn. for Humanities (Humanist scholar 1979-80), Wash. Libr. Assn. (legis. rep. 1972), U. Wash. Grad. Sch. Libr. and Info. Sci. Alumni Assn. (1st v.p. 1986-87, pres. 1987-88), Community Coll. Librs. and Media Specialists, Seattle Community Coll. Fedn. Tchrs. Baptist. Home: 3032 NE 87th St Seattle WA 98115 Office: Seattle Cen Community Coll 1701 Broadway Seattle WA 98122

BISSELL, BETTY DICKSON, stockbroker; b. Salina, Kans., Sept. 9, 1932; d. Henry Shields and Alta May Dickson; m. Buford Lyle Bissel, Jr., Nov. 1, 1952; 1 child, Bradford Dickson. Student, U. Kans., 1949-52; cert. fin. planner, Coll. Fin. Planning, 1976. With Dean Witter Reynolds Inc., Menlo Park, Calif., 1975—, asst. br. mgr., 1978-82, asso. v.p. investments, 1980-82, 1st v.p. investments, 1982-86, sr. v.p. investments, 1986—. Pres. Jr. League San Jose (Calif.), 1963-64. Mem. Internat. Assn. Fin. Planners, Peninsula Stock and Bond Club, Pi Beta Phi, Commonwealth Club Calif., Summit League Club (Saratoga-Los Gatos), Jr. League Club (San Jose, Calif.), Menlopolitans Club (Menlo Park, Calif.). Republican. Episcopalian. Office: 1010 El Camino Real Ste 200 Menlo Park CA 94025

BISSELL, ELEANOR AMORET, retail executive; b. Norwalk, Conn., Apr. 6, 1960; d. Louis Garner Bissell and Martha Lawrence (Lewis) Kingsford. BA in Sociology, Goucher Coll., Towson, Md., 1982. Counselor Luther Gulick Camps, South Casco, Maine, 1977-78; head lifeguard Goucher Coll., Towson, Md., 1979-82; sales assoc. Hechts, Balt., 1982-83, selling asst., 1983-84, group mgr., 1984-85; sales mgr. Macy's, Lawrenceville, N.J., 1985-89, asst. buyer, 1989—. Author, editor Men's Monthly, 1988—; author, editor: Men's Dress Shirts, 1987. Republican. Episcopalian. Home: 72 Fair Oaks Ct Newtown PA 18940 Office: Macys 151 34th St New York NY 10001

BISSETT, BARBARA ANNE, steel distribution company executive; b. Cleve., Sept. 27, 1950; d. George Jr. and Helen (Kirkwood) B.; m. Kerry Mark Kitchen, Oct. 6, 1979; children: Mark Jeffrey, Lauren Brooke. BFA, U. Denver, 1974. Inside sales rep. Bissett Steel Co., Cleve., 1977-78, inside sales mgr., 1978-80, v.p., 1980-88, pres., 1988—; mentor strategic planning course Greater Cleve. Growth Assn., 1987—. Mem. bd. dirs. Coun. of Smaller Ent., 1990—. Mem. Am. Soc. Metals, Steel Svc. Ctr. Inst. (com. mem. Young Execs. Forum 1987—, v.p. programming young leadership forum 1989), Coun. Smaller Enterprises (mem. leadership coun. 1989, bd. dirs. 1990—), Assn. Women in Metals Industries, Cleve. Yacht. Club, Women's City Club Cleve. Republican. Presbyterian. Home: 1994 Coe's Post Run Westlake OH 44145 Office: The Bissett Steel Co 9005 Bank St Valley View OH 44125

BISSEX, JANICE NEWELL, dietitian; b. Salem, Mass., Dec. 15, 1959; d. David Ellsworth and Carol (Thoms) N.; m. Donald Abeel Bissex, Mar. 5, 1988. BS, U. Maine, 1981; MS, Boston U., 1984. Nutrition dir. New Eng. Heart Ctr., Boston, 1982-85; regional sales mgr. Practorcare, Inc., San Diego, 1985-88, div. sales mgr., 1988-89; consulting dietitian U.S. Senate Restaurants, Washington, 1989—; pres. JNB Assocs., Boston, 1990—; seminar leader Nat. Restaurant Assn. Ednl. Found., 1990—. Contbg. author: The Exercising Adult, 1987. Mem. NAFE, Am. Dietetic Assn. (registered dietitian), Mass. Dietetic Assn. (bd. dirs. 1984-85). Home and Office: JNB Assocs 40 Glen St Melrose MA 02176

BISSLAND, MARY LOU, chiropractic assistant, radiological technologist; b. Angels, Pa., Oct. 20, 1935; d. Charles Scott and Emma Grace (Burrus) Weitzel; m. James Ronald Bissland, Dec. 28, 1957; children: James Scott, Deborah Elaine, Robin ONallie, David MArtin, Ronald Paul. Cert. in nursing, James Martin Sch. of Nursing, Phila., 1956. Lic. practical nurse; cert. acupuncture asst., chiropractic physician's asst., X-ray technologist. Nurse Overbrook Sch. for Blind, Phila., 1956-57, Lankanau Hosp., Phila., 1957, Drs. Hosp., Bethlehem, Pa., 1958-59; chiropractic asst. Chiropractic Intensive Care Ctr., Tulsa, 1972-77; chiropractic asst. Bissland Chiropractic, Eldridge, Iowa, 1963-65, Kalona, Iowa, 1965-72, Titusville, Fla., 1977—. Republican. Baptist. Lodge: Order Ea. Star. Office: Bissland Chiropractic 1410 S Washington Ave Titusville FL 32780

BISZICK, DORIS ANNA MARIA, international fixed income sales broker; b. N.Y.C., Sept. 24, 1963; d. Mychajlo and Romana (Peruc) Luczkiw; m. Craig Michael Biszick, Oct. 10, 1987. BA in Polit. Sci, SUNY, Albany, 1985; MIA, Columbia U., 1987. Soviet analyst CIA, Washington, 1985; internat. credit analyst Salomon Bros. Inc., N.Y.C., 1986-87; internat. investment broker Goldman Sachs & Co., N.Y.C., 1987—. Nat. City Found. scholar, 1981-85, W. Avery Harriman Inst. scholar, 1986-87, Columbia U. Sch. Internat. Affairs fellow, 1986-87. Home: 330 E 38th St Apt 35P New York NY 10016 Office: Goldman Sachs & Co 85 Broad St 27th Fl New York NY 10004

BITLER, CATHY FITZPATRICK, economic development and public affairs executive; b. Ft. Benning, Ga., Apr. 24, 1958; d. Benjamin Elbert and Barbara (Hayman) Fitzpatrick; m. David Levi Bitler, Sept. 11, 1982; 1 child, Sarah Kathryn. BS in Communications, Ohio U., 1980. Reporter Sta. WHOK Inc., Lancaster, Ohio, 1980-83; dir. news Sta. WHOK Inc., Lancaster, 1983-88, dir. promotions, 1985-88; econ. devel. asst. South Cen. Power, Lancaster, 1988—. Author: Fairfield Monthly, 1984. Pres. United Cerebral Palsy Lancaster, 1986-89; mem. adv. com. Southeastern Correctional Inst., 1983-87; mem. adv. bd. Fairfield County Youth, 1985-87, Special Wish Found., 1986-88. Mem. Ohio Assoc. Press (bd. dirs. 1984-85, best regularly scheduled news award 1986), Unity Singers, Ohio U. Alumni Assn. (Disting. Svc. award 1989). Republican. Home: 566 Lynnwood Ln Lancaster OH 43130 Office: South Cen Power 2780 Coonpath Rd Lancaster OH 43130

BITTEL, MURIEL HELENE, managing editor; b. N.Y.C., Mar. 22; d. Ernest Henry and Helen Minnie (Seibel) Albers; m. Robert Gifford Walcutt, June 15, 1946; children—Lynn Lowell Walcutt, Mark James Walcutt, Judith Anne Walcutt; m. Lester Robert Bittel, May 8, 1973. B.A., Douglass Coll. Feature writer Daily Home News, New Brunswick, N.J.; editor Fawcett Pubs., N.Y.C., 1940-46; pub. relations dir. Electrovox/Walco Inc., East Orange, N.J., 1946-62; mng. editor Acad. Hall Pubs., Bridgewater, Va., 1974—. Mng. editor: Ency. Profl. Mgmt., 1978; Handbook Profl. Mgrs., 1985. Home: 106 Breezewood Terrace Bridgewater VA 22812

BITTEN, MARY JOSEPHINE, Township clerk; b. Brighton, Mich., May 20, 1942; d. William Frederick and Josephine Grace (Wright) Belz; m. Gerald A. Bitten, (div. Dec. 1982); children: Joann, Mark, Scott. Student, Howell High Sch., 1960. Bookkeeper Bitten Brothers, Brighton, Mich., 1963-67; v.p. Holiday Of Hartland (Mich.), 1977-88; acct. Taylor Bldg., Detroit, 1978-79; pres. Mar-Bar Ins., Brighton, Mich.; real estate mgr. C-21, Howell, Mich., 1979-86; township clk. Township of Brighton (Mich.), 1987--; self-employed builder Brighton, Mich., 1986--. Mem. Republican Women, dir. Livingston County Clks., treas. Livingston County Township Assn., 1988, chmn. Brighton Township Recycling, 1988, Mich. Township Assn., Brighton Area C. of C. Lutheran.

BITTMANN, SUSAN WILKINS, social studies educator; b. Lumberton, N.C., Nov. 10, 1946; d. William Earl and Leslie Daniel (McNeill) Wilkins; m. Christopher Jacob Bittmann, Jr., Apr. 20, 1973. Student, Meredith Coll., 1964-66; AB in Edn., U. N.C., 1968, MA in History, 1971; postgrad., U. South Fla., 1979-80. Cert. social studies tchr. Tchr. social studies Gt. Bridge High Sch., Chesapeake, Va., 1968-69, J. P. Moore Jr. High Sch., Lumberton, 1971-72, Chamberlain High Sch., Tampa, Fla., 1972-89, Hillsborough High Sch. Internat. Baccalaureate Program, Tampa, 1989—; mem. social studies textbook selection com. Fla. Dept. Edn., Hillsborough County, 1985-86, mem. revision com. for social studies, 1988; reader Ednl. Testing Service, Princeton, 1986—, test developer, 1987—; mem. Fla. Content Area Exam. Devel. Com. on History and Humanities, 1987-88. Co-editor: Limited English Proficient Manual, 1986. Sec. Carrollwood Service League, Tampa, 1974-76, mem. ways and means com., 1978-79; mem. pres. council U. South Fla., Tampa, 1983—. Named Social Studies Tchr. of Yr., Hillsborough County, 1986, Tchr. of Yr. Chamberlain High Sch., 1987, 89; Fla. Humanities grantee, 1985-86; recipient Master Tchr. award, 1986. Mem. NEA, Fla. Teaching Profession, Nat. Coun. for Social Studies, Fla. Coun. for Social Studies, Assn. for Supervision and Curriculum Devel., Phi Delta Kappa, Alpha Delta Kappa (treas. 1989—), Pi Sigma Kappa, Phi Mu (sec. alumna Tampa 1975-77), Hillsborough Classroom Tchrs. Assn. Democrat. Methodist. Office: Hillsborough High Sch 5000 Central Ave Tampa FL 33603

BITTNER, KATHERINE LOUISE, industrial/organizational psychologist, professor; b. Allentown, Pa., Nov. 9, 1960; d. Frank David and Janet Fay (Romberger) B.; m. Dale Linwood Reichert, June 14, 1986. BA, Bucknell U., 1982; MA, Fairleigh Dickinson U., 1984; PhD, Pa. State U., 1990. Rsch. cons. AT&T, N.Y.C., 1982-84; rsch. asst. Applied Rsch. Lab., Univ. Pk., 1984-86, Office of Planning Studies, Univ. Pk., 1986-87; devel. cons. Phila. (Pa.) Electric Co., 1988-89; organizational behavior and indsl. psychology professor Moravian Coll., 1989—; cons. Applied Psychol. Inst., Univ. Pk., 1988, Landy, Jacobs & Assocs., State Coll., Pa., 1987-88. Supporter Planned Parenthood, Washington, 1990. Mem. Am. Psychol. Assn. (assoc. div. 14), Humane Soc., Penn. PIRG, Psi Chi, Phi Beta Kappa. Republican. Lutheran. Home: 1221 Timothy Dr Phoenixville PA 19460

BITTNER, MARY ELLEN, judge; b. Lake Forest, Ill., May 15, 1947; d. Ralph H. and Mary Elizabeth (Ewing) Rockwood; m. David J. Benard, Aug. 17, 1968 (div.); 1 child, Mary Elizabeth; m. Herbert E. Bittner, Feb. 20, 1987. BS in Math., U. Ill., 1969, JD, 1972. Bar: Ill. 1972, D.C. 1975. Counsel NLRB, Washington, 1972-76, asst. chief counsel, 1976-80, adminstrv. law judge, 1980-87; adminstrv. law judge Drug Enforcement Adminstrn., Washington, 1987—. Mem. outreach com. St. John's Ch., Lafayette Sq., Washington, 1976-88; bd. dirs. Coop. Urban Ministry Ctr. Inc., Washington, 1983-85. Recipient cert. of commendation NLRB, 1977, 80. Author: (with Herbert Bittner) The Labor Lawyer, vol. 1, no. 4, 1985. Mem. ABA (com. devel. law under Nat. Labor Rels. Act 1979—), Nat. Assn. Women Judges, NLRB Profl. Assn. (pres. 1975-76), Forum of U.S. Adminstrv. Law Judges (pres. 1985-87), Zonta of Washington (bd. dirs. 1983—, chmn. fin. com. 1983-85, chmn. pub. affairs com 1985-88, chmn. mem. com. 1988-89, 2d v.p. 1987-88, 1st v.p. 1988-89, pres. 1989—). Democrat. Episcopalian. Home: 4819 Morgan Dr Chevy Chase MD 20815 Office: Drug Enforcement Adminstrn 1405 I St NW Washington DC 20537

BIVENS, CONSTANCE ANN, educator; b. Madison, Ind., June 26, 1938; d. Nelson and Virginia (Cole) B. BS, George Peabody Coll. for Tchrs., 1960, MA, 1966; EdD, Nova U., Ft. Lauderdale, Fla., 1982. Cert. educator. Tchr. Broward County Schs., Ft. Lauderdale, Fla., 1960-61, 65—, Jefferson County Schs., Louisville, Ky., 1961-62, Ft. Knox (Ky.) Schs., 1962-64, Madison (Ind.) Consol. Schs., 1964-65; chmn. K-Adult Council, Nova Schs., Ft. Lauderdale, 1976-78; cons. 1978-80. Author: Boots, Butterflies, and Dragons, 1982. Mem. Hollywood Hills United Meth. Ch., 1966—, Children's Cancer Caring Ctr. Inc., Broward County, 1986—. Mem. AAUW, Fla. Reading Assn., Nat. Edn. Assn., Assn. of Supervision and Curriculum Devel., Kings Daughters, Irish Cultural Inst., Hollywood Hist. Soc., Zool. Soc. Fla., Nat. Audubon Soc., Delta Kappa Gamma Soc. Internat. Republican. Methodist. Home: 5516 Arthur St Hollywood FL 33021 Office: Nova Blanche Forman Elem Sch 3521 Davie Rd Fort Lauderdale FL 33314

BIVENS, LYNETTE, government official; b. Groom, TEx., Apr. 6, 1952. BS, W. Tex. State U., Canyon, 1974; postgrad., Okla. State U. Officer-in-chg., postmaster U.S. Postal Svc., Wewoka, Okla.; div. supr. delivery and vehicle progs. U.S. Postal Svc., Oklahoma City. With USAR, 1979-86. Recipient Postal Svc. Safety awards, Postal Svc. Achievement award. Mem. Nat. Assn. Postmasters, Nat. Assn. Postal Suprs. Home: PO Box 580 Luther OK 73054

BIX, HELEN HELMAN, manufacturing company executive; b. Celle, Germany, May 6, 1935; came to U.S., 1948; d. Heinrich and Berta (Nass) Hellmann; m. Harold Charles Bix, Dec. 19, 1954; children: Cindy J., Barbara C., Brian S. B in Bus., U. Minn., 1954. Trainee buyer's program Dayton-Hudson Corp., Mpls., 1952-54; pres. Beco-Helman Co., Inc., Mpls., 1954—. Bd. dirs. Washington U., St. Louis, 1982-84; mem. planning com. Shanghai Re-Union, Los Angeles; chmn. Beth El Synagogue, Mpls., 1979-85; chmn. scholarship com. Sch. of Adult Jewish Studies, Mpls., 1980. Recipient Humanitarian award Jewish Nat. Fund, 1974, Golden Book award. Mem. Nat. Assn. Female Execs., League of Women Voters, Walker Art Ctr., Solomon Guggenheim Mus., Mus. Modern Art of N.Y.C., Jewish Mus. N.Y.C., Council of Jewish Women, U. Minn. Alumni Assn. Jewish. Club:

Northwest Tennis. Lodge: B'nai B'rith, Hadassah. Office: Beco-Helman Inc 801 Washington Ave N Minneapolis MN 55401

BIXBY, KATHERINE COSTLOW (MRS. E. REW BIXBY), civic worker; b. Lusk, Wyo., Feb. 8, 1920; d. Jesse Patrick and Anna (Thompson) Costlow; m. E. Rew Bixby, May 30, 1942; children: Patrick William, Jean Bixby Hennessy. Student, Cottey Coll., 1937-38; BA, Doane Coll., 1941. Tchr. elem. schs., Lusk, 1941-42; exec. dir. Vol. Ctr., Los Angeles, 1971-84; tchr. vol. mgmt. U. So. Calif., Marymount Coll., Valley Coll.; cons. Exec. Service Corps, 1984-86; trainer Ctr. Non-Profit Mgmt., 1984-86. Bd. dirs. Welfare Planning Council 1962-72, USO, 1965-71, Comprehensive Health Planning Los Angeles County, 1969-72, United Crusades Calif., 1968-72, Mayor's Com. on Aging, 1970-72, Los Angeles Mental Health Commn., 1967-72, Planned Protective Services, 1969-71, Camp Fire Girls, 1950-59, United Way, Inc., 1963-71, Calif. Social Welfare Archives, 1979-88. Recipient Gold Key award United Way, 1963, Armed Forces Vol. award, 1966, Luther Gulick award Camp Fire Girls, 1959, Gold Medallion award USO, 1970, Koshland Found. award, 1977. Mem. Nat. Conf. Social Welfare (bd. dirs. 1976-78), Assn. Vol. Adminstrs. (regional chmn. 1981-82), U. So. Calif. Sch. Social Work (bd. councillors 1988—) Calif. Social Welfare Archives, Exec. Svc. Corps. Home: 920 Crestview Ave Glendale CA 91202

BIXLER, LOIS JANE, custom services executive; b. Harrisburg, Pa., June 25, 1958; d. Leon Lemar and Mary Helen (Holland) B. BSBA, Shippensburg U. Pa., 1980. Systems analyst Unisys, Radnor, Pa., 1981-82, project mgr., 1983-85; corp. program mgr. Unisys, Detroit, 1986-87, Bell Bell, Pa., 1988-89; mgr. custom svcs. Unisys, Camarillo, Calif., 1989—. Republican. Methodist. Home: 5684 Recodo Way Camarillo CA 93010 Office: 747 Calle Plano Camarillo CA 93010

BIZUB, JOHANNA CATHERINE, law librarian; b. Denville, N.J., Apr. 13, 1957; d. Stephen Bernard and Elizabeth Mary (Grizzle) B. BS in Criminal Justice, U. Dayton, 1979; MLS, Rutgers U., 1984. Law libr. Morris County Law Libr., 1981-83, Clapp & Eisenberg, Newark, 1984-86; dir. libr. Sills Cummis, 1986—. Mem. Assn. Legal Adminstrs., N.J. Law Librarians Assn. (treas. 1987-89, v.p., pres. elect 1989-90, pres. 1990—), Am. Assn. Law Librs., N.J. Libr. Assn., Spl. Librs. Assn. (treas. 1990—), Law Libr. Assn. Greater N.Y., Am. Legion Aux. (treas. Rockden unit 175 1983—). Democrat. Roman Catholic. Home: 11 Elm St Rockaway NJ 07866 Office: Sills Cummis Legal Center 1 Riverfront Pla Newark NJ 07102-5400

BJORNSON, MARIA, theatrical designer. Designer London. Designer The Phanton of the Opera (Antoinette Perry awards for best scenic design and best costume design 1988), The Cunning Little Vixen. *

BLACK, APRIL MARIE, clinical laboratory official; b. Valparaiso, Ind., Apr. 11, 1961; d. Lester Paul and Mary Pauline (Mathews) Pullins; m. Thomas Alan Black. BS in Mktg. and Mgmt., Ind. U., 1983; postgrad., Ind. Weslyan U., 1990—. Mgr. Peoples Drug, Indpls., 1983-86; adminstrv. asst. Capitol Drilling Co., Indpls., 1987-88; supr., coord. ops. project SciCor, Indpls., 1988—. Office: SciCor 8200 SciCor Dr Indianapolis IN 46234

BLACK, CATHLEEN PRUNTY, newspaper company executive; b. Chgo., Apr. 26, 1944; d. James Hamilton and Margaret (Harrington) B. B.A., Trinity Coll., 1966. Advt. sales rep. Holiday mag., N.Y.C., 1966-69, Travel & Leisure mag., N.Y.C., 1969-70; advt. sales rep. New York mag., 1970-72, assoc. pub., 1977-79, pub., 1979-83; pres. USA Today, 1983, now publisher; advt. dir. Ms. mag., 1972-75, assoc. pub., 1975-77. Home: 2915 Woodland Dr NW Washington DC 20008 Office: USA Today 1000 Wilson Blvd Arlington VA 22209

BLACK, COBEY, journalist, corporate executive; b. Washington, June 15, 1922; d. Elwood Alexander and Margaret (Beall) Cobey; m. Edwin F. Black; children: Star, Christopher, Noel, Nicholas, Brian, Bruce. BA, Wellesley Coll., 1944; postgrad., U. Hawaii. Exec. sec. to Irene, designer Metro-Goldwyn-Mayer, 1944; actress Fed. Republic Germany, 1945-46; women's editor Washington Daily News, 1947-50; columnist Honolulu Star Bull., 1954-65, Honolulu Advertiser, 1972-85; cons. HEW, Peace Corps, 1960-61; v.p. Mandalay Imports Corp.; bd. dirs. Pacific and Asian Affairs Coun., 1986—, Honolulu Com. on Fgn. Rels., 1987—; pres. Black & Black, Inc. Author: Birth of A Princess, 1962, Iolani Luahine, 1986; travel editor Bangkok World, 1968-69; publicist CBS-TV series Hawaii Five-O, 1978. Mem. Hawaii State Commn. on Status of Women, 1978-86. Democrat. Episcopalian. Clubs: Nat. Press, Royal Bangkok Sports, Outrigger Canoe, Waialae Country. Office: Black & Black Inc 1152 Koko Head Ave Ste 102 Honolulu HI 96816

BLACK, DAWN, Canadian legislator; b. Vancouver, B.C., Can., Apr. 1, 1943; d. John Edmund and Virginia Lorraine Whitty; m. Peter James Black, Aug. 28, 1965; children: David Christopher, Matthew Wayne, Stuart Anthony. Mem. Ho. of Commons, Ottawa, Ont., Can., 1988—; bd. dirs. Westminster Community Legal Svcs. Mem. New Dem. Party. Anglican. Office: House of Commons, Parliament Bldgs, Ottawa, ON Canada K1A 0A6*

BLACK, EILEEN MARY, teacher; b. Bklyn., Sept. 20, 1944; d. Marvin Mize and Anne Joan (Salvia) B. Student, Grossmont Coll., El Cajon, Calif., 1964; BA, San Diego State U., 1967; postgrad., U. Calif., San Diego, Syracuse U. Cert. tchr., Calif. Tchr. La Mesa (Calif.)-Spring Valley Sch. Dist., 1967—. NDEA grantee Syracuse U., 1968. Mem. Calif. Tchrs. Assn., Calif. Young Reps. Roman Catholic. Home: 9320 Earl St Apt 15 La Mesa CA 92042 Office: Northmont Elem Sch 9405 Gregory St La Mesa CA 92042

BLACK, FRANCES PATTERSON, library administrator; b. Huntsville, Ala., July 27, 1949; d. Fred C. and Mary Jane (Baird) Patterson; m. Larry David Black, Aug. 29, 1970; 1 child, Amy Susan. BA, U. Ala., 1971, MLS, 1972. Dir. Fairhope (Ala.) Pub. Library, 1972-77; rsch. asst. State Libr. Ohio, Columbus, Ohio, 1977-78; head tech. and extension svcs. Southwest Pub. Librs. (formerly Grove City Pub. Libr.), Grove City, Ohio, 1978-86; asst. dir. pub. svcs. Southwest Pub. Librs., Grove City, Ohio, 1986-88, dir., 1988—; mem. libr. adv. bd. Orient (Ohio) Correctional Instn., 1988—. Mem. planning Grove City Arts in the Alley, 1988—. Mem. ALA, Pub. Libr. Assn., Libr. Adminstrn. and Mgmt. Assn., Ohio Libr. Assn. (mem. legis. network 1987—, chpt. coord. 1985-86), Grove City Area C. of C., Westland Area Bus. Assn., AAUW. Office: SW Pub Librs 3359 Park St Grove City OH 43123

BLACK, KAYLENE SLAY, finance executive; b. Santa Barbara, Calif., July 31, 1945; d. Kay Parker Slay and Gwendolyn (Milliron) Montgomery; m. Harold Ray Black, July 08, 1989; children by previous marriage: William Parker, Russell Slayton, Sara Lorene. Student, Huntingdon Coll., 1963-65, 84. Bookkeeper, designer Dunn's Inc., Prattville, Ala., 1968-76; pres., owner, mgr. Dunn's, Inc., Prattville, Ala., 1976-81; office mgr., system control operator Profl. Billings, Inc., Montgomery, Ala., 1982-90; pres. Provider Claims & Collection Mgmt., Inc., Dothan, Ala., 1990—. Cubmaster Boy Scouts Am., bd. dirs. Cub Scout Dist. Day Camp, Montgomery, Autauga, Elmore and Chilton Counties, 1972. Mem. NAFE, Ala. Bus. Profl. Women's Assn. (state-wide display artist 1976-78), Ala. Wholesale Floral Assn. (bd. dirs. 1979-81) S.E. Ala. Florist Assn., MDS Client Support Group. Republican. Clubs: Jr. Women's (Prattville), Phoenix Christian Singles, Camden Study. Home: 103 Raintree Ct Dothan AL 36303

BLACK, KELLY HUNTER, media supervisor; b. N.Y.C., Nov. 4, 1960; d. Thomas Howard and Elizabeth (Hunter) B. BA, Stanford U., 1983. Media asst. Busse & Cummins, San Francisco, 1983-84, media buyer, 1984-86; media planner J. Walter Thompson Agy., San Francisco, 1986-87; media supr. J. Walter Thompson, San Francisco, 1987—. Recipient Media Shooting Star, Mktg. and Media Decisions, N.Y.C., 1988. Mem. Ad Softball League (San Francisco). Office: J Walter Thompson Agy 4 Embarcadero Ste 800 San Francisco CA 94111

BLACK, KELLY MARIE, credit manager, consultant; b. Monterey Park, Calif., Jan. 24, 1960; d. Jim and Catherine (Fernsler) Ryan; m. Murrell A. Black, Oct. 9, 1977; children: Heather, Bryan. AA in Bus., Mesa (Ariz.) Community Coll., 1979. Credit mgr. E&C Mfg., Fullerton, Calif., 1980-83, CLS Corp., Brea, Calif., 1983-86, Orco Tool & Equipment, Santa Ana, Calif., 1986—; cons. Arak Welter Snipper, L.A., 1983—; chmn. Solar Energy Exch., L.A., 198-485, Plumbing and Heating, L.A., 1986-87. Coach, mgr. West Am. Bobby Sox, Anaheim, Calif., 1983-86; coach Loara Little League, Anaheim, 1986—; vol. St. Justin Ch., Anaheim, 1987—. Mem. Soc. Profl. Credit Mgrs., Bldg. Industry Credit Assn. (asst. chmn. Orange County chpt. 1988—). Republican. Roman Catholic.

BLACK, LYNDA KAY, insurance company executive; b. Oklahoma City, Mar. 26, 1959; d. James R. and Catherine C. (Highberger) B. BA and BBA, Wichita State U., 1982, MBA, 1986. CPCU; assoc. in premium audit, assoc. in loss control mgmt. Ins. auditor USF&G Ins., Wichita, 1986-87, sr. ins. auditor, 1986-87; asst. mgr. USF&G Ins., Balt., 1987—. Mem. NAFE, Soc. CPU, Nat. Assn. Ins. Premium Auditors, Balt. Coun. on Fgn. Affairs, Coun. on Internat. and Fgn. Affairs. Republican. Roman Catholic.

BLACK, MARTHA SUSAN LOWE, lawyer; b. Maryville, Tenn., Sept. 18, 1945; d. Ernest Broyles and Esther Charlotte (Carlson) Lowe; B.A. with honors, Mount Holyoke Coll., 1967; postgrad. (NDEA fellow), Rice U., 1967-69; J.D. (Green scholar), U. Tenn., 1973; m. David T. Black, June 7, 1975; children—Charlotte Carlson, Elizabeth Cannon. Admitted to Tenn. bar, 1974; asst., then asso. prof. U. Tenn. Coll. Law, Knoxville, 1973-81; mem. firm Kizer & Black, P.C., Maryville, Tenn., 1981—; chmn. U. Tenn. Commn. Women, 1979-80. Chmn., Blount County Foster Care Review Bd., 1976-83; bd. dirs., chmn. Blount County Children's Home; mem. community adv. council Maryville Coll.; mem. Blount County Hist. Trust. Recipient Am. Jurisprudence and Corpus Juris Secundum awards, 1972; named Grad. of Yr., U. Tenn., 1973. Mem. Am. Bar Assn., Tenn. Bar Assn., Blount County Bar Assn. (pres. 1987), Order Coif. Office: 329 Cates St Maryville TN 37801

BLACK, MAUREEN, realty company executive; b. Manchester, Eng., Feb. 4, 1937; came to U.S., 1957, naturalized, 1962; d. William Henry and Kathleen Mary (Cleaver) Jackson; grad. Felt and Tarrant Comptometer Sch., Eng., 1953; student Alamogordo br. N.Mex. State U., 1959-60, 62-63; m. Charles J. Dugan, Nov. 1979; 1 dau., Karen Elizabeth Black. Office mgr., personnel dir. J.C. Penney Co., Alamogordo, 1958-66; exec. sec. to project mgr. Re-entry System div. Gen. Electric Co., Holloman AFB, 1967-68; soc. editor, columnist Alamogordo Daily News, 1968-73; regional corr. El Paso (Tex.) Times, 1968-75; free lance writer and photographer; script writer Film Unit 505, Alamogordo, 1971; realtor asso. Shyne Realty, Alamogordo, 1975-77, West Source Realtors, 1977-80; owner, broker Hyde Park West Realty Co., 1980—. Pres., Alamogordo Music Theatre, 1971-72. Mem. planning com. tourism, recreation, convs. Gov. of N.Mex., 1965; mem. N.Mex. State Film Commn., 1973-74; life mem. Aux. of Zia Sch. for Handicapped Children, pres. Aux., 1975-76, 80-82; mem. Zia Sch. Bd., 1988-89; pres. Zia Found., 1988-89. Recipient service award Nat. Found., March of Dimes, 1971; Americanism medal DAR, 1972; named Career Woman of Yr., Alamogordo chpt. Am. Bus. Women's Assn., 1971. Mem. Alamogordo C. of C. (chmn. convs. and motion picture com. 1965—), Nat. Assn. Realtors, Realtors Assn. N.Mex., Internat. Realtors Assn. Alamogordo Bd. Realtors (chmn. public relations com., v.p. 1981-82, pres. 1983-84), N.Mex. Opera Guild. Home: 1206 Desert Eve Dr Alamogordo NM 88310 Office: PO Box 2021 Alamogordo NM 88310

BLACK, NAOMI RUTH, writer, editor; b. Springfield, Mass., Oct. 19, 1957; d. Henry Arnold and Zelda Edith (Hodosh) B.; m. John Ian Bralower, July 22, 1990. BA in Anthropology, Beloit Coll., 1979. Project coordinator, editor Woodward-Clyde Cons., San Francisco, 1978-80; asst. editor, travel editor William Morrow Co., N.Y.C., 1980-83; mng. editor Quarto Mktg. Ltd., N.Y.C., 1983-85; freelance writer N.Y.C., 1985—. Author: Seashore Entertaining, 1987, Dude Ranches of the American West, 1988, Small Parties, 1990, (as N.R. Gordon) Seashells, 1990; co-author: The American Mail-Order Gourmet, 1986, East Coast Bed and Breakfast Guide, 1986, West Coast Bed and Breakfast Guide, 1989, The New England Companion, 1990; contbr. articles to periodicals. Bd. dirs. Writers and Pubs. Alliance for Nuclear Disarmament, N.Y.C., 1987-88. Office: 378 W End Ave New York NY 10024 Office: 378 W End Ave #1001 New York NY 10024

BLACK, PAGE MORTON, civic worker; b. Chgo.; d. Alexander and Rose Morton; m. William Black, Mar. 27, 1962. Student, Chgo. Mus. Coll. Singer, pianist, Pierre Hotel, N.Y.C., Warwick Hotel, One Fifth Ave. Sherry Netherland Hotel; singer radio show and comml. Chock Full o' Nuts Corp.; rec. artist Atlantic Records; co-founder Page and William Black Post-Grad. Sch. Medicine, Mt. Sinai Med. Sch., 1965—; chmn., mem. exec. bd. Parkinsons' Disease Found., Columbia U. Med. Ctr. (mem. adv. coun.); mem. nat. vis. coun. Columbia U. Health Scis. Faculties, hon. chmn. Chock Full O' Nuts Corp., 1983—. Recipient Ann. award Parkinsons' Disease Found., 1987. Home: Premium Point New Rochelle NY 10801

BLACK, PATTI CARR, museum administrator; b. Sumner, Miss., May 18, 1934; d. Samuel Bismarck and Velma Lewis (Carnathan) Carr; m. D. Carl Black, Feb. 10, 1957 (div. 1968); 1 child, Elizabeth. B.A., Miss. U. for Women, 1955; M.A., Emory U., 1968. Research librarian Miss. Dept. Archives and History, Jackson, 1957-63; research librarian Met. Mus. Art, N.Y.C., 1968-69, Time Inc., N.Y.C., 1969-70; curator of exhibits Miss. State Hist. Mus., Jackson, 1976—, dir., 1976—; mem. nat. adv. bd. Ctr. for Study So. Culture, 1978—, Smithsonian Nat. Mus. Act, 1984—. Editor: Mules and Mississippi, 1978, 81, Made by Hand: Mississippi Folk Art, 1980, Documentary Portrait of Mississippi: The Thirties, 1982, Eudora, 1984, The Natchez Trace, 1986, Approaching the Magic Hour, 1989. Founder New Stage Theatre, Jackson, 1965, bd. dirs., 1965—; bd. dirs. Miss. Inst. Arts and Letters, 1984—; mem. devel. panel So. Arts Fedn.; bd. dirs. Southeastern Mus.' Council. NEA fellow, 1975. Mem. Miss. Hist. Soc. (merit award 1980), Am. Assn. Mus. for State and Local History (awards com. 1976-80, exec. council 1983-85), Miss. Mus. Assn. (pres. 1979-80). Democrat. Episcopalian. Home: 1157 Quinn St Jackson MS 39202 Office: Miss State Hist Mus Box 571 Jackson MS 39205

BLACK, ROSALIE JEAN, human resources executive, university official; b. Dunsmuir, Calif., Dec. 29, 1938; d. Allen B. Henry and Margaret R. Albonico Luther Lea (stepfather); m. James H. Black, June 12, 1956 (div. 1965); 1 child, Kimberly Elaine. AA equivalent, Foothill and Ohlone, 1964-74. Contracts adminstr. USAF, L.A. and Shelby, Ohio, 1956-58; ops. planner/adminstr. Lockheed Missiles & Space Co., Inc., Sunnyvale, Calif., 1958-81; dir. human resources Dialog Info. Svcs., Inc., Palo Alto, Calif., 1981—; instr. Supervisory program, 1982-84; mem. Lockheed Univ. Rels. and Mgmt. Adv. Couns., Calabassas, Calif., 1982-88; lectr., guest panel mem. Contbr. articles to profl. jours. Recipient Cert. Human Resources Inst., 1982, Achievement award in English, Bank of Am., 1956. Mem. Am. Soc. Pers. Adminstrn., No. Calif. Human Resources Coun. (mem. orgn. planning com. 1967-68), Calif. Scholarship Fedn. (life), Bay Area Human Resources Forum, Henry and Worthington Descendent Assn. Democrat. Lutheran. Home: 1400 Fallen Leaf Ln Los Altos CA 94022 Office: Dialog Info Svcs Inc 3460 Hillview Ave Palo Alto CA 95014

BLACK, SARAH COLLEEN, book editor; b. Mpls., May 28, 1961; d. Robert John and Phyllis Rose (Gleason) Fabiny; m. Graham Spence Black, June 20, 1987. BA, Smith Coll., Northampton, Mass., 1983. Editorial asst. Putnam Pub. Group, N.Y.C., 1983-84, mng. editor, 1984-85; prodn. editor Berkley Pub. Group, N.Y.C., 1985-86; asst. editor Bantam Books, N.Y.C., 1986-87; sr. editor Joshua Morris Pub., Wilton, Conn., 1987—. Office: Joshua Morris Pub 221 Danbury Rd Wilton CT 06897

BLACK, SHIRLEY RENEÉ, medical technologist; b. DeQueen, Ark., Aug. 28, 1960; d. Charles Leo and Shirley Yvonne (Head) Eudy; m. Jeffrey Allen Black, Mar. 1, 1986. BS in Med. Tech., U. Ark., 1983; student, So. Ark. U., 1978-81. Med. technologist Wilhelmina Med. Ctr., Mena, Ark., 1982-85, Community Hosp., DeQueen, 1985-88, McCurtain Meml. Hosp., Idabel, Okla., 1988-89, Dr. THomas A. Jones Family Practice, Valliant, Okla., 1989—. Mem. Am. Soc. Clin. Pathologists (assoc.), Am. Soc. Med. Tech., Okla. Soc. Med. Tech., P.E.O. Methodist. Home: Rt 3 Box 49 Idabel OK 74745

BLACK, SHIRLEY TEMPLE (MRS. CHARLES A. BLACK), ambassador, former actress; b. Santa Monica, Calif., Apr. 23, 1928; d. George Francis and Gertrude Temple; m. John Agar, Jr., Sept. 19, 1945 (div. 1949); 1 dau., Linda Susan; m. Charles A. Black, Dec. 16, 1950; children: Charles Alden, Lori Alden. Ed. under pvt. tutelage; grad., Westlake Sch. Girls, 1945. Rep. to 24th Gen. Assembly UN, N.Y.C., 1969-70; amb. to Ghana Accra, 1974-76; chief of protocol White House, Washington, 1976-77; amb. to Czechoslovakia Prague, 1989—; mem. U.S. Delegation on African Refugee Problems, Geneva, 1981; mem. public adv. com. UN Conf. on Law of the Sea; dep. chmn. U.S. del. UN Conf. on Human Environment, Stockholm, 1970-72; spl. asst. to chmn. Pres.'s Council on Environ. Quality, 1972-74; del. treaty on environment USSR-USA Joint Commn., Moscow, 1972; mem. U.S. Commn. for UNESCO, 1973—. Began film career at age 3 1/2; first full-length film was Stand Up and Cheer; other films included Little Miss Marker, Baby Take a Bow, Bright Eyes, Our Little Girl, The Little Colonel, Curly Top, The Littlest Rebel, Captain January, Poor Little Rich Girl, Dimples, Stowaway, Wee Willie Winkie, Heidi, Rebecca of Sunnybrook Farm, Little Miss Broadway, Just Around the Corner, The Little Princess, Susannah of the Mounties, The Blue Bird, Kathleen, Miss Annie Rooney, Since You Went Away, Kiss and Tell, 1945, That Hagen Girl, War Party, The Bachelor and the Bobby-Soxer, Honeymoon, 1947; narrator, actress: TV series Shirley Temple Storybook, NBC, 1958, Shirley Temple Show, NBC, 1960; author: Child Star: An Autobiography, 1988. Dir. Bank of Calif.; dir. Fireman's Fund Ins. Co., BANCAL Tri-State Corp., Del Monte Corp.; Mem. Calif. Adv. Hosp. Council, 1969, San Francisco Health Facilities Planning Assn., 1965-69; Republican candidate for U.S. Ho. of Reps. from Calif., 1967; bd. dirs. Nat. Wildlife Fedn., Nat. Multiple Sclerosis Soc., UN Assn. U.S.A.; bd. dirs. exec. com. Internat. Fedn. Multiple Sclerosis Socs. Appointed col. on staff of Gov. Ross of Idaho, 1935; commd. col. Hawaiian N.G.; hon. col. 108th Rgt. N.G. Ill.; dame Order Knights Malta, Paris, 1968; recipient Ceres medal FAO, Rome, 1975, numerous other state decorations. Mem. World Affairs Council No. Calif. (dir.), Council Fgn. Relations, Nat. Com. for U.S./China Relations. Club: Commonwealth of Calif. Office: US Embassy Prague US Dept of State Washington DC 20520*

BLACK, SUSAN HARRELL, federal judge; b. Valdosta, Ga., Oct. 20, 1943; d. William H. and Ruth Elizabeth (Phillips) Harrell; m. Louis Eckert Black, Dec. 28, 1966. B.A., Fla. State U., 1964; J.D., U. Fla., 1967. Bar: Fla. 1967. Asst. state atty. 4th Jud. Ct. Fla.; asst. gen. counsel City of Jacksonville, Fla.; judge County Ct. of Duval County, Fla.; judge 4th Jud. Circuit Ct. of Fla.; U.S. dist. judge Mid. Dist. Fla., Jacksonville, 1979-90, chief judge, 1990—; faculty Fed. Jud. Ctr.; mem. U.S. Judicial Conf. Com. on Judicial Improvements; bd. trustees Am. Inns. Ct. Found. Trustee emeritus Law Sch. U. Fla.; past pres. Chester Bedell Inn of Ct. Mem. Am. Bar Assn., Fla. Bar Assn., Jacksonville Bar Assn. Episcopalian. Office: US Dist Ct PO Box 53135 Jacksonville FL 32201-3135

BLACK, SUZANNE ALEXANDRA, clinical psychologist, researcher; b. N.Y.C., May 6, 1958; d. Lawrence E. and Aline R. (Amsellen) B. BA in Psychology, Clark U., 1980; MA in Gen. Psychology, Yeshiva U., 1984, D in Clin. Psychology, 1987. Lic. psychologist, Calif. Rsch. assoc. Inst. for Study of Exceptional Children Roosevelt Hosp. Ctr., 1980-82; rsch. cons. Sch. Pub. Health Columbia U., N.Y.C., 1982-83; clin. psychology extern Albert Einstein Coll. of Medicine Bronx Psychiat. Ctr., 1983-84; clin. psychology, neuropsychol. extern N.Y. U. Med. Ctr./Bellevue Hosp., N.Y.C., 1985-86, Jewish Bd. Family and Children's Svcs., N.Y.C., 1984-85; pre-doctoral clin. psychology/neuropsychology intern Rusk Inst. Rehabilitation NYU Med. Ctr., N.Y.C., 1986-87; post-doctoral clin. psychology fellow in emergency room and in-patient psychiatry Harbor/UCLA Med. Ctr., Torrance, 1987-89; pvt. practice clin. psychology Torrance, 1989—; clin. asst. prof. psychology Fuller Grad. Sch. Psychology, Pasadena, Calif., 1987-88; clin. supr. psychiat. residents and psychology externs Harbor/UCLA Med. Ctr., 1987-89; lectr. in field. NIMH grantee, 1986-87. Mem. Am. Psychol. Assn. (women membership com., clin. neuropsychology com.), Calif. State Psychol. Assn. Office: 24445 Hawthorne Blvd #105 Torrance CA 90505

BLACKBURN, CATHERINE ELAINE, lawyer, pharmacist; b. Columbus, Ohio, Nov. 5, 1953; d. Robert Jerome and Patricia Ann (Buchman) B. BS in Pharmacy with high distinction, U. Ky., 1978; JD with honors, Ohio State U., 1982. Bar: Ohio 1982, U.S. Dist. Ct. (so. dist.) Ohio 1983. Chief pharmacist Louisa (Ky.) Community Hosp., 1978; pharmacist Riverside Meth. Hosp., Columbus, 1978-82; law clk. Michael F. Colley Co., L.P.A., Columbus, 1980-82, assoc., 1982-87; asst. prof. law U. Louisville Sch. Law, 1987—; workshop leader Ohio Drug Studies Inst., Columbus, 1982, 83, 14th Nat. Conf. on Women and the Law, Washington, D.C., 1983, 15th Nat. Conf., 1985; lectr./speaker Iowa Trial Lawyers Assn., Iowa City, 1984; speaker Nat. Assn. for Rights Protection and Advocacy Systems, Nat. Conf., Boston, 1986; lectr. legal writing Coll. Law Ohio State U., 1986; mem. aids edn. task force, subcom. on legal ethical issues U. Louisville, 1988—; speaker Nat. conf. Nat. Assn. Protection and Advocacy Systems, Washington, 1988, 16th Internat. Congress on Law and Mental Health, Toronto, 1990; cons. Ohio Legal Rights Svc., 1985—, Mich. Protection and Advocacy Svc., Lansing, 1988—, Advocacy Inc., Austin, Tex., 1989—. Staff writer, editor Ohio State U. Law Jour., 1980-82; contbr. articles to profl. jours. Trustee Women's Outreach for Women, Columbus, 1982-85, Amethyst, Inc., 1985-87; incorporator, treas. Columbus Career Women Inc., 1986-87. Fellow Am. Soc. Pharmacy Law; mem. ABA, Assn. Trial Lawyers Am. (lectr., speaker 1982—), Order of Coif, Phi Beta Kappa, Rho Chi Soc. Democrat.

BLACKBURN, ELIZABETH HELEN, molecular biologist; b. Hobart, Australia, Sept. 26, 1948; 1 child. BS, U. Melbourne, Australia, 1970, MS, 1971; PhD in Molecular Biology, Cambridge (Eng.) U., 1975. Fellow in biology Yale U., New Haven, 1975-77; fellow in biochemistry U. Calif., San Francisco, 1977-78; from asst. prof. to prof. molecular biology U. Calif., Berkeley, 1978—. Recipient Eli Lilly award in microbiology, 1988, NAS award in microbiology, 1990. Office: U Calif Dept Molecular Biology Berkeley CA 94720*

BLACKBURN, MARTHA GRACE, corporate executive, publisher; b. London, Ont., Can., Oct. 9, 1944; d. Walter Juxon and Marjorie Ludwell (Dampier) Blackburn; children—Richard Antony Frederick, Sarah Dampier, Annabelle Grace. B.A. in French, U. Western Ont., London, 1969. Chmn. bd., pres. Blackburn Group Inc, London, Ont., 1984, also bd. dir.; chmn. Blackburn Mktg. Svcs. Inc., Blackburn Holdings Ltd.; pub. London Free Press Printing Co. Ltd., 1984, also dir.; dir. CFPL Broadcasting Ltd., London, Netmar Inc. (formerly Pennysaver Publs.), CKNX Broadcasting Ltd., Compusearch Market and Social Research Ltd.; pres. Kilbyrne Investments Inc. Founding mem. Walter J. Blackburn Found.; dir.-at-large Jr. Achievement of Can., Can. Equestrian Team; hon. patron Kidney Found. Can.; mem., hon. bd. dirs. Alan Thicke Centre for Juvenile Diabetes Rsch. adv. bd. Vanier Cup; past chmn. adv. bd. Performing Arts Ctr.; mem. adv. coun. Orch. London; bd. dirs. World Wildlife, 1985—; mem. nat. adv. coun. IMAGINE, Can. Ctr. for Philanthropy; mem. adv. coun. Elgin and Winter Garden Project. Mem. Can. Press, Internat. Assn. for Students in Econs. and Bus. Mgmt. (western adv. com.), Can. Assn. Family Enterprises, U. Western Ont. Women in Mgmt. (adv. com. rsch. project), London Hunt and Country Club. Anglican. Office: PO Box 2280, London, ON Canada N6A 4G1

BLACKER, HARRIET, public relations executive; b. N.Y.C., July 23, 1940; d. Louis and Rebecca (Siegel) B.; m. Roland Algrant, Aug. 6, 1970 (div. Jan. 1981); m. Matthew E. Harlib, Aug. 25, 1988. B.A., U. Mich., 1962. Exec. asst. Nat. Book com., N.Y.C., 1965-67; dir. publicity Hawthorn Books, N.Y.C., 1967-69, Coward-McCann & Geoghegan, N.Y.C., 1969-74; exec. dir. publicity Random House, N.Y.C., 1974-79; East Coast v.p. Pickwick Maslansky Koenigsberg, N.Y.C., 1980-81; v.p. pub. relations Putnam Pub. Group, N.Y.C, 1981-85; pres. Harriet Blacker, Inc., N.Y.C., 1986-90; ptnr. Blacker Hunter Pub. Rels. Inc., N.Y.C., 1990—. Mem. Publishers Publicity Assn. (sec. 1973-75, treas. 1982-83, pres. 1983-85), Women's Media Group. Home: 310 E 75th St New York NY 10021 Office: Blacker/Hunter Pub Rels 381 Park Ave S New York NY 10016

BLACKERT, VIRGINIA ROSE, publisher, editor; b. Teaneck, N.J., Aug. 4, 1948; d. Charles Maynard and Rose Marie (Ferraro) B.; m. Matthew R. Englert, Mar. 10, 1968 (div. 1971); 1 child, Hilary Jane Englert. Staff artist Rutland (Vt.) Daily Herald, 1974-75; advt. dir. Entertainment Enterprises,

Inc., Rutland, 1975-79; writer Phillip C. Camp Assocs., Inc., Woodstock, Vt., 1979-81; freelance writer, 1980-82; writer Vt. Ski Areas Assn., Woodstock, 1981-82; pub., editor Prosper Hill Pub., Inc., Barnard, Vt., 1982—; also pres. Prosper Pub., Inc., Barnard, Vt., 1987—. Editor, pub. Essence of Stowe, 1979-80, Woodstock Common, 1982, Stowe Country, 1984, Rutland Seasons, 1986, Vermont Seasons, 1988; contbg. writer Bantam Doubleday Books' Guide to the Soviet Union, 1991, Guide to Ireland and Northern Ireland, 1991. Bd. dirs. Woodstock Learning Clinic, 1986—; mem. Children's Art Exchange (Soviet-Am.), Middlebury, Vt.; advisor Woodstock Union High Sch. Endowment Assn., 1988—. Mem. Stowe Area Assn., Woodstock C. of C., Woodstock Hist. Soc., Woodstock Sister City Coalition. Home: PO Box 206 Barnard VT 05031 Office: Prosper Hill Pub Inc Rte 12 Barnard VT 05031

BLACKFIELD, CECILIA MALIK, teacher, civic volunteer; b. Oakland, Calif., Jan. 18, 1915; d. Benjamin Malik and Mollie Saak; m. William Blackfield, Dec. 25, 1941; children: Leland Gregory, Pamela Esther, Karen Ann. BA, U. Calif., Berkeley, 1936; MEdn., San Francisco State Tchrs Coll, 1937. cert. elem. tchr. Calif. (lifetime). Tchr. Albany (Calif.) Sch. Dist., 1938-43; rep. NEA, Alameda County, Calif., 1938-43. Pres. Calif. Tchrs. Assn., Alameda County, Calif., 1939; mem. (charter) Territorial Hosp. Aux., Kauikeolani Children's Hosp. (bd. dirs.); bd. dirs. Hastings Law Sch. Found., San Francisco, Calif., McCoy Pavilion Park, Honolulu, Hi., Daughters of the Nile, Honolulu, Temple Emmanuel; mem. Mayor's Citizen Advisory Com. for Diamond Head, Wakiki, Honolulu, Mayor's Adv. Com. for Community & Urban Renewal, Beautification Com., League of Women Voters; chmn. Hawaii Cancer Fund Crusade and many more. Named Woman of the Year for Nat. Brotherhood Week, Honolulu, 1972. Mem. Hawaii Chpt. Women's Aux. Nat. Assn. Home Builders (pres.), Outdoor Circle (pres.), Friends of Foster Gardens, Washington Palace State Capitol, Hadassah (past pres. Oakland chpt.), Women's Com. Brandeis Univ. Home: 901 Kealaolu Ave Honolulu HI 96816

BLACKHAM, ANN ROSEMARY (MRS. J. W. BLACKHAM), realtor; b. N.Y.C., June 16, 1927; d. Frederick Alfred and Letitia L. (Stolfe) DeCain; m. James W. Blackham Jr., Aug. 18, 1951; children: Ann C., James W. III. AB, Ohio Dominican Coll., 1949; postgrad., Ohio State U., 1950. Mgr. br. store Filene & Sons, Winchester, 1950-52; broker Porter Co. Real Estate, Winchester, 1961-66; sales mgr. James T. Trefrey, Inc., Winchester, 1966-68; pres., founder Ann Blackham & Co. Inc., Realtors, Winchester, Mass., 1969—. Mem. bd. econ. advisors to Gov., 1969-74; participant White House Conf. on Internat. Cooperation, 1965; mem. Presdl. Task Force on Women's Rights and Responsibilities, 1969; mem. exec. coun. Mass. Civil Def., 1965-69; chmn. Gov.'s Commn. on Status of Women, 1971-75; regional dir. Interstate Assn. Commn. on Status of Women, 1971-74; mem. Gov. Task Force on Mass. Economy, 1972; mem. Gov.'s Jud. Selection Com., 1972, Mass. Emergency Fin. Bd., 1974-75; corporator, trustee Charlestown Savs. Bank, 1974-84; corporator Winchester Hosp., 1983—; mem. Winchester 350th Anniversary Commn.; mem. design rev. commn. Town of Winchester; bd. dirs. Phoenix Found., Bay State Health Care, Mass. Taxpayers Found., Speech and Hearing Found.; mem. regional selection panel White House Fellows, 1973-74; mem. com. on women in svc. U.S. Dept. Def., 1977-80; 2d v.p. Doric Dames, 1971-74, bd. dirs., 1974—; dep. chmn. Mass. Rep. State Com., 1965-66; sec. Mass. Rep. State Conv., 1970, del., 1960, 62, 64, 66, 70, 72, 74, 78, 90; state vice chmn. Mass. Rep. Fin. Com., 1970; alt. del.-at-large Rep. Nat. Conv., 1968, 72, del., 1984; pres. Scholarship Found., 1976-78, Mass. Fedn. Women's Clubs. Recipient Pub. Svc. award Commonwealth of Mass., 1978, Merit award Rep. Party, 1969, Pub. Affairs award Mass. Fedn. Women's Clubs, 1975; named Civic Leader of Yr., Mass. Broadcasters, 1962. Mem. Greater Boston Real Estate Bd. (bd. dirs.), Mass. Assn. Real Estate Bds. (bd. dirs.), Nat. Assn. Real Estate Bd. (women's coun.). Brokers Inst., Coun. Realtors (pres. 1983-84), Winchester C. of C. (bd. dirs.), Greater Boston C. of C., Nat. Assn. Women Bus. Owners, ENKA Soc., Capitol Hill Club, Ponte Vedra Club, Winchester Boat Club, Winchester Country Club, Wychemere Harbor Club, Womens City Boston Club, Winton Club (sec., bd. dir.). Home: 60 Swan Rd Winchester MA 01890 Office: Ann Blackham & Co Inc 11 Thompson St Winchester MA 01890

BLACK-KEEFER, SHARON KAY, telecommunications executive; b. Denver, Jan. 23, 1949; d. Benoni Franklin and Loretta Marie (Meals) Black; m. Stephen Malone Keefer, Aug. 3, 1974; children: Sean M., Craig L., Elisabeth A. Student, U. Costa Rica, 1969; BA in Internat. Affairs magna cum laude, U. Colo., 1971, MS in Telecommunications, 1972. Rsch. positions U. Colo., Boulder, 1968-71; analyst telecommunications policy Office Telecommunications U.S. Dept. Commerce, Boulder, Colo., 1971-76; sr. systems analyst Norwest Info. Services Inc., Mpls., 1976-84, cons. data ops., 1984-85; mgr. voice communications Northwestern Nat. Life Ins. Co., Mpls., 1985-88; v.p. telecommunications svcs. COREMAR/Northwestern Nat. Life Ins., Mpls., 1989; sr. cons. Hatfield Assocs., Boulder, Colo., 1989—; adj. faculty mem. U. Denver Grad. Sch., Pace U., U. Minn. Sch. Mgmt., St. Mary's Coll. Grad. Ctr., and telecommunications adv. bd., mem. adv. bd. U. Colo. Telecommunications Program. Chairperson Community Action Com., Stillwater, Minn., 1984-86; mem. communications adv. com. Met. Coun. Twin Cities, St. Paul, 1977-78; pack chairperson Cub Scouts Am., Stillwater, 1987-89; elder 1st Presbyn. Ch., Stillwater, 1984-86. Mem. Internat. Communications Assn. (academic devel. com.), Nat. Rolm Users Group (chair Maintenance com. 1985-88), Minn. Telecommunications Assn. Office: Hatfield Assocs 4840 Riverbend Rd Boulder CO 80301

BLACKLER, SHARON RENDA, hospital program director; b. Coventry, Eng., Dec. 11, 1947; d. Gerald William and Renda Winifred (Robson) B.; m. Stanford Bingham Jr., Mar. 16, 1974 (div. Oct. 1979); 1 child, Jason A. Registered diagnostic X ray technician, Stanford U. Med. Ctr., 1968, registered therapy technician, 1969; BS in Health Services Adminstrn. cum laude, U. Phoenix, 1982. Staff technologist Santa Clara Valley Med. Ctr., San Jose, Calif., 1969-70, 1972; jr. radiographer Manchester (Eng.) Royal Infirmary, 1971; staff technologist Peninsula Hosp., Burlingame, Calif., 1972-76; sr. technologist Sequoia Hosp., Redwood City, Calif., 1976-81, tech. dir. Radiation Oncology sect., 1981—. Mem. Am. Assn. Med. Dosimetrists (recording sec. 1987-90), Soc. Radiographers, Radiologists Bus. Mgrs. Assn., Soc. Radiation Oncology Adminstrs., Am. Soc. Radiologic Technologists. Republican. Episcopalian. Home: 4454 Junipero Serra Ln San Jose CA 95129 Office: Sequoia Hosp Dept Radiation Oncology Whipple and Alameda Redwood City CA 94062

BLACKMAN, GHITA WAUCHETA, natural energy consultant; b. Chgo., Feb. 19, 1932; d. William Harveston Joseph and Zelda (Booth) Harris; m. David Edward Blackman, June 7, 1953 (div. Oct. 1976); children—Anasa, Anthony, Cynthia, Tracy. Student NYU, 1949-50, U. Dayton, 1952-53. Various secretarial positions U.S. Air Force, Dayton, Ohio, then Am. Humanist Assn., Yellow Springs, Ohio, 1950-64; sec. Antioch Coll., Yellow Springs, 1964-66, Fels Research Inst., Yellow Springs, 1966-70; cons. direct sales Fashion Two Twenty, Dayton, 1966-72; mem. sales staff Prophet & Friends Inc., New Britain, Conn., 1972-76; customer relations clk. Conn. Natural Gas Corp., Hartford, 1976-80, natural energy cons., 1980—. Mem. Dayton Jr. Philharm. Orch., 1947-53, second violin Springfield Symphony, Ohio, 1956-64; v.p. Conn. Capitol Area chpt. Older Women's League, Hartford, 1985-87; sec. Spiritual Assembly of the Baha'is of West Hartford, Conn., 1977-78; corr. sec. Spiritual Assembly of the Baha'is of Hartford, 1982—. Mem. Nat. Assn. Female Execs., Nat. Assn. Profl. Saleswomen. Avocation: music. Home: 31 Woodland St Hartford CT 06105 Office: Conn Natural Gas Corp 100 Columbus Blvd Hartford CT 06103

BLACKMAN, JEANNE A., lobbyist; b. Decatur, Ill., Sept. 23, 1943; d. Robert Russell and Elizabeth Irene (DeWolfe) Shulke; m. Gary L. Blackman, Apr. 16, 1963 (div. Aug. 1983); children: Jeffrey Lynn, Stephanie Sue. BS Elem. Edn., Ind. U., 1965; MS in Edn. Adminstrn., Eastern Ill. U., 1979. Cert. tchr. and administr.; lic. real estate salesperson. Elem. tchr. Taylorville (Ill.) Community Sch. Dist., 1965-86; real estate salesperson Craggs-Adams Realtors, Taylorville, 1985-87; adminstrv. asst. to chief of staff Ill. Dept. of Aging, Springfield, 1986-87, consumer adv., 1987-89; lobbyist Ill. Guardianship and Advocacy Commn., Springfield, 1989—; pres. Taylorville Edn. Assn., 1983-85; mem. adv. council Gov.'s Rehab., Springfield, 1987—. Co-founder, treas. Ill. Vol. Optometry Services to Humanity, Taylorville, 1976—; pres. Capitol City Rep. Women's Club, 1988—, Women in Mgmt., 1989— ; fundraiser, chairperson Ill. Women's Polit. Caucus, Springfield, 1985—; pres. Am. Field Service Student Exchange Program, Taylorville, 1985-87; bd. dirs. LWV Springfield chpt. 1984—; trustee Lincolnland Community Coll., 1989; mem. Mayor's Commn. International Visitors. Mem. AAUW (edn. chairperson Taylorville chpt. 1985—), DAR, Sister Cities Assn. Springfield, Ill. Women in Govt. (bd. dirs. 1988—, v.p.), Women's Legis. Network, Ill. Fedn. Rep. Women (bd. dirs. 1988—, ways and means com. 1987—), Greater Springfield C. of C., Delta Delta Delta. Presbyterian. Home: #19 Washington Pl Springfield IL 62702 Office: Ill Guardianship and Adv Commn 421 E Capitol Springfield IL 62701

BLACK-RHODES, DIANA KAREN, public affairs director; b. Tulsa, Okla., Nov. 22, 1953; d. Jackson Robert and Barbara Jean (Parkinson) Black; m. John Van Rhodes, Sept. 2, 1984. BS in Radio-TV-Film, Okla. State U., 1976. Program coord. KWTV, Oklahoma City, 1978-86, asst. program dir., 1986-90, pub. affairs dir., 1990—; vis. instr. U. Okla. Sch. Journalism, Norman, Okla., 1986. Named in Ladies in the News, Okla. Hospitality Club, Okla. City, 1988; recipient Hal Phillips Meml. Journalism, Broadcasting Scholarship, Okla. State U., 1975. Mem. Am. Women in Radio & TV, Nat. Assn. of TV Program Execs. Home: 2719 NW 47th St Oklahoma City OK 73112 Office: KWTV Griffin Television Inc 7401 N Kelley Oklahoma City OK 73111

BLACKSHEAR, HELEN F., retired educator; b. Tuscaloosa, Ala., June 5, 1911; d. Samuel and Annie Laurie (Longshore) Friedman; m. William Mitchell Blackshear, Apr. 21, 1934 (dec. Sept. 1986); children: Anne Spragins-Harmuth, Sue Blackshear-Bowen, Helen M. Stevenson. BA, Agnes Scott Coll., 1931; MA, U. Ala., Tuscaloosa, 1932. Visitor social work Child Welfare Dept., Ala., 1937-39; English tchr. Montgomery County, Ala., 1942-73. Author: Robert Loreman, Belated Romanticist, 1932, Mother Was A Rebel, 1973, Southern Smorgasbord, 1974, Creek Captives and Other Alabama Stories, 1975, (poems) Along Alabama Roads, (poems) And Time Remembered. Named Poet of Yr. Ala. State Poetry Soc., 1985. Mem. Ala. Writers Concave (pres. 1985-87), Ala. State Poetry Soc. (treas. 1980-82), Nat. League Am. Penwomen (pres. Montgomery br. 1982-84, Creative Writers Montgomery (v.p. 1978-80), Art Coun. Montgomery (sec. 1983-88). Republican. Presbyterian. Home: 334 Felder Ave Montgomery AL 36104

BLACKSHEAR, MARGARET RUTH BONHAM, retired secondary school educator; b. Jellico, Tenn.; d. Samuel Robert and Hattie Jeanette (McClellan) Bonham; m. Julian Ward Blackshear Sr., June 29, 1940; 1 child, Julian Ward, Jr. BS, Knoxville Coll., 1932; MA, Northwestern U., Evanston, Ill., 1938. Instr. in math. Swift Meml. Jr. Coll., Rogersville, Tenn., 1933-35; tchr. math., sci. Howard High Sch., Chattanooga, 1936-41, 43-83, head dept. math. and sci., 1976-83. Active Venture, 1986, Pace, 1989; bd. dirs. Crime Alert/Law Enforcement, 1971; treas. Presbyn. Ch. of Reconciliation, 1969—, elder, 1978—. Named Chattanooga Tchr. of Yr., Evans Found., 1970, Disting. Alumni of Yr., 14th Nat. Conf. on Blacks in Higher Edn., Washington, 1989. Mem. NEA, AARP, AAUW, Math. Assn. of Am., Nat. Coun. Tchrs. of Math, Tenn. Tchrs. of Maths. (chmn. east fin. com. 1978—), Tenn. Ret. Tchrs. Assn., Chattanooga Tchrs. of Math (charter, v.p.), Knoxville Coll. Alumni Assn. (treas. 1971—), Northwestern U. Alumni Assn. (class rep. 1978—), Alpha Kappa Alpha (Pi Omega chpt., pres. 1938-47, outstanding creative arts award 1986). Democrat. Home: 5005 North Hwy 58 Chattanooga TN 37416 Office: Chattanooga Pub Schs Ret Tchrs Chattanooga TN 37408

BLACKSTEN-PLANTZ, ANNA MARIE, public safety officer, investigator; b. Fargo, N.D., Dec. 23, 1948; d. Ove Harold and Florence Mildred (Holsinger) Anderson; m. Ralph H. Plantz; children: David, Angela, Brooke. Student Lane Community Coll., 1972-74; criminology cert. of competancy Inst. Applied Sci., 1978; grad. Oregon Police Acad., 1984. Cert. radiol. monitoring, 1982; cert. State of Oregon first responder, 1984-87, gen. level law enforcement data system operator, 1987. Crime prevention officer, lab. technician Eugene (Oreg.) Police Dept., 1974-79; fire prevention technician, investigator Seaside Fire Dept., Seaside, Oreg., 1980-83; pub. safety lt., Oreg. Health Scis. U., 1985—. Bus. and Profl. Women's Club scholar, 1976-77. Mem. Oreg. Fire Marshal's, Bus. and Profl. Women, Internat. Assn. Arson Investigators, Exec. Females, Inc., Oreg. Fire Edn. Assn., Oreg. Peace Officers Assn. Home: 237 NW Merle Dr Hillsboro OR 97124 Office: Oreg Health Scis U 3181 SW Sam Jackson Park Rd Portland OR 97201

BLACKSTOCK, VIRGINIA LEE LOWMAN (MRS. LEROY BLACKSTOCK), civic worker; b. Bixby, Okla., July 2, 1917; d. Joseph Arthur and Winifred (Lundy) Lowman; student Tulsa Coll. Bus., 1935-37; m. Leroy Blackstock, Dec. 29, 1939; children—Vincent Craig, Priscilla Gay (Mrs. Richard S. Kurz), Birch Lee, Lore Anne (Mrs. Dwight Mitchell), Trena Jan (Mrs. Frank Dale). Legal sec. law firm, Tulsa, 1937-41. Chmn. program Internat. Students in Tulsa, 1955-65; mem. Tulsa Council Camp Fire Girls, 1963-66; mem. youth com. Tulsa Philharmonic Soc., 1969-70; now mem. women's assn.; pres. Eliot Elementary P.T.A., 1961-62, Edison High Sch. P.T.A., 1971-72; mem. Tulsa Opera Guild. Co-chmn. Democratic precinct No. 132, 1960-67. Mem. Tulsa County Bar Aux. (pres. 1954-55, sec. 1962-63, chaplain 1966-67). Baptist. Clubs: Summit, Petroleum. Home: 7213 S Atlanta St Tulsa OK 74136

BLACKSTONE, SANDRA LEE, lawyer, educator, former government official; b. Washington; d. Fred J. and Madeline S. Blackstone; B.A., U. Vt., 1969; J.D., U. Denver, 1977; Ph.D., Colo. Sch. Mines, 1979. Systems analyst Martin Marietta Aerospace, Denver, 1969-74; cons. legal, econ. and regulatory matters W.R. Grace & Co., Colo. Energy Research Inst., Colo. Sch. Mines, Sherman & Howard, Denver, 1976-79; mgr. bus. devel. for synthetic fuels Rocky Mountain Energy subs. Union Pacific Corp., Denver, 1979-81; dep. dir. energy and mineral resources Bur. Land Mgmt., Dept. Interior, Washington, 1981-83; prof. Denver Coll. Law, 1983—; mem. Colo. Adv. Council on Energy and Energy-Related Mineral Research, 1980-82; mem. Colo. Supreme Ct. Task Force on Gender Bias, 1988-89; mem. Nat. Coal Coun., 1984—; mem. Colo. Women's Forum; Rep. precinct committeewomen, 1970-74; del. Denver County Rep. Conv., 1971, 74, Colo. State Rep. Conv., 1972. Colo. Energy Rsch. Inst. fellow, 1974-76, Natural Resources fellow Mobil Oil Co., 1975-76, Kennecott Corp. fellow, 1976-77. Mem. ABA (natural resource and environment com. 1985-89), NAS (com. on nat. water quality assessment 1988-90, com. on abandoned mine lands 1985-86, com. on paleontol. collecting 1985-87, bd. on mineral and energy resources, 1983-88). Office: U Denver Coll Law 1900 Olive St Denver CO 80220

BLACKWELL, ANNA DERBY, public relations consultant; b. Honolulu, Aug. 12, 1932; d. Stephen Arthur and Dora (Cooke) Derby; m. Charles Hoffman Bond, Nov. 26, 1952 (div. Sept. 1970); children: Caroline Bond Dvojacki, Suzi, Boyd Davis, Sarah Bond Langan, Elizabeth; m. Robert Douglas Howe, Oct. 22, 1974 (dec. Apr. 1981); m. Jesse Eugene Blackwell, June 12, 1984. Student, Vassar Coll., 1950-52, U. Hawaii, 1952-53, U. Canterbury, New Zealand, 1985, Hawaii Pacific U., 1988—. Writer/reporter Waikiki Beach Press, Waihe'e, Hawaii, 1960-64; pub. rels. dir. YWCA of Oahu, Honolulu, 1966-72; first exec. dir. Moanalua Gardens Found., Honolulu, 1972-82; mng. editor Trade Pub. Co., Honolulu, 1987-88; pub. rels. and advt. coord. Chaney, Brooks and Co., Honolulu, 1988-89; account mgr. AdCorp Internat., Honolulu, 1989; cons. ANNAgram, Honolulu, 1960—. Editor: Wilders of Waikiki, 1980. Sec. outreach com. St. Andrew's Cathedral, Honolulu, 1984—, choir mem. 1946—, co- chmn. Inst. Human Svcs. Supper Com., 1987—; founder Women's Fund in Hawaii, Honolulu, 1989—; trustee, sec. Cooke Found., Ltd., Honolulu, 1989—. Mem. Pub. Rels. Soc. of Am. (accredited), Women in Communications Inc., Orgn. of Women Leaders. Episcopalian.

BLACKWELL, ANTOINETTE LYNN, systems analyst, consultant; b. Anderson, Ind., Apr. 14, 1960; d. Donald Hugh and Janet Louise (Slaughter) B. Student in Computer Sci., Purdue U., 1978-79, Anderson Coll., 1980. Programmer/analyst Community Hosp., Anderson, Ind., 1979-81, Dynamic Control, Boston, 1981-82, project leader, Winter Park, Fla., 1982-84, mgr. implementations, Longwood, Fla., 1984-85, sr. tech. cons., Longwood, 1985—; developer spl. project internat. services Baxter Systems Div., 1986-88, sr. analyst tech. cons., 1988-89, Spectrum Healthcare Solutions (formerly Baxter Systems Div.), 1989—. Recipient Vocat. Edn. award, Anderson Rotary Club, 1978. Mem. Office Edn. Assn. (parliamentarian 1977-78, awards 1977-78), Electronic Computing Health Oriented, Common-IBM Users Group, Nat. Assn. Female Execs. Avocations: photography, writing, reading, volleyball, racquetball. Office: Spectrum Healthcare Solutions 587 E Sanlando Springs Dr Longwood FL 32750

BLACKWELL, JUDITH ELLEN, marketing executive; b. N.Y.C., July 5, 1956; d. Oliver Thomas and Marie Elizabeth (Prutzman) B.; m. Paul Alan Konowitch, Nov. 3, 1984; 1 child, Jeffrey Oliver. BA cum laude, Duke U., 1978; M in Internat. Mgmt., Am. Grad. Sch. Internat. Mgmt., 1979. With Avon Products, N.Y.C., 1979-85; mktg. mgr. bus. svcs. Prodigy Svcs. Co., White Plains, N.Y., 1985—. Mem. Am. Mktg. Assn. Republican. Office: Prodigy Svcs Co 445 Hamilton Ave White Plains NY 10601

BLACKWELL, LUCY WHITE, retired state official; b. Jackson, Tenn., Apr. 22, 1912; d. William Francis and Ethel (White) Blackwell; A.B., Lambuth Coll., 1933; postgrad. West Tenn. Bus. Coll., 1934-35. Stenographer, Tenn. Emergency Relief Adminstrn., Jackson, 1935; accounting clk. FSA, Jackson, Brownsville, Tenn., 1936-39; stenographer Tenn. Dept. Pub. Welfare, Jackson, 1939-40; clk., interviewer, local office mgr. Tenn. Dept. Employment Security, Jackson, 1940-73. Comdr. Am. Cancer Soc., Madison County, Tenn., 1943-54, dist. comdr. W. Tenn., 1947-48, rec. sec. Tenn. div., 1954-56, bd. dirs., 1945—, organizer Madison County unit, 1954, pres., 1954-55; bd. dirs. Jackson Community Chest, 1955-57; pres. League Women Voters, 1951. Treas., chmn. bd. trustees Jackson Free Library, 1948-57. Recipient R.E. Womack Alumni Achievement award Lambuth Coll. Alumni Assn., 1956; named Jackson-Madison Woman of Year, 1955. Mem. Internat. Assn. Personnel Employment Security (pres. Jackson chpt. 1956), Lambuth Coll. Alumni Assn. (pres. 1962-63). Presbyterian. Clubs: Pilot Internat. (past pres. Jackson, dist. gov. Tenn., internat. dir. exec. com.). Altrusa Internat. (chmn.). Home: 45 Belle Haven Dr Jackson IN 38305

BLACKWELL, MARY ANN, speaker, educator; b. Woburn, Mass., May 19, 1932. BS in Edn., Lesley Coll., 1954; postgrad., Am. U., 1955, U. Va., 1963, Tufts U. Founder, pres. Blackwell & Assocs., Washington, 1988—; conductor workshops in field; cons. in field. Bd. dirs. Friends of the Nat. Mus. African Art, Smithsonian Inst.; v.p. for devel. Woman's Nat. Dem. Club, Georgetown Hosp. Ladies Bd.; active U.S. Ho. of Reps. Day Care Ctr. Com., 1987; arranger reception and dinner conv. site com. Dem. Nat. Com., Washington, 1986; official liaison for U.S. Asst. Sec. for Maritime Affairs. Mem. Va. Assn. Female Execs. (bd. advisory), Am. Soc. for Tng. and Devel., Washington Internat. Trade Assn. (embassy com.), U.S. Internat. Cultural & Trade Ctr. Commn. (conf./tng./edn. adv. com., club/reception adv. com.), Tng. Officer's Conf., Higher Edn. Group Washington D.C., D.C. C. of C. (relocation svc.). Office: Blackwell & Assocs 626 A St SE Washington DC 20003

BLACKWOOD, LOIS ANNE, teacher; b. Denver, Sept. 18, 1949; d. Randolph William and Eloise Anne (Green) Burchett; m. Clark Burnett Blackwood, June 26, 1971; children: Anna Colleen, Courtney Brooke. BA, Pacific U., 1971. Tchr. Forest Grove (Oreg.) Pub. Schs., 1971-72, Clarksville (Tenn.) Pub. Schs., 1972-73, Dept. of Defense Schs., Frankfurt, Germany, 1973-76, St. Vrain Alley Schs., Longmont, Col., 1977—; presenter at inservices and symposiums St. Vrain Valley Schs., Longmont, Colo., 1978-88, tchr. of tchrs.; cons. to Brush Pub. Schs., 1985; presenter U. N. Colo. symposium, 1987. Mem. Longmont Symphony Guild. Recipient Sustained Superior award, U.S. Army, Frankfurt, Germany, 1975, Outstanding Performance award, Dept. of Army, 1976; Hon. Mention for Colo. Tchr. of Year, Colo. Dept. Edn., 1984. Mem. NEA, Colo. Edn. Assn., St. Vrain Valley Tchrs. Assn. Republican. Home: 1175 Winslow Circle Longmont CO 80501 Office: Cen Elem Sch 425 Bross St Longmont CO 80501

BLADE, MELINDA KIM, educator, researcher, archaeologist; b. San Diego, Jan. 12, 1952; d. George A. and Arline A. M. (MacLeod) B. BA, U. San Diego, 1974, MA in Teaching, 1975, MA, 1975, EdD, 1986. Cert. secondary tchr., Calif.; cert. community coll. instr., Calif.; registered profl. historian, Calif. Instr. Coronado Unified Sch. Dist., Calif., 1975-76; head coach women's basketball U. San Diego, 1976-78; instr. Acad. of Our Lady of Peace, San Diego, 1976—, chmn. social studies dept., 1983—, counselor, 1984—, co-dir. student activities, 1984—, coord. advanced placement program, 1986—, dir. athletics, 1990; mem. archaeol. excavation team U. San Diego, 1975—, hist. researcher, 1975—; lectr., 1981—. Author hist. reports and research papers. Editor U. San Diego pubs. Vol. Am. Diabetes Assn., San Diego, 1975—; coord. McDonald's Diabetes Bike-a-thon, San Diego, 1977, 78; bd. dirs. U. San Diego Sch. Edn. Mem. Nat. Council Social Studies, Calif. Council Social Studies, Soc. Bibl. Archeology, Assn. Supervision and Curriculum Devel., Assn. Scientists and Scholars Internat. for Shroud of Turin, Medieval Acad. Am., Medieval Assn. Pacific, Am. Hist. Assn., Western Assn. Women Historians, Renaissance Soc. Am., San Diego Hist. Soc., Phi Alpha Theta (sec.-treas. 1975-77), Phi Delta Kappa. Office: Acad Our Lady of Peace 4860 Oregon St San Diego CA 92116

BLADES, BARBARA OAKEY, marketing and management consultant; b. Roanoke, Va., Jan. 11, 1951; d. Clarence Milton Oakey and Dorothea (Cheves) Oakey McCallum; m. Stephen G. Blades Sr. July 1, 1968 (div. 1976); children: Stephen G. Jr., Windy Shannon Blades Pepin. Student, Va. We. Coll., 1968-74. Lic. real estate broker, Ga. Adminstr. personnel and purchasing McFadden Tool and Engring., Roanoke, 1975-78; legal adminstr., mgr. property Katz, Paller & Land Attys. at Law, Atlanta, 1978-82; mgr. multi tenant and comml. property Ferpace Corp., Coppedge & Co., Atlanta, 1982-84; cons. mktg., mgmt. The Blades Group, Atlanta, 1985—. Co-chmn. Ga. State Kids Know, 1988; active in Youth at Risk, Atlanta, 1989, Charis House Project Holy Innocents Episc. Ch., Atlanta, 1988-89. Mem. Smyrna Bus. Assn. (co-chmn. image com. 1987-88), Cobb County C. of C. Exec. Women, Beta Sigma Phi. Republican.

BLADES, JANE M., educator; b. Jersey City, Dec. 1, 1953; d. Nunzio Thomas and Evelyn Rose (Spizzirro) Savino; m. Brian Hilton Blades, Sept. 20, 1980; children: Adam Hilton, Erik Thomas. BA, Kean Coll., 1983. Cert. handicapped tchr., N.J. Staff asst. Am. Telephone and Telegraph Co., Parsippany, N.J., 1979-81; spl. edn. tchr. Perth Amboy Pub. Schs., N.J., 1984; mgmt. cons. J. Anthony and Assocs., Inc., Hillsborough, N.J., 1986, project mgr., 1987; cons. Datanomics, Inc., Piscataway, N.J., 1987-88; tchr. of the handicapped Edison (N.J.) Twp. Bd. Edn., 1988—; cons. in field. Mem. Nat. Assn. Female Execs., Soc. for Tech. Communication, Kappa Delta Pi, Phi Kappa Phi. Republican. Presbyterian. Home: 27 Hill Ave Somerset NJ 08873

BLAESI, MARY VIRGINIA, real estate agent, appraiser; b. Prairie Grove, Ark., Nov. 16, 1953; d. Franklin Martin and Betty Jean (Alexander) Blair; m. John Edward Blaesi, Sept. 10, 1988. BEd, U. Ark., 1974. lic. broker, master sr. appraiser. Realtor Bartlesville, Okla., 1980—; sr. appraiser Land Rush Real Estate Appraisal, Bartlesville, 1988—. Mem. AAUW, Nat. Assn. Realtors, Okla. Assn. Realtors, Bartlesville Bd. Realtors, Nat. Assn. Master Appraisers, Women's Council of Realtors.

BLAESS, DONNA ADELE, counselor, educator; b. Detroit, Dec. 17, 1948; d. Marvin Julius and Mildred Catherine (Konka) B. BA, U. Tampa, Fla., 1970; MA, U. of South Fla., 1972; PhD, U. Iowa, 1976. Rsch. evaluator Boston U., 1976-77; project dir. Contract Rsch. Corp., Belmont, Mass., 1977-79; adj. prof. Peabody Coll. of Vanderbilt U., Oxford, 1980-81; clin. staff mem. Assocs. for Human Resources, Concord, Mass., 1982-84; program coord., asst. prof. St. Thomas U., Miami, Fla., 1985—; psychotherapist Ctr. for Family Learning, Ft. Lauderdale, Fla., 1986-88; pvt. practice psychotherapist Miami, 1988—; Mem. Dept. Profl. Regulation, Bd. Clin. Social Work, Marriage and Family Therapy and Mental Health Counseling, 1990. Edn. cons. homelsess program New Horizons Mental Health Ctr., Miami, 1988; mem. adv. com. Parent to Parent, Miami, 1988-89; gov.'s appointee Fla. Dept. Profl. Regulation; bd. clin. social work Marriage and Family Therapy, and Mental Health Counseling, 1990—. Mem. Am. Assn. for Counseling and Devel. (media rev. bd. 1986—), Am. Mental Health Counselors Assn., Fla. Mental Health Counselors Assn. (sec. 1988-89, treas. 1989—). Home: 15665 Miami Lakeway N Miami Lakes FL 33014

BLAGER, FLORENCE BERMAN, voice pathologist. Student, W.Va. Wesleyan Coll., 1946-47; PhD, Ohio U., 1970; MA, U. Denver, 1966. Assoc. prof. dept. otolaryngology and psychiatry U. Colo. Health Scis. Ctr., Denver, 1978—; chief speech pathology and audiology John F. Kennedy Child John F. Kennedy Ctr., Denver, 1971-89; chief speech pathology and audiology svcs. Nat. Jewish Ctr. for Immunology and Respiratory Medicine, Denver, 1985—; rsch. assoc. Recording and Rsch. Ctr. Denver Ctr. for the Performing Arts, 1985—, dir. workshops Recording and Rsch. Ctr., 1986—; asst. prof. dept. otolaryngology U. Colo. Med. Ctr., 1971-78; adj. assoc. prof. dept. communication disorders U. Colo., Boulder, 1971-80; adj. assoc. prof. dept. communication disorders U. Denver, 1971-86; del. XV Internat. Congress of Logopedics and Phoniatrics from Am. Speech and Hearing Assn., Buenos Aires, 1971. Contbr. numerous articles to profl. jours. Mem. Am. Speech-Lang. and Hearing Assn., Colo. Speech and Hearing Assn., N.Y. Acad. Sci., Soroptimists (bd. dirs. 1980-82), Zeta Phi Eta (pres. 1987). Home: 2338 S Jasmine Pl Denver CO 80222

BLAHA, MARGARET WIRTH, elementary educator; b. N.Y.C., Feb. 27, 1909; d. Louis and Margaret (Feid) Wirth; m. John F. Blaha, May 10, 1934; children: Robert L., John W. BA, Hunter Coll., 1929; MA, Columbia U., 1933. Elem. sch. tchr. N.Y.C. Bd. Edn., 1929-70; reading cons., tchr. English to Immigrants N.Y.C., 1970—. Mem. legis. adv. com. Queens County, N.Y., 1966—; regional coord. Diocesan Coun. Cath. Women, Bklyn., 1960—; bd. dirs. St. Anastasia'a Ladies Aux., Douglaston, N.Y., 1965— (Woman of Yr. 190); active Douglaston Woman's Club, pres. 1985-86. Recipient Builder of Brotherhood award Nat. Coun. Christians and Jews, 1972, Our Lady of Good Counsel award Coun. Cath. Women, 1974; elected to Hunter Coll. Hall of Fame, 1975. Mem. AAUW, Phi Delta Kappa, Delta Kappa Gamma (State Achievement award 1989), Alpha Delta Pi (Outstanding Alumni award 1967). Home: 242-17 54th Ave Douglaston NY 11362

BLAINE, DOROTHEA CONSTANCE RAGETTÉ, lawyer, b. N.Y.C., Sept. 23, 1930; d. Robert Raymond and Dorothea Ottilie Ragetté; BA, Barnard Coll., 1952; MA, Calif. State U., 1968; EdD, UCLA, 1978; JD, Western State U., 1981; postgrad. in taxation Golden Gate U. Bar: U.S. Dist. Ct. (ea., so. and cen. dists.) Calif., 1982. Mem. tech. staff Planning Rsch. Corp., L.A., 1964-67; assoc. scientist Holy Cross Hosp., Mission Hills, Calif., 1967-70; career devel. officer and affirmative action officer County of Orange, Santa Ana, Calif., 1970-74, sr. adminstrv. analyst, budget and program coord., 1974-78; spl. projects asst. CAO/Spl. Programs Office, 1978-80, sr. adminstrv. analyst, 1980-83; pvt. practice, 1982—; instr. Am. Coll. Law, Brea, Calif., 1987; judge pro tem Orange County Mcpl. Ct., 1988; bd. dirs. Orange County Lawyers Referral, del. to state bar conv., 1985-89. Bd. dirs. Deerfield Community Assn., 1975-78, Orange YMCA, 1975-77. Mem. ABA, ACLU, Trial Lawyers Am., Calif. Trial Lawyers Assn., Orange County Trial Lawyers Assn., Calif. Women Lawyers, Nat. Women's Polit. Caucus, Calif. Bar Assn., Orange County Bar Assn. (Orange County del. to Calif. State Bar Conv. 1985-90, bd. dirs. Orange County Lawyers Referral Svc. 1988—), Delta Theta Phi, Phi Delta Kappa. Office: 6 Hutton Centre Dr Ste 845 Santa Ana CA 92707

BLAINE, KATHLEEN ELAINE, information systems professional; b. Manchester, N.H., Oct. 7, 1953; d. Kenneth Arthur and Jennie (Bongers) B. BA in Microbiology, U. N.H., 1975, MS in Microbiology, 1979; postgrad., U. Mass., 1984-86. Sr. research technician DANA-Farber Cancer Inst., Boston, 1979-81; sr. research technician Beth Israel Hosp., Boston, 1981-83; chief technologist St. Elizabeths Hosp., Brighton, Mass., 1983-86; cons. Med. Info. Tech. Inc., Westwood, Mass., 1986-87; patient care system mgr. Choate-Symmes Health Svcs., Wilmington, Mass., 1987-88; asst. dir. mgmt. info. systems Choate-Symmes Health Svcs., 1988—. Contbr. articles to profl. jours. Mem. Nat. Assn. for Female Execs., Healthcare Info. & Mgmt. Systems Soc., Healthcare Fin. Mgmt. Assn. Republican. Presbyterian. Office: Choate Symmes Health Svcs Regional Health Ctr 500 Salem St Wilmington MA 01887

BLAIR, BARBARA ANNE, educator; b. Gastonia, N.C., Oct. 21, 1926; d. James Luther and Annie Maude (Smith) B. BA, Agnes Scott Coll., 1948; MS, U. Tenn., 1953, PhD, 1956. Lab. analyst Union Carbide, Oak Ridge, Tenn., 1948-49; rsch. assoc. Med. Sch. U. Buffalo, 1956-57, U. Va., Charlottesville, 1957-61; asst. prof. chemistry Wilson Coll., Chambersburg, Pa., 1961-62; with Sweet Briar (Va.) Coll., 1962—, acad. dean, 1974-77, prof. chemistry, 1980—; vis. lectr. Women's Christian Coll., Madras, India, 1968-69. Contbr. articles to profl. jours. Fellow AAAS; mem. Am. Chem. Soc. (local sec. 1971-74, officer); AAUP, AAUW, Phi Beta Kappa, Sigma Xi. Democrat. Presbyterian. Office: Sweet Briar Coll PO Box P Sweet Briar VA 24595

BLAIR, BETTY STEPP, marketing consultant; b. Odessa, Tex., July 2, 1947; d. William Fleming and Barbara Jane (Thompson) Stepp; m. Stephen Randolph Blair, Mar. 25, 1968 (div. 1978); children: Stacy Rae, Brian Randolph. BBA, SW Tex. State U., 1970. Sales rep. stas. KYXY and XETV, San Diego, 1975-77; owner, mgr. Royal Suite, San Diego, 1977-79; internat. design cons. T. Goodrich & Assocs., Del Mar, Calif., 1979-80; acct. Sickels O'Brien Co., San Diego and La Jolla, Calif., 1980-81; property mgr. Total Office/Koll, San Diego, 1981-83; asst. devel. dir. Am. Cancer Soc., San Diego, 1983-86, also bd. dirs.; assoc. D'Agostino, Underwood & Assocs., 1986-87; dir. devel. Combined Arts and Edn. Council of San Diego County, 1987, spl. event prodn. and mktg., Blair & Assocs., 1987—; cons. Poway Firewood Co., Calif., 1980-84, Starflight Prodns., San Diego, 1985-86. Mem. Republican Central Com., San Diego, 1977, steering com. Young Connoisseurs, San Diego Mus. of Art, 1982-84, San Diego Rep. Businesswomen, 1984-86; bd. dirs. Rep. Bus. and Profl. Club, San Diego, 1986; adv. bd. The Sports Club San Diego Aventine, The Soc. Club, Am. Cancer Soc., Single Profl. Soc. for Arts; vol. charitable orgns. and theaters. Recipient State award Am. Cancer Soc., 1985. Mem. Nat. Soc. Fund Raising Execs., Chi Omega. Avocation: tennis. Home: PO Box 174 La Jolla CA 92038 Office: Blair & Assocs 620 State St San Diego CA 92101

BLAIR, DANA MILLER, physician; b. Berkeley, Calif., Nov. 4, 1957; d. Daniel Holmes and Natalie (Cake) Miller; m. Gregory Robb Blair, June 30, 1979; children: Jeffrey Alden, Katherine Jeanne. BS, U. Calif., Davis, 1979; MD, St. Louis U., 1983. Intern U. Utah, Salt Lake City, 1983-84; resident U. Utah, 1984-86; resident internal medicine U. Utah, Salt Lake City, 1983-86; internist Pub. Health Svc./IHS, Talihina, Okla., 1986-88, Tahlequah, Okla., 1988-90; vis. postdoctoral fellow in rheumatology U. Calif. at Davis, Sacramento. Lt. comdr. USPHS, 1986-90. Recipient Isloated Hardship Svc. award USPHS, 1986, Physicians Recognition award AMA, 1987, Achievement citation AMWA, St. Louis, 1983, Achievement medal USPHS, 1989. Mem. Am. Coll. Physicians, Alpha Omega Alpha, Phi Kappa Phi. Methodist. Office: U Calif Div Rheumatology/Allergy Clin Immunology Sch Medicine TB 192 Davis CA 95616

BLAIR, ELAINE JUDITH, management consultant; b. Flint, Mich., Aug. 9, 1957; d. Ada Mae (Temple) B. BSc., Mich. State U., 1980, MA, 1986. Graduate asst. Upward Bound, Mich. State U., East Lansing, 1985-86; employment counselor Youth Devel. Corp., Lansing, Mich., 1987--, employment trainer, 1988; social services supr. Radiant Living Inc., Detroit, 1988; social worker, therapist Spaulding for Children, Southfield, Mich., 1989—; prof., instr. C.H. Mason Bible Coll., Lansing, 1986. Editor: Newspaper, Main Artery 1985. Cons. Adolescent Sch. Bd. Prevention Task Force, Lansing Mich. 1988. Recipient MSU Scholarship for Acad. Excellence award Mich. State U., 1975.

BLAIR, JANE COLEMAN, retired educator; b. N.Y.C., Apr. 7, 1928; d. Leighton Hammond and Jane (Fraser) Coleman; m. William Draper Blair, Jr., June 25, 1949; children: Jane Blair Gelston, Elizabeth Blair Jones. Student, Bryn Mawr Coll., 1946-49; BA, Am. U., 1974, MEd, 1976. Cert. secondary tchr., Md. Tchr., dir. admissions Stone Ridge Country Day Sch. of the Sacred Heart, Bethesda, Md., 1976-86. Pres., bd. dirs. Jr. League of Washington; bd. dirs. Columbia Hist. Soc., Meridian House Internat., Hillcrest Children's Ctr.; mem. Am. Hist. Soc. Mem. Visiting Nurse Assn., Am. Hist. Soc. (bd. dirs.), Visiting Nurse Assn. (bd. dirs.). Democrat. Episcopalian. Club: F St. (bd. dirs. 1986—). Home: 118 E Melrose St Chevy Chase MD 20815

BLAIR, KATHIE LYNN, social services worker; b. Oakland, Calif., Sept. 29, 1951; d. Robert Leon Webb and Patricia Jean (Taylor) Peterson; m. Terry Wayne Blair, Dec. 29, 1970 (div. 1972); 1 child, Anthony Wayne. Eligibility worker Dept. Social Services, San Jose, Calif., 1974-76; adult and family services worker State of Oreg., Portland, 1977-89; guest speaker welfare advocacy groups, Portland, 1987. Contbr. articles to mags. Mem. Nat. Geog. Soc. Democrat.

BLAIR, MARIE LENORE, educator; b. Maramec, Okla., Jan. 9, 1931; d. Virgil Clement and Ella Catherine (Leen) Strode; m. Freeman Joe Blair, Aug. 26, 1950; children: Elizabeth Ann Blair Crump, Roger Joe. BS, Okla. A&M Coll., 1956; MS, Okla. State U., 1961, postgrad., 1965-68. Reading specialist Pub. Schs. Stillwater (Okla.), 1966-88. Past bd. dirs. Okla. Reading Council. Mem. Internat., Okla., Cimarron (past pres.) reading assns., NEA, Okla. Edn. Assn., Stillwater Edn. Assn., Kappa Kappa Iota. Democrat. Mem. Disciples of Christ. Lodges: Demoley Mothers, Rainbow Mothers, Lahoma, White Shrine Jerusalem (past worthy high priestess). Order White Shrine Jerusalem (past supreme queen's attendant), Internat. Order of Rainbow for Girls (Okla. exec. com.), Order Eastern Star (past grand Martha, past grand rep. of Nebr. in Okla.). Home: Route 1 Maramec OK 74045

BLAIR, MARY ELLEN, author; b. Orange, N.J., Dec. 29, 1921; d. John Wesley Marden and Louella Fay Stubblefield; m. Laurence Robert Blair; children: Laurence R. Jr., Ellen E. B. Lamb, Joanne B., William J. BA, Rutgers U., 1943. Author: Margaret Tafoya, 1986, Nampeyo Fannie, 1990. Judge pottery exhibitions.

BLAIR, MATTIE D., city official, consultant, small business owner; b. Chgo., Nov. 26; d. James and Geraldine (Oliver) Cannon; div.; 1 child, Lisa Marie. B.S. in Bus. Adminstrn. in Acctg., Roosevelt U., 1979; M.B.A. in Fin., DePaul U., 1985. Pub. auditor Arthur Andersen & Co., Chgo., 1978-81; controller Johnson Products & Co., Chgo., 1981-82; mgr. fiscal policies United Way of Chgo., 1982-86; dir. devel. fin. City of Chgo., 1986-88, mng. commr., 1988-89; deputy inspector Gen. Housing Authority, Chgo., 1989—; cons. on fin. and mgmt. to small non-profit orgns. Developer network to assist black profls. in fin. and acctg. Mem. League of Black Women (v.p. 1983—). Democrat. Mem. United Ch. of Christ. Avocations: tennis; jogging; sports. Office: Gen Housing Authority 105 W Madison St Ste 1103 Chicago IL 60602

BLAIR, PATRICIA JEAN, corporate personnel executive; b. Fairhaven, Minn., Mar. 17, 1939; d. Earl Philip and Doris Elizabeth (Seeley) B. BS in Mgmt., U. San Francisco, 1978; MBA in Human Resources, Golden Gate U., 1982. Jr. escrow officer Transam. Title Co., Phoenix, 1965-68; adminstr. Transam. Info. Services, Los Angeles, 1968-72; mgr. adminstrn. Synergraphics, Inc., San Francisco, 1972-80; dir. adminstrv. svcs. Transam. Corp., San Francisco, 1980—, dir. corp. personnel, 1985—; dir. personnel Transam. Realty Svcs. Group, San Francisco, 1989—; bd. dirs. Calif. Employment Law Coun. Contbr. articles to profl. jours. Night unit leader LWV, Alameda, Calif., 1980-82; advisor Dance Action, Inc., San Francisco, 1983—; mem. corp. action com. San Francisco Sch. Vol. Program; bd. dirs. Calif. Employment Law Coun., Philharmonia Baroque, San Francisco, 1985—; bus. vol. for the arts San Francisco C. of C., 1983—. Mem. Am. Compensation Assn. (cert. compensation profl.), Am. Soc. Personnel Adminstrs., No. Calif. Human Resources Conf., Bay Areas Human Resource Profls. Republican. Lutheran. Office: Transamerica Corp 600 Montgomery St San Francisco CA 94111

BLAIR, VIRGINIA ANN, public relations executive; b. Kansas City, Mo., Dec. 20, 1925; d. Paul Lowe and Lou Etta (Cooley) Smith; m. James Leon Grant, Sept. 3, 1943 (dec. July 1944); m. 2d, Warden Tannahill Blair, Jr., Nov. 7, 1947; children: Janet, Warden Tannahill, III. B.S. in Speech, Northwestern U., 1948. Free-lance writer, Chgo., 1959-69; writer, editor Smith, Bucklin & Assocs., Inc., Chgo., 1969-72, account mgr., 1972-79, account supr., 1979-80, dir. pub. relations, 1980-85; pres. GB Pub. Rels., 1985—; judge U.S. Indsl. Film Festival, 1974, 75; instr. Writer's Workshop, Evanston, Ill., 1978; dir. Northwestern U. Library Council, 1978—. Emmy nominee Nat. Acad. TV Arts & Scis., 1963; recipient Service award Northwestern U., 1978, Creative Excellence award U.S. Indsl. Film Festival, 1976, Gold Leaf merit cert. Family Circle mag. and Food Council Am., 1977. Mem. Pub. Rels. Soc. Am. (counselors acad.), Am. Advt. Fedn. (lt. gov. Ill. 6th dist.), Women's Advt. Club Chgo. (pres.), Publicity Club Chgo., Nat. Acad. TV Arts & Scis., Woman's Club Evanston (pres.), Zeta Phi Eta (Service award 1978), Alpha Gamma Delta. Author dramas (produced on CBS): Jeanne D'Arc: The Trial, 1961; Cordon of Fear, 1961; Reflection, 1961; If I Should Die, 1963; 3-act children's play: Children of Courage, 1967. Home and Office: 463 Highcrest Dr Wilmette IL 60091

BLAIR-LARSEN, SUSAN MARGARET, educator; b. Plainfield, N.J., May 28, 1950; d. Adam Craig and Edith Elizabeth (Wessel) Blair; m. Bruce Osborn Larsen, July 15, 1989. BS, Castleton (Vt.) State Coll., 1972; MS, U. Scranton, Pa., 1974; EdD, U. Pa., 1984. Tchr. Palisades Sch. Dist., Kintnersville, Pa., 1973-75; reading specialist Lakewood (N.J.) Sch. Dist., 1975-84; prof. U. Minn., Morris, 1984-85, Rutgers U., Newark, 1985-88, Trenton (N.J.) State Coll., 1988—; evaluator Literacy Vols. of Am., Toms River, N.J. Editor: Higher Education and Reading Instruction, 1988. Mem. Mantoloking and Bay Head (N.J.) Women's Rep. Club. Mem. N.J. Assn. Tchr. Educators (exec. bd. 1989-90, v.p. 1990-91), N.J. Reading Assn. (bd. dirs. 1988-91), Internat. Reading Assn., Ocean County Coun. Reading, Ea. Ednl. Rsch. Assn., Phi Delta Kappa (Ten Yr. award 1990), Pi Lambda Theta. Roman Catholic.

BLAIS, ALLISON SCHAU, guidance counselor, volunteer; b. Erie, Pa., Apr. 25, 1943; d. Alfred Isham and Anna Eleanor (Pearson) Schau; m. Jeffrey David Blais, July 27, 1974; children: Jennifer Allison, Benjamin Jeffrey. BA, U. Fla., 1966, M.Ed., 1968; postgrad., Oswego State Coll. Tchr.Head Start Volusia Sch. System, Ormond Beach, Fla., 1967-68; tchr. Ormond Jr. High Sch., Ormond Beach, 1967-69; dir. guidance Southwestern Sch., DeLand, Fla., 1969-77; high sch. guidance counselor Fulton (N.Y.) Sch. System, 1986—. Chmn. bd. deacons. Ormond Beach Presbyn. Ch., 1970-73; confirmation tchr., v.p. parish council, eucharistic minister St. Mary's Ch., Baldwinsville, N.Y.; leader Girl Scouts U.S., Baldwinsville; counselor, tutor Teen Ctr., Baldwinsville. Mem. AAUW (pres. 1970-72, 79-81), N.Y. State Assn. for Counseling and Devel., Oswego County Counselors Assn., Am. Fedn. Tchrs., Columbiettes Aux. (pres. 1985-87), Alpha Delta Kappa. Republican. Roman Catholic. Home: 2 Gettman Dr Baldwinsville NY 13027 Office: G Ray Bodley High Sch 6 William Gilland Dr Fulton NY 13069

BLAISE, MRS. CLARK See MUKHERJEE, BHARATI

BLAKE, ANN BETH, psychologist; b. Hibbing, Minn., Dec. 31, 1944; d. James Edward Foutz and Betty Helen (Blake) Smith; adopted d. Edmund Carl Drinkwitz; m. John Peter Hennes, June 10, 1978 (div. Nov. 1979). AA, Hibbing State Jr. Coll., 1964; PhB, U. N.D., 1966; MEd, U. Wash., 1978, PhD, 1983. Lic. psychologist, Wash. With house staff Seattle Children's Home, 1966-67; caseworker, case reviewer Wash. Dept. Social and Health Svcs., Everett and Seattle, 1967-75; group and individual facilitator Human Alternatives N.W., Seattle, 1975-79, 84; teaching asst. in curriculum and instrn. U. Wash., 1978-80; contract counselor Luth. Social Svcs., 1982-84; counselor Highland Community Coll., Midway, Wash., 1984; therapist Thurston-Mason Community Mental Health Ctr., Olympia, Wash., 1984-87; asst. prof. psychology St. Martin's Coll., Lacey, Wash., 1987-90, pres. faculty, 1988-89; pvt. practice, Olympia, 1987—; grad. faculty advisor Antioch Coll., Seattle, 1985-88, 88-90, Vt. Coll., Montpelier, 1989—. Mem. Am. Psychol. Assn., Deschutes Psychol. Assn. (treas. 1985-87). Democrat. Home: 1323 Eskridge Blvd SE Olympia WA 98501 Office: PO Box 5944 Lacey WA 98503

BLAKE, DARLENE EVELYN, political worker, consultant, educator; b. Rockford, Iowa, Feb. 26, 1947; d. Forest Kenneth and Violet Evelyn (Fisher) Kuhlemeier; m. Joel Franklin Blake, May 1, 1975 (dec. Jan. 1989); 1 child, Alexander Joel. AA, North Iowa Area Community Coll., Mason City, 1967; BS, Mankato (Minn.) State Coll., 1969; MS, Mankato (Minn.) State U., 1975. Cert. profl. tchr., Iowa; registered art therapist. Tchr. Bishop Whipple Sch., Faribault, Minn., 1970-72; art therapist C.B. Wilson Ctr., Faribault, 1972-76, Sedgwick County Dept. Mental Health, Wichita, Kans., 1976-79; cons. Batten, Batten, Hudson & Swab, Des Moines, 1979-81; pres. J.F. Blake Co., Inc., Des Moines, 1984—; polit. cons. to Alexander Haig for Pres., 1987-88; mgmt. tng. specialist Communications Data Svcs., Inc., Des Mointes, 1988-90; exec. mgr. customer svc. spl. interest fulfillment div. and diversified svcs. div., 1990—; mem. nat. adv. bd. Alexander Haig for Pres., 1987-88. Exhibited in one-woman show at local libr., 1970. Chmn. U.S. Selective Svc. Bd. 27, Polk County, Iowa, 1981—; sustaining mem. Rep. Nat. Com.; Rep. candidate Polk County Treas., Des Moines, 1982; chmn. Polk County Rep. Party, 1985-88; commr. Des Moines Commn. Human Rights and Job Discrimination, 1984-89; mem. Martin Luther King Scholarship Com., 1986-88; mem. Iowa State Bd. Psychology Examiners, 1983-90; mem. 5th Dist. Jud. Nominating Commn., 1990-96. Mem. Am. Art Therapy Assn., (cert., standards com. 1986—), Am. Soc. Tng. Devel., Iowa Art Therapy Assn. (pres. elect. 1984-85, founder), Internat. Platform Speakers Assn., Toastmasters. Lutheran. Clubs: Des Moines Garden (pres. 1984-85), Polk County Rep. Women (pres. elect 1983-85). Home and Office: 2301 Glenwood Dr Des Moines IA 50321

BLAKE, IRENE ELVIN, management consultant; b. Paterson, N.J., Aug. 6, 1947; d. Charles Russell and Irene (Crawford) Elvin; m. LeRoy Carl Blake, Feb. 14, 1982. BA, Montclair State, 1968; MM, New Eng. Conservatory Music, 1970. Asst. mgr. data svcs. Broadway Bank & Trust, Paterson, N.J., 1973-80; controller Travelong, Inc., Union, N.J., 1980-82; mgr. ops. analysis system planning Mfrs. Hanover Trust Co., N.Y.C., 1982-85; sr. system analyst United Jersey Bank, Hackensack, 1985-86; mgr. cons. svcs. Automated Fin. Systems, Inc., Exton, Pa., 1986—. Choir mem. Kings Chapel Boston, 1970-72; soloist St. Mary's Episc. Ch., North Halledon, N.J., 1975-80. Mem. Am. Mgmt. Assn., NAFE, Am. Guild Musical Artists. Home: 150 W Shoen Rd Exton PA 19341 Office: Automated Fin Systems 123 Summit Dr Exton PA 19341

BLAKE, JANE SALLEY, publishing executive; b. Tallahassee, Fla., Sept. 3, 1937; d. George Lawrence Salley and Eleanor (King) Hookham; m. Arthur Copeland Blake Jr., Sept. 5, 1959; children: A. Copeland III, Tarrant Salley. BA in Fine Arts, Fla. State U., 1958. Exec. sec. Hist. Homes Found., Louisville, 1975-76; chair Ky. Heritage Bicentennial, Louisville, 1976; founder, pres., chmn. Arts Forum, Inc., Louisville, 1978-84; pres. Blake Publs., Inc., Louisville, 1983-86; pres., prin. The Center mag., Inc., Louisville, 1986—, J.S. Blake Communications Group, Louisville, 1986—. V.p. Art Ctr. Assn., Louisville, 1967-72; bd. dirs., publicity chair Children's Theatre, 1968; v.p., bd. dirs. Crusade vs. Crime, 1972-74; bd. dirs. Farmington Hist. Home, 1973-75, 77-80, actor/singer Actors' Theatre, Lunchtime Theatre, 1974; mem. theatre a la carte troupe, 1976-77; founder, chmn. Potpourri of the Arts, 1979-83; mem. pub. rels. com. Jefferson County Police, 1987-88. Recipient Gov's. Arts award, 1989. Mem. Pub. Rels. Soc. Am. (Landmark of Excellence award 1988, 89), Advt. Club Louisville (13 Louie awards for publs. 1981-84), Women in Communications, The Entrepreneur Soc. (exec. com., bd. dirs., chair 1990 Horizon awards, Above and Beyond the Call of Duty award 1990), Bus. Advocates, Ky. C. of C., Louisville C. of C., Soc. Profl. Journalists, Women's Club Louisville, Women's Alliance. Democrat. Office: The Center Mag Inc 118 Bauer Ave Louisville KY 40207

BLAKE, JOAN JOHNSTON WALLMAN, playwright; b. Nashville, May 14, 1930; d. Graham Walpole Johnston and Emilie (Wright) Roberts; m. John Christian Wallman, May 13, 1950 (div. 1960); children: Joan, Tia, Chris, Chellie, Parker, Peter; m. Octave Blake, Jan. 28, 1962 (dec. Jan. 1969). Student, Finch Jr. Coll., N.Y.C., 1948-49, Concordia U., Montreal, Que., Can., 1973-76. Author, host radio sta. WEEB, Southern Pines, N.C., 1949-50; co-founder, owner Double Hook Book Shop, Montreal, 1974—; freelance journalist, broadcaster; dir. LePiggerie Theatre, Que., 1964-67; founder Amanda Theater, 1990. Author: (play) Amanda and Atwater Square, 1985, Amanda and the Northern Lights, 1990; author, hostess (documentary) Vermont PBS, 1983. Recipient award of Merit Assn. for Can. Studies, 1988. Mem. Can. Booksellers Assn.

BLAKE, LAURA, architect; b. Berkeley, Calif., Dec. 26, 1959; d. Igor Robert and Elizabeth (Denton) B. BA in Art History, Brown U., 1982; MArch, UCLA, 1985. Architect The Ratcliff Architects, Berkeley, 1986-90, IDG Architects, Oakland, Calif., 1990—. Organizer charity ball Spinsters San Francisco, 1988, sec., 1988-89, mem. adv. bd., 1989-90; alumni interviewer Brown U. Recipient Alpha Rho Chi bronze medal, 1985. Mem. AIA, The Spinsters of San Francisco (adv. bd. 1989—). Republican. Episcopalian. Office: IDG Architects 1730 Franklin St Oakland CA 94612

BLAKE, MARGARET TATE, psychologist, educator; b. Cyril, Okla., Jan. 17, 1927; d. Joseph Clifford and Luella (Anderson) Tate; m. Duane L. Blake, Dec. 1945 (div. 1974); children: Richard Duane, Barbara Gwen, Debra Dawn; m. Charles H. Jansen, Aug. 15, 1986. BS, Okla. U., 1947; MS, Iowa State U., 1963, PhD, 1966. Lic. marriage and family therapist, Colo. Asst. prof. Drake U., Des Moines, Iowa, 1964-66, Colo. State U., Ft. Collins, 1966-68; prof. psychology U. No. Colo., Greeley, 1968-89; pvt. practice Greeley, 1989—. Producer videotapes in field. Fellow Am. Assn. Marriage and Family Therapy (bd. dirs. 1989—, pres. Colo. chpt. 1986-89); mem. Colo. Assn. Counseling and Devel. (pres. 1980-81), Rocky Mountain Coun. Family Rels. (pres. 1984-87), Am. Bd. Vocat. Experts (diplomate). Home: 1912 29th Ave Greeley CO 80631

BLAKE, TRUDI ODELLA, odemaker; b. Itaaca, Mich., Apr. 21, 1921; d. Leo Charles Lepley and Grace Cornelia (Street) Lepley-Reed; m. George Blake; children: Russell, Kevin, Lorene, Suzanne, Philip. Student, Detroit Sch. of Bus., 1941, Hollywood Sch. of Comedy Writing, 1966. Former writer local and nat. TV stas.; former writer for Phyllis Diller. Author: (odes) Forever Grand and Glorious, Ode to Soapy, a Huckleberry Friend, Ode to the Tigers, Dear Hearts and Republican People, A Voyage That's Socko, to Spain and Morocco, Over the Rainbow to Liberal, We The People - 200, Ode to a Bunch of Swells, From Sauks to Saginaw, A Ode to Michigan, To Conquer Tomorrow, Michigan City Ode, A Miracle in Our Midst; contbr. odes to various bus. Recipient Cert. of Special Tribute State of Mich., 1988. Mem. Nat. Speakers Assn. (named Official Odemaker 1984), Oakland County Writers Assn. Home and Office: Box 2842 Farmington Hills MI 48333

BLAKELEY, LINDA, psychotherapist; b. Bklyn., July 26, 1941; d. Charles and Blanche (Josephson) Berkow; m. Dec. 17, 1961 (div. 1983); children: Stacey, Scott. BA, UCLA, 1964; PhD, Calif. State U., Northridge, 1977, Calif. Grad. Inst., 1985. Founder, dir. Parents Sharing Custody, Beverly Hills, Calif., 1984-87; pvt. practice Beverly Hills, 1984—; trainer Calif. Assn. Marriage and Family Therapists, 1988, 89. Author: Positive Parenting After Separation & Divorce, ABC's of Stress Management, The Man-Woman Dance. Mem. Calif. Psychol. Assn. (state bd. dirs. media com. 1989-90), Calif. Assn. Marriage and Family Therapists (L.A. chpt. chairperson ethics com. 1988), Beverly Hills C. of C. (pres. women's network 1989-90, chairperson health care com. 1989—). Office: 420 S Beverly Dr Ste 100 Beverly Hills CA 90212

BLAKELY-SCOTT, SANDRA GAIL, management consultant; b. Cleve., Jan. 16, 1949; d. Julius Leonard and Myrtle Lucille (Bell) Blakely; m. Buddy Scott; children: Dana Michele, Jason Michael. Student, Dillard U., 1966-69, Kent (Ohio) State U., 1970-71. Counselor Neighborhood Youth Corps, Cleve., 1971-73; personnel mgr. Kimball Systems/Litton Industries, Cleve., 1973-74; employment interviewer, tng. specialist Am. States Ins., Indpls., 1976-79; foreman Internat. Harvester, Indpls., 1979-80; instr. tng. inc. Ind. Vo-Tech. Coll., Indpls., 1981-86; cons. tng. and econ. devel. Cuyahoga Community Coll., Indpls., 1986-87; pvt. practice cons. Plainsboro, N.J., 1987-89; tng. projects mgr. UJB Fin. Corps, Princeton, N.J., 1988-90; pres. Up-Over Prodns., Inc., Plainsboro and Naples, Fla., 1989—; mem. employment com. Indpls. Urban League, 198486; mem. basic skills com. State Commn. on Higher Edn., Indpls., 1985-86. Mem. YWCA Child Care Task Force, Indpls., 1982-85, Coun. of Black Execs., Indpls., 1985-86; mem., chmn. Ind. Black Expo Art Exhibition and Competition, Indpls., 1985-86. Recipient Key to the City, Mayor of Indpls., 1985. Mem. Cen. Jersey Network Profl. Women, NAFE, Naples Area C. of C., Alpha Kappa Alpha.

BLAKEMORE, SALLY GAY, graphic designer; b. Odessa, Tex., Apr. 15, 1947; d. William Saundrs and Annelle (Frazier) B.; m. Michael Prochoroff; m. Paul D. Turner; m. John Russell Storbeck, July 13, 1989. BFA, U. Tex., 1970; postgrad., U. New Orleans, 1986-89. Animal caretaker zoology dept. U. Tex., Austin, 1972-78, dept. artist zoology dept., 1978-79; typesetter, designer Valiant Art Svcs., Falls Church, Va., 1979-81; freelance illustrator Betty Binns Graphics, N.Y.C., 1981-82; art dir. Theatre Crafts Mag., N.Y.C., 1982-84; art prodn. mgr. N.Y. Mag., N.Y.C., 1984-85; illustrator, freelance designer New Orleans, 1985-87; creative svcs. dir. Design Ptnrs., New Orleans, 1987-89; designer John Muir Publs., Santa Fe, 1990—. Author: I Really Want a Dog, 1990; illustrator: Kidding Around NY, 1988, Kidding Around Boston, 1990, Kidding Around Chicago, 1990. Mem. Doris Day Animal League, 1989-90, Concerned Citizens Nuclear Power, Santa Fe, 1990, Internat. Copier Soc., N.Y.C., 1988-89; vol. Soc. for Prevention Cruelty to Animals, Santa Fe, 1990—. Recipient 1st pl. painting Deutsche Welle Radio, Cologne, Fed. Republic Germany, 1972, Amy Freeman Lee watercolor honorable mention, Austin, Tex., 1974, honorable Art Dirs. and Designers Assn., New Orleans, 1989. Mem. Spiritual Cruise Control Ctr. (pres. 1982—, pub. DADA newspaper). Hindu. Home: 3012 Siringo Rondo S Santa Fe NM 87505 Office: John Muir Publs Railroad Yard Santa Fe NM 87501

BLAKESLEE, TAMMY LYNNE, industrial hygienist; b. Key West, Fla., Sept. 6, 1961; d. Charles Maynard Jarrell and Peggy Lou (Wiggins) Morris; m. Jeffrey Allen Blakeslee, June 11, 1983; 1 child, Sarah Elizabeth. BS summa cum laude, Quinnipiac Coll., Hamden, Conn., 1983. Pers. coordinator Data Documents, North Haven, Conn., 1983-84; indsl. hygiene, safety engr. Shipley Co., Inc., Newton, Mass., 1984-87; corp. indsl. hygienist Shipley Co., Inc., Marlborough, Mass., 1987—. Sunday sch. tchr. 1st Congl. Ch., Shrewsbury, Mass., 1987—. Mem. Am. Indsl. Hygiene Assn., New Eng. Am. Indsl. Hygiene Assn., Am. Chem. Soc., Semiconductor Safety Assn. Office: Shipley Co Inc 455 Forest St Marlborough MA 01752

BLAKNEY-RICHARDS, BETTYE RUTH, biology educator; b. Shubuta, Miss., Sept. 5, 1939; d. Willie and Alma (Britton) B.; m. Robert Richards, Feb. 19, 1970 (div. July 1978); 1 child, Benita Wonjiku. BS, Tougloo (Miss.) Coll., 1961; MS, Chgo. State U., 1974; PhD, So. Ill. U., 1988. Cert. med. technologist. Clin. microbiologist Chgo. Bd. Health, 1966-67, U. Chgo., 1967-77; prof. biology City Colls. Chgo., 1977—; vis. prof. biology Northeastern U., Chgo., 1979-80; vis. asst. prof. pathology Nat. Coll. Naprapathy, Chgo., 1979-80; vis. asst. prof. biology U. Ill., Chgo., 1989—, Nat. Louis U., Chgo., 1990—; vis. prof. pathophysiology Auroro U., 1990—. Author: Clinical Microbiology, 1989; contbr. articles to profl. jours. Edn. com. LWV, Chgo., 1975, 84; mental health chair Delta Sigma Theta Sorority, Inc., Chgo., 1974; bd. dirs. YMCA, Lawrence, Mass., 1962; exec. com. Faculty Coun. City Colls. Chgo., 1987-88; Christian edn. chairperson Neighborhood United Meth. Ch., 1988—. Named Fellow Ill. Consortium for Ednl. Opportunity, 1986-88, Achievement Scholar NSF, 1960; recipient Acad. Achievement award Black Affairs Coun., 1986, 87, Master Tchrs. award City Colls. Chgo., 1978, Innovation in Teaching award, 1981, Commendation award Chgo. Pub. Schs., 1974. Mem. Am. Soc. Microbiology, Am. Soc. Pathology, Ill. Soc. Med. Technology (bd. dirs. 1989-90), Am. Soc. Med. Technology, Nat. Sci. Tchrs., Ill. Soc. Microbiology. Democrat. Methodist. Home: 342 Hyde Pk Ave Bellwood IL 60104

BLANCHARD, CAROL KLINE, artist, art gallery owner; b. Reading, Pa., Apr. 14, 1937; d. Richard Kershner and Pauline (Whitaker) Loewen; m. David Gellinger Kline, Mar. 1, 1958 (div. 1979); children: Susan Kline Komitsky, Robert David, Nancy Kline Rathman; m. Gerald Joseph Blanchard, Nov. 28, 1981. BS, U. Pa., 1959. Asst. dir. hematology lab. U. Pa. Hosp., Phila., 1959-61; med. researcher U. Mich., Ann Arbor, 1961-63; owner, dir. Old Quarter Gallery, New Orleans, 1977—; presenter workshops, various mus. and art guild groups, Ala. and La., 1980—. One woman batik shows include: LeDon Art Gallery, Bay Minette, Ala., 1980, Eastern Shore Fine Art Mus., Fairhope, Ala. Mem. LePetite Art Guild, Studio D'Artiste (pres. 1978-84). Democrat. Roman Catholic. Home: 3870 Mimosa Dr New Orleans LA 70131 Office: Old Quarter Gallery 621 Chartres St New Orleans LA 70130

BLANCHETTE, JEANNE E. MAXANT, artist, educator, performer; b. Chgo., Sept. 25, 1944; d. William H. and L. Barbara (Martin) Maxant; m. Yasuo Shimizu, Apr. 28, 1969 (div. 1973); m. William B. Blanchet, Aug. 21, 1981. BA summa cum laude, Northwestern U., 1966; MFA, Tokyo Fine Arts U., 1971; MA, Ariz. State U., 1978; postgrad., Ill. State U., 1979-80. Instr. Tsuda U., Kodaira, Japan, 1970-71; free-lance visual, performing artist various cities, U.S., 1973—; artist in residence YMCA of the Rockies, Estes Park, Colo., 1976-81 summers; prof. fine arts Rio Salado Coll., Surprise, Ariz., 1976—; lectr. Ariz. State U. West, Sun City, 1985—; featured entertainer various Phoenix clubs, 1975—. Author: Original Songs and Verse of the Old (And New) West, 1987, A Song in My Heart, 1988, Reflections, 1989, The Bug in the Rug, 1990; contbr. articles to newspapers, jours., 1975—; featured entertainer various Phoenix clubs, 1975—. Founding mem. Del Webb Hosp. Woodrow Wilson fellow, 1966; ADA B.C. Welsh scholar, 1980; recipient numerous art, music awards including 2d in Show Tokyo Budokan Exhbn., 1970. Mem. Nat. League Am. Pen Women (sec. chpt. 1987—, v.p. 1988, pres. 1990), Nat. Art Edn. Assn., Nat. Rifle Assn. (disting. expert 1983), Ariz. Press Women (numerous awards in original graphics and writing 1980-90), Nat. Fedn. Press Women, Northwestern U.'s John Evans Club, Henry W. Rogers Soc., Phi Beta Kappa. Roman Catholic. Office: Rio Salado Coll Area West 12213 W Bell #210 Surprise AZ 85374

BLANCO, JOSEFA JOAN-JUANA (JOSSIE BLANCO), social services administrator; b. Havana, Cuba, Jan. 31, 1954; came to U.S., 1962; d. Oscar Manuel and Josefa (Rodriguez) B.; m. John Franklin Hurt III, Nov. 18, 1979 (div. June 1985); children: John Franklin IV, Jeaninne Bernadette. BA in Psychology and Religion, Fla. Internat. U., 1975, MA in Sch. Psychology, 1976, postgrad. in pub. adminstrn., 1983—; MS in Human Resource Adminstrn., Villanova U., 1979. Lic. tchr., Fla.; tng. lic. clin. and child care svcs. Psychometrician Mailman Ctr. for Child Devel., U. Miami, 1975-76; supr. adoptions Health and Rehabilitative Svcs. Fla., Miami, 1972-75, 76-80; instr. psychology Draughons Jr. Coll., Memphis, 1980-81; spl. project dir. Children's Psychiat. Ctr., Miami, 1981-84; exec. dir. Community Habilitation Ctr., Miami, 1984-86; shelter dir. Miami Bridge, Inc., Miami, 1986-89; regional dir. Luth. Ministries Fla., Ft. Lauderdale, 1989-90; exec. dir. Residential Pla. at Blue Lagoon Inc., Miami, 1990—; facilitator nat. confs. Nat. Justice Dept. Bd. dirs. S.E. Region Com. To Study AIDS and AIDS Prevention; mem. Adult Congregate Living Facility. Recipient award for svc. to runaways Fla. Network, 1989, plaque for work with troubled youth Friends Fla. Network, 1989; Miami Herald scholar, 1969. Mem. Residential Child Car Assn. (bd. dirs., chmn. advocacy com.), Fla. Network Youth and Family Svcs. (quality assurance com., tng. com.), NAFE. Republican. Roman Catholic. Home: 13679 SW 62nd St Miami FL 33183 Mailing Address: 10521 SW 48th St Miami FL 33165 Office: Residential Pla at Blue Lagoon Inc 5617 NW 7th St Miami FL 33183

BLAND, EVELINE MAE, real estate broker; b. Hughesville, Pa., Aug. 24, 1939; d. Burton Anthony and Mary Margaret (Mack) Morgan; m. Theodore D. Bland; 1 child, Susanna Elisabeth. BA, Mansfield (Pa.) U., 1961; Orff Schulwerk cert., Royal Conservatory, Toronto, Ont., Can., 1976. Tchr. Newburgh (N.Y.) Jr. High Sch., 1961-62, Cedar Grove (N.J.) Bd. Edn., 1962-66, West Caldwell (N.J.) Bd. Edn., 1973-76, Covenant Christian Sch., North Plainfield, N.J., 1976-77; salesperson Janett Realtors, Verona, N.J., 1977-79; sales mgr. Degnan Boyle Realtors, Caldwell, 1979-88, Schlott Realtors, Montclair, 1988—; prin. Camp Shawnee, Waymart, Pa., 1961-71. Organist, choir dir. 1st Conglist Ch., Verona, 1978—; trustree Montclair Hist. Soc., 1970-87; bd. dirs. State Repertory Opera. Mem. Nat. Realtors Assn. (cert.), N.J. Assn. Realtors (profl. stds. and edn. coms. 1987), West Essex Bd. Realtors (v.p., sec. 1985-86, pres. 1987, career trainer 1987, Realtor of Yr. 1987), West Essex C. of C., Montclair C. of C., FIABCI-USA, Lambda Mu. Republican. Baptist. Lodge: Gideons Aux. (various offices 1982-87), Kiwanis.

BLANDIN, NANETTE MARIE, political scientist; b. Seattle, May 10, 1948; d. J. Julien and Evelyn B. Baget; m. Don Michael Blandin, Sept. 2, 1972. Diplome, Institut d'Etudes Politques Universite de Bordeaux (France), 1969; BA in Polit. Sci. and French with honors, U. Calif., Davis, 1970; MPA, Washington Pub. Affairs Ctr. U. So. Calif., 1976. Hdqrs. personnel officer Dept. Mental Hygiene, Sacramento, 1970-72; program dir. Calif. Adv. Coordinating Council Pub. Personnel Mgmt., Sacramento, 1972; budget examiner, mgmt. analyst Exec. Office Pres. Office Mgmt. Budget, Washington, 1973-79; spl. asst. to insp. gen. Dept. Labor, Washington, 1979-80; chief div. assessment and tech. dir. div. program and policy assessment Office of Insp. Gen., Washington, 1980-84; sr. staff mem. Ctr. Pub. Policy Edn. The Brookings Instn., Washington, 1984—; founder, co-chmn. Washington Young Profls Forum, 1974-76; bd. dirs. Nat. Ctr. Pub. Services Internship Programs, 1972-73; prof. adv. bd. George Mason U., 1978-79. Contbr. articles in field; bd. editors Pub. Adminstr. Rev.; bd. dirs., series editor The Bureaucrat. Mem. Am. Soc. Pub. Adminstrn. (chmn. fin. and adminstrn. com. 1979-80, nat. council 1978-81, v.p. Nat. Capital Area chpt., Leadership award Nat. Capital Area 1978), World Future Soc., Pi Sigma Alpha (life). Home: 1913 Shepherd St NW Washington DC 20011 Office: 1775 Massachusetts Ave NW Washington DC 20036

BLANEY, CAROLE ANN, mortgage banking company executive; b. Cheltenham, Eng., Mar. 15, 1946; came to U.S., 1952; d. Matthew Francis and Joan (Barker) B.; m. James Lenners, Jan. 16, 1965 (div. 1980); children: Gregory M., Kathryn M. Lenners McCabe. Student, Anchorage Community Coll., 1974-82; mortgage banker's cert., Northwestern U., 1979; comml. banking cert., U. Wash., 1982. Mgr. mortgage servicing, v.p. Nat. Bank Alaska, Anchorage, 1973-84; mgr. mortgage lending, v.p. United Bank Alaska, Anchorage, 1984-88; owner, pres. Mgmt. Solutions, Alamogordo, N.Mex., 1988—; loan systems officer, cons. mortgage system devel. MAI Data Svcs., Milw. Mem. Nat. Assn. Bank Women, Nat. Assn. Female Execs. Republican. Office: Mgmt Solutions 7050E N Presidio Dr Milwaukee WI 53223

BLANEY, CONNIE GAYLE, jewelry importer and broker; b. Houston, July 21, 1955; d. William Robert Jr. and Billie Beatrice (DicKerson) Henderson; m. William Joseph Blaney, Dec. 1980; children: William Ryan, Kristen Nicole. Postgrad. (hon.), Santa Fe Community Coll., Gainesville, Fla., 1974; AA (hon.), Hillsborough Community COll., Tampa, Fla., 1975; postgrad. (hon.), U. South Fla., 1975; BS (hon.), Middle Tenn. State U., 1977-78. Assoc. tchr. Plant City (Fla.) High Sch., 1978-79; dir. admissions Lakeland (Fla.) Coll., 1979-81; mktg. cons. WVFM Broadcasting, Lakeland, Fla., 1981-82; jewelry importer and broker Jewelry Etcetera, Tampa, 1984—. Contbr. articles to various publs.; jewelry exhibitor, 1st place creative arts, 1987. Mem. Ladies Guild Resurrection Ch., Lakeland, 1984-85, devel. coun. St. Joseph's Hosp., Tampa, Tampa Bay Investment Club, homeroom mother Carrollwood Day Sch., classmother Dancemakers, Tampa, 1988—, team mother Citrus Park Little League. Finalist Arthur Young Entrepreneur of the Yr. award Inc. mag., 1989. Mem. Bus. and Profl. Women's Club Inc. (charter), Profl. Assn. Cert. Divers, YMCA Divers Assn., Boca Ciega Yacht Club, Cleve. Heights Women's Tennis Assn., Phi Theta Kappa (sec. 1975-76), Gamma Beta Phi. Democrat. Roman Catholic.

BLANEY, ELIZABETH CHARLOTTE, journalist, tennis professional; b. Evanston, Ill., May 3, 1954; d. Joseph Addison and Elizabeth Charlotte (von Kahler) Blaney. Student, So. Meth. U., 1975-77; BA in Journalism summa cum laude, Tex. Woman's U., 1990. Asst. tennis profl. Brookhaven Racquet Club, Dallas, 1972-74, Centre Tennis Club, Richardson, Tex., 1977; head tennis profl. Centre Tennis Club, Arlington, Tex., 1978-79, 81-82; player on internat. tennis circuit, 1980-81; tennis profl. Brookhaven Racquet Club, Dallas, 1983-84, Denton (Tex.) Country Club, 1984-90. Recipient Karen Krantacke Sportsmanship award Women's Sports Found., 1980; winner Swedish Open Tennis Tournament, 1981. Mem. Women in Communication Inc., Nat. Assn. Black Journalists, Pi Sigma Alpha. Home: 321 Lake Park Rd Lewisville TX 75057-2307

BLANEY, NANCEE LOU, retirement community executive; b. Hinckley, Ohio, July 29, 1951; d. Edwin Thomas and Alice Josephine (Skorepa) Kolarek; m. Tom William Blaney, July 2, 1972; children: Kevin, Mindy, Megan. Student, Ohio State U., 1972-73; BS, Heidelberg Coll., 1973. Lic. Nursing Home Adminstr., Ohio. Adminstr. Heritage Care Ctr., Shelby, Ohio, 1983-84; pres., chief exec. officer The Good Shepherd, Ashland, Ohio, 1984—. Bd. dirs. Ashland (Ohio) YMCA, 1990-93. Mem. AAUW (sec. local chpt., 1987-89), Altrusa Club of Ashland (Ohio) (treas. 1988-90). Methodist. Office: The Good Shepherd 622 Center St Ashland OH 44805

BLANKE, GAIL ANN, communications executive; b. Cleve., Jan. 20, 1941; d. Warren J. and Isabelle (Voigt) B.; m. Franklin James Cusick, Feb. 22, 1969; children—Katharine Jennings, Abigail Jennings. A.B., Sweet Briar Coll., 1963. Mgr., Lifetime Sports Found., Washington, 1965-66, CBS, N.Y.C., 1966-69; v.p. Allen & Dorwood Advt., N.Y.C., 1969-72; v.p. communications Avon Products, Inc., N.Y.C., 1972—. Mem. YWCA's Acad. Women Achievers, 1984; bd. dirs. Child Care Action Campaign. Recipient Gold Key award PR News, 1987. Mem. Am. Women in Radio and TV (bd. dirs. 1971), Internat. Assn. Bus. Communicators, Assn. Nat. Advertisers (bd. dirs. 1989), Fashion Group Internat. (bd. dirs. 1990), Women's Forum of N.Y., Soc. of Mayflower Descendants, Met. Club, Lawrence Beach Club, Rockaway Hunt Club. Office: Avon Products Inc 9 W 57th St New York NY 10019

BLANKENBAKER, VIRGINIA MURPHY, state legislator; b. Indpls., Mar. 29, 1933; d. Charles J. and Francis June (Hesler) Murphy; m. Richard Blankenbaker, 1959; children: Susan, Sharon, David, Betty, James. BS, Purdue U., 1955; MS, Butler U., 1979. Tchr. Pensacola, 1955-56, Indpls., 1976-81; in pub. relations Colonial Food Store, 1957-59; investment broker A.G. Edwards & Sons, Inc., 1987—; mem. Ind. State Senate, 1981—. Mem. Ch. Health & Human Svcs. Com., 1988—. Republican. Methodist. Office: 5019 N Meridian St Indianapolis IN 46208

BLANKENSHIP, LETHA PEARL, airline flight attendant; b. Grand Junction, Colo., Dec. 6, 1966; d. Glenn Gerald and Margaret Jean (Laymon) B. Postgrad., Arkansas Tech. U., 1987. Cert. tng. flight attendant, American Airlines. Cashier, bookkeeper The Treasure Chest, Dover, Ark., 1979-84, florist, wedding cons., 1979-84; photographer freelance, Russellville, Ark., 1984-85; cashier McDonalds, Russellville, Ark.; receptionist Findley Tanning Salon, Russellville, Ark., 1985-86; sec., receptionist Dan Findley Constrn., Ark., 1986; clerk K-Mart #9711, Russellville, Ark., 1986-87; flight attendant American Airlines, Dallas, 1987—; candidate In-flight tng. instr., Dallas. Active Ark. Tech. U. Theatre, 1984-86, Russellville Community Theatre. Supporter, organizer Walter Hartfield dist. rep., Russellville, 1985. Miss Ark. Tech. U. Pageant contestant, 1985-86, Miss Lake Dardanelle (Ark.) contestant, 1987. Mem. Assn. of Profl. Flight Attendants, Nat. Assn. Female Execs. Methodist. Home: 2635 Verandah Ln #1924 Arlington TX 76006

BLANKENSHIP, NANCY CAROL, state official; b. Springfield, Mo., Apr. 5, 1946; d. Raymond T. and Velda Valeria (Richardson) B.; m. Charles B. Kinser, Dec. 6, 1969 (div. Dec. 1975). Student, Parkview Coll., Springfield, 1964. Cert. nursing home adminstr., Mo. Record technician Springfield Gen. Hosp., 1972-75; dir. med. records Burell, Springfield, 1975-82; adminstr. Mary E. Wilson Home, Springfield, 1982-88; record technician II, Springfield Regional Ctr., State of Mo., 1988—; cons. Ash Grove (Mo.) Nursing Home, 1974-86, also others. Investigator Springfield Commn. on Human Rights, 1984—. Mem. Am. Med. Record Assn. (accredited), Mo. Med. Record Assn., Order Eastern Star, White Shrine Jerusalem. Democrat. Methodist. Home: 1740-B S Kentwood Ave Springfield MO 65804 Office: Springfield Regional Ctr 1515 and Pythian Sts Springfield MO 65802

BLANKERTS, BETH ANN, director food nutrition and support services, educator; b. Toledo, May 30, 1954; d. Justice James and Ruth Eleanor (Boldt) B. BS, Bowling Green State U., Bowling Green, 1977; MPA, Ind. U., Gary, 1988. Lic., registered dietitian, Ohio. Student mgr. Harshman Dorm Bowling Green State U., 1975-77; directory asst. Ohio Bell Telephone Co., Toledo, 1972-76; water safety instr. West Toledo YMCA, Toledo, 1973-78; mgr. Wendy's Internat., Toledo; dir. food svcs. Ara Healthcare Nutrition Svcs., Inc., Phila., 1978-87; dir. food & nutrition Mercy Hosp., Toledo, 1987-90; dir. support svcs. Plazacare Ctr., Toledo, 1990—; part-time faculty Bowling Green State U.; bd. dirs. Mobile Meals Toledo 1989; mem. adv. bd. Macomber Whitney High Sch. Food Program Toledo 1988—; co-chmn. food com. Mercy Hosp. 1988-89. Mem. Am. Dietetic Assn., Toledo Dietetic Assn. (chmn. mgmt. com. 1988-89, pres.-elect), Am. Soc. Hosp. Food Svc. Adminstrs. (pres. N.W. Ohio chpt. 1988-89), Round Table Women in Food Svc., Am. Coll. Healthcare Execs. Republican. Luthern. Home: 3004 Barrington Dr Toledo OH 43606 Office: PlazaCare Ctr 2005 Ashland Toledo OH 43624

BLANKINSHIP, KATHLEEN FLO, personal and professional development company executive, cleaning service executive, cosmetologist; b. Loma Linda, Calif., Nov. 5, 1947; d. Boyde Jefferson and Nell (Miller) Henderson; m. Floyd Jerome Smith, Oct. 25, 1969 (div. 1972); m. 2d Edwin Allen Blankinship, Oct. 15, 1977; 1 child, Robert Allen Smith. Cert. bookkeeping/acctg. Calif. Bus. Sch., San Bernardino, 1966; AA, San Bernardino Valley Coll., 1975; student Riverside (Calif.) City Coll., 1985. Lic. Cosmetologist. Bookkeeper Laurentide Fin. Co., San Bernardino, 1969-70; loan officer Avco Thrift, San Bernardino, 1972-74; waitress Agro Land & Cattle, Colton, Calif., 1974-76; mem. advt. staff Holcombe Pub., San Bernardino, 1976-80; stylist, mgr. Mane St. Hair Design, Loma Linda, Calif., 1980-84; owner, profl. speaker, cons. U.&I Enterprises, Grand Terrace, Calif., 1983—; organizational analyst Pomona Valley Praise Temple, Calif., 1985; rep. Equitable Life Assurance Soc. U.S., 1986; mentor Positive Force, Highland, Calif., 1985; owner Higher Image Hair, Riverside, 1988—; fin. cons. BancVest Fin. Services Inc., 1986; stylist Ann & Friends, 1986-88. Author: Seasons of My Times, 1980, Winning Isn't For Everyone, 1986; contbr. monthly make-over column to mag., 1980-84. Mem. Vols. in Child Abuse and Neglect, 1978; campaign worker McCartney for Judge, 1969-70; Trainer Choices Program Riverside County Sch. Dist., 1986—. Mem. Nat. Assn. Female Execs., Equitable Life Assurance Soc. U.S. (registered rep.), Women in Networking, Greater Riverside C. of C. (bd. dirs. 1986—, chmn. Bus. in Action, chmn. edn. com. 1987—), Redlands C. of C. (ambassador). Republican. Club: S.B. Pro-Club (bd. dirs.). Lodge: Toastmasters. Avocations: skiing, reading, personal development. Home: 3985 Pierce St #320 Riverside CA 92505

BLANKMEYER, BONNIE LOU, psychologist, educator; b. Council Bluffs, Iowa, Oct. 20, 1937; d. Milbourn Lee Chambers and Edna Mae (Bell) Porter; m. Charles E. Blankmeyer, May 21, 1955; children: Charles E. Jr., Diana Marie Knight. BA summa cum laude, U. Tex., San Antonio, 1978; MA, U. Tex., Austin, 1983, PhD, 1985. Lic. psychologist, Tex. Psychometrist dept. psychiatry Health Sci. Ctr. U. Tex., San Antonio, 1973-80, instr., 1985-86, asst. prof., 1986—, coord. inpatient psychol. svcs., 1986—, program dir. eating disorders program, 1990—. Editor psychology news column Med-Line News, 1989-90; contbr. articles to profl. publs. Chair bd. dirs. Crisis Ctr. San Antonio Area, 1974-76. Mem. Bexar County Psychol. Assn., Tex. Psychol. Assn. (continuing edn. com. 1988—), Am. Psychol. Assn., Internat. Neuropsychol. Soc., Soc. Personality Assessment, Nat. Register Health Svc. Providers in Psychology. Office: U Tex Health Sci Ctr 7703 Floyd Curl Dr San Antonio TX 78284-7792

BLANTON, BARBARA, state legislator; b. Crystal Springs, Miss., Sept. 8, 1937; m. Terrell Blanton. Grad., Hinds Jr. Coll. Mem. Hinds Jr. Coll. Alumni Assn. (pres.), Miss. Seat Belt Coalition, Miss. 2001. Baptist. *

BLANTON, PATRICIA LOUISE, periodontal surgeon; b. Clarksville, Tex., July 9, 1941; d. Ben E. and Mildred L. (Russell) B. MS, Baylor U., 1964, PhD, 1967, DDS, 1974, cert., 1975. Diplomate Am. Coll. Bd. Oral Medicine. Teaching asst. Baylor Coll. of Dentistry, Dallas, 1963-67, asst. prof., 1967-70, spl. instr., 1970-73, assoc. prof., 1974-76; resident periodontics VA Hosp., Dallas, 1975; prof. Baylor Coll. of Dentistry, Dallas, 1976-85, Baylor U. Grad. Sch., Dallas, 1976—; prof., chmn. Baylor Coll. of Dentistry, Dallas, 1983-85; cons. VA Hosp., Dallas, 1979-82; adj. prof. Baylor Coll. of Dentistry, Dallas, 1985—; cons. Commn. on Dental Accreditation and Coun. of Dental Edn., 1981—; v.p. State Anatomical Bd., Tex., 1983-85; mem. ADA-AADS Liaison Com., 1983—; chmn. Nat. Insts. Health, Oral Biology and Medicine Study Sect. II, 1985-86. Author: Periodontics for the G.P., 1977, Current Therapy in Dentistry, 1980, An Atlas of the Human Skull, 1980 (1st place honors 1981). Invited participant Am. Coun. on Edn., Austin, 1984; mem. liaison com. Dallas County Dental Soc.-Am. Cancer Soc., Dallas, 1976-78. Named one of Outstanding Young Women in Am., 1976. Fellow Am. Coll. Dentists, Internat. Coll. Dentists; mem. Am. Assn. Anatomists, Am. Acad. Periodontology, Southwest Soc. Periodontology, ADA, Am. Acad. Oral Medicine, Am. Acad. Osseointegration, Xi Psi Phi, Omicron Kappa Upsilon. Office: 4514 Cole Ave Ste 902 Dallas TX 75205

BLASKO, JANICE MARIE, marketing professional; b. Homestead, Pa., Jan. 30, 1958; d. Julius James and Irene Marie (Chorba) B. Lic. pvt. pilot. Coordinator constrn. Catalina Homes, Orlando, Fla., 1982-84; regional mgr. Avian Corp., Orlando, 1984-86; mgr. sales, mktg. Hangar One Inc., Orlando, 1986-89; exec. asst. land devel. and acquisitions Catalina Homes, Inc., Orlando, 1989—. Vol. Goals 2000 Arts Task Force, Orlando, 1987-89; scouting coord. Boy Scouts Am. Mem. Greater Orlando C. of C., Tampa C. of C., Fla. Bus. Travel Assn. Roman Catholic. Club: Aviation Council (Orlando) (sec. 1986-87). Home: 421 Poplar Ct Maitland FL 32751 Office: Catalina Homes Inc 644 Ferguson Dr Orlando FL 32805

BLATNER, SHERRY DIANE, legal administrator; b. N.Y.C., July 4, 1947; d. Fred and Frances (Winer) B.; m. Keith F. Senft, June 14, 1981. BA, Adelphi U., 1969; MA, U. Pa., 1970. Bar: N.Y., 1978. Law clk., then assoc. Shea & Gould, N.Y.C., 1972-79; assoc. Simpson, Thacher & Bartlett, N.Y.C., 1979-81; legal adminstr. Sacks, Tierney & Kasen, Phoenix, 1981-85, Plattner, Silhasek & Schneidman, Phoenix, 1985-87, Winston & Strawn, Phoenix, 1987-88, Bohm, Broder & Koudelka, P.C., Phoenix, 1988—; bd. advisors Nat. Inst. for Paralegal Tng., N.Y.C., 1980-81. Mem. ABA, Assn. Legal Adminstrs., Ariz. Bar Assn. (econs. of law practice sect.). Office: Bohm Broder & Koudelka PC 2141 E Camelback Rd Ste 222 Phoenix AZ 85016

BLATT, ALLISON QUENSEN, business manager; b. Manhattan, Kans., Mar. 28, 1962; d. Jeremiah Lion and Elizabeth Marie (Kempske) B. BA, Concord Coll., Athens, W.Va., 1982, BA in Interdisciplinary Studies, 1982. Mktg. asst. Stage One, Louisville, 1985-86; mktg. intern Pepsico Summerfare, Purchase, N.Y., 1986; dir. ticket svcs. Pa. Stage Co., Allentown, 1986-88; bus. mgr. Dept. Theatre, Lehigh U., Bethlehem, Pa., 1988—. Dir.: (plays) The Cocktail Party, 1983, Tequila, 1984, Bad Habits, 1985, Crossing The Bar, 1989. Named to Outstanding Young Women of Am., 1988. Mem. AAUW, Alpha Psi Omega. Home: 101 N 11th St Apt BB Allentown PA 18102 Office: Lehigh U Dept Theatre 203 Chandler-Ullmann 17 Bethlehem PA 18015

BLATT, BEVERLY FAYE, biologist, consultant; b. Pitts., Mar. 17, 1944; d. Simon and Sadie (Skigen) B.; m. Marc Harry Lavietes, Aug. 13, 1966 (div. June 1987); children: Bryan Ross, Jonathan David; m. David Herman Filipek, Dec. 28, 1987. AB magna cum laude, Vassar Coll., 1965; PhD, Case Western Res. U., 1969; postdoctoral, NYU, 1969-70. Asst. prof. pathology Sch. Medicine NYU, 1971-80; asst. prof. medicine Sch. Medicine SUNY, Bklyn., 1980-84, Stony Brook, 1984-88; sect. head clin. immunology rsch. L.I. Jewish Med. Ctr., New Hyde Park, N.Y., 1986-88; cons. BFB Biocons., Alameda, Calif., 1988—. Co-chair spl. gifts class of 1965 25th reunion, 1988-89, chair 25th reunion gift class of 1965 Vassar Coll., 1989-80. NSF fellow, 1967-69, Am. Cancer Soc. fellow, 1969-70, NIH fellow, 1970-71; N.Y. Arthritis Found. grantee SUNY, 1981-87, NIH grantee, 1971-77, 81-85. Mem. AAAS, Am. Soc. Cell Biology, Am. Women in Sci., Fedn. Am. Scientists, Harvey Soc., N.Y. Acad. Scis. Office: BFB Biocons 3265 Central Ave Alameda CA 94501

BLATT, MELANIE JUDITH, commercial food equipment sales professional; b. Phila., Sept. 29, 1946; d. Jack and Rose (Ginsburg) Weinberger; children: Marnie, Keath, Lindsay. BA, Antioch U., 1980; MA, U. Phoenix, 1989. Cert. human service worker. Social worker Dept. Pub. Welfare Pa., Doylestown, 1977-80; mgr. customer service Qualidine Inc., Lansdale, Pa., 1980-81; sales rep. Sharp Products, Tempe, Ariz., 1982-83, Hobart Corp., Tempe, 1984—. Bd. dirs. Bucks County Jewish Family Service, Bucks City, 1982. Mem. Retail Grocers Assn. Ariz. Home: 9705 E Mountaint View unit 1120 Scottsdale AZ 85258 Office: Hobart Corp 929A Hobokam Dr Tempe AZ 85281

BLATT, NANCIE M., medical company executive; b. Detroit, May 9, 1938; d. Samuel Albert and Bernice Roma (Smokler) Miller; m. Martin Jay Blatt, Aug. 14, 1957; children: Lauren, Susan, Stephanie. BA in Edn., U. Mich., 1962, MA in Edn., 1968; AA (hon.), Schoolcraft Community Coll., 1988. Tchr. Livonia (Mich.) Pub. Schs., 1962-74; collector Stewart Oxygen Svc., Detroit, 1974-76, dir. rsch. and records, 1977-79; asst. to pres. Oxygen Therapy Inst., Oak Park, Mich., 1980-82; adminstrv. dir. Unimed, Ltd., Highland Park, Ill., 1982-87, v.p. adminstrn., 1988—. Trustee Schoolcraft Community Coll., Livonia, 1972-81; candidate Mich. State Ho. of Reps., Livonia, 1977. Democrat. Jewish. Home: 370 D Park Ave E Highland Park IL 60035 Office: Unimed Ltd 555 Vine Ave Highland Park IL 60035

BLATTNER, MEERA MCCUAIG, educator; b. Chgo., Aug. 14, 1930; d. William D. McCuaig and Nina (Spertus) Klevs; m. Minao Kamegai, June 22 1985; children: Douglas, Robert, William. B.A., U. Chgo., 1952; M.S., U. So. Calif., 1966; Ph.D., UCLA, 1973 . Research fellow in computer sci. Harvard U., 1973-74; asst. prof. Rice U., 1974-80; asso. prof. applied sci. U. Calif. at Davis, Livermore, 1980—; adj. prof. U. Tex., Houston, 1977—; vis. prof. U. Paris, 1980; program dir. theoretical computer sci. NSF, Washington, 1979-80. NSF grantee, 1977-81. Mem. Soc. Women Engrs., Assn. Computing Machinery, IEEE Computer Soc. Contbr. articles to profl. jours. Office: U Calif Davis/Livermore Dept Applied Sci Livermore CA 94550

BLATZ, LINDA JEANNE, marketing professional; b. N.Y.C., Dec. 8, 1950; d. William Edmund and Jeanne Grace (Hyman) B. BS, U. Md., 1972. Mgr. sales Milliken & Co., N.Y.C., 1972-81; retail market mgr. Greenwood Mills Mktg. Co., N.Y.C., 1981-89; dist. mgr. Steelcase Inc., N.Y.C., 1989—. Contbr. articles to profl. jours. Mem. N.Y.C. Ballet guild; PEO; mem. jr. com. N.Y.C. Ballet; tng. mgr., membership v.p. N.Y. Jr. League. Mem. Nat. Assn. Uniform Mfrs. and Distbrs., U. Md. Alumni Assn., Am. Woman's Econ. Devel. Corp., Alpha Gamma Delta. Congregationalist. Club: Sandbar Beach (membership bd.).

BLAU, HELEN MARGARET, biology professor; b. London, May 8, 1948; (parents Am. citizens); d. George E. and Gertrude Blau; m. David Spiegel, July 25, 1976; children: Daniel Spiegel, Julia Spiegel. BA in Biology, U. York (Eng.), 1969; MA in Biology, Harvard U., 1970, PhD in Biology, 1975. Predoctoral fellow dept. biology Harvard U., Cambridge, Mass., 1969-75; postdoctoral fellow div. med. genetics U. Calif. Dept. Biochemistry and Biophysics, San Francisco, 1975-78; asst. prof. dept. pharmacology Stanford (Calif.) U., 1978-86, assoc. prof. dept. pharmacology, 1986—; co-chmn. meeting regulation of tissue specific gene expression Fedn. Am. Societies for Experimental Biology, Copper Mountain, Colo., 1990; editorial bd. Jour. of Cell Biology, Somatic Cell Molecular Genetics and Exptl. Cell Rsch. Contbr. articles to profl. jours. Mem. molecular cytology study sect. (ad hoc) NIH, 1987-88; mem. five-yr. planning com., genetics and teratology br. Nat. Inst. for Child Health and Devel./NIH, 1989—. Mellon Found. Faculty fellow, 1979-80; William M. Hume Faculty scholar, 1981-84; grantee NIH, NSF, MDA, March of Dimes, 1978-90; recipient Rsch. Career Devel. award NIH, 1984-89, Smith Kline & Beckman award, 1989-91. Mem. Am. Soc. for Cell Biology (program com. 1990, nominating com. 1985-86). Democrat. Home: 580 Cotton St Menlo Park CA 94025 Office: Stanford U Sch Medicine Pharmecology Dept Stanford CA 94305-5332

BLAU, VICTORIA JEWEL, nurse; b. Lewiston, Idaho, Nov. 9, 1944; d. Earl Joseph and Virginia Josephine (Frazier) Vannoy; m. Jack Lawrence Blau, Aug. 18, 1984; children from previous marriage: Christina Lynn, Melanie Ann. AA, San Joaquin Delta Coll., 1980; BS in Nursing, Calif. State U., 1985. RN, Calif. Med. sec./libr. Kaiser Permenete Clinic, Hayward, Calif., 1963-70; staff nurse-med. surg. Lodi (Calif.) Meml. Hosp., 1980-86, Dameron Hosp., Stockton, Calif., 1986—. Sec., letter writing chair Christian Community Concerns, Lodi, 1985—; letter writer Citizens Leading Effective Action Now, Modesto, Calif., 1986—; mem. Concerned Women for Am., Am. Family Assn., Sacramento, 1988—. Mem. Calif. Nurses Assn. Republican. Baptist. Home: 1216 Devine Dr Lodi CA 95240 Office: Dameron Hosp 525 W Acacia Stockton CA 95210

BLAUVELT, MELINDA, photographer; b. Northampton, Mass., Sept. 15, 1949; d. Theodore Orlando and Melba (Miller) B.; m. Edwin E. Jr. Wells, July 3, 1982; children: Winthrop, Townsend. Student, Mt. Holyoke Coll., 1967-69; BA, Yale Coll., 1971; MFA, Yale Sch. Art, 1973. Lectr. art Smith Coll., Northampton, Mass., 1974; lectr. visual and environ. arts Harvard U., Cambridge, Mass., 1975-76; rsch. fellow Harvard U., Cambridge, 1977-78; asst. prof. art U. Va., Charlottesville, 1978-83. One-woman shows include Harvard U., 1977, 78, Bayly Mus., 1980, Wright Art Ctr. 1981, Southeastern Ctr. Contemporary Art, Winston-Salem, 1981; group shows include Yale Art Gallery, 1973, Addison Gallery Am. Art, 1975, Harvard U., 1975, Va. Mus. Richmond, 1980, Corcorcan Gallery Art, Washington, 1981, 82, 87, Mus. Fine Arts, Houston, 1982; permanent collections include Mus. Fine Arts, Houston, Dallas Mus. Fine Arts, High Mus. Atlanta; contbr. articles to profl. jours. Home and Office: 5 Stanwich Ln Greenwich CT 06830

BLAZON, DENISE G., sales executive; b. Manchester, N.H., Jan. 5, 1952; d. Paul G. and Jeanne (Croteau) Blazon; 1 child, Christina Blazon. AA, U. N.H., Durham, 1976; postgrad., U. Conn., Stamford. Lic. real estate salesperson, N.Y. Food and beverage mgr. Bostma Inc., Concord, N.H., 1976-81; sales coord. Matco Products, Inc., Bedford Hills, N.Y., 1982-85; mfrs. sales rep. Waterline Inc., Butler, N.J., 1985-88; N.E. ter. factory rep. Hydro Air Industries, Inc., Orange, Calif., 1988—. Contbr. Planned Parenthood Fedn. Am., Ea. Paralyzed Vet.'s Assn. Mem. NAFE, NOW (contbr.), Nat. Irrigation Assn., Nat. Spa and Pool Inst., Vietnam Vets. Am. (assoc.). Home and Office: 41 Wenonah Rd Putnam Valley NY 10579

BLEAM, DONNA LEES, real estate executive; b. Quakertown, Pa., June 17, 1944; d. Harry Lawrence and Dorothy (Clark) Lees; m. Howard John Bleam, June 23, 1962; children: Karl David, Kurt Tyler. Student, James Madison U. With sales dept. Home Land Realty Co., Inc., Harrisonburg, Va., 1978-82, assoc. broker, 1982-84; broker, owner Buyers Brokerage, Harrisonburg, 1985—; lectr. in field; chmn. Real Estate Resources, Harrisonburg, 1985—. Author various mag. articles on hist. Va. country property, 1981-82. Bd. dirs. Welcome Wagon, Harrisonburg, 1977-79. Mem. Am. Assn. Real Estate Appraisers (cert.), Va. Assn. Realtors (membership com. 1986-87, profl. standards com. 1987-89, cert. ethics instr. 1987-89, bd. dirs. 1989), Harrisonburg-Rockingham Bd. Realtors (bd. dirs. 1985—, Realtor of Yr. 1987), Real Estate Securities and Syndication Inst., Working Women's Forum (founding mem.), DAR. Office: Buyers Brokerage 420 E Market St Harrisonburg VA 22801

BLECK, PHYLLIS CLAIRE, surgeon, musician; b. Oak Park, Ill., Mar. 10, 1936; d. William Fred and Mildred A. (Jones) B. BS, U. Ill., 1958; MM, Northwestern U., 1968; DMA, U. So. Calif., 1970; postgrad., Autonoma U., Guadalajara, Mex., 1973-76; MD, Rush Med. Coll., 1979; MS in Surgery, U. Ill., 1983. Diplomate Am. Bd. Surgery, Am. Bd. Thoracic Surgery. Prin. trumpet Fla. Symphony Orch., 1960-66, Orch. Sinfonica Nat. de Peru, 1965; instr. Thornton Jr. Coll., 1966-68; lectr. U. So. Calif., 1969-73; asst. prof. Whittier Coll., 1973; asst. in gen. surgery Rush Presbyn. St. Luke's Med. Ctr., Chgo., 1979-82, instr. gen. surgery, 1982-84; resident in cardiothoracic surgery U. Medicine and Dentistry N.J., 1984-87; pvt. practice medicine specializing in cardiothoracic surgery, Aurora, Ill., 1987—. Editor: Mozart Divertimento for Winds; research on vascular ischemia. Fellow Am. Coll. Chest Physicians; mem. Kappa Delta Pi, Pi Kappa Lambda, Sigma Alpha Iota.

BLECK, VIRGINIA ELEANORE, illustrator; b. Waukegan, Ill., Dec. 22, 1929; d. George William and Eugenia (Van Honder) Pavlik; m. Thomas Frank Bleck, June 16, 1951; children: Thomas G., James H., Catherine Bleck-Muschler, Marilynn Bleck-Cobbs, Robert F., Susan M., Linda Bleck-Mai, John W., Charles D. Student, U. Ill., 1947-48, Art Inst. Chgo., 1948-50. Free lance artist Waukegan, Ill., 1950-86; artist Merrill-Chase Galleries, Chgo., 1972-77, Hallmark Cards Inc., Kansas City, Mo., 1977—; owner, operator Bleck Tree Farms, Waukegan, Green Oaks, Grayslake, Ill., 1972—. Republican. Roman Catholic. Home and Office: 10330 W Yorkhouse Rd Waukegan IL 60087

BLECKER, NAOMI PERLE, credit manager; b. N.Y.C., Mar. 3, 1956; d. Sidney and Zelda (Pologe) B. Student, CUNY, 1973-77. Credit mgr. new accounts Gimbel's Dept. Store, N.Y.C., 1975-78; credit mgr. Eue/Screen Gems div. Columbia Pictures Corp., N.Y.C., 1977-82; credit mgr. Trans Am. Video, Inc. AME, Inc., N.Y.C., 1982—. Mem. Nat. Assn. Credit Mgmt. (chmn. motion picture and t.v. group 1982—), Nat. Assn. Female Execs., Am. Jewish Congress. Democrat. Home: 141-30 Pershing Crescent Briarwood New York NY 11435

BLECK-MUSCHLER, CATHERINE MARY, illustrator; b. Waukegan, Ill., Sept. 11, 1956; d. Thomas Frank and Virginia (Pavlik) Bleck; m. George Fredrick Muschler, Nov. 25, 1982; 1 child, Carolyn. BFA, U. Ill., Champaign-Urbana, 1978. Assoc. art dir. Chgo. Tribune, 1979-82; staff illustrator Dallas Times Herald, 1982-83; freelance illustrator Dallas, 1983-86, N.Y.C., 1986-88, Cleve., 1988—. Illustrator: (children's books) Family Skills Series, 1985-86. Recipient Print Regional Design Annual award, Print Mag., 1983, 84, 88, Communications Arts Illustration Annual award, Communication Arts, 1984, 86, 87, Am. Illustrator Annual award, Am. Illustration, 1984, 85, 88, Graphis Internat. award, Graphis, 1983, 84. Mem. Soc. of Illustrators (Annual award 1984, 86).

BLEDSOE, JANE KATHRYN, art museum director, art historian; b. Independence, Mo., Sept. 9, 1937; d. Byron Vickery and Nell Louise (Schroeder) Elerick; m. Charles Edward Bledsoe, Oct. 7, 1956; children: James King, Julie Annette Bledsoe Ainley. BA, Calif. State U., Long Beach, 1974, cert. in mus. studies, 1976, MA, 1981; cert., Mus. Mgmt. Inst., 1981. From asst. to assoc. dir. Univ. Art Mus., Long Beach, 1974-88; dir. Ga. Mus. Art, U. Ga., Athens, 1988—; part-time instr. Christ Coll., Irvine, Calif., 1975-85, Calif. State U., Long Beach, 1974-88; cons. Archtl. Digest mag., L.A., 1982-88. Curator/editor exhbn. and catalog: Anders Zorn Rediscovered, 1984, Figurative Sculpture, 1984 (NEA grant). Mem. Am. Assn. Mus., COll. Art Assn., ArtTable, Inc. (founding mem. L.A. chpt. 1985), Athens Area C. of C. (CVB bd. 1988—), Vintage MG Club So. Calif., Assn. Art Mus. Dirs., Rotary Internat. Home: 594 Caldwell Circle Athens GA 30605 Office: U Ga Ga Mus Art Jackson St-N Campus Athens GA 30602

BLEIDT, BEVERLY JEAN, clinical psychologist, consultant; b. Danville, Ky., July 8, 1948; d. John William Brown and Dorothy Alene (Southwood) Hanks; m. John Justin Bleidt, June 7, 1969; children: John Justin, Lindsey Rutherford. BA, U. Louisville, 1969, MA, 1976, PhD, 1978. Lic. psychologist, Ky. Tchr. Jefferson County Bd. Edn., Louisville, 1969-72, psychometrist, 1974; psychol. cons. Psychol. Consultation Svcs., Louisville, 1979-84; dir. div. support svcs. Office Edn. for Exceptional Children Ky. Dept. Edn., Frankfort, 1984-85; dir. clin. svcs. The Family Place: A Child Abuse Treatment Agy., Louisville, 1985-89; pvt. practice, Louisville, 1979—; psychol. cons. Psychol. Consultation Svcs., Louisville, 1979-84; mem. Child Protection Community Coun., Louisville, 1984-90, Jefferson County Child Victims Treatment Found. Task Force, Louisville, 1988-90; pres., dir., bd. dirs. Exploited Children's Help Orgn. (E.C.H.O.), Louisville, 1989—; psychologist Office Edn. for Excellence in Programming for Students with Emotional Disabilities, Ky. Dept. Edn., Frankfort, 1985-87, Jefferson County Child Abuse Multidisciplinary Team, 1985-87. Bd. dirs. Salvation Army Boys and Girls Club, Louisville, 1979-80, Harvey Brown Counseling Ctr., Louisville, 1985-87; trustee Chance Sch., Inc., Louisville, 1987—. Mem. Am. Psychol. Assn., Ky. Psychol. Assn. Office: Nolan Bldg 2100 Gardiner Ln Ste 307 Louisville KY 40205

BLESSEN, KAREN, free-lance illustrator, designer. BFA, U. Nebr., 1973. Freelance illustrator Dallas Morning News, 1973-86, designer, 1986-89, freelance illustrator, designer, 1989—. Recipient Pulitzer prize Columbia U., 1989; also awards N.Y. Art Dirs. Club, Soc. Newspaper Design, Dallas Press Club. Office: care Dallas Morning News Communications Ctr Dallas TX 75265*

BLESSING-MOORE, JOANN CATHERINE, physician; b. Tacoma, Wash., Sept. 21, 1946; d. Harold R. and Mildred (Benson) Blessing; m. Robert Chester Moore; 1 child, Ahna. BA in Chemistry, Syracuse U., 1968; MD, SUNY, Syracuse, 1972. Diplomate Am. Bd. Pediatrics, Am. Bd. Allergy Immunology, Am. Bd. Pediatric Pulmonology. Pediatric intern, then resident Stanford U. Sch. Medicine, Palo Alto, Calif., 1972-75, allergy pulmonology fellow, 1975-77, co-dir. allergy pulmonology dept. Children's Hosp., 1977-84, clin. asst. prof. dept. pediatrics, 1977-84, co-dir. pulmonology lab., 1977-84; clin. asst. prof. dept. immunology Stanford U. Hosp., 1987—; allergist Palo Alto Med. Clinic, 1984-90; pvt. practice allergy immunology-pulmonary Palo Alto, Calif., 1990—; dir. ednl. program for children with asthma Camp Wheeze, Palo Alto, 1975—; cons. in field. Author handbooks, camp program manuals; co-editor jour. supplements; contbr. articles to sci. publs. Leader Med. Explorer troop Boy Scouts Am., 1987-90; bd. dirs., commr. San Mateo and Santa Clara County Lung Assn., 1978-89; mem. coms. Woodside (Calif.) Elem. Schs., 1989—. Fellow Am. Acad. Allergy Immunology (various offices 1980—), Am. Coll. Allergy Immunology, Am. Coll. Chest Physicians (com. mem. 1980—), Am. Acad. Pediatrics (mem. com. 1980—); mem. Am. Thoracic Soc., Am. Lung Assn., N. Calif. Allergy Found. (bd. dirs., pres.), Penninsula Women's Assn., Santa Clara County Med. Soc., Chi Omega. Republican. Presbyterian. Office: 770 Welch Rd #232 Palo Alto CA 94301 also: 29 Baywood Ste #1 San Mateo CA 94402 also: Stanford Univ Hosp Dept Immunology Palo Alto CA 94304

BLETTER, ROSEMARIE HAAG, architectural history educator; b. Heilbronn, Germany, Feb. 27, 1941; came to U.S., 1956; d. Karl and Johanna (Bischoff) Haag; m. Robert Bletter, Nov. 28, 1964 (dec. 1975); 1 child, Nathaniel; m. Martin Filler, June 3, 1978. BS cum laude, Columbia U., 1962, MA, 1967, PhD, 1973. Guest lectr. Yale U., New Haven, 1973-74; asst. prof., assoc. prof. Columbia U., N.Y.C., 1974-83; guest curator Whitney Mus. Am. Art, N.Y.C., 1983-85; adj. assoc. prof. Inst. Fine Arts, NYU, N.Y.C., 1984-87; prof. archtl. history Grad. Ctr., CUNY, 1987—; vis. assoc. prof. Rutgers U., New Brunswick, N.J., 1986-87; guest curator Bklyn. Mus., 1975; panelist Dept. Cultural Affairs, N.Y.C., 1985, Pennsylvania Avenue Devel. Corp., Washington, 1988; reviewer div. pub. programs NEH, Washington, 1979—. Author: Skyscraper Style, 1975, Venturi, Rauch and Scott Brown, 1984; co-author: El Arquitecto Josep Vilaseca i Casannovas, 1977; contbr. numerous articles onn modern architecture to profl. jours.; writer, cons. documentary films Beyond Utopia, Arata Isozaki, James Stirling, 1983-87. Fellow Am. Coun. Learned Socs., 1977-78, Rockefeller Found., 1984-85; grantee Graham Found. for Advanced Studies in Fine Arts, 1980-81, N.Y. State Coun. on Arts, 1983-84, Nat. Endowment for Arts, 1985. Mem. Soc. Archtl. Historians (bd. dirs. 1981-84), Coll. Art Assn. Am. Home: 200 East End Ave Apt 11B New York NY 10128 Office: CUNY Grad Ctr 33 W 42d St New York NY 10128

BLEVINS, FLORENCE EVELYN, banker; b. Gainesville, Tex., Apr. 5, 1933; d. Joseph Bernard and Anna (Walterschied)Walter; m. Barry Eugene Blevins, Nov. 26, 1953; children: Belinda, Thomas, Philip, Joseph and Susan. BBA in Acctg., U. Tex., Odessa, 1977. CPA, Tex.; cert. fin. planner. Acct., office mgr. Graham & Assocs., Odessa, Tex., 1977-82; trust office First State Bank, Odessa, 1983-85; asst. v.p., trust officer Bank One, Tex. (formerly M-Bank), Odessa, 1985—. Vol. Rep. Party,Odessa, 1988; treas. Permian Playhouse, Inc., Odessa, 1986-88; sec. Cath. Charities, Inc., Odessa, 1987—. Named Vol. of the Yr., Permian Playhouse, Inc., Odessa, 1988. Mem. AAUW (membership chmn. 1984-89), Tex. Soc. CPA's, Permian Basin CPA's. Republican. Roman Catholic. Home: 3602 Maple Odessa TX 79762

BLEVINS, KIMBERLY ANN, communications executive; b. Tulsa, Oct. 19, 1964; d. Larry Dwight and Sybil Mae (Snow) Markle; m. Jack Douglas Blevins, May 26, 1984; 1 child, Kayla Marie. BS in Mktg., S.W. Mo. State U., 1987. Mktg. dir. Acqua-Mist Cleaning Sys., Nixa, Mo., 1987-88; communications asst. Baird, Kurtz & Dobson, CPAs, Springfield, Mo., 1988—. Contbr. articles to profl. jours. Mem. Women in Communications (newsletter editor/sec. 1989-90), Springfield C. of C. (women's div. publicity chmn. 1988-89), Pub. Rels. Soc. Am. Office: Baird Kurtz & Dobson 901 Saint Louis PO Box 1900 Springfield MO 65801

BLEWITT, JOAN MCGUINESS, college administrator; b. Wilkes-Barre, Pa., Sept. 11, 1952; d. William and Marion (Schmidle) McGuiness; m. Charles George Blewitt, Sept. 18, 1982; 1 child, John Charles. BS, Coll. Misericordia, Dallas, Pa., 1974; MA, Marywood Coll., Scranton, Pa., 1980; PhD, U. Pa., 1985. Nat. cert. counselor. Tchr. Bridgewater-Raritan (N.J.) Sch. Dist., 1974-77; reading diagnostician Wilkes Coll., Wilkes-Barre, 1977-80, counselor, 1978-81; adminstr. Coll. Misericordia, 1981; dir. career planning and placement King's Coll., Wilkes-Barre, 1982—. Bd. dirs. Salvation Army, Wilkes-Barre, 1988—. Mem. AACD, Am. Assn. for Sch., Coll. and Univ. Staffing, Am. Assn. for Tng. and Devel., Coll. Placement Coun., Mid. Atlantic Assn. for Sch., Coll. and Univ. Staffing, Mid. Atlantic Placement Assn., Wilkes-Barre C. of C. (bd. dirs. exec. women's coun. 1989—, mem. grad. leadership program), AAUW. Office: King's Coll 133 N River St Wilkes-Barre PA 18711

BLEYMAN, LEA KANNER, biology educator, genetics researcher; b. Halle, Germany, Nov. 9, 1936; came to U.S., 1946; d. Salomon David and Amalia Kanner; 1 child, Anne. BA magna cum laude, Brandeis U., 1958; MA, Columbia U., 1961; PhD, Ind. U., 1966. Rsch. assoc. U. Ill., Urbana, 1964-69, U. N.C., Chapel Hill, 1970-72; assoc. prof. biology Baruch Coll., CUNY, 1973-78, prof., 1979—, chmn. dept. natural scis., 1981-83. Co-author: (lab. manual) General Biology, 1982; asst. editor Protozoological Actualities, 1979; mem. editorial bd. Jour. Protozoology, 1985—; contbr. articles to profl. jours. Bd. dirs. Aux. Enterprises Corp., N.Y.C., 1983—, CUNY Women's Rsch. and Devel. Fund, 1986—, 305 E 24th Street Corp., N.Y.C., 1989—. Grad. fellow USPHS, 1961-64, rsch. fellow Sigma Xi, 1974, Max Planck Inst., Berlin, 1974, Chancellors faculty fellow CUNY, 1985-86; scholar Baruch Coll., 1987. Mem. AAAS, Am. Assn. Women in Sci., Am. Genetics Assn., Am. Soc. Cell Biology, Genetics Soc. Am., Soc. Protozoologists (exec. com. 1981-86), N.Y. Acad. Scis. Office: Baruch Coll CUNY 17 Lexington Ave New York NY 10010

BLINN, LORENA VIRGINIA, natural sciences educator; b. East Chicago, Ind., Sept. 8, 1939; d. Ralph Hastings and Edith (Harwell) Stoops; m. Gerald H. Martin, Aug. 21, 1971 (div. May 1982); children: Matthew Christopher, Elizabeth Ashley; m. Walter Craig Blinn, May 18, 1985. BS in Pre-Med./Chemistry, U. Ga., 1961, MS in Zoology/Sci. Edn., 1964; PhD in Sci. Edn./Geology, Mich. State U., 1971. Biology tchr. McIntyre Park Sr. High Sch., Thomasville, Ga., 1961-62; instr. dept. natural sci. Mich. State U., East Lansing, 1964-71, assoc., 1971-80, prof., 1985-89, prof. Ctr. Integrative Studies Gen. Sci., Ctr. Natural Sci., 1989—. Co-editor: Natural Science Lab Manual, 1976; contbr. articles to profl. jours. Founder, pres. Friends of Historic Williamston (Mich.), 1974; founder Williamston Mine Reclamation Com., 1982; sec. bd. dirs. Capital Area Wildlife Rehab. Assn., Lansing, Mich., 1989—. Recipient Leaders in Am. Sci. award, 1968. Mem. Nat. Sci. Tchrs. Assn., AAAS. Office: Mich State U 117 N Kedzie Hall East Lansing MI 48823

BLISS, DOROTHY CRANDALL, biologist, educator; b. Westerly, R.I., Feb. 20, 1916; d. Frank Henry and Alice Addie (Arnold) Crandall; m. Paul Bayton Bliss, Mar. 6, 1969 (dec.); 1 stepchild, Dorothy Bliss Raines. BS, U. R.I., 1936, MS, 1938; PhD, U. Tenn., 1957. Instr. sci. Westerly (R.I.) Jr. High Sch., 1936-37, Greebrier Coll., Lewisburg, W.Va., 1941-43, So. Sem. & Jr. Coll., Buena Vista, Va., 1943-47, U. Wyo., Laramie, 1947-49; adj. prof. Biology Randolph-Macon Woman's Coll., Lynchburg, Va., 1949-59; assoc. prof. Biology Randolph-Macon Woman's Coll., Lynchburg, 1959-68; prof. Biology Randolph-Macon Women's Coll., Lynchburg, 1968-83. Contbr. numerous articles to profl. jours. Mem. bd. dirs. Friends Lynchburg Streams & Valleys, 1984-90. Recipient So. Fellowship Fund, Ea. Nat. Park & Monument Assn., 1955-56, rsch. grantee, 1966-69, John Shelton Horsely rsch. award, VAS, 1959; grantee U.S. Forest Svcs., 1962; Outstanding Educator Am., 1974-75. Fellow Va. Acad. Sci. (elected award, 1980, Shelton Horsely rsch. award 1959, grant 1975); mem. Am. Fern Soc., So. Appalacian Bot. Club (v.p. 1964, pres. 1966), Assn. Southeastern Biologists (sec. 1967-70, v.p. 1972-73), Ecol. Soc. Am. Va. Native Plant Soc. (botany chmn.), Phi Kappa Phi, Sigma Xi. *-. Home: 322 Sumpter St Lynchburg VA 24503

BLISS, TAMARA COLLEEN, dance educator; b. Newport, Wash., Sept. 23, 1952; d. Gordon Frazey and Patricia Alice (Nevers) B.; m. Dennis Seymour Diamond, July 4, 1985. Student, Spokane Falls Coll., 1970-73; BA in Dance Theatre, Western Wash. State U., 1975; AAS in Fashion Design, Fashion Inst. Tech., N.Y.C., 1987; cert. fitness, Marymount Manhattan Coll., 1988. Modern dance instr. Community Assn. Schs. for Arts, St. Louis, 1976-78; dancer, performer Metro Theatre Circus, St. Louis, 1976-78, Wimmer, Wimmer & Dancers, Salt Lake City, Phila., 1979-83; jazz dance instr. Sch. Pa. Ballet, Phila., 1981-84; ind. arts in edn. tchr. Pa. Coun. on Arts, Gettysburg, York, 1984-85; dance tchr. Tappan Zee Dance Group, Tarrytown, N.Y., 1985-89; adj. instr. Marymount Manhattan Coll., N.Y.C., 1989—; dancer, performer Rachel Lampert & Dancers, N.Y.C., 1986—; personal fitness instr., N.Y.C., 1987—; costume cons. Marymount Manhattan Coll., 1988—; fabric rep. Alta Moda Textiles, Montreal, 1990—. Choreographer, performer: In the Gallery, On My Own, 1984. Western States Arts Found. grantee, 1974. Mem. Internat. Dance Exercise Assn. Democrat. Office: Marymount Manhattan Coll 221 E 71st St New York NY 10021

BLISS, VALERIE ELIZABETH, marketing director, consultant; b. Elmhurst, Ill., Oct. 18, 1964; d. James Victor and Carole Joyce (Baker) B. BS in Mktg., Ill. State U., 1987. Ins. agt. MONY Fin. Svcs., Chgo., 1987-88; sales rep. Southwestern Bell, Darien, Ill., 1987-88; dir. mktg. Rhodes/Am., Chgo., 1988—; mktg. cons. N.Y. Bronze, Newark, 1988—. Poll judge Ill. State U., Normal, 1987. Mem. Am. Furniture Mfg., Am. Concrete Inst., Am. Mktg. Assn., Am. Hardware Mfr., Am. Silver Inst., Pi beta Phi Alumni Assn. Republican. Adventist. Home: 1800 Vista Ct #102 Schaumburg IL 60193 Office: Rhodes Am Steel Wool 2825 W 31st St Chicago IL 60623

BLISSERT, JULIE HARRISON, public relations adminstrator; b. Cottage Grove, Oreg., Mar. 23, 1954; d. Wilfred James and Marjorie Frances (Stennick) Harrison; m. Albert Duryea Blissert, June 25, 1977. Student, U. Sussex, Eng., 1974-75; AB summa cum laude, Occidental Coll., 1976; cert., Radcliffe Coll., 1976. Editorial asst. Simon & Schuster Pocket Books, N.Y.C., 1976-77; prodn. asst. U. Okla. Press, Norman, 1977-79; copy editor Post-Standard, Syracuse, N.Y., 1979-80; reporter Syracuse Newspapers Oswego (N.Y.) Bur., 1980-83; asst. dir. pub. affairs SUNY, Oswego, 1983-84, dir. pub. affairs, 1984—; freelance editor U. Okla. Press, Norman, 1978-79, Health Awareness Publs., East Syracuse, N.Y., 1979-87, Syracuse U. Press, 1982-83. Mem. Women in Communications, Inc., Nat. Issues Forum of Oswego (steering com. 1983—, convenor 1984, 85), Greater Oswego C. of C. (mem. com. 1986—, com. chair 1990—), SUNY Coun. Univ. Affairs and Devel., Oswego County Press Club, Phi Beta Kappa. Office: SUNY 509 Culkin Hall Oswego NY 13126

BLISSITT, PATRICIA ANN, nurse; b. Knoxville, Tenn., Sept. 23, 1953; d. Dewitt Talmadge and Imogene (Bailey) B. BS in Nursing with high honors, U. Tenn., 1976, MS in Nursing, 1985. RN, cert. critical care nurse, cert. neurosci. nurse. Staff nurse neurosci. unit City of Memphis Hosp., 1976-78, head nurse neurosci. unit, 1978-79; physician's asst. Dr. John D. Wilson, Columbus, Miss., 1979-81; staff nurse med.-surg.-trauma intensive care unit U. Tenn. Meml. Hosp., Knoxville, 1982-83; staff nurse neurosci. intensive care unit Bapt. Meml. Hosp., Memphis, 1985-86, clin. nurse specialist neurosci., 1986—; nurse cons. neurosci. VA Hosp., Memphis, 1986; mem. adv. com. Tenn. Bd. Nursing Practice. Contbr. articles to profl. jours. Mem. editorial cons. bd. Focus on Critical Care, 1990—. Mem. Am. Assn. Neurosci. Nurses (pres. local chpt. 1989-90, treas. local chpt. 1987-89, nat. lectr., resource devel. com., continuing edn.-annual sci. program com., chair patient edn. com.), Am. Assn. Spinal Cord Injury Nurses, AACCN (lectr., CCRN corp. exam devel. com. 1989—, editorial cons. bd. Focus on Critical Care 1990—, pres.-elect Greater Memphis area chpt. 1989-90, pres. 1990-91), Am. Nurses Assn. (coun. med. and surg. nurses, coun. clin. nurse specialists), Tenn. Nurses Assn., Nat. Head Injury Found., Nat. Stroke Assn. Methodist. Avocation: music. Home: Blair Tower 810 Washington Ave Apt 315 Memphis TN 38105 Office: Bapt Meml Hosp 899 Madison Ave Memphis TN 38146

BLITZ, PEGGY SANDERFUR, corporate travel management company official; b. Pitts., Apr. 12, 1940; d. Charles I. and Rebecca Polk (McBride) Wallace; m. Clark L. Blitz, Aug. 25, 1962 (div. Apr. 1974); children: Danette

L., Jonathan D. BS, Ball State U., 1962; postgrad., No. Ill. U., 1976-77. Cert. speech therapist, spl. edn. tchr. Tchr. mentally retarded Anderson (Ind.) Pub. Schs., 1962-64; speech therapist Elgin (Ill.) Pub. Schs., 1964-66; pvt. practice speech therapy Elgin, 1966-68; tchr. mentally retarded Easter Seal Rehab. Ctr., Elgin, 1968-77; account exec. Whitehall Hotel, Chgo., 1977-79; regional mgr. IVI Travel Inc., Milw., 1979-85; sr. v.p. IVI Travel Inc., Dallas, 1985-88; pres. Travelmasters, Inc., Chgo., 1988—, 1989—; mem. adv. bd. Pan Am., 1988-90. Presbyterian. Home: 505 N Lake Shore Dr #1913 Chicago IL 60611 Office: Travelmasters Inc 450 W Algonquin Rd Arlington Heights IL 60005

BLIZNAKOV, MILKA TCHERNEVA, architect; b. Varna, Bulgaria, Sept. 20, 1927; came to U.S., 1961, naturalized, 1966; d. Ivan Dimitrov and Maria Kesarova (Khorozova) Tchernev; m. Emile G. Bliznakov, Oct. 23, 1954 (div. Apr., 1974). Architect-engr. diploma, State Tech. U., Sofia, 1951; Ph.D., Engring.-Structural Inst., Sofia, 1959; Ph.D. in Architecture, Columbia U., 1971. Sr. researcher Ministry Heavy Industry, Sofia, 1950-53; pvt. practice architecture Sofia, 1954-59; assoc. architect Noel Combrisson, Paris, 1959-61; designer Perkins & Will Partnership, White Plains, N.Y., 1963-67; project architect Lathrop Douglass, N.Y.C., 1967-71; assoc. prof. architecture and planning Sch. Architecture, U. Tex., Austin, 1972-74; prof. Coll. Architecture, Va. Poly. Inst. and State U., Blacksburg, 1974—; prin. Blacksburg, 1975—; bd. dirs., founder Internat. Archives Women in Architecture, Va. Poly. Inst. and State U. Prin. works include Speedwell Ave. Urban Renewal, Morristown, N.J., 1967-69, Wilmington (Del.) Urban Renewal, 1968-70, Springfield (Ill.) Central Area Devel, 1969-71, Arlington County (Va.) Redevel, 1975-77. William Kinne scholar, summer 1970; vis. scholar Inst. Advanced Russian Studies, The Wilson Ctr. of Smithsonian Instn., 1988; NEA grantee, 1973-74; Am. Beautiful Found. grantee, 1973; Fulbright Hays research fellow, 1983-84; Internat. Research and Exchange Bd. grantee, 1984. Mem. Internat. Archive Women in Architecture (founder, chair bd. dirs.), Am. Assn. Tchrs. Slavic and East European Langs., Soc. Archtl. Historians, Nat. Trust Hist. Preservation, Am. Assn. Advancement of Slavic Studies, Assn. Collegiate Schs. of Planning, Inst. Modern Russian Culture (chairperson architecture, co-founder, dir.), Assn. Collegiate Schs. of Architecture. Home: 2813 Tall Oaks Dr Blacksburg VA 24060 Office: Va Poly Inst and State U Coll Architecture Blacksburg VA 24061

BLOCH, ANDREA LYNN, physical therapist; b. Cleve., Nov. 25, 1952; d. Sanford and Nadalane Lee (Benchell) B. BA in Zoology, Miami U., Oxford, Ohio, 1974; MA, Kent State U., 1975; Cert. in Phys. Therapy, Ohio State U., 1977. Lic. phys. therapist, Ohio. Asst. dir. phys. therapy The Mt. Sinai Med. Ctr., Cleve., 1977-86; dir. rehab. therapy svcs. Marymount Hosp., Garfield Heights, Ohio, 1986-88; pres., owner Bloch Phys. Therapy, Inc., University Heights, Ohio, 1988—. Editor newsletter Cleve. Phys. Therapy Orthopedic Study Group, 1989—; contbr. articles to profl. jours. Chmn. essays/posters contest University Heights Meml. Day Parade, 1985-87, com. mem., 1985—. Mem. NAFE, Am. Phys. Therapy Assn., Am. Alliance for Health, Phys. Edn., Recreation, and Dance, Am. Back Soc., Am. Soc. Profl. and Exec. Women, Delta Zeta Cleve. Eastside Alumnae Assn. (chmn. ways and means program 1987, v.p. 1988-90, pres. 1990—), Eta Sigma Gamma. Home: 2586 Warrensville Ctr Rd University Heights OH 44118

BLOCH, BARBARA JOYCE, author, editor; b. N.Y.C., May 26, 1925; d. Emil William and Dorothy (Lowengrund) B.; m. Joseph B. Sanders, Aug. 3, 1944 (div. 1961); children: Elizabeth Sanders-Hines, Ellen Janice Benjamin; m. 2d, Theodore S. Benjamin, Sept. 20, 1964. Student, NYU, 1943-45, New Sch. Social Rsch., 1966. Office mgr. Writers War Bd., N.Y.C., 1943-45, Westchester Dem. Com., White Plains, N.Y., 1955-56; mgr. Westchester Symphony Orch., 1957-62; mng. editor Cooking Ency., Rutledge Books, N.Y.C., 1970-71; pres. Internat. Cookbook Services, White Plains, 1978—; columnist House Beautiful, 1984-87; cons. in field; tchr. cooking classes White Plains, 1975-80; lectr. in field. Author: Anyone Can Quilt, 1975; Meat Board Meat Book, 1977; If It Doesn't Pan Out, 1981; Garnishing Made Easy, 1983; editor/author: All Beef Cookbook, 1973; In Glass Naturally, 1974; Fresh Ideas with Mushrooms, 1977; Holly Farms Complete Chicken Cookbook, 1984; Gulden's Cookbook, 1985, A Centennial Celebration-Recipes from Solo, 1988, Salute to the Great American Chefs, 1988, Microwave Party Cooking, 1988, TCBY and More, 1989, A Little Jewish Cookbook, 1989; Am. adapter The Cuisine of Olympe, 1983, Baking Easy and Elegant, 1984, Best of Cold Foods, 1985, Cakes and Pastries, 1985, series of 12 Creative Cuisine books, 1985, The Art of Cooking, 1986, The Art of Baking, 1987, A Century of Recipes from Solo, 1988; editor contbr. various books; contbr. articles to profl. jours. Nat. bd. dirs. Emcampment for Citizenship, N.Y.C., 1966-72; bd. dirs. YWCA Central Westchester, 1965-71, Westchester Ethical Humanist Soc., 1968-70; exec. com., pres. Internat. Student Exchange of White Plains, 1955-70; bd. dirs. Westchester Chamber Music Soc., 1986—. Jewish. Home and Office: Internat Cookbook Svcs 21 Dupont Ave White Plains NY 10605

BLOCH, JULIA CHANG, government official; b. Chefoo, Peoples Republic of China, Mar. 2, 1942; came to U.S., 1951, naturalized, 1962; d. Fu-yun and Eva (Yeh) Chang; m. Stuart Marshall Bloch, Dec. 21, 1968. BA, U. Calif., Berkeley, 1964; MA, Harvard U., 1967, postgrad. in mgmt., 1987; DHL (hon.), Northeastern U., Boston, 1986. Vol. Peace Corps, Sabah, Malaysia, 1964-66, tng. officer East Asia and Pacific region, Washington, 1967-68, evaluation officer, 1968-70; mem. minority staff U.S. Senate Select Com. on Nutrition and Human Needs, Washington, 1971-76, chief minority counsel, 1976-77; dep. dir. Office of African Affairs, U.S. Internat. Communications Agy., Washington, 1977-80; fellow Inst. Politics, Harvard U., Cambridge, Mass., 1980-81; asst. adminstr. Bur. for Food for Peace and Voluntary Assistance, AID, Washington, 1981-87, asst. adminstr. Bur. for Asia and Near East, 1987-88; assoc. U.S.-Japan Rels. Program, Ctr. for Internat. Affairs, Harvard U., Cambridge, Mass., 1988-89; ambassador to Kingdom of Nepal, 1989—; U.S. Senate rep. World Conf. on Internat. Women's Yr., Mex., 1975; advisor U.S. Del. to Food and Agr. Orgn. Conf., Rome, 1975; rep. Am. Council Young Polit. Leaders, Peoples Republic China, 1977; charter mem. Sr. Exec. Service, 1979; head U.S. del. Biennial Session World Food Programme, Rome, 1981-86, Devel. Assistance Com. Meeting on Non-Govtl. Orgns., Paris, 1985, Intergovtl. Group on Indonesia, The Hague, The Netherlands, 1987, World Bank Consultative Group Meeting, Paris, 1987; mem. com. to visit art mus., 1989—; mem. U.S. Nat. Com. for Pacific Econ. Cooperation, 1984—; mem. adv. bd. Women's Campaign Fund, 1976-78; exec. bd. mem. Internat. Ctr. for Research on Women, 1974-81; bd. dirs. Minority Legis. Edn. Prgoram, 1976-78; pres. Nat. Peace Corps counsel, 1988-89; trustee Shriver Peace Worker program. Co-author: Chinese Home Cooking, 1986. Mem. exec. bd. Internat. Ctr. for Research on Women, 1974-81; mem. adv. bd. Women's Campaign Fund, 1976-78, Nat. Women's Polit. Caucus, 1978-84, Nat. Presdl. Debate Forum, 1987—; mem. nat. adv. council Experiment in Internat. Living, 1981—; bd. dirs. Minority Legis. Edn. Program, 1976-78. Recipient Hubert Humphrey award for internat. service, 1979, Humanitarian Service award AID, 1987, Leader for Peace award Peace Corps, 1987, Asian Am. Leadership award, 1989; named Outstanding Woman of Color, Nat. Inst. for Women of Color, 1982, Woman of Distinction, Nat. Conf. for Coll. Women Student Leaders and Women of Achievement, 1987, Woman of Yr. Orgn. Chinese Am. Women, 1987, Disting. Pub. Svc. award Nat. Assn. Profl. Asian Pacific Am. Women, 1989; Ford Found. Study fellow for internat. devel. Harvard U., 1966. Mem. Exec. Women in Govt., Orgn. Chinese Am. Women (founder, chair 1977—, bd. dirs., Woman of Yr. 1987), Asia Soc. (pres. coun. 1989—), Prytannean Honor Soc., Mortar Bd. Republican. Avocations: ceramics, gourmet cooking, collecting art. Office: US Dept State NEA/INS Rm 5251 NS Washington DC 20523

BLOCK, DIANE ZUERN, manager; b. N. Y., Nov. 1, 1946; d. Herman and Lillian (Zuern) Block. Student, Am. Acad. of Dramatic Arts, N.Y.C., 1962-64, Xavier U., Cin., 1981. Asst. sec. Exec. Office Environ., Boston, 1972-74; v.p. Kellerman Corp., Miami, Fla., 1974-76; adminstrv. dir., cons. The Talbott Group, N.Y., 1976-82; dir. proxy services Chruchill Communications Corp., N.Y., 1982--. Auhtor: (anthology) From Sea to Sea, 1986; (book, poetry) Nonentity, 1974. Mem. Vietman Vet. Am., Queens, N.Y., Newtown Civic Orgn., Queens. With U.S. Navy, 1967-69. Mem. Nat. Investor Relations Inst., Am. Soc. Corp. Secs., Security Industry Assn., Internat. Platform Assn., Acad. Poets. Democrat. Home: 84-49 Elmhurst Ave New York NY 11373 Office: Churchill Communications 500 8th Ave New York NY 10018

BLOCK, JANET LEVEN (MRS. JOSEPH E. ROSEN), public relations consultant; b. Chgo.; d. Benjamin J. and Rosebud (Goldsmith) Leven; student Brenau Coll. for Women, Gainesville, Ga., Northwestern U.; m. Albert William Block, Sept. 27, 1947 (div.); m. Joseph E. Rosen, Dec. 5, 1985; children: Mitchell, Stephanie Block McEwen. Reporter, Chgo. Am. Newspaper, 1939-40; catalog advt. Alden's Chgo. Mail Order Co., N.Y.C., Chgo., 1940-42; stylist and public relations dir. Fashion Advt. Co., N.Y.C., 1942-44; asst. account exec., stylist Buchanan & Co., Advt. Agy., N.Y.C., 1944-46; advt. agy account exec. Abbott Kimball Co., Chgo., 1946-47; free-lance merchandising and public relations rep., Cin., 1960-64; v.p. public relations, spl. events Lazarus (previously Shillito's), Cin., 1964-87; cons. pub. relations and advt. Cin., 1987—. Bd. dirs. Children's Heart Assn., 1975—; bd. dirs. Friends of Hamilton County Parks, 1979-80, treas., 1982; vice chair adv. bd. Hoxworth Blood Ctr., 1986-88; bd. dirs. ARC, 1984-86, Salvation Army, 1983-85; Great Rivers council Girl Scouts U.S.A., 1980-83, Family Service, 1985-88; Cin. Commn. on the Arts, Cin. Ballet 1985—; mem. licensing com. Cin. Bicentennial Com., 1985-87; trustee Wood Hudson Cancer Rsch. Lab., 1988—. Recipient Silver Medal award Advertisers' Club Cin., 1976; named YWCA Career Woman of Achievement, 1982. Mem. Fashion Group Cin. (past regional dir.), Downtown Council (promotion chmn. 1975-76, 80-81), Public Relations Soc. Am. (dir. 1974-75, sec. 1976, treas. 1977), TV Soc. Am., Bus. and Profl. Women's Club, Advt. Club. Cin. (dir. 1967—, v.p. 1972, Advt. Woman of Yr. 1972, mem. Speakers Bur. 1973—, pres. 1973-74, AAF Silver medal 1976), Women in Communications. Home: 2324 Madison Rd #1107 Cincinnati OH 45208

BLOCK, LYNNE WOOD, accountant; b. New Orleans, July 13, 1943; d. John Sorber and Emilie Douglas (Poe) Wood: m. Lawrence Richard Block, Oct. 2, 1983. Student, Ursuline Acad., 1957-61, Hunter Coll., 1968-69, Pace U., 1978-79. Clk. Dunn & Bradstreet, New Orleans, 1961-64; fashion model Stewart Model's, N.Y.C., 1965-70; prin. The Real Tinsel Antiques, N.Y.C., 1970-75, Other World Furniture Imports, W. Hampton, N.Y., 1976, The Lynne Wood Co., N.Y.C., Ft. Myers Beach, Fla., 1976—; owner Lynne's Studded Jackets, 1988—; seminar leader, Ft. Myers Beach, 1983-88; cons. Cross and Desire Corp., N.Y.C., 1980—. Author: Evelyn the Raccoon, 1984, Photos in American Heritage Magazine, 1990; one-man shows include VCCA, 1989, 90, Chuck Levitan Gallery, N.Y.C. of Port-A-Shrines. Named Model of Yr., Photography Annual, 1968; Va. Ctr. for Creative Arts fellow, 1990. Mem. Pilot Internat., Am. Bus. Women's Assn. (sec. 1986—).

BLOCK, MAURINE, retired business owner; b. Ft. Worth, Aug. 23, 1914; d. Louis Block and Rae (Goldsmith) Adler. BJ, U. Mo., 1935. Book reviewer Dallas News, Dallas Times Herald, 1936-40; copywriter retail group Sears Roebuck & Co., Dallas, 1940-41, advt. mgr., 1941-49; advt. and pub. rels. mgr. Dallas Iron & Wire Wks., Dallas, 1949-61; editor Bankers Digest, Dallas, 1961-65; corr. Advt. Age, Printing Impressions Bus. Ins., Dallas, 1960-77; owner Maurine Block Advt. and Editing, Dallas, 1965-77. Active in past various civic orgns. Recipient Silver medal Am. Advt. Fedn., Dallas, 1984; Benjamin Franklin fellow Royal Soc. Arts Eng., London, 1959. Mem. Dallas Advt. League (hon. life, Most Valuable Mem. 1956), Press Club Dallas (bd. dirs. 1989-91), Women in Communications (Matrix award 1957). Home: 4015 Stonebridge Dr Dallas TX 75204

BLOCK, PAMELA JO, vocational training administrator; b. Freeport, Ill., May 25, 1947; d. Carl and Leona Mae (Stukenberg) B. BS, Iowa State U., 1969; MEd, U. Ill., 1973. Tchr. Palatine (Ill.) High Sch., 1969-85, dept. chairperson, 1973-85; mgr. N.W. Suburban Career Coop., Palatine, 1985—; cons. Household Internat., Prospect Heights, Ill., 1982-83; evaluator Ill. State Bd. Edn., 1976—. Contbr. articles to profl. jours. Mem. suburban adv. coun. United Way, 1984-87; mem. exec. bd. N.W. suburban coun. Boy Scouts Am., 1989—, Schaumburg-Elk Grove (Ill.) Mental Health Ctr., 1990—; bd. dirs. Ill. Women's Agenda, Chgo., 1986-87. Named Outstanding Young Woman of Ill., 1982, Charlotte Danforth Woman of Achievement, Women in Mgmt., 1989. Mem. AAUW (pres. Wheeling-Buffalo Grove, Ill. br. 1982-84, chairperson Ill. div. found. 1985-87, mem. program com., mem. nat. found. 1987—, mem. rsch. adv. panel 1989—), Am. Vocat. Assn., Rotary (chairperson vocat. svc. com. Buffalo Grove lub 1987-88). Home: 190 Woodstone Dr Buffalo Grove IL 60089 Office: NW Suburban Career Coop 1750 S Roselle Rd Palatine IL 60067

BLOCKSOM, RITA VERLENE HAYNES, special education educator; b. Decatur, Ill., Sept. 13, 1952; d. Verne Floyd Haynes and Lura Emily (Wiley) Brockett; m. Richard Brian Day, June 21, 1970 (div. Apr. 1976); m. Bruce Willard Blocksom, Nov. 22, 1978; children: Jason Matthew, Jaimee Erickа. BS, Eastern Ill. U., 1984; MA, Wright State U., 1988. Cert. elem., spl. and gifted edn. tchr., Ill., Ohio. Dir. Engine City Sta., Olney, Ill., 1980-84; author, cons. Pinâroo Pub., Bend, Oreg., 1987-88; author, editor D.O.K. Publs., East Aurora, N.Y., 1986-88; ednl. cons. Sch. Profl. Psychology Wright State U., Dayton, Ohio, 1986-87; dir., cons. Children's program, Wright State U., Dayton, Ohio, 1987—. Author: Nurturing Early Promise, 1988; (with others) Gifted Education, 1988; co-editor: Pre-primary/Primary Center, 1988; (ednl. series) Create-A-Kid Series, 1986-88. Recipient Cert. of Merit Ohio Assn. Gifted Children, 1986-88. Mem. Assn. Supervision and Curriculum Devel., Nat. Assn. Gifted Children, Phi Delta Kappa. Home: PO Box 310 Logansport IN 47649

BLOEMER, ROSEMARY CELESTE, bookkeeper, accountant; b. St. Louis, Jan. 26, 1930; d. Edward J. and Leslie F. (McCreary) Walsh; m. Edward H. Bloemer, Sept. 4, 1948; children: Stephen, Diane, Janet. Cert. in court reporting, Bayside Coll., San Francisco, 1948; student, U. Mo., St. Louis, 1949-51, 83. Teller Roosevelt Savs. & Loan, 1967; income tax sec. Boatmen's Nat. Bank, St. Louis, 1968-73; sec. psychology dept. Washington U., St. Louis, 1978; beverages contr. Chase-Park Plaza Hotel, St. Louis, 1977-81; owner Bloemer Tax Service, St. Louis, 1975—; legal sec. Lickhalter Law Office, St. Louis, 1970-88, Law Office of James K. Steitz, St. Louis, 1981-83; bookkeeper, tax advisor Mo. Hwy. Patrol Assn., Inc., St. Louis, 1981-83; bookkeeper, tax acct. Mo. State Hwy. Patrol Civilian Employees Assn., St. Louis, 1983—; acct. Clarion Hotel, St. Louis, 1986, Bel-Air Hilton Inn, St. Louis, 1984-85; consignment standard stock machine screws, contr. accounts receivable Consol. Aluminum Co., 1973-75; sec. to 5 fin. specialists Community Devel. Agy., St. Louis, 1980-81. Arbitrator, shopper, speaker Bur. Bus. Bur. St. Louis, 1980—; sec. to pres. Bd. Higher Edn., Christian Ch., 1975-77; vol. in choir Shrine of St. Joseph, St. Louis. Mem. Nat. Soc. Tax Profls., Nat. Assn. Tax Practitioners, Am. Soc. Notaries; Internat. Platform Assn. Roman Catholic. Home and Office: 1435 Trampe St Saint Louis MO 63138

BLOESCH, MAUREEN LEE, jewelry designer and manufacturer, educator; b. Bronx, N.Y., Dec. 17, 1942; d. Milton Radison Rappaport and Harriette Dorothy (Tag) Becker; m. Melvyn Bernstein (div.); children: David Lawrence, Daniel Glenn, Aaron Leonard; m. Frederic Stuart Bloesch, Apr. 1, 1981. Student, Saunders Trade Sch., 1960, Flushing Beauty Sch., Queens, N.Y., 1969, N.Y.C. Community Coll., CUNY, 1974. Lic. child care provider, cosmetologist, N.Y.; cert. CPR responder. Owner Lee the Traveling Barber & Beautician, Putnan Valley, N.Y., 1969—; jewelry designer, owner, mfr. Bloesch & Bloesch Originals, Putnan Valley, 1985—; art dir. Splty. Industries Inc., Bronx, 1970-78; asst. installer All County Security Inc., Putnam Valley, 1984; mgr. No. Lights Crystal Co., Westchester, N.Y., 1984; personal sec. Century 21 Richard Harris Realty, Peekskill, N.Y., 1985-90; tchr. crafts Bedford (N.Y.) Correctional Instn., 1990—, Tandy Leather Co., N.Y., 1st Presbyn. Ch., N.Y. Mem. Putnam Valley Ambulance Corps, 1990—, Putnam Valley Women's Orgn., 1990—. Recipient cert. of appreciation Sta. PBS-TV, Tex., 1990. Democrat. Home: PO Box 273 Putnam Valley NY 10579 Office: 47 Trail to the Hemlocks Putnam Valley NY 10579

BLOISE, LINDA ELIZABETH, film company director, educator; b. Chgo., Oct. 2, 1948; d. Harry Joseph and Elizabeth Agnes (Gordon) Fanning; m. Robert John Bloise, Jan. 19, 1974 (div. May 1989); children: Rosemary, Robert, Suzanne. BS, Loyola U., Chgo., 1971. Educator Chgo. Pub. Schs., 1972-77; asst. dir. Terra Nova Film, Chgo., 1985—; pres. Beverly Family Ctr., Chgo., 1982-84. Contbr. articles to profl. jours. Mem. Women in the Dir.'s Chair, Nat. Coun. on Aging, Mid Am. Congress on Aging, Am. Soc. on Aging, Am. Film and Video Assn. Democrat. Roman Catholic. Home: 2557 W 117th St Chicago IL 60655 Office: Terra Nova Films 9848 S Winchester Ave Chicago IL 60643

BLOMME, KAY LYNN, marine service and supply company executive; b. Mt. Clemens, Mich., Aug. 25, 1959; d. William C. and Patricia Ann (Strunk) B. Student, MacComb Community Coll., Warren, Mich., 1977-80, Oakland Community Coll., Auburn Hills, Mich., 1981-84, Coll. Charleston, S.C., 1985-86. Cashier Ponderosa Restaurant, Warren, 1975-76; sales clk., asst. mgr. Sears Roebuck and Co., Troy, Mich., 1976-78; asst. restaurant mgr. Burger Chef Systems, Inc., Hazel Park, Mich., 1978; area mgr., buyer Korvettes, Inc., Madison Heights, Mich., 1978-80; promotional clk. Warner, Elektra, Atlantic Rcd., Southfield, Mich., 1981; account exec. Lieberman Enterprises, Elk Grove, Ill., 1981-83, Bus. Resources, Inc., Ann Arbor, Mich., 1983-84; pres., owner Kay's Marine Svc. and Supply Co., Inc., Mt. Pleasant, S.C., 1984—. Asst. editor Way Point Guide, 1988. Organizer, worker C.A.R.E., Carter Jr. High., 1971-74. Recipient Award of Excellence U.S. Pres. Nixon, Warren, 1974. Fellow NAFE, NABER, Low Country Womens Network; mem. NOW. Home: #99 St Phillips St Unit 115 Charleston SC 29403 Office: Kay's Marine Svc and Supply 215 Coleman Blvd Mount Pleasant SC 29464

BLOMQUIST, SUSAN GAIL, graphic artist; b. Chgo., Dec. 25, 1953; d. Howard Joseph and Evelyn Gene (Reynolds) B. A.A., Am. Acad. Art, 1973. Apprentice prodn. artist Am. Graphics, Chgo., 1973-74; prodn. mgr. Graphic Services, Chgo., 1974-77; gen. mgr. Graphic Connections, Chgo., 1977-80; freelance prodn. artist Source/Inc., Chgo., 1980-82, Perception, Chgo., 1982-84; prodn. art dir. Robert Case & Assoc., Chgo., 1984-86; freelance prodn. artist, 1986—. Illustrations pub. in Talk to Yourself, Why Not, 1976. Recipient of Robert Allerton Art Scholar., U. of Il., 1969, auto crossing first place award, 1979, 80, 81. Mem. Nat. Assn. Female Execs. Club: Porsche of Am. (sec. 1981-82) (Chgo.). Avocations: auto racing; skiing; community theater. Home: 401 Fullerton Pkwy Apt 603 E Chicago IL 60614

BLONDIN, ETHEL, Canadian legislator; b. Ft. Norman, N.W.T., Can., Mar. 25, 1951; d. Cecilia Modeste; children: Troy Zanl, Tanya, Timothy George. Asst. dept. minister of culture N.W.T.; mem. from Western Arctic riding Ho. of Commons, Ottawa, Ont., Can., 1988—. Mem. mcpl. couns. and sch. adv. bds.; bd. dirs. Can. Native Arts Found., Arctic Inst. N.Am. Liberal. Roman Catholic. Office: House of Commons, Parliament Bldgs, Ottawa, ON Canada K1A 0A6*

BLOOD, KAREN A., data processing executive; b. Springfield, Mass., Nov. 11, 1959; d. James Clayton and Dorothy Virginia (Walters) B. Student, U. Md., Hood Coll., Frederick, Md. Pres. Scorpion Sys., Inc., Frederick, 1980—. Past pres. Women's Ctr. Council, 1985—; gubernatorial appointee Jud. Nominating Commn. for 6th Dist., 1988—; elected del. Dem. Nat. Conv., 1988; speaker, exhibitor, organizer Frederick Women's Fair, 1985-90; bd. dirs. Women Entrepreneurs Balt., 1989—. Named Outstanding Young Marylander; named Bus. and Profl. Women Woman of the Yr. Mem. IEEE (western Md. subsection past chair), Internat. Electrical and Electronics Engrs., Frederick County C. of C. (past v.p.). Office: 40 E Patrick St Frederick MD 21701

BLOOM, BARBARA L., office services company executive; b. Cleve., Jan. 19, 1939; m. Louis D. Tuber, Dec. 19, 1976; children: Kevin Margolis, Vicki Margolis. Student, Ohio State U. Pres. Statler Office Svcs. and Exec. Suite, Cleve., 1981—. Recipient Greater Cleve. Enterprising Women Pace Setter award. Mem. NAFE, Women Bus. Owners Assn., Exec. Suite Network, Nat. Assn. Sectl. Svcs., Cleve. Exec. Assn., Profl. Secs. Internat., Rotary. Office: 1127 Euclid Ave #375 Cleveland OH 44115

BLOOM, CLAIRE, actress; b. London, Feb. 15, 1931; d. Edward Max and Elizabeth (Grew) Blume; m. Rod Steiger, Sept. 19, 1959 (div. Jan. 1969); 1 child, Anna Justine; m. PHilip Roth, April 29, 1990. Student, Badminton Sch., Bristol, Eng., Fern Hill Manor, New Milton, Eng., Guildhall Sch. Music and Drama, London. Appeared as Ophelia, Stratford-Upon-Avon, 1948; plays include also Ring Around the Moon, London, 1949-51, Romeo and Juliet, also as Juliet in Old Vic tour of U.S.; film roles in limelight Richard III, 1956, Alexander the Great, 1956, The Brothers Karamazov, 1958, Look Back in Anger, 1958, The Brothers Grimm, 1962, The Chapman Report, 1962, The Haunting, 1963, 80,000 Suspects, 1963, Alta Infidelita, 1963, Il Maestro di Vigeuono, 1963, The Outrage, 1964, The Spy Who Came in from the Cold, 1965, The Illustrated Man, 1969, Three into Two Won't Go, 1969, A Severed Head, 1971, A Doll's House, 1973, Islands in the Stream, 1976, Clash of the Titans, 1981, Always, 1984, Sammy and Rosie, 1987, Crimes and Misdemeanors, 1989; Broadway prodns. include Rashomon, 1959; other theatre appearances include Altona, Royal Court Theatre, London, 1960, A Doll's House, Hedda Gabler, 1971, Vivat! Vivat Regina!, 1972; N.Y. appearance The Innocents, 1976; London appearances A Doll's House, 1973, A Streetcar Named Desire, 1974, Rosmersholm, 1977, The Cherry Orchard, 1981, These are Women, 1982-83, When We Dead Awaken, 1990; many roles Brit. and U.S. TV including In Praise of Love, 1975, A Legacy, 1975, Henry VIII, 1979, Hamlet, 1979, The Ghost Writer, 1983, Cymebeline, 1983, King John, 1983, Brideshead Revisited, 1981, Shadowlands, 1984, Time and the Conways, 1985, Queenie, 1987, Anastasia, 1987, Shadow in the Sun, 1988; author: Limelight and After, 1982. Recipient Evening Standard award, London, 1974, Brit. Film and TV award, London, 1984. Office: William Morris Agy 1350 6th Ave New York NY 10019

BLOOM, OLIVE ZOE, office manager; b. Sterling, Kans., Jan. 5, 1933; d. Archie J. and Virginia Mae (Hutchins) Selfridge; m. Lewis Theil Bloom; children: R. Lamont, Barry T., James E. BS in Home Econs., Sterling Coll., 1965. Sec. physician's office Pratt, Kans., 1980—. Campaign worker Nancy Kasselbaum race for U.S. senator, Kans.; mem. Hosp. Aux., pres., 1979-80. Mem. Kans. Med. Soc. Aux. (sec. 1989-90), AAUW (pres. 1982-83), Ninnescah Med. Soc. Aux. (pres. 1989-90). Republican. Methodist. Home and Office: 1408 E Maple Pratt KS 67124

BLOOM, SUSAN, computer executive; b. Dorchester, Mass., Jan. 24, 1951; d. Stephen and M. Elaine (Doran) Vlachos; m. William D. Doyle, Sept. 21, 1974 (div. 1979); m. J. Robert Bloom, July 22, 1982. B in Econs., Smith Coll., 1976. Merchandiser Zayer Corp., Framingham, Mass., 1976-79; mgr. agy. automation Comml. Union, Boston, 1979-82; lead analyst Southeast Bank, Miami, Fla., 1982-85; mgr. bus. design Am. Express, Great Neck, N.Y., 1985-86; officer, system devel. TIAA-CREF, N.Y.C., 1986—; v.p. Cambridge Bus. Services, Miami, Fla. and N.Y.C., 1983—. Contbr. articles to profl. jours.; editor: Handbook of Business Strategies, 1986. Tchr. SETA-Women Off Welfare, Boston, 1981, tutor, 1987. Mem. Nat. Assn. Female Execs., Nat. System Design Analysts (co-founder, dir.), Nat. Assn. Ins. Women. Roman Catholic.

BLOOMER, ELIZABETH MARY, economist; b. Dallas, Nov. 3, 1962; d. Herbert Allan and Elizabeth Jane (Baker) B.; m. Christopher James Phelan, Jan. 2, 1988. BA in Econs., Mills Coll., 1985; MA in Econs., U. Chgo., 1987, postgrad., 1987—. Staff cons. Planmetrics, Inc., Chgo., 1987-88; industry economist IRS, Chgo., 1988—. Vol. Cook County Rep. Party, 1990, Lynn Martin for Cook County Rep. U.S. Senate, 1990; vol. adult literacy tutor Chgo. Literacy Project. Mem. Am. Mgmt. Assn., Am. Friends of London Sch. Econs., NAFE, Mills Coll. Alumnae Assn. (vol. Chgo. chpt. 1985—). Roman Catholic. Office: IRS 230 S Dearborn DPN 19-5 Chicago IL 60604

BLOOMFIELD, GEORGETTA SNYDER, healthcare marketing company executive, consultant; b. Chambersburg, Pa., July 28, 1952; d. Mark Philip and Ruby (Harbor) Snyder; m. James C. Bloomfield, June 17, 1977; children: Rebecca A., James C. Jr. BSW, Shippensburg U., 1975. Community svc. rep. Manor Healthcare Corp., Silver Spring, Md., 1987-87; with Vis. Nurse Assn. York County, York, Pa., 1987-88; dir. community rels. Sr. Lifestyels, Inc., Phila., 1988—. Mem. Acad. Health Svcs. Mktg., Women in Communication. Home: 2ll8 Sycamore Rd York PA 17404 Office: Sr Lifestyles Inc 3377 Fox Run Rd Dover PA 17315

BLOOMFIELD, SERENA LURIE, psychologist; b. Petersburg, Va., Aug. 26, 1953; d. Robert and Elizabeth (Franklin) Lurie; m. Stephen I. Bloomfield, Oct. 22, 1983; children: Rachel M., Sophie A. BA, Smith Coll., 1975; MEd, U. Mass., 1978, EdD, 1985. Coord. family therapy tng. Franklin County Mental Health Assn., Greenfield, Mass., 1979-83; clin. dir. Ctr. for

Human Devel., Springfield, Mass., 1983-86; pvt. practice psychologist Amherst, Mass., 1986—; co-owner Bloomfield Assocs., Amherst, 1989—; cons. psychologist Mass. Dept. Social Svcs., Springfield, 1983—, People's Bridge Action, Athol, Mass., 1987—, Crossroads Community Growth Ctr., 1986-88. Mem. Am. Assn. for Marriage and Family Therapy (clin.), Am. Psychol. Assn., Assn. Family and Conciliation Cts., Zonta (bd. dirs. Northampton, Mass. chpt. 1989). Office: 441 West St Ste C Amherst MA 01002

BLOOMGARDEN, KATHLEEN FINN, public relations executive; b. N.Y.C., June 9, 1949; d. David and Laura (Zeisler) Finn; m. Zachary Bloomgarden; children: Rachel, Keith, Matthew. BA, Brown U., 1970; MA, Columbia U., PhD. Pres. Rsch. & Forecasts, N.Y.C., Ruder Finn, N.Y.C., 1988—. Bd. dirs. N.Y. Arthritis Found. Mem. Pub. Rels. Soc. Am., Nat. Investor Rels. Inst., Women's Forum, Young Pres.'s Orgn., Pharm. Advt. Coun., Swedish-Am. C. of C, CARE (bd. dirs.). Jewish. Home: 1084 North Ave New Rochelle NY 10804 Office: Ruder Finn 301 E 57th St New York NY 10022

BLOOMQUIST, EUNICE I., physiologist; b. Worcester, Mass., Sept. 9, 1940; d. Rudolph Adrian and Carrie Helen (Stone) B.; m. Al-Walid I. El-Bermani, June 27, 1970 (div.); children: Noah El-Bermani, Alia El-Bermani. BS, Simmons Coll., Boston, 1963; PhD, Boston U., 1968. Fellow Tufts U., Sch. Medicine, Boston, 1968-69, instr., 1969-70, asst. prof., 1970-75; assoc. prof. Tufts U., Sch. Medicine, Dental Medicine, Vet. Medicine, Boston, 1975-84; assoc. prof. Tufts U., The Sackler Sch. Grad. Biomed. Scis., Boston, 1975-84, acting chmn. physiology dept., 1980-84, prof., 1984—. Contbr. articles to profl. jours. Grantee Nat. Heart, Lung and Blood Inst. Mem. Am. Physiol. Soc., Soc. Gen. Physiologists. Office: Tufts U 136 Harrison Ave Boston MA 02111

BLOS, JOAN W., author, critic, lecturer; b. N.Y.C., Dec. 9, 1928; m. Peter Blos, Jr., 1953; 2 children, 1 deceased. B.A., Vassar Coll., 1950; M.A., CCNY, 1956. Asso. publs. div., mem. tchr. edn. faculty Bank St. Coll. Edn., N.Y.C., 1958-70; lectr. Sch. Edn., U. Mich., Ann Arbor, 1972-80; U.S. editor Children's Literature in Education, 1976-81. Author: "It's Spring!" She Said, 1968, (with Betty Miles) Just Think!, 1971, A Gathering of Days: A New England Girl's Journal, 1830-32, 1979 (Newbery medal ALA, Am. Book award 1980), Martin's Hats, 1984, Brothers of the Heart: A Story of the Old Northwest, 1837-1838, 1985, Old Henry, 1987, Lottie's Circus, 1989, The Grandpa Days, 1989, One Very Best Valentine's Day, 1990. Office: care Curtis Brown Ltd Ten Astor Pl New York NY 10003

BLOSSER, PATRICIA ELLEN, science educator; b. Wayne County, Ohio, Apr. 17, 1931; d. Russell Ford and Mabel Ellen (Kastor) B. BA, Wooster Coll., 1953; MA, U. No. Colo., 1956; MA in Liberal Studies, Wesleyan U., 1962; PhD, Ohio State U., 1970. Cert. secondary sch. sci. tchr., Ohio, Colo., Ill. Tchr. secondary sch. sci., 1953-67; teaching and research assoc. Ohio State U., Columbus, 1967-70, prof. sci. edn., 1970—; rsch. assoc. Edn. Resources Info. Ctr. Clearing House for Sci., Math. and Environ. Edn., 1970; dir. user svcs. Edn. Resources Info. Ctr., 1979—; presenter in-service tchr. workshops. Editor: Investigations in Science Education, 1978-89; mem. editorial bd. Sci. Edn.; contbr. articles to profl. jours. Named Master Tchr. Jennings Found., 1964; U.S. Office Edn. grantee, 1970, 72. Mem. Am. Edn1. Rsch. Assn., Assn. Edn. Tchrs. in Sci. (pres. 1976-77), Assn. Supervision and Curriculum Devel., Assn. Tchr. Educators, Nat. Sci. Tchrs. Assn. (bd. dirs. 1966-68, 76-77, 78-80, 88-89), Nat. Assn. Rsch. in Sci. Teaching (bd. dir. 1984-87, pres. 1988-89), Nat. Sci. Suprs. Assn., Phi Delta Kappa (pres. Ohio State U. chpt. 1976-77), Delta Kappa Gamma (Margaret I. White fellowship awards 1967, 69). Office: 249 Arps Hall 1945 N High St Columbus OH 43210

BLOSSOM, BETH, public relations consultant; b. Babylon, N.Y., June 14, 1926; d. Sumner Newton and Edna (Stroh) B.; m. Robert Roy Metz, Aug. 16, 1952 (div. Dec. 1976); children: Robert Sumner, Christopher Roy. Student, U. N.H., 1944-46; grad. diploma, Am. Acad. Dramatic Arts, N.Y.C., 1948. Editorial asst. Celebrity Svc. Inc., N.Y.C., 1948; producer/writer Sta. WNBC, N.Y.C., 1949-52; writer/publicist press dept. NBC, N.Y.C., 1952-56; pub. rels. cons., ptnr. Pub. Libr. Prodns., Inc., N.Y.C., 1965-73; assoc. dir. Communications Ctr., Population Inst., N.Y.C., 1974-77; pub. rels. dir. Toy Mfrs. of Am., N.Y.C., 1978-82; ind. pub. rels. cons. Babylon, 1982—. Mem. Pub. Rels. Soc. Am. Home and Office: 71 Independence Ave Babylon NY 11702

BLOUNT, EVELYN, religious organization administrator; b. Winder, Ga., Oct. 20, 1942; d. Willie Brown and Ouida (Pool) B. BS, Woman's Coll. Ga., 1964; MRE, So. Bapt. Theol. Sem., 1969. Tchr. Blue Mountain (Miss.) Coll., 1964-66, Berkman High Sch., Gwinnette County, Ga., 1966-67; group leader Bapt. Ctr., Louisville, Ky., 1967-69; min. edn. 1st Bapt. Ch., Auburn, Ala., 1969-70; Acteens dir. Woman's Missionary Union, Aux. Ga. Bapt. Conv., Atlanta, 1970-73; youth dept. supr., field svcs. dir., nat. enlargement plan dir., program design specialist Woman's Missionary Union Aux. So. Bapt. Conv., Birmingham, Ala., 1973-85; exec. dir. Woman's Missionary Union Aux. S.C. Bapt. Conv., Columbia, 1985—; mem. prenatal mission project adv. group S.C. Dept. Health and Environ. Control; bd. dirs. Teen Pregnancy Reduction Network, Inc. Author: Code E and Teachers Guide for Code E, 1973, (with others) Youth Ministry Missions Projects, 1978. Named hon. life mem. USAF Air Def., 1959. Mem. NAFE, Exec. Dirs. Democrat. Home: 300 Friarsgate Blvd Irmo SC 29063

BLOXHAM, ELEANOR JOAN EARLE, manager investment operations; b. Joliet, Ill., Oct. 28, 1957; d. John Sutherland and Eleanor Grace (Lee) E., m. Robert Alan Bloxham, May 31, 1975. BA in English magna cum laude, Louisiana State U., 1980; MBA in Fin., NYU, 1985. From acceptance tester to assoc. mgr. Prudential Asset Mgmt. Co., Florham Park, N.J., 1980-87, mgr., cost acctg., budgeting, 1987-88; mgr., investment op. Prudential Gateway Investors, Newark, N.J., 1988—. Mem. Nat. Orgn. Women, 1989, SEECQ, literacy trainer Op. Upgrade, 1980, Baton Rouge, La., 1979, 1980. Stern scholar NYU, 1990. Mem. Nat. Assn. Female Execs., NYU Fin. Club, Soc. Presbyterian. Home: 105 White Meadow Rd Rockaway NJ 07866 Office: Prudential Plaza Bldg Newark NJ 07109

BLUE, CATHERINE ANNE, lawyer; b. Boston, Feb. 17, 1957; d. James Daniel and Angela Devina (Savini) Mahoney; m. Donald Sherwood Blue, Oct. 4, 1980; children: Mairead Catherine, Edward Pierce. BA, Stonehill Coll., North Easton, Mass., 1977; JD, Coll. William and Mary, 1980. Bar: Pa. 1980. Atty., Aluminum Co. Am., Pitts., 1980-83, Pa. Dept. Revenue, Harrisburg, 1983-85, State Workmen's Ins. Fund, Pitts., 1985-87, Met. Pitts. Pub. Broadcasting (name now QED Communications Inc.), 1987—. Mem. Pa. Bar Assn., Allegheny County Bar Assn. Democrat. Home: 118 Washington St Pittsburgh PA 15218 Office: QED Communications Inc 4802 Fifth Ave Pittsburgh PA 15213

BLUE, ROSE, author, educator; b. N.Y.C.; d. Irving and Frieda (Rosenberg) Bluestone. BA, Bklyn. Coll.; postgrad. Bank St. Coll. Edn., 1967. Tchr., N.Y.C. Public Schs., 1967—; writing cons. Bklyn. Coll. Sch. Edn., 1981-83. Author: A Quiet Place, 1969; Black, Black Beautiful Black, 1969, How Many Blocks Is The World, 1970, Bed-Stuy Beat, 1970, I Am Here (Yo Estoy Aqui), 1971, A Month of Sundays, 1972, Grandma Didn't Wave Back, 1972 (teleplay 1983), Nikki 108, 1973, We are Chicano, 1973, The Preacher's Kid, 1975, Seven Years from Home, 1976, The Yo Yo Kid, 1976, The Thirteenth Year, 1977, Cold Rain on the Water, 1979, My Mother The Witch, 1981 (teleplay 1984), Everybody's Evy, 1985, Heart to Heart, 1986, Goodbye Forever Tree, 1987, The Secret Papers of Camp Get Around, 1988; lyricist: Drama of Love, 1964, Let's Face It, 1961, Give Me a Break, 1962, My Heartstrings Keep Me Tied To You, 1963, Homecoming Party, 1966. Contbg. editor: Teacher mag., Day Care mag. Mem. Authors Guild Am., Authors League Am., PEN, Mensa, Profl. Women's Caucus, Broadcast Music, Inc. Home and Office: 1320 51st St Brooklyn NY 11219

BLUE, SHANDA GENEVIEVE HANSMA, controller; b. Grand Rapids, Mich., Mar. 26, 1948; d. Willard Ray and Evelyn Gene (Leech) Hansma; m. Lare Dillman Heckman, Mar. 1971 (div. May 1974); 1 child, Danyi Hansma Heckaman; m. Courtney Allen Blue, Aug. 23, 1975; children: Morgan Genevieve, Graydon Courtney. Student, Western Mich. U., 1969, Ancilla Coll., Donaldson, Ind., 1970-71, Goshen Coll., 1973, 1983, I.U. Purdue U., Indpls., 1976. Dentist's asst. Stephen P. Hunt D.D.S., Cromwell, Ind., 1976-77; computer coordinator Starcraft, Goshen, Ind., 1982-85; controller The Local Craftsman, Syracuse, Ind., 1985—. Guest author, theatre review River City, 1982; author poems. Bd. treas. Lakeland Community Services, 1985—, democrat candidate, Syracuse Town Bd., 1986, 89, election bd. Democrat mem., 1987-90, trustee, Syracuse Library Bd., 1988—. mem. NAFE, Internat. Women's Writing Guild, American Acad. Poets. Lutheran. Office: The Local Craftsman Syracuse Webster Rd Syracuse IN 46567

BLUESTEIN, JUDITH ANN, rabbi, educator, diversified industry executive; b. Cin., Apr. 2, 1948; d. Paul Harold and Joan Ruth (Straus) Bluestein; BA, U. Pa., 1969; postgrad. Am. Sch. Classical Studies, Athens, Greece, 1968, Vergilian Soc., 1970, 76, 77, 78, Hebrew Union Coll., Jewish Inst. Religion, Jerusalem, 1971, 1979-80, Am. Acad. in Rome, 1975; MA in Religion, Case Western Res. U., 1973, MA in Latin, 1973; MEd, Xavier U., 1984; MAHL, Hebrew Union Coll.-Jewish Inst. Religion, Cin., 1983; MPhil Hebrew Union Coll., 1989. Ordained rabbi, 1984. Sec., Paul H. Bluestein & Co., Cin., 1964—; v.p. Panel Machine Co., 1966—, Blujay Corp., 1966—, Ermet Products Corp., 1966—; ptnr. Companhia Engenheiros Indsl. Bluestein do Brasil, Cin., 1971—; tchr. Latin, Cin. Public Schs., 1973-79; rabbi Temple Israel, Marion, Ohio, 1980-84, Temple Sholom, Galesburg, Ill., 1985-86; co-chmn. Interfaith Plea for Soviet Jews, 1986; lectr. Hebrew Union Coll.-Jewish Inst. Religion, 1986-89; vis. lectr./Jewish chaplain Denison U., 1987-88; vis. lectr. Ind. U., Bloomington, 1989—; bd. dirs. Cin. Council for Soviet Jews, 1982-84, 85—, sec. 1985-87. Fellow Case Western Reserve U., 1970-73, Hebrew Union Coll.-Jewish Inst. Religion, 1985—; Revson fellow Jewish Theol Sem. Am., 1984-85; Hausmon Meml. fellow Hebrew Union Coll. Jewish Inst. Religion, 1985-86; Isadore and Goldie Millstone fellow Hebrew Union Coll., 1986-87, Julia and Leo Forchheimer fellow, 1987-89., Mrs. Henry Morganthau fellow Hebrew Union Coll., 1989—. Mem. Archeol. Inst. Am., Assn. Jewish Studies, Am. Acad. Religion, Classical Assn. Middle West and South (v.p. Ohio 1976-79), Central Conf. Am. Rabbis, Am. Classical League, Ohio Classical Conf. (council 1976-79), Vergilian Soc., Soc. Bibl. Lit., Cin. Assn. Tchrs. Classics (pres. 1976-78), Am. Philol. Assn. Address: 2300 Lincoln Rd Apt 99 Hattiesburg MS 39401

BLUESTEIN, VENUS WELLER, psychologist, educator; b. Milw., July 16, 1933; d. Richard T. and Hazel (Beard) Weller; m. Marvin Bluestein, Mar. 7, 1954. BS, U. Cin., 1956, MEd, 1959, EdD, 1966. Diplomate Am. Bd. Examiners in Profl. Psychology. Psychologist-in-tng. Longview State Hosp., Cin., 1956-58; sch. psychologist Cin. Pub. Schs., 1958-65; asst. prof. psychology U. Cin., 1965-70, assoc. prof., 1970-79, prof., 1979—, dir. undergrad. studies, 1976—, dir. sch. psychology program, 1965-70, co-dir. sch. psychology program, 1970-75; cons. child psychologist. Sec., U.S. exec. com. rsch. Children's Internat. Summer Villages, 1964-68; chmn. Ohio Interuniv. Coun. Sch. Psychology, 1967-68. Editor Ohio Psychologist, 1961-68, coeditor, 1972-79; contbr. articles to profl. publs. Vol. various ednl. programs Cin. Zoo, 1983—. Recipient George B. Barbour award, 1985. Mem. AAUP, Am. Psychol. Assn., Cin. Psychol. Assn. (sec. 1961-62), Ohio Psychol. Assn. (citation 1972, Disting. Svc. award 1968), Sch. Psychologists Ohio, Forum for Death Edn. and Counseling, Kappa Delta Pi, Sigma Delta Pi, Psi Chi (award for outstanding mentor 1985). Office: U Cin Dept Psychology Cincinnati OH 45221

BLUITT, KAREN, computer program manager; b. N.Y.C., Oct. 25, 1957; d. James Bertrand and Beatrice (Kaufman) B.; m. Kenneth Mark Curry, Nov. 24, 1979. BS, Fordham U., 1979; MBA, Calif. State Poly. U., 1982. Software engr. Hughes Aircraft Co., Fullerton, Calif., 1979-81; microprocessor engr. Beckman Instruments Co., Fullerton, 1981-82, Singer Co., Glendale, Calif., 1982-83; sr. software engr. Sanders Assoc., Nashua, N.H., 1983-85; software project mgr. GTE Corp., Billerica, Mass., 1985-86; sr. software engr. Wang Labs, Lowell, Mass., 1986-87; project task leader Vanguard Rsch., Lexington, Mass., 1987-88; program mgr. Applied Rsch. & Engring., Bedford, Mass., 1989—. 1st lt. USAR, 1979-88. Scholar Gov. N.Y. Scholarship Com., 1975-79; Beta Gamma Sigma scholar, 1978—. Mem. NAFE, NOW, LWV, AAUW, Am. Brokers Network, Civil Affairs Assn., Boston Computer Soc. Execs. Office: Applied Rsch & Engring 3 Preston Ct Bedford MA 01730

BLUM, ALEXANDRA LYNNE, banker; b. Robbinsdale, Minn., Feb. 18, 1956; d. Rudolph Edward Grabmeier and June Harriet (Dunham) Kuklok; m. Michael Antonio Andreottola, Aug. 4, 1979 (div. July 1986); 1 child, Marc; m. John Stanley Blum, July 7, 1990. BS in Fin., Northeastern U., 1983; MBA, St. Cloud State U., 1988. Cert. fin. planner. Staff aide to U.S. Senator Floyd Haskell, Denver, 1976-77; accounts payable clk. Kraft, Inc., Needham, Mass., 1977-78; comml. credit investigator Bank New Eng., Boston, 1978-79, comml. loan analyst, 1982-84; installment loan collector Shawmut Bank, Boston, 1980-82; comml. loan officer 1st Am. Nat. Bank, St. Cloud, Minn., 1984-88, asst. v.p. comml. loans, 1988-89, asst. v.p. comml. real estate, 1989—. Fundraiser United Way, St. Cloud, 1984—, St. Cloud State U. Found., 1988-89. Mem. Fin. Women Internat. (v.p. Cen. Lakes chpt. 1989-90, pres. and state exec. bd. 1990-91), Forum Exec. Women, St. Cloud C. of C. Democrat. Lutheran. Office: 1st Am Nat Bank 1100 W St Germain Saint Cloud MN 56301

BLUM, BARBARA DAVIS, banker; b. Hutchinson, Kans., July 6, 1939; d. Roy C. and Jo (McKinnon) Davis; children: Devin, Hunter, Ragan, Davis. Student, U. Kans., 1955-56; B.A., Fla. State U., 1958, M.S.W., 1959. Mem. faculty Pediatric Psychiatry Clinic, U. Kans. Med. Center, Lawrence, 1960-62; acting adminstr. Suffolk County (N.Y.) Mental Health Clinic, Huntington, L.I., 1963-64; founder, partner Mid-Suffolk Center for Psychotherapy, Hauppage, L.I., N.Y., 1964-66; v.p. Restaurant Associates of Ga., Inc., Atlanta, 1966-74; dep. adminstr. U.S. EPA, Washington, 1977-81; mem. Pres.'s Interagy. Coordinating Council; pres., chief exec. officer Adams Nat. Bank; adv. U.S. Del. to UN Environment Program Governing Coun., Nairobi, Kenya, 1978, 79; chairperson U.S. Del., U.S./Japan Environ. Agreement, Tokyo, Japan, 1977-79; head 1st U.S. Environ. Del. to Peoples' Republic of China, 1979; chmn. Environ. Policy Inst., 1981-84; sr. adviser UN Environment Program; bd. dirs., exec. com. Washington Bd. Trade. Chmn. D.C. Econ. Devel. Fin. Corp., Leadership Washington; pres. Save America's Vital Environment, Atlanta, 1972-76, Friends of the River, Inc., 1972-75; vice chairperson Fulton County (Ga.) Planning Commn., 1973-76; chmn. Nat. Adv. Commn. Resource Conservation and Recovery; del. UN Mid Decade Conf. on Women, 1980; bd. dirs., pres. UN U. for Peace Found.; mem. adv. bd. UN Audio-Visual Trust; bd. dirs. Kaiser Permanente Mid Atlantic, Ctr. for Policy Alternatives; dep. polit. dir. Carter-Mondale U.S. presdl. campaign, 1976, nat. dep. dir., 1976; dir. ops. Carter/Mondale Transition Team, Washington, 1976-77. Decorated comdr.'s cross Order of Merit W. Ger.; recipient Disting. Service award Federally Employed Women, 1978, Spl. Conservation award Nat. Wildlife Fedn., 1976, Orgn. of Yr. award Ga. Wildlife Fedn., 1974, Disting. Service award Americans for Indian Opportunity, 1978. Mem. Washington Women's Network (dir., founder). Democrat. Club: Cosmos.

BLUM, BARBARA MEDDOCK, association executive; b. Oil City, Pa., Nov. 8, 1938; d. Marvin Lee and Hazel Genevieve (Jackson) Meddock.; m. Stuart Hollander Blum, Sept. 21, 1963. BA in Psychology, Allegheny Coll., 1960. Psychometrist, researcher Hofstra U., Hempstead, N.Y., 1960-62; adminstrv. asst., editor The Asia Soc., N.Y.C., 1962-66, exec. asst., 1966-72, adminstrv. officer, 1972-85, dir. adminstrn., 1985-88, ret. 1988. Mem. Am. Mgmt. Assn. Office: The Asia Soc 725 Park Ave New York NY 10021

BLUM, CARYN ELIZABETH, paralegal; b. Parkersburg, W.Va., June 28, 1959; d. Harold Frederick and Jeanne Katherine (Powers) Blum. BA, Calif. State Poly. U., 1981. Calendar clk. Memel Jacobs Pierno & Gersh, L.A., 1981-82, paralegal, 1983-85; paralegal Hirschtick Chenen Lemon & Curtis, Marina del Rey, Calif., 1985—; adminstrv. asst. LWV of L.A., 1990. Mem. AAUW (legis. chmn. 1986, v.p. membership 1987). Democrat. Office: Hirschtick Chenen et al 4720 Lincoln Blvd Suite 200 Marina del Rey CA 90292

BLUM, JOAN KURLEY, fund raising executive; b. Palm Beach, Fla., July 27, 1926; d. Nenad Daniel and Eva (Milos) Kurley; m. Robert C. Blum, Apr. 15, 1967; children: Christopher Alexander, Martha Jane, Louisa Joan, Sherifa Carolyn, Paul Helmuth. BA, U. Wash., 1948. Cert. fund raising exec. U.S. dir. Inst. Mediterranean Studies, Berkeley, Calif., 1962-65; devel. officer U. Calif. at Berkeley Alumni Assn., 1965-67; pres. Blum Assocs., Fund-Raising Cons., San Anselmo, Calif., 1967—; mem. faculty U. Calif. Extension, Inst. Fund Raising, SW Inst. Fund-Raising U. Tex., U. San Francisco, U.K. Vol. Movement Group, London, Australasian Inst. Fund Raising. Contbr. numerous articles to profl. jours. Recipient Golden Addy award Am. Advt. Fedn.; Silver Mailbox award Direct Mail Mktg. Assn., Best Ann. Giving Time-Life award, others. Mem. Nat. Soc. Fund-Raising Execs. (dir.), Nat. Assn. of Hosp. Devel., Women Emerging., Tamalpa Running Club, Rotary. Office: 292 Red Hill San Anselmo CA 94960

BLUM, NANCY K., company executive; b. Keokuk, Iowa; d. Charles Frederick and Gwyneth Irene (Lough) B. BA, Oakland U., Rochester, Mich., 1981. Producer/dir. Checkmate Prodns., L.A.; mgr. residuals Cannon Group, Inc., L.A.; exec. asst. Victoria Principal Prodns., Beverly Hills, Calif.; mgr. Harry A. Glassman, Nova Surgicenter, Beverly Hills. William T. Morris Found. scholar. Mem. NAFE, Plastic Surgery Adminstrn. Assn., Am. Film Inst., Golden Key.

BLUM, PAULA LOUISE, executive assistant; b. Altoona, Pa., Apr. 20, 1959; d. Robert Homer and Mary Louise (Coveney) B. Cashier Country Garden Market, Altoona, Pa., 1973-76, head of deli dept., 1976-77; waitress Parks Seafood Restaurant, Daytona Beach, Fla., 1977-80; with promotions Hawaiian Tropic Inc., Honolulu, 1980-81; with sales Hawaiian Tropic Inc., Perfumes of Hawaii, Honolulu, 1981-86; asst. to v.p. Langer Hawaii Corp., Honolulu, 1986—. Republican. Roman Catholic. Home: 144 Royal Circle Honolulu HI 96816 Office: Langer Hawaii Corp 1430 Hart St Honolulu HI 96815

BLUMBERG, ADELE ROSENBERG, community volunteer; b. Harrisburg, Pa., Jan. 19, 1916; d. Robert and Mary (Katzman) Rosenberg; m. Leonard Blumberg, June 16, 1940; children: Joyce Kozloff, Bruce, Allen. AB, Dickinson Coll., Carlisle, Pa., 1937; grad., Froelich Sch. Music, Harrisburg, 1932. Tchr. piano various cities, 1933-47; with Pa. Dept. Pub. Assistance, Harrisburg, 1937-40; assoc. pubr. Somerset Star, Somerville, N.J., 1951-55; sec. Raritan Valley Pub. Co., Manville, N.J., 1950-88. Bd. dirs. People Care Ctr., Finderne, N.J., 1985—, Arts Found. N.J., New Brunswick, 1986—; pres. Somerville Girl Scout Coun., 1954-55, Rolling Hills Girl Scout Coun., 1966-72, Jewish Fedn. Somerset County, 1974-76; pres., sec., bd. dirs. Bridgewater (N.J.) Local Assistance Bd., 1957—, many others in past. Recipient Hannah G. Solomon award, Nat. Council Jewish Women, 1969, Community Patriot, Bridgewater Edn. Assn., 1976, Teraentenary award, Bd. Freeholders and Cultural and Heritage Commn. Somerset County, 1988. Mem. Zonta (v.p. 1970-71). Democrat. Jewish. Address: 1820 Woodland Ter Bound Brook NJ 08805

BLUMBERG, ALYSE NEIBURG, financial services planner; b. Phila., Dec. 17, 1946; d. Sidney Aaron and Deborah Pearl (Burstein) Neiburg; m. Peter S. Blumberg; children: F. Scott, Sarah Beth. BS, Pa. State U., 1968; MEd, Temple U., 1971; CLU, Am. Coll., 1989. CLU, chartered fin. cons. Tchr. North Pa. Sch. Dist., Lansdale, 1969-75; owner The Enchanted Closet, Spring House, Pa., 1980-82; pres. Soft Power, North Wales, Pa., 1984—; brokerage mgr. Transam. Occidental Life Cos., Lansdale, 1986—; agy. securities coordinator Transam. Fin. Resources, Lansdale, 1987—; gen. agt. Transamerica Life Cos., 1988—, CNA Kife Cos., 1990—; ins. com. North Pa. Sch. Dist., Lansdale, 1969-72; moderator Life Underwriters Tng. Course, 1990—. Mem. mother's com. Germantown Acad., Ft. Washington, Pa., 1975—, 10K race dir., 1979-84, computer com., 1984-86. Mem. NAFE, AAUW (bd. dirs. 1972-78), NYSE, Nat. Assn. Life Underwriters, Nat. Assn. Security Dealers, N.Y. Stock Exschange, Am. Soc. CLUs and Chartered Fin. Cons., Montgomery CountyWomen's Network, Montgomery County Estate Planning Coun., Montgomery County Assn. Life Underwriters (bd. dirs. 1990—), Jaycettes (com. 1969-74), Pa. State U. Alumni Assn., Rotary. Republican. Jewish. Home: 121 Crestwood Dr Lansdale PA 19446 Office: PO Box 728 Lansdale PA 19446

BLUMBERG, BARBARA MARILYN, history educator, writer; b. Bronx, N.Y., Oct. 27, 1936; d. Albert A. and Yvette (Beneck) Schneck; m. Paul Marvin Blumberg, Aug. 25, 1955 (div. 1973); 1 child, Ira Joseph; m. Alan L. Krumholz, Apr. 12, 1974; 1 child, Mark Reuben. A.B. in History, U. Calif.-Berkeley, 1968, M.A. in History, 1962; Ph.D. in History, Columbia U., 1974. Prof. history Adelphi U., Garden City, N.Y., 1967-68, Queens Coll., Flushing, N.Y., 1968-75, Pace U., N.Y.C., 1971—. Author: The New Deal and the Unemployed: The View from NYC, 1979; Celebrating the Immigrant: An Administrative History of the Statue of Liberty National Monument, 1952-82, 1985, A National Park Emerges: The Statue as Park and Museum in Liberty: The French- American Statue in Art and History, 1986; editor NYC: Readings in History, Literature, and Culture, 1982, From World War to Cold War: Readings in Foreign and Domestic Policy, 1988. Mem. Am. Hist. Assn., Inst. Research in History (dir. 1983-84, mem. exec. com., sec. 1985-86), Women in the Hist. Profession (co-chmn. coordinating com. N.Y. 1983-84), Orgn. Am. Historians, Phi Beta Kappa. Office: Pace Univ Pace Plaza New York NY 10570

BLUMBERG, BARBARA SALMANSON (MRS. ARNOLD G. BLUMBERG), housing consultant, retired state housing official; b. Bklyn., Oct. 2, 1927; d. Sam and Mollie (Greenberg) Salmanson; m. Arnold G. Blumberg, June 19, 1949 (dec. June 1989); children: Florence Ellen Schwartz, Martin Jay, Emily Anne. BA, De Pauw U., 1948; postgrad., New Sch. for Social Rsch., N.Y.C. With pub. rels. Nate Fein & Co., N.Y.C., 1948-51; freelance pub. rels. cons., 1960—; councilwoman North Hempstead, N.Y., 1975-82; adviser to energy com. N.Y. State Assembly, N.Y.C., 1982-84; dir. spl. needs housing Div. Housing and Community Renewal, State of N.Y., 1984-89; ret. Pres. UN Assn. Great Neck, N.Y., 1967-69, chmn. China Study Workshop, 1966-67; pres. Shalom chpt. Hadassah, 1955-57; exec. v.p. Lakeville P.T.A., Great Neck, 1963-65; exec. v.p. Great Neck S. Jr. High Sch., 1965-66; co-chmn. Great Neck UNICEF, 1968-70, mem. speakers bur., 1971—; v.p. Herricks Community Life Ctr., 1976-77, B'nai B'rith, Lake Success, N.Y.; coord., 6th Congl. Dist., N.Y. McGovern for Pres.; bd. dirs. New Dem. Coalition of Nassau, Am. Jewish Congress, Am. Jewish Com., Day Care Coun. of Nassau County, The Inn, Mental Health Assn. Nassau County; v.p. Reform Dem. Assn. Great Neck; bd. dirs. Citizen's Sch. Com., Great Neck; mem. platform com. Nassau Dem. Com.; mem. adv. com. to speaker N.Y. State Assembly; mem. Community Advocates resource coun. Recipient award Anti-Defamation League, New Hyde Park, N.Y., 1975, Alumni award DePauw U., 1977, Hadassah New Life award, 1980. Mem. N.Y. Alumni Club DePauw U. (trustee), North Shore Archeol. Assn. (chmn. study group), Women in Communication, Internat. Platform Assn., L.I. Women's Network (co-convenor), Interfaith Nutrition Network (bd. dirs.), Community Advocates (bd. dirs.), Mental Health Assn. of Nassau County (bd. dirs.), Alpha Lambda Delta. Home: 12 Birch Hill Rd Great Neck NY 11020

BLUMBERG, GRACE GANZ, law educator, lawyer; b. N.Y.C., Feb. 16, 1940; d. Samuel and Beatrice (Finkelstein) Ganz; m. Donald R. Blumberg, Sept. 9, 1959; 1 dau., Rachel. B.A. cum laude, U. Colo., 1960; J.D. summa cum laude, SUNY, 1971; LL.M., Harvard U., 1974. Bar: N.Y. 1971, Calif. 1989. Confidential law clk. Appellate Div., Supreme Ct., 4th Dept., Rochester, N.Y., 1971-72; teaching fellow Harvard Law Sch., Cambridge, Mass., 1972-74; prof. law SUNY, Buffalo, 1974-81, UCLA, 1981—; cooperating atty. ACLU. Editorial bd.: Am. Jour. Comparative Law, 1977; contbr. articles to profl. jours. Baldy Summer Research fellow in law and social policy, 1977-78; SUNY research Found. summer faculty fellow, 1975. Mem. Am. Soc. Comparative Law, Am. Assn. Law Schs., NOW, ACLU. Office: UCLA Sch Law 405 Hilgard Ave Los Angeles CA 90024

BLUMBERG, JULIA BAUM, community leader, educator; b. Hazleton, Pa.; d. Benjamin and Ida Ruth (Lurie) Baum. PhB summa cum laude, Muhlenberg Coll., Allentown, Pa.; postgrad. NYU, Columbia U.; m. Leo Blumberg, Aug. 9, 1938. Mem. faculty Bethlehem (Pa.) Sr. High Sch. Life mem. B'nai B'rith Women, organized Bethlehem group, 1938, pres. Bethlehem, 1938-39, pres. Dist. 3, 1945-46, mem. nat. exec. bd., 1957-59, rep. nat. orgn., 1957-59, chmn. nat. career and counseling svcs. 1957-59, chmn. dist. 3 Klutznick scholarship award, 1966-69, mem. bd. B'nai B'rith Women of Wilmington, pres. nat. career and counseling svcs., 1962-64; life mem. Temple Beth Emeth Sisterhood, pres., 1952-53, mem. bd., 1949-59, 70-90;

treas. Dist 8, Nat. Fedn. Temple Sisterhoods, 1952-56; mem. nat. exec. bd. nat. fedn., 1953-57; gen. chmn. Dist. 8 conv., Wilmington, 1957; pres. community adv. bd. Hillel Counselorship, U. Del., 1979-82, bd. dirs., 1982-90; mem. bd. Wilmington City Fedn. Women's Clubs and Allied Orgns., 1951—, 1st v.p., 1961-63, pres., 1963-65; mem. bd. mgrs. Florence Crittendon Home of Del., 1955-61; mem. Women's div. Brandeis U.; life mem. Aux. Kutz Home for Aged, also bd. dirs. aux., 1972-90, named Hon. Life Chmn. Bd., 1983; mem. Nat. Career and Counseling Svcs., 1957-59, Mayor's Com. for Christmas, Mayor's Com. for UN; mem. bd. UNICEF, 1972-82; mem. steering com. CARE, Inc., 1971-82; mem. Del. Nature Edn. Soc., Inc., 1963-90 (charter mem.), Del. Coun. on Crime and Justice; chmn. bldg. and furniture com., dedication com. Hillel Found. at U. Del., 1963-64, hon. life chmn. community adv. bd. B'nai B'rith Hillel Counselorship, U. Del.; mem. women's div. Jewish Fedn. Del.; mem. bldg. fund com. St. Francis Hosp., 1973; v.p. bd. dirs. Kutz Home Aux.; mem. Friends of the Grand Opera House. Apptd. chmn. survey com. for accreditation by Mid. Atlantic States Assn. for Accreditation of Colls. and High Schs. Bethlehem (Pa.) Sr. High Sch. Author: (accrediting guide) The Philosophy and Aims & Objectives of Secondary Education. Recipient Citation of Merit, Nat. Commn. B'nai B'rith Career & Counseling Svc., Citation award Bur. Jewish Women's Orgns. of Wilmington, Del. Mem. Nat. Coun. Jewish Women (life), Greater Wilmington Fedn. Women's Orgns. (bd. dir. 1965-69, 69-73, 73-77, 77-86, pres. Past Officers Club 1965-67, historian 1973-75, bd. dir. 1975—), Del. Mental Health Assn., Crippled Children and Adults Soc. Del., Hadassah (life), B'nai B'rith Women (life), Phi Sigma Iota. Jewish (life mem., pres. Sisterhood 1952-53, mem. bd. 1970-90, bd. dir. temple 1952-55). Clubs: Widener U. Faculty Wives (hon. life), Wilmington New Century (edn. com. 1978-86, internat. affairs com. 1978-89, art and music com. 1988-90, chmn. admissions com.). Home: 1401 Pennsylvania Ave Apt 406 Wilmington DE 19806

BLUMBERG, RENA JOY, broadcast executive; b. Cleve., Oct. 31, 1934; d. Ezra and Sylvia (Lamport) Shapiro; m. Michael Blumberg, Mar. 6, 1964; children: Catharyn Blumberg Gildesgame, David, Stuart. Bachelors, Brandeis U., 1956; Humane Letters (hon.), Baldwin Wallace Coll., 1987. Community rels. dir. WDOK-FM, Cleve., 1972—; bd. dirs. Blue Cross and Blue Shield of Ohio, McDonald & Co. Securities Inc., Providence House, A Crisis Nursery, Playhouse Sq. Found., North Coast Devel. Corp., Women-Space, United Labor Agy., WVIZ, Channel 25, others; community rels. cons., host various media series; chmn. numerous exhibits, community celebrations. Author: Headstrong, 1982. Trustee Brandeis U., 1978—, chmn. of the Fellows, 1984-88, chmn. hon. degree com., 1985—, sec. of the bd. trustees, 1990; active numerous civic projects including co-chmn. Heartstring, The Nat. Tour/Western Res. AIDS Found., 1989, Black Tie Slumber Party for Rainbow Babies and Children's Hosp., 1989; chmn. Three Spl. Events/United Way Campaign, 1989; hon. chmn. Ronald McDonald Benefit: The Houses that Love Built, 1988, others. Recipient numerous svc. awards including No. Ohio Live Award of Achievement in Community Events, 1987-89, Downtown Bus. Coun. Recognition Award for Communication, Greater Cleve. Growth Assn., 1990, Disting. Leadership award Nat. Assn. Community Leadership Orgns., Women in Communications Matrix award, 1981, first place 1985, 86, 89, Ohio State Media award Am. Cancer Soc., 1979, radio and TV awards 1980, 81, 82, 84, 86, 89, Courage award Ohio Div. Am. Cancer Soc., 1982, others. Home: 18910 S Woodland Rd Shaker Heights OH 44122 Office: WDOK-FM 1250 Superior Ave Cleveland OH 44114

BLUME, ELIZABETH RENEE, office manager, clinical research coordinator; b. Warren, Pa., Aug. 29, 1953; d. William Wesley and Betty Josephine (Anderson) B. Grad. Little Valley Central Sch. Motor vehicle acct. Cattaraugus County, Little Valley, N.Y., 1971-76; asst. office mgr. Dr. Widger and Dr. Gutierrez, Salamanca, N.Y., 1976-80; adminstrv. sec. The U. Tex. Med. Sch., Houston, 1980; exec. sec. Stanley J. Dudrick, M.D., Houston, 1980-87; office mgr. Joseph J. O'Donnell MD, Livingston, Tex., 1988-89; exec. dir. Med. Transitional Assn., Houston, 1989—. Co-author Annals of Surgery, 1983, Transactions of the So. Surg. Assn., The Yearbook of Surgery and Gastroenterology. Co-chmn. United Way Campaign dept. surgery The U. Tex. Med. Sch., Houston, 1980; mem. Big Brothers and Sisters of Houston, 1990. Recipient Sorosis Literary Guild award for English N.Y. State Fed. Women's Clubs, 1971, Eastern Star award, 1971. Mem. Stanley J. Dudrick Found. and Soc., Am. Soc. for Nutritional Support Svcs. (exec. sec., bd. dirs. 1983-87, co-author Sci. poster session 1982, 84, 85, Exceptional Contbrn. award 1986), Am. Soc. for Parenteral and Enteral Nutrition (co-author sci. poster session 1982, 84), Eur. Soc. Parenteral and Enteral Nutrition (co-author sci. poster session 1985), Theta Rho (pres. 1969-70). Home and Office: 5939 Sanford Houston TX 77096

BLUME, JUDY SUSSMAN, author; b. Elizabeth, N.J., Feb. 12, 1938; d. Rudolph and Esther (Rosenfeld) Sussman; m. John M. Blume, Aug. 15, 1959 (div. Jan. 1976); children: Randy Lee, Lawrence Andrew; m. George Cooper, June 6, 1987; 1 stepchild, Amanda. B.A. in Edn., N.Y. U., 1960; LHD (hon.), Kean Coll., 1987. Author: fiction books including Are You There God, It's Me Margaret (selected as outstanding children's book 1970), Then Again, Maybe I Won't, 1971, It's Not the End of the World, 1972, Tales of a 4th Grade Nothing, 1972, Otherwise Known as Sheila the Great, 1972, Deenie, 1973, Blubber, 1974, Forever, 1976, Superfudge, 1980, Tiger Eyes, 1981, Just As Long As We're Together, 1987, Fudge-a-mania, 1990, others; adult novels Wifey, 1978, Smart Women, 1984; Letters to Judy: What Kids Wish They Could Tell You, 1986; exec. prod. (25 min. film) Otherwise Known As Sheila The Great, Calico Films. Founder, trustee The Kids Fund, 1981. Recipient Carl Sandburg Freedom to Read award Chgo. Pub. Library, 1984, the Civil Liberties award ACLU, 1986, John Rock award Ctr. for Population Options, 1986; numerous Children's Choice awards, U.S.A., Europe, Australia. Mem. Authors Guild, Soc. Children's Book Writers, PEN (bd. dirs.), Soc. Children's Book Writers. Office: care Harold Ober Assocs 40 E 49th St New York NY 10017

BLUME, SHEILA BIERMAN, psychiatrist; b. Bklyn., June 21, 1934; d. Benjamin and Rose (Lazar) Bierman; m. Martin Blume, June 12, 1955; children: Frederick, Janet. Student Cornell U., 1951-54; MD cum laude, Harvard U., 1958. Intern, Children's Hosp. Med. Ctr., Boston, 1958-59; Fulbright fellow to Tokyo U., 1959-60; resident in psychiatry Central Islip Psychiat. Center, 1962-65; dir. Charles K. Post Alcoholism Rehab. Center, Central Islip Psychiat. Ctr., 1964-79; dir. N.Y. State Div. Alcoholism and Alcohol Abuse, 1979-83; med. dir. Nat. Coun. on Alcoholism, 1984; med. dir. Alcoholism, Compulsive Gambling and Chem. Dependency Programs, South Oaks Hosp., 1984—; clin. assoc. prof. psychiatry Albany Med. Ctr., 1979-82; clin. prof. psychiatry SUNY-Stony Brook, 1984—; apptd. to Nat. Commn. Alcoholism and Other Alcohol Related Problems, 1980; mem. Nat. Commn. Confidentiality of Health Records, 1976-80, Nat. Coun. on Compulsive Gambling, adv. bd., 1972—; bd. dirs. Children of Alcoholics Found., 1983—. Recipient Dr. Milton Helpern Disting. Physicians award for contbn. field of alcoholism, 1980, Harold Riegelman award for contbn. to field of alcohol policy, 1983. Mem. L.I. Coun. Alcoholism and Other Drug Dependencies (dir. 1972-79), Am. Soc. Addiction Medicine (dir., pres. 1979-80), Nat. Coun. Alcoholism, (dir.). Editor: (with S. Zimberg and J. Wallace) Practical Approaches to Alcoholism Psychotherapy, 1978; editor Bull. Suffolk County Med. Soc., 1969-76; contbr. articles profl. jours., chpts. in books. Home and Office: 284 Greene Ave Sayville NY 11782 also: South Oaks Hosp Amityville NY 11701

BLUMENFELD, ANITA, community relations director; b. London, Oct. 30, 1933; came to U.S. 1955; d. Samuel and Eva (Lehrman) Leigh; m. George Blumenfeld, Dec. 30, 1956; children: Michael Russell, Vincent Joseph. Student, City of London Coll., 1949-51. Adminstrv. asst. Jewish Nat. Fund & Mogen David Adom (Israeli Red Cross), London, 1951-55; field cons. AMIT Women, L.A., 1978-81; pub. relations rep. Mercury Savs. & Loan, Long Beach, Calif., 1981-84; community relations dir. Ams. AMIT Women for Torah & Israel, L.A., 1986—. Editor, collator: British Evacuees during World War II, 1977-79; compiler: Social Action Conference Reports, 1977, 79, 85. Social action chmn. Temple Menorah, 1970-79; co-pres. Vols. for Israel, 1988-89; active various other civic orgns. Mem. Amnesty Internat., Ams. for Safe Israel, Hadassah. Democrat. Jewish. Home: 2743 W 233 St Torrance CA 90505 Office: AMIT Women 6505 Wilshire Blvd Los Angeles CA 90048

BLUMENFELD, SHARNA FAYE, service executive; b. Decatur, Ill., June 8, 1934; d. Sewell and Natalie Marion (Appelbaum) Susler; m. Stewart Norman Blumenfeld, Aug. 15, 1954; children: Debora Ruth, David Bruce. BS in Edn. cum laude, U. Kans., 1958. Elem. sch. tchr. Lawrence (Kans.), L.A. Pub. Schs., 1958-72; travel counselor Esquire Travel Svc., Encino, Calif., 1977-79, Jet Set Travel, Potomac, Md., 1979-80; mgr. Globetrotter Travel, Wheaton, Md., 1980-84; pres. Conference Connections, Rockville, Md., 1984--; sr. travel cons. The Travel Place, Potomac, Md., 1984-86; mgr. Uniglobe the Travel Profls., Rockville, 1986-88; dir. bus. devel. Uniglobe MidAtlantic Region, Rockville, 1988--; coord. Inst. of Cert. Travel Agts., Rockville, 1983-88; school bd. chmn., speech therapy cons., speaker, Accra, Ghana, 1973-77. Co-author Women in National Development in Ghana, 1975. Life mem. Inst. of Cert. Travel Agts., Am. Women's Assn., Accra (spl. projects chmn. 1974-76), AAUW. Democrat. Jewish. Home: 6 Candlelight Ct Potomac MD 20854 Office: Uniglobe Travel 2440 Rsch Blvd Ste 312 Rockville MD 20850

BLUMENTHAL, BARBARA ANNE, marketing executive; b. Washington, Jan. 23, 1949; d. Lester Sylvan Blumenthal and Violet Magaret (Smith) David. BA cum laude, Boston U., 1971; JD, New England Sch. of Law, 1975. Bar: Mass., 1975. Asst. dist. atty. Suffolk County, Boston, 1975-78, Middlesex County, Cambridge, Mass., 1978-79; mgr. exec. programs/direct sales devel. Apple Computer, Inc., Cupertino, Calif., 1981-85; v.p. sales and mktg. Mentor Learning Systems, Santa Clara, Calif., 1986; mgr. mktg. communications 3Com Corp., Santa Clara, 1987-88; dir. corp. mktg. Software Pub. Corp., Mountain View, Calif., 1988—. Recipient various advt. video awards. Office: Software Publishing Corp 1901 Landings Dr Mountain View CA 94039

BLUMENTHAL, RONNIE, lawyer; b. Passaic, N.J., Nov. 27, 1944; d. Paul and Marga (Stern) B. BA, George Washington U., 1966, JD, 1969. Bar: D.C. 1969. Gen. atty. EEOC, Washington, 1969-71, spl. asst. to acting chmn., 1971-78, sr. atty., 1978-82, dir. spl. services, 1983-85, dir. compliance programs, 1985—; legis. fellow U.S. Senate, 1982. Mem. ABA, D.C. Bar Assn., Exec. Women in Govt. Home: 3315 Wisconsin Ave NW Washington DC 20016 Office: EEOC 1801 L St NW Washington DC 20507

BLUMENTHAL, SUSAN JANE, physician; b. N.Y.C., June 29, 1952; d. Stanley Robert and Eloyse Shirlee (Levine) B.; m. Edward John Markey, June 26, 1988. BA, Reed Coll., 1971; MD, U. Tenn., 1976; MPA, Harvard U., 1982. Diplomate Am. Bd. Psychiatry and Neurology. Intern. Stanford U. Sch. of Medicine, 1976-77, residency and fellowship, 1977-80; fellow NIMH, 1980-81, assoc. dir. Psychiatry Tng. Rev., head suicide rsch. unit and coord. of project depression, 1982-85, chief behavioral medicine program, 1985—; clin. asst. prof. Tufts Med. Ctr., 1981-82; clin. asst. prof. psychiatry George Washington Sch. Medicine, 1982-86; clin. assoc. prof. psychiatry Georgetown Sch. Med., 1986—. Editor: Suicide over the Life Cycle, 1989, Premenstral Syndrome, 1985; contbr. articles to sci. jours.; advice columnist. Commdr. USPHS, 1984—. Decorated Outstanding Svc. medal USPHS, Commendation medal. Mem. Am. Psychiat. Assn. (cons. Joint Coun. on Pub. Affairs), AMA, Am. Coll. Psychiatrists (membership com.), Group for the Advancement Psychiatry, Am. Med. Women's Assn. (chairperson com. on publicity and pub. rels.), Congl. Club (Washington), Harvard Club (bd. dirs.)Soc. Women's Health Rsch., Nat. Women's Health Resource Ctr. (bd. dirs.). Office: NIMH 5600 Fishers Ln Rm 11-C-06 Rockville MD 20857

BLUMER, ANNE M., educator; b. Tigerton, Wis., Sept. 2, 1956; d. Anthony R. and Bernadine G. (Donder) Spolar. Student, Fox Valley Tech. Inst., Appleton, Wis.; grad. gemologist, Gemol. Inst. Am., 1989. Buyer/clock repair Spolars Jewelry, Appleton; instr. Extension div. Gemol. Inst. Am., Santa Monica, Calif. Mem. NAFE, Gemology Inst. Am. Alumni Assn., Am. Gem Soc. Home: 6161 N Rosewood Dr Appleton WI 54915 Office: 1660 Stewart St Santa Monica CA 90404

BLUM-GOLDSTEIN, SUSAN RUTH, French educator; b. Boston, May 25, 1963; d. Haywood and Evelyn (Rauch) Blum; m. Seth Lewis Goldstein, Aug. 20, 1989. BA in French/Anthropology, Dickinson Coll., Carlisle, Pa., 1985; BA in Secondary Edn. Fgn. Lang., U. Md., 1988; tchrs. cert., Gratz Coll., Phila, 1981; Lettres Modernes, U. Paul Valery, Montpellier, France, 1984. English asst. to French law students Faculte de Droit et Des Scis. Economiques, Montpellier, 1983-84; park ranger div. interpretation and hist. svcs. U.S. Dept. Interior, Nat. Park Svc., Phila., 1985; park ranger, White House liaison U.S. Dept. Interior, Nat. Park Svc., Washington, 1986; social studies/lang. tchr. Temple Beth Ami, Rockville, Md., 1987-88; French/social studies tchr. Psychiat. Inst. Montgomery County and Washington, Rockville, 1987-88; tchr. French Paint Branch High Sch., Burtonsville, Md., 1988; tchr. ESL Wildcat Svc. Corp., N.Y.C., 1988-89; tchr. French and English as a Second Lang. Intermediate Sch. 77, N.Y.C. Bd. Edn., Ridgewood, N.Y., 1989—; French tutor High Grade Tutoring Svc., N.Y.C., 1988—. Vol., counselor, med. asst. Planned Parenthood of Met. Washington, Rockville, 1987-88. Mem. Am. Fedn. Tchrs., Am. Assn. Tchrs. French (mem. com. N.Y.C. pub. schs. 1990—), United Fedn. Tchrs., N.Y. State United Tchrs., Phi Sigma Iota. Home: 110-45 71st Rd Apt 5E Forest Hills NY 11375 Office: Intermediate Sch 77 976 Seneca Ave Ridgewood NY 11385

BLUMSTEIN-ELDER, RENÉE, research and statistical consultant; b. Bklyn., Apr. 1, 1957; d. Robert and Rosalie (Burak) Blumstein; m. Martin Charles Elder, June 23, 1985. BA, Queens Coll., N.Y., 1978; MA, Columbia U., 1980, MEd, 1982, MPhil, 1984, PhD, 1986. Rsch. psychologist CCNY, 1980-85; rsch. cons. AT&T, N.Y.C., 1986; rsch. analyst Citibank, N.Y.C., 1986-87, rsch. and statis. cons., 1987—; rsch. and statis. cons. Informed Decision Svcs., Englewood, N.J., 1987-90; adj. prof. rsch. methods CUNY, 1990—. Scholar Columbia U., 1981. Mem. Am. Psychol. Assn., Am. Soc. Tng. and Devel., Metro. Office: Informed Decision Svcs 51 W Hudson Ave Ste 5 Englewood NJ 07631

BLYTH, ANN MARIE, educator; b. Sharon, Pa., June 18, 1949; d. Chester Stanley and Mary Clara (Romian) Kacerski; m. Lynn Allan Blyth, June 26, 1976 (dec. June 1983); 1 stepchild, Breton Alan Blyth; 1 child, Amanda Lynn. BS in Edn., Kent (Ohio) State U., 1971; postgrad., Loyola U., New Orleans, 1973-74; MS in Teaching, John Carroll U., 1978. Cert. comprehensive sci., maths. and physics tchr., Ohio. Jr. high math. tchr. New Philadelphia ((Ohio) Bd. of Edn., 1971-72; high sch. sci. and math. tchr. Hubbard (Ohio) Exempted Village Bd. of Edn., 1972-76, Painesville (Ohio) City Bd. of Edn., 1976—; instr. math. Morton Salt, Painesville, 1979-80. Mem. Adv. Bd. Western Res. Br. of Am. Lung Assn. of Ohio, Painesville, 1986-89, sec. 1988-89, Northeastern Br., Youngstown, Ohio, 1989—. Martha Holden Jennings Found. scholar, 1984-85; named Tchr. of the Yr., Harvey High Sch. Key Club, 1981-82. Mem. NEA, Ohio Edn. Assn., Northeastern Ohio Edn. Assn., Painesville City Tchrs. Assn., Am. Assn. Physics Tchrs., Nat. Sci. Tchrs. Assn., Cleve. Regional Coun. of Sci. Tchrs., Sci. Edn. Coun. of Ohio. Democrat. Episcopalian. Home: 8545 Willow Ln Chardon OH 44024 Office: Thomas W Harvey High Sch 167 W Washington St Painesville OH 44077

BLYTH, MYRNA GREENSTEIN, publishing director, editor, author; b. N.Y.C., Mar. 22, 1939; d. Benjamin and Betty (Austin) Greenstein; m. Jeffrey Blyth, Nov. 25, 1962; children: Jonathan, Graham. B.A., Bennington (Vt.) Coll., 1960. Sr. editor Datebook mag., N.Y.C., 1960-62, Ingenue mag., N.Y.C., 1963-68; book editor Family Health mag., 1968-71; book and fiction editor, then assoc. editor Family Circle mag., N.Y.C., 1972-78; exec. editor Family Circle mag., 1978-81; editor-in-chief Ladies' Home Jour., 1981—, pub. dir., 1987—; freelance writer, contbr. mags. Author: (novels) Cousin Suzanne, 1975, For Better and For Worse, 1978; contbr. articles to New Yorker mag., New York mag., Redbook mag., Cosmopolitan mag., Reader's Digest. Bd. dirs. Child Care Action Campaign, N.Y.C., 1989—. Mem. Am. Soc. Mag. Editors (exec. com. 1989—), N.Y. Women In Communications, Inc., Women's Media Group, Authors League. Office: Ladies' Home Jour 100 Park Ave New York NY 10017

BLYTHE, ANGELA D., small business owner; b. Salt Lake City, Nov. 9, 1960; d. James Dale and Nancy Hope (Moore) Smith; m. Walter M. Blythe, Aug. 20, 1981; children: James, Nicole. Pres. The New Race, Inc., Colorado Springs, Colo.; owner The Branch Restaurant, Cripple Creek, Colo.; writing and mktg. rep. Interrace Mag., Schenectady, N.Y. Contbr. articles to profl. jours. Methodist. Home: PO Box 312 Green Mountain Falls CO 80819 Office: 236 E Bennett Ave Cripple Creek CO 80813

BOADEN, LUCILLE ANN, editor, English educator; b. Moline, Ill., Nov. 27, 1945; d. Rhys Bartlett and Evelyn Euseba (Nowers) B. AB, Augustana Coll., 1967; AM, U. Chgo., 1968, PhD, 1976. Instr. English Augustana Coll., Rock Island, Ill., 1970-79, asst. prof. English, 1979—; editor Augustana Coll. mag., Rock Island, 1979—. Author: (with Youngberg) The Mystery of the Singing Mermaid, 1987; contbr. articles and short stories to various publs. Pres. Augustana Hist. Soc., Rock Island, 1983-86, editor newsletter 1983-88, bd. dirs. 1980—. Ford Found. fellow, 1968. Mem. Phi Beta Kappa. Lutheran. Office: Augustana Coll 639 38th St Rock Island IL 61201

BOARDMAN, EUNICE, music educator; b. Cordova, Ill., Jan. 27, 1926; d. George Hollister and Anna Bryson (Feaster) Boardman. B. Mus. Edn., Cornell Coll., 1947; M. Mus. Edn., Columbia Tchrs. Coll., 1951; Ed.D., U. Ill., 1963. Tchr. music pub. schs., Iowa, 1947-55; prof. music edn. Wichita State U., Kans., 1955-72; vis. prof. mus. edn. Normal State U., Ill., 1972-74, Roosevelt U., Chgo., 1974-75; prof. mus. edn. U. Wis., Madison, 1975-89, dir. Sch. Music, 1980-89; prof. music edn. U. Ill., Urbana, 1989—. Author: Musical Growth in Elementary School, 1963, 5th rev. edit., 1986, Exploring Music, 1966, 3d rev. edit., 1975, The Music Book, 1980, 2d rev. edit., 1984, Holt Music, 1987, Dimensions of Musical Thinking, 1989. Mem. Soc. Music Tchr. Edn. (chmn. 1984-86), Music Educators Nat. Conf. Office: U Ill 3000 Music Bldg Urbana IL 61801

BOARDMAN, ROSANNE VIRGINIA, logistics consultant; b. Twin Falls, Idaho, Oct. 4, 1946; d. Gordon Ross and Garnet Othalia (Peterson) Tobin; m. Lowell Jay Boardman, May 12, 1973; 1 child, Christina Garnet. BA cum laude, Occidental Coll., 1968; MA with honors, Columbia U., 1969; postgrad., U. Calif., Irvine, 1971-72, U. Calif., Los Angeles and Santa Barbara, 1969, 73-74. Cert. jr. coll. tchr., Calif., cert. secondary tchg., Calif. Instr. U. Calif., Irvine, 1971-72, Ventura (Calif.) Community Coll., 1973-77; tech. writer Raytheon Service Co., Ventura, 1977-78; engring. analyst John J. McMullen Co., Ventura, 1978-80; sr. logistics specialist Raytheon Co., Ventura, 1977-78, 80-83; civilian tech. writer, editor USN, Port Hueneme, Calif., 1983-84, civilian logistics mgr., 1984-88; cons. Support Mgmt. Systems, Oxnard, Calif., 1988—. Author numerous manuals and logistics guides. Internat. fellow Occidental Coll., 1967; recipient Outstanding Performance award Naval Ship Weapon Systems Engring. Sta., 1985, 86. Mem. Soc. Logistics Engrs., Phi Beta Kappa.

BOATENG, ADWOA ACHIA, information specialist and executive; b. Elmira, N.Y., Nov. 28, 1955; d. George Kwadwo Boateng and Dorothy (Collins) Vinluan. BS, Elmira Coll., 1976, MS, 1981; MLS, SUNY, Buffalo, 1985. Lab. technician Corning (N.Y.) Glass Works, 1976-81, libr. asst., 1981-85, bus. libr., 1985-87; mgr. Bausch & Lomb, Rochester, N.Y., 1987—. Spl. Librs. Assn. scholar, 1984-85. Mem. Am. Soc. for Info. Sci., Spl. Librs. Assn. (affirmative action liaison rep. 1989—), Soc. Competitive Intelligence Profls., Altrusa, NAFE. Home: 220 Meigs St Apt 2 Rochester NY 14607

BOATRIGHT, ANN LONG, dancer, pianist, music educator, choreographer; b. Louisville, Jan. 11, 1947; d. William Frazier and Mary Madolin (Hagan) Long; m. Ned Collins Boatright Jr., June 15, 1968; 1 child, Elizabeth. Student, Jordan Coll. Music, 1960-65, Butler U., 1965-68; BA, SUNY, Plattsburgh, 1970; MusM, Ithaca Coll., 1974. Cert. tchr. N.Y., Ohio. Music tchr. pub. schs., Plattsburgh, Ithaca, and Rochester, N.Y., 1970-76; head dance program Columbus (Ohio) Sch. for Girls, 1977-82; instr. Suzuki piano Capital U., 1982-85, instr. eurythmics, 1982—, developer tchr. tng. for music and movement, 1985-88; past tchr. eurythmics, music, movement Lake Forest Coll., Capital U., Wittenberg U., Ohio State U., Eastern Mich. U., Denison U., Utah State U.; tchr. Suzuki and traditional piano, Columbus, 1985—; instr. Suzuki Summer Music Insts. Capital U., clincian 1982-88; clinician classical dance Wittenberg U., 1989; ballet soloist with Jordan Coll. Music Co., Butler U., Ithaca Ballet Co.; dancer with Indpls. Civic Ballet Co., Columbus Theatre Ballet Co.; pianist with Butler U. String Trio. Choreographer: (ballets, mus. comedies) Odds 'n Ends, 1980, Little Match Girl, 1979, Crusades, 1982, Ballet of Unhatched Chicks, 1982, Wheels, 1979, Marathon, 1981. Mem. Arts For Peace-Unify Ohio, 1986, women's service bd. Grant Med. Ctr., Franklin Park Conservatory, St. Mark's Episcopal Ch., jr. council Columbus Mus. Art, Zephyrus League. Mem. Music Tchrs. Nat. Assn. (nat. cert.), Ohio Music Tchrs. Assn. (condr. various workshops, clinician 1986-87, 89, faculty summer camp 1988-90), Nat. Guild Piano Tchrs., Am. Coll. Musicians (faculty), Suzuki Assn. Am., Suzuki Assn. Ohio, Alpha Chi Omega, Sigma Alpha Iota. Republican.

BOATWRIGHT, CHARLOTTE JEANNE, hospital marketing and public relations executive; b. Chattanooga, Dec. 12, 1937; d. Clifton Gentry and Veltina Novella (Braden) Blevins; m. Robert W. Boatwright; children: Lynn Kay, Janis Ann, Karen Jean, Mary Ruth, Melody Susan, April Celeste. Diploma, Erlanger Sch. Nursing, Chattanooga, 1963; BS, U. Tenn., Chattanooga, 1976, MEd, 1981; PhD, Columbia Pacific U., San Rafael, Calif., 1987. RN, Tenn. Surgeon's asst. William Robert Fowler, M.D., Chattanooga, 1963-64; instr. med.-surg. nursing Baroness Erlanger Hosp. Sch. Nursing, 1964-67, instr. fundamentals nursing, 1971-74, chmn. dept. mental health-psychiat. nursing, 1977-81; staff nurse Meml. Hosp., Chattanooga, 1967-68, nursing supr., 1968-70; dir. inservice edn. Hutcheson Med. Ctr., Ft. Oglethorpe, Ga., 1970-71; youth work cons. Sewanee Dist. Episcopal Chs., Chattanooga, 1975-76; dir. spl. projects North Park Hosp., Chattanooga, 1984-87, dir. mktg. and pub. rels., 1987—. mem. dept. youth work Episcopal Diocese Tenn., 1975-77; condr. adult ch. sch. groups St. Martin's Episcopal Ch., Chattanooga; vice chmn. Brynewood Park Community Assn., 1985, 86. Mem. Am. Coll. Healthcare Execs. (nominee), Tenn. Hosp. Assn., Tenn. Soc. for Hosp. Mktg. and Pub. Rels., Chattanooga C. of C., U. Tenn. Alumnae Assn., Columbia Pacific U. Alumnae Assn., Chi Sigma Iota. Republican. Office: North Park Hosp 2051 Hamill Rd Chattanooga TN 37343

BOAZ, DONIELLA, psychotherapist, consultant; b. Grand Junction, Colo., Apr. 8, 1934; d. Leon T. and Marian (Fonder) Hutton; m. Richard Boas, Apr. 7, 1956 (div. 1983); children: Roxanne, Annika, Becca. Cert. pastoral ministry Seattle U., 1978; cert. clin. pastoral edn. Va. Mason Hosp., 1979; BA, Antioch West, 1980; postgrad. Lan Ting Inst., Fujian Province, China, 1986, C.G. Jung Inst., Zurich, 1986, 87, 89. Cert. neuro-linguistic programmer, 1983. Owner Donalee's Studio of Dance, Kirkland, Wash., 1952-63; adminstrv. asst. Ch. of Redeemer, Kenmore, Wash., 1974-76; counselor Eastside Mental Health, Bothell, Wash., 1976-79; psychotherapist, Seattle, 1979—; owner, cons. Optimum Options, Seattle, 1979—; mem. DISCOVERIES Seminars, various other govt., bus., non-profit orgns., nat. and internat. trainer, cons.; mem. adj. faculty Seattle U. Northwest Coll. Holistic Studies and Huston Sch. Theology, 1980-87. V.p. Episcopal Ch. standing com. on stewardship, 1979-81; active in local politics., 1968-80. Assoc. mem. Clin. Pastoral Edn., Wash. Assn. Counseling and Devel. Avocations: philosophy; carpentry; bridge; entertaining; traveling. Office: Optimum Options Grosvenor House 500 Wall St Ste 309 Seattle WA 98121

BOBAN, KATHLEEN, company executive; b. Joliet, Ill., May 13, 1962; d. Richard Edward and Christine (Kirincich) B. BS, No. Ill. U., 1984. Cons. Software Architects, Chgo., 1984-86; sr. cons. Interactive Bus. Sys., Oak Brook, Ill., 1986-89; devel. ctr. analyst Hewitt Assocs., Lincolnshire, Ill., 1989—. Home: 1251 W Grace Apt 2E Chicago IL 60613

BOBBITT, HELEN DAVIS, educator; b. Kansas City, Mo., Dec. 2, 1913; d. Robert and Georgia Helen (Lucas) Davis; m. George Presley Bobbitt, Apr. 9, 1938; 1 child, Charles Robert. BS in Edn., Cen. Mo. State U., Warrensburg, 1941; MS, Emporia (Kans.) State U., 1964. Cert. tchr., Mo., Kans. Tchr. Camden County, Mo., 1933-35, Stoutland (Mo.) Schs., 1936-39, Clinton (Mo.) Schs., 1942-44, Hutchinson (Kans.) Schs., 1945-48; tchr. El Dorado (Kans.) Schs., 1960-83, ret., 1983. Mem. AAUW, (sec. 1953-54, pres. 1958-61), Ret. Tchrs. Butler County (courtesy chmn. 1984—, treas. 1989—), Book Lovers Club, Delta Kappa Gamma Internat. (chmn. 1979-89, Phi State Scholar, Helen D. Bobbitt Hostelship award 1989). Home: 900 W Third El Dorado KS 67042

BOCCI, MARILYN KATHLEEN, physical therapist; b. St. Paul, Feb. 9, 1949; d. George Reinhold and Emilie Katherine (Gerhardt) Stahnke; m. Paul Michael Bocci, May 16, 1981; children: Daniel Joseph, Amanda Ruth, Jeffrey Michael. BA in Biology, Dana Coll., 1971; cert., Mayo Found. Sch. Phys. Therapy, Rochester, Minn., 1973. Staff phys. therapist Rockford (Ill.) Meml. Hosp., 1973-76; staff phys. therapist Alexian Bros. Med. Ctr., Elk Grove Village, Ill., 1976-79, sr. phys. therapist, 1979-82, 84—, supr., 1982-83. Mem. AAUW, Am. Phys. Therapy Assn. Lutheran. Office: Alexian Bros Med Ctr 800 W Biesterfield Elk Grove Village IL 60007

BOCCIA, ANN MARIE, paralegal; b. San Pedro, Calif., Apr. 23, 1958; d. Franklin S. and Julia (Mattera) B. AA, Harbor Coll., 1983; paralegal cert., Continental Tech. Inst., L.A., 1986. Invoicing/sales rep. Bronson of Calif., Gardena, 1976-78; traffic mgr. GSC Athletic Equipment, San Pedro, 1978-81; exec. legal sec. Stein, Shostak, Shostak & O'Hara, L.A., 1981; paralegal, computer adminstr. Silver, McWilliams, Stolpman, Mandel, Katzman et al, Wilmington, Calif., 1981—; cons. San Pedro Chiropractic Ctr., 1989—. Recipient Presdl. award Calif. Trial Lawyers Assn., 1988. Mem. Nat. Paralegal Assn., L.A. Trial Lawyers Assn. (speaker 1989-90, voter registration com. 1988-89), L.A. Paralegal Assn. Democrat. Roman Catholic. Office: Silver McWilliams et al 1121 N Avalon Blvd Wilmington CA 90744-3598

BOCCIA, MARIA LIBORIA, biologist; b. Bronx, Dec. 5, 1953; d. Silvio Mario and Emily (Russo) B. BA, SUNY, Geneseo, 1974; MS, U. Mass., 1979, PhD, 1981. Rsch. asst. dept. psychology U. Mass., Amherst, 1976-81; teaching asst. dept. zoology U. Mass., 1976-79, teaching assoc., 1979-81; postdoctoral fellow U. Denver, 1981-83; asst. prof. Okla. Bapt. U., Shawnee, 1983-86; rsch. assoc. U. Colo. Health Scis. Ctr., Psyciatry, Denver, 1986; asst. prof. U. Colo. Health Scis. Ctr., Psychiatry, 1986—; mem. spl. study sect. NIMH, Washington, 1988-89; outside reviewer NSF, 1988-90; reviewer various profl. jours. Editor Jour. Bibl. Equality, 1989—; contbr. articles to profl. jours. Bd. dirs. Front Range Christians for Bibl. Equality, Denver, 1989—. SUNY Regents scholar, 1971-74. Mem. AAAS, Am. Psychol. Assn., Animal Behavior Soc., Am. Soc. Primatologists (prog. com. 1986-90, R&D com. 1990—), Devlopmental Psychobiology Rsch. Group (exec. com. 1989—). Office: UCHSC Campus Box C268R 4200 E 9th Ave Denver CO 80262

BOCCIO, BARBARA ANN, advertising executive; b. Bronx, N.Y., Apr. 19, 1958; d. William Graves and Ann Teresa (O'Neill) Armstrong; m. Joseph Thomas Boccio, Nov. 8, 1980; children: Gina Marie, Eva Ann. Student, N.Y. Inst. Tech., 1982-84, SUNY, Farmingdale, 1984-87. Artist Co-Art Assoc., Floral Park, N.Y., 1981-83; art dir. Garvan Advt., Hicksville, N.Y., 1983-85, AM & P Svcs., Elmont, N.Y., 1985-87; pres. Boccio Design, Bethpage, 1987—. Mem. Occupational Edn. Graphic Arts Com. for Sewanka Cen. High Sch. dist. (adv. coun.). Mem. L.I. Network Entrepreneurs (v.p.), L.I. Ad Club, L.I. Assn., Nat. Assn. Women's Bus. Owners, Am. Bus. Assocs. Republican. Roman Catholic. Home and Office: 7 Manchester Dr Bethpage NY 11714-3203

BOCCUZZI, NANCY KOWA, hospital administrator; b. Olney, Ill., July 18, 1945; d. Carl Edwin Kowa and Sarah Elizabeth (Van Cleve) Scott; m. Salvatore R. Boccuzzi, June 6, 1970; 1 child, Ellen Elizabeth. RN, St. Luke's Hosp., St. Louis, 1966; BA, Jersey City State Coll., 1976; MA, Fairleigh Dickinson U., 1978; MPH, Columbia U., 1983. Nursing supr. Presbyn. Hosp., N.Y.C., 1967-79, asst. dir. nursing, 1979-81; adminstr. dept. ob-gyn. Columbia U., N.Y.C., 1981-84; mgr. Nutritional Mgmt., Boston, 1984-86; healthcare cons. Equicor/Equitable HCA Corp., N.Y.C., 1986-88; corp. adminstr. dept. medicine St.Luke's Roosevelt Hosp. Ctr., N.Y.C., 1988—. Contbr. articles to profl. jours. Recipient Outstanding Managerial Performance award Jour. Nursing Adminstrn., 1980. Mem. Am. Nurses Assn., Am. Pub. Health Assn., Adminstrs. in Internal Medicine. Roman Catholic. Home: 971 Cordes Ct Oradell NJ 07649 Office: St Lukes Roosevelt Hosp Ctr 425 W 59th St Ste 5D New York NY 10019

BOCHICCHIO-AUSURA, JILL ARDEN, photographer; b. Indpls., Jan. 22, 1951; d. Anthony Joseph and Claire Gilbert (Parkin) Bochicchio; m. Robert Vincent Ausura Apr. 21, 1979; 1 child, Bret Anthony Bochicchio-Ausura. AA, Montgomery Coll., 1971; BS, Ind. State U., 1974, MS, 1976. Instr. photography Montgomery Coll., Rockville, Md., 1976-79; prin. Bochicchio Photography, Gaithersburg, Md., 1983—; lectr. in field. Contbr. photographs to So. Exposure. Recipient Kodak Gallery award Eastman Kodak Co., 1987, 88, 89. Fellow Md. Profl. Photographers Assn. (bd. dirs. 1984-90, pres. 1988, chmn. of bd. 1989, Photographer of Yr. 1984—, Creative Photographer of Yr., 1984, 85, 86, 87, Hartig Meml. award, 1985, 86, 87, 88, 89, Carolyn Yen Meml. Nature award 1989, travel loan collection 1985, 86, 87, 88, 89); mem. Profl. Photographers Am. (cert., master photographer 1987, craftsman photographer 1989), Southeastern Profl. Photographers Assn. (1st pl. creative photograph 1985, 1st pl. wedding photograph 1985), Upper Montgomery County C. of C. Home and Office: Bochicchio Photography 808-101 Quince Orchard Blvd Gaithersburg MD 20878

BOCK, CAROLYN ANN, education materials company consultant, writer, lecturer; b. New Bavaria, Ohio, Jan. 25, 1942; d. Wilfred Ignatius and Marcella Mary (Birkemeier) Gerschutz; m. Donald Charles Bock, Sept. 7, 1974; 1 son, Jonathon Edward. Student Notre Dame Coll., 1960-62, 87, John Carroll U., 1962-66. With sales and promotions dept. Schaffer Diversified Corp. and other cos., Cleve., 1962-74; columnist, writer West Life Newspaper, Westlake, Ohio, 1980-83, Westlaker Times, Lorain, Ohio, 1983-84; owner Dynamic Living Assocs., Westlake, 1986—. Feature writer, bus., arts, families. Author: Authors, Artists and Auras, 1988, Gerschutz family history, 1989. Co-founder, trustee Community Action Team, Westlake, 1980-85, Westlake Arts Council, 1984—, co-founder, 1983-84, pres., 1984-85; chmn. Morning Seminar, Rocky River, Ohio, 1981-85; pres. Westlake PTA Council, 1980-82, Parkside Jr. High PTA, Westlake, 1983-84; active Boy Scouts, Cub Scouts, Westlake, 1977-82; mem. Clague Playhouse, Westlake, 1983—, Westlake Hist. Soc., 1985—, Nuclear Freeze Campaign, Cleve., 1984—. Recipient Outstanding Service award Westlake Cub Scouts, 1980; hon. life mem. Ohio PTA, 1982; Ohio Arts Council grantee, 1984, 85; Notre Dame Coll. scholarship, 1960. Mem. Am. Entrepreneurs Assn., Westlake C. of C., Sigma Delta Chi. Republican. Unitarian Universalist. Avocations: traveling; reading; sewing; cooking. Home and Office: 23553 Belmont Dr Westlake OH 44145

BOCK, J. KATHRYN, psychology educator; b. Bellefonte, Pa., Mar. 29, 1948; d. Richard Harry and Evalyn June (Shoup) B.; m. David Edmund Irwin, Dec. 26, 1981. BA, Bucknell U., 1969; AM, U. Ill., 1973, PhD, 1975. Asst. prof. Mich. State U., East Lansing, 1976-82, assoc. prof., 1984-87, prof. psychology, 1988—; vis. asst. prof. U. Oreg., Eugene, 1975-76; asst. prof. Cornell U., Ithaca, N.Y., 1983-84; vis. lectr. MIT, Cambridge, 1987-88. Contbr. articles to profl. jours. Sloan Found. fellow U. Pa., 1982-83; Max Planck Inst. Psycholinguistics fellow, Nijmegen, The Netherlands, 1983, 88. Mem. Psychonomic Soc. Office: Dept Psychology Mich State U East Lansing MI 48824

BOCKEWITZ, ALETA JUNE, office manager; b. Muscatine, Iowa, June 29, 1945; d. Wilbur David and Dorothy Elizabeth (Smull) Ripley; div.; children: William Joseph, Christine Elizabeth. Student, No. Nev. Real Estate Sch., 1987, Barbizon Modeling Sch., Reno, 1990, Scott Community Coll., Bettendorf, Iowa, 1984, Black Hawk Coll., 1975-76, 83-84, Western Nev. Community Coll., 1986—. Sec., social svc. rep. Friendship Manor, Rock Island, Ill., 1984-86; companion pvt. party, Rock Island, Ill., 1986; sec./clk. Carson Postal Dept., Carson City, Nev., 1986-87; com. sec. Nev. Legis., Carson City, 1987-88; adminstrv. aide II State of Nev., Carson City, 1987-88, to mgmt. asst. II, 1989—. Active St. Patrick's Ch., past pres. Rosary Soc., choir mem., others; chmn. Miss. Valley Girl Scouts; pres. Rockridge High Sch. Band Boosers, others. Republican. Baptist.

BOCKEWITZ, WILMA GERTRUDE, teacher; b. Atlanta, Ill.; d. William Riley and Etta Mae (Orr) Foster; m. Harry Urban Bockewitz, 1929; children: Carol Lou, Mary Suzanne. BS, U. Ill., 1927. Tchr. Belleville High Sch.; substitute tchr. Morton High Sch. Recipient art award Oak Park Show. Mem. AAUW, La Grange Art League, Allied Art. Republican.

BOCKEY, PAMELA SUE, writer, festival administrator; b. Van Wert, Ohio, Feb. 27, 1952; d. Dal eLeRoy and Dolores Ellen (Burkholder) Keysor; m. Thomas Eugene Bockey, Dec. 2, 1972. Student, Bowling Green State U., 1971. Dir. D&D Farm, Inc., Van Wert, Ohio; office mgr. Centralized Data Processing, Aeroquip Corp.; input sys. specialist Aeroquip Corp./Trinovio Corp., Van Wert; adminstrv. assoc. Wassenberg Art Ctr., Van Wert. Coord. Van Wert County Peony Festival. Mem. NAFE, Am. Bus. Women's Assn. (bull. editor Peony chpt. 1989, v.p. 1990), Van Wert C. of C. (mem. visitors bur.). Republican. Home: RR 2 Box 58B Van Wert OH 45891

BOCKIAN, DONNA MARIE, data processing executive; b. N.Y.C., June 4, 1946; d. Forrest Mager and Mary C. (Lovelace) Hastings; m. James Bernard Bockian, Sept. 16, 1984; children: Vivian Shifra, Adrian Adena, Lillian Tova. BA in Psychology, Vassar Coll., 1968; diploma in systems analysis NYU, 1978. Computer programmer RCA, N.Y.C., 1968-71; systems analyst United Artists Corp., N.Y.C., 1971-78; project leader Bradford Nat. Corp., N.Y.C., 1978-81; project mgr. Mfrs. Hanover Trust, N.Y.C., 1981-83; project mgr. Chem. Bank, N.Y.C., 1983-86; mgr. fin. systems Salomon Bros., N.Y.C., 1986-87; v.p. James B. Bockian and Assocs., 1987—; mgr. systems quality assurance GAB Bus. Svcs., Inc., Parsippany, N.J., 1989—. Mem. Assn. Women in Computing (exec. com. 1982-83), Vassar Club. Avocation: photography. Home: 26 Farmhouse Ln Morristown NJ 07960

BODA, VERONICA CONSTANCE, lawyer; b. Phila., Oct. 8, 1952; d. Louis Paul and Helen Ann (Zwigaitis) B. AB, Wilson Coll., 1974; JD, Vermont Law Sch., 1978; LLM in Taxation, Villanova U., 1989. Staff atty. Cape-Atlantic Legal Services, Atlantic City, 1978-79; sole practice Phila., 1980—; tchr. Am. Inst. for Paralegal Studies, Phila., 1982-86; instr. bus. adminstrn. program Pa. State U., Media, Pa., 1987—; ins. agt. Prudential Ins. Co., Wayne, Pa., 1985-86; ins. broker V C Boda & Co., Phila., 1986—; coord. planned giving Wilson Coll., Chambersburg, Pa., 1985—; title ins. atty. Neshaminy Abstract Co., Doylestown, Pa., 1987—. Author: (with others) Newberg on Class Actions, 1985; contbr. articles to profl. jours. Bd. dirs. Colonial Phila. Hist. Soc., 1983, pres., 1984—; asst. treas. Independence Hall Assn., 1989—. Mem. Nat. Assn. Women Lawyers (treas.), Phila. Bar Assn. (com. chair real estate section 1984-86). Democrat. Roman Catholic.

BODINE, CHARLENE LOUISE, civic worker; b. Ekalaka, Mont., Sept. 23, 1942; d. Charles Henry and Eldora Hope (Bailey) Kittelmann; m. Richard Peter Bodine, Sept. 8, 1962; children: Todd, Melanie. BS in Office Mgmt., U. Wyo., 1987. Sec. Ryan Lab., Mont. State U., Bozeman, 1961-68; census taker, Billings, Mont., 1970; tchr.'s aide Sch. Dist. 2, Sheridan, Wyo., 1974-77, substitute tchr., 1977-83. Fundraiser Sheridan Coll., 1989-90, trustee, 1990; sec. Sheridan Newcomers, 1975; pres. Sheridan Svc. League, 1976-77. Mem. AAUW (historian 1989-90). Republican. Roman Catholic. Home: 1217 Lewis St Sheridan WY 82801

BODINE, DELLA L., nursing administrator; b. Trenton, Oct. 16, 1951; d. Richard Stauffer and Jessie Mae (Beck) White; m. Wayne H. Bodine, July 2, 1972; 1 child, Jessica Leigh. Diploma Helene Fuld Sch. Nursing, Trenton, 1972; B.S.N., Trenton State Coll., 1980; M.S.N., U. Pa., 1983. Lic. nursing home adminstr., N.J. Dir. nursing Lakewood House, Burlington, N.J., 1972-73, Moorestown Nursing Home, N.J., 1973-78; staff nurse Burlington County Meml. Hosp., N.J., 1978-80, head nurse, 1980-81; dir. nursing Mt. Holly Ctr., N.J., 1981-82; assoc. dir. nursing Hamilton Hosp., Trenton, 1983-85; nursing supr. Hickory House Nursing Home, Honeybrook, Pa., 1986-87, asst. dir., 1987-88; owner, mgr. Marsh Creek Campground, Lyndell, Pa., 1984—; owner Star Nursing Home Staffing Svc., Lyndell, 1988—, also bd. dirs. Home: PO Box 257 Lyndell PA 19354 Office: Star Nursing Home Staffing Svc PO Box 273 Lyndell PA 19354

BODINE, MICHELLE DAWN, medical center director; b. Atchison, Kans., July 11, 1964; d. Donald Lee and Carol Ann (McConnaughey) Hubach; m. Paul Mitchell Bodine, May 14, 1988. BS with nursing honors, Washburn U., 1986; postgrad., Cen. Mich. U., 1989—. RN, Kans. Staff nurse St. Francis Hosp. and Med. Ctr., Topeka, 1986-87; staff nurse Employees' Benefit Assn. Med. Ctr., Topeka, 1987-88, supr., 1988; dir. med. ctr. A.T. & S.F. Employees' Benefit Assn. (EBA Med. Ctr.), Topeka, 1988—. Bd. dirs. Am. Diabetes Assn.-Kans., Topeka, 1990—. Mem. Am. Nurses Assn., Kans. Nurses Assn. (publicity com. dist. 1, 1987-89), Sigma Theta Tau. Republican. Roman Catholic. Office: Employees' Benefit Assn 620 SE Madison St Topeka KS 66607

BODINE, SARAH ELLIOTT, educator; b. Detroit, July 12, 1930; d. Ray Earl and Harriet (Weston) Elliott; m. Marc W. Bodine Jr., June 6, 1953 (dec. Jan. 1988); children: Marc W. III, Robert W. Student, DePauw U., 1948-50; BS, U. Ill., 1952; MA, Northwestern U., 1961. Tchr. Sch. Union 46, Topsham, Me., 1958-61, Princeton (N.J.) Pub. Schs., 1961-63, Binghamton (N.Y.) Pub. Schs., 1963-75, Socorro (New Mex.) Pub. Schs.; instr. Denver Auraria Community Coll., 1981-85; dir. vol. Denver Symphony Orch., 1978-80; program specialist Fla. Conv. Svcs. Sec. N.Mex. Fedn. Tchrs., Albuquerque, vice chair, Socorro County Rep. Group, Socorro, 1979-80, pres. sec., founder, Friends Evergreen Library, 1982-88. Mem. AAUW. Republican. Episcopalian. Home: 101 Palm Ct Naples FL 33942

BODKIN, RUBY PATE, corporate executive, real estate broker, educator; b. Frostproof, Fla., Mar. 11, 1926; d. James Henry and Lucy Beatrice (Latham) P.; m. Lawrence Edward Bodkin Sr., Jan. 15, 1949; children: Karen Bodkin Snead, Cinda, Lawrence Jr. BA, Fla. State U., 1948; MA, U. Fla., 1972. Lic. real estate broker. Banker Barnett Bank, Avon Park, Fla., 1943-44, Lewis State Bank, Tallahassee, 1944-49; ins. underwriter Hunt Ins. Agy., Tallahassee, 1949-51; tchr. Duval County Sch. Bd., Jacksonville, Fla., 1952-77; pvt. practice realty Jacksonville, 1976—; tchr. Nassau County Sch. Bd., Jacksonville, 1978-83; sec., treas., v.p. Bodkin Corp., R&D/Inventions, Jacksonville, 1983—; assoc. Brooke Shields Innovative Designer Products, Inc., Kendall Park, N.J., 1988—; substitute tchr. Duval County Sch. Bd., 1980—. Mem. Jacksonville Symphony Guild, 1985—, Mus. Sci. And History Guild, Jacksonville, 1959—, Southside Woman's Club, Jacksonville, 1957—, Garden Club Jacksonville, 1976—. Recipient 25 Yr. Service award Duval County Sch. Bd., 1976, Tchr. of Yr. award Bryceville Sch., 1981. Mem. Ponte Vedra Inn and Club, San Jose Country Club. Home: 1149 Molokai Rd Jacksonville FL 32216 Office: Bodkin Jewelers & Appraisers PO Box 16482 Jacksonville FL 32216

BODMAN, HELENE DUNN, musicologist; b. N.Y.C., Nov. 22, 1936; d. Kempton and Susan Barret (Gill) Dunn; m. Richard S. Bodman, Jan. 28, 1961; children: Taylor, James Martyn. Ed. New Eng. Conservatory, 1957-60; B.Mus., San Francisco Conservatory of Music, 1968; M.A. in Music, Am. U., 1982. Dir. Opera and Symphony Previews, San Francisco, 1966-67; instr. piano, music theory, San Francisco, 1969-71, Wilmington, Del., 1973-76; case dir. Congressman William S. Mailliard, Washington, 1973; arts coord. Del. State Arts Coun., 1977-78; music libr. Am. U., Washington, 1981-84; pres. Music Info. Specialists, 1984—, dir. Discovering Music, 1984—; dir. Rsch. Ctr. for Chinese Mus. Iconography, 1984—; cons. Boys Clubs of Am. Young Artists Program. Author: Chinese Musical Iconography: A History of Musical Instruments Depicted in Chinese Art, 1987, Chinese Musical Iconography: A Catologue, 1988, National Symphony Orchestra: A Discography, 1988; program annotator Dumbarton Concert Series; Handel Festival Orch., Nat. Chamber Orch., Smithsonian Inst. Bd. dirs. Spring Opera of San Francisco, 1967-71, Wilmington Music Sch., 1973-78, Washington Performing Arts Soc., 1980—, Nat. Symphony Orch., Washington, 1979-82; trustee San Francisco Conservatory of Music, 1967-71; bd. overseers New Eng. Conservatory, 1985—. Mem. Smithsonian Instn. (steering com. Friends of Music), Am. Musicol. Soc. Office: 205 E 95th St Ste 31-D New York NY 10128

BODNER, M. GAYLE, lawyer; b. Louisville, May 29, 1963; d. Thomas L. and Mary M. (Becker) Bodner. BA with high distinction, U. Ky., 1984; JD cum laude, U. Louisville, 1988. Asst. programmer Jefferson County Bd. Edn., Louisville, 1984-86; legal clk. Wyatt, Tarrant & Combs, Louisville, 1986-87, Ky. Fried Chicken Corp., Louisville, 1987-88; assoc. atty. Tex. Gas Transmission Corp., Owensboro, Ky., 1988—; legal counsel, bd. dirs. Tex. Gas Employees Credit Union, Owensboro, Ky. Bd. dirs. Theater Workshop of Owensboro. Scholar U. Louisville, 1985-88. Mem. ABA, Ky. Bar Assn., Fed. Energy Bar Assn., Daviess County Bar Assn., Phi Beta Kappa, Delta Theta Phi. Republican. Office: Tex Gas Transmission 3800 Frederica St Owensboro KY 42301

BOE, ANNE CAROL, networking counselor; b. Seattle, May 10, 1946; d. Milton and Lenore (Wolf) Weis; m. May 26, 1970 (div. 1980). BE in Speech, Western Wash. State Coll., 1972; MEd in Counseling, S.D. State U., 1978; MA in Career Devel., U. Minn., 1979. Instr., counselor Normandale Community Coll., Bloomington, Minn., 1976-78; placement dir. Grossmont Coll., San Diego, 1978-80; pres., owner Career Networks, San Diego, 1980—; motivational and keynote speaker. Author: Is Your Net-Working?, 1989; producer video Networking For Your Personal and Financial Growth in the 1990's. Named Speaker of Yr., Nat. Mgmt. Assn., 1986. Mem. Nat. Speakers Assn. (pres. San Diego 1987-88, Mem. of Yr. award 1987), San Diego Career Guidance Assn. (pres. 1984-85), Greater San Diego C. of C., Golden Triangle C. of C. (bd. dirs. 1987-88). Home: 607 Summer View Circle Encinitas CA 92024

BOECKMANN-ROSS, LAVERNE, publishing executive, foundation executive; b. Glendale, Calif., Oct. 14, 1949; d. Herbert F. and Jane Boeckmann; m. Steven A. Ross, Apr. 14, 1984. A.A., Glendale Jr. Coll., 1969; B.A., San Diego State U., 1971; teaching credential, U. So. Calif., 1975. Elem. tchr. Los Angeles Sch. Dist., 1974-78; account exec. Valley Mag., Granada Hills, Calif., 1978-86; v.p. Tara Labs., Panorama City, Calif., 1982-89; account exec. KABC Let's Talk Mag., Granada Hills, Calif., 1985-86; co-founder World Research Found., Sherman Oaks, Calif., 1983—, v.p., 1989—. Coordinator Beauty Contest, Northridge, Calif., 1983. Mem. San Fernando Valley Exec. Assn. (bd. dirs. 1982-83), NAFE, Women's Network Assn. Republican. Avocations: painting, dancing, skiing, travel, singing. Office: World Research Found 15300 Ventura Blvd #405 Sherman Oaks CA 91403

BOEDECKER, ANNE L., psychologist, business owner; b. Poughkeepsie, N.Y., Jan. 20, 1951; d. Ray F. and Elizabeth (Hutchinson) B.; m. Terrence P. Kimper, Aug. 19, 1979; 1 child, Wendy. Student, Dartmouth Coll., 1971-72; BA, Vassar Coll., 1973; MS, Pa. State U., 1975, PhD, 1978. Lic. psychologist, N.H. Adj. prof. Pa. State U., College Park, 1977-78; intern U. Tex. Counseling Ctr., Austin, 1978-80; staff psychologist Cen. N.H. Community Mental Health Svcs., 1980-81; prof. Grad. Sch. Antioch Coll., Keene, N.H., 1981-83; counselor, cons. Ruadlett Jr. High Sch., Concord, N.H., 1983-85; adj. prof. New Eng. Coll., Hennifer, N.H., 1985-86, Notre Dame Coll., Manchester, N.H., 1986-87; pvt. practice Concord, 1981—; exec. dir. Wellspring Ctr. for Human Devel., Concord, 1987—; mem. adv. coun. counseling program Notre Dame, Manchester, 1985-88; cons. Rape & Domestic Violence Crisis Ctr., Concord, 1986-88; mem. psychiatry dept. Concord Hosp., 1989—. Editor: Women Therapists Resource Directory, 1986; contbr. articles to profl. jours. Founder, sec. Coalition Against Sexual Exploitation, Concord, 1987-89; mem. Bow (N.H.) PTA, 1989—. Rufus Choate scholar Dartmouth Coll., 1972. Fellow N.H. Psychol. Assn. (chair women and minorities com. 1986-89); mem. Am. Psychol. Assn. Home: 4 One Stack Dr Bow NH 03304 Office: Wellspring Ctr Human Devel 38 Warren St Concord NH 03301

BOEDECKER, ERIN ELAINE, industrial engineer; b. Corning, N.Y., Dec. 31, 1959; d. Charles Harold Shattuck and Stella Anastasia (Polyniak) B.; m. David Lynn Boedecker, May 30, 1987. BS, Va. Poly. and State U., 1981; MS in Engring., U. Tex., 1989. Seismic analyst Seimograph Svc. Corp., Houston, 1981-85; indsl. engr. USAF, San Antonio, 1987—. Recipient Alumni Presdl. scholarship Va. Poly. Inst., 1977-81. Mem. Kelly Mgmt. Assn., Ops. Rsch. Soc. Am., Omega Rho, Phi Eta Sigma. Republican. Baptist. Home: 7506 Ledgebrook San Antonio TX 78244

BOEGNER, MARY ELIZABETH BLANCHE, artist; b. Mpls., Sept. 23, 1925; d. Gordon Raymond and Anna Marie (Schwegmann) Blanche; m. Allan Patrick Boegner, Apr. 29, 1947; children: Patricia Ann Boegner Grote, John Gordon. Student, St. Cloud (Minn.) Tchrs. Coll., 1943-45, State Tchrs. Coll., Duluth, Minn., 1943-46. Performing artist various studios, 1937-51; free lance artist Bryan, Tex., 1977—; artist Tex. Renaissance Festival, Magnolia, 1978-85, Exhibit Paris, 1982. Exhibited in group shows at Brazos Valley Mus., 1986 (award), Messina Hof Wine Cellars, 1988. Mem. Brazos Valley Art League, Brazos Valley Arts Coun., Houston Art League, VFW Auxiliary (past sec., pres., Community Svc. award 1967-68). Home and Studio: 2200 S College Ave Bryan TX 77801

BOEHM, MARGARET STITT, accountant; b. Detroit, Sept. 29, 1944; d. Ralph Frank and Ella (Marks) Stitt; m. Edward W. Harris III, June 11, 1966 (div. June 1974); children: Deborah DePrez Harris, David Edward Harris; m. Theodore R. Boehm, Jan. 27, 1985. BA, Mt. Holyoke Coll., 1966. CPA, Ind., Ohio. Owner Peggy Harris, CPA, Indpls., 1976-81; commr. Pub. Service Commn. of Ind., Indpls., 1981-85; head dept. fin. Meth. Hosp., Indpls., 1985-86; dep. dir. State Budget Agy., Indpls., 1986-89; fin. dir. YWCA of Cin., 1989—. Treas. Meridian Kessler Neighborhood Assn., Indpls., 1977. Mem. Am. Inst. CPA's, Ind. CPA Soc., Govt. Fin. Officers Assn. Democrat. Home: 3789 Country Club Pl Cincinnati OH 45208

BOEHME, SARAH ELIZABETH, museum curator; b. Orange, Tex., Aug. 3, 1948; d. Lawrence Herbert and Gwendolyn (Dixon) B. BA, Sarah Lawrence Coll., 1970; MA, Bryn Mawr Coll., 1973. Curator, instr. St. Lawrence U., Canton, N.Y., 1973-77; curator Stark Mus. Art, Orange, 1978-82; John S. Bugas curator Whitney Gallery Western Art Whitney Gallery Western Art Buffalo Bill Hist. Ctr., Cody, Wyo., 1986—; guest curator U. Wyo., Laramie, 1987, 88. Author: Rendezvous to Roundup: The First 100 Years of Art in Wyoming, 1990; co-author: Frontier America: Art and Treasures of the Old West, 1988; contbr. articles to profl. pubs. Bd. dirs. Park County (Wyo.) Arts Coun., 1989—. Smithsonian predoctoral fellow, 1983-86; Whiting fellow, 1984-85, Samuel H. Kress fellow. Mem. AAUW, Coll. Art Assn., Am. Assn. Mus. Methodist. Home: 2013 Newton Ave Cody WY 82414 Office: Buffalo Bill Hist Ctr 720 Sheridan Ave PO Box 1000 Cody WY 82414

BOEHMER, RAQUEL DAVENPORT, television producer, newsletter editor; b. Bklyn., Feb. 24, 1938; d. John Joralemon Davenport and Fanny (Barberis) Allison; m. Peter Joseph Boehmer; children: Kristian Ludwig, Louisa, Timothy Joralemon. BA, Wells Coll., 1959. Radio producer Maine Pub. Broadcasting Network, Bangor, 1977—; developer, editor consumer newsletter Seafood Soundings, Monhegan, Maine, 1986—; speaker Seafare, 1986, Los Angeles; keynote speaker Beyond Wells Day, Wells Coll., Aurora, N.Y., 1988. Writer, producer (weekly radio spot) Whole Foods for All People, 1977—; producer, host (TV cooking program) Different Kettle of Fish, 1984; author: A Foraging Vacation, 1982, Raquel's Main Guide to New England Seafoods, 1988. Writer legislation, Maine legis., 1985, 87; treas. Monhegan Plantation, 1970-72, chair bicentennial com., 1976; chair Monhegan Sch. Bd., 1973-74; co-chair Monhegan Solid Waste Com., 1988-90. Recipient Pub. Service award Maine Nutrition Assn.; named Gt. New Eng. Cook Yankee mag., 1986. Mem. Nat. Newsletter Assn., Women's Fisheries Network, Colonial Dames Am., Women's Strike for Peace. Home and Office: Lobster Cove Rd Monhegan Island ME 04852

BOEING, MARCIA DELANO COMLEY, advertising executive; b. Hartford, Conn., July 13, 1946; d. Winthrop Delano and Mary-June (Bowes) Comley; m. Peter Alan Boeing, Sept. 23, 1973 (div. July 1978); 1 child, Carl Delano. BA, Regis Coll., 1968. Advt. mgr. Allyn and Bacon, Inc., Boston, 1971-74; dir. creative svcs. Graphics Unltd., Westwood, Mass., 1981-84; pres., chief executive officer Design Ad Cetera, Inc., Norwood, Mass., 1984—; tchr. Boston Ctr. for Adult Edn., 1985. Recipient Desi award, N.Y. Art Dirs., 1988, Bronze award, Internat. Hotel, Sales and Mktg. Assn., 1986. Mem. Builders Assn. Boston (sales and mktg. coun. 1987—, Prism awards com. 1988, chmn. Prism awards 1989). Roman Catholic. Home: 11 J William Hgts Millis MA 02054 Office: Design Ad Cetera Inc 1426 Providence Hwy Norwood MA 02054

BOEMER, LOIS E., public relations executive; b. St. Louis, Jan. 2, 1934; d. Edward Frederick and Marie Elizabeth (Joeckel) Hoffmann; m. Allen James Boemer, Jan. 28, 1956; children: Susan Sullivan, Cheryl, Lisa Byrne, Eric. Grad. high sch., St. Louis. Exec. sec. Ge. Am. Life Ins. Co., St. Louis, 1951-56; office mgr. Evang. Children's Home, St. Louis, 1957-62; asst. rsch.

U. Wis., Madison, Wis., 1963-65; weekly columnist Newton (Mass.) Times, 1968-72; Office/mktg. mgr. Good Clancy & Assocs., Boston, 1974-84; prin. Boerner Assocs., Newton, Mass., 1984-88; pres. BA Communications, Newton, Mass., 1988—. Adv. bd. Tng. Inc./Greater Boston YMCA; parent's coun. Hartwick Coll., Oneonta, N.Y., 1989-91; pres. Luth. Ch. Newton, Mass., 1985-87. Mem. Soc. Mktg. Profl. Svcs. (founding mem., NE regional dir., 1982-83), NE Women in Real Estate, Boston Soc. Arch. Democrat. Office: BA Communications Inc 12 Mt Ida Terrace Newton MA 02158

BOERNER, JO M., real estate trainer; b. Wayne, Okla., Apr. 17, 1944; d. James Olman and Virgie M. (Jones) Whitaker; m. Buddy Dennis Boerner, July 3, 1964; children: Christopher Alexander, James Dennis, Edward Floyd. Assoc. Abide Realtors, Oklahoma City, 1976-83; br. mgr. Merrill Lynch Realtors, Oklahoma City, 1983-86; dir. career devel. Marolyn Pryor & Assocs., Oklahoma City, 1986-87, Long & Foster, Realtors, Fairfax, Va., 1987—; regional v.p. Women's Coun. of Realtors, Chgo., 1987; bd. dir. Oklahoma City Bd. Realtors, 1984-85; instr. Realtors Inst. Okla. State U., 1987. Contbr. articles to profl. jours. Bd. govs. Wednesday's Child Found., Oklahoma City, 1987; mem. Allied Arts Coun., Oklahoma City, 1985-87, Realtors Polit. Action Com., Okla., 1984-87. Recipient State of Excellance award Okla. State Gov., 1987, Omega Tau Rho medal. Mem. Nat. Women's Coun. of Realtors (gov. bd. 1985-87), Nat. Assn. Realtors, Women's Coun. of Realtors (pres. 1985, gov. 1986), Va. Assn. Realtors, Siga Internat. (trustee 1982-83), Toastmasters. Republican. Office: Long & Foster Realtors 11351 Random Hills Rd Fairfax VA 22030

BOESEL, ELIZABETH PARKS, editor of periodical; b. Toledo, July 9, 1962; d. Milton Charles Jr. and Lucy Laughlin (Mather) B. BA in English and Theatre Arts, Hollins Coll. Asst. stage mgr. Va. Stage Co., Norfolk, 1984-86; asst. prodn. stage mgr. Va. Opera Assn., Norfolk, 1986-88; stage mgr. Manhattan Class Co., N.Y.C., 1988-89; asst. to editor-in-chief Lear Pub., N.Y.C., 1988-90, spl. projects editor, 1990—; stage mgr. Lime Kiln Arts, Lexington, Va., summers 1986, 87; bd. dirs. Michabo Inc., Manhattan Class Co. Mem. N.Y. Jr. League. Episcopalian. Office: Lear Publishing 655 Madison Ave 7th Flr New York NY 10021

BOESKE, ADELE CLAIRE, quality control executive; b. Boston, Dec. 1, 1947; d. John Joseph and Adela Mary (Wistejunas) Wilkalis; div. Dec. 1979; 1 child, Steven Jason. Assoc. in Chemistry, Lowell Tech. Inst., 1969; Assoc. in Computer Sci. with honors, No. Essex Community Coll., Haverhill, Mass., 1979. Chem. lab. technician Raytheon, Lowell, Bedford, Mass., 1967-70, Honeywell, Inc., Billerica, Mass., 1970-71; final test supr. Spectrametrics, Inc., Andover, Haverhill, Mass., 1979-84; quality control mgr. Amdev, Inc., Danvers, Mass., 1984—. Mem. Am. Soc. for Quality Control, Nat. Assn. for Female Execs.

BOETTCHER, NORBE BIROSEL, chemist; b. Manila, June 6, 1932; d. Dionisio Martinez and Filomena (Cuaresma) Birosel; m. Robert Arnold Boettcher, June 6, 1961; 1 child, Heidi Noriko. BS in Chemistry, Philippine Women's U., 1953; postgrad., U. Iowa, 1955-57. Chemist, rsch. and devel. Lawry's Foods, Inc., L.A., 1957-61; chemist, quality control, rsch. and devel. Sunsweet Products, San Jose, Calif., 1964-68; teaching asst., rsch. chemist Coe Coll., Cedar Rapids, Iowa, 1969-77; chemist, rsch. and devel. Penford Products Co., Cedar Rapids, 1977—; sci. writer FISH, San Francisco. Mem. Brucemore, Inc., Cedar Rapids, Met. Opera Guild, N.Y.C. Recipient Golden Poet award, 1990, World of Poetry, 1987, 88, Silver Poet award, 1989. Mem. AAAS, AAUW, Cedar Rapids Art Mus., Philippine-Am. Club (social chmn. pres. Linn County, Iowa 1989—). Republican. Roman Catholic. Home: 348 7th St Marion IA 52302 Office: Penford Products Co 1st St SW Cedar Rapids IA 52406

BOETTGER, SUSAN DORIS, organic chemist; b. Two Rivers, Wis., Oct. 6, 1952; d. Hilary L. and Mary J. (Beitzel) B. BS, U. Wis., 1974; MS, Cornell U., 1977, PhD, 1979. Postdoctoral fellow dept. chemistry Cornell U., Ithaca, N.Y., 1979, U. Rochester, N.Y., 1979-81; rsch. scientist A indsl. div. Bristol-Myers Squibb Co., Syracuse, N.Y., 1981-82, rsch. scientist pharm. rsch. and devel., 1983-84, sr. rsch. scientist, 1984—. Contbr. articles to profl. jours.; patentee in field. Bd. dirs. Onondaga Audubon Soc., 1990; mem. Adirondack Coun. Helfaer scholar U. Wis., 1973; fellow Cornell U., 1974. Mem. Am. Chem. Soc. (chmn. nominations Syracuse sect. 1984, sec. 1986-88), Phi Beta Kappa, Phi Kappa Phi, Sigma Delta Epsilon. Office: Bristol-Myers Squibb Co PO Box 4755 Syracuse NY 13221-4755

BOFINGER, PAMELA LYNN, sales executive; b. Alhambra, Calif., Apr. 28, 1964; d. Richard Anthony and Marjorie Ruth (Hovey) Pellerito; m. Robert T. Bofinger, June 4, 1988. Student, U. Calif., Irvine, 1986; MBA, Pepperdine U., 1990. Pub. defender interviewer Orange County Pub. Defender, Santa Ana, Calif., 1984-86; legal asst. Sitheris Chebithes Law Firm, Irvine, Calif., 1985-87; advt. specialist So. Calif. Network, Newport Beach, 1985-87; sr. sales rep. NEC Home Electronics, Wood Dale, Ill., 1987-90; account exec. NEC Techs., Irvine, Calif.; mem. internat. performing group Up With People. Pres. Arts in the Inner City The Pram Group. Recipient Best Presentation award, NEC Home Electronics. Mem. NAFE, Am. Mgmt. Assn., U. Calif. Irvine Alumni Assn., Pi Beta Phi. Republican. Home: 24231 Grayston Dr El Toro CA 92630 Office: 30 Executive Pk Ste 200 Irvine CA 92714

BOGAN, KATHLEEN MAY, lawyer; b. West Roxbury, Mass., Nov. 25, 1947; d. Arthur John and Regina Rose (Hafer) B.; m. Louis Raymond Barnett Jr., Jan. 17, 1969 (div. Aug. 1974). AB, Syracuse U., 1969; JD, Lewis and Clark Coll., Portland, Oreg., 1980. Bar: Oreg., 1982, U.S. Dist. Ct. Oreg. 1982. City desk editor Anchorage Daily Times, 1969-71; creative group head Panasonic Inc., N.Y.C., 1972-73; mgr. creative svcs. The Irvine Co., Newport Beach, Calif., 1973-76; law clk. Oreg. Ct. Appeals, Salem, 1980-82, Oreg. Supreme Ct., Salem, 1982; legal counsel Oreg. State Legislature, Salem, 1983-85; mgr. human resource bur. City of Portland, 1985; exec. dir. Oreg. Criminal Justice Coun., Portland, 1985—; asst. prof. adminstrn. justice Portland State U., 1987—; Fulbright sr. prof. law, West Berlin, 1990. Bd. dirs. Outside-In Med. Clinic, 1985-89, Oreg. Coun. on Crime and Delinquency, 1983-86; mem. Mayor's Task Force on Alcoholism, Portland, 1985; mem. adv. com. City-County Task Force on Homelessness, Portland, 1985; exec. com. Multnomah County Dem. Party, Portland, 1985; mem. Oreg. ACLU Commn. on Gay and Lesbian Rights, 1985-90; mem. State Juvenile Svcs. Commn. Secure Custody Alternatives Com., 1983-84. Mem. Nat. Criminal Justice Assn., Nat. Assn. Criminal Justice Planners, Criminal Justice Stats. Assn., Am. Correctional Assn., Oreg. State Bar (affirmative action com. 1984-87), Nat. Lesbian and Gay Law Assn. Office: Oreg Criminal Justice Coun PO Box 751 Portland OR 97207

BOGAN, MARY FLAIR, stockbroker; b. Providence, July 9, 1948; d. Ralph A.L. and Mary (Dyer) B.; B.A., Vassar Coll., 1969. Actress, Trinity Sq. Repertory Co., R.I., Gretna Playhouse, Pa., Skylight Comic Opera, Milw., Cin. Playhouse, Playmakers' Repertory, Va.; mem. nat. co. No Sex, Please, We're British; also TV commls., 1970-77; account exec. E.F. Hutton & Co., Inc., Providence, 1977-86; account v.p. Paine Webber, 1986—; econ. reporter Sta. WPRI-TV, 1982-85, Sta. WJAR-TV, 1987—. Treas. Red Bridge Council Rep. Women; chmn. new mems. com. R.I. Fedn. Rep. Women. Recipient Century Club award, 1980, 81, 82, 83, 85; Blue Chip Sales award, 1983, 85, Pacesetter Sales Award, 1986, 87. Mem. Internat. Platform Assn., Newport Preservation Soc., Providence Preservation Soc. Clubs: Turks Head, Brown Faculty. Home: 18 Cooke St Providence RI 02906 Office: Paine Webber 1520 Hospital Trust Tower Providence RI 02903

BOGARDUS, SARAH EMILY RAY, volunteer; b. Eugene, Oreg., June 25, 1920; d. Leonard Leon and Florence Venus (Dugan) Ray; m. Robert Anthony Bogardus, Jan. 12, 1946 (dec. Feb. 1983); children: Robert Anthony Jr., John Harker, Jane Roberts. BA, U. Oreg., 1941; MS, NYU, 1942. Exec. trainee Bloomingdale's, N.Y.C., 1942-43. Mem. Tillamook County Election Bd., Neskowin, Oreg., 1988—; bd. dirs. North Lincoln Hosp. Aux., Lincoln City, Oreg., 1984—, v.p., 1989; bd. dirs., treas. Neskowin Regional San. Dist., 1984—; mem. Columbia River coun. Girl Scouts U.S., 1965-71. Lt. supply corps WAVES, USNR, 1943-46. Mem. AAUW, DAR (regent 1986-88, treas. 1990—), Neskowin Ladies Golf Club (pres. 1988—), Devils Lake Ladies Golf Club Lincoln City (sec. 1986), Sigma Kappa (state alumnae officer, 1975-79, del. Portland Panhellenic 1962-66). Republican. Episcopalian. Home: 46495 Terrace Dr Neskowin OR 97149

BOGART, JUDITH SAUNDERS, public relations executive; b. Batesville, Ind., Nov. 16, 1936; d. David Rodman and Anne Eva (Kohles) Saunders; m. William Robert Bogart, Oct. 22, 1971. BA, Baldwin-Wallace Coll., 1958. Dir. pub. relations Greater Cin. Girl Scout Council, 1958-61, Nation's Capital Girl Scout Council, Washington, 1963-65; Gt. Rivers Girl Scout Council Cin., 1965-68; account rep. Edn. Funds Inc., Providence, 1967-68; dir. community relations Cin. Human Relations Commn., 1968-76; community relations cons. Cin., 1976-77; v.p. pub. relations Jewish Hosp. Cin., 1977-85; exec. v.p. Diversified Communicatons Inc., Cin., 1985-88; pres. Judith Bogart Assocs., Cin., 1989—. Bd. dirs. Girl Scouts U.S. 1987—, pres. Gt. Rivers council, Cin. 1984-87; bd. dirs. Nat. Council Internat. Visitors, Washington, 1988—, chair-elect, 1990-91; trustee Cin. Internat. Visitors Ctr. 1981-87; co-chair pub. relations Greater Cin. Bicentennial 1985-88; mem. United Way Planning Bd., Cin. 1987—, Xavier Univ. Community Relations Bd., Cin., 1983—. Named Career Woman of Achievement, YWCA, 1983. Fellow ARP; mem. Women in Communications Inc. (nat. headliner 1983, nat. pub. relations com., Outstanding Woman in Communications 1976), Pub. Relations Soc. Am. (nat. pres. 1983, pres. Cin. chpt. 1976, Outstanding Mem. 1977) N.Am. Pub. Relations Council (pres. 1989). Office: 617 Vine St Ste 1418 Cincinnati OH 45202

BOGART, SUSAN ALEXANDER, interior designer; b. Paterson, N.J., May 10, 1959; d. Frederick William and Olive Rose (Vehrkens) Alexander; m. Adrian Thomas Bogart III, Nov. 8, 1986. BS, Drexel U., 1982. Jr. designer Tom Lee Ltd., N.Y.C., 1980, 82-83; tenant estimator Radnor Corp., Phila., 1981-82; dir. rehab. N.Y. Hilton Hotel, N.Y.C., 1983-86; sr. designer Bogart Cons., Locust Valley, N.Y., 1986-87; prin., interior designer Susan Alexander, N.Y.C., 1988—; guest lectr., Cornell U., Ithaca, N.Y., 1985-86; interior designer, Nat. Arts Club, N.Y.C., 1988—. Mem. Am. Soc. Interior Designers, Am. Womens Econ. Devel. Assn., Nat. ARts Club. Republican. Roman Catholic. Office: 277 Ave C Ste 4E New York NY 10009

BOGART, WANDA LEE, interior designer; b. Ashville, N.C., Feb. 26, 1939; d. Bob West and Virginia Elizbeth (Worley) McLemore-Snyder; m. Sterling X. Bogart, Feb. 12, 1962; children: Kevin Sterling, Kathleen Elizabeth. BA, San Jose (Calif.) State U., 1961. Tchr. Redondo Beach (Calif.) Sch. Dist., 1962-65; free-lance interior designer Ladera, Calif., 1970-75; designer MG Interior Design, Orange, Calif., 1975-80; prin., pres. Wanda Bogart Interior Design Inc, Orange, 1980—. Contbr. articles to profl. jours. Named on of Top 20 Interior Designers in So. Calif. Ranch and Coast Mag., 1987. Mem. Internat. Soc. Interior Design, Orange C. of C. Office: Wanda Bogart Interior Design Inc 1440 E Chapman Ave Orange CA 92666

BOGATAY, LYNNE MARIE, health science facility administrator; b. Euclid, Ohio, Dec. 1, 1955; d. Edward Lawrence and Elizabeth Therese (Kulfan) B. BS, John Carroll U., 1977, MBA, 1988. Rsch. technologist Cleve. Clinic Found., 1977-89, rsch. adminstr., 1989—. Provisional mem. Jr. League of Cleve., Inc., 1989-90, mem. 1990—. Mem. Am. Coll. Healthcare Execs., Healthcare Adminstrs. Assn. N.E. Ohio, Toastmasters Internat., Beta Gamma Sigma. Roman Catholic. Office: Rsch Inst Cleve Clinic 9500 Euclid Ave NN1-06 Cleveland OH 44195

BOGATY, LISA BRADFORD, college dean; b. Winchester, Tenn., Aug. 15, 1952; d. James Houston Bradford and Katherine (Valenti) Aho; m. David William Bogaty, Sept. 18, 1971; children: Katherine Elaine, Lauren Amber, Sharon Rebecca. BSBA in Mktg., U. Tenn., 1979, MBA in Mktg., Fin., 1983, doctoral student, 1989—. With paste-up/layout Winchester Herald Chronicle, 1971; asst. buyer Miller's Dept. Store, Knoxville, 1971-74; mktg. cons. Bradford & Assocs., Knoxville, 1978—; prof. mktg. Pellissippi State (formerly State Tech.), Knoxville, 1983—, asst. dean bus., 1985-88, dean applied scis./tech., 1988—; tech. rsch. U. Tenn. Tech. Assistance Ctr., Knoxville, 1980, 81; Small Bus. Devel. Ctr. cons. SBA, Knoxville, 1986-88. Mem. Women in Higher Edn. Today (pres. 1988-90), Am. Assn. Women in Jr. and Community Colls. (regional rep. 1989-90, Leaders award 1989), Am. Mktg. Assn. (profl., Svc. award), Am. Coun. Edn. (steering coun. 1989-90), Knoxville Assn. Women Execs., PSTCC Pres.'s Club, Knoxville C. of C. (subcom. chair 1988-90), Phi Kappa Phi, Beta Gamma Sigma. Republican. Roman Catholic. Home: 5325 Hickory Hollow Rd Knoxville TN 37919 Office: PSTCC 10915 Hardin Valley Knoxville TN 37933

BOGDAN, CAROLYN LOUETTA, financial specialist; b. Wilkes-Barre, Pa., Apr. 15, 1941; d. Walter Cecil and Ethna Louetta (Kendig) Carpenter; m. James Thomas Bogdan, May 5, 1961; 1 child, Thomas James. Grad. high sch., Kingston, Pa. Head bookkeeper Forty Ft. (Pa.) State Bank, 1959-63, U.S. Nat. Bank, Long Beach, Calif., 1963-65; office mgr. United Parts Exchange, Long Beach, 1976-81; contract adminstr. Johnson Controls, Inc., Rancho Dominguez, Calif., 1981-88; credit coord. Johnson Controls, Inc., 1989—; co-owner, acct. Bogdan Elec. R & D, Lakewood, Calif., 1981—. Officer, records keeper, Radio Amateur Civil Emergency Svc., Los Angeles County Sheriff dept., 1980—. Mem. Nat. Notary Assn., Am. Inst. Profl. Bookkeepers, Tournament of Roses Radio Amateurs (pin chmn. 1975—). Republican. Home: 3713 Capetown St Lakewood CA 90712 Office: Johnson Controls Inc 19118 S Reyes Ave Rancho Dominguez CA 90221

BOGDANOFF, PHYLLIS SWEED, publishing executive; b. N.Y.C., Dec. 6, 1931; d. Paul and Frances (Spitzer) Sweed; m. Leonard Bogdanoff Feb. 15, 1957 (wid. Oct. 1975); children: Patricia, James Alan. BA, NYU, 1950. Asst. editor Fox-Shulman Publs., N.Y.C., 1951-57; asst. editor/prodns. McGraw-Hill Publs., N.Y.C., 1957-61; mng. editor Haire Publs., N.Y.C., 1961-66; editor Geyer-McAllister Publs., N.Y.C., 1966—, sr. v.p., 1976—, co-pub., 1978—; seminar speaker in field, 1985—. Recipient Indsl. Mktg. award Indsl. Mktg. Mag., 1965, Dallas Market Editorial award, Dallas Market Ctr., 1969, Gift Mktg. Editorial award. Mem. Nat. Assn. Limited Edition Dealers, Nat. Home Fashions League (now Internat. Fedn. of Design Assocs.), Cooper-Hewitt Mus. Home: 505 Laguardia Pl New York NY 10012 Office: Geyer-McAllister Publs 51 Madison Ave New York NY 10010

BOGEDAIN, CAROL SIENSKI, dietitian; b. Detroit, July 30, 1952; d. Theodre Stanley and Jennie Dolores (Pielecha) Sienski; m. David Dalko, Dec. 11, 1976 (dec. Feb. 1979); m. William Bogedain, Aug. 15, 1981. BS, Mich. State U., 1974; MS, U. N.C., Greensboro, 1982. Dietetic intern Henry Ford Hosp., Detroit, 1974-75; rsch. dietitian Duke U. Med. Ctr., Durham, N.C., 1975-76; clin. dietitian VA Med. Ctr., Durham, N.C., 1976-77; chief clin. dietitian VA Med. Ctr., Salisbury, N.C., 1977-85, chief adminstrv. dietitian, 1985—; adj. instr. U. N.C., Greensboro, 1982—. Mem. Am. Dietetic Assn., N.C. Dietetic Assn. (pres.-elect 1988-89, pres. 1989-90), Greensboro Dietetic Assn., Omicron Nu, Sigma Kappa. Republican. Episcopalian. Home: Route 17 Box 78 Salisbury NC 28144 Office: VA Med Ctr 1601 Brenner Ave Salisbury NC 28814

BOGGS, ANGELA ROSALIE, occupational health and safety administrator; b. Phila., Dec. 27, 1947; d. Nicolas Concetto and Benedetta (Graci) Muni; m. Roger Alan Boggs, Nov. 1, 1970; children: Derek Ethan, Jared Christian. BA magna cum laude, The Cath. U. Am., 1969; MS, Harvard U., 1983. Cert. safety profl. Jr. chemist Smith, Kline & French Labs., Phila., 1969; analytical chemist WARF Inst., Madison, Wis., 1970-72; environ. analyst IEP, Inc., Northboro, Mass., 1982-83; research asst. Harvard U., Boston, 1983-84; environ. chemist, pub. health specialist Geotech. Engrs., Inc., Winchester, Mass., 1984; engr. hazardous materials Shipley Co., Newton, Mass., 1984-85, supr. environ. health and safety, 1985, mgr. safety health and security, 1986-88; mgr. indsl. and environ. health Adams-Russell, Inc., Waltham, 1988-89, M/A-COM, Inc., Burlington, Mass., 1989—; mem. program com. Am. Conf. on Chem. Labeling, 1986—. Mem. Am. Chem. Soc., Soc. for Risk Analysis, Am. Electronics Assn. (environ. and occupational health com. and clean air task force), Semiconductor Safety Assn., Risk and Ins. Mgmt. Soc., Sigma Xi. Roman Catholic. Home: 305 Concord Rd Wayland MA 01778 Office: M/A COM Inc 63 South Ave Burlington MA 01803

BOGGS, CORINNE CLAIBORNE (LINDY BOGGS), former congresswoman; b. Brunswick Plantation, La., Mar. 13, 1916; d. Roland Philoman and Martha Corinne (Morrison) Claiborne; m. Thomas Hale Boggs, Jan. 22, 1938 (dec.); children—Barbara (Mrs. Paul E. Sigmund, Jr.), Thomas Hale Jr., Corinne (Mrs. Steven V. Roberts), William Robertson (dec.). BA, Sophie Newcomb Coll., Tulane U., 1935, LLD (hon.); LittD, U. St. Thomas; DPub Svc. (hon.), Trinity Coll., Washington, 1975; hon. degree, St. Mary of Woods; LLD, Loyola U. Tchr. history and English St. James Parish, La., 1936-37; elected to 93d Congress to fill vacancy caused by death of husband, 1973; re-elected to 94th-101st Congresses from 2d La. Dist., 1973-91; ret., 1991; mem. appropriations com. majority mem. from Ho. of Reps., Am. Revolution Bicentennial Adminstrn. Bd., chmn. Commn. Ho. of Reps. Bicentenary; mem. campaign com. Democratic Nat. Com., 1974; chairwoman Dem. Nat. Conv., 1976; mem. Com. on Bicentennial of U.S. Constn. Pres., Dem. Congl. Wives Forum, 1954, Womans Nat. Democratic Club, 1958-59, Congl. Club, 1971-72; co-chmn. Inaugural Balls for Presidents John F. Kennedy, 1961, Lyndon Johnson, 1965; mem. Nat. Hist. Publs. and Records Com.; bd. dirs. La. Council for Music and Performing Arts; hon. bd. dirs. Met. New Orleans chpt. Nat. Found. March of Dimes; bd. advisers. CLOSE-UP and Presdl. Classroom; regent emeritus Smithsonian Instn.; mem. president's council Tulane U. Recipient Weiss Meml. award NCCJ, 1974; Nat. Oak award La. Assn. Ind. Colls. and Univs., Disting. Service medal Saint Mary's Dominican Coll., 1976, Humanitarian award AMVETS Nat. Aux., Torch of Liberty award B'nai B'rith, 1976, Gala IV award Birmingham So. U., 1976, Eleanor Roosevelt Humanitarian award, 1977, E. Roosevelt Centennial award, 1984, 1st woman recipient Disting. Alumna award Tulane U., 1986; 1st woman recipient VFW Congl. award, 1986. Mem. Nat. Soc. Colonial Dames, LWV, Internat. Fedn. Catholic Alumni. Office: Rayburn House Office Bldg Rm 2353 Washington DC 20515*

BOGGS, DEBBIE-SUE, office administrator; b. Phila., May 7, 1956; d. Jack D. and Janet (Conston) Miller; m. Jerry A. Boggs, Dec. 26, 1982. BA, BS in Social Welfare and Spanish, Pa. State U., 1977. VISTA paralegal So. Ariz. Legal Aide, Tucson, 1978-79; youth counselor VisionQuest, Tucson, 1979; gen. edn. instr. Tucson Job Corps Ctr., 1979-81; legal sec. Molloy, Jones & Donahue, Tucson, 1981-85, paralegal, 1985-86; office adminstr. Murphy, Goering, Roberts and Berkman P.C., Tucson, 1986—. Vol. fitness instr. Lighthouse City YMCA, 1988—. Mem. ABA, Nat. Assn. Legal Adminstrs., Tucson Assn. Legal Adminstrs., Pa. State Club Greater Tucson (pres. 1987—), So. Ariz. Fitness Assn. Democrat. Jewish. Home: 3000 W Treeline Dr Tucson AZ 85741 Office: Murphy Goering Roberts & Berkman PC 1840 E River Rd Ste 302 Tucson AZ 85718

BOGGS, ELIZABETH MONROE, civic worker; b. Cleve., Apr. 5, 1913; d. Frank Adair Jr. and Elizabeth (McNairy) Monroe; m. Fitzhugh Willets Boggs, Sept. 20, 1941 (dec. Jan. 1971); 1 child, Jonathan David. BA summa cum laude, Bryn Mawr Coll., 1935; PhD in Theoretical Chemistry, Cambridge U., Eng., 1941; LLD (hon.), Ohio State U., 1972; DSc (hon.), U. Medicine and Dentistry of N.J., 1984; DHL (hon.), Kean Coll. of N.J., 1986. Rsch. assoc. dept. chemistry Cornell U., 1940-42; lectr. physics U. Pitts., 1942-43; rsch. assoc. Explosives Rsch. Lab. OSRD, Bruceton, Pa., 1943-45. Del. White House Conf. on Children and Youth, 1950, White House Conf. on Edn., 1955; mem. Pres.'s nat. com. White House Conf. Children and Youth, 1960; bd. dirs. Nat Health Coun., 1958-61; mem. Pres.'s Panel on Mental Retardation, 1961-62; bd. dirs. Nat. Assn. Retarded Children, 1950-63, 2d v.p. 1957, 1st v.p., 1957-58, pres., 1958-60; mem. bd. N.J. Welfare Coun., 1952-59, 61-66, 71—, pres., 1956-58; 1st v.p. N.J. Assn. Mental Health, 1964-66; pres. N.J. Assn. Retarded Children, 1966-67; mem. Joint Commn. on Mental Health of Children, 1967-71; mem. Nat. Adv. Child Health and Human Devel Coun., 1967-71; adv. coun. Grad. Sch. Social Work, Rutgers U., 1964-68, chmn., 1971-77; mem. Pa. Adv. Coun. Mental Health and Mental Retardation, 1968-71, N.J. Mental Retardation Planning Bd., 1970-71, N.J. Gov.'s Task Force on Welfare Mgmt., 1969-71; vice chmn N.J. State Devel. Disabilities Coun., 1971-79, mem., 1979-90; chmn. Nat. Adv. Coun. on Svcs. and Facilities for Developmentally Disabled, 1971-74; mem. Pres.'s Com. on Mental Retardation, 1975-76; mem. tech cons. panel on long term care data set USPHS, 1976-78; mem. N.J. State Adv. Com. on Title XX, 1974-79; chmn. Task Group on Implementation of UN Declaration of Rights of Mentally Retarded Persons, Internat. League of Socs. for Mentally Handicapped, 1972-78; bd. dirs. Nat. Assn. for Retarded Citizens, 1978-79; presdl. appointee Nat. Coun. on the Handicapped, 1980-82; acting dir. N.J. State Office on Prevention of Mental Retardation, Trenton, 1988; mem. tech. adv. group to asst. sec. for planning and evaluation U.S. HHS, 1988-90; co-chair Congl. Task Force on Rights & Empowerment of People with Disabilities, 1988-90; vice chair N.J. Gov.'s Task Force on Svcs. for Disabled Persons, 1986-87; expert advisor on Social Security Info. Modernization Project, U.S. Social Security Adminstrn., 1990—. Home: RD 2 Box 439 Hampton NJ 08827

BOGHOSIAN, PAULA DER, educator, consultant; b. Watervileit, N.Y., Nov. 11, 1933; d. Harry and Osgi (Piligian) der B. BS magna cum laude, Syracuse U., 1964, MS, 1967; postgrad., SUNY, Oswego, 1972, SUNY, Albany, 1974. Cert. profl. sec., 1974. Asst. prof. Cazenovia (N.Y.) Coll., 1964-73; instr. Bd. of Coop., Syracuse, N.Y., 1973-76, dir. bus. careers, 1976—; cons. computer bus., prin. Syracuse, 1984—. Zonta scholar, 1964; Jessie Smith Noyes grantee Syracuse U., 1965. Mem. Assn. Info. Systems Profl. (com. chmn.), Bus. Tchrs. Assn. of N.Y. State, Adminstrv. Mgmt. Soc., Eastern Bus. Tchrs. Assn., Assn. for Supervision and Curruculum Devel., Assn. of Am. Jr. Colls., Assn. of Am. U. Profs., Nat. Assn. for Armenian Studies and Research Harvard U., Internat. Tng. Communications (v.p. 1985-86), Delta Pi Epsilon, Beta Gamma Sigma, Phi Kappa Phi, Pi Lambda Theta, Sigma Lambda Delta. Republican. Mem. Armenian Apostolic. Home: 3181 B Bellevue Ave Syracuse NY 13219

BOGNER, MARGARET ANN, health service executive; b. Joliet, Ill., Apr. 19, 1947; d. Harold R. and Dolores R. (Telfer) B. BA, No. Ill. U., 1972; M in Mgmt., Northwestern U., 1983. Adminstrv. asst. Northwestern Meml. Hosp., Chgo., 1972-79; bus. mgr. The Thresholds, Chgo., 1981—. Mem. Lincoln Park Conservation Assn., Chgo., Art Inst., Chgo., Chgo. Arch. Found., Chgo., Lincoln Park Zool. Soc., Chgo., Mus. of Sci. and Industry, Chgo.; mem. Shakespearan Festival, Stratford, Ont. Mem. Nat. Alliance for Mentally Ill. Club: Chgo. Met. Ski Council (regional v.p. 1984-85, 87-88 (credential chmn. 1985-86), Pine Point Ski (midwest chmn. 1987—, pres. 1988—). Office: The Thresholds 2700 N Lakeview Chicago IL 60614

BOGRAD, MICHELE LOUISE, clinical psychologist; b. Denver, Mar. 12, 1952; d. Nathan Bograd and Ruth (Parker) Kaufman. BA, Colo. Coll., 1970-74; PhD, U. Chgo., 1983. Cons. Nat. Inst. of Mental Health, Northwestern U. and U. Chgo., 1978-79; psychology intern South Shore Mental Health Ctr., Quincy, Mass., 1979-80; child psychologist Harvard Community Health Plan, Cambridge, Mass., 1980-81; research ad tng. coordinator Family Svc. Unit of the Dist., Atty.'s Office, Quincy, Mass., 1980-82; research assoc. Family Inst. of Cambridge (Mass.), 1983-84, assoc. faculty, 1986-90; lectr. in psychiatry Harvard Med. Sch., Boston, 1985-87; core faculty Kantor Family Inst., Somerville, Mass., 1985—. Co-editor: book Feminist Perspectives on Wife Abuse, 1988, Abuse, 1988; editor: Theories, Politics and Practices of Treating Men in Family Therapy, 1990; contbr. articles to profl. jours. Mem. American Psychological Assn., American Orthopsychiatry Assn., Mass. Psychological Assn., Soc. for Family Therapy and Rsch., Feminist Therapy Inst., Am. Assn. Marriage and Family Therapists, Am. Family Therapy Assn. Democrat. Jewish.

BOGSTAHL, DEBORAH MARCELLE, market research consultant; b. Irvington, N.J., June 5, 1950; d. Marcel and Helena Christina (de Jaroszynsky) Bogstahl; m. Richard Neil Press, Mar. 20, 1976; children: Alexandra Boman, Michelle Boman. BA in English Edn., Trenton State Coll., 1972. Cert. tchr., N.J. Project dir. U.S. Testing Co., Hoboken, N.J., 1973-75; project dir. J. Walter Thompson Co., N.Y.C., 1975-77; rsch. account exec. Dancer Fitzgerald Sample, N.Y.C., 1977-80; group rsch. mgr. Bristol-Myers Co., N.Y.C., 1980-87; dir. rsch. Med. Econs. Co., Inc., Oradell, N.J., 1987-90; market rsch. cons., 1990—. Contbr. poetry to anthology. Mem. Am. Mktg. Assn., Pharm. Adv. Coun., Healthcare Bus. Women's Assn. Democrat. Roman Catholic. Avocations: sailing, reading, writing, horticulture, guitar.

BOGUE, CARRIE ANNE, manufacturing company executive; b. Paris, Ill., Aug. 13, 1952; d. Marion Leon and Lillie Evelyn (Miller) Davis; m. John Lyodd Keep, May 26, 1985; children: Robert Leon, Christina Lynn. Beautician, Technique Sch. Beauty Culture, Paris, Ill., 1970. Inventory analyst J.I. Case, Terre Haute, Ind., 1977-85; prodn. mgr. Standard Locknut and Lockwasher, Inc., Carmel, Ind., 1985-87; materials mgr. TES, Bay City, Mich., 1987-90, now ops. mgr., 1990—. Mem. Am. Prodn. and Inventory Control Soc., (named outstanding member of the yr. Region XIII), NAFE, Soc. Mfg. Engrs. Home: 2323 Center Ave Bay City MI 48708

BOHANNON, SHARI ANN, business executive; b. Bakersfield, Calif., July 27, 1946; d. Vernon David and Jacqueline Sharon (Kramer) Hobbs; AA, West Valley Jr. Coll., 1968; BS, San Jose State U., 1972; children by previous marriage: Michelle, Richard, Garld. Asst. dir. core area devel. San Jose (Calif.) C. of C., 1969-71; asst. dir. health occupations Modesto Jr. Coll., 1971-75; mgr. Microwave Assocs. Communications Co., Sunnyvale, Calif., 1978-81; field engrng. supr. Four Phase Systems, Inc., Cupertino, Calif., 1981-83; mgr. Rayne Plumbing & Sewer Service Inc., 1983-84; mgr. M/A COM MAC, Inc., San Jose, 1984-89; sales mgr. RACON, Inc., San Jose, 1989—. Mem. NAFE (network dir.). Home: 6571 American Ct San Jose CA 95120 Office: PO Box 20190 San Jose CA 95160

BOHANNON, VERSIE DARNELL, retired social worker; b. Memphis, Mar. 15, 1931; d. Robert and Willa Mae (Govan) Minor; m. Garland Bohannon, Apr. 14, 1951; children: Garland Jr., Rodney. BA in Psychology, U. Toledo, 1980. Lic. social worker. Fellow AAUW, Alpha Kappa Alpha. Democrat. Methodist. Home: 2518 Hartwell Ave Toledo OH 43607

BOHLE, SUE, public relations executive; b. Austin, Minn., June 23, 1943; d. Harold Raymond and Mary Theresa (Swanson) Hastings; m. John Bernard Bohle, June 22, 1974; children: Jason John, Katie Christine. BS in Journalism, Northwestern U., 1965, MS in Journalism, 1969. Tchr. pub. high schs Englewood, Colo., 1965-68; account exec. Burson-Marsteller Pub. Relations, Los Angeles, 1969-73; v.p., mgr. pub. relations J. Walter Thompson Co., Los Angeles, 1973-79; founder, pres. The Bohle Co., L.A., 1979—; former exec. v.p. Ketchum/Bohle Pub. Relations, Los Angeles; freelance writer, instr. communications Calif. State U. at Fullerton, 1972-73; instr. writing Los Angeles City Coll., 1975-76; lectr. U. So. Calif., 1979—. Contbr. articles to profl. jours. Dir. pub. rels. L.A. Jr. Ballet, 1971-72; pres. Panhellenic Advisers Coun., UCLA, 1972-73; mem. adv. bd. L.A. Valley Coll., 1974-75, Coll. Communications Pepperdine U., 1981-85, Sch. Journalism U. So. Calif., 1987—, Calif. State U., Long Beach, 1988—; bd. visitors Medill Sch. Journalism Northwestern U., 1984—. Univ. scholar, 1961-64, Panhellenic scholar, 1964-65. Mem. Pub. Rels. Soc. Am. (L.A. chpt., bd. dirs. 1981-90, v.p. 1983, pres. 1989, del. to nat. assembly, 1980, exec. com. 1984-86, sec.-treas. 1990), Women in Communications, Shi-ai, Delta Zeta (editor The Lamp 1966-68), Kappa Alpha Tau. Office: The Bohle Co 1901 Ave of the Stars Ste 1925 Los Angeles CA 90067

BOHLKEN, DEBORAH KAY, data processing executive; b. Anchorage, Nov. 16, 1952; d. Darrell Richard and Gertrude Ann (Merkel) B. BA, U. Ark., 1975, MSW, 1977. Specialist community devel. State of Ark., Little Rock, 1976-77, supr. community area, 1977-78, mgr. evaluation and data processing, 1978-80; corp. analyst Systematics, Inc., Little Rock, 1980-83, mgr. corp. planning and rsch., 1983-85, group mgr. planning, rsch., Washington Congl. liasion, 1985-89, 90—; mktg., planning and devel. mgr. Systematics, Inc. Contbr. articles and papers to profl. publs. Bd. dirs. Cen. Ark. Radiation Therapy Inst. Hotline, Little Rock, 1980-82, Cancer Soc., Little Rock, 1986-89; state chair Cansurmount, Little Rock, 1985-89. Nat. Juvenile Justice Law Enforcement Adminstrn. explimary data processing grantee, 1976-78. Mem. NAFE, Nat. Assn. Bank Svcs., Cash Mgrs. Assn., Fin. Mgrs. Assn., Mortgage Bankers Assn., U.S. Savs. and Loan Assn., Am. Mgmt. Assn. Democrat. Methodist. Office: Systematics Inc 4001 Rodney Parham Rd Little Rock AR 72212

BOHLS, SALLY RUTH, musician, educator; b. Odessa, Tex., Sept. 16, 1956; d. Billy James and Addie Belle (Anderson) Whitlock; m. Jon Mark Bohls,. MusB, B of Edn., Tex. Tech. U., 1979; MusM, Southern Meth U., 1981. 2nd oboe Midland Odessa Symphony, Odessa, Tex., 1973-75, Lubbock (Tex.) Symphony, 1975-79; 1st oboe Lewisville (Tex.) Symphony, 1986—, Richardson Symphony, Dallas, 1987—; judge Univ. Interscholastic League, Tex. Band Masters Assn. Mem. Dallas Fed. Musicians, Internat. Double Reed Soc., Tex. Music Educators Assn. (judge). Home: 1921 Kentwood Carrollton TX 75007

BOHN, CHARLOTTE GALITZ, real estate executive; b. Chgo., Aug. 7, 1930; d. Chester Charles and Sarah Madelyn (McCarthy) B; m. Robert Allan Galitz, Nov. 25, 1955; children: Charles Robert, Thomas Allan, Madelyn Clare, (div. Sept. 1965). Student, Northwestern U., 1955, City Coll., Chgo., 1989. Lic. real estate salesperson, N.C. Lab. tech. Kraft Foods Rsch. Lab., Glenview, Ill., 1950-56; researcher data processing control Kemper Ins. Co., Chgo., 1967-70; jr. acct. Tractor Supply Co., Chgo., 1970-75; real estate salesman MGM Realty Co., Chgo., 1975-81, 85-88; broker Bohn Real Estate Agy, Raleigh, N.C., 1981-85; founder, pres. Pvt. Rsch., Chgo., 1985—; researcher, zoning map City of Raleigh, 1980-81. Contbr. various rsch. projects and sci. proposals. Vol. Chgo. Boy's Club; treas. Churchwomen of St. Mary's, Crystal Lake, Ill.; vol. Lifeguard Easter Seal Soc.-Multiple Sclerosis, Raleigh, 1983-84, PTA, 1967-77. Recipient Adviser Emblem of Merit award Jr. Achievement, 1955. Assoc. mem. Smithsonian Inst., Nat. Trust Hist. Preservation, Raleigh C. of C., Jaycee Aux. (restaurant mgr.), Chgo. N. Side Realty Bd., Nat. Geog. Soc., Wilson Ctr. Assn., Mensa (nominating), Am. Assn. Ret. Persons, Irish Am. Heritage Ctr., Am. Assn. Advancement of Sci. Episcopalian. Home: 6126 Roscoe Chicago IL 60634 Office: Private Rsch 6126 Roscoe St Chicago IL 60634

BOHN, SARAH A, psychologist; b. Visalia, Calif., Mar. 20, 1956; d. Paul Hallam and Jane (Anderson) B. BA in Psychology, U. Ariz., 1978; MA in Clin. Psychology, Bowling Green (Ohio) State U., 1981, PhD, 1984. Lic. psychologist, Calif. Intern Mercy Med. Ctr., San Diego, Calif., 1983-84, post-doctoral fellow, 1984-85; staff psychologist, cons. VAMC, La Jolla, Calif., 1985-86; pvt. practice, cons. San Diego, Oceanside, Calif., 1986—; intern, dir. Capistrano By the Sea Hosp., Dana Point, Calif., 1986—; oral examiner Psychology Examining Commn., Sacramento, Calif. 1988—; jour. reviewer Jour. of Emergency Med. Svc., Solana Beach, Calif., 1987—; adj. prof. Calif. Sch., San Diego, 1987—; presenter in field. Mem. San Diego Zool. Soc., 1989, Project Wildlife, San Diego, 1989. NIMH fellowship Bowling Green State U., 1982; Sigma Xi Rsch. grant, 1982. Mem. Am. Psychol. Assn. (site advisor 1990—), Nat. Registry for Mental Health Providers, Calif. State Psychol. Assn., Phi Beta Kappa, Phi Kappa Phi. Democrat. Presbyterian. Home: 4507 Sierra Morena Carlsbad CA 92008

BOHNE, MILDRED THOMPSON, antique company owner, retired anesthesiologist; b. Chgo., June 29, 1917; d. O.C. Thompson and Mildred Manley; m. Edmund Louise Bohne, Apr. 11, 1942; chidren: William, Nancy, Philip. BA, U. Miss., 1937; MD, Cornell U., 1941. Diplomate Am. Bd. Anesthesiology. Rotating intern Jersey City Med. Ctr., 1941-42; anesthesiology resident Columbia-Presbyn. Hosp., N.Y.C., 1942-43; pvt. practice anesthesiology Balt., 1943-46; chief anesthesiology dept. Overlook Hosp., Summit, N.J., 1946-66; pres. staff, anesthesiologist John E. Runnells Hosp., Scotch Plains, N.J., 1950-66; retired from med. practice, 1966; co-owner antique bus. Newmanstown, Pa., 1966—. Contbr. articles to profl. jours. Mem. AMA, N.J. Med. Soc., N.J. Anesthesiology Soc. (pres. 1954-55). Republican. Mem. Soc. of Friends. Home and Office: RD 1 Box 160 Box 160 Newmanstown PA 17073

BOHOSKEY, BERNICE FLEMING, mineral-land owner, writer; b. Seattle, Feb. 9, 1918; d. Katherine Elizabeth Emmeluth; m. Woodward Bohoskey, Aug. 6, 1942 (dec.); children: Charles W., Katherine A., Michael J., Constance E. Student, Mills Coll., Oakland, Calif., 1935-36, Cornish Sch. Arts, Seattle, 1936-38. Model various newspapers. mags., 1936-38; mem. Earl Carroll's Vanities; actress various movies, choreographer Hollywood, Calif.; ptnr. Yakima Ranches Ltd. Composer: (hymn) Blessed Trinity, 1948, (song) Just Give Me the Merry-Go-Round, 1949; contbr. articles to profl. jours. Founder, pres. Young First Voters Groups, 1940; spkr., organizer, Yakima County, Wash.; pres. Young Reps. Club, Wash., 1940. Mem. Jr. League (sustaining). Republican. Catholic.

BOHRER, BETTY, nurse, medical sales representative; b. Orlando, Fla., Feb. 15, 1962; d. LeRoy Preston and Ruth (Davis) B. ASN, Weber State Coll., 1982; student, U. Utah, 1982-85. RN, Calif., Utah. Nurse Dr. Kent M. Hardy, Ogden, Utah, 1976-82; ski instr. Powder Mountain Ski Resort, Eden, Utah, 1979-82; nurse ICU U. Utah Med. Ctr., Salt Lake City, 1982-85, Hoag Meml. Hosp., Newport Beach, Calif., 1985-87; nurse Sullivan Nursing Svc., Huntington Beach, Calif., 1985—; profl. rep. SIGVARIS, Branford, Conn., 1988-90; sales rep. Medi U.S.A., 1990—. Mem. Am. Assn. Critical Care Nurses, Jaycees.

BOHUNICKY, DEBRA ANN, nurse; b. Binghamton, N.Y., May 5, 1954; d. Anthony and Elizabeth (Stank) B. BS in Nursing, Cath. U., Washington, 1982; MS, SUNY, Binghamton, 1987. RN, Va., Fla., N.Y.; lic. rehab. provider, Fla. Staff nurse bone marrow transplant unit St. Francis Hosp., Honolulu, 1982-83; pub. health nurse Twin Tier Home Health, Inc., Binghamton, 1983-84, community awareness coord., 1984-85, hospice coord., 1983-85; utilization rev. and quality assurance coord. James G. Johnston Meml. Nursing Home, Johnson City, N.Y., 1985-87; nurse mgr. Winter Park (Fla.) Home Health, 1987-88; regional case mgmt. supr. VPS Case Mgmt., Inc., Orlando, Fla., 1988-89; corp. supr. Fortis Corp., Richmond, Va., 1989—; owner Bohun & Assocs., Richmond, Va., 1990—; cons. Profl. Home Care, Binghamton, 1985, Gilbert Chiropractic Clinic, Richmond, 1989—; coord. Health Awareness Day for Spanish Am. Franciscan Sisters, Washington, 1981, Sydney (N.Y.) Sr. Health Fair, 1986. Mem. Am. Nurses Assn., N.Y. State Nurses Assn., Cen. Va. Assn. Rehab. Nurses (pres.-elect 1989-91), Nat. Assn. Rehab. Nurses, Va. Nurse Assn. for Rehab. Nurses, Nat. Hospice Assn., Managed Care Assn., Sigma Theta Tau. Office: Bohun & Assocs PO Box 31792 Richmond VA 23294-1792

BOICE, ANN KELLEY, elementary school educator; b. Flagstaff, Ariz., May 7, 1932; d. Victor H. and Mary (Pinckard) K.; m. Fred Tait Boice, Dec. 23, 1952; children: Henry Kelley, Mariann Tait, Jennifer Lynn, Fred Tait Jr., Margaret Ellen. Student, Pomona Coll., 1950-53; BA in Education, U. Ariz., 1953, MA in Education, 1971. Tchr. Sopori Sch., Pima County, Ariz., 1952-53, 60-61, Adventure Sch., Tucson, 1971-72, Tucson Community Sch., 1966-68, 72—. Pres. Jr. League of Tucson, 1971-72, Peter Howell Sch. PTA, Tucson, 1973-74; chairperson Tucson Women's Commn., 1978-80; v.p., sec. Casa de los Ninos for Child Abuse, Tucson, 1985-86; v.p. bd. dirs. Casa de los Ninos Abuse Ctr.; pres. Planned Parenthood So. Ariz., 1987-88, mem. edn. com.; sec. bd. dirs. First Steps Daycare, 1990—; bd. dirs. women's studies adv. coun. U. Ariz., 1990—. Named Woman of Yr., Tucson C. of C., 1970; recipient Jr. League Sustainer award Women of Yr., Tucson, 1988. Republican. Home: 4741 Paseo del Bac Tucson AZ 85718 Office: Tucson Community Sch 2109 E Hedrick Dr Tucson AZ 85719

BOIMAN, DONNA RAE, artist, art academy executive; b. Columbus, Ohio, Jan. 13, 1946; d. George Brandle and Donna Rae (Rockwell) Hall; m. David Charles Boiman, Dec. 8, 1973 (div. Aug. 1990). BS in Pharmacy, Ohio State U., 1969; student, Columbus Coll. Art & Design, 1979-83. Registered pharmacist, Ohio. Pharmacist, mgr. various retail stores, Cleve., 1970-73, Columbus, 1973-77; owner L'Artiste, Reynoldsburg, Ohio, 1977-81; pres. Cen. Ohio Art Acad., Reynoldsburg, 1981-90, Art Acad. Cen. Ohio, Reynoldsburg, 1990—; owner Big Red Designs, Reynoldsburg, 1989—, Art Acad. of Granville (Ohio), 1990—; cons. to Mayor City of Reynoldsburg, 1986-87. Represented in permanent collections including Collector's Gallery Columbus Mus. Art, Gallery 200, Columbus Art Exch., The Huntington Collection, Dean Witter Reynolds Collection, Zanesville Art Ctr., Mt. Carmel East Hosp., Columbus, Corp. 2005, Radisson Hotels, Mich. and Ohio, Fifth 3d Bank, Bexley, Ohio, On Line Computer Libr., Dublin, Ohio; author: Anatomy Made Easy: Draw, Color and Learn, Anatomy and Structure: A Guide for Young Artists, 1988. Recipient John Lennon Meml. Award for the Arts, Internat. Art Challenge com., 1987. Mem. Pa. Soc. Watercolorists, Nat. Soc. Layerists in Multimedia, Columbus Art League, Cen. Ohio Watercolor Soc. (pres. 1983-84), Am. Quarter Horse Assn., Ohio Quarter Horse Assn., Allied Artists of Am. (assoc.), Licking County Art Assn., Nat. Wildlife Fedn., Ohio State U. Alumni Assn., Ohio State U. Pharmacy Alumni Assn. (charter), Mid-Ohio Dressage Assn. Office: Art Acad of Cen Ohio 7297 E Main St Reynoldsburg OH 43068

BOINEAU, ELIZABETH LLOYD, marketing and public relations company executive; b. Columbia, S.C., Apr. 19, 1956; d. Robert Trippett and Dotsy (Lloyd) B. BA in Psychology, Randolph-Macon Woman's Coll., 1977. Mgr. Linning House Galleries, Inc., Charleston, S.C., 1977-78; pub. rels. asst., asst. mktg. officer Citizens & So. Nat. Bank S.C., Charleston, 1979-81, mktg. officer, 1982-84; dir. Office Pub. Rels., Charleston County Sch. Dist., Charleston, 1984-90; owner, mgr. E. Boineau and Co., Charleston, 1990—; cons. Mobile (Ala.) Jr. League, 1990, Bapt. Coll., Charleston, 1990, Statewide Polit. Movement, Charleston, 1990, Med. U. S.C. Wellness, Charleston, 1990, Coll. of Charleston, 1990, Coastal Engring. & Testing, 1990; nat. workshop presenter, regional coord. bus.-edn. partnership program S.C. Dept. Edn., 1984-86. Contbr. articles to profl. jours. Bd. dirs. Juvenile Restitution Program, Charleston, 1987-91, Cities-in Schs., 1989-90, Children's Hosp. Fund, Med. U. S.C., 1988-90; exec. advisor Jr. Achievement; advisor Future Bus. Leaders Am.; mem. Jr. League Charleston, 1987—. Mem. Nat. Sch. Pub. Rels. Assn. (nat. rsch. com. 1989-90, 6 nat, Golden Achievement awards 1987-89, numerous awards S.C. chpt. including gold award for best total pub. rels. program 1990), Am. Advt. Fedn. (nat. pub. svc. com. 1987-90), Advt. Fedn. Charleston (bd. dirs., pres. 1986-87, gold, 4 silver, bronze Addy awards), Charleston C. of C., Sales and Mktg. Execs. Charleston, UDC (state and nat. officer), Randolph-Macon Woman's Coll. Alumnae Assn. (treas. Charleston chpt.). Home: 55-B Montagu St Charleston SC 29401 Office: 14 N Market St Charleston SC 29401

BOISE, AUDREY LORRAINE, educator; b. Hackensack, N.J., Feb. 12, 1933; d. Paul George and Lillian Rose (Goedecker) B. BA, Wellesley (Mass.) Coll., 1955; MA, Fairleigh Dickinson U., 1977. Cert. tchr., K-8, learning disabilities supervision. Tchr. Township of Berkeley Heights (N.J.), 1958-67; learning cons. Borough of New Providence (N.J.), 1978-82, 1986—, Scotch Plains/Fanwood (N.J.), 1984-86; instr. Fairleigh Dickinson U., Madison, N.J., 1983, 1975-76; several other short-term teaching positions; supr. student tchrs. 1975-78; lectr. on fgn. countries and U.S. History, N.J., 1980—; travel agt. (part-time) 1967—. Mem. Republican Nat. Com., Washington, U.S. Senatorial Club, Washington, Republican Presidential Task Force, Washington, N.J. State Republican Com., Trenton, N.J., Nat. Fedn. of Republican Women, Washington. Mem. NEA, N.J. Assn. of Learning Cons., Assn. for Children with Learning Disabilities, N.J. Edn. Assn., Coll. Club of Summit, Fortnightly, Hist. Soc. of Summit. Methodist. Office: Dept of Spl Svcs New Providence Bd of Edn 340 Cen Ave New Providence NJ 07974

BOITEL, ANA MARIA, company executive; b. Cuba, Aug. 13, 1952; d. Oscar J. and Dulce Maria (Reyes) Boitel. Dir. bus. devel. Cooper Carry & Assocs., Washington, 1989—. Active in community orgns.; adv. com. Leadership Fairfax; bd. dirs. McLean Orch.. Mem. Fairfax County C. of C. Home: 7523 Old Dominion Dr McLean VA 22102

BOJARSKI, JEANNE FRANCES, technical writer; b. N.Y.C., Dec. 20, 1951; d. Frank J. and Theodosia H. (Trzcinski) B.; children: Jessica James (dec.), Alexandra Jeanne Bojarski-Stauffer. BA in Philosophy, New Coll., Sarasota, Fla., 1974; postgrad. in econs., U. Chgo., 1979-81. Adminstrv. asst. Nat. Bus. Lists, Inc., N.Y.C., 1974-76; freelance writer, N.Y.C., 1976-77; asst. to pres. Tribal Arts Gallery, N.Y.C., 1977-78; instr. econs. Roosevelt U., Chgo., 1980-83; sr. cons. Cooley/Baker, Inc., Chgo., 1981-85; dir. tech. writing and proposal coordination Control Systems Internat., Overland Park, Kans., 1986—. Editor: The Grackle (jazz criticism), 1976. Bd. dirs. Studio Infinity Ltd., N.Y.C., 1976-77; hon. parent Gillis Home for Children, Kansas City, 1985. Mem. NRA, Soc. for Tech. Communication, Mut. Musician's Found. Libertarian. Avocations: hunting, photography, bicycling, jazz, trap shooting.

BOK, SISSELA, writer, philosopher; b. Stockholm, Dec. 2, 1934; d. Gunnar and Alva (Reimer) Myrdal; m. Derek Bok, May 7, 1955; children—Hilary, Victoria, Tomas. BA, George Washington U., 1957, MA, 1958, LHD (hon.), 1986; PhD, Harvard U., 1970; LLD (hon.), Mt. Holyoke Coll., 1985, Clark U., 1988. Lectr. Simmons Coll., Boston, 1971-72; lectr. Harvard-MIT Div. Health Scis. and Tech., Cambridge, 1975-82, Harvard U., Cambridge, 1982-84; assoc. prof. philosophy Brandeis U., Waltham, Mass., 1985-89, prof. philosophy, 1989—; mem. ethics adv. bd. HEW, 1977-80; bd. dirs. Population Council, 1971-77, Hastings Inst., 1976-84. Author: Lying: Moral Choice in Public and Private Life, 1978 (Melcher award, George Orwell award), Secrets: On the Ethics of Concealment and Revelation, 1982, Alva: Ett kvinnoliv, 1987, A Strategy for Peace, 1989; mem. editorial bd. Ethics, 1980-85, Criminal Justice Ethics, 1980—. Mem. adv. bd. Cultural Survival, 1986—; bd. dirs. Inst. for Philosophy and Religion, Boston U.; mem. Pulitzer Prize Bd., 1989—. Recipient Abram L. Sachar Silver medallion Brandeis U., 1985. Fellow Hastings Ctr. (dir. 1976-84); mem. Am. Philos. Assn. Office: Brandeis U Dept Philosophy Waltham MA 02254

BOKULIC, CHRISTINE ANN, sales representative; b. Paris, France, June 7, 1965; came to U.S., 1965.; d. Frank John and Dorothy Ann (Mrdeza) B. BS, Frostburg State U., Frostburg, 1987. Sales rep. GTCO Corp., Columbia, M.D., 1987-89; Nat. Assn. Female Exect M.D., 1988-89. Mem. Exec. V.P. Am. Mktg. Assoc. Collegiate Chpt. (v.p. 1986-87). Republic. Roman Catholic. Home: 11923 Tildenwood Dr Rockville MD 20852

BOLA, MARYBETH MARX, business inventory planner, chemical engineer; b. Bridgeport, Conn., Sept. 10, 1959; d. Andrew Charles and Sheila Margaret (Greaney) Marx; m. James Joseph Bola, May 27, 1984. BSCE, U. Notre Dame, 1981; MS in Chem. Engring., U. Va., 1983; MBA in Fin., U. Rochester, N.Y., 1988. Devel. engr. consumer div. Mobil Chem. Co., Macedon, N.Y., 1983-85; product devel. engr., scientist Eastman Kodak Co., Rochester, 1985-89, sales forecaster, demand planner, consumer imaging div., 1990—. Mem. Notre Dame Club of Rochester (alumni schs. com. 1988—, sec. 1990—). Roman Catholic. Home: 30 Mountain Rise Fairport NY 14450 Office: Eastman Kodak Co 343 State St Rochester NY 14650-1018

BOLAFFI, JANICE LERNER, endocrinologist; b. Boston, Dec. 12, 1933; d. Nathan and Estelle (Caen) Lerner; m. Andre Bolaffi, Sept. 12, 1954; children: David, Miriam. BA, Brandeis U., 1954; MA, Boston U., 1973, PhD, 1978; postgrad., Tufts U./New Eng. Med. Ctr., 1978-81. Asst. rsch. biochemist U. Calif., San Francisco, 1984-89, assoc. rsch. biochemist, 1989—; vis. asst. prof. Tufts U. Med. Sch., Boston, 1981-83. Contbr. articles to profl. jours., chpts. to books in field. Active NAACP (Westchester County 1963-70), New Dem. Coalition, Westchester County, N.Y., 1966-70, various polit. campaigns, Boston, 1971-83, San Francisco, 1984—, Urban League, Westchester County, 1963-70. Grantee Charlton Fund, Tufts Med. Sch., 1982, Calif. Am. Diabetic Assn., 1989; recipient postdoctoral award NIH, 1978-81. Mem. AAAS, Endocrine Soc., Am. Diabetes Assn., NAACP, Sigma Xi, Phi Beta Kappa. Office: Metabolic Rsch Unit Univ Calif San Francisco PO Box 0540 San Francisco CA 94143

BOLAND, JANET LANG, judge; b. Kitchener, Ont., Can., Dec. 6, 1924; d. George William and Miriam Janet (Geraghty) Lang; m. John Brown Boland, Oct. 1, 1949; children: Michael, Christopher, Nicholas. B.A., Waterloo Coll., 1946; law degree, Osgoode Hall, 1950; hon. doctorate of law, Sir Wilfred Laurier U. Bar: Ont. 1950, named Queen's counsel 1965. Mem. firm White, Bristol, Beck & Phipps, Toronto, Ont., 1959-69; partner firm Lang Michener, Toronto, 1969-72; county ct. judge Toronto, 1972-76; judge Supreme Ct. of Ont., Toronto, 1976—; co-chmn. Penal Reform for Women Joint Com., 1956-58. Mem. Jr. League Toronto. Roman Catholic. Office: Osgoode Hall, Queen St, Toronto, ON Canada M5H 2N7

BOLD, MARY ELLENDER, publisher; b. Fayetteville, Ark., Nov. 21, 1952; d. Ann (Moore) Brown; m. Thomas James Bold, Sept. 23, 1972; children: Ethan Thomas, Katherine Ann. Student, Syracuse U., 1970-72. Owner, pub. Bold Prodns., Fla., 1983-88, Arlington, Tex., 1988—; presenter pub. seminars. Author: How to Improve Your Mind over Summer Vacatiopn, 1987, Kids in Orlando, 1985, The Decision to Publish, 1987, 89; editor: Handmade Christmas Gifts that Are Actually Usable, 1987. Mem. Nat. Assn. Ind. Pubs. (adv. bd. 1988-, exec. dir. Tex. State chpt. 1989-), Fla. Pubs. Group (exec. bd. 1986-88). Democrat. Office: Bold Prodns PO Box 152281 Arlington TX 76015

BOLDEN, ROSAMOND, state official; b. Beggs, Okla., May 5, 1938; d. Benjamin James and Mary Crosby; m. James Alan Bolden, Jan. 27, 1963 (dec. Dec. 1973); 1 child, Stacie Lenore. B.S., U. Calif.-Berkeley, 1961, MA 1971. Employment counselor to office mgr. Calif. Dept. Employment, Sacramento, 1965-75; asst. civil rights officer Calif. Dept. Health, Sacramento, 1976-77; chief Office Bldg. and Grounds, Calif. Dept. Gen. Services, Sacramento, 1977—; chmn. merit award bd. dept. personnel adminstrn., State of Calif. Sacramento, 1979-84; mem. women's adv. bd. Calif. Personnel Bd., Sacramento, 1980-84. Bd. dirs. Tierra Del Oro coun. Girl Scouts U.S., Sacramento, 1984, Sacramento Urban League, 1986-89, treas.; mem. citizen rev. bd., chmn. admission/allocation subcom. United Way, Sacramento, 1984; founding mem. Sacramento Black Women's Network, 1981. Recipient award of appreciation United Calif. State Employee Campaign, 1980; cert. of appreciation Nat. Assn. Retarded Citizens, 1981 United Way, 1984; named Outstanding Pub. Adminstr., Am. Soc. for Pub. Adminstrs., 1989. Mem. Bldg. Owners and Mgrs. Assn. (co-founder Calif. chpt. 1986, mem. govt. bldg. com., chairwoman bldg. ops. div. 1987—), NAACP, Black Advocates in State Svc., Alpha Kappa Alpha. Home: PO Box 22457 Sacramento CA 95831 Office: State of Calif 915 Capital Mall Room 106 Sacramento CA 95831

BOLDRIN, LAURIE-ANNE, translator, educator; b. Dearborn, Mich., Nov. 8, 1964; d. Lorenzo Ettore and Piera Maria (Zanotti) B. BA, Lake Erie Coll., 1986; teaching cert., Cleve. State U., 1988; postgrad, Oakland U., 1989—. Cert. tchr., Ohio. Translator, sec. Dewal Group, Birmingham, Mich., 1986; temporary worker Olsten Temporary Svc., Cleve., 1987; asst. mgr. Decor Mktg., Mentor, Ohio, 1988; sales support assoc. Kelly Kitt, Beachwood, Ohio, 1989; tchr. Pan Am. Langs., Troy, Mich., 1989—; guest tchr. Mohawk Elem. Sch., Utica, Mich., 1990; bi-lingual adminstrv. asst. The Woodbridge Group, Troy, Mich., 1990—. Mem. Great Lakes Invitational Conf. Assn. (bd. dirs. 1986—).

BOLDT, DENNISE M., nurse; b. Cuero, Tex., Nov. 23, 1951; d. August Joseph and Sophie Geneva (Hermes) Polasek; m. Michael Wayne Boldt, Feb. 19, 1977; children: Sarah, Steven. RN, Brackenridge Hosp. Sch. Nrsg, Austin, 1973; postgrad., U. Tex., Austin, Victoria (Tex.) Coll. Staff nurse Brackenridge Hosp., Austin, Tex.; field nurse Coastal Bend Home Health, Victoria, Tex.; ICU-CCU supr. DeTar Hosp., Victoria; dir. patient svcs. Crossroads Home Health, Victoria; v.p. Crossroads Home Health; v.p. Crossroads Nursing Svc. Mem. ANA, Tex. Nurses Assn., Tex. Assn. Home Health Agencies, (chmn. peer rev. ethics com.), Nat. Assn. Home Health Agencies. Home: 412 Sun Valley Dr Victoria TX 77904 Office: 1501 Mockingbird 403A Victoria TX 77904

BOLEBRUCH, LORI ANN, navy officer; b. Gloversville, N.Y., Aug. 10, 1957; d. Frank and Beverly June (Daniels) B. BA in Theatre Arts, SUNY, Oswego, 1979; MS in Systems Mgmt., U. So. Calif., 1988. Commd. ensign USN, 1980, advanced through grades to lt. comdr., 1990; pub. affairs officer Fleet Logistics Support Squadron-30, San Diego, 1980-82; student naval aviator Schs. Command, Pensacola, Fla., 1982-83; pilot under tng. Helicopter Anti-Submarine Warfare Squadron-10, San Diego, 1983-84; schedules officer, maintenance div. officer Fleet Composite Squadron-5, Philippines, 1984-86; asst. ops. officer Helicopter Combat Support Squadron-1, San Diego, 1986-88; flight deck officer USS Lexington, Pensacola, 1988—. Contbr. articles to profl. jours. Ptnrs. in Edn. coord. USS Lexington/AA Dixon Sch., Pensacola, 1989—; USS Lexington vol. coord. Spl. Olympics, Pensacola, 1990; pub. rels. Pensacola Little Theatre, 1990; v.p. membership JET SET/Nat. Mus. Naval Aviation, Pensacola, 1990—. Named regional finalist White House Fellowship, 1990. Mem. Women Officers' Profl. Assn. (symposium com. San Diego chpt. 1986-88), Tailhook Assn. (conv. com. 1987—, Membership award 1989), Naval Helicopter Assn. (chpt. membership 1987-88), Oswego Alumni Assn., U. So. Calif. Inst. Safety and Systems Mgmt., Alumni Assn., Blue Hare-on Hash House Harriers, Pensacola Runners Assn. Home: 11550 Haven Wood Rd Pensacola FL 32514 Office: USS Lexington AVT 16 NAS Pensacola FL 32508

BOLENE, MARGARET ROSALIE STEELE, bacteriologist, civic worker; b. Kingfisher, Okla., July 11, 1923; d. Clarence R. and Harriet (White) Steele; student Oreg. State U., 1943-44; B.S., U. Okla., 1946; m. Robert V. Bolene, Feb. 6, 1948; children—Judith Kay, John Eric, Sally Sue, Janice Lynn, Daniel William. Technician bacteriology dept. Okla. Dept. Health, Oklahoma City, 1946-48; asst. bacteriologist Henry Ford Hosp., Detroit, 1948-49; bacteriol. cons., also asst. bus. mgr. Ponce Gynecology and Obstetrics, Inc., 1956—. Organizing dir. Bi-Racial Council, 1963; lay adviser Home Nursing Service, 1967-68; mem. exec. bd. PTA, 1956-71; active various community drives; sponsor Am. Field Service; patron Ponce Playhouse; bloodmobile vol. ARC; vol. Helpline. Republican precinct organizer, 1960. Mem. AAUW (treas. 1964-66), DAR (sec.-treas. 1961-67, 1st vice regent 1972-73, chpt. treas. 1974-84), Kay-Noble County Med. Aux. (treas. 1957-58, 66-67), Ponca City Art Assn., Pioneer Hist. Soc., Okla. Heritage Assn., Daus. Founders and Patriots (state pres. 1980-84), Nat. Huguenot Soc., Hereditary Order First Families Mass. Daus. Am. Colonists (chpt. pres. 1982-84), Magna Charta Dames (treas. Okla. chpt. 1984), Order Colonial Physicians and Chirurgiens (life), Ancient and Honorable Arty. Co. Women Descs. Okla. Ct. (treas. 1983-84, registrar 1986—), Dames of Ct. of Honor, Colonial Dames of 17th Century, Hereditary Order of First Families of Mass., U. Okla. Assn. (life), Lambda Tau, Phi Sigma, Alpha Lambda Delta. Presbyterian (elder 1983-86). Clubs: Ponca City Country, Ponca City Music, Red Rose Garden (pres. 1983-84), Twentieth Century. Home: 2116 Juanito Ave Ponca City OK 74604

BOLES, JANET KAY, political science educator; b. Burkburnett, Tex., July 26, 1944; d. Stark Simpson and Edith Lois (Ross) B.; m. Franklin Evans, Aug. 23, 1975; 1 child, Christine Elaine. BA, U. Okla., 1966; MA in Libr. Sci., U. Mich., 1967; PhD, U. Tex., 1976. Asst. libr. N.Y. State Libr., Albany, 1967-68; librar. Johnson Presdl. Libr., Austin, Tex., 1969; asst. prof. polit. sci. Corpus Christi (Tex.) State U., 1975-77, U. Tex., Austin, 1977-80; asst. prof. polit. sci. Marquette U., Milw., 1980-88, assoc. prof., 1988—, dir. urban affairs, 1988—; co-dir. Inst. for Citizenship and Pub. Policy, Milw., 1984-85; mem. edn. bd. Women and Politics, 1986-88, 89—; adv. bd. MS. Mag., N.Y.C., 1980-84. Author: The Politics of the E.R.A., 1979; editor: The Egalitarian City, 1986; contbr. articles to profl. publs. Active Day Care com. Wis. Dept. Health and Social Svcs., Madison, 1985-88; troop leader Girl Scouts U.S., Glendale, Wis., 1988—; polling worker Farenthold for Gov. campaign, Austin, 1972. Rsch. grantee NSF, 1973-74, Milw. Found., 1985, Ctr. for Am. Woman and Politics, 1988—. Mem. Am. Polit. Sci. Assn. (rsch. grantee 1988—), Women's Caucus for Polit. Sci. (sec. 1981-82), Midwest Polit. Sci. Assn. (mem. exec. council 1986-89), Midwest Women's Caucus (pres. 1983-84), Policy Studies Orgn., NOW, Nat. Women's Polit. Caucus, LWV, Phi Beta Kappa, Pi Sigma Alpha. Democrat. Unitarian. Home: 6535 N Range Line Rd Glendale WI 53209 Office: Marquette U Dept Polit Sci Milwaukee WI 53233

BOLEY, DONNA JEAN, state legislator; b. Bens Run, W.Va., Dec. 9, 1935; d. Glen A. and Grace (Jones) Northcraft; m. Jack Edward Boley, 1956; children: Kari Lynn, Brian Lee. Student, Parkersburg Community Coll. Sec. Pleasants County Rep. Exec. Com., 1970-75, vice-chmn., 1978-82, chmn., 1982—; state senator from dist. 3 State of W.Va., 1986—. Mem. St. Marys Women's Club (pres. 1972-74, 80-81). Republican. Methodist. *

BOLEY, JACQUELINE, language educator; b. Columbus, Ohio, Apr. 14, 1954; d. Bruno A. and Sara R. Boley. Student, Columbia U., 1966-68; BA with distinction, Cornell U., 1970; MA, Cambridge (Eng.) U., 1978; postgrad., U. London, 1973-80; harpsichord studies, Trinity Coll. of Music, London, 1975-79. Lectr. Classics Trinity Coll., Hartford, Conn., 1983-85; lectr. Italian Cen. Conn. State U., New Britain, Conn., 1985—. Author: The Hittite Hark-Construction, 1984, The Sentence Particles and the Place Words in Old and Middle Hittite, 1989; contbr. articles to profl. jours.; writer Latin poetry. NEH grantee, 1986, 88, Trinity Coll. grantee, 1984. Mem. Am. Oriental Soc. Home: 69 Atlantic Dr Old Saybrook CT 06475

BOLEY BOLAFFIO, RITA, artist; b. Trieste, Italy, June 7, 1898; d. Angelo Luzzatto and Olga Senigaglia; came to U.S., 1939, naturalized, 1944; studied with Joseph Hoffmann, Kunstgewerbe Schule, Vienna, Austria; diploma violin Music Conservatory, Vienna; student of F. Ondricek; m. Orville F. Boley; children: Lucius R., Bruno A. Fashion and textile and interior designer Wiener Werkstatte, Vienna and Milan, Italy; murals and displays throughout U.S., maj. exhns. collage and assemblage include Mus. of Art, Columbia, S.C., Am. House, N.Y.C., J.L. Hudson Gallery, Detroit, Pen and Brush Club, N.Y.C., Richard Kollmar's Gallery, N.Y.C., Guild Hall Mus., East Hampton, N.Y., James Pendleton Gallery, N.Y.C. Washington Art Assn. Conn., Galerie St. Etienne, N.Y.C., Hudson River Mus., Yonkers, N.Y.; represented in pvt. collections, also represented in European and Am. publs. Mem. arts group ARC, 1942-44. Mem. Composer, Author and Artists Am. Studio: 310 W 106th St New York NY 10025

BOLGER, FRANCINE JO, marketing executive; b. N.Y.C., Dec. 9, 1956; d. Francis Joseph and Kathleen Rose (Hyland) B. BS in Bus. and Fin., Bloomsburg (Pa.) State U., 1979. Group sales rep. The New Eng., N.Y.C., 1979-84; group pension cons. The New Eng., Chgo., 1984-87; regional mktg. dir. The New Eng., Fairfax, Va., 1987—. Tutor, Project Literacy, Chgo., 1985-86. Mem. Women in Employee Benefits, Chgo. Soccer Club. Republican. Roman Catholic. Office: The New Eng 11130 Main St Ste 301 Fairfax VA 22030

BOLI, SARAH COLLINS, property manager; b. Warren, Pa., July 18, 1958; d. Hugh C. and Elizabeth (Harper) Wood; m. Robert McPherson Boli, Dec. 22, 1982; 1 child Jonathan William. AA in Liberal Arts, Jamestown Community coll., N.Y., 1978; BA in Environ. Science, Alfred U., N.Y., 1980; postgrad., U. Wash., 1988—. Lab. asst. Jamestown Community Coll., Jamestown, N.Y., 1976-78; dir. commercial ops. Tech and Turf Inc., Madison, N.J., 1980-81; mgr. King's Motel Pacific Land Assoc., Enumclaw, Wash., 1985—; owner Plan'dscape; mem. design rev. bd. City of Enumclaw. Author: Jamestown Community College Preserve, 1978. Tourism com. C. of C., Enumclaw, Wash., 1985—. Served as sgt. U.S. Army, 1981-85. Mem. Assn. U.S. Army, Am. Soc. Landscape Architects (Student Merit awards Washington chpt. 1988), Bus. and Profl. Women (Young Career Woman award Wash. state dist. 4 1986), Sigma Lambda Alpha, Tau Sigma Delta (pres. Iota chpt. 1989). Republican. Methodist. Home and Office: 1334 Roosevelt Way East Enumclaw WA 98022

BOLING, BETH A., manufacturing executive; b. Indpls., Dec. 21, 1960; d. Fred F. and Miriam (Query) B. BS in Indsl. Engring., Purdue U., 1983; M in Engring., Cornell U., 1984; MBA, Stanford (Calif.) U., 1989. Coop. engr. Western Electric, Indpls., 1980-83; indsl. engr. GE, Schenectady, N.Y., 1984-87; bus. analyst GE, Fairfield, Conn., 1988; product mgr. GE, Louisville, 1989—. Office: GE Appliances AP4-104 Louisville KY 40225

BOLING, CAROLE JEAN, educator; b. North Pointe, Nebr., Dec. 15, 1943; d. Lawrence Keith and Nellie Rose (Annis) B. BA, Sioux Falls (S.D.) Coll., 1967; MS, Emporia (Kans.) State U., 1979. Cert. elem. tchr. Tchr. Sioux Falls Sch. Dist., 1967-72; spl. programs coord. project headstart Bismarck (N.D.) Sch. Dist., 1973-75, title I resource coord., 1975-77; lectr. Emporia State U., spring 1979; mem. part-time faculty Maricopa Community Coll., Phoenix, 1984-87, mem. faculty, 1987-88; program specialist, facilitator Creighton Sch. Dist., Phoenix, 1988—; mem. adj. faculty Ariz. State U., Tempe, summer 1990; team tchr. Chusila Boarding Sch., Tonatanie, N.Y., spring 1984, DilCon (Ariz.) Boarding Sch., summer 1984; utoring cons. Literacy Vol., Phoenix, 1985-88; developer materials spl. English as second lang. grant program, Phoenix, spring 1986. Mem. Internat. Reading Assn., Ariz. Reading Assn., Ocotillo Reading Assn., Nat. Coun. Tchrs. of English, Grad. Students in Reading Edn. Republican. Roman Catholic.

BOLING, JEWELL, retired government official; b. Randleman, N.C., Sept. 26, 1907; d. John Emmitt and Carrie (Ballard) B. Student, Women's Coll., U. N.C., 1926, Am. U., 1942, 51-52. Interviewer N.C. Employment Service, Winston-Salem, Asheboro, 1937-41; occupational analyst U.S. Dept. Labor, Washington, 1943-57, placement officer, 1957-58, employment service adviser, 1959-61, occupational analyst, 1962, employment service specialist counseling and testing, 1963-69, manpower devel. specialist, 1969—. Author: Counselor's Handbook, 1967; Counselor's Desk Aid, Eighteen Basic Vocational Directions, 1967; Handbook for New Careerists in Employment Security, 1971; contbr. articles to profl. publs. Recipient Meritorious Achievement award U.S. Dept. Labor, 1972. Mem. AAAS, N.Y. Acad. Scis., Am. Assn. Counseling and Devel., Nat. Career Devel. Assn., Am. Rehab. Counseling Assn. (archivist 1964-68), Assn. Measurement in Counseling and Devel., Assn. for Supervision and Curriculum Devel., Assn. Humanistic Psychology, Planetary Soc., Smithsonians, Sierra Club, Nature Conservancy, Internat. Platform Assn., Audubon Naturalist Soc., Nat. Capital Astronomers (editor Star Dust 1949-58), Wilderness Soc. Address: Rte 2 Box 176 Randleman NC 27317

BOLING, JUDY ATWOOD, civic worker; b. Madras, India, June 19, 1921 (parents Am. citizens); d. Carroll Eugene and Marion Frances (Ayrer) Atwood; A.A., San Antonio Jr. Coll., 1940; student Rogue Community Coll., Grants Pass, Oreg., 1978-79, So. Oreg. State Coll., Ashland, 1982—; m. Jack Leroy Boling, Apr. 8, 1941 (dec. July 1988); children: Joseph Edward, Jean Ann, James Michael, John Charles. First aid instr. ARC, various locations, 1940-65, chmn. vols., Calif., 1961-62, Eng., 1964-65; den mother cub scouts Boy Scouts Am., Monterey, Calif., 1951-52; active Girl Scouts U.S., 1953—, coun. pres., Winema (Oreg.) Coun., 1971-73, 79-82, del. to nat. council, 1966, 72, 81, cons. for nat. pubs., 1971, 79; Sunday sch. tchr. Base Chapel, Pyote, Tex., 1949-51, choir dir., 1951; Sunday sch. adminstr. Base Chapel, Morocco, 1954-55; Sunday sch. tchr. Hermon Free Meth. Ch., L.A., 1956-57; active United Way campaign, 1967-84, Childrens Festival, 1974-88; former liaison with local people in Japanese-Am., Franco-Am., Anglo-Am. orgns.; mem., patron Rogue Craftsmen Bd., Grants Pass, 1972-85, sec., 1972-78, v.p., 1978-85; bd. dirs. Rogue Valley Opera Assn., 1978-85, sponsor/mem., 1978—; bd. dirs. Community Concert, 1979-88; historian Josephine County Rep. Women, 1982-86, treas., 1986—; frequent public speaker; mem. KSYS, KSOR TV. Recipient Thanks badge Girl Scouts U.S., 1957, 60, 73, Girl Scouts Japan, 1959, United Kingdom Girl Guides, 1982; others; cert. of appreciation USAF, 1959, City of Hagi, City of Fukuoka (Japan), Gov. of Fukuoka Prefecture; 2 citations Internat. Book Project; Oreg. Vol. award Sen. Packwood, 1983; Community Woman of Year award Bus. and Profl. Women, 1984. Mem. Josephine County Hist. Soc., So. Oreg. Resources Alliance, Am. Host Found., Friends of Library, Women's Investment Group (pres. 1987, v.p.), Grants Pass Art Mus. Republican. Club: Knife and Fork. Contbr. articles to profl. jours. Address: 3016 Jumpoff Joe Creek Rd Grants Pass OR 97526

BOLING, KATHLEEN MARY, executive secretary; b. St. Paul, Sept. 14, 1950; d. Ernest Ard and Mary Matilda (Paulsen) Robotti; m. E. Ronald Boling, May 20, 1984; children: Scott T. Burke, Kari K. Burke. AA, Lakewood State Jr. Coll., White Bear Lake, Minn., 1970; postgrad., Southwestern Adventist Coll., Keene, Tex., 1988—. Clk.-typist Nat. Car Rental, Inc., Mpls., 1970-72; supr. customer svc. Kelly Svcs. Inc., Flint, Mich., 1972-73; exec. sec. sales svc. Win Schuler Foods, Inc., Marshall, Mich., 1974-75; exec. sec. St. Regis Paper Co., Battle Creek, Mich., 1976-80; exec. sec., office mgr. Calhoun County Community Mental Health Svcs., Battle Creek, 1983-88, asst. adminstr., 1988-89; exec. sec. Battle Creek Adventist Hosp., 1989—. Trustee Mental Health Vol. Coun., Battle Creek, 1989—; supt. local ch., 1988—, co-dir. youth dept., 1989—. Named Vol. of Yr., Mental Health Vol. Coun. and Calhoun County Community Mental Health Svcs. Bd., 1989. Mem. Profl. Secs. Internat. (v.p. Greater Battle Creek chpt. 1988-89, pres. 1989—, editor Hospitality City chpt., 1976-78, treas. 1977-78). Office: Battle Creek Adventist Hosp 165 N Washington Ave Battle Creek MI 49017

BOLINGER, BECKY LYNN, personnel specialist, business owner; b. Honolulu, Apr. 4, 1959; d. Terry Lee and Patricia Ann (Toering) Shaw; m. Richard Allen Bolinger, Mar. 29, 1981; children: James Bradley, Cale Evan, Kacey William, Garrett Richard. Grad. high sch., Portage, Ind. Mgr. Victorian Bridal Salon, Valparaiso, Ind., 1979-82; formal wear dept. mgr. Ferndales Bridal Village, Englewood, Colo., 1982-83; mgr. Sir Knight Formal Wear, Denver, 1983; br. mgr. Career Forum, Inc., Wheatridge, Colo., 1983-89; owner Absolute Employment Agy., Westminster, Colo., 1989—. Mem. PTA, Arvada, Colo., 1986—. Mem. Nat. Assn. Personnel Cons., NAFE, Westminster C. of C. Home: 7579 Jay Cord Arvada CO 80003 Office: Absolute Employment Agy 8120 Sheridan B304 Westminster CO 80003

BOLINGER, BONNIE LOU, nurse; b. Frenchburg, Ky., Mar. 7, 1938; d. Butler and Bessie (Hackney) Rothwell; m. James D. Bolinger, Aug. 30, 1957 (div. June 1982); children: Michelle, Keith, Douglas. Cert. practical nursing, Dayton (Ohio) Sch. Practical Nursing, 1971; cert. enterostomal therapy, Ferguson-Droste-Ferguson Clinic, Grand Rapids, Mich., 1972; AD in Nursing, St. Petersburg Jr. Coll., Clearwater, Fla., 1978. Patient educator, enterostomal therapist Miami Valley Hosp., Dayton, 1972-77, Meml. Hosp., Hollywood, Fla., 1978-79; sales rep. ConvaTec, Princeton, N.J., 1981-84; dir. patient edn. Nightingale Med., Cin., 1984-87; profl. svc. mgr. Coloplast, Inc., Tampa, Fla., 1987—. Author: Teenagers Ostomy Guide, 1978; contbg. author: Principles of Ostomy Care, 1982. Recipient Svc. and Rehab. award Ohio div. Am. Cancer Soc., 1976, Community Svc. award Aux. to Montgomery County Med. Soc., Dayton, 1975. Mem. Internat. Assn. Enterostomal Therapy (pres. 1979-81, coodinator mid-east region 1974-75, mid-east region pres. award 1988), World Coun. Enterostomal Therapy. Democrat. Unitarian. Home: 13113 Oregon Ave N Tampa FL 33612 Office: Coloplast Inc 5610 N Sligh Tampa FL 33634

BOLITHO, LOUISE GREER, educational administrator, consultant; b. Wenatchee, Wash., Aug. 13, 1927; d. Lon Glenn and Edna Gertrude (Dunlap) Greer; m. Douglas Stuart, June 17, 1950 (div. Dec. 1975); children: Rebecca Louise, Brian Douglas. BA, Wash. State U., 1949. With Stanford (Calif.) U., 1967-86, adminstrv. asst. physics labs., 1974-77, mgr. ctr. for research in internat. studies, 1977-84, law sch. fin. and adminstrv. services dir., 1984-86; computer cons., Palo Alto, Calif., 1984—; acting mgr. Inst. for Internat. Studies, 1987-88, fin. analyst, 1988—. Mem. Peninsula vols., Menlo Park, Calif., 1986—; budget com. chmn., bd. dirs. Mid-Peninsula Support Network, Mountain View, Calif., 1984-86; chairwoman active older adults com. YMCA; pres. 410 Sheridan Ave. Homeowners Assn., 1989—. Mem. AAUW (bd. dirs. 1987-88), Stanford/Palo Alto IBM Personal Computer User's Group, Palo Alto C. of C. Home and Office: 410 Sheridan Ave #445 Palo Alto CA 94306

BOLLINGER, PAMELA BEEMER, health facilities administrator; b. Chgo., Apr. 7, 1947; d. Eldred Harlan and Shirley Pearl (Olsen) Beemer; m. Gary Allen Bollinger, Aug. 23, 1969. BS, Millikin U., 1969. Med. technologist Rush-Presbyt. St. Luke's Med. Ctr., Chgo., 1969-70, exec. technologist, 1975-77; hematology supr. Meml. Hosp. DuPage County, Elmhurst, Ill., 1970-75; chief med. technologist U. Tex.-M.D. Anderson Hosp., Houston, 1977-88; lab. dir. Northeast Med. Ctr. Hosp., Humble, Tex., 1988—; cons. Technicon Instruments Corp., Tarrytown, N.Y., 1984-88, Coulter Electronics, Inc., Hialeah, Fla., 1978-83. Contbg. author: Clinical Laboratory Annual, 1984, Phlebotomy Handbook, 1984, Clinical Hematology: Principles, Procedures, Correlations, 1988. Vol. Ponderosa Forest Civic Assn., Houston, 1985, Muscular Dystrophy Assn., Houston, 1980-81. Mem. Am. Soc. Clin. Pathology (cert.), Am. Soc. Med. Tech. (Joseph J. Kleiner meml. award 1985), Tex. Soc. Med. Tech. Home: 1914 Big Horn Dr Houston TX 77090 Office: NE Med Ctr Hosp 18951 Memorial N Humble TX 77338

BOLMARCICH, VIRGINIA DEVLIN, radiologist, educator; b. East Falls, Pa., June 22, 1944; d. Lawrence and Elizabeth (McHale) Devlin; m. Lawrence J. Bolmarcich, Aug. 3, 1968; children: Sarah, Mary. BA, U. Pa., 1966; MD, Med. Coll. Pa., 1971; postgrad., Drexel U., 1989—. Diplomate Am. Bd. Radiology. Intern Grad. Hosp. of U. Pa., Phila., 1971-72; staff radiologist, instr. Med. Coll. Pa., Phila., 1975-76, Phila. Gen. Hosp., 1976-77; resident in radiology Mercy Cath. Med. Ctr., Darby, Pa., 1972-75, staff radiologist, clin. asst. prof., 1977—. Mem. Am. Coll. Radiology, Pa. Med. Soc., Pa. Radiologic Soc., Delaware County Med. Soc.

BOLOGNA, JOANNE DENISE, systems development supervisor; b. Albany, N.Y., Mar. 22, 1961; d. Matthew Joseph and Viola Theresa (Audi) B. BA in Computer Sci., LeMoyne Coll., 1983; postgrad. Rensselear Poly. Inst., 1983, Russel Sage Coll., 1984, 1986—. Documentation specialist McAuto Systems Group, Inc., Menands, N.Y., 1983-84, sr. programmer/analyst, 1984-85; systems analyst Empire Blue Cross & Blue Shield, Albany, N.Y., 1985-86; lead systems analyst Computer Scis. Corp., Menands, 1986-88, supr. systems devel., 1988—. Mem. Nat. Assn. Female Execs. Roman Catholic. Avocations: jogging, skiing, reading, computers, tax consulting. Home: 4066 Albany St Schenectady NY 12304 Office: Computer Scis Corp 800 N Pearl St Menands NY 12204

BOLOTIN, LORA M., business owner, electronics executive; b. Dallas; d. Joseph and Bertha Marshall; m. M. L. Bolotin, June 21, 1953; children: Linda Susan, Scott Evan, Kent Carter. BA in Edn., Roosevelt U., 1952; postgrad., UCLA, 1980, Calif. State U., Northridge, 1988. Cert. tchr., Ill. Tchr. Chgo. Bd. Edn., 1952-55; v.p. Bolotin Assocs., Inc., Woodland Hills, Calif., 1973-83, pres., 1984—. Art Inst. of Chgo. scholar, 1946; recipient 2 Sterling Silver Art medals, Am. Legion, 1946, 47. Home: 16663 Calneva Dr Encino CA 91436 Office: Bolotin Assocs Inc 21241 Ventura Blvd Ste 268 Woodland Hills CA 91364

BOLSEN, BARBARA ANN, association newspaper editor; b. Cin., Aug. 27, 1950; d. William Dornette and Ida Louise (Krueck) B.; m. Roy Austin Petty, May 19, 1979. BS, Northwestern U., 1971. Reporter Aroostook County Times, Presque Isle, Maine, 1972; copy editor, reporter Lerner Newspapers, Chgo., 1972-73; assoc. editor Am. Med. News., Chgo., 1973-75, sr. editor, 1975-77, 78-81, sr. editor Washington, 1981-82, exec. editor, 1982—; editorial dir. Book Developers, Inc., Chgo., 1977-78; assoc. editor med. news. sect. Jour. AMA Washington, 1981-82. Recipient Gold Circle award Am. Soc. Assn. Execs., 1984, 87. Office: Am Med News 535 N Dearborn St Chicago IL 60610

BOLSTER, JACQUELINE NEBEN (MRS. JOHN A. BOLSTER), communications consultant; b. Woodhaven, N.Y.; d. Ernest William Benedict and Emily Claire (Guck) Neben; student Pratt Inst., Columbia U.; m. John A. Bolster, May 8, 1954. Promotion mgr. Photoplay mag., 1949-53; merchandising mgr. McCall's, N.Y.C., 1953-64; dir. promotion and merchandising Harper's Bazaar, N.Y.C., 1964-71; dir. advt. and promotion Elizabeth Arden Salons, N.Y.C., 1971-76; dir. creative services Elizabeth Arden, Inc., 1976-78, dir. communications Elizabeth Arden Salons, 1978-87, communication cons., 1987—. Recipient Art Director's award 1961, 66. Mem. Fashion Group, Fashion Execs. Roundtable, Inner Circle, Advt. Women N.Y. (life), Women's Nat. Rep. Club (life), Mag. Promotion Assn. Episcopalian. Home and Office: 8531 88th St Woodhaven NY 11421 also: Halsey Neck Ln Southampton NY 11968

BOLT, KATHERINE HEYM, software engineer; b. Bronxville, N.Y., July 12, 1944; d. Harold C. and Katherine (Burgess) Heym; 1 child, Bevin Barbara. BA in Math., Ohio Wesleyan U., 1966; MA in Math., U. Mich., 1967. Tchr. Lahser High Sch., Mich., 1968; staff engr. Charles Stark Draper Lab., Cambridge, Mass., 1968-78; sr. programmer ModComp, Ft. Lauderdale, Fla., 1978-81; sr. software engr. Autech Data Systems, Ft. Lauderdale, 1981-85, Emergent Tech., Boca Raton, Fla., 1985-86, Motorola, Inc., Boynton Beach, Fla., 1987—. Mem. Computer Soc. of IEEE, Soc. for Indls. and Applied Math., Gulfstream Sailing Club, Kappa Alpha Theta, U.S. Yacht Racing Union, J24 Class Assn. Democrat. Episcopalian. Home: 401 Lincoln Ct Pompano Beach FL 33073 Office: 1500 NW 22d Ave Boynton Beach FL 33426-8753

BOLTE, CANDICE REGINA, communications administrator; b. Jersey City, Oct. 18, 1948; d. George John and Frances Margaret (Hawkridge) B. BA in Math. Edn., Jersey City State Coll., 1970, MA in Math. Edn., 1972. Cert. systems profl. Tchr. high sch. math. Belleville (N.J.) Bd. Edn., 1970-79; developer system devel. tng. AT&T Long Lines, Piscataway, N.J., 1979-84; system planner AT&T Communications, Piscataway, 1984-87; system mgr. AT&T, Basking Ridge, N.J., 1987—. Head usher Marble Collegiate Ch., N.Y.C., 1986-88. Mem. Assn. for Systems Mgmt. (pres. N.Y. chpt. 1983-86, div. dir. 1987-88, adv. com. internat. edn. 1984-86, internat. com. chair 1986-87, internat. dir. 1988—, Outstanding Service 1981, 87, 88, Disting. Service award 1988). Mem. Dutch Reformed Ch. Office: AT&T 295 N Maple Ave Basking Ridge NJ 07920

BOLTON, BARBARA DIANE, chemical dependency program administrator; b. Ft. Madison, Iowa, Nov. 24, 1950; d. Francis Edward and Fern June (Miller) B.; 1 child, Emily Anne Brotherton. BS in Social Work, S.W. Mo. State U., 1981; MS in Social Work, U. Ark., 1982. Cert. Acad. Cert. Social Workers; cert. substance abuse counselor, Mo. Social work intern VA, Little Rock, 1981-82; family therapist St. John's Reg. Health Ctr. Bridgeway Program, Springfield, Mo., 1982-84; sr. counselor St. John's Reg. Health Ctr. Bridgeway Program, 1984-85, clin. dir., 1985-87, program dir., 1987—; faculty S.W. Mo. State U., Springfield, 1987; mem. drug. edn./referral CORE Com. S.W. Mo. State U., Springfield, 1986—; chmn. treatment Community Consortium Com., Springfield, 1988-89. Mem. regional adv. coun. State Div. Alcohol & Drug Abuse, Springfield, 1988—; steering com. "The Ozarks Fights Back" Community Effort for Prevention Alcohol & Drug Abuse, Springfield, 1989. Mem. Nat. Assn. Social Workers, Alpha Delta Mu, Alpha Kappa Delta. Office: Bridgeway 2828 N National Springfield MO 65803

BOLTON, MARTHA O., writer; b. Searcy, Ark., Sept. 1, 1951; d. Lonnie Leon and Eunice Dolores Ferren; m. Russell Norman Bolton, Apr. 17, 1970; children: Russell Norman II, Matthew David, Anthony Shane. Grad. high sch., Reseda, Calif. Freelance writer for various comedians, 1975-86; newspaper columnist Simi Valley Enterprise, Simi, Calif., 1979-87; staff writer Bob Hope, 1986—. Author: A Funny Thing Happed to Me on My Way Through the Bible, 1985, A View from the Pew, 1986, What's Growing Under Your Bed?, 1986, Tangled in the Tinsel, 1987, (help book) So, How'd I Get to be in Charge of the Program?, 1988, Humourous Monologues, 1989, Let My People Laugh, 1989, If Mr. Clean Calls Tell Him I'm Not In, 1989, Journey to the Center of the Stage, 1990, If You Can't Stand the Smoke, Get Out of My Kitchen, 1990. Pres. Vista Elem. Sch. PTA, Simi, 1980-81. Recipient Emmy award nomination for outstanding achievement in music and lyrics NATAS, 1988, Angel award, 1990. Mem. Nat. League of Am. Pen Women (br. pres. 1984-86, Woman of Achievement award Simi Valley br. 1984), Writers Guild Am. West, ASCAP, Soc. Children's Book Writers. Office: PO Box 1212 Simi CA 93062

BOLTON, MARY JANE, educational consultant; b. McCloud, Calif., Nov. 29, 1934; d. Edwin Elsworth and Frances Ione (Turner) Day; m. Harry Procter Bolton Jr., Jan. 24, 1955; children: Linda, Harry, Kenneth, David, Dale. BS in Home Econs., U. Calif., Davis, 1957; MA in Edn. Adminstrn., Calif. State U., Sacramento, 1978. Tchr. Placer Hills Elem. Sch. Dist., Meadow Vista, Calif., 1959-84, adminstr., 1972-82; ednl. cons. Sacramento County and Placer County, 1982-89; cons. Region 4 Tech. Edn. Ctr., Sacramento, 1985-86, Placer County Office Edn., Auburn, Calif., 1987-89; instr. Sierra Coll., Rocklin, Calif., 1973-80, trustee, 1981-89, pres. bd. dirs. 1982, 89. Chmn. bd. dirs. Auburn Youth Svc. Ctr., 1988-89. Mem. 99's Women's Pilot Assn., Assn. Calif. Sch. Adminstrs., AAUW (pres. 1983-84), Bus. and Profl. Women (v.p. 1980-81), Delta Kappa Gamma (pres. 1980-82), Phi Delta Kappa. Republican. Home: 1180 Grange Rd PO Box 1238 Meadow Vista CA 95722

BOLTZ, CAROL HOFMANN, school system administrator; b. Warren, Pa., Oct. 26, 1934; d. James Ray and Romayne Elizabeth (Lesser) Barrett; m. John Thomas Hofmann, Aug. 18, 1959 (div. June 1980); children: Paul Barrett, Lynn Hoffmann Ottney; m. David James Boltz; 1 stepson, David James. MusB, Oberlin Coll., 1956; MS in Edn., SUNY, Fredonia, 1981. Cert. elem. edn. and reading tchr. Chapel organist Vassar Coll., Pughkeepsie, N.Y., 1956-59; dir. music Lafayette Ave. Prebyn. Ch., Buffalo, 1959-64; pvt. practice specializing as organ and piano tchr. Buffalo and Fredonia, 1959-89; organist 1st United Meth. Ch., Fredonia, 1967-89; organ instr. SUNY, Fredonia, 1970-71; reading tutor Fredonia Migrant Program, 1975-79; reading specialist Dunkirk (N.Y.) Schs., 1980—; organ recitalist in field. Founder Organ Vesper Recital Series, Fredonia, 1970—; mem. exec. bd. Fredonia Chamber Players, 1986—. Mem. AAUW, Am. Guild Organists, Internat. Reading Assn., Oberlin Alumni Assn. (pres. Buffalo chpt. 1960-62), Phi Delta Kappa, Sigma Alpha Iota, Phi Kappa, Lambda. Republican.

BOLTZ, MARY ANN, aerospace materials company executive, travel agency executive; b. Far Rockaway, N.Y., Jan. 12, 1923; d. Thomas and Theresa (Domanico) Caparelli; m. William Emmett Boltz; children: Valerie Ann Boltz Austin, Beverly Theresa, Cynthia Marie Boltz O'Rourke. Grad. high sch., Lawrence, N.Y., 1941. Publicist CBS, N.Y.C., 1943-48; mgr. Coast-Line Internat. Distbrs. Ltd., Lindenhurst, N.Y., 1961-80, v.p., 1980-86, pres., 1987—; chief exec. officer Air Ship 'N Shore Travel, Woodmere, N.Y. and Marco Island, Fla., 1978—. Formerly radio and TV editor local publs., writer Gotham Guide mag. Sec. Inwood Civic & Businessmen's Assn., 1952-64, pres., 1964-66, chmn. bd., 1967-68; pres. Lawrence Pub. Schs. System PTA, 1956-58; pres., life mem. Cen. Coun. PTA, 1958-60; founder Inwood Civic Scholarship Fund, 1964; v.p. Econ. Opportunity Coun., Inwood; mem. fundraising bd. yearly ball St. Joachim Ch., Cedarhurst, N.Y.; gift chmn. L.I. Bd. Boys Town of Italy; bd. dirs. Marco Island Cancer Fund Dr.; dir., promoter Marco Island Philharmonic Symphony; dir. polit. campaign William Sieffert, Oceanside, N.Y. Recipient awards Nassau Herald Newspaper, Cedarhurst, Inwood Civic Assn., PTA, 25 Yr. Silver Medallion Boys Town of Italy. Mem. Marco Island C. of C. Republican. Roman Catholic. Home: 323 Livingston Pl Cedarhurst NY 11516 Office: Coast-Line Linternat Distbrs 274 Bangor St Lindenhurst NY 11757

BOMBA, MARGARET ANN, lawyer; b. Bklyn., July 1, 1947; d. Fred S. and Mary (Alban) Bomba; B.S., St. Francis Coll., 1975; postgrad. Columbia U., 1977; J.D., Bklyn. Law Sch., 1982; m. John N. Pizzuto, May 27, 1978. Sec., adminstrv. asst. Fieldcrest Mills, Inc., N.Y.C., 1966-71, product mgr. textiles for the home 1973-84; sole practice, N.Y.C., 1984—; sales and product mgmt. Wamsutta Mills Inc., N.Y.C., 1972-73; prof. law Parsons Sch. Design, 1985—; arbitrator N.Y. Stock Exchange, 1987—; sole practice, N.YC., Newark, 1984—. Mem. N.Y. County Lawyers Assn. (trade regulation com. 1985, real property com. 1986), ABA, Assn. Bar City of N.Y., Assn. Trial Lawyers Am., N.Y. State Bar Assn. Office: 14 Wall St New York NY 10005 also: 99 Chapel St Newark NJ 07105

BOMBECK, ERMA LOUISE (MRS. WILLIAM BOMBECK), author, columnist; b. Dayton, Ohio, Feb. 21, 1927; d. Cassius Edwin Fiste and Erma (Fiste) Harris; m. William Lawrence Bombeck, Aug. 13, 1949; children: Betsy, Andrew, Matthew. BA, U. Dayton, 1949; holder 15 hon. degrees. Columnist Newsday Syndicate, 1965-70, Pubs.-Hall Syndicate (now N.Am. Syndicate), 1970-85, Los Angeles Times Syndicate, 1985-88, Universal Press Syndicate, Kansas City, Mo., 1988—; contbg. editor: Good Housekeeping mag., 1969-74. Author: At Wit's End, 1967, Just Wait Till You Have Children of Your Own, 1971, I Lost Everything In The Post-Natal Depression, 1974, The Grass Is Always Greener Over The Septic Tank, 1976, If Life is a Bowl of Cherries, What Am I Doing in the Pits?, 1978, Aunt Erma's Cope Book, 1979, Motherhood: The Second Oldest Profession, 1983, Family: The Ties That Bind... and Gag!, 1987, I Want To Grow Hair, I Want To Grow Up, I Want To Go To Boise, 1989. Mem. Am. Acad. Humor Columnists, Theta Sigma Phi (Headliner award 1969). Office: Universal Press Syndicate 4900 Main St Kansas City MO 64112

BOMGAARS, MONA RUTH, physician, educator; b. Orange City, Iowa, Feb. 15, 1939; d. Arie John and Artha H. (Korver) B. BA, Westmar Coll., 1960; MD, U. Nebr.-Omaha, 1963; MPH, U. Calif.-Berkeley, 1972. Diplomate Am. Bd. Family Practice, Am. Bd. Geriatrics. Intern Wayne County Gen. Hosp., Eloise, Mich., 1963-64; resident U. Nebr. Hosp., Omaha, 1964-66; fraternal worker United Presbyn. Ch., N.Y.C., 1967-76, staff physician Francis Newton Hosp., Ferozepore, Punjab, India, 1968-69, chief med. officer Bhagwant Meml. Hosp., Christian Med. Coll., Ludhiana, Punjab, India, 1969-71, dir. Lalitpur Community Health Svcs., Kathmandu, Nepal, 1972-75; exec. officer for devel. health mgmt. devel. staff U. Hawaii Sch. Medicine, Honolulu, 1976-81; chief communicable disease div. Hawaii Dept. of Health, Honolulu, 1981-84, acting med. dep. dir., 1983-84. asst. prof. dept. family practice and community medicine U. Hawaii Sch. Medicine, 1976-79, assoc. prof., 1979-81, clin. prof., 1982-84; assoc. prof. dept. family medicine, coord. U. Medicine and Dentistry N.J.-Rutgers, 1984-86; chairperson Dept. Family Practice Cook County Hosp., Chgo., 1986—. Contbr. articles to med. jours., chpts. to books. Bd. dirs. Ch. World III, 1988—; trustee Westmar Coll., 1986; active Presbyn. Med. Mission Fund, 1989—. Fellow Am. Acad. Family Physicians (sec. Hawaii chpt. 1983, pres.-elect 1984; trustee N.J. chpt. 1986); mem. AAFP, Am. Pub. Health Assn., Soc. Tchrs. Family Medicine.

BONALDI, JANE GAYLE, educator; b. Evansville, Ind., Mar. 4, 1942; d. A. Lloyd and Martha (Moore) Culley; m. Alfred R. Bonaldi, Oct. 29, 1943 (div. Apr. 1990); children: Alfred Ronald Jr., Donna Jane. BFA, U. Ill., 1964, MA in Art Edn., 1969. Designer Mallory, Smith & Tilford Advt., Evansville, Ind., 1965; paste-up artist Creative Press Printing Co., Evansville, 1965-66; advt. mgr. Mt. Vernon (Ind.) Dem., 1966-67; art tchrs. Met. Sch. Dist. of Mt. Vernon, 1967-68; substitute tchr. pub. schs., Rockville, Md., 1970-71, Belleville, Ill., 1984-90; with sales dept. Elder Cadillac Inc., Belleville, Ill., 1990—. Pres., St. Clair County Legal Aux., Belleville, 1986; bd. dirs. St. Clair County Cancer Bd., 1982—; pub. info. chmn. Belleville Twp. High Sch. West Band Parents Assn., 1987-89. Mem. AAUW, U. Ill. Athletic Assn. United Ch. of Christ.

BONAR, LINDA LOUISE, arts administrator; b. Upland, Calif., May 22, 1949; d. Kenneth Robert and Rosemary (Val Perga) Bonar; m. John Morton Stratton, Oct. 4, 1947; children: Lauren Gabrielle, John Morton. BA magna cum laude, U. Utah, 1976, MA in Art History, 1980; student, U. Calif., Berkeley, 1970. Ski instr. Snowbird Ski & Summer Resort, Snowbird, Utah, 1974-80; research project mgr. Utah Hist. Soc., Salt Lake City, 1976-80; exec. dir. Snowbird Inst., 1981-85; exec. dir. arts and entertainment Snowbird Corp., 1981-86; assoc. instr. arch. U. Utah, 1981; exec. dir. Utah Arts Festival, Salt Lake City, 1987—; lectr./cons. Utah Arts Council Conf., 1988, grants review panel, 1981—; lectr. in field. Editor Utah Arts Festival mag., 1987-89; contbr. articles to profl. jours. Invited juror Nat. Documentaries, KUED-TV, Salt Lake City, 1986. Recipient Archtl. Restoration Merit award, Utah Heritage Found., 1981, Civic Beautification award, Deseret News, 1978. Mem. Assn. Performing Art Presenters, We. States Art Fedn., Am. Fedn. Arts, Utah Fundraisers Soc., Utah Presenters Network, The New Yorker, Snowbird Club. Democrat. Office: Utah Arts Festival 168 W 500 North Salt Lake City UT 84103

BONAZINGA, MARIE THERESE, manufacturing company executive; b. Bklyn., May 10, 1948; d. Bartholomew and Ann (Palermo) B. AA, Gloria K. Bus. Sch., 1967, U. Louisville, 1975. Adminstrv. asst. Gallard-Schlesinger Chem. Mfg. Corp., Carle Place, N.Y., 1967-75; v.p. Accurate Chem. & Scientific Corp., Westbury, N.Y., 1975—; pres. Accurate Surg. & Scientific Instruments Corp., Westbury, 1979—, Leeches USA Ltd., Westbury, 1986—. Recipient Boli award L.I. Advt. Club, 1981. Mem. Nat. Assn. Women Bus. Owners, Roslyn Heights Civic Assn. Office: Accurate Surg & Sci Instruments 300 Shames Dr Westbury NY 11590

BONCHER, MARY, talent agent; b. Green Bay, Wis., Jan. 19, 1946; d. Anthony Peter and Bernice Mary (Lannoye) Williams; m. Joseph Phillip Boncher, Jan. 7, 1967; children—Yvette, Noelle. Diploma, Rosemary Bischoff Sch. Modeling, Milw., 1965. Dir. Mary Boncher Model Agy. & Sch. Ltd., Bloomington and St. Charles, Ill., 1970-80, Mary Boncher Model Agy. Ltd., St. Charles, 1980-84, Mary Boncher Model Mgmt. Ltd., Chgo., 1985—; fashion reporter TV and radio Men's Fashion Assn., N.Y.C., 1975-80, Eleanor Lambert's Am. Designer, N.Y. Fashion Press, N.Y.C., 1975-80; fashion corr. Green Bay Daily News, 1975-76. Lector Cath. mass, 1983—. Mem. Ill. Women in Film, Advt. Photographer's Assn., Internat. Platform Assn., Advt. Photographers Assn. Republican. Roman Catholic. Office: Mary Boncher Model Mgmt Ltd Presidential Towers Ste 810 575 W Madison St Chicago IL 60606

BOND, ALINE BLAKELY, educator; b. Memphis, Dec. 31, 1940; d. Tom Blakely and Mary Etta Phillips; m. Elroy Bond, Dec. 24, 1961; children: Patricia Ann, Elroy, Karen Danise. BA, Le Moyne-Owen Coll., Memphis, 1962; postgrad., Tuskegee (Ala.) Inst., 1965-66; MEd, Memphis State U., 1976. Tchr., chmn. dept. English Memphis City Schs., 1963—; cons. Mary Kay Corp., 1989—; writing cons.; lectr. in field. Dir. Christian edn. Ellis Grove Bapt. Ch. Mem. NAFE, United Teaching Profession (faculty rep.), Women in Edn. (2d v.p. Memphis chpt. 1989—), Nat. Coun. Tchrs. of English, Contemporary Bus. Women's Assn. (charter), Alpha Kappa Alpha. Home: 1865 Benning St Memphis TN 38106 Office: Northside High Sch 1212 Vollintine Memphis TN 38107

BOND, A(MANDA) ODESSA, educator; b. Phila., Dec. 4, 1942; d. Noah and Elizabeth (Watlington) B. BA, Morgan State U., Balt., 1965; MA, Villanova U., 1979; postgrad., U. Pa., 1986—. Cert. tchr. Pa. Tchr. Bd. Edn., Phila., 1969—; pres. Watlington O Bond Ednl. Corp., Wilmington, Del., 1979—. Author: The Double Tragedy, 1970; contbr. articles to newspapers, mags. and profl. jours. Active Rep. Presdl. Task Force, 1982—, World Affairs Council, 1976—, Goodwill Industries, life mem., 1981. Club: Peale.

BOND, AUDREY MAE, real estate broker; b. New Orleans, June 17, 1932; d. Melvin and Ann Thomas (Freeman) Respert; m. Robert M. Bond, Aug. 16, 1975; children: Betty Lee, Deborah Huggins. AA, Oxnard (Calif.) Coll., 1977. Lic. real estate broker, Calif. Benefit authorizer Dept. HEW, San Francisco, 1955-75; pvt. practice realty, 1977-88; owner/broker A. Bond Realty, Oxnard, Calif., 1988—. Sec./treas. Channel Islands confs. Evang. Luth. Ch. in Am., 1989—. Mem. Profl. Coll. Women's Orgn. (v.p.), Nat. Assn. Ret. Fed. Employees (1st v.p.), Calif. Assn. Realtors, Nat. Bd. Realtors, ELC in Am. (sec., treas.). Home: 3420 Taffrail Ln Oxnard CA 93035

BOND, CATHY LOUISE ELIZABE, nurse, counselor; b. Beech Grove, Ind., Apr. 17, 1952; d. Sherman Michael and Evelyn Ann (Wessling) Gatchell; m. Robert D. Bond, May 30, 1974 (div. 1985); children: Andrew Warren, Aaron Michael. BSN, Ind. U., 1974, MS in Nursing Adminstrn., 1983. Pediatric staff nurse Meth. Hosp., Indpls., 1974-77, mgr. pediatric ICU, 1977-83; asst. prof. Wabash Valley Coll., Mt. Carmel, Ind., 1983-84; assoc. prof. Vincennes (Ind.) U., 1984-86; perinatal clin. nurse specialist St. Francis Hosp. Ctr., Beech Grove, 1986-87; perinatal clin. nurse specialist, coord. and counselor Bereavement Program, Meth. Hosp., Indpls., 1987—; lectr. in field; mem. faculty St. Francis Hosp. ACLS Course, 1986-90, Meth. Hosp., 1987—. V.p., conf. chairperson Ind. Coun. for Adolescent Pregnancy, 1989-90. Mem. Nat. Assn. Neonatal Nurses, Nat. Assn. for Obstetric, Gynecologic and Neonatal Nurses, Am. Soc. of Psychoprophylaxis in Obstetrics. Office: Meth Hosp Ind 1701 N Senate Blvd Indianapolis IN 46202

BOND, ELIZABETH HUNT, social worker; b. Hartsville, Tenn., Sept. 11, 1953; d. C.H. Hunt and Pearl Calvert Cotton; m. David Farrar Bond, Sept. 7, 1986. AA, Martin Methodist Coll., Pulaski, 1971-73; BA, Scarritt Coll., Nashville, 1973-75; MSW, U. Tenn, 1975-77. Am. Assn. Trainers in Clin. Hypnosis, Advanced Training, 1979-81. Asst. tchr. St. Luke's Day Care, Nashville, 1974-75; resident counselor Tenn. Prison for Women, Nashville, 1975-76; therapist Dede Wallace Mental Health Ctr., Nashville, 1977; adult outpatient therapist Eastside Mental Health Ctr., Birmingham, 1977-78; adult and child therapist Harriett Cohn Mental Health Ctr., Clarksville, Tenn., 1978-79; adult outpatient therapist Eastside Mental Health Ctr., 1979-80; community edn. instr. Avondale Community Sch., Birmingham, 1980-83; personal counselor Birmingham Southern Coll., Birmingham, 1984-88; therapist Adult & Child Devel. Profls., Brimingham, 1980—; Adult and Child Devel. Profls.; cons. Adult & Child Devel. Birmingham, 1980-89. Ptrn. Conscience Amnesty Internat. Nat.; contbr. Planned Parenthood Nat., 1988, Ala. Pub. TV. Recipient Outstanding Young Women of Am. Nat., 1985; Nat. Honor Soc. High Sch. Shelbyville, Tenn., 1980, Who's Who in Am. Jr. Colls. & Univs. Scarritt Coll. 1975. Mem. Nat. Trust for Hist. Preservation, Nat. World Wildlife Fund, Environ. Defense Fund. Democrat. Methodist. Home: 8333 Third Ave S Birmingham AL 35206

BOND, JANICE SACHIKO, English educator; b. Lihue, Hawaii, Aug. 4, 1941; d. Tooru and Yukiko (Miura) Yamane; m. David Edward Stem, June 25, 1962 (div. Jan. 1977); children: John David, Lawrence Edward; m. Jerry Don Bond, Feb. 3, 1978 (dec. June 1987). BEdn, Kansas State Tchrs. Coll., 1963; postgrad., Brigham Young U., Laie, Hawaii, 1967, 68, U. Hawaii Manoa, 1976, Kauai Community Coll., Lihue, 1976. Cert. tchr. English and speech, Hawaii. Receptionist Coll. Info. Office, Emporia, Kans., 1960-62; distbr. Tupperware, Kapaa, Hawaii, 1966-69, Amway, Kapaa, 1974—; disc jockey Sta. KTOH, Lihue, 1960, 67; tchr. English Kauai High and Intermediate Schs., Lihue, 1967-68, 70-71, 88—, Kapaa High and Intermediate Schs., 1971-74, 75-87; salesperson The Westin Kauai (golf shop), Lihue, 1987—; advisor Nat. Honor Soc., Kapaa, 1984-87. Dir. publicity, mother's march March of Dimes, Kauai, 1980—, coordinator bid for bachelors, 1988, 89, rep. telethon, Honolulu, 1984; foster family mother, Dept. Human Services, 1981-90; program chmn. Girl Scouts U.S., Kauai, 1972-74, advisor Girl Scouts Srs., Kapaa, 1966-69, career cons., N.Y.C., 1972, del. Dallas, 1972, Honolulu, 1972, 73, 74; vol. Kapaa Missionary Ch. Vacation Bible Sch., mem. prayer line, 1984-85, choir, 1978, tchr. 2-yr. olds, dir. cradle roll., 1980-82; chmn. hospitality com. Kapaa Missionary Ch., 1986—; den mother Boy Scouts Am., 1977-79, mem. troop com., 1980-88; facilitator Am. Cancer FreshStart Clins., 1981-87, vol. neighborhood canvass; participant Big Sisters/Big Bros., Kauai, 1968-74, bd. dirs. nominating com. 1970-72; mem. Kapaa High Band Boosters, 1973-88, pres. 1986-88, Children's Home Steering Com., 1988—; co-chmn. cocktail reception DKG Internat. Film Festival, 1988, chmn. profl. affairs com., hospitality com., 1989. Mem. Nat. Council of Tchrs. English, Hawaii Council of Tchrs. English, Hawaii State Tchrs. Assn., Delta Kappa Gamma (state conv. com. 1988-89). Home: 3920 Hunakai St Lihue HI 96766

BOND, LORA, retired biology educator; b. Bryan, Tex., May 17, 1917; d. J. David and Leila (McGregor) B. BA, U. Tenn., 1938; MA, Wellesley Coll., 1941; PhD, U. Wis., 1945. Acting instr. botany U. Tenn., Springfield, Mo., 1943; faculty mem. Drury Coll., Springfield, Mo., 1943-45, 48-62; instr. botany Wellesley Coll., 1945-48; prof. biology emeritus Drury Coll., Springfield, 1962—. Mem. AAAS, AIBS, Bot. Soc. Am., Am. Genet. Assn., Mo. Acad. Sci., Assn. SE Biologists, Sigma Xi. Home: 1512 N Washington Ave Springfield MO 65803 Office: Drury Coll 900 N Benton Ave Springfield MO 65802

BOND, MARY LOU, title company executive; b. Enid, Okla., Nov. 29, 1936; d. Harold Earnest and Nellie Maude (Cowles) Taft; m. Charles D. Bond, July 25, 1956; children: Michael Lowell, Bryan Timothy, Mark Stephen. Student, Okla. State U., 1954-56. Exec. sec. Shell Oil Co., Midland, Tex., 1960-63, Gordon Knox & Assocs., Midland, 1963-64; escrow sec. Tarrant Title Co., Ft. Worth, 1978-83, mgr. Airport Freeway br., 1988-89; escrow officer Safeco Land Title Co., Hurst, Tex., 1983-88; asst. v.p., escrow officer Am. Title Co., Bedford, Tex., 1989—; escrow officer, br. mgr. Safeco Land Title, Hurst, Tex., 1989—; br. mgr., escrow officer United Title Co., 1989—. Del. Hurst-Euless-Bedford Ind. Sch. Dist., P.T.A Bd.; rep. L.D. Bell High Sch. Mem. Tex. Land Title Assn. (assoc.), N.E. Tarrant County Bd. Realtors (assoc.; mem. women's council 1983-90), Hurst-Euless-Bedford C. of C., Pi Beta Phi Alumni Assn. Republican. Mem. Christian Ch. (Disciples of Christ). Home: 1101 Springdale Rd Bedford TX 76021 Office: United Title Co 1600 Airport Frwy FNB Tower Ste 103 Bedford TX 76022

BOND, SARAH ANN, lawyer; b. Kansas City, Mo., Dec. 27, 1955; d. Marcus Buster and Roberta Marie (Brennan) B. BA in History, Colo. State U., 1975; MA in History and Econs., U. Colo., 1978, JD, 1981; postgrad., U. Mont., 1978-79. Bar: Colo. 1981, Mont. 1984, U.S. Ct. Appeals (9th and 10th cirs.), U.S. Dist. Ct. Legal staff Mont. Dept. Natural Resources and Conservation, Helena, 1981-83; assoc. Ireland, Stapleton, Pryor, P.L., Denver, 1983-85; hearings examiner Mont. Dept. Natural Resources and Conservation, 1985—. Mem. Lewis and Clark Bar Assn. (bd. dirs. lst dist.). Home: 1020 8th Ave Helena MT 59601 Office: Mont DNRC 1520 E 6th Ave Helena MT 59620-2301

BOND, VICTORIA ELLEN, conductor, composer; b. Los Angeles, May 6, 1945; d. Philip and Jane (Courtl) B.; m. Stephan Peskin, Jan. 27, 1974. B Mus. Arts, U. So. Calif., Los Angeles, 1968; M Mus. Arts, Juilliard Sch. Music, 1975, D Mus. Arts, 1977. mem. N.Y. State Coun. Arts Music Panel, 1987-90; bd. dirs. Am. Music Ctr., 1987—. Guest condr. Cabrillo Music Festival, Calif., 1974, White Mountains Music Festival, N.H., 1975, Aspen (Colo.) Music Festival, 1976, Shenandoah Music Festival, W.Va., 1977, Colo. Philharm., 1978, Houston Symphony, 1979, 86, Buffalo Philharm., 1979, Pitts. Symphony, 1980, Anchorage Symphony, 1980, N.W. Chamber Orch., Seattle, 1980, Ark. Symphony, 1981, Hudson Valley Philharm., N.Y., 1981, Newton Symphony, Boston, 1982, Hartford Symphony, 1982, RTE Symphony, Dublin, Ireland, 1983, Albany Symphony Orch., 1984-85, Houston Symphony Orch., 1986, Richmond Symphony Orch., 1987, Williamsburg Symphony Orch., Greenville Symphony Orch., Des Moines Symphony Orch., Utah Symphony Orch., Cape Cod Symphony Orch., Tallahassee Symphony Orch., Va. Symphony Orch, 1988-90; music dir. New Amsterdam Symphony Orch., N.Y.C., 1978-80, Pitts. Youth Symphony Orch., 1978-80, Empire State Youth Orch., 1982-86, Southeastern Music Ctr., 1983-84, Bel Canto Opera, 1983-86, Roanoke (Va.) Symphony Orch., 1986—; artistic dir. S.W. Va. Opera, 1989—; Exxon/Arts Endowment condr., Pitts. Symphony, 1978-80; recs. include Twentieth Century Cello, Two American Contemporaries, The Frog Prince; commd. by Pa. Ballet, 1978, Jacob's Pillow Dance Festival, 1979, Am. Ballet Theater, 1981, Empire State Inst. Performing Arts, 1983, 84, Stage One, Louisville, 1986, Ga. State U.; artistic dir. Bel Canto Opera Co., 1986-88. Recipient Victor Herbert award 1977, Perry F. Kendig award, 1988, ASCAP Composition award, 1973—; Nat. Inst. for Music Theater grantee in opera conducting N.Y.C. Opera, 1985, Martha Baird Rockefeller grantee, 1978-79, Meet-The-Composer grantee in Composition, 1973; Juilliard scholar 1972-77; Juilliard fellow, 1975-77, Aspen Music Festival fellow, 1973-76; named Exxon/Arts Endowment Conductor, 1978-80, Woman of Yr. in Va., 1990. Mem. ASCAP (recipient awards 1975—), Am. Symphony Orch. League, Am. Fedn. Musicians, Mu Phi Epsilon. Office: Roanoke Symphony Orch PO Box 2433 Roanoke VA 24010

BONDAR, ROBERTA LYNN, Canadian astronaut; b. Sault Sainte Marie, Ont., Can., Dec. 4, 1945. BS in Zoology and Agr., U. Guelph, 1968; MS in Exptl. Pathology, U. Western Ont., 1971; D in Neurobiology, U. Toronto, 1974; MD, McMaster U., 1977. Intern Toronto Gen. Hosp.; resident in neuro-opthalmology Tufts's New Eng. Med. Ctr., Boston, Playfair Neurosci. Unit, Toronto Western Hosp.; postdoctorate fellow Nat. Rsch. Coun. Can., 1974; asst. prof. medicine, dir. Multiple Sclerosis Ctr. McMaster U., 1982; Canadian astronaut Govt. of Can., Ottawa, Ont., 1983—, chairwoman Canadian Lifescis. Subcom. for Space Sta., 1985, payload specialist Canadian astronaut program, 1989—. Recipient Career Scientist award Ont. Ministry Health, 1982, Vanier award Jaycess of Can., 1985; fellow U. Western Ont., 1971, Ont. Ministry Health, 1981; Nat. Rsch. Coun. Canada scholar, 1971-74. Fellow Royal Coll. Physicians and Surgeons Can.; mem. Am. Acad. Neurology, Canadian Neurol. Soc., Canadian Aeros. and Space Inst., Canadian Soc. Aerospace Medicine, Coll. Physicians and Surgeons Ont., Flying Ninety-Nines Internat. Women Pilots Assn., Canadian Stroke Soc., Aerospace Med. Assn., Royal Astron. Soc. Can., Canadian Fedn. Univ. Women (hon.), Zonta (hon.). Office: Canadian Astronaut Program, care Nat Rsch Coun, Ottawa, ON Canada

BONDAREW, BEVERLY ANN, communications company executive; b. Detroit, Dec. 19, 1949; d. Harry and Henrietta (Englander) King; m. Helmut Bondarew Sr., Oct. 19, 1979; children: Helmut Jr., Robyn Amanda, Mikhail Harrison. BA in Sociology, U. South Fla., 1971, M in Secondary Edn., 1974. Adminstrv. position Wilson & Co., Chgo., 1975-77; asst. to comptroller TSC Industries, Chgo., 1977-79; from staff adminstr. to facility mgr. MCI Telecommunications Corp., Chgo. and Atlanta, 1979—. Mem. Internat. Facility Mgr. Assn., Mail Mgmt. Assn. Democrat. Jewish. Office: MCI Telecommunications Corp 400 Perimeter Ctr Terr NE Atlanta GA 30346

BONDI, KATHLEEN, social worker; b. Hammond, Ind., Sept. 7, 1952; d. Del and Anna (Uher) Bondi. BA, Purdue U., 1974; MSW, Ind. U., Indpls., 1987. Caseworker Youth Svc. Bur., Kokomo, Ind.; hotline dir. Voluntary Action Ctr., South Bend, Ind.; social worker Ind. State Devel. Ctr., South Bend; therapist Madison Ctr., South Bend. Mem. Nat. Assn. Social Workers (reg. rep.), Nat. Assn. for Dually Diagnosed, Internat. Soc. for Study of Multiple Personality and Dissociation, Alpha Delta Mu. Office: 1025 Widener Ln South Bend IN 46614

BONDI, NIKKI C., company executive; b. Cleve., Aug. 28, 1950; d. August and Lucille (Hammond) Bondi; m. James B. McPolin, July 11, 1975; children: Molly Anne, Benjamin James. BA, John Carroll U., University Heights, Ohio. Selling group mgr. The Higbee Co., Cleve., 1972-75; fin. placement div. mgr. Champion Personnel Sys., Inc., Cleve., 1976-84; asst. v.p., dir. human resources adminstrn. Progressive, Mayfield Village, Ohio, 1984—. Mem. Nat. Assn. Personnel Cons., Am. Soc. Personnel Adminstrn., Ohio Assn. Personnel Cons. Office: Progressive 6000 Parkland Blvd Mayfield Heights OH 44124

BONDINELL, STEPHANIE, counselor, former educational administrator; b. Passaic, N.J., Nov. 22, 1948; d. Peter Jr. and Gloria Lucille (Burden) Honcharuk; m. Paul Swanstrom Bondinell, July 31, 1971; 1 child, Paul Emil. BA, William Paterson Coll., 1970; MEd, Stetson U., 1983. Cert. elem. educator, Fla.; guidance counselor grades K-12, Fla. Tchr. Bloomingdale Bd. Edn., N.J., 1971-80; edn. dir. Fla. United Meth. Children's Home, Enterprise, 1982-89; guidance counselor Volusia County Sch. Bd., Deltona, Fla., 1989—. Sec. adv. com. Deltona Jr. High Sch., 1984-88; sec. Deltona Jr. PTA, 1982; vice-chmn. adv. com. Deltona Middle Sch., 1988, chmn., 1989—; mem. secondary sch. task force Volusia County Sch. Bd., 1986—; mem. Volusia County Rep. Exec. Com., Rep. Presdl. Task Force. Acad. scholar Becton, Dickinson & Co., N.J., 1966; N.J. State scholar, 1966-70; named girls state rep. Am. Legion, N.J., 1966; recipient Vol. Svc. award Volusia County Sch. Bd., Deland, 1985. Mem. Am. Assn. for Counseling and Devel., Assn. for Curriculum Devel., Coun. for Exceptional Children, Div. for Learning Disabilities, Fla. Pers. and Guidance Assn., N.J. Edn. Assn., Internat. Platform Assn., Deltona Civic Assn. Republican. Avocations: painting, creative writing, dancing. Home: 1810 W Cooper Dr Deltona FL 32725 Office: Volusia County Sch Bd 2022 Adelia Blvd Deltona FL 32725

BONDS, JEAN FULTON, nurse; b. Harriston, Miss.; d. John Rivers and Ava Adine (Wade) Fulton; widowed; 1 child, John Christian. Diploma, Holy Name of Jesus Hosp. Sch. Nursing, Gadsden, Ala., 1956; BS in Nursing, Incarnate Word Coll., 1959; MS in Nursing, Tex. U., 1966. RN, Ala. Draftsman Ill. Cen. R.R., Vicksburg, Miss., 1945-48; stenographer Child Welfare Dept., Fayette, Miss., 1951-53; clk. County Health Dept., Fayette, 1952-53; staff nurse VA Hosp., Jackson, Miss., 1956-57; asst. dir. nursing svcs. Grace Luth. Hosp., San Antonio, 1958-61, S.W. Tex. Meth. Hosp., San Antonio, 1962-65; edn./quality assurance coord. Holy Name of Jesus Med. Ctr., Gadsden, Ala., 1965—. Mem. Nat. Assn. Quality Assurance Profls., Assn. for Practitioners in Infection Control, Sigma Theta Tau (Alpha Delta chpt.). Roman Catholic. Office: Holy Name of Jesus Med Ctr PO Box 268 Gadsden AL 35902

BONDS, THYRA VERLE, retired civilian military employee; b. Des Moines, Dec. 1, 1927; d. Charles Christopher and Haley Dell (Evans) Johnson; m. Melvin Bonds, Dec. 26, 1952 (div. 1969); children: Kasandra Verle, Gayle Denyse. AS in Commerce (Bus. Adminstrn.), St. Louis U., 1974; student, Drake U., 1947-52. With Dept. Def., 1957-84; chief program mgmt. Aircraft Surviability Equipment Aviation Command, St. Louis, 1971-84; ret. Aviation Command, St. Louis, 1984; mentor St. Louis Pub. Schs., 1986—. Contbr. articles to nat. mags. Amb. good will of women Louisville C. of C., 1967-68; vol. Telephone Reassurance Program, St. Louis, 1980; adv. mem. Mo. Commn. Status of Women, 1982—; bd. govs. Army Aviation Scholarship Found., Westport, Conn., 1984-90; mem. Community Adv. Coun., Webster Groves, Mo., 1985-90. Decorated Meritorious Civilian Svc.; recipient Career and Community Svc. award, 1978, Yes I Can award, 1979. Mem. Nat. Army Aviation Assn. Am. (v.p. 1981-83), Coalition of 100 Black Women (v.p. 1988-90), Assn. U.S. Army (adv. coun. 1985-90), Nat. Affiliation for Literacy Advance, Nat. Drifters, Inc. (v.p., treas.), Order Eastern Star, Phi Chi Theta. Home: 15 Marvin Ct Webster Groves MO 63119

BONE, JANET WITMEYER (JAN BONE), author; b. Shamokin, Pa., Dec. 19, 1930; d. Paul Eugene and Kathryn (Bender) Witmeyer; BA, Cornell U., 1951; MBA, Roosevelt U., 1987; m. David P. Bone, Oct. 27, 1951; children: Jonathan, Christopher, Robert, Daniel. Newspaper and trade mag. writer, freelance writer, 1962—; sr. writer spl. advt. sects. Chgo. Tribune, 1986—; writer newsletter Rand McNally, 1988—; writer articles Nat. Safety Coun., 1989—; tchr. creative writing adult edn. Sch. Dist. 211, Palatine, Ill., 1974—. Co-author: Understanding the Film, 4th edit., 1990; author: Opportunities in Film Production, 2d, 1990, Opportunities in Cable Television,

1983, Opportunities in Telecommunications, 1984, rev. edit., 1989, Opportunities in Computer-Aided Design and Computer-Aided Manufacturing (CAD/CAM), 1986, Opportunities in Robotics, 1987, Opportunities in Laser Technology, 1988. Trustee William Rainey Harper Community Coll., Palatine, 1977-85, sec. bd. trustees, 1979-85. Recipient Chgo. Working Newsman's award, 1968, Sch. Bell award Ill. Edn. Assn., 1968, Am. Polit. Sci. Assn. award disting. reporting pub. affairs, 1970. Mem. Phi Theta Kappa, Alpha Omicron Pi. Address: 353 N Morris Dr Palatine IL 60067

BONGIORNO, SANDRA L., health counselor; b. Worcester, Mass.; d. Gerald Michael and Janet (Gentile) Turturo; children: Justin Leigh, Brooke Yuka. BA in Edn., Anna Maria Coll., 1967; MS in Counseling, SUNY, Albany, 1968; MA in Psychology, Rosebridge Inst., 1982. Cert. counselor Nat. Bd. Cert. Counselors. Dir. counseling Elizabeth Seton Coll., Yonkers, N.Y., 1968-70; adminstr. asst. U. Hawaii Sch. Med., Honolulu, 1971-73; adminstr. officer U. Hawaii Sch. Medicine, Honolulu, 1973-75; drug and alcohol counselor U.S. Army Hosp., Nuremburg, Fed. Republic Germany, 1975-76; counseling instr. Solano Community Coll., Susuin City, Calif., 1980-82; dir. family support specialist Family Support Ctr. Yokota AFB, Tokyo, 1983-85, dir., 1983-85; adolescent therapist Christ Our Shepherd Luth. Ch., Peachtree City, Ga., 1987—; pvt. practice adolescent therapy Peachtree City, 1987—. Bd. dirs. YMCA, Fayette County Mental Health Assn.; councilwoman City of Peachtree City, 1988—. Mem. Am. Bus. Women's Assn. (named Woman of the Yr. 1989). Lutheran. Office: Christ Our Shepherd Luth Ch PO Box 2189 Peachtree City GA 30269

BONHAM-YEAMAN, DORIA, law educator; b. Los Angeles, June 10, 1932; d. Carl Herschel and Edna Mae (Jones) Bonham; widowed; children: Carl Q., Doria Valerie-Constance. BA, U. Tenn., 1953, JD, 1957, MA, 1958; EdS in Computer Edn., Barry U., 1984. Instr. bus. law Palm Beach Jr. Coll., Lake Worth, Fla., 1960-69; instr. legal environment Fla. Atlantic U., Boca Raton, 1969-73; lectr. bus. law Fla. Internat. U., North Miami, 1973-83, assoc. prof. bus. law, 1983—. Editor: Anglo-Am. Law Conf., 1980; Developing Global Corporate Strategies, 1981; editorial bd. Attys. Computer Report, 1984-85, Jour. Legal Studies Edn., 1985—. Contbr. articles to profl. jours. Bd. dirs. Palm Beach County Assn. for Deaf Children, 1960-63; mem. Fla. Commn. on Status of Women, Tallahassee, 1969-70; mem. Broward County Democratic Exec. Com., 1982—; pres. Dem. Women's Club Broward County, 1981; mem. Marine Council of Greater Miami, 1978—, Service award, 1979. Recipient Faculty Devel. award Fla. Internat. U., Miami, 1980; grantee Notre Dame Law Sch., London, summer 1980. Mem. U.S. Council for Internat. Bus., Am. Bus. Law Assn., No. Dade C. of C., Am. Acctg. Assn., AAUW (pres. Palm Beach County 1965-66), Alpha Chi Omega (alumnae club pres. 1968-71), Tau Kappa Alpha. Episcopalian. Office: Fla Internat U North Miami FL 33181

BONI, MIKI, artist; b. Bklyn., Nov. 10, 1938. BA, U. Guanajuato, 1974; divorced; children: Andrew, Viki. Dir. advt. and pub. relations Kebo, Inc., Natick, Mass., 1965-74; tchr. painting and drawing U. Guanajuato (Mex.), 1974-76; exec. dir. Kreativ Assos., Watertown, Mass., 1976-82; prin. Miki Boni Assocs., 1982-86; editor, designer publ. Interface Found., Watertown, 1987-89, program dir., 1989—. Recipient spl. painting award Lincoln Center, 1978. Mem. Nat. Assn. Neurolinguistic Programming (master practitioner), Women Art Profls. (co-founder, v.p.).

BONIFAS, BARBARA J., human resources executive; b. Delphos, Ohio, Apr. 2, 1947; d. Robert Eugene and Alice (Hoelderle) B. BS in Social Welfare, Ohio State U., 1971; postgrad., Harvard Bus. Coll., 1980-85. Field dir. Appleseed Ridge Girl Scout Coun., Lima, Ohio, 1971-73; program dir. Heart of Ohio Girl Scout Coun., Zanesville, Ohio, 1973-75; exec. dir. Pennyroyal Girl Scout Coun., Owensboro, Ky., 1975-76; asst. exec. dir. Kentuckiana Girl Scout Coun., Louisville, 1976-80; chief exec. officer Girl Scout Coun. St. Croix Valley, St. Paul, 1980-88; exec. dir. Great Rivers Girl Scout Coun., Cin., 1988—; Instr. Jr. High Religious Edn., 1983-85. Agy. champaign chair United Way, St. Paul, 1987, mem. cabinet, 1985; pres., v.p. treas. Council Agency Dirs., St. Paul, 1981-85; mem. fin. com. local Ch., 1983-84; mem. fin. com. Home Owners' Assn., 1987. Mem. Assn. Girl Scout Exec. Staff, Am. Mgmt. Assn., Exec. Dirs. Refugee Orgns., St. Paul C. of C. Roman Catholic. Lodge: Rotary. Office: Great Rivers Girl Scout Coun 4930 Cornell Rd Cincinnati OH 45242

BONILLA, MARY ANN, pediatrician; b. Riobamba, Ecuador, Mar. 6, 1956; came to U.S., 1959; d. Fidel G. and Maria Elia (Moyano) B. BS, St. Peter's Coll., 1977; MD, Loyola U., Chgo., 1981. Intern, then resident in pediatrics Brookdale Hosp. Med. Ctr., Bklyn., 1981-84; fellow in pediatric hematology and oncology Meml. Sloan Kettering Cancer Ctr., N.Y.C., 1984-88, asst. clin. pediatrician hematology and oncology dept., 1989—. Mem. Am. Acad. Pediatricians, Am. Soc. Hematology, Am. Soc. Clin. Oncology. Office: Meml Sloan Kettering 1275 York Ave New York NY 10021

BONILLA, SHARI LOUISE, staff assistant; b. Santa Barbara, Calif., Mar. 20, 1965; d. Arthur George Bonilla and Donna Mildred (Mee) Mee. Student, U. Nev., Las Vegas. Staff asst. Reynold's Electrical & Engring., Co., Inc., Las Vegas, 1983—. Counselor Community Action Against Rape, Las Vegas, 1985. Mem. Student Accting. Assn. Republican. Roman Catholic. Office: REECo 2501 Wyandotte Las Vegas NV 89102

BONINE, JOAN MARLYN GRIFFEN, director accounting, accountant; b. Detroit, Mar. 19, 1942; d. Richard S. and Hazel L. (McLean) Griffen; m. Edward E. Corl, Dec. 21, 1963 (div. Nov. 1971); m. Jerome L. Bonine, Mar. 1, 1982; 1 child, Lenee Lyn. Student, Hillsdale (Mich.) Coll., 1960-62, Cleary Coll., 1973, Lansing (Mich.) Community Coll, 1983. Bookkeeper Midwest Vendall, Inc., Howell, Mich., 1962-71; with McPherson Hosp., Howell, 1971—, mgr. acctg. div., 1983—, dir. acctg. div., 1988—; treas. C.H.C. Credit Union, Howell, 1980-86. Mem. Hosp. Fin. Mgmt. Assn., Am. Bus. Woman's Assn. (pres. Achates, Mich. chpt. 1979), Livingston Conservation and Sportsmans Assn. Office: McPherson Hosp 620 Byron Rd Howell MI 48843

BONIS FAST, FRANCINE DALE, lawyer; b. N.Y.C., Feb. 19, 1951; d. Henry Bernard and Florence May (Greinsky) Bonis; m. Mark Joel Fast, Oct. 18, 1987; 1 stepchild, Ronald. BA with honors, Rutgers U., 1973; JD, U. Louisville, 1977. Bar: N.J. 1977, U.S. Dist. Ct. N.J. 1977. Chief tech. writer Great A&P Tea Co., Nat. Data Ctr., Piscataway, N.J., 1973-74; chief atty., acting mgr. Disaster Relief Office U.S. SBA, Newark, 1978-79; assoc. Unger and Unger, attys. at law, Newark, 1979-81, Jennings & Waxman, attys. at law, East Orange, N.J., 1981-82; instr. matrimonial and bus. law Horizon Paralegal Inst., Linden, N.J., 1983-87; pvt. practice Bloomfield, N.J., 1982—. Active community social svc. and fundraising orgns. including United Jewish Appeal Metro West, N.J., 1982—, Myeloma Cancer Rsch. Fund, West Orange, N.J., 1989, Living with Cancer Support Group, St. Claire's-Riverside Hosp., Denville, N.J.; vol. various local, state and fed. polit. campaigns, 1978-85; writer Inst. Paralegal Studies Mahwah, N.J. Named one of Outstanding Women in Am., Outstanding Am. Soc., 1983—. Mem. N.J. State Bar Assn., Essex County Bar Assn., Myeloma Soc. Am. (Little Rock) (founding mem.). Office: 332 Gettysburg Way Lincoln Park NJ 07035

BONK, SHARON CATHERINE, librarian; b. North Tonawanda, N.Y., Nov. 28, 1943; d. Joseph J. and Ann (Danylow) B. BS in Edn., SUNY, Geneseo, 1965; MA in Am. Studies, U. Minn., 1969, MA in Libr. Sci., 1969. High sch. libr. Sch. Dist. 3, Huntington, N.Y., 1965-67; social scis. selector Northeastern U. Librs., Boston, 1969-81, head, periodicals dept., 1978-82; head acquisitions dept. SUNY Albany Librs., Albany, 1978-83; asst. dir. tech. svcs. SUNY Librs., Albany, 1984-88, interim dir., 1988-89, asst. dir. rsch. svcs., 1989-90; asst. direct user svcs. Albany, 1990—. Contbr. articles to profl. jours.; author chpts. in monographs; assoc. editor Serials Rev. Trustee Sand Lake (N.Y.) Town Libr., 1987-89. Recipient Fulbright Fellowship, 1989, Chancellor's Award for Excellence in Librarianship, SUNY, 1986, Lambert Scholarship, Blackwells Coll. of Libr. Wales, U.K., 1981. Mem. Assn. for Libr. Collections and Tech. Svcs./ALA (bd. dirs. 1989-91), Beta Phi Mu. Office: Univ Librs/SUNY Albany NY 12222

BONNELL, VICTORIA EILEEN, sociologist; b. N.Y.C., June 15, 1942; d. Samuel S. and Frances (Nassau) B.; m. Gregory Freidin, May 4, 1971. B.A. Brandeis U., 1964; M.A., Harvard U., 1966, Ph.D., 1975. Lectr. politics U. Calif.-Santa Cruz, 1972-73, 74-76; asst. prof. sociology U. Calif.-Berkeley, 1976-82, assoc. prof., 1982—. AAUW fellow, 1979; Regents faculty fellow, 1978; Fulbright Hays faculty fellow, 1977; Internat. Research and Exchanges Bd. fellow, 1977, 88; Stanford U. Hoover Instn. nat. fellow, 1973-74; Guggenheim fellow, 1985; fellow Ctr. for Advanced Study in Behavioral Scis., 1986-87; grantee Am. Philos. Soc., 1979, Am. Council Learned Socs., 1976. Mem. Am. Sociol. Assn., Am. Assn. Advancement Slavic Studies. Author: Roots of Rebellion: Workers' Politics and Organizations in St. Petersburg and Moscow, 1900-1914, 1983; editor: The Russian Worker: Life and Labor under the Tsarist Regime, 1983; contbr. articles to profl. jours. Office: U Calif Dept Sociology Berkeley CA 94720

BONNER, BERNADETTE MAE, TV producer, director; b. Honolulu, Hawaii, Mar. 7, 1963; d. Horace Teddlie and Florence Ayson (Suyat) B. Student, Loyola Marymount U., 1981-82; BS in Broadcast Journalism, U. Ill., 1985. Prodn. asst. KITV-TV (ABC), Honolulu, 1984; studio technician WCIA-TV (CBS), Champaign, Ill., 1984; programming coord. People's Choice TV, Rantoul, Ill., 1985; dir., tech. dir. WICS-TV (NBC), Springfield, Ill., 1985-89; producer, dir. KPLR-TV, St. Louis, 1989—; producer Children's Miracle Network Telethon, Springfield, 1988, 89, dir., St. Louis, 1990; speaker St. Louis Sch. Partnership Program, 1990. Mem. NAFE, NATAS, Kappa Tau Alpha, Phi Kappa Phi. Roman Catholic. Office: KPLR-TV 4935 Lindell Blvd Saint Louis MO 63108

BONNER, BESTER DAVIS, educator; b. Mobile, Ala., June 9, 1938; d. Samuel Matthew and Alma (Davis) Davis; m. Wardell Bonner, Nov. 28, 1964; children: Shawn Patrick, Matthew Wardell. BS, Ala. State Coll., 1959; MS in Library Sci., Syracuse U., 1966; PhD, U. Ala., 1982. Cert. tchr. Librarian Westside High Sch., Talladega, Ala., 1959-64; librarian, tchr. lit. Lane Elem. Sch., Birmingham, Ala., 1964-65; head librarian Jacksonville (Ala.) Elem. Lab. Sch., 1965-70; asst. prof. library media Ala. A&M U., Huntsville, 1970-74; adminstv. asst. to pres. Miles Coll., Birmingham, 1974-78, chmn. div. edn., 1978-85; specialist media Montgomery County Pub. Schs., Md., 1987-88; dir. library & media services div. of ednl. technology Dist. of Columbia Pub. Schs., 1988—; forum leader Nat. Issues Forum, Domestic Policy Assn. U. Ala., Birmingham 1983-84. Contbr. writer The Developing Black Family, 1975. Chmn. ethics commn. St. Ala., Montgomery 1977-81; radiothorn site coordinator United Negro Coll. Fund, Birmingham 1981. Mem. Ala. Instructional Media Assn. (pres. dist. II, 1971-72), Am. Library Assn., Assn. Women Deans and Adminstrs., Montgomery County Edn. Assn., Montgomery County Media Specialists Assn., Com. 100, Alpha Kappa Alpha, Ala. St. Alumni Assn. (sec. Talladega chpt. 1964-65). Democrat. Methodist.

BONNER, BRIGID ANN, marketing professional; b. Mpls., Apr. 27, 1960; d. John Patrick and R. Jeanne (Crahan) B. BS in Journalism and Indsl. Adminstrn., Iowa State U., Ames, 1982; MBA, Harvard U., 1988. Mktg. statistician Fingerhut, Minnetonka, Minn., 1982-83; mktg. rep. IBM Corp., Mpls., 1983-88, exec. cons., 1988-90, mktg. mgr., 1990—. Mem. com. United Way of Minn., Mpls., 1989—. Mem. Harvard Bus. Sch. Club Minn. (bd. dirs. Mpls. chpt. 1989—, mgmt. assistance program cons. 1990—). Republican. Roman Catholic. Home: 2601 Sunset Blvd Minneapolis MN 55416 Office: IBM Corp 100 Washington Sq 8th Fl Minneapolis MN 55401

BONNESS, PATRICE MARIE, publishing company executive; b. Milw., Dec. 4, 1964; d. Joseph Denny and Virginia Mary (Haas) B. AA, U. Fla., 1987; BA with honors, Fla. Atlantic U., 1989. Sec. Highway Pavers, Inc., Naples, Fla., 1986; congl. intern U.S. Congress, Washington, 1986; corp. sec. Bonness, Inc., Naples, 1987-88; pres., owner Naples Desktop Pub. Co., Naples, 1990—; bd. dirs. Bonness, INc., Naples, Better Rds., Inc., Naples. Guardian pro tem Guardian Ad Litem, Naples, 1984; vol. Alachua County Older Am.'s Coun., Gainesville, Fla., 1986, Literacy Vols. of Am., Naples, 1990—. Mem. Women in Communications, Inc. (scholar 1989), Naples C. of C., Fla. Free-lance Wirter's Assn. Roman Catholic. Office: Naples Desktop Pub Co 501 Goodlette Rd D-100 Naples FL 33940

BONNET, BEATRIZ ALICIA, interpreter, translator, flutist; b. Nueva Helvecia, Uruguay, Nov. 2, 1959; came to U.S., 1982; d. Alvaro Ismael and Violete Irma (Felix) B.; m. Michael Walter O'Connor, Jan. 23, 1988. Student, Conservatorio Universitario, Montevideo, Uruguay, 1978-81, U. Ark., Little Rock, 1982-83; MusB, MusM, Rice U., 1988. Flute recitalist Uruguay Ministry Edn. and Culture, Montevideo, 1980-82; tchr. flute Spring Branch Ind. Sch. Dist., Houston, 1983-87, Klein Ind. Sch. Dist., Houston, 1983—, Aldine Ind. Sch. Dist., Houston, 1988—; interpreter, translator Global Communication Svcs., Houston, 1986—, pres., 1988—; stage musician Comedia Nacional, Montevideo, 1981-82; freelance flutist, Houston, 1985—; instr. music theory Rice U., Houston, 1986-88. Am. Field Svc. scholar, 1977-78, Rice U. scholar, 1983-86, Inst. Hispanic Culture scholar, 1987; Rice U. fellow, 1986-88. Mem. Am. Translators Assn. Home and Office: 8026 Ridgeview Dr Houston TX 77055

BONNIWELL, KATHERINE, magazine executive. Grad., Vassar Coll., 1969, Stanford U. With Morgan Guaranty Trust Co., 1969—; corp. analyst, then asst. circulation dir. Time, Inc., 1976-78; circulation dir. Money mag., 1978-80; v.p. Time-Life Films, 1980-81; v.p., dir. mktg. and communications Sotheby Park Bernet, 1981—; pub. LIFE, N.Y.C., 1988—; gen. mgr. People mag. Office: Life Mag Time & Life Bldg New York NY 10020*

BONOW, RAYSA ROSE, television producer; b. Monesson, Pa., Sept. 27, 1930; d. Samuel Sydney and Esther (BeermanS) B. BS, W. Va. U., Morgantown, 1952. Writer, producer WFMJ-TV, Youngstown, Ohio, 1955-59; producer WNBC-TV, N.Y.C., 1963-69, WBZ-TV, Boston, 1970-74; exec. producer KDKA-TV, Pitts., 1974; producer Sta. WCBS-TV, N.Y.C., 1974-75; creator, producer People CBS, 1977; producer Am. Alive NBC, 1978; producer, 1979-80; exec. producer KYW-TV, Phila., 1980-83, WNEV-TV, Boston, 1983-86, Look, N.Y.C., 1986-89; producer Everyday, 1989—; cons. Numerous TV shows, Calif., N.Y., Boston, 1975-89. Author: How to Be A Thin Person, 1976, Raysa Bonow's Complete Guide to Feeding Your Dog, 1989, TV Guide, Ladies Home Jour., 1971-76; creator Not for Women Only, Sta. WNBC-TV, 1965; creator, producer Yes We Can, Sta. WBZ-TV, 1974; writer Syn. Preview, 1990. Vol., Mem. Animal rights Orgn., Phila, 1960-. Recipient 2 Emmy awards Nat. Assn. TV, Arts and Sci., 1984, Iris awards Nat. Assn. TV Broadcasters, 1983, 84. Mem. Am. Women Radio & TV, Acad. TV Art & Sciences, ASPCA Greenpeace, MSPCA Bide-A-Wee. Home: RR 1 #301 Water Mill NY 11976

BONTEZ, MARIA, nurse; b. Boston, Mar. 28, 1933; d. Robert Bontez and Carmel (Brannon) Lopes. AAS, Brooklyn Coll., 1960; BS, Pace U., 1979; MS, New Rochelle Coll., 1981; postgrad., Columbia U., 1988—; D (hon.), U. Fla., 1973. RN, cert. gerontologist, nursing home adminstr. Dir. nursing Gramercy Park Nursing Home, N.Y.C., 1963-71, Morris Park Nursing Home, Bronx, N.Y., 1971-76; adminstr. Throgs Neck Nursing Home, Bronx, 1976; asst. adminstr. Park Cresant Nursing Home, N.Y.C., 1980-81; dir. nursing St. John's Episcopal Home for the Aged, Bklyn., 1982-84; pres., cons. Collybonco Inc., Mt. Vernon, N.Y., 1984—; agt. N.Y. State Ins. Dept., 1976—; patient assessor N.Y. State, 1986. Served with U.S. Army, 1952-54. Mem. Am. Pub. Health Assn., Veterans Assn. Democrat. Club: New Eng. (N.Y.C.). Lodge: Rosicrucians (chairperson bd.). Office: Collybonco Inc 10 Fiske Pl Mount Vernon NY 10550

BONYNGE, JEANNE REDFIELD, law librarian; b. Bronxville, N.Y., Feb. 10, 1925; d. Humphrey Fuller and Amy Louise (Cowing) Redfield; m. Russell Bonynge, Jr., May 15, 1948 (dec. Aug. 1971); children: Terry, Jeffrey. BA, Denison U., 1946; MALS, Rosary Coll., River Forest, Ill., 1970. Asst. librarian Schiff, Hardin and Waite, Chgo., 1971-73, IRS, Washington, 1974-78; librarian U.S. Tax Ct., Washington, 1978—. Pres. Greater Chgo. Com. for UNICEF, 1969-73; mariner leader coun. Girl Scouts U.S. Named Outstanding Citizen Village of Wilmette, Ill., 1972. Mem. Am. Assn. Law Libraries, Law Librarians Soc. Washington, LWV (pres. Wilmette 1965-67, chmn. Lake Michigan inter-league group 1967-69). Office: US Tax Ct 400 2d St NW Washington DC 20217

BOOHER, ALICE ANN, lawyer; b. Indpls., Oct. 6, 1941; d. Norman Rogers and Olga (Bonke) B. BA in Polit. Sci., Butler U., 1963; LLB, Ind. U., 1966, JD, 1967. Bar: Ind. 1966, U.S. Dist. Ct. (so. dist.) Ind. 1966, U.S. Tax Ct. 1970, U.S. Ct. Customs and Patent Appeals 1969, U.S. Ct. Mil. Appeals 1969, U.S. Ct. Appeals (D.C. cir.) 1969, U.S. Supreme Ct. 1969; cert. tchr., Ind. Research asst., law clk. Supreme and Appellate Cts. Ind., Indpls., 1966; legal intern, atty., staff legal advisor Dept. State, Washington, 1966-69; staff legal adviser Bd. Vets. Appeals, Washington, 1969-78, sr. atty., 1978—; former counselor D.C. Penal Facilities and Shelters. Author: The Nuclear Test Ban Treaty and the Third Party Non-Nuclear States, also children's books; ocntbr. articles to various publs., chpts. to Whiteman Digest of International Law; exhibited crafts, needlepoint in juried artisan fairs. Bd. dirs. numerous community groups, including D.C. Women's Commn. for Crime Prevention, 1980-81. Recipient various awards; named Ky. Col., 1988. Mem. ABA, DAV Aux, VFW Aux., Women's Bar Assn. D.C., D.C. Sexual Assault Coalition (chmn. legal com.), Butler U. Alumni Assn., LWV, Nat. Mus. Women in Arts, Bus. and Profl. Women's Club (pres. D.C. 1980-81, nat. UN fellow 1974, nat. bd. dirs. 1980-82, 87—, Woman of Yr. award D.C. 1975, Marguerite Rawalt award D.C. 1986), USO, Women Profl. Assn., Navy League USA, Am. Legion Aux., Vietnam Vets. Am., Task Force on Women of the Mil. and Women Vets. (chmn. 1986—), Alpha Chi Omega, Women's Dem. Club, Nat. Lawyers Club, Army-Navy Club.

BOOKER, BETTY MAE, writer; b. Allentown, Pa., Nov. 26, 1948; d. Harold George and Bessie (Bealer-Miller) Bartholomew; m. Samuel Efford Booker III, June 27, 1970; children, Liesel Tamarah, Dacey Justin. BA in English, Millersville State Coll., 1970. Contbr. poetry to jours. and lit. mags. including Plainsong, America, The Christian Century, Poetry Now. Home: 3511 Valley View Ave NW Roanoke VA 24012

BOOKER, BEVERLY BEVILLE, research chemist; b. Savannah, Ga., Oct. 26, 1954; d. Herschel Ray and Ida Marie (Bove) Beville; 1 child, Matthew Anthony. BS in Med. Tech., Med. Coll. Ga., 1976; MS in Clin. Lab. Sci., U. Ala., Birmingham, 1977, BS in Acctg., 1989. Blood bank technologist U. Ala. Hosp., Birmingham, 1976-77; asst. supr. physiology Bapt. Med. Ctr., Montclair, Birmingham, 1977-79; rsch. chemist Nephrology Rsch. and Tng. Ctr. U. Ala., Birmingham, 1979—; presenter at sci. meetings. Mem. Am. Soc. Clin. Pathology, Alpha Aeta, Phi Kappa Phi. Roman Catholic.

BOOKER, DEIDRE ELIZABETH, freelance writer, advertising executive; b. Gastonia, N.C., Sept. 24, 1965; d. James and Elizabeth Jenelle (Froneberger) B. BA in Journalism, U. N.C., 1987. Writer U. N.C. News Bur., Chapel Hill, 1986-87; copywriter, account exec. Sumner & Wells Advt., Gastonia, 1987-89; copy adminstr. Barclays Am., Charlotte, N.C., 1989-90; freelance writer Cramerton, N.C., 1990—; pres., chief exec. officer DB Advt.; chmn. publicity Fish Camp Jam, Gastonia, 1990. Recipient Gold award Admissions Mktg. Report, 1989, Silver award, 1989, 1st Place awards Club Mgrs. Assn., 1988. Mem. NAFE, Alpha Kappa Alpha. Democrat. Baptist. Home: 571 Baltimore Dr Cramerton NC 28032

BOOKER, NANA LAUREL, public relations executive; b. Waco, Tex., Aug. 5, 1946; d. Karl and Helen Dorothy (Keene) B. BA, Baylor U., 1968; MA, U. Fla., 1970; MBA, Pepperdine U., 1980. Accredited by Pub. Relations Soc. Am. Asst. prof. communications U. New Orleans, 1970-74, 1977-78; pub. relations cons. New Orleans, 1974-78; dir. pub. relations Touro Infirmary, New Orleans, 1976-78; dir. communications Lifemark Corp., Houston, 1978-81; pres. Communications Alliance, Houston, 1981-82, Nana Booker & Assocs., Houston, 1984—; dir. internat. relations, communications mayor's office City of Houston, 1982-84. Co-author: Introduction to Theatrical Arts, 1972. Mem. South Tex. Dist. Export Council, Houston, 1988—; press aide campaign K. Whitmire for Mayor, Houston, 1982; mem. exec. adv. bd. coll. bus. adminstrn. Houston U., 1990—; bd. dirs. Escape Ctr., 1990—. Mem. Internat. Pub. Rels. Assn., Pub. Rels. Assn. Am. (accredited, Excalibur award 1988), Houston World Trade Assn. (bd. dirs. 1986—), Houston-Shenzhen Sister City Assn. (bd. dirs. 1987—), Swiss-Am. C. of C. (bd. dirs. 1987—), River Oaks Breakfast Club.

BOONE, DEBORAH ANN (DEBBY BOONE), singer; b. Hackensack, N.J., Sept. 22, 1956; d. Charles (Pat) Eugene and Shirley (Foley) B.; m. Gabriel Ferrer, 1979; children: Jordan Alexander, Gabrielle Monserrate and Dustin Boone (twins), Tessa Rose. Student Calif. schs. Singer with father, Pat Boone, and family group, 1970—, profl. rec. artist, 1977—; numerous appearances on TV talk and variety programs; appeared in ABC-TV Movie of the Week, Sins of the Past, 1984; star children's video Hug Along Songs; author: Debby Boone--So Far, (children's book) Bedtime Hugs for Little Ones, 1988; co-author: Tomorrow is a Brand New Day, 1989; starred in nat. tour and Broadway Seven Brides for Seven Brothers , 1981-82, nat. tour Sound of Music, 1987, 88. Recipient Am. Music award (Song of Year), Grammy award (Best New Artist), 1977, Grammy award for best inspirational performance, 1980, Grammy award for best Gospel performance for Keep the Flame Burning, 1984, Nat. Assn. Theatre Owners award (Best New Personality), Dove award, 1980, Dove award for album Surrender, 1984, Country Music award for Best New Country Artist, 1977; named Singing Star of Yr. AGVA, 1978, Working Mother of Yr., 1982. Mem. Ch. on the Way. Address: 12001 Ventura Pl Ste 201 Studio City CA 91604

BOONE, DEBRA GEORGE, accountant; b. Coral Gables, Fla., Dec. 2, 1958; d. William George (stepfather) and Mildred Elizabeth (Wells) Preston. AA, Daytona Beach (Fla.) Community Coll., 1977; BS in Acctg., Fla. So. Coll., 1980. CPA, Fla. Sr. staff acct. Geller, Ragans, James, Oppenheimer & Creel, CPA's, Orlando, Fla., 1980-83; controller Br. Properties, Inc., Ocala, Fla., 1983-88; acctg. supr. Disney Devel. Co., Orlando, Fla., 1988—. Bd. dirs., treas., mem. various coms. Marion County United Way, Ocala, 1984-88. Named Outstanding Young Woman of Am., 1985; recipient Alumni Achievement award Fla. So. Coll. Mem. Am. Inst. CPA's, Fla. Inst. CPA's (local chpt. treas. 1985-86, state bd. govs. 1986—, v.p. 1986-87, pres. 1987-88), Altrusa (treas. Ocala club 1986-87), Phi Chi Theta, Kappa Delta. Baptist. Home: 840 Rosemere Circle Orlando FL 32811 Office: Disney Devel Co 8801 Vistana Centre Dr Ste 200 Orlando FL 32821

BOONE, DOROTHY MAE, county official; b. Gordon, Nebr., May 29, 1919; d. C. H. and Ethel Mae (Lewis) Perkins; m. M. H. Boone, Oct. 2, 1943. AA, Iowa Western Community Coll., Council Bluffs, 1977; grad., Am. Legion Officers Sch., Indpls., 1973. Nat. VA accredited svc. rep. Office Gen. Counsel, Washington, 1976—; exec. sec., adminstrv. asst., adminstrv. sec. Pottawattamie County Veterans' Affairs Commn., Council Bluffs, Iowa; dir. Veteran Affairs Commn., Pottawattamie County, 1987—; nat. svc. officer DAV, 1989—; local bd. mem. U.S. Nat. Selective Svc. System, Washington, 1982—; notary pub. Recipient Cert. of Appreciation, Kiwanis, 1985, Commendation, DAV, 1987, Nat. Svc. Officers award, County Svc. award Nat. VA, 1986. Home: 1320 N 21st St Council Bluffs IA 51501 Office: Veterans Affairs Commn 223 S 6th St Court House Council Bluffs IA 51501

BOONE, FRANCES LAVONNE, technical engineer; b. L.A., Jan. 28, 1929; d. E. Frank Smith and Frances J. (Weber) Way; m. Herbert E. Mills, Mar. 17, 1953 (div. July 1971); children: Katherine Denise, Carol Diane; m. Charles C. Boone, Feb. 20, 1983. Grad. high sch., L.A. Operator Pacific Bell Telephone Co., San Francisco, 1949-61; engring. assoc. Pacific Bell Telephone Co., Sacramento, 1961-68, engr., 1968-83; tech. engring. asst. Roseville (Calif.) Telephone Co., 1984—. Republican. Mormon. Home: 7531 Clovis Ct Citrus Heights CA 95610-2438

BOONE, JANICE FOWLER, nurse; b. Bklyn., June 25, 1945; d. Earl Justice and Mary Jean (Fisher) Fowler; m. Larry Dean Boone, Apr. 26, 1986; children: Ted Muncy, Toni B., Terri B. Student, Asheville Buncombe Tech.Coll., Asheville, N.C., 1981; BSN, U. N.C., 1970. Psychiatric staff nurse, 1970-71, occupational health nurse, 1973-75, safety and health adminstr., 1975—, supr. environ. control, 1980—, supr. Republican. Baptist. Home: PO Box 957 Mars Hill NC 28754 Office: Hwy 70 Black Mountain NC 28711

BOONE, KAY LANIER, public relations consultant, writer; b. Ft. Worth, Sept. 3, 1941; d. John David and Reba Louise (Smith) Lanier; m. William T. Boone, July 22, 1967 (div. June 1988); children: Katherine, Suzanne, Lisa. Student, Abilene (Tex.) Christian U., 1959-60; BA in Journalism, North Tex. State U., 1964. Reporter Daily Oklahoman/Oklahoma City

Times, 1964-66; feature writer Houston Post, 1967; info. rep. Okla. Dept. Inst., Social and Rehab. Services, Oklahoma City, 1967-73; dir. pub. info. United Way Mecklenburg-Union, Charlotte, N.C., 1974-76; account mgr., sr. writer Epley Assocs./Pub. Relations, Charlotte, 1977-78; account mgr. Yarbrough Co./Advt., Pub. Relations, Dallas, 1979-82; owner Boone & Assoc./Pub. Relations and Advt., Richardson, Tex., 1982-88; v.p. Yarbrough Co./Advt., Dallas, 1988-90; owner The Creative Solution, Dallas, 1990—. Author, editor History of Child Welfare In Oklahoma, 1976. Mem. SBA (region VI adv. coun. 1990—), Pub. Rels. Soc. Am., Assn. Women Entrepreneurs of Dallas (pres. 1987-88), Richardson C. of C. (editor newsletter 1986-87), Dallas Women in Bus. (Advt. of Yr. 1988), Small Bus. Congress in Dallas (co-chair 1988). Unitarian.

BOONE, KIMBERLIE ANN, television producer, director; b. Chgo., Dec. 1, 1960; d. Phillip B. and Verma D. (Coleman) B. BA in Media Communications, U. Ill., Chgo., 1983. Lic. radiotelephone operator. With video tech. dept. Am.'s Shopping Channel, Harahan, La., 1983-85; producer, dir. Sta. WVUE-TV, New Orleans, 1985-89, Sta. TKN-TV, River Grove, Ill., 1990—; producer Leukemia Televent, New Orleans, 1989, UNCF Telethon, New Orleans, 1987-88. Mem. NAFE, Greenpeace Internat. Home: 7734 S Langley Ave Chicago IL 60619

BOONE, LOIS RUTH, legislator; b. Vancouver, B.C., Can., Apr. 26, 1947; d. George Charles Bearne and Ruth (Lindberg) Chudley; m. Arthur Edward Boone, Nov. 28, 1970; children: Sonia, Tanis. Tchr.'s cert., Simon Fraser U., 1969. Tchr. Sch. Dist. 57, Prince George, B.C., 1969-71, Sch. Dist. 27, Williams Lake, B.C., 1971-72; office mgr. Prince George YM-YWCA, 1972-73; case aide worker Vancouver YWCA, 1973-74; adminstrv. asst. Gov. B.C., Prince George, 1978-86; mem. legis. assembly Gov. B.C., Victoria, 1986—. Trustee Sch. Dist. 57, Prince George, 1981-85. Mem. New Democratic Party. Office: BC Legislature, Parliament Bldgs, Victoria, BC Canada V8V 1X4

BOONE, MARY ANN, veterinarian; b. Buffalo, Sept. 18, 1961; d. William Howard and Jeanne Marie (Kuhn) Schemel; m. Harold Craig Boone, May 16, 1987. DVM, La. State U., 1986. Assoc. vet. Town & Country Vet. Clinic, Russellville, Ark., 1986-87, Ark. Vet. Clinic, Ft. Smith, 1986-89; owner, veterinarian Pointer Trail Animal Clinic, Van Buren, Ark., 1989—. Program cons. Girl Scouts U.S.A., Ft. Smith, 1989—. Mem. Am. Vet. Med. Assn., Ark. Vet. Med. Assn., Ft. Smith Vet. Med. Assn. Roman Catholic.

BOOREM, MARY TERESA, direct marketing buyer; b. Chgo., Nov. 3, 1955; d. Robert Thomas and Mary Teresa (Mannion) B.; m. Darrel A. Gornik, Oct. 1, 1978 (div. May 1986); 1 child, Alexandra Shannon Gornik. BA in Psychology, Loyola U., Chgo., 1977; postgrad., U. Mo., Kansas City, 1990—. Asst. buyer Montgomery Ward, Chgo., 1977-79, assoc. buyer, 1979-81, buyer, 1981-87; buyer House of Lloyd, Grandview, Mo., 1987—; Alumni recruiter Loyola U., 1989—; mem. Parents Without Ptnrs., 1988—; pres. Cath. Single Parents, 1988-89. Roman Catholic. Home: 15712 W 125th Terr Olathe KS 66062 Office: House of Lloyd 301 Duck Rd Grandview MO 64030

BOORKMAN, JO ANNE, librarian; b. San Jose, Calif., July 21, 1947; d. Charles John and Ruth Ellen (Reuss) B. BA, Scripps Coll., 1969; MS, U. Ill., 1971. Bibl. search analyst biomed. library UCLA, 1971-73, reference librarian Darling biomed. library, 1973-77; head pub. svcs. health scis. library U. N.C., Chapel Hill, 1977-80, head collections devel. health scis. library, 1980-84; head pub. svcs. Carlson health scis. library U. Calif., Davis, 1985-86, acting asst. univ. librarian health scis., 1986-87, head Carlson library, 1988—. NSF fellow, 1969-70. Mem. ALA, Spl. Libraries Assn., Med. Library Assn. (bd. dirs. 1988—), No. Calif. and Nev. Med. Library Group (pres. 1988-89), Mid-Atlantic chpt. Med. Library Assn. (pres. 1983-84), P.E.O. Office: U Calif Carlson Health Scis Library Davis CA 95616-5291

BOOTH, BARBARA RIBMAN, civic worker; b. N.Y.C., May 2, 1928; d. Benjamin C. and Ceclia (Lowe) Ribman; m. Mitchell B. Booth, July 13, 1952; 1 child, Brian S. AA, Centenary Jr. Coll., Hackettstown, N.Y., 1948; BA, Barnard Coll., 1950. Pres. women's alliance, chmn., Christmas fair 1st Congl. Ch. of City of N.Y., 1959-63; mem. vol. com. Sheltering Arms Children's Svc., N.Y.C.; vol., coord. high sch. visits, pres. aux. N.Y. Hosp.; trustee Florence K. Griswold Meml. Fund. Com., All Souls Unitarian Ch., N.Y.C.; bd. dir. women's div. Jefferson Dem. Club. N.Y.C.; committeewoman N.Y. County Dem. Com.; bd. govs., v.p. N.Y. Fruit and Flower Mission, Inc.; del. city conv., chmn. East Manhattan br. LWV. Home: 75 East End Ave New York NY 10028

BOOTH, GLENNA GREENE, club woman, genealogical researcher; b. Jacksonville, Fla., Feb. 25, 1928; d. Aubrey Madison and Ruth Thelma (Leymaster) Greene; m. John Newton Booth, Mar. 25, 1967. Student, Fla. So. Coll., 1946-48; B Design, U. Fla., 1953. Exec. sec., editor co. newspaper Stockton, Whatley, Davin & Co., Jacksonville, 1955-67. Capt. residential campaign United Appeal Oklahoma City, 1968-71; bd. dirs. 1st Ch. of Christ, Scientist, Oklahoma City, 1981-83, chmn. bd., 1982-83, treas., 1983-85, 2d reader, 1985-88, presiding officer, 1988-91. Mem. DAR (state rec. sec. 1984-86), Women Desc. Ancient and Hon. Arty. Com. (nat. pres. 1989-92), Children Am. Colonists (rec. sec. gen. 1989-92), Soc. Colonial Dames XVII Century (nat. historian 1985-87), Soc. Colonial Daus. 17th Century, Daus of 1812, Gen. Soc. Mayflower Desc. (gov. Okla. soc. 1986-88), Nat. Huguenot Soc. (state pres. 1979), Nat. Soc. Magna Charta Dames (state pres. 1978-80), Hereditary Order Des. Colonial Govs., U. Fla. Alumni Assn., P.E.O., Zeta Tau Alpha, numerous others. Home: 3223 NW 18th St Oklahoma City OK 73107-3810

BOOTH, HEATHER TOBIS, social action organization executive; b. Brookhaven, Miss., Dec. 15, 1945; d. Jerome Sanford and Hazel (Weisband) Tobis; s. Paul R. Booth, July 2, 1967; children: Eugene Victor, Daniel Garrison. BA, U. Chgo., 1967, MA, 1970. Dir. Midwest Acad., Chgo., 1972-78, Citizen Labor Energy Coalition, Chgo., 1978-82, State and Local Leadership Project, Chgo., 1982-85, Citizen Leadership Found., Chgo., 1982-87; co-dir. Citizen Action, Chgo., 1985-89, pres., 1990—; dir. Coalition for Dem. Values, Washington, 1990—; pres. Midwest Acad., Citizen Leadership Found. Author: Citizen Action and the New American Populism, 1986; contbr. articles to profl. jours. Office: Coalition for Dem Values 1007 Ripley St Silver Spring MD 20910

BOOTH, MARGARET A(NN), communications company executive; b. N.Y.C., Dec. 25, 1946; d. Herbert and Alice (Traum) B.; m. Marvin E. Schechter, Jan. 22, 1984. BS, U. Wis., 1968. Editorial asst. Bantam Books, N.Y.C., 1968-70; publicity asst. Ruder & Finn Inc., N.Y.C., 1970-71, dir. radio and TV, 1971-76, v.p., 1974-76; pres. Pub. Interest Pub. Rels., N.Y.C., 1976—, M. Booth & Assocs., Inc., N.Y.C., 1983—. Author: Promoting Issues and Ideas, 1987; contbr. articles to profl. jours. Bd. dirs. The Village Nursing Home, N.Y.C., 1985—, Ctr. for Population Options, N.Y.C., 1986—, Citizens Union Found., 1989. Recipient YWCA Salute to Women Achievers, City of N.Y., 1985. Mem. Women in Communications (Matrix award for Pub. Rels. 1987), Pub. Rels. Soc. of AM., Women Execs. Pub. Rels. Office: M Booth & Assocs Inc 225 W 34th St Ste 1500 New York NY 10001

BOOTHE, URSULA YVONNE, retired public housing manager; b. Glen Ridge, N.J., Feb. 19, 1931; d. Frederick Winfield and Louise Gertrude (Knight) Rainer; m. Richard Harold Boothe, June 16, 1956; children: Yvonne Victoria, Richard Alan, Natasha Dawn. BA, Morgan State U., 1954. Children's counselor Dept. Social Svc., N.Y.C., 1954-60; housing asst. N.Y.C. Housing Authority, Bklyn., 1960-78; asst. mgr. N.Y.C. Housing Authority, Bklyn, 1978-87; pub. housing mgr. N.Y.C. Housing Authority, Long Island City, 1987-89, ret., 1989. Democrat. Roman Catholic. Home: 117-31 239th St Elmont NY 11003

BOOTS, SHARON GRAY, editor; b. Grand Rapids, Mich., May 5, 1939; d. Robert Thomas and Roma Margareta (West) Gray; m. Marvin R. Boots, Dec. 28, 1964 (div. 1977); 1 child, Katherine Margaret. BA in Chemistry, U. Wis., 1960; PhD in Organic Chemistry, Stanford U., 1964. Postdoctoral fellow MIT, Cambridge, Mass., 1964; rsch. fellow Med. Coll. Va. Va. Commonwealth U., Richmond, 1968-76, Stanford (Calif.) U., 1978-81, U. Wis., Madison, 1981-82; editor jour. Pharm. Sci. Am. Pharm. Assn., Washington, 1982-86; rsch. chemist Midwest Rsch. Inst., 1965-66; rsch. assoc. Am. Tobacco Co., 1966-68; mng. editor analytical chemistry Am. Chem. Soc., Washington, 1987—; chair, editorial policy com. Coun. Biology Editors, Bethesda, Md., 1990—. Author: (with others) Ethics and Policy in Scientific Publication, 1990. Mem. Am. Chem. Soc., AAAS, Nat. Wildlife Fedn., Smithsonian Instn. (contbg. mem.), Friends of Kennedy Ctr., Audubon Soc., Sierra Club, Phi Beta Kappa. Office: Am Chem Soc 1155 16th St NW Washington DC 20036

BOOZ, GRETCHEN ARLENE, marketing executive; b. Boone, Iowa, Nov. 24, 1933; d. David Gerald and Katherine Bevridge (Hardie) Berg; m. Donald Rollett Booz, Sept. 3, 1960; children: Kendra Sue (dec.), Joseph David, Katherine Sue. AA, Graceland Coll., 1955. Med. asst. Robert A. Hayne M.D., Des Moines, 1955-61; mktg. services mgr. Herald Pub. House, Independence, Mo., 1975—. Author: (book) Kendra, 1979. Mem. Citizens Adv. Bd., Blue Springs, Mo., 1979—, Mayor's Christmas Concert Com., Independence, 1987—; bd. dirs. Child Placement Services, Independence, 1987—, Hope House, Inc., Independence, 1987—; trustee Graceland Coll., Lamoni, Iowa, 1984—. Mem. Leadership Edn. Action Devel. (L.E.A.D.), Independence C. of C. (diplomat, Outstanding Mem. award 1981). Republican. Mem. Reorganized Ch. Jesus Christ Latter Day Saints. Home: 1200 Crestview Dr Blue Springs MO 64015 Office: Herald Pub House 3225 S Noland Rd Independence MO 64055

BOOZER, LINDA SHIELDS, reading specialist; b. Columbia, Pa., Mar. 28, 1944; d. H. Morrell and Ruth (Ludwig) Shields; m. Larry D. Boozer, July 2, 1966 (div. May 1990); children: Kellie Jo, Gregory Dale. BSEd, Kutztown (Pa.) State U., 1966; MSEd, Millersville (Pa.) U., postgrad. Chair processing writing dept. summer writing workshop Northeastern U., Boston, 1990; RIF coordinator Donegal Sch. Dist., Mt. Joy, Pa.; reading supr. Donegal Sch. Dist.; reading specialist Donegal Sch. Dist., Marietta, Pa. Recipient Reading is Fundamental chpt. I grant. Mem. Assn. for Supervision and Curriculum Devel., Lancaster Lebanon Reading Coun., Keystone State Reading Assn., Internat. Reading Assn. Home: 133 Frank St Mount Joy PA 17552

BORANYAK, SHARON ETZEL (MRS. MARK BORANYAK), editor, writer; b. Topeka, Kans., May 2, 1951; d. Raymond Francis and Julia Elizabeth (Porubsky) Etzel; BS, Kans. State U., 1973; m. Mark Boranyak, Apr. 20, 1974. Assoc. editor Capper's Weekly, Topeka, Kans., 1973-76; pub. info. specialist Stormont-Vail Hosp., Topeka, 1976; informational writer Water Quality Mgmt. sect. Kans. Dept. Health and Environment, Topeka, 1976-77, pub. relations dir. div. environment, 1977-79; editor Kans. Legis. Div. of Post-Audit, 1979-83; sr. tech. editor McDonnell Douglas Corp., St. Louis, 1983-89, freelance tech. editor, St. Louis, 1989—; cons. Topeka Broadcast Council. Mem. Women in Communications (treas. Topeka chpt. 1975-79), Nat. Fedn. Press Women (v.p. Topeka chpt. 1978-79, pres. 1980—), Topeka Home Econs. Assn., People to People. Republican. Roman Catholic. Contbr. articles to profl. jours. Home and Office: 5808 Mango Dr Saint Louis MO 63129

BORCHERS, REBA JEANETTE, programmer, analyst; b. Columbia, Ky., Jan. 11, 1939; d. James Lyle and Nellie Kathryn (Hale) Blair; (div. 1977); children: Patricia, Stewart, Kevin Johnson; m. Lowell Jacob Borchers. AS in Bus. cum laude, Columbus (Ohio) Tech. Inst., 1983; BBA cum laude, Otterbein Coll., 1989. Quality control insp. Edmont-Wilson, Inc., Mt. Vernon, Ohio, 1967-83; engring. technician Am. Electric Power Svc. Corp., Columbus, 1984-86; programmer, analyst Adria Labs., Columbus, 1986-89; programmer, analyst II Huntington Svc. Corp., Columbus, 1989—. Mem. Am. MENSA, Ltd., Rake and Hoe Garden Club (pres. Howard, Ohio chpt. 1970, 73, 79), East Knox Band Boosters (pres. Howard chpt. 1971). Home: 8 Avalon Rd Mount Vernon OH 43050

BORDA, DEBORAH, symphony orchestra executive; b. N.Y.C., July 15, 1949; d. William and Helene (Malloy) B. BA, Bennington Coll., 1971; postgrad., Royal Coll. Music, London, 1972-73. Program dir. Mass. Coun. Arts and Humanities, Boston, 1974-76; mgr. Boston Musica Viva, Boston, 1976-77; gen. mgr. Handel and Haydn Soc., Boston, 1977-79, San Francisco Symphony, 1979-86; pres. St. Paul Chamber Orch., 1986-88; exec. dir. Detroit Symphony Orch., 1988—. Office: Detroit Symphony Orch Ford Auditorium Detroit MI 48226

BORDACS, KRISZTINA, environmental engineer; b. Budapest, Hungary, Feb. 24, 1956; came to U.S., 1984; d. Ferenc and Ilona Bordacs. BSCE, Budapest Tech. U., 1976, MS in Bioengring., 1979; PhD in Environ. Engring., U. Minn., 1988. Registered profl. engr. Hungary, Pa. Environ. lab. mgr. mcpl. waste water treatment plant City of Budapest, 1979-84; prin. rsch. engr. Air Products & Chems., Inc., Allentown, Pa., 1988-90; sr. environ. engr. Rhone-Poulenc, Inc., Princeton, N.J., 1990—; Contbr. articles to profl. jours. Mem. Water Pollution Control Fedn., Internat. Assn. on Water Pollution Control and Rsch. Roman Catholic.

BORDALLO, MADELEINE MARY (MRS. RICARDO JEROME BORDALLO), wife of former governor of Guam; b. Graceville, Minn., May 31, 1933; d. Christian Peter and Mary Evelyn (Roth) Zeien; m. Ricardo Jerome Bordallo, June 20, 1953; 1 dau., Deborah Josephine. Student, St Mary's Coll., South Bend, Ind., 1952; A.A., St. Katherines Coll., St. Paul, 1953; A.A. hon. degree for community service, U. Guam, 1968. Presented in voice recital Guam Acad. Music, Agana., 1951, 62; mem. Civic Opera Co., St. Paul, 1952-53; mem. staff KUAM Radio-TV sta., Agana, 1954-63; freelance writer local newspaper, fashion show commentator, coordinator, civic leader, 1963, nat. Dem. committeewoman for Guam, from 1964, 1st lady of Guam, 1974-78, from 1983; senator 16th Guam Legislature, 1981-82, 19th and 20th Guam Legislature, 1988—, 20th Guam Legislature, 1989—; del. Nat. Dem. Conv., 1964, 68, 72, 76, 80, 84; pres. Women's Dem. Party Guam, 1967-69; rep. Presdl. Inauguration, Washington, 1965, 77, 85; del. Dem. Western States Conf., Reno, 1965, Los Angeles, 1967, Phoenix, 1968, conf. sec., 1967-69; del. Dem. Women's Campaign Conf., Wash., 1965. Pres. Guam Women's Club, 1958-59; del Gen. Fedn. Women's Clubs Convs., Miami Beach, Fla., 1961, New Orleans, 1965, Boston, 1968; v.p. Fedn. Asian Women's Assn., 1964-67, pres., 1967-69; pres. Guam Symphony Soc., 1967-73, del. convs., Manila, Philippines, 1959, Taipei, Formosa, 1960, Hong Kong, 1963, Guam, 1964, Japan, 1968, Taipei, 1973; chmn. Guam Christmas Seal Drive, 1961; bd. dirs. Guam chpt. ARC, 1963, sec., 1963-67; pres. Marianas Assn. For Retarded Children, 1968-69, 73-74, 84—; bd. dirs. Guam Theatre Guild, Am. Cancer Soc.; mem. Guam Meml. Hosp. Vols. Assn., 1966—, v.p., 1966-67, pres., 1970-71; chmn. Hosp. Charity Ball, 1966; pres. Women for Service, 1974—, Beauty World Guam Ltd., 1981—, First Lady's Beautification Task Force of Guam, 1983—; pres. Palace Restoration Assn., 1983—; nominee Dem. party for Gov. of Guam. Mem. Internat. Platform Assn., Guam Rehab. Assn. (assoc.), Guam Lytico and Bodig Assn. (pres. 1983—). Clubs: Spanish of Guam, Inetnon Famalaoan (pres. 1983-86). Home: PO Box 1458 Agana GU 96910

BORDELEAU, NANCY VIVIAN, human services executive, consultant; b. Boston, Aug. 30, 1934; d. Edmund and Dorothy (Goldstein) McIntosh; m. Roland John Bordeleau, June 18, 1955; children: John Michael, Lisa Marie, Michele Denise. EdB, R.I. Coll., 1955; MBA, Bryant Coll., 1985. Tchr. Hugh B. Bain Jr. High Sch., Cranston, R.I., 1955-57; social caseworker R.I. Dept. Social Welfare, Cranston, Johnston, Scituate and Foster, 1957-60; dir. Dept. Pub. Welfare, Cranston, 1966-85, R.I. Dept. Human Svcs., Cranston, 1985-89. Trustee Butler Hosp., Providence, 1968-84; chairperson State Employees Combined Charitable Campaign, R.I., 1987; mem. com. on ministry Am. Bapt. Chs. R.I., 1990—, steering com. Gov's. Health Care Conf., 1989—, Nat. Conf. Christians & Jews; founder Eastman House, Inc., Cranston; bd. dirs. Greater Providence YMCA; 1st pres. Eastman House, Inc. Recipient Charles B. Willard Achievement award Alumni Assn. R.I. Coll., Providence, 1978, Exemplary Program award Council for Community Service, 1982, Outstanding Woman award YWCA Greater R.I., 1985, 87; Henry Toll fellow Council State Govts., Lexington, Ky., 1986. Mem. Am. Pub. Welfare Assn. (Pres.'s award 1988), Nat. Leadership Conf. Women Execs. State Govt. Republican. Baptist. Home: 70 Poppy Dr Cranston RI 02920

BORDELON, CHERYL ANN, educational administrator; b. Graceville, Minn., Aug. 5, 1947; d. John Edmund and Lois Ramona (Olson) Paulsen; m. Leslie Lewis Bordelon, Aug. 10, 1968; 1 child, Steven Lewis. BA in Sociology magna cum laude, St. Louis U., 1969; MA in Ednl. Counseling, Calif. State U., San Bernardino, 1982. Cert. tchr., in pupil pers. and adminstrv. svcs., Calif. Tchr. St. Louis City Schs., 1969-70, Dept. of Def. Schs., Wiesbaden, Fed. Republic Germany, 1970-74; tchr. Redlands (Calif.) Adult Sch., 1980-89, counselor, 1983-89, prin., 1989—. Recipient cert. of recognition for outstanding community svc. Wiesbaden Air Base, 1973. Mem. Calif. Adult and Continuing Edn. Counselors Assn. (sec., Pres. 1985-88), Calif. Coun. for Adult End. (chpt. pres. 1988-89, Tchr. of Yr. award 1987), Calif. Assn. for Counseling and Devel., Assn. for Calif. Sch. Adminstrs., AAUW, East Valley Mental Health Assn., Phi Beta Kappa. Office: Redlands Adult Sch 33 W Lugonia Ave Redlands CA 92374

BORDEN, BRENDA JANE, technical writer; b. Newark, Feb. 2, 1958; d. Irving and Sonya (Spade) Gertzog; m. Craig Scott Borden, June 21, 1986. BS in Bus/Mktg., Fairleigh Dickinson U., 1980. Mktg. asst. AgfaGevaert, Teterboro, N.J., 1980-81; product support specialist CompuScan, Fairfield, N.J., 1982-83; tech. writer Ambi Corp., Stamford, Conn., 1984-86, Dictaphone Corp., Stratford, Conn., 1986-88, ChannelNet, Shelton, Conn., 1988—. Treas. Circle K. Spl. Olympics, Madison, N.J., 1978-80. Mem. Soc. for Tech. Communication, Nat. Assn. for Female Execs. Home: 178 Austin Ryer Ln Branford CT 06405 Office: ChannelNet 230 Long Hill Cross Rd Shelton CT 06484

BORDEN, KATHLEEN ELIZABETH PEDDER, health services nurse; b. Fall River, Mass., May 13, 1955; d. William F. and Josephine B. (Hanna) Pedder; m. Richard D. Borden, July 3, 1984; 1 child, Derek R. Student, Bristol Community Coll., Fall River, Mass., 1978-86; diploma, Diman Regional Sch. Nursing, Fall River, 1982; BS in Nursing magna cum laude, Southeastern Mass. U., 1988. RN, Mass. Dental asst. Edward J. Steinhof DDS, Fall River, 1971-73; lic. practical nurse, weekend staff dept. nursing Middlesex County Hosp., Waltham, Mass., 1982-85; staff lic. practical nurse dept. nursing Nichols House Nursing Home, Fairhaven, Mass., 1986; staff RN inpatient chem. dependency detoxification unit Stanley St. Treatment and Resources, Fall River, 1988-90; staff RN Rosewood Rest Home, Fall River, 1989—; presenter health promotion project for preschool children, 1987, nursing rsch. seminar, 1987; participant adopt a resident program Rosewood Rest Home, Fall River, 1983—. Vol. nursing svcs. to residential care facility, 1986—. Mem. Sigma Theta Tau. Roman Catholic. Home: 53 Hambly St Fall River MA 02721

BORDEN, NANCY, portfolio manager; b. L.A., Aug. 4, 1939; d. Robert F. and Kathryn (Moore) M.; children: Mark Elliot, Robin Lane. BA, U. S.C., L.A., 1960; postgrad., Cypress Coll., 1974, Anthony Schs., Colton, 1982, Am. Sch., Riverside, Calif., 1988. Cert. CREA, NREA. Rsch. psychologist Pacific State Hosp., Pomona, Calif., 1960-63; bus. mgr. Hosp., Los Alamitos, 1974-76; real estate sales Lake Perris Real Estate, Riverside, 1976-82, real estate broker, co-owner; tax preparer H&R Block, Riverside, 1982-85; cert. real estate appraiser Lake Perris Real Estate, Riverside, 1988—; v.p. Tryland Corp. Perris, 1980. Author: Beginning Bridge, 1964. Recipient NSF Scholarship award 1960, Calif. Credential for Real Estate Instrn., 1983, Calif. Cert. Tax Preparer. Mem. Nat. Assn. of Real Estate Appraisers, Inland Empire bridge Assn. (pres. 1980), Alpha Gamma Delta, Am. Contract Bridge Life Master. Republican. Presbyterian. Office: Lake Perris Real Estate 4645 Wade St Perris CA 92370

BORDEN, SANDRA MCCLISTER, day care center administrator, dancer; b. Trenton, Oct. 18, 1946; d. Harry Arthur and Ruth West McClister; m. Robert Stetson Borden, Mar. 23, 1968; children: Robert Freeman, Randolph McClister, David Buckley, Christian Delano. BA, Eastern Nazarene Coll., Quincy, Mass., 1968; MA, Nova U., 1986. Tchr. kindergarten Doves Nest Day Care Ctr., Rockland, Mass., 1979-84, owner, adminstr., 1979-90; owner, adminstr. Dove's Nest Day Care Ctr., Weymouth, Mass., 1980-82, Abington, Mass., 1980-83; owner, editor Barter & Trade Jour., Rockland, 1980-83; owner Dove's Nest Family Day Care System, Rockland, 1984—; co-owner Carriage House Day Care Ctr., Brockton, Mass., 1986—, Commonwealth Child Care Cons., 1987—, Bevell Assocs., Stoughton, Mass., 1987-89, Beginning Roots Day Care Ctr., Stoughton, 1987—; pres. Ednl. Videos of New England; ptnr. Tender Loving Child Care Inc., 1988-89, Dancer Foggs Dancers, Boston, 1980—; dir. Country Dance Soc., Boston, 1982—, v.p. 1986—, dancer, 1984-85, pres. 1988; co-founder, dancer Rapscallion Rapper Sword Team, 1985—. Foster mother for Helping Hands monkey, Boston U. Sch. Medicine; bd. dirs. LWV, Rockland, 1972-73. Mem. NAFE, Nat. Assn. Young Children, Royal Scottish Dance Soc., Country Dance Soc., Rose Galliard N.W. Clog Team, 1989), Assn. for Childhood Edn. Internat., Women Aglow Club (sec., bd. dirs.), New Eng. Folk Festival Assn. Baptist. Home: 1040 Plymouth St Abington MA 02351

BOREN, LYNDA SUE, university educator; b. Leesville, La., Apr. 1, 1941; d. Leonard and Doris (Ford) Schoenberger; m. James Lewis Boren, Sept. 1, 1961; 1 child, Lynda Carolyn. BA, U. New Orleans, 1971, MA, 1973; PhD, Tulane U., 1979. Visiting prof. Newcomb Coll. Tulane U., New Orleans, 1979-81, 82-83, U. Erlangen-Nuremburg, W. Germany, 1981-82, Middlebury (Vt.) Coll., 1983-84, Ga. Inst. Tech., Atlanta, 1985-87; prof. Northwestern State U., Natchitoches, La., 1987—; visiting prof. Srinakharinwirot U., Bangkok, Thailand, 1989-90; planning com. First Kate Chopin Internat. Conf., Natchitoches, La., 1987-89. Author: Eurydice Reclaimed: Language, Gender and Voice in Henry James, 1989; contbr. numerous articles to profl. jours. Founding mem. John F. Kennedy Library. Recipient Mellon Fellowship Tulane U., 1977-78, Fulbright Lectureship USIA & Bd. Foreign Scholars, 1981-82, 1989-90, Seminar Fellowship Nat. Endowment for Humanities, 1986. Mem. Am. Studies Assn., MLA, Fulbright Alumni Assn., AAUP, The Nat. Museum Women in the Arts, Art Guild. Democrat.

BOREN, SUSAN S., retail executive. Sr. v.p. for personnel Dayton-Hudson Corp., Mpls. Office: Dayton-Hudson Corp 777 On the Mall Minneapolis MN 55402*

BORG, MICHELE LEE, research analyst, consultant; b. Lincoln, Nebr., Oct. 13, 1958; d. Verl Rodger and Deloris Louise (Brown) B. BA, U. Nebr., 1983, postgrad., 1985—. Intake specialist Lancaster County Dept. of Corrections, Lincoln, 1980; dispatcher, jailer Brown County Sheriff's Dept., Ainsworth, Nebr., 1982; state probation officer Cass County Probation Office, Plattsmouth, Nebr., 1983-84; criminal justice field rep. Nebr. Crime Commn., Lincoln, 1984-87; specialist U.S. Justice Dept. Nat. Inst. Corrections, Boulder, Colo., 1987-89; rsch. analyst Nebr. Crime Commn., Lincoln, 1989—; criminal justice cons. Nat. Inst. Corrections, U.S. Justice Dept., 1990—; coord. small jail initiative Nat. Inst. Corrections, 1987-89. Contbr. articles to profl. jours. Mem. Cass County Mental Health Adv. Bd., Plattsmouth, 1983-84, Lancaster County Coalition in Response to Domestic Violence, Lincoln, 1986-87, Nebr. Spl. Edn. and Corrections Subcom., Lincoln, 1986-87. Mem. Am. Jail Assn., Am. Correctional Assn., Nebr. Sheriff's Assn., Colo. Correctional Assn., Am. Soc. for Pub. Adminstrn. Republican. Methodist. Office: Nebr Crime Commn PO Box 94946 Lincoln NE 68509-4946

BORGESE, ELISABETH MANN, political science educator, author; b. Munich, Apr. 24, 1918; arrived in U.S., 1938, naturalized, 1941, became Can. citizen, 1983; d. Thomas and Katia (Pringheim) Mann; m. Giuseppe Antonio Borgese, Nov. 23, 1939; children: Angelica, Dominica. Diploma, Conservatory of Music, Zurich, 1937; PhD (h.c.), Mt. St. Vincent U., 1986. Research assoc., editor Common Cause, U. Chgo., 1945-51; editor Perspective USA; Diogenes (Intercultural Publs.), 1952-57; exec. sec. bd. editors Ency. Brit., Chgo., 1964-66; sr. fellow, assoc. Ctr. for Study Dem. Instns., Santa Barbara, Calif., 1964-79; Killam sr. fellow Dalhousie U., Halifax, N.S., Can., 1979-80; prof. dept. polit. sci. Dalhousie U., 1980—; chmn. planning coun. Internat. Ocean Inst. 1986; chmn. Internat. Ctr. for Ocean Devel.; advisor Austria del. 3d UN Conf. on Law of Sea, 1976-82; Prep. Commn. Jamica, 1983-86. Author: To Whom It May Concern, 1962, Ascent of Woman, 1963, The Language Barrier, 1965, The Ocean Regime, 1968, The Drama of the Oceans, 1976, Seafarm: The Story of Aquaculture, 1980, The Mines of Neptune, 1985, The Future of the Oceans: A Report to the Club of Rome, 1986; (plays) Only the Pyre, 1987; contbr. short stories, essays to mags. Decorated medal of High Merit, Austria; Order of Can.; recipient

Sasakawa Internat. Environ. prize UN, 1987. Mem. Acad. Polit. Sci., AAAS, Am. Soc. Internat. Law, World Acad. Arts and Scis., Third-World Acad. Sci. Office: Dahlousie U, Dept Polit Sci, Halifax, NS Canada B3H 4H6

BORGESON, AMY LOUISE, lawyer; b. Virginia, Minn., Oct. 12, 1953; d. Oliver Whitaker and Helen Marie (Bradt) B. BA, McGill U., Montreal, Can., 1975; JD, U. Minn., 1978. Bar: Minn. 1979, U.S. Dist. Ct. Minn. 1979. Jud. clk. State Dist. Ct., 6th Jud. Dist., Virginia, 1980; assoc. Trenti Law Firm, Virginia, 1980-83; ptnr. Vincent & Borgeson, Mpls., 1983-85; assoc. Law Offices of Louis D. Bass, Mpls., 1985-87; workers' compensation atty.-prin. Minn. Dept. Employee Relations/Safety & Workers Compensation, St. Paul, 1987-89; compensation judge Dept. Labor & Industry, St. Paul, 1989—. Editor Comp Report, Comp Corp, Inc., St. Paul, 1989—. Bd. dirs. Iron Range Rehab. Ctr., Virginia, 1981-83, Women Helping Offenders, Mpls., 1986-88. Office: Dept Labor & Industry 443 Lafayette Rd Saint Paul MN 55155

BORGOS, DENISE MARTHA, systems analyst; b. N.Y.C., Aug. 4, 1948; d. Felipe and Marie (Carrasquillo) Borgos; div. Diploma, Paralegal Inst., Phoenix, 1983; BA cum laude, U. P.R., 1969. Sales/reservations agt. Eastern Airlines, San Juan, Fla., 1970-79, Tampa, Fla., 1979-85, Miami, Fla., 1985-87; customer svc. rep., systems analyst System One Corp., Miami, 1987—. Recipient French award U. P.R., 1969. Mem. Alliance Francaise, Am. Soc. Notaries. Republican. Roman Catholic.

BORGSTAHL, KAYLENE DENISE, health facility administrator; b. Hampton, Iowa, May 21, 1951; d. Harry Dell and Berniece Irene (Muhlenbruck) Crabb; m. Michael Lowell Borgstahl, Aug. 19, 1972; children: Elliot Michael, Brett Andrew. BS in Nursing, U. Iowa, 1973; MPA, Iowa State U., 1986. Asst. adminstr. Linn County Vis. Nurse Assn., Cedar Rapids, Iowa, 1975-85; v.p. program svcs. Voluntary Hosps. Iowa Home Health Care, Cedar Rapids, 1985-86; adminstr. Norell Home Health Svcs., Edina, Minn., 1986-87; case mgr. In Home Health Svcs., Mpls., 1987-88; adminstr. Sundance Med. Clinic Ltd., Shakopee, Minn., 1988—. Mem. Sigma Theta Tau. Republican.

BORGSTEDT, AGNETA DAGMAR, pediatrician, medical educator; b. Hamburg, Fed. Republic Germany, May 31, 1931; came to U.S., 1956; d. Werner Robert and Else Charlotte (Scherer) V. Rehren; m. Harold H. Borgstedt, May 11, 1957; children: Eric V.R., Astrid Anne. Abitur, Heilwigschule, Hamburg, 1950; MD, U. Hamburg, 1955. Diplomate Am. Bd. Pediatrics. Intern Rochester (N.Y.) Gen. Hosp., 1956-57, resident, 1957-59, chief resident, 1959-60; assoc. resident Strong Meml. Hosp., Rochester, 1960, fellow pediatric neurology, 1960-63; instr. U. Rochester Med. Sch., 1968, asst. prof., 1968-69, clin. asst. prof., 1969—. Contbr. numerous articles on pediatric neurology and devel. disabilities profl. jours. Mem. profl. adv. bd. Epilepsy Assn. Rochester, 1978—. Mem. Med. Soc. County of Monroe, Rochester Pediatric Soc., Acad. Pediatrics (com. children with disabilities, neurology and devel. sect.). Home and Office: PO Box 38 Henrietta NY 14467

BORISKIE, HELEN ANN (HEFLEY BORISKIE), corporate executive, educator, inventor; b. Port Arthur, Tex., Dec. 5, 1949; d. John Martin and Wanda Ion (Hines) Hefley; m. Donald Leslie Boriskie, Dec. 27, 1968; children: Amy Lynne, Laurie Ann, Barry James. BS, N. Tex. State U., 1971, MEd, 1979. Tchr. elem. Bullock Elem. and Garland (Tex.) Ind. Sch. Dist., 1971-76; supr. network admissions Southwestern Bell Tel., St. Louis, 1977-78; supr. bus. svcs. Southwestern Bell Tel., Dallas, 1978-79, customer svcs. supr., 1979-80, customer svcs. staff supr., 1980-83, asst. staff mgr. corp. communications div., 1983-85; pres., chief exec. officer ASHLAR Products, Inc., Dallas, 1985-86, Raleigh, N.C., 1988-89; chief exec. officer Tot-Safe, Inc., Raleigh, N.C., 1989—; pres. Annie, Ltd., Raleigh, 1989, 90; chief exec. officer Holland Grill Co., APEX, N.C., 1990—. Author, editor: Buckle Up With Beary, 1988; inventor seat belt buckle guard, tag-a-long, safety Id badge, porta-potty. Vol. home for aged Dallas Vol. Orgn., 1985. Named Tchr. of Yr., Garland Fedn. Women's Clubs, 1974, 75, Young Educator of Yr. Garland C. of C., 1974. Mem. Garland Classroom Tchrs. (pres. 1975), Garland Edn. Assn. (sec. 1976), Tex. State Tchrs. Orgn. (voting del. 1974, 75, 76), Coun. for Entrepreneurial Devel., N.C. World Trade Assn. (Triangle chpt. hospitality com. 1989, Barringer Meml. com. 1990), Nat. Edn. Assn., Phi Delta Kappa. Home and Office: 608 Hawick Rd Raleigh NC 27615

BORK, MILDRED ELLEN MARSHALL, nursing educator; b. Covington, Ky., Feb. 6, 1933; d. Arthur J. and Cora E. (Grover) Marshall; m. William R. Clark, Oct. 4, 1958 (div. Dec. 1978); children: Ellen Torbeck, William R. Clark, Craig M. Clark, Brian B. Clark; m. Robert L. Bork, Feb. 18, 1984. BS in Nursing, U. Cin., 1955, MS in Nursing, 1971. Staff, head nurse VA Hosp., Cin., 1955-57; head nurse, sr. clin. instr. Univ. Hosp., Cin., 1957-59, charge nurse, 1967-68; instr. N. Ky. Community Coll., Covington, 1968-69; instr. No. Ky. U., Highland Heights, 1971-77, asst. prof., 1977-89, assoc. prof., 1989—; cons. faculty No. Ky. U., Highland Heights, 1979-80; cons. med. policies New Perceptions, Inc., Newport, Ky., 1983-84; presenter in field. Bd. dirs. New Perceptions, Inc., no. Ky., 1981—, No. Ky. Mental Health Assn., Covinton, 1981-84; mem. speakers bur. No. Ky. Mental Health, Covington, 1985—, Riverside Good Coun. Found. Bd., no. Ky., 1988—. Named Ky. Col., 1986; recipient Alumnae Appreciation award U. Cin., 1989; summer fellow No. Ky. U., 1988; rsch. grantee No. Ky. U., 1988. Mem. Am. Nursing Assn. (psychiat./mental health com.), Ky. Nurses Assn. (dist. 3 bd. dirs. 1988—, state conv. com., 1989—, nominating com., 1980-82, pres. dist. 3 1990—), AAUP (No. Ky. U., acad. freedom and tenure 1987), Nat. League Nursing Psychiat. Nurses, Am. Psychiat. Nurses Assn., U. Cin. Nursing Alumnae (treas. 1956-57, nominating com. 1984, awards com. 1988-90), Sigma Theta Tau, Alpha Alpha Pi. Roman Catholic. Home: 1013 Carpenters Trace Villa Hills KY 41017 Office: No Ky U Highland Heights KY 41076

BORMAN, CAROL JEAN, nurse; b. St. Cloud, Minn., Oct. 10, 1933; d. Joseph Frank and Clothilda Mary (Weyrens) Zabinski; m. Donald James Borman, Aug. 11, 1962; 1 child, Helen Carol. Diploma in nursing, St. Cloud Hosp., 1954. RN, Minn. Staff nurse St. Joseph's Hosp., Phoenix, 1956-57, Midway Hosp., St. Paul, 1962-64; staff to head nurse St. Cloud Hosp., 1954-56, asst. head nurse, 1957-62, head nurse, 1964-68, 71-72, staff nurse, 1968-71, asst. dir. nursing, 1972-82; nursing supr. St. Gabriel's Hosp., Little Falls, Minn., 1983-84, asst. dir. med., surg., pediatrics depts., 1984-89; nurse mgr. St. Benedict's Ctr., St. Cloud, 1989—. Nat. League of Nursing, Am. Legion Aux. Republican. Roman Catholic. Home: 2016 N 13th St Saint Cloud MN 56303 Office: St Benedict's Ctr 1810 Minnesota Blvd SE Saint Cloud MN 56303

BORN, BROOKSLEY ELIZABETH, lawyer; b. San Francisco, Aug. 27, 1940; d. Ronald Henry and Mary Ellen (Bortner) B.; m. Alexander Elliot Bennett, Oct. 9, 1982; children: Nicholas Jacob Landau, Ariel Elizabeth Landau. A.B., Stanford U., 1961, J.D., 1964. Bar: D.C. 1966. Law clk. U.S. Ct. Appeals, Washington, 1964-65; legal researcher Harvard Law Sch., 1967-68; asso. firm Arnold and Porter, Washington, 1965-67, 68-73; partner Arnold and Porter, 1974—; lectr. law Columbus Sch. Law, Cath. U. Am., 1972-74; adj. prof. Georgetown U. Law Center, Washington, 1972-73. Pres. Stanford Law Rev, 1963-64. Chairperson bd. visitors Stanford U. Law Sch., 1987; bd. dirs. Nat. Legal Aid and Defenders Assn., 1972-79, Am. Bar Found., 1989—; chairperson bd. dirs. Nat. Women's Law Ctr., 1981—; trustee Ctr. for Law and Social Policy, Washington, 1977—, Women's Bar Found., 1981-86. Mem. ABA (chairperson sect. individual rights and responsibilities 1977-78, chairperson fed. judiciary com. 1980-83, chairperson consortium on legal services and the pub. 1987-90, bd. govs. 1990—), D.C. Bar (sec. 1975-76, bd. govs. 1976-79), Am. Law Inst., Lawyers' Com. for Civil Rights Under Law (trustee 1978—), Am. Judicature Soc. (bd. dirs. 1984-88), Order of Coif. Office: Arnold & Porter 1200 New Hampshire Ave NW Washington DC 20036

BORN, ETHEL WOLFE, church worker; b. Kasson, W.Va., Jan. 6, 1924; d. Otto Guy and Nancy Grace (Nestor) Wolfe; m. Harry Edward Born, Apr. 4, 1944; children: Rosemary Ellen (dec.), Barbara Anne Born Craig. Student, Ecumenical Inst., Geneva, 1983, Mary Baldwin Coll., 1987—. Author: A Tangled Web--A Search for Answers to the Question of Pelestine, 1989, By My Spirit, Methodist Protestant Women in Mission, 1879-1939, 1990; contbr. articles to religious publs. Va. pres. United Meth. Women, 1972-76; bd. dirs. United Meth. Gen. Bd. Global Ministries, N.Y.C., 1976-84, v.p. women's div., 1980-84, v.p. com. on relief, 1980-84, Mid. East cons. women's div., 1984-88; chmn. N.Am. Coordinating Com. for Non-govtl. Orgns. on Question of Palestine, 1986-87; chmn. UN Symposium for Non-govtl. Orgns. on Question of Palestine, N.Y.C., 1986, 87; pres. N.Am. area, asst. world treas. World Fedn. Meth. Women, 1986—; mem. United Meth. Gen. Commn. on Christian Unity and Inter-Religious Concerns, N.Y.C., 1988—. Home: 6995 Malinda Rd Salem VA 24153

BORNAND, RUTH CHALOUX, antique music box specialist; b. N.Y.C., Oct. 13, 1901; d. Frank and Ruby (Forsyth) Chaloux; m. Adrian V. Bornand (dec.); children: Hilaire Bornand Coy, Elise Bornand Wegener. Student, Woods Bus. Coll., 1920-21. Proprietor Bornand Music Box Co., Pelham, N.Y., 1945—. Organizer Handicapped Children's Group, N.Y.C., 1950-51; mem. ladies guild Ch. of the Redeemer, Pelham, 1947-48. Mem. Musical Box Soc. Internat. (co-founder 1949, corresponding sec., trustee 1978, historian 1959, museum com. 1980—), Order Eastern Star. Republican. Home and Office: Bornand Music Box Co 139 4th Ave Pelham NY 10803

BORNEMAN, ALICE GREGORY, educator; b. Wilkes-Barre, Pa., June 15, 1940; d. Dwight Lewis and Margaret Elizabeth (Wolfe) Gregory; m. Edward Leo Borneman, Dec. 29, 1962; children: Margaret Ann, Linda Marie, Edward Gregory, Clayton Gregory. BS in Edn., Rider Coll., Lawrenceville, N.J., 1962; MA in Edn., Rider Coll., 1989. Bus. edn. tchr. Woodstown (N.J.) High Sch., 1962-64, Interboro High Sch., Glenolden, Pa., 1966-67, Parkland High Sch., El Paso, Tex., 1967-69, Lower Cape May (N.J.) High Sch., 1972-73; bus. edn. tchr. Wildwood (N.J.) High Sch., 1979—, chmn. dept. computer and bus., 1990—; adj. prof. Atlantic Community Coll., 1990—. Sec. Wildwood Civic Club, 1983-88; adv. coun. Cape May County Vocat. Sch., 1989—; mem. mastectomy support group Burdette Tomlin Meml. Hosp. Recipient Walter A. Brower award for devotion to excellence in field of bus. edn., Rider Coll., 1989. Mem. AAUW, Delta Pi Epsilon, Delta Kappa Gamma. Republican. Roman Catholic. Home: 8504 Seaview Ave Wildwood Crest NJ 08260 Office: Wildwood High Sch 4300 Pacific Ave Wildwood NJ 08260

BORNHOLDT, LAURA ANNA, university administrator; b. Peoria, Ill., Feb. 11, 1919; d. John and Barbara (Kohl) B. A.B., Smith Coll., 1940, M.A., 1942; Ph.D., Yale U., 1945. Asst. prof. history Smith Coll., Northampton, Mass., 1945-52; internat. relations asso. AAUW, Washington, 1952-57; dean Sarah Lawrence Coll., Bronxville, N.Y., 1957-59; dean women, adj. prof. history U. Pa., Phila., 1959-61; dean coll., prof. history Wellesley (Mass.) Coll., 1961-64; v.p. Danforth Found., St. Louis, 1964-73; sr. program officer Lilly Endowment Inc., Indpls., 1973-76; v.p. for edn. Lilly Endowment Inc., 1976-84; spl. asst. to pres. U. Chgo., 1984—; Nat. adv. com. on black higher edn. and black colls. and univs. Dept. Edn., 1977-82; mem. Yale U. Council, 1977-82; emerita life trustee Coll. of Wooster, Ohio, 1967-77; trustee St. Louis U., 1971-75; mem. bd. Nat. Council on Library Resources, 1983-80. Contbg. editor Change Mag., 1980—. Recipient Yale U. Wilbur Cross medal, 1976, Smith Coll. Alumnae medal, 1987. Mem. Am. Assn. Higher Edn., Phi Beta Kappa. Home: 5000 S East End Ave Apt 25A Chicago IL 60615 Office: U Chgo 5801 S Ellis Ave Chicago IL 60637

BORNSTEIN, LINDA UPHAM, company official, educational administrator; b. Boston, June 27, 1952; d. Horace Emerald and Betty Hope(Lawrence) Upham; m. Peter Hartwell Bornstein, Aug. 7, 1976; children: Alison Lawrence, Christopher Alexander. BA, U. Mass., Boston, 1977. Research asst. U. Mass., 1975-77; sec. Prog. of Applied Sci., Coll. William and Mary, Williamsburg, Va., 1978-80; lectr. Weight Watchers of N.H., Nashua, 1983-89; bookkeeper Bergeron, Hanson & Bornstein, Berlin, N.H., 1987—; ednl. advocate Parent Info. Ctr., Concord, N.H., 1985—; surrogate parent State of N.H., Dept. Edn., Concord, 1986—; learning resource coordinator Sch. for Lifelong Learning, Berlin, N.H., 1988—. Incorporator No. N.H. Found., 1986—; bd. dirs. Androscoggin Valley Hosp., Berlin, 1986-88; auditor Milan Meth. Ch., 1986—; chmn. Androscoggin Valley Hosp. Gov. Golf Tournament, 1989—; mem. adv. com. to Sch. Bd., Berlin, 1988—; mem. adv. bd. Salvation Army, 1990—. Mem. AAUW, Androscoggin Valley Hosp. Aux. (pres. 1986-88). Republican. Methodist. Office: Bergeron Hanson & Bornstein 110 Pleasant St Berlin NH 03570

BORNT, DOROTHY ELLEN, small business owner; b. Bklyn, Aug. 7, 1961; d. George and Carol Ann (Kramer) DeNoto; m. Scott J. Bornt, June 26, 1987; 1 child, Scott John II. BA, SUNY, Stonybrook, 1983; MLS, SUNY, Albany, 1984. Info. specialist Urbach, Kahn & Werlin P.C., Albany, 1984-88; owner Bornt Trucking, Nassau, N.Y., 1988—. Mem. Spl. Libraries Assn., Am. Soc. Info. Sci. Republican. Roman Catholic. Home and Office: RR 1 Box 218 East Nassau NY 12062

BOROS, ANDREA CLARE, insurance company executive; b. Cleve., Oct. 14, 1958; d. Paul and Edith K. (Marotta) Boros; m. Phillip Raymond Capone, May 27, 1983 (div. 1987); 1 child, Jesse Lee. BS, Kent State U., 1980. Police adminstr.'s asst. Kent (Ohio) State U. Police Dept., 1979-80; juvenile correction worker Parmadale/St. Anthony's Children's Home, Parma, Ohio, 1980-81; communications specialist Cleveland Hts./Shaker Hts. Fire Dept., 1982-83; legal asst. Hyatt Legal Svcs., Maple Hts., Ohio, 1983-86; compliance analyst Progressive Ins. Co., Mayfield Village, Ohio, 1986, compliance supr., 1986-88; compliance mgr. Interstate Svc. Ins. Agy., Columbus, Ohio, 1988—. Leadership group St. Paul's Cath. Ch. Single Again Ministry, Westerville, Ohio, 1990—. Mem. NAFE, Am. Soc. Profl. and Exec. Women, Life and Health Compliance Assn. Republican. Office: Interstate Svc Ins Agy 7720 Riversedge Dt Columbus OH 43235

BOROWSKI, JENNIFER LUCILE, corporate administrator; b. Jersey City, Oct. 23, 1934; d. Peter Anthony and Ludwika (Zapolska) B. BS, St. Peter's Coll., 1968; postgrad., Pace Coll., 1976-77. Mgr. benefits Amerada Petroleum Corp., N.Y.C., 1951-66, Mt. Sinai Hosp., N.Y.C., 1966-67; mgr. payroll and payroll taxes Haskins & Sells, N.Y.C., 1967-74; mgr. payroll and payroll tax Cushman & Wakefield, Inc., N.Y.C., 1975-89. Mem. Am. Payroll Assn. (bd. dirs. 1979-81, cert.), Am. Mgmt. Assn., Am. Soc. Payroll Mgrs., Internat. Platform Assn. (hon.), Am. Soc. Profl. Exec. Women, NAFE. Republican. Roman Catholic. Home: 36 Front St North Arlington NJ 07032

BORRY, CAROL ANN, trade association administrator, music educator; b. Lancaster, Pa., Dec. 14, 1925; d. William Earle and Mary Winifred (Maurer) Hickman; m. H. Kenneth Borry, Dec. 27, 1947 (dec.); children: Barrett Earle, Kendace Carol, April Winifred. Student, West Chester (Pa.) State U., 1943-46. Tchr. piano Oxford Sch. Music., N.Y.C., 1946; tchr. Warwick Twp., Lititz, Pa., 1946-47, Palmer Twp. Schs., Easton, Pa., 1948-49, Elizabethtown (Pa.) Elem. Sch., 1960-61; supr. Nat. Assn. States Dept. Agr., Harrisburg, Pa., 1973—; dir. choir 1st Meth. Ch., Centerville, Md., 1950-53, Luth. Ch., Bainbridge, Pa., 1953-57; min. music. Bapt. Ch., Delmar, Del., 1948-49, Glossbrenner United Meth. Ch., Mt. Joy, Pa., 1976—. Leader 4-H Club, 1963-73; bd. dirs. Bible Sch., Centerville, 1954; pres. PTA, Bainbridge, 1956; active on Rep. com., Mt. Joy, 1974-80, insp. of elections, 1989; sunday sch. tchr., 1975-85; law disciple, speaker Meth. Ch., 1976-86; chairperson adminstrv. bd. Glossbrenner United Meth. Ch., 1988—. Mem. Am. Guild Handbell Ringers, Elizabeth Hughes Soc. (pres. 1982-84), Meth. Women Elizabethtown (pres. 1980-82), Homemaker's Club (pres. 1952). Methodist. Home: RD 2 Box 196 Mount Joy PA 17552

BORST-MANNING, DIANE GAIL, management consultant; b. Rochester, N.Y., Nov. 5, 1937; d. Howard Louis and Emily Kathleen (Crew) Borst; m. Steven Manning, Sept. 11, 1979. B.A. cum laude, Wagner Coll., 1959; M.B.A., N.Y.U., 1966. Planner N.Y.U. Med. Ctr., N.Y.C., 1962-76, assoc. dir. planning, 1976-78, dir. mgmt. services, 1978-80; dir. human resources Mt. Sinai Med. Ctr., N.Y.C., 1980-85, dir. planning, 1985-86; sr. v.p. The Manning Orgn., Inc., 1986—; pres. Diane Borst Manning Assocs., Inc., 1986—; inst. dept. health care mgmt. Mt. Sinai Sch. Medicine, CUNY, 1982—; adj. faculty Orange County Community Coll., Sarah lawrence Coll., New Sch. Social Research, 1986—. Editor: Managing Non-Profit Organizations, 1979. Author: (cassette) Managers and Secretaries - How to Achieve Teamwork, 1980. Chairperson grants Port Jervis Council for Arts; mem. Health Systems Agy. Bd., N.Y.C., 1976-79; trustee Helene Fuld Sch. Nursing, N.Y.C., 1989—. Fullbright fellow, 1959. Mem. N.Y. Personnel Mgmt. Assn. (bd. dirs. 1974-76), Greater N.Y. Hosp. Assn., Am. Compensation Assn., Bur. Nat. Affairs (personnel policy forum 1983-84), Am. Assn. Hosp. Planners, Assn. Am. Med. Colls. Group on Instrl. Planning. Club: City (N.Y.) Avocations: gardening; auto mechanics; carpentry, real estate. Office: 40 W 55 St Suite 9D New York NY 10019

BORTNER-WANDLING, DEBORAH ANN, financial planning specialist; b. York, Pa., Apr. 14, 1949; d. James Cyrus and Delores (Kinard Bortner; m. Robert Bruce Wandling, July 12, 1986. BA in Psychology and Sociology, Western Md. Coll., 1971; MA in Teaching with honors, Trenton State Coll., 1973. Cert. tchr. of hearing impaired, Pa., N.J.; cert. tchr. of speech correction, Pa.; cert. tchr. of mentally and/or physically handicapped, Pa.; cert. tchr. of handicapped, N.J.; cert. tchr. of psychology, N.J. Tchr. Katzenbach Sch. for Deaf, West Trenton, N.J., 1973-79; adj. prof. sign lang. skills Mercer County Community Coll., Trenton, N.J., 1982-84; resource high sch. tchr. Hamilton Bd. Edn., Trenton, 1979-84; interpreter for deaf, coord. interpreter referral svcs. Div. of Deaf, N.J. Dept. Labor, Trenton, 1979-86; instr. learning resource ctr. Fleming-Reading Mid. Sch., Flemington, N.J., 1985-87; fin. planning specialist A.L. Williams, Morrisville, Pa., 1985; fin. planner Waddell and Reed, Langhorne, Pa., 1986—; presenter on devel. and implementation of fin. planning programs to various ednl. instns., bus. and individual clients. Home: 656A Rose Hollow Dr Yardley PA 19067 Office: Waddell and Reed 307 One Oxford Valley Langhorne PA 19047

BORTZ, PHYLLIS E., accountant; b. N.Y.C., Feb. 23, 1926; d. Jacob G. Elkin and Jennie Solomon; m. Bernard J. Brotz, July 3, 1947; children: Joyce G. Fiedler, John G., Jean G. BA, Hunter Coll., N.Y.C., 1948; grad., Therese Aub Secretarial Sch., N.Y.C., 1949. Office mgr. Ross & Barnett, CPA, N.Y.C., Bond-Margolis Projects, Inc., Jericho, N.Y., Monitoring and Evaluation Svcs., Wantagh, N.Y.; pres. Philber Projects Ltd., Jericho. Chmn. Scholarship Awards Com., Scarsdale, N.Y.; rec. sec. Hadassah, 1988—.

BORUT, JOSEPHINE, insurance executive; b. Bridgeport, Conn., Aug. 3, 1942; d. Frank and Catherine (Russo) Occhipinti; m. Arthur Lee Borut, Nov. 22, 1963; 1 child, Adam Seth. BS in Art, Hofstra U., 1964, MA in Humanities, 1971; cert. in mgmt., Adelphi U., 1984. Cert. art tchr., N.Y. Art tchr. Cen. Islip (N.Y.) Elem., 1964-65; coord. art dept. Mineola (N.Y.) Jr. High, 1965-70; art tchr., coord. Brandeis Sch., Lawrence, N.Y., 1979-81; mgr. community rels. Empire Blue Cross/Blue Shield, N.Y.C., 1984-85, mgr. conf. planning, 1985—; freelance artist, East Meadow, 1978-79; lectr. meeting planning. Contbr. articles to Meeting Mgr. Mag., 1989-90. Recipient hon. mention L.I. Art Tchrs. Assn. Art Show, 1966, 3d Place art show Hofstra U., 1966, 2d Place East Meadow Pub. Libr. Juried Art Show, 1979. Mem. NAFE, Am. Soc. Assn. Execs., Meeting Planners Internat. (treas., bd. dirs. Greater N.Y. chpt., com. chmn.), Am. Soc. Profl. and Exec. Women, Ins. Conf. Planners. Home: 1823 Kent St Westbury NY 11590 Office: Empire Blue Cross/Blue Shield 622 3d Ave New York NY 10017

BORYSEWICZ, MARY LOUISE, editor; b. Chgo.; d. Thomas J. and Mabel E. (Zeien) O'Farrell m. Daniel S. Borysewicz, June 11, 1955; children: Mary Adele, Stephen Francis, Paul Barnabas. B.A., Mundelein Coll., 1970; postgrad. in English lit., U. Ill, 1970-71; grad. exec. program, U. Chgo., 1982. Editor sci. publs. AMA, Chgo., 1971-73; exec. mng. editor Am. Jour. Ophthalmology, Chgo., 1973—; asst. sec., treas Ophthalmic Pub. Co., 1985—; guest lectr. U. Chgo. Med. Sch., 1979, Harvard U. Med. Sch., 1978, Northwestern U. Med. Sch., 1979, Am. Acad. Ophthalmology, 1976, 81. Editor: Ophthalmology Principles and Concepts, 6th edit., 1986; contbr. articles to sci. publs. Active vol. svcs. Art Inst. Chgo. Mem. Am. Soc. Profl. and Exec. Women, Council Biology Editors (fin. com. 1985—, bd. dirs. 1988—), Bus. Vols. for the Arts (1988—), Chgo. Women in Pub. Home: 4415 N California Ave Chicago IL 60625 Office: 435 N Michigan Ave Chicago IL 60611

BOS, MARILYN WHITNEY, educator; b. Fredricksburg, Va., Oct. 3, 1940; d. D. Ransom and Marian Whitney; m. Charles Anthony Bos, Feb. 24, 1964; children: Margot Bos Stambler, Karla Bos-Strata, Lisa Bos Grewell. BA, Oberlin Coll., 1962; MA in Edn., Va. Tech., 1980. Elem. tchr. Fairfax (Va.) County Schs., 1965-71, Loudoun County Schs., Round Hill, Va., 1971-75; founding tchr. gifted program grades 4-5 Futura Loudoun County Schs., Leesburg, Va., 1975-83, founding tchr. grades K-5, 1983—; presenter at conf. No. Va. Coun. for G/T Edn., 1979, 81, 83, 88, 90, at state conf. Va. Assn. for Edn. of Gifted, Roanoke, Va., 1985, 87, 89; program organizer 14th annual NVCG/TE conf., Sterling Va., 1989; inservice Loudoun County Pub. Schs., 1975—. Co-author: (with Diana Herrmann) Loudoun, Our County, 1979, revision 1982, 90. Pres. bd. dirs. AAUW, Leesburg, 1986-88; pres. bd. dirs. The Loudoun Mus., Leesburg, 1989-90; mem. nominating com. LWV, Leesburg, 1988-90. Named Outstanding Tchr. of the Gifted, No. Va. Coun. for Gifted/Talented Edn., 1986-87. Mem. Va. Assn. for the Edn. of Gifted, Coun. for Exceptional Children-Talents and Gifts Div., Loudoun Edn. Assn., Va. Edn. Assn., NEA, Talents Unlimited (Va. trainer, cert. 1989), Adults for Gifted And Talented Edn. (founder 1975), Loudoun Book Club. Home: 211 N King St Leesburg VA 22075

BOSHIER, MAUREEN LOUISE, health facilities administrator; b. Elizabeth, N.J., Oct. 1, 1946; d. John Henry and Mary Hanora (McGarry) B.; m. Robert Hall Rea, May 23, 1987. BSN, Coll. Misericordia, Dallas, Pa., 1968; MS in Psychiat. Nursing, U. Colo., 1973; MBA, U. Phoenix, 1987. Clin. specialist psychiat. nursing Denver Gen. Hosp., 1973-74; dir. rehab. services N.Mex. Cancer Control, Albuquerque, 1976-80; exec. dir. N.Mex. State Bd. Nursing, Albuquerque, 1980-84; exec. v.p. N.Mex. Hosp. Assn., Albuquerque, 1984-88; adminstr. surg. services, sr. nursing adminstr. U. N.Mex. Hosp., Albuquerque, 1988—; dir. Profl. Seminar Cons., Inc., Albuquerque, 1982—; v.p. exec. bd. N.Mex. Health Resources, Albuquerque, 1981—, pres., 1989; vice chmn., bd. dirs. Hosp. Home Health Care, Albuquerque, 1978—; dir. Acad. Seminars, Inc., 1982—. Contbr. articles to profl. jours. Sec. N.Mex. Ballet Co., Albuquerque, 1982-87; vice chmn. Gov.'s Task Force on Nursing Issues, Albuquerque, 1982-88; adv. bd. Subarea Coun. Health Systems, Albuquerque, 1980-84. Capt. U.S. Army, 1967-71. Mem. N.Mex. Orgn. for Nurse Execs. (treas. 1988-89, pres. 1990), N.Mex. League Nursing, N.Mex. Nurses Assn. (nurse adminstr. award 1984), Sigma Theta Tau. Democrat. Home: 6408 Prairie Ave NE Albuquerque NM 87109 Office: U NMex Hosp 2211 Lomas Blvd NE Albuquerque NM 87106

BOSLEY, KAREN LEE, English educator; b. Beech Grove, Ind., Sept. 23, 1942; d. Lowell Holmes and Kathryn Gertrude (Drake) Foley; AB in Lang. Arts summa cum laude, U. Indpls., 1965; MA in English, Northwestern U., 1967; MA in Journalism, Ball State U., 1984; postgrad. (Newspaper Fund fellow), U. Mo., 1973, Ohio U., 1977; m. Norman Keith Bosley, Dec. 21, 1964; children: Mark Harold, Rachael Kathryn, Keith Lowell, Sidney Clark. Copy editor, reporter Indpls. News, 1963-65; English tchr., yearbook adviser Beech Grove (Ind.) Jr. High Sch., 1965-66; English tchr. So. Regional High Sch., Manahawkin, N.J., 1967-68; assoc. prof. humanities, journalism and English, student newspaper adviser Ocean County Coll., Toms River, N.J., 1971—; part time reporter Daily Times-Observer, Toms River, 1972-77. Trustee Long Beach Island Hist. Assn., Friends of Island Library, 1975-79; pres. Long Beach I. PTA; chmn. Long Beach Twp. Dem. Mcpl. Com., 1971-78; Dem. committeeman Long Beach Twp. Dist. 2, 1971-78, 85—; mem. Long Beach Twp. Recreation Commn., 1972-77, chmn., 1972-75; bd. dirs. Ocean County Red Cross, 1972-78, Ocean County Family Planning, Inc., 1972-78, Student Press Law Ctr., 1989—; chmn. Cub Scout pack 32, Ocean County council Boy Scouts Am.; founder, bd. dirs. Long Beach I. Hist. Assn., Island Democrats, Inc.; adminstrv. bd. First United Meth. Ch. Beach Haven Terrace (N.J.). Mem. AAUW (pres., dir. Barnegat Light Area br.), NEA, N.J. Edn. Assn., Ocean County Edn. Assn., Faculty Assn. Ocean County Coll. (v.p. 1984-85), Coll. Media Advisers (disting. newspaper adviser for U.S. 2-yr. colls. 1978, dir., sec.), Assn. Edn. in Journalism and Mass Community., Journalism Assn. (dir., v.p.), Soc. Profl. Journalists, Sigma Delta Chi. Contbr. article to publ. in field. Home: 9 E Old Whaling Ln Long Beach Twp NJ 08008-2930 Office: Ocean County Coll College Dr CN2001 Toms River NJ 08754-2001

BOSS, KATHLEEN ALICE, art director, graphic designer; b. Burbank, Calif., July 9, 1957; d. Kenneth Howard and Narlene Wallace (Barr)

B. Student, Coastline Coll., 1976-79, Glendale Coll., 1976-77; AA, Orange Coast Coll., 1982; BFA, Art Ctr. Coll., Pasadena, Calif., 1985. Photographer Figge Photography, Newport Beach, Calif., 1975-80; designer Ocean Pacific Sportswear, Anaheim, Calif., 1983; art dir. Ogilvy & Mather Advt., L.A., 1986; designer Eisaman, Johns & Laws Advt., L.A., 1987-89; designer, beauty and personal care products Epi Products, Inc., Santa Monica, Calif., 1989—; cons. Andresen Typographics, L.A., 1985—. design theme cons. Pasadena Centennial Celebration, 1985; design cons. Children's Hosp., L.A., 1987—, Dorothy Goldeen Gallery, Santa Monica, Calif., 1987-88, ARC, L.A., 1988—. Vol. Concern II, cancer rsch., L.A., 1986—, Mus. Contemporary Art, L.A., 1987—. Recipient awards of merit Art Dirs. Club L.A., 1986, Western Art Dirs. Club, 1986, cert. of excellence Advt. Club Orange County, 1986, award of excellence L.A. Advt. Women, 1987, merit awards Photo Design, 1987. Democrat.

BOSSERT, CAROL JO, museum administrator; b. Richmond, Ind., Nov. 25, 1956; d. W. Richard and Nancy Lou (Bardonner) B.; m. Douglas Emery Brough, Feb. 11, 1987. BA, DePauw U., 1978; MS, U. Tex., Dallas, 1983, PhD, 1985. Rsch. asst. U. Tex., Dallas, 1978-85, teaching asst., 1978-85; postdoctoral fellow U. Utah Med. Ctr., Salt Lake City, 1985-86; dir. sci. dept. Newark Mus., 1986—. Mem. AAAS, Alliance N.J. Environ. Edn. (adv. com. 1989—), Soc. Preservation Natural History, Mus. Coun. N.J. (pres. bd. trustees 1988—), AAUW, Alpha Phi. Office: Newark Mus 49 Washington St PO Box 540 Newark NJ 07101

BOST, THEDA KERBY, travel agency manager; b. Sweetwater, Tex., July 27, 1928; d. Leslie George and F. Lorene (Price) Kerby; m. Howard William Bost, Sept. 10, 1950; children: Janet Elizabeth, Barbara Suzanne, Carole Anne. BA, U. Tex., 1950, MEd, 1955. Cert. travel counselor, 1985. Tchr. Austin (Tex.) Pub. Sch., 1953-55, AAUW Preschool, Bartlesville, Okla., 1972-75; travel agt. Spears World Travel Svc., Bartlesville, 1975—; mgr.-counselor Spears/Carlson Travel Network, Bartlesville, 1985—. Bd. dirs. Bluestem Girl Scout Coun., Bartlesville, 1967-69, Bartlesville (Okla.) Pub. Libr., 1975-78. Mem. AAUW (v.p. 1967-69, bd. dirs. 1972-75), Inst. Cert. Travel Agts. Republican. Methodist. Home: 1334 Quail Dr Bartlesville OK 74006 Office: Carlson Travel Network 500 S Keeler Ave Bartlesville OK 74006

BOSTED, DOROTHY STACK, public relations executive; b. Newark, Apr. 6, 1953; d. Richard Joseph and Dorothy Marie (Irvin) S.; m. Kenneth James Bosted, Aug. 22, 1976; 1 child, Danielle Whitney. Student, Lyndon State Coll., 1971-73; BA, NYU, 1975. Reporter The Daily Advance, Succasunna, N.J., 1974-75; producer, tech. intern Manhattan Cable TV, N.Y.C., 1975; editorial asst. Calif. Sch. Employees Assn., San Jose, 1975-76; news dir., anchor UA-Columbia Cablevision, Oakland, N.J., 1977-79; dir. pub. relations Overlook Hosp., Summit, N.J., 1981-84; pres. Dorothy Bosted Pub. Relations, Harding Twp., N.J., 1984-86; dir. pub. relations, communications Middlesex County Coll., Edison, N.J., 1986-88; mgr. corp. communications Hoechst Celanese Corp., Bridgewater, N.J., 1988-89; ptnr. Bosted-Burton Assocs., Bridgewater, N.J., 1986—; cons. Bridgewater, 1986—. Co-author: Writing with Impact, 1986; contbr. articles to N.Y. Times, various mags. Seminar leader Kinnelon (N.J.) Enrichment Program, 1978; trustee Middlesex County Coll. Found., Edison, 1986-88; bd. dirs. Middlesex County Coll. Alumni Assn., 1986-88. Recipient News Program ACE award Nat. Cable TV Assn., 1979, Spectrum of Talent merit award Internat. Assn. Bus. Communicators, 1982, Percy award N.J. Hosp. Mktg. and Pub. Relations Assn., 1982, 84, Tribute to Women and Industry award YWCA, Ridgewood, N.J., 1979; Mennen Co. scholar, 1971, Neighborhood House scholar, 1971, KP scholar, 1971. Mem. Tribute to Women and Industry Mgmt. Forum (v.p. pub. rels. Ridgewood chpt. 1986-87, bd. dirs. cen. N.J. chpt 1989—), Pub. Rels. Soc. Am. (editor N.J. chpt. newsletter 1987-89, bd. dirs. N.J. chpt. 1989—). Republican. Methodist. Home: 732 Cedarbrook Rd Bridgewater NJ 08807

BOSTEK, EVA MARIA, veterinarian; b. Passaic, N.J., June 21, 1961; d. Charles and Stella (Stepien) B. BS with distinction, Cornell U., 1983; DVM summa cum laude, Ohio State U., 1987. Lic. N.J., N.Y., Mass., N.H., Vt. Veterinarian Anchor Animal Hosp., North Dartmouth, Mass., 1987-89, Madison (N.J.) Vet. Hosp., 1989—; consulting veterinarian The Seeing Eye, Inc., Morristown, N.J., 1989—, St. Hubert's Giralda, Madison, N.J., 1989—; vet. coll. tutor Ohio State U., Columbus, 1985; coll. teaching asst. Cornell U., Ithaca, N.Y., 1981-83. Team capt. Ohio State U. Fund Raising Campaign, Mass., 1989; fin. aid. com. grad. profl. coun., Columbus, 1983-85. Scholarship Am. Soc. of Animal Sci., 1983; named Presdl. Scholars finalist U.S. Office Edn., 1979. Mem. Am. Vet. Med. Assn., Am. Animal Hosp. Assn., Met. N.J. Vet. Med. Assn., Ohio State Vet. Medicine Alumni Assn., Cornell Agrl. and Life Scis. Alumni Assn., Cornell Clubs, Phi Kappa Phi, Phi Zeta, Omega Tau Sigma (class rep. 1983-86). Democrat. Roman Catholic. Home: 2467 Rte 10 E #7-6A Morris Plains NJ 07950 Office: Madison Vet Hosp 262 Main St Madison NJ 07940

BOSTIC, MARY LOUISE PRICE, sculptor, educator; b. Portales, N.Mex., Nov. 28, 1939; d. Kit M. and Alma G. (Hackley) Price; m. Doyle L. Bostic, Oct. 22, 1965 (div. 1989); children: John L., Kitty L. BS, Southeastern Okla. State U., 1966; MA, Fla. State U., 1969; PhD, East Tex. State U., 1981. Edn. minister 1st Bapt. Ch., Ardmore, Okla., 1962-65; tchr. art Ardmore Pub. Schs., 1965-66; instr., grad. asst. Fla. State U., Talahassee, 1966-67; from instr. to asst. prof. Southeastern Okla. State U., Durant, 1971-89; assoc. prof. Southeastern La. U., Hammond, 1989—; artist-in-residence State Arts coun. Okla., Oklahoma City, 1981-89. One-man shows include Southeastern Okla. State U., 1987, Guyman, Fairview, Fairland, Woodward, Seiling, Frederick, Putnam City, Ardmore, Ponca City, Hugo, Durant, 1981-88. Coord. Fun Country Arts Festival, Durant, Okla., 1984-86; bd. dirs. Renaissance Faire & Parade, Durant, 1987; grants evaluation com. Arts & Humanities coun. Okla., 1989. Mem. Nat. Art Edn. Assn., Internat. Tech. Edn. Assn., Kiwanis Internat. Baptist. Office: Southeastern La U PO Box 847SLU Hammond LA 70402

BOSTIC, STEPHANIE EVON, public relations executive; b. Jamaica, N.Y., Mar. 22, 1953; d. Joseph Edward and Maud Gertrude (Wilson) B.; 1 child, Charly Evon Simpson. BS in Pub. Communications, Boston U., 1975. Pub. relations asst. U.S. Tennis Assn., N.Y.C., 1975-77, asst. dir. pub. relations, 1977-80, pub. relations coordinator women's circuit, 1983-85; media relations mgr. ASME, 1985-86; pres. Bostic & Small Cons., Inc., 1985; editor, writer and pub. info. specialist Stone & Webster Engring. Corp., 1986-87, Doremus Porter Novelli, 1987-88, Bostic & Small Cons., Inc., Garden City. 1985—; editorial asst. U.S. Tennis Assn. Player Records, 1975, 76, stats. coordinator U.S. Tennis Assn. Tennis Yearbook, 1976, project editor U.S. Tennis Assn. Player Records, 1977, 78, 79, U.S. Open Tennis Championships Media Guides, 1976, 77, 78, 79; dir. pub. relations Women's Tennis Assn., 1980, D. Parke Gibson Assocs., Inc., N.Y.C., 1981-82; feature writer Queens Tribune, 1981; press-publicity coordinator Mercedes Tournament Champions, World Championship Tennis, 1984. Chmn. pub. relations com., gen. vol. com. 4th Ann. United Negro Coll. Fund/Arthur Ashe Tennis Benefit, 1978; pub. relations-publicity co-coordinator Forest Hills/Pro-Celebrity Tennis Tournament-Juvenile Diabetes Found., 1984; com. mem. Harlem Jr. Tennis Tournament, 1984. Mem. Nat. Assn. Media Women (dir. publicity Met. N.Y. chpt. 1979), Nat. Coalition 100 Black Women, Pub. Relations Soc. Am. (com. on minorities), Boston U. Sch. Pub. Relations Alumni Assn., (CEBA awards judge), Delta Sigma Theta. Home: 412 Old Country Rd Garden City NY 11530

BOSTON, LEONA, organization executive; b. Joliet, Ill., Aug. 4, 1914; d. Dorie Philip and Margaret (Mitchell) B. Student LaSalle Extension U., 1936-37, 1946, U. Chgo., 1944-45. Tchr., Nat. Stenotype Sch., Chgo., 1937; stenotypist Rotary Internat., Evanston, Ill., 1937-44, sec. to comptroller, 1944-50, head personnel dept., 1950-65, exec. asst. to gen. sec., 1965-77; mem. exec. com. North Shore Festival of Faith, Northfield, Ill., 1978. Bd. dirs. YWCA, Evanston, 1961-63. Mem. Bus. Profl. Women's Club Evanston (chmn. fin. com. 1977-78). Evangelical (fin. sec. Bible Ch., Winnetka 1965-68, treas. 1979-80). Club: Zonta (Evanston)(v.p., chmn. program com. 1969-70, pres. 1970-71, chmn. membership com. 1976-78, historian 1979-84, mem. past pres.' com. 1972—, mem. fin. com. 1985-89, chmn. fin. com. 1987-89, mem. club history and archives com. 1989—). Home and Office: 350 W Schaumburg Rd Schaumburg IL 60194 also: 2025 San Marcos Dr SE #34 Winter Haven FL 33880

BOSTON, MARTHA BIBEE, psychologist, educator; b. L.A., Sept. 16, 1948; d. Ernest Arnold Bibee and Elise (Fryling) Vincent; m. Daniel G. Coston, August 17, 1968 (div. 1982); 1 child, Seth Bibee; m. Christopher B. McKenney, Aug. 29, 1987; 1 child, Amy Jo. BS, Harding U., 1970; MS, U. Del., 1982, PhD, 1984. High sch. tchr. Indian River Sch. Dist., Georgetown, Del., 1970-79; rsch. asst. U. Del., Newark, Del., 1980-84; instr. U. Del., Newark, 1982-84; asst. prof. Allentown Coll., Center Valley, Pa., 1984-87, Newmann Coll., Aston, Pa., 1987—; Clinical internship in psychology, Allentown Coll., Counseling Ctr., Center Valley, Pa., 1984-87. Conbtr. several articles for profl. jours. 1985—. Adult edn. coord. St. Paul's United Meth. Ch., Wilmington, Del., 1988—, Grace United Meth. Ch., Georgetown, Del., 1974-79, bd. dir. Christian edn., 1975-79. Recipient Pres. Award for Dissertation, U. Del., Newark, 1984, Runner-up Woodrow Wilson Award for Dissertation, 1984. Mem. NOW (pres. Bucks County chpt. 1986-87), Am. Psych. Assn., Pa. Psych. Assn., Am. Psych. Soc., Jean Paiget Soc. Democrat. Home: 6 Hurst Rd Wilmington DE 19803 Office: Newmann Coll Convent Rd Aston PA 19014-1279

BOSWELL, WINTHROP PALMER, writer; b. Bklyn., Dec. 17, 1922; d. Carleton Humphries and Winthrop (Bushnell) Palmer; BA, Smith Coll., 1943; postgrad. U. S.C., 1956-58; MA, San Francisco State Coll., 1969; m. James Orr Boswell, Oct. 26, 1946; children: James Lowell, Rosalind Palmer, John Winthrop. Rsch. asst. G-2 Spl. Br., U.S. Army, 1943-46; rsch. asst. Hoover Instn., Stanford, Calif., 1976; docent Filoli, 1979-80; books include The Roots of Irish Monasticism, 1970; Irish Wizards in the Woods of Ethiopia, 1971; The Snake in the Grove, 1972; The Killing of the Snake King in Abyssinia, 1973; Hisperica Famina or The Garden of God, 1974; Bruce and the Question of Geomancy at Axum: The Evidence from the Norman Bayeux Tapestry, 1986. Mem. Soc. History of Discoveries, Peninsula Country Club (San Mateo, Calif.), Francisca Club (San Francisco).

BOSWORTH, MARY ANNSENETTA, nurse anesthetist; b. Lexington, S.C., Jan. 7, 1950; d. Odell and Agnes Willeeze (Warner) Kaminer; m. Terry Wayne Bosworth, Oct. 24, 1970 (div. 1977); 1 child, Darlene Annsenetta. AA in Nursing, U. S.C., 1970; cert. in anesthesia, Richland Meml. Hosp., 1978. Anesthetist Richland Meml. Hosp., Columbia, S.C., 1978-79, Midlands Anesthesia Assocs., West Columbia, S.C., 1979—. Mem. S.C. Assn. Nurse Anesthetists, Am. Assn. Nurse Anesthetists. Republican. Methodist. Home: 312 Willow Winds Dr Columbia SC 29210 Office: Midlands Anesthesia Assocs 160 Medical Circle Ste A West Columbia SC 29169

BOTHWELL, CHUNG THI NGUYEN, resource manager; b. Saigon, Vietnam, Nov. 19, 1949; came to U.S., 1969, naturalized, 1978; d. Tang Van and Nghi Thi (Tran) Nguyen; BBA, U. Miami (Fla.), 1974, MBA, 1980; m. Anthony Peirson Xavier Bothwell, Dec. 22, 1973; children: Anthony Peirson Xavier II, Thomas Theodore Nguyen. Budget analyst Fla. Power & Light Co., Miami, 1973-78; asst. to assoc. dean grad. program Sch. Nursing, U. Wis., Madison, 1978-79; mgr. budgets and costs Central Life Assurance Co., Madison, 1980-83; sr. budget analyst Lawrence Livermore Nat. Lab., Calif., 1983-84, prin. acct., 1984-85, asst. to ops. mgr., laser isotope separation program, 1985-86, asst. ops. mgr. free electron laser optical sci. and tech. program, 1986-87, resource mgr. laser advanced applications program, 1987—. Project chmn. Madison chpt. ARC, 1978-79; human services commr. City of Madison, 1982-83; mem. City of Livermore Social Concerns Com., 1984-85, chairperson, 1985-86; mem. Alameda County Human Relations Commn., 1985., sec., 1989—. Internat. student scholar, 1973. Mem. Nat. Assn. Accts. (bd. dirs., newsletter editor 1984-85, assoc. dir. hospitality 1985-86, dir. community responsibility 1986-87, pres. 1989—, S. Alden Pendleton award 1987, Pub. Rels. award 1988), Am. Acad. Mgmt., AAUW (corp. relations chairperson 1984-85, membership v.p. 1985-86). Republican. Roman Catholic. Home: 1320 Spring Valley Common Livermore CA 94550-6760 Office: Lawrence Livermore Nat Lab Box 5508/L-465 Livermore CA 94550

BOTHWELL, LINDA ANN, sales executive; b. Mpls., Sept. 22, 1954; d. Leon Robert and Royal Mae (Johnson) B. BA in Bus. Adminstrn., Winona State U., 1976. Sales rep. Del Monte, Mpls., 1976-78, Armour Pharm. Co., Rockford, Ill., 1978-80, Am. Druggist, Chgo., 1980-81, Patient Care, Chgo., 1981-82, Steven Herlitz, Inc., Chgo., 1982-83, Lebbar-Friedman, Chgo., 1983-85, McKnight Med. Communications, Chgo., 1985-86; nat. sales mgr. U.S. Pharmacist, Chgo., 1986—. Named Space Rep. of the Yr., McCann Healthcare Advt., Inc., 1987. Mem. Midwest Pharm. Advt. Council, Women in Health Care (v.p. 1982-83). Office: US Pharmacist 352 Park Ave S New York NY 10010

BOTKIN, NANCY GALLEY, nursing educator, volunteer, fundraiser; b. Dickerson Run, Pa., Nov. 14, 1935; d. Allen Quitman and Elsie Mae (Ware) Galley; m. Robert Filcer Botkin, June 19, 1976 (dec. Aug. 1982). Diploma, Allegheny Gen. Hosp. Sch. Nurs, 1958; BSN, Chatham Coll., 1958; flight nurse wings, Sch. Aerospace Med., 1962; MS in Nursing Edn., U. Pitts., 1966. Staff nurse Allegheny Gen. Hosp., Pitts., 1958-59, instr. sch. nursing, 1959-64, chmn. med.-surg. dept., 1966-67, coord. exec. phys. program, 1987-88, pres. bd. dirs., 1988—; assoc. prof. Community Coll. Allegheny County, Pitts., 1967-72; dir. nursing program Westmoreland County Community Coll., Youngwood, Pa., 1972-76; cons. spl. events Allegheny Health Systems, Inc., Pitts., 1985-86; mem. nursing adv. com. Community Coll. Allegheny County, 1979-82. Author: History of the Galley Family, 1968. Mem. Pitts. Symphony Assn., 1976—, Commonwealth bd. Med. Coll. Pa., 1988—; chmn. Centennial Ball Allegheny Gen. Hosp. Aux., 1984-85, pres. 1981-84. Mem. DAR, Pa. Assn. Hosp. Auxs. (rec. sec. s.w. dist. 1984-86), Allegheny County Med. Soc. Aux., Galley Family Assn. (v.p. 1975—), Twig and Blossom Garden Club, Sigma Theta Tau. Republican. Baptist. Home: 1505 W Ingomar Rd Pittsburgh PA 15237

BOTSFORD, SUSI, realtor; b. Las Vegas, Nev., Aug. 5, 1947; d. Peryl Dean and Jacqueline Jean (Ford) B.; m. James J. Blascovich, Sept. 5, 1970 (div. June 1979); 1 child, Elizabeth Marie. BA, U. Nev., 1969. Realtor Purtell & Wigdale, Milw., 1976-79, Coldwell Banker, Reno, 1980-90, Re/Max, Reno, 1990—; bd. dirs. Reno Realtors Credit Union, 1982-85. Vol. Crisis Call Ctr., Reno, 1982. Mem. Nat. Assn. Realtors, Reno-Sparks Assn. Realtors, U. Nev.-Reno Alumni Assn. (treas. 1990). Democrat. Home: 1238 Gilly Ln Sparks NV 89434 Office: Re/Max Realty Profls 15 Continental Dr Reno NV 89509

BOTT, E. JOYCE, accountant; b. Sewickley, Pa., Aug. 30, 1957; d. Marshall Joseph and Connie Joyce (Snyder) Bennett; m. Mark E. Bott, Aug. 25, 1979. BS, Clarion (Pa.) State Coll., 1979. Mgr. gen. acctg. Westinghouse Elec. Corp., Bettis Atomic Power Lab., West Mifflin, Pa. Mem. NAFE, Am. Mgmt. Assn. Home: 3010 Main St Munhall PA 15120

BOTT, EMILY O'NEIL, insurance company salesperson; b. N.Y.C., Apr. 2, 1922; d. Francis Edward and Mary Frances (Moore) O'Neil; m. Robert A. Bott, Aug. 11, 1952 (div. 1973); children: Brian D., Eric D., Kathleen A., Martha D., Daniel C., Aimee S., Sarah V. student, St. Mary's Coll., 1941; BS in English, St. Louis U., 1943, MA in Am. History, 1947. Traffic dir. KMVI Radio Sta., Wailuku, Hawaii, 1971-72; sales dept. head Liberty House, Kahului, Hawaii, 1972-74; special agt. Northwestern Mut. Life Ins. Co., Island Maui, Hawaii, 1974—. Vol. Maui Philharm. Soc., Wailuku, 1986—; vol. emergency rm. Maui Meml. Hosp.; d. dirs. Big Bros./Big Sisters, 1988—. Mem. Maui Assn. Life Underwriters. Roman Catholic.

BOTTERO, LAURA ANN, communications trainer, consultant; b. San Francisco, Jan. 19, 1961; d. Joel Louis Bottero and Joan Patricia (Walsh) Gallicano. BA in English, U. San Diego, 1983. Recruiting asst. Bain and Co., Palo Alto, Calif., 1984-85; profl. devel. coord. Bain and Co., San Francisco, 1985-86; coach, assoc. trainer Decker Communications, Inc., San Francisco, 1986-87, resource developer, 1988-89, trainer, speaker, cons., 1987-90; sr. trainer Decker Communications, Inc., Chgo., 1990—. Cons. to agy. vols. United Way, San Francisco, 1988, 89. Mem. Am. Bus. Women's Assn. (corr. sec. 1984-85), Nat. Soc. for Performance and Instrn. Democrat. Roman Catholic. Home: 2300 Lincoln Park W #310 Chicago IL 60614 Office: Decker Communications Inc 70 W Madison St Ste 1400 Chicago IL 60602

BOTTGE, PEGGY ANN, gas company administrator; b. Mount Kisco, N.Y., Sept. 7, 1956; d. Otto William and Anna Marie (Mazza) B. Service mgr. Suburban Propane Gas, Millerton, N.Y., 1981-82, office-service mgr., 1982-83, dist. mgr., 1983-86; dist. mgr. Suburban Propane Gas, Saratoga Springs, N.Y., 1986—. Mem. NAFE, N.Y. Gas Assn., Saratoga C. of C., Rotary. Republican. Baptist. Office: Suburban Propane Gas 610 Maple Ave PO Box 364 Saratoga Springs NY 12866

BOTTGER, TRACY ANN, amusement company executive; b. Keokuk, Iowa, May 26, 1956; d. Cecil Aubrey Bottger and Betty (Lehman) Maltby. Line assembler Motorola, Inc., Quincy, Ill., 1972-73; finish operator Shellor Globe, Inc., Keokuk, 1973-75; sec., route technician, v.p., collector Bottger Novelty Co., Keokuk, 1973-86; music program dir., collector, route technician Status Vending Corp., Las Vegas, 1986-87; v.p., sec., music program dir., route supr. Iowa Coin Ltd., Keokuk, 1987—. Contr. Nat. Land Enforcement Officers Meml. Fund, Harlan, Iowa, 1989, Sea Turtle Rescue Fund, Washington, Iowa, 1989. Mem. Pacemakers (sec. 1980-81, 3rd place Spring Run 1981). Republican. Roman Catholic. Home: 1120 Orleans Keokuk IA 52632 Office: Iowa Coin Ltd 1611 Blondeau Keokuk IA 52632

BOTTORFF, MICHELE LYNETTE STANFORD, historical museum director; b. Perrysburg, Ohio, Mar. 8, 1952; d. Frederick Warren and Geraldine Winona (Coolidge) Stanford; div.; children: Erin, Jonathan, Christopher. BS in Edn., Bowling Green State U., 1974. Dir. Wayne County Hist. Mus., Richmond, Ind., 1986—. Bd. dirs., Whitewater Opera Co., Richmond. Mem. Am. Assn. Museums, Am. Assn. State and Local History, Wayne County Arts Consortium (pres.), Kiwanis, Kappa Kappa Kappa (past pres.). Republican. Methodist. Office: Wayne County Hist Mus 1150 North A St Richmond IN 47374

BOTTS, ELLEN ALBERTA, human resources executive; b. Ada, Okla., Feb. 10, 1947; d. Chalmer Fredrick Barbee and Ima Ellen (Eberhardt) Ryel; children: Thomas E. Orr, Charles David Orr; m. Bill Raymond Botts, Aug. 27, 1982. Student, Parsons (Kans.) Jr. Coll., 1965-66, Wichita State U., 1977-80. Personnel clk. Kreonite, Inc., Wichita, Kans., 1976-77, personnel asst., 1977-80, personnel mgr., 1980-84; dir. human resources Fidelity Cos., Wichita, 1984-86, B&D Instruments, Valley Center, Kans., 1986—, Avionics, Inc., Valley Center, 1986—; mem. adv. bd. Wichita C. of C., 1983, United Tech. Inst., Wichita, 1988—. Mem. Civil Rights EEOC, Wichita, 1982. Mem. Am. Soc. Personnel Adminstrs., Nat. Assn. Suggestion Systems. Office: B&D Instruments & Avionics 209 W Main St Valley Center KS 67147

BOUCHER, ANNE CAREY, public relations consultant; b. Balt., Feb. 1, 1938; d. James III and Mary Lewis (Hall) Carey; m. William Boucher III, May 26, 1962. Student, Sarah Lawrence Coll., 1955-56, Md. Inst. Art, 1956-58. Asst. fashion stylist Hutzler Bros., Balt., 1956-57; mgr. Dorothy Lamour Cosmetics, Balt., 1960-61; pres. Jolie Maison Inc., Balt., 1963-66, Anne Boucher & Assocs., Balt., 1983-85, Boucher & Assocs., Balt., 1986—; ptnr. Boucher, Boucher & Yuhanick, Balt., 1988—; cons. communications RTKL Inc., Balt., 1966-67; advt. dir./owner Balt. Scene mag., 1980-83; sec./treas. Westfalls Devel. Corp., Balt., 1986-88. Bd. dirs. Med. Eye Bank Md. Inc., 1967-85, chmn. 1970-75; bd. dirs. Commerce and Industry Combined Health Appeal, 1968, Balt. Forward Trust Inc., 1972-74, Balt. Assn. for Visually Handicapped, 1976, Balt. chpt. ARC, 1983-89, S.T.E.P. Inc.; chmn. Md. Commn. on Status of Women, 1970-75; chmn./co-chmn. CARE Com. Greater Balt., 1975-84, hon. chmn., 1986—; treas. Friends of Govt. House, 1979-87; trustee Balt. Mus. Art, 1982-85; active other civic orgns. Named One of Outstanding Women Balt. County, AAUW, 1976; honoree Action for the Homeless, Inc., 1990, S.T.E.P. Inc. Mem. Delta Kappa Gamma (life hon.). Democrat. Home: 1900 Western Run Rd Cockeysville MD 21030 Office: Boucher & Assocs 15 Charles Pla Ste 300 Baltimore MD 21201

BOUCHER, CELESTE SUZETTE, human resources executive; b. Great Lakes, Ill., Mar. 23, 1956; d. Thomas Louis Sr. and Mary Helen (Marr) B. Cert. in Profl. Mgmt., Lake Forest Coll., 1988. Human resources asst. MCC Powers, Northbrook, Ill., 1980-82, supr. human resources adminstrn., 1982-84, mgr. human resources, 1984-86, mgr. dept. benefits and compensation, 1986-87; mgr. dept. benefits and compensation Dynascan Corp., Chgo., 1987-88, dir. human resources, 1988—. Mem. Am. Soc. for Personnel Adminstrn., Soc. Human Resources Profl., Am. Compensation Assn. (cert.), Midwest Personnel Mgmt. Assn., Nat. Assn. Female Execs. Republican. Roman Catholic. Office: Dynascan Corp 6460 W Cortland St Chicago IL 60635

BOUCHER, MILDRED EILEEN, state agency administrator; b. Chelsea, Mass., Dec. 8, 1928; d. William Brennan and Lillian Beatrice (Baggs) Hudson; m. Lawrence Clifford Boucher, Oct. 4, 1947 (dec. 1980); children: Katherine, Lawrence, Deborah, Jayne, Lyle, Constance. AA with honors, Indian River Community Coll., Fort Pierce, Fla., 1982, AS, 1983; BS in Applied Tech. magna cum laude, Fla. Inst. Tech., 1984. Tchr., head sci. dept. Peace Corps, Republic of Kiribati, 1984-85; environ. health specialist State of Fla., Port St. Lucie, 1989—; chmn. St. Lucie County Environ. Control. Hearing Bd., Fort Pierce, 1985-89. Editor: The Electrolyte, 1982. Active diabetic screening, Fort Pierce, Port St. Lucie, 1982, 83; mem. village coun. Rongorongo Maneaba, Beru Island, Republic of Kiribati, 1985. Mem. Am. Soc. Clin. Pathologists (registrant), Fla. Pub. Health Assn., Alpha Epsilon Soc. Republican. Methodist. Home: 1879 SE Vesthaven Ct Port Saint Lucie FL 34952 Office: HRS-Saint Lucie County Health Unit 9356 S US Hwy 1 Port Saint Lucie FL 34952

BOUCHER, MIRIAM CHERNY, professional society administrator; b. Boston, Mass., Sept. 12, 1954; d. Lester and Naomi (Orenberg) C.; m. Robert Cyrille, Oct. 13, 1979. Student, Brandeis U., Waltham, Mass., 1972, Exeter U., England, 1974; BA in English, NE. U., Boston, 1976; Post Grad., Study Harvard Extension, Cambridge, 1986. Sr. sec. Mass. Inst. Tech., Cambridge, 1978-83, adminstr. sec., 1983-84; adminstr. sec. Whitehead Inst. for Biomed., Cambridge, 1984-88, adminstr. asst. Chemn. vol. com., asst. regional coord., CPR instr. trainer, first aid instr. ARC Mass. Bay/Cambridge Region, 1978—. Recipient Numerous Cert. Appreciation from the Red Cross. Mem. Mass. Chap. Am. Soc. for Trainers and Devel. Jewish.

BOUCHER, ROBERTA MARY, social service director; b. New Haven, Oct. 12, 1951; d. George Thomas and Julia (Hughes) B. BS, Sacred Heart U., 1974; MS, U. New Haven, 1984; cert. bus. and personnel, St. Joseph's Coll., West Hartford, Conn., 1984. Work release counselor Conn. Dept. Corrections (Vista), Bridgeport, 1974-76; social investigator New Haven Dept. Welfare, 1976-81, social work supr., 1981-82, dep. dir., 1982-86; asst. dir. Norwalk (Conn.) Social Svcs., 1986-87, dir., 1987—; relocation officer City of Norwalk, 1986—. Mem. Norwalk Anti-Drug Task Force, 1986—, Norwalk Community Mental Health Com., 1987—; bd.d irs Norwalk Kiwanis Emergency Shelter, 1986—; bd. dirs. human svcs. dept. Norwalk Community Coll., 1989—. Recipient Commendation of Excellence, Mayor City of New Haven, 1981, 82, 83, 84. Mem. Conn. Assn. Local Gen. Assistance Adminstrs., Greater Norwalk Community Coun., Am. Pub. Welfare Assn., Conn. Housing Coalition, Conn. Assn. Human Svcs. Roman Catholic. Office: Norwalk Social Svcs 137 East Ave Norwalk CT 06851

BOUCHER, ROSEMARIE, retail business owner; b. Danbury, Conn., Sept. 5, 1940; d. Anthony J. and Mary T. (Caruso) Germinaro; m. Richard W. Boucher, Oct. 8, 1960 (div. Sept. 1983); children: Diana Lynn Boucher Callahan, Michael David. Student, Western Conn. State U., 1979. Office mgr. Household Fin. Corp., Danbury, 1958-64; interior decorator The Stone Co. Inc., Danbury, 1969-78, office mgr., 1978-81, corp. sec., 1981-85, part owner, mgr., 1985—. Exec. v.p. Downtown Coun., Danbury, 1984—; cert. counselor Rape Crisis Svc., Danbury, 1984-87; bd. dirs. Danbury Parking Authority, 1988—, chmn. bd. 1990—; chmn. bd. City Ctr. Tax Dist. Mktg. Commn., Danbury, 1989—; pres. Vol. Bur. Greater Danbury, 1990-91, Jr. Achievement, Danbury, 1990-91; sec.-treas. Taste of Danbury, 1987—. Recipient Outstanding Svc. award Jr. Achievement, 1987, 88, 89. Mem. Nat. Assn. Accts. (pres. Danbury 1984-85, Disting. Svc. cert. 1986), Nat. Decorating Products Assn. (cert. wallpaper cons.), Danbury Sch. and Bus. Collaborative. Republican. Roman Catholic. Office: The Stone Co Inc 11 Ives St Danbury CT 06810

BOUCK, NOËL PATRICK, genetics educator, researcher; b. San Francisco, Oct. 23, 1936; d. J. Howard and Vivian M. (Brennan) Patrick; m. G. Benjamin Bouck, Aug. 19, 1961; children: Julia, John, Laura. BA, Pomona Coll., 1958; MA, Columbia U., 1960, Harvard U., 1962; PhD, Yale U., 1969. Instr. U. Ill., Chgo., 1973-76; vis. prof. Salk Inst., La Jolla, Calif., 1977-78; asst. prof. microbiology-immunology Northwestern U., Chgo., 1979-85, assoc. prof., 1985—; bd. dirs. Leukemia Rsch. Found., Chgo, 1981-85; study sect. NIH, Washington, 1987-88; cons. Greenwald Found., N.Y.C., 1990. Contbr. rsch. papers to profl. jours. Pegram fellow Columbia U., 1961, Merrill fellow Radcliffe Inst., Cambridge, Mass., 1967-68. Mem. AAAS, Am. Assn. Cancer Rsch., Am. Soc. Microbiology, Tissue Culture Assn., Am. Soc. Cell Biology, Genetics Soc. Am., Sigma Xi. Office: Northwestern U Dept Microbiology/Immunol 303 E Chicago Ave Chicago IL 60611

BOUCKLEY, SANDRA LYNN, automobile company executive; b. Oshawa, Ont., Can., Apr. 17, 1959; came to U.S., 1985; d. Frederick Charles and Helen (Zochodne) B. BME, GM Inst., Flint, Mich., 1982, MS in Mfg. Mgmt., 1987. Registered profl. engr., Ont. Exptl. test engr. GM Can., Oshawa, 1982-83, power train design engr., 1983-85; mktg. svc. engr. C-P-C group GM, Warren, Mich., 1985-86, asst. engring. bus. mgr., 1986-87, engring. bus. mgr., 1987-89; advt. mfg. program mgr. Mfg. Tech. Ctr. Chrysler Motors, Detroit, 1989-90; ops. mgr. Dodge truck assy. Chrysler Motors, Warren, 1990—; assy. mgr. Jefferson North assy. plant Chrysler Motors, Detroit, 1990—. Mem. Jr. League Birmingham, Mich., 1987—. Mem. Soc. Automotive Engrs. (nat. women engrs. com. 1989—, nat. hwy. vehicle mfg. com. 1989—, nat. membership com. 1990—, editor Detroit Supercharger 1990—),Soc. Women Engrs. (v.p. Detroit 1989-90), Engring. Soc. Detroit. Home: 1834 Quincy Dr Rochester Hills MI 48306 Office: Chrysler Motors Jefferson North Assy Plant 2101 Conner Ave Detroit MI 48215

BOUCOUVALAS, MARCIE, adult learning educator; b. Boston, Mar. 22, 1947; d. Stellios Efstathios and Georgia (Foundas) B.; m. Nicholas Gregory Gianourakos, May 17, 1970; 1 child, Anastasia Starr Boucouvalas-Gianourakos. BS, Boston State Coll., 1968; MEd, Boston U., 1971; PhD, Fla. State U., 1980. Social worker Roxbury Neighborhood House, Boston, 1966; rsch. assoc. Postgrad. Med. Inst., Boston, 1968-71; program info. coord. Bd. Health Columbia, S.C., 1971-72; human resources devel. staff Dept. Corrections, Columbia, 1972-76; editor Career Edn. Ctr., Fla. State U., Tallahassee, 1978; tutor, cons. Adult Pub. Sch., Charlottesville, Va., 1978-79; freelance editor, Tallahassee, 1979-80; asst. prof. adult learning Va. Poly. Inst. and State U., No. Va. Grad. Ctr., Falls Church, 1980-86; assoc. prof. 1986— . Field editor Jour. Transpersonal Psychology, 1981—; author: Interface: Lifelong Learning and Community Education, 1979; Adult Education in Greece, 1988; contbr. articles to profl. jours. Counselor, trainer Contact-help, Columbia, S.C., 1972-76; rape educator YWCA, 1975-76; mem. Soc. for Rsch. in Adult Devel. Inst. for Noetic Scis. Recipient Golden Key award, 1986; Kellogg faculty devel. grantee, 1987; Fla. State U. fellow, 1977; Kellogg exchange prof., Eng., 1984. Mem. AAAS, Am. Assn. Adult and Continuing Edn. (head commn. on status of women 1977-78, head adult psychology 1980-83, 89-90, recipient Service awards 1978, 82, program chair Nat. Conf. Empowering the Adult Learner 1987), Commn. on Profs. Adult Edn. (co-chmn. task force on internat. adult edn. 1984—, exec. com. 1986-88), Va. Assn. Adult and Continuing Edn., Met. Washington Area Assn. Adult and Continuing Edn., Am. Soc. Tng. and Devel. (elected to nat. exec. rsch. bd. 1990—), Am. Psychol. Assn., Transpersonal Psychology Interest Group, Assn. Transpersonal Psychology (field editor jour.), World Future Soc., N.Y. Acad. Scis., Internat. Assocs. in Adult Edn. (program com. 1986-88, apptd. head of exec. com. 1990—), Psi Chi, Phi Delta Kappa (pres. 1989-90 Disting. Svc. award, rsch. rep. 1981-86). Greek Orthodox. Avocations: Music, dancing, ice skating. Office: Va Poly Inst and State U Grad Ctr 2990 Telestar Ct Falls Church VA 22042

BOUDREAU, NANCY ANNA, banker; b. Portola, Calif., Oct. 29, 1947; d. William Ellis and Hazel Harriett (Sanders) Bennett; m. James Louis Boudreau, 1966; children: Rene' Christine, Jamie Danielle. Student, U. Wis., River Falls, 1965, U. Wis., Stevens Point, 1965-67; BA, Winona State U., 1975. Instr. evening sch. Western Wis. Tech. Inst., La Crosse, 1972-75; youth placement specialist Job Svc. Wis., La Crosse, 1975-82; human resource officer First Bank La Crosse, 1982-83, asst. v.p. ops. and human resources, 1983-84, asst. v.p., 1984-86; v.p. ops. First Bank of Platteville (Wis.), 1986-87, exec. v.p., 1987-89, pres. banking and adminstrn., 1989—, also bd. dirs.; instr. Am. Inst. Bankers, Madison, Wis., 1985—; corp. sec. First Nat. Bank of Platteville, 1988—; bd. dirs. Platteville Area Indsl. Devel. Corp., treas., 1989—; bd. dirs. S.W. Wis. Tech. Coll. Found., 1989, Wis. Bankers Assn. Benefits and Ins.; pres., sec. First Shares, Inc., bd. dirs. Contbr. articles to profl. jours. Pres. YMCA, La Crosse, 1985; co-chmn. YM-YW Joint Exec. Com., La Crosse, 1985; div. chmn. United Way, La Crosse, 1980-86; bd. dirs. Luth. Hosp. Corp., La Crosse, 1986. Grantee Coop. Ednl. Svcs. Agy., 1974-75. Mem. Am. Soc. Pers. Adminstrs., Wis. Bankers Assn. (bd. dirs., treas. bank mktg. sect. 1988, vice-chmn. 1989, chmn. 1990), La Crosse Area Pers. Assn. (pres. elect 1986), Greater L Crosse C. of C., Platteville C. of C. (bd. dirs., pres. 1989), Bank Mktg. Assn. (adv. coun.). Republican. Methodist. Club: AVANT Women in Bus. Leadership (La Crosse). Lodges: Rotary (Platteville), Rotary Internat. Office: First Nat Bank of Platteville 170 W Main St Platteville WI 53818

BOUDREAUX, GLORIA MARIE, nurse, educator; b. Lafayette, La., May 2, 1935; d. Simon Zepherin and Orta Marie (Pierret) B. Diploma in nursing, Charity Hosp. Sch., 1962; BA, St. Edward's U., 1974; MS, Tex. Women's U., 1976. Head surg., med. nurse Lafayette (La.) Charity Hosp., 1962-65; psychiat. staff nurse VA Hosp., New Orleans, 1968-72; psychiatric nurse U.S. Army Nurse Corp., San Francisco and Augusta, Ga., 1966-67; instr. Tex. Woman's Univ. Sch. of Nursing, Houston, 1976-80; clin. specialist VA Med. Ctr., Houston, 1980-87; psychiatric nursing coordinator Spring Shadows Glen, Houston, 1987-88; instr. assoc. degree nursing program Houston Community Coll., 1988—; instr. assoc. degree nursing program Houston Community Coll., 1988—. Served to col. with U.S. Army, 1966—. Recipient Army Res. Component medal, 1972, Army Commendation medal, 1978. Mem. Reserve Officers Assn. (chpt. pres. 1981-83), Assn. Mil. Surgeons of U.S., Am. Nurses Assn. (cert. in psychiatric mental health nursing), Sigma Theta Tau. Home: 509 Brand Ln #104 Stafford TX 77477

BOUDRIA, CHERYLANNE, day care director; b. Limstone, Maine, Dec. 12, 1959; d. Albert and Lydia Anne (Silvia) Oliveira; m. David Timothy Boudria, June 9, 1984. BA in Humanities, Southeastern Mass. U., 1984. Cert. sec. educator, health asst., Mass. Field transcriber Bankers & Tradesman, Boston, 1978-84; sch. tchr. Swansea (Mass.) Pub. Schs., 1984-87; social day care dir. Swansea Coun. on Aging, 1987—; counselor Outreach, Fall River, Mass., 1988-90; tutor in field. Campaign promoter Bristol County Politics, Mass., 1978-80; fund raiser Swansea Coun. on Aging, 1989; writer weekly press releases Swansea Social Day Care, 1988-90. Recipient Award for Enriching the Lives of the Elderly Swansea, 1989. Home: 141 Angell St Fall River MA 02723

BOUER, JUDITH, executive search counselor; b. Jersey City, Oct. 15, 1942; d. Louis and Eleanor (Rosenfeld) B.; m. David Allen; children: Stephen, Louis. BS, U. Bridgeport, 1964; MS, Kean Coll., 1980. Placement counselor Baker Scott & Co., Parsippany, N.J., 1979—. Mem. Nat. Assn. Exec. Recruiters, Nat. Assn. Personnel Cons., Women in Cable, Nat. Cable TV Assn., Cable TV Adminstrn. and Mktg. Soc. Office: Baker Scott & Co 1259 Rte 46 Parsippany NJ 07054

BOUGHTON, LERONIA, manager; b. Bklyn., June 30, 1952; d. Leroy and Ruthie (Hill) Basnight; m. Rhenard Boughton, Sep. 21, 1985. BA, Hunter Coll., N.Y.C., 1982; MSc., Bklyn. Coll., 1984. Asst. prodn. mgr. Holt, Rinehart & Winston, N.Y.C., 1984-85; product control planner Ashland Electric Products, Blyn., 1985; pub. relations adminstr. Continental Airlines, Houston, 1986-87; supr. mktg. info. dept. NW Ayer (Advt. Co.), Houston, 1987-; pres. Bklyn. Coll. Graduate Students Assn., 1981-82. Treas. Devoe St. Baptist Ch., Bklyn. 1980-85. With U.S. Army Reserve. Democratic. Baptist. Home: 2331 Quail Place Dr Missouri City TX 77489

BOUGHTON, LORALEE GEORGIA, research assistant; b. Aberdeen, Wash., Feb. 10, 1963; d. Fred Warren and Shirley M. (Voelker) B. AAS, Paul Smith's Coll., 1983; BA, Widener U., 1985; postgrad., U. Nev. Las Vegas. Asst. exec. housekeeper Radisson Hotel, Wilmington, Del., 1985; asst. mgr. Days Inn, Albany, N.Y., 1985-87; asst. to the pres. Albany Conv. and Vis. Bur., 1987-88; sec. Atlas Copco Comptec, Voorheesville, N.Y., 1988-89; personal mgr. One Step Mgmt., Las Vegas, 1990—; tour guide USA Hosts, Las Vegas, 1989—; rsch. asst. U. Nev. Las Vegas Health Care Adminstrn., 1989—. Pub. affairs officer Civil Air Patrol, Albany, 1987-89. Democrat. Home: 4325 S Bruce #75 Las Vegas NV 89119

BOUHOUTSOS, JACQUELINE COTCHER, clinical psychologist, educator; b. Phila.; d. David Jacob and Bertha (Blagman) Cotcher; m. Dimitri C. Bouhoutsos, June 11, 1948 (dec. 1983); 1 child, Elene Bouhoutsos Brown. BA cum laude, UCLA, 1944; MSW, U. Calif., Berkeley, 1950; PhD with highest honors, U. Innsbruck, Austria, 1956. Lic. psychologist, lic. clin. social worker, Calif. Caseworker Alameda County Pub. Welfare, 1949-50, San Francisco City and County Pub. Welfare Dept., 1950-53; chief social work svcs. French and Am. zones of Austria, 1953-54; staff psychologist Toledo State Hosp., 1958-59, Toledo Mental Hygiene Clinic, 1959-60; dir. Calif. Family Guidance Ctr., 1964-67; dir. psychol. svcs. DePaulo Med. Group, 1974-77; pvt. practice clin. psychology Santa Monica, Calif., 1960—; mem. staff CPC Westwood Hosp., 1987—; mem. faculty Klinik Neurologie Psychiatrie, Innsbruck, 1954-56, Inst. Angewandte Psychologie Diagnostik, Innsbruck, 1954-55; asst. prof. Sch. Social Work UCLA, 1957-58, clin. prof. psychology, 1982—; adj. assoc. prof. community mental health, U. Wis., Green Bay, 1975-78; mem. faculty Calif. Sch. Profl. Psychology, 1974-81; cons. L.A. County Dept. Mental Health, 1968-74, Motion Picture Assn. Am., 1969-74, Jerry L. Pettis Meml. Vets. Hosp., 1979, Masi Rsch. Cons., Inc., Washington, 1985—, others. Author: Sexual Intimacy Between Therapists and Patients (with K. Pope), 1986; contbr. chpts. to books, articles to profl. publs.; cons. editor Profl. Psychology: Rsch. and Practice; editorial bd. Jour. of Imagination, Cognition and Personality; reviewer for Psychol. Abstracts, Am. Psychologist; guest TV and radio programs; producer documentary films. Chair Mental Health Info. Coord. Coun., 1968-69; mem. adv. com. Project Search, U. So. Calif., 1969-71, Allied Health Professions project, UCLA, 1969-71; chair acad. com. Modern Greek Studies Ctr., Loyola-Marymount U., 1979—; manpower adv. panel Calif. Dept. Mental Health, co-chair, 1980-85; mem. mental health adv. bd. County of Los Angeles, 1979-86; adv. bd. Psychologists for Social Responsibility, 1984—; chair Calif. State Senate Task Force on Sexual Involvement Therapists and Patients, 1986. Grantee John and Mary Markle Found., N.Y., 1981-82, 82-83, Ctr. Mental Health Initiatives, Washington, 1984, Simon Found., Beverly Hills, Calif., 1985, others; recipient Cine Golden Eagle award to TV documentary: A System in Shambles; recipient Outstanding Contbn. award City of L.A., Recognition award County of Los Angeles, others. Fellow Am. Psychol. Assn. (chair com. internat. rels. in psychology, 1986, Champus peer reviewer 1980-84, bd. dirs. 1986—); mem. Assn. for Media Psychology (exec. dir. 1986-88), Calif. State Psychol. Assn. (chair ethics com. 1986-88, exec. coun. 1986—, pres. 1981, mem., chair coms.), L.A. County Psychol. Assn. (pres. 1970), Psychol. Ctr. (bd. dirs. 1971-73, pres. 1973-74), Acad. Cert. Social Workers, AAAS, Am. Orthopsychiat. Assn. Office: 228 Santa Monica Blvd Ste 4 Santa Monica CA 90401

BOULANGER, DEBRA ANN, marketing and communications executive; b. Pawtucket, R.I., Oct. 9, 1956; d. Robert N. and Joyce P. (DeFontes) B.; m. Paul Thomas Miner, July 7, 1979 (div. Nov. 1984); m. Neal Marshall Goldsmith, Sept. 21, 1986. BS in Edn. and Clin. Psychology, Lesley Coll., 1978. Master tchr. Coop. Ednl. Services, Wilton, Conn., 1978-82; adminstrv. asst. N. Dean Meyer & Assocs., Ridgefield, Conn., 1983-84, mktg. mgr., 1984-86; account rep. Western region Gartner Group, Inc., Stamford, Conn., 1986-88, account exec. So. New England, 1987-89; mgr. mktg. & communications Gartner Group, Inc., 1989—. Home: 90 Hudson St #7E New York NY 10013 Office: Gartner Group Inc 56 Top Gallant Rd Stamford CT 06902

BOULANGER, MARY JANET, accountant; b. Martin, S.D., Sept. 7, 1950; d. James Mike and Claradel (Tellifero) Pich; m. Floyd Terkildsen, Mar., 1967 (div. 1969); 1 child, Larry Paul; m. Loren Lee Boulanger, Aug. 11, 1972; 1 child, Jon Christian. BS in Math., Natural Sci., U. Wyo., 1986. Dental asst. Jerome L. Behounek, DDS, Casper, 1973-74; teller Hilltop Nat. Bank, Casper, 1974-75; accts. maintenance clk. Soil Conservation Service, Casper, 1975-76; acctg. clk. U.S. Geol. Survey, Casper, 1976-79; acctg. technician U.S. Dept. Energy, Casper, 1979-85, staff acct., 1985-89, fin. mgr., 1989—; Dept. of Energy rep. Women's Exec. Leadership Program, 1988. Active vol. Big Bros./Big Sisters, Casper, 1977-78, Home Sch. Assn. Cresthill Elem. various programs, Casper, 1983-88, Casper Jr. Baseball league, 1986—, Casper Amateur Hockey Assn., 1986—; instr. Presidential Classroom for Young Ams., Alexandria, Va., 1987. Recipient Outstanding Performance award Naval Petroleum and Oil Shale Res., Washington, 1983, 84; named Outstanding Tech. Employee, Fed. Exec. Council, 1985, Female Civil Servant of the Yr., Fed. Exec. Council, 1986. Mem. Nat. Assn. Female Execs., Am. Legion Aux. (Martin). Republican. Baptist. Office: US Dept of Energy 800 Werner Ct Suite 342 Casper WY 82601

BOULDEN, JUDITH ANN, federal judge; b. Salt Lake City, Dec. 28, 1948; d. Douglas Lester and Emma Ruth (Robertson) Boulden; m. Alan Walter Barnes, Nov. 7, 1982; 1 child, Dorian Lisa. BA, U. Utah, 1971, JD, 1974. Bar: Utah 1974. Law clk. to A. Sherman Christianson U.S. Cts., Salt Lake City, 1974; assoc. Roe & Fowler, Salt Lake City, 1975-81, McKay Burton Thurman & Coudie, Salt Lake City, 1982-83; Chpt. 7 trustee U.S. Trustee, Salt Lake City, 1976-82, Standing Chpt. 12 trustee, 1987-88, Standing Chpt. 13 trustee, 1988-89; sr. ptnr. Boulden & Gillman, Salt Lake City, 1983-88; U.S. Bankruptcy judge U.S. Cts., Salt Lake City, 1988—. Mem. Utah Bar Assn.

BOULDING, ELISE MARIE, sociologist, educator; b. Oslo, Norway, July 6, 1920; came to U.S., 1923, naturalized, 1929; d. Joseph and Birgit (Johnsen) Biorn-Hansen; m. Kenneth Boulding; Aug. 31, 1941; children: John Russell, Mark David, Christine Ann, Philip Daniel, William Frederic. B.A., Douglass Coll., 1940; M.S., Iowa State Coll., 1949; Ph.D., U. Mich., 1969. Research asso. Survey Research Inst., U. Mich., 1957-58, Mental Health Research Inst., 1959-60; research devel. sec. Center for Research on Conflict Resolution, 1960-63; prof. sociology, project dir. Inst. Behavioral Sci., U. Colo., Boulder, 1967-78; Montgomery vis. prof. Dartmouth Coll., 1978-79, chmn. dept. sociology, 1979-85, prof. emerita, and sr. fellow Dickey Endowment, 1985—; sec. gen. Internat. Peace Rsch. Assoc., 1989-91; mem. program adv. council Human and Social Devel. Program, UN Univ., 1977-80; mem. governing council, 1980-86. Translator: Polak Image of the Future, 1961; author: From a Monastery Kitchen, 1976, (with Nuss, Carson and Greenstein) Handbook of International Data on Women, 1976, The Underside of History: A View of Women Through Time, 1976, Women in Twentieth Century World, 1977, (with Passmore and Gassler) Bibliography on World Conflict and Peace, 1979, (with Burgess and K. Boulding) Social System of Planet Earth, 1980, Children's Rights and the Wheel of Life, 1980, (with Moen, Lilleydahl and Palm) Women and the Social Costs of Economic Development, 1981, Building a Global Civic Culture: Education for an Interdependent World, 1988, One Small Plot of Heaven: Reflections of a Quaker Sociologist on Family Life, 1989. Internat. chairperson Womens Internat. League for Peace and Freedom, 1967-70; mem. Exploratory Project on Conditions for Peace, 1984—, chmn. bd. 1988-89; mem. U.S. Commn. for UNESCO, 1978-84, mem. UNESCO Peace Prize jury, 1980-87; chmn. bd. Boulder Community Parenting Ctr. Recipient Disting. Achievement award Douglass Coll., 1973, Ted Lentz Peace prize, 1977, Nat. Woman of Conscience award, 1980; Danforth fellow, 1965-67. Mem. AAAS, AAUP, Am. Sociol. Assn. (Jessie Bernard award 1982), Internat. Sociol. Assn., Internat. Peace Rsch. Assn. (newsletter editor 1983-87), World Future Studies Fedn., World Future Soc., Colo. Women's Forum. Quaker. Home: 624 Pearl St Apt 206 Boulder CO 80302

BOULTINGHOUSE, BEATE CAROLA, sales executive; b. Marburg, Hessia, Fed. Republic Germany, Nov. 26, 1949; came to U.S. 1952; d. George Woodward and Marlene Gertrude (Rettig) Ireton. BA, Glassboro (N.J.) State Coll., 1973. Office mgr./cons. Marshall Gerson DDS, Glassboro, 1971-80; sr. account mgr. Levi Strauss & Co., San Francisco, 1981—; grad. asst. Dale Carnegie courses, Syracuse, N.Y., 1988—. Mem. NAFE, Am. Mktg. Assn., Women in Sales, Mensa. Office: Levi Strauss & Co 8512 Sextant Dr Baldwinsville NY 13027-8905

BOULTON, SHAUNA DEE, educator; b. Salt Lake City, May 29, 1949; d. Melvin and Afton Lillie (Davidson) Boulton. BS, U. Utah, 1971, MEd, 1981, PhD in Edn. (hon.) World U., Benson, Ariz., 1986. Cert. elem., severely handicapped, spl. resource tchr., Utah. Tchr. Habilitation Ctr. for Multiple Handicapped, Salt Lake City, 1971-73, Hartvigsen Sch. for Multiple Handicapped, Salt Lake City, 1973-79, William Penn Elem. Sch., Salt Lake City, 1979-83, East Mill Creek Elem. Sch., 1983-88, Canyon Rim Elem. Sch., Salt Lake City, 1988—. Vol., Spl. Olympics. Mem. NEA, Utah Edn. Assn., Granite Edn. Assn., Nat. Mus. of Women in Arts and Greenpeace. Home: 1516 Glen Arbor St Salt Lake City UT 84105 Office: Canyon Rim Elem Sch 3005 S 2900 E Salt Lake City UT 84109

BOUNDAS, LOUISE GOOCH, editor; b. Yazoo City, Miss.; d. James Clifford and Anne (Butler) Gooch; m. George Basil Boundas, Sept. 29, 1966. BA, U. N.C., 1959; MS, Yeshiva U., N.Y.C., 1969. Mng. editor Electro-Tech. mag., N.Y.C., 1962-68, Pub. Affairs Com, N.Y.C., 1970-72; mng. editor Stereo Rev. mag., N.Y.C., 1972-86, editor in chief, 1987—; editorial dir. Car Stereo Rev., Sound and Image, Stereo Rev. Spl. Publs., N.Y.C., 1987—. Named to YWCA Acad. Women Achievers. Mem. Am. Soc. Mag. Editors, Overseas Press Club. Office: Stereo Rev 1633 Broadway New York NY 10019

BOUNDS, JULIA-ANNA GREEN, nurse anesthetist; b. Monroe, La., Dec. 15, 1946; d. James Legrande and Ruth Eddy (Brown) Green; divorced; 1 child, Courtney Elizabeth. BS in Nursing, La. State U., 1978; diploma in anesthesia, Charity Hosp. Sch., 1985. RN, La. Nurse Hotel Dieu Hosp., New Orleans, 1978-80, charge nurse, 1981-82; supr., nurse St. Charles Gen. Hosp., New Orleans, 1980; supr., charge nurse Delaronde Hosp., Chalmette, La., 1982-85; nurse anesthetist Orleans Anesthesia Assocs., New Orleans, 1985—. Bd. advisors Audubon Trace Condiminium Assn., Jefferson, La., 1986. Mem. Am. Assn. Nurse Anesthetists, La. Assn. Nurse Anesthetists (bd. dirs. 1987-88, sec. 1988-89, pres.-elect 1989-90, pres. 1990—). Democrat. Roman Catholic. Home: 2502 Aububon Trace Jefferson LA 70121

BOUNDS, MARY LOU, nurse; b. Queens, N.Y., May 30, 1949; d. William Boykin and Ruth Elizabeth (Manning) Williams; m. Eldon Bounds; children: Wendy, Timothy; stepchildren: Vicki, Rita. BSN, U. So. Miss., 1983. Med. asst. Dr. E.P. Reeves, Collins, Miss., 1968-79; med. sec. Dr. C.C. Tyler, Collins, 1968-79; subrural mail carrier U.S. Post Office, Seminary, Miss., 1979-90; RN Forrest Gen. Hosp., Hattiesburg, Miss., 1983-90, St. Luke's Episcopal Hosp., Houston, 1990—. Active PTA, Seminary, Miss., 1980-85. Mem. Am. Nursing Assn., Miss. Nursing Assn., Miss. Student Nursing Assn. (second v.p. 1981-82, first v.p. 1982-83, elected cons. 1983-84), Nat. Student Nurses Assn. (del. 1983), U.S. Rural Letter Carriers Assn., Athletic Booster Club (sec. 1983-85), Sigma Theta Tau. Democrat. Roman Catholic. Home: Rte 1 Box 133 Alvin TX 77511

BOUNDS, NANCY, modeling and talent company executive; b. Rodney, Ark.; d. William Thomas and Mary Jane (Fields) Southard; m. Robert S. Bounds, 1960 (div. 1965); 1 child, Ronnie Jean; m. Mark Curtis Sconce, Nov. 28, 1972. Student Northwestern U., 1950. Exec. dir. Internat. Fashion/Modeling Assn., N.Y.C., 1978; founding pres. Internat. Talent and Model Schs. Assn., N.Y.C., 1979-80; pres. Nancy Bounds Internat., Omaha, 1959—. Contbr. articles to profl. jours. Producer TV Heart Fund Auction, 1965; chairperson Douglas/Sarpy County Heart Assn., Omaha, 1966, 73-74. Recipient Nat. Tchr.'s award MiLady Pub. Co., 1965, Outstanding Service award Mayor of Omaha, 1984, Uta Halee Girls Village, 1983-87, March of Dimes service award, 1977, 84, Toys for Tots service award, 1986, Muscular Dystrophy citation of merit, 1982. Mem. Internat. Models and Talent Assn. Unitarian. Avocations: reading, painting, travel, golf, tournament bridge. Home and Office: 4803 Davenport Omaha NE 68132

BOUNDS, SARAH ETHELINE, historian; b. Huntsville, Ala., Nov. 5, 1942; d. Leo Deltis and Alice Etheline (Boone) Bounds; AB, Birmingham-So. Coll., 1963; MA, U. Ala., Tuscaloosa, 1965, Ed.S. in History, 1971, PhD, 1977. Tchr. social studies Huntsville City Schs., 1963, 65-66, 71-74; residence hall adv., dir. univ. housing U. Ala., Tuscaloosa, 1963-65, 68-71; instr. history N.E. State Jr. Coll., Rainsville, Ala., 1966-68; instr. history U. Ala., Huntsville, 1975, 78-80, 85—, dir. Weeden House Mus., 1981-83; asst. prof. edn., supr. student tchrs. U. North Ala., Florence, 1978. Mem. AAUW, Assn. Tchrs. Educators, Nat. Council Tchrs. Social Studies, NEA, Ala. Hist. Assn., Ala. Assn. Historians, Ala. Assn. Tchrs. Educators, Huntsville Hist. Soc., Historic Huntsville Found., Alpha Delta Kappa (state pres. Ala. 1990—), Kappa Delta Pi, Phi Alpha Theta. Methodist. Club: Huntsville Pilot (pres. 1990). Home: 1100 Bob Wallace Ave SE Huntsville AL 35801

BOURBEAU, NINA MARIE, insurance exective; b. Camplejeune, N.C., Sept. 2, 1957; d. David and Jane (Tardiff) B. Student, Scottsdale Community Coll., 1976-87. Typist United Way, Phoenix, 1976-77; various positions Sentry Ins., Scottsdale, Ariz., 1977-86; computer operator and typist Skanco Ins., Scottsdale, 1986-87; agy. asst. Scottsdale Ins. Co., 1987—. Author: Time-Out, 1979, Poetry Workshop, 1988. Mem. Earthwatch, 1984—, Smithsonian Inst., 1984—, Phoenix Zoo, 1988—, Scottsdale Ctr. for Arts., 1989—. Democrat. Office: Scottsdale Insurance Co 8370 Via De Ventura Scottsdale AZ 85258

BOURGAIZE, LINDA HARPER, school administrator; b. Tacoma, Wash., May 1, 1947; d. Donald William and Helen (Harper) Bourgaize; 1 child, Matthew Harris. BA, San Jose State U., 1971, MS, 1973. Psychologist Whisman Sch. Dist., Mountain View, Calif., 1972; psychologist, coordinator, dir. pupil personnel svcs. Mt. Pleasant Sch. Dist., San Jose, 1972-81; dir. San Benito/Santa Cruz Counties Spl. Edn. Local Plan Area, Aptos, Calif., 1981—; cons. State Dept. Edn., Sacramento, 1977—, Whisman Sch. Dist., 1987-88; pvt. practice psychology, Calif., 1975—. Chmn. steering com. Coalition for Adequate funding for Handicapped Children, Sacramento, 1987—; mem. self-estem task force County Bd. Suprs., Santa Cruz, Calif., 1989; chmn. La Selva Beach Recreation Dist., 1984-88. Mem. PEO, Assn. for Supervision and Curriculum Devel., Council for Exceptional Children, Calif. SELPA Adminstrs. (chmn. 1989—), Assn. Calif. Sch. Adminstrs., League Women Voters, Phi Delta Kappa. Democrat. Home: 27 Altivo Ave La Selva Beach CA 95076 Office: San Benito/Santa Cruz 9055 D Soquel Dr Aptos CA 95003

BOURGAULT, LISE, Canadian legislator; b. St. Pamphile, Que., Can., June 5, 1950. Student, U. Laval, École Nat. d'Adminstrn. Pub. Mem. Can. Ho. of Commons, 1984—. Contbr. articles to profl. publs. Mem. Homeowners Assn. Que. (dir. gen.), Assn. des Proprietaires de Logements Locatifs du Que. (founding pres.), Que. Bus. Men and Women's Assn., Montreal C. of C. Mem. Progressive Conservative Party. Address: 230 Mary St, Lachute, PQ Canada J8H 2C6*

BOURGEOIS, LOUISE, sculptor; b. Paris, Dec. 25, 1911; came to U.S., 1938, naturalized, 1953; d. Louis and Josephine (Fauriaux) B. Student, Sorbonne U., 1936-37; baccalaureate, Ecole des Beaux Arts, 1936-38; postgrad., Ecole du Louvre, 1936-38, Academie Julian, Ranson, Grande Chaumiere, Colarossi, Paul Colin, Friz, Leger, Vaclav Vytlacil; D.F.A. (hon.), Yale U., 1977, Calif. Coll. Arts and Crafts, 1988, Moore Coll. Art, Mass. Coll. Art. Docent Louvre, 1937-38; teaching asst. Atelier Yves Brayer, Grande Chaumiere, 1937-38; tchr. Great Neck (NY) Schs., program, 1960, Bklyn. Coll., 1963-68, Pratt Inst., 1965-67; Sch. Visual Arts, 1977. One-woman shows include Norlyst Gallery, 1947, Peridot Gallery, 1949, 50, 53, Allan Frumkin Gallery, Chgo., 1953, White Art Mus., Cornell U., Ithaca, N.Y., 1959, Stable Gallery, 1964, Rose Fried Gallery, 1964, 112 Greene St., N.Y.C., 1978, Xavier Fourcade Gallery, N.Y.C., 1978, Renaissance Soc., 1981, Mus. Modern Art, N.Y.C., 1982, Akron Art Mus., 1983, Contemporary Art Mus., Houston, 1983, Daniel Weinberg Gallery, Los Angeles, 1984, Robert Miller Gallery, 1984, Serpentine Gallery, London, 1985, Maeght-Lelong, Zurich, 1985, Paris, 1985, Taft Mus., Cin., 1987-89 (travelled to The Art Mus. at Fla. Internat. U., Miami, Fla., Laguna Gloria Art Mus., Austin, Tex., Gallery of Art, Washington U., St. Louis, Henry Art Gallery, Seattle, Everson Mus. Art, Syracuse, N.Y.), Mus. Overholland, Amsterdam, The Netherlands, 1988, Dia Art Found., Bridgehampton, N.Y., Frankfurter Kunstverein, Frankfurt, Fed. Republic Germany, 1989 (travelled to Städtische Galerie im Lenbachhaus, Fed. Republic Germany, 1990, Riverside Studios, London, 1990, Musée St. Pierre, Lyon, 1990, Fondacion Tapies, Barcelona, Spain, Kunstmuseum, Lucerne, Switzerland, Kröller-Müller Mus., Otterio, The Netherlands); exhibited in numerous group shows,

U.S., Europe, including 64th Whitney Biennial, 1987, Centre Georges Pompidou, Paris, Mus. Ludwig, Cologne, Fed. Republic Germany; represented in permanent collections Mus. Modern Art, N.Y.C., Whitney Mus., Met. Mus. Art, Hirshorn Mus., Musée Nat. D'Art Moderne, Paris, R.I. Sch. Design, NYU, Albright-Knox Art Gallery, Buffalo, Australian Nat. Gallery, Canberra, Kunstmuseum Luzern, Switzerland, Musée d'Art Moderne, Paris, Mus. Fine Arts, Houston, Storm King Art Ctr., Mountainville, N.Y., also pvt. collections; works reproduced in Contemporary Sculpture (Giedion Welker), 1955, Sculpture of This Century (Michel Seuphor), 1959, Form and Space (Trier), 1961, A Concise History of Modern Sculpture, (Herbert Read), 1964, Modern American Sculpture (Dore Ashton), 1968, History of Modern Art (H.H. Arnason), 1968, What is Modern Sculpture, 1969, Sculpture in Wood (J.C. Rich), 1970, numerous others, also various mags. Recipient Outstanding Achievement award Women's Caucus, 1980, Pres.'s Fellow award R.I. Sch. Design, 1984, Skowhegan medal for sculpture Skowhegan (Maine) Sch. Painting and Sculpture, Creatvie Arts Medal award for sculpture Brandeis U., 1989. Fellow Am. Acad. Arts and Scis.; mem. Am. Acad. and Inst. Arts and Letters, Sculptors Guild, Am. Abstract Artists, Coll. Art Assn. (Disting. Artist award for lifetime achievement 1989). Office: care Robert Miller Gallery 41 E 57th St New York NY 10022-1908

BOURGEOIS, PEGGY R., health care executive; b. Baton Rouge, Oct. 31, 1939; d. Samuel Edward and Ruth Mae (Franklin) Boudinot; m. Benjamin Frank Bourgeois Sr., Jan. 26, 1962; children: Benjamin Frank, Rebecca Ruth. BSN, Northwestern State U., Natchitoches, La., 1985; MN, La. State U., New Orleans, 1989. Cert. diabetes educator. Staff nurse/charge nurse, relief supr. Baton Rouge Gen. Med. Ctr., diabetes edn. coord. dept. edn., dir. diabetes Ctr.; cons. and researcher in field. Recipient Citation, Am. Diabetes Assn., Vol. of the Yr., 1987, recognition at program meeting Nat. Standards of Diabetes Patient Edn. progs., 1989, Citation for Svc. Rendered to Summer Camp Prog., 1986, Delores M. Scherle Entrepreneural award LSUMC, 1989, Legis. Internship in Nursing award AADE, 1990, Leadership in Nursing award Baton Rouge Dist. Nurses Assn., 1990. Mem. ANA, Am. Assn. Diabetes Educators, Am. Diabetes Assn., Juvenile Diabetes Found., Myasthenia Gravis Found. Episcopalian. Office: Diabetes Ctr Baton Rouge Gen Med Ctr Box 2511 Baton Rouge LA 70821

BOURNE, MARY BONNIE MURRAY (MRS. SAUL HAMILTON BOURNE), music publishing company executive; b. Salix, Iowa, Sept. 13, 1903; d. Thomas William and Kathryn (McDermott) Murray; student Morningside Normal Coll., 1922-23; student Am. Banking Inst., N.Y.C.; m. Saul Hamilton Bourne, Apr. 12, 1928; 1 dau., Mary Elizabeth. Appeared with George White Scandals, Ramblers, Cocoanuts, Ziegfield Follies, 1925-28; owner, mgr. Bourne Co., N.Y.C., 1960—. Mem. social work recruiting com. United Hosp. Fund. Trustee S.H. Bourne Found., Coll. New Rochelle; trustee N.Y. Infirmary, 1945—, chmn. social service youth bd., 1947—, bd. visitors Sch. Music, Catholic U. Am., Washington. Mem. A.S.C.A.P. (dir., pubs. adv. com.). Home: 14 E 75th St New York NY 10021 Office: 5 W 37th St New York NY 10016

BOUTELLE, JANE CRONIN, fitness consultant; b. Arlington, Mass., Nov. 3, 1926; s. William Francis and Sara (Gillis) Cronin; m. G. William Boutelle, 1953 (dec. 1973); children—Jeanne E., William R., James G. B.S., Boston U., 1948; M.A., Columbia U., 1953. Cert. tchr., Mass. Tchr. dance and health edn. Newton High Sch., Mass., 1948-51, Scarsdale High Sch., N.Y., 1951-55, Marymount Coll., Tarrytown, N.Y., 1955-58, Manhattanville Coll., Purchase, N.Y., 1958-59; pres., fitness cons. The Boutelle Method, Inc., Greenwich, Conn., 1973—. Author: Lifetime Fitness for Women, 1978. Contbr. articles to mags. Pres Westchester Dance Council, Westchester County, N.Y., 1956-57; mem. Nat. Alumni Bd. Boston U., 1981— (chmn. 40th reunion); mem. woman's com. Lighthouse, Westchester County, N.Y., 1983. Recipient Bravo award Greenwich YWCA, 1978. Mem. AAUW (chmn. edn. 1963-68), Soroptimists Internat. (chmn. scholarship com.) , Greenwich Woman's Club Gardeners (chmn. scholarship com.) Assn. Women in Phys. Edn. (chmn. 1954-55), Greenwich Assn. Pub. Schs. (chmn. 1968-73). Home: Huckleberry Ln Greenwich CT 06831 Office: The Boutelle Method Inc Huckleberry Ln Greenwich CT 06831

BOUTON, JANET LAURA, health facilities administrator; b. Pearl River, N.Y., Sept. 25, 1943; d. George Edward and Laura Grace (Hanna) B.; 1 child, Jessie McDade. BA, Tufts U., 1965; MS, London Sch. Econs., 1966; DSc, Johns Hopkins U., 1982. Rsch. asst. Boston U. Med. Sch., 1968-70, Harvard U. Med. Sch., Boston, 1970-71; grants mgr. Columbia Point Health Ctr., Boston, 1971-72; health plan analyst Kaiser Found. Health Plan, L.A., 1972-73; assoc. dir. Met. Atlanta Found. for Med. Care, 1973-74; staff asst. Inst. Medicine, Washington, 1977-78; sr. health planner Md. Health Planning Agy., Balt., 1978-79; dir. planning Good Samaritan Hosp., Balt., 1979-84, v.p. for planning and mktg., 1984—; sr. project cons. Policy Rsch., Inc., Balt., 1984; asst. prof. U. Balt., 1981; mem. Gov.'s Coun. Trauma Rehab., Balt., 1987-88. Active Leadership Assn., Balt., 1988—; v.p. planning Lupus Found. Am., Washington, 1988—; chmn. adv. bd. Peopls's Community Health Ctr., 1989—; bd. dirs. Md. Lupus Found., Balt., 1982-88, N.E. Community Orgn., Balt., 1978-82. Mem. Md. Hosp. Assn., Am. Pub. Health Assn. (pub. policy com., Md. food com.), Soc. for Hosp. Planning and Mktg., Md. Soc. for Hosp. Planning (v.p. 1982-83). Office: Good Samaritan Hosp 5601 Loch Raven Blvd Baltimore MD 21239

BOUTRIS, WENDY JOSEPH, banker; b. Phila., May 9, 1963; d. Barry Elliot and Linda Jane (Dorr) Joseph; m. Demetrios Aristides Boutris, May 29, 1988. AB, Harvard U., 1985; postgrad., UCLA. V.p. Hon. Fed. Bank, L.A., 1985—. Active in Big Sisters of L.A., 1988—. Mem. Mortgage Bankers Assn. Am., Calif. Mortgage Bankers Assn., So. Calif. Mortgage Bankers Assn., Harvard Club So. Calif. Democrat. Home: 3472 Oak Glen Dr Los Angeles CA 90068 Office: First Collateral Svcs 3575 Cahuenga Blvd W Ste 250 Los Angeles CA 90068

BOUZIANIS, MELISSA FARRAH, plastics engineer, consultant; b. Lawrence, Mass., Nov. 20, 1957; d. Albert Louis and Jeanne Viola (LeClerc) Farrah; m. James Dean Bouzianis, Oct. 18, 1987. BS in Biol. Scis., U. Lowell, 1979, MS in Plastics Engring., 1983. Tech. mktg. specialist Plastics div. Gen. Electric, Pittsfield, Mass., 1981-82, mgr. resins programs, 1982-84; computer and bus. equipment specialist Plastics div. Gen. Electric, Selkirk, N.Y., 1984-85; mgr. mktg. programs Plastics div. Gen. Electric, Pittsfield, Mass., 1985-86; mktg. mgr. ChemFab, Merrimack, N.H., 1986; sr. cons. Arthur D. Little, Inc., Cambridge, Mass., 1986-88; cons., pres. Bouzianis Consultants, Stratham, N.H., 1988—; adj. prof. U. Lowell, 1982-84. Editor: Structural Foam, 1984; contbr. articles to profl. jours. Tchr. St. Anthony's Ch., Lawrence, 1986; tutor Literacy Vols. Am., Exeter, N.H., 1988; math tutor Exeter High Sch., 1989. Mem. Soc. Plastics Engrs. (bd. dirs. Eastern Regional chpt.). Home: 9 Brookside Dr Stratham NH 03885

BOVARNICK, ELLEN, utility company executive; b. Boston, Jan. 2, 1954; d. Bennett and Evelyn (Singer) B. BSBA, Boston U., 1975, MBA, 1976. CPA, Mass., Fla., cert. internal auditor. Auditor U.S. Gen. Acctg. Office, Boston, 1976-81; internal auditor Fla. Power and Light Co., Miami, 1981-82; oper. analyst Fla. Power and Light Co., Juno Beach, 1982-84, sr. oper. analyst, 1984-85, sr. mgmt. analyst, 1985-87, supervising analyst, 1987—. Bd. dirs. Jewish Family and Children's Svc., West Palm Beach, Fla., 1984-85, v.p. bd. dirs. 1985—; mem. various coms. Jewish Fedn. Palm Beach County, 1983—. Mem. NAFE, AICPA, Am. Soc. of Women CPAs, Fla. Inst. of CPAs, Beta Gamma Sigma. Jewish. Home: 5204 Celery Ln Palm Beach Gardens FL 33418 Office: Florida Power & Light Co 700 Universe Blvd Juno Beach FL 33408

BOWDEN, ANN, bibliographer, educator; b. East Orange, N.J., Feb. 7, 1924; d. William and Anna Elisabeth (Herrstrom) Haddon; m. Edwin Turner Bowden, June 12, 1948; children: Elisabeth Bowden Ward, Susan Turner, Edwin Eric; m. 2d, William Burton Todd, Nov. 23, 1969. BA, Radcliffe Coll., 1948; MS in Library Services, Columbia U., 1951; PhD, U. Tex., 1975. Cataloger, reference asst. Yale U., 1948-53; manuscript cataloger, rare book librarian, librarian Humanities Research Ctr., librarian Acad. Ctr., U. Tex., Austin, 1958-63, lectr., sr. lectr. Grad. Sch. Library and Info. Sci., 1964-85, 88-89; coordinator adult services Austin Pub. Library, 1963-67, asst. dir., 1967-71, dep. dir., 1971-77, assoc. dir., 1977-86; bd. dirs. Tex. Info. Exchange, Houston, 1977-78; bd. dirs. AMIGOS Bibliog. Council, Dallas, 1978-82, chmn. bd., 1980-81, trustee emeritus, 1986—; chmn. AMIGOS '85 Plan, 1984-86; scholar in residence Rockefeller Found. Villa Serbelloni, Bellagio, Italy, 1986, Ransom Ctr. scholar U. Tex., Austin, 1990—; Zachariah Polson fellow Libr. Co. of Phila., 1990. Author (with W.B. Todd) Tauchnitz International Editions in English, 1988; editor: T.E. Lawrence Fifty Letters: 1921-1935, 1962; Maps and Atlases, 1978; assoc. editor Papers of the Bibliographical Soc. Am., 1967-82; contbr. articles to profl. jours. Served as cpl. USMC Women's Res., 1944-46. Mem. ALA (council 1975-79), Assn. Coll. and Research Libraries (chmn. rare book and manuscript sect. 1975-76), Tex. Library Assn. (chmn. publs. com. 1965-71), Bibliog. Soc. Am., Phi Kappa Phi, Kappa Tau Alpha. Club: Grolier (N.Y.C.).

BOWDEN, MAXINE, chef, minister; b. N.Y.C., Mar. 7, 1943; d. Philip and Frieda (Silverman) Aaron; m. Henry Earl Bowden, Aug. 22, 1983. BA, Bklyn. Coll., 1967, postgrad., 1967-69; student, Art Student's League, 1970. Tchr. Narcotic Addiction Control Commn., Staten Island, N.Y., 1967-70; writer, educator Appleton Century Crafts Pub., N.Y.C., 1970-74, Mind, Inc., N.Y.C.; chef, owner Cuisine by Maxine, N.Y.C., 1977-80; chef La Fogata Restaurant, N.Y.C., 1980-83, The Ballroom Restaurant, 1983-88, Citibank, N.Y.C.; owner Cuisine By Maxine, Queens, N.Y., 1990—; minister Hope Life, Inc.-Noah's Ark Ch., N.Y.C., 1980—. Mem. Coun. for Common Consciousness, N.Y.C., 1989—. Mem. NAFE. Republican. Home and Office: 9740 62d Dr Rego Park NY 11374

BOWEN, BARBARA, systems engineer; b. Bourne, Mass., Feb. 28, 1961; d. Joseph John and Lena (Carella) Bowen. BS, SUNY, Stony Brook, 1983; MS, Adelphi U., Garden City, N.Y., 1985. Lectr. SUNY, Stony Brook; assoc. and asst. sys. engr. Grumman Electronic Systems, Bohemia, N.Y.; systems engr. Grumman Electronic Systems. NAFE. Home: 64 Tracy Ln East Islip NY 11730

BOWEN, BARBARA LYNN, computer company executive; b. Toledo, May 19, 1945; d. John Thomas and Grace Elizabeth (Spaulding) B. AB, Oberlin Coll., 1967; M.S., So. Conn. U., 1968; PhD, Cornell U., 1972. Asst. prof. Queens Coll., Flushing, N.Y., 1979-81; mgr. mktg. support-tng. Logo Computer Systems, Inc., N.Y.C., 1981-83; dir. Apple Edn. Found., Apple Computer, Inc., Cupertino, Calif., 1983-84; program dir. edn. affairs Apple Computer, Inc., Cupertino, 1984-86, mgr. external rsch., 1986—; mem. Nat. Task Force on Ednl. Tech., 1984-86; bd. advisers N.E. Regional Exch. Teleconf. Project, Bolton, N.H., 1984-85, Nat. Ctr. on Computer Equity, N.Y.C., 1985-88. Author: Apple Logo Training Manual, 1983. Mem. editorial bd. Nat. Rural Spl. Edn. quar., 1986-88, Edn. & Computing Jour., 1988—. Bd. dirs. Ctr. for Econ. Conversion, Mountain View, Calif., 1985, 86, pres. bd. dirs., 1986. Mem. Am. Ednl. Rsch. Assn., Bus. Execs. for Nat. Security, Computer Profls. Social Responsibility, Leadership Am. Home: 749 Ramona Ave Sunnyvale CA 94087 Office: Apple Computer Inc 20525 Mariani Ave #76-3C Cupertino CA 95014

BOWEN, CHRISTINE LYN, computerized healthcare billing company executive; b. Troy, N.Y., July 23, 1952; d. Joseph William and Evelyn Ann (Webster) Sneden; m. Alan Leslie Deyo, May 20, 1974 (div. Dec. 1977); 1 child, Jason Alan Deyo; m. Robert Charles Bowen, Sept. 12, 1981. B in Applied Social Sci., SUNY-Binghamton, 1979. Office mgr. Maine Med. Group, N.Y., 1977-78; med. edn. coord. Binghamton Gen. Hosp., 1978-82; systems op. mgr. Med. Office Systems of So. Tier, Inc., Binghamton, 1983-85, chief oper. officer, systems ops. mgr., med. edn. coord., med. office mgr., 1985—; account rep. 3M Health Info. Systems, Binghamton; past owner, operator tanning co.; owner, pres. CSB Assocs., 1986-88; cons. N.Y. and Pa. Editor Erudition Digest newsletter, 1982. Mentor B-R-I-D-G-E, Binghamton, 1981-84; active Port Dickinson Community Assn., Binghamton, 1984—; co-chairperson disaster svc., bd. dirs. Broome County chpt. ARC, 1984—. 1st lt. U.S. Army, 1970-73. Mem. Women's Network, MOSST User Group (bd. dirs. 1983—), Altrusa (local treas. 1982-83). Democrat. Avocations: cross-country skiing, antique hunting, camping, swimming, golfing. Home and Office: MR 90 Krager Rd Binghamton NY 13904

BOWEN, DEBRA JEAN, computer programmer, systems analyst; b. Laurinburg, N.C., Sept. 12, 1955; d. George Taylor and Betty Jean (Hart) B. Student, Coll. of Charleston, 1975-79, Trident Tech. Coll., 1984-86. Computer operator Charleston Meml. Hosp., 1986, computer programmer, 1986-87, programmer, analyst, 1987—; cons. in field. Mem. System 3/X Users Group. Methodist. Office: Charleston Meml Hosp 326 Calhoun St Charleston SC 29401

BOWEN, JOAN MARTIN, education council president; b. San Francisco, Feb. 13, 1939; d. Charles Martin and Janet Martinl m. Arden R. Bowen; children: Mark, Robin, Scott, Julie Weigand. BS, U. Calif., Berkeley, 1961; MS, U. Calif., 1978; PhD, U. San Francisco, 1981. Tchr. K-12 various sch. dists., various locations, 1961-80; pres. Nat. Info Resource Cons., Hayward, Calif., 1984-87; mgr. Pacific Tel. & Tel., San Francisco, 1981-85, AT&T, San Francisco, 1985-89; pres. Industry Edn. Coun. of Calif., Pleasanton, 1989—; lectr. in field. Chmn. Bay Area Corp. Edn. Roundtable, 1988—; chmn. budget Salvation Army Adv. Coun., 1984—; mem. Bay Area Coun., San Francisco, 1988-89; active Easter Seal Soc. Alameda County; bd. dirs. Pacific Grad. Sch. Psychology. Mem. AAUW, Calif. Tchrs. Assn. (pres. 1979), Nat. Assn. Industry Edn., Prytanean Honor Soc., Phi Delta Kappa. Home: 17257 San Franciscan Dr Castro Valley CA 94552 Office: Industry Edn Council Calif 6000 Stoneridge Mall Rd Pleasanton CA 94588

BOWEN, KELLEY BAILEY, artist, gallery director; b. Houston, Mar. 17, 1962; d. Myron Edgar Bailey and Georgia Numsen (Reynolds) White; m. Robert Ted Bowen, Dec. 3, 1982. Student, Columbia Sch. Broadcasting, Houston, 1982-83, Glassell Sch. Art, Houston, 1986, Southwest Tex. State U., 1986-88, The Womens Inst., Houston, 1989, U. Houston, 1989-90, U. St. Thomas, 1990—. Lic. Fed. Communications Commn. Broadcasting. Owner Bowen Interior Accessory Design, New Braunfels, Tex., 1985-86; asst. to the dir. AIR Gallery, Austin, Tex., 1988; dir. Heartworks Co. Paper Bear Gallery, San Marcos, Tex., 1988; dir. Hays County Art Exhibition, Joey Waldon Live With His Art, The Macabre Show Exhibition, Altered Spatial Patterns Exhibition, San Marcos, 1988. Exhibiting artist, paintings, Gotham Fine Arts, 1989, Emerging Artists Show, Notes from the Underground, The Green Parrot, 1988, Eleganza, Houston, Texas, 1990. Juror Youth Fair Art Exhibition, asst. Nat. Arts Week Republic Plaza Exhibition, Austin, Tex., 1988, com. mem. Sights and Sounds of Christmas Festival, San Marcos, Tex., 1987, 1988, pres., 1988, social chmn., Student Art Forum, Southwest Tex. State U., 1987; mem. Jr. League of Houston, Inc., 1990—. Presbyterian. Home and Office: 1839 Lexington Houston TX 77098

BOWEN, MARCIA KAY, customs house broker; b. Bradford, Pa., July 20, 1957; d. George W. Allen Jr. and Katherine (Jema) Allen; m. Glenn Edward Rollins, June 26, 1975 (div. 1979); m. Michael James Bowen, Dec. 27, 1983; children: James Derek, Kodie Ann. Student Houston Community Coll., 1978-81; student Am. Mgmt. Assn., 1984-85. Lic. customs house broker. Asst. mgr. W.R. Zanes & Co. of La., Inc., Houston, 1975-76; sec. Westchester Corp., Houston, 1973-75; import br. mgr. Schenkers Internat., Inc., Houston, 1976-85; br. mgr. F.W. Myers & Co., Inc., El Paso, 1985-88, regional mgr., 1989—. Mem. Houston Customs House Brokers Assn. (sec. 1977-79, mem. U.S. customs com. 1979-83), El Paso Customs House Brokers Assn., Houston Freight Forwarders Assn., El Paso Fgn. Trade Zone Assn., Nat. Assn. Female Execs., Soc. Global Trade Execs., El Paso/Juarez Transp. and Distbn. Assn., Inc. Roman Catholic. Office: FW Myers & Co Inc 9801 Carnegie St El Paso TX 79925

BOWEN, NANCY LYNN, electrical engineer; b. Las Vegas, Nev., July 15, 1955; d. Edward Robert and Shirley Jean (Krug) Johnston; m. Bruce Keefe Bowen, June 3, 1978. BS magna cum laude, U. Mo., 1977; MS in Elec. Engring., MIT, 1979. Design engr. Analog Devices, Inc., Wilmington, Mass., 1979-82, Palo Alto, Calif., 1983-84; sr. design engr. Advanced Micro Devices, Sunnyvale, Calif., 1982-83; staff design engr. Micro Linear Co, San Jose, Calif., 1984-88; sr. design engr. Silicon Systems, Inc., San Jose, Calif., 1988—. Contbg. mem. Sempervirens Fund, Los Altos, Calif., 1986-88. Mem. Ice Skating Inst. Am., Underwater Photography soc., Sierra Club (life mem.). Democrat. Home: 1484 Chukar Ct Sunnyvale CA 94087 Office: Silicon Systems Inc 1641 N First St Ste 275 San Jose CA 95112

BOWER, CINDY LOU, property management and resort hotel company executive; b. Scottsbluff, Nebr., Apr. 6, 1957; d. Raymond Eugene and Kathleen Coila (Roberts) B. B.S. in Psychology, U. Wyo., 1980. Profl. basketball player Washington Metros, 1979; asst. to mng. dir. Western Services Corp., Silver Springs, Md., 1980-82; v.p., gen. mgr. Key Resort Mgmt., Crested Butte, Colo., 1982—. Mnr. Crested Butte Soccer Team, 1982—; capt. Crested Butte Softball, 1982—; mem. Crested Butte/Mount Crested Butte Adv. Bd., 1983—. Named to Women's Collegiate All-Am. Basketball Team, region VII Nat. Scouting Assn. and Women Pro Basketball League, 1979. Mem. Nat. Assn. Female Execs., Denver/Colo. Conv. Bur., Colo. Soc. Assn. Execs., Am. Hotel/Motel Assn., Colo./Wyo. Hotel/Motel Assn., Crested Butte/Mount Crested Butte C. of C., Gunnison County C. of C., Crested Butte Bus. and Profl. Women's Club (v.p.). Republican. Lutheran. Home: 712 Seagull Ave Altamonte Springs FL 32701 Office: Key Resort Mgmt 21 Emmons Rd Mount Crested Butte CO 81225

BOWER, FAY LOUISE, nurse; b. San Francisco, Sept. 10, 1929; d. James Joseph and Emily Clare (Andrews) Saitta; BS with honors, San Jose State Coll., 1965; MSN, U. Calif., 1966, DNSc, 1978; children: R. David, Carol Bower Tomei, Dennis James, Thomas John. Office nurse Dr. William Grannis, Palo Alto, Calif., 1950-55; staff nurse Stanford Hosp., 1964-72; asst. prof. San Jose State U., 1966-70, asso. prof., 1970-74, prof., 1974-82, coord. grad. program in nursing, 1977-78, chairperson dept. nursing, 1978-82; dean U. San Francisco, 1982-89, v.p. acad. affairs, 1988-89, dir. univ. planning, 1989—, speaker; cons. univs.; vis. prof. Harding Coll., 1977, U. Miss., 1976; lectr. U. Calif., San Francisco, 1975. Cert. pub. health nurse, sch. nurse, Calif. Fellow Am. Acad. Nursing; mem. Calif. Nurses Assn., Nurses Assn. Coll. Ob-Gyn, Calif. Tchrs. Assn., AAUP, Pub. Health Assn. Calif., Nat. League Nursing (bd. dirs.), Calif. League for Nursing (pres.), Western Gerontol. Assn., Sigma Theta Tau (pres. Beta Gamma chpt.), Jesuit Deans in Nursing (chair). Democrat. Roman Catholic. Club: Commonwealth (San Francisco). Author: (with Em O. Bevis) Fundamentals of Nursing Practice: Concepts, Roles and Functions, 1978; (with Margaret Jacobson) Community Health Nursing, 1978; The Process of Planning Nursing Care, 3d edit., 1982; Theoretical Foundations of Nursing I, II, and III, 1972; editor: Normal Development of Body Image, 1977; Distortions in Body Image in Illness and Disability, 1977; Foundations of Pharmacologic Therapy, 1977; Nursing Assessment, 1977. Home: 1820 Portola Rd Woodside CA 94062 Office: U San Francisco Sch Nursing San Francisco CA

BOWER, JEAN RAMSAY, court administrator, lawyer; b. N.Y.C., Nov. 25, 1935; d. Claude Barnett and Myrtle Marie (Scott) Ramsay; m. Ward Swift Just, Jan. 31, 1957 (div. 1966); children: Jennifer Ramsay, Julia Barnett; m. Robert Turrell Bower, June 12, 1971. A.B., Vassar Coll., 1957; J.D., Georgetown U., 1970. Bar: D.C. 1970. Exec. dir. D.C. Dem. Cen. Com., Washington, 1969-71; pvt. practice, Washington, 1971-78; dir. Counsel for Child Abuse and Neglect Office, D.C. Superior Ct., 1978—; mem. mgmt. bd. Child Advocacy Ctr., 1980-87. Mem. Mayor's Com. on Child Abuse and Neglect, 1973—, vice chmn., 1975-79; mem. Family Div. Rules Adv. Com., 1977—; pres., bd. dirs. C.B. Ramsay Found., 1984—. Mem. mgmt. bd. Child Advocacy Ctr., 1980-87. Named Washingtonian of the Yr. Washing. Mag., 1978. Mem. Women's Bar Assn. (found. 1986—, Woman Lawyer of Yr. 1986), D.C. Bar Assn., Women's Bar Assn. Found (bd. dirs. 1986). Office: DC Superior Ct Rm 4235 500 Indiana Ave NW Washington DC 20007

BOWER, KATHLEEN ANN, communications executive; b. Stanford, Calif., Feb. 10, 1962; d. E. George and Joan Martine (Sorensen) B. BS in Bus. Adminstrn. and Mktg., San Jose State U., 1984. Editorial specialist Regis McKenna, Inc., Palo Alto, Calif., 1980-82; market researcher Dudley-Anderson-Yutzy Pub. Rels., Los Altos, Calif., 1982-84; dir. mktg. InterSight Communications, Inc., Los Gatos, Calif., 1985; account exec. Rudolph Design, Inc., Santa Cruz, Calif., 1986; promotional programs mgr. 3Com Corp., Santa Clara, Calif., 1986-88; advt., promotions and creative svcs. mgr. Software Pub. Corp., Mountain View, Calif., 1988—. Columnist, editor newsletters; co-founder, Connect-Jour. of Computer Networking, 1987. Mem. Am. Mktg. Assn., Am. Mgmt. Assn., Peninsula Women in Advt., Pub. Rels. Soc. Am., San Jose Film Commn., San Francisco Film and Video Commn., Profl. Media Network (bd. dirs. 1985-86), Beta Gamma Sigma. Home: 509 26th Ave Santa Cruz CA 95062 Office: Software Pub Corp 1901 Landings Dr Mountain View CA 94309

BOWER, R. JANET, retired college educator; b. Pitts., Mar. 13; d. Alvin Lionel and Rose Clementine (Saller) B. BA, Waynesburg (Pa.) Coll., 1941; MA, U. Chgo., 1950, PhD, 1953. Head psychology dept. Centenary Coll. for Women, Hackettstown, N.J., 1955-58; rsch. dir. for study on aging Cath. Charities, Washington and Milw., 1958-59; rsch. assoc. Bank St. Coll. Edn., N.Y.C., 1959-61; assoc. prof. psychology and edn. Jersey City State Coll., 1961-68, prof. psychology and edn., 1968-83, prof. emeritus, 1986—; vis. assoc. prof. edn. U. So. Calif., L.A., 1966-67. Home: 35 Robert Gardens #7 Queensbury NY 12804

BOWER, SANDRA IRWIN, communications executive; b. Cin., Oct. 4, 1946; d. Max Tooley and Sara Ruth (Long) Irwin; m. Jack Lee Bower, June 13, 1965; children: Carrie Lyn, Chad Quentin. Grad., Ind. U., 1989. With dept. pub. relations Eli Lilly and Co., Indpls., 1969—, head creative svcs., 1989—. Mem. Women in Communications, Internat. Assn. Bus. Communicators. Office: Eli Lilly and Co Lilly Corp Ctr Indianapolis IN 46285

BOWERMAN, COLENE LYNETTE WATKINS, physician assistant; b. Council Bluffs, Iowa, Nov. 5, 1963; d. Robert Paul and Linda Joann (Morrow) Watkins; m. Richard Michael Bowerman, Sept. 24, 1988. BS, U. Nebr., 1988. Physician asst. State of Nebr., Lincoln, 1988-89, Hastings (Nebr.) Family Practice, PC, 1989—, Hastings Family Planning, 1989—. Tutor Hastings Literacy Program, 1989—; merit badge counselor Boy Scouts Am., Hastings, 1989—; human and legal rights com. Mid Nebr. Mental Retardation Svcs., Hastings, 1989—; treas. Loran Schmitt Soc., Omaha, 1986-87. Fellow Nebr. Acad. Physician Assts.; mem. Nat. Commn. Cert. Physician Assts., Am. Acad. Physician Assts., NAFE, Soroptimists Internat., Alpha Phi Omega (U. Iowa Omicron chpt., life mem., v.p. 1985). Lutheran. Home: 2020 N 2d Ave Hastings NE 68901 Office: Hastings Family Practice PC 606 N Minnesota Ave Hastings NE 68901

BOWERS, BARBARA A., educator; b. Morristown, N.J., Aug. 14, 1938; d. Bertha (Opitz) Dambeck; m. George V. Bowers, June 7, 1958; children: Thomas, Margaret, Deborah, RoseMarie, Lisa, Robert. BS, U. Ala., 1960; MA, U. South Fla., 1974; EdS, Fla. State U., 1988, EdD, 1989. cert. tchr. Fla. Tchr. Choctawatchee High Sch., Shalimar, Fla., 1960-62, Okaloosa-Walton Jr. Coll., Valparaiso, Fla., 1965-68, St. Mary's Parochial Sch., Fort Walton Beach, Fla., 1970; tchr., dept. chmn. Ft. Walton Beach High Sch., Ft. Walton Beach, 1970—; instr. Okaloosa-Walton Community Coll., Niceville, Fla., 1982—; com. mem. Fla. Bus. Edn. Instructional Materials Coun., Tallahassee, 1985-87, Fla. Task Force for Writing Test Bank Items, 1987-90. Organist St. Mary's Cath. Ch., Ft. Walton Beach, Fla., 1975-89, Corpus Christi Catholic Ch., Destin, Fla., 1989—; mem. St. Mary's Parish Coun., Ft. Walton Beach, Fla., 1989-91. Named Tchr. of Year Ft. Walton Beach (Fla.) High Sch., 1974, Region 1 Adviser ofYear Fla. FBLA, Tallahassee, 1974; cited for Outstanding Contribution to Bus. Edn., State of Fla., Tallahassee, 1975-77. Mem. Am. Vocat. Assn., Fla. Vocat. Assn., Okaloosa Vocat. Assn., Nat. Bus. Edn. Assn., Southern Bus. Edn. Assn., Fla. Bus. Edn. Assn. (chmn. county membership com. 1979—), Assn. for Supervision and Curriculum Devel., Delta Pi Epsilon (sec. 1990-92). Roman Catholic. Home: 145 Linstew Dr NW Fort Walton Beach FL 32548 Office: Fort Walton Beach High Sch 400 Hollywood Blvd Fort Walton Beach FL 32548

BOWERS, ELOISE B., civic worker; b. Meredith, N.Y., Jan. 1, 1912; D. Charles and Elizabeth (McDonnell) Bechtel; m. Paul A. Bowers, Apr. 1, 1945; children: Paul A. Jr., Peter Clark, Patricia Eloise. RN, Yonkers (N.Y.) Gen. Hosp. Sch. of Nursing, 1932. bd. dir. health careers program Pa. Health Coun., Camp Hill, 1963-70. Contbr. articles to profl. jours. Historian women's bd. Thomas Jefferson U., Phila. 1984, pres. 1981-84; trustee Thomas Jefferson U., 1981-84; v.p. Women's Aux. Phila. County Med. Soc., 1958, pres., 1960. 1st lt. U.S. Army, 1941-45. Mem. Friends of Independence Victorian Soc., Pa. Hist. Soc., Phila. Orch. Assn., Am. Legion, Acorn Club (Phila.). Republican.

BOWERS, JANE ANN, food scientist; b. Fredonia, Kans., Aug. 19, 1940; d. Clarence Edward and Bernice Elnora (Howe) Raymond; m. Clinton Darrel Bowers, Nov. 29, 1963; children: Miriam Ruth, Janel Lea. AA, Independence Community Coll., Kans., 1960; BS, Kans. State U., 1962, MS, 1963, PhD, 1967. Rsch. assoc. Iowa State U., Ames, 1963-64; asst. prof. food sci Kans. State U., Manhattan, 1967; assoc. prof. to prof. and dept. head food sci. Kans. State U., 1975—. Contbr. over 70 articles and book chpts. Mem. Inst. Food Technologists (editorial bd.), Am. Home Econs. assn., Am. Meat Sci. Assn., Coun. Agrl. Sci. and Tech., Gamma Sigma Delta (Award of Merit). Methodist. Office: Kansas State U Dept Food and Nutrition Manhattan KS 66506

BOWERS, JANICE L., school assistant superintendent; b. Dodge City, Kans., July 16, 1947; d. Chris William and Lois (Moore) Langvardt; m. George Alden Bowers, Mar. 9, 1974; 1 child, Jessica. BS, Emporia State U., 1969, MA, 1970; PhD, Kans. State U., 1982. Div. prin. Highland Park High Sch./Topeka (Kans.) pub. schs.; prin. Topeka pub. schs.; prin. Mesa (Ariz.) pub. schs., asst. supt.; mem. Mesa Pub. Sch. Com. Cert. Task Force, Lang. Arts Textbook Selection Com. Contbr. articles to profl. jours. Recipient Kamelot award. Mem. Am. Assn. Sch. Pers. Adminstrs., ARiz. Sch. Pers. Adminstrs. Assn., Nat. Assn. Ednl. Negotiators, Kans. Assn. for Middle Level Edn., Nat. Mid. Sch. Assn., Pi Gamma Mu, Phi Delta Phi, Delta Kappa Gamma, Phi Delta Kappa. Office: 546 N Stapley Mesa AZ 85203

BOWERS, M. DEANE, biology educator; b. Portchester, N.Y., Mar. 19, 1952; d. Richard and Katharine (Semon) Bowers. BA, Smith Coll., 1974; PhD, U. Mass., 1979. Postdoctoral fellow Stanford (Calif.) U., 1979-81; asst. to assoc. prof. Harvard U., Cambridge, Mass., 1981-89; assoc. prof. biology U. Colo., Boulder, 1989—. Contbr. articles to profl. jours. Mem. Ecol. Soc. Am., Soc. for Study of Evolution, Lepidopterists Soc. (exec. council 1981-84, 86-89), AAAS, Phytochem. Soc., Chem. Ecology Soc. Office: U of Colo Dept EPO Biology Boulder CO 80216

BOWERS, MARY ELLEN KATHRYN, quality control executive, chemist; b. Cleve., Nov. 3, 1949; d. Arthur L. and Dorothy Virginia (DeLura) Jaklic; 1 child, Matthew Anthony. A.A. with honors Lakeland Community Coll., 1985, student, Lake Erie Coll., Painesville, Ohio. Lab technician W.S. Tyler, Inc., Cleve., 1969-71, C-E Tyler, Cleve., 1974-76; quality control mgr. Morton Salt, Painesville, Ohio, 1977—. Treas. com. mem. Boy Scouts Am., 1988-90, sr. mem. explorer scouts marksmanship post, 1987-90, sec. local com., 1987-90; mem. Lake County Indsl. Community Awareness Emergency Response Adv. Panel, 1987-90. Mem. NAFE, AAAS. Republican. Roman Catholic. Avocations: traveling, photography, tutoring math. Home: 1651 Mentor Ave Bldg 6 Unit 604 Painseville OH 44077 Office: Morton Salt Div Morton Internat Inc PO Box 428 Grand River OH 44045-0428

BOWERS, NORMA JEAN, music educator; b. Wichita, Kans., Sept. 28, 1929; d. William Edward and Helen Marie (Braniff) Bingman. BMusEdn, James Millikin U., Decatur, Ill., 1950; MMus, No. Ill. U., 1964. Music tchr. Norris City (Ill.) Community Unit Sch., 1951-54, Aurora (Ill.) Sch. Dist. 131, 1955-57, Batavia (Ill.) Pub. Schs. #101, 1958-90. Artist watercolor paintings, portraits on commn. Choir dir. Congl. Ch., Geneva, Ill. Mem. Ill. Edn. Assn., Batavia Edn. Assn. (pres. 1968-69, 82-85), NEA, Acad. Am. Educators (named outstanding educator 1973-74), Delta Kappa Gamma, Sigma Alpha Iota. Office: Batavia Pub Schs 12 W Wilson St Batavia IL 60510

BOWERS, PATRICIA ELEANOR FRITZ, economist; b. N.Y.C., Mar. 21, 1928; d. Eduard and Eleanor (Ring) Fritz. Student scholar, Goucher Coll., 1946-48; B.A., Cornell U., 1950; M.A., NYU, 1953, Ph.D., 1965. Statis. asst. Fed. Res. Bank N.Y., N.Y.C., 1950-53; lectr. Upsala Coll., East Orange, N.J., 1953-59; researcher Fortune mag., N.Y.C., 1959-60; teaching fellow NYU, N.Y.C., 1960-62, instr., 1962-64; mem. faculty Bklyn. Coll., 1964—, prof. econs., 1974—. Author: Private Choice and Public Welfare, 1974. Sec. Friends of the Johnson Mus., Cornell U., 1989—. Mem. Am. Econ. Assn., Econometric Soc., N.Y. Acad. Scis., Fgn. Policy Assn., Women's Econ. Round Table, Met. Econ. Assn. (sec. 1963-68, pres. 1974-75), Am. Statis. Assn. (univs. chmn. ann. forecasting confs. 1970-71, 71-72), City Island Yacht Club, Cornell Club N.Y., Kappa Alpha Theta. Home: 145 E 16th St New York NY 10003 Office: CUNY Bklyn Coll Dept Econs Brooklyn NY 11210

BOWERS, PATRICIA NEWSOME, public relations executive; b. Baton Rouge, June 21, 1944; d. Carl Allen and Sue Mayre (Powell) Newsome; m. Robert Lloyd Bowers Jr., Aug. 19, 1967 (div. Nov. 1979); children: Paige Ivy, Katherine Elizabeth. BJ, La. State U., 1967. Sr. writer, editor Litton Industries, Pascagoula, Miss., 1978-80; sr. presentations supr. Martin Marietta Aerospace, Orlando, Fla., 1980-81; mgr. presentations Martin Marietta Aerospace, Balt., 1981-85, mgr. pub. rels., 1985-90; dir. pub. rels. and corp. communications Contraves USA, Pitts., 1990—. Coach Parkville Recreation Council, Balt., 1985-87; bd. dirs. Salvation Army, Human Resources Devel. Agy. Balt. County; adv. bd. Nat. Aquarium in Balt. Mem. Pub. Rels. Soc. Am. (bd. dirs. Chesapeake conf. 1987), Navy League (bd. dirs. Balt. council 1986-87), Balt. County C. of C. (leadership program 1986-87), Pitts. Press Club. Republican. Episcopalian.

BOWERS, SUSAN KATHLEEN, data processing executive; b. Waukesha, Wis., Feb. 17, 1964; d. Henry Max and Patricia (Bandlow) B.; 1 child, Ryan William Bowers. AAS, Waukesha County Tech. Inst., 1985. Pro shop mgr. Edgewood Golf Course, Big Bend, Wis., 1980-85; data entry operator T.A. Chapman, Brookfield, Wis., 1984-85; ops./data processing mgr. Calif. Hawaii Promotions, Gardena, 1985—. Office: Calif Hawaii Promotions 1935 W 139th St Gardena CA 90249

BOWERS, ZELLA ZANE, real estate broker; b. Liberal, Kans., May 24, 1929; d. Rex and Esther (Neff) Powelson; m. James Clarence Bowers, Aug. 12, 1949; (div. 1977); 1 child: Dara Zane. BA, Colo. Coll., 1951. Cert. real estate brokerage mgr. Sec. Bowers Ins. Agy., Colorado Springs, Colo., 1955-59, Cen. Colo. Claims Service, Colorado Springs, 1959-63; pres. Premium Budgeting Co., Colorado Springs, 1962-67; pres., owner Monument Valley Realty, Inc., Colorado Springs, 1981-89; mng. broker The Buick Co. Buyer's Market; pres. Realtor Svcs. Corp., 1989. Hon. trustee The Palmer Found., Colorado Springs, 1980—, pres., 1983-84; trustee Pikes Peak United Way, 1988-91, Colo. Assn. Realtors Edn. Found., 1988—; pres. Vis. Nurse Assn., Colorado Springs, 1966-67, 74; dir. Colo. League Nurses, Denver, 1968; steering com. The Kennedy Ctr. Imagination Celebration, Colorado Springs, 1989, chmn., 1990; sec. Care & Share, Colorado Springs, 1984; chmn. McAllister House Mus., Colorado Springs, 1973-74; docent chmn. Colorado Springs Fine Arts Ctr., 1969-70; pres. Friends of the Library, 1971-72; pres. Woman's Ednl. Soc. Colo. Coll., 1974-77; civil adminstrv. staff asst. Air Def. Filter Ctr., 1956-57, ground observer, 1956, others. Recipient Women's Trade Fair Recognition award, 1987. Mem. Nat. Assn. Realtors, Colo. Assn. Realtors, Colorado Springs Bd. Realtors (pres. 1987-88), Children of the Am. Revolution (pres. 1956-57, hist. preservation bd. 1989-92, chmn. 1989-90), Gamma Phi Beta. Avocations: genealogy, travel. Home: PO Box 7894 Colorado Springs CO 80933 Office: 102 S Tejon St Ste #1100 Colorado Springs CO 80903

BOWERSOX, JUDITH JEANE, university administrator; b. Camden, N.J., Nov. 21, 1949; d. F. Louis and Regina Marguerite (Browne) Ligouri; m. James P. Bowersox, Apr. 8, 1967; (div. 1975); 1 child, Julie Diane. BS, Johns Hopkins U., Baltimore, 1981; MAS, John Hopkins U., Baltimore, 1984. Admission coordinator Johns Hopkins U., Sch. of Hygiene & Pub. Health, Baltimore, 1972-85; assoc. dir. div. adminstrn. and bus. Johns Hopkins U., Sch. of Continuing Studies, Balt., 1985-; scholarship com. Johns Hopkins U. Sch. Continuing Studies, Balt., 1985—, tech. com., 1986-87; hospitality com. Am. Assn. Collegiate Registrars and Officers Admision, 1986. Mem. Exec. Women's Network (hospitality com. 1988, chair membership com. 1989), Delta Sigma Pi. Home: 8129 Kirkwall Court Towson MD 21204

BOWES, ARLENE DANNENBERG, dentist; b. Phila., Aug. 8, 1950; d. Arthur Milton Jr. and Aileen (Hart) Dannenberg; m. Stephen Mallory Bowes III, Apr. 21, 1979; 2 children. AB, Swarthmore (Pa.) Coll., 1972; DMD, U. Pa., 1977. Pvt. practice Lutherville, Md., 1979—. Hist. dist. treas. Lutherville Community Assn., 1986—, zoning chmn., 1989—. Lt. USPHS, 1977-79. Home: 1603 Francke Ave Lutherville MD 21093

BOWES, FLORENCE (MRS. WILLIAM DAVID BOWES), writer; b. Salt Lake City, Nov. 19, 1925; d. John Albreckt Elias and Alma Wilhelmina (Jonasson) Norborg; student U. Utah, 1941-42, Columbia, 1945-46, N.Y. U., 1954-55; grad. N.Y. TV Workshop, 1950; m. Samuel Ellis Levine, July 15, 1944 (dec. July 1953); m. 2d, William David Bowes, Mar. 15, 1958 (dec. 1976); 1 son, Alan Richard. Actress, writer Hearst Radio Network, WINS, N.Y.C., 1944-45; personnel and adminstrv. exec. Mut. Broadcasting System, N.Y.C., 1946-49, free-lance editor, writer, 1948-49; freelance writer NBC and ABC, 1949-53; script editor, writer Robert A. Monroe Prodns., N.Y.C., Hollywood, Calif., 1953-56; script and comml. dir. KUTV-TV, Salt Lake City, 1956-58; spl. editor, writer pub. relations dept. U. Utah, Salt Lake City, 1966-68, editor, writer U. Utah Rev., 1968-75; author: Web of Solitude, 1979; The MacOrvan Curse, 1980; Interlude in Venice, 1981; Beauchamp, 1983. Mem. Beta Sigma Phi. Home: 338 K St Salt Lake City UT 84103

BOWKER, ANN MARTA, art educator, artist; b. Yakima, Wash., July 2, 1935; d. Donald Archie and Jessie Beryl (Bennington) B.; 1 child, Erin. BA, Cen. Wash. U., 1957; MA, U. Wash., 1968. Tchr. art Yakima Pub. Schs., 1957-58; tchr. English, journalism Naches Sch. Dist., Naches, Wash., 1961-64; producing artist Seattle, L.A., 1970-71; tchr. art South Kitsap Sch. Dist., Port Orchard, Wash., 1971-73; tchr. creatively talented students Yakima Pub. Schs., 1973-85; producing artist Yakima, 1985-86; tchr. gifted students, enrichment tchr. Yakima Pub. Schs., 1986—. Fiber artist quilted ensemble Fairfield Corp. Fashion Show, 1987, 88, 89. Mem. Wash. Assn. for the Edn. Talented & Gifted. Home: PO Box 10445 Yakima WA 98909-1445

BOWLES, BARBARA LANDERS, food company executive; b. Nashville, Sept. 17, 1947; d. Corris Raemone Landers and Rebecca Aima (Bonham) Jennings; m. Earl Stanley Bowles, Nov. 27, 1971; 1 son, Terrence Earl. B.A., Fisk U., 1968; M.B.A., U. Chgo., 1971. Chartered fin. analyst, 1977. Banker to v.p. First Nat. Bank of Chgo., 1968-81; asst. v.p. Beatrice Cos., Chgo., 1981-84; v.p. investor relations Kraft Inc., Chgo., 1984-89; pres., founder The Kenwood Group Inc., Chgo., 1989—; bd. dirs. Hyde Pk. Bank. Recipient Salute to Am.'s Top 100 Black Bus. and Profl. Women award Delta Sigma Theta and Dollars & Sense Mag., 1985; United Negro Coll. Fund scholar, 1989. Mem. NAACP (life), Assn. for Investment Mgmt. and Rsch., Fin. Analysts Fedn., Nat. Assn. Investment Clubs, Nat. Investor Relations Inst., Chicago Fisk Alumni Assn. (pres. 1983-85). Mem. United Ch. of Christ. Club: University (Chgo.). Avocations: tennis, bridge.

BOWLES, DEBORAH ANN, educator; b. Guymon, Okla., Aug. 24, 1949; d. James H. and Willie Mae (Duckett) Armstrong; m. Gerald Bowles, June 10, 1972; children: Ryan, LeAnne. BS in Elem. Edn., U. Tex., 1971; MS in Spl. Edn., U. Tex., Dallas, 1978. Tchr. jr. high spl. edn. Mpls. pub. schs.; tchr. emotionally disturbed Plano (Tex.) Ind. Sch. Dist., 1976-80; tchr./dir. pre-sch. The Learning Tree, Plano, 1980-81; 3rd grade tchr./team leader Plano Ind. Sch. Dist., 1982—. Children/youth counselor and tchr. Christ United Meth. Ch., Plano, 1977—. Named Tex. Computer Tchr. of Yr., IBM, 1988. Mem. ASCD, Internat. Reading Assn., Nat. Coun. Tchrs. of English, Nat. Coun. Tchrs. of Math., Delta Kappa Gamma (hon. tchr. Mu Beta chpt., chair profl. affairs). Office: Jackson Elem Sch Plano ISD 1101 Jackson Dr Plano TX 75075

BOWLES, MARTHA THOMAS, performing arts administrator; b. Greensboro, N.C., Dec. 29, 1952; d. Hargrove Jr. and Jessamine Woodward (Boyce) B.; m. Geoffrey McKewen Curme, Dec. 31, 1977; children: Jonathan Woodward Bowles Curme, Margaret Erkskine Bowles Curme. BA, U. N.C., 1975; MBA, Harvard U., 1979. Asst. treas. Chem. Bank, N.Y.C., 1975-77; mgr. spl. projects Belk Stores Svcs., Charlotte, N.C., 1979; sr. fin. analyst Duke Power Co., Charlotte, 1980-84, sr. fin. analyst long term fin., 1984-85, sr. fin. analyst cash mgmt., 1985-87, dir. cash ops., 1986-87; vice chmn. Mecklenburg Co. Indsl. Facilities Pollution Control Fin. Authority, Charlotte, 1983-87, adminstr. spl. projects, 1987-88; campaign dir. N.C. Performing Arts Ctr., Charlotte, 1988—. Mem. Charlotte Community Concert Assn., 1981-84; mem. Com. of 100 Women Johnson C. Smith U., 1989—; trustee Sacred Heart Coll., Belmont, N.C., 1983-84; mem. community adv. bd. Sta. WTVI, 1986—; bd. dirs. Planned Parenthood Greater Charlotte, 1987—, pres., 1989-90. Mem. Women Execs., Women for Peace, Phi Beta Kappa. Democrat. Episcopalian. Office: NC Performing Arts Ctr 400 S Tryon St Ste 1946 Charlotte NC 28285

BOWLING, ANN TROMMERSHAUSEN, genetics educator; b. Portland, Oreg., June 1, 1943; d. William Ernst and Helen Claire (Bowen) Trommershausen; m. Lloyd H. Smith, Sept. 1967 (div. 1972); m. Michael Bowling, Feb. 2, 1980; 1 child, Lydia. BA, Carleton Coll., 1965; PhD, U. Calif., Davis, 1969. Asst. prof. Occidental Coll., Eagle Rock, Calif., 1969-73; asst. rsch. geneticist U. Calif., Davis, 1973-75, asst. adj. prof., 1975-77, assoc. adj. prof., 1977-85, adj. prof., 1985—. Mem. AAAS, Internat. Soc. Animal Genetics, Am. Genetics Soc. Office: U Calif Serology Lab Davis CA 95616

BOWLING, EVELYN BURGE, speech pathologist; b. Champion Height, Ohio, Jan. 24, 1931; d. George Reginald and Ethel (Thompson) Burge; m. Donald Bowling, Oct. 6, 1950; children: Melodie Anne, David Mark. AB, UCLA, 1958; MA, Sacramento State U., 1968; PhD, Sierra U., 1985. Cert. speech pathologist; elem. educator. Speech pathologist Santa Ana (Calif.), 1958-59; deaf & hearing educator Long Beach (Calif.) Schs., 1959-60; speech pathlgist chief Fairviews State Hosp., Costa Mesa, Calif., 1960-67; speech pathologist Lanterman Hosp., Pomona, Calif., 1967-70; cons., therapist Davis (Calif.) Med. Ctr., 1970-75; owner, dir. Sunrise Lang. & Speech Edn. Svcs., Fair Oaks, Calif., 1975—; exec. voice, trainer and cons. Author: Voice Power, 1980, After Your First Six Words, I Know You, 1988; contbr. various articles to profl. jours. Mem. Am. Lang. Speech and Hearing, Calif. Speech and Hearing Assn., Calif. Speech Pathologists and Audiologists, Internat. Assn. for Logopedics and Phonictrics, Assn. for Transpersonal Psychology, Am. Penwomen, Nat. Speakers Assn. Democrat. Home: 6155 Carolinda Dr Roseville CA 95661 Office: Sunrise Language Speech Edn 7806 Madison Ave Fair Oaks CA 95661

BOWLING, KATHLEEN E., company executive; b. Balt., June 22, 1946; d. Gustav Herman and Mary Elizabeth (Marse) Pfeifer; children: Kathleen Miller, Karol Bowling, Kristine Bowling. Clk. then sec. Levenson & Klein, Inc., Balt., 1977-87; asst. svc. mgr. Levenson & Klein, Inc., 1988-90; customer svc. mgr. Shaivitz Furniture, 1990—. Mem. NAFE, Am. Heart Assn., MADD. Democrat. Presbyterian.

BOWMAN, BARBARA SHERYL, banker; b. Cleve., Sept. 2, 1953; d. Bert and Shirley Marie (Regan) B. BS magna cum laude, Calif. State U., Fresno, 1976; postgrad., Am. Grad. Sch. Internat. Mgmt., 1976; MBA magna cum laude, Loyola-Marymount U., 1980. Asst. to pres. Aerol Co., L.A., 1976-77; mgmt. trainee First Interstate Bank of Calif., L.A., 1977-78; mgr. consumer credit First Interstate Bank of Calif., Brentwood, Calif., 1978-79; asst. v.p. First Interstate Bank of Calif., Beverly Hills, Calif., 1979-82, v.p., team leader, 1982-84, v.p., sales mgr., 1985—; sr. v.p. Fimsa subs. First Interstate Bancorp, West Los Angeles, 1988, Fimsa S.W. subs. First Interstate Bancorp, Houston, 1989—; v.p. Mercantile Nat. Bank, L.A., 1982; v.p. asst. mgr. Real Estate div. Fical, San Diego, 1986-87; speaker San Diego Mortgage Bankers Assn., 1986. Mem. NAFE, Am. Bus. Women's Assn., Nat. Assn. Bank Women (v.p. L.A. chpt. 1984-86), Loyola-Marymount Alumni Assn., Bldg. Industry Assn., St. Mary's Acad. Alumni Assn., Phi Kappa Phi. Republican. Roman Catholic. Office: Fimsa 650 N Sam Houston Pkwy Houston TX 77060

BOWMAN, BEVERLY ANN, accountant; b. Kansas City, Mo., Aug. 10, 1958; d. Virgil William and Modean (Aston) B. BS, Ark. Tech. U., 1980. CPA. Staff acct. Russell Brown & Co., Little Rock, 1980-83; mgr. Richard Bell & Co., North Little Rock, 1983-88; pres., ptnr. B.A. Bowman, P.A., Little Rock, 1988—; fin. adv. Phi Mu Epsilon Lambda, Russellville, Ark., 1986—. Mem. ACTS Touring Group, Little Rock, 1985—. Mem. AICPA, Ark. Soc. CPA's (MAS chmn. 1986). Baptist. Office: B A Bowman PA 315 Dryad Ln Little Rock AR 72205

BOWMAN, BEVERLY ANN HATFIELD, English educator; b. Kenova, W. Va., July 11, 1946; d. Roy Edward and Joyce Mae (Adkins) Hatfield; m. Max N. Bowman, Aug. 16, 1969; children: Kimberli, Bryce. BA, Houghton Coll., 1968; MS, U. Bridgeport, 1979; postgrad., So. Ill. U. Cert. tchr., N.Y., Ill. Tchr. English N.Y. St. Pub. Schs., New City, 1968-73; instr. Lees McRae Coll., Banner Elk, N.C., 1979-80; lectr. Boston Coll., 1980, Kent (Ohio) State U., 1981-82; cons. pub. rels. El Paso Community Coll., 1982-83; lectr. English U. Tex., El Paso, 1983-85; chair El Paso Assn. Gifted, 1985-86; tchr. English Bond Community Schs., Greenville, Ill., 1986—. Pianist Coronado Ch., El Paso 1983-86, Greenville Meth. Ch., 1987; vol. Cancer Assn., El Paso 1984. Fellow Mid Ill. Edn., 1987. Mem. Nat. Assn. Tchrs. English, Tchrs. Union, El Paso Assn. Gifted and Talented (chmn. dirs. 1984-87), Christian Women's. Republican. Methodist. Home: 409 S Fourth St Greenville IL 62246 Office: Bond Schs Community Vandalia Rd Greenville IL 62246

BOWMAN, DEBORAH ANNE, sales executive; b. Lansing, Mich., Dec. 20, 1957; d. Norman James and Christine Ruth (Levring) B. BSBA, U. Fla., 1980. Sales rep. D. Van Nostrand Co., Gainesville, Fla., 1980-81, Benjamin-Cummings Pubs., Dallas, 1981-84, Mc-Graw Hill Book Co., Dallas, 1984-85, sales mgr., L.A., 1985-86; br. sales mgr. Norrell Svcs., Dallas, 1986—. Active United Way; active mentor program YWCA. Named one of Outstanding Young Women in Am., 1983, Young Career Woman Yr., 1987, Las Colinas Woman of Yr. Las Colinas Bus. and Profl. Women's Club, 1990. Mem. NAFE, Assn. for Computing Machinery (assoc.), Recognition Tech. User's Assn., Bus. and Profl. Women's Club (pres. Las Colinas chpt., named Pres. of Yr. Tex. State chpt. 1989), Irving C. of C. (women's div., diplomat, named Super Achiever 1989), Downtown Dallas Career Women's Network, Irving Women's Career Network, Irving Symphony League, Irving Theatre Guild, The 500, Inc., Dallas Gator Club (sec.), Phi Kappa Phi, Alpha Lambda Delta, Alpha Omicron Pi. Roman Catholic. Office: Norrell Svcs Inc 350 N Saint Paul #2875 Dallas TX 75201

BOWMAN, DOROTHY MARIE, librarian; b. North Tazewell, Va., May 20, 1937; d. Roy and Thelma Vivian Ann (Shrader) Brewster; m. John LeRoy Bowman, Dec. 28, 1957; children: Annette Toner, Kathleen Rader, Alice. BS in Edn., Radford (Va.) Coll., 1958; MLS, Cath. U. Am., 1989. Tchr., librarian Virginia Beach (Va.) Pub. Schs., 1958-59; tchr. Norfolk (Va.) City Schs., 1959-60; librarian Albemarle Pulp & Paper Mfg. Co., Richmond, Va., 1961-64; tchr. Henrico (Va.) Pub. Schs., 1966-67, asst. librarian, 1967-70; librarian Chickahominy Acad., Henrico County, 1972-73, Nasemond-Suffolk (Va.) Acad., 1975—. Pres. Highland Springs (Va.) United Meth. Women, 1973-74; residential campaign chmn. Am. Cancer Soc., Richmond, 1972-73; co-chair Nansemond-Suffolk Acad. Evaluation Steering Com., 1984-85, Main St. United Meth. Ch. Coun. on Ministries, Suffolk, 1983-85. Mem. AAUW (br. treas. 1983-87), Va. Library Assn., Sans Souci Lit. Club (pres. Suffolk chpt. 1985-87), Highland Springs Jr. Woman's Club (pres. 1970-71), Delta Kappa Gamma (chpt. pres. 1986-88). Republican. Home: 100 Ayers Creek Ln Suffolk VA 23434 Office: Nansemond Suffolk Acad 3373 Pruden Blvd Box 1249 Suffolk VA 23434

BOWMAN, ELIZABETH SUE, psychiatrist, educator; b. Roanoka, Va., Mar. 9, 1954; d. Edward David and Mildred Lenora (Miller) B.; m. Philip Meredith Coons, Sept. 5, 1981. BS, Purdue U., 1976; MD, Ind. U., Indpls., 1980; STM summa cum laude, Christian Theol. Sem., Indpls., 1987. Diplomate Am. Bd. Psychiatry and Neurology. Resident in psychiatry sch. of medicine Ind. U., 1980-84, chief resident sch. of medicine, 1984, asst. prof. sch. of medicine, 1984—; asst. dir. inpatient psychiatry dept. Ind. U. Hosp., 1984-90; staff psychiatrist Indpls. VA Hosp., 1986-89; mem. community adv. bd. Buchanan Counseling Ctr., Indpls., 1989-. Contbr. articles to med. jours. Mem. Am. Psychiat. Assn., Am. Med. Women's Assn., Assn. Women Psychiatrists, Ind. Psychiat. Soc. (sec. 1985-86, editor newsletter 1985-88), Ind. U. Psychiat. Assocs. (bd. dirs. 1986—). Methodist. Office: Ind U Hosp N-604 926 W Michigan St Indianapolis IN 46202-5250

BOWMAN, ERIN GARDNER, professional fundraiser; b. Carrizo Springs, Tex., Sept. 5, 1948; d. Edward O'Meara and Thetis (Sanderford) Gardner; children: Charles Buchanan Tennison, Jr., Casey Gardner Tennison, Marrs McLean Bowman. Student, U. Tex., 1966-68, U. Ams., Mexico City, 1967; BA, Incarnate Word Coll., San Antonio, 1972. St. Luke's Episcopal Sch., San Antonio, 1971-73, Cambridge Elem. Sch., San Antonio, 1974-76, R.F. Dini and Assocs., Houston, 1987, Condra and Co., San Antonio. Mem. exec. com., bd. dirs. Santa Rosa Children's Hosp. Found., 1979-89; bd. dirs. Santa Rosa Children's Hosp., 1988—; chmn. adv. bd. U. Tex. Health Scis. Ctr. Nursing Sch.;; pres. Cancer Ctr. Coun., 1985. Mem. S.W. Found. Forum, San Antonio Mus. Assn., San Antonio Zoo Assn., Assistance Guild San Antonio (charter), San Antonio Livestock Expn., Friends Kennedy Ctr., McNay Art Mus., Smithsonian Assocs., Pan Tex. Assembly, Tex. Wildlife Assn., Argyle Club, San Antonio Country Club, Club Girard, Frontier Club (bd. dirs. 1988-90). Republican. Episcopalian. Home: 627 E Olmos Dr San Antonio TX 78212

BOWMAN, FRANCINE LORRAINE, diplomat; b. Bayonne, N.J., May 3, 1940; d. Edward Bowman and Mary (Grzyb) Bera. Student, Seton Hall U., 1957-60, U. Md., 1964-65, Fgn. Svc. Inst., Washington, 1974-75. Fgn. svc. officer numerous cities worldwide U.S. Dept. State, Washington, 1961—. Mem. Nat. Wildlife Fedn. Office: US Dept State Virginia Ave Washington DC 20520

BOWMAN, HAZEL LOIS, educator; b. Plant City, Fla., Feb. 18, 1917; d. Joseph Monroe and Annie (Thoman) B.; A.B., Fla. State Coll. for Women, 1937; M.A., U. Fla., 1948; postgrad. U. Md., 1961-65. Tchr., Lakeview High Sch., Winter Garden, Fla., 1939-40, Eagle Lake Sch., Fla., 1940-41; welfare visitor Fla. Welfare Bd., 1941-42; specialist U.S. Army Signal Corps, Arlington Hall, Va., 1942-43; recreation worker, asst. procurement officer ARC, CBI Theater, 1943-46; lab. technician Am. Cyanamid Corp., Brewster, Fla., 1946-47; instr., asst. prof. gen. extension div. U. Fla., Fla. State U., 1948-51; free-lance writer, editor, indexer, N.Y., Fla., 1951-55; staff writer Tampa (Fla.) Morning Tribune, 1956; staff writer, telegraph editor Winter Haven (Fla.) News-Chief, 1956-57; registrar/admissions officer U. Tampa, 1957-59; coll. counselor, Atlantic states, 1959-60; registrar/freshman adviser Towson State Tchrs. Coll., Balt., 1960-62; dir. student personnel, guidance, admissions Harford Jr. Coll., Bel Air, Md., 1962-64; instr. York (Pa.) Coll., 1965-66, asst. prof. English, journalism, 1966-69; tchr. S.W. Jr. High Sch., Lakeland, Fla., 1969-70; tchr. learning disabled Vanguard Sch., Lake Wales, Fla., 1970-82; libr. asst. Polk County Hist. and Geneal. Libr., Bartow, Fla., 1986—. Editor Tampa Altrusan, 1958-60, Polk County Hist. Calendar, 1986-90. Mem. AAUW, NOW, Nat. Geneal. Soc., Mortar Bd., Alpha Chi Alpha, Chi Delta Phi. Home: 511 NE 9th Ave Mulberry FL 33860

BOWMAN, JACQUELINE BONNIE, school superintendent. BA in Sociology, La Verne (Calif.) U., 1959; MA, Pasadena (Calif.) Coll., 1967; PhD in Psychology, U. So. Calif., 1974. Cert. elem. and secondary tchr., Calif.; lic. counselor, psychologist and ednl. psychologist, Calif. Elem. tchr. Charter Oak Unified Sch. Dist., Covina, Calif., 1958-63, counselor, psychometrist, 1963-66, sch. psychologist, 1966-69, coord. spl. edn., 1969-71, prin. elem. and secondary schs., 1971—, dir. pupil personnel svcs., spl. edn. and staff devel., 1982-85, asst. supt. support svcs., 1985-87, asst. supt. ednl. svcs., 1987—; instr. UCLA, 1960-63; psychologist Whittier (Calif.) Guidance Ctr., 1966-69; prin. high sch. Charter Oak Found., Covina, 1974-79; instr. La Verne (Calif.) U., 1969, 71, cluster leader doctoral program, 1978-80; presenter Qualified Increasing Human Effectiveness Workshop, 1982—. Author: (with others) East San Gabriel Valley Special Education Cooperative Handbook; contbr. articles to profl. jours. V.p., bd. dirs. Edgewood Counseling Ctr.; supt. Sunday Sch. Luth. Ch.; active in PTA. Mem. AAUW, Nat. Assn. Sch. Psychologists, Nat. Sch. Adminstrs. Assn., Calif. Assn. Sch. Adminstrs., Nat. Speakers Assn., Assn. for Supervision and Curriculum Devel., Calif. Assn. Sch. Psychologists (chmn.), Coun. for Exceptional Children, Calif. Assn. for Neurologically Handicapped Children, Calif. Assn. for Gifted (chmn.), Assn. Sch. Adminstrs. Bd. Dirs., Assn. Calif. Sch. Adminstrs. Supt.'s Acad., East San Gabriel Valley Coop. for Spl. Edn., East San Gabriel Valley Coop. Edn. Programs (chmn.), Toastmistresses Club, Native Daughters of the Golden West, Phi Lambda Theta (sec. Sigma chpt.).

BOWMAN, MARTHA ALEXANDER, librarian; b. Washington, June 8, 1945; d. Lyle Thomas and Helen (Goodwin) Alexander; m. David Henry

Bowman, June 11, 1965 (div. 1982); 1 child, Elaine. B.A., U. Md., 1967; M.S. in Library Sci., Cath. U. Am., 1969. Librarian U. Md., College Park, 1969-72, head acquisitions, 1973-75; asst. univ. librarian George Washington U., Washington, 1975-78, assoc. univ. librarian, 1978-82; univ. librarian U. Louisville, 1983-90; dir. libraries U. Mo., Columbia, 1990—; chmn. bd. dirs. SOLINET (Southeastern Library Network), 1987-88. Coordinator U. Louisville United Way, 1987. Mem. ALA (chmn. poster sessions 1983-85, co-chmn. nat. conf. in Cin. 1989), Am. Assn. Higher Edn., Athletic Assn. U. Louisville (vice chmn., bd. dirs.), D.C. Library Assn. (pres. 1981-82), Women Acad. Libr. Dirs. Exch. Network. Episcopalian. Home: 1830 Woodfill Way Louisville KY 40205 Office: Univ Louisville Libraries Louisville KY 40292

BOWMAN, MARVIS, program analyst, military career officer; b. Phenix City, Ala., Dec. 19, 1936; d. Willie Lee and Lillie Mae (Fleming) Pugh; m. Raymond Bowman, Nov. 17, 1960; children: Darell Alan, Pamela Kay, Tracy Dafina. Assoc's., Sinclair Coll., 1980; BS in Bus., Wright State U., 1981; postgrad., U. Dayton, 1983, Cen. Mich. U., 1988. With USAF, Wright-Patterson AFB, Ohio, 1957—, mgmt. analyst, 1974-76, fin. specialist, 1976-84, cost performance analyst, 1984-86, supervisory program analysis officer, 1988—. Mem. Am. Mgmt. Assn., Nat. Assn. Female Execs., Am. Soc. Mil. Comptrollers, Blacks in Govt. (chmn. publicity com.). Baptist. Home: 5301 Pinnacle Rd Dayton OH 45418

BOWMAN, NANCY MOFFETT, counselor; b. Harrisonburg, Va., Feb. 20, 1942; d. John Guthrie and Florence Ellen (Reese) Moffett; m. Wayne St. Clair, Aug. 17, 1965; children: John Moffett Stuart, George Holland Dudley. BA, High Point Coll., 1963; MS, Va. Commonwealth U., 1965. lic. profl. counselor. Dean women Vardell Hall, Red Springs, N.C., 1964-65; asst. dir. St. Andrews Presbyn. Coll., Laurinburg, N.C., 1965; counselor Bon Air Sch. for Girls, Richmond, Va., 1966-69; vocat. evaluator Bon Air Sch. for Girls, Richmond, 1969-70; disability specialist State Dept. Vocat. Rehab., Richmond, 1970-72; counselor Union Theol. Sem., Richmond, 1983—, Next Step, Inc., Richmond, 1984-85; owner, counselor Bowman Counseling Assocs., Richmond, 1985—; vol. counselor St. John's Vianny Ctr., Richmond, 1980; vol. counselor Project Jump St., Richmond, 1977-79; bd. dirs. Brookfield, Inc., Richmond. Author: Mental Deficiency, 1969, Psychological Testing, 1969, Assertiveness Training, 1984, Children of Alcoholics, 1988. Bd. dirs. Historic Richmond Found., 1978—; pres. West End Community Ctr., Richmond, 1973-74; ofcl. electoral bd. City of Richmond, 1976—; deacon 1st Presbyn. Ch., Richmond, 1986-89; cons. Big Bros./Big Sisters of Richmond, 1988—. Mem. Am. Assn. Counseling and Devel., Va. Counselors Assn., Va. Assn. Drug and Alcohol Progs., Richmond Area Women Bus. Owners, Richmond Area Mental Health Counselors Assn., Stonewall Ct. Club. Office: Bowman Counseling Assocs 3108 Parham Rd #502B Richmond VA 23229

BOWMAN, PATRICIA ANN, real estate executive; b. Potsdam, N.Y., Oct. 20, 1949; d. Wilton and Shirley Ann (Hay) B. BS in Bus. Adminstrn., Susquehanna U., 1971; cert. in real estate, Inst. for Paralegal Tng., Phila., 1972. Registered pub. acct. Legal asst. Weinberg & Green, Balt., 1972-74; real estate closing officer Callahan, Caldwell & Laudeman, Balt., 1974-77; asst. dir. mortgage financing Monumental Properties Trust, Balt., 1977-79; sr. real estate analyst The Equitable Live Assurance Soc., N.Y.C., 1979-82; project mgr. real estate Chem. Bank, N.Y.C., 1982—. Mem. Young Mortgage Bankers Assn., Bldg. Owners and Mgrs. Inst. Republican. Episcopalian. Office: Chem Bank NY 633 3d Ave 8th Fl New York NY 10017

BOWMAN, SUSAN A., artist; b. Boston, Mass., Jan. 10, 1956; d. Edward H. and Ann (Semple) B. BFA, San Francisco Art Inst., 1979; MFA, Rutgers U., 1985. Teaching asst. Rutgers U., New Brunswick, N.J., 1984-87; freelance artist N.Y., 1985-87; asst. art dir. Woman Mag. Harris Pub., N.Y., 1987-88; assoc. art dir. Child Mag. N.Y. Times Mag. Group, N.Y.; adj. prof. Baruch Coll., N.Y.C., 1989. Fellow: Art Fellowship.

BOWMAN-DALTON, BURDENE KATHRYN, educator, computer consultant; b. Magnolia, Ohio, July 13, 1937; d. Ernest Mowles and Mary Kathryn (Long) Bowman; B.M.E., Capital U., 1959; MA in Edn., Akron U., 1967, postgrad. 1976—; m. Louis W. Dalton, Mar. 13, 1979. Profl. vocalist, various clubs in the East, 1959-60; music tchr. East Liverpool (Ohio) City Schs., 1959-62; music tchr. Revere Local Schs., Akron, Ohio, 1962-75, elem. tchr., 1975-80, elem. team leader/computer cons., 1979-85, tchr. middle sch. math., gift-talented, computer literacy, 1981—, dist. computer specialist, 1987—; local and regional dir., Olympics of the Mind, also World Problem Captain for computer problem, 1984-86; cons., workshop presenter State of Ohio, 1987—. Mem. Citizen Com., Akron, 1975-76; profl. rep. Bath Assn. to Help, 1978-80; mem. Revere Levy Com. 1986; audit com. BATH, 1977-79; volunteer chmn. Antique Car Show, Akron, 1972-81; dist. advisor MidWest Talent Search, 1987—; dist. statistician of standardized test results. Martha Holden Jennings Found. grantee, 1977-78; Title IV ESEA grantee, 1977-81. Mem. Assn. for Devel. of Computer-Based Instructional Systems, Assn. Supervision and Curriculum Devel., Ohio Assn. for Gifted Children, Phi Beta. Republican. Lutheran. Home: 353 Retreat Dr Akron OH 44313 Office: 3195 Spring Valley Rd Bath OH 44210

BOWNE, MARTHA HOKE, magazine editor, consultant; b. Greeley, Colo., June 9, 1931; d. George Edwin and Krin (English) Hoke; children: Gretchen, William, Kay, Judith. BA, U. Mich., 1952; postgrad., Syracuse U., 1965. Tchr. Wayne (Mich.) Pub. Schs., 1953-54, East Syracuse and Minoa Cen. Schs., Minoa, N.Y., 1965-68; store mgr. Fabric Barn, Fayetteville, N.Y., 1969-77; store owner Fabric Fair, Oneida, N.Y., 1978-80; producer, owner Quilting by the Sound, Port Townsend, Wash., 1987—, Quilting by the Lake, Cazenovia, N.Y., 1981—; organizer symposium Am. Quilters Soc. Workshops, Paducah, 1984—. Contbr. articles to profl. jours. Mem., pres. Minoa Library, 1960-75; mem. Onondaga County Library, Syracuse, 1968-71. Mem. Nat. Quilting Assn., Am. Quilters Soc. (editor newsletter 1985—), New Eng. Quilt Mus. Home: 88 Lincklaen St Cazenovia NY 13035

BOWSER, EMILIE LOUISE, nurse, educator, dress designer; b. Newark, Ohio, July 16, 1941; d. James Elbert and Geraldine Mae (Utts) Drumm; m. Gary L. Bowser, June 6, 1964 (div. July 1980); children—Deborah, Diana, David. B.S.N. in Nursing, Ohio State U., 1964; M.S. in Nursing, Wayne State U., 1984. R.N., Ohio. Charge nurse West Paces Ferry Hosp., Atlanta, 1972-73; clin. instr. St. Vincent's Hosp., Toledo, Ohio, 1976; staff nurse Toledo Hosp., part time 1976—; staff nurse Flower Hosp., Toledo, 1978-79; clin. instr. U. Toledo, 1979; assoc. prof. nursing Owens Tech. Coll., Toledo, 1979—, cons. continuing edn., 1981-87; owner Emilie's Original Bridal Creations; advisor Nat. Student Nurses Assn., Toledo, 1981-87. Cub scout com. chmn. Wolverine council Boy Scouts Am., 1983-86; mem. youth com., tchr., acolyte advisor Trinity Episcopal Ch. Mem. Ohio Nurses Assn. (publicity com. 1980-82), Bedford Band Boosters, Alpha Delta Pi. Republican. Club: Tamaron Country (Toledo). Office: Owens Tech Coll Oregon Rd Toledo OH 43699

BOWYER, JOAN ELIZABETH, medical technologist, realtor; b. Ellensburg, Wash., July 11, 1944; d. Chester Joseph and Rita Geneva (Newell) Howarth; 1 child, Suzanne Elise. BA, Ft. Wright Coll. of Holy Names, 1966; grad., Real Estate Sch. Oreg., 1982; PhD, Claremont McKenna Coll., 1990. Lic. med. technologist. Med. technologist Lab. of Clin. Medicine, Seattle, 1967-69, Sacred Heart Gen. Hosp., Eugene, Oreg., 1969-73, 74-76, McKenzie Willamette Hosp., Springfield, Oreg., 1976-77, Mid-Columbia Hosp., The Dalles, Oreg., 1977-82; realtor Red Carpet/Rick Hall Realty, Hillsboro, Oreg., 1982-85, Century 21 Columbia Realty, Portland, 1985—; med. technologist ARC, Portland, 1982-89, Physicians Med. Lab., 1989—; mem. exec. bd. dirs. Calif. Community Coll. Coun. on Staff Devel., 1989—. Co-editor: The Dalles Gen. Hosp. Newspaper, 1980-82. Pres. Wasco County Edn. Service Dist. Parents Group, The Dalles, 1978-82; founder, pres. Mid-Columbia Parents of Deaf, 1978-82; parental spokesperson Spl. Edn. Adv. Com., Salem, Oreg., 1980-82; activist parent for deaf/hearing impaired, 1977—. Mem. Med. Technologists of Am. Soc. Pathologists, Nat. Assn. Realtors, NAFE, Century 21 Investment Soc., Million Dollar Club. Republican. Avocations: photography, dancing, hiking, travel. Home: 704 SE 38th St Portland OR 97214 Office: Century 21 Columbia 2208 SE 182d St Portland OR 97233

BOXER, BARBARA, congresswoman; b. Bklyn., Nov. 11, 1940; d. Ira and Sophie (Silvershein) Levy; m. Stewart Boxer, 1962; children: Doug, Nicole. B.A., Bklyn. Coll., 1962. Stockbroker N.Y.C., 1962-65; journalist, assoc. editor Pacific Sun, 1972-74; congl. aide to rep. 5th Congl. Dist. San Francisco, 1974-76; mem. Marin County Bd. Suprs., San Rafael, Calif., 1976-82; mem. 98th-102nd Congresses from 6th dist. Calif., 1983—, mem. budget com., armed services com., select com. children, youth and families; chairwoman budget com. task force on AIDS, majority whip at large, co-chair Mil. Reform Caucus. Pres. Marin County Bd. Suprs., 1980-81; mem. Bay Area Air Quality Mgmt. Bd., San Francisco, 1977-82, pres., 1979-81; bd. dirs. Golden Gate Bridge Hwy. and Transport Dist., San Francisco, 1978-82; founding mem. Marin Nat. Women's Polit. Caucus, Marin Community Video; pres. Dem. New Mems. Caucus, 1983. Recipient Open Govt. award Common Cause, 1980. Jewish. Office: 307 Cannon House Office Bldg Washington DC 20515

BOXLER, DOROTHY BACINO, dental hygienist; b. Del., Mar. 7, 1956; d. Evro James and Josephine (Camoirano) B.; m. Daniel Leo Boxler, June 22, 1955; 1 child, Anthony. Cert. dental hygiene, Temple U., 1976; BS, West Chester U., 1981. Clin. dental hygienist Group Dental Assocs., Wilmington, Del., 1976-1987; dental health educator Avon Grove Sch. Dist., West Grove, Pa., 1984-90; clin. instr. Temple U., Sch. Dental Hygiene, Phila., 1982, Del. Tech. Community Coll., Sch. Dental Hygiene, Wilmington, 1982; implementor, coord. sch. fluoride tablets, cons., promoter Nat. Children's Dental Health month, Avon Grove Sch. Dist, West Grove, Pa., 1984-90. Mem. Am. Dental Hygiene Assn., New Castle County Dental Hygiene Assn., New Garden Art Assn. (pres., 1987-89), Sigma Phi Alpha, Kappa Delta Pi. Roman Catholic. Home: 141 Cold Springs Dr Kennett Square PA 19348

BOXX, RITA MCCORD, banker; b. Greenwood, S.C., Aug. 10, 1930; d. John Thomas Logan and Dempsie (Dixon) McCord; student public schs.; m. John Douglas Boxx, Apr. 17, 1949; children—John Stephen, Eric Wesley, Merry Christine. Asst. mgr. Greenwood Ins. Agy., 1951-65, mgr., 1967-80; with Bankers Trust S.C., Greenwood, 1951—, (name now NCNB) asst. v.p. charge ins. dept., 1980—; tchr. ins. seminars. Mem. Nat. Assn. Ins. Women, Ind. Ins. Agts. Greenwood, Ind. Ins. Agts. S.C., Ind. Ins. Agts. Am., Greenwood Assn. Ins. Women, Greenwood C. of C. (dir. 1974-76, chmn. environ., energy and conservation com. 1974, chmn. edn. com. 1977). Baptist. Club: Greenwood Country. Home: 434 Dogwood Dr Greenwood SC 29646 Office: PO Box 1058 Greenwood SC 29648

BOYAR, LEA A., advertising executive; b. Boothbay Harbor, Maine, Sept. 9, 1958; d. Harold Charles and Josephine Julia (Cislo) B. BA in French magna cum laude, Tufts U., 1979. Asst. buyer Abraham & Strauss, Bklyn., 1979-80; asst. account exec. Ogilvy & Mather, N.Y.C., 1981-82, account exec., 1982-85, account supr., 1985-86, v.p., account supr., 1987-88; v.p., account supr. Lord, Geller, Federico, Einstein Inc., N.Y.C., 1988-90, v.p., mgmt. supr., 1990—. Office: Lord Geller Federico Einstein Inc 655 Madison Ave New York NY 10021

BOYCE, DOREEN ELIZABETH, educational foundation executive; b. Antofagasta, Chile, Apr. 20, 1934; d. George Edgar and Elsie Winifred Vaughan; B.A. with honors, Oxford (Eng.) U., 1956, M.A. with honors, 1960; Ph.D., U. Pitts., 1983, D. in Hum. Lit., Westminster Coll., 1986; m. Alfred Warne Boyce, Aug. 11, 1956; children: Caroline Elizabeth, John Trevor Warne. Lectr. and tutor in econs. U. Witwatersrand, South Africa, 1960-62; provost and dean of faculty, prof. econs. Chatham Coll., Pitts., 1963-79; prof. econs., chmn. dept. econs. and mgmt. Hood Coll., Frederick, Md., 1979-82; exec. dir. Buhl Found., Pitts., 1982—; dir. Duquesne Light Co., Dollar Bank, FSB, Microbac Labs., Inc., Orbeco Analytical Svcs., Inc., Rsch. for Better Schs., Del. White House Conf. on Small Bus., 1980; mem. Gov.'s Conf. Small Bus., 1979-82; trustee Franklin and Marshall Coll., 1982—, Clark U. Pres.'s Coun., 1989—, Frick Edn. Commn., 1980—, Buhl Sci. Ctr., 1982—; mem. citizens sponsoring com. Allegheny Conf. Community Devel., 1982—; mem. Fed. Jud. Nominating Commn., 1977-79, Pa. Gov.'s Commn. on Financing of Higher Edn., 1983-85 bd. dirs. World Affairs Coun., 1984—. Mem. Am. Econs. Assn., Exec. Women's Coun., Am. Assn. Higher Edn. (mem. com. prof. devel. Coun. Founds.), Grantmakers of Western Pa. (pres. 1984). Office: The Buhl Found 4 Gateway Ctr Rm 1522 Pittsburgh PA 15222

BOYCE, EMILY STEWART, library and information science educator; b. Raleigh, N.C., Aug. 18, 1933; d. Harry and May (Fallon) B. BS, East Carolina U., 1955, MA, 1961; MS in Library Sci., U. N.C., 1968; postgrad., Cath. U. Am., 1977. Librarian Tileston Jr. High Sch., Wilmington, N.C., 1955-57; children's librarian Wilmington Pub. Library, 1957-58; asst. librarian Joyner Library East Carolina U., Greenville, N.C., 1959-61, librarian III, 1962-63; ednl. supr. II ednl. media div. N.C. State Dept. Pub. Instrn., Raleigh, 1961-62; assoc. prof. dept. library and info. scis. East Carolina U., Raleigh, 1964-76, prof., 1976—, chmn. dept., 1982-89; cons. So. Assn. Colls. and Schs., Raleigh, 1975—. Mem. Pitt County Hist. Preservation Soc., Greenville, Pitt County Mental Health Assn. Mem. ALA, AAUW, N.C. Library Assn., Southeastern Library Assn., Assn. Library and Info. Sci. Educators, Spl. Libraries Assn., LWV, NOW. Democrat. Home: 1406 Rondo Dr Greenville NC 27858 Office: East Carolina U Dept Libr & Info Studies Greenville NC 27878-4353

BOYCE, TRACY DAVENPORT, corporate publications executive; b. Charlotte, N.C., Aug. 18, 1966; d. Juston Burns III and Brenda (Bostian) Davenport; m. J. Donovan Boyce, Mar. 18, 1989. BA, U. N.C., 1988. Asst. mgr. corp. pub. rels. NCNB Corp., Charlotte, 1988-90, asst. mgr. corp. publs., 1990—. Corp. contact and coord. Teen-Age Parent Svcs., Teen Outreach Program/Cities in Schs., 1989—; mem. pub. and media rels. com. Mecklenburg County Bond campaign, 1989; mem. pub. rels. com. Jazz Charlotte, 1990; vol. Habitat for Humanity; mem. corp. vol. coun. United Way, Charlotte, 1990—; event coord. Discovery Place Festival of Trees. Mem. Internat. Assn. of Bus. Communications, Women in Communication, Inc., Charlotte Pub. Rels. Soc. Republican. Presbyterian. Home: 415 K West 8th St Charlotte NC 28202 Office: NCNB Corp 1 NCNB Pla Charlotte NC 28255

BOYD, BARBARA ANN, information systems executive; b. Columbus, Ohio, Aug. 7, 1956; d. William Thomas and Eunice Lucille (Seeliger) B.; m. Robert Bruce Wright, Apr. 16, 1983. BA, Capital U., 1978. Programmer Nationwide Ins. Co., Columbus, 1978-80, lead programmer, analyst, 1981-82, supr., 1982-87, planning specialist, 1987-88, planning mgr., 1988-90, data ctr. mgr., 1990—. Mem. steering com. Nationwide Operation Feed Campaign, Columbus, 1986-88; instr. CPR, 1986-89; mem. placement com. Cen. Ohio Rehab. Ctr., Columbus, 1987—. Mem. Am. Mgmt. Assn., NAFE, Fox Fire Golf League, Bash Golf League, Toastmasters. Democrat. Lutheran. Office: Nationwide Ins Co One Nationwide Plaza Columbus OH 43216

BOYD, BOBBIE MARGUERITE, college alumni administrator; b. Kirksville, Mo., Aug. 30, 1957; d. John Maurer and Hattie Mae (Myers) B. BBA, So. Meth. U., 1979; Grad. in Comml. Art., U. Ariz., 1980; student, Scottsdale Community Coll., 1983-84; CIS, Ariz. State U., 1984. Intern Nordensson Advt. and Pub. Rels., Tucson, 1980; fund raising coord. So. Ariz. Div. Am. Heart Assn., Tucson, 1980-82; dir. devel. svcs. Am. Grad. Sch. of Internat. Mgmt., Glendale, Ariz., 1983-85, dir. alumni rels., 1985—. Vol. Crisis Nursery, Phoenix, 1988—. Mem. Coun. for Advancement and Support of Edn. (1 silver, 2 bronze medals 1987), Am. Soc. Assn. Execs., Nat. Soc. Fundraising Execs. (conf. com. 1985), AAUW, Phi Theta Kappa, Alpha Lambda Delta, Phi Eta Sigma. Republican. Presbyterian. Home: 888 E Clinton St #2089 Phoenix AZ 85020 Office: Am Grad Sch Internat Mgmt Alumni Rels Dept 15249 N 59th Ave Glendale AZ 85306

BOYD, CONSTANCE DOROTHY, educator; b. Wilkes-Barre, Pa., July 23, 1943; d. John A. and Constance D. (Olpinski) Novinski; m. John E. Boyd, Feb. 23, 1980; children: Linda Maximowicz, Richard Maximowicz. BS in Edn., Wilkes Coll., 1965; MS in Edn., Millersville (Pa.) U., 1970; postgrad., Pa. State U., 1988—. Cert. elem. tchr., reading specialist, reading supr., Pa. Tchr. West York (Pa.) Sch. Dist., 1966-68; tchr. Owen J. Roberts Sch. Dist., Pottstown, Pa., 1968-72, reading specialist, 1972-86, dist. reading coordinator, 1986—; adj. instr. Manor Jr. Coll., Jenkinstown, Pa., 1985-88; speaker in field. Editor: (newsletter) The Book, 1988—. Mem. Internat. Reading Assn., Keystone State Reading Assn. (chmn. newspaper in edn. com. 1984-89), Tri-County Reading Assn. (charter, pres. 1983-84, treas. 1979—), NEA, Pa. Edn. Assn. Home: 1071 Penn Cir King of Prussia PA 19406 Office: Owen J Roberts Sch Dist RD #1 Pottstown PA 19464

BOYD, DAWN MICHELE, vocational consultant, psychotherapist; b. N.Y.C., Dec. 30, 1952; d. Alonzo Fredrick and Kathlyn Marie (Hunter) Morrow. BA, NYU, 1974; MA, Columbia U., 1975, MEd, 1976. Cert. ins. rehab. specialist, Calif.; lic. marriage and family therapist, Calif. Asst. family counselor Boys Harbor, Inc., N.Y.C., 1973-74; tchr. Upward Bound program Columbia U., N.Y.C., 1974-75, vocat. counselor Psychol. Consultation Ctr., Tchrs. Coll., 1975-76; rehab. counsel Neurol. Inst., Columbia-Presbyn. Med. Ctr., N.Y.C., 1975-76; psychologist II, team leader Washington Heights Community Mental Health Ctr., N.Y.C., 1977-81; vocat. cons. Vocat. Exploration Svcs., L.A. and Van Nuys, Calif., 1984-89; vocat. cons., rehab. economist, psychotherapist Dawn Boyd Cons., Sherman Oaks, Calif., 1989—. Mem. Nat. Assn. Rehab. Profls. in Pvt. Sector, Calif. Assn. Marriage and Family Therapists, NAFE, Women's Referral Svc., Nat. Head Injury Found. Republican. Roman Catholic. Office: 13601 Ventura Blvd Ste 250 Sherman Oaks CA 91423

BOYD, DEBORAH ANN, pediatrician; b. Urbana, Ohio, Jan. 30, 1955; d. John A. Sr. and Juanita Jean (Routt) B. BA cum laude, Wittenberg U., 1977; MD, U. Cin., 1982. Diplomate Am. Bd. Pediatrics, Nat. Bd. Med. Examiners. Intern Children's Hosp. Med. Ctr., Cin., 1982-83, pediatric resident, 1982-85; pediatrician Nat. Health Svc. Corps, Springfield, Ohio, 1985-89, Community Hosp. Health Care Ctr., Springfield, 1989—; mem. Continuing med. edn. com. Mercy Med. Ctr., Springfield, 1989—, infection control com., 1987—. Adv. com. Miami Valley Child Devl. Ctr., Springfield, 1985—, New Parents as Tchrs., 1986—. Democratic. Home: 2310 N Limestone 118 Springfield OH 45503 Office: Community Hosp Health Care 144 W Pleasant St Springfield OH 45506

BOYD, JANE ELIZABETH, accountant; b. Sapulpa, Okla., Aug. 13, 1946; d. Ralph Edward and Betty Jo (Walker) Bray; m. Don Ray Boyd, June 24, 1972; children: Barbara, Bradley. BSBA, U. Tulsa, 1969; postgrad in human resource mgmt., Houston Bapt. U. Acct. Duval Corp., Houston, 1971-74, Relco Constrn., Houston, 1976-78; owner, mgr. Jane's Wall Creations, Houston, 1982—, Money Mgr. Am., Houston, 1986-87; acct. Enron Corp., Houston, 1987—; cons. in field. Recipient Pace Award Enron Corp., 1988. Mem. Svcs. Cooperative Assn. (v.p. 1987), Toastmasters (adminstrv. v.p. 1988-89). Office: Enron Corp 1400 Smith Room 814 Houston TX 77251-1188

BOYD, LEONA POTTER, retired social worker; b. Creekside, Pa., Aug. 31, 1907; d. Joseph M. and Belle (McHenry) Johnston. Student Las Vegas Normal U., N.Mex., 1933, Carnegie Inst. Tech. Sch. Social Work, 1945, U. Pitts. Sch. Social Work, 1956-57; m. Edgar D. Potter, July 16, 1932 (div.); m. Harold Lee Boyd, Oct. 1972. Tchr. Creekside (Pa.) Pub. Schs., 1927-30, Papago Indian Reservation, Sells, Ariz., 1931-33; caseworker, supr. Indiana County (Pa.) Bd. Assistance, 1934-54, exec. dir., 1954-68, ret. Bd. dirs. Indiana County Tourist Promotion, hon. life mem.; former bd. dirs. Indiana County United Fund, Salvation Army, Indiana County Guidance Ctr., Armstrong-Indiana Mental Health Bd.; cons. assoc. Community Rsch. Assocs., Inc.; mem. Counseling Ctr. Aux., Lake Havasu City, Ariz., 1978-80; former mem. Western Welcome Club, Lake Havasu City, Sierra Vista Hosp. Aux., Truth or Consequences, N.Mex. Recipient Jr. C. of C. Disting. Svc. award, Indiana, Pa., 1966, Bus. and Profl. Women's Club award, Indiana, 1965. Mem. Am. Assn. Ret. Persons, Daus. Am. Colonists, Sierra County Hist. Soc., Common Cause (Washington and N.Mex.). Lutheran. Home: 507 N Foch St Truth or Consequences NM 87901

BOYD, LINDA JOYCE (LINDA JOYCE HICKS), school system administrator; b. Annapolis, Md., Dec. 10, 1946; d. James Melcar and Evelyn (Johnson) Hicks; m. Gerald Bernard Boyd, Jan. 2, 1969; 1 child, Kimberly Elaine. BS, Morgan State U., 1968; MEd, Bowie (Md.) State Coll., 1978; EdD, Nova U., 1986. With Anne Arundel County Pub. Schs., Annapolis, 1968-69, 71-87, asst. prin., 1980-81, prin., 1981-87; counselor, test proctor Edn. Devel. Agy., Worms, Fed. Republic of Germany, 1969-71; supr. elem. schs. Carroll County (Md.) Pub. Schs., 1987—; participant Madeline Hunter Tchr. Effectiveness Tng., Anne Arundel County, 1981-85; bd. dirs., co-chairperson New Wave of Entertainment, Annapolis, 1986-88. Registrar St. Philip's Episcopal Ch. Vestry, Annapolis, 1985—; co-supt. St. Philip's Ch. Sch., 1988—; mem. task force Anne Arundel County At-Risk Youth, 1989—, citizens adv. com. Bates Mid. Sch. Recipient award George Cromwell faculty, 1983, Tyler Heights faculty, 1986. Mem. NEA, Assn. for Suprs. Curriculum Devel., Assn. for Ednl. Leadership (sec. 1985-86), Internat. Reading Assn., Nat. Assn. Elem. Sch. Prins., Nat. Assn. Sec. Schs. (assessor 1982—), Md. Assn. Elem. Sch. Prins. (com. on profl. devel. 1986-87), Links Internat. (chmn. ways and means com. Annapolis chpt.), Md. State Tchrs. Assn., NAFE, Delta Sigma Theta, Epsic. Women's Club (sec. 1977—). Democrat. Club: Episc. Women's (Annapolis) (sec. 1977—), Links Internat. Home: 613 Marti Ln Annapolis MD 21401

BOYD, LOUISE YVONNE, software systems engineer; b. Newburgh, N.Y., July 24, 1959; d. Charles Carter and Louise Yvonne (Lewis) B. BS in Math., U. Fla., 1981. Software systems engr. NASA, Kennedy Space Ctr., Fla., 1982—; adj. prof. of computer sci. Brevard Community Coll., Cocoa, Fla., 1984-88; mentor NASA Nurture Program, 1984—, NASA SHARP Program, 1988—, Kennedy Space Ctr.; NASA judge regional, state and internat. sci. fairs, 1987—; pub. speaker NASA, Kennedy Space Ctr., 1988—. Named in Black Achievers in Sci. exhibit, Chgo. Mus. Sci. and Industry, 1989, 30 Leaders of the Future, Ebony Mag., 1989. Mem. Nat. Tech. Assn. (region III dir. 1989—), Soc. Women Engrs. (treas. space coast sect. 1989-90, v.p. 1990—), Assn. Computing Machinery, Math/Sci. Network, NAFE, Nat. Mgmt. Assn., IEEE Computer Soc., Toastmasters Internat. (area 29 gov. 1990, area 11 gov. 1989, space coast div. gov. 1990—, Disting. Toastmaster award 1990).

BOYD, MARGARET LOUISE, educator; b. Ardmore, Va.; d. John H. and Geneva (Brown) Smith; m. Donald G. Boyd, June 5, 1959 (div. 1980); 1 child, Gilbert L. BS, Langston U., 1958; MS, Va. Poly. Inst., 1975; postgrad., Vanderbilt U. Tchr. pub. schs., Tacoma, 1960-62, Ft. Rucker, Ala., 1962-63, Ardmore, Okla., 1963-64; tchr. pub. schs. Chgo., 1964-65; tchr. Heidelberg DOD, Fed. Republic Germany, 1965-70, Fairfax County Pub. Schs., Reston, Va., 1970—; bus. mgr., Elegant Weddings by Margaret, Reston, 1986. Bd. dirs. No. Va. Juvenile Detention Commn.; active nat. steering com. Nat. Readership Conf. Am. Youth Found., Reston Town Coun. Mem. AAUW, NEA, Bus. Prof. Women, Bus. Va. Women's Club, AAUW, NEA, Nat. Coun. Negro Women, Va. Assn. Female Execs. (adv. bd.), Phi Delta Kappa, Delta Kappa Gamma, Alpha Kappa Alpha. Home: 2033 Lake Winds Dr Reston VA 22901

BOYD, MARY DEXTER, newspaper editor; b. Columbus, Ga., Feb. 5, 1913; d. Charles Amory and Lydia Cook (Folwell) Dexter; m. Francis William Boyd, Jr., Sept. 1, 1934 (dec. July 1972); children—Robert Alexander, Richard Dexter, Mary Frances Boyd Logback, Elizabeth Folwell Boyd James. Student Agnes Scott Coll., 1930-31; B.S., Kans. State U., 1934. Cert. tchr., Kans. Tchr., Kensington High Sch., Kans., 1934-35; asst. editor Jewell County Record, Mankato, Kans., 1940-72, editor, 1972—. Mem. Comml. Devel. Assn., Mankato, 1972—, Mankato Endowment Assn., 1972—, Housing Authority City of Mankato, 1975—, Jewell County Fair Bd., 1980—. Mem. Kans. Press Assn., Kans. Press Women, Omicron Nu, Kappa Alpha, Xo Chi Omega (v.p. 1932-33). Clubs: Modern Minerva (pres. 1939-40), Desire Tobey Sears, DAR, P.E.O.. Home: 405 S Center St Mankato KS 66956 Office: Jewell County Record 111 Main St Mankato KS 66956

BOYD, PATSY JEAN, accountant; b. Houston, Nov. 2, 1940; d. William Andrew and Stella Agnes (Nichols) Scott; m. Charles J. Boyd Jr., Aug. 27, 1960; children: Blair Vali Boyd Upchurch, Eric Austin. BBA, U. Tex., Tyler, 1981. CPA, Tex. Payment clk. United Mercantile Security Life, Dallas, 1960-63; sec. T.C. Wilson, PA, Jacksonville, Tex., 1965-67; sec. legal Norman, Hassell, Spiers, Jacksonville, 1967-79; controller, analyst Allied Tex. Bank, Jacksonville, 1980-83; controller Pizza Systems, Inc., Tyler, 1983—, v.p. fin., 1987—. Organist First Bapt. Ch., Jacksonville, 1985—. Mem. Tex. Soc. CPA's. Office: Pizza Systems Inc 3808 Old Jacksonville Rd Tyler TX 75701

BOYD, VIRGINIA ANN, biomedical educator, cancer researcher; b. Shreveport, La., Nov. 15, 1944; d. Fletcher W. and Bess J. (Sherman) Lewis; m. James Pierce Boyd, June 4, 1964 (div. May 1973); children: Kathryn Ann, David Greogry. BS, Northwestern State U., La., 1965, MS, 1968; PhD, La. State U., 1971. Instr., Jacksonville State U., Ala., 1968-69; postdoctoral fellow Baylor U. Coll. Medicine, Houston, 1971-73; scientist II, Litton Bionetics-FCRF, Frederick, Md., 1973-82, prin. scientist, 1976-82; prin. scientist Program Resources Inc., Nat. Cancer Inst., Frederick, 1982-88; assoc. prof. biology Hood Coll., Frederick, 1982-88, prof., chmn. dept., 1988—; virology cons. Biol. Abstracts, 1983—; cons. Biol., Rockville, Md., 1985; microinjection specialist PRI-FCRF. Active Girl Scouts U.S., bd. dirs., 1980-83; vestry Catoctin Episcopal Ch., Thurmont, Md., 1978-85; mem. to Europe People to People delegation for Tissue Culture, 1984; mem. People to People Biothch. and Cell Biology Del. to Japan and China, 1987. Recipient Teaching Excellence award Hood Coll., 1983-84; Nat. Cancer Inst. grantee, 1984—. Mem. AAUW (fellowship panelist 1988—), Am. Soc. Virology, Am. Soc. Microbiology, Tissue Culture Assn., N.Y. Acad. Scis., Internat. EBV Soc., Sigma Xi (chpt. dir. 1982—), Phi Kapp Phi. Republican. Avocations: reading, tennis, fishing, camping, travel. Office: Hood Coll Rosemont Ave Frederick MD 21701

BOYD-FOY, MARY LOUISE, engineering and construction executive; b. Memphis; d. Ivory and Mamie (Grey) Boyd; m. James Arthur Foy, Mar. 16, 1975; stepchildren: Lisa D., Steven M. BS in Sociology, Columbia U., 1975; postgrad., Boston U., 1989—. Asst. to dir. United Negro Coll. Fund., Inc., N.Y.C., 1958-60; adminstrv. asst. Fgn. Policy Assn., N.Y.C., 1960-70; exec. asst. Columbia U., N.Y.C., 1970-78; sales mgr. Internat. Paper Co., N.Y.C., 1978-80; corp. mgr. Ebasco Svcs. Inc., N.Y.C., 1980—. Mem. United Negro Coll. Fund, Inc.; bd. dirs. YWCA, N.Y.C., 1989—; chmn. nat. MED week U.S. Dept. Commerce, 1989. Recipient recognition award United Negro Coll. Fund, Inc., 1984, Disting. Svcs. plaque, 1985, 8, 87, 88, Outstanding Achievement award N.Y. State Senate, 1984; named to Queens County Registry Disting. Citizens, 1987. Mem. Am. Assn. Blacks in Energy (nat. 1st vice chmn.), Nat. Assn. Univ. Women (charter mem. L.I. branch, Woman of Yr. 1984), Coalition of 100 Black Women (award 1984, 86, 87, 89). Home: 117-20 232d St Cambria Heights NY 11411 Office: Ebasco Svcs Inc 2 World Trade Ctr New York NY 10048-0752

BOYER, KAYE KITTLE, association management executive; b. Peoria, Ill., July 5, 1942; d. Keith Howard and Evelyn Pearl (Benson) K.; m. Jon Frederick, March 20, 1965; children: Tristan Donna, Kristine Monique. Student, Merrill Palmer Inst., Detroit, 1964; BS in Home Economics, The Pa. State U., University Park, 1964; MA in Sociology, Rutgers State U., New Brunswick, 1967. Cert. Assn. Exec., Cert. Home Economist. Creative researcher Nat. Inst. Drycleaning, Silver Spring, Md., 1963; extension home economist Md. Cooperative Extension Service, Westminster, 1964-65; coord. human resources N.J. Cooperative Extension Service, New Brunswick, 1966-67; instr. Douglass Coll., Rutgers U., New Brunswick, 1967-70; coord., instr. pilot project Urban Coalition of Met. Wilmington Inc., Wilmington, Delaware, 1972; asst. to chmn. 4-H Youth Devel. Dept., Cook Coll., 1973-74; feasibility study dir. Ocean County Coll., Toms River, N.J., 1975; exec. dir. N.J. Home Economics Assn., Manalapan, 1975-86; pres. Boyer Mgmt. Svcs., Manalapan, N.J. and Earleville, Md., 1984—; mgr. Costume Soc. Am. Earleville, Md., 1984—; cons. Plumpton Park Zool. Gardens Rising Sun, 1988-89, N.J. White House Conf., Trenton, 1980; bd. dirs. N.J. Soc. Assn. Execs., Belle Mead, 1985-86, Md. Soc. Assn. Execs., Balt., 1989—. Editor Exchs. Newsletter Resource Dir., N.J. Programs and Svcs. Related to Adolescent Pregnancy. Adv. com. Dept. Community Edn. Rutgers, New Brunswick, 1979-84; vol. Soroptimists Internat. of Elkton, Md., 1987—; player U.S. Pub. Links Amateur. Mem. Am. Home Econs. Assn.(Ruth O'Brien Project grant), Md. Home Econs. Assn., Am. Soc. Assn. Execs., AAUW, Com. Library of Cecilton, Kappa Omicron Nu. Democrat. Home: 55 Edgewater Dr PO Box 73 Earleville MD 21919

BOYER, LAURA MERCEDES, librarian; b. Madison, Ind., Aug. 3, 1934; d. Clyde C. and Dorcas H. (Willyard) Boyer. A.B., George Washington U., 1956; A.M., U. Denver, 1959; M.L.S., George Peabody U., 1961. Pub. sch. tchr., Kankakee, Ill., 1957-58; asst. circulation librarian U. Kans., Lawrence, 1961-63; asst. reference librarian U. of Pacific Library, Stockton, Calif., 1963-65, head reference dept., 1965-84, coordinator reference services, 1984-86; reference librarian Calif. State U.-Stanislaus, Turlock, 1987-90, ref. coord., 1990—. Compiler of Play Anthologies Union List, 1976. Author article in profl. jour. Mem. Am. Soc. Info. Sci., ALA, Calif. Library Assn., AAUP, Nat. Assn. Female Execs., Nat. Assn. for Edn. and Advancement of Cambodian, Laotian and Vietnamese Ams., DAR, Daughters of Am. Colonists, Phi Beta Kappa, Kappa Delta Pi, Beta Phi Mu. Republican. Episcopalian. Home: 825 Muir Rd Modesto CA 95350

BOYER, LILLIAN BUCKLEY, artist, educator; b. Paterson, N.J., Mar. 1, 1916; d. George and Adele (Roomy) Buckley; m. Floyd E. Boyer, Jr., Sept. 7, 1935; 1 child, Karen Boyer Lloyd. BA in Art Edn., U. Ky., 1975. Field interviewer Survey Rsch. Ctr., U. Mich., 1963-68; 20 regional one-woman shows; instr. art U. Ky., Lexington; Ky. reporter for Sunshine Artists mag., 1976-85. Crusade chmn. Am. Cancer Soc., Anaheim, Calif., 1958, Orange County, Calif., 1959; active, hon. life mem. PTA, 1950-62; mem. Lexington Arts & Cultural Coun., Ky. Citizens for the Arts, Ky. Women's Heritage Mus., Cin. Art Mus., Friends of Ky. Ednl. TV, JB. Speed Art Mus., Headley Whitney Mus., Friends of Lexington Pub. Libr.; pres., dir., life mem. Lexington Art League, 1976-80, 82-83, 84-86. Recipient 56 awards for printmaking, painting and sculpture. Mem. U. Ky. Alumni Assn., Living Arts and Sci. Ctr., Friends of U.K. Art Mus., Nat. Mus. Women in Arts. Methodist. Address: 969 Holly Springs Dr Lexington KY 40504

BOYETTE, MARSHA ANN, credit union administrator; b. Hahira, Ga., Nov. 4, 1952; d. John Gilbert and June Marsh (Giddens) B. BS in Elem. Edn., Ga. So. Coll., 1975; cert., Valdosta (Ga.) State Coll., 1977-78, Ga. So. Coll., 1981; postgrad., U. Mo., 1981—. Tchr. Ga. Pub. Sch. System, 1975-83; personnel cons. Fin. Mgmt. Personnel, Atlanta, 1983-84; trainer, quality control coord. Elrick and Lavidge Mktg. Rsch. div. Equifax, Atlanta, 1985-87; presonnel adminstr. TechSouth Inc. subs. BellSouth Enterprises, Atlanta, 1987; tng. and mktg. dir. First R.R. Community Fed. Credit Union, Waycross, Ga., 1987-88, v.p. human resources, 1988—. Chmn. employers com. for State of Ga. Dept. Labor, Waycross, 1989—; commr. Waycross/Ware County Planning Commn., Waycross, 1988—. Mem. Fin. Mktg. Assn., ASTD, Friends of the Library. Episcopalian. Office: First RR Community Union 505 Haines Ave Waycross GA 31501

BOYKIN, FRANCES LEWIS, retired social worker; b. Boston; d. Joel Randolph and Frances Virginia (Kenney) Lewis; m. Herbert Charles Boykin Jr., Dec. 23, 1951 (div. 1958). BS, Simmons Coll., 1945, MS, 1946. Cert. social worker, N.Y. Caseworker Family Service of Orange County, Maplewood, N.J., 1946-47; child welfare worker Riverdale Children's Assn., N.Y.C., 1946-51; supr., casework coordinator Assoc. Day Care Services of Greater Boston, 1952-53; caseworker, advancing to sr. caseworker Salvation Army-Family Service, N.Y.C., 1955-74; psychiat. researcher, 1957-62; student supr. NYU Sch. Edn., 1969-74, field supr. student unit, 1976-79; field supr. for student unit Salvation Army Corps and Community Ctrs., N.Y.C., 1974-79, adv. orgn. mem. Salvation Army N.Y. State, 1979-86 (meritorious service award); adj. asst. prof. NYU Sch. Social Work, 1977-79. Bd. dirs. Assn. Bronx Community Orgns., 1964-73, v.p., 1968-69, treas., 1970-73; bd. dirs. N.Y.C. region NCCJ, 1976-85, mem. exec. com., 1977-85; mem. Bronx adv. com. Urban League, 1966-69; pres. corp. body 12th Ch. Christ Scientist, N.Y.C., 1988; active mother ch. 1st Ch. Christ Scientist, Boston. Recipient Service plaque for 30 yrs. with Salvation Army N.Y.C., 1986. Mem. Nat. Assn. Social Workers, Acad. Cert. Social Workers, Internat. Conf. Social Work (del. 1964-84). Home: 2235 Fifth Ave New York NY 10037

BOYLAN, ELIZABETH SHIPPEE, biology educator, academic administrator; b. Shanghai, China, Nov. 29, 1946; d. Nathan M. and Elizabeth (Little) Shippee; m. Robert J. Boylan, Oct. 2, 1971; children: Elizabeth B., Emily A. AB, Wellesley Coll., 1968; PhD, Cornell U., 1972. Postdoctoral fellow U. Rochester (N.Y.) Sch. Medicine, 1972-73; asst. prof. Queens Coll.-CUNY, Flushing, 1973-78, assoc. prof., 1978-82, prof. biology, 1983—, acting asst. provost, 1988-89, asst. provost, 1989-90, assoc. provost, 1990—; mem. grad. faculty Grad. Ctr. CUNY, N.Y.C., 1977—; vis. investigator Sloan-Kettering Inst. Cancer Rsch., N.Y.C., 1979-80; trustee N.Y. Met. Reference and Rsch. Libr. Agy., Bklyn., 1989—. Contbr. articles to profl. publs.; patentee in field. Grantee Nat. Cancer Inst., 1975-83, Am. Inst. Cancer Rsch., 1987-90, Am. Fedn. Aging Rsch., 1988-89. Mem. AAAS, Endocrine Soc., Soc. Devel. Biology, Am. Assn. Cancer Rsch., Sigma Xi. Office: Queens Coll CUNY 65-30 Kissena Blvd Flushing NY 11367

BOYLAN, KATHRYN CARNES, nurse, city official; b. Bellefontaine, Ohio, Dec. 8, 1938; d. John Kindel and Mary Frances (Brennan) Carnes; m. Timothy Virgil Boylan, June 10, 1961; children: John T.J., Mary Frances, Anne Virginia. BSN, Coll. Mt. St. Joseph, Cin., 1960; MEd, U. Cin., 1975. RN, Ohio; cert. advanced adminstrv. nursing. Pub. health nurse City of Cin., 1960-61; instr. M.B. Johnson Sch. Nursing, Elyria, Ohio, 1961-62, 69-85; staff nurse Elyria Meml. Hosp., 1966-69; adminstr. Elyria Health Dept., 1985-86, health commr., 1986—. Bd. dirs., past pres. W.G. Nord Mental Health Bd., Elyria, 1967—; chmn. Lorain County AIDS Task Force, 1988—; bd. dirs. Lorain County Free Clinic, 1986—, Cath. Social Svc., Lorain, Ohio, 1988—; mem. Lorain County Child Abuse and Neglect Adv. Bd.; com. mem. Lorain County Solid Waste Plan, 1989, St. Mary Ednl. Found., 1988, Diocese of Cleve. Office of Women in the Ch. Named Woman of Achievement, Lorain YWCA, 1983; recipient Disting. Alumnae award Mt. Notre Dame High Sch., Reading, Ohio, 1986, Disting. Alumnae award Leadership Lorain. Mem. Am. Pub. Halth Assn., Assn. Ohio Health Commrs. (pub. affairs com. 1987—), AAUW (pres. Elyria 1975-77), Lorain County Hist. Soc., Phi Delta Kappa. Democrat. Roman Catholic. Home: 239 Eastern Heights Blvd Elyria OH 44035 Office: Elyria City Health Dept 202 Chestnut St Elyria OH 44035

BOYLAN, MARYANN HARR, educational administrator; b. Porterville, Calif., June 15, 1949; d. Lester Eugene and patricia Ann (Jinnett) Harr; m. Jerry David Boylan, July 19, 1969 (div. 1980); 1 child, Karl Ann. AA, Reedley Coll., 1969; BS, Northwest Missouri State, 1971, MS, 1976. Tchr., counselor Hanford Unified Sch., Hanford, Calif., 1979-82, Kings County Dept of Educ., Hanford, Calif., 1982-84; dir. counselling Dinuba Pub. Sch., Dinuba, Calif., 1984-88; prin. Sierra Vista High Sch., Dinuba, Calif., 1988—; counselor, tchr. Iowa Western Comm. Coll., Clarinda, 1976-78. Mem. Tulare County Delinquency Prevention Bd., Tulare County Alcohol Bd., H. B. McDaniel Bd., Stanford, 1988. Mem. Profl. Women in Edn., Calif. Counselors Assn. (chmn., area rep. Fullerton 1988), Tulare King Guidance Assn. (pres. 1988-89). Democrat. Home: 5638 W Cambridge Visalia CA 93277 Office: Dinuba Pub Sch 1327 E El Monte Dunuba CA 93618

BOYLAN, VIRGINIA WALKER, lawyer; b. Washington, Dec. 29, 1941; d. Robert D. and Dorothy Elizabeth (Compton) Walker; B.A., Am. U., 1964; J.D., Cath. U. Am., 1979; 1 child, Kaithlin Janine. Admitted to Va. bar, 1979; resource specialist LWV of U.S., 1968-71; legis. asst. to Rep. John Melcher, 1971-76; sr. counsel Select Com. on Indian Affairs, U.S. Senate, Washington, 1979—. Trustee, Nat. Reyes Syndrome Found., 1980-85. Democrat. Office: 838 Hart Senate Office Bldg Washington DC 20510

BOYLE, BARBARA DORMAN, motion picture company executive; b. N.Y.C., Aug. 11, 1935; d. William and Edith (Kleiman) Dorman; m. Kevin Boyle, Nov. 26, 1960; children: David Eric, Paul Coleman. BA in English with honors, U. Calif., Berkeley, 1957; JD, UCLA, 1960. Bar: Calif. 1961, N.Y. 1964, U.S. Supreme Ct. 1964. Atty. bus. affairs dept, corp. asst. sec. Am. Internat. Pictures, L.A., 1960-65; ptnr. Cohen & Boyle, L.A., 1967-74; exec. v.p., gen. counsel, chief op. officer New World Pictures, L.A., 1974-82; sr. v.p. prodn. Orion Pictures Corp., L.A., 1982-85; exec. v.p. prodn. RKO Pictures, L.A., 1986-87; pres. Sovereign Pictures, Inc., L.A., 1988—; lectr. in field. Exec. producer (film) Eight Men Out, 1987; contbr. articles to profl. jours. Bd. dirs. UCLA Law Fund Com., Ind. Feature Project/West, L.A. Women's Campaign Fund; founding mem. entertainment adv. coun. sch. law UCLA, co-chmn. 1979-80; mem. adv. bd. Am. Film Inst., Womens Directing Workshop. Mem. Acad. Motion Picture Arts and Scis., Women in Film (pres. 1977-78), Hollywood Women's Polit. Com., Women Entertainment Lawyers Assn., Calif. Bar Assn., N.Y. State Bar Assn. Office: Sovereign Pictures Inc 11845 W Olympic Blvd Los Angeles CA 90064

BOYLE, BARBARA JANE, insurance company executive; b. Shenandoah, Iowa, Mar. 1, 1936; d. Thomas Henry and Hazel Ingred (Gell) Hill; m. Richard F. Smith, Jan. 6, 1990; children: Jill, Chris Richardson. BA, Iowa State Tchrs. Coll., Cedar Falls, 1960. Tchr. elem. United Community Schs., Boone, Iowa, 1975-79; mgr. dist. sales World Book Ency., St. Paul, 1980-83; ins. agt. Allstate Ins. Co., St. Paul, 1983-84; mgr. market sales Allstate Ins. Co., Eden Prairie, Minn., 1985-88, mgr. ind. agy., 1989—. Fellow Life Underwriting Tng. Coun.; mem. Nat. Assn. Life Underwriters, Minn. Assn. Profl. Ins. Agts. Methodist.

BOYLE, JOANNE WOODYARD, college president; b. White Plains, N.Y., Oct. 27, 1935; d. George Gordon and Josephine (Tschinkel) Woodyard; m. Arthur J. Boyle Jr.; children: Arthur III, Elizabeth, B. Patrick, John W., Terence G., J. Teig, Morgan. BA, Seton Hill Coll., 1957; MAT, Harvard U., 1959; PhD, U. Pitts., 1983. Instr. English dept. Seton Hill Coll., Greensburg, Pa., 1958-59, asst. prof., 1960-67, assoc. prof., 1968-85, prof., 1985-87, pres., 1987—; Bd. visitors Coll. Arts and Scis., Sch. Library/Info. Sci., U. Pitts, 1978—; exec. com., bd. trustees U. Pitts, 1978-85; exec. com. Women's Coll. Coalition, Washington, 1988—. Bd. dirs. Greensburg Area Cultural Coun., 1988, Citizen's League S.W. Pa., Pitts., 1988, Westmoreland Mus. Art, Greensburg, 1988, Sewickley Acad., Pitts., 1989; adv. bd. Laurel Initiative, Pitts., 1988; adv. com. Secretariat for Cath. Jewish Rels., Washington, 1988. Named Pa. Prof. of Yr. Coun. for the Advancement and Support Higher Edn., 1985. Mem. Am. Assn. Higher Edn., Commn. for Ind. Colls. and Univs. (exec. com. 1990), World Affairs Coun. (bd. dirs. 1990). Office: Seton Hill Coll Office of Pres Greensburg PA 15601

BOYLE, KAY, writer; b. St. Paul, Feb. 19, 1902; d. Howard Peterson and Katherine (Evans) B.; m. Richard Brault, June 24, 1923 (div.); m. Laurence Vail, Apr. 2, 1931 (div.); children: Sharon Walsh, Apple-Joan, Kathe, Clover, Faith Carson, Ian Savin; m. Baron Joseph von Franckenstein (dec. 1963). Student, Ohio Mechanics Inst., 1917-19; LittD (hon.), Columbia U., 1971; LHD (hon.), Skidmore Coll., 1977, So. Ill. U., 1978, Bowling Green State U., 1986, Ohio State U. Prof. English and creative writing San Francisco State U., 1963-79. Author: poems A Glad Day, 1930, Wedding Day; short stories, 1930, Plagued by the Nightingale; novel, 1931, Year Before Last; novel, 1932, Gentlemen, I Address You Privately; novel, 1933, My Next Bride; novel, 1934, Death of a Man; novel, 1936, The White Horses of Vienna; short stories, 1937, Monday Night; novel, 1938, His Human Majesty: novel, 1939, The Crazy Hunter; 3 short novels, 1940, Primer for Combat; novel, 1942, Avalanche, 1943, A French Man Must Die; novel, 1945, American Citizen; poem, 1944, Thirty Stories, 1946; 1939, novel, 1947, His Human Majesty, 1949, The Smoking Mountain; essays, 1951, The Seagull on the Step; novel, 1955, Three Short Novels, 1958, children's book The Youngest Camel, 1959, novel, Generation Without Farewell, 1960, Collected Poems, 1962, essay, Breaking the Silence, 1962, Nothing Ever Breaks Except the Heart; short stories, 1966, (children's book) Pinky, the Cat Who Like to Sleep, 1966, editor: The Autobiography of Emanuel Carnevali, 1967, Being Geniuses Together; memoir, 1968, (children's book) Pinky in Persia, 1968, Testament For My Students; poems, 1970, The Long Walk at San Francisco State; essays, 1970, The Underground Woman; novel, 1975, Fifty Stories, 1980, Words That Must Somehow Be Said: The Selected Essays of Kay Boyle 1927-1984, 85, This is Not a Letter, Life Being the Best, Short Stories, 1988, Poems, 1985; contbr. short stories to mags. Recipient O. Henry Meml. prize, 1936, 1941; San Francisco Art Commn. award, 1978, Columbus Found. Am. Book award 1983, The Los Angeles Times Robert Kirsch award, 1986, Lannan Found. award, 1989; Guggenheim fellow, 1934, 61; sr. citizen grantee Nat. Endowment for Arts, 1980. Mem. Am. Acad. Arts and Letters. Address: 40 Camino Alto #2306 Mill Valley CA 94941-2976

BOYLE, PATRICIA JEAN, judge. Student, U. Mich., 1955-57; B.A., Wayne State U., 1963, J.D., 1963. Bar: Mich. Practice law with Kenneth Davies, Detroit, 1963; law clk. to U.S. Dist. judge, 1963-64; asst. U.S. atty., Detroit, 1964-68; asst. pros. atty. Wayne County; dir. research, tng. and appeals Wayne County, Detroit, 1969-74; Recorders Ct. judge City of Detroit, 1976-78; U.S. dist. judge Eastern Dist. Mich., Detroit, 1978-83; justice Mich. Supreme Ct., Detroit, 1983—. Active Women's Rape Crisis Task Force, Vols. of Am. Named Feminist of Year Detroit chpt. NOW, 1978; recipient Outstanding Achievement award Pros. Attys. Assn. Mich., 1978; Spirit of Detroit award Detroit City Council, 1978. Mem. Women Lawyers Assn. Mich., Fed. Bar Assn., Mich. Bar Assn., Detroit Bar Assn., Wayne State U. Law Alumni Assn. (Disting. Alumni award 1979). Office: Mich Supreme Ct PO Box 30052 Lansing MI 48909*

BOYLE, RENÉE KENT, cultural organization executive, translator, editor; b. Cairo, July 4, 1926; came to U.S., 1946; d. Maurice Colin and Victoria Smith; m. John E. Whiteford Boyle, Feb. 2, 1950; children: Vanessa Whiteford Wayne, Christopher, Andrea Heller, Mara Whiteford. Diploma, St. Clare's Coll., Heliopolis, Egypt, 1944; postgrad., Rice U., 1947-48, Santa Monica Coll., 1950-51. Dep. dir. Am. Friends of Mid. East, Tehran, Iran, 1959-62, Les Amis Americains du Maghreb, Tunis, Tunisia, 1962-64; v.p. Fgn. Services Research Inst., Washington, 1964—; v.p. Whiteford Internat. Enterprise, Villars sur Ollon, Switzerland, 1967-74; pres. Wheat/Forders Press. Editor: Primers for the Age of Inner Space series, Beyond the Present Prospect, 1978, The Indra Web, 1982, Graffiti on the Wall of Time, 1982, Of the Same Root: Heaven, Earth & I, 1989. Mem. Dem. Nat. Com., Washington, 1982—. Mem. Acad. Ind. Scholars (exec. dir.), Ams. for Dem. Action, People for Ethical Treatment of Animals, Sierra Club. Unitarian. Avocation: cordon bleu cooking. Home: 2718 Unicorn Ln NW Washington DC 20015-2234 Office: Fgn Svcs Rsch Inst Box 6317 Washington DC 20015-0317

BOYLE, SUSAN JEANNE, medical sales professional; b. Evanston, Ill., Dec. 31, 1952; d. John E. and Annette (Kleinman) B.; m. Jack Richard Henry, Oct. 11, 1986. BS, Colby-Sawyer Coll., 1974. Med. technologist Northwestern Meml. Hosp., Chgo., 1974-75, Assocs. Internal Medicine, Chgo., 1975-81; mgr. dist. sales Am. Diagnostics, Newport Beach, Calif., 1981-83; specialist tech. sales Coulter Electronics Inc., Hialeah, Fla., 1983—. Mem. Jr. League of Monmouth County, Inc. Mem. Am. Assn. Clin. Pathologists (cert.), Phi Theta Kappa. Republican. Roman Catholic. Home: 198 Spruce Dr Shrewsbury NJ 07702 Office: 98 Mayfield Ave Edison NJ 08818

BOYLES, BEATRICE C., educator; b. Phila., Jan. 9, 1915; d. Harald Julius and Maren A. Christiansen; m. Elmer Woodrow Boyles, July 13, 1940. BS, State Coll., Glassboro, N.J., 1939; MS, U. Del., 1951. Tchr. sci./English pub. schs., Pennsgrove, N.J., 1936-46, Wilmington, Del., 1946-54; prin. pub. schs., Wilmington, 1954-60; prin. grades K-6 plus blind and handicapped pub. schs., 1960-68, prin., 1968-72. Contbr. articles to profl. jours. Mem. Gov.'s Coun. on Aging, Del., 1981—, Coun. on Handicapped, 1983—, RSVP Bd., Del., Bd. Nursing, 1983-89. Recipient Vol. award, Kiwanis, 1986. Mem. Del. Ret. Sch. Personnel (past pres.), AAUW, Older Women's League, Common Cause. Home: 704 Wilson Rd Wilmington DE 19803

BOYLES, DONNA LOU COCHRAN, tour director; b. Dexter, Kans., July 15, 1935; d. Fay Felix and Sarah Opal (Yeager) Cochran; m. Murry Lee Boyles, June 5, 1955; children: Belinda Erin, Bryan Murry, Blaine Lou. AA, Cowley Co. Comm. Coll., 1956; BS in Bus. Adminstrn.-Mktg., San Jose St. U., 1975. Instr. word processing Santa Clara Adult Educ., Calif., 1983; real estate agent Real Estate World, Sunnyvale, Calif., 1979-83, Midtown Realty, Sunnyvale, Calif., 1983-85, Fox and Carskadon, Cupertino, Calif., 1986-87; tour dir. Saga Holidays, Boston, Mass., 1987--. Chaplain's aid El Camino Hosp., Mountain View, Calif., 1983. Mem. Internat. Tour Mgmt. Inst. Alumni Group. Home: 776 Henderson Ave Sunnyvale CA 94086

BOYRIVEN, MARIETTE HARTLEY See HARTLEY, MARIETTE

BOYSEN, MELICENT PEARL, finance company executive; b. Houston, Dec. 1, 1943; d. William Thomas and Mildred Pearl (Walker) Richardson; m. Stephen M. Boysen, Sept. 10, 1961 (dec. 1973); children: Marshella, Stephanie, Stephen. Student, Cen. Mo. State, 1973-75. Owner, pres. Boysen Enterprises, Kansas City, Mo., 1973—, Boysen Agri-Services, Kansas City, 1984—; fin. cons., underwriter New Eng. Life Ins. Co., Kansas City, 1978-81; cons. San Luis Rey (Calif.) Tribal Water Authority, Wind River (Wyo.) Reservation, Cheyenne River (S.D.) Sioux, Iroquois Nations (N.Y.) 1983—; founding bd. dirs. Visible Horizons 1987—. Founding bd. dirs. Rose Brooks Ctr. battered women, Kansas City, 1979—, treas., 1979-81; founding bd. dirs. Am. Indian Youth. Mem. Internat. Fin. Planners Assn., Internat. Agri-Bus. Assn., DAR, Kans. C. of C. and Industry, Kansas City C. of C. Republican. Methodist. Office: Boysen Enterprises PO Box 9104 Shawnee Mission KS 66201

BOYTER, ANGELA MARIE, federal government official; b. Balt., Dec. 9, 1944; d. Lewis John and Genevieve (Payne) DiCarlo. BA, Goucher Coll., 1964; MS, Johns Hopkins U., 1968, MSE, 1972; postgrad., MIT, 1988. CPA, Md. Tech. mgr. U.S. Dept. Def., Ft. Meade, Md., 1964—; pvt. practice acctg., Ellicott City, Md., 1978-85; bd. dirs. Tower Fed. Credit Union, Annapolis Junction, Md. Bd. dirs. Sexual Assault Ctr. Howard County, Md., 1978-84, St. John's Community Assn., Ellicott City, 1969—; pres. Howard County Citizens' Assn., 1970-75, bd. dirs., 1989—; active on Howard County Charter Rev. Commn., 1980, 88, Howard County Criminal Justice Task Force, 1974-75; activist for tax reform and repeal of marriage tax, 1977-83. Mem. AICPA, Inst. Mgmt. Sci., Ops. Research Soc. Am. Home: 3914 MacAlpine Rd Ellicott City MD 21043

BOYTIM, JOAN FREY, singer, musician, educator; b. Sheridan, Pa., May 6, 1933; d. Norman L. and Ruth Mae (Lambert) Frey; m. James Alvin Boytim, Aug. 4, 1961. BS in Music Edn., Indiana U. Pa., 1955, MEd, 1964; postgrad. Staatliche Hochschule für Musik, Munich, 1955-56, 58, Ind. U., summers 1967, 70, 71. High sch. music tchr., Carlisle, Pa., 1956-59, choral dir., 1959-65; pvt. voice tchr., Carlisle, 1965—; lectr.; recitalist. Editor: Solo Vocal Repertoire for Young Singers, 1980, 82; med. illustrator; contbr. articles to profl. jours. Rotary fellow, 1955-56. Mem. Nat. Assn. Tchrs. of Singing (past state gov.; membership com.), Internat. Horn Soc. (life), Music Educators Nat. Conf. (life), Delta Omicron (life), Mus. Arts Club Carlisle (treas. 1982-84). Republican. Methodist. Avocations: sewing, painting, gardening. Home: 160 Glendale St Carlisle PA 17013

BOZA, CLARA BRIZEIDA, marketing professional, arts management consultant; b. Havana, Cuba, Apr. 18, 1952; came to U.S., 1957; d. Eduardo Otmaro and Hubedia Marta (Garcia) B.; m. J. Phillip Carver, Oct. 6, 1989. BA in English summa cum laude, Barry Coll., 1973, MA in Communication Media, 1988. Legal asst. supr. Steel Hector & Davis, Miami, Fla., 1978-80; program adminstr. Dade County Council Arts & Scis., Miami, 1980-82; dir. program devel. Nat. Found. for Advancement in Arts, Miami, 1982-85; exec. dir. Bus. Vols. for Arts/Miami, 1985-86; dir. communications and client rels. Steel Hector & Davis, Miami, 1986—; S.E. regional cons. Arts and Bus. Coun., N.Y.C., 1986-88; bd. advisors Mary Luft and Co./Tigertail Prodns., Miami, 1987—, continuing legal edn. program Fla. Internat. U., Miami, 1988—; panelist So. Arts Fedn., Atlanta, 1983-84, Fla. Arts Council, 1983-84, 86-87; panelist and speaker various local, state and nat. orgns. and assns. Recipient ednl. scholarship Barry Coll., Miami, 1969-73, Fla. Bd. Regents, 1969-73. Mem. ABA (law practice sect.), Women in Communications Inc., Greater Miami C. of C., Nat. Assn. Law Firm Mktg. Adminstrs., Am. Mktg. Assn. Office: Steel Hector & Davis 4000 SE Fin Ctr 200 S Biscayne Blvd Miami FL 33131-2398

BOZONE, BILLIE RAE, librarian; b. Norphlet, Ark., Oct. 7, 1935; d. Guy Samuel and Vera (Jones) B. B.S. in Library Sci, Miss. State Coll. for Women, 1957; M.A., George Peabody Coll. for Tchrs., 1958. Asst. ref. librarian Miss. State U., State College, 1958-61, serials librarian, 1961-63; asst. ref. librarian U. Ill. at Urbana, 1963-65; asst. librarian New Eng. Mut. Life Ins. Co., Boston, 1965-67; sr. ref. librarian U. Mass., Amherst, 1967-68; head circulation dept. Smith Coll., Northampton, Mass., 1968-69; asst. librarian Smith Coll., 1969-71, coll. librarian, 1971—; Bd. dirs. Hampshire Inter-library Center, Amherst, 1971—; mem. exec. com. NELINET, 1977-79; chmn. Five Coll. Librarians Council, 1980-82. Mem. ALA, Assn. Coll. and Research Libraries, Alpha Beta Alpha, Alpha Psi Omega. Home: 47 Red Gate Lane Amherst MA 01002 Office: Smith Coll Libr William Allan Neilson Libr Northampton MA 01063

BOZSA, DEBORAH ANN, advertising company executive; b. Belleville, Ill., Aug. 8, 1953; d. James Andrew and Clara Elizabeth (Buescher) B.; m. Charles Alan Mecum, Jan. 18, 1975. BA, So. Ill. U., 1974, MS, 1978. Mgmt. info. specialist Office of Manpower Devel., Edwardsville, Ill., 1976-78; territorial advt. mgr. CPI Corp., St. Louis, 1979-81; media buyer D'Arcy, Masius, Benton & Bowles, St. Louis, 1981-83, media supr., 1983-85, media mgr., 1985-87, assoc. media dir., 1987-88, v.p., assoc. media dir., 1988-90, v.p., communications dir., 1990—,; instr. Belleville (Ill.) Area Coll., 1978-81; cons. McKendree Coll., Lebanon, Ill., 1979. V.p., bd. dirs. Madison County Info. Line, Edwardsville, 1975-76; bd. dirs., dir. project rev. com. St. Louis Health Systems Agy., 1978-82; vol. area 12 Ill. Spl. Olympics, 1982—. Fellow So. Ill. U., 1975-76. Office: D'Arcy Masius Benton & Bowles 1 Memorial Dr Saint Louis MO 63102

BOZSAN, JACQUELINE ANN, furniture manufacturing company executive; b. Mt. Pleasant, Pa., May 2, 1946; d. Clarence Edward and Agnes Veronica (Lynch) Kirchner; m. William James Bozsan, Aug. 24, 1963 (div. 1974); 1 child, Gentry William. Attended pub. schs., Library, Pa. Admissions rep. Median Sch., Pitts., 1973-75; sales rep. Western Union, Pitts., 1975-77, Exxon Corp., Houston, 1977-79, Translux Corp., Pitts., 1979-81, Natco Corp., Hyattsville, Md., 1981-83; prin. W.P. Furniture Design, Alexandria, Va., 1983-85; govt. sales rep. The Hon Co., Muscatine, Iowa, 1985-86; govt. sales mgr. GF Corp., Youngstown, Ohio, 1986-88; v.p. sales Crown Furniture Mfg. Co., Rockville, Md., 1988—. Republican. Lutheran. Home: 2230 George C Marshall Dr Ste 401 Falls Church VA 22043

BRAASCH, JUDI RAE, travel executive; b. Jamestown, N.D., Nov. 9, 1941; d. Carl F. and Fern L. (Murphy) Frey; m. Benny G. Braasch; children: Jeffrey, Jody, Nicole, Robyn. BS, N.D. State U., 1966. Cert. travel cons. Dir. info. svcs. Jamestown (N.D.) Coll., 1964-75; owner, mgr. Yesteryear Inc., Jamestown, 1975-82; mgr. Satrom Travel, Bismarck and Minot, N.D., 1982-86; gen. mgr. Biltmore Travel, Phoenix, 1986—. Active Landmark Network, Mesa, Ariz. Mem. Internat. Cert. Travel Cons., Am. Soc. Travel Agts., Ariz. Travel Agts. Assn., Rotary. Home: 405 E Scott Gilbert AZ 85234 Office: Biltmore Travel 1201 S Alma School Rd #1750 Mesa AZ 85210

BRACE, BARBARA ANN, management consultant, accountant; b. Chgo., June 19, 1936; d. Robert J. and Norine (McConville) McKenzie; m. F.R. King, Nov. 19, 1955 (div. 1959); m. Regis L. Brace, Aug. 6, 1960; children: Lawrence, Karen, Kevin. Student, UCLA, 1954-55. Cons., tax preparer Brace & Assocs., Burbank, Ill., 1981—. Parade lady City of Burbank, 1975—. Mem. Nat. Assn. Tax Practitioners (pres. Ill. chpt. 1987—), Nat. Soc. Pub. Accts. (fellow), Burbank C. of C. (treas. 1979—). Democrat. Roman Catholic. Office: 6215 W 79th St Burbank IL 60459

BRACEY, COOKIE FRANCES LEE, minister; b. Phila., Mar. 14, 1945; d. John Daniels and Evelyn (Jarvis) Bracey. B in Social Work, Temple U., 1983; MDiv, Wesley Theol. Sem., 1990. Adminstrv. asst. United Meth. Ch., Phila., 1963-86, parish community devel., 1984-86; local pastor United Meth. Ch., Catonsville, Ellicott City, Md., 1986-90; champlain Meth. Hosp., Phila., 1990—. Mem. Multi-Cultural Task Force, Phila. 1980, Victims& Crime Task Force,. Mem. Temple Univ. Soc. Adminstrn. Alumni Assn., Nat. Fellowship Local. Democrat. Home: 1419 W Cayuga St PO Box 9756 Philadelphia PA 19140

BRACHER, KATHERINE, astronomy educator; b. San Francisco, Oct. 26, 1938; d. Frederick G. and Agnes Hargreaves (Nuttall) B. AB cum laude, Mt. Holyoke Coll., 1960; AM, Ind. U., 1962, PhD, 1966. Instr. astronomy U. So. Calif., L.A., 1965-66, asst. prof., 1966-67; asst. prof. Whitman Coll., Walla Walla, Wash., 1967-72, assoc. prof., 1972-81, prof., 1981—. Column editor Mercury, 1983—; contbr. articles to profl. jours. Recipient Town and Gown award Whitman Coll., 1980, Lange award for Sci. Teaching, 1989. Mem. Am. Astron. Soc., Hist. Astronomy Div. (council mem. 1985—, vice-chair, 1987-89, chair 1989—), Astron. Soc. Pacific, AAUP. Office: Whitman Coll Dept Astronomy Walla Walla WA 99362

BRACKEN, KATHLEEN ANN, nurse; b. Chgo., Mar. 14, 1947; d. Thomas James and Catherine Anastasia (Cowal) B.; RN, CNA, Little Company of Mary Hosp., Evergreen Park, Ill., 1968; BSN, Lewis U., 1984, MBA, 1989. Mem. staff Little Company of Mary Hosp., Evergreen Park, 1968-69, 71—, supr. ICUs, 1976-79, dir. ICUs, 1979—; staff nurse coronary care unit Little Co. of Mary Hosp., Torrence, Calif., 1969-70; staff nurse Chgo. Lying-In Clinic, U. Chgo., 1970-71; instr.-trainer cardiopulmonary resuscitation; bd. dirs., mem. CPR tng. com., chmn. nursing cardiovascular com. South Cook Heart Assn., 1977-83, recipient Meritorious Service award, 1979, 81, 82, 83, 84, 85, 86. Mem. Am. Nurses Assn., Council on Nursing Adminstrn., Chgo. Heart Assn., Assn. for Advancement Med. Instrumentation, Am. Assn. Critical Care Nurses (pres. Southside Chgo. Area chpt. 1983-84, rec. sec. 1984-85), Am. Heart Assn. (cardiovascular nursing council), Ill. Orgn. Nursing Execs., Nat. Assn. Female Execs., Delta Epsilon Sigma, Sigma Theta Tau. Home: 10321 S Campbell Ave Chicago IL 60655 Office: Little Co of Mary Hosp 2800 W 95th St Evergreen Park IL 60642

BRACKEN, PEG, author; b. Filer, Idaho, Feb. 25, 1918; d. John Lewis and Ruth (McQuesten) B.; m. Parker Edwards, Mar. 17, 1966; 1 dau., Johanna Kathleen. A.B., Antioch Coll., 1940. Author: The I Hate to Cook Book, 1960, The I Hate to Housekeep Book, 1962, I Try to Behave Myself, 1963, Peg Bracken's Appendix to The I Hate to Cook Book, 1966, I Didn't Come Here to Argue, 1969, But I Wouldn't Have Missed It for the World, 1973, The I Hate to Cook Almanack - A Book of Days, 1976, A Window Over the Sink, 1981, The Compleat I Hate to Cookbook, 1986. Mem. AFTRA, Screen Actors Guild, Authors Guild, PEN.

BRACKETT, GAIL BURGER, budget administrator, political science educator; b. Bloomington, Ind., June 25, 1950; d. Clifford Robert and Opal June (McKinnon) Burger; m. Denis C. Brackett, July 14, 1973. BS, So. Ill. U., 1971, MS, 1972, PhD, 1984. Project coordinator instnl. research and studies So. Ill. U., Carbondale, 1972-80, budget analyst, 1980-81, adminstrv. asst. budget office, 1981-87, adj. asst. prof. polit. sci., 1987; sr. budget analyst Commonwealth of Va., Richmond, 1987—; mem. adminstrv. profl. staff coun., 1978-80; speaker Coll. and Univ. Machine Records Conf., 1979, 84, 87; referee Assn. for Computing Machinery Jour., 1978. Active Friends Sallie Logan Library, 1986-87, sta. Friends WSIU pub. radio, 1985-87, pres. Lydia Unit United Meth. Ch., 1987. Fellow Post-doctoral Acad. Higher Edn. (bd. dirs. 1986-87); mem. Bus. and Profl. Women, Nat. Assn. Female Execs., Assn. Instl. Research, Ill. Assn. for Instl. Research (panel 1983), Pi Omega Pi, Phi Kappa Phi, Phi Delta Kappa. Home: 21 Chase Gayton Circle #518 Richmond VA 23233 Office: Commonwealth of Va Dept Planning and Budget PO Box 1422 Richmond VA 23211

BRACKMANN, ANTOINETTE ELIZABETH, accountant; b. St. Louis, Sept. 16, 1923; d. Anton and Theresa (Schnitzmeier) Schumack; m. Roy Brackmann, Apr. 3, 1948 (dec.); children: William, Joan, Gail, Gloria. BSBA, U. Mo., 1977; AA, Jefferson Coll., 1973. CPA, Mo. Treas. High Ridge (Mo.) Fire Protection Dist.; acct. Zielinski and Assocs., Inc., St. Louis; prin. Brackmann CPAs, High Ridge. Mem. Mo. Soc. CPAs, Am. Woman's Soc. CPAs, St. Louis County Bus. and Profl. Women's Club. Roman Catholic. Office: PO Box 640 High Ridge MO 63049

BRACKMANN, HOLLY JEAN, art history educator, artist; b. Elmhurst, Ill., Aug. 27, 1947; d. Stanley Emil Edward and Shirley Elizabeth (Schray) B.; m. Michael Leroy Kelley, July 23, 1977 (dec. Dec. 1987). AA in Art with high honors, Foothill Coll., 1967; BA in Art History with great distinction, San Jose State U., 1969; MA in Art History, UCLA, 1972. Docent Triton Mus. Art, Santa Clara, Calif., 1969; instr. art history Ohlone Coll., Fremont, Calif., 1972; instr. art Coll. of the Sequoias, Visalia, Calif., 1972-73; instr. art history, textiles Mendocino Coll., Ukiah, Calif., 1973—; lectr. various orgns., 1975-89; guest curator Grace Hudson Mus., 1988; study tour leader, Mendocino Coll., 1983-90; mem. various comms., Mendocino Coll., 1974-84, 86-89. One woman show Hopland, Calif., 1984; exhibited in group shows at San Jose (Calif.) State U. Gallery, 1969, San Jose Mus. Art, 1976, Mendocino County Mus., Willits, Calif., 1980, Humboldt Cultural Ctr., Eureka, Calif., 1986, Loveland Mus., 1987, Grace Hudson Mus., Ukiah, Calif., 1988, Carnegie Art Mus., Oxnard, Calif., 1989, Calif. Mus. Art, Santa Rosa, 1989, Salt Lake Art Ctr., 1989, Mid. Tenn. State U., Murfreesboro, 1989. Pres. Parks, Recreation and Cultural Arts Commn., 1985, mem. 1982-86; mem. Sun House Guild of the Grace Hudson Mus., San Francisco Mus. Soc., San Francisco Mus. Modern Art. Recipient numerous awards, Redwood Empire Fair, Mendocino County Fair. Mem. AAUW, Conf. No. Calif. Handweavers (pres. 1988-89, numerous awards 1976, 77, 79, 82-89), Yokayo Spinners and Weavers Guild (coord. 1980-89), Coll. Art Assn., Am. Craft Coun., Calif. Tchrs. Assn., Handweavers Guild Am. (Third Place award 1986), Surface Design Assn., Made in Mendocino Coop. Gallery, Sigma Kappa. Office: Mendocino Coll 1000 Hensley Creek Rd Ukiah CA 95482

BRACY, KATHERINE BRANFIELD, educator, musician; b. Alliance, Ohio, Mar. 13, 1938; d. Richard W. and Katherine Sophia (Untch) Branfield; m. Carl Cluster Bracy, Feb. 17, 1968 (dec. 1977). BM, Oberlin Conservatory Music, 1959; MM, Baylor U., 1965. Harp instr. U. Tex., Austin, 1960-65; tchr. Alliance (Ohio) Pub. Schs., 1965-68, Columbus (Ohio) Pub Schs., 1968—; prin. harpist Ft. Worth Symphony Opera and Ballet, 1959-60, Austin Symphony, 1960-65, Youngstown (Ohio) Symphony, 1967-68, Columbus Symphony, 1969-85, Lakeside (Ohio) Summer Symphony, 1964-67, 71—; solo harpist Sounds of Hope European Concert Tours, North Webster, Ind., 1978, 80—. Mem. Am. Harp. Soc., Am. Guild Organists, NEA, Ohio Edn. Assn., Cen. Ohio Tchrs. Assn., Columbus Edn. Assn., Mu Phi Epsilon. Republican. Lutheran. Home: 6612 Merry Ln Columbus OH 43229

BRADBURY, KATHLEEN CHARLOTTE, librarian; b. Ft. Worth, June 19, 1949; d. Leonard Stanley George and Maureen (Davidson) Hart. BA, Tex. Woman's U., 1971, MLS, 1972. With Ft. Worth Pub. Libr., 1972—, br. mgr. Meadowbrook br., 1985-88, head of media dept., 1990—. Membership v.p. AAUW, Ft. Worth, 1982-84, cultural chmn., 1987. Mem. ALA, Tex. Libr. Assn. (chair dist. 7, 1982-83, chmn. continuing edn. div. 1990—), Librs. of Tarrant County (vice-chair 1990—), Beta Phi Mu chpt. Beta Lambda (chair 1985-86). Home: 701 Timberview Ct N Fort Worth TX 76112-1715

BRADBURY, LORRE JO, sales professional; b. Ridgewood, N.J., Apr. 17, 1957; d. Joseph and Doris (Simmons) Distasio; m. W. David Bradbury, May 7, 1983. BS, Drexel U., 1982; grad., Chevrolet Dealership Mgmt. Acad., 1987. Mktg. asst. Video Systems Corp., Pennsauken, N.J., 1977-80; mgr. leasing and sales Distasio Chevrolet, Marlton, N.J., 1980—. Office: Distasio Chevrolet 444 Rt 73 S Marlton NJ 08053

BRADEN, BETTY JANE, legal association administrator; b. Sheboygan, Wis., Feb. 5, 1943; d. Otto Frank and Betty Donna (Beers) Huettner; children: Jennifer Tindall, Rebecca Leigh; m. Berwyn Bartow Braden, Nov. 5, 1983. BS, U. Wis., 1965. Cert. elem. tchr., Wis. Tchr. Madison (Wis.) Met. Sch. Dist., 1965-70, 71-72, sub. tchr., 1972-75; adminstrv. asst. ATS-CLE State Bar of Wis., Madison, 1978, adminstrv. asst. Advanced Tng. Seminars-Continuing Legal Edn., 1979, coordinator, 1980, adminstr. coordinator, 1980-84, adminstrv. dir., 1984-87, dir. adminstrn., bar svcs., membership, 1987—; speaker Bar Leadership Inst. of ABA. Mem. Meeting Planners Internat. (sec. Wis. chpt. 1981-82, pres. 1982-83); Adminstrv. Mgmt. Soc., Am. Mgmt. Assn., Am. Soc. for Personnel Adminstrn., Am. Soc. of Assn. Execs., Wis. Soc. of Assn. Execs., LWV, Nat. Assn. Bar Execs. Home: 52 Golf Course Rd Madison WI 53704 Office: State Bar of Wis 402 W Wilson St Madison WI 53703

BRADEN, BETTY L., communications executive, business owner; b. Hibbing, Minn., Nov. 9, 1944; d. George Phillip and Rose (Ruzynski) Krier; divorced; 1 child, Beth Michaela. BS in English cum laude, U. Minn., 1966. With editorial prodn. Harbrace Publs., Duluth, Minn., 1969-70; assoc. editor Bruce Pub. Co., Mpls., 1970-71; mng. editor Master Publs., Inc., Mpls., 1972-78; project dir., copywriter Communication Arts, Inc., Mpls., 1979-80, Adhouse Corp., Mpls., 1980-81; pres., owner Braden Communications, Mpls., 1982—; mem. adv. coun. Internat. Biog. Centre, Cambridge, Eng., 1989—. Mem. pub. affairs com. Greater Mpls. C. of C., 1984-85; campaign worker Dem. Party, Mpls., 1988. Mem. Bus. and Indsl. Advt. Assn., Minn. Meeting, Minn. Press Club. Home and Office: 2701 Brunswick Ave N Minneapolis MN 55422

BRADEN, JOAN KAY, mental health counselor; b. Easton, Pa., Apr. 14, 1934; d. W.F. and J.H. (Snover) Ebner. AA, George Washington U., 1973, BA in Gen. Studies with distinction, 1976; MA, Hood Coll., Frederick, Md., 1979. Cert. clin. mental health counselor, Md. Staff psychologist Gt. Oaks Ctr. Md. Dept. Health and Mental Hygiene, Silver Spring, 1980-86; instr. Cath. Univ. Am., 1981-82; behavioral cons. U. Md. Hosp., Balt., 1986-87; therapist Montgomery County Abused Persons Program, Bethesda, Md., 1987—; pvt. practice mental health counseling Kensington, Md., 1979—; cons., group leader Am. Lung Assn., Rockville, Md., 1983-85, Lupus Found., Alexandria, Va., 1984-87. Editor: Help for Families of Chronic Lung Disease, 1985. Mem. Am. Psychol. Assn., Md. Assn. Counseling and Devel., Md. Mental Health Counseling Assn. (pres. 1988-89), Am. Mental Health Ccounselors Assn. (profl. recognition award 1989), Psi Chi, Alpha Sigma Lambda. Office: 3720 Farragut Ave Kensington MD 20895

BRADESCA, DONNA MARIE, nun, religious educator; b. Cleve., Mar. 12, 1938; d. Joseph Thomas and Ruth Mary (Kilbane) B. BS in Edn., St. John Coll., Cleve., 1961, MEd, 1969; DMinistry, United Theol. Sem., Dayton, 1988. Joined Order of Ursuline Nuns of Cleve., 1956. Tchr. elem. schs. Roman Catholic Diocese Cleve., 1961-70; dir. religious edn. St. Charles Parish, Parma, Ohio, 1970-76; tchr., adminstr. St. Mary Sem., Cleve., 1976—; tchr., Ursuline Coll., Pepper Pike, Ohio, St. John Coll., Cleve., 1969-72; coord. Ohio Field Educators Supervisory Tng. coun., Columbus, 1976-79; mem. Adult Edn. Bur., Diocese of Cleve., 1968—. Contbr. articles on edn. to theol. publs. Mem. Cath. Assn. Theol. Field Educators (coord. 1979-81), Midwest Assn. Theol. Schs. (pres. 1986-88), Assn. Nat. Field Educators. Democrat. Office: Saint Mary Sem 1227 Ansel Rd Cleveland OH 44108

BRADFORD, BARBARA TAYLOR, author, journalist, novelist; b. Leeds, Eng.; came to U.S., 1964; d. Winston and Freda (Walker) Taylor; m. Robert Bradford, Dec. 24, 1963. Student pvt. schs., Eng.; LittD (hon.), U. Leeds, Eng., 1990. Women's editor Yorkshire (Eng.) Evening Post, 1951-53, reporter, 1949-51; editor Woman's Own, 1953-54; columnist London Evening News, 1955-57; exec. editor London Am., 1959-62; editor Nat. Design Center Mag., 1965-69; syndicated columnist Newsday Spls., L.I., 1968-70; nat. syndicated columnist Chgo. Tribune-N.Y. (News Syndicate), N.Y.C., 1970-75, Los Angeles Times Syndicate, 1975-81. Author: Complete Ency. Homemaking Ideas, 1968, A Garland of Children's Verse, 1968, How to be the Perfect Wife, 1969, Easy Steps to Successful Decorating, 1971, Decorating Ideas for Casual Living, 1977, How to Solve Your Decorating Problems, 1976, Making Space Grow, 1979; novel A Woman of Substance, 1979, Luxury Designs for Apartment Living, 1981, Voice of the Heart, 1983, Hold the Dream, 1985, screen adaptation, 1986, novel Act of Will, 1986, To Be the Best, 1988, novel The Women in His Life, 1990. Recipient Dorothy Dawe award Am. Furniture Mart, 1970, 71, Matrix award N.Y. Women in Communications, 1985. Mem. Authors Guild, Nat. Soc. Interior Designers (Distinguished Editorial award 1969, Nat. Press award 1971), Authors Guild Am. (coun. mem. 1989—), Am. Soc. Interior Designers. Office: 450 Park Ave New York NY 10022

BRADFORD, CAROL SCHLOSNAGLE, communications executive; b. Carlisle, Pa., Dec. 23, 1950; d. Eugene Stanley and Ethel Mae (Smeltzer) S.; B.A. in English Lit., Hood Coll., 1972; MBA, U. Wash., 1988. Photojournalist, feature writer Carlisle Evening Sentinel, Carlisle, 1968-71, Frederick (Md.) News-Post, 1971-72; v.p. public rels. Cole & Weber, Inc., Seattle, 1974-82; v.p. communications Group Health Coop., Seattle, 1982-90l mng. dir. Ogilvy & Mather Pub. Rels., Kuala Lumpur, Maylaysia, 1990—. Publicity dir., fund raiser Am. Expdn. to K2, Pakistan, 1978; v.p. bd. dirs. Pike Market Community Clinic; mem. recruitment and pub. rels. coms. Leadership Tomorrow; bd. dirs. Nat. Coop. Bus. Found. Mem. Seattle Advt. Fedn., Public Rels. Soc. Am. (Wash. State chpt. award of Merit, 1978), Am. Hosp. Assn., Mktg. Communicators Exec. Internat. Republican. Presbyterian. Clubs: Washington Athletic, Seattle Press, Seattle. City publicity and travel writer and photographer for consumer and trade mags., newspapers. Home: 107 Jalan Ara, Bangsar Barv, 59100 Kuala Lumpur Malaysia Office: Ogilvy & Mather Wisma MCIS, Jalan Barat, Petaling Jaya, Selangor Malaysia

BRADFORD, CHRISTINA, newspaper editor; b. Dec. 23, 1942; d. J. Robert and Lesley (Jones) Merrill; m. Alan Bradford, Sept. 24, 1966 (div. 1973). AA, Stephens Coll., Columbia, Mo., 1962; BS in Journalism, U. Mo.-Columbia, 1964. Asst. city editor Detroit Free Press, 1975-80; asst. mng. editor Democrat and Chronicle, Rochester, N.Y., 1980-82, mng. editor, 1982-86; mng. editor/news Detroit News, 1986-89, mng. editor, 1989—. Mem. AP Mng. Editors, Am. Soc. Newspaper Editors, Detroit Athletic Club. Home: 208 Main Sail Ct Detroit MI 48207 Office: Detroit News 615 W Lafayette Detroit MI 48231*

BRADFORD, LOUISE MATHILDE, social worker; b. Alexandria, La., Aug. 3, 1925; d. Henry Aaron and Ruby (Pearson) Bradford; B.S., La. Poly. Inst., 1945; cert. in social work La. State U., 1949; M.S., Columbia U., 1953; postgrad. Tulane U., 1962, 64, La. State U., 1967; cert. U. Pa., 1966. Diplomate Clin. Social Work. With La. Dept. Public Welfare, Alexandria, 1945-78, welfare caseworker, 1950-53, children's caseworker, 1957-59, child welfare cons., 1959-73, social services cons., 1973-78, state cons. day care, 1963-66; dir. social services St. Mary's Tng. Sch., Alexandria, La., 1978—; del. Nat. Day Care Conf., Washington, 1964; mem. early childhood edn. com. So. States Work Conf., Daytona Beach, Fla., 1968; mem. La. adv. com. 1970 White House Conf. on Children, also del.; mem. So. region planning com. Child Welfare League Am., 1970-73; mem. profl. adv. com. Cenla chpt. Parents Without Partners, 1970—; adj. asst. prof. sociology La. Coll., Pineville, 1969-85, lectr. Kindergarten workshop, 1970-72; mem. La. 4-C Day Care Licensing Rev. Com., Central La. 4-C Steering Com.; social services cons. La. Spl. Edn. Ctr., Alexandria, 1980-86; del. Internat. Conf. on Social Welfare, Nairobi, 1974, Jerusalem, 1978, Hong Kong, 1980, Brighton, 1982, Montreal, 1984. Pres., Les Soignees, Alexandria, 1947-48. Bd. dirs. Cenla Community Action Com., Alexandria, 1966-68. Mem. Acad. Cert. Social Workers, Nat. Assn. Social Workers, La. Bd. Cert. Social Worker, So. La. Assns. Children under Six, La. Conf. Social Welfare, Internat. Council on Social Welfare, Am. Pub. Welfare Assn. (S.W. region planning com. 1965), Am. Assn. on Mental Retardation, DAR, Central La. Pre-Sch. Assn. (dir. 1967-70), Marquis Biog. Library Assn. (adv.), Rapides Golf and Country Club. Methodist (kindergarten bd. 1967-87), ofcl. bd. 1974-75, 77-81, 83-85). Home: 5807 Joyce St Alexandria LA 71302 Office: PO Box 7768 Alexandria LA 71306

BRADFORD, ORCELIA SYLVIA, infosystems specialist; b. Kansas City, Mo., Apr. 28, 1953; d. Thomas Wayne and Sylvia (Fueston)Ryan; m. Stanley Lynn, Sept. 26, 1975; children: Richard Lee, April Orcelia. Grad., Belleville Area Coll., 1979. Operator Fin. Data Systems, St. Louis, 1979-81; operator Community Fed. Savs. and Loan, St. Louis, 1981-82, scheduler, 1982-84; prodn. control scheduler Citicorp Person-to-Person, Inc., St. Louis, 1984-87; tech. cons. Cap Gemini Am., Overland Park, Kans., 1987; data analyst Source EDP, Overland Park, 1987-88; prodn. control analyst US Sprint, Kansas City, Mo., 1989—. Mgr. local youth girls' softball team. Republican. Baptist. Home: 9303 Alden Rd Lenexa KS 66215 Office: US Sprint 1300 E 104th Kansas City MO 64131

BRADLEY, AMY LORRAINE, psychotherapist; b. Little Rock, May 29, 1949; d. Arthur Ervin and Mildred Helen (Hoeltzel) B. BA, U. Ark., 1972, MSW, 1973. Lic. social worker, Ark. Pvt. practice Little Rock, 1983—; mem. clin. staff Bridgeway Hosp., North Little Rock, Ark., 1989—; cons. employee assistance programs 3M, 1988—, Planned Behavioral Health Care, Inc., 1988—. Mem. Nat. Assn. Social Workers, Acad. Cert. Social Workers. Office: 2723 Foxcroft Ste 310 Little Rock AR 72207

BRADLEY, BONNIE, mezzo soprano; b. Wilmington, Del.; d. Archie Merill and Blanche Ruth Bradley; Certs. in Oratorio, Song, Opera, Britten-Pears Sch. Advanced Musical Studies, Snape-on-Maltings, Eng.; cert. in Opera, Inst. Musical Studies, Graz, Austria, Mozarteum Sommerakadamie, Salzburg, Austria; B.Mus. in Voice, Westminster Choir Coll.; M.Mus. in Opera Performance, Manhattan Sch. Music, N.Y.C., 1975; m. Nicholas Nicosia, June 28, 1975; children: Francesca Maria Aida, Jonathan Gregory. Operatic and concert artist performing with opera cos. and maj. symphony orchs., recitalist U.S., Eng., Germany, Austria, the Caribbean, 1975—; instr. master classes colls. and univs.; adjudicator maj. vocal competitions. Helene Rubenstein Found. grantee; winner Artists Internat. Competition, Liederkranz Found. competition, N.Y. Oratorio solo competition; recipient Minna Kauffman Ruud Found. competition award. Mem. Am. Guild Musical Artists, Nat. Assn. Tchrs. of Singing, Coll. Music Soc., Washington Arts Group. Office: care Metropolitan Musical Artists 1872 Kirby Rd McLean VA 22101

BRADLEY, CAROL ANN, nursing administrator; b. Genoa, Nebr., July 7, 1953; d. John Martin and Marguerite (Leonard) Brower; m. Jonathan R. Bradley, Nov. 30, 1985; children: Amanda, Emma. Assoc. Nursing, U. Nebr., Omaha, 1974, BS in Nursing, 1977; MS in Nursing, U. Ariz., 1978. Staff charge nurse U. Nebr., Omaha, 1974-77; mem. faculty, staff nurse U. Ariz., Tucson, 1977-78; clin. nurse specialist VA, San Diego, 1978-80; dir. nursing med. Good Samaritan Med. Ctr., Phoenix, 1980-85; v.p. patient care United Western Med. Ctr., Santa Ana, Calif., 1986-87; dir. nursing Rancho Los Amigos Med. Ctr., Downey, Calif., 1987—. Contbr. articles to profl. jours. Mem. Am. Orgn. Nurse Execs., Orgn. Nurse Execs. Calif. (bd. mem. 1987-91), Assn. Rehab. Nursing, Calif. Assn. Hosp. and Health Systems. Democrat.

BRADLEY, CHARLOTTE ANN, pharmacist; b. Aiken, S.C., Mar. 19, 1959; d. Parmer Thomas and Helen (Pike) B. BS in Pharmacy, U. S.C., 1982. Staff pharmacist Bapt. Med. Ctr., Columbia, S.C., 1982—. Mem. S.C. Soc. Hosp. Pharmacist, Am. Pharm. Assn., Am. Soc. Hosp. Pharmacist, Fifth Dist. Pharm. Assn. Home: 1120 Butler St Columbia SC 29205

BRADLEY, DIANE ROSE, lawyer, service company executive; b. N.Y.C., Nov. 14, 1956; d. Augustine and Rosemary (Dineen) Farfone; m. Stephen D. Bradley, Apr. 24, 1982. BA, Boston Coll., 1978; JD, Bklyn. Law Sch., 1986; Student, N.Y. Inst. Tech., 1988—. Bar: N.Y. 1986. Lawyer Sharretts, Paley, Carter & Blauvelt, P.C., N.Y.C., 1985-87; dir. internat. legal and fin. svcs. Paramount Communications, Inc., N.Y.C., 1987—. Tchr., Peace Corps, 1978-79. Faculty scholar Bklyn. Law Sch., 1985. Mem. ABA, Can. Bar Assn., Ct. Internat. Trade, Internat. Bar Assn., Am. Corp. Coun. Assn. Office: Paramount Communications 15 Columbus Circle New York NY 10023

BRADLEY, EDNA PYGATT, educator; b. Effingham, S.C., July 8, 1925; d. Lemuel George and Fannie (Melton) Pygatt; m. Luther Alexander Bradley, Sept. 21, 1950; children: Joan, Lucinda, Luther, Everett, Melody. BS in Elem. Edn., S.C. State Coll., 1949; postgrad., Temple U., 1962-63; MA in Elem. Edn., Ball State U., Muncie, Ind., 1973. Tchr. Chaves Sch., Hemingway, S.C., 1952-54, East End Elem. Sch., Greenwood, S.C., 1953-68; tchr. Garfield Elem. Sch., Muncie, 1969-88, ret., 1988. Author: Biographical Sketches of Afro American Role Models from Muncie, Indiana; contbr. articles to profl. jours. Bd. dirs. City Human Rights Bd., Muncie, 1988-89; sec. Meals on Wheels, Muncie, 1979-85; bd. dirs. Drug Abuse Bd., Muncie, 1988-89; communion steward bd. Trinity Ch., Muncie, 1969—, sanctuary choir, 1969—, chmn. Global Concern Com., 1988-89; treas. North Ind. Meth. Conf. Bd., Epworth Forest, 1977-84. Recipient Community Svc. award Muncie Newspaper, 1976, Sagamores of the Wabash award Gov. of Ind., 1989, many others. Mem. AAUW (sec. 1971—), Coalition 100 Women (sec. 1985—), Fedn. Colored Women (state chmn. 1986—), S.C. State Coll. Alumni Assn. (sec. 1983—), Nat. Assn. Afro Am. Women (sec. 1987—), Mr. and Mrs. Club (asst. sec. 1974-89), Ind. Tchrs. Assn. (state rep. 1985-87, bd. dirs. 1987-88), Delta Sigma Theta (Great Ret. Tchr. of Yr. Lake City Alumni chpt. 1990). Addresss: Rte 4 Box 54B Hemingway SC 29554

BRADLEY, EILEEN, federal agency administrator, lawyer; b. Phila., Jan. 26, 1948. AB, Trinity Coll., 1969; JD, George Washington U., 1979. Bar: D.C. 1980, Pa. 1984. Program analyst, staff asst. Adminstrn. on Aging, Dept. of Health, Edn. and Welfare, Washington, 1969-74, dir. div. State and Area Agy. Programs on Aging, 1974-76; dir. age discrimination study U.S. Commn. on Civil Rights, Washington, 1976-78, spl. asst. to staff dir., 1978-

79, dir. div. housing and federally assisted programs, 1979-80; dir. policy and planning Adminstrn. on Aging, Dept. Health and Human Svcs., Washington, 1981-82; regional adminstr. Office of Human Devel. Svcs. Dept. Health and Human Svcs., Phila., 1982-86, Atlanta, 1986; assoc. commr. Office of Hearings and Appeals, Social Security Adminstrn. Dept. Health and Human Svcs., Falls Church, Va., 1987—. Recipient Honor award Miss. Head Start Assn., 1986. Mem. D.C. Bar Assn. (adminstrv. law and agy. practice sect.), Adminstrv. Conf. of U.S. Office: HHS-Social Security One Skyline Tower 5107 Leesburg Pike #1600 Falls Church VA 22041

BRADLEY, GWENDOLYN, opera singer, soprano; b. N.Y.C.; degree N.C. Sch. Arts, Curtis Inst., Acad. Vocal Arts. Debut with Lake George Opera as Nanette in Falstaff, 1976; debut with Met. Opera as Le Rossignol in Ravel's L'Enfant et les Sortileges, 1981; Met. Opera performances include Ariadne auf Naxos, Rigoletto, Porgy and Bess, Tales of Hoffmann, Le Rossignol, Siegfried, Abduction from the Seraglio, Arabella, L'Enfant et les Sortilèges, Die Frau ohne Schatten, 1980-88 seasons; internat. operatic debut Corfu Festival, Greece, summer 1981; other European engagements include Netherlands Opera, Paris Radio, Hamburg Staatsoper, Glyndebourne Festival, Berlin Deutsch Opera, Monte Carlo Opera, Nice Opera; has appeared with Phila., Cleve., Central City Operas, Mich. Opera Theater; recitalist, concert performer; soloist Phila. Orch., Nat., Seattle, Denver, Honolulu, St. Louis Symphonies, Kansas City Philharm., Aspen Festival Chamber Orch.; recitals include Carnegie Recital Hall, Phillips Gallery, Dumbarton Oaks, Washington, community concerts. Nat. finalist Met. Opera Guild auditions; winner 26 competitions and awards. Office: care Columbia Artists Mgmt Inc 165 W 57th St New York NY 10019*

BRADLEY, INEZ MAYO, pathologist; b. New Orleans, July 29, 1935; d. Eugene and Emily (Veans) Mayo; m. William George Bradley Jr., May 30, 1964; children: Linda, William III. BA, So. U. A&M, 1957; postgrad., Iowa U., 1957-58, La. State U., 1959-60, Cath. U. Am., 1962-65, Trinity Coll., 1978-85. Tchr. East Baton Rouge Sch. System, 1958-59, speech-hearing therapist, 1959-63; speech-hearing therapist Gallautet U. for Deaf, Washington, 1963-64; speech-lang. pathologist Washington pub. schs., 1964—. Chair Howard U. Cancer Rsch. Cen., Washington, 1985-89; benefit chair Club 20, 1987—, scholarship chair 1988-89. Recipient merit awards D.C. pub. schs., 1980-88; NIH grantee, 1965. Mem. AAUW, Am. Speech and Hearing Assn. (cert.), Coun. for Exceptional Children (Outstanding Achievement in Edn. 1979), Dist. Speech-Lang., Hearing Assn. (chairperson 1966-68), So. U. Alumni (life), Delta Sigma Theta (life, sgt. at arms & historian 1976, 82, Excellence in Edn. award 1983), Omega Wives (Woman of Yr. 1975), D.C. Hook-up of Women (scholarship chair 1980). Democrat. Roman Catholic. Home: 1824 Varnum St N E Washington DC 20018

BRADLEY, LYNN PENCE, information services administrator; b. Washington, Pa., Dec. 24, 1962; d. Harry Edmund and Virginia Lee (Walliser) Pence. BS Computer Sci., Acctg. magna cum laude, SUNY, Plattsburgh, 1984. Programmer, analyst Tandy Corp., Ft. Worth, 1984-87, applications mgr., 1987—. Democrat. Methodist. Office: Tandy Corp 400 Two Tandy Ctr Fort Worth TX 76102

BRADLEY, MARIE LANE, business owner; b. Easton, Md., Mar. 25, 1940; d. Marion Francis and Mary Virginia (Howell) Lane; m. Kit M. Bradley, Jan. 30, 1960; children: Kit M. Jr., Lance T. RN, Md. Office mgr. Van Scoyac and Assocs., Irvington, Va.; word processing mgr. Sovran Bank, Richmond; exec. sec. Rappahannock-Westminster Canterbury, Irvington; owner Secretarial Svcs., Cambridge, Md. Mem. NAFE, Nat. Assn. Secretarial Svcs., Profl. Secs. Internat. (sec.), Dorchester C. of C. (bd. dirs.), Ladies of Elks (pres. club #1272). Democrat. Methodist. Home: 304 Belvedere Ave Cambridge MD 21613

BRADLEY, MARILYNNE GAIL, advertising executive; b. Rockford, Ill., Apr. 12, 1938; d. Sherwin S. and Lillian (Leopold) Gersten; m. Charles S. Bradley, Dec. 28, 1959; children: Suzanne, Scott. BFA, Washington U., 1960; MAT, Webster U., St. Louis, 1975; MFA, Syracuse U., 1981. With Essayons Studio, St. Louis, 1968-69; tchr. Webster Groves High Sch., St. Louis, 1970—; instr. Webster Coll., St. Louis, 1973-82, Washington U., St. Louis, 1984-87; advt. exec. C. Bradley & Assocs., St. Louis, 1965—; sec. Mo. Art. Edn., State of Mo., 1986-87. Author, illustrator: Arpens and Acres, 1976, Packets on Parade, 1980; illustrator: St. Louis Silhouettes, 1977; editor (video) 12 Water Color Lessons, 1987. Bd. govs. Webster Groves (Mo.) Hist. Soc., 1965-72; mem. St. Louis Philharmonic Soc., 1956-72. Named Tchr. of Yr., 1987. Mem. So. Watercolor Soc. (sec. 1978-80), St. Louis Woman Artists, St. Louis Artist Guild (sec. 1985-86, pres. 1989—), Disting. Woman 1987), Monday Club (chmn. 1979-83). Office: C Bradley & Assocs 817 S Gore Saint Louis MO 63119

BRADLEY, PENELOPE HARTFORD, real estate sales executive; b. L.A., Feb. 18, 1940; d. Harold and Elva (Hartford) Hartley; divorced; children: C. Scott, Mark, Tracy. Student, UCLA, 1957-60, San Diego State U., 1961-62. Realtor, assoc. Earl Thacker, Ltd., Honolulu, 1972; pres. Bradley Properties, Ltd., Honolulu, 1975—; instr. Grad. Real Estate Inst., Honolulu.; bd. dir. Econ. Devel. Corp., Honolulu, 1989, Hawaii Conv. Park Coun., Honolulu, 1989; state instr. in investments; speaker in field. Sponsor Honolulu Symphony, 1988-89, chmn. fund raising, real estate div. Aloha United Way, Honlulu, 1979, 80, 90; mem. Better Bus. Bur.; bd. dirs. Realtors Polit. Action Com. Recipient Leader award YWCA, Honlulu, 1989. Mem. Nat. Assn. Realtors (urban affairs and pub. affairs com.), Hawaii Visitors Bur., Hawaii C. of C., Downtown Improvement Assn., Young Pres.' Orgn. (edn. chairperson 1988-89, chpt. chairperson 1989-90), Honlulu Bd. of Realtor (pres. 1989, v.p., treas., bd. dir., chmn. of strategic planning com., chmn. of fin. and audit com.), Hawaii Assn. Realtors (v.p. 1989), Comml. Investment Inst. (cert. real estate mgr., cert. residential specialist), Japanese-Am. Soc. of Honolulu, Downtown Improvement Assn., Pres.' Club. Office: Bradley Properties Ltd 1177 Kapiolani Blvd Honolulu HI 96814

BRADLEY, VELMA JEAN, insurance company executive; b. Ft. Wayne, Ind., Dec. 22, 1951; d. Vincent Joseph Lijewski and Vera Caroline (Strange) Reardon; m. Alan D. Bradley, Jan. 26, 1974; children: Jacob, Jared. Student, Indiana U., Ft. Wayne, 1971, Davenport Coll., Grand Rapids, Mich., 1975, Luth. Coll. Health Professions, Ft. Wayne, Ind., 1990—. Office mgr. Ash Brokerage Co., Ft. Wayne, Ind., 1971-74; asst. supr. collection dept. Old Kent Bank, Grand Rapids, Mich., 1975-79; mgr. sub-standard dept. Ash Brokerage Co., Ft. Wayne, 1982-86; dir. spl. markets Mut. Security Life, Ft. Wayne, 1986-88, asst. v.p., dir. spl. markets, 1988—. Cons. Jr. Achievement Project Bus., Ft. Wayne, 1987; participant Grandma's Marathon, Duluth, Minn., 1989, N.Y.C. Marathon, 1989. Mem. Nat. Assn. Life Underwriters, Ft. Wayne chpt. Nat. Assn. Life Underwriters (bd. dirs. 1988—). Roman Catholic.

BRADLEY, WANDA LOUISE, librarian; b. Havre de Grace, Md., June 6, 1953; d. William Smith and Josephine Viola (Miller) B. BA, U. Md., 1975; MSLS, Atlanta U., 1976; postgrad., Cath. U.; MPA (scholar), U. Balt., 1986. Libr. Harford County Pub. Libr., Bel Air, Md., 1976, Harford County Bd. Edn., Bel Air, Md., 1977-81, Nat. Grad. U., Arlington, Va., 1982, Md. State Dept. Edn., Balt., 1982-83, U.S. Dept. Labor, Washington, 1984, Balt. Gas and Electric Co., 1984-85, Morgan State U., Balt., 1985, Coppin State Coll., Balt., 1985-86, Montgomery County Pub. Sch. System, Rockville, Md., 1985-86, Community Coll., Balt., 1987-88; grant adminstr. Howard County Pub. Libr., 1988; acad. advisor George Mason U., Fairfax, Va., 1981-82. Dept. Edn. fellow, 1983-84; U. Balt. Merit scholar, 1975, 84, Atlanta U. scholar, 1976; Howard County Pub. Libr. grantee, 1988. Mem. ALA, ASIS, Md. Libr. Assn., Spl. Librs. Assn., Med. Libr. Assn. Methodist.

BRADLEY-RIPPEY, JACKIE, graphic designer; b. Fountainhead, Tenn., May 5, 1952; d. Jack Lillard Bradley and Betty Shaw (Saylors) Bradley Harris; m. Allen Rhea Rippey, Nov. 3, 1980. BFA, Middle Tenn. State U., Murfreesboro, 1978. Owner, graphic designer Bradley-Rippey Design, Nashville, 1982—. Recipient Addy So. Dist. Advt. Fedn., 1989; Diamond award Nashville Advt. Fedn., 1989; award of excellence Consol. Paper, 1989, Prinding Industry Assn., 1989, Nashville Advt. Fedn., 1990. Mem. Creative Forum (pres. 1989-90). Home: PO Box 50093 Nashville TN 37205

BRADMILLER, LINDA LOUISE, lawyer; b. Cin., June 29, 1953; d. Richard William and Helen Mary (Sohmer) B. BA with high honors, U. Fla., 1975; MSW, U. Ky., 1977; JD, U. Pa., 1987. Bar: Pa. 1987, U.S. Dist. Ct. (ea. dist.) Pa. 1988, U.S. Ct. Appeals (3d cir.) 1988; lic. social worker, Pa. Adj. asst. prof. psychiat. social work Coll. Medicine U. Cin., 1977-84; assoc. Schnader, Harrison, Segal & Lewis, Phila., 1987—. Contbr. articles to profl. publs. Vol. atty. Support Ctr. for Child Advs., Phila., 1987—, Women's Law Project, Phila., 1989. Grad. fellow U. Ky., 1976-77; NIMH trainee, 1975-76. Mem. Pa. Bar Assn., Phila. Bar Assn., Nat. Assn. Social Workers, Acad. Cert. Social Workers, Phi Kappa Phi. Democrat. Office: Schnader Harrison et al 1600 Market St Ste 3600 Philadelphia PA 19103

BRADSHAW, BEVERLY JEAN, counselor; b. Denver, Dec. 25, 1946; d. William Heartsel and Shirley Marie (Powell) B. BA, U. No. Colo., 1970; MA, U. Denver, 1984; postgrad., Webster State Coll., U. No. Colo. Cert. Type B profl. tchr., Colo. Recreation supr. City of Englewood (Colo.), 1968-76; communications bd. chmn. U. No. Colo., Greeley, 1968-70; tchr. Englewood Schs., 1970-83, counselor, tchr., 1984-87, counselor, 1987—; guest speaker Colo. Assn. Sch. Bds., 1984; dist. rep. State Title IX Commn., 1971-73. Mayor pro tem Englewood City Council, 1980-87; chmn. Mcpl. Issues Com., Colo. Mcpl. League, 1986; mem. Human Devel. Policy Com., Nat. League of Cities, 1984-87, South Suburban Parks and Recreation Found., 1984—. Mem. Greater Englewood C. of C., Am. Assn. Counseling and Devel., NEA, Colo. Edn. Assn. (legis. liaison, 1988), Englewood Educators (negotiations chmn. 1974-75), Assn. Humanistic Edn. and Devel., Nat. Peer Helpers Assn., Alpha Kappa Delta. Republican. Roman Catholic. Home: 2910 S Marion St Englewood CO 80110

BRADSHAW, CYNTHIA HELENE, educator; b. S.I., N.Y., May 9, 1954; d. Frederick Thomas and Audrey Helene (Stetter) B. BS in Elem. Edn., Wagner Coll., 1975; MS in Edn., U. Miami, 1979. Cert. elem. tchr., adminstr., and supr. Tchr. Young Scholars Montessori Sch., S.I., 1975-76; tchr. Lutheran Schs., Mo. Synod, S.I., 1976, Hialeah and North Miami, Fla., 1976-80; tchr. Dade County Pub. Schs., Miami, Fla., 1980-88, Rahway (N.J.) Pub. Schs., Bayonne (N.J.) Pub. Schs., 1988—; reliability study subject Fla. Dept. Edn., Tallahassee, 1984—; participated in 3 videos in cooperation with Wagner Coll., S.I., N.Y., Bayonne (N.J.) Bd. Edn.; co-produced videos with Wagner Coll. and S.I. Continuum, 1988—. Sch. chairperson United Way, Miami, 1983—. Recipient Cert. of Recognition Dade County Pub. Schs., 1984. Mem. United Tchrs. Dade, United Tchrs. Dade Polit. Orgn., Order Ea. Star, U. Miami Sch. Edn. Allied Professions Alumni Assn. (mem. alumni telephone funding campaign 1984), Wagner Coll. Alumni Assn. (alumni telephone funding campaign 1988—), Alpha Delta Kappa. Republican. Lutheran. Home: 34 Douglas Ave Staten Island NY 10310 Office: Robinson Sch 31st St and Kennedy Blvd Bayonne NJ 07002 also: Roosevelt Sch 28th St and Ave C Bayonne NJ 07002

BRADSHAW, LILLIAN MOORE, retired librarian; b. Hagerstown, Md., Jan. 10, 1915; d. Harry M. and Mabel E. (Kretzer) Moore; m. William Theodore Bradshaw, May 19, 1946. B.A., Western Md. Coll., 1937, DLitt (hon.), 1987; B.L.S., Drexel U., 1938, Litt.D. (hon.), 1978; LHD, So. Meth. Univ., 1990—. Asst. adult circulation dept. Utica (N.Y.) Pub. Libr., 1938-41, asst. head, 1941-43; adult libr. Enoch Pratt Free Libr., Balt., 1943-44; asst. coord. work with young adults Enoch Pratt Free Libr., 1944-46; br. libr. Dallas Pub. Libr., 1946-47, readers adviser, 1947-52, head dept. circulation, 1952- 55, coord. work with adults, 1955-58, asst. dir., 1958-62, dir., 1962-84; asst mgr. City of Dallas, 1984-85; mem. adv. group on librs. Libr. of Congress, 1976-77. Mem. bd. publs. So. Meth. U., 1970-78; mem. curriculum com. Leadership Dallas, 1978-79, mem. adv. com., 1978-82; mem. Tex. Gov.'s Commn. on Status of Women, 1970-72, Tex. Com. for Humanities, 1980-84, Nat. Reading Coun., Washington, 1970-73; pres. Tex. Humanities Alliance, 1986-88—; conferee, asst. task force leader Goals for Dallas, 1966-69, vice chmn. achievement com. for continuing edn., 1971, chmn., 1972, chmn. citizen info. and participation com., 1976-77, trustee, 1977-78, sec., 1977, treas., 1979-83, exec. com., 1977-84; hon. chair Literacy Vols. Am., Dallas, 1987—; mem. Com. to Plan the Future Goals for Dallas, 1973-74, Dallas County Hist. Found., 1987—; mem. adv. bd. Tex. Library Systems Act, 1974-77; del. White House Conf. on Library and Info. Services; mem. ad hoc com. for planning and monitoring White House Conf. follow-up activities, 1980; bd. dir. Hoblitzelle Found., 1971—, Univ. Med. Ctr., 1984-87, Urban Design Adv. Coun. Dallas, Friends of Fair Park; trustee Lamplighter Sch., 1974-81, Friends of Dallas Pub. Library, 1984—, Dallas Ballet, 1986-88, Dallas Arboretum and Bot. Garden, 1986-88; bd. trustees Employees Retirement Fund, Dallas, 1989—. Named Tex. Libr. of Year, 1961; recipient Disting. Alumnus award Drexel U. Libr. Sch., 1970; Titche's Arete award for epitome of excellence in chosen field, 1970; Public Adminstr. of Yr. award, 1981; Excellence in Community Svc. award Dallas Hist. Soc., 1981; citation of honor Dallas chpt. AIA, 1982; Lillian Moore Bradshaw chair in libr. and info. studies established in her honor Tex. Woman's U. Mem. ALA (v.p. adult svcs. div. 1966-67, pres. adult svcs. div. 1967-68, council 1968-69, pres. 1970-71, endowment trustee 1984-88), Tex. Libr. Assn. (pres. 1964-65, chmn. pub. librs. div. 1955-56, chmn. awards com. 1973-74, 79-80, Disting. Svc. award 1975), Tex. Soc. Architects (hon. 1982), Dallas Hist. Soc. (trustee 1984-87), Dallas County Hist. Found. Club: Zonta (pres. Dallas I 1976-77, Svc. award 1981). Home: 6318 E Lovers Ln Dallas TX 75214

BRADSHAW, NANCI MARIE, business executive; b. Schenectady, Aug. 21, 1940; d. Leo Arthur and Angela Bertha (Bonk) Bradshaw; m. William Clayton Hoehn, Oct. 12, 1963 (div. 1979); children: Sharon Ann, Theresa Lynn. BS, Skidmore Coll., 1977. Asst. to pres. Schenectady Indsl. Drafting, 1978-79; bus. exec. math dept. SUNY, Albany, 1979-86, sec. council on acad. freedom and ethics, 1983-85; Evangelist Newspaper, Albany, 1986-89; cons., lectr. trustee, v.p., sec. Help Ctr., Inc., Troy, N.Y., 1982-897 lectr., cons. Organizational Mgmt., Albany, Schenectady and Troy, 1984—. Coord., originator Pre-Kindergarten PTO, Schenectady, 1976-78, Sunday sch. program Immaculate Conception Ch., Schenectady, 1970-79; mem. Pruyn Cultural Ctr., N.Y. Mem. Nat. Assn. Female Execs., N.Y. Acad. Scis., Math. Assn. Am., Am. Mgmt. Assn. Republican. Roman Catholic. Lodge: Soroptimist Internat. Avocations: refinishing antiques, reading, music, fitness. Home: 157 Maple Ave Troy NY 12180

BRADY, ADELAIDE BURKS, public relations agency executive, giftware catalog executive; b. N.Y.C., June 27, 1926; d. Earl Victor and Audrey (Calvert) Burks; B.S., Boston U., 1946; m. James Francis Brady, Jr., June 22, 1946 (div. 1953); 1 son, James Francis. Exec. v.p. Media Enterprises, 1952-55; dir. group relations Save the Children Fedn., N.Y.C., 1955-59; dir. pub. affairs div. Girl Scouts U.S.A., N.Y.C., 1959-69; pres. Communication Internat., Inc., Washington, 1969-73, Burks Brady Communications, N.Y.C., 1972—, Adelaide's Angel Shopper Catalog Inc., Wilton, Conn., 1976—; exec. v.p. Arts in the Parks Inc., Washington, 1971—; bd. dirs. Lenox Hill Hosp., N.Y.C.; past bd. dirs. Achievement Rewards for Coll. Scientists Found.; pres. Animal Lovers Inc. Mem. Nat. Womens Rep. Club., N.Y.C. Recipient Silver Reel award for film The Children of Now, Save the Children Fedn.; decorated cmmdr. Order St. John of Jerusalem (Eng.), 1974. Mem. Nat. Assn. Women Bus. Owners, Public Relations Soc. Am., AAUW, NEA, Am. Women in Radio and TV, Nat. Ednl. Broadcasters Assn., Am. Soc. Profl. and Exec. Women, Women Execs. in Public Relations, N.Y. Press Women, Nat. Fedn. Press Women (state pres.), Women's Econ. Roundtable, Nat. Assn. Profl. Women, Nat. Assn. Female Execs., DAR. Episcopalian. Club: Capitol Hill (Washington), Officers (Wash.). Home: 267 Westport Rd Wilton CT 06897 Office: 785 Park Ave New York NY 10021 also: Box 647 Wilton CT 06897

BRADY, HOLLY WHEELER, magazine editor; b. Evanston, Ill., Apr. 28, 1947; d. Warren Calvin and Doris (Wise) Wheeler; m. Cyrus Townsend Brady, Apr. 12, 1969; 1 child, Caitlin. BA, Stanford U., 1969; MA, Miami U., 1971. Cert. secondary educator. Tchr. Northmont High Sch., Englewood, Ohio, 1972-74; advt. writer Rike-Kumler Co., Dayton, Ohio, 1974-76; editor, mgr. Mazer Corp., Dayton, 1976-81; editor Learning mag., Palo Alto, Calif., 1981-84; editor-in-chief Classroom Computer Learning mag., San Rafael, Calif., 1983—. Contbr. articles to profl. jours., mags. including Parents, Parenting and Mademoiselle. Office: Classroom Computer Learning 2169 E Francisco Blvd #A4 San Rafael CA 94901

BRADY, SISTER JANE FRANCES, hospital executive; b. White Plains, N.Y., Nov. 14, 1935; d. Joseph Andrew and Helen Louise (Mooney) B. BS summa cum laude, Coll. St. Elizabeth, 1957; MBA, Seton Hall U., 1965; MS in Hosp. Adminstrn., Columbia U., 1969. Lic. nursing home adminstr., N.J. Exec. sec. AT&T, White Plains, 1957-58; asst. Office of Sec. Gen., Convent Station, N.J., 1958-66; adminstrv. asst. St. Joseph's Hosp., Paterson, N.J., 1966-67; adminstrv. resident The Bklyn. Cumberland Med. Ctr., 1968-69; asst. adminstr. St. Joseph's Hosp. and Med. Ctr., Paterson, 1969-72; pres., chief exec. officer St. Joseph's Hosp. and Med. Ctr., &, 1972—; trustee St. Joseph Hosp. and Med. Ctr., Paterson, N.J., Irvington (N.J.) Gen. Hosp., rep. to N.J. Dept. Health; mem. Bergen-Passaic Hosp. Adminstrs.' Coun., vice chmn. Commn. on Legal and Ethical Problems in Delivery of Health Care, State of N.J., N.J. Health Care Adminstrn. Bd., select com. Ind. Care Cath. Health Assn. U.S.; bd. dirs. No. New Jersey Health Planning Coun., Health Care Ins. Exchange, Princeton Ins. Co. Contbr. articles to profl. jours. Recipient Paterson Community Svc. award Great Falls dist. Boy Scouts Am., 1987, Citation of Merit, N.J. Assn. Non-Profit Homes for Aging, 1987, 1st Citizen of Yr. award Paterson Community Support Fund Inc., 1987; named Hon. Rotarian, 1989, Woman of the Yr., Am. Legion Post 438, 1990. Fellow Am. Coll. Health Care Execs.; mem. Am. Hosp. Assn., Kappa Gamma Pi. Roman Catholic. Home: 703 Main St Paterson NJ 07503 Home and Office: St Joseph's Hosp & Med Ctr 703 Main St Paterson NJ 07503

BRADY, JEAN VICK, education educator; b. Rocky Mount, N.C., Mar. 4, 1937; d. Ernest Telfair and Carrie Elizabeth (Baker) Vick; m. William Thomas Brady, Apr. 2, 1939; children: Arlan Thomas, William Tyler. AB in Eng. & Elem. Edn., Atlantic Christian Coll., Wilson, N.C., 1961; MA in Edn., East Carolina U., Greenville, 1963. Cert. Tchr., N.C. Tchr. Fayetteville (N.C.) City Schs., 1960-61, Rocky Mount City Schs., 1961-64, Raleigh (N.C) City Schs., 1964-66, Campbell County Schs., Brookneal, Va., 1966-68; dir. Homeplace Inc., Laurinburg, N.C., 1972-74; tchr. Scotland (N.C.) County Schs., 1981-82, Nash County (N.C.) Schs., 1981-82, Round Rock (Tex.) Schs., 1982-84; instr. Coll. Lake County, Grayslake, Ill., 1986—. Author, Editor: Directory, Adult Edn. Classes in Lake County 1988. Elected mem. bd. edn. Libertyvill (Ill.) High Sch., 1989—. Recipient Scotland County Mental Health Assn. award, Laurinburg, N.C., 1974. Democrat. Baptist. Home: 633 Innsbruck Ct Libertyville IL 60048

BRADY, JENNIE M., service specialist; b. Tampa, Fla., May 4, 1948; d. William Jackson and Mattie Estelle (Garrett) Amason; m. Walter Edward Brady Jr., Mar. 27, 1982; children: Roger Dwaney, Walter Edward III, Faith René Brady Smith, Velma Mychelle Amann, Lydia Diane Emerson, Theresa Victoria; 1 adopted child, David Lamar Ogilvie. Student, Mo. Western State Coll., Coastal Tng. Svc. Nurse's aide Manhattan ConvalescentCtr., Tampa, Fla., 1983-84; secretarial worker Sun Saver Solar Glass Tinting, Tampa, 1986; technician Westshore Grooming Inc., Tampa, 1987-88, Holiday Pet Inn, Tampa, 1987-88; owner, mgr. Bradamas Farms and Myjoy Kennels, Heflin, Ala. Bd. dirs. Pony Express Hist. Assn., 1972-78; legis. chmn., girls' counselor, parliamentarian Am. Legion Aux., 1972-81; jr. activities chmn., legis. chmn. DAV Aux., 1981-90; jr. vice comdr., sr. vice comdr. VFW Aux., 1981-90; bd. dirs., pres., sec., treas., archivist Buchanan County Hist. Soc., 1974-78; vol. VA Hosp., Tampa, 1987, Birmingham, Ala., 1988-90. Mem. NAFE, Wildlife Rescue. Home: Bradamas Farms Rte 1 Box 106A-9 Heflin AL 36264

BRADY, LINDA CAROL, architect; b. N.Y.C., May 18, 1949; d. John Joseph and Irene H. (Olawska) B.; B.Arch., Pratt Inst., 1971. Staff technician, draftsperson Gruzen & Partners, 1970-72; staff designer Warner, Burns, Toan, Lunde, 1973-75; archtl. cons. Citibank N.A., N.Y.C., 1976-77, staff architect, 1977—, asst. v.p., 1981-86, v.p., sr. project mgr. corp. facilities, 1986—; corp. sec. Citidel, Inc., 1982-86. Registered architect, N.Y. Mem. Am. Legion Aux., Pratt Alumni Assn., Nat. Classical Soc., Internat. Facilities Mgmt. Assn. (charter mem. N.Y. chpt.). Office: One Citicorp Center New York NY 10043

BRADY, MARY THERESE, psychologist, educator; b. Springfield, Mass., Nov. 28, 1959; d. William and Elizabeth (McDonnell) B.; m. William Carey Cole. BA, Holy Cross Coll., Worcester, Mass., 1981; MA, Wright Inst., 1986, PhD, 1988. Lic. psychologist, Calif. Postdoctoral fellow, psychologist out-patient psychiatry Children's Hosp. of San Francisco, 1988-89; dean of students Profl. Sch. Psychology, San Francisco, 1989-90; adj. faculty Calif. Sch. Profl. Psychology, Alameda, 1990—; pvt. practice psychotherapy San Francisco, 1989—; adj. clin. faculty, field placement liaison Wright Inst., Berkeley, Calif., 1988-89. Mem. No. Calif. Soc. for Psychoanalytic Psychotherapy, Am. Psychol. Assn. Office: 1736 Divisadero St San Francisco CA 94115

BRADY, MAUREEN O'KEEFE, product evaluation professional; b. RockvilleCentre, N.Y., June 27, 1945; d. Frank Xavier O'Keefe and Olga Marie (Scheim) Galgano; m. Thomas Joseph Brady, June 11, 1966; children: Matthew, Elizabeth. Diploma, Bellevue Sch. Nursing, 1966; AA in Data Processing, Cen. Piedmont Community Coll., 1983; BA in Computer Sci., U. N.C., Charlotte, 1988. R.N., N.Y. Staff nurse N.Y. Infirmary, N.Y.C., 1966-68, Nassau Hosp., Minneola, N.Y., 1969-72, Presbyn. Hosp., Charlotte, N.C., 1979-84; systems analyst Unisys Corp., Charlotte, 1984-86; sr. analyst Unisys Corp., 1986-87, mgr. product evaluation, 1987-89; coord. order communication Cabarrus Meml. Hosp., 1989—. Mem. Domicilliary Home Com., Mecklenburg County, 1988. Mem. Am. Nurses Assn., N.C. Nurses Assn., Phi Kappa Phi. Republican. Roman Catholic. Home: 6749 Brookmede Dr Charlotte NC 28226

BRADY, NANCY SAMMARTINO, dentist; b. Phila., Sept. 8, 1955; d. Frank John and Kathryn Lenora (Schatzle) Sammartino; m. John Joseph Brady, Jr., Jan. 23, 1982; children: Jennifer Kathryn, John Joseph III. BA, Villanova U., 1976; DDS, Temple U., 1981. Clin. instr. sch. dentistry Temple U., Phila., 1981-83; pvt. practice gen. dentistry Phila., 1981-83, Freeland, Pa., 1984—. Co-author: Into the Future, 1990. Mem. AAUW (sec. Hazleton chpt. 1987-89, fundraising chair Hazleton chpt. 1988, hospitality 1989—, transp. 1989—, program v.p. 1990-91, Betty Harlor Meml. award 1989), ADA, Pa. Dental Assn., Hazleton Area Dental Soc. (v.p. 1989, pres. 1990), Daisy Girl Scout leader, 1989-90. Roman Catholic. Home: 22 Providence Rd Hazleton PA 18201 Office: 450 Washington St Freeland PA 18224

BRADY, PRISCILLA MAE, nursing administrator, researcher; b. Worcester, Mass., Jan. 4, 1940; d. Earl Haywood and Madalene (Traver) Dunton. RN, Worcester City Hosp., 1961; BS in Health Studies, Anna Maria Coll., 1983. RN, Mass. Staff nurse surg. ICU Worcester City Hosp., 1963-65, head nurse med. ICU and critical care unit, 1965-73; nurse coord. Worcester Found. of Exptl. Biology, 1973-77, nurse coord. Ea. coop. oncology group, 1977-78; rsch. asst. clin. pharmacology Med. Sch. U. Mass., Worcester, 1979-83, clin. rsch. coord. div. cardiovascular medicine Med. Sch., 1983-87, project coord. Worcester heart attack study Med. Sch., 1987-89; dir. nursing svcs. Ariz. Cancer Ctr. U. Ariz., Tucson, 1990—, mem. faculty, 1990—; chairwoman exec. com. Cen. Mass. chpt. Am. Heart Assn., Worcester, 1987-89. Mem. editorial bd. Clin. Rsch. Practice Jour., 1985-87. Named one of Outstanding Vols., Am. Heart Assn., 1988-89; recipient Outstanding Svc. award City of Worcester, 1989. Mem. Nat. Oncology Nurses Soc., S.C. Oncology Nurses Soc., So. Ariz. Am. Heart Assn., Am. Bus. Womens Assn. (Woman of the Yr. 1989). Democrat. Office: U Ariz Cancer Ctr 1501 N Campbell Ave Tucson AZ 85724

BRADY, SHARON ELIZABETH, editor; b. Omaha, Feb. 9, 1963; d. William Joseph and Frances Anne (Fredlake) B. BA, Princeton U., 1985. Editor Tech. News of Am., N.Y.C., 1985—; trustee news-weekly NASSAU, Inc., Princeton, N.J., 1985—. Co-author: Big Blue and You, 1989; editor monthly newsletter computer industry Inforperspectives, 1987—, The Four Hundred, 1990—, The Businessweek newsletter for info. execs., 1990; contbr. articles to mags. Office: Technology News of Am 110 Greene St New York NY 10012

BRADY, SUE CAROL PIPES, graphics company executive; b. Lynchburg, Va., Apr. 5, 1947; d. John Eugene and Jean Erle (Bruffey) Pipes; m. Louis Bevier Basten III, Nov. 24, 1973 (div. 1983); children: John Austin Slausen Basten, Catherine Serena Bevier Basten. Student, U. Va., 1968-70; BA,

Mary Washington Coll., 1970. Owner, pres. As You Like It, Lynchburg, 1977-83; v.p. Am. Graphics, Inc., Lynchburg, 1988—. Gov.'s regional appointee Bravo Arts and Bravo Arts Edn., Richmond, Va., 1978-79; trustee Seven Hills Sch., Lynchburg, 1988—; pres. Lynchburg Fine Arts Ctr. Art Div., 1976-80; bd. dirs. Lynchburg Fine Arts Ctr., 1978-80. Mem. Boonsboro Country Club, Long Cove Club, Jr. League of Lynchburg (sustaining advisor). Republican. Episcopalian. Home: Plumbroque 1301 Wakefield Lynchburg VA 24503

BRAGA, LINDA JEAN, lawyer; b. Nottinghamshire, Eng., Dec. 15, 1953; came to U.S., 1955; naturalized, 1961; d. Douglas Colin and Jean (Sampson) B. BA summa cum laude, SUNY-Buffalo, 1974, JD, 1978. Bar: Tex. 1978, N.Y. 1989, U.S. Dist. Ct. (no. dist.) Tex. 1979, U.S. Dist. Ct. (ea. dist.) Tex. 1981. Title lawyer S.W. Land Title Co., Dallas, 1977-78; assoc. Green, Gilmore & Rothpletz, Dallas, 1979-82, ptnr., 1983-86; ptnr. Linda J. Braga, A Profl. Legal Corp., Dallas, 1986—; commr. City of Garland Plan Commn., 1987-89, chmn., 1989; vice chmn. City of Garland Utility Adv. Bd., 1989—. N.Y. State Regents scholar; SUNY-Buffalo undergrad. research asst., and grad. teaching asst. grantee. Mem. ABA, State Bar Tex., Dallas Bar Assn., N.Y. State Bar Assn., Am. Immigration Lawyers Assn., Good Samaritans of Garland, Inc. (bd. dirs. 1988—), SUNY-Buffalo Alumni Assn., SUNY-Buffalo Law Alumni Assn., Erie County Trial Lawyers Assn. (Excellence award 1977), Noon Garland Exchange Club, Garland Bus. Profl. Women's Club, Garland C. of C. (bd. dirs. 1989—), Phi Beta Kappa. Office: 12820 Hillcrest Rd Ste 116 Dallas TX 75230 also: 3321 Broadway Blvd Ste 101 Garland TX 75043

BRAGG, ANNA LOU SPENCER, real estate broker; b. Denton, Tex., May 25, 1943; d. Thomas Morris and Betty Lou Rachel (Bradham) Spencer; m. Bobby J. Bragg, Sept. 5, 1964; children—Robert Morris, Jennifer Suzanne. A.A., San Jacinto Coll., 1962; B.S., U. Houston, 1964. Aerospace engr. NASA Johnson Space Center, Houston, 1964-66, reliability and quality assurance engr., 1966-69; instr. adult edn. Coll. Mainland, Texas City, Tex., 1974-76, Alvin Community Coll. (Tex.), 1975-76; agt. Jim Baker Realtors, Dickinson, Tex., 1976-80; pres. Bayou Realtors, Inc., Dickinson, Tex., 1980—. Trustee Dickinson Ind. Sch. Dist., 1989—. Mem. Tex. Assn. Realtors, Gulf Coast Bd. Realtors (dir. 1983-86), Dickinson C. of C. (bd. dirs. 1983-87, pres. 1986-87), Nat. Assn. Realtors, AAUW (v.p.), Mortar Bd., Tex. Garden Clubs (bd. dirs. 1979-84, treas. 1981-83, dist. vice dir. 1983-85; master flower show judge). Home: 2706 Mt Vernon Dr Dickinson TX 77539 Office: Bayou Realtors Inc 1613 Pine Dr Dickinson TX 77539

BRAHAM, DELPHINE DORIS, government accountant; b. L'Anse, Mich., Mar. 16, 1946; d. Richard Andrew and Viola Mary (Niemi) Aho; m. John Emerson Braham, Sept. 23, 1967 (div. Dec. 1987); children: Tammy, Debra, John Jr. BS summa cum laude, Drury Coll., 1983; M in Mgmt., Webster U., St. Louis, 1986. Bookkeeper, Community Mental Health Ctr., Marquette, Mich., 1966-68; credit clk. Remington Rand, Marietta, Ohio, 1971-72; acctg. technician St. Joseph's Hosp., Parkersburg, W.Va., 1972-74; material mgr. U.S. Army, Ft. Leonard Wood, Mo., 1982-86, accountant, 1986—; instr., adj. faculty Columbia Coll., 1987—, Park Coll., 1988—. Leader Girls Scouts U.S., Williamstown, W.Va., 1972-74, Hanau, W.Ger., 1977-79. Mem. AAUW (treas. Waynesville br. 1986-90), NAFE, Assn. Govt. Accts., Am. Soc. Mil. Comptrollers, Waynesvill Bus. and Profl. Women's Orgn. Home: Rte 2 Box 248L #28 Waynesville MO 65583

BRAHNEY, CAROLYN ANN, art educator; b. Struthers, Ohio, Aug. 16, 1939; d. Ralph and Mary L. (Ramun) Peluso; m. James Henry Brahney, May 16, 1964; children: Mary Frances, James Eric, Scott Mitchell. BS in Fine Art and Edn., Youngstown (Ohio) State U., 1962; MA in Art Edn., U. Pitts., 1982. Cert. tchr., Pa. Art instr. Youngstown U., 1962-64, Sinclair Coll., Dayton, Ohio, 1972-79, Community Coll. of Allegheny County, Pitts., 1983-88, LaRoche Coll., Pitts., 1988; art tchr. Youngstown Sch. Dist., East High Sch., 1962-64, South High Sch., 1966-67, No. Area Sch. Dist. Substitute Tchrs., Pitts., 1983-85; exec. dir. North Hills Art Ctr., Pitts., 1986-90; juror Ann. Mountain State Forest Festival Juried Art Exhibit, W.Va., 1990. One woman shows Latin Cultural Found., Youngstown, Ohio, 1963, Youngstown State U. Gallery, 1964, Sinclair Community Coll. Gallery, Dayton, Ohio, 1972, North Hills Art Ctr. Gallery, Pitts., 1990; three-person exhibit Sinclair Community Coll. Gallery, 1978; exhibited in group shows Creative Treasures Beavercreek, Ohio, 1977-79, Penn Hills Art Festival, Verona, Pa., 1989, North Hills Art Festival, Pitts., 1989, Pitts. Watercolor Soc., Pitts. Ctr. for Arts, 1990, North Hills Art Ctr. Gallery, Pitts., 1984-90, others. Juror 18th Congl. Dist. Art Competition, 1989, 90, N. Allegheny Sch. Dist., Invention Am., 1990, Ann. Mountain State Forest Festival Juried Art Exhibit, W.V., 1990; bd. dirs. North Hills Arts Festival, 1987—, v.p., 1990. Recipient Best of Show award Butler Art Inst., 1962, North Hills Art Ctr., 1990. Mem. AAUW (illustrator book 1988), Artists Equity, Pa. Art Assn., Artists' and Craftsmen's Guild, Inc., Pitts. Watercolor Soc. (bd. mem.), Pitts. Ctr. for the Arts. Home: 1966 Lammerton Dr Allison Park PA 15101 Office: North Hills Art Ctr 432 Babcock Blvd Pittsburgh PA 15237

BRAIDWOOD, LINDA SCHREIBER, archaeologist; b. Grand Rapids, Mich., Oct. 9, 1909; d. F. Robert and Mathilde (Neumann) Schreiber; m. Robert J. Braidwood, Jan. 4, 1937; children: Gretel, Douglas. Student, Wellesley Coll., 1927-28, U. Munich, Germany, 1928-29; AB, U. Mich., 1932; MA, U. Chgo., 1943. Field asst. Syrian expdn., Oriental Inst. U. Chgo., 1937-47, prehistoric project field asst., Oriental Inst., 1947—, assoc. Oriental Inst., 1947—, instr. home study dept., 1957-63. Author: Digging Beyond the Tigris, 1953; co-author: Excavations in the Plain of Antioch I, 1960, Prehistoric Archeology Along The Zagros Flanks, 1983; contbr. articles and revs. to profl. jours.; mem. adv. bd. jour. Archaeology, 1952-67. Fulbright rsch. fellow, Turkey, 1963-64. Office: Oriental Inst U Chgo Chicago IL 60637

BRAILOW, NORMA LIPTON, artist; b. N.Y., Apr. 30, 1916; d. Leon Israel Lipton and Estelle (Laiken) Rich; m. Alexander A. Brailow, Apr. 26, 1941; children: Anthony George, David Gregory. BA, Keuka Coll., 1963; MA, State U., 1970. Lic. tchr. Fashion artist Berger's Dept. Store, Buffalo, 1941-44; tchr. II, Penn Yan Acad., 1967-69; sculptor, Keuka Park, N.Y., 1970—. One woman shows include Lightner Gallery, Keuka Coll., N.Y., 1978, 1982, Arnot Art Mus., Elmira, N.Y., 1979, Yates County Arts Coun., Penn Yan, N.Y., 1988; exhibited in two-sculptor show Benedict and Brailow, Yates County Arts Coun., 1989; exhibited in numerous group shows Keuka Coll. Penn Yan Coun. Bd. dirs. Yates County Arts Coun., Yates Performing Arts. Mem. AAUW (bd. dirs. Yates County). Home and Office: Box 36 212 Cherry St Keuka Park NY 14478

BRAILSFORD, JUNE EVELYN, musician, educator; b. Wiergate, Tex., Apr. 11, 1939; d. Lonnie and Jessie (Coleman) Samuel; m. Marvin Delano Brailsford, Dec. 23, 1960; children: Marvin Delano, Keith, Cynthia. BA in Music, Prairie View A & M U., Tex., 1960; MA in Music, Trenton (N.J.) State Coll., 1981; postgrad., Jacksonville State U., summer 1971, Lamar U., Beaumont, Tex., summer 1963. Jr. high music tchr. Lincoln Jr. High Sch., Beaumont, Tex., 1960-61; organist/choir dir. various chs., various locations, 1962-82; kdir. adult edn. Morris County Human Resources, Dover, N.J., 1980-82; band and choral dir. Zweibruecken Am. High Sch., Ger., 1982-84; vocal soloist and pianist Am. Women's Activities, Ger., 1986-87; dir. female coir U.S. Army War Coll., 1978-79, U.S. Air Force Skylarks, Sembach, Ger., 1976-77. Hostess/fundraiser Quad City Symphony Guild 75th Yr., Rock Island, 1989, Links, Inc. Beautillion Scholarship, 1989, active many other charitable orgns. Recipient Molly Pitcher award U.S. Army Field Arty. Officers, 1986, Outstanding Civilian Svc. award Dept. of Army, 1990. Mem. AAUW, Music/Etude Club, Rock Island Arsenal Hist. Soc. (hon. mem.), Quad City Symphony Guild (USO com.). Baptist. Home: 2 Fairfax Dr Fort Belvoir VA 22060

BRAISTED, MADELINE CHARLOTTE, military officer, personnel administrator; b. Jamaica, N.Y., Nov. 23, 1936; d. Melvin Vincent and Charlotte Marie (Klos) B. A.A.S., Nassau Community Coll., 1968; B.A., Hofstra U., 1973, M.A., 1975. Enlisted, U.S. Marine Corps., Cherry Point, N.C., 1954-57; reservations agt. Airline Industry, N.Y.C., 1957-64; reservations controller Auto Lease Industry, N.Y.C., 1964-66; nuclear medicine technician Queens Gen. Hosp., Jamaica, N.Y., 1969-70; lab. mgr. CUNY, 1970-80; commd. capt. U.S. Army Reserve, 1980, advanced through enlisted grades to major, 1984; cons. Energy Etcetera, Flushing, N.Y., 1979-85; capt. U.S. Army Res., Fort Totten, N.Y., 1977-80; major AMEDD Health Profl. Support Agy., U.S. Army, Washington, 1980—. Author, pub. Energy Etcetera catalog, 1981-85; artist On Shore painting (hon. mention 1974). Merit badge counselor Boy Scouts Am., Queens County, N.Y., 1980-83; active mem. PTA, Jamaica, 1980-84. Decorated Army Commendation medal with one oak leaf, Army Achievement medal with one oak leaf cluster; named Community Leader and Noteworthy Am., Hist. Preservation of Am., 1976. Mem. Assn. Mil. Surgeons of U.S., Res. Officers Assn., Nat. Assn. Female Execs., Am. Pub. Health Assn., Soc. Nuclear Medicine. Roman Catholic. Avocations: painting; sculpture. Office: US Army Med Dept Officer Procurement PO Box 4649 Bay Terrace NY 11360

BRAITERMAN, THEA GILDA, economics educator, state legislator; b. Balt., Md., Sept. 11, 1927; d. Isaac E. and Clara (Fink) Bloom; m. Marvin Braiterman, Mar. 21, 1948; children: Kenneth, Marta, David. BS, Johns Hopkins U., 1949; MA, U. Md., 1966; PhD, Union Inst., 1977. Assoc. prof. econs. Balt. Coll. of Commerce, 1966-73; prof. econs. New England Coll., Henniker, N.H., 1973—; mem. N.H. Ho. of Reps., 1988—; cons. on retirement, 1988—. Author: Workbook on Economic Theory, 1966; contbr. articles to profl. jours. Sec., bd. govs. United Way of Merrimack County, Concord, N.H., 1984—; v.p., bd. govs. Community Svcs. Coun., Concord, 1980-84. Recipient Jane Addams Grant, Jane Addams Peace Assn., 1976-77, Gilmore Grant, New England Coll., 1988—. Mem. Am. Econ. Assn., Ea. Econ. Assn. Home: PO Box 686 Henniker NH 03242 Office: New England Coll Henniker NH 03242

BRAKE, BARBARA WHITAKER, public relations executive; b. Nashville, Jan. 13, 1946; d. Robert Clayton and Sara Virginia (Omchundro) Whitaker; m. Delmas Carter Brake, Dec. 14, 1974. BS in Journalism, U. Tenn., 1970. Pub. rels. asst. Union Planters Nat. Bank, Memphis, 1970-71; mkgt. officer 1st Am. Nat. Bank, Nashville, 1971-76, v.p., dir. pub. rels. dept., 1976—. Contbr. numerous articles to profl. jours. Recipient Excellence award Gov. of Tenn., 1974. Mem. Pub. Rels. Soc. Am. (bd. dirs. Nashville chpt. 1981-85), Soc. Profl. Journalists. Presbyterian. Office: 1st Am Nat Bank First American Ctr Nashville TN 37237

BRAKE, ELIZABETH J., librarian; b. Superior, Nebr., Oct. 8, 1925; d. John Knox and Lottie Frances (Touzalin) McKee; m. William M. Brake, June 13, 1947; children: Michael S., W. Randolph, Robert C. BA, U. Denver, 1946; MLS, Rutgers U., 1970. Librarian VA Hosp., Lyons, N.J., 1962-64; sch. librarian Cranford (N.J.) pub. schs., 1965-69, Millburn (N.J.) pub. schs., 1969-70; cataloger U. Tex., Arlington, 1970-77, head cataloging dept., 1977-87; ret. Mem. ALA, AAUW, Tex. Libr. Assn. Republican. Methodist. Home: 1209 Riverview Dr Arlington TX 76012

BRAKHAN, JUTTA JOHANNESSON, business owner, furniture designer; b. Berlin, Germany, Sept. 5, 1942; came to U.S., 1960; d. Benno and Brigitte (Niemoeller) Johannesson; m. Andrew Albrecht Brakhan, May, 1963 (div. Nov. 1979); children: Markus, Naomi Vanessa. BA, Sarah Lawrence Coll., 1971. Owner Finished Interiors, Ltd., Westport, Conn., 1980—. Mem. Am. Soc. Designers, LWV. Lutheran. Office: Finished Interiors Ltd 11 Riverside Ave Westport CT 06880

BRAM, ISABELLE MARY RICKEY MCDONOUGH (MRS. JOHN BRAM), civic worker; b. Oskaloosa, Ia., Apr. 4; d. Lindsey Vinton and Heddy (Lundee) Rickey; B.A. in Govt., George Washington U., 1947, postgrad., 1947-49; m. Dayle C. McDonough, Jan. 20, 1949; m. 2d, John G. Bram, Nov. 24, 1980. Dep. tax assessor and collector Aransas Pass Ind. Sch. Dist., 1939-41; sec. to city atty., Aransas Pass, Tex., 1939-41; info. specialist U.S. Dept. State, Washington, 1942-48. Treas. Mo. Fedn. Women's Clubs, Inc., 1964-66, 2d v.p., 1966-68, 1st v.p., 1968-70, pres., 1970-72; bd. dirs. Gen. Fedn. Women's Clubs. Mem. steering com. Citizens Com. for Conservation; mem. exec. com. Missourians for Clean Water. Pres., DeKalb County Women's Democratic Club, 1964. Bd. dirs. DeKalb County Pub. Library, pres., 1966; bd. dirs. Mo. Girls Town Found.; dir. DeKalb County Little Theater Players. Mem. AAUW, Nat. League Am. Pen Women, DeKalb County Hist. Soc., Internat. Platform Assn., Law Soc. U. Mo., Jefferson Club of U. Mo., Zeta Tau Alpha, Phi Delta Delta, Phi Delta Gamma. Democrat. Episcopalian. Mem. Order Eastern Star. Clubs: Tri Arts, Shakespeare, Wimodausis, Gavel, Ledgers, Jefferson. Editor: Mo. Clubwoman mag. Home: Sloan and Cherry Sts Box 156 Maysville MO 64469

BRAMAN, HEATHER RUTH, technical writer; b. Wilmington, Ohio, Apr. 27, 1934; d. William Barnett and Violet Ruth (Davis) Hansford; m. Barr Oliver Braman, June 29, 1957 (div.); children: Sean Robert, Heather Paige. BA, Hiram Coll., 1956; postgrad., Sinclair Community Coll., Dayton, Ohio, 1977-85, Wright State U., Dayton, 1986. Personnel clk. USAF, Wright-Patterson AFB, Ohio, 1956, specification editor, 1956-57, publs. editor, writer, 1957-63; homemaker, vol. children's med. ctr. Dayton Pub. Schs., 1963-73; tchr. Gloria Dei Montessori Sch., Dayton, 1973-77, asst. mgr., actg. mgr., mgr. tennis club, 1977-81; asst. mgr., acctg. mgr., mgr. tennis club USAF, Wright-Patterson AFB, Ohio, 1977-81; tech. writer Miclin, Inc., Alpha, Ohio, 1982, Indsl. Design Concepts, Dayton, 1982-83; tech. writer, cons. Belcan Corp., Cin., 1984—; real estate investor. Founder, bd. dirs. Trotwood (Ohio) Women's Open Tennis Tournament, 1976-81; mem. Harrison Twp. Parks Bd., 1980-82; ballpersons coord., Dayton Pro Tennis Classic, 1977-80; pres. Dayton Tennis Commn., 1978-80; mem. parents exec. com. Hiram (Ohio) Coll., 1985—; ct.-appointed Spl. Advocate/Guardian Ad Litem (CASA GAL), 1988—. Mem. NOW, NAACP, Dayton Pub. Schs. Orgns., Dayton Tennis Umpires Assn., Mothers Against Drunk Drivers., AARP, WWF, HALT, Sigil of Phi Sigma. Democrat. Quaker. Home: 320 Elm Hill Dr Dayton OH 45415 Office: Belcan Corp 10200 Anderson Way Cincinnati OH 45242

BRAME, MARILLYN A., technical communications executive; b. Indpls., Sept. 17, 1928; d. David Schwalb and Hilda (Riley) Curtin; 1 child, Gary Mansour. Student, Meinzinger Art Sch., Detroit, 1946-47, U. N.Mex., 1963, Orlando (Fla.) Jr. Coll., 1964-65, El Camino Coll., Torrance, Calif., 1974-75; PhD in Hypnotherapy, Am. Inst. Hypnotherapy, 1989, PhD, 1989. Cert. and registered hypnotherapist. Color cons. Pitts. Plate Glass Co., Albuquerque, 1951-52; owner Signs by Marillyn, Albuquerque, 1952-53; design draftsman Sandia Corp., Albuquerque, 1953-56; designer The Martin Co., Orlando, 1957-65; pres. The Arts, Winter Park, Fla., 1964-66; supr. tech. publs. Gen. Instrument Corp., Hawthorne, Calif., 1967-76; pres. Camart Design, Westminster, Calif., 1977-86, Visual Arts, El Toro, Calif., 1978—; mgr. tech. publs. Archive Corp., Costa Mesa, Calif., 1986—; adj. instr. Orange Coast Coll., Costa Mesa, 1985—; hynotherapist, El Toro, 1986—. Author: (textbook) Folkdancing is for Everybody; prodn. editor; (newsletter) Techniscribe, 1986, 1987; inventor, designer dance notation system MS Method. Mem. bd. govs. Lake Forest II Showboaters Theater Group, 1985-88. Mem. Soc. Tech. Communication (v.p. programs, 1987—, newsletter editor 1986-87, newsletter prodn. editor 1985-86). Office: Visual Arts 25422 Trabuco Rd 105 El Toro CA 92630

BRAMHALL, SHIRLEY ANNE (BILLIE BRAMHALL), city planner, city official; b. N.Y.C., Dec. 8, 1926; d. Isadore and Kate (Gluck) Willinger; m. Marvin Scilken, Apr. 1946 (div. June 1947); m. David F. Bramhall, Aug. 13, 1948; children: Martha Ann, Frederick Paul, Jenny Rachel, Rebecca Laura. BA, U. Colo., 1947; MA, U. Pitts., 1972. Rsch. assoc. Morton Hoffman & Co., Balt., 1961-64; cons., 1964-69; neighborhood planner Pitts. Planning Dept., 1979-71, dep. dir., 1971-75; div. chief Small Area Planning div., Denver, 1975-79; chief planner Community Devel. Agy., Denver, 1979-81; program officer Piton Found., Denver, 1981-84; pres. Bramhall & Assocs., Denver, 1984-87; dep. dir. Denver Planning and Community Devel. Office, 1987—; former instr. urban studies Johns Hopkins U., U. Balt., Notre Dame Coll. Balt.; adj. prof. planning U. Colo. Sch. Architecture and Planning, Denver, 1984-87. Pres., v.p., mem. Denver Housing Authority Bd., 1984-87. Recipient Disting. Svc. award U. Colo., 1983, Denver Regional Coun. Govts., 1982. Mem. Am. Planning Assn., Nat. Assn. Housing and Redevel. Ofcls., Denver City Club (v.p. 1985-86). Home: 2324 Eudora St Denver CO 80207 Office: Planning and Com Del Office 200 W 14th Ave Denver CO 80104

BRAMNICK, LEA SHAPIRO, educational materials company executive; b. Phila., Aug. 23, 1938; d. Irving Benjamin and Sylvia (Bloom) Shapiro; B.S. in Edn., Temple U., 1959, M.S. in Edn., 1962; children—Michael Richard, Gary David. Tchr. elem. schs., Phila. Bd. Edn., 1959-65; project mgr., designer ednl. materials Instructo, McGraw Hill, Paoli, Pa., 1971-74; dir. home products unit Research for Better Schs., Phila., 1974—; pres. The Lobster Factory, Inc., designers ednl. materials, Merion Station, Pa., 1976—; dir. corp. communications AJ Wood, corp. dir. Direct Mail div., 1985, dir. Customer Service div., 1986. Creator Cooking for Kids program. Author: The Great Cook's Guide to Children's Cookery, 1976; The Kid's Kitchen Encyclopedia, 1979; The Parents Solution Book, 1983.

BRAMSON, BERENICE LOUISE, soprano, teacher; b. Omaha, Nebr., May 29, 1929; d. Harry Lazarus and Irene (Schiffer) Sommer.; m. Alan Lewis Bramson, Sept. 10, 10, 1950; children: Barbara E. Bramson Dodge, Steven S. Grad. high sch., Omaha, Nebr. Co-dir. The Center for Music in Westchester, Westchester, N.Y., 1980—; founder, dir. The Sch. for Singers, Katonah, N.Y., 1981—; guest instr. Skidmore Coll., SUNY Binghamton, Cornell U. Opera appearances: Vancouver Opera Assn., N.Y. Grand Opera, Bklyn. Opera Soc.; soloist with: Denver Symphony, Buffalo Philharmonic, Wichita Symphony, Amarillo Symphony, Caramoor Festival Orchestra, Goldman Band, New Orchestra of Westchester, Chappaqua (N.Y.) Orchestra and others; solo appearances Weill Hall at Carnegie Hall, Merkin Hall, Alice Tully Hall, Town Hall, N.Y.C. and others; premiered music of American composers; recordings: Gemini Hall "Women's Work", 1975 and oth ers. Mem. The Bohemians. Home: 24 Hillside Ave Katonah NY 10536

BRAMWELL, MARVEL LYNNETTE, nurse; b. Durango, Colo., Aug. 13, 1947; d. Floyd Lewis and Virginia Jenny (Amyx) B. Diploma in lic. practical nursing, Durango Sch. Practical Nursing, 1968; AD in Nursing, Mt. Hood Community Coll., 1972; BS in Nursing, BS in Gen. Studies cum laude, So. Oreg. State Coll., 1980; cert. edn. grad. sch. social work, U. Utah, 1987. RN, LPN, cert. counselor alcohol, drug abuse. Staff nurse Monument Valley (Utah) Seventh Day Adventist Mission Hosp., 1973-74, La Plata Community Hosp., 1974-75; health coordinator Tri County Head Start Program, 1974-75; nurse therapist, team leader Portland Adventist Med. Ctr., 1975-78; staff nurse Indian Health Service Hosp., 1980-81; coordinator village health services North Slope Borough Health and Social Service Agy., 1981-83; nurse, supr. aides Bonneville Health Care Agy., 1984-85; staff nurse Latter Day Saints Adolescent Psychiat. Unit, 1985-86; coordinator adolescent nursing CPC Olympus View Hosp., 1986-87; charge and staff nurse adult psychiatry U. Utah, 1987-88; nursing supr. St. Joseph Villa, Salt Lake City, 1989—; assisted with design and constrn. 6 high tech. health clinics in Ala. Arctic, 1982-83; creator after care program Greatest Love, 1986-87. Contbr. articles to profl. jours. Active Mothers Against Drunk Driving; mem. acad. rev. com. Community Health Assn. Program U. Alaska Rural Edn., 1981-83. Recipient Cert. Appreciation Barrow (Alaska) Lion's Club, 1983, U.S. Census Bur., Colo., 1970. Mem. NOW, Nat. League Nurses, Assn. Women Sci., Am. Soc. Circumpolar Health, Casandra. Home: PO Box 511282 Salt Lake City UT 84151

BRANAN, CAROLYN BENNER, accountant, lawyer; b. Wiesbaden, Fed. Republic Germany, Mar. 7, 1953; came to U.S., 1958; d. Huebert Harrison and Kathryn Wilfreda (Diggs) Benner; m. Robert Edwin Branan, Oct. 3, 1981 (div. Aug. 1988); 1 child, Lynn. BA in Philosophy, U. S.C., 1973, JD, 1976. Bar: S.C. 1977, U.S. Dist. Ct. S.C. 1977, U.S. Ct. Appeals (4th cir.) 1977; C.P.A., N.C. Sole practice law, Columbia, S.C., 1977-79; sr. mgr. Deloitte Haskins & Sells, Charlotte, N.C., 1979-89; exec. fin. counseling regional dir., 1987-89; sr. mgr. in charge personal fin. planning practice KPMG Peat Marwick, 1989—; cons. Gov.'s Bus. Council Task Force on Infrastructure Financing, 1983. Contbr. articles to profl. jours. Former mem. exec. com., former treas., v.p., chmn. budget com., bd. dirs. Charlotte Opera Assn., 1981-89; v.p. Opera Carolina 1985-87; exec. com., chmn. annual funding campaigns N.C. Opera, 1982, 83, 88; exec. com. mayor's study com. Performing Arts Ctr., Charlotte, 1983-85; former mem. adv. coun., bd. dirs., chmn. performing arts Springfest, Charlotte, 1982-86; fin. chmn. Opening of New Charlotte Transit Mall, 1984-85; bus. adv. coun. Queens Coll., Charlotte, 1984—; mem. endowment bd. St. Peter's Ch., 1988—. Mem. ABA (former chmn. important devels., chmn. gen. acctg. matters, regulated pub. utilities tax sect. 1984—), N.C. Bar Assn., S.C. Bar Assn., Women Execs., N.C. Assn. Women Attys., Charlotte Estate Planning Council, Nat. Assn. Accts. (bd. dirs., dir. profl. devel., dir. community affairs 1979-84), N.C. Assn. CPAs, Women Execs., Founders Soc. of Charlotte Opera Assn. (life), Golden Circle (bd. dirs.), Charlotte City Club, Rotary (treas., Charlotte). Episcopalian. Home: 530-A N Poplar St Charlotte NC 28202 Office: KPMG Peat Marwick 2800 Two First Union Ctr Charlotte NC 28282

BRANAND, DYANNE MARIE, import/export company executive; b. Chgo., Aug. 11, 1950; d. Robert Eugene and Lorraine Helen (Lauterbach) Brandt; m. Robert Edwin Branand, Nov. 26, 1974; children: Brandt, Brian, Brittany. BS in Psychology, Loretto Heights Coll., Denver, 1972; BA, Parks Coll., Denver, 1973. Adminstrv. asst. U.S. Ho. of Reps., Washington, 1973-80; v.p. Columbia Diversified Energies, Washington, 1980-83; ptnr. Robert Branand Internat., Washington, 1983—. Chmn. bd. Capitol Hill Montessori Sch., Washington, 1989. Mem. Women in Internat. Trade, Washington Internat. Trade Assn. Republican. Roman Catholic. Office: Robert Branand Internat Four E St SE Washington DC 20003

BRANCAFORTE, CHARLOTTE LANG, language educator; b. Munich, Fed. Republic Germany, July 26, 1934; came to U.S., 1958; d. Christoph and Marielouise (Unglert) Lang; m. Benito Brancaforte, Nov. 11, 1961; children: Elio Christoph, Daniela Beatrix, Stephanie Andrea. D in Teaching, Landshut Coll., Germany, 1954; BA in Edn., Denver U., 1958; PhD in German and Polit. Sci., U. Ill., 1967. Asst. prof. German, U. Wis., Madison, 1966-73, assoc. prof., 1973-78, prof., 1978—, chair Dept. of German, 1980-84, dir. Max Kade Inst. German-Am. Studies, 1984-89. Author: Venus, critical study, 1974; Partial Latin Translation of Lazarillo De Tormes, 1983; co-author: Lazarillo De Tormes, 1977; editor: Max Kade Series of German-American Studies, The German Forty-Eighters in the United States, 1989. Chmn., Western European Area Studies Program, U. Wis., 1980-86. Mem. Modern Lang. Assn., Soc. Renaissance and Baroque Studies, Nat. Assn. Dept. Fgn. Langs. (pres. 1984). Home: 1727 Summit Ave Madison WI 53705 Office: U Wis Dept German 1220 Linden Dr Madison WI 53706 also: U Wis Max Kade Inst German-Am Studies 901 University Bay Dr Madison WI 53705

BRANCH, CYNTHIA LYNN, veterinarian; b. St. Petersburg, Fla., Apr. 2, 1957; d. Lloyd Lamar and Frances Lowe (Arrington) B; m. Gregory Robinette, Jan 13, 1962. BS, Univ. Fla., 1980; DVM, U. Fla., 1984. Veterinarian Animal Health Care Clinic, Virginia Beach, Va., 1986—; cons. Tidewater Humane Soc., Virginia Beach, 1988—. Mem. Am. Veterinary Medicine Assn., Va. Veterinary Medicine Assn. Home: 4192 Charity Neck Rd Virginia Beach VA 23456 Office: Animal Health Care Clinic 1485 General Booth Blvd Virginia Beach VA 23454

BRANCH, ERICA DANIELLE, broadcasting executive; b. N.Y.C., Feb. 2, 1966; d. B. Lawrence and Elva C. (Rawls) B. BS, Syracuse U., 1987. Prodn. asst. Positively Black, WNBC-TV, N.Y.C., 1987, WNBC-TV Essence, N.Y.C., 1987, WNBC-TV Christmas Spl., N.Y.C., 1987; prodn. sec. WCBS-TV 48 Hours, N.Y.C., 1987-88, asst. to exec. producer, 1988-89, broadcast assoc., 1989—. Recording sec. Delta Sigma Theta Sorority Inc., Montclair, N.J., 1990—. Named Outstanding Young Women of Am., 1987. Mem. Black Filmakers Soc. Home: 458 Centre St South Orange NJ 07079

BRAND, MARCIA CEPERLY, marketing executive; b. N.Y.C., Mar. 1, 1962; d. Douglas Bechtel and Linda Barclay (Ceperly) Smith; m. Laurence T. Brand, Sept. 7, 1987. BA in Urban Studies, Brown U., 1984. Mktg. mgr. The Rouse Co., Balt., 1984-86; mgr. leasing ops. Corcoran Jennison, Inc., Laurel, Md., 1986-87, regional dir., 1987-88; v.p. corp. mktg. CFM Mgmt. Svcs., Inc., McLean, Va., 1989-90; pres. Creative Mktg. Concepts, McLean, Va. and Balt., 1990—. Tutor/literacy coord. Coalition of Peninsula Orgns. Literacy Project, Balt., 1990; mem. Fed. Hill Neighborhood Assn., Balt., 1989—, Interagency Fair Housing Coordinating Group, Rockville, Md., 1989—. Mem. Am. Mgmt. Assn., NAFE, Property Mgmt. Assn., Condominium Assns. Inst. Episcopalian. Office: Creative Mktg Concepts 6849 Old Dominion Dr Ste 400 McLean VA 22101

BRAND, MARY LOU, nurse; b. Colorado Springs, Colo., Apr. 19, 1934; d. Frederick William and Clara Irene (Morriss) B. BS, U. Denver, 1957; MA, U. Colo., 1963; postgrad., U. No. Colo., 1969-77. Cert. in spl. svcs., Colo. Staff nurse Presbyn. Med. Ctr., Denver, 1957-68; staff sch. nurse Denver Pub. Schs. Dist. I, 1958—, counselor, 1963—; co-dir. sch. nurse workshop U. Wyo. Summer Sch., Laramie, 1967, U. No. Colo., 1969, 70; RN, Nat. Coun. for Sch. Nurses, pres., 1968-69. Contbr. articles to profl. jours. Profl. mem. Colo. div. ARC, 1958—; mem. Rep. Nat. Com., 1982—. Recipient Florence Nightingale award U. Colo. Sch. Nursing, 1988. Fellow Am. Sch. Health Assn.; mem. AAHPERD (conf. dir. 1968, Nat. Sch. Nurse award 1972), ANA, NEA, Colo. Nurses Assn. (chmn. sch. nurses sect. 1963-68), Colo. Edn. Assn., Colo. Sch. Health Coun. (sec. 1981-82, v.p. 1983-84, pres., bd. dirs. 1984-87, newsletter editor, recognition award 1986), Denver Classroom Tchrs. Assn. (area rep. 1987-89, award for svc. to children 1971), Presbyn. Med. Ctr. Sch. Nursing Alumni Assn., Statue of Liberty-Ellis Island Found. Home: PO Box 2650 Littleton CO 80161 Office: John F Kennedy High Sch 2855 S Lamar ST Denver CO 80227

BRANDANO, PHYLLIS TERESA, teacher; b. Boston, Oct. 26, 1952; d. Carmen James and Ann Marie (Rossi) Licciardi; m. James Lenin, Feb. 14, 1987. BS, Salem State Coll., 1974; M in Edn., Northeastern U., 1979; postgrad., Suffolk U., 1989. Reading tchr., sch. coord. profl. devel. sch. sites Melrose Pub. Schs., Mass., 1974—; lang. cons. Tuffs U., Medford, Mass., 1986—. Author: song, 1981, Am. Music awards; Literature Kits, patent office U.S., 1986 (copywright); poetry Treasury of Children Poetry, 1988 (Hon Mention). Mem. Sons of Italy, Melrose, 1980—. Recipient: Horace Mann Grant, Dept. of Edn., 1986-87. mem. Internat. Reading Assn., Nat. Edn. Assn. Convention (del., 1979), Mass. Edn. Assn. Convention (del., 1979), Assn. of Supervision & Curriculum Devel. Republican. Roman Catholic.

BRANDENBERG, PEARLINE, retired office manager; b. Aug. 3, 1934; d. Johnnie Brandenberg and Josephine (Williams) Johnson; m. Harold Jefferson, Sept. 15, 1956; children: Joyce Theresa, Roslyn Renee. Student, Manhattan Dental Sch., N.Y.C., 1973. Dental asst. Drs. Epstein and Digregorio, Bklyn., 1974-76, office mgr., 1976-89. Home: 691 Crawford St NE Orangeburg SC 29115

BRANDES, ZITA JUDITH MILLER, psychologist, psychotherapist; b. N.Y.C.; d. Solomon and Pauline (Rosenthal) Miller; m. Irwin Wolf Brandes, June 15, 1952; children: Mark, Jed, Paul. BA in Early Childhood Edn. cum laude, Bklyn. Coll., 1954; MS in Counseling, Queens Coll., 1970, cert. sch. psychology, 1977; PhD in Sch. Psychology, Fordham U., 1982; cert. in psychoanalysis and psychotherapy, Inst. for Contemporay Psychotherapy, 1987. Lic. Psychologist, N.Y.; nat. cert. sch. psychologist. Second grade tchr. El Paso (Tex.) Pub. Sch., 1954-55; early childhood tchr. West Side Day Nursery, N.Y.C., 1955-56; sch. counselor N.Y.C. (N.Y.) Sch. Dist., 1970-76; staff psychologist North Shore Child Guidance Ctr., Manhasset, N.Y., 1977-84; sch. psychologist Robert L. Stevenson Sch., N.Y.C., 1988-89; pvt. practice psychotherapist and psycho-diagnostician N.Y.C., 1983—; supr. to psychotherapists, 1986—. Rsch. asst. (book) Pets and Human Behavior, 1969. Founding mem., bd. dirs. Southride Nursery Sch., Jackson Heights, N.Y., 1962-64; mem. Nat. Found. for Ileitis and Colitis, 1975—, Amnesty Internat., 1985—, Simon Wiesenthal Ctr., 1980—, Women Strike for Peace, 1960's. Mem. Am. Psychol. Assn., Nassau County Psychol. Assn., Soc. Inst. for Contemporary Psychotherapy. Office: 21 West 86th St New York NY 10024

BRANDES-BOWEN, ILA ANN, entrepreneur; b. Charlotte, Apr. 3, 1954; d. Roddy Arthur and Marguerite (Johnson) Brandes; m. Timothy Ray Bowen, July 1, 1984. B.A., U. N.C., Greensboro, 1977. Asst. supr. quality control Ball Corp., Asheville, N.C., 1977-79, indsl. engr., Muncie, Ind., 1979-80, methods and standards engr., 1980-82, materials handling engr., 1982-85, customer service engr., 1983-85; cons. Porsche Market Group, Rockaway, N.J., 1985-86; owner, pres. IAM, Asheville, N.C., 1985-87; owner PIP, Statesville, N.C., 1986—; addressed 1984 Internat. Exposition Food Processors (speech pub.). Counselor Young Life, Greensboro, 1972-77, Jr. Achievement, Muncie, 1979-81; bd. dirs. Muncie Symphony Membership Dr., 1981, Corp. Challenge, Muncie, 1981-83, United Way Fund Dr., Muncie, 1982-83, DSDC, Statesville, 1988—, Fox Creek Farms, Inc., Troutsdale, Va., 1989—. Mem. NAFE. Republican. Presbyterian.

BRANDIS, PAMELA, sociologist; b. Chgo., Oct. 14, 1946; d. Theodore and Esther Ruth (Doege) B. BA, U. Wash., 1972, MA, 1977; MS, U. Oreg., 1982, PhD, 1989. Cert. secondary tchr., Wash. Instr. Edmonds Community Coll., Wash., 1977-79; teaching fellow U. Oreg., Portland, 1979-83; research analyst Columbia Info. Systems, Portland, 1984-86; evaluation sociologist Bonneville Power Adminstrn., Portland, 1986—; cons., free-lance researcher, Portland, 1986—. Contbr. Energy Conservation Program Evaluation Proc.1988—, The Christian Science Periodicals, articles to newspapers. Swimming coach U.S.A. Paraplegic Assn., Seattle, 1969. Recipient cash award for outstanding work Bonneville Power Adminstrn., 1988, 90. Mem. Soc. for Applied Sociology, Pacific Sociol. Soc., Pi Gamma Mu. Republican. Christian Scientist. Home: 4211 SW Woodside Circle Lake Oswego OR 97035

BRANDOLINI, ANITA JEAN, chemist, researcher; b. Chester, Pa., Mar. 4, 1956; d. Guy and Josephine (DeBerardinis) B. BS, Drexel U., 1979; MA, U. Del., 1981, PhD, 1983. Chemist Mobil Chem. Co., Edison, N.J., 1983—. Contbr. articles to profl. jours. Mem. Am. Chem. Soc. (chair Cen. N.J. chpt. 1985, councilor 1989—, chair pub. affairs com. N.J. chpt. 1990—), Soc. for Applied Spectroscopy, Soc. Plastics Engrs., Phi Lambda Upsilon. Office: Mobil Chem Co PO Box 3029 Edison NJ 08818-3029

BRANDON, KAREN NICOLE, legal assistant; b. Atlanta, Apr. 10, 1965; d. Gene and Erna (Britzelmeier) Gardner; m. Ronald Austin Brandon, Dec. 15, 1989. BS in Justice & Law Adminstrn., Western Conn. State U., 1987; MBA, U. D.C., 1989. Front end supr., store auditor Bradlees Dept. Store, Danbury, Conn., 1981-86; pre-trial diversion counselor Danbury Superior Courthouse, 1984; legal asst. Secor, Cassidy & McPartland, Danbury, 1985-87; legal sec. Gager, Henry & Narkis, Waterbury, Conn., 1987-88, Lane and Edson, P.C., Washington (D.C.), 1988-89, Dewey, Ballantine, Bushby, Palmer & Wood, Washington, 1989-90, Melrod, Redman & Gartlan, P.C., Washington (D.C.), 1990—. Mem. Jr. Achievement, Danbury, 1981. Home: 3522 Peartree Ct Apt 34 Silver Spring MD 20906 Office: Melrod Redman and Gartlan 1801 K St NW Washington DC 20006

BRANDON, SUZANNE, lawyer, educator; b. Millville, Wis., Dec. 18, 1928; d. James Laurence and Annabelle (Scott) B.; m. (dec. Mar. 1970); children: Margaret, Donna, David, Daniel; m. Paul Gerog Slaton, Aug. 26, 1983; children: Eric, Ellen. BA in Sociology, U. Wis., 1974, MS in Sociology, 1976; JD, U. Minn., 1985, PhD in Sociology, 1987. Ins. underwriter N.Am. Life and Casualty Co., Madison, Wis., 1961-62; gen. mgr. adminstrn. Stenjem Bldg. Corp. and Stenjem Realty Co., Madison, 1963-66; payroll auditor U. Wis., Madison, 1966-68; office supr., bd. tech. and adult edn. State of Wis., Madison, 1968-70; staff mem. Jour. Law and Inequality, U. Minn. Law Sch., Mpls., 1983-84, exec. editor, 1984-85; pvt. practice Hopkins, Minn., 1985—; tutor juvenile delinquency and social disorganization Athletic Dept. U. Wis., Madison, 1973-74, teaching asst. criminology, 1975; instr. Met. State U., 1987; instr. Coll. of St. Catherine, St. Paul, 1987-88, asst. prof., 1988—; instr. U. Minn., Mpls., 1982, asst. prof., 1989—. Contbr. articles to profl. jours. Arbitrator Better Bus. Bur.; bd. mem. Legal Advice Clinics, Inc., quality control com.; vice-chmn. Hopkins Zoning and Planning Comm., Hopkins, Minn.; vol. Sojourner Shelter (for battered women); vol. atty. Legal Advice Clinics, Minn. Aids Project, Hennepin County Guardianship Project; social action com. Temple Israel. Recipient Trewartha Honors Undergrad. Rsch. award, U. Wis., 1974, Alfred Reschke Social Sci. scholarship, U. Wis., 1974, NIMH fellowship, U. Minn., 1978-81, Nat. Inst. of Justice fellowship, U. Minn., 1981-82. Mem. ABA, Minn. Bar Assn., Minn. Women Lawyers (social action com.), Assn. Trial Lawyers Am., Minn. Justice Found., Wis. Criminal Justice Edn. Assn., Minn. Criminal Justice Edn. Found., Am. Sociol. Assn., Sociologists of Minn., Midwest Sociologists for Women in Soc., Nat. Women's Studies Assn., Nat. Coun. Family Relations, Minn. Coun. Family Relations, Alpha Kappa Delta. Jewish.

BRANDSTATER, LYNN BOURDON, clinic administrator; b. Muskegon, Mich., May 1, 1958; d. Joseph Jerome and Dolores Jane (Brogren) Bourdon; m. Allen E. Brandstater, Nov. 26, 1988. BA in Psychology, UCLA, 1980. Child advocate Children's Bur. L.A., Van Nuys, Calif., 1980-82; group travel coord. Guide Cardillo Travel, Culver City, Calif., 1982-84; dir. adminstrv. svcs. Verdugo Mental Health Ctr., Glendale, Calif., 1984—; chmn. interagency com. L.A. county Dept. Mental Health, L.A., 1985-86; mem. com. execs. L.A. Northangeles Region United Way, 1984-89. Third v.p. Days of the Verdugos Assn., Glendale, Calif., 1989—; 1st v.p. L.A. Foothill Republican Women Federated, Glendale, 1989—. Mem. NAFE, Assn. Mental Health Info. Officers, Nat. Cath. Devel. Conf. (assoc.), Bus. and Profl. Women (pres. Verdugo Hills chpt. 1988-89). Office: Verdugo Mental Health Ctr 417 Arden Ave Glendale CA 91203

BRANDT, BLANCH MARIE, health care facility administrator; b. Dryden, Ont., Can., Apr. 12, 1937; came to U.S., 1964; d. Frederick William and Mary Elizabeth (Gamble) Morton; m. Les W. Brandt, Dec. 12, 1958. BA, Southwestern Bapt. Bible Coll., Tucson, 1983. Dir. Vision Enhancement Ctr., Riverside, Calif.; adminstr. vision clinic San Bernardino County Probation, Calif.; ednl. and career cons. Recipient Outstanding Project award Am. Pub. Health Assn., Nat. Jewel Young award, 1990. Mem. Am. Correctional Health Svcs., UCM Ministers. Home: 2686 W Mill St #13 San Bernardino CA 92410 Office: 5051 Canyon Crest Dr Ste 102 Riverside CA 92507

BRANDT, BRENDA JOYCE, veterinarian; b. Emporia, Kans., Jan. 20, 1961; d. Jean Lee and Joyce Ann (Griffith) B.; m. James Carey Lane, Feb. 14, 1988. BS, Kans. State U., 1984, DVM, 1986. Assoc. veterinarian Animal Med. Clinic, Fayetteville, Ark., 1986-88; pvt. practice Best Friends Mobile Vet. Svc., Emporia, 1988—. Mem. Am. Vet. Med. Assn., Kans. Vet. Med. Assn., Altrusa. Home and Office: Rte 1 Box 104 Emporia KS 66801

BRANDT, CONNIE MARIE, management consultant; b. Akron, Ohio, Jan. 16, 1947; d. Beryl Howard Jr. and Jean Mary (Cunin) Haught; m. David L. Feathers, 1968 (div. 1988); m. Thomas Kergan Brandt, Mar. 29, 1990. BA magna cum laude, U. Akron, 1968. Br. mgr. Citizens Savs. & Loan Co., Akron, Ohio, 1972; sr. sales exec. Xerox Corp., Akron, 1972-78; sales dir. Mary Kay Cosmetics, Dallas, 1978-81; exec. search cons. Woodruff Mgmt. Group, Akron, 1981-82; pres. Womanomics, Akron, 1982-84; sales planning mgr. Westco Group, Inc., Akron, 1984-86; regional mgr. Profitwatch Systems, Inc., Ft. Wayne, Ind., 1986-87; dir. profl. devel. Westco Group, Inc., Akron, 1987—. Author: Selling It Like It Is, 1983, Come the Rest of the Way, Baby, 1983. Mem. Zonta, Am. Bus. Women Assn., Am. Soc. Tng. and Devel. Office: 35 N Harbour Dr Ocean Ridge FL 33435-6212

BRANDT, SUSAN GARBEE, journalist; b. Lynchburg, Va., Dec. 28, 1956; d. Walter Addison and Betty Ruth (Mitchell) Garbee; m. Ralph Leon Brandt Jr., June 19, 1982; 1 child, Timothy Ryan. BA, Va. Tech. Coll., 1979. Reporter The News and Daily Advance, Lynchburg, 1979-83, staff writer, 1983-85, religion writer, 1985-86, bus. writer, 1986—. Bd. dirs. Lynchburg Newspaper Fed. Credit Union, 1987—, Nelson County Child Care Ctr., Lovingston, Va., 1988—. Recipient 1st pl. writing awards Va. Press Assn., 1981, 87, 88. Mem. Investigative Reporters & Editors, Va. Press Women, Nat. Press Women, Soc. Profl. Journalists, Lioness Club (bd. dirs. 1986—), Delta Zeta.

BRANIGAN, HELEN MARIE, educational administrator; b. Albany, N.Y., Sept. 24, 1944; d. James J. and Helen (Weaver) B. BS in Bus. Edn., Coll. St. Rose, Albany, 1967, MA in English, 1972; postgrad., SUNY, Albany, 1973-81. Tchr., chair dept. bus. edn. S. Colonie Sch. Dist., Albany, 1968-81; assoc. Bur. Bus. Edn. N.Y. State Edn. Dept., Albany, 1981-87, assoc. Bur. Occupational Edn. Program Devel., 1987—; mem. adv. coun. SUNY-Cobbleskill, 1985—; lectr. in field. Editor McGraw-Hill Book Co., N.Y.C., 1986-88; contbr. articles to profl. jours. Lay vol. Archdiocese of Anchorage, 1967-68; mem. N.Y. State Staff Devel. Coun. Mem. Nat. Assn. State Suprs. Bus. Edn., Bus. Tchrs. Assn. N.Y. State, Ea. Bus. Edn. Assn., Nat. Bus. Edn. Assn., Nat. Assn. for Supervision and Curriculum Devel., Delta Pi Epsilon. Democrat. Roman Catholic. Home: 540 New Scotland Ave Albany NY 12208 Office: NY State Edn Dept Bur Occupational Edn Program 1 Commerce Plaza Rm 1623 Albany NY 12234

BRANNAN, PEGGY L., small business owner; b. Springfield, Mo., Sept. 17, 1937; d. Francis Leo and Bernadine Colletta (Blaes) Lehar; m. Donald Joseph Brannan, June 24, 1961 (div. 1984); children: Karen Colleen, Michael John, Nanci Ann, Erin Marie, Mary Susan. Student, Meadows-Draughon Sch., New Orleans, 1957, Loyola U., New Orleans, 1958, Southeastern La. U., Hammond, La., 1984-85. Sec. Johnson Constrn. Co., Springfield, Mo., 1954; editor yellow pages So. Bell Telephone Co., New Orleans, 1955-56; stenographer, asst. chief steno FBI, New Orleans, 1956-62; sec. Spl. Investigations, New Orleans, 1963-64; realtor/assoc. Derbes Real Estate, Wagner & Traux Real Estate, Merrill Lynch, Covington, La., 1975-82, 84-86; owner Progressive Sectl. Svc., Covington, 1987—. Vol. Spl. Olympics, Denver, 1982-84, Rep. Women's Assn., Covington, La., 1988-89; sec. Nat. Orgn. Prosthesis Implants, Inc., Metairie, La., 1989—. Mem. Referral Assocs. of La., Am. Bus. Women's Assn., Franco's Athletic Club. Republican. Roman Catholic. Home: 812 S Monroe St Covington LA 70433 Office: Progressive Secretarial 812 S Monroe St Covington LA 70433

BRANNICK, ELLEN MARIE, management consultant; b. Rochester, Minn., Aug. 10, 1934; d. Daniel Ryther and Grace Ellen (Mills) Markham; m. Thomas L. Brannick,. BS in Health, Phys. Edn., MacMurray Coll., 1956, MS, 1959. Elem. phys. edn. Ritenour Consol. Sch. Dist., Overland, Mo., 1958-61; head tchr., summer dir. Civic League Day Nursery, Rochester, 1961-64; recreation therapist Rochester State Hosp., 1964-68; rehab. dir. Rochester State Hosp., 1968-70; rehab. therapist Napa State Hosp., Calif., 1971; indsl. therapy con. Napa State Hosp., 1971-73, community liaison rep., 1973—. Mem. Friends Napa County Library, 1977,, Napa County Humane Soc., 1978,. Mem. Nat. Coun. for Therapeutic Recreation, Calif. Alliance for the Mentally Ill, Napa Valley AIDS project, Napa County Hist. Soc. Democrat. Office: Napa State Hosp 2100 Napa Vallejo Hwy Napa CA 94558

BRANNON, FRANCES JOAN, professor of exercise physiology; b. Parcoal, W.Va., Jan. 24, 1935; d. Doy Alton and Lona Margaret (Armstrong) B. BA, Berea Coll., 1956; MS, U. Tenn., 1961; PhD, U. Md., 1968. Cert. tchr., Ky. Instr. Berea (Ky.) Coll., 1956-61, U. Md., College Park, 1965-68; asst. prof. Macalester Coll., St. Paul, Minn., 1968-69; prof. Slippery Rock (Pa.) U., 1969—; founder Brannon Health Resources Mgmt., Prospect, Pa., 1976—, founder, cons. Bio-Energetics Rehab., Prospect, 1976-89. Author: Exercise Physiology, 1978, (with others) Cardiac Rehabilitation, 1988 (Pres. award 1988). Founder Tigger Neutering Fund, Butler Humane Soc., 1971. Recipient Commonwealth Disting. Teaching chair, State of Pa., 1974. Mem. Am. Coll. of Sports Medicine, Tri-State Assn. of Cardiac Rehab., Am. Assn. of Health, Phys. Edn. and Recreation, Pa. Assn. of Health, Phys. Edn. and Recreation, Phi Kappa Phi. Republican. Home: RD1 Box 70 Prospect PA 16052 Office: Slippery Rock U Field House Slippery Rock PA 16057

BRANNON, RACHEL ANN, nurse executive; b. Nashville, Sept. 17, 1954; d. John Benjamin and Lillian (Rittenberry) Brannon. BSN, Vanderbilt U., 1976; MSN, U. Ala., Birmingham, 1982. Cert. in hosp. adminstrn., 1982. Staff nurse I & II Methodist Hosp., Memphis, 1976-80; adminstrv. resident Miami Valley Hosp., Dayton, Ohio, 1982-83; dir. nursing Miami Valley Hosp., 1983-87; v.p. for nursing svcs. Nashville Meml. Hosp., Madison, Tenn., 1987—. Vice pres. Social Health Assn., Dayton, 1984-87; bd. dirs. Hospice of Dayton, 1987; post advisor Explorers, Dayton, 1985-87; mem. joint coordinating com. for the Wright State U./Miami Valley Sch. of Nursing, Dayton, 1987; mem. adv. com. Tenn. State U. Sch. Nursing, 1988-90, Austin Peay State U. Sch. Nursing, 1989-90; chairperson, mem. hosp. consortium Tenn. Poison Ctr., 1989-90; mem. Sun Health Nursing Coun., 1989—. Mem. Am. Orgn. Nurse Execs., Tenn. Orgn. Nurse Execs., L.R. Jordan Healthcare Execs. Assn., Sigma Theta Tau. Mem. Ch. of Christ. Office: Nashville Meml Hosp 612 W Due West Ave Madison TN 37115

BRANNON, WINONA EILEEN, electrical contractor; b. Austell, Ga., Jan. 3, 1948; d. John Milton and Vera Inez (Banks) McDaniel; m. Harold Wallace Smith, May 9, 1966 (div. June 1967); m. Jerry Edward Weddington, Feb. 24, 1968 (div. Feb. 1984); children: Michael Richard, Paula Daniell; m. David Lee Brannon, Dec. 9, 1985; 1 step-child, Kimberly Lorraine. Cert. in data processing, DeKalb Tech., Chamblee, Ga., 1968; cert. in keypunch, Ga. State, 1969; cert. in elec. codes, Cobb Voc. Tech., Marietta, Ga., 1983. Lic. hair stylist, Ga.; lic. elec. contractor, Ga. Hair stylist Casa Di Bella and Modella, Atlanta and Mableton, Ga., 1965-68; sec. and keypunch operator Ga. Sec. of State, Atlanta, 1968-70; data transcriber IRS, Chamblee, Ga., 1969-73, data processor, 1978-79, IDRS operation, 1980-82; sch. bus driver Cobb County Bd. Edn., Marietta, 1974-77; meat packer Cudahy (Bar-s Meats), Atlanta, 1979-80; electrician J&J Electric, Mableton, 1982-85; elec. contractor Watts New Electric, Mableton, 1985—. Recipient First Pl. Hair Styling award, Mableton, 1965, 66. Mem. Adams Rainbow (worthy advisor 1965), Ea. Star (Assn. matron 1983). Republican. Methodist. Home and Office: 5923 Ridge Dr Mableton GA 30059

BRANSCOMB, ANNE WELLS, lawyer, communications consultant; b. Statesboro, Ga., Nov. 22, 1928; d. Guy Herbert and Ruby Mae (Hammond) Wells; m. Lewis McAdory Branscomb, Oct. 13, 1951; children: Harvie Hammond, Katharine Capers. BA, Ga. Coll., 1949, U. N.C., 1949; postgrad., London Sch. Econs., 1950; MA, Harvard U., 1951; JD with honors, George Washington, 1962. Bar: D.C. 1962, Colo. 1963, N.Y. 1973, U.S. Supreme Ct. 1972. Research assoc. Pierson, Ball and Dowd, Washington, 1962; law clk. to presiding judge U.S. Dist. Ct., Denver, 1962-63; assoc. Williams & Zook, 1963-66; pvt. practice Boulder, 1966-69; assoc. Arnold and Porter, Washington, 1969-72; communications counsel Teleprompter Corp., N.Y.C., 1973; v.p. Kalba-Bowen Assocs. Inc., communication cons., Cambridge, Mass., 1974-77, chmn. bd., 1977-80, sr. assoc. dir., 1980-82; pres. The Raven Group, Concord, Mass., 1986—; trustee Pacific Telecommunications Council, 1981-83, 86—; mem. tech. adv. bd. Dept. Commerce, 1977-81; WARC adv. com. Dept. State, 1978-79; mem. Carnegie Corp. Task Force on Pub. Broadcasting, 1976-77; mem. overseers, vis. com. Harvard U. Office of Info. Tech., 1977-83; vis. scholar Yale U. Law, 1981-82; mem. program on information resources and pub. policy Harvard U., 1986—; chmn. program com. Legal Symposium Telecom '87, Internat. Telecommunications Union, 1986-87; bd. dirs. Pub. Interest Radio, 1986-88; adj. prof. internat. law Tufts U., 1987-89; mem. adv. bd. Atwater Inst., Ottawa, Can., 1988—; mem. Carnegie Corp. task force on nongovtl. orgns, 1990—. Contbr. articles to profl. jours.; mem. editorial bd. Info. Soc.; editor: Toward a Law of Global Communications Networks; contbg. editor Jour. Communications, 1980—. Housing commr. Boulder Pub. Housing Authority, 1969-70; bd. dirs. Nat. Pub. Radio, 1975-78; trustee EDUCOM, Interuniv. Communications Council Inc., 1975-78; vice chmn. Colo. Dem. State Cen. Com., 1967-69; del. mem. permanent orgn. com. Dem. Nat. Conv., 1968; trustee, exec. com. Rensselaer Poly. Inst., 1980-89; active Carnegie Corp. Task Force on Nongovtl. Orgns., 1990—. Recipient Alumni Achievement award Ga. Coll., 1980; recipient Rotary Found. fellowship, 1950-51; inaugural fellow Gannett Ctr. for Media Studies Columbia U., 1985. Mem. ABA (Nat. Conf. Lawyers and Scientists ABA/AAAS 1985—, chmn. communications com. sci. and tech. sect. 1980-82, chmn. communications law div. 1982-84, mem. coun. and tech. sect. 1981-85), Am. Polit. Sci. Assn., Internat. Communications Assn., Internat. Inst. Communications, Soc. Preservation of First Wives and First Husbands (nat. pres. 1981—), Order of Coif, Valkyries, Phi Beta Kappa, Alpha Psi Omega, Chi Delta Phi, Pi Gamma Mu.

BRANSCOMBE, NYLA RUTH, social psychology educator; b. Sussex, N.B., Can., Oct. 6, 1956; came to U.S., 1982; d. Leslie Arthur and Edna Ida (Parlee) B.; m. Robin Edward Price, July 17, 1982 (div. Feb. 1990). BA, York U., Toronto, Ont., Can., 1980; MA, U. of W. Ont., London, Can., 1982; PhD, Purdue U., 1986. Vis. asst. prof. dept. psychology U. Ill., 1986-87; asst. prof. U. Kans., 1987—; statis. cons. Purdue U., West Lafayette, Ind. 1985-86. Author: (chpts in books with others) Affect, Cognition and Social Behavior, 1988, Emotion and Social Judgments, 1990; contbr. articles to profl. jours. Bd. dirs. First Step House, Lawrence, Kan., 1990-93. Grantee U. Kans., 1989-90; fellow Soc. Scis. and Humanities Rsch. Coun. of Can., 1982-87. Mem. Am. Psychol. Assn., Midwest Psychol. Assn., Clinton Marina and Yacht Club. Office: U Kans Dept Psychology Lawrence KS 66045

BRANSON, BRENDA SULLENS, accountant; b. Dahlonega, Ga., July 22, 1961; d. Joseph L. and Sammie L. Sullens; m. James E. Branson, Dec. 20, 1980. BBA in Acctg., BBA in Fin., North Ga. Coll., 1986. Lic. real estate agt., Ga. Asst. v.p. Bank of Dahlonega, 1978-87; fin. officer Health Systems Mgmt., Inc., Dahlonega, 1987-90; staff acct. Walker & Smith, CPAs, Gainesville, Ga., 1990—; owner Branson Acctg. Svcs., Dahlonega, 1989—. Mem. Dahlonega/Lumpkin County C. of C., NAFE. Baptist. Home: Rt 7 PO Box 830 Dahlonega GA 30533 Office: Walker & Smith PO Box 385 Gainesville GA 30503

BRANSON, MARY LOU, family therapist, military agency administrator; b. Tulsa, June 11, 1932; d. Clarence Leo and Peg (McDonald) Jester; m. Robert K. Branson, Sept. 8, 1956 (div. Dec. 1976); children: Malinda, Scott, Craig. BA, Okla. State U., 1956; MS, Tex. Woman's U., 1981, PhD, 1984. Cert. drug and alcohol counselor, marriage and family therapist. Claims rep. Social Security Adminstrn., Ohio, La., N.Mex., 1957-63; reconsideration specialist State of Fla. Disability Determinations, Tallahassee, 1975-79; intern Office Families, Washington, 1982; sr. regional employee assistance program counselor Control Data Corp., Dallas, 1983-85; dir. Family Svc. Ctr. Naval Air Sta., Dallas, 1985-87, 89—; dep. dir. Family Svc. Ctr. Naval Support Activity, Holy Loch, Scotland, 1987-89; mem. com. single parent families Nat. Council Family Relations, Mpls., 1984-85, co-op edn. bd. Tex. Woman's U., Denton, 1985-86. Author, editor: (book) Tallahassee Coloring Book, 1972. Dir. Cerebral Palsy Nursery Sch., Baton Rouge, 1961; bd. dirs. Diablo Valley Montessori Sch., Lafayette, Calif., 1966; pres. La. State U. Faculty Wives, Baton Rouge, 1962. U. Tulsa scholar, 1950, Texas Woman's U. scholar, 1980-85. Mem. Am. Assn. Marriage and Family Therapy (clin.), Nat. Council on Family Relations, Assn. Labor-Mgmt. Adminstrs. and Cons. on Alcoholism, Internat. Family Therapy Assn., Kappa Alpha Theta Alumni Club (v.p. 1973). Office: Family Svc Ctr Naval Air Sta Bldg 12 Dallas TX 75211

BRANTLEY, WILLA JOHN, educational administrator; b. Carthage, Miss., Aug. 24, 1956; d. Rena John; m. Harlon Dwight Bell, May 15, 1974 (div. 1979); children: Chassidy Georgina, Gerrard Dwight; m. Nicky Paul Brantley, Jan. 5, 1985. Student, East Cen. Jr. Coll., 1975, Wood Jr. Coll., 1975-76; BEd magna cum laude, Jackson State U., 1979; postgrad., Miss. State U., 1979-81, 83—. Cert. elem. tchr., Miss. Counselor Miss. Bank Choctaw Indian, Phila., Miss., 1979; elem. tchr. Standing Pine Sch., Walnut Grove, Miss., 1979-81; prin. Standing Pine Sch., Walnut Grove, 1983-87; ednl. specialist Chcotaw Agy., Phila., 1981-83, 87—, acting agy. supr. for edn., 1981-88, agt. supt. for edn., 1988—; tchr. evaluator State Dept. Edn., Phila., 1985—; trainers of tng. Nat. Indian Sch. Bd., Phila., 1987—; curriculum specialist Bur. Indian Affairs-Choctow, Phila., 1987—, staff devel. coord., 1986—. Vol. program implementation Save the Children Fedn., Cherokee, N.C., 1981—; planning participant nat. issues forum Kettering Found., Dayton, Ohio, 1987; mem. task force com. Office of Indian Edn. Program, Washington, 1985. Named to Outstanding Young Woman Am., 1987; recipient Cert. of Recognition Save the Children Fedn., 1986. Fellow Internat. Reading Assn., Miss. Staff Devel. Coun.; mem. Minn. Edn. Computer Consortium, Assn. Supr. and Curriculum, Red Water Basketball Club, Red Water Community Devel. Club, Phi Theta Kappa. Democrat. Methodist. Home: PO Box 161 Carthage MS 39051

BRANTON, CAMILE B., counselor, educator; b. Greenwood, Miss., Aug. 30, 1950; d. Don Otho and Sarah (Goodpasture) Baker; children: Irene, Sarah. BS, MS, Miss. State U., 1972, PhD, 1989; MEd, MS, Delta State U., Cleveland, Miss., 1987. Lic. counselor, Miss.; cer. counselor; Diplomate Am. Bd. Med. Psychotherapists. Asst. prof. behavioral scis. Delta State U., Cleveland, Miss., 1989—. Author: Coercive Sexual Behavior among College Students: A Causal Model, Coercive Sexual Behavior Rating Scale. Mem. Am. Assn. for Counseling and Devel., Nat. Bd. Cert. Counselors, Coun. for Exceptional Children, Assn. for Children with Learning Disabilities, Am. Mental Health Counselors Assn., Miss. Counseling Assn., Am. Psychol. Assn., DAR, Phi Delta Kappa, Kappa Delta Pi, Delta Gamma. Home: 1303 College St Cleveland MS 38732 Office: Delta State U PO Box 3142 Cleveland MS 38733

BRASHEAR, DIANE LEE, marital and sex therapist; b. Parkersburg, W.Va., July 21, 1933; d. Ralph Elijah and Dorothea Esther (McDade) Blake; m. Richard Evers Brashear, aug. 31, 1956; children: Allison Donaldson, Meredith Kay. BS in Social Adminstrn., Ohio State U., 1955, MSW, 1957; PhD, Purdue U., 1971. Chief social worker Ind. Sch. for Blind, Indpls., 1965-68; asst. prof. social work Ind. U., Indpls., 1970-72; dir. Brashear Ctr., Inc., Indpls., 1972-84; news reporter marriage & family coun. WTHR-Channel 13, Indpls., 1980—; asst. prof. ob/gyn Ind. U. Sch. Medicine, Indpls., 1984—; vis. prof. Purdue U., West Lafayette, Ind., 1971-72; bd. dirs. Alan Guttmacher Inst., National, 1985—. Author: Social Worker as Sex Educator, 1977; editor Indpls. Mo., 1975—; contbr. articles, book chpts. and video tapes. Pres. Planned Parenthood Greater Indpls., 1985-87, bd. dirs. Planned Parenthood Fedn. Am., 1983-88; vice chmn. Greater Indpls. Progress Community, 1989—, United Way, Indpls., 1989—; pres. Community Svc. Coun., Indpls., 1989—. Recipient Pauline Selby award, Big Sisters Greater Indpls., 1986, Leadership award YWCA, Ind., 1986. Mem. Am. Assn. Marriage & Family, Am. Coll. Ob/Gyn, Am. Soc. Psychosomatic Ob/Gyn, Soc. Scientific Study Sex, Soc. Sex Therapy & Rsch. Office: Ind U 926 W Michigan St Indianapolis IN 46202

BRASLEY, AMY JORDAN, school psychologist; b. Spokane, Jan. 7, 1956; d. Everett Junior and Helen Susan (Fountain) Jordan); m. Robert Lawrence Brasley, Jr., June 4, 1983; children: Nathan Jordan, Ann Elise. BA, U. Idaho, 1977; MS, Utah State U., 1980. Cert. sch. pscyhologist; lic. counselor, Idaho; nationally cert. sch. psychologist. Sch. psychologist Prairie View Spl. Svcs., Glendive, Mont., 1980-82, Union County Edn. Svc. Dist., La Grande, Oreg., 1982-83, Malheur County Edn. Svc. Dist., Ontario, Oreg., 1984-86, Nampa (Idaho) Sch. Dist., 1986-87, Boise (Idaho) Sch. Dist., 1987—. Mem. Idaho Sch. Psychology Assn., Nat. Assn. Sch. Psychologists, Idaho Soc. Individual Psychology, Am. Psychology Assn., Phi Beta Kappa.

BRASSELL, ROSELYN STRAUSS, lawyer; b. Shreveport, La., Feb. 19, 1930; d. Herman Carl and Etelka (McMullan) Strauss. BA, La. State U., 1949; JD, UCLA, 1962. Bar: Calif. 1963. Legal sec. Welton P. Mouton, Lafayette, La., 1949-50; office sec. Leake, Henry, Golden & Burrow, Dallas, 1950-57; atty. CBS, Los Angeles, 1962-68, sr. atty., 1968-76, asst. gen. atty., 1976-83, broadcast counsel, 1983—. Co-writer: Life After Death for the California Celebrity, 1985; bd. editors U. Calif. Law Rev., 1960-62. Named Angel of Distinction Los Angeles Cen. City Assn., 1975. Mem. Calif. Bar Assn., Los Angeles County Bar Assn. (exec. com. 1970—, sect. chmn. 1980-81), Beverly Hills Bar Assn., Los Angeles Copyright Soc. (treas. 1977-78, sec. 1978-79, pres. 1981-82), Am. Women in Radio and TV (nat. dir.-at-large 1971-73, nat. pub. affairs chmn. 1977-78, Merit award So. Calif. chpt. 1989), NATAS, Women in Film, Los Angeles World Affairs Coun., U. Calif. Law Alumni Assn. (dir. 1971-74), Order of Coif, Alpha Xi Delta, Phi Alpha Delta. Republican. Home: 631 N Wilcox Ave Los Angeles CA 90004 Office: 7800 Beverly Blvd Los Angeles CA 90036

BRASSIL, JEAN ELLA, psychologist; b. New Haven, Conn., June 4, 1933; d. Joseph Eugene and Ella Eve (Lindhardt) B. BS, So. Conn. State U., 1955; MA, Columbia U., 1957; PhD, Adelphi U., 1971. Cert. tchr., Conn., N.Y. Tchr. pub. schs. North Haven, Conn., 1955-58, 60-62, Casper, Wyo., 1958-59, Montebello, Calif., 1959-60; psychol. examiner Meriden (Conn.) Pub. Schs., 1962-63; instr. Adelphi U., Garden City, N.Y., 1964-67; asst. prof. So. Conn. State U., New Haven, 1967-68; psychologist Child Guidance Clin. Greater Bridgeport (Conn.), 1968-73; psychologist, counselor Fairfield (Conn.) Pub. Schs., 1973—; pvt. practice psychology Derby, Conn., 1972—. Mem. Am. Psychol. Assn., Conn. Psychol. Assn. (bd. dirs. 1971-81, sec. 1981-82, pres. 1983). Home: 7 Orangewoor Dr Derby CT 06418 Office: Roger Sherman Sch Fern St Fairfield CT 06430

BRASWELL, LAURA DAY, periodontist; b. Bowling Green, Ky., July 22, 1958; d. Lawson Moyers and Bettye (Braswell) Wall B. DDS, U. N.C., 1982; cert., Emory U., 1988. Staff dentist Sam Rudd DDS, Raleigh, N.C., 1982-83; mem. faculty Emory U., Atlanta, 1983—; primate dentist Yerkes Regional Primate Ctr., Atlanta, 1984—; zoo dentist Zoo Atlanta, 1986—; periodontist Michael Fritz DDS, Atlanta, 1988—. Vol. Healing for the Poor, Kingston, Jamaica, 1986, Cen. Presbyn. Health Ctr., Atlanta, 1986—; bd. dirs. Arthritis Found., Ga. Mem. Am. Acad. Periodontology, IAOR, Psi Omega. Episcopalian. Home: 586 Emory Oaks Way Decatur GA 30033 Office: Emory U 1462 Clifton Rd NE Atlanta GA 30322 also: 3316 Piedmont Rd NE Atlanta GA 30305

BRASWELL, PEARL EVA, jeweler, researcher; b. Anchor, Ill., Oct. 25, 1914; d. Arthur and Anna Maria (Berlet) Troyer; m. Daniel E. Braswell II, June, 1945; childen: John Braswell (dec.), Daniel E. III. Student, Ill. Comml. Coll., 1943, Gemological Inst. Am., 1954-55. Owner Pearl Braswell Antiques, Champaign, Ill., 1948-56; pres., owner Pearl Braswell Jeweler, Inc., Palm Beach, Fla., 1956-86; executor Gems, Ltd. Breakers Hotel, Palm Beach, 1986-89; trustee William Barringer Found., Palm Beach, 1989—. Fundraiser Leukemia Soc., Palm Beach, 1975—; bd. dirs. Prairie AIDS Found., Urbana, Ill., 1988-89. Republican. Home: 901 Cheshire Dr Champaign IL 61821 also: 401 Peruvian Ave Palm Beach FL 33481 Office: Braswell Jewelers Gems Ltd Breakers Hotel Palm Beach FL 33480

BRATAAS, NANCY, state senator; b. Mpls., Jan. 19, 1928; d. John Draper and Flora (Warner) Osborn; m. Mark Gerard Brataas, 1948; children—Mark, Anne. Ed. U. Minn. First elected to Minn. Senate, 1975, re-elected. 76, 80, 82, 86—; pres. Brataas Systems. Minn. Republican state chairwoman, 1963-69; state chairwoman Minn. Rep. Fin. Com., 1969-71. Mem. League Women Voters, AAUW, Zonta Internat. Episcopalian. Home: 839 10-1/2 St SW Rochester MN 55902 Office: Minn Senate Saint Paul MN 55155

BRATCHER, CARLA ELIZABETH, obstetrician, gynecologist; b. Wichita, Kans., Sept. 18, 1942; d. Carl E. and Armilda Elizabeth (Salmans) Dillon; m. Carl E. Bratcher III, Apr. 9, 1983. Student, U. Wash., 1960-62; BS, U. Fla., 1966; MD, U. Pa., 1979. Diplomate Am. Bd. Ob-Gyn. Rsch. technician Nat. Cancer Inst.-NIH, Bethesda, Md., 1967-73, Wistar Inst., Phila., 1973-75; ob-gyn intern Madigan Army Med. Ctr., Tacoma, 1979-80, resident in ob-gyn, 1980-83; chief ambulatory care svc. ob-gyn. 2d Gen. Hosp., Landstuhl, Fed. Republic Germany, 1984-87; pvt. practice, Grand Prairie, Tex., 1988-89; pvt. practice ob/gyn. Redmond, Oreg., 1990—; vol. instr. dept. ob-gyn Dallas-Ft. Worth Med. Ctr., 1988-89. Maj. M.C., U.S. Army, 1979-87. Fellow Am. Coll. Obstetricians and Gynecologists; mem. AMA, Dallas County Med. Soc., Oreg. Med. Assn., Am. Med. Women's Assn. Democrat. Office: Redmond Ob/Gyn 1228 N Canal Redmond OR 97756

BRATCHER, TWILA LANGDON, conchologist, malacologist; b. Smoot, Wyo.; d. Willis G. and Pearl (Graham) Langdon; m. Ford F. Bratcher, Sept. 10, 1942. Research assoc. Los Angeles Mus. Natural History, 1965—; mem. Ameripages Sci. Expedition to Galapagos Islands, 1971; author stories for blind children about skin diving, sea shells, creatures of the sea pub. Braille Inst., 1964-72; work with schs. for blind. Mem. Conchological Club So. Calif. (pres. 1966, 88; life hon. mem.), Am. Malacological Union (councilor at large 1971), Western Soc. Malacologists (pres. 1973), Hawaiian Malacological Soc., Conchologists Am. (exec. bd. 1985-88), San Diego Shell Club, Pacific Shell Club (life hon. mem.). Club: So. Calif. Woman's Press (pres. 1977-79). Author: Living Terebras of the World; contbr. articles to sci. jours. Home: 8121 Mulholland Terr Hollywood CA 90046

BRATHWAITE, HARRIET LOUISA, nursing educator; b. Rye, N.Y., Aug. 28, 1931; d. James Pierce and Mattie (Collins) Bowling; m. Leroy L. Brathwwaite, Feb. 18, 1950; 1 child, Helene Ann Brathwaite Ward. AAS in Nursing, Bklyn. Coll., 1959; BSN, L.I. U., 1965; postgrad., Tchrs. Coll. of Columbia U., 1965-68; MSN, Adelphia U., 1973. Staff nurse Kings County Hosp., Bklyn., 1959; head nurse City Hosp. at Elmhurst, Queens, N.Y., 1959-62; instr. Kings County Hosp. Sch. Nursing, 1963-65, Downstate Med. Ctr. Sch. Nursing, 1965-69; nurse community mental health South Beach Psychiat. Ctr., 1969-73; cons. psychiat. nursing service HEW and N.Y. State Health Dept., Albany, 1973-74; chief of service Creedmoor Psychiat. Ctr., Queens Village, N.Y., 1974-87; asst. prof. nursing L.I. U., Queens, 1987—. Co-leader Allied Dems., Jamaica, N.Y., 1959-62; bd. dirs. South Queens Dems., Howard Beach, N.Y.; mem. adv. bd. Transitional Services, Queens, 1983-85. Recipient Cert. of Appreciation, Nat. Black Nurses, 1989. Mem. Nat. Black Nurses Assn. (chmn. legis. com. Queens chpt. 1981—, Cert. of Appreciation 1989), Am. Nurses Assn., N.Y. State Nurses Assn. (dist. 14, 25 Yr. Membership award 1986), Orthopsychiatry Assn., AAUW, NAACP, 100 Black Women of L.I. Club: Knickerbocker (chmn. fin. and scholarship com.). Home: Cuffee Dr PO Box 1841 Sag Harbor NY 11963

BRATHWAITE, MELLISSA ANNETTE, radio announcer, producer; b. Bklyn., Aug. 2, 1961; d. Erskine and Virginia (Higgins) B. BBA, Howard U., 1985, postgrad. Mgmt. asst., assoc. producer Sta. WHUR-Radio, Washington, 1982-85; mgmt. asst. Sta. WBLS/WLIB Radio, N.Y.C., 1983, NBC/WKYS Radio, Washington, 1985; announcer, engr. Sta. WOL-Radio, Washington, 1985; mktg. rep. Diaspora Records, Washington, 1985-86; music dir., announcer, engr. Sta. WYCB Radio, Washington, 1985-87; promotions rep. A&M/Word Records, Washington, 1986-87; producer, announcer, engr. Sta. WOL-Radio, 1987-90; asst. community affairs dir. Sta. WHUR-FM Radio, Washington, 1990—; radio monitor Video Monitoring Services, Washington, 1986. Author, publisher: Sunshine: A Collection of Poetry, 1985. Counselor Cath. Charities, Washington, 1986; counselor/recruiter Nat. Council on Negro Women, Washington, 1986; adv. bd. mem. SPECTRUM: Cobra Assocs., 1984; coord. Just Say No To Drugs program YMCA, vol. Big Sister Growin'Up program, intergeneration program; vocal minister, eucharistic minister St. Augustine Gospel Choir; aerobic instr. Roman Catholic.

BRATSOS, DIANE, artist, consultant, sculptor; b. Boston, Apr. 29, 1958; d. Gary and Adella Laura Bratsos; m. Leon Curtis Shaffer, June 30, 1985 (div. 1989); m. Scott David Shaw, Sept. 8, 1990. BA in History, Worcester State Coll., 1982; MA in Fine Arts, Assumption Coll., 1986. Cert. art tchr., K-12, Mass. Dir./curator Artemis Prodns.-Bratsos Gallery, Boston, 1986-87; art tchr. Immaculate Conception Elem. Sch., Everett, Mass., 1988-89; owner, pres., art cons. Gallery Without Walls, Reading, Mass., 1987—; tchr. art history Massasoit Community Coll., Canton, Mass., 1990—. Office: Gallery Without Walls 242 Main St Ste A Reading MA 01867

BRATTAIN, ARLENE JANE CLARK, interior designer; b. Phila., July 27, 1938; d. Franklin Corning Clark and Nora May Robertson; children: Kathy, Kurt, Karen, David. Cert. in interior design, N.Y. Sch. Interior Design, 1975; BS, U. Minn., 1986. Exec. United Way, Mpls., 1980; interior designer AB Interiors, Minnetonka, Minn., 1982—; pvt. practice color analyst, Minnetonka, 1984—; cons. showroom Rollin B. Child Tile, Plymouth, Minn., 1985; interior designer Room & Bd. Stores, Minnetonka, 1985-86. Designer Window Fashions mag., 1988—, Am. Soc. Interior Designers Showcase Home, 1987, Showcase Home for March of Dimes, 1988, Showcase Vignette, 1989. Trainer dist. Camp Fire Girls, Minnetonka, 1967-78; trainer, leader Boy Scouts Am., Mpls., 1967-80; pres. PTA, Minnetonka, 1970, Music Boosters, Minnetonka, 1976-84. Recipient Silver Fawn award Boy Scouts Am., 1973. Mem. Am. Soc. Interior Designers (assoc.), Internat. Furnishings and Design Assn. (exec. 1988—), Nat. Trust for Hist. Preservation, Mensa.

BRATTAIN, HARRIET JANE, architect; b. Greenville, S.C., Oct. 15, 1951; d. Richard Vassar and Eleanor Ruth (Groves) B. B Environ. Design, N.C. State U., 1973; M Urban Studies, Old Dominion U., 1980. Sr. planner Atlantic div. Naval Facilities Engrng. Command, Norfolk, Va., 1974-79; architect Naval Facilities Engrng. Command, 1979-89, head ops. br. facilities planning div., 1989—. Editor, Shore Facilities Planning Manual, 1987. Mem. Am. Planning Assn., Am. Inst. of Certified Planners, Toastmasters. Home: 5901 Mount Eagle Dr Alexandria VA 22303 Office: Facilities Engrng Command 200 Stovall St Alexandria VA 22332

BRATTIN, KATHLEEN ANN, telecommunications company financial executive; b. Oak Park, Ill., Apr. 30, 1957; d. William Robert and Dorothy Catherine (Morrison) Marks; m. Bruce Alyn Brattin, Oct. 6, 1979; childen: Meghan Christine, James Michael. BA in Fin., U. Ill., 1979. Fin. analyst Wis. Electric Power Co., Milw., 1979-81; supr. treasury Wis. Bell, Milw., 1981-83, asst. mgr. budgets, 1983-84; supr. cash mgmt. Ameritech Svcs., Inc., Arlington Heights, Ill., 1984-85; assoc. fin. planning Ameritech Svcs., Inc., Schaumburg, Ill., 1985-87; sr. treasury analyst Ameritech Svcs., Inc., Arlington Heights, 1987-88, mgr. treasury, 1988-89; mgr. corp. planning Ameritech Svcs., Inc., Schaumburg, 1989—. Mem. Bartlett (Ill.)-Walnut Hills Homeowners Assn., 1988—. Mem. NAFE, Nat. Corp. Cash Mgrs. Assn. (cert.), U. Ill. Alumni Assn., Delta Zeta. Republican. Roman Catholic. Home: 648 Hazelnut Ct Bartlett IL 60103 Office: Ameritech Svcs Inc 1900 E Golf Rd l0th Fl Schaumburg IL 60178

BRATTON, IDA FRANK, educator; b. Glasgow, Ky., Aug. 31, 1933; d. Edmund Bates and Robbie Davis (Hume) Button; m. Robert Franklin Bratton, June 20, 1954; 1 son, Timothy Andrew. B.A., Western Ky. U., 1959, M.A., 1962. Cert. secondary tchr., Ky. Tchr. math. and sci. Gottschalk Jr. High Sch., Louisville, 1959-65; tchr. math. Iroquois High Sch., Louisville, 1965-79, Waggener High Sch., Louisville, 1979—. Mem. NEA, Ky. Edn. Assn., Jefferson County Tchrs. Assn., AAUW. Democrat. Methodist. Avocations: travel; needle crafts. Home: 304 Paddington Ct Louisville KY 40222 Office: Waggener High Sch 330 S Hubbards Ln Louisville KY 40207

BRATTON, KATHLEEN WILSON, mutual fund executive, lawyer; b. Wilmington, Del., Oct. 29, 1949; d. William Wilson and Julie Clare (Hallahan) B.; m. Brian F. Wruble, Apr. 20, 1985; 1 child, Henrietta Zane Bratton Wruble. A.B., Radcliffe Coll., 1971; J.D., U. Chgo., 1974. Bar: N.Y. 1975, Md. 1979, U.S. Dist. Ct. (so. dist.) N.Y. 1975, U.S. Ct. Appeals (2d cir.) 1975, U.S. Supreme Ct. 1978. Assoc. firm Reid & Priest, N.Y.C., 1974-78, William Wilson Bratton, Elkton, Md., 1979-80; asst. counsel Equitable Life Assurance Soc. U.S., N.Y.C., 1980, assoc. counsel, 1980-81, asst. gen. counsel, 1981-84, v.p. counsel, 1984-87, sector head mut. fund product devel., 1987—, sector head product devel.; pres. The Equitable Funds, N.Y.C., 1987—, The Hudson River Trust, 1990—; exec. v.p. Equico Securities, 1987—; mem. 1933 and 1934 Act Subcom. Am. Council Life Ins., Washington, 1982-87. Mem. ABA, N.Y. State Bar Assn., DAR (head Elk chpt., Elkton, Md.). Democrat. Home: 320 West End Ave Apt 5A New York NY 10023 Office: Equitable Life Assurance Soc US 1755 Broadway 3d floor New York NY 10019

BRATYANSKI, DORIS MADELINE (DORI BRYANT BRATYANSKI), magazine advertising executive; b. Perth Amboy, N.J., Oct. 8, 1952; d. Adolph Joseph and Frances Mae (Griffin) B. BA, Douglass Coll., 1974. Tchr. Perth Amboy Bd. Edn., 1974-75; dist. sales mgr. Hertz Corp., N.Y.C., 1975-80; adv. acct. exec. N.Y. Daily News, N.Y.C., 1980-81, Omni Mag., Penthouse, N.Y.C., 1981-82; travel advt. mgr. USA Today/Gannett, N.Y.C., 1981-85; advt. mgr. Hanover Pub., N.Y.C., 1985-86, N.Y. advt. mgr. So. Mag., dir. Ark. Writer's Project, Little Rock, 1986-88, northeastern advt. mgr., 1987—; Ea. advt. mgr. Shape mag., Men's Fitness mag. div. Weider Health and Fitness, N.Y.C., 1988—. Morris Goldfarb scholar, 1970. Mem. Advt. Club N.Y., NAFE, Am. Soc. Travel Agts., Caribbean Tourism Assn., Travel and Tourism Research Assn., Travel Industry Assn. Can. Republican. Roman Catholic. Avocations: languages, writing plays and musical scores. Office: Weider Health & Fitness 6 E 46th St New York NY 10017

BRAUCH, MERRY RUTH MOORE, consultant on gifted education; b. Hubbard, Iowa, Jan. 28, 1920; d. Orville Freneau and Jenny Leona (Thurston) Moore; m. George Pierson Brauch, June 29, 1947. BA, U. Iowa, 1939; MA, Ind. U., 1945; postgrad., Drake U., 1960-61, Western Ill. U., 1965-77. Cert. secondary tchr., spl. supr. lang. arts, Ill. Tchr. Des Moines Pub. Schs., 1954-62; tchr. to gifted, English tchr. Rock Island (Ill.) Pub. Schs., 1962-88; cons. on gifted edn., 1988—. Bd. dirs. Rock Island Art Guild, 1964—, Friends of Chamber Music, 1978-82, Rock Island Pub. Libr., 1990—; mem. Friends of Art, Davenport Mus. Art, 1968—, Focus Bethan Children's Home, Moline, Ill., 1982—. Mem. NEA (life), AAUW (br. pres. 1981-83, br. named gift Ednl. Found. 1983-84), Presbyn. Women (life), Etude Music Club (sec. 1986-89), PEO (v.p. 1989—), Delta Kappa Gamma, Phi Delta Kappa. Republican. Home: 4517 13th Ave Rock Island IL 61201

BRAUCHT, CAROL JEAN, management consultant; b. Millersburg, Ill., Dec. 1, 1939; d. Weber Arthur Von and Gertrude (Weeks) B. Student, St. Ambrose U., Davenport, Ill., 1987. Contr. prodn. Hdqrs. AMCCOM, Rock Island, Ill., 1982--. Contbr. poems Great World Poetry, 1989. Mem. NAFE, Am. Soc. Mil. Contrs., Woodrow Wilson Internat. Ctr. for Scholars, Smithsonian Inst., Audubon Soc. Lutheran.

BRAUCHT, STEPHANIE ANN SIROTNAK, counselor, consultant; b. Streator, Ill., Apr. 11, 1948; d. Albert Joseph and M. Virginia (Cameron) Sirotnak; m. Blaine Clair Braucht, June 14, 1970; children: Morgan, Jared. BA, Western Ill. U., 1970, MS in Edn., 1980; primary cert., Inst. for Rational-Emotive Therapy, 1989. Exec. coord. Mercer County Dist. 708 Mental Health, Aledo, Ill., 1980-82; sch. counselor Westmer Community Unified Sch. Dist., Joy, Ill., 1984-88; pvt. practice ednl. cons. Joy, Ill., 1988—; sch. counselor Rockridge Community Unit Sch. Dist., Taylor Ridge, Ill., 1989—. Contbr. articles to profl. jours. Mercer county chairperson Am. Cancer Soc., 1979-81; v.p. Youth Svcs. Planning Bd., Henry Mercer and Rock Island Counties, 1983, 84, 88—. Recipient award of Merit Ill. State Bd. Edn., 1988. Mem. Am. Assn. for Counseling Devel., Am. Sch. Counselor Assn., Ill. Assn. Counseling and Devel., Ill. Sch. Counselor Assn., Elem. Sch. Guidance and Counseling (editorial bd.). Methodist. Home: Rt 1 Box 134 Joy IL 61260 Office: 14114 134th Ave W Taylor Ridge IL 61284

BRAULT, G(AYLE) LORAIN, healthcare executive; b. Chgo., Jan. 3, 1944; d. Theodore Frank and Victoria Jean (Pribyl) Hahn; m. Donald R. Brault, Apr. 29, 1971; 1 child, Kevin David. AA, Long Beach City Coll., 1963; BS, Calif. State U.-Long Beach, 1973, MS, 1977. RN, Calif. Dir. nursing Canyon Gen. Hosp., Anaheim, Calif., 1973-76; dir. faculty critical care masters degree program Calif. State U., Long Beach, 1976-79; regional dir.. nursing and support svcs. Western region Am. Med. Internat., Anaheim, Calif., 1979-83; v.p. Hosp. Home Care Corp. Am., Santa Ana, Calif., 1983-85; pres. Hosp. Home Health Care Agy. Calif., Torrance, 1986—; invited lectr. China Nurses Assn., 1983; cons. AMI, Inc., Saudi Arabia, 1983; advisor dept. grad. nursing Calif. State U., L.A., 1988, advisor Nursing Inst., 1990-91; guest lectr. Dept. Pub. Health UCLA, 1986-87; assoc. clin. prof. U. So. Calif., 1988-90. Contbr. articles to profl. jours., chpts. to books. Commr. HHS, Washington, 1988. HEW advanced nurse tng. grantee, 1978. Mem. Women in Health Adminstrn. (sec. 1989, v.p. 1990), Nat. Assn. Home Care, Am. Orgn. Nursing Execs., Calif. Assn. Health Svcs. at Home (task force chmn. 1988, bd. dirs. 1989, chmn. bd. dirs. 1990-91), Calif. League Nursing (bd. sec. 1983, program chmn. 1981-82), Am. Coll. Health Care Execs., Phi Kappa Phi, Sigma Theta Tau. Republican. Methodist. Home: 1032 Andrews Dr Long Beach CA 90807

BRAUN, EUNICE HOCKSPEIER, author, religious order executive, lecturer; b. Alta Vista, Iowa; d. George Phillip and Lydia (Reinhart) Hockspeier; student Gates Coll., 1932-34, Coe Coll., 1937-39, Northwestern U., 1944-47; m. Leonard James Braun, May 29, 1937. Freelance writer for mags., newspapers, 1947-52; bus. mgr. Baha'i Publishing Trust, Wilmette, Ill., 1952-55, mng. dir., 1955-71; internat. news editor Baha'i News, 1952-70; tchr. Baha'i schs., Alaska, Can., Europe and U.S., 1958—; lectr. Baha'i Faith in U.S., Central Am., Europe, Africa, Asia, 1953—; cons. Baha'i Pub. Trust, New Delhi, India, 1972; mem. aux. bd. Continental Bd. Counselors, Baha'i Faith in the Ams., 1972—. Mem. Nat. League Am. Pen Women, Baha'i Faith, Iota Sigma Epsilon. Author: Know Your Baha'i Literature, 1959; The Dawn of World Peace, 1963; Baha'u'llah: His Call to the Nations, 1967; From Strength to Strength, Half Century of the Formative Age of the Baha'i Faith, 1978; A Crown of Beauty, 1982; The March of the Institutions, 1984; A Reader's Guide: The Development of Baha'i Literature in English, 1986; contbr. essays to Baha'i World, Internat. Record. Home: 1025 Forestview Ln Glenview IL 60025

BRAUN, MARY ANN DOROTHY, nurse; b. Altoona, Pa., Oct. 24, 1942; d. Cyril Joseph and Mary Mildred (Kimmel) Lambour; m. John Gary Braun (div.); children: Sandra Suzanne, Jeffrey Galen. Diploma in nursing, Meth. Hosp., Lubbock, Tex., 1982; BSN, West. Tex. State, 1984; MSN, U. Ala., 1986. RN, Tex., Kans., Mo. Post anesthesia recovery room nurse Meth. Hosp., Lubbock, 1981-83; RN R.H. Hinz, M.D., Lubbock, 1983-85, U. Ala. Hosp., Birmingham, 1985-86; ob.-gyn. nurse practitioner Truman Med. Ctr., Kansas City, 1986-88; dir. women's svcs. The St. Mary Hosp., Manhattan, Kans., 1988-90; dir. practice and legis. Orgn. for Obstetric, Gynecologic & Neonatal Nurses, 1990—; affiliate faculty, U. Mo., Kansas City, 1987-90. Contbr. articles in profl. jours. Community advisor U. Mo.-Kans. City Sch. Nursing, 1989. Recipient scholarship, Am. Bus. Women's Assn., Lubbock, 1984. Mem. Perinatal Assn. Kans. (bd. dirs. 1989-90), Assn. Nurse Practitioners in Reproductive Health, Nurses Assn. Am. Coll. Ob.-Gyn. (adv. coun. 1987-90), Internat. Childbirth Edn. Assn., Kans. State Nurses Assn. (chmn. pub. rels. 1989-90). Home: 2201 Russell Rd Alexandria VA 22301 Office: 409 12th St SW Washington DC 20024

BRAUN, VIRGINIA VICKERS, publications professional; b. Little Falls, N.Y., Nov. 22, 1947; d. Harry Dan and Frances (Steele) Vickers; m. Eric R. Braun, Mar. 26, 1971. BA in English, St. Lawrence U., 1969; MJ, U. Mont., 1984. Features editor The Lebanon (Tenn.) Democrat, 1974-78; editorial asst. U.S. Forest Svc., Missoula, Mont., 1978-80; news writer U. Mont., Missoula, 1981-83, publs. editor, 1983-89, publs. mgr., 1989—. Editor mags. including The Montanan, 1983-90, Vision, 1984-90. Recipient 1st place Lifestyles, Tenn. Press Assn., 1976, 77, 78, 2d place, 1975, 3d place U. Network Pub., 1984, 1st place Coun. for Advancement and Support of Edn., 1987. Mem. Missoula C. of C. (bd. dirs. conv. and visitors bur. 1989—), Missoula Bus. Women's Network. Home: 21 Greenbriar Ln Missoula MT 59802 Office: U Mont 321 Brantly Hall Missoula MT 59812

BRAUN-BRASHARES, BARBARA SUE, realtor; b. Painesville, Ohio, Nov. 23, 1948; d. David Jennings and Eleanor Patricia (Swan) Braun; m. Jeffrey R. Brashares, May 23, 1975 (div. 1987). Student, Adrian Coll., 1966-69; BA in Art, Baldwin Wallace Coll., 1971. Order editor Union Carbide Corp., Cleve., 1971; supv. order dept. Modern Curriculum Press, Cleve., 1971-78; claims adminstr. Rail-Van Consolidated, Inc., Columbus, Ohio, 1979-87; realtor, assoc. Red Carpet Keim Realty (formerly Keim Group Realty), Marco Island, Fla., 1987—. Editor: (newspaper) Views from the Hills, 1980-83. Mem. Young Reps. of Collier County, Naples, Fla., 1989; bd. dirs., sec. Sunset House Condominiums of Marco Island, Inc., 1987—; mem. Citizen's Adv. Com. to Sheriff of Collier County, Fla. Mem. Women's Coun. Realtors, Women's Rep. Club, POLO Club. Home: 830 H Meadowland Dr Naples FL 33963 Office: Red Carpet Keim Realty Gulf Coast 1069 N Collier Blvd Marco Island FL 33937

BRAUNER, PHYLLIS AMBLER, retired chemistry educator; b. Natick, Mass., Oct. 2, 1916; d. Albert Warren and Pauline (Parker) Ambler; m. William Brauner, Aug. 14, 1943 (dec. 1948); children: Susan, Catherine. BA, Wheaton Coll., Norton, Mass., 1938; MA, Wellesley Coll., 1940; PhD, Purdue U., 1943, Boston U., 1959. Head sci. dept. Wynnwood Sch., Lake Grove, N.Y., 1938-39; chem. analyst Bellevue Hosp., N.Y.C., 1940-41; rsch. scientist GE Co., Lynn, Mass., 1943-44; chem. instr. Northeastern U., Boston, 1945-46, Swarthmore (Pa.) Coll., 1946-49; from instr. to prof. chemistry Simmons Coll., Boston, 1949-83; prof. chemistry U. Md. Overseas Program, Japan, Guam, 1984, Framingham (Mass.) State Coll., 1985—; prof. chemistry Boston U., U. So. Calif., Simmons Coll., summers 1959-77; dir. Nat. Sci. Found. Summer Insts., 1968-74. Contbr. to sci. publs. Mem. Am. Chem. Soc. (chair Northeastern sect. 1973-74, Hill award 1985), Ouroboros. Home: 15 Benton St Wellesley MA 02181 Office: Framingham State Coll State St Framingham MA 01701

BRAUNSTEIN, NADINE SUSAN, nutrition consultant; b. Camden, N.J., July 10, 1957; d. Ronald Frederick and Pearl (Bunks) B. BS, Drexel U., 1979; MS, MGH Inst. Health Professions, Boston, 1984. Registered dietitian. Student aide Food and Nutrition Svc., USDA, Robbinsville, N.J., 1977; research dietitian Temple U. Hosp., Phila., 1979-80; clin. dietitian Temple U. Hosp., 1980-82; cardiovascular nutrition specialist MGH-Harvard Cardiovascular Health Ctr., Boston, 1983-88; nutritionist Harvard Community Health Plan, Watertown, Mass., 1988—; pres. Nadine Braunstein MS, RD, Nutrition Cons., Chestnut Hill, Mass., 1988—; mem. program peer rev. com. Mass. Heart Assn., Needham, 1989—. Editor Perspective Mag., 1977-79; producer/host cable TV program Nutrition in the 90's, 1990—. Membership chairperson Temple Ohabei Shalom, Brookline, Mass., 1986-88; mem. Girl Scouts U.S., 1966—; vol. Project Place Soup Kitchen, Boston, 1989; vol. nutritionist Crittenden Hastings Shelter for Homeless Pregnant Women, Brighton, Mass., 1989-90. Named Recognized Young Dietitian of the Year Am. Dietetic Assn., 1987; recipient Diamond award Harvard

Community Health Plan, 1989. Mem. Mass. Dietetic Assn. (chair coun. on practice 1989-90), Am. Heart Assn., NAFE. Democrat. Jewish. Office: 25 Boylston St Ste 309 Chestnut Hill MA 02167

BRAUSE, DONNA CARLENE, small business owner; b. Columbus, Ohio, Aug. 23, 1958; d. Donald Eugene and Carlene Amanda (Marckhoff) Brown; m. R. Tim Brause, Aug. 23, 1980; 1 child, Nathan K. BA in History Edn., Bluffton (Ohio) Coll., 1980; postgrad., Marion (Ohio) Tech. Inst., 1989—. Instr. Mansfield Bus. Coll., Marion, 1981-82; promotion asst. Mktg. Unltd., Bucyrus, Ohio, 1983-84; owner, mgr. dbc Enterprises, Bucyrus, 1984—; salesperson Hydrocepts Inc./Swim Co., Bucyrus, 1984-90; adminstrv. asst., sec. corp. Fischer Hardware Inc., Bucyrus, 1986-90. Named Outstanding Young Career Woman, Bucyrus Bus. and Profl. Women, 1983. Mem. NAFE, Ohio Geneal. Soc. (pres. Crawford County chpt. 1985-86), Sulphur Springs Homemakers (pres. 1985). Home and Office: 4755 Ziegler Rd Bucyrus OH 44820

BRAVERMAN, DONNA CARYN, fiber artist; b. Chgo., Apr. 4, 1947; d. Samuel and Pearl (Leen) B.; m. William Stanley Knopf, Jan. 21, 1990. Student, U. Mo., 1965-68; BFA in Interior Design, Chgo. Acad. Fine Arts, 1970. Interior designer Ascher Dental Supply-Healthco., Chgo., 1970-72, Clarence Krusinski & Assocs. Ltd., Chgo., 1972-74, Perkins & Will Architects, Chgo., 1974-77; fiber artist Fiber Co-op Fibrecations, Chgo., 1977, Scottsdale, Ariz., 1977—. Exhibited in group shows at Mus. Contemporary Crafts, N.Y.C., 1977, James Prendergast Library Art Gallery, Jamestown, N.Y., 1981, Grover M. Herman Fine Arts Ctr., Marietta, Ohio, 1982, Okla. Art Ctr., 1982, Middle Tenn. State U., Murfreesboro, 1982, Redding (Calif.) Mus., 1983, Tucson Mus. Art, 1984, 86, The Arts Ctr., Iowa City, 1985, The Wichita Nat., 1986; in traveling exhibitions Ariz. Archtl. Crafts, 1983, Clouds, Mountains, Fibers, 1983; represented in permanent collections Phillips Petroleum, Houston, Metro. Life, Tulsa, Directory Hotel, Tulsa, Keys Estate Ariz. Biltmore Estates, Phoenix, Sohio Petroleum, Dallas, Reichold Chem., White Plains, N.Y., Rolm Telecommunications, Colorado Springs, Mesirow & Co., Chgo., Exec. House Hotel, Chgo., Cambell Estate, Ariz., Dictaphone Worldhead Quarters, Stratford, Conn., Davenport Bldg., Boston; contbr. articles to profl. jours. Home and Office: 1041 E Glenrosa Phoenix AZ 85014

BRAVERMAN, LOUISE MARCIA, architect; b. N.Y.C., Nov. 23, 1948; d. Don S. and Madlyn (Barotz) B.; m. Steven Z. Glickel, July 1, 1984; 1 child, Jennifer Liberty. BA, U. Mich., 1970; MArch, Yale U., 1977. Registered architect, N.Y. Ptnr., architect Austin Braverman Patterson, Architects, N.Y.C. and Southport, Conn., 1982—; guest design critic Yale U., Columbia U., U. Pa., Cooper Union U., Syracuse U., Bryn Mawr Coll., Ohio State U. Bd. dirs. Diller Quaile Sch. Music. Mem. Am. Inst. Architects, Archtl. League, Assn. Real Estate Women, Nat. Women's Mus. (charter). Club: Yale (N.Y.C.). Office: Austin Braverman Patterson Architects 39 E 31 St New York NY 10016

BRAVERMAN, SUSAN PLAVIN, nutrition educator; b. N.Y.C., Mar. 14, 1937; d. Victor and Rose (Garber) Plavin; m. Edward I. Braverman, Sept. 9, 1962 (dec. 1984); children: Andrew Michael, Louise Ellen. BS, Cornell U., 1958; MS, Hunter Coll., 1967. Registered dietitian, N.Y. Clin. dietitian Beth-El Hosp., Bklyn., 1959-62; nutrition instr. N.Y. Hosp. and Cornell U. Sch. Nursing, N.Y.C., 1962-64; nutrition cons. Convalescent Home N.Y., Far Rockaway, 1966-68; pub. health nutritionist Nassau County Dept. Health, Mineola, N.Y., 1970-71; pvt. practice cons., 1972—; program dir. Queens Coll., CUNY, Flushing, 1987—; mem. nutrition com. Nassau Heart Assn., Mineola, 1977—. Co-author: L.I. Diet Manual, 1989. Pres. South Side High Sch. PTA, Rockville Centre, 1983-85, Rockville Centre Coun. PTA's, 1985-87; chmn. nutrition com. Nassau Dist. PTA, Hicksville, N.Y., 1986-87; mem. Rockville Centre Human Relations Com., 1984-86. Recipient Jenkins Meml. award Rockville Centre PTA, 1986, Disting. Svc. award Rockville Centre PTA, 1987, Dietitian of Yr. award L.I. Dietetic Assn., 1988. Mem. Am. Dietetic Assn. (dir. at large 1987—), N.Y. State Dietetic Assn. (treas. 1974-76, pres. 1976-77, chmn. dels. 1978-80), Human Ecology Alumni Assn. Cornell U. (pres. 1989—). Jewish. Home: 106 Andover Rd Rockville Centre NY 11570

BRAVO, ROSE MARIE, retail executive; b. N.Y.C., Jan. 13, 1951; d. Biagio and Anna (Bazzano) LaPila; m. Charles Emil Bravo, June 13, 1971 (div. 1977); m. William Selkirk Jackey, Oct. 9, 1983. B.A. in English, Fordham U., 1971. Exec. trainee, dept. mgr. A&S, Bklyn., 1971-74; assoc. buyer Macy's, N.Y.C., 1974-75, buyer, 1975-79, councillor, 1979-80, adminstr., 1980-84, group v.p., 1984-85, sr. v.p. 1985-88; chmn., chief exec. officer, I. Magnin, San Francisco, 1988—. Chmn. retail com. March of Dimes Birth Defects Found., 1980-81. Office: I Magnin & Co 135 Stockton St San Francisco CA 94108

BRAWN, LINDA CURTIS, state legislator; b. Rockland, Maine, June 16, 1947; d. Charles Samuel and Alice (Jenkins) Curtis; m. William Preston Brawn, Aug. 19, 1969; children: Charles, Michael. A in Liberal Studies, U. Maine, Augusta, 1978; BS in Edn., U. Maine, Orono, 1981. Tchr. Mother Goose Nursery Sch., Camden, Maine, 1973-82; kindergarten tchr. Rockland, Maine, 1983-85; mem. Maine State Senate, Augusta, 1986—. Author: Festival Memories, 1987. Mem. Camden Conservation com., 1984—; bd. dirs., chmn. pub. issues Am. Cancer Soc., 1986—; chmn. Knox County Rep. Com., 1985-86. Mem. Maine Fedn. Women's Clubs (pres. elect), Order Eastern Star. Baptist. Home: 59 Park St Camden ME 04843 Office: Maine State Senate PO Box 4952 Augusta ME 04330*

BRAWNER, COLLEEN COLBERT, manager; b. Wash., Apr. 25, 1957; d. M.B. and P.K. (Smith) Colbert: m. Larry F. Brawner, Nov. 26, 1949. BA in Econmics, Minor Urb, Va. Tech., Blacksburg, 1979; postgrad., U. Va. Sch. Retail Bank Mgmt., Charlottesville, 1989. Mgmt. trainee Sovran Bank N.A., Fairfax, Va., 1979-82; br. mgr. Sovran Bank N.A., Alexandria, Va., 1982-85; account exec., bus. devel. officer Perpetual Savings Bank, Wash., 1985--; asst. v.p. comml. lending Cen. Fidelity Bank, Vienna, Va. Mem. The Leadership Inst., City of Alexandria 1984, Franklin Park Assn., Wash. 1985--, Nat. Neighborhood Coalition, Wash. 1988. Recipient Olive Scott Benzie award Fin. Women Internat., Potomac Group, 1987, Va. State Scholarship, 1988. Mem. Fin. Women Internat. (regional chair 1988-89, state pres. 1987-88), Sales and Mktg. Assn., Toastmasters Club. Roman Catholic. Home: PO Box 8171 Falls Church VA 22182 Office: Cen Fidelity Bank 8117 Leesburg Pike Vienna VA 22180

BRAXTON, JUANITA LOUISE HARRIS, management consultant; b. Newburgh, N.Y., Sept. 10, 1960; d. Charlie and Mamie Lee (Revels) Harris; m. Andrew Larry Braxton, Sept. 20, 1981; children: Tristian Adam Lawrence, Tory D'Angelo. BA, Nat. Coll. Edn., 1988; AS, Central Tex. Coll., 1987; AA, Community Coll. of Air Force, 1987. Sr. mgmt. cons. Tidewater Cons., Inc., Arlington, Va., 1987-89, prin. mgmt. cons., 1989—. Sec. PTA, Prince George's, Md., 1988. With USAF, 1979-87. Mem. Nat. Contract Mgrs. Assn., NAFE, Nat. Assn. Bus. Women, Heroines of Jericho. Baptist. Home: 4092-1 Edgebrook Dr Andrews AFB MD 20335 Office: Tidewater Cons Inc 2700 S Quincy St Ste 400 Arlington VA 22206

BRAXTON, MARY ELLEN, quality assurance professional, consulting firm executive; b. Magnolia, Ark., Sept. 10, 1946; d. Sam G. and Leta (Rhodes) Serio; children: Felice, Lynnette. BS, Coll. of St. Francis, Joliet, Ill., 1983. Diplomate Am. Bd. Quality Assurance and Utilization Rev. Utilization rev. and qualty assurance dir. U. Hosp., Little Rock; area rev. coord. A.R. Found. for Med. Care, Ft. Smith, Ark.; pres. MedQual Rev. Systems, Inc., Little Rock. Contbr. articles to profl. jours. Chmn. uniform com. Our Lady of Good Counsel Sch., 1982; leader renew group Our Lady of Good Counsel Ch., 1986-88. Mem. Nat. Assn. Quality Assurance Profls. (cert., del. 1986, 88, 89), Ark. Assn. Quality Assurance (del. to nat. conv. 1986, 88, 89, pres.-elect 1987-89, pres. 1989-90). Office: 415 N McKinley Ste 810 Little Rock AR 72205

BRAY, BONNIE ANDERSON, biochemist; b. Lincolnton, Ga., Oct. 27, 1929; d. Roy Stephen and Bonnie (New) Anderson; m. Richard Connell Bray, May 17, 1965. BS in Chemistry, U. Ga., 1950; PhD in Biochemistry, Columbia U., 1963. Chemist Union Carbide, Oak Ridge, Tenn., 1950-52; jr. biologist Oak Ridge Nat. Lab., 1952-59; predoctoral fellow depts. medicine and biochemistry Columbia U., N.Y.C., 1959-63, rsch. assoc. depts. medicine and biochemistry, 1963-66, rsch. assoc. dept. biochemistry, 1969-70, rsch. assoc., assoc. rsch. scientist dept. medicine, 1970-86; staff fellow lab. of biophys. chemistry NIH, Bethesda, Md., 1966-67; rsch. assoc. Community Blood Coun. Greater N.Y., N.Y.C., 1967-69; assoc. rsch. scientist dept. medicine Columbia U. and St. Luke's- Roosevelt Hosp. Ctr. Contbr. articles to profl. publs. Mem. Biochem. Soc., Am. Soc. Biochemistry and Molecular Biology, Soc. Exptl. Biology and Medicine, Am. Chem. Soc., Soc. Complex Carbohydrates (by-laws com. 1972), Sigma Xi, Phi Kappa Phi. Office: St Luke's-Roosevelt Hosp Ctr 428 W 59th St Antenucci Bl New York NY 10019

BRAY, CAROLYN SCOTT, educational administrator; b. Childress, Tex., May 19, 1938; d. Alonzo Lee and Frankie Lucille (Wood) Scott; m. John Graham Bray, Jr., Aug. 24, 1957 (div. May 1980); children: Caron Lynn, Kimberly Anne, David William. BS, Baylor U., 1960; MEd, Hardin-Simmons U., 1981; PhD, U. North Tex., 1985. Registered med. technologist. Rsch. asst. Fairleigh-Dickinson Rsch. Ctr., Hardin-Simmons U., Abilene, Tex., 1979; adj. prof. bus. communication Hardin-Simmons U., 1981-84; dir. career placement, 1979-82, assoc. dean students, 1982-85; assoc. dir. career planning and placement U. North Tex., Denton, 1985—, adj. prof. higher edn. adminstrn., mem. Mentor program; cons. univs.; organizer, mem. Abilene Women's Network, 1982-85; mem. Abilene Art Mus., 1975-86, Abilene Philharm. Assn., 1969-79; mem. scholarship com. U. North Tex. League for Profl. Women, v.p. 1988-89. Mem. Assn. Sch., Coll. and Univ. Staffing (bd. dirs. 1989—, chair. mem. com. 1988-90, conf. planning com. 1988—), S.W. Placement Assn. (chair ann. conf. registration, profl. devel. and adv. com. liberal arts network), Tex. Assn. Sch., Coll. and Univ. Staffing (v.p. 1986-87, pres. 1987-88), Coll. Placement Coun., North Cen. Tex. Assn. Sch. Personnel Adminstrs. and Univ. Placement Personnel (pres. 1987-88, sec. 1988-89), Tex. Assn. Coll. and Univ. Student Personnel Adminstrs., Denton C. of C. (pub. rels. com., chair new mem. orientation), Dallas Human Resources Mgmt. Assn., Leadership Denton (co-dir. curriculum 1988-89, chair membership selection com. 1990), Friend of theSymphony, Denton Cultural Arts Assn., Pi Lambda Theta, Kappa Kappa Gamma (chpt. advisor, chmn. adv. bd. Zeta Sigma chpt.). Republican. Avocations: skiing, water skiing, tennis, golf, reading. Office: PO Box 13378 Denton TX 76203

BRAY, CYNTHIA ANN, nurse specialist; b. Easton, Pa., Dec. 15, 1943; d. Earl Douglas and Pauline (Lang) Bray. BA cum laude, U. Pa., 1977; MS in Edn., St. Joseph's U., Phila., 1982; RN, Hahnemann Hosp. Sch. Nursing, 1964. Supr. and head nurse operating rm. Hahnemann U. Hosp., Phila., 1964-74; head nurse, instr. Hosp. of the Univ. of Pa., Phila., 1974-86; nurse specialist, dir. edn. perioperative nursing, trauma coord., laser safety officer Hahnemann U. Hosp., Phila., 1986—. Active Women Against Rape. Mem. Am. Nurses Assn., Assn. Operating Rm. Nurses, Pa. Nursing Assn., Phila. Coun. Operating Rm. Nurses, AAUW, Hahnemann Honor Soc. For Nursing, Malignant Hyperthermia Assn. of U.S. (profl. adv. coun.), MADD. Republican. Methodist. Home: 2424 Avon Rd Ardmore PA 19003 Office: Hahnemann U Broad/Vine Sts Philadelphia PA 19102

BRAY, DEBORAH KUREK, nursing administrator; b. Elyria, Ohio, June 19, 1956; d. John Richard Jr. and Ann Gertrude (Dunn) Kurek; m. Lavoy Bray Jr., June 27, 1987. BSN, Med. Coll. of Va., 1985, MSN, 1987. Staff nurse, head nurse CICU, 1981; asst. head nurse emergency rm. Stuart Circle Hosp., Richmond, Va., 1983; adminstrv. supr. Retreat Hosp., Richmond, 1987, assoc. dir. nursing svcs., 1988; v.p. nursing svcs. Southampton Meml. Hosp., Franklin, Va., 1989—. Author: Relationship Between Job Satisfaction and Flexible Scheduling. Mem. Va. Orgn. Nurse Execs. (sec.).

BRAZEAL, DONNA SMITH, psychologist; b. Greenville, S.C., Feb. 10, 1947; d. G.W. Hovey and Ollie Occena (Crane) Smith; m. Charles Lee Brazeal, June 27, 1970 (div. May 1980). BA, Clemson U., 1971, MEd, 1975; postgrad., Western Carolina U., 1974, Furman U., Greenville, 1977, Columbia Pacific U., 1988—. Lic. sch. psychologist, S.C., N.C. Instr., head med. record dept. Greenville Tech. Coll., 1971-73; chief psychologist Greenville County Schs., 1975-80, Union County Schs., Monroe, N.C., 1980—; pvt. practice psychology Monroe and Charlotte, N.C., 1986—; mem. learning disabilities com. Greenville County Schs., 1978-79; co-founder, bd. dirs. Ctr. for Spiritual Awareness of N.C., Monroe, 1982—. Co-author, co-editor: School Psychologist, 1980. Child find program coordinator Union County, 1980-85; mem. various coms. Assn. for Retarded Citizens, Monroe; mem. interagy. council Piedmont Mental Health, Monroe, 1983—. Catawba Bus. Women scholar, 1965; N.C. Dept. Pub. Instrn. Pre-Sch. Incentive grantee, 1984. Mem. Nat. Assn. Sch. Psychologists, N.C. Assn. Sch. Psychologist (mem. pub. relations com. 1984-85), Animal Protection Inst. Am., Greenpeace, Union County Humane Soc., River Hills Community Ch. (mem. adult edn. com. 1985-86), Delta. Libertarian. Unitarian. Home: PO Box 240173 Charlotte NC 28224

BRAZEE, LOUISE ANN, communications company marketing executive; b. Milford, Conn., Nov. 23, 1956; d. John Ashley and Eleanor Arlyle (Wood) B. BS in Home Econs., U. N.C., Greensboro, 1978; postgrad., Kennesaw Coll., 1979-82; MBA in Mktg., U. Ga., 1984. Quality control technician RJR Foods, Inc., Atlanta, 1979-80; quality assurance technician Federated Foods, Inc., Norcross, Ga., 1980-82; trade cons. Internat. Trade Devel. Ctr., Athens, Ga., 1982-83; new products mgr. Scovill Apparel Fasteners Inc., Watertown, Conn., 1984-87; product mgr. Holt Lloyd Corp., Tucker, Ga., 1987-88; mgr. product mgmt. OKI Telecom, Norcross, Ga., 1988—. Loaned exec. Waterbury (Conn.) United Way, 1984, group chairperson, 1985, mem. speaker's bur., 1985-86; adv. Jr. Achievement of Waterbury, 1984-85, advisor ctr. mgr., 1985-86, Cambodian Refugee Relocation Com., Naugatuck, Conn., 1985-86, Northside Hosp. Aux., Atlanta, 1987—, High Mus. Young Careers. Mem. Inst. Food Technologists, Am. Mktg. Assn., U. N.C.-G Alumni Assn., U. Ga. Alumni Assn., Norcross-Peachtree Corners Jaycees (pres. 1988-89, chmn. bd. 1989-90). Republican. Presbyterian. Home: 4645 Warners Trail Norcross GA 30093 Office: OKI Telecom 437 Old Peachtree Rd Suwanee GA 30174

BRAZER, MARA HOPE, public relations executive; b. Detroit, Apr. 21, 1955; d. Harvey Elliott and Marjorie Louise (Cahn) B. BA, U. Mich., 1977. Dir. pub. info. Nat. Commn. on Unemployment Compensation, Washington, 1978-80; spl. asst. media rels. U.S. Consumer Product Safety Commn., Washington, 1980-81; exec. dir., founder Parkfriends, Inc., Washington, 1982-85; dir. fed. rels. Yale U., New Haven, 1981-82; publicist Sta. KPIX-TV, San Francisco, 1985-86; prin. Mara Brazer Communications, San Francisco, 1986-88; sr. v.p. Edelman Pub. Rels. Worldwide, San Francisco, 1988—. Participant Women's Campaign Fund, San Francisco and Washington, 1978; v.p. City Celebration, Inc., San Francisco, 1986—. Recipient Spl. citations Conn. State Legis., 1984, Elm-Ivy award New Haven Found., 1983. Mem. Women in Communcations, Inc., Silicon Valley Entrepreneurs Club (co-founder Santa Clara, Calif. chpt. 1986), Commonwealth Club of San Francisco. Office: Edelman Pub Rels Worldwide 456 Montgomery St Ste 800 San Francisco CA 94104

BRAZIER, MARY MARGARET, psychology educator, researcher; b. New Orleans, Feb. 4, 1956; d. Robert Whiting and Margaret Long (Mc Waters) B. BA, Loyola U., New Orleans, 1977; MS, Tulane U., 1985, PhD, 1986. Asst. prof. psychology Loyola U., 1986—. NSF grantee, 1987. Mem. Am. Psychol. Assn., Southeastern Psychol. Assn., Midwestern Psychol. Assn., Southwestern Psychol. Assn. (coun. 1988—), So. Soc. Philosophy and Psychology (exec. coun. 1989—). Roman Catholic. Office: Loyola U Dept Psychology 6363 St Charles Ave New Orleans LA 70118

BRDLIK, CAROLA EMILIE, accountant; b. Wuerzburg, Germany, Mar. 11, 1930; came to U.S., 1952; d. Ludwig Leonard and Hildegard Maria (Leipold) Baumeister; m. Joseph A. Brdlik; children: Margaret Louise, Charles Joseph. BA, Oberrealschule Bamberg, Fed. Republic Germany, 1948; MA, Bavarian Interpreter Coll., Fed. Republic Germany, 1949; Cert., Internat. Accts. Soc., Chgo., 1955. Interpreter, exec. sec. NCWC Amberg, Schweinfurt, Ludwigsburg and Munich, Fed. Republic Germany, 1949-52; exec. sec. Red Ball Van Lines, Jamaica, N.Y., 1952; interpreter Griffin Rutgers Inc., N.Y.C., 1952-53; office mgr., exec. sec. Rehab. Ctr. Summit Co., Inc., Akron, 1953-56; pvt. practice acctg. Cuyahoga Falls, Ohio, 1956-61, Uniontown, Ohio, 1961-82; fin. and tax cons. Omaca, Inc., Uniontown and Deerfield Beach (Fla.), 1982-86, sec., treas., 1981-86; pres. Omaca, Inc., Uniontown and Deerfield Beach, Fla., 1986—; sec.-treas. Shipe Landscaping, Inc., Greensburg, Ohio, 1968—, Sattler Machine products, Copley, Ohio, 1981-87; asst. treas. Mar-Lynn Lake Park, Inc., Streetsboro, Ohio, 1969—. Bd. dirs., trustee Czechoslovak Refugees, Cleve. and Cin., 1968. Mem. Nat. Soc. Tax Profls. (cert., accredited taxation and accountancy), Pub. Accts. Soc. Ohio, Nat. Soc. Pub. Accts., Nat. Assn. Tax Preparer's, Ohio Soc. Pub. Accts., Fla. Assn. Ind. Accts., Nat. Assn. Enrolled Agts. Roman Catholic. Home: 2026 SW 17th Dr Deerfield Beach FL 33442

BREAKSTONE, KAY LOUISE, public relations executive; b. Allentown, Pa., Sept. 9, 1936; d. Morris H. and Mabel (Gruber) Senderowitz; B.S., N.Y. U., 1967; m. Jules L. Breakstone, Dec. 3, 1960; children—Enid, Jessica. With N.Y. Conf. Bd., 1967-69, Bache, Halsey Stuart, N.Y.C., 1969-70; securities analyst Dean Witter, N.Y.C., 1970-71; vice-pres. Burson Marsteller, Inc., N.Y.C., 1971-79; dir. investor relations Kennecott Corp., Stamford, Conn., 1979-81; sr. v.p. Burson-Marsteller, 1981-87, exec. v.p., 1987—; dir. First Women's Bank. Mem. Nat. Investor Relations Inst. (pres. 1980-81). Office: 230 Park Ave S New York NY 10003

BREAUX, LAURA LANE, registered nurse; b. Pensacola, Fla., Nov. 23, 1940; d. Wray Whitten and Sue Evelyn (Hanshaw) Lane; m. Chadwick Paul Breaux, Mar. 6, 1965 (div. 1987); children: Chadwick Paul Jr., Matthew Sean, Andrew Patrick, Stephen Lane. BA in English, Speech, Judson Coll., Marion, Ala., 1962; Assoc. degree in Nursing, Northwestern State U., Shreveport, La., 1988. RN, La. Tchr. Okaloosa County Schs., Ft. Walton Beach, Fla., 1962-65; ind. childbirth educator Alexandria, La., 1974-88; staff nurse, childbirth educator La. State U. Med. Ctr., Shreveport, 1988—. Pub. rels. com. Jr. League Alexandria, 1975-76; mem. Shreveport Symphony Bd., 1978-79; mem. child devel. task force Jr. League Shreveport, 1978-79, community affairs coun., 1981; bd. dirs. East Ridge Country Club Swim Team, Shreveport, 1980-82. Mem. Am. Soc. Psychoprophylaxis in Obstetrics (Lamaze coord. Shreveport 1982-85), Am. Coll. Childbirth Educators, U.S. Masters Wimming (bd. dirs. 1983-87), So. Masters Swimming (chmn. La. and Miss. sect. 1983-87, newsletter editor 1983-87). Republican. Home: 5 Crystal Springs Rd #258 Greenville SC 29615

BRECHBILL, SUSAN REYNOLDS, lawyer, educator; b. Washington, Aug. 22, 1943; d. Irving and Isabell Doyle (Reynolds) Levine; B.A., Coll. William and Mary, 1965; J.D., Marshall-Wythe Sch. Law, 1968; m. Raymond A. Brechbill, June 29, 1973; children—Jennifer Rae, Heather Lea. Admitted to Va. bar, 1969, Fed. bar, 1970; atty. AEC, Berkeley, Calif., 1968-73, indsl. relations specialist AEC, Las Vegas, 1974-75; atty. ERDA, Oakland, Calif., 1976-77; atty. Dept. Energy, Oakland, 1977-78, dir. procurement div. San Francisco Ops. Office, 1978-85, asst. chief counsel for gen. law, 1985—; mem. faculty U. Calif. Extension; speaker Nat. Contract Mgmt. Assn. Ann. Symposiums, 1980, 81, 83, 84, 88; speaker on doing bus. with govt. Leader Girl Scouts U.S.A., San Francisco area. Named Outstanding Young Woman Nev., 1974. Mem. Va. State Bar Assn., Fed. Bar Assn., Nat. Contract Mgmt. Assn. (pres. Golden Gate chpt. 1983-84, N.W. regional v.p. 1984-86), Nat. Assn. Female Execs. Republican. Contbr. articles to profl. jours. Home: 67 Scenic Dr Orinda CA 94563

BRECHNER, BEVERLY L., mathematics educator; b. N.Y.C., May 27, 1936; d. Herman and Goldie (Zimmerman) B. BS, U. Miami, Coral Gables, Fla., 1957, MS, 1959; PhD, La. State U., 1964. Instr. La. State U., New Orleans, 1962-64, asst. prof., 1964-68; asst. prof. U. Fla., Gainesville, 1968-71, assoc. prof., 1971-83, prof., 1983—; vis. assoc. prof./scholar U. Mich., Ann Arbor, 1977-78; vis. assoc. prof. U. Tex., Austin, 1980. Contbr. over 20 rsch. papers to profl. jours. Faculty Devel. grantee U. Fla., 1977, Conf. grantee NSF, 1988. Mem. Math. Assn. Am. (pres. Fla. sect. 1977-78, gov. Fla. sect. 1980-83, nat. bd. govs., George Polya prize 1989), Am. Math. Soc., Soc. for Indsl. & Applied Mathematicians, AAAS, Sigma Xi. Democrat. Jewish. Home: 4003 NW 17th Ave Gainesville FL 32605-3513 Office: U Fla Dept Math Gainesville FL 32611-2082

BRECHT, SALLY ANN, quality assurance executive; b. Trenton, N.J., Aug. 5, 1951; d. Charles L. and Helen (Orfeo) B. BBA, Coll. William & Mary in Va., 1973; MBA, Rider Coll., 1981. Electronic data processing auditor McGraw Hill, Inc., Hightstown, N.J., 1976-79, State of N.J., Mercerville, 1979-80, NL Industries, Hightstown, 1980-84; systems tech. planning specialist Ednl. Testing Service, Princeton, N.J., 1984-85, acting div. dir. application devel., 1985-87, mgr. computer standards and security, 1987-88, asst. dir. office corp. quality assurance, 1988—. Contbr. articles to popular publs. Office: Ednl Testing Svc Rosedale Rd Princeton NJ 08520

BRECKEL, ALVINA HEFELI, librarian; b. Chgo., Dec. 6, 1948; d. William Christ and Liselotte (Herrmann) Hefeli; m. Theodore A. Breckel, Feb. 10, 1973. BFA cum laude, Bradley U., 1970; MALS, Rosary Coll., River Forest, Ill., 1973. Cert. art tchr., medial libr., Ill. Tchr. art Chgo. Pub. Schs., 1971-84; libr. Oakton Community Coll., Des Plaines, Ill., 1988—. Editor News & Notes, 1988-89. Rep. election judge, New Trier Twp., Ill., 1988; com. mem. Villagers for a Safe Winnetka, 1989. Mem. NEA, Ill. Edn. Assn., AAUW (bd. dirs. New Trier chpt. 1989—), Sandwich (Mass.) Hist. Soc., Winnetka Hist. Soc., Art Inst. Chgo. (life), Nat. Greentown Glass Assn., Nat. Early Am. Glass Club (chpt. founding mem.), Greater Chgo. Area Glass Collectors Club, Pi Lambda Theta (life, art editor chpt. Notes 1977-84), Delta Zeta (v.p. Chgo. North Shore chpt. 1987-90). Home: 185 Fuller Ln Winnetka IL 60093 Office: Oakton Community Coll 1600 E Golf Rd Des Plaines IL 60016

BRECKENRIDGE, BETTY GAYLE, industrial psychologist consultant; b. Austin, Tex., Dec. 8, 1945; d. Glen Floyd and Mary Margaret (Stone) B. BA, Baylor U., 1966; MA, So. Meth. U, 1984. Cons. Devel. Dimensions Internat., Pitts., 1985—. Mem. Soc. for Indsl. Orgnl. Psychology. Office: 332 W Fairmount State College PA 16801

BREDAHL, JANICE ANN, automotive corporation executive; b. Mpls., Sept. 4, 1957; d. George Franklin and Loraine May (Graham) Lunger; m. John Patrick Bredahl, Mar. 9, 1980 (div. Jan. 31, 1985). BA in Phys. Edn., Point Loma Coll., 1979. Clk. typist San Diego Econ. Devel. Corp., 1978-79; CPT operator, customer rels. sec. BMW of N.Am., Inc., Los Angeles, 1979-82, sec. to reg. svc., reg. parts mgrs., 1982-84; info. ctr. trainer BMW of N.Am., Inc., Montvale, N.J., 1984-87; info. ctr. analyst BMW of N.Am., Inc., Westwood, N.J., 1987—; tchr. computers The Berkley Sch., White Plains, N.Y., 1986; substitute tchr. The Berkley Sch., White Plains, 1987; sec. to regional svc. and regional parts mgrs. Sec. bd. mgrs. Mountainview Condo Assn., Valley Cottage, N.Y., 1987-88, pres. bd. mgrs., 1988-89; mem. Statue of Liberty-Ellis Island Found., 1984-89. Mem. MVC Assn. (pres. 1988-89). Republican. Lutheran. Clubs: Bergen County General. Soc. (Bergen, N.J.); Rockland Lake Runners' Assn. (N.Y.). Office: BMW of N Am Inc PO Box 1227 Westwood NJ 07675-1227

BREDEWEG, JUDITH SENKEL, county official; b. Milw., May 19, 1941; d. Vernon Hoyt and Jeanette W. (Wenzel) Senkel; m. William D. Bredeweg, Aug. 17, 1963; children: Catherine, Daniel. BA, Lakeland Coll., 1963; postgrad., San Diego State U., 1965. Cert. secondary edn. tchr., Ill. Tchr. secondary edn. Valley View Sch. Dist., Romeoville, Ill.; exec. officer Bur. of Employee Svc. Ill. Dept. Corrections, Springfield, Ill.; elected official Will County Bd., Joliet, Ill.; chmn. Will County Pub. Bldg. Commn.; speaker in field. Hist. columnist for newspapers. Past pres. Bolingbrook (Ill.) Local Devel. Corp., bd. dirs.; past trustee Village of Bolingbrook; bd. dirs. Trailways coun. Girl Scouts U.S. Named Rep. Woman of the Yr., Will County, 1982, Woman of the Yr., S.W. Bus. and Profl. Women, 1989; recipient Disting. Svc. award Bolingbrook Jaycees. Mem. Ill. Fedn. Bus. and Profl. Women (pres.). Home: 529 Concord Ln Bolingbrook IL 60440

BREDT, CAROL, engineering management; b. Phila., Dec. 22, 1939; d. Lester and Helen Segal; m. Allen B. Bredt, Aug. 28, 1960; children: Robert, David, Paul. BA in Physics, Temple U., 1960; postgrad., U. So. Calif., L.A., 1970-72. Programmer Autologic, Inc., Newbury Pk., Calif., 1973-76; systems analyst HW Systems, Van Nuys, Calif., 1976-77; software engr. Pertec, Inc., Chatsworth, Calif., 1977-79; dir. product devel. Micom Systems, Inc., Simi Valley, Calif., 1979-87; engring. mgr. Transtream, Inc., Agoura, Calif., 1987-88; cons. Bredt Enterprises, Northridge, Calif., 1988—. Home: 9501

Donna Ave Northridge CA 91324 Office: Bredt Enterprises Northridge CA 91324

BREED, HELEN ILLICK, ichthyologist, educator; b. New Cumberland, Pa., Mar. 12, 1925; d. Joseph Simon and Della May (Brotzman) Illick; m. Henry Eltinge Breed, Jr., Nov. 23, 1957; children: Henry E., Joseph I., Brenda E. BS, Syracuse U., 1947, MS, 1949; PhD, Cornell U., 1953. Tchr. sci. Lyons (N.Y.) Cen. High Sch., 1949-50; instr. zoology and physiology Akron (Ohio) U., 1953-54; postdoctoral Ford Found. fellow, instr. physiology Vassar Coll., Poughkeepsie, N.Y., 1954-55; asst. prof. biology Russell Sage Coll., Troy, N.Y., 1955-57; asst. dir. systematic biology NSF, Washington, 1957; assoc. prof. conservation Cornell U., Ithaca, N.Y., 1957-61; rsch. assoc. biology Rensselaer Poly. Inst., Troy, 1964-68; environ. cons. Eltick Rsch. Corp., Troy, 1971-90; ichthyology cons. Ichthyological Assocs., Ithaca, N.Y., 1971-80, Lima Peru, 1972-73, Lake George Project, Troy, 1969. Contbr. articles to profl. jours. Capital dist. mem. Syracuse U. campaign for excellence, Troy, 1988-90. Nat. Wildlife Fedn. fellow, 1950, Sports Fishing Inst. fellow, 1951-53, Am. Scandinavian Found. fellow, Trondheim, Norway, 1959-60. Mem. AAAS, Am. Soc. Zoologists, Soc. Systematic Zoology, Am. Soc. Ichthyologists and Herpetologists, Am. Fisheries Soc., Brunswick Hist. Soc. Republican. Lutheran. Home and Office: RD 3 Box 245B Troy NY 12180

BREEDLOVE, CINDY LEA, editor; b. Plainview, Tex., Nov. 28, 1944; d. Robert and Nancy Elizabeth (Jones) Graham; m. J. Pat Breedlove, Sept. 1, 1968. BA in Social Work, U. Tex., 1966. Social worker Parkland Meml. Hosp., Dallas, 1966-68; child welfare, intake worker Dept. Human Svcs., Corpus Christi, Tex., 1973-76; editor, mgr. Tikal Prodns., Inc., San Antonio, Tex., 1978-82, Mountain Prodns., Inc., Albuquerque, 1982—; dir., co-host Fine Art Workshops, Mex., Europe, 1984—, Art Show, Am. Cancer Soc., Santa Fe, N.Mex., 1985, Art Show, Ronald McDonald House, Lubbock, Tex., 1987, and other fine art and charity shows, 1984—. Editor fine art catalogues, community and univ. publs. Sec. Spirit of Ruidoso, N.Mex., 1985-86. Recipient Brochure of Yr. award, Hotel-Motel Assn. N.Mex., 1986. Mem. Altrusa. Home: PO Box 54 Alto NM 88312 Office: Mountain Productions Inc 3323 Princeton Dr NE Albuquerque NM 87107

BREEN, FAITH FEI-MEI LEE, economist, management consultant; b. Burbank, Calif., Feb. 3, 1951; d. John Quong and Eleanor S.G. (Choy) Lee; m. George Edward Breen, Jr., Nov. 30, 1974; children: Erika Lee, George Edward III. BA, U. Md., 1972; MA, U. Pitts., 1975; PhD, U. Md., 1990. Asst. dir. Ctr. for Health Policy Rsch., Am. Enterprise Inst. Pub. Policy, Washington, 1975-77; economist U.S. Dept. Labor, Bur. Internat. Labor Affairs, Washington, 1978; Nat. Gov.'s Assn., Ctr. Pub. Policy Rsch., Washington, 1978-79; expert cons., economist Pres.'s Adv. Com. Women, Washington, 1979-81; polit. econ. cons. Nat. Assn. State and Territorial Solid Waste Mgmt. Ofcls., Washington, 1981-82; expert cons., economist to dep. under sec. mgmt. U.S. Dept. Edn., Washington, 1980-83; adj. faculty dept. econs. Central Mich. U., Washington, 1978—; assoc. prof. Sch. Bus. and dept. econs. Prince Georges Community Coll., Largo, Md., 1985—; pres. Systems Resources Mgmt., Inc., 1988—; lectr. in field. Contbr. articles to profl. jours.; exec. producer TV program: Saccharin and the Public Interest, 1978. past pres. Inner Wheel of College Park, 1986-87, chmn., bd. dirs. Orgn. Chinese Am. Women, 1990, del. Women-to-Women Exchange program, 1987; chair fin. com. University Park Rep. Women's Club, 1985; controller Nat. Rep. Com.'s Nat. Rep. Heritage Group Council, 1985—. Recipient Nat. Def. Lang. fellow, 1973-75; cert. of appreciation Sec. U.S. Dept. Edn., 1983; Fulbright-Hays Seminar Abroad, 1986. Mem. Am. Econ. Assn., Fulbright Alumni Assn., Ashton Swim Club. Roman Catholic. Avocations: tennis, swimming, bridge. Home: 2021 Avoca Ln Oak Hill Estates MD 20905 Office: Systems Mgmt Inc 3 Bethesda Metro Ctr Ste 700 Bethesda MD 20814

BREEN, MARILYN, mathematics educator; b. Anderson, S.C., Nov. 8, 1944; d. Marvin and Martha Louise (Lesser) B.; m. Walter Gill Kelley, May 24, 1975; 1 child, Joyce Elizabeth. BA, Agnes Scott Coll., 1966; MS, Clemson U., 1968, PhD, 1970. Mem. faculty dept. math. U. Okla., Norman, 1971—, instr., 1971-73, asst. prof., 1973-77, assoc. prof., 1977-82, prof., 1982—. Contbr. rsch. articles to math. jours. Mem. Am. Math. Soc., Math. Assn. Am., Phi Beta Kappa, Sigma Xi, Phi Kappa Phi. Presbyterian. Office: U Okla Dept Math 601 Elm Ave Norman OK 73019

BREHM, JUANITA R(OSE), entrepreneur; b. Pulaski Twp., Wis., Oct. 10, 1947; d. Arnold and Mary Gertrude (Neff) Richter; m. Michael Robert Brehm, May 5, 1946; children: Eric Michael, Kevin Michael. AA, Madison (Wis.) Bus. Coll., 1969. Legal sec. Lawrence Hall, Atty., Madison, 1969-70; computer operator Interstate Electric, Racine, Wis., 1978-79, system adminstr., 1979-85; owner, pres. Software City, Racine, 1985—. Mem. Wis. Women Entrepreneurs, Data Processing Mgmt. Assn. (bd. dirs. 1983-84). Roman Catholic. Home: 2818 Orchard St Racine WI 53406 Office: Software City 4700 Washington Ave Racine WI 53406

BREHMAN, PENNY ANN, educator; b. Chgo., Feb. 22, 1947; d. Lyle Cleveland and Anna Martha (Tkach) Wilson; m. Thomas Ralph Brehman, Aug. 5, 1967 (div. 1980). BA, Northeastern Ill. U., 1968. Secondary educator Notre Dame High Sch. for Girls, Chgo., 1969-87; educator Lake Forest (Ill.) Country Day Sch., 1987—, coord. interdisciplinary studies, 1989—; resource specialist St. Ignatius Coll. Prep., Chgo., 1990—; editorial cons. Ency. Britannica Ednl. Corp., Chgo., 1989. Vol. cataloger Evanston (Ill.) Hist. Soc., 1986-89. Named Outstanding Tchr. U. Chgo., 1988; recipient Golden Apple award Found. for Excellence in Teaching, Chgo., 1986, Fellowship Coun. for Basic Edn., Washington, 1985. Fellow Acad. Educators, Coun. for Basic Edn.; mem. Ill. Assn. Tchrs. English. Home: 2429 W Greenleaf Chicago IL 60645

BREITBACH, STEPHANIE HANNELORE, travel executive; b. Battle Creek, Mich., May 5, 1959; d. Herbert Walter and Inge Rosa (Hoffman) B. Vice pres. Ermisch Travel Battle Creek, 1975—. Office: Ermisch Travel Battle Creek 26-28 E Michigan Ave Battle Creek MI 49017

BREITENBACH, MARY LOUISE MCGRAW, psychologist, drug rehabilitation counselor; b. Pitts., Sept. 26, 1936; d. David Evans McGraw and Louise (Schoch) Neel; m. John Edgar Breitenbach, Apr. 15, 1960 (dec. 1963); m. Joseph George Piccoli III, Aug. 15, 1987. Postgrad., Oreg. State Coll., 1960-61; BA, Russell Sage Coll., Troy, N.Y., 1958; MEd, Harvard U., 1983. Lic. profl. counselor, Wyo. Paraprofessional psychologist St. John's Episc. Ch., Jackson, Wyo., 1963-82; pvt. practice Wilson, Wyo., 1983—; counselor Curran/Seeley Found. Addiction Svcs., Jackson, 1989—, Van Vleck House/Tri-County Group Home, Jackson, 1986-89, others. Trustee Teton Sci. Sch., Kelly, Wyo. 1960-76; pres. bd. govs. Teton County Mus. Bd., Jackson; vestry mem. St. John's Ch., Jackson. Mem. Am. Psychol. Assn., Wyo. Psychol. Assn., Wyo. Assn. Counseling and Devel., Wyo. Assn. Addiction Specialists. Democrat. Episcopalian. Home and Office: Star Rte Wilson WY 83014

BREITMEYER, JO ANNE, computer specialist, graphic artist; b. Ann Arbor, Mich., Mar. 25, 1947; d. Philip and Joan Clista (Thomas) B. Student, U. Tex., 1965-66, Boston U., 1966-67, U. Md., 1967-68; AA, BA, Canada Coll., Redwood City, Calif., 1970. Mktg. sec. Fairchild Camera & Instrument Co., Mountain View, Calif., 1969-70; sec. to v.p. Optimum Systems, Inc., Palo Alto, Calif., 1970-72; sec. to pres. Advanced Memory Systems, Sunnyvale, Calif., 1972-74; asst. to pres. Ness Time, Inc., Mountain View, 1974-75; art dir. Collage, Inc., Mountain View, 1975-76; owner, mgr. Briteday, Inc., Mountain View, 1976-87; with mktg. communications dept. PANAGEA, Cupertino, Calif., 1987-89; with Hewlett Packard Co., Palo Alto, 1989; mgr. adminstrn. Micro Intgration Corp., San Jose, Calif., 1989—. Bd. dirs. Peninsula Little Club, Palo Alto, 1981-87, mem. pub. rels. com., 1984-87; bd. dirs. Peninsula Children's Ctr., Palo Alto, 1984-87, printing chmn. charter aux., 1984—; sec. Cypress Point Homeowners Assn., Mountain View, 1978-80, treas., 1988; mem. No. Calif. Arthritis Found., 1970—; printing chmn. Menlo Circus Club Charity Horse Show, 1983—, Festival of Trees, 1984—. Mem. Bus. Profl. Advt. Assn., Peninsula Mktg. Assn., Mountain View Women in Bus. (steering com. 1986-87), Alpha Omicron Pi (chpt. advisor 1988—, v.p. philanthropy Palo Alto alumnae 1988-89, mem. internat. conv. com. 1986-87). Home: 209 Horizon Ave Mountain View CA 94043 Office: Micro Integration Corp 1015-C E Brokaw Rd San Jose CA 95131

BRELAND, ANITA LESSER, strategic planner, librarian; b. Hattiesburg, Miss., Aug. 17, 1947; d. William Jasper Lee and LaVerne (Isaacson) Yancey; m. Joseph Martin Breland, Mar. 4, 1989. BA, U. Tex., 1969, M of Libr. and Info. Sci., 1980. Communications coord. Tex. State Libr., Austin, 1978-79; systems libr. Austin Pub. Libr., 1981-83, data systems mgr., 1983-84; tech. libr. IBM, Austin, 1984-85, info. ctr. mgr., 1985-87; libr. planning cons. IBM, Milford, Conn., 1987-89, chief libr. strategist, 1989—; Mem. Organizing Task Force Coalition for Networked Info., Washington, 1990—, Libr. Steering Com. IBM, Thornwood, N.Y., 1987—, Learning Ctr. Task Force IBM, Thornwood, N.Y., 1986—. Author and illustrator: Come to Chimera: a librarian's planning handbook, 1978; contbr. articles to profl. jours.; speaker and conductor of seminars, workshops in field. Mem. ALA, Libr. and Info. Tech. Assn., Am. Women Entrepeneurs, Spl. Libr. Assn., INFORMA Steering Com. IBM, Greenpeace, Sierra Club, Beta Phi Mu, Phi Kappa Phi. Office: IBM 472 Wheelers Farms Rd Milford CT 06460

BREMER, CHRISTINE DODGE, human factors engineer; b. N.Y.C., Mar. 19, 1952; d. Berton Bernard and Marie Augusta (Schomaker) B.; m. Raleigh Keith Little, Sept. 30, 1978; children: Keith Bremer, Jonathan Berton, Katherine Marie. BA in Psychology, SUNY, Plattsburg, 1972; postgrad., U. Minn., 1972-77. Rsch. asst. SUNY, Plattsburg, 1969-72, teaching asst., 1970-71; instr. U. Minn., Mpls., 1974-76, rsch. asst., 1976-77; rsch. assoc. Honeywell Inc., Mpls., 1977-80, human factors engr., 1980-81, sr. human factors engr., 1981-89, loaned exec. to community program Phillips TLC, 1989—. Contbr. articles profl. jours. Bd. dirs. Community Child Care Ctr., Mpls., 1984-86; del. Nat. Adv. Panel of the Child Care Action Campaign, N.Y.C., 1988—. Named Honoree YWCA Leader Luncheon, Mpls., 1986; recipient fellowship Ctr. for Rsch. in Human Learning, U. Minn., 1972-76, commendation State of Minn., St. Paul, 1988. Mem. Honeywell Women's Coun. (chmn. rsch. com. 1987, chmn. Coun. 1988), Honeywell Women in Technology and Sci. (chmn. 1983), Human Factors Soc. (bd. dirs. Upper Midwest chpt. 1988—). Unitarian. Office: Honeywell Inc MN12-5131 2701 4th Ave S Minneapolis MN 55408

BREMER, ELAINE ROSS, marketing executive; b. Bronx, N.Y., July 6, 1950; d. Irving Leon and Lillian Zelda (Obrentz) Ross; m. Robert William Bremer, Nov. 20, 1973. BA, Queens Coll., 1971; MS, Bklyn. Coll., 1975. News writer, reporter Sta. WLIR-FM, Hempstead, N.Y., 1972-73; asst. TV editor Homelife mag., N.Y.C., 1973-74; prodn. asst. Stuart Publs., N.Y.C., 1974-75; promotion supr. Smith-Sternau Orgn., Inc., N.Y.C., 1975-79; mktg. dir. Fairchild Books & Visuals, N.Y.C., 1979—. Democrat. Jewish. Home: 57-44 Little Neck Pkwy Little Neck NY 11362 Office: Fairchild Books & Visuals 7 E 12th St New York NY 10003

BRENCHLEY, JEAN ELNORA, microbiologist, researcher, director biotechnology institute; b. Towanda, Pa., Mar. 6, 1944; d. John Edward and Elizabeth (Jefferson) B.; m. Bernard Asbell, July 21, 1990. BS, Mansfield U., 1965; MS, U. Calif., San Diego, 1967; PhD, U. Calif., Davis, 1970. Research assoc., Biology Dept. MIT, Cambridge, 1970-71; from asst. prof. to assoc. prof. microbiology Pa. State U., Univ. Pk., 1971-77; head. Dept. Molecular and Cell Biology, dir. Biotech. Inst. Pa. State U., University Park, 1984-87, prof. microbiology, dir. Biotech. Inst., 1984—; assoc. prof. then prof. biology Purdue U., West Lafayette, Ind., 1977-81; research dir. Genex Corp., Gaithersburg, Md., 1981-84; mem. bioprocess com. Nat. Acad. Sci.; bd. trustees Biosis, 1983-88. Recipient Waksman award Theobald Smith Soc., 1985. Mem. AAAS (biol. scis. nominating com. 1987—), Am. Soc. Microbiology (pres. 1986-87), Assn. Women in Sci., Am. Soc. Biol. Chemists, Am. Chem. Soc. (com. Toxic Substances Control Act), Sigma Delta Epsilon (hon.). Office: Pa State Univ 519 Wartik Lab University Park PA 16802

BRENDLE, ALISON SMITH, sales executive; b. Mason, Mich., Aug. 30, 1954; d. Richard Lyle and Genevieve Louise (Stevens) Smith. Student, St. Petersburg (Fla.) Jr. Coll., 1974. Salesperson Mr. Donut, St. Petersburg, Fla., 1969-70; nursing asst. Pasadena Manor, South Pasadena, Fla., 1970-73; office mgr. Walter Collins Ins., St. Petersburg, 1973; underwriter Bennett, Wallace, Welch & Green Ins., St. Petersburg, 1973-76; co-owner, sales exec. Pro Svc. Inc., Largo, Fla., 1976—; cons. Ind. for Dental Groups, St. Peterburg, 1985—. Author: Where Riches Lie, 1988-89; illustrator Karate Forms, Store Front, 1988, Graphic Design and Logo, 1989; photographer. Mem. NAFE, Nat. Fed. Internat. Bus., Concerned Women. Democrat. Office: Pro Svc Inc 11701 S Belcher Rd Ste 124 Largo FL 34643

BRENNA, CAROL DIANE, beauty consultant; b. Lancaster, Pa., Dec. 2, 1959. BS (psychology), Elizabethtown Coll., 1982. Dir. patient care Talbot Pl., Hummelstown, Pa., 1982-84; dir. aftercare ARC, Terr., Ephrata, Pa., 1984-86; beauty cons. Mary Kay Cosmetics, Lancaster, 1985—; bridal cons. May Kay Cosmetics, Lancaster, 1985—. Recipient Nat. Hon. Soc. Psychology Psi Chi, 1982, Who's Who Students Am. U. & Coll., 1982, Star Cons., Mary Kay Cosmetics, 1988. Mem. Nat. Assoc. Female Exec., Order of Ea. Star, Lancaster. Lutheran. Home and Office: 302 Pearl St Lancaster PA 17603

BRENNAN, BARBARA TAYLOR, nurse administrator; b. Neptune, N.J., June 14, 1950; d. Stanley and Marietta Elizabeth (Van Eesteren) Taylor; m. Patrick Douglas Barnes, Jan. 3, 1969 (div. July, 1977); 1 child, Marilyn Elizabeth; m. Thomas Joseph Brennan, Oct. 6, 1979. BSN, U. N.C., 1974; MS in Nursing Adminstrn., U. Pitts., 1984. Staff nurse, instr. nursing edn. Forsyth Meml. Hosp., Winston-Salem, N.C., 1974-79; surg. nurse clinician Mercy Hosp., Charlotte, N.C., 1979-80; asst. dir. nursing Divine Providence Hosp., Pitts., 1980-86; v.p. nursing Bapt. Hosp., Nashville, 1986—; adv. bd. Tenn. Donor Svcs., Nashville, 1988—, Bapt. Home Health Svcs., Nashville, 1986—. Mem. Am. Orgn. Nurse Execs., Tenn. Orgn. Nurse Execs., Emergency Nurses Assn., Sigma Theta Tau. Office: Bapt Hosp 2000 Church St Nashville TN 37236

BRENNAN, CARROLL ANN, pediatrician; b. New Brunswick, N.J., Feb. 28, 1956; d. Robert Thomas and Janet Marie (Deinzer) B.; m. William Eric Carlson, June 13, 1981; children: Sean William, Brynn Rachel. BS magna cum laude, Muhlenberg Coll., 1977; MD, St. Louis U., 1981. Diplomate Am. Bd. Pediatrics. Resident pediatrics Wayne State U., Detroit, 1981-85, fellow pediatric hematology-oncology Children's Hosp. Mich., 1985-86; fellow pediatric hematology-oncology U. Minn., Mpls., 1986-89, instr. pediatrics, 1989—. Author: (abstract) Jour. Cellular Biochemistry, 1990. Alternate del. Local Ind.-Rep. Com., Fridley, Minn., 1990. Grantee NIH, 1978, Children's Cancer Rsch. Fund, 1989, Ronald McDonald Children's Charities, 1990. Fellow Am. Acad. Pediatrics (author, presentor abstract 1985); mem. AMA, Northwestern Pediatric Soc., Am. Soc. Pediatric Hematology-Oncology, Am. Soc. Clin. Oncology. Republican. Roman Catholic. Office: U Minn Hosp & Clin 420 Delaware St SE Minneapolis MN 55455

BRENNAN, DOROTHEA ELIZABETH, bank executive; b. Bridgeport, Conn., Mar. 14, 1950; d. Daniel Edward and Emily (Tabor) B. BA cum laude, Loyola U., New Orleans, 1972; MA in Communications, Fairfield (Conn.) U., 1981. Clk. elections com. Conn. Gen. Assembly, Hartford, 1973; mgmt. trainee First Bancorp, Inc., New Haven, 1974-75, asst. comptr., 1975-78, asst. v.p., asst. comptr., 1978-79, asst. v.p. mktg., 1979, v.p., corp. banking officer, 1980-83, v.p., dir. info. resources, 1983-84; sr. cons. Peat Marwick Main & Co., Hartford, 1986-88, mgr. mgmt. consulting, 1986-88; v.p. asset quality/risk mgmt. People's Bank, Bridgeport, Conn., 1989—. Active New Haven Preservation Trust, 1980-84, New Haven Bus. Vol. for Art, 1986—; bd. dirs. New Haven Boys and Girls Club, 1983-84, Arts Coun. of Greater New Haven, exec. com., chmn. strategic planning commn., 1989—, bd. dirs., 1989—, Vol. Achievement award, 1990. Recipient Women in Leadership award YWCA, New Haven, 1990. Republican. Roman Catholic. Office: People's Bank 850 Main St Bridgeport CT 06604

BRENNAN, EILEEN HUGHES, nurse; b. Atlanta, Sept. 26, 1951; m. David Lee Altizer, May 11, 1974 (div. Dec. 1978); m. Scott Curtis Brennan, Feb. 6, 1982. Student, North Ga. Coll., 1969-70; diploma, Ga. Bapt. Sch. Nursing, 1973; student, Tift Coll., 1970-73, Ga. State U., 1980-85, SUNY, Albany, 1986-90. Cert. nurse operating room, registered nurse. Orthopedic charge nurse Grady Meml. Hosp., Atlanta, 1974; operating room pvt. circulator DePaul Hosp., Norfolk, Va., 1974-76; nurse orthopedics Cabell Huntington (W.Va.) Hosp., 1976; surg. charge nurse VA Hosp., Huntington, 1976-77; mem. operating room open heart team VA Hosp., Deatur, Ga., 1986-90; orthopedic nurse specialist Peachtree Orthopedic Clinic, Atlanta, 1982; operating rm. charge nurse Doctors Meml. Hosp., Atlanta, 1982-85, chmn. operating rm. policy and procedures, 1982-84; vascular rsch. coordinator #141 Co-operative Study - a multi-ctr. VA Study, Decatur, Ga., 1988-89. Editor: Urology Pamphlet, 1986, Open Heart Instrumentation, 1987. Vol. ARC, Atlanta, 1970-88, Am. Heart Assn., Atlanta, 1987-88, Atlanta Lung Assn., 1985-88, Am. Lung Assn., Atlanta, 1988. Recipient Cert., United Fund Campaign, Atlanta, 1981, Spl. Incentive award VA Med. Ctr., Decatur, Ga., 1981, Performance award Nurse Profl. Standards Bd., Decatur, 1987, Achievementaward, 1987. Mem. Assn. Operating Room Nurses (co-chmn. Project Alpha 1986-87), Nurses Orgn. of Va. Episcopalian. Club: East Lake Country (Atlanta). Home: 9250 Brumbelow Crossing Way Alpharetta GA 30202 Office: VA Med Ctr Surg Svc 1670 Clairmont Ave #112 Decatur GA 30033

BRENNAN, NORMA JEAN, professional society publications director; b. Helena, Mont., Apr. 16, 1939; d. Harland Sanford Herrin and Elizabeth (Wardlaw) Brumfield; m. Anthony E. Brennan, Dec. 4, 1964 (div. Mar. 1986); children: Christopher E., Kimberly A. BA, U. Pacific, 1960. Editorial asst. Am. Rocket Soc., N.Y.C., 1961-62, asst. mng. editor, 1962-65; mng. editor AIAA, N.Y.C., 1978-80; publs. dir. AIAA, N.Y.C., Washington, 1980—. Mem. Young Republicans, Stockton, Calif., 1958-60; vol. Mt. Sinai Hosp., N.Y.C., 1962-64. Mem. Soc. for Scholarly Pub., Coun. Biology Editors, Assn. Am. Pubs., European Assn. Sci. Editors, Coun. Engring. and Sci. Soc. Execs., Wash. Women's Info. Network, AIAA (sr., Space Shuttle Flag award). Home: 11551 Links Dr Reston VA 22090 Office: AIAA 370 Lenfant Promenade SW Washington DC 20024

BRENNAN, PATRICIA ANNE, marketing executive; b. Port Chester, N.Y., Oct. 21, 1953; d. John Patrick and Barbara Louise (Kolb) B. BS, U. Conn., 1975. Mem. investment dept. staff State Nat. Bank of Conn., Greenwich, 1975-77; mgr. pension investment ops. Union Carbide Corp., Danbury, Conn., 1977-85; cons. Rogers, Casey & Barksdale, Inc., Stamford, Conn., 1985-88; pres. Greylyn Fin. Corp., New Canaan, Conn., 1988—. Home: 67 Sherwood Pl Greenwich CT 06830 Office: Greylyn Fin Corp 39 Pine St New Canaan CT 06840

BRENNAN, PATRICIA VIOLET, banker; b. New Haven, Mar. 14, 1961; d. James Patrick and Violet (Lord) B. BA, U. Vt., 1983; postgrad. in bus., Boston Coll., Newton, Mass., 1988. Sec. U.S. Trust Co., Boston, 1984-85, asst. to pres., 1985-87; mgmt. trainee USTCorp, Boston, 1987-88; comml. loan officer USTrust/Norfolk, Quincy, Mass., 1988—. Mem. NAFE, NOW, South Shore C. of C. Office: USTrust/Norfolk Batterymarch Pk Quincy MA 02169

BRENNER, BEVERLY ANN, educator, health club owner; b. Youngstown, Ohio, Feb. 1, 1936; d. Michael Robert and Delia (Merletti) Tucci; m. William Edward Brenner, Dic. 21, 1957; children: William Jr., Beverly Ann, Brian. BA, Case Western Res. U., 1957. Cert. tchr., Ohio, N.C. Tchr. Euclid (Ohio) Sr. High Sch., 1957-61, Shaker Heights (Ohio) High Sch., 1961-63, Chapel Hill (N.C.) High Sch., 1979—; owner, mgr. Triangle Women's Health Ctr., Chapel Hill, 1983—. Pres. Rep. Women's Club Chapel Hill, 1986—; dist. rep. 4th Congl. Dist. N.C. Fedn. Rep. Women, 1987—; mem. exec. bd. Orange County Liberacy Coun., 1989—. Mem. Delta Phi Alpa, Chapel Hill Swim Club. Lutheran. Office: Chapel Hill Bd Edn Merritt Mill Rd Chapel Hill NC 27514

BRENNER, ESTHER LERNER, fundraiser; b. Washington, July 27, 1931; d. Mayer and Ethel Sarah (Kawarsky) Lerner; children: Mayer Alan, Saul Daniel, Matthew H. BA with distinction, George Washington U., 1953; MBA, U. Judaism, L.A., 1987. Speech therapist Alexandria area schs. for handicapped, Va., 1952-54; speech therapist, pvt. practice L.A., 1954-62; tchr. L.A. area pvt. schs., 1962-72; exec. dir., lobbyist Mfrs. Assn., L.A., 1980-82; exec. dir. Citizens for Constl. Rights, Beverly Hills, Calif., 1982-86; regional coord. U.S. Holocaust Meml. Council, Washington, 1986-89; pres. L.A. Hebrew High Sch., 1987-89; bd. dirs. Bur. Jewish Edn., L.A. Pres. Beverly-Angeles Homeowners Assn., 1978-87; sec., bd. dirs. Westside Civic Fedn., L.A., 1978-89; bd. dirs. Meals on Wheels, Beverly Hills, Friends of Beverly High Sch. Endowment Fund, 1939 Club. Mem. Nat. Soc. Fund Raising Execs., Soc. of Calligraphers, So. Calif. Council of Jewish Communal Service, Phi Beta Kappa. Home: 1264 Beverly Green Dr Beverly Hills CA 90212

BRENNER, MARY ELLEN, delivery service professional; b. Patchogue, N.Y., May 11, 1960; d. William G. and Mary (Duane) B. BS in Communication Arts, St. John's U., 1982. Editorial asst. Parade Mag., N.Y.C., 1982-84; mktg. mgr., bank officer Mfrs. Hanover, N.Y.C., 1984-88; sr. staff writer Merrill Lynch Relocation, White Plains, N.Y., 1988-89; tng. supr. United Parcel Svc., Greenwich, Conn., 1989—. Home: 41 Cedar Ln Ossining NY 10562

BRENNER, RENA CLAUDY, communications executive; b. Camden, N.J.; d. John Lawler and Louretta (Du Fresene) Morgan; m. Edgar W. Claudy (div. 1968); 1 child, Renee; m. Millard Brenner, Nov. 6, 1971 (dec. 1975); children: Sally, Malcolm, Hugh. Student, U. Pa., 1978, U. Mich., 1983. Reporter Tribune-Telegram, Salt Lake City, 1943-45, Times Chronicle, Jenkintown, Pa., 1950-55; free-lance writer Enfield, Pa., 1955-60; pub. relations dir., advt. mgr. Gen. Atronics/Magnavox, Phila., 1960-70; mgr. corp. pub. relations ITE-Imperial, Phila., 1970-73, dir. corp. communications, 1973-76; dir. corp. communications Parker-Hannifin Corp., Cleve., 1976-83, v.p. corp. communications, 1983-85; pres. Brenner Assocs., Clearwater, Fla., 1986—. Recipient Creative Direction award Phila. Club Advt. Women, 1970, Clarion award Women in Communications, 1982, Gold Key award Pub. Relations News, 1984. Mem. Bus. Profl. Advt. Assn. (life), Pub. Relations Soc. Am. (life), Nat. Investors Relations Inst.. Office: Brenner Assocs 1501 Gulf Blvd #607 Clearwater FL 34630

BRENNESSEL, BARBARA ANNE, biology educator, researcher; b. Bklyn., Aug. 15, 1948; d. Warren William and Providence Rosalie (Cataldo) B.; m. Nicholas Francis Picariello, Sept. 17, 1977; children: Adriana, Gianina, Marisa. BS in Biology, Fordham U., 1970; PhD in Biochemistry, Cornell U., 1975. Rsch. fellow, instr. microbiology and immunology Med. Sch. Tulane U., New Orleans, 1975-77; rsch. fellow oral biology and pathophysiology Harvard Sch. Dental Medicine, Cambridge, Mass., 1977-78, Aid for Cancer Rsch. fellow, 1978-80; asst. prof. biology Wheaton Coll., Norton, Mass., 1980-86, assoc. prof., 1986—; vis. lectr. oral biology and pathophysiology Harvard Sch. Dental Medicine, 1983-85. Author: (software) DNA Synthesis and Replication, 1986, DNA Sequence Analysis, 1989; contbr. articles to sci. jours. NIH grantee, 1970-74, Acad. Rsch. Enhancement award, 1987-89; Rsch. Corp. rsch. grantee, 1985-87. Mem. AAAS, N.Y. Acad. Scis., Am. Soc. Cell Biology, Am. Soc. Zoologists. Office: Wheaton Coll Norton MA 02766

BRENT, DONITA MAY, state agency administrator; b. Bloomington, Ill., Sept. 21, 1939; d. Charles Lewis and Evelyn Lois (Stevens) Simpson; m. Thomas David Walters, June 12, 1959 (dec. Apr. 1970); children: Whitney Thomas, Diana Thomasine; m. William Lee Brent, Oct. 3, 1975; 1 child, Bradi Gene. BS in Bus. Adminstrn., U. No. Colo., Greeley, 1981; student, Ill. Wesleyan U., Bloomington, 1957-59. Lice. real estate broker, Colo. Legal sec. Wall and Ulbrich, Bloomington, 1958-60; exec. sec. Ft. Bragg (N.C.) Exchange, 1960-63; owner, mgr. Mister Donut Franchise, Denver, 1968-72; vol. bus. coord. Non Profit Christian Orgns., Southeastern Colo., 1968-72; corp. sec., adminstrv. asst. Ark. River Power Authority, Lamar, Colo., 1986—. Home: 403 Willow Valley Lamar CO 81052 Office: Ark River Power Authority 3409 S Main St PO Box 70 Lamar CO 81052

BRENT, JENNIFER KAY, social welfare administrator; b. Rolla, Mo., Aug. 28, 1960; d. Bill Mac and Emma Lou (Bivens) B. BS, Southeast Mo. State U., Cape Girardeau, 1982, cert. in psychology. Tchr. Mountain View Pub. Sch., Mo., 1982-83; counselor Div. of Youth Svcs., Cape Girardeau,

Mo., 1983-85; juvenile placement Div. of Youth Svcs., Cape Girardeau, 1985-87; mktg. coord. New Beginnings Chem. Dependency Treatment Ctr., Kirksville, Mo.; program dir. New Beginnings Chem. Dependency Treatment Ctr., 1987—; Mem. Mo. State Cert. Oral Rev. Bd. Bd. dirs., Mo. Substance Abuse Certification Bd., Columbia, Mo., 1989. Outstanding Svc. Award, Nat. Crime Commission, speaker, Nation Osteopathic Conv. Mem. NAFE, Mo. Assn. Alcoholism Counselors, Mo. Juvenile Justice Assn., Mo. Police Juvenile Officers Assn., Am. Businesswomen's Assn., Mo. Speakers' Bur. for Chem. Dependency Edn., Jaycees. Avocations: outdoor recreation, writing, music, photography, travel. Home: 2107C S Franklin Kirksville MO 63501 Office: 900 E Laharpe Kirksville MO 63501

BRENT, MARY HARTEL, lawyer; b. New Orleans, La., July 24, 1943; d. Stephen Camille and Rosary (Nix) Hartel; m. Robert James Brent Jr., May 1966; children: Robert, Stephen, John, Michael. Degree, U. Grenoble, France, 1964; BA, Barat Coll., 1965; JD, Loyola U., New Orleans, 1987. Bar: La.1987, U.S. Dist. Ct. (we. dist., ea. dist., middle dist.) 1987. Law clk. Supreme Ct. La., New Orleans, 1987-88; assoc. Hartel & Kenny, PLC, New Orleans, 1988—; legal cons., Guild of St. Clement of Rome Parish, Metairie, La., 1987—. Pres. New Orleans YWCA, 1982-84; bd. dirs., legal cons. SE La. coun. Girls Scouts U.S.A., 1987-89. Mem. ABA, La. State Bar Assn., Fed. Bar Assn., Orleans Club, Causeries du Lundi. Home: 7 Tara Pl Metairie LA 70002 Office: Hartel & Kenny PLC 1600 Pere Marquette Bldg New Orleans LA 70112

BRESLIN, BARBARA LEE, system support specialist, accountant; b. Coalddale, Pa., July 27, 1958; d. John Archibald and Barbara (Tronosky) B. BSBA in Acctg., Shippensburg (Pa.) U., 1980, MBA, 1988. Asst. staff auditor Prudential Ins. Co., Millville, N.J., 1980-81, staff auditor, 1981-83, audit sr., 1983; staff analyst Pa. Blue Shield, Camp Hill, 1983-85, sr. staff analyst, 1985-88, sr. project mgr., 1988-89, info. system mgr., 1989—. Mem. Jr. League of Harrisburg (Pa.). Home: 2711 High St Grantham PA 17027

BRESLIN, MARY, college president; b. Chgo., Sept. 27, 1936; d. William J. and Margaret D. (Hession) B. B.A., Mundelein Coll., Chgo., 1958; M.A., Marquette U., 1961; J.D., Loyola U., Chgo., 1977. Bar: Ill., Fed. Ct.; joined Sisters of Charity of Blessed Virgin Mary, Roman Cath. Ch., 1961. Internal auditor Fed. Res. Bank, Chgo., 1958-59; asst. bus. mgr. Mundelein Coll., Chgo., 1964-67, bus. mgr., treas., 1967-75, v.p. bus. affairs, treas., 1975-85, pres., 1985—; cons., evaluator North Central Accreditation Assn., Chgo., 1978—, Middle State Accreditation Assn., Phila., 1981—. Home & Office: Mundelein Coll 6363 N Sheridan Rd Chicago IL 60660

BRESLOW, ESTHER MAY GREENBERG, biochemistry educator, researcher; b. N.Y.C., Dec. 23, 1931; d. Harry Daniel and Lillian (Solomon) Greenberg; m. Ronald Charles David Breslow, Sept. 4, 1955; children: Stephanie Ruth, Karen Ann. BS with distinction, Cornell U., 1953; MS in Biochemistry, NYU, 1955, PhD in Biochemistry, 1959; postgrad., Radcliffe Coll., 1954-55. Postdoctoral fellow Cornell U. Med. Coll., N.Y.C., 1959-61, rsch. assoc., 1961-64, asst. prof., 1964-72, assoc. prof., 1972-78, prof. biochemistry, 1978—; mem. rev. panels NIH, Bethesda, Md., 1973-77, NSF, Bethesda, 1981-84. Mem. editorial bd. Jour. Biol. Chemistry, 1982-87, Internat. Jour. Peptide and Protein Rsch., 1981: contbr. articles to profl. jours. Mem. Englewood (N.J.) Bd. Health, 1986—; mem. Dem. Mcpl. Com., Englewood, 1985—. Eli Lilly fellow, 1954-55; USPHS fellow, 1959-61; NIH grantee, 1961—. Fellow AAAS; mem. Am. Soc. for Biochemistry and Molecular Biology, Am. Chem. Soc. (sec. div. biol. chemistry 1972-76), Harvey Soc., Sigma Xi. Home: 275 Broad Ave Englewood NJ 07631 Office: Cornell U Med Coll 1300 York Ave New York NY 10021

BRESSANT, MICHELE RENÉE, government official; b. Perth Amboy, N.J., Aug. 7, 1956; d. Ronald and Evelyn Pauline (Hall) Bressant. BS in Psychology, U. Pitts., 1978. Undergrad. teaching fellow U. Pitts., 1978; info. operator Greyhound Buslines, Pitts., 1978; med. clk. typist VA Hosp., Houston, 1979-81, patient services asst., 1981-82, psychology technician, 1982; revenue officer IRS, Houston, 1982—. Vol. Rape Crisis Ctr., Houston, 1980, Income Tax Assistance Program, Houston, 1984. Recipient Golden Panther award U. Pitts., 1978, Suggestion award VA Hosp., Houston, 1981; named Employee-of-the Month group 1400 IRS, Oct., Nov., Dec. 1985, June 1986. Mem. Nat. Assn. Female Execs., Fed. Bus. Assn., Federally Employed Women. Democrat. Baptist. Office: IRS PO Box 1299 Newark NJ 07101

BRETON, TRACY ANN, journalist; b. N.Y.C., July 16, 1951. BA in Journalism, Polit. Sci., Syracuse U., 1973. Reporter Danbury (Conn.) News-Times, summer 1972; reporter in legal affairs Providence Jour.-Bull., 1973—; past vis. prof. U. R.I., Kingston. Past contbg. editor, Auto Week mag; contbr. articles to N.Y. Times, New Woman mag., other profl. and popular publs. mem. R.I. Supreme Ct. Com. on Cameras in Courtroom, Providence, 1980—, Italian Food and Wine Commn., N.Y., 1985—; fundraiser Internat. House of R.I., Providence, 1986—. Recipient Best Feature Story for large met. newspaper award UPI, 1976, Service to Women in R.I. award Gov.'s Permanent Adv. Commn. on Women, 1977. Mem. Providence Newspaper Guild (mem. exec. bd.), Kappa Kappa Gamma Alumni Group (past pres. social dir.), Phi Kappa Phi Honor Soc. Home: 174 Columbia Ave Cranston RI 02905 Office: Providence Jour-Bull 75 Fountain St Providence RI 02902

BRETSCHNEIDER, ANN MARGERY, histotechnologist; b. Newton, Mass., May 11, 1934; d. Herman Frederick and Elizabeth Louise (Brady) B.; B.S., Northeastern U., Boston, 1957; M.S., Rutgers U., 1979. Histopathologic technician NIH, Bethesda, Md., 1957-58; chief histologic technician U. Ala. Med. Center, Birmingham, 1958-61; chief med. technologist in histology, instr. Muhlenberg Hosp., Plainfield, N.J., 1961-67; instr. anatomy Northeastern U., 1967-68; research-teaching specialist U. Medicine and Dentistry-Rutgers U. Med. Sch., 1968—; workshop leader, cons. in field. Mem. Am. Soc. Clin. Pathologists (affiliate), Nat. Soc. Histotech., Electron Microscopy Soc. Am., N.J. Soc. Histotech. Co-author: Thin Is In: Plastic Embedding of Tissue for Light Microscopy, 1981. Home: 96 Lennox Ct Piscataway NJ 08854 Office: Teaching Labs UMDNJ R W Johnson Med Sch Piscataway NJ 08854

BRETT, JACQUELYN ANN, state agency administrator; b. Chgo., Apr. 4, 1947; d. Robert and Catherine (Gaughan) B.; m. Harley E. Akers, July 6, 1980. BS in Communications, U. Ill., 1970. Pub. rels. dir. Lady Luck Casino, 1977-78; publicity dir. Silverbird Hotel/Casino and Silver City Casino, 1978; mktg. and publicity dir. Ipi-Tombi, Las Vegas, Nev., 1978-79; mktg. dir. Royal Am. Americana Hotel/Casino, 1979; ad rep. Ben Stepman Advt., 1979-81; pub. rels./mktg. dir. Circus Circus Enterprises dba Silver City Casino, Las Vegas, 1981-83, 84-87, Herb Pastor's Casinos, Las Vegas, 1983-84; print media buyer Circus Circus Enterprises, Las Vegas, 1987; Las Vegas rep. Nev. Commn. on Tourism and Nev. Mag., Las Vegas, 1987—; freelance writer Holiday Internat. Casino, Airliners Party, Ron Smith and His Celebrity Look Alikes, Boys' Club of Clark County, Broadway Dept. Stores, 1978, Nev. Pl. Casino, 1981, Clark County Community Coll., 1985; Vegas corr. Dallas Times Herald, Denver Post, Fun and Gaming, 1987—; beauty coord. and judge for pateants in L.A., Chgo., Las Vegas, 1965—; guest appearance on radio and TV shows in Chgo., L.A., Las Vegas, 1965—. Contbr. articles to profl. jours. Hon. bd. dirs., adv. com. Disting. Women in So. Nev., Las Vegas, 1988, 89, 90. Mem. Women in Communication, Inc., Museums and Attractions in Nev. (bd. dirs. 1988-89), Receptive Operators Assn. (appreciation award 1989), Las Vegas Tourism Coun. (planning com. 1988-89), Hotel Sales Mgmt. Assn., Screen Actors Guild, AFTRA, Screen Extras Guild. Office: Nev Commn on Tourism 3150 Paradise Rd Las Vegas NV 89109-9096

BRETT, LISA FARRELL, financial analyst; b. Plainfield, N.J., Feb. 25, 1956; d. Edward Asa and Elsie (Schweighardt) F.; m. William J. Brett, Apr. 19, 1980 (dec. 1982). BS in Math., Westminster Coll., New Wilmington, Pa., 1978; MBA, Pace U., N.Y.C., 1984. Actuarial analyst Crum & Forter Ins Comp., Basking Ridge, N.J., 1978-80; pricing analyst Emery Air Freight, Wilton, Conn., 1980-81; fin. analyst Data Switch, Shelton, Conn., 1984-85; sr. fin. analyst Playtex, Inc., Stamford, Conn., 1985—. Budget rep. Ridgebury PTA, 1988-89. Mem. AAUW (legis chmn., treas. 1988-89). Republican. Roman Catholic. Office: Playtex Inc Fairfield Ave Stamford CT 06902

BRETT, MARY L., mental health specialist; b. N.C., June 25, 1940; d. Zollie Brett and Sadie (Lawrence) Brett Stiff; divorced; children: Roderick Devan, Terence Quinton, Lauren DeNichola. AA, AS, Laramie County Community Coll., 1978; B of Social Work, U. Wyo., 1980; MS, Wright State U., 1982. Peer counselor Laramie County Community Coll., Cheyenne, Wyo., 1977-78; case worker Nat. ARC, Cheyenne, 1977-80; grad. asst. Wright State U., Dayton, Ohio, 1980-82; counselor Day Mont West CMHC, Dayton, 1982-86; spl. svc. counselor Wilberforce (Ohio) U., 1983-86; spl. svc. dir. Cen. State U., Wilberforce, 1986-87; contract specialist Def. Electronic Supply Ctr., Dayton, 1987-89, Naval Air Test Ctr., Patuxent River, Md., 1989—; mental health therapist St. Mary's County Health Dept., Leonardtown, Md., 1989—; mem. social com. Nat. Contract Mgmt. Assn., Lexington Park, Md., 1989—. Author: (poem) My Man, 1989. Mem. Am. Bus. Women, Chi Sigma Iota. Home: PO Box 1667 Lexington Park MD 20653 Office: 5511 Towey Ct Great Mills MD 20634

BRETT-MAJOR, LIN, lawyer; b. N.Y.C., Sept. 21, 1943; d. B.L. and Edith H. Brett; children from previous marriage: Dania S., David M. BA, U. Mich., 1965; JD cum laude, Nova Law Ctr., 1978. Bar: Fla. 1978, U.S. Ct. Appeals (5th and 11th cirs.) 1981, U.S. Tax Ct. 1981, U.S. Dist. Ct. (so., mid. and no. dist.) Fla. 1982, U.S. Supreme Ct. 1984, Trial Bar of U.S. Dist. Ct. (mid. and no. dists.) Fla., U.S. Mil. Ct. Appeals 1990. Internat. communications asst. Mitsui and Co., Ltd., N.Y.C., 1962; with dept. pub. relations and devel. St. Rita's Hosp., Lima, Ohio, 1965-66; reporter The Lima News, 1969-70; intern U.S. Atty.'s Office, Miami, 1977; sole practice Ft. Lauderdale, Fla., 1980—; participant Gov.'s Conf. on World Trade, Mia and Jacksonville, Fla., 1984—; speaker trial and negotiating techniques, internat. negotiation trade Bus. Owner's Conf., Hollywood, Fla., 1986, Nova U. Law Ctr., 1988, ABA Nat. Conv., Toronto, 1988, Fla. Atlantic U., 1989; bd. dirs. Neurol. Rehab. Ctr. Contbr. articles to profl. jours. on internat. anti-trust law. Mem. Ft. Lauderdale Opera Soc., 1985—, Ft. Lauderdale Mus. of Art, 1985—. Recipient Silver Key award ABA, 1977. Mem. ABA, Assn. Trial Lawyers Am., Fed. Bar Assn., Fla. Bar Assn. (mil. law com. 1989—, chmn. legis. issues subcom., 1990—), Broward County Bar Assn., Internat. Platform Assn., U. Mich. Alumni Assn., U. Mich. Gold Coast Alumni Assn. (pres. 1988-90, SE U.S. dist. scholarship chmn. 1990-91), Ft. Lauderdale C. of C. Republican. Club: U.S. Propeller (nat. del. Port Everglades, Fla. 1981—). Office: Victoria Park Ctr 1401 E Broward Blvd Ste 200 Fort Lauderdale FL 33301

BRETZ, (ALMA) LINDA M., library administrator; b. Far Rockaway, N.Y., Sept. 22, 1934; d. Rocco Joseph and Linda Alma (Ley) Mazza; B.S. in L.S., SUNY, Geneseo, 1956; M.F.A. in Dramatic Arts, Columbia U., 1959; m. Robert Lawrence Bretz, June 10, 1961; children—Erika Katharine, John Michael, David Reinhard. Librarian, N.Y.C. Public Library, 1956-59; asst. prof. library edn. SUNY Coll., Geneseo, 1959-66; librarian Lincoln br. Rochester (N.Y.) Public Library, 1966-67, head br., 1967-72; inservice tng. cons. Monroe County (N.Y.) Library System, Rochester, 1972-73, children's services cons., 1973-75, asst. dir. system, 1976-78, dir. Rochester Public Library and Monroe County Library System, 1978-89; adv. com. Community Savs. Bank, 1981-84; del. N.Y. Gov.'s Conf. Libraries, 1978, White House Conf. on Library and Info. Scis., 1979; trustee Reynolds Libr., 1979-89; mem. N.Y. State Profl. Librarians Cert. Exam. Com., 1973-78, chmn. 1977; mem. N.Y. State Edn. Commr.'s Adv. Com. Equal Opportunity for Women, 1985-89. Registrar, Rochester Bach Festival, 1975-89, bd. dirs., 1975—, chmn., 1990—; bd. dirs. Opera Theatre of Rochester, 1981-85, Rochester Health Network, 1982-88, Genesee Health Svc., 1986—, Rochester Area Health Maintenance Orgn., 1987—, Rundel Libr. Found., 1989—, Rochester Primary Care Network, 1990. Mem. ALA, N.Y. Libr. Assn. (councilor-at-large 1976-80, pres. 1982), Am. Soc. Pub. Adminstrn. (pres. Rochester-Monroe County chpt. 1979-80), Rochester Area Ednl. TV Assn. (nominating com. 1987-88), Rotary, Delta Kappa Gamma. Office: Rochester Pub Libr 115 South Ave Rochester NY 14604

BRETZLAFF, KATHERINE NELLE, veterinarian, educator; b. Champaign, Ill., Aug. 11, 1956; d. Robert William Bretzlaff and Celeste Marie (Quick) Taylor. BS, U. Ill., 1978, DVM, 1980, MS, 1982, PhD, 1986. Diplomate Am. Coll. Theriogenologists; lic. vet. Ill., Tex. Assoc. research U. Ill., Urbana, 1980-85; asst. prof. Tex. A&M U., College Station, 1986—. Contbr. articles to profl. jours. Mgr. 4-H Club, Bryan, Tex., 1986—. Mem. Tex. Vet. Med. Assn., Am. Vet. Med. Assn., Am. Coll. Theriogenologists, Soc. Theriogenology, Am. Soc. Animal Sci. Republican. Presbyterian. Office: Tex A&M U Dept Large Animal Medicine College Station TX 77843-4475

BREUER BACULIS, DIANA RUTH, community relations executive, business owner; b. Burlington, Iowa, Mar. 14, 1949; d. William H. and Dorothy M. (Nelson) B.; m. George J. Baculis, Aug. 9, 1986; 1 child, Kimera L. BS in Journalism, U. Iowa, 1981. Advt. sales mgr. Sta. KNIA of Leighton Enterprises, Knoxville, Iowa, 1976-80; sr. staff asst. community rels. dept. Mercy Hosp., Cedar Rapids, Iowa, 1982-88; supr. community rels. dept. Cedar Rapids Pub. Libr., 1988—. Treas. fundraising Iowa Women's Polit. Caucus, Johnson County, 1973-75; v.p. Am. Women in Radio and TV, Iowa, 1975-79. Recipient John Cotton Dana award ALA, 1989. Mem. Pub. Rels. Soc. Am. (bd. dirs. 1988—), Downtown Promotion Com. Cedar Rapids, Friends Cedar Rapids Libr., U. Iowa Alumni Assn., Beta Sigma Phi. Office: Cedar Rapids Pub Libr 500 First St SE Cedar Rapids IA 52401

BREWER, CHERYL ANN, obstetrical and gynecological educator; b. New Rochelle, N.Y., Oct. 31, 1959; d. John Paul and Marie Elizabeth (Royance) B. BS, Miss. U. for Women, 1981; MD, Ind. U., Indpls., 1985. Resident in ob-gyn. SUNY Health Scis. Ctr., Syracuse, 1985-89, asst. prof. ob-gyn., 1989—. Fellow Am. Coll. Ob-Gyn. (jr.); mem. AMA, Am. Med. Women's Assn. Home: 129 Iron Oak Circle Liverpool NY 13088 Office: SUNY Health Scis Ctr 750 E Adams St Syracuse NY 13210

BREWER, GLORIA ANN, systems engineer; b. Albany, N.Y., May 29, 1954; d. Clair Edward and Theresa Jane (Pasqualitti) B. BS, Coll. of Mt. St. Vincent, Bronx, N.Y., 1976; MA, St. John's U., 1981. Systems engr. Data Gen. Corp., Westborough, Mass., 1978—. Office: Data Gen Corp 255 Washington St Ste 280 Newton Corner MA 02158

BREWER, JANICE KAY, state legislator, property and investment firm executive; b. Hollywood, Calif., Sept. 26, 1944; d. Perry Wilford and Edna Clarice (Bakken) Drinkwine; m. John Leon Brewer, Jan. 1, 1963; children—Ronald Richard, John Samuel, Michael Wilford. Med. asst. cert. Valley Coll., Burbank, Calif., 1963, practical radiol. technician cert., 1963; D. Humanties, (hon.), Los Angeles Chiropratic Coll., 1970. Pres., Brewer Property & Investments, Glendale, Ariz., 1970—; mem. Ariz. Ho. of Reps., Phoenix, 1983-86, Ariz. Senate, 1987—. Committeeman, Republican Party, Phoenix, 1970, 1983; legis. liaison Ponderosa Rep. Women, Phoenix, 1980; bd. dirs. Westside Mental Health Agy., Phoenix, 1983—. Named Woman of Yr., Chiropractic Assn. Ariz., 1983. Mem. Nat. Fedn. Rep. Women, Am. Legis. Exchange Council. Lutheran. Home: 6835 W Union Hills Dr Glendale AZ 85308 Office: Office of Sate Senate State Capitol Phoenix AZ 85007*

BREWER, JEANNE PICKERING, communications professional; b. Dec. 8, 1962; d. James Herman and Annie Lou (Ferguson) Pickering; m. L. Gordon Brewer Jr., May 28, 1983. BA, Mars Hill (N.C.) Coll., 1983. Advt. mgr. Gregory Poole Equipment Co., Raleigh, N.C., 1985-87, Century Data Systems, Raleigh, N.C., 1987-89; dir. communications Rsch. Triangle Found., Research Triangle Park, N.C., 1989—. Mem. Pub. Rels. Soc. Am., Western Wake Jaycees (past officer), Triangle Advt. Fedn., United Daus. of Confederacy, Mars Hill Alumni Assn. Office: Rsch Triangle Found 2 Hanes Dr PO Box 12255 Research Triangle Park NC 27709

BREWER, JOYCE MARIE, nursing administrator; b. New Orleans, Jan. 23, 1949; d. Harrison J. Holloway and Melvey Raye Coyle Langston; m. John Money Brewer, July 22, 1972. ADN, Hinds Jr. Coll., Raymond, Miss., 1978; MS, U. Miss., 1982. RN, Miss. Nurse midwife Kuhn Meml. Hosp., Vicksburg, Miss.; dir. nurse midwifery svcs. Meth. Hosp. of Mid-Miss., Lexington; clin. supr. Miss. Bapt. Med. Ctr., Jackson; instr. in CPR and first aid. Mem. Am. Nurses Assn., ACNM, NAACOG, ARC, Miss. Nurses Assn., CEAMJ, ICEA.

BREWER, TERRI EVELYN, psychologist; b. Savannah, Ga., June 13, 1959; d. William C. and Virginia (Finley) B. BS with high honors, Auburn U., 1981, MS, 1982; D in Psychology, Wright State U., 1988. Lic. psychologist, Ala.; cert. legal asst. Counselor Far Hills Bapt. Ch., Dayton, 1983-85; inpatient therapist Dartmouth Psychiat. Hosp., Dayton, 1983-84; psychology intern Greene Meml. Hosp., Xenia, Ohio, 1985-86; child psychology intern Montgomery County Childrens Svcs., Dayton, 1986-87, U. Ark. for Med. Scis., Little Rock, 1987-88; pvt. practice Montgomery, Ala., 1990—; dir. psychol. svcs. Ala. Youth Svcs., Montgomery, Ala., 1988—; psychology cons. Humana Hosp. Teen Unit, Montgomery, 1990—; adj. prof. Auburn (Ala.) U., 1989—; bd. dirs. Legal Asst. Adv. Com., Montgomery. Author: Psychological Diagnosis Treatment Planning and Intervention, 1989. Scholarship Wright State U., 1985. Mem. Am. Psychol. Assn. Baptist.

BREWSTER, ELIZABETH WINIFRED, English language educator, poet, novelist; b. Chipman, N.B., Can., Aug. 26, 1922; d. Frederick John and Ethel May (Day) Brewster. B.A., U. N.B., 1946; M.A., Radcliffe U., 1947; B.L.S., U. Toronto, Ont., Can., 1953; Ph.D., Ind. U., 1962; D.Litt., U. N.B., 1982. Cataloger Carleton U., Ottawa, Ont., 1953-57; cataloger Ind. U. Library, Bloomington, 1957-58, N.B. Legis. Library, 1965-68, U. Alta. Library, Edmonton, Can., 1968-70; mem. English dept. Victoria U., B.C., 1960-61; reference libr. Mt. Allison U. Libr., Sackville, N.B., 1961-65; vis. asst. prof. English U. Alta., 1970-71; mem. faculty U. Sask., Saskatoon, Can., 1972—, asst. prof. English, 1972-75, assoc. prof., 1975-80, prof., 1980-90, prof. emeritus, 1990—. Author: East Coast, 1951, Lilloot, 1954, Roads, 1957, Passage of Summer, 1969, Sunrise North, 1972, In Search of Eros, 1974, Sometimes I Think of Moving, 1977, The Way Home, 1982, The Sisters, 1974, It's Easy to Fall on the Ice, 1977, Digging In, 1982, Junction, 1982, A House Full of Women, 1983, Selected Poems (2 vols.), 1944-84, 1985, Visitations, 1987, Entertaining Angels, 1988, Spring Again, 1990. Recipient E.J. Pratt award for poetry U. Toronto, 1953, Pres.' medal for poetry U. Western Ont., 1980. Mem. League Can. Poets, Writers' Union Can., Assn. Can. Univ. Tchrs. English. Office: U Saskatchewan, Dept English, Saskatoon, SK Canada S7N 0W0

BREWSTER, LOUISE S., public relations executive; b. Boston, Jan. 28, 1961; d. Dudley Nichols and Cynthia Story (Bishop) B. BA in English with honors, Wellesley Coll., 1983. Publicity asst. Houghton Mifflin Co., N.Y.C., 1984-85; pub. relations assoc. Viacom Enterprises, N.Y.C., 1985-87; assoc. dir., publicity Dodd Mead & Co., Inc., N.Y.C., 1987-88, dir. publicity, 1988-89; sr. account exec. Lynn Goldberg Communications, N.Y.C., 1989—. Playwright: (drama) The Tamer Tamed, 1983, (musical) Juliet & Romeo, 1982; reporter, writer: Viacom Enterprises, Viacomments mag., 1985-87. Class fundraiser Wellesley (Mass.) Coll., 1987-89; tutor English, Queens, N.Y., 1984-86. Named Wellesley Coll. scholar, 1983, Wellesley Town scholar, 1979-83. Mem. Pubs. Publicity Assn.

BREWSTER, OLIVE NESBITT, retired librarian; b. San Antonio, July 19, 1924; d. Charles Henry and Olive Agatha (Nesbitt) B.; B.A., Our Lady of Lake Coll., 1945, B.S. in L.S., 1946. Asst. librarian aeromed. library U.S. Air Force Sch. Aviation Medicine, Randolph AFB, Tex., 1946-60, chief cataloger aeromed. library Sch. Aerospace Medicine, Brooks AFB, Tex., 1960-83, chief tech. processing, 1983-88; ret., 1988. Mem. ALA, Am. Soc. Indexers, Mensa. Anglican. Home: 1906 Schley Ave San Antonio TX 78210

BREYER, CAROL ANN, state agency administrator, consultant; b. Rochester, N.Y., Feb. 26, 1934; d. Charles and Caroline (Gleichauf) Strobel; m. Lee John Breyer, Aug. 16, 1969. BA, Mt. St. Agnes Coll., 1957; MA, Notre Dame U., 1968; PhD, Walden U., 1977. Dir. pub. rels. Mt. St. Agnes Coll., Balt., 1967-69; asst. coord. world justice and peace office U.S. Cath. Conf., Washington, 1969-70; tng. specialist U.S. Civil Svc. Commn., Washington, 1970-72; asst. dir. external tng. Prince Georges Community Coll., Largo, N.D., 1972-75, dir. publs., 1975-79; asst. dir. Fla. Div. Community Coll.s, Tallahassee, 1979-83; exec. dir. Fla. Gov.'s Employment Alliance, Tallahassee, 1983—. Roman Catholic. Home: 2929 Tipperary Ct Tallahassee FL 32308 Office: Fla Govs Employment Alliance 345 S Magnolia Dr Tallahassee FL 32301

BREYMAIER, ANN MEREDITH (MEREDITH CHENEY), writer, poet, educator; b. Elyria, Ohio, June 17, 1925; d. Harvey Chapman and Ethel Josephine (Steffen) Cheney; m. Robert William Breymaier, May 24, 1952; 1 foster child, Christina Lipe Torres; 1 adopted child, Walter William II. BA, Ohio State U., 1947; MA, Eastern Mich. U., 1972, MA in Lang. and Lit., 1986. Provisional secondary teaching cert., Mich. Asst. to editor Clintonville Booster, Columbus, Ohio, 1947-48; copywriter, performer continuity Sta.-WLEC, Sandusky, Ohio, 1948-49; typist Sta.-WERE, Cleve., 1950; record librarian, music shows producer Sta.-WDOK, Cleve., 1950-51, traffic mgr., 1951-52, also performer, writer, producer children's show, 1951-52; writer pub. info. Sta.-WEMU, Eastern Mich. U., Ypsilanti, 1977-80, also on-air work, 1978-80; substitute tchr. Ypsilanti Pub. schs., 1981—; coordinator newsletter writer Ypsilanti Food Coop., 1981-85; Latin tutor. Contbr. poems to lit. jours. and anthologies. Recipient 4th prize Seven Mag. Jesse Stuart Internat. poetry contest, 1975, 2d Place award Terre Haute Poetry Soc. Winter Contest, 1975, 2d prize Seven Mag. Jesse Stuart Internat. poetry contest, 1978, 4th prize Mich. Poetry Soc., 1974, 1st prize Mich. Poetry Soc., 1974, 2d prize Mich. Poetry Soc., 1975, spl. mention certs. World of Poetry contests, 1984—, Golden Merit award World of Poetry Conv., 1985-89. Mem. Women in Communications, Inc., Chimes, Mich. Reading Assn., Washtenaw Reading Council, Poetry Soc. of Mich., Alpha Epsilon Rho, Phi Mu. Club: Ypsilanti Area Garden (pres. 1981). Presbyterian. Avocations: reading, radio, television, writing for newsletters, gardening. Home and Office: 1376 Skyway Dr Ypsilanti MI 48197

BRIAN, SHARON LYNN, information systems technician; b. El Dorado, Ark., Nov. 23, 1946; d. Raymond Elbert and Beulah Lynn (Cook) Smith; m. Alfred Thomas Brian, Aug. 10, 1968; children: Christopher Aron, Kelly Lynn. BS in Math., So. Ark. U., 1968; postgrad., U. Houston, 1971-73, So. Meth. U., 1974-75. Tchr. math. El Dorado Pub. Schs., 1968-69; computer programmer, systems analyst, systems mgr. Tex. Instruments, Dallas, 1969-85, sr. mem. tech. staff, 1985-86; cons. dental offices, Tex., 1985—. Publicity chmn. PTA, Allen, Tex., 1985-86, pres., 1986-88; treas. United Meth. Women, Allen, 1976; adv. bd. New Parents as Tchrs, Indigent Health Care; sec. Allen Swim Team. Mem. Am. Mgmt. Assn., Guide Internat. (group mgr. 1984-86), Allen Sports Assn. (treas.). Club: Plano Maple (Tex.) (pres. 1985-86). Avocations: reading, needlework, water skiing. Home and Office: Box 1137 Allen TX 75002

BRICKER, VICTORIA REIFLER, anthropology educator; b. Hong Kong, June 15, 1940; came to U.S., 1947, naturalized, 1953; d. Erwin and Henrietta (Brown) Reifler; m. Harvey Miller Bricker, Dec. 27, 1964. A.B., Stanford U., 1962; A.M., Harvard U., 1963, Ph.D., 1968. Vis. lectr. anthropology Tulane U., 1969-70, asst. prof., 1970-73, assoc. prof., 1973-78, prof., 1978—, chmn. dept. anthropology, 1988—. Author: Ritual Humor in Highland Chiapas, 1973, The Indian Christ, The Indian King: The Historical Substrate of Maya Myth and Ritual, 1981 (Howard Francis Cline meml. prize Conf. Latin Am. History), A Grammar of Mayan Hieroglyphs, 1986; book rev. editor: Am. Anthropologist, 1971-73; editor: Am. Ethnologist, 1973-76; gen. editor: Supplement to Handbook of Middle American Indians, 1977—. Guggenheim fellow, 1982; Wenner-Gren Found. Anthropol. Rsch. grantee, 1971; Social Sci. Rsch. Coun.l grantee, 1972; NEH grantee, 1990. Fellow Am. Anthrop. Assn. (exec. bd. 1980-83); mem. Am. Soc. Ethnohistory (exec. bd. 1977-79), Linguistic Soc. Am., Seminario de Cultura Maya, Societe des Americanistes. Office: Tulane Univ Dept Anthropology New Orleans LA 70118

BRICKEY, IRIS ANN, construction company executive; b. Roanoke, Va., Feb. 24, 1941; d. Bernie Roscoe and Alice Mary (Quinn) Lee; m. James Monteray Brickey, Aug. 29, 1958; 1 child, Andrea. Payroll clk. New Castle Mfg. Co., 1959-66; corp. officer, office mgr. Thor Inc., Roanoke, 1967—. Mem. Nat. Assn. Women in Constrn. (pres. 1989-90), Roanoke Moose. Republican. Office: Thor Inc PO Box 13127 Roanoke VA 24031

BRICKEY, KATHLEEN FITZGERALD, law educator; b. Austin, Tex., Sept. 16, 1944; d. Robert Bernard and Ina Marie (Daw) Fitzgerald; m. James Nelson Brickey, Aug. 22, 1969. BA, U. Ky., 1965, JD, 1968. Criminal law specialist/cons. Ky. Crime Commn., Frankfort, Cin., 1968-71; exec. dir. Ky.

Judicial Conf. and Coun., Frankfort, 1971-72; adj. prof. law U. Ky., Lexington, 1972; asst./assoc. prof. law U. Louisville, 1972-76; assoc. prof. law Washington U., St. Louis, 1976-80; prof. law Washington U., 1980—, George Alexander Madill prof. law, 1989—; cons. U.S. Sentencing Commn., 1988; witness U.S. Senate Com. on Judiciary, Washington, 1986. Author: Kentucky Criminal Law, 1974, Corporate Criminal Liability, 1984, Corporate and White Collar Crime, 1990; contbr. articles to profl. jours. Mem. Am. Law Inst., Soc. for Reform of Criminal Law, Assn. Am. Law Schs. (sect. on criminal justice chair 1989, exec. com. 1985—). Office: Washington U Sch Law Campus Box 1120 Saint Louis MO 63130

BRICKMAN, JANE PACHT, history educator; b. N.Y.C., Feb. 5, 1946; d. Sol and Beatrice (Lereah) Pacht; m. John M. Brickman, Feb. 26, 1972; children: Elizabeth A., Suzanna P. BA, Queens Coll., 1968, MA; PhD, CUNY, 1978. Part-time tchr. Hofstra U., Queens Coll., Pace U., U.S. Mcht. Marine Acad., 1970-83; asst. prof. history U.S. Mcht. Marine Acad., Kings Point, N.Y., 1983-86, assoc. prof. history, 1986—, women's advisor, 1983—. Contbr. articles to profl. jours. Office: US Mcht Marine Acad Kings Point NY 11024

BRIDGER, BARBARA B., controller; b. Laurinburg, N.C., Feb. 26, 1957; d. Hilburn and Hazel Pauline (Presley) Barber; m. Armand Dale Bridger, Apr. 7, 1977; 1 child, Robert Dale. BS in Math., Pembroke State U., 1981; postgrad., U. Kans., Overland Pk., 1984-85. Payroll, acctg. control clk. Butler Mfg. Co., Laurinburg, 1980-82, cost acct., programmer, 1982-83; plant contr. Butler Mfg. Co., Grandview, Mo., 1983-85; sr. fin. analyst Butler Mfg. Co., Kansas City, Mo., 1985-86, acctg. mgr., internat. contr. bldgs. div., 1986-87; contr. Walker div. Butler Mfg. Co., Parkersburg, W.Va., 1987—; treas. Butler Employee Credit Union, Kansas City, 1985-87. Advisor Jr. Achievement, Kansas City, 1985-86, In Roads, Kansas City, 1985-87; bd. advisors Parkersburg Community Coll., 1989; v.p. Laurinburg Jaycettes, 1982, pres., 1983; pres. Young Dems., Laurinburg, 1982. Recipient N.C. Speak Up award N.C. Jaycettes, 1982; named Outstanding Local Pres. N.C. Jaycettes, 1983. Mem. Parkersburg C. of C. Republican. Baptist.

BRIDGES, BERYL CLARKE, marketing executive; b. N.Y.C., Oct. 27, 1941; d. David and Edith (Foster) Clarke; m. R. Shaw Bridges, Sept. 2, 1962 (div. May 1985); chldren: Robert Shaw Jr., Margaret Clarke, John Morrison. BA in English, Philosophy, Wheaton Coll., 1963. Acct. exec. McMoran-Redington Pub. Rels., Greenwich, Conn., 1975-77; mgr. sales promotion Lindenmeyr Graphic Resource Ctr., Greenwich, 1977-79; corp. mgr. promotions Lindenmeyr Paper Corp., Greenwich, 1979-81; mgr. southeastern region Paper Sources Internat. subs. Lindenmeyr Paper Corp., 1981-83, v.p. mktg., 1983-84; pres., dir. Paper Sources Internat. div. Cen. Nat. Gottesman, Rutherford, N.J., 1984—; cons. and lectr. in field. V.p. Greenwich Hist. Soc., 1974-77; mem. Jr. League, Greenwich, 1971-78. Mem. Am. Inst. Graphic Arts. Republican. Episcopalian. Clubs: Jupiter Island, Hobe Sound Yacht. Home: 214 S Beach Rd Hobe Sound FL 33455 Office: 125 Gates Ave Montclair NJ 07042

BRIDGES, LINDA, educator, union administrator; b. Corpus Christi, Tex., Dec. 19, 1949; d. Frederick J. and Doris (Lee) Schneider. AA, Del Mar Coll., 1970; BS in Edn., Tex. Agrl. and Indsl. U., 1971. Cert. tchr., Tex. Tchr. Corpus Christi Ind. Sch. Dist., 1971-78; exec. v.p. Corpus Christi Am. Fedn. Tchrs., 1978-80, pres., 1980—; adv. bd. Dos Mundos Day Sch., Corpus Christi, 1987—, Tex. Edn. and Economy Com., 1990; mem. strategic planning team Corpus Christi Ind. Sch. Dist., 1989-90. Regent Del Mar Coll., Corpus Christi, 1984-90. Mem. Am. Fedn. Tchrs. (pres. 1980—, mem. at-risk task force 1989—), Tex. Fedn. Tchrs. (exec. com., chair legis. com. 1984—), Assn. Supervision and Curriculum Devel. Democrat. Office: Am Fedn Tchrs 1001 Louisiana Ave Ste 401 Corpus Christi TX 78404

BRIDGMAN, ELIZABETH KLEIN (BETTY BRIDGMAN), journalist; b. Mpls.; d. William and Katherine Louise (Chromy) K.; m. Donald Elliott Bridgman, June 26, 1937 (dec.); children: George Henry, Katherine Urwick Ellgen, John Elliott, William Lewis, Thomas Willson, Arthur Kirby. AB summa cum laude, Hamline U., 1936; postgrad., U. London, 1936-37, U. Minn., 1941, 56. Instr. Hamline U., St. Paul, 1958-64; with Community Resource Vols. (changed to WISE) Mpls. Pub. Schs., 1966—; speaker, instr. writer's confs., Minn., Wis., 1969—; speaker women's groups, 1955—. Author: Lullaby For Eggs, 1955, Chorus For American Women, 1957, This is Minnesota, 1958; contbr. over 150 poems and 30 articles to nat. mags. and newspapers. Chmn. academicians Rep. Women, 1964, chairwoman Legis. Campaign, Minn., 1962-68, chairwoman of ward Morningside and Edina, 1962-65; chmn. poetry com. Minn. Centennial Celebration, 1958. Recipient Good Neighbor Community Chest, 1952, Newsmaker Recognition award Suburban Press, 1966, Disting. Alumni award Hamline U., 1990, numerous poetry prizes. Mem. Nat. League of Am. Pen Women (treas. Minn. br., 1975-86, 89—, AAUW (Mpls. br.), Mpls. Poetry Soc., League of Minn. Poets. Republican. Christian Scientist. Home: 4306 Grimes Ave S Minneapolis MN 55424

BRIERTON, CHERYL L. WOOTTON BLACK, lawyer; b. Hartford, Conn., Nov. 11, 1947; d. Charles Greenwood and Elizabeth (Grechko) Wootton; m. David Martin Black, Oct. 12, 1968 (div. 1978); m. John Thomas Brierton, Sept. 6, 1982 (div. 1988); 1 child, John Greenwood. BA, Wellesley Coll., 1969; JD, U. San Diego, 1982. Bar: Calif. 1983. Tchr., librarian Anglican High Sch., Grenada, West Indies, 1972-74; dep. dir. Transalpino Student Travel, Paris, 1975-76; asst. dir. adminstn. Project OZ, YMCA, San Diego, 1976-78; asst. coordinator policy and advocacy Community Congress San Diego, 1978-81; field dir. Calif. Child, Youth and Family Coalition, San Diego, 1981-83; asst. exec. dir. Community Congress San Diego, 1984-85; exec. dir. Calif. Child, Youth and Family Coalition, Sacramento, 1985-86; lawyer Defense Logistics Agency, Defense Depot Tracy, Calif., 1986-88, Dept. of the Navy, Mare Island Naval shipyard, Vallejo, 1988-89, San Diego Superior Ct., 1989—; faculty Nat. Juvenile Judges Conf. Dispositional Alternatives Serious Offenders, 1982, 6th and 7th Nat. Conf. Juvenile Justice 1979-80; cons. San Diego Youth Involvement Project 1983-84, San Diego Youth and Community Services 1983-84, S. Bay Community Services, Chula Vista 1983. Scholar U. San Diego 1979. Mem. Juvenile Justice Commn., Golden Hill Neighborhood Justice Cen. Planning Bd, Regional Criminal Justice Planning Bd. Com. Judicial Process, MENSA. Home: 1329 Bancroft St San Diego CA 92102

BRIFFEL, MEYANNE PUTNAM, optometrist; b. Waverly, N.Y., June 9, 1950; d. J. David and Jane (Barry) Putnam; m. Harry Briffel, June 26, 1973; children: Henry, Clark. BS, Franklin & Marshall, 1972; OD, Pa. Coll. Optometry, 1976. Staff optometrist Internat. Ladies Garment Worker Union Health Ctr., N.Y.C., 1976-78; optometric cons. Pearl Optical, N.Y.C., 1978-80; staff optometrist Grand Opticians, N.Y.C., 1980-85; ptnr. pvt. practice optometry Long Beach, N.Y., 1978—; ptnr. Stahl Eye Assocs./Garden City Optics, Garden City, N.Y., 1986—. Pres. Lawrence Country Day Sch. Parent Assn., Hewlett Bay Park, N.Y., 1987-88; bd. trustees Lawrence Country Day Sch., 1987-90, Lawrence Country Day Sch./Woodmere Acad., 1990—; mem. chmn.'s adv. panel N.Y. State Com. on Commerce and Industry, 1990—. Home: 44 Cheltenham St Lido Beach NY 11561 Office: 612 E Park Ave Long Beach NY 11561

BRIGANCE, REBECCA ELIZABETH, educator; b. Martin, Tenn., Feb. 7, 1945; d. Maurice Leon and Johnie Rebecca (Stoker) Compton; m. Jerry Lee Brigance, Aug. 7, 1965; children: Steven Leon, Jason Lee. BS, U. Tenn., Martin, 1966, MS, 1979. Cert. tchr. Tchr. jr. high Weakley Bd. Edn., Sharon, Tenn., 1966-67, 88—, tchr. 1st grade, 1975-88; tchr. 5th grade Hardeman County Bd. Edn., Grande Junction, Tenn., 1967-68. Mem. projects com. PTA, Sharon, 1970—; com. mem. Homecoming '86, Sharon, 1985-86; sponsor alumni reunion City of Sharon, 1983, 85; sponsor high sch. and jr. high cheerleaders, Sharon, 1980—; pres. Delta Kappa Gamma, 1985-87. Named Tenn. Tchr. of Yr., Tenn. State Dept. Edn., Nashville, 1990. Mem. NEA, Tenn. Edn. Assn., Tenn. Assn. Mid. Schs. (West Tenn. Tchr. of Yr. 1989), Weakley County Edn. Assn. (com. chmn. 1983-84, sec. 1985), Parent-Tchr. Club (treas. 1974-76), Booster Club (projects officer 1985—). Democrat. Presbyterian.

BRIGGS, E. JANETTE, accountant; b. Leachville, Ark., Sept. 24, 1931; d. John Henry and Gertha (Milligan) Hawkins; m. Robert M. Briggs, Aug. 7, 1954 (div. June 1979); children: Robert M. III, John A., Douglas S., Todd E. Corp. contr. Firetrol, Inc., Cary, N.C., 1971—. Mem. Nat. Assn. Accts., Controller's Council, Raleigh Bridge Club (sec. 1983-88). Republican. Methodist. Home: 8321-201 Hempshire Pl Raleigh NC 27612

BRIGHT, BETTY SUIDA, air pollution control official; b. Harbor Beach, Mich.; d. David Frank and Suzanne (Olshove) Suida. A.A. in Bus., Eastern Mich. Coll. Commerce; A.A. in Liberal Arts, Macomb Coll.; B.A. in Polit. Sci., Wayne State U., later postgrad.; postgrad. U. Detroit, Cranbrook U.; grad. Congl. Sch., Washington, 1980; M.B.A., Central Mich. U. With product design office Chrysler Corp.; commr. Mich. Air Pollution Control Commn., 1982—; speaker to women's groups. Congl. candidate 18th Congl. Dist., 1980; mem. Mich. State budget com., 1982, state issues com., 1972; mem. Oakland County Exec. Com., 17th Congl. exec. com.; bd. dirs. Lincoln Republican Club; nat. del., Kansas City, 1976; nat. hon. sgt.-at-arms, Miami Beach, Fla., 1972; Rep. precinct del.; mem. Oakland County campaign com.; mem. Mich. State com., 1980—; past v.p. Royal Oak Area Rep. Com. (Mich.); sponsor Mich. Opera Theatre; bd. dirs. women's com. Am. Lung Assn.; mem. Project Hope, Founders' Soc., Detroit Art Inst.; mem. women's assn. Detroit Symphony Orchestra. Recipient Women to Watch award Cobo Hall, 1980. Mem. Bus. Women's and Profl. Assn. (legis. liaison), Women of Wayne, Jr. League (past pres.), Internat. Platform Assn., Rep. Women's Bus. and Profl. Forum, Gold Key, Beta Sigma Phi, Pi Sigma Alpha, Sigma Iota Epsilon. Clubs: Detroit Yacht, Women's Econ. (publicity com.), Economic, Chrysler Mgmt. (Detroit, mem. photographic com.). Address: 32608 Inkster Rd Franklin MI 48024

BRIGHT, DEBRA ANN, environmental consultant; b. L.A., Sept. 17, 1957; d. Donald Bolton and Patricia Jean (McLaughlin) B. BS in Biology, U. So. Calif., 1979; MPH in Epidemiology, UCLA, 1982. Registered environ. assessor, Calif. Rsch. asst. Alpha Therapeutics, Pasadena, Calif., 1979; environ. specialist Bright & Assocs., Placentia, Calif., 1980-83, v.p., 1983-88; sr. v.p. Environ. Audit, Inc., Placentia, 1988—; guest lectr. U. Calif., Irvine, 1986—. Pub. Health Svc. grantee, 1981-82. Mem. Am. Pub. Health Assn., Air Pollution Control Assn., Harbor Assn. of Industry and Commerce. Republican. Methodist. Office: Eviron Audit Inc 1000 Ortega Way Ste A Placentia CA 92670-7125

BRIGHT, JERLENE ANN, information systems programs administrator; b. Norman, Okla., July 4, 1942; d. Hoyt David and Pearl J. Little; Asso. in Bus., Okla. Sch. Banking and Bus., 1964; student U. Okla., 1974-76; m. James Bright, July 25, 1959; children—Bridget, Michelle, Erika. Project coordinator U. Okla. Computing Center, 1965-68, dir. info. systems programs U. Okla., Norman, 1968-84; data processing dir. Dwight's Energydata, Inc., 1984—; participant UN energy meetings and workshops to third world meetings. Contbr. numerous papers and articles to profl. jours. Mem. Soc. Petroleum Engrs. Home: 4317 Lyrewood Ln Norman OK 73072

BRILES, JUDITH, writer, speaker, consultant; b. Pasadena, Calif., Feb. 20, 1946; d. James and Mary Tuthill; MBA, Pepperdine U., 1980; children: Shelley, Sheryl. Brokers asst. Bateman, Eichler, Hill, Richards, Torrance, Calif., 1969-72; account exec. E. F. Hutton, Palo Alto, Calif., 1972-78; pres. Judith Briles & Co., Palo Alto, 1978-85, Briles & Assocs., Palo Alto, 1980-86; ptnr. The Briles Group, Inc., 1987—; instr. Menlo Coll., 1986-87, Skyline Coll., 1981-86; instr. U. Calif.-Berkeley Sch. Continuing Edn., U. Calif.-Santa Cruz Sch. Continuing Edn., U. Hawaii; mem. adv. coun. Miss Am. Pageant, 1989—, No-nonsense Panty Hose, 1989—. Pres., v.p., sec., bd. dirs. Foothill-DeAnza Coll. Found., Los Altos Hills, Calif., 1979-90; mem. adv. bd. Flint Ctr., Cupertino, Calif. Mem. NAFE (adv. bd. bus. woman's mag. 1981-86), Peninsula Profl. Women's Network, Nat. Speaker's Assn. (bd. dirs.). Republican. Club: Commonwealth. Author: The Woman's Guide to Financial Savvy, 1981; Money Phases, 1984, Woman to Woman: From Sabotage to Support, 1987, Dollars and Sense of Divorce, 1988, Faith and Savvy Too!, 1988, When God Says No, 1990, The Confidence Factor, 1990. Home and Office: 558 Cambridge Ave Palo Alto CA 94306

BRILEY, MARTHA CLARK, insurance company executive; b. Glen Ridge, N.J., May 31, 1949; d. David Ormiston and Marion Jane (Drury) Clark; m. Richard Keith Dentel, Dec. 29, 1972 (dec. Feb. 1974); m. Joseph Coyle Briley, Mar. 25, 1978; children: Christopher, Alexis. AB, Brown U., 1971; MBA, Harvard U., 1978. CLU, 1986, chartered fin. cons., 1987. Asst. treas., trainee Chase Manhattan Bank, N.Y.C., 1971-74, 2d v.p. corp. fin., 1974-76, v.p., team leader corp. lending, 1978-81; v.p. corp. fin. Prudential Ins. Co., Newark, 1981-83, v.p., treas., 1983-89; pres., chief exec. officer Prudential Power Funding Assocs., Newark, 1989—. Trustee Brown U., 1987—, Ind. Coll. Fund. N.J., 1988—; bd. dirs. Stuart Country Day Sch. of Sacred Heart, 1989—. Recipient Alumni Svc. award Brown U., Providence, R.I., 1984. Mem. Fin. Women's Assn., Com. of 200. Republican. Presbyterian. Office: Prudential Power Funding Assocs 100 Mulberry St 4 Gateway Ctr Newark NJ 07102

BRILL, BONNIE, physical therapist; b. Charleston, S.C., Nov. 2, 1948; d. Harry Harris II and Virginia Brill. Lic. phys. therapist. Pediatric phys. therapist Ga. State Health Agys., Atlanta, 1972-73; staff phys. therapist Peachtree Orthopedic Clinic, Atlanta, 1974; contractor Ga. Health Care Orgns., Atlanta, 1975-79; engr., cons. Medicas Systems Corp., Houston, 1979-81, Bay Area Hosps., San Francisco, 1981-82; chief phys. therapist San Francisco Gen. Hosp., 1982-83; dir. phys. therapy Ralph K. Davies Med. Ctr., San Francisco, 1983-84; contractor Calif. Health Care Orgns., San Francisco area, 1984-86; founder Peak Relief, San Francisco, 1986—; cons. in field. Mem. Am. Phys. Therapy Assn. (Calif. chpt., pvt. practice sect.), Eckankar.

BRILL, YVONNE CLAEYS, engineer, consultant; b. St. Norbert, Manitoba, Canada, Dec. 30, 1924; d. August and Julienne (Carette) Claeys; m. William Franklin Brill, Dec. 15, 1951; children: Naomi, Matthew, Joseph. BS, U. Manitoba, Canada, 1945; MS, U. So. Calif., 1951. Mathematician Douglas Aircraft, Santa Monica, Calif., 1945-46; research analyst Rand Corp., Santa Monica, 1946-49; group leader Marquardt Corp., Van Nuys, Calif., 1949-52; staff engr. UTC Research, East Hartford, Conn., 1952-55; project engr. Wright Aeronautical, Wood Ridge, N.J., 1955-58; mgr. propulsion systems RCA AstroElectronics, Princeton, N.J., 1966-81, staff engr., 1983-86; mgr. solid rocket motor NASA Hdqrs., Washington, 1981-83; with space engring segment Internat. Maritime Satellite Orgn., London, 1986—; mem. USAF Sci. Adv. Bd., Washington, 1982-83. Contbr. articles to sci. jours.; patentee in field. Bd. dirs. Princeton YWCA, 1981-82. Recipient Engr. of Yr. award Cen. Jersey Engring. Councils, 1979, Diamond Superwoman award Harpers Bazaar/DeBeers Corp., 1980. Fellow AIAA, Soc. Women Engrs. (dir. student affairs 1979-80, 83-84, treas. 1980-81, Engring. Achievement award 1986); mem. Internat. Astronautical Acad. (academician, edn. com. 1983-85), U.S. Nat. Acad. Engring. (elected 1987), Sigma Xi, Tau Beta Pi. Republican. Home: 914 Rte 518 RD 1 Skillman NJ 08558 Office: Internat Maritime Satellite Orgn, 40 Melton St, London NW1 2EQ, England

BRILLANTES, DOROTHY ANN, hospital services director; b. N.Y.C., Oct. 15, 1950; d. Anthony and Dorothy (Lang) Begley; m. John Brillantes, May 4, 1979; 1 child, Kristin Hope; stepchildren: John Eric, Paul. BA in Mgmt., Coll. of Notre Dame, Balt., 1984. Claims examiner Blue Cross/Blue Shield, N.Y.C., 1968-75, sr. utilization rev. analyst, 1975-76, div. chief utilization rev., 1976-79; mgr. med. records Johns Hopkins Hosp., Balt., 1979-80, dir. admitting, 1980-85, cons./dir. med. records, 1985-87, sr. dir. hosp. svcs., 1987—; chairperson Dunbar High Sch. program Johns Hopkins Hosp., Balt., 1987—. Home: 10213 Clubhouse Ct Ellicott City MD 21043 Office: Johns Hopkins Hosp 600 N Wolfe St Baltimore MD 21205

BRINCKS, CYNTHIA ANN, oil and gas company executive; b. Calmar, Iowa, July 23, 1958; d. Vernon Paul and Mary Gertrude (Smith) Frana; m. Daniel Lee Brincks, Mar. 8, 1980; children: Joshua, Nicholas. Diploma, N.E. Iowa Tech. Inst., Calmar, 1977; postgrad., Ins. Inst. Am., Malvern, Pa., 1988—. Lic. Claim Adjuster, Tex. Pharmacy sec. North Iowa Med. Ctr., Mason City, 1977-79; sec. to supt. N.E. Iowa Tech. Inst., Calmar, 1979-81; sec. III Tex. Oil & Gas Corp., Dallas, 1981-83, sec. II, 1983-84, ins. adminstr., 1984-87, ins. analyst, 1987—. Coach Forney Youth Assn., Tex. 1984-85. Mem. Dallas-Ft. Worth Risk and Ins. Mgmt. Soc. (soc. dir. 1988—). Roman Catholic. Office: Tex Oil & Gas Corp 1700 Pacific Ave Dallas TX 75201

BRINE, DOLORES RANDOLPH, chemist; b. Marion, N.C., Nov. 26, 1945; d. Carl Lee and Addie (Ritter) Randolph; m. George Atkins Brine, Aug. 31, 1968. BS, Duke U., 1968. Rsch. chemist Research Triangle Inst., Research Triangle Park, N.C., 1968—. Contbr. articles to profl. jours., chpts. to books. Mem. Am. Chem. Soc. Episcopalian. Home: 6505 Hunters Ln Durham NC 27713

BRINER, PAMELA JOAN, banker; b. Vancouver, B.C., Can., Apr. 21, 1950; came to U.S., 1953; d. James Henry and Margaret Elaine (Withrow) Pitman; m. Michael Charles Wasmann, Nov. 21, 1970 (div. Jan. 1975); m. John Gaylord Briner, May 17, 1975. Grad. high sch., San Mateo, Calif. Sales clk. Melart's, San Mateo, 1966-69; note clk. Wells Fargo Bank, San Mateo, 1969-70, 72-73; flight attendant Hughes Air West, San Francisco, 1970; receptionist Harris & Stroh, Hayward, Calif., 1970-72; office mgr. Sky Climber, Inc., Brisbane, Calif., 1973; new accounts to cashier Placer Nat. Bank/Bank of Alex Brown, Auburn, Calif., 1974-82; exec. officer The Bank of Commerce, N.A., Auburn, 1983—; bd. dirs. Auburn Palm Terr. Episcopalian. Office: The Bank of Commerce NA 540 Wall St PO Box 5770 Auburn CA 95604

BRINK, JUDITH KAY, investment company executive; b. Decatur, Ill., Mar. 23, 1947; d. Richard James Winwood and Priscilla Elizabeth (Warner) McClure; m. John Mason, 1966 (dec. 1966); m. Joe Brink, Aug. 21, 1971. Student, Western Ill. U., 1968-71. Registered rep. Nat. Assn. Security Dealers. Sales asst. Bear Stearns Corp., Chgo., 1976-78; registered sales asst. Chgo. Corp., 1978-80; investment broker A.G. Edwards & Sons, Merrillville, Ind., 1980-84; v.p. investments A.G. Edwards & Sons, Merrillville, 1984-87, v.p. investments, mgr., 1987—. Mem. Internat. Assn. Fin. Planners, Lakeshore Bus. & Profl. Women (various offices). Office: AG Edwards & Sons 405 W Northmoor Rd Peoria IL 61614-3542

BRINK, MARION ALICE, alcohol and drug programs consultant; b. Boston, Feb. 15, 1928; d. Martin Bernhard and Astrid Marie (Bjaastad) Windedal; m. A. Rudie Shobaken, Feb. 5, 1947 (div. 1963); children: Richard Michael, Ron Eric; m. James A Brink, Jan. 29, 1977. Student, Cambridge Jr. Coll., 1945-47, Framingham State Coll., 1967, Boston U., 1967-69; BA, U. N.H., 1983; M in Theol. Studies, Harvard U., 1987. From lab tech. to chemist Liberty Mut. Rsch., Hopkinton, Mass., 1963-77; asst. to mgr. Rec. Sec. Office Harvard U., 1977-79; sec. Sloan Sch. MIT, 1980-82; owner tech. typing svc. New Castle, N.H., 1982-84; counseling intern Green Pastures Counseling Ctr., Dover, N.H., 1984-85; alcohol educator Freedom From Chem. Dependency Found., Inc., Needham, Mass., 1985-87; dir. devel., editor News Bulletin Freedom From Chem. Dependency Found., Inc., Needham, 1987-88; ptnr. Palmerbrink, Charlestown, Mass., 1989—. Counselor Women's Resource Ctr., Portsmouth, 1980; treas., bd. dirs. Friends of Erich Lindemann Mental Health Ctr.; bd. dirs. Canteen Com. Mem. Older Women's League, Community Assn. Serving Alcoholics, Newton-Needham C. of C., Ctr. for Process Studies. Democrat. Unitarian. Home: 35 Monument Ave Charlestown MA 02129

BRINKER, RUTH MARIE, social services executive; b. Hartford, S.D., May 1, 1922; d. Peter Rudolph and Marie Rose (Wenger) Appel; widowed, June 1974; children: Lisa Flanagan, Sara Dorsey. Asst. book buyer Sears, Roebuck & Co., Chgo., 1945-47; dog columnist San Francisco Examiner, Chronicle, 1948-60; antique shop owner San Francisco, 1960-73; mgr. Meals On Wheels, San Francisco, 1973-86; with food program Trinity Ch., San Francisco, 1980-83; founder, exec. dir. Project Open Hand, San Francisco, 1985—. Recipient Ams. Who Care award Nat. AIDS Network, 1987, For Those Who Care award KRON (NBC affiliate), 1987, Dorothy Langston Human Rights award Cable Car Awards, 1987, Achievement award The Alliance, 1988. Office: Project Open Hand 2720 17th St San Francisco CA 94109

BRINKLEY, BETSY ANNE, purchasing administrator; b. Richmond, Va., May 11, 1959; d. Martha Lou (Caplinger) B. BBA, James Madison U., 1981, MBA, 1983. Procurement analyst Calculon Corp., Germantown, Md., 1983-85; agt. purchasing, subcontracts ORI/Calculon Corp., Rockville, Md., 1986-87; adminstr. contracts ORI/Calculon Corp., Rockville, 1987-89; sr. contracts adminstr. ARC Profl. Svcs. Group subs. ORI/Calculon Corp, Rockville, 1989—. Mem. beautification com. Watkins Mill Homeowner's Assn., Gaithersburg, Md., 1986—. Mem. Nat. Contract Mgmt. Assn. Democrat. Presbyterian. Home: 10232 Millstream Dr Gaithersburg MD 20879 Office: ARC Profl Svcs Group 2440 Research Blvd Rockville MD 20850

BRINKLEY, PHYLLIS, speaker, program artist; b. Madison, Wis., May 28, 1926; d. Reynale R. and Florence (Jarvis) Crosby; B.A. in Speech and English, U. Wis., 1948, postgrad. in speech and oral interpretation of lit., 1949; m. William Malry, Jr., Aug. 5, 1949. Speaker, program artist, 1956—, current programs include First Ladies of our Land, Women of Worth, Portrait of the Lincolns, Mary and Abraham, Stained Glass: Gift of Light; radio artist Focus on Books, Sta. WHA, 1967-72; tchr. speech, 1951-56; interpretative reader, 1950-58. Vol. hosp. aux.; public affairs chmn. Madison Civics Club; pres. Madison Women's Mcpl. Golf League, 1959; chmn. Little Sisters of Sisters of St. Benedict, 1968-69; pres. E.L.C. Women, Our Savior's Luth. Ch., dir. lay ministry. Recipient award of excellence Wis. Fedn. Women's Clubs; named hon. cannoneer St. Louis Civil War Roundtable. Mem. Internat. Platform Assn., Nat. League Am. Pen Women, Phi Beta. Author: Abraham Lincoln and His Wife, Mary: Two Human Beings, 1975; The Lincolns: Targets for Controversy, 1986. Home: 6115 Imperial Dr Rt 2 Waunakee WI 53597

BRINSON, ELAINE KOGER, real estate and securities broker; b. Charleston, S.C., Nov. 21, 1936; d. James Edgar and Hazel Elizabeth (Martin) Koger; m. Thomas Woodrow Brinson, Apr. 6, 1958 (div. 1979); children: Thomas Benjamin, Alise Michele; m. David Morris Wiggs, Mar. 27, 1983. B.A., Furman U., 1957; M.A.T., The Citadel, Charleston, S.C., 1978. Cert. secondary sch. tchr., S.C.; lic. real estate, securities, ins. broker. Tchr., instr. jr. and sr. high sch. and tech. coll., 1972-83; ind. contractor comml. and investment real estate, 1981-84; assoc. realtor/broker Charleston Comml., Inc., 1984-86, Spectrum Properties, Charleston, 1986-87; owner, broker-in-charge Excel Properties, Inc., 1987-89; fin. adviser NYLiF Advisers, Inc., 1990—. Founder, pres. Meml. Soc. of Charleston, 1969—, Givens Found. (local investment group), 1983-84; model Citadel Mall Trend Bd., 1987-88; bd. dirs. My Sister's House, 1988—; active various community activities, programs committee chairmanships; bd. dirs., transp. coord. HELP, 1969-71; rep. Luth. Svc. Ctr., 1967-69; Luther League advisor, nursery chmn., adult Sunday sch. tchr., pres. and v.p. Churchwomen, Faith Luth. Ch., 1962-70. Named Mrs. S.C., 1969; mem. Charleston County Bus. Adv. Bd., 1988—. Mem. Nat. Assn. Realtors, Trident Bd. Realtors, Comml. and Investment Properties Coun. of Charleston, Cert. Comml. Investment, Realtors Nat. Mktg. Inst., NAFE, Am. Congress Real Estate Investors, Am. Soc. Prevention Cruely to Animals, NEA (del. 1983), S.C. Edn. Assn. (rep. 1982-83), Charleston County Edn. Assn. (rep. 1982-83), Charleston Women's Network, Trident C. of C. (mem. leadership coun. 1986-87, legis. task force, mem. Transpn. com. 1987—, chmn. scholarship com. 1987—), Beta Sigma Phi (pres. Alpha Tau chpt. 1965-66, pres. city-wide 1966-67). Avocations: rare coin collecting, gardening, gourmet cooking, sailing, swimming. Lodge: Kiwanis (bd. dirs. North Charleston club, pres. elect 1989, green light com. 1989, 1st v.p. 1989-90). Home: 16 Edenwood Ct Charleston SC 29407 Office: NYLiF Advisers Inc 1 Poston Rd Parkshore Ctr Ste 190 Charleston SC 29407

BRINTON, TINA REE, cardiology product line administrator; b. Claremore, Okla., Apr. 25, 1956; d. Max William Jr. and Jacquline Berneice (Christian) Johns; m. William C. Brinton, Jr., Oct. 18, 1977; children: Matthew Charles, Rebecca Ruth. AS in Nursing, Mo. Western State Coll., 1976, BS in Nursing, 1989. RN, Mo. Staff nurse ICU, St. Joseph (Mo.) Hosp., 1976-80; head nurse, unit coord. Heartland Hosp. East, St. Joseph, 1980-86, dept. dir. med.-surg. nursing unit, 1986-88; dir. cardiology and critical care svcs. Heartland Hosps., St. Joseph, 1988-90, also mem. Speaker's Bur.; adminstr. cardiac svcs. Lehigh Valley Hosp. Ctr., Allentown, Pa., 1990—. Past pres. Humboldt Sch. PTA; mem. properties com., Sunday sch.

tchr. Wyatt Park Bapt. Ch.; pres. Buchanan County div. Am. Heart Assn., also past chmn. ednl. com., mem. Mo. task force on women and cardiology issues. Mem. Am. Acad. Med. Adminstrs., Am. Acad. Cardiovascular Adminstrs., Am. Assn. Critical Care Nurses. Home: 3022 Louise Ct Allentown PA 18103 Office: Lehigh Valley Hosp Ctr 1200 S Cedar Crest Blvd Allentown PA 18103

BRISCOE, JOYCE ELIZABETH, accountant; b. Pampa, Tex., Aug. 28, 1950; d. Joseph Frank and Martha Enna (Cox) Fischer; m. Barry Bernard Briscoe, July 2, 1971; 1 child, Brian. B of Bus. Adminstrn., Tex. Tech. U., 1972, postgrad., 1973. CPA. Acct. Tenneco Chems., Houston, 1974-75; acct. metals div. Duval Corp. subs. Pennzoil Co., Houston, 1976-78, staff acct., 1978, sr. staff acct., 1978-81, mgr. staff acctg., 1981-82, mgr. corp. acctg., 1982-85; mgr. corp. acctg. Pennzoil Sulphur Co., Houston, 1985, mgr. acctg., 1985-86; mgr. oil revenue and royalty Pennzoil Co., Houston, 1986—. Mem. Am. Inst. CPA's, Tex. Soc. CPA's (and Houston chpt.). Office: Pennzoil Co 700 Milam PO Box 2967 Houston TX 77252-2967

BRISCOE, MARY LOUISE, English educator; b. Hutchinson, Kans., May 24, 1937; d. Arthur D. and Charlotte B. B.; B.A., Kans. State U., 1959; M.A., Bowling Green State U., 1961; Ph.D., U. Wis., 1968; 1 dau., Brenna. Asst. prof. U. Wis., Whitewater, 1967-72; coordinator women's studies program U. Pitts., 1972-77, assoc. prof., chmn. dept. English, 1977-85, prof., 1985—, now dean Coll. Arts and Scis. Mem. MLA. Author: Up Against the Wall, Mother, 1971; American Autobiography: A Bibliography, 1945-1980, 1982; assoc. editor: First Person Female American, 1980. Office: Univ of Pitts Office of Dean Coll Arts and Scis Pittsburgh PA 15260

BRISENTINE, CECILIA KAY, educator; b. Ft. Lee, Va., Feb. 10, 1952; d. Robert Allen Jr. and Mercedes (Glinsceg) B. BA, U. Md., 1974; MS, Johns Hopkins U., 1980. Advanced profl. cert., Md. Pharmacy clk. Dart Drug Corp., Landover, Md., 1969-75; Sales clk. Woodward and Lothrop, Landover, 1970; swimming pool supr., operator, lifeguard Offenbacher Aquatics, Rockville, Md., 1971-73; fgn. lang. tchr. Balt. City Pub. Schs., 1974—; sanitarian Prince Georges County Health Dept., Cheverly, Md., 1974-76; assembler Balt.'s Biol. Labs., Hunt Vally, Md., 1977-78; asst. mgr. Princess Shops, Inc., Balt., 1979-81; tchr. Tchr.'s Resource Svc., Pikesville, Md., 1979-80; chmn. fgn. lang. dept. Roland Park Pub. Sch., 1990; field test tchr. Harcourt Brace Jovanivich, Inc., Orlando, Fla., 1987-88; dept. chmn. North East Middle Sch., Balt., 1980-82, co-operating tchr., 1981-82; faculty adv. bds. W. Balt. & North East Middle Schs., Balt., 1977-82. Co-author: (curriculum) Communication Activities, 1984. Mem. Coun. on Fgn. Affairs, Balt., 1988; participant Embassy of the Fed. Republic of Germany, Washington, 1989. Mem. NEA, MSTA, United German-Am. Com. of the U.S.A., Inc., Am. Assn. Tchrs. German, Am. Coun. Tchrs. Fgn. Langs., Md. Fgn. Lang. Assn., Balt. Tchrs. Union, Assn. for Supervision and Curriculum Devel., Johns Hopkins Alumni, Jobs Daus. (past honored Queen), U. Md. Alumni Assn., Kappa Delta Pi. Democrat. Methodist. Office: Roland Park Pub Sch 233 5207 Roland Ave Baltimore MD 21210

BRISSETTE, ESTELLE COOK, travel agency owner; b. Liverpool, N.S., Can., Apr. 15, 1936; d. Walter Henry and Elizabeth (Clow) Cook; m. Paul A. Brissette Jr., Oct. 10, 1953 (div. 1981); children: Gregory, Stephen, Pamela. BA, U. N.C., 1975. Founder, ptnr. Tennis with Love, Ltd., Wilmington, N.C., 1976-79; ptnr. D. Ecols, Wilmington, 1978-80; adminstrv. rep. King's Coll., Charlotte, N.C., 1978-79; mgr. tourism Greater Wilmington C. of C., 1979-82; dir. sales Ramada Inn, Wilmington, 1982-83; account rep. WMFO Radio, Wilmington, 1983-84; exec. dir. Cape Fear Voluntary ActionCtr., Wilmington, 1984; owner, pres. Travel Agts. Internat., Wilmington, 1984—; owner, adinstr. T.A.I. Travel Acad., Wilmington, 1987—; lectr. in field. Mem. Am. Soc. Travel Agts., Greater Wilmington C. of C., Wilmington Execs. Club, Cape Fear Country Club, Landfall Country Club. Home: 1939 Prestwick Ln Wilmington NC 28405 Office: Travel Agents Internat 902 S College Rd Wilmington NC 28403

BRISTOL, LOUISE FITZGERALD, nurse; b. Moorestown, N.J., Mar. 24, 1935; d. Edward William and Katherine (D'Arcy) Fitzgerald; children: John Edward, Eric Charles. RN, W. Jersey Hosp., 1956; BS in Nursing, U. Pa., 1975; MS, U. Del., 1985; postmaster's cert. in nursing adminstrn., Villanova U., 1987. RN, N.J. Nurse West Jersey Hosp., Camden, N.J., 1956-57, Mount Holly (N.J.) Hosp., 1957-59, Good Samaratin Hosp., Syracuse, N.Y., 1959-61, Syracuse VA Med. Ctr., 1961-64; med. staff nurse Phila. VA Med. Ctr., 1967-80, staff nurse ICU, 1969-70, surg. staff nurse ICU, 1970-73, night coord., 1973-78; nurse Wilmington (Del.) VA Med. Ctr., 1980-86; headnurse/supr. Coatesville (PA.) VA Med. Ctr., 1986-89; geriatric gerontol. clin. nurse specialist VA Med. Ctr., Coatesville, Pa., 1989—. Mem. Nurses of the VA (pres. Coatsville chpt., nat. membership com., nat. publicity com.), Am. Nurses Assn. (gerontology coun.), Kansas City, Am. Nurses Assn. (cert.). Roman Catholic. Club: Brandywine Valley Assn. Office: Coatesville Vet Adminstn Med Ctr Coatesville PA 19320

BRISTOL, SHARON LEE, educator; b. Morganton, N.C., Sept. 29, 1942; d. Robert Lambert and Alma Jane (Vickrey) B. BS, U. N.C., Greensboro, 1964; MEd, Johns Hopkins U., 1974. Tchr. Greensboro Pub. Sch., 1964-65, Baltimore County (Md.) Pub. Schs., 1965-78; tchr., co-chmn. phys. edn. dept., dir. women's athletics Woodlawn High Sch., Baltimore County, 1978—; basketball chmn. dist. 6, State of Md., 1974—, mem. state basketball com., 1974—, site chmn. girl's state basketball tournament, 1974—. Poll worker Balt. Dem. Com., 1984, 86, 88. Named Tchr. of Yr., Westview Rotary Club, 1989. Mem. NEA, Md. Tchrs. Assn., Tchrs. Assn. Baltimore County, Md. Athletic Dirs. Assn. (Md. rep. to nat. rules com. 1982, Dist. 6 Athletic Dir. of Yr. award 1990), Women Coaches Assn. Baltimore County (pres. 1970-71), NOW (lobbyist pro choice 1990), NAGWS (basketball rules com. 1982-83, Md. rep. to nat. basketball rules com. 1982). Office: Woodlawn High Sch 1801 Woodlawn Dr Baltimore MD 21207

BRISTOR, VALERIE JAYNE, educator; b. Elyria, Ohio, Dec. 16, 1954; d. Ben Leight and Joyce Minerva (Stackhouse) B. BA, Evangel Coll., 1977; MEd, U. South Ala., 1981; PhD, Ball State U., 1988. Cert. elem. educator. Educator Evangel Christian Sch., Mobile, Ala., 1977-78, Mobile County Pub. Schs., 1978-86; doctoral fellow Ball State U., Muncie, Ind., 1986-88; asst. prof. Fla. Atlantic U., Boca Raton, 1988—; cons. Broward County Pub. Schs., Fort Lauderdale, Fla., 1988—; presenter Fla. Reading Assn., Fort Lauderdale, 1989, Internat. Reading Assn., Atlanta, 1990. Contbr. articles to profl. jours. 010Vol. Gil Carmichael for Gov., Meridian, Miss. Named Most Promising Tchr. Evangel Coll., 1977; recipient Doctoral Fellowship Ball State U., 1986-87, Rsch. Doctoral Fellowship, 1987-88, Elem. Edn. award for Disting. Doctoral Dissertation Ball State U., 1988. Mem. Am. Reading Forum, ASCD, Broward County reading Coun., Fla. Reading Assn., Internat. Reading Assn. (commendation 1984), Kappa Delta Pi (sec. 1983-86). Republican. Home: 8577 NW 61st St Tamarac FL 33321

BRISTOW, JOAN HALBLEIB, healthcare facility administrator; b. Lancaster, Pa., June 15, 1935; d. George S. Halbleib and Barbara E. (Sload) Malone; children: Quentin Daniel, Nadene, Eric Paul, Gretchen. Diploma in nursing, Jefferson Med. Coll., 1956; BS, St. Joseph's Coll., 1982; MA, Rider Coll., 1985. R.N., Pa., N.J. Nurse Cancer Inst., NIH, Bethesda, Md., 1956-58, Blood Bank Inst., NIH, Bethesda, 1958-60; nurse, supr. Jeanes Hosp., Fox Chase, Pa., 1960-64, Mayo Skilled Care, Somerton, Pa., 1970-73; nurse, supr., then patient care coord. St. Mary Hosp., Langhorne, Pa., 1973-77; risk mgmt., quality assurance coord. St. Mary Hosp., 1977-85; dir. risk mgmt., quality assurance St. Francis Med. Ctr., Trenton, N.J., 1985-90; v.p. quality svcs. Community Gen. Hosp., Reading, Pa., 1990—. Contbr. articles to profl. jours. Home: 662A Rose Hollow Dr Yardley PA 19067 Office: Community Gen Hosp 145 N Sixth St Reading PA 19603-1728

BRITE, K. JANE, advertising agency executive. Exec. v.p., group gen. mgr. Young & Rubicam, N.Y.C. Office: Young & Rubicam 285 Madison Ave New York NY 10017*

BRITKO-LEESE, KIMBERLY LYNN, convention services executive; b. Greensburg, Pa., Feb. 21, 1962; d. Edwin D. and Luci Barbara (Natale) B.; m. May 26, 1990. BS, U. N.H., 1984. Front desk clk. Howard Johnson Hotel and Conf. Ctr., Portsmouth, N.H., 1985, reservations mgr., 1985, sales asst., 1986, sales mgr., 1987-88, asst. hotel mgr., 1989-90; conv. svcs. mgr. Clarion Maxwell House Hotel, Nashville, 1990—. Recipient Cert. of Appreciation White House Communications, 1988, 89, U.S. Army Recruiting Battalion, 1988-90, Pub. Safety award Durham N.H. Police Dept., 1983. Mem. NAFE, C. of C., Rotary (asst. sgt. at arms 1988-89, Svc. Merit 1989). Republican. Home: 493 Creek Point Dr Mount Joliet TN 37122 Office: Clarion Maxwell House Hotel 2025 Metro Ctr Blvd Nashville TN 37228

BRITT, CHRISTINA LYNN, management recruiter; b. Fullerton, Calif., Aug. 25, 1962; d. Chester Fay and Virginia Lee (Morris) B. BA in Psychology, UCLA, 1984. Mgr. br. ops. Bank of Am., various locations, 1984-88; asst. v.p., mgmt. recruiter First Interstate Bank, L.A., 1988—. Mem. UCLA Alumni Assn., UCLA Prytanean Assn., Kappa Kappa Gamma Alumni Assn. Republican. Home: 1128 Highview Ave #3 Manhattan Beach CA 90266 Office: First Interstate Bank 707 Wilshire Blvd W33-40 Los Angeles CA 90017

BRITT, ERLINDA ORNELAS, international sales specialist; b. MacAdoo, Tex., Feb. 23, 1939; d. Pablo Carrasco and Nieves (Mercado) Ornelas; m. Arnold J. Britt (div. Aug. 1975); children: Ron, Byron, James, Tolmy. BA, N.C. State U., 1972; MBA, Tampa Coll., 1989. Cert. tchr., N.C., Fla. Tchr. Cumberland County Schs., Fayetteville, N.C., 1972-75, Hillsborough County Schs., Tampa, Fla., 1975-83; specialist internat. sales McNichols Co., Tampa, 1983—; cons. Field Crest Mills, Whiteville, N.C., 1972-73. Columnist Tampa Bay Bus., 1988-89. Mem. com. pastoral search 1st Baptist Ch., Tampa, 1988, com. pub. relations, 1989; internat. homemaker NATO, 1956-75. Mem. Tampa Bay Trade Coun. (trade task force 1986-88), Grandmother Club (chmn. sunshine 1988-89). Republican. Home and Office: Ornelas Cons 305 S Westland Tampa FL 33606

BRITT, GEORGETTA LEE CULTON, corporate executive; b. Junction City, Ky., Feb. 21, 1932; d. James Thomas and Anabel (Nevius) Culton; m. William Edward Britt, Dec. 25, 1955; children: James Edward, Susan Lee, Laura Anne. Degree in acctg., Spencerian Comml. Coll., Louisville, 1952. Acct. George C. Baird & Co., Augusta, Ga., 1963-65, E.H. Bridger, Raleigh, N.C., 1970-72; acct., asst. sec. Saleeby, Inc., Raleigh, 1972-74; corp. sec.-treas. Saieed Constrn. Co., Inc., Raleigh, 1974-77; sec.-treas., office mgr. Associated Fire Protection, Inc., Raleigh, 1977-88; owner Acctg. by George, Raleigh, 1988—. Co-chair Precinct for Rep. Party, Raleigh, 1970-73. Mem. Nat. Assn. Accts., Am. Soc. Women Accts. (charter), Nat. Assn. Women in Constrn. (bd. dirs. Raleigh chpt. 1976-77, 84-85, treas. 1977-78). Presbyterian. Avocations: swimming, dance, bicycling, bridge. Home: 425 Millbrook Rd Raleigh NC 27609 Office: Acctg by George 425 Millbrook Rd Raleigh NC 27609

BRITT, JULIE, freelance editor, designer; b. Metuchen, N.J.. Cert. in Graphic/Advt. and Fine Art, Parson's Sch. Design, N.Y., 1958. Asst. to coms. The Fashion Group, N.Y.C., 1960-63; asst. editor, fashion looks editor Glamour Mag., N.Y.C., 1963-73; fashion settings editor Harper's Bazaar, N.Y.C., 1973-75; freelance editorial stylist, producer, conceptual designer N.Y.C., 1975—. Home: 12 E 97th New York NY 10029 Office: 787 Madison #3R New York NY 10021

BRITT, MAISHA DORRAH, protective services official; b. S.C.; d. Charles Joseph Britt and Versena (Kennedy) Dorrah; m. W. Benjamin Williams, Dec. 14, 1963 (div. June 1976); children: Terri Rochelle, Trina Michelle. AS, BS, Phila Coll. Textiles and Sci.; MA, Antioch U., Phila., 1986. Cert. in Electronic Surveillance. Physician's asst. Dr. Leonard B. Segal, Phila., 1973-76; police officer Phila. Police Dept., 1976-79; sgt. county detective Phila. Dist. Atty's Office, 1979-90; spl. agt. Bur. Consumer Protection Office of Atty. Gen., Phila., 1990—; founder, dir. Creative Awareness Workshop, Phila., 1978—. Sec. bd. Horizon House, Phila., 1988—; vol. Women Against Abuse, Phila., 1983—, youth adv. New Gethsemane Bapt. Ch., Phila., 1978—; mem. bd. trustees Ctr. for Literacy, 1990—. Recipient award of Appreciation Dobbins High Sch. Alumni Assn., 1985. Mem. Am. Soc. for Indsl. Security, County Detectives Assn., Fraternal Order of Police, Internat. Police Assn., Internat. Assn. of Women Police, Nat. Womens Hall of Fame, Nat. Assn. Chiefs of Police, Bus. and Profl. Women's Club. Republican. Office: Office Atty Gen Commonwealth of Pa 1009 State Office Bldg Philadelphia PA 19130

BRITTON, ALICE FAYE, secretarial services company owner, executive; b. St. Louis, Aug. 6, 1952; d. Rufus and Lena (Richard) Manuel; children: LeAnn DaShon, Heather Nicole. Student, Florissant Valley Coll., 1971-73, Harris Stowe State Coll., 1973-75. Inventory sec. St. Louis Bd. Edn., 1973-77; engring. sec. McDonnell Douglas Corp., St. Louis, 1977-87; exec., dir., owner Britton Secretarial Svcs., St. Louis, 1987—. Mem. NAFE, St. Louis Met. Minority Supplier Coun., Nat. Assn. Women Bus. Owners, Mothers Against Drunk Drivers, Sigma Gamma Rho. Democrat. Home: 1233 Walt Bowers Ln Saint Louis MO 63106 Office: Britton Secretarial Svcs 1948A Benton St PO Box 7917 Saint Louis MO 63106

BRITTON, BARBARA ANN, medical technologist; b. Ft. Knox, Ky., Sept. 15, 1959; d. Cleveland and Evelyn (Graham) B. Student, Coll. of William and Mary, 1977-78; BA in Biology, Coker Coll., 1982; cert. med. tech., McLeod Regional Med. Ctr., 1982; postgrad., Med. USC, 1989—; BS in Nursing. Med. technologist McLeod Regional Med. Ctr., Florence, S.C., 1982, Georgetown (S.C.) Meml. Hosp., 1982-83; salesperson Pantry, Inc., Maryville, S.C., 1983; med. technologist Trident Regional Med. Ctr., Charleston, S.C., 1983—, Colleton Regional Hosp., Walterboro, S.C., 1985—. Organist, pianist Sandy Grove Missionary Bapt. Ch., Myrtle Beach, S.C., 1982-83, Union Bapt. Ch., Charleston, 1983-88; organist Lovely Mountain Bapt. Ch., Charleston, 1988-89. Med. USC fellow in nursing, 1989—. Mem. NAACP (awards), Young Women's Missionaries, Zeta Phi Beta. Democrat. Baptist. Home: 1742 Sam Rittenberg Blvd #19A Charleston SC 29407 Office: Trident Regional Med Ctr 9330 Medical Pla Dr Charleston SC 29418-9195

BRITTON, MARGUERITE ANN, public relations executive; b. Chgo., July 7, 1937; d. Leonard C. and Marguerite (Walther) Phillips; m. Harold F. Britton, Sept. 23, 1961; children: Cynthia, Joseph, Marjorie, John, James, Christine. BA, Mundelein Coll., 1959. Feature editor The News, Skokie, Ill., 1958-62; freelance writer, editor, 1962-82; staff 48th Ward Alderman, Chgo., 1984-85, Marge Britton Pub. Rels. Svcs., Chgo., 1985—; dir. pub. rels. North Side Real Estate Bd., Chgo., 1983—; cons. Edgewater/Uptown Builders Assn., Chgo., 1985—, Halsted River Triangle Assn., Chgo., 1987—, Ind. Schs. Fair, Chgo., 1988—. Contbr. articles to newspapers. Mgr. citizens for Maion Volini, Chgo., 1972-84; v.p., chmn. Edgewater Community Coun., Chgo., 1974-85; pres. Lakewood/Balmoral Residents Coun., Chgo., 1970-72; organizer taxpayers United for Fairness, Chgo., 1989. Mem. Publicity Club of Chgo. Democrat. Roman Catholic. Office: Pub Rels Svcs 5414 N Magnolia Chicago IL 60640

BRITTON, MARLA LYNN, real estate broker; b. Moline, Ill., Mar. 28, 1960; d. Clement Otis and Constance Ann (Little) Sutton; m. Dan Michael Britton, May 12, 1984; children: Alyssa Michelle, Katlyn Christine, Kayla Christine. BS, U. Ill., 1982. Constrn. laborer Clement Sutton Corp., Westby, Wis., 1973-78, sec. corp. hdqrs., 1978-82, gen. mgr. mfg. div., 1982-85, v.p. heading real estate div., 1985—. Active Prairie Women's Civic Club. Mem. Wis. Assn. Assessing Officers, Westby Bus. Assn. Methodist. Office: Clement Sutton Corp 210 High Echo Ln Westby WI 54667

BRITZ, DIANE EDWARD, investment company executive; b. York, Pa., June 15, 1952; d. Everett Frank and Billie Jacqueline (Sherrill) B.; m. Marcello Lotti, Sept. 9, 1978 (dec. Apr. 1990); children: Ariane Elizabeth, Samantha Alexis. BA, Duke U., 1974; MBA, Columbia U., 1982. Asst. mgr. Columbia Artists, N.Y.C., 1974-76; gen. mgr. Eastern Music Festival, Greensboro, N.C., 1977-78; v.p. Britz Cobin, N.Y.C., 1979-82; pres. Pan Oceanic Mgmt., Inc., N.Y.C., 1983—; also bd. dirs Pan Oceanic Mgmt., N.Y.C.; pres. Pan Oceanic Advisors, Ltd., N.Y.C., 1988—, also bd. dirs; bd. dirs. QualiTech, Inc. Bd. advisors, Turtle Bay Music Sch.; class chmn. Duke U. Ann. Fund Dr. Mem. NAFE, Fin. Women's Assn. (bd. dirs.), Caramoor Garden Guild (bd. dirs.), Columbia Bus. Sch. Club of N.Y. (reunion chmn.), Doubles Club, Wings Club, LaFayette Club. Mem. Soc. of Friends. Office: Pan Oceanic Mgmt Ltd 122 E 42d St Ste 205 New York NY 10168

BROADBENT, AMALIA SAYO CASTILLO, graphic arts designer; b. Manila, May 28, 1956; came to U.S., 1980, naturalized, 1985; d. Conrado Camilo and Eugenia de Guzman (Sayo) Castillo; m. Barrie Noel Broadbent, Mar. 14, 1981; children: Charles Noel Castillo, Chandra Noel Castillo. BFA, U. Santo Tomas, 1978; postgrad. Acad. Art Coll., San Francisco, Alliance Francaise, Manila, Karilagan Finishing Sch., Manila, Manila Computer Ctr.; BA, Maryknoll Coll., 1972. Designer market research Unicorp Export Inc., Makati, Manila, 1975-77; asst. advt. mgr. Dale Trading Corp., Makati, 1977-78; artist, designer, pub. relations Resort Hotels Corp., Makati, 1978-81; prodn. artist CYB/Young & Rubicam, San Francisco, 1981-82; freelance art dir. Ogilvy & Mather Direct, San Francisco, 1986; artist, designer, owner A.C. Broadbent Graphics, San Francisco, 1982—. Works include: Daing na Isda, 1975, (Christmas coloring) Pepsi-Cola, 1964 (Distinctive Merit cert.), (children's books) UNESCO, 1973 (cert.). Pres. Pax Romana, Coll. of Architecture and Fine Arts, U. Santo Tomas, 1976-78, chmn. cultural sect., 1975; v.p. Atelier Cultural Soc., U. Santo Tomas, 1975-76; mem. Makati Dance Troupe, 1973-74. Recipient Merit cert., Inst. Religion, 1977. Mem. Alliance Francaise de San Francisco, Nat. Assn. Female Execs. Roman Catholic. Office: AC Broadbent Graphics 407 Jackson St Ste 302 San Francisco CA 94111

BROADHEAD, LESA ROGERS, performing artist; b. Conway, S.C., Sept. 17, 1956; d. William Barry Rogers and Carolyn (Inman) Lyons; m. Richard Dowell Barrow III, May 20, 1978 (div. 1983); m. Geoffrey David Broadhead, Aug. 15, 1987. BFA, East Carolina U., 1982; MFA, So. Meth. U., 1985. Ballet instr. La. State U., Baton Rouge, 1985-86; dance instr. Huntingdon Coll., Montgomery, Ala., 1986-87, Kent (Ohio) State U., 1988—, Wadsworth (Ohio) Sch. of Ballet, 1989—; artistic dir. La. State U. Ballet Ensemble, Baton Rouge, 1985-86, The Company Dancers, Montgomery, Ala., 1986-87; dancer Cleveland Opera, 1988-89. choreographer (modern dance), 1987, 88, 89. Meadows Sch. of the Arts scholar So. Meth. U., 1984. Mem. Nat. Dance Assn., Indian Music Cir. (bd. dirs.). Republican. Meth.

BROADWATER, SHIRLEY MARIE, psychologist; b. Rosemont, W.Va., May 8, 1937; d. Robert Brooks and Irma Pearl (Wimer) Riffle; children: Cheryl Lynn Daugherty Johnson, Robert L. Daugherty Jr.; m. J. Rodney Broadwater, Aug. 28, 1982. Student, Indiana U. Pa., 1965, 66, U. Pitts., Johnstown, Pa., 1966-67, 68-69; AB in Secondary Edn. with highest honors, West Liberty State Coll., 1972; MS in Psychology, Shippensburg (Pa.) U., 1983. Cert. secondary tchr., Pa. Psychotherapist Contemporary Psychol. Svcs., Chambersburg, Pa., 1984-88; pvt. practice psychology, Chambersburg, 1988—; psychologist to dep. coroner, Chambersburg, 1988—. Vol. Piney Mountain Nursing Home, Fayetteville, Pa., 1981; telephone worker Contact Teleministry 24 Hour Hotline, Chambersburg, 1981-84, support worker, 1984—; bd. dirs. Family Health Svcs., Chambersburg, 1984-89. Mem. APA (assoc.), Pa. Psychol. Assn., Chambersburg C. of C. Republican. Methodist. Office: 394 Floral Ave Chambersburg PA 17201

BROADWAY, NANCY RUTH, landscape design and construction company executive; b. Memphis, Tenn., Dec. 20, 1946; d. Charlie Sidney and Patsy Ruth (Meadows) Adkins. BS in Biology and Sociology cum laude, Memphis State U., 1969; postgrad., Tulane U., 1969-70; MS in Horticulture, U. Calif.-Davis, 1976. Lic. landscape contractor, Calif. Claims adjuster Mass. Mut. Ins., San Francisco, 1972-73; community garden coord. City of Davis, Calif., 1976; supr. seed propagation Bordier's Wholesale Nursery, Santa Ana, Calif., 1976-78; owner, founder Both Co., Both Landscape Constrn. & Design Mgmt., 1978-88, Design & Man Consultare, 1988—. NDEA fellow Tulane U., 1969-70. Fellow Am. Hort. Soc.; mem. Nat. Assn. Gen. Contractors, Calif. Native Plant Soc., Stockton C. of C. Democrat. Office: Desert Samaritan Med Ctr Mesa CA 95254 Address: 520 Stagg Ln Santa Cruz CA 95062

BROADWAY, ROXANNE MEYER, entomology educator, researcher; b. Maywood, Calif., Mar. 31, 1951; d. Philip and Sylvia (Pelta) Meyer; m. James Edwin Broadway, Feb. 29, 1984. BA, UCLA, 1973; PhD, U. Calif., Davis, 1985. Lab technician VA Hosp., Northridge, Calif., 1973-77; postdoctoral researcher U. Calif., Davis, 1985-86, Wash. State U., Pullman, 1986-87; asst. prof. Cornell U., N.Y. State Agrl. Expt. Sta., Geneva, 1987 --. Patentee (pending) porteinase inhibitory agents; Contbr. articles to profl. jours. Mem. AAAS, Entomological Soc. Am. Office: NY State Agr Exp Sta Entomology Dept Geneva NY 14456

BROCK, BEVERLY EUGENIE, director of media services and photography; b. Houston, Aug. 3, 1950; d. Howard George and Milady Elizabeth (Skalnik) B. BFA, Stephen F. Austin State U., Nacogdoches, Tex., 1970-74, MA, 1974-75. Lic. broadcast endorsement, 1972; Nikon Sch. Photography, 1985. Gen. mgr. Sta. KSAU-FM, instr. radio, TV and film Stephen F. Austin State U., Nacogdoches, Tex., 1974-76; dir. pub. info. Tex. A&M U., Galveston, Tex., 1977-79; from asst. media specialist to mgr. communications, pub. affairs Galveston (Tex.) Coll., 1979-88, dir. media services, photography, 1988—; mem. Stephen F. Austin State U. A Capella Choir, Nacogdoches, Tex., 1971-73, sponsor, dir., Galveston Coll. Student Newspaper, "The Barometer," 1982-85; speaker Galveston Independent Sch. Dist. Speakers Bur., 1983-88. Author: Standard Operating Procedure for Ednl. Radio Sta., KSAU-FM, 1974. Chief photographer American Cancer Soc., 1983-85, Galveston Sesquicentennial Com. 1986, American Heart Assn., 1986—; mem. U.S. Postal Service Council, Galveston C. of C. Edn. Com., 1986-88, United Way, West End Bus. Div., 1987—. Mem. Nat. Council on Community Relations, Tex. Intercollegiate Press Assn., Profl. Photographers of Am., NAFE, Mu Phi Epsilon Internat. Music Sorority, Humane Soc. of the US, Press Club of Galveston County, Distributive Edn. Clubs of Am., American Cetacean Soc., Cousteau Soc. Republican. Home: 446 Buoy Dr Webster TX 77598 Office: Galveston Coll 4015 Ave Q Galveston TX 77550

BROCK, BRENDA GAIL, association executive, word processing consultant; b. Peoria, Ill., Jan. 25, 1950; d. Charles Franklin and Mary Jeanette (Hardy) Hendrickson; m. Hal Wayne Brock Sr.; children: Monica Rae, Hal Wayne Jr., Nicholas Scott. AS, Ill. Cen. Coll., 1974; student Inst. Orgn. Mgmt., 1986—. Adminstrv. asst. Greater Detroit C. of C., 1978; with Detroit Compact. Author Supervisors Guide to Word Processing, 1980, Word Processing Training Course, 1983. Mem. Phi Theta Kappa. Avocations: baseball, reading, writing. Home: 3108 Castle Ct Sterling Heights MI 48310 Office: Detroit Compact 2751 E Jefferson Detroit MI 48207

BROCK, JUDITH ANNE, marketing professional, magazine editor; b. McAlester, Okla., July 8, 1950; d. Eddie W. and Irene Laverne (Hicks) Lee; m. James Lavern Hodge, Jan. 30, 1970 (div. Dec. 1977); 1 child, Joshua Lee. AA in Bus., Crowder Coll., 1972; student, Mo. So. State Coll., Boston U., 1988. Pres. J.L.I., Neosho, Mo., 1981—; v.p., dir. mktg. The Brock Corp., Neosho, 1982—; founder, editor In... Joplin (Mo.) Metro mag., 1984—; founding pres. The Apricotery, Neosho and Boston, 1987—; founder The Epicenter, Joplin, 1987—; dir. mktg. Techmark Ltd., Neosho, 1987—; bd. dirs. Ozark Ctr., Joplin, 1983, Am. Heart Assn., Joplin, 1987. inventor card games Josh, 1982, E.W. Lee, 1988. Pres. Neosho PTA, 1982-84; Cub Scout leader troop 34, 1982-84; host parent Internat. Ednl. Found., 1983-88; pres. Gifted Assn., Neosho, 1985-86. Named Woman of Yr., Beta Sigma Phi, Neosho, 1983-84; recipient Bringing Out Your Best award Budweiser Light, 1983. Mem. Am. Mktg. Assn. (exec.), Neosho C. of C. (retail dir. 1983-84), Kansas City Mktg. Assn., Joplin Advt. Club (Addy Award of Merit 1987, Addy Award of Excellence 1988), Mensa Internat. Club, Soroptimist Club (treas. 1984-85). Home: 23 Brimmer St TH 1 Boston MA 02108

BROCK, KATHERINE MIDDLETON, publisher; b. Keokuk, Iowa, June 3, 1938; d. Thomas Michael and Eleanor Mary (Serat) Middleton; m. Thomas Dale Brock, Feb. 20, 1971; children: Emily Katherine, Brian Thomas. BA, Vassar Coll., 1960; MA, U. Calif., Berkeley, 1963; PhD, U. Mass., 1967. Scientific asst. Tech. U., Trondheim, Norway, 1963-64; asst. prof. San Francisco State Coll., 1967-70; postdoctoral fellow Ind. U., Bloomington, 1970-71; rsch. assoc. U. Wis., Madison, 1971-73; mng. editor, v.p. Sci. Tech. Pub., Inc., Madison, 1973—. Author: (with others) Basic Microbiology with Applications, 1973. Nancy Skinner Clark fellowship Vassar Coll., 1960. Mem. Sierra Club (trip leader 1969—). Home: 1227 Dartmouth Rd Madison WI 53705 Office: Sci Tech Pubs Inc 701 Ridge St Madison WI 53705

BROCK, MARY ANNE, research biologist, consultant; b. Aurora, Ill., June 29, 1932; d. Paul Peter and Helen Anna (Mattas) B. BA, Grinnell Coll., 1954; MA, Harvard U., 1956, PhD, 1959. Teaching fellow Harvard U., Cambridge, Mass., 1954-58; rsch. assoc. Harvard Med. Sch., Boston, 1959-60; rsch. biologist Nat. Inst. Aging, NIH, Balt., 1960—; vis. scientist Stanford U., Calif., 1977; cons. NASA, 1981—. Contbr. articles to profl. jours. Bd. dirs. Cross Keys Condo Assn., Balt., 1980-85. Fellow Gerontol. Soc. Am.; mem. AAAS, Cryobiology Soc. (bd. govs. 1973-76, sec. 1971-72), Chesapeake Soc. Electron Microscopy (council 1979-82), Am. Soc. Cell Biology, Am. Soc. Zoologists, Internat. Hibernation Soc., Soc. Rsch. Biogl. Rhythms, Acad. Sci., Internat. Soc. Chronobiology, Sigma Xi, Phi Beta Kappa. Office: Gerontology Rsch Ctr NIA NIH 4940 Eastern Ave Baltimore MD 21224

BROCKER, SANDRA LEE POTISH, nurse administrator; b. Scranton, Pa., Mar. 20, 1947; d. John and Joan (Casoria) Potish; m. Marc Tadeu Bocker, Aug. 8, 1982; 1 child, Lindsay M. RN, Robert Packer Hosp. Sch. of Nursing, Sayre, Pa., 1967; BSN, Evangel Coll., 1976; MBA, Mercer U., 1982. RN, Ga., Pa., Conn., Calif., Mo. Staff nurse Robert Packer Hosp., Sayre, Pa., 1968-69; staff nurse, ICU and recovery room Greenwich (Conn.) Hosp., 1969-70; head nurse, program coord., acting asst. dir. of nursing Silver Hill Found., New Canaan, Conn., 1970-78; v.p. nursing Ridgeview Inst., Smyrna, Ga., 1978—; clin. placement coord. Ga. Baptist Sch. of Nursing, Atlanta, 1978—. Fund raiser, health fairs Am. Lung Assn., Smyrna, 1989. Mem. Am. Nurses Assn., Ga. Nurses Assn., Ga. Hosp. Assn. Nursing Execs., Am. Hosp. Assn. Nursing Execs., NAFE. Office: Ridgeview Inst 3995 S Cobb Dr Smyrna GA 30080

BROCKMANN, HELEN JANE, zoologist, educator; b. Louisville, Feb. 25, 1947; d. Maxwell Curtis and Helen (Easton) B. BS, Tufts U., 1967; MS, U. Wis., 1972, PhD, 1976. Asst. prof. dept. zoology U. Fla., Gainesville, 1976-83, assoc. prof. dept. zoology, 1983-89, prof. dept. zoology, 1989—; vis. rsch. biologist Princeton U., 1985; postdoctoral fellow Oxford (Eng.) U., 1977-78. Contbr. chpts. to books, articles to profl. jours. NSF grantee, 1983-86, 1990—; Harry Frank Guggenheim Found. grantee, 1978-80. Mem. Animal Behavior Soc. (treas. 1982-88, pres. elect 1-89—), Soc. Study Evolution (assoc. editor 1987-90), United Faculty Fla. (chpt. pres. 1989—). Home: 415 NW 19th St Gainesville FL 32603 Office: Dept Zoology U Fla Bartram Hall Gainesville FL 32611

BROCKWAY, LAURIE SUE, journalist; b. N.Y.C., Dec. 18, 1956; d. Lee L. and Shirley Ruth B. AA, Laguardia Community Coll., 1978; student, Hunter Coll., 1978-81. Features editor The Bklyn. Paper, 1978-81; editor-in-chief The Iniator, N.Y.C., 1982-83; pub., editor The Transformer, N.Y.C., 1983-84; co-producer, writer The Brockway Good News Report, N.Y.C., 1984-85; N.Y. bur. chief Women's News, N.Y.C., 1983-85, Manhattan corr., 1985—; account supr., Brockway Assocs., Inc., N.Y.C., 1985-88; free lance editor, writer, 1988—; co-producer, writer, host, news anchor/writer, moderator This Is the New Age, The One Show, Whole Life Expo. Contbr. articles to mags., newspapers. Recipient LaGuardia Meml. award, 1978, Laguardia Student Coun. scholar, 1978, Expository Writing award, LaGuardia English Dept., 1978.

BRODBECK, NANCY ELIZABETH, environmental engineer; b. Bakersfield, Calif., Mar. 9, 1962; d. William Charles and Mary Ellen (Hancock) B. BS in Petroleum Engring., U. Okla., 1984. Cert. engr. intern, Okla. Petroleum engr. Liberty Nat. Bank and Trust Co., Oklahoma City, 1984-86, Lindsey & Miller, Inc., Oklahoma City, 1987-89; environ. engr. G & E Engring. Inc., Oklahoma City, 1989—. Named Nat. Merit finalist Nat. Merit Scholarship Corp., 1980; Univ. scholar U. Okla., 1980. Mem. Soc. Petroleum Engr. (jr.), Delta Gamma (1st v.p. Okla. City alumnae chpt. 1988—). Methodist. Home: 10224 Eastlake Dr Oklahoma City OK 73162 Office: G & E Engring Inc 5601 NW 72nd Ste 154 Oklahoma City OK 73132

BRODER, PATRICIA JANIS, art historian, writer; b. N.Y.C., Nov. 22, 1935; d. Milton W. and Rheba (Mantell) Janis; m. Stanley H. Broder, Jan. 22, 1959; children: Clifford James, Peter Howard, Helen Anna. Student, Smith Coll., 1953-54; B.A., Barnard Coll., Columbia U., 1957; postgrad., Rutgers U., 1962-64. Stock brokerage trainee A.M. Kidder & Co., N.Y.C., 1958; registered rep. Thomson & McKinnon, N.Y.C., 1959-61; ind. registered investment advisor, 1962-64; art cons.; art investment advisor. Art cons., art investment advisor; writer on art history; books include Bronzes of the American West (Best Art Book award Nat. Acad. Western Art, 1975), Great Paintings of the Old American West, American Indian Painting and Sculpture, Taos: A Painter's Dream (Western Heritage Wrangler award for best art book Nat. Cowboy Hall of Fame and Western Heritage Ctr., 1980, Art Book award Border Regional Libr. Assn., 1981), Hopi Painting: The World of the Hopis, Dean Cornwell: Dean of Illustrators, The American West: The Modern Vision (Western award 1984, Trustees award Cowboy Hall of Fame 1984), Shadows on Glass: The Indian World of Ben Wittick, 1990. Recipient Herbert Adams Meml. medal for svc. to Am. sculpture Nat. Sculpture Soc., 1975, Western Heritage Wranglers award for best article on Am. west Nat. Cowboy Hall of Fame and Western Heritage Ctr., 1975, Trustees Gold medal for outstanding contbn. to the west Nat. Acad. Western Art, 1984. Mem. Western History Assn., AAUW. Home: 488 Long Hill Dr Short Hills NJ 07078

BRODERICK, GERTRUDE CATHERINE CREEDON, retired educator, administrator; b. Boston, July 3, 1926; d. William Joseph and Gertrude C. (Boylen) Creedon; m. Thomas Francis Broderick, May 2, 1970 (dec. Aug. 23, 1989). AB, Emmanuel Coll., 1948; MA, Harvard U., 1949; postgrad., Boston U., 1965-66, U. Hartford, 1967-68. Tchr. New Britain (Conn.) Pub. Schs., 1949-51; tchr., housemaster Newton (Mass.) Pub. Schs., 1951-67; asst. supt. of schs. Southington (Conn.) Pub. Schs., 1967-70; chair, dept. edn. Emmanuel Coll., Boston, 1970-74; ednl. specialist Mass. Dept. Edn., Quincy, 1974-89; asst. curriculum and instruction Watertown (Mass.) High Sch., 1988-89; ret., 1989; tchr. part time Franciscan Children's Hosp. and Rehab. Ctr., Brighton, Mass., 1989—; com. mem. Curriculum and Instl. Commn., Watertown, Mass., 1989—, Guidance Adv. Commn., Watertown, 1989—, Structure and Facilities Commn., Watertown, 1989—. Bd. dirs. Coun. on Aging, Watertown, 1989—; v.p. Watertown LWV, bd. dirs. 1984—, chair edn. 1984—; moderator Candidates Night, Watertown; co-chair St. Patrick's Synod, Watertown, 1988. Roman Catholic.

BRODERICK, PATRICIA CATHERINE, school psychologist, educator; b. Phila., Oct. 13, 1947; d. Louis B. and Helen (Yurkanin) Mezalick; m. Robert D. Broderick, Oct. 4, 1975; children: Evan, Meredith. BA, Alvernia Coll., Reading, Pa., 1972; MA in Counseling Psychology, Villanova U., 1978; PhD, Temple U., 1983. Cert. tchr., in counseling, sch. psychology, Pa.; lic. clin. psychologist, Pa. Tchr. Mitchell-Main Line Day Sch., Haverford, Pa., 1974-76; mem. adj. faculty, researcher Villanova (Pa.) U., 1982—; sch. psychologist Lower Merion Sch. Dist., Gladwyne, Pa., 1985, Wissahickon Sch. Dist., Ambler, Pa., 1986—; researcher, cons. Day Care Orgn. NE Pa., Phila., 1987-90. Contbr. articles to psychol. jours. Grantee Spanish Heritage Assn., 1974. Mem. APA, Phila. Assn. Neuropsychologists. Home: 277 Huntsman Ln Blue Bell PA 19422

BRODKIN, ADELE RUTH MEYER, psychologist; b. N.Y.C., July 8, 1934; d. Abraham J. and Helen (Honig) Meyer; m. Roger Harrison Brodkin, Jan. 26, 1957; children: Elizabeth Anne, Edward Stuart. BA, Sarah Lawrence Coll., 1956; MA, Columbia U., 1959; PhD, Rutgers U., 1977. Lic. psychologist, N.J. Sch. psychologist pub. schs., River Edge, Norwood, 1961-66, Morristown, Chatham, N.J., 1967-73; cons. psychologist United Hosp. Newark, 1973; assoc. dir. Infant Child Devel. Ctr. St. Barnabas Med. Ctr., Livingston, N.J., 1977-79; clin. asst. prof. dept. psychiatry U. Medicine and Dentistry N.J., Newark, 1979-90, assoc. prof., 1990—; vis. scholar Hastings (N.Y.) Ctr. for Life scsi., 1979; mem. Essex County Mental Health Adv. Bd., Essex City, N.J., 1985-87; cons. Scholastic, Inc., 1988—. Co-author: The Meaning of Psychotherapy in the Teacher's Life and Work, 1962; author, producer: (videotape documentary) Competing Commitments, 1984 (Best Ednl. Videotape award N.J. Cable); co-author, producer: Passage to Physicianhood, 1985, The Insidious Epidemic, 1986; columnist Between Tchr. and Parent, Pre-K Today mag., 1988—, You and Today's Child, Instructa Mag., 1990—. Columbia U. Adelaide M. Ayer scholar, 1961; grad. fellow Rutgers U., 1976-77, Yale U. postdoctoral fellow, 1978-79, Rutgers U., Princeton U. postdoctoral fellow, 1981-83. Fellow Am. Orthopsychiat. Assn.; mem. Am. Psychol. Assn., N.J. Psychol. Assn. (Psychol. Recognition 1982, 86, 90), Am. Sociol. Assn., N.Y. Acad. Scis. Jewish. Home: 520 White Oak Ridge Rd Short Hills NJ 07078

BRODMAN, ESTELLE, retired educator, librarian; b. N.Y.C., June 1, 1914; d. Henry and Nettie (Sameth) B. A.B., Cornell U., 1935; B.S., Columbia U., 1936, M.S., 1943, Ph.D., 1954; post-doctoral study, UCLA, 1959, U. N.Mex., 1960; D.Sc. (hon.), U. Ill., 1975. Asst. librarian Cornell U. Sch. Nursing Library, N.Y.C., 1936-37; asst. med. librarian Columbia Libraries, N.Y.C., 1937-49; asst. librarian for reference services Nat. Library Medicine, Washington, 1949-61; librarian, assoc. prof. med. history Washington U. Sch. Medicine, St. Louis, 1961-64; librarian, prof. med. history Washington U. Sch. Medicine, 1964-81, librarian, prof. med history emerita, 1981—; documentation expert UN Tech. Assistance program UN, Central Family Planning Inst., New Delhi, 1967-68; documentation expert WHO, New Delhi, 1970, Manila, 1983; documentation expert ECAFE, Bangkok, 1973, AID, 1975, UNFPA, 1976; Mem. Pres.'s Commn. Libraries, 1968-70, Mo. Gov.'s Adv. Commn. Libraries, 1977-78; study sect. NIH, 1971-75, chmn., 1973-75; instr. Columbia U., 1946-52, 84, Cath. U. Am., 1957; vis. prof. Keio U., Tokyo, 1962, U. Mo., 1971, 73, Washington U. Med. Sch., 1964-81. Author: Development of Medical Bibliography, 1954, Bibliographical Lists for Medical Libraries, 1950; Editor: Bull. Med. Library Assn, 1947-57; guest editor N.J. Medicine, 1988. Mem. Med. Library Assn. (spl. award 1957, Noyes award 1971, Gottlieb award 1977, Frank B. Rogers info. advancement award 1985; pres. 1964-65), Spl. Libraries Assn. (dir. 1949-52, John Cotton Dana award 1981), Am. Assn. History Medicine, N.J. Med. History Soc. (treas. 1985-88, v.p. 1988—). Home: 19-09 Meadow Lakes Hightstown NJ 08520

BRODNAX, MARGARET O'BRYAN, educator; b. Ark., Sept. 26, 1932; d. Edgar Ray and Willie Bell (Graves) O'Bryan; m. Charles Teddy Brodnax; children: Mary Margaret, Faulkner Eugene (dec. Nov. 1989). BS in Edn., U. Cen. Ark., 1954; MA, Tex. Christian U., 1959, PhD, 1968. Tchr. English Pine Bluff (Ark.) Jr. High Sch., 1954-56; instr. English Tex. Tech. U., Lubbock, 1959-60; instr., asst. prof. English N.E. La. U., Monroe, 1960-69; prof. English Samford U., Birmingham, Ala., 1969—; exchange prof. English Anhui Normal U., Wuhu, Anhui, China, 1989; vis. fellow in English Harvard U., Cambridge, Mass., 1979. Contbr. articles to profl. jours.; editor: Ala. Writers Conclave Jour., 1984—; editorial bd. Delta Kappa Gamma Internat. Soc. Jour. for Tchrs., 1988—. Recipient Univ. fellowship, Tex. Christian U., Fort Worth, 1966-68. Mem. MLA, Southeastern Medieval Assn., Midwest Medieval Assn., Ala. Coll. English Tchrs. Assn., Ala. Coun. Tchrs. English, AAUW, Delta Kappa Gamma (pres. Beta Upsilon chpt. 1986-88, Beta state scholarship, 1979). Episcopalian. Office: Samford U Box 2205 Birmingham AL 35229

BRODRICK, LOIS HUNTER, real estate broker; b. Altoona, Pa., Aug. 31, 1920; d. Frank Mathew and Faye (McKague) Hunter; m. Richard Boyd Brodrick, Apr. 20, 1946 (dec.); children—Victoria, Barrie Bea. BA, Pa. State U.-State College, 1942; postgrad. U. Calif.-Berkeley, extensions, 1978. Lic. real estate broker. Prin., Brodrick Real Estate and Devel., Shingle Springs, Calif., 1980-82; Brodrick Real Estate Co., Shingle Springs, 1982-84; rep. Titan Capital Corp., Sacramento, 1983—; prin. Brodrick Toy Svc. Pres. Calif. Rep. Assembly, Lamorinda unit, Orinda, Calif., 1978; v.p. Orinda Rep. Women, 1977; bd. dirs. Hacienda Del Orinda Homeowners, 1978-79. Mem. Internat. Fin. Planners, Nat. Assn. Security Dealers (registered rep.), Kappa Kappa Gamma (past pres. Bay Area). Club: Cameron Park Country (Calif.). Home: 3490 Fairway Dr Shingle Springs CA 95682

BRODY, ANITA BLUMSTEIN, judge; b. N.Y.C., May 25, 1935; d. David Theodore and Rita (Sondheim) Blumstein; m. Jerome I. Brody, Oct. 25, 1959; children—Lisa, Marion, Timothy. AB, Wellesley Coll., 1955; JD, Columbia U., 1958. Bar: N.Y. 1958, Fla. 1960, Pa. 1972. Asst. atty. gen. State N.Y., 1958-60; sole practice, Ardmore, Pa., 1972-79; ptnr. Brody, Brown & Hepburn, Ardmore, 1979-81; judge Pa. Ct. Common Pleas 38th Jud. Dist., Norristown, 1981—; lectr. in law U. Pa., Phila., 1978-79. Mem. ABA, Pa. State Trial Judges Assn., Pa. Bar Assn., Montgomery Bar Assn. (bd. dirs. 1979-81). Republican. Jewish. Office: Court House Swede St & Airy Sts Norristown PA 19404

BRODY, JANE ELLEN, journalist; b. Bklyn., May 19, 1941; d. Sidney and Lillian (Kellner) B.; m. Richard Engquist, Oct. 2, 1966; children: Lee Erik and Lorin Michael Engquist (twins). B.S., N.Y. State Coll. Agr., Cornell U., 1962; M.S. in Journalism, U. Wis., 1963; HHD (hon.), Princeton U., 1987. Reporter Mpls. Tribune, 1963-65; sci. writer, personal health columnist N.Y. Times, N.Y.C., 1965—; mem. adv. council N.Y. State Coll. Agr., Cornell U., 1971-77. Author: (with Richard Engquist) Secrets of Good Health, 1970, (with Arthur Holleb) You Can Fight Cancer and Win, 1977, Jane Brody's Nutrition Book, 1981, Jane Brody's The New York Times Guide to Personal Health, 1982; Jane Brody's Good Food Book, 1985. Recipient numerous writing awards, including; Howard Blakeslee award Am. Heart Assn., 1971; Sci. Writers' award ADA, 1978; J.C. Penney-U. Mo. Journalism award, 1978; Lifeline award Am. Health Found., 1978. Jewish. Office: NY Times 229 W 43nd St New York NY 10036

BRODY, NANCY LOUISE, lawyer; b. Chgo., Nov. 17, 1954; d. Mitchell and Grace Yaden (Williams) Block; m. Daniel Matthew Brody, Oct. 28, 1979. BA, U. Mich., 1975; JD, Loyola U., Chgo., 1979. Bar: Ill. 1979, Pa. 1980, Ariz. 1981. Sec., gen. counsel Block & Co., Inc., 1981—, also bd. dirs., 1981—; bd. dirs. Insmed Pharms., Inc. Bd. dirs. Ind. YMCA, 1986-87, Charlottesville YMCA, 1989-90; mem. Jr. League, Charlottesville. Named one of Outstanding Young Women Am., 1983. Fellow Am. Bar Found. (life), Pa. Bar Found. (bd. dirs. 1984-88); mem. ABA (ho. dels. 1986-88, state membership chmn. Pa. 1986-88), Ill. State Bar Assn., Pa. Bar Assn. (bd. govs. 1984-87, treas. 1983-84, chairperson 1985-86 young lawyers div.), Zonta (parliamentarian Ind. chpt. 1985-86, 87-88), Pi Beta Phi (alumnae adv. coun. 1989—). Republican.

BROER, EILEEN DENNERY, management consultant; b. Phila., Sept. 7, 1946; d. Vincent Paul and Jane Dorothy (Knight) Dennery; m. Paul Alan Broer, Nov. 26, 1970 (div. 1980); m. Charles Kenneth ReCorr, Sept. 10, 1981; 1 child, Matthew Vincent; stepchildren: Kenneth, Christopher. BA, Coll. Mt. St. Vincent, 1969. Media dir., control mgr. Merrill Anderson Co., N.Y.C., 1970-72; adminstrv. asst. fin. McCall Pattern Co., N.Y.C., 1972-74, personnel specialist, 1974-77, mgr. employee rels., 1978; dir. personnel Notions Mktg. Inc., N.Y.C., 1978-79; 2nd v.p. personnel Manhattan Life Ins. Co., N.Y.C., 1979, v.p. human resources, 1980-82; v.p. human resources McM Corp., Raleigh, N.C., 1982-85; pres. The Human Dimension, 1985—; bd. dirs. Ctr. For Health Edn. Inc.; adj. faculty writing NYU, 1975-78. Mem. Human Resource Planning Soc., Orgn. Devel. Network, Nat. Assn. Women Bus. Owners (pres. N.C. chpt. 1988-89), Am. Soc. for Tng. and Devel., Raleigh C. of C., Gestalt Inst. Cleve. Office: The Human Dimension PO Box 5367 Cary NC 27511

BROERS, KIMBERLY ANN, editor, writer; b. Dayton, Ohio, Sept. 20, 1956; d. Deryl Dean and Valerie Carol (Devine) B. Cert., Univ. Bordeaux, France, 1977; BA in Writing and French summa cum laude, William Jewell Coll., 1978. Editor, proofer Johnson City Community Coll., Overland Park, Kans., 1978-79; sr. staff writer Women in Bus. mag., Kansas City, Mo., 1979-81; freelance writer, editor Kansas City, 1981-90; assoc. editor nat. mag. VFW Aux., Kansas City, 1984—; copywriter Tappan Design, Shawnee Mission, Kans., 1989—. Author, editor: Celebrate 75 Years, 1989; contbr. numerous articles to mags. Nat. publs. judge VFW, 1987-90; vol. Sta. KCPT Pub. TV., 1990; newsletter editor Nat. Soc. for the Protection of Animals, 1989-90. Mem. Women in Communications Inc. (newsletter editor 1987-88, roster editor 1988-91), Women for Progressive Art (founding mem., publs. dir. 1988-89). Home: 3730 Bell Kansas City MO 64111 Office: VFW Aux 406 W 34th St Kansas City MO 64111

BROGAN, RITA, marketing company executive; b. Tokyo, Oct. 11, 1951; (father Am. citizen); d. William Joseph and Toshiko (Yamaki) B.; m. H. Stuart Elway, Sept. 11, 1976 (div. 1985); 1 child, Zachary Elway; m. Michael Richards, May 24, 1987; 1 child, Hunter Richards. BA summa cum laude, U. Wash., 1972, MA, 1975, EdD, 1978. Community affairs cons. Wash. Office Community Devel., Olympia, 1974-75; instr. Fairhaven Coll., U. Wash., Seattle, 1974-76; pres. Communication Design, Inc., Seattle, 1976-82; exec. asst. King County Exec., Seattle, 1982-84; supt. Municipality of Metro Seattle, 1984-87; pres., chief exec. officer Pacific Rim Resources, Inc., Seattle, 1989—; legis. asst. Seattle City Coun. 1978; mem. task force Wash. Gov.'s Transition Team, Seattle, 1984; com. mem. Transp. Rsch. Bd., Washington, 1988—. Contbr. articles on transp. mktg. to profl. publs. Mem. Wash. State Women's Coun., Olympia, 1975-77, chmn., 1977; mem. President's Internat. Women's Yr. Commn., 1977-78; co-chmn. Seattle Sch. Levy Campaign, 1980; com. chmn. Wash. Gov.'s Task Force on Hunger, Spokane, 1986-89; chmn. Capital Asian Counselling and Referral Svc., Seattle, 1988—. Recipient Leadership Tomorrow award Seattle C. of C. Mem. Womens Transp. Seminar, Phi Beta Kappa (trustee Puget Sound chpt. 1980-86, pres. 1985-86). Office: Pacific Rim Resources 10700 Meridian Ave N 506 Seattle WA 98133

BROGAN-WERNTZ, BONNIE BAILEY, police officer, municipal agency administrator; b. Pine Grove Mills, Pa., Mar. 28, 1941; d. Gilbert Chester and Rosalie Evelyn (Reed) Bailey; m. Donald M. Brogan, Aug. 12, 1960 (div. Oct. 1971); children: Donna Lynn Gregory, Rodney Marshall Brogan; m. Robert R. Werntz, Aug. 28, 1982. A in Criminal Justice, Ind. U., 1976, BS, 1981. Cert. instr. law enforcement tng., Ind. Stenographer South Bend (Ind.) Police Dept., 1970-73, police officer, 1973—, cpl. accident investigation, 1975-80, detective sgt., investigator sex crimes, 1980-85, field tng. officer administr., shift comdr. lt., 1985-88, dir. tng., lt., 1988—; bd. dirs. Women's Com. on Sex Offenses, South Bend; vol., trainer rape crisis Sex Offense Services, South Bend, 1980-87; recorder, treas. Child Sexual Abuse Consortium, South Bend, 1982-85; mem. Giarretto Task Force/Family and Children Ctr., Mishawaka, Inc., 1985. Iniator ordinance St. Joseph County Funds for Examinations and Victims of Sex Crimes, 1983. Bd. dirs. Parents Anonymous, South Bend, 1982, Women's Shelter for Battered Women, South Bend, 1985, South Bend Credit Union Supervisory Commn., 1983; mem. Children and Adolescent Adv. Council, South Bend, 1984. Recipient Joseph J. Newman award Protective Bd./Council for Retarded St. Joseph County, 1982, Child Abuse Investigator award The Breakfast Exchange Club, 1982, award for Exceptional Quality in Investigative Child Abuse/Neglect, Child Protective Services of St. Joseph County Dept. Pub. Welfare, 1983, Outstanding Service award Women's Com. on Sex Offenses, 1983, Outstanding Officer of Yr. award, St. Joseph County Council of Clubs, 1985, Police Officer of Yr. award, Ind. Council Fraternal Vets. and Social Scis., 1985, Outstanding Achievement award YWCA Tribute to Women, 1986. Mem. Internat. Assn. of Women Police (Hon. Mention Officer of Yr. 1985), Fraternal Order of Police. Democrat. Home: 1709 E Altgeld St South Bend IN 46614 Office: South Bend Police Dept 701 W Sample St South Bend IN 46625

BROGDON, BRENDA KAY, occupational therapist, supervisor; b. Oregon, Ill., Sept. 19, 1959; d. Robert Bartow and Virginia Lee (Simon) Noble-Westerdale; m. Rocky Dwain Brogdon, July 1, 1989; children: Ryan, Katie. BS, Tex. Woman's U., 1984. Registered occupational therapist, Tex. Staff therapist St. Joseph's Hosp., Ft. Worth, 1984-85; dept. head All Saints Hosp., Ft. Worth, 1985-86; staff therapist Ergomedic, Inc., Ft. Worth, 1986; clin. supr. Ctr. Neuro Skills, Irving, Tex., 1986—. Mem. Am. Congress Rehab. Medicine, Tex. Occupational Therapy Assn. (sec. Trinity North dist. 1988-89), Am. Occupational Therapy Assn. Office: Ctr Neuro Skills Ste 200 3501 N MacArthur St Irving TX 75062

BROGLIATTI, BARBARA SPENCER, television and motion picture executive; b. Los Angeles, Jan. 8, 1946; d. Robert and Lottie (Goldstein) Spencer; m. Raymond Haley Brogliatti, Sept. 19, 1970. BA in Social Scis. and English, UCLA, 1968. Asst. press. info. dept. CBS TV, L.A., 1968-69, sr. publicist, 1969-74; dir. publicity Tandem Prodns. and T.A.T. Communications (Embassy Communications), L.A., 1974-77, corp. v.p., 1977-82, sr. v.p. worldwide publicity, promotion and advt. Embassy Communications, Los Angeles, 1982-85; sr. v.p. worldwide corp. communications Lorimar Telepictures Corp., Culver City, Calif., 1985-89; pres., chmn. Brogliatti Co., Burbank, Calif., 1989—; bd. govs. TV Acad., L.A., 1984-86. Bd. dirs. KIDSNET, Washington, 1987—. Recipient Gold medallion Broadcast Promotion and Mktg. Execs., 1984. Mem. Dirs. Guild Am., Publicists Guild, Acad. TV Arts and Scis. Office: Brogliatti Co 4000 W Alameda Blvd Ste 200 Burbank CA 91505

BROMENSHENK, GAIL LUCILLE, civic worker; b. St. Paul, Sept. 17, 1944; d. George Norman and Muriel Lucille (Byus) Page; m. Jerry J. Bromenshenk, Aug. 14, 1971. Student, U. Southampton, Eng., 1964-65; BA, Beloit Coll., 1966. Elem. tchr. St. Paul Pub. Schs., 1966-71; elem. tchr. Bozeman (Mont.) Pub. Schs., 1971-73, tchr. summer arts program, 1972. Trustee Missoula Pub. Libr., 1982-88, past chmn.; trustee Missoula Mus., 1989-91; mem. Leadership Missoula, Missoula C. of C., 1983. Mem. AAUW (pres. Missoula br. 1976-80, chmn. Ednl. Found. programs Mont. div. 1980-82, named gift honoree Missoula br. 1987). Home: 200 Rimrock Way Missoula MT 59803

BROMET, EVELYN JUNE, professor of psychiatry; b. New Britain, Conn., Nov. 10, 1944; d. Max and Ruth Bromer; m. David Keim Parkinson, Jan. 27, 1985; 1 child. BA, Smith Coll., 1966; PhD, Yale U., 1971. Rsch. assoc. Stanford (Calif.) U., 1972-76; asst. to assoc. prof. U. Pitts., 1976-86; prof. of psychiatry SUNY, Stony Brook, 1986—; reviewer NIMH, Rockville, Md., 1978—; scientific adv. com. VA Nat. Study, Bethesda, 1987-89; cons. in field. Contbr. articles to profl. jours. and book chpts. Recipient Rema LaPouse award Am. Pub. Health Assn., 1989. Office: SUNY Putnam Hall-South Campus Stony Brook NY 11794

BROMM, SARAH JEAN, sales representative; b. St. Anthony, Ind., Aug. 13, 1966; d. Ralph Joseph and Norma Jean (Krodel) B. BS, Ind. State U., 1988. Pharm. sales rep. Eli Lilly and Co., Indpls., 1988—. Mem. Am. Mktg. Assn., A Network of Evansville Working Women, Evansville Zool. Soc. (bd. dirs. 1989—).

BRONN, LESLIE JOAN BOYLE, radiologist, medical administrator; b. White Plains, N.Y., Aug. 23, 1948; d. Myles Joseph and Harriet Geib (Warburton) Boyle; m. Donald George Bronn, Aug. 21, 1973; children: Jay Alexander, Natasha Nisa. BS, Ohio State U., 1970, MD, 1976. Diplomate Am. Bd. Radiology. Intern internal medicine Ohio State U. Hosp., Columbus, 1976-77, resident internal medicine, 1977-78, resident diagnostic radiology, 1978-81; chief radiology service VA Outpatient Clinic, Columbus, 1981-86; chief diagnostic radiology service Allen Park (Mich.) VA Hosp. Med. Ctr., 1986-87, chief nuclear medicine and diagnostic radiology services, 1987—; clin. asst. prof. radiology Ohio State U. Coll. Medicine, 1981-86, Wayne State U. Sch. Medicine, 1986—. mem. Am. Coll. Radiology, Radiol. Soc. N.Am., Assn. VA Chiefs of Radiology, Am. Assn. Women Radiologists, Am. Inst. Ultrasound in Medicine, Phi Beta Kappa, Alpha Lambda Delta. Office: VA Med Ctr Chief Radiology Svc Outer Dr and Southfield Rd Allen Park MI 48101

BRONNER, ELLEN PATRICIA, food service director; b. Bronxville, N.Y., May 1, 1954; d. Francis X. and Diana C. (Tully) B. BS in Food and Nutrition, Marymount Coll., 1976; MBA, U. Conn., 1983. Dietetic intern U. Nebr., Lincoln, 1976-77; patient svc. dietitian Bridgeport (Conn.) Hosp., 1977-79, asst. dir. dietary dept., 1979-84; instr. part-time Marymount Coll., Tarrytown, N.Y., 1983-84; asst. dir. dietary dept. Rex Hosp., Raleigh, N.C., 1985-87, dir. dietary svcs., 1987—. Mem. Am. Dietetic Assn., N.C. Dietetic Assn., Raleigh Dietetic Assn., Am. Soc. for Hosp. Food Svc. Adminstrs. Republican. Roman Catholic. Home: 207 Norham Dr Cary NC 27513 Office: Rex Hosp 4420 Lake Boone Trail Raleigh NC 27607

BRONOCCO, TERRI LYNN, telecommunications company executive; b. San Antonio, Jan. 7, 1953; d. Lawrence and Jimmie Doris (Mears) B.; m. Martin L. Lowy, July 5, 1975 (div. Jan. 1979). Student in communications U. Tex.-Austin, 1970-73. Pub. relations mgr. Assocs. Corp., Dallas, 1976-79; editor-in-chief Nat. Tax Shelter Digest, Dallas, 1979; fin. editor Dallas/Ft. Worth Bus., Dallas, 1979-80; pub. affairs dir. Gen. Telephone Co., Lewisville, Tex., 1980-82; pub. info. mgr. GTE Corp., Stamford, Conn., 1982-83, media communications mgr., 1983-84, media relations and communications mgr., 1984-86; v.p. external affairs U.S. Sprint Communications Co., Dallas, 1986-88; v.p. external affairs U.S. Sprint, Washington, 1988—. Fundraiser, pub. relations counsel Am. Shakespeare Theatre, Stratford, Conn., 1984-86; bd. dirs. Music Found. for the Handicapped, Bridgeport, Conn., 1984-86;

precinct chmn. Dallas County Dem. Party, 1982; bd. dirs. Far Mill River Assn., Stratford, 1983-86; mem. adv. commn. State Tex. Emergency Communications, 1987—. Recipient award for Newspaper Series Dept. Transp., 1980. Mem. Internat. Assn. Bus. Communicators (Best Photograph award 1977), Women in Communications (Matrix award 1985), Women in Mgmt., Am. Mgmt. Assn., Dallas C. of C. (telecommunications com. 1987, Spl. Recognition award 1978). Roman Catholic. Home: 1600 N Oak St Arlington VA 22201 Office: US Sprint Communications Co 2002 Edmund Halley Dr Reston VA 22091

BRONSDON, MELINDA ANN, microbiologist; b. Seattle, May 15, 1940; d. Horace Greeley and Frances Mayes (Jordan) Rahskopf; m. Lincoln Parker Bronsdon, Jr., Aug. 19, 1967 (div. 1982); children: Carl Sterling, Keith Jordan. Cert., LaChatelainie, Neuchatel, Switzerland, 1958; BA, Pomona Coll., 1963; postgrad., U. Wash., 1963-64, 81-82, MS, 1987. Registered microbiologist, Am. Acad. of Microbiology. Laboratorian U. Wash., Seattle, 1959-62; teaching asst. Pomona Coll., Claremont, Calif., 1963; histologist U. Wash. Regional Primate Rsch. Ctr., Seattle, 1965, clin. technologist, 1966-87, clin. supr., 1988, rsch. scientist, 1988—; clin. microbiologist U. Hosp., Seattle, 1981-83. Contbr. articles to profl. jours. Vol. PTA, Kirkland, Wash., 1974-78. Grantee US Pub. Health Svc., U. Wash., 1963. Mem. Am. Soc. for Med. Tech., Am. Soc. for Microbiology, Campylobacter Soc., Internat. Campylobacter Workshop., US Amateur Ballroom Dance Assn. Democrat. Office: U of Wash HSB SJ-50 Seattle WA 98195

BRONSKI, BETTY JEAN, health science facility administrator; b. Chgo., Mar. 21, 1952; d. Joseph Jacob and Helen Margaret (Hruby) B. BS, Marquette U., Milw., 1974, MS, 1975; MS, Cardinal Stritch Coll., Milw., 1987. Speech pathologist Sch. Dist. BrownDeer, 1974-79; project analyst Eaton Corp., Milw., 1979-82; mktg. rsch. dir. SSM- Mgmt. Services, Milw., 1982-86; adminstr. asst. SSM-Ministry Corp., Milw., 1986-87; dir. planning & devel. St. Mary's Hill Hosp., Milw., 1987-89; pres. Carefinders, Inc., 1989—. Vol. Greater Milw. Area Spl., Olympics 1979-82. Mem. Am. Assn. Mental Health Adminstrs. Roman Catholic. Home: 5150 North Berkeley Blvd Whitefish Bay WI 53217 Office: Carefinders Inc Suite 146 PO Box 17900 Milwaukee WI 53217

BRONSON, CLAIRE SEKULSKI, finance educator; b. Memphis, Oct. 14, 1947; d. Julian Bernard and Opal Geneva (Scruggs) Sekulski; m. George D. Bronson, May 28, 1968; children: Christopher, Kevin, Meredith. BA, Conn. Coll. for Women, 1969; MA, U. Conn., 1971, PhD, 1982. Substitute tchr. Enfield pub. schs., Conn., 1979-82; asst. prof. econs. Western New Eng. Coll., Springfield, Mass., 1983, vis. asst. prof. fin., 1983-84, asst. prof. fin., 1984—, chmn. acctg. and fin. dept., 1989—; mem. investment inst. adv. com., 1983-84; mem. adv. bd. Suffield Bank, 1983-89; assoc. bd. dir. Enfield Nat. Bank, 1989—; part-time instr. econs. Manchester Community Coll., Conn., 1974-76, Asnuntuck Community Coll., Enfield, 1975-79; cons. small bus. Contbr. articles to profl. jours.; book editor for various pubs. Mem. Enfield Cultural Arts Commn., 1983-86; mem. adv. com. Enfield Bd. Edn., 1981-83; bd. dirs. Enfield Girls Softball Assn., v.p., 1989, pres., 1990; sec. St. Bernard's Parish Coun., 1988-89, v.p., 1989-90; pres. Nathan Hale PTO, Enfield, 1980-81. Mem. Am. Fin. Assn., Am. Econ. Assn., Eastern Fin. Assn., Fin. Mgmt. Assn., Fin. Mgmt. Assn. Twin Mothers Club (Hartford, Conn.). Republican. Roman Catholic. Avocations: collecting antique jewelry, tennis, reading. Home: 21 S Meadow Ln Enfield CT 06082 Office: Western New Eng Coll Wilbraham Rd Springfield MA 01119

BRONSTEIN, LEONA BARTEL, educator; b. Lansing, Mich., Nov. 10, 1932; d.John and Mary Augusta (Kolp) Bartel; m. Daniel A. Bronstein, Mar. 27, 1975. BS, Siena Heights Coll., 1959, MS, 1967; MA, Bowling Green State U., 1972. Cert. permanent tchr., Mich.; joined Adrian Dominican Sisters, 1950, resigned, 1971. Tchr. parochial schs., Adrian, Mich.; tchr. parochial schs. Mich. and Ill., 1950-71; tchr. chemistry East Lansing (Mich.) High Sch., 1971—, chmn. sci. dept., 1974-81, 89—, coord. gifted and talented, 1988—; manuscript reviewer Amsco Sch. Publs., N.Y.C., 1985; article reviewer Jour. Chem. Edn., 1983; mem. mentor tchr. program Mich. State U., East Lansing, 1987—. Author chemistry lab. manuals, 1982, 83; contbr. articles to profl. jours. Named Outstanding High Sch. Sci. Tchr. Mich. State U. chpt. Sigma Xi, 1982; recipient award Mich. Dept. Edn., 1984, U.S. Dept. Edn., 1984; NSF grantee, 1969-72. Mem. Nat. Sci. Tchrs. Assn., Am. Chem. Soc., AAAS, Mich. Sci. Tchrs. Assn., Nat. Audubon Soc., Sierra Club. Home: 1650 Sylvan Glen Rd Okemos MI 48864 Office: East Lansing High Sch 509 Burcham Dr East Lansing MI 48823

BRONSTON, EDYTHE LEE, lawyer; b. Scranton, Pa., Jan. 2, 1936; d. Arthur and Eve (Shocker) Rubin; m. William E. Bronston, Mar. 7, 1968; 1 child, Pamela S. Bronston Hinojosa. BA, Calif. State U., Northridge, 1977; JD, Loyola U., L.A., 1980. Bar: Calif. 1980, U.S. Dist. Ct. (cen., so. ea. and no. dists.) Calif. 1981, U.S. Ct. Appeals (9th cir.) 1981. Assoc. Lipofsky & Lande, L.A., 1980-82, Robinson, Wolas & Diamant, L.A., 1982-85; assoc. Cox, Castle & Nicholson, L.A., 1985-89, ptnr., 1989—. Mem. ABA (bus. bankruptcy com., bus. law sect.), LWV (bd. dirs. L.A. 1974-75, dir. corp. and community affairs Calif. chpt. 1985-89), L.A. County Bar Assn. (pres. prejudgment remedies sect. 1987-88), Beverly Hills Bar Assn., Women Lawyers L.A., Comml. Credit League, L.A. Bankruptcy Forum (editorial bd. Calif. Bankruptcy Jour., bd. dirs. 1987—), chpt. 1985-89), Calif. Bankruptcy Forum (bd. dirs. 1989—). Office: Cox Castle & Nicholson 2049 Century Park E Ste 2800 Los Angeles CA 90067

BROOKE, PATRICIA CYNTHIA, lawyer; b. Conn., Oct. 30, 1953; d. Louis S. and Patricia S. B. BS, Union Coll., 1975; JD, St. Mary's U., San Antonio, 1981. Bar: Tex. 1981, U.S. Dist. Ct. (no. and we. dists.) Tex. 1984, U.S. Ct. Appeals (5th cir.) 1984. Assoc. Roy L. Bell Law Office, Odessa, Tex., 1983-86, ptnr., 1986; ptnr. Bell & Jatko, Odessa, 1987; pvt. practice Odessa, 1987—; asst. county atty. County of Ector, Tex., 1989; bd. dirs. Permian Basin Bankruptcy Bar, Midland, Tex., 1987—; alternate judge Odessa Mcpl. Ct., 1984-86. Bd. dirs., chmn. legal com. Our New Beginnings, 1984-86; mem. charter revision com. City of Odessa, 1984; v.p., bd. dirs. Planned Parenthood of West Tex., Odessa, 1988—. Fellow Tex. Bar Found.; mem. ABA (alternate dispute resolution com. 1988—), Tex. Young Lawyers Assn. (bd. dirs. 1987—, chmn. profl. ethics com. 1987-88, chmn. alternate dispute resolution com. 1988-89), Ector County Young Lawyers Assn. (pres. 1986-87), State Bar Tex. (alternate dispute resolution com. 1988—), Leadership Odessa, Leadership Odessa Alumni Assn., Tex. Leadership Conf., Assn. Jr. Leagues, Mission Country Club, Odessa Petroleum Club. Office: 620 N Grant Ste 906 Odessa TX 79761

BROOKER, PATRICIA LEE, accountant, financial consultant, director; b. Helena, Mont., Sept. 28, 1956; d. Clifford and Phyllis Ruth (Wolf) Madsen; m. Edwin Dale Brooker, Dec. 25, 1975; 1 child, Stephanie Lee. Student, Gustavus Adolphus Coll., 1974-75, U. Mont., 1975; diploma in acctg., McGraw Hill Coll., 1988. Teller Am. Fed. Savs. & Loan, Helena, Mont., 1976-77; from office asst. to asst. mgr. fin. ITT, Orlando, Fla., 1977-86; acctg. supr. Plantscape House Inc., Orlando, Fla., 1986-87; exec. dir. acctg. Mars Inc., Missoula, 1987-89; staff accountant Edward C. Kerins CPA, 1989; office mgr., exec. accountant Outpost Marine, 1989—; acct. B&B Enterprises, Missoula, 1985-89. Dir. adminstrn. and leadership courses CAP, Orlando, 1980-87. Recipient membership ribbons and unit citations CAP, 1980-87. Mem. Nat. Assn. Female Execs. Republican. Home: PO Box 871 East Helena MT 59635 Office: Mars Inc 7525 York Rd Helena MT 59601

BROOKER, SUSAN GAY, personnel executive; b. Washington, Sept. 4, 1949; d. Robert Morris and Mildred Ruby (Parler) B. BA, St. Mary's Coll., St. Mary's City, Md., 1971. News editor WPGC Radio, Lanham, Md., 1971; mgr. trainee Household Fin. Corp., Silver Spring, Md., 1972; career counselor Place-All, Betnesda, Md., 1972-73; exec. v.p. New Places, Inc./Get-A-Job, Washington, 1973—, also bd. dirs.; mem. Emploibank, Washington, 1978-79. Recipient Cert. Appreciation U.S. Fish and Wildlife Assn., 1985. Mem. Pell-Capital Personnel Services Assn. (cert.), NOW, St. Mary's Coll. Alumni Assn. (bd. dirs. 1987—). Democrat. Home: 9902 Sidney Rd Silver Spring MD 20901 Office: New Places Inc 1925 K St Suite 407 Washington DC 20006

BROOKINS, GERALDINE KEARSE, psychology educator; b. Bklyn., May 3, 1946; d. Lee Andrew and Mary Alice (Toles) Kearse; m. Phillip Johnson, Sept. 8, 1973; 1 child, David Phillip. BA, Oberlin (Ohio) Coll., 1968; PhD, Harvard U., 1977. Rsch. asst. dept. human devel. Harvard Grad. Sch. Edn., Cambridge, Mass., 1969-70; head program ops. Brookline (Mass.) Early Edn. Project, 1971-72; rsch. asst. Lab. Human Devel., Harvard Grad. Sch. Edn., Cambridge, 1972-73; rsch. assoc. Ednl. Devel. Ctr., Newton, Mass., 1973-74; sr. rsch. asst. Huron Inst., Cambridge, 1974; dir. Rsch. Inst. Jackson (Miss.) State U., 1980-84, asst. prof. psychology, 1975-80, assoc. prof. psychology, 1980-86, prof. psychology, 1986; vis. prof. psychology and Afro-Am. studies U. Miss., Oxford, 1988-89; cons. W.T. Grant Found., N.Y.C., 1989, Office Children and Youth, Jackson, Miss., 1984-88, J.F. Kennedy Sch. Govt., Cambridge, Mass., 1986-88. Co-editor: Beginnings, 1985. Pres. Planned Parenthood, Jackson, 1985; panel mem. United Way, Jackson, 1986-88; com. chair United Negro Coll. Fund Dr., Jackson, 1989. Mem Soc. Rsch. in Child Devel., Am. Psychol. Assn., Am. Ednl. Rsch. Assn., Jack and Jill of Am. Inc. (recording sec. 1989-91). Home: 6075 Holbrook Dr Jackson MS 39206 Office: Jackson State U 1400 Lynch St Jackson MS 39217

BROOKLERE, ANNA MARIA, pharmacist; b. Birmingham, Ala.; d. Anthony John and Sara Jean (Gagliano) B. BS, Auburn U. Pharmacy intern Brooklere Pharmacy, Birmingham, 1983; pharmacy intern Univ. Hosp., Birmingham, 1983-84, pharmacist, 1984—; pharmacist Brooklere Pharmacy, Birmingham, 1984—. Vol. St. Patricks Cath. Ch., Birmingham, 1984-85. Mem. Ala. Pharm. Assn., Ala. Soc. Hosp. Pharmacists, Jefferson County Pharm. Assn., Auburn U. Pharmacy Alumni Assn. (life), U.S. Tennis Assn. (so. region chpt.), Ski CLub, Park West Tennis Club, Phi Delta Chi Alumni Assn. Clubs: Ski, Park West Tennis (Birmingham).

BROOKMAN, MARILYN K., dean; b. Centralia, Ill.; d. William O. and Lularose (Trumbo) Armstrong; m. Joseph H. Brookman; 1 child, Lucretia. BS with honors, So. Ill. U., Carbondale, 1975, MS with honors, 1980, PhD with honors, 1987. Instr. Kaskaskia Coll., Centralia, Ill., 1974-76, asst. to pres., affirmative action officer, 1975-81, dir. counseling, 1981-88, dean student devel., 1988—; adj. instr. So. Ill. U., Carbondale, 1981-88; co-chmn. North Cen. Accredition self study, Kaskaskia Coll., 1988-89, 25/50 Anniversary Project, Kaskaskia Coll., 1990—; editor Ill. Statewide Articulation Transfer Coords. Adv. Newsletter. Contbr. articles to profl. jours. Pres. bd. Centralia Cultural Soc., 1988-90; mem. St. Mary's Hosp. Devel. Coun. Named Outstanding Young Woman of Am., 1977, Outstanding Career Guidance Program, Ill. Dept. Adult Vocat. Tech. Edn., 1989, Girl of Yr., Beta Sigma Phi, 1970. Mem. AAUW (award), Ill. Assn. Counseling/Devel. (sec. 1985-86, pres. 1990, Okaw Valley Chpt.), Ill. Community Coll. Coun. Adminstrs., So. Ill. U. Alumni Assn., Nat. Bd. Cert. Counselors (cert. counselor 1985), Rotary (speaker 1988, 89, 90), Delta Kappa Gamma, Phi Delta Kappa, Pi Lambda Theta. Lutheran. Office: Kaskaskia Coll Shattuc Rd Centralia IL 62801

BROOKOVER, BARBARA RUTH, crime analyst; b. Albuquerque, N.Mex., Sept. 29, 1956; d. Edward Raymond and Ruth Evelyn (Lanning) Stepka; m. Bruce Allen Brookover, June 26, 1982; children: Derek Allen, Danica Lynne. BA in Geography, U. N.Mex., 1978; postgrad., San Diego State U., 1978-81. Sr. analyst Criterion, Inc., San Diego, Calif., 1982-85; crime analyst City of Oceanside (Calif.)úPolice Dept., 1985-87; sr. crime analyst City of Chula Vista (Calif.) Police Dept., 1987—. Mem. Calif. Law Enforcement Assn. of Records Suprs., San Diego Crime Analysis Assn. (v.p. 1988-89, pres. 1990), NAFE. Office: City of Chula Vista Police 276 Fourth Ave Chula Vista CA 92010

BROOKS, ANDREE NICOLE, journalist, journalism educator, author; b. London, Feb. 2, 1937; d. Leon Luis and Lillian (Abrahamson) Aelion; m. Ronald J. Brooks, Aug. 16, 1959 (div. Aug. 1986); children—Allyson, James. Journalism cert., N.W. London Poly., 1958. Reporter Hampstead News, London, 1954-58; story editor Photoplay mag., N.Y.C., 1958-60; N.Y. corr. Australian Broadcasting Co., N.Y.C., 1961-68; elected rep. Elstree, Eng., 1973-74; columnist N.Y. Times, N.Y.C., 1978—; free-lance journalist, 1978—; adj. prof. journalism Fairfield U., Conn., 1983-87. Author: Children of Fast Track Parents, 1989 (Best Non-fiction Book award 1990). Mem. exec. bd. Am. Jewish Com., 1987—. Recipient numerous awards including 1st place for news writing Conn. Press Women, 1980, 83, 85, 86, Outstanding Achievement award Nat. Fedn. Press Women, 1981, 1st place award Fairfield County chpt. Women in Communications, 1982, 83, 86, 87, 2d place award in mag. writing Nat. Assn. Home Builders, 1983, Spl. Service award Conn. chpt. Am. Planning Assn., 1983, 1st place award for mag. writing Nat. Fedn. Press Women, 1983; named one of Am. Women of Achievement Am. Jewish Com., 1989; assoc. fellow Yale U., 1989. Mem. Conn. Press Women (chmn. nominating com. 1983-86), Women in Communications (contest co-chmn. 1983-84). Home: 15 Hitchcock Rd Westport CT 06880

BROOKS, ANITA HELEN, public relations executive; b. N.Y.C.; d. Arthur and Bertha (Stewart) Sayle; m. Arnold Brooks, July 1, 1954 (div.). BA, Hunter Coll., 1950; MA, Columbia U., 1952, MLS, 1954. Tchr. Latin Hunter Coll. High Sch., N.Y.C., 1955; publicity rep. WOR Radio, N.Y.C., 1955; writer King Features Syndicate, N.Y.C., 1955-59; pub. relations writer NBC-TV, N.Y.C., 1956; dir. pub. relations N.Y. State Mental Health Fund Campaign, 1956, WMCA Radio, N.Y.C., 1957; account exec. various pub. rels. agys., N.Y.C., 1957-65; pres. Anita Helen Brooks assocs., Pub. Relations, N.Y.C., 1965—; lit. agt. Anita Brooks Lit. Agt., N.Y.C., 1956—. Writer radio-TV shows. Vice chair Sinatra for Meml. Sloan-Kettering Cancer Hosp. Benefit; mem. patronesscom. Harkness Ballet Found., benefit com. Mannes Coll. of Music, N.Y.C. Decorated Dame Cmmdr. Knights of Malta; named hon. citizen Venezuela. Mem. Am. Women in Radio and TV, Pub. Rels. Soc. Am., Internat. Radio and TV Soc., Publs. Publicity Assn., Assn. Motion Picture Advertisers, Mystery Writers Am., Columbia U. Alumni Assn., Sisters in Crime Soc., Smithsonian Assocs., N.Y. Press Club, Eta Sigma Phi, Latin/Greek Honor Soc. Office: 155 E 55th St New York NY 10022

BROOKS, ANTOINETTE MARIE, real estate executive; b. Worcester, Mass., Dec. 3, 1940; d. Philip F. and Madeline (Rondinone) Inangelo; m. Richard E. Brooks, Dec. 27, 1958; children: Richard E. Jr., Marlo J., Jeffrey Paul. A in Bus., Cen. NE Coll., 1958; student, Thomas Edison Sch., 1959, Am. Inst. Banking, 1973, Lee Inst. Real Estate, 1965. Credit clk. Pub. Finance Co., Worcester, Mass., 1958-61; asst. treas. Trans Ea. Corp., Worcester, Mass., 1961-65; pres. Antoinette M. Brooks Real Estate Assocs., Worcester, 1965-79; sales rep. Dennison's Mfg. Co., Framingham, Mass., 1979-81; mgr. N.E. Indsl. Park, Holliston, Mass., 1982-83; residential mgr. Coldwell Banker, Northborough, Mass., 1983-89; pres. Re/Max 1st Choice Real Estate, Northborough, 1989—. Justice of the Peace, Mass., 1983—. Mem. Women's Coun. Realtors (pres. 1981), Greater Worcester Bd. Realtors (com. mem. 1977—), Nat. Assn. Realtors, Mass. Assn. Realtors, Worcester Bd. Realtors (profl. standards com. 1987—, speaker 1987), 100 Percent Club, NAFE (bd. dirs. local chpt. 1987), Worcester Order Sons Italy. Democrat. Roman Catholic. Home: 293 Davis St Northborough MA 01532 Office: Re/Max 1st Choice RE 276 W Main St Northborough MA 01532

BROOKS, BETH ANN, marketing executive, nurse; b. Oak Lawn, Ill., Feb. 4, 1962; d. John N. and Carol A. (Vander Meeden) B. BSN, Valparaiso (Ind.) U., 1984; MS, Northwestern U., 1989. RN, Ill. Staff nurse Rush Presbyn.-St. Luke's Med. Ctr., Chgo., 1984-86; clin. nurse mgr. St. Francis Hosp., Evanston, Ill., 1986-87; dir. mktg. Myerscough Med. Staffing, Inc., Chgo., 1987-89; account exec. Bentley, Barnes & Lynn Advt., Chgo., 1989—. Northwestern U. scholar, 1987-88, 88-89. Mem. Am. Nurses Assn., Nat. League Nursing, Chgo. Yacht Club, U.S. Yacht Racing Union. Office: Bentley Barnes & Lynn Inc 420 N Wabash St Chicago IL 60611

BROOKS, CAROLINE DELL VOGEL, business owner; b. Wichita Falls, Tex., June 10, 1938; d. Irvin John and Mary Caroline (Meredith) Vogel; m. Kenneth Lee Brooks, Mar. 31, 1961; children: Amy Brooks Johnson, Mary Caroline. BJ, U. Tex., 1960; postgrad., Cen. Mich. U., 1975-77. Interim editor Liberty Tribune, 1969; editor progress editions Dispatch Newspapers, North Kansas City, Mo., 1972-73; dir. pub. rels. William Jewell Coll., Liberty, Mo., 1963-66, 70-71, Maple Woods Community Coll., Kansas City, Mo., 1971-77; pub. rels. exec. corp. hdqrs. H&R Block, Kansas City, 1977-78; tech. transfer specialist Argonne (Ill.) Nat. Lab., 1978—; owner, mgr. Reunion Organizers, Dallas, 1989—. Contbr. numerous articles to profl. jours. Mem., pub. rels. bd. Vol. Ctr. for Plano, Tex., 1990—. Winner (4) 1st Place awards Mo. Press Women Assn., 1970, 1st Place award Nat. Fedn. Press Women, 1971, 72, 1st Place award Mo. Press Women's Assn., 1973. Mem. Women in Communications, Inc. (v.p. 1976-77, pres. 1978). Home: 2501 Buttercup Dr Richardson TX 75082

BROOKS, CHRISTINE ANN, business forms manufacturing accountant; b. Quantico, Va., May 5, 1953; d. Chestine Lewis and Annie Laurie (Edwards) B. BA in Psychology, Mary Washington Coll., 1977, BLS in Bus. Adminstrn., 1981. Sr. acct., then group leader, acctg. and data processing Moore Bus. Forms & Systems Div., Fredericksburg, Va., 1977-82; career cons. Contax Career Cons., Dallas, 1982-83; programmer analyst Moore Bus. Forms & Systems Div., Denton, Tex., 1983-85; plant acct. Moore Bus. Forms & Systems Div., Modesto, Calif., 1985-89; product acct. Moore Bus. Forms & Systems Div., Glenview, Ill., 1989-90; plant controller Moore Bus. Forms & Systems Devel., Atlanta, 1990—. Democrat. Home: 325 Oak Creek Dr Apt 103 Wheeling IL 60090 Office: Moore Bus Forms & Systems 1519 Mitchell Ave Albany GA 31705-3225

BROOKS, CLAUDIA A., software executive, consultant; b. Atlanta, Jan. 18, 1957; d. John William and Annette (Thompson) B.; m. Robert A. Davis, Mar. 22, 1974 (div. Aug. 1978); 1 child, Robert. Student, Coastal Carolina Community Coll., Jacksonville, N.C., 1977-78; AA in Computer Sci., Clayton Jr. Coll., Morrow, Ga., 1980; BBA in Info. Systems, Ga. State U., 1984. Cert. in Info. Systems, Bus. Adminstrn. Data processing, fin. coord. UFCW Union and Employers Trust Fund, Atlanta, 1981; programmer, analyst, asst. data ctr. mgr. Davidson Mineral Properties, Inc., Atlanta, 1981-82; product specialist, programmer Info. Systems Am., Inc., Atlanta, 1982-83; programmer, analyst Software Shop Systems, Inc., Atlanta, Farmingdale, N.J., 1983-85; mgr. product devel. Software Shop Systems, Inc., Farmingdale, 1985-88; pres. Computer Assistance Group, Atlanta, 1988—. Vol. Op. New Life USN, Guam, 1975, vol. asst. Indochina refugee effort ARC, Guam, 1975. Mem. NAFE, Mensa, Cousteau Soc., Internat. Cessna 120/140 Assn. Presbyterian.

BROOKS, CLAUDIA MARIE, lawyer; b. Oakland, Calif., Aug. 2, 1952; d. Rex E. and Colleen M. (Walker) Brooks; m. James A. Smith. AB, U. Calif.-Berkeley, 1974; JD, U. Calif. Hastings Coll. of Law San Francisco, 1979; postgrad. Monterey Inst. Fgn. Studies (Calif.), 1974, Institut de Francais, Villefranche-sur-Mer, France, 1979, 84, Oxford U. (Eng.), 1973, Hague Acad. Internat. Law (Netherlands), 1980. Bar: Calif. 1979, U.S. Dist. Ct. (no. dist.) Calif. 1979, U.S. Ct. Appeals (9th cir.) 1979. Extern for Calif. Supreme Ct., San Francisco, 1978; assoc. Smith & Brooks, Attys. at Law, Redlands, Calif., 1979-82, ptnr., 1982—. Editor-in-chief Hastings Internat. and Comparative Law Rev., 1978-79; contbr. article to law rev. Pub. mem. Fgn. Service selection bds. U.S. Dept. State, Washington, 1983; del. U.S./China Joint Session on Trade, Investment, Econ. Law, Beijing, 1987, U.S./Japan Bilateral Session, Tokyo, 1988. Mem. State Bar Calif., San Bernardino County Bar Assn., San Francisco Press Club. Office: Smith & Brooks 130 W Vine St PO Box 672 Redlands CA 92373

BROOKS, DAISY, graphic artist, secretary; b. Monroe, La., Apr. 10; d. Bennie Clifton and Annie Mae (Wright) Pruitt; m. Ronald I. Brooks, Oct., 1963; children: Charmine, Kenneth, Ronald. Student, City Coll. of San Francisco, 1977-78, U. San Francisco, 1975. Claims examiner Calif. Physician Svcs., San Francisco, 1965-68; bookkeeping and coding clk. Associated Bus. Svcs., San Francisco, 1968; computer clk. Budget Unit, San Francisco, 1968-70; emergency check typist-spl. needs, 1971-73; unit clk. Aid to Families With Dependent Children, 1974-76; gen. svcs. unit clk. Dept. Social Svc., 1976-78; sr. typist supr. Mcpl. Railway, 1978-79; graphic artist, sec. Crown Zellabach, San Francisco, 1979-80; reports clk. AT&T, Pleasanton, Calif., 1981-90. Mem. Bernal Height Com. Bd.; charter mem. Rep. Presdl. Task Force, 1982, Rep. Presdl. Citizen's Adv. Commn., Nat. Rep. Senatorial Commn.; bd. dirs., sec., treas. sch. for handicap and deficiency for children Christian Welfare Growth and Devel. Ctr., 1974-79; mem. task force Commn. on Status of Women's-Women Owned Bus., 1977-79; mem. Multi-Cultural and Bilingual Edn. Com for San Francisco schs., 1969-74; co-chairperson adv. com. Emergency Sch. Aid Act, 1972; mem. Human Rights Commn's. Youth and Edn. Com., 1972-79; mem. Rep. County Cen. Com. San Francisco; vol., mem. San Francisco Coun. Rep. Woman; del.-at-large Calif. Rep. Assembly; charter founder, one of chief architects Rep. Ronald Reagon Ctr., Washington; charter mem. rep. nat. com. Presdl. Campaign Trust, 1990; tng. sponsor Ronald Reagon Presdl. Found. Ctr. for Pub. Affairs; sustaining mem. Rep. Nat. Com.; mem. Whitney Young Child Devel. Ctr., Inc., 1987—. Mem. AFL-CIO COPE Union, Smithsonian Nat. Assocs. (hon.), Am. Biog. Inst. (hon., rsch. bd. advisors 1990), Nat. Mus. Women in Arts (charter), U.S. Senatorial Founder's Club, Cable Car Club (bd. dirs. 5th congressional dist. 1967-79).

BROOKS, DAWNE LEA, clergywoman; b. St. Paul; d. Clinton Joseph Williamson and Beatrice (Gilbertson) Sorensen. AA in Psychology, Bellevue Community Coll., 1977; BA in Religion and Counseling, Ottawa (Kans.) U., 1982; MA in Human Rels. and Mgmt., Webster U., 1984. Ordained to ministry Unity Ch., 1982. Dir. ch. groups, counselor Unity Ch. of Practical Christianity, Seattle, 1975-79; adminstr. youth edn. Community Unity Ch., Kansas City, Kans., 1981; hostess radio programs Unity Sch. Christianity, Unity Village, Mo., 1981-82; assoc. minister, dir. edn., counselor Christ Ch. Unity, Kansas City, 1984-86, chmn. Unity Ministerial Alliance, 1984-89; sr. minister, counselor Christ Unity Ch., Chattanooga, 1989—; spiritual leader U.S. Armed Forces Retreat, Ft. Jackson, S.C., 1983. Editor: Policy Manuel for a Unity Ministry, 1988. Named Vol. of Month, Assn. Unity Chs., 1988. Mem. Toastmasters (sec. 1988-89). Office: Christ Unity Ch 105 McBrien Rd Chattanooga TN 37411

BROOKS, DIANA D., auction house executive; b. Glen Cove, N.Y., 1950. Grad. Yale U. Formerly exec. v.p. Sotheby's, Inc., N.Y.C., now pres., dir. Office: Sotheby's Inc 1334 York Ave New York NY 10021

BROOKS, DONNA LYNNE, food service company executive; b. Manhattan, Kans., Mar. 19, 1957; d. Paul George and Marjorie Lee (Davis) Mugler; m. William Randall Brooks, July 21, 1979; 1 child, Carly Lynne. BS in Home Econs. magna cum laude, Southwestern Coll., Winfield, Kans., 1979. Catering mgr. Saga Food Svc., Fla. State U., Tallahassee, 1979-84; food svc. mgr. Marriott Edn. div., Tuskegee U., Ala., 1985-87; food svc. dir. Marriott Food & Svc. Mgmt., Boca Raton, Fla., 1987—. Sponsor United Meth. Youth Fellowship, Delray Beach, Fla., 1987-88; active PTA, Delray Beach, 1987—. Mem. Fla. Atlantic U. Women's Club, Kappa Omicron Phi. Home: 10374 Boca Entrada Blvd Apt 226 Boca Raton FL 33428 Office: Whitehall Boca 7300 Del Prado South Boca Raton FL 33433

BROOKS, GLADYS SINCLAIR, public affairs consultant; b. Mpls.; d. John Franklin and Gladys (Phillips) Sinclair; m. Wright W. Brooks, Apr. 17, 1941; children: Diane (Mrs. Roger Montgomery), Johm, Pamela (Mrs. Jean Marc Perraud). Student U. Geneva, Switzerland, 1935; BA, U. Minn., 1936; LLD, Hamline U., 1966. Dir. Farmer's and Mechanics Bank, 1973-82; mem. Met. Council, 1975-83; lectr. world affairs, 1939—; mem. Mpls. City Council, 1967-73; mem. Met. Airports Commn., 1971-74; pres. World Affairs Ctr. U. Minn., 1976-83; instr. continuing edn. for women U. Minn.; lectr. on world tours as Am. specialist U.S. Dept. State, 1959-60; pres. Brooks/Ridder & Assocs. Mem. Mpls. Charter Commn., 1948-51; pres. YWCA, 1953-57, mem. nat. bd., del. world meeting, Denmark; pres. Minn. Internat. Ctr., 1953-63; chmn. Minn. Women's Com. for Civil Rights, 1961-64; mem. U.S. Com. for UNICEF, 1959-68; mem. Gov.'s Adv. Com. Children and Youth, 1953-58, Minn. Adv. Com. Employment and Security, 1948-50; Midwest adv. com. Inst. Internat. Edn.; mem. nat. com. White House Conf. Children and Youth, 1960; chmn. Gov.'s Human Rights Commn., 1961-65; dir. Citizens Com. Delinquency and Crime, 1969-90; chmn. Mpls. Adv. Com. on Tourism, 1976-82, Ctr. Women in Govt.; vice chmn. Nat. Community Partnerships Seminars, 1977-82; mem. Midwest Selection Panel, White House Fellows, 1981. Del. Rep. Nat. Conv., 1952; state chmn. Citizens for Eisenhower, 1956; founder, pres. Rep. Workshop; co-chmn. Mpls. Bicentennial Commn., 1974-76; pres. Internat. Center for Fgn. Students; dir. Minn. Alumni Assn.; trustee United Theol. Sem., YWCA, Met. State U.; del. dirs. Hamline U., Midwest China Ctr., Walker Health Services; mem. pres.'s adv. council St. Catherine's Coll. Recipient Centennial Women of Minn. award Hamline U., 1954; Woman of Distinction award AAUW, Mpls. 1956;

Woman of Yr. award YWCA, 1973; Brotherhood award NCCJ, 1975; Service to Freedom award Minn. State Bar Assn., 1976; Community Leadership award YWCA, 1981. Mem. World Affairs Council (pres. 1942-44), Minn. LWV (dir. 1940-45), Mpls. Council Ch. Women (pres. 1946-48), Nat. Council of Chs. (mem. gen. bd., v.p. 1961-69), Minn. Council of Chs. (1st woman pres. 1961-64, Christian service award 1967), Mpls. Council of Chs. (v.p. 1946-48), United Ch. Women (bd. mgrs.), Minn. UN Assn. (dir.), Nat. League Cities (human resources steering com. 1972-73), Am. Acad. Polit. Sci., Mpls. C. of C., Minn. Women's Polit. Caucus, Minn. Women's Econ. Roundtable, AAUW, Women's Symphony Assn., Delta Kappa Gamma (hon.). Presbyn. Clubs: Horizon 100, Women's. Home: 5056 Garfield Ave S Minneapolis MN 55419

BROOKS, GWENDOLYN, writer, poet; b. Topeka, June 7, 1917; d. David Anderson and Keziah Corinne (Wims) B.; m. Henry L. Blakely, Sept. 17, 1939; children: Henry L., Nora. Grad., Wilson Jr. Coll., Chgo., 1936; L.H.D., Columbia Coll., 1964. Instr. poetry Columbia Coll., Chgo., Northeastern Ill. State Coll., Chgo.; mem. Ill. Arts Council; cons. in poetry Library of Congress, 1985-86. Author: poetry A Street in Bronzeville, 1945, Annie Allen, 1949, Maud Martha; novel, 1953, Bronzeville Boys and Girls; for children, 1956, The Bean Eaters; poetry, 1960, Selected Poems, 1963, In the Mecca, 1968, Riot, 1969, Family Pictures, 1970, Aloneness, 1971, To Disembark, 1981; autobiography Report From Part One, 1972, The Tiger Who Wore White Gloves, 1974, Beckonings, 1975, Primer for Blacks, 1980, Young Poets' Primer, 1981, Very Young Poets, 1983, The Near-Johannesburg Boy, 1986, Blacks, 1987, Gottschalk and the Grande Tarantelle, 1988, Winnie, 1988. Named one of 10 Women of Yr., Mademoiselle mag., 1945; recipient Creative Writing award Am. Acad. Arts and Letters, 1946; Guggenheim fellow, 1946, 47; recipient Pulitzer prize, 1950, Anisfield-Wolf award, 1969, Essence award, 1988, Frost medal Poetry Soc. Am., 1989; named Poet Laureate of Ill., 1968; recipient Lifetime Achievement award Nat. Endowment for the Arts, 1989; inducted into Nat. Women's Hall of Fame, 1988. Mem. Soc. Midland Authors. Home: 7428 S Evans Ave Chicago IL 60619

BROOKS, HELENE MARGARET, editor-in-chief; b. Jersey City, Apr. 1, 1942; d. Sinclair Duncan and Helen Margaret (McDermott) B.; m. Joseph F. Olivieri, Dec. 10, 1987. BA, C.W. Post Coll., 1977. Asst. editor McCall's Mag., N.Y.C., 1969-72, assoc. editor, 1972-75, editor features and travel, 1975-83; managing editor 50 Plus Mag. Whitney Commn., N.Y.C., 1983; exec. editor 50 Plus Mag. Whitney Comm., N.Y.C., 1983-87; editor in chief Network Mag./Internat. Airlines Travel Agt. Network, N.Y.C., 1987—; editorial cons. Am. Hairdressing Industry , N.Y.C. 1983. Mem. Am. Soc. Mag. Editors, Am. Assn. Travel Editors, Phi Eta. Democrat. Presbyterian. Home: 84 Trellis Ln Wantagh NY 11793 Office: Internat Airlines Travel 300 Garden City Plaza Ste 342 Garden City NY 11530

BROOKS, JANE PEYSER, school psychologist; b. N.Y.C., Oct. 11, 1936; d. Melvin W. and Ruth (Israelson) Peyser; m. Frederic H. Brooks, June 10, 1957; children: Frederic H., Kate M., Mark J. BA, Barnard Coll., 1958; MA, Tchrs. Coll., 1960, Fairfield U., 1975; EdD, St. John's U., 1989. Nat. cert. sch. psychologist. Tchr. Bd. Edn., N.Y.C., 1960-62; sch. psychologist Bd. Coop. Ednl. Svcs., Yorktown Heights, N.Y., 1976-79, Bd. Edn., Stamford, Conn., 1979—. Bd. mem. Eisman Found. for Children, N.Y.C. Mem. Am. Psychol. Assn., Conn. Psychol. Assn., Nat. Assn. Sch. Psychologists, Conn. Assn. Sch. Psychologists, Am. Assn. Counseling and Devel., Sch. Psychologists Internat. Home: 189 Shore Rd Old Greenwich CT 06870 Office: Stamford Sch System Hillandale Ave Stamford CT 06902

BROOKS, JANET EILEEN, librarian; b. Muskogee, Okla., July 24, 1957; d. James Neal and Helen Eileen (Gardner) Brown; m. David Shaffer Brooks, Aug. 2, 1980. BA, Anderson (Ind.) Coll., 1979; MEd, Okla. City U., 1988. Tchr. St. Mary's Elem. Sch., Ponca City, Okla., 1979-80; pub. svc. libr. Met. Libr. System, Okla. City, 1980-89, materials selector, 1989—. Mem. Okla. Libr. Assn., Okla. Sch. Librs. and Media Specialists Assn., ALA, Mountain Plains Libr. Assn., Young Adult Sequoyah Com., Intellectual Freedom Com. Office: Met Libr System 131 Dean A McGee Oklahoma City OK 73102

BROOKS, JEANNE ELLEN, health information services executive; b. Washington, Mo., Apr. 2, 1950; d. Hugh Joseph and Margaret Evelyn (Schroeder) Roetheli; m. Robert Louis Brooks, Aug. 1, 1970; children: Robert Joseph, Michael Christopher. B Sociology, Benedictine Coll., Atchison, Kans., 1972. Cert. in health info. mgmt., 1985; accredited record technician, 1975. Clk. St. Francis Hosp., Washington, Mo., 1966-68; clk. Gibson Store, Atchison, 1970-71; sec. SAGA Food Svc., Atchison, 1971-72; accredited record technician St. John's Mercy Hosp., Washington, 1973-78; transcriptionist Med. Transcription Svc., Ellisville, Mo., 1978-83; accredited record technician St. John's Mercy Hosp., Washington, 1983-84; dir. health info. St. John's Mercy Hosp., 1984—; mem. adv. bd. East Cen. Coll., Union, Mo., 1986; mem. search com. Stephens Coll., Columbia, Mo. 1985. Mem. Am. Med. Record Assn., Ea. Mo. Med. Records, Mo. Med. Record Assn., Ladies Sodality (v.p. 1984-86). Roman Catholic. Office: St Johns Mercy Hosp 200 Madison Ave Washington MO 63090

BROOKS, JO ANNE WHITE, medical records administrator; b. St. Augustine, Fla., Nov. 25, 1928; d. James Oren and Fannie Mae (McKenzie) White; m. Wiley Truett Brooks, Oct. 21, 1950; children: Wiley Truett, James David, Susan Diane, Leslie Joan. AA, Lees McRae Jr. Coll., Banner Elk, N.C., 1947; student, St. Joseph Coll., Windham, Maine, 1987—. Mgr. med. record dept. Gaston Meml. Hosp., Gastonia, N.C., 1948-60, West Volusia Meml. Hosp., Deland, Fla., 1961-68; dir. med. record dept. Wake Med. Ctr., Raleigh, 1968—; cons. in field; clin. instr. E. Carolina U., Greenville, 1975—, W. Carolina U., Cullowee, N.C., 1988—, Pitts. U., 1984—; lectr. in field. Panel mem. United Way, Raleigh, 1986-87; mem. Child Advocacy, Raleigh, 1986-87; active in past various charitable orgns. Mem. Am. Med. Record Assn., N.C. Med. Record Assn. (pres. 1975-76), Southeastern Med. Record Conf. (pres. 1974-75), Altrusa (pres. 1987-89, treas. 1989—). Democrat. Baptist. Home: 3100 Shadwell Ct Raleigh NC 27613 Office: Wake Med Ctr 3000 New Bern Ave Raleigh NC 27610

BROOKS, JOAN LOGAN, educator, consultant; b. Lynchburg, Va., Oct. 21, 1940; d. Lewis Wilson and Macie Turner (Logan) B.; 1 child, Frederick Marshall Williams; m. Craig Moller Hove, Apr. 18, 1981. BA cum laude, Lynchburg Coll., 1979, MEd, 1989; postgrad., Union Theol. Sem., 1980-81, 82-83; MA, Presbyn. Sch. Christian Edn., 1987. Sales clk. J.P. Bell Co., Lynchburg, 1960-61; adminstrv. asst. Cen. Fidelity Bank, Lynchburg, 1961-68; engring. aide Babcock and Wilcox Co., Lynchburg, 1968-78, engring. applications programmer, 1979-80; adj. instr. Va. Sem. and Coll., Lynchburg, 1987-89, assoc. prof. ednl. ministry, 1989—; pvt. practice ednl. cons. in Christian Edn. Lynchburg, 1987—; itineration organizer Blue Ridge Presbytery, Lynchburg, 1985-86, workshop organizer, 1987; educator, organizer St. Andrew Presbyn. Ch., Lynchburg, 1984-89. Designer, creator (needlework banner) Chrismon Cross, 1986 (1st prize, 1986). Pres. Georgetown Forest Homeowners' Assn., Lynchburg, 1990-93. Mem. Va. Div. UDC (v.p. 1989-91), Kirkwood Otey Chpt. UDC (historian 1978-80, 85-91, pres. 1989-91, Jefferson Davis Medal, 1990), Nat. Soc. DAR (Red Hill chpt.), Religious Edn. Assn., Lynchburg Hist. Found., Campbell County Hist. Soc. Presbyterian. Home: 408 West Cadbury Dr Lynchburg VA 24501-2331

BROOKS, JULIE AGNES, psychiatrist; b. Grand Rapids, Mich., Apr. 16, 1941; d. Wesley Clyde and Janet Niven (Nicol) B. BA in Bacteriology, Fla. State U., 1963; Degree in Med. Tech., Mercy Hosp., San Diego, 1968; MD, U. Autonoma, Guadalajara, 1980. Cert. med. tech. Am. Soc. Clin. Pathologists. Intern U. Iowa, Iowa City, 1980; resident U. Iowa, 1980-81, Cherokee (Iowa) Mental Health Inst., 1982-83; practice medicine specializing in psychiatry Aberdeen, S.D., 1984-86, Ft. Myers, Fla., 1987—; mem. staff Ga. State Mental Hosp., Savannah, 1986-87, G. Pierce Wood Meml. Hosp., Arcadia, Fla., 1987-89; vol. physician Mexican Govt., 1979; cons. psychiatrist Sioux reservations, Eagle Butte, Sisseton, 1984-86; med. dir. Columbus (Ga.) Mental Health, Mental Retardation, Substance Abuse Program, 1987. Mem. Am. Psychiat. Assn., NAFE, U. Autonoma Guadalajara Alumni Assn. Home: PO Box 50280 Fort Myers FL 33905 Office: 2243 D McGregor Blvd Fort Myers FL 33905

BROOKS, KIMBERLY A., accountant; b. Norfolk, Va., June 10, 1955; d. S. Alan and Barbara (Cooper) Yulsman; m. Donald M. Brooks, Sept. 21, 1985; 1 child, Justin. BS in Acctg., U. Pa., 1977. CPA. From jr. to sr. auditor Laventhol & Horwath, Phila., 1977-82; audit supr. Goldenberg/Rosenthal, Phila., 1982-84; dir. internal audit Siemens Med. Systems, Inc., Iselin, N.J., 1984-89; pvt. practice Horsham, Pa., 1990—. Mem. AICPAs, Pa. Soc. CPAs, Inst. Internal Audit. Home: 310 Saw Mill Ln #10E Horsham PA 19044

BROOKS, LEANNE RUTH, educator; b. Muncie, Ind., Nov. 11, 1961; d. H. Terrence and Ruth Margaret (Hunter) Hurt; m. Ivan Roderick Brooks, Sept. 1, 1984. BA, Anderson U., Ind., 1984. Dist. mgr. Sujen, Chattanooga, 1984-87; tchr. computer aide Sch. Dist. #61, Decatur, Ill., 1987-90; CCP faciliator Job Tng. Partnership, Decatur, 1990—. Mem. Camarada Club, Kappa Mu Epsilon, Phi Eta Sigma, Sigma Zeta, Alpha Chi, Delta Mu Delta. Republican. Ch. of God. Home: 1423 N Walnut Grove Decatur IL 62526

BROOKS, MARY CAMPBELL, singer, songwriter; b. Houston, Feb. 29, 1964; d. George McNielle and Lisbeth (Gibson) B. BA in Journalism, Trinity U., San Antonio, 1986. Pres. Assn. Residence Hall Students, Trinity U., San Antonio, 1984-85; pres. Sopris Records, Aspen, Colo., 1986-88; pres. Seven Castles Music, Aspen, 1986—, Austin, Tex., 1988—; pres. Mary Brooks Prodns., Aspen, 1986-88, Austin, 1988—. Writer, producer, artist (record album) Mountain Angel, 1987 (Colo. Composer's Classic award 1987), (video) Live on 6th St, 1989. Performer Pitkin County Fair-Benefit, Aspen, 1987, Redstone Fair-Benefit, Redstone, Colo., 1987, Sta. KDNK-FM Benefit, Cardondale, Colo., 1987, Benefit Save the Ledge, Redding, Conn., 1988. Mem. Nat. Assn. for Campus Activities (assoc.), Austin Music Industry Coun., Broadcast Music, Inc. Office: Mary Brooks Prodns 1508 Southport Ste 236 Austin TX 78704

BROOKS, MRS. MEL See BANCROFT, ANNE

BROOKS, NAOMI WILLIAMS, nurse educator; b. Union Bridge, Md., Nov. 23, 1937; d. Patrick Henry and Ruth Isabel (Richter) Williams; m. Luther Preston Brooks, Nov. 23, 1960 (dec. 1973); children: Gordon Patrick, Angela Ruth. BS, U. Md., 1961; MS, U. Md., Balt., 1977; postgrad., U. Md., College Park. Staff nurse Washington Hosp. Ctr., Washington, 1958-62; head nurse Washington Hosp. Ctr., 1962, instr., 1962-63; instr. to asst. prof. nursing U. Md., Balt., 1976—. Mem. ch. coun. Zion Evang. Luth. Ch., Takoma Park, Md., 1981—, chmn. evangelism com., 1988—. Mem. Md. League for Nursing (legis. health policy com. 1983—, bd. dirs. 1989—), Md. Nurses Assn. (chmn. nominating com. 1988-89), AAUW, U. Md. Alumni Assn., Sigma Theta Tau (nominating chmn. 1986-88, counselor 1981-83, 88—), Phi Kappa Phi. Lutheran.

BROOKS, PAMELA MARIE, materials executive; b. Oklahoma City, Mar. 15, 1964; d. William Charles and Elizabeth (Waters) B. BS, BA, Boston U., 1986. Mfg. inventory control supr. Analog Devices Semiconductor, Wilmington, Mass., 1986-87; prodn. control mgr. Acoustic Tech., Boston, 1987-88, 1987-88; materials mgr. Acoustic Tech., Boston, Mass., 1988--. Career adv. mem. Boston U. CAP, Nat. Marfan Syndrome Found., Detroit, 1987—. Mem. Nat. Assn. Female Executives. Roman Catholic. Office: Acoustic Tech 30 Jeffries St East Boston MA 02128

BROOKS, RENANA ESTHER, clinical psychologist, consultant, researcher; b. Bethesda, Md., July 18, 1956; d. David Abraham and Harriet (Kahn) B.; m. Robert Benjamin Rouirsky, Jan. 1, 1989. Student, Princeton U., 1978; BA, Barnard Coll., 1980; PhD, George Washington U., 1989. Staff neuropsychologist, faculty mem. Harvard Med. Sch., Cambridge, Mass., 1985-88; dir. psychol. svcs. Commonwealth Mental Health Assocs., Va., 1985-90; post-doctoral fellow U. Mass. Med. Ctr., Worcester, 1988-89; dir., creator High Profile/Peek Performance Cons. Co., Washington, 1990—; dir. neuropsychol. svcs. Kingsburg Sch. for Learning Disabilities, Washington, 1990—; cons. Ctr. for Memory Impairment and Neurobehavioral Disorders, Cambridge. Contbr. articles to profl. jours. Fellow Am. Psychol. Assn. (also div. of Cons. Psychologists, Clin. Psychologists); mem. AAMFT (clin.). Home: 2440 Virginia Ave D 205 Washington DC 20037

BROOKS, ROBERTA DELORES, school psychologist; b. Kitts Hill, Ohio, July 9, 1933; d. George L. and Alma (Chafin) B. Assoc. in Liberal Arts, Ashland Jr. Coll., 1952; BSc in Edn., Ohio State U., 1954; MA in Psychology, Marshall U., 1964; EdD, U. Cin., 1974. Lic. psychologist, Ohio; nat. cert. sch. psychologist; cert. secondary tchr., sch. counselor, provisional adminstr. specialist in spl. edn. Tchr. English, Rock Hill High Sch., Pedro, Ohio, 1955-57; tchr. history, Ironton (Ohio) City Schs., 1957-63, tchr. English,, 1963-67, counselor, psychologist Title I program, 1968-78, dist. sch. psychologist, 1978-86, part-time chief psychologist, 1987—; clin. supr. Family Guidance Ctr., Ironton, 1990; pres. Ironton Edn. Assocs., 1965-66; psychologist Meigs County Schs., Pomeroy, Ohio, 1986-87; psychologist, cons. Ohio Ctr. for Youth and Famiy Devel., Pedro, 1986—; lectr. Morehead (Ky.) State U., 1987. Mem. alumni bd. U. Cin. Coll. Edn., 1983-90; mem. Ironton Coun. for Arts, 1985—. Recipient Outstanding Svc. award Arthritis Found. Southwestern Ohio, 1968, Outstanding Young Educator award Ironton Jaycees, 1967; U. Cin. doctoral scholar, 1970-74. Mem. Nat. Assn. Sch. Psychologists (charter mem.), Coun. on Exceptional Children, Ohio Psychol. Assn., Ohio Sch. Psychologists Assn. (chmn. nominating com., at-large rep. mem. exec. bd. 1982-85), Sch. Psychologists Assn. S.E. Ohio (hon. life, pres. 1978-79, Disting. Svc. award 1986), AAUW, Ohio Ret. Tchrs. Assn. (life), Psi Chi. Republican. Office: Ironton City Schs 105 S 5th St Ironton OH 45638

BROOKS, SUSAN ANN, accountant; b. Exeter, N.H., Aug. 20, 1963; d. Peter Grant and Carolyn (Goss) B. BBA in Managerial Acctg., Hofstra U., Hempstead, N.Y., 1985; MBA in Bus. Adminstrn., N.H. Coll., Manchester, 1990. Cert. managerial acct. Acct. C.H. Sprague & Son, Portsmouth, N.H., 1985-87; staff acct. Harris Graphics, Dover, N.H., 1987-88; sr. staff acct. Timberland, Hampton, N.H., 1988—. Mem. Nat. Assn. Accts. Home: 440 Winnacunnet Rd Apt 3 Hampton NH 03842 Office: Timberland 11 Merrill Dr Hampton NH 03842

BROOKS, VERA RAMEY, business educator; b. Southside, Tenn., Jan. 10, 1952; d. Cleveland and Virgie (Moore) Ramey; m. Enoch Melvin Brooks, Dec. 21, 1974; children: John, Christopher, Clinton. BS in Bus., Edn., Austin Peay State U., 1974; M Bus. Edn., Middle Tenn. State U., 1981. Cert. profl. sec. Machine transcriptionist Jasten Am. Yearbook, Inc., 1974; sec. ARO, Inc., Arnold AFB, Tenn., 1975-78; instr. bus. Coffee County Cen. High Sch., Manchester, Tenn., 1978-80; asst. prof. Motlow State Community Coll., Tullahoma, Tenn., 1980—. Sunday sch. tchr. Cabin Row Missionary Bapt. Ch., 1970-74, Atlantic Temple, 1982—; faculty coun. mem., Motlow, 1988-90. Named to Outstanding Young Women of Am., 1984. Mem. Nat. Bus. Edn. Assn., Tenn. Bus. Edn. Assn., Atlantic Temple Ch. of God in Christ Edn. Club (Outstanding Leadership award 1981), Delta Pi Epsilon (pres. Gamma Eta chpt. 1988-90). Home: Rt 4 Box 4576 Tullahoma TN 37388

BROOME, CLAIRE VERONICA, epidemiologist, researcher; b. Tunbridge Wells, Kent, England, Aug. 24, 1949; came to U.S., 1951; d. Kenneth R. and Heather C. (Platt) B.; m. John F. Head, Apr. 2, 1988; 1 child, Gabriel K. BA, Harvard U., 1970, MD, 1975. Diplomate Am. Bd. Internal Medicine. Dep. chief spl. pathogens br. Ctrs. for Disease Control, Atlanta, 1979-80, chief meningitis, spl. pathogens br., 1981—; cons. vaccine devel. AID, 1988—, WHO, NIH, various universities; mem. steering com. on encapsulated bacterial vaccines, WHO, Geneva, 1989—, adv. com. on vaccines FDA, Washington, 1990—. Contbr. numerous articles to profl. jours. Recipient M. C. Rockefeller fellowship, 1970-71, Meritorious Svc. medal USPHS, 1986, rsch. grants NIH, FDA, Dept. of State. Fellow Infectious Diseases Soc. Am.; mem. ACP, Am. Epidemiologic Soc., Am. Soc. Microbiology, Common Cause, Phi Beta Kappa, Alpha Omega Alpha. Office: Ctrs for Disease Control CO9 Atlanta GA 30333

BROOME, L. ELIZABETH, psychotherapist; b. Denver, Apr. 16, 1939; d. LeRoy Laurence and Lillian Thulin Broyles; children: Christine Broome-Plemons, Barbara Broome. BA, U. Colo., 1973, MA, 1975; PhD, Walden U., 1982. Cert. Nat. Bd. Cert. Counselors. Dir. Gregg Bemis Child Care Ctr., Colorado Springs, Colo., 1973-76; therapist Pikes Peak Mental Health Ctr., Colorado Springs, 1976-82; pvt. practice psychotherapist Colorado Springs, 1982-88; co-founder, team mem. Family Devel. Project, Colorado Springs, 1985-87; pvt. practice psychotherapist Everett, Wash., 1988—. Mem. NOW. Mem. Am. Assn. for Counseling & Devel., Am. Psychol. Assn., Internat. Soc. for Prevention of Child Abuse & Neglect, Am. Profl. Soc. on the Abuse of Children. Office: 3020 Rucker Ave Ste 308 Everett WA 98201

BROPHY, MARY NONA, computer software consultant; b. Phoenixville, Pa., Feb. 7, 1959; d. Eugene Michael and Mary Catherine (Garrett) B. Student, Drexel U., 1981; BA summa cum laude, Rochester Inst. Tech., 1981; M Libr. and Info. Sci., U. Tex., 1983. Programmer Systems and Computer Technology, Malvern, Pa., 1984-86, assoc. cons., 1986-87, cons., 1987-89, sr. cons., 1989—. Archaeologist, developer mus. display case Rosehill Mansion, Geneva, N.Y., 1981. Mem. Valley Forge Ski Club. Democrat. Roman Catholic. Home: 272 Kimbel Dr Phoenixville PA 19460 Office: Systems and Computer Tech 4 Country View Rd Malvern PA 19355

BROSA, CAROL JOANNE, corporate professional; b. Baldwin, Kans., May 20, 1933; d. Murlin Lewis and Orpha Phyllis (Cunningham) Cook; m. Julius Albert Brosa, July 6, 1958; children: Cynthia Irene Brosa Irvine, Melinda Jean Brosa Rittgers. BA, Baker U., 1955. Office mgr. C.B. Willey R.E. and Ins. Agy., Baldwin, Kans., 1952-55; ins. salesman Farmers Mutual Ins. Co., Marysville, Kans., 1954-55; office mgr. Treasurer's Office Baker U., Baldwin, 1955-56; sec. acct. Paden, Bartlett, West, Engrs., Topeka, 1956-58; sec. N.Mex. State U., Las Cruces, 1958-59; acct. sec. Seaborn Collins Agy., 1959-61; office mgr. Barbara Bartocci Agy., Overland Park, Kans., 1978-81; acct. Accountemps, Kansas City, Mo., 1981-82; corp. sec. lending agy. mgr. Savs. Bond and Mortgage Co., Topeka, 1985-89; trustee Savs. Bond and Mortgage Co., Topeka 1986-89. Organized Bookkeeping System, Wesley Fellowship Group 1956. Sustaining mem. Rep. Nat. Com., 1979—, newsletter editor AAUW, Topeka 1987-89, leader Girl Scouts Am., Overland Park, vol. Social Svcs., Overland Park. Mem. Am. Shorthorn Assn., Pie In The Sky Investment Group, Investment Club, Home and Garden. Republican. United Methodist. Home: 2790 Jewell Ave Topeka KS 66611 Office: Brosa Shorthorn Farm Rte 1 Box 136C Valley Falls KS 66088

BROSE, PAULA LYNN, advertising media buyer, planner; b. Detroit, June 25, 1942; d. Max and Jean (Miller) B. BA, NYU, N.Y.C., 1964. Tape editor, rec. engr. NYU, N.Y.C., 1961-65; promotion copywriter WJBK-TV, Detroit, 1965-68; copywriter, staff asst. Jonathan, James and Alan, 1968-69; sr. staff asst., broadcast media estimator Campbell Ewald Co., 1969-78; media buyer, traffic and prodn. coord. Wilding Advt., 1978-80; media buyer, traffic coord. Starr Advt., 1980; media buyer Robert Solomon & Assocs., 1980-83; ptnr., cons. Media Svcs., 1983-87; owner, cons. Brose Media Svcs., Southfield, Mich., 1987—. Mem. Founders Soc., Detroit Inst. Arts, 1979—. Mem. Am. Women in Radio and TV (treas. 1990-1991), Adcraft Club, Met. Assn. Bus. Women. Jewish. Office: Brose Media Svc 23237 Providence #205 Southfield MI 48075

BROSNAN, CAROL RAPHAEL SARAH, arts administrator, musician; b. Paterson, N.J., July 19, 1931; d. Basil Roger Warnock and Mary Ellen Carroll (McDonald) B. Student, George Washington U., Washington, 1956-61, U. Va., 1975, U. Oxford (Eng.), 1975; B.A. in History, George Washington U., 1981, postgrad., 1983-87; studied with Iris Brussels and Helen Yakobson, 1983-87. Adminstrv. clk. Dept. of Army, Def., Pentagon, Office of asst. chief of staff intelligence, Washington, 1955-58; clk. fgn. sci. info. program NSF, Washington, 1958-60, adminstrv. clk., 1960-65, adminstrv. fellowship clk. grad. fellowship program, 1965-72; deputy chmn. for mgmt. Nat. Found. Arts and Humanities, Nat. Endowment for Arts, Washington, 1972—; music tchr. piano, Paterson, N.J., 1945-53; piano recitalist U.S., Heidelberg, W. Ger. Served with WAC, 1953-55. Recipient Young People's Concerts award, 1945. Hon. fellow Harry S. Truman Libr. Inst. Nat. and Internat. Affairs, 1975. Fellow Intercontinental Biog. Assn.; mem. Am. Assn. for Advancement Slavic Studies, Am. Hist. Assn., Am. Philol. Assn., Acad. Polit. Sci. (contbg.), Am. Classical League, Friends of Bodleian Libr. (Oxford U.), Luther Rice Soc. of George Washington U. (life), Phi Alpha Theta. Home: 7523 McWhorter Pl Apt 303 Annandale VA 22003 Office: Nat Endowment for Arts 1100 Pennsylvania Ave NW Washington DC 20506

BROSSEAU, IRMA FINN, business executive, management consultant; b. Boston, Sept. 4, 1930; d. Harry Miller and Alfreda (Zimmerman) Dyer; m. George Brosseau, Jan. 14, 1977; children by previous marriage—Hester, Jonathan, Sarah. B.S., Simmons Coll., 1952; hon. doctorate, Hawthorne Coll., 1984. Cert. assn. exec. Asst. to prodn. mgr. Houghton Mifflin Pub. Co., Boston, 1952-56; desk editor, women's editor Quincy (Mass.) Patriot Ledger, 1956-58; desk editor, reporter, feature writer, women's editor Anchorage Times, 1958-60, 66-71; desk editor Anchorage News, 1965-66; program dir. Nat. Fedn. Bus. and Profl. Women's Clubs, Inc., Washington, 1972-77; exec. dir. Nat. Fedn. Bus. and Profl. Women's Clubs, Inc., 1977-84; chief exec. officer Fedn Bus. and Profl. Women and Bus. and Profl. Women Found., Washington, 1984-87; pres. The Brosseau Group, Reston, Va., 1987—; founder Women's Exec. Groups, 1987, Double Track Mgmt. Coaching System, Mgmt. Assitance Program; cons. vol. leadership devel., mgmt., writer and workshop leader; speaker, trainer in mgmt. and strategic mgmt. planning; bd. dirs. Nat. Coun. on Future of Women in Workplace. Mem. Reston Bd. Commerce. Recipient Alumnae Achievement award Simmons Coll., 1987. Mem. Am. Soc. Assn. Execs. (trustee found.), Greater Washington Soc. Assn. Execs., Network Entrepeneurial Women, Reston Rotary Club, ACLU, Common Cause. Office: 11345 Sunset Hills Rd Reston VA 22090

BROTHERS, JOYCE DIANE, television personality, psychologist; b. N.Y.C.; d. Morris K. and Estelle (Rapoport) Bauer; m. Milton Brothers, July 4, 1949; 1 child, Lisa Robin. BS, Cornell U., 1947; MA, Columbia U., 1950, PhD, 1953; LHD (hon.), Franklin Pierce Coll., Gettysburg Coll. Asst. in psychology Columbia U., N.Y.C., 1948-52; instr. psychology Hunter Coll., N.Y.C., 1948-52; ind. psychologist, writer, 1952—. Co-host: TV program Sports Showcase, 1956; appearances: TV program Dr. Joyce Brothers, 1958-63, Consult Dr. Brothers, 1960-66, Ask Dr. Brothers, 1965-75; hostess (TV syndication) Living Easy with Dr. Joyce Brothers, 1972-75; columnist TV syndication, N.Am. Newspaper Alliance, 1961-71, Bell-McClure Syndicate, 1963-71, King Features Syndicate, 1972—, Good Housekeeping mag., 1962—; appearances Sta. WNBC, 1966-70; radio program Emphasis, 1966-75, Monitor, 1967-75, Sta. WMCA, 1970-73, ABC Reports, 1966-67, NBC Radio Network Newsline, 1975—; news analyst radio program, Metro Media-TV, 1975-76, news corr., TVN, Inc., 1975-76, Sta. KABC-TV, 1977-82, Sta. WABC-TV, 1980-82, , 86-88, Sta. WLS-TV, 1980-82, NIWS Syndicated News Service, 1982-84, The Dr. Joyce Brothers Program, The Disney Channel, 1985, Sta. WKBS-TV News, 1987—; spl. feature writer Hearst papers, UPI; author: Ten Days to a Successful Memory, 1959, Woman, 1961, The Brothers System for Liberated Love and Marriage, 1975, How to Get Whatever You Want Out of Life, 1978, What Every Woman Should Know About Men, 1982, What Every Woman Ought to Know About Love and Marriage, 1988, The Successful Woman, 1989. Co-chmn. sports com. Lighthouse for Blind; door-to-door chmn. Fedn. Jewish Philanthropies, N.Y.C.; mem. fund raising com. Olympic Fund; mem. People-to-People Program. Winner $64,000 Question TV Program, 1956, $64,000 Challenge, 1957; recipient Mennen Baby Found. award, 1959, Newhouse Newspaper award, 1959, Am. Acad. Achievement award, Am. Parkinson Disease Assn. award, 1971, Sigma Delta Chi Deadline award, 1971, Pres.'s Cabinet award U. Detroit, 1975, Woman of Achievement award Women's City Club Cleve., 1981, award Calif. Home Econs. Assn., 1981, award Distributive Edn. Clubs Am., 1981, Pub. Service award Ridgewood Women's Club, 1987, Women Who Make a Difference award, Sen. Bill Bradley, 1990. Mem. Sigma Xi. Office: NBC 30 Rockefeller Pla New York NY 10020

BROTHERS, KAREN ELIZABETH, software development company executive; b. Hackensack, N.J., July 25, 1946; d. William Herman and Lorraine Olive (Nelsen) Ellers; m. Dennis Frederick Brothers, Nov. 12, 1967; children: Michael, Shannon. BS in Maths., MIT, Cambridge, 1969. Ptnr. Consultus, Cambridge, Mass., 1972-80; v.p., software devel. Warner Eddison Assocs., Inc., Cambridge, 1981-83; pres. Inmagic, Inc., Cambridge, 1984--; trustee Mass. Computer Software Coun., 1987—. Mem. Wayland Fin.

Com., 1979-85, chair, 1983-84; founding mem. Emerge; mem. Govs. Export 90's Coun., 1989. Mem. Assn. Computing Mach. Office: Inmagic Inc 2067 Mass Ave Cambridge MA 02140

BROTHERTON, MAUREEN SALTZER, newspaper executive; b. Winchester, Mass., Mar. 21, 1959; d. William Charles Saltzer and Janet Ann (Quigley) Child; m. O. Lee Brotherton, June 27, 1981 (div. 1984). BS in Journalism summa cum laude, Boston U., 1981; postgrad., Northeastern U., Boston, 1984. Freelance corr. Concord (N.H.) Monitor, 1981-82; advt. sales rep. N.H. Times, Concord, 1981-82, circulation mgr., 1982-83; circulation and promotion mgr. Century Publs. Inc., Winchester, Mass., 1983-84, asst. gen. mgr., 1984-85; ad dir., ops. mgr. Provincetown (Mass.) Adv., 1985-86; gen. mgr. Healdsburg (Calif.) Tribune, Lesher Communications, 1986-87, Valley Times, Lesher Communications, Pleasanton, Calif., 1987—; corp. oper. bd. dirs. Lesher Communications Inc., Walnut Creek, Calif. Vol. Granite State Pub. Radio, Concord, 1982-83; bd. dirs. Tri-Valley YMCA, Pleasanton, 1989—; chairperson Wings for Charity Fundraising Com., Pleasanton, 1989. Mem. Calif. Newspaper Pubs. Assn., Internat. Newspaper Mktg. Assn., Internat. Newspaper Advt. and Mktg. Execs. Assn., Admark-East Bay, Calif. Newspaper Advt. Execs. Assn., Pleasanton C. of C. (leadership com.). Democrat. Home: 460 Bollinger Cyn Ln #285 San Ramon CA 94583 Office: Valley Times Lesher Communications 127 Spring St PO Box 607 Pleasanton CA 94566

BROTMAN, PHYLLIS BLOCK, advertising and public relations executive; b. Balt., Mar. 23, 1934; d. Sol George Block and Delma (Herman) Brotman; student Balt. Jr. Coll., U. Va., Mary Washington Coll.; m. Don N. Brotman, Aug. 16, 1953; children: Solomon G., Barbara Gay. Assoc., Channel 13 TV, 1953-55; free-lance pub. relations, 1960-66; coordinator pub. relations Md. Council Ednl. TV, 1965-66; pres. Image Dynamics, Inc., Balt., 1966—; lectr., cons. Lectr. pub. relations Johns Hopkins; spl. lectr. pub. schs., Baltimore County, Inst. Politics, Miss., Ark., N.C., La.; cons. legis. info. program Md. Gen. Assembly, 1970; former coordinator spl. events Balt. Jr. Coll.; former program coordinator Wine Inst. Internat. pres. B'nai B'rith Girls, 1952-53. Bd dirs. Nat. Council Jewish Women, 1969-71, former coordinator pub. affairs, chmn. coll. program, program intellectual enrichment; bd. dirs. Levindale Home and Infirmary Ladies Aux., 1963-64, Assoc. Placement and Guidance Bur., 1964-65, Sinai Hosp. Aux., 1964-65, Chamber Symphony of San Francisco, Balt. Symphony Orchestra; state chmn. U.S. Olympics; former bd. dirs. Assoc. Jewish Charities, Nat. Jewish Welfare Fund; vice chmn. Nat. UN Day Com.; rep. to UN; nat. commr. B'nai B'rith Youth Orgn.; trustee Loyola Coll., Mary Washington Coll.; bd. vis. Towson State U.; chmn. econ. devel. commn. Balt. County, bd. govs. Center Club, Balt. Symphony Orch., Chamber Symphony San Francisco; mem. compensation com. Md. Gen. Assembly. Recipient certificate of achievement Md. Ho. of Dels., Md. Senate, Asso. Jewish Charities, 1965, award for outstanding community service Beta Omega Kappa, 1952; Woman of Yr. award Balt. Cancer Ctr.-U. Md., 1984, Pres.'s award for Pvt. Sector Initiatives, Mayor's award for Outstanding Pub. Service. Mem. Pub. Relations Soc. Am. (assoc., sec. Md. chpt., cert. of achievement Md. chpt.), Am. Assn. Polit. Consultants (dir., nat. pres.), Md. C. of C. (bd. dovs.), Am. Assn. Advt. Agys. (bd. dirs., chmn. Eastern region, govt. affairs com.), Internat. Assn. Polit. Cons., McDonough-Field Assn. (pres.), Balt. Council Pub. Relations, Md.-Del.-D.C. Press Assn., Council State Govts., Advt. Assn. Balt. (past bd. dirs.), Chesapeake Bay Flyers, Advt. Club D.C. (co-chmn. communications com. Am. Advt. Fedn.), Md. C. of C., Beta Omega Kappa (past pres.). Democrat. Jewish (pres. parents assn. 1968-70, mem. religious sch. com., bd. congregation). Mem. B'nai B'rith Women (v.p. Balt.), Hadassah (past chmn., speaker rep.). Instrumental in legislation to create state-wide endl. TV network. Home: 8105 McDonogh Rd Baltimore MD 21208 Office: Image Dynamics Inc 1101 N Calvert St Baltimore MD 21202

BROUGH, KAREN TANASSY, accountant; b. Plainfield, N.J., May 13, 1946; d. Louis Julius and Katharyn (Drake) Tanassy; m. Charles Nelson Brough, Aug. 29, 1970; children: John Tanassy, Christine Katharyn, Jessica Marie. Student, C.Z. Coll., 1964-67; BA in Anthropology, Calif. State U., Fresno, 1971, postgrad., 1982-83. CPA, Calif. Sec. hdqrs. South Command U.S. Army, Ft. Amador, C.Z., 1965-67, Quarry Heights, C.Z., 1967-68; real estate saleswoman Fresno and Clovis, Calif., 1976-78; loan agt. Wells Fargo Mortgage Co., Fresno, 1978-80; co-owner Applied Real Estate Seminars, Clovis, 1980-82; acct. KMG Main Hurdman, CPA, Fresno, 1983; internal auditor office auditor-contr.-treas. County of Fresno, 1983-87, sr. acct. computer svcs., 1987-89; asst. auditor contr. Modera County, 1989—. Contbr. articles to real estate publs. Chmn. Ft. Washington SheArea Rsch. Team, 1978-80; pres. scheduling com. Clovis Jr. Soccer League, 1980-83, sec., 1983-84, registrar, 1984-85, treas., 1985-87. C.Z. Soc. CPA's scholar, 1965. Mem. Phi Kappa Phi, Beta Alpha Psi. Democrat. Episcopalian. Home: 481 McArthur Ave Clovis CA 93612

BROUGHTON, BEVERLY JANE, construction executive; b. Detroit, Oct. 8, 1927; d. Donald John and Ida Mae (Coller) Garpow; m. Howard Millar Trerice, Jan. 3, 1953 (div. Mar. 1974); children: Howard Owen, Bruce Whitney. BA, Wayne U., 1949, cert. in teaching, 1951. Free-lance lectr., 1951-54; ins. agt. Donald Garpow Agy., Detroit, 1954-64; ptnr. Mobile Office Equipment Co., Detroit, 1979-85; owner, pres. Best Mobile Office/Modulars, Waterford, Mich., 1985—. Acrylic art represented in pvt. collections. Alt. del. Mich. Reps., Grand Rapids, 1984. Mem. Nat. Assn. for Self-Employed, Nat. Assn. for Female Execs., Constrn. Assn. Mich. Christian Scientist. Office: Best Mobile Office Modulars 4080 Dixie Hwy Waterford MI 48329

BROUN, ELIZABETH, art historian, museum administrator; b. Kansas City, Mo., Dec. 15, 1946; d. Augustine Hughes and Roberta Catherine (Hayden) Gibson; m. Ronald Broun, June 5, 1968; 1 dau., Katherine. B.A., U. Kans., 1968, Ph.D., 1976; cert. advanced study, U. Bordeaux, France, 1967. Curator prints and drawings Spencer Mus. Art, Lawrence, Kans., 1976-83; asst. prof. U. Kans., Lawrence, 1978-83; asst. dir. chief curator Nat. Mus. Am. Art, Washington, 1983-88; acting dir., 1988-89; dir. Nat. Mus. Am. Art, Washington, 1989—. Author: exhbn. catalogues Prints of Zorn, 1979, Prints and Drawings of Pat Steir, 1983, Patrick Ireland; Drawings 1965-85, 1986, Albert Pinkham Ryder, 1989; co-author: Benton's Bentons, 1980, Engravings of Marcantonio Raimondi, 1981. Woodrow Wilson fellow, 1968-69; Ford. Found. fellow, 1970-72. Mem. Phi Beta Kappa. Home: 7702 Marbury Rd Bethesda MD 20817 Office: Nat Mus Am Art 8th & G Sts NW Washington DC 20560

BROUSSARD, CAROL MADELINE, writer, photographer; b. Albany, Calif.; d. Roy E. and Adele (Belfils) Avila; m. Marvin E. Broussard; children: Valerie Madeline, Sean Hunter Rutledge. Student, West Hill Coll., Coalinga, Calif., Coll. Sequoias, Visalia, Calif., Inst. Metaphysics, La Brea, Calif. Pub. TV Watch, Tyler, Tex., 1969-74; resource sec. John C. Fremont Sch., Corcoran, Calif., 1974-77; editor Coalinga (Calif.) Record, 1978-81; pub. Kern Valley Chronicle, Lake Isabella, Calif., 1981-84; freelance writer, 1990—. Author poetry; song lyrics video to be aired Cajun Hoedown Man Century Cablevision, summer 1990. Recipient Photo-Journalist award Calif. Newspaper Assn., 1983, Best Feature Photo award Calif. Justice System, 1984, World of Child Photo award Fresno City and County Offices, 1980, Poetic Achievemnt award Amherst Soc., 1990, Award of Merit World of Peotry, 1990, Golden Poet award, 1990, Iliad Literary award '90, 1990. Republican. Home and Office: 445 W Nees Ave #105 Fresno CA 93711

BROUSSARD, MARGARET FAYE, office manager; b. Lafayette, La., Nov. 26, 1952; d. Chester Joseph and Mary Broussard; m. Steven Edmond, June 2, 1973 (div.). Student, U. Southwestern La., 1970-73; cert., San Jacinto Jr. Coll., Houston, 1975; BS, Tex. So. U., 1978; postgrad. in liberal arts, Houston Bapt. U., 1990. CRT operator, sr. terminal operator 1st City Nat. Bank, Houston, 1974-75; sec., librarian Tex. So. U. Banking Ctr., Houston, 1975-78; part-time sec. Tex. So. U. Day Care Ctr. and Temporaries Inc., Houston, 1978-79; adminstrv. sec., accounts payable clk. Temporaries Inc., Houston, 1979-80; accounts payable clk., in-house temp. Met. Transit Authority, Houston, 1980-81; office asst., word processing specialist Houston Oil & Minerals, Houston, 1981-82, Tenneco Oil Corp. (acquired Houston Oil & Minerals 1982), Houston, 1982-83; adminstrv. asst. Hoover Keith & Bruce Inc., Houston, 1983-87; office mgr. Collaboration in Sci. and Tech. Inc., Houston, 1987—. Vol. Sheltering Arms, Houston, 1981-83, March of Dimes 12 Mile Walk, Houston, 1985, Head Start & Food Pantries, Houston, 1985—. Recipient Nat. Def. grantee U. Southwestern La., 1970-73. Mem. Nat. Assn. Female Execs. Office: Collaboration in Sci and Tech Inc 15835 Park Ten Pl Ste 105 Houston TX 77084-5131

BROWDER, JEANNETTE ZENO, teacher; b. New Orleans, Sept. 15, 1946; d. Edgar Edward Zeno and Marguerite (Farue) DeSilva; m. Sylvester Leon Browder, Apr. 4, 1970; children: Darrin Bernard, Andrea LeRita. BA in Early Childhood Edn, U. N.C., Wilmington, 1985. Cert. kindergarten tchr., N.C. Sales clk. Levine's Dept. Store, New Orleans, 1967-68; substitute tchr. Orleans Parish Pub. Sch., New Orleans, 1968-72; title 7 aide Ferguson (Mo.) Florissant Reorganized, 1976-79; tchr. 2d grade Silverdale (N.C.) Elem. Sch., 1986-87; tchr. kindergarten Morton Elem. Sch., Jacksonville, N.C., 1987—; tutor below average students, Onslow and Jacksonville, N.C., 1986—. Mem. NEA, Onslow County Assn. Educators, Onslow Lejeune Reading Assn., Non-Commd. Officers Wives Club (v.p., mem.-at-large New River and Jacksonville, N.C. chpts. 1980—), Montford Point Marine Corps Assn. Ladies Aux. (parliamentarian), Tau Gamma Delta (chmn. scrapbook com. Jacksonville chpt. 1987—). Democrat. Baptist. Home: 10 Langtry St Jacksonville NC 28540 Office: Onslow County Schs Rt 2 Morton Elem Sch Jacksonville NC 28546

BROWER, JANET SUE, small business owner; b. Toledo, Apr. 8, 1944; d. Kenneth Reber and Mattie (Erb) Elmerna; m. Thomas Edwin Brower, June 23, 1962; children: Jeanette S. Wade, Joy S. Pipkin. Grad. high sch., Ceres, Calif. Loan sec. State Mortgage, San Jose, Calif., 1976-79; owner TPS Agy., Redding, Calif., 1980—. Mem. NAFE, C. of C., Nat. Assn. of Pers. Cons., Soroptimist Internat (charter pres. 1987-88, del. 1988-89). Redding Bus. Club (founder), Trade Club. Republican. Office: TPS Agy 1900 Churn Creek Ste 119 Redding CA 96002

BROWER, JOY DANIELS, public affairs officer, consultant; b. Seattle, June 28, 1941; d. Joseph Arthur and Pearl (Klenman) D.; m. John R. Brower, June 28, 1990. BA, Smith Coll., 1963; MBA, Seattle U., 1988. Prodn. asst. Seattle Repertory Theatre, 1963-65; stage mgr. Va. Mus. Theatre, Richmond, 1965-66; office asst. Seattle Symphony Orchestra, 1966-67; freelance sec., 1968-70; office mgr. Joe Daniels Agy., Seattle, 1970-73; pub. affairs officer Can. Consulate, Seattle, 1974-90; officer pub. rels. spl. events DanCo, Seattle, 1990—. Mem. Seattle Art Mus., Seattle Opera Guild. Mem. Am. Mktg. Assn., Pub. Rels. Soc. Am., Women in Communications, Inc., Women's Univ. Club, City Club, World Affairs Coun., World Trade Club, Jr. League. Home: 100 Ward St #306 Seattle WA 98109 Office: DanCo Pub Rels Spl Events PO Box 19382 Seattle WA 98109

BROWES, PAULINE, Canadian legislator; b. Harwood, Ont., Can., May 7, 1938; d. Robert Earle and Clara (Sandercock) Drope; m. George Harold Browes, Sept. 12, 1961; children: Tammy, Janet, Jeffrey. Student, Toronto Tchrs. Coll., York U., McLaughlin Coll. Mem. for cen. Scarborough Can. Ho. of Commons, 1984—. Chmn. Scarborough Bd. Health, 1979-84. Mem. Progressive Conservative Party. Anglican. Club: Albany of Toronto, U. Women's Club, Scarborough Golf and Country Club. Office: Ho of Commons, 409 W Block, Ottawa, ON Canada K1A 0A6*

BROWN, ADRIENNE JEAN, microbiology diagnostic testing company official; b. Balt., June 10, 1950; d. Richard James and Lorraine Mary (Braun) Whitely; m. Wayne Timothy Brown, June 4, 1972; 1 child, Craig Alexander. BA, Towson State U., 1972. Cert. purchasing mgr. Regional ter. rep. Avon Products, Inc., Newark, Del., 1966-69; adminstrv. asst. LDKP, Inc., Balt., 1973-76; adminstrv. asst. Becton Dickinson Microbiology Systems, Cockeysville, Md., 1976-79, jr. buyer, 1979-81, buyer, 1982-84, sr. buyer, 1985—, supr., 1986—, corp. polystyrene negotiator, 1987—. Sec., editor Walnut Hills-Blue Ridge Estates Improvement Assn., Kingsville, Md., 1975-78; den leader Boy Scouts Am., Bradshaw, Md., 1987-88. Republican. Roman Catholic. Home: 11901 Caspian Rd Kingsville MD 21087 Office: Becton Dickinson Micro Sys 250 Schilling Circle Cockeysville MD 21030

BROWN, ALICE MARIE, loss prevention specialist; b. Teaneck, N.J., Nov. 12, 1955; d. James Joseph and Alice (Farr) B. BA, William Paterson Coll., 1977; postgrad., Montclair State U., 1989—. Tchr. Elizabeth (N.J.) High Sch., 1982-87; security supr. Fortunoff, Wayne, N.J., 1987-89; loss prevention mgr. NBO Stores, Carlstadt, N.J., 1989—; police officer Ridgefield Park (N.J.) Spl. Police, 1980-90. Mem. Soc. Investigators of Newark, Am. Soc. Indsl. Security, NAFE, Ridgefield Park Jr./Sr. High Sch. Alumni Assn. (editor newsletter 1990—). Office: NBO Stores 100 Industrial Rd Carlstadt NJ 07072

BROWN, ALICE PRATT, museum executive; b. Toledo, Ohio, Dec. 17, 1908; d. John Sherring and Genevieve (Doyle) Pratt; m. William Weston Brown, May 25, 1934; children: Hayden William, William Weston, Alice Sherring. Student, Lasell Jr. Coll., Newton, Mass., 1927-29. Sec. Mattatuck Mus., Waterbury, Conn., 1970—; justice of the peace, 1975—. pres. Middlebury Hist. Soc., 1970-82; corporator, trustee Lasell Coll., Newton, 1979—; sustaining mem. Jr. League. Mem. Colonial Dames of Am. Republican. Congregationalist. Home: 193 Crest Rd Middlebury CT 06762

BROWN, ALICE ROBERTA, transportation company executive; b. Pottsville, Pa., July 5, 1952; d. Emmett Franklin and Ruth Minnie (Nagle) Miller; divorced; children: Jeremy Scott, Travis Edward. BS in Psychology, Millersville U., 1973; MS in Human Resource Mgmt., U. Utah, Stuttgart, W.Ger., 1978. Lab. technician, Bio-Med. Labs., Friedensburg, Pa., 1969-71; mgr. Sico, Lancaster, Pa., 1971-73; quality control mgr. Berkley Products Co., Akron, Pa., 1974-75, order dept. clk., 1978-79, customer svc. mgr., 1979-89, safety and health officer, 1979-89, pers. employment counselor, 1980-89, gen. mgr. chmn. mgmt. div., 1988-89; ops. mgr. Keystone Block Transp. Co., Temple, Pa., 1989—; switchboard operator U.S. Army, Stuttgart, 1975-77. Mem. NAFE. Republican. Avocations: camping; gardening; motorcycling; reading. Office: Keystone Block Transp Co PO Box 9 Temple PA 19560

BROWN, ALISON A., computer center administrator; m. Kenneth G. Wilson, 1982. With Cornell U., Ithaca, N.Y., 1968-88, assoc. dir. for advanced computing & networking Theory Ctr.; assoc. dir. Ohio Supercomputer Ctr. Ohio State U., Columbus, 1988—. Office: Ohio State U Ohio Supercomputer Ctr Columbus OH 43210*

BROWN, ANNE BARBARA, financial executive; b. Bronxville, N.Y., Sept. 22, 1949; d. Paul Robert and Anne (Brady) B.; m. William Lawrence Farrell, Sept. 28, 1975; 2 children. BA, Trinity Coll., Washington, 1971; MBA, U. Pa., 1973. Fixed income salesperson Goldman, Sachs & Co., N.Y.C., 1973-78, v.p., 1978-83, v.p., fin. futures specialist, Dallas, 1983-87; v.p. fixed income div., N.Y.C., 1987—. Trustee Coun. Pa. Women U. Pa. Mem. women's com. Girl Scouts of N.Y., N.Y.C., 1982-83. Heubner fellow Wharton Grad. Sch., U. Pa., 1972. Mem. Trinity Coll. Alumni Assn. N.Y., Wharton Grad. Alumni Assn., Phi Beta Kappa. Roman Catholic. Club: Wharton (N.Y.C.) (officer 1975-79). Office: Goldman Sachs & Co 85 Broad St 25th Fl New York NY 10004

BROWN, ANNIE MARIE VEDEL, real estate associate; b. Hellerup, Denmark, May 12, 1941; came to U.S., 1961; d. Tage Vedel and Karen Wium (Jensen) Taaning; m. Joseph Edward Brown III, Dec. 27, 1960; children: Christian, Eric, Lars. Student, U. Copenhagen, 1959-61; BS, Trenton State Coll., 1983. Lic. med. sec., Denmark, lic. in real estate, N.J. Med. sec. Burlington County Hosp., Mt. Holly, 1962-64; nursery sch. tchr. Cranberry House Sch., Medford, N.J., 1974-75; substitute tchr. Lenape Regional High Sch. System, Medford, 1978-84, Medford Twp. Schs., Medford, 1982-85; real estate assoc. B. Gary Scott Realtors, Etc., Medford, 1985—; self-employed appraiser, Medford, 1987—; bd. dirs. The Central Record. Weekly columnist The Central Record, 1985-89. Exec. bd. Medford Home and Sch. Assn., 1981-89. Recipient Million Dollar award Better Homes & Gardens Real Estate, 1987, 88, B. Gary Scott 2 Million Dollar award, 1989. Mem. AAUW (officer Medford chpt. 1989—), Burlington County Bd. Realtors (edn. com. 1990—, bi-laws com.), Nat. Residential Appraisers Inst., Pinelands Garden Club. Home: 32 Friar Tuck Dr Medford NJ 08055 Office: B Gary Scott Realtors 510 Stokes Rd Medford NJ 08055

BROWN, ARLENE ANN, data communications company executive; b. Cleve., Feb. 21, 1951; d. Lawrence Francis and Irene Marie (Kandzer) Tamasovich; m. William David Brown, June 25, 1977; children—Raymond Noel, Lawrence Joseph. B.S., Notre Dame Coll., Cleve., 1971; postgrad. Baldwin-Wallace Coll., 1974-76. System analyst Ohio Bell Telephone Co., Cleve., 1971-76; mktg. specialist So. Bell Telephone Co., Atlanta, 1977-78; acct. exec. Teletype Corp., Skokie, Ill., 1978-79, sales mgr., 1979-80, regional sales mgr., 1980-82; v.p. sales David Brown Assoc., Atlanta, 1982; computer cons. Notre Dame Coll., 1972-73. Sec. Stonehaven Homeowners Assn., Ga., 1986. NSF grantee, 1970; recipient Digilog Sales award Digilog, Inc., 1984-85. Mem. Am. Mgmt. Assn., Ga. Telecommunications Assn., Nat. Assn. Female Execs. Roman Catholic. Avocations: golfing, tennis, sailing, traveling. Office: David Brown Assos Inc PO Box 1048 Stone Mountain GA 30086

BROWN, ARLENE PATRICIA THERESA, artist; b. Elizabeth, N.J., Jan. 3, 1953; d. William J. and Adelaide Elizabeth (Von Krasa) B.; student Union Coll., 1971. BA, Kean Coll., 1980. Owner, pres. Reni Co., Roselle, N.J., 1979—; pvt. tchr. art, artist glass etching, airbrush artist designer, Roselle Park, 1979—; owner Twinks Trademark and Associated Characters. Exhibited in The Children's Mus., Ind.; patentee in field. Recipient 3d Place award Custom Car and Van Show, Meadowlands, N.J., 1981, 2d place award Custom Car and Van Show, Asbury Park, N.J., 1982. Mem. Graphic Artists Guild, Artists' Equity Assn., Summit Art Assn., Princeton Art Assn., Am. Women's Econ. Devel. Assn., Found. Christian Living, Positive Thinkers Club, N.J. Art Dirs. Club, Westfield Art Assn., Alumni Assn. Kean Coll. Mailing Address: PO Box 186 Roselle Park NJ 07204

BROWN, AVA COLLEEN, health consultant; b. Queens, N.Y., Oct. 19, 1952; d. Leon Francis and Vera Naomi (Holmes) Fountain; m. Larry Arnold Brown, July 10, 1971; children: Kydan, Jenaya. BSN, Stockton State Coll., Pomona, N.J., 1980; MSN, Oral Roberts U., 1985. Pediatric rehab. nurse Hill Crest Med. Ctr., Tulsa, 1980-81; paramed. examiner Lifedata Med. Svcs., Tulsa, 1981-85; maternal child health nurse clinician Atlantic City (N.J.) Health Dept., 1986-89; ind. health cons. Atlantic City, 1989—. Treas. Blacks Against AIDS, Atlantic City, 1987-89, exec. dir., 1989—; instr. AIDS edn.; vol. AIDS support svcs. Mem. NAFE, N.J. State Nurses Assn. Office: 1700 Arctic Ave 1st Fl Atlantic City NJ 08401

BROWN, BARBARA GENE, principal; b. Circleville, Kans., Jan. 9, 1938; d. George Thomas and Edity Marie (Cole) Morris; m. George Nelson Brown, Aug. 29,1957 (div. June 1985); children: Luther Cole, Georgia Nelsene Brown Flood, Douglas Spencer. BS, Washburn U., 1963; MA, Emporia State U., 1974. Tchr. elem. schs., Kans., 1958-81; sch. libr. St. Marys (Kans.)/Rossville, 1982-88; elem. prin. Hawthorne Elem. Sch., Ottawa, Kans., 1988—; mem. selection com. William Allen White Children's Book Award, 1986-88, No. Cen. Evaluation team, 1987. Recipient Ottawa Edn. Grant Warrensburg Children's Literature Festival trip, 1989. Mem. Kans. Assn. Elem. Sch. Prins. (com. rep.), Kans. Assn. Elem Sch. Librs.(dist. dir.) Kans. Reading Assn.(literacy com.), U. Sch. Adminstrs.(communications com. rep.), Am. Bus. Women (sec., pub. rels., 1982-86), U. Women (program com.), Beta Sigma Phi (banner com., 1989), Delta Kappa Gamma (legis. com., 1988), Zeta Tau Alpha (sports chmn., 1957). Methodist. Office: 501 S Poplar Ottawa KS 66067

BROWN, BEATRICE, symphony conductor; b. Leeds, Eng., May 17, 1917; came to U.S., 1921, naturalized, 1927; d. Abraham and Sarah (Levinson) B.; m. Morris Rothenberg, Jan. 29, 1961. BA, Hunter Coll., 1937; MA, N.Y.U., 1939; Berkshire Music Center scholar, 1948-49; Condr. Chamber Music Assocs., N.Y.C., 1950-53; music dir., condr. Scranton (Pa.) Philharm. Orch., 1963-70, NE Pa. Philharm., 1970-72, Ridgefield (Conn.) Orch., 1969—, Western Conn. Symphony Orch., Danbury, 1981—, Housatonic Chamber Orch., 1982—; condr. N.Y., N.J., Conn. opera cos.; TV appearances; lectr.; violist symphony orchs., 1944—, Chamber Music Group, Musique Vivante, Am. Symphony Orch., N.Y. Pops Orch., 1979—; guest conductor, Brazil, 1989; instr. music Hunter Coll., 1937-43; tchr. music N.Y.C. Pub. Schs., 1944-61; adj. asst. prof. Lehman Coll., 1972-74; tchr. music Bronx High Sch. Sci., N.Y.C., 1970-79. Fulbright grantee, 1953-55, Martha Baird Rockefeller grantee, 1957-59, Peace award UN, 1980, Wellington award, 1981; named to Hunter Coll. Hall of Fame, 1972; named One of 100 Disting. Women in Conn., 1976, One of 5 outstanding Women in Ridgefield, Conn., 1979. Mem. Am. Symphony Orch. League (bd. dirs.), Condrs. Guild Am. (bd. dirs. 1985—), Phi Beta Kappa. Home and Office: 3 Seir Hill Rd Apt C2 Norwalk CT 06850-1328

BROWN, BEVERLY JEAN, educator; b. Pensacola, Fla., Jan. 24, 1943; d. Elisha and Melanie Alfreda (Creal) Jones; m. Ozie Marion Portis, May 1, 1963 (div. Apr. 1976); 1 child, Diedra LaShalle; m. Ernest Arnell Brown, Oct. 13, 1978. BS, Fla. A&M U., 1966; M of Edn., U. North Fla., 1986. Cert. in adminstrn. and supervision. Tchr. Meriwether County Sch. Dist., Greenville, Ga., 1966-67, Hamilton County Sch. Dist., Jasper, Fla., 1968-69; tchr. Duval County Sch. Dist., Jacksonville, Fla., 1969-82, primary resource tchr., 1982-87; adminstrv. intern Duval County Sch. Bd., 1987-88; tchr. in instrnl. support Fla. Reading Assn., 1988—. Mem. Duval County Reading Assn., Order Ea. Star. Democrat. Home: 5135 Chivalry Dr Jacksonville FL 32208

BROWN, BILLIE, public relations executive; b. Portsmouth, Ohio; d. John William and Lillian (Mitchell) B. Student, Yale U., New Haven Conn., MusB, MusM; postgrad. mgmt., Harvard U., 1984. V.p. Cunningham and Walsh, N.Y.C., 1965-79, Corning Glass Works, Corning, N.Y., 1979-82; v.p Westinghouse Brdctg., N.Y.C., 1982-84; pres. Billie Brown, Inc., N.Y.C. Mem:Yale Club of NYC. Office: Billie Brown Inc 681 Lexington Ave New York NY 10022

BROWN, BILLIE AUGUSTINE, educator, artist; b. Pangburn, Ark., Aug. 1, 1924; d. Prince Colombus and Icy May Wood; children: Terry Wood, Dawn Elizabeth, Benjamin McLove, Laura Delphine. BA in Edn., Harding Coll., Searcy, Ark., 1962, MS, 1966; MA in Guidance and Counseling, U. Central Ark., 1974. Librarian, White County, Ark. 1947-52; U.S. postal clk., 1954; pub. sch. tchr., 1959-78; art specialist Pulaski County (Ark.) Spl. Sch. Dist., 1978-79, instructional coordinator art, 1979-87 ; sculptor, Little Rock, 1987—; lectr. art edn. U. Ark., Little Rock, 1987—; co-founder, bd. advisers Ark. Young Artists Assn.; mem. Very Spl. Arts Bd., 1986—, treas., 1987-89, U.S.A. Art Mentor Handicapped in Art. Recipient 1st place award in pastel White County Art Show, 1957, 1st place in illus. poetry Ark. Festival Arts, 1973, Patron of Arts award Ark. Young Artists Assn., 1985, Spl. Achievement award, Phi Delta Kappa, 1985. Mem. Nat. Art Edn. Assn., Ark. Art Educators, Mid-So. Watercolorists (chair profl. growth com.), Ark. for Arts, Delta Kappa Gamma. Democrat. Baptist. Home and Office: 2805 N Grant Little Rock AR 72207

BROWN, CAROL ANN, dentist, alcohol and drug abuse consultant; b. Webster, S.D., Oct. 12, 1944; d. Harry Elmer and Flossie Blanche (Fausch) B.; children: Laura Lee Phelps Deitsch, Brett G. Phelps. BS in Secondary Edn. summa cum laude, No. State U., Aberdeen, S.D., 1972; postgrad., Rutgers U., 1976; DDS, U. Minn., 1986. Tchr. Groton (S.D.) High Sch., 1973-74; health planner, asst. dir. div. alcohol and drug abuse S.D. Health Dept., Pierre, 1974-77, acting div. dir., 1977-78; pvt. practice, Colorado Springs, Colo., 1987—; cons. Living with Solutions, Sioux Falls, S.D., 1980—, U. Minn., Mpls., 1982-86. Mem. United Family Farmers, Aberdeen, 1969-74; legis liaison Commn. on Alcoholism, S.D. Health Dept., 1974-78. Mem. ADA, Colo. Dental Assn. (com. mem. 1988—), Colorado Springs Dental Assn., Colo. Concerned Dentists (sec. 1987—). Roman Catholic. Home: 63 Newport Circle Colorado Springs CO 80906 Office: 1855 S Nevada Colorado Springs CO 80906

BROWN, CAROL ROBERTSON, librarian; b. Anamosa, Iowa, Oct. 27, 1943; d. William Ferman and Grace Viola (Klumph) Robertson; m. Eric Ramsay Brown, Aug. 25, 1965 (div. July 1987); children: Ian Robertson, Kevin William. BA, Cornell Coll., Mt. Vernon, Iowa, 1965; MA, Ind. U., 1966. Reference librarian Undergrad. Library, Ind. U., Bloomington, 1966-68, asst. undergrad. librarian, 1968-70; adult materials specialist Houston Pub. Library, 1975-77, mgr. Jungman br., 1977-79, asst. chief br. svcs., 1979-88; cons. Carol Brown Assocs., Houston, 1988—; freelance cons., Houston, 1976-88. Author: Selecting Library Furniture, A Guide for Librarians, Designers and Architects, 1989; contbr. articles to profl. jours. Mem.

AAUW, Library Adminstrn. and Mgmt. Assn., Pub. Library Assn., ALA, Tex. Library Assn., Phi Beta Kappa, Beta Phi Mu. Office: Carol Brown Assocs 5500 N Braeswood Suite 112 Houston TX 77096

BROWN, CAROLYN ELIZABETH, educational administrator, consultant; b. Liberty, Tex., Aug. 11, 1943; d. Jack Edwin and Octavia Elizabeth (Fahring) Stanley; m. Walter Lamar Brown, July 10, 1961 (div. 1981); children: Michael Lamar, Carolyn Elizabeth, Samuel Stuart. BA, Sam Houston State U., Huntsville, Tex., 1969, MEd, 1977. Cert. tchr., profl. counselor, ednl. adminstr., Tex. English tchr. Huntsville Ind. Sch. Dist., 1969-79, asst. prin., 1980-82; prin. Alief (Tex.) Ind. Sch. Dist., 1982—; exec. dir. Edgemoor Sch., Houston, 1989—. Mem. adv. bd. Odessy Ho. of Tex., 1989—; vol. Palmer Drug Abuse Program, Houston, 1983-86, Alief Parents In Action, 1984-87, Houston Mus. Fine Arts, 1987-88. Mem. Nat. Assn. Secondary Sch. Adminstrs., Nat. Assn. Counseling Devel., Assn. Curriculum Devel., Tex. Assn. Secondary Sch. Adminstrs. Office: Brown and Assocs 2001 Holcombe Blvd Ste 205 Houston TX 77030

BROWN, CAROLYN MARGUERITE HUTCHINSON, management consultant; b. Hampton, Va., Dec. 6, 1936; d. Mark Edwin and Myrtle Rowena (Wood) Hutchinson; m. Ronald Lee Taylor, Sept. 28, 1957 (div. Mar. 1961); m. Sidney James Brown, Feb. 15, 1969; adopted children: Debra Kathleen Brown Peters, Stephen Paul, Gregory Lawrence, Tracy Lynn Brown Bullock. Student, Va. Poly. Inst., 1956-57, Fla. Tech. Coll., 1964-65. Cost acct. Boeing Aerospace Co., Cape Canaveral, Fla., 1967-69; acct. Bechtel Power Corp., Morgantown, Md., 1969-70; engring. aid Bechtel Power Corp., Gaithersburg, Md., 1970-72; planning engr. Bechtel Power Corp., Grand Gulf, Miss., 1975-77; systems analyst Pacific Internat. Corp., Gaithersburg, 1972-74; field engr. Canadian Bechtel Ltd., Ft. McMurray, Alta., Can., 1974; systems analyst Bechtel Corp., San Francisco, 1979-80; project scheduler TERA Corp., Berkeley, Calif., 1980-81; mgr. automated systems, program planning, and control Electro-Mech. div. Northrop Corp., Anaheim, Calif., 1987-89; sr. staff cons. customer base Systonetics, Inc., Fullerton, Calif., 1981-87, nat. mgr. cons. and ednl. svcs., 1989-90; with Systonetics Customer Base, 1981-90; project mgmt. cons. TECHCO, Placentia, Calif., 1990—; speaker in field. Author: The Dictionary of Power Plant, 1973, Project Management Techniques, 1984, VISION Planning and Schedule Guide, 1985, VISION Resource and Cost Guide, 1986. Sec. Project Mgmt. Inst., Orange Co. Chpt., 1989, New Eng. Geneal. Hist. Soc., Gen. Soc. of Mayflower Descendents, nat. Geneal. Soc., Soc. Genealogists. Mem. Project Mgmt. Inst. (sec. Orange County chpt. 1989-90), New Eng. Geneal. Historic Soc., Gen. Soc. of Mayflower Descendents, Nat. Geneal. Soc., Soc. Genealogists. Republican. Home: 1956 Brookhaven Ave Placentia CA 92670 Office: TECHCO 1956 Brookhaven Ave Placentia CA 92670

BROWN, CAROLYN SMITH, communications educator, consultant; b. Salt Lake City, Aug. 12, 1946; d. Andrew Delbert and Olive (Crane) Smith; m. David Scott Brown, Sept. 10, 1982. BA magna cum laude, U. Utah, 1968, MA, 1972, PhD, 1974. Instr. Salt Lake Ctr., Brigham Young U., Salt Lake City, 1976-78; vis. asst. prof. Brigham Young U., Provo, 1978; asst. prof. Am. Inst. Banking, Salt Lake City, 1977—; prof., chmn. English, communication and gen. edn. depts. Latter Day Saints Bus. Coll., Salt Lake City, 1973—, acad. dean, 1986—; founder, pres. Career Devel. Tng., Salt Lake City, 1979—; field mktg. dir. Systems Internat./Performas Inc., Mpls., 1978—; cons. inhouse seminars First Security Realty Services, USDA Soil Conservation Service, Utah Power & Light, Utah State Social Services, HUD, Intermountain Health Care, Continental Bank; chmn. centennial coordination com. Latter Day Saints Bus. Coll., 1986-87, N.W. accreditation self-study com. 1980-82, 87, Title IX self-evaluation com., 1977, 79, grievance com., 1979—. Author: Writing Letters & Reports That Communicate, 6 ed., 1985; contbr. articles to profl. jours. Demi-soloist Utah Civic Ballet (now Ballet West), Salt Lake City, 1964-68; active Mormon Ch. Named Tchr. of Month, Salt Lake City Kiwanis, 1981; NDEA fellow, U. Utah, 1972. Mem. Am. Bus. Communications Assn. (lectr. West/N.W. regional chpt. 1987), Delta Kappa Gamma (2d v.p. 1977-79), Lambda Delta Sigma (Outstanding Woman of Yr. 1983), Kappa Kappa Gamma (Outstanding Alumnus in Lit. 1974). Republican. Clubs: Alice Louise Reynolds Literary (Salt Lake City) (v.p. 1978-79, sec. 1985-86). Office: LDS Bus Coll 411 E South Temple Salt Lake City UT 84111

BROWN, CATHY FRANKLIN, real estate broker; b. Knoxville, Tenn., Oct. 10, 1947; d. Otho Franklin and Maude Blanche (Worthington) B. BS, U. Tenn., 1968. Licensed real estate broker, Tenn. Social worker Tenn. Dept. Human Svcs., Clinton, 1969-72, office dir., 1972-75; real estate broker, investor, owner Otho Brown Realty Co., 1969—; alderman Town of Clinton, 1975-85, mayor, 1985—; State of Tenn. Indsl. and Agrl. Devel. Commn. State of Tenn., Nashville, 1989—. Active ARC, Clinton Port Authority (bd. dirs. 1989—), Clinton Reg. Planning Commn. Methodist. Home and Office: 445 Eagle Bend Rd Clinton TN 37716

BROWN, CHARLINA PIERCE, education educator; b. Ironton, Ohio, Feb. 8, 1935; d. Charlton Louian and Ina (Hill) Pierce; m. July 29, 1961 (div. Aug. 1981); children: Heather Pierce, Stacia Ketchersid. BS, Fla. State U., 1957, MS, 1961; PhD, Tex. Women's U., 1977. Elem. tchr. Leon County Bd. Pub. Instrn., Tallahassee, 1957-59, 61-64; grad. asst. Inst. Human Devel., Fla. State U., Tallahassee, 1959-61; asst. prof. div. edn. Tift Coll., Forsyth, Ga., 1960-61, North Tex. State U., Denton, 1977-78; instr. Jacksonville (Fla.) U., 1965-66; cons. HEW, Livingston, Ala., 1967-68; grad. asst., adj. asst. prof. Tex. Woman's U., Denton, 1978-81; asst. prof. edn. Bethune-Cookman Coll., Daytona Beach, Fla., 1988—; developer, dir. Coop. Presch., Livingston, Ala., 1967-68; owner, cons. Pupils, Parents, Preschs., Denton, 1980-81; asst. head tchr. Rsch. Ctr. for Child Devel., Tallahassee, 1987. Officer Denton Woman's Club, 1970-76. Tex. Woman's U. fellow, 1976-77. Mem. Assn. for Childhood Edn. Internat. (tchr. edn. com.), Assn. for Supervision and Curriculum Devel., AAUW (pres. Tallahassee br. 1986-87), Alpha Delta Kappa, Pi Lambda Theta, Delta Gamma (alumni pres. 1957-59). Democrat. Baptist. Home: 2271 W Lake Hall Rd Tallahassee FL 32308 Office: Bethune-Cookman Coll 640 2d Ave Daytona Beach FL 32017

BROWN, CHARLOTTE FRANCES, retail executive; b. Thomasville, Ga., July 18, 1956; d. Robert Curtis and Mary Frances (Simpson) B. ABJ, U. Ga., 1978. Account exec. Savannah (Ga.) News-Press, 1978-84, supr. retail sales, 1980-82; account exec. Sta. WECA-TV and W17AB-tV, Tallahassee, Fla., 1984; advt. mgr. Wilbro Jewelers Catalog Showrooms, Dothan, Ala., 1985—; co-chmn. Addy Awards Tallahassee Advt. Fedn., 1984-85; so. region rep. T.R.I.P. program Family Weekly mag., 1983-84. Performer, editor prologue Savannah Theatre Co., 1979-80; performer Thomasville on Stage & Co., 1984. Editor of prologue and performer Savannah Theatre Co., 1979-80; mem. Savannah Striders Track Club, 1982-84; performer Thomasville On Stage & Co., 1984; bd. dirs. Dothan Advt. Fedn. 1985-86. Recipient Addy awards Dothan Advt. Fedn., 1985, 86. Democrat. Methodist. Home: 173 Fox Run Apts Dothan AL 36301 Office: Wilbro Inc 3121 Ross Clark Circle NW Dothan AL 36303

BROWN, CLAIRE LOUISE, software engineer; b. Providence, Aug. 30, 1947; d. Arthur and Lucille Jeanne (Levesque) Durand; m. Richard Guy Brown, July 11, 1966 (div. Sept. 1980); children: Barbara Anne, Robert Thomas. AS, No. Va. Community Coll., Annandale, Va., 1976; BS, George Mason U., 1977. Software engr. Adaptronics, Inc., McLean, Va., 1977-80; software engr. mgr. ENSCO, Springfield, Va., 1980-83; system engr. Ventana Scis., Inc., Springfield, Va., 1983-84; software engr. E-Systems, Inc., Falls Church, Va., 1984; software engr. mgr. Engring. Rsch. Assocs., Vienna, Va., 1984-90. Patentee System for Nondestructive evaluation, 1979, 1980. Mem. Alpha Chi, Va. chpt., Sigma Pi Sigma, GMU chpt., Fairfax, Va. Office: Engring Rsch Assocs 1595 Springhill Rd Vienna VA 22182-8005

BROWN, COLLEEN MARY, civil engineer; b. Lancaster, Pa., Apr. 1, 1961; d. John Herman and Sonya Arlene (Wetzel) B. BS magna cum laude, U. Pitts., 1983, postgrad., 1986. Engr.-in-tng. N.M. Lake Inc. Surveyors, Lancaster, 1983-84; civil engr.-in-tng. Pa. Dept. Transp., Harrisburg, 1984-85, civil engr. II, 1985-87, cons. engr., 1987—. Alcoa Aluminum Co. Found. scholar, 1979. Home: 4808 Count St Harrisburg PA 17109

BROWN, CONNIE YATES, small business owner; b. Carthage, Mo., Apr. 29, 1947; d. Charles Lee and Eunice Jane (Farmer) Yates; m. Larry Edward Brown, June 19, 1982; 1 step-dau., Tammy Lynn Brown. BS, Pittsburg State U., 1969. Cert. home economist. With White Shield Oil and Gas/Petro-Lewis, Tulsa, 1969-74, dept. supt., 1971-74; with Southwestern Bell Telephone Co., 1975-79; owner, mgr. Abbyco, Inc., rental, sales carpet cleaning equipment, Tulsa, 1977—; sec. R.D.R. Assn. Inc.; lectr. in field. Active Okla. Rep. Party. Named Rookie of Yr., Tulsa div. Southwestern Bell Yellow Pages, 1976; sales award winner Rug Doctor Licensee of Yr., 1981, 85. Mem. Home Economists in Bus., Am. Home Econs. Assn., Met. Tulsa C. of C., Equipment Rental Dealers Assn. Eastern Okla., Tulsa Alumnae Panhellenic (bd. dirs., membership chmn.), Pitts. State U. Alumni Assn. (past pres. Tulsa chpt.), Tulsa Area Women Bus. Owners, Tulsa Women's Found., Resonance, Order of Rainbow for Girls, Phi Upsilon Omicron, Alpha Gamma Delta (nat. dir. alumnae devel. 1984-86, coord. alumnae philanthropy 1990—). Home: 7806 S Evanston Ave Tulsa OK 74136 Office: Abbyco Inc 8600 S Lewis Ave Tulsa OK 74137

BROWN, DALE SUSAN, government administrator, writer; b. N.Y.C., May 27, 1954; d. Bertram S. and Beatrice Joy (Gilman) B. B.A., Antioch Coll., 1976. Research asst. Am. Occupational Therapy Assn., Rockville, Md., 1976-79; writer Pres.' Com. on Employment of People with Disabilities, Washington, 1979-82, program mgr., 1982—; cons. in field; gen. assembly speaker nat. conv. Gen. Fedn. Women's Clubs, 1981; mem. Rehab. Services Adminstrn. Task Force on Learning Disabilities, 1981—. Author: Steps to Independence for People with Learning Disabilities, 1980; writer film: They Could Have Saved Their Homes, 1982; editorial bd. Perceptions, 1981-83. Pres. Assn. Learning Disabled Adults, Washington, 1979-80; bd. dirs. Closer Look Nat. Info. Ctr., Washington, 1980—, Am. Coalition of Citizens with Disabilities, 1985-86. Found. for Children with Learning Disabilities grantee, 1982. Recipient Margaret Byrd Rawson award, 1989, Personal Achievement award, 1989. Mem. Nat. Network of Learning Disabled Adults (founder, pres. 1980-81, rep. Inter-agy. com. on computer support handicapped employess 1988—), Nat. Assn. Govt. Communicators (Blue Pencil award 1986, rep. inter-agy. com. on handicapped employees 1989—), Learning Disabilities Assn. (bd. dirs. 1986—), ALA. Democrat. Jewish. Office: Pres' Com on Employment People with Disabilities 1111 20th St NW Rm 600 Washington DC 20036

BROWN, DARMAE JUDD, librarian; b. Jefferson City, Mo., Sept. 14, 1952; d. William Robert and Dorothy Judd (Curtis) B. BA, W.Va. Wesleyan Coll., 1974; MA, U. Denver, 1975; postgrad. Odessa Coll., 1982-84, U. No. Ia., 1984-88, U. Denver, 1989. Searching assoc. Bibliog. Ctr. for Rsch., Denver, 1975-76; libr. N.E. Colo. Regional Libr., Wray, 1976-81; head tech. svcs. Ector County Libr., Odessa, Tex., 1981-84, Waterloo (Iowa) Pub. Libr., 1984-89; coord. computer libr. svcs. Aurora (Colo.) Pub. Libr., 1989—. Mem. ALA, Iowa OCLC Users Group (pres. 1986-87), Colo. Libr. Assn., Libr. & Info. Tech. Assn., Beta Phi Mu, Sigma Alpha Iota. Home: 15651 E Caspian Cir #13-102 Aurora CO 80013

BROWN, DEBORAH M.S., writer; b. Woodstock, Va., Apr. 29, 1953; d. Jack M. and Mary Ellen (Myers) Showalter; m. E. Allen Brown, Aug. 29, 1987. BA in Am. History, Radford (Va.) Coll., 1975; cert. in publishing, George Washington U., 1981. Tour guide Voice of Am. Div. U.S. Info. Agy., Washington, 1975-76, writer, 1976-77, tech. info. specialist, 1977-81; bibliographic specialist U.S. Info. Agy., Washington, 1981-85, media specialist, 1985-86, writer, editor, 1986—. Mem. Mid-Atlantic Germanic Soc. (bd. dirs. and editor newsletter 1982-88). Office: US Info Agy 301 4th St SW Rm 410 Washington DC 20547

BROWN, DENISE SCOTT, architect, urban planner; b. Nkana, Zambia, Oct. 3, 1931; came to U.S., 1958; d. Simon and Phyllis (Hepker) Lakofski; m. Robert Scott Brown, July 21, 1955 (dec. 1959); m. Robert Charles Venturi, July 23, 1967; 1 child, James C. Student, U. Witwatersrand, South Africa, 1948-51; diploma, Archtl. Assn., London, 1955; M of City Planning, U. Pa., 1960, MArch, 1965; DFA (hon.), Oberlin Coll., 1977, Phila. Coll. Art, 1985, Parsons Sch. Design, 1985; LHD (hon.), N.J. Inst. Tech., 1984. Registered architect, U.K. Asst. prof. U. Pa., Phila., 1960-65; assoc. prof., head urban design program UCLA, 1965-68; with Venturi, Rauch and Scott Brown, Phila., 1967—, ptnr., 1969-89; prin. Venturi, Scott Brown and Assocs. Inc., Phila., 1989—; vis. prof. architecture U. Calif., Berkeley, 1965, U. Pa., 1982-83; vis. prof. architecture Yale U., 1967-70, 87; Eliot Noyes design critic in architecture Harvard U., Cambridge, 1989-90; mem. vis. com. MIT, 1973-83; mem. adv. com. dept. architecture Temple U., 1980—; policy panelist design arts program Nat. Endowment for Arts, 1981-83. Author: Urban Concepts, 1990; co-author: Learning from Las Vegas, 1972, rev. edit., 1977, A View from the Campidoglio: Selected Essays, 1953-84, 85; contbr. numerous articles to profl. jours. Mem. curriculum and adult edn. com. Phila. Jewish Children's Folkshul, 1980-86; mem. bd. advisors Architects, Designers and Planners for Social Responsibility, 1982—; mem. capitol preservation com. Commonwealth of Pa., Harrisburg, 1983-87; bd. dirs. Cen. Phila. Devel. Corp., 1985—, Urban Affairs Partnership, Phila., 1987—; trustee Chestnut Hill Acad., Phila., 1985-89. Recipient numerous awards, citations, commendations for design, urban planning, Chgo. Architecture award, 1987, Order of Merit Republic of Italy, 1987. Mem. Am. Planning Assn., Archtl. Assn. London, Alliance Women in Architecture N.Y., Soc. Archtl. Historians (bd. dirs. 1981-84), Royal Inst. Brit. Architects. Democrat. Jewish. Office: Venturi and Scott Brown Assocs Inc 4236 Main St Philadelphia PA 19127

BROWN, DIANE ROBINSON, sociology educator; b. Newark, Aug. 11, 1944; d. Eugene Jasper and Mary Rochelle (Davis) Robinson; m. Lafayette Brown, Jr., July 29, 1972 (div. 1979); m. Arthur D. Rogers, Nov. 25, 1987. AB in Sociology, Ind. U., 1966; MA in Sociology, U. Mass., 1968; PhD in Sociology, U. Md., 1984; postgrad., Johns Hopkins U., 1984-86. Programmer Prudential Ins. Co., Newark, 1967; system engr. IBM, Cambridge, Mass., 1968-70; info. coord. Community Devel. Adminstrs., Newark, 1970-72; staff assoc. Mass. State Coll. System, Boston, 1972-75; rsch. assoc. Inst. for Urban Affairs and Rsch., Washington, 1975-79, sr. rsch. assoc., 1979-86, acting dir., 1986-87, dir. rsch., 1987-90; assoc. prof. Howard U., Washington, 1990—. Assoc. editor Humanity and Society, 1988—, Jour. Health and Social Behavior, 1989—. HUD grantee, 1986—, U.S. Dept. Edn. grantee, 1987-88; Ford Found. fellow, 1985-86. Mem. Assn. Social and Behavioral Scientists (exec. com. 1987—), Am. Pub. Health Assn. (coun. mental health sect. 1987—), D.C. Sociol. Soc. (exec. com. 1987—). African Methodist Episcopalian. Home: 8904 Talbot Ave Silver Spring MD 20910 Office: Howard U Washington DC 20059

BROWN, DOLORES CONNOR, medical association administrator; b. Cumberland, Md., Mar. 7, 1937; d. George Conrad and Sara Regina (Sidaway) Connor; m. Timothy C. Brown Jr., Aug. 2, 1958; children: Thomas Charles, Sara Ann, Teresa Lynn. BS, U. S. C., 1983; MBA, U.S.C., 1988. Chief technologist Hazelwood TB Hosp., Louisville, 1958-59; med. technologist Gerald Greenfield, Louisville, 1960-65, Kentucky Med. Soc., Louisville, 1965, Hendon, Blodgett, Minish, Graves & Ward, Louisville, 1965-73; head instr. Atlanta (Ga.) Coll. of Med. Asst., 1973-74; supr. technologist Richland Meml. Hosp., Columbia, S.C., 1974-85; asst. chief technologist Richland Mem. Hosp., Columbia, 1985-89, adminstrv. dir., 1989—; adv. Midland Tech. Coll., 1987--. Mem. Am. Soc. Med. Tech., S.C. Am. Soc. Med. Tech., ASMT, Am. Soc. Clin. Home: 6028 Yorkshire Dr Columbia SC 29209 Office: Richland Meml Hosp 5 Richland Medical Pk Columbia SC 29203

BROWN, DONNA LYNN, service executive; b. Bklyn., Aug. 15, 1955; d. Myles Harris and Iris Georgia (Misroch) Goldberg; m. John M. Brown, Sept. 15, 1979. BA in English, Franklin & Marshall Coll., 1977. Adminstrv. asst. Planned Parenthood, Bristol, Pa., 1980-81, Phoenix Mut., Phila., 1981-83; claims examiner Phila. Life Ins. Co., 1983-84; mktg. coord. Bayly, Martin & Fay, Inc., Phila., 1984-88; customer svc. mgr. Boockford & Co., Oakbrook Terrace, Ill., 1989—. Mem. Bensalem (Pa.) Coalition, 1987-88, coord. Am. Heart Assn., 1988, Greater Phila. chpt. Employee Benefits Specialists, 1988. Mem. NAFE. Democrat. Jewish. Home: 736 Ridgeview St Downers Grove IL 60516 Office: Boockford & Co One Oakbrook Terrace Oakbrook Terrace IL 60181

BROWN, DOREEN LEAH HURWITZ, development company executive; b. Marseille, France, June 11, 1927; came to U.S., 1939, naturalized, 1941; d. Nathan and Anne (Silverstone) Hurwitz; m. Donald L. Brown, Dec. 30, 1951 (dec.); children: Claudia Geraldine, Nicole Deborah. BA cum laude, Bryn Mawr Coll., 1947. Adminstrv. asst., interpreter, translator FAO, Washington, 1949-51; exec. Aldon Constrn. & Mgmt. Corp., Washington, 1951—, v.p., exec. officer, 1977—; consumer liaison Nat. Acad. Scis., 1973; del. ann. US-EC Conf. on Agriculture C. of C., US-Japan Conf.; mem. impoters and retailers textile adv. com. Internat. Trade Adminstrn. U.S. Dept. Commerce. Author: Window on Washington, The Trade Deficit. Nat. chmn. nat. affairs Nat. Coun. Jewish Women, N.Y.C., 1971-75; pres. Consumer Edn. Coun. on World Trade, 1973-78, Consumers for World Trade, Washington, 1977—; mem. Women's Nat. Dem. Club, 1960—; mem. Internat. Trade Importers and Retailers Textile Adv. Com., Dept. Commerce. Mem. Bryn Mawr Coll. Alumnae Assn., World Trade Forum. Democrat. Jewish. Office: Consumers for World Trade 1726 M St NW Ste 1002 Washington DC 20036

BROWN, DOROTHEA WILLIAMS, technology consulting company executive; b. Austin, Tex., Dec. 23, 1918; d. Van Wilford and Ethel Lee (Connor) Williams; m. Ira Harper Brown, Aug. 23, 1943; 1 child, Michele Brown Scott. BA, Huston-Tillotson Coll., Austin, 1939; MA, John Carroll U., 1959; PhD, U. Akron, 1980. Cert. counselor, supr., adminstr., Ohio. Tchr., counselor, prin. Cleve. Pub. Schs., 1952-70; chief program officer Kent Ctr. for Ednl. Devel. and Strategic Svcs., Kent (Ohio) State U., 1970-75; dean, dir. Cuyahoga Community Coll., Cleve., 1975-79; assoc. dir. Nat. Inst. Staff and Orgn. Devel., U. Tex., Austin, 1979-82; dir., cons., co-owner Tapit, Inc. (Theory and Practice in Tech.), Washington and Newark, 1983—; cons. Cleve. Commn. for Higher Edn., 1968-71; sec. vol. com. Austin Ind. Sch. Dist., 1987-89. Contbg. editor New Lady, 1963-70; contbr. articles to ednl. jours. Mem. nat. bd. dirs. Girl Scouts U.S., 1977-83, bd. dirs., chmn. nominating com. Lone Star coun., 1981-85; chmn. Austin Commn. for Women, 1981-85; v.p. Laguna Gloria Art Mus., Austin, 1983—; mem. Higher Edn. Commn. Austin, 1983—; trustee Cen. Tex. chpt. ARC, 1988-89; community advisor Jr. League of Austin, 1987-89; docent Tex. Gov.'s mansion, 1983-87, Lyndon Baines Johnson Libr./Mus., 1988—; Am. Inst. for Learning (Creative Rapid Learning Ctr.); sec. Women and World Issues, 1984-87; trustee ADOPT-A-SCH., 1990—. Recipient Martin Luther King Community award Bergstrom AFB, Austin, 1984, Woman of Austin award Austin Commn. for Women, 1989, Outstanding Woman award Girl Scouts U.S.A., 1989; named to Austin Women Hall of Fame, 1985, 87, Tex. Women's Hall of Fame nominee, 1986, 88. Mem. AAUW, Links (program dir. western area 1987-89, contbn. award 1987), Order Eastern Star (Bronze Star award Mt. Olive grand chpt. 1987), Phi Delta Kappa, Pi Lambda Theta, Alpha Kappa Alpha. Episcopalian. Home: 5406 Pendleton Ln Austin TX 78723 Office: TAPIT Inc 12 Brophy Dr Ewing Twp Trenton NJ 08638

BROWN, DOROTHY JEAN, educational consultant; b. Kansas City, Mo., Mar. 12, 1927; d. Orville and Lessie Mae (Smith) Fitzgerald; m. Lewis Frank Brown, Mar. 29, 1956; children: Lewis Gene, Orville Frank. BEd, Washburn Mcpl. U., 1951; MA, Sonoma State Coll., 1975. Gen. elem. life diploma, Calif. Tchr. Fresno (Calif.) City Schs. Child Care, 1951-54; tchr. Vallejo City (Calif.) Unified Sch. Dist., 1954-87, cons., 1987—. Mem. exec. bd. YWCA; community adv. bd. Tanner Project; coord. edn. dept. No. Calif. First Ecclesiastical Jurisdiction Ch. of God in Christ. Recipient Community Svc. award Elma Hayson Club, 1987, Flosden, Highland, Lincoln, Fed. Terace, McKinley, Steffan Manor, Cave Sch. Parent Tchr. Appreciation awards, Community Svc. award Tanner Project of Vallejo City Sch. Dist., 1988, 89. Mem. Nat. Assn. Bench and Bar Spouses Inc., NEA (life), Vallejo Edn. Assn. (human rels. chmn.), Solano County Lawyer's Wives, Nat. Congress Parents and Tchrs., NAACP (Golden Heritage-life), North Bay Transcribing Guild, Solano County Black Educators, Delta Kappa Gamma (Chi State area 1 treas.), Alpha Kappa Alpha (life, founding pres. Kappa Beta Omega local chpt.). Democratic. Home: 400 Lakeside Dr Vallejo CA 94589

BROWN, DOROTHY MCKENNA, academic administrator; b. July 19, 1938; m. James Earl Brown Jr.; children: Mary Marguerite, Sheila Ann. BS in Biology, Coll. Misericordia, Dallas, Pa., 1960; MS in Biology, Villanova U., 1962; EdD in Sci. Edn., U. Pa., 1973. From instr. to prof. biology Cabrini Coll., Radnor, Pa., 1962-79, chairperson, 1964-72, v.p. acad. affairs, 1972-79; pres. Rosemont (Pa.) Coll., 1979—; treas. Commn. for Ind. Colls. and Univs., 1980-82, 1st vice-chmn. 1982-83, chmn. commn., 1983-84, past chmn., 1984-85, mem exec. com. 1987—; mem. com. on pers. affairs, commn. on higher edn. study com. on off-campus programs Pa. Assn. of Colls. and Univs., 1979; chmn. acad. policies task group Pa. region 1, continuing edn. project Compact for Life Long Ednl. Opportunities, 1977-79; chmn. Pa. Dept. Edn. Program Approval, 1972-80, Md. Dept. Edn., 1979; trustee, chmn. exec. com., mem. nominating com., mem. acad. affairs com. Hahnemann U., 1979—; bd. dirs. Inst. Planning Com.; mem. nominating com., corp. responsibility com. Provident Mutual Life Ins. Co., 1982—. Bd. dirs. Mayor's Commn. for Women, Phila., 1981-83, dir., 1984—, mem. ad hoc com. long range planning, 1986-88, profl. svcs. com., 1984—, chmn. profl. svcs. com. 1986—; trustee St. Charles Sem., 1989—, chmn. acad. affairs, 1989—, instl. planning com., 1985—. Mem. Assn. Cath. Colls. and Univs. (bd. dirs. 1985—), Mid. States Assn. of Colls. and Schs. (chmn. 4 accrediting teams, mem. 2 accrediting teams). Home: 16 Meredith Rd Green Hill Farms PA 19151 Office: Rosemont Coll Rosemont PA 19010

BROWN, DRENDA KAY, psychologist; b. Carrollton, Mo., Jan. 15, 1952; d. Ethan Lyle Pracht and Wilma Estelene (Henderson) Lucas; m. David Kent Brown, June 23, 1973; 1 child, Matthew Kent. BA in Psychology, William Jewell Coll., 1974; MS in Clinical Psychology, Cen. Mo. State U., 1976; postgrad. in clin. psychology, Fielding Inst., Santa Barbara, Calif., 1987—. Lic. psychologist, Minn. Therapist Briscoe Carr Cons., Kansas City, Mo., 1978-79; psychologist Crittenton Ctr., Kansas City, 1979-81, Cen. Minn. Mental Health Ctr., St. Cloud, 1981-85, St. Cloud Hosp., 1985-87; gen. practice psychology St. Cloud, 1985—; cons. St. Benedicts Ctr., St. Cloud, 1984—, Country Manor, 1986-90. Mem. Cen. Minn. Child Abuse Team, St. Cloud, 1981-85; bd. dirs. Cen. Minn. Child Care Assn., St. Cloud, 1982-83. Mem. Cen. Minn. Psychological Assn. (pres. 1984-85), Minn. Licensed Psychologists, Minn. Psychol. Assn., Alpha Delta Pi Alumni Assn. Presbyterian. Office: 2025 Stearns Way Ste 111 Saint Cloud MN 56303

BROWN, EDITH, healthcare, community development agency administrator; b. Milw., Nov. 25, 1935; d. Anton J. and Elizabeth K. (Kribitsch) Volk; m. Edward S. Brown. BS, U. Wis., 1958, MS in Social Work, 1964; MS in Mgmt., Cardinal Stritch Coll., Milw., 1985. Hosp. admissions worker, 1958-60; welfare worker, 1960-62; with Kiwanis Children's Ctr. and Children's Hosp. Psychiat. Clinic, Milw., 1962-64; social worker Lutheran Social Services, Milw., 1964-67; foster care supr. Milwaukee County Dept. Social Services, 1967-71, social services adminstr. child protection and parent services, comprehensive emergency services and a coordinated community edn. and support services, 1971-79; assoc. dir. Community Devel. Agy., City of Milw., 1979—; tech. advisor for child abuse, neglect, woman abuse, domestic violence; grants writer, tchr., cons. in field. Mem. Summerfest Adv. Council, Mayor's Beautification Com.; chmn. Summerfest Planting, 1972—; chmn. Milwaukee County Child Abuse and Neglect Task force, 1976-78; chmn. adv. council Milw. Boy's Club, 1981-84; vice chmn. Internat. Yr. for Disabled Persons, 1982; liaison Nat. Yr. for Disabled Persons, City of Milw., 1982-83; asst. chairperson City of Milw. United Way Campaign, 1983; mem. Mayor's Youth Initiatives Task Force, 1984-85; mem. adv. panel M.P.A. degree program U. Wis., 1984—. Office of Vocat. Rehab. scholar, 1962-64; Successful Women in Mgmt. award J. Wis., 1977; award Community Tchrs. Corps, 1977; Changemaker award Wis. Fed. Jr. Women's Clubs, 1978; Outstanding Community Services award Milwaukee County, 1979, Outstanding Services award, 1979, Exemplary Service award, 1982; Woman of Yr. award Mcpl. Women's Assn., 1981. Mem. Acad. Cert. Social Workers, Nat. Assn. Social Workers, Internat. Council on Social Welfare, Internat. Fedn. Social Welfare, Am. Soc. for Pub. Adminstrn. (pres. Milw. chpt., Outstanding Service and Dedication award 1984-85), Research Clearinghouse, Am. Bus. Women's Assn. (Woman of Yr. award 1975), Internat. Graphoanalysis Soc. (pres. Wis. chpt., 1988 Citation of Merit), Variety of Wis. Tech. Club. Contbr. to profl., community, resource documents, 1971—; author print and broadcast programs. Office: Community Devel Agy 200 E Wells St Milwaukee WI 53202

BROWN, EDITH TOLIVER, educator retired; b. Mize, Ky., Dec. 26, 1916; d. Manford Clarence and Snowy May (McGuire) Toliver; m. James Link Brown, Mar. 14, 1948; 1 child, Pamela Jo Brown Elick. BA in Elem. Edn., Ky. Weslyan U., 1947. Permanent tchr. cert., Ohio. Tchr. Mapleton Elem.

Sch., Mt. Sterling, Ky., 1939-44; chief of personnel records sect. Office of InterAm. Affairs, Washington, 1944-46; personnel staff Lockbourne (Ohio) AFB, 1951; tchr. Groveport (Ohio) Elem. Sch., 1957-73; substitute tchr. Pickaway and Franklin Counties, 1973-77; chmn. Textbook Com. Groveport (Ohio) Elem. Sch., 1960-65; mem. Curriculum Guide com., Columbus, Ohio, 1965-66. Trustee United Way of Pickaway County, 1984-87; chmn. Cancer Crusade Madison Township, Heart Fund Drive, Madison Township; counselor Buckeye Girls's State, Columbus, 1955. Named Ky. Col. by Ky. Gov. Brown, 1982. Mem. AAUW, Ohio Retired Tchrs. Assn. (pres. 1989), Pickaway County Retired Tchrs. Assn., Am. Legion Aux. #730, Nat. Retired Tchrs. Assn. (del. to 5 conventions AARP). Democrat. Methodist. Home: 6341 Perrill Rd Ashville OH 43103

BROWN, EILEEN CLARE, business executive; b. N.Y.C., Nov. 28, 1943; d. Gordon John and Effie Carolyn (Hanlon) Brown; m. Leo Edmund Cobb, Aug. 7, 1980 (div. 1986). Mem. portfolio mgmt. team Lepercq, de Neuflize & Co., N.Y.C., 1972-76; v.p. Clarens Assocs., Inc., N.Y.C., 1976-90, also bd. dirs.; exec. asst. to pres. Grow Group, Inc., N.Y.C., 1990—. Republican. Roman Catholic. Home: 333 E 69th St Apt 9K New York NY 10021 Office: Grow Group Inc 200 Park Ave New York NY 10166

BROWN, ELEANOR MOORE, research chemist; b. East Liverpool, Ohio, Mar. 19, 1936; d. Wilbert Swan and Ruth (Garwood) Moore; m. Alfred Gene Brown, June 11, 1960; 1 child, Carolyn. BA, Ohio Wesleyan U., 1958; MS, Drexel U., 1967, PhD, 1971. Analytical chemist Harshaw Chem. Co., Cleve., 1958-61; chemist Calbiochem, L.A., 1961-62; rsch. asst. Mich. State U., Lansing, 1963-64; NRC fellow Eastern Regional Rsch. Ctr./U.S. Dept. Agr., Phila, 1971-73, dairy rsch. co. fellow, 1973-75, rsch. chemist, 1975—. Mem. Am. Soc. Biochemistry and Molecular Biology, Protein Soc., Am. Chem. Soc., Assn. for Women in Sci., Internat. Assn.Women Bioscientists. Office: Eastern Regional Rsch Ctr US Dept Agr 600 e Mermaid Ln Philadelphia PA 19118

BROWN, ELIZABETH TAYLOR, psychology educator; b. Cleve., Jan. 2, 1930; d. Talmadge Andrew and Alberta Lois (Carter) Guy; m. Eugene Donaldson Taylor, Sept. 9, 1954 (div. Sept. 1963); 1 child, Eugene Guy; m. Dallas Coverdale Brown, Jr., Sept. 5, 1985. BA, Ohio State U., 1952; PhD, Washington U., St. Louis, 1968. Lic. clin. psychologist, Ohio, W.Va. Staff psychologist Standard Oil Ohio, 1963-65; lectr. Case Western Res. U., Cleve., 1964-66, asst. prof., 1968-71; instr. Cleve. State U., 1964-68, assoc. prof., 1971-85; prof., chairperson dept. psychology W.Va. State Coll., Institute, 1985—; cons. psychologist Juvenile Ct. Cuyanoga County, Cleve., 1966-67; mem. personnel Rsch. Inc., Cleve., 1966-81. Contbr. articles to profl. jours. Bd. dirs. LWV, St. Louis, 1960-63, Arts & Edn. Coun., St. Louis, 1960-63. Mem. Am. Psychol. Assn., Links, Inc., Alpha Kappa Alpha. Home: 400 Bibby St Apt E Charleston WV 25301 Office: WVa State Coll Campus Box 170 Institute WV 25112

BROWN, ELLEN ZERVOS, day care facility administrator; b. Orlando, Fla., July 5, 1930; d. Alfred Henry and Polly Rosella (Higgs) Corbett; m. Robert Hall Brown, Dec. 1, 1988; children: John, Mark, Kenneth, Zervos. Diploma, So. Coll., 1949; RN, Fla. Sanitarium and Hosp., 1952; diploma, Patricia Stevens Finishing Sch, 1957. Surg. nurse oper. rm. Garfield Meml. Hosp., Washington, 1952-53; charge nurse Walter Reed Army Med. Ctr., Washington, 1955-62; team leader oncology unit Washington Adventist Hosp., Takoma Park, Md., 1966-77; adminstr. Concord Adult Day Care Ctr. Coun. on Aging, Inc., Orlando, Fla., 1977-81; team leader neo-natal unit Fla. Hosp., Orlando, 1982-84. Author: Coping With Cancer, Kidney Stones, Bonnie, Our Angel in White. Vol. patient rels., chaplain Fla. Hosp. Aux. Mem. Takoma Park Nurses Club, Soc. Nursing Profls., Am. Nursing Assn., Assn. Seventh-Day Adventist Nurses, Am. Cancer Soc., ARC, Am. Heart Assn., Cen. Fla. Mental Health Assn.

BROWN, FAITH GIDEON, public relations professional; b. Phila., Apr. 7, 1942; d. Winfred S. III and Marie (DeForest) Gideon. BA in Eng., Montclair State Coll., Upper Montclair, N.J., 1977, postgrad., 1978-80; postgrad., Syracuse U., N.Y.C., 1978-79. Pub. relations coordinator Bamberger's N.J., Newark, 1964-67; asst. dir. community relations United Hosp. Newark, 1967-69; dir. pub. relations United Way of Essex & West Hudson, Newark, 1975-80; dir. devel. Newark Boys Chorus Sch., 1980-82; sub-contractor Miller Poor Assocs., Verona, N.J., 1983—; pres. FGB Enterprises, 1983—; cons. Approtech Health Systems Inc., Washington and St. Thomas, V.I., 1985-89, Affinity Card Mktg., Inc., South Orange, N.J., 1987—, Imbuia Ventures, Inc., St. Thomas, 1990—. Trustee Greater Newark Christmas Fund, 1983—, Community Day Nursery, East Orange, 1984—; bd. mem. Community Adv. Bd. Fairleigh Dickinson U., Rutherford, N.J., 1980-85; jr. Warden, vestry Ch. St. Andrew & Holy Communion, South Orange, 1988—. Mem. N.J. Chap. Nat. Assn. Media Women (Treas. 1987--), Nat. Assn. Female Execs. Democrat. Episcopal. Home and Office: 759 Stirling Dr East South Orange NJ 07079

BROWN, FRANCES ANNE, therapist; b. Newport News, Va., Feb. 13, 1946; d. Quincy and Frances (Williams) B. AA in Nursing, Chowan Coll., 1968; BS in Profl. Arts, St. Joseph's Coll., North Windham, Ma., 1980. Staff nurse in psychiatry Duke U. Med. Cen., Durham, N.C., 1968-71; head nurse in psychiatry Duke U. Med. Cen., Durham, 1971-76; pvt. practice counseling Chapel Hill, N.C., 1976—; trainer assertiveness Durham (N.C.) Tech. Inst., Duke U. Med. Ctr., Piedmont Tech. U., 1980-83; cons. Ctr. Wellbeing, Carrboro, 1987; photographer Alderman's Galleries, Durham, House of Frames, Durham. Co-chair Orange County Domicilliary Home Adv. Com., 1985-87; bd. dirs. Orange County Rape Crisis Cen., chair 1986-87. Mem. Hillsborough Historical Soc., NOW (publicity/photography com. 1981—), Nat. Assn. Women Bus. Owners (cons. 1987, sec. 1987—), Am. Psychol. Assn. (assoc.), Chapel Hill/Carrboro C. of C. (mem. speakers bur., cons. 1981-87), N.C. Soc. Clin. Hyponosis, Internat. Platform Assn. Baptist. Lodge: Women Moose. Home: 29 Bluff Trail Chapel Hill NC 27516 Office: 104 S Estes Dr Ste 304 Chapel Hill NC 27514

BROWN, MRS. GARDNER RUSSELL See GILLICE, SONDRA JUPIN

BROWN, GAYE ROBINSON, labor analyst, social worker; b. Roanoke, Va., Sept. 21, 1938; d. Nelson Warren and Edna Frances (Cloyd) Robinson; m. Perry Walker Brown, Apr. 20, 1985; children: Robert Spencer, Andrew Spencer, Sharon, Perry Walker Jr., Anne Leaphart, Deborah Morse. BA, Coll. of William and Mary, 1960; MSW, U. S.C., 1984. Mgr. young New Yorker div. Lord & Taylor, Falls Church, Va.; dir. human resources Santee Lynches Coun. of Govts., Sumter, S.C.; planner employment and tng. div. Office of the Gov., Columbia, S.C.; rsch. analyst S.C. State Devel. Bd., Columbia. Active policy com. United Way of the Midlands, 1988-90, allocations panel 1984-88; vol. Lowman Home for the Aged, 1990; pres. Capital BPW, 1987-89. Mem. NAFE, LWV, S.C. Econ. Devel. Assn., Bus. and Profl. Women (pres.), Kappa Alpha Theta (pres. alumnae dis. 1989-90). Democrat. Lutheran. Home: 4 Cheryse Ct Chapin SC 29036

BROWN, GEORGIA WATTS, librarian; b. St. Francisville, La., Oct. 1, 1934; d. Edward Watts and Mary Alice (Jones) Calvin; m. Ollie J. Brown, Aug. 23, 1958; children: Pamela Karen, Oliver Joseph. BA, So. U., Baton Rouge, 1957; MS, La. State U., 1969. Asst. serials libr. So. U., Baton Rouge, 1957-62, serials libr., 1962-69, jr. div. libr., 1969-72, acting directory of libraries, 1972—. Mem. East Baton Rouge Libr. Bd., Govs. Com. of One Hundred, 1986-87, La. Centeseptequinary Commn., La., 1987-88, Art and Humanities Coun., Baton Rouge. Recipient Public Svc. award Baton Rouge Bicentennial Commn. and Mayor, City of Baton Rouge, 1976. Mem. La. Libr. Assn. (chmn. acad. sect. 1979-80), ALA, Southeastern Libr. Assn, Delta Sigma Theta. Democrat. Baptist. Office: So U John B Cade Libr Baton Rouge LA 70813

BROWN, GERALDINE, nurse, free lance writer; b. Clemson, S.C., Nov. 1, 1945; d. Isaac and Gladys (Patterson) B. AS in Nursing, U. D.C., Washington, 1973; real estate cert., Long and Foster Inst., College Park, Md., 1984; cert. in TV broadcasting, Columbia Sch., Bailey's Crossroads, Va., 1987; BS in Nursing, Bowie State U., 1989. RN, D.C., FCC Third Class License. Supr. staff nurse Walter Reed Hosp., Washington, 1970-76; supr. clin. nurse Dept. Human Svcs., Washington, 1976-78, community health nurse, 1978-84; nursing instr. Phillips Bus. Sch., Alexandria, Va., 1984-85; pvt. nurse pvt. practice, Washington, 1973—; dir. pub. affairs Bible Way Chs. Worldwide, Inc., Washington, 1978—; society columnist As It Happens, Charlotte (N.C.) Post, 1964-66; society editor Washington Cafe. Soc. mag., 1971; contbr. feature stories Capital Spotlight newspaper, 1978—. Asst. organizer DC Mayor's United Nations Day, 1980; vol. Met. Boys and Girls Clubs, Washington, 1980—; vol. Nursing Instr., The Washington Saturday Coll., 1982-84; Co. ARC, 1973—, Big Sisters of the Washington Met. Area, 1988—. Recipient certs. of excellence Govt. of D.C., 1978-84; cert. of appreciation Mayor of D.C., 1980, meritorious pub. svc. award, 1980; svc. trophy Washington Saturday Coll., 1984. Mem. Am. Nurses Assn., Fraternal Order of Police, Smithsonian Inst. (assoc.), NAACP, Wash. Urban League. Democrat. Apostolic.

BROWN, GERALDINE REED, lawyer, consulting executive; b. L.A., Feb. 18, 1947; d. William Penn and Alberta Vernice (Coleman) Reed; m. Ronald Wellington Brown, Aug. 20, 1972; children: Kimberly Diana, Michael David. BA summa cum laude, Fisk U., 1968; JD, Harvard U., 1971, MBA, 1973. Bar: N.Y. 1974, U.S. Dist. Ct. (so. and ea. dists.) N.Y. 1974, U.S. Ct. Appeals (2d cir.) 1974, U.S. Supreme Ct. 1977. Assoc. White & Case, N.Y.C., 1973-78; atty. J.C. Penney Co., Inc., N.Y.C., 1978-88; pres. The Reed-Brown Cons. Group., Montclair, N.J., 1989—; asst. prof. bus. law Montclair State Coll., 1990—; adj. prof. bus. law Kean Coll. N.J., 1989—. Bd. dirs. Coun. Concerned Black Execs., N.Y.C., 1977-88, Studio Mus. in Harlem, N.Y.C., 1980-81; mem. Montclair (N.J.) Devel. Bd., 1985-88, ad hoc com. on Montclair Econ. Devel. Corp., 1985-88; trustee Montclair YWCA; trustee United Hosps. Med. Ctr., chmn. bylaws com., vice chair strategic planning com., pers. com.; chair bylaws com. N.J. United Minority Bus. Brain Trust.; mem. Essex County Ct. Apptd. Spl. Advocates. Mem. ABA (several coms. sect. corp., banking and bus. law, sect. internat. law and practice), N.Y. State Bar Assn. (continuing legal edn. com., legis. liason 1981-90, vice chmn. 1988-90, exec. com. of corp. counsel sect., chmn. com. on SEC, fin. corp. law and governance), Assn. of Bar of City of N.Y. (corp. law com. 1978-81), N.Y. County Lawyers Assn. (corp. law com.), Women's Econ. Roundtable, Exec. Women of N.J., Harvard Bus. Sch. Club, Harvard Law Sch. Assn., Coalition 100 Black Women, Harvard Bus. Sch. Black Alumni Assn., Harvard Law Sch. Black Alumni Assn., Harvard Club (N.Y.C.), Phi Beta Kappa, Delta Sigma Theta (chair social action com. Montclair alumnae chpt., chair bylaw com., parlimentarian). Home and Office: The Reed-Brown Cons Group 180 Union St Montclair NJ 07042

BROWN, GERRYANNE, homecare agency executive; b. Phila., Mar. 21, 1945; d. Harold J. and Anne M. (McCormick) B. BA, U. Conn., 1967. Lic. social worker, Mass. Dir. recreation svcs. Dept. of Army, Seoul, Korea, 1968-69, Schwabisch Gmünd, Ger., 1969-74; dir. Ret. Sr. Vol. prog. Action, Inc., Gloucester, Mass., 1975-88; dir. Homemaker Svcs. of Greater Cape Ann Action, Inc., 1988—. Author cookbook: Indigestion for 20 People or More, 1973. Adv. bd. Sr. Home Care Svcs., Gloucester, 1981-89; tour dir. Ret. Sr. Vol. Prog., Gloucester, 1985-88; ct. mediator Salem Dist. Ct., 1984—; mem. Ipswich Dem. Town Com., 1979—; income tax counselor AARP, Ipswich, 1977—. Mem. Nat. Assn. RSVP Dirs. (reg. del. 1984-88, treas. 1988), Kappa Alpha Theta. Office: Homemaker Svcs of Cape Ann 24 Elm St Gloucester MA 01930

BROWN, GLENDA CAROL, insurance executive, small business owner; b. Jackson, Miss., June 30, 1949; d. Troy Snow and Bonnie Glenn (Gill) Brown Jr., A.A. in Radio and TV, Marjorie Webster Jr. Coll., 1969; B.A. in Radio and TV, U. Md., 1974; M.A. in Bus. Mgmt. and Supervision, Central Mich. U., 1975. Adminstrv. asst. Dept. Navy (NTDA), Washington, 1970-78; tech. writer, editor VSE Engring., Alexandria, Va., 1979; agt. Aetna Life Ins. Co., McLean, Va., 1979-84; gen. agt. Western Fidelity Ins. Co., Washington, 1985—; real estate agt. Century 21 BNR Realty, Washington. Mem. NAFE, D.C. Assn. Life Underwriters, Profl. Ins. Agts., Arlington C. of C., No. Va. Bd. Realtors. Avocations: reading, piano, tennis, ice skating, phys. fitness. Home and Office: 7561 Vogels Way Springfield VA 22153

BROWN, HELEN BENNETT, biochemist; b. Greenwich, Conn., Oct. 6, 1902; d. John Lansingh and Susan Jessie (Bronson) Bennett; m. John James Brown, June 16, 1928 (div. Jan. 1977); children: Susan Jessica Brown Girardeau, Margaret Bronson Brown Bevington. BA, Mt. Holyoke Coll., 1924; PhD, Yale U., 1930; ScD (hon.), Mt. Holyoke Coll., 1974. Technician dept. pediatrics Grace Hosp., New Haven, Conn., 1924-27; rsch. asst. dept. physiology Yale U., New Haven, Conn., 1927-28; rsch. assoc. dept. pediatrics Western Res. Univ., Cleve., 1928-31; rsch. assoc. Ben Venue Labs., Cleve., 1944-48; staff rsch. div. Cleve. Clinic, 1948-68, dir. dietary rsch., 1958-68, resident emeritus staff in rsch., 1968—; cons. Am. Dietetic Assn., Chgo., 1970-82, Am. Heart Assn., Dallas, 1968-77, Nat. Heart, Lung, Blood Inst., Bethesda, 1968-82, AMA, Chgo., 1982-83, Blue Shied Sr. Adv. Com., Cleve., 1983-90. Author ednl. materials on diets, blood lipids, others.; assoc. editor Coronary Club Health Letter, 1972-90. Pres. Nutrition for Greater Cleve., 1979-84; mem. Ohio Episcopal Diocese Ministry on Aging, Cleve., 1986-90; cons. Judson Retirement Community, Cleve., 1984—. Named Woman of Profl. Excellence, Cleve. Clinic, 1983, Lifetime Achievement award, 1990, Cleve. Career Woman of Achievement, YWCA, 1990. Fellow Coun. on Atheriosclerosis, Coun. on Epidemiology; mem. Am. Inst. Nutrition, Am. Dietetic Assn. (hon. mem.), Am. Heart Assn., NEO Affiliate, Sigma Xi. Home: 1890 E 107th St #527 Cleveland OH 44106 Office: Cleveland Clinic Found One Clinic Ctr 9500 Euclid Ave Cleveland OH 44195-5255

BROWN, HELEN GURLEY, writer, editor; b. Green Forest, Ark., Feb. 18, 1922; d. Ira M. and Cleo (Sisco) Gurley; m. David Brown, Sept. 25, 1959. Student, Tex. State Coll. for Women, 1939-41, Woodbury Coll., 1942. Exec. sec. Music Corp. Am., 1942-45, William Morris Agy., 1945-47; copywriter Foote, Cone & Belding (advt. agy.), Los Angeles, 1948-58; advt. writer, account exec. Kenyon & Eckhardt (advt. agy.), Hollywood, Calif., 1958-62; editor-in-chief Cosmopolitan mag., 1965—; editorial dir. Cosmopolitan internat. edits., 1972—. Author: Sex and the Single Girl, 1962, Sex and the Office, 1965, Outrageous Opinions, 1967, Helen Gurley Brown's Single Girl's Cook Book, 1969, Sex and the New Single Girl, 1970, Cosmopolitan's Love Book: A Guide to Ecstasy in Bed, 1978, Having It All, 1982. Named 1 of 25 most influential women in U.S., World Almanac, 1976-81; recipient Francis Holmes Achievement award for outstanding work in advt., 1956-59, Disting. Achievement award U. So. Calif. Sch. Journalism, 1971, Spl. award for editorial leadership Am. Newspaper Woman's Club, Washington, 1972, Disting. Achievement award in Journalism Stanford U., 1977, Matrix award in mag. category, N.Y. Women in Communications, 1985; Helen Gurley Brown Rsch. Professorship established in her name Northwestern U. Medill Sch. Journalism, 1986. Mem. Authors League Am., Am. Soc. Mag. Editors, AFTRA, Eta Upsilon Gamma. Office: Cosmopolitan The Hearst Corp 224 W 57th St New York NY 10019

BROWN, HELENE GURIAN, health science facility administrator; b. N.Y.C., May 3, 1929; d. Elias Jerome and Ethel (Lipman) Gurian; m. Robert L. Brown, Nov. 27, 1947; children: Jeffrey, Brian. BS, UCLA, 1957. Coord. spl. svcs. Birmingham VA Hosp., Van Nuys, Calif., 1947-50; dir. Coun. Health Agys., L.A., 1968-72, Community Cancer Control, L.A., 1972-82; dir. Cancer Control Ctr. UCLA, 1982—; conf. presenter in field. Vol. educator Am. Cancer Soc., San Francisco, 1950—, bd. dirs., Atlanta, 1969—; bd. dirs. Nat. Cancer Inst., Washington, 1984—. Recipient Ewing Laymen's award Soc. Surg. Oncology, Award of Excellence medal Pub. Health Assn. L.A., bronze medal Am. Cancer Soc., Women of Yr. award Assoc. In-Group Donors, award of excellence Soc. Oral Pathology. Fellow Am. Pub. Health Assn.; mem. Soc. Pub. Health Educators. Office: UCLA Cancer Control Ctr 1100 Glendon Ave #711 Los Angeles CA 90024

BROWN, IONA, violinist, orchestra director; b. Salisbury, Wiltshire, England, Jan. 7, 1941. Studied w. Hugh Maguire, London, Remy Principe, Rome, Henryk Szeryng, France. Violinist Nat. Youth Orch. of Gt. Britain, 1955-60, Philharmonia Orch. of London, 1963-66; violinist Acad. of St. Martin-in-the-fields, 1964—, concertmaster, dir., 1974—; artistic dir. Norwegian Chamber Orch., Oslo; prin. guest dir. City of Birmingham Symphony Orch., Birmingham, England; music dir. Los Angeles Chamber Orch., Los Angeles, 1987—. Office: Los Angeles Chamber Orch 315 W 9th St Suite 300 Los Angeles CA 90015*

BROWN, ISABELLE RUTH, civic leader; b. Mobile, Ala., Aug. 18, 1910; d. Benjamin and Sarah Gup; m. Ronald Brown, Feb. 24, 1933; children: Bennett, Barry. Student, Goucher Coll., 1927; BS, Case Western Res. U., 1932. Del. White House Conf. for Children and Youth, 1960, White House Conf. on Aging, 1961; chmn. Greater Cleve. Women's Com. for Civil Rights, 1963; mem. Ohio Gov.'s Com. on Status of Women, 1965-69;; project dir. Women in Community Svc., Cleve., 1965; pres. Internat. Coun. Jewish Women, 1966-69, hon. life v.p.; chmn. women's orgn. Jewish Community Fedn. Cleve.; mem. nat. exec. coun. Am. Jewish Com., 1966—; hon. life v.p. Nat. Coun. Jewish Women. Recipient Disting. Svc. award Cleve. Community Fedn., 1966, Hannah G. Solomon award Nat. Coun. Jewish Women, 1969. Home: 13435 N Park Blvd Cleveland OH 44118

BROWN, JAN W., small business owner, legislator; b. Roundup, Mont., Mar. 16, 1942; d. John Estes and Janet Lillian (Snyder) Dahl; m. William A. Brown III; children: Erik Lane, Kimberly Elise. BA in Sociology, Social Work, Carroll Coll., 1976. Sec. 1st Nat. Bank, Bozeman, Mont., 1962, Office of Gov., Helena, Mont., 1963-69; pub. info. coord. Helena Model City Program, 1969-73; pub. relations and assn. mgmt. Mont. Bar Assn., Helena, 1973-76, Mont. Assn. Life Underwriters, Helena, 1973-76; legis. liaison Mont. Religious Legis. Coalition, Helena, 1975-81; exec. dir. Helena Food Share Inc., 1987; co-owner Jorud Photo and Gifts, Helena, 1971—; legislator Mont. St. Legislature, Helena, 1983—; mem. legis. coun. Helena, 1989; bd. dirs. Helena Food Share, Inc., Bus. Improvement Dist.; chmn. state adminstrn. com. Mont. Ho. Reps. Chmn. Mont. Medal of Valor Com., Helena, 1986-89; pres. United Way, helena, 1982; bd. dirs. Mont. area Health Edn. Ctr., Bozeman, 1988—, Mont. Hunger Coalition, Helena, 1988-89. Recipient Disting. Svc. award Mental Health Assn., 1976, Disting. Community Svc. award Jayceens, 1982, Annual Appreciation award Child Support Enforcement award United Way, 1988, Community Svc. award VFW, 1988. Mem. Toastmasters, Helena Unltd. Democrat. Episcopalian. Office: Jorud Photo and Gifts 327 N Last Chance Gulch Helena MT 59601

BROWN, JANE MARTIN THORNTON, health science center administrator; b. Elberton, Ga., Mar. 6, 1951; d. Laurie William and Mary Frances (Martin) Thornton; m. Donald McCarty Brown Jr., June 14, 1980; children: Laurie Elizabeth, Judson McCarty. Student, U. Ala., 1969-70, Georgetown Coll., 1970-71; BS, Minot State Coll., 1973, MS, 1974. Speech-lang. pathologist Duval County Sch. System, Jacksonville, Fla., 1974-77, Newberry (S.C.) County Schs., 1977-78, Tri-County Spl. Edn. Coop., Murphysboro, Ill., 1978-79; speech-lang. pathologist Ga. Retardation Ctr., Atlanta, 1980-82, dir. speech-lang. pathology, 1982-87, coordinator of quality circles, 1983-86, coordinator of interdisciplinary habilitation, 1986-87, dir. programs, evaluation, research and tng., 1987-90; coord. disciplines Ga. Retardation Ctr., Athens, 1990—; chairperson Ga. Mental Retardation, Developmentally Disabled Network, Atlanta, 1987—; expert panel mem. Speech Pathology Assessment Instrument Team, Athens, 1986-87, Ga. Dept. Edn., Atlanta, 1987. Presentor: (paper) Developmental Disabilities: Where do we go from Here?. Pres. Citizen's Adv. Com., Atlanta, 1985—; mem. Gainsbor. Civic Assn., Atlanta, 1985—, Gov's. Edn. com., N.D., 1972-74, Com. for Networking Conf., Atlanta, 1985—. Grantee Minot State Coll., 1973-74. Mem. Ga. Speech-Lang.-Hearing Assn., Retarded Citizens of Atlanta (Vital Svc. award 1987), Am. Assn. Mental Deficiency, Coun. for Exceptional Children, Mental Retardation Inst. (finalist mgr. of year Ga. 1989, leadership dept. Human Resources 1989). Democrat. Methodist. Office: Ga Retardation Ctr-Athens 850 College Station Rd Athens GA 30601

BROWN, JANET, educator; b. Detroit, Dec. 4, 1936; d. William and Grace J. (Roughgarden) Van Der Sluys; m. Nail E.C. Eminson, May 28, 1958 (div. 1971); children: Alexander E. Brown, Leila G. Eminson Atkins; m. E.A. Brown (dec. 1973). BA, Knox Coll., 1958; MS, Chgo. State U., 1973; PhD, U. Wis., Milw., 1987. Tchr. Galesburg (Ill.) Schs., 1958-60, Peoria (Ariz.) Schs., 1960-61; reading specialist Park Forest (Ill.) Schs., 1962-63. 68-73; ESL instr. Waukesha County Tech. Inst., Waukesha, Wis., 1975-79; reading specialist U. Wis. Ctr., Waukesha, 1978-83, mgr. Learning Lab. Student Support Svcs., 1983—. Bd. dirs. Great Blue Heron council Girl Scouts U.S., 1988—; bd. dirs., scholarship chmn. Milw. Council for Adult Learning, 1988—. Mem. Internat. Reading Assn., Wis. Assn. Equal Opportunity Program Personnel, PEO Sisterhood (v.p. 1988-90), Phi Kappa Phi. Office: U Wis Ctr-Waukesha 1500 University Dr Waukesha WI 53188

BROWN, JANINE LOUISE, assistant professor; b. Los Angeles, Feb. 15, 1954; d. Richard George and Lois (Rohrs) B.; m. Herman Martin Schoenemann, Aug. 9, 1986. AA, Los Angeles Pierce Coll., 1974; BS with honors, N.D. State U., 1977; MS, Washington State U., 1980, PhD, 1984. Research asst. Wash. State U., Pullman, Wash., 1978-80; research technologist Wash. State U., Pullman, 1980-81, research asst., 1981-84; research assoc. Uniformed Svcs. U., Bethesda, Md., 1985-87; asst. prof. Uniformed Svcs. U., Bethesda, 1987—; research assoc., cons. Smithsonian Nat. Zoo, Washington, 1987—; adj. prof. George Mason U., Manassas, Va., 1988—. Co-author: Global Tiger Survival Plan, 1986; contbr. numerous articles to profl. jours. Recipient Grad. Student Competition award Am. Soc. Animal Sci., 1983, Research Grant Dept. Defense, 1987, Research Grant Ringling Bros. Circus, 1989. Mem. Am. Soc. Animal Sci., Soc. for the Study of Reproduction. Democrat. Home: 12609 Gould Rd Wheaton MD 20906 Office: Uniformed Svcs Univ 4301 Jones Bridge Rd Bethesda MD 20814

BROWN, JEAN BUSH, speech and language pathologist, audiologist; b. Springfield, Mo., Jan. 22, 1947; d. Denzil Lee and Betty Jean (Smith) Bush; 1 child, Larry G. Brown II. BA, Memphis State U., 1973, MA, 1974, PhD, 1981. Cert. speech and lang. pathologist, audiologist, counselor. Instr., coord. audiol. svcs. U. Minn., Duluth, 1981-82, instr., dir. audiol. programs, 1981-83, coord. coop. tng. program, Duluth component, 1981-83, asst. prof., dir. audiology programs, 1981-83; clin. group practice and direct patient care Albuquerque Aphasia and Speech Consultants, 1983-86; pvt. practice direct patient care Vocal Point Therapies, Inc., Albuquerque, 1986—; dir. Communication and Cognitive Treatment Ctr., Albuquerque; mem. auditory verbal com. Let the Children Hear Found., 1988—. Grantee U. Minn., 1980, 81, Blandin, Inc., 1981. Mem. Am. Speech-Lang.-Hearing Assn., N.Mex. Speech-Lang.-Hearing Assn., Nat. Head Injury Found., N.Mex. Head Injury Found. Home: 11901 El Dorado Pl NE Albuquerque NM 87111 Office: Vocal Point Therapies Inc 3900 Juan Tabo NE Ste 17 Albuquerque NM 87111

BROWN, JENNIFER JANE, medical assistant; b. Wilmington, Del., Apr. 11, 1959; d. Joseph James and Paula Jane (Sutton) B. BS in Plant Sci., U. Del., 1981; BS in Health Sci., George Wash. U., 1988, student, 1988. Vol. Wilmington Med. Ctr., 1972-75, Tilton Terr. Nursing Home, Wilmington, 1976-77; nurses aide Little Sister's Nursing Home, Newark, 1978-80; nurses asst. Atlantic City Med. Ctr.; horticulturist Longwood Gardens, Kennett Square, Pa., 1978-79; horticulture tchr. Del. Pub. Sch., 1979-80; floral designer Floralies Garden Ctr., Washington, 1980-81; landscape designer Bloomin Newmans, Bethesda, Md., 1981-86; asst. to physicians Drs. Richard Katon, Melinda Wolf, Germantown, Md., 1988—; provider basic life support Am. Heart Assn., Washington, 1988—; provider advanced cardiac life support Am. Heart Assn., Washington, 1988—. Leader Girl Scouts Am., Md., 1989. Fellow: Nat. Assn. Physician Assts.; mem. Md. Assn. Physician Assts., Md. Physician Quality Assurance. Republican. Home: PO Box 251 Poolesville MD 20837 Office: Drs Katon & Wolf 20528 Germantown Rd Ste 104 Germantown MD 20874

BROWN, JOAN MAZZAFERRO, telephone company executive; b. Greenport, N.Y., Jan. 1, 1956; d. Joseph Anthony and Sophia (Kroleski) M. BS, SUNY-Brockport, 1978; MS, Purdue U., 1980. Sr. tech. assoc. Bell. Tel. Labs., Whippany, N.J., 1978-79, mem. tech. staff, 1979-83; staff analyst Pacific Bell Co., San Francisco, 1983-84, staff mgr., 1984-85, dist. staff mgr., San Ramon, Calif., 1985—. Kodak scholar, 1978. Mem. NAFE. Roman Catholic. Club: Young Adults (San Ramon). Avocations: skiing, sailing, aerobics, theatre, dance. Office: Pacific Bell 221 W Winton Ave Rm C318 Ramon CA 94544

BROWN, JOYCE CHRISTINE, sales professional; b. Uniontown, Pa., Nov. 17, 1956; d. Howard Wendell Sr. and Bessie Christine (Hennen) Dennis; m. Walter Lee Brown Jr., Oct. 10, 1987; 1 child, Lindsay Lee. BSBA with honors, Tampa (Fla.) Coll., 1990. Various positions in adminstrn. U.S.

Govt., Washington, 1974-82; with Navy Regional Data Automation Ctr., Washington, 1980-83, adminstrv. asst. to comdg. officer, 1982-83; mgr. adminstrv. svcs. Capital Systems, Inc., Arlington, Va., 1983-84; sales adminstrn. mgr. Coloplast, Inc., Tampa, 1985—. Mem. NAFE, Am. Soc. for Quality Control, Health Industry Mfrs. Assn. Republican. Methodist. Home: 406 Maplewood Dr Oldsmar FL 34677

BROWN, JUANITA ORA LUCKETT, financial manager; b. Chgo., July 31, 1948; d. Clifford Homer and Irma Jean (Maxwell) Luckett; m. Oddie Lee Brown, July 17, 1971; children: Odili Njoli, Chapelle Beth. BS in Math., U. Chgo., 1969; MBA, Columbia U., 1971. Cons. Union Carbide, N.Y.C., 1971-74, sr. cons., 1974-77, supr. client service, 1977-79, sr. fin. analyst, 1979-80; mgr. ops. analysis Am. Can Co., Greenwich, Conn., 1980-81, Mgr. corp. analysis standards and measurements, 1981-82, dir. fin., 1983-84, dir. asset mgmt., 1984-85, dir. resource analysis, 1985-86; mgr. fin. analysis Bristol-Myers Co., N.Y.C., 1987—; v.p., asst. treas. Bidermann Industries Corp., N.Y.C., 1990—; seminar leader Assn. for Integration Mgmt., N.Y.C. and Washington, 1976-79. Active Twp. of Teaneck (N.J.) Facilities Com., 1986—, Friends of the Teaneck Libr., 1986; treas. Working Parents Assn., 1985-87, Lowell Sch. PTO, 1981-83; fundraiser U. Chgo., Newark, 1986; pianist Sunday sch. Varick Meml. AMEZ Ch., Hackensack, N.J., 1979—. Recipient Black Achiever award Harlem YMCA, 1978. Mem. Nat. Assn. Female Execs., Nat. Black MBA Assn. (nat. pres. 1977-78), Alumni Assn. Columbia U. (dir. 1976-77). Methodist. Club: Toastmasters (treas. N.Y.C. chpt. 1973-75). Office: Bristol-Myers Co 345 Park Ave New York NY 10154

BROWN, JUDY MARIE, sales executive; b. Shreveport, La., Sept. 7, 1957; d. James H. and Billie Lucille (Alford) B. BA, Northeast La. U., 1977. Continuity dir. Sta. KEEL/KMBQ Radio, Shreveport, 1978-79; mgr., part owner New South Advt. Ltd., Shreveport, 1979-83; from local sales to nat. sales mgr. Sta. KSLA TV, Shreveport, 1983-89; nat. regional sales mgr. Sta. KATV TV, Little Rock, 1989—. Bd. dirs. NCCJ, Shreveport, 1989, Little Rock, 1990—; chair sacramental instr. Cath. Rite of Christian Initiation of Adults Adopted for Children, St. Mary of the Pines Cath. Ch., Shreveport, 1979-89; lay eucharistic minister, lector, communication com. Diocese of Shreveport and Little Rock, 1979-89; 2d v.p. Shreveport Ad Fedn., 1982-83; swim instr. ARC, Shreveport, 1979-89; communications bd. Diocese of Little Rock, 1989—; dir. Rites of Christian Initiation of Adults, Cathedral of St. Andrews, Little Rock, 1989—. Mem. Associated Gen. Contrators. Office: Sat KATV TV PO Box 77 Little Rock AR 72203

BROWN, JULIE ANN, actress, singer; b. Aug. 31, 1958; d. Leonard Francis Brown and Celia Jane (McCann) Arden; m. Terrence E. McNally, June 11, 1983 (div. Aug. 1988). AA in Theater, Valley Coll., Van Nuys, Calif., 1977; Degree (hon.), Am. Conservatory Theatre, San Francisco, 1978. Performed as lead singer on albums including Goddess in Progress, 1984, Trapped in a Body of a White Girl, 1987; co-writer, appeared in movie Earth Girls Are Easy, 1987; star of MTV's Just Say Julie, 1989. Mem. Writer's Guild Am., Screen Actors Guild, AFTRA. Democrat.

BROWN, JUNE GIBBS, government agency official; b. Cleve., Oct. 5, 1933; d. Thomas D. and Lorna M. Gibbs; children: Ellen Rosenthal, Linda Gibbs, Victor Janezic, Carol Janezic. B.B.A. summa cum laude, Cleve. State U., 1971, M.B.A., 1972; postgrad., Cleve. Marshall Law Sch., 1973-74; J.D., U. Denver, 1978; postgrad. Advanced Mgmt. Program, Harvard U., 1983. Real estate broker, officer mgr. N.E. Realty, Cleve., 1963-68; staff acct. Frank T. Cicirelli, C.P.A., Cleve., 1970-71; asst. to comptroller S.M. Hexter Co., Cleve., 1971; grad. teaching fellow Cleve. State U., 1971-72; dir. internal audit Navy Fin. Ctr., Cleve., 1972-75; dir. fin. systems design Bureau of Land Mgmt., Denver, 1975-76; project mgr. Bureau of Reclamation, 1976-79; insp. gen. Dept. Interior, Washington, 1979-81, NASA, Washington, 1981-85; v.p. fin. and adminstrn. Systems Devel. Corp., a Burroughs Co., 1985-86; assoc. adminstr. for mgmt. NASA, 1986-87; insp. gen. U.S. Dept. Def., Arlington, Va., 1987-90; dep. insp. gen. USN-CINCPACFLT, 1990—; bd. dirs. Fed. Law Enforcement Tng. Ctr., 1984-85, Interagy. Auditor Tng. program Dept. Agrl. Grad. Sch., 1983-85; chmn. interagy. com. on Ifon. Resource Mgmt., 1984-85; mem. bd. advs. Nat. Contract Mgmt. Assn., 1987-89. Mem. bd. advisors Howard U. Sch. Bus., 1987-89. Recipient award Am. Soc. Women Accts., 1969, 70, 71, Raulston award Cleve. State U., 1971, Pres.'s award Cleve. State U., 1971, Outstanding Achievement award U.S. Navy, 1973, Career Svc. award Chgo. region Fed. Exec. Bd., 1974, Outstanding Contbn. to Fin. Mgmt. award Denver region Fed. Exec. Bd., 1977, Fin. Mgmt. Improvement award Joint Fin. Mgmt. Improvement Program, 1980, Outstanding Service award Nat. Assn. Minority CPA Firms, 1980, NASA exceptional service medal, 1985, Outstanding Achievement in Aerospace award, 1987, Woman of Yr. award Bur. Land Mgmt., Dept. Interior, 1975, Robert W. King Meml. award Assn. Govt. Accts., 1988, Disting. Pub. Svc. award Dept. Def., 1989; named Disting. Alumni Cleve. State U., 1990. Fellow Nat. Acad. Pub. Adminstrn.; mem. Assn. Govt. Accts. (nat. pres. 1985-86, nat. exec. com. 1977-87, vice chmn. nat. ethics com. 1978-80, chmn. fin. mgmt. standards bd. 1981-82, service award 1973, 76, outstanding achievement award 1979, King award 1988, nat. ethics com. 1990), Am. Inst. CPAs, Am. Accts. Assn., Assn. Fed. Investigators, Nat. Contract Mgmt. Assn. (bd. advisors), NASA Alumni Assn., Women in Aerospace, Am. Soc. for Pub. Adminstrn. (Profl. Responsibility Exemplery Practice award 1990, pres.-nat. capitol area chpt. 1989), Exec. Women in Govt., Beta Alpha Psi. Office: CINCPACFLT 03B Pearl Harbor HI 96860

BROWN, JUNE WILCOXON, writer; b. W. Lafayette, Ohio, Aug. 14, 1914; d. Ralph Foster and Pearl Almeda (Marx) Wilcoxon; B.A., U. Md., 1935; m. Albert W. Brown, Nov. 3, 1938; 1 son, Peter Wilcoxon. Freelance writer, 1945-60, 81—; editor Select mag., Madison, Wis., 1959-65; radio script writer Beverly Stark Radio Show, 1963-68, John Doremus Show, 1971-72; sit-in hostess Mary Brooks Jackson radio show, St. Thomas, V.I., 1966-75, Louise Noble Radio Show, St. Thomas, 1975-81; author monthly column Caribbean Corner, 1977-78; author: Inside American Paradise, 1990 (hon. mention Internat. Literary awards 1988); author fiction and articles in nat. magazines. Mem. Nat. League Am. Pen Women (pres. Madison 1954), St. Thomas Community Music Assn. (v.p. 1970-71), Women in Communications (Writers cup Madison 1951), Kappa Kappa Gamma. Republican. Address: Box 7396 Saint Thomas VI 00801

BROWN, KAREN KAY, microbiologist, corporate executive; b. Manhattan, Kans., July 25, 1944; d. Clarence Christian and Edna Dorothy (Spiecker) Kilker; m. Harold G. Brown, June 18, 1966. BS in Chemistry and Biology, Washburn U., 1966; PhD in Molecular Biology and Microbiology, Okla. State U., 1972. Quality assurance microbiologist Haver-Lockhart, Shawnee, Kans., 1972; rsch. scientist Cutter-Haver-Lockhart, Shawnee, 1972-80; prin. scientist Bayvet div. Miles Labs., Merriam, Kans., 1981-84; mgr. biol. rsch. Mobay Animal Health, Merriam, 1984—; pres. Pair O' Docs Investments, Kansas City, Mo., 1984—; cons. Limburg Investments, Ltd., Englewood, Colo., 1988—; biohazards officer Mobay Animal Health, 1974—; patent liaison Mobay Animal Health and Diamond Sci., Des Moines, 1988—; mem. USDA;/DNA task force, Washington, 1985-90. Contbr. articles to profl. jours.; holder 10 U.S. patents, 25 fgn. patents; radio interviewer Pub. Radio, 1986. Election judge Rep. Party, Stillwater, Okla., 1967-72; CPR instr. Am. Heart Assn., Kansas City, 1985—; mem. Emergency Med. Svcs. Team, Kansas City, 1985—; bd. dirs. Animal Care Inst., Maple Woods Community Coll., 1988—. Recipient Miles Sci. and Tech. award, 1984, Mobay Sci. and Tech award, 1985-86; USPHS fellow. Mem. AAAS (invited speaker 1986), N.Y. Acad. Sci., Am. Assn. Lab. Animal Scientists (bd. dirs. Kansas City chpt. 1981-83, regional examining bd., 1981-85), Am. Soc. for Microbiology, Tissue Culture Assn., Sigma Xi, Phi Kappa Phi. Office: Mobay Corp Animal Health Div 9009 W 67th St Merriam KS 66202

BROWN, KATHLEEN, lawyer, state treasurer; d. Edmund G. and Bernice B.; m. George Rice (div. 1979); children: Hillary, Alexandra, Zebediah; m. Van Gordon Sauter, 1980; 2 stepsons. BA in History, Stanford U., 1969; grad., Fordham U. Sch. Law. Mem. L.A. Bd. Edn., 1975-80; with O'Melveny & Myers, N.Y.C., then L.A.; commr. L.A. Bd. Pub. Works, 1987—; elected treas. of Calif., 1990. Democrat. Address: Office of State Treas PO Box 942809 Sacramento CA 94209*

BROWN, KAY (MARY KATHRYN BROWN), state official; b. Ft. Worth, Tex., Dec. 19, 1950; d. H.C., Jr. and Dorothy Ruth (Ware) B.; m. William P. Dougherty, Dec. 15, 1978 (div. 1984). B.A., Baylor U., 1973. Reporter, UPI, Atlanta, 1973-76; reporter, feature writer Anchorage Daily Times (Alaska), 1976-77; reporter, co-owner Alaska Advocate, Anchorage, 1977; aide, researcher Alaska State Legislature, Juneau, 1979-80; dep. dir. div. of oil and gas (formerly div. minerals and energy mgmt.) Alaska Dept. Natural Resources, Anchorage, 1980-82, dir., 1982-86. Chmn. ways and means com. Alaska Woman's Polit. Caucus, 1982-84, mem. steering com., 1982-86; bd. dirs. Blood Bank Alaska, 1984-86 ; del. Alaska Democratic Conv., 1984; elected Alaska Ho. of Reps., 1986.

BROWN, KORIE BETH, English educator; b. Los Angeles, Apr. 1, 1962; d. Kenneth Sydney and Marilyn Ruth (Solomon) B. BA in English, Mills. Coll., 1983, BA in Legal Processes, 1983; MA in English, U. Calif., Santa Barbara, Calif., 1986. Cert. English tchr., Calif., community coll. instr., Calif. Journalist Santa Barbara (Calif.) Weekly, 1985; temporary worker Kelly Svcs., Santa Barbara, 1986-87; tchr. Duarte (Calif.) Unified Sch. Dist., 1987—; instr. Mt. San Antonio Coll., Walnut, Calif., 1988-90; coord. advanced placement program, writing proficiency testing, advisor literary mag., Duarte High Sch., 1987—, advisor drama club and newspaper. Author: Walrus Literary Mag., 1982, 83; contbr. articles to mag. Mem. Amnesty Internat., 1989, Nat. Parks Conservation Fund Assn., Washington, 1989. Mem. Nat. Coun. Tchrs. English, NEA, Caif. Tchrs. Assn., Duarte Unified Edn. Assn. Democrat. Jewish. Office: Duarte High Sch 1565 Central Ave Duarte CA 91101

BROWN, LARITA EARLY DAWN MA-KA-RE, publisher, computer and educational products manufacturing executive; b. Santa Monica, Calif., Dec. 21, 1937; d. Robert Walter and Lela Shirley (Sims) B. AA, Santa Monica City Coll., 1956; BA, Los Angeles State U., 1973; D (hon.), Boston U., 1977; Masters, LaSalle U., postgrad. Tchr. parochial sch. Gardena, Calif., 1968-70; supr. Early Childhood programs/tchr. L.A. City Schs.-Headstart Program, 1970-72; project asst. Mayor's Office Employment and Job Devel., L.A., 1972-76; community svcs. specialist U.S. Dept. Commerce, Washington, 1976-81; owner, founder N and Out Pub. Co., Richardson, Tex., 1984—; dir. tutorial programs resource learning ctrs.; cons. human resources, Dallas area, 1985—; contractor Reading Is Fundamental assn., 1984; robot programmer; computer scis. specialist, cons.; founder, dir. Skooter Sam Ednl. Software Co., Dallas; founder Electronics Tech. Consortium; founder (pvt. sch.) Skooter Sam New Age Space Sch. Author: Ginalyn's Surprise, 1984, Skooter Sam in Texas, 1985, Skooter Sam Series, Queens/Kings of African Heritage, African American Inventors, Skooter Sam: Key to the Future, Skooter Sam: White Scholar, Princess Ebony, Queens and Kings, Queens and Kings of Africa, Collectible Dolls, Skooter Sam: Esteem Team, others; patentee numerous childrens' computer products. Active Dallas PTA Council; supr. various polit. campaigns, Calif. and Tex., 1970—; advisor youth and coll. student div. NAACP, 1981-82; media cons. Nat. Womens Polit. Caucus, Hollywood, Calif., 1976; vol. Bridge Over Troubled Waters project for homeless. Recipient trophy from Los Angeles County Community Colls., 1980, Service award U. So. Calif., 1970, Dallas Kiwanis Clubs, 1984, Silver Poet award, 1986, Sesquicentennial Tex. Logo award, 1986, Gold Seal award Gov. State of La., Mayor City of New Orleans; named hon. citizen S. Dallas. Mem. Anthropol. Assn. Am., Phi Beta Alpha Gamma. Methodist. Office: N & Out Pub-Mfg PO Box 74-1082 Dallas TX 75374-1082

BROWN, LAVELLE SHELLY, accountant; b. Watsonville, Calif., Aug. 1, 1961; d. Firman E. Brown and Radeene Sibyll (Kusalich) Anguiano. BS in Acctg., Coll. Notre Dame, 1989, postgrad., 1989—. Bookkeeper Pixie Pla., Aptos, Calif., 1975-80, mgr., 1980-84; clk. Chiorini Hunt & Buchard, Santa Cruz, Calif., 1977; acctg. clk. Port-O-Net, Inc., Santa Cruz, 1977-79; operator Pacific Telephone, Santa Cruz, 1980; sales rep. No. Light, Castro Valley, Calif., 1984-85; acct. Coll. of Notre Dame, Belmont, Calif., 1985—; model, rep. Mari Smith Presents, San Jose, Calif., 1988—. Del. Calif. Community Jr. Coll. Assn., 1981, 82, Calif. Community Coll. Student Govt. Assn., 1981, 82; model Nordstron-Lupis Benefit, Palo Alto, Calif., 1987. Mem. Nat. Assn. Accts., Inst. Internal Auditors, Aerobics and Fitness Assn. Am. (instr.), Am. Soc. Women Accts., Alpha Gamma Sigma, Gamma Chi Sigma. Republican. Baptist. Home: 1050 Ralston Ave #14 Belmont CA 94002-2240 Office: Coll of Notre Dame 1500 Ralston Ave Belmont CA 94002-1908

BROWN, LEANNA, state senator; b. Providence, 1935; d. Harold and Esther Young; m. W. Stanley Brown; children: William, Stephen. BA with honors, Smith Coll., 1956. Coun. mem. Ednl. Testing Svc., Princeton, N.J., 1956-60, Chatham Borough, 1969-72; mem. taxation and fin. com. Nat. Assn. Counties, 1976-79; mem. Morris County Bd. Chosen Freeholders, 1972-81, bd. dirs., 1976; bd. dirs. Chatham Trust Co., 1982—; pres. N.J. Assn. Counties, 1978; chmn. N.E. N.J. Transp. Coordinating Com., 1979-80; mem. N.J. Assembly, 1980-83, N.J. Senate, 1984—; mem. Casino Revenue Fund Study Commn., 1984-86, Madison YMCA Capitol Campaign Com., 1986—, chmn., Primary Gifts com., 1987—; trustee Ctr. for Nonprofit Corps., 1985—; mem. Gov.'s Commn. on Internat. Trade, 1986—; vice chmn. Congressman Dean Gallo's Small Bus. Export Opportunity Task Force, 1987—; coord. Kean for Gov., County of Morris, 1985. Vice chmn. N.J. Hist. Commn., 1986-89; trustee Morris Mus. Arts and Sci., 1975—, Arts Coun. Morris Area, 1973—; del. White Ho. Conf. on Children, 1970; devel. coun. N.J. Sci. and Tech. Ctr., Liberty State Park, 1986—. Mem. N.J. Assn. Elected Women (pres. 1982, 83). Home: 7 Dellwood Ave Chatham NJ 07928 Office: Cory Commons 123 Columbia Turnpike Florham Park NJ 07932 Other: NJ State Senate State Capitol Trenton NJ 08625

BROWN, LESLIE ANN, biologist; b. Tucumcari, N.Mex., Nov. 28, 1961; d. David Elmer and Charlotte Suzanne (Six) B. BA in Biology, Kans. State U., 1983. Ward attendant Oak Park Vet. Clinic, Lenexa, Kans., 1978-79; undergrad. lab. tech. Div. Biology, Kans. State U., Manhattan, 1981-83; receptionist Service Merchandise, Houston, 1985; sales rep. LKB Instruments, Houston, 1986-87; sr. tech. specialist Pharmacia LKB Biotech., Piscataway, N.J., 1987-89, assoc. mgr. electrophoresis tech. svc., 1990—. Com. chmn. Fone Crisis Ctr., Manhattan, Kans., 1981-83. Vanderbilt fellow, 1983-85; named one of Outstanding Young Women of Am., 1984, 87, 88. Republican. Presbyterian.

BROWN, LINDA ANNE, government program administrator; b. Washington, May 11, 1953; d. Gilbert James and Helen Lucille (Elliott) Gordon; m. John Michael Brown; 1 child, Laura Kimberly. Cert., U. Denver. Chief civilian med. care br. Naval Med. Commd., Washington; mgr. mktg. div. Hosp. Corp. of Am., Washington; dir. govt. programs Acumenetics, Inc., McLean, Va. Mem. NAFE. Home: 7483 Little River #204 Annandale VA 22003

BROWN, LINDA COCKERHAM, quality assurance scientist; b. Durham, N.C., Dec. 4, 1946; d. Harry Lee and Amanda Emmaline (Parks) Cockerham; divorced; children: Eva Angelique, Benjamin James Jr. BS, Agrl. and Tech. U. of N.C., 1970. Lab. technician Burlington Industries, Greensboro, N.C., 1969; tchr. Wayne Community Coll., Goldsboro, N.C., 1976-77; lab. technician ICI Americas Inc., Goldsboro, 1978-80, sr. lab. technician, 1980-82, quality assurance scientist, 1982-88; quality assurance scientist Radian Corp., Research Triangle Park, N.C., 1989—; mem. Council Agrl. Sci. and Tech., 1983—. Sec., pres. Protestant Women of Chapel, Goldsboro, 1972, 75; mem. City Planning Com., Goldsboro, 1987; sec./treas. Goldsboro Wayne Youth Bowling Assn.; bd. dirs. Community Concert Council, Goldsboro, 1987, bd. dirs. admissions and budget com. United Way, Goldsboro, 1987. Recipient research stipend NSF, 1966, Saslow award, 1970. Mem. Soc. Quality Assurance, NAFE, Agrl. and Tech. U. N.C. Alumni Assn. (sec. 1982-87), N.C. Quality Assurance Discussion Group. Baptist. Club: Officers' Wives (newspaper editor 1973). Office: Radian Corp PO Box 13000 Chapell Hill Rd & Nelson Hwy Research Triangle Park NC 27709

BROWN, LINDA CURRENE, small business executive; b. Clovis, N.Mex., Oct. 28, 1942; d. Currie Oscar and Minnie Irene (Rodgers) Bell; m. Harvey Robert Brown, June 11, 1961; 1 child, Christopher Robert. Student, Ea. N.Mex. U., 1960-63. Youth dir. Sandia Bapt. Ch., Clovis, 1969-76; v.p. Linda's Orna-Metal, Clovis, 1974—; portrait cons. Triangle Home Ctr., Clovis, 1977-81, dept. supr., 1979-81, customer rels. rep., 1981-82, advt. dir., 1982-83; merchandising mktg. dir., advt. dir., customer relations rep. Holands Office Equipment, Clovis, 1983-85; office mgr. Poka Lambro Telecommunications, Clovis, 1985. Patentee in field. Active Clovis High Plains Hosp. Aux., 1983. Democrat. Baptist. Home and Office: 1940 Cameo Clovis NM 88101

BROWN, LINDA LOCKETT, school food service administrator, nutrition consultant; b. Jacksonville, Fla., Jan. 8, 1954; d. Willie James and Katie Lee (Taylor) Lockett; m. Thomas Lee Brown, Dec. 18, 1982; children: Ashanti, William, Timothy. BS in Agr., U. Fla., 1975, M of Agr., 1981. Lic. profl. nutritionist. Chemist/microbiologist Green Giant Co., Alachua, Fla., 1975-77; lab. technologist II U. Fla., Gainesville, 1977-81, extension agt. I, Ft. Myers, 1981-85, extension agt. II, 1985-87, West Palm Beach, 1987-88; area supr. Palm Beach County Sch. Food Svc., 1988—; nutrition cons. Congregate Meals, Ft. Myers, 1984-87, Serenity House, Ft. Myers, 1985-87; cons. Performax, 1989—. Columnist Palm Beach Post, 1989—; contbr. articles to profl. jours. Mem. exec. bd. Community Coordinating Coun., Ft. Myers, 1985; co-founder Friends of Hearing Impaired Youth, Gainesville, 1976; tutor-coord. Sampson, Gainesville, 1973; mem. Jr. League, Ft. Myers, 1987; mem. Jr. League, Palm Beach, Fla., 1987—, mem. edn. tng. com., community rsch. com. 1989-90; mem. nutrition com. Am. Heart Assn., Palm Beach, 1989—. State U. System Bd. Regents grantee, 1980. Mem. Soc. Nutrition Edn. (legis. network chmn.), Am. Dietetic Assn. (network of blacks in nutrition, chair legis. com. 1988-89, chair nominating 1989, sec. 1989-90), Fla. Dietetic Assn. (chair minority issues com., chair membership 1987-88, chair edn. and registration 1988-90), Palm Beach Dietetic Assn. (community nutrition chair 1988-89, chair legis. com. 1989-90), Caloosa Dietetic Assn. (sec.), NAFE, Nat. Assn. Extension Home Econs. Agts., Internat. Platform Assn., Nutrition Today Soc., Alpha Zeta, Epsilon Sigma Phi. Club: Greater Palm Beaches Bus. and Profl. Women (minority student mentor, role model mentor). Avocations: singing, violin. Office: Palm Beach County Sch Food Svc 7061 Garden Rd Riviera Beach FL 33404

BROWN, LINDA ODESSA, home economist; b. Monroe, Ga., Dec. 2, 1957; d. L.J. and Odessa (Smith) B. Cert., Athens (Ga.) Tech. Coll., 1976; BS, Ft. Valley (Ga.) State Coll., 1982; MS, Iowa State U., 1984. Cert. tchr., Mo., Iowa. Rsch. asst. Iowa State U., Ames, 1982-84; urban agt., home economist Ky. Coop. Extension, Erlanger, 1985-86; area coord. Ky. Coop. Extension, Frankfort, 1986—. Recipient Cert. of Appreciation, Minority Affairs Office of State of Iowa, 1984. Mem. Am. Home Econs. Assn., Ky. Assn. Home Economists, Nat. Assn. Home Economists, Ft. Harrod chpt. Assn. Home Economists (pub. rels. chmn. 1988—), AAUW, Ky. State U. Women's Club. Democrat. Baptist. Office: Kenton County Extension Svc PO Box 97 5272 Madison Pike Independence KY 41051

BROWN, LINDA RUTH, uniform company executive; b. Richmond, Ind., May 18, 1952; d. Virgil Howard and B. Jean (Mosier) Colbath; m. Steve Nichols, Jr., May 10, 1969 (div.); children: Rodney Dwayne, Ryan David; m. Ernest Lee Brown, Oct. 22, 1977; children: Heather Nicole, Waylon Shayne; stepchildren: Christine L., Carol Renee. Bank teller, acctg. clk. Union Fin., New Albany, Ind., 1969-74; bookkeeper, office mgr. Jeff Elks Club, Jeffersonville, Ind., 1975-77; asst. personnel dir. Hyatt Regency Louisville, 1974-82; personnel dir., office mgr. NuYale, Jeffersonville, 1982-87; personnel dir., denim mgr. Universal Uniforms, Louisville, 1987-89, controller, office mgr., 1989, asst. v.p., 1989—. Home: 214 Hopkins Ln Jeffersonville IN 47130 Office: Universal Uniforms 1721 S 7th St Louisville KY 40208

BROWN, LIZZIE PEARL, chemistry educator; b. Newberry, S.C., Oct. 13, 1931; d. Delton Bibbs and Elvira Elbina (Reeder) Boyd; m. John Percy Brown, Nov. 15, 1959; 1 child, David Albercrombie. BS, S.C. State Coll., Orangeburg, 1954; MS, Howard U., 1960; Student, Ill. Inst. Tech., Chgo., 1962-64; PhD, Howard U., Wash., 1970. Science tchr. Norfield High Sch., Norway, S.C., 1954-57; teaching asst. Howard U., Washington, 1957-59, teaching fellow, 1966-67; chemistry tchr. So. U. and A&M Coll., Baton Rouge, 1959-61; rsch. technician Hoekton Inst. Med. Rsch., Chgo., 1961-64, U. Chgo. Med. Sch., Chgo., 1964-66; lab. scientist U. Md. Hosp., 1966-66; prof. chemistry Morgan State U., Balt., 1970—; cons. Howard U. Wash., 1973-75; mentor Mt. Royal Middle Sch. Balt., 1986-87. Contbr. articles to profl. jours. Mem. Urban League, Balt., 1972—, Balt. Zool. Soc., 1975—, Nat. Aquarium Balt., 1984—, Hillen Rd. Improvement Assn. Balt. Recipient NASA Traineeship Howard U. Wash., 1967-69, Rsch. Stipend Argonne Nat. Lab. Lamont Ill., 1973, Faculty Internship Environ. Protection Agy. Chgo., 1986, Faculty Internship U.S. Dugway Proving Ground, Utah, 1987. Fellow Am. Inst. Chemists; mem. AAAS, Am. Chem. Soc., AAUW, N.Y. Acad. Scis., Beta Kappa Chi, The Coll. Club (Balt.). Office: Morgan State U Hillen Rd Coldspring Ln Baltimore MD 21239

BROWN, LOIS HEFFINGTON, health facility administrator; b. Little Rock, Mar. 28, 1940; d. Carl Otis and Opal (Shock) Heffington; M. Ivy Roy Brown, June 21, 1984; children: Carletta Jo Rice, Roby Lynn Rice, Pherby Allison Graham, Phelan Missy Graham. Student, Guilford Tech. Community Coll., Jamestown, N.C., 1974-75, 77, 80. Cert. hearing aid specialist. Sec. Berger Enterprises, West Memphis, Ark., 1962-65; office mgr. Beltone Hearing Care Ctr., Greensboro, N.C., 1975-81; owner Hearing Care Ctr., Cullman, Ala., 1982-85, Miracle-Ear Ctr., Cullman, Decatur, Fultondale, Jasper and Birmingham, Ala., 1985-87; pres. L&I Corp., Cullman, Decatur, Fultondale, Jasper and Birmingham, 1987—. Gov.-appointed Ala. Bd. Hearing. Mem. Nat. Hearing Aid Soc., Ala. Hearing Aid Dealers Assn. (sec. 1984-86, v.p. 1986-88, bd. dirs. 1988—), Women of the Moose. Republican. Baptist. Home: Rte 1 PO Box 113A Danville AL 35619 Office: L&I Corp 2109 A Danville Rd SW Decatur AL 35601

BROWN, LORETTA ANN PORT, physician, geneticist; b. Kingston, N.Y., July 30, 1945; d. Frank and Sophie (Hormann) Port; m. Robert Don Brown, Aug. 22, 1970; 1 child, Adrian Robert. BS, SUNY, New Paltz, 1967; MS, U. Mich., 1968, postgrad., 1969; MD, Ea. Va. Med. Sch., Norfolk, 1981. Diplomate Am. Bd. Med. Examiners. Lab. tech. U. Mich., Ann Arbor, 1969-70; rsch. asst. M.D. Anderson Hosp. and Tumor Inst., Houston, 1970; rsch. instr. Baylor Coll. Medicine, Houston, 1971-76; resident internal medicine Ea. Va. Med. Sch., Norfolk, 1981-84; asst. prof. medicine Med. Coll. Hampton Rd, Norfolk, 1984—; physician Health America, Hampton, Va., 1984-87, Tidewater Pulmonary Assocs., Newport News, Va., 1987-88; chief, admitting and screening VA Med. Ctr., Hampton, 1988—; trainee genetics USPHS, Ann Arbor, Mich., 1967-69; rsch. participant NSF, Albion, Mich., 1966; cons. VA Med. Ctr., 1984-88. Contbr. articles to profl. jours. Recipient Achievement award Am. Med. Women's Assn., 1981, Am. Chem. Soc., 1966. Mem. Am. Morgan Horse Assn., Am. Horse Show Assn., Old Dominion Morgan Horse Assn. (v.p. 1987-89), Va. Carolinas Morgan Horse Assn., Delmarva Morgan Horse Assn., Potomac Morgan Horse Club, Nu Pi Sigma. Roman Catholic. Office: VA Medical Ctr 590/170 Hampton VA 23667

BROWN, LORRAINE ANN, administrative services coordinator; b. Providence, Mar. 15, 1947; d. Leonard Francis and Elaine Frances (Pettis) Millen; m. Jeffrey Schofield Brown, May 22, 1976 (div. 1983); 1 child, Kaneeta Sage; m. Dieter Paul Wuennenberg, July 14, 1965; 1 child, Desiree Jacqueline Wuennenberg. Student, Manhattan Sch. Printing, 1972, L.A. Trade Tech. Coll., 1981-83. Communications rep. TransAmerica Occidental, Los Angeles, 1973-77; owner, jewelry designer The Lorraine Brown Co., El Segundo, Calif., 1979-83; mgr. Silk Lingerie Outlet, Sherman Oaks, Calif., 1982-83; office mgr. Am. Silk Label, L.A., 1984; asst. prodn. coordinator Pacific Coast Mills, L.A., 1984-85; asst. designer jr. wear Judy Knapp Inc., L.A., 1986-87; sales exec. Integrated Aquatic Systems, Marina Del Rey, Calif., 1987-88; adminstrv. svcs. coord. Contel Fed. Systems, Marina Del Rey, Calif., 1988—. Asst. leader Girl Scouts U.S., El Segundo, 1985-87. Mem. Young Exec. Singles, Advanced Degrees, Sierra Singles. Home: 756 Main St El Segundo CA 90245

BROWN, LOUISE DONA, human rights advocate; b. Inglewood, Calif., Sept. 19, 1959; d. Robert Edward Fleischmann and Donna May (Paris) Woods; m. Steven Ross Brown; children: Kimberlee, Geoffrey. AA, Antelope Valley Coll., 1986. Sales and svc. rep. Lyle Parido Ins. Agy., Inc., Palmdale, Calif., 1982-88, promotion coord., 1985-88; human rights activist, 1989—; art cons. Collectors Corner of Calif.; pub. speaker Antelope Valley Hosp. Eating Disorders Unit, Lancaster, Calif., 1985—. Founding editor (monthly jour.) E.D.E.N. News, 1985—; founding pres. Network, columnist; author (short story) Success, 1985. Chairperson solicitation Desert Haven Auction, 1989—. Mem. Amnesty Internat. (founder, area coord. Antelope Valley br. 1988—), Antelope Valley Bus. Breakfast Club (founder, pres.),

Antelope Valley Progressive Voice (charter). Democrat. Lodge: Optimists (pres. Palmdale club). Office: PO Box 500097 Palmdale CA 93550-0097

BROWN, LUCINDA ANN, library administrator; b. Marietta, Ohio, Feb. 22, 1956; d. William Dorsey and Margaret (Wittner) B. BS in History, Marshall U., 1980; MLS, U. Ky., 1982. Pub. svcs. libr. Campbell County Pub. Libr., Newport, Ky., 1982-85; dir. Boone County Pub. Libr., Florence, Ky., 1985—; mem. various coms. Ky. Dept. for Librs. and Archives, Frankfort, 1985—; v.p., pres. Ky. Libr. Network, Frankfort, 1988-90. Group campaign leader No. Ky. chpt United Way, Florence, 1988-90. Recipient Outstanding Svc. award Greater Cin. Libr. Consortium, 1989. Mem. NAFE, ALA, Ky. Libr. Assn. (chair elect, chair pub. libr. chpt. 1987-89), Greater Cin. Libr. Consortium (v.p., pres. 1986-88), Southeastern Libr. Assn., No. Ky. Adult Reading Coun., Inc. (founder 1986, pres. 1988-90). Office: Boone County Pub Libr 7425 US 42 Florence KY 41042

BROWN, LYNETTE RALYA, journalist, publicist; b. Beloit, Wis., Dec. 15, 1926; d. Lynn Louis and Ethel Clara (Meeker) Ralya; m. Donald Adair Brown, Jr., Dec. 20, 1947; children: Donald Adair III, Alison Laura, Julia Carol. BA in Journalism, Mich. State U., 1948; MA in Journalism, Michigan State U., 1985; MA in Mass Communication, Wayne State U., 1983. Actress, publicist Grand Traverse Playhouse, Traverse City, Mich., 1946 (summer), N.Y. Summer Playhouse, Mackinac Island, Mich., 1947 (summer); writer WILS Radio, Lansing, Mich., 1947-48; writer, performer WJBK Radio, TV, Detroit, 1948-49; editor Denby Ctr. News, Detroit, 1949-51; free lance writer Oakland County, Mich., 1952-78; editor Henry Ford Mus., Dearborn, Mich., 1979-81; writer, reporter Legal Advertiser Newspaper, Detroit, 1983-85; publicist Bloomfield (Mich.) Birmingham (Mich.) Pub. Librs., 1986-89; free lance writer, publicist Lynette Brown Communications, Birmingham, Mich., 1989—. Columnist: (newspaper) At the Libraries, 1986-89. Probation sponsor Dist. Ct. Mich., 1960-70; publicist Oakland County Vol. Bur., 1979-82; leader sr. high/jr. high youth group Drayton Ave. Presbyn. Ch., Oakland County, 1952-54, 62-66, Pine Hill Congl. Ch., Oakland County, 1968-71, Northbrook Presbyn. Ch., Oakland County, 1976-77; polit. campaign worker Rep. candidates and non-partisan jud. candidates, 1952—; Cub Scout leader Royal Oak Emerson Sch., Oakland County, 1961-64; Girl Scout troop leader Bloomfield Twp. Meadow Lake Sch., Oakland County, 1966-71. Mem. AAUW (chair women's issues), Rep. 300 Club, Lincoln Club (bd. dirs.). Home and Office: 6120 Westmoor Birmingham MI 48010

BROWN, MARCIA J., author, artist, photographer; b. Rochester, N.Y., July 13, 1918; d. Clarence Edward and Adelaide Elizabeth (Zimber) B. Student, Woodstock Sch. Painting, summers 1938, 39; student painting, New Sch. Social Research, Art Students League; B.A., N.Y. State Coll. Tchrs., 1940; student Chinese calligraphy, painting, Zhejiang Acad. Fine Arts, Hangzhou, Peoples Republic China, 1985, 87. Tchr. English, dramatics Cornwall (N.Y.) High Sch., 1940-43; library asst. N.Y. Pub. Library, 1943-49; tchr. puppetry extra-mural dept. U. Coll. West Indies, Jamaica, B.W.I., 1953; tchr. workshop on picture book U. Minn.-Split Rock Arts Program, Duluth, 1986, workshop on Chinese brush painting Brush Artists Guild, 1988; sponsor Chinese landscape painting workshops with Zhuo HeJun, 1988-89. Illustrator: The Trail of Courage (Virginia Watson), 1948, The Steadfast Tin Soldier (Hans Christian Andersen), 1953, Anansi (Philip Sherlock), 1954, The Three Billy Goats Gruff (Asbjornsen and Moe), 1957, Peter Piper's Alphabet, 1959, The Wild Swans (Hans Christian Andersen), 1963, Giselle, 1970, The Snow Queen (Hans Christian Andersen), 1972, Shadow (Blaise Cendrars), 1982 (Caldecott award 1983), (with others) Sing a Song of Popcorn, 1988; author, illustrator: The Little Carousel, 1946, Stone Soup, 1947, Henry Fisherman, 1949, Dick Whittington and His Cat (retold), 1950, Skipper John's Cook, 1951, The Flying Carpet (retold), 1956, Felice, 1958, Tamarindo, 1960, Once a Mouse (retold), 1961 (Caldecott award), Backbone of the King, 1966, The Neighbors, 1967, The Bun (retold), 1972, All Butterflies, 1974 (Boston Globe Honor Book, Horn Book), The Blue Jackal (retold), 1977, Walk Through Your Eyes, 1979, (with photographs) Touch Will Tell, 1979, (with photographs) Listen to a Shape, 1979, Lotus Seeds; Children, Pictures and Books, 1985; translator. illustrator: Puss in Boots, 1952, Cinderella (Charles Perrault), 1954 (Caldecott award), How, Hippo!, 1969 (honor book Book World Spring Book Festival); author, photographer: film strip The Crystal Cavern, 1974; woodcut prints exhibited, Bklyn. Mus., Peridot Gallery, Hacker Gallery, Library Congress, Carnegie Inst., Phila. Print Club; Chinese brush painting and calligraphy exhibited at Hammond Mus., North Salem, N.Y., 1988; prints in permanent collection, Library of Congress, N.Y. Pub. Library, pvt. collections; art work in Mazza Gallery Findlay (Ohio) Coll. Recipient Disting. Service to Children's Lit. award U. So. Miss., 1972; Regina medal Cath. Library Assn., 1977; Disting. Alumnus medal SUNY, 1969; U.S. nominee Andersen award illustration, 1966, 75; Life fellow Internat. Inst. Arts and Letters, 1961. Mem. Authors Guild, Print Council of Am., Art Students League, Oriental Brush Artists Guild, Sumi-e Soc. Am.

BROWN, MARGARET DEBEERS, lawyer; b. Washington, Sept. 24, 1943; d. John Sterling and Marianna Hurd (Hill) deBeers; m. Timothy Nils, Aug. 28, 1965; children—Emeline Susan, Eric Franklin. B.A. magna cum laude, Radcliffe Coll., 1965; postgrad. Harvard U. Law Sch., 1965-67; J.D., U. Calif.-Berkeley, 1968. Bar: Calif. 1969, U.S. Ct. Appeals (9th cir.) 1971, U.S. Supreme Ct. 1972, U.S. Ct. Appeals (D.C. cir.) 1986, U.S. Ct. Appeals (2d cir.) 1987. Assoc. White, Hamilton, Wyche, Shell & Pollard, Petersburg, Va., 1968-70, Heller, Ehrman, White & McAuliffe, San Francisco, 1970-73; sole practice, San Francisco, 1973-77; atty. Pacific Telephone (name changed to Pacific Bell 1984), San Francisco, 1977-83, sr. atty., 1983-85; sr. counsel Pacific Telesis Group, 1985—; speaker McGeorge Law Sch., Sacramento, 1983. Mem. ABA, Am. Corp. Counsel Assn., San Francisco Bar Assn., Phi Beta Kappa. Office: Pacific Telesis Group 130 Kearny St Rm 3659 San Francisco CA 94108

BROWN, MARGARET JEAN, sales executive; b. Pitts., June 5, 1947; d. Edward George and Margaret (Resko) Couch; 1 child, James Ralph Brown. AA, Prince George's Community Coll., 1974. V.p. sales Benchmark Systems Inc., Arlington, Va., 1979-89; chmn. bd. dirs. Accent Bus. Interiors, Gambrills, Md., 1989—. Mem. NAFE, Nat. Assn. Profl. Saleswomen. Republican. Home: 1804 Lang Dr Crofton MD 21114

BROWN, MARGARET REE, nurse; b. Sandersville, Ga., Mar. 1, 1949; d. Roger Lee Brown and Gladys Olee (Lawson) Arp; m. Bruce Edward Brown. BS, Northeastern U., 1975. RN, Mass. Asst. team leader Mass. Rehab. Hosp., Boston, 1975-77; head nurse Jewish Meml. Hosp., Boston, 1977-81; med. nurse coordinator Roxbury (Mass.) Comprehensive Community Health Ctr., 1981-83; clin. nurse coordinator Mattapan (Mass.) Community Health Ctr., 1983-86; dir. staff devel. Fuller Men. Health Ctr., Boston, 1985—; nursing educator Concord Bapt. Ch. Nurses Unit, Boston, 1977—. Site coordinator Nat. Health for Vol. Orgns., Dorchester, Mass., 1981-84; bd. dirs. Am. Cancer Soc., Mattapan, 1981, Hawthorne Youth and Community Ctr., Roxbury, 1986. Mem. NAACP, Mass. Nurses Found., Mass. Nurses Assn., New Eng. Regional Black Nurses Assn. (sec. 1984-88, v.p. 1988-89, bd. dirs.), Nat. Black Nurses Assn. (nominating com. chair 1988-90). Democrat. Baptist. Home: 103 Homestead St Dorchester MA 02121 Office: Fuller Mental Health Ctr 85 E Newton St Boston MA 02118

BROWN, MARGARET RUTH ANDERSON, state legislator; b. Scottsbluff, Nebr., Oct. 11, 1944; d. Everett Howard and Ruth (Nichols) Anderson; m. Kermit Campbell Brown, 1966. BA, U. Wyo., 1966, postgrad. 1971-73; postgrad. Pepperdine Coll., 1967-68. Mem. Legis. Exec. Commn. on Reorgn. of State Govt., 1974-78; mem. Wheatland (Wyo.) Town Council, 1974-75, Carbon County Council of Govts., 1976-83, chmn., 1980-83; mem. adv. council for Div. of Community Programs, 1979-85, chmn., 1983-85, adv. council Dept. Health and Social Services, 1982-85; mem. bd. dirs. Nat. Assn. Regional Councils, 1982-86; mem. Wyo. Ho. of Reps., 1983-87. Mem. AAUW, LWV (bd. dirs. Wyo. chpt. 1973-82, pres. 1979-81), P.E.O., Soroptomists. Republican.

BROWN, MARIE A., tourism company executive; b. Jamaica, N.Y., Nov. 2, 1936; d. Giuseppe Orlando and Florence (Verderese) Calabrese; m. William E. Brown, June 29, 1957; 1 child, Christopher William Brown. BA, NYU, 1957. Cons. Gulliver's Travel, Garden City, N.Y., 1973-80; regional mgr. Bhutan Travel Svc., N.Y.C., 1980-87; founder, owner Bhutan Travel Inc., N.Y.C., 1987—; mng. dir. Bhutan Travel Inc., N.Y.C., 1987—. Contbg. photographer (book) Bhutan, 1989, (video) The Door Opens, 1987; cover photographer (book) Feminine Ground, 1989; photographer (video segments) Arthur Frommers Travel Channel, 1987, 89. Mem. Greenpeace, People for the Ethical Treatment of Animals, Internat. Fund for Animal Welfare. Recipient 1st prize travel writing Travelscene Mag., 1978, 1st prize honorable mention photography Winter Arts Festival, Bethpage, N.Y., 1986. Mem. Pacific Asia Travel Assn., Asia Soc. Office: Bhutan Travel Inc 120 E 56th St 1430 New York NY 10022

BROWN, MARIE MAGDALEN JENKINS, biology educator, writer; b. Eldorado, Ill., Sept. 26, 1909; d. B. Robert and Clara Ann (Rhine) Jenkins; m. Harley P. Brown, Dec. 20, 1989. AB in English and Edn., Phillips U., 1929; MS in Biology, Cath. U. Am., 1951; PhD in Zoology, Okla. U., 1961. Cert. tchr., Okla., Va. Prof. biology James Madison Coll., Harrisonburg, Va., 1962-75, ret., 1975; chmn. biology dept. Benedictine Heights Coll., Guthrie, Okla., 1952-55, registrar, 1954-57; lectr. in field. Author 7 books. NIH Rsch. grantee, 1966-69. Mem. Am. Soc. Zoologists, Soc. Children's Book Writers, Phi Sigma (sec.), Sigma Xi. Democrat. Roman Catholic. Home: 504 Dakota St Norman OK 73069

BROWN, MARILYN BRANCH, social service executive; b. Richmond, Va., Apr. 11, 1944; d. Elbert LeRoy and Edna Harriett (Eley) Branch; m. Winfred Wayland Brown, Jr., June 19, 1982; 1 dau., Lesli Antoinette; 1 dau. by previous marriage, Kara Rachelle Lancaster. B.S., Va. State U., 1966; M.S., U. Nebr., 1968. Nat. Tchr. Corps intern U. Nebr. at Omaha and Omaha Pub. Schs., 1966-68; tchr. McKlenburg County Pub. Schs., Boydton, Va., 1968-71; community organizer model cities health planning Capital Area Comprehensive Health Planning Coun., Richmond, Va., 1971-72; asst. dir. com. mental health mental retardation svcs. bd. Va. Dept. Mental Health & Mental Retardation, Richmond, 1972-75, spl. edn. dir., 1975-76; civil rights coord. Va. Dept. Social Svcs., Richmond, 1976-88, dir. spl. edn. compliance, 1988—; chmn. EEO adv. com., 1984-88; supr. spl edn. compliance Va. Dept. Edn., 1988—; chmn. adv. com. on Black adoption Va. Dept. Social Svcs. Program coord. Swansboro Bapt. Ch., Richmond, 1979—; mem. Swansboro Ensemble, 1974—. Recipient Youth Motivation Commendation, Nat. Alliance of Bus., 1983. Fellow Am. Orthopsychiat. Assn.; mem. Am. Assn. Affirmative Action, Black Adminstrs. in Child Welfare, Alliance for Black Social Welfare, Psi Chi, Alpha Kappa Alpha. Baptist. Home: 5500 Larymore Rd Richmond VA 23225 Office: Va Dept Social Services 8007 Discovery Dr Richmond VA 23288

BROWN, MARY ELEANOR, physical therapist, educator; b. Williamsport, Pa., Jan. 1, 1906; d. Sumner Locher and Mary Kate (Eagles) Brown. Student U. Wis.-Madison, 1927-28; B.A., Barnard Coll., 1931; M.A., NYU, 1941, postgrad., 1942-45, Western Reserve U., 1960-61; postgrad. U. Miami, Miami-Dade Jr. Coll., 1971-72, Cuesta Community Coll., 1977-79. Supervising phys. therapist, rsch. asst. Inst. for Crippled and Disabled, N.Y.C., 1941-46; instr. edn. N.Y.U., 1942-46; phys. therapist Childrens Rehab. Inst., Cockeysville, Md., 1946; organizing dir. phys. edn. State Rehab. Hosp., West Haverstraw, N.Y., 1946-47; phys. therapy cons. Nat. Soc. for Crippled Children and Adults, Chgo., 1947-49; physical therapy cons., dir. prof. svcs., dir. cerebral palsy sch. N.Y. State Dept. Health, Albany, N.Y. and Eastern N.Y. Orthopedic Hosp. Sch., Schenectady, N.Y., 1949-53; chief phys. therapist Bird S. Coler Hosp. for Chronic Diseases, N.Y.C., 1953-54; chief phys. therapist, instr. edn. St. Vincents Hosp. and N.Y.U., 1954-58; chief rsch. assoc. hand rsch. Highland View Hosp., Cleve., 1958-64, cons. on kinesiology, hand rsch., 1964-65; supr. continuing edn. for phys. therapists, asst. prof. phys. therapy Case Western Res. U., Cleve., 1964-68; dir. phys. therapy Margaret Wagner House of Benjamin Rose Inst., Cleve., 1968-70; free lance writer, 1970—; 1st Mary Eleanor Brown lectr. clin. phys. therapy rsch. Inst. Rehab. and Rsch., Tex. Med. Center, Houston, 1979; Adv. bd. Community Svcs. Dept. Cuesta Community Coll., San Luis Obispo, Calif., 1977—; vol. UN and Univ. for Peace, Costa Rica, 1982—. Author: Therapeutic Exercise and Recreation: Group Activities for Fitness and Well-Being, 1989, Therapeutic Recreation and Exercise: Range-of-Motion Activities for Health and Well-Being, 1989; contbr. articles in field to profl jours. Recipient Award of Merit, Case-Western Res. U., 1970; award for clin. rsch. Inst. Rehab. and Rsch., Tex. Med. Ctr., Houston, 1979; Lucy Blair Svc. award Am. Phys. Therapy Assn., 1984, Disting. Alumna award Lancaster Country Day Sch., 1987. Mem. Inst. Gen. Semantics, Internat. Soc. Gen. Semantics, Am. Phys. Therapy Assn., Planetary Citizens, Better World Soc., Morro Bay Art Assn. Home: 659 Bernardo Ave Morro Bay CA 93442

BROWN, MOLLIE MARGARET, psychotherapist, social organization administrator; b. Rochester, N.Y., Jan. 4, 1931; d. Raymond J. and Marie (Fournaise) B. BSN, Duquesne U., 1965; M Nursing Edn., U. Pitts., 1967; PhD, U. Chgo., 1982. RN. Tchr. Notre Dame High Sch., Elmira, N.Y., 1956-63; adminstr. Sisters of Mercy, Rochester, N.Y., 1969-72; psychiat. nurse St. James Hosp./County Mental Health, Hornell, N.Y., 1967-69; asst. prof. nursing U. Rochester (N.Y.), 1970-72; dir. out-patient svc. Genesee Community Mental health Ctr., Rochester, 1975-78; acting chair dept. nursing, pvt. practice Nazareth Coll., Rochester, 1978-80; pvt. practice psychotherapy Rochester, 1978—; exec. dir. Spirit House, Inc., Rochester, 1981—. Editor: Readings in Gerontology, 1973-78, 80; contbr. articles to profl. jours. Bd. dirs. Regional Coun. on Aging, Rochester, 1970-75, East House Corp., Rochester, 1984-89. Roman Catholic. Office: Spirit House Therapeutic Community 72 Dorvid Rd Rochester NY 14617

BROWN, NANCY ALICE, human resources management executive, association executive; b. Chgo., Feb. 14, 1934; d. Daniel Webster and Mary Ella (Earls) Hampton; m. James D. Brown (div.); children: Robert Anthony Hebert, Donna Marie Hebert-Parker, Lawrence A. Brown. BA, DePaul U., MA. Personnel mgr. Martin Luther King Health Ctr., Chgo., 1974-81; staff specialist Am. Hosp. Assn., Chgo., 1981-85; employee relations mgr. Chem. Bank, Chgo., 1985-87; dir. Am. Hosp. Assn., Chgo., 1987—. Bd. dirs. Chgo. met. chpt. So. Christian Leadership Conf., 1979-84, Community Leadership Orgn., Chgo., 1984-85. Mem. Am. Soc. Personnel Adminstrn., Human Resources Mgmt. Assn. of Chgo. (com. mem.), NAACP, Operation People United to Save Humanity, Am. Soc. Dirs. of Vol. Services, Am. Soc. Assn. Execs., Chgo. Soc. Assn. Execs, League of Black Women. Democrat. Baptist. Home: 756 E 167 Pl South Holland IL 60473

BROWN, NANCY J., state representative; b. Chgo., Sept. 3, 1942; d. Herman Hugo Becker (dec.) and Katherine Evelyn (Gralund) Johnson; m. Myron Douglass Brown, June 7, 1968; children: Derek Douglass, Jason Alan. BS, Barat Coll., 1978; postgrad., U. Mo., 1982—. Treas. Village of Riverwoods (Ill.), 1975-76, trustee, 1976-78, 79-80, plan commr., 1978; twp. trustee, mem. zoning bd. Oxford (Kans.) Twp. Johnson Co., 1981-84; mem. Kans. Ho. of Reps., 1984—; cons. TRW Credit Data, Chgo., 1978-80; extension asst. U. Kans., Lawrence, 1980-81, office mgr. Gubernatorial Campaign, Kans., 1981-82. Mem. Nat. Hazardous Mat. Transp. Adv. Council, 1985-87, State Task Force on Autism, Kans., State Emergency Response Commn., Kans.; chmn. Community Devel. Block Task Force, Kans.; former bd. dirs. LWV. Recipient Excellence in Edn. award Blue Valley Sch. Dist., 1984. Mem. Nat. Assn. Towns & Twps. (bd. dirs.), Kans. Assn. of Twps. (exec. dir. 1983—), Blue Valley Community Council (chmn.), Blue Valley Hist. Soc., Am. Soc. Pub. Adminstrn. Republican. Address: PO Box 23314 15429 Overbrook Ln PO Box 23314 Stanley KS 66224

BROWN, NAOMI, laboratory technician; b. Sparta, Ga., Oct. 15, 1954; d. Clinton and Lillie Gay (Pearson) B. BS in Biology, Ga. Coll., Milledgeville, 1976; cert., Ga. State U., 1978. Lic. waste water analyst. Gas chromatograph operator Sewell Plastic, Atlanta, 1978-83; lab. technician II City of Atlanta, 1978—. Home: 1660 Harbin Rd Atlanta GA 30311

BROWN, NATALIA TAYLOR, former contract specialist, secondary educator; b. St. Louis, Mar. 3, 1928; d. Gentry and Olivia (Webb) Taylor; diploma with honors, Hubbard Bus. Coll., St. Louis, 1949; B.S., St. Louis U., 1983; m. Edward Brown, Sept. 30, 1951. Civilian with Dept. of Def., St. Louis, 1957-86, contract specialist U.S. Army Troop Support Command and U.S. Army Aviation Systems Command, 1969-86; substitute tchr. St. Louis Pub. Schs., 1986—. Mem. Coalition 100 Black Women, John N. Doggett Scholarship Found., St. Englebert Sch. Bd; life mem. NAACP. Recipient Sustained Superior Performance award U.S. Army, 1970. Mem. Knights of St. Peter Claver, Ladies Aux., Internat. Tng. in Communication, Women's Assn. of St. Louis Symphony Soc., Gamma Phi Delta (Elizabeth Garner Meml. award 1966). Roman Catholic.

BROWN, OLLIE DAWKINS, psychotherapist, scientific researcher; b. Martin County, Tex., May 30, 1941; d. David G. and Wilma Loree (Turner) Dawkins; m. Robert Jerry Brown, Sept. 28, 1958 (div.); children: Mark Allen, James Russell. BS, Tex. Tech U., 1965; MEd, North Tex. State U., 1973; MS, East Tex. State U., 1983. Cert. tchr., Tex. Tchr. Eastfield Community Coll., Dallas; diagnostician Lillian Solomon, Ph.D., Dallas, 1972-82; with Environ. Health Ctr., Dallas;, 1982—; psychotherapist Counseling and Edn. Ctr., Dallas, 1985—; researcher U. Tex., Dallas, 1988—. Contbr. articles to profl. jours., chpts. to med. textbooks. Mem. Prestwood Bapt. Ch., Dallas, 1985. Fellow Am. Biog. Rsch. Assn. (life, nat. adviser); mem. Am. Psychol. Assn., Tex. Psychol. Assn. Republican. Clubs: Toastmasters, Townnorth Trendsetters (treas. 1984-85). Home: 634 Williams Way Richardson TX 75080 Office: Pastoral Counseling and Edn Ctr 4525 Lemmon Ave Dallas TX 75219

BROWN, PATRICIA ANNE, cleaning service company executive; b. Dallas, May 14, 1939; d. Collin Drumheller and Gussie Mae (Garner) Skinner; 1 child, James Patrick Gordon. Student, St. Petersburg (Fla.) Jr. Coll, 1957-58, So. Meth. U., 1970-71. Airline stewardess Eastern Airlines, Miami, Fla., 1958-61; sec. United Svcs. Auto Assn., San Antonio, 1961-64, George Peabody Coll. for Tchrs., Nashville, 1964-65, Vanderbilt U. Hosp., Nashville, 1965-67, Hilton Hotels, Dallas, 1968-70; legal sec. Wynne, Jaffe & Tinsley, Dallas, 1970-72, Stalcup, Johnson, Myers & Miller, Dallas, 1972-74; owner apt. properties San Antonio, 1974-84; pres. Corridor Cleaning Svc., Inc., Boerne, Tex., 1984—. Republican. Methodist. Home: Route 1 Box 1699 Boerne TX 78006 Office: Corridor Cleaning Services 27112 Bent Trail Boerne TX 78006

BROWN, PATRICIA COCHRAN, artist, educator; b. Pitts., Nov. 16, 1955; d. Paul Edmund and Patricia Wilson (Cochran) B. BS, Purdue U., 1979; MS, East Tenn. State U., 1983. State park naturalist State of Ind., Indpls., 1975; botanist Carnegie Mus. Natural HIstory, Pitts., 1977-79; instr. chemistry East Tenn. State U., Johnson City, 1981-83; instr. biology U. Pitts., 1984-87; instr. art South Arts, Bethel Park, Pa., 1987—; botany artist Bayberry Studio, Upper St. Clair, Pa., 1987—; instr. art Lincoln Community Ctr., West Lafayette, Ind., 1974. Exhibited in group shows Pitts. Soc. Artists, 1987, Am. Artists Profl. League, N.Y.C., 1987 Salmagundi Club, N.Y.C., 1987. Winner Pa. Dept. Transp. graphics design contest for signs to designate wildflower areas along state roads, 1989. Mem. Soc. Econ. Botany, Ft. Pitt. Soc., DAR, Nat. Soc. DAR (chmn. Am. Heritage and Conservation, Pitts. chpt. 1989—), Am. Rabbit Breeders Assn., Inc., Beta Beta Beta. Republican. Episcopalian. Home and Office: Bayberry Studio 1531 Redfern Dr Upper Saint Clair PA 15241

BROWN, PATRICIA FORTINI, educator, art historian; b. Oakland, Calif., Nov. 16, 1936; d. Jack Gino Fortini and Mary Lillian (Wells) Forester; m. Peter Claus Meyer, May 28, 1957 (div. 1979); children: Paul Wells, John Jeffrey; m. Peter Robert Lamont Brown, Aug. 16, 1980 (div. 1989). AB in Polit. Sci., U. Calif., Berkeley, 1959, MA in History of Art, 1978, Phd in History of Art, 1983. Studio artist San Rafael, Calif., 1963-75; lectr. Mills Coll., Oakland, spring 1983; asst. prof. art and archaeology Princeton (N.J.) U., 1983-89, assoc. prof. art and archaeology, 1989—. Author: Venetian Narrative Painting in the Age of Carpaccio, 1988; contbr. articles to profl. jours. Commr. Cultural Affairs Commn., City of San Rafael, 1975-77; co-curator Falkirk Community Cultural Ctr., 1976-77. Social Sci. Rsch. Coun. fellow, 1980-81, Am. Acad. in Rome fellow, 1989-90, Guggenheim fellow, 1989; Fulbright-Hayes grantee, Italy, 1980-81. Mem. Coll. Art Assn., Renaissance Soc. Am. (adv. coun., rep. discipline of visual arts 1988—). Episcopalian. Office: Princeton U Dept Art and Archaeology Princeton NJ 08544-1018

BROWN, PATRICIA IRENE, lawyer, law librarian; b. Boston; d. Joseph Raymond and Harriet A. (Taylor) B. BA, Suffolk U., 1955, JD, 1965, MBA, 1970; MTS, Gordon Conwell Theol. Sem., 1977. Bar: Mass. 1965. Library asst. Suffolk U., Boston, 1951-60, asst. librarian, 1960-65, asst. law librarian, 1965-85, assoc. law libr., 1985—. Dir. Referral/Resource Ctr., Union Congl. Ch., Winthrop, Mass. First Woman inducted into Nat. Baseball Hall of Fame, Cooperstown, N.Y., 1988, All- Am. Girls Profl. Baseball League, 1950-51. Mem. Mass. Bar Assn., Boston Bar Assn., Assn. Am. Law Libraries. Office: Suffolk U Law Libr 41 Temple St Boston MA 02114

BROWN, PATRICIA MARY, real estate appraiser, broker; b. Detroit, May 28, 1945; d. Daniel Loren McCoubrey and Patricia Marie (MacLean) Myles; m. Charles William Borst, Jan. 27, 1965 (dec. 1966); children: Charles William Borst II, Robert Scott Brown. AA summa cum laude, Oakland Community Coll., 1976; Cert. in Real Estate, U. Mich., 1980; student, Madonna Coll., 1981—. Real estate sales appraiser Tower Appraisal Co., Farmington, Mich., 1966-77; fee appraiser FHA, Detroit, 1977—; pres. Internat. Appraisal and Investments, Inc., Plymouth, Mich., 1980—. Campaign worker, Rep. Nat. Com., Mich., 1979—; fundraiser, Northville chpt. Am. Cancer Soc., 1988, 89. Mem. Nat. Assn. Realtors, Mich. Assn. Realtors, Am. Inst. Real Estate Appraisers. Episcopalian. Office: Internat Appraisal Invest 689 N Mill St Plymouth MI 48170

BROWN, PATRICIA METZGER, hospital nurse executive; b. Balt., May 25, 1945; d. Melvin Lincoln and Elsie Marie (Schneider) Metzger; m. Robert John Brown, July 24, 1964; children: Robert Durry, Erin Lynn. Nursing diploma, Md. Gen. Hosp., 1968; BS, Coll. Notre Dame, 1982; MBA, Loyola Coll., Balt., 1984. RN. Cert. nurse adminstr. Staff nurse Md. Gen. Hosp., Balt., 1968-74; day clin. supr. Fallston (Md.) Gen. Hosp., 1974-77, acting dir. nursing, 1977-78, assoc. dir nursing, 1978-79, v.p. patient care svcs., 1979-87; v.p. nursing Md. Gen. Hosp., Balt., 1987—; bd. dirs. mem. Md. Hosp. Ctr., Balt., 1987—, Williams & Wilkens Pub., Balt., 1987—, Md. Hosp. Assn. Ctr. for Nursing. Adv. bd. mem. Harford (Md.) Community Coll., 1987—, Union Chapel Ch., Joppa, Md., 1984—; legis. com. mem. Md. Hosp. Assn., Lutherville, 1983—. Mem. ANA, ACHE, Md. Hosp. Ctr. for Nursing Adv. Bd., Am. Coll. Health Care Execs., Am. Orgn. Nurse Execs. (dir. mem. 1987-90), Md. Orgn. Nurse Execs. (legis. com. chair 1981—), Sigma Theta Tau. Democrat. Methodist. Home: 1003 Brookwood Dr Joppa MD 21085-1501 Office: Maryland Gen Hosp 827 Linden Ave Baltimore MD 21201

BROWN, PAULA KINNEY, heating and air conditioning contractor; b. Portsmith, Va., June 19, 1953; d. Curtis Wade and Joan (Glascoe) Kinney; m. Wayne Howard Brown, Feb. 12, 1983; children: Rebecca Jo, Raina Jaye. AS, Lake Sumter Community Coll., 1973, 77; student Lake County Area Vocat. Ctr., 1979, 80. Pres. Kinney's Air Conditioning and Heating, Leesburg, Fla., 1981—; head computer system operator, 1986—, office mgr. Mem. adv. com. for Area Lake Air Conditioning and Heating Vo-Tech. Sch., Eustis, Fla., 1981-82. Mem. Ch. of Christ. Home: 1838 Lynn Ave Fruitland Park FL 34731 Office: Kinney's Air Conditioning and Heating 409 N 13th St Leesburg FL 32748

BROWN, PHYLLIS SMILEY, school system administrator; b. Mpls., Mar. 14, 1943; d. Bernard J. and Rena (Stillman) Smiley; m. Jay A. Brown, Aug. 29, 1965; children: Barbara, Richard. BA, UCLA, 1965; MS, SUNY, New Paltz, 1978; SAS, SDA, SUNY, 1984. Tchr. Enlarged City Sch. Dist., Middletown, N.Y., 1975--; instructional leader Enlarged City Sch. Dist. Liberty St & Albert St. Schs., Middletown, N.Y., 1978--; remedial math tchr. Liberty St., Middletown, N.Y., 1985--; summer elem. prin. Enlarged City Sch. Dist., Middletown, dist. math pilot coordinator, 1988-89; cons. Cope, Phila., 1983, Holt Mathematics, 1983; chmn. Liberty St. Sch. Study Team, 1978—. Mem. Assn. of Mathematics Tchrs., ABC Reading Council, Phi Delta Kappa, Delta Kappa Gamma. Democrat. Office: Liberty Street Sch 6 Liberty St Middletown NY 10940

BROWN, QUINCALEE, association executive; b. Wichita, Kans., Nov. 9, 1939; d. Quincy Lee and Lorene (York) B.; m. James Parson Simsarian, June 24, 1978. B.A., Wichita State U., 1961; M.A., U. Pitts., 1963; Ph.D., U. Kans., 1975. Asst. prof. speech communications, dir. debate Wichita State

U., 1963-69, Ottawa U., 1970-73; adminstrv. asst. Montgomery County (Md.) Commn. for Women, 1973-74, exec. dir., 1975-80; mgr. fed. women's program Govt. Printing Office, Washington, 1974-75; exec. dir. AAUW, Washington, 1980-85, Gen. Fedn. of Women's Clubs, 1986, Water Pollution Control Fedn., 1986—. Contbr. articles to profl. jours. Recipient award for contbn. to public service Women for Equality, award for contbn. to public service Montgomery County Govt., 1975, Outstanding Contbn. to Sex Equity, 1979, Career Achievement award Profl. Fraternity Assn., 1981. Fellow Am. Soc. Assn. Execs. (bd. dirs. 1985-88, vice chmn. 1990—, cert. assn. exec.); mem. Greater Washington Soc. Assn. Execs., Speech Communications Assn., AAUW, Kappa & Delta Epsilon (hon.), Zeta Phi Eta (Outstanding Svc. award 1975). Office: 601 Wythe St Alexandria VA 22314-1994

BROWN, RITA MAE, author; b. Hanover, Pa., Nov. 28, 1944; d. Ralph and Julia Ellen B. AA, Broward Jr. Coll., 1965; BA, NYU, 1968; cinematography degree, Sch. Visual Arts, N.Y.C., 1968; PhD, Inst. Policy Studies, 1976. Lectr. Fed. City Coll., 1970-71; mem. faculty Goddard Coll., 1973—; pres. Am. Artists Inc., Charlottesville, Va., 1980—; mem. lit. panel Nat. Endowment Arts, 1978-81; Hemingway judge for 1st fiction PEN Internat., 1983; blue ribbon panelist Prime Time Emmy Awards, 1984, 86. Author: The Hand that Cradles the Rock, 1971, Rubyfruit Jungle, 1973, Songs to a Handsome Woman, 1973, A Plain Brown Rapper, 1976, Six of One, 1978, Southern Discomfort, 1982, Sudden Death, 1983, High Hearts, 1986, Starting From Scratch: A Different Kind of Writer's Manual, 1988, Bingo, 1988, Wish You Were Here, 1990; TV series include I Love Liberty, ABC-TV, 1982, Long Hot Summer, NBC, 1985, My Two Loves, ABC, 1986, The Alice Marble Story, Gross-Weston Prodns., 1986, Southern Exposure, NBC, 1990; TV films include The Girls of Summer, 1989, Selma, Lord, Selma, 1989, Rich Men, Single Women, 1989, The Thirty Nine Year Itch, CBS, 1990, Home, Sweet, Home, FKA, 1990; (for cable TV) The Mists of Avalon, 1986; scriptwriter film, Sweet Surrender, 20th Century Fox, 1986, Table Dancing, Universal Studios, 1987. Bd. dirs. Human Rights Campaign Fund, N.Y.C., 1986. Recipient Award for Best Variety Show on TV Writers Guild Am., 1982, Literary Lion award N.Y. Pub. Library, 1986, Emmy award nomination for "The Long Hot Summer", ABC mini-series, 1985; Emmy nomination for Best Variety Show "I Love Liberty", 1982; named Charlottesville favorite author The Observer, 1990, Athlete of the Week, The Observer, 1990. Mem. PEN Internat. Office: Am Artists Inc PO Box 4671 Charlottesville VA 22905

BROWN, ROBERTA DORR, higher education administrator; b. Batesville, Ark., Aug. 10, 1922; d. Claude G. and Ouida L. (Thomas) Dorr; m. Edmund Burke Brown, Dec. 26, 1957; children: Sarah, Ed. B. Jr. BA, Ark. Coll., Batesville, 1944; MA, U. Ark., 1951, EdD, 1966; cert., Harvard U. Inst. Ednl. Mgmt., Boston, 1978, George Washington U., 1980; LittD (hon.), Ark. Coll., 1989. Registrar Ark. Coll., Batesville, 1946-66, asst. acad. dean, 1964-66, acad. dean, 1966-73, dean inst. rsch. devel., 1973-77, acting dean, 1977-78, v.p. planning, 1977-88, dean, prof. edn. emerita, 1988—; acting acad. dean, Ark. Coll. 1962-64; field reader U.S. Dept. Edn., Washington, 1980—; cons. Ark. Coll., 1988—. 1st Congl. Dist. alt. Dem. Conv., San Francisco, 1984. Mem. Am. Coun. Edn. Nat. Identification Program Women, Ark. Women's History Inst. (bd. dirs. 1988), Presbytery Ark. Com. Prep. Ministry, Independence County Hist. Soc. (past pres.), Batesville Collector Club (past pres.), Duplicate Bridge Club. Home: 764 Josephine Dr Batesville AR 72501

BROWN, RUBYE GOLSBY, educator; b. Youngstown, Ohio; d. Clifford and Augusta Bell (Blalock) Golsby; m. Robert L. Brown; children: Harlean J. Preston, Charles, Louis, Carson, Gloria, Robin, Debbie. BS, Youngstown (Ohio) State Coll., 1979, MS, 1981; Cert. in History and Govtl. Econs., Youngstown State U., 1989. Credit mgr. Klivan's, Youngstown, 1953-56; sec. City Hall, Treasurer's Office, Youngstown, 1956; substitute tchr. Chaney High Sch., Youngstown, 1981—. Mem. Ohio State Bd. Health, 1980—; pres. Mahoning County Courtwatch, 1987—; ednl. specialist Police Dept. Task Force, Youngstown, 1989—. Recipient Health Care award, Columbus State Bd. Health, 1988. Mem. Am. Soc. Curriculum and Devel., Am. Univ. and Coll. Women. Democrat. Baptist.

BROWN, RUTH, rhythm and blues singer. Known as Miss Rhthym, 1950's; star original Paris prodn. Black and Blue; first major artist signed to Atlantic Records, recorded Teardrops from My Eyes (No. 1 Billboard Hit); later No. 1 hits include 5-10-15 Hours, Mama Treats Your Daughter Mean; appeared on stage in Guys and Dolls, Aladdin Theatre, Ruth Brown and Friends, Gilded Cage, Las Vegas; played role of Mahalia Jackson in stage play, Selma, L.A.; European and Asian tours with Monterey Jazz Festival; regular performer TV series Hello Larry; star off-Broadway in Staggerlee; co-star with Divine in film Hairspray; featured on Showtime spl. Atlantic Records 40th Anniv.; host nat. syndicated radio series Harlem Hit Parade Sta. WGBO Jazz 88; star That Rhythm Those Blues for PBS; latest album, Have a Good Time, Fantasy Records. Recipient Antoinette Perry award for performance by leading actress in a mus. for Black and Blue, 1989. Office: care Black & Blue Minskoff Theatre 200 W 45th St New York NY 10036*

BROWN, RUTH CARDWELL, pediatrician; b. Ironton, Ohio, Aug. 11, 1943; d. Chester Eichert and Mary Elizabeth (Lawless) Cardwell; m. Jimmy Sheppard Brown, Dec. 9, 1971; children: Andrew Cardwell, Laura Elizabeth. BSc cum laude, Ohio State U., 1965, MD summa cum laude, 1969. Diplomate Am. Bd. Pediatrics. Intern and resident Emory U. Sch. Medicine, Atlanta, 1969-73; staff physician Ga. Retardation Ctr., Atlanta, 1973-82; pvt. practice Northside Pediatrics, Atlanta, 1982—; clin. instr. dept. pediatrics Emory U., Atlanta, 1974—; med. dir. Easter Seals Ctr., Atlanta, 1982-83; pres. med. staff Scottish Rite Children's Hosp., Atlanta, 1989. Bd. dirs. Down Syndrome Assn., Atlanta, 1987—, Socttish Rite Children's Hosp., Atlanta, 1988-89. Fellow Am. Acad. Pediatrics, Am. Acad. Cerebral Palsy; mem. Phi Beta Kappa, Alpha Omega Alpha. Methodist. Office: Northside Pediatrics D-14 6500 Vernon Woods Dr Atlanta GA 30328

BROWN, SANDRA JEAN, banker; b. Bridgeport, Conn., June 10, 1936; d. Victor James and Mildred Lillian (Norbeck) B. Various positions Poeple's Bank, Bridgeport, 1953-72; corp. sec. People's Bank, Bridgeport, 1972—; dir. Conn. Housing Fin. Authority, 1985—. Bd. dirs. Barnum Mus. Found., YWCA Greater Bridgeport, Internat. Inst. Conn., Greater Bridgeport Symphony. Recipient Community Leadership award Sacred Heart U., Bridgeport, 1983; Salute to Women award YWCA Greater Bridgeport, 1984. Mem. Nat. Assn. Bank Women (state pres. 1981-82), Assn. Savs. Bank Women Conn., Fin. Women Internat.

BROWN, SANDRA LOUISE PALMER, marketing representative, consultant; b. Royal Oak, Mich., Dec. 2, 1957; d. Michael Peter and Elizabeth Louis (Hampers) Palmer; m. Gregory Jacob Brown, June 9, 1990. BBA, Iowa State U., 1982. Transp. analyst Mass. Bay Transp. Authority, Boston, 1982-85; tech. support rep. Project Software & Devel., Cambridge, Mass., 1985-86; self-employed computer cons. Newton, Mass., 1986-87; account rep. IBM, Boston, 1987—. Mem. Mus. Fine Arts, Boston, 1987—, Jr. League Boston, 1985—; vol. Young Life, Westwood, Mass., 1984—, Mass. Spl. Olympics, Boston, 1988. Mem. NAFE, Boston Computer Soc., Lexington Club. Republican. Club: Mt. Auburn Tennis (Watertown, Mass). Office: IBM One Copley Pl Boston MA 02116

BROWN, SANDRA MARIE, dog breeder, consultant; b. LaFollette, Tenn., July 10, 1958; d. Gene and Beaulah M. (Letner) Hale; m. Thomas Garrett Brown, Dec. 12, 1981. Student, Lincoln Meml. U., 1973-76. Asst. restaurant and catering mgr. Holiday Inns. Inc., Knoxville, 1975-80; singer and TV personality Knoxville, 1976-80; dog breeder and designer of pet clothes Paw Pals Inc., Knoxville, 1987—; cons. Humane Soc., Knoxville, 1986, K-9 Acad., Knoxville, 1986, Little Bits Creations, LaFollette, 1985—. Author: Life in Applachia, 1973. Mem. Nat. Rep. Com., 1987; spokesperson Crestwood Hills Orgn., 1982-87, Knox County Homeowners Assn., 1986—; mem. Harmony Internat. Women's Barbershop Chorus; bd. dirs. Knoxville Harmony Internat. Mem. Knox County Humane Soc. (top breeder poodles 1984), Northshore Animal League, Greenpeace, Deane Hill Country Club, Vol. Rep. Club, Young Women's Aux. (pres. 1970-73), Sweet Adelines. Baptist. Home: 308 Bridgewater Rd Knoxville TN 37923

BROWN, SARA LOU, accounting firm executive; b. Houston, Oct. 11, 1942; d. William Hale and Ruth Elizabeth (Hearon) Rutherford; m. Joseph Kurth Brown, Dec. 21, 1965 (div. Mar. 1979); 1 child, Derek Kurth. B.A., Rice U., 1964; M.B.A., U. Tex., 1966. C.P.A., Tex. Mem. staff Peat, Marwick, Mitchell & Co., Houston, 1966-69, mgr., 1969-73, ptnr., 1973—; asst. treas. Zool. Soc. of Houston, 1986, 87. Treas. Houston Grand Opera, 1973-74, Parks and Recreation Bd., City of West University Place, Tex., 1983, 84. Mem. Am. Inst. C.P.A.s, Tex. Soc. C.P.A.s. Home: 2404 Stanmore Houston TX 77019 Office: KPMG Peat Marwick PO Box 4545 Houston TX 77210*

BROWN, SARAH E., lawyer; b. Topeka, Kans., Aug. 9, 1936; d. Paul Shannon and Alice (Rafter) B.; A.B., Vassar Coll., 1958; JD, Georgetown U., 1963; m. Ralph J. Temple, July 17, 1960 (div. 1983); children—Katherine Esme, John Anthony. Admitted to D.C. bar, 1964; staff mem. U.S. Senator Estes Kefauver, Washington, 1958; legis. aide U.S. Senator Vance Hartke, Washington, 1959-60; staff asst. John F. Kennedy Presdl. Campaign, Washington, 1960; asst. to dir. compliance surveys and research Pres.'s Com. on EEO, Washington, 1961-65; cons. Migrant div. Office Econ. Opportunity, Washington, 1965-66; practiced in Washington, 1968-71; staff atty. Pub. Defender Service, Washington, 1971—; adj. prof. criminal law George Washington U. Grad Sch., Washington, 1974-76; faculty Nat. Inst. Trial Advocacy Georgetown U. Law Center, 1980-81; mem. D.C. Bar Com. on D.C. Cts.; treas., dir. N.W. Investment Co., Washington, 1964-66; bd. dirs. Women's Legal Def. Fund, 1976-77; past mem. criminal justice com. D.C. Commn. on Status of Women; bd. dirs. Washington Halfway House for Women; bd. dirs., Law Students in Ct., 1979—. Mem. ABA, Bar Assn. D.C., Criminal Practice Inst. Com., Women's Bar Assn., Judicial Conf. for D.C. Cts., Nat. Assn. Criminal Def. Attys., Washington Council Lawyers (dir. 1979-82), Women's Legal Def. Fund, Lawyers Com. of Washington Opera. Home: 8132 Inverness Ridge Rd Potomac MD 20854 also: Dillons Run Rd Capon Bridge WV 26711 Office: 451 Indiana Ave NW Washington DC 20001

BROWN, SARAH S., auditor; b. Lafayette, Ind., Jan. 16, 1932; d. Harry H. and Nell G. (Hiett) Stewart; m. Robert E. Brown, Mar. 28, 1954; children: James D., Barbara Jo Brown Ritchie, Rodger S. Office mgr., investigator Fairfield Tairfield Twp., Lafayette, 1952-68; mgr. West Lafayette (Ind.) License Br., 1969; mem. bd. registration Tippecanoe County, Lafayette, 1970-74, clk. cir., county and superior cts., 1975-82, auditor, 1983—. Sec. Tippecanoe County Young Reps., 1954-55, vice chmn., 1955-66, 2d Congl. Young Reps., 1960-66, Nat. Fedn. Young Reps., 1964. Recipient Sagamore of the Wabash award Gov. Orr and Gov. Bowen of Ind., 1978, Tribute to Women award Ind. State Fedn. of Rep. Wome, Salute to Women award Purdue Women's Cacaus. Mem. Am. Legion Aux., Ind. Fedn. Home Hosp. Aux. Soc. of Friends. Office: Tippecanoe County Court House Lafayette IN 47901

BROWN, SHANNON ARLEEN, sales executive; b. Florence, Ala., Aug. 12, 1965; d. Thomas H. and Iva (Curtis) B. BA in Communications, U. Ala. Tourism rep. C. of C., Florence, Ala., 1987-89; sales rep. Paper & Chem. Supply, Sheffield, Ala., 1989—. AAUW, Kiwanis Internat. Home: Rt 5 Box 458 Florence AL 35630 Office: Paper & Chem Supply PO Box J Sheffield AL 35660

BROWN, SHARON ELIZABETH, computer science administrator; b. Lynn, Mass., Nov. 23, 1960; d. Leland James Brown and Vail (Wilkinson) Bartelson. BSChemE, U. Mass., 1982. Software engr. K&L Automation div. Daniel Industry, Tucson, 1983-86, sr. software engr., 1986-87, asst. mgr. software systems, 1987; software mgr. Daniel Automation, Houston, 1987-. Mem. NSPE, Am. Inst. Chem. Engrs. Republican. Home: 2851 Wallingford Dr Apt 1222 Houston TX 77042 Office: Daniel Automation 19203 Hempstead Hwy Houston TX 77065

BROWN, SHARON GAIL, company executive, consultant; b. Chgo., Dec. 25, 1941; d. Otto and Pauline (Lauer) Schumacher; B in Gen. Studies, Roosevelt U.; m. Robert B. Ringo, Aug. 2, 1984; 1 dau. by previous marriage, Susan Ann. Info. analyst Internat. Minerals & Chems., Northbrook, Ill., 1966-71, programmer analyst, 1971-74; programmer analyst Procon Internat. Inc. subs. UOP Inc., Des Plaines, Ill., 1974-76, systems analyst, 1976-77, project leader, 1977-78; mgr. adminstrv. services, 1978-82; spl. cons. to pres. IPS Internat., Ltd., 1982-83; spl. cons. to pres. CEI Supply Co. div. Sigma-Chapman, Inc., 1984-87, ptnr. and co-founder Brown, Ringo & Assocs., 1987—; data processing cons. Mem. Buffalo Grove (Ill.) Youth Commn., 1978-82; mem. adv. com. UOP Polit. Action Com., 1979-82; Mem. Rep. Senatorial Com. Inner Circle. Mem. Am. Mgmt. Assn., Chgo. Council on Fgn. Rels., Lake Forest-Lake Bluff Hist. Soc. Home: 121 N Sheridan Rd Lake Forest IL 60045

BROWN, SHARON HENDRICKSON, broadcasting company executive; b. Malta, Mont., Mar. 27, 1944; d. Elmer Theodore and Dorothy Harriet (Flom) Hendrickson; m. Monty Charles Brown, Oct. 24, 1962; children—Michael Charles, Misty Dawn. Cert. med. lab. technologist, Profl. Bus. Inst., 1962; student Alaska Meth. U., Meth. Coll. Lic. 3d class broadcaster, FCC. On-air, traffic, copywriter various radio stas., Alaska, Tex., Mont., 1967-73; asst. news dir., prodn. mgr. Sta. KIXS-Radio, Killeen, Tex., 1973-74; prodn. mgr., continuity dir. Cape Fear Broadcasting, Fayetteville, N.C., 1978-81, account exec., 1981-85; gen. mgr. Ad Channel (Time/Life TV), Fayetteville, 1985-86, market cons., 1986; sales mgr. Sta. WFAI-Radio (Beasley Broadcasting Group), Fayetteville, 1986-87; prin. Two-ShA Art Gallery, Columbus, N.Mex. 1988-89; judge Miss Ft. Bragg Pageant, N.C., 1983; mem. parade com. Dogwood Festival, Fayetteville, 1983, mem. publicity com., 1984-85, mem. Deming (N.Mex.) Arts Council, 1988-89. Painting included in The Gov.'s Show, Santa Fe, 1988. Festival coord. Columbus Day Festival, 1988-89; dir. pub. rels. Spirit of Columbus Com., 1988-89; mem. city coun. Village of Columbus, 1989—. Mem. Tex. Press Women (pres. Dist. 10 1973-74, 1st place award 1973), Fayetteville Area Advt. Fedn. (Gold ADDY award 1984, Silver ADDY award 1984), Nat. Assn. Female Execs., Assn. U.S. Army, Fayetteville Area Bd. Realtors, Fayetteville C. of C. Lutheran. Avocations: painting, writing, photography. Home: PO Box 506 Columbus NM 88029

BROWN, SHIRLEY ANNE, nurse; b. San Diego, Jan. 8, 1955; d. Martin Laurel and Beverly Jean (Eacock) B. BS in Nursing, Seattle Pacific U., 1979; M Nursing, U. Wash., 1984. RN, Wash. Staff nurse Swedish Hosp. Med. Ctr., Seattle, 1979-80, Ballard (Wash.) Community Hosp., 1980-83; nurse clinician Community Home Health Care, Seattle, 1983-89; clinician ambulatory care and specialist occupational health CHEC Med. Ctr., Seattle, 1989—; cons. in field; historian USAFR, Washington, 1988—, jr. v.p., 1989—. Vol. ARC, 1988. Capt. USAFR, 1985—. Mem. Am. Assn. Occupational Health Nurses (edn. chmn. 1984-85), USAF Assn., Reserve Officers Assn. (historian dept. Wash, 1988—, jr. v. p. 1989—, Seattle chpt. USAF committeeman, 1987—), Assn. Mil. Surgeons U.S., Order of Eastern Star, Sigma Theta Tau. Methodist. Home: 8014 18th Ave NW Seattle WA 98117 Office: CHEC Med Ctr 8313 Aurora Ave N Seattle WA 98103

BROWN, SHIRLEY M., science administrator; b. Phila., Apr. 25, 1924; d. Paul and Bertha Evelyn (Zucker) M.; m. Bernard Beau, Sept. 1, 1947; children: Eric Joel, Aimee Susan. BA, Temple U., Phila., 1945, MA, 1947. Rsch. chemist U. Mich., Ann Arbor, 1947-50; instr. Upsala Coll., East Orange, 1960-74; acad. planner Rutgers U., New Brunswick, N.J., 1974-80, assoc. dir. Waksman Inst., 1980-88; exec. dir. Rutgers Rsch. and Ednl. Found., New Brunswick, 1980—; assoc. dir. Office of Corp. Liaison and Technol. Transfer Rutgers U., 1988—. sec. Joint Civic Com. Westfield 1962-66, Com. for Human Rights Westfield 1967-70; publicity chairperson. PTA Westfield 1963-67. Mem. LWV, Assn. Univ. Technol. Mgrs., Nat. Coun. Univ. Rsch. Adminstrs., Soc. Rsch. Adminstrs. Home: 146 Tudor Oval Westfield NJ 07090

BROWN, SUZANNE WILEY, museum director; b. Cheyenne, Wyo., Aug. 28, 1938; d. Robert James and Catharine Helen (Schroeder) Wiley; BS with honors, U. Wyo., 1960, MS, 1964; postgrad. U. Cin. Med. Sch., 1965-66, U. Ill., 1969-72; m. Ralph E. Brown, July 19, 1968; 1 dau., Nina M. Rsch. asst. Harvard Med. Sch., 1962-63; rsch. asst. U. Cin. Med. Sch., 1964-65; sr. lab. asst. U. Chgo., 1966-67; rsch. assoc. U. Colo. Med. Sch., 1968; teaching asst. U. Ill., 1971-73; exec. asst. Chgo. Acad. Scis., 1974-82, asst. dir., 1982-84, assoc. dir., 1984—. mem. adv. bd. Mitchell Indian Mus., Evanston, Ill. NDEA fellow, 1960-62. Mem. Mus. Educators of Greater Chgo., Am. Assn. Mus., Internat. Coun. Mus., Brookfield Zool. Soc. (bd. govs.), Midwest Mus. Conf., Phi Beta Kappa, Sigma Xi, Phi Kappa Phi. Office: 2001 N Clark St Chicago IL 60614

BROWN, TINA, magazine editor; b. Maidenhead, Eng., Nov. 21, 1953; d. George Hambley and Bettina Iris Mary (Kohr) B.; m. Harold Evans, Aug. 20, 1981; 1 child, George Frederick. M.A., Oxford U. Columnist Punch Mag., London, 1978; editor in chief Tatler Mag., London, 1979-83, Vanity Fair Mag., N.Y.C., 1984—. Author: (play) Under the Bamboo Tree, 1973 (Sunday Times Drama award), (play) Happy Yellow, 1977, (book) Loose Talk, 1979, (book) Life As A Party, 1983. Named Most Promising Female Journalist, recipient Kathrine Pakenham prize Sunday London Times, 1973; named Young Journalist of Yr., 1978, Mag. Editor of Yr. Advt. Age mag., 1988. Office: Vanity Fair Mag 350 Madison Ave New York NY 10017

BROWN, VALERIE ANNE, psychiatric social worker, educator; b. Elizabeth, N.J., Feb. 28, 1951; d. William John and Adelaide Elizabeth (Krasa) B.; B.A. summa cum laude (fellow), C.W. Post Coll., 1972; M.S.W. (Silberman scholar), Hunter Coll., 1975. Social work intern Greenwich House Counseling Center, N.Y.C., 1973-74, Metro Cons. Center, N.Y.C., 1974-75; sr. psychiat. social worker, co-adminstr. Saturday Clinic, Essex County Guidance Center, East Orange, N.J., 1975-80; pvt. practice psychiat. social work, psychotherapy, 1979—; sr. psychiat social worker John E. Runnells Hosp., Berkeley Heights, N.J., 1980-86; dir. social work Northfield Manor, West Orange, N.J., 1987; clin. coord. Project Portals East Orange Gen. Hosp., 1987-88; asst. dir. ARS/Century House Riverview Med. Ctr., Red Bank, N.J., 1988—; co-founder Women's Growth Ctr., Cedar Grove, N.J., 1979; counselor Passaic Drug Clinic, 1978-80; field instr. Fairleigh Dickinson U., Madison, N.J., 1981-86; field supr. Union Coll., Cranford, N.J., 1986; instr. Sch. Social Work, NYU, N.Y.C., 1980-83, asst. prof., 1983-85; evaluator Intoxicated Driver Resource Ctr., Essex County, N.J., 1987-88; asst. dir. Addiction Recovery Svcs./Century House, Riverview Med. Ctr., Red Bank, N.J., 1988—. Fundraiser Am. Heart Assn. Mem. Nat. Assn. Social Workers (diplomate in clin. social work, listed in nat. register of clin. social workers), N.J. Assn. Clin. Social Workers, Nat. Assn. Social Workers, N.J. Assn. Women Therapists, Am. Soc. Tng. and Devel., Psi Chi, Pi Gamma Mu, Sigma Tau Delta. Office: 40 Ave of the Commons Shrewsbury NJ 07702

BROWN, VICTORIA ANN, communications equipment company executive; b. Lancaster, Ohio, Apr. 16, 1947; d. Albert and Dorothy Brown; m. Edward Botwinick, Apr. 6, 1986; stepchildren: Andrew, Eric. BS summa cum laude, Ohio U., 1969, MBA, 1972. Various positions Polaroid Corp., 1969-76; asst. v.p. field svc. Timeplex Inc., Woodcliff Lake, N.J., 1976-79, v.p. sales, 1979-83, v.p. corp. devel., 1983-84, sr. v.p. sales & mktg., 1984-88, pres., 1988—. Chairwoman Wider Opportunity for Girl Scouts, Paramus, N.J., 1988; pres. Women in Network Girl Scouts, Paramus, 1988; mem. Harvest Ball for Chestnut Ridge March of Dimes, 1988; bd. dirs. Bergen County coun. Girl Scouts U.S., Paramus, 1988, Bergen County United Way, Paramus, 1989—; trustee Manhattan Coll., N.Y.C., 1989—. Mem. Altrusa Club (Bergen County), Mortar Bd., Phi Beta Kappa. Democrat. Roman Catholic. Office: Timeplex Ave 400 Chestnut Ridge Rd Woodcliff Lake NJ 07675

BROWN, VIRGINIA LILLIE, retired educator; b. Lafayette, Ind., Apr. 25, 1920; d. Francis Leo and Violet Marie (Klinger) Cassman; m. Harrison Margerum Brown, June 12, 1943; children: John Harrison, Richard Lee, Francis Alan. BS, Purdue U., 1942. Engr. trainee GE, Schenectady, N.Y., 1943; math tchr. Lafayette Sch. System, 1943-44, Chatham-Savannah, Savannah, Ga., 1965-76; writer, lectr. govt. revenues topics. Contbr. taxation articles to profl. jours. Pres. LWV, Savannah, 1978-81 (Leadership awards Gov. of Ga. 1988), bd. dirs., taxation LWV Ga., Atlanta, 1983-84, treas., 1989-92; mem., vice chmn. Chatham-Savannah Authority for the Homeless, 1989-91. Mem. AAUW (editor newsletter Ga. div. 1989-91, v.p. program Savannah chpt. 1970s). AAUW (editor newsletter Ga. div. 1989-91, v.p. program Savannah chpt. 1970s). Democrat. Home: 99 Tall Pine Ave Savannah GA 31404

BROWN, MRS. WALSTON SHEPARD See REGAN, ELLEN FRANCES

BROWN, WANDA MARIE, financial consultant, educator; b. Birmingham, Ala., July 18, 1945; d. Earlie and Vivian Lee (Doby) Suttles. BS, Calif. State U., Long Beach, 1969; MBA, UCLA, 1973. Acct. various acctg. firms, 1968-75; sr. systems analyst Security Pacific Bank Corp., L.A., 1975-76; asst. prof. Calif. State U., L.A., 1975—; city treas. City of Inglewood (Calif.), 1981—; mng. dir. Mgmt. Control Systems, Inglewood, 1979—; cons. SBA, L.A., 1978-81. Vol. coord. Inglewood Police Dept., 1982; bd. dirs. Inglewood Philharmonic Assn., 1988—; mentor-advisor Inglewood Unified Sch. Dist., 1985. Mem. NAFE, Nat. Assn. of Accts., Nat. Assn. of Black Accts., Calif. Mcpl. Treas. Assn., Am. Acctg. Assn., Beta Gamma Sigma, Top Ladies of Dist., Inc. Home: 2611 W 78th Pl Inglewood CA 90305 Office: Mgmt Control Systems 8443 S Crenshaw #206 PO Box 2302 Inglewood CA 90305

BROWN, WANDA YVETTE, consultant; b. Emporia, Va., Sept. 10, 1959; d. Willie Mason and Marion (Edwards) B. BS, Va. Commonwealth, 1981. Account exec., cons. Bidnet/Dun & Bradstreet, Rockville, Md., 1985-90; tech. specialist GE Info. Svcs., Rockville, Md., 1990—. Mem. United Black Culture, Rockville, 1988. Mem. NAFE, Toastmasters. Democrat. Baptist. Home: 450 Girard St #204 Gaithersburg MD 20877

BROWN, WENDY ELAINE, systems programmer; b. Los Alamos, N.Mex., Apr. 28, 1956; d. Leon J. and Dorothy (Stern) B. B.A., Northwestern U., 1978. Software engr. Prime Computer Inc., Natick, Mass., 1978-80; systems programmer Dialcom, Silver Spring, Md., 1980-85; systems programmer, analyst APA, Falls Church, Va., 1985-86; mem. tech. staff Corp. for Open Systems, McLean, Va., 1986-89; systems analyst PSC Internat. Inc., McLean, 1989—. Mem. Prime User's Group, (sec. treas. 1986), Electronic Networking Assn. Democrat. Jewish. Avocations: sewing, theatre/stage crew, electronic networking. Home: 2248 Washington Ave #203 Silver Spring MD 20910 Office: PSC Internat Inc 2010 Corporate Ridge Ste 700 McLean VA 22102

BROWN-BUCHANAN, DEBORAH ANN, insurance and investment producer, paralegal; b. Camden, N.J., Dec. 26, 1956; d. Robert James and Audrey Ann (Deso) Brown; m. Stephen Timothy Buchanan, April 25, 1987. AA, Gloucester County Community Coll., 1980; cert., Am. Inst. Paralegal Studies, Mahwah, N.J., 1983. Skip tracer W.T. Grants, Woodbury Heights, N.J., 1975-78; recovery supr. Princeton Bank (formerly Bank of N.J.), Moorestown, N.J., 1979-82; asst. sec. 1st People's Bank of N.J., Westmont, 1982-85; asst. v.p. Equibank, Pitts., 1985-86; asst. sec. Continental Bank of N.J., Haddonfield, 1986-88; ins. and investment producer Prudential Ins. Co. Am., Marlton, N.J., 1989—; lectr. Asst. to author/editor: Compliance Book on Banking Regulations, 1986. Sec. fin. com. St. Margaret Mary Cath. Ch., 1985-88. Mem. Nat. Assn. Life Underwriters, Nat. Assn. Securities Dealers, South Jersey C. of C. Home: 1151 Walnut Ave Woodbury Heights NJ 08097 Office: Prudential Ins Co Am Lake Center Executive Park 401 Rte 73 N Ste 150 Marlton NJ 08053

BROWN-COCHRANE, ANDREA KANE, underwriter; b. Dhahran, Saudi Arabia, Jan. 30, 1962; came to U.S., 1963; d. Andrew Jackson and Elizabeth Jeannine (Kane) Brown; m. Mark Anthony Cochrane, June 29, 1985. BS, Humboldt State U., 1985; MBA, U. Phoenix, 1990. Mgmt. trainee Western Fed. Savs., Marina Del Rey, Calif., 1985-86, computer systems and inventory control specialist, 1986-87; commitment coord. Calif. Fed. Bank, L.A., 1987-89, underwriter, 1989—. Mem. Network for Profl. Devel., NAFE. Republican. Roman Catholic.

BROWNE, ANN APRIL, purchasing manager; b. Washington, Apr. 9, 1945; d. Benjamin and Sarah (Barr) Mudrick. BA in Bus. Mgmt., Eckerd Coll., 1987. Purchasing mgr. Gen. Kinetics, Rockville, Md., 1972-73; assoc. buyer Control Data Corp., Rockville, 1973-74; outside sales rep. Mid Atlantic Industries, Bladensburg, Md., 1974, U.S. C. of C., San Antonio,

1975; inside sales coord. Frabimore Equipment & Controls, Inc., Elk Grove Village, Ill., 1976-77; customer svc. rep. Viracon, Inc., Bensenville, Ill., 1977; purchasing mgr. Vectrol div. Westinghouse Elec. Corp., Oldsmar, Fla., 1978-83; purchasing agt. Helen Ellis Meml. Hosp., Tarpon Springs, Fla., 1987—. Mem. Material Mgmt. Assn., Nat. Assn. Purchasing Mgmt. (cert.), Phi Theta Kappa.

BROWNE, ANNA THERESE, editor, writer; b. L.I., N.Y., Mar. 30, 1958; d. Thomas Bernard and Rade Therese (Lawrence) Browne; m. William B. Muzzall, Aug. 1, 1980 (div.). AA, Muskegon Community Coll., 1978; BA, Mich. State U., 1980. Mng. editor Oreg. Dept. Transp., Salem, 1980-83; editor Fred Meyer, Inc., Portland, Oreg., 1983-87; communications dir. World Forestry Ctr., Portland, 1988—; freelance reporter Media, Inc., Seattle, 1990—. Mem. com. United Way, Portland, 1986—; vol. escort Feminist Women's Health Ctr., Portland, 1989—. Recipient publ. honors United Way, 1984-88, Individual award, 1990. Mem. Internat. Assn. Bus. Communicators (dist. bd. 1990—, pres. Portland chpt. 1987-88), Women In Communications Inc. (pres. Portland chpt. 1990—, Pres.'s citation 1989). Democrat. Office: World Forestry Ctr 4033 SW Canyon Rd Portland OR 97221

BROWNE, BEVERLY ANN, marketing educator, educational psychologist; b. Seattle, Dec. 2, 1938; d. Egil Reinert and Pearl Leola (Murie) Berg; m. William Griest Browne, Oct. 1963, children: William Russell, Amy Elizabeth. BA cum laude, U. Wash., 1961, tchr. cert., 1964; MA, Oreg. State U., Corvallis, 1979; PhD, U. Oreg., 1985. High sch. tchr. Chelsea (Mich.) High Sch., 1965-68; teaching asst. psychology dept. Oreg. State U., Corvallis, 1976-84, instr. psychology dept., 1984-85, asst. prof. psychology dept., 1985-88, asst. prof. mktg. dept., 1988—; vis. prof. U. Oreg., Eugene, 1990; reviewer various texts McGraw Hill, N.Y.C., 1987, Knopf, N.Y.C., 1988. Contbr. articles to profl. jours., papers to profl. assns. Rsch. support grantee NIH, 1986. Mem. Soc. Rsch. in Child Devel., Am. Psychol. Assn., Am. Psychol. Soc., Western Psychol. Assn., Phi Kappa Phi, Lambda Chi. Office: Coll Bus Oreg State U Corvallis OR 97331

BROWNE, DIANA GAYLE, artist, social services; b. San Francisco, Aug. 31, 1924; d. Clarence Luther and Elsa Henrietta (Ericson) Sidelinger; m. Alfred B. Britton Jr., Sept. 2, 1942 (div. 1960); children: Alfred B. Britton III, Kathryn H. Lumbert, Patrick Luther Britton; m. James Stuart Browne M.D., May 19, 1963; children: Bruce Petter Browne, Julia Regina Browne. BA Magnum Cum Laude, San Jose State U., 1949; MSW, U. Calif., 1958; BFA, San Francisco Art Inst., 1973. Lic. Clinical Social Worker, Calif. Clinical social worker Dept. of Mental Health, Sacramento, 1958-59; clinical social worker U. Calif. Med. Ctr., San Francisco, 1960-61, Langley Porter Inst., San Francisco, 1961-66, Napa (Calif.) State Hosp., 1980-85; freelance artist Mill Valley, Calif., 1966-80, Mill Valley, 1985—. Named Best of Show Hon. Mention, Cash award Marin Arts Guild, Larkspur, Calif., 1977, 78, 79, Best of Show, Merit awards (7), Marin County Fair, San Rafael, Calif., 1977, 78, 89, 90. Mem. AAUW (v.p. San Francisco chpt. 1963), Calif. Soc. of Printmakers, Marin Soc. of Artists (adv. coun. 1987-89, Cash and Merit awards 1974-79), San Francisco Women Artists (sec. 1978-79), Artisans Mill Valley, Acci Gallery, Berkeley, Eastbay Watercolor Soc. (mem. chmn. 1986-88, Merit award 1987), Outdoor Art Club, Alpha Chi Omega Alumnae (pres. 1949-51, 1966-68), Family Svc. League (Mill Valley).

BROWNE, JENNIFER LYNN, electronics technician; b. London, Ont., Can., Mar. 18, 1954; d. Thomas Patrick Brown and Norah Theresa (O'Toole) Lewrey. Student, Fanshawe Coll., London, 1975; BA, U. S.C., 1979. Audio visual coordinator Keuka Coll., Keuka Park, N.Y., 1978-79; asst. mgr. tech. svcs. U. S.C., Columbia, 1979-80; communications technician AT&T, Atlanta, 1980-90, tech. support supr. accunet svcs., 1990—. Editor newspaper CWA Local 3250, 1986. Mem. NOW. Roman Catholic. Home: 3007 Stone Mountain St Lithonia GA 30058

BROWNE, JOY, psychologist; b. New Orleans, Oct. 24, 1950; d. Nelson and Ruth (Strauss) B.; Carter Thweatt, June 9, 1966 (div. 1979); 1 child, Patience. BA, Rice U.; PhD, Northeastern U.; postgrad., Tufts U. Registered psychologist, Mass. With research/optics dept. Sperry Rand, Boston, 1966-68; engr. space program Itek, Boston, 1968-70; head social services dept. Boston Redevel. Authority, 1970-71; staff psychologist South Shore Counselling Assocs., Boston, 1971-82; on-the-air psychologist Sta. WITS, Boston, 1978-82, Sta. KGO, San Francisco, 1982-84; host, news Sta. KCBS, San Francisco, 1984-85; on-the-air psychologist Sta. WABC, N.Y.C., 1985-87, ABC Talkradio, N.Y.C., 1987—; dir. Town of Hull Adolescent Outreach Program. Author: The Used Car Game, 1971, The Research Experience, 1976, Nobody's Perfect, 1988, Why They Don't Call When They Say They Will and Other Mixed Signals, 1989. Mem. Am. Psychol. Assn., Phi Kappa Phi (Communicator of Yr.). Office: ABC Talkradio 125 W End Ave New York NY 10023

BROWNE, LESLIE, dancer, actress; b. N.Y.C., June 29, 1957; d. Kelly and Isabel (Mirrow) B. Grad., Profl. Children's Sch., N.Y.C. Mem. corps de ballet N.Y.C. Ballet, 1974-76; soloist Am. Ballet Theatre, 1976-86, Prin., 1986—; appearances in films Turning Point, 1977, Nijinsky, 1980. Recipient Dance Edn. of Am. award. Mem. Acad. Motion Picture Arts and Scis. Office: Am Ballet Theatre 890 Broadway New York NY 10003*

BROWNE, MARY ANITA, television promotion executive; b. Miami, Fla., Feb. 14; d. Samuel J. and Lottie C. Browne. BA, Mich. State U., 1985. Creative svcs. asst. Sta. WPTV, West Palm Beach, Fla., 1986-89, pub. affairs dir., 1988—. Bd. dirs. Episcopal Ministry Mich. State U., East Lansing, 1982-85; youth speech cons. St. Patrick's Episcopal Ch., West Palm Beach, 1988-89; mem. Nat. Black Coalition, Washington, 1986—. Mem. NAFE, Broadcast Promotion & Mktg. Execs., Palm Beach Assn. Black Journalists, Mich. State Alumni Assn., NAACP, Nat. Assn. Black Journalists. Home: 1505 N Mangonia Dr West Palm Beach FL 33401

BROWNE, SHIRLEY ANNETTE, anesthesiologist; b. Port Arthur, Tex., May 26, 1952; d. William Benjamin and Mildred Annette (Stephens) B. BS, Lamar U., 1974; MD, U. Tex., 1977. Resident in anesthesiology U. Tex. Med. Sch., Houston, 1981; asst. anesthesiologist, instr. anesthesiology M.D. Anderson Hosp. and Tumor Inst., Houston, 1981-83, Alief Gen. Hosp., Houston, 1983-85, West Houston Med. Ctr. Hosp., 1985-87; dir. anesthesia and anesthesiology, asst. anesthesiologist Polly Ryon Meml. Hosp., Houston, 1987—. Mem. AMA (physicians recognition award 1981, 83, 87), Am. Soc. Anesthesiologists, Tex. Soc. Anesthesiologists, Tex. Gulf Coast Soc. Anesthesiologists, Internat. Anesthesia Rsch. Soc. Tex. Med. Assn., Harris County Med. Soc. Office: 6862 Hwy 6 S Houston TX 77083

BROWNELL, ANNA GALE, biology educator; b. Leipzig, Germany, June 17, 1942; came to U.S., 1945; d. Ruth Louise (Rademacher) Sargent; m. William B. Brownell, July 1, 1970 (div. Apr. 1985). BA in Chemistry, Bowling Green (Ohio) State U., 1964; PhD in Biochemistry, Northwestern U., 1975. Biologist Syntex Labs., Palo Alto, Calif., 1965-66; organic chemist Stauffer Research Labs., Richmond, Calif., 1966-70; research asst. prof. U. So. Calif., Los Angeles, 1977-81; research biochemist UCLA, 1982-85; asst. prof. dept. biology Chapman Coll., Orange, Calif., 1985-88, assoc. prof., chair dept. biology, 1988—. Lay minister Episcopal Diocese Los Angeles, Laguna Niguel, Calif., 1986. NIH grantee, 1977, 86; NIH postdoctoral fellow, 1975. Mem. Am. Soc. for Bone and Mineral Res., Am. Soc. for Cell Biology, Tissue Culture Soc. Democrat. Home: 220 W Escalones San Clemente CA 92672 Office: Chapman Coll Dept Biology 333 N Glassell Orange CA 92666

BROWNER, FRANCINE, clothing manufacturer; b. N.Y.C., Sept. 10, 1945; d. Arnold and Chickie (Ulrich) Lehrer; divorced; children—Stacy Lyn, Jacqueline Beth. Student Syracuse U., 1963-64, Parsons Sch. Design, 1964-66, Queens Coll., 1973-76. Designer Organically Grown, Los Angeles, 1978-79; designer, merchandiser Bronson of Calif., Gardena, Calif., 1979; designer Robyn's Nest, Los Angeles, 1979-80, Calif. Class, Los Angeles, 1982-83; dir. merchandising and design Spare Parts, Los Angeles, 1983-84; owner, pres. Rue de Reves, Los Angeles, 1984—. Founder Los Angeles Mus. Contemporary Art. Democrat. Jewish. Avocations: sailing, cars, films, tennis. Office: Rue de Rêves 4480 Pacific Blvd Los Angeles CA 90058

BROWNHILL, TONI ROBECK, director, program or activities; b. Langdon, N.D., Sept. 29, 1946; d. Ralph James and Mary Frances (Backes) Robeck; m. James Edward, Nov. 8, 1968; children: Jason, Ryan, Katie. BA in anthropology, Colo. State U., 1988. Bilingual citizenship tchr. Adult Basic Edn. Amnesty Program, 1988—; literacy mentor coord. Vols. Clearing House, Ft. Collins, Colo., 1988—. Co-chmn. Soth Cluster CAP Task Force, 1980-85; mem. Ft. Collins Area Council for Gifted & Talented, 1980-84, Sch. Bd. Liaison Team, 1983, Leadership, Fort Collins, 1984-85, Steering Com., 1985-86; vol. Colo. State U. Host Family/Internat. Friends, 1972—; U.S. Dept. of Edn./Ctr. for Ednl. Devel., 1985-87. Mem. Phi Beta Kappa. Democrat. Roman Catholic. Home: 2006 Winfield Ct Fort Collins CO 80526 Office: Vols Clearing House 401 Linden Fort Collins CO 80526

BROWNING, BEVERLY ANN, grants consultant; b. Flint, Mich., Nov. 21, 1948; d. Sherman L. and Gladys Bernice (Wright) Mitchell; m. John B. Browning, Dec. 30, 1966; 1 child, Lara Suzanne. Assoc., Mott Community Coll., 1981; BA in Mgmt., Spring Arbor Coll., Flint, 1985; M Pub. Adminstrn., U. Mich., Flint, 1988. Instr. Lapeer (Mich.) Intermediate Sch. Dist., 1980-83, Flint (Mich.) Bd. Edn. Mott Adult High Sch., 1980-84, Baker Coll., Flint, 1985-86; project specialist Jobs Central, Flint, 1984-86; rsch. intern U. Mich., Flint, 1986; major prof. Spring Arbor Coll., Flint, 1987—; project specialist grants and devel. dept. Genesee Intermediate Sch. Dist., Flint, 1986-89; owner, cons. Innovative Creations, Flint, 1986—; cons., owner Grant$line, Flint, 1986—. Editor Grant$Line, 1988. Pres., v.p. Vol. Action Ctr., 1986, 87; v.p. Newspapers for the Blind, 1987; mem. com. YWCA, 1987; mem. long range planning com. Shelter for Women, Inc., 1987. C.S. Mott fellow, 1986, King/Parks grad. scholar, 1987; recipient Take Charge award Clairol Corp., 1987. Mem. Assn. Grant Writers, Nat. Assn. Fund Raising Execs., Am. Soc. Tng. and Devel., Mich. Assn. State and Fed. Program Specialists. Democrat. Roman Catholic. Home: 1902 Park Forest Flint MI 48507 Office: Grant$line 119 N Grand Traverse Flint MI 48503

BROWNING, CAROL ANNE, pediatrician, educator; b. Appleton, Wis., June 1, 1936; d. Bertie Lee and Margaret (Loscher) B. BA, Oberlin Coll., 1958; MD, U. Wis., 1962. Diplomate Am. Bd. Pediatrics, Am. Bd. Neonatal-Perinatal Medicine. Intern Highland-Alameda County Hosp., Oakland, Calif., 1962-63; resident Children's Hosp. East Bay, Oakland, 1963-65; pediatrician Kaiser-Permanente Med. Ctr., Walnut Creek, Calif., 1965-68; neonatologist Med. Coll. Wis., Milw., 1970-89; mem. staff Sinai Samaritan Med. Ctr., Milw., 1970—; assoc. prof. pediatrics U. Wis. Sch. Medicine, Milw., 1989—; bd. dirs. Perinatal Found., Madison, Wis., 1988—. Bd. dirs. Unitarian Ch. North, Mequon, Wis., 1987-89, St. Francis Children's Ctr., Milw., 1987-90. Fellow Am. Acad. Pediatrics; mem. Nat. Perinatal Assn., Wis. Assn. for Perinatal Care (bd. dirs. 1985—, Callon-Leonard award 1989). Democrat. Office: Sinai Samaritan Med Ctr 950 N 12th St Milwaukee WI 53233

BROWNING, DEBBIE SUE, civil engineer; b. Columbia, May 9, 1958; d. Walter Beyard and Alice Virginia (George) B. BS in Civil Engring., U. S.C., 1980, Master in Engring., 1988. Environ. engr. S.C. Dept. Health and Environ. Control, Columbia, 1981-85; chemical engr. U.S. Dept. Energy Savannah River Ops., Aiken, S.C., 1985-88; chief non-reactor nuclear safety br. U.S. Dept. Energy, Aiken, 1988; environ. engr. Chem-Nuclear Systems, Inc., Columbia, 1989—.

BROWNING, NITA SPARKS, university administrator; b. Fayette, Mo., Jan. 17, 1929; d. Walter Edward and Juanita (Gibson) Sparks; m. Robert W. Browning, June 10, 1950; children: Robert Walter, Jeanne Elizabeth, Nancy Anne, John Winston. AA, Christian Coll., Columbia, Mo., 1949; BJ, U. Mo., 1951. Accredited in pub. relations. Dir. pub. info. Webster Coll., St. Louis, 1969-74, Lindenwood Coll., St. Charles, Mo., 1977-78; dir. pub. relations Parks Coll. of St. Louis U., Cahokia, Ill., 1978—; v.p. St. Louis Journalism Found., 1988—. Bd. dirs. St. Louis Aviation Mus., 1984—. Mem. Pub. Relations Soc. Am. (accredited; pres. St Louis chpt. 1984, pres.'s award 1980(, Women in Communications, St. Louis Press Club, Aviation/Space Writers Assn., Wednesday Club of St. Louis, Kappa Tau Alpha, Delta Delta Delta. Office: Parks Coll of St Louis U Cahokia IL 62206

BROWNING, REBA SMITH, bus contractor; b. Jacksonville, Fla., Dec. 5, 1926; d. Reuben F. and Emmie Ruth (Hopkins) Smith; m. Richard McGuire, July 26, 1945 (div. July 1949); children—Michael Vernon, Patricia Gail; m. Elwood Likens Browning, Aug. 17, 1957; 1 child, Bruce Morgan. Ed. pub. schs., Jacksonville. Bus owner, contractor Duval County Schs., Jacksonville, 1969-75; owner, pres. Browning Transp., Inc., Jacksonville, 1975—; driver tng. instr. Mem., sec. Fla. Vol. Chaplain Cert. Com., Jacksonville, 1984-85. Recipient Outstanding Christian of Yr. award Hogan Baptist Brotherhood, Jacksonville, 1971; Nat. Safety Slogan of Yr. award Gateway Transp., 1972. Mem. Nat. Fedn. Ind. Bus., U.S. C. of C., Duval County Sch. Bus Contractor's Assn. (pres. 1970-73, 81-83, bd. dirs.), Nat. Save-the-Children Club, Jacksonville Be-a-Friend Club. Republican. Baptist. Avocations: public speaking; poetry; furniture refinishing. Office: Browning Transp Inc 8655 Phillips Hwy Jacksonville FL 32216

BROWNING-SLETTEN, MELISSA ANN, mechanical engineer; b. Steubenville, Ohio, Aug. 31, 1947; d. Milton M. and Mabel (Steele) Trudix; m. Darwin N. Sletten; 1 child, Erik Darby. B.S. in M.E., U. Colo., Boulder, 1977. Purchasing agt. Eastman Kodak, Windsor, Colo., 1971-73; mech. engr. Public Service Co. of Colo., Denver, 1978-85, supr. prodn. standards, 1985-87; maintenance services mgr., 1987—. cons. Hvar Service, Inc. Mem. ASME, CSE. Episcopalian. Home: 11023 Tennyson Pl Westminster CO 80030 Office: 5900 E 39th Ave Denver CO 80201

BROWNLEE, JUDITH MARILYN, Wiccan minister; b. Beaumont, Tex., May 16, 1940; d. Alvin Maurice and Juanita M. (Whittington) B.; m. Theodore Blakey Peak, Apr. 12, 1974 (div. 1981); 1 child, Daniel David Brownlee Peak. BA, Lamar U., Beaumont, Tex., 1962; postgrad., U. Denver, 1971, Avalon Inst., Boulder, Colo., 1989. Tchr. Deer Trail (Colo.) High Sch., 1963-64, Lutcher Stark High Sch., Orange, Tex., 1967-69; library technician Denver Pub. Library, 1970-73; bus. exec. Weight Watchers Rocky Mtn., Denver, 1974; mailorder div. mgr. Mile High Comics and Books, Denver, 1975-81; religious student Our Lady Perpet. Responsibility, The Silent Cir., 1975-79; religious tchr. The Silent Cir., Denver, 1979-83; gov. employee Colo. Atty. Gen. Office, Denver, 1983--; minister Fortress Temple, Denver, 1984--; pub. speaker, Denver, 1988--, workshop leader, Spring Mysteries Festival, Seattle, 1988, lectr. Isis Metaphysical Ctr., workshop leader, 1985--, organizer Front Range Pagan Festival, 1985, workshop leader Dragonfest Pagan Festival, Denver, 1987--. Author: Pagan Parenting The Wheel of the Year, 1988. Contbr. articles to profl. jours. Interviewee KOA Radio, 1984, KUSA Channel 9, 1987, ; community producer Mile High Cablevision, 1987; telephoner counselor Lifeline of Colo., Denver, 1988. Mem. Assn. Past Life Rsch. and Therapy, Women's Spiritual Leadership Alliance, Daus. the New Moon, Soc. for Creative Anachronism (founder ceo 1970-73, treas. 1981-83), Denver Area Sci. Fiction Assn. (editor, 1969-70, dir. 1974-75, convention chair, 1970-75), Covenant Unitarian Universalist Pagans. Office: Fortress Temple PO Box 65 1525 Sherman C S 6 Denver CO 80203

BROWNLEE, MARLYS KAY, education educator; b. Frazee, Minn., May 9, 1940; d. Theodore and Doris May (Long) Flaten. BA, Upper Iowa U., 1961; postgrad., So. Colo. State Coll., 1973. Ch. musician missionary, 1960—; tchr. pub. schs. various pub. schs., Ariz. and Colo., 1961-75; music tchr. Marlys Brownlee Music, Gainesville, Va., 1961—; editor U.S. Dept. Interior, Washington, 1975-88; mgmt. analyst Vint Hills Farm Sta., Warrentown, Va., 1989—. Credit com. Interior Credit Union, Wash., 1985-88; christian life com. Va. So. Baptists, 1986-89. Mem. Nat. Assn. Investors, C. of C., Va. Fed. Music, Nat. Fed. Musicians. Home: RR 1 Box 409E Gainesville VA 22065 Office: Marlys Brownlee Music PO Box 83 Gainesville VA 22065

BROWNLEE, PAULA PIMLOTT, association president; b. London, June 23, 1934; came to U.S., 1959; d. John Richard and Alice A. (Ajamian) Pimlott; m. Thomas H. Brownlee, Feb. 10, 1961; children: Kenneth Gainsford, Elizabeth Ann, Clare Louise. B.A. with honors, Somerville Coll., Oxford (Eng.) U., 1957; D.Phil. in Organic Chemistry, Oxford (Eng.) U., 1959; Postdoctoral fellow, U. Rochester, N.Y., 1959-61. Research chemist Am. Cyanamid Co., Stamford, Conn., 1961-62; lectr. U. Bridgeport, Conn., 1968-70; from asst. to assoc. prof. chemistry Rutgers U., N.J., 1970-76, assoc. dean, then acting dean Douglass Coll., 1972-76; dean faculty, prof. chemistry Union Coll., Schenectady, N.Y., 1976-81; pres., prof. chemistry Hollins (Va.) Coll., 1981-90; pres. Assn. Am. Colls., Washington, 1990—. Author articles, lab. manual. Bd. dirs. edn. testing svc. C & P Tel. Co. of Va.; vice chair Assn. Religion in Intellectual Life. Mem. Am. Chem. Soc., Royal Chm. Soc. London, Soc. Values in Higher Edn., Sigma Xi. Episcopalian. Office: 1818 R St NW Washington DC 20009

BROWNLOW, SHEILA ESTHER, psychologist, educator; b. Beverly, Mass., Nov. 13, 1961; d. William Russell and Antoinette Maria (Iarossi) B. Student, Boston State Coll., 1979-82; BA, U. Mass., 1984; PhD, Brandeis U., 1990. Supr. Friendly's, Wilbraham, Mass., 1978-88; postdoctoral rsch. assoc. Brandeis U., Waltham, Mass., 1989-90; asst. prof. psychology Catawba Coll., Salisbury, N.C., 1990—; vis. lectr. U. Lowell, Mass., 1987; lectr. psychology Brandeis U., 1989-90, teaching fellow, 1985-88. Mem., activities coord. Mass. Pub. Interest Rsch. Group, Boston, 1983-85. Rosenhirsch fellow Brandeis U., 1984-85, Goldstein fellow, 1986-87, Barr fellow, 1988-89. Mem. A.m Psychol. Assn. (Travel award 1988), Am. Psychol. Soc., Psi Chi Honor Soc. Office: Dept Psychology Catawba Coll Salisbury NC 28144

BROWNMILLER, SUSAN, author, feminist activist; b. Bklyn., Feb. 15, 1935. Student, Cornell U., 1952-55. Reporter NBC-TV, Phila., 1965; network newswriter ABC-TV, N.Y.C., 1965-67; formerly researcher Newsweek, N.Y.C.; staff writer Village Voice, N.Y.C.; free-lance writer. Author: Shirley Chisholm, 1970, Against Our Will: Men, Women and Rape, 1975, Waverly Place, 1989. Office: care Simon & Schuster 1230 6th Ave New York NY 10020*

BROWN-MOHR, KAREN LEE, paper company executive, former state legislator; b. Rumford, Maine, Apr. 14, 1953; d. Leland Richard and Barbara May (Dougherty) B.; B.A. in Psychology, U. Mass., 1975. Mem. Maine Ho. of Reps., 1976-84; public relations cons. Boise Cascade Corp., Portland, Maine, 1983, mgr. govtl. affairs for Maine, 1984—; mem. Oxford County Republican Com., 1975-80; vice chmn. 2d Congressional Dist. Conv., 1978-80, chmn., 1986—; chmn. Sen. William Cohen's U.S. Mil. Acad. selection com. Home: 37 Kenwood St Portland ME 04102 Office: Boise Cascade Corp One Portland Sq Portland ME 04101

BROWN-OLMSTEAD, AMANDA, public relations executive; b. Jackson, Miss., Oct. 7, 1943; d. J.A. and Iris (Williams) Brown; m. George T. Olmstead; children: Vanessa, Blake. Student in Liberal Arts, U. Miss., 1965. In pub. relations, fashion direction and coordination Rich's, J.P. Allen, and Saks Fifth Ave., 1965-71; founder, pres., owner A. Brown-Olmstead Assocs., Atlanta, 1972—; v.p. Pinnacle Group; instr. courses Emory U. and SBA. Bd. dirs. Atlanta chpt. Muscular Dystrophy, 1968-73, pres., 1972-73; adv. bd. YMCA Women of Achievement, 1983; founder Young Careers div. High Mus. Art, 1970; mem. annual ball com. Bot. Gardens, 1981-82, Piedmont Ball Com., 1975, 78; mem. Atlanta Clean City Commn., 1978-81, Leadership Atlanta, 1978, Central Atlanta Progress, 1983; active Atlanta Ballet, 1969-76. Recipient Gold Medal N.Y. Film and TV Festival, 1968; named one of Ten Outstanding Young People of Atlanta, 1976; featured as one of six young tycoons in fashion in U.S., Mademoiselle mag., 1970. Mem. Pub. Relations Soc. Am., Fashion Group, Atlanta C. of C. (Phoenix House award adv. bd. 1983). Democrat. Episcopalian. Clubs: Atlanta City, World Trade. Writer, dir. TV spl.: The Land of Cotton, 1968. Office: A Brown-Olmstead Assocs 127 Peachtree St NE #200 Atlanta GA 30303*

BROWNRIGG, JUDITH HAMILTON, nurse, institutional sales executive; b. Roanoke, Va., June 14, 1950; d. Carl Cannaday and Mary Lee (Anderson) H.; m. W. Grant Brownrigg, Apr. 28, 1984. BS in Nursing, U. Va., 1972, MBA, 1982. RN, Va. Staff, charge nurse No. Va. Drs. Hosp., Falls Church, 1972; librarian John Hopkins Sch. Internat. Studies, Bologna, Italy, 1974-75; English instr. Politzer Sch. Langs., Bologna, 1975-76; staff, charge nurse Alexandria (Va.) Hosp., 1975, Roanoke (Va.) Meml. Hosp., 1972, 76-77; head nurse intensive care U. Va. Hosp., Charlottesville, 1972, 77-79, staff nurse clinic, 1979-80; mgmt. assoc. Equitable Life Assurance Soc., N.Y.C., 1982-84, product mgr., 1984-86; v.p. product devel. Equitable Real Estate Investment Mgmt., Inc., N.Y.C., 1986-87; v.p. instl. sales Equitable Real Estate, N.Y.C., 1987—. Mem. Fin. Women's Assn. N.Y., Montclair-Newark Jr. League. Baptist. Home: 305 N Mountain Ave Upper Montclair NJ 07043 Office: Equitable Real Estate Investment Mgmt Inc 787 7th Ave New York NY 10019

BROWNSTONE, CAROLINE TAYLOR, marketing executive; b. Toledo, Sept. 11, 1941; d. Richard and Isabel (Safian) Taylor; m. Louis H. Brownstone III; children: Kim, John, Stephanie, Louis. AA, U. Toledo, 1962; BA in Mgmt. and Retailing, Simmons Coll., 1977. Cert. tchr., Calif. Adj. faculty mem. Coll. Profl. Studies U. San Francisco, grad. fellow intenat. orgn. devel.; pres. San Francisco Ballet Aux.; dir. internat. mktg. Casto Corp., Palo Alto, Calif. Mem. exec. com., chair media and pub. rels. com., organizer eastern European study tour, former bd. trustees World Affairs Coun.; bd. dirs. internat. host com. State of Calif. Mem. UN Univ. Assn., Friends of Vieilles Maison Francais (bd. trustees), Polish Arts and Culture Found. (bd. trustees), San Francisco Symphony Assn., San Francisco Ballet Assn. (former bd. trustees, pres. San Francisco Ballet Aux.), Simmons Coll. Alumni Assn.

BROYLES, NINA SUE, lawyer; b. Aurora, Ill., Dec. 10, 1944; d. J. Otis and Ann (Colford) Broyles; m. Edwin Wyatt Fleshman, June 6, 1981; children: Kristen Noelle (dec.), Steven Broyles, Christopher Reed, Elizabeth Ann, David Clayton. BA, So. Miss. U., Hattiesburg, 1975; MSW, So. Miss. U., 1976; JD, So. U., Baton Rouge, 1983. Clin. social worker Bossier Parish Sch. Bd., Bossier City, La., 1976-78; coordiantor women's bur. St. of La., Baton Rouge, 1980-81; exec. dir. Spl. Delivery Adoption Svcs., Baton Rouge, 1988—; pvt. practice law Baton Rouge, 1983—. Bd. dirs. Family Counseling, Baton Rouge, 1989—, Friends of LA. Council on Child Abuse, 1989—, chmn. legis. com.; rep. Baton Rouge Community Bd., 1977. U. So. Calif. fellow, 1975. Mem. Fed. Bar Assn., La. Bar Assn., ABA, Baton Rouge Bar Assn., Acad. Cert. Social Workers, La. Assn. Family Mediators, Acad. Family Mediators, La. Competent Authority. Home: 3141 Moss Point Baton Rouge LA 70808 Office: 7809 Jefferson Hwy #D1 Baton Rouge LA 70809

BROZMAN, TINA L., federal judge; b. 1952. BA, NYU, 1973; JD, Fordham U., 1976. Ptnr. Anderson Russell Kill & Olick, 1976-85; bankruptcy judge U.S. Ct. So. Dist. N.Y., N.Y.C., 1985—; lectr. Practicing Law Inst., 1987. Mem. Assn. of Bar of City of N.Y. Office: US Dist Ct Custom House 1 Bowling Green New York NY 10004*

BRU, GEORGINA-ANN DOROTHEA, nurse, health science facility administrator; b. Bristol, England, Jan. 18, 1945; came to U.S., 1946; d. Malcolm Simon and Dorothea Thelma (Bird) B. BA, Hartwick Coll., 1966; BS in Nursing, Columbia U., 1973, MA, 1984. RN, N.Y. Nurse Boston Children's Hosp., 1973-75; nurse Meml. Sloan-Kettering Cancer Ctr., N.Y.C., 1975-78, head nurse, 1978-84, asst. dir., 1984-90, project mgr., 1990—. Contbr. articles to nursing jours., 1981—. Mem. Assn. Pediatric Oncology Nurses (pres. 1987-89), Sigma Theta Tau. Unitarian. Home: 55 East End Ave 5E New York NY 10028 Office: Meml Sloan Kettering Ctr 1275 York Ave New York NY 10021

BRUBAKER, KAREN SUE, manufacturing executive; b. Ashland, Ohio, Feb. 5, 1953; d. Robert Eugene and Dora Louise (Camp) B. BSBA, Ashland Coll., 1975; MBA, Bowling Green State U., 1976. Supr. tire ctr. ops. BF Goodrich Co., Akron, Ohio, 1976-77, supr. tire ctr. acctg., 1977-79, asst. product mgr. radial passenger tires, 1979-80, product mgr. broadline passenger tires, 1980-81, group product mgr. broadline passenger and light truck tires, 1981-83, mktg. mgr. T/A high tech radials, 1983-86; product mgr. B.F. Goodrich T/A radials The Uniroyal Goodrich Tire Co., Akron, Ohio, 1986—. Sect. chmn. indsl. div. United Way, Akron, 1983-86. Recipient Alumni Disting. Service award Ashland Coll., 1986; Alpha Phi Clara Bradley Burdette scholar, 1975. Mem. NAFE, Am. Mktg. Assn. (pres. Akron/Canton chpt. 1982-83, Highest Honors award 1983, v.p. bus. mktg., elected to nat. bd. dirs., v.p. profl. chpts., 1987-89), Susan B. Anthony Soc.

of Akron Women's Network, Zonta, Beta Gamma Sigma, Omicron Delta Epsilon. Home: 1862 Indian Hills Tr Akron OH 44313 Office: The Uniroyal Goodrich Tire Co 600 S Main St Akron OH 44397-0001

BRUBAKER, VICKIE LEE, civic worker; b. Balt., July 6, 1962; d. James Albert and Judy Earleen (Collins) Franklin; m. Philip Loren Brubaker, May 28, 1983; children: Alexander Colin, Kyle Anthony, Jeffrey Thomas. Student, U. Md., 1980-82. Personnel dir. R.B. Enterprises, Pasadena, Md., 1980-83; sales coord. Am. Phone Ctrs., Atlanta, 1983-85; with customer rels. dept. The William House, Dallas, 1985. Contbr. articles to local newspapers. Pres. Teen-Age Reps., Pasadena, 1976-80; active Coll. Reps., College Park, Md., 1980-81, Young Reps., Atlanta, 1983-84. Mem. Jaycess (dist. dir. State Conn. 1990—, pres. Tri-Bury chpt. 1989-90). Mem. Christian Ch. Home: 2715 E Main St Waterbury CT 06705 Office: Tri-Bury Jaycees PO Box 21 Southbury CT 06488

BRUCE, ABBI JAN, oncology nurse; b. Concord, N.H., Oct. 24, 1957; d. Mitchell and Bernice Frances (Katz) Backon; m. Kevin Andrew Bruce, Apr. 7, 1990. BS, U. N.H., 1979; MS, Columbia U., 1987. RN, Va., N.Y. Staff nurse NYU Med. Ctr., N.Y.C., 1979-81; sr. staff nurse Meml. Sloan-Kettering Cancer Ctr., N.Y.C., 1981-87; head nurse Med. Coll. of Va., Richmond, 1987-89, clin. oncology nurse, 1989—. Rudin Meml. Found. Fellow, 1986-87; Jewish Found. for the Edn. of Woman scholar, 1986-87. Mem. Assn. for Study of Childhood Cancer (bd. dirs. Richmond chpt. 1989-90), Oncology Nursing Soc., Sigma Theta Tau. Office: Med Coll of Va Box 7 MCV Sta Richmond VA 23298

BRUCE, DANIA GAYLE, interior decorator; b. Morristown, Tenn., Mar. 4, 1937; d. Fred W. and Katye (Jones) Hartman; m. Paul Love Bruce, 1961; children: Paula Ann Combs, John Richard, Ronald Powell. Student, Draughon's Bus. Coll., Knoxville, Tenn., 1957. Interior decorator Morristown, Tenn., 1961—. Life mem. Witt PTA of Hemblen County, Morristown, 1981; pres. jr. reading circle, Morristown, 1971-72; 2nd v.p. ladies reading circle Morristown, 1989. Mem. Beta Sigma Phi (first lady of Morristown 1972). Democrat. Methodist. Home: 865 Rouse Rd Morristown TN 37813

BRUCE, ELIZABETH ALICE (BETSEY BRUCE), broadcast journalist; b. Gary, Ind., Dec. 27, 1948; d. Kenneth Ashel Barnette and Mary Elizabeth (Lasher) Myers; m. Robert S. Bruce, Dec. 11, 1971; 1 child, Whitney Elizabeth Anne. B.J., U. Mo., 1970. Writer, editor Sta. KMOV-TV (formerly Sta. KMOX-TV), St. Louis, 1970-71, staff reporter, 1971-89, 5 P.M. News co-anchor, 1973, 74-76, host Newsmakers program, 1976-89, polit. editor, 1978-89, weekend news anchor woman, 1978-89; anchor, reporter Sta. KTVI-TV, St. Louis, 1989—; pub. speaker; seminar instr. Jr. League, St. Louis, 1980, 82, 86; journalism advisor St. Louis Med. Soc., 1983. Trustee Cystic Fibrosis Found., 1979—, treas., sec., v.p.; pres. adv. council Girl Scouts U.S.A., St. Louis, 1979—; trustee, pres. Carrswold Subdiv., Clayton, Mo., 1979-87. Recipient honor cert. for broadcast reporting Valley Forge Freedom Found., 1982, Media award Mental Health Patient Advocacy Group, 1982, Emmy award, St. Louis chpt. Nat. Acad. TV Arts and Scis., 1981, 84, cert. of leadership St. Louis YWCA, 1983, Spl. Leadership award for communications, 1984. Mem. Soc. Profl. Journalists (2d v.p. 1982-84), Women in Communications (Philpott-Collins award 1978), Investigative Reporters and Editors, AFTRA, Women's Polit. Caucus, U. Mo. Alumni Assn. (publs. com.), Kappa Alpha Theta. Office: Sta KTVI-TV 5915 Berthold Ave Saint Louis MO 63110

BRUCE, JUDITH WINSOR, nursing home administrator; b. Paterson, N.J., May 21, 1948; d. Lawrence Hunt and Margaret Ruth (Ruppe) B.; m. Stephen James Smith, June 2, 1972 (div. 1976). BS in Secondary Edn. cum laude, U. Vermont, 1970; MPH, NYU, 1977. Adminstrv. asst. Hanover (N.H.) Terr. Healthcare, 1972-74; med. care evaluation asst. Cabrini Med. Ctr., N.Y.C., 1974-76, supr. utilization rev., 1976-77, asst. adminstr., 1977-78, v.p. long term care, 1978-82; assoc. exec. dir. Met. Jewish Geriatric Ctr., Bkln., 1982-87, sr. v.p., chief operating officer, 1987—; cons. Akin, Gump, Hauer, Strauss, Feld, Washington, 1983. Chair liaison Blue Cross-Blue Shield of Greater N.Y., N.Y.C., 1981-82; mem. adv. bd. Elizabeth Seton Coll., Yonkers, N.Y., 1981-82; trustee First Unitarian Ch., Bklyn., 1986-89. Mem. Am. Coll. Health Care Adminstrs., Am. Soc. Profl. and Exec. Women, Hosp. Fin. Mgmt. Assn., N.Y. Assn. Homes and Services on Aging (bd. dirs. 1980-82, chair program com. 1982), Phi Beta Kappa. Republican. Unitarian. Home: 305 Hicks St Brooklyn Heights NY 11201 Office: Met Jewish Geriatric Ctr 4915 Tenth Ave Brooklyn NY 11219

BRUCE, LINDA FAYE, industrial engineer; b. Laurens, S.C., Nov. 8, 1946; d. William Edward and Doris Alta (Culbertson) B. AS in Indsl. Engring., Piedmont Tech. Coll., Greenwood, S.C., 1975. Various positions Am. Lava div. 3M Co., Laurens, 1965-73, assoc. indsl. engr., 1973-77; jr. indsl. engr. Security Pacific Nat. Bank, L.A., 1977-78; indsl. engr., cost engr. Mattel, Inc., Hawthorne, Calif., 1978-79; indsl. engr. Power Products, Boca Raton, Fla., 1979-80; mfg. engr. II, electronics div. Mattel, Inc., Hawthorne, 1980-83; mfg. engr. II Excellon Automation, Torrance, Calif., 1983-84; sr. indsl. engr. Mattel, Inc., Hawthorne, Calif., 1984—, cons. world-wide mfg. facilities, 1985—; programmer computer system SEWDATA, 1987. Mem. Soc. Mfg. Engrs. Presbyterian. Home: 554 25th St Hermosa Beach CA 90254 Office: Mattel Toys 5150 Rosecrans Ave Hawthorne CA 90250

BRUCE, MARY BETH, electronics executive; b. Hartford, Conn., Apr. 21, 1956; d. Lawrence Alvin and Marie Agnes (Shea) B.; m. Ali Asghar Mosleh, Nov. 26, 1977 (div. June 1987). Acctg. cert., Lowell Regional Vocat., 1980; student, N. Va. Coll., 1985-87. Vice pres. Integrated Systems Designers, Alexandria, Va., 1984-86; asst. acct. Nat. Ctr. Missing & Exploited Children, Washington, 1987-88; pres. Precision Test Equipment, Woburn, Mass., 1988—. Mem. NAFE, NOW, New England Native Am. Inst. Office: Precision Test Equipment 175 T New Boston St Woburn MA 01801

BRUCE, NADINE CECILE, internist, educator; b. Oak Park, Ill., Apr. 6, 1942; d. Roy Alford and Henrietta Hedwige (Denk) B. BS in Chemistry, Coll. St. Francis, 1964; MD, U. Ill., 1970. Diplomate Nat. Bd. Internal Medicine, Nat. Bd. Med. Examiners. Resident in internal medicine St. Francis Integrated Med. Program, Honolulu, 1970-74; pvt. practice Honolulu, 1974-77; assoc. program dir. med. residency program U. Hawaii, Honolulu, 1974-87, dep. program dir., 1987-90, program dir., 1990—; mem. staff Queens Med. Ctr., 1974—. V.p. bd. trustees Hawaii Bound Sch., 1977-80; bd. govs. Hawaii Med. Libr., 1980-85, Hawaii Blood Bank, 1983; mem. drug product selection bd. State of Hawaii, 1984—, chmn., 1987-89. Fellow ACP (gov. 1989—); mem. AMA, Hawaii Med. Assn. (councillor 1979-82), Honolulu County Med. Soc. (pres. 1983-84), Am. Soc. Internal Medicine, Assn. Program Dirs. in Internal Medicine, AAUP, N.Y. Acad. Scis., Soc. Gen. Internal Medicine. Republican. Roman Catholic. Office: U Hawaii Dept Medicine 1356 Lusitana St Honolulu HI 96813

BRUCE, WENDY LOUISE, accountant; b. Md., July 15, 1966; d. Malcolm Charles and Marcia Mae (Thomas) B. BS, Calif. State Poly. U., Pomona, 1989. Corp. mgmt. trainee Hyatt Regency, Dallas; with mgmt. info. systems dept. Hyatt Tech. Ctr., Oak Brook, Ill. Mem. NAFE, Sigma Kappa (1st v.p., fund raising chair). Home: 44 Miners Trail Irvine CA 92720 Office: Hyatt Tech Ctr Oak Brook Terrace Tower One Tower Ln Ste 400 Oak Brook IL 60521

BRUCK, PHOEBE ANN MASON, landscape architect; b. Highland Park, Ill., Nov. 26, 1928; d. George Allen and Louise Townsend (Barnard) Mason; m. F. Frederick Bruck, June 30, 1956. Student Bard Coll., 1946-49; B.S., Ill. Inst. Tech., 1954; M.L.A., Harvard U., 1963. Trainee, Nat. Gallery of Art, Washington, 1947, Mus. Modern Art, N.Y.C., 1948; head design dept. Design Research Inc., Cambridge, Mass., 1955-60; cons. The Architects Collaborative & Sert, Jackson Assocs., Inc., 1960-63; v.p. F. Frederick Bruck, Architect & Assoc., Inc., Cambridge; vis. design critic dept. landscape architecture Harvard U. Grad. Sch. Design, 1971-79. Contbr. to New Landscapes for Living, 1980. Judge, New Eng. Flower Show, Mass. Hort. Soc., 1971-79, Thoreau Awards, Assn. Landscape Contractors, 1980; mem. Sci. Adv. Group for Edn., Cambridge Pub. Schs., 1981-82; chair Harvard Sq. Adv. Commn., 1987—. Mem. Mass. Bd. Registration of Landscape Architects (vice chmn.), Am. Arbitration Assn., Am. Soc. Landscape Architects, Boston Soc. Landscape Architects (pres. 1973-75, examining bd. 1978-81), Mass. Soc. Mayflower Descendants, Harvard Sq. Def. Fund (chmn. adv. ocm. 1987, bd. dirs. 1984-85, pres. 1985-86), Harvard U. Grad. Sch. Design Alumni Assn. (officer 1972-78), Soc. for Protection of New Eng. Antiquities (design adv. com). Episcopalian. Home: 148 Coolidge Hill Cambridge MA 02138

BRUCKART, BERNICE CAROL, elementary educator; b. Portland, Oreg., June 21, 1935; d. Samuel Marion and Neva Arlene (Iler) Cereghino; m. John Ray Bruckart III, Aug. 15, 1970; children: Ralph Richard, Roger Scott. BS Lewis and Clark Coll., 1958. Cert. elem tchr., Oreg. Elem. tchr. Portland Pub. Sch. Dist., 1958-68, Tigard (Oreg.) Pub. Sch. Dist. 23J, 1968—; student tchr. supr. Lewis and Clark Coll., 1964, 66, Portland State U., 1975, 1977, George Fox Coll., Newberg, Oreg., 1988. Mem. NEA, Oreg. Edn. Assn., Tigard Edn. Assn. (faculty rep. 1987-88), Delta Kappa Gamma (recording sec. 1988-90). Republican. Methodist. Home: 10595 SW Kiowa St Tualatin OR 97062

BRUCKEN, ELEANOR ELIZABETH, speech/language pathologist; b. Cleve., June 18, 1929; d. Rudolph Joseph and Bertha Elizabeth (Bruckner) George; m. John Philip Brucken, Mar. 22, 1975. BA, Ohio U., 1951; MA, Kent State U., 1975. Speech, lang. pathologist Parma (Ohio) Bd. Edn., 1951-53; svc. club dir. U.S. Army Spl. Svcs., Germany, 1953-55; speech, lang. pathologist W.Va. U., Morgantown, W.Va., 1956-58, Lorain (Ohio) Bd. Edn., 1958-62, Cleve. (Ohio) Bd. Edn., 1962-82, PSI, Twinsburg, Ohio, 1987-90. Geneal. com. Western Reserve Hist. Soc., Cleve., 1985—. Mem. Ohio Geneal. Soc., Ohio Speech/Hearing Assn., Am. Speech-Lang.-Hearing, Ohio Palatines to Am. Geneal Soc. (sec. 1988—), 7 Ohio County Geneal. Socs. Home: 6814 Somerset Dr Brecksville OH 44141

BRUCKER, CONNIE, police officer, consultant; b. Detroit, June 29, 1946; d. Joseph Schwenk and Errawanna Coates; 1 child, Debra June Huegel. Student San Jose State Coll., 1980, East Los Angeles Coll., 1978. Legal sec. Lapin & Chester, West Los Angeles, Calif., 1972-75; police officer Santa Monica Police Dept., Calif., 1977—, mem. "K9 bite" rev. bd., mem. various award coms.; instr. Santa Monica Jr. Coll.; speaker, lectr. Lady Beware Programs, Los Angeles Area; cons. Safety Products, Calgary, Can., Calif. Council Hosps., Los Angeles, TV movies and spls. and interviews, Los Angeles. Author writings in field. Bd. dirs. ARC, Santa Monica, 1984—. Recipient Medal of Courage, City of Santa Monica, 1979, Mayor's Commendation, 1982. Mem. Internat. Police Assn., Women Peace Officers Assn., Los Angeles Peace Officers Assn., Santa Monica Police Officers Assn., Sexual Assault Investigators Assn., Calif. Sexual Assault Investigators Assn. (pres. 1987). Office: Santa Monica Police Dept 1685 Main St Santa Monica CA 90401

BRUCKER, JANET MARY, nurse; b. London, May 26, 1946; came to U.S., 1953; d. George Edward and Elsie Maud (Sharp) Blain; m. Dennis Jack Brucker, July 8, 1967 (div. 1978); children: Stephen Jack (dec.), Denise Michelle. Diploma in nursing, Kent State U., 1967; student, San Jacinto Coll., 1979-82; BSN, U. Tex., Houston, 1984; MS in Nursing Adminstrn., Tex. Woman's U., 1988. RN, Tex. Staff nurse pediatrics Mount Sinai Hosp., Cleve., 1967-71; staff nurse Rainbow Babies and Children's Hosp., Cleve., 1971-73; night charge nurse pediatrics Clear Lake (Tex.) Hosp., 1973; head nurse Bay Area Pediatric Assocs., Clear Lake City, 1973-78; staff nurse, night charge nurse pediatric intensive care Tex. Children's Hosp., Houston, 1978, unit tchr., pediatric intensive care, 1978-79, charge nurse Jr. League Clinic, 1979-80, asst. nurse mgr. pediatric neurosurgery/neurology, 1980-86, staff devel. coord., 1986-90, asst. dir. nursing, 1990—; clin. instr. pediatrics Houston Bapt. U., 1988—, U. Tex. Health Sci. Ctr. Sch. Nursing, Houston, 1988—; speaker in field. Contbr. numerous articles to profl. jours. Mem. Am. Assn. Neurosci. Nurses (chmn. social activity southeast Tex. chpt. 1985, membership chmn. 1984), Continuing Edn. League, Health Meeting Planners Houston, Nat. Assn. Female Execs., Sigma Theta Tau. Episcopalian. Home: 15304 Tadworth Dr Houston TX 77062 Office: Tex Children's Hosp 6621 Fannin St Houston TX 77030

BRUCK-LIEB, LILLY, consumer advisor, broadcaster, columnist; b. Vienna, Austria, May 13, 1918; came to U.S., 1941, naturalized, 1944; d. Max and Sophie M. Hahn; Ph.D. in Econs., U. Vienna; postgrad. Sorbonne, Paris, Sch. of Econs., London, Sch. of Bus., Columbia U., 1941-42, Sch. of Social Work, N.Y. U., 1964-66; m. Sandor Bruck, Mar. 7, 1943; 1 child, Sandra Lee (Mrs. John David Evans III); m. David L. Lieb, Dec. 7, 1985. Dir. consumer edn. Dept. Consumer Affairs, City of N.Y., 1969-78; project dir. Am. Coalition of Citizens with Disabilities, 1977-78; consumer advisor, broadcaster In Touch Networks, N.Y.C., 1978—; consumer affairs commentator Nat. Public Radio, 1980-82. Chmn. Westchester County, Bonds for Israel, 1960-64. V.p. Jewish Community Ctr., White Plains, N.Y. Recipient Eleanor Roosevelt award Bonds for Israel, 1963; Woman of Yr. award Anti Defamation League, 1972; Community Service award local council Girl Scouts U.S.A., 1974. Mem. Soc. of Consumer Affairs Profls. Democrat. Author: Access, The Guide to a Better Life for Disabled Americans, 1978; contbr. articles on disability and rehab. to books, ency., and mags. Home: 25 Murray Hill Rd Scarsdale NY 10583 Office: In Touch Networks 15 W 65th St New York NY 10023

BRUDERLE, LOUISE MARIE, magazine editor and publisher; b. Darby, Pa., July 24, 1956; d. Charles Paul and Edith (Holmes) B.; m. Jack Michael Zamorski, Oct. 3, 1981. BFA, Villanova U., 1978; cert. advt./pub. relation, Charles Morris Price Sch., Phila., 1979. Artist/typesetter Argus Printing Co., Wayne, Pa., 1980-82; freelance artist, writer and photographer Sarasota, Fla., 1982-87; staff writer Sarasota Sun newspaper, 1987-88; mng. editor West Coast Woman, Sarasota, 1988—, assoc. pub., 1989, pub., 1990—. Editor newsletter Artbeat, 1986—, Libretto, 1988—. Bd. dirs. crisis counselor Safe Place and Rape Crisis Ctr., Sarasota, 1986—. Democrat. Roman Catholic. Home: 3475 Huntington Pl Dr Sarasota FL 34237 Office: West Coast Woman PO Box 3047 Sarasota FL 34230-3047

BRUDNAK, PEGGY HELENE, fast-food chain executive; b. Chgo., Jan. 8, 1923; d. Michael and Theresa (Hricisin) Kundrat; m. George Andrew Brudnak, June 16, 1946; children—Teresa M. Brudnak Luddy, George A. II, Catherine A. R.N., Englewood Hosp. Sch. Nursing, Chgo., 1944; B.A. with distinction, U. Redlands, Calif., 1977, MA, 1988; cert. occupational health nurse, U. Calif.-Riverside, 1977-79. Occupational health nurse Kaiser Cement Co., Lucerne Valley, Calif., 1971-73, City of San Bernardino, Calif., 1974-79; instr. trainer CPR, San Bernardino County Am. Heart Assn., 1973-78; franchisee, dir. ops. Burger King Restaurant, Hesperia, Calif., 1979—; cons., Victorville Burger King Restaurant, 1974—. Choir mem. Holy Family Ch., Hesperia, 1970-72, Sunday sch. tchr., 1971-72. Served as 2d lt. Nurses' Corps, U.S. Army, 1944-45, PTO. Recipient Key to City, San Bernardino, 1977; Service award Am. Heart Assn., 1977. Mem. Inland Ctr. Assn. Occupational Health Nurses (treas. 1974-75), Burger King Franchisee Orgn. Republican. Roman Catholic. Club: Shoreline Yacht (Long Beach, Calif.). Avocations: boating; scuba diving; swimming; hiking; golf. Home: 17433 Aspen St Box 104 Hesperia CA 92345

BRUEHL, MARGARET ELLEN, human relations consultant; b. Phila., Nov. 22, 1935; d. George Martin and Virginia (Fowler) Gauger; m. William Justice Bruehl, Aug. 4, 1956; children—Amelia Susan, Alexandra Anne. B.S., West Chester U., 1956. Elem. tchr., pub. schs., Lindenhurst, N.Y., 1956-58, 59-60, Ridley Park, Pa., 1958-59; trainer Margaret Bruehl Assocs., N.J., N.Y., Pa., 1976-80; ptnr. Pneumaa/Bruehl/Assocs., Ohio, N.Y., 1981-87; coordinator, leader of human-relations programs Princeton Theol. Sem.'s Ctr. for Continuing Edn., N.J., 1980—; sr. cons. conflict dept. The Alban Inst., Washington. Co-author: Managing Conflict, 1982. Mem. Assn. Creative Change (profl., coord. 1990 Conflict Conf. with Alban Inst.), Soc. for Profls. in Dispute Resolution (profl.), People and People Dispute Resolution Del. to the People's Republic of China. Democrat. Avocations: cooking, film and video, jazz, classical music, gardening. Home and Office: 107 Main St PO Box 2826 Setauket NY 11733

BRUEL, IRIS BARBARA, psychologist; b. N.Y.C., June 10, 1933; d. Herman and Anna (Cohen) Goldstein; m. Robert Bruel, Apr. 1953 (div. 1957); adopted children: Michael Abraham, Russell Emanuel. BA in Psychology, CCNY, 1956, MS in Sch. Psychology, 1961; PhD in Clin. Psychology, U. Miami, Fla., 1972. Cert. profl. psychologist, Fla. Child supr. Linden Hill Sch., Hawthorne, N.Y., 1957-59; tchr., therapist The League Sch. for Severely Disturbed Children, Bklyn., 1959-61, Assn. for Mentally Ill Children, Yonkers, N.Y., 1961-63; asst. psychology rsch. U. Miami, Coral Gables, Fla., 1964-67; trainee VA Hosp., Miami, 1967-68; intern diagnostic testing and psychotherapy Henderson Clinic, Ft. Lauderdale, Fla., 1968-69; intern child psychol. svcs. San Fernando Valley Child Guidance Clinic, Van Nuys, Calif., 1970-71; cons. Sorensen Group, N.Y.C., 1972; clin. psychologist Dade County Dept. Youth Svcs., Miami, 1972-77; co-dir. Ctr. for the Whole Family, Inc., Coral Gables, 1976-79; pvt. practice clin. psychology, South Miami, Fla., 1979—; cons. Jewish Vocat. Svc., 1980—; mem. affiliate staff Grant Ctr. Hosp., 1977—; allied health staff Highland Park Hosp., 1988—; adj. prof. Nova U., Ft. Lauderdale, 1977; field supr. practicum students So. Fla. Sch. Profl. Psychology, Miami, 1978—; clin. psychologist Juvenile Ct. Mental Health Clinic, Miami, 1989; cons. Guardian Ad Litem program, 1988—. Sec. Reform Dem. Club, N.Y.C., 1962-63. Mem. Am. Psychol. Assn., Am. Soc. Clin. Hypnosis, Nat. Acad. Neuropsychology, Fla. Soc. Clin. Hypnosis (sec., newsletter editor), Dade County Mental Health Assn., Cousteau Soc., Amnesty Internat. Jewish. Home: 2869 Shipping Ave Miami FL 33133 Office: 7800 Red Rd South Miami FL 33143

BRUEMMER, LORRAINE VENSKUNAS, funeral director, real estate broker, nurse; b. Waterbury, Conn., Jan. 25; d. Anthony George and Mary Agnes (Kritchman) Venskunas; m. Jay Porter Bruemmer, Oct. 28, 1973; 1 child by previous marriage: Linda L. Rocco Sovak. R.N., St. Francis Hosp. Sch. Nursing, 1950; B.S., Columbia U., 1958; M.Ed., U. Hartford, 1961. Head nurse pediatrics Cook Hosp., Hartford, Conn., 1953-56; instr. pediatrics Bellevue Hosp., N.Y.C., 1958-59; instr. med. surg. nursing New Britain Gen. Hosp., 1959-62; hosp. supr. New Britain Gen. Hosp., 1962-63; owner Venskunas Funeral Home, New Britain, 1962—; owner Bruemmer Venskunas Real Estate, New Britain, 1974—; commr. New Britain Health Dept., 1965-74; nurse blood bank ARC, N.Y.C., 1957-59, New Britain, 1960-69. Vol. Republican Party, New Britain. Mem. New Britain Funeral Dis. Assn. (pres. 1975-78), Conn. Funeral Dirs., Nat. Funeral Dirs., New Britain Bd. Realtors, Hartford Bd. Realtors, Nat. Bd. Realtors, Multiple Listing Service Greater Hartford. Roman Catholic. Clubs: Ladies Guild (pres. 1969), Shuttle Meadow Country. Avocations: antiques; golf; tennis; swimming; bicycling; gardening. Home: 36 Roslyn Dr New Britain CT 06052 Office: Venskunas Funeral Home 665 Stanley St PO Box 1612 New Britain CT 06051

BRUER, JACQUELYN JEAN, production planning executive; b. Indpls., May 13, 1957; d. Ralph Arthur Bruer and Arlou (Scott) Schmidt; m. Lawrence Hughbanks Jr., May 13, 1978 (div. Nov. 1984). AA, Purdue U., 1981, BS, 1981; postgrad., Ind. U., Ft. Wayne, 1983. With Manpower Temp. Services, Terre Haute, Ind., 1978, Ft. Wayne, Ind., 1981-83; procurement analyst Gen. Foods Co., Lafayette, Ind., 1983-88, sr. procurement analyst, 1987-88; prodn. scheduler Chesebrough-Pond's Inc., Jefferson City, Mo., 1988—. Advisor Jr. Achievement, Lafayette, 1984-87, (exec. advisor 1986-87); dir. Brandonwood Community Assn., Ft. Wayne, 1982-83. Mem. Am. Production Inventory Control Soc. (treas. 1989-90., v.p. adminstn. 1986-87, dir. 1985-86, cert.), Jefferson City Jaycees, NAFE. Lutheran. Lodge: Am. Legion, (historian 1982-83). Office: Chesebrough-Pond's Inc 8900 Truman Blvd Jefferson City MO 65109

BRUESEWITZ, GAIL CECELIA, marketing professional; b. N.Y.C., May 17, 1956; d. Arthur George and Blanche Juliana (Dobos) B.; m. Joseph LoPinto, Sept. 1990. BA in Eng. Lit., SUNY, Binghamton, 1978. Exec. sec. promotion and artist devel. Columbia Records/CBS Records, Inc., N.Y.C., 1979-82, dir. nat. dance music mktg., 1982-89; v.p., power station promotion Crossover Mktg. Inc., N.Y.C., 1989-90; pres. Brueser Prodns., 1990; dir. promotion/artist devel. Ear Candy Records, 1990—; rep. record div. Women's Orgn. Coun. CBS, Inc., N.Y.C., 1980-82; adv. bd., dance/music, New Music Seminar, N.Y.C., 1989—. Editor: (newsletter) Brueser's Boogie Backpage, 1983—. Bd. dirs. Mt. Tremper (N.Y.) Lutheran Camp and Retreat Ctr., 1976-78, Camp Wilbur Herrlich, Pawling, N.Y., 1990; active Big Sisters, Binghamton (N.Y.) Social Svcs. dept., 1975-78. Named N.Y. rep. for Mademoiselle mag., 1975. Democrat. Lutheran. Office: Ear Candy Records care Skyline Studios 36 W 37th St 3d Fl New York NY 10018

BRUESEWITZ, LYNN JOY, computer executive; b. Milw., July 6, 1952; d. Frank Alexander and Wanda Marie (Behmke) Bonczkiewicz; m. Ralph James Cheske, July 19, 1972 (div. July 1975); m. Stephen Roland Bruesewitz, May 19, 1979; children: Wendy Sue, Jessica Rose. Student, Milw. Area Tech. Coll., 1969-71. Mgr. loan service Wauwatosa (Wis.) Savs. & Loan, 1969-71; mgr. ops. McCreedy Art Studio, Milw., 1971-72; office mgr. Schellgell Food Service, Milw., 1974-80; office and systems mgr. Wiviott's, Milw., 1980-82; cons. software support systems St. Charles, Ill., 1982-84; dir. computer services, systems analyst midwest regional office Real Estate, Glendale Heights, Ill., 1984-87; pres. FSN Computer Services, Naperville, Ill., 1986-87; owner, pres. Software Support Systems, St. Charles, 1987—; mgr. system conversion DATA Intelligence Systems, Boston, 1976, Montalbano Builders, Westmont, Ill., 1983, Ptnrs. Midwest, 1984-86; mgr. system design ADC, Milw., 1978-80; advisor 1st Computers, Chgo., 1984-86. Mem. Greater O'Hare Assn. (pres.), Nat. Assn. for Female Execs. Roman Catholic. Office: Software Support Systems Saint Charles IL 10174

BRUETT, KAREN DIESL, sales and fundraising consultant; b. N.Y.C., May 15, 1945; d. Francis J. and Dorothy (Peterson) Diesl; m. William H. Bruett, Jr., Mar. 18, 1967; 1 child, Lindsey Diesl. BA in English, St. Lawrence U., 1966; MA, Hunter Coll., 1971. Tchr. English Freeport (N.Y.) pub. schs., 1966-70; exec. interviewer, researcher Louis Harris & Assocs., N.Y.C., 1970-72; dir. adult edn. West Side YMCA, 1972-76, mem. bd. mgrs., 1978-83; v.p. new bus. devel. Gaylord Adams & Assocs., Inc., N.Y.C., 1976-81; account exec. John Blair Mktg., N.Y.C., 1981-83, v.p. sales, 1983-84, sr. v.p., gen. sales mgr., 1984-86; ind. sales and fundraising cons.; bd. dirs. Resolution, Inc., Winsooki, Vt. Trustee St. Lawrence U., 1978—, chmn. devel. com., 1988—, chmn. alumni fund, 1983-84, chmn. annual giving, 1984-88, chmn. planning com., 1987-88, mem. exec. com., 1987—, chmn. devel. com., 1988—; trustee Vt. Council on Arts, 1986—, vice chmn. bd. trustees, chmn. devel. coms., 1988—; del. Am.-Soviet Youth Forum, Baku, USSR, 1974. Home and Office: RR 1 Box 1740 Hinesburg VT 05461

BRUFF, BEVERLY OLIVE, public relations consultant; b. San Antonio, Dec. 15, 1926; d. Albert Griffith and Hazel Olive (Smith) B. BA, Tulane U., 1948; postgrad. Our Lady of Lake Coll., 1956, Okla. Center for Continuing Edn., 1960-70. Asst. dir. New Orleans Theatre Guild, 1948-50; dist. dir. San Antonio Area coun. Girl Scouts Am., 1958-70, public rels. dir., 1970-83; free-lance pub. rels., 1983—; mem. Coun. of Pres., v.p., 1981-82, 84—; mem. Coun. of Internat. Rels. Zoning commr. Hill Country Village, Tex., 1973-76, 83-85, 88-90; councilwoman Hill Country Village, 1985-88; bd. dirs. Animal Def. League, 1989—, Camp Fire, Inc. Mem. Pub. Rels. Soc. Am., Tex. Pub. Rels. Assn. (Silver Spur award), Women in Communications (historian 1969-70, v.p. 1970-71, treas. 1971-73), Tex. Press Women (recipient state writing contest awards 1971, 72, 73, 74, mem. exec. bd. dirs. 1970-71, 73-74, dist. treas. 1972-73, dist. v.p. 1973), Nat. Fedn. Press Women, Internat. Assn. Bus. Communicators, Speech Arts of San Antonio (pres. 1964-66, 70-72, 84—, dir. 1964-72, 88—, chmn. bd. dirs. 1966-69), Am. Women in Radio and TV (dir. chpt. 1974, sec. 1975, pres. 1979-80), San Antonio Soc. Fund Raising Execs., Assn. Girl Scout Exec. Staff. (exec. bd. 1963-72, nat. bd. 1972-74), Animal Def. League (bd. dirs.). Home: 508 Tomahawk Tr San Antonio TX 78232

BRUIN, LINDA LOU, lawyer; b. Grandville, Mich., June 7, 1938; d. John and Tena (Groeneveld) B. A.A., Grand Rapids Jr. Coll., 1958; A.B., Hope Coll., 1961; postgrad. U. Stockholm, Sweden, 1963-64; A.M., U. Mich., 1967; J.D., Wayne State U., 1973. Bar: Mich. 1973, U.S. Dist. Ct. (we. dist.) Mich. 1980, U.S. Ct. Appeals (6th cir.) 1984. Tchr. Georgetown Pub. Sch., Jenison, Mich., 1959-63, Bullock Creek Area Sch., Midland, Mich., 1964-70; legal supr. Legis. Service Bur., Mich. State Legis., Lansing, 1973-79; legal counsel Mich. Assn. Sch. Bds., Lansing, 1979—. Monthly columnist Mich. Sch. Bd. Jour., 1981—. Mem. Citizen's Commn. to Improve Mich. Courts, 1986. Fellow Inst. Ednl. Leadership, 1982. Mem. ABA (com. mem. 1983—), Women Lawyers Assn. Mich. (pres. 1984-85), Mich. State Bar Assn. (com. chmn. 1982-87, State Bar Rep. Assembly 1985—), LWV. Democrat. Office: Mich Assn Sch Bds 421 W Kalamazoo Lansing MI 48933

BRUINS, AMY CONANT, management consultant, insurance consultant; b. N.Y.C., Mar. 10, 1959; d. William Henry and Charlotte (Heavens) B. AB in Pub. Policy and French, Duke U., 1980; MBA, Dartmouth Coll., 1987; cert., Xerox Corp., 1981. With Chubb Group of Ins. Cos., 1980-81; br. auditor Chubb Group of Ins. Cos., Warren, N.J., 1982-83; unit mgr. Chubb Group of Ins. Cos., New Providence, N.J., 1983-85; cons. The MAC Group, Chgo., summer 1986; sr. cons. Price Waterhouse, Washington, 1987-88, mgr., 1988—. Vol. Voter Registration Drives, D.C. and Va., 1987—; recruiter on behalf Price Waterhouse, Dartmouth Coll. Amos Tuck Sch., 1987—; assoc. Smithsonian Mus., Washington, 1987—; treas. Reynolds Prospect Condominium Assn., Alexandria, Va., 1989—. #D. Mem. Am. Mgmt. Assn., NAFE, Ins. Acctg. Systems Assn. Episcopalian. Office: Price Waterhouse 1801 K St NW 7th Fl Washington DC 20006

BRUKER, DEBORAH WILLIS, graphic designer; b. Memphis, Apr. 10, 1951; d. Albert Clyde and Phyllis (Hoffman) Willis; m. Davenport Sanford Bruker, Mar. 16, 1973 (div. Sept. 1979). BFA, U. Ga., 1973. Staff artist Perry Communications, Atlanta, 1973-76; designer John Muhlhausen Design, Inc., Atlanta, 1976-79, Hauser Assocs., Atlanta and Houston, 1981-83; sr. graphic artist Atlanta Regional Commn., 1979-81; prin. DWB Design, Atlanta, 1983-85; pres. RWB Environ., Inc., Atlanta, 1985-87; v.p., prin. designer Wagner Bruker Design Assocs. Inc., Atlanta, 1987-88; pres., prin. designer Bruker Design Assocs., Inc., Atlanta, 1988—; instr. Portfolio Ctr., Atlanta, 1985. Work pub. in nat. books. Mem. Soc. Environ. Graphic Designers (S.E. regional rep. 1988-90), Art Dirs. Club Atlanta (membership dir. 1984-85, show chmn. 1985-86), Am. Inst. Graphic Artists (Atlanta bd. mem.). Presbyterian. Office: 2135-D De Foor Hills Rd NW Atlanta GA 30318

BRULÉ, A. LORRAINE, commercial property manager; b. Yakima, Wash., Aug. 16, 1925; d. Arthur E. and Helen (Auvé) Brulé; m. Nolan D. Roach, Oct. 24, 1959 (div. Jan. 1978); children: Dusty Dean, Susan Marie, Dean Patrick, Gaylen Leigh Brulé. Student, Seattle U., 1943-44, Dominican Coll. San Rafael, 1944-45; BS in Sociology, Seattle U., 1947. Bookkeeper, Harper Meggee, Inc., Seattle, 1947-48; sec. bookkeeper Griffin Envelope Co., Seattle, 1948-50; with Yukon Investment Co., Inc., Seattle, 1950-59, 75-85, treas., 1977-85, mgr. comml. properties, 1975-85, asst. sec., 1975-85; cons. property mgmt., 1985—. Mem. Seattle Art Mus. Mem. Seattle U. Alumni Assn. Roman Catholic. Home and Office: Seven Highland Dr Unit 703 Seattle WA 98109-3215

BRUMBACK-HENRY, SARAH E., industrial psychologist, management consultant; b. Columbus, Kans., Dec. 5, 1948; d. F. L. Brumback and Alice (Bossi) Eggeman; m. J. P. Henry, June 24, 1974 (div. 1980). BS, U. Kans., 1970, MA, 1972; PhD, Stevens Inst. Tech., 1987. Cons. U. Kans., Lawrence, 1968-72; exec. dir. Community Svcs. Consortium, Dodge City, Kans., 1972-73; adminstr., mgr. San Francisco Opera, 1973; asst. dir. U.S. com. UNICEF, N.Y.C., 1973-76; asst. v.p. Irving Trust Co., N.Y.C., 1976-86; sr. cons. Towers Perrin, N.Y.C., 1986—; program chmn. Am. Soc. Tng. & Devel., N.Y.C., 1980; cons. Mayor's Pvt. Sector Survey, N.Y.C., 1988. Contbr. article to profl. jours. Mem. Am. Psychol. Assn., Am. Psychol. Soc., Human Resource Planning Soc., Orgn. Devel. Network (dir. N.Y. chpt. 1989), Soc. Indsl./Organizational Psychology (workshop com. 1989—), Met. Assn. Applied Psychology. Home: 162 W 56th St #602 New York NY 10019 Office: Towers Perrin 100 Summit Lake Dr Valhalla NY 10595

BRUMM, MARCIA COWLES, pharmacist; b. Cleve., Nov. 22, 1921; d. Forest Eugene and Vivian Curtis (Bonnallie) Cowles; m. Joseph Norris Brumm, Apr. 27, 1962. BS, Case Western Res. U., 1944. Lic. pharmacist, Ohio, Calif., Ariz., Colo. Pharmacist Am. Pharm. Assn., Washington, 1944-70. Treas. Am. Assn. Hosp. Pharmacists in Ohio, 1952-56; mem. Gen. Fedn. Woman's Club, Ft. Pierce, 1980, AAUW, Port St. Lucie, Ft. Pierce, Fla., 1978, United Meth. Women, Point St. Lucie, 1976. Recipient Cert. 500 Hours Vol. Work, U. Fla., Port St. Lucie, 1989. Republican. Methodist. Home: 502 SE Seahouse Dr Port Saint Lucie FL 34983

BRUMMUND, FRANCINE ANN, public relations specialist; b. Tacoma, Apr. 7, 1960; d. Arnold Raymond Brummund and Georgia Lenore (Fischer) Holmstrom. B in Univ. Studies, N.D. State U., 1985. Seminar coord. YMCA of N.D. State U., Fargo, 1980-83; coord. Knorr for U.S. Senate campaign, Fargo, N.D., 1982; intern U.S. Senator Mark Andrews, Washington, 1983; interviewer Job Service of N.D., Fargo, 1983-84; with pub. rels. GTE-Sylvania Corp., Orange, Calif., 1985-89; southwest sales supr. consumer svcs. GTE-Sylvania Corp., Orange, 1989—. Youth mem. Gov.'s Employment and Tng. Forum, Bismarck, N.D., 1980-82; vol. pub. rels. coord. Altenburg for Congress., Fargo, 1984. Republican. Roman Catholic. Home: 17676 Cameron St #1 Huntington Beach CA 92647 Office: GTE Sylvania Consumer Svcs 6505 E Gayhart St Commerce CA 90040

BRUMUND, LORALEE ANN, transportation planner, emergency medical technician; b. Waukegan, Ill., Dec. 26, 1949; d. Alvin Lorenz and Dorthe Mae (Maxwell) B.; m. Ronald Eugene Mengel, June 10, 1972 (div. Apr. 1989); children: Wade W., Brooke B. Student, U. Wis., 1972, George Washington U., 1968-69, George Washington U., 1986. Transp. planner Bi-State Regulatory Planning Commn., Rock Island, Ill., 1973-75; surveyor Fuqua George Survey, Gallatin, Tenn., 1978-80; transp. planner U. Wis. Parking and Transp., Madison, 1980-85; emergency med. technician Dane County Regulatory Planning Commn., Madison, 1987—, Curtis Ambulance, Madison, 1987—. Mem. Iowa Citizens Adv. Commn., Davenport, 1975-76. Mem. AAUW (studies dir. Davenport, Iowa chpt. 1973-75), Wis. Women in Transp. Lutheran. Home: 908 Woodward Dr Madison WI 53704

BRUN, JUDY KAY, nutrition education consultant; b. Petoskey, Mich.; d. Lester Jasper and Beatrice Winona (Hoar) Kalbfleisch; m. Torben Otto Brun, June 29, 1968; 1 child, Christian Tor Brun. BS, Mich. State U., 1964; MS, Iowa State U., 1967, PhD, 1970. Cert. home economist; lic. nutritionist. Tchr. Clarkston (Mich.) High Sch., Clarkston, 1964-66, James Madison Mem. High Sch., Madison, Wis., 1967-68; asst. prof. Chgo. State Univ., 1971-74, U. Ill., Champaign, 1974-78; dir. rsch. and evaluation Nat. Dairy Coun., Ill., 1978-86; v.p. div. Nutrition Edn. Nat. Dairy Coun., Rosemont, Ill., 1986-89; pres. Brun and Assocs., Sante Fe, 1989—; prof., chair Iowa State U., Ames, 1990—; pres., bd. dirs. Soc. for Nutrition Edn., Oakland, 1987-90, pres. Soc. for Nutrition Edn. Found., editorial bd. Jour. of Nutritional Edn., 1981-87. Contbr. rsch. articles to mags. Recipient Prof. Achievement award, Iowa State U., 1986. Mem. Soc. for Nutrition Edn. (pres. 1987-90), Am. Home Econs. Assoc. Office: Brun and Assocs 3228 Calle Celestial Santa Fe NM 87501

BRUNDAGE, PATRICIA LOUNSBURY, art gallery director; b. Orange, N.J., Sept. 11, 1953; d. John Denton and Ann (Lounsbury) Brundage; m. William Bryant Copley, Nov. 12, 1983; children: Bryant, Caroline Ann. Student Washington & Jefferson Coll., 1971-73; B.F.A., U. Ga., 1975. Asst. to dir. Castelli-Sonnabend Tapes and Films, Inc., N.Y.C., 1976-77, dir., 1977—; dir. Leo Castelli Gallery N.Y.C., 1984—. Episcopalian. Club: Jr. League (N.Y.C.). Home: 38 W 9th St New York NY 10011 Office: Leo Castelli Gallery 420 W Broadway New York NY 10012

BRUNDIGE, LINDA ANN, photographer; b. South Gate, Calif., Dec. 3, 1946; d. Ernest Richard and Mary Elisabeth (James) B. BA in Journalism, Long Beach (Calif.) State U., 1969. Photographer L.A. Herald Examiner, 1972-78; owner/operator Line of Sight Photography, Lynwood, Calif., 1971—; judo instr. City of Huntington Park, 1971—; reserve dep. L.A. County Sheriff's Dept., 1977—; photographer Sanford Studios, Whittier, Calif., 1988—. Mem. Women in Communications, Press Photographers of Greater L.A. (bd. dirs.), Calif. Res. Peace Officers Assn., Profl. Peace Officers of L.A. County, Sheriff's Relief Assn., L.A. Republican. Home and Office: 11021 Bullis Rd Lynwood CA 90262

BRUNEAUX, DEBRA LOUISE, costume designer; b. Orange, Calif., Oct. 19, 1953; d. James Fredricksen and Carol Gwen (Cashner) B. BA in Exptl. Psychology, U. Calif., Santa Barbara, 1975. Residents women's cutter/draper Ctr. Theatre Group, Los Angeles, 1978-79; asst. to resident costume designer Oreg. Shakespearean Festival Assn., Ashland, 1980-82; costume shop supr. Sacramento Theatre Co., Calif., 1982-83; resident costume designer Sacramento Theatre Co., 1983-88; costume designer, costume mgr. Oreg. Shakespeare Festival, Portland Ctr. Stage, 1988—; costume shop mgr., cons. Berkeley Repertory Theatre, Calif., 1979. Home: 2031 NW Johnson #9 Portland OR 97209 Office: Oreg Shakespeare Festival PO Box 9008 Portland OR 97207

BRUNELL-KAECHELE, DIANE J., securities company executive, realtor; b. Pitts., May 24, 1952; d. August and Jean (Rosso) Jucha; m. Charles Brunell, Mar. 5, 1978 (div. Dec. 1985); m. Thomas T. Kaechele, May 5, 1989. BS cum laude, Point Park Coll., Pitts., 1974. Registered investment advisor SEC; lic. realtor, Conn. Mktg. cons. Southport (Conn.) Advisors, Inc., 1980-84; nat. wholesale mgr. Cheshire Mgmt. Co., Wallingford, Conn., 1984-85; v.p. Cheshire Securities, Inc., Wallingford, 1984-85; pres., bd. dirs. Colonial Equities Corp., West Hartford, Conn., 1985-88; cons. to major real estate developers and owners Washington, Conn., 1988—; co-owner, pres., bd. dirs. Sponsors Securities Corp., Washington, 1989—. Mem. Washington Environ. Coun., 1987. Recipient cert. of recognition Coll. Fin. Planning, Denver, 1989. Mem. Nat. Assn. Securities Dealers, Real Estate Securities and Syndication Inst. (pres. Conn. chpt. 1989—), Internat. Assn. Fin. Planners, Nat. Soc. Compliance Profls., Conn. Bd. Realtors, Waterbury Bd. Realtors, NAFE. Republican. Congregationalist. Home and Office: 134 Nettleton Hollow Rd Washington CT 06793

BRUNER, ANN CRADDOCK, art educator, artist; b. Owensboro, Ky., Oct. 29, 1947; d. Marshall Wells and Alice (Craddock) Bruner. BA summa cum laude, Ky. Wesleyan Coll., Owensboro, 1969; MA, Western Ky. U., 1978. Art cons. Follow Through Program Owensboro Pub. Schs., 1971-74; art tchr. Owensboro Middle Sch., 1974-81, 1983-88; art tchr. Owensboro Jr. High/High Sch., 1981-83, Owensboro High Sch., 1988—; two-man exhibit at Owensboro Mus. Fine Art, 1978; paintings accepted Ky. Watercolor Soc. "Totally Transparent VII," Bowling Green, 1987, Paducah Art Guild '87 Show, Owensboro Mus. Fine Art, Christmas in Ky., 1987. Recipient various art awards. Mem. Ky. Watercolor Soc., Owensboro Art Guild, NEA, Ky. Edn. Assn., Owenboro Edn. Assn., Owensboro Mus. Fine Art, Owensboro Saddle Horse Assn. (pres. 1976-78), Alpha Chi. Republican. Presbyterian. Home: 2527 Iroquois Dr Owensboro KY 42301 Office: Owensboro High Sch Owensboro KY 42301

BRUNETT, RUTH ANGELA, adult education educator; b. Detroit, Sept. 2, 1948; d. Raymond Henry and Cecilia (Gill) B.; children: James, Joseph, Melanie. BA, Wayne State U., Detroit, 1970, MA, 1975. Tchr. Eng. and Brit. lit. Hillsborough County Schs., Varico, Fla.; adult educator ESL East Bay Adult Ctr./Hillsborough County Schs., Gibsonton, Fla. Mem. NAFE, Nat. Coun. Tchrs. of English, Am. Assn. Adult and Community Edn., Fla. Assn. Community Edn., Fla. Adult Edn. Assn., Assn. Supervision and Curriculum Devel., Macomb-St. Clair Soc. for Autistic Children (bd. dirs.), Nat. Assn. Pers. Cons. Office: East Bay Adult & Community Ctr 770 Big Bend Rd Gibsonton FL 33534

BRUNETTE, MARQUA LEE, music therapist; b. Evanston, Ill., May 1, 1950; d. Harold Thomas and Margaret Louise (Wharf) B. Student, U. Hawaii, 1972; MusB in Edn., Ind. U., 1973; postgrad., Loyola U., New Orleans, 1973-75. Adminstrv. asst. to dean, instr. in piano Coll. Music, Loyola U., 1973-75; pvt. practice music therapy, instr. piano New Orleans, 1975—; sales rep. Pro Travel, Inc., New Orleans, 1986-89, Pontchartrain Travel, 1989—; mktg. cons. Internat. Component Mfg. Inc., Grand Prairie, Tex.; lectr. in field of music and dyslexia, 1987—. Bd. dirs., mem. vol. com. New Orleans Symphony, 1979—; bd. dirs. Jr. Philharm. Soc., New Orleans, 1977-81, pres., 1980-81; bd. dirs. Young Audiences, Inc., 1984—; bd. dirs. Overture to the Cultural Season, 1983—, pres. 1985-86; mem. New Orleans Opera Assn., 1983, bd. dirs. jr. com., 1984-86. Mem. Orton Dyslexia Soc. (bd. dirs. La. br. 1988—), Nat. Assn. Music Therapy, Inc. (registered), Music Tchrs. Nat. Assn., La. Music Tchrs. Assn., Ind. U. Alumni Assn. (mem. 1973, pres. New Orleans chpt. 1976—), Mu Phi Epsilon. Republican. Methodist. Home: 1036 Napoleon Ave New Orleans LA 70115

BRUNEY, LAURA ANN, association administrator, consultant; b. Detroit, June 17, 1957; d. James E. and Marian Patricia (Clancy) B. BS, U. Fla., 1979; M in Pub. Adminstrn., U. Miami, 1988. Med. TV producer U. Miami, 1979-83, dir. instructional resources, 1983-88; exec. dir. Bus. Vols. for Arts, Miami, 1988—; tng. Bd. dirs. Parent Resource Ctr., 1987—; mem. Leadership Miami, 1988, com. chmn., 1989; mem. Directions, Am. Cancer Soc., Miami, 1988—; founding mem. Dade County Cultural Alliance; mem. adv. bd. Kids in Crisis, Miami, 1987; founding chmn. Theatre Coalition Miami, 1990. Mem. Women in Communications (seminar chmn. 1990), Am. Mktg. Assn., Women's Network Miami. Office: Bus Vols for Arts 150 W Flagler St Ste 2500 Miami FL 33130

BRUNGARDT, HELEN RUTH, minister; b. Littlefield, Tex., Sept. 2, 1931; d. Isaac Henry and Helen Irene (Hanna) Pelt; m. Guido Milton Brungardt, July 22, 1950 (div.); children: Karla Kay, Linda Gail, Mark Douglas, Celeste Dawn. Student, Tex. Christian U., 1948-49, U. N.Mex., 1969, Divine Sci. Ednl. Ctr., 1976-80. Tchr. Napoleon Hill Acad., Albuquerque, 1964-66; practitioner First Ch. Religious Sci., Albuquerque, 1969-72, tchr., 1971-72; founder, minister Symphony of Life Ch., Albuquerque, 1972-81; founder, dir., pres. Inst. for the Emerging Self, Albuquerque, 1981—; cons. ministers, individuals, 1977—; lectr. various orgns., radio, tv, 1975—; instr. Profl. Leadership Tng., Albuquerque, 1965-82; bd. dirs., co-founder Grand Teton Retreat. Author: Contemplation, 1975, Mystical Meaning of Jesus, 1980, Beyond Liberation, 1985; contbr. articles to profl. jours. Mem. Divine Sci. Fedn., Internat. New Thought Alliance. Republican. Mem. Ch. Divine Sci. Home: 159 Meadowlark Ln Corrales NM 87048

BRUNI, KATHY DIANNE, marketing professional; b. Colville, Wash., Feb. 6, 1957; d. Vern Oliver and Neta Evelyn (Duff) Stebbins; m. Francis Guy Bruni, Apr. 26, 1980 (div. 1990); 1 child, Jason Eric. BA, Wash. State U., 1979. Clk. Coast to Coast Stores, Camas, Wash., 1974-78; packager Guardian Industries, Portland, Oreg., 1979-81; prodn. worker Hewlett-Packard, Camas, 1981-82, order processing clk., 1982, order processing support person, 1983-84, mktg. support person, 1984-86; computer svcs. coord. Seattle (Wash.) Pacific U., 1986-87; mktg. support specialist Zenith Data Systems, Bellevue, Wash., 1987-89, sr. mktg. support specialist, 1989-90, regional trainer, 1990—. Mem. Northwest Folk Dancers Inst. (v.p. 1987-89). Office: Zenith Data Systems 300 120th Ave NE Bldg 1 Ste 205 Bellevue WA 98005

BRUNNER, LILLIAN SHOLTIS, nurse, author; b. Freeland, Pa., Mar. 29; d. Andrew J. and Anna (Tomasko) Sholtis; m. Mathias J. Brunner, Sept. 8, 1951; children: Janet Brunner Hoch, Carol Ann, Douglas Mathias. Diploma, U. Pa., 1940, BS, 1945, LittD (hon.), 1985; MS in Nursing, Case-Western Res. U., 1947; ScD (hon.), Cedar Crest Coll., 1978. Registered nurse. Operating room supr. U. Pa. Hosp., Phila., 1942-45; head, fundamentals of nursing dept. U. Pa., 1945-46; asst. prof. surgical nursing Yale U. Sch. Nursing, New Haven, Conn., 1947-51; surgical supr. Yale-New Haven Hosp., 1947-51; research project dir. Sch. Nursing Bryn Mawr Hosp., Pa., 1973-77; co-founder History of Nursing Mus., Pa. Hosp., Phila., 1974; mem. bd. overseers Sch. Nursing, U. Pa., 1982—, bd. dirs. emeritus; chmn. nursing adv. Presbyn.-U. Pa. Med. Ctr., Phila., 1970-88, trustee, 1976-88, vice chmn., bd. trustees, 1985-88. Author: Manual of Operating Room Technology, 1966, (with others) Lippincott Manual of Nursing Practice, 1974, 4th edit., 1986, Textbook of Medical and Surgical Nursing, 1964, 6th edit., 1988; mem. editorial bd. Jour. Nursing and Health Care, Nursing '90', Nursing Photobook Series, 1978—. Bd. dirs. Presbyn. Med. Ctr. Found., Phila., 1985—. Recipient Disting. Alumnus award Frances Payne Bolton Sch. Nursing, Case Western Res. U., 1980. Fellow Am. Acad. Nursing; mem. Am. Nurses Assn., Nat. League for Nursing (judge nat. writing contest 1982-84, Disting. Service award 1979), Nat. League Am. Pen Women (sec. Phila. chpt. 1972-76, nat. sec. 1984-86), Am. Med. Writers Assn., Assn. Operating Room Nurses, Nurses Alumni Assn. U. Pa. Hosp., Ben Franklin Soc., Internat. Old Lacers Soc., Sigma Theta Tau. Home and Office: 1247 Berwyn-Paoli Rd Berwyn PA 19312

BRUNNER, MARY MARTINEZ, sales executive; b. Orem, Utah, June 27, 1945; d. Manuel C. and Tina (Montoya) Martinez; m. David H. Brunner (div. Dec. 1984); children: Matthew, Daniel. Student, LaSalle Extension U., Chgo., 1979-80. Svc. asst. AT&T, 1963-65; stewardess United Air Lines, 1965-67; night mgr. Hertz, Chgo., 1968-69; sales and distbn. mgr. Azoplate div. Am. Hoechst, Murry Hill, N.J., 1969-76; dist. sales mgr. Itek Graphix Systems, Nashua, N.H., 1976-88; regional sales mgr. Pagitek Internat., Boston, 1987-88, Qubix Graphic Systems, San Jose, Calif., 1988; regional systems cons. Linotype Co., 1989—; regional sales mgr. VAR/Co-op; owner Park & Martinez Exporter, Arlington Heights, Ill., 1986—. Mem. NAFE, NOW, Arlingting Heights Hist. Soc., Greenpeace, Sierra Clu. Republican. Roman Catholic. Office: PO Box 1970 Arlington Heights IL 60006

BRUNO, AUDREI ANN, nurse; b. Pitts., Oct. 31, 1946; d. Vincent Joseph and Julia Elizabeth (Karaffa) Mataya; m. Edward Orlando Bruno, Apr. 30, 1966; children: Brent Edward, Bradley Edward. AA, Community Coll. Allegheny County, 1976; B, Pa. State U., 1984; MSN, U. Pitts., 1988. Cert. nurse adminstr. Psychiat. nursing supr. Western Psychiat. Clinic and Inst., Pitts., 1976-81; staff charge nurse Magee Women's Hosp., Pitts., 1981-82; charge team leader Central Med. Pavillion, Pitts., 1982-84; clin. specialist Vis. Nurse Assn. of Alleghany County, Pitts., 1984—; instr., mem. speakers bur. Community Coll. Allegheny County, West Mifflinb, Pa., 1986—; project developer WPIC Adolescent Module, 1980-81; chief exec. officer Psycho-Ednl. Cons., 1989—. Chmn. North Huntington (Pa.) Suicide Awareness and Prevention Com., 1986-88; fieldworker Project Star, Pitts., 1986-88; mem. Pa. Task Force on Elder Abuse, Nurses Interest in Care of Elderly, Geriatric Ednl. Networi; mem. adv. com. Nat. Project DART. Mem. Nat. Nursing Orgn., Grad. Student Orgn. Nursing Quality Assurance (cons.), Internat. Platform Assn., Sigma Theta Tau. Home: 14071 Ridge Rd North Huntingdon PA 15642 Office: Vis Nurse Assn Allegheny Co 1000 Jacks Run Rd 6th fl North Versailles PA 15187

BRUNO, CATHY EILEEN, state official; b. Binghamton, N.Y., Apr. 5, 1947; d. Martin Frank and Beverly Carolyn (Hamlin) Piza; BA, SUNY, Binghamton, 1968; M.S.W., Syracuse (N.Y.) U., 1976; m. Frank L. Delaney, June 28, 1969 (div.); m. Paul R. Bruno, May 5, 1990. Psychiat. social worker Willard (N.Y.) Psychiat. Center, 1968-73, Broome Devel. Center, Binghamton, 1973-74, 76; congl. legis. aide, 1975; asst. dir. bur. program and fiscal audits N.Y. State Office Mental Retardation and Devel. Disabilities, Albany, 1976-80, asst. dir. bur. program and fiscal audits, 1976-80, statewide coordinator intermediate care facilities for developmentally disabled, 1980, cert. coordinator Western County service group, 1980-83, Upstate unit dir. Bur. Cert. Control, 1983-85; dir. ICF/DD Survey and Rev., 1985-89; area dir. Bur. Program Cert., 1989—; adj. instr. SUNY Sch. Social Welfare, Albany, 1982-83. Grantee HEW, 1975-76. Mem. Upstate Assn. Psychiat. Social Workers in State Schs. and Hosps. (sec. 1970), Am. Mgmt. Assn. Office: PO Box 3153 Albany NY 12209-0153

BRUNO, GRACE ANGELIA, accountant, educator; b. St. Louis, Oct. 11, 1935; d. John E. and Rose (Goodwin) B. BA, Notre Dame Coll., 1966; MEd, So. Ill. U., 1972; MAS, Johns Hopkins U., 1983; PhD, Walden U., 1985. CPA, Mo., Md., N.J. Tchr. Sisters of Notre Dame, St. Louis, 1962-80; pres. Bruno-Potter, Inc., Avon-By-The-Sea, N.J., 1981—; asst. treas., instr. acctg. Coll. of Notre Dame of Md., Balt., 1978-79, treas., 1979-80; asst. prof. acctg. Georgian Ct. Coll., Lakewood, N.J., 1985—; fin. advisor James Harry Potter Gold Medal Award, N.Y.C., 1980—. Elected to Internat. Platform Assn., 1987. Mem. Am. Inst. CPA's, N.J. Soc. CPA's, N.J. Bus. Educators, St. Louis Bus. Educators (treas. 1972-73). Democrat. Roman Catholic. Home and Office: 419 Third Ave Avon By The Sea NJ 07717

BRUNO, JUDYTH ANN, chiropractor; b. Eureka, Calif., Feb. 16, 1944; d. Harold Oscar and Shirley Alma (Farnsworth) Nelson; m. Thomas Glenn Bruno, June 1, 1968; 1 child, Christina Elizabeth. AS, Sierra Coll., 1982; D of Chiropractic, Palmer Coll. of Chiropractic West, Sunnyvale, Calif., 1986. Diplomate Nat. Bd. Chiropractic Examiners. Sec. Bank Am., San Jose, Calif., 1965-67; marketer Memorex, Santa Clara, Calif., 1967-74; order entry clk. John Deere, Milan, Ill., 1977; system analyst Four Phase, Cupertino, Calif., 1977-78; chiropractic asst. Dr. Thomas Bruno, Nevada City, Calif., 1978-81; chiropractor Chiropractic Health Care Ctr., Nevada City, 1987—. Area dir. Cultural Awareness Coun., Grass Valley, Calif., 1977—; vol. Nevada County Library, Nevada City, 1987-88, Decide Team III, Nevada County, 1987—. Mem. Am. Chiropractic Assn., Toastmasters (sec. 1988, pres. 1989, edn. v.p. 1990), Calif. Chiropractic Assn., Soroptimists (chair environ. com. 1989-90, 90—). Republican.

BRUNO, KAY ANDERSON, pharmaceutical executive, speaker; b. Casper, Wyo., Aug. 4, 1941; d. James D. and Rhea (Wadsworth) Anderson; m. N.J. Bruno, Feb. 6, 1966 (div. 1985); children: James, Thomas, Michael. BS in Journalism, Northwestern U., 1963; cert. in advanced mgmt., Emory U., 1989. Assoc. editor Jour. Am. Med. Assn., Chgo., 1963-66; account exec. Gardner, Jones & Cowell, Chgo., 1966-69, Pub. Communications, Inc., Chgo., 1980; account supr. Hill & Knowlton, Chgo., 1981-85; sr. dir. pub. affairs Searle, Chgo., 1985—; guest lectr. Medill Sch. Journalism Northwestern U., 1989; lectr. to various groups. Bd. dirs. Juvenile Protective Assn., 1983—. Mem. Medill Sch. Journalism Alumni (v.p. 1989). Office: Searle 5200 Old Orchard Rd Skokie IL 60077

BRUNS, MARIA REYES, core pins manufacturing company executive; b. Rio Grande City, Tex., June 23, 1947; d. Manuel L. and Maria G. (Vela) Lopez; m. Dennis F. Bruns, Oct. 29, 1966; children: Dennis, Angela and Andrew (twins). Student pub. schs., La Grulla, Tex. Lic. real estate agt., Calif. Real estate agt. Tarbell Realtors, Norco, Calif., 1979-81, Devel. Dimensions, Covina, Calif., 1981-82, Republic Devel., Covina, 1982-83; office mgr., pres. Cal Pin Corp., Norco, 1982—. Coord., Neighborhood Watch, Norco. Recipient cert. of appreciation, Cal-Vet Paralyzed Vets., 1986, Missing Children Network, 1986, West Coast Vietnam Vets., 1988, Riverside Sheriff Assn. Mem. Nat. Fedn. Bus., Norco C. of C. Republican. Roman Catholic. Home: 3986 Center Ave Norco CA 91760 Office: Cal Pin Corp Ste 307 2059 Hamner St Norco CA 91760

BRUNSDALE, ANNE E., federal official; b. Mpls., Oct. 1, 1923. BA, U. Minn., 1945, MA, 1946; MA, Yale U., 1949. With Cen. Intelligence Agy., 1947-50, 56, Craig-Hallum Corp., Mpls., 1957-65; assoc. dir. publs. Free Soc. Assn., Washington, 1966-67, v.p. rsch.; rsch. assoc. Am. Enterprise Inst. for Pub. Policy Rsch., Washington, 1967-70, dir. of publs., 1970-77, mng. editor Regulation, 1977-85, resident fellow, 1984-85; vice chmn. U.S. Internat. Trade Commn., Washington, 1986-88, acting chmn., 1988-89, chmn., 1989—. Office: US Internat Trade Commn 500 E St SW Washington DC 20436*

BRUNSON, DOROTHY E., broadcasting executive; b. Glensville, Ga., Mar. 13, 1938; d. Wadis and Naomi (Ross) Edwards; children: Edward, Daniel. BS, Empire State Coll. Entered print communications industry, 1960-62; asst. gen. mgr. radio sta. WWRL, N.Y.C., 1964-68, corp. coordinator, liason dir., 1968-72; v.p. Howard Sanders Advt., Inc., N.Y.C., 1972-79; corp. v.p. Inner City Broadcasting Corp., N.Y.C., 1973-79, corp. gen. mgr., 1979; pres. Sta. WEBB, Balt., 1979, Sta. WIGO, Atlanta, 1979, Sta. WBMS, Wilmington, N.C., 1979—; lectr., speaker bus., econ. devel., affirmative action, communications, women rights, religious and human issues throughout country; panelist bus. and communications White House, 1977. Contbr. articles to Vogue, Black Enterprise, Newsweek. Recipient awards including citation NCCJ. Methodist. Office: Brunson Communication Inc Brunson Broadcasting Co 300 Druid Park Dr Baltimore MD 21215 also: Sta WIGO-AM 1532 Howell Mill Rd Atlanta GA 30318

BRUNTON, LINDA ANN, vacation center executive; b. Buffalo, May 30, 1942; d. Robert Thomas and Alice Elsa (Guttman) B. BS, SUNY, Cortland, 1964; MEd, Springfield (Mass.) Coll., 1970; postgrad., NYU, 1980-87. Cert. therapeutic recreation specialist. Phys. edn. tchr. Lewiston (N.Y.)-Porter Jr. High Sch., 1964-68; camp coord. Niagra County (N.Y.) Coun. Girl Scouts, 1970-71; dir. membership svcs. Freedom Valley Girl Scouts, Valley Forge, Pa., 1971-79; program dir. Camp Sun Mountain, Shawnee on Delaware, Pa., 1979-80; asst. dir. Capital Care Ctr., Columbus, Ohio, 1979-80; therapeutic recreation worker Phila. State Hosp., 1980-81; vacation ctr. dir. The Lighthouse, N.Y.C., 1981—; cons. Catholic Charities Community Residences, Amityville, N.Y., 1989-90; standards visitor Am. Camping Assn., 1979—.

BRUSH, SALLY ANDERSON, social services administrator; b. Cleve., Nov. 3, 1934; d. William Ervin and Marian Lois (Hagler) Anderson; m. Thomas Bart Brush, June 28, 1958; children: Bart Anderson, Andrew

Warren, Lisa Ann, Mark Thomas. AB, Smith Coll., 1956; MEd, U. Cin., 1982. Human svc. worker various pub., pvt. and religious agys., N.Y.C., Detroit and Cin., 1956-59; tchr. Mariemont Community Pre-Sch., Cin., 1972-74; divorce investigator Hamilton County Domestic Rels. Ct., Cin., 1974-76, counselor, 1976-78; founder, dir. Strengthening Families After Divorce, Cin., 1978-82; program coord. Aring Inst. Beech Acres, Cin., 1982-89, dir., 1990—; workshop presenter to cos., schs. and agys., Cin., 1978—; divorce mediator, Cin., 1978—; cons., Cin., 1978—. Polit. worker various candidates and tax levy campaigns, Cin., 1967—; campaign mgr., asst. mgr. for city coun. candidates, Cin., 1969-81; pres. class of 1956, Smith Coll., 1986-91. Recipient Disting. Alumnae award for women's studies U. Cin., 1983; grantee Dept. Justice and other orgns., 1978-81. Mem. AACD, Nat. Coun. for Children's Rights, Nat. Coun. on Family Rels., Ohio Assn. for Counseling and Devel. (Meritorious svc. award 1988), Greater Cin. Assn. for Counseling and Devel. (Disting. Svc. award 1988), Woman's City Club. Democrat. Home: 3804 Broadview Dr Cincinnati OH 45208 Office: Aring Inst Beech Acres 6881 Beechmont Ave Cincinnati OH 45230

BRUSS, KATHERINE VIVIAN, psychologist; b. Bloomington, Minn., Oct. 22, 1961; d. Franklin Alvin and Diane Vivian (Brehmer) B. BA, U. Minn., 1983; D in Psychology, Baylor U., 1988. Lic. psychologist, Ga. Psychol. fellow Mexia State U., Waco, Tex., 1984-85, Baylor U., Waco, 1985-86, McClennan County Juvenile Probation, Waco, 1986-87; psychologist Ga. State U., Atlanta, 1987—; psychologist Atlanta Women's Counseling Ctr., 1989—. Activist Pro-Choice Rally, Atlanta, 1989. Herber Joseph Reynolds Presdl. scholar Baylor U., 1985. Mem. Am. Psychol. Assn., Ga. Psychol. Assn. Home: 469 Oakdale Rd #10 Atlanta GA 30307 Office: Ga State U University Pla Atlanta GA 30303

BRUSSELL, MARY SUE, graphic arts company executive; b. Milw., Dec. 24, 1961; Mem. Printers Industry Am.; d. James William and Theresa Cecilia (Breclau) B. BA, U. Wis., 1984. Asst. mgr. Lerner Co., Thornton, Colo., 1986-87; sec. Stivers Temporary Pers., Aurora, Colo., 1987; advt. svcs. mgr. Cardiff Pub. Co., Englewood, Colo., 1987-89, Rocky Mountain Embossing Co., 1989—. Mem. Denver Advt. Fedn., Denver C. of C. Roman Catholic.

BRUST, SUSAN MELINDA, telecommunications executive; b. N.Y.C., Sept. 27, 1951; d. Stanley Milton and Preva Joan (Simons) B.; m. William S. Boorstein; children: Jon Bradley, Leigh Rachel. BA in Geology, Hunter Coll., 1973; postgrad., Bernard Baruch Coll., 1988—, Tel Aviv U., 1971, U. Colo., 1973. Sales rep. Burroughs Corp., N.Y.C., 1976-81; pvt. network specialist Tymnet, Inc., N.Y.C., 1981-85; regional sales mgr. Dama Telecommunications, N.Y.C., 1985-87; account exec. Network Equipment Tech., N.Y.C., 1987—; ind. telecommunications cons. Brust & Assocs., N.Y.C., 1983—. Exec. bd. mem. Jewish Guild for the Blind, N.Y.C., 1975; assoc. Spl. Olympics, N.Y.C., 1984—. Mem. Nat. Tay-Sachs Found., NAFE, Assn. Women in Computing, Empire Wo/Men in Telecommunications. Democrat. Home: 21 Dante St Larchmont NY 10538 Office: Network Equipment Tech 33 Whitehall St New York NY 10004

BRUZELIUS, CAROLINE ASTRID, art historian; b. Stockholm, Apr. 18, 1949; arrived in U.S., 1965; d. Axel Sture Bruzelius and Constance (Brickett) Brereton; m. Robert Weldon Wallace, May 15, 1982; 1 child, Anders Edward Axel. Wellesley Coll.; BA, Wellesley U., 1971; MA, Yale U., 1973, MPhil, 1974, PhD, 1977. Asst. prof. Dickinson Coll., Carlisle, Pa., 1977-79; researcher NEH, Paris, 1979-80; Mellon fellow and asst. prof. Harvard U., Cambridge, Mass., 1980-81; Mellon fellow, asst. prof. Duke U., Durham, N.C., 1982, assoc. prof., 1986—, chmn. art dept., 1989—. Author: Longpont and the Architecture of the Cistercian Order in the Thirteenth Century, Analecta cisterciensia, 1979, The Thirteenth Century Church at St.-Denis, 1985, The Brummer Collection in the Duke University Museum of Art, 1990. Recipient Summer award NEH, 1984, Rome Prize Am. Acad. on Rome, 1985-86, Dir.'s award Duke Mus., 1988.

BRYAN, APRIL BETH, food service executive; b. North Richland Hills, Tex., June 29, 1964; d. William Clarence Bryan and Avalon Marvelle (Johnson) Smith; m. Orville J. Smith, 1982. Grad. high sch., North Richland Hills. Various positions Steak and Ale Corp., Dallas, 1980-85; svc. capt. Pinnacle Club Corp. Am., Dallas, 1986-87, svc. dir., 1987-88; svc. mgr. Loews Anatole Hotel, Dallas, 1988-89, mgr. Nana Grill restaurant, 1989-90, tower food and beverage dir., 1990—; mem. Bacchus Wine Group, Loews Anatole Hotel, 1990; employee recognition mayor Loews Anatole Twp., Dallas, 1989—. Mem. Dallas Mus. Art, 1989-90. Mem. NAFE. Democrat. Office: Loews Anatole Hotel 2201 Stemmons Fwy Dallas TX 75207

BRYAN, BILLIE MARIE (MRS. JAMES A. MACKEY), biologist; b. Norfolk, Va., Dec. 30, 1932; d. William B. and Marie (Fortescue) Bryan; B.A. in Biology, U. Richmond, 1954; M.Ed., Am. U., 1966; m. James A. Mackey. Bacteriologist, Arlington County Health Dept., Arlington, Va., 1954-58; med. bacteriologist Walter Reed Army Inst. Research, Walter Reed Army Med. Center, Washington, 1959-62; tchr. Fairfax (Va.) High Sch., 1962-66; biologist NIH, Washington, 1966—. Mem. Am. Pub. Health Assn., Am. Soc. Info. Sci., Am. Med. Writers Assn., DAR. Contbr. articles to profl. jours. Home: 201 Quaint Acres Dr Silver Spring MD 20904 Office: NIH-NIDDK Westwood Bldg Rm 606 Bethesda MD 20892

BRYAN, CHRISTINA HELEN, labor relations specialist; b. Jamaica, N.Y., Dec. 29, 1948; d. Albert James and Margaret Mary (Jones) Bowers; m. John Warren Bryan, Oct. 17, 1970. BA, Hofstra U., 1976. Adjustment's coord. Hecht/May Co., Laurel, Md., 1971-73; asst. dir. continuing edn. Hofstra U., Hempstead, N.Y., 1976-78; asst. cataloguer Hofstra U., Hempstead, 1978-82; grad. intern personnel Blue Cross/Blue Shield, N.Y.C., 1983-84; personnel rep. The Bank of N.Y., Valley Stream, 1984-85; human resource devel. cons. The Port Authority of N.Y. and N.J., N.Y.C., 1985-87, labor relations specialist, 1987—; cons. L.I. Railroad, Hollis, N.Y., 1987—, Chase Manhattan Bank, N.Y.C., 1987—. Calligrapher posters, 1978—; seminar lectr. Mem. Am. Soc. Personnel Adminstrs. (bd. dirs. N.Y. 1987-88), Am. Mgmt. Soc., NAFE, N.Y. State Banker's Assn. (mem. personnel rels. com.). Roman Catholic. Home: 157 Sherman Ave Merrick NY 11566 Office: The Port Authority NY-NJ Labor Rels One World Trade Ctr 61S New York NY 10048

BRYAN, CLARICE ADINA, lawyer; b. St. Thomas, V.I., Apr. 30, 1923; d. C. Arthur and Iza Anita (Lanclos) B.; A.B., Howard U., 1943; LL.B., Columbia U. and Howard U., 1949; 1 dau., Charlene Smith. Admitted to V.I. bar, 1950; tax assessor Govt. of V.I., 1950-60, asst. atty. gen., 1961-65, asst. commr. of labor, 1965-68, dir. consumer affairs, 1968-73; individual practice law, St. Thomas, 1950—; dir. People's Bank, 1971-75; trustee V.I. Retirement System. Vice pres. V.I. Constl. Conv., 1977, del., 1964, 81; mem. UN Status of Women Commn. Mem. ABA, Internat. Women Lawyers Assn., V.I. Bus. and Profl. Women (state pres. 1964-65). Roman Catholic. Home: 245A Bourne Field Saint Thomas VI 00801 Office: Rm B2 Professional Bldg Saint Thomas VI 00801

BRYAN, EDNA EUGENIE, nursing administrator; b. Two River Bridge, W.I., Feb. 21, 1936; came to U.S., 1967; d. Samuel Uriala and Brenda (Wellington) Distant; m. Everton Wesley Bryan, Mar. 25, 1961; children: Sheila, Angus. BS, Mercy Coll., 1978; MS in Health Care Mgmt., Biscayne Coll., 1983. RN N.Y. Charge nurse Southwestern Hosp., London, 1962-63, Purley Hosp., Surrey, Eng., 1963, Wilson Hosp., Mitchum, Eng., 1963-64; supr. St. Heliers Hosp., Surrey, 1964-65; vis. nurse Croydon Dist. Nursing Assn., Surrey, 1965-67; charge nurse Mt. Sinai Hosp., N.Y.C., 1967-68, Bronx Lebanon Hosp., N.Y.C., 1968-69; asst. head nurse Westchester Square Hosp., N.Y.C., 1970-71; supr. No. Med. Group, N.Y.C., 1971-73; asst. dir. nursing Waring Nursing Home, N.Y.C., 1973-85; head nurse Miami (Fla.) VA Hosp., 1985—; supr. nursing Miami Jewish Home and Hosp. for Aged, 1985-89, staff devel. coord., 1989—; cons., inservice instr., N.Y.C., 1974-75. Mem. pub. edn. com. Cancer Soc., 1982—. Mem. Nat. Assn. Female Execs. Republican. Mem. Assembly of God Ch. Home: 19445 NW 19th Ct Miami FL 33056 Office: Miami Jewish Home & Hosp for Aged 151 NE 52d St Miami FL 33137

BRYAN, GLORIA JANE, legal assistant; b. Montreal, Que., Can., Feb. 5, 1959; came to U.S., 1963; d. Earl John and Gloria Ruth (Bohart) Peters; m. Richard E. Bryan, July 17, 1979 (div. Aug. 1983); 1 child, Sara Jayne. Student, Broward Community Coll., Ft. Lauderdale, Fla., 1989—. Sec. Simons & Schlesinger, Ft. Lauderdale, 1981-82; legal asst. Chidnese & McCollem, Ft. Lauderdale, 1982—. Mem. Peace Luth. Sch. PTA, Ft. Lauderdale, 1989—, Am. Heart Assn., Ft. Lauderdale, 1989—. Mem. Aerobics and Fitness Assn. Am., NAFE. Office: Chidnese & McCollem 201 SE 12th St Fort Lauderdale FL 33316

BRYAN, MARY ANN, interior designer; b. Dallas, Nov. 16, 1929; d. William C. and Harriet E. (Carter) Green; m. Frank Wingfield Bryan, Aug. 31, 1957; children: Frank Wingfield, Elizabeth F. BS in Interior Design U. Tex., 1950. Head of stock Foleys Dept. Store, Houston, 1952-53, asst. buyer, 1953-54, buyer, 1955-60, exec. tng. dir., 1960-61; owner, pres. The Bryan Design Assocs., Inc., Houston, 1961—; mem. adv. bd. Houston Art Inst. Active Bluebird Circle; U.S. del. Friendship Among Women. Mem. Am. Soc. Interior Designers (nat. bd., 1984-86, pres. Gulf Coast chpt. 1975), Chi Omega. Republican. Home: 10023 Locke Ln Houston TX 77042 Office: The Bryan Design Assocs 1502 Augusta St 100 Houston TX 77057

BRYANT, ANN ALEACE, recreation therapist; b. Roanoke, Va., Apr. 13, 1961; d. John Junior Bryant and Alice Margaret (Davis) Rice. BS, Longwood Coll., 1983; M of Pub. Adminstrn., Auburn U., 1988. Cert. therapeutic recreation specialist. Recreation therapist VA Med. Ctr., Tuskegee, Ala., 1983-89; therapeutic recreation cons. VA Med. Ctr., Montgomery, Ala., 1984-89, recreation therapist, Houston, 1989—; adj. prof. Ala. State U., Montgomery, 1988-89. Recipient Superior Performance award VA Med. Ctr. Recreation Service, Tuskegee, 1983, Outstanding Performance award, 1984, 86, 87, 88; Spl. Recognition cert. U.S. Congress, 1985. Mem. AAUW, Nat. Therapeutic Recreation Soc., Nat. Recreation and Parks Assn., Am. Therapeutic Recreation Assn., Alpha Sigma Phi, Delta Psi Kappa, Phi Kappa Phi. Avocations: reading, cooking, crossword puzzles, walking. Home: 3401 Ocee St #805 Houston TX 77063 Office: VA Med Ctr Recreation Service (11K) 2002 Holcombe Blvd Houston TX 77030

BRYANT, BARBARA EVERITT, public information officer; b. Ann Arbor, Mich., Apr. 5, 1926; d. William Littell and Dorothy (Wallace) Everitt; m. John H. Bryant, Aug. 14, 1948; children: Linda Bryant Valentine, Randal E., Lois B. AB, Cornell U., 1947; MA, Mich. State U., 1967, PhD, 1970. Editor art Chem. Engring. mag. McGraw-Hill Pub. Co., N.Y.C., 1947-48; editorial rsch. asst. U. Ill., Urbana, 1948-49; free-lance editor, writer, 1950-61; with continuing edn. adminstrn. dept. Oakland Univ., Rochester, Mich., 1961-66; grad. rsch. asst. Mich. State Univ., East Lansing, 1966-70; sr. analyst to v.p. Market Opinion Rsch., Detroit, 1970-77, sr. vp., 1977-89; dir. Bur. of the Census, U.S. Dept. of Commerce, 1989 —. Author: High School Students Look at Their World, 1970, American Women Today & Tomorrow, 1977; contbr. articles to profl. jours. Mem. U.S. Census Adv. Com., Washington, 1980-86, Mich. Job Devel. Authority, Lansing, Mich., 1980-85; state editor LWV of Mich., 1959-61. Mem. Detroit Chpt. of Women in Communications, Inc. (pres. 1974-75, Nat. Headliner award 1980), Detroit Chpt. of Am. Mktg. Assn. (pres. 1976-77), Am. Mktg. Assn. (midwestern v.p. 1978-80, v.p. mktg. rsch. 1982-84). Republican. Presbyterian. Avocation: swimming. Home: 400 N St SW Washington DC 20024 Office: Bur Census Fed Ctr Suitland MD 20233 also: Bur of the Census Washington DC 20233

BRYANT, DEBORAH REID, university official, counselor; b. Elmira, N.Y., Dec. 31, 1950; d. Wilbur James and Beatrice (Bonner) Reid; m. Cleveland Walker Bryant, Jr., July 3, 1976; 1 child, Jason Reid. B.S. in Phys. Edn., Health, Recreation, Boston U., 1972; M.Ed. in Counseling, SUNY-Brockport, 1975. Cert. counselor. Asst. dir. ednl. opportunity program Corning Community Coll., N.Y., 1972-73; child devel. practitioner, cons. Comprehensive Interdisciplinary Devel., Elmira, N.Y., 1973-74; asst. dir. student activities Monroe Community Coll., Rochester, N.Y., 1975-77; asst. dean student devel. U. New Orleans, 1978-81; dir. ctr. commuter services Loyola U., New Orleans, 1981-86; assoc. dir. career devel. U. Md., College Park, 1987—. Bd. dirs., family life task force S. Central Conf. United Ch. of Christ. Afro-Am. scholar Boston U., 1972. Mem. So. Assn. Coll. Student Affairs, La. Assn. Women Deans, Adminstrs. and Counselors, Assn. Coll. Unions Internat., Nat. Entertainment and Campus Activities Assn., Am. Assn. Counseling and Devel., Am. Coll. Personnel Assn. (mem. various coms.), La. Coll. Personnel Assn. (mem. exec. bd.), Delta Sigma Theta. Democrat. Avocations: walking; exercising; reading. Office: U Md Career Devel Ctr 3121 Hornbake College Park MD 20742

BRYANT, DONNA LOUISE, employee benefits specialist, consultant; b. Waltham, Mass., May 2, 1946; d. Allen Clifford and Shirley Ethyl (Hartwell) Durgin; children: Adam, Benjamin. BA, R.I. Coll., 1969. Adminstrv. asst. Am. Edn. Rsch. Assn., Washington, 1969-72; tech. editor Policy Rsch. Inst. Syracuse U., Washington, 1972-74; adminstrv. asst. Citizens for Hwy. Safety, Washington, 1975-77; sales trainee traffic control div. 3M Corp., St. Paul, 1977; mktg. dir. Park-Nicollet Health Plan, Mpls., 1977-82; mktg. cons. Bryant Mktg., Austin, Tex., 1982-89; employee benefits mgr. Lincoln Nat. Life, Austin, 1990—; cons. United Healthcare Corp., Austin, Lincoln Nat. Author poetry and songs. Treas. La Leche League, Mpls. and Austin; copres. Forest North Neighborhood Assn., Austin. Mem. Nat. Assn. Exec. Women, Bus. and Profl. Women, Austin Assn. Life Underwriters.

BRYANT, EVA LOU, sales executive; b. Orrick, Mo., Aug. 15, 1941; d. William Maurice and Lena Mae (Gooch) Hall; m. David Lynn Bryant, Aug. 20, 1960; children—Alan, Karen, James, Diane, Jason, Zane. A.A., Purdue U., Ft. Wayne, 1982; A.A., Ind. U., 1982, B.S., 1983. Owner Day Nursery, Colorado Springs, Colo., 1973-76; asst. mdse. coordinator House of Fabrics, Hastings, Nebr., 1978-79; with GTE Directories Corp., Ft. Wayne, 1980-81, service rep., 1981-83, telephone sales rep., 1983-85, dist. sales mgr., 1985-86; telemktg. mgr. Stas. WMEE/WQHK, 1986-88; discount brokerage mgr. Lincoln Nat. Bank and Trust Co., Ft. Wayne, 1987-89; with sales dept. Warren's Fashion Fabrics, Orangeburg, 1989—; owner, mgr. Mo. farm. Vestry chmn. St. Alban's Episcopal Ch., Ft. Wayne, 1986—, (lic. layreader and chalice-bearer of Episcopal diocese), active PTA, Episcopal Ch. Women, Girl Scouts U.S.A., Boy Scouts Am., 4-H, Little League, Am. Arthritis Found., Am. Cancer Soc., Am. Heart Assn. Recipient Pres.'s award, GTE, 1984, Top Gen. Sales award, 1984, Top Sales Travel Incentive, 1985, 86. Mem. Am. Bus. Women's Assn., AAUW, Nat. Assn. Female Execs., Delta Zeta. Republican. Episcopalian. Avocations: needlework, reading, sports.

BRYANT, FRANCES JANE, newspaper editor; b. Cushing, Okla., Dec. 10, 1933; d. Edward Glahn and Dorothy Evelyn (McLean) B. AA, Christian Coll., Columbia, Mo., 1953; BJ, U. Mo., 1955. Reporter The Norman (Okla.) Transcript, 1955-57, wire editor, 1957-59, city editor, 1959-67, mng. editor, 1967—. Bd. dirs. Juvenile Services, Inc., Cleveland County, Okla., 1981-87, pres., 1984-85; bd. dirs. Cleveland County chpt. ARC, 1987—. Named Oustanding Bus. Woman Bus. and Profl. Women, Norman, 1971, State Woman of Year Theta Sigma Phi, U. Okla., 1968; recipient Disting. Alumni award Columbia Coll. (formerly Christian Coll.), 1980. Mem. AP/Okla. News Execs. (pres. 1970-71), Soc. Profl. Journalists, Altrusa Internat. (pres. Norman chpt. 1969-71). Democrat. Episcopalian. Home: 606 Sherwood Dr Norman OK 73071 Office: The Norman Transcript 215 E Comanche Norman OK 73069

BRYANT, GAY, magazine editor, writer; b. Newcastle, Eng., Oct. 5, 1945; came to U.S., 1970; d. Richard King and Catherine (Shiel) B.; m. Charles Childs, Apr. 10, 1982. Student, St. Clare's Coll., Oxford, Eng., 1961-63. Sr. editor Penthouse Mag., N.Y.C., 1968-74; assoc. editor Oui mag., N.Y.C., 1974-75; founding editor New Dawn mag., N.Y.C., 1975-79; exec. editor Working Woman mag., N.Y.C., 1979-81, editor, 1981-84; editor, v.p. Family Circle mag., N.Y.C., 1984-86; editor in chief Infashion mag., N.Y.C., 1987-88, New Woman mag., N.Y.C., 1988-90, Mirabella mag., N.Y.C., 1990—; adj. prof. Sch. Journalism, NYU, 1982-87. Author: The Underground Travel Guide, 1973, How I Learned To Like Myself, 1975, The Working Woman Report, 1984. Recipient award Acad. Women Achievers, YMCA, N.Y.C., 1982. Mem. Women's Media Group, Am. Soc. Mag. Editors. Home: 34 Horatio St New York NY 10014 Office: Mirabella Mag 10 E 53d St 14th Fl New York NY 10022

BRYANT, JEANNETTE MARIE, educator, writer; b. Cumberland, Md., Jan. 11, 1939; d. Scott and Mabel Jeannette (Swisher) Davis; m. James C. Bryant, Aug. 12, 1960; children: Chet, Stephanie. BA, Shepherd Coll., Shepherdstown, W.Va., 1967; postgrad., George Mason U., 1989—. Editor, writer Nat. Wildlife Fedn., County of Fairfax, Vienna, 1978-85; tchr. Fairfax, Va., 1964-70, 89; primary coord. Carol Morgan Sch., Santo Dominco, Dominican Republic; tchr. gifted and talented ctr. Forest Edge Elem. Sch., Reston, Va., 1985—. Author, editor: (tchrs. guide) Wildlife Week, 1984, Teachers Guide, 1985, Conservation Directory, 1979-85. Leader 4-H Club, Great Falls, Va., 1978. Mem. Nat. Assn. Environ. Edn., Nat. Assn. for Gifted and Talented, Nat. Assn. Sci. Tchrs. Methodist. Home: 759 Aplewood Ln Great Falls VA 22066

BRYANT, JOANNE CATHERINE, educator; b. North English, Iowa, May 17, 1930; d. Vincent A. and Margaretta Jane (Johnston) Donahoe; m. Harvey Lee. BS in Edn., Avila Coll., 1951; MEd, U. Ill., 1953. Tchr. East Whitier (Calif.) Sch. Dist., 1953-56, Creole Petroleum Corp., Tiajuana, Venezuela, 1956-58, Internat. Petroleum, Talara, Peru, 1963-68, Internat. Sch., Tripoli, Libya, 1971; founder of Beginning English Class Needs Ctr., Taft, Calif., 1987--; vol., translator Kern County Dept. Welfare & Public Health, Taft, 1983—, NEEDS Ctr., Flying Samaritans, 1988—. Co-chmn. Jr. Red Cross, New Canaan, Conn., 1976-78; bd. dirs. Salvation Army, Taft, West Side Dist. Hosp., Taft, Community Health Ctrs., Kern County, Bakersfield, Calif., Assistance League of Bakersfield, 1990. Mem. AAUW (v.p. 1972-73), Concerned About Petroleum (bd. dirs. 1985—), Petroleum Engring. Wives (bd. dirs. 1988-89), Soroptimist Internat. of Taft (Women Helping Women award, 1988). Home: 829 Philippine Taft CA 93268

BRYANT, KAREN WORSTELL, financial consultant; b. Cadillac, Mich., Sept. 7, 1942; d. Harley Orville and Rose Edith (Bell) Worstell; children: Lynda Jean, Tracey Jo, Cynthia Jill, Troy Thomas; m. Robert Melvin Bryant, Nov. 29, 1968. Student, Cen. Mich. U., 1963-67, Mich. State U., 1966, Johns Hopkins U., 1982-83. Sales rep. Xerox Corp., Southfield, Mich., 1972-74; specialist cons. and employment contracts policy study Policy Study Group, Johnson & Johnson, IBM World Trade Asia and others, Tokyo, 1974-79; area sales mgr. Universal Plastics, McLean, Va., 1979-81; exec. product mgr. The Western Union Telegraph Co., Upper Saddle River, N.J., 1981-86; dir. mktg. and sales support The Nat. Guardian Corp., Greenwich, Conn., 1986-88; fin. cons. Shearson Lehman Bros., Paramus, N.J., 1988—. Mem. NAFE, Internat. Platform Assn., N.Y. State Horse Coun., Nature Conservancy. Republican. Home: 19 Sky Meadow Rd Suffern NY 10901 Office: Shearson Lehman Bros E 130 Ridgewood Ave Ground Fl Paramus NJ 07653

BRYANT, LINA ANTONETTA, advertising copywriter; b. Louisville, June 6, 1960; d. Jules E. and Maria Garcia (Gentile) Brackett; m. Richard Earl Bryant, Mar. 3, 1984. BA, B. Applied Sci., U. Louisville, 1982. Photo editor, mng. editor Thinker Mag., Louisville, 1980-82; editor Workforce Newspaper, Louisville, 1984; culinary mgr. Amelia Brown Frazier Harrods Creek, Ky., 1984-87; asst. mgr. Words Today, Louisville, 1987-88; adminstrv. sec./pub. rels. coord. Green Valley Conv. Ctr., New Albany, Ind., 1988-89; advt. copywriter Westminster/John Knox Press, Louisville, 1989—; co-founder, pub. rels. coord. Feathered Friends Soc., Louisville, 1988—. Contbr. articles and photographs to newspapers, mags., jours. Mem. Deer Park Neighborhood Assn., Louisville, 1987—, Louisville Zool. Soc., 1987—, Friends of Animals of Ky., Louisville, 1986—, Kentuckiana Cage-Bird Club, Louisville, 1989—. Mem. Women in Communications, Am. Heart Assn. (com. mem. Ky. affiliate 1989—). Democrat. Office: Westminster/John Knox Press 100 Witherspoon St Louisville KY 40202-1396

BRYANT, LYNDA JEAN DARDEN, infosystems computer/security program manager; b. Washington, Oct. 13, 1941; d. Jesse Robert Darden and Virginia Mae (Lamm) Darden Zierdt; m. 1960 (div. 1984). BA in Mgmt. Info. Systems, Eckerd Coll., 1984. Cert. info. systems auditor. Statis. officer U.S. Bur. Census, Washington, 1961-67; program analyst Gen. Electric Co., Largo, Fla., 1967-71, systems analyst, 1971-78, dept. mgmt. and resource analyst, 1978-82, computer security and system designer, 1982-87; EDP auditor Planters Nat. Bank, Rocky Mount, N.C., 1987-88; program mgr. Office Tech. Assistance/Fed. Systems and Integration Mgmt., Falls Church, Va., 1988—. Contbr. articles to profl. jours. Mem. EDP Auditors (publs. chmn. 1987-88). Democrat. Methodist. Home: 7409 Meadowleigh Way Alexandria VA 22310 Office: US GSA-OTA-FEDSIM 5203 Leesburg Pike Ste 400 Falls Church VA 22041

BRYANT, MARTHA J., accountant; b. Jersey Shore, Pa., May 3, 1949; d. Paul E. and Carolina M. (Vairo) B. BS in Health and Phys. Edn., Lock Haven U., 1975; AA, Williamsport Area Cmmnty Coll., 1977, AS in Acctg. and Bus. Mgmt., 1977, AA, 1978. Cert. health and phys. edn. tchr. Office worker Citizens Cable Co., Williamsport, Pa., 1967-71, Lock Haven (Pa.) U., 1973-74; accounts payable clerk Williamsport Area Community Coll., 1977-78, sec. gen. svcs., 1978-83, sec. transp., 1983-86; acct. I West Branch Drug and Alcohol Abuse Commn., Williamsport, 1986-88; acct. Radiant Steel Products Co., Williamsport, 1988—; instr. personal computer Williamsport Area Community Coll., 1984-85. Developer (computer programs) Departmental Budget Tracking, 1984, Patient Information System, 1987. Dir. swimming YWCA Day Camp, Williamsport, 1971-72; instr. swimming YWCA, Williamsport, 1975-84, YMCA, Williamsport, 1985—, ARC (10 yr. pin 1985); coach varsityfield hockey Williamsport Area Community Coll., 1978-81; cantor St. Boniface Ch., Williamsport, 1977; pres. Williamsport Civic Chorus, 1986-88; cast mem. Community Theatre League, Williamsport, 1986-89. Recipient Bishop Hafey award St. Lawrence Ch. Cath. Daus., 1965, acad. scholarship Williamsport Area Community Coll., 1977. Mem. Greater Williamsport Arts Coun., Wililamsport Music Club (treas. 1989—), Repaz Elks Bank. Democrat. Roman Catholic. Home: 330 E Mountain Ave South Wililamsport PA 17701 Office: Radiant Steel Products Co 205 Locust St Williamsport PA 17701

BRYANT, MARY SNELL, aircraft sales management executive; b. Mexico, Mo., Feb. 27, 1949; d. William Ernest and Marie Louise (Austin) Snell; m. Timothy Clark Bryant, Jan. 17, 1981. BA Northwestern U., 1971; MBA U. Ill., 1973. CPA, Ill., Tex. Dir. eval. and projects G.D. Searle & Co., Skokie, Ill., 1977-78, spl. asst. to exec. v.p. fin., 1979; dir. planning Searle Med. Products, Dallas, 1980, controller ventures, 1981; dir. planning Pearle Health Services, Inc., Dallas, 1981-83, v.p. internat., 1983-85; mgr. mgmt. cons. services Alexander Grant & Co. (now known as Grant Thornton), Tampa, Fla., 1985-87; gen. mgr. R&B Aviation, Clearwater, Fla., 1987-88; instr. pilot Piper Aircraft Corp., Vero Beach, Fla., 1988-89, mgr. ea. region, 1989—; trustee Am. Stage Co., 1986-89. Treas., bd. dirs. St. Petersburg YWCA, 1986-88. Winner Great So. Air Race, 1988. Mem. AICPA, Tex. Soc. CPAs, Ill. Soc. CPAs, Fla. Race Pilots Assn., Air Race Classic Ltd., Aircraft Owners and Pilots Assn., The 99s Club (membership chmn. Suncoast chpt. 1987-88). Home: 307 Brightwaters Blvd NE Saint Petersburg FL 33704

BRYANT, MELISSA DUNBAR, registered investment advisor; b. Paducah, Ky., Oct. 16, 1957; d. Oscar Sims and Nancy Lee (Stevens) B. B in Gen. Studies, U. Ky., 1979. Fgn. currency teller Liberty Nat. Bank & Trust, Louisville, 1981-83; investment adv. Morton H. Sachs & Co., Louisville, 1983--. Republican. Office: Morton H Sachs & Co 1346 S 3d St Louisville KY 40208

BRYANT, PAMELA KAYE, registered nurse; b. Cullman, Ala., Aug. 19, 1953; d. James Franklin and Dorothy Marie (McAfee) Hancock; m. Patrick Dwight Bryant, Oct. 22, 1971; children: Joshua Patrick, Jody Lee. AAS in Nursing cum laude, Wallace State Community Coll., 1978; BS in Nursing with honors, U. Ala., Birmingham, 1982. Registered nurse, Ala. Nursing asst. Cullman Med. Ctr., 1975-76; RN Ensor, Baccus, Williamson OB/GYN, Cullman, 1978-80, Carraway Meth. Med. Ctr., Birmingham, 1982-85, Cullman Internal Medicine, 1985-89; RN GI lab. Cullman Med. Ctr., 1990—. RN ARC, Birmingham, 1983. Recipient various awards Ala. State Fair, local county fairs for pen, ink and pencil drawings. Mem. Sigma Theta Tau. Democrat. Baptist. Home: 401 Arnold St SE Cullman AL 35055

BRYANT, RUTH ALYNE, banker; b. Memphis, Jan. 12, 1924; d. James Walter and Leola (Edgar) B. Student, Rhodes Coll. (formerly Southwestern Coll.), Memphis, 1941-43. Clk. Fed. Res. Bank of St. Louis (Memphis Br.), 1943-47, exec. sec., 1947-68, asst. cashier, 1968-69, asst. v.p., 1969-73, v.p., 1973—. Trustee chancellor's coun. U. Mo., St. Louis, 1979—, chmn., 1985-88; mem. adv. bd. Salvation Army, St. Louis, 1983—, DePaul Health Ctr., St. Louis, 1984-87; mem. adv. coun. Hope Ctr., 1987, chmn., 1990—; chmn. adv. coun. Riverway Sch., 1989—; bd. dirs. Assocs. of St. Louis U. Librs.,

1977—, pres., 1983-85; bd. dirs. The Vanderschmidt's Sch., 1980-86, Internat. Edn. Consortium, 1988—, St. Louis Merc. Libr., 1989—; trustee Mo. Coun. on Econ. Edn., 1989—. Mem. Am. Inst. Banking (nat. women's com. 1962-63, pres. Memphis chpt. 1968-69), Mo. Bankers Assn. (mktg. and pub. relations com. 1974-76), Nat. Assn. Bank Women (editor Woman Banker 1959-62, v.p. so. region 1967-68, v.p. 1969-70, pres. 1970-71, trustee ednl. found. 1974-75), English Speaking Union (bd. dirs. 1989—), Bank Mktg. Assn. (dir. Mo.-Ill. chpt. 1976-79). Home: 4466 W Pine Blvd Apt 15E Saint Louis MO 63108 Office: Fed Res Bank of St Louis 411 Locust St Saint Louis MO 63102

BRYANT, TARA ANN, training specialist; b. Smithtown, N.Y., Nov. 3, 1963; d. Thomas Nelson and Kathleen Mary (Repetto) B. BA, SUNY, Stony Brook, 1985, MS in Tech. Systems Mgmt., 1986; EdM, Harvard U., 1990, Harvard U., 1990. Cert. secondary sch. social studies tchr., N.Y. Substitute tchr. Three Village Central Sch. Dist., Stony Brook, N.Y., 1984-86; grad. teaching asst. SUNY, Stony Brook, 1985-86; exec. asst. to dir. mgmt. info. systems unit City of N.Y., dept. of parks and recreation, N.Y.C., 1986-87, fiscal auditor, 1987; tng. and orientation adminstr. Price-Waterhouse, N.Y.C., 1987-89. Vol. Spl. Olympics, Hauppauge, N.Y., 1984, Three Village Dem. Club, Stony Brook, 1986; campaign worker, Hochbrueckner for Congress, Stony Brook, 1986; roadrace organizer, Mfr.'s Hanover Corp. Challenge, Price Waterhouse, 1989; co-chmn., dean's adv. com., Harvard Grad. Sch. Edn., 1989-90. Mem. Nat. Assn. Exec. Women, MASS-11 User's Group, Digital Equipment Computer User Group. Roman Catholic.

BRYNER, LOIS CATHARINE, educator; b. Wrightsville, York, Pa., Apr. 25, 1923; d. Charles Wilbur and Carrie Catharine (Waltman) B. BS, Bloomsburg (Pa.) U., 1944; MA, Bucknell U., 1948; postgrad., Pa. state U., 1963. Cert. elem. tchr., Pa. Tchr. 4th, 5th, 6th graders Danville (Pa.) Area Sch., from 1944, head tchr., 1951-89, ret., 1989. Mem. Trinity United Meth. Ch., Danville Women's Club; cert. lay speaker Meth. Ch.; vol. Medicare and Medicaid, AARP. Recipient Am. Legion award; named Outstanding Elem. Tchr. Am., 1972. Mem. NEA, Pa. State Edn. Assn., Am. Assn. Ret. Persons Pa., Bus. Profl. Women's Club (charter mem., pres. 1955-56), College Club (pres. 1962-63, 82-83, 90), Soroptomist Club (v.p. 1962-63), Cen. Susquehanna Intermediate Unit, Insvc. Coun., Nat. Ret. Tchrs. Assn., Beta Sigma Phi (Lady of yr.1986), Delta Kappa Gamma.

BRYSON, DOROTHY PRINTUP, retired educator; b. Britton, S.D., Dec. 2, 1894; d. David Lawrence and Marion Harland (Gamsby) Printup; m. Archer Butler Hulbert, June 16, 1923 (dec. Dec. 1933); children: Joanne Woodward, Nancy Printup; m. Franklin Fearing Wing, Sept. 15, 1938 (dec. Mar. 1942); m. Arthur Earl Bryson, Feb. 15, 1964 (dec. Apr. 1979). AB, Oberlin Coll., 1915; AM, Radcliffe Coll., 1916; LHD (hon.), Colo. Coll., 1989. Instr. Latin, Tenn. Coll., Murfreesboro, 1916-18; tchr. Latin, prin. high sch., Britton, 1918-20; instr. classics Colo. Coll., Colorado Springs, 1921-22, 23-25, sec., instr., head resident, 1951-60; tchr. latin San Luis Prep. Sch., Colorado Springs, 1934-36, 41-42, Sandia Sch., Albuquerque, 1937-39, Westlake Sch., L.A., 1946-49; exec. dir. YWCA, Colorado Springs, 1942-46, 49-51; editor western history Stewart Commn., Colorado Springs, 1934-41; ret., 1960. Editor: Overland to the Pacific, 5 vols., 1934-41. Pres., bd. dirs. Day Nursery, Colorado Springs, 1933-37. Fellow Aelioian Lit. Soc., 1920-21; scholar U. Chgo., 1920-21. Mem. LWV (v.p., bd. dirs. Colorado Springs 1943-45), Women's Ednl. Soc. Colo. Coll. (pres., bd. dirs. 1955—), Reviewers' Club (officer 1923—), Woman's Lit. Club (officer 1924-34), Phi Beta Kappa. Republican. Episcopalian. Home: 107 W Cheyenne Rd Apt 610 Colorado Springs CO 80906

BRYSON, JOYCE, transportation executive; b. Mt. Clemens, Minn., Apr. 21, 1928; d. Arthur and Norma (Watson) Champion; m. John Bryson (div.); children: David, Robert, Arthur. Student, Mich. State U., 1949, Sullins Coll., 1950. Sales Real Estate One, Algonac, Mich., 1973-77; owner, pres. Champion Auto Ferry, Harsens Island, Mich., 1977—; owner Port Welcome, 1989—. Mem. Harsens Island Garden Club (pres. 1989—). Republican. Home: 1664 N Channel Harsens Island MI 48028

BUATTI, MARYANNE, lawyer; b. Bronx, N.Y., Feb. 25, 1956; m. Carlos Ramos, Aug. 14, 1977; children: Lauren Buatti Ramos, Alexis Buatti Ramos. BA in Sociology cum laude, St. John's U., 1977; JD with distinction, Hofstra U., 1982. Bar: N.Y. 1983. Assoc. Generosa & Carusona, Malverne, N.Y., 1983-85, Golden, Upton, Generosa & Carusona, Lynbrook, N.Y., 1985-87, Golden, Wexler & Sarnese, Garden City, N.Y., 1987—. Mem. N.Y. State Bar Assn., Nassau County Bar Assn. Office: Golden Wexler & Sarnese 377 Oak St Garden City NY 11530

BUBEN, ARLENE CAROL, state agency administrator; b. Rochester, N.Y., Aug. 8, 1948; d. Joseph and Isabelle (Krol) B; m. Lawrence Hurless, Dec. 20, 1980. BS in Modern Lang. and English, Northeastern U., 1969, MBA, 1975. Program facilitator Salt Lake Community Coll., Salt Lake City; planning and project mgr. S.E. Idaho Coun. of Govts., Pocatello; dir. S.E. Idaho Pvt. Industry Coun., Pocatello. Mem. NAFE, Community Svcs. Coun., Zonta. Home: 1651 Alvin Ricken Dr Pocatello ID 83201

BUBENIK, PATRICIA JEAN HADLE, assistant superintendent; b. Denver, Jan. 12, 1947; d. H. Paul and Allie Hadle; B.A., Colo. State U., 1969; M.A., U. Calif., Santa Cruz, 1970; Ed.D., U. San Francisco, 1981; m. David M. Bubenik, June 21, 1969. Tchr. Madrone Sch., Sunnyvale Sch. Dist. (Calif.), 1970-77; tchr. Demonstration Sch. for Gifted, San Jose State U., 1977; lang. arts specialist Sunnyvale Sch. Dist., 1977-78, vice prin., Madrone Sch., 1978-79, prin. summer sch., 1979, prin. Lakewood Sch., 1979-82; prin. Columbia Community Sch., Sunnyvale, 1982-85; asst. supt. Mountain View Sch. Dist., 1985—; ednl. cons., Calif., 1977—; creator Kids Can Write Project, Kids' View mag.; founder Jr. Scribe, dist. wide student mag., Challenge Team; co-dir. Project Cause; chair in-sch. scouting div. Bd. dirs. Calif. Young People's Theatre, Umbrella House; founder Mayor's Youth Coun., 1964. IDEA Fellow, 1986—, Bay Area Writing Project fellow, U. Calif., Berkeley, 1978; Boettcher Found. scholar, 1965. Recipient Vol. award Calif. Parks and Recreation Assn., 1983, Award of Merit, Boy Scouts Am.; named one of 100 Exec. Educators, 1988. Mem. Assn. Calif. Sch. Adminstrs. (exec. bd., chair curriculum and instruction leaders com.), Women Leaders in Edn. (pres.), Assn. Curriculum and Supervision Devel., Santa Clara Reading Coun. (exec. bd.), Calif. Reading Assn., Calif. Assn. Gifted, Calif. Assn. Tchrs. English, Internat. Reading Assn., Am. Assn. Sch. Adminstrs., Phi Delta Kappa, Phi Beta Kappa, Phi Kappa Phi, Phi Sigma Iota. Club: Women Leaders in Edn. Author: A New Direction: Focusing on the Whole Person Through the Affective Domain, 1977; Effects of Principal-Delivered Written Positive Reinforcement on Teacher and Class Behavior, 1981; contbr. articles to profl. jours. Office: 220 View St Mountain View CA 94041

BUBIER, ELLEN STEWART, publishing executive; b. Atlanta, Nov. 2, 1962; d. Herbert Ledyard and Mary Ellen (Luttrell) Stewart. Student, U. Paris, 1983; BA, U. of the South, 1984. Intern Atlanta Art Papers Inc., summer 1984, mng. editor, 1984-86; free-lance cons., 1986-87; gen. mgr. Southline Press Inc., Atlanta, 1987-88; office mgr. In-House Design, Atlanta, 1989, The Writers Group, Atlanta, 1989—. Mem. The Nature Conservancy, The Arts Exchange (bd. dirs. 1985-86), Atlanta Art Papers Inc. (bd. dirs. 1984-87). Episcopalian. Home: 1140 Springdale Rd NE Atlanta GA 30306 Office: The Writers Group 40 Inwood Circle Atlanta GA 30309

BUBNIC, ANNE MARIE, nonprofit organization administrator; b. Springfield, Mass., Jan. 17, 1949; d. Stephen Borowiec and Marcelle (Denis) Weitzel; m. Brian J. Bubnic, May 23, 1979. BS in Biology and Chemistry, Coll. of Our Lady of the Elms, Chicopee, Mass., 1970; MPA, U. San Francisco, 1987. Cert. fund raising exec. Med. tech. Monson State Hosp., Palmer, Mass., 1970; biochemist Purdue U., West Lafayette, Ind., 1970-73; indsl. microbiologist Hazleton Labs., Vienna, Va., 1974-75; med. tech. No. Va. Tng. Ctr., Fairfax, 1975-76; research physiologist Cutter Labs., Berkeley, Calif., 1977-82; exec. dir. Nat. Found. Ileitis and Colitis, San Francisco, 1982-87; dir. sustaining gifts U. San Francisco, 1987-88; exec. dir. Marine World Found., Vallejo, Calif., 1988—. Contbr. articles to profl. jours. Pres. Nat. Found. for Ileitis and Colitis, 1982; mem. adv. bd. Community Edn. Found., Novato Unified Sch. Dist., 1989—, Vol. Ctr. Solano County, 1989—; bd. dirs. Self-Help Clearing House of the Bay Area, San Francisco, 1982-86. Recipient Grad. Student Rsch. award 1988, Pres.'s award Nat. Found. Ileitis and Colitis, 1988, Founder's award, 1990. Mem. AAUW, NAFE, Nat. Soc. Fund Raising Execs. (bd. dirs. 1987—, treas. 1989—, Abel Hanson award 1986, 87, President's award 1988, 89), Am. Soc. Assn. Execs., Soc. Nonprofit Orgns., Women in Computing, Community Entrepreneurs Orgn., Nat. Assn. Desk Top Pubs., Zonta, Rotary. Democrat. Home: 3 Oak Forest Rd Novato CA 94949 Office: Marine World Found Marine World Pkwy Vallejo CA 94589

BUC, NANCY LILLIAN, lawyer; b. Orange, N.J., July 27, 1944; d. George L. and Ethel (Rosenbaum) B. AB, Brown U., 1965; LLB, U. Va., 1969. Bar: Va. 1969, N.Y. 1977, D.C. 1978. Atty. Fed. Trade Commn., Washington, 1969-72, atty., adviser to chmn., 1971-72; assoc. Weil, Gotshal & Manges, N.Y., 1972-77, ptnr., 1977-80; ptnr. Weil, Gotshal & Manges, Washington, 1981—; chief counsel FDA, Rockville, Md., 1980-81; mem. adv. com. on new devels. in biotech. Office of Tech. Assessment, Washington, 1986-89. Mem. editorial bd. Food Drug and Cosmetic Law Jour., 1981-87, Jour. of Products Liability, 1981—, Health Span: The Jour. of Health, Bus. & Law, 1984—. Trustee Brown U., Providence, 1973-78, Va. Law Sch. Found. Fellow Brown U., 1980—; recipient Disting. Svc. award Fed. Trade Commn., Washington, 1972, Merit award FDA, Rockville, 1981, Sec.'s Spl. citation HHS, Washington, 1981. Mem. ABA (spl. com. to study the FTC Washington 1988-89), Com. of 200, Alan Guttmacher Inst. (bd. dirs.). Office: Weil Gotshal & Manges 1615 L St NW Ste 700 Washington DC 20036

BUCCI, ELAINE THERESA, lawyer, state legislator; b. Providence, Sept. 6, 1957; d. Anthony Joseph and Theresa (Garganese) B. BA in Elem. Edn. summa cum laude, Boston Coll., 1979; JD cum laude, Suffolk U., 1982. Bar: U.S. Dist. Ct. R.I. 1982. Atty. Bucci Law Offices, North Providence, R.I., 1982—; mem R.I. Ho. of Reps., Providence, 1985—; clk. Providence Probate Ct., 1988. Mem. R.I. Legal/Ednl. Partnership Program, 1985—. Mem. ABA, R.I. Bar Assn., R.I. Trial Lawyers Assn., Assn. Trial Lawyers Am., Phi Delta Phi. Lodge: Sons of Italy. Home: 25 Prosper St Providence RI 02904 Office: 1920 Mineral Spring Ave North Providence RI 02904

BUCCITELLI, MARCIA DENISE, lawyer; b. New Britain, Conn., Mar. 28, 1949; d. Alfred J. and Marie T. (Monterosso) Bak; m. Anthony J. Buccitelli, Jan. 16, 1971; children: Anthony, Bianca, Nicole. BA with honors, U. Conn., 1970; JD cum laude, U. Md., 1980. Bar: Mass. 1980. Claims rep. Liberty Mut. Ins. Co., Boston, 1970-71; tchr., mem. faculty St. Joseph Sch., Wakefield, Mass., 1971-73; mem. faculty and English dept. Stoneham (Mass.) High Sch., 1973-76; mem. faculty USDA, Washington, 1980—; assoc. Amrhein & Amrhein, Hingham, Mass., 1986—; mem. faculty U. Md., College Park, 1980-85; instr. U.S. Dept. Justice, Washington, spring 1983. Mem. Mass. Bar Assn., Phi Beta Kappa, Phi Kappa Phi. Democrat. Roman Catholic. Office: Amrhein & Amrhein 20 Downer Ave Hingham MA 02043

BUCH, KIMBERLY KREISLER, industrial psychology educator; b. Mayfield, Ky., Jan. 30, 1956; d. Carl William and Dorothy May (Covington) Kreisler; m. Alan Leo Buch, June 25, 1977; 1 child, Carl Alexy. BS, Western Ky. U., 1977, MA, 1982; PhD, Iowa State U., 1987. Rsch. asst. Iowa State U., Ames, 1983-87; asst. prof. U. N.C., Charlotte, 1987—; cons. Urban Inst., Charlotte, 1987-88. Vol. Equal Rights Amendment, Iowa, 1979. U. N.C. rsch. grantee, 1988. Mem. Am. Psychol. Assn., Acad. Mgmt., Assn. Quality and Participation, PEO Club. Office: U NC Dept Psychology Charlotte NC 28223

BUCHANAN, BRENDA J., computer manufacturing executive; b. San Diego; d. Fred and Annie M. (Winston) B. BS in Math., Physics and Chemistry, U. Denver; MA in Math., Washington U., 1973; postgrad., McGill U., 1973-75, U. Cologne, Fed. Republic Germany, 1973-75. Math. instr. Washington U., St. Louis, 1969-71; programmer/analyst United Aircraft of Can., Longueil, Que., 1971-73; ops. research analyst Consol. Bathurst Ltd., Montreal, Que., 1973-76; corp. new product planning mgr. Digital Equipment Corp., Maynard, Mass., 1976-80; new product program mgr. Digital Equipment Corp., Springfield, Mass., 1980-84, tapes bus. mgr., 1984-88; corp. purchasing program office mgr. Northboro, Springfield, Mass., 1986-88; dist. mfg. mgr. Northboro, Marlboro, Mass., 1988-89, area mfg. mgr., 1989—; mem. Digital Equipment Women's Adv. Com., 1986—. Leader, Can. Girl Guides, Montreal, 1972-74; mem. mayor's blue ribbon com. Dept. Pub. Works, Springfield, 1983. Fulbright fellow, Fed. Republic Germany; recipient Experiment in Internat. Living award Fed. Republic Germany. Mem. Can. Ops. Research Soc., LWV (bd. dirs.), Strathmore Shire Assn. (trustee 1987—), The Profl. Council, Alpha Kappa Alpha (Basileus, Ivy of Yr., Denver chpt.). Democrat. Baptist Club: Links, Inc. (Springfield) (treas. 1984-86). Home: 4E Strathmore Shire PO Box 49 North Uxbridge MA 01538 Office: Digital Equipment Corp 3 Results Way (MR03-2/J20) Marlborough MA 01752-9103

BUCHANAN, DEBRA ANN, program coordinator, consultant; b. Oxberry, Miss., Sept. 13, 1956; d. Victor and Mary Louise (Gary) B.; 1 child, Terance Arnaz. BA, Miss. Valley State U., Itta Bena, 1978; MA, U. No. Iowa, 1980; EdD, Okla. State U., Stillwater, 1988. Bursar, acct. Langston (Okla.) U., 1984-85; rsch. assoc. Grad. Coll. Okla. State U., Stillwater, 1988-89, minority programs coord. Coll. Arts & Scis., 1989—; mem. adj. faculty dept. psychology Okla. State U., Stillwater, 1989—. mem. Task Force on Affirmative Action, Stillwater, 1989-90; field reader U.S. Dept. Edn., Washington, 1990—; co-chair Multicultural Awareness Program, Stillwater, 1988—. Mem. Women's Polit. Caucus, Stillwater, 1988—. Mem. Black Alumni Assn. Okla. State U. (nat. treas. 1989-90).

BUCHANAN, DIANNE JEAN JOHNSON, human resources executive; b. Harvey, Ill., Sept. 12, 1948; d. Virgil Albert and Jean (Armstrong) Johnson; m. Dennis Michael Buchanan, May 7, 1988. BBA in Mktg., U. Tex., 1970. Mktg. rsch. asst. Belden Assocs., Dallas, 1970-72; personnel staff Meisel Photochrome Co., Dallas, 1972-75; personnel staff Geosource, Inc., Houston, 1975-77, corp. compensation specialist, 1977-78; personnel officer, compensation and benefits mgr. Capital Bank, Houston, 1978-79; compensation specialist Anderson Clayton & Co., Houston, 1979-81, dir. human resources Ranger Ins. subs., 1981-84, corp. compensation dir., 1984-87; v.p. human resources NBC Bank, Houston, 1987-89; asst. v.p., mgr. compensation Tex. Commerce Bancshares, Houston, 1989-90; human resources cons., 1990—. Mem. assoc. vestry Saint John the Divine Ch., Houston, 1983; bd. dirs. Meadowbriar Home for Girls, Houston, 1978-79. Mem. Houston Compensation Assn. (bd. dir. 1983-87, pres. 1985-86, v.p. 1984-85), Houston Personnel Assn. (com. 1982-84), Am. Soc. Personnel Adminstrs., Am. Compensation Assn. (com. 1983, 85-87), River Oaks Breakfast Club (Houston, v.p. membership 1988).

BUCHANAN, EDNA, journalist; b. Paterson, N.J.. Journalist Miami Beach (Fla.) Daily Sun, 1965-70, The Miami (Fla.) Herald, 1970—. Author: Carr: Five Years of Rape and Murder, 1979, The Corpse Had a Familiar Face: Covering America's Hottest Beat, 1987, Nobody Lives Forever, 1990; contbr. articles to Family Circle mag., Cosmopolitan mag., Rolling Stone mag., Fame mag. Recipient Green Eye Shade award Soc. Profl. Journalists, 1982, Pulitzer prize for gen. reporting, 1986. Mem. United Ch. of Christ. Office: The Miami Herald One Herald Pla Miami FL 33101

BUCHANAN, GLORIA JEAN, retail executive; b. Bowling Green, Ky., Nov. 3, 1950; d. Albert M. and Lenora (Hayes)Paschal; m. Michael C. Moonan (div.); 1 child, Shelly; m. Andrew George Buchnan. Mgr. Alexander Wallcovering, Falls Church, Va., 1976-81; decorator Duron Paints and Wallvocering, Beltsville, Md., 1982-84, sales rep., 1984-85, archtl. rep., 1985-86, dir., 1986—. Mem. Constrn. Specification Inst., Interior Design Soc., Nat. Assn. Female Execs., Washington Sales and Mktg. Council. Republican. Episcopalian. Home: 7488 Tangier Way Manassas VA 22110 Office: Duron Paints and Wallcoverings 10406 Tucker St Beltsville MD 20705

BUCHANAN, JENNIFER LEE, financial analyst; b. Pitts., Aug. 5, 1957; d. William Keegan and Celeste Hazel (Wolfe) B.; m. Daryl Lee Hollnagel, Oct. 18, 1986; 1 child, Katharine Foster. BA, Washington & Jefferson Coll., 1979; MBA in Fin., U. Hartford, 1981. Assoc. fin analyst-B Ohio Edison Co., Akron, 1982-83, assoc. fin.analyst-A, 1983-85, fin analyst, 1985—. Fund raiser Jr. Achievement. Mem. LWV, DAR, Am. Mgmt. Assn., Hudson Book Club. Presbyterian. Home: 6740 Pinebrooke Dr Hudson OH 44236 Office: Ohio Edison Co 76 S Main St Akron OH 44308

BUCHANAN, PEGGY CARR, treasurer; b. Newton, Miss., Dec. 3, 1925; d. Cecil Anderson and Edna (Steinwinder) Carr; m. John Felder, May 29, 1954; 1 child John Elliott. BA, Millsaps Coll., 1947. Adminstrv. asst. The Houston Post, 1960-67; treas. The Hobby Foundn., Houston, 1967—. Democrat. Home: 6255 Cedar Creek Houston TX 77057 Office: The Hobby Found 3050 Post Oak Blvd Houston TX 77056

BUCHANAN, SHERRIE LEE KOROUS, auditor; b. Salt Lake City, Mar. 25, 1949; d. Howard Charles and Neva Gae (Downs) Korous; m. Warren Bernell Buchanan, Apr. 12, 1968 (div. 1986); children; Sean Edward, W Clark. AAS in Acctg., Clark County Community Coll., Las Vegas, Nev., 1976; BS in Bus. Adminstrn., U. Nev., Las Vegas, 1978, MPA, 1990. CPA, Nev. Part time acctg. instr. Clark County Community Coll., Las Vegas, 1974-78; bus. lic. auditor Clark County, Las Vegas, 1978-80; internal auditor City of Las Vegas, 1980-85, sr. internal auditor, 1985-89, chief, internal audit div., 1989—; tutor in acctg. Clark County Community Coll., Las Vegas, 1974-78. Mem. Nev. Soc. CPA's, Nev. Govt. Fin. Officer Am., U. Nev. at Las Vegas Alumni, Alpha Kappa Psi. Home: 1926 Randa Ln Las Vegas NV 89104 Office: City of Las Vegas 400 E Stewart Las Vegas NV 89104

BUCHANAN, TERI BAILEY, public relations executive, marketing agency owner; b. Long Beach, Calif., Feb. 24, 1946; d. Alton Hervey and Ruth Estelle (Thompson) Bailey; m. Robert Wayne Buchanan, Aug. 14, 1964 (div. May 1979). BA in English with highest honors, Ark. Poly. Coll., 1968. With employee communications AT&T, Kansas City, Mo., 1968-71; free-lance writer Ottawa, Kans., 1971-73; publs. dir. Ottawa U., 1973-74; regional info. officer U.S. Dept. Labor, Kansas City, 1974; owner, operator PBT Communications, Kansas City, 1975-79; sr. pub. affairs rep., sr. editor, exhibit supr., communications specialist Standard Oil/Chevron, San Francisco, 1979-84; owner The Resource Group/Mktg. Pub. Relations, San Francisco, 1984—; adv. bd. Golden Gate U. Hosp. Mgmt. Dept., San Francisco, 1984—; mem. faculty Golden Gate U. Pub. Relation Masters Program, San Francisco, 1987. Pub. relations trainer Bus. Vols. for Arts, San Francsico, 1985—; pro-bono cons. Black Tie Soc.-Mayor's Fund-Homeless, San Francisco, 1987. Recipient Internat. Assn. Bus. Communicators Bay Area Gold and Silver awards, 1984. Mem. Publicity Club, Pub. Relations Round Table, San Francisco Conv. and Visitors Bur., San Francisco C. of C., Commonwealth Club Calif. (vice chmn. pub. relations com. 1984—). Democrat. Congregationalist. Office: The Resource Group 555 De Haro #340 San Francisco CA 94107

BUCHANAN-DAVIDSON, DOROTHY JEAN, medical editor and writer, retired; b. Monmouth, Ill., Dec. 22, 1925; d. John Dales and Helen Barr (Huey) Buchanan; m. Max Arthur Davidson, May 31, 1957; children: Scott Arthur, Janet Rae, Nancy Jean. Student, Monmouth Coll., 1943-45; BS, Washington State U., 1947; MS, U. Cin., 1949, PhD, 1951. Instr. dept. biochemistry Vanderbilt U., Nashville, 1950-53; project assoc. dept. biochemistry U. Wis., Madison, 1956-60; abstractor Chem. Abstracts, Columbus, Ohio, 1960-76; abstractor water resources ctr. U. Wis., Madison, 1974-76; tchr. Madison Area Tech. Coll., 1974-76; sci. writer Wis. Clin. Cancer Ctr., Madison, 1976-80; editor, curriculum coord. adminstrv. medicine program U. Wis., Madison, 1980-83, program coord. ctr. for affective disorders, 1983-86, editor sch. nursing, 1987-90; numerous freelance writing and editing jobs. Contbr. articles, tech. publs., and feature stories to profl. jours.; contbr. news releases to Wis. newspapers; columnist Wis. Med. Jour. Elder, deacon Presbyn. Ch., Oregon, Wis., 1962—; mem. Oregon (Wis.) Hist. Soc., 1988—. Fellow USPHS, Paris, 1955-56, Children's Hosp. Rsch. Found., Cin., 1948-50, Wash. State Coll., 1945-47, Lilly Postdoctoral fellow in med. scis., London, 1953-55. Mem. Am. Med. Writers Assn., Anciens Eleves de l'Institut Pasteur, Madison MacIntosh Users Group (v.p. 1988, editor 1988-89), Sigma Xi, Iota Sigma Pi. Home: 6278 Sun Valley Pkwy Oregon WI 53575

BUCHBINDER, SHARON BELL, professional association executive; b. Washington, Nov. 27, 1951; d. James Wright and Effie Naomi (Rhodes) Bell; m. Dale Buchbinder, May 9, 1976; 1 child, Joshua. BA in Psychology, U. Conn., 1973; MA in Psychology, U. Hartford, 1976; AAS in Nursing, SUNY, Albany, 1981; postgrad., U. Ill., Chgo., 1986—. RN. Intravenous technician Hartford (Conn.) Hosp., 1974-76; supr. Albany Med. Ctr. Hosp., 1976-80; asst. rsch. scientist N.Y. Dept. Mental Hygiene, Albany, 1980-81; staff specialist Nat. Commn. on Nursing, Chgo., 1982-83, Am. Hosp. Assn., Chgo., 1983-84; sr. rsch. assoc. AMA, Chgo., 1984-86, exec. asst., 1986-88, mktg. exec., 1988-89, asst. dept. dir. dept. preventive medicine, 1989-90; instr. sch. pub. health U. Ill. Contbr. articles to profl. jours. Recipient rsch. grant Mut. Life Ins. Co. of N.Y., 1986. Mem. N.Y. Acad. of Scis., NAFE, Am. Pub. Health Assn., Phi Kappa Phi. Democrat. Jewish.

BUCHER, CAROL ANNE, educator; b. Goshen, N.Y., Mar. 16, 1948; d. Gordon Edwin and Ethel Louise (Butterweck) Bucher; BA cum laude, Slippery Rock (Pa.) State Coll., 1970; MEd with honors, Johns Hopkins U., 1977, CASE degree with honors, 1987. Presch. tchr. Running Brook Children's Nursery, Columbia, Md., 1975-77; learning specialist for severe and profoundly handicapped Howard County Bd. Edn., Columbia, 1978-88, resource/Diagnostic-Prescriptive tchr., 1988—. Mem. NEA, Md. State Tchrs. Assn., Howard County Edn. Assn. (chmn. spl. edn. task force 1983-85, sec. rep. assembly, sec. bd. dirs.), Howard County Pilots Assn., Aircraft Owners and Pilots Assn., Phi Delta Kappa, Mu Kappa Gamma, Pi Gamma Mu.

BUCHERRE-FRAZIER, VERONIQUE, international development company executive, project director; b. Casablanca, Morocco, Nov. 20, 1951; came to U.S., 1967; d. Maurice Daniel Bucherre and Lucette Jaqueline Piani; m. Douglas Lee Frazier; 1 child, Marc Andrew. Diploma Para Profesores, Gregorio Maranon, Madrid, 1972; MA, San Francisco State U., 1974; PhD in Latin Am. Affairs, U. Paris-Sorbonne, 1980; diploma in conf. interpreting, London Sch. of Poly., 1983. Lic. real estate broker, Md. Instr. French Peace Corps, Baker, La., 1968; editorial asst. Newsweek mag., San Francisco, 1970-72; mem. faculty San Francisco State U., 1972-74, 77; conf. interpreter-translator France and U.S., 1974-85, rural developer, 1976-86; pres. Bucherre & Assocs., Washington, 1985-88; inventor The Rainbank System, 1985; bd. dirs. Rainbank Project, 1986-88, chief exec. officer; pres. Rainbank Group Ltd., 1988—; mem. bd. mgmt. Institut des Hautes Etudes de L'Amerique Latine, Paris, 1975-76; mem. Lab III, Centre National de Recherche Scientifique, Paris, 1975-77; mem. Inter-Am. Def. Bd. Internat. Civilian Staff Assn., pres. 1987—. Author: Florence, 1979, Uruguay, 1980. Mem. Droit Humain Club, G.I.T.E. Club (Paris). Office: 6404 Western Ave Chevy Chase MD 20815

BUCHHOLZ, BARBARA B., free-lance writer; b. N.Y.C., Jan. 17, 1949; d. Joseph and Estelle Ruth (Cohen) Ballinger; m. Edward John Buchholz, Oct. 23, 1971; children: Joanna Emily, Lucy Rebecca. BA, Barnard Coll., 1971; MA, Hunter Coll., 1976; postgrad., NYU, 1978-80, Washington U., 1982-85. Editor House and Garden Guides mag., N.Y.C., 1972-80; reporter St. Louis Post-Dispatch, 1980-88; free-lance writer bus. and food publs. Chgo., 1988—. Co-author: Needlepoint Designs for Amish Quilts, 1977, Corporate Bloodlines: The Future of the Family Firm, 1989; author, editor: People's Emergency Guide, 1980, The Aviator's Source Book, 1982. Democrat.

BUCHHOLZ, CAROLYN LEIGH, lawyer; b. Boulder, Colo., Dec. 10, 1955; d. Glen Elvis and Alice Joy (McIntosh); m. Roger Alan Buchholz, Oct. 4, 1980; BA cum laude, Middlebury Coll., 1978; JD, U. Colo., 1981. Bar: Colo. 1981, U.S. Dist. Ct. Colo. 1981, Mont. 1988, U.S. Dist. Ct. Mont. 1989. Rsch. asst. Rocky Mountain Mineral Law Found., Boulder, Colo., 1979-80; assoc. Sisk, Foley, Hultin, & Driver, Denver, 1981-83, Hultin, Driver & Spaanstra, Denver, 1983-85, Hultin & Spaanstra, Denver, 1985-86; asst. atty. gen. Colo. Dept. of Law, Denver, 1986-88; assoc. Cogswell & Wehrle, Denver, 1988-89, shareholder, 1989—; spl. asst. atty. gen. Mont., 1988—; with Cogswell & Eggleston, P.C., 1989—; mem., atty. program to provide legal svcs. to indigent, Denver, 1982-86. Mem. procedural rules subcom. Colo. Air Quality Control Commn., 1983-84; mem. Lafayette Planning Commn., 1986-87, Lafayette (Colo.) City Council, 1987—, mayor pro tem, 1989—. Mem. ABA (natural resources sect.), Colo. Bar Assn., Denver Bar Assn. (legal fees arbitration com. 1983-84, 86-87), Mont. Bar

Assn., Am. Bus. Women's Assn, Lafayette Louisville Downtown Revitalization, Inc. (pres. 1986-89), Boulder County Long Range Planning Commn., Alliance Profl. Women (bd. dirs. 1986—), Am. Planners Assn. Democrat. Methodist. Office: Cogswell & Eggleston PC 1700 Lincoln St Ste 3500 Denver CO 80203

BUCHHOLZ, MONICA FINNIGAN, publisher; b. Oneonta, N.Y., Sept. 15, 1961; d. John and Eleanor (Henrich) Finnigan; m. Theodore O. Buchholz, May 24, 1987. BA in Communications, Marist Coll., Poughkeepsie, N.Y., 1983. Editor IBM, East Fishkill, N.Y., 1983; asst. editor Reston (Va.) Pub. Co., 1983-85; advt. dir. Page Avjet Corp., Orlando, Fla., 1985-86; mng. editor Intertec Pub., White Plains, N.Y., 1986-89; pub. Automotive Svc. Assn., Bedford, Tex., 1989—. Contbr. numerous articles to various publs. Mem. NAFE. Office: Automotive Svc Assn PO Box 929 Bedford TX 76095

BUCHHOLZ, TERRI ANNE, investment company executive; b. Burlington, Colo., Dec. 30, 1958; d. Marvin Henry and Judith Anne (Neidig) B. BS, Colo. State U., 1981. From registered rep. to div. mgr. First Investors Corp., Westminster, Colo., 1986—. Mem. NAFE, Nat. Assn. Securities Dealers (lic.). Office: First Investors Corp 8704 Yates Dr Ste 210 Westminster CO 80030

BUCHMAN, HELENE MARCIA, transportation planner; b. Balt., July 25, 1950; d. Henry Leon and Marceline (Karsh) B. BA, U. Md., 1968; M Environ. Planning, Ariz. State U., 1982. Planner Ariz. Dept. Transp., Phoenix, 1982-85; transit planner Maricopa Assoc. of Govts., Phoenix, 1985-86, sr. transit planner, 1986-88; mgr. transp. planning City of Burbank, Calif., 1988-89; cons. L.A., 1989—; staff Kosmont & Assoc., Inc., Burbank, CA, 1990—. Mem. Am. Planning Assn., Inst. Transp. Engrs. (affiliate), Women's Transp. Seminar.

BUCHMAN, MARION, poet, educator; b. Balt.; d. Jacob Solomon and Mildred (Valinski) Friedmond. Poetry reader Rider Coll., Trenton, N.J., 1963; instr. prosody Community Coll. Balt., 1970, Am. U., Washington, 1976, Johns Hopkins U., Balt., 1976-82, Balt. Free U., 1976-82. Author: A Voice in Ramah, 1960, America, 1976, In His Pavilion, 1986; contbr. numerous poems to mags., newspapers, anthologies, jours. including The N.Y. Times, Md. Eng. Jour., Ariz. Quar., Poet Lore, Stanza, Cats, Poetry View, Redbook; poems and books housed in Spl. Collection Dept. John Hopkins U. Recipient Cheltenham prize Arts Coun. Gt. Britain, John Masefield award, Al Di La prize Franklin Coll. Switzerland, Golden Poet award, 1st prize World of Poetry, 1989. Mem. Poetry Soc. Am. (awards 1978—), London Poetry Secretariat, Poetry Soc. G.B., N.Y. Poetry Forum, Nat. Fedn. State Poetry Socs., Md. Council English Tchrs. (hon.), Nat. Council Tchrs. English (affiliate), Author's Guild Am., Author's League Am. Home: 11 Slade Ave Apt 315 Baltimore MD 21208

BUCHWALD, JENNIFER SULLIVAN, neurophysiologist, educator; b. Okmulgee, Okla., Oct. 20, 1930. AB, Lindenwood Coll., 1951, LLD (hon.), 1970; PhD, Tulane U., 1959. Rsch. asst. dept. anatomy UCLA, 1959-62, asst. prof. pediatrics, 1963-66, asst. prof. physiology, 1966-67, assoc. prof. physiology, 1967-73, prof. physiology, 1973—, vice chair dept. physiology, 1985-87, assoc. dir. Brain Rsch. Inst., 1978-89; mem. programs adv. NIH, 1982-86, counselor, 1977-81. Recipient Career Devel. award NIH, 1965-69, Parkinson Found. award USPHS, 1963-69, Women of Sci. award U. Calif., Los Angeles, 1969. Mem. Neurosci. Soc. (treas. 1975-77). Office: UCLA Sch Medicine Dept Physiology Los Angeles CA 90024

BUCHWALD, NAOMI REICE, federal magistrate; b. Kingston, N.Y., Feb. 14, 1944; BA cum laude, Brandeis U., 1965; LLB, cum laude, Columbia U., 1968. Bar: N.Y. 1968, U.S. Ct. Appeals (2d cir.) 1969, U.S. Dist. Ct. (so. and ea. dists.) N.Y. 1970, U.S. Supreme Ct. 1978. Litigation assoc. Marshall, Bratter, Greene, Allison & Tucker, N.Y.C., 1968-73; asst. U.S. atty. So. Dist. N.Y., 1973-80, dep. chief civil div., 1976-79, chief civil div., 1979-80; U.S. magistrate U.S. Dist. Ct. (so. dist.) N.Y., N.Y.C., 1980—. Recipient spl. citation FDA Commrs., 1978. Mem. ABA, Fed. Bar Council (v.p. 1982-84), Assn. of Bar of City of N.Y. (trademarks and unfair competition com. 1988-89), N.Y. State Bar Assn., Phi Beta Kappa, Omicron Delta Epsilon. Editor, Columbia Jour. Law and Social Problems, 1967-68. Office: US Courthouse Foley Sq Rm 1602 New York NY 10007

BUCK, ALISON JENNIFER, technical writer; b. Bangor, Maine, Dec. 11, 1952; d. George Hill and Anna (Komisaruk) B. BS, U. Maine, Orono, 1974; MA, Brigham Young U., 1978. Cert. tchr., Maine, Mass. Vol. program coordinator Head Start/Hampshire Community Action Commn., Northampton, Mass., 1980; career edn. specialist, job developer Hampshire Ednl. Collaborative, Northampton, 1981; documentation specialist Amherst (Mass.) Assocs., 1981-84; sr. tech. writer Visual Intelligence Corp., Amherst, 1984-85; tech. documentation specialist Video Communications Inc., Feeding Hills, Mass., 1986-87; contract tech. writer Digital Equipment Corp., Westfield, Mass., 1987; mktg. coordinator, tech. publs. mgr. Millitech Corp., South Deerfield, Mass., 1988; contract tech. writer Carrier Corp., Farmington, Conn., 1988-89; author computer-based tng. materials AMS Courseware Developers, Manchester, Conn., 1989—. Co-author: The Coffee Maker Cookbook, 1988. Mem. Soc. for Tech. Communication. Democrat. Office: Carrier Corp 4 Farm Springs Farmington CT 06032

BUCK, ANNE MARIE, library director, consultant; b. Birmingham, Ala., Apr. 12, 1939; d. Blaine Alexander and Marie Reynolds (McGeorge) Davis; m. Evan Buck, June 17, 1961 (div. Apr. 1977); children: Susan Elizabeth Buck Rentko, Stephen Edward. BA, Wellesley (Mass.) Coll., 1961; MLS, U. Ky., 1977. Bus. mgr. Charleston (W.Va.) Chamber Music Soc., 1972-74; dir. Dunbar (W.Va.) Pub. Libr., 1974-76; tech. reference libr. AT&T Bell Labs., Naperville, Ill., 1977-79; group supr. libr. AT&T Bell Labs., Reading, Pa., 1979-83; group supr. support svcs. AT&T Bell Labs., North Andover, Mass., 1983; dir. libr. network Bell Communications Rsch. (Bellcore), Morristown, N.J., 1983-89; dist. mgr. corp. support, human resources devel. Bell Communications Rsch. (Bellcore), Livingston, N.J., 1989—; adj. prof. Rutgers U., New Brunswick, N.J., 1989—; instr. U. Wis., Madison, 1988—; bd. dirs. Engring. Info. Inc., N.Y.C.; speaker profl. assn. confs., 1982—; libr. cons. North Port (Fla.) Area Libr., 1990—. Contbr. articles to profl. jours. Sect. mgr. United Way of Morris County, Cedar Knolls, N.J., 1984—; advisor Family Svc. Transitions Coun., Morristown, 1987—; libr. trustee Lisle (Ill.) Pub. Libr. Dist., 1978-80; bd. dirs. Kanawha County Bicentennial Commn., Charlestown, 1974-76. Mem. ALA (Grolier Nat. Libr. Week grant 1975), Am. Soc. Info. Sci. (chpt. chmn. 1987-89, chpt. of yr. 1988), The Conf. Bd. Inc. (chmn. info. svcs. adv. coun. 1987-89), Spl. Libr. Assn., Indsl. Tech. Info. Mgrs. Group, N.J. Wellesley Club (regional chmn. 1986-89), Sierra Club, N.J. Schola Cantorum, Beta Phi Mu. Unitarian. Home: 43 Washington Ave Chatham NJ 07928 Office: Bellcore PO Box 486 Livingston NJ 07039-0486

BUCK, KATHLEEN ANN, lawyer; b. South Bend, Ind., Nov. 14, 1948; d. Betty Jo and Cecil and Betty Jo (Parfitt) B.; m. Raymond Donald Battocchi, Aug. 20, 1975; children: Adam, Brian. B.A. cum laude, St. Mary's Coll., Notre Dame, Ind., 1970; J.D., Ind. U., 1973; student U. Iberoamericana, Mexico City, 1968. Bar: D.C., Fla. Trial atty. F.R.L.S., Delray Beach, Fla., 1973-75; atty. Swift & Co., Washington, 1975-77; atty., asst. dir. govt. relations Esmark, Inc., Washington, 1977-81; asst. gen. counsel U.S. Dept. Def., Washington, 1981-86; gen. counsel USAF, Washington, 1986-87, Dept. Def., Washington, 1987-89, Kirkland & Ellis, Washington, 1989—. Recipient Disting. Pub. Svc. medal Dept. Def., Exceptional Civilian Svc. medal USAF. Mem. ABA (standing com., com. on law and nat. security), D.C. Bar, Fla. Bar, Women in Govt. Relations (Most Disting. Mem. award 1979), Capitol Hill Equestrian Soc., Pi Sigma Alpha. Home: 2094 Van Tuyl Pl Falls Church VA 22043 Office: 655 15th St NW Washington DC 20005

BUCK, LINDA DEE, executive recruiting company executive; b. San Francisco, Nov. 8, 1946; d. Sol and Shirley D. (Setterberg) Press; student Coll. San Mateo (Calif.), 1969-70; divorced. Head hearing and appeals br. Dept. Navy Employee Rels. Svc., Philippines, 1974-75; dir. human resources Homestead Savs. & Loan Assn., Burlingame, Calif., 1976-77; mgr. VIP Agy., Inc., Palo Alto, Calif., 1977-78; exec. v.p., dir. Sequent Personnel Svcs., Inc., Mountain View, Calif., 1978-83; founder, pres. Buck & Co., Burlingame, 1983—. Publicity mgr. for No. Calif., Osteogenesis Imperfecta Found. Inc., 1970-72; cons. Am. Brittle Bone Soc., 1979-88. Jewish. Office: Buck & Co 330 Primrose Rd Ste 302 Burlingame CA 94010

BUCK, LORRAINE, sales representative; b. Columbus, Ohio, Sept. 15, 1968; d. Norman Whitney and Delphine Lorraine (Zelinski) B. BA in Journalism, Ind. U., 1990. Day care instr. Tabernacle Acad., Indpls., 1985-88; sales intern Sherwin-Williams, Indpls., 1989; sales rep. E.J. Brach, Inc., Cin., 1990—. Mem. Women in Communications, Inc. (v.p. Ind. U. student affiliation 1988-90), Gamma Phi Beta. Republican. Methodist. Home: 9230 Deercross Pkwy #3D Blue Ash OH 45236

BUCK, LOUISE ZIERDT, psychologist; b. Edgewood, Pa., Nov. 21, 1919; d. Conrad Henry and Nancy Leora (Harshberger) Zierdt; div. 1954; children: David Randall, Susan Buck Sutton. BS, Pa. State U., 1940; MEd, U. Pitts., 1954; EdD, Columbia U., 1978; advanced cert., Bklyn. Coll., 1984. Lic. sch. psychologist, N.Y. Tchr., dir. Chatham Village Nursery Sch., Pitts., 1953-55; tchr., dir. Yellow Springs (Ohio) Community Nursery Sch., 1955-58; tchr. Oak Lane Country Day Sch., Phila., 1958-59, Walden Sch., N.Y.C., 1959-60, Bank St. Sch. for Children, N.Y.C., 1960-61; early childhood tchr., coord. sch. psychology Bd. Edn., City of N.Y., 1961-87; asst. prof. Bklyn. Coll., 1978-80; rsch. fellow Albert Einstein Coll. Medicine, Bronx, N.Y., 1988-89; psychotherapist Fifth Ave Ctr. for Psychotherapy, N.Y.C., 1989, Met. Ctr. for Mental Health, N.Y.C., 1990—; psychologist cons. Bd. Edn., City of N.Y., 1987-88. Contbr. articles to profl. jours. Mem. Am. Psychol. Assn., Soc. for Psychoanalytic Psychotherapy, Nat. Assn. for Edn. Young Children. Democrat. Home: 444 E 86th St Apt 34C New York NY 10028 Office: Met Ctr for Mental Health 130 W 97th St New York NY 10025

BUCK, NATALIE SMITH, former state official; b. Carlsbad, N.Mex., Jan. 10, 1923; d. Milton R. and Rosa Adele (Binford) Smith; student Coll. William and Mary, 1940-41; BBS, U. Colo., 1943; postgrad. U. Tex., 1945-46; m. C. B. Buck, Sept. 12, 1948; children: Warren Z., Barbara Anne. Chief clk., State Senate, N.Mex., 1951-53; sec. of state, N.Mex., 1955-59; chief personnel adminstr. N.Mex. Health and Social Services Dept., 1959-73. Democrat. Home: 108 W Alicante Rd Santa Fe NM 87501

BUCK, SARAH MAY, banking professional; b. Freemont, Ohio, Dec. 29, 1964; d. John William and Jane Wilson (Wassell) K. BSBA, Bowling Green State U., 1987; MBA, Baldwin-Wallace U., 1989. Office supr. Bowling Green (Ohio) State U., 1984-87; comml. loan officer Nat. City Bank, Cleve., 1987—. Coach Cathlic Youth Orgn. Volleyball, Avon Lake, Ohio, 1988; mem. Flats Racing League, Crew Team, Cleve., 1988-89; vol. Jr. Achievement, Cleve., 1989. Mem. Delta Sigma Pi. Republican. Mem. United Ch. of Christ. Home: 313 Janice Dr Berea OH 44017

BUCKLAND, ANN ELIZABETH, editor; b. Windsor, Ont., Can., May 17, 1933; d. John Raymond and Grace Elizabeth (Mason) B.; m. Miguel Angel Hidalgo, Aug. 3, 1956 (div. 1974); children: Daniel Norman, Kathleen Mercedes. Student, Wesley Hosp. Northwestern U., Chgo., 1954; BSci., Mercy Coll., Det., 1979; MA in Adminstrn. Health C, Cen. Mich. U., Mt. Pleasant, 1985. Cert. Med. Record Adminstrn. High sch. principal Am. Sch. Guayaquil, Ecuador, S. Am., 1958-62; dir. med. records Saginaw Community Hosp., Mich., 1980-83; dir. med. records and distbg. coord. St. Joseph's Hosp., Minot, N.D., 1983-86; editor, journal Am. Med. Record Assn., Chgo.; sec. founding bd. Mich. Quality Assurance Coordinators, Mich. 1976; editor Newsletter N.D. Med. Record Assn., Minot 1984-85. Editor: Monthly Mag. 1986—; Author: Contbr. articles to profl. jours. 1986—. Recipient Citation award Bd. Dirs. AMRA 1987. Mem. Am. Med. Record Assn., Ill. Med. Record Assn., Chgo. and Vicinity Med. Record Assn. Democratic. Roman Catholic. Office: Am Med Record Assn 919 N Michigan Ste 1400 Chicago IL 60611

BUCKLE, JUNE M., researcher; b. Coatesville, Pa., June 5, 1951. Diploma in nursing, St. Joseph Hosp., Lancaster, Pa., 1972; BS in Nursing, Fla. Internat. U., 1977; MS in Nursing, U. N.C., 1979; ScD, Johns Hopkins U., 1990. Staff nurse Coral Gables Hosp., Miami, 1974-75; asst. head nurse Larkin U., Miami, 1975-77; clin. faculty Duke U., Durham, N.C., 1980-81; nursing coord. VA Med. Ctr., Durham, 1979-81; asst. dir. nursing Sinai Hosp., Balt., 1981-84, Johns Hopkins Hosp., Balt., 1984-86; sr. rsch. coord. Ctr. for Hosp. Fin. and Mgmt. Johns Hopkins U., Balt., 1986-89; dep. dir. Robert Wood Johnson Faculty Fellowhships in Health Care Fin., Balt., 1988—; rsch. assoc. Ctr. for Hosp. Fin. and Mgmt. Johns Hopkins U., Balt., 1989—; cons. in health care, 1986—. Contbr. articles to profl. jours. Rsch. fellowship NIH Ctr. for Nursing Rsch., 1988-90, nursing fellowship in repiratory care Am. Lung Assn. of Md., 1988-90. Mem. Am. Nurses Assn., Md. Nurses Assn., Am. Pub. Health Assn., Sigma Theta Tau. Home: 46 Abbey Bridge Ct Baltimore MD 21093 Office: Ctr Hosp Fin & Mgmt 327 Hampton House 624 N Broadway Baltimore MD 21205

BUCKLES-DEANS, DELORA ELIZABETH, educational diagnostician, consultant; b. Houston, Apr. 19, 1940; d. Joseph Bernhardt and Helen Elizabeth (Phillips) Blazek; m. Richard George Buckles, June 26, 1962 (div. Oct. 1969); children: Gregory, Deborah; m. 2d, Harry Alexander Deans, Jan. 1, 1975; 1 dau., Catherine; stepchildren: Laurie, Daniel, Melissa, Andrew. BA, U. Tex., 1962; postgrad. Cornell U., 1962; MEd, Boston U., 1966, cert. advanced grad. study, 1966; EdD, U. Houston, 1981. Instr., Boston U., 1964-66; coordinator Harris County Dept. Edn., Houston, 1969-72; dir. resource services Klein Ind. Sch. Dist., Spring, Tex., 1972-75; coordinator, ednl. diagnostician area 6 Houston Ind. Sch. Dist., 1975-78; inservice coordinator Coll. Edn. U. Houston, 1979-81; ednl. diagnostician Vocat. Evaluation Ctr. for Handicapped, Houston, 1981-84; coordinator ednl./vocat. evaluation Houston Ind. Sch. Dist., 1984-86; cons. Aldine Ind. Sch. Dist., Houston, 1981-82, Harlingen Ind. Sch. Dist. (Tex.), 1982-83, Houston Learning Acad., 1987-89, Humble Ind. Sch. Dist., 1986—, ednl. diagnostician, 1986—; adj. prof. U. Houston at Clearlake, 1984-89, prof. U. Wyo., Laramie, 1989—. Contbr. articles to profl. jours.; patentee in field. Campaign worker Democratic Party Tex., Houston, 1979-86. Named Outstanding Student, U. Tex., Austin, 1962. Mem. Council Ednl. Diagnostics Services (sec. 1981-83), Tex. Council Exceptional Children (chmn. 1980-82), Tex. Ednl. Diagnostics Assn. (pres. 1981-82), Tex. Div. for Career Devel. (pres. 1986-87), Phi Delta Kappa, Zeta Tau Alpha. Democrat. Episcopalian. Home: 2505 Skyview Ln Laramie WY 82070

BUCKLEY, BETTY BOB, journalist, consultant; b. Tonkawa, Okla., Nov. 1, 1925; d. Clinton Sawyer and Mary Powell (Barnes) Diltz; m. Ernest Lynn Buckley, Aug. 17, 1946 (dec. Aug. 1989); children: Betty Lynn, Patrick Joe and Michael Jay (twins), Norman Lee. Student, Tex. Tech U., 1943-46, S.D. State U., 1946, Tex. Christian U., 1966; BA in Communication, U. Tex., Arlington, 1983. Reporter Big Spring (Tex.) Herald, 1942-43; society reporter Lubbock (Tex.) Avalanche Jour., 1944; reporter Mercury-Chronicle, Manhattan, Kans., 1948, Ft. Worth Press, 1951; columnist Moroccan Courier, Casablanca, Morocco, 1953; asst. editor Gen. Dynamics News, Ft. Worth, 1968-71; dir. pub. rels. Casa Manana Theatre, Ft. Worth, 1975-82; tchr. pub. rels. S.D. State U., Brookings, 1986; freelance pub. relations cons. Brookings, 1988—. Mem. AAUW, PEO, Women in Communication (pres. Ft. Worth chpt. 1957-59, Outstanding Mem. Ft. Worth chpt. 1977). Methodist. Home: 803 Harvey Dunn Brookings SD 57006 also: 4128 Locke Ave Fort Worth TX 76107

BUCKLEY, CAROL JOY, media specialist; b. Evanston, Wyo., Sept. 18, 1931; d. Frank Earl and Maude Annie (Hutchinson) Wirig; m. Jack H. Buckley, Mar. 18, 1930; children: John William, Jill, Heidi Ann, Mark Wirig, Michael Duke, Jay Harry. BS in Home Econs. with honors, U. Wyo., 1953, BS in Nursing with honors, 1954. Cert. elem. tchr.; RN. Grad. nurse Uinta County Meml. Hosp., Evanston, Wyo., 1954-55, Ivinson Meml. Hosp., Laramie, Wyo., 1956-57; asst. instr. U. of Wyo. Coll. of Nursing, Laramie, Wyo., 1955-57; elem. tchr. Daggett County Sch. Dist., Manila, Utah, 1958-59; acting health officer Daggett County, Manila, Utah, 1958-61; sch. nurse Uinta County Sch. Dist. 6, Lyman, Wyo., 1961-74, tchr. 5th grade, 1961-64; remedial reading kindergarten tchr. Reading Devel., Lyman, 1964-67; media specialist K-12 Remedial and Devel. Reading and English Lyman, 1972-83; libr., media specialist Lyman High Sch., 1983—. Contbg. author: Those Good Years at Wyoming U., 1965. Pres. Lyman PTA, 1964-65; chmn. Unita County Mental Health Adv. Bd., 1976; co-chmn. Uinta County Rep. Com.; mem. Wyo. Coun. for Children and Youth, 1977-82; mem, Wyo. Gov.'s Conf. on Libr. and Info. Svcs., 1978. Named Outstanding Young Educator, Evanston Jaycees, 1966, Wyo. Jaycees, 1966; Utah State U. grantee, 1971. Mem. Wyo. Libr. Assn. (constn. and by-pass com. 1977), Wyo. Ednl. Media Assn., Lyman Edn. Assn. (pres. 1969-70), Xadena Homemakers Club (v.p. 1965-87), Pi Beta Phi, Delta Kappa Gamma (pres. 1982-84), Sigma Theta Tau. Republican. Home: 3991 N Hwy 414 Lyman WY 82937 Office: Uinta County Sch Dist 6 127 Franklin Lyman WY 82937

BUCKLEY, ESTHER GONZALEZ-ARROYO, federal commissioner, educator; b. Laredo, Tex., Mar. 29, 1948; d. Hector and Amalia Margarita (Ayala) Gonzalez-Arroyo; m. Elmer Buckley; children: Trina, James, Catherine, Christopher, Rebecca, George, Jennifer. AA, Laredo Jr. Coll., 1965; BA in Math., U. Tex., 1967; postgrad., Southwestern Med. Sch., 1967-69; MS in Secondary Edn., Laredo State U., 1975. Tchr. math. Christen Jr. High Sch., Laredo, 1970, tchr. sci., 1971-74; tchr. adult basic edn. Laredo Jr. Coll., 1970-75, tchr. ESL, 1978-81; head sci. dept. Dr. Leo Cigarroa High Sch., Laredo, 1982; commr. on civil rights U.S. Govt., Washington, 1983—; sec., tchr. migrant youth program Laredo Ind. Sch. Dist., 1970, 71, 74, writer curricula for gifted and talented programs and English lang. devel., 1975, 82; presenter, presider in-svc. workshops, campus rep., 1978—, chmn. supr.'s tchr. adv. com., 1983-89. Mem. Tchr's. Profl. Practices and Ethics Commn. Tex., 1982-83, Webb County Select Com. on Higher Edn., Laredo, 1986; mem. commn. on women State of Tex., Austin, 1987-89, task force on career ladder, 1987—. Named Outstanding Hispanic Educator U.S. Dept. Edn., 1984, Meritorious Tchr. Laredo C. of C., 1989. Mem. Assn. for Supervision and Curriculum Devel., Assn. Tchrs. and Profl. Educators, Soc. Internat. Bus. Fellows, Phi Delta Kappa (charter mem. Laredo chpt.), Kappa Delta Pi (charter mem. Laredo chpt.), Webb County Reps. Women's Club (v.p. 1976-77). Republican. Roman Catholic. Home: 101 Century Circle Laredo TX 78043 Office: US Commn on Civil Rights 1121 Vermont Ave NW Washington DC 20425

BUCKLEY, HELEN ANN, federal judge, lawyer; b. San Francisco, June 12, 1926; d. Martin Joseph and Helen Bernice (Kuhl) B. AB, U. Calif., Berkeley, 1951; JD, U. Calif., 1954. Bar: Calif. 1955, D.C. 1956, Iowa 1977. Assoc. in law U. Calif., Berkeley, 1954-55; trial atty. tax div. U.S. Dept. Justice, Washington, 1955-60; tax counsel Hunt Foods, Fullerton, Calif., 1961-63; ptnr. Pacht, Ross, Warne, Berhardt and Sears, Los Angeles, 1963-71; assoc. Norton Simon Inc., Los Angeles, 1971-74; prof. law U. Iowa Coll. Law, Iowa City, 1974-81; vis. prof. law Pepperdine U., Malibu, Calif., 1981-82; prof. law Temple U., Phila., 1982-83; spl. trial judge U.S. Tax Ct., Washington, 1983—; instr. law U. So. Calif. Law Ctr., 1973; vis. prof. law Hastings Coll., San Francisco, 1976. Mem. adv. com. Mus. Art, Iowa City, 1974-81. Mem. D.C. Bar Assn., Calif. Bar Assn., Iowa Bar Assn., Am. Inn of Ct., Nat. Assn. Women Judges. Office: US Tax Ct 400 2nd St NW Washington DC 20217

BUCKLEY, JOAN MARIE, meeting planner; b. Bronx, N.Y., Oct. 20, 1958; d. William and Edna Ruth (Schwarz) Stephens; m. Kevin Edward Buckley, Aug. 9, 1980 (div. Apr. 1990). Student, Hardbarger Bus. Coll., 1977. Sec. CCB, Durham, N.C., 1977-80; sec. Burroughs Wellcome Co., Research Triangle Park, N.C., 1980-86, speakers program coord., 1986-90, meeting planning coord., 1990—. Mem. NAFE, Jr. Civinettes, Unicorn Club (pres. 1977-78). Republican. Roman Catholic. Office: Burroughs Wellcome Co 3030 Cornwallis Rd Research Triangle Park NC 27709

BUCKLEY, LEA MARIE, employment specialist; b. Jackson, Mich., Oct. 14, 1952; d. Norman A. and Mildred J. (Brousek) B. BA in Psychology, U. Wis., 1974; MA in Expressive Therapy, U. Louisville, 1978, MBA, 1982. Expressive therapist Bridgehaven, Inc., Louisville, 1977-79; program dir., cons. Seven Counties Svcs., Louisville, 1979-82; ins. advocate student health dept. U. Louisville, 1982-83; instr., trainer Jefferson County Schs., 1983-87; mgr. Hampton Assocs., Inc., 1987—. Mem. Am. Soc. Tng. and Devel., Ky. Assn. Specialists in Group Work (membership chmn. 1978-81), Toastmasters (ednl. v.p. 1989, pres. 1990), 55 Works (chair 1988-90). Office: Hampton Assocs Inc 410 W Chestnut St Ste 552 Louisville KY 40205

BUCKLEY, LISA LOUISE, quality assurance executive; b. Cin., Nov. 22, 1958; d. Gene Lamont and Audrey Lou (Gilcher) B.; m. Barnard Jack Prenner, Apr. 27, 1985. BS in Human Relations, Fla. State U., 1980, MSW, 1982. Cons. planner/evaluator Nova U. Clinic, Coral Springs, Fla., 1983-84; chief evaluation planning, grants & statis. Henderson Mental Health Ctr., Ft. Lauderdale, Fla., 1982-84; dir. planning and evaluation Gulfstream Area Agy. on Aging, Lantana, Fla., 1984-85; dir. quality assurance ops. Emergency Med. Svcs. Assocs., Plantation, Fla., 1986—; cons. Nova U. Mental Health Clinic, Coral Springs, 1983-84; cons. on quality assurance trauma/emergency svcs. to 100 hosps.; cons., speaker Area II Quality Assurance Profls., Bradenton, Fla., 1989; workshop speaker Fla. State U., Tallahassee, 1984; lectr. nat. conf. on quality assurance & risk mgmt. Am. Coll. Emergency Physicians, Orlando, Fla., 1989, Pa chpt. Am. Coll. Emergency Physicians Scientific Assembly, on trauma/emergency svcs quality assurance Emergency Dept. Med. Dirs. nat. confs. Author: Quality Assurance Manual, 1986, 90; editor (newsletter) The Quality Connector, 1987—; contbr. articles to profl. jours. and chpt. to book. Campaign participant Elect Bob Butterworth to Fla. Atty.-Gen., Southeast Fla., 1986; French horn player Hollywood (Fla.) Symphony Orchestra, 1982-84, Sunrise (Fla.) Symphony Orchestra, 1982-84. Mem. Broward Assn. Quality Assurance Profls. (sec. 1986-88, pres. 1989), Fla. Assn. Quality Assurance Profls. (bd. dirs. 1988-90), Am. Soc. for Quality Control, Nat. Assn. Quality Assurance Profls. Am. Med. Record Assn., Omicron Nu (nat. officer and nat. fin. com., 1981-83, pres. Fla. State U. chpt. 1981-82) Phi Kappa Phi. Democrat. Unitarian. Home: 2771 NE 5 St Pompano Beach FL 33062 Office: EMSA Ltd Partnership 100 NW 70th Ave Plantation FL 33317

BUCKLEY, LORRAINE MADSEN, biology educator; b. Memphis, Feb. 22, 1953; d. Grant Chesley and Doris Virginia (Christenbury) Madsen; m. Jay Benedict Buckley, June 27, 1980; 1 child, Crystal Dawn. BS, U. Tenn., 1976; MS, La. State U., 1979. Instr. lab. Biology Dept. U. Tenn., Martin, 1975-76, Zoology and Physiology Dept. La. State U., Baton Rouge, 1976-79; asst. research Mus. Natural History La. State U., Baton Rouge, 1978-79; curatorial technician Bernice P. Bishop Mus., Honolulu, 1979-81; research and adminstrv. asst. Hawaiian Shrimp Co., Honolulu, 1980-81; instr. Chapman Coll., Pearl Harbor, Hawaii, 1980-81; instr., marine coordinator Windward Community Coll., Kaneohe, Hawaii, 1980-84; marine sci. specialist Blue Water Marine Lab. U. Hawaii, Honolulu, 1982; instr. biology Jackson (Tenn.) State Community Coll., 1984—; assoc. investigator Hawaiian Backyard Aquaculture Program, Kaneohe, 1983-84; staff mem. Maui Underwater Transect Workshop U. Hawaii, 1983, 84; capt. dive team Data Acquisition Project, Puako, Hawaii, 1983. Contbr. articles on aquaculture, botany, ichthyology and behavioral ecology to profl. jours. Judge Hawaii Sci. Fair, 1980-84, county/city sci. fairs, Jackson, 1985—; mem. membership com. YMCA, Jackson, 1986—. Marine edn. grantee Sea Grant Agy., 1982-84; recipient cert. appreciation marine and aquaculture edn. Marine Option Program U. Hawaii, 1984. Mem. Am. Soc. Ichthyologists and Herpetologists, Animal Behavior Soc., Assn. Southeastern Biologists, Audubon Soc., Tenn. Acad. Sci. Office: Jackson State Community Coll 2046 North Pkwy Jackson TN 38301

BUCKLEY, MARY ELIZABETH, clinical social worker; b. Providence, July 25, 1950; d. Cornelius Robert and Elizabeth Anna (Clarke) B. BA in Anthropology, U. R.I., 1972; MSW, R.I. Coll., Providence, 1985. Drug counselor City of Providence, 1975; sr. ctr. dir. The Salvation Army Corps. Community Ctr., Providence, 1976-79; field worker R.I. Dept. of Elderly Affairs, Providence, 1980-81; clinical social worker, geriatric specialist R.I. Commnity Mental Health Ctr., Woonsocket, R.I., 1985-86; coord. elderly svcs. Providence Ctr. for Counseling and Psychiatric Svc., 1986—; clinical social worker Counseling Resource Assoc., Woonsocket, 1989—; cons. Bayberry Commons Nursing Home, Pascoag, R.I., 1985-86, Govs. Commn. on Domestic Violence Against Elders, Providence, 1990; facilitator Family Care Giver Support Groups, Woonsocket and Providence, 1985—; clinical social worker, Human Resource Inst., Fall River, Mass., 1989—. Co-chmn. Statewide Key Counsel, R.I., 1986—. Mem. Nat. Assn. of Social Workers, Acad. Cert. Social Workers. Home: 35 Larch St Providence RI 02906

BUCKLEY, PRISCILLA LANGFORD, magazine editor; b. N.Y.C., Oct. 17, 1921; d. William Frank and Aloise (Steiner) B. B.A., Smith Coll., 1943.

Copy girl, sports writer U.P., N.Y.C., 1944; radio rewrite staff mem. U.P., 1944-47; corr. U.P., Paris, France, 1953-56; news editor Sta. WACA, Camden, S.C., 1947-48; reports officer CIA, Washington, 1951-53; with Nat. Rev. Mag., N.Y.C., 1956—; mng. editor Nat. Rev. Mag., 1959-86, sr. editor, 1986—; Mem. U.S. Adv. Commn. Pub. Diplomacy, 1984—. Columnist: One Woman's Voice Syndicate, 1976-80. Club: Sharon (Conn.) Country (sec. 1973-77, pres. 1978-80). Home: Great Elm Sharon CT 06069 Office: Nat Review 150 E 35th St New York NY 10016

BUCKMASTER, DEBORAH LEE, marketing professional; b. Newark, Feb. 13, 1953; d. Robert William and Marliese (Esser) B.; m. Melvin K. Buckmaster, Oct. 6, 1990; stepchildren: Kimberly, Janet, Beth. BA in Psychology, U. Colo., 1975, MBA, 1977. Assoc. indsl. analyst Solar Energy Rsch. Inst., Golden, Colo., 1977-80; mktg. rsch. analyst First Nat. Bank Denver, 1980-82; asst. product mgr. Rocky Mountain Bank Note Co., Lakewood, Colo., 1982-86; mktg. rsch. evaluation supr. Wis. Pub. Service Corp., Green Bay, 1986—; instr. mktg. N.E. Wis. Tech. Coll., Green Bay, 1989—. Mem. Am. Mktg. Assn. (v.p. communications Colo. chpt. 1980-83), Wis. Dressage and Combined Tng. Assn. (chpt. del. 1986-88), U.S. Dressage Fedn. Methodist. Office: Wis Pub Svc Corp PO Box 19001 Green Bay WI 54307

BUCKNAM, MARY OLIVIA, artist; b. Modesto, Calif., Feb. 6, 1914; d. Charles Henry and Helen Anne (Cross) Caswell; m. William Nelson Bucknam, June 22, 1946 (dec. 1966); children: William Nelson Jr., Charles Henry. BA, Calif. State U., San Jose, 1936; postgrad., U. Calif., Berkeley, 1938, Calif. State U., Stanislaus, 1968-75, U. San Francisco, 1968-75. Tchr. Stanislaus County (Calif.), 1936-38, Modesto (Calif.) Schs., 1938-43, San Bernardino (Calif.) City, 1943-46; art tchr. Klamath Union Schs., Klamath River, Calif., 1960-61; co-owner Bigfoot Ranch and Resort, Klamath River, 1960-66; art tchr., tchr. Riverbank (Calif.) City Schs., 1966-79; art cons. Riverbank Elem., 1986; gallery artist Cen. Calif. Art League, Modesto, 1986—. Group shows include Siskiyow Artists Assn., 1961-66 (Best of Show award, First award and other awards), Stanislaus County Shows, 1975-90 (Best of Show award, First award and other awards); over 100 paintings held by pvt. individuals and pub. orgns. Donor with Caswell family of land for Caswell State Park, San Joaquin County, Calif., 1955; pres. Caswell Sch. PTA, Ceres, Calif., 1956-57, Ceres Study Club, 1952-53; v.p. Siskiyou Artists Assn., Yreka, Calif., 1963-65; pres. Modesto Tchrs. Assn., 1940-41. Mem. Cen. Calif. Art League (chmn. bank shows Modesto 1988—, co-chair young artists show Modesto 1986, 88, 89, 90), Calif. Retired Tchr. Assn., Stanislaus County Hist. Soc., AAUW (Modesto br., fellowships chair 1959-60, historian 1956), Tuolumne River Lodge, Delta Kappa Gamma (hist.-photography 1985—), Kappa Delta Pi. Republican. Presbyterian. Home: 2704 La Palma Dr Modesto CA 95354

BUCKNER, LINDA IVERSON, insurance, software, and marketing consultant, writer; b. Lincoln, Nebr., July 14, 1950; d. Joseph Thomas and Henrietta Mae (McClure) Fisher; m. David Lynn Iverson, Dec. 29, 1967 (div. May 1980); children: Rachelle, Meggan, Elyssa; m. John David Buckner, Apr. 17, 1981. BS in Bus., U. S.D., 1974; student in Direct Mktg., Northwestern U., 1986-87. Lic. life, accident and health ins. agt., 1980, property and casualty agt., 1985. Mktg. rep. ESCO, Northfield, Ill., 1975-76; sales mgr. Safecom, Inc., Schaumburg, Ill., 1976-79; account exec. CNA, Inc., Chgo., 1979-81; mktg. mgr. Computer Sci. Corp., Chgo., 1981-83; ptnr., v.p. mktg. Buckner & Assocs., Wheaton, Ill., 1981—; account exec., mgr. nat. accounts devel. Marsh-McLennan Group, 1984-86; pres. Buckner & Assocs., 1986—; cons. Ins. Agy. Automation, 1979-81, CARA Corp., Lombard, Ill., 1983-84. Dem. election judge, DuPage County, Ill., 1977—; mem. DuPage County Citizens Adv. Com., 1978-80; mem. Hoffman Hallmark Choir, 1978-80, fundraiser Acad. Performing Arts, Chgo., 1981—. Mem. NAFE, Nat. Assn. Ins. Women, Soc. Mgmt. Info. Systems (assoc.), Data Processing Mgmt. Assn., Am. Mgmt. Assn., Am. Soc. Assn. Execs., Chgo. Soc. Assn. Execs., Direct Mktg. Assn. Home and Office: Buckner & BCB/Bay Path 505 W Union St Wheaton IL 60187

BUCUZZO, ESTELLE LEMIRE, machine and tool company executive; b. Manchester, N.H., Apr. 3, 1927; d. William Joseph and Eva Marie (Racette) Lemire; m. James Michael Bucuzzo; children: William, Andrea, Lisa, Laura. BS, Simmons Coll., Boston, 1947. Sec. Sta. WEEI Radio, Boston, 1947, Sta. WLAW Radio, Lawrence, Mass., 1947-52; buyer's clk. Western Electric Co., North Andover, Mass., 1953-59; v.p. J.M.B. Machine Tool Co., Haverhill, Mass., 1962—. Republican. Roman Catholic. Home: 41 Eudora St Haverhill MA 01830 Office: JMB Machine & Tool Co Inc 15 Hale St Haverhill MA 01830

BUCZYNSKI-SMITH, DONNA MARIE, healthcare consultant; b. Newark, Jan. 14, 1958; d. Chester Frank and Martha Theresa (Dombrowski) B. BA in Psychology, U. Rochester, 1980; MBA in Healthcare Adminstrn., CUNY, 1982, MS in Computer Info. Systems, 1986. Adminstrv. resident Luth. Med. Ctr., Bklyn., 1981, adminstr. on duty, 1981-84; unit mgr. St. Luke's-Roosevelt Hosp. Ctr., N.Y.C., 1983-84; adminstr., dept. ambulatory care Mt. Sinai Hosp., N.Y.C., 1984-85, asst. dir., dept. ambulatory care, 1985-87; sr. cons., healthcare info. systems practice Ernst & Young, N.Y.C., 1987-89, mgr. healthcare info. systems practice, 1989; mgr. healthcare info. systems practice Ernst & Young, Miami, Fla., 1990—. Recipient Foster G. McGaw scholarship in Hosp. Adminstrn., CUNY/Am. Hosp. Supply Corp., 1981. Mem. Am. Coll. Healthcare Execs., Healthcare Info. and Mgmt. Systems Soc. (Am. Hosp. Assn.), ECHO (IBM's User Group), Health Care Fin. Mgmt. Assn., CUNY Alumni Assn. Roman Catholic. Office: Ernst & Young 100 Chopin Pla Ste 1800 Miami FL 33131-2373

BUDD, BERNADETTE SMITH, newspaper executive, public relations consultant; b. N.Y.C., Feb. 23, 1948; d. Stanley Allen and Toby (Percak) Smith; children: Amy Bernadette Rose, Karen Wendy, Paige Elizabeth, Kelly Lyn Budd Tinsley; m. Thomas Witbeck Budd, July 4, 1988. B.A. in History and English, Bucknell U., 1964; M.A. in Liberal Studies, SUNY-Stony Brook, 1971; Ed.M., Columbia U., 1982. Tchr. history N.Y., 1964-69; innovator pre-sch. programs, Shoreham, N.Y., 1975-79; editor, pub. Community Jour., Wading River, N.Y., 1978—, advt. mgr., 1978—; editor Shoreham-Wading River Newsletter, 1978-88; profl. breeder, shower A.K.C. golden retriever dogs; cons., workshop leader, 1979—; owner CJ Typesetting and Printing. Editor: C. of C. Directory, Shoreham, 1983, 84; contbr. articles N.Y. Times, Reader's Digest, Psychology Today Mag.; columnist N.Y. Times, 1986-89. Advisor Teen Recreation Adv. Com., Rocky Point, N.Y., 1979-82; mem. Nuclear Emergency Evacuation Com., 1979-82; pres. PTA, Wading River, 1980-83; v.p. Spl. Edn. PTA, Wading River, 1979-80; active Com. Gifted and Talented Children, Wading River, 1979-80, Occupational Edn. Commn., 1979-80; mem. Suffolk County Human Rights Commn. Recipient Disting. Service award Am. Cancer Soc., 1982-83; award of merit N.Y. State Pub. Relations Assn., 1982-83; award of honor Nat. Sch. Pub. Relations Assn., 1981. Mem. Wading River C. of C. (bd. dirs. 1979-80), Suffolk County Bus. and Profl. Women's Assn., Women's Equal Rights Congress, East End Women's Network, N.Y.C. Press Assn., Rocky Point C. of C. (bd. dirs.), Soc. Profl. Journalists, Sigma Delta Chi, Kappa Kappa Gamma. Roman Catholic. Club: L.I. Press. Home: PO Box 619 Wading River NY 11792 Office: Community Jour PO Box 619 Wading River NY 11792

BUDDING, ANITA, retired educator; b. The Hague, Netherlands, July 30, 1929; came to U.S., 1956; d. Sally and Reina (Stibbe) Meyer; m. Antonius Jacob Budding, Mar. 30, 1953; children: Karin Elisabeth, Ingrid Helen. BSc in Geology, U. Amsterdam, 1951; MS in Teaching, New Mex. Tech., Socorro, 1971. Cert. educator State of N.Mex. Geologist Saskatchewan Geol. Survey, Regina, 1953-55; tchr. Socorro Consolidated Schs., 1968-84. Mem. AAUW (dir. 1987-), Socorro Beautification Com. (pres. 1985-).

BUDEN, ROSEMARY VIDALE, geoscientist, educator; b. New Haven, Mar. 27, 1931; d. Henry George Martin and Geraldine (Ruckman) Jacobson; m. Guido Vidale (dec. Apr. 1961); children: Linda, Ann, John; m. David Buden, Apr. 13, 1984; children: Susan, Janice, Barry. BA, Oberlin (Ohio) Coll., 1952; MSc, U. Mich., 1955; PhD, Yale U., 1968. Rsch. assoc. chemistry U. So. Calif., L.A., 1955-56; assoc. prof. SUNY, Binghamton, 1968-75; fellow Geophys. Lab. Carnegie Instn., Washington, 1974-75; assoc. group leader Los Alamos (N.Mex.) Nat. Lab., 1975-85; sr. geochemist Sci. Applications Int. Corp., Albuquerque, 1985; adj. prof. U. N.Mex., Albuquerque, 1985—; program dir. NSF, Washington, 1988-90; prin. scientist EG&G, Idaho Nat. Engring. Lab., Idaho Falls, 1990—; Chmn. U.S. Nat. Com. for Geochemistry, Washington, 1978-81; mem. earth sci. adv. bd. Stanford U., 1983-85; mem. vis. com. MIT, Cambridge, 1984-89. Contbr. articles to profl. jours. Fellow AAAS, Mineral. Soc. Am. (councilor 1990—), Geol. Soc. Am., Am. Geophys. Union, Geochem. Soc., Sigma Xi. Office: EG&G Idaho Nat Engring Lab PO Box 1625 Idaho Falls ID 83415-2107

BUDIN, BEVERLY R., lawyer; b. Phila., Jan. 20, 1945; d. Max and Evelyn Rutman; m. Michael A. Budin, Aug. 23, 1964; children: Eric, Katherine. BA, U. Pa., 1965; JD, Stanford U., 1969. Bar: Mass. 1970, Pa. 1975, Fla. 1983. With Ctr. Law and Edn. Harvard U., Cambridge, Mass., 1970; assoc. Maloney, Williams and Baer, Boston, 1972-75, Wolf, Block, Schorr and Solis-Cohen, Phila., 1975-78, Spector Gadon & Rosen, Phila., 1978—; speaker, panelist in field Estate Planning Coun. Northeastern Pa., Dickinson Coll. Law Sch., Inst. for Paralegal Tng., Phila., U. Pa. Wharton Sch., Pa. Bar Inst., Profl. Edn. Sys., Inc., also others, 1980—; lectr. Villanova U. Sch. Law, 1987, 88, now adj. prof.; mem. tax mgmt. adv. bd. Estates, Gifts and Trusts Jour. Contbr. articles to legal publs.; author bur. of Nat. Affairs, Life Insurance, 1987. Vice pres. Phila. Dance Alliance. Fellow Am. coll. Trust and Estate Counsel; mem. ABA (chmn. estate tax includability subcom. estate and gift tax com. sect. taxation), Phila. Bar Assn. (exec. com. orphans' ct. sect. 1986-87, taxation com.). Office: Spector Gadon & Rosen 1700 Market St 29th Fl Philadelphia PA 19103

BUDKE, CAMILLA EUNICE, educator; b. Diller, Nebr., Nov. 9, 1928; d. Rudolph Elmer and Abbie Lena (Zarybnicky) Hubka; m. Larry Francis Budke, Sept. 13, 1952; children: Laurie, Mary, David, Mark. BA cum laude, Duchesne Coll., Omaha, 1950; MS summa cum laude, Kans. State U., 1978; reading specialist, Kans. SAtate U., 1980. Tchr. English/history pub. schs., Blue Springs, Nebr., 1950-51; tchr. English/history Junction City, Kans., 1951-52, Marysville, Kans., 1969-73; tchr. English/reading Unified Sch. Dist. 383, Manhattan, Kans., 1974—. Mem. Parent and Sch. Involvement Com., Manhattan, Kans., 1988—. Mem. AAUW, NEA (bldg. rep. 1986—), Internat. Reading Assn., Riley County Hist. Soc., Kans. Tchrs. English, Atheneum, Cath. Daus., Delta Kappa Gamma, Kappa Gamma Pi. Democrat. Roman Catholic. Home: 1312 Nichols Manhattan KS 66502

BUDOFF, PENNY WISE, physician, author, researcher; b. Albany, N.Y., July 7, 1939; d. Louis and Goldene Wise; m. Seymour L. Budoff, June 24, 1962; children: Jeff, Cynthia. Student U. Wis.; B.A., Syracuse U., 1959; M.D., SUNY-Upstate Med. Sch., 1963. Intern, St. Luke's Meml. Hosp., Utica, N.Y., 1963-64; practice medicine specializing in family practice and women's health, Woodbury, N.Y., 1964-85, 85—; founder, dir. Penny Wise Budoff Women's Med. Ctr., Bethpage, N.Y.; lectr., TV guest on women's medicine; mem. Nat. Com. on Women in Family Medicine; clin. rsch. on menstrual pain and women's health problems. Author: No More Menstrual Cramps and Other Good News, 1980, No More Hot Flashes and Other Good News, 1983; contbr. articles to profl. jours. Bd. dirs. Coalition Against Domestic Violence; adv. bd. Nassau County Physicians for Reproductive Health. Named Women of Yr., C.W. Post Coll., L.I., 1981; recipient Nat. Consumers League award, 1983, Max Cheplove award Erie chpt. N.Y. State Acad. Family Physicians, 1983. Fellow Nassau County Med. Soc., Am. Acad. Family Physicians (nat. com. on pub. rels.); mem. AMA, NOW (Equality Award in Health 1988, Unsong Heroine award), Am. Med. Women's Assn. (co-chmn. nat. women's health com., liason), Nassau Acad. Family Physicians (past pres.). Home: 11 Fairbanks Blvd Woodbury NY 11797 Office: Women's Med Ctr 4300 Hempstead Turnpike Bethpage NY 11714

BUDSON, SUSAN BEHE, legal assistant; b. Detroit, Nov. 20, 1943; d. Daniel and Rose (Swatlo) Budson; children: Leslie M. Rosenberg, Julie Ellen Rosenberg. BA, U. Mich., 1965; Teaching. Cert., SUNY, New Paltz, 1966; Paralegal Cert., Marist Coll., Poughkeepsie, N.Y., 1980. Tchr. Beacon (N.Y.) City Schs., 1966-68; clk. to judge Justice Ct., Town of Poughkeepsie, 1980; legal asst. Corbally, Gartland & Rapleyea, Poughkeepsie, 1979; legal asst./adminstr. Van DeWater & Van DeWater, Poughkeepsie, 1981—; mem. paralegal adv. council Marist Coll., 1986—. Bd. dirs. Mid-Hudson Modern Dance Studio, Poughkeepsie, 1982-84, Commons Bd. of Mgrs., Poughkeepsie, 1987; mem. Clearwater, Poughkeepsie, 1989—; bd. dirs., treas. Alzheimer's Assn., Poughkeepsie, 1987-90. Mem. Legal Profls. Dutchess County, Mid-Hudson Personnel Assn., Dutchess County Bar Assn. (assoc.). Home: 2A Downing Pl Poughkeepsie NY 12603 Office: Van DeWater & Van DeWater 40 Garden St Poughkeepsie NY 12601

BUDWICK, JEANINE ELSTER, diagnostic and remediation therapist; b. Poland, Apr. 14, 1948; came to U.S., 1951; d. Sam and Sally Simone (Schmaltz) Elster; m. Max Jason Budwick, Dec. 31, 1965; children: Mitchell Bernard, Philip Howard. BA with honors, Coll. of S.I., 1986; postgrad., Rutgers U. Pvt. diagnostic therapist S.I., N.Y.; substitute tchr. math. and scis. Holmdel (N.J.) Pub. Schs. Reading vol., S.I.; vol. Silver Lake Nursing Home, S.I., 1980-85; v.p. fin. sect. Women's Am. Orgn. and Rehab. through Tng., pres., 3 yrs. Recipient letter of recognition Clove Lake Nursing Home, S.I., 1984. Mem. Psi Chi.

BUECHLER, JEAN ANN, music educator, composer, publisher; b. Mason City, Iowa, Aug. 8, 1945; d. Bert Roscoe and Pauline Elizabeth (Rieman) Nolin; m. Russell Neal Buechler, Dec. 1, 1973; children: Ryan Kirk, Jalyn Marie. BS, Iowa State U., 1968. Cert. elem. edn. and music tchr., Iowa. Elem. tchr. pub. schs., Muscatine, Iowa, 1968-71, Ames, Iowa, 1971-76; pvt. tchr. piano Ames, 1976—, Huxley, Iowa, 1978-84, Randall, Iowa, 1987—; owner, mgr. Willow Lake antique Shop, Huxley, Iowa, 1980-84, Major Music Studio, Ames, 1987—. Composer Patterns for Piano, 4 vols., 1988. Performer Randall Fine Arts Coun., 1988—, Ames Hosp. Aux., 1988—. Mem. NEA, Nat. Music Tchrs. Assn., Iowa Music Tchrs. Assn., Questers Club, Rush Light Club, Sigma Alpha Iota, Omicron Nu. Republican. Home: RR 1 Box 55 Huxley IA 50124 Office: Major Music Studio 706 Clark St Ames IA 50010

BUEGELER, BARBARA STEPHANIE, accounting and business executive, consultant; b. Lawrence, Kans., Mar. 29, 1945; d. Kimball Drexel and Sara Patricia (Cook) Poland; m. Gregory E. Brown, Jan. 27, 1967 (div. Dec. 1981); 1 child, Katherine P.; m. David M. Buegeler, Feb. 14, 1986. BS magna cum laude, St. Edward's U., 1989, postgrad., 1989—. Acct., controller Schlotzsky's Inc. Corp and Schlotzsky's, Inc., Austin, Tex., 1978-80; ind. ins. agt. New Eng. Life and Cen. Life, Austin, 1980-81; exec. v.p., controller, cons. Supreme Ct. Racquet Clubs, Inc., Austin and San Antonio, 1980-85; pvt. practice Austin, 1984—; asst. controller, cons. Bob Clark Builders Tex., Inc., Round Rock, 1985-87; cons., acct. D. Abernethy Constrn. Corp., Austin, 1987—, Philanthroprises, Inc., Austin, 1987—; controller C.D. Sprague Constrn. Corp., Austin, 1988—. Mem. Inst. Internal Auditors, NAFE, Assn. for Systems Mgmt. (assoc.), Bus. and Profl. Women's Clubs. Democrat. Presbyterian. Home: 911 Mockingbird Manchaca TX 78652 Office: Philanthroprises Inc 911 Mockingbird Manchaca TX 78652

BUEHNER, HEIDI RENATA, Veterinarian; b. Portland, Oreg., Apr. 17, 1958; d. Henry Albert Buehner and Betty Ann Mateer; m. Ron Jay Dickey, Aug. 15. BS, Oreg. State U., Corvallis, 1981, MA, 1987, DVM, 1986; DVM, Wash. State U., Pullman, 1986. Veterinarian Beaverton Pet Clinic, Beaverton, Oreg., 1986-87, Redwood Vet Hosp., Grants Pass, Oreg., 1987--; veterinarian, WildLife Images, Grants Pass, Oreg., 1987--. Mem., Am. Vet. Med. Assn., Am. Animal Hosp. Assn., Soc. of Theriogenology. Rep. Presbyterian. Home: 1326 A Dowell Rd Grants Pass OR 97527

BUELL, CYNTHIA LOUISE, communication educator; b. Ravenna, Ohio, Nov. 24, 1944; d. Franklin Burt and Sara Marie (Bonham) B.; m. Gene Szigeti, Jr., May 19, 1984; 1 child, Franklin Kyle. BA in English, Lake Erie Coll., Painesville, Ohio, 1966; MA in Speech, Kent State U., 1970; MA in Communication, Marshall U., 1981; PhD in Communication, Fla. State U., 1983. Cert. in communicatons, Ohio. Lectr. speech Case Western Res. U., Cleve., 1967-77; asst. prof. So. W.Va. Community Coll., Williamson, 1977-80; instr. English, Tallahassee Community Coll., 1983-84; grad. teaching asst. in communication Fla. State U., Tallahassee, 1981-83; assoc. prof. communication Wesleyan U., Macon, Ga., 1984—; trainer, cons. various cos., Macon, 1990—. Author: Persuasive Public Speaking: A Liberal Arts Approach, 1990. Avcocate Hospice Cen. Ga., Macon, 1988—; Wesleyan Coll. campaign chmn. United Way, Macon, 1989, 90. Grantee Marshall U., 1978, Wesleyan Coll., 1986, 90. Mem. Speech Communication Assn. (vice chmn.-elect sr. coll. sect. 1989), Internat. Assn. for Bus. Communication, So. Speech Communication Assn., Ga. Speech Communication Assn. (pres. 1989). Republican. Methodist. Home: 180 Castlegate Rd Macon GA 31210 Office: Wesleyan Coll 4760 Forsyth Rd Macon GA 31297

BUETTNER, CAROL ANN, state legislator; b. Madison, Wis., Jan. 16, 1948; d. John J. and Lucy (Kraner) Murphy; m. Douglas William Buettner, 1976. BS, U. Wis., Oshkosh, 1972. Dir. nutrition program for older adults County of Winnebago, Wis., 1973-82; state rep. dist. 81 State of Wis., 1983-87, state senator, 1987—; instr. pre-retirement planning Fox Valley Tech. Inst., 1978-81. Bd. dirs. Oshkosh Found., 1976-82. Home: 232 Fulton St Oshkosh WI 54901*

BUFFINGTON, AUDREY VIRGINIA, educator, consultant, author; b. Westminster, Md., Oct. 6, 1931; d. Martin Luther and Elsie Virginia (Heltibridle) Myers; m. John David Buffington, June 20, 1953 (div. 1963); 1 child, A. Virtina Buffington Hunter. BA, Western Md. Coll., 1952; MEd, Pa. State U., 1968. Cert. tchr., supr., Md., Mass. Tchr. math. Carroll County Pub. Schs., Westminster, 1952-68, supr. math., 1968-73; state math. supr. Md. Dept. Edn., Balt., 1973-79; program mgr. Ginn & Co., Lexington, Mass., 1979-81; tchr. math Wayland (Mass.) Pub. Schs., 1982—; speaker, workshop leader numerous local and state edn. meetings. Author: Meters, Liters and Grams, 1973, textbook series Merrill Mathematics, 1985, 87, math. comic books King Features Comic Math. Libr., 1979; creator NASCO Algebra Models. Pres. Carroll County Gen. Hosp. Aux., Westminster. Recipient Math. Educator of Yr. award Md. Coun. Tchrs. Math., 1978, Trustee Alumni award Western Md. Coll., 1979. Mem. NEA, Nat. Coun. Tchrs. Math., Assn. State Suprs. Math., Assn. Tchrs. Math. in Mass., Mass. Tchrs. Assn. Republican. Lutheran. Home: 2 Old Farm Rd Wayland MA 01778

BUFFKIN, BEVERLY EDITH, government agency administrator; b. Sonoma, Calif., Nov. 3, 1961; d. Lawrence Robert and Anna Olivia (Anderson) J.; m. Mark D. Buffkin, Dec. 12, 1987; 1 child, Beaufort John. BS in Fin., Marist Coll., 1983. Fin. mgmt. trainee Navy Fin. Ctr., Long Beach, Calif. and Cleve., 1984-86; budget dir. USN, Long Beach, 1986-89; budget analyst Naval Air Sta., Alameda, Calif., 1989; dep. controller Naval Air Res., Alameda, 1989—; counselor EEO, Dept. of the Navy, Long Beach, 1987-89. Mem. Am. Soc. Mil. Comptrollers (v.p. 1984-86, sec. 1986-87, pres. 1987-89), Fed. Mgrs. Assn., NAFE, Delta Zeta (v.p. 1982). Club: Long Beach Rowing. Lodge: Circle K (lt. gov. 1983-84). Office: Naval Air Res Cod 60 NAS Alameda CA 94501

BUFFUM, NANCY KAY, interior designer; b. Portland, Oreg., Aug. 10, 1941; d. William Cheely and Wanda (Camblin) Whitman; student Shasta Coll., 1959-60, U. Calif.-Berkeley, 1960-63; m. Jack Erwin Buffum, Mar. 24, 1961 (div. 1981); children—Andrew Lewis, Airenne. Exec. sec. Pacific Mut. Life Ins. Co., San Francisco, 1961-63; gen. cashier N.Am. Brokers, San Francisco, 1963-64; mgr. So. area office Lindsey & Co., Sacramento, 1964-65; escrow office, sales rep. Kennicott Constrn. Co., Redding, Calif., 1967-69; office mgr., gen. ptnr. Buffum & Assocs., Redding, 1969-72; asst. designer Penthouse Interiors, Redding, 1973-75; owner, designer The Design Works, Redding, 1975—; lectr. on design and antiques to community groups and colls. Pres. Shasta County Easter Seals Soc., 1971-73; pres. Redding Elem. Sch. PTA, 1973-77, trustee, adv. com. sch. bd., 1975-77; bd. dirs. Redding Mus. League; adviser KIXE Pub. TV Sta.; mem. Redding Planning Commn., 1981-87; mem. adv. bd. Riverfront Playhouse, 1980, Mercy Hosp., 1989; v.p. Sacramento Div. League of Calif. Cities, 1989; mem. Calif. Devel. Coun., 1988—; mem. Redding City Coun., 1988, mayor, 1990—; bd. dirs. Pvt. Industry Coun., 1985—. Recipient Pub. Svc. award Rotary Internat., 1976, named Business Woman of Yr., 1982, Woman of Yr., Bus. and Profl. Women Assn., 1988, Woman of Achievement, AAUW, 1989. Mem. DAR (hon. pub. svc. award), Redding C. of C. (v.p. 1984-85; Bus. Woman of Year 1982), Soroptimists, Redding Main Club. Republican. Avocations: snow skiing, scuba diving, entertaining, sewing, reading. Office: 1600 California St #100 Redding CA 96001

BUFORD, EVELYN CLAUDENE SHILLING, printing company executive; b. Fort Worth, Sept. 21, 1940; d. Claude and Winnie Evelyn (Mote) Hodges; student Hill Jr. Coll., 1975-76; m. William J. Buford, Mar. 1982; children by previous marriage: Vincent Shilling, Kathryn Lynn Shilling Vassar. With Imperial Printing Co., Inc., Ft. Worth, 1964-70, 77—, gen. sales mgr. comml. div., 1982—, corp. sec., 1977—; with Tarrant County Hosp. Dist., Fort Worth, 1973-77, asst. to asst. adminstr., 1981-84. Mem. adv. bd. Bus. Profls. Am., Ft. Worth Ind. Sch. Dist. Mem. Exec. Women Internat. (dir., publs. chmn., v.p. 1984, pres. 1985, chmn. adv. com. 1986, 87, scholarship dir. 1988-90, corp. publ. com. 1988-89), NAFE, Presidents Club Tex. Republican. Methodist. Home: 1025 Kenneth Ln Burleson TX 76028 Office: Imperial Printing Co Inc 1429 Hemphill Fort Worth TX 76104

BUGBEE, MYRA JANE, educator; b. Middlesboro, Ky., May 25, 1952; d. Leon Morris and Wilma Ethel (Pennington) Ball; m. Richard Lee Bugbee, Jr., May 6, 1978. BS, Va. Poly. Inst. and State U., 1974; teaching credential, U.Calif., Davis, 1980; postgrad., Rider Coll., Lawrenceville, N.J. Lic. pvt. pilot. Dept. supr. J.C. Penney Co., Del Rio, Tex., 1974-77; instr. sewing Singer Sewing Co., Altus, Okla., 1977-78; tchr. 1st grade Scandia Elem. Sch., Travis AFB, Calif., 1980-83, Mill Lake Sch., Monroe Twp. Bd. Edn., Spotswood, N.J., 1984-88; pre-first tchr. Mill Lake Sch., Monroe Twp. Bd. Edn., Spotswood, 1988—; mem. sch. coms. Vol. Am. Cancer Fund Dr., 1990; brownie scout leader Girl Scouts U.S., 1978-80. Mem. NEA, Monroe Twp. Ednl. Assn. (exec. bd.), Middlesex County Ednl. Assn. (county rep.), Phi Upsilon Omicron. Home: 5 Mill Rd Jamesburg NY 08831 Office: Mill Lake Sch Monmouth Ave Spotswood NJ 08884

BUGBEE-JACKSON, JOAN, sculptor; b. Oakland, Calif., Dec. 17, 1941; d. Henry Greenwood and Jeanie Ogden (Abbot) B.; B.A. in Art, San Jose (Calif.) State Coll., 1964, M.A., 1966; student Nat. Acad. Sch. Fine Arts, N.Y.C., 1966-72, Art Students League, N.Y.C., 1968-70; m. John Michael Jackson, June 21, 1973; 1 child, Brook Bond. Apprentice to Joseph Kiselewski, 1970-72; Instr. art Foothill (Calif.) Jr. Coll., 1966-67; instr. design De Anza Jr. Coll., Cupertino, Calif., 1967-68; instr. pottery Greenwich House Pottery, N.Y.C., 1969-71, Craft Inst. Am., N.Y.C., 1970-72, Cordova (Alaska) Extension Center, U. Alaska, 1972-79, Prince William Sound Community Coll., 1979—; one-woman exhbns. in Maine, N.Y.C., Alaska and Calif.; group exhbns. include Allied Artists Am., 1970-72, Nat. Acad. Design, 1971, 74; pres. Cordova Arts and Pageants Ltd., 1975-76; commns. include Marie K. Smith Commemorative plaque, 1973, Bob Korn Pool Commemorative Plaque, 1975, Eyak Native Monument, 1978, Anchorage Pioneer's Home Ceramic Mural, 1979, Alaska Wildlife Series Bronze Medal, 1980, sculpture murals and portraits Alaska State Capitol, 1981, Pierre De Ville Portrait commn., 1983, Robert B. & Evangeline Atwood, 1985, Armin F. Koernig Hatchery Plaque, 1985, Cordova Fishermen's Meml. Sculpture, 1985, Alaska's Five Govs., bronze relief, Anchorage, 1986, Reluctant Fisherman's Mermaid, bronze, 1987, Charles E. Bunnell, bronze portrait statue, Fairbanks, 1988, Alexander Baranof monument, Wally Noerenberg, Sitka, Alaska, 1989, Hatchery Plaque, Prince William Sound, Alaska, 1989; also other portraits. Scholarship student Nat. Acad. Sch. Fine Arts, 1969-72; recipient J.A. Suydam Bronze medal, 1969; Dr. Ralph Weiler prize, 1971; Helen Foster Barnet award, 1971; Daniel Chester French award, 1972; Frishmuth award, 1971; Allied Artists Am. award, 1972; C. Percival Dietsch prize, 1973; citation Alaska Legislature, 1981, 82. Fellow Nat. Sculpture Soc. Address: Box 374 Cordova AK 99574

BUGG, JUNE MOORE, state legislator; b. Altoona, Ala., Oct. 7, 1919; d. Sims Smith and Bertie Edith (Powell) Moore; m. Bill Knight Bugg (dec. 1987); children: Barbara Bugg, Bill Jr. BA in Edn., U. Ala., 1940, postgrad., 1970; MS in Edn., Jacksonville (Ala.) State U., 1970. Librarian Gadsden (Ala.) High Sch., 1941-46, tchr. English, 1952-65; librarian Ala. Tech. Coll., Gadsden, 1949-51; mem. Ala. Ho. of Reps., Montgomery, 1983—; librarian Gadsden Ctr., U. Ala.; student-tchr. supr., U. Ala., Birmingham, 1975-80. Chair Project Our Town, Gadsden; mem. Ala. Dem. Exec. Com., 1982—; mem. adv. coun. Ret. Sr. Vol. Program, Etowah County, Ala.; adv. bd. Community Intensive Treatment for Youth of Etowah County. Recipient

Pres.'s award Downtown Action Council, 1976-77, award AAUW, 1981; inducted into Ala. Sr. Citizens' Hall of Fame, 1990. Mem. Alpha Xi Delta (Order of Rose 1987). Methodist. Office: Ala Ho Reps Union St Montgomery AL 36130

BUIST, JEAN MACKERLEY, veterinarian; b. Newton, N.J., Dec. 24, 1919; d. Ackerson Jacob and Mary Morris (Morford) Mackerley; m. Richardson Buist, Oct. 2, 1948; children: Peter Richardson, Jean Morford Buist Earle, Mary Elizabeth Buist Forbes. DVM, Cornell U., 1942. Veterinarian Summit (N.J.) Dog and Cat Hosp., 1942-48; pvt. practice Sparta, N.J., 1948—. Mem. Sparta Twp. Bd. Health, 1962-82; mem., chmn., sec. N.J. State Bd. Vet. Med. Examiners. Recipient Gaines award Newton Kennel Club, 1970, Disting. Svc. award Assn. Women Veterinarians, 1989. Mem. Nat. Assn. State Bds. (pres.-elect 1984, pres. 1985-86), Am. Vet. Med. Assn. (nat. bd. exam. com. 1987—, chmn. 1990—), N.J. Vet. Med. Assn. (treas. 1982—), N.J. Acad. Vet. Medicine and Surgery (bd. dirs. 1972—, sec. 1975-82), Sussex County 4-H Horse Club Leaders Assn. (pres. 1970-76), Sussex County Horse Show Assn. (v.p. 1980-82, pres. 1982-90), Sussex County Farm and Horse Show Assn. (v.p. 1980—). Home: 143 Old Stanhope Rd Sparta NJ 07871

BUKAR, MARGARET WITTY, administrator, civic leader; b. Evanston, Ill., June 21, 1950; d. LeRoy and Catherine Ann (Conrad) Witty; m. Gregory Bryce Bukar, June 5, 1971 (dec. 1989); children: Michael Bryce, Caroline Nicole. BS, DePaul U., 1972, MBA, 1981. Staff med. technologist The Evanston (Ill.) Hosp., 1972-75, immunopathology lab. supr., 1975-77, lab. mgr., 1977-84, dir. lab. adminstrn., 1984-85; bookkeeper Ronald Knox Montessori Sch., Wilmette, Ill., 1986-87. Den leader Cub Scouts, Boy Scouts Am., Wilmette, 1985-87, den leader coach, 1987-88; active PTA of St. Francis Xavier Sch., 1985—, chair rummage sale, 1987-88; mem. sch. bd. St. Francis Xavier Sch., 1986-87, sec. 1988-89, vice chmn., 1989-90. Recipient Emily Withrow Stebbins award Evanston Hosp., 1985. Mem. NAFE, Am. Soc. Clin. Pathologists, Wilmette Hist. Soc. Avocations: knitting, restoring old homes, interior design. Home: 1611 Greenwood Ave Wilmette IL 60091

BUKLEY, ANGELIA P., control systems engineer; b. Natchez, Miss., Feb. 3, 1957; d. Flavius H. and Pauline (Day) Smith; m. Jerry W. Bukley, Feb. 4, 1984. BSBE, BEE, Miss. State U., 1980, MEE, 1981; postgrad., U. Ala., Huntsville. Engr. Control Dynamics Co., Huntsville, 1982-85; engring. mgr. BDM Internat., Huntsville, 1985-89; instr. U. Ala., Huntsville, 1989-90; engr. Marshall Space Flight Ctr. NASA, Huntsville, 1990—. Contbr. articles to profl. jours. CPR instr. ARC, Huntsville, 1983-88; moderator Scholars' Bowl, Ala. Ednl. Opportunity Ctr., Huntsville, 1989-90. Mem. AIAA, IEEE (Engr. of Yr. 1990), Control Systems Soc. of IEEE (chmn. 1988-90), Spring City Cycling Club, (pres. 1989-90).

BUKOVSAN, LAURA ANN, professor of microbiology; b. Norfolk, Va., Jan. 2, 1940; d. Robert Hunter and Grace Elizabeth (Grabman) Colgin; m. William Bukovsan, Aug. 29, 1964; children: William Hunter, James Richard. BS, U. Richmond, 1961; MA, Ind. U., 1963, PhD, 1969. Lectr. SUNY, Oneonta, 1974-75, Hartwick Coll., Oneonta, N.Y., 1979-80; asst. prof. SUNY, Oneonta, 1980-86, assoc. prof., 1986-90, prof. biology, 1990—. Author: Laboratory Exercises in Microbiology, 1987. Trustee Otego (N.Y.) Libr., 1989-94. Ford grant SUNY, 1985, 87. Mem. AAAS, Am. Soc. Microbiology, Soc. of Protozoologists, Genetics Soc. Am., Sigma Xi (sec. 1970-80). Office: SUNY Dept Biology Oneonta NY 13820

BUKOWSKI, ELAINE LOUISE, physical therapist; b. Phila., Feb. 18, 1949; d. Edward Eugene and Melanja Josephine (Przyborowski) B. BS in Phys. Therapy, St. Louis U., 1972; MS, U. Nebr., 1977. Licensed phys. therapist, N.J., Mo., Pa. Clk. City of Phila., 1967; staff phys. therapist St. Louis Chronic Hosp., 1973, Cardinal Ritter Inst., St. Louis, 1973-74; dir. campus ministry musicals Creighton U., Omaha, 1974-75; teaching asst. U. Nebr. Med. Ctr., Omaha, 1975-76; lectr. in anatomy U. Sci. and Tech., Kumasi, Ghana, 1977-78; chief physical therapist Holy Family Hosp., Berekum, Ghana, 1978-79; coordinator info. & guidance The Am. Cancer Soc., Phila., 1979-81; staff phys. therapist Holy Redeemer Vis. Nurse Assn., Phila., 1981-83; rehab. supr. Holy Redeemer Vis. Nurse Assn., Swainton, N.J., 1983-87; asst. prof. phys. therapy Stockton State Coll., Pomona, N.J., 1987—; bd. dirs. The Bridge, Phila., 1979-80; vacation relief phys. therapist in N.J. summers 1988—; mem. profl. adv. coun. Holy Redeemer VNA, Swainton, N.J., 1982—, chmn., 1985—, mem. personnel com., cons. hospice program, 1985-88, rehab. cons., 1987-88; legis. adv. coun. subcom. on edn. and health care Cape May & Cumberland Counties, 1988—. Co-author slide study program, 1976, (video) Going My Way? The Low Back Syndrome, 1976; contbr. articles to profl. jours. Vol. Am. Cancer Soc., Phila., 1979-82, Walk-a-Day-in-My Shoes prog. Girl Scouts Am., Cape May County, N.J., 1983-86; task force phys. therapy prog. Stockton State Coll., Pomona, N.J., 1985-88. U.S. Govt. trainee, 1971, 72; Physical Therapy Fund grantee, 1975, 76; recipient Vol. Achievement award Am. Cancer Soc., 1981. Mem. Am. Phys. Therapy Assn. (community health, edn. traineeship, geriatric sects., orthopedic sect.), N.J. Soc. of Am. Phys. Therapy Assn. (key contact voting dist. 1, legis. network State of N.J. 1989—), Smithsonian Assn., Phys. Therapy Club (sec. 1971-72). Office: Stockton State Coll Phys Therapy Program Pomona NJ 08240

BULAT, MARILYN ELLEN, educator, lecturer; b. Davenport, Iowa, Aug. 10, 1926; d. Carl Nicholas and Eleanor Elizabeth (Linehan) Stutz; m. Thomas Joseph Bulat, Sept. 1, 1949; children: Kathleen, Thomas, Carl, Christine, John, Anne. BA, Marycrest Coll., 1948, MA, 1974. Counselor Iowa State Employment Svc., Davenport, 1948-49; rsch. asst. State U. Iowa, Iowa City, 1950-51; sub. tchr. Bettendorf (Iowa) Pub. Schs., 1974—; lectr. Sci. Assocs., Bettendorf, 1980—. Bd. dirs. Putnam Mus. Roundtable, Davenport, 1987—, chmn. Vol. Rsch. Study, 1985-87; pres. Cath. Svc. League, 1987-89; pres. PTA, Davenport, 1968-70, life mem. 1971—; vol. tutor coord. Davenport Pub. Schs., 1967-73. Mem. AAUW (pres. 1970-71, grant given in her honor 1987), Iowa State Tchrs. Assn. (cert.), Kappa Gamma Pi (pres. 1963-64).

BULEY, MARY THERSE, telecommunications analyst; b. New Prague, Minn., June 28, 1956; d. Charles Henry and Mary Catherine (O'Brien) Buley. BA in Bus. Adminstrn., Coll. St. Benedict, 1978; MBA, Coll. St. Thomas, 1985. Pub. utility rate analyst Minn. Dept. Pub. Svc., St. Paul, 1978-87, 88-89, acting telecommunications mgr., 1987-88; telecommunications/regulatory analyst Minn. Dept. Adminstrn., St. Paul, 1989—; bd. dirs. Telecommunications Access for Communicatively Impaired Persons, St. Paul, 1988-90. Bd. dirs. Coll.St. Benedict Alumni Bd., St. Joseph, Minn., 1982-83; lector, Eucharistic minister St. Olaf Cath. Ch., Mpls.; 2d vice chmn. precinct Dem. Farmer Labor Party, Mpls., 1990. Mem. Women in State Employment (bd. dirs., co-chmn. programs 1990), Trout Unltd. Home: 3509 Colfax Ave S Apt 2 Minneapolis MN 55408

BULFORD, SALLY FARRAN, social services administrator, writer; b. Cleve., May 12, 1939; d. John Frederick Farran and Jeanne Marie (Tresch) Shaw; m. George S. Bulford, Sept. 10, 1960 (div. 1970); 1 child, Anne Farran. Student, Wittenberg U., 1957-58; BA, Ohio State U., 1960, MA, 1962, postgrad., 1987—. Editor Mother Earth News, Hendersonville, N.C., 1971-72; ptnr. Parameter, Columbus, Ohio, 1972-75; editor Ohio Bur. Employment Svcs., Columbus, 1973, Linc Resources, Columbus, 1977-86; dir. Amethyst, Inc., Columbus, 1985-89; devel. dir. Nat. Assault Prevention Ctr., Columbus, 1989—. Contbr. articles to profl. jours. Mem. parent adv. com. Learning Unlimited Sch. for Gifted and Talented, 1977-80, Nat. Inservice Network, 1982, Women's Outreach for Women, 1980-83, sec. 1981-82, Cave Inc., 1983—, Gentlepeople, Inc., 1984—. Mem. Nat. Soc. Fundraising Execs., Nat. Writer's Club, Verse Writer's Guild. Office: Nat Assault Prevention Ctr PO Box 02005 Columbus OH 43202

BULGER, RUTH ELLEN, science administrator, analyst; b. Kansas City, Oct. 21, 1936; d. Tom and Helene (Burnson) Grouse; m. Roger James Bulger, June 8, 1960; children: Faith, Grace. AB, Vassar Coll., Poughkeepsie, N.Y., 1958; AM, Radcliffe Coll., Cambridge, Mass., 1959; PhD, U. Wash. Instr. Sch. Medicine U. Wash., Seattle, 1962-66, asst. prof. Sch. Medicine, 1967-70; assoc. prof. anatomy U. N.C., Chapel Hill, 1970-72; assoc. prof. pathology U. Md., Balt., 1972-74, prof., 1974-76; prof. anatomy U. Mass., Worchester, 1977-78, U. Tex. Health Sci. Ctr., Houston, 1978-88; div. dir. health scis. policy Inst. Medicine, NAS, Washington, 1988—. Contbr. numerous rsch. articles to sci. jours., chpts. to books. Bd. dirs. Found. for Children, 1980-86; moderator 1st Congl. Ch. Houston, 1986-88. Recipient John Freeman award, 1958, Olive Lambert Chemistry prize, 1958, Minnie Stevens Piper award; Matthew Vassar scholar, 1958-59; Andelot fellow Radcliffe Coll., 1959; NIH predoctoral fellow, 1959-62; NIH RCDA, 1969. Mem. Am. Soc. for Nephrology (councillor 1979-83, sec.-treas. 1984-87), Phi Beta Kappa (Greater Houston chpt. councillor 1984-88, sec.-treas. 1986-87, pres. 1987-88, Merck Chemistry award 1957). Office: NAS Inst Medicine 2101 Constitution Ave Washington DC 20418

BULKELEY, CHRISTY CLAIRE, foundation executive; b. Galesburg, Ill., Feb. 10, 1942; d. Gerald Clough and Patricia Ann (Pettingell) Bulkeley; m. Perry David Finks, Sept. 6, 1975. B.J., U. Mo., 1964. Reporter, The Times-Union, Rochester, N.Y., 1964-72, editorial page editor, 1973-74; pres., pub., editor Saratogian, Saratoga Springs, N.Y., 1974-76, 84; pres., pub., editor Comml. News, Danville, Ill., 1976-84; v.p. central region newspaper div. Gannett Co. Inc., 1981-84, v.p. spl. corp. projects, 1984; v.p. Gannett Found., 1985—; dir. WRI Inc., Albany and N.Y.C. Contbg. author: New Guardians of the Press, 1983. Bd. dirs. Danville Area Econ. Devel. Corp., 1981-84, Community Coll. Found., Danville, 1979-84, Vermilion County OIC, Danville, 1978-82, Travers Com., Saratoga, N.Y., 1984; leadership giving capt., nominating com. Greater Rochester United Way, 1986-89; adv. bd. U. Mo. Sch. Journalism, 1986—; v.p. Rochester Grantmakers Forum, 1986-88; mem. steering com. Rochester Womens Fund, 1986-88. Recipient awards Gannett Co. Inc., 1984; Outstanding Contbns. Ill. Mcpl. Human Relations Assn., 1981; Young Achiever Nat. Council Women, 1976. Mem. Women in Communications Inc. (pres. 1975-76, headliner 1978), Am. Soc. Newspaper Editors (bd. dirs. 1983-84), Inland Daily Press Assn. (bd. dirs. 1983-84), AP (nominating com. 1979-84), Women and Found/Corp. Philanthropy (program com. 1988-89), Soc. Profl. Journalists., Danville Area C. of C. (bd. dirs. 1980-84), Carolina Trace Club. Home: 3001 Veasey Terr NW 1611 Washington DC 20008 Office: Gannett Found Inc 1101 Wilson Blvd Arlington VA 22209

BULLARD, JUDITH EVE, psychologist, systems engineer; b. Oneonta, N.Y., Oct. 5, 1945; d. Kurt and Herta (Deutsch) Leeds; divorced; children: Nicholas A., Elizabeth A. BA in Polit. Sci., Spanish U., Oreg., 1966, MA in Psychology, 1973. Supr. residential program Skipworth Juvenile Home, Eugene, Oreg., 1966-68; research asst. Oreg. Research Inst., Eugene, 1968-69, 83-85; supr. residential program Ky. Correctional Facility, Lexington, 1969-70; research asst. U. Oreg., Eugene, 1970-73; asst. dir. Regional Mental Health Clinic, Frankfort, Ind., 1974-76; dir. mental health Lane County Mental Health, Eugene, 1977-80; cons. Managerial Communications, Eugene, 1980-83; systems engr. AT&T Bell Labs., Holmdel, N.J., 1985—; instr. mental health subjects, various ednl. instns.; mem., chmn. compensation and appraisal com. Consumer Product Lab. Bd. dirs. Asbury Park 10K, Jersey Shore 1/2 Marathon, 1985—, Women's Resource and Survival Ctr., Keyport, N.J., 1986—. Recipient Affirmative Action award Bell Lab. Mem. Women's Profl. Network (trustee Holmdel br. 1987—), Partnership in Edn. & Bus., Corrections in Mental Health, Human Factors Soc. Office: AT&T 1K505 Crawfords Corner Rd Holmdel NJ 07733

BULLARD, MARY BOYKIN, educator; b. Perote, Ala., Oct. 24, 1933; d. Estell and Minnie (Rodgers) Boykin; 1 child, Bernadette Maria. BS magna cum laude, Ala. State U., 1955; MS, Troy State U., Montgomery, Ala., 1973. Tchr. Paterson Elem. Sch., Montgomery, 1955, Fews Elem. Sch., Montgomery, 1955-68, Bear Elem. Sch., Montgomery, 1968-77; adminstrv. asst. Dozier Elem. Sch., Montgomery, 1977-78, Wares Ferry Elem. Sch., Montgomery, 1978-79; prin. Highland Ave. Elem. Sch., Montgomery, 1979-80, Vaughn Rd. Elem. Sch., Montgomery, 1980-87; supr.instrn. Montgomery County Bd. Edn., 1987—; adj. instr. Ala. State U., Montgomery, 1988; lectr. in field; conductor seminars in field. Contbr. to book: African Cultures, 1978. Mem. Montgomery Community Concert Assn., 1975—, Montgomery Mus. Fine Arts, 1988—, YMCA, 1979—. Mem. Montgomery County Edn. Assn. (bd. dirs. 1975-82), NEA, Ala. Council for Sch. Adminstrn. and Supervision, Montgomery Sch. Adminstrs. Assn. (pres. 1980-81), Ala. Assn. Elem. Sch. Adminstrsn. (dist. rep. 1983-85, treas. 1985-86, pres. 1986-87), So. Assn. Colls. and Schs., Ten Times One is Ten Federated Club, Kappa Delta Pi. Office: Montgomery County Bd Edn PO Box 1991 Montgomery AL 36102-1991

BULLARD, SHARON WELCH, librarian; b. San Diego, Nov. 4, 1943; d. Dale L. and Myrtle (Sampson) Welch; m. Donald H. Bullard, Aug. 1, 1969. B.S.Ed., U. Central Ark., 1965; M.A., U. Denver, 1967. Media specialist Adams County Sch. Dist. 12, Denver, 1967-69; tchr., libr. Humphrey pub. schs., Ark., 1965-66, libr., 1969-70; catalog libr. Ark. State U., Jonesboro, 1970-75; head documents cataloging Wash. State U., Pullman, 1979-83; head serials cataloging U. Calif.-Santa Barbara, 1984-88, head circulation dept., 1988—; cons. Ctr. for Robotic Systems Microelectronics Rsch. Libr., Santa Barbara, 1986, Calif. State Libr. retrospective conversion project, 1987, Ombudsman's Office U. Calif., Santa Barbara, 1988; distributor Amway, 1985—. Canvasser, Citizens for Goleta Valley, 1985-86. Mem. ALA, Calif. Libr. Assn. (tech. svcs. chpt. southern Calif. sect.), Libr. Assn. U. Calif.-Santa Barabara (mem. subcom. on advancement and promotion 1987—), NAFE, So. Calif. Tech. Processes Group (membership com. 1987). Avocations: t'ai chi chih, walking, hiking, camping, swimming.

BULLEN, MARTHA MAHON, marketing consultant; b. Oakland, Calif., Sept. 23, 1960; d. Bruce Allan and Mary Willis (Waters) Mahon; m. Martin Rixon Bullen, May 28, 1983; 1 child, Claire Mary. BA summa cum laude, Carleton Coll., 1982. Mktg. asst., coordinator Scott, Foresman and Co., Glenview, Ill., 1982-86; mktg. mgr. Bonus Books, Chgo., 1986-88; prin. Bullen Pub. Svcs., Glen Ellyn, Ill., 1989—. Mem. AAUW (bd. dirs. 1983—, newsletter co-editor 1983—, Best in State award 1988), Publishers Mktg. Assn., Phi Beta Kappa. Home and Office: 247 Sawyer Ave Glen Ellyn IL 60137

BULLINS, SANDRA ELAINE, veterinarian; b. Washington, Mar. 8, 1955; d. Joseph Melvin and Mary Kathleen (Fisher) Odell. BS, Radford U., 1977; DVM, Va.-Md. Regional Coll. Vet. Medicine, 1985. Assoc. veterinarian Everhart Animal Hosp., Balt., 1985-87; pvt. practice, Altavista, Va., 1988—. Mem. AVMA, Piedmont Vet. Assn., Altavista Jaycees (bd. dirs. 1989—), NOW, Sierra Club. Democrat. Methodist. Home: Rte 1 Box 165-V Lynch Station VA 24571 Office: Altavista Animal Hosp Rte Box 216-A Altavista VA 24517

BULLIS, FLORENCE EVELYN, small business owner; b. Juneau County, Wis., July 18, 1919; d. John Henry and Edith Aurelia (Wilson) Luth; m. Harvey Leon Bullis, Sept. 23, 1944; children: Lawrence, Richard. BS in Home Econs., U. Cin., 1966, BA in Edn., 1966, MA in Edn., 1971. Evening and night child supr. Orthogenic Sch. at U. Chgo., 1940-42, Billings Hosp./U. Chgo., 1942-45; x-ray tech. Dr. Benjamin Braun, Chgo., 1945-47; home econs. tchr. Cin. pub. schs., 1966-71, writer tchrs. manual, 1970-71; owner Pins, Needles n' Stuff, Cin., 1971-83; ret. Author Students in the Child Care Unit. Active ch. choir. Mem. AAUW. Republican.

BULLOCK, ANNA MAE See TURNER, TINA

BULLOCK, GALE JEANEANE, nurse; b. Charleston, S.C., Nov. 25, 1954; d. Jean Henderson and Elizabeth Ruth (Bendt) B. BS in Nursing, Med. U. of S.C., 1978. RN, S.C. Staff nurse Med. U. Hosp., Charleston, 1978; staff nurse, emergency room Roper Hosp., Charleston, 1978-82, asst. head nurse, emergency room, 1982-83, gen. duty nursing supr., 1983-87; staff nurse Doctors' Home Health Care, Inc., Charleston, 1987-88; staff nurse Roper Home Health Care, Charleston, 1987—, coord. home health care; staff nurse Fairview Southdale Hosp., Edina, Minn., 1990—; dean's search com. Med. U. of S.C. of Nursing, Charleston, 1984-86. Mem. Med. U. of S.C. Coll. of Nursing Alumni Assn. (pres. 1984-86), Sigma Theta Tau. Home: 6400 Barrie Rd #1302 Edina MN 55435

BULLOCK, GAYLE NELSON, hospital administrator; b. Mpls., Sept. 16, 1952; d. Leslie A. and Joyce (Olson) Nelson; m. William J. Bullock; 1 child, Leslie. Student, U. Santa Clara, 1970-72; BA, UCLA, 1974; MPA, U. So. Calif., 1976. Rsch. assoc. Tech. Systems Inst., L.A., 1975-76; asst. adminstr. Cedars-Sinai Med. Ctr., L.A., 1976-79; assoc. adminstr. South Bay Hosp., Redondo Beach, Calif., 1979-84; sr. v.p. corp. devel. Robert F. Kennedy Med. Ctr., Hawthorne, Calif., 1984-85; pres., chief exec. officer St. Jude Hosp., Yorba Linda, Calif., 1985-89; regional v.p. St. Joseph Health System, Orange, Calif., 1989; sr. v.p. Long Beach (Calif.) Meml. Med. Ctr., 1989—. Fellow Am. Coll. Healthcare Execs. (Calif. regents adv. com., Robert S. Hudgens Meml. award com., 1989—); mem. Healthcare Execs. So. Calif. (bd. dirs.), Hosp. Coun. So. Calif. (bd. dirs.), Hosp. Home Health Care Agy. Calif. (bd. dirs.), Women in Health Adminstrn. So. Calif. (bd. dirs.), Delta Gamma Alumnae. Republican. Roman Catholic. Home: 136 Starcrest Irvine CA 92715 Office: Long Beach Meml Med Ctr PO Box 1428 Long Beach CA 90801-1428

BULLOCK, GWENDOLYN A., retired city official; b. N.Y.C., Oct. 18, 1930; d. Herman and Mary (Barnes) Williams; m. John A. Bullock, Dec. 22, 1951 (div. 1960). BA in Pub. Bus. Adminstrn, Antioch Coll., Yellow Springs, Ohio, 1975; M.Urban Studies, Occidental Coll., L.A., 1975; PhD in Pub. Adminstrn., Am. U., Washington, 1983. With VA, Washington, 1948-52, U.S. Dept. Labor, Washington, 1952-64; sec., prog. analyst U.S. Office Econ. Opportunity, Washington, 1964-67; urban policy specialist U.S. HUD, Washington, 1967-70; community svcs. officer U.S. HUD, 1968-69; exec. asst. Dept. Human Resources, D.C. Govt., 1969—; spl. asst. to dep. mayor D.C. Govt., 1971-72; personnel mgr. U.S. Personnel Mgmt., Washington, 1980-84; adminstrv. officer Housing & Community Devel., D.C. Govt., 1984-89; ret.; adj. prof. Am. U., 1989—. Bd. dirs. Hosp. for Sick Children, Washington, 1985—; pres. Big Sisters of D.C., Washington, 1970; active various other charitable orgns. Nat. Urban fellow, Nat. League Cities, 1969-70; Ford Found. fellow, 1969, others. Mem. Am. Soc. Pub. Adminstrn., AAUW, D.C. Group of Am. Soc. Pub. Adminstrn.

BULLOCK, MARIE, real estate investment executive, educator; b. Washington, Aug. 18, 1941; d. Jerry John and Anna Marie (Horstkamp) McCarthy; m. Patrick Ettien, May 31, 1965 (div. Sept. 1969); m. 2d, Charles Edward Bullock, Mar. 3, 1973; children—Ryan, Bennett. BA in Spl. Edn., Marymount Coll., 1984, MA in Counseling, Trinity Coll., 1987. Cert. in spl. edn., Va. Sec., treas. McCarthy Mfg. Co. Inc., Alexandria, Va., 1969-82; v.p. EduTrainer, Inc., Alexandria, 1979-83; mng. ptnr. C&E Partnership, Alexandria, 1971—. Pres. St. Andrew's Episcopal PTA, Bethesda, 1981; bd. dirs. Bethesda Acad. Arts. Mem. Montgomery County Assn. for Children with Learning Disabilities, Council Exceptional Children (v.p. 1984), Psi Chi. Democrat. Christian. Clubs: Kenwood Country (Bethesda, Md.); Zonta Internat. Avocations: reading; theater; cooking; biking; skiing. Home: 5118 Dalecarlia Dr Bethesda MD 20816

BULLOCK, NORMA KATHRYN RICE, chemical research professional; b. Bartlesville, Okla., Sept. 24, 1945; d. Robert Bruce and Norma Elaine (Fanshier) Rice; m. Kenneth Richard Bullock, Feb. 4, 1967; children: Kerry Robin, Kevin Royce. BA, Colo. U., 1967; MS, Northwestern U., 1969, PhD, 1972. Rsch. specialist The Gates Co., Denver, 1972-76; sr. electrochemist Johnson Controls, Inc., Milw., 1977-80, mgr. chem. rsch., 1980—; adj. asst. prof. U. Wis.-Milw., 1979. Editor symposium procs.; contbr. tech. papers to profl. publs. NIH fellow, 1969-72. Fellow Royal Soc. Chemists (London), Am. Inst. Chemists; mem. Am. Chem. Soc. (treas. Colo. sect. 1974-76), Internat. Union Pure and Applied Chemistry (U.S. rep. 1987-91), Electrochem. Soc. (div. sec.-treas. 1988-90, bd. dirs. 1985-87, chmn. coun. local sects. 1985-86, chmn. contbg. membership 1983-85, chmn. Rocky Mountain sect. 1973-74), Internat. Soc. Electrochemistry. Office: Johnson Controls Inc 5757 N Green Bay Ave Milwaukee WI 53209

BULLUCK, JANICE DENISE, insurance company representative; b. Rocky Mount, N.C., Mar. 27, 1958; d. Estee B. and Julia (Israel) B. BA in Psychology, N.C. Cen. U., 1980. Ins. agt. N.C. Mut. Life Ins. Co., Rocky Mount, 1985-87, sales mgr., 1987—. Active NAACP. Lt. USAF, 1980-84. Mem. Rocky Mount Life Underwriters Assn., Life Underwriters Tng. Coun. (grad.), NAFE, Alpha Kappa Alpha Sorority Inc. Democrat. Home: 528 Antioch Rd Rocky Mount NC 27801 Office: 420 N Parker St Rocky Mount NC 27801

BULMAHN, LYNN, journalist, free-lance writer; b. Waco, Tex., Feb. 18, 1955; d. Franklin Harrold and Louise (Stolte) B. BA, SW Tex. State U., 1977. Med., health, and gen. assignment reporter Waco Tribune Herald, 1977—, city desk rewrite person, 1977-78, editor/reporter religion page, 1978-81, human svcs. reporter, 1978-83, med. reporter, 1978—, Help-Line columnist, 1981-86 ; free-lance writer, 1975-77; gen. assignment reporter, 1977-88, med./health features writer, Waco Tribune-Herald, 1988—. Voter registration chmn. Waco area LWV, 1977-80; vol. Family Abuse Ctr., Waco, 1982—. Recipient Anson Jones Merit citation, Tex. Med. Assn., 1978, Outstanding Contbn. award Nat. Found. March of Dimes, 1980, Pub. Health award for media excellence Tex. Pub. Health Assn., 1980, 85, 88, 89, First Place award Readers Digest Mag. Workshop Tex. Competition, 1981, Feature Writing award North and East Tex. Press Assn., 1983, Media Appreciation award McLennan County Med. Assn., 1985, Journalism Excellence award Am. Cancer Soc., 1989, Silver Star of Tex. award Tex. Hosp. Assn., 1989, Newspaper award, Mental Health Assn., 1985, Medic award, 1985. Mem. Central Tex. Journalists, Waco Jaycees (Outstanding New Mem. of Month 1985), Sigma Delta Chi. Office: Waco Tribune-Herald 900 Franklin Ave Waco TX 76702

BUMPUS, LINDA DOSTER, teacher; b. Buffalo, May 11, 1946; d. Carlton Herman and Evelyn Amelia (Leight) Doster; m. Richard James Bumpus, Jr., June 24, 1967; children: Scott Allen, Heidi Michelle. BS, SUNY, 1968, MS, 1971. Tchr. SUNY at Buffalo Campus Sch., 1968-70, N.Y. State Div. for Youth, Johnstown, 1975--; steward, counsel leader Pub. Employees Fedn., 1980—, mem. exec. bd., 1989—. Troop advancement chmn. Boy Scouts Am., 1989, com. chmn. Explorer post, 1988—. Mem. AAUW (past pres.), Assn. Math. Tchrs. N.Y. State, N.Y. State United Tchrs. Home: RD 1 Box 555 Gloversville NY 12078 Office: NY State Div for Youth Box 605 Johnstown NY 12095

BUMSTEAD, SUSAN, insurance/financial services company public relations consultant; b. Boston, July 3, 1963; d. Robert Martin and Lou Ann (Neth) B. BA, U. N.H., 1985. Pub. rels. cons. New England Mut. Life Ins. Co., Boston, 1985—. Fund raiser Hammond Castle Mus., Gloucester, Mass., 1987, 88. Mem. Women in Communications, Publicity Club New England (merit award 1987), Phi Beta Kappa. Republican. Office: New Eng Mut Life Ins Co 50l Boylston St Boston MA 02117

BUNCH, KAREN SHORE, marketing professional; b. Greensboro, N.C., Apr. 12, 1957; d. Ralph B. and Bettie Majette (Brickhouse) Shore; m. Keith Whitfield Bunch, Aug. 31, 1985. BSBA, Appalachian State U., 1979. Sales svc. specialist Stevens Graphics, Greensboro; bus. mgr. Guilford Bus. Forms, Greensboro; dir. adminstrn. Keith Bunch Assocs., Greensboro. Mem. winning women in the workplace com. YWCA; mem. Piedmont Triad Coun. for Internat. Visitors; bd. elders Fellowship Presbyn. Ch. Mem. NAFE, Am. Bus. Women's Assn. (newsletter editor Carolina Piedmont chpt. 1989, v.p. 1990—, Merit award 1990, named Bus. Assoc. of Yr. 1990), Greensboro Area Incentives Network (founder, bd. dirs., Woman of Yr 1990), Twin City Female Execs. (bd. dirs.), Greensboro C. of C. (chair small bus. coun., named Small Bus. Adv. of Yr. 1990), Triad Women's Profl. Devel. Conference Steering Com., Triad Masters Swimming (bd. dirs.). Office: 1901-G Ashwood Ct Ste 258 Greensboro NC 27408

BUNCH, LUANN VICTORY, marketing executive; b. Mpls., May 3, 1955; d. John F. and Theresa A. (Otten) Victory; m. Dennis Bunch, Dec. 24, 1986. AA, North Hennepin Community Coll., Brooklyn Park, Minn., 1975; BA magna cum laude, St. Cloud State U., 1976; MA with high honors, Southwestern Mo. State U., 1978. Dir. pub. rels. Park Cen. Hosp., Springfield, Mo., 1977-79; dir. community rels. and devel. Mt. Carmel Med. Ctr., Pittsburg, Kans., 1980-82; dir. physician mktg. and recruiting Coord. Svcs., Wichita, 1982-85; mgr. profl. rels. Rep. Health Corp., Dallas, 1985-86; dir. mktg. Timberlawn Psychiat. Hosp., Dallas, 1987—. Editor: Insight (Telestar award 1988), 1987, Direct Mail Piece (Telestar award 1988, Bronze Quill award of Excellence for Brown Bag lectr. series Internat. Assn. Bus. Communicators 1989), 1987, Inner View, 1977-78, Spectrum, 1980; host radio and TV talk shows, Pittsburg. Bd. dirs. ARC, Pittsburg, 1981; dir. Pittsburg Community Theatre, 1981; instr. Pittsburg Children's Theatre Workshop, 1981; pub. relations cons. Am. Diabetes Assn., Springfield, 1979.

Recipient Applause award Tex. Soc. Mktg. and Pub. Rels., 1988-89, 90-91, Telestar award and merit award Brown Bay Series, 1990, First Pl. award Nat. Assn. Pvt. Psychiat. Hosps., 1990. Mem. Am. Mktg. Assn., Am. Soc. Mktg. and Pub. Rels., Am. Soc. Planning and Mktg., Women in Communications, Tex. Soc. Hosp. Mktg. and Pub. Rels. Roman Catholic. Home: 4421 Sterling Ln Plano TX 75024 Office: Timberlawn Psychiat Hosp 4600 Samuell Blvd Dallas TX 75223

BUNDESEN, FAYE STIMERS, teacher, investment/management company owner; b. Cedarville, Calif., Sept. 16, 1932; d. Floyd Walker and Ermina Elizabeth (Roberts) Stimers; m. Allen Eugene Bundesen, Dec. 27, 1972; children—William, David, Edward Silvius; Ted, Eric Bundesen. B.A., Calif. State U.-Sacramento, 1955; M.A., Calif. State U.-San Jose, 1972. Licensed real estate broker, Calif. Elem. sch. tchr. San Francisco Pub. Schs., 1955-60; elem. and jr. high sch. tchr., lang. arts specialist Sunnyvale (Calif.) Schs., 1978-83; cons. Santa Clara County Office of Edn. and Sunnyvale Sch. Dist., 1983-86; v.p. Bundesen Enterprises, Elk Grove, Calif., 1975-81, pres., 1981—. Bd. dirs. Sunnyvale Sch. Employees' Credit Union, 1983-86, v.p., 1984-86; mem. City of San Jose Tenant/Landlord Hearing Com., 1983-86, v.p., 1984-85. Mem. Assn. Supervision and Curriculum Devel., Calif. Scholarship Fedn. (life), AAUW, Tri-County Apartment Assn., Calif. Apartment Assn., Nat. Apartment Assn., Santa Clara County Real Estate Bd., Calif. Assn. Realtors, Nat. Assn. Realtors, Sacramento Assn. Realtors. Presbyterian. Office: PO Box 2006 Elk Grove CA 95759-2006

BUNDSCHUH, MARJORIE GUREVITZ, clinical laboratory technologist, chemist; b. Columbus, Ohio, July 27, 1952; d. Norman and Norma Jean (Stetelman) Gurevitz; m. David Alan Clayman, June 5, 1977 (div. June 1981); m. John Phillip Bundschuh, May 25, 1986. Student, Ohio U., 1970-72; BS in Med. Tech., U. Cin., 1976; postgrad., Cen. Mich. U., 1978, Calif. Coll. Arts and Crafts, 1981-82. Registered med. technologist Am. Soc. Clin. Pathologists; lic. clin. lab. technologist, Calif. Computer programmer, operator svcs. div. Amron co., 1971-72, 74-77; cell biology and immunology rsch. asst. Shriner's Burn Inst., Cin., 1974-75; spl. chemistry lab. technician Doctor's Hosp. North, Columbus, Ohio, 1975, hematology med. technologist, 1977; chemistry and microbiology med. technologist Children's Med. Ctr., Dayton, Ohio, 1977-81; microbiology and chemistry clin. lab. asst. U. Calif. San Francisco Gen. Hosp., 1982-86, chemistry clin. lab. technologist, 1987—; sales cons. computer software packages Amron Systems, Columbus and San Francisco, 1981-82. Co-chmn. fundraising Women's Twig of Children's Med. Ctr., Dayton, 1980; vol. youth at risk program Breakthrough Found., San Francisco, 1983, fin. sponsor 1986—, Holiday Project, San Francisco, 1983-84; chpt. pres. Women's Am. ORT, Dayton, 1979-80; fin. family sponsor The Hunger Project, San Francisco, 1983—; active San Francisco Mus. Modern Art. Mem. Am. Assn. Clin. Chemistry, Am. Assn. for Med. Tech., Am. Assn. for Clin. Pathology (assoc.), Iota Sigma Pi. Jewish. Home: 730 Bay Rd Mill Valley CA 94941 Office: San Francisco Gen Hosp U Calif Clin Labs 1001 Potrero St Rm 2M San Francisco CA 94110

BUNDY, ELIZABETH CAMPBELL, electronics consulting company executive; b. N.Y.C., May 15, 1960; d. Clifford Blaine and Jeanne (Maher) Campbell; m. Christopher Bruce Bundy, Aug. 30, 1980; children: Christopher Douglass, Patricia Elizabeth, Victoria Frances. BSBA, Calif. State U., Chico, 1981. Rsch. mgr. The Bradbury Mgmt. Group, San Jose, Calif., 1981-84, dir. rsch., 1984-85; dir. rsch. MSL Internat., Ltd., San Francisco, 1985-86; cons. Holland Rusk & Assocs., San Francisco, 1986; pres. Connect Worldwide, Palo Alto, Calif., 1986—; bd. dirs. DC Systems, Pleasanton, Calif. Mem. NAFE. Republican. Episcopalian.

BUNE, KAREN LOUISE, criminal justice official; b. Washington, Mar. 6, 1954; d. Harry and Eleanor Mary (White) B. BA in Am. Studies cum laude, Am. U., 1976, MS in Adminstrn. of Justice with distinction, 1978. Notary pub., Va. Case mgr. Arlington (Va.) Alcohol Safety Action Program, 1979—; case mgr. regional rep. of case mgmt. com. of Dirs. Assn. Commn. on Va. Alcohol Safety Action Program, Richmond, 1980-81, 84-85, 88-89, mem. subcom. studying treatment issues, 1988—. Sch. of Justice rep. alumni adv. com. Coll. Pub. Affairs, Am. U., Washington, 1982-86, chmn. student rels., 1982-86. Recipient spl. achievement award Dept. Navy, 1973, merit award Arlington County, 1986. Mem. Nat. Assn. Chiefs Police (Award of Merit 1986), Nat. Criminal Justice Assn., Am. Pub. Health Assn., Am. Police Hall of Fame (Cert. of Appreciation 1985), No. Va. Fraternal Order of Police, Acad. Criminal Justice Scis., So. Criminal Justice Assn., Am. Soc. Criminology, NAFE, Phi Kappa Phi, Phi Alpha Alpha, Phi Delta Gamma (2d v.p. 1978-80, 82, 1st v.p. 1981-82). Home: 926 S 16th St Arlington VA 22202 Office: Arlington Alcohol Safety 1400 N Courthouse Rd N Arlington VA 22201

BUNIM, MARY-ELLIS, television producer; b. Northampton, Mass., July 9, 1946; d. Frank Roberts and Roslyn Dena (LaMontagne) Paxton; m. Robert Eric Bunim, Jan. 31, 1971; 1 dau., Juliana. Pres. MEP Prodns. Inc., 1976—; ptnr. Bunim-Murray Prodns., N.Y.C., 1988—; exec. producer daily CBS TV series Search for Tomorrow, 1976-81, As the World Turns, 1981-84, NBC-TV's Santa Barbara, 1984-86, Crime Diaries, 1988, ABC's Loving, 1989-90, FBC series American Families, 1990—; v.p. tape programs New World TV, L.A., 1986-87.

BUNN, DOROTHY IRONS, court reporter; b. Trinidad, Colo., Apr. 30, 1948; d. Russell and Pauline Anna (Langowski) Irons; m. Peter Lynn Bunn; children: Kristy Lynn, Wade Allen, Russell Ahearn. Student No. Va. Community Coll., 1970-71, U. Va., Fairfax, 1971-72. Registered profl. reporter; cert. shorthand reporter. Pres., chief exec. officer Ahearn Ltd., Springfield, Va., 1970-81, Bunn & Assocs., Glenrock, Wyo., 1981—; cons. Bixby Hereford Co., Glenrock, 1981-89, co-mgr., 1989—. Del., White House Conf. on Small Bus., Washington, 1986. Mem. NAFE, Am. Indian Soc., Nat. Shorthand Reporters Assn., Wyo. Shorthand Reporters Assn. (chmn. com. 1984—), Nat. Fedn. Ind. Businesses, Nat. Assn. Legal Secs., Nat. Fedn. Bus. and Profl. Women, Nat. Assn. Legal Secs. Internat. Avocations: art, music. Home: PO Box 1602 Bixby Hereford Co Glenrock WY 82637 Office: Bunn & Assocs 81 Bixby Rd Glenrock WY 82637

BUNNER, PATRICIA ANDREA, lawyer; b. Fairmont, W.Va., Sept. 16, 1953; d. Scott Randolph and Virginia Lenore (Keck) B. AB in History and English, W.Va. U., 1975, JD, 1978. Bar: W.Va. 1978, U.S. Dist. Ct. (so. dist.) W.Va. 1978, U.S. Dist. Ct. (no. dist.) W.Va. 1985, U.S. Supreme Ct. 1989. Mem. staff Dem. Nat. Com., Washington, 1978-79; assoc. Gailor, Elias & Matz, Washington, 1979-81, N.Y. State Bankers Assn., N.Y.C., 1981-83; ptnr. Bunner & Bunner, Fairview, W.Va., 1984—; exec. dir. N.Y. State Consumer Mortgage Rev. Bd.; chmn. dist. VIII Consumer Mortgage Rev. Com., N.Y.C., 1982-83; cons. atty. Energy Cons. Assocs., Spring Harbor, N.Y., 1981; of counsel Monongahela (W.Va.) Soil Conservation Dist., 1985. Author: N.Y. State Bankers Assn. Legis. Directory, 1983. Pres. Monongalia County Dem. Women, 1987—; sec. Monongalia County Devel. Authority, 1984—; pres. United Taxpayers Assn., Inc., W.Va., 1985-88; bd. dirs. W.Va. U., Morgantown, 1974-75. Rilla Moran Woods fellow Nat. Fedn. Dem. Women, Washington, 1978. Mem. ABA (vice chmn. legal econs. and new lawyers coms. 1986-87, litigation sect., 1st amendment rights and media law com., gen. practice com., corps. and banking com.), W.Va. Bar Assn. (com. econs. of law practice 1987—), Assn. Trial Lawyers Am., W.Va. Trial Lawyers Assn., N.Y. State Bar Assn., Monongalia County Bar Assn., Marion County Bar Assn., W.Va. Criminal Def. Lawyers Assn., Women's Info. Ctr. (founding), LWV, NAFE, W.Va. Alliance for Women's Studies (founding), Bus. and Profl. Women (bd. dirs.), Climates, Inc., Monongalia County Hist. Soc., Clay-Battelle Alumni Assn., W.Va. Coll. Law Alumni Assn., Nat. Rifle Assn. (life), Nature Conservancy, Nat. Arbor Day Found., World Wildlife Fund, Am. Farmland Trust, AAUW, Sierra Club, Audobon Soc., Young Dems. Club W.Va. (sec. 1976), Phi Alpha Theta (chpt. pres. 1974-75), Phi Beta Kappa, Zeta Phi Eta, Alpha Rho (chpt. pres. 1974). Mem. Ch. of Christ. Club: Woman's (bd. dirs. Morgantown chpt. 1986—). Home: Rt 2 Box 341 Fairview WV 26570 Office: 818 Monongahela Bldg 235 High St Morgantown WV 26505

BUNT, LYNNE JOY, insurance broker; b. Corning, N.Y., Sept. 25, 1948; d. William Henry and Cleo Ann (Williams) Prentice. A.A., Foothill Coll., 1969; ins. studies IIAAC, IEA, WAIB; C.P.C.U. Vice-pres., account exec. Jardine Emmett & Chandler, Inc., San Francisco, 1979—; tchr. ins. seminars. Mem. Western Assn. Ins. Brokers, Underwriters Forum, Ins. Forum (program chair). Congregationalist. Republican. Office: 333 Bush St San Francisco CA 94120

BUNTING, SUSAN ETHEL, auditor; b. Chgo., Aug. 29, 1956; d. Roy R. Breitenbach Sr. and Cecilia J. (Cunha) Cass; m. Russell R. Dworzack, Nov. 3, 1973 (div. Aug. 1978); 1 child, Neil Eric; m. Thomas Garnet Bunting, Feb. 1979; children: Roy Garnet, Jordan Arthur. BS, Calif. State U., Hayward, 1982, MBA, 1988. CPA, Tex. Acctg. clk. Pacific Stereo, Emeryville, Calif., 1975-80; fin. auditor Safeway Stores, Inc., Oakland, Calif., 1982-85; electronic data processing auditor Safeway Stores, Inc., Oakland, 1985-87; internal auditor Pacific Gas and Electric, San Francisco, 1987-88, computer resource and tng. coord., 1989—. Mem. EDP Auditors Assn., Am. Inst. CPA's. Office: Pacific Gas and Electric 4 Embarcadero Ctr #200 San Francisco CA 94111

BUNTON, MILDRED SETTLE, dietitian; b. Uniontown, Pa., Sept. 30, 1906; d. Reuben and Mary Belle (Watkins) Settle; m. Ansel Sumter Bunton, July 1, 1935 (div. 1937); 1 child, Mary Adebonojo. BS in Home Econs., Pa. State U., 1932; MNS, Cornell U., 1953. Registered dietician. Dietetic intern Freedmen's Hosp., Washington, 1932-33; dietitian Provident Hosp., Chgo., 1933-35; staff dietitian VA Hosp., Tuskegee, Ala., 1937-40, asst. chief dietitian, 1940-47; dir. internship Howard U. Hosp., Freedmen's Hosp., Washington, 1947-73; ret., 1973—; Advisor Life at Sixty Clubs-Change, Inc., Washington, nursing adv. com. Washington Tech. Inst. Contbr. articles to profl. jours. Active Mayor's Commn. on Food, Nutrition and Health, Washington, 1969, United Ch. Women, Washington, Nineteenth. St. Bapt. Ch., deaconess, ch. sch. tchr., choir mem.; women's hosp. aux. Howard U., life mem.; vol. Thomas House; Mildred S. Bunton ann. scholarship given annually to Coll. Allied Sci., Howard U. State Fedn. Pa. Women scholar, 1930-31; named Disting. Alumna Pa. State U., 1973, Black Achiever Order Eastern Star, 1976. Mem. Am. Dietetic Assn. (Medallion 1976), D.C. Home Econs. Assn. (Plaque of Distincton 1972), AAAS, Soc. for Nutrition Edn., AAUW, Am . Heart Assn., Assn. Schs. Allied Health Professions, Am. Diabetes Assn., N.Y. Acad. Sci., NAACP (life), Nat. Coun. Negro Women (life, liaison), Zeta Phi Beta (Beta Zeta chpt., life, past liaison). Democrat. Home: 1330 Massachusetts Ave NW Apt 621 Washington DC 20005

BUNZEL, TRACY L., sales manager; b. Sept. 20, 1962; d. Kenneth W. and Dawn (Camillo) B. BA, Mills Coll., 1985; postgrad., Golden Gate U. Sales rep. IBM, San Francisco, 1984-85, CPT, San Francisco, 1985-87; sales mgr. Informix, San Francisco, 1987—; pres. TLB Consulting, Oakland, Calif., 1990—. Grantee Ford Found., 1984. Mem. NAFE. Home: 130 Glenwood Hercules CA 94577

BUPP, CHANDLER MEENEN, speech language pathologist; b. St. Louis, Oct. 12, 1954; d. Vernon Henry and Ethel Harriet (Metheny) Meenen; m. Christopher Lee Bupp, Aug. 6, 1977; 1 child, Jennifer Michelle. BSEd, Cen. Mo. State U., 1977, MS, 1978. Speech pathologist LaMonte (Mo.) Sch. Dist., 1978-79, Escambia County Sch. Dist., Pensacola, Fla., 1979-80, Sch. of Hope, Ft. Walton Beach, Fla., 1980-81. Sec. Cherry Run Sch. PTA, 1989—; Brownie troop leader Girl Scouts U.S., 1989—. Mem. AAUW, Am. Speech-Lang.-Hearing Assn. (cert. in speech pathology), Greater Newington Wives' Club. Republican. Presbyterian. Home: 7321 Outhaul Ln Burke VA 22015

BURAS, BRENDA ALLYNN, public affairs executive; b. New Orleans, May 1, 1954; d. Allen Anthony and Gloria Violet (Short) B. BA in Commerce, Loyola U., New Orleans, 1976, MBA, 1984. Stenographer Texaco Inc., New Orleans, 1974-76, engr.'s asst., 1976-78, natural gas contracts analyst, 1978-80, pub. affairs asst., 1980-83, pub. and govt. affairs coord. S.E. region, 1983-89; banking officer, mgr pub. rels. and mktg. promotion Am. Bank & Trust Co. (name now Alerion Bank), New Orleans, 1990, asst. v.p., community reinvestment act officer, 1990—; owner Achievements Unltd.; cert. lectr. Silva Method Mind Devel. and Stress Control. Loaned exec. United Way Greater New Orleans, 1978-79, mem. speakers bur., 1979-83, vol. leadership devel. program, 1987; cons. Jr. Achievement Project Bus., 1979-80; voting commr. St. Bernard Parish, 1976-80; mem. Friends of Audubon Zoo; chmn. subcom. United Way Corp. Recognition/Thank-You, 1988-89; vice chairwoman United Way Yr.-Round Communication Com., 1989-90, United Way External Communication Com., 1990; mem. cen. svc. budget com. United Way, 1990; speaker explorers program Boy Scouts Am., New Orleans, 1984-89; host, media com. for Rep. Conv. 1988; chairwoman pub. rels. com., mem. grants and membership coms., bd. dirs. New Orleans Food Bank for Emergencies, 1989. Producer Bringing Out the Best Awards Show, 1988. Named Outstanding Communication Com. Vol., United Way, 1988. Mem. Pub. Rels. Soc. Am., Press Club New Orleans, Inst. Noetic Scis., U.S. Figure Skating Assn., Dixieland Figure Skating Club. Republican. Office: Alerion Bank 200 Carondelet St New Orleans LA 70130

BURATTI, BONNIE J., space scientist; b. Bethlehem, Pa., Mar. 24, 1953; d. Ralph J. and Hildegard M. (Singles) B.; children: Nathan, Reuben, Aaron. MS, MIT, 1976, Cornell U., 1980; PhD, Cornell U., 1983. Summer intern Maria Mitchell Observatory, Nantucket, Mass., 1973; assoc. scientist Am. Sci. and Engring., Cambridge, Mass., 1974-76; rsch. asst. MIT, Cambridge, 1977-83; rsch. and teaching asst. Cornell U., Ithaca, N.Y., 1977-83; post-doctoral nat. rsch. coun. jet propulsion lab. Calif. Inst. Tech., Pasadena, 1985—; cons. NASA, Washington, 1989—. Contbr. articles to profl. jours. Mem. MIT Ednl. Coun., Internat. Astro. Union, Am. Astro. Soc., Am. Women in Sci., Am. Geophys. Union. Office: Jet Propulsion Lab Calif Inst Tech 4800 Oak Grove Dr 183-501 Pasadena CA 91109

BURBIDGE, ELEANOR MARGARET PEACHEY, astronomer, educator; b. Davenport, Eng.; d. Stanley John and Marjorie (Stott) Peachey; m. Geoffrey Burbidge, Apr. 2, 1948; 1 child, Sarah. B.S., Ph.D., U. London; Sc.D. hon., Smith Coll., 1963, U. Sussex, 1970, U. Bristol, 1972, U. Leicester, 1972, City U., 1973, U. Mich., 1978, U. Mass., 1978, Williams Coll., 1979, SUNY, Stony Brook, 1985, Rensselaer Poly. Inst., 1986, U. Notre Dame, 1986. Mem. staff U. London Obs., 1948-51; research fellow Yerkes Obs., U. Chgo., 1951-53, Calif. Inst. Tech., Pasadena, 1955-57; Shirley Farr fellow Yerkes Obs., 1957-59, assoc. prof., 1959-62; mem. Enrico Fermi Inst. for Nuclear Studies, 1957-62; prof. astronomy dept. physics U. Calif.-San Diego, 1964—, univ. prof., 1984—; dir. Royal Greenwich Obs. (Herstmonceaux Castle), Hailsham, Sussex, Eng., 1972-73; Lindsay Meml. lectr. Goddard Space Flight Ctr., NASA, 1985; Abby Rockefeller Mauze prof. MIT, 1968; David Elder lectr. U. Strathclyde, 1972; V. Gildersleeve lectr. Barnard Coll., 1974; Jansky lectr. Nat. Radio Astronomy Observatory, 1977; Brode lectr. Whitman Coll., 1986. Author: (with G. Burbidge) Quasi-Stellar Objects, 1967; editor: Observatory mag., 1948-51; mem. editorial bd.: Astronomy and Astrophysics, 1969—. Recipient (with husband) Warner prize in Astronomy, 1959, Bruce Gold medal Astronomy Soc. Pacific, 1982; hon. fellow Univ. Coll., London, Girton Coll., Lucy Cavendish Coll., Cambridge; U.S. Nat. medal of sci., 1984; Sesquicentennial medal Mt. Holyoke Coll., 1987, Einstein medal World Cultural Coun., 1988. Fellow Royal Soc., Nat. Acad. Scis. (chmn. sect. 12 astronomy 1986), Am. Acad. Arts and Scis., Royal Astron. Soc.; mem. Am. Astron. Soc. (v.p. 1972-74, pres. 1976-78; Henry Norris Russell lectr. 1984), Internat. Astron. Union (pres. commn. 28 1970-73), Grad. Women Sci. (nat. hon. mem.). Office: U Calif-San Diego Ctr Astrophysics & Space Scis Mail Code C-011 La Jolla CA 92093

BURBRIDGE, KATHERINE ANN, economist, researcher; b. Peoria, Ill., June 18, 1953; d. Lloyd Hubert and Genevieve Ann (Vaster) B. BS in Environ. Biology, Eastern Ill. U., 1974; MA in Math., Ops. Research, 1984; M in Pub. Adminstrn., Sangamon State U., 1984. Vol. U.S. Peace Corps, Philippines, 1974-77; technician biology Northern Regional Research Ctr. USDA, Peoria, 1977-78; intern mgmt. ops. analysis Dept. Adminstrv. Services State of Ill., Springfield, 1979-81; asst. chief Commerce Commn. State of Ill., Springfield, 1981-86; rate cons. Tampa (Fla.) Electric Co., 1986—; cons. Jr. Achievement Project, Tampa, 1988. Vol. Planned Parenthood, Springfield, 1985-86; marshal math. program com. Sangamon State U., 1981. Mem. AUW, Beta Beta Beta. Roman Catholic. Office: Tampa Electric Co PO Box 111 Tampa FL 33601

BURCH, DANNETTE KATHLEEN, audit supervisor; b. Holloman AFB, N.Mex., Oct. 17, 1960; d. Richard E. Burch and Patricia C. (Sanchez) Flavian. B in Acctg., N.Mex. State U., 1983. CPA, N.Mex. Staff auditor State of N.Mex., Santa Fe, 1983—. Mem. N.Mex. Soc. CPAs, AICPAs, Assn. Govt. Accts., Friends of Santa Fe Opera. Democrat. Roman Catholic.

BURCH, RUTH MARIE, legal secretary; b. Ypsilanti, Mich., July 8, 1940; d. Harold Paul and Rita Alice (Pierce) Townsend; m. Thomas M. Burch, Sept. 9, 1961; children: Daniel, Colleen, James, Cathy. Cert., AC3 Computer Sch., 1989. Legal and exec. sec. plastics tech. group Johnson Controls Inc., Manchester, Mich.; med. receptionist Drs. Bauer, Kivi and Peterson, Ann Arbor, Mich. Mem. NAFE. Home: 6655 Jackson Rd #517 Ann Arbor MI 48103

BURCHAM, BARBARA JUNE, health program coordinator; b. Franklin, Ind., Aug. 14, 1952; d. Charles W. Sr. and Marchetta (Mann) B. BA in Psychology, Ind. U., 1975; postgrad., Ind. U. Purdue U., Indpls., 1976, Butler U., 1981, Ball State U., 1987. Registered sanitarian; lic. real estate assoc. Vocat. devel. technician Marion County Assn. for Retarded Citizen, Indpls., 1975-77; caseworker Marion County Welfare Dept., Indpls., 1977; environ. health specialist Marion County Health Dept., Indpls., 1978-89, asst. HIV/AIDS Program coord., 1989—; v.p., bd. dirs. B.C.B. Corp., Indpls., 1979-85. Active Indpls. Clean City Comml. Prodn. and Spl. Events, 1983-84; coord. Irvington Ann. Spring Clean-up, 1986-87; vol. 10th Pan Am. Games, 1987, Air Pollution Enforcement, 1988, Tox-a-way Day, 1987-88; lay-min. Unity of Indpls., 1988—, co-chmn. steering com. for community projects, choir; pres. Marion County HIV/AIDS Coalition. Recipient Cert. of Commendation Corwin Guardianship Case, 1985, Irvington Spring Clean-Up, 1986, 87, Clerkin and Miller Cases, 1988. Mem. Ind. Environ. Health Assn. (chmn. legis. com.), Ind. Pub. Health Assn. (ligis. com.), Nat. Environ. Health Assn., NAFE, Am. Bus. Women Am., Assn. Humanistic Psychologists. Office: Marion County Health Dept 1101 W 10th St Indianapolis IN 46202

BURCHAM, EVA HELEN (PAT BURCHAM), electronics technician; b. Bloomfield, Ind., Apr. 11, 1941; d. Paul Harold and Hazel Helen (Buzan) B. Grad., Blackstone Sch. of Law, 1988. With Naval Weapons Support Ctr., Crane, Ind., 1967-76, 78-80, electronics technician, 1980—. With U.S. Army, 1976-77, with Res. 1977-81. Named to Am. Women's Hall of Fame. Mem. NAFE, SOLE, ASWE, Am. Legion., Am. Biographical Inst. (hon., adv. bd.). Roman Catholic. Home: 200 W Washington Loogootee IN 47553

BURCHELL, MARY CECILIA, surgeon; b. Haverhill, Mass.; d. William P. Burchell and Helen R.; m. Austin E. Givens, Jan. 29, 1968. AB, Barnard Coll., N.Y.C, 1947-51; MD, U. Md., Baltimore, 1957. Diplomate Am. Bd. Surgery, Am. Bd. Colon and Rectal Surgeons. Surgeon Martinez VA Med. Ctr., Martinez, Calif.; assoc. clin. prof. surgery U. Calif.-Davis Sch. Medicine; cons. Bd. Med. Quality Assurance, State of Calif. Cons., United Ostomy Assn., Contra-Costa County, Calif. Named: Excellence in Teaching, Dept. Surgery, UC Davis Sch. of Med. Sacramento, Calif., 1982. Fellow Am. Soc. Colon and Rectal Surgeons; mem. ACS, N.W. Soc. Colon and Rectal Surgeons (treas. 1984-85, v.p. 1987-88, pres. 1988-90). Home: Box 769 Alamo CA 94507 Office: Martinez VA Med Ctr Dept Surgery 150 Muir Rd Martinez CA 94553

BURCHER, HILDA BEASLEY, librarian; b. Va., June 5, 1938; d. Andrew and Virgie (Hall) Beasley; m. Eugene Stearns Burcher, June 18, 1960; children: Eugene Andrew, Mark Eric. BA in English, U. Va., 1960; MSLS, U. Md., 1967. Tchr's. profl. cert., libr's. cert. Va. English tchr. Fairfax (Va.) County Pub. Schs., 1960-65, reference libr., 1969-75; head libr. St. Agnes Sch., Alexandria, Va., 1975—. Mem. Alexandria (Va.) Symphony Guild, 1987-90. Mem. ALA, Va. Ednl. Media Assn., Met. Washington Ind. Sch. Libr's Assn., Beta Phi Mu.

BURCHETT, BETTY MARTELA, science education educator; b. Stambaugh, Ky., Nov. 16, 1934; d. Eddie and Beaunie (Van Hoose) B. AB in Chemistry, Berea Coll., 1955; MA in Edn., Morehead U., 1963; MA in Natural Sci., Middle Tenn. State U., 1964; EdD in Sci., Ind. U., 1971. Tchr. sci. and math. Paintsville (Ky.) High Sch., 1955-64; asst. prof. biology and chemistry Morehead (Ky.) U., 1964-69; grad. teaching asst. Ind. U., Bloomington, 1969-71; assoc. prof. sci. edn. U. Mo., Columbia, 1971—; sci. cons. pvt. and pub. schs., Mo., 1971—. Mem. Nat. Sci. Tchrs. Assn. (life), Elem. Sci. Internat. (dir. svcs.), Pi Lambda Theta. Baptist. Office: Dept of Curriculum and Instrn 212 Townsend Hall Columbia MO 65211

BURCHFIELD, SUSAN ELIZABETH, televsion specialist; b. Columbia, Mo., Nov. 23, 1958; d. Charles Edward and Jacqueline E. (Lowry) B. AB, U. Mo., 1981, MA, 1982; MA, U. So. Calif., L.A., 1986. Promotion mgr. Sta. KMIZ-TV, Columbia, 1982-84; mgr. MTM Distbn., Studio City, Calif., 1986—. Mem. Acad. TV, Arts and Scis., Am. Film Inst. Methodist. Office: MTM Distbn 12001 Ventura Pl Studio City CA 91604

BURDA, MARIANNE LOUISE, emergency room physician; b. Pitts., May 31, 1959; d. Philip Charles and Anna (Koltek) B. BS in Biology, Marquette U., 1981; MD, Med. Coll. Pa., 1985; postgrad., Duquesne U., 1989—. Resident Mercy Hosp., Pitts., 1985-87; emergency room staff physician McKeesport (Pa.) Hosp., 1987-89, The Med. Ctr., Beaver, Pa., 1989-90; staff physician Peter's Med. Care Ctr., McMurray, Pa., 1989-90. Mem. AMA, Am. Med. Women's Assn., Pa. Med. Soc., Allegheny County Med. Soc., Phi Beta Kappa.

BURDEN, JEAN (PRUSSING), poet, writer, editor; b. Waukegan, Ill., Sept. 1, 1914; d. Harry Frederick and Miriam (Biddlecom) Prussing; m. David Charles Burden, 1940 (div. 1949). B.A., U. Chgo., 1936. Sec. John Hancock Mutual Life Ins. Co., Chgo., 1937-39, Young & Rubicam, Inc., Chgo., 1939-41; editor, copywriter Domestic Industries, Inc., Chgo., 1941-45; office mgr. O'Brion Russell & Co., Los Angeles, 1948-55; adminstr. pub. relations Meals for Millions Found., Los Angeles, 1955-65; editor Stanford Research Inst., South Pasadena, Calif., 1965-66; propr. Jean Burden & Assocs., Altadena, Calif., 1966-82; lectr. poetry to numerous colls. and univs., U.S., 1963—; supr. poetry workshop Pasadena City Coll., Calif., 1960-62, 66, U. Calif. at Irvine, 1975; also pvt. poetry workshops. Author: Naked as the Glass, 1963, Journey Toward Poetry, 1966, The Cat You Care For, 1968, The Dog You Care For, 1968, The Bird You Care For, 1970, The Fish You Care For, 1971, A Celebration of Cats, 1974, The Classic Cats, 1975, The Woman's Day Book of Hints for Cat Owners, 1980, 84; Poetry editor: Yankee Mag, 1955—; pet editor: Woman's Day Mag, 1973-82; Contbr. numerous articles to various jours. and mags. MacDowell Colony fellow, 1973, 74, 76; Recipient Silver Anvil award Pub. Relations Soc. of Am., 1969, 1st prize Borestone Mountain Poetry award, 1963, Gold Crown award for lit. achievement, 1989. Mem. Poetry Soc. Am., Acad. Am. Poets, Authors Guild. Address: 1129 Beverly Way Altadena CA 91001

BURDETT, KELLY, retired ambassador; b. Bluffton, Ind., Oct. 10, 1928; d. Winston and Pamela (Salisbury) B.; m. Patrick Ivanov Romanov, July 16, 1952; children: Stephen Roosevelt, Jacqueline Catherine, Paddington Yeats. BS with honors in Econs., U. Ill., 1949; MS summa cum laude in Polit. Sci., Wellesley Coll., 1950; MA in Modern Langs., Trinity Coll., Washington, 1952; JD, Northwestern U., 1959. Bar: Ill. 1959, Tenn. 1959, D.C. 1961, U.S. Ct. Appeals (D.C. cir.) 1963. Asst. staff mem. Senator Calhoun Davis, Washington, 1951-52; campaign mgr. Pritchert for Gov. Com., Nashville, 1953-54; gubernatorial aide State of Tenn., Nashville, 1954-56, asst. state atty., 1959-61; pros. atty. criminal div. Dept. Justice, Washington, 1961-64; gen. counsel Fgn. Svc., Dept. State, Washington, 1964-68; internat. corp. counsel Am. Embassy, Bern, Switzerland, 1968-72; sec. to amb. Am. Embassy, Cairo, 1972-76; assoc. prof. law SUNY, Albany, 1976-79; assoc. dir. S.W. region Rep. Nat. Com., Phoenix, 1979-80; asst. to amb. Am. Embassy, Ulan Bator, Mongolian People's Republic, 1980-83; amb. to Mongolian People's Republic Am. Embassy, Ulan Bator, 1983-89; cons. N.J. Associated Banks, Trenton, 1963-68, Lockerbie Exports, N.Y.C., 1965-68; bd. dirs. Phoenix Internat. Corp., 1978—, S.W. Fin. Inst., 1977-80; lectr. Brookings Inst., Washington, 1989—. Author: Mongolian Politics, 1989. Sec. Cambridge (Mass.) Rep. Cen. Com., 1949-50; co-chmn. fin. and funding com. Nashville Rep. Com., 1959-61, active pub. rels. com., publs. com., 1953-56; tech. liaison GOP Tenn., 1960-61; chmn. fundraising com. Rep. Party Md., 1963-65, legal advisor, 1962-65, sec. ideology com., 1965-66; active Washington Rep. Com., 1964-68; ops. coord. Friends of Nixon Com., Washington, 1965-68; v.p. Reps. Abroad Coun., Rome, 1973-75, legal counsel image com., 1972; mem. N.Y. Reps., Albany, 1977-78, 89—. Decorated Order of the Khan, Mongolian People's Republic; recipient Outstanding Am. Overseas award European Ambs. Soc., 1975, Presdl. citation, 1988. Mem. ABA, NOW, AAUW, Nat. Soc. Fundraisers, Internat. Conservative Assn., Tenn. Bar Assn., Washington Bar Assn., Smithsonian Assocs., Phi Beta Kappa. Methodist. Home: Werik Towers 21 N Gate Dr Albany NY 12203

BURDETTE, JANE ELIZABETH, association executive; b. Huntington, W.Va., Aug. 17, 1955; d. C. Richard and Jewel Kathryn (Wagner) B. AAS, Parkersburg Community Coll., W.Va., 1976; BA, Glenville State Coll., W.Va., 1978; MA, W.Va. U., 1984. Fund raiser, recruiter Muscular Dystrophy Assn., Charleston, W.Va., 1973, 74, 75; sec., bookkeeper Nationwide Ins. Co., Parkersburg, 1975; v.p. Burdette Funeral Home, Parkersburg, 1976-85; intake and referral specialist Wood Sheltered Workshop, Parkersburg, 1984-85; exec. dir. YWCA, Parkersburg, 1985—. Bd. dirs. Sheltered Workshop, Parkersburg, 1982-86, Western Dist. Guidance Ctr., Parkersburg, 1984—; bd. advisors Parkersburg Community Coll., 1980-89, Domestic Violence Interdisciplinary adv. com., 1987, Just Say No, 1987—; mem. Wood County Commn. on Crime, Delinquency and Corrections, Parkersburg, 1985—; chmn. Mid Ohio Valley United Fund Agy., 1986 Heads, Community Svc. Coun., 1985; liaison Gov. Commn. on Disabled Persons, Charleston, W.Va.; mem. Career Adv. Network, 1987—; treas. W.Va. Women's Conf., 1987; exec. com. W.Va. chpt. Muscular Dystrophy Assn., 1987—; mem. We've Been There Parent Support Group, 1987—; mem. A Spl. Wish Found., 1988, Horizon's Ind. Living Coun., 1990—; mem. Parkersburg Consumer Adv. Group, founding com. Banquet of Wealth, 1988—; past transition plan team leader Wood County Bd. Edn.; past liason Internat. Yr. Disabled Persons; past treas. and program chmn. Gov.'s Conf.; former pres. Y Teen Club, YWCA; former adv. com. Mountwood Pk. White Oak Village; mem. Jr. League Parkersburg, 1988—, Organ Donor Com., 1989. Named Miss Wheelchair W.Va., 1981, Outstanding Young Woman of Yr. for W.Va., 1981, Outstanding Young Woman of the Yr, 1986; recipient Kenneth Hieges award Muscular Dystrophy Assn., 1982, Outstanding Citizen award Frat. Order of Police, 1984, Community Service award Moose Lodge, 1987, Cert. Appreciation State W.Va., Gov. Jay Rockefeller, Cert. Appreciation Am. Legion Aux., Trail of New Beginning award, Banquet of Wealth Trial Blazer award YWCA/Altrusa, 1989; named W.Va.'s Disabled Profl. Woman of Yr. Pilot Internats., 1989. Mem. NAFE, World Communication Assn., W.Va. Women in Higher Edn., W.Va. Funeral Dirs. Assn., AAUW, Jr. League, Toastmasters (Communications and Leadership award 1989). Democrat. Roman Catholic. Avocation: designing. Home: 2500 Brooklyn Dr Parkersburg WV 26101 Office: Young Women's Christian Assn 2501 Dudley Ave Parkersburg WV 26101

BURDICK, CAROLYN JANE, physiologist; b. Westerly, R.I., Jan. 10, 1938; d. Thomas John and Amy (Eaton) B.; B.A., Smith Coll., 1959; Ph.D., Harvard U., 1965. NIH fellow Harvard U., Cambridge, Mass., 1962-64, dept. cell biology Rockefeller U., N.Y.C., 1964-66; lectr. physiology Hunter Coll., N.Y.C., 1966; asso. prof. biology Bklyn. Coll., 1966—; mem. corp. Marine Biol. Lab, Woods Hole, Mass., 1972—. Mem. Am. Soc. Zoologists, Phi Beta Kappa, Sigma Xi. Author: Laboratory Manual for General Physiology, 1978; contbr. numerous articles in field to profl. jours. Office: CUNY Bklyn Coll Dept of Biology Brooklyn NY 11210*

BURFORD, ANNE MCGILL, lawyer; b. Casper, Wyo., Apr. 21, 1942; d. Joseph John and Dorothy Jean (O'Grady) McGill; m. David Gorsuch, June 4, 1964 (div. 1982); children: Neil, Stephanie, J.J.; m. Robert Fitzpatrick Burford, Feb. 20, 1983. Student, Nat. U. Mex., 1955-56, 58, Regis Coll., Denver, 1959; BA, U. Colo., 1961, LLB, 1964. Bar: Colo. 1964, D.C., 1985. Asst. trust adminstr. 1st Nat. Bank of Denver, 1966-67; instr. Metro State Coll., 1966-67; asst. dist. atty., Jefferson County, 1968-71; dep. dist. atty., Denver, 1971-73; hearing officer Real Estate Commn., State Bds. Cosmetology, Optometric Examiners, Profl. Nursing and Vet. Medicine, 1974-75; corp. counsel Mountain Bell Telephone Co., Denver, 1975-81; mem. Colo. Ho. of Reps., 1977-81, chmn. state affairs com., 1979-80, chmn. legal svcs. com., 1980; del. Nat. Conf. State Legislators; mem. Nat. Conf. Commrs. on Uniform State Law, 1979, 80; presdl. del. to Kenya's Independence, 1983; loaned exec. mgmt. and efficiency task force Colo. Dept. Regulatory Agys., 1976; adminstr. EPA, Washington, 1981-83; now lectr. Author: Are You Tough Enough, 1986. Former bd. dirs. YMCA. Fulbright scholar, Jaipur, India, 1964-65. Mem. D.C. Bar Assn., Mortar Bd., Phi Alpha Delta, Delta Delta Delta. Republican. Roman Catholic. Home and Office: 3853 S Hudson St Denver CO 80237

BURFORD, ANNETTE, investment counselor; b. Enid, Okla., Apr. 8, 1919; d. George Evarde and Alice (Cordt) Burford. BS in Bus., Columbia U., 1956; Dipl., Juilliard Sch., N.Y.C., 1946; student, Oklahoma City U., 1935-39, U. Okla., 1936-37. Chartered investment counselor. Assoc. Scudder, Stevens & Clark, N.Y.C., 1956-70; v.p. investments Scudder, Stevens & Clark, 1970-85; ret.; bd. dirs. Investor Responsibility Research Ctr., Washington, 1974-85, chmn. bd., 1983-85. Chmn. instl. rev. theol. edn. com. Presbyn. Ch. U.S.A., Louisville, 1985—. Recipient Disting. Alumni Award, Oklahoma City U., 1972. Mem. Am. Arbitrage Assn. (panel mem.) Corp. Forum (pres. 1982—), Investment Counsel Assn. Am. (chmn. corp. responsibility com. 1975-85), Womens Bond Club of N.Y. (exec. com. 1981-84). Presbyterian. Address: 150 E 61st St Apt 14C New York NY 10021

BURG, RUTH COOPER (THELMA BURG), administrative judge; b. Phila., Mar. 29, 1926; d. Philip and Rose Anna (Applebaum) C.; m. Max Gunter Breslauer, Dec. 21, 1946 (dec. Aug. 1964); m. Maurice Benjamin Burg, Dec. 30, 1967; children—Elizabeth, Lawrence, Joan, Robert. B.S. in Chemistry, George Washington U., 1945; postgrad., George Washington U. Sch. Medicine, 1945-46; J.D. cum laude, George Washington U., 1950. Bar: D.C. 1950, Md. 1954, U.S. Supreme Ct. 1968. Report Analyst Naval Research Lab., Washington, 1946-48; clk. U.S. Tax Ct., Washington, 1950-53; sole practice Washington, 1953-65; asst. to chairman Bd. Contract Appeals, Energy Commn., Bethesda, Md., 1965-72; adminstrv. judge Armed Services Bd. Contract Appeals, Falls Church, Va., 1972—; adv. bd. Nat. Contract Mgmt. Assn.; lectr. in field. Taxation editor George Washington Law Rev., 1949-50. Contbr. articles to legal jours. Bd. advisors Harriet B. Burg Found., Washington, 1983—. Recipient John Bell Larner medal George Washington U., 1950. Fellow Am. Bar Found.; mem. ABA (chmn. pub. contract law sect. 1984-85, standing com. on jud. selection, tenure and compensation, 1987-89, rep. to Nat. Conf. Lawyers and Scientists 1989—), Phi Sigma Sigma (internat. pres. 1954-56). Democrat. Jewish. Lodge: B'nai B'rith (dist. 5 pres.-elect 1968, founding pres. Kroloff chpt. 1960). Home: 3106 Q St NW Washington DC 20007 Office: Armed Service Bd Contract Appeals 5109 Leesburg Pike Rm 700 Falls Church VA 22041

BURGER, AMY LOUISE, psychologist; b. Glen Cove, N.Y., Nov. 10, 1956; d. Chester and Hannah Jacqueline (Kaufman) B. BS, U. Iowa, 1979; MA, U. N.C., 1985, PhD, 1987. Lic. psychologist, N.C. Intern in clin. psychology W.S. Hall Psychiat. Inst., Columbia, S.C., 1984-85; staff psychologist John Umstead Hosp., Butner, N.C., 1987—; sr. psychologist I in tng. Dorothea Dix Hosp., Raleigh, N.C., 1988. Mem. Am. Psychol. Assn., N.C. Psychol. Assn., Phi Beta Kappa.

BURGER, ISABEL CUELLAR, manufacturing executive; b. Havana, Cuba, Aug. 4, 1960; came to U.S., 1970; d. Armando Tomas and Marta Eduviges (Pulles) Cuellar; m. Sanford Jay Burger. AA, Miami-Dade Community Coll. Bank teller Biscayne Fed. Savs. and Loan, Miami, 1978-80; sec. Pan Am. Exterminating Co., Inc., Miami, 1980-82; sec.-treas. Michelin Canvas Products, Inc., Miami, 1982—; pres. Michelin Svc. Co., 1988—. Democrat. Roman Catholic. Home: 7975 SW 69 Terr Miami FL 33143 Office: Michelin Canvas Products 7254 NW 34 St Miami FL 33122-1124

BURGER, JANETTE MARIE, data processing executive; b. Union City, Ind., July 9, 1958; d. William Bronson and Janet Sue (Boyle) B.; m. Dan Micheal Mraz, Nov. 14, 1980 (div. May 1985). BA, Hanover Coll., 1980; M in Liberal Sci., Northern Ill. U., 1985. Subs. tchr. Dist. 300 Sch. Corp., Dundee, Ill., 1980-82; libr. Gail Borden Pub. Library, Elgin, Ill., 1982-83, Follett Software Co., 1984—. Democrat. Roman Catholic. Home: 1850 W Highland #F203 Elgin IL 60123 Office: Follett Software Co 809 First St Mc Henry IL 60050

BURGES, MARY MARGARET, nursery executive; b. San Antonio, Jan. 27, 1921; d. John Hardy and Mamie Jefferson (Guinn) Morris; m. Ellis Gray Burges, Feb. 26, 1944; children: Elisabeth Lee Wilson, William Rust. BA, Southwest Tex. State U., 1943; MEd, Incarnate Word U., 1960. Cert. tchr., Tex. Math. tchr. Tex. Pub. Schs., various cities, 1943-83; owner, operator Medina Valley Greenhouses, Castroville, Tex., 1963—. Columnist in local newspaper, 1985—. Bd. dirs. Castro Colonies Heritage Assn., Castroville, 1985-87. Named Outstanding Bus./Profl. Individual Medina County Soil and Water Conservation Dist., 1988, Woman of Yr. Medina County Home Demonstration Club, 1956. Mem. Tex. Assn. Nurserymen (cert.), San Antonio Nurserymans Assn., Alamo Orchid Soc. (sec. 1960-61), San Antonio Cactus and Xerophyte Soc., Alsatian Dancers Tex., DAR, Native Plant Soc. Tex., Delta Kappa Gamma (pres. 1984-86). Home and Office: Medina Valley Greenhouses PO Box 504 Castroville TX 78009

BURGESON, JOYCE ANN, resource center official, travel agency official; b. Jamestown, N.Y., Sept. 10, 1936; d. Walter Edward and Marion (Cree) Van Horn; m. David G. Burgeson, Sept. 10, 1955; children: Kathalene, Donna, Jeffrey, Karen, Christine. AS, Empire State Coll., SUNY, Saratoga Springs, 1990. Bookkeeper Burgeson Wholesale, Jamestown, 1962-88; realtor assoc. Kote Realty, Jamestown, 1982-89; real estate appraiser Goldome Bank, Jamestown, 1986-89; travel saleswoman, tour escort Cert. Travel Tours, Jamestown, 1983-90, Travelhost of Jamestown, 1990—; payroll supr. The Resource Ctr., Jamestown, 1988—. Mem. bd. Maple Grove High Sch., Bemus Point, N.Y., 1979-82; mem. adminstrv. bd. 1st United Meth. Ch., Jamestown, 1985—, cert. lay speaker, 1987—. Mem. NAFE, Am. Payroll Soc., Toastmasters Internat., Order of Vikings. Home: 3280 W Oak Hill Rd Jamestown NY 14701 Office: The Resource Ctr 880 E 2d St Jamestown NY 14701

BURGESS, ANN BAKER, biology educator; b. Madison, Wis., Sept. 20, 1942; d. John Gordon and Elizabeth (Nelson) Baker; m. Richard Ray Burgess, June 17, 1967; children: Kristin, Andreas. BS in Chemistry, U. Wis., 1964; PhD in Biochemistry & Molecular Biology, Harvard U., 1969. Postdoctoral fellow Inst. for Molecular Biology, U. Geneva, 1969-71; postdoctoral fellow Mcardle Lab., U. Wis., Madison, 1971-72, asst. scientist, 1972-73; lectr. biology core curriculum U. Wis., Madison, 1973-84; vis. scientist dept. genetics U. Wash., Seattle, 1983-84; sr. lectr. biology core curriculum U. Wis., Madison, 1987—, assoc. chair biology core curriculum, 1980-90, dir. biology core curriculum, 1990—; undergrad. advisor faculty advising svc. U. Wis., Madison, 1978—. Pres. bd. dirs. Wingra Sch., Madison, 1986-88. Postdoctoral fellow Am. Cancer Soc., 1969-71; recipient teaching award Golden Key Honor Soc., 1986. Office: U Wis Biology Core Curriculum 361 Noland Hall Madison WI 53706

BURGESS, JANET HELEN, interior designer; b. Moline, Ill., Jan. 22, 1933; d. John Joseph and Helen Elizabeth (Johnson) B.; student Augustana Coll., Rock Island, Ill., 1950-51, U. Utah, Logan, 1951-52, Marycrest Coll., 1959-60; m. Richard Everett Guth, Aug. 25, 1951; children: John Joseph, Marshall Claude, Linnea Ann Guth Layman Sinclair; m. Milan Andrew Vodick, Feb. 16, 1980. One-person shows: El Pao, Bolivar, Venezuela, 1952-62; represented in pvt. collections, U.S., Europe, S.Am.; producer, designer Playcrafters Barn Theatre, Moline, Ill., 1963-65; designer, gen. mgr. Grilk Interiors, Davenport, Iowa, 1963-87; dir. Fine Arts Gallery, Davenport, 1978-84; chmn. bd. Product Handling, Inc., Davenport, 1981-88; owner mail order bus. Amazon Vinegar & Pickling Works Drygoods, Davenport. Contbr. articles to profl. jours.; design work featured in Gift & Decorative Accessories mag., 1969, 80, Decor mag., 1979. Bd. dirs. Rock Island Art Guild, 1974—, Quad Cities Arts Council, 1980-84 ; bd. dirs. Village of East Davenport (Iowa) Assn., 1973-84 , pres., 1981; bd. dirs. Neighborhood Housing Services, Davenport, Davenport Area Conv. and Tourism Bur., 1981; mem. adv. bd. interior design dept. Scott Community Coll., 1975-80; mem. Mayor's Com. Historic Preservation, Davenport, Iowa, 1976-77, 85—; bd. dirs. retail com. Operation Clean Davenport, 1981; mem. 16th Iowa Civil War Re-enactment Union. Mem. Gift and Decorative Accessories Assn. (nat. merit award 1969), Am. Soc. Interior Designers (assoc.), Nat. Trust Hist. Preservation, Preservation Group, State Iowa Hist. Soc. Home: 2801 34th Ave Ct Rock Island IL 61201 Office: 2218 E 11th St Davenport IA 52803

BURGESS, JEANNE LLEWELLYN, retired international consumer products corporation executive, research foundation executive; b. New Albany, Ind., Aug. 6, 1923; d. Jesse Joel and Lydia Ann (Young) Llewellyn; m. Quentin F. Burgess, Dec. 24, 1941 (dec. Nov. 1984). Student, Ind. U., 1948-49, Ind. U. SE, New Albany, 1979, 89-90. Supr. policy dept. Wabash Life Ins. Co., Indpls., 1952-53; claim examiner Acacia Mut. Life Ins. Co., Washington, 1954-61; exec. sec. System Devel. Corp., Falls Church, Va., 1962-64; mgr. stockholder relations Brown-Forman Corp., Louisville, 1965-89, ret., 1989; sec., treas. Airline Mushroom Producers, New Albany, 1977-84; exec. dir. Sylvan Forest Inst., Louisville, 1984—. Co-editor Corporate Fact Book, 1987; mgr. Brown-Forman Ann. Report, 1970-88; contbr. numerous poems and articles for mags. and newspapers. Active arts coun. Floyd County, Ind. and met. Louisville 1977—; mem. adv. bd. Gov.'s Task Force on Forest Mgmt., Indpls., 1980; mem. Speed Mus. Alliance, Louisville, 1989-90; cons. Jr. Achievement, Floyd County, 1981-82, judge nat. essay contest, 1983; bd. dirs. Fairview Historic Cemetery, New Albany; mem. Dodrasquicentennial Celebration Com. New Albany, 1988; del. citizens ambassador program People to People Internat., 1988; chmn. centennial com. Edwardsville United Meth. Ch., 1989, writer ch.'s history, 1989. Recipient Clarion Merit award Women In Communications, 1982, Cert. of Accomplishment Four Seasons Wine Symposium, N.Y.C., 1970, Woman of Achievement award Floyd City Bus. and Profl. Women, 1989. Mem. So. Ind. C. of C., Svc. Corps of Retired Execs., Am. Forestry Assn., Nat. Assn. Investors (corp. adv. bd. 1981-83), Purdue U. Extension Master Gardeners. Republican. Methodist. Home: 4000 Persimmon Ln New Albany IN 47150

BURGESS, JUDITH GRISSINGER, utilities executive; b. Harrisburg, Pa., May 28, 1948; d. John Philip and Virginia (Houser) Grissinger; m. Gary R. Burgess, July 20, 1968 (div. 1978); children: G. Tyge, Philip E. AAS, Harrisburg Community Coll., 1985; BA, Farleigh Dickinson U., 1989—. Fashion and retail cons. Pomeroys Inc., Harrisburg, 1967-68; acct. rep. cons. Adeptic Services Inc., Harrisburg, 1969-75; asst. bus. mgr. Jewish Community Ctr., Harrisburg, 1975; asst. controller Sta. WITF-TV, Hershey, Pa., 1976; prin., cons. Accudata Inc., Harrisburg, 1976-80; adminstr., analyst GPU Nuclear Inc., Middletown, Pa., 1981-85; analyst GPU Nuclear Inc., Parsippany, N.J., 1985-87, sr. analyst, 1989—; economist GPU Service Corp., Parsippany, 1987-89. Active Internat. Wildlife Found., Washington, 1988—, Smithsonian Inst., Washington, 1984—, Rep. Nat. Com., Washington, 1985. Mennon scholar, 1989. Mem. Nat. Assn. Female Execs., Nat. Assn. Bus. Economists, Atlantic Economists Assn., Omicron Delta Epsilon. Lutheran. Home: 200 Baldwin Rd Apt G-33 Parsippany NJ 07054 Office: GPU Nuclear Corp 1 Upper Pond Rd Parsippany NJ 07054

BURGESS, MARY ANN, university administrator; b. Detroit, May 15, 1937; d. George T. and Felixa (Piontek) Smith; m. Laroy C. Burgess, Aug. 11, 1956; children: Laroy Jr., Susan Styborski, Blaine. BS, SUNY, Fredonia, 1982; MS, SUNY, Buffalo, 1987. Lic. real estate agt. Adminstr. SUNY, Fredonia, 1967—; assoc. ERA Larson Real Estate, Fredonia, 1989—. Treas. Kosciuszko Polish Home Assn., Inc., Dunkirk, N.Y., 1974—. Mem. AAUW. Roman Catholic. Home: 325 Hoyt St Dunkirk NY 14048 Office: SUNY Fredonia NY 14063

BURGESS, MARY JOHANNAH, art educator; b. Pensacola, Fla., Dec. 29, 1925; d. Burl R. and Ervie Ella (Davis) B. BA in Art and Edn., George Peabody Coll., 1947, postgrad., 1948-50; postgrad., U. Tenn., 1948-50, U. West Fla., 1967; MA in Elem. Edn. Supervision and Adminstrn., U. West Fla., 1971. Art tchr. Linden Elem. Sch., Oak Ridge, Tenn., 1947-51, Tate High Sch., Gonzalez, Fla., 1951-58; tchr. art and journalism Escambia High Sch., Pensacola, 1958-66; art supr. Sch. Dist. for Escambia County, Pensacola, 1966—; art cons., workshop coord. ednl. orgns., Fla.; mem. So. Accredation of Colls. and Schs. Coms., Fla. Author, editor several ednl. guides, 1971-88. Mem. steering com. Pensacola Art Coun., 1966-67; bd. dirs. Pensacola Mus. Art, 1975—. Mem. Nat. Art Edn. Assn., Fla. Art Edn. Assn. (State Art Career award 1989), Fla. Assn. for Supervision and Curriculum Devel., Escambia Art Educators Assn., Escambia Assn. Adminstrs. in Edn., Delta Kappa Gamma Internat. Home: 1310 N 18th Ave Pensacola FL 32503 Office: Sch Dist Escambia County 30 E Texar Dr Pensacola FL 32503

BURGESS, MARY RUTH, construction executive; b. Birmingham, Ala., Nov. 20, 1948; d. Harold Herman and Ruth Elizabeth (Bagwell) Hollis; m. A.E. Burgess, Nov. 22, 1975. Student, Walker Coll. Pres. Squaw Supply, Birmingham. Recipient Bronze Hope Chest award State Multiple Sclerosis Soc. Home: 2870 Old Rocky Ridge Rd 107 Birmingham AL 35243

BURGESS, MARY SCHIDING, education educator; b. Lancaster, Pa., Apr. 30, 1932; d. Harry Wilmer Schiding and Mattie Ruth (Shook) Hillard; m. Theodore M. Warner, July 14, 1941 (div. Dec. 1976); children: Thomas M., Scott M.; m. Keith R. Burgess, Jan. 20, 1978. BS, Millersville U., 1972, MS, 1977. Reading specialist Lancaster-Lebanon I.U. 13, E Petersburg, Pa., 1973--; reading tchr. Conestoga Valley Sch. Dist., Leola, Pa., 1972-73; learning styles; chmn. learning Lancaster Leb. I.U. 13, E. Petersburg 1987--. Author: Explore: A Manual to Improve Learning, 1986, Gifts, 1986. Mem. League of Women Voters, Lancaster, Pa., 1978—, Common Cause, 1980—, Amnesty Internat., Lancaster chpt., 1978—. Mem. Lancaster Lebanon Reading Council, Keystone State Reading Assn., Internat. Reading Assn., Assn. for Suprs. Curriculum Devel. Democrat. Lutheran. Home: 3224 Pinewyn Cir Lancaster PA 17601

BURGESS, MYRTLE MARIE, lawyer; b. Brainerd, Minn., May 3, 1921; d. Charles Dana and Mary Elzaida (Thayer) Burgess. B.A., San Francisco State U., 1947; J.D., Hastings Coll. Law, 1950. Bar: Calif. 1951. Pvt. practice law, San Francisco, 1951-52, Reedley, Calif., 1952—; judge pro tem Fresno County Superior Ct., 1974-77; now owner/operator Hotel Burgess. Bd. dirs. Reedley Indsl. Site Devel. Found., 1970-81; dir., 2d v.p. Kings Canyon unit Calif. Republican Assembly, 1973-75; pres., bd. dirs. Sierra Community Concert Assn., Reedley council Girl Scouts U.S.A., 1955-56; commr. Fresno City-County Commn. Status of Women; bd. dirs., treas. Reedley Downtown Assn., 1983—; bd. dirs. Kinship Program, 1988; bd. dirs., sec. Kings View Found. Recipient award for remodeling and preservation of old bldg. Fresno Hist. Soc., 1975, others. Mem. ABA, Calif. Bar Assn., Fresno County Bar Assn., World Peace Through Law Internat., Am. Trial Lawyers, Reedley C. of C. (bd. dirs. 1958-63, 87—, Woman of Yr. 1971, Athenian award 1988). Republican. Presbyterian. Clubs: Bus. and Profl. Women's (pres.). Lodge: Order Eastern Star. Office: 1107 G St Reedley CA 93654

BURGESS, PATRICIA ANN, nurse, educator; b. Carson City, Nev., Oct. 20, 1938; d. Joseph Cecil and Victorine Virginia (Sciarini) Morrison; children: Heather, Michael. Diploma, Mary's Help Coll. Nursing, 1959; B.S.N. (Profl. Nurse trainee), U. Nev., 1974, M.S., 1981. Cert. rural nurse practitioner, child and adolescent nurse, pediatric nurse. Staff nurse Marin Gen. Hosp., San Rafael, Calif., 1959; staff nurse Washoe Med. Ctr., Reno, 1959, head nurse emergency room, 1960, staff nurse ICU, 1961-64, head nurse ICU, 1965-66, staff nurse pediatrics, 1978, 82—; lectr. U. Nev., 1974-81, asst. prof. pediatrics, 1982-88; metabolic screening coord. State Nev., 1988-89; instr. Truckee Meadows Community Coll., 1989-90. Contbr. articles in profl. jours. Mem. Nev. Task Force on Child Abuse and Neglect; mem. health profls. adv. group March of Dimes. Mem. Am. Nurses' Assn., Nev. Nurses' Assn. (bd. dirs. dist. #1), Orvis Sch. Nursing Hon. Roman Catholic. Home: 1479 Coronet Circle Reno NV 89509 Office: U Nev Orvis Sch Nursing Reno NV 89557

BURGESS, SUSIE MAE, photographer; b. KingStree, S.C., Oct. 20, 1959; d. Dave Irvin and Fannie Amanda (Porcher) B. BA, Columbia Coll., S.C., 1981. With The Children's Outlet, Burlington, N.C., 1983-89; machine operator Injectronic Inc., Burlington, N.C., 1983-86; boxer, inspector Perfection Hy-Test, Burlington, N.C., 1986—. Mem. Alpha Psi Omega (treas. 1980-81). Democrat. Baptist.

BURGESS FONGSAM, CAROLE SHARON, dentist; b. St. Andrew, Jamaica, Jan. 24, 1956; came to U.S., 1978; d. Ferdinand A. and Edna May (Moore) Burgess; m. Patrick Randolph Fong Sam, Sept. 9, 1978; children: Michelle Alicia Fong Sam, Jason Patrick Fong Sam. BS with honors, U. of the West Indies, Jamaica, 1974-78; DDS with honors, Howard U., 1986. Technician biochem. rsch. Cornell U. Med. Coll., N.Y.C., 1979-82; resident D.C. Hosp., Washington, 1986-87; assoc. Dr. Bertha Martin, Washington, 1987-88; employee dentist Dr. Roy Baptiste DDS, PC, Silver Spring, Md., 1987-89; civilian contract dentist Walter Reed Army Med. Ctr., Washington, 1989; assoc. Dr. Robert Kelly DDS, PA, Kensington, Md., 1989—; proprietor, gen. dentist Wheaton, Md., 1990—. Mem. PTA, Md., 1985—; cookie chair Girl Scouts U.S., Md. Troop 1630, 1986-87, meetings parent asst., 1986-89. Mem. ADA, Acad. Gen. Dentistry (recruitment aid), Oral Cancer Soc., Am. Assn. Women Dentist (Acad. Excellence and Leadership award 1986), Omicron Kappa Upsilon (Acad. Excellence award 1986). Roman Catholic. Home: 14923 Ladysmeade Circle Silver Spring MD 20906 Office: 2416 Blueridge Ave Wheaton MD 20902

BURGETT, DOLORES MARY, municipal treasurer; b. Lorain, Ohio, Sept. 9, 1935; d. Albert and Mary Katherine (Farkas) Zalog; m. Daniel Arnold Burgett, May 4, 1957 (div. 1972); 1 child, Diane M. Zaleski. Student, Lorain Community Coll., Elyria, Ohio, 1979-80. With accounts payable Thew Shovel Co., Lorain, 1954-63; engring. coord. Relience Electric Co., Lorain, 1972-77; treas. City of Lorain, 1977-90. Pres. Democratic Women, Lorain, 1975-76; mem. Ohio State Democrat Women, Columbus, 1974—. Mem. Firelands Tax Assn. (pres. 1988—), Mcpl. Treasurers U.S. Can., Ohio Mcpl. Treasurers, Zonta Club (pres. 1978-79) Hungarian Coun. (trustee 1985—), Hungarian Citizens Club (pres. 1986-87). Byzantine Catholic. Home: 3944 Ivanhoe Dr Lorain OH 44053

BURGIO, JANE, state government official; b. Nutley, N.J.; m. John Burgio; children: John E., James. Student, Newark Sch. Fine and Indsl. Arts. Mem. N.J. State Assembly, Trenton, 1974-82; sec. of state State of N.J., Trenton, 1982—; chief election officer State of N.J.; chmn. N.J. Bd. Canvassers; alt. del. Rep. Nat. Conv., 1972, 88, del. and mem. platform com., 1984, del., 1988; past mem. arts, tourism, and cultural resources com. Nat. Conf. State Legis.; mem. Nat. Leadership Conf. Women in State Govt. Former mem. bd. Trustees for the Support of Free Pub. Schs.; trustee Caldwell Coll., Rider Coll., Planned Parenthood of Essex County; former trustee North Essex Devel. Council; former mem. MBA adv. bd. Seton Hall U.; past trustee Arts Council Essex area, Julie Maloney Dance Co.; former mem. St. Barnabas Hosp. Devel. Com.; past pres. James Caldwell High Sch. PTA; participant Rotary Internat. Exchange Student Program; adv. bd. Sch. Fine and Performing Arts, Montclair State Coll.; mem. long range planning com. N.J. Symphony; charter mem. Nurses House, Inc. Recipient Alumni Recognition award Univ. Coll., Rutgers U., Newark, Hist. award N.J. League Hist. Socs., Cert. N.J. Humane Soc., Newark, Sol Stetin award Am. Labor Mus., Peter Rodino award Seton Hall U. Sch. Law, numerous other awards from culutral, hist., ednl., charitable orgns. Mem. Nat. Assn. Secs. of State (mem. exec. com., mem. archives com., former chmn. by-laws and constitution com.), Nat. Conf. State Legislature, Millburn-Short Hills Bus. and Profl. Women, Women's Polit. Caucus N.J., West Essex LVW (trustee). Office: NJ State Dept State House CN 300 Trenton NJ 08625

BURGMAN, DIERDRE ANN, lawyer; b. Logansport, Ind., Mar. 25, 1948; d. Ferdinand William Jr. and Doreen Yvonne (Walsh) B. BA, Valparaiso U., 1970, JD, 1979; LLM, Yale U., 1985. Bar: Ind. 1979, U.S. Dist. Ct. (so. dist.) Ind. 1979, N.Y. 1982, D.C. 1989, U.S. Dist. Ct. (so. dist.) N.Y. 1982, U.S. Ct. Appeals (7th cir.) 1982, U.S. Ct. Appeals (D.C. cir.) 1984, U.S. Ct. Appeals (2d cir.) 1984, U.S. Supreme Ct. 1985, D.C. 1989. Law clk. to chief judge Ind. Ct. Appeals, Indpls., 1979-80; prof. law Valparaiso (Ind.) U., 1980-81; assoc. Dewey, Ballantine, Bushby, Palmer & Wood, N.Y.C., 1981-84, Cahill Gordon & Reindel, N.Y.C., 1985—. Note editor Valparaiso U. law rev., 1978-79; contbr. articles to law jours. Mem. bd. visitors Valparaiso U. Sch. Law, 1986—, chmn., 1989—. Ind. Bar Found. scholar, 1978. Mem. ABA (trial evidence com., profl. liability com.), Assn. of Bar of City of N.Y. (com. profl. responsibility), N.Y. County Lawyers Assn. (asst. chmn. com. Supreme Ct. 1987-88, Outstanding Svc. award 1988, exec. vice chmn. 1990, chmn. 1990—), Law and Humanities Inst. Home: 164 E 61st St New York NY 10021 Office: Cahill Gordon & Reindel 80 Pine St 17th Fl New York NY 10005

BURGO, JANICE ELIZABETH, nurse; b. Thibodaux, La., July 8, 1938; d. Donald L. and Yvonne Marie (Adams) LeBlanc; m. Edward C. Burgo Sr., Oct. 22, 1960 (dec. Apr. 1984); children: Edward Jr., Karen Burgo Adams, David, John, Richard. Student, Loyola U.; B of Nursing, Hotel Dieu Sch. of Nursing, New Orleans, 1959. Indsl. nurse McDermott, Morgan City, La., 1960-62; clin. coordinator Thibodaux (La.) Gen. Hosp., 1962-87—, critical care coordinator, 1987—. Mem. choir St. John Cath. Ch. Mem. Critical Care Assn., Am. Diabetes Assn., Ed White Alumni Assn. Home: 617 Waverly Rd Thibodaux LA 70301 Office: Thibodaux Gen Hosp 602 N Acadia Rd Thibodaux LA 70301

BURK, MADGE BERNADINE, librarian; b. Nacogdoches, Tex., May 16, 1924; d. Tyra Hulen and Madge (Christopher) B. BS, Stephen F. Austin State U., Nacogdoches, 1954, MEd, 1957; postgrad., Am. U., 1945-46, Tex. Woman's U., 1985, 87, 88. Cert. elem. and secondary tchr., Tex. Clk.-typist U.S. Dept. Labor Libr., Washington, 1943-45, 48-50; teletypist Braniff Airlines, Dallas, 1946-47; typist Libr. of Congress, Washington, 1947; libr. asst. U.S. Dept. Def. Spl. Svcs. Libr., Korea, Japan, 1947-48, 50-52; tchr., libr. Hamshire-Fannett Ind. Sch. Dist., Beaumont, Tex., 1954-60, 63-64; libr. U.S. Dept. Def. Dependent Schs., Okinawa, Germany, Japan, 1960-63, 64-71, Washington Pub. Schs., 1971-72, U.S. Dept. Def. Pub. Schs., Okinawa, 1972-84; critic, cons. BZZ Theater Showcase Prodns., Nacogdoches, 1989—. Author: Sweet Thang is My Bloodhound, 1965. Candidate sch. bd., Central Heights Ind. Sch. Dist., 1986. Mem. Nat. Ret. Tchrs. Assn., NAFE, Nat. Geographic Soc., Assn. for Supervision and Curriculum Devel., NOW, NEA (life). Democrat. Home: RR 5 Box 3570 Nacogdoches TX 75961

BURK, MARTHA GERTRUDE, software company executive, psychologist; b. Tyler, Tex., Oct. 18, 1941; d. Ivan Lee Burk and Dorothy May (White) Dean; m. Eddie C. Talley, Sept. 2, 1960 (div. Sept. 1985); children: Edward, Mark; m. Ralph Estes, July 3, 1986. BS, U. Houston, 1962; MS, U. Tex., Arlington, 1968, PhD, 1974. Lic. psychologist, Tex. Asst. prof. mgmt. U. Tex., Arlington, 1976-79, rsch. dir. Grad. Sch. Social Work, 1974-76; ptnr. Sch. Psychology Cons. U. Tex., 1979-80; pres. A.U. Software, Inc., Wichita, Kans., 1981—. Author (software) Talley Spl. Edn. Mgmt. System, 1984, Testlab 2000, 1988. Mem. Kans. Child Care Adv. Com., Topeka, 1989, Commn. Responsive Democracy, Washington, 1990. Rsch. grantee U.S. Dept. Edn., 1989, 90. Mem. NOW (nat. bd. dirs. 1988-90). Democrat. Office: AU Software Inc PO Box 33608 Washington DC 20033-0608

BURK, SYLVIA JOAN, petroleum landman, free lance writer; b. Dallas, Oct. 16, 1928; d. Guy Thomas and Sylvia (Herrin) Ricketts; m. R. B. Murray, Jr., Sept. 7, 1951 (div. Jan. 1961); children: Jeffery Randolph, Brian BeVaughn; m. Bryan Burk, Apr. 26, 1973. B.A., So. Meth. U., Dallas, 1950, M.L.A., 1974; postgrad. U. So. Calif., 1973-74. Landman, E. B. Germany & Sons, Dallas, 1970-73; asst. mgr. real estate Atlantic Richfield Co., L.A., 1973-74; landman GoldKing Prodn. Co., Houston, 1974-76; oil and gas cons./landman, co-owner Burk Properties, Burk Ednl. Properties, Houston, 1976—. Author: Petroleum Lands and Leasing, 1983, Sovereignty of Title; contbr. articles to jours. and photographs. Mem. The Author's Guild, Inc., Foremost Women 20th Century, Am. Assn. Petroleum Landmen (dir. 1980-82, 2d v.p. 1982-83), Houston Assn. Petroleum Landmen (dir. 1978-79), Dallas Woman's Club, Sweetwater Country Club. Republican. Presbyterian. Office: Burk Ednl Properties PO Box 1501 Stafford TX 77497-1501

BURKA, MARIA KARPATI, chemical engineer; b. Ujpest, Hungary, June 24, 1948; came to U.S., 1958; d. Jozsef and Katalin (Szentirmai) Karpati; m. Robert Alan Burka, Dec. 22, 1968; children: Jacqueline, Michael, Jennifer. BA, MIT, 1969, MS, 1970; MA, Princeton U., 1972, PhD, 1978. Process design engr. Scientific Design Co., N.Y.C., 1970-71; asst. prof. U. Md., College Park, 1978-81; environ. scientist EPA, Washington, 1981-82; program dir. NSF, Washington, 1984—. Mem. AAUW, AIChE (sec., treas. CAST div. 1988—), Sigma Xi. Home: 5056 Macomb St NW Washington DC 20016 Office: NSF 1800 G St NW Washington DC 20550

BURKE, B. MEREDITH, demographer; b. Los Angeles, Feb. 14, 1947; d. Louis Harold and Sylvia (Roseman) Goldberg. BA, UCLA, 1967; MA, U. So. Calif., 1971, U. Pa., 1973; PhD, U. Pa., 1979. Cons. economist 1st Nat. Bank Boston, 1971-72; cons. economist World Bank, Washington, 1974, Maseru, Lesotho, 1981; instr. internat. stats. program U.S. Census Bur., Washington, 1977; project dir. United Mine Workers Health and Retirement Funds, Washington, 1977-78; dir. Population Ctr. Nat. Coun. on Aging, Washington, 1980-81; cons. economist Electric Power Rsch. Inst., Calif., 1984-85; rsch. assoc. Stanford Med. Sch., Palo Alto, Calif., 1986; coord. health mgmt. tng. Health Mgmt. Tng., San Diego State U., 1987; coord. mgmt. info. Family Planning Internat. Asst., N.Y.C., 1988-90; manpower economist Interam. Devel. Bank, Jamaica, 1978, U.S. Agy. for Internat. Devel. eastern Caribbean, 1979, UN Devel. Program, Maseru, 1986; health economist Pan Am. Health Orgn., Washington, 1982. Contbr. articles to profl. jours. Vice chmn. allocation com. Untied Way Santa Clara County, Calif., 1984, Maternal Child and Adolescent Health Adv. Bd., San Mateo County, Calif., 1986-87; pres. Nat. Women's Polit. Caucus, San Diego, 1987-88; bd. dirs. Girls Club San Diego, 1987-88. Mem. Population Assn. Am., AAAS. Democrat.

BURKE, BARBARA CLARK, management; b. Culpeper, Va., July 13, 1953; d. John Marshalla nd Annie Irene (Pullen) Clark. Grad. high sch., Sperryville, Va., 1971. Office mgr. Rappahannock News, Wash., 1978-82, bus. mgr., 1982-84, gen. mgr., 1984—; cons. Sperryville Antique Market, 1987—, Sperryville Bus. Council, 1989. Office: Rappahannock News 59 Main St Washington VA 22747

BURKE, BARBARA FLORENCE, university administrator; b. Norwood, Mass., Jan. 20, 1935; d. Walter Pryce and Florence Lorraine (Sullivan) B. AA, Fisher Jr. Coll., Boston, 1954; student, Northeastern U., 1967—. Legal sec. Hale and Dorr, Boston, 1954-56, Hoffman & Schwartz, Walpole, Mass., 1956-58; office mgr., bookkeeper George Iverson, Dedham, Mass., 1958-66; campaign sec. Dukakis for Atty. Gen., Boston, 1966; sec. Senate Pres. Maurice Donahue, Boston, 1967; campaign coord. Dukakis for Lt. Gov., Boston, 1969-70; dir. placement Sch. Law Northeastern U., Boston, 1967-69, 71-75, exec. asst. to pres., 1975-89, exec. dir. centennial celebration, 1989—; bd. dirs. Northeastern U. Fed. Credit Union, Boston. Pres. St. Jude Cath. Women's Club, Norfolk, Mass., 1958-59; v.p. Women on Wheels of Mass., 1965-66; chairperson Dem. Town Com., Norfolk, 1962-72. Roman Catholic. Office: Northeastern U 360 Huntington Ave Boston MA 02115

BURKE, BEVERLY GAIL, industrial and organizational psychologist; b. Vicksburg, Miss., Jan. 22, 1952; d. William Ottis and Elizabeth Rebecca (Birdsong) B.; 1 child, Jennifer Erin White; m. Richard Gilbert Moffett III, Nov. 27, 1988. BA, U. So. Miss., 1974, MS, 1975; MS, Auburn U., 1981. Psychologist Searcy Hosp., Mt. Vernon, Ala., 1975-79; instr. Auburn (Ala.) U., 1983-85, Auburn U., Montgomery, Ala., 1987-89; rsch. analyst Litton Computer Svcs., Ft. Benning, Ga., 1985-87; sr. rsch. assoc. Econ. Devel. Inst. Auburn (Ala.) U., 1989—. Contbr. articles to profl. jours. Mem. APA (assoc.), Soc. for Indsl. and Orgnl. Psychology (assoc.), Acad. Mgmt., Southeastern Psychol. Assn., So. Mgmt. Assn. Office: Auburn U Econ Devel Inst 3554 Haley Ctr Auburn AL 36849-5252

BURKE, CHERYL LEA, advertising and public relations executive; b. Bryan, Tex., Aug. 23, 1963; d. Horace Reagan and Shirley Elaine (Darrow) Burke. BS magna cum laude, Tex. A&M U., 1986. Mgr. editorial svcs. Nat. Cattlemen's Assn., Denver, 1986-88; mng. editor Nat. Cattlemen's Mag., Denver, 1986-88; gen. mgr. Brangus Publs., Inc., San Antonio, 1988-89; account exec. S&C Advt. and Pub. Rels., San Antonio, 1989—. Contbr. articles to newspapers, mags., jours. and newsletters. Vol., United Way Big Bros./Big Sisters, San Antonio, 1990. Recipient pub. awards Livestock Publs. Coun., 1989. Mem. Women in Communications Inc. (com. chmn. 1987-88, numerous writing awards), Tex. Press Women, Nat. Press Women, Greater C. of C., North San Antonio C. of C., Phi Kappa Phi. Home: 4934 Woodstone Apt 608 San Antonio TX 78230 Office: S&C Advt and Pub Rels 100 NE Loop 410 Ste 540 San Antonio TX 78216

BURKE, CHRISTINE FRANCES, state legislator; b. Boston, June 3, 1956; d. Gerald Francis and Helen Margaret (McColgan) Hughes; m. John Edmund Burke, Apr. 22, 1979; children: Jackson Hughes, Daniel Joseph. Diploma in Nursing, Mass. Gen. Hosp. Sch. Nursing, Boston, 1978; BA in Govt., Colby Coll., 1989. RN United Engrs. and Constructors, Boston, 1978-79, Emory U. Hosp., Atlanta, 1979-82, Colby Coll., Waterville, Maine, 1985-88; state legislator State of Maine, Augusta, 1989—. Treas. Maine Common Cause, 1983-84. Recipient Harry S. Truman award Harry S. Truman Scholarship Com., 1987. Mem. Am. Coun. Young Polit. Leaders, Am. Nurses' Assn., Maine State Nurses' Assn. (legis. com. 1985), Phi Beta Kappa. Home: PO Box 11 Vassalboro ME 04989 Office: State House Sta #2 Augusta ME 04333

BURKE, ELLEN SMITH, health science facility human resources director; b. Mt. Kisco, N.Y., Apr. 23, 1952; d. Eugene Andrew and Florence Johanna (Tirkot) Smith; widowed; 1 child, Allison Ambler. BA in Writing Arts and English cum laude, Oswego State U., 1974; MBA in Indsl. Relations, Pace U., 1979. Service rep. N.Y. Telephone Co., White Plains, 1974-76; wage and salary asst. Albert Einstein Coll. Med., Bronx, N.Y., 1977-78; asst. dir. personnel Beth Abraham Hosp., Bronx, 1978-84, dir. human resources, 1984—. Scholar U.S. Nat. Merit Soc., N.Y., 1970, N.Y. State Bd. of Regents, 1970-74; grantee Mellon Found. Soc., 1976-79. Mem. DAR, Internat. Found. Employee Benefits Plan, Assn. Hosp. Human Resources Adminstrs. (chmn. spl. projects com. Bronx chpt. 1987-88, editor newsletter 1989-90, dir. programs 1990—), Am. Soc. Hosp. Human Resources Adminstrs., Mensa, Human Resources Systems Profls., Am. Soc. Human Resource Adminstrs., Assn. Vol. Nursing Homes (chairperson). Republican. Presbyterian. Home: Raymond Rd North Salem NY 10560 Office: Beth Abraham Hosp 612 Allerton Ave Bronx NY 10467

BURKE, JACQUELINE YVONNE, telecommunications executive; b. Newark, Apr. 10, 1949; d. Trim and Viola (Smith) Russell; m. Harry Clifford Burke Jr., Aug. 20, 1968 (div. 1977); 1 child, Terence Christopher. Student, Howard U., Washington, 1966-67. Teaching asst. Barringer High Sch., Newark, 1967; course developer Prudential Property and Casualty Ins., Newark, 1968-74; exec. Ad-A-System, Avenel, N.J., 1974-77; staff mgr. AT&T, Basking Ridge, N.J., 1977-83; quality assurance mgr. ops. and engring. Bell Communications Rsch., Morristown, N.J., 1984-86, dir. traffic routing adminstr., mem. tech. staff, 1986—; instr. Summer Tech. Edn. Program, Morristown, 1987. Instr. Youth for Christ, Fanwood, N.J., 1984-86; cons., instr. Black Achievers/YMCA, Newark, 1985; pres. Archway Pregnancy Ctr., Elizabeth, N.J., 1985-89; counselor Restoration House Youth Ctr., 1988—, Teen Crisis Hot-Line, 1988-89; mem. Faith Fellowship Ministries World Outreach Ctr., 1987—, tchr. neighborhood Bible study, 1989—; mem. bd. advisors Bros. and Sisters, Inc., 1989—; apptd. bd. advisors Am. Biog. Inst. Rsch., 1989. Recipient Tribute to Woman in Industry award YWCA, 1985, Black Achiever award, 1985, Sojourner Truth award Nat. Assn. Negro Bus. and Profl. Women, 1989, Bellcore Synergy III cert., 1989, Recognition award YWCA, 1986, Cert. of Recognition Urban Women's Ctr., 1990; named Outstanding Young Woman Am., 1985. Mem. Nat. Assn. Negro Bus. and Profl. Women's Club, Inc., Career Options/YWCA, Am. Mgmt. Assn., Tribute to Women and Industry (speaker, mem. forum 1985—), Internat. Platform Assn., Am. Biog. Inst. (rsch. bd. advisors 1989—). Democrat. Home: 229 West Ave South Plainfield NJ 07080 Office: Bell Communications Rsch 435 South St Rm 1J325 Morristown NJ 07960

BURKE, JOYCE M., realty executive; b. Sparta, Wis., Aug. 30, 1939; d. Arnold and Vessie (Hanson) Westby; m. Joseph Burke, Dec. 30, 1959 (div. 1980); children: Michael, John. Grad. high sch., Sparta, 1957. Pres. First United Realtors, Naperville, Ill., from 1980; dir. Talman Savs. and Loan, Chgo., 1989—; trustee Dozen, Dallas, 1989—. Recipient Athena award Naperville Area C. of C., 1988. Home: 1186 Le Provence Naperville IL 60540

BURKE, KATHRYN BRYANT, artist; b. Chattanooga, Tenn., Aug. 1, 1920; d. Louis Charlton and Mabel (Hodges) B.; John Alvin, Feb. 20, 1944; children: Kathryn Dianne, John Michael. Student, High Museum Sch. of Art, Atlanta, 1941; BFA, Atlanta Coll. of Art, 1967; postgrad., Oglethorpe U., 1967, Emory U. Grad. Sch. of Arts &, 1989. Artist designer Grizzard Advtg., Atlanta, 1941-45; freelance artist Kathryn Burke Studio, Atlanta, 1945-57; sec., treas. Art Dirs. Club, Atlanta, 1955; studio dir., instr. in painting Kathryn Burke Studio-Workshop, Atlanta. Painter: art exhibitions, solo, 1969-86. mem. High Museum of Art, Emory U. Museum of Art and Archaeology, The Drawing Soc. Emory U. Museum, Metropolitan Museum of Art. Republican. Episcopalian. Office: Kathryn Burke Studio Worksh 1300 Indian Trail NW Atlanta GA 30327

BURKE, LUCILLE PENNUCCI, systems analyst, programmer; b. Morristown, N.J., Jan. 31, 1938; d. Bernard and Pauline Lucy (Corea) Pennucci; m. Eugene E. Burke Jr., Nov. 1984. Student, parochial schs., Morristown and Madison, N.J. Sr. console operator Beneficial Mgmt. Co., Morristown, 1955-66; asst. keypunch supr. Cessna, Inc., Morristown, 1966-68; control supr., keypunch supr. Keuffel & Esser, Morristown, 1968-71; encoding (data entry) mgr. Newsweek mag., Livingston, N.J., 1971-73; mgr. data entry, Litton Publs., Oradell, N.J., 1973-75; sr. systems analyst, trainer Gen. Computer Systems, N.Y.C., 1975-76; regional tng. coordinator, sr. system engr., customer rep. No. Telecom Systems Corp., Houston, 1976-79; contract programmer Houston Ind. Sch. Dist., 1979; contract programmer Bechtel Corp., Houston, 1979, data entry supr., 1979-81, sr. system analyst, 1981-90, supr. group, 1990—. Vol. The Sheltering Arms, Houston, 1978—. Democrat. Roman Catholic. Home: 3 Town Oaks Pl Bellaire TX 77401 Office: Bechtel Inc 3000 Post Oak Blvd Houston TX 77056

BURKE, MARGARET ANN, computer and communications company specialist; b. N.Y.C., Feb. 25, 1961; d. David Joseph and Eileen Theresa (Falvey) B. BS in Computer Sci., St. John's U., Jamaica, N.Y., 1982. Cert. data processor. Software specialist Bell Atlantic, Washington, 1983—. Commr. C&P Telephone Softball League, 1986—; mem. Corcoran Gallery of Art, 1989—, Smithsonian Resident Assoc. Program, League Rep. Women D.C., Premier. Mem. NAFE, Alliance Francaise, Nat. Fedn. Rep. Women, Am. Film Inst., Data Processing Mgmt. Assn., Internat. Platform Assn. Roman Catholic. Home: 6652 A Hillandale Rd Chevy Chase MD 20815 Office: Bell Atlantic 13101 Columbia Pike Silver Spring MD 20904

BURKE, MARJORIE HARDMAN, state legislator, farmer; b. Nov. 14, 1932; m. Billy B. Burke; children: Roberta Diane, Carolyn Sue. AB, Glenville State Coll., 1953. House mem. 9th Del. Dist. State of W.Va., Sand Fork, 1980—; majority whip 68th legislature; speaker pro tem 69th legislature; former chmn. state com. Agrl. Stabilization and Conservation Svc.; dir., sec., treas. W.Va. Livestock Round-up. Chair women's caucus Gilmer County Recreation Coun., 1985-86; mem. Dem. State Exec. Com. Mem. W.Va. Fedn. Dem. Women (pres.), Gilmer County Dem. Women's Club, Cen. W.Va. Livestock Mktg. Assn. (mgr.), W.Va. Simmental Assn., Gilmer County 4-H Leaders, Future Farmers of Am. Alumni, Order Eastern Star, Glenville Extension Homemakers Club. Baptist. Home: Titan Farms Sand Fork WV 26430 Office: PO Box 300 Sand Fork WV 26430

BURKE, MARY JOAN THOMPSON, psychiatric social worker; b. Louisville, Apr. 1, 1933; d. Thomas Earl and Imelda C. (Mattingly) Thompson; B.S., Nazareth Coll., 1955; M.S.W., U. Pitts., 1969; m. Joseph Charles Burke, Sept. 1, 1956; children: Anne Maura, Colleen Elizabeth. Psychiat. social worker Homestead Community Mental Health Center, Pitts., 1969-70, Mental Hygiene Instr., Montreal, Que., Can., 1971-73, Champlain Valley Physicians Hosp., Plattsburgh, N.Y., 1973-79; pvt. practice psychol. counseling, 1977-89; instr. Empire State Coll., 1988—. Bd. dirs. Assn. Retarded Children, Center Emotionally Disturbed, 1974-76, Clinton County Community Services, 1974—, Alice T. Miner Colonial Collection; mem. profl. adv. com. Clinton County Health Dept.; co-chmn. Conf. on Psychiatry and Medicine, 1974-82; mem. Lake Champlain Com. Bd. Mem. Nat. Assn. Social Workers, Am. Assn. Marriage and Family Counselors, Am. Acad. Certified Social Workers, LWV, Internat. Coll. Psychomatic Medicine, N.Y. State Assn. Community Service Bds. (1st v.p.). Roman Catholic. Home: 473 State St Albany NY 12203

BURKE, MARY VERONICA, economist; b. N.Y.C., Nov. 14, 1945; d. James Michael and Marie Alyce (McElroy) B. BA, CCNY, 1967; MA, George Mason U., 1979. Mgmt. intern Pres.'s Com. Consumer Interests, Washington, 1970; economist U.S. Dept. Commerce, Washington, 1970-77, NSF, Washington, 1977—; adminstr. Indsl. Panel on Sci. and Tech., Washington, 1982—. Del. neighborhood conservation adv. com., Arlington, Va., 1978—. Mem. Inst. Theological Encounter with Sci. and Tech. Office: NSF 2000 L St NW #602 Washington DC 20036

BURKE, MICHELLE MARY, travel industry consultant; b. L.A., Feb. 24, 1947; d. Edward DeWood and Marianne (Lang) Corey; m. Jeremiah Joseph Healy, Nov. 24, 1972 (div. Apr. 1984); m. James Francis Burke, Sept. 22, 1984. BA in Sociology, Calif. State U., Northridge, 1979. Wine broker Calif. Wine Mktg., Long Beach, 1982-84; wine columnist Las Virgenes Ind. Jour., Calabasas, Calif., 1983-85; owner, operator Wine Discovery, Agoura Hills, Calif., 1983-85; travel cons. ETA Travel, Century City, Calif., 1985-86; restaurant staff trainer Shenandoah Cellars, Northridge, Calif., 1984-86; travel cons. Let's Travel, Santa Monica, Calif., 1986—; freelance writer Malibu, Calif., 1986—; restaurant/travel editor Ind.-Jour. Newspapers, Santa Monica, 1988—; corp. sec. Travelbank USA, Inc., Santa Monica, 1988—; dir. Travelbank USA, Inc., Santa Monica, 1988—; wine/travel tour dir. Wine Discovery/Let's Travel, 1983—. Contbr. Windows to the World, 1989; editor: (newsletter) Serendipity, 1988—; contbr. travel articles to newspapers and mags. Mem. Internat. Assn. Wine, Food and Travel Writers (awards com. 1988-89), ARCS (L.A.). Republican. Roman Catholic. Home: 1781 Latigo Canyon Rd Malibu CA 90265 Office: Travelbank USA Inc 1541 Ocean Ave 2d Fl Santa Monica CA 90401

BURKE, PATRICIA H. See ROSE, ELIZABETH

BURKE, REBECCA LEE, clothing shop owner; b. East Liverpool, Ohio, Oct. 27, 1951; d. Robert Lee and Lenora Van Fossen; m. Keith Hal Burke, Aug. 16, 1969; children: Keith Robert, Kevin Charles. Diploma Cosmetology, A&H Sch. of Cosmetology, East Liverpool, Ohio, 1969. Lic. cosmetology instr., mgr. Salesman advt. Evening Review, East Liverpool, 1983-84, Buckeye Pub., Lisbon, Ohio, 1984-85; owner Little Bit More, East Liverpool, 1985—, Salem, Ohio, 1986-88, Steubenville, Ohio, 1986—. Speaker Salem YWCA, 1987; cons., speaker Obesity Counciling Group, Salem, 1987; pres. East Liverpool Bus. Assn.; mem. Steubenville Bus. Assn., East Liverpool High Sch. Ban Boosters; mem. adv. bd. Ohio Valley Bus. Coll. Mem. NAFE, Bus. and Profl. Women of Am., Salem C. of C., East Liverpool C. of C. (bd. dirs.), Calcutta (Ohio) C. of C., East Liverpool High Sch. Alumni Assn., Quota Club, Rotary (Calcutta chpt.). Republican. Home: 775 Center St East Liverpool OH 43920 Office: Little Bit More 16761 St Clair Ave East Liverpool OH 43920

BURKE, ROSANN MARGARET, public relations specialist; b. Ypsilanti, Mich., July 29, 1927; d. Omer B. and Grace E. (Riley) Spratt; m. William Monroe Burke, Mar. 14, 1957 (dec. Feb. 1967); 1 child, Martin William. BS, Northwestern U., Evanston, Ill., 1949. Editor Commerce Clearing House, Chgo., 1949-52; women's editor Associated Newspapers, Wayne, Mich., 1952-55, Ann Arbor (Mich.) News, 1956-58; pub. rels. specialist, libr. technician children's dept. Ypsilanti Dist. Libr., 1976-89. Editor Libr. Life, 1988; playwright The Invitation, 1960. Mem. Historic Eastside Assn., Ypsilanti. Mem. AAUW, Ypsilanti Heritage Found., Central Bus. Community, Delta Zeta Alumni. Home: 217 Oak St Ypsilanti MI 48198

BURKE, VIRGINIA MAY, teacher; b. Falls City, Nebr., Oct. 13, 1933; d. Wesley Raymond and Opal Louise (Klein) Ferguson; m. Robert L. Lade, Jan. 24, 1954 (dec. Aug. 1973); children: Robert, Thomas, Darcie Votipka, Douglas; m. Willis Reed Burke, Sept. 17, 1977 (dec. Dec. 1984). BS in Edn., Peru State U., 1959; postgrad., Colo. State U., 1966, N.W. Mo. State U., 1971-72, 80, 87. Tchr. Tarkio R#1 Sch., Tarkio, Mo., 1960-89. Mem. Mo. State Tchrs. Assn., Tarkio Classroom Tchrs. (pres., Hon. Alumnus of Tarkio High 1989), PEO. Lutheran.

BURKE, YVETTE MARIE, data processing official, computer programmer, consultant; b. Independence, Mo., Aug. 14, 1965; d. Ralph Lawrence and Jeanetta Faye (Drury) B. Student, Electronic Computer Programming Inst., Kansas City, Mo., 1985, AS in Computer Sci./Bus. Adminstrn., 1988. Quality control computer clk. DST Systems, Inc., Kansas City, 1983-84; computer operator/programmer Kimberly Services Inc., Overland Park, Kans., 1985-86; computer programmer Lawrence Photog. Inc., Kansas City, Kans., 1986-88; mgr. data processing Vasos, Kugler and Dickerson Law Office, Kansas City, Kans., 1986—. Mem. Nat. Assn. Female Execs. Democrat. Baptist. Office: 923 NW 60th Terr Kansas City MO 64118

BURKE, YVONNE WATSON BRATHWAITE (MRS. WILLIAM A. BURKE), lawyer; b. Los Angeles, Oct. 5, 1932; d. James A. and Lola (Moore) Watson; m. William A. Burke, June 14, 1972; 1 dau., Autumn Roxanne. A.A., U. Calif., 1951; B.A., UCLA, 1953; J.D., U. So. Calif., 1956. Bar: Calif. 1956. Mem. Calif. Assembly, 1966-72, chmn. urban devel. and housing com., 1971, 72; mem. 93d Congress from 37th Dist. Calif., 94th-95th Congresses from 28th Dist. Calif., House Appropriations Com.; chmn. Congl. Black Caucus, 1976; ptnr. Jones, Day, Reavis & Pogue, Los Angeles; dep. corp. commr., hearing officer Police Commn., 1964-66; atty., staff McCone Commn. (investigation Watts riot), 1965; bd. dirs. Ednl. Testing Svc.; chair L.A. br. Fed. Res. Bank; U.S. adv. bd. Nestle. Vice chmn. 1984 U.S. Olympics Organizing Com.; bd. dirs. or bd. advisers numerous orgns.; regent U. Calif., Bd. Ednl. Testing Service; Amateur Athletic Found.; bd. dirs. Ford Found., Brookings Inst. Recipient Profl. Achievement award UCLA, 1974, 84; named one of 200 Future Leaders Time mag., 1974; recipient Achievement awards C.M.E. Chs.; numerous other awards, citations.; fellow Inst. Politics John F. Kennedy Sch. Govt. Harvard, 1971-72; Chubb fellow Yale, 1972. Office: Jones Day Reavis & Pogue 355 S Grand Ave Ste 3000 Los Angeles CA 90071 also: Jones Day Reavis & Pogue 901 Lakeside Ave Cleveland OH 44114

BURKEN, RUTH MARIE, retail company executive; b. Kenosha, Wis., Sept. 25, 1956; d. Richard Stanley and Anne Theresa (Steplyk) Wojtak; m. James H. Burken, Oct. 15, 1988. AAS, Gateway Tech. Inst., 1976; BA, U. Wis.-Parkside, 1980. Transp. aide Kenosha Achievement Ctr. (Wis.), 1977; lifeguard U. Wis.-Parkside, Kenosha, 1980, library clk., 1978-80; asst. mgr. K Mart Corp., Troy, Mich., 1980-88, regional office supr., 1988, internal auditor, 1989—. Mem. NAFE, Distributive Edn. Clubs Am. (parliamentarian 1976), U. Wis.-Parkside Alumni Assn., Career Guild. Roman Catholic.

BURKES, LEISA JEANOTTA, company executive; b. Fairfield, Ohio, May 30, 1961; d. Will Robert and Rethel Jeanotta (Russell) Fights; m. Michael Edward Burkes, Aug. 23, 1985. BA in Chemistry, Miami U., Oxford, Ohio, 1982; MS in Med. Technology, Miami U., 1983; MBA in Internat. Bus., Duke U., 1991. Registered med. technologist. Med. technologist Mercy Hosp., Hamilton, Ohio, 1982-85; analytical chemist Procter & Gamble Co., Cin., 1985-87, products rsch. chemist, 1987-88; new products anlyst Glaxo Inc., Rsch. Triangle, N.C., 1988-90; internat. product mgr.-dermatology Glaxo Inc., Research Triangle Park, 1990—. Co-author: Supercritical Fluid Extraction and Chromatography, 1988; contbr. articles to profl. jours. Named Woman of the Days, 1979; recipient many acad. scholarships, 1980-82, including Phi Beta Kappa scholar, 1980, Phi Kappa scholar, 1981. Mem. NAFE, Am. Chem. Soc., Am. Soc. Medical Technology, Am. Soc. Clin. Pathology. Home: 4129 Worley Dr Raleigh NC 27613

BURKES, LYNN JOY, psychiatrist, educator; b. N.Y.C., Aug. 10, 1945; d. Albert and Adele (Mishkin) B.; m. Marvin Leifer; children: Jennifer, Michael. BS, CCNY, 1966; MD, Med. Coll. Pa., 1970. Diplomate Am. Bd. Psychiatry and Neurology, Am. Bd. Child Psychiatry. Intern in npediatrics L.I. Jewish Hosp., 1970-71; resident Albert Einstein Coll. Medicine, Bronx, N.Y., 1971-74; resident psychiatry Albert Einstein Coll. of Medicine, Bronx, N.Y., 1971-73; fellow NYU Med. Ctr., N.Y.C., 1974-75, asst. prof. psychiatry, 1975-76; pvt. practice N.Y.C., 1975-; dir. pediatric liaison svc. NYU-Bellevue Med. Ctr., 1975-83, dir. devel. clinic, 1983—. Fellow Am. Acad. Child Psychiatry; mem. Acad. Psychiatry. Office: 185 W End Ave New York NY 10023

BURKET, GAIL BROOK, author; b. Stronghurst, Ill., Nov. 1, 1905; d. John Cecil and Maud (Simonson) Brook; A.B., U. Ill., 1926; M.A. in English Lit., Northwestern U., 1929; m. Walter Cleveland Burket, June 22, 1929; children—Elaine (Mrs. William L. Harwood), Anne, Margaret (Mrs. James

Boyce). Pres. woman's aux. Internat. Coll. Surgeons, 1950-54, now bd. dirs. Mus.; nat. vice chmn. Am. Heritage of DAR, 1971-74; pres. Northwestern U. Guild, 1976-78; sec. Evanston women's bd. Northwestern U. Settlement, 1979-81, pres., 1984-86; mem. cen. com., 1986—. Recipient Robert Ferguson Meml. award Friends of Lit., 1973. Mem. Nat. League Am. Pen Women (Ill. state pres. 1952-54, nat. v.p. 1958-60), Soc. Midland Authors, Poetry Soc. Am., Women in Communications, AAUW (pres. N. Shore br. 1961-63), Ill. Opera Guild (bd. dirs. 1982—, 1st v.p. 1986—), Daus. Am. Colonists (state v.p. 1973-76), Colonial Dames Am. (chpt. regent 1974-80), Phi Beta Kappa, Delta Zeta. Author: Courage Beloved, 1949; Manners Please, 1949; Blueprint for Peace, 1951; Let's Be Popular, 1951; You Can Write a Poem, 1954; Far Meadows, 1955; This is My Country, 1960; From the Prairies, 1968. Contbr. articles, poems to lit. publs. Address: 1020 Lake Shore Dr Evanston IL 60202

BURKETT, CATHY CRAPPS, owner, operator; b. Columbia, S.C., Feb. 16, 1959; d. Horace Edward and Harriet Henriette (Miller) Crapps; 1 child, Edwin Joseth; 1 step child, Abbey Elizabeth. A in Retail Mgmt., U.S.C., 1979, BA magna cum laude, 1981. Sales person, sec. WBLR Radio, Batesburg, S.C., 1981-87; owner Cagney's Fashions, Leesville, S.C., 1988--. Mem. Leesville Merchants Assn., Nat. Fed. Small Bus. Owners. Home: PO Box 460 Leesville SC 29070 Office: Cagney's Fashions 102 Main St Leesville SC 29070

BURKETT, JOSEPHINE RUTH, performing art inventor, educator; b. San Diego, Nov. 16, 1927; d. Joseph and Frances (Nunez) Novotne; m. Paul Burket , Mar. 10, 1950 (div. July 1981). BA, L.A. State U., 1959; postgrad., Long Beach State U., 1960. Cert. tchr., Calif. Tchr. Benicia High Sch., San Francisco Bay area, 1982; inventor of performing art Poetry in Motion, 1983. Democrat. Home: 5353 Geneva Ave San Diego CA 92114

BURKHALTER, LELA MERLE, banker; b. Red Oak, Iowa, Jan. 18, 1947; d. Arthur F. and Merle I. (Bunting) B. BS in Music, Faith Bapt. Bible Coll., Ankeny, Iowa, 1970. Computer programmer Guardsman Life Ins. Co., West Des Moines, Iowa, 1968-71; sec. Campus Bapt. Ch., Ames, Iowa, 1971-74; word processor Free Meth. Hdqrs., Winona Lake, Ind., 1974-77; loan officer, retirement savs. officer 1st Fed. Savs. & Loan, Creston, Iowa, 1977-90; piano tchr., 1970—. Mem. bldg. and trades adv. com. Southwestern Community Coll., Creston, 1981-89, chmn., 1989; mem. music com. 1st Bapt. Ch., Creston, 1981—, choir dir., 1982-88; mem. com. RR Heritage Com., Creston, 1980-85, chmn., 1982. Home: 908 N Spruce Creston IA 50801

BURKHARDT, DOLORES ANN, library consultant; b. Meriden, Conn., July 28, 1932; d. Frederick Christian and Emily (Detels) Burkhardt; B.A., U. Conn., 1955; M.S., So. Conn. State Coll., 1960; postgrad. Cen. Wash. State Coll., 1962, Columbia, 1964—; 6th yr. diploma U. Conn., 1972. Asst. librarian So. Conn. State Coll. Library, summers 1960, 62; sch. library tchr. Farmington High Sch., Unionville, Conn., 1955-65; library cons.; media specialist East Farms Sch., Farmington, Conn., 1967-70; sch. library coordinator K-12, Durham-Middlefield, Conn., 1970-72; media specialist regional dist. 10, Burlington-Harwinton, Conn., 1972-78; ednl. media cons., 1978—. Instr. Boston U. Media Inst. Spl. cons. Conn. Dept. Edn., 1965—. Mem. AAUW (sec. 1956-58), NEA, Conn. Edn. Assn., New Eng. (pres. 1969-70), Conn. (2d v.p. 1965—, chmn. sch. library devel.; chmn. standards com. 1970-72, chmn. instructional materials selection policy com. Region 10) sch. library assns., Am. Assn. Sch. Librarians, New Eng. Sch. Devel. Council, Phi Delta Kappa. Lutheran. Home and Office: 812 Savage St Southington CT 06489

BURKHART, BEVERLY JOANNE, associate professor; b. Martinsburg, W.Va., Feb. 8, 1947; d. Joseph Cleveland and C. Marie (Henry) B.; m. Kenneth M. Green Jr., Aug. 6, 1977 (div. 1987). BA, Shepherd Coll., 1969; MED, Shippensburg U., 1975, Shippensburg U., 1983. Sec. Shepherd Coll. Student Ctr., Shepherdstown, W.Va., 1965-69; secretarial instr. James Rumsey Vo-Tech Ctr., Martinsburg, W.Va., 1974, Mineral County Vo-Tech Ctr., Keyser, W.Va., 1969-75; assoc. prof. Hagerstown Jr. Coll., Hagerstown, Md. Named Outstanding Young Woman of Am., 1983; recipient Cert. of Appreciation, Hagerstown, 1982, Faculty Recognition award Community Coll. Consortium, U. Mich., U. Toledo, Mich. State U., 1989. Mem. AAUP, Nat. Bus. Edn. Assn., Profl. Sec. Internat. (chair edn. and cert. profl. sec. com. Hager chpt. 1988—), Md. Bus. Edn. Assn., Md. Vocat. Assn., Delta Pi Epsilon (v.p. 1988—), Kappa Delta Pi. Democrat. Roman Catholic. Office: Hagerstown Jr Coll 751 Robinwood Dr Hagerstown MD 21740

BURKHART, BOBBIE NEWMAN, hospital financial management executive; b. Dandridge, Tenn., Sept. 11, 1948; d. David Harding Newman and Bonnie (Cate) Hudgens; m. Charles Monroe Burkhart, Feb. 21, 1970; children: Creed, Kacy, Caryn. BS, U. Tenn., 1969; MBA, Samford U., 1981. CPA, Tenn.; cert. mgmt. analyst. In-charge acct. Ernst & Ernst, Knoxville, Tenn., 1969-71; dir. fin. U. Ala. Hosp., Birmingham, 1972—; treas., nat. exec. com. bd. Nat. Coalition Burn Ctr. Hosps., Washington, 1986—; fin. advisor Univ. Hosp. Aux., Birmingham, 1976—. Curriculum com. mem. Hoover (Ala.) Bd. Edn., 1988—; coach, team mom Hoover-Shades Mountain Ball Park, Hoover, 1979—. Mem. AICPA, Healthcare Fin. Mgmt. Assn., Inst. Mmgt. Acctg., Nat. Assn. Accts. Republican. Baptist. Home: 1501 Verdure Circle Birmingham AL 35226 Office: U Ala Hosp 619 S 19th St Birmingham AL 35233

BURKHART, LINDA SUE, management executive; b. San Francisco, Aug. 22, 1953; d. Charles Monroe and Lorraine (Kindler) Deaderick; m. Jeffrey Scott Burkhart; children: Danielle, Brittany. BBA, San Diego State U., 1975; postgrad., UCLA, 1977-78. Sales mgr. Universal/Rusco Corp., San Gabriel, Calif., 1977-81; reg. mgr. Nestle/Alcon, Dallas, 1981; dir. sales/mktg. Ladd-Fab, El Monte, Calif., 1981-83; mgr. regional sales Ela Co., City of Industry, Calif., 1983-88; prin. owner Burkhart & Assocs., Arcadia, Calif., 1988—. Recipient Cert. of Achievement, Action in Mgmt., L.A., Million Dollar Sales award Environ. Lighting for Architecture, 1989. Mem. NAFE, AAUW, Internat. Material Mgmt. Soc. Conf. (Achievement award 1980), Am. Lighting Assn. Republican. Office: Burkhart & Assocs 37 E Huntington Dr Arcadia CA 91006

BURKHEAD, CHERYL ELAINE, educational administrator; b. Seattle, Feb. 1, 1958; d. Beryl Jackson and Elaine (Hagen) B. BA in Anthropology, U. Wash., 1986, BA in Sociology, 1986. Counselor United Cerebral Palsy, Seattle, 1974; mgr. West Coast Theater Corp., Seattle, 1974-79; coord. Youth Job Svcs., Edmonds, Wash., 1979-83; tchr. Edmonds Sch. Dist., 1979-83; restaurant mgr. LaConcha Restaurant, Seattle, 1985-89; attendance specialist Marysville (Wash.) Sch. Dist., 1989—; mental health cons. (abuse) Marysville Middle Sch., 1985—, presenter Cen./S.Am., 1989—; presentor Cen./S.Am. Edmonds Sch. Dist., 1989—; outdoor cons. Marysville Sch. Dist., 1985—. Bd. dirs., staff dir. Jr. Citizens Camp., Wash., N. Idaho, 1980—; chair Peace Fellowship of First Bapt. Ch., Seattle, 1989—, mem. sister ch. com. 1988—; bd. dirs. Outreach Commn., Seattle, 1989—. Mem. Am. Bus. Women's Assn., Am. Univ. Women's Assn. Home and Office: 6053 25th Ave NE Seattle WA 98115

BURKHOLDER, ROSEMARY ROSENBERGER, chef; b. Reading, Pa., June 4, 1958; d. Melvin Joseph and Mildred L. (Rosenberger) B. A.O.S. in Culinary Field, Culinary Inst. Am., 1984. Apprentice Berkshire Country Club, Reading, 1981-82; apprentice Cattails Restaurant, Cathedral City, Calif., 1983; tournant The Greenbrier Resort, White Sulphur Springs, W.Va., 1984; demi chef Century Plaza Hotel, L.A., 1984-86; sous chef Grand Champions Resort, Indian Wells, Calif., 1986—; instr. Epicurean Cooking Sch., L.A., 1985-87, Uppercrust Cooking Co., Palm Desert, Calif., 1988-89, Chinese Ministry Commerce, People's Republic China, 1988. Recipient Gold Cert. So. Calif. Restaurant Writers Assn., 1989; named for Chocolate Sculpture & Display, Guittard Chocolate Show, L.A.X. Hilton, L.A., 1986. Mem. Am. Culinary Fedn., So. Calif. Chef's Assn. Republican.

BURLESON, CAROLYN ODOM, educator, minister, consultant; b. Phila., Aug. 1, 1942; d. Frederick and Cornelia Alice (Veney) Odom; m. Richenel Johan Burleson, May 16, 1981; 1 child, Cornell Douglas Williams. BS in Edn., Cheyney State Coll., 1965; postgrad., Temple U., 1971; PhD, Columbia Pacific U., 1986. Cert. English tchr., Pa.; cert. psychotherapist, Pa. Instr. English Audenried Jr. High Sch., Phila., 1965-72; instr. English University City High Sch., Phila., 1972-87, dir. intercultural learning project, 1983-87; instr. English ESL Lauds., 1988—; pres., cons. seminar leader COB Assocs., Inc., Phila., 1985—; asst. minister Christ Unity Ctr., L.A. Author: Lifestream-Your Flow of Creative Living, 1985, From The Eye of The Hurricane, 1985. Recipient citation Phila. Commn. on Human Relations, 1986; Phila. Alliance for Teaching Humanities in the Schs. grantee, 1984. Mem. Nat. Council Tchrs. English, Nat. Assn. Supervision and Curriculum Devel., Am. Assn. Religious Counselors, Internat. New Thought Alliance, Nat. Assn. for Female Execs., Clergy Women United, Alpha Kappa Alpha. Democrat. Mem. Unity Ch. Lodge: Rosicrucian (sec. bd. 1976-78, lectr. mid. Atlantic region 1978—, master 1980-81, regional monitor Pa. and Del. 1985-87). Home: 430 S Gramercy Pl #102 Los Angeles CA 90020 Office: COB Assocs PO Box 76383 Los Angeles CA 90076

BURLESON, KAREN TRIPP, lawyer; b. Rocky Mount, N.C., Sept. 2, 1955; d. Bryant and Katherine Rebecca (Watkins) Tripp; m. Robert Mark Burleson, June 25, 1977. BA, U. N.C., 1976; JD, U. Ala., 1981. Bar: Tex. 1981, U.S. Dist. Ct. (so. dist.) Tex. 1982, U.S. Ct. Appeals (fed. cir.) 1983. Law clk. Tucker, Gray & Espy, Tuscaloosa, Ala., 1978-81, to presiding justice Ala. Supreme Ct., Montgomery, summer 1980; atty. Exxon Prodn. Rsch. Co., Houston, 1981-86, coord. tech. transfer, 1986-87; assoc. Arnold, White and Durkee, Attys. at Law, Houston, 1988—. Contbr. articles to profl. jours. Recipient Am. Jurisprudence award U. Ala., 1980, Dean's award, 1981. Mem. ABA, Houston Bar Assn. (internat. transfer tech. com. 1983-84, interprofl. rels. com. 1988-90, intellectual property law sect. ethics com. 1989-90), Houston Intellectual Property Lawyers Assn. (outstanding inventor com. 1982-84, chmn. student edn. com. 1986, sec. 1987-88, bd. govs. 1987-88, chmn. awards com. 1988-89, chmn. program com. 1988-91), Tex. Bar Assn. (antitrust law com. 1984-85, chmn. Internat. Law com. of Intellectual Property Law Sect. 1987-88), Am. Intellectual Property Lawyers Assn., Phi Alpha Delta (clk. 1980). Republican. Methodist. Office: Arnold White & Durkee PO Box 4433 Houston TX 77210

BURLEY, NANCY TYLER, ecology, ethology and evolution educator; b. Syracuse, N.Y., July 5, 1949; d. Carlton Edwin and Christine Culver (Duell) B.; m. Richard Symanski, July 3, 1975; l child, Cole Tyler. BS, Syracuse U., 1971; MS, U. Cin., 1973; PhD, U. Tex., 1977. Asst. prof. biology McGill U., Montreal, Que., Can., 1977-79; asst. prof. ecology, ethology and evolution U. Ill., Urbana, 1979-84, assoc. prof., 1984-89, prof., 1989—; assoc. profl. scientist Ill. Nat. History Survey, Urbana, 1985—; vis. sr. rsch. fellow La-Trobe U., Melbourne, Australia, 1986-87. Author: (with W.M.F. Willson) Mate Choice in Plants, 1983; mem. editorial bd. Am. Naturalist, 1990-82; contbr. articles to profl. jours. Fellow NDEA Title IV, 1971-73; rsch. and travel grantee NSF, 1976, 81, 83, 85, 88-90, English Rsch. Coun., 1978, 79, Whitehall Found., 1986. Mem. AAAS, Am. Ornithologists Union, Am. Soc. Naturalists, Animal Behavior Soc., Human Behavior Evolution Soc. (steering com. 1988-90), Soc. for Study Evolution, Internat. Soc. for Behavioral Ecology (exec. com. 1988-90). Office: U Ill Dept EEE 606 E Healey St Champaign IL 61821

BURLIN, ZERITA G., school system administrator; b. Mansfield, Mass., June 19, 1921; d. Francis Dee and Ethel L. (Fayant) G.; m. Willard Crowell, Aug. 21, 1921; children: Francis Dee, Dorinda J., Kendra Burlin-Brown. Student, Burdett Coll., Boston, 1940-42; -. Exec. sec. Boston City Club, 1942-43; sec. Bliss & Laughlin, Mansfield, 1945-49, SW Card Tap & Die, Mansfield, 1949-52; receptionist Sturdy Hosp., Attleboro, 1952-58; adminstrv. sec. Foxboro (Mass.) Pub. Schs., 1958-83. Co-Dir. Foxboro Adult Edn. 1968-78; Chairperson Foxboro Recreation Com. 1980-84; Vol. Fish Foxboro 1983-88. Recipient Outstanding Citizen award Town of Foxboro Sta. WJCC Norfolk Mass., 1983. Protestant. Home: 22 Putnam Rd Foxboro MA 02035

BURLINGAME, DENISE ONUFREY, corporate administrative assistant, actress; b. Phila., Jan. 31, 1953; d. Stephen Anthony and Florence (Palodoro) Onufrey; m. Joseph M. Cherry, Feb. 23, 1974 (div. Aug. 1983); m. Richard H. Burlingame, Aug. 29, 1987. Student, Temple U. Exec. sec. to med. dir. Eagleville (Pa.) Hosp., 1974-80; exec. sec. to atty. Sperry Corp., Blue Bell, Pa., 1981-84, exec. sec. to gen. counsel, 1984-86; exec. sec. to sr. v.p. and gen. counsel Unisys Corp., Blue Bell, 1987-88, exec. sec. to exec. v.p. and chief fin. officer, 1988-89, corp. adminstrv. asst. to vice chmn., 1989—. Actress TV mini-series George Washington I & II, 1985-86, movie Trading Places, 1983, Blow Out, 1981. Mem. SAG. Republican. Home: 116 Patriot Circle Norristown PA 19401 Office: UNISYS Corp PO Box 500 Blue Bell PA 19424

BURMAN, BETH JULIANNA, retired educator; b. Goshen, Ind., Feb. 2, 1912; d. August Louis and Julia Henrietta (Bauch) Burman. AB, Capital U., 1934; MED, U. Toledo, 1964; student, Columbia U., summer 1940, U. Mich., summer 1961. Cert. tchr., Ohio. Tchr. Lucas County Schs., Toledo, 1935-39; tchr. Toledo City Pub. Schs., 1939-60, supr. jr. high, 1960-65, supr. math. K-12, 1965-70. Mem. AAUW, Delta Kappa Gamma (v.p.). Lutheran. Home: 2618 Gloria Ct Toledo OH 43614

BURMAN, DIANE BERGER, organization development consultant; b. Pitts., Dec. 7, 1936; d. Morris Milton and Dorothy June (Barkin) Berger; m. Sheldon Oscar Burman, Dec. 15, 1926; children: Allison Beth, Jocelyn Holly, Harrison Emory Guy. BA, Vassar Coll., 1958; MA, Middlebury Coll., 1961. Tchr. of French Allderdice High Sch., Pitts., 1960-61, Mamaroneck (N.Y.) High Sch., 1961-64; personnel specialist G.D. Searle & Co., Skokie, Ill., 1972-77, orgn. devel. tng. cons., 1977-78; personnel and orgn. devel. cons. Abbott Labs., North Chgo., 1978-82; orgn. devel. cons., v.p. Harris Bank, Chgo., 1982—. Mem. edit. bd. Orgn. Devel. Jour., 1987. Mem. Am. Soc. Tng. and Devel. (bd. dirs. Chgo. career devel. profl. practice area 1987—), Orgn. Devel. Network (exec. dir. Chgo. chpt. 1986—), Assn. Psychol. Type Bd.-Nat. Conf., Orgn. Devel. Inst. (adv. bd. 1987—, chmn. nat. conf. 1990), Nat. Assn. Bank Women, Vassar Club (bd. dirs. 1975-80). Jewish. Home: 247 Prospect Ave Highland Park IL 60035 Office: Harris Bank 111 W Monroe Chicago IL 60690

BURMAN, JULIE ANN, dancer, choreographer; b. Chgo., June 28, 1957; d. Marshall Lyle Burman and Marian Sylvia (Sondheimer) Schwartz. BA, U. Colo., 1979. Dancer Colo. Caravan, Boulder, 1979, Hubbard St. Dance Co., Chgo., 1980-85, James P. Dance Co., Chgo., 1986—; pres., dir., owner River North Dance Studio, Chgo., 1986—; v.p. River North Dance Co., 1989—; bd. dirs. discovery bd. Goodman Theatre, Chgo., Chgo. Performing Arts Ensemble. Redmond scholar U. Colo., 1978; Ill. Arts Coun. fellow, 1978. Mem. Chgo. Dance Coalition, Standard, Chi Omega Soc. Office: River North Dance Studio 400 W Erie Chicago IL 60610

BURMAN, MARSHA LINKWALD, lighting manufacturing executive, marketing development professional; b. Balt., Jan. 9, 1949; d. William and Lena (Ronin) Linkwald; m. Robert Schlosser, July 2, 1972 (div. 1980); m. John R. Burman, June, 1986; children: Melanie, David, Heather, Richard. BS in Edn. cum laude, Kent State U., 1970, MA in Sociology summa cum laude, 1971. Cert. secondary edn., Ohio. Spl. project dir. Tng. and Rsch. Ctr., Planned Parenthood, Chgo., 1978; with mgmt. edn. ctr. Gould, Inc., Chgo., 1979, program adminstr., 1979-80; systems trainer Lithonia Lighting, 1981, mgr. tng. and edn., 1981-86, dir. mktg., tng. and devel., corp. tng. and presentation facility, 1986—. Author: (booklet) Putting Your Best Foot Forward (award Am. Soc. Tng. and Devel.), 1982; author, editor: Dictionary of Lighting Industry Terminology, 1988, 2d edit., 1990. U.S. Office Edn. grantee, 1971. Mem. Lithonia Lighting Mgmt. Club (v.p. 1982-83), Am. Soc. of Tng. and Devel. (bd. dirs. 1982, spl. projects. dir. Atlanta chpt. 1982, Vol. of Yr., Community Leader Am. 1987, 89), Tng. Dirs. Roundtable (founding mem.), Toastmasters. Avocation: reading. Office: Lithonia Lighting Div Nat Svc Industries 1400 Lester Rd Conyers GA 30207

BURNES, LINDA JANE, testing professional; b. Big Rapids, Mich., Sept. 14, 1949; d. Robert Fay and Verena (Hotchkiss) B. BA, Olivet Coll., 1972. Testing clk. Ferris State U., Big Rapids, Mich., 1974-76, testing technician, 1976-87, testing asst., 1987—. Exec. com. mem. Mecosta County Republican Com., Big Rapids, 1986—, 10th Congl. Dist. Republican Com., Big Rapids, 1988—; legis. chair Mecosta County Gen. Hosp. Aux., Big Rapids, 1989—; active in numerous campaigns. Mem. AAUW (Mich. div. legis. programme 1986-87, Mich. div. bylaws chair 1987-89), Mecosta County Area C. of C. (chair govtl. affairs coun. 1985), Ferris Profl. Women. Congregationalist. Home: 620 Clark Apt A Big Rapids MI 49307 Office: Ferris State U Alumni 228 Big Rapids MI 49307

BURNETT, ANNE BERKELEY AXTON, bank executive; b. Louisville, July 15, 1960; d. Edwin Dymond and Jane Hamilton (Host) Axton; m. Michael Kenneth Burnett, Oct. 12, 1985. BA, Vanderbilt U., 1981; MBA, Coll. William and Mary, 1984. Banking rep. Cen. Fidelity Bank, Richmond, Va., 1984-85; banking officer Centerre Bank, St. Louis, 1986-88; asst. v.p. Centerre/Boatmen's Bank, St. Louis, 1988-89, Sovran Bank, Richmond, 1989—. Active Jr. League, 1985—. Mem. Nat. Corp. Cash Mgmt. Assn., Robert Morris Assn. (assoc.). Office: 12th and Main Sts Richmond VA 23219

BURNETT, BRENDA BULLOCK, government agency official; b. Red Mountain, Calif., Apr. 12, 1941; d. Miles Wallace and Harriet Jane (Wittmeyer) Bullock; M. Daniel George Burnett, Oct. 3, 1970. Student U. Redlands, 1959-60, 61-62; B.A., U. Md., 1967. With U.S. Navy, various locations, 1969—, assoc. head budget div. Naval Weapons Center Office Fin. and Mgmt., China Lake, Calif., 1975-77, head reports and analysis br., 1977-78, head fin. mgmt. Br. A, 1978-81, mem. staff Hdqrs. Dept. Def. Schs. Ger., 1982-84, head plans and programs br., 1984-88. Mem. Ridgecrest City Council, 1980-81; instr. Stop Smoking Clinic, Am. Cancer Soc.; founding mem. Maturango Mus., Ridgecrest, ins. treas. and trustee 1987, v.p., 1989. Mem. NAACP. Democrat. Home: 735 Sonja Ave Ridgecrest CA 93555 Office: Naval Weapons Ctr Code 0835 China Lake CA 93555

BURNETT, CAROL, actress, comedienne, singer; b. San Antonio, Apr. 26, 1936; d. Jody and Louise (Creighton) B.; m. Joseph Hamilton, 1963 (div.); children: Carrie Louise, Jody Ann, Erin Kate. Student, UCLA, 1953-55. Introduced comedy song I Made a Fool of Myself Over John Foster Dulles, 1957; Broadway debut in Once Upon a Mattress, 1959; regular performer in Garry Moore TV show, 1959-62; appeared several CBS-TV spls., 1962-63; star Carol Burnett Show, CBS-TV, 1966-77, Carol & Co., 1990; appeared on Broadway, play Fade Out-Fade In, 1964, play Plaza Suite, 1970, musical play I Do, I Do, 1973, Same Time Next Year, 1977, television miniseries Fresno; films include Pete 'n' Tillie, 1972, Front Page, 1974, A Wedding, 1977, Health, 1979, Four Seasons, 1981, Chu Chu and the Philly, 1981, Annie, 1982; TV movies Friendly Fire, 1978, The Grass is Always Greener Over the Septic Tank, 1979, The Tenth Month, 1979, Life of the Party, 1982, Between Friends, 1983, Hostage, 1988; club engagements, Harrah's Club, The Sands, Caesar's Palace, MGM Grand. Recipient outstanding comedienne award Am. Guild Variety Artists, 5 times; Emmy award for outstanding variety performance Acad. TV Arts and Scis., 5 times; TV Guide award for outstanding female performer, 1961, 62, 63; Peabody award, 1963; Golden Globe award for outstanding comedienne of year Fgn. Press Assn., 8 times; Woman of Year award Acad. TV Arts and Scis.; People's Choice award favorite all-around female entertainer, 1975, 76, 77; 1st ann. Nat. TV Critics Circle award for outstanding performance, 1977; San Sebastian Film Festival award for best actress for A Wedding, 1978; Horatio Alger award Horatio Alger Assn. Disting. Ams., 1988; named One of 20 Most Admired Women Gallup Poll, 1977. Address: ICM 8899 Beverly Blvd Los Angeles CA 90048*

BURNETT, DEBORAH BECHER, sales executive; b. Chgo., July 2, 1949; d. Donald Fredrick and Marily Ann (Lutz) B.; m. John Edward Burnett, Sept. 28, 1970 (div. July 1990); children: Christopher, Cassandra. BS, Wright State U., 1981; MS, Hartford Grad. Ctr., 1986. Mgr. Sambo's Restaurant, Owensboro, Ky., 1975-78; prin. Talbott Terrace Cafeteria, Dayton, 1978-81; programmer analyst GM, Dayton, 1981-83; systems analyst GM, Lockport, N.Y., 1983-85; systems engr. Electronic Data Systems, Bristol, Conn., 1985; project mgr. Electronic Data Systems, Detroit, 1985-86, account mgr., 1986-88, fin. adminstrn. mgr., 1986-89, sales exec., 1989—. coach girl's soccer traveling team. GM fellow, 1985. Mem. NAFE, Am. Bus. Women Assn., Soc. Automotive Engrs. Republican. Lutheran.

BURNETT, RITA MARLINE, dentist; b. Oswego, Kans., Apr. 29, 1954; d. Elizabeth Ann (Bassett) B.; m. Brett LaMarr Ferguson, Dec. 31, 1984; children: Brittny, Helene-Cole, Brett LaMarr Jr. Student, Blackburn Coll., 1972-73; BS, U. Kans., 1976; DDS, U. Mo., Kansas City, 1983. Diplomate Am. Bd. Dentistry. Jr. biologist Midwest Rsch. Inst., Kansas City, Mo., 1976-77; rsch. toxicologist Mobay Chem. Corp., Stillwell, Kans., 1977-79; assoc. in gen. dentistry Anne Johnson DDS, Kansas City, Mo., 1983-84; pvt. practice family dentistry Kansas City, Kans., 1984—. Mem. ADA, Assn. Am. Women Dentists, Am. Soc. Dentistry for Children, Kans. Dental Soc., Mo. Dental Soc., Heart of Am. Dental Soc., Greater Kans. City (Mo.) Dental Soc., Wyandotte County Dental Soc., Am. Bus. Women's Assn. (pres. Women in Action chpt., Kans. City, Mo. 1986-87). Baptist. Home: 9920 Antioch Rd Overland KS 66212 Office: 4631 Orville Ste 217 Kansas City KS 66102

BURNETT, SUSAN WALK, personnel service company owner; b. Galveston, Tex., Aug. 21, 1946; d. Joe Decker and Ruth Corinne (Lowe) Walk; m. Rusty Burnett, Dec. 27, 1973; stepchildren—Barbara, Sara. B.A. in Journalism, U. Ark.-Fayetteville, 1968. Asst. pub. relations mgr. sta. KATV, Little Rock, 1968-69; speech writer Assoc. Milk Producers, Inc., Little Rock, 1969-70; mgr. Allied Personnel, Houston, 1970-74; owner Burnett Cos. Consol., Inc., Houston, 1974—. Speaker Job Search Seminars, Houston, 1984; worker Easter Seals Telethon. Recipient Appreciation awards Lyndon Johnson Space Ctr., NASA, 1983, State of Tex., 1984. Mem. Tex. Assn. Personnel Cons. (v.p. 1985), Houston Assn. Personnel Cons. (pres. 1986, v.p. 1985), Nat. Assn. Personnel Cons., Houston C. of C., Chi Omega Alumnae. Republican. Methodist. Avocations: Reading; golf; flying; sailing. Office: Burnett Cos Consol Inc 9800 Richmond Suite 800 Houston TX 77042

BURNEY, ANDREA JOYCE, public relations executive; b. Danville, Va., May 7, 1953; d. George Anderson and Symantha Lucinda (Bennett) B.; 1 child, Cedric Earl. BS, Boston U., 1975. Reporter Registered Pub. Co., Danville, 1975-79; editor Aetna Life & Casualty Co., Hartford, Conn., 1979-80; media specialist Nat. 4-H Coun., Chevy Chase, Md., 1980-85; pres. pub. rels. Daville Community Coll., 1985—. Bd. dirs. ARC, Danville, 1987—, Daville Voters League, 1987—; sec., del. Dem. Com., Danville, 1987—; mem. Danville Commn. on Youth and Children, 1988—. Mem. Nat. Coun. for Mktg. and Pub. Rels., Internat. Assn. Bus. Communicators (v.p. profl. devel. 1984, job bank coord. 1982-84), Va. Community Colls. Assn. (bd. dir., parliamentarian 1987—), Delta Sigma Theta. Office: Danville Community Coll 1008 S Main St Danville VA 24541

BURNEY, VICTORIA KALGAARD, business consultant, civic worker; b. Los Angeles, Apr. 12, 1943; d. Oscar Albert and Dorothy Elizabeth (Peterson) Kalgaard; children: Kim Elizabeth, J. Hewett. BA with honors, U. Mont., 1965; MA, U. No. Colo., 1980; postgrad. Webster U., St. Louis, 1983-84. Exec. dir. Hill County Community Action, Havre, Mont., 1966-67; community orgn. specialist ACCESS, Escondido, Calif., 1967-68; program devel. and community orgn. specialist Community Action Programs, Inc., Pensacola, Fla., 1968-69; cons. Escambia County Sch. Bd., Fla., 1969-71; pres. Kal Kreations, Kailua, Hawaii, 1974-77; instr., dir. office human resources devel. Palomar Coll., San Marcos, Calif., 1978-81; chief exec. officer IDET Corp., San Marcos, 1981-87; cons. County of Riverside, Calif., 1983. Mem. San Diego County Com. on Handicapped, San Diego, 1979; cons. tribal resource devel., Escondido, Calif., 1979; mem. exec. com. Social Services Coordinating Council, San Diego, 1982-83; mem. pvt. sector com. and planning and rev. com. Calif. Employment and Tng. Adv. Council, Sacramento, 1982-83; bd. mgrs. Santa Margarita Family YMCA, Vista, Calif., 1984-86; bd. dirs. North County Community Action Program, Escondido, 1978, Casa de Amparo, San Luis Rey, Calif., 1980-83; mem. San Diego County Pub. Welfare Adv. Bd., 1979-83, chairperson, 1981; assoc. mem. Calif. Rep. Cen. Com., Sacramento, 1984-85, 89—; ofcl. San Diego County Rep. Cen. Com., 1985—, exec. com., 1987—; chmn. 74th Assembly Dist. Rep. Caucus, 1989—; chmn. Working Ptnrs., 1987—. Mem. Nat. Assn. County Employment and Tng. Adminstrs. (chairperson econ. resources com. 1982-85), Calif. Assn. Local Econ. Devel., San Diego Econ. Devel. Corp., Oceanside Econ. devel. Council (bd. dirs. 1983-87), Oceanside C. of C., San Marcos C. of C. (bd. dirs. 1982-85), Carlsbad C. of C. (indsl. council 1982-85), Escondido C. of C. (comml. and indsl. devel. council 1982-87), Vista C. of C. (vice chairperson econ. devel. com. 1982-83), Vista Econ. Devel. Assn.,

Nat. Mgmt. Assn. (charter mem. North County chpt.), Nat. Job Tng. Partnership, Job Tng. Assn. San Diego, Am. Mgmt. Assns., San Diego County Golden Eagle Club, Rancho Santa Fe Rep. Women's Club Federated.

BURNHAM, PATRICIA WHITE, management consultant; b. Omaha, July 30, 1933; d. William Max and Berniece Irene (Shockey) Orr; m. William L. White, June 18, 1955 (div. Nov. 1979); children: Lucinda, Christopher, Duncan; m. Robert A. Burnham, Feb. 23, 1980. BA in English, DePauw U., Greencastle, Ind., 1955; MA in English, Ill. State U., 1966, PhD in Adminstrn., 1977. Tchr. Morton Grove (Ill.) and Evansville (Ind.) pub. schs., 1955-60; instr. Ill. State U., Normal, 1963-71, dir. Nat. Student Exchange, 1971-74, dir. continuing edn., 1974-76, asst. dean, 1976-79; assoc. dir. Ill. Bd. Higher Edn., Springfield, 1979-80; assoc. vice provost Ohio State U., Columbus, 1980-81; specialist bus. ins. Nationwide Ins. Co., Columbus, 1981-83; v.p. pvt. banking Chase Manhattan Bank, N.A., N.Y.C., 1983-88; nat. and internat. cons. mkt. rsch., bus. devel. Transitions Group, Inc., Wilton, Conn., 1986—; cons. profl. devel. Ill. area community colls. Contbr. articles to profl. jours. Bd. dirs. Mennonite Hosp., Bloomington, Ill., Ind. Coll. Fund, N.Y. Mem. AAHE, AERA, Am. Mktg. Assn., Fairfield County Exec. Women (bd. dirs. 1987-89), PEO (pres. Evansville 1959-61), Phi Beta Kappa, Phi Delta Kappa. Presbyterian. Office: Transitions Group Inc 367 Chestnut Hill Rd Wilton CT 06897

BURNHAM, SHEILA KAY, accountant; b. Alliance, Ohio, May 7, 1955; d. Donald Everald and Marilyn Arlene (Datz) B. AS, Cen. Ohio Tech. Coll., 1977. CPA, Ohio. Staff acct. E.A. Guelde & Assocs., Newark, Ohio, 1973; staff acct., sr. acct. Wells & Snyder, Newark, 1973-78; mgr. Wells, Snyder, Digman & Co., Newark, 1978-83; acctg. instr. Cen. Ohio Tech. Coll., Newark, 1982-83; prin. Digman, Burnham & Co., Newark, 1983-84, Sheila K. Burnham, CPA, Newark, 1984—; acctg. instr. Cen. Ohio Tech. Coll., 1990—; panelist Tax Facts Radio and TV program, Columbus, Ohio, 1983—. Bd. dirs., treas. The Easter Seal Soc. of Licking County, Newark, 1983—, pres. 1987—; treas. Ohio Easter Seal Soc. 1988-89, v.p. 1989—; pres. The Ctr. for Alternative Resources, Newark, 1987—, treas. 1988—; bd. dirs. YWCA, 1988—, treas., 1988—; Big Sister, Newark, 1984—; mem. adv. com. for acctg. tech. Cen. Ohio Tech. Coll., Newark, 1984—; instr. Vol. Income Tax Assistance Program, Newark, 1985—; trustee, mem. adminstrv. bd., chairperson fin., choir mem., Sunday Sch. tchr. Christ United Meth. Ch., Newark, 1969—; mem. Leadership Tomorrow, 1988-89; bd. dirs. The Vol. Ctr., 1989; home program host Crisis Pregnancy Ctr., 1990; vol. Crisis & Intervention Hotline, 1990. Recipient Outstanding Alumni award Cen. Ohio Tech. Coll., 1983. Mem. Ohio Soc. CPA's, Am. Women's Soc. CPA's. Am. Soc. Women Accts., Newark Area C. of C., Mental Health Assn., Soroptimist Internat., Zonta Internat. Republican. Methodist. Home: 345 Central Ave Newark OH 43055 Office: 51 N Third St Ste 102 Newark OH 43055

BURNHAM, SOPHY, writer; b. Balt., Dec. 12, 1936; d. George Cockran and Sophy Tayloe (Snyder) Doub; m. David B. Burnham, Mar. 12, 1960 (div. 1984); children: Sarah Tayloe, Molly Bright. BA cum laude, Smith Coll., 1958. Aquisitions editor David McKay, Inc., N.Y.C., 1971-73; contbg. editor Town and Country mag., N.Y.C., 1975-80, New Art Examiner mag., Washington, 1985-86; staff writer Mus. & Arts/Washington, Washington, 1987—; contbg. editor New Woman mag., 1984—; freelance writer, author, playwright, Washington, 1970—. Author: The Art Crowd (Book of the Month Club alt. selection), 1973, The Landed Gentry, 1978, (novels) Buccaneer, 1977, The Dogwalker, 1979, A Book of Angels, 1990; plays include The Study, The Nightingale, Beauty and the Beast, The Witch's Tale (named Best Children's Radio Play), Penelope (3d Prize Episcopal Drama award); films include The Smithsonian's Whale, The Leaf Thieves: contbr. 105 articles, essays to nat. mags. and jours. Mem. lit. panel D.C. Arts and Humanities Commn. 1986, 87; founding mem. The Studio Theatre, 1978-85, chmn. bd. dirs. 1979-80; vice chairperson D.C. Community Humanities Coun., 1979-80, founding mem., 1979-85. Recipient Award of Excellence Communications Arts mag., 1980, Pub. Humanities award D.C. Community Humanities Coun., 1988; D.C. Arts and Humanities Coun. grantee, 1980-81, Helene Wurlitzer Found. of Taos grantee, 1981, 83; Office of Advanced Drama Rsch. grantee U. Minn., 1976. Mem. Women's Internat. Theatre Alliance (sec. 1979-81), Octagon Com. (bd. dirs. 1984-89). Home and Office: 1405 31st St Washington DC 20007

BURNISTON, KAREN SUE, nurse; b. Hammond, Ind., May 20, 1939; d. George Hubbard and Bette Ruth (Ambler) B. RN, Parkview Methodist Hosp., Ft. Wayne, Ind., 1961; BS in Nursing, Purdue U., 1974; MS, No. Ill. U., DeKalb, 1976. Staff nurse Parkview Meml. Hosp., 1961-63, 71-73; physician office and operating room nurse, 1963-67; nurse N.W. Ind. Home Health Services, 1974; mem. faculty Michael Reese Hosp. Sch. Nursing, Chgo., 1977-79; asst. dir. nursing Mt. Sinai Hosp. Med. Center, Chgo., 1977-79; asst. adminstr. patient services St. Margaret Hosp., Hammond, 1980-85; asst. adminstr. patient services St. Catherine Hosp., East Chgo., Ind., 1985-86, chief operating officer, 1986-88; v.p. nursing St. Joseph Hosp. and Health Ctr., Kokomo, Ind., 1988—; vis. assoc. prof. Purdue U. Sch. Nursing. Bd. dirs. South Lake Ctr. Mental Health, Ancilla Home Health, Inc., Chgo., 1987-88, Hospice of N.W.Ind., 1987-88. Served with Nurse Corps, USAF, 1967-71. Mem. Am. Nurses Assn., Am. Orgn. Nurse Execs., Ind. Orgn. Nurse Executives (pres. 1984), Sigma Theta Tau. Mem. Christian Ch. (Disciples of Christ). Home: 3312 Woodhaven Trail Kokomo IN 46902

BURNS, BARBARA ANN MAYS, civil engineer; b. Jasper, Ala., Dec. 17, 1951; d. Wallace and Margie Evelyne (White) Mays; m. Printice Ronald Howton, Nov. 20, 1968 (div. 1972); 1 child, Ronald David Howton; m. Stephen Dale Burns, Oct. 11, 1988. AS, Walker Jr. Coll., Jasper, 1975; BS, U. Ala., 1979. Asst. environ. coordinator State of Ala. Hwy. Dept., Birmingham, 1976-78; project engr. M.C. West, Inc., Columbia, Tenn., 1978-80, Tillett Bros. Constrn. Co., Inc., Shelbyville, Tenn., 1980-86; subcontractor GRW Engrs., Lexington, Ky., 1986-88; civil engr. Endicott & Assocs., Lexington, 1988-90; pres. The Dixie Atali Co., Inc., Lexington, 1990—; chmn. bd. The Dixie Atali Co., Inc., 1989—. Mem. The Echota Cherokee Tribe, Birmingham, 1988—. Mem. Soc. Women Engrs. (charter mem.). Democrat. Baptist. Home: 3125 Rolling Hills Ct Lexington KY 40516 Office: The Dixie Atali Co Inc 3125 Rolling Hills Ct Lexington KY 40516

BURNS, BARBARA BELTON, investment company executive; b. Fredericktown, Mo., Dec. 10, 1944; d. Clyde Monroe and Mary Celestial (Anderson) Belton; m. Larry J. Bohannon; Mar. 27, 1963 (div.); 1 child, Timothy Joseph; m. Donald Edward Burns, Nov. 1, 1980; stepchildren: Brian Edward, David Keone. Student, Ohio State U., 1970-75. Dir. nat. sales Am. Way, Chgo., 1976-77; recruiter Bell & Howell Schs., Columbus, Ohio, 1978-80; pres., founder Bardon Investment Corp., Naples, Fla., 1980—; founder Cambridge Mgmt. Co., Columbus, 1983-86; pres., chief exec. officer Charter's Total Wardrobe Care, Columbus, 1984-89. Treas. Vicace/Columbus Symphony, 1981-82; fund raiser Grant Hosp., Columbus, 1986; chairperson Impresarios/Opera Columbus, 1986-87; founding mem. Columbus Women's Bd. 1986-87; mem. devel. com. Babe Zaharias/Am. Cancer Soc.; auction chair Opera Ball-Opera/Columbus, 1989; tennis tournament chair NABOR Scholarship fund, 1990. Named Entrepreneur of Yr. Arthur Young/Venture mag., 1988; recipient Design award Reynoldsburg C. of C., 1988. Mem. Naples C. of C. (new bus. com. 1990—). Republican.

BURNS, BARBARA M., volunteer; b. Evanston, Ill., July 4, 1929; d. Martin Hughes and Miriam (Miller) B. BA, Smith Coll., 1951; diploma, U. London, 1954, Evanston Bus. Coll., 1958. Researcher for dir. Presdl. Appointments Office White House, Washington, 1959; personal sec. to Senator Jacob Javits, Washington, 1959-60; exec. asst. to asst. chmn. Rep. Nat. Com., Washington, 1960-62; adminstrv. asst. to Hon. John Clifford Folger, Washington, 1962-63; spl. asst. to John F. Kennedy Ctr., Washington; spl. asst. to Pres. on Arts White House, Washington, 1963-66; dir. confs. for corp. execs. Sch. Advanced Internat. Studies Johns Hopkins U., Washington, 1966-69; dep. asst. sec. for consumer svcs. HEW, Washington, 1969-73; asst. to sec. interior for internat. activities Dept. Interior, Washington, 1973-77; Washington editor Bus. and Soc. Rev., 1978-82; chmn. Wadsworth Preservation Fund, 1983-85; mem. consumer coun. Am. Nat. Standards Inst., 1969-73, nominating com. Am. Stock Exchange, 1972. Profl. chmn. vol. svc. bd. Washington Jr. League, 1965-66; profl. chmn. bd. dirs. 1966-67, mem. project rsch. com., 1967-68, adv. planning com., 1968-69, mem. nominating com., 1969-70; sustaining mem. Rep. Nat. Com.; mem. rector's com. St. John's Ch.-Lafayette Sq., Washington 1989—. Mem. Exec. Women in Govt. (founding mem.), Smithsonian Assocs., Nat. Cathedral Assn., Colonial Dames Am. (bd. dirs. 1985-88), Sulgrave Club (Loadsworth fund Washington 1983-85, bd. dirs. 1987—, 1st v.p. 1989—), Georgetown Rep. Club (v.p., co-founder 1964). Episcopalian. Home: 6 Pomander Walk Washington DC 20007

BURNS, CAROL J., architect, educator; b. Cedar Rapids, Iowa, Nov. 24, 1954; d. Robert Joseph and Alice T. (Neuhaus) B. Student, Bryn Mawr Coll., 1973-75; BA, Yale Coll., 1980, MArch, 1983. Designer Osborne and Stewart, San Francisco, 1975-77; project architect Hunter Smith and Assocs., New Haven, 1983-85; project designer A.M. Kinney and Assocs., Cin., 1985-86; asst. prof. U. Cin., 1984-86; adj. prof. R.I. Sch. Design, Providence, 1986-87; asst. prof. Harvard U., Cambridge, Mass., 1987—; prin. C. Burns, Architect, Guilford, Conn., 1986—. Editor jour. Yale Sch. Architecture Perspecta 21, 1984; designer bank br. (Soc. Am. Reg. Architects award 1988); group shows include Erector Sq. Gallery, New Haven, 1987, Tangeman Gallery, Cin., 1986, Canessa Gallery, San Francisco, 1985, Norfolk 4 Plus 4: Architects and Sculptors, Norfolk, Conn., 1983. Mem. Guilford Land Trust, 1987—, Women's Nat. Art Mus., Washington, 1988—. Grantee U. Cin. Research Council, 1985, 86, Graham Found., 1983; Eero Saarinen fellow, 1983. Mem. Shoreline Alliance Arts. Club: Yale (New Haven). Office: Harvard U 48 Quincy St Cambridge MA 02148

BURNS, CATHERINE ELIZABETH, art dealer; b. Winnipeg, Man., Can., June 21, 1953; came to U.S., 1955; d. Robert Franklin and Claire Margaret (Lillington) B. BA, U. Calif., Davis, 1975; MA in Museology, U. Minn., 1978. Adj. prof., curator univ. gallery U. Mass., Amherst, 1978-80; curator gallery of art Washington U., St. Louis, 1981-82; dealer in 19th and early 20th century prints and drawings Catherine E. Burns Fine Prints, Oakland, Calif., 1982—; also appraiser Catherine E. Burns Fine Prints, Oakland. Organizer San Francisco Fine Print Fair; mem. Nat. Trust for Hist. Preservation, Oakland Heritage Alliance. Grantee Nat. Endowment for Arts, 1981-82. Mem. Graphic Arts Coun., Art Deco Soc. Calif. Office: PO Box 11201 Oakland CA 94611

BURNS, DEBORAH DENISE, financial planner, broker; b. Houston, Mar. 15, 1953; d. Allie (Burns) Sneed; divorced; 1 child, James E. Beard. BS in Psychology, U. Houston, 1983. Collection clk. Foley's Dept. Store, Houston, 1973-76; clk. U.S. P.O., Houston, 1976-81; office mgr. LFA, Inc., Houston, 1981-83; ind. sales agt. First Continental Ins. Co., Houston, 1983-86; unit mgr. Summit Mktg. Group, Houston, 1985—, broker, 1985—. counselor Julia C. Hester House United Way Agy., Houston, 1984. Roman Catholic. Office: First Continental Ins Co 2303 Smith Houston TX 77006

BURNS, ELLEN BREE, federal judge; b. New Haven, Conn., Dec. 13, 1923; d. Vincent Thomas and Mildred Bridget (Bannon) Bree; m. Joseph Patrick Burns, Oct. 8, 1955 (dec.); children: Mary Ellen, Joseph Bree, Kevin James. BA, Albertus Magnus Coll., 1944, LLD (hon.), 1974; LLB, Yale U., 1947; LLD (hon.), U. New Haven, 1981, Sacred Heart U., 1986. Bar: Conn. 1947. Dir. legis. legal services State of Conn., 1949-73; judge Conn. Cir. Ct., 1973-74, Conn. Ct. of Common Pleas, 1974-76, Conn. Superior Ct., 1976-78; judge U.S. Dist. Ct. Conn., New Haven, 1978—, chief judge, 1988—. Trustee Fairfield U., 1978-85, Albertus Magnus Coll., 1985—. Recipient John Carroll of Carrollton award John Barry Council K.C., 1973, Judiciary award Conn. Trial Lawyers Assn., 1978, Cross Pro Ecclesia et Pontifice, 1981, Law Rev. award U. Conn. Law Rev., 1987, Judiciary award Conn. Bar Assn., 1987. Mem. ABA, Am. Bar Found., New Haven County Bar Assn. Roman Catholic. Office: US Dist Ct 208 US Courthouse 141 Church St New Haven CT 06510

BURNS, GLENNA MARIE, retired educator; b. Arlie, Tex., Aug. 11, 1928; d. James Goodman and Nancy Irene (Covey) Beavers; m. Glen Storrs Johnston, June 1, 1947 (dec. July 1960); children: Ted Wayne, James Glen; m. Buck Burns, Jan. 21, 1967. BS in Elem. Edn., Tex. Tech U., 1963. Cert. elem. tchr., Tex. Tchr. Community Ctr. Sch., Childress, Tex., 1946-47, Lubbock (Tex.) Ind. Sch. Dist., 1963-88. Writer 12 advanced acad. tng. workshops. Mem. Tex. Dem. Women's Assn., Lubbock; vol. Dem. Party, Lubbock; bd. dirs. Lubbock Labor Coun., 1988—, People First, Lubbock, 1988-89; bd. dirs. Young Parents prgram LISD. Grantee AAUW, 1990-91. Mem. Lubbock Fedn. Tchrs. (pres. 1984-87, workshop coord. 1985—), AAUW (pres. 1988-89, 89-91), Lubbock Ret. Tchrs. Assn. (edn. chmn. 1988-89, 89—, pres. elect 1990-91), Lubbock Classroom Tchrs. (pres. 1983-84, v.p. 1984-85), LWV (bd. dirs. Lubbock chpt. 1988—, edn. chmn.), Lubbock Woman's Club, Ladies Bible Class. Home: 4215 51st St Lubbock TX 79413 Office: Lubbock Fedn Tchrs 1901 University Ave Lubbock TX 79410

BURNS, HELENE BARBARA, accountant; b. Bronx, N.Y., Oct. 16, 1953; d. Joseph and May (Klapp) Burstein; m. Dennis M. Burns, July 1, 1979; 1 child, Rebeka Nicole. BS in Acctg. cum laude, Bklyn. Coll., 1975; MBA in Fin. with hons., St. John's U., 1986. Staff acct. Price Waterhouse & Co., N.Y.C., 1975-76; acctg. supr. Joseph E. Seagram & Sons, Inc., 1976-78; asst. to controller Petroleum div. St. Joe Minerals Corp., 1978-82; cons. The Oved Group, S.I., N.Y., 1985-87; owner, pres. Temporary Solutions, S.I., 1987-89; ptnr. Cotton Club for Kids, S.I., 1990—. Mem. Nat. Assn. Female Execs., Omicron Delta Epsilon, Beta Gamma Sigma. Republican. Jewish. Home and Office: 46 Purdue St Staten Island NY 10314

BURNS, SISTER JACQUELINE, academic administrator; b. Kearny, N.J., Sept. 1, 1927; d. John Francis and Elizabeth Louise (Calmar) B. BA, Coll. St. Elizabeth, Convent, N.J., 1957; MA, Cath. U. Am., Washington, 1964; PhD in History, Cath. U. Am., 1968; LHD (hon.), Seton Hall U., 1988. Secondary sch. tchr. St. John Cathedral High Sch., Paterson, N.J, 1957-64; instr., asst. prof. Coll. of St. Elizabeth, Convent, N.J., 1967-71, asst. dean of studies, 1971-76, dean of studies, 1976-81, pres., 1981—; bd. dirs. Chestnut Hill Coll., Phila., 1990—. Trustee N.J. Ind. Coll. Fund (treas. 1985-87); mem. N.J. Com. for Humanities, New Brunswick, 1982-86; bd. dirs. N.J. Coun. on Econ. Education, Trenton, 1984-88, Morris County Consumer Credit Union, Morristown, 1984-88; mem. N.J. Bd. Higher Edn., Trenton, 1988—; trustee St. Joseph Hosp. and Med. Ctr., Paterson, 1984-88; bd. dirs. Nat. Assn. Ind. Colls. & Univs., 1985-88. Recipient Pres.'s award for ednl. leadership Northeast Coalition of Ednl. Leaders, 1987, Woman of Achievement award Bus. and Profl. Women's Clubs N.J., Morris County, 1984, Fulbright scholarship, France, 1964. Mem. Assn. Ind. Colls. and Univs. of N.J. (bd. dirs. 1978—, chmn. 1985-87), Morris County C. of C. (bd. dirs. 1988—). Address: Coll St Elizabeth Office of Pres Convent Station NJ 07961

BURNS, JOAN COULON, retired educator; b. Pioneer, Ohio, Dec. 18, 1921; d. William W. and Bernice Winifred (Ely) Coulon; m. Robert K. Burns, May 30, 1942; children: Carole, David. BS, Bowling Green (Ohio) State U., 1944; MS, Miami (Ohio) U., 1967. Tchr. Latin grammar Bowling Green State U., 1944; tchr. Latin and English Gibsonburg (Ohio) Bd. of Edn., 1945; tchr. English and French Midland Park (N.J.) Bd. of Edn., 1961; sec. aerospace med. rsch. div. Wright-Patterson AFB, Dayton, Ohio, ret.; tchr. French, Latin, English Kettering, Ohio, 1956-60, 1962-87. Named Martha Jennings scholar. Mem. ACTFL, OFLT, NEA, OEA, KCTA, AAUW, Am. Assn. Tchrs. French, Phi Delta Kappa, Delta Kappa Gamma, Sigma Pi Rho, Beta Pi Theta. Home: 3550 Echo Spring Trail Kettering OH 45429

BURNS, KATHLEEN JOYCE, commissioner of public works; b. New Bedford, Mass., Nov. 7, 1953; d. Manuel Fernandes Jr. and Maria Julia (Pereira) Camacho; m. Daniel Francis Burns, May 16, 1975; 1 child, Jollian Anne. BS in Indsl. Tech., Roger Williams Coll., 1989. With City of New Bedford, 1973—, adminstrv. asst. to commr. pub. works, 1985-86, commr. pub. works, 1986—; mem. Olmsted adv. com. City of New Bedford, 1984—, mem. mayor's devel. group, 1986—, chairperson Pub. Facilities Group, 1987—, mem. zoning adv. com., 1989—. Tree warden City of New Bedford Forestry Div., 1986—, sec. planning bd., 1986—. Mem. Am. Farmland Trust, Nat. Trust for Hist. Preservation, Water Pollution Control Fedn. Democrat. Roman Catholic. Home: 139 Fisher Rd Westport MA 02747

BURNS, LUCY DENISE, newspaper publisher, editor; b. Jamaica, N.Y., Nov. 23, 1956; d. Perry and Marjorie (Johnson) B. Student, Bernard M. Baruch Coll., 1974-77, Pace U., 1977-78. Bookkeeper various orgns., N.Y.C., 1978-84; enforcement officer N.Y.C. Dept. Sanitation, 1984-86; spl. patrolman N.Y.C. Bd. Edn., 1986—; pub., editor in chief Women Mean Bus., N.Y.C., 1988—; cons. Ch. Women United, Jamaica, 1989—; produce QPTV Cable TV, promoter, air personality. Mem. communications com. Big Apple Sickle Cell, Jamaica, 1989—; dir. communications Ch. Women United, 1988—. Recipient Ann. Salute to Women Entrepreneurs, Caribbean-Am. C. of C. and Industry, Inc., Bkyn., 1989, appreciation award Mulcare Beauty Studio, Inc., St. Albans, 1990. Mem. NAFE, Cambria Heights Civic Assn., NAACP, Lions. Baptist. Home: 120-43 223d St Cambria Heights NY 11411 Office: Women Mean Bus PO Box 00J Cambria Heights NY 11411-0399

BURNS, MARIAN LAW, legal adminstrator; b. Drexel Hill, Pa., Jan. 10, 1954; d. Vincent Charles and Agatha M. (Paoletti) Law; m. Lawrence Joseph Burns, Sept. 29, 1979; children: Peter Andrew, Rita Marie. Paralegal, legal sec. Tuso & Gruccio, Vineland, N.J., 1972-74; legal sec. Swartz, Campbell & Detweiler, Phila., 1974-80; adminstrv. mgr. Drinker Biddle & Reath (formerly Smith, Lambert, Hicks & Beidler, P.C.), Princeton, N.J., 1980-88; legal adminstr. Sherr, Joffe & Zuckerman, P.C., West Conshohocken, Pa., 1988-90, Groen, Laveson, Goldberg & Rubenstone, Bensalem, Pa., 1990—. Mem. ABA (assoc., sect. econs. of law practice), Nat. Assn. Legal Adminstrs., Phila. Assn. Legal Adminstrs. Office: Groen Laveson Goldberg & Rubenstone Ste 200 4 Greenwood Sq PO Box 5018 Bensalem PA 19020

BURNS, MICHELE, caterer; b. Jamaica, N.Y., Oct. 11, 1960; d. Richard and Mary Ann (Cormano) B. Grad., Hillcrest High Sch. Gen. mgr. Heskel's Restaurant, N.Y.C., 1979-82, Vanessa Restaurant, N.Y.C., 1982, Met. Improvement Co., N.Y.C., 1982-83; mgr. Jay Robert Caterers, N.Y.C., 1984-86; owner Exciting Affairs Caterers, N.Y.C., 1986—. Office: Exciting Affairs Caterers 119-50 Metropolitan Ave Kew Gardens NY 11415

BURNS, NORMA DECAMP, architect; b. N.Y.C., Dec. 14, 1940; d. Cyrus and Stella (Werner) DeCamp; m. Robert Paschal Burns, Dec. 4, 1973; 1 child, Linda Paige. BS, Fla. State U., 1962; MArch, N.C. State U., 1976. Registered architect, N.C. Tchr. high schs., Fla., Md., 1962-73; pres., owner Burnstudio Architects P.A., Raleigh, N.C., 1977—, WorkSpace, Inc., Raleigh, 1981—. Past chmn. City of Raleigh Appearance Commn.; mem. land use com Triangle J Council Govts.; mem. Downtown Adv. Com., Raleigh; bd. advisers Preservation Found. N.C., Raleigh, 1985—; mem. bus. adv. coun. Peace Coll., Raleigh, 1985-88; councilman-at-large Raleigh City Coun., 1985-89, mem. law and fin. com., 1987-88, chmn. comprehensive planning com., 1988-89, downtown com., 1988-89, univ. liaison; mem. exec. bd., pres. elect N.C. State U. Sch. Design Found., 1989—. Recipient numerous awards including Owens-Corning Energy award, 1984; Adaptive Reuse award Durham Preservation Soc., 1983, 84, Spectator Architecture award, 1983-89, Triangle Devel. award, 1984-88, 89; cited in Ten Best Designs of 1984, TIME mag. Loeb fellow, Harvard U. 1986-87. Mem. AIA (nat. interiors com. 1981-84, nat. design com. 1985-88, nat. housing com. 1988, chmn. N.C. historic resources com. 1983-85, selected exhibitor 1988 exhbn. by Women in Architecture), Nat. Trust Historic Preservation. Office: Burnstudio Architects PA PO Box 25688 Raleigh NC 27611

BURNS, PAT ACKERMAN GONIA, infosytems specialist, software engineer; b. Birmingham, Ala., July 16, 1938; d. Richard Lee and Hattie Eugenia (Bragg) Ackerman; m. Robert Edward Gonia, June 4, 1957 (div. Jan. 1973); children: Deborah Hayes, Junita Kayler, Ronald Gonia; m. James Clayton Burns, June 23, 1984. BS in Math., U. Ala., 1970, postgrad., 1971-77. Cert. secondary tchr., Ala. Missionary United Meth. Bd. of Missions, Sumatra, Indonesia, 1961-64; homebound tchr. Huntsville (Ala.) City Schs., 1970-75; mem. tech. staff Gen. Rsch. Corp., Huntsville, 1975-79; rsch. scientist Nichols Rsch. Corp., Huntsville, 1979-84, mgr. personnel div., 1984-87, mgmt. info. systems dept. head, 1987—; mem. adv. com. Drake Tech. Sch., Huntsville, 1988—. Mem. PTA, Huntsville, Ch. Women United, Huntsville, Community Chorus, Huntsville. Mem. NAFE, Data Processing Mgmt. Assn., Assn. Personnel Adminstrs., IEEE, Am. Computer Soc., Huntsville C. of C. (speaker 1986—). Republican. Methodist. Office: Nichols Rsch Corp 4040 S Memorial Pkwy Huntsville AL 35802

BURNS, ROBERTTA JEAN, assistant county administrative officer; b. El Centro, Calif., July 20, 1949; d. Robert Jess and Mary Blanche (Evans) Rosenbaum; m. James Gerald Burns Jr., Feb. 1, 1969; children: Jacquilyn, Brooke. AA, Imperial (Calif.) Valley Coll., 1971; BA, San Diego State U., 1978. Audit clk. Sears Roebuck & Co., El Centro, 1969-70; computer operator Philco-Ford, Seeley, Calif., 1970-71; with County of Imperial, El Centro, 1972—, sr. adminstrv. analyst, 1984-87, asst. county adminstrv. officer, 1987—; mem. Salton Sea Task Force, Sacramento, 1986—; alternate Aging Agy. Adv. Bd., El Centro, 1989; bd. dirs. FEMA Local Emergency Bd., El Centro, 1985—. Mem. adv. task force on Imperial Valley Coll. Mus., Imperial, 1986; mem. Imperial Valley Chorus, El Centro. Mem. AAUW (sec. 1988—), Native Daus. of Calif., Imperial Valley Pioneer's Soc., Imperial Valley Archael. Soc. (pres. 1976), Soroptimist Internat. Republican. Methodist. Office: County of Imperial 940 W Main St El Centro CA 92243

BURNS, ROBIN, cosmetics company executive. Student, Syracuse U. Formerly with Bloomingdale's, N.Y.C., v.p.; pres. Calvin Klein Cosmetics; pres., chief exec. officer Estee Lauder USA, N.Y.C., 1990—. Office: Estee Lauder USA 767 Fifth Ave New York NY 10153*

BURNS, RUTH ANN MARY, television executive; b. New Brunswick, N.J., Nov. 7, 1944; d. Chester Patrick and Mary Francis (Norko) Shea; m. Carl William Burns, Sept. 6, 1965; children: Christopher Carl, Heather Shea. BA, Douglass Coll., 1967; MA, Rutgers U., 1976. War corr. AP, N.Am. Newspaper Alliance, Vietnam, 1967; editor News Tribune, Woodbridge, N.J., 1967-70; writer, cons. Star Ledger, N.Y. Times, Parade mag., 1970-76; sr. research and program assoc. Eagleton Inst. of Politics, New Brunswick, 1976-81; project dir. Ctr. for Am. Woman & Politics, New Brunswick, 1978-81; v.p. Sta. WNET, N.Y.C., 1982-84, sr. v.p., 1984—. Author: Women in Municipal Management, Choice, Challenge, Change, 1980 (HUD award); contbg. author: Women and the American City, 1981; also articles. V.p. Edison (N.J.) Bd. Edn., 1975-82; advisor Sch. Communications Rutgers U., 1985-87; trustee Rutgers U., 1987—. Recipient Nat. Writing award William Randolph Hearst Found., 1967, Achievement award Am. Soc. Pub. Adminstrn., 1981, Woman of Yr. award Raritan Valley Regional C. of C., 1982; named to Rutger's U. Hall Disting. Alumni. Mem. Nat. Assn. TV Arts and Scis., Am. Soc. Women in Radio and TV, Eastern Ednl. Network, Douglass Soc. Democrat. Roman Catholic. Home: 6 Longview Rd Edison NJ 08820 Office: Sta WNET 356 W 58th St New York NY 10019

BURNS, SALLY ANN, medical association administrator; b. Findlay, Ohio, Dec. 13, 1959; d. Van Larson and Marian (Delia) B. Student, Findlay Coll., 1980-82, Bowling Green State U., 1982-83; AAS, Houston Community Coll., 1985. Lic. physical therapist asst., Tex. Intern in clin. studies various Hosps., Houston, 1984-85; patient care Spring Br. Meml. Hosp., Houston, 1985-86; pres. Burns Phys. Therapy Clinic, Inc., Houston, 1986—; pres. Phys. Therapy Plus, Inc., Houston, 1988—, also bd. dirs. Author: Physical Therapy for Multiple Sclerosis. Mem. Inst. for Profl. Health Svc. Adminstrs. (charter mem.), Am. Judicature Soc., Am. Phys. Therapy Assn., Tex. Phys. Therapy Assn., Community Health Adminstrn. Home: 1601 Hollyhurst E-22 Houston TX 77056 Office: Burns Phys Therapy Clinic 5220 Travis Houston TX 77002

BURNS, SHARON RYAN, information systems manager; b. Detroit, Jan. 13, 1957; d. Gordon Thomas and Lorraine (Lanzon) Ryan; m. David John Burns (dec. 1988); children: Kendra Marie, Brian David. BS in Acctg., No. Mich. U., 1979. Software specialist Digital Equipment Corp., Chgo., 1984-87; infosystems mgr. Lindberg Corp., Rosemont, Ill., 1988—. Office: Lindberg Corp Ste 700 6133 N River Rd Rosemont IL 60612

BURNS, VICKI HILL, marketing professional; b. Nashville, Nov. 30, 1949; d. John Benjamin and Nellie (Collier) Hill; m. Granville Goodloe Waggoner Jr., Mar. 12, 1971 (div. Aug. 1987); 1 child, Jennifer Peyton; m. Alfred Michael Burns, June 23, 1989; 1 child, Brandon Micaiah. BA in Secondary

Edn., Vanderbilt/Peabody Coll., Nashville, 1970, postgrad., 1970. Sec. to dir. food svc. Vanderbilt/Peabody Coll., Nashville, 1970-71; interviewer food stamp program Tenn. Dept. Welfare, 1972; dividend asst., sec. Tenn. Securities, 1972-73; med. librarian Met. Health Dept., 1973-76; freelance profl. model, 1976-87; editorial advisor, prodn. asst. Athlon Publs., 1978-83; mktg. rep. Westside Athletic Club, 1988; mktg. cons. Gracie & Co., Nashville, 1988-89; mktg. asst. Gracie & Companie subs. S.E. Venture Cos., Nashville, 1989—; owner Kingpins, Inc., Nashville, 1989; subs. secondary tchr. Met. Sch. System, 1971; participant Am. Bus. Seminars; chmn. spl. projects Action Auction program Sta. WDCN-TV, 1987-88. Vol., solicitor Friends of Children's Hosp., 1979—; fundraiser, sec. bd. dirs. Santa's Helpers; creator, performer children's puppet shows Cumberland Mus., 1984-87, puppeteer, 1989; promotional vol. various projects Nashville Symphony, 1985-90. Republican. Methodist. Office: Gracie and Companie PO Box 210348 Nashville TN 37221

BURNS, VIRGINIA LAW, writer; b. Redford, Mich., May 23, 1925; d. Alvin John and Leola Miriam (Wadley) Law; divorced; children: James Ritchie, Duncan Ritchie, Margaret Ritchie. Student, Cranbrook Acad. Art, Bloomfield Hills, Mich., 1943, U. Mich., 1943-47; BA, Mich. State U., 1956. Cert. tchr., Mich. Tchr. elem. schs. State of Mich., 1969-87; editor, publisher Enterprise Press, Laingsburg, Mich., 1987—; vis. author, writer Mich. Council for Humanities. Contbr. articles to newspapers, mags.; author (juvenile biographies) Frontier Doctor, 1978, Frontier Soldier, 1980, First Frontiers, 1985, Tall Annie, 1987. Leader Boy Scouts Am., DeWitt, Mich., Girl Scouts U.S., East Lansing, Mich., 4-H Club, Onaway, Mich. Recipient Literary award of Excellence Historical Soc. of Mich.; nominated one of Michigan's First Ladies for promoting state history in literature. Mem. Soc. Children's Book Writers, Detroit Women Writers Assn. Home: 8600 S Fenner Laingsburg MI 48848 Office: Enterprise Press 8600 Fenner Rd Laingsburg MI 48848

BURNS-LOVE, DARLENE LOUISE, aesthetician cosmetologist; b. Phoenix, Mar. 27, 1959; 1 child, Kyndra Louise. Student, Internat. Beauty, Scottsdale, Ariz., 1977; AAS, Scottsdale Community Coll., 1989. Freelance model, actress, voice overs, 1974--, freelance make up artist, 1977--; cosmetologist Louis Anthony Salons, Scottsdale, Ariz., 1977-80; aesthetician Elizabeth Arden Salons, NYC; owner Darlene Louise Cons., Scottsdale, Ariz., 1981--, Darlene Louise Skin Care, Ariz., 1982--. Author: Natural Skin Care, 1984, guest Radio and TV appearances for beauty profession, 1984--. Recipient Best Facial, New Times Weekly Paper, Ariz., 1985. Mem. Ariz. Aestheticians Assn. (founder, pres.), American Skin Care Assn., American Bus. Women's Orgn., American Legion Women's Aux.

BURNSTEIN, FRANCES, chamber of commerce executive; b. N.Y.C., Oct. 13, 1935; d. Benny and Yetta Kirshenbaum; m. Barry Burnstein, Oct. 16, 1955; children: Steven, Barbara, Lori. Student, CCNY, 1953-55; grad., Insts. Orgn. Mgmt., 1983. Dep. mayor Twp. of Cherry Hill, N.J., 1975-77; exec. dir. Cherry Hill C. of C., 1977-88, pres., 1988—; commr. Camden County Parks, 1986-88. Trustee Cooper Found. Med. Ctr., Camden, N.J., 1980-89, Police Athletic League, 1976—; bd. dirs. ARC, Camden County, 1981—, Guidance Ctr., 1982-84; trustee Ronald McDonald House of Kids, Camden County United Way, 1981—, v.p., 1981-84, pres.'s cabinet, 1982-84; co-chair Del. River Region Tourism Council, 1983; exec. adv. coun. Rutgers U. Sch.Bus., 1985—; bd. dirs. Disaster Appeal Com., 1981—. Named Newsmaker of Yr., Cherry Hill C. of C., 1984; Frances Burnstein Little League Softball Field dedicated to her, 1980; selected for cover of N.J. Woman Mag., 1986; named one of seven Women to Watch in 1986, State of N.J., Bus. Watch 1989 Bus. Jour. N.J. Mem. NAFE, N.J. Assn. C. of C. (v.p.), N.J. Assn. C. of C. Execs. (v.p. 1987—), Am. Assn. C. of C., Am. Assn. C. of C. Communications Coun., World Affairs Coun., Nat. Assn. Membership Dirs., Am. Mgmt. Assn., Am. Heart Assn. (bd. dirs. Cherry Hill chpt. 1987—). Republican. Jewish. Lodge: Garden State Rotary (Person of Yr. 1980). Office: Cherry Hill C of C 1060 Kings Hwy N Cherry Hill NJ 08034

BURR, LAURIE DIANE, business systems consultant; b. Bath, N.Y., Jan. 29, 1953; d. Jonathan Williams and Dorothy Evelyn (Daines) B.; m. Jeffrey Howard Halpern. AB, Vassar Coll., 1974; MBA, U. Va., 1983. Fin. planner Burlington, Vt., 1975-76; mktg. rep. IBM, Burlington, 1976-80; fin. planner IBM/Lab.-Mfg., Poughkeepsie, N.Y., 1983-84; marketer, analyst IBM/Regional & Br. Offices, Balt., 1984-86; proposal mgr. IBM/Pub. Sector Group, Balt., 1986-88; bus. systems cons. pub. sector industry IBM, Bethesda, Md., 1988—. Mem. Eastport Yacht Club (Annapolis, Md.). Republican. Episcopalian.

BURRI, BARBARA ANNE, software company official; b. Mineola, N.Y., July 24, 1953; d. Robert Alexander and Mary (Christ) B.; m. Thomas Gerard Bechard, May 8, 1982 (div. Mar. 1989). AS in Engring., Nassau Coll., Garden City, N.Y., 1973; BSCE, Union Coll., 1975; MBA, Syracuse U., 1978; advanced cert., Northeastern U., 1983. Asst. dir. Oswego County Coun. on Arts, Oswego, N.Y., 1978-79; ops. analyst TASC, Reading, Mass., 1979-84; product mgr. personal computers WSI, Bedford, Mass., 1984-86; sr. bus. analyst Wang Labs., Lowell, Mass., 1986-88; product mgr. software Execaire, Dorval, Que., Can., 1988—; owner, mgr. Bayside Cons., Plaistow, N.H., 1983—. Trainer, leader, nat. del. Girl Scouts U.S.A., Boston, 1962—. Recipient Thanks Badge, Girl Scouts U.S.A., 1989; grantee NSF, 1975. Home: 135 Forrest St Apt 22 Plaistow NH 03865 Office: 10255 Ryan Ave, Dorval, PQ Canada

BURRIS, BETTY PRICE, banker; b. High Point, N.C., Oct. 22, 1942; d. Samuel and Eloise (Little) Walls; m. Ray T. Price, Jan. 3, 1963 (div. 1977); children: Melinda Ann Price Cheek, Teresa Gail Price; m. James C. Burris, Jr., Dec. 20, 1980. BSBA and Econs., High Point Coll., 1987; MS in Adult Edn., N.C. Agr. and Tech. State U., 1989. Sr. collections coord. Wachovia Bank & Trust Co., N.A., Greensboro, N.C., 1973—. Treas. Friends High Point Theatre, 1979—. Mem. AAUW (treas. High Point 1987—). Democrat. Methodist. Home: 1454 Finsbury Ln High Point NC 27260 Office: Wachovia Bank & Trust Co NA PO Box 21048 Greensboro NC 27420

BURRIS, FRANCES WHITE, personnel director; b. Cuero, Tex., Oct. 18, 1933; d. Marian Cecil and Dorothy Christine (Pruetz) White; m. Berlie Burris Jr, Mar. 8, 1958 (div. 1982); children: William Alan, Joel Maurice. BA, Mary Hardin Baylor Coll., Belton, Tex., 1955; M in Eng., Trinity U., San Antonio, 1959. Cert. tchr., Tex. Elem. tchr. East and Mt. Houston Independent Sch. Dist., 1956, Edgewood Ind. Sch. Dist., San Antonio, 1956-57, 58-59; tchr. Edna (Tex.) Ind. Sch. Dist., 1957-58; elem. tchr. Northside Ind. Sch. Dist., San Antonio, 1960-62, Southside Schs., San Antonio, 1962-63; mgr. Michael's Dept. Store, Houston, 1980-81; eligibility worker Tex. Dept. Human Resources, Houston, 1981—. Mem. Meridith Manor Civic Club, Houston, 1966-78, Settlers Valley Civic Club, Katy, Tex., 1979-81. Mem. Tex. State Employees Union (exec. bd. 1984—, del. gen. assembly 1984-90, lobbyist 1985-89). Democrat. Baptist. Club: Bridge (Houston).

BURRIS, HARRIETT COLEMAN, educational administrator; b. Chestertown, Md., June 5, 1920; d. Charles P. and Myrtle S. (Usilton) Coleman. Grad., M.G.W. Sch. Nursing, Easton, Md., 194l; BS in Edn., U. Del., 1960, MEd, 1964. RN, Del.; cert. tchr., adminstr., Del. Nurse, supr. Kent Gen. Hosp., Dover, Del., 194l-56; elem. tchr. Rose Valley Sch., Dover, 1956-59; tchr. Smyrna (Del.) Elem. Sch., 1959-76; Title I dir., kindergarten prin. Smyrna Sch. Dist., 1976-78, prin. Clayton (Del.) Elem. Dist., 1978-89, ret., 1989. Mem. NEA (life), Del. Assn. Sch. Adminstrs. (membership and program coms. 1987-89), Am. Nurses Assn., AAUW, Am. Assn. Ret. Persons, VFW Aux., Delta Kappa Gamma (past charter pres. Theta chpt.), Phi Delta Kappa. Democrat. Methodist. Home: Box 207 Clayton DE 19928

BURRIS, KATHRYN ANN, professional association administrator; b. Fredricksburg, Tex., Dec. 1, 1957; d. Bryon Curthburn and Sara Lee (Matthews) Rinehart; m. Charles Anthony Burris, Nov. 4, 1989. BS, Howard Payne U., 1979; diploma, Ranger Jr. Coll., 1982. Cert. Okla. Bd. Nurse Registration and Nursing Edn. Educator Brownwood (Tex.) Home and Sch., 1979-80; critical care nurse Brownwood Regional Hosp., 1981-83; home healthcare nurse Healthcare, Inc., Tulsa, 1983-85; staff nurse Broken Arrow (Okla.) Med. Ctr., 1984-85; state dir. Am. Chronic Pain Assn., Tulsa, 1987—. Feature columnist (newspaper) The Tulsa Tribune, 1988—; contbg. writer (newsletters) Nat. Chronic Pain Outreach Assn. Lifeline, 1988, Am. Chronic Pain Assn. Chronicle, 1989—. Make-up artist Brownwood Theater Co., 1980-81, wardrobe dir., 1980. Mem. Reflex Sympathetic Dystrophy Syndrome Assn. (state dir. 1988-90). Democrat. Unitarian. Home: 10061 S Sheridan Rd Ste 615 Tulsa OK 74133 Office: Am Chronic Pain Assn PO Box 55372 Tulsa OK 74155

BURRIS, LAUREN BAYLERAN, business owner; b. Detroit, Mar. 30, 1952; d. Haig Aram and Dirouhi (Halajian) Bayleran; m. William James Burris, Feb. 4, 1981; children: Taron, Ian. BBA, U. Mich., 1973; MBA, Wayne State U., 1978. Sales rep. IBM Corp., Detroit, 1973-76; assoc. dir. U. Mich., Dearborn, 1976-78; owner Bayleran & Burris, Inc., Orchard Lake, Mich., 1978—, L.B. Burris & Co., Inc., Orchard Lake, 1982—, Servicelease, Inc., Orchard Lake, 1989—; cons. Rapidata, Southfield, Mich., 1980-82. Editor: A Practical Armenian & English Book, 1971. Head pub. rels. com. Oakland County C. of C., Pontiac, Mich., 1983. mem. Wayne State U. Alumnae Assn. (pres. Detroit chpt. 1981-83), Alpha Phi. Republican.

BURRIS, SHIRLEY KAY, legal systems coordinator; b. Pleasant Plains, Ill., Feb. 1, 1940; d. Elba M. and Lela P. (Dunkel) Gabbert; children: David L., Donna K. Gillette. Student, Lincolnland Community Coll., Springfield, Ill. Sec. Sangamo Electric Co., Springfield, 1958-65; legal sec. G. William Horsley, 1973-74; legal systems coord. Heyl, Royster, Voelker and Allen, Edwardsville, Ill., 1975—. Named Legal Sec. Yr. Sangamon County Legal Sec., 1980-81. Mem. NAFE. Home: 9 Carriage Ln Edwardsville IL 62025

BURROUGHS, BONNIE LEIGH, advertising executive; b. Appleton, Wis., July 4, 1950; d. Robert J. and Charlotte (Clausen) B.; children from previous marriage: John Burroughs, Paul Burroughs. Student Marian Coll., Fond du Lac, Wis. Media dir., artist understudy James Spallas & Assocs., Fond du Lac, 1969-75; artist, art dept. Mercy Marine, Fond du Lac, 1970-73; pres., owner Burroughs & Assocs., Fond du Lac, 1980—. Mem. County Bd. Suprs., Fond du Lac, 1979-81; bd. dirs., pres. Fond du Lac County Legal Aux.; bd. dirs. Fond du Lac County Hist. Soc., 1980-89, Wau Bon Council Girl Scouts U.S., 1987, 89—. Avocations: reading, swimming, golf. Office: Burroughs & Assocs 76 S Macy Ste 215 Fond du Lac WI 54935

BURROWS, CYNTHIA JANE, chemistry educator; b. St. Paul, Minn., Sept. 23, 1953; d. Donald W. and Phyllis I. Burrows. BS, U. Colo., 1975; MS, Cornell U., 1978, PhD, 1982. Postdoctoral rsch. assoc. U. Louis Pasteur, Strasbourg, France, 1981-83; asst. prof. dept. chemistry SUNY, Stony Brook, 1983-89, assoc. prof. dept. chemistry, 1989—. Fellow NSF-CNRS, 1981, Bourse Chateaubriand, Strasbourg, 1982, Japan Soc. for Promotion of Sci. Rsch., Okazaki, 1989. Mem. Am. Chem. Soc., AAAS. Office: Dept Chemistry SUNY Stony Brook NY 11794

BURROWS, DEBRA GABRIELLE, adult education educator; b. New Brunswick, N.J., Feb. 10, 1954; d. Mario R. Casale and Setphanie (Firczuk) Ur; m. Arnold Eugene Burrows Jr., Dec. 3, 1977. BS in Math., Westminster Coll., New Wilmington, Pa., 1976; MEd in Ednl. Adminstrn., Pa. State U., University Park, 1985. Underwriter Liberty Mut. Ins. Co., Williamsport, Pa., 1977-78; program coord. Lycoming/Clinton STEP, Williamsport, 1983-84; summer program dir. Clinton County Tng. Office, Lock Haven, Pa., 1985-87; tchr., counselor Central Intermediate Unit 10, Lock Haven, 1982-87, adult edn. coord., 1987—; cons. Inst. Adult Literacy, University Park, 1989—. Columnist Keep Learning, 1989-90. Vice-chmn. Lamar Twp. (Pa.) Zoning Hearing Bd., 199—; instr., leader West Br. Riders 4-H Club, South Renovo, Pa., 1983-86; mem. Lamar Twp. Planning Commn., 1989. Recipient Community Svc. award South Renovo (Pa.) Borough, 1983. Mem. AAUW, Pa. Assn. Adult Continuing Edn. (treas. 1990—), Pa. Assn. Single Parent/Homemaker and Sex Equity Program Coords. (sec. 1989—), Clinton County Coalition for Lit., Phi Delta Kappa. Democrat. Home: RD 1 Box 251E Mill Hall PA 17751

BURROWS, ELIZABETH MACDONALD, religious organization executive; b. Portland, Oreg., Jan. 30, 1930; d. Leland R. and Ruth M. (Frew) MacDonald. Certificate, Chinmaya Trust Sandeepany, Bombay; PhD (hon.), Internat. U. Philosophy and Sci., 1975. Ordained to ministry First Christian Ch., 1976. Mgr. credit Home Utilities, Seattle, 1958, Montgomery Ward, Crescent City, Calif., 1963; supr. Oreg. Dist. Tng. West Coast Telephone, Beaverton, 1965; pres. Christian Ch. Universal Philosophy, Seattle, 1971—, Archives Internat., St. Louis, 1971—; v.p. James Tyler Kent Inst. Homeopathy, 1984—, Internat. Coll. Universal Psychology, 1986—. Author: Crystal Planet, 1979, Pathway of the Immortal, 1980, Odyssey of The Apocalypse, 1981, Maya Sangh, 1981, Harp of Destiny, 1984, Commentary for Gospel of Peace of Jesus Christ according to John, 1986, American Poetry Anthology, 1989. Mem. Internat. Speakers Platform, Internat. New Thought Alliance, Cousteau Soc., Internat. Order of Chivalry. Home: 10529 Ashworth Ave N Seattle WA 98133 Office: Christian Ch Universal Philosophy 10529 Ashworth Ave N Seattle WA 98133

BURROWS, LEE R., art director; b. Sacramento, July 5, 1935; d. Walter and Dorothy (Meadows) Toulou; m. Curtis Burrows, Mar. 14, 1951; children: Linda, Lannette, Michael, Angela, Shaunee. Student, Yuba Coll. Freelance recording studio owner Wheatland, Calif.; tchr. children arts program Yuba City (Calif.) Recreation Dept.; arts program coord. MSV Recreation Dept., Marysville, Calif.; exec. dir. Yuba/Sutter Regional Arts Coun., Marysville. Producer weekly cable TV program, 1983-89. Mem. Nat. Assembly of Local Arts Agys., Nat. Inst. Arts and Disabilities, Calif. Confederation Local Arts, Rural Arts Svcs., Yuba-Sutter C. of C., Yuba-Sutter Hist. Assn. Home: PO Box 150 Marysville CA 95901

BURRY, GAIL BLACK, educational association administrator; b. Dunnellon, Fla., Oct. 5, 1939; d. Givohn Black and Eva Lou (Daniel) Black Medard; m. James Albert Burry, May 11, 1958; children: James Albert Jr., Lou Ann. BA in Bus. Edn., Fla. So. Coll., 1961; MEd, U. Fla., 1967. Tchr. Lake County Schs., Tavares, Fla., 1961-82; pres., bus. agt. Lake County Edn. Assn., Leesburg, Fla., 1982—; bd. dirs. Pvt. Industry Coun., Tavares, 1983—. Sec., United Way, Leesburg, 1983—. Mem. Fla. Edn. Assn. (v.p. 1982—), Fla. Edn. Leaders Forum, Edn. Found. Lake County (sec. 1987—), P.E.O. Sisterhood (charter), Altursa Club Lake County (past pres), Delta Kappa Gamma. Democrat. Methodist. Office: Lake County Edn Assn PO Box 490816 Leesburg FL 34749-0816

BURRY, JUDITH MESNICK (ANNE BURRY), education educator; b. Cleve., July 19, 1942; d. Harry and Alice (Baine) Mesnick; m. June 1, 1968 (div. Apr. 1977); children: Steven, Christine, Heidi. BS in English and Elem. Edn., Bowling Green State U., 1964; EdM in Reading, SUNY, Buffalo, 1968; EdS in Ednl. Psychology, U. No. Colo., 1984, PhD in Applied Stats. and Rsch. Methods, 1984. Tchr. South Euclid (Ohio)-Lyndhurst Pub. Schs., 1964-66, jr. high sch. reading cons., 1966-67; instr. SUNY, Buffalo, 1967-68; ednl. cons., Buffalo, 1968-78; cons. internship program U. No. Colo., Greeley, 1978-81, rsch. asst., 1981-84; asst. prof., rsch. assoc. U. Kans., Lawrence, 1984-88; asst. prof. behavioral studies Coll. Edn., U. Ala., Tuscaloosa, 1988—; cons. on student and tchrs. assessment States of Colo., Kans., Fla., and Ala., also Ednl. Testing Svc.; conf. presenter, 1983—. Editor Jour. Pers. Evaluation in Edn., 1990; contbr. articles to profl. jours., chpts. to books. Scholar NDEA, 1966; grantee Nat. Inst. Edn., 1985, Office Ednl. Rsch. and Improvement and Kans. Dept. Edn., 1985-88, NSF, 1987, S.D. Div. Edn., 1988, U. Ala. Coll. Edn., 1988. Mem. APA, Am. Ednl. Rsch. Assn. (reviewer 1985—), Am. Evaluation Assn., Nat. Coun. in Measurement in Edn., Mid-South Ednl. Rsch. Assn., Phi Delta Phi, Phi Delta Kappa, Phi Lambda Theta. Unitarian. Office: U Ala Behavioral Studies PO Box 870231 Tuscaloosa AL 35487-0231

BURSEY, JOAN TESAREK, chemist; b. Omaha, Mar. 25, 1943; d. Frank William and Helen (Koznarek) Tesarek; m. Maurice Moyer Bursey, Dec. 28, 1970; children: John Thomas Kieran, Sara Helen. BS in Chemistry, Creighton U., 1965; PhD in Chemistry, U. Calif., Berkeley, 1969. Postdoctoral fellow U. N.C., Chapel Hill, 1969-71; scientist Rsch. Triangle Inst., Research Triangle Park, N.C., 1971-84; sr. staff scientist Radian Corp., Research Triangle Park, 1984—. Fellow Royal Soc. Chemistry; mem. Am. Chem. Soc. (treas. 1987—), Alpha Chi Sigma. Democrat. Roman Catholic. Home: 101 Longwood Pl Chapel Hill NC 27514 Office: Radian Corp PO Box 13000 Research Triangle Park NC 27709

BURSIK, CAROL JEAN, librarian; b. Chgo., Dec. 13, 1948; d. George and Doris Loraine (Klecka) B. BA in Spanish, U. Ky., 1970, MA in Libr. Sci., 1973. Asst. libr. Coun. of State Gov., Lexington, Ky., 1971-73; rsch. asst. Nat. Legis. Conf., Lexington, 1973-74; libr. Armor Sch. Library, Ft. Knox, Ky., 1974-76, Post Library, Ft. Eustis, Va., 1976-78, Natick (Mass.) R&D Command, 1978-80; acquisition libr. HQs U.S. Army Europe, Heidelberg, Fed. Republic Germany, 1980-84; chief libr. Natick (Mass.) RDT&E Ctr., 1984-86; systems libr. Pentagon Library, Washington, 1986—. Mem. coord. com. Spl. Interest Group on Libraries and Info. Tech., Washington. Mem. ALA (sec.-treas. fed. librs. roundtable 1989—), Libr. and Info. Tech. Assn., D.C. Libr. Assn. Home: 2200 Columbia Pike Arlington VA 22204 Office: The Pentagon Pentagon Libr Rm 1A518 Washington DC 20310-6080

BURSINGER, JOELLEN, public relations executive; b. Tomah, Wis., Nov. 29, 1958; d. John R. and Carol Geane (Nahley) B. BA, U. Wis., 1981; JD, John Marshall Law Sch., 1987. Bar: Ill. 1987, U.S. Dist. Ct. (no. dist.) Ill. 1987. Promotion coordinator Playboy Enterprises, Inc., Chgo., 1981-83; staff dir. communications and pub. affairs ABA, Chgo., 1984—. Mem. ABA, Internat. Assn. Bus. Communicators, Chgo. Bar Assn., Chgo. Council of Lawyers, U. Wis. Club (communications v.p. Chgo. chpt. 1983).

BURSLEY, KATHLEEN A., lawyer; b. Washington, Mar. 20, 1954; d. G.H. Patrick and Claire (Mulvany) B. BA, Pomona Coll., 1976; JD, Cornell U., 1979. Bar: N.Y. 1980, U.S. Dist. Ct. (ea. and so. dists.) N.Y. 1980, U.S. Ct. Appeals (5th and 11th cirs.) 1981, Fla. 1984, U.S. Dist. Ct. (middle dist.) Fla. 1984., Tex. 1985. Assoc. Haight, Gardner, Poor & Havens, N.Y.C., 1979-81; counsel Harcourt Brace Jovanovich, Inc., N.Y.C. and Orlando, Fla., 1981-85; v.p. and counsel Harcourt Brace Jovanovich, Inc., Orlando, 1985—. Mem. Target 90, San Antonio, 1985—. Mem. Maritime Law Assn. (proctor). Office: Harcourt Brace Jovanovich Inc 6277 Sea Harbor Dr Orlando FL 32887*

BURSTEIN, KAREN SUE, auditor general, lawyer, city official; b. Bklyn., July 20, 1942; d. Herbert and Beatrice (Sobel) B. B.A., Bryn Mawr Coll., 1964; postgrad. Fisk U., 1964-65; New Sch. Social Research, 1965; J.D., Fordham U., 1970. Bar: N.Y. 1971, U.S. Dist. Ct. (ea. and so. dists.) N.Y. 1971. Instr. Fisk U., Nashville, 1965; film editor Colorvision, Inc., N.Y.C., 1966; staff atty. Nassau County Law Service, N.Y., 1970-72; mem. N.Y. Senate, 1973-78; spl. prof. law Hofstra U., N.Y.C., 1976-78; commr. Pub. Service Commn., Albany, N.Y., 1978-80; exec. dir., chmn. Consumer Protection Bd., Albany, 1981-83; pres. CSC, Albany, 1983-87; auditor gen. N.Y.C., 1987—; co-chmn. N.Y. Gov.'s Commn. on Domestic Violence, 1979—; co-leader N.Y. State study group to Japan, 1984; chmn. Temp. Commn. on Workers' Compensation, Albany, 1984-86, Gov.'s Blue Ribbon Panel on Pub. Power, 1986. Contbr. articles to profl. publs., chpts. to books. Del. Democratic Nat. Conv., 1976, Am. Council Young Polit. Leaders' del. to USSR, 1979, Nat. Women's Conv., Houston, 1977; mem. exec. bd. Coalition to Free Soviet Jews; mem. governing council Am. Jewish Congress. Recipient Outstanding Service award South Shore div. Am. Jewish Congress, Personal Devel. award Bus. and Profl. Women's Club, Humanitarian award L.I. Rehab. Assn., Myrtle Wreath Achievement award Nassau region Hadassah, Women of Action award B'nai B'rith Women, Benjamin Potokin award N.Y. State Employees Brotherhood Com. Mem. Hadassah (life), ACLU, Nassau County Bar Assn., NAACP, Nat. Council Jewish Women, Wilderness Soc., Ctr. Women in Govt., NCCJ, Democrat. Office: Auditor Gen 217 Broadway Ste 206 New York NY 10007

BURSTEIN, RENA BENSON, career and educational counselor, consultant; b. N.Y.C., July 12, 1926; d. Joshua and S. Faigel (White) Benson; m. Elias Burstein, Sept. 19, 1943; children: Joanna, Sandra, Miriam. Student, Brown U., 1943-45; BA in Chemistry, George Washington U., 1948; MS in Edn., U. Pa., 1967. Lab. asst. U.S. Naval Rsch. Lab., Washington, 1945-47; substitute, sec. sch. counselor Phila. Sch. Dist.; counseling psychologist B'nai B'rith Career and Counseling Svcs., Phila., 1969-85; pvt. practice Phila., Narberth, Pa., 1986—; cons. Phila. Sch. Dist. Grant, 1989; workshop presenter various community and ednl. groups. Contbr. articles to local newspapers. Mem. AAUW (bd. dirs.), Am. Psychol. Assn., Am. Assn. Counseling and Devel., Pa. Counseling Assn., Counseling Assn. Greater Phila. (pres. 1988-89, Svc. award 1989).

BURSTEIN, SHARON ANN PALMA, corporate communications specialist; b. Schenectady, N.Y., July 18, 1952; d. Harold Edward and Lois Ida (Hesner) Rieck; m. Joseph Carmen Palma, May 17, 1975 (div. Sept. 1982); m. Richard Lyle Burstein, Sept. 8, 1985; 1 child, Alexandra Blaire. BA, Nat. Coll. Edn., 1974; postgrad., Russell Sage Coll., 1974-78, Union Coll., 1980. Cert. tchr., N.Y. Elem. tchr. Saratoga Springs (N.Y.) Schs., 1974-80; ednl. cons. Whitcomb Assocs., Boston, 1980-81; ednl. mktg. specialist Monroe Systems for Bus., Newington, Conn., 1981-83; nat. mktg. mgr. Victor Techs., Hartford, Conn., 1983, Exclusives, Boston, 1984-85; dir. pub. rels. Lawrence Group, Albany, N.Y., 1985-87, dir. corp. communications, 1987-88; v.p. Lawrence Group, Albany, 1988-89; v.p investors rels. Lawrence Group, N.Y.C., 1987-89; pres. S.A. Burstein & Assocs., Albany, 1989—; cons. N.Y. Assn. Bus. Ofcls., 1982-83. Editor: Helpline newspaper, 1985, 87; co-producer: Playing It Safe, 1986 (Nori award 1987), To Be As Independent As You Can Be (Nori award 1989), Cookbook Capital Connoisseur (Nori award 1989); acted in TV comml., 1981 (Addy award 1982). Bd. dirs. Multiple Sclerosis Soc., Albany, 1986—, Mohawk Pathways Girl Scouts U.S.; active in N.Y. Spl. Olympics, 1987, Capital Women's Charity Found., Albany, 1987—. Mem. NAFE, Nat. Investor Relations Inst., Am. Mgmt. Assn., Assn. Profl. Communicators, Nat. Assn. Investment Clubs, Albany C. of C. (mem. women's bus. coun.), Kappa Delta Pi. Democrat. Clubs: Steuben, Womens Press. Home: 46 Greenway S Albany NY 12208

BURSTYN, ELLEN (EDNA RAE GILLOOLY), actress; b. Detroit, Dec. 7, 1932; m. Paul Roberts; m. Neil Burstyn; 1 child, Jefferson. LHD (hon.), Dowling Coll.; DFA (hon.), Sch. Visual Arts. Artistic dir. The Actor's Studio, N.Y.C., 1982-88. Appeared regularly on Jackie Gleason TV show, 1956-57; made Broadway debut in Fair Game, 1957-58; other play appearances include summer stock John Loves Mary, 1960, Broadway prodns. of Same Time, Next Year, 1975 (Tony award as best actress, Drama Desk award, Outer Circle Critics award), 84 Charing Cross Road, 1982, (off-Broadway) Park Your Car in Harvard Yard with Burgess Meredith, Driving Miss Daisy, Chgo., 1988, Broadway prodn. Shirley Valentine, 1989 and Chgo., 1990; film appearances include Goodbye Charlie (under name Ellen McRae), 1964, For Those Who Think Young, 1965, Tropic of Cancer, 1969, Alex in Wonderland, 1971 (named Best Supporting Actress N.Y. Film Critics, Nat. Soc. Film Critics, Acad. Award nominee for Best Supporting Actress), The Last Picture Show, 1971 (Acad. award nominee Best Actress), The King of Marvin Gardens, 1972, The Exorcist, 1973 (Acad. Award nominee for Best Actress), Harry and Tonto, Alice Doesn't Live Here Anymore, 1974 (Acad. Award as Best Actress, Golden Globe award, Brit. Acad. award), Providence, 1977, Dream of Passion, 1978, Resurrection, 1980, Silence of the North, 1980, Twice in a Lifetime, 1986, Hannah's War, 1987; TV movies include Thursday's Game, 1974, The People vs. Jean Harris, 1981 (Emmy nomination), Act of Vengeance, Into Thin Air, Surviving, Something in Common, 1986, Pack of Lies, 1987 (Emmy nomination); dir. off-Broadway play Judgement, 1981, Into Thin Air, 1985; star TV series The Ellen Burstyn Show, 1986; narrator segment TV show Dear America: Letters Home from Vietnam, 1988; appearance documentary film Balls of Grace; original photography work featured in Darkroom Photography mag., June, 1989. Mem. individual artists grants and policy overview panels Nat. Endowment for the Arts, Theater Adv. Council City of New York. Mem. Actors Equity Assn. (pres. 1982-85). Office: PO Box 217 Palisades NY 10964*

BURSZTAJN, SHERRY, neurobiologist, educator; b. Lodz, Poland, Feb. 19, 1946; came to U.S., 1959; d. Abraham and Miriam (Bricks) B.; m. Stephen A. Berman, July 29, 1984. BS, Fairleigh Dickinson U., 1969; PhD, Syracuse U., 1974. Postdoctoral fellow Cornell Med. Sch., N.Y.C., 1974-76, Yale Sch. of Medicine, New Haven, Conn., 1976-77; resident assoc. Harvard Med. Sch., Boston, 1977-80; asst. prof. Baylor Coll. Medicine, Houston, 1980-90; assoc. biochemist Harvard Med. Sch./McLean Hosp., Belmont, Mass., 1990—; grant reviewer Nat. Multiple Sclerosis Found., N.Y.C., 1985-89. Contbr. articles to profl. jours. Recipient Med. Found. Fell, Harvard U., 1977-79, Muscular Dystrophy Fell, 1979-80, grants NIH, 1983—, rsch. career devel. award NIH, 1983-88; named Harvard U. Scholar, 1987-88.

Mem. AAAS, Soc. Neuroscience, Am. Soc. for Cell Biology, Marine Biol. Lab (corp. mem.). Office: Harvard Med Sch Mailman Rsch Ctr 115 Mill St Belmont MA 02178

BURT, BARBARA SWETT, founder and general manager; b. Hinsdale, Ill., Oct. 21, 1955; d. Philip E. and Ann (Parkhurst) Swett; m. Richard F. Burt, Aug. 21, 1977; children: Jenna Joscelyn, Anita Mills. Student, Middlebury Coll., 1973-75; BA, Boston U., 1978. Editorial asst. Winthrop Pubs., Cambridge, Mass., 1977-78; coll. traveler McGraw-Hill Book Pubs., N.Y.C., 1978-80; editor Mass. Council for Children, Concord, Mass., 1981-84; founder, gen. mgr. Telltales Fine Children's Books, Bath, Maine; bd. dirs. Maine Writers & Pubs. Alliance, Brunswich, Maine, 1988--. Mem. Am. Booksellers Assn., Am. Booksellers for Children, Direct Mktg. Assn., Catalog Council of Direct Mktg. Assn. Office: Telltales PO Box 614 Bath ME 04530

BURT, LINDA K., hospital controller; b. Hastings, Nebr., Oct. 7, 1951; d. Keith Remy and Marjorie Lucille (Lovegrove) B. BBA, U. Nebr., 1973; MS Acctg., Bentley Coll., 1979. CPA. Dir. cost anaylsis St. Elizabeth Community Health Ctr., Lincoln, Nebr., 1974-78; audit mgr. Arthur Andersen & Co., Chgo., Omaha, 1979-86; from v.p./corp. dir. internal audit to v.p. fin. Ancilla Systems, Inc., Elk Grove, Ill., 1986-89; v.p. fin. Luth. Gen. Hosp., Pk. Ridge, Ill., 1989-90; contr. N.W. Meml. Corp., Chgo., 1990—; bd. dirs. Private Home Car, Chgo., Geneva (Nebr.) Implement Co., Ancila Ins. Trust, Elk Grove Village, Ill., Evanston (Ill.) Northshore Home Health, Inc. Mem. AICPA, Ill. Soc. CPA, Healthcare Fin. Mgmt. Assn. Republican. Methodist. Home: 1660 N Hudson Ave Unit 2J Chicago IL 60614

BURTIN, MARGARET IRENE, architectural designer, business owner; b. Colne, Lancashire, England, June 26, 1939; d. George Miller and Irene (Wilson) Bassnett; m. James Darrel Burtin, May 18, 1963; children: Jennifer M., Jill R., J. Matthew. BA, Lindenwood Coll., 1961. Ind. archtl. designer Lebanon, Mo., 1972-81; v.p. Niangua Industries Corp., Conway, Mo., 1982-88; co-owner McCalmont-Burtin, Cin., 1990—. Mem. Lebanon Planning and Zoning Commn., 1980-81; mem. Lebanon City Coun., 1982-88; bd. dirs. Charles and Ethel Hughes Found., Lebanon, 1983-90. Mem. AAUW. Methodist. Home: 4157 Fox Run Trail Unit 2 Cincinnati OH 45255

BURTON, ALICE JEAN, biology educator; b. Beijing, May 19, 1934; (parents Am. citizens); d. Myron Simmons and Esther Annette (Smith) B. BS, U. Mich., 1957; PhD, U. Ill., 1961. Postdoctoral fellow Calif. Inst. Tech., Pasadena, 1961-64; asst. biochemist, assoc. biochemist, biochemist Brookhaven Nat. Lab., Upton, N.Y., 1964-70; assoc. prof. biology St. Olaf Coll., Northfield, Minn., 1970-87, prof., 1987—. Contbr. articles to profl. jours. Grantee Rsch. Corp., 1972, 85, NSF, 1986, Howard Hughes Med. Inst., 1988. Mem. AAAS, Biophys. Soc. (coun. 1972-75), Am. Microbiol. Soc., Sigma Xi. Office: St Olaf Coll Biology Dept Northfield MN 55057

BURTON, ANNA MARJORIE, nurse; b. Pontiac, Mich., May 1, 1931; d. Harold Vale and Sophia (Eaton) Kelly; widowed; children: Julie A. Burton Stone, William A., Rory R., Kenneth G. Student Mich. State U., 1949-51; A.A., Fla. Keys Community Coll., 1976, A.S. in Nursing, 1983; R.N., Fla., Calif., N.Y. Orthodontic technician Birmingham, Mich., 1960-67; claims rep. Social Security Adminstrn., Lexington, Ky., 1967-71, Key West, Fla., 1972-79; pvt. duty nurse specializing in internat. handicap travel, 1979—. Recipient Appreciation award Vets. Council, 1974; hon. Conch and Key, City of Key West, 1974. Mem. U.S. Coast Guard Aux. (permanent) (comdr. 1976), U.S. Power Squadron, Key West Power Squadron (sec. 1984-85), Am. Nurses Assn., Fla. Nurses Assn., Dist. 25 Nurses Assn., Bus. and Profl. Women (treas. 1988—), Handicapped Boaters Assn., Boat Owners Assn. of U.S., U.S. Yacht Racing Union, Key West Art and Hist. Soc., Am. Cancer Soc., Am. Diabetes Assn., Juvenile Diabetes Assn., Am. Heart Assn. Travelers Century Club, Key West Yacht Club (hon.). Home: 1420 Von Phister St Key West FL 33040

BURTON, BARBARA ANNE, plumbing and heating company executive; b. Flushing, N.Y., Nov. 28, 1948; d. Victor Arthur and Anne (Inglima) Schettini; m. Maurice John Burton, Mar. 10, 1973; children: Anthony John, Christopher Maurice. Acad. diploma, Flushing High Sch., 1966. Loan payers. Household Fin. Corp., N.Y.C., 1966-67; sec. P.F. Collier Inc., London, 1968-69, exec. sec., 1969-70; sec. Bill Lutz Assocs., N.Y.C., 1970-72; exec. sec. merchandising Courtaulds N.Am., N.Y.C., 1972-75; sec.-treas. M. Burton Plumbing & Heating Corp., N.Y.C., 1975—. Republican. Roman Catholic. Home: 53-42 211 St Bayside NY 11364 Office: M Burton Plumbing & Heating 206-0148th Ave Flushing NY 11364

BURTON, BARBARA RICHARDS, company executive; b. Stamford, Tex., Oct. 19, 1933; d. Okey Frank and Myrtle Dorothy (Olson) Richards; m. Donald Gene Burton, Nov. 20, 1954; children: David Richards, E. Suzanne, Paul Wayne. RN, Hardin-Simmons U., Abilene, Tex., 1954; BS, E. Tex. State U., Commerce, 1976. Operating rm. nurse Hendrick Meml. Hosp., Abilene, 1954-56, Harris Hosp., Ft. Worth, 1957-60; operating rm. head nurse Harris Hosp., 1960-61; office mgr. Ramsey County Hist. Soc., St. Paul, 1964-68; sch. nurse Garland Ind. Sch. Dist., Garland, Tex., 1972-84; v.p. adminstrn. Alexander & Alexander of Tex., Inc., Dallas, 1984—. Recipient Behrens award, Hendrick Meml. Hosp., 1954. Mem. AAUW (v.p. 1976-77), Dallas Area Sch. Nurses Assn. (pres. 1971-72), Talespinners Story League (pres. 1982). Republican. Baptist. Office: Alexander & Alexander 2711 N Haskell Ste 800 LB8 Dallas TX 75204

BURTON, KAREN POLINER, physiology professor; b. Albug, N. Mex., Feb. 18, 1952; d. Saul and Mary (With) Poliner; m. Michael David Burton, June 19, 1978; children: Christopher David, Kevin Michael. BS, So. Meth. U., 1974; PhD, U. Tex., 1978. Instr. U. Tex. Health Sci. Ctr., Dallas, 1979-81; asst. prof. U. So. Ala. Coll. Medicine, Mobile, 1981-82; from asst. prof. to assoc. prof. U. Tex. SW Med. Ctr., Dallas, 1983—. Contbr. articles to profl. jours., book chpts. in field. Recipient New Investigator Rsch. award NIH, 1982-85, rsch. grant Am. Heart Assn., 1982-83, 1983-86, NIH, 1986-91. Mem. AAAS, Internat. Soc. Heart Rsch., Am. Physiological Soc., Am. Heart Assn., Electron Microscopy Soc. Am., The Oxygen Soc., Sigma Xi (sec.-treas. 1986-87). Roman Catholic. Office: U Tex SW Med Ctr 5323 Harry Hines Blvd Dallas TX 75235

BURTON, KATHRYN CURRAN, advertising public relations and publishing executive; b. N.Y.C., Oct. 7, 1941; d. George A. and Dorothy A. (Stillwell) McKeon; B.A., N.Y.U., 1961; postgrad. Russian Inst., Fordham U.; m. James L. Burton, Dec. 17, 1986. Account exec., pub. relations B.B.D.O., 1969-71; v.p. pub. relations Wisser & Sanchez, Inc., N.Y.C., 1971-75; v.p. BritAm Promotions, N.Y.C., 1975-78; exec. v.p. Inter Americas Advt., N.Y.C., 1978—; pres. Curran Assocs Advt./Pub. Relations, N.Y.C., 1970; pub. Southwestern Woman mag., 1988—; cons. in field. Bd. trustees Okla. Mus. of Arts, Okla. City Art Mus. Mem. Am. Women in Radio and TV, N.Y. Women in Communications, Am. Platform Assn., Okla. Zoologic Soc. (bd. trustees), Colonial Dames XVII Century, Publicity Club. Republican. Home: 8514 Waverly Ave Oklahoma City OK 73120

BURTON, MARGARET ANN, educational professional, consultant; b. Washington, Pa., Mar. 23, 1926; d. Lawrence George and Blanche Lulu (Van Kirk) Gideon; m. Foster Job, Margaret Jean, Elizabeth Lee. BFA, Ariz. State U., 1972, MFA, 1980, postgrad., 1981-86. Founding dir. hist. mus. Tempe (Ariz.) Hist. Soc., 1972-78; dir. children summer program Phoenix Zoo, 1979-80; art. dir., tchr. ceremics Scottsdale (Ariz.) Parks and Recreation Dept., 1981; dir. Stevens House Heritage Sq. Project Ariz. State U., Tempe, 1981-87, asst. to exec. dir., 1987-89; archivist exhibits coord. Ariz. State U. Grady Gammage Auditorium, 1989—; cons. Guadalupe (Ariz.) Hist. Soc., 1977-79, Winslow (Ariz.) Hist. Soc., 1986-87, pilot program Arts for the Spl. Edn. Children, Tempe, 1979-80; mem. steering com. Heritage Sq. Matsuri Festival, Phoenix, 1985-88. Coordinator documentary Sta. KAET-TV, 1978; dir. video documentary Southwest Heritage, 1988. Chairperson heritage com. Tempe Bi-Centennial Commn., Tempe, 1976; vol. Sta. KAET, Tempe, 1974—; vol., del. Mike Dukakis for Pres., Tempe, 1988; mem. Citizens Bond Com., Tempe, 1976; apptd. cadre program Ariz. Dept. Edn., Phoenix, 1974. Recipient Al Merito award Ariz. Hist. Soc., 1974, merit award Ariz. State U., 1986; named Citizen of Yr. Meyer Elem. Sch., 1976, All-Am. Woman City of Tempe, 1985. Mem. Cen. Ariz. Mus. Assn. (founder, v.p. 1978-79), Adult Continuing Edn. Assn. (charter, pres. 1983-84), Women Interest Now (charter), Faculty Women, Women in Higher Edn. (adv. council). Democrat. Presbyterian. Office: Ariz State U Pub Events Gammage 105 Tempe AZ 85287-0105

BURTON, SHIRLEY THRASHER, state agency administrator; b. Rosebud, Tex., Apr. 12, 1935; d. Frank Burkett and Nettie (Bailey) Thrasher; m. Thomas D. Ford, Sept. 2, 1955 (div. June 26, 1982); children: Thomas C. and Jennifer R.; m. David L., July 8, 1984. BA Summa cum laude, Southwest Tex. State U., San Marcos, 1975; postgrad, Southwest State U., San Marcos, 1989. Coord. human rels. Lockhart Intermediate Sch., 1975-76; bus. mgr. Sch. of Am. Rsch., Santa Fe, New Mexico, 1976-78; real estate broker Chaparral Realty, Inc., Santa Fe, 1978-82; adminstra. asst. Tex. Savs. & Loan Dept., Austin, Tex. Bd. dirs. League of Women Voters, Austin, 1984, Family Outreach, Austin, 1986. Democrat. Presbyterian. Home: 8813 Honeysuckle Trail Austin TX 78759

BURWELL, JULIE ANN, personnel executive; b. Hartford, Conn., Nov. 2, 1957; d. Matthew David and Judith B. (Burwell) Mermelstein. BBA, U. Ky., 1979, MBA, 1986—. Employee St. Joseph Hosp., Lexington, Ky., 1980-86; dir. personnel Good Samaritan Hosp., Lexington, 1986-88; dir. human resources Good Samaritan Hosp., 1988—. Vol. March of Dimes, Lexington, 1989, Lexington Tourism Cabinet, 1987—; co. rep. United Way, Lexington, 1988-89. Mem. Ky. Soc. Hosp. Personnel Adminstrn., Am. Soc. Healthcare Human Resources Adminstrn., Ky. Safety & Health Network. Office: Good Samaritan Hosp 310 S Limestone St Lexington KY 40508

BUSBY, SHANNON NIXON, educator; b. Gainesville, Tex., Nov. 30, 1955; d. James H. and Helen M. (Ross) Nixon; m. Larry W. Busby, Apr. 3, 1982; 1 child, James Ross. BS in Home Econs. Edn., Tex. Tech U., 1977; MEd, Sul Ross State U., Alpine, Tex., 1982. Cert. profl. ednl. diagnostian, tchr. of lang. and/or learning disabilities, tchr. of vocat. homemaking. Home econ. tchr. Pecos (Tex.)-Barstow-Toyah Ind. Sch. Dist., 1978-83, ednl. diagnostian spl. edn. dept., 1983—; interior design cons. L.W. Busby and Co., Pecos, 1989—; bd. dirs. Dept. Mental Health and Mental Retardation, Pecos, 1980-83. Chairperson Tex. War on Drugs, Pecos, 1980-83. Mem. AAUW (local pres. 1982-86, local v.p. 1978-81, Tex. state bd. dirs. 1982-83), Tex. Ednl. Diagnosticians Assn., Tex. Soc. for Autistic Citizens. Home: 1519 Mary St Pecos TX 79772

BUSBY, STACY DORTCH, sales executive; b. Charlotte, N.C., Nov. 23, 1964; d. Robert Cleveland and Charlotte (Book) Dortch; m. Eric Oneal Busby, Dec. 2, 1989. BA in Polit. Sci., N.C. State U., 1987. Mfrs. rep. Bob Dortch Enterprises, Cary, N.C., 1987—. Vol. Young Dems., Charlotte, 1988—. Mem. Chi Omega Alumni Assn., Wolfpack Club, N.C. State Young Alumni (pres.). Presbyterian. Home and Office: 5407 Two Moons Dr Charlotte NC 28212

BUSCH, JOYCE IDA, small business owner; b. Madera, Calif., Jan. 24, 1934; d. Bruno Harry and Ella Fae (Absher) Toschi; m. Fred O. Busch, Dec. 14, 1956; children: Karen, Kathryn, Kurt. Student, Calif. State U., Fresno, 1982—. Stewardess United Air Lines, San Francisco, 1955-57; prin. Art Coordinates, Fresno, 1982—, Busch Interior Design, Fresno, 1982—; art cons. Fresno Community Hosp., 1981-83; docent Fresno Met. Mus., 1981-84. Treas. Valley Children's Hosp. Guidance Clinic, 1975-79, Lone Star PTA, 1965-84,; mem. Mothers Guild Jan Joaquin Mem. Hosp., 1984-88. Mem. Am. Soc. Interior Designers (student), Illuminating Engring. Soc. N.Am. Republican. Roman Catholic. Club: Sunnyside Garden (pres. 1987-88).

BUSCH, KAREN LOUISE, marketing company executive; b. Madera, Calif., July 28, 1958; d. Fred O. and Joyce (Toschi) B. BA, Calif. State U., Fresno, 1981; postgrad., U. Calif., San Diego. Product mgr. Home Fed. Savs. & Loan, San Diego; v.p. TNT Mktg., San Diego. Mem. Am. Mktg. Assn., Jr. Achievement of San Diego. Home: 10669 SD Mission Rd#107 San Diego CA 92108

BUSCH, RITA MARIE, educational administrator; b. Rock Rapids, Iowa, Oct. 4, 1956; d. Ronald Henry and Evelyn Marie (Brandt) B. BA, Westmar Coll., 1978; MA, U. S.D., 1982, EdS, 1987. Cert. elem. tchr., Iowa. Tchr. Everett Elem. Sch., Sioux City, Iowa, 1978-88, prin., 1988—; also prin. Roosevelt Elem. Sch., Sioux City. Named Bus. Assoc. of the Yr., Am. Bus. Women's Assn., 1989. Mem. NEA, LWV, AAUW, Phi Delta Kappa. Democrat. Methodist. Home: 1331 S Maple C-26 Sioux City IA 51106 also: Roosevelt Elem Sch 2015 W 6th Sioux City IA 51103

BUSCHER, JUDITH GAY, psychotherapist; b. Omaha; m. Robert B. Buscher; children: Robert B. Jr., Elizabeth, Julie Ann. BGS, U. Nebr., 1975, MSW, 1976. Lic. social worker, alcohol and drug counselor, Nebr. Program coord. Immanuel Med. Ctr., Omaha; psychotherapist Rizzo and Assocs., Omaha. Mem. Acad. Nat. Social Workers. Home: Rt 4 Box 23 Elkhorn NE 68022

BUSCHER, NANCY, freelance writer; b. Middletown, Ohio, Oct. 12, 1941; d. Michael E. and Dorothy I. (Bennett) Tancey; m. H. Kenneth Buscher, Apr. 28, 1962 (dec. 1978); children: Lisa, Angi, Kevin, Valerie; m. John M. Williams, Sept. 8, 1990. Student, Ind. U. Owner, pres. Superior Gage Co. Inc., Kokomo, 1978-85, Tanci Ladies Apparel, 1980-83; host TV talk show Kokomo, Ind.; freelance writer, poet, playwright Charleston, S.C.; assoc. staff mem. Byline mag. Author: (plays) The Big Parade, The Birthday Caper, The Christmas Cat-Astrophe (2d pl. in nat. contest); contbr. numerous articles to profl. jours. Mem. NAFE, Nat. League Am. Pen Women (sec. Charleston chpt. 1990—), Soc. Children's Book Writers, Poetry Soc. S.C. (chmn.), Quills and Nibs (founder), N.C. Writer's Network, N.Y. Dramatists Guild. Home and Office: 1106 Seccessionville Rd Charleston SC 29412

BUSCHMANN, MARYBETH TANK, educator; b. Evanston, Ill., Oct. 10, 1942; d. Marvin H. and Elizabeth Jane (Lind) Tank; m. Robert J. Buschmann, Sept. 5, 1970. Grad. with honor, Augustana Hosp. Sch. Nursing, 1964; BSN, Augustana Coll., Rock Island, Ill., 1965; MS in Biology, U. Ill., Champaign-Urbana, 1968; PhD in Anatomy, U. Ill., Chgo., 1975. RN, Ill. Staff nurse McKinley U. Hosp., Urbana, 1966-67, Mercy Hosp., Urbana, 1967-68; rsch. dir. U. Wis., Madison, 1969-70; USPHS predoctorate trainee nurse-scientist program U. Ill. at Med. Ctr., Chgo., 1970-75, asst. prof., 1975-79; assoc. prof. U. Ill., Chgo., 1979-84, prof., 1984—. Contbr. articles to profl. jours. Judge Luth. Sci. Congress, River Forest, Ill., 1987-90. Fellow NIH, 1975; scholar Am. Nurses Found., 1979. Mem. AAAS, Am. Assn. Anatomists, Am. Soc. on Aging, Soc. for Neurosci., Gerontol. Soc. Am., Nat. Gerontol. Nursing Assn., Midwest Nursing Rsch. Soc., Midwest Soc. Electron Microscopists (exec. com. 1980-85, pres. 1982-83, bd. dirs. 1980-81, awad for leadership 1983, Founder's award 1988), N.Y. Acad. Scis., Sigma Xi, Sigma Theta Tau. Republican. Lutheran. Office: U Ill 845 S Damen Ave Chicago IL 60612

BUSE, SHARON ELAINE, clinical laboratory administrator; b. Piqua, Ohio, Mar. 2, 1951; d. Harold William and Pauline Evelyn (Brokaw) Hess; m. Douglas Keith Buse, May 9, 1949; children: David Preston, Benjamin Wesley, Timothy Robert, Elizabeth Elaine. BS in Med. Technology, Miami U., 1973; MBA, Wright State U., Dayton. Staff technologist Mt. Carmel Med. Ctr., Columbus, Ohio, 1973-75; microbiologist V.A. Med. Ctr., Dayton, Ohio, 1975-78; lab. mgr. Stouder Hosp. Upper Valley Med. Ctr., Troy, Ohio, 1978—; mem. adv. bd. Montgomery Co. Joint Vocat. Sch., Dayton, Ohio, 1984—, Sch. Med. Tech., Kettering Med. Ctr., 1985-88. Author: Laboratory Quality Assurance, 1985. Pres. La Sertoma, bd. dirs. Miami County ARC; coach Odyssey of the Mind, Casstown, Ohio, 1988, 1989. Mem. American Soc. Clin. Pathologists, Clin. Lab. Mgmt. Assn. United Methodist. Office: Upper Valley Med Ctr 920 Summit Ave Troy OH 45373

BUSEY, DIANE FAYE, art gallery director; b. Stockton, Calif., Oct. 30, 1954; d. Norman and Alice (Lee) Hong; 1 child, Daniel K. AA, San Joaquin Delta U., 1974; BA, San Francisco State U., 1976. Clerk typist II Dept Motor Vehicles, Stockton, 1972-78; sales cons. Princess House Crystal, Stockton, 1977-78; sales, book-keeper Kailua Bay (Hawaii) Goldsmith, 1978-80, Village Goldsmith, Kailua Kona, Hawaii, 1980-83; dir., cons. Connoisseur's Gallery, Kaiwaihae, Hawaii, 1983-86; interior designer D. Busey Designs, Scottsdale, Ariz., 1984-87; art dir. Magadini Galleries, Scottsdale, Ariz., 1987—. Mem. Ariz. Action Network, NAFE. Democrat. Office: Magadini Galleries 4160 N Craftsman Ct Scottsdale AZ 85251

BUSH, ANN KATHLEEN, marketing executive; b. Wausau, Wis., Dec. 19, 1960; d. Frank Jerome and Mary Joan (Chapiewsky) Tucek; m. Cary Joseph Bush, Feb. 19, 1958. BS, U. Minn., 1985, MBA, 1988. Asst. mgr. The Art Store, Northfield, Minn., 1983-84; mktg. rsch., graphics tech. Custom Rsch., Inc., Mpls., 1984-85; sr. project coord. Arthur Shuster, Inc., St. Paul, 1985-87; teaching asst. mktg. dept. U. Minn., Mpls., 1987-88; mgr. mktg. Swiss Colony Stores, Inc., Monroe, Wis., 1988—. Vol. Bloomington Art Ctr., 1986-88. Mem. AMA, Beta Gamma Sigma, Phi Kappa Phi. Lutheran. Office: Swiss Colony Stores Inc One Alpine Ln Monroe WI 53566

BUSH, BARBARA PIERCE, wife of President of the United States; b. Rye, N.Y., June 8, 1925; d. Marvin and Pauline (Robinson) Pierce; m. George Herbert Walker Bush, Jan. 6, 1945; children: George Walker, John Ellis, Neil Mallon, Marvin Pierce, Dorothy Walker. Student, Smith Coll., 1943-44; hon. degrees, Stritch Coll., Milw., 1981, Mt. Vernon Coll., Washington, 1981, Hood Coll., Frederick, Md., 1983, Howard U., Washington, 1987, Judson Coll., Marion, Ala., 1988, Bennett Coll., Greensboro, N.C., 1989, Smith Coll., 1989, Morehouse Sch. Medicine, 1989. Hon. chair adv. bd. Reading is Fundamental; hon. mem. Bus. Coun. for Effective Literacy; mem. adv. coun. Soc. of Meml. Sloan-Kettering Cancer Ctr.; hon. mem. bd. dirs. Children's Oncology Svcs. of Met. Washington, The Washington Home, The Kingsbury Ctr.; hon. chmn. nat. adv. coun. Literacy Vols. of Am., Nat. Sch. Vols. Program; sponsor Laubach Literacy Internat.; nat. hon. chmn. Leukemia Soc. of Am.; hon. mem. bd. trustees Morehouse Sch. of Medicine; hon. nat. chmn. Nat. Organ Donor Awareness Week, 1982-86; pres. Ladies of the Senate, 1981-88; mem. women's com. Smithsonian Assocs., Tex. Fedn. of Rep. Women, life mem., hon. mem.; hon. chairperson for the Nat. Com. on Literacy and Edn. United Way, Barbara Bush Found. for Family Literacy, Washington Parent Group Fund, Girls Clubs of Am., 10th anniversay Harvest Nat. Food Bank Network; hon. chmn. Nat. Com. for the Prevention of Child Abuse and Childhelp U.S.A.; hon. pres. Girl Scouts U.S; hon. chair Nat. Com. for Adoption. Recipient Nat. Outstanding Mother of Yr. award, 1984, Woman of Yr. award USO, 1986, Disting. Leadership award United Negro Coll. Fund 1986, Disting. Am. Woman award Coll. Mt. St. Joseph, 1987. Mem. Tex. Fedn. Rep. Women (life), Internat. II Club (Washington), Magic Circle Rep. Women's Club (Houston). Episcopalian. Address: White House 1600 Pennsylvania Ave Washington DC 20501

BUSH, BETTY JEAN, education educator; b. Barnard, Mo., Dec. 28, 1938; d. William Wyatt and Lucile E. (Agee) Johnson; m. Robert E. Bush, June 3, 1960; children: Gregory Robert, Jeffrey Brian, Traci Ann. BS in Edn., Northwest Mo. State U., 1960, MS, 1970; PhD, U. Mo., Kansas City, 1985. Tchr. St. Joseph (Mo.) Pub. Schs., 1961, Hillsdale (Okla.) Pub. Schs., Columbia (Mo.) Pub. Schs.; reading dir. Stephens Coll., Columbia; coordinator elem. edn. Northwest Mo. State U., Maryville, 1989--; dir. freshman program Northwest Mo. State U., 1989--; pub. sch. cons. Area Pub. Schs., Mo., Ks., Ia., Nebr., 1989--. Author, editor A Freshman Year Handbook, 1987. Contbr. articles to profl. jour. Pres. United Way Nodaway CO., 1980, v.p. Wesley Found., 1982, youth coordinator American Red Cross, Project Plus Adult Literacy, St. Francis Hosp. Found., Maryville, Mo., 1989--. Mem. AAUW, Internat. Reading Assn., Nat. Tchrs. of English, Mo. Tchrs. of Reading, Phi Delta Kappa, P.E.O. Democrat. Methodist. Office: NW Mo State U Brown Hall 221 Maryville MO 64468

BUSH, JUDY LYNN, administrator of church volunteers; b. Madison, Wis., Aug. 6, 1938; d. Marvin Leonard and Alberta Ruth Martha (Wagner) Anderson; m. James Paul Rasmussen (div.); children: Linda Bradley, Nancy Carlisle, Dan Rasmussen; m. George L. Bush. BS, U. Wis., 1960, MS, 1979; Cert. vol. mgmt. program, U. Colo., 1987. Tchr. Neenah Pub. Schs., Neenah, Wis., 1960-61; tchr. Menasha Pub. Schs., Menasha, Wis., 1961; med. sec. U. Wis. Hosp., Madison, 1974-77, 79-81; adminstrv. sec. Luth. Campus Ministry, Madison, 1981-83; coord. vol. ministries Luther Meml. Ch., Madison, 1984—. Founding mem. Capitol City Opera Co., Madison, 1983; adv. to bd. Madison Opera Guild, 1987-88; bd. dirs., edn. chair Friends of Univ. Hosp., Madison, 1987-88; pres. Madison-Freiburg Sister City Com., Madison, 1988-89, v.p., 1989—). Mem. Vol. Adminstrs. Dane County (bd. dirs., chair edn. com. 1988-89). Lutheran. Home: 3420 Valley Creek Circle Middleton WI 53562

BUSH, JUNE LEE, real estate executive; b. Philippi, W.Va., Sept. 20, 1942; d. Leland C. and Dolly Mary (Costello) Robinson; m. Jerry Lee Coffman, June 15, 1963 (div. 1970); 1 child, Jason Lance; m. Richard Alfred Bush, May 20, 1972. Grad., Fairmont State Coll., 1962, Dale Carnegie, Anaheim, Calif., 1988. Exec. sec. McDonnell Douglas, Huntington Beach, Calif., 1965-72; adminstrv. asst. Mgmt. Resources, Inc., Fullerton, Calif., 1978-80; bldg. mgr. Alfred Gobar Assocs., Brea, Calif., 1980—; treas. Craig Park E., Fullerton, 1982, bd. dirs. 1982—. Author instrn. manual Quality Assurance Secretarial Manual, 1971. Sec. PTA, La Palma, 1974. Mem. Gamma Chi Chi. Home: 2517 Biscayne Pl Fullerton CA 92633 Office: Alfred Gobar Assocs Inc 201 S Brea Blvd Brea CA 92633

BUSH, LORI HERMELIN, marketing executive; b. Cleve., June 9, 1956; d. Meyer and Barbara Rose (Rapport) H.; m. Steven Val Bush, Feb. 14, 1987; 1 child, Zachary. BA in Allied Medicine, Ohio State U., 1978; MBA in Mktg., Temple U., 1985. Med. technologist Ball Meml. Hosp., Muncie, Ind., 1978-80; rsch. assoc. Bio/Data Corp., Hatboro, Pa., 1980-82, group mgr., 1982-86; dir. mktg. Minnetonka (Minn.) Med., 1986-88; v.p. mktg. Tsumura Med. div. Tsumura Internat., Inc., 1988—. Contbr. articles to profl. jours. Mem. Am. Soc. Clin. Pathologists (faculty). Jewish. Office: Minnetonka Med Inc PO Box 1A Minnetonka MN 55343

BUSH, MARJORIE ANN, broadcasting executive; b. Cleve., Sept. 13, 1925; d. Frank Victor and Helen (Stepnik) Dabkowski; m. John S. Bush, Nov. 13, 1948; children: Cynthia Bush Haynes, Victoria Bush Humpal. G-rad. high sch., Cleve. Sec. Cleve. Rec. Co., 1943-50; with Sta. WIXY (formerly Sta. WDOK), Cleve., 1950-76, pub. svc. dir., 1969-74, music dir., 1970-76; adminstrv. asst., placement dir. Ohio Sch. Broadcast Technique, Cleve., 1976—; music coord. Globetrotter Communications, Inc., 1975—; sec. Ednl. Broadcast Svcs., Inc., 1976—. Bd. dirs. Bill Gavin Conv. ans Awards Com., Bill Gavin Report in San Francisco, 1974. Recipient Kal Rudman's Froday Morning Quarterback in Phila., 1975, Bobby Poe's Music Survey in Washington, 1975. Roman Catholic. Home: 6774 Oakwood Dr Independence OH 44131 Office: Ohio Sch Broadcast Technique 5500 S Marginal Dr Cleveland OH 44103

BUSH, STEPHANIE REGINA, state legislator; b. East Orange, N.J., Mar. 16, 1952; d. Alonzo Charles and Dora (Weathersbee) B. B in Psychology and Polit. Sci., Cornell U., 1971; JD, Am. U., 1978. Bar: N.J. 1978, Pa. 1979. Pvt. practice law, East Orange, 1978—; mem. State of N.J. Assembly, East Orange, 1988—; mem. select com. on drug abuse, standing com. on housing State of N.J. Assembly, 1988—; vice-chmn. commn. on criminal disposition State of N.J., chair com. on alternatives to incarceration; atty. East Orange Bd. Adjustment and Planning; speaker NOW, N.J. Black Issues Conv., Nat. Polit. Congress Black Women, numerous schs. and colls. Recipient Black and Profl. Women's Achievement award Southeastern Chester County, 1980, Garnett's Achievement award City of East Orange, 1988. Mem. Nat. Bar Assn., Pa. Bar Assn., N.J. Bar Assn., Garden State Bar Assn, Essex County Bar Assn., Assn. Trial Lawyers Am., Assn. Black Women Lawyers of N.J. (past pres.). Home: 44 Glenwood Ave Ste 103 East Orange NJ 07017

BUSHEE, ELEANOR JANE, dental educator; b. Monticello, Ill., Feb. 3, 1922; d. Ralph Waldo and Bessie Elinor (Fitzwater) B.; m. Joseph D. Padula, July 10, 1948 (dec. 1955)); m. Vernon E. Thomas, June 1, 1958 (div. 1964). BS, U. Ill., 1944; DDS, Northwestern U., 1948; postgrad., So. Ill. U., 1968-69. Pvt. practice gen. dentistry Hartford, Conn., 1948-58, N.Y.C., 1958-63; asst. prof. So. Ill. U., Carbondale, 1963-66, assoc. prof., supr. dental hygiene, 1967-72, prof., chmn. div. allied health, 1972-75, assoc. dean, 1975-79; prof. Sch. Dental Medicine So. Ill. U., Alton, 1979-88, asst. dean Sch. Dental Medicine, 1980-88, prof. emerita, prof. part time, 1988—; cons.

commn. on accreditation, ADA, 1975-81; editorial cons., adviser dental publs. Contbr. chpt.: Current Concepts in Dental Hygiene, 1979, Comprehensive Review of Dental Hygiene, 1980; editor: Mosby's Comprehensive Review of Dental Hygiene, 1986, 2d edit., 1991. Bd. advisers, vol. Caravan Women's Oasis Ctr., Alton, 1987—. Fellow Am. Coll. Dentists, Acad. Dentistry Internat.; mem. ADA (mem. coun. dental practice 1988—), Ill. Dental Soc., Am. Assn. Dental Schs., Am. Assn. Women Dentists (pres. 1987), Fedn. Dentaire Internat., Zointa Club of Alton-Wood River (sec. 1988), Alton Community Women's Svc. League (chair prog. com. 1990—). Presbyterian. Home: 417 Prospect St Unit D Alton IL 62002 Office: So Ill U Sch Dental Medicine 2800 College Ave Alton IL 62002

BUSHNELL, CATHARINE, marketing consulting firm executive; b. Pullman, Wash, July 2, 1950; d. David and Catharine Howe (Goodfellow) B.; m. H. Michael Sisson, Oct. 31, 1975. BS in Speech, Northwestern U., 1972. Prodn. mgr. Mike White Advt., Chgo., 1972; stage actress, Chgo., 1972-73; ptnr., dir. photography Mome, Raths & Outgrabe, Chgo., 1973-75; exec. v.p. Sisson Assocs., N.Y.C., 1975—; pres. Illusion Gallery, Creative Resource Co., N.Y.C., 1981—, The Sisson Group Inc., 1986—; faculty New Sch.-Parsons Sch. of Design, 1985-86. Photographer motion picture stills for various films, N.Y.C., 1975—; author: Raggedy Ann and Andy in the Tunnel of Lost Toys, 1980; Raggedy Ann and Andy and the Pirates of Outgo Inlet, 1981; Linda's Magic Window, 1981; Frannie's Magic Kazoo, 1982. Judge ann. student photog. portfolio rev. High Sch. of Art and Design, N.Y.C., 1979-83. Mem. Licensing Industry Assn., Internat. Photographers Motion Picture Industry, Internat. Soc. Photography (charter), Actors Equity Assn., Northwestern U. Alumnae Assn., Delta Zeta. Office: The Sisson Group Inc 300 E 40th St New York NY 10016

BUSHNELL, MARGARET MARY, business owner; b. New Haven, Apr. 27, 1945; d. Francis and Helen (Sullivan) Macksey; m. George Bushnell, Apr. 11, 1969. Cert. real estate, Manchester (Conn.) Community, 1972. Lic. broker, Conn. Broker, co-owner Curtin and Bushnell Realty, Wethersfield, Conn.; owner, broker Century 21 Bushnell Realty, Wethersfield. Recipient Outstanding Svc. award. Mem. Greater Hartford Assn. of Realtors, Nat. Assn. Realtors. Home: 644 Silas Deane Hwy Wethersfield CT 06109

BUSSE, LU ANN, audiologist; b. Peru, Ind., Jan. 11, 1956; d. Louie M. and Isol Ann (Johnston) B.; 1 child, Brittany Isol Clifton. BA, U. Cen. Fla., 1975; MA, Northwestern U., 1977. Pediatric audiologist Lake-McHenry Regional Program, Gurnee, Ill., 1977-80; cons. pvt. clin. practice Arlington, Tex., 1979—; research assoc. Northwestern U., Evanston, Ill., 1980-84; regional audiologist Cochlear Corp., Arlington, 1985—; pres. Audiological Svcs., Inc., Arlington, 1982—; guest lectr. various univs. and profl. orgns., 1980—. Co-author: Adult Learning Disabilities, 1985, Cochlear Implants in Children, 1986; contbr. articles to profl. jours. Pres. Sunday sch. class First United Meth. Ch., Arlington, 1988-89. Univ. scholar Northwestern U., 1975-77; univ. fellow Northwestern U., 1980-81, 83-84. Mem. Am. Speech-Lang. Hearing Assn. (cert. clin. competency), Acoustical Soc. Am. (assoc.), Nat. Assn. for Female Execs., Sigma Xi (assoc.). Home and Office: 1805 Donna St Arlington TX 76013

BUSSELL, ANNETTE TROUP, accountant; b. Ocilla, Ga., Sept. 21, 1945; d. Hardy Thomas and Evelyn (Downing) Troup; m. Bily C. Bussell, June 20, 1965 (div. Aug., 1975); children: Michele, Carla. BBA, U. Fla., 1981, M in Acctg., 1984. CPA, Fla. Office mgr. Bus. Control Svc., Jacksonville, Fla., 1972-73, ptnr., 1973-80, owner, 1980-84; pvt. practice Jacksonville, 1984—. Mem. AICPA, Fla. Inst. of CPAs, Beta Gamma Sigma. Republican. Office: 767 Stockton St Jacksonville FL 32204

BUSSEY, HOLLY JEAN, infosystems executive; b. Takoma Park, Md., Dec. 9, 1954; d. Alfred Gordon and Dorothy Ann (McElvenny) B.; m. James B. Sanders. AA, Bucks County Community Coll., Newtown, Pa., 1975; AB magna cum laude, Wheaton Coll., Norton, Mass., 1978; M in Libr. and Info. Mgmt., Rutgers U., 1981. Info. documentalist N.W. Ayer ABH Internat., N.Y.C., 1978-80; info. specialist N.W. Ayer, Inc., N.Y.C., 1980-81, computer info. specialist, 1981-82, v.p., mgr. Info. Ctr., 1982—. Co-author: Guide to Design and Renovation of Libraries and Archives, 1989. Mem. Am. Mgmt. Assn., Am. Mktg. Assn., Spl. Librs. Assn., Assn. Info. Mgrs., Demographic Inst., Phi Beta Kappa. Unitarian. Office: N W Ayer Worldwide Pla 825 Eighth Ave New York NY 10019-7498

BUSTER, LISA B., export/import company executive, promotion company executive; b. Phila., June 26, 1959; d. Leonard David and Arlene Linda (Segal) B. Student Georgetown U., 1977-79; BA in Spanish, U. N.C., 1981. Asst. to sports dept. WDVM-TV, Washington, 1978-79; sports reporter WCHL Radio, Chapel Hill, N.C., 1980; sports reporter, anchor WDCG-WDNC Radio, Durham, N.C., 1980-81; anchor, reporter KTVG-TV, Helena, Mont., 1982-83; dir. celebrity promotions, Starpower, Feasterville, Pa., 1984; pres., owner Promotion in Motion Internat., Ltd., Jenkintown, Pa., 1984—, Dakota Internat. Corp., 1989—. Mem. The Athletics Congress, U. N.C. Alumni Assn. Avocations: horseback riding, travel, languages, music. Address: Promotion in Motion Internat Ltd PO Box 181 Jenkintown PA 19046

BUSTIN, BEVERLY MINER, state senator; b. Morrisville, Vt., Feb. 14, 1936; d. Donald Haze and Della Mae (Kenfield) Miner; children: Catherine Margaret, David Wayne. BS, Thomas Coll. Maine state senator, 1979—, chair joint select com. on alcoholism services, 1982-84, chair instl. services com., 1983-84, chair bus. and commerce commn., 1985-87. Mem. Kennebec County (Maine) Dem. Com., Hollowell (Maine) Dem. Com.; treas. Uplift, Inc., 1980-86; vice chair Kennebec County Regional Health Agy., 1984-88, chair audit program rev., 1987—, mem. banking and ins. com., 1987—, chair joint select com. on corrections, 1987—, chair Commn. on Overcrowding at AMHI-BMHI, 1987-89. Office: Maine State Senate Augusta ME 04330

BUSWELL, DEBRA SUE, small business owner, programmer/analyst; b. Salt Lake City, Apr. 8, 1957; d. John Edward Ross and Marilyn Sue (Patterson) Potter; m. Randy James Buswell, Aug. 17, 1985. BA, U. Colo., Denver, 1978. Programmer, analyst Trail Blazer Systems, Palo Alto, Calif., 1980-83; data processing mgr. Innovative Concepts, Inc., San Jose, Calif., 1983-86; owner Egret Software, Milpitas, Calif., 1986—. Mem. IEEE, No. Calif. Pick Users, Commonwealth Club of Calif. Home and Office: 883 Del Vaile Ct Milpitas CA 95035

BUSWELL, SUSAN ROWE, state legislator; b. Denver, Sept. 13, 1935; d. Kenneth Wyer and Leone (Krumling) Rowe; children—Janice, Scott. B.A., Carleton Coll., 1957; postgrad. U. Copenhagen, 1958. Analyst, Dept. Def., Washington, 1959-62; officer mgr. Green Street Coalition, Annapolis, Md., 1980-81; exec. dir. Md. Assn. Elem. Sch. Adminstrs., College Park, 1981-83; del. Md. Gen. Assembly, Annapolis, 1983—; exec. dir. Md. Assn. Nonpub. Spl. Edn. Facilities, 1985—. Mem. Howard County Bd. Edn. (Md.), 1973-83, Howard County Recreation and Parks Bd., 1975-79; bd. dirs. Howard County Commn. on Arts, 1975-80. Recipient Mortar Board award Carleton Coll., Northfield, Minn., 1957. Mem. LWV, Delta Kappa Gamma. Democrat. Mem. United Ch. of Christ. Club: Soroptimists. Office: Md Assn Bds Edn 133 Def Hwy ste 204 Annapolis MD 21401

BUTA, MARY OPRITZA, retired business education educator; b. Youngstown, Ohio, Jan. 2, 1913; d. Daniel Pamfilie and Marina (Neaga) Opritza; m. Serafin Simon Buta, Mar. 5, 1949 (dec. 1989); 1 child, Mary Jeanette Buta Lomuscio. BS in Edn., Miami U., Oxford, Ohio, 1935; MA in Edn., NYU, 1940; postgrad., Youngstown (Ohio) State U., 1932-33, 73, Westminster Coll., New Wilmington, Pa., 1962. Cert. apprentice pharmacist, Ohio State Bd. Tchr. Bryan High Sch., Yellow Springs, Ohio, 1935-37, Meml. High Sch., Campbell, Ohio, 1937-43, Bliss Coll., Columbus, Ohio, 1944, Struthers (Ohio) High Sch., 1946-49, 53-81; tchr., treas. North High Sch., Youngstown, Ohio, 1952-53; confidential sec. Am. Embassy U.S. State Dept., Bucharest, Romania, 1949-50; dept. chmn. Struthers High Sch., 1976-81. Sponsor Nat. Honor Soc., Struthers High Sch.; active Struthers Girl Scouts, 1962-65. Named One of Outstanding Secondary Educators by Outstanding Secondary Educators of Am., 1973. Mem. AAUW (editor Youngstown chpt. bull. 1968-70), NEA (life), Mahoning Ret. Tchrs. Assn. (sec. 1981-83), Salem Hist. Soc. (life), Ohio Ret. Tchrs. Assn. (life), Nat. Ret. Tchrs. Assn., Office Strategic Svcs. Vets. (life), Raymond Molyneaux Hughes Soc. (personal accomplishmensts recognition cert. Miami U.), FDR Pensioners Club, Carmen Sylva Aux., Frat. Bus. Edn. (hon.), Delta Kappa Gamma Internat. Soc. (Gamma Epsilon chpt. honoring women educators 1974), Delta Pi Epsilon. Mem. Holy Trinity Romanian Orthodox Ch.

BUTCHER, AMANDA KAY, university administrator; b. Lansing, Mich., Oct. 25, 1936; d. Foster Eli and Mayme Lenore (Taft) Stuart; m. Claude J. Butcher, Aug. 24, 1957; 1 child, Mary Beth. BS in Bus., Cen. Mich. U., 1981. Office asst. Dept. Dairy Sci., East Lansing, Mich., 1966-76; bus. mgr. dept. Dept. Pathology, Mich. State U., East Lansing, 1976—. Mem. Adminstrv. Profl. Suprs. Assn. (v.p. 1982), Adminstrv. Profl. Assn. East Lansing (pres. 1976-80). Democrat. Home: 610 Emily Lansing MI 48910 Office: Mich State U Dept Pathology 622 E Fee East Lansing MI 48824-1316

BUTCHER, SUSAN H., dog kennel owner, sled dog racer; b. Boston, Dec. 26, 1954; d. Charles and Agnes (Young) B.; m. David Lee Monson. Driver 1st dog team to summit Mt. KcKinley, Alaska, 1979; winner among top 10 finishers Long Distance Sled Dog Races, Alaska and Minn., 1978-87; 5th pl. Iditarod Race, Anchorage and Nome, Alaska, 1980, 81, 2d pl., 1982, 84, champion, winner 1st pl., 1986, 87, world record holder, 1986-87; champion, winner 1st pl. Coldfoot Classic Race, Brooks Range, Alaska, 1985; winner Iditarod, Alaska, 1988, Kusho 300, Bethel, Alaska, 1988, Portage 250, Alaska, 1988; bd. dirs. Iditarod Trail Com., Wasilla, Alaska, 1980-86, ambassador of good will Iditarod Sport of Sled Dog Racing, 1982—; mem. nutrition adv. panel Purina Pro Plan, St. Louis, 1986—; tech. advisor Allied Fibers, N.Y.C., 1985—. Contbr. articles to profl. jours. Hon. chmn. March of Dimes, Anchorage, 1986, Spl. Olympics, Anchorage, 1987. Named Musher of Yr. Team and Trail, N.H., 1987, one of Profl. Sports Women of Yr. Womens Sports Found., N.Y.C., 1987, Sports Woman of Yr., W.S.F, 1988, Sportswomen of Yr. U.S. Sports Acad.; recipient Victor award, Las Vegas, Nev., 1987, 88, legis. commendation States of Alaska and Mass., 1986-87, Moniqo Bedeaux prize French Sport Acad., 1989, Athletic Achievement award Tanguray, N.Y., 1989. Mem. Iditarod Trail Com., Iditarod Trail Blazers (life), Beargrease Race Com., Kuskokwim 300 Race Com. Club: Interior Dog Mushers (Manley, Alaska); Nome Kennel; Norton Sound Sled Dog. Home and Office: Trail Breaker Kennel 1 Eureka Eureka AK 99756

BUTEAU, MICHELLE DIANE, energy company executive; b. Oakland, Calif., Mar. 6, 1952; d. Bernard Lamonthe and June (Dowler) B.; m. Barry Crawford Anderson, Nov. 1974 (div. 1982); 1 child, Damon Buteau-Anderson. BA in Liberal Arts, Cath. U. Am., 1974, MBA, Loyola/Notre Dame Coll., 1989. Dir. U.S. Summer Sch. Inst., U.S. Dept. State/USIA, Posnan, Poland, 1975-76; bookkeeper Internat. Energy Assocs. Ltd., Washington, 1980-83, rsch. assoc., 1983-85, project mgr., 1984—, sr. cons., 1987—. Actress and dir. dinner theatres, 1974—. Intern to Senator Everett M. Dirksen, Washington, 1968; pres. Cath. Youth Orgn., Bethesda, Md., 1968-70. Mem. NAFE, Am. Mgmt. Assn. Buddhist. Avocations: acting, dancing, singing, writing. Office: ERC Environ and Energy Svcs Co 3211 Jermantown Rd Fairfax VA 22030

BUTEL, JANET SUSAN, virology eductor; b. Overbrook, Kans., May 24, 1941; d. Floyd Charles and Berniece (Humbert) B.; m. David Yates Graham, Mar. 31, 1967; children: Susan Kathleen, David Peter. BS summa cum laude, Kans. State U., 1963; PhD with honors, Baylor U., 1966. Postdoctoral fellow Baylor Coll. Medicine, Houston, 1966-68; asst. prof. Baylor U. Coll. Medicine, Houston, 1968-72, assoc. prof., 1972-76, prof., 1976—, head div. of molecular virology, 1989—; Joseph L. Melnick prof. virology Houston, 1986; study sect. mem. NIH, Bethesda, Md., 1980-84; bd. sci. counselors Nat. Cancer Inst., Bethesda, 1985-89. Contbr. editor: Lange Med. Microbiology, 1987—; contbr. sci. articles to profl. jours. Grad. fellow NSF, 1963-66; rsch. grantee NIH, 1973—. Mem. AAAS, Am. Assn. for Cancer Rsch., Am. Soc. for Cell Biology, Am. Soc. for Microbiology (div. chair 1990-91), Am. Soc. for Virology, N.Y. Acad. Scis., Internat. Assn. Breast Cancer Rsch. (bd. govs. Lakewood, Colo. 1987-91), Soc. of Sigma Xi. Office: Baylor Coll Medicine One Baylor Plaza Houston TX 77030

BUTERA, ANN MICHELE, consulting company executive; b. Bayside, N.Y., Apr. 27, 1958; d. Gaetano Thomas and Josephine (Inserro) B. BA, L.I. U., 1979; MBA, Adelphi U., 1982. Dept. mgr. Abraham & Straus Stores, Huntington, N.Y., 1978-80; mgmt. cons. Chase Manhattan Bank N.A., Lake Success, N.Y., 1980-83, Nat. Bankcard Corp., Melville, N.Y., 1983-84; pres. Whole Person Project, Elmont, N.Y., 1984—. Bd. dirs. Nassau County coun. Girl Scouts U.S., 1985—. Mem. NAFE, L.I. Networking Entrepreneurs (pres. 1984—), North Shore Bus. Forum, L.I. Ctr. for Bus. and Profl. Women. Republican. Roman Catholic. Home and Office: Whole Person Project 82 Cerenzia Blvd Elmont NY 11003

BUTLER, BETTY RAE, educator; b. Albuquerque, N.M., June 7, 1948; d. Charles Clinton and Annetta Rae (Kuenzler) Haralson; m. Frank Forrest, Sept. 16, 1967; children: Shane, Quinn C., Stace E., Lance, Darce C., Travs, Kryss C., D'Lany, Jessy. Student, U. N.M., Albuquehque, 1967. Sec., copy-writer KRZY-AM KRST-FM Radio, Albuquerque, 1966-68; landscape artist SW Saint, Albuquerque, 1971-81; columnist SW St. Newspaper, Albuquerque, 1981-83; workshop facilitator Safe and Sound at Home Program Chaparell Girl Scouts, Albuquerque; cons., trainer Safe Haven Program, Pub. Svc. Co., Albuquerque, 1984-86, Safe Haven Program, 1985-87; cons., puppeteer trainer APS Safety Smart Programs, Albuquerque, 1985-87; exec. dirs. Safety Smart Programs, Albuquerque, 1982-89; dir. N.M. Missing Children's Clearinghouse & Child Safety Info. S, Albuquerque, 1988—; publicity chmn. N.Mex. Assn. for Community Edn. Devel., Albuquerque, 1982-83; juvenile protection dir. Bernalillo County PTA, Albuquerque, 1986—; chmn. health and welfare N.Mex. Congress Parents & Tchrs., 1990—; curriculum reviewer Task Force for Nat. Ctr. for Missing and Exploited Children, Washington, 1987-89; youth protection trainer Great Southwest coun. Boy Scouts Am., Albuquerque, 1988—; lectr. to women's confs., 1982—. Author: Survivor's Handbook, 1982. Community svc. leader after sch. programs Albuquerque Pub. Schs. Community Edn., 1977-82. Office: Identi Find A Child Safety PO Box 6806 Albuquerque NM 87197

BUTLER, CANDACE GAYLE, advertising executive; b. Bloomington, Ind., Jan. 5, 1951; d. Garwood and Beatrice Eileen Judah; m. John D. Butler, June 16, 1973; children: Tobias John, Lindsey Kay. BS, DePauw U., 1973; MS, Ind. U., 1980. Instr. in vocal music South Bend (Ind.) Community Sch. Corp.; exec. v.p. Butler's Bolt and Nut Co., Sturgis, Mich., pres., co-owner. Active numerous community, ednl. and ch. orgns. Named Hon. Woman of the Yr. Mem. Ind. Bus. and Profl. Women (state pres.). Home: 1705 Portage Ave South Bend IN 46616 Office: Butler's Bolt & Nut Inc 3922 W Cleveland Rd South Bend IN 46628

BUTLER, CAROL KING, small business owner; b. Charlotte, N.C., May 29, 1952; d. Charles Snowden Watts and Marion (Thomas) King; m. James Rodney Butler, Aug. 12, 1972 (div. 1975). Student U. N.C., Greensboro, 1970-72. Sales rep. Sta.-WKIX, Raleigh, N.C., 1978-82, N.C. Box, Inc., Raleigh, 1982-84; radio sales account exec. WRAL-FM, Raleigh, 1984-88, team sales mgr., 1988; prin. Butler-Smith Assocs., Raleigh, 1988—. Mem. Nat. Assn. Female Execs. Republican. Episcopalian. Avocations: water skiing, snow skiing, tennis, boating, bicycling. Home: 11917 Shooting Club Rd Raleigh NC 27613 Office: Butler-Smith Assoc Greystone Office Pk 901-D Paverstone Dr Raleigh NC 27615

BUTLER, CYNTHIA CALIBANI, lawyer; b. Lawton, Okla., June 20, 1959; d. Robert John Calibani and Diane (Hart) Renfro; m. Gregory Scott Butler, Nov. 8, 1986. BA, Okla. State U., 1981; JD, Okla. City U., 1986. Lawyer John W. Norman Inc., Oklahoma City, 1986-87, Mark S. Clark Inc., Lawton, 1987-90, Johnson, Livshee & Tayloe, Lawton, 1990—. Vol. Lawton Community Theater, 1986-. Mem. Okla. Bar Assn., ABA, Am. Trial Lawyers Assn., Alpha Epsilon Rho. Office: Johnson Livshee & Tayloe 816 W Gore Blvd Lawton OK 73501

BUTLER, DEBORAH ANN, director teacher education; b. Hampton, Va., Dec. 29, 1949; d. Carson Jr. and Mary Morton (Cole) B.; m. Thomas S. Dickinson, Jan. 2, 1981; children: Cortney Wilson, Kathleen Dickinson. BA in English, Christopher Newport, 1972; MEd in English Edn., U. Va., 1978, EdD in English Edn., 1980. English tchr. Lindsay Jr. High Sch., Hampton, 1973-77; grad. instr. english edn. U. Va., Charlottesville, Va., 1978-80; asst. prin., supervising tchr., english edn. Model Lab Sch., Ea. Ky. U., Richmond, Ky., 1980-82; asst. prin., coord. middle grades tchr. edn. N.C. Wesleyan Coll., Rocky Mount, N.C., 1982-85; assoc. prof., dir. tchr. edn. Wabash Coll., Crawfordsville, Ind., 1985—. Author: (reference book) American Women Writers on Vietnam: Unheard Voice, 1990; contbr. articles to profl. jours. Mem. Nat. Middle Sch. Assn. (folio reviewer, 1990—), Nat. Coun. Tchrs. English, Ind. Middle Sch. Assn. (bd. mem. 1987—, newsletter editor 1989—, chair info. and publs. com.), Delta Kappa Gamma. Democrat. Presbyterian. Office: Wabash Coll 301 W Wabash Ave Crawfordsville IN 47933

BUTLER, GLORIA DEAN, promotion director; b. Vicksburg, Miss., Jan. 29, 1958; d. Burl and Dean (Clark) B. BS in Social Rehab., U. So. Miss., 1979; postgrad., Reformed Theol. Sem., 1988—. Program devel. specialist Miss. Vocat. Rehab. for the Blind, Jackson, 1980; profl. employment counselor Snelling & Snelling, Jackson, 1980-81; sales asst. ITT Telecommunication, Corinth, Miss., 1982-83; creative services producer Sta. WTOK-TV, Meridian, Miss., 1983-86; exec. coordinator Keep Am. Beautiful, City of Meridian, 1986-88; promotion dir. Sta. WDBD-TV, Jackson, 1988—. Contbr. articles to newspapers; contbr. poetry to So. Poetry Rev., 1987—(Blue Ribbon award 1988). Grad. asst. Dale Carnegie, Meridian, 1987. Recipient 1st Place State Distributive Edn. Clubs Am., 1976, Human Relations award Dale Carnegie Inst., 1987, Commendation award City of Meridian, 1986-88. Mem. Jackson Advt. Club, Nat. Assn. Female Execs., Meridian C. of C. (area appearance com., 1986—). Republican. Baptist. Club: Pilot (Jackson).

BUTLER, GRACE CAROLINE, medical administrator; b. Lima, Peru, Dec. 19, 1937; (parents Am. citizens); d. Everett Lyle and Mary Isabella (Sloatman) Gage; m. William Langdon Butler, Dec. 28, 1961; children: Mary Dyer, William Langdon Jr. AA, Stephens Coll., 1957; BS in Nursing, Columbia U., 1960; postgrad., Union County Coll., 1984. Head nurse N.Y. State Psychiat. Inst., N.Y.C., 1960-61; clin. instr. Columbia U., N.Y.C., 1960-61; staff nurse, educator Vis. Nurse Service, Summit, N.J., 1962-63; health adminstr. Eagle Island Girl Scout Camp, Tupper Lake, N.Y., 1964; evening supr. Ashbrook Nursing Home, Scotch Plains, N.J., 1968-72; teaching asst. Scotch Plains-Fanwood (N.J.) Sch. System, 1975-78; staff nurse Westfield (N.J.) Med. Group, 1980-82, head nurse, 1982-83, supr., 1983-84; office adminstr. Harris S. Vernick, MD, PA, Westfield, 1984-86, corp. v.p., office adminstr., 1986-88; corp. v.p., office adminstr. Assocs. in Medicine, Westfield, 1988-90; diabetes educator Boehringer Manneheim Diagnostics, 1984—, Eli Lilly and Co., Indpls., 1984—; microbiologist tester Med. Technol. Corp., Somerset, N.J., 1984—; computer advisor Cordis Corp., Miami, 1985—. Asst. leader Girl Scouts of America, Fanwood, N.J., 1970-73; religious educator All Saints Episcopal Ch., Scotch Plains, 1967-82; bd. dirs. PTA, Scotch Plains, Fanwood, 1973-79; social dir. Highland Swim Club, Scotch Plains, 1973-78. Mem. League For Ednl. Advancement for Registered Nurses, Am. Soc. of Notaries, Columbia U./Presbyn. Hosp. Sch. of Nursing Alumni Assn. Republican. Episcopalian. Home: 125 Russell Rd Fanwood NJ 07023 Office: Assocs in Medicine 128 S Euclid Ave Westfield NJ 07090

BUTLER, HEIDI LORD, management executive; b. Salisbury, Md., Nov. 24, 1958; d. William Loux and Virginia Louise (Dick) Lord; m. Daniel Wallace Butler, May 30, 1987. Student, Meredith Coll., Raleigh, N.C., 1976-78; BSBA, Salisbury State U., 1981. Pres. Heidi A. Lord Acctg. Services, Ocean City, Md., 1981-82; acctg. supr. Perdue Inc., Salisbury, 1982-86; acctg. mgr. Genzyme, Boston, 1986-87; dir. bus. devel. Silvester Design, Inc., Norwalk, Conn., 1988—; instr. Wor-Wic Coll., Salisbury, 1983-86; speaker in field. Active Newcomers Club of Ridgefield, Conn., 1988—; contbr. Colonial Williamsburg (Va.) Found., 1985—. Mem. Soc. for Mktg. Profl. Services, Women in Mgmt., Internat. Facility Mgmt. Assn. (promotion com. 1989—), Am. Bus. Assocs. (chmn. membership com. 1988-89), Internat. Alliance for Women, Norwalk C. of C. Republican. Episcopalian. Office: Silvester Design Inc 18 Marshall St Norwalk CT 06854

BUTLER, HELEN J., adminstrative assistant, consultant; b. West Blocton, Ala., Oct. 1, 1931; d. Charlie and Mary Ella (Powell) Johnson; m. Ruben T. Graham, Jan. 1952 (div.); children: Ronald (dec.), Marilyn (dec.); m. George Hill Jr., Jan. 11, 1958 (div. June 1960); 1 child, Deborah A.; m. Ike Butler, July 7, 1962 (div. Feb. 1967); 1 child, Kevin M. Student, Detroit Inst. Commerce, 1948-50, Wayne State U., Detroit, 1950-53, H&R Block, $, 1986-88. Legal sec. U.S. Dist. Ct., Detroit, 1967-69, adminstrv. asst., 1969-77, 77-79; adminstrv. asst. U.S. Ct. Appeals, Cin., 1977-79; legal stenographer Perdue & Morris Law Firm, Detroit, 1979; legal sec. Harry Philio, Detroit, 1980-81; med. sec. Conant Garden Med. Ctr., Detroit, 198182, Long Life Med. Ctr., Detroit, 1984-85, Evergreen Med. Ctr., Detroit, 1985-86; adminstrv. asst. Avis Wrecking Co., Detroit, 1986—. Recording sec. Ferndale (Mich.) Bd. Edn., 1952; ct. reporter Women's Aux. Med. Conv., Detroit, 1982. Mem. NAFE, Pi Tau Nu. Democrat.

BUTLER, KAREN LEIGH HAYES, educational administrator; b. Sioux City, Iowa, Mar. 22, 1950; d. Otis Calvin and Delores LaVonne (Hall) Hayes; m. John Edwin Butler, June 17, 1972; children: Carmen DeAnn, Carri Lynne, James Jordan. BS, U. Nebr., 1972, MS, 1982, specialist degree, 1989, postgrad., 1990—. Tchr. Omaha Pub. Schs., 1972-82, prin., 1982-87, adminstrv. asst. to supt., 1987-90; prof. dept. tchr. edn. U. Nebr., Omaha, 1990—; instr. Met. Tech. Coll., Omaha, 1972-76, Coll. of St. Marys, Omaha, 1976-78; Danforth speaker Auburn (Ala.) U., 1990. Contbr. articles to newspaper, Edn. Jour. Deaconess, mission leader Pilgrim Bapt. Ch., 1972—; program chmn. Social Settlement, 1986-90; bd. dirs. YWCA, Omaha, 1990—; mem. Leadership Omaha, Omaha C. of C., 1989-90. Recipient Tribute to Black Women award Nat. Coun. Negro Women, 1990; fellow Inst. for Devel. Ednl. Activities, 1990. Mem. Am. Assn. Sch. Adminstrs., Nat. Coun. Sch. Adminstrs., Nebr. Coun. Sch. Adminstrs., Assn. for Supervision and Curriculum Devel., Omaha Sch. Adminstrs. Assn., Caring and Concerned Educators, NAACP (edn. com. 1986—), Phi Delta Kappa, Delta Sigma Theta. Democrat. Home: 6328 Country Club Rd Omaha NE 68152 Office: U Nebr Tchr Edn Kayser Hall 514E 60 Dodge St Omaha NE 68182

BUTLER, LESLIE ANN, advertising agency owner; b. Salem, Oreg., Nov. 19, 1945; d. Marlow Dole and Lala Ann (Erlandson) Butler. Student Lewis and Clark Coll., 1963-64; BS, U. Oreg, 1969; postgrad. Portland State U. 1972-73. Creative trainee Ketchum Advt., San Francisco, 1970-71; asst. advt. dir. Mktg. Systems, Inc., Portland, Oreg., 1971-74; prodn. mgr., art dir., copywriter Finzer-Smith, Portland, 1974-76; copywriter Gerber Advt., Portland, 1976-78; freelance copywriter, Portland, 1983-84, 83-85; copywriter McCann-Erickson, Portland, 1980-81; copy chief Brookstone Co., Peterborough, N.H., 1981-83; creative dir. Whitman Advt., Portland, 1984-87; prin. L.A. Advt., 1987—. Co-founder, v.p., newsletter editor Animal Rescue and Care Fund, 1972-81. Recipient Internat. Film and TV Festival N.Y. Finalist award, 1985, 86, 87, 88, Internat. Radio Festival of N.Y. award, 1984, 85, 88, Hollywood Radio and TV Soc. Internat. Broadcasting award, 1981, TV Comml. Festival Silver Telly award, 1985, TV Comml. Festival Bronze Telly, 1986, AVC Silver Cindy, 1986, Los Angeles Advt. Women LULU, 1986, 87, 88, 89 Ad Week What's New Portfolio, 1986, N.W. Addy award Seattle Advt. Fedn., 1984, Best of N.W. award, 1985, Nat. winner Silver Microphone award, 1987, 88, 89. Mem. Portland Advt. Fedn. (Rosey Finalist award 1986), Portland Art Assn., Assn. Research and Enlightenment, Nat. Wildlife Fedn., ASPCA, Friends and Advocates of Urban Natural Areas, People for Ethical Treatment of Animals. Home and Office: 6005 SE 21st Ave Portland OR 97202

BUTLER, MARGARET KAMPSCHAEFER, computer scientist; b. Evansville, Ind., Mar. 7, 1924; d. Otto Louis and Lou Etta (Rehsteiner) Kampschaefer; m. James W. Butler, Sept. 30, 1951; 1 child, Jay. A.B., Ind. U., 1944; postgrad., U.S. Dept. Agr. Grad. Sch., 1945, U. Chgo., 1949, U. Minn., 1950. Statistician U.S. Bur. Labor Statistics, Washington, 1945-46, U.S. Air Forces in Europe, Erlangen and Wiesbaden, Germany, 1946-48; statistician U.S. Bur. Labor Statistics, St. Paul, 1949-51; mathematician Argonne (Ill.) Nat. Lab., 1948-49, 51-80, sr. computer scientist, 1980—; dir. Nat. Energy Software Center, Dept. Energy Computer Program Exchange,

1960—; cons. AMF Corp., 1956-57, OECD, 1964, Poole Bros., 1967. Editor: Computer Physics Communications, 1969-80; Contbr.: chpt. to The Application of Digital Computers to Problems in Reactor Physics, 1968, Advances in Nuclear Science and Technology, 1976; also articles to profl. publs. Treas. Timberlake Civic Assn., 1958; rep. mem. nominating com. Hinsdale (Ill.) Caucus, 1961-62; coord. 6th dist. Equal Rights Amendment, 1973-80; del. Rep. Nat. Conv., 1980; bd. mgrs. YWCA DuPage dist. of Met. Chgo.; mem. computer and info. systems com. Coll. DuPage, 1987—; mem. industry adv. bd. Computer Sci. Dept. Bradley U.; vice chairperson Ill. Women's Polit. Caucus, 1987—. Recipient Cert. Leadership Met. YWCA. Chgo., 1985, Merit award Chgo. Assn. Technol. Socs., 1988. Fellow Am. Nuclear Soc. (mem. publs. com. 1965-71, chmn. math and computation div. 1966-67, dir. 1976-79, exec. com. 1977-78, chmn. bylaws and rules com. 1979-82, reviewer for publs.); mem. Assn. Computing Machinery (exec. com., sec. Chgo. chpt. 1963-65, publs. chmn. nat. conf. 1968, reviewer for publs.), Assn. Women in Sci. (pres. Chgo. area chpt. 1982, exec. bd. 1985-87), Nat. Computer Conf. (chmn. Pioneer Day com. 1985, tech. program chmn. 1987). Republican. Home: 17W139 Hillside Ln Hinsdale IL 60521 Office: Argonne Nat Lab 9700 S Cass Ave Argonne IL 60439

BUTLER, MARILYN ANN, nursing administrator; b. Crosby, Tex., Sept. 23, 1937; d. Frank Marin and Myrtle Lee (Becker) Smith; children: Kimberly Lynn, Richard Scott. Diploma in nursing Lillie Jolly Sch. Nursing, Houston, 1958; BS U. Tex., 1986. RN, Tex. Surg. asst. C. M. Ashmore, M.D., Houston, 1958-61; head nurse, nursing supr. Meml. Hosp. System, Houston, 1962-77; nursing adminstr. Navarro Regional Hosp., Hosp. Corp. Am., Corsicana, Tex., 1981—. Bd. dirs. County Mental Health/Mental Retardation Com., Corsicana, 1988—, Navarro County Child Evangelis, 1987—. Mem. Am. Coll. Healthcare Execs., Am. Orgn. Nurse Execs., Tex. Orgn. Nurse Execs. (bd. dirs. 1983-85, pres., 1986-87, exec. com. 1987-88). Republican. Baptist. Office: Nararro Regional Hosp 3201 W Hwy 22 Corsicana TX 75110

BUTLER, MARY ANNE, school principal; b. Savannah, Ga., Dec. 13, 1946; d. John George and Mary Catherine (Winters) B. BS, Armstrong State Coll., 1967; MEd, Ga. State U., 1972; edn. specialisst, Ga. So. Coll., 1984. Cert. tchr., Ga. Tchr. Chatham-Savannah Bd. Edn., 1969-70, spl. edn. tchr., 1970-73, coord. behavior disorders, 1973-81; prin. Blessed Sacrament Sch., Savannah, 1981—; cons. pre-sch. and extended-day sch. programs. Grantee Ga. Dept. Edn., 1970, U.S. Dept. Edn., 1971. Mem. NEA, Mental Health Assn. Coastal Empire (sec. 1975, pres. 1978), Coun. Exceptional Children, Nat. Cath. Edn. Assn., Delta Kappa Gamma, Phi Kappa Phi. Democrat. Roman Catholic. Home: 517 E 53d St Savannah GA 31405 Office: Blessed Sacrament Sch 1003 E Victory Dr Savannah GA 31405-2499

BUTLER, MICHELLE ANN, advertising executive, artist; b. Orange, N.J., Jan. 29, 1963; d. Gerald Leroy and Nancy Ann (Mahoney) B. BA cum laude, Cath. U. Am., 1985. Media dir. Bryant, Inc., N.Y.C., 1985-86, account exec., bus. mgr., 1986-87; account exec. Stone Alexander Advt., Montville, N.J., 1987-88; v.p. account svcs. Stone Alexander Advt., Mountain Lake, N.J., 1988-89; pres. Signature Communications, Inc., Montville, 1989—; freelance historical cartographer L'Enfant Trust, Washington, 1984, graphic artist George Washington U. Med. Ctr., 1984-85, illustrator Smithsonian Institution Mus. Natural History, 1985; mktg. cons. Silk Cocoon, Morristown, N.J., 1988—. Commd. artist Allied Signal Corp., Morristown, N.J., 1985, Cath. U. Am., Washingon, 1985; freelance artist Army Mag., N.Y.C. 1988—. Hon. mention trade ad Art Dirs. Club N.J., 1989. Mem. NAFE, Women in Arts, Art Dirs. Club Met. Washington, Morris County C. of C., Psi Chi. Republican. Roman Catholic. Home: 1 Washington Ave 14-4A Morristown NJ 07960

BUTLER, OCTAVIA ESTELLE, free-lance writer; b. Pasadena, Calif., June 22, 1947; d. Laurice and Octavia Margaret (Guy) B. AA, Pasadena City Coll., 1968; student, Calif. State U., Los Angeles, 1969—. Free-lance writer Los Angeles, 1975—. Author: Patternmaster, 1976, Mind of My Mind, 1977, Survivor, 1978, Kindred, 1979, , Wild Seed, 1980, Clay's Ark, 1984, Dawn, 1987, Adulthood Rites, 1988, Imago, 1989; also sci. fiction short stories. Recipient fifth prize Writer's Digest Short Story Contest, 1967, Creative Arts Achievement award Los Angeles YWCA, 1980, Sci. Fiction (Hugo) Best Novelette award World Sci. Fiction Conv., 1985, Best Short Story award World Sci. Fiction Conv., 1984, Nebula Best Novelette award Sci. Fiction Writers Am., 1985, Locus Best Novelette award, 1985, Best Novelette award Sci. Fiction Chronicle Reader, 1985. Mem. Sci. Fiction Writers Am. Address: PO Box 6604 Los Angeles CA 90055

BUTLER-BURNETTE, CATHY DELORES, editor; b. Guntersville, Ala., July 7, 1960; d. Henry Oliver and Eula Beatrice (Hedgepeth) Butler; m. Larry Ecter Burnette, Mar. 12, 1988; 1 child, Lucas Robert. Ba, U. Ala., Tuscaloosa, 1982; MDiv., So. Bapt. Theol. Sem., 1987. Intern Western Recorder, Middletown, Ky., 1981-82; editor Woman's Missionary Union, Birmingham, Ala., 1987—. Mem. Greenpeace, 1990, World Wildlife Fund, 1990. Mem. NAFE, Square Table Book Reviewers (pres. 1989—). Baptist.

BUTLER-TURNER, JANICE ILENE, chemistry and physics educator; b. Lincolnton, Ga., Dec. 1, 1936; d. Ellis Raymond and Katherine Butler; m. Thomas A. Turner Jr., Aug. 24, 1958; 1 child, Thomas A. III. AB, Ga. Coll., 1958; MS, Emory U., 1959; PhD, U. S.C., 1970. Instr. dept. chemistry and physics Augusta (Ga.) Coll., 1959-61, asst. prof., 1961-70, assoc. prof., 1970-76, prof., 1976—, chmn. dept. chemistry and physics, 1976—; cons. Darpa, Huntsville, Ala., 1987-90. Contbr. articles to profl. publs. Mem. Am. Chem. Soc. (chmn. 1989), Ga. Acad. Sci. (state acad. com. on chemistry 1980-86, chmn. 1986-87, chmn. subcom. on prog. assessment 1989-90), Sigma Xi (v.p. local chpt. 1982-83, pres. 1983-84, chmn. nat. assy. dels. 1984), Phi Kappa Phi (pres. local sect. 1976-77, mem. admissions com., audit com. 1987-89). Office: Augusta Coll Dept Chemistry and Physics 2500 Walton Way Augusta GA 30910

BUTMAN, GRACE ANNA, retired adult education educator; b. Sharon, Wis., Oct. 29, 1908; d. Martin and Katherine Adelaide (Roth) Kelhofer; m. Burel Stark Butman, June 2, 1934 (dec. May 1969); 1 child, Cecile Katherine Butman Michael. BS, U. Wis., 1930, MS, 1966. Food supr. Wis. State Girls Sch., Milw., 1930-31, Marshall Field & Co., Chgo., 1931-33, DeMet's Restaurants, Chgo., 1933-34; instr. home econs. high sch., Dodgeville, Wis., 1951-54, Kaukauna, Wis., 1954-60, Kewaunee, Wis., 1960-64; div. coordinator home econs. N.E. Wis. Tech. Coll., Green Bay, 1964-72. Author: New Fabrics, New Clothes and You, 1966; (course study) Child Care Assistant, 1970. Mem. AAUW (pres. 1988-89). Republican. Congregationalist.

BUTNER, BONNIE JEAN, nurse, educator; b. Starkville, Miss., Sept. 12, 1952; d. Otis Len and Opal (Adams) Malone; m. Philip Charles Butner, June 11, 1976; children: Bridgette Ann-Marie, Brittany Lynn. Student, Miss. State U, 1971; BSN, Miss. Coll., 1977. Registered nurse. Nurse tech. Hinds Gen. Hosp., Jackson, Miss., 1972-76; nurse St. Dominic's Hosp., Jackson, 1976-78; nurse supr. Forrest Gen. Hosp., Hattiesburg, Miss., 1978-82; edn. dir. Southeast Miss. Air Ambulance, Hattiesburg, 1982-85; adminstrv. supr. Meth. Hosp., Hattiesburg, 1985-87; clin. dir. for dialysis Hattiesburg Clinic, 1987—. Chmn. blood pressure Am. Heart Assn., Hattiesburg, 1982—. Maj. U.S. Army N.G., 1975—. Mem. Pinebelt Assn. Critical Care Nurses, Southeast Miss. Emergency Nurses Assn. Republican. Baptist. Home: Rt 3 Box 300-P Purvis MS 39475

BUTNER, MARY BOEMKER, social services administrator; b. Louisville, Ky., Feb. 18, 1954; d. Norbert James and Hattie (Hagan) Boemker; divorced, 1979; 1 child, Victoria Leigh. BS, Spalding U., Louisville, 1976, Ind. U., New Albany, 1983; MS, Ind. U., New Albany, 1980; Specialist Degree in Counseling Psych., Spalding U., 1986. Cert. tchr., Ind., Ky., sch. psychologist, Ind., counselor and ednl. tester, Ky.; registered nurse, Ky., Ind. Ednl. psychologist Ky. Bapt. Hosp., Louisville, 1976-77; substance abuse counselor River Region, Louisville, 1977-78; nurse cons. Changing Patterns, Inc., Louisville, 1981-84; academic counselor, lectr. Ind. U. Sch. Nursing, New Albany, 1985-88; edn. intervention specialist, rsch. coord. youth/family activity, cons. Choice, Inc., Louisville, 1988—; advisor in field. Contbr. articles to profl. jours. Panel mem. Gatorade Sports Medicine. Fellow World Assn. Social Psychiatry, Internat. Biog. Assn.; mem. Am. Biog. Assn. (dep. gov.), Am. Assn. Counseling and Devel., Am. Assn. Profl. Hypnotherapists, Ky. Nurses Assn. (mem. coun.), Am. Assn. Social Psychiatry, Internat. Coun. Nurses, Assn. for Humanistic Orthopsychiatry, Gatorade Panel Sports Medicine, Nat. Wildlife Fedn., Sierra Club, Sigma Theta Tau, Kappa Delta Phi, Pi Lambda Theta. Roman Catholic. Home: 1209 Curlew Ave Louisville KY 40213

BUTRIN, JOANN ELIZABETH, nurse; b. Canton, Ohio, Aug. 31, 1950; d. Geroge and Evelyn Winafred (Kuepfer) B. RN, Geisinger Sch. Nursing, 1971; BSN, Evangel Coll., 1975; MSN, Pa. State U., 1982; PhD, U. Minn., 1990. Supr. Allied Rehab. Ctr., Scranton, Pa., 1973-74; dir. med. svcs. Assemblies of God Fgn. Missions, Zaire, 1974-85; mem. adminstrv. staff health Care Ministries, Lakeland, Fla., 1986—; cons. Health Care Ministries Internat., Lakeland, 1986—. Contbr. articles to profl. jours. Mem. Transcultural Nursing Soc., Bicultural Nursing Ci. Assn., Sigma Theta Tau. Republican. Assemblies of God. Home: 707 Carpenters Way #38 Lakeland FL 33809 Office: Health Care Ministries Box 90819 Lakeland FL 33804

BUTSKO, JESSICA JUAREZ, customer service professional; b. Kerrville, Tex., Dec. 30, 1957; d. Gerald C. and Santa (Medina) Juarez; m. Alan Dale Butsko, Sept. 12, 1981; 1 child, Jason Michael. BBA, Stephen F. Austin U., 1979; student, Dale Carnegie, 1985. V.p. sales dept. Flex Temp Inc., Irving, Tex., 1984-87; customer svc. supr. ACI Glass Products, Farmers Branch, Tex., 1987—. Mem. NAFE, Phi Chi Theta. Home: 524 Tipton Rd Irving TX 75060

BUTSON, ELIZABETH, corporate marketing executive; b. Istanbul, Turkey, Mar. 30, 1938; came to U.S., 1957; d. Alexander Margarities and Katy Halepli; m. Thomas G. Butson; 1 child, Alexander. BS, Boston U., 1960. Pub. rels. coord. Philip Morris Internat., 1965, spl. project mgr., 1968-71, mgr. mktg. svcs., 1972, dir. mktg. svcs., 1973-82, 1983, v.p. new products mktg. svcs., 1984-89. Named Honorary Delegate of the Caribbean Horse Racing Federn., 1984, Outstanding Woman of Yr., 1980. Mem. Boston Univ. Club, Lambda Theta Pi. Office: Phillip Morris USA 120 Park Ave New York NY 10017

BUTTEL, PATRICIA ANN, industrial engineer; b. Ottumwa, Iowa, Nov. 20, 1960; d. Theodore Lyle and Nancy Beth (Wright) B.; m. Barrett Scott Lazarus, Aug. 15, 1987 (div. Oct. 1989). BS in Indsl. Engring., Iowa State U., 1984; postgrad., U. Denver, 1988-90. Mfg. engr. Tex. Instruments, Dallas, 1984-87; mfg. engr. Martin Marietta, Denver, 1988-89, systems analyst, 1989-90, 1990—. Mem. Nat. Mgmt. Assn., Career Women's Assn. (membership chair 1990-91). Home: 8356 Russet Ct Bldg 33 Highlands Ranch CO 80126 Office: Martin Marietta PO Box 179 Mail Sta P9770 Denver CO 80201

BUTTERFIELD, DIANE MARIE, financial executive, accountant, consultant; b. Albert Lea, Minn., Aug. 24, 1950; d. William Roland and Genevieve Elaine (Mahowald) B. BA in Acctg., S.W. Minn. U., Minn., 1972. CPA, Minn. Various positions Peat Marwick Mitchell and Co., Mpls., 1972-80; sr. mgr. Peat Marwick Mitchell and Co., N.Y.C., 1980-83; cons. Edmond, Okla., 1983-84; dir. acctg. Policy and Rsch. dept. Household Internat., Prospect Heights, Ill., 1984-89; dep. contr. Mfrs. Hanover Trust Co., N.Y.C., 1989—; alt. mem. emerging issues task force Fin. Acctg. Standards Bd., 1984-87; mem. fn. instruments dept., 1986-89. Mem. AICPA, Nat. Assn. Accts. (mgmt. acctg. practices com. 1989—).

BUTTERFIELD, LAURA LOUISE, psychologist; b. Istanbul, Turkey, Nov. 14, 1952; came to U.S., 1961; d. Robert Emmett and Shirley (Jackson) B.; m. Peter David Wolfson, Aug. 8, 1976; children: Joanna, David. MEd, Columbia U., 1976; D in Psychology, Pace U., 1989. Lic. psychologist. Therapist DeVeaux Sch., Niagara Falls, N.Y., 1976-77, Lincoln Hall, Lincolndale, N.Y., 1977-79; rehab. counselor Silver Hill Found., New Cannan, Conn., 1979-80; psychology extern various schs. and med. ctrs., N.Y., 1980-84; psychology intern Jewish Bd. of Family and Children's Svcs., N.Y.C., 1984-85; psychologist Astor Child Guidance Ctr., Bronx, N.Y., 1989—; instr. Pace U., N.Y.C., 1981-83. Leader consciousness-raising group NOW, Westchester, N.Y., 1979-88. Mem. NOW, Am. Psychol. Assn., Westchester Psychol. Assn. Democrat. Home: 77 Soundview Ave White Plains NY 10606

BUTTERS, NANCY LEE, clinical social worker; b. Boston, Dec. 29, 1950; d. J. Keith and Helena (Renaud) B. BA, Brown U., 1973; MSW, Simmons Coll., 1978. Social worker Thom Clinic, Boston, 1978-81; chief social worker Lang. and Cognitive Devel. Ctr., Boston, 1981-83; dir. mental health svcs. Little House Health Ctr., Boston, 1983-89; pvt. practice, Lexington and Reading, Mass., 1989—. Mem. Nat. Assn. Social Workers, Am. Assn. Group Psychotherapy, Acad. Cert. Social Workers, Northeastern Soc. for Group Psychotherapy (exec. com. 1988-91, bd. dirs. 1989-92). Home: 52 Meriam St Lexington MA 02173 Office: 18-A Auburn St 18-A Woburn St Reading MA 01867

BUTTERWORTH, JANE ROGERS FITCH, physician; b. Louisville, Aug. 3, 1937; d. Howard Mercer and Jane Rogers (McCaw) Fitch; m. William Butterworth, Sept. 5, 1958 (div. Feb. 1968); children: Jane Rogers, William Stoddard, Robert Mercer, Benjamin Richard Mallory, Anne Lewis. BS, U. Louisville, 1971, MD, 1974. Rotating intern Humana Hosp. Audubon (formerly St. Joseph's Hosp.), Louisville, 1974-75, resident in radiology, 1975-76; resident in phys. medicine and rehab. Frasier Rehab. (formerly Inst. of Phys. Medicine and Rehab.), Louisville, 1976-80; staff physiatrist Rockford (Ill.) Meml. Hosp., 1980-83; clin. instr. Rockford Sch. Medicine, 1980-83; med. dir. phys. medicine and rehab. Western Res. Care System, Youngstown, Ohio, 1983—, mem. teaching staff residency program, 1983—; clin. instr. Northeastern Ohio U. Coll. of Medicine, Rootstown, 1983—, chairperson phys. medicine subcoun., mem. acad. rev. and promotions com., 1985—; adj. faculty Youngstown State U., 1984—; regional med. advisor Rehab. div. Ohio Indsl. Commn., Youngstown, 1985—; mem. admissions com. Northeastern Ohio U. Coll. Medicine, 1988. Mem. choir St. John's Episcopal Ch., Youngstown, 1985—, mem. vestry, 1989; bd. dirs. Goodwill Industries, Youngstown, 1985—, rehab. div. advisor, 1986—; mem. med. rev. staff Hospice, Youngstown, 1984—; dir. med. svcs. Easter Seals Soc., Youngstown, 1987—; mem. med. bd. pub. TV, Youngstown, 1986—; violinist Youngstown State U. Orch, 1985. Recipient Community Svc. award St. John's Episcopal Ch., 1988. Mem. AMA, Ohio State Med. Assn., Mahoning County Med. Soc. (mem. coun. 1989), Jefferson County Med. Soc., Ky. Med. Assn., Am. Congress of Rehab. Medicine, Colonial Dames Soc. Am., Phi Beta, Chi Delta Phi, Kappa Alpha Theta. Republican. Home: 186 Rockland Dr Boardman OH 44512 Office: Western Res Care System Southside Hosp 345 Oakhill Youngstown OH 44501

BUTTI, LINDA, visual artist, educator; b. Bklyn., Jan. 15, 1951; d. Vincent and Philomena (Canobbio) B. BA, CUNY, 1972, MFA, 1975. asst. prof. art LaGuardia Community Coll., CUNY, Seton Coll., Yonkers, N.Y. One-woman shows include Ward Nasse Gallery, N.Y.C., 1984, 86, Newhouse Ctr. for Contemporary Art, N.Y.C., 1985, Princeton (N.J.) U., 1989; exhibited in group shows at Bklyn. Mus., 1986, Pace U., 1989, 88, Nancy Stein Gallery, 1989, Guild Hall Mus. , E. Hampton, N.Y., 1989, Nabisco Brands Gallery, N.J., 1989, Lincoln Ctr., N.Y.C., 1987, Newhouse Gallery, 1987, Marywood Coll., Pa., 1987, S.I. Mus., 1988, Paul VI Inst., 1988, Phoenix Gallery, N.Y.C., 1988, Aart Vark Gallery, Phila., 1990, Lever House, N.Y, C., 1990, St. John's U., N.Y.C., 1990; represented in permanent collections Bell Atlanta, Smith Barney, Upham and Harris, N.Y.C., NBC Studios, N.Y.C., Brenau Coll., Ga., Cath. Telecommunications Ctr. of Am., N.Y.C., Sterling Drug Art Collection, Pa., Mitsubish Capital, N.Y.C., Iona Coll., The Art Network S.I., N.Y. Recipient Creative Artist award CAM Competition, 1979; Com. for Visual Arts grantee, 1980, 85, 89, Chase Manhattan Bank grantee, 1981, Guild Hall Mus. Honorable award, 1989. Mem. Women in the Arts (sec. 1984—), Cath. Artists of the 80's (coord. spl. projects 1985—), Women Caucus for Art.

BUTTI, MARY MADELINE, principal; b. N.Y.C., Nov. 20, 1921; d. Ernest Charles and Anna (Mazzoni) Fusi; m. Lewis Charles Butti, Apr. 6, 1947; children: Claire Butti Myers, Lawrence Richard. BA, Hunter Coll., 1943; MA, Columbia U., 1945. Tchr. English N.Y.C. Sch. System, 1947-67; asst. prin. N.Y.C. Sch. System, Bklyn., 1967-76; prin. Jr. High Sch. 223, Bklyn., 1976—; v.p. Council Suprs. and Adminstrs., Bklyn., 1978—, trustee/sec. welfare fund, 1980—, retirees welfare fund, 1983—.ž. V.p. New Hyde Park (New Hyde Park) Health Ins. Plan Consumer Council, 1976—; pres. Commonwealth Civic Assn., Douglaston, N.Y., 1981—; mem. Community Bd. 11, Bayside, N.Y., 1983—; bd. dirs. Highpoint Condominion, Douglaston, 1985—. Mem. Nat. Assn. Secondary Sch. Prins., Jr. High Sch. Prins. Assn. (exec. bd. 1981-83), Delta Kappa Gamma (Elizabeth Turbin Pi award 1981), Phi Delta Kappa (St. John's U. chpt.). Roman Catholic. Home: 244-16 73d Ave Douglaston NY 11362

BUTTINGER, CATHARINE SARINA CAROLINE, psychiatrist; b. Bruchsal, Fed. Republic Germany, July 23, 1951; came to U.S., 1982; d. John Levine and Juliana Magdalena Buttinger; m. Roger L.M. Dunbar, Oct. 7, 1982; 1 child, Emma Magdalena. Abitur, Schuldorf-Bergstrasse, Jugenheim, Fed. Republic Germany, 1973; MD, U. Heidelberg, Fed. Republic Germany, 1980, Med.Sc.D., 1982; postgrad., Columbia U., 1985-88. Neurosurgeon U. Hosp. Heidelberg, 1980-82; researcher Albert Einstein Coll. Medicine, N.Y.C., 1982-83, internship, 1984-85; researcher NYU, N.Y.C., 1983-84; psychiatrist Coll. Physicians and Surgeons Columbia U., N.Y.C., 1985-88, rsch. fellow eating disorders, 1988-90; candidate Columbia U. Ctr. for Psycho-Analytic Tng. and Rsch., 1985—; pvt. practice, 1988—. Ginsburg fellow Group for Advancement of Psychiatry, 1986-88. Mem. AMA, Am. Psychiatric Assn., Am. Psychoanalytic Assn., German Med. Assn. Home: 100 Bleecker St New York NY 10012 Office: 300 Central Park W New York NY 10024

BUTTON-SHAFER, JANICE, physicist; b. Cin., Sept. 13, 1931; d. Charles Titsworth and Anita Blanche (Wolever) Button; m. John Shafer; children: Christina Mae, Charles Frederick, John Christopher (twins). B in Engring. Physics, Cornell U., 1954; postgrad., U. Goettingen, Fed. Republic of Germany, 1955; PhD in Nuclear Physics, U. Calif., Berkeley, 1959. Rsch. physicist Lawrence Radiation Lab., Berkeley, 1959-66; lectr. in physics U. Calif., Berkeley, 1962-66; assoc. prof. physics U. Mass., Amherst, 1966-70, prof. physics, 1970—. Contbr. numerous articles to profl. jours. Participant peace and world security studies MIT, Harvard U., U. Md. 1983-89. Fulbright fellow, 1954-55, Gen. Electric Coffin fellow, 1956-57. Fellow Am. Phys. Soc.; mem. AAAS, Am. Phys. Soc. Commn. on the Status of Women in Physics, Am. Assn. Physics Tchrs., Cornell Club (bd. dirs. Western Mass. 1987-89), Tau Beta Pi, Sigma Xi. Home: 62 Stony Hill Rd Amherst MA 01002 Office: U Mass Dept Physics LGR Tower C Amherst MA 01003

BUTTS, PAMELA DENISE, marketing executive; b. Atlanta, Apr. 1, 1965; d. Eddie Lee and Sallie Cornelius (Banks) B. BS in Info. Systems, DeVry Inst., Atlanta, 1985. PC operator CBI/Equifax, Atlanta, 1986-87; project support specialist Equifax Mktg. Svcs., Atlanta, 1987-88; tng. resources coord. Equifax, Inc., Atlanta, 1988-89; support analyst Equifax, Inc., 1989-90, end user support cons., 1990—. Editor Tech. News; co-editor newsletter CB-Eye. Mem. Phoenix Users Group.

BUTTS, VIRGINIA, corporate public relations executive; b. Chgo.. B.A., U. Chgo. Writer Dave Garroway radio show NBC, N.Y.C., 1953; writer, producer, talent Sta. WBBM-TV, Chgo.; midwest dir. pub. relations for mags. Time, Fortune, Life and Sports Illustrated, Time Inc., 1956-63; dir. pub. relations Chgo. Sun-Times and Chgo. Daily News, 1963-74; v.p. pub. relations Field Enterprises Inc., Chgo., 1974-84, The Field Corp., 1984—; mem. pub. affairs adv. com. Art Inst. Chgo. Contbr.: Lesly's Public Relations Handbook, 1978, 83. Pub. affairs adv. com. Art Inst. Chgo.; bd. dirs. Landmarks Preservation Coun. Ill. Recipient Clarion award Women in Communications, Inc., 1975, 76, Businesswoman of the Yr. award Lewis U., 1976. Mem. Pub. Rels. Soc. Am. (nat. bd. ethics 1987—), Publicity Club Chgo. (Golden Trumpet award 1968, 69, 75, 76, 80), Nat. Acad. TV Arts and Scis., The Chgo. Network. Club: Mid-Am. (Chgo.). Office: The Field Corp 333 W Wacker Dr Chicago IL 60606

BUTZ, GENEVA MAE, pastor; b. Emmaus, Pa., May 11, 1944; d. Edwin F. and Arlene E. (Engler) B. BA, Hood Coll., 1966; MRE, Union Theol. Sem., 1968. Ordained clergywoman United Ch. of Christ, 1972. Dir. Christian edn. United Ch. of Christ, Palos Verdes, Calif., 1968-72; mng. editor Youth mag., United Ch. Bd. for Homeland Ministries, Phila., 1972-75; affiliate rep. Ecumenical Community of Taizé, France, New Zealand, Australia, Indonesia, India and others, 1975-77; parish worker Temple Presbyn. Ch., Phila., 1978-83; pastor Old First Reformed Ch., United Ch. of Christ, Phila., 1984—; bd dirs. exec. com. Met. Christian Coun. of Phila., 1985—; cons. Auburn Theol. Sem., N.Y., 1988-89. Author: Color Me Well, 1986, Christmas Comes Alive, 1988; contbr. Women Pray, Karen Roller, Ed, 1986. Mem. Old City Civic Assn., Phila., 1984—, Pledge of Resistance, Phila., 1985—; bd. dirs. Bethesda Project, Inc., Phila., 1986; del. Gen. Synod-United Ch. of Christ, Cleve., Ft. Worth, 1987-89; bd. dirs. Phila. Religious Leadership Devel. Fund, 1988—, Protestant adv. bd. Temple U., Phila., 1987; mem. dialogue group Reformed Ch. in Am./United Ch. of Christ. Recipient Human Rels. award Nt. Conf. of Christians and Jews, Phila., 1985; named One of 85 People to Watch Phila. mag., 1985, One of 7 Clergy Leading U.S. Constl. BIcentennial Parade, 1987. Mem. Nat. Orgn. of Women, Ch. Women United of Greater Phila. (bd. mgrs. 1985-87), Old Phila. Clergy (v.p. 1986-87), Assn. Uniting Arts and Religion (steering com.), Phila. Assn. (ministrial standing). Democrat. Office: Old First Reformed Ch 4th & Race St Philadelphia PA 19106

BUTZ, MARY E., loan originator; b. Milw., Sept. 5, 1957; d. Kenneth H. and Ida (Oribiletti) B. Student, Alverno Coll., 1985—. Loan processor Norwest Mortgage Corp., Milw., 1979-87; loan originator Chase Home Mortgage, Milw., 1987-88, Mid-States Mortgage, Milw., 1988-90, Republic Capital Mortgage, Milw., 1990—. Mem. Milw. Bd. Realtors, Ozaukee Bd. Realtors, Milw. Art Mus. (new mem. com.).

BUTZLAFF VOSS, BAMBI LYN, association executive; b. Fond du Lac, Wis., July 24, 1962; d. Ervin George and June Ann (Schwarze) Butzlaff; m. James Henry Voss, Sept. 22, 1984, 1 child, Le'erin Olyssa. BJ, U. Wis., 1984. Cert. by the Wis. Hosp. Pub. Relations and Mktg. Soc. Radio announcer Stas. WBEV, WXRO, Beaver Dam, Wis., 1979-83; dir. mktg. and pub. rels. Horicon (Wis.) State Bank, 1981-84; prodn. coord. Authur, Downers Grove, Ill., 1984-85; pub. rels. mktg. dir. Lakeland Hosp., Elkhorn, Wis., 1985-89; exec. dir. Brookfield (Wis.) C. of C., 1989-90; pub. rels. practitioner U. Wis., Waukesha, 1990—; medallion campaign coord. Milw. Boys, Girls Club, 1985; children's telethon prodn. worker, coord. Channel 12, Milw., 1985. Writer, editor Here's News, 1985—, Hospice Newsletter, 1985—, Communiqué, 1987—; facilitator Guest Rels. Prog. Bldg. Bridges, 1986—. County Sec. Dem. Party Waukesha County, 1987—. Named Employee of the month Lakeland Hosp., Elkhorn, Wis., 1987. Mem. Wis. Hosp. Pub. Rels. & Mktg. Soc., Wis. Soc. Healthcare Planning & Mktg., Am. Soc. Hosp. Mktg. & Pub. Rels. Democrat. Lutheran. Home: W258 S6860 Ivy Ct Waukesha WI 53186 Office: U Wis Waukesha Dept Pub Rels 1500 University Dr Waukesha WI 53188

BUXBAUM, ALEXANDRA, photographer; b. Evanston, Ill., Mar. 1, 1962; d. Brigitte (Zenger) Kaeske; m. Michael Victor Buxbaum, Nov. 7, 1982. Student, Truman Coll., 1982-83, Columbia Coll., 1983-86. Photographer Pioneer Press, Wilmette, Ill., 1986-88, ADA, Chgo., 1988—, Black Star Pub. Co., N.Y.C., 1988—, Christian Sci. Monitor, Boston, 1988—, Kraft Gen. Foods, Glenview, Ill., 1989—, Agence France Presse, Washington, 1988—, L.A. Times, 1989—; freelance photographer Chgo., 1986—; career day guest panel Forest Hosp., Des Plaines, Ill., 1988—, Women Employed, Chgo., 1989. Exhibited in group show at Chgo. Pub. Libr., 1986. Recipient Award of Excellence Photographers Forum, 1986. Mem. Women in Communications, Inc. Home: 88 W Schiller Chicago IL 60610

BUXBAUM, LINDA ZELFMAN, manufacturing executive; b. New Haven, Conn., Aug. 26, 1937; d. Albert A. and Esther (Rozen) Zelfman; m. Paul Joseph Buxbaum, Sept. 7, 1958 (dec. Aug. 1976); children: Laurel, Mark, Rebecca; m. Welles Thompson Hotchkiss, Oct. 23, 1977. BA, Smith Coll., 1959; MA, Farleigh Dickinson U., 1968; MBA, Clark U., 1983. Tchr. Roxbury High Sch., Succasunna, N.J., 1964-68; advt. writer William C. McDade Assocs., Morristown, N.J., 1968-69; pub. relations cons. Coll. Entrance Exam. Bd., Waltham, Mass., 1970-73; editor, writer Internat. Biomed. Info., Acton, Mass., 1973-75; pubs. mgr. Digital Equipment Corp., Maynard, Mass., 1977-79; mktg. communications mgr. Digital Equipment

Corp., Hudson, N.H., 1979-83; mktg. mgr. Digital Equipment Corp., Marlboro, Mass., 1983-85; program mgr. Digital Equipment Corp., Merrimac, N.H., 1985-88; industry mgr. Digital Equipment Corp., N.Y.C., 1988—. Editor: (reference book) Biomedical Health Care Marketplace Guide, 1973. Trustee Congregation Beth El, Sudbury, Mass., 1973-83; chmn. Bd. of Assessors, Sudbury, Mass., 1985-88. Mem. NAFE, Paper Industry Mgmt. Assn., Bus. Profl. Advt. Assn., Am. Mktg. Assn., Beth Haverim (trustee 1990—), Women's Club (Ridgewood, N.J.). Democrat. Jewish. Office: Digital Equipment Corp 2 Penn Plaza New York NY 10121

BUZALJKO, GRACE WILSON, editor, writer; b. Cambridge, Mass., Nov. 4, 1922; d. Charles and Elizabeth (Douglas) Wilson; m. Ahmed Buzaljko, Mar. 9, 1963 (div. Mar. 1980). BA cum laude, St. Mary Coll., Leavenworth, Kans., 1944; postgrad., U. Pitts., 1946-47, New Sch. for Social Rsch., 1949-50. Promotions asst. Pitts. Press, 1945-48; manuscript editor John Wiley & Sons, N.Y.C., 1948-52, Harcourt Brace Jovanovich, N.Y.C., 1952-60, U. Calif. Press, Berkeley, 1960-67; adminstrv. editor Harcourt Brace Jovanovich, San Francisco, 1967-72; editor dept. anthropology U. Calif., Berkeley, 1973-88, ret., 1988. Editor: Yurok Myths (A.L. Kroeber), 1976, Karok Myths (A.L. Kroeber and E.W. Gifford), 1980; contbr. articles to profl. jours. Co-clk. Berkeley Soc. of Friends Meeting, 1988-90. Mem. AAUW (v.p., program chmn. Berkeley br. 1981-83, legis. chmn. 1988—), Kroeber Anthrop. Soc., Miwok Archeol. Preserve of Marin. Home: 612 Albemarle St El Cerrito CA 94530

BUZZA, BONNIE WILSON, communication educator; b. Mpls., Feb. 23, 1944; d. Henry Woodrow and Bonnie Laurette (Carlson) Wilson; m. David Thomas Buzza, Mar. 19, 1967. BA, Macalester Coll., St. Paul, 1966; MA, U. Denver, 1967, PhD, 1970. Prof. weekend and evening coll. Met. State Coll., Denver, 1970-73; prof., dept. chmn. Ripon (Wis.) Coll., 1974-88; prof. communications, chmn. dept. Coll. of Wooster, Ohio, 1988-90; asst. dean, coll. fine arts and humanities St. Cloud State U., 1990—; cons. Communication Mgmt. Assocs.; dir. London-Florence program ACM, London, 1983. Contbr. articles to profl. publs. Mem. exec. bd. Wayne County Women's Network, Wooster, 1989; vol. Every Woman's House, Wooster, 1990. Recipient Outstanding Young Tchr. award Cen. States Speech. Assn., 1977, Disting. Citizen award Macalester Coll. Alumni Assn., 1981, Severy award for teaching excellence Ripon Coll., 1988. Mem. Speech Communication Assn., Assn. for Communication Adminstrn., Cen. States Communication Assn. (Program of Excellence award small coll. com. 1990), AAUP, NAFE, Ripon Coll. Soc. Scholars (co-founder, life), Pi Kappa Delta, Alpha Psi Omega. Office: Saint Cloud State U Coll Fine Arts & Humanities Kiehle 101 Saint Cloud MN 56301

BYAM, M(ARIE) ELIZABETH, data processing management consultant; b. Cooperstown, N.Y., Oct. 31, 1949; d. Harmon Leigh and Elizabeth Virginia (Baldo) B. BA, Ga. State U., 1972; postgrad., Columbia So. Sch. Law, 1976-78. Cert. systems profl. Programmer Coastal States Life Ins. Co., Atlanta, 1973-75; programmer, analyst So. Airways, Atlanta, 1975-76; cons. computer programming Atlanta, 1978-82; sr. cons., field mgr. Computer Dynamics, Woodland Hills, Calif., 1983-84; owner, prin. cons. MEB Assocs., Canoga Park, Calif., 1984—; frequent speaker on career planning and info. processing techs. for schs., profl. confs. and meetings. Guest co-host Ms. Biz radio show, 1987. Bd. dirs. Opera Guild So. Calif., Los Angeles, 1984-88. Mem. Data Processing Mgmt. Assn. (publs. dir. 1988, treas. 1989, pres. 1990), Assn. Women in Computing (pres. L.A. chpt. 1985-87, nat. conf. chmn. 1986), Sierra Club. Republican. Home and Office: MEB Assocs 6846D Hatillo Canoga Park CA 91306

BYARS, ILA PEARL, social services administrator, civic worker; b. Travis, Tex., June 25, 1908; d. William Lafayette and Sibyl Allen (Massey) B.; student public schs. With Mid-west States Telephone Co., Blanco, 1924-53; with Bigden Ins. and Real Estate, Tex., 1953-55; pvt. kindergarten tchr., Blanco, 1955-56; waitress various restaurants, 1956-62, 63-65; with Wall Furniture, also Wall Funeral Home, Blanco, 1952-53, 65-66; staff food dept. Blanco Mill Nursing Home, 1966—. County chmn. Am. Heart Assn., 1957-72, meml. and campaign mgr., 1957-72; bd. dirs. Blanco County unit Am. Cancer Soc., 1959-72, unit sec., 1971-74, 86—, pres., 1974-76; trustee Blanco Library, 1950-53, librarian, 1952-53; bd. dirs. Blanco County Tb Assn., 1951-53; sec. Council on Ministries, United Meth Ch., 1986—, sec. chancel choir, 1985-86, mem. nominating com., 1982—, parish com., 1986, Sunday Sch. tchr., 1949—, dir. Vacation Bible Sch., from 1968, asst. dir., 1986, chmn. children's dept., 1986—, bd. dirs., sec. to bd. 1989—; chmn. birthday parties at Will Nursing Home, 1988-89. Recipient Achievement citations Am. Heart Assn., 1970, 71, 73; citation Am. Cancer Soc., 1971, 25-yr. pin., 1985, Yellow Rose Tex. award Gov. Tex., 1988. Mem. Blanco C. of C. (sec. 1967-72, dir. 1967-71), Daus. of Nile, Wesleyan Service Guild (co-founder 1952, pres. 1968—), Nat. Trust Hist. Preservation, Tex. Hist. Found., The Smithsonian Assocs. United Meth. Women (reporter 1986, chmn. nominating com. 1988—). Lodges: Daus. of Nile, Order Eastern Star (past matron; organist, sec. 1986, 87). Home: PO Box 246 Blanco TX 78606

BYE, ROSEANNE MARIE, marketing professional; b. Chgo., Nov. 27, 1946; d. Paul David and Gwendalynn Luciell (Hipp) Forrester; BS in Foods and Nutrition, Western Ill. U., 1969; m. Richard Wayne Bye, June 14, 1969. Banquet mgr. Western Ill. U., 1967-69; new product home economist Hunt/Wesson Foods, Fullerton, Calif., 1969-73; retail and restaurant home economist Lawry's Foods, L.A., 1973-74; mgr. product devel. Carl Karcher Enterprises, Anaheim, Calif., 1974-81; v.p. R & D Denny's Restaurants, La Mirada, Calif., 1981-88; owner, cons. Roseanne Bye & Assocs., Orange, Calif., 1988-89; v.p. foodsvc. div. TG Mktg. and Advt., Inc., Anaheim, 1989—; mem. speakers bur. mktg. fast food Industry/Edn. Coun. Mem. food svc. adv. com., Calif. State U., Long Beach, Chapman Coll., adv. com. Santa Ana Jr. Coll., Garden Grove Sch. Dist. Recipient Nat. Mktg. award for devel. of Charbroiler Steak Sandwich, 1975-76, serve-yourself salad bar, 1978-79. Mem. Am. Home Econs. Assn., Calif. Home Econs. Assn. (Outstanding Economist in Bus. 1977, 79, 86, pres. 1977-79), Home Economists in Bus. (award of excellence, Western regional adv. 1976-78, nat. pub. rels. chmn. 1983-85), Women in Mgmt., Nat. Restaurant Assn. (chmn. mktg. rsch. div., nat. conf. speaker), NOW, Anaheim C. of C. (publicity chmn. 1977-78), Soc. Advancement Food Svc. Rsch. (bd. dirs. 1986-88, co-chair regional meetings 1988—, Fellowship award 1987), Internat. Food Svc. Editorial Coun., Multi Unit Food Svc. Ops., Chain Ops. Execs., Internat. Platform Assn. Republican. Presbyterian. Clubs: Tennis and Swim, Gourmet/Wine, Teddy Bear, Lit. Guild, Newport Harbor Art Mus., Bower's Art Mus., Gem Theatre Guild. Office: TG Mktg & AdvtInc 3943 E La Palma Ave Anaheim CA 92807

BYERS, DONNA JEAN, educator; b. Chgo., Jan. 8, 1956; d. Donald Lee and Shirley Jeanine (Hawbaker) Elzy; m. Robin Wayne Byers, Nov. 24, 1979; 1 child, Kathryn Olivia. BS, Ind. U., 1978; MS, Ind. U., South Bend, 1983; postgrad., Richardson (Tex.) Coll., 1979. Spl. educator Grand Prairie (Tex.) Ind. Sch. Dist., 1978-79; with Interior Design Etc. Assocs., Carmel, Ind., 1979-80; spl. educator Crestwood Sch. Dist., Paris, Ill., 1980-82, Indpls. Pub. Schs., 1983—; workshop presenter Indpls. pub. schs., 1988—, mem. least restrictive environment adv. com., 1986-88. Mem. Jr. League of Indpls. Named Tchr. of Yr., Susan Roll Leach Sch., 1988-89; recipient Leadership and Devel. fellowship, 1989-90. Mem. NEA, Ind. Tchrs. Assn., Council for Exceptional Children, Assn. for Children with Learning Disabilities, Ind. U. Alumni Assn., Kappa Kappa Gamma. Republican. Home: 5635 N Pennsylvania St Indianapolis IN 46220 Office: Indianapolis Public Schs 2107 N Riley Ave Indianapolis IN 46218

BYERS, ROSEMARIE, library director; b. Pitts., Sept. 6, 1936; d. John William and Angeline Virginia (Patton) Bilotta; m. Ronald Gerard Byers; children: Barbara, Thomas, Mary, Carol. BA in Math., Duquesne U., 1957; MLS, Carnegie Mellon U., 1959. Cert. profl. libr., Mich. Reference libr. Duquesne U., Pitts., 1957-59, Grace A. Dow Meml. Libr., Midland, Mich., 1960-77; supr. of user svcs. Grace A. Dow Meml. Libr., Midland, 1977-79; assoc. dir., 1979-80, dir., 1981—. Developer Libr. Circulating System Rosemaries Baby, 1979. Bd. dirs. ARC Midland (Mich.) County Chpt., 1985—, White Pine Libr. Coop., chmn. 1989—; vice chmn. Theatre Guild Midland Ctr. for the Arts, 1989—. Mem. Saginaw Valley Press Club (bd. dirs. 1987—), Zonta Club of Midland (bd. dirs. 1989—). Home: 6208 Pebblestone Midland MI 48640 Office: Grace A Dow Meml Libr 1710 W St Andrew's Rd Midland MI 48640-2698

BYERS, VIRGINIA BULLARD, nursing educator; b. Clemmons, N.C., Aug. 29, 1928; d. John Sidney and Fannie Eliza (Sheets) Bullard; m. Donald Conley Byers, Aug. 16, 1958; children: James Donald, Judith Louise. BSN, U. Pa., 1952, MSEd in Nursing, 1960; PhD in Higher Edn., U. Pitts., 1978. Asst. head nurse Lawrence Meml. Hosp., New London, Conn., 1952-53; clin. instr. Bryn Mawr (Pa.) Hosp. Sch. Nursing, 1953-55; instr. nursing U. Pa., Phila., 1955-58, Ohio State U., Columbus, 1958-61; asst. prof. nursing U. Pitts., 1961-65, 69-72, assoc. prof. nursing, 1972-76; assoc. prof. nursing SUNY Coll. Tech., Utica, 1979-86, SUNY Health Sci. Ctr., Syracuse, 1987—. Author: Nursing Observation, 1968, 3d edit., 1978. Elder, Presbyn. Ch. U.S.A., Dewitt, N.Y., 1987—. Mem. AAUW, Nat. League for Nursing, N.Y. State Nurses Assn. (chmn. coun. on ethical practice 1987), Sigma Theta Tau, Omicron (v.p. 1989—), Iota Delta Xi (pres. 1986-88), Pi Lambda Theta. Home: 7695 Clark Ln Manlius NY 13104

BYHAM, CAROLYN MENTZER, facilities planner, designer, city official; b. Easton, Pa., Nov. 11, 1941; d. Robert E. and Helena (Aagaard) Mentzer; m. William C. Byham, Feb, 11, 1967; children; Tacy M., Carter W. AB, W. Va. U., 1963; MA, The Ohio State U., 1964. Exec. B.B.D.O. Advt., NYC, 1964-68; exec. v.p., designer planner Devel. Diminsions Internat., Pitts., 1971—; commr. City of Mt. Lebanon (Pa.), 1983—. Bd. dirs. Local Govt. Acad., Pitts., 1988—, Uptown Mt. Lebanon, Pitts., 1984—, Pitts. Pub. Theatre, 1989—, Performing Arts for Children, Pitts. 1975—; co-founder Pitts. Children's Festival, 1985—; candidate Pa. Legis., 1990. Mem. Pa. Elected Women's Assn., AAUW (pres. 1973-75, Outstanding Woman award 1980). Republican. Protestant. Office: DDI 1225 Washington Pike Bridgeville PA 15017

BYINGTON, SALLY RUTH, association administrator; b. Grand Rapids, Mich., Apr. 16, 1935; d. George and Evangeline (Boerma) Meyer; m. S. John Byington, Nov. 27, 1964 (div. Dec., 1988): children: Nancy Lee, Barbra Ann. BA, Western Mich. U., 1957; MA, U. Md., 1962. Cert. tchr. k-8, Md. Grad. asst. U. Md., College Pk., 1959-60; tchr. U. Chgo. Lab. Sch., 1963-64, Grand Rapids, Mich., 1957-59. 64-65, Montgomery County Md. Pub. Schs., Rockville, Md., 1961-63; learning specialist Endeavor Learning Ctr., Rockville, 1987-88; asst. to pres. Women in Militry Svc., Arlington, Va., 1988-89; exec. asst. Korean War Vets. Meml. Adv. Bd., Washington, 1989—; cons. Handicapped Children Early Edn. Program, Bur. Edn. for Handicapped, Dept. edn., Washington, 1975-80; diagnostician pvt. practice. Pres. Greater Springfield Rep. Women's Clubs, Springfield, Va., 1980's, v.p. 1980's; dist. dir. Fairfax County Rep. Com. 1988; vol. Fairfax County Pub. Schs. Enrollment Study, 1985. Recipient vol. recognition award Fairfax Pub. Schs., 1985. Mem. League of Women Voters (study rep. 1980's). Home: 1231 Maryland Ave NE Washington DC 20002 Office: Korean War Vets Meml Adv Bd 18th & C Sts NW Rm 7023 MIB Washington DC 20002

BYLSMA, CAROL ANN, environmental education administrator; b. Los Angeles, Dec. 5, 1941; d. Carl Minke and Anna (Testa) Bylsma; m. Leo C. Jones Jr., June 23, 1961, (div. Nov., 1979); children: Lauran Marie, Lynell Ann. BS, U. Colo., Boulder, 1970; MA, U. No. Colo., Greeley, 1978; postgrad., U. Colo., 1984—, Rocky Mountain Bio Lab., Gothic, Colo., 1984. Tchr. Tchr. Douglas County Schs., Castle Rock, Colo., 1970-79, Cherry Creek Schs., Englewood, Colo., 1979-81; naturalist Colo. Div. of Parks & Recreation, Denver, 1978-81; dir. Barr Lake Nature Ctr., Brighton, Colo.; instr. Met. State Coll., Denver, 1982-84; environ. edn. cons. Aerie Nature Series, 1982-85; environ. edn. coordinator Colo. Div. of Wildlife, Denver, 1985—; dir. Nature Adventures Internat., Denver, 1985—; project WILD coordinator Colo. Div. of Wildlife, Denver, 1985—, E.E. cons., 1985—, aquatic edn. dir., 1990—; bd. dirs. Wild Colo. Fund, 1987—; instr. environ. edn. Colo. State U., 1985—, Colo. Sch. Mines, 1990—. Actor: Cottonwood Kid, 1986, By Grace of Man, 1981; editor (newsletter) Wild Colorado, 1985—; feature page Outdoors Colorado. Pres. Western Interpreters Assn., Denver, 1981-83, western region Environ. Edn. Council, 1985—; Field Trip Coordinator Denver Audubon Soc., Denver, 1979-82;. Recipient Service award Western Regional Environ. Edn. Council, San Francisco, 1988. Mem. Project Wild (nat. steering com.), N.Am. Environ. Edn. Assn., Colo. Alliance for Environ. Edn. (bd. dirs.), Nat. Sci. Tchrs. Assn., Assn. for Supervision and Curriculum Devel., Windstar, Xerces Soc. Democrat. Office: Colo Div of Wildlife 6060 Broadway Denver CO 80216

BYNUM, BARBARA STEWART, health scientist administrator; b. Washington, June 13, 1936; d. Oliver Walton and Mabel (Easton) Stewart; m. Elward Bynum, Apr. 4, 1959; 1 son, Christian. B.A. in Chemistry, U. Pa., 1957; postgrad. in biochemistry, Georgetown U., 1958-60. Chemist Nat. Cancer Inst. NIH, Bethesda, Md., 1958-71; adminstrv. asst., office assoc. dir. for adminstrn. NIH, Bethesda, 1971-72, sci. grants program specialist div. rsch. grants, 1972-75, health scientist adminstr. div. rsch. grants, 1975-78, asst. chief for spl. programs, sci. rev. br. div. rsch. grants, 1978-81, dir. div. extramural activities Nat. Cancer Inst., 1981—; reviewer, cons. AAAS, Washington, 1974—; chmn. HHS Task Force Working Group on Cancer in Minorities, 1986—. Recipient Dirs. award NIH, 1980; recipient Sr. Exec. Service Superior Performance award HHS, 1982, 1987. Mem. Am. Assn. Cancer Research, Am. Assn. Pathologists, AAAS, Biophys. Soc. Democrat. Roman Catholic. Office: Nat Cancer Inst Extramural Activities Bldg 31 9000 Rockville Pike Bethesda MD 20892

BYRAM, ZOOEY JOAN, editor health newsletter; b. Hollywood, Calif., June 12, 1949; d. John Pohly Myers and Joelle (Kaufmann) Kornell; m. Jerry Lee Jackson, Apr. 29, 1969 (div. Jan. 1984); 1 child, Elijah Andrew Jackson; m. Dennis Clark Byram, Feb. 14, 1988. AA, Donsbach U., Huntington Beach, Calif., 1984, BS, 1986; postgrad., Columbia Coll., 1984; student, Coll. of the Desert, 1977-78. Tchrs. asst. Steele Ln. Annex, Santa Rosa, Calif., 1968; ch. sec. Presbyn. Ch., Coachella, Calif., 1973-75; tchrs. asst. Desert Sands Unified Schs., Indio, Calif., 1975-77; desk clk. La Quinta (Calif.) Hotel and Golf Resort, 1980-81; pharmacy clk. Twain Harte (Calif.) Pharmacy, 1983; gourmet caterer All-Around Catering, Sonora, Calif., 1984-85; nutritional cons. C.Z. & Assocs., Carmel, Calif., 1985-87; travel agt. George Morello Travel, San Mateo, Calif., 1989; editor For the Health of It, Coeur d'Alene, Idaho, 1989—. Author: Everyday Children, 1978; producer pub. svc. message Hear the Hungry Children, 1986. Vol. Disaster ARC, Watsonville, Calif., 1989, Change 4 the Hungry, Calif., 1989, Habitat for Humanity Internat., Americus, Ga., 1989, Paralyzed Vet. of Am., Boston, 1989, Hunger Project, San Francisco, 1985-87. Office: For the Health of It PO Box 1624 Coeur d'Alene ID 83814-1624

BYRD, HARRIETT ELIZABETH, state legislator; b. Cheyenne, Wyo., Apr. 20, 1926; d. Robert C. Rhone and Sudie E. Smith; m. James W. Byrd; children: Robert C., James W. II, Linda C. BS in Edn., W.Va. State Coll., 1949; MEd, U. Wyo., 1977. Former elem. sch. tchr. Sch. Dist. 1 City of Cheyenne; state rep. State of Wyo., from 1981, state senator, 1989—; del. Dem. Nat. Conv., 1980, alt. del., 1984. Bd. dirs. Laramie County Sr. Citizens; adv. bd. U. Wyo. Pub. Radio-Sta. KUWR. Mem. LWV, Dem. Women's Club., Altrusa Internat., Inc. (pres. Cheyenne chpt. 1974-75), Wyo. Wildlife Fedn., Kappa Delta Pi, Delta Kappa Gamma. Roman Catholic. Home: 6400 Antelope Ave Cheyenne WY 82009*

BYRD, JOANN KATHLEEN, newspaper editor; b. Baker, Oreg., Jan. 5, 1943; d. Joe Bryant and Anne Bradford (Dickson) Green; m. James Douglas Byrd, Mar. 11, 1978 (dec. 1988); 1 child by previous marriage: Drew Joseph Gibbs. BS in Journalism, U. Oreg., 1964. Student reporter East Oregonian, Pendleton, 1956-64; reporter Spokane Daily Chronicle, 1964-69, 72-74, asst. city editor, 1974-78; city editor The Herald, Everett, Wash., 1978-81, mng. editor, 1981, exec. editor, 1981—; bd. dirs. New Directions for News, 1987—; juror 1988, 89, Pulitzer prizes. Bd. visitors John S. Knight Fellowships, Stanford U., 1983-84, program com., 1984—; continuing studies chmn. Wash. AP News Execs., 1984-85, v.p. 1986-87, pres. 1987-88; judge Ernie Pyle awards, 1984. Fellow Gannett Ctr. for Media Studies Columbia U. 1989. Mem. Am. Soc. Newspaper Editors, Am. Press Inst., Women in Communications, Soc. of Profl. Journalists, Sigma Delta Chi. Home: 7930 53d Ave W #203 Mukilteo WA 98275 Office: The Herald Grand and California Sts Everett WA 98206

BYRD, KATHLEEN MARY, state archeologist; b. Stamford, Conn., Feb. 2, 1949; s. Daniel Lester and Catherine Ruth (Byrne) Byrd; m. Robert Walter Neuman, May 4, 1980. B.A., Marquette U., 1971; M.A., La. State U., 1974; Ph.D., U. Fla., 1976. Archaeol. and zooarchaeol. cons. Baton Rouge, 1976-78; archaeologist II, State of La., Baton Rouge, 1978-79, state archaeologist, 1979—. Contbr. articles to profl. jours. Mem. La. Archaeol. Survey & Antiquities Commn., 1979—. Mem. Soc. Am. Archaeology, Soc. for Hist. Archaeology, La. Archaeol. Soc., Sigma Xi.*

BYRD, MARY LAAGER, life science researcher; b. N.Y.C., Apr. 7, 1935; d. Creston Frederick Laager and Mary King (Poteat) Lindgren; m. Mark Willard Byrd, Dec. 17, 1954 (div. Apr. 1967); children: Carolyn Byrd Hill, Christopher M., Cynthia Byrd Becker. Student, U. Pa., 1952-55, U. Madrid, Spain, 1964-65, Mitchell Coll., 1965-66. Researcher Zool. Soc., San Diego, Calif., 1974-87; researcher Found. for Endangered Animals, La Jolla, Calif., 1985—, also bd. dirs., sec./treas., 1985—; cons. South Fla. Aguaculture, Florida City, 1989—; cons. Save the Manatee, Orlando, Fla., 1990. Editor: One Medicine, 1984; contbr. articles to profl. jours. Active Fla. Keys Land Trust, Marathon, 1989—. Recipient grant Zool. Soc. of San Diego, Chaco, Paraguay, 1985-90. Mem. The Nature Conservancy, Zool. Soc. of San Diego, Found. Moises Bertoni de Paraguay, Key Largo Sailing Club. Republican. Home: 1924 Stancel Dr Clearwater FL 34624 Office: South Fla Aquaculture 40801 SW 232nd Ave Florida City FL 33034

BYRD, MICHAELE ABNER, computer software company executive; b. Bklyn., June 22, 1949; d. Philip Russell and Yvonne Edythe (Dixon) Abner; student U. Pa., 1966-68, Marymount Coll., 1968-69; B.A., U. Pa., 1971; m. David Caulbert Byrd, III, July 24, 1976. Mktg. support rep. IBM, Washington, 1971-74, mktg. support rep. staff instr., Dallas, 1974-78, mktg. support mgr., McLean, Va., 1978-79, adminstrv. systems ops. mgr., Gaithersburg, Md., 1979-81, mktg. support rep. sch. tng. mgr., Dallas, 1981-82, office systems edn. specialist, 1982-84; info. systems mktg. cons., Bethesda, Md., 1984-85; nat. tng. mgr. Temporaries, Inc., Washington, 1985-88; owner, pres. Software Edn., Inc., Silver Spring, 1988—. Mem. adv. com. Hannah Harrison Career Sch.; bus. edn. adv. com. D.C. Pub. Schs. Mem. NAFE, Nat. Assn. Profl. Saleswomen, Nat. Assn. Women Bus. Owners. Office: 5523 Englishman Pl Rockville MD 20852-4657

BYRD, SANDRA JUDITH, payroll executive; b. Detroit, July 14, 1960; d. Brian Kenneth and Ruth (Jocius) Paukstys; m. Michael Keith Byrd, Nov. 23, 1985; 1 child, Kristin Michelle. Student, So. Ill. U., 1979-84. Asst. mgr. Colony West Swim Club, 1979, mgr., summers, 1980-82; aquatic supr. So. Ill. U., Carbondale, 1982; asst. mgr. Body Shop, Vero Beach, Fla., 1984; office mgr. Insta-Med Clinics, Inc., Vero Beach, 1984; receptionist Redgate Communications Corp., Vero Beach, 1985, circulation asst., 1985-87, circulation mgr., 1987-88; circulation dir. TT Pubs., Inc., Longwood, Fla., 1988-89; supr. of nursing payroll Orlando (Fla.) Regional Med. Ctr., 1989—; bus. mgr. Treasure Coast Diagnostics, Inc., 1987-88. Ill. State scholar, 1979-82. Mem. NAFE. Home: 1013 Pond Apple Ct Oviedo FL 32765 Office: Orlando Regional Med Ctr 1414 S Kohl Ave Orlando FL 32806

BYRD, SUE GIBSON, fashion merchandising educator; b. Loudon, Tenn., June 19, 1953; d. Henry Eugene and Carrie Lou (Simpson) Gibson; m. Robert Glen Byrd, Dec. 23, 1983; 1 child, Martha Marie. BS in Fashion Merchandising, U. Tenn., 1974, MS in Extension Edn., 1975, PhD in Human Ecology, 1986. Cert. home economist, Tenn. Extension agt. Tenn. Extension Svc., Jacksboro, 1975-81, Dunlap, 1981-84; grad. teaching asst. U. Tenn., Knoxville, 1984-86, lectr., 1987; asst. prof. fashion merchandising U. Tenn., Martin, 1987—. Mem. planning com. West Tenn. Revitalization Conf., Martin, 1988; fashion judge Obion County Extension Svc., Union City, Tenn., 1988, 89, 90. Sadie Katherine Stanton scholar and Ida A. Anders scholar U. Tenn., Knoxville, 1986; grantee U. Tenn., Martin, 1988, 89. Mem. Am. Home Econs. Assn., Tenn. Home Econs. Assn. (state bd. dirs. 1988-90, chmn.-elect dist. 1 1988-89, chmn. 1989-90), Assn. Coll. Profs. Textiles and Clothing, Tenn. Assn. Extension Home Econs. (dist. bd. dirs. 1983), Gamma Sigma Delta, Omicron Nu. Presbyterian. Home: 109 Park St Martin TN 38237 Office: U Tenn 340 Gooch Hall Martin TN 38238

BYRNE, GAYLE ELIZABETH, foundation administrator; b. Medford, Oreg., July 6, 1939; d. Walter Lewis and Naomi Mary (Fraley) Childress; m. James Robert Smith, July 4, 1970 (div. 1981); m. Michael Edward Byrne, Apr. 3, 1982; 1 child, Natalie Susan. BS, U. Oreg., 1971, MS, 1973. Dir. Neighborhood Youth Corps, Eugene, Oreg., 1967-68; grad. tchr. U. Oreg., Eugene, 1972-73; coord. Crisis Clinic, Mary Bridge Children's Hosp., Tacoma, Wash., 1974-75; coun. U. Hawaii, Honolulu, 1975-76; rehab. dir. So. Oreg. Goodwill, Medford, Oreg., 1977-80; pres. So. Oreg. Goodwill, Medford, 1981—; treas of bd. Oreg. Assn. Rehab. Facilities, Salem, Oreg., 1984-86; pres. of bd. Living Opportunities, Medford, 1985-88; bd. dirs. Am. Red. Cross, Medford, 1986. Adv. com. Dept. of Vocat. Rehab., Salem, 1984—. Mem. Nat. Rehab. Assn., Medford Rogue Rotary. Democrat. Office: So Oreg Goodwill Ind 604 N Fir Medford OR 97501

BYRNE, VIRGINIA MARIE, clothing executive; b. Southfield, Mich., Jan. 13, 1967; d. Howard Edmund Jr. and Mary Ellen (Crusoe) B. BA in Fashion and Bus. Adminstrn., Siena Heights Coll., 1989. Mktg. rsch. assoc. Opinion Search, Southfield, Mich., 1988-89; asst. to pres. Profl. Image, Ltd., Chgo., 1989—. Mem. Children Am. Revolution (past 2d v.p. Mich. chpt.), Phi Sigma Sigma (pres. Adrian, Mich. chpt. 1988-89). Republican. Roman Catholic. Home: 625 W Wrightwood Apt 414 Chicago IL 60614 Office: Profl Image Ltd 221 E Cullerton Chicago IL 60616

BYRON, BEVERLY BUTCHER, congresswoman; b. Balt., July 27, 1932; d. Harry C. and Ruth Butcher; m. Goodloe E. Byron, 1952 (dec.); children: Goodloe E. Jr., Barton Kimball, Mary McComas; m. B. Kirk Walsh, 1986. Student, Hood Coll., 1962-64. Mem. 96th-102nd Congresses from 6th Md. Dist., 1979—; mem. armed services com., chmn. subcom. on military personnel and compensation. State treas. Md. Young Democrats, 1962, 65; bd. assocs. Hood Coll.; bd. visitors U.S. Air Force Acad., 1980-87; trustee. St. Mary's Coll.; bd. dirs. Frederick County chpt. ARC; sec. Frederick Heart Assn., 1974-79; mem. Frederick Phys. Fitness Commn.; chmn. Md. Phys. Fitness Commn., 1979-89; mem. Frederick County Landmarks Found.; bd. dirs. Am. Hiking Soc. Episcopalian. Home: 306 Grove Blvd Frederick MD 21701 Office: 2430 Rayburn House Office Bldg Washington DC 20515

BYRON, SISTER MICHAEA, college president; b. Waseca, Minn., Aug. 7, 1927; d. Arthur and Marion (Burns) B. BS, Coll. St. Teresa, 1954; MS, Iowa State U., 1955; PhD, U. Minn., 1974. Tchr. St. Peter Sch., St. Paul, 1948-52; mem. faculty, chairperson dept. family life Coll. St. Teresa, Winona, Minn., 1955-85, pres., 1985—; mem. alumnae bd. St. Theresa's Coll.; mem. accreditation team for secondary schs., Minn. Mem. LWV, Tri-Coll./Tri-County Poverty Program, Winona Area Hospice Coalition, Community Meml. Hosp. Pastoral Team, Winona Sr. Citizens Advocacy Bd.; mem. exec. council Sisters of St. Francis; chmn. bd. trustees St. Anne's Hospice; mem. sponsorship bd. St. Mary's Hosp., Mayo Med. Ctr. Mem. Nat. Council Aging, Am. Gerontol. Soc., Nat. Council Family Relations, Am. Home Econ. Assn., Nat. Cath. Council Home Econs., Acad. Polit. and Social Scis., Minn. Home Econ. Assn., Minn. Home Econs. Tchr. Educators, Minn. Council on Family Relations, Winona County Home Economists, AAUW, Winona C. of C. (mem. higher edn. task force), Pi Gamma Mu, Omicron Mu, Phi Kappa Beta, Phi Lambda Theta. Roman Catholic. Office: Coll of St Teresa Winona MN 55987-0837

BYRUM-ELLERMAN, KAY FRANCES, certified financial planner; b. Dover, Ohio, Jan. 29, 1942; d. Charles Woodrow Stahl and Marjorie Augusta (Knight) Simonson; m. Ron Eugene Byrum, Mar. 12, 1968 (div. 1976); children: Karen Kay, Robert Allen; m. James Howard Ellerman, Oct. 13, 1984. Student, Cerritos Jr. Coll., 1959-61, Coll. for Fin. Planning, Denver, 1987—. Asst. to chmn., chief exec. officer Denny's, Inc., La Mirada, Calif., 1973-79; career agt. N.Y. Life Ins. Co., Fullerton, Calif., 1979-81; pres. Fin. Svcs. Unltd., Inc., Laguna Hills, Calif., 1981—, Newport Beach, Calif., 1989—; seminar speaker Fin. Svcs. Unltd., Inc., Laguna Hills, 1982—. Bd. dirs. YWCA, Santa Ana, Calif., 1986—. Named Orange County Woman of Excellence Woman's World Internat., 1985. Mem. Internat. Assn. Fin. Planners, WeCan Club (pres. 1987—), Women in Bus. Club (bd. dirs. 1984-86), Cert. Fin. Planners Assn. (cert.). Republican. Home: 2175 Via Teca San Clemente CA 92672 Office: Fin Svcs Unltd Inc 24411 Ridge Rt Ste 220 Laguna Hills CA 92653

BYSIEWICZ, SHIRLEY RAISSI, lawyer, educator; b. Enfield, Conn.; d. Kyriakos and Anna (Gavala) Raissi; m. Stanley J. Bysiewicz, July 18, 1959; children: Susan, Walter John, Karen, Gail. B.A., J.D., M.S. in L.S. U. Conn. Bar: Conn. 1954. Mem. firm Raissi & Raissi, Enfield, 1954—; faculty U. Conn., West Hartford, 1956—; prof. law U. Conn., law librarian., 1956-83; Mem. Permanent Commn. on Status Women for Conn., 1976-80, pres., 1978-79; mem. Conn. Law Library Adv. Com., 1976—; mem. Conn. Law Revision Commn., 1980—, co-pres., 1987—; Superior Ct. referee; mem. Conn. Law Revision Commn., 1980—; founder Conn. Women's Edn. and Legal Fund. Author: (with Max White) Forms of Town Government in Connecticut, 1954, Survey of County Law Libraries in Connecticut, 1967, Dictionary of Legal Terms, 1983, Selected Annotated Bibliography on Education for Professional Responsibility, 1968, (with Weckstein) Effective Legal Research, 1979; bus. mgr.: Law Library Jour, 1968-72; editor: Connecticut Juvenile Law Handbook, 1985, Sources of Conneticut Law, 1987; co-editor: (with Whitman) Materials on Estate Planning, 1969. Contbr. law articles to profl. jours. Mem. Bar Assn. Conn. (treas. 1975-78), Nat. Assn. Women Lawyers, ABA, Hartford County Bar Assn. (exec. com.), Conn. Bar Assn. (presider juvenile justice coms. 1982-85, women lawyers sect.), Am. Assn. Law Schs. (co-presider sect. on status of women, sect. legal research 1974), Am. Assn. Law Librarians (law library jour. com., sec. 1980-83), U. Conn. Law Sch. Alumni Assn. (exec. sec. 1958-68), New Eng. Law Librarians (pres. 1970), Women's Equity Action League, Delta Zeta. Greek Orthodox. Home: S Plumb Rd Middletown CT 06457 Office: 65 Elizabeth St Hartford CT 06105

BYWATERS, CANDACE LEAH, oil and gas company executive; b. Omaha, Aug. 29, 1947; d. John Lawrence and Virginia Marie (Barton) Trapp; m. Emil Jean Fullmer, Oct. 10, 1975 (dec. Mar. 1979); m. Lloyd Edward Bywaters Sr., Aug. 31, 1979; children: Carey Ann, Toby Barton. Student, Upper Iowa U., 1978-83. Various acctg. and adminstrv. positions Enron Corp., Omaha, 1965-80; dir. contracts Enron Gas Processing Co., Houston, 1980—. Pres. Henry W. Yates Elem. Sch. PTA, Omaha, 1982-84; bd. dirs. Dundee Elem. Sch. PTO, 1984-85. Mem. Natural Gas Assn. Houston, Tex. Mid-Continent Oil and Gas Assn. Libertarian. Roman Catholic. Home: 15519 Pebble Bend Dr Houston TX 77068

CABANAS, ELIZABETH ANN, food service administration executive; b. Port Arthur, Tex., Oct. 27, 1948; d. William Rosser and Frances Merle (Block) Thornton. BS, U. Tex., 1971; MPH, U. Hawaii, 1973. Registered dietitian. Clin. nutritionist Family Planning Inst., Honolulu, 1972-74; dietitian Kauikeolani Hosp., Honolulu, 1974-75; dietitian San Antonio Ind. Schs., 1975-84, asst. food service adminstr., 1984-89; coord. equipment and facilities Dallas Ind. Sch., 1990—; lectr. nutrition U. Hawaii, Honolulu, 1974-75; lectr. St. Mary's U., San Antonio Coll., 1984—; cons. dietitian, 1980—. Contbr. articles to profl. jours. Mem. Allegro San Antonio Symphony Orch., 1984—, Texans for Barerra, San Antonio, 1986. Mem. Assn. Sch. Bus. Officials Internat., Nutrition and Food Svc. Mgmt. Com., Am. Dietetic Assn., Am. Sch. Food Service Assn., Tex. Sch. Food Service Assn. (dist. bd. dirs. 1977-78), San Antonio Sch. Food Service Assn. (com. chmn. 1975—), Tex. Assn. Sch. Bus. Ofcls., Tex. Restaurant Assn., San Antonio Area Food Svc. Adminstrs. Assn. (pres. 1989—), Assn. Profls. in Positions Leaderships and Edn., San Antonio Mus. Assn., Randolph C. of C. Republican. Methodist. Clubs: Hawaii (chmn. entertainment com. 1983), Los Amigos Ski (San Antonio). Home: 8745 Southwestern Blvd #110 Dallas TX 75206 Office: Dallas Ind Sch Dist Dallas TX 75204

CABELL, ELIZABETH ARLISSE, psychologist; b. Bryan, Tex., Apr. 14, 1947; d. John David Kernodle and Jeanne Forrest (McCluer) Dabbs; m. Kent E. Johnson, Dec. 23, 1967 (div. May 1972); m. Donald Allen Cabell, May 19, 1978; children: Ryan, Andrew. BA with honors, U. Tex., 1968; MA, U. Colo., 1973, PhD, 1977. Cert. sch. psychologist. Vocat. trainer Mary Lee Sch. Spl. Edn., Austin, Tex., 1968-69; employment counselor Colo. Div. Employment, Denver, 1971-73; sch. psychologist Aurora (Colo.) Mental Health Ctr./Aurora Pub. Schs., 1974-76, Douglas County Schs., Castle Rock, Colo., 1976-77, Jefferson County Schs., Lakewood, Colo., 1977-80, Denver Pub. Schs., 1980-82; coord. spl. learning support program/learning disabled adult Community Coll. of Denver, 1983-89; sch. psychologist Denver Pub. Schs., 1990—; mem. faculty part-time Met. State Coll., Denver, 1984-86; mem. grad. faculty part-time U. Colo., Denver, 1977-81, 86—; presenter in field. Mem. parent adv. coun. Logan Sch. for Creative Learning, 1987-89. U.S. Dept. Edn. grantee, 1987-89. Mem. Am. Psychol. Assn., Nat. Assn. Sch. Psychologists, Coll. Reading and Learning Assn., Coun. for Learning Disabilities, Colo. Assn. for Gifted and Talented. Democrat. Home: 3930 S Wabash St Denver CO 80237 Office: Denver CO 80204

CABILLONAR, MARGO NAOMI, infosystems specialist; b. Summit, N.J., June 19, 1941; d. Egmedio Lachica and Grazia (Catanio) C.; m. Gregory S. Toffic (div. Dec. 1975). BA, Rutgers U., 1963; student, Chubb Inst. Computer Tech., 1976. Statis. clk. Bankers Trust Co., N.Y.C., 1963-64; with Sherbourne Corp., Killington, Vt., 1964-65; programmer Clary Datacomp Systems, San Gabiel, Calif., 1966-69, Monroe div. Litton Corp., Morris Plains, N.J., 1970-73, Symbolic Systems, Summit, N.J., 1974-75, 1st Nat. Bank, Totowa, N.J., 1976-77, Bencom-Beneficial Mgmt. Corp., Morristown, N.J., 1977-78; sr. systems analyst TWA, Kansas City, Mo., 1978-87; sr. programmer analyst Pars Svcs. Partnership, Kansas City, 1987—. Adv. Jr. Achievement, Kansas City, 1981-83; treas. Springs Homeowners Assn., Kansas City, 1987—. Roman Catholic. Home: 4914 NW Barry Rd Kansas City MO 64154 Office: Pars Svcs Partnership 7300 Tiffany Springs Rd 26D Kansas City MO 64153

CABLE, CAROLE LAW-GAGNON, university development officer; b. New Orleans, Jan. 21, 1944; d. Stewart Paul and Mary Jean (Law) Gagnon; m. Thomas Monroe Cable, Sept. 1, 1966; 1 child, Amory Law Cable. BA, Tulane U., 1965; MA, U. Ill., 1972; MLS, U. Tex., 1968, PhD, 1983. Head architecture libr. U. Tex., Austin, 1977-79; head fine arts library U. Tex., 1979-88, devel. officer, 1988—. Contbr. articles to Book Collector, Library Quar., Art Documentation, Research Strategies. Mem. Austin Lyric Opera Guild, 1987—, Planned Parenthood, 1989—. Mem. Art Libraries Soc./N. Am. (chair Texas chpt. 1976-77, nat. chair membership com. 1983), Book Club Tex. Democrat. Episcopalian. Home: 902 Live Oak Ridge Austin TX 78746 Office: U of Texas Gen Librs Austin TX 78713-7330

CABRAL, ELIZABETH BARBARA, management consultant; b. Oxnard, Calif., Nov. 25, 1964; d. Chuck Michael and Barbara Elizabeth (DeSoto) C. BA/Broadcast Journalism Mgmt./Polit. Sci, U. So. Calif., 1986. Community rels. Office of the President U. So. Calif., L.A., 1985-86; employment specialist Job Tng. Office City of Oxnard, 1982-86; advt. coord. Petoseed Corp., Ventura, Calif., 1986-87; cons. Fontaine, Quintanilla and Assocs., Oxnard, 1987—; project dir. On The Job Tng. Program, Santa Barbara, Calif., 1989—; govt. mktg. cons. Cabral & Assocs., Ventura, 1989—. Author bus. plans and govt. proposals in field. Bd. dirs. Tri-County Purchasing Outreach Network, Santa Barbara, 1988—. Recipient merit scholarship, U. So. Calif., 1982, J.M. Meml. scholarship, 1986. Mem. Oxnard C. of C. Roman Catholic. Office: Fontaine Quintanilla & Assocs 451 W 5th St Oxnard CA 93030

CABRAL, JUDITH ANN, telecommunications executive; b. London, Aug. 15, 1951; came to U.S., 1953; d. Frank and Evelyn Joy (Blanchard) C. BA, Salisbury State U., 1973; MEd, Bowie State U., 1979. Cert. elem. sch. educator, voice mail system adminstr. Elem. educator Anne Arundel County Pub. Schs., Annapolis, Md., 1973; adminstr. U.S. Naval Inst., Annapolis, 1973-78; project mgr. Associated Enterprises, Inc., Annapolis, 1980-85, dir. Tel. media and voice processing, 1985—; speaker in field. Contbg. author: Business Ownership for People With Disabilities, 1984. Contbr. various articles to profl. jours. Author Legislation Chpt. 650 and 675 Laws of Md., 1983; task force rep. Md. Investment in Job Opportunities Program, 1986. Recipient Cert. of Appreciation Archdiocese of Balt., 1989. Mem. NAFE, Am. Mgmt. Assn., Voice Mail Assn. Europe, Info. Industries Assn. Roman Catholic. Office: AEI TeleSonic 120 Admiral Cochrane Dr Annapolis MD 21401

CABRINETY, PATRICIA BUTLER, software company executive; b. Earlville, N.Y., Sept. 4, 1932; d. Eugene Thomas and Helen Sylvester (Fulmer) Butler; m. Lawrence Paul Cabrinety, Aug. 20, 1955; children: Linda Anne, Margaret Marie, Stephen Michael. BS in Elem. Edn. and Music, SUNY, Potsdam, 1954. Cert. tchr. N.Y., Pa., Minn., Mass. Asst. tchr. music Hamilton (N.Y.) Cen. Sch., 1948-50; tchr. Cherry Lane Sch., Suffern, N.Y., 1954-56; instr. music Towanda, Pa., 1960-63, Sayre, Pa., 1963-79; pres. Superior Software Inc., Mpls., 1981—, Mizen Products, Mpls., 1988—; poet and illustrator, Edina, Minn., 1981—; cons. in field. Composer, artist numerous compositions; inventor: Musical for Computer, 1981; author monthly column on Boy Scouts, 1975-78, also more than 101 pub. poems and 40 pub. illustrations; author: CHARIS series; composer of "Pauletter Fry" and "Mi Cazone"; creator of The Professional Writers' MAIL-IT Kit and Name in Notes. Recipient Golden Poet award World of Poetry, 1985-88, Poet of Month award All Season's Poetry, 1986, Vantage Press Invitational award, 1985-88, Poet of Month award Editor's Desk, 1986, Internat. Poet award, 1986. Mem. NAFE, AAUW, DAR, Am. Soc. Profl. and Exec. Women, Nat. Assn. Bus. and Profl. Women, Nat. Writers Assn., Am. Mgmt. Assn., Pioneers, Computer History Inst. for the Preservation of Software (bd. dirs.), Legion of Mary, Third Order Carmelite, Mpls. Music Tchrs. Forum, Edina C. of C., Worcester County Music Assn., Worcester County Poetry Assn. Home: 925 Pearl Hill Rd Fitchburg MA 01420

CACCAMISE, GENEVRA LOUISE BALL (MRS. ALFRED E. CACCAMISE), retired librarian; b. Mayville, N.Y., July 22, 1934; d. Herbert Oscar and Genevra (Green) Ball; m. Alfred E. Caccamise, July 7, 1974. BA, Stetson U., DeLand, Fla., 1956; MLS, Syracuse U., 1967. Tchr. grammar sch., Sanford, Fla., 1956-57, elem. sch., Longwood, Fla., 1957-58; tchr., libr. Enterprise (Fla.) Sch., 1958-63; libr., media specialist Boston Ave. Sch., DeLand, 1963-82; head media specialist Blue Lake Sch., DeLand, 1982-87, ret., 1987. Author Volusia County manual Instructing the Library Assistant, 1965. Charter mem. West Volusia Meml. Hosp. aux., DeLand, 1962—; leader Girl Scout U.S., 1955-56; area dir. Fla. Edn. Assn., Volusia county, 1963-65; bd. dirs. Alhambra Villas Home Owners Assn., 1972-75; trustee, pres., DeLand Pub. Library; v.p. Friends of DeLand Pub. Library, 1987, pres., 1989, 90; charter mem. Guild of the DeLand Mus. Art, v.p., 1990. Mem. AAUW (2d v.p. chpt. 1965-67, rec. sec. 1961-65, 78-80, pres. 1980-82, parliamentarian 1982-84), Assn. Childhood Edn. (1st v.p. 1965-66, corr. sec. 1963-65), DAR (chpt. registrar 1969—, asst. chief page Continental Congress, Washington 1962-65), Fla. Libr. Assn., Bus. & Profl. Women's Club (corr. sec. DeLand 1968-71, 2d v.p. 1969-70), Stetson U. Alumni Assn. (class chmn. for ann. fund drive 1968), Volusia County Assn. Media in Edn. (treas.), Volusia County Retired Educators Assn. (pres. Unit II 1988-90), Soc. of Mayflower Descendants (lt. gov. Francis Cook Colony 1988-90), Pilgrim John Howland Soc., Colonial Dames XVII Century, Magna Charta Dames, Nat. Soc. New Eng. Women (v.p. Daytona Beach Colony 1990—), Hibiscus Garden Circle (treas. 1988-89, v.p. Daytona Beach Colony 1990—), Delta Kappa Gamma (pres. Beta Psi chpt.), Nat. Soc. of U.S. Daus. of 1812. (rec. sec. Peacock chpt. 1989-90). Democrat. Episcopalian. Address: PO Box 241 De Land FL 32721

CADE, CHERYL A., trade association executive; b. El Paso, Tex., Nov. 15, 1946; d. Benjamin T. Jr. and Dorothy L. (Ruff) Baird; m. Robert M. Cade, Dec. 17, 1984; children: Cheryl Lynn, Thomas Wade, Jessica. Student, Tex. Western Coll., 1965, Durham Bus. Coll., El Paso, 1966, Florissant (Mo.) Valley Coll., 1977. Freelance exec. sec., bookkeeper Tettaton and Assocs., Dallas; sec. to chmn. Internat. Assn. Merger and Acquisition Cons., Dallas; adminstr. Internat. Assn. Merger and Acquisition Cons., Burr Ridge, Ill., also editor Intermac Network News. Home: 6307 Walnut Ave Downers Grove IL 60516 Office: Internat Assn Merger and Acquisition Cons 200 S Frontage Rd Ste 103 Burr Ridge IL 60521

CADLE, NANCY MASSEY, medical-surgical nurse; b. Oneida, Tenn., July 19, 1953; d. James Fenton and Erma (Phillips) Massey; 1 child, Treye. Diploma, St. Mary's Sch. Nursing, Knoxville, Tenn., 1974. RN, Tenn.; registered ACLS nurse. Nursing supr. Fentress County Gen. Hosp., Jamestown, Tenn.; supr. Scott County Hosp., Oneida. Mem. Am. Nurses Assn. Home: PO Box 83 Oneida TN 37841

CAESAR, SHIRLEY, gospel singer, evangelist; b. Durham, N.C., 1938; d. James and Hallie Caesar; m. Harold Williams, 1983. BSBA, Shaw U., 1984. Mem. gospel group Caravan, until 1966; formed gospel group The Caesar Singers, 1968; founder Shirley Caesar Outreach Ministries, Durham, 1968—. Albums include Love Parade, 1985, Christmasing, 1986, Her Very Best, 1987, Live in Chicago, 1988, I Remember Mama, 1989. Coun. mem. City of Durham, from 1987. Recipient Grammy awards NARAS, 1971, 80, 84, 85, Image Achievement award NAACP, 1985, 87; named to Gospel Hall of Fame. Office: Shirley Caesar Outreach Mins PO Box 3336 Durham NC 27702*

CAFFERATA, PATRICIA ANN, advertising executive; b. Smithville, Mo., Sept. 6, 1944; d. Jack and E. Agnes (Sims) Shepherd; m. D. Michael Cafferata, Mar. 27, 1976; 1 child, Diane L. BS in Home Econs. cum laude, N.W. Mo. State U., 1969. Research assoc. Barickman Advt., Kansas City, Mo., 1969-73; research assoc. Needham, Harper and Steers, Chgo., 1973-74, assoc. research dir., 1974-82, sr. v.p., research dir., 1982-87; pres., chief exec. officer Young and Rubicam, Chgo., 1987—. Mem. The Adv. Council J.L. Kellogg Grad. Sch. Mgmt. Northwestern U., Evanston, Ill., 1987, pres. council Museum Sci. and Industry, Chgo., 1987; bd. dirs. James Webb Young Fund U. Ill., 1987, Chgo. Area Council Boy Scouts Am., 1987, Mus. Broadcast Communicatins, Chgo., 1987. Named Woman of Yr., Women's Advt. Club Chgo., 1986. Mem. Am. Psychol. Assn., Am. Mktg. Assn., The Chgo. Network. Clubs: Chgo. Advt. (bd. dirs. 1986-87), Women's Advt., Econ. of Chgo. Office: Young & Rubicam Chgo 1 S Wacker Dr Ste 1800 Chicago IL 60606*

CAFFEY, DONAJEAN SMITH, educator; b. Brady, Tex.; d. Aubrey Eugene and Alice Bertha (Williams) Smith; m. William Stewart Caffey, July 20, 1963; children: Shana, Terri, Michael. BS, Howard Payne U., Brownwood, Tex., 1964; MEd, Tarleton State U., Stephenville, Tex., 1978. Cert. lang.-learning disability tchr., reading supr., Tex. Prin. Comanche Primary Sch.; tchr. lang. arts Sidney (Tex.) Schs.; elem. tchr. reading Comanche (Tex.) Sch. Dist. Mem. Classroom Tchrs. Assn. (pres.), Delta Kappa Gamma. Home: Rte 5 Box 38C Comanche TX 76442

CAFFIE, BARBARA JEAN, community relations specialist, consultant; b. Ohio, Jan. 8, 1938; d. Jacob and Flossie (Sutton) Richardson; m. Linell R. Hollins, Aug., 1956 (div. Jan. 1960); children: Brian Justin, Lori Linell C.; m. Jacob R. Caffie, Jan. 25, 1964 (div.); children: Douglas, Jacob R. Student, Baldwin Wallace Coll., 1987-88. With Ea. Greyhound Lines, Cleve., 1960-68, Ohio Civil Rights Commn., Cleve., 1968-69; reporter, producer, host Sta. WJW-TV, Cleve., 1969-77; dir. communications CETA program City of Cleve., 1977-81; pub. info. officer Coun. for Econ. Opportunity, Cleve., 1981-83; pub. rels. specialist, interviewer Cuyahoga Metro Housing Authority, Cleve., 1983-87; asst. mktg. mgr. St. Clair Mgmt. Galleria, Cleve., 1987-88; dir. community affairs North Coast Cable, Cleve., 1989-90; coord. community affairs Cleve. Regional Transit Authority, 1990—; pvt. practice cons., Berea, Ohio, 1990—. Vol. Am. Cancer Soc., Cleve., 1990—, United Negro Coll. Fund, Cleve., 1990—, Project Friendship, Cleve., 1990—, Berae Adv. Cable Commn., 1990—. Recipient Vol. award Forrest City Hosp. Assn., 1973, Cleve. Bd. of Edn., 1976, Nat. Assn. Bus. and Profl. Women, 1975, J.F.K. Alumni Assn., 1976, Am. Cancer Soc., 1977. Baptist. Office: Greater Cleve Transit 615 Superior Ave NW Cleveland OH 44113

CAFINI, REGENIA DAYREE, federal administrator; b. Fayetteville, N.C., Aug. 16, 1962; d. Edward L. and Mary E. (Davis) C. Student, George Mason U., 1985. CPA; cert. mgmt. acct. Staff investigator com. on appropriations U.S. Ho. Reps., Washington; fin. specialist FSLIC, Washington; svc. rep. C&P Telephone Co., Arlington, Va. Mem. Nat. Assn. Accts. (dir. CMA programs, Rookie of Yr. 1989), Phi Theta Kappa.

CAGGINE, CAROLYN CASSANDRA, publishing executive; b. Bklyn., Nov. 12, 1932; d. Charles Cosmo and Rose Louise (Daversa) C. BA cum laude, St. John's U., Jamaica, N.Y., 1954. Reprint editor Prentice-Hall, Inc., Englewood Cliffs, N.J., 1954-58; asst. editor Dun & Bradstreet, Inc., N.Y.C., 1958-59; mng. editor Promenade Mags., Inc., N.Y.C., 1959-70; dir. publs. and graphics Girl Scouts U.S.A., N.Y.C., 1970-88, 1988—, editor-in-chief, 1984-88, editor in chief, 1989—. Democrat. Roman Catholic. Office: Girl Scouts USA 830 Third Ave New York NY 10022

CAGGINS, RUTH PORTER, nurse, educator; b. Natchez, Miss., July 11, 1945; d. Henry Chappelle and Corinne Sadie (Baines) Porter; m. Don Randolph Caggins, July 1, 1978; children: Elva Rene, Don Randolph, Myles Thomas Chapelle. BS, Dillard U., New Orleans, 1967; MA, NYU, 1973; doctoral candidate Tex. Woman's U., 1987—. Staff nurse Montefiore Hosp., Bronx, 1968-70, head nurse, 1970-72; nurse clinician Met. Hosp., N.Y.C., 1973-74, clin. supr., 1974-76; asst. prof. U. So. La., Lafayette, 1976-78; assoc. prof. Prairie View A&M U. Coll. Nursing, Houston, 1978—. Mem., The Links Inc., Houston, 1982—, Cultural Arts Coun., Houston. Mem. Am. Nurses Assn. (clin. ethnic/racial minority fellow 1989-90), Am. Group Psychology Assn., A.K. Rice Inst., Houston Group Psychotherapy Soc., Sigma Theta Tau, Delta Sigma Theta. Democrat. Baptist. Avocations: singing, sewing, traveling, aerobics, writing. Home: 5602 Goettee Circle Houston TX 77091 Office: Prairie View A&M U Coll Nursing 6436 Fannin Houston TX 77030

CAGLE, DIANE DAY, county official; b. Greenville, S.C., Jan. 29, 1946; d. Ivey Edward and Carrie (Gossett) Day; m. Allan Bill Cagle, Apr. 17, 1971; 1 child, Allan Ivey. Student, Draughon's Bus. Coll., Greenville, 1966. Sec. Indian Head Yarn Co., Greenville, 1964-69; v.p., sec. Dixie Iron & Metal Co., Greenville, 1969-84; chief magistrate Greenville County, 1984—. Mem. S.C. Magistrtaes Assn., Westcliff Community Club, Greenville Profl. Women, S.C. Numismatic Assn. Baptist. Club: Greenville Coin. Home: 521 Westcliffe Way Greenville SC 29611 Office: Greenville County Magistrate's Office 6247 White Horse Rd Greenville SC 29611

CAHILL, LISA SOWLE, educator, author, lecturer; b. Phila., Mar. 27, 1948; d. Donald Edgar and Gretchen Elizabeth (MacRae) Sowle; m. Lawrence R. Cahill, Mar. 25, 1972; children: Charlotte Mary, James Donald, Donald Robert, William MacRae. B.A., U. Santa Clara, 1970; M.A., U. Chgo., 1973, Ph.D., 1976. Instr., Concordia Coll., Moorhead, Minn., 1976; asst. prof. theology Boston Coll., Chestnut Hill, 1976-82, assoc. prof. theology, 1982-89, prof. theology, 1989—; vis. scholar Kennedy Inst. Ethics Georgetown U., fall 1986. Author: Between the Sexes: Toward a Christian Ethics of Sexuality, 1985, (with Thomas A. Shannon) Religion and Artificial Reproduction: An Inquiry into the Vatican Instruction, 1988; contbr. articles to profl. jours.; assoc. editor Religious Studies Rev., 1981—, Jour. Religious Ethics, 1981—, Jour. Medicine and Philosophy, 1989—, Concillium, 1989—; adv. bd. Logos: Philos. Issues in Christian Perspective, Jour. of Law and Religion, 1983—, Interpretation, 1989—; assoc. editor Horizons: A Publ. of the Coll. Theology Soc., 1983—; mem. editorial bd., bd. dirs. Jour. Religion and Philosophy. Active Instnl. Rev. Bd. Harvard Community Health Plan, 1979-85; mem. bioethics com. March of Dimes, 1985—; mem. theology and ethics com. Cath. Hosp. Assn., 1985—. Boston Coll. Summer Rsch. grantee, 1977; Faculty fellow, 1986. Mem. Am. Acad. Religion (program com. 1979-82), Soc. Christian Ethics (dir. 1983-86). Cath. Theol. Soc. Am. (moral theology steering com. 1984-87), Coll. Theology Soc. Democrat. Office: Boston Coll Dept Theology Chestnut Hill MA 02167

CAHILL, PAMELA LEE, state legislator; b. Belfast, Maine, Apr. 22, 1953; d. B.D. and Catherine (Snow) Sanborn; m. Bradley W. Cahill; children: Veronica Lynn, Brandon. Student, U. Maine. Former mem. Maine Ho. of Reps.; mem. Maine State Senate. Exec. dir. Reagan-Bush campaign, Maine, 1984. Republican. Office: Maine State Senate State House Sta 3 Augusta ME 04330*

CAHILL, PHYLLIS HENDERSON, marketing executive, educator; b. Phila., Nov. 5, 1954; d. Phyllis Henderson Garofalo; m. Peter Joseph Cahill, Mar. 26, 1977 (div. June 1982). B.S. in Food Mktg., St. Joseph's Coll., Phila., 1976; postgrad., Carnegie Inst., 1982-83. Cert. instr. numerous Dale Carnegie courses. Account rep. Quaker Oats Co., Cranford, N.Y., 1976-77; mktg. mgr. Lumex, Inc., Bayshore, N.Y., 1978, Foodmaker, Inc., Hauppauge, N.Y., 1979, Yorkshire Food Sales, New Hyde Park, N.Y., 1980-84, CutCo Industries, Jericho, N.Y., 1984-86; mgr. advt. and sales promotion Nutri/System, Willow Grove, Pa., 1986—. Home: 333 Norris Hall Ln West Norriton PA 19403 Office: Nutri/System 3901 Commerce Ave Willow Grove PA 19090

CAHILL, ROSALIE MARIE, writer/publisher; b. N.Y.C., Oct. 11, 1923; d. Peter A. and Grace (Callahan) Saitta; m. James Q. Cahill, May 31, 1957; children: Joseph, Stephen, Christopher. BA, St. Joseph's Coll., Bklyn., 1940; MLS, Columbia U., 1941; postgrad., U. Dubuque, 1969-70. Asst. librarian Pace Coll., NYC, 1941-42, Equitable Life Assn. Soc., NYC, 1942-45; librarian Lenox Hill Hosp., NYC, 1945-52; chemistry, physics librarian Columbia U., NYC, 1952-58; freelance research writer NYC, 1959-67, Iowa, 1967-71; librarian Dubuque (Iowa) Pub. Sch. System, 1971-72, Clear Creek Dist. Sch. System, Iowa City, 1972-79; freelance research writer publisher, 1980--. Co.-mgr. West Br. Food Pantry, 1981—; mem. Citizens Adv. Bd. Iowa Dept. Human Svcs., 1981-84, Cedar (Iowa) Task Force on Needs of Mentally Retarded, 1983-85, Iowa Bd. of Examiner Nursing Home Adminstrs., 1985-88. Mem. AAUW (pres. Tipon chpt. 1989—), Iowa Farm Bur. Women (chmn. Cedar County div. 1986-88). Democrat. Roman Catholic. Home and Office: Rt 2 Box 92 West Branch IA 52358

CAICEDO, JUANA ESTHER, bank executive; b. Portoviejo, Ecuador, July 25, 1949; came to U.S., 1982; d. Miguel Felipe Caicedo Lamar and Orfa Cedeno. B in Econs., Catholic U., Guayaquil, Ecuador, 1974. Acctg. trainee Delloitte Haskins & Sells, N.Y.C., 1975-76; asst. mgr., sr. account officer Bank of Am., Guayaquil, 1976-80; gen. mgr. Asesores Financieros subs. Greyhound Leasing & Fin. Corp., Guayaquil, 1980-82; minister, counselor comml. affairs Ecuadorean Govt. Trade Office, N.Y.C., 1982-88; v.p., mgr. Cen. Bank of Ecuador, N.Y.C., 1986-88; v.p. Mfrs. Hanover World Trade Corp., N.Y.C., 1989—; mem. adv. bd. Cath. U. Sch. Econs., Guayaquil, 1971-74, instr. sources fin., 1979-80, instr. credit analysis Banking Sch., 1980-81. treas. Fundacion Para Pacientes Quemados, Guayaquil, 1979-82. Mem. Econs. Assn., Ecuadorean-Am. Assn. N.Y. (dir. 1984-88, v.p. 1988—), Pan Am. Soc. N.Y. (dir. 1985-88). Roman Catholic. Club: Guayaquil Tennis. Office: Mfrs Hanover World Trade Corp 270 Park Ave 8th Fl New York NY 10017

CAIN, CONSTANCE MARIE, advertising agency executive; b. Chgo., Feb. 5, 1955; d. Thomas Murchison and Mary Louise (Johnson) C. BJ, U. Mo., 1977. Art. dir. Bernard Hodes Advt., Chgo., 1977-78, Jordan/Tamraz/Caruso Advt., Chgo., 1978-79; owner, pres. Chrysalis Advt. & Design, Inc., Elmhurst, Ill., 1979—. Mem. Women Entrepreneurs of DuPage, Elmhurst C. of C., Leads Club (dir. 1987—, leader of yr. 1988). Democrat. Mem. United Ch. of Christ. Home: 653 Euclid Elmhurst IL 60126 Office: Chrysalis Advt 489D Spring Rd Elmhurst IL 60126

CAIN, DEBRA LYNN, social service administrator; b. El Paso, Tex., Apr. 23, 1954; d. George William Cain and Patricia Carole Freeman; m. Luther Blue Jr., Dec. 21, 1979; 1 child, Matthew Luther Blue. BS in Psychology, Iowa State U., 1977; M.S.A., Cen. Mich. U., 1989—. Program dir. Haven YWCA, Pontiac, Mich., 1977-82, exec. dir., 1977—; faculty Mich. Jud. Inst., Lansing, 1985—; chmn. Tri-County Coalition Against Domestic Violence, 1981-84; bd. dirs. S.E. Mich. Anti-Rape Network, Oakland County Coun. for Children at Risk. Pres. exec. coun. United Way, Oakland County, Mich., 1987-88; mem. PTA, Bloomfield Hills, Mich., 1986-88, West Bloomfield, 1988—; vol. Campaign for Judges, since 1984. Named Exec. of Yr. United Community Svcs., 1987. Mem. Am. Mktg. Assn., Nat. Assn. Female Execs., United Way Execs. Assn. (pres. 1987-88), S.E. Mich. Anti-Rape Network, Sexual Assault Info. Network, Mich. Coalition Against Domestic Violence (v.p., bd. dirs. Berkley chpt. 1978-89, treas. 1979—, spl. recognition 1989), Mich. Interdisciplinary Profl. Assn., Altrusa. Office: Haven 92 Whittemore Pontiac MI 48058

CAIN, GLORIA C, guidance counselor; b. Winston-Salem, N.C., July 11, 1950; m. Larry Cain, Jan. 2, 1972. BA, Winston-Salem State U., 1986; MS, N.C. A&T State U., 1988. Rsch. tchr., supervisory counselor, fin. aid counselor N.C. A&T State U., Greensboro; guidance counselor Winston-Salem State U. Recipient merit award Winston-Salem State U. Mem. Am. Assn. for Counseling and Devel., N.C. Assn. for Women Deans, Adminstrs.

and Counselors, N.C. Assn. Counseling and Devel., N.C. Coll. Pers. Assn., Pi Gamma Mu, Chi Sigma Iota. Home: PO Box 12204 Winston-Salem NC 27117

CAIN, KIMBERLY JUNE, sales executive; b. Austin, Tex., Nov. 26, 1961; d. Orvil Lee and Rosalie Mae (Kelln) Miller; m. Steven Allen Cain, July 26, 1980. Student, U. Tex., 1984; AA, North Harris County Coll., Houston, 1986; BS, U. Houston, Clear Lake, 1988. Receptionist Waggoner Carr, Atty. at Law, Austin, 1979-80; acct. Miller's Rest Home, Inc., Austin, 1976-80; with sales dept. Venus de Milo Health Club, Houston, 1984; substitute tchr. Clear Creek Ind. Sch. Dist., League City, Tex., 1988-89; exec. cons. Nat. Revenue Corp., Houston, 1989—, Houston Post, 1989—; cons. student bus. inst. SBA, Houston, 1988; sec., bd. dirs. Barton Heights Nursing Home, Houston. Vol. Lloyd Doggett for Senate, Austin, 1974. Recipient Area Merit award Vocat. Office Edn., 1980. Mem. Assn. for Promotion of Profl. Women, Phi Theta Kappa (pres. 1986). Lutheran.

CAIN, MADELINE ANN, state representative; b. Cleve., Nov. 21, 1949; d. Edward Vincent and Mary Rita (Quinn) C. BA, Ursuline Coll., 1973; MPA, Cleve. State U., 1985. Tchr. St. Augustine Acad., Lakewood, Ohio, 1973-75; clk. coun. legis. aide Lakewood City Coun., 1981-85; legis. liaison Cuyahoga County Bd. Commrs., Cleve., 1985-88; mem. Ohio Ho. of Reps., Columbus, 1989—. Mem. Community Devel. Block Grant Citizens Adv. Com., Human Svcs. Task Force, Lakewood Hosp. Adv. Com., Lakewood Citizens Fin. Adv. Com., Cuyahoga County Indigent Care Task Force. Mem. Lakewood Bus. and Profl. Women. Democrat. Roman Catholic. Home: 15555 Hilliard Rd Lakewood OH 44107 Office: Ohio Ho of Reps State House Columbus OH 43215

CAIN, MARCENA JEAN BEESLEY, retail store executive; b. Kingman, Kans., May 1, 1935; d. Albert Eugene and Stella Wanda (Ruthowski) Beesley; m. Kenneth B. Cain, Aug. 4, 1951; children—Kenneth Thomas, David Raymond. With AMVETS Thrift Stores, D.C., 1971—, asst. dir., 1971-87, exec. adminstr., 1987—, asst. dir. Amvets Value Village Thrift Stores, Balt.; ptnr. Bank St. Joint Venture Realty, Del-Mar Realty, Oakland Ctr. Partnership Ltd., 1987; pres. Family Thrift Ctr., Inc.; v.p. 4 corps. Mem. Bus. and Profl. Women's Club, Highlandtown Businessmen Assn., DAV Aux. (past nat. historian), PTA Valley Forge Mil. Acad. (D.C. area rep.), Highlandtown Mchts. Assn. (pres. 1983-84), Govanstown Mchts. Assn. (rec. sec.), Affiliated Mchts. Assn. Balt. (past pres.). Republican. Christian Scientist. Office: 3424 Eastern Ave Baltimore MD 21224

CAIN, PATRICIA JEAN, accountant; b. Decatur, Ill., Sept. 28, 1931; d. Paul George and Jean Margaret (Horne) Jacka; m. Dan Louis Cain, July 12, 1952; children: Mary Ann, Timothy George, Paul Louis. Student, U. Mich., 1949-52, Pasadena (Calif.) City Coll., 1975-76; BS in Acctg., Calif. State U., L.A., 1977, MBA, 1978; M in Taxation, Golden Gate U., Los Angeles, 1988. CPA, Calif.; cert. personal fin. planner; cert. advanced fin. planner. Tax supr. Stonefield & Josephson, L.A., 1979-87; chief fin. officer Loubella Extendables, Inc., L.A., 1987—; participant program in bus. ethics U. So. Calif., L.A., 1986; trainer for A-Plus in house tax Arthur Andersen & Co., 1989-90. Bd. dirs. Sierra Madre Girl Scout Coun., Pasadena, 1968-73, treas., 1973-75, elected nat. del., 1975; mem. Town Hall, L.A., 1987—. Listed as one of top six tax experts in L.A. by Money mag., 1987. Mem. AICPA (chairperson nat. tax teleconf. 1988), Am. Women's Soc. CPA's (bd. dirs. 1986-87, v.p. 1987-90), Calif. Soc. CPAs (chairperson free tax assistance program 1983-85, high rd. com. 1985-86, chairperson pub. rels. com. 1985-89, microcomputer users discussion group, taxation com., fin. com./speaker computer show and conf. 1987-89, planning com. and speaker San Francisco Tax and Microcomputer show 1988), Internat. Arabian Horse Assn., Beta Alpha Psi. Democrat. Episcopalian. Club: Wrightwood Country (Calif.). Home: 3715 Fairmeade Rd Pasadena CA 91107 Office: Loubella Extendables Inc 2222 S Figueroa St Los Angeles CA 90007

CAIN, RHONDA MAUREEN, small business owner; b. Grand Junction, Colo., Mar. 10, 1956; d. Stephen Donald Cain and Phyllis Ann (Eisenbeis) Skinner; m. Ted Emerson Hudgins, Jan. 31, 1975 (div. July 1978); 1 child, Rebekah Michelle. AA, Lane Community Coll., Eugene, Oreg., 1980. Legal sec. Heiman-Miller, Eugene, 1977-79, Thorp, Dennett, Purdy, Golden & Jewett, Springfield, Oreg., 1979-81, Clyde, Pratt, Gibbs & Cahoon, Salt Lake City, 1981-83; pvt. practice Eugene, 1983-86; legal sec. Wyman, Bautzer, Kuchel & Silbert, Irvine, Calif., 1986-88; owner Briefs a'La Carte, San Clemente, Calif., 1988—. Bd. dirs. Capistrano Unified Sch. Dist. Found.; rescue diver Profl. Assn. Diving Instrs., Santa Ana, 1988. Mem. San Clemente C. of C. (co-chairperson parade com., 1990, legis. action com., 1990, amigos, 1990, fiesta com. 1990). Republican. Office: Briefs a'La Carte 302 N El Camino Real Ste 209 San Clemente CA 92672

CAIN, RUTH, media relations coordinator, columnist; b. Detroit; d. Emil Walter and Lydia (Sanquist) Edstrom; m. Charles C. Cain III, Aug. 26, 1946 (dec. Sept. 1988); children: Nancy, Charles, Bradford, Christopher, Carol, Laura, Janice. BA, Wayne State U., 1945. Writer Detroit Bur. AP, 1945-46, Bus. Week, 1946-48; promotions writer Detroit Free Press, 1966-69; coor. media rels. Blue Cross/Blue Shield of Mich., Detroit, 1969—; sr. columnist Adams Pub. Co., Mt. Clemens, Mich., 1990—. Mem. Christian svc. com. St. Peter the Apostle Ch., Harper Woods, Mich., 1989—. Mem. AAUW, Women in Communications (pres. 1977-78, Headliner award 1983), Pub. Rels. Soc. Am., Cranbrook Writers Guild (bd. dirs. 1989—), Mich. Women's Hist. Ctr. and Hall of Fame (charter mem.), Detroit Press Club, Soc. Profl. Journalists. Roman Catholic. Home: 1066 Woodbridge Saint Clair Shores MI 48080 Office: Blue Cross/Blue Shield of Mich 600 Lafayette E Detroit MI 48226

CAINE, CAROL WHITACRE, business owner; b. Vandergrift, Pa., Mar. 14, 1925; d. Guy Alvin and Genevra Madeline (Lash) Whitacre; m. Charles Clyde Caine, Dec. 27, 1948; children: Christopher, Charles Lash. BS, Ohio State U., 1951. Part-time med. and x-ray technician Internal Medicine Lab., 1950-70; co-owner Transceiver Ctrs. of Columbus, Ohio, 1968-79, PIP Printing, Cheyenne, Wyo., 1981—. Mem. AAUW (bd. dirs. Cheyenne chpt. 1984-86), Wyo. Media Profls., Am. Soc. Radiol. Technologists, Am. Soc. Med. Tech., Nat. Fedn. Press Women, Zonta (bd. dirs. Cheyenne chpt. 1988—), Order of Eastern Star, Alpha Phi (life). Home: 3304 Sunrise Hills Dr Cheyenne WY 82009 Office: PIP Printing 1718 Capitol Ave Cheyenne WY 82001

CAIRNS, MARION GRACE HUEY, state legislator; b. Sparta, Ill., June 8, 1928; d. Frank McClellan and Pertie (Boyington) Huey; m. Donald F. Cairns, Sept. 2, 1950; 1 child, Douglas Scott. BA, Monmouth Coll., 1950; LLD (hon.), Webster U., 1989. Prin. Ellis Grove (Ill.) Elem. Sch., 1951-52; tchr. Nebr. High Sch., Falls City, 1952-54; layout designer Hallmark Corp., Kansas City, Mo., 1954-55; instr. evening sch. Washington U., St. Louis, 1959; substitute tchr. Webster Groves (Mo.) High Sch., 1960-66; instr. Hickey Bus. Sch., St. Louis, 1966-70; state legislator State of Mo., Webster Groves, 1977—; adj. prof. Webster U., Webster Groves, 1978—, adv. bd. to paralegal studies; mem. Children's Svcs. Commn., State of Mo., Jefferson City, 1980—; bd. dirs. Edgewood Children's Ctr., Webster Groves. Advocate crime victims Mo. Victim Assistance Network. Named Citizen of Yr., Webster Groves C. of C., 1984, Child Advocate of Yr. Mo. Child Care Assn., 1985, St. Louis Coun. Child Abuse and Neglect, 1987; recipient YWCA Women in Leadership award, 1989. Mem. Nat. Conf. State Legislators, Nat. Order Women Legislators, Nat. Fedn. Rep. Women. Presbyterian. Home: 17 E Swon Ave Webster Groves MO 63119 Office: State Capitol Bldg Webster Groves MO 65101

CAIRNS, ROBERTA ANNE ELIZABETH, librarian; b. Waltham, Mass., Feb. 1, 1945; d. Robert H. and Elizabeth F. (Peck) C. BA, Stonehill Coll., 1966; MS, U. R.I., 1969. Libr., Fiske Pub. Libr., Wrentham, Mass., 1966-71; dir. Barrington Pub. Libr. (R.I.), 1971-79; dir. libr. svcs. East Providence Pub. Libr. (R.I.), 1979—; producer, host East Providence Inside, 1984—. Author: History of St. Mary's Church, 1978. Bd. dirs. Am Cancer Soc., East Providence, 1983, Bradley Hosp., 1985; chairperson Citizens Adv. Commn. Cable TV, East Providence, 1983-88; coord. pub. rels. City of East Providence, 1985-88; mem. Cable TV Statewide Adv. Coun., 1984-85; mem. East Providence Vets. Meml. Com., 1985-87, Legis. Commn. on Funding of Librs., 1987-89. Named East Providence Woman of Yr., 1985, Women in Leadership award, 1988. Mem. ALA, East Providence Profl. Managerial and Tech. Employees Assn. (v.p. 1983-86), New Eng. Libr. Assn., R.I. Libr. Assn. (pres. 1986), Pub. Libr. Assn. (v.p., pres. elect mktg. of pub. libr. svcs. sect. 1990—), State Adv. Coun. on Librs., East Providence C. of C. (pres. 1988-90), Greater Providence C. of C. (bd. dirs. 1988—), East Providence C. of C. (bd. dirs. 1985—, v.p. 1983-85, pres. 1988-90), Rotary. Roman Catholic. Home: 1355 Wampanoag Trail East Providence RI 02915 Office: East Providence Pub Libr 41 Grove Ave E Providence RI 02914

CAIRO, SALLY J., educational administrator; b. Mt. Clemens, Mich., Mar. 15, 1944; d. Herbert Anthony and Sally Davis (Knight) Maison; m. Richard Cairo, July 24, 1981; children: Sean, Gary, Thomas. BA, U. Detroit, 1977; MA, Ea. Mich. U., 1984, EdS, 1988. Cert. tchr., Mich. Spl. edn. tchr. Chippewa Valley Schs., Mt. Clemens; adminstrv. asst. Richmond (Mich.) Community Schs., dir. spl. svcs.; coord. spl. edn. Livingston Ednl. Svc. Agy., Howell, Mich. Mem. Coun. for Exceptional Children, Mich. Assn. for Spl. Edn. Adminstrs., NAFE, Phi Delta Kappa. Home: 13037 Whitfield Dr Sterling Heights MI 48312

CALABIA, DAWN T., migration services director; b. Bklyn., May 22, 1941; d. Thomas Michael and Alice Brady (Diver) Tennant; B.A., St. John's U.; M.S.W., Fordham U., 1969; m. Florentine Calabia; children: Florentine Christopher, Theodore Rizal, Alison Maria Clara. Local area analyst N.Y.C. Planning Commn., 1967-68; urban planner Manoussoff Assos., 1969-72; fundraiser, cons. N.Y. State ADA, 1973-74; legis. asst. to Rep. Solarz (N.Y.), Washington 1978-84; staff cons. House Fgn. Affairs Com., 1984-89; assoc. dir. refugees and migration U.S. Cath. Conf., Washington, 1989—. Mem. Nat. Assn. Social Workers, Ams. for Democratic Action (nat. bd. dirs.), St. John's U. Alumni Assn. (v.p.), Coun. on Fgn. Rels., NOW, Lambda Kappa Phi. Office: US Cath Conf 3211 4th St NE Washington DC 20017

CALABOTTA, LINDA CAROL, retail executive; b. Buffalo, Sept. 27, 1953; d. Thomas Joseph and Ruth Mary (Rauhenstein) Doeseckle; m. John Russell, Sept. 29, 1971 (div. 1982); 1 child, Juliet Patricia, 1 foster child, Shannon Skinner; m. Samuel J. Ciccia, May 8, 1990; stepchildren: Samuel Jr., Mary Jo, Shirley Stepp. Grad. high sch. Various positions Quaker Bonnet, Buffalo, 1968-81; mgr. Chi-Chi's Tool Rental Inc., Buffalo, 1981—; owner A Party Extravaganza, 1990—. Recipient 1st place award Culinary Arts, 1978. Mem. Bison City Yacht Club (1st women commodore 1987—), West N.Y. Rental Assn. (sec. 1985-86). Roman Catholic. Home: 268 Potomac Ave Buffalo NY 14213

CALABRESE, DIANE MARIE, entomologist, writer; b. Erie, Pa., Apr. 1, 1949; d. Albert Robert and Lucy (Salorino) C.; m. Peter Tallerico, Aug. 1, 1980. BS, Gannon Coll., 1971; MS, U. Conn., 1974; PhD, 5, 1977. Instr. Kans. State U., Manhattan, 1977-78; lectr. U. Tex., El Paso, 1978-80; asst. prof. Trinity Coll., Washington, 1980-81, Dickinson Coll., Carlisle, Pa., 1981-87; assoc. Papillons: Diversified Endeavors, Dedham, Mass., 1988—; rsch. assoc. Coordinating Bd. Higher Edn., Jefferson City, Mo., 1990—; mem. adv. panel NSF Systgematic Biology, Washington, 1987—. Series editor: Iowa State U. Press, 1989—; sect. editor: Women in Natural Resources, 1988—; editor: Women in Entomology, 1981—; contbr. articles to profl. jours. Vol. Bethesda Mission, Harrisburg, Pa., 1987-88, Kingston House Merrimac Mission, Boston, 1988-89. W.K. Kellogg Found. fellow, 1983-86, Noyes fellow The Bunting Inst., 1987-88. Fellow Royal Entomol. Soc. of London; mem. Entomol. Soc. of Am., Ecol. Soc. of Am., Soc. for Systematic Biology (councillor 1978-81), Soc. for Conservation Biology. Democrat. Office: Papillons: Diversified Endeavors 22 Anderson Ave Columbia MO 65203-2673 also: Coordinatin Bd Higher Edn Jefferson City MO 65201

CALABRETTA, MARTI ANN, senator; b. Sandusky, Ohio, Dec. 14, 1940; d. Wilfred and Ida (Gerding) Beutler; m. Joseph Miller, Feb. 2, 1963 (div. Mar. 1976); m. Bennie G. Calabretta, Dec. 18, 1976; children: Joseph, Patrick, Rebecca, Debora, John, Ben, Lisa. Student, Case Western Res. U., 1961-63; BA, U. Utah, 1963, MSW, 1966; cert. mental health mgmt., U. Wash., 1981. Mental health specialist 4 Corners Mental Health Services, Moab, Utah, 1972-75, Idaho Mental Health Services, Coeur d'Alene, Idaho, 1975-81; sch. social worker Wallace (Idaho) Sch. Dist., 1981-85; state senator Boise, Idaho, 1984—. Pres. Valley Coordinating Corp., Kellogg, Idaho, 1982-86; mem. Pvt. Industry Council, Coeur d'Alene, 1984—, Idaho State Council on Developmental Disabilities, 1986—; vice chmn. Silver Valley Human Resources task force, Kellogg, 1982—. Mem. Idaho Edn. Assn. (del. 1983-84), Nat. Conf. State Legis. (health and welfare com.). Democrat. Episcopalian. Home: Nuchols Gulch Box 784 Osburn ID 83849 Office: Wallace Sch Dist 393 Wallace ID 83849*

CALAFIORE, LINDA C., school director; b. Chgo., Nov. 11, 1952; d. Michael and Jennie (Gibilisco) C. BS, U. Ill., 1974; MBA, Loyola U., Chgo., 1980. Planner Champagne Regional Planning Commn., Chgo., 1974-76; adminstr. Ill. State Bd. Edn., Chgo., 1976-83; pres. Cooking and Hospitality Inst., Chgo., 1983—. Author, editor: (newsletter) Under the Canopy, 1985—. Bd. dirs. River North Assn., Chgo., 1990. Named one of top 100 women making an impact in 1990's in Chgo. Today's Chgo. Woman, 1990. Mem. Ill. Restaurant Assn., Nat. Restaurant Assn., Internat. Assn. Cooking Profls. (chmn. 1987), Am. Inst. Wine and Food (bd. dirs. 1990—), Chgo. Culinary Guild (pres. 1989—). Office: Cooking Hospitality Inst 361 W Chestnut Chicago IL 60610

CALDERON, CYNTHIA ANN, management services company executive; b. El Paso, Tex., Sept. 28, 1964; d. Samuel Israel Calderon and Maria Lilia (Ontiveros) Rogers; m. James Allan Checkalski, Apr. 26, 1985 (div. Oct. 1986); m. Henry Horn Adams, Jr., Dec. 9, 1988; 1 child, Andre Enrique. Grad. high sch., Mpls. Ops. asst. Paine Webber Jackson & Curtis Inc., Mpls., 1980-83; office mgr. European Imports Co., Mpls., 1984; asst. investment mgr., office mgr. Mpls. Tchrs. Retirement Fund, 1985-89; propr., mgr. The Organized Exec., Plymouth, Minn., 1989—. Facilitator Chrysalis, women's crisis ctr., Mpls., 1985; advisor Minnitonka (Minn.) Pub. Sch. System, 1986-87; vol. St. Joseph's Home for Children, Mpls., 1986. Republican. Roman Catholic. Office: The Organized Exec 14615 Gleason Lake Dr Plymouth MN 55447

CALDERON, HAZEL G., career counseling company executive; b. Snowhill, Md., Dec. 13, 1938; d. Alfred L. and Elizabeth C. (Hoggard) Watford; children: Angela A. Mosby, Felipe A. III. Student, Temple U.; MEd, U. Mass., U. Amherst, 1981; communications cert., Personal Dynamics Inst., Mpls., 1979. Lic. real estate agt.; cert. col. adminstr. Mgr. fed. women's program Dept. Navy, Phila., mgr. fed. equal opportunity recruitmant EEO Office; exec. dir. Phila. Affirmative Action; pres. Exquisite Splty. Co. Mem. NAFE, Nat. Assn. Media Women, United Minority Enterprise Assn. Recipient Superior Performance award Dept. Navy.

CALDERONE, MARY STEICHEN, physician; b. N.Y.C., July 1, 1904; d. Edward J. and Clara (Smith) Steichen; m. Frank A. Calderone, Nov. 1941 (dec. 1987); children: Linda Steichen Hodes, Francesca Calderone-Steichen, Maria S. B.A., Vassar Coll., 1925; M.D., U. Rochester, 1939; M.P.H., Columbia U., 1942; D.Med. Sci. (hon.), Women's Med. Coll., 1967; L.H.D. (hon.), Newark State Coll., 1971, Dickinson Coll., 1981, Jersey City State Coll., 1982; Sc.D. (hon.), Adelphi U., 1971, Worcester Found. Exptl. Biology, 1974, Brandeis U., 1975, Haverford Coll., 1978, Columbia U., 1985; LL.D., Kenyon Coll., 1972; Ped.D. (hon.), Hofstra U., 1978; D. Hum. (hon.), Bucknell U., 1982. Intern Bellevue Hosp., N.Y.C., 1939-40; med. dir. Planned Parenthood-World Population, 1953-64; co-founder, exec. dir., pres. Sex Info. Edn. Council U.S., N.Y.C., 1964-82; adj. prof. program in human sexuality NYU, N.Y.C., 1982-88; lectr. human sexuality; 33d Lower lectr. Acad. Medicine and Cleve. Clinic, 1970; Rufus Jones lectr. Friends Gen. Conf., 1973; Hundley lectr. gynecology, Balt., 1973; Pres.'s Disting. visitor Vassar Coll., 1983; 7th ann. Bronfman lectr. Am. Pub. Health Assn., 1967. Author: Release From Sexual Tensions, 1960; co-author: Family Book about Sexuality, 1981 (pub. Japan and Germany), rev. edit. May, 1989 (named best trade book Am. Med. Writers Assn. 1990); co-author: Talking with Your Child about Sex, 1982 (pub. Japan, Germany and Brazil); editor: Abortion in U.S, 1958, Manual of Family Planning and Contraceptive Practice, 1964, rev. edit., 1970, Sexuality and Human Values, 1974; contbr. articles to profl. jours., mags., textbooks, encys. Recipient 4th Ann. Disting. Svc. to Humanity award Women's Aux. Albert Einstein Med. Ctr., Phila., 1966, Woman of Conscience award Nat. Council Women, 1968; citation Merrill-Palmer Inst. Human Devel. and Family Life, Detroit, 1969, Woman of Achievement award Greater N.Y. chpt. women's div. Albert Einstein Coll. Medicine, Yeshiva U., 1969, Haven Emerson award N.Y.C. Pub. Health Assn., 1970, Ann. award Soc. Sci. Study of Sex, 1976, Elizabeth Blackwell Disting. Svc. to Humanity award Hobart and Wm. Smith Coll., 1977, Margaret Sanger award Planned Parenthood Fedn. Am., 1980, Abram Sachar Silver medal Brandeis U. Nat. Women's Com., 1983, Mcdonald House award Univ. Hosps. Women's Com., Cleve., 1983, Human Svc. award Mental Health Assn. New York and Bronx Counties, 1983, Lifetime Achievement award Schlesinger Libr. Radcliffe Coll., 1983, Disting. Alumni award Columbia U., 1984, Jake Gimbel hon. lectr. award U. Calif. Sch. Medicine, 1984, Cert. of Commendation Am. Acad. Pediatrics, 1985, Living Legacy award Women's Internat. Ctr., San Diego, 1988, Richard J. Cross award for Disting. Contbn. to Sexuality, Robert Wood Johnson Med. Sch., 1988; named one of America's 75 Most Important Women Ladies Home Jour., 1971, one of 50 most influential women in U.S. Newspaper Enterprises Assn., 1975. Fellow Am. Public Health Assn. (Edward W. Browning award for prevention of disease 1980), Soc. Sci. Study Sex (hon. life mem.); mem. Am. Coll. Sexologists, Am. Assn. Marriage and Family Counselors (hon. life mem.), Am. Assn. World Health, AMA (hon. life), Soc. Sex Therapy and Research, Alpha Omega Alpha. Quaker.

CALDINI, MARIA PIA, physician; b. Florence, Italy, Aug. 8, 1931; d. Alessandro and Laura (Fornari) Poltri-Tanucci; m. Paolo Caldini, Apr. 11, 1956; children: Carolina, Filippo. MD, Florence U., 1956. Diplomate Am. Bd. Anesthesiologists. Intern U. Hosp., Florence, 1955-56; resident in anesthesiology U. Padua (Italy) Med. Sch., 1958-59, Winnipeg (Can.) Hosp., 1960-61, Denver Gen. Hosp., 1964; intern Mercy Hosp., Balt., 1965-66; resident instr., asst. prof. Johns Hopkins Hosp., Balt., 1967-72; anesthesiologist Lahey Clinic Found., Boston, 1972-81, New England Bapt. Hosp., Boston, 1981—. Fellow Am. Coll. Anesthesiologists; mem. NAFE, Mass. Med. Soc., Mass. Soc. Anesthesiologists, Suffolk Med. Soc., Am. Soc. Anesthesiologists, Internat. Anesthesia Rsch. Soc., Nat. Italian-Am. Found., Smithsonian Inst. Office: New England Bapt Hosp 92 Parker Hill Ave Boston MA 02102

CALDOW, JUNE A., office equipment company official; b. Washington, Dec. 7, 1928; d. William Roy and Susan Olive (Bruner) Gregory; m. Samuel C. Caldow, Mar. 1, 1952; children: Laurie Sue, Christy Leigh, Samuel Colburn. BS, Wilson Tchrs. Coll., Washington, 1951. Cert. tchr., Washington. Tchr. pub. schs., Va., Washington Pub. Schs.; customer svc. mgr. Xerox Corp., Silver Spring, Md.; equipment planning and control mgr. Xerox Corp., Washington; br. mgr. Xerox Corp., Norfolk, Va., adminstrv. nat. account mgr. Mem. President's Adv. Coun. for Mgmt. Improvement. Mem. Nat. Contract Mgmt. Assn., President's Club Xerox Corp., All Star Club Xerox Corp. Home: 1140 Chatmoss Dr Virginia Beach VA 23464 Office: Xerox Corp 8 Koger Ctr Norfolk VA 23400

CALDWELL, ALETHEA OTTI, health care systems executive; b. British Guyana, May 27, 1941; d. Charles Manoram. BS, Pacific Union Coll., Angwin, Calif., 1961; MS, U. Calif.-Irvine, Orange, 1973. Asst. dir. to dir. Intercommunity Hosp., Covina, Calif., 1963-71; contracts officer Orange County, Santa Ana, Calif., 1972-73; assoc. hosp. adminstr. Cedars-Sinai Med. Ctr., L.A., 1974-77, assoc. adminstr., 1977-80; exec. assoc. dir. U. Calif.-Irvine Med. Ctr., Orange, 1980-84; chief exec. officer Univ. Med. Ctr., Tucson, Ariz., 1984-87; pres., chief exec. officer Ancilla Systems Inc., Chgo., 1987—; cons. John Dempsey Hosp., Farmington, Conn., 1985; trustee Mercy Health System, 1988—; mem. health adv. com. Sch. Mgmt. Brigham Young U., 1988; bd. dirs. Health Alliance, 1988—. Contbr. to profl. publs., newspapers. Bd. dirs. Cath. Community Svcs., Tucson, 1984-85, United Way, Tucson, 1984-85; nat. bd. advisors Univ. Ariz. Coll. of Bus. & Pub. Adminstrn.; bd. trustees Mercy Health System, 1988—; health adv. com. Brigham Young U. Sch. of Mgmt., 1988; bd. dirs. Health Alliance. Recipient Women in Business and Industry award YMCA, Orange County, Calif., 1983, Women on the Move award YMCA, Tucson, 1984; Yr. of Ariz. Women award Ariz. Press Women, 1985; named one of Top 25 Turnaround Execs., Healthweek. Mem. Health Insights (bd. dirs. 1984—), Health Alliance (bd. dirs. 1988—), Univ. Hosp. Consortium (bd. dirs. 1984-87), Am. Coll. Healthcare Execs., Council of Teach Hosps., Am. Hosp. Assn. (com. hosp. closures), Cath. Health Assn. (multi-instl. systems com. 1988-89). Office: Ancilla Systems Inc 111 E Wacker Dr Ste 1910 Chicago IL 60601

CALDWELL, BARBARA HART, medical association administrator; b. Balt., Feb. 19, 1940; d. Godwin Waring Hart and Elizabeth (Callister) Hart Porter; children: Cheryl, Stephen. BA, U. North Fla., Jacksonville, 1981; MS, Cen. Mich. Coll., Mt. Pleasant, 1986. Rsch. asst. Rutgers U., New Brunswick, N.J., 1963-67; lab. mgr. Belle Baruch Inst. Coastal Rsch. U. S.C., Columbia, 1969-73; med. tech. Meml. Hosp., Jacksonville, Fla., 1974-80; from lab. supr. to computer coord. U. Med. Ctr., Jacksonville, Fla., adminstrv. dir. lab. svs., 1984—. Amb. C. of C., 1986-87, projects dir. Port of Jacksonville-Pilot Club, 1988—; bd. dirs. Hubbard House Shelter for Battered Women and Children, 1989-90. Mem. Am. Soc. for Med. Tech. (Fla. div. pres. elect 1987-88, pres. 1988—), Clin. Lab. Mgrs. Assn. (chmn. clin. lab. coun. 1989). Democrat. Episcopalian. Office: U Med Ctr 655 W 8th St Jacksonville FL 32209

CALDWELL, DONNA MOTE, finance administrator, accountant; b. Gainesville, Ga., Jan. 28, 1962; d. Ralph Tilman and Catherine (Teague) Mote; m. Troy Roland Caldwell, Sept. 4, 1982; children: Jared Matthew, Kaeli Brooke. BBA, North Ga. Coll., 1984. Acct. St. Joseph's Hosp. Dahlonega (Ga.), Inc., 1985-86, asst. bus. office mgr., 1986-87, acctg. mgr., 1987-88, adminstrv. asst. fin., dir. materials mgmt., 1988—. Mem. Mother Catherine McAuley Award Com., 1987-89. Office: St Joseph's Hosp 1111 Mountain Dr Dahlonega GA 30533

CALDWELL, JEAN LEONORA, public relations executive, consultant; b. Sandusky, Ohio, Nov. 22, 1928; d. Paul Arthur Gallagher and Elizabeth Leonora (Senn) Shambaugh; m. Walter Glen Caldwell, June 5, 1948; children: Sharon Elizabeth, Cynthia Jean, Walter Glen III. BA, Miami U., Oxford, Ohio, 1950. News editor Geauga Rep. Record, Chardon, Ohio, 1950-51; with advt. and promotion dept. Paula Black Advt., Cleve., 1962-65; promotion dir. Westgate Mall, Fairview, Ohio, 1965-68; dir. pub. rels. Olive Advt., Lakewood, Ohio, 1968-69; freelance pub. rels. Cleve., 1969-70; account exec. Wendell Advt., Cleve., 1970-73; dir. pub. rels. Cleve. Inst. Music, 1973-89; pres. Caldwell & Co. div. Caldwell Internat., Rocky River, Ohio, 1989—; cons. Performers & Artists for Nuclear Disarmament, Cleve., 1982—, Tom Evert Dance Co., Cleve., 1988—, Nat. Pub. Radio-Sta. WCPN, Cleve., 1989—. Vice pres., mem. bd. trustees NOVA, Cleve., 1982-85; mem. bd. trustees PAND, Cleve., 1982—, Tom Evert Dance Co., Cleve., 1988—, Cleve. Philharmonic Orch., 1985—; pres. children's bd. Lakewood Hosp., 1958-59; bd. dirs. Lyric Opera Theater Bd., 1981-84. Mem. Pub. Rels. Soc. Am., Press Club of Cleve., Jr. Women's Club (pres. Lakewood, Ohio chpt. 1956-57). Democrat. Episcopalian. Home and Office: 20341 Glendale Dr Rocky River OH 44116

CALDWELL, JUDY CAROL, advertising executive, public relations executive; b. Nashville, Dec. 28, 1946; d. Thomas and Sarah Elizabeth Carter; m. John Cope Caldwell; 1 child, Jessica. BS, Wayne State U., 1969. Tchr. Bailey Mid. Sch., West Haven, Conn., 1969-72; editorial asst. Vanderbilt U., Nashville, 1973-74; editor, graphics designer, field researcher Urban Observatory of Met. Nashville, 1974-77; account exec. Holden and Co., Nashville, 1977-79; bus. tchr. Federated States of Micronesia, 1979-80; dir. advt. Am. Assn. for State and Local History, Nashville, 1980-81; dir. prodn. Mktg. Communications Co., Nashville, 1981-83; owner, pres. Ridge Hill Corp., Nashville, 1983—. Office: Ridge Hill Corp 4004 Hillsboro Rd Ste A-201 Nashville TN 37215

CALDWELL, L. SCOTT, actress. Mem. Milw. Repertory Theatre, 1981-82. Appeared in Negro Ensemble Co. prodns. The Daughters of the Mock, 1978, A Season to Unravel, 1979, Old Phantoms, 1979, Plays from Africa, 1979, Home, 1979, 80, Colored People's Time, 1982, About Heaven and Earth, 1983; other theater appearances include A Raisin in the Sun, Buffalo, 1982, Joe Turner's Come and Gone, New Haven, 1985, Boston, 1986, N.Y.C., 1988 (Antoinette Perry award for best featured actress in a play 1988), A Month of Sundays, N.Y.C., 1987; appeared in films Without a Trace, 1983, Exterminator 2, 1984, God Bless the Child, 1988, various TV appearances. Office: Bauman Hiller & Assocs 250 W 57th St New York NY 10107*

CALDWELL, MARIE ELLEN, graphic designer, design studio owner, executive; b. Hillsboro, Ill., Nov. 8, 1954; d. Donald Gene and Betty Irene (Fahs) Murphy; m. Matthew Allen Caldwell, Aug. 6, 1977 (div. 1989). BS in Journalism, English Edn., U. Ill., 1977. Asst. pub. relations dir. Ill. State Fair Agency, State of Ill., Springfield, 1974, publicity dir., 1975-76; publs. editor Caradco Window and Door Mfgs., Rantoul, Ill., 1977-78; community educator Devel. Svcs. Ctr., Champaign, Ill., 1978-80; gen. mgr. Timber Lake Playhouse, Mt. Carroll, Ill., 1981-83; pub. relations dr. Mt. St. Clare Coll., Clinton, Iowa, 1984; pres., owner, creative dir. Caldwell Graphic Design and Communications, Mt. Carroll, Ill., 1984—; cons. Family Svcs. of Champaign County, 1984. Designer, writer Annual Report Publ. Devel. Svcs. Ctr. (div. winner U.S. and Can.1979), 1978. Bd. dirs. County Health and Human Svcs. Bd., Carroll County, Ill., 1986; promotion com. chair Mayfest Annual Preservation Festival, Mt. Carroll, 1987. Mem. Pub. Rels. Soc. Am., Bus. and Profl. Women, Internat. Assn. Bus. Communicators. Republican. Home: 105 W Wall St Morrison IL 61270 Office: Caldwell Graphic Design and Communications 106 E Market St Mt Carroll IL 61053

CALDWELL, MARY PERI, counseling psychologist, educator; b. Cleve., Aug. 21, 1935; d. Francesco and Gerlanda (Gagliano) Peri; m. Robert Joseph Caldwell, 1956 (div. 1962); children: Deborah Ann, Thomas Robert. BS in Edn., Kent State U., 1961; MA in Counseling Psychology, Alfred Adler Inst., Chgo., 1981. Cert. clin. mental health counselor; lic. mental health counselor, Fla., clin. counselor, Ohio. Tchr. various sch. systems Cleve., 1957-85; pvt. practice as counseling psychologist Brunswick, Ohio, 1980-87, Coral Springs, Fla., 1987—; mem. faculty, dir. Cleve. Inst. Adlerian Studies, 1983—, exec. sec., 1978-82, pres., 1982-84; mem. med. staff Care Unit, Coral Springs; mem. mental health profl. staff. Univ. Pavillion Hosp., Tamarac, Fla.; lectr. U.S. and Can. Author: Stress/Distress/Burnout: Resolving the Puzzle of Stress, 1983; editor: Adlerian Psychology Bull., 1983-86; contbr. articles to profl. jours. Leader various parent edn. groups, 1981—. Jennings Found. grantee, 1979; recipient Disting. Service award N.E. Ohio Tchrs. Assn., 1983, Nat. Disting. Svc. award Registry Counseling and Devel., 1990. Mem. N.Am. Soc. Adlerian Psychology (clin. mem., assembly del., Outstanding Woman award 1980), Am. Assn. Counseling and Devel., Am. Mental Health Counselors Assn., Fla. Assn. Counseling and Devel., Broward County Mental Health Assn., Exec. Women Coral Springs, Am. Bus. Women's Assn., Fla. Speakers Assn., Rotary, Gamma Phi Beta (pres. 1967-70). Home: 8208 NW 100th Way Tamarac FL 33321 Office: 3300 University Dr Ste 615 Coral Springs FL 33321

CALDWELL, PATTY JEAN GROSSKOPF, advocate, educator; b. Davenport, Iowa, Sept. 28, 1937; d. Bernhard August and Leontine Virginia (Carver) Grosskopf; m. Donald Eugene Caldwell Mar. 29, 1956 (dec. Feb. 1985); children: John Alan, Jennifer Lynn Caldwell Lear. BA, State U. Iowa, 1959. Hearing officer Ill. State Bd. Edn., Springfield, 1979—, appellate, 1986—; pres., bd. dirs. adv. Tri-County Assn. for Children with Learning Disabilities, Moline, Ill., 1972-79; adv. vol., Iowa nd Ill., 1979—; mem. adv. coun. Prairie State Legal Svcs., Inc., Rock Island, Ill., 1984—; mem. profl. svcs. com. United Cerebral Palsy NW Ill., Rock Island, 1986-88; arbitrator Am. Arbitration Assn., Chgo., 1986—, Better Bus. Bur., Davenport, 1986—. Founder, pres. Quad-Cities Diabetes Assn., Moline, 1969-72, bd. dirs., 1973—; mem. com. Moline Internat. Yr. Disabled, Moline, 1981; mem. Assn. for Retarded Citizens, Rock Island, 1987; mem., vol. Coun. on Children at Risk, Moline, 1988—; reader for the blind on Sta. WVIK, Rock Island, 1989—. Mem. Ill. Assn. for Children with Learning Disabilities (bd. dirs., adv. 1980-83). Methodist. Home and Office: 5006 46th Ave Ct Moline IL 61265 Address: 4169 via Marina #315 Marina del Rey CA 90292

CALDWELL, PAULA DAY, telecommunications executive; b. Colorado Springs, Colo., Nov. 11, 1954; d. Taylor Arnold Day and Constance Theo (Jenkins) Day Pearson; m. Michael Anthony Caldwell, Feb. 21, 1981. BS, Lindenwood Coll., 1981; MBA, Dallas Bapt. U., 1986. Exec. sec. Minority Econ. Devel. Agy., St. Louis, 1974-76; adminstrv. asst. New Age Fed. Savs. and Loan, St. Louis, 1976-78; bookkeeper Family Planning Council, 1978-81; account exec., cons. AT&T Corp., Dallas, 1981—; co-owner Jewelry Connection. Mem. Nat. Assn. Female Execs. Dallas Women's Found. Democrat. Baptist. Home: PO Box 763845 Dallas TX 75376 Office: AT&T Corp 5525 LBJ Frwy 3d Fl Dallas TX 75240

CALDWELL, RUTH MARGARET, nurse; b. Memphis, Jan. 2, 1956; d. Alva Edwin and Jo Helen (Powers) Boatwright; m. Terence John Caldwell, May 7, 1988; 1 child, Jonathan Patrick. Assoc. Nursing, Memphis State U., 1980. Cert. inpatient obstetric nurse, cert. childbirth educator. Nurse labor and delivery Meth. Hosp., Memphis, 1980-81; staff nurse, specialist St. Jude's Children's Rsch. Hosp., Memphis, 1981-84; nurse, childbirth educator Bapt. Meml. Hosp., Memphis, 1984-85, 5th Gen. Hosp., Bad Cannstatt, Fed. Republic of Germany, 1985-87, Lexington Med. Ctr., West Columbia, S.C., 1987-88, Humana Hosp. Alaska, Anchorage, 1989—. Author: Prenatal Handbook, 1987. Mem. Orgn. for Obstet., Gynecol. and Neonatal Nurses, Internat. Childbirth Edn. Assn., Am. Soc. Psychoprophylaxis in Obstetrics. Home: 116B Iliamna Ave Fort Richardson AK 99505

CALDWELL, SANDRA MARIE, accountant; b. Lexington, Ky., Apr. 11, 1959; d. Francis Mark and Frances Jane (Thomas) C. B.S. in Acctg., U. Ky., 1983; M.B.A., Xavier U., Cin., 1987. Record clk. Good Samaritan Hosp., Lexington, 1976-85; acctg. clk. Semicon Assocs., Lexington, 1985-86, acctg. analyst, 1986-87, fin. planner Cox Fin. Corp., Cin., 1987—, partnership analyst Pizza Huts Cin., 1987—; contr. The Nickert Group, Cin., 1989—. Mem. NAFE, Nat. Assn. Accts., Nat. Soc. MBAs. Office: Pizza Huts of Cin 800 compton Rd Unit 37 Cincinnati OH 45231

CALDWELL, SARAH, opera producer, conductor, stage director and administrator; b. Maryville, Mo., Mar. 6, 1924. Student, U. Ark., Hendrix Coll., New Eng. Conservatory, Berkshire Music Ctr., Tanglewood, Mass.; D. Mus. (hon.), Harvard U., Simmons Coll., Bates Coll., Bowdoin U. Mem. faculty Berkshire Music Ctr.; dir. Boston U. Opera Workshop, 1953-57; created dept. music theater Boston U.; founded Boston Opera Group (later became Opera Co. of Boston), 1957, sinced served as artistic dir. and condr. Asst. to Boris Goldovsky in direction of New Eng. Opera Co.; operatic directorial debut with Rake's Progress, Opera Workshop, 1953; operatic debut as condr. with Opera Group of Boston, 1957, Carnegie Hall debut with Am. Symphony Orch., 1974; condr. and/or dir. maj. opera cos. in U.S., including N.Y. Met. Opera, Dallas Civic Opera, Houston Grand Opera, N.Y.C. Opera; condr. with maj. orchs. including: Indpls. Symphony, Milw. Symphony, Am. Symphony, N.Y. Philharmonic; condr. at Ravinia Festival, 1976. Recipient Rogers and Hammerstein award. Office: Opera Co Boston Inc PO Box 50 Boston MA 02112

CALDWELL, ZOE, actress, director; b. Hawthorn, Victoria, Australia, Sept. 14, 1933; m. Robert Whitehead, 1968; 2 sons: Sam, Charlie. Attended, Meth. Ladies Coll., Melbourne, Australia. Theater debut as mem. of Union Theatre Repertory Co., Melbourne, 1953; other appearances in Colette, N.Y.C., 1970, A Bequest to the Nation, London, 1970, The Creation of the World and Other Business, N.Y.C., 1972, Love and Master Will, Washington, 1973, The Dance of Death, N.Y.C., 1974, Long Day's Journey Into Night, N.Y.C., Washington, 1976, Medea, N.Y.C., 1982 (Tony award for best actress); plays directed include: An Almost Perfect Person, N.Y.C., 1977, Richard II, Stratford, Ont., 1979, These Men, N.Y. off-Broadway, 1980, The Taming of the Shrew, Hamlet, Am. Shakespeare Theatre, 1985; appeared in The Madwoman of Chaillot, Goodman Theater, Chgo., 1964, repertory theater Stratford-on-Avon, 2 seasons, The Way of the World and The Caucasian Chalk Circle, Mpls., Slapstick Tragedy (Tony award for best supporting actress), N.Y.C., 1966; appeared in Antony and Cleopatra, Richard III and The Merry Wives of Windsor at Stratford, Ont. Shakespeare Festival, 1967; appeared in The Prime of Miss Jean Brodie (Tony award for best actress 1968), one-woman play Lillian, 1986; one-woman theater presentation, Come A-Waltzing With Me; Dorothy F. Schmidt Vis. Eminent Scholar in Theatre, Fla. Atlantic U., Boca Raton, 1989. Decorated Order Brit. Empire; recipient Word award, 1966. Address: care Whitehead-Stevens 1501 Broadway New York NY 10036*

CALESTINO, KAREN JOAN, construction company executive; b. Providence, R.I., Sept. 18, 1952; d. Astillodore and Maria (Micheletti) Diodati; m. Peter George Calestino, Apr. 11, 1976; children: Maria, Peter A. Student, R.I. Jr. Coll., Warwick, 1972. Notary Public. Exec. sec. A&D Constrn. Co., Inc., Cranston, R.I., 1974-87, asst. treas., 1980-87, also bd. dirs. Recipient Honor award Hist. Preservation Soc., Providence, 1983. Mem. Women in Constrn. Bldg. Trades Assn., Greater Boston C. of C., NAFE. Roman Catholic. Office: A&D Constrn Co Inc 116 Preston Dr Cranston RI 02910

CALFEE, ANNETTE, telecommunications company official; b. Enterprise, Ala., Feb. 14, 1947; d. Lessie F. and Irene (McCray) Rogers; divorced; children: Sandra R., Sharif. AA in Gen. Edn. and Psychology, Ocean County Coll., Toms River, N.J., 1978; BA in Psychology, Rutgers U., 1982; cert., Am. Ctr. for Mgmt. Devel., 1987. Asst. tng. specialist Ocean County Coll., 1978-81; customer sales rep. N.J. Bell Telephone Co., Newark, 1981-84; mgr. sales ops. Bell Atlanticom Systems, Inc., Princeton, N.J., 1984-87, implementation mgr., 1985-87, mgr. methods and procedures, 1987—. Mem. NAFE, Coun. Action for Minority Profls. Office: Bell Atlanticom Systems Inc 105 Carnegie Ctr Princeton NJ 08540

CALHOUN, CHERYL, convention services and sales professional; b. Macon, Miss., Jan. 26, 1950; d. Prentiss Lee and Betty (Weaver) Parks; m. Harry Cole Barnes, Sept. 11, 1968 (div. 1980); children: Rome Bradley, Brian Hudson; m. Ross B. Calhoun, Nov. 15, 1981; stepchildren: Ross Blake Jr., Kimberley Frances. BBA, U. Tex., Arlington, 1981. Sec. Beaver Dam Cattle Plantation, Clarksdale, Miss., 1972-73, Bapt. Meml. Hosp., Memphis, 1973-74; exec. sec., office mgr. Arlington Convention and Visitors Bur., 1975-77, convention svcs. mgr., 1977-81; meeting planner Convention and Meeting Coords., Ft. Worth, 1981-82; convention coord. Arlington (Tex.) Hilton Hotel, 1982-83, catering sales mgr., 1983-84; state sales mgr. Arlington Conv. and Visitors Bur., 1984-88, dir. conv. sales and svcs., 1988-90, exec. dir. Arlington conv. and visitors bur., 1990—. Mem. Am. Soc. Assn. Execs., Tex. Soc. Assn. Execs., Internat. Assn. Convention and Visitors Burs., Nat. Assn. Exec. Mgrs., Hotel Sales and Mktg. Assn., Religious Conf. Mgrs. Assn., Tex. Assn. Convention and Visitors Burs. Republican. Methodist. Office: Arlington Convention and Visitors Bur Ste 650 1250 E Copeland Rd Arlington TX 76011

CALHOUN, EVELYN WILLIAMS, social worker; b. Tyler, Tex., Sept. 12, 1921; d. James Stanley and Norma (Skelton) Williams; m. William Benjamin Calhoun, Jr., Mar. 15, 1942 (div. Mar. 1949); children: William Benjamin III, Anne Stanley (Mrs. Donald Elliot Loyd). B.A., Baylor U., 1941; M.S.W., Worden Sch. Social Work, 1960; postgrad., U. Chgo., 1955-56. Lic. social psychotherapist, Tex.; cert. social worker, advanced clin. practitioner, Tex. Field worker Tex. Dept. Pub. Welfare, Tyler, 1953-55; field placement Salvation Army Family Svc., Chgo., 1955-56; child welfare worker Tyler-Smith County Child Welfare Unit, 1957-59; field placement Tex. Inst. Rehab. and Research, Baylor U., Houston, 1959-60, med. social worker, 1960-64; research social worker pre-natal research project dept. ob-gyn. U. Tex. Med. Br., Galveston, 1964-66, supr. social svc. dept. ob-gyn., 1966-74, cons. satellite clinics, 1967-74, cons. family planning project, 1969-74, cons., supr. head and neck cancer svc., ear, nose and throat, chest surgery and neurosurgery, 1974-78, cons., supr. plastic surgery and oral surgery svc., 1975-78, supr. internal medicine svcs., otolaryngology, ophthalmology and dermatology, 1978-81; field instr. U. Houston Grad. Sch. Social Work, 1968-81. Bd. dirs. Galveston County Community Action Coun., 1966-68, Galveston chpt. Am. Cancer Soc., 1974-81; trustee Houston Intergroup Assn., 1974-76. Mem. Nat. Assn. Social Workers (chmn. research coun. San Jacinto chpt. 1963-64, dir. chpt. 1964-67, chmn. Galveston br. 1964-67, sec. 1967-68; group leader so. regional inst. 1966, alt. Tex. del. 1969-71, Tex. del. 1971-73, dir. 1969-73; alt. del. Tex. state coun. 1967), Acad. Cert. Social Workers, Galveston County Soc. Social Svc. Dirs. (sec. 1979-80), AAUW, Baylor Alumnae Assn., Daus. King (pres. 1976-78), Order De Moley, Toastmistress, Delta Alpha Pi. Episcopalian. Home: 405 Hodencamp Rd Hillcrest Inn #230 Thousand Oaks CA 91306 also: PO Box 7662 Thousand Oaks CA 91359

CALHOUN, KENDALL RUSSELL, lawyer, nurse; b. Chestertown, Md., Feb. 26, 1948; d. Harry Simmons Russell and Rebecca Rigley (Anthony) Forman; m. Manley Paul Calhoun Jr., Apr. 25, 1971; children: Manley Paul III, Rachel Kendall. BSN, U. Md., 1970; JD, U. Balt., 1978. Bar: Md. 1978, U.S. Dist. Ct. Md. 1984. Staff nurse City of Balt. Dept. of Health, 1970-73, nursing supr., 1973-75; legal intern Edelman, Levy & Rubenstein, P.A., Balt., 1977, with, 1977-78, assoc., 1978-79; staff atty. Legal Aid Bur., Inc., Balt., 1979-81; asst. bar counsel Atty. Grievance Commn. of Md., Annapolis, 1981—. Mem. ABA (faculty 1990—), Md. Bar Assn., Nat. Orgn. Bar Counsel. Office: Atty Grievance Commn of Md 580 Taylor Ave Rm 404 Annapolis MD 21401

CALHOUN, MADELEINE S. ABLER, orchestra manager; b. Bronx, N.Y., Dec. 26, 1961; d. Morton and Mildred (Gates) Abler. MusB in Music Edn., SUNY, Potsdam, 1983; MBA in Arts Adminstrn., SUNY, Binghamton, 1986. Cert. tchr., N.Y. House mgr. Anderson Ctr. for Arts, Binghamton, 1984-85; intern Sydney (Australia) Opera House Trust, 1986; dir. audience svcs. New Orch. Westchester, Hartsdale, N.Y., 1987-89, asst. dir., 1989—; mgmt. asst. Tanglewood Berkshire Music Ctr., 1983; grad. asst. SUNY, Binghamton, 1984-85. Mem. Am. Symphony Orch. League (conf. del. 1987, 89). Democrat. Jewish. Home: 170 Honey Ln Wappingers Falls NY 12590 Office: New Orch Westchester Ill N Central Ave Hartsdale NY 10530

CALINSKY, ANNE CONSTANTIN, protective services official; b. Seattle, Sept. 3, 1952; d. James Alford and Wanda Anita (Moyer) Constantin; children: Holly Kay, Guy Andrew, Christian Burke. BS, U. Okla., 1977; AS, Valley Coll., 1987. Cert. tchr., Calif. Community svc. officer San Bernardino (Calif.) County Sheriff, 1982-85, dep. sheriff, 1985-89, detective, 1989—; trainer Birge & Assoc., Lake Arrowhead, Calif., 1989; instr. in hostage negotiations and stress mgmt. techniques, 1987—. Author: An Anthology of Poetry, 1976. Bd. dirs. Chaffey Community Coll. Found., Rancho Cucamonga, Calif., 1986-87. Recipient Proclamation award City of Rancho Cucamonga, 1985. Mem. Internat. Soc. for Prevention of Child Abuse and Neglect, Am. Profl. Soc. on Abuse of Children, Calif. Assn. Hostage Negotiation, So. Calif. Hostage Negotiators Assn., Assn. Exec. Women, Calif. Women Peace Officers Assn., Internat. Footprinters Assn., Calif. Peace Officers Assn., Calif. State Sheriffs Assn., Women Peace Officers Assn. Episcopalian. Office: San Bernardino County Sheriff 655 E 3d St San Bernardino CA 92415

CALISHER, HORTENSE (MRS. CURTIS HARNACK), author; b. N.Y.C., Dec. 20, 1911; d. Joseph Henry and Hedvig (Lichtstern) C.; m. Curtis Harnack, Mar. 23, 1959; children by previous marriage: Bennet Hughes, Peter Heffelfinger. A.B., Barnard Coll., 1932; LittD (hon.), Skidmore Coll., 1980, Grinnell Coll., 1986; LittD, Hofstra U., 1988. Adj. prof. English Barnard Coll., N.Y.C., 1956-57; vis. lectr. State U. Iowa, 1957, 59-60, Stanford U., 1958, Sarah Lawrence Coll., Bronxville, N.Y., 1962, 67; adj. prof. Columbia U., N.Y.C., 1968-70, CCNY, 1969; vis. prof. lit. SUNY, Purchase, 1971-72, Brandeis U., 1963-64, U. Pa., 1965; Regent's prof. U. Calif., 1976; vis. prof. Bennington Coll., 1978, Washington U., St. Louis, 1979, Brown U., spring 1986; lectr., W. Ger., Yugoslavia, Rumania, Hungary, 1978; guest lectr. U.S./China Arts Exch., Republic of China, 1986. Author: (novels) False Entry, 1961, Textures of Life, 1962, The Railway Police and the Last Trolley Ride, 1966, The New Yorkers, 1969, Journal from Ellipsia, 1965, Queenie, 1971, Standard Dreaming, 1972, Eagle Eye, 1973, On Keeping Women, 1977, Mysteries of Motion, 1984, The Bobby-Soxer, 1986 (Kafka prize 1987), Age, 1987; short stories include In The Absence of Angels, 1951, Tale for the Mirror, 1962, Extreme Magic, 1963, Collected Stories, 1975, Saratoga Hot, 1985; autobiography: Herself, 1972; memoir: Kissing Cousins, 1988; contbr. short stories, articles, revs. to Am. Scholar, N.Y. Times, others. Guggenheim fellow, 1952, 55; Dept. of State Am. Specialists's grantee to S.E. Asia, 1958; recipient Acad. of Arts and Letters award, 1967, Nat. Council Arts award, 1967, Lifetime Achievement award Nat. Endowment for the Arts, 1989. Mem. Am. Acad. and Inst. Arts and Letters (pres. 1987-90), PEN (pres. 1986-87). Office: c/o Candida Donadio & Assoc 231 W 22nd St New York NY 10011

CALKINS, JOANN RUBY, nursing administrator; b. Mich., June 28, 1934; d. William Russell and Imajean (Dunkle) Armentrout; m. James W. Calkins, 1952; children: Russell, Jill, Cindy; m. W. Arthur Brindle, May 7, 1983. AS, Delta Coll., 1964, BS, Cen. Mich. U., 1972, MA, 1977. Staff nurse, L.P.N. clin. instr., asst. dir. Sch. Nursing, Midland (Mich.) Hosp., 1964-71; dir. nursing, dir. substance abuse unit Gladwin (Mich.) Hosp., 1972-76; prin. Calkins Profl. Counseling & Cons., Harrison, Mich., 1976-78, part-time, 1978-83; dir. nursing service Central Mich. Community Hosp., Mt. Pleasant, 1978-83; dir. nursing Oaklawn Hosp., Marshall, Mich., 1983-87; asst. adminstr. for nursing Betsy Johnson Meml. Hosp., Dunn, N.C., 1987—; part-time prin. W. Arthur and Assocs. Cons.; conducted workshops Mich. Dept. Public Health, Mich. Hosp. Assn.; exec. dir. Holistic Health Agy., 1977-82. Trustee Mid-Mich. Community Coll.; mem. adv. bd. to schs. of nursing Johnston Community Coll., Sampson Community Coll., Cen. Carolina Community Coll.; mem. adv. bd. St. Joseph of the Pines Home Health Agy. Recipient Murial A. Grimmason Nursing Scholarship award, 1962; Cert. nursing adminstr. Mem. Mich. Soc. Hosp. Nursing Adminstrs. (mem. steering com. 1979-80, dir., 14 county rep. 1980-83, pres. 1983-84, chmn. devel. com.), Mich. Nurses Assn., Am. Nurses Assn., Am. Orgn. Nurse Execs., N.C. Orgn. Nurse Execs., N.C. Nurses Assn. (bd. dirs. Dist. V rep. 1990-92, Johnston Community Coll.), NAFE. Methodist. Lodge: Lioness Internat. (3d v.p. 1985). Home: 513 Argyll Dr Sanford NC 27330 Office: 800 Tilghman Dr Dunn NC 28334

CALKINS, JUDITH MORITZ, financial executive; b. New Haven, May 31, 1942; d. George Carl and Amelia Elinor (Pluta) Moritz; m. Peter W. Calkins, May 4, 1974; children: Adam, Seth, Rachel. AA, Concordia Coll., Bronxville, N.Y., 1962; student, N.H. Coll., 1989—. Staff adminstr. Treas. Office, Carling Brewing Co., Waltham, Mass., 1971-76; bus. mgr. PR Pub. Co. Inc., Exeter, N.H., 1977-90; fin. mgr. Jackson, Jackson & Wagner, Exeter, 1987—. Dist. and coun. leadership trainer Boy Scouts Am. Mem. NAFE, Am. Mgmt. Assn., Seacoast Women's Network. Lutheran.

CALLAGHAN, MARY ELLEN, law marketing professional; b. Phila., Jan. 20, 1950; d. John Paul and Eleanor Elaine (Murphy) C. BBA in Mktg. and Mgmt. summa cum laude, Temple U., 1990. Sec. First Pa. Bank, Phila., 1967-69; sec. I-T-E Imperial Corp., Ardmore, Pa., 1969-71; legal sec. Dechert Price & Rhoads, Phila., 1972-76; sec., office mgr. Dechert Price & Rhoads, London, 1976-79; legal sec. Dechert Price & Rhoads, Phila., 1979-81; personal sec. to Hon. Arlen Specter U.S. Senate, Washington, 1981; legal sec. Dechert Price & Rhoads, Phila., 1981-85, client devel. coord., 1985—. Mem. Nat. Assn. Law Firm Mktg. Adminstrs., Beta Gamma Sigma. Office: 4000 Bell Atlantic Tower 1717 Arch St Philadelphia PA 19103

CALLAHAM, BETTY ELGIN, librarian; b. Honea Path, S.C., Oct. 8, 1929; d. John Winfred and Alice (Dodson) C. B.A., Duke U., 1950; M.A., Emory U., 1954, Master Librarianship, 1961. Tchr. pub. schs. N.C., Ga. and S.C., 1951-60; field svcs. libr. S.C. State Libr., 1961-64, adult cons., 1964-65, dir. field svcs., 1965-74, dep. libr., 1974-79, dir., 1979-90, ret., 1990; Conf. coord. Gov.'s Conf. on Pub. Librs., 1965, S.C. White House Conf. Libr. and Info. Svcs., 1978-79; del. White House Conf. Libr. and Info. Svcs., 1979; mem. OCLC Users Coun., 1982-84, 86-87; chair del. SOLINET, 1983-84; bd. dirs. Southeastern Libr. Network, 1984-88, vice chmn., 1985-86, chmn. bd. 1986-87. Mem. Hist. Columbia Found. Mem. ALA (coun. 1977-80), S.C. Libr. Assn. (fed. rels. coord. 1976-80, chmn. pub. libr. sect. 1965, mem. legis. com. 1984-90, v.p., pres.-elect 1987-88, pres. 1988-89, Intellectual Freedom award 1986, Educator of Yr. award 1987), Southeastern Libr. Assn., S.C. Assn. Pub. Libr. Dirs., S.C. Women in Govt., South Caroliniana Soc., Riverbanks Zool. Soc., Hist. Columbia Soc., Friends S.C. State Mus. Home: 733 Poinsettia Pl Columbia SC 29205

CALLAHAN, DONNA MARIE, logistics specialist; b. Johnson City, N.Y., Nov. 14, 1948; 040Nicholas and Evelyn (Belensky) Polowitz; widowed Oct. 1987; children: Lisa Renee, Laurie Anne, Amy Marie. AAS, Broome Community Coll., Binghamton, N.Y., 1968; BSBA, Lemoyne Coll., Syracuse, N.Y., 1990. Sec. IBM Corp., Endicott, N.Y., 1968-71; software libr. GE, Syracuse, 1979-84, data mgmt. specialist, 1984-88, logistics specialist, 1988-90, requirements and planning coord., 1990—. Mem. Bus. Profl. Women, NAFE. Roman Catholic. Home: 4688 The Post Rd Manlius NY 13104 Office: GE PO Box 4840 Syracuse NY 13221

CALLAHAN, JEAN MARIE, furniture manufacturing executive; b. Weymouth, Mass., Jan. 15, 1956; d. William Francis and Mildred Anne (Robertson) C.; m. Stuart Baker, Nov. 14, 1987. BA, Franklin Pierce Coll., 1978. Sec. to pres. mgr. Shimazaki Corp., N.Y.C., 1980-82; asst. to v.p. mktg. Bing & Grondahl Inc., Elmsford, N.Y., 1982-83; mgr. A&B Am., Yonkers, N.Y., 1983-86; mng. dir. U.S. ops. A&B Sweden Inc., Plymouth, Mass., 1986—. Actress Mt. Vernon (N.Y.) Scholar Program, 1980-83, St. Peter and Paul PLayers, Mt. Vernon, 1985; asst. Andy Spano Campaign, White Plains, N.Y., 1985. Mem. Plymouth C. of C. Democrat. Roman Catholic. Clubs: Irish Am. of Westchester, Ferry Sloop. Office: A&B Sweden Inc 29 North St Plymouth MA 02360

CALLAHAN, PIA LAASTER, research virologist; b. Chapell-lez-Herlaimont, Belgium, Sept. 21, 1955; came to U.S., 1956; d. Heino and Helga (Sepp) Laaster; m. Lynn T. Callahan III, June 26, 1981. BS in Microbiology, Cornell U., 1977; M in Clin. Microbiology, Hahnemann U., 1979. Registered microbiologist. Research asst. Temple U. Med. Coll., Phila., 1979-80; microbiologist Thomas Jefferson Hosp., Phila., 1980-81; staff virologist Merck Sharp & Dohme Rsch. Labs., West Point, Pa., 1981-84, research virologist, 1984—. Contbr. articles to profl. jours. Mem. NAFE, Am. Soc. Microbiology. Republican. Lutheran. Home: 41 Laubert Rd Conshohocken PA 19428 Office: Merck Sharp and Dohme Rsch Labs Sumneytown Pike West Point PA 19486

CALLAHAN, REBECCA LYNNE, computer company executive; b. Boston, Jan. 10, 1965; d. Robert Stephen and Dixie Leigh (Jones) Wood; m. Richard Dean Callahan, June 22, 1989. BA in Internat Rels., Brigham Young U., 1987; cert. in Essentials of Indsl. Security M, Dept. of Def. Security Inst., 1989. Mgr. trainee McDonald's, Middletown, R.I., 1983-85; test info. mgr. Syscon Corp., Middletown, 1987-88, analyst, supr., 1988 --. Vol. music instr. Utah State Hosp., Provo, 1986; chmn. 5-state single adult conf. LDS Ch., Hingham, Mass, 1987-89; exec. sec. LDS Ch. Regional Orgn. for Teenage Girls, 1988-90; music trainer LDS Ch. Regional Children's Orgn., 1990--; pres. LDS Ch. Parish Women's Orgn., 1987--; mem., asst. coach Newport Athletics, 1989 --. Recipient Award for Patriotism Daughters of Patriots and Founders of Am., Provo, 1985. Mem. NAFE. Home: PO Box 133 Foxboro MA 02035 Office: Syscon Corp 10 John Clarke Rd Middletown RI 02840

CALLAN, CLAIR MARIE, physician, laboratory director, educator; b. Sleaford, Lincolnshire, Eng., May 18, 1940; d. Joseph Edward and Margaret Mary (Hart) Mills; m. John Patrick Callan, Apr. 4, 1964; children—Eoin, Grainne, Colm, Maeve. M.B., B.Surgery, B. in Art of Obstetrics, Univ. Coll., Dublin, Ireland, 1963. Intern Mater Hosp., Dublin, 1963-64, resident in anesthesia, 1964-65; staff physician State of Conn., Middletown, 1966-68; anesthesiologist St. Francis Hosp., Hartford, Conn., 1972-76; med. dir. Dept. of Income Maintenance, State of Conn., Hartford, 1978-84; dir. med. affairs Abbott Labs., Abbott Park, Ill., 1985—; clin. asst. prof. med., Chgo. Med. Sch./U. Health Scis., 1987—. Contbr. articles to profl. jours. Pres. PTA, Wethersfield, Conn., 1974, Capitol Region Assn. of Pvt. Swim Clubs, Hartford, 1978. Mem. Am. Med. Women's Assn. (pres. 1984-85, councillor 1981-83), AMA (pres. Conn. aux. 1979-81), Am. Acad. Med. Dirs. Republican. Roman Catholic. Avocations: tennis; golf; needlework. Home: 816 Paddock Ln Libertyville IL 60048 Office: Abbott Labs D970 1 Abbott Park Rd Abbott Park IL 60064

CALLAN, MELINDA ANN, Mental Health teamleader; b. Moultrie, Ga., July 24, 1954; d. James Pete and Violette (Jones) C. BS, Shorter Coll., 1978; MSPA, West Ga. Coll., 1989. Therapeutic recreation N.W. Ga. Regional Hosp., Rome, 1978-83, mental health teamleader, 1983-88; mental health teamleader Bainbridge (Ga.) State Hosp., 1988—; recreation cons. Review Nursing Home, Rome, 1979-82, handicap awareness commn., Floyd Recreation Dept., 1980-81, chairperson Qmrp Council, Bainbridge State Hosp., 1988—. Fellow Am. Assn. Mental Retardation. Home: 222 Bruton St A-3 Bainbridge GA 31717 Office: Bainbridge State Hosp Bainbridge GA 31717

CALLANAN, KATHLEEN JOAN, electrical engineer, airplane company executive; b. Detroit, Feb. 10, 1940; d. John Michael and Grace Marie (Kleehammer) C. BSE in Physics, U. Mich., 1963; postgrad. in physics Northeastern U., 1963-65; MSEE, U. Hawaii, 1971; diploma in Japanese lang. St. Joseph Inst. Japanese Studies, Tokyo, 1973; cert. in mgmt. Boeing Mil. Airplane Co. Employee Devel., 1985. Vis. scholar Sophia U., Tokyo, 1976-79; elec.-electronic components engr. Boeing Mil. Airplane Co., Wichita, Kans., 1979-83, instrumentation design engr., 1983-85, strategic planner for tech., 1985-86, research and engring. tech. supr., 1986-87 ; electromagnetic effects Avionics mgr., 1987-89, elec. and electronics mgr., 1989—, design tech. support mgr., 1990—. Contbr. articles to profl. jours. Mem. Rose Hill Planning Commn., Kans., 1982-85; coordinator Boeing Employees Amateur Radio Soc., Wichita, 1982-83. Fellow Soc. Women Engrs. (sr. mem., sect. rep. 1981-83, sec. treas. 1985-86, regional bd. dirs. 1983-85, sect. pres. 1987-88); mem. AIAA, Bus. and Profl. Women, Quarter Century Wireless Assn. (communications com. 1985-86). Lodge: Toastmasters (local pres. 1985-86, competent toastmaster 1985). Avocations: amateur radio, singing, bowling. Home: 1201 N West St Rose Hill KS 67133 Office: PO Box 7730 Wichita KS 67277-7730

CALLANDER, KAY EILEEN PAISLEY, educator, writer; b. Coshocton, Ohio, Oct. 15, 1938; d. Dalton Olas and Dorothy Pauline (Davis) Paisley; m. Don Larry Callander, Nov. 18, 1977. BSE, Muskingum Coll., 1960; MA in Speech Edn., Ohio State U., 1964, postgrad., 1964-84. Cert. elem., gifted, drama, theater tchr., Ohio. Tchr. Columbus (Ohio) Pub. Schs., 1960-70, 80-88, drama specialist, 1970-80, classroom, gifted/talented tchr., 1986-90, ret., 1990; pres. The Ali Group, Inc., Columbus, 1990—; pres. Ali Group, Inc., Kay Kards; coord. Artists-in-the-Schs., 1977-88; cons., presenter numerous ednl. confs. and sems., 1971—. Producer-dir., Shady Lane Music Festival, 1980-88; dir., tchr. (nat. distbr. video) The Trial of Gold E. Locks, 1983-84; rep., media pub. relations liason Sch. News., 1983-88; author, creator Trivia Game About Black Americans (TGABA). Benefactor, Columbus Jazz Arts Group; v.p., bd. dirs. Neoteric Dance and Theater Co., Columbus, 1985-87; tchr., participant Future Stars sculpture exhbt, Ft. Hayes Ctr., Columbus Pub. Schs., 1988; tchr. advisor Columbus Coun. PTA's, 1983-86, ch-chmn. reflections com., 1984-87; mem. Humane Soc. of U.S., Statue of Liberty-Ellis Island Found., Inc., Columbus Mus. Art; mem. call and worship coms. Old Trinity Luth. Ch., Columbus, Ohio PTA; supt.'s adv. coun., Columbus Pub. Schs., 1967-68; presenter Young Author Sem., Ohio Dept. Edn., 1988; cons. and workshop leader for sem./workshop Teaching about the Constitution in Elem. Schs., Franklin County Ednl. Coun., 1988; presenter for Illustrating Methods for Young Authors' Books, 1986-87;. Named Educator of Yr., Shady Lane PT, 1982, Columbus Coun. PTAs, 1989; Sch. Excellence grantee Columbus Pub. Schs.; Commendation Columbus Bd. Edn. and Ohio Ho. of Reps. for Child Assault Prevention project, 1986-87. Mem. NEA, NAFE, NOW, The Smithsonian Assoc., Ohio Edn. Assn., Columbus Edn. Assn., Capital Area Humane Soc., Cen. Ohio Tchrs. Assn., Better Bus. Bur. Cen. Ohio, Inc., Ohio State U. Alumni Assn., Friends of Sta. WOSU-TV Ohio State U., Nat. Trust for Hist. Preservation, U.S. Army Officers' Club (def. constrn. supply ctr., Columbus), The Navy League, Liturgical Art Guild Ohio, Columbus Jazz Arts Group, Columbus Mus. of Art, Humane Soc. of U.S., Internat. Platform Assn., Assn. for Supervision and Curriculum Devel., Nat. Coun. for the Social Studies. Republican. Home: 570 Conestoga Dr Columbus OH 43213 Office: The Ali Group Inc PO Box 13093 Columbus OH 43213

CALLARD, CAROLE CRAWFORD, librarian, educator; b. Charleston, W.Va., Aug. 8, 1941; d. William O. and Helen (Shay) Crawford; m. Donald Pope Callard, Apr. 20, 1966; children: Susan Lynne, Annie Laurie. BA in Am. History, U. Charleston, 1963; MLS, U. Pitts., 1966; MA in Social Founds., Ea. Mich. U., 1978. Tchr. Blessed Sacrament Sch., South Charleston, W.Va., 1962-64; grad. trainee W.Va. Libr. Commn., Charleston, 1964-65; reference libr. Tompkins County Pub. Libr., Ithaca, N.Y., 1966-69; head libr. U.S. Embassy, Addis Ababa, Ethiopia, 1969-70; head govt. documents Haile Sellassie U., Addis Ababa, 1970-71; br. libr. Ann Arbor (Mich.) Pub. Libr., 1973-83; documents libr. U. Mich., Ann Arbor, 1983-84; spl. collections libr. Libr. of Mich., Lansing, 1984—, spl. collections supr., 1989—; chair around the world, around the campus U. Mich. Faculty Women's Club, Ann Arbor, 1974-76. Author: Index to 150th Anniversary Issue Ithaca Jour., 1967, Guide to Local History, Sources in the Huron Valley, 1980; editor: Sourcebook of Mich., 1986; coordinator project Mich. Cemeteries: Comprehensive Guide and Mich. 1870 Census Index; contbr. articles to profl. jours. Membership chair LWV, Ann Arbor; pres. Geneal. Soc. Washtenaw County, Mich., 1977-78, Washtenaw Libr. Club, 1982-83, Libr. Mich. Staff Assn., Lansing, Mich., 1985-86. Grantee U. Pitts., 1966, prof. staff grantee Ann Arbor Pub. Schs., 1980, edn. found. grantee Mich. Libr. Assn., 1982. Mem. Mich. Libr. Assn. (chmn. govt. documents sect. 1982-84), Spl. Librs. Assn., AAUW (corr. sec., historian 1973-74, 82-83), Fedn. Genealogy Socs. (del., corr. sec. 1986-87, v.p. regional affairs 1989-90), Nat. Genealogy Soc. (instr. devel. com. 1988-90), Mich. Geneal. Coun., DAR, Friends Ann Arbor Pub. Libr. (chmn. book sale).

CALLAWAY, ANITA MARIA, entrepreneur; b. Paterson, N.J., July 3, 1964; d. Joseph Milliard and Teressa Alice (Carmichael) C. Student, Electronic Computer Programming Inst., Paterson, 1983, Montclair State Coll., 1984-86. Computer operator Laura Ashley, Mahwah, N.J., 1983-85; computer programmer Keystone Camera, Clifton, N.J., 1985-86; lead computer operator Gucci Am., Secaucus, N.J., 1986-89; v.p. data processing R.S. Assocs., Montclair, N.J., 1989—; pres. Ind. Bus. Cons., Montclair, N.J., 1990—; data processing cons. Candace Enterprises, Plainfield, N.J., 1989—. Baptist. Home: 255 18th Ave Paterson NJ 07504 Office: Ind Bus Cons 504 Bloomfield Ave Montclair NJ 07042

CALLBECK, CATHERINE, Canadian legislator; b. Central Bedeque, P.E.I., Can., July 25, 1939; d. Ralph and Ruth Callbeck. Student, Mt. Allison U., Dalhousie U., Syracuse U. Dir. Can. Inst. Rsch. and Pub. Policy; mem. legislature Province of P.E.I., from 1974; mem. Ho. of Commons, Ottawa, Ont., Can., 1988—. Liberal. Mem. United Ch. of Can. Office: House of Commons, Parliament Bldgs, Ottawa, ON Canada K1A 0A6*

CALLENDER, NORMA ANNE, educator; b. Huntsville, Tex., May 10, 1933; d. Cleburn William Carswell and Nell Ruth (Collard) Hughes Bost; m. B.G. Callender, July, 1951 (div. 1964); remarried 1967 (div. 1973); children: Teresa Elizabeth, Leslie Gemey, Shannah Hughes, Kelly Mari; m. E. Purfurst, June 1965 (div. Aug. 1965). BS in Edn., U. Houston, 1969; MA, U. Houston at Clear Lake, 1977; postgrad. Lamar U., 1972-73, Tex. So. U., 1971, St. Thomas U., 1985, 86, U. Houston-Clear Lake, 1979, 87, 89-91, San Jacinto Coll., 1988, 89. Aerospace Inst., NASA, Johnson Space Ctr., 1986. Cert. reading specialist, Tex. Tchr., Houston Ind. Schs., 1969-70; co-counselor and instr. Ellington AFB, Houston, 1971; tchr. Clear Creek Schs., Seabrook, Tex., 1970-75; part-time instr. San Jacinto Coll., Pasadena, Tex., 1980-81; tchr. Clear Creek Schs., Webster, Tex., 1975-86; univ. adj., U. Houston, Clear Lake, Tex., 1986—; owner, dir. Bay Area Tutoring and Reading Clinic, Clear Lake City, Tex., 1970—; mem. adv. bd. Clear Creek Ednl. Resource Ctr. Publ., League City, 1976-77; mem. Prin's Council of Excellence, 1985-86. Contbr. poetry to profl. jours. Mem. Bay Area Rep. Women's Fedn., 1987—, Rep. Presdl. Task Force (chari. jours. Mem. Bay Area Rep. Women's Fedn., 1987—, Rep. Presdl. Task Force (charter), 1982; state advisor U.S. Congl. Adv. Bd., 1985-87; bd. dirs. Ballet San Jacinto, 1985-87; vol. Family Outreach Ctr., 1989—; adv. bd. Community Ednl. Television, 1990—. Recipient Franklin award U. Houston, 1965-67; Delta Kappa Gamma/Beta Omicron scholar, 1967-68; PTA scholar, 1973; Berwin scholar, 1976; Mary Gibbs Jones scholar, 1976-77; Found. Econ. Edn. scholar, 1976; Insts. Achievement Human Potential scholar, Phila., 1987-88. Mem. Clear Creek Educators Assn. (honorarium 1976, 77, 85), Internat. Reading Assn. (rsch. com. chpt. 1976-77), Houston World Affairs Coun., Leadership Clear Lake Alumni Assn. (charter, program and projects com mem. 1986-87, edn. com. 1985), Tex. Soc. Coll. Tchrs. Edn., Kappa Delta Pi, Phi Delta Kappa, Phi Kappa Phi. Mem. Life Tabernacle Ch. Home: 963 Seagate Ln Houston TX 77062 Office: PO Box 890932 Houston TX 77289-0932

CALLISTER, LYNN CLARK SCOTT, nurse educator; b. Washington, Oct. 19, 1942; d. Harold Glen and Virginia Louisa (Driggs) Clark; m. William Harris Scott, June 30, 1964 (div. Apr. 1987); children: Carolyn, Suzanne, William Jared, Christine, Jenilynn; m. Reed Richards Callister, Aug. 18, 1989. BS summa cum laude, Brigham Young U., 1964; MSN, Wichita State U., 1988. RN, Kans., Utah. Critical care nurse St. Mark's Med. Ctr., Salt Lake City, 1964-66, nursing adminstrn., 1966-69; ARC maternal/child educator, pediatric nurse Misawa (Japan) Air Force Base Hosp., 1969-72; commn. on the status of women City of Wichita (Kans.), 1977-80; chmn., substance abuse prevention program Wichita (Kans.) Pub. Schs., 1983-86; faculty, coll. nursing Brigham Young U., Provo, 1988—; nursing workshops and presentatations Utah, Calif., N.Mex., Kans., Nebr., Mo., 1980-89. Contbr. articles to profl. jours. Recipient scholarship, Kans. Nurses Assn., 1988. Mem. NAACOG, Nat. League of Nursing, Utah State Nurses Assn., Am. Nurses Assn., Sigma Theta Tau (Epsilon Gamma and Iota Iota chpts.). Republican. Mormon. Home: 2525 N 860 E Provo UT 84604 Office: Brigham Young U 436SWKT Provo UT 84602

CALLOWAY, DORIS HOWES, nutrition educator; b. Canton, Ohio, Feb. 14, 1923; d. Earl John and Lillian Ann (Roberts) Howes; m. Nathaniel O. Calloway, Feb. 14, 1946 (div. 1956); children: David Karl, Candace; m. Robert O. Nesheim, July 4, 1981. BS, Ohio State U., 1943; PhD, U. Chgo., 1947. Head metabolism lab., nutritionist, chief div. QM Food and Container Inst., Chgo., 1951-61; chmn. dept. food sci. and nutrition Stanford Rsch. Inst., Menlo Park, Calif., 1961-63; prof. U. Calif., Berkeley, 1963—, provost profl. schs. and colls., 1981-87; mem. expert adv. panel on nutrition WHO, Geneva, 1972—, tech. adv. com. Consultative Group on Internat. Agrl. Rsch., 1989—, Internat. Commn. on Health Rsch. for Devel., 1987-90, adv. coun. Nat. Inst. Arthritis, Metabollic & Digestive Diseases, Nat. Inst. Aging, NIH, Bethesda, Md., 1974-77, 78-82; trustee Internat. Maize and Wheat Improvement Ctr., 1983-88; trustee, bd. dirs. Winrock Internat. Inst.; cons. FAO, UN, Rome, 1971, 74-75, 81-83; lectr. Cooper Meml., 1983. Author: Nutrition and Health, 1981, Nutrition and Physical Fitness 11th edit., 1984; mem. editorial bd. Am. Dietetic Assn. Jour., 1974-77. Recipient Meritorious Civilian Service Dept. Army, 1959; named Disting. Alumna Ohio State U., 1974, Wellcome vis. prof. Fedn. Am. Soc. Exptl. Biol., U. Mo., 1980. Fellow Am. Inst. Nutrition (pres. 1982-83, sec. 1969-72, editorial bd. 1967-72; Conrad A. Elvehjem award 1986); mem. Inst. Medicine NAS, Sigma Xi. Office: U Calif Morgan Hall Berkeley CA 94720

CALLOWAY, MAUREEN, fundraiser; b. Houston, May 5, 1964; d. Clifford Clyde Calloway Jr. and Diane (Chamness) Upchurch. BA in Polit. Sci. & History, So. Meth. U., 1986. Staff asst. U.S. Congressman Mac Sweeney, Washington, 1987, exec. asst., 1987; dep. dist. dir. U.S. Congressman Mac Sweeney, Georgetown, Tex., 1987-88; fin. dir. Texans for Sweeney, Round Rock, Tex., 1988-89; house coun. coord. Nat. Rep. Congl. Com., Washington, 1989—. Mem. Fed. City Rep. Women, Washington, 1990; provisional mem. Jr. League of Washington, 1990; vol. Local Area Student Recruitment for So. Meth. U., Washington, 1986—. Mem. So. Meth. U. Alumni Assn., Tex. State Soc., Alpha Delta Pi Sorority Alumnae Assn., Capitol Hill Club. Republican. Methodist.

CALMESE, LINDA, computer training center executive, consultant; b. East St. Louis, Ill., June 3, 1947; d. Lonnie Daniel and Louise (Anderson) C. BS, So. Ill. U., 1969, MS, 1972, specialist degree counselor edn., 1978. Tchr. bus. edn. St. Teresa Acad., East St. Louis, 1969-73, DODDS, Madrid, 1973-84; computer cons. Scott AFB, Ill., 1984-87, Norton AFB, Calif., 1986, Navy Fin. Ctr., Cleve., 1987, Billy Mitchell Air Field, Milw., 1987, Richards Gebaur AFB, Kansas City, Mo., 1988, NASA, Cleve., 1988, Army Corps Engrs., St. Louis, 1988, Nat. U. San Diego, 1988; pres. Bits and Bytes Computer Tng. Ctr., Belleville, Ill., 1985—; instr. State Community Coll., East St. Louis, 1986-87, Office Pers. Mgmt. San Diego, San Francisco, L.A.; computer cons. Army Aviation Systems Command, St. Louis, 1986-87, Ohio Army N.G., Worthington, Ohio, 1986, 88, Mil. Personnel Records Ctr., St. Louis, 1986, 90, City of San Francisco, 1988, City of San Diego, 1988, Port Hueneme (Calif.) Naval Base, 1988, Corona (Calif.) Naval Weapons Sta., 1989, FAA, Kansas City, Mo., 1989, 90, Sharpe Army Depot, Stockton, Calif., 1989, Mare Island Naval Shipyard, Vallejo, Calif., 1989, Rock Island (Ill.) Arsenal, 1989, Ft. Leavenworth (Kans.) Army Base, 1990, Fed. Crop Ins. Corp., Kansas City, 1990, FDIC, Chgo., 1990, VA Hosp., Chgo., 1990. Contbr. chpt. to book: Business Education for the 70's, 1969. Clk. Mt. Zion Bapt. Mission East Ch., East St. Louis, 1987—. Mem. NAFE, Delta Pi Epsilon, Pi Omega Pi. Avocations: travel, computing, reading, aerobics. Office: Bits and Bytes Computer Tng Ctr 7705 W Main St Ste 7 Belleville IL 62223

CALTAGIRONE, CARMEN LILLIAN, educational administrator; b. Tampa, Fla., Jan. 22, 1950; d. Joe G. and Mary Jane (Reina) Caltagirone. BA, U. South Fla., 1971, MEd, 1976. Tchr. theology Tampa Cath. High Sch., 1971-83, chmn. dept. theology, 1973-83; asst. prin. Acad. of Holy Names, Tampa, 1983—, pastoral minister, 1989—; asst. chaplain Tampa Gen. Hosp., 1981-84; cons. Cath. ch. groups, 1978—. Author: The Catechist As Minister, 1981; Friendship As Sacrament, 1988; contbr. to religious periodicals. Coordinator Respect Life, Tampa, 1979-83. Recipient Up and Comers award Price Waterhouse/Tampa Bay Bus.Jour., 1989. Mem. Assn. for Supervision and Curriculum Devel., Nat. Middle Sch. Assn. Democrat. Office: Acad of the Holy Names 3319 Bayshore Blvd Tampa FL 33629

CALVERT, LOIS WILSON, civic worker; b. Hartford, Conn., Sept. 12, 1924; d. Royal Wouldhave and Evelyn Charlotte (Danielson) Wilson; m. Wallace Erdix Calvert, Mar. 29, 1947; children: Pamela, Gary, Craig and David (twins). Grad., Bryant Coll., 1943. Registrar of voters Town of Simsbury, Conn., 1982—. Hist. columnist Imprint Publs., West Hartford, Conn., 1986-87. Bd. dirs. Simsbury Hist. Soc., 1978—; mem. Simsbury Com. on Aging, 1980-89, Dem. Town Com., Simsbury, 1982—, also archivist, Simsbury Cemetery Assn., 1987—, Friends of Simsbury Library; del. 6th dist. Dem. Conv., Bristol, Conn., 1984, 86; trustee Simsbury Land Trust, 1984-88; justice of the peace Town of Simsbury, 1985—, mem. design rev. bd., 1989—; mem. constl. conv. bicentennial commn., Hometown Hero, 1986; alt. Conn. Dem. Conv. for Gov., Hartford, 1986—; mng. dir. Simsbury Hist. Soc.; del. State Dem. Conv., Hartford, 1990. Named a Simsbury Woman Hartford Woman mag., 1987. Mem. Registrar of Voters Assn. Conn. Congregationalist. Home: 28 Riverside Rd Simsbury CT 06070

CALVET, CORINNE, actress, therapist; b. Paris, 1925; came to U.S., 1949; d. Pierre and Juliette (Munier) Dibos de Mailly; m. John Fontaine; children: Robert Fontaine, Michael Calvet. Student, U. Sorbonne, Paris, Arica Inst., N.Y.C. Actress, 1950—; hypnotherapist Santa Monica, Calif., 1980—. Actress: (films) Rope of Sand, My Friend Irma, Petrus, Front and Center, We are Not Married, What Price Glory, On the Riviera, Peking Express, Sailor Beware, Powder River, Flight to Tangier, So This is Paris, The Far Country, The Sins of Casanova, Mail Order Bride, One Step to Eternity, Bluebeard's Tenth Honeymoon, Quebec, Dr. Jeckell and Mr. Hype, Hemingway: Adventures of a Young Man, Sword and the Sorcerer, Road House, (TV shows) Batman, Police Story, Hart to Hart, General Hospital, various game shows, (TV movies) Phantom of Hollywood, CBS, Dressed to Kill, NBC, French Atlantic Affair, ABC, (stage prodns.) Comedie Francaise, Personal Appearances, Mourning Becomes Electra; author: The Kirlan Aura, 1974, (autobiography) Has Corinne Been a Good Girl, 1983. Recipient Look award, Golden Globe award; named Dame of Malta. Mem. N.Y. Acad. Arts and Scis. Home and Office: Pacific Plaza Towers 1431 Ocean Ave Santa Monica CA 90401

CALVIN, DOROTHY VER STRATE, computer company executive; b. Grand Rapids, Mich., Dec. 22, 1929; d. Herman and Christina (Plakmyer) Ver Strate; m. Allen D. Calvin, Oct. 5, 1953; children: Jamie, Kris, Bufo, Scott. BS magna cum laude, Mich. State U., 1951; MA, U. San Francisco, 1988. Mgr. data processing. Behavioral Rsch. Labs., Menlo Park, Calif., 1972-75; dir. Mgmt. Info. Systems Inst. for Prof. Devel., San Jose, Calif. 1975-76; systems analyst, programmer Pacific Bell Info. Systems, San Francisco, 1976-81; staff mgr., 1981-84; mgr. applications devel. Data Architects Inc., San Francisco, 1984-86; pres. Ver Strate Press, San Francisco, 1986—. Instr., Downtown Community Coll., San Francisco, 1980-84, Cañada Community Coll., 1986—; mem. computer curriculum adv. coun. San Francisco City Coll., 1982-84. V.p. LWV, Roanoke, Va., 1956-58; pres. Bulliss Purissima Parents Group, Los Altos, Calif., 1962-64; bd. dirs. Vols. for Israel, 1986-87. Mem. NAFE, Assn. Systems Mgmt., Assn. Women in Computing. Democrat. Avocations: computing, gardening, jogging, reading. Office: Ver Strate Press 1645 15th Ave San Francisco CA 94122

CALZETTA, FRANCES ANNETTE, educator; b. New Haven, Dec. 19, 1935; d. Carmine and Assunta (Parente) C. BS, So. Conn. State U., 1957, MS, 1960; cert. advanced study, Fairfield U., 1968, postgrad., 1968-75. Cert. elem. tchr., reading specialist, Conn. Elem. tchr. Woodbridge (Conn.) Bd. Edn., 1957-78, lit. cons., 1978-86, lit. specialist, 1986—. Dir. essay contest Columbus Day Com., Inc., New Haven, 1979-84, cultural chmn. Christoforo Colombo 1992 Celebration Com.; rep. cand. town clk. New Haven, 1985, 87; scholarship chmn. Am. Com. on Italian Migration, New Haven and N.Y.C., 1984-90; co-chmn. Forbes Area Comml. and Resdl. Assn., New Haven, 1972—; 3d v.p. New Haven Coun. Cath. Women, 1965-67, pres., 1989—; bd. dirs. Cath. Charities, Cath. Family Svcs., New Haven, Archdiocese of Hartford. Mem. Am. Soc. Curriculum and Devel., Nat. Italian-Am. Found., Theater and Youth Alliance Am. Home: 239 Forbes Ave New Haven CT 06512 Office: Woodbridge Bd Edn 40 Beecher Rd Woodbridge CT 06525

CAMARDA, ROSE MARIE, teacher; b. Charleroi, Pa., Aug. 26, 1947; d. Nicholas Edward and Laura Bell (Peters) C. BS, Suny U., Brockport, 1969; MS, Syracuse U., Syracuse, 1973. Edn. (N-12). Elem. Syracuse (N.Y.) City Sch., 1969-70; elem. Syracuse City Sch., 1970-77, tchr., 1973-85, with, 1985-89, mentor tchr., 1990—; master tchr. Urban Tchr. Prog. Syracuse 1973; master tchr. Tchr. Corps Prog. Syracuse 1975-77; coaching Syracuse City Sch. Syracuse 1980-87; science dept. chairperson Shea Middle Sch. Syracuse 1985—; presenter Super Sci. Conf., 1989; author's cons. Den Mother Cub Scouts of Am. Syracuse 1961-63; Site Dir. Peace Inc. Syracuse 1975-76; Community Edn. Supr. Merrick Sch. Syracuse 1975-76. Recipient Newmast Scholarship Nasa and Nat'l Science Tchr. Assoc. 1985, Grant Statellite Station Syracuse City Sch. Shea Middle Sch. 1987, Citation Nasa Tchr. in Space Prog. 1984-85; Named One of N.Y. top 100 Science Tchr.- Opticle Soc. of Am. 1986. Mem. N.Y. State United Tchr., Nat'l Science Tcchr. Assoc., Syracuse Tchr. Assoc. (rep. 1972-75). Dem. Catholic. Home: 142 Mather St Syracuse NY 13203 Office: Shea Middle Sch 1607 S Geddes St Syracuse NY 13207

CAMERON, COLLEEN IRENE, alcoholism counselor; b. Stillwater, Minn., Nov. 3, 1952; d. Lyle James and Mary Rose (Jesse) C.; 1 child, Natalie Irene. Grad. high sch., Lindstrom, Minn. Cert. alcohol and drug counselor III, Wis. Counseling supr. St. Croix Health Ctr., New Richmond, Wis., 1977-83; dir. Our Lady's Inn, St. Louis, 1984; dir. ops. Carpenter Health Care Systems, St. Louis, 1984-86; supr. Edgewood Program St. John's Mercy Med. Ctr., St. Louis, 1986—, St. Elizabeth Med. Ctr., Granite City, Ill., 1986—. Mem. Am. Coll. Addiction Treatment Adminstrs. Roman Catholic. Office: Edgewood Program 1121 University Dr Edwardsville IL 62025

CAMERON, IRMA KYLLIKKI, small business owner, consultant; b. Rovaniemi, Finland, Dec. 25, 1948; came to U.S., 1967; d. Antti Antero Napankangas and Laura Vappu (Karvonen) Makkyla; m. Matt Kullervo Kosola, Dec. 24, 1964 (div. July 1972); 1 child, Jari; m. Jerry Lee Massmann, Aug. 25, 1984. BA in Mid Mgmt., Hennepin County Community Coll., 1982; postgrad. in bus. mgmt., Coll. of St. Thomas, 1983-85. Supr. sales Gen. Mills, Inc., Mpls., 1970-75; mgr. sales office Tampa, Fla., 1975-77; mgr. customer service Mpls., 1977-80, mgr. consumer relations, 1980-88; prin. Customer Relations Cons., Plymouth, Minn., 1988—. Contbg. author: Business Communication Today, 1986. Arbitrator Better Bus. Bur. Minn., Mpls., 1981—; mem. exec. com. Community Action Team Gen. Mills., Mpls., 1985-88, chmn. Adopt-A-Highrise Project, 1986-88. Recipient Leadership award Mpls. YWCA, 1981. Mem. Grocery Mfrs. Am., Soc. Consumer Affairs Profls., Nat. Assn. Female Execs. Republican.

CAMERON, JUDITH ELAINE MOELLERING, jewelry designer and manufacturer; b. Eagle Grove, Iowa, May 26, 1943; d. Albert Edwin and Marion (Trask) Moellering; m. William Ewen Cameron, Aug. 13, 1966 (div. 1970). BA, Drake U., 1965. Polit. intern, Washington, 1965; model, asst. buer, copywriter, Yonkers, Des Moines, 1962-66; asst. to columnist Harlan Miller, 1962-65; dir. pers. 4th Northwestern Nat. Bank, Mpls., 1966; head copywriter SPF Advt., Mpls., 1966-68; dir. spl. projects program U. Minn., Mpls., 1968-70; cons. pub. rels. Fed. Republic of Germany, Italy, Spain, 1970-71; mgr. Jetset Sportswear, Footville, Wis., 1971-72; artist Almunecar, Spain, 1972-74; dir. pub. rels. Topspin, Totalplan Sports Internat., A.G., Madrid, 1974-76, mng. dir., Madrid and London, 1976-80; European mgr. Siam Internat. Amalgamated Mfrs. Ltd., London, 1977-80; European rep. Siam Cement Trading Co., London, 1979-80; European mgr. Third Wave Electronics Co., Inc., London, 1980-82; exec. v.p., dir. Electronic Specialty Products, Inc., N.Y.C., 1983-84; pres. Q.E.D., Ltd., Hong Kong, 1981-85, Comml. Brain, Inc., N.Y.C. and N.Mex., 1984—, Judith Cameron of Santa Fe, 1988—. Bd. dirs. N.Mex. Repertory Theater; mem. N.Mex. Task Force, Arts Advocacy, Fashion Coun., Rep. Nat. Com. 4 one-woman shows, Spain; 4 group exhbns., Europe. Mem. NAFE, Republicans Abroad, Women Bus. Owners of N.Y., Iowa Soc. N.Y. (founding mem., pres.), Coun. Internat. Rels., Spotlighters, Am. Crafts Coun., Alpha Phi.

CAMERON, JUDITH LYNNE, educator, hypnotherapist; b. Oakland, Calif., Apr. 29, 1945; d. Alfred Joseph and June Estelle (Faul) Moe; m. Richard Irwin Cameron, Dec. 17, 1967; 1 child, Kevin Dale. AA in Psychol., Sacramento City Coll., 1965; BA in Psychol., German, Calif. State U., 1967; MA in Reading Specialization, San Francisco State U., 1972; postgrad., Chapman Coll.; PhD, Am. Inst. Hypnotherapy, 1987. Cert. tchr., Calif. Tchr. St. Vincent's Catholic Sch., San Jose, Calif., 1969-70, Fremont (Calif.) Elem. Sch., 1970-72, LeRoy Boys Home, LaVerne, Calif., 1972-73; tchr. Grace Miller Elem. Sch., LaVerne, Calif., 1973-80, resource specialist, 1980-84; owner, mgr. Pioneer Take-out Franchises, Alhambra and San Gabriel, Calif., 1979-85; resource specialist, dept. chmn. Bonita High Sch., LaVerne, Calif., 1984—; mentor tchr. in space sci. Bonita Unified Sch. Dist., 1988—; owner, therapist So. Calif. Clin. Hypnotherapy, Claremont, Calif., 1988—; bd. dirs., recommending tchr., asst. dir. Project Turnabout, Claremont, Calif.; Teacher-in-Space cons. Bonita Unified Sch. Dist., LaVerne, 1987—; advisor Peer Counseling Program, Bonita High Sch., 1987—; advisor Air Explorers/Edwards Test Pilot Sch., LaVerne, 1987—; mem. Civil Air Patrol, Squadron 68, Aerospace Office, 1988—; selected amb. U.S. Space Acad.-U.S. Space Camp Acad., Huntsville, Ala., 1990; named to nat. teaching faculty challenger Ctr. for Space Edn., Alexandria, Va., 1990. Vol. advisor Children's Home Soc., Santa Ana, 1980-81. Named Tchr. of Year, 1988-89, Bonita High Sch., La Verne, Calif., Space Ambassador U.S. Space Camp, 1990, Nat. Teaching Faculty Challenger Ctr. for Space Edn., 1990. Mem. Council Exceptional Children, Calif. Assn. Resource Specialists, Calif. Elem. Edn. Assn., NEA, Calif. Teacher's Assn., Calif. Assn. Marriage and Family Therapists, Planetary Soc., Com. Scientific Investigation L5 Soc., Challenger Ctr. for Space Edn., Calif. Challenger Ctr. Crew for Space Edn. Republican. Clubs: Chinese Shar-Pei Am., Concord, Rare Breed Dog, Los Angeles. Home: 3257 La Travesia Dr Fullerton CA 92635 Office: Bonita High Sch 115 W Allen Ave San Dimas CA 91773

CAMEY, PAMELA S., sales official; b. Princeton, Ill., Mar. 28, 1962; d. William R. and Sharon A. (Borg) C. BS, So. Ill. U., Carbondale, 1984, MS, 1985. Cert. emergency medicine technician; cert. in wilderness search and rescue. Asst. field hockey coach So. Ill. U.; sales rep. Electro Therapeutics, N.Y.C., South East Med. Corp., Sem Corp., Charlotte, N.C., Miles Pharm., Miles Inc., West Haven, Conn. Mem. Women Self Def. Coun., Victim Prevention Inc. Mem. NAFE. Home: 1233 12th Ave Moline IL 61265

CAMMACK, CAROLINE, fashion designer; b. Abilene, Tex., Nov. 4, 1951; d. James Willard and Mary (Booth) Steward; m. William White Cammack II, May 24, 1980. AA in Fashion Design, Stephens Coll., 1971; BS in Fashion Design, Tex. Tech., 1972; AA in Interior Design, El Centro Coll., 1980. Freelance fashion designer Dallas, 1975-80; interior designer Paul Toomey Inc., Dallas, 1980-81, Joyce Browning Co., Dallas, 1982-83; freelance fashion and interior designer Dallas, 1983, 85-86; space planner Regency Devel., Dallas, 1983-85; ptnr., owner Flowers/Cammack Designs, Dallas, 1986—. Author (poems): The Hot-House Lily, 1976. Mem. Jr. League, Dallas, 1976—, Poetry Soc., Tex., 1976—. Mem. Fashion Group, Am. Soc. Interior Designers, Bach Soc. Republican. Episcopalian. Office: Flowers/Cammack Designs 5518 Dyer St Ste 15 Dallas TX 75206

CAMMERMEYER, MARGARETHE, nurse; b. Oslo, Mar. 24, 1942; came to U.S., 1951; d. Jan and Margrethe (Grimsgaard) C.; m. Harvey H. Hawken, Aug. 1965 (div. 1980); children: Matthew, David, Andrew, Thomas. BS, U. Md., 1963; MA, U. Wash., 1976, postgrad., 1987—. RN, Wash. Staff nurse VA Hosp., Seattle, 1970-73, clin. nurse specialist in neurology, epilepsy, 1976-81; clin. nurse specialist in neuro-oncology VA Med. Ctr., San Francisco, 1981-86; clin. nurse specialist in neuroscis. VA Med. Ctr., Tacoma, Wash., 1986—; asst. chief nurse, supr. Army Res. Hosp., Seattle, 1972-81; chief nurse Army Res. Hosp., Oakland, Calif., 1985-88, Wash. Army N.G. and N.G. Hosp., Tacoma, 1988. Co-author: Neurological Assessment for Nursing Practice, 1984 (named Book of Yr. Am. Nurses Assn.); co-editor, contbg. author: Core Curriculum for Neuroscience Nursing, 1990; contbr. articles to profl. publs. Served to capt. nurse corps U.S. Army, 1963-68, Vietnam, other locations. Decorated Bronze Star medal; recipient presdl. cert. for outstanding community achievement of Vietnam era vets., 1979, "A" Proficiency designation Office of Surgeon Gen. Dept. of Army, 1986; named Woman of Yr. Woman's Army Corps Vets. Assn., 1984, Nurse of Yr. VA, 1985. Mem. Am. Assn. Neurosci. Nursing (former chair core curriculum), Am. Nurses Assn., Wash. State Nurses Assn., Assn. Mil. Surgeons of U.S., Sigma Theta Tau. Home: 1715 S 234th St Des Moines WA 98198 Office: VA Med Ctr American Lake Tacoma WA 98493

CAMP, ALETHEA TAYLOR, state agency administrator; b. Wingo, Ky., Nov. 12, 1938; d. Wayne Thomas and Ethel Virginia (Austin) Taylor; children: Donna Paul, Sean Richard. BA, Murray State U., 1961; MA, So. Ill. U., 1975. Tchr. McClean and Hopkins (Ky.) County Schs., 1961-64; instr. homebound Harrisburg (Ill.) Community Sch. Dist., 1971-73; counselor evaluation Coleman Rehab. Ctr., Shawneetown, Ill., 1974-75; counselor corrections and parole Dept. Corrections, State Ill., Springfield, 1975-77, supr. casework, 1977, supr. parole, 1977-80; asst. warden programs Dept. Corrections, State Ill., Hillsboro, 1980-84, warden, 1984—. Mem. Am. Correctional Assn., Ill. Correctional Assn., N. Am. Wardens Assn. Office: Ill Dept Corrections Graham Correctional Cen Hillsboro IL 62049

CAMP, BARBARA ANN, municipal government official; b. Lancaster, Pa., Feb. 13, 1943; d. Linton Ferguson and Anna (Wills) Mennig; m. Nils Victor Anderson, Nov. 25, 1961 (div. 1972); children: Barbara Jean, Susan Michelle, Jennifer Eileen; m. Robert Tomlin Camp, Dec. 29, 1973. Registered mcpl. clk., N.J. Sec., Sun Oil Corp., Phila., 1960-61; sales clk. Thomas Jewelers, Ocean City, N.J., 1969-71; composite typist Avalon Herald, N.J., 1971-72; exec. sec. Publs. Press., Pleasantville, N.J., 1972-74; clk.-typist Twp. of Upper Tuckahoe, N.J., 1977-78, mcpl. clk., 1978—. Editor twp. calendar, 1984-86. Mem. Mcpl. Clks. Assn. of N.J. (asst. treas. 1985-87, treas. 1987, asst. sec. 1988, sec. 1989, 2d v.p. 1990), Internat. Inst. Mcpl. Clks., Cape May County Clks. Assn. (past sec., past v.p., past pres.), Assn. Twps. (sec.). Avocations: snow skiing, boating. Home: 223 Laurel Dr Marmora NJ 08223

CAMP, HAZEL LEE BURT, artist; b. Gainesville, Ga., Nov. 28, 1922; d. William Ernest and Annie Mae (Ramsey) Burt; m. William Oliver Camp, Jan. 24, 1942; children: William Oliver, David Byron. Student, Md. Inst. Art, 1957-58, 62-63. One-woman shows at Ga. Mus. Art, Rockville Art Mus., Coll. Notre Dame (Balt.), U. Md., Balt. Vertical Gallery, Cleveland Meml. Gallery (Balt.), Unicorn Gallery, 1982, Hampton Ctr. for Arts and Humanities (Va.), 1985, others; exhibited in juried shows at Peale Mus., Balt., Wilmington (Del.) Fine Arts Ctr., Smithsonian Instn., Turner Gallery, Balt., Bendann Art Gallery, Balt., 1980, City Hall Gallery, Balt., 1982, Balt. Watercolor Soc., 1983, Miniature Painters, Sculptors and Gravers Soc. at the Arts Club, Washington, 1987, 88, 89, Hampton Bay Days Raddison Hotel Gallery, 1988, Twentieth Century Gallery, Williamsburg, Va., 1989, D'Art Ctr., Norfolk, Va., 1989, others; represented in permanent collections: Ga. Mus. Art, Peabody Inst. (Balt.), Rehoboth Art League, numerous pvt. collections; contbr. illustrations to mags., booklets. Mem. 20th Century Gallery, Williamsburg, Va. Recipient 1st prize Md. chpt. Artists' Equity, 1967, St. Marys County Art Assn., 1964, 67, 1st prize still life Cape May, N.J., 1969, Catonsville (Md.) Community Coll., 1969, St. John's Coll., 1969, Best in Show York (Pa.) Art Assn. Gallery, 1972, 2d award Md. Inst. Alumni Founding Chpt., Balt., 1976, Best in Show Three Arts Club, 1978, Honorable Mention, Rehoboth Art League, 1983, Purchase award Old Point Nat. Bank, Hampton, Va., 1985, Merit award Hampton (Va.) City Hall, 1986, Juror's Choice award Twentieth Century Gallery, Williamsburg, Va., 1987, Award of Excellence Md. State Biennial Eliminations at Essex Community Coll., 1989, Montgomery Coll., Rockville, Md., 1987. Mem. Nat. League Am. Pen Women (pres. Carroll br. 1968-70, editor The Quill 1975-76, editor for Carroll br. 1982-83, rec. sec. nat. exec. bd. 1979-80, nat. nominating com. 1982, Md. art chmn. 1982, Watercolor award 1966), Artists' Equity, Rehoboth Art League, Va. Watercolor Soc., Md. Inst. Alumni Assn., Balt. Watercolor Soc. (hon. mention 1982, sec. 1978-80), Peninsula Fine Arts Ctr., Nat. League Am. Pen Women. Methodist. Home: 2 Bayberry Dr Newport News VA 23601

CAMP, LAURIE SMITH, lawyer; b. Omaha, Nov. 28, 1953; d. Edson and Virginia Elizabeth (Abbott) Smith; m. Jon Allan Camp, May 12, 1975; children: Jonathan Scott, Abigail Anne. BA with honors, Stanford U., 1974; JD, U. Nebr., 1977. Bar: Nebr. 1977, Kans. 1979. In-house counsel 1st Nat. Bank, Lincoln, Nebr., 1977-78; assoc. Turner & Boisseau, Great Bend, Kans., 1978-80; gen. counsel Nebr. Dept. Correctional Svcs., Lincoln, 1980—; gen. ptnr., counsel Haymarket Historic Real Estate Rehab., Lincoln, 1982—. Editor-in-chief Nebr. Law Rev., 1976-77; contbr. articles to profl. jours. Mem. Nebr. Bar Assn., Nebr. Correctional Assn. (pres. 1982-83). Office: Nebr Dept Correctional Services PO Box 96441 Lincoln NE 68509

CAMP, LINDA JOYCE, government official; b. Plattsburgh, N.Y.; d. Maurice B. and Katherine E. (Trombley) C. BS, Cornell U., 1973, M of Pub. Sci., 1977. Media specialist N.Y. Sea Grant Program, Ithaca, 1973-76; mgr. communications, cable communications officer City of St. Paul, 1980-87, purchasing systems mgr., 1988—; mem. met. council telecommunicaions task force, St. Paul, 1982-85; mem. Minn. Telecommunications Council, St. Paul, 1984-85. Vol. Big Sister Program, St. Paul, 1980-83. Bush fellow, 1987. Mem. Nat. Assn. Telecommunications Officers (pres. 1983, Pres.'s award 1985), Am. Mgmt. Assn., St. Paul Women in City Mgmt. Club: Cornell U. (Minn.). Office: City of St Paul 233 City Hall Saint Paul MN 55102

CAMP, ROSE ELIZABETH THOMAS, commissioner; b. Lake Forest, Ill., Oct. 2, 1952; d. Gordon Ward and Rose Lorraine (Crossett) Thomas; m. Jack Tarpley Camp, Jr., Apr. 24, 1976; children—Thomas Henry, Sophia Rose. A.B., Sweet Briar Coll., 1974; J.D., Woodrow Wilson Coll. Law, 1981. Counselor, Ferry Hall Day Camp for Girls, Lake Forest, 1967-71; congl. intern Congressman Henry B. Gonzalez of Tex., San Antonio and Washington, 1973-74; legis. asst. Senator John L. McClellan of Ark., Washington, 1974-76; exec. asst. Glover and Davis, P.A., Newnan, Ga., 1976-78; office mgr. Congressman Newt Gingrich, Newnan, 1978-83, congl. adminstr., 1983-88; commr. Coweta County Clean and Beautiful Commn., 1988—. Editor-in-chief Sweet Briar News, 1974; contbr., author to families histories. Del. to Republican Conv., State of Ga., Atlanta, 1984, Sixth Dist., Newnan, Ga., 1984; tour guide vol. Hist. Male Acad. Mus., Newnan, 1984; vol. ARC, Fort Sam Houston and Washington, 1972-76; mem. Rep. Women's Club, Newnan, 1979—. Served with USAR, 1973-74. Mem. LWV, DAR (page continental congress 1974), AAUW, Ga. Trust for Hist. Preservation, United Daus. of Confederacy (pres. Newnan 1981-83), Newnan-Coweta Hist. Soc., Nat. Soc. U.S. Daus. of 1812, Soc. Daus. of U.S. Army, Colonial Dames of XVII Century, Daughters of the Am. Colonists, Sweet Briar Alumnae Assn. (class rep. 1974—). Presbyterian (elder). Club: Driftwood Garden. Home: 1615 Handy Rd Newnan GA 30263

CAMPANA, ANA ISABEL, architect; b. Banes, Oriente, Cuba, Jan. 16, 1934; came to U.S., 1967, naturalized, 1974; d. Abelardo Joaquin and Amparo (Cabrera) C. BS, Instituto del Vedado, Havana, Cuba, 1953; postgrad., Havana U., 1962, Albany (N.Y.) Inst. History and Art, 1970. With Ministry of Pub. Works Havana, 1962-67, architect designer various firms, 1967-74; sr. architect Gen. Electric Co., Schenectady, N.Y., 1974-89; architect LaBerge Group, Albany, 1989—. Recipient 1st nat. award Nat. Mus. Com., Havana, 1948, 1st Province award, 1948, several international archtl. performance awards. Mem. AIA (assoc.). Roman Catholic. Home: 422 Sand Creek Rd Apt 506 Albany NY 12205 Office: LaBerge Group 4 Computer Dr W Albany NY 12205

CAMPANARO, LURANA TUCKER, industrial relations specialist; b. Los Angeles, Mar. 29, 1935; d. Leon William and Elizabeth W. (Taylor) Tucker; m. Lawrence A. Spanier, June 28, 1958; (div. July 1967); children: Douglas, Ava, Shana; m. Rocco, Jan 13, 1973; stepchildren: Doralea, Anthony. Postgrad., Mt. St. Mary's Coll., Los Angeles, 1955, Marymount Coll., Los Angeles, 1956; BA in Sci., Labor Studies, SUNY, 1977; Masters in Pub. Adminstrn, Long Island U., Greenvale, 1980. Training specialist Nassau County Bur. of Career Planning, Garden City, N.Y., 1967-70; human relations specialist Nassau County Vocat. Ctr. for Women, Garden City, 1970-71, dir., 1971-75; advisor to county exec. Nassay County Co. Exec. Office, Garden City; exec. dir. Nassau County Office of Women's Services, Garden City, 1977-83; legis. advisor N.Y. State Assembly Ways & Means Com., 1984-87, N.Y. State Senate, Albany, 1987-88; special community advisor Nassau County Com. on Human Rights, Garden City, 1988--.; tchr. N.Y. Inst. Tech., Commack, 1978-80, Cornell U. Sch. Indsl. Rels., Farmingdale, 1980-81; pres. CARLU Assn., Ltd., L.I., 1987—; with Corp. Communications, Group Health Ins., N.Y.C., 1985-89. Contbr. articles to profl. jours. Bd. dirs. Nassau County Legal Aid Soc., Garden City, 1979-80; Governing Bd. Long Island Health Systems Agy., Melville, 1979-82. Recipient Community Contbn. Long Island Lighting Co., 1983, Career Counseling Program L.I. U. C.W. Post Campus, 1978, Good Govt. award Nat. Assn. of Counties, 1974-75, 1978-79. Mem. Pi Alpha Alpha Nat. Hon. Soc. Republican. Roman Catholic. Office: Nassau County Commn on Human Rights 320 Old Country Rd Garden City NY 11530

CAMPANELLA, ALICE, retirement benefits administrator; b. Tamgiers, Morrocco, Oct. 2, 1955; d. Sam And Guillermina Campanella. Student, Boise State U., 1977. Actuarial svcs. adminstr. Boise (Idaho) Cascade Corp.; retirement benefits adminstr. J.R. Simplot Co., Boise. Vol. program YWCA. Mem. Am. Soc. for Pub. Adminstrn., Soc. Human Resources Mgmt., Human Resources of Treasure Valley, Western Pension Conf. Home: 1206 Michigan Ave Boise ID 83706

CAMPANELLA, DONNA MADELINE, advertising agency executive; b. N.Y.C., May 22, 1952; d. Dominic Salvatore and Lillian Theresa (Agatone) C. BA magna cum laude, Fordham U., 1974, postgrad. in bus. adminstrn., 1980-81. Asst. spot TV buyer Young & Rubicam, Inc., N.Y.C., 1974-75, media planner, 1975-77, media supr., 1977-84; v.p., media dir. Cato Johnson/Young & Rubicam, N.Y.C., 1984-88; sr. v.p., group media planning dir. Lintas, N.Y.C., 1988—; presenter, trainer Young & Rubicam Advt. Skills Workshop, N.Y.C., 1983-87; tchr., lectr. Advt. Women N.Y., 1987-88. Contbr. articles to trade publs. Sec. Baydale Tenants Assn., Bayside N.Y., 1985, pres. 1986. Mem. NAFE. Home: 686 Ascan Rd Franklin Square NY 11010 Office: Lintas 1 Dag Hammarskjold Pla New York NY 10017

CAMPBELL, ALMIRA TAYLOR, retired librarian; b. Hyde Park, Mass., May 26, 1920; d. Arthur Balcom and Mildred Victoria (Fuller) Taylor; m. Vincent Alexander Douglas Argyle Campbell, June 26, 1953 (dec. 1985); 1 child, Faith Campbell Bacastow. AA, Colby Jr. Coll., 1940; BA, Mt. Holyoke Coll., 1942; BS Sch. Libr. Sci., Simmons Coll., 1943. Acquisitions asst. Yale Law Sch. Libr., New Haven, 1943-45; prof. asst. accessions dept. Williston Meml. Libr./Mt. Holyoke Coll., South Hadley, Mass., 1945-48; head libr. Mt. Hermon (Mass.) Sch., 1948-53; head libr., tchr. French Stoneleigh Prospect Hill Sch., Greenfield, Mass., 1961-70; cataloguer F.L. Boyden Libr./Deerfield (Mass.) Acad., 1970-79; now ret.; vol. Ormond Beach (Fla.) Pub. Libr., 1983-89. Vol. Meml. Hosp., Ormond Beach, 1981—, Halifax Humane Soc., Ormond Beach, 1988—; Circle leader, mem. choir Christ Presbyn. Ch., Ormond Beach, 1986—; leader Alzheimer Assn. Support Group, Daytona Beach, Fla., 1987—, Ormond Beach, 1989—. Mem. AAUW (chmn. lit. group 1988-90). Republican. Home: 28 Niagara Falls Circle Ormond Beach FL 32174

CAMPBELL, AVRIL KIM, Canadian minister of state; b. Port Alberni, B.C., Can., Mar. 10, 1947; m. Howard Eddy. BA in Polit. Sci., U. B.C., 1969, LLB, 1983. Lectr. polit sci. U. B.C., Vancouver, 1975-78; lectr. polit. sci. and history Vancouver Community Coll., Langara, 1978-81; articled student, lawyer Ladner Downs, Vancouver, 1983-85; exec. dir. Office of Premier, 1985-86; candidate for leader Social Credit Party, 1986; mem. legis. assembly Vancouver Point Grey, 1986-88; chmn. govt. caucus intern program; M.P. from Vancouver Centre Ho. of Commons, Ottawa, Ont., Can., 1988, chmn. builder's lien act hearings, mem. caucus strategic planning coms., chmn. select standing coms. on labor, justice and intergovtl. rels., mem. select standing com. on edn., health and social svcs., on forests and lands, chmn. task force on heritage conservation Project Pride, minister of state for Indian affairs and No. devel., 1989-90, minister of justice, atty. gen. Can., 1990—; co-founder, co-owner Bridges Restaurant, Vancouver, 1978-89. Trustee Vancouver Sch. Bd., 1980-84, chmn. bd., 1983, vice-chmn., 1984. Can. Coun. doctoral fellow London Sch. Econs., 1970-74. Office: House of Commons, Parliament Bldgs, Ottawa, ON Canada K1A 0A6*

CAMPBELL, BARBARA ANN, editor; b. Portland, Oreg., July 17, 1935; d. Clarence Fontaine and Roberta Bessie (Mount) Bogart; m. Milton Gray Campbell, Jan. 25, 1958 (div. July 1983); children: Milton Gray Jr., Julie Melinda, Justin Garrett. Student, San Diego State Coll., 1954-55. Customer svc. rep. Harrison-Bell, Inc., South Plainfield, N.J., 1979-81, area rep., 1981-84; editor Daisy Publs., Seattle, 1984-86; editor, mng. editor Scott Publs., Livonia, Mich., 1986—. Office: Scott Publs 30595 West 8 Mile Rd Livonia MI 48152

CAMPBELL, BETTY JEAN, pediatrician; b. Indpls., July 9, 1951; d. William Arthur and Margaret Marie (Shaefer) C. MD, Ind. U., 1976. Diplomate Am. Bd. Pediatrics. Intern, then resident in pediatrics Riley Hosp., Ind. U. Med. Ctr., Indpls., 1976-79; pvt. practice Terre Haute, Ind., 1979—; pres. med. staff Regional Hosp., Terre Haute, 1987, trustee, 1989—. Active Terre Haute Ctr. Med. Edn. Fellow Am. Acad. Pediatrics, Ind. Chpt. Am. Acad. Pediatrics; mem. AMA, Ind. State Med. Assn., Vigo County Med. Soc. (pres. 1990). Office: 501 Hospital Ln Terre Haute IN 47802

CAMPBELL, BEVERLY-CLAIRE, non-profit literacy corporation executive; b. Detroit, Jan. 21, 1954; d. Theodore R. and Mary Frances (Parks) C. BA in Speech and Theatre, Newberry Coll., 1976. Advt. dir. The Weekly Observer, Hemingway, S.C., 1976-77; family editor The Press and Standard, Walterboro, S.C., 1977-78; pub. info. dir. Sherman Coll. Straight Chiropractic, Spartanburg, S.C., 1978-80; exec. dir. Adult Writing And Reading Edn., Inc. (AWARE), Spartanburg, 1980—; adv. com. Inst. for the Study of Adult Literacy, Pa. State U., State College, 1988-89. Editor SCLA News, 1986-88. Press sec. Ann Hicks for County Coun., Spartanburg, 1988; bd. dirs. Little Theatre, Spartanburg, 1984-88, publicity chair, 1984-87. Recipient Elizabeth J. Patterson Pub. Svc. award Women's History Month Com., Spartanburg County, 1988, Internat. Communications Achievement, Toastmasters, Spartanburg, 1987; named Literacy Coord. of Yr. State Dept. Edn., S.C., 1986. Mem. Leadership Spartanburg Alumni Assn., Spartanburg County Coun. Internat. Reading Assn. (state literacy chair, 1989—). Office: Spartanburg AWARE Inc PO Box 308 Spartanburg SC 29304

CAMPBELL, BONNIE JEAN, lawyer, state official; b. Norwich, N.Y., Apr. 9, 1948; d. Thomas Glenn and Helen Henrietta (Slater) Pierce; m. Edward Leo Campbell, Dec. 24, 1974. BA summa cum laude, Drake U., 1982, JD, 1984. Bar: Iowa 1985, U.S. Dist. (no. and so. dist.) Iowa 1985, U.S. Ct. Appeals (8th cir.) 1989, U.S. Supreme Ct. 1989. Clk. U.S. Dept. Housing and Urban Devel., Washington, 1965-67, U.S. Senate Subcom. on Inter Govtl. Relations, Washington, 1967-69; case worker Hon. Harold E. Hughes, Washington, 1969-74; field rep. U.S. Senator John C. Culver, Des Moines, 1974-80; assoc. Wimer, Hudson, Flynn & Neugent, P.C., Des Moines, 1984-89; of counsel Belin, Harris, Helmick, Des Moines, 1989-91; atty. gen. State of Iowa, 1991—. Mem. awareness com. Powell III, Iowa Meth. Hosp., Des Moines, 1984; mem. adv. com. Des Moines Community Coll., Ankeny, Iowa, 1985; mem. adv. bd. The Assistance Ctr., Des Moines, 1985; state chmn. Iowa Dems., Des Moines, 1987-89. Mem. Iowa Bar Assn. (lawyers helping lawyers 1985—), Phi Beta Kappa. Home: 300 Walnut #187 Des Moines IA 50309 Office: Office Atty Gen Hoover State Office Bldg 2nd fl Des Moines IA 50319

CAMPBELL, BONNIE MARIE, real estate professional; b. Belle Fourche, S.D., Mar. 2, 1944; d. James Julius and Anita Marie (Nelsen) Wiessner; m. Scott Harrison Campbell, Sept. 17, 1977; children: Keith Edward, Kimberly Denise, Tyson Scott; 1 stepchild, Shad Harrison Campbell. Student, Portland (Oreg.) State U., 1966. Lic. real estate agt., Oreg., Wash. Asst. to dir. Dept. Vocat. Rehab., Portland, 1966-69; asst. to pres. Reddaway Truck Lines, Portland, 1973-75; mgr. procurement Notestine Enterprises, Portland, 1976-80; salesman real estate Realty World, West Linn, Oreg., 1980-83, Profls. 100, Inc., Portland, 1983—. Mem. Nat. Assn. Realtors, Nat. Council Exchangers (Gold Card mem.), Comml.-Investment Real Estate Council, Clackamas County Bd. Realtors (Million Dollar Club), Portland Bd. Realtors, Nat. Assn. Female Execs. Hist. Preservation. Roman Catholic. Club: Toastmasters (Portland). Office: Profls 100 Inc Realtors 5285 SW Meadows Dr #161 Lake Oswego OR 97035

CAMPBELL, CAROLINE KRAUSE, drug company executive; b. Praha, Tex., May 5, 1926; d. Charles Joseph and Mary Victoria (Havrde) Krause; student, U. N.Mex., 1958-63; diploma Alexander Hamilton Inst., 1966-69; m. Richard E. Campbell, Dec. 30, 1946; children—Richard E., Don Michael, Scott Gary, Jonathan Miles, Candace Kay. Survey researcher Winona Research Co., Mpls., 1953-54; merchandiser, buyer Campbell Drug Inc., Albuquerque, 1961-77, gen. mgr., 1978—, pres., 1978—, dir., 1978—. Mem. Nat. Assn. Corp. Dirs., Assn. Commerce and Industry of N.Mex., C. of C. Albuquerque (bd. dirs.), Small Business Roundtable, Nat. Assn. Retail Druggists (impaired pharmacist com.), Medicine/Bus. Coalition, N.Mex. Pharm. Assn., Internat. Platform Assn., Albuquerque Symphony Women's Assn. Republican. Clubs: Albuquerque Rose Soc., Italian Cultural. Lodge: Elks. Office: Campbell Drug Inc 8252 Menaul Blvd NE Albuquerque NM 87110

CAMPBELL, CLAIRE PATRICIA, nurse, educator; b. Jan. 10, 1933; d. Hugh Paul and Clara Louise (Bell) Campbell. Student So. Meth. U., 1956-57; BS in Nursing, U. Tex. Sch. Nursing-Galveston, 1959, Family Nurse Practitioner, 1979, cert., 1984; MS in Nursing, Tex. Woman's U. Sch. Nursing, 1971. Staff nurse Parkland Meml. Hosp., Dallas County Hosp. Dist., 1955-70, head nurse gen. surgery, chest surgery, neurosurgery, orthopedics, and internal medicine, until 1970; instr. nursing Tex. Woman's U. Sch. Nursing, Dallas, 1971-72; researcher nursing diagnosis, Dallas, 1972-77; family nurse practitioner pain mgmt. program Otis Engring. Health Service, Dallas, 1979-86, Dallas Rehab. Inst., 1986—; adj. asst. prof. U. Tex. Sch. Nursing, Arlington, 1976—; cons. nursing diagnosis. Author: Nursing Diagnosis and Intervention in Nursing Practice, 1st edit., 1978, 2d edit., 1984. Mem. Am. Nurses Assn., Tex. Nurses Assn. - Dist. 4, North Am. Nursing Diagnosis Assn., Sigma Theta Tau. Roman Catholic.

CAMPBELL, COLINE, Canadian legislator; d. Samuel J. Campbell and Cecile Theriault; m. Ronald T. Whitman. Student, St. Francis Xavier U., Laval U., U. Ottawa, Harvard U. Lawyer, educator; mem. Ho. of Commons, 1974-79, 80-84, 88—. Liberal. Roman Catholic. Office: House of Commons, Parliament Bldgs, Ottawa, ON Canada K1A 0A6*

CAMPBELL, DEBORAH KAYE, secondary school guidance counselor; b. Richlands, Va., Aug. 22, 1955; d. Robert Allen and Betty Ann (Boswell) Surber; m. Ted McKinley Campbell, June 26, 1982. BS in Social studies, Radford Coll., 1977, MS in Guidance, 1980. Social studies tchr. Russell County Schs., Lebanon, Va., 1977-81, guidance counselor, 1981—. Home: Rt 4 Box 6 Lebanon VA 24266 Office: Lebanon High Sch PO Box 217 Lebanon VA 24266

CAMPBELL, DEBRA LYNN, marketing consultant; b. Phoenix, Apr. 8, 1954; d. Joseph David and Elaine Lucinda (Krueger) C.; m. J. Frederick Stillman, III, Oct. 26, 1985. BS, U. Ariz., 1975; MBA, Harvard U., 1980. Brand mgr. Procter & Gamble Co., Cin., 1975-78; project mgr. Dunham & Marcus, N.Y.C., 1980-81; v.p. Cox, Lloyd Assocs., N.Y.C., 1981-83; cons. Am. Cons. Corp., N.Y.C., 1983-85, dir., 1985-87, dir., chief fin. officer, 1987-88, pres., chief operating officer, 1988-90; pres. DCA, 1990—. Recipient Reggie award Promotion Mktg. Assn. Am. (Reggie award 1986, 87, 90). Mem. Am. Mktg. Assn. Office: Am Cons Corp 55 Fifth Ave New York NY 10003

CAMPBELL, DONNA WAUGH, diplomat, Soviet issues consultant; b. N.Y.C., Nov. 19, 1937; d. Donald Byers Waugh and Marjorie (Pace) Covell; m. Richard C. Campbell, June 10, 1967 (div. Jan. 1971). Student, Green Mountain Coll., 1955-56. Owner br. office Fin. Network Investment Corp., Palm Springs, Calif., 1982-89; owner earthpeace, Newfane, Vt., 1989—; Del. Soviet-Am. Forum for Life with Human Rights, 1988; active Odessa-Kiev Peacewalk, 1988, Uggarod-Kuv Peacewalk, 1989, Am. Soviet Coast to Coast Friendship, 1989, Kazakhstan Auti Nuclear Walk, 1990. Participant L.A.-San Francisco Am.-Soviet Peace Walk, 1988, Odessa-Kiev Peace Walk, 1988, Uzgarod-Kiev Peace Walk, 1989, Anti-Nuclear Walk-Kezochstan, 1990; coord. Brattleboro (Vt.) Earth Day, 1990; chairperson Hands Across Am., Coachella Valley, Calif., 1986; bd. dirs. Coachella Valley Women's Network, 1982-89, Angel View Crippled Children's Aux., Coachella Valley, 1984-86, Food in Need of Distbn., Palm Springs, 1986-89, Peace Coun. of the Desert, Coachella Valley, 1988-89. Lt. USCG, 1964-67. Recipient Golf Lifesaving medal Treasury Dept., 1965, One of Fifteen Women You Make a Difference, minorities and Women in Bus. Mag., 1989, Athena award for Outstanding Women in Coachella Valley, 1987. Mem. Rotary. Home: RFD#1 Box 2342 Newfane VT 05345

CAMPBELL, DORIS KLEIN, psychology educator, retired; b. Tazewell County, Ill., Oct. 28; d. Emil L. and Cora M. (Osterdock) Klein. AB, Augustana Coll., Rock Island, Ill., 1930; MA, U. Ill., 1931; EdD, U. Fla., 1962. Instr. in psychology and edn. Arlington Hall, Washington, 1931-33, Cen. Acad. and Coll., McPherson, Kans., 1933-37; supr. practice teaching Seattle Pacific Coll., Seattle, 1937-39; elem. tchr. The Harris Schs., Chgo., 1939-41; instr. to prof. of psychology East Tenn. State U., Johnson City, 1960-77; Fulbright prof. Silliman U., Dumaguete City, The Philippines, 1968-69, 77-80. Vol. telephone and support worker Contact Ministry, Johnson City, 1980-81, tchr.UPWARD Cerebral Palsy Sch., Lakeland, Fla., 1982-86, counselor Help and Resource Line Mental Health Ctr., Winter Haven, Fla., 1987-89. Mem. Am. Psychol. Assn., Fulbright Alumni Assn., Phi Kappa Phi, Delta Kappa Gamma, Tau Kappa Alpha. Home: Asbury Ctr Appalachian Ste 7 400 N Boone St Johnson City TN 37604

CAMPBELL, ELNORA FRANCES, data processing executive; b. Omaha, Jan. 3, 1948; d. George Edward and Rosina Frances (Fiest) McMullen; m. Robert B. Campbell, Jr., Sept. 14, 1968 (div. 1976); 1 child, Robert P. LPN, St. Mary's Hosp., Kansas City, Mo., 1967; Cert., Computer Programming Inst., Kansas City, Mo., 1979. LPN St. Mary's Hosp., Kansas City, 1967-68, St. John's Hosp., Lansing, Kans., 1968-69, Kans. U. Med. Ctr., Kansas City, Kans., 1971-79; dir./programmer Gynecology and Obstetrics Chartered, Kansas City, 1979—; dir. computer ops. Kans. U. Gynecol. & Obs. Found., Kansas City, 1985—.

CAMPBELL, FRANCES HARVELL, foundation administrator; b. Goldston, N.C.; d. George Henry and Evelyn (Meggs) Harvell; m. John T. Campbell, Jr., Apr. 27, 1968 (div. Aug. 1973). BS magna cum laude, U. Md., 1982. Asst. to Congressman Claude Pepper, U.S. Ho. of Reps., 1968-80, staff dir., 1980-89; exec. dir., curator Mildred and Claude Pepper Libr.; chmn. bd., pres. Mildred and Claude Pepper Found., 1989—; exec. dir. Franklin D. Roosevelt Meml. Commn. Author: Young America Speaks, 1957. V.p. Dem. Women of Capitol Hill, 1982-83. Mem. NAFE, Women in Govt. Rels., Nat. Dem. Club, Internat. Platform Assn., Fla. State Soc. (bd. dirs. 1982-85), Phi Kappa Phi, Alpha Sigma Lambda. Avocations: orchid culture, gourmet food preparation, gardening. Home: 6222 Hardy Dr McLean VA 22101 Office: Congl Office Bldg Rm 347-H2 Washington DC 20515

CAMPBELL, GLORIA MAE, freelance designer; b. Ely, Minn., Dec. 19, 1925; d. Jacob Leonard and Selma Adena (Willman) Pete; m. John Malcolm Campbell, May 1, 1954; children: Morna Selma, Moira Mary. BFA, Art Inst. Chgo., 1951, MFA, 1951. Interior designer Glass-Huebner Assn., Chgo., 1951-52; textile design Cannon Mills, N.Y.C., 1954-65; freelance designer N.Y.C., 1954-65; self-employed designer Edmonds, Wash., 1965—;

sec. Nat. Home Fashions League, Seattle, 1978-80, pres., 1980-82. Arts commr. Edmonds Arts Commn., 1981-88, vice chmn., 1982-85, chmn., 1986. Daniel D. Vandergrift scholar, 1947-48, Joseph S. Snydacker scholar, 1948-49, Art Inst. Chgo. Mem. Internat. Furnishings & Design Assn., Handweavers Guild Am., Am. Tapestry Alliance, Artist Trust, Ctr. for Wooden Boats, Delta Phi Delta. Home and Office: 9414 216th St SW Edmonds WA 98020

CAMPBELL, HELEN LOUISE, state agency official; b. Austin, Tex., Aug. 26, 1939; d. Herbert Louis and Hattie Louise (Schwartfeger) Benner; m. R.M. Johnson, Sept. 22, 1956 (dec. June 1963); children: Ronald M., Rhonda Louise; m. Lonnie Campbell (div. 1983). Student in mgmt., Austin Community Coll., 1981-84; grad. Exec. Fire Officer Program, Nat. Fire Acad., Emmitsburg, Md., 1987; student, St. Edwards U., 1987—. Office mgr. E&W Inc., Austin, 1970-71; adminstrv. asst. Austin Fire Dept., 1971-87; firemen's pension commr. State of Tex., 1987—; commr. Fire Protection Personnel Standard and Edn. State of Tex., 1985. Del. State of Tex. Dem. Conv., 1982, 84; pres. bd. dirs. United Action for the Elderly Inc., Austin, 1985-86; bd. dirs. Austin Groups for Elderly, 1987; chmn. State of Tex. Higher Edn. Commn. Fire Svc., 1985-87; life mem. Tex. PTA. Recipient Award for Excellence United Action for Elderly, 1986, Achievement award U. Tex. YWCA, 1986. Mem. Tex. Firemen's and Fire Marshals' Assn. Baptist. Home: 2562 Stoutwood Circle Austin TX 78745 Office: Firemen's Pension Commr 3910 S 1-35 Suite 235 Austin TX 78704

CAMPBELL, JEAN, retired, human services organization administrator; b. Fairhaven, Mass., Mar. 4, 1925; d. Elwyn Gilbert and Marion Hicks (Dexter) C. AA, Lasell Coll., Auburndale, Mass., 1944; BA, Brown U., 1946; MEd, U. Hartford, 1963. Field dir. Waterbury Area Council Girl Scouts, Inc., Waterbury, Conn., 1946-52; exec. dir. Manchester (Conn.) Girl Scouts, Inc., 1952-60; dist. dir. Conn. Valley Girl Scout Council, Inc., Hartford, 1961-63; dir. field services Plymouth Bay Girl Scout Council, Taunton, Mass., 1963-64, exec. dir., 1964-68; exec. dir. New Bedford (Mass.) YWCA, 1968-87; mem. adv. bd. Bay State Ctrs. for Displaced Homemakers, Southeastern Mass., 1982-87, Southeastern Mass. U. Women's Studies, North Dartmouth, Mass., 1987. Trustee Millicent Library, Fairhaven, 1970—; corporator Compass Bank for Savs., 1976—; bd. dirs. Greater New Bedford Concert Series, 1978—; hon. trustee St. Luke's Hosp. of New Bedford, 1986—; mem. adv. bd. Bierstadt Art Soc., New Bedford, 1987-88, investment com. YWCA, 1975—; deacon First Congl. Ch. Fairhaven, 1989; reunion coord. Coll. Class #44 1989; com. mem., past pres. Interchurch Council of Greater New Bedford, 1973—; bd. dirs., former treas. ICC Svcs. Corp., 1973—. Recipient Sidney Adams Community Service award Interchurch Council of Greater New Bedford, 1984, AAUW Achievement award, 1987, Thanks badge Girl Scouts U.S., 1956; named Woman of Yr., Internat. Women's Day Com., 1987. Mem. Delta Kappa Gamma Soc. (pres. Eta chpt. 1986-88). Club: Moneta Assocs. Investment (New Bedford) (pres. 1982-84, 86—).

CAMPBELL, JEANNE MARIE, public relations executive; b. Chgo.; d. John and Wilhelmina Evelyn (Powers) Kruzic; widowed; children—Keith Maclean, Scott McElroy. B.A., B.S., No. Ill. U., 1966; M.S. in Edn., 1971; M.A., Loyola U., Chgo., 1975; postgrad. Am. U., Washington. Mem. faculty Am. U., Washington, Loyola U., Chgo., 1973-77, George Washington U.; speechwriter Congressman Dan Rostenkowski, 1977-79; press sec. Congresswoman Margaret Heckler, 1979-80; v.p. New Eng. Council, Inc., Washington, 1981-85; sr. assoc. Martin Haley Cos., 1981-85; pres. Campbell-Raupe, Inc., Washington, 1985—. Vol. tutor Laubach Lit. Assn., Ill. and Washington, 1965—. Mem. Tax Coalition, Am. League Lobbyists (sec. 1983, bd. dirs.), Women in Govt. Relations. Avocation: writing. Office: Campbell Raupe Inc 1010 Pennsylvania Ave SE Washington DC 20003

CAMPBELL, JILL FROST, academic administrator; b. Buffalo, July 29, 1948; d. Jack and Elaine Mary (Hamilton) Frost; m. Gregory H. Campbell, May 31, 1969; children: Geoffrey, Kimberly, Kristina. BS, SUNY, Brockport, 1970, MS in Edn., 1981; postgrad., SUNY, Buffalo, 1989—. Acct. clk. bursar's office SUNY, Brockport, 1974-75, sr. acct. clk., 1975-78, instl. rsch. asst., 1978-82, asst. dir. instl. rsch. office, 1982-86, acting assoc. pers. office, 1986-87, dir. contract and grant adminstrn., sponsored rsch. dept., 1987—. Mem. exec. com. Nativity Home Sch. Assn., Nativity Blessed Virgin Mary Sch., Brockport, 1985-87, mem. sch. bd. pub. rels. and mktg. com., 1985-88; active Friends of Brockport Athletics, 1985—; coach Brockport Youth Summer Soccer, 1988, 89, 90; mem. com. Chancellor's Award for Excellence in Profl. Svc., Brockport, 1989, 90. Grantee United Univ. Professions, 1985, 90. Mem. NAFE, Nat. Assn. Instl. Rsch. (mem. exec. com., co-originator and discussion leader books and current issues 1985-87, co-author profl. file, presenter papers, presenter panels 1979-87), SUNY Assn. Instl. Rsch. and Planning Officers (mem. exec. com., presenter papers, presenter panels 1984-87), Nat. Coun. Univ. Rsch. Adminstrs., North East Assn. Instl. Rsch. (mem. exec. com., sec. 1985-87, presenter papers, presenter panels 1978-87), SUNY Brockport Alumni Assn., Brockport Profl. Women's Group, Rsch. Found. Cen. Office Systems Users Group, 1987-89, sponsored program communications com. 1990—, SUNY Labor Mgmt. Excellence award 1990). Home: 5129 Redman Rd Brockport NY 14420 Office: SUNY Rsch Found 521 Allen Adminstrn Bldg Brockport NY 14420

CAMPBELL, JO, educational administrator; b. Brookings, S.D., Feb. 25, 1950; d. Robert Dexter and Margaret Rose (Lins) Stewart; m. Lee Arthur, Nov. 30, 1974. Bachelors, S.D. State U., 1972; postgrad., U. Wyoming, 1977-; Masters, Bank Street Coll., NYC, 1985; postgrad., Parson's Sch. Design, NYC, 1985. Travel agt. Nervig Travel Service, Brookings, S.D., 1970-72; mgr., buyer Mountain Co. Inc., Mt. Rushmore, Keystone, S.D., 1972-75; purchasing agt. Thunderbasin Coal Co., Gillette, Wy., 1975-77; art tchr., art curriculum facilitator Campbell County Sch. Dist., Gillette, Wyo., 1977-87, elem. prin., 1987—; initiating bd. mem. Assn. Profl. Artists, 1977-84, Powder River Arts Council, Gillette, Wy., 1979-88, Wy. Arts Alliance, 1981-87, bd. mem. Wy. Arts for Youth, 1977-83. Arts in pub. bldgs., stained glass, misc. pieces, 1983, 1984. Gov. appointed bd. mem. Wy. Council on the Arts, Cheyenne, 1985--. Mem. Nat. Assn. Elem. Prins., Wyo. Assn. Elem. Sch. Prins. (state editor 1987-89), NAFE, Stained Glass Assn. Am. Home: Four Fawn Ct Gillette WY 82716 Office: Campbell County Sch Dist 1000 W 8th Gillette WY 82716

CAMPBELL, JUDITH LOWE, child psychiatrist; b. Indpls., Jan. 21, 1946; d. Albert St. Clair and Adele V. (Lobraico) Lowe; m. Robert Frank Campbell, Nov. 30, 1968; children: Christiaan Robert, Kevin Lowe, Geoffrey Ford. B.S. in Zoology, Butler U., 1967; M.D., Ind. U., 1971. Resident in psychiatry Ind. U. Sch. Medicine, 1971-73, fellow in child psychiatry 1973-75; asst. dir. Riley Child Guidance Clinic, Indpls., 1975-79, dir. child psychiatry consultation, liaison service to pediatrics, 1975-79; dir. child psychiatry services Riley Hosp. for Children, 1979-85; pvt. practice child psychiatry, Indpls., 1985—; child psychiatry cons. Center for Mental Health of Madison County (Ind.), Anderson, 1975-77, Lutheran Child Welfare Assn., Indpls., 1974—, Lutherwood Children's Home, Indpls., 1974—, Jewish Family and Children's Services, 1983-84, child and adolescent div. Midtown Community Mental Health Center, 1983-85; assoc. med. dir. child and adolescent psychiat. svcs. Community Hosps. of Indpls., Inc., 1989-90; med. dir. children unit Arbor Hosp. Greater Indpls., 1990—; instr. Ind. U. Sch. Medicine, Indpls., 1974-75, asst. prof. dept psychiatry, 1975-89, clin. assoc. prof., 1989—. V.p. precinct committeeman Rep. Party, 1990—. Recipient Physician's Recognition award in Continuing Edn. AMA, 1974, 77; Helen McQuiston award in sci., 1967. Fellow Am. Psychiat. Assn., Ind. Psychiat. Soc. (councilor 1978-80, 90-91, sec. 1981-83, editor newsletter 1981-83, chmn. com. women 1983—), Am. Burn Assn., Am. Acad. Pediatrics (Ind. br.), Am. Med. Women's Assn., Am. Acad. Child and Adolescent Psychiatry, Am. Assn. Psychiat. Services for Children, Ind. Coun. Child and Adolescent Psychiatry (sec. 1986-87, pres.-elect 1987-88, pres. 1988-89, Smithsonian Assocs., Field Mus. Natural History, Indpls. Mus. Art, Indpls. Zool. Soc., Pi Beta Phi, Beta Sigma Phi. Clubs: Carmel Racquet, Eastern Star, Woodland Country. Contbr. articles on child psychiatry to profl. jours. Research on emotional aspects of burns in children, craniofacial anomalies in children, also sex differences in child and adolescent population groups. Office: 11075 N Pennsylvania Indianapolis IN 46280

CAMPBELL, KARLYN KOHRS, speech and communication educator; b. Blomkest, Minn., Apr. 16, 1937; d. Meinhard and Dorothy (Siegers) Kohrs; m. Paul Newell Campbell, Sept. 16, 1967. BA, Macalester Coll., 1958; MA, U. Minn., 1959, PhD, 1968. Asst. prof. SUNY, Brockport, 1959-63, Calif. State U., L.A., 1966-71; assoc. prof. SUNY, Binghamton, 1971-72, CUNY, 1973-74; prof. communication studies U. Kans., Lawrence, 1974-86, dir. women's studies, 1983-86; prof. speech-communication U. Minn., Mpls., 1986—; inaugural Gladys Borchers lectr. U. Wis., Madison, 1974. Author: Critiques of Contemporary Rhetoric, 1972, Form and Genre, 1978, The Rhetorical Act, 1982, The Interplay of Influence, 1983, rev. edit., 1987, Man Cannot Speak for Her, 2 Vols., 1989, Deeds Done in Words, 1990; mem. editorial bd. Communication Monographs, 1977-80, Quar. Jour. Speech, 1981-86, Philosophy and Rhetoric, 1988-; contbr. articles to profl. jours. Recipient Woolbert Rsch. award, 1987; Tozer scholar Macalester Coll., 1958, Tozer fellow, 1959. Mem. Speech Communication Assn., Central States Speech Communication Assn., Ctr. Study of the Presidency, Phi Beta Kappa, Pi Phi Epsilon. Office: U Minn Dept Speech-Communication Minneapolis MN 55455

CAMPBELL, LESLEY ANN, environmental specialist II; b. Des Moines, Iowa, July 30, 1959; d. Robert Frederick and Sherrill Ann (Cox) Kryselmire; m. Douglas Alan Campbell, Aug. 14, 1949. AA, Iowa Western Community Coll., 1979; BS, U. of South Dakota, 1981. County inspector Polk County Phys. Planning, Des Moines, Iowa, 1988; environmental specialist State of Iowa Dept of Natural Resources, Des Moines, 1988--. Bd. mem. Polk County Victim Svcs., Des Moines, 1988—. Mem. Women in Natural Resources, Delta Cpt. of Beta Sigma Phi. (treas.). Presbyterian. Office: Iowa Delta of Natural Resou Wallace State Off Bldg Des Moines IA 50319

CAMPBELL, LINDA ANN, pharmacist; b. Boston, Dec. 17, 1961; d. Norman Ambrose and Mary (Hodde) C. BS in Pharmacy, U. R.I., 1985. Lic. pharmacist, R.I. Chief pharmacist Cameron's Pawtuxet Pharmacy, Inc., Cranston, R.I., 1986—. Vol. tutor Literacy Vols. of R.I., North Kingstown, 1988—; mem. Girl Scouts U.S. Mem. R.I. Pharm. Assn. (chmn. pub. rels. 1987-88, chmn. membership 1988-89, Disting. Young Pharmacist award 1988), Am. Pharm. Assn. (del. to nat. conv. 1988), Am. Soc. for Pharmacy Law. Roman Catholic. Home: 15 Avice St Narragansett RI 02882 Office: Cameron's Pawtuxet Pharmacy 2206 Broad St Cranston RI 02905

CAMPBELL, LOU ELLEN, sales and marketing executive; b. Richlands, Va., Nov. 3, 1943; d. Harman and Gladys Maye (Meadows) Allison; m. Robert Thomas Campbell, Sept. 1, 1978. AA, East Tenn. State U., 1966; BS, U. Md., 1975; MS, Cen. Mich. U., 1980. With sales and mktg. dept. 3M Co., St. Paul and Balt., 1972-85; mktg. mgr. Shopsmith, Inc., Dayton, Ohio, 1986, Easco Hand Tools, East Windsor, Conn., 1987; area mgr. KAR Products, Mass., 1988—. Contbr. articles to various publs. Mem. Forest Park Civic Assn., Springfield, Mass., 1988—. Mem. AAUW, NAFE, Internat. Maintenance Inst., Nat. Assn. for Profl. Saleswomen, Toastmasters (pres. 1990, Competent Toastmaster award), Sales and Mktg. Execs. Western New Eng., Sport Divers Western Mass., Order Ea. Star. Republican. Methodist. Home and Office: 66 Fairfield St Springfield MA 01108

CAMPBELL, MARGARET M., academic dean; b. New Orleans, Dec. 1, 1928; d. Walter and Caroline Louise (Seither) C. BA, St. Mary's Dominican Coll., 1950; MSW, Boston Coll., 1952; 3d yr. cert. clin. practice, N.Y. Sch. Social Work, 1959; DSW, Columbia U., 1970. Caseworker Charity Hosp., New Orleans, 1951-53, Cath. Social Services, San Francisco, 1953-55; supr. Spl. Service Club sect. U.S. Army Europe, 1956-58; caseworker Children's Bur., New Orleans, 1959-60, Associated Cath. Charities, New Orleans, 1960-63; lectr. Dominican Coll., New Orleans, 1961-66; spl. projects worker Associated Cath. Charities, New Orleans, 1964-65; dir. Fla. Family Ctr., New Orleans, 1965-67; asst. prof. Tulane U. Sch. Social Work, New Orleans, 1968, assoc. prof., 1971; dir. continuing edn. programs Tulane U., New Orleans, 1976-80; dir. Child Welfare Services Tng. Ctr. Region IV, New Orleans, 1979-82; dean Tulane U. Sch. Social Work, New Orleans, 1982—, prof., 1986—; chmn. various coms. sch. social work including Advanced Programs Admissions, Continuing Edn., Family and Children Task Report, Library, Ednl. Policy, Direct Services to Individuals Sequence, NASW Student Liaison, Priorities Com. Author numerous publications and articles in profl. jours. in field. Recipient Alumnae award Dominican Coll., 1970, Dominican Coll. Torchbearer award, 1985. Mem. Nat. Assn. Social Workers (chpt. pres. 1973-75, bd. dirs., treas., program dir., membership com., 1955-85; social worker of yr. Southeastern La. chpt. 1976; La. chpt. award 1978), Acad. Cert. Social Workers, Internat. Conf. on Social Welfare, New Orleans Children's Council, Child Welfare Info. Exchange Panel for La., Task Force on Adolescent Treatment Ctr., New Orleans Collaborative Tng. Program, Child Welfare League (chmn. southeastern conf. 1980-83), Council on Social Work Edn. (steering com. 1980-81, coordinator 1985), La. State Med. Soc. (geriatrics subcom. 1985-86), Nat. Council on Aging, Gerontological Soc. Am. (conf. com. 1985), Southern Gerontology Soc., Adult Protection Services Network. Office: Tulane U Sch of Social Work New Orleans LA 70118

CAMPBELL, MARIA BOUCHELLE, banker, lawyer; b. Mullins, S.C., Jan. 23, 1944; d. Colin Reid and Margaret Minor (Perry) C. Student, Agnes Scott Coll., 1961-63; AB, U. Ga., 1965, JD, 1967. Bar: Ga. 1967, Fla. 1968, Ala. 1969. Pvt. practiced law Birmingham, Ala., 1968—; law clk. U.S. Cir. Ct. Appeals, Miami, Fla., 1967-68; assoc. Cabaniss, Johnston and Gardner, 1968-73; sec., counsel Ala. Bancorp., Birmingham, 1973-79; sr. v.p., sec., gen. counsel AmSouth Bancorp., 1979-84, exec. v.p., gen. counsel, 1984—; exec. v.p., gen. counsel AmSouth Bank, 1984—; lectr. continuing legal edn. programs; cons. to charitable orgns. Exec. editor Ga. Law Rev, 1966-67. Bd. dirs. St. Anne's Home, Birmingham, 1969-74, chancellor, 1969-74; bd. dirs. Children's Aid Soc., Birmingham, 1970—, 1st v.p., 1988-90, pres., 1990—; bd. dirs. Positive Maturity, 1976-78, Mental Health Assn., 1978-81, YWCA, 1979-80, NCCJ, 1985—, state chair, 1990—, Op. New Birmingham, 1985-87, pers. com., 1987—; bd. dirs. Soc. for the Fine Arts U. Ala., 1986-89; commr. Housing Authority, Birmingham Dist., 1980-85, Birmingham Partnership, 1985-86, Leadership Birmingham, 1986—, program com., 1989—, co-chair program com., 1990—; mem. pres. adv. coun. Birmingham So. Coll, 1988—, chair bd. overseers Masters Program, 1990—; mem. pres.'s cabinet U. Ala., 1990—; trustee Ala. Diocese Episcopal Ch., 1971-72, 74-75, mem. canonical revision com., 1973-75, 89—, liturg. commn., 1976-78, treas., chmn. dept. fin., 1979-83, mem. coun., 1983-87, chancellor, 1987—, cons. on stewardship edn., 1981—, dep. to gen. conv., 1985, 88; mem. Standing Commn. on Constn. and Canons, 1988—; bd. advisors So. region of Am. Soc. Corp. Secs. Named One of Top Ten Women in Birmingham, 1989. Mem. ABA, State Bar Ga., Fla. Bar, Ala. Bar Assn., Birmingham Bar Assn., Am. Corp. Counsel Assn. (bd. dirs. Ala. 1984-89), Assn. Bank Holding Cos. (chmn. lawyers com. 1986-87), Greater Birmingham C. of C. (bd. dirs. 1988—), Kiwanis, Mountain Brook Club, Downtown Club, Summit Club. Home: 141 Camellia Circle Birmingham AL 35213 Office: AmSouth Bancorp PO Box 11007 Birmingham AL 35288

CAMPBELL, MARSHA MARIE, business executive; b. Washington, Iowa, Mar. 6, 1952; d. David Elwood and Ada Beth (Dennison) Kleese; m. James Richard Campbell, July 7, 1972; children: Clayton Kleese, Jesse David. BBA, U. Iowa, 1975; MS, Utah State U., 1978. Bookkeeper Schoonover's Drug Store, Washington, 1975; payroll analyst NE Mo. State U., Kirksville, 1976; teaching asst. Utah State U., Logan, 1978; bus. tchr. Box Elder/Logan City Schs., Logan and Brigham City, Utah, 1978-79; systems procedures analyst Thiokol Corp., Brigham City, 1979-83; mgr. policies and adminstrn. Thiokol Corp., Ogden, Utah, 1989—; supr. policies and adminstrv. resources Morton Thiokol, Brigham City, 1983-87; supr. bus. systems procedures Morton Thiokol, Ogden, 1987-89. Mem. Assn. for Systems Mgmt., Bus. Forms Mgmt. Assn., Am. Records Mgmt. Assn., Assn. for Info. and Image Mgmt., Am. Assn. Contingency Planners. Office: Thiokol Corp 2475 Washington Blvd Ogden UT 84401

CAMPBELL, MARSHA MULFORD, public affairs executive; b. Princeton, N.J., Feb. 13, 1946; d. James Maurice and Barbara (Heinrich) Mulford; m. Jack Lee Campbell, Nov. 18, 1978. BA, U. Mo., Columbia, 1969. Buyer Macy's, Kansas City, Mo., 1969-79; territory mgr. Bonne Bell Cosmetics, Kansas City, 1979-82; regional mgr. Woods for Senate, Kansas City, 1982; campaign mgr. Heeter for Coun., Kansas City, 1983; fin. and office mgr. Kansas City 1/2 Cent Sales Tax Campaign, 1983; state and local affairs coordinator Hallmark Cards, Inc., Kansas City, 1984—. Bd. govs. Citizen's Assn., Kansas City, 1985-86; v.p. Com. for County Progress, Kansas City, 1988—; pres. Mo. Assn. Social Welfare, WDAF TV Love Fund for Children; bd. dirs. Spofford Home for Children; chmn. coun. ministries Country Club United Meth. Ch.; mem. gov.'s statewide task force steering com. MO. Youth 2000 Steering Com.; vice chmn., screening com. co-chmn. Countywide Dem. Polit. Club, Citizens for County Progress; mem. nat. adv. panel Child Care Action Campaign; mem. legis. com. United Way. Mem. Greater Kansas City C. of C. (met. affairs com. 1985—), U. Mo. Bus. and Pub. Adminstrn. Alumni Assn. (bd. dirs. Kansas City div.). Democrat. Methodist. Home: 445 Westover Rd Kansas City MO 64113 Office: Hallmark Cards Inc PO Box 419580 Kansas City MO 64141

CAMPBELL, MARTHA JEAN (JEAN F. CAMPBELL), retired public relations consultant; b. Indpls., Oct. 13, 1926; d. Matthew Stanley and Rachel Nell (Campbell) Farson; m. Donald Guy Campbell, Oct. 15, 1949; children: Scott Guy, Jennifer Lee. BA, Butler U., 1962. Dir. media relations St. Joseph Med. Ctr., Phoenix, 1970-72; feature writer N.Am. Newspaper Alliance, N.Y.C., 1972-74; communications specialist Samaritan Health Service, Phoenix, 1974-77; sr. v.p. Ralph Jackson Assocs., Los Angeles, 1979-82; prin. Jean Campbell Pub. Relations, Phoenix, 1977-79, Los Angeles, 1982-87; press sec., cons. senator Barry Goldwater, Phoenix, 1968, mayor John Driggs, Phoenix. 1969; media cons. Scottsdale (Ariz.) Pub. Schs., 1969-70, Ariz. Commn. Arts/Humanities, Phoenix, 1971-74. Recipient 1st Pl. "Lulu" award Los Angeles Advt. Women, 1978. Mem. Pub. Relations Soc. Am. (Los Angeles newsletter editor 1980, reception chmn. 1985, chmn. spouse tours for nat. conv. 1987), Publicity Club Los Angeles, LWV (dir. publs. Ind. chpt. 1960, founder, pres. Brownsburg, Ind. chpt. 1959). Republican. Presbyterian. Home and Office: 4426 E Vermont Ave N Phoenix AZ 85018

CAMPBELL, MARY A., social worker; b. Springfield, Mass., Aug. 10, 1950; d. Carmino A. and Laura E. (Dion) Yacovone; m. Thomas C. Campbell, June 22, 1979; children: Francis, Timothy, Thaddeus. Student, Smith Coll.; BA in Sociology, Internat. Coll., Springfield, 1972; MS in Social Work, U. Wis., Milw., 1974. Ct. investigator Mass. Soc. for Prevention Cruelty to Children, Greenfield; med. social worker, dir. Franklin Med. Ctr., Greenfield; social worker Greenfield Ob-Gyn Assn. Mem. Nat. Assn. Social Workers, Acad. Cert. Social Workers. Home: PO Box 247 Charlemont MA 01339 Office: Greenfield OB-GYN Assocs PC 5 Park St Greenfield MA 01301

CAMPBELL, MARY KATHLEEN, mortgage banker; b. Torrance, Calif., Aug. 5, 1944; d. David F. and Katherine I. (Norton) Shields; m. John Alan Campbell, Aug. 19, 1963; children—Lisa Marie Campbell Mitchell, John Andrew. B.B.A. in Acctg., Nat. U., San Diego, 1984. Head cashier Navy Exchange, San Diego, 1968-69; customer relations mgr. J.M. Fields, Norfolk, Va., 1970-72; acct. Hart Enterprises, San Diego, 1973-76; asst. treas. Midwest Pacific Fin., Inc., San Diego, 1976-80, treas., 1980-84, v.p., treas., 1984—; asst. sec. Midwest Fed. Savs. of Eastern Iowa, Burlington, 1978—, asst. v.p., 1985—; treas., dir. Burlington Fin., San Diego, 1984—. Vol. worker Girl Scouts U.S.A., San Diego, 1970-77, Boy Scouts Am., San Diego, 1972-79, Am. Cancer Soc., San Diego, 1978-82; student-family liaison Am. Field Service, Poway, Calif., 1983—. Mem. Fin. Mgrs. Soc., Assn. for Profl. Mortgage Women, Am. Bus. Women's Assn. (treas. 1980-81, Woman of Yr. Poway 1982). Office: Midwest Pacific Fin Inc 5405 Morehouse Dr San Diego CA 92121

CAMPBELL, MARY KATHRYN, chemistry educator; b. Phila., Jan. 20, 1939; d. Henry Charles and Mary Kathryn (Horan) C. A.B. in Chemistry, Rosemont Coll., 1960; Ph.D., Ind. U., 1965. Instr. Johns Hopkins U., 1965-68; asst. prof. chemistry Mt. Holyoke Coll., South Hadley, Mass., 1968-74; assoc. prof. Mt. Holyoke Coll., 1974-81, prof., 1981—; vis. scholar U. Paris VII, 1974-75; vis. prof. U. Ariz., 1981-82, 88-89; mem. panel on grad. fellowships NSF, 1979-81. Contbr. articles to profl. jours. Fellow Woodrow Wilson Found., 1960, NSF, 1960-64, NIH, 1964-65; grantee in field. Mem. Am. Chem. Soc., AAAS, AAUP, AAUW, Sigma Xi. Office: Mount Holyoke Coll Carr Lab Dept Chemistry South Hadley MA 01075

CAMPBELL, NANCY EDINGER, nuclear engineer; b. Washington, May 9, 1957; d. Ralph Joseph and Eleanor (Brabble) Edinger; m. Larry Alan Campbell, Feb. 25, 1984. BS in Nuclear Engring. with honors, Ga. Inst. of Tech., 1978; MBA, U. Pitts., 1985. Nuclear safety engr. Westinghouse Nuclear Tech. Div., Monroeville, Pa., 1978-81; nuclear fuel proposal engr. Westinghouse Nuclear Fuel Div., Monroeville, 1981-86; nuclear fuel project engr. Westinghouse Comml. Nuclear Fuel Div., Monroeville, 1986-90; reactor engr. U.S. Nuclear Regulatory Commn., Washington, 1990—; chmn. hospitality, rep. nuclear fuel div. Westinghouse Women's Career Devel. Com., Pitts., 1985-87. Assoc. advisor Westinghouse Explorer Post 258, Monroeville, 1980-81. Mem. Am. Nuclear Soc., Soc. of Women Engrs., Engring. Soc. Balt., Nat. Trust Hist. Preservation, Phi Kappa Phi, Tau Beta Pi, Phi Eta Sigma. Episcopalian. Office: US Nuclear Regulatory Commn Washington DC 20555

CAMPBELL, NANCY IRENE BARR, assistant blood bank manager; b. Washington Co., Va., Aug. 17, 1955; d. Charles Ray and Carol Ann (Vestal) Barr; m. Samuel Henry Campbell, May 2, 1974; 1 child, Samuel H. II. Cert. med. technology, Bristol (Tenn.) Meml. Hosp., 1976; BS cum laude, King Coll., 1988; MA, Tusculum Coll., 1990. Med. technologist Bristol Regional Med. Ctr., 1976—; life support instr., Am. Heart Assn., Roanoke, Va., 1985—; licensee lab. supr., State of Tenn., Nashville, 1988—. Hon. mem. Damascus (Va.) Vol. Rescue Squad, 1988. Mem. Am. Soc. Clin. Pathologists, VFW Aux., King Coll. Alumni Assn., High Point PTA. Democrat. Methodist. Home: 417 Greenbriar Circle Bristol VA 24201 Office: Bristol Regional Med Ctr 209 Memorial Dr Bristol TN 37620

CAMPBELL, PATRICIA BARBARA, educational research company executive, consultant; b. Worcester, Mass., Dec. 9, 1947; d. Philip Stephen and Barbara M. (McCarthy) C.; m. Tom R. Kibler, Jan. 19, 1977; 1 child, Kathryn. BS in Math., LeMoyne Coll., 1969; MS in Instrnl. Tech., Syracuse U., 1971, PhD in Tchr. Edn., 1973. Rsch. programmer Thomas J. Watson Rsch. Ctr., IBM, Yorktown Heights, N.Y., 1968-69; instr. computer uses in edn., asst. to dir. rsch. Syracuse (N.Y.) U., 1970-72; evaluator Tchr. Cons. Inc., Syracuse, 1971-72; asst. prof., assoc. prof. ednl. founds. Ga. State U., Atlanta, 1973-77; dir. project on sex stereotyping in edn. Women Educators, Red Bank, N.J., 1976-79; dir. grants, rsch. and acad. devel. William Paterson Coll., Wayne, N.J., 1979-80; dir. Campbell-Kibler Assocs., Groton, Mass., 1980—; program and evaluation cons. to numerous orgns., including Bklyn. Coll., CUNY, Rutgers U., Harvard U., Douglass Coll., Cities in Schs., Youth Bur. City N.Y., pub. schs.,Boston, N.Y., N.J., nonprofit groups throughout US. Co-author: What Will Happen If...Young Children and the Scientific Method, 1985; author: (monograph) The Hidden Discriminator, 1989, also chpts. to books. Recipient merit award Ednl. Press Assn. Am., 1987; grantee U.S. Dept. Edn., 1976-90. Mem. Am. Ednl. Rsch. Assn. (chmn. com. on spl. interest groups 1984-85, bd. dirs. profs. ednl. rsch. 1975-78, Willystein Goodsell award 1990), Women Educators (chmn. 1976-78, 85-86). Office: Groton Ridge Heights Groton MA 01450

CAMPBELL, PATRICIA CAWLEY, nurse; b. Newark, Mar. 10, 1949; d. Richard Patrick and Bridget (Maloney) Cawley; m. Ruel Campbell, June 20, 1970; 1 child, Kerry. BA, Georgian Ct. Coll., 1987. RN, N.J. Nurse Greystone Park Hosp., Morristown, N.J., 1969-72; program supr. Jersey Shore Med. Ctr., Neptune, N.J., 1974-87; asst. v.p. patient care svcs. Kimball Med. Ctr., Lakewood, N.J., 1987—; mem. Ocean County Task Force for Nursing Shortage, Toms River, N.J., 1988—. Vice pres., Point Pleasant (N.J.) Bd. Edn., 1987—. Mem. Orgn. Nurse Execs. Roman Catholic. Home: 548 Oak Terr Point Pleasant NJ 08742 Office: Kimball Med Ctr 600 River Ave Lakewood NJ 08700

CAMPBELL, RENODA GISELE, personal management executive; b. L.A., May 4, 1963; d. Rumby D. and Margarete (Alexander) C. BA, Loyola Marymount U., L.A., 1985. Sec. Warner Brothers Records, Burbank, Calif., 1985-87, exec. sec., 1987-89; mgmt. exec. Direct Mgmt. Group, L.A., 1989—. Office: Direct Management Group 947 N La Cienega Blvd #G Los Angeles CA 90069

CAMPBELL, SELAURA JOY, lawyer; b. Oklahoma City, Mar. 25, 1944; d. John Moore III and Gyda (Hallum) C., m. Robert H. Goldberg, Apr. 1984 (div. Nov. 1985). AA, Stephens Coll., 1963; BA, U. Okla., 1965; MEd, Chapel Hill U., 1974; JD, N.C. Cen. U., 1978. Bar: Ariz 1983; lic. real estate broker, N.C.; cert. tchr. N.C. With flight svc. dept. Pan Am. World Airways, N.Y.C., 1966-89; lawyer Am. Women's Legal Clinic, Phoenix, 1987; charter mem. Sony Corp. Indsl. Mgmt. Seminar, 1981. Mem. N.C. Cen. U. Law Rev., 1977-78; del. People's Republic China, People to People, 1987. Mem. State Bar Ariz., Ariz Hist. Soc., Delta Gamma, Phi Alpha Delta. Republican. Episcopalian. Home: 206 S Taft St Cleveland TX 77327

CAMPBELL, SHEILA HOOD, architect; b. Montclair, N.J., Nov. 1, 1952; d. William Parsons and Jean (Smith) C.; m. Elwood Evans Reynolds, Sept. 22, 1985; children: Matthew, Margot. BA, Mt. Holyoke Coll., 1974; MArch, U. Pa., 1978. Registered architect, Pa. Architect Environ. Design Collaborative, Phila., 1979-80, Lyman S.A. Perry, Architects, Newtown Square, Pa., 1981-82, Jacobs/Wyper, Architects, Phila., 1982-84, Venturi, Rauch & Scott Brown, Phila., 1984-86, Dagit, Saylor, Architects, Phila., 1986, Schmidt-Copeland, Cleve., 1986-87; cons. architect Sheila Campbell, Architect, Cleveland Heights, Ohio, 1987—. Mem. Cleveland Heights Babysitting Coop. Mem. Mt. Holyoke Club Cleve.

CAMPBELL, SHERRY ANITA, computer scientist; b. Sumiton, Ala., Dec. 29, 1947; d. Amos and Bertha Louise (Pugh) Grammer; m. Dennis Keith Moxley, May 16, 1964 (div. 1979); children: Dennis Keith Jr., Alan Jason; m. Bruce Scott Campbell, June 17, 1980. AA in Computer Sci., Pensacola Jr. Coll., 1983; BS in Systems Sci., U. West Fla., 1985. Sec. Am. Gen. Life Ins. Co., Pensacola, Fla., 1977-78, Riggs & Dunaway, CPAs, Pensacola, 1978-79, U. West Fla., Pensacola, 1979-80; computer scientist Eglin AFB, Simulation, Fla., 1985—. Mem. NAFE, Eglin AFB Aerobics Team, Eglin AFB Archery Club. Methodist. Home: 321 Goldenrod Ct Niceville FL 32578 Office: 3200Sptw/KRSRS Eglin AFB FL 32542

CAMPBELL, SHERRY DAWN, small business owner; b. Longview, Tex., Dec. 10, 1951; d. Donald Woods and Wanda Allene (Russell) Braley; m. James Brian Campbell, Dec. 31, 1985. Grad. high sch., Oklahoma City. Paste up artist Evans Furniture Co., Oklahoma City, 1972-79, photo set designer, 1975-77; paste-up and overlay artist Evans Furniture, Oklahoma City, 1981-85; TV set designer Adco Advtg. Co., Oklahoma City, 1976-79, exec. electronic media, 1976-79, TV and radio copywriter, 1976-79, producer and director, 1976-79; owner Tile Designs, Oklahoma City, 1979-85; prin. Campbell Bros., Oklahoma City, 1984—, Victorian Lady Stained Glass Co., Oklahoma City, 1987—, Medieval Glassworks, Oklahoma City, 1989—. Exhibited at group shows including Norman (Okla.) Renaissance Festival, Paseo Art Festival, Oklahoma City, 1989, Cantebury Art Festival, Edmond, Okla., 1989, Walnut Valley Festival, Winfield, Kans., 1989. Episcopalian. Home: 94 W Shore Dr Lake Hiwassee OK 73007 Office: Campbell Bros Rte 1 Lake Hiwassee OK 73007

CAMPBELL, SUSAN CUNNINGHAM, communications consultant; b. Boston, July 18, 1942; d. John Ray and Gertrude (Cunningham) C. AB, U. Wis., 1965; MA, U. Mass., 1968; MEd, Lesley Coll., Cambridge, Mass., 1978. Social worker/field rep. Pub. Welfare, Boston, 1967-69; welfare cons. Master Tax Plan Comm., Boston, 1969-72; mgmt. analyst Social Security Adminstrn., Balt., 1972-73; asst. dep. mgr. Filene's, Wellesley, Mass., 1973-74; exec. trainee, dept. mgr. Sears, Roebuck & Co., Natick, Mass., 1974-80; sr. distribn. analyst Digital Equip. Corp., Hudson, Mass., 1980-82; retail mktg. mgr. Sml. Bus. Sys. Group, Westford, Mass., 1982-83; communications cons. Wellesley, 1984—; lectr./instr. Northeastern U., 1985-87, Lesley Coll., 1986-87; instr. North Shore Community Coll., Beverly, Mass., 1989-90; lectr. in field. Contbr. articles to profl. jours. Chmn. Marblehead (Mass.) Recycling Com., 1989—. Carnegie fellow, 1965. Mem. North Shore C. of C. Home and Office: 29 Franklin St Marblehead MA 01945

CAMPBELL, SUSAN PANNILL, banker; b. Richmond, Va., May 28, 1947; d. Raymond Brodie and Lucie Courtice (McDonald) C. A.B., Coll. William and Mary, 1969; M.Ed., U. Va., 1970, postgrad., 1974-75; postgrad. Summer Inst. of Coll. Admissions, Harvard U., 1972. Counselor, instr. Thomas Nelson Community Coll., Hampton, Va., 1970-71; asst. dean admissions U. Va., Charlottesville, 1971-78; banking officer, asst. v.p. Tex. Commerce Bank, Houston, 1978-82; asst. v.p. First City Tex., Houston, 1982-85, v.p., 1985—. Loaned exec. United Way, Houston, 1978; v.p. EnCorps, div. Houston Symphony League, 1981-82, pres., 1982-83, bd. dirs., 1983-85; bd. dirs. Houston Symphony League, 1982-83; bd. advisors Houston Symphony Soc., 1982—. Honor award scholar Mary Baldwin Coll., Staunton, Va., 1965-66. Mem. Nat. Assn. Bank Women, Am. Symphony Orch. League (vol. council), Houston Bus. Forum, Coll. William and Mary Alumni Assn., Kappa Alpha Theta. Democrat. Methodist. Office: First City Tex PO Box 2557 Houston TX 77252

CAMPBELL, SUZANN KAY, physical therapy educator; b. New London, Wis., Apr. 19, 1943; d. Martin J. and Virginia May (Schoenrock) Reetz; m. Richard T. Campbell, Feb. 6, 1965; children: Dianne Elizabeth, Deborah Carol. BS in Phys. Therapy, U. Wis., 1965, MS, 1968, PhD in Neurophysiology, 1973. Lic. phys. therapist; cert. neurodevel. therapist, Brazelton instr. Staff therapist Cen. Wis. Colony, Madison, 1965-68; instr. U. Wis.-Madison, 1968-70; asst. prof. phys. therapy U. N.C., Chapel Hill, 1972-77, assoc. prof., 1977-84, prof., 1984-87; prof. phys. therapy and community health scis. U. Ill., Chgo., 1987—, Charles E. Culpeper fellow in med. scis., 1985-87. Editor: Pediatric Neurologic Physical Therapy, 1984; editor Phys. and Occupational Therapy in Pediatrics jour., 1979—; mem. editorial adv. bd. Churchill Livingstone Pubs., N.Y.C., 1983—; contbr. articles to profl. jours. Mem. Am. Phys. Therapy Assn. (adv. coun. on phys. therapy edn. 1983-86, rsch. fellow 1980, Golden Pen 1978, rsch. award pediatrics sect. 1984, Worthingham fellow 1987, Disting. Educator award edn. sect., 1988), Wis. Phys. Therapy Assn. (pres. 1971-72), N.C. Phys. Therapy Assn. (treas. 1984-85). Democrat.

CAMPBELL, SYLVIA JUNE, music educator; b. Dyersburg, Tenn., Jan. 13, 1957; d. Ernest Martin and Shoko (Okuyama) Stanley; m. Paul Timothy Campbell, June 14, 1980; 1 child, Colin Blair. B Music Edn., Baylor U., 1979. Cert. tchr. instrumental music, all levels, Tex. Band dir. Edward H. White Mid. Sch., San Antonio, 1979-80, Richfield High Sch., Waco, Tex., 1980-83, Midway Ind. Sch. Dist., Waco, Tex., 1987-88, Lake Air Middle Sch., Waco, Tex., 1988-90, China Spring (Tex.) Ind. Sch. Dist., 1990—. Adminstrv. bd. Austin Ave United Meth. Ch., Waco, 1990, choir mem., 1988-90, pre-sch. choir dir., 1989-91; flutist Waco Community Band, 1981-90. Mem. Tex. Music Educators Assn., Tex. Bandmasters Assn., AAUW (legal advocacy fund laison 1990—, exec. bd.). Republican. United Methodist. Home: 4228 Mitchell Rd Waco TX 76710

CAMPBELL, TERESA ANN, military officer; b. Ashiya AFB, Fukuoka, Japan, 1957; came to U.S.A., 1957; d. Hugh Richard and Gertrude Mary (Gorman) C. BS in Nursing, U. S Fla., 1979; postgrad., Squadron Officer's Sch., Maxwell AFB, Ala., 1984, Sch. Health Care Scis., Sheppard AFB, Tex., 1986, Sch. Aerospace Medicine, Brooks AFB, Tex., 1987. Cert. Inpatient Obstetric Nurse. Enlisted USAF, 1979, advanced through grades to maj., 1989—. Mem. Nurse's Assn. of American Coll. Obstetricians and Gynecologists, Air Force Assn. Democrat. Roman Catholic. Home: 4949 Country View Ln Fair Oaks CA 95628 Office: FTW Hosp Mather AFB CA 95655

CAMPBELL, VIRGINIA GWEN RUSH, small business consultant; b. Des Moines, Dec. 24, 1939; d. Wilbur A. and Genevieve E. (Townsend) Rush; m. George S. Campbell, Feb. 16, 1963 (div. July 1975). BS, Iowa State U., 1961; MBA, U. Mo., St. Louis, 1985. Asst. buyer Neiman Marcus, Dallas, 1961-63; instr. Eunice Farmer Fabrics, St. Louis, 1969-73; sales rep. Leiter Fabrics, Portsmouth, Ohio, 1973-75; buyer Famous Barr, St. Louis, 1975-82; mgr. mktg. communications Interface Tech., St. Louis, 1983-85; dir. St. Louis Small Bus. Devel. Ctr., 1985—; assoc. dir. Mo. Small Bus. Devel. Ctr., St. Louis, 1987-89; adv. bd. Small Bus. Coalition, St. Louis, 1987—; exec. com. Regional Commerce & Growth Assn., St. Louis, 1989—. Bd. dirs. Child Day Care Assn., St. Louis, 1989—, Grace Hill Child Devel. Bd., St. Louis, 1988—; bd. dirs. Grace Hill Neighborhood Health Ctr., St. Louis, 1985—, v.p., 1988—; pres. Episcopal Neighborhood Sch., St. Louis, 1988—, Home Health Care Adv. Bd., St. Louis, 1986-88; 1st v.p. Diocesan Episcopal Ch. Women, St. Louis, 1971-73; vestry St. Timothy's Episcopal Ch., St. Louis, 1976, 82-85, 90—, pres. Episcopal Ch. women, 1969-70. Recipient Cert. Appreciation SBA, 1989, Svc. award Small Bus. Coalition, 1989. Mem. Nat. Assn. Women Bus. Owners, St. Louis Regional Commerce and Growth Assn., St. Louis Forum. Office: Small Bus Devel Center 3642 Lindell Saint Louis MO 63108

CAMP-BREWER, LAURA MARIE, educator; b. Memphis, Nov. 15, 1962; d. John Francis and Donna Elizabeth (Borsch) C.; m. Philip E. Brewer, May 21, 1988. B, Memphis State U., 1988. Ins. asst. Prudential Ins. Co., Memphis, 1981-84, Fed. Express Corp., Memphis, 1984-88; tchr. Shelby County Sch. System, Memphis, 1989—; owner, mgr. Flowers on Terr., Memphis. Puppet Ministry Dir. Union Avenue Baptist Ch., Memphis, 1988-, Girls in Action Dir. Union Avenue Baptist Ch., Memphis, 1988; Sunday Sch. Tchr. Union Avenue Baptist Ch., Memphis, 1988; Section Leader Union Avenue Baptist Ch. Choir, Memphis, 1988-89; Pres.Jr. Achievement Co., Memphis, 1979. Repubican. Southern Baptist. Home: 3943 Philwood Ave Memphis TN 38122 Office: Shelby Bd of Edn 160 South Hollywood Memphis TN 38111 also: Flowers on the Terr 477 High Point Terr Memphis TN 38111

CAMPOLI, ELLA FRANCES, mortgage company executive; b. New Castle, Pa., Nov. 5, 1906; d. Domenico and Michelina (Perretta) Faraone; m. James Campoli, May 4, 1925. Student, New Castle Bus. Coll., 1923. Office, traffic mgr. Harper Furniture Co., Cinn., 1948-50; asst. to pres. Harper Furniture co., Cinn., 1951-62; ptnr. Campoli Partnership, Oldsmar, Fla., 1968--. Pres. Cinn. Chpt. Pilot Internat., 1961-62; publicity, chairparson, Pilot Internat., Cinn., 1962--. Mem. Am. Bus. Women's Assn., Oldsmar C. of C., Oldsmar Civic Club. Democrat. Roman Catholic. Home and Office: 327 E Shore Dr Oldsmar FL 34677

CAMRON, ROXANNE, editor; b. Los Angeles; d. Irving John and Roslyn (Weinberger) Spiro; m. Robert Camron, Sept. 28, 1969; children: Ashley Jennifer, Erin Jessica. B.A. in Journalism, U. So. Calif., 1967. West Coast fashion and beauty editor, Teen mag., Los Angeles, 1969-70; sr. editor Teen mag., 1972-73, editor, 1973—; pub. relations rep. Max Factor Co., 1970; asst. to creative dir. Polly Bergen Co., 1970-71; lectr. teen groups; freelance writer. Active Homeowners Assn. Mem. Women in Communications., Am. Soc. Exec. Women. Office: Teen Mag 8490 Sunset Blvd Los Angeles CA 90069*

CANAN, ELIZABETH LEVY, health care administrator; b. Coffeyville, Kans., Feb. 26, 1963; d. Joe Lynn and Patsy Sue (Pote) Levy. BA in Pers. Adminstrn., U. Kans., 1985; M of Hosp. and Health Care Adminstrn., U. Minn., 1987. Adminstrv. resident Rochester (Minn.) Meth. Hosp., 1986; adminstrv. trainee Mayo Found., Rochester, 1987-90; systems analyst Mayo Clinic, Rochester, 1990—. Mem. Am. Hosp. Assn., Am. Coll. Healthcare Execs., P.E.O. (chaplain), Kiwanis, Kappa Alpha Theta (corr. sec. Rochester alumni chpt. 1989—). Republican. Methodist. Home: 805 1st St SW #4 Rochester MN 55902 Office: Mayo Clinic 200 SW 1st St Rochester MN 55905

CANAVAN, ELLEN MCGEE, realtor; b. San Antonio, Dec. 26, 1941; d. Edward Francis and Eleanor Mary (Mullen) McGee. B.A., Regis Coll., 1963; M.Ed., Boston Coll., 1975, C.A.E.S., 1978; M.P.A., Harvard U., 1985; m. M. Christopher Canavan, Jr., Apr. 18, 1965; children: Elizabeth Ann, Michael Edward. Personnel asst. Avco-Everett Rsch. Lab., Everett, Mass., 1963-65; dir. rehab. Mass. Rehab. Commn., Chestnut Hill, 1977-78; dir. community edn. Norfolk Mental Health Assn., Norwood, Mass., 1978-80; mem. Mass. Ho. of Reps., 1980-88, mem. coms. on banking, human svcs., elderly affairs. Mem. Gov.'s Spl. Commn. on Mental Health Facilities, Gov.'s Spl. Commn. on Violence Against Children, Spl. Commn. on Alcohol and Drug. Edn.; bd. dirs. YMCA; adv. bd. Glover Meml. Hosp., Mount Pleasant Hosp.; mem. Town Meeting, 1976-88, chmn. spl. com. on mental health, 1976-77; mem. Needham (Mass.) Planning Bd., 1975-80. Mem. Nat. Fedn. Republican Women, Today's Women, Mass. Legislators Assn., Brae Burn Country Club. Roman Catholic. Office: Room 22 State House Boston MA 02133

CANE, PAULA P., speech and language pathologist, scriptwriter; b. Cin., Feb. 16, 1945; d. Paul J. and Pauline Albia (Patti) Weber; children: Adam, Miguel. BS, Purdue U., 1967, MS, 1971. Lic. speech and lang. pathologist, Fla., Conn. Instr. communications U. Bridgeport, Conn., 1974-75; speech and lang. pathologist Lee County Bd. Edn., Ft. Myers, Fla., 1986; cons. Cedar Montessori Schs., Naples, Fla., 1986-87; asst. casting dir. prodn. mgmt. Suncoast Films, Inc., Clearwater, Fla., 1989; pvt. practice speech and lang. pathology St. Petersburg Beach, Fla., 1967—; screenwriter, playright Naples, Fla., 1986—; acting, voice instr. Pass-A-Grille Actors Studio, St. Petersburg, co-founder, 1989; condr. numerous workshop onn spl. needs of gifted and talented children. Contbr. numerous articles to newsletters. Cofounder, pres. Parents and Friends Gifted and Talented Children. Recipient Ind. Speech and Hearing Found. awards, 1966-67; grad. teaching fellow Purdue U., 1970-71. Mem. Am. Speech-Lang.-Hearing Assn. (cert. clin. competence 1972—), Fla. Motion Picture and TV Assn. Home and Office: 1404 Pass-A-Grille Way Saint Petersburg FL 33706

CANEVA-BIGGANE, TERRI DENISE, sales executive; b. Brush, Colo., Apr. 17, 1955; d. Eugene Lee and Bonnie Jean (Scott) Caneva; m. Dennis James Biggane, Sept. 27, 1986. BA in Speech Communications, U. Denver, 1976, MA in Organizational Communications, 1978. Sales rep. Sandoz, Inc., East Hanover, N.J., 1979-80; sales trainer Sandoz, Inc., Colorado Springs, Colo.; regional sales mgr. Critikon, Inc. div. Johnson & Johnson, Tampa, Fla., 1980-83; product specialist Critikon, Inc. div. Johnson & Johnson, San Francisco; sales mgr. Howmedica div. Pfizer, Rutherford, N.J., 1983-84; with Hosp. Satelite Network, L.A., 1984-88, regional sales mgr., 1984-87; product specialist Hosp. Satellite Network, Boston, 1987-88; area mgr. Hosp. Satellite Network, Denver, 1987-88; regional sales mgr. Mobile Tech., Inc., Boca Raton, Fla., 1989—; area sales mgr. Mobile Tech., Inc., L.A., 1989—. Mem. Nat. Orgn. Female Execs. Democrat. Methodist. Home: 1936 NW 8th St Boca Raton FL 33486

CANFIELD, LOUISE MONETTE, biochemist; d. Rollie Tomlinson Grounds and Maggie Mae (Hortman) Alvord; m. Eugene G. Sander, Feb. 24, 1979; children: Jay Kenneth, Kathy Lee. AB with distinction, U. Calif., Berkeley, 1970; MS, U. Ala., Huntsville, 1972; PhD in Biochemistry, Vanderbilt U., 1976. Instr., rsch. asst. U. Ala., Huntsville, 1969-72; NIH postdoctoral fellow dept. biochemistry U. Wis., Madison, 1976-80; asst. prof. depts. medicine and biochemistry W.Va. U. Sch. Medicine, Morgantown, 1979-80; asst. prof. depts. animal sci. and biochemistry Tex. A&M U., College Station, 1980-86, assoc. dir. honors program, 1985-87, dir. honors program, 1987-88, assoc. prof. dept. animal sci., 1986-87; assoc. prof. dept. biochemistry U. Ariz. Coll. Medicine, Tucson, 1987—. Contbr. articles to profl. jours., chpts. to books. Grantee NIH, 1976-78, 79-84, 86-89, Am. Cancer Soc., 1980-81, Robert A. Welch Found., 1982-88, Thrasher Found., 1988-89. Mem. AAAS, Am. Chem. Soc., AAUW (scholar 1987), Am. Dietetics Assn., Am. Soc. for Biochemistry and Molecular Biology, Internat. Assn. Women Biochemists, Am. Inst. Nutrition, Sigma Xi (dir. at large, bd. dirs. 1987-90, exec. com. 1987-89). Democrat. Methodist. Office: U Ariz Dept Biochemistry 1501 N Campbell Ave Tucson AZ 85724

CANFIELD, LYNDA RAE, writer; b. Elmira, N.Y., June 15, 1947; d. Raymond Frank and Doris Rae (Kilbourne) C.; m. William U. Hensel, IV, Sept. 10, 1967 (div. Oct. 1975); children—Jason William, Aaron David. B.A., Albany State U., 1969; M.S., Pa. State U., 1972. Cert. psychologist, Wis. Psychologist, Madison Pub. Schs., 1972-77; realtor Lyons Romo Inc., Tucson, 1978-83; writer bus. publs., Tucson, 1983—. Contbr. articles on tourism, sci., bus. to mags. Pres. bd. Avra Water Coop., Avra Valley, Tucson, 1982-88; pres. Picture Rocks Fire Aux., 1978-80. Recipient Merit award Met. Tucson C. of C. Rodeo Com., 1985. Mem. Internat. Platform Assn. Democrat. Roman Catholic. Avocations: softball, banjo. Home: 9800 W Rudasill Rd Tucson AZ 85743

CANFIELD, MURIEL JEAN NIXON, Spanish linguistics educator; b. Batavia, N.Y., Apr. 12, 1928; d. Robert and Amy Beatrice (Coultas) Nixon; m. Delos Lincoln Canfield, Aug. 2, 1971; children: Gerald Richard, Susan Nixon. BA, U. Rochester, 1949, MA, 1965; PhD, So. Ill. U., 1984. Prof. English Colegio Metodista Cen., Havana, Cuba, 1949-50; tchr. Spanish and Latin N.Y. State Pub. Schs., 1950-59; dir., owner Tutoring Sch., Rochester, N.Y., 1960-64; instr. English linguistics U. Rochester, 1964-65, dir. internat. student and scholar affairs, 1967-69; instr. Spanish and English, chmn. fgn. langs. Rochester Inst. Tech., 1964-67, assoc. registrar, dir. fgn. students, 1965-67; asst. dir. pub. info. City of Rochester, 1969-71; researcher, writer, translator, evaluator Am. Assn. Tchrs. Spanish and Portuguese, Chgo. Press.; researcher, writer, translator, evaluator So. Ill. U., Carbondale, 1973-87, prof. Spanish linguistics, 1981-89; prof. Spanish, Linguistics Grupo Canfield, 1986—; prof. Spanish linguistics Grupo Canfield. Author: Adjustment Experiences of Non-Immigrant Foreign Students, 1968, Criminal Justice Standards for a Nonmetropolitan Area, 1977, Vocational English as a Second Language Guidelines, 1981, Latin American Institute at Southern Illinios University at Carbondale, 1958-73, 85; translator Criminology in Spain, Criminology in Mexico, 1983; producer, writer various multi cultural shows for IBE?DAVTE, State of Ill., 1981. Pres., editor yearbook Carbondale Garden Club, 1971—; pres., treas. Carbondale Found. for Better Environ., 1973-81; coord. George Bush for Pres. Campaign, Jackson County, Ill., 1980; Rep. candidate for county clk. and recorder, Jackson County, 1978; fund raiser Jackson County Boosters Club, 1979—; pres. Carbondale Coun. Garden Clubs, 1980-81. Recipient Bicentennial award State of Ill., 1976, Disting. Svc. award City of Carbondale, 1977; Genesee scholar, 1945, Vassar Coll. scholar, 1945, U. Rochester scholar, 1963. Mem. Am. Assn. Tchrs. Spanish and Portuguese (program evaluator 1973-75, researcher, writer, translator, evaluator), Nat. Assn. Fgn. Student Affairs (bd. dirs. 1969-70), AAUW, LWV (chmn. criminal justice Carbondale 1975-84), Phi Kappa Phi, Phi Sigma Iota (life). Episcopalian.

CANGUREL, SUSAN STONE, personnel executive; b. Madison, Wis., Sept. 11, 1946; d. John Mather and Lois Marie (Wiessinger) Murray; m. Melih Cangurel; children—Lora Rae, Julie Lynn. Student U. Wis., 1964-66, U. Wis., Milw., 1976-78, U. Tex., El Paso, 1981-84. Adminstrv. asst. Madison C. of C., 1967-72; v.p. loan adminstrn.Kensington Mortgage & Fin. Corp., Milw., 1972-79; ; v.p. adminstrn. Mortgage Investment Co., El Paso, 1979-85; mgr. personnel svcs. Summa Corp., Las Vegas, 1985-88, v.p. MGM Desert Inn, 1988—. Mem. NAFE, Am. Soc. Personnel Adminstrs., Inst. Internal Auditors, Am. Mgmt. Assn., Am. Soc. for Tng. & Devel., Nev. Hotel & Motel Assn. Author poems and short stories. Home: 2329 Mohigan Way Las Vegas NV 89109

CANION, KIMBERLY ANN, broadcast television engineer; b. San Antonio, Dec. 17, 1963; d. Doyle Lewis and Rhoda Nadine (Merkens) C. BA, Trinity U., San Antonio, 1986; MBA, U. Tex., San Antonio, 1988. TV remote crew Trinity U., 1983-86; pub. rels. intern Atkins & Assocs., San Antonio, 1986; mktg. asst. Regnier, Valdez & Assocs., San Antonio, 1989; broadcast TV engr. KENS-TV, San Antonio, 1982—; engrng. rep. KENS-TV adv. coun., 1990-91. Mem. pub. rels. com. Trinity U. Coll. Reps., 1985-86. Named to Outstanding Young Women of Am., 1987; recipient Donald J. Douglas Entrepreneurship award Trinity U., 1986, Presdl. scholarship, Trinity U., 1982-86. Mem. U. Tex. at San Angelo MBA Assn., Am. Mktg. Assn., Trinity U. Mgmt. Assn., Women in Communications, Blue Key, Mortar Bd., Alpha Lambda Delta, Alpha Chi, Alpha Epsilon Rho (alumni chairperson 1984-85, pres. 1985-86), Zeta Chi. Lutheran. Home: 1015 San Angelo Blvd San Antonio TX 78201 Office: KENS-TV 5400 Fredericksburg Rd San Antonio TX 78229

CANN, NANCY TIMANUS, retail yacht sales executive; b. Balt.; d. E. Frank Timanus and Ruth F. (Herman) Schell; m. Jerrold R. Cann, Mar. 25, 1967; 1 child, Justin Ronald. Grad., Balt. Bus. Coll., 1967. Pres. Crusader Yacht Sales, Inc., Annapolis, Md., 1982—. Mem. Yacht Architects and Brokers Assn. (v.p. 1989—, chmn. membership com. 1989—), Bayfarers (chmn. 1987-88, bd. dirs. 1988—). Home and Office: 7078 Bembe Beach Rd Annapolis MD 21403

CANN, SHARON LEE, health science librarian; b. Ft. Riley, Kans., Aug. 14, 1935; d. Roman S. and Cora Elon (George) Foote; m. Donald Clair Cann, May 16, 1964. Student Sophia U., Tokyo, 1955-57; B.A., Sacramento State U., 1959; M.S.L.S., Atlanta U., 1977. Cert. health scis. librarian. Recreation worker ARC, Korea, Morocco, France, 1960-64; shelflister Library Congress Washington, 1967-69; tchr. Lang. Ctr., Taipei, Taiwan, 1971-73; library tech. asst. Emory U., Atlanta, 1974-76; health sci. librarian Northside Hosp., Atlanta, 1977-85; library cons., 1985-86; librarian area health edn. ctr., learning resource ctr. Morehouse Sch. Medicine, 1985-86; edn. librarian Ga. State U., 1986—. Editor Update, publ. Ga. Health Scis. Library Assn., 1981; contbr. articles to publs. Chmn. Calif. Christian Youth in Govt Seminar, 1958. Named Alumni Top Twenty, Sacramento State U., 1959. Mem. ALA, Med. Library Assn., Spl. Library Assn. (dir. South Atlantic chpt. 1985-87), Ga. Library Assn. (spl. library div. chmn. 1983-85), Ga. Health Scis. Library Assn. (chmn. 1981-82), Atlanta Health Sci. Library (chmn. 1979), Am. Numis. Assn., Am. Overseas Assn. Club: Toastmasters (Atlanta) sec.-treas. 1983-84). Home: 5520 Morning Creek Circle College Park GA 30349

CANNAVA, MARIE ELIZABETH, educator; b. San Juan, Puerto Rico, Dec. 17, 1946; d. Bernard and Isabel (Gilot) C.; m. Peter Philip Cannava; children: Peter Matthew, Richard Michael. BA in English, Hunter Coll, 1968; MS, Queens Coll., 1972. Tchr. English, Cen. Comml. High Sch., N.Y.C., 1968-69, Carey High Sch., Sewanhaka Cen. High Sch. Dist., Franklin Square, N.Y., 1969--. Den mother pack 373, Cub Scouts Am., Smithtown, N.Y., 1986-88, also com. chmn. Mem. Nat. Coun. Tchrs. English, AAUW (chmn. pub. rels. 1987). Democrat. Roman Catholic. Home: 12 Harding St Hauppauge NY 11788

CANNISTRA, LINDA M., hospital official; b. Waltham, Mass., Sept. 10, 1955; d. Francesco and Mary A. (Cincotta) C. BS, Providence Coll., 1977; MBA, Bryant Coll., Smithfield, R.I., 1987. Cert. microsurg. specialist. Rsch. project devel. coord. R.I. Hosp., Providence, 1983—. Contbr. articles to profl. jours. Mem. AAAS, NAFE, Orthopaedic Rsch. Soc., Am. Mgmt. Assn., N.Y. Acad. Sci., Delta Mu Delta. Home: 12 Jefferson Rd North Smithfield RI 02895 Office: RI Hosp Orthopaedic Rsch 593 Eddy St Providence RI 02903

CANNON, CHRISTINE ANNE, veterinarian; b. Chgo., Nov. 13, 1952; d. Joseph Phillip and Mildred Eileen (Toll) C.; m. Robert L. Van Grinsven, Mar. 25, 1989. BS in Animal Sci., Purdue U., 1974; BS in Vet. Medicine, U. Ill., 1975, DVM, 1977. Vet. Bellemore Small Animal Hosp., Granite City, Ill., 1977-79, Humane Soc. of Mo., St. Louis, 1979-81, Wheaton Way, Bremerton, Wash., 1981-82, Rose Hill Animal and Bird Hosp., Kirkland, Wash., 1982-83; relief vet. Wash., 1983-87; vet., owner Bird and Exotic Pet Care Clinic, Lynnwood, Wash., 1987—. Asst. editor Avian Emergency Care A Manual for Emergency Clinics, 1990. Group leader Canine Coll., Kirkland, 1986-87; mentor Project Discovery, Edmonds, Wash., 1989; leader Explorer Scouts troop Boy Scouts Am., St. Louis, 1981. Mem. Assn. Avian Vets., Am. Vet. Med. Assn., Wash. State Vet. Med. Assn., Seattle-King County Vet. Med. Assn. (rep. South Snohomish chpt. 1990—), Finch Lovers of Puget Sound (co-founder, sec.-treas. 1987—), Avicultural Soc. Puget Sound, Northwest Exotic Bird Soc. Office: Bird & Exotic Pet Care Clin 19713 Scriber Lake Rd Lynnwood WA 98036

CANNON, DEBORAH LYNN, hotel management company executive; b. Richmond, Va., Mar. 7, 1961; d. Norman H. and Pauline Pearl (Stewart) C. AA, Catonsville Community Coll., 1981. Sales asst. Hyatt Regency, Balt., 1981-83; sales mgr. Brookshire Hotel, Balt., 1983-84; front office mgr. Lincoln Plaza, Oklahoma City, Okla., 1984-85; sales dir. Peabody Ct., Balt., 1985-86; mgr. corp. rels. Brookshire Hotels, Columbia, Md., 1986—, dir. sales & mktg., 1986—, corp. dir. sales & mktg., 1986—. Mem. Am. Soc. Assn. Execs., Hotel Sales & Mktg. Assn. Internat. (pres. 1986-88; most outstanding mem., 1986-87). Republican. Home: 8397 L Montgomery Run Rd Ellicott City MD 21043 Office: Brookshire Hotels 9705 Patuxent Woods Dr Columbia MD 21046

CANNON, MARLENE HUTTON, foundation administrator; b. Ann Arbor, Mich., Sept. 24, 1934; d. Merl Noyer and Helen (Foster) Hutton; m. Samuel Phillips Cannon, June 26, 1953 (div. Aug. 1983); children: Steven Phillips, Anne Foster. BS, Northwestern U., 1953. Exec. dir. Danville (Ill.) Area Community Coll. Found. Chmn. Women's Spl. Div. United Way,

Danville, 1970-85, bd. dirs., 1975-85; bd. dirs. local YWCA, 1965-68; head bookkeeper Vol. Gift Shop Lakeview Meml. Hosp., Danville, 1962-87; discussion leader Great Books Program Danville Elem. Schs., 1960-70; chmn. Tri-Found. Charity Pro Am, 1981-89 (Dedicated Svcs. award 1988). Mem. Nat. Coun. Resource Devel., Clover Club, Danville Country Club. Home: 1300 Park Haven Ct Danville IL 61832 Office: DACC Found 2000 E Main St Danville IL 61832

CANNON, NANCY GLADSTEIN, insurance agent; b. San Francisco; d. Richard and Caroline (Decker) Gladstein; m. Robert L. Cannon, Dec. 21, 1971; 1 child, Richard Michael. BA, San Francisco State U., 1964; JD, U. West Los Angeles, 1980. Tchr. San Bruno (Calif.) Park Schs., 1964-69, Inglewood (Calif.) Unified Schs., 1969-75; exec. dir. Henrico Edn. Assn., Richmond, Va., 1975-76; agt. Blue Cross So. Calif., 1981-84, State Farm Ins. Co., Pacific Palisades, Calif., 1984—; pres. Cannon Ins. Agy., Pacific Palisades, 1984—. Del. Dem. Nat. Conv., Chgo., 1968; mem. bd. govs. Pacific Palisades Civic League, 1987—, Community Coun., 1988-89; bd. dirs. YMCA, Palisades-Malibu, 1989-92. Mem. Pacific Palisades C. of C., Santa Monica C. of C., Rotary, L.A. Athletic Club. Republican. Office: Cannon Ins Agy Inc 1027 Swarthmore Pacific Palisades CA 90272

CANNON, YOLANDA J., legal assistant; b. Camp Pendleton, Calif., Sept. 7, 1957; d. Carl R. and Lille M. (Hanible) Cannon. BA, Howard U., 1979; JD, Tex. So. U., 1983. Legal ast. Liddell, Sapp, Zivley, Hill & LaBoon, Houston, 1985—. Mem. State Bar Tex. Legal Assts., Nat. Fedn. Paralegals, Houston Legal Assts. Assn., Howard U. Alumni Assn., Phi Alpha Delta. Home: 2626 Holly Hall 1101 Houston TX 77054

CANNONE-MCGILL, ROSALIE A(NTOINETTE), lawyer; b. Elizabeth, N.J., June 28, 1943; d. Nicola and Anna (LaMonica) C. B.A., Rutgers U., 1965; J.D., Seton Hall U., 1977. Bar: N.J. 1977, U.S. Dist. Ct. N.J. 1977, U.S. Supreme Ct. 1983. Employment interviewer N.J. State Dept. Labor and Industry, Elizabeth, 1965-66; tchr., supr., reading specialist Elizabeth Sch. Dist., 1966-77; atty. Office Gen. Counsel, Prentice-Hall, Inc., Englewood Cliffs, N.J., 1977-81; asst. gen. counsel Alfa-Laval, Inc., Ft. Lee, N.J., 1981-87; sec. bd. dirs. Imo, Inc., Ft. Lee, 1984-85, Stal Refrigeration, Ben Saleem, Pa., 1982-83, Celleco, Inc., Atlanta, 1982-87; asst. sec. Alfa-Laval, Inc., Ft. Lee and subs., 1981-87; with Pirelli Cable Corp., Union, N.J., 1987—. Mem. ABA, N.J. Bar Assn., Am. Arbitration Assn. (arbitrator). Office: Pirelli Cable Corp Florham Park NJ 07932

CANNY, PAULA KAY, lawyer; b. Washington, Mar. 8, 1955; d. Robert William and Catherine (Carlson) C. B.A. in Econs., Kirkland Coll., 1977; J.D., U. San Francisco, 1980. Bar: Calif. 1980, U.S. Ct. Appeals (9th cir.) 1980. Assoc., Wald, Brown & Knoll, Oakland, Calif., 1980-82; dep. dist. atty. Ventura County (Calif.), 1982-83, San Mateo (Calif.), 1983-84; pvt. practice, Burlingame, Calif., 1989—. Active NOW, Women's Sports Found. Mem. Calif. Pub. Defenders Assn., Calif. Attorneys for Criminal Justice, U.S. Powerlifting Assn. Democrat. Office: 1450 Chapin Ave Burlingame CA 94010

CANON, NANCY ANNE, school superintendent; b. Goshen, Ind., Apr. 20, 1939; d. Ernest Elemer and Hazel Bell (Cain) Ferguson; m. Joseph Michael Canon; children: Patrick Allen, Michael Bryan. BS, We. Oreg. State Coll., 1961, MS, 1964; PhD, U. Oreg., 1975. Tchr. Jefferson (Oreg.) Elem. Sch., 1961-63, Monmouth (Oreg.) Elem. Sch., 1963-64; supervising tchr. Campus Elem. Sch., We. Oreg. State Coll., 1964-69; head tchr., supervising tchr. Ashland (Oreg.) pub. schs., 1970-71; supr. student tchrs. U. Oreg., Eugene, 1972-74; prin., curriculum coordinator, supt. intern Roseburg (Oreg.) Pub. Sch., 1975-80; substance abuse prevention specialist Juvenile Svc. Commn., Medford, Oreg., 1983-84; supr. student tchrs. So. Oreg. State Coll., Ashland, 1984-86; teaching prin. Irish Bend Grad Sch., Monroe, Oreg., 1986-88; supt. Dayville (Oreg.) Sch. Dist., 1988—; conductor workshops in field; cons. in field; sr. counselor Oreg. Assn. Activity Advisors, Salem, 1988—. Contbr. articles to profl. jours. Bd. dirs. We. Oreg. State Coll. Pendleton Arts Council. Mem. Organizing Oreg. Women for Ednl. Adminstrn., Roseburg Adminstrs. Assn. (pres. 1977), AAUW, Oreg. Assn. Activity Advisors, Oreg. Assn. Sch. Execs., Oreg. Elem. Prins. Assn. (regional pres. 1977-78), Toastmasters (pres. 1976, 83, Outstanding Toastmaster 1978). Republican. Presbyterian. Home: PO Box 301 Dayville OR 97825 Office: Dayville Pub Schs PO Box C Dayville OR 97825

CANOVA, CAROL JOY, public relations specialist; b. Syosset, N.Y., Mar. 8, 1965; d. Ralph Michael and Mary Ellen (Maloney) Della Ratta; m. Eugene J. Canova, July 14, 1990. BA, Ind. U., 1987. Tourism and promotions intern Bloomington (Ind.)/Monroe County Convention Bur., 1987; sr. chairperson pub. info. Ind. U. Student Found., Bloomington, 1987; communications and spl. events dir. Peninsula Housing & Builders Assn., Newport News, Va., 1988-89; vol. pub. rels. asst. James City County Govt., Williamsburg, Va., 1989, communications asst., 1990—, rideshare coord., 1990—. Editor, researcher: Restaurant Guide, 1987; editor sales Parade of Homes Plan Book, 1988; editor The Peninsula Builder, 1988-89. Roman Catholic. Home: 112 E Chippenham Dr Yorktown VA 23693

CANTALUPO, BARBARA ANNE, language professional; b. Rochester, N.Y., Dec. 7, 1947; d. Anna May Dorosh; children from previous marriage: Elizabeth, Christopher; m. Charles Roger Cantalupo III, Oct. 29, 1988; 1 child, Alicia. AB, U. Rochester, 1969; MSW, SUNY, Buffalo, 1973, MA, 1984, PhD in English, 1988. Social work supr. Cath. Charities, Buffalo, 1976-78; cons. to Head Start Chautauqua Opportunities, Mayville, N.Y., 1979-81; teaching asst. SUNY, Buffalo, 1983-87; lectr. SUNY, Fredonia, 1987; instr. of English Pa. State U., DuBois, 1987-88, asst. prof. of English, 1988-89; asst. prof. of English Pa. State U., Allentown, 1989—. Author: Ghost City, 1987. Recipient Fulbright teaching fellowship, Morocco, 1989-90. Mem. MLA, N.E. MLA, Ctr. for Exploratory and Perceptual Arts (bd. dirs. 1987), AAUW. Democrat. Office: Pa State U Allentown Fogelsville PA 17960

CANTARUTTI, TRACEY LERCH, management consultant, marketing specialist; b. Rock Island, Ill., Apr. 4, 1955; d. Donald Roy and Dorothy Jean (Myers) Lerch; m. Robert Cantarutti, May 21, 1983; children: Michael, Angela, Alexandra. BA in Spanish, U. Ill., Urbana, 1977; cert., Alliance Francaise, Paris, 1979; M in Internat. Mgmt., Am. Grad. Sch. of Internat. Mgmt., 1980. Asst. to cultural attache Inst. of North Am. Studies, Barcelona, Spain, 1978-79; grad. asst. Am. Grad. Sch. of Internat. Mgmt., Glendale, Ariz., 1980; mktg. analyst Motorola, Inc., Schaumburg, Ill., 1981-82, mktg. planner, 1982-84, sr. product planner, 1984-86; sr. cons. Chgo. Cons. Group, Arthur Young, 1986-87, mgr., 1987—. Vol. Septemberfest Com. March of Dimes, Schaumburg, 1984-86; vol. village election support Schaumburg United Party, 1987. Recipient Amalio Suarez fellowship Am. Grad. Sch. of Internat. Mgmt., 1980, Celia Howard scholarship Ill. Fedn. Bus. and Profl. Women, 1980. Mem. Woodfield Bus. and Profl. Women's Club (treas. 1987—), Am. Mktg. Assn., Nat. Assn. Female Execs. Office: Arthur Young 1 IBM Pla Chicago IL 60611

CANTELMO, PATRICIA ANN, principal; b. Jersey City, N.J., Feb. 13, 1944; d. Joseph Anthony and Josephine Elizabeth (Parisi) C. BA in Elem. Edn., Jersey City State Coll., 1965, MA in Early Childhood, 1974; postgrad., Wm. Patterson Coll., 1976. Team tchr. Teaneck (N.J.) Twp. Pub. Schs., 1965-69, tchr., 1969-70, team leader, 1970-77, emergency sch. aid act team coordinator, 1977-78, elem. prin., 1978-84, primary prin., 1986-88, elem. prin., 1988—; middle sch. prin. East Hanover (N.J.) Pub. Schs., 1984-86; adj. tchr. Jersey City State Coll., 1981-82, Fairleigh Dickinson U., Teaneck, 1982-83; workshop leader Macmillan Pubs., 1978-80. Vol. Englewood Cliffs (N.J.) Dem. Assn., 1972—. Mem. Assn. for Supervision and Curriculum Devel., Nat. Assn. Elem. and Secondary Sch. Prins., Nat. Prins. Assn., Phi Delta Kappa. Home: 235 Prospect Ave Hackensack NJ 07601

CANTER, DEBORAH DEAN, dietetics educator; b. Detroit, Aug. 2, 1950; d. John Raymond and Maggie Eulala (Housden) C. BS, U. Tenn., 1972, MS, 1974, PhD, 1977. Clin. instr. in dietetics U. Tenn., Knoxville, 1974-77; from asst. prof. in dietetics to assoc. prof. Kans. State U., Manhattan, 1977—; dir. Coordinated Program Dietetics, Manhattan, 1988—. Vol. Big Bros. and Big Sisters, 1980, Am. Heart Assn., 1987—; bd. dirs. edn. Manhattan Hospice Care, Inc., 1985-86. Mem. The Am. Dietetic Assn. (bd. dirs. 1986-87), Am. Sch. Food Svc. Assn., Commn. Dietetic Registration (chmn. 1990—), Zeta Tau Alpha. Office: Kans State Univ Justin Hall 106 Manhattan KS 66506

CANTER, PAMELA S., nurse; b. Dover Township, Oh., Mar. 12, 1963; d. Everett Dean and Carolyn Jean (Dauterman) H.; m. Hall G. Canter, May 18, 1985; 1 child, Callie Jean. Student, Assoc. Sci. Nursing, Westerville, 1981-82. Advanced Cardiac Life Support, Basic Life Support Instr., Advanced Cardiac Life Support Instr. Nursing aide Grant Hosp., Cols., 1982; rn Grant Hosp., Columbus, 1982-85, Bethesda Hosp., Zanesville, Oh., 1985--, Perry County Family Practice, New Lexington; nurse rep., charge nurse Inservice Edn. Com. Grant Hosp. Columbus 1983-85; clinical student nurse preceptor Grant Hosp.; outpatient cardiac rehab. charge nurse Bethesda Hosp. Zanesville 1987--; coordinator Perry County Family Practice New Lexington, 1986-87. Republican. Methodist. Home: 929 Convers Ave Zanesville OH 43701

CANTLIFFE, JERI MILLER, art educator, artist; b. Alliance, N.C., Nov. 25, 1927; d. Rufus Faye Miller and Viola Elizabeth (Ireland) Miller Smith; m. Lawrence R. Cantliffe Jr., Sept.1, 1949; children: Eileen M., David L., Geri Lyn, Lisa Ann, Jonathan M. BA, Meredith Coll., 1949; M in Art Teaching, Wesleyan U., 1967; postgrad., Paier Sch. Art, New Haven, 1974-76. Designer Stephenson Appliance Co., Raleigh, N.C., 1949-50; lab. asst. N.C. State Coll., Raleigh, 1950, Hoffman-LaRoche Pharms., Clifton, N.J., 1951-52; art tchr. Horace Wilcox Tech. Sch., Meriden, Conn., 1962-66; workshop tchr. Park & Recreation Dept., Haddam and Wallingford, Conn., 1970-84, YWCA, Meriden, 1970-85, Middletown (Conn.) Art Guild, 1970-90, instr. in arts and crafts, 1989; workshop tchr. Community Art Ctr., Kensington, Conn., 1977-79; freelance artist specializing in home portraits, 1980—. One woman shows include Cen. Bank, Meriden, 1977, 79, 82, Meriden Pub. Library, 1981, 84 (commd. artist, Women of Yr. in Arts award 1979), Cheshire (Conn.) Pub. Library, 1982, Phoenix Mut. Life Ins. Co., Hartford, Conn., 1982, N. Haven (Conn.) Pub. Library, 1983, 86, Greene Art Gallery, Guilford, Conn., 1984, Meredith Coll., Raleigh, 1984, Lord Proprietor's Inn, Edenton, N.C.; juried mem. shows include Salamagundi, N.Y.C., New Haven Paint & Clay, Friends of New Britain (Conn.) Mus., Meriden Arts & Crafts (Frederick Flatow award 1979, Butler Paint award 1980, Alan Reid Meml. prize watercolor 1986), Middletown (Conn.) Art Guild (1st prize watercolor 1977, 78), Brush & Palette, New Haven, Milford (Conn.) Fine Arts, Mt. Carmel Art Assn., Hamden, Conn., Wis. Watercolor Show, Glastonbury (Conn.) Art Guild, The New Group, New Haven, Conn. Classic Arts, Conn. Acad. Fine Arts, Am. Penwomen, Faifield, Conn.; invitational shows include Jewish Home for the Aged, New Haven, Art-on-the Mountain, Wilmington, Vt., Wesleyan Showcase, Middletown Showcase (Most Popular award 1979), Glastonbury C. of C., AAUW Art Show, Soundview Ann. Art Show; illustrator Meriden Calendar, Meriden City Hall Christmas card. Co-chmn. Commn. on Arts, Meriden, 1975-76. Recipient Redstone Mfg. award "Mum" Art Festival, Bristol, Conn., 1978, Best in Show award Middletown Ann. Winter Show, 1978, Judges Tri-color award Community Art League, Kensington, 1978, Most Popular Vote award Middletown Showcase, 1979, Rick Ciburi 1st prize award Cheshire Art League, 1981, Best in Show (watercolor) Bridgeport Art League, 1982; named Woman of Yr. in Arts Meriden Girls Club, 1982, Meriden-Record Jour., 1981, Meriden YWCA, 1983, Meredith Coll., 1984. Mem. Rotary (youth exch. com., internat. com. chair youth exch. officer Meriden chpt.), Nat. League Am. Pen Women (state art co-chair 1988-89, nat. art bd. 1990—, chmn. nat. assistance membership 1990—, pres. Fairfield County br. 1988—). Congregationalist. Lodge: Rotary.

CANTO, DIANA CATHERINE, nurse; b. Antioch, Calif., Mar. 20, 1939; d. William Light and Emma Catherine (Disher) Clark; children: Paul Petroni, Peter Petroni, Patrick Canto, Alexander Canto. AS with honors, Contra Costa Coll., San Pablo, Calif., 1982; BSN summa cum laude, Holy Name Coll., Oakland, Calif., 1984; MS, U. Calif., San Francisco, 1987. RN, Calif.; cert. PNP, FNP, CPR. RN Children's Hosp. Oakland, Calif., 1984-86, Merrithew Meml. Hosp., Martinez, Calif., 1986-87; family nurse practitioner Contra Costa County Detention Facility, Martinez, Calif., 1987, Berkeley (Calif.) City Pub. Health Dept., West Berkeley (Calif.) Health Clin., 1987-88, Maxicare Health Svcs., Calif., 1988—, U. San Francisco, 1989—, Homeless Program Alameda, San Leandro, Calif., 1989—; with San Francisco Pub. Health Dept., 1989—; researcher Contra Costa County P.H.D., Pitts., 1984, Ctr. for New Americans, Concord, Calif., 1985, UCSF, 1986-87, edn. program developer, Children's Hosp. Oakland, 1984-85, other ctrs. Mem. Walnut Creek Com. on Aging. Mem. AAUW, LWV, NOW, Am. Nurses Assn., Calif. Nurses Assn., Calif. Coalition Nurse Practitioners, Nat. Assn. Pediatric Nurse Practitioner Assn., Council Nursing and Anthropology, Intercultural Interest Group of the Bay Area, Am. Pub. Health Assn., Kappa Gamma Pi, Sigma Theta Tau. Home: 117 Jose Ln Martinez CA 94553 Office: San Francisco Pub Health Dept Health Ctr #3 1525 Silver Ave San Francisco CA 94134

CANTOR, ELEANOR WESCHLER, medical association executive; b. N.Y.C., Dec. 30, 1913; d. Samuel Peter and Anna (Rauchwerger) W.; m. Alfred Joseph Cantor, June 9, 1938; children—Pamela Corliss, Alfred Jay. B.A., Hunter Coll., N.Y.C., 1938. Producer radio quiz show CBS, N.Y.C., 1936-41; exec. officer Internat. Acad. Proctology, N.Y.C., 1948—, Internat. Bd. Proctology, 1950—; co-founder Acad. Psychosomatic Medicine, 1954.

CANTOR, MURIEL GOLDSMAN, sociologist, educator; b. Mpls., Mar. 2, 1923; d. Leo and Bess Goldsman; m. Joel M. Cantor, Aug. 6, 1944 (dec. 1988); children: Murray Robert, Jane Cantor Shefler, James Leo. B.A., UCLA, 1964, M.A., 1966, Ph.D., 1969. Lectr. dept. econs. and sociology Immaculate Heart Coll., L.A., 1966-68; faculty Am. U., Washington, 1968—; instr. Am. U., 1968-69, asst. prof. sociology, 1969-72, assoc. prof., 1972-76, dept. chmn., 1973-75, 77-79, prof., 1976-89; vis. prof. communication studies UCLA, 1982; dir. women's studies Am. U., Washington, 1989—; cons. agencies including NIMH; cons. Corp. for Pub. Broadcasting, 1974-75, 80-81. Author: The Hollywood TV Producer: His Work and His Audience, 1971, 2d edit. with new intro., 1987, Prime Time Television: Content and Control, 1980, (with Phyllis L. Stewart) Varieties of Work Experience, 1974, 82, (with Suzanne Pingree) The Soap Opera, 1983, (with Sandra Ball-Rokeach) Media, Audiences, and Social Structure, 1986; editor Nat. SWS newsletter, 1977-78. Bd. dirs. Population Inst., 1978-80; trustee WETA, 1972-76. NIMH grantee, 1979-81; recipient Premio Diego Fabbri for Soap Opera in Rome, 1988. Mem. Am. Sociol. Assn. (chair-elect soc. culture sect. 1989—), D.C. Sociol. Soc. (pres. 1977-78, Stewart A. Rice Merit award 1987), Sociologists for Women in Society, Eastern Sociol. Soc. (exec. council 1981-84, 89—). Home: 8408 Whitman Dr Bethesda MD 20817 Office: Am U Dept Sociology Washington DC 20016

CANTOR, PAMELA CORLISS, psychologist; b. N.Y.C., Apr. 23, 1944; d. Alfred Joseph and Eleanor (Weschler) C.; m. Howard Feldman, Sept. 11, 1969; children: Lauren Jaye, Jeffrey Lee. BS cum laude, Syracuse U., 1965; postgrad. in medicine, Johns Hopkins U., 1969-70; MA, Columbia U., 1967, PhD, 1972; postgrad., Harvard U.-Children's Hosp. Med. Ctr., 1973-74. Instr. Radcliffe Inst., Harvard U., 1977-78; assoc. prof. psychology Boston U., 1970-80; pvt. practice clin. psychology, Chestnut Hill, Mass., 1980—; faculty Med. Sch., Harvard U.; lectr. in field, also TV and radio appearances. Author: Understanding A Child's World- Reading in Infancy through Adolescence, 1977; cons. editor: Suicide and Life-Threatening Behavior; columnist: For Parents Only; contbr. chpts. to handbooks and numerous articles to profl. jours. Apptd. mem. Mass. Gov.'s Office for Children Statewide Adv. Bd., 1980—; adv. bd. Samaritans of Boston; pres. Nat. Com. Youth Suicide Prevention; mem. HHS Presdl. Task Force on Youth Suicide. Mem. Am. Psychol. Assn., Am. Assn. Suicidology (pres. 1985-86), Am. Orthopsychiat. Assn., Mass. Psychol. Assn., Am. Assn. Suicidology (bd. dirs.). Home: 65 Essex Rd Chestnut Hill MA 02167

CANTRELL, ANDREA, library administrator; b. Springfield, Mo., Jan. 1, 1948; d. A.J. Cantrell and Wilma (Snowden) Cave; m. Stephen J. Chism, 1989. BA, Am. U., 1970; MLS, U. Md., College Park, 1971. Young adult svcs. libr. Thomas Jefferson Regional Libr., Jefferson City, Mo., 1971-72; reference libr. Springfield-Greene County Libr. (Mo.), 1972-74; coord. Libr. resources Mo. State Libr., Jefferson City, 1974-78; chief cons. svc. Wash. State Library, Olympia, 1978-79; dir. Joplin Pub. Libr. (Mo.), 1979-81; dir. libr. resources div. Okla. Hist. Soc., Oklahoma City, 1981-85; spl. collections libr. U. Ark., Fayetteville, 1985—. Author: Manuscript Resources for Women's Studies, 1989; contbr. articles to profl. jours. Mem. ALA (chmn. staff devel. com. 1977-78; genealogy com. 1983-85), Ark. Libr. Assn. (chmn. coll. and Univ. div. 1986-87), Assn. Specialized and Coop. Libr. Agys. (chmn. 1978-79), Mo. Libr. Assn. (mem. various coms.), Zeta Tau Alpha. Lodge: Soroptimist Internat. Office: Spl Collections Dept U Ark Libraries Fayetteville AR 72701

CANTRELL, COLEEN SHARON, nursing administrator; b. Williamsport, Pa., Feb. 8, 1952; d. William Francis and Natalie Elizabeth (Musser) Caldwell; 1 child, Christopher William Cantrell. BS in Nursing, Indiana U. of Pa., 1974; MS in Adminstrn., Cen. Mich. U., 1988. Commd. 1st lt. U.S. Army Nurse Corps, 1974, advanced through grades to capt., 1980; maj. USAR; orthopedic staff nurse, Fort Polk, La., Seoul, Korea, 1974-77, head nurse urology, Fort Bragg, N.C., 1977-78, evening, night supr., 1978-79, infection control nurse, 1979-80; head nurse urology St. John's Regional Med. Ctr., Joplin, Mo., 1981-84, staff nurse, 1980-81, dir. med. nursing svc., 1984—. Asst. leader Explorer Scouts MoKan coun. Boy Scouts Am., 1984-85, 87-88. Recipient U.S.A. Commendation award, 1977, 80, cert. of award St. John's Regional Med. Ctr., 1983. Mem. Am. Nurses Assn. (cert.), Mo. Assn. Nursing Svc. Adminstrs., Mo. Nurses Assn. (bd. dirs. local dist. 1985-87, treas. 5th dist. 1988—), Oncology Nursing Soc. Lutheran. Avocations: playing piano, camping, reading. Office: St Johns Regional Med Ctr 2727 McClelland Blvd Joplin MO 64804

CANTRELL, CONSTANCE, pension funds representative; b. Oklahoma City, Oct. 31, 1945; d. John Bara and Elizabeth Catherine (Carman) C. BA in English, Northeastern State U., 1967; MA in English, Pepperdine U., 1976. Ghostwriter Gov.'s Office, Sacramento, 1967-69; dist. rep. Calif. Legislature, Los Angeles, 1969-72; research assoc. Supreme Ct. Calif., San Francisco, 1972-74; bus. devel. specialist URS Cor., San Francisco, 1974-77; v.p. First Nat. Bank & Trust. Co., Tulsa, 1978-84, Boatmen's Trust Co., St. Louis, 1984—. Mem. Assn. Investment Mgmt. Sales Execs., S.W. Pension Conf., Nat. Council on Tchr. Retirement, Mo. Assn. Pub. Employee Retirement Systems. Office: Boatmen's Trust Co 100 N Broadway Saint Louis MO 63102

CANTRELL, LAVONNE OPAL (LEE CANTRELL), water treatment company executive; b. Pontiac, Mich., Dec. 27, 1935; d. Archiebald Hugh and Pearl Marie (Heath) Warden; m. Willis Walter Cantrell, Sept. 11, 1979. AA in Aerospace Tech. with honors, Glendale (Calif.) Community Coll., 1975. Lic. comml. pilot, FAA. Telegrapher Western Union Telegraph Co., Pontiac and Rochester, Mich., 1955-57; surgery aide Dr.'s Hosp., Cleve., 1958-60; dep. sheriff Los Angeles County Sheriff's Dept., 1967-71; aircraft mechanic Airresearch Aviation Co., Los Angeles, 1978-79; owner Hill Country Services, Kendalia, Tex., 1982—; pres. L&W Water Systems, Inc., Kendalia, 1985—. Res. dep. sheriff Kendall County Sheriff's Dept., Boerne, Tex., 1981—. Served with USN, 1960-67. Mem. Water Quality Assn., Am. Water Works Assn., Ninety Nines, Wirly Girls, Am. Legion (adjudant 1983-86, comdr. 1986-87), Alpha Gamma Sigma. Republican. Mormon. Home: PO Box 302 Kendalia TX 78027 Office: Hill County Svcs 106 Fawn Circle Kendalia TX 78027

CANTRELL, MARY, mental health association administrator; b. Grafton, W.Va., Jan. 10, 1915; d. John and Olga (Meister) Robinson; 1 child, Suzanne Herbert. BS in Nursing, Baylor U., 1955; MS in Nursing, U. Tex., 1960; doctoral student, North Tex. U. RN. Head nurse St. Elizabeth Hosp., Washington, 1937-40; dir. nursing svc. U. Okla., Norman, 1942-51; dir. nursing edn. Waco (Tex.) VA Hosp., 1952-74; dir. mental health assoc. program McLennan Community Coll., Waco, 1974-85; dir. Heart of Tex. chpt. Mental Health Assn., Waco, 1985—; cons. Community Career Ctr. for Displaced Homemakers, Tex. Coordinating Bd.; nursing cons. Brazos Ctr. for Psychiatry; mem. speakers' pool continuing edn. in the health scis. Baylor U. Med. Ctr., adv. com. faculty tng. project So. Regional Edn. Bd., Coun. for Standards in Human Svc. Edn.; site visitor for So. Regional Edn. Bd. accreditation of mental health programs in colls. and univs. Mem. women's issues forum com. YWCA, Heart of Tex. Coun. Govts. Exec. Health Planning Com., vol. svcs. coun. Waco Ctr. for Youth, Retired Sr. Vol. Program Adv. Bd., Adaptive Living Ctr. Adv. Bd., Cen. Tex. Coun. for the Deaf Adv. Bd., Assn. for the Advancement Community Welfare; past mem. Freeman House Bd., adv. com. Area Agy. on Aging, com. on drug abuse Heart of Tex. Coun. Govts.; mem. Waco YWCA Pathfinder, 1985; elected to Silver Haired Legis., com. chair, mem. exec. com., 1987. Recipient Jr. C. of C. Annual award for community svc., 1986, Gov. of Tex. award for vol. svc. to the handicapped, 1986, Appreciation award VFW, 1988, Miriam Klubok award for outstanding and continuous leadership in the nat. orgn. for human svc. edn., 1989, Waco Unit Annual award Nat. Assn. Social Workers, 1989; named nominee Tex. Dept. Mental Health-Mental Retardation's Vol. of Yr., Waco Ctr. for Youth, 1986, Tex. Vol. award Waco United Way, 1986. Mem. Tex. Nurses Assn. (past dir., every office except treas., chmn. of every com. Dist. 10, Nurse of Yr. 1990), Am. Nurses' Assn. (past sec., exec. com. on psychiat. nursing practice), Nat. Orgn. Human Svc. Educators (immediate past pres., bd. dirs., Lenore McNeer award 1984), Tex. Mental Health Assn., Tex. Jr. Coll. Tchr.'s Assn., Tex. Orgn. Human Svc. Edn., Nat. Mental Health Assn., Nat. Assn. for Mental Health (staff coun.), Sigma Theta Tau. Home: 1517 Royal Oaks Dr Waco TX 76710 Office: Mental Health Assn 305 Londonderry Ste 10 Waco TX 76712

CANTRELL, SHARRON CAULK, educator; b. Columbia, Tenn., Oct. 2, 1947; d. Tom English and Beulah (Goodin) Caulk; children—Christopher, George English, Steffenee Copley; m. William Terry Cantrell, Mar. 18, 1989. BA George Peabody Coll. Tchrs., 1970; MS Vanderbilt U., 1980; EdS Mid. Tenn. State U., 1986. Tchr., Ft. Campbell Jr. High Sch., Ky., 1970-71, Whitthorne Jr. High Sch., Columbia, Tenn., 1977-86, Spring Hill (Tenn.) High Sch., 1986—; chmn. edn. Homecoming '86 Maury County Schs., Columbia, 1984-86. Mem. Maury County Edn. Assn. (pres. 1983-84), Tenn. Edn. Assn., NEA, AAUW (pres. Tenn. div. 1983-85), Nat. Council Tchrs. English, Maury County C. of C., Phi Delta Kappa. Mem. Ch. of Christ. Home: 1090 Rolling Fields Columbia TN 38401 Office: Spring Hill High Sch School St Spring Hill TN 37174

CANTWELL, ALICE CATHERINE, industrial lobbyist; b. Bar Harbor, Maine, Mar. 30, 1927; d. John Francis and Bridget Mary (Finnegan) C. BA, Russell Sage Coll., 1972. Stenographer, office asst. Pub. Health Nursing Assn., Bar Harbor, 1945-46; stenographer for advt. news Cities Service Oil Co., N.Y.C., 1946-47; legal sec. Law Office Ralph C. Masterman and chmn. State of Maine Rep. party, Bar Harbor, 1947-51; sec. purchasing then sec. plant ops. Allegheny Ludlum Steel Corp., Watervliet, N.Y., 1952-61; from sec. to mgr. NE regional govtl. relations Ford Motor Co., Albany, N.Y., 1961—; mem. steering com. Associated Industries of Mass., Boston, 1985—; mem. various coms. Bus. Council of State of N.Y., Albany, 1981—. Mem. Albany Symphony Orchestra, Vanguard, Albany Inst. History and Art. Roman Catholic. Clubs: City of Albany, Ladies of Charity, University. Lodge: Soroptomists (Woman of Distinction 1986). Office: Ford Motor Co 111 Washington Ave Ste 206 Albany NY 12210

CANTWELL, LINDA WALSH, civic worker; b. Franklin, N.J., Aug. 19, 1938; d. James Peter and Mary Agnes (Kerin) Walsh; m. Howard Danforth Cantwell, Sept. 1, 1962; children: Kerin Louise, Christopher Danforth, Kevin Walsh. BA, Rutgers U., 1960. Actuarial asst. Home Life Ins. Co., N.Y.C., 1960-62. Benefit chmn. Pasadena (Calif.) Jr. Philharm. Com., 1983-84, pres., 1985-86; chmn. San Gabriel (Calif.) Valley Med. Ctr. Found., 1987-89; pres. Almansor Ctr. Aux., 1989—; concert chmn. Pasadena Area Youth Music Coun., 1989—; trustee Almansor Ctr., South Pasadena, Calif., 1988—, San Gabriel Valley Med. Ctr., 1989-90; bd. dirs. Music Ctr. Opera League, L.A., 1988—. Democrat. Roman Catholic. Home: 1409 Hillcrest Ave Pasadena CA 91106

CANTWELL, LOIS, writer, editor; b. Jersey City, June 16, 1951; m. Robert Sefcik, Oct. 3, 1981; children: Teddy, Zoe. BA, U. Wis., 1973. Editor Ideal Pub., N.Y.C., 1977-78; editor-in-chief children's div. Parents mag., N.Y.C., 1978-81; editor-in-chief Careers mag. E.M. Guild Inc., N.Y.C., 1987-89; freelance writer N.Y.C., 1981-87; v.p., dir. internal communications Kidder, Peabody and Co., Inc., N.Y.C., 1989-90; mgr. internal communications Sony Corp Am., Park Ridge, N.J., 1990—; cons. AT&T, Morristown, N.J., 1985, CNR Ptnrs., N.Y.C., 1987. Author: Money and Banking, 1984, Freedom,

1985, Modeling, 1986, Blackstone's Magic Adventures, 1986. Pres. Midtown Manor Coop., N.Y.C., 1985, treas., 1986. Mem. So. Profl. Jours., Sigma Delta Chi, Nat. Acad. TV Arts and Sci., Fred Lewis Allen Room, Writers Room. Home: 42 Walnut Ave Millburn NJ 07041

CANTY, EILEEN MAXWELL, human resources consultant; b. N.Y.C., June 1, 1933; d. Edward Gerard and Anne Miriam (Morahan) Maxwell; m. James J. Canty, Jr., Sept. 3, 1960; children: Anne Elizabeth, Kathleen Marie (dec.), James Joseph III, Edward Maxwell. BA, Coll. of New Rochelle, N.Y., 1955; MA, Fordham U., 1956, PhD, 1962. Rsch. asst. The Psychol. Corp., N.Y.C., 1956-60; with ITT, N.Y.C., 1960-61, 77-87; dir. personnel devel. ITT-Continental Baking Co., Rye, N.Y., 1980-81; dir. employee rels. ITT, N.Y.C., 1981-87; from asst. prof. to acting chair dept. counseling and svcs. Seton Hall U., South Orange, N.J., 1962-68; assoc. prof. Fairleigh Dickinson U., Teaneck, N.J., 1968-70; assoc. prof. Coll. of New Rochelle, 1970-77, chair psychology dept., 1976-77; dir. orgn. devel. and staffing N.Y. Hosp., N.Y.C., 1987-88; assoc. prof. Schs. Bus., Adelphi U., Garden City, N.Y., 1988-89; prin. Mercer Meidinger Hansen, N.Y.C., 1989—. Contbr. articles to profl. jours. Mem. youth career subcom. Nat. Urban League, N.Y.C., 1978-80; mem. com. N.Y. Alliance for Pub. Schs., N.Y.C., 1984—. Mem. Am. Psychol. Assn., Am. Soc. Personnel Adminstrs., Human Resources Planning Soc., Met. Assn. Applied Psychologists, Psi Chi, Sigma Xi. Democrat. Roman Catholic. Home: 518 Cortlandt Ave Mamaroneck NY 10543 Office: Mercer Meidinger Hansen 1166 Ave of Americas New York NY 10036

CAPELL, CYDNEY LYNN, editor; b. Jacksonville, Fla., Dec. 20, 1956; d. Ernest Clary and Alice Rae (McGinnis) Capell; m. Garrick Philip Martin, July 16, 1983 (div. Jan. 1988). BA, Furman U., 1977. Mktg. rep. E.C. Capell & Assocs., Greenville, S.C., 1977-80; sales rep. Prentice-Hall Publs., Cin., 1980-81; sales, mktg. rep. Benjamin/Cummings, Houston, 1981-83; sales rep. McGraw-Hill Book Co., Houston, 1983-85, engring. editor, N.Y.C., 1985-87; acctg. and infosystems editor Bus. Pubs., Inc., Plano, Tex., 1988-89; sr. editor Gorsuch Scarisbrick Pubs., Scottsdale, Ariz., 1989—; editor lit. mag. Talon, 1972; news editor Paladin newspaper, 1977. Named Rookie of Yr., McGraw-Hill Book Co., 1985. Mem. NOW, NAFE, Women in Pub., Women in Communications, Mensa. Republican. Avocations: tennis, ballet.

CAPELLE, BARBARA FREDERICA, freelance writer; b. Stamford, Conn., Aug. 30, 1927; d. Henry Herman and Matilda Barbara (Specht) Goossen; m. Robert Henry Capelle, Feb. 10, 1951; children: Stacey Elizabeth Mathis, Barbara Hughes Bennette, Robert Henry Jr., Christopher Andrew. BA in English, U. Conn., 1950; MA in Profl. Svcs., Fairfield (Conn.) U., 1980. Coord. N.Y. Arbitration Com., N.Y.C., 1950-54; Middle East program officer Save the Children Fedn., Westport, Conn., 1970-73, program dept. coord., 1973-75; coord. vol. svcs. Norwalk (Conn.) Hosp., 1975-79; first coord. pre-trial diversion program Voluntary Action Ctr. and Norwalk Superior Ct., Norwalk, 1979-80; asst. dir. Voluntary Action Ctr., Stamford, Conn., 1980-81; freelance writer Darien and New Canaan, Conn., 1981—. Sr. writer Greenwich mag., 1990—; contbr. numerous articles to nat. publs. Mem.-at-large, mem. adminstrv. bd. United Meth. Ch., New Canaan, 1971—, pub. rels. officer, 1984—; v.p. bd. A Better Chance, New Canaan, 1980-82. Mem. AAUW (pres. Norwalk-Westport br., 1987—, pub. info. officer Conn. div. 1990—), Directory Vol. Svcs., Conn. Assn. Dirs. Vols. and Svcs. Hosps. Home: 458 White Oak Shade Rd New Canaan CT 06840

CAPELLI, ELIZABETH A., manufacturers representative; b. Phila., June 23, 1963; d. John Placido and Patricia (Verna) Capelli. BA in English/ Comm., Villanova (Pa.) U., 1985. Editorial asst., staff writer Auto. Industries, Radnor, Pa., 1984-85; bus. devel. specialist Greater Phila. C. of C., 1985-86; sr. sales rep. Dupli-Fax, Inc., Phila., 1986-87; promotional cons., exec. sales S. Walter Packaging Corp., Phila., 1987-89; mfrs. rep. Lewis Assocs., Inc., White Plains, N.Y., 1989—. Com. mem. Am. Cancer Soc., Burlington County, N.J., 1988—. Mem. Young Exec. Specialty Advt., Nat. Exec. Network, Phila. C. of C. (ambassador chmn. 1987-89), Villanova Club of South Jersey, Main Line Alumni Club. Republican. Roman Catholic. Home: 312 S Hinchman Ave Haddonfield NJ 08033 Office: Lewis Associates Inc 405 Tarrytown Rd #417 White Plains NY 10607

CAPERTON, DEE KESSEL, former state legislator, civic worker; b. Ripley, W.Va.; d. Oliver D. and Catherine (Hartman) Kessel; children: William Gaston IV, John Ambler. BA in Lit. and Polit. Sci., W.Va. U., 1964, MA in Guidance Counseling, 1979; postgrad., Marshall U., 1978; PhD in Counseling, U. Pitts., 1983. Interior decorator Stone & Thomas, Charleston, 1974-76; founder, prin. Caperton Devel. (interior decorating firm), Charleston, 1976-79; intern individual and group counseling Charleston Job Corps, 1978-79; intern group therapy, behavior med. unit Charleston Area Med. Ctr., 1979; psychology intern, researcher Charleston Area Med. Ctr. and W.Va. U, 1983; mem. W. Va. Ho. of Delegates, 1986-88; now advocate for women and children; aide Hon. Ken. Hechler, Congressman, 1960. Co-chair Gov. Task Force on Children, Youth & Families; bd. dirs. Charleston Domestic Violence Ctr., Inanna Fund for W.Va. Women, W.Va. Edn. Fund, W.Va. Humanities Found., W.VA. Com. for Prevention of Child Abuse, W.Va. Goodwill Industries; mem. adv. com. Women's Health Ctr., Charleston, 1979; mem. adv. coun. Charleston Job Corps; del. White House Conf. on Children and Youth, 1960; bd. visitors Coll. Creative Arts W.Va. U.; mem. W.Va. Coll. Grad. Studies Found.; mem. steering com. W.Va. Women's Agenda; trustee UC.; bd. visitors Coll. Creative Arts; founder kindergartens under Fed. Community Action Program Charleston and Emmons, W.Va., 1965, 66; charter mem., bd. officer Vandalia Housing Ctr., 1968-73; founder, pres. Charleston Children's Theatre, 1977-79. Mem. Am. Psychology Assn., W.Va. Psychology Assn., W.Va. Human Resources Assn. Office: 405 Charleston National Pla Charleston WV 25301

CAPLAN, DENISE BOORSTEIN, lawyer; b. Grand Rapids, Mich., July 7, 1958; d. Ronald Lee and Debra (Block) Boorstein; m. Michael Scott Caplan, Aug. 9, 1980; children: Jeremy, Gregory. BA, U. Ill., 1980; JD, U. Chgo., 1983. Bar: Ill. Assoc. Kirkland & Ellis, Chgo., 1983-86; ptnr. Goldberg, Kohn, Bell, Block, Rosenbloom & Monte, Chgo., 1986—. Mem. ABA, Chgo. Bar Assn. Home: 355 Lincolnwood Rd Highland Park IL 60035 Office: Goldberg Kohn Bell et al 55 E Monroe Chicago IL 60603

CAPLAN, ELINOR, cabinet minister, Canadian provincial legislator; b. Toronto, Ont., Can., 1944; m. Wilf Caplan; children: David, Mark, Zane, Meredith. Pres. Elinor Caplan and Assocs., 1973-78; alderman Ward 13 City of North York, 1978-85; legislator Ont. Legislature, 1985-87; minister Ministry of Health, Toronto, 1987—; chmn. Mgmt. Bd. of Cabinet, chmn. of cabinet Peterson Govt.; minister Govt. Svcs. Past chmn. North York Coun. Com., Human Resources Adv. Coun., Rapid Transit Subcom.; past mem. North York Bd. of Health; past vice chmn. North York Interagy. Coun. Mem. North York Bus. Assn. (founder, past chmn. devel. and econ. growth com.). Office: Ministry of Health, Hepburn Block Queens Pk, Toronto, ON Canada M7A 2C4

CAPLAN, VERLA LOUISE, educator; b. Oskaloosa, Iowa, Nov. 1, 1914; d. Curtis Ernest and Lois Mozelle (Carr) Van Voorhis; m. Lewis Henry Caplan, Apr. 4, 1939; children: Constance, Roberta, Lewis, Laurence, Gerald, Barbara. Nursery-primary cert., Ann Reno Teaching Inst., N.Y.C.; BA in History and Govt., Kansas City (Mo.) U., 1961; MA, U. Mo., Kansas City, 1969, postgrad. Cert. nursery-primary tchr., N.Y.; cert. tchr., Iowa; life cert. elem. tchr., Mo. Elem. tchr. Kansas City Sch. Bd.; tchr. gifted children sci., elem. tchr. Independence (Mo.) Sch. Dist.; cons. and vol. tchr., Kansas City. Grantee NSF. Mem. Internat. Reading Assn., Nat. Sci. Tchrs. Assn., Am. Childhood Educators, Mo. Tchrs. Assn., Independence Classroom Tchrs. (past pres.), Mo. Math. Tchrs. Assn., Sci. Tchrs. Mo., Assn. Supervision Curriculum Devel. Home: 6017 Wornall Rd Kansas City MO 64113

CAPLIN, BARBARA ELLEN, dancer; b. Framingham, Mass., May 1, 1954; d. Samuel and Frances (Zichek) C. AS in Early Childhood Edn., Mass. Bay Community Coll., 1974; BS in Early Childhood Edn., Boston State Coll., 1977. Student tchr. Jonathan Maynard Sch., Framingham, 1977; encoding clk. Framingham Assessor's Office, 1979; U.S. census taker Framingham, 1980; bookkeeper Frances Caplin, Framingham, 1980—; dancer, 1982—. Dancer (concert) Joy of Movement, 1985-86. Active mem. Humane Soc. USA, Washington, 1987—, Doris Day Animal League. Mem. Nat. Assn. Unknown Players for the Film, TV and Print Modeling Arts, NAFE, Am. Film Inst., Internat. Tap Assn., World Wildlife Fund. Democrat. Jewish. Home and Office: 26 McAdams Rd Framingham MA 01701

CAPLIN, JO ANN, communications company executive; b. Indpls.; d. Irvin and Mildred Shirley (Brodsky) C. B.A., U. Mich.; M.A., Yale U., NYU. TV producer ABC News, N.Y.C., 1972-79, CBS News, N.Y.C. and Washington, 1979-85; pres. Caplin Communications, Inc., N.Y.C., 1986—; instr. New Sch. for Social Rsch., N.Y.C., 1980-81. Producer numerous TV shows, including: (documentary) Incest: The Best Kept Secret, 1979 (Emmy award 1980); (series) 30 Minutes, 1978-82 (Emmy award 1982), 20/20, CBS Mag., HBO Consumer Reports Spl., Adam Smith's Money World. Bd. dirs. Nat. Found. for Advancement in the Arts, 1985—. Mem. NATAS, NAFE, Martha Graham Guild (mem. steering com.), Yale U. Alumni Assn. (rep).

CAPLINGER, PAULA RUTH, music educator; b. Sacramento, Calif., Sept. 10, 1948; d. Gerald Lavell and Evelyn Ruth (Wanner) C.; divorced. BA, Calif. State U., Sacramento, 1973. Cert. elem. tchr., Calif. Traveling music tchr. Sacramento Unified Sch. Dist., 1973—; commr. Calif. Tchr. Competency Panel, 1988; co-coord. Pacific Telesis Shared Decision Making project Will C. Wood Middle Sch.; mem. restructuring com. Sacramento City Unified Sch. Dist. 1st trumpet Sacramento Valley Wind Ensemble, 1986—, El Doroado Brass, 1989—. Mem. NEA, Sacramento City Tchrs. Assn. (v.p., Golden Apple award 1986), Calif. Tchrs. Assn. (adv. panel for legal svcs.), Music Educators Nat. Conf. Office: Sacramento City Tchrs Assn 2564 21st St Sacramento CA 95818

CAPLOVITZ, IRIS ANN SMITH, executive assistant; b. San Antonio, Apr. 1, 1944; d. Aaron Eugene and Selma Rose (Schwartz) Smith; m. Nathan Caplovitz, Aug. 15, 1965; children: Bryan David, Michael Alan, Cathryn Diane. Student, San Antonio Coll., 1962-63, U. Houston, 1963, 77, 88—; AA, Houston Community Coll., 1977. Secretarial positions, 1963-64; exec. sec. Baylor U. Coll. Medicine, Houston, 1964-66; sec. to CPA Houston, 1977-79; sec., acct. John S. Turner, CPA, Houston, 1979-86; exec. asst. U. Tex. Sch. Allied Health, Houston, 1986—; part-time bookkeeper Houston Vet. Svcs., 1979-86. Mem. Golden Key. Jewish. Home: 7911 Mobud Dr Houston TX 77036

CAPO, HELENA FRANCES, comedienne; b. N.Y.C., July 29, 1959; d. Frank Remo Capo and Rose Nellie (Aguilar) Richards; m. William Patterson, Oct. 18, 1986; 1 child, W. Spencer Patterson. BA, Queens Coll., 1981. Engr., disc jockey Sta WQMC-AM, N.Y.C., 1980; writer Sta. WBLS-FM, N.Y.C., 1984-86; assoc. editor Laugh Factory Mag., Los Angeles, 1985—; pres. Precision Production Inc., N.Y.C., 1985—; producer N.Y.C. 1st Official Comedy Day, 1984; tchr. Learning Annex, N.Y.C., 1984; creator Availiabilities Hotline, N.Y.C., 1985. Author: Training Your Pet Flea, 1984, Dogslapping, 1987, Fast Talking for Fun & Profit, 1990; video tape Microwave Sex, 1988; record album Rappin' Mae, 1985; producer: Stand-Up for Animals, 1988. Named Worlds Fastest Talker Guinness Book World Records, N.Y.C. and London, 1989. Roman Catholic. Office: Precision Productions Inc 85-20 167th St Jamaica NY 11432

CAPOBIANCO, EVA MARY, sculptor; b. N.Y.C., Dec. 10, 1954; d. Ferdinand and Evelyn (Kriska) C. BFA summa cum laude, Long Island U., 1977. Self-employed sculptor N.Y.C., 1977—; artist in residence Artpark, Lewiston, N.Y., 1987, Tompkins Square Libr., N.Y.C., 1980-81; sculptor's asst. to Alice Aycock, 1976, Mon Levinson, 1977, Jerome H. Zimmerman, 1976-77. Prin. works include Security with Flower Boxes, Jamaica, N.Y., 1987; one-woman show The Lower Manhattan Cultural Coun., N.Y.C., 1990; represented in group shows at The First Women's Bank, N.Y.C., 1981, Tompkins Sq. Libr., N.Y.C., 1981, NYU, 1983, Ceres Gallery, N.Y.C., 1985, Bklyn. Arts and Culture Assn., 1985, Gallery at the Old Post Office, Dayton, Ohio, 1986, Amos Eno Gallery, N.Y.C., 1987, Jon Taner Gallery, Fairlawn, N.J., 1989, Nabisco Hdqrs., East Hanover, N.J., 1990. vol. The Astraea Found., N.Y.C., 1988-90; bd. dirs. Friends of Tompkins Sq. Libr., N.Y.C., 1981-82; mem. commn. Artists in the Gardens Operation Greenthumb, N.Y.C., 1987. Recipient Juror's award Charlotta Kotik, juror, Positive/ Negative IV, East Tenn. State U., 1988, Juror's Honorable Mention, The Artist Views the City, Dayton, Ohio, 1986; full 4-yr. scholar C.W. Post Ctr. Long Island U., 1973-77. Mem. Internat. Sculpture Ctr., Women's Caucus for Art. Home: 33 Rockland Ave Staten Island NY 10306

CAPODILUPO, ELIZABETH JEANNE HATTON, public relations executive; b. McRae, Ga., May 3, 1940; d. Lewis Irby and Essee Elizabeth (Parker) Hatton; m. Raphael S. Capodilupo, Jan. 21, 1967. Grad., Dale Carnegie Inst., 1976. Sec. A.R. Clark Acct., Fernandina Beach, Fla., 1958-59; receptionist, girl Friday Sta. WNDT-TV, N.Y.C., 1960-62, Coy Hunt and Co., N.Y.C., 1962-69; clk. Woodlawn Cemetery, Bronx, N.Y., 1969-71, historian, community affairs coord., 1971—, editor newsletter, 1979—, asst. to pres., 1984, dir. pub. rels., 1984; grad. asst. Dale Carnegie Inst., 1977-78. Researcher Woodlawn Cemetery's Hall of Fame. Chairwoman Ann. Adm. Farragut Honor Ceremony, Bronx, 1976—; founder, chairperson Toys for Needy Children, 1983-90; bd. dirs. Bronx Mus. Arts, v.p., 1983-84; pres. Bronx Coun. Arts, 1987-90; mem. adv. bd. Salvation Army, 1985, Bronx Arts Ensemble, 1985; bd. mgrs. Bronx YMCA, 1985, life mem.; bd. dirs. Bronx Urban League, 1985, Bronx Coun. on the Arts, 1985, pres., 1987-90. Recipient award citation VFW, 1976, Voice of Democracy Program judge's citation, 1980, Disting. Community Service award N.Y.C. Council, II Leone di Sanmarco award Italian Heritage & Culture Com. Bronx, 1989; named Woman of Yr., YMCA, Bronx, 1986, Woman of Yr., Network Orgn. of Bronx Women, 1986, Jeanne and Ray Capodilupo named as Mr. & Mrs. Bronx 1989-90 proclaimed by Borough Pres.; cert. appreciation Dale Carnegie Inst., 1977; Outstanding Citizenship award Bronx N.E. Kiwanis Club, 1981; Service to Youth award YMCA of Bronx, 1983; recipient proclamation City Council of N.Y., Italian Heritage and Culture Com. of the Bronx, 1989; Outstanding Cemeterian award Am. Cemetery Assn., 1987-88; Citation of Merit Bronx Borough Pres.'s Office, 1988; Spl. Hons. for Outstanding Vol. Work Ladies Aux. Our Lady of Mercy Med. Ctr.; named Hon. Grand Marshall Bronx Columbus Day Parade, 1987-89, Bronx Meml. Day Parade, 1989; apptd. to commn. celebrating 350 yrs. of the Bronx Borough Pres. Mem. Bronx County Hist. Soc., Network Orgn. Bronx Women, Women in Communication, Bronx C. of C. (sec. 1988), YMCA (life mem.), N.Y. Press Club, Italian Big Sisters Club, Women's City Club, Order Eastern Star. Methodist. Office: Woodlawn Cemetery PO Box 75 Bronx NY 10470

CAPONE, ANNETTE, editor. BA, Pa. State U., 1966. Articles editor Seventeen mag., 1971-76; assoc. articles editor Ladies' Home Jour., 1979-81; assoc. editor Mademoiselle, 1981-83; editor-in-chief Redbook mag., 1983—. Mem. Women in Communications, Am. Soc. Mag. Editors. Office: Redbook Mag 224 W 57th St New York NY 10019

CAPONE, MARGARET LYNCH, civic worker, parliamentarian; b. Wilkinsburg, Pa., May 21, 1907; d. John Edward and Anna Freda (Dunstrup) Lynch; m. Carmen R. Capone, July 21, 1936 (dec. May 1983); children: David Michael, Mary Ann Capone Sperling, Donald William. Student U. Pitts., 1925-33, 1949-53, Carnegie Inst. Tech., 1955-56. Parliamentarian Pa. Nurses Assn., 1960-68, Allegheny County Law Wives, Pa., 1975-89; treas. Allegheny County LWV, 1965-69, v.p., 1969-73, pres., 1973-79, parliamentarian, 1979—, historian, 1980; parliamentarian St. Lucy Guild to Blind, Pitts., Allegheny County Lawyers Aux., Diocese Coun. Cath. Women, Marian Manor Guild; cons. parliamentarian. Author: So You've Joined A Club, 1954; Parliamentary Pointers, 1972; editor Clea News, 1954-72. Named Woman of Yr., Clea News, 1973; Personality of Yr., Pitts. chpt. K.C., 1979. Mem. Nat. Assn. Parliamentarians (profl. registered parliamentarian, local pres. 1959-61, state pres. 1963-64, nat. v.p. 1977-79), Am. Inst. Parliamentarians (cert. profl. parliamentarian), Duquesne U. Women's Guild. Republican. Roman Catholic. Lodges: K.C. Women's Guild, Toastmistresses (pres. local club 1950-51, nat. bd. dirs. 1953-63, nat. sec. 1954-56, nat. v.p. 1956-57, editor Toastmistress Mag. 1958-62). Home: 6530 Zupancic Dr Pittsburgh PA 15236

CAPORRINO, CHARLOTTE KATHERINE, designer; b. St. Catherines, Ont., Can., Aug. 8, 1954; came to U.S., 1957; d. Stanley Stachura and Lottie (Marczewski) Cardullias; m. Carmen Caporrino, Sept. 2, 1988. BA, Kent State U., 1986. Design coord. Christian Dior div. Jones Apparel Group, N.Y.C., 1987-89; designer, merchandiser womens sportswear San Andre, N.Y.C., 1989—. Kent State U. scholar, 1983-86; named Young Women of Am. Ohio chpt., 1986. Republican. Roman Catholic. Home: 1 Doris Pl Bloomfield NJ 07003 Office: 3423 Kennedy Blvd Jersey City NJ 07307

CAPOWICH, SUZANNE, contract development specialist; b. Waterbury, Conn., Mar. 20, 1961; d. Raymond Sr. and Anne (Rigon) C. BBA in Mktg., U. Ga., 1982; MS in Mgmt., Ga. State U., 1987. CPCU. Exec. mgt. trainee Burdines, Miami, Fla., 1982-83; mgr. evening sch. Branell Coll., Atlanta, 1984; market underwriter Allstate Ins. Co., Atlanta, 1984-87; analyst Ins. Svcs. Office, Inc., N.Y.C., 1987-90, contract devel. specialist, 1990—; dept. chmn. United Way Allstate Ins. Co., Atlanta, 1985, 86, mem. helping hands com., 1987. Loaned exec. United Way of Dade County, Miami, 1982. Recipient Community Svc. award United Way Dade County, 1982. Mem. Soc. CPCU's (N.Y. chpt.), Toastmasters Internat. (sgt.-at-arms), Gamma Iota Sigma (exec. bd. 1990). Office: Ins Svcs Office Inc 160 Water St 15-9 New York NY 10038

CAPOZZI, CAROLYN ANN, computer systems professional; b. Jamestown, N.Y., Apr. 6, 1947; d. Elmer Herbert and Goldie (Tomaswick) Davis; m. William Joseph Capozzi, Oct. 30, 1970; children: James, William. AAS, Jamestown Community Coll., 1967; BA, SUNY, Albany, 1969. Statistician N.Y. State Higher Edn. Svcs. Corp., Albany, 1964-74, sr. rsch. analyst, 1974-77, data processing project assoc., 1977-82, supr. data processing, 1982-84, dir. systems devel., 1984—. Mem. Assn. Systems Mgmt., Data Processing Mgmt. Assn. Roman Catholic. Office: NY State Higher Edn Services Corp 99 Washington Ave Albany NY 12255

CAPOZZI, DELLA MARIE, nursing administrator; b. Phila., June 23, 1963; d. Alfred Charles and Elaine Mary (Granieri) C. Diploma in Nursing, Bryn Mawr Hosp. Sch. Nursing, Pa., 1984; BS in Nursing, Eastern Coll., St. David's, Pa., 1989; postgrad., Temple U. Sch. Law, Phila., 1990—. Critical care RN; cert. advanced cardiac life support. Staff nurse Suburban Gen. Hosp., Norristown, Pa., 1984-87; med. rev. specialist Intracorp, Plymouth Meeting, Pa., 1987-88; staff nurse, asst. nurse, mgr., acting nurse mgr. Presbyn. Med. Ctr. Phila., 1988-90. Roth Found. scholar, 1981-84, Charlotte Newcombe Found. scholar, 1988. Mem. Am. Assn. Critical Care Nurses. Republican. Roman Catholic.

CAPPEL, CONSTANCE, author, consulting company executive; b. Dayton, Ohio, June 22, 1936; d. Adam Denison and Mary Louise (Henry) C.; m. R.A. Montgomery Jr., June 16, 1962 (div. Apr. 1980); children: Ramsey, Anson, Montgomery. BA, Sarah Lawrence Coll., 1959; MA, Columbia U., N.Y.C., 1961; postgrad., The Union Inst., Cin., 1975-80, 89—. Editor Newsweek, N.Y.C., 1961-63, Vogue, N.Y.C., 1964-66; grad. prof. Goddard Coll., Plainfield, Vt., 1975-79; founder, chief exec. officer, pub. Vt. Crossroad Press, Waitsfield, 1972-82; comml. realtor Investmark, Dayton, 1985-87; prin. Cappel Cons., San Francisco, 1986—. Author: Hemingway in Michigan, 1966, Vermont School Bus Ride, 1977. Founder Women's Rights Project/ACLU, Vt., 1973-74. McDowell Colony fellow, Peterborough, N.H., 1972, 74. Mem. Am. Mgmt. Assn., Commonwealth Club Calif., Bodega Harbour Club, Little TRaverse Yacht Club. Episcopalian. Office: PO Box 553 Bodega Bay CA 94923

CAPPELLETTI, MARIETTA, management consultant; b. Elkhart, Ind., Sept. 28, 1940; d. Anthony James and Helen (Ciavarelli Minelli. BS Psychology, Ind. U., South Bend, 1980; student, Rutgers U., New Brunswick, N.J., 1981; MS in Counseling & Guid, Ind. U., South Bend, 1984; MS in Mgmt., Lesley Coll., Cambridge, Mass., 1986. Placement coord. Goodwill Industries, Inc., South Bend, 1980-81; cons. Michiana EAP, South Bend, 1981-86; clin. coord. Pathways Chem. Dependency Program, South Bend, 1986-87; cons. Employee Assistance Plus, South Bend, 1987-89; program mgr. workwell EAP Welborn Bapt. Hosp., Evansville, Ind., 1989—; focus group mem. chem. dependency United Way of St. Joseph County, Inc. S. Bend Ind. 1988. Bd. Mem. YMCA S. Bend Ind., 1986-, Ind. U. Adv. Bd. Counseling & GUidance S. Bend Ind., 1988-. Recipient Honorary Tribute to Women award Young Women's Christian Assn.. Mem. Employee Assistance Soc. N. Am., No. Ind. Assn. Counseling. Home: 831-C Erie Ave Evansville IN 47715

CAPPELLO, EVE, business consultant; b. Sydney, Australia, Dec. 4, 1922; d. Nem and Ethel Shapira; children from previous marriage: Frances Soskins, Alan Kazdin; came to U.S., 1940, naturalized, 1944; AA, Santa Monica City Coll., 1972; BA, Calif. State U.-Dominguez Hills, 1974; MA, Pacific Western U., 1977, PhD, 1978. Singer, pianist, L.A., 1956-76; pvt. practice profl. and personal devel., corp. tng., various locations, 1976-85 ; instr. Calif. State U. Extension, Dominguez Hills, 1977-86; Mt. St. Mary's Coll., U. of Judaism, U. So. Calif., Loyola Marymount U., 1976—; founder, pres. A-C-T Inst.; invited lectr. World Congress Behavior Therapy, Israel, Melbourne U., Australia; mem. Calif. Community Coll. Placement Assn. Mem. Calif. State U.-Dominguez Hills Alumni Assn., Women's Internat. Network (founder, chmn. bd. 1st pres.), Inc., Assn. Advancement Behavior Therapy, Assn. Behavioral Analysis, Internat. Platform Assn., Century City C. of C., Alpha Gamma. Author: Let's Get Growing, 1979, The New Professional Touch, 1983, 2d edit., 1988, Dr. Eve's Garden, 1984, Act, Don't React, 1985, 3d edit., 1988, The Game of the Name, 1985, The Perfectionist Syndrome, 1990, newspaper columnist, 1976-79; contbr. articles to profl. jours. Home: 10600 Eastborne Ave #16 Los Angeles CA 90024 Office: PO Box 25544 Los Angeles CA 90025

CAPPIELLO, ANGELA, conference and meeting planner; b. New Hyde Park, N.Y., July 6, 1954; d. Augustine and Angela (Tamburello) C. Mgmt. and conv. cert., NYU, 1988, cert. in assn., food and beverage mgmt., 1989, cert. in travel mgmt., 1990. Mgr. meetings and convs. N.Y. Libr. Assn., N.Y.C., 1987-89; conf. coord. ASCE, N.Y.C., 1989; mgr. meetings and confs. Coun. Cons. Orgns., N.Y.C., 1990—. Mem. Am. Soc. Assn. Execs., Meeting Planners Internat., Internat. Soc. Pres. Non-Profit Orgns., N.Y. Soc. Assn. Execs., NAFE, Profl. Conf. Mgrs. Assn., Internat. Soc. Meeting, Planners, Nat. Assn. for Advancement of Fat Acceptance (bd. dirs. 1983-86). Office: 36 New Hyde Park Rd New Hyde Park NY 11040 Office: 230 Park Ave Ste 544 New York NY 10169

CAPPS, KATHERINE HERRING, healthcare executive, health education consultant; b. Dallas, Sept. 7, 1957; d. Clinton Gaye and Adele (Harper) Herring; m. John Gordon Capps, Apr. 16, 1983; 1 child, John Eric Harper. BS in Health Edn., U. Ala., Tuscaloosa, 1982; postgrad., Auburn U., Montgomery, Ala., 1989—. Exec. dir. West Ala. Profl. Svcs., Selma, 1982-85; adminstrv. dir. Vaughan Regional Med. Ctr., Selma, 1985-90, Healthsouth Med. Ctr., Birmingham, Ala., 1990—; edn. cons. Wallace Community Coll., Selma, 1986-87; speaker in field, 1983—. Contbr. articles to profl. publs. Mem. allocations com. United Way, Selma, 1985-90. Mem. Ala. Hosp. Assn. Mktg. Soc. (v.p. 1988-90, pres. 1990—), Am. Soc. Pers. Adminstrs., Ala. Hosp. Assn. Pers. Adminstrs., Ala. Hosp. Assn. Pub. Rels. and Mktg. Soc. (bd. dirs.), Ala. Gerontol. Soc., Selma and Dallas County Pers. Assn., Selma-Dallas County C. of C. (edn. task force 1985, bd. dirs. 1988-90). Home: 2306 Old Orrville Rd Selma AL 36701 Office: Healthsouth Med Ctr 1127 12th St S Birmingham AL 35205

CAPSALIS, BARBARA DAMON, banker; b. Washington, Apr. 22, 1943; d. Wallace Carver and Gertrude Marie (Larson) Damon; m. John N. Capsalis, Aug. 7, 1965. B.S. cum laude in Math, Ohio U. Dep. commr. N.Y.C. Dept. Gen. Services; chief technology officer Chem. Banking Corp., N.Y.C. Recipient Catalyst Women of Yr. award, Woman of Achievement award YWCA. Office: Chem Bank 277 Park Ave 4th Fl New York NY 10172

CAPUANO, CHRISTINE MARIE, medical researcher; b. N.Y.C., Dec. 24, 1953; d. Nicholas Edward and Val-Jeán Marie (Loseman) C. BS, York Coll./CUNY, 1976. Lic. emergency med. technician, N.Y. Tech. specialist dept. pediatrics, ob.-gyn. SUNY Bklyn., N.Y.C., 1977, tech. specialist dept. neurosurgery, 1977-82, instructional support specialist dept. anesthesiology, 1982—. Contbr. articles to profl. publs. CPR instr. ARC, N.Y.C., 1979—; recording sec. Canarsie Vol. Ambulance Corp., Bklyn., 1981, bd. dirs., 1982, newsletter editor, 1988-89, pres., 1990. Winner, N.Y.State Excellence award,

1990. Republican. Roman Catholic. Office: Dept Anesthesiology SUNY HSC Bklyn 450 Clarkson Ave Brooklyn NY 11203

CAPUTO, ANNE SPENCER, information science educator; b. Eugene, Oreg., Jan. 14, 1947; d. Richard J. and Adelaide Bernice (Marsh) Spencer; m. Richard Philip Caputo, July 15, 1977; 1 child, Christopher Spencer Caputo. BA in History, Lewis and Clark Coll., Portland, Oreg., 1969; MA, U. Oreg., 1971; MALS, San Jose State U., 1976. Librarian San Jose State U., Calif., 1972-76; online instr. DIALOG Info. Services, Palo Alto, Calif., 1976-77, chief info. scientist, Washington, 1977-85, mgr. classroom instrn. program, 1986-89, dir. ednl. outreach svcs., 1990—; asst. prof. info. sci. Catholic U. Am., Washington, 1978—; online cons. Nat. Com. Library-Info. Sci., Washington, 1980-82; bd. dirs. ASK!, Washington, 1981—. Author: Brief Guide to DIALOG Searching, 1979. Contbr. articles to profl. jours. Named Info. Sci. Tchr. of Yr., Catholic U. Am., 1983. Mem. Am. Soc. for Info. Sci. (officer, chair Potomac Valley chpt. 1985-86), ALA, Spl. Library Assn., D.C. Library Assn., Am. Assn. Sch. Librarians. Republican. Episcopalian. Avocation: photographing architectural details on National Trust buildings. Home: 5314 26th Rd N Arlington VA 22207 Office: DIALOG Info Svcs 1901 N Moore St Ste 500 Arlington VA 22209

CARADJA, PRINCESS CATHERINE, speaker to veterans organizations; b. Romania, 1893; came to U.S. 1955; d. Prince Kretulesco and Princess Cantacuzene; m. Prince Caradja, 1914; children. Proprietor hosp. for typhus cases, Romania, 1916-19, St. Catherine's Crib found. for orphan children, Romania, 1919-49; speaker on life behind Iron Curtain and the value of freedom France, England, Algeria, Morocco, Canada, U.S., 1952—; speaker variuos POW and vet. groups. Recipient Freedom award of the Order of Lafayette, 1966, award Valley Forge Freedom Found., 1977. Home and Office: care Armour Home 8100 Wornall Rd Kansas City MO 64114

CARAMELLO, ANNE OLSZEWSKI, graphic artist; b. Milw., July 14, 1951; d. Eugene Raymond and Nanette Madeleine (Beyer) Olszewski; m. Charles Caramello, Apr. 30, 1979; 1 child, Dagmar. BFA in Printmaking and Art History, U. Wis., Milw., 1973, MA in Graphic Design, 1978. Staff designer Sch. Fine Arts U. Wis., Milw., 1976-78; graphic designer Newsletter Svcs., Inc., Washington, 1979-83; art dir. Smith-Sternau Orgn., Inc., Washington, 1983-86; sr. art dir. Nat. Geog. Soc., Washington, 1986—. Recipient Silver Internat. ECHO award, 1989, Direct Mktg. Assn. of Washington Silver MAXI award, 1989. Mem. Am. Inst. Graphic Arts, Univ. and Coll. Designers Assn., Coll. Art Assn., Samuel Beckett Soc. Office: Nat Geog Soc 16th and M Sts NW Washington DC 20036

CARAWAY, BETTY JONES, former governor's assistant; b. Wichita Falls, Tex., Sept. 30, 1928; d. Ivey Lee and Lou (Jones) Sides; m. Charles E. Caraway (div. 1965); 1 child, Judith Caraway Buttrill. Student Mrs. Cuykendall Bus. Sch., summer 1944; diploma Hardin Jr. Coll., 1946; BBA, U. Tex., 1949; postgrad. Stanford U. Asst. to gen. counsel Library of Congress, Washington, 1967-68; asst. to dir. Pacific Missile Range, Dept. of Navy, Washington, 1968-69; asst. to sr. ptnr. Pittman, Lovett & Hennessee, Washington, 1969-77; asst. campaign mgr. Chuck-Robb campaigns, Va.; asst. to campaign mgr. for Jimmy Carter, Washington; asst. to dir. Alcohol Fuels Dept., Dept. Energy, Washington, 1981-82; adminstrv. asst. to dir. Job Tng. Partnership Act program for Gov. White of Tex., Austin, 1983-87. Social chmn. Houston Jr. Forum; chmn. Cherry Blossom Festival, Washington, 1977; active polit. campaigns, Mus. Fine Arts. Mem. U. Tex. Exes, Stanford Exes of Houston. Democrat. Methodist. Avocations: oil painting; scuba diving. Home: 2244 Albans Rd Houston TX 77005-1520

CARBALLO-RICARDO, NEYDA, English educator; b. Oriente, Cuba, Oct. 7, 1941; came to U.S., 1971; d. Benito and Melba (Oliveros) Carballo; children: Neyda, Francisco Jose. Student, U. Havana, 1963-64; BA, Montclair State Coll., 1981; MA, Jersey City State Coll., 1986. Cert. ESL tchr., N.Y., naturopathic physician., nutritional cons., nat. aerobic instr. Instr. ESL, Hudson County Community Coll., West New York, N.J., SUNY, N.Y.C.; founder Neyda Figure Salon, 1973, Sisana Health Ctr., 1986. Recipient award for Best Figure Salon in N.J., 1983, for Best Health Ctr. in N.J., 1988. Mem. Lions (charter mem. Weehwaken club). Home: 561 60th St West New York NJ 07093 Office: Ctr for Natural Therapies 145 W 30th St 2d Fl New York NY 10001

CARBERRY, DEIRDRE, ballerina; b. Manhasset, N.Y., Nov. 7, 1965; d. Larry Paul and Marilyn (Monsour) C. Student pub. schs., Fla., pvt. schs., Fla. and N.Y.C. Corps Am. Ballet Theatre, N.Y.C., 1980-83, soloist, 1983—. Youngest person to join Am. Ballet Theatre to dance solo and prin. roles, prin. artist, U.S., Europe, Mid-East, S.Am., Cen. Am., 1979—; soloist Am. Ballet Theatre, 1983—; ptnrs. have included Mikhail Baryshnikov, Fernando Bujones, Patrick Bissell, Kevin McKenzie; created lead female role in world premier The Little Ballet (choreographed for her and Mikhail Baryshnikov by Twyla Tharp, 1983). Videotapes include: Tharp by Baryshnikov, ABT at the Met, ABT in San Francisco, Sleeping Beauty, Baryshnikov Dances Balanchine, all televised on PBS. Toured U.S. with Baryshnikov and Co., 1984, 85, 87. Recipient Silver medal 1st U.S. Internat. Ballet Competition, Jackson, Miss., 1979; Harkness House scholar, 1978-79, N.Y. State Dance Summer program scholar, 1979, Sch. Am. Ballet scholar, 1979-80. Office: Am Ballet Theater 890 Broadway New York NY 10003

CARBO, KIMBERLY MONIQUE, public relations executive; b. New Orleans, Aug. 29, 1960; d. Claude Joseph Jr. and Rosina (Dickerson) C. BA in Communications, U. New Orleans, 1981, postgrad., 1982. Editorial asst. La. State U. Med. Ctr., New Orleans, 1980-82; news intern Sta. WDSU-TV affiliate NBC, New Orleans, 1980; customer ops. adminstrv. asst. Cox Cable New Orleans, Inc., 1982, pub. relations asst., 1982-85; mktg. exec. sec., writer Standard Coffee Svc. Co., New Orleans, 1985-86; pub. info. specialist, film liaison Mayor's Office Pub. Info., New Orleans, 1986-87, head pub. info. specialist, film liaison, 1987-88, acting dep. dir., film liaison, 1988-89, dep. dir., film liason, 1989—; prodn. asst. Sta. WGNO-TV program Black Is, New Orleans, 1979, Sta. WYES-TV Documentary on New Orleans, 1983; publicity coord. So. Rep. Theatre Festival, New Orleans, 1987; liaison to State Film Commn., New Orleans, 1986—; fl. mgr. DRC Prodn., New Orleans, 1986-88. Author various poems and short stories. Vol. numerous polit. campaigns, New Orleans, 1986—, So. Rep. Leadership Conf., New Orleans, 1988; media and hospitality vol. Rep. Nat. Convention, New Orleans, 1988. Mem. Am. Film Inst., New Orleans Assn. Film and Tape Profls. (hon.), New Orleans Film Commn. (staff liaison). Democrat. Roman Catholic. Home: 4015 Urquhart St New Orleans LA 70117 Office: Mayor's Office Pub 1300 Perdido St City Hall Rm 2W17 New Orleans LA 70112

CARBONE, CLAUDIA, investment company executive, editor, writer; b. Denver, Dec. 30, 1941; d. John Anthony and Ada (Aiello) C.; m. John L. Chambers, Aug. 12, 1961 (div. Jan. 1985); children: Susan, David, Michael, Kathleen, Nicholas; m. Howard W. Mansell, June 23, 1990. BA, Met. State Coll., Denver, 1984. Program dir. Ski & Recreation Channel, Denver, 1984-85; copywriter Ski Directory Am. Ski Assn., Denver, 1985-86, mem. promotions staff, 1985-87; ski columnist Villager Newspaper Group, Englewood, Colo., 1987-88, ski editor, 1988—; gen. ptnr. Carbone Investment Co., Denver, 1987—; freelance, 1989—. Contbr. articles to Skiers Adv. Newspaper, 1986-87, and popular ski mags. Chairperson dinner fundraiser Atty. Gen. Campaign, Denver, 1974. Colo. scholar Met. State Coll., 1983, 84. Mem. Rocky Mountain Ski Media (v.p. 1989—), N.Am. Ski Journalists (com. chair 1989, bd. dirs.), The Gathering Pl., Hospice of St. John.

CARCEDO, JO ZENAIDA, city official; b. Nashville, June 8, 1956; d. Jose Antonio and Minnie Ella (Compton) C. BA, Vanderbilt U., 1978; MPA, U. Tex., 1982. Health extentionist U.S. Peace Corps, Mariano Acosta, Ecuador, 1982-84; provider rels. cons. Prudential Ins. Co., Memphis, 1985-88; chief grants adminstrn. Houston Dept. Health and Human Svcs., 1989—. Task force mem. United Way, 1990; bd.mem. Fed. Emergency Mgmt. Assistance, Amigos Vols. Edn. Svcs., 1990. Recipient Beyond War award Peace Corps, 1987. Mem. NAFE, Am. Pub. Health Assn.,Am. Soc. Pub. Adminstrn. Roman Catholic. Home: 7520 Brompton Apt 734 Houston TX 77025 Office: 8000 N Stadium Dr Houston TX 77054

CARDENAS, NORMA ALICIA, teacher; b. Edinburg, Tex., May 1, 1952; d. Jesus Maria and Rose Mary (Hon) C. BA, Pan American U., 1974. Orch. dir. North Jr. High Sch., Edinburg, 1974-80, Edinburg Jr. High Sch., 1980-85, South Jr. High Sch., Edinburg, 1985—; violist, violinist Valley Symphony Orch., Edinburg, 1966—, South Tex. Chamber Orch., Edinburg, 1980—; mem., mgr. The Silken Strings, Edinburg, 1974—. Mem. South Tex. Symphony Assn., Edinburg, 1976—. Mem. Tex. Music Educators Assn. (treas. 1982-86), Tex. Orch. Dirs. Assn., Am. Strings Tchrs. Assn., Tex. Classroom Tchrs. Assn., Mu Phi Epsilon (sec. 1978-82). Democrat. Roman Catholic. Home: 303 W Fay St Edinburg TX 78539

CARDENAS, PATRICIA LORAIN HICKS, advertising executive; b. Mpls., July 2, 1939; d. Patrick Ambrose and Dorothy Lorraine (Simonson) Hicks; m. Hugh Thomas Cardenas, Oct. 20, 1962; children: Christiana Lorain, Cory Hugh. Postgrad., Northwestern U. Chgo., 1958-59. Actress Beverly Hills (Calif.) Child Theatre, 1944-45, MGM, Culver City, Calif., 1944-45, WDGY Radio, Mpls., 1945-46; TV personality WTCN/WCCO TV, Mpls., 1948-56; state teen chmn. Nat. Found., Mpls., 1956-57, nat. teen chmn., 1957-58; adminstr. Nat. Found., Chgo., 1958-60; free lance radio and TV talent Mpls., 1960-62; owner Cardenas Corp., Spring Park, Minn., 1962—; cons. pub. rels., Figure Skating Club of Mpls., 1972-83, Twin Cities Figure Assn., Mpls., 1980-81, Archtl. Assn., Mpls., 1980-83, Cable Value Network, 1988—; mgmt. adv. svcs. for talent and various bus. Author short stories; writer bus. profiles for pub. rels. Sec., exec. com. The Blake Schs., Wayzata, Hopkins, Mpls., 1977-79. Mem. U.S. Figure Skating Assn. (life), Figure Skating Club Mpls. (pres. 1980-83, bd. dirs. 1977-80), Phi Beta (pres. 1968-70). Home and Office: 2400 Interlachen Rd #309 Spring Park MN 55384 Office: Cardenas Corp PO Box 414 Excelsior MN 55331

CARDILICCHIA, TINA GAIL, health association administrator; b. N.Y.C., Mar. 26, 1944; d. David and Anna (Lionetti) Simon. BS summa cum laude, Mercy Coll., 1986. Lead girl Household Fin. Corp., N.Y.C., 1961-65; asst. dir. quality control Revlon Research Ctr., Bronx, N.Y., 1965-71; ops. contr. Vis. Nurse Svc. of N.Y., 1974-88; adminstr. Palmetto Med. Ctr., Miami, 1988—. Mem. Med. Group Mgmt. Assn., Alpha Chi. Roman Catholic. Office: Palmetto Med Ctr 7950 NW 53rd St Miami FL 33166

CARDIN, SHOSHANA SHOUBIN, non-profit organization administrator, consultant; b. Tel Aviv, Oct. 10, 1926; came to U.S., 1927; d. Sraiah and Chana (Barbalot) Shoubin; m. Jerome Stanley Cardin, Aug. 17, 1958; children: Steven Harris, Ilene Marcia, Nina Beth, Sanford Ronald. Student, Johns Hopkins U., 1942-45; BA, UCLA, 1946; MA, Antioch U., 1979; LHD (hon.), Western Md. Coll., 1985, Jewish Theol. Seminary, 1989. Tchr. elem. schs. Balt., 1946-50; pres. Fedn. of Jewish Women's Org., Md., 1965-67; sec. Voluntary Action Ctr. Cen. Md., 1973-75; vice chmn. Gov.'s Vol. Coun., N.Y.C., 1985—; chmn. Nat. Conf. on Soviet Jewry, Md., 1988—; gov. Jewish Agy. for Israel, 1985—. Co-Editor: Leadership Logic, 1974, Volunteerism: Moving into the 1980's, 1979, Strategies for Success-Surviving the New Federalism, 1982; contbr. editor, author of numerous pubs. Bd. dirs. Am. Jewish Joint Distbn. Com., United Israel Appeal, United Way Cen. Md., 1983-85, Health Welfare Council Cen. Md., 1980-85, Jewish Community Ctr. Balt., 1970-76, Balt. County Gen. Hosp. Aux., 1972-74, Park Sch. Parent's Assn., 1966-71, Md. Assn. Mental Health, 1965-66, March of Dimes Balt. Chpt., 1966-68, Levindale Ladies Aux., 1961-65, Chizuk Amuno Sch. Bd., 1963-65; Balt. Jewish Council, 1963-70, 1980-82 (sec. 1967-70) ; pres. Chizuk Amuno PTA, 1964-65, Jewish Community Ctr. Assocs. 1969-71 (exec. com. 1969—); chmn. Md. State Employment and Trng. Council, 1979-83, Md. Vol.Network, 1980-82, Md. Comm. Women, 1974-79 (commr. 1968-79), Maryland Women's Conf., 1977; trustee United Jewish Appeal, Nat. Retinitis Pigmentosa Found., Loyola-Notre Dame Library, 1980-84, Balt. Hebrew Coll., 1979-82, Antioch U., 1977-78, Nat. Assn. Comms. for Women, Edn. and Research Fund, 1976-77; sec. Voluntary Action Ctr. Cen. Md., 1973-76 (exec. com. 1971-76); commr. Md. Comm. Human Relations, 1979-82; coordinator Women's Fair Balt., 1975; co-founder Women Together, 1973 (exec. com. 1973-76); co-chmn. Md. Interfaith Conf. Peace, 1966; del. Md. Constln. Conv., 1967; mem. Md. Jr. League (hon. life). Recipient Louise Waterman Wise award Am. Jewish Congress, 1970, Citizen Civics Affairs award B'nai B'rith, 1968, Jimmie Swartz medallion, 1983, Governor's Citation State of Md., 1982, Cert. of Merit U.S. Congress, 1979, Cert. of Distinguished Citizenship State of Md., 1969, Na'Amat Golda Meir award, 1989; named Outstanding Citizen of Md. Jewish War Vets., 1978, Woman of Yr. B'nai B'rith Women Md., 1967, one of Women of Distinction Fashion Group Balt. Inc., 1975, Honored and Outstanding Citizen City of Balt., 1969; inductee Md. Jewish Hall of Fame Jewish Hist. Soc. Md., 1979; Organizational and Community Devel. Fellow Johns Hopkins, 1976-77. Mem. Md. Assn. Parliamentarians (bd. dirs. 1976-77), Nat. Coun. Jewish Women (bd. dirs. 1963-65, 68-72, 73-74, Hannah G. Solomon award 1975), Coun. Jewish Fedns. (pres. 1984-87), Assn. Voluntary Action Scholars. Democrat. Office: Nat Conf on Soviet Jewry 10 E 40th St New York NY 12016

CARDINAL, SHIRLEY MAE, educator; b. Morann, Pa., May 6, 1944; d. Thomas Joseph and Mary Louise (Nemish) Giza; m. Charles Edward Cardinal, June 11, 1966; children: Julie Ann, Karen Lee. BS, Lock Haven U., 1966; MEd, Pa. State U., 1970. Tchr. Bald Eagle Nittany, Mill Hall, Pa., 1966-68; tchr., supr. Pa. State U., University Park, 1968-76; tchr., chairperson State Coll. (Pa.) Area Schs., 1968-76; primetime educator Oreg.-Davis Corp., Hamlet, Ind., 1984—; instr., cons. Dept. of Edn., Indpls., 1979—, cons. energy edn., 1980-85, educator linker, 1981—, rep. prime time, 1987—; instr. Ancilla Coll., Donaldson, Ind., 1976—. Author: Energy Activities with Learning Skills, 1980. Chmn. publicity com. Rep. Orgn. Plymouth, Ind., 1983—; mem. Teacher Talk, Ind. Gov's. Com., 1988-89. Recipient Mankind and Edn. award U.S. Jaycees and Ind. Jaycees, 1981. Mem. Ind. State Tchr. Assn., Marshall County Reading Assn., Pa. State U. Club, Phi Delta Kappa, Pi Lamba Theta, Sigma Kappa, Tri Kappa. Roman Catholic. Home: 10101 Turf Ct Plymouth IN 46563

CARDINALE, KATHLEEN CARMEL, medical center administrator; b. Donegal, Ireland, July 13, 1933; came to U.S., 1958, naturalized, 1966; d. Denis and Mary (Cannon) O'Boyle; m. Anthony Cardinale, Aug. 28, 1965; BA, Jersey City State Coll., 1971, MA, 1973; RN, N.Y., U.K. nurse Walton Hosp., Liverpool, Eng., 1955; staff nurse, acting-in-charge Manhattan Gen. Hosp., N.Y.C., 1958-59; charge nurse, acting-in-charge, Met. Hosp., N.Y.C., 1959-60; charge nurse, relief supr. Manhattan Gen. Hosp., N.Y.C., 1960-64, asst. dir. nursing, 1964-68, staffing coord., 1968-70; acting assoc. dir. nursing Bernstein Inst., N.Y.C., 1970; clin. supr., clin. specialist Beth Israel Med. Ctr., N.Y.C., 1971-73; asst. dir. nursing Cabrini Med. Ctr., N.Y.C., 1974-77, assoc. dir. nursing, 1977-78, v.p. nursing svcs., 1978—. Mem. Am. Nurses Assn., Greater N.Y. Hosp. Assn. (mem. mental hygene com.), Am. Hosp. Assn., Am. Orgn. Nurse Execs. Home: 545 E 14th St New York NY 10009 Office: 227 E 19th St New York NY 10003

CARDONA, FLORENCIA BISENTA DE CASILLAS MARTINEZ See CARR, VIKKI

CARDONA, MARI LOURDES, model, educator, speaker, certified image consultant; b. Mayaguez, P.R., Dec. 9, 1963; d. Angel C. and Carmen Haydee (Jimenez) C. AA, IFAC, Miami, Fla.; BBS, U. Sacred Heart, Santurce, P.R. Prof. model, instr. Barbizon Internat., P.R., 1983-86, fashion and pageant coord., 1984-86; asst. dir. D'Rose Internat. Modeling and Finishing Sch., Miami, 1986-88; program dir. Miami Health Club and Spa, 1988-89; admissions dir. Barbizon Internat., Miami, 1990—; pres., seminar coord. Ambiance Image Cons. Inc., Miami, 1990—; pres. Comite Jovenes Club Civico, San Sebastian, P.R., 1975-76; seminars, workshop presenter Modelaje de Verano summer camp, 1985-88. Prodn. asst.: (radio program) La Cocina en su Casa, 1989 (Best Cooking Show 1989); producer Miss Dorado Teen-Ager Pageant 1977 (Best Local Show 1977). Recipient Jean Comp. award Internat. Modeling and Talent Assn. Conv., N.Y.C., 1987. Mem. NAFE. Roman Catholic.

CARDONE, BONNIE JEAN, photojournalist; b. Chgo., Feb. 21, 1942; d. Frederick Paul and Beverly Jean (Johnson) Rittschof; m. David Frederick Cardone, June 9, 1963 (div. 1978); children: Pamela Susan, Michael David. BA, Mich. State U., 1963. Editorial asst. Mich. State Dental Assn. Jour., Lansing, 1963-64; asst. editor Nursing Home Adminstr. mag., Chgo., 1964-65; asst. editor Skin Diver Mag., L.A., 1976-77, sr. editor, 1977-81, exec. editor, photographer, 1981—. Co-author: Shipwrecks of Southern California, 1989. Mem. Am. Soc. Mag. Photographers, Soc. Profl. Journalists, Santa Monica Blue Fins Club (treas. 1975-76, pres. 1977-78, sec. 1985-86, v.p. 1987-88), Calif. Wreck Divers Club. Office: Skin Diver Mag 8490 Sunset Blvd Los Angeles CA 90060

CARDOZA, ANNE DE SOLA, screenwriter, scriptwriter, producer, sculptor, novelist; b. N.Y.C., Nov. 18, 1941; d. Sara Nunez de Sola and Michael Cardoza. B.S. in Creative Writing, English, NYU, 1964; M.A. in Creative Writing, English, San Diego State U., 1979; diploma Hollywood Scriptwriting Inst., 1984; diploma Alexandra Inst. Painting, San Diego, 1988. Pres. Anne Cardoza Prodns. Author of 33 books including In The Chips: 101 Ways to Make Money with your Personal Computer, 1985, High Paying Jobs in Six Months or Less, 1984, Understanding Robotics, 1985, Careers in Robotics, 1985, Careers in Aerospace, 1985, (novels) Psyche Squad; co-author: Winning Tactics for Women Over 40, 1988, (screenplay and novel) Midnight Shift, 1989, Playpen Eyes, 1989, (screenplay) Black Snow Melting, 1990, (comedy) How To Be A Play Men's Woman; author 17 screenplays; contbr. articles to various publs., film scripts, 2 novelettes and collections of short stories. Office: PO Box 4333 San Diego CA 92104

CARDULLO, ALICE CECILIA, dermatologist, educator; b. N.Y.C., Jan. 10, 1955; d. Hugo Maria and Claire June (Moore) C. BA, Barnard Coll., 1977; MS, Columbia U., 1978; MD, Mt. Sinai Sch. Medicine, N.Y.C., 1982. Diplomate Am. Bd. Pediatrics, Am. Bd. Dermatology. Resident in pediatrics Mt. Sinai Hosp., N.Y.C., 1982-85; rsch. fellow in dermatology Columbia-Presbyn. Med. Ctr., N.Y.C., 1985-86, resident, 1986-89; pvt. practice, Wayne and Butler, N.J., 1989—; clin. instr. Columbia U. Coll. Physicians and Surgeons, 1989—. Contbr. articles to med. jours. Mem. Am. Acad. Dermatology, Soc. for Pediatric Dermatology, N.J. Med. Soc., Passaic County Med. Soc., Phi Beta Kappa. Roman Catholic. Office: 9 Carey Ave Butler NJ 07405

CARDWELL, SANDRA GAYLE BAVIDO, real estate broker; b. Vinita, Okla., July 14, 1943; d. Amos Calvin Wilkins and Gretta Odell (Pool) Wilkins Kudlemyer; m. Phillip Patrick Bavido, Nov. 26, 1964 (div. Dec. 1973); 1 child, Phillip Patrick Bavido Jr.; m. Max Loyd Cardwell, Jan. 18, 1979; 1 child, Vicky Ann Cardwell Herr. AA, Tulsa Jr. Coll., 1973; BS cum laude, U. Tulsa, 1975. Sec. with various cos., 1966-69; sec. U.S. Dept. Fgn. Langs., West Point, N.Y., 1969-70; dep. ct. clk. civil div. Tulsa County Dist. Ct., Tulsa, 1975-76, dep. ct. clk. U.S. Passport Office, 1976-77; broker-assoc. Gordona Duca, Inc., Realtors, Tulsa, 1977—. Mem. Polit. Action Com., Tulsa, 1980—. Mem. AAUW, Tulsa Met. Bd. Realtors, Okla. Bd. Realtors, Tulsa Christian Women's Club (contact advisor 1988-89), Stonecroft Ministries (life pubs. 1987-88), United Meth. Women (bd. dirs. 1986-87), Phi Theta Kappa (pres.), Pi Sigma Alpha (treas. 1974). Republican. Methodist. Home: 4212 E 98th St Tulsa OK 74137-4827 Office: Gordona Duca Inc Realtors 7103 S Yale Tulsa OK 74136

CARDWELL, SUE POOLE, reclamation services company executive; b. Clearfield, Pa., Oct. 31, 1952; d. Robert Thomas Poole and Alice Katz Jost, Mary B. (Edwards) (stepmother) and Patricia Alice (Coleman) (stepmother) P.; m. Charles Howard Cardwell, Nov. 24, 1979; children: Jonathon Aaron, Jacqueline Leigh. Clk.-typist Ky. Dept. Mines and Minerals, 1974; sr. reclamation insp. div. reclamation Ky. Dept. Natural Resources, Madisonville, 1974-77; pres. Reclamation Svcs. Unltd., Inc., Madisonville, 1977—; chmn. West Ky. adv. group Office Surface Mining, Dept. Interior, 1979—; adv. bd. U. Ky. Symposium on Surface Mining Reclamation and Hydrology, also mem. exec. adv. com.; mem. Ky. Adv. Com. on Strip Mine Regulation, 1979—; mem. exec. bd. Ky. Task Force on Exploited and Missing Children; bd. dirs., sec. Ky. Alliance for Missing and Exploited Children; mem. Rep. Senatorial Inner Circle, 1984—; mem. fin. com. St. Joseph's Ch., Central City, Ky.; pres. PTA, Madison, Ky, 1989—. Served with WAC, 1972-73. Named hon. Ky. col.; named to W.Va. Ship of State. Mem. West Ky. Coal Operators Assn. (dir.), West Ky. Assn. Gen. Contractors, Hazardous Materials Control Rsch. Inst., Mining and Reclamation Council Am. (chmn. reclamation subcom.), Profl. Reclamation Assn. Am. (bd. dirs., charter), World Safety Assn., W.Va. Surface Mine Assn., Nat. Reclamation Assn. West Ky., West Ky. Constrn. Assn. of Associated Gen. Contractors, West Ky. Constrn. Assn. (bd. dirs.); contbg. editor Ky. Coal Jour. Office: 12 Hartland Ave Madisonville KY 42431

CAREY, CYNTHIA, physiology educator; b. Denver, July 17, 1947; d. Raymond Giddens and Faye Vivian (Kingsbury) C. AB, Occidental Coll., 1969, MA, 1970; PhD, U. Mich., 1976. Teaching fellow U. Mich., Ann Arbor, 1970-74, research asst., 1974-76; asst. prof. physiology U. Colo., Boulder, 1976-82, assoc. prof., 1982—; cons. NASA, Washington, 1984, NSF, Washington, 1983-86. Contbr. articles to profl. jours. Fellow AAAS; mem. Am. Ornithologists Union, Am. Soc. Zoologists, Am. Soc. Ichthyologists and Herpetologists, Am. Physiol. Soc., Cooper Ornithol. Soc. (bd. dirs.). Home: 2649 Juniper Ave Boulder CO 80302 Office: U Colo Dept EPO Biology Boulder CO 80309

CAREY, ERNESTINE GILBRETH (MRS. CHARLES E. CAREY), writer, lecturer; b. N.Y.C., Apr. 5, 1908; d. Frank Bunker and Lillian (Moller) Gilbreth; m. Charles Everett Carey, Sept. 13, 1930; children: Lillian Carey Barley, Charles Everett. B.A., Smith Coll., 1929. Buyer R. H. Macy & Co., N.Y.C., 1930-44, James McCreery, N.Y.C., 1947-49; lectr. book reviewer, 1949—, syndicated newspaper articles, 1951; Co-recipient (with Frank B. Gilbreth, Jr.) (Prix Scarron French Internat. humor award for Cheaper by the Dozen 1951), (with Lillian Moller Gilbreth) (McElligott medallion Assn. Marquette U. Women 1966); Author: Jumping Jupiter, 1952, Rings Around Us, 1956, Giddy Moment, 1958, (with Frank B. Gilbreth, Jr.) Cheaper by the Dozen, 1949, Belles on Their Toes, 1951; also mag. articles and book revs. Bd. dirs. Right to Read, Inc., 1968—, co-chmn., 1967; lay adv. com. Manhasset (N.Y.) Bd. Edn.; trustee Manhasset Pub. Library, 1953-59, v.p., 1956-59; trustee Smith Coll., 1967-72. Montgomery award Friends of Phoenix Public Library, 1981. Mem. Authors Guild Am. (life mem., mem. guild council 1955-60), P.E.N. Republican. Conglist. Clubs: North Shore, Smith College (L.I.) (asst. chmn. scholarship com. 1950-59); Smith Coll. (N.Y.); Smith College Phoenix (Phoenix) (vice chmn. scholarship com. 1967), 7 College Conf. Council (Phoenix). Home: 6148 E Lincoln Dr Paradise Valley AZ 85253

CAREY, FRANCES ELIZABETH, physicist; b. Balt., Mar. 16, 1945; d. Luther Wells and Catherine Rose (Hyson) C. Student, Internat. Corr. Sch., 1984, Internat. Corr. Sch. Bus. Mgmt., 1990. Supr. Westinghouse, Balt., 1964-69; supr. applied physics lab. Johns Hopkins U., Laurel, Md., 1969—. Participant Animal Rights, Md., 1989, GreenPeace, 1989, M.A.D., Md., 1989, Gun Control, Md., 1989. Recipient Group Achievement award, NASA, 1981. Mem. NAFE. Republican. Roman Catholic. Home: 5924 1/2 Johnnycake Rd Baltimore MD 21207 Office: Johns Hopkins U Applied Physics Lab Johns Hopkins Rd Laurel MD 20707

CAREY, JANE QUELLMALZ, printing company executive; b. Albany, N.Y., May 6, 1952; d. Henry and Marion Agar (Lynch) 1979. Student, Stephen's Coll., 1969-70; cert., Katherine Gibbs Sch., Boston, 1971. Sec. to headmaster St. Agnes Sch., Albany, 1971-72; exec. sec. Dwight Bldg. Co., Hamden, Conn., 1972-73; v.p. Q Corp., U.S. Agt. for WHO Pubs., Albany, 1973-77, pres., 1978—. Bd. dirs. Next Step, Inc., Albany, 1976-79, Mohawk Hudson Humane Soc., Menands, N.Y., 1988—. Mem. Printing Industries East and Cen. N.Y. (bd. dirs. 1985—), Am. Assn. World Health (bd. dirs. 1977-78), Alumnae Assn. Doane Stuart Sch. (bd. dirs. 1988). Episcopalian. Clubs; Traffic (N.Y.C.), Hudson River (Albany). Home: 12 Strathmore Dr Loudonville NY 12211 Office: Boyd Printing Co Inc 49 Sheridan Ave Albany NY 12210

CAREY, JEAN LEBEIS, management consulting executive; b. Charleston, W.Va., June 2, 1943; d. Edward H. and Marian (Lendved) Lebeis; m. Robert W. Carey (dec. Mar. 1990), Nov. 1971; 1 child, Megan Rose. BA, Pa. State U., 1965. Programmer Penn Mut. Life Ins., Phila., 1967-68; sr. analyst/programmer U. Pa., Phila., 1969-72; sr. systems analyst Acme Markets, Phila., 1972-74; programming mgr. Bryn Mawr Coll., Pa., 1976-77; project adminstr. Smith Kline Beckman, Phila., 1977-83; project mgmt. cons. Arco Chem. Co., Phila., 1983-87; chief exec. officer Carey Project Orgn., Ardmore, Pa., 1987—; chmn. Systems Methodology Users Mid-Atlantic, 1984-86, PMI Systems Tech. Papers, 1983; co-dir. Cobol project, U. Pa., Phila., 1969-72; Pa. Counc. on Children's Svcs., 1988—; lectr. in field. Contbr. articles to profl. jours. Bd. dirs. Scan/Child Abuse Treatment Ctr., Phila., 1983—, Danceteller/Dance Theater, Phila., 1985-88; mem. Leadership, Phila. vol. svcs. group, 1985—, World Affairs Coun.; trustee SCAN Devel. Fund, Inc., 1989—. Recipient Excel award, Arco, 1986. Mem. Project Mgmt. Inst. Soc. of Friends. Home and Office: Carey Project Orgn 663 Cricket Ave Ardmore PA 19003

CAREY, JEANNE GRACE, computer consulting firm executive; b. N.Y.C., Apr. 19, 1957; d. Richard John and Ruth (Brown) C. Student, SUNY, Oswego, 1980. Sales rep. Computerland of Ithaca, N.Y., 1981-83; store mgr. CompuShop, San Jose, Calif., 1983-85; account rep. Computerland of San Francisco, 1985-86, CPT Corp., San Francisco, 1986-87; owner, computer cons. The Computer Link, San Francisco, 1987—, Optimum Computing, Inc., San Francisco, 1987—. Mem. Summit Workshops Inc.

CAREY, KATHRYN ANN, corporate philanthropy, advertising and public relations executive, editor, writer, consultant; b. Los Angeles, Oct. 18, 1949; d. Frank Randall and Evelyn Mae (Walmsley) C.; m. Richard Kenneth Sundt, Dec. 28, 1980. BA in Am. Studies with honors, Calif. State U., L.A., 1971. Tutor Calif. Dept. Vocat. Rehab., L.A., 1970;teaching asst. U. So. Calif., 1974-75, UCLA, 1974-75; claims adjuster Auto Club So. Calif., San Gabriel, 1971-73; corp. pub. rels. cons. Carnation Co., L.A., 1973-78; cons., adminstr. Carnation Community Svc. Award Program, 1973-78; pub. rels. cons. Vivitar Corp., 1978; sr. advt. asst. Am. Honda Motor Co., Gardena, Calif., 1978-84; exec. dir. Am. Honda Found., 1984—; adminstr. Honda Matching Gift and Vol. Program; mgr. Honda Dealer Advt. Assns., 1978-84; cons. advt., pub. rels., promotions. Editor: Vivitar Voice, Santa Monica, Calif., 1978, Honda Views, 1978-84, Found. Focus, 1984—; asst. editor Friskies Research Digest, 1973-78; contbg. editor Newsbriefs and Momentum, 1978—, Am. Honda Motor Co., Inc. employees publs.; Calif. Life Scholarship Found. scholar, 1967. Mem. Advt. Club L.A., Pub. Rels. Soc. Am., So. Calif. Assn. Philanthropy, Coun. on Founds. of Washington, Ninety-Nines, Am. Quarter Horse Assn., Aircraft Owners and Pilots Assn., Los Angeles Soc. for Prevention Cruelty to Animals, Greenpeace, German Shepherd Dog Club Am., Ocicats Internat., Am. Humane Assn., Humane Soc. U.S., Elsa Wild Animal Appeal. Avocation: private pilot. Democrat. Methodist. Office: Am Honda Found 700 Van Ness Ave Torrance CA 90509-2205

CAREY, MARCIA J., service executive; b. Willmar, Minn., Feb. 13, 1941; d. Franklin N. and Thelma L (Portinga) Fanberg; m. Donald L. Carey, June 23, 1962 (div. May 1976); children: Michelle C., Matthew S. Student, Trinity Coll., 1959-61, Calif. State U., Chico., 1961-62. Cert. med. transcriptionist; accredited record technician. Med. transcriptionist Hillcrest Hosp., Petaluma, Calif., 1972-73; med. care evaluation coordinator Santa Teresa Community Hosp., San Jose, Calif., 1973-79; med. transcriptionist San Jose, 1979-84; dir. pub. relations Dictation West, South San Francisco, Calif., 1984-85, dir. ops., 1985-87; pres. United Transcription Services, San Jose, 1987—. Mem. Am. Assn. Med. Transcription, (treas. 1981, v.p. 1982, bd. dirs. 1979-82, pres. South Bay chpt. 1979-80, 85-86), Am. Med. Record Assn. Home: 1638 La Terrace Circle San Jose CA 95123 Office: United Transcription Svcs 5899 Santa Teresa Blvd San Jose CA 95123

CAREY, MARGARET THERESA LOGAN, newspaper education consultant; b. Phila., May 8, 1931; d. Michael Francis and Margaret Mary (Meehan) Logan; m. William Emmett Carey, June 21, 1952; children: William Edward, Michael Patrick, Peggy Ann. AA, Bucks County Community Coll., 1968; student, Temple U., 1968-69; BS, U. Bridgeport, 1971; MEd in Reading, U. N.C., 1973. Reading resource tchr. Wake County Sch. Dist., Raleigh, N.C., 1971-76; newspaper in edn. cons. The News & Observer, Raleigh, 1976-77; ednl. cons. U.S. News and World Report, Washington, 1977-78; newspaper in edn. cons. N.Y. Times, N.Y.C., 1978, Times Newspaper, Trenton-Princeton, N.J., 1979—; cons. N.J. Dept. Edn., Trenton, 1978-79. Editor, founder (children's page) Funtimes, 1981-88, (supplement) Create-An-Ad, 1984-88. State rep. for N.J. Am. Newspaper Pubs. Assn. Found., Reston, Va., 1983—; dir. Reading Is Fundamental, Washington, 1984—. Mem. Internat. Reading Assn. (literacy 1986), N.J. Reading Assn. (award 1986), Tri-County Reading Assn. (award 1984), N.J. Assn. for Lifelong Learning, Mercer County Assn. for Lifelong Learning, N.J. Press Assn. (chmn. newspaper in edn. com. 1983—), Assn. Supervision and Curriculum Devel. Roman Catholic. Clubs: Princeton Ski, Princeton Racquet. Office: Times Newspaper 500 Perry St Box 847 Trenton NJ 08605

CAREY, NANCY BUNTING, telecommunications executive, lawyer; b. Salisbury, Md., Apr. 18, 1949; d. Asher Burton and Pauline (Bunting) C. AB, Mt. Holyoke Coll., 1971; JD, Temple U., 1974. Bar: Md., 1974, Pa., 1974, D.C., 1975. Intern to U.S. Rep. Donald Riegle, Washington, 1969; law clk. Cathel & Ewell, Ocean City, Md., 1972, 73; atty. broadcast bur. renewal br. FCC, Washington, 1974-75, atty. office of Gen. Counsel, Legal Rsch. and Treaties, 1975-77, legal asst. to Commr. Abbott Washburn, 1977-82; dir., fed. and regulatory liaison MCI, Washington, 1982-85; v.p. human resources United Telephone System, Inc., Overland Park, Kans., 1985-87; v.p. intrastate revenues United Telecommunications, Inc., Overland Park, 1987-88; v.p. mktg. U.S. Sprint, Kansas City, 1988-89; v.p. bus. devel. Audio Info. Scis., Horsham, Pa., 1989-90; dir. strategic planning and market devel. UNISYS Corp., Blue Bell, Pa., 1990—; bd. dirs. United Telephone System, Inc., Overland Park, United Telephone NW, Hood River, Oreg., United Telephone Midwest Group, Kansas City, United Telephone Ind., Inc., Warsaw, United Telespectrum, Kansas City, United Telephone Systems, Inc., Overland Park. Bd. dirs. WGR Leader Found., Washington. Mem. ABA, D.C. Bar Assn., Women in Govt. Rels. (dir. Leader found. 1985-87). Republican. Methodist. Office: UNISYS Corp PO Box 500 Blue Bell PA 19424

CAREY, PATRICIA ELAINE STEDMAN, hospital administrator; b. Ft. Wayne, Ind., July 17, 1944. BBA, U. Houston; MS, U. Houston, Clear Lake. Corp. resident Hosp. Corp. of Am., Nashville, 1981-82; asst. adminstr. Longview (Tex.) Regional Hosp., 1982-84; adminstr. Barstow (Calif.) Community Hosp., 1984-87, Shriners Hosp., Shreveport, La., 1987—. Mem. Women's Polit. Fund, Shreveport, 1988—, Shreveport Women's Commn. Mem. Am. Coll. Healthcare Execs., N.W. La. Hosp. Assn. (pres. Shreveport chpt. 1990—), Rotary, Toastmasters, River Cities Network, Quota Club Shreveport. Unitarian. Home: 5801 Lovers Ln Shreveport LA 71105 Office: Shriners Hosp for Children 3100 Samford Ave Shreveport LA 71103

CAREY, SARAH COLLINS, lawyer; b. N.Y.C., Aug. 12, 1938; d. Jerome Joseph and Susan (Atlee) Collins; m. James J. Carey, Aug. 28, 1962 (div. 1977); 1 child, Sasha; m. 2d John D. Reilly, Jan. 27, 1979; children—Sarah, Katherine. B.A., Radcliffe Coll., 1960; LL.B., Georgetown U., 1965. Bar: D.C. 1966, U.S. Supreme Ct. 1977. Soviet specialist USIA/U.S. Dept. State, 1961-65; asso. Arnold & Porter, Washington, 1965-68; asst. dir. Lawyers Com. for Civil Rights, Washington, 1968-73; ptnr. Adams Duque & Hazeltine and predecessor cos., Washington, 1973-87, Heron, Burchette, Ruckert & Rothwell, Washington, 1987—; cons. Ford Found., 1975-83, Carnegie Corp., 1984-88. Contbr. articles to profl. jours. Bd. dirs. New Transcentury Found., Washington, 1982—, Overseas Edn. Fund., 1982—, Inst. for Soviet-Am. Relations, 1983—, Carribean Cen. Am. Action, 1987—, Georgetown U. Sch. Law Inst. for Pub. Representation, 1971-85, Am. Arbitration Assn., 1975-82, Vis. Nurses Assn., 1976-81. Mem. ABA (internat. law com.), D.C. Bar Assn. (sect. internat. law), Womens Bar Assn., Washington Internat. Trade Assn., others. Democrat. Office: Heron Burchette Ruckert & Rothwell 1025 Thomas Jefferson St NW #700 Washington DC 20007

CARGILE, SUSAN WALTER, manufacturing executive; b. Cleve., Apr. 9, 1942; d. Paul William and Susan Elizabeth (Hamilton) Walter; m. Michael Edward Cargile, Nov. 26, 1966; children: Christopher, Heather. BA, Denison U., 1964. With devel. Hawken Sch., Cleve., 1967-74; adminstrv. position Fuller, Sadeo & Zung, Cleve., 1977-79; asst. dir. Women's City Club, Cleve., 1979-81; with pub. relations Fuller, Sadeo & Zung Assocs., Cleve., 1981-84; pres. Sheet Metal Products, Willoughby, Ohio, 1984—. Active Leadership Cleve., 1988-89; pres. bd. trustees Laurel Sch., 1985-89, exec. com. 1985—; mem. pub. affairs com. City of Shaker Heights, Ohio, 1987—; sec. Cleve. Coun. Ind. Schs., 1985—; mem. Hist. Soc.; bd. dirs. Govt. Rsch. Inst., 1990—. Mem. Ohio Motorist Assn. (bd. dirs. 1990—), Assn. Women in Metal Industry, Garden Club. Presbyterian. Home: 20725 Shaker Blvd Shaker Heights OH 44122 Office: Sheet Metal Products 4764 Topps Ind Pkwy Willoughby OH 44122

CARGILL, PAULA MARIE, social worker; b. Henrietta, N.C., Sept. 18, 1943; d. John Edwin and Mabel Anne (Bridges) C. BA in Sociology/French, Winthrop Coll., 1965; MSW, So. Bapt. Theo. Sem., 1973; MS in Social Work, U. Louisville, 1975; grad. in gerontology, U. Mich., 1983. Lic. profl. counselor, ind. social worker, S.C. Social worker Connie Maxwell Children's Home, Greenwood, S.C., 1965, 70-71; tchr. French secondary pub. schs., N.C., S.C., 1965-70; instr. sociology and French North Greenville Coll., Tigerville, S.C., 1973-74; adj. assoc. instr. North Greenville Coll., Tigerville, 1973-85; clin. social worker S.C. Dept. Mental Health, Simpsonville, 1975-77; social work supr. J Health Care Ctr., Inc., Simpsonville, 1977-84, S.C. Dept. Corrections, Greenville, 1984-89; exec. dir. Grady H. Hipp Nursing Ctr., Greenville, S.C., 1989—; cons. Cargill Cons. Svc., Greenville; social worker, nursing home cons. Aging Cons. Svc., Greenville, 1982-89, rehab. agy. cons., 1984. Contbr. articles to religious mag. Bd. dirs. Greenville County Alcohol/Drug Abuse Commn., 1981-84, Ch. Community Ministries, Greenville Bapt. Assn., 1982—, Grady H. Hipp Nursing Ctr., 1985-89; mission action cons. So. Bapt. Conv., 1982-83; coun. mem. Bapt. Women, Greenville, 1979-81, 88—; flutist Greenville Civic Band. Mem. Nat. Assn. Social Workers (diplomate, bd. dirs. S.C. chpt. 1976-77, 79-81, 83-85), Am. Correctional Assn., S.C. State Employees Assn., Aging Svcs. Network, Am. Aging Network Svcs., Mensa, Greenville Forum, Alumni Leadership Greenville, Wellington Green Community Club. Home and Office: 1 Kenilworth Dr Greenville SC 29615-2320

CARIC, HELEN LORA, health science specialist; b. Skopje, Macedonia, Yugoslavia, Jan. 1, 1939; came to U.S., 1972; d. Miladin and Hedy (Hem) Milicevic; m. Ernst Anzbock, Dec. 14, 1959 (div. 1971); children: Harald, Evelyn; m. Ranko Caric, Nov. 3, 1973 (div. 1981); 1 child, Peter. Student, Molloy Coll., 1979-81, L.I. U., 1981-82, Rockland Community Coll., 1985, Vt. Coll., 1985-86, Orange County Community Coll., 1988, Empire State Coll., 1990—. Ordained to ministry Universal Spiritualist Assn. U.S.A., 1985; lic. notary pub., real estate agt., N.Y.; registered and cert. reflexologist, N.Y. Owner Walter's Bake Shop, 1973-79; nurse's aide Hillside Manor, 1980; clerical worker Molloy Coll., 1980-81, L.I. U., 1981-82; chiropractor asst. Steven R. Siegel D.C., 1982; owner Linden Motel, 1983; lectr. on Shiatsu and reflexology New Age Ctr., 1985-86; v.p. Universal Ctr. New Age Consciousness, Inc., Monroe, N.Y., 1985-89, min., 1985—; with Abatelli Realty, 1988; gen. agt. Intern Cons. Exchange, San Diego, Calif., 1986. Chairperson Rep. Nat. Hispanic Assembly for Orange County, N.J. Mem. Am. Massage Therapy Assn., Alliance of Massage Therapists, Inc., Universal Spiritualist Assn., N.Y. State Soc. Med. Massage Therapists, Orange County C. of C., Internat. Platform Assn., Warwick Art League. Home: 16 Grand Ave Middletown NY 10940 Office: Universal Ctr New Age 1-3 Stage Rd 1 Stage Rd Monroe NY 10950

CARICATO, JOAN LEEDY, service executive; b. Trenton, N.J., Aug. 9, 1957; d. James Bachman and Sara Ann (Kearney) Leedy; m. Victor Daniel Caricato, June 5, 1982; children: Joseph James, Rachael Alexandria. BS in Med. Records, York (Pa.) Coll., 1979. Instr. York Coll. of Pa., 1979-81; health record analyst York Hosp., 1979-81; dir. med. records Copley Meml. Hosp., Aurora, Ill., 1981-87, dir. patient adminstrn., 1988—; clin. instr. Coll. of DuPage, Glen Ellyn, Ill., 1981—, Ill. State U., Bloomington, 1982—, U. Ill., Chgo., 1985—. Mem. Am. Med. Record Assn., Chgo. and Vicinity Med. Record Assn., Ill. Med. Record Assn., Hosp. Fin. Mgrs. Assn. Office: Copley Meml Hosp 502 N Lincoln Ave Aurora IL 60505

CARITA, LOIS ROXANE, health facility administrator; b. Phila., Jan. 13, 1949; d. Louis Rocco and Helen Marie (DiOrio) C. BA, Temple U., 1970. Child care vol. coord. So. Home for Children, Phila., 1968-70; mgr. communications First Investment Annuity Co, Valley Forge, 1970-72; tchr. Phila. Pub. Schs., 1972-73; adminstrv. asst., then adminstr. Div. Plastic Surgery, U. Pa., Phila., 1975-87; adminstrv. dir. Ctr. Human Appearance, U. Pa., Phila., 1987—; sec.-treas. rsch. and edn. fund, Ctr. for Human Appearance, 1988—. Mem. Amnesty Internat.; sec.-treas. Plastic Surgery Edn. Found., 1979—. Mem. Plastic Surgery Adminstrs. Assn. (bd. dirs. 1985-87). Office: Ctr Human Appearance 3400 Spruce St Philadelphia PA 19104

CARL, JEAN GERALYN, marketing communications executive; b. Chester, Pa., Mar. 9, 1959; d. Charles Joseph and Longina (Michaylytza) Kraus; m. Frederick James Carl, May ll, 1985. BA in English, Bloomsburg U., 1977. Communications asst. FDI Mgmt. Corp., Chadds Ford, Pa., 1981-83, Day & Zimmerman, Inc., Phila., 1983-86; communications specialist SEI Corp., Wayne, Pa., 1986-87; mgr. mktg. communications Lucas Sensing Systems, Pennsauken, N.J., 1987—. Mem. Am. Mgmt. Assn., Phila. Writers Assn., Phi Kappa Phi. Office: Lucas Sensing Systems 7905 N Rte 130 Pennsauken NJ 08110

CARL, JUDITH LEE, psychologist; b. L.A., Aug. 26, 1944; d. Herbert Frank and June Pauline (Culler) Malone; m. Richard Allen Carl, Aug. 15, 1969 (div. Jan. 1989). BA, Calif. State U., L.A., 1968, MS, 1975; PhD, U. So. Calif., L.A., 1983. Lic. psychologist, Calif. Tchr. Hawaii Bd. of Edn., Honolulu, 1969-70; tchr. Torrance (Calif.) Unified Sch. Dist., 1970-75, counselor, 1975-82; pvt. practice marriage, family and child counselor Torrance, 1978-88; psychol. asst. dr. Melvyn Lewin, Palos Verdes Estate, Calif., 1980-88; pvt. practice Palos Verdes Estate, 1988—; clin. dir. Pev-Mar Recovery, Torrance, 1984-85, Place in the Valley, Grants Pass, Oreg., 1989—. Named Woman of the Yr., YWCA, 1981. Mem. APA, Calif. State Psychol. Assn., CAP-PAC. Office: 716 Yarmouth Rd Palos Verdes Estates CA 90274

CARL, TOMMIE EWERT, composer; b. Marion, Kans., Sept. 23, 1921; d. Andrew A. and Orpha (Ratzlaff) Ewert; m. Leo D. Carl, Jan. 1, 1943; 1 child, David Richard. BA, Am. U., 1970, MA, 1972. Acct. comptrollers' office Hammer Galleries/Dant Distilling, N.Y.C., 1946-48; chief acctg. div. Cen. Purchasing Office, Tokyo, 1949-52; instr. Medieval Theory Am. U., Washington, 1971-72; mem. com. to obtain charter for a women's bank Washington, 1974-76. Composer electric music Anagrams, 1972, Bells, 1974, Illusions, 1974, Chromosynthesis, 1974, Futurama I, 1974, Futurama II, 1974. Mem. Bus. Women No. Va., Composers' Forum, Inc., Am. Women Composers, Inc. (founder, pres. 1976-88), Sigma Alpha Iota. Home: 7315 Hooking Rd McLean VA 22101 Office: Am Women Composers 1690 36th St NW Ste 410 Washington DC 20007

CARLBERG, NANCY ELLEN, writer; b. L.A., Aug. 8, 1947; d. Robert Eugene and Evelyn Elaine (Rollier) C. BA, Chapman Coll., 1969; MLS, Calif. State U., Fullerton, 1974. Libr. asst. Orange County Pub. Libr. System, Orange, Calif., 1969-74; genealogist Inst. Family Rsch., Salt Lake City, 1974-77; genealogist for Alex Haley, author of Roots, L.A., 1977-80; self-employed genealogist Anaheim, Calif., 1980-86; pub. Carlberg Press, Anaheim, 1986—; self-employed writer Anaheim, 1985—. Author: Climbing the Family Tree with Nancy, 1986, Researching in Salt Lake City, 1987, Teaching Genealogy, 1988, Beginning Swedish Research, 1989, Nancy's Easy Filing System, 1987, Preserving Your Family Heritage, 1987, Using the Los Angeles Family History Center, 1987, Travelling to England to Find Your Roots (Cheap), 1990, Using the Family History Library Computer System, 1990. Mem. com. Task Force on the Persistently Homeless, Anaheim, 1990. Mem. AAUW (br. pres. 1989-90), COSMEP, Orange County Calif. Geneal. Soc. (life), Nat. Writers Club, Brit. Family History Soc., Mensa, Optimist Club. Democrat. Home: 1782 Beacon Ave Anaheim CA 92804-4515

CARLETON, GAYE, public relations executive; b. Phila., Apr. 21, 1952; d. George Norman and Mary Patricia (Vandergrift) C.; m. James Tyrone Copening, June 16, 1984. BA, U. Iowa, 1974. Asst. to dir. City Spirit Arts Project, New Hope, Pa., 1975-77; dir. Arts Alliance Buck County, New Hope, 1977-79; pres. Pressing Matter Pub. Relations, San Francisco, 1979-81, Rockit Pub. Relations, N.Y.C., 1982-87, Carleton and Co., Pub. Relations, N.Y.C., 1987—. Mem. Women in Music, Women in Bus. Network (v.p. 1988—). Home: 343 Bleecker St New York NY 10014 Office: Carleton and Co 580 Broadway Ste 504 New York NY 10012

CARLETON, MARY RUTH, television news anchor, consultant; b. Sacramento, Feb. 2, 1948; d. Warren Alfred and Mary Gertrude (Clark) Case; m. Bruce A. Hunt, Jan. 21, 1989. B.A. in Polit. Sci., U. Calif.-Berkeley, 1970, M.J., 1974. TV news anchorwoman, reporter Sta. KXAS-TV, Ft. Worth, 1974-78, Sta. KING-TV, Seattle, 1978-80, Sta. KOCO-TV, Oklahoma City, 1980-84; news anchor, reporter Sta. KTTV-TV, L.A., 1984-87; news anchor Sta. KLAS-TV, Las Vegas, Nev., 1987—; broadcast instr. U. Okla., 1982-84, Okla. Christian Coll., 1981-84, UCLA, 1985-87; cons. Positive Image, Las Vegas, 1989—. Bd. dirs. World Neighbors, Oklahoma City, 1984-89, Allied Arts Coun. So. Nev., Las Vegas, 1988—; mem. Nathan Adelson Hospice, 1989—, Nev. Inst. for Contemporary Art, 1989—, Exec. bd. MDA, 1989—. Named Communicator of Yr., Okla. Wildlife Fedn., 1983, Women in Communication Byliner, 1984, Disting. Woman of So. Nev.; recipient Broadcasting award UPI, 1981, Emmy award, L.A., 1986, L.A. Press Club award 1986; named Okla. Woman in News, Hospitality Club, 1981. Mem. Women in Communications (Clarion award 1981), Sigma Delta Chi. Democrat. Roman Catholic. Avocations: tennis, gourmet cooking. Office: Sta KLAS-TV 3228 Channel 8 Dr Las Vegas NV 89109

CARLEY, JONI MARIE, psychic, talk show hostess; b. Camden, N.J., June 9, 1955; d. Joseph Loran and Marie Elizabeth (Aspell) C.; m. Keiji Yamaguchi, Mar. 29, 1941. B Music Therapy, Combs Coll., Phila., 1978; postgrad., Temple U., 1985-86. Pvt. practice Phila., 1978—; talk show hostess WRTI, Phila., 1986—; actress stage, film, radio Annenberg Ctr., Phila., 1979—; musician, vocalist various nightclubs, 1982-84. Vol. Youth at Risk, Phila., 1988. Mem. Nat. Assn. Music Therapy, Macrobiotic Assn. Pa. (bd. dirs. 1989), Inst. Noetic Scis., Greenpeace, One Peaceful World Fedn.

CARLEY, ROBIN MICHELE, public relations counselor; b. Teaneck, N.J., Mar. 3, 1955; d. Victor Haig and Adele May (Trado) C.; m. Carl James Tagliaferro, May 21, 1983. B.S., U. Fla., 1977; M.A., William Paterson Coll., 1981. Asst. creative dir. Dialog, Inc., Haworth, N.J., 1977; account exec. BSY Assocs., Caldwell, N.J., 1978; community relations officer Rahway Hosp., (N.J.), 1979-81; account exec. Doremus & Co., N.Y.C., 1981-84; account mgr. Marketshare, div. Doremus and BBD&O, N.Y.C., 1984—; cons. Pub. Service Council. Recipient 1st place ann. report competition award N.J. Hosp. Assn., 1981. Mem. Pub. Relations Soc. Am., Women in Communications, Inc., Counselor Acad. Home: 800 Kinder Komack Rd Oradell NJ 07649

CARLIN, ANNE ILISHABETH, pastor, educator, evangelist; b. San Antonio, Sept. 12, 1949; d. Otha Hart and Connie Colbert (Weathers) McClain; m. Nolon Calvin Dawson Carlin, Nov. 26, 1968. Assoc. in Fgn. Lang., Brown's Acad., Sem., Houston, 1974; B of Biblical Studies, Grace Miracle Faith Sem., 1980, MDiv magna cum laude, 1989, D of Leadership (hon.), 1989. Extension worker La. State U., Baton Rouge, 1967-68; owner, operator Connettes Beauty Salon, Plaquemine, La., 1969-72; bookkeeper, acct. Gilbert Gertner Enterprise, Houston, 1973-80, Blums Importers, Houston, 1977-80; designer, dressmaker Mother and Daughter Touch, Plaquemine, 1980-89; pub., author First Black Christian Newspaper, Plaquemine, 1980-85; coord., centrifuger The Damon Project, Baton Rouge, 1985-87; evangelist, counselor Holy Ghost Temple, Baton Rouge, 1980-89; program dir. Herman Graham Ctr., Plaquemine, 1987—; pastor, tchr. Grace Miracle Faith C.O.G.I.C., Baton Rouge, Houston, 1980—; coord. UpJohn Med. Svcs., Baton Rouge, 1986—; sec. and vocalist Radio Ministry, San Antonio. Author: Pastor's Manual, 1983, Guide for Intercessors, 1983. V.p., counselor East Baton Rouge Prayer Assn., 1982—; dir. Children's Ministry Grace Miracle Faith Outreach, 1980-84. Named Mother of Yr. East Baton Rouge Prayer Assn., 1987, Herman Graham Community Ctr., Plaquemine, 1989. Fellow Regiae Socius Sanctissimus (royal ring 1988); mem. Houston Women on Bus. for Christ (prayer min. 1979—, Grace award 1981, 84, 87), Corps Ambs. for Christ (capt. 1982-85, purple stole 1982), Grace Miracle Faith Sem. Alumni (pres. bd. dirs. 1980—, Gospel award 1984-86, 88), Women A'Glow (watchman 1976-78), Eastern Star (chaplain 1960, 84-85). Democrat. Baptist.

CARLISLE, LILIAN MATAROSE BAKER (MRS. E. GRAFTON CARLISLE, JR.), author, lecturer; b. Meridian, Miss., Jan. 1, 1912; d. Joseph and Lilian (Flournoy) Baker; student Dickinson Coll., 1929-30, Pierce Coll. Bus. Adminstrn., 1930-31; B.A., U. Vt., 1981, M.A., 1986; m. E. Grafton Carlisle, Jr., Jan. 9, 1933; children: Diana, Penelope. Legal sec. A. W. Sanson, Phila., 1931-35; adminstrv. sec. RAF Ferry Command, Montreal, Que., Can., 1942; exec. staff mem. in charge collections, research Shelburne (Vt.) Mus., 1951-61; exec. sec. Burlington Area Community Health Study, 1963, coordinator, 1964; asst. coordinator Vt. Mental Retardation Planning Project, 1965; project dir. 4-county Champlain Valley Medicare Alert, 1966; dir. public relations Champlain Valley Agrl. Fair, 1968-77; lectr. U. Vt. Elder Hostel program, 1976-77, mem. faculty Vacation Coll., 1980-83. Pres., Burlington Community Council for Social Welfare, 59-61, 71-73; chmn. bd. Interfaith Sr. Citizens, 1977-79; justice of peace, 1979-81; pres. Chittenden County Extension Adv. Com., 1977-78; lay mem. Gov.'s Conf. on Problems of Aging for White House Conf., 1960; chmn. publs. com. Vt. Bicentennial Commn., 1974-77; mem. Gov.'s Commn. on Mobile Homes, 1973-79; mem. Vt. Ho. of Reps., 1968-70. Recipient Community Council Disting. Citizen award, 1978. Mem. Vt. (trustee, chmn. mus. com. 1967), N.Y. (faculty seminar) Chittenden (pres. 1969-72, editor Heritage Series of 10 books about Chittenden County towns 1972-76) hist. socs., Vt. Old Cemetery Assn., Vt. Folklore Soc., League Vt. Writers (dir. 1962; v.p., pres. 1967-69). Am. Pen Women (pres. Green Mountain br. 1980-82), Order Women Legislators (pres. Vt. br. 1972-74), Mem;l. Soc. Vt. (pres. 1989—), Chi Omega. Conglist. Club: Zonta (pres. 1964-65). Co-author: The Story of the Shelburne Museum, 1955; Profile of the Community, 1964; Environmental and Personal Health of the Community, 1964; Vermont Clock and Watchmakers, Silversmiths and Jewelers, 1970; also numerous catalogs on collections at Shelburne Mus.; editorial cons. Burlington Social Survey, 1967; contbr. articles to profl. jours. Home: 117 Lakeview Terr Burlington VT 05401

CARLISLE, MARGO DUER BLACK, research foundation executive; b. Providence; d. Thomas F. Jr. and Margaret MacCormick Black; m. Miles Carlisle; children: Mary Hamilton, Tristram Coffin. BA, Manhattanville Coll. Legis. asst. Senator James A. McClure, Washington, 1973; staff mem. budget commn. task force U.S. Senate, Washington, 1974-75, exec. dir. steering com., 1976-80; staff dir. Senate Rep. Conf., Washington, 1981-85; exec. dir. Coun. for Nat. Policy, Washington, 1985-86; asst. sec. for legis. affairs Dept. Def., Washington, 1986-89; v.p. for govt. rels. The Heritage Found., Washington, 1989—; staff dir. nat. security and fgn. policy subcoms. for Rep. platform, 1984, Washington. Contbr. articles on govt. policy to profl. jours. Trustee Phila. Soc., Washington, 1987-88. Mem. Nantucket Yacht Club (Mass.). Roman Catholic. Home: 3221 Garfield St Washington DC 20008 Office: The Heritage Found 214 Massachusetts Ave NE Washington DC 20002

CARLISLE, PATRICIA KINLEY, mortgage company executive; b. Royston, Ga., Sept. 21, 1949; d. Luther Clark Kinley and Ann Busby Carey; children: Angela Renee, William Clark, Matthew Vincent. Grad., Suburban Inst. Real Estate, Tucker, Ga., 1978; grad. with honors, Lanier Tech. Sch., Oakwood, Ga., 1983; postgrad., Gainesville Coll., 1986, Maryville Coll., 1986. Lic. real estate salesperson, Ga. Fin. analyst, then pers. mgr., coord. Citicorp Acceptance Co., Inc., St. Louis, 1983-89; exec. v.p., v.p. purchasing, regional sales mgr. George-Ingraham Corp., Stone Mountain, Ga., 1989-90; sr. loan officer Terrace Mortgage Co., Atlanta, 1990—. Mem. NAFE, Forsyth County Bd. Realtors, Aircraft Owners and Pilots Assn. Home: PO Box 467364 Atlanta GA 30346 Office: Terrace Mortgage Cok 900 Ashwood Pkwy Ste 130 Atlanta GA 30338

CARLSEN, DEBORAH EILEEN BETTRAY, data base administrator; b. Chgo., Nov. 6, 1956; d. Theodore Walter and Patricia Ann (Knorr) Bettray; divorced; 1 child, Alana Lee. BS in Mgmt., Ill. Inst. Tech., 1978. Jr. systems analyst Milw. R.R., Chgo., 1978-79; programmer/analyst St. Paul Fed., Chgo., 1979-80; data base adminstr. Schwinn Bicycle, Chgo., 1980—. Mem. NAFE, Assn. Systems Mgmt., Chgo. Area Software A.G. User's Group (co-chairperson, v.p. midwest region). Roman Catholic. Office: Schwinn Bicycle Co 217 N Jefferson Chicago IL 60606

CARLSEN, JANET HAWS, insurance company owner, mayor; b. Bellingham, Calif., June 16, 1927; d. Lyle F. and Mary Elizabeth (Preble) Haws; m. Kenneth M. Carlsen, July 26, 1952; children: Stephanie L. Bagnani, Scott Lyle, Sean Preble, Stacy K., Spencer J. Cert., Armstrong Bus. Sch., 1945;

student, Golden Gate Coll., 1945-46. Office mgr. Cornwall Warehouse Co., Salt Lake City, 1950-55, Hansen's Ins., Newman, Calif., 1969-77; owner Carlsen Ins., Gustine, Calif., 1978—. Mem. city council City of Newman, 1980-82, mayor, 1982—; bd. dirs. ARC, Stanislaus, Calif., 1982-88; vice chair Dem. Cen. Com., Calif., 1982-83; grand marxhall Newman Fall Festival, 1989; v.p. cen. div. League of Calif. Cities, 1989-90, pres., 1990—. Named Soroptimist Woman of Achievement, 1987, Soroptimist Woman of Distinction, 1988, Outstanding Woman, Stanislaus County Commn. for Women, 1989. Morman. Club: Booster (Newman). Lodge: Soroptimist. Home: 1215 Amy Dr Newman CA 95360 Office: 377 5th St Gustine CA 95322

CARLSEN, LAURIE BETH, trade association administrator; b. Milton, Mass., Feb. 10, 1961; d. Mervin L. and Marion A. Carlsen. BS, U. R.I., 1982. Sec. Fidelity Investments, Boston, 1982-83, regional office adminstr., 1983-85, nat. conf. coord., 1985-89, dir. trade shows and confs., 1987-89, assoc. market mgr., 1989—. Mem. Internat. Exhibitors Assn., Meeting Planners Internat. Office: Fidelity Investments 82 Devonshire St Boston MA 02109

CARLSEN, MARY BAIRD, clinical psychologist; b. Salt Lake City, Aug. 31, 1928; d. Jesse Hays and Susannah AManda (Bragstad) Baird; m. James C. Carlsen, May 1, 1949; children: Philip, Douglas, Susan, Kristine. Student, St. Olaf Coll., 1946-47; BA, Whitworth Coll., 1950; MA, U. Conn., 1967; PhD, U. Wash., 1973. Profl. organist, piano tchr. Wash., Oreg., Ill., Conn., 1949-68; staff counselor Presbyn. Counseling Svc., Seattle, 1976-79; pvt. practice clin. psychologist, marriage therapist, career devel. specialist Seattle, 1978—; chmn. sr. adult adv. coun. Seattle Parks Dept., 1975-76. Grantee PEO Rsch., 1972, U. Wash. Women's Guidance Ctr., 1972. Mem. Am. Psychol. Assn., Wash. State Psychol. Assn., Assn. Humanistic Psychology, Am. Assn. Marriage and Family Therapy.

CARLSON, ANITA HOKE, home economics educator; b. Upland, Calif., Oct. 1, 1942; d. William R. and Mary S. (Hess) Hoke; m. Jon O. Carlson, June 20, 1964; children: Heather Lynn, Jennifer Sue. Student, Messiah Coll., Grantham, Pa., 1960-63; BS in Home Econs., Drexel U., 1964; MS, Carnegie Mellon U., 1971; MA in Teaching, Jacksonville U., 1990. Cert. home economics. Tchr. Butler (Pa.) Jr. High Sch., 1964-67, Goessel (Kans.) High Sch., 1967-69, Franklin Jr. High Sch., Champaign, Ill., 1969-71; asst. ombudsman Greater Anchorage Borough, 1974-75; tchr. Chappell Schs., Jacksonville, Fla., 1981-82, Arlington Country Day Sch., Jacksonville, 1983-84, John Gorrie Jr. High Sch., Jacksonville, 1984-88; tchr. home econs. Terry Parker High Sch., Jacksonville, 1988—. Mem. Fla. Home Econs. Assn. (v.p. dist. 1989—), AAUW (bd. dirs. 1988-89). Home: 3213 Hermitage Rd Jacksonville FL 32211

CARLSON, ANITA LYNNE, healthcare company executive, pharmacist; b. Chgo., June 7, 1952; d. Clayton Arthur and Sharon Natalie (Abrams) Hembree; m. Roger Paul Carlson, Feb. 26, 1977; 1 child, Staci. BS in Pharmacy, U. Ill., Chgo., 1982. Lic. pharmacist, Ill.; cert. substance abuse counselor. Dir. pharm. purchasing Evanston (Ill.) Hosp., 1983-86; v.p. group svcs. Zahn Drug Inc., Chgo., 1986-88; dir. instnl. sales and mktg. Pharm. Basic, Inc., Chgo., 1987-88; plan mgr. Health Care Pharmacy Providers, Jacksonville, Fla., 1988-90; mgr. Managed Prescription Svcs., St. Louis, 1990—; mem. adv. bd. RX Net, Alexandria, Va., 1987-88; pres., cons. Carlson Agy., Inc., Jacksonville, 1988—. Author: Reasons To Eat on a Diet, 1986; contbr. to newsletters. Tchr. community drug edn. courses Chgo. Pub. Schs., 1980-88; CPR instr. Am. Heart Assn., 1982—. Mem. Am. Pharmacy Assn., Am. Hosp. Hosp. Pharmacists, Nat. Assn. Retail Drugists, Fla. Pharmacy Assn., Ga. Pharmacy Assn., Ala. Pharmacy Assn., N.C. Pharmacy Assn., S.C. Pharmacy Assn., Greenpeace, Sierra Club, Rho Psi, Lambda Kappa Sigma. Home: 13226 Greenbough Saint Louis MO 63146 Office: Managed Prescription Svcs 11701 Borman Dr Saint Louis MO 63146

CARLSON, BARBARA BIGGER, planning analyst; b. Bklyn., Apr. 21, 1939; d. John Howard and Martha Barbara (Seaman) Bigger; m. Brian Bennett Carlson, June 25, 1960; children: David Arnold, Sarah Frances, John Bennett. BA, U. Wis., 1961, MA, 1980. Writer Pub. Radio, Madison, Wis., 1960-62; writer, editor Ednl. Pub., Middleton, Wis., 1974-77; planning analyst State of Wis., Madison, 1977—. Sch. bd. mem. Middleton-Cross Plains Area, 1972-81. Mem. Wis. Correctional Assn. Democrat. Presbyterian. Office: State of Wis Dept Corrections 1 W Wilson Box 7925 Madison WI 53707

CARLSON, BARBARA JEAN, education educator; b. Milwaukee, Wis., July 26, 1926; d. Howard McKinley and Ruth E. (Morgan) Zoerb; children: Kevin Morgan Werner, Kerry Jo Werner Fitzpatrick; m. Robert Frederick Carlson, Aug. 20, 1975. BS, U. Wis., 1949; postgrad., Calif. State U., 1969. Sec. Campbell Soup Co., Sacramento, 1950-52; lab. tech. Morse Lab., Sacramento, 1952-53; asst. chem. testing engr. Dept. Transp. State of Calif., Sacramento, 1953-55; high sch. tchr. San Juan Unified Sch. Dist., Carmichael, Calif., 1969-70; adult sch. tchr. San Juan Unified Sch. Dist., Carmichael, 1970--; cons. (textbook) Contemporary's Ged The Sci. Test, 1985. Treas. Calif. Council Adult Edn., Sacramento, 1973-85. Mem. AAUW, Calif. Coun. Adult Edn., Nat. Coun. Tchrs. of Math. Republican. Presbyterian. Home: 2120 Lambeth Way Carmichael CA 95608

CARLSON, CARMEN ELIZABETH, information systems consultant; b. Mpls., May 23, 1963; d. Kenneth Leonard and Darlene Ruth (Lundquist) C. BA, Wheaton (Ill.) Coll., 1984; MBA, U. Minn., 1989. Banker asst. Bank of Wheaton, 1984-85; consumer banker Norwest Bank Minn., N.A., Mpls., 1985-87; product mktg. officer First Bank, Mpls., 1989-90; info. systems cons. Andersen Cons., Mpls., 1990—. Mem. U. Minn. Alumni Assn., Omicron Delta Epsilon. Office: Anderson Cons 45 S 7th St Minneapolis MN 55402

CARLSON, CAROL SUE, nursing administrator; b. Bay City, Mich., Jan. 15, 1946; d. Donald L. and Marjorie E. (Brown) Gillette; m. John H. Carlson, June 23, 1968; children: Kristen, Emily, Derek. BS in Nursing, Mich. State U., 1968; MS in Nursing, U. So. Miss., 1982. Staff nurse St. Joseph Hosp., Pontiac, Mich., 1968, Mercy Hosp., Bay City, 1968, Ind. Univ. Med. Ctr., Indpls., 1969-70; instr. nursing Ind. Vocat. Tech. Coll., Bloomington, 1970-72, Lafayette, 1973-78; staff nurse Community Home Health, Ocean Springs, Miss., 1980-81; instr. nursing Miss. Gulf Coast Jr. Coll., Gautier, 1982-87; staff nurse Ocean Springs Hosp., 1980, dir. nursing, 1987—. Inst. basic cardiac life support Miss. Heart Assn., 1985-88; treas. Taconi Elem. Sch. PTO, Ocean Springs, 1983-84, Gulf Coast Youth Orch., Inc., Ocean Springs, 1989—, treas., 1989-90; children's coord. St. Paul United Meth. Ch., Ocean Springs, 1985, mem. adminstrv. bd., 1987-89, chmn. health and welfare, 1989-90; chmn. Christian Women's Club, Lafayette, Ind., 1975-76. Mem. Am. Nurses Assn., N.Am. Nursing Diagnosis Assn., Miss. Nursing Diagnosis Conf. Group (co-founder 1985), Miss. Nurses Assn. (active continuing edn. rev. 1986-88), Miss. Hosp. Assn. Orgn. Nurse Execs. (pres. S.E. Coun. 1989—, chmn. edn. com.), Dist. 6 Nurses Assn. (sec. 1987-88), Duchess Club (v.p. 1987-88), Sigma Theta Tau. Home: 124 Watersedge Dr Ocean Springs MS 39564 Office: Ocean Springs Hosp 3109 Bienville Blvd Ocean Springs MS 39564

CARLSON, CAROL WEBER, mechanical engineering; b. Tampa, Fla., Jan. 17, 1960; d. Conrad Raymond and Joan Mary (Thurston) W.; m. Chris C. Carlson, Feb. 20, 1988. BS in Mech. Engring., U. Fla., 1983; postgrad., U. Cen. Fla., 1989—. Registered profl. engr., Fla. Test engr. Pratt & Whitney, W. Palm Beach, Fla., 1983-84, design engr., 1984-85; student asst. U. Cen. Fla., Fla. Solar Energy Ctr., Cape Canaveral, 1985; design engr. EG&G Fla., Kennedy Space Ctr., Fla., 1986-88, sr. engr., 1988—. Vol. Space Coast Physically Handicapped Benefit, Brevard, Fla., 1986, 87. Mem. ASME (treas. 1987-88, sec. 1988-89, v.p. 1989-90, chmn. Canaveral sect. 1990—), Team Rocket Triathlon (pres. 1986-87). Office: EG&G Fla Kennedy Space Center FL 32815

CARLSON, CHARLOTTE BOOTH, technical illustrator; b. Brigham City, Utah, July 1, 1920; d. Robert Edwin and Mary Alice (Carhartt) B.; m. Gerald Luther Carlson, Nov. 11, 1943 (div. June 1969); children: Joel Koch, Elaine Marie Seldner, Kris Donald. Student, Omaha U., 1937-39; cert. in Engring., Nebr. State U., 1941; student, Fine Arts Ctr., Colorado Springs, 1941-42. Background painter, title bd. operator Alexander Film Co., Colorado Springs, 1943-44; draftsman Bell Telephone Co., N.Y.C., 1944-47; founder Carlson Graphic Services, Princeton, N.J. Contbr. poetry to local newspapers. Mem. Order of Eastern Star (organist 1984-86, line officer 1986-90, worthy matron 1989-90). Mem. Soc. Friends. Home: 5F Holly House Princeton NJ 08540

CARLSON, DALE BICK, writer; b. N.Y.C., May 24, 1935; d. Edgar M. and Estelle (Cohen) Bick; children: Daniel, Hannah. BA, Wellesley Coll., 1957. Author children's books, adult books 1961—, including: Perkins the Brain, 1964, The House of Perkins, 1965, Miss Maloo, 1966, The Brainstormers, 1966, Frankenstein, 1968, Counting is Easy, 1969, Your Country, 1969, Arithmetic 1, 2, 3, 1969, The Electronic Teabowl, 1969, Warlord of the Genji, 1970, The Beggar King of China, 1971, The Mountain of Truth (Spring Festival Honor book, named Am. Library Assn. Notable Book), 1972, Good Morning Danny, 1972, Good Morning, Hannah, 1972, The Human Apes, 1973 (named Am. Library Assn. Notable Book), Girls Are Equal Too, 1973 (named Am. Library Assn. Notable Book), Baby Needs Shoes, 1974, Triple Boy, 1976, Where's Your Head?, 1977, The Plant People, 1977, The Wild Heart, 1977, The Shining Pool, 1979, Lovingsex for Both Sexes, 1979, Boys Have Feelings Too, 1980, Call Me Amanda, 1981, Manners that Matter, 1982, The Frog People, 1982, Charlie the Hero, 1983, 1984-85: The Jenny Dean Science Fiction Mysteries, The Mystery of the Shining Children, The Mystery of the Hidden Trap, The Secret of the Third Eye, The James Budd Mysteries, The Mystery of Galaxy Games, The Mystery of Operation Brain, 1985, Miss Mary's Husbands, 1988, others; editor-in-chief Parents League Bull., 1967-72. V.p. Parents League N.Y. Mem. Authors League Am., Authors Guild, Nature Connection. Address: 307 Neck Rd Madison CT 06443

CARLSON, DAWN MARIE, advertising executive; b. Milw., Oct. 25, 1956; d. Donald Andrew and Mary Joyce (Hogan) C. AS, Indian Valley Coll., Novato, Calif., 1982; BA in Mgmt., Sonoma State U., 1985. Exec. tng. program Emporium Capwell Co., San Francisco, 1978; dept. sales mgr. Emporium Capwell Co., 1974-79; sales mgr. Olan Mills, Scottsdale, Ariz., 1980-81; asst. v.p. C.R. Seaton Co./Colossal Group, Sonoma, 1986; dir. Novato (Calif.) Human Needs Ctr., 1987-88; account exec. Majestic Co., San Rafael, Calif., 1989—. Bd. dirs. Am. Heart Assn., chair cardiac arrest com.; bd. dirs. Exodus Home for Autistic Children, Marin Mus. Am. Indian, v.p.; bd. dirs. Symphony League, historian, publicity chair, Olompali People and State Park; mem. community adv. panel pub. broadcasting channel Sta. KRCB. Mem. Golden Gate Advt. Specialty Assn., Advt. Specialty Inst., AAUW, NAFE, Marin Interconnect Networking Group (membership chair), Soroptimist Internat., San Rafael C. of C. (chair bus. alliance group), Marin County C. of C., Novato C. of C. Democrat. Roman Catholic. Home: 230 B San Andreas Dr Novato CA 94945

CARLSON, DEBORAH ANN, educator; b. Faribault, Minn., Mar. 6, 1948; d. Lawrence Burton and Selma Louisa Theresa (Boldt) C. AB, St. Olaf Coll., Northfield, Minn., 1969; MA, Coll. of St. Thomas, St. Paul, 1970, U. Minn., 1972. Tchr. Stillwater (Minn.) Sr. High Sch., 1969-70, Anoka (Minn.)-Hennepin Schs., 1972-74, Mpls. Pub. Schs., 1974—; tchr. English, Internat. Fine Arts Magnet Sch., Washburn High Sch., 1989—; prin. violist 1st Unitarian Soc. Orch., Mpls., 1973-78, Civic Orch. Mpls., 1979—; violist Mt. Curve String Quartet, Mpls., 1973—; mem. program com. Conf. on History of Women, 1980, 82. Editor: Women's History Tour of the Twin Cities, 1982. Pres. Civic Orch. Mpls., 1980-82. Mem. Minn. Hist. Soc., Women Historians Midwest (pres. St. Paul 1978-80). Democrat. Lutheran. Home: 624 Morgan Ave S Minneapolis MN 55405

CARLSON, JANET FRANCES, psychologist, educator; b. Newport, R.I., Oct. 3, 1957; d. Robert Carl and Alice Marion (Orina) C.; m. Kurt Francis Geisinger, Sept. 22, 1984. BS in Psychology/Biology, Union Coll., Schenectady, 1979; MA in Clin. Psychology, Fordham U., 1982, PhD in Clin. Psychology, 1987. Lic. psychologist, N.Y.; cert. sch. psychologist, N.Y., Conn. Clin. psychology intern Conn. Valley Hosp., Middletown, Conn., 1983-84; research fellow Schering-Plough Found., Bronx, N.Y., 1984-85; psychologist I Creedmoor Psychiat. Ctr., Queens Village, N.Y., 1985-86; psychologist Hallen Sch., Mamaroneck, N.Y., 1986-88; asst. prof. psychology Fordham U., Bronx, N.Y., 1988-89; asst. prof., div. of sch. and applied psychology program Fairfield (Conn.) U., 1989—; adj. asst. prof. psychology Fordham U., Bronx, 1987-88. Recipient Sugarfree scholarship, 1984-85, Sigma Xi Grant-in-Aid of Research, 1984-85. Mem. Conn. Psychol. Assn., Eastern Psychol. Assn., Am. Psychol. Assn., Nat. Assn. Sch. Psychologists, Conn. Assn. Sch. Psychologists, Northeastern Ednl. Rsch. Assn., Sigma Xi, Psi Chi (charter), Phi Kappa Phi.

CARLSON, JANET LYNN, chemistry educator; b. Mpls., Aug. 31, 1952; d. Donald S. and Katheryn F. (Kubo) Maeda; m. James G. Carlson, June 26, 1976. BA, Hamline U., 1974; PhD, Stanford U., 1978. Asst. prof. Macalester Coll., St. Paul, 1978-87, assoc. prof., 1987—. Contbr. articles to profl. jours. Office: Macalester Coll 1600 Grand Ave Saint Paul MN 55105

CARLSON, JEANNIE ANN, writer; b. Bklyn., Jan. 13, 1955; d. Lloyd Arthur and Ruth Frances (Riley) C.; 1 child, Carl Philip; m. H. Daniel Hopkins, Dec. 16, 1987. BA, Randolph-Macon Woman's Coll., 1977. Mktg./editing rep. Harris Pub., White Plains, N.Y., 1982; adminstrv. asst. Ray Fried Assocs., Inc., Eastchester, N.Y., 1980-84; proofreader Nat. Pennysaver, Elmsford, N.Y., 1983-84; chief writer Profl. Resume and Writing Service, St. Petersburg, Fla., 1984-87; exec. writer, pres. Viking Communications, Inc., 1987—; feature writer Ashbury News, Crestwood, N.Y., 1983-84; editorial asst. Children's Rights Am., Largo, Fla., 1984; pub. rels. coord. The Renaissance Cultural Ctr., Clearwater, Fla., 1985; com. mem. work area on communications Pasadena Community Ch., St. Petersburg, Fla., 1986-88. Recipient Golden Poet award World of Poetry, 1985, 88, 89, Silver Poet award, 1986, 90, Recognition award Nat. Soc. Poets, 1979, poetry awards Internat. Publs., 1976-77, Achievement Certs. Profl. Resume and Writing Service, 1985, 86, 87, 6 World of Poetry awards of merit, 1983 (2), 85, 87, 88 (2). Mem. City News Service (affiliate writer). Lutheran. Avocations: theatre, culinary arts. Office: Viking Communications Inc 300 31st St N Ste 212 Saint Petersburg FL 33713

CARLSON, KRISTI MORK, professional association executive; b. Grand Forks, N.D., Mar. 5, 1955; d. Kendall Eugene and Eileen Lucille (Osking) Mork; m. Timothy Lynn Chartier (div. 1977); m. Wallace James Carlson; children: Celeste, Clark, Adam. BS in Communications, N.D. State U., 1979. With N.D. State U. Phys. Plant, Fargo, 1979, Melroe div. Calrk Equip., Gwinner, N.D., 1979-80; dir. Women's Advocacy Network, Lisbon, N.D., 1980—; farmer Lisbon, 1980—. Bd. dirs. Food Pantry, Lisbon, 1989—, Mental Health Assn. Ransom County, Lisbon, 1989—. Recipient Mental Health Award of Merit, N.D. mental Health Assn., 1988. Democrat. Lutheran. Home: RR 2 Box 86 Lisbon ND 58054 Office: Womens Advocacy Network Box 919 Lisbon ND 58054

CARLSON, MARIAN BILLE, geneticist, researcher, educator; b. Princeton, N.J., Oct. 19, 1952; d. B.C. and L.W. Carlson; m. Stephen P. Goff, Oct. 15, 1977; children: Sarah Carlson, Thomas Carlson. BA summa cum laude, Harvard U., 1973; PhD with distinction, Stanford U., 1978. Asst. prof. genetics Columbia U., N.Y.C., 1981-86, assoc. prof., 1987-88, prof., 1988—. Assoc. editor Genetics, 1988—; mem. editorial bd. Molecular and Cellular Biology, 1987-92; contbr. chpts. to books, articles to profl. jours. NSF fellow, 1973-76, Jane Coffin Childs fellow, 1978-81; recipient Irma T. Hirschl Career Sci. award, 1982-87, Lamport award for basic rsch. Columbia U., 1987, Faculty Rsch. award Am. Cancer Soc., 1988—. Mem. Genetics Soc. Am., Am. Soc. for Microbiology, Phi Beta Kappa, Sigma Xi. Office: Columbia U 701 W 168th St New York NY 10032

CARLSON, MARY ANN, state legislator, hotel executive; b. Palo Alto, Calif., Jan. 22, 1944; m. Wesley H. Carlson; 5 children. BA, Marquette U., 1965; postgrad., Fordham U., 1977. Co-owner, operator West Mountain Inn, Arlington, Vt.; mem. Vt. State Senate, Montpelier, 1989—; mem. Gov.'s Commn. on Women; trustee United Counseling Svc. Bd. dirs. Arlington Libr. Mem. Women Bus. Owners Vt., Northshire Women's Collective. Democrat. Home: PO Box 465 Arlington VT 05250 Office: Vt State Senate Montpelier VT 05602*

CARLSON, MARY ANNE JEROW, sales executive; b. Cin., Oct. 7, 1957; d. James Edward and Joyce Ann (Burris) Jerow; m. Raymond Hjalmar Carlson, Jr., Nov. 25, 1989. BBA, U. Cin., 1979. Sales rep. paper products Procter & Gamble, Flint, Mich., 1981-82; dist. field rep. paper products Procter & Gamble, Cleve., 1982-83; unit mgr. paper products Procter & Gamble, Phila., 1983-87, unit mgr. spl. assignment nat. accounts, 1987-88; unit mgr. spl. assignment sales merchandising Procter & Gamble, Cin., 1988-89; unit mgr. spl. spl. assignment nat. account Procter & Gamble, N.Y.C., 1989—. Mem. NAFE, Delta Delta Delta (pres. 1977-78). Republican. Methodist. Home: 717 Tupelo Crossing Chesapeake VA 23320 Office: Procter & Gamble Distbg Co 100 Walnut Ave Clark NJ 07066

CARLSON, NANCY LEE, English language educator; b. Spokane, Wash., June 1, 1950; d. Alfred William and Geneva May (Conniff) C. BS, Wash. State U., 1973; MEd, curriculum specialist, Ea. Wash. U., 1987. Tchr. Stevenson-Carson Sch. Dist., Wash., 1973-74, Spokane Sch. Dist., 1974—; vis. faculty Ea. Wash. U., 1989—. Spokane County co-chmn. Sen. Slade Gordon campaign, 1988; Rep. precinct committeesperson, 1988-90; bd. dirs. Spokane Civic Theater, 1986—; mem. Spokane Human Svcs. Adv. Bd., 1986—, chmn., 1990—; treas. Inland Empire for Africa, Spokane, 1985-86; vice chmn. Ea. Wash. phone bank for Sen. Dan Evans, Spokane, 1984; mem. Mayor's Task Force on the Homeless, 1987-88; mem. adv. com. for Sen. Slade Gorton's campaign, 1989—. Mem. NEA, Nat. Coun. Tchrs. English, Wash. Coun. Tchrs. English, Assn. for Supervision and Curriculum Devel., Am. Mgmt. Assn., Wash. Edn. Assn., Spokane Edn. Assn., Wash. State U. Alumni Assn. (area rep. 1987—). Republican. Presbyterian. Office: Rogers High Sch Sch Dist #81 E 1622 Wellesley Spokane WA 99207

CARLSON, RIA MARIE, public relations executive, writer; b. Los Angeles, Apr. 8, 1961; d. Erick Gustaf and Roberta Rae (Bandelin) C.; m. James Bradley Gerdts, May 19, 1985. BA cum laude, U. So. Calif., 1983. Assoc. producer NBC, Burbank, Calif., 1982-85; account exec. Kerr & Assocs. Pub. Rels., Huntington Beach, Calif., 1985-86; pub. rels. mgr. Orange County Performing Arts Ctr., Costa Mesa, Calif., 1986-88; dir. pub. rels. and mktg. Bowers Mus., Santa Ana, Calif., 1988-90; dir. pub. rels. FHP Internat. Corp., Fountain Valley, Calif., 1990—; free-lance writer, 1985—. Scriptwriter award ceremony Latin Bus. Assn., 1985; author, editor newsletter Am. Sch. Food Svc. Assn. Bus. Report, 1985-86; assoc. editor Revue mag., 1987; editor Artifacts mag., 1988—; contbr. articles to publs; cast mem. Disneyland, Anaheim, Calif. Prodn. asst. Profiles in Pride, Black History Month, Burbank, 1985. Named one of Outstanding Young Women in Am., 1985. Mem. AAUW (bd. dirs. pub. rels., br. officer), Pub. Rels. Soc. Am., NAFE, Women in Communications, Am. Film Inst., U. So. Calif. Alumni Assn., Blackstonians Pre-Law Hon. Soc. (life), Calif. Scholarship Fedn. (sealbearer, life). Republican. Roman Catholic. Avocations: writing short stories, reading, skiing, softball, travel. Office: FHP Corp Hdqrts 9900 Talbert Ave Fountain Valley CA 92708

CARLSON, RUTH ELLEN, health care company executive; b. Geneva, Ill., Jan. 21, 1952; d. Frederick William and Ann Marie (Hookham) C. Student, Iowa State U., 1970-72; MBA, U. Chgo., 1976. Brand mgr. Procter & Gamble Co., Cin., 1976-82; mktg. dir. Wm. Wrigley Jr. Co., Chgo., 1982-86; v.p. footcare product mgmt. Schering-Plough Health Care Inc., Liberty Corner, N.J., 1987—. Office: Schering-Plough Health Care Products Inc Allen Rd Liberty Corner NJ 07938

CARLSON, SARAH ANN, state representative; b. Jamestown, N.D., Oct. 13, 1966; d. Ervin Adolph and Phyllis Jean (Layton) C. BA in Polit. Sci., U.N.D., 1988, postgrad., 1988—. Mem. N.D. Ho. of Reps., Bismarck, 1988—. Pres. U. N.D. Dems., Grand Forks, 1986, 87, N.D. Young Dems., Grand Forks, 1987, 88 (named Outstanding N.D. Young Dem. 1988). Lutheran. Home: 1324 2nd Ave N Grand Forks ND 58203

CARLSON, TINA MARIE, company executive; b. St. Charles, Ill., Feb. 3, 1958; d. Ivan Alfred and Blanche Ione (Scott) C. Student, No. Ill. U., 1976-77, Columbia Coll., Chgo., 1977-81. Catering mgr. Galleon, St. Charles, 1980-83; v.p. mktg. Ivan Carlson & Assocs., Chgo., 1983-87, pres., 1987—; lectr. in field. Author newsletter column; mem. adv. bd. Spl. Event Mag., 1987—. Mem. Internat. Spl. Events Soc. Republican. Episcopalian. Home: 415 Covington Terr Buffalo Grove IL 60089 Office: Ivan Carlson & Assocs 225 N Racine Chicago IL 60607

CARLTON, CAROL LEE, librarian; b. Williamson, W.Va., Mar. 19, 1941; d. Samuel Howard and Edna Lorraine (Moore) C.; m. Jim Charles Harris, Mar. 16, 1963 (div. Mar. 1968). AS in Med. Tech., Bluefield (Va.) Coll., 1961; BS in Secondary Edn., Pikeville (Ky.) Coll., 1966; MS in Community Devel., U. Louisville, 1972; MS in Libr. Sci., U. Ky., 1978. Supr. bacteriology dept. Harlan (Ky.) Appalachian Regional Hosp., 1963-64; social worker Juvenile Ct. Ky. Dept. Child Welfare, Pikeville, 1966-67; asst. chief technologist ARC Regional Blood Ctr., Louisville, 1967-68; social svc. worker W.Va. Dept. of Welfare, Williamson, 1968-73; quality control reviewer, state hearing officer W.Va. Dept. of Welfare, Charleston, 1973-74; supr. family svcs. W.Va. Dept. of Welfare, Williamson, 1974-77; grad. asst. U. Ky., Lexington Tech. Inst., 1977-78; asst. libr. U. Ky., S.E. Community Coll., Cumberland, 1978-80; libr. So. W.Va. Community Coll., Williamson, 1980-90, head libr., 1990—. Mem. Am. Bapt. Conv. Devel. Faculty grantee Ky. Coun. Higher Edn., 1980, Coll. Libr. Tech. and Cooperation Networking grantee U.S. Dept. Edn., 1990. Mem. AAUW (chair various coms. Williamson chpt. 1982—), Registry Med. Technologists, Ky. Libr. Assn. W.Va. Libr. Assn., W.Va. Community Coll. Assn., Women of the Moose, Beta Phi Mu, Phi Alpha Theta, Phi Theta Kappa. Democrat. Office: So WVa Community Coll Dept Librs Armory Rd Williamson WV 25661

CARLTON, CLAUDIA DOWDY, library automation consultant; b. Richmond, Va., May 20, 1955; d. Carroll Burns and Caroline Byerly (Putney) Dowdy; m. Marvin McCray Spencer, May 17, 1973 (div. June 1980); m. James John Carlton, June 28, 1983; children: Justin Stafford, Amy Shay. BS in Art Edn. and Library Sci., Longwood Coll., 1976. Librarian Cumberland County (Va.) Schs., 1976-79, Goochland County (Va.) Schs., 1979-80; media specialist Seminole County Schs., Sanford, Fla., 1980-81; software cons. Follett Library Book Co., Crystal Lake, Ill., 1981-83; pvt. practive library automation cons. Fla., 1983—. Leader Girl Scouts U.S.A., Cumberland, Va., 1976-77; coordinator Boy Scouts Am., 1977-79; pres. Cumberland County PTA, 1977-78; mem. pub. relations com. Cumberland Vol. Rescue Squad, 1979-80. Mem. NEA, Va. Edn. Assn., Ga. Library/Media Dirs., Fla. Assn. Instrnl. Materials. Home and Office: PO Box 1318 Mount Dora FL 32757

CARLTON, MARION CLADE, educator; b. New Orleans, June 6, 1917; d. Edward Jacob and Magdelena (Gleber) Clade; m. John Powell Carlton, 1940; children: John Jr., Claire Schneider, Edward, Marion Hebbler, Michael, Carol Exnicios. PhB, Loyola U., New Orleans, 1937, MEd, 1971; tchr.'s diploma, New Orleans Sch. Speech Drama, 1937. Tchr. St. Stephen's Sch., New Orleans, 1937-38; substitute tchr. New Orleans Pub. Schs., 1938-40; tchr. St. Joseph's Acad., New Orleans, 1940-42, Acad. Holy Angels, New Orleans, 1960—. Mem. AAUW, Cosmopals, Aux. of Cosmopolitan Internat., Kappa Delta Pi. Democrat. Roman Catholic. Home: 4619 Schindler Dr New Orleans LA 70127

CARMACK, PAULA LENORA, education educator; b. East Chicago, Ind., May 10, 1951; d. John Edward and Mittie Marie (Brown) Jones; m. Everett Carmack, Oct. 14, 1972 (div. June 1981); children: Erin Joi Carmack, Amen-Ra Banks. BS, Chgo. State U., 1972; MS, DePaul U., Chgo., 1976. Credut collector Sears Roebuck and Credit Co., Chgo., 1970-72; reservationist Conrad Hilton Hotel, Chgo., 1971-72; educator Chgo. Bd. Edn., 1974--; delegate Chgo. Tchrs. Union, 1987--. Mem. Chgo. Assn. Black Sch. Educators, Eastern Star. Democrat.

CARMAN, HOLLY LYNN, food processing professional; b. Montpelier, Ohio, Oct. 28, 1953; d. William Lewis and Willene (Childers) Mead; m. Leroy Junior Carman, Jan. 15, 1972; 1 child, Eric Christopher. Lic. stationary engr., Ohio. Bookkeeper, cook W. and W. Truck Stop, Montpelier, 1970-72; mgr. D. and M. Cafe, Edon, Ohio, 1974-76; sales rep. Avon Products, Edon, 1975-77; boiler operator Dimension Veneers, Edon, 1978-79;

bus. mgr. Bishop and Kell Personnel, Edon, 1985-87; lead stationary engr. LaChoy Food Products, Archbold, Ohio, 1979-86; prodn. lead person Fox Packaging, Montpelier, 1986-87; quality assurance mgr. Classic Food Products, Montpelier, 1987-89; sanitation supr. Rich Products Corp., Hilliard, Ohio, 1989—. Adviser, counselor 4-H Club, Edon, 1970-75; cubmaster Boy Scouts Am., Edon, 1981-82; chair St. Jude's Bike-a-Thon, Edon, 1982-85; dir., instr. ice skating program Bryan (Ohio) Parks Dept., 1986—. Mem. NAFE, Ice Skating Inst. Am. (performer, choreographer 1985—). Office: Rich Products Corp 4600 Northwest Pkwy Hilliard OH 43026

CARMAN, LAURALEE, computer company executive, consultant; b. Phoenix, May 28, 1964; d. John W. Peters and Janet May (Muder) Hiscoe; m. Brian S. Carman, July 23, 1983. Student, Portland (Oreg.) Community Coll., 1980-82. Asst. project mgr. No. Telecom, Santa Maria, Calif., 1981-82; customer svc. Savenet, Portland, 1982-84; acct. exec. Finzer Bus., Portland, 1984-86; western sales mgr. Abaton Tech., San Francisco, 1986-87; prin. DTP Cons., San Francisco, 1986-87; western sales mgr. DEST Corp., San Francisco, 1987-88; founder, pres. Adelphi Corp., San Ramon, Calif., 1988—. Mem. Nat. Assn. Female Execs. Home: 73 Chancellor Ct Alamo CA 94507 Office: Adelphi Corp 2420 Camino Ramon Ste 140 San Ramon CA 94583

CARMICHAEL, ANN CROCKER, academic administrator; b. Union, S.C., Oct. 11, 1955; d. Arthur William and Ruth (O'Shields) Crocker; m. Ernest Ray Carmichael, Jr.; 1 child, Catherine O'Shields. AA, Anderson Coll., 1975; BS, Lander Coll., 1977; MEd, Clemson U., 1978; PhD, U.S.C., 1986. Lic. profl. counselor;. Administrv. asst. Anderson Coll., S.C., 1979; dean of students Judson Coll., marion, Ala., 1979-80; dir. Counseling Ctr., Charleston, S.C., 1980-88; dean of students Baptist Coll., Charleston, 1986-88, assoc. v.p., asst. prof. of edn, 1988—. Mem. Nat. Bd. Cert. Counselors, S. C. Coll. Personnel Assn., Am. Assn. for Counseling and Devel., Southern Assn. for Coll. Student Affairs. Baptist. Office: Baptist Coll Box 10087 Charleston SC 29411

CARMICHAEL, CHARLOTTE MARIE BREEDEN, telecommunications consultant, realtor; b. Warrenton, Va., Mar. 24, 1945; d. Albert Aldine and Winnie (Hensley) Breeden; m. Michael William Carmichael, Feb. 6, 1965; children: Kathy Lynn, Bryan William. BS with High Honors, Va. Commonwealth U., 1967; postgrad., U. Va., 1971-72. Owner Intercontinental Telecommunications, Inc., Houston, 1983—, Carmichael Communications Cons., Inc., Houston, 1982—, ITI of Utah, Salt Lake City, 1985—. Mem. NAFE, Am. Soc. Profl. and Exec. Women. Republican. Mormon. Office: ITI 4900 Woodway Suite 950 Houston TX 77056

CARMINES, PAMELA KAY, physiologist; b. Hampton, Va., May 6, 1955; d. John Sterling Carmines and Janet Celeste Leffers. BS, Longwood Coll., Farmville, 1977; PhD, Ind. U., Indianapolis, 1982. Postdoctoral fellow U. Ala., Birmingham, Ala., 1982-85; research instr. U. Ala., Birmingham, 1984-86, research asst. profr., 1986-88; asst. prof. Tulane U. Sch. Medicine, New Orleans, 1988—; bd. med. adv. Ala. Kidney Found., Birmingham, 1986-88. Contbr. articles to profl. jours. Recipient First Award NIH-Nat. Inst. Diabetes and Digestive and Kidney Diseases, 1987-90, Established Investigatorship award, Am. Heart Assn., 1990-95. Mem. Am. Physiol. Soc., Microcirculatory Soc., Am. Soc. Nephrology, Am. Heart Assn., Internat. Soc. Nephrology, AAAS, Sigma Xi, Phi Mu. Office: Tulane U Sch Medicine Psysiology Dept 1430 Tulane Ave New Orleans LA 70112

CARMODY, SUSAN DOLORES, sales professional; b. Phila., Apr. 26, 1953; d. Thomas James and Dolores Theresa (Stewart) C. AS, Harcum Jr. Coll., Bryn Mawr, Pa., 1979; student, Phila. Coll. Sci. and Textiles, 1983-84. Asst. store mgr. Hit or Miss, Dresner, Pa., 1979-80; dept. mgr. Pomeroy's Allied Corp., Levittown, Pa., 1980-83, asst. buyer, 1983-84; co-mgr. Victoria's Secret Stores div. Ltd. Inc., Willow Grove, Pa., 1984-85, store mgr., 1985-86; store mgr. Victoria's Secret Stores div. Ltd. Inc., Balt., 1986-88; dist. sales mgr. Victoria's Secret Stores div. Ltd. Inc., Phila., 1988—. Office: Victoria's Secret Stores 2300 E Lincoln Hwy Langhorne PA 19047

CARMODY-AREY, CHRISTINE, educator; b. N.Y.C., Dec. 29, 1938; d. John Joseph and Mary Agnes (Daly) Carmody; m. Robert A. Arey, July 14; 1 child, Howard John Arey. BA, Jersey City State Coll., 1980, postgrad. cons. women's rights, Jersey City, 1985—; prof. Katharine Gibbs Sch., Montclair, N.J., 1989. Adminstrv. asst. W.R. Grace & Co., N.Y.C., 1967-69; pres. NOW of N.J., Trenton, 1981-85; prof. Jersey City (N.J.) State Coll., 1985—; cons. women's rights, Jersey City, 1985—. Del. Dem. Conv., San Francisco, 1984; legis. cons. Nat. Assn. for Advancement of Psychoanalysis, N.Y.C., 1986. Recipient Jersey Jour. Woman of Achievement, Jersey Jour., 1978, Jersey City Parents Coun. award, Traffic, Health and Safety Chair, 1979; named N.J. Most Powerful Women, N.J. Mag., 1983, One of Six Jersey Women to Watch in 1985, Jersey Woman Mag., 1985. Mem. N.J. Assembly (pres. 1981-85, Dedicated Svc. award, 1985), Am. Fedn. Tchrs., Phi Delta Kappa. Democrat. Roman Catholic. Home: 44 Broadman Pkwy Jersey City NJ 07305

CARNAHAN, FRANCES MORRIS, magazine editor; b. Evergreen, Ala., Oct. 28, 1937; d. Houston DeLeon and Rene Vester (Bass) Morris; m. Peter Malott Carnahan, Feb. 13, 1960; children—Brian Morris, Edmund Malott. Student, U. Ala., 1956-58. With Mobile Press-Register, 1956-58; with H.L. Green Co., N.Y.C., 1958-60, J.H. Lewis Advt. Agy., Mobile, 1960-61, Early Am. Life mag., Cowles Mags. Inc., Hist. Times, Inc., Harrisburg, Pa., 1972—; editor Early Am. Life, 1975—. Costume designer, Harrisburg Community Theatre, 1961-71, Gov. Pa. Sch., 1976-77; Author articles. Mem. Am. Soc. Mag. Editors. Home: 1524 Greening Ln Harrisburg PA 17110 Office: Early American Life Box 8200 2245 Kohn Rd Harrisburg PA 17105

CARNERA, GIOVANNA MARIA, hospital executive; b. Sequals, Udine, Italy, June 5, 1947; came to U.S., 1949; d. Primo and Giuseppina Pina (Kovacic) Carnera; m. Philip Barry Alderson, Feb. 8, 1966 (dec. 1976); children: Anne Marie, Karl Umberto; m. Virgil Joseph Hamilton, Aug. 19, 1983. BA, UCLA, 1969; Laureata, Educadato Uccellis, Italy, 1965; postgrad., Sangamon State U., Springfield, Ill. Cert. alcoholism counselor. Adminstrv. asst. Glendale Fed. Savs., Los Angeles, 1976-78, Sitmar Cruises, Los Angeles, 1978-80; internat. relations specialist Bernardin SpA, Milan, 1980-82; employee assistance program specialist Sangamon-Menard Alcoholism & Drugs Council, Springfield, Ill., 1982-87, St. John's Hosp., Springfield, 1987—; cons. in field. Contbr. articles to profl. jours. Chmn. Mother's Against Drunk Drivers, Springfield, 1982; bd. dirs. The Parent Place, Springfield, 1988—. Mem. Nat. Assn. Female Execs., Assn. Labor and Mgmt. (cons. on alcoholism), Springfield C. of C. Democrat. Roman Catholic. Home: 1837 Hastings Rd Springfield IL 62702 Office: St John's Hosp 800 E Carpenter St Springfield IL 62729

CARNEVALE, SALLY LONDON, textile sales and marketing executive; b. Newark, Mar. 17, 1954; d. Allen Jay and Elaine (Rose) London; m. Louis Michael Carnevale, May 25, 1980. BS in Textiles and Chemistry, U. Del., 1976; MBA, U. Wis., 1978. Consultant/auditor, Business Advisory Center, Wausau, Wis., 1977-78 Market planner Celanese Corp., Charlotte, N.C., 1978-80, market research analyst, Celanese Fibers operations, N.Y.C., 1980-82, planning coordinator, 1982-83, fiber sales and home furnishings merchandising rep., 1983-84; product mgr. home furnishings Collins & Aikman Corp., N.Y.C., 1984-85, nat. sales mgr. home furnishings, 1985-87, dir. sales, 1987—. Mem. Big Bro./Big Sister Program, Newark, Del., 1973-76, program coordinator, Madison, Wis., 1976-78; vol. tutor Dept. Social Services, various locations, 1975-80; Com. mem., life mem. Hadassah, 1981—. Mem. Am. Mktg. Assn., Am. Field Service, Mu Kappa Tau. Home: 253 E Palisade Ave Englewood NJ 07631 Office: Collins & Aikman Corp 210 Madison Ave New York NY 10016

CARNEY, CLAIRE T(HERESE), real estate executive; b. New Bedford, Mass., June 18, 1922; d. Philippe and Rose Anna (Belhumeur) Galipeau; m. Hugh J. Carney, Feb. 19, 1944 (dec. May 1962); children: Doreen, Patrick, Mark, Hugh Jay. BA, Southeastern Mass. U., 1973, LHD, 1990. Dep. collector IRS, New Bedford, 1945-47; cost acct. Morse Twist Drill and Machine Co., New Bedford, 1961-68; treas. Claremont Corp., New Bedford and Quincy, Mass., 1968—, Claremont Devel. Assocs., Quincy, 1968—. Chmn. Dartmouth (Mass.) Hist. Soc., 1981-89, New Bedford Whaling Mus., 1986—; trustee, vice-chmn. Southeastern Mass. U., Dartmouth, 1981-89; mem. adv. bd. New Bedford Symphony Orch., 1985-88; advisor Bierstadt Art Soc., 1986-90; mem. adv. bd. Share, 1989—; bd. dirs. Ctr. for Rehab. Engring., 1989—. Recipient Share Found. award, 1989; named 1st Woman of Yr., YWCA Tribute, 1984. Mem. Cath. Womens Club, Southeastern Mass. Alumni Assn. (ex-officio 1979-89, svcaward 1982). Home: Broken Sound 2451 NW 63 St Boca Raton FL 33496 Office: Claremont Regency 800 Pleasant St New Bedford MA 02742

CARNEY, JEAN KATHRYN, psychologist; b. Ft. Dodge, Ia., Nov. 10, 1948; d. Eugene James and Lucy (Devlin) C.; m. Mark Krupnick, Jan. 1, 1977; 1 child, Joseph Carney Krupnick. BA, Marquette U., Milw., 1970; MA, U. Chgo., Chgo., 1984; PhD, U. Chgo., 1986. Registered Clin. Psychologist, Ill. Reporter Milw. Jour., 1971-76, editorial writer, 1976-79; asst. prof. psychology St. Xavier Coll., Chgo., 1985-86; dir. Lincoln Park Clinic, Chgo., 1986-87; pvt. practice psychotherapist Chgo., 1987--; mem. med. staff Michael Reese Hosp. Med. Ctr., Chgo., 1987-. Recipient Best Series Articles, 1975, Best Editorial, 1978, Milw. Press Club, William Allen White Nat. Award for Editorial Writing, 1978, Robert Kahn Meml. Award for Research on Aging, Univ. Chgo., 1985. Mem. Am. Psychol. Assn., Ill. Psychol. Assn. Home: 5526 S Cornell Ave Chicago IL 60637 Office: 55 E Washington Ste 1219 Chicago IL 60602

CARNEY, KATHLEEN L., interior designer; b. Cleve., Dec. 19, 1947; d. Joseph Smythe and Irene (Smith) Walsh; m. James A. Carney, July 18, 1970; 1 child, James Kenneth. BA, Barat Coll. Sacred Heart, Lake Forest, Ill., 1969. Cert. interior designer, Ohio, Ill. Tchr. Cleve. Bd. Edn., 1969-71; owner The Mart - Antiques & Interiors, Rocky River, Ohio, 1985—. Jr. League Cleve., 1978—; fundraiser, liaison Malachi House Cleve., 1987—; patron mem. women's com. Cleve. Orch.; active Pioneer Womens bd. Western Res. Acad., Hudson, Ohio, 1987-88; bd. dirs. Cleve. Montessori Assn. Cleve., 1977—; active ARC. Mem. Am. Women's Econ. Devel. Corp., Allied Bd. Trade, Westwood Country Club. Democrat. Roman Catholic. Home: 65 Kensington Oval Rocky River OH 44116 Office: The Mart 28691 Center Ridge Rd Westlake OH 44145

CARNEY, KAY, actress, director, educator; b. Rice Lake, Wis., Aug. 2, 1933; d. Rexford Hugh and Margot Caroline (Haanstad) C. B.S., U. Wis., 1955; M.A., Mt. Holyoke Coll., 1958; postgrad., Centre du Théâtre National, 1970, Columbia U. and Case-Western Res. U., 1957-63; Creative Arts fellow U. Colo., 1963. Actress performing in London, Paris, Istanbul, Ankara, Tel Aviv and Nicosia, 1970-72, performing in Off Off-Broadway! An Anthology with Kay Carney, N.Y.C., Chgo., San Francisco, Vancouver, Balt., Phila., Boston and various U.S. colls., 1973—, The Mothers by Maria Irene Fornes, Ubu Repetory Theatre, N.Y.C., 1987; performed Tonques, 1985, Camptown Ladies, 1986, Age of Enlightenment, 1986, Vacancy, 1987; dir. Mourning Pictures, Broadway and Lenox Arts Ctr., 1974, A Pretty Passion, Interart Theatre, N.Y.C., 1982, Quilt Pieces, Theatre of Open Eye, N.Y.C., 1983, Superwoman Bites the Dust, Playwright's Platform, Boston, 1984, The Mothers, Ubu Repetory Theatre, Airport, Theater at St. Peter's, 1988, A Good Time, Playwright's Horizons, N.Y.C., 1988, Sleep Disturbances, Am. Renaissance Theatre, N.Y.C., 1989, numerous others; tchr. acting, directing and psychophys. work Hunter Coll., Henry St. Playhouse, SUNY, Purchase, U. Calif.-Santa Cruz, 1977-80; assoc. prof. dept. theatre Smith Coll., Northampton, Mass., 1980-82, Bklyn. Coll., 1983-87; tchr. Ensemble Studio Theatre Inst., 1987, Brandeis U., 1989—; condr. workshops for profls. in U.S. and abroad, Coll. of Charleston, 1989, Marymount Manhaltan Coll., 1988; organizer, trainer La Mama theatre groups, Paris and Tel Aviv; bd. dirs. Bear Rep. Theatre, 1977-79; performed with Open Theater, 1965-67; seminarian with Jerzy Grotowski, 1970. Moratorium organizer, performer Angry Artists Against the War, 1966-70; mem. Performing Artists for Nuclear Disarmament, 1981—, St. Clements Arts in Religious Action Com., 1972-75; organizer Bay Area Women in Theatre Orgn., 1978-80; contbr. articles to profl. jours. Kosciuszko Found. grantee, 1979, SUNY Rsch. Found. grantee, 1976. Mem. Soc. Stage Dirs. and Choreographers, Actors Equity, AFTRA, East Cen. Theatre Conf., Women and Theatre Program, Assn. for Theatre in Higher Edn. (presenter nat. convs.), League Profl. Theatre Women/N.Y. Democrat. Episcopalian.les to profl. jours. Office: Brandeis U Theatre Arts Dept Box 9110 Waltham MA 02254-9110

CARNEY, PHILLITA TOYIA, marketing communications management company executive; b. Chgo., Apr. 18, 1952; d. Phillip Leon Carney and Margaret Clarice (Ewing) Brown. Student, U. Utah, 1971-74; BS in Bus., Westminster Coll., 1976. Ordained to ministry Full Gospel Ch., 1989. Corp. tng. dir. U&I Sugar Corp., Salt Lake City, also Moses Lake, Wash., 1976-77; program coordinator Div. on Aging, Seattle, 1977-78; bus. devel. officer Del Green Assoc., Foster City, Calif., 1978-79; regional v.p. Equitec Fin. Group, San Francisco, Irvine and Oakland, Calif., 1979-84, United Resources, Oakland, San Francisco, Nev., 1984-86; owner, mgr. Carney & Assocs., Oakland, 1986; regional v.p. Eastcoast Ops. Benefits Communications Corp. div. Great West Life Assurance Co., Washington, 1986-87; nat. dir. enrollment services, nat. plan adminstr. U.S. Conf. Mayors Fringe Benefits Program, MCW Internat., Ltd., 1988—; dir. pub. rels. nat./internat. Liberty Temple Full Gospel Ch. and World Out Reach Ministries, Chgo., 1989—; dir. Total One, San Francisco; corp. cons., advisor Am. Intermediation Services, San Francisco, 1986; nat. dir. communications and enrollment services for U.S. Conf. Mayor's flexible benefits plan MCW Internat., Ltd., 1988—; cons. Washington Literacy Council; sr. bus. cons., prnr. Performance Strategies Inc., San Diego, 1986. Moderator, creator pub. affairs radio program, 1975-76 (Best Pub. Affairs Program award Nat. Pub. Radio 1976). Del. White House Conf. on Small Bus., Washington, 1986; mem., lobbyist Concerned Women for Am., 1987; dir. communications U.S. Conf. Mayors, MCW Internat., Nat. Adminstrs. Recipient award Am. Legion, 1970, DAR, 1970. Fellow Am. Biog. Inst. Research Assn. (assoc., nat. advisor); mem. Internat. Assn. Fin. Planning, Women Entrepreneurs, Internat. Biog. Ctr., Bus. and Profl. Women, Sales Mktg. Exec. Assn., Zonta Internat. (pres. 1985—). Avocations: jogging, swimming, reading, writing. Home: 10925 S Wood Chicago IL 60643

CARNICKE, SHARON MARIE, theatre specialist and director; b. Bridgeport, Conn., July 28, 1949; d. Stephen J. and Evelyn (Furjesz) C. Cert. Russian Lang., Moscow U., USSR, 1970; AB, Barnard Coll., 1971; MA, NYU, 1973; PhD, Columbia U., 1979. Asst. prof. Sch. Visual Arts, N.Y.C., 1980-83; coord., core curriculum Columbia U., N.Y.C., 1978-83; asst. dean, curriculum NYU, 1983-86, asst. prof., English, 1984-87; asst. prof., drama U. So. Calif., L.A., 1987—; Russian evaluator, Nat. Endowment of the Arts, Washington, 1984-87; cons. core curriculum Sch. Visual Arts, N.Y.C., 1980-83; interpretor Soviet Dirs. at Actors Studio, N.Y.C., 1978. Contbr. articles to profl. jours.; author: The Theatrical Instinct, 1989; translator plays from Russian, Chekhov and New Soviet, 1970—; adaptor, trans. plays: The Storm, Blackforest, 1978, 89. Interpretor Am. Soviet Youth Forum, USA, USSR, 1973-74. Fellowship Am. Coun. Learned Socs., 1988-89, Rockefeller Found., U. Wis., Madison, 1988, Mogilat-Mihaly fellowship, USSR, 1978; grantee Institut d'etudes slaves, La Sorbonne, France, 1979. Mem. Am. Lit. Translators Assn., Dramatists Guild, MLA. Office: U So Calif Div Drama-DRC Los Angeles CA 90089-0791

CARNIE, MARY CATHERINE, television station executive; b. Clayton, Ala., Oct. 25, 1938; d. Ories Kendall and Harriet Catherine (Scheffer) White; m. Gary Miles Carnie, Dec. 22, 1958 (div. May 1969); 1 child, Kendall Joanne. Cert. in Acting, Pasadena Playhouse Coll. Theatre Arts, 1959. Profl. actress Turn of the Century Cabaret Theatre, El Paso, Tex., 1962-73; co-author stage play A Story Of Tender Love, Or Mass Entanglement In The Tender Trap, 1964; continuity asst. KROD-TV, El Paso, 1968-69; drama critic El Paso Jour., 1977-78; continuity dir. KDBC-TV, El Paso, 1969—; continuity/promotion mgr. KDBC-TV, El Paso, 1982—; tchr.'s aide El Paso Pub. Schs., 1967; researcher Biog. Dictionary, Notable Women in Am. Theatre, 1982; scriptwriter Your Chamber and You, 1981, Your Zoo Needs You, 1973. Contbr. articles to profl. jours. Mem. task force Cultural Planning Project, El Paso, 1985; dir. edn. El Paso Zool. Soc. Bd., 1974; bd. dirs. Delta Day Care Ctr., 1973-78; mem. scholarship com., vocat. placement adv. com. El Paso/Ysleta Ind. Sch. Dist., 1979—; ruling elder Presbyn. Ch., 1971-77. Flat Rock Playhouse scholar, 1960. Mem. Actor's Fund Am. (life), Broadcasting Promotion and Mktg. Execs., Tex. Press Women (recording sec. 1983-85), Nat. Fedn. Press Women. Club: United Presbyn. Women. Avocations: reading; traveling. Home: 315 S Ascarate St El Paso TX 79905 Office: Sta KDBC-TV 2201 Wyoming El Paso TX 79903

CARNIGLIA, SHERRY, advertising agency executive. V.p., then sr. v.p. J. Walter Thompson U.S.A., Inc., San Francisco, now sr. v.p., dep. gen. mgr. Office: J Walter Thompson USA Inc 4 Embarcadero Ctr Ste 900 San Francisco CA 94111*

CAROLIN, CAROL ANNE, service executive; b. Syracuse, N.Y., July 23, 2348; d. Michael and Carmel Frances (Masterpol) Wuzela; m. Robert E.; children Douglas Charles, Christine Anne. Postgrad., syracuse U., 1981. Cert. Hotel Adminstr. Food & Beverage supr. Holiday Inns, Syracuse, 1971-73; sales & catering mgr. Holiday Inns, E Syracuse, N.Y., 1973-75; hotel gen. mgr. Holiday Inns, E Syracuse, 1975-77, Holiday Inns., Baldwinsville, N.Y., Holiday Inns, N Syracuse, N.Y., 1979-82; hotel, devel. cons. Tygate Hotel Corp., Vt., 1982-85, Uccellini United Group of Cos., Albany, N.Y., 1985—; hotel gen. mgr. Uccellinin United Group of Cos., DBA Quality Inn, Fulton, N.Y., 1987--; cons. in field. Bd. dirs. Onon. County Commission on Tourism, Syracuse, N.Y., 1978-80, Oswego County Commission on Tourism, 1988--. Recipient: Distinguished Service Cert., United State Air Force, 1974, Class VP award, Holiday Inn U., 1975; named: Honorary Brewmaster, Anheuser Busch, 1978. mem. Greater Syrcacuse C. of C. (bd. dirs., 1975-82; v.p., 1979-80; pres. 1980-81) Greater Fulton C. of C. (bd. dirs. 1988--), Internat. Mgmt. Council. Roman Catholic. Office: Quality Inn 930 S First St Fulton NY 13069

CARON-PARKER, LAURA MARIE, occupational therapist; b. Seattle, July 27, 1959; d. Charles William and Gwendolyn Mary (Carlson) C. BA in Occupational Therapy, Coll. St. Catherine, St. Paul, 1981. Registered occupational therapist. Mem. occupational therapy staff Meml. Med. Ctr., Long Beach, Calif., 1982; occupational therapist Marina Profl. Services, Long Beach, 1982-84; mem. occupational therapy staff Meml. Health Techs., Long Beach, 1983-84, coordinator stroke rehab. team, 1983-84; dir. occupational therapy Intermountain Health Care Rehab. Services, Orange, Calif., 1984-87, regional dir. L.A. area, 1987-88; regional coordinator Los Angeles area Intermountain Health Care Therapy Mgmt., Orange, 1988—; cons. Am. Heart Assn., L.A., 1986—; founder, coordinator Gerontic Network, L.A., 1987—; co-founder, coordinator P.D.R. Walkers, L.A., 1987—; recruiter Coll. St. Catherine, Newport Beach, Calif., 1983-88. Mem. Am. Occupational Therapy Assn., Occupational Therapy Assn. Calif. (pub. relations liaison 1986-87, key person to legislature 1987 SELAC chpt., govt. affairs subcom. 1988, rep. on spl. interest sect. gerontology, mem. practice com.), Los Angeles Occupational Therapy Dirs. Forum (mem. edn. com. 1988-89, exec. com. 1988-89), World Fedn. Occupational Therapy, Am. Soc. on Aging, Nat. Citizen's Coalition for Nursing Home Reform, Inst. for Profl. Health Service Adminstrs. (charter mem.), Coll. St. Catherine Alumni Assn. (v.p. Orange County chpt.). Home: 2021 Ocean Ave #225 Santa Monica CA 90405 Office: IHC Therapy Mgmt 1915 W Orangewood Ave Ste 212 Orange CA 92668

CAROZZOLO, SHIRLEY JEAN, clergywoman; b. Buffalo, Nov. 21, 1935; d. Albert A. and Jean Louise (Hanna) La Chiusa; m. Vito A. Carozzolo, Sept. 17, 1966; children: Michael John Kurban, David Charles Kurban. Various secretarial positions, 1953-55, 68-74; office mgr. Haney Erection Services Inc., Tonawanda, N.Y., 1975-76, corp. sec., 1976-84, EEO officer, 1980-84; ordained minister of gospel Full Gospel Assemblies Internat.; corp. sec.-treas. New Covenant Evang. Ministries Inc., 1984-87; fin. adminstr. World Outreach Conf., 1985; treas. New Covenant Tabernacle, 1985—. Mem. Niagara Frontier Subcontractors Assn. (membership chmn. 1978), Leadership Council Western N.Y., Prison Fellowship Local Council of Western N.Y., Am. Mgmt. Assn., Am. Soc. Profl. and Exec. Women, Christian Ministries Mgmt. Assn. (1st v.p. 1985-87), Nat. Assn. Ch. Bus. Adminstrs., Christian Found. for the Performing Arts (treas. 1986-87, univ. pres. 1989), Zonta (1st v.p. 1979-81, pres. 1981-82). Republican. Home: 426 Ashford Ave Tonawanda NY 14150 Office: 1 World Ministries Ctr Buffalo NY 14223

CARPENTER, CAROL SETTLE, banker; b. Schenectady, Oct. 22, 1953; d. Carl Oscar and Ursula Elsen (McEldowney) Settle; m. R. Jay Carpenter, May 4, 1985; 1 child, Reilly. BBA, Rochester Inst. Tech., 1975, postgrad. Inst. Children's Lit., 1988-90. Mgmt. trainee Lincoln First Bank, Rochester, N.Y., 1976-77; investment sec. Blyth Eastman Dillon, Scottsdale, Ariz., 1977-79; stockbroker E.F. Hutton, Scottsdale, 1979; stockbroker Rauscher Pierce Refsnes, Scottsdale, 1979-81; exec. v.p. RL Kotrozo Inc., Scottsdale, Ariz., 1981-85; asst. v.p. United Bank Ariz., Phoenix, 1985-88; asst. v.p. investments Citibank, Phoenix, 1988—. Staff vol. Crisis Nursery, Phoenix, 1987; mem. Contemporary Art Forum. Mem. Nat. Assn. Female Execs., Phi Gamma Nu. Republican. Presbyterian. Clubs: Plaza (Phoenix) (promotion chmn. 1986-87 , membership devel. 1988), Phoenix Country. Avocations: music, art, writing for children. Home: 374 E Verde Ln Phoenix AZ 85012 Office: Citibank 302 N First Ave Ste 300 Phoenix AZ 85003

CARPENTER, CHRISTY, public relations executive; b. Washington, Dec. 15, 1949; d. Leslie Elisha and Liz (Sutherland) C. BA, Brown U., Providence, 1972; JD, Am. U., Washington, 1975. Law clk. to presiding justice U.S. Supreme Ct., Washington, 1976-77; spl. asst. to asst. sec. of commerce U.S. Dept. Commerce, Washington, 1977-79; dir. market devel. Warner Amex Cable Communications, N.Y.C., 1979-84; mgr. market devel. Trintex Corp. (name changed to Prodigy Svcs. Co.), White Plains, N.Y., 1984-86; dir. internat. devel. Telaction Corp., N.Y.C., 1986-87; v.p., group dir. Hill & Knowlton, N.Y.C., 1987—. Apptd. bd. dirs. Women's Action Alliance, N.Y.C., 1988—; del. Albert Gore Presdl. Campaign, N.Y.C., 1988; fundraiser U.S. Senatorial Candidates, N.Y.C., 1984-88. Democrat. Home: 50 Central Park W New York NY 10023 Office: Hill & Knowlton 420 Lexington Ave New York NY 10017

CARPENTER, DOROTHY FULTON, state legislator; b. Ismay, Mont., Mar. 13, 1933; d. Daniel A. and Mary Ann (George) Fulton; B.A., Grinnell Coll., 1955; m. Thomas W. Carpenter, June 12, 1955; children: Mary Ione, James Thomas. Tchr. elem. schs., Houston, and Iowa City, 1955-58; mem. Iowa Ho. Reps., 1980—, asst. minority floor leader, 1982-88. Pres. Planned Parenthood of Iowa, 1970; bd. dirs. Planned Parenthood Fedn. Am., 1977-80; fin. chmn. Episcopal Diocese of Iowa, 1979-80. Recipient Grinnell Coll. Alumni award, 1980. Mem. NOW, Common Cause. Republican.

CARPENTER, ELIZABETH JANE, digital equipment company communications executive; b. Cleve., Mar. 29, 1949; d. Robert E. and Joan Jaffe. BA, Western Coll., Oxford, Ohio, 1970. Pub. relations asst. Lennen & Newell/Pacific, Honolulu, 1970-73; account exec. Marschalk Advt., Cleve., 1973-76; cons. Carpenter Advt. & Pub. Relations, Cleve., 1976-80; internat. pub. relations mgr. Wang Labs., Inc., Boston, 1980-82, advt. mgr., 1982-87; mgr. worldwide communications CSS, Digital Equipment Corp., Merrimack, N.H., 1987—; assoc. producer Am. Treasure, TV spl., 1986, The Entrepreneurs, TV spl., 1986-87; owner Carpenter Antiques, Dennis, Mass. Trustee Nashua Ctr. for Arts. Mem. Cape Cod Antiques Dealers Assn., Boston Advt. Club, Boston Club. Office: CSS Digital Equipment Corp Continental Blvd Merrimack NH 03062

CARPENTER, ELIZABETH SUTHERLAND, journalist, author, equal rights leader; b. Salado, Tex., Sept. 1, 1920; d. Thomas Shelton and Mary Elizabeth (Robertson) Sutherl; m. Leslie Carpenter, June 17, 1944; children: Scott Sutherland, Christy. B.J., U. Tex., 1942; hon. doctorate, Mt. Vernon Coll. Reporter, UP, Phila., 1944-45; propr. with husband of news bur. representing nat. newspapers Washington, 1945-61; exec. asst. to Vice Pres. Lyndon B. Johnson, 1961-63; pres. sec., staff dir. to Mrs. Johnson, 1963-69; v.p. Hill & Knowlton, Inc., Washington, 1972-76; cons. LBJ Library, Austin, Tex.; asst. sec. Dept. Edn., 1980-81; co-chmn. ERAmerica, 1976-81. Author: Ruffles and Flourishes, 1970, Getting Better All The Time, 1987. Recipient Woman of Year award in field of politics and pub. affairs Ladies Home Jour., 1977. Named to Tex. Women's Hall of Fame, 1985. Mem. Nat. Women's Polit. Caucus (founding mem., nat. policy council 1971—), Women's Nat. Press (pres. 1954-55), Alpha Phi, Theta Sigma Phi (Nat. Headliners award 1962). Clubs: Press (Washington); Headliners (Headliner award), Univ. (Austin). Home and Office: 116 Skyline Dr Austin TX 78746

CARPENTER, KATHRYN LYN, public relations company executive; b. Casper, Wyo., Sept. 15, 1961; d. Hugh Lewis and Kathryn Estelle (Pepper) C. BS in Mass Communications, U. Utah, 1983. Mcht. rep. Tracy Collins Bank & Trust, Salt Lake City, 1983-84; communications specialist Arthur Young & Co., Salt Lake City, 1984-88; officer, dir. pub. rels. 1st Interstate Bank Utah, Salt Lake City, 1988-89; pres. KC Communications, Corona del Mar, Calif., 1989—; cons. Mountain West Venture Group, Salt Lake City, 1984-87, Catheter Tech. Inc., Salt Lake City, 1986-89, Sta. KTVX, Salt Lake City, 1986, Inter Therapy, Inc., Costa Mesa, Calif., 1990. Mem. Jr. League, Salt Lake City, 1988-89, Orange County, Calif., 1989—. Mem. Pub. Rels. Soc. Am. (accredited, officer 1988-89), Women in Communications (officer 1988-89), Kappa Kappa Gamma. Home and Office: 1127 Goldenrod Ave Corona del Mar CA 92625

CARPENTER, LINDA LEIGH, telecommunications executive; b. Atlanta, Nov. 19, 1960; d. James Robert and Eloise (Stephens) C. BSBA, Western Carolina U., 1984. Mktg. mgr. Media Mktg., Inc., Atlanta, 1984-86; sales person Executone (Isoetec) Info. Systems, Atlanta, 1986-88, Velobind, Atlanta, 1988-89; sales mgr. Tie Systems, Inc., Atlanta, 1989-90; location mgr. Tie Systems, Inc., Raleigh, N.C., 1990—. Mem. High Mus. Art, Atlanta, 1985. Mem. NAFE, Western Carolina Alumni Assn., Zeta Tau Alpha Fraternity, Kappa Alpha Order Little Sister. Republican. Home: 8210 Innsbruck Dr Atlanta GA 30350 Office: Tie Systems Inc 809 Spring Forest Rd Ste 1200 Raleigh NC 27609

CARPENTER, MARY LAURE, hospital administrator; b. South Bend, Ind., Oct. 17, 1953; d. Daniel Pierre and Elizabeth Ann (Arigan) Laure; m. Gregory John Ingrassia, Oct. 26, 1974 (div. 1981); m. David James Carpenter, Dec. 30, 1983. Student, U. Mo., St. Louis, 1972-74; BA, DePaul U., Chgo., 1988. With Christian Hosp. N.E., St. Louis, 1974-78; patient account mgr. Faith Hosp., Creve Coeur, Mo., 1978-81; telephone collector Tri-County Accounts Bur., Wheaton, Ill., 1981; Medicaid supr. Ingalls Meml. Hosp., Harvey, Ill., 1981-82; owner Medicare Claims Svc., Berkeley, Ill., 1982-84; ops. mgr. Superior Med. Supply, Elmhurst, Ill., 1984-85; bus. mgr. Forest Health Sys.-Forest Hosp., Des Plaines, Ill., 1985-86; asst. adminstr. Vencor/Sycamore (Ill.) Hosp., 1986-89; patient accounts mgr. Linden Oaks Hosp., Naperville, Ill., 1989—; lectr. in field. Mem. Am. Guild Patient Acctg. Mgrs. (v.p. 1979-80, Pres.'s award, 1980, Journalism award 1979), Health Care Fin. Mgmt. Assn., Midwest Hosp. Credit Mgr. Assn. (bd. dirs. 1976-79). Office: Linden Oaks Hosp PO Box 2198 Naperville IL 60567-2198

CARPENTER, MARY PAIGE ABEEL, consultant; b. Petersburg, Va., May 26, 1950; d. Elmer Raymond and Paige Bolyn (Sharpe) Abeel; m. Kent Dee Carpenter, Mar. 16, 1974; 1 child, Margaret Elizabeth. BA in Journalism, Mich. State U., 1972. Reporter Richmond (Va.) News Leader, 1973-74; head edn. svcs. Ga. Dept. Archives and History, Atlanta, 1974-77; communications specialist Jud. Coun. Ga., Atlanta, 1977-80; mgmt. procedures analyst Pan Am World Svcs., Ft. Gordon, Ga., 1980-84; mgr. communications Pan Am World Svcs., Martinez, Ga., 1984-87; ind. cons. Charlotte, N.C., 1987—. Mem. Women in Communications, Soc. Tech. Communication. Methodist. Home and Office: 9207 Willowglen Trail Charlotte NC 28215

CARPENTER, MIRIAM CHARLOTTE, nurse; b. Milbrooke, Ala., Aug. 30, 1932; d. Alton Kimbrough and Edna Lee (Cheves) Helton; m. Oran Gerald Carpenter, Jan. 23, 1970; children: Nanette Weimer, Jenna Ormsbee, Joey Culbreth. AA, Coll. Mainland, Texas City, Tex., 1977; BS, East Tex. State U., 1979, MS, 1985; BSN, U. Tex., 1982. RN; lic. nursing home adminstr., Okla. Various pos. U. Tex. Med. Br., Galveston, 1975-76, patient care coordinator for internal medicine, 1976-77; house supr. nurse tng. coordinator St. Joseph Hosp., Paris, Tex., 1977-79, dir. quality assurance hosp.-wide, 1980-84; house supr., quality assurance coordinator VA Hosp., Bonham, Tex., 1984-85; dir. nurses Delta Home Health Care, Inc., Cooper, Tex., 1985-86; dir. quality assurance, infection control nurse Choctaw Meml. Hosp., Hugo, Okla., 1986-87, operating room supr., 1988—; dir. nurses Leisure Lodge Skilled Nursing Facility, Sulphur Springs, Tex., 1988-89; asst. dir. Paris (Tex.) Outreach Ctr., 1989—; health occupations com. Paris Jr. Coll., 1988; bd. dirs. Med. Plaza Home Health, Paris, 1984-85. Vol. St. Joseph Hosp., Paris, 1982-87. Recognized for acad. achievements and nursing mgmt. Soc. Nursing Profls. Am., 1988, 84; named one of Notable Women Tex., 1984. Mem. U. Tex. Alumni Assn., East Tex. State U. Alumni Assn., Quota Club (sec. 1968-70), Lions (Detroit, Tex. chpt., sec./treas. 1990-91) Kappa Delta Phi, Phi Theta Kappa. Democrat. Methodist. Home: 200 Key West Rd Paris TX 75460 Office: Paris Outreach Ctr 625 W Washington St Paris TX 75460

CARPENTER, NANCY CAROL, travel agency executive; b. Huntington, W.Va., Mar. 31, 1956; d. Leonard Cecil and Mary (Scott) Rice; m. Lonnie Theron Carpenter, May 30, 1975; 1 child, Krystal Rae. Student, Marshall U., 1975. Travel counselor Huntington (W.Va.) Auto Club, 1976-85; ticket agt. Huntington Auto Club Worldwide Travel, 1985-86; mgr. br. office Huntington Auto Club Worldwide Travel, Ceredo, W.Va., 1986—. Active Huntington Mus. Art. Mem. Am. Automotive Assn. (cert. domestic travel counselor). Republican. Methodist. Lodge: Jobs Daughters (hon. queen 1974). Office: AAA World Wide Travel US Rt 60 and 2d St W Ceredo WV 25530

CARPENTER, PATRICIA, clinical psychologist, poet; b. Detroit, May 16, 1920; d. William Henry and Kathryn Virginia (Dix) Humphrey; m. Warren H. Carpenter, Mar. 29, 1958. AB, Oberlin Coll., 1941; BS in LS, Western Res. U., 1943; MA, Wayne State U., 1958, PhD, 1961. Diplomate in clin. psychology ABEP. Libr. Detroit Pub. Libr., 1943-49; rsch. libr. United Automobile Workers-CIO, Detroit, 1950-56; rsch. fellow, grad. asst. Wayne State U., Detroit, 1956-58; psychologist Clinic for Child Study, Wayne County Juvenile Ct., Detroit, 1959-63, dir. psychol. svcs., 1963-81; dir. Psychol. Svcs. for Youth, Brighton, Mich., 1981—; cons. Wayne County Juvenile Ct., Detroit, 1981-83; cons. North Suburban Counseling Assocs., Mt. Clemens, Mich., 1974-81, Genesee County Child and Adolescent Svc., Flint, Mich., 1980-82; leader intensive juvenile workshops Dialogue House, N.Y.C., 1985—. Contbr. articles to profl. jours., poetry to various publs. Home: 3875 W Coon Lake Rd Howell MI 48843 Office: Psychol Svcs for Youth 121 W North St Brighton MI 48116

CARPENTER, R(OBERTA) LYNN, cosmetic industry executive; b. Fall River, Mass., July 23, 1948; d. Robert Leonard Carpenter and Alice E. (Raphael) Carpenter Zais. BA, Southeastern Mass. U., 1970. Cosmetic rep. Cherry & Webb, Newport, R.I., 1970-71, Jordan Marsh, Boston, 1971-73; account mgr. Etherea/Norell div. Revlon-N.Y., Atlanta & Ft. Lauderdale, Ga. & Fla., 1973-77, Vidal Sassoon, Inc., Ft. Lauderdale, 1977-78; mfr.'s rep. Renauld Sunglasses, Ft. Lauderdale, 1978-79; account mgr., regional mgr. Alfin Fragrances, Ft. Lauderdale, 1980-87; regional mgr. Parfumes Pierre Cardin, Chgo., 1987-89, Trina, Inc., Chgo., 1990—; ptnr. Mystery Mail; ptnr. Mystery Mail. Mem. NAFE, Fla. Cosmetic Assn. Roman Catholic.

CARPENTER, SUSAN KAREN, defender; b. New Orleans, May 6, 1951; d. Donald Jack and Elise Ann (Diehl) C. B.A. magna cum laude with honors in English, Smith Coll., 1973; J.D., Ind. U., 1976. Bar: Ind. 1976. Dep. pub. defender of Ind. State of Ind., Indpls., 1976-81, pub. defender of Ind., 1981—; chief pub. defender Wayne County, Richmond, Ind., 1981; bd. dirs. Ind. Pub. Defender Council, Indpls., 1981—, Ind. Lawyer's Commn., Indpls., 1984—; trustee Ind. Criminal Justice Inst., Indpls., 1983—. Mem. Criminal Code Study Commn., Indpls., 1981—, Supreme Ct. Records Mgmt. Com., Indpls., 1983—. Mem. Ind. State Bar Assn. (criminal justice sect.), Nat. Legal Aid and Defender Assn. (mem. Amicus com. 1984—), Nat. Assn. Defense Lawyers, Phi Beta Kappa. Office: State Pub Defender 309 W Washington St Ste 501 Indianapolis IN 46204

CARPENTER, WENDY JOAN, English educator; b. Bridgeport, Conn., Jan. 8, 1955; d. Robert Arnold and Joan Audrey (Crespo) C. BA in English, Fairfield (Conn.) U., 1977, MA in English Edn., 1985, CAS in Adminstrn., 1989. Lic. English tchr., intermediate adminstr. Tchr. English Rippowam High Sch., Stamford, Conn., 1980, Stamford High Sch., 1980-82, J.M. Wright Voc. Tech. High Sch., Stamford, 1982-84, Extraordinary Learning Program, Stamford, 1984—; freelance writer, 1977—; cons. Conn. Writing Project, 1985—; presenter Writing Inst., Fairfield U., 1986; producer 13 Mag. ann. extraordinary learning program lang. arts showcase, Stamford, 1989—. Contbr. articles to profl. jours. Stamford Bd. Edn. mini-grantee, 1985, 89, Outstanding Achievement in Media award Conn. Assn. Bds. Edn., 1989, Utilization of TV in Edn. award WNET Channel 13, N.Y.C., 1990. Mem. Nat. Coun. Tchrs. English, Nat. Assn. Young Writers, NEA, Greenpeace. Democrat. Home: 14 Waterbury Ave Stamford CT 06902

CARPENTER-GORKA, BARBARA JO, social services administrator; b. Warren, Ohio, May 22, 1951; d. Claude Ceylon and Alice Pauline (Thornston) C. BS, Kent State U., 1974. Cert. phys. edn. tchr. Program tchr. Lake County YMCA, Madison, Ohio, 1974-86, br. exec., 1986—; cluster pres. Northeast Ohio YMCA Phys. Dir., Madison, 1984-85; field coord. Great Lakes Zone YMCA Leaders Clubs, Madison, 1983-85; sch. dir. Great Lakes YMCA Leaders Sch., Muskingham, Ohio, 1974-85; sr. dir. YMCA of USA, 1980, advanced mgr., 1989. Pub. Great Lakes Leaders Newsletter, 1983-85 (Merit award 1983-85). Mem. Madison Community Devel., 1985—. Mem. Assn. of Profl. Dir. (treas. chpt. 71 1985, zone sec. 1986), Madison-Perry C. of C., Bus. & Profl. Women (v.p. and pres. Unionville, Ohio 1980-86). Democrat. Methodist. Home: 2380 Forest Glen Madison OH 44057 Office: East End YMCA 730 Lake St Madison OH 44057

CARPENTER-MASON, BEVERLY NADINE, executive health care quality assurance nurse; b. Pitts., May 23, 1933; d. Frank Carpenter and Thelma Deresa (Williams) Smith; m. Sherman Robert Robinson Jr., Dec. 26, 1953 (div. Jan. 1959); 1 child, Keith Michael; m. David Solomon Mason Jr., Sept. 10, 1960; 1 child, Tamara Nadina. RN, Shadyside Hosp. Sch. Nursing, Pitts.; BS, St. Joseph's Coll., North Windham, Maine, 1979; MS, So. Ill. U., 1981; postgrad., Columbia Pacific U., 1990—. Staff nurse med. surgery, ob-gyn neontology and pediatrics Pa., N.Y., Wyo., Colo. and Washington, 1954-68; mgr. clinician dermatol. svcs. Malcolm Grow Med. Ctr., Camp Spring, Md., 1968-71; pediatric nurse practitioner Dept. Human Resources, Washington, 1971-73; asst. dir. nursing Glenn Dale Hosp., Md., 1973-81; nursing coord. medicaid div. Forest Haven Ctr., Laurel, Md., 1981-83, spl. asst. to supr. for med. svcs., 1983-84; spl. asst. to supt. for quality assurance Burr. Habilitation Svcs., Laurel, 1984-89; exec. asst. quality assurance coord. Mental Retardation Devel. Disabilities Adminstrn., Washington, 1989—; also bd. dirs.; cons. and lectr. in field. Contbr. articles to profl. jours. Mem., star donor ARC Blood Drive, Washington, Md., 1975—; chair nominations com. Prince Georges Nat. Coun. Negro Women, Md., 1984-85. Recipient awards Dept. Air Force and D.C. Govt., 1966—, Della Robbia Gold medallion Am. Acad. Pediatrics, 1972, John P. Lamb Jr. Meml. Lectureship award East Tenn. State U., 1988. Mem. NAFE, Am. Assn. Mental Retardation (conf. lectr. 1988), Am. Coll. Utilization Rev. Physicians, Am. Bd. Quality Assurance and Utilization Rev. Physicians (case study editor, mem. jour. editorial bd. 1985—, chmn. publs. com. 1987—, asst. treas. 1988—), Assn. Retarded Citizens, Top Ladies of Distinction, Inc. (1st v.p. 1986—), Internat. Platform Assn., Chi Eta Phi. Democrat. Baptist. Home: 11109 Winsford Ave Upper Marlboro MD 20772 Office: MR/DDA Bundy Bldg Ste 202 429 O St NW Washington DC 20001

CARPER, DIANE CLEMENTS, business and property manager; b. Erie, Pa., Sept. 28, 1945; d. Harold Ralph and Ida Marie (Chimenti) Clements; married; 1 child, Rebecca Elizabeth. Student, So. Methodist U., 1969-72, Tulsa Jr. Coll., 1973-74; MBA, Barry U., 1988, BS in Psychology, 1987, postgrad. in bus., 1987—; postgrad. in bus., Nova U., 1987—. Dept. mgr. Neiman Marcus, Dallas, 1965-69; asst. to v.p. mfg. Lowrance Electronics, Tulsa, 1972-74; flight attendant Braniff Internat., Dallas, 1976-82, night mgr., crew scheduler, 1976-82; coordinator for AIDS Research Labs. U. Miami, Fla., 1984-85; adminstr. Cordis Corp., Miami, 1986-88, supr. adminstrv. and tech. ctr., co. quality coord., 1988-89; bus. and property mgr. Carrollton Sch. Sacred Heart, Miami, 1989—; cons. Valeries and Valeries Too, Abilene, Tex., 1969-76, Stout Fashions, Midland, Tex., 1976—. Vol. Project Literacy for Every Adult in Dade County; treas. Convent of the Sacred Heart of Miami, Inc. Mem. Nat. Acad. Mgmt., So. Acad. Mgmt., Assn. Pers. Adminstrs., Internat. Platform Assn., MADD, Mensa, Miami Runners Club. Republican. Roman Catholic. Home: 4110 Hardie Rd Miami FL 33133

CARPER, FREDA SMITH, bank marketing director; b. Roanoke, Va., Aug. 19, 1953; d. Samuel E. and R. Violet (Wilson) Smith; m. Charles R. Carper, June 18, 1978 (div. 1990). AAS in Mgmt., U. Ky., Prestonburg, 1980. Sales dir. Ramada Inn, Roanoke, 1975-76; account exec. mgr. Am. Hotel Mgmt., Raleigh, N.C., 1976-78; asst. v.p., mktg. dir. Pikeville (Ky.) Nat. Bank, 1980-83; v.p., mktg. dir. First Fed. Roanoke (name changed to CorEast Savs. Bank), 1983-88, Colonial Am. Bank, Roanoke, 1988-89; asst. v.p., mktg. mgr. Western region Crestar Bank, Roanoke, 1989—. Bd. dirs. Mt. Pleasant Civic League; chmn. YMCA membership com., Roanoke; chmn. mktg. adv. coun. ARC; mktg. com. United Way; mem. regional bd. Am. Lung Assn., 1990. Recipient Addy award Charleston/Huntington Ad Club, W.Va., 1982, 83, 87, 88. Mem. Sales Mktg. Execs. (pres. 1986-87), Sales Mktg. Execs. Internat. (regional bd. dirs. 1986-87), Am. Advt. Fedn. (chairperson 3d dist. govt. rels. 1990), Advt. Fedn. Roanoke (treas. 1986-87, v.p. 1987-88, pres. 1989-90, Addy award 1984, 87, 88), Bank Mktg. Assn., Roanoke C. of C. (co-chair bus. after-hour com.). Democrat. Baptist. Office: Crestar Bank 10 Franklin Rd Roanoke VA 24011

CARPER, GERTRUDE ESTHER, artist, marina owner; b. Jamestown, N.Y., Apr. 13, 1921; d. Zenas Mills and Virgie (Lytton) Hanks; m. J. Dennis Carper, Apr. 5, 1942; children: David Hanks, John Michael Dennis. Student violinist, Nat. Acad. Mus., 1931-41; diploma fine arts, Md. Inst. Art, 1950; voice student, Frazier Gange, Peabody Inst. Music, 1952-55. Interior decorator O'Neill's (Importers), Balt., 1942-44; auditor Citizens Nat. Bank, Covington, Va., 1945-46; owner, developer Essex Yacht Harbour Marina, Balt., 1955—; owner, developer St. Michael's Sanctuary, widllife preserve Essex Yacht Harbor Marina, Balt., 1965—. Jewelry designer, 1987—; portrait artist, 1947—; exhibited one-woman shows Ferdinand Roten Gallery, Balt., 1963, Highfield Salon, Balt., 1967, Le Salon des Nations a Paris, 1985, Ducks and Geese of North Am., 1986; exhibited group shows Md. Inst. Alumni Show, 1964, Essex Libr., 1981, Hist. Preservation of Am., Hall of Fame, 1989, others; Author: Expressions for Children, 1985; contbr. articles and poetry to ch. publs. and newspapers. Vol. tchr. of retarded persons, 1942—; leader Women's Circle at local Presbyn. chs., 1952—, mem. 40 yrs. of choir svc. Mem. Md. Inst. Art Alumni Assn. (life), Grand Coun. World Parliament of Chivalry (Nobless of Humanity citation). Office: Essex Yacht Harbour Marina 500 Sandalwood Rd Baltimore MD 21221-5830

CARPIEN, JANNET SIEGLE, corporate executive, financial planner; b. Reading, Pa., Jan. 24, 1943; d. Robert Eugene and Helen (Jablonski) Siegle; m. Alan Hugh Carpien, Oct. 4, 1969; children: Juliette M., Seth M. BS, Kutztown (Pa.) State U., 1964; postgrad., George Washington U., U. Madrid, San Diego State U. Tchr. Spanish and phys. edn. Holy Name High Sch., Reading, Pa., 1964-65; tchr. English, reading and speech Western High Sch., Washington, 1966-68; tchr. English Meml. Jr. High Sch., San Diego, 1968-70, Ballou High Sch., Washington, 1971-72; account exec. Johnston, Lemon & Co., Inc., Washington, 1976-84; corp. v.p., fin. planner Smith Barney Harris Upham & Co., 1984—; mem. adj. faculty Coll. Fin. Planning George Washington U., Denver, 1983—. Contbr. articles to profl. jours. Chmn. com. on seminar Womens Nat. Bank Adv. Bd., Washington, 1979-80, 81-84; mem. bus. com. D.C. Commn. for Women, Washington, 1982—; 1st v.p. bd. dirs. Florence Crittenton of Greater Washington, 1987. Recipient Profl. Service award Washington Pub. Accts., 1979, Pres.'s Club Profl. Achievement award Johnston, Lemon & Co. Inc., 1983. Mem. Internat. Assn. Fin. Planning (sec. 1980-81, exec. v.p. 1985-86, pres. 1986-87, Ea. regional bd. dirs. 1986—, chmn. 1988—, bd. dirs. 1987—), Stockbrokers Soc., Bond Club of Washington, Nat. Assn. Securities Dealers (broker). Democrat. Jewish. Office: Smith Barney Harris Upham & Co 1776 Eye St #600 Washington DC 20006

CARR, AUDRI JOAN, computer company executive; b. N.Y.C., Oct. 8, 1936; d. Samuel and Lillian (Snyder) Friedlander; m. Alan N. Carr, June 8, 1957; children: Allison, Evan. BS, Hunter Coll., 1957. Chemist Charles Pfizer, N.Y.C., 1957-60; prof. Med. Coll. Va., Richmond, 1964-66; analyst Horizons Rsch., Cleve., 1972-76; mgr. MBIS, Cleve., 1976-78; purchasing mgr. Technicare, Cleve., 1978-83, quality assurance mgr., 1983-86; purchasing mgr. Hauserman, Cleve., 1986-88; dir. materials Cumulus Corp., Cleve., 1988—. Contbr. articles to profl. jours. Pres. Womens Am. Orgn. for Rehab. through Tng., Richmond, 1966, Cleve., 1970, nat. bd. dirs., N.Y.C., 1966-72, v.p. dist., Cleve., 1970-74. Mem. Nat. Assn. Purchasing Mgmt., Am. Product and Inventory Control Soc., Am. Soc. Quality Control, Am. Chem. Soc. Democrat. Jewish. Home: 23863 Wimbledon Rd Shaker Hgts OH 44122 Office: Cumulus Corp 23500 Mercantile Rd Cleveland OH 44122

CARR, BARBARA J., hospital administrator; b. Miami, Fla., Oct. 16, 1950; d. Charles Ray and Evelena (Gordon) C.; 1 child, Charles Richard Seifert. Student, Miami Dade Jr. Coll., 1968-74, U. Miami, 1972-74, Nova U., 1982-83, Barry U., 1988—. Asst. dir. heart sta. Jackson Meml. Med. Ctr., Miami, 1972-76; mktg. dir. Cardio Svcs. Union Carbide, Miami, 1976-80; adminstrv. dir. cardiovascular svcs. Miami Vascular Inst. Bapt. Hosp. of Miami, 1981—. Mem. Am. Heart Assn., Acad. Med. Arts and Scis., Am. Coll. Cardiovascular Adminstrs., Am. Acad. Med. Adminstrs., Nat. Alliance Cardiovascular Techs. (v.p. 1987, state pres. 1987-88), Nat. Soc. Cardiovascular Techs. (nat. pres. 1976-78, chmn.), Am. Coll. Cardiovascular Adminstrs.

CARR, BARBARA KUNKEL, psychotherapist, consultant; b. Garfield, N.J., Mar. 17, 1945; d. Everett Edward and Florence Hilda (Davidsen) K.; m. John E. Carr, Nov. 4, 1988; children: Tasha Jade Decker, Lara Ashley Decker, Audrey Carr, Edward John Carr. BA in Psychology and Pre-Theology, Elmira Coll., N.Y., 1966; MA in Human Devel., Fairleigh Dickinson U., 1983; PhD in Transpersonal Psychology and Alcholism Studies, Union Inst., 1988. Income maintenance supr. Sussex County Welfare, Newton, N.J., 1975-79; dept. supr. Colonial Penn Ins. Co., Phila., 1979-81; adminstrv. mgr. Velo-Bind, Inc., Mt. Laurel, N.J., 1982-83; mgmt., human relations cons. pvt. practice, N.J., Mass. and Maine, 1983—; co-founder, psychologist Carr Counseling, Waltham, Mass., 1989—; clk. Supreme Jud. and Superior Cts., York County, Maine, 1985-88; cons. Ctr. for Addictive Behaviors, Inc., Salem, Mass., 1988—; treas., psychotherapist Circle Counseling Assocs., Waltham, 1988-89; mem. faculty Nasson Coll., Springvale, Maine, 1986-87. Artist stained glass windows. Teaching fellow Fairleigh Dickinson U., 1983-84. Mem. Am. Psychol. Practitioners Assn. (founding mem.), Northeastern Soc. for Group Psychotherapy (affiliate mem.), Mensa. Avocations: canoeing, photography, furniture restoration. Home: 1526 Mystic Valley Pkwy Medford MA 02155 Office: Carr Counseling 371 Moody St Ste 102 Waltham MA 02154

CARR, BERNADETTE PATRICIA, editor, publisher; b. N.Y.C.; d. Francis and Elizabeth (O'Donnell) C. BA in English Lit, Mercy Coll., Dobbs Ferry, N.Y., 1966; MA in Am. Lit, Fordham U., 1968. Mng. editor Photoplay mag., N.Y.C., 1969-70; editor Photoplay mag., 1971-73; editor-in-chief MacFadden Fan Titles mag., N.Y.C., 1973-74; editor Weight Watchers mag., N.Y.C., 1975-80; editor-in-chief Every Woman mag., N.Y.C., 1980-82; assoc. pub., editor CPDA News, N.Y.C., 1982-84; v.p. Rosnick/Carr Communications, Durham, N.C., 1985—. Mem. NOW, Soc. Consumer Affairs Profls., AAAS. Home: 13 Durbin Pl Durham NC 27705

CARR, BEVERLY ANNE, business manager; b. Phila., July 31, 1942; d. Fred and Rose (Rucco) Carrara; m. George E. Carr, June 3, 1961; children: Raymond, David. AA in Acctg., Pa. State U., Ogontz, 1972. Adminstr. Hassinger & Schwam Architects, Phila., 1968-80, Gerald F. Schwam Assocs., Elkins Park, Pa., 1980-86; bus. mgr. Penn's Grant Realty Corp., Doylestown, Pa., 1986—; mgmt. cons. various architectural firms, Phila., 1986—. Elected mem. Pa. State Rep. Com., Bucks County, 1988—; active in Bucks County Drug, Alcohol Com., 1980-88, Bucks County Community Devel. Citizens Com., 1988-90, Am. Heart Assn. (Outstanding Vol. of Yr. 1985); bd. dirs. Bucks County Am. Cancer Soc., 1987—. Mem. NAFE, Bucks County Bd. Realtors (com. and legis. R-Pac 1988), Soroptomist Internat. (pres. Bucks county chpt. 1988-90). Roman Catholic. Home: 3015 Swamp Rd Doylestown PA 18901 Office: Penns Grant Realty Corp 350 S Main St Ste 303A Doylestown PA 18901

CARR, BONNIE JEAN, professional skater; b. Chgo., Sept. 29, 1947; d. Nicholas and Agnes Marie (Moran) Musashe; m. James Bradley Carr, Dec. 8, 1984; children: Brittany Jean, James Bradley II. BS, Northwestern U., 1969; JD (hon.), Loyola U., Chgo., 1978. Skater Adventures on Ice, Mpls., 1961; prin. skater Jamboree on Ice, Chgo., 1961-68; society editor The Free Press, Colorado Springs, Colo., 1969; prin. skater, publicist on tour, asst. lighting dir., tour ednl. tutor Holiday on Ice Internat., 1970-74; skating dir. William McFetridge Sports Ctr., Chgo., 1975-86; choreographer, prin. skater Ice Time, USA, Mundelein, Ill., 1975—; skating coach St. Bronislava Athletic Club, Chgo., 1967-69; publicity dir. Amateur Skating Assn. Ill., Chgo., 1968; founder, dir. skating programs for blind, hearing impaired and mentally handicapped, Chgo., 1975-85; physical fitness advisor Exec. Health Seminars, Chgo., 1979; founder, dir. skating programs Fred Hutchinson Cancer Research Ctr., Seattle, 1985-86; guest speaker Am. Cancer Soc., Columbia, S.C., 1973; conditioning coach over 50 programs Riverside Wellness and Fitness Ctr., Richmond, Va., 1989—. Recipient Key to City, Mobile, Ala., 1973, Service Recognition award Special Olympics, Chgo., 1984. Mem. Am. Guild Variety Artists, Internat. Dance-Exercise Assn. Found. (cert. 1990). Methodist. Home: 1931 Albion Rd Midlothian VA 23113 Office: Ice Time USA 28800 Gilmer Rd Mundelein IL 60060

CARR, BRENDA SUE, health science facility administrator; b. New Castle, Ind., Sept. 17, 1955; d. Robert G. Carr and Wilma Renita (Richardson) Lindsey. BS in Radiologic Tech., Minot (N.D.) State U., 1982. Registered radiologic technologist, Am. Registry of Radiologic Technologists; lic. med. radiologic technologist. Instr. West Fla. Hosp., Pensacola, 1982-84; chief technologist Evergreen (Ala.) Hosp., 1984-85; asst. dir. Irving (Tex.) Healthcare System, 1985—. Sgt. USAF, 1974-78. Mem. Am. Soc. Radiologic Technologists, Tex. Soc. Radiologic Technologists (com. edn. spl. procedures 1989-90), Dallas Area Radiologic Technologists (pres. 1990—), Tex. Hosp. Assn. Democrat. Office: Irving Healthcare System 1901 N MacArthur Blvd Irving TX 75061

CARR, DIANE COLE, human resources specialist; b. Atlanta, Sept. 30, 1952; d. Robert J. and Bonnie Jean (Marler) C. BBA, Ga. State U., 1973. Asst. v.p. mktg. United Airlines, Cleve.; dir. sales and mktg. Hotel Oro Negro, Tenerife, Canary Island, Spain; mgr. human resources Stonebridge Devel., Chattanooga. Recipient Outstanding Community Stewardship award Atlanta C. of C., Outstanding Pub. Rels. Disting. Svc. award Atlanta C. of C. Mem. Am. Assn. Records Mgrs., NAFE, Bus. and Profl. Women Chattanooga, Nat. Bd. Realtors and CHA. Home: 1414 Continental Dr #309 Chattanooga TN 37405

CARR, GERALDINE MARIE, lawyer; b. Boston, Jan. 31, 1955; d. Thomas Joseph and Grace Marie (Havlin) C.; m. Robert G. Josephs, July 30, 1983; 1 child. AB, Mt. Holyoke Coll., 1977; JD, U. Calif., Davis, 1984. Bar: Calif. 1984, D.C. 1987. Assoc. Duncan, Weinberg, Miller & Pembrooke, Washington, 1985-86, Birch, Horton, Bittner & Cherot, Washington, 1986—. Bd. dirs. Rollingwood Citizens Assn., Chevy Chase, Md., 1987-90. Mt. Holyoke Coll. fellow, 1976. Mem. ABA, D.C. Bar Assn., Washington Coun. Lawyers. Democrat. Office: Birch Horton Bittner & Cherot 1155 Connecticut Ave NW Ste 1200 Washington DC 20036

CARR, GLENNA DODSON, educator; b. Asheville, N.C., Jan. 7, 1927; d. Harry D. and Ruth (Gatling) Dodson; m. Thomas Deaderick Carr, May 20, 1961; 1 child, Susan Catherine. BS, James Madison U., Harrisonburg, Va., 1948; MS, Fla. State U., Tallahassee, 1951; EdD, U. Fla., 1959. Asst. prof. to prof. U. Fla., Gainesville, 1951—; prof., dir. Ctr. for Econ. Edn. U. Fla., 1977—; bd. dirs., corp. treas. Santa Fe Healthcare, Inc., Gainesville, 1982—. Contbr. numerous articles to profl. jours. Active various local and state task forces in govt. Democrat. Presbyterian. Home: 1546 SW 35th Pl Gainesville FL 32608 Office: Center for Economic Edn 186 Norman Hall Gainesville FL 32611-2053

CARR, JOSEPHINE SUSSMAN, writer, teacher; b. Washington, July 21, 1952; d. King and Josephine (Skinner) C.; m. Elliot J. Sussman; children: Rachel, Daniel. BA, Mt. Holyoke Coll., 1974; MA, Bryn Mawr Coll., 1980. Author: No Regrets, 1982, My Beautiful Fat Friend, 1988. Mem. Children's Book Soc., Poets and Writers, Inc. Address: 4837 S Kimbark Ave Chicago IL 60615

CARR, KATHRYNE ELIZABETH, management company executive; b. Albuquerque, Jan. 31, 1955; d. James Henry and Maureen (Morrissey) Ford; m. David Wilkinson Jr. Carr, Aug. 2, 1981; children: Wilkinson Micajah, Martha Maureen Doran. BA, Allegheny Coll., 1978. Mkt. analyst Mktg. Corp. Am., Westport, Conn., 1979; systems engr. MITRE Corp., McLean, Va., 1979-82; case worker Darden Bus. Sch. U. Va., Charlottesville, 1982-83; asst. to pres., chief exec. officer Genetic Systems Corp., Seattle, 1984-86; dir. mktg. U. Tech. Corp., Charlottesville, 1987-88; project mgr. Innotage Mgmt., Inc., Charlottesville, 1989—; cons. Pacific Gas & Electric, Portland, Oreg., 1982, Insmed Corp., Charlottesville, 1988, Pharm. Rsch. Assoc., 1989. Author corp. brochures, 1984—; co-author: Biomass Handbook for Developing Countries, 1981. Mem. Jr. League Charlottesville. Roman Catholic. Home: 1007 Cottonwood Rd Charlottesville VA 22901 Office: Innotage Mgmt 1575 State Farm Blvd Charlottesville VA 22901

CARR, MARIE PINAK, import/export company executive; b. Buffalo, June 17, 1954; d. Henry and Hildegard (Poech) Pinak; m. Richard Wallace Carr, Oct. 18, 1980; children: Katherine Marie, Ann Louise, Elizabeth Ashby. BS, Syracuse U., 1976. Cancer microbiologist Nat. Cancer Inst., Rockville, Md., 1976-78; mktg. specialist sci. equipment Precision Scientific, Washington, 1978-80; art importer Dicmar Trading Co., Inc., Washington, 1981-83; book dist. Dicmar Trading Co., Inc., Silver Spring, Md., 1983—. Co-author: The Willard Hotel, 1986. Bd. dirs. Salvation Army Aux., Washington, 1982-89; com. mem. Wolf Trap Assocs., Va., 1990, Am. Cancer Soc., Washington, 1988—; co-chmn. Nat. Cancer Ball, 1989-90; active Jr. League Washington, 1987-90. Mem. Washington Club. Republican. Roman Catholic. Office: Dicmar Trading Co Inc 8880 Brookville Rd Silver Spring MD 20910

CARR, PATRICIA WARREN, adult education educator; b. Mobile, Ala., Mar. 24, 1947; d. Bedford Forrest and Mary Catherine (Warren) Slaughter; m. John Lyle Carr, Sept. 26, 1970; children: Caroline Elise, Joshua Bedford. BS in Edn., Auburn U., 1968, MEd, 1971. Tchr. DeKalb County Schs., Atlanta, 1969-70; counselor Dept. Defense Schs., Okinawa, Japan, 1972-75; tchr. Jefferson County Schs., Jefferson, Ga., 1975-76; counselor Clarke County Schs., Athens, Ga., 1976-78; tchr. Fairfax County Schs., Adult and Community Edn., Fairfax, Va., 1980—; resource specialist Vol. Learning Program; coordinator Enrichment for Srs. Program Fairfax Area Agy. on Aging and Adult and Community Edn., 1985-89; cons. State Va. Dept. Edn., 1984—, Va. Assn. Adult and Community Edn., 1987, Commn. on Adult Basic Edn., 1988; instr. George Mason U., Fairfax, 1985. Tchr. Met. Meml. United Meth. Ch., Washington, 1981—; co-leader McClean, Va. troop Girl Scouts U.S., 1985-88. Mem. Am. Assn. Adult and Community Edn., Smithsonian Nat. Assocs., No. Va. Assn. Vol. Adminstrs., Va. Assn. Adult and Community Edn. Methodist. Office: Fairfax County Adult and Community Edn 7510 Lisle Ave Falls Church VA 22043

CARR, PHYLLIS MAE, mortgage company executive, real estate broker; b. Bklyn., Aug. 23, 1943; d. Max and Anne (Epstein) Edelstein; divorced; 1 child, Melanie Jan; m. Stuart Burton Carr, Apr. 17, 1977. Lic. real estate broker, N.Y.; lic. mortgage broker, N.Y. Real estate agt. Heino Real Estate Inc., Bklyn., 1981-85; real estate broker Coldwell Banker/Neuhaus Realty, S.I., N.Y., 1985-87; pres. Carr Investors Planning, Ltd., S.I., 1986—, internat. collateral dealer, 1989—; owner, mgr. Carr Investors Planning Ltd., S.I.; internat. investment banker. Recipient gold award President's Real Estate Club, 1987. Mem. S.I. C. of C., S.I. Bd. Realtors, N.Y. State Bd. Realtors. Democrat. Jewish. Home and Office: 88 Mulberry Circle Staten Island NY 10314

CARR, RUTH ANNE, judge; b. Athens, Ga., July 22, 1947; d. James Fletcher and Bennie Lou (Blakely) C.; 1 child, Lisa Raye Rissmiller. Student U. Ga., 1966; JD, Woodrow Wilson Coll., 1978; LLM, 1987. Bar: Ga. 1978, U.S. Dist. Ct. (no. dist.) Ga. 1982, U.S. Ct. Appeals (11th cir.) 1982. Pvt. practice, Atlanta, 1978-84; gen. mgr. Am. Seal and Stamp Co., Atlanta, 1980-81; atty. State of Ga., Atlanta, 1982-86, adminstrv. law judge; legal services officer Ga. Div. Mental Health/Mental Retardation, 1986—; legal services officer, dir. forensic services Ga. Div. Mental Health, Mental Retardation and Substance Abuse, 1987—; vis. tchr. Woodrow Wilson Coll., Atlanta, 1982; guest speaker DeKalb High Schs., Decatur. Bd. dirs. Terraces Condominium Assn., Atlanta; state rep., 1987—; mem. Bd. Govs., 1989. Mem. ABA, State Bar Ga., Nat. Assn. State Mental Health Attys. (state rep. 1987—), Nat. Assn. State Mental Health Forensic Dirs. (state rep. 1987—). Avocations: horses, gardening. Home: 2527 Terrace Tr Decatur GA 30035 Office: Div Mental Health/Mental Retardation and Substance Abuse Rm 306 878 Peachtree St Atlanta GA 30309-3999

CARR, SANDRA GOTHAM, advertising executive; b. Tokyo, June 9, 1948; d. Fred Calvin and Evelyn (Dirr) Gotham; m. James P. Jenkins, June 15, 1970 (div. 1989); m. Dayton T. Carr, Dec. 27, 1986 (div. 1989). Student, Stanford-in-France, Tours, 1968-69; BA, Stanford U., 1970, MA, 1971. Account exec. Young & Rubicam Inc., N.Y.C., 1972-78, account supr., 1978-80; pres., Gotham Prodns., N.Y.C., 1980-82; v.p., mgmt. supr. Ogilvy & Mather, 1982-85; v.p. Steuben Glass, N.Y.C., 1985-88; sr. v.p. Siegel & Gale, N.Y.C., 1988—; cons. Congl. coms., FDA, FTC for exec. program Am. Assn. Advt. Agys., Washington, 1978-80; cons. Ctr. Arctic Studies Sorbonne, Paris, in U.S. and Can., 1980-82; seminar dir. N.Y. chpt. Women in Bus., N.Y.C., 1983-84. Writer and editor 4-part TV documentary script Invit! The Universal Cry of the Eskimo People, 1981. Writer speeches for Georgetown Ctr. Strategic and Internat. Studies, also newsletter for Am. Assn. Advt. Agys. Bd. dirs. Rensselaerville (N.Y.) Inst., trustee; fund raiser Stanford U., N.Y.C., promotion coord. of benefits and advt. Medic Alert, N.Y.C., 1983-84; mem. exec. com. Youth Counseling League, N.Y.C., 1984. Mem. Writers Guild Am., Young Profls. Group of Fgn. Policy Assn. (organizing chmn. 1980-81), N.Y. Women in Communications, Stanford Club. Home: 220 E 73d St New York NY 10021 Office: Siegel & Gale 1185 Ave of the Americas New York NY 10036

CARR, VIKKI (FLORENCIA BISENTA DE CASILLAS MARTINEZ CARDONA), singer; b. El Paso, Tex.; d. Carlos and Florence (Martinez) Cardona. Grad. high sch.; hon. doctorate, St. Edwards U., 1974, U. San Diego, 1975. Soloist with, Pepe Callahan Mexican-Irish Band, Los Angeles, Palm Springs, rec. star 37 Liberty and Columbia Albums; hit records Can't Take My Eyes Off You, It Must Be Him, With Pen in Hand; recorded 12 albums CBS-Mex.including hits Disculpame, Total, Ni Princesa; 12 Gold Records; guest appearances on TV including Dean Martin, Ed Sullivan, Jackie Gleason, Smothers Bros., Jerry Lewis, Jonathan Winters, Carol Burnett, spls. with Bob Hope, Jim Nabors, Johnny Carson; hostess of Tonight show several times; appeared in 5 TV Spls. for Mex. and various nightclubs, U.S., Europe, Australia, Japan; toured mil. bases in Vietnam; debut in mus. comedy as Lt. Nellie Forbush in South Pacific, Kansas City; starred in Unsinkable Molly Brown, Ohio; lead role I'm Getting My Act Together and Taking It on the Road, St. Louis; debut as TV dramatic star in Mod Squad, 1972; sang at royal command performance for Queen Elizabeth, 1967; performance at Inaugural Celebration, Kennedy Music Center, 1973; hostess Mrs. America Pageant, TV, 1981-87, Mrs. World Pageant, TV, 1984-87, Hispanic World Vision, 1989, 90. Founder, pres. Vikki Carr Scholarship Found., 1971. Named Woman of Yr. L.A. Times, 1970, Vis. Entertainer of Yr. Mexico City, 1972, Singer of Yr. Am. Guild Variety Artists, 1972, Woman of World, 1974; recipient Humanitarian award Nosotros, 1981; named Number 1 Female Selling Album Artist for CBS Mex., 1982, 83, 84; recipient Woman of Yr. award League United Latin Am. Citizens, 1983, Hispanic Woman of Yr. award Hispanic Women's Council, 1984; Grammy award for best Mexican-Am. performance, 1985, Silver Achievement award YWCA, 1989, Golden Eagle award Nosotros, 1989. Office: Vi-Car Enterprises Inc care Dianne Forthman PO Box 5126 Beverly Hills CA 90210

CARRAGHER, AUDREY ANN, state legislator; b. Jamaica Plain, Mass., Jan. 27, 1924; d. Daniel Joseph and Frances Louise (Wright) McLeod; R.N., Faulkner Hosp., 1945; postgrad. Northeastern U., 1968-76; B.Gen. Studies, U. N.H., 1978, postgrad., 1979; m. John C. Carragher, Nov. 11, 1947; children—John C., Janice, Daniel, Lawrence. Library trustee, mem. Bicentennial Commn., 1974; mem. New Eng. Bd. Library Trustees, 1975; chmn. Chelmsford Hist. Commn., 1975; mem. Growth Policy Commn., 1976; student rep. Lifelong Learning Council U. N.H., 1977; planner Nashua (N.H.) Human Services Council, 1978; mem. county Adv. Council on Aging, 1979; mem. N.H. Ho. of Reps., 1980-86; candidate N.H. State Senate, 1986—, mem. exec. dept. com., adminstrn. com., 1980-84, constl. revision com., 1980-82, subcom. chmn. for state reapportionment and for children and youth legislation, vice chmn. state instns. com., 1982-84, mem. joint com. on exec. reorgn., mem. policy com., Rep. floor leader, vice chairperson Health and human servs. com., 1984-86, mem. state/fed. relations com., 1984-86, vice chairperson joint com. on ann. sessions, 1985, elected del. N.H. Constitutional Conv., 1984-94; mem. health and human resources com. Nat. Conf. State Legislatures, 1984-86. Pres., Chelmsford Friends of Library, 1973, Rep. Women's Club of Nashua, 1980-82; bd. dirs. N.H. Sch. Vols., 1980-85; mem. State Conf. on Aging-Social Services, 1981; pres. N.H. Fedn. Rep. Women, 1986-88; mem. nominating com. Nat. Fedn. Rep. Women, 1988—, Nashua Fedn. Rep. Women; mem. exec. com., mem. at large Nat. Fedn. Rep. Women, 1988-89, pres., vice chmn. by-laws, 1990—; founder Nashua Friends of Library, 1982-83; mem. planning bd. City of Nashua, 1984—, mem. long range master plan com. 1984—; New Eng. Found. Arts Bd., New Hampshire, 1988—, New Hampshire Stat Coun. Arts, 1987—; vice chmn. Women's Orgn. Adv. com. 1989 Inaugural Pres. Bush; active ARC Blood Bank, 1970-82; mem. Jackson Ski Touring Found. Served with Cadet Nurses Corps, 1945. Mem. Nat. Order Women Legislators, Nashua Vis. Nurses Assn. Parliamentarians, N.H. Order Women Legislators, Vis. Nurse Assn. (exec. bd. 1987), Portsmouth Yacht Club, Women's Guild of Parish Club. Roman Catholic. Office: State Coun on the Arts 40 N Main St Concord NH 03301

CARRÉ, SARA MCDOWELL, research center administrator; b. Lancaster, Pa., Apr. 29, 1950; d. Robert James and Louise (Pool) McDowell; m. Edwin V. Carré Jr., Jan. 23, 1982. BA, Temple U., 1971. Cert. tchr., Pa. Acct. U. Pa., Phila., 1979-81; asst. to the dir. Univ. Press (U. Pa.), Phila., 1981-82; analysis and rev. acct. U. Pa., Phila., 1982, supr. trust acctg., 1982-83, mgr. cen. gifts processing, 1983-84; asst. dir. info. systems Fox Chase Cancer Ctr., Phila., 1985-86, dir. adminstrv. systems, 1986-87, dir. ops. and gift planning, 1987-89; sr. adminstr. Fels Inst. for Cancer Rsch. and Molecular Biology, Phila., 1989—. Mem. NAFE, Nat. Soc. Fund Raising Execs., Am. Mgmt. Assn., Soc. for Rsch. Adminstrs., Nat. Coun. Univ. Rsch. Adminstrs. Presbyterian. Office: Temple U Sch Medicine 3420 N Broad St Philadelphia PA 19140

CARRELL, BETTY LOU, laser company executive; b. St. Louis, Oct. 8, 1941; m. Felix DeLuca, Oct. 8, 1960 (dec. Dec. 1964); children: Vincent A., Laura M. DeLuca McMullan. Cert. operating rm. technician, U.S. Army, Ft. Sam Houston, 1961; BS, U. Mo., 1970; AS in Nursing, Araphoe Community Coll., Littleton, Colo., 1979. RN, Colo. Rsch. chemist Monsanto Chem. Co., St. Louis, 1965-70; operating rm. technician various hosps., Kans.,, 1962-65, 70-79; operating rm. supr. Denver, 1979-81; adminstr., cofounder Inst. for Laser Medicine, St. Joseph Hosp., Denver, 1981-84; nat. sales mgr. Infra-Med Laser Co., Boston, 1985-86, dir. edn., 1984-86; laser cons. Aurora, Colo., 1990—; pres., founder Laser Resource, Inc., Aurora, 1986—; edn. advisor Laser Inst. Am. Contbr. numerous articles to profl. jours. With U.S. Army, 1959-61. Mem. Am. Soc. for Laser Medicine and Surgery, Assn. Operating Rm. Nurses, Am. Nat. Standard Inst. (bd. dirs.), Med. Laser Safety Officer Soc. (founder), Cons. Consortium of Laser Tech. Office: Laser Resource Inc 14221 E 4th Ave #325 Aurora CO 80011

CARREY, RANDI LEE, computer company owner; b. Bklyn., Nov. 27, 1958; d. Abe and Joyce (Davidowitz) C. BS, NYU, 1979, MBA, 1980. Product mgr. Citibank, N.Y.C., 1980-84; cons. Kenneth Leventhal, N.Y.C., 1984-85; owner Savant Solutions, N.Y.C., 1985—. Vol. DOROT, N.Y.C., 1985—. Mem. Nat. Assn. Women Bus. Owners. Office: Savant Solutions 315 W 57th St New York NY 10019

CARRICK, PAULA S., lawyer; b. Phila., Feb. 29, 1944; d. Joseph Warren Carrick and Agnes Dorothea Strecker. Diploma, St. Francis Hosp. Sch. Nursing, 1965; BS, Troy State U., 1979; cert., Air Command and Staff Coll., 1978; JD, Walter F. George Sch. Law, 1982. Bar: S.C., Ga.; RN, Del., S.C. Sr. risk mgmt. cons. Va. Ins. Reciprocal, Richmond; quality assurance/risk mgmt. coord. Med. U. S.C., Charleston; sr. cons. Va. Profl. Underwriters, Inc., Richmond; cons. Am. Assn. Critical Care Nurses, Charleston; cons. to chief nurse USAF, surgeon gen.; adjunct faculty Shenandoah Coll. and Conservatory, Winchester, Va.; speaker in field. Contbr. articles to profl. publs. Col. USAFR, 1990. Mem. ABA, Am. Nurses Assn., Am. Soc. Healthcare Risk Mgmt., Va. Assn. Quality Assurance Profls., Am. Soc. Law and Medicine, Phi Delta Phi. Home: PO Box 3971 Fort Smith AR 72913

CARRICO, CHRISTINE KATHRYN, health sciene administrator; b. Charlottesville, Va., Apr. 25, 1950; d. John Harper and Claire Kathryn (Johnston) C.; m. Wallace Oles Keene, Oct. 5, 1986. BA, Hollins Coll., Roanoke, Va., 1971; PhD, Yale U., 1976. Pharmacology rsch. assoc. Nat. Cancer Inst. NIH, Bethesda, Md., 1977-79; program adminstr. pharm. scis. program NIH, Bethesda, 1979-84, dep. dir. Nat. Inst. Gen Med. Scis., 1984-85, dir., 1984—. Tutor Rockville (Md.) Youth Svcs., 1978—; CPR instr. Am. Heart Assn., Bethesda, 1980-83; class fund chmn. alumnae ann. fund Hollins Coll., 1989—. Mem. Am. Soc. Pharmacology and Exptl. Therapeutics (nominating com. 1989), Sr. Execs. Assn., N.Y. Acad. Scis., Smithsonian Resident Assocs., Friends Nat. Zoo, Nat. Space Soc., Hollins Coll. Alumnae Club Washington (treas. 1979-81), Phi Beta Kappa. Office: Nat Inst Gen Med Scis-NIH 5333 Westbard Ave Rm 919 Bethesda MD 20892

CARRIE, DOREEN, personal care industry executive; b. N.Y.C., Apr. 20, 1958; d. Stanley and Stella Weiss, m. Allen Eisdorfer, June 22, 1986. BA, Rutgers U., 1980. Cert. tchr. Concept Therapy Inst., 1986. Mgr. Johnson and Johnson, North Brunswick, N.J., 1980-81; exec. creator Life Zones Inc., Woodbridge, N.J., 1982 --; speaker conventions and corps. Mem. Concept Therapy Club (pilot 1990-91). Home: 105 C Keystone Ct 1 Woodbridge NJ 07095 Office: Life Zones 520 W 8th St Plainfield NJ 07060

CARRIGAN, MARTHA LORETTO, management; b. Suffern, N.Y., June 25, 1961; d. John Walter and Mary Pat (O'Brien) Boyer; m. Jeffrey Gerard Carrigan, Dec. 28, 1984. BA in Communication, U. Wis. - Milw., 1983. Training asst. Payco Am., Brookfield, Wis., 1984, training coordinator, 1984-85; training cons. Crawford & Assocs., Milw., 1986-88; office automation support specialist Manpower Inc., Milw., 1988--; Speaker, Presenter Campus Crusade & InterVarsity, Milw. 1986--; Coordinator Eastbrook Ch., Milw. 1987-88; authorized office automation specialist Bus. Ptnr. Program, Milw. 1988--. Co-author, editor: Training Programs and Documents, Manpower, 1986—. Bd. Dirs. Vol. Ctr. Greater Milw., 1987--; Del. Wis. Rep. Caucus & Convention, Appleton Racine 1987--; Mem. Zoological Soc. Milw. 1988--, Wis. Right to Life, Milw. 1988--. Mem. East Side Rep. Club Milw., Century Club U. Wis. Republican.

CARRILLO, ANA C., counselor; b. Miami, Fla., Aug. 27, 1963; d. Jose I. and Mercedes (Real) C. BA in Polit. Sci., Chestnut Hill Coll., 1985; EdM in Counseling, Boston U., 1989. Cert. counselor, Mass., Fla. Counselor Dept. Def. Dependent Schs., Torrejon AFB, Madrid, 1988-89, Our Lady of Lourdes Acad., Miami, 1989—. Mem. Young Vizcayans. Republican. Roman Catholic. Home: 9901 SW 139th St Miami FL 33175

CARRILLO, DONNA GRIBBEN, insurance company official; b. N.Y.C., Mar. 21, 1954; d. James Gribben and Helen Patricia (Baumann) Jardine; m. Luis A. Carrillo, Sept. 30, 1989. AA, Hillsborough Community Coll., Tampa, Fla., 1977; BA, U. South Fla., 1980. Clk. Met. Life Ins. Co., Tampa, 1973-81; asst. bus. mgr. Chgo. Tribune Co., New Port Richey, Fla., 1981; bus. mgr. Chgo. Tribune Co., Naples, Fla., 1981-82; stock broker Merril Lynch Pierce Fenner & Smith, Springfield, Mo., 1982-83, Paine Webber, Tampa, 1983-384; spl. agt. Northwestern Mut. Life Ins. Co., Tampa, 1984—. Mem. Nat. Assn. Life Underwriters (nat. sales achievement award 1988, nat. quality award 1988, 89, health ins. quality award 1989), Tampa Assn. Life Underwriters, Westshore Midday Bus. and Profl. Women (rec. sec. 1990-91), Small Bus. Networking (rec. sec. 1985-86). Democrat. Office: Northwestern Mut Life One N Dale Mabry Ste 1100 Tampa FL 33609

CARRILLO-ABBOTT, CHERYL LEE, account executive; b. Wyandott, Mich., Apr. 29, 1953; d. Raymond Fedelis and Evelyn Elizabeth (Gibson) Zenk; m. Martin G. Carrillo, June 23, 1974 (div. 1985); children: Sara Elizabeth, Amy Lee; m. Timothy Abbott, Dec. 24, 1989. Student, Fullerton Coll., 1974. Estimator Zenk Carbide Prod., Wmstn., Calif., 1969-74; instrumentation designer Fluor Corp., Irvine, Calif., 1974-77; pvt. Vasona Interiors, Orange, Calif., 1977-85; acct. exec. Madden Enterprises, San Diego, Calif., 1985-89; dir. sales Classic/Lensol Decorative Fabrics, Inc., Commerce, Calif., 1989—. Author, book, "Exposed To The Reflextive Form Of I". Mem. Internat. Soc. of Int. Design., Internat. Drapery Assn. Republican. Roman Catholic. Home: 17741 Collins Circle Huntington Beach CA 92647

CARRINGTON, MARY ANN, telecommunication executive; b. Kankakee, Ill., Feb. 20, 1957; d. Adam M. and Mary Lu (Paulson) Leon; m. Paul William Carrington July 14, 1953. AS, Coll. Dupage, 1977; BS, Elmhurst Coll., 1979. Mgr. Ponderosa Steak Ho., Wheaton, Ill., 1980; asst. Evangelical Health System, Oakbrook, Ill., 1981-84; mgr. Osco Drug Store, Oak Brook, Ill., 1984—, Ill. Bell Telephone, Chgo.; owner, pres. Spangles Original Jewelry, Mama's Secret Fudge, Carrington Enterprises. Home: 2844 Vail Ct Lisle IL 60532 Office: Ill Bell Telephone 225 W Randolph Chicago IL 60606

CARRINGTON, SUSAN SCHELL, chemical company executive; b. Allentown, Pa., Nov. 14, 1951; m. Edward T. Carrington, Aug. 25, 1979. BS in Chemistry, Bucknell U., 1973. Rsch. chemist Dow Chem. Co., Midland, Mich., 1973-75, prodn. supr. plastic resins and agrl. chems., 1975-82, environ. specialist, 1982-84, supt. plastics resins pilot plant, 1984-86, rsch. mgr. fabricated consumer products, 1986-88, mgr. investor relations, 1988—. Councilman City of Midland, 1985-87; vice chmn. Midland County Solid Waste Adv. Com., 1987—; chmn. Midland City Solid Waste Com. Mem. Am. Chem. Soc., Alpha Chi Omega. Home: PO Box 2340 Midland MI 48641

CARRINGTON, SYLVIA, freelance broadcast engineer; b. N.Y.C., May 1, 1960; d. George Joshua Tynes and Florence (Stewart) Carrington. Student, Glassboro State Coll., 1978-81; cert., Announcers Tng. Studios, N.Y.C., 1984-86; BA in Journalism, Thomas A. Edison Coll., 1989. cert. in electronics FCC Gen. Radio Telephone Operators License. Announcer Sta. NBS, Phila., 1982-83; gen. assignment reporter Phila. Spirit, 1982-85; prodn. asst. Greenpoint Gazette, Bklyn., 1984; asst. engr. Sta. WNYE-FM, Medger Evans Coll., Bklyn., 1984; freelance broadcast camera/audio engr. Channel 44 and Channel C,D, N.Y.C., 1984—; engrng. apprentice CBC, N.Y.C., 1985. Mem. Exec. Networks, Soc. Motion Picture and TV Engrs. (assoc.), Nat. Assn. Radio and Telecommunications Engrs., Internat. Soc. Cert. Electronics Technicians, Assn. Communication Technicians, NAFE. African Methodist Episcopalian. Home: 30 3d Ave Brooklyn NY 11217

CARRION, TANNER RAE, insurance executive; b. Hartsville, S.C., Nov. 11, 1945; d. William Lawton McCoy and Doris Louise (Seeby) Davila; m. Jose Antonio Carrion, Feb. 17, 1964 (div.); 1 child, Rhapsody Annette Carrion Williams. Grad. high sch., West Columbia, S.C. Flexibility clk. Blue Cross/Blue Shield of S.C., Columbia, 1966-71; title I reading and math. tutor Congaree Elem. Sch., West Columbia, 1975-77; dir. group ins. S.C. Auto & Truck Dealers Assn., Columbia, S.C., 1982—. Mem. Capital Bus. and Profl. Women (treas. 1988-89, pres. 1989—). Republican. Episcopalian.

CARRIS, MARCIA LYNN, marketing professional; b. Jackson, Mich., Jan. 7, 1956; d. Earl Junior and Betty Jane (Long) C. Student, Jackson Community Coll., 1973-75; BBA, U. Mich., 1978, MBA, 1983. CPA, Ill. Acct. Ford Motor Co., Dearborn, Mich., 1978-81; intern Xerox Corp., Rochester, N.Y., 1982; staff cons. Peterson and Co., Chgo., 1983-84, sr. cons., 1984-86, exec. cons., 1986-87; dist. mgr. fin. Ameritech Pub., Troy, Mich., 1987-88, venture analyst, 1988, dir. mktg. planning and analysis, 1988—. Active Big Bros./Big Sisters, Oakland, Mich., 1987—. Mem. Planning Forum. Office: Ameritech Pub Inc 100 E Big Beaver Rd 14th Floor Troy MI 48083

CARRITHERS, ROBIN CAROLE, nurse; b. Louisville, Apr. 26, 1955; d. Carl Garnett and Mildred Louise (Wibbels) C. BSN, Vanderbilt U., Nashville, 1981; MSN, U. Louisville, 1985. RN. Staff charge Humana Hosp., Louisville, 1981-84, nurse coord., 1984-86; nurse coord. Vanderbilt U. Hosp., Nashville, 1986; adj. faculty Vanderbilt Sch. Nursing, Nashville, 1986—. Mem. Am. Assn. Critical-care Nurses (program chmn. Middle Tenn. chpt. 1988), Sigma Theta Tau. Democrat. Methodist. Office: Vanderbilt U Hosp D-2120 MCN Nashville TN 37232

CARROLL, ADORNA OCCHIALINI, real estate executive; b. New Britain, Conn., Aug. 24, 1952; d. Antonio and Mary Ida (Reney) Occhialini; m. Christoper P. Buchas, Sept. 7, 1974 (div. Nov. 1982); 1 child, Jenna Rebecca; m. John Francis Carroll, Oct. 15, 1983; children: Jordan Ashley, Sean William. BA in Philosophy, Cen. Conn. State U., 1974; grad., Realtors Inst., 1989. Lic. real estate broker, real estate agt. Dir. therapeutic recreation program Ridgeview Rest Home, Cromwell, Conn., 1974, Meadows Convalescent Home, Manchester, Conn., 1975, Andrew House Health Care, New Britain, 1976; owner, mgr. Liquor Locker, Newington, Conn., 1977-87; owner, broker A.O. Carroll & Co., Newington, 1985—; ptnr. Marco Realty & Devel. Co., Newington, 1978—. Mem. Nat. Assn. Realtors, Conn. Assn. Realtors (mem. polit. affairs com. 1988, 89), Greater New Britain Bd. Realtors (pres. 1990, chmn. polit. affairs 1988, 89, chairperson bd. programming 1989, mem. edl. orientation com. 1989, mem. budget com. 1989), Nat. Package Store Assn., Conn. Package Store Assn. (legis. lobbyist 1984-88, pres. 1986-88, Disting. Svc. award 1985), Greater Hartford Package Store Assn. (pres. 1981-82), Newington C. of C. (bd. dirs. 1987-88, chmn. legis. 1988). Home: 22 Hickory Hill Ln Newington CT 06111 Office: 976 W Main St New Britain CT 06053

CARROLL, ANN FOLEY, personnel consultant; b. Fitchburg, Mass., Feb. 17, 1962; d. Bernard James and Martha Jane (Hazel) Foley; m. Charles Bernard Carroll, Oct. 5, 1986; 1 child, Shannon Foley. BA in English, U. N.H., 1985. Supr. mdse. div. Lenox, Inc., Kittery, Maine, 1985, asst. mgr., 1985-86, store mgr., 1986-89; pers. cons. New Perspective Pers., Woburn, Mass., 1989—. Active York Hist. Soc. Mem. Kittery Bus. Council, 1986—. Democrat. Roman Catholic. Home: 4 Wildwood Ln Salem NH 03079

CARROLL, BARBARA ANNE, radiologist, educator; b. Beaumont, Tex., Oct. 20, 1945; d. Theron Demp and Annette Ione (Anderson) C.; m. Olaf T. von Ramm. BA, U. Tex., 1967; MD, Stanford U., 1972. Intern, Stanford Hosp., Palo Alto, Calif., 1972, resident, 1973-76; research asst. Genetics Found., U. Tex., Austin, 1963-67; teaching asst. NSF Summer Biology Workshop, Austin, 1967; clinician Planned Parenthood, Santa Clara, Calif., 1973-76; instr. extension div. U. Calif.-Santa Cruz, 1972-76; asst. prof. radiology Stanford U. Med. Sch., Palo Alto, 1977-84, assoc. prof. radiology, 1984-85; chief diagnostic ultrasound, 1977-85; assoc. prof. radiology Duke U., Durham, N.C., 1985—; cons. Searle, Santa Clara, 1977-78, Diasonics, Inc., Santa Clara, 1979-83, NIH, 1981-84, Acuson, 1984—; mem. commn. on Ultrasound Am. Coll. Radiology, 1989—. Contbr. articles to various publs.; reviewer numerous med. jours., 1982—; assoc. editor Radiology Jour., 1986—, Investigative Radiology, 1989—, Jour. of Ultrasound in Medicine, 1990—. Bd. dirs. Planned Parenthood Santa Clara County, 1975-76. Agnes Axtell Moule Faculty scholar, 1979-84; recipient Cancer and Med. Research Found. award, 1980. Fellow Am. Inst. Ultrasound in Medicine (bd. govs. 1987—); mem. Soc. Radiologists in Ultrasound, Am. Coll. Radiology, Assn. Women Radiologists, Assn. Univ. Radiologists, Venezuelan Ultrasound Soc., N.C. Ultrasound Soc. (faculty adv. 1986—), Phi Beta Kappa. Democrat. Presbyterian. Office: Duke U Med Sch Dept Radiology Box 3808 Durham NC 27710

CARROLL, BONNIE, publisher, editor; b. Salt Lake City, Nov. 20, 1941. Grad. high sch., Ogden, Utah. Owner The Peer Group, San Francisco, 1976-78; pub., editor The Reel Directory, Cotati, Calif., 1978—. Pub., editor The Reel Thing newsletter, San Francisco, 1977-78. Mem. Assn. Visual Communicators (bd. dirs. 1987—), No. Calif. Women in Film, San Francisco Film Tape Council (exec. dir. 1979-81). Office: The Reel Directory PO Box 866 Cotati CA 94931

CARROLL, DIAHANN, actress, singer; b. N.Y.C., July 17, 1935; d. John and Mabel (Faulk) Johnson; m. Monte Kay (div.); m. Fredde Glusman (div.); m. Robert DeLean, 1975 (dec. 1977); m. Vic Damone, 1987. Student, N.Y. U. Began career as model; actress: motion pictures, including Claudine (Nominated for Acad. award as best actress by the Acad. Motion Picture

Arts and Scis. 1974), Carmen Jones, Porgy and Bess, Hurry Sundown, Paris Blues, The Split; on Broadway in No Strings, House of Flowers; appeared in: play Same Time, Next Year; TV series Julia, Dynasty, 1984-87; TV movies Death Scream, 1975, I Know Why the Caged Bird Sings, 1979, Sister, Sister, 1982. Address: care Triad Artists 10100 Santa Monica Blvd 16th Fl Los Angeles CA 90067*

CARROLL, ELIZABETH JOAN, real estate developer, broker; b. Ft. Wayne, Ind., July 19, 1944; d. George Perry and Mildred (Rawles) Shaffer; m. James Frederick Carroll, July 24, 1965 (div. May 1985); children: David, Kristin, Stephen, Brian. RN, Toledo Hosp. Sch. Nursing, 1964. Cert. comml. investment mem. Nurse Toledo Hosp., 1964; head nurse St. Vincent Hosp., Toledo, 1965-71; residential sales rep. Grogan Co., Toledo, 1972-73, Gallanger Real Estate, Syracuse, N.Y., 1973; pres. Multiple Listing Svc., Spartanburg, 1980; mem. internat. adv. bd. Univ. S.C., Spartanburg, 1986—. Bd. dirs. United Services council, Spartanburg, 1984-86; active Asian Ioga Trade Missions, Korea, Republic of China, Hong Kong, Singapore, 1981-82; mem. N.C. Outward Bound, 1985. Recipient Nat. Creative Nursing award Colgate-Palmolive, 1971. Mem. Internat. Real Estate Fedn., Soc. Indsl. and Office Realtors (computer com. internat. commn. 1987—), Cert. Comml. Investment of Nat. Assn. Realtors, Leadership S.C. Alumni, Japan-Am. Assn. West S.C., West S.C. Internat. Trade Assn. (v.p., S.C. Econ. Developers Assn., S.C. State Ports Authority (adv. com. 1989), Spartanburg Bd. Realtors (pres. 1980-81), Spartanburg Exec. Women's (pres. 1986). Republican. Roman Catholic. Home: 1340 Pinecrest Rd Spartanburg SC 29302 Office: Carroll Properties Corp 1151 Cedar Crest Rd Spartanburg SC 29301

CARROLL, GENEVA BARR, public management educator; b. Silver Point, Tenn., June 15, 1930; d. Roe and Bertha (Hutchings) Barr; m. Barby Ray Carroll, June 21, 1952; children: Connie Carroll Feehan, Elise Carroll Scanlan, Barry. BS, Okal. State U., 1954; MA, U. Miss., 1961; PhD, La. State U., 1972. Vocat. home econs. tchr. Glenco (Okla.) High Sch., 1955-56, Calument (Okla.) High Sch., 1956-57; asst. prof. U. Miss., Oxford, 1963-66; cons. to state depts. La. State U., Baton Rouge, 1973-80, grants mgr., 1984—; La. State U. planning cons. State Planning Office, Baton Rouge, 1973-77; La. State U. human. Author: Data Locator Guide, 1976, revised edit., 1979, 82, Development and Maintenance of the La. Occupational Information System, Vol. I-IV, 1981-84. Planning cons. YMCA, Baton Rouge, 1982-84, Long Range Planning Com. for State and Local Govt., Baton Rouge, 1982-84. La. Dept. Labor grantee, Baton Rouge, 1980-84, Regional Office Labor fin. mgr. tng. grantee, Dallas. 1981-82, Nat. Occupational Info. Coord. Com. career counseling grantee, Washington, 1983-84. Mem. Women in Mgmt. (pres. 1985-87), Nat. Family Relations Coun., La. Family Relations Coun. (treas. 1982-87), Phi Kappa Phi (chpt. pres. 1986-87), La. State U. Women's Faculty Club (v.p. 1985-86). Baptist. Home: 553 Castle Kirk Dr Baton Rouge LA 70808 Office: La State U 385 Pleasant Hall Baton Rouge LA 70803

CARROLL, GRETCHEN LOU, assistant principal; b. Bad Axe, Mich., Jan. 15, 1950; d. Lloyd Ferris adn Eva Jean (Gilbert) Reimann; m. Michael James Carroll, Aug. 23, 1969; children: Aaron Michael, Adam Lloyd. BA, Saginaw Valley State U., 1980; MA, Cen. Mich. U., 1985, EdS, 1988. Cert. adminstrn., tchr. Tchr. Birch Run (Mich.) Schs., 1981-82; tchr. South Intermediate Sch., Saginaw (Mich.) Pub. Schs., 1983-90; asst. prin. Lake Ville Community Schs., Otisville, Mich., 1990—; advisor Journalism, Saginaw, 1983-87. Mem. NEA, Mich. Ednl. Assn., AAUW (membership chairperson Frankenmuth, Mich. 1984-90, acad. track chairperson Frankenmuth 1990), Phi Delta Kappa (rsch. chairperson 1989-90, membership chairperson 1990, Rsch. award 1989). Lutheran. Home: 165 Sunburst Frankenmuth MI 48734 Office: Lake Ville Community Schs 12455 Wilson Rd Otisville MI 48463

CARROLL, INEZ RICHARDSON, editorial assistant; b. Oklahoma City, Aug. 25, 1929; d. L.E. and Inez (Williams) R.; m. Herbert S. Carroll, Nov. 21, 1951 (dec. Jan. 1983); 1 child, Rhonda Lynne. BA, Fisk U., 1950; MEd, North Tex. State U., 1960. Tchr. grade 2 Ft. Worth Ind. Sch. Dist., 1959-69, curriculum specialist, 1969-72, resource tchr. cen. cities project, 1969-72, resource tchr., editorial asst., 1975—. Bd. dirs. Planned Parenthood, Ft. Worth, 1978-80, Ft. Worth Plumbing Bd., 1986-88; vol. Ft. Worth Growth Ctr., 1982-90. Mem. AAUW, Prog. Literary and Arts Club (v.p. 1990), Delta Sigma Theta. Presbyterian. Office: Ft Worth Ind Sch Dist Carlson Bldg 3320 W Cantey Fort Worth TX 76109

CARROLL, JEANNE, public relations executive; b. Oak Park, Ill., May 20, 1929; d. John P. and Mary (Noonan) Carroll; B.A., U. London, 1950; M.A., Northwestern U., 1951; m. Harold M. Kass, Apr. 1966. Bus. girls editor Charm Mag., N.Y.C., 1951-53; pub. relations dir. Rosary Coll., River Forest, Ill., 1953-66; chmn. publicity Am. Cancer Soc., bd. dirs. W. and S.W. Suburban Unit, 1967—; med. adminstr., asst. to Dr. Harold Kass, Oak Park, Ill., 1969—. Pub. relations counselor in Midwest for Brown U., 1962; dir. pub. relations Mundelein Coll., 1968; producer radio show for teen-agers, Chgo., 1954; lectr. sci. devels. Bell Labs. for AT&T, 1954; participant annual Sun-Times seminars for coll. journalists MacMurray Coll., Jacksonville Ill. Chmn. March of Dimes campaign for Chgo., ednl. TV Channel 11, River Forest, 1963; trustee DePaul U., Chgo., chmn. Soc. Fellows dinner; chmn. Oak Park Hosp. Ben Din Dan, 1971-80; mem. com. library Internat. Relations, 1975-82; mem. bd. Arden Shores, sch. for boys, 1984—; bd. dirs. Globe Theatre Ctr. Recipient Excellence award for coll. brochures Am. Coll. Pubs. Com., 1957; medal of recognition for work in pub. relations Bishop Fulton Sheen, 1960; Humanitarian award Performing Arts Ctr. and Citizens Com., Chgo., 1976; award DuSalbe Mus., 1978. Mem. Ill. Assn. Coll. Admissions Counsellors (pres.), Assn. Coll. Pub. Relations Assn., Family Service Assn. Am. (past bd. dirs.), Acad. Hosp., Pub. Relations, Ill. (pres.), Chgo. (pub. relations dir., med. soc. auxs.), Oak Park Hosp. (pres. women's aux. 1986-89), West Suburban Hosp. Med. Ctr. Aux. (life). Mailing Address: 712 Courtland Circle Springdale Western Springs IL 60558 Office: 715 Lake St Oak Park IL 60301

CARROLL, KIM MARIE, nurse; b. Ottawa, Ill., Feb. 13, 1958; d. John J. and Charin E. (Reilley) Marmion; m. Thomas Christopher Carroll, Aug. 25, 1979; 1 child, Christopher John. B.S.N., U. Denver, 1983; diploma Copley Meml. Hosp. Sch. Nursing, Aurora, Ill., 1979. R.N., Ill., Ind., Colo.; critical care practitioner. Staff nurse Penrose Hosp., Colorado Springs, Colo., 1979-83, asst. head nurse cardiac floor, 1983-84; asst. dir. nurses Big Meadows Nursing Home, Savanna, Ill., 1985-86, dir. nurses, 1986-88; clin. mgr. Ind. Heart Physicians, Inc., Beech Grove, Ind., 1989—. Mem. NAFE, Am. Cancer Soc. (v.p. Carroll County, Ill., 1988, pub. edn. chmn. 1987-88), Ind. Coun. on Cardiovascular Nursing, Beta Sigma Phi (chpt. pres. 1988-89), Sigma Theta Tau. Roman Catholic. Avocation: skiing. Home: 8229 Autumn Mill Ln Indianapolis IN 46256 Office: Ind Heart Physicians Inc 112 N 17th Ave Ste 300 Beech Grove IN 46107

CARROLL, LLAWANNA FAYE, manager; b. Jackson, Ala., May 15, 1955; sd. Enoch Roosevelt and Rosa Lyn (White) Todd; m. Philip Lee Carroll, June 5, 1981; children: Sydney Nicole, Shannon Patrice. BS, Auburn U., 1976; MPH, U. Ala., Birmingham, Ala., 1985. Registered med. technologist. Lab technician, med. technologist Carraway Meth. Med. Ctr., Birmingham, Ala., 1976-78; chief technologist Jackson (Ala.) Hosp., 1975-80; night svc. med. technologist Bapt. Med. Ctr. Montclair, Birmingham, 1980-81, sr. med. technologist, 1981-83; med. technologist II Good Samaritan Hosp. & Health Ctr., Dayton, Ohio, 1983-87; processing lab. supr. Community Blood Ctr., Dayton, 1983-85, tech. svcs. supr., 1985-89, compliance mgr., 1989—; safety com. chairperson Community Blood Ctr., Dayton, 1989—, on-site radiation safety officer, 1989—. Mem. Victory Theatre Assn. Mem. Am. Pub. Health Assn., Am. Assn. Blood Banks, Ohio Assn. Blood Banks, Dayton Area Blood Bankers, NAACP, Delta Sigma Theta Sorority, Gamma Sigma Sigma. Democrat. Baptist. Home: 838 Manhattan Ave Dayton OH 45406 Office: Community Blood Ctr 349 S Main St Dayton OH 45402

CARROLL, MARGARET ANN, chemist; b. Clearfield, Pa., Nov. 16, 1929; d. William J. and Margaret R. (Rosenhoover) C. BS magna cum laude, Coll. Misericoria, Dallas, 1951; MS, St. Joseph U., Phila., 1963. Control chemist Winthrop Stearns, Rensselaer, NY, 1951-53; from microanalytical chemist to sr. chemist Smith Kline and French Labs, Phila., 1953-79; assoc. sr. investigator Smithkline and French Labs, Phila., 1979—. Contbr. articles to profl. jour. contbr. chpt. The Analytical Approach, 1983. Mem. Am. Chem. Soc., Chromatography Forum, Microchemical Soc. Office: Smithkline and French Labs PO Box 1539 King of Prussia PA 19406

CARROLL, MARILYN JEANNE, medical technologist, educator; b. San Pedro, Calif., Feb. 20, 1950; d. Wayne E. and Katherine M. (Hepburn) Arnold; m. Shawn Michael Carroll, Aug. 2l, 197l; children: Michael J., Megan J. AA, L.A. Harbor Coll., Wilmington, Calif., 1970; BA, Calif. State U., Dominiguez, 1972. Med. technologist Martin L. King Hosp., L.A., 1975, Harbor Gen. Hosp., Torrance, Calif., 1975-79, Rsch. and Edn. Inst., Torrance, 1979-88; teaching asst. UCLA, 1980-88; v.p., lab. mgr. J.A. Turner Diagnostic Parasitology Lab., Carson, Calif., 1984—; lectr. Harbor-UCLA Med. Ctr., Torrance, 1975—; teaching asst. UCLA, 1980—. Mem. Am. Soc. Microbiology, Am. Soc. Clin. Pathologists, Am. Soc. Parasitologists, So. Calif. Soc. Parasitologists, Sports Car Club Am. Democrat. Office: JA Turner Diagnostic Parasitology Lab 519 W Carson St Ste 104 Carson CA 90745

CARROLL, PATRICIA MARY, marketing and sales executive; b. N.Y.C., Dec. 5, 1939; d. Patrick Michael and Bridget Patricia (Ginnelly) Curran; m. Thomas Michael Carroll, Jan. 26, 1963; children: Matthew Thomas, Jeanne Anastasia. BS, Fordham U., 1961; MS, Coll. New Rochelle, 1975; postgrad., NYU, 1972, CUNY, 1983—. Cert. tchr. spl. edn. and English, N.Y. Exec. confidential sec. N.Y. Daily News, 1961-66; tchr. White Plains (N.Y.) Adult Edn. Ctr. and Westchester Devel. Ctr., 1975; asst. dir. nursing and allied health edn. March of Dimes Birth Defects Found., White Plains, 1976-84; sales/mktg. mgr. Stoffel Seals Corp., Nyack, N.Y., 1984-87; mgr. mktg. McGraw-Hill, N.Y.C. and Washington, 1988-89, Faulkner & Gray, Inc., 1989—; copy editor Pergamon Press, Elmsford, N.Y., 1979; editor texts Appleton-Century-Crofts. Assoc. editor The First Six Hours of Life series, 1978-82, Prenatal Care series, 1978-82, 1978-85, Intrapartal Care series, 1980-82, The Birth Defects Original Article Series, 3 vols., 1984; editor: Concepts of Human Development (B. Raff and C. Windwer); contbr. articles to profl. jours. and newspapers. Legis. adv. com. N.Y. State Assembly, 1980-84; mem. Mamaroneck (N.Y.) Beautification Com., 1983; nominating com. for assoc. mems. Internat. Festivals Assn., 1986-87. Coll. scholar, 1957. Mem. AAUW, Women In Communications (program com. 1983-90), Women's Nat. Book Assn., Am. Coll. Healthcare Mktg. Inst. Roman Catholic. Home: 171 Maple Ave Mamaroneck NY 10543 Office: Faulkner & Gray Inc 106 Fulton St New York NY 10038

CARROLL, PAULA MARIE, security company executive; b. Fresno, Calif., July 17, 1933; d. Paul Edward Mikkelsen and Helen Marie (Anderson) Mack; m. Herman S. Carroll Jr., April 25, 1954. V.p., co-owner Cen. Valley Alarm Co., Inc., Merced, Calif., 1963—; pres., co-owner Cen. Valley Alarm Co., Inc., Merced, 1988—. Author: Life Wish, 1986. Mem. Hospice of Merced and Mariposa Counties, Calif., 1979; pres., founder Consumers for Med. Quality Inc., Merced, 1981; chair Ombudsman, Merced, 1982-85. Recipient Celebrating Women award Merced County, 1987, Pres.'s award Calif. Trial Lawyers Assn., 1987; named Woman Distinction Soroptimist Internat., 1986; Consumers for Med. Quality grantee Calif. Trial Lawyers Assn., 1987. Mem. Western Burglar and Fire Alarm Assn., Soc. Law and Medicine, Hastings Ctr. Inst. of Soc., NAFE, Internat. Platform Assn., Inst. Rsch. Assn. (assoc.), Beta Sigma Phi. Home: 3271 Alder Ave Merced CA 95340 Office: Cen Valley Alarm Co Inc 620 W 14th St Merced CA 95340

CARROLL, REBECCA ANN, quality engineering specialist; b. Shelbyville, Ind., Sept. 17, 1946; d. Morgan Robert and Katherine (Comstock) Hendrickson; m. Ronald Lee Higdon, May 28, 1966 (div. 1972); children: Hayley Rhome, Tasha Noel; m. Bobby Eugene Carroll, June 1, 1974; 1 child, Tonia Renee. Student, Purdue U. Extension, Indpls., 1970-72. Engrng. technician P.R. Mallory Co., Indpls., 1967-70; quality analyst RCA Corp., Indpls., 1970-73; engrng. technician Union Carbide Corp., Indpls., 1973-77; quality engr. No. Telecom, Nashville, 1978-89; mgr. quality engrng. Cumberland Swan Inc., Smyrna, Tenn., 1989—. Active Nashville mayoral campaign, 1987. Mem. Am. Soc. Quality Control (sect. chair 1987-88, technical program chair 1989; named Vol. of Month 1989), Tenn. Quality Coalition (conf. com. chair 1987—). Roman Catholic. Home: 132 Beulah Blvd Pleasant View TN 37146 Office: Cumberland Swan Inc One Swan Dr Smyrna TN 37167

CARROLL, REBECCA LOIS, flute and piano educator; b. Phila., Dec. 22, 1952; d. Lewis Richard and Doris May (Benjamin) C. BS in Elem. Edn., Nyack (N.Y.) Coll., 1975; pvt. study flute, piano, voice. Pvt. tchr. flute and piano, Nyack and Audubon, N.J., 1968—; tchr. Bellmawr (N.J.) Nursery Sch., 1975-80, Lad & Lassie Pre-Sch., Kirkwood, 1981-85; piccoloist Haddonfield (N.J.) Symphony, 1968—; lectr., panelist, performer music for assns. and schs. Mem. Nat. Flute Assn., South Jersey Music Tchrs. Assn. (bd. dirs. 1988-90), Flute Soc. Greater Phila., Phila. Mus. Soc., NAFE. Home and Office: 333 Walnut St Audubon NJ 08106

CARROLL, ROSEMARY LALEVÉE, public relations executive; b. Philadelphia, Sept. 12, 1945; d. Russell Reeve and Anne (Hiney) Lalevée; m. Edward Francis Carroll, July 31, 1969; children: Edward Jr., Brian Russell, Patrick Liam. BA, Coll. St. Elizabeh, Convent Sta., N.J., 1967; postgrad., Syracuse U., 1967-68. Managing editor The Lawrence (N.J.) Ledger, Inc., 1968-70; dir. community relations and devel. Mercer Med. Ctr., Trenton, N.J., 1971-77; dir. community relations Westlake Community Hosp., Melrose Park, Ill., 1978-79, Southeastern Regional Planning and Econ. Devel. Dist., Taunton, Mass.; mgr. pub. info. and community relations Plimoth Plantation, Plymouth, Mass., 1981-85; dir. mktg. and devel. Jordan Hosp., Inc., Mass., 1985-89; dir. devel. and pub. rels. The Seeing Eye, Inc., Morristown, N.J., 1990—; contbr. editor, The Aluma, Coll. St. Elizabeth, N.J., 1972-79, managing dir., The Portiuncula, Cardinal Cushing Sch. and Tng. Ctr., Hanover, Mass., 1979-81. Pres. Plymouth Philharm. Orch., 1983-85; vol. publicist Town's ann. tree-lighting ceremony, art guild show, town 4th of July parade; religious edn. tchr. Ch. Blessed Kateri Tekakwitha. Mem. N.J. Press Women (v.p. 1974-76), Mass. Media Women (founding pres. 1980-82), Nat. Fedn. Press Women (New Eng. regional dir. 1982, 3d v.p. 1983-85, 2d v.p. 1985-87, 1st v.p. 1987-89, nat. pres. 1989-91), New Eng. Assn. Hosp. Devel., Acad. Health Svcs. Mktg. Avocation: travelling. Office: The Seeing Eye Inc Morristown NJ 07963

CARROLL LANGE, MONICA, psychologist, consultant; b. Santa Monica, Calif., Nov. 2, 1951; d. Jack and Elizabeth Bergal (Longaker) Kahlenberg; m. Stephen D. Lange, June 30, 1989; children: Mailan, James, Michael, Michael. AA with honors, El Camino Coll., 1980; BA summa cum laude, U. Calif., Dominguez Hills, 1982, MA, 1984; PhD, The Claremont Grad. Sch., 1987. Editor various orgns. L.A., 1969-80; instr. Calif. State U.-Dominguez Hills, Carson, 1983—; pvt. practice cons. Calif., 1983—; psychol. asst. Long Beach (Calif.) Counseling Ctr., 1985-87; pvt. practice psychologist Manhattan Beach, Calif., 1987—; psychologist Project Touch, Hermosa Beach, Calif., 1987-89, Lakewood (Calif.) Counseling Ctr., 1987-89, Fairview Devel. Ctr., Costa Mesa, Calif., 1989—; mem. adv. bd. learning disabilities dept. El Camino Coll., Torrance, 1987-88. Coun. for Exceptional Children grantee, 1989—. Mem. Am. Psychol. Assn., Calif. State Psychol. Assn., Coun. for Exceptional Children (rep. for multi handicapped), Assn. for Children and Adults with Learning Disabilities, Psychology Honor Soc. Democrat.

CARROLL-VAN NORMAN, DONNA LEE, health care executive; b. McKeesport, Pa., Dec. 6, 1958; d. Clyde Irwin and Lillian Gertrude (Lee) C.; m. Scott Alan Van Norman, May 12, 1984; children: Shawna Cortney, Craig Jeffrey David. BA in Natural Scis., LaRoche Coll., Pitts., 1981; EMT, St. Alex. Med. Ctr., Bismarck, N.D., 1984; postgrad., Kennedy Western U., Agoura Hills, Calif. Radiologic tech. St. Francis Med. Ctr., Pitts., 1978-80, Presbyn. U. Hosp., Oakland, Pa., 1980-81, Health Examinetics, San Diego, 1982-83, St. Alexius Med. Ctr., Bismarck, 1983-86; EMT Forsyth Ambulence Co., Forsyth, Mont., 1986-87; radiologic tech. mgr. Rosebud Health Care Ctr., Forsyth, 1986-89, risk mgr., 1989—. Mem. NAFE, Am. Soc. Radiologic Technologists, Mont. Soc. Radiologic Technologists, Mont. Soc. Emergency Med. Technologists, Rosebud health Care Ctr. Aux. (pres. 1988-89), Spouses Support Group (v.p. 1986), N.D. Soc. Radiologic Technologists. Methodist. Home: Box 1029 3 Wibaux Pl Forsyth MT 59327 Office: Rosebud Healthcare Ctr Box 268 383 N 17th St Forsyth MT 59327

CARRUTHERS, SARA PROCTER, sales assistant; b. Cin., Ohio, June 23, 1962; d. Ralph Rogan and Donna (Young) C. Student, Miami U., 1980-83. Field tech. P.M. Mag., Cin., Ohio, 1983-85; natl. sales asst. WKRC TV, Cin., 1985-87; sales asst., traffic asst. WKRC Radio, Cin., 1987--. Founder, Dir., "Little Peoples Theatre", 1985, Luisa, Theatre "The Fantasticks", "Sound of Music", Annie, Theatre, "Annie Get Your Gun". Volunteer, Merry Hosp., Hamilton, 1980--, Westover Retirement Home, 1983--. Recipient Internat. Thespian Soc. Hamilton Taft, 1977-80, Omega, State Voice Ofcls., Interstate, 1978-79, Cin. Debutante, City of Cin. Soc., 1980-81. Mem. Am. Fedn. TV and Radio Artists, Little Harbor Club, Delta Zeta (nat. social chmn. 1988—, nat. rush com.). Republican. Episcopal. Home: 601 Glenway Dr Hamilton OH 45013

CARSCH, RUTH ELIZABETH, consulting librarian; b. London, May 3, 1945; came to U.S., 1949; d. Harry and Ellen Margot (Adler) C.; 1 child, Zachariah Robert. BA, CUNY, 1967; MS in Libr. Sci., Columbia U., 1968. Cert. libr., N.Y., Calif. Reference libr., YA specialist N.Y. Pub. Libr., 1968-70; arts resource assoc. N.Y. State Coun. on the Arts, N.Y.C., 1970-72; tech. info. specialist Bechtel, Inc., San Francisco, 1972-75; rsch. assoc. Erick & Lavidge Mkt. Rsch., San Francisco, 1980-86; reference libr. Burlingame (Calif.) Pub. Libr., 1986—; cons. Ruffin Cooper, Photographer, San Francisco, 1978—, Peterson, Skolnick & Dodge, 1978—, Port Authority N.Y., N.J., 1982-84, Camp, Dresser, McKee, Engrs., Boston, 1988; file coord. Community Info Program PLS, Belmont Calif, 1986-87; reference libr. Skyline Coll., 1988—. Researcher: Cubist Books & Cubist Prints, 1984 (Art Libr. Assn. award, 1986). Mem. No. Calif., Bus. Librs. Roundtable, Bay Area Architecture-Engring. Librs. Roundtable.

CARSELL, CAROLYN KAY, teacher; b. Davenport, Iowa, Nov. 18, 1938; d. Edward Joseph and Esther Naomi (Vergo) Karasek; m. James Herbert Carsell, Aug. 21, 1960; children: James Patrick, Jon Christopher, Susanne Kay. BA, Marycrest Coll., 1961; MS, Western Ill. U., 1989. Tchr. elem. Ericcson Sch., Moline, Ill., 1959-62, Blackhawk Sch., Moline, 1965-68, Seton Cath. Sch., Moline, 1975-81, Jefferson Sch., Bettendorf, Iowa, 1981—. Mem. NEA, Iowa State Edn. Assn., Internat. Reading Assn., Nat. Coun. Tchrs. of English, World Orgn. Porcelain Artists, Internat. Porcelain Artists, Porcelain Portrait Soc., World Orng. Porcelain Tchrs., Phi Kappa Phi. Home: 5101 8th Ave Moline IL 61265 Office: Jefferson Sch 610 Holmes Bettendorf IA 52722

CARSEY, MARCIA LEE PETERSON, television producer; b. South Weymouth, Mass., Nov. 21, 1944; d. John Edwin and Rebecca White (Simonds) Peterson; m. John Jay Carsey, Apr. 12, 1969; children: Rebecca Peterson, John Peterson. B.A. in English Lit., U. N.H., 1966. Exec. story editor Tomorrow Entertainment, Los Angeles, 1971-74; sr. v.p. prime time series ABC-TV, Los Angeles, 1978-81; founder Carsey Prodns., Los Angeles, 1981; co-owner Carsey-Werner Co., 1982—; co-exec. producer TV series Oh Madeline, 1983; exec. producer The Cosby Show, 1984—, A Different World, 1987—, Roseanne, 1988—, Chicken Soup, 1989—, Grand, 1990. Office: Carsey-Werner Co 4024 Radford Ave Studio City CA 91604

CARSON, CAROL S., economist; b. 1939. BA, Coll. of Wooster, 1961; MA, Fletcher Sch. Law and Diplomacy, Tufts U., 1962; PhD, George Washington U., 1971. Asst. to dir. Bur. Econ. Analysis, Commerce Dept., Washington, 1972-76, chief current bus. analysis, 1976-82, chief economist, 1982-85, dep. dir., 1985—; adj. asst. prof. Pace Coll. at Westchester, 1971-72. Office: Commerce Dept Bur Econ Analysis 1401 K St NW Washington DC 20230

CARSON, CHERYL DAWN, fixed income assistant; b. Galion, Ohio, Aug. 8, 1961; d. Richard Leroy and Marvel Rose (Kurtz) Broka; m. Donald Scott Carson, Aug. 1, 1959; 1 child, Andrew Scott. BA, Anderson Coll., 1979-83. From member benefits clk. to investment mortgage asst. State Tchrs. Retirement System, Columbus, Ohio, 1983-86, fixed income asst., 1986--. Republican. Home: State Tchrs Retirement Syst 275 E Broad St Columbus OH 43215

CARSON, DONITA FAYE, accountant; b. Tell City, Ind., Oct. 10, 1956; d. Donald Henry and Naomi Faye (Richard) Cassidy; m. David Earl Carson, Dec. 27, 1975; children: David Jason, Jamie Kristine. BS in Acctg., U. So. Ind., 1983; cert. in Real Estate, Ind. U., 1984. Realtor Hollinden Realty, Tell City, 1985-87, Key Assocs., Tell City, 1987-90; acct. Consol. Refineries, Troy, Ind., 1986-90; substitute tchr. Tell City Sch. Corp., 1981-90; lectr. Weight Watchers Kentuckiana, Louisville, 1982-84; owner Pure Water Perry County, Tell City, 1985-90. Mem. Prime Time Com., Tell City, 1984-85; bd. dirs., treas. Tot-Lots Inc., Tell City, 1984-85; aux. Perry County Community Coun. for Riley Childrens Hosp., Perry County Meml. Hosp.; chmn. James Whitcomb Riley Childrens Hosp. Community Coun., Marksmen Booster Club; chmn. rm. mothers Mill Creek PTA, 1990-91; mem. Tates Creek PTA. Named Outstanding Young Woman Am. 1985, 87, 88. Mem. NAFE, Women's Bus. Initiative, Perry County LWV, Hoosier Heights Country Club (chmn. 1985, auctioneer 1984-86, invitational chmn. 1989), Oak Meadows Country Club, Beta Sigma Phi (pres. Mu Gamma chpt. 1988-89, Woman of Yr. 1986). Lutheran. Home: 2105 Hawkesbury Way Lexington KY 40515

CARSON, FLORIDA PEARL, educator; b. Ardmore, Okla., Dec. 27, 1906; d. John Anthony and Margaret Elizabeth (Bond) Heartsill; m. Guy Edward Carson, Mar. 4, 1934 (dec. 1974); children: Carole Pearl, Duane Alan. BA, Southeastern Coll., 1933. Cert. elem. tchr., Okla. Tchr. elem. Springer (Okla.) Pub. Sch., 1926-27, Wilson (Okla.) Pub. Schs., 1927-28; primary tchr. Mt. Washington Pub. Sch., Ardmore, 1929-34; with light and power co. Pontiac, Mich., 1942-44; with torpedo plant St. Louis, 1944-45; tchr. elem. Ardmore Pub. Schs., 1945-69, ret., 1969; basketball coach Springer High Sch., 1926-28, Mt. Washington Jr. High Sch., Ardmore, 1932-34. Insp. Carter County Election Bd., Ardmore, 1970—. AAUW fellow, 1989. Mem. AAUW (ofcl. bd., chmn. reservations com. 1980—), Goddard Ctr. Visual and Performing ARts. Democrat. Methodist. Home: 1410 W Broadway Ardmore OK 73401

CARSON, JULIA M., state legislator; b. Louisville, July 8, 1938; 2 children. Ed. Ind. U., 1960-62, St. Mary of the Woods, 1976-78. Mem. In. Ho. of Reps., Indpls., 1972-76; mem. Ind. Senate, 1976—. Vice pres. Greater Indpls. Prog. Com.; nat. Democratic committeewoman; trustee YMCA; bd. dirs. Pub. Service Acad. Recipient Woman of Yr. Ind. award, 1974; Outstanding Leadership award AKA; Humanitarian award Christian Theol. Sem. Mem. NAACP, Urban League, Nat. Council Negro Women. Baptist. Office: State Senate Indianapolis IN 46205 Other: 2530 N Park Ave Indianapolis IN 46205*

CARSON, MARGARET MARIE, gas industry executive, marketing professional; b. Windber, Pa., Dec. 30, 1944; d. Peter and Margaret (Olenik) Buben; m. Claude Carson, Dec. 30, 1967 (div. 1974); m. Brian Charles Scruby, June 6, 1975; stepchildren: Debbie, Victor, Chris, Kenneth. BA, U. Pitts., 1971; MS in Mgmt., Houston Bapt. U., 1985. Petroleum analyst Gulf Oil Co., Pitts., 1973-75, crude oil analyst, 1971-74, environ. coordinator, 1974-79, mgr. oil acquistition, Houston, 1980-84, mktg. dir., 1985; sales dir. Cabot Cons. Group, Houston, 1985-86; dir. competitor analysis, Enron Corp., Houston, 1987—; adj. prof. bus tech. Houston Community Coll., 1985—. Columnist: The Collegian, 1984-85; contbr. to Cathedral Poets, 1976. Mem. Young Reps., Houston, 1980-85; sponsor Classical Guitar Soc., Houston; bd. dirs. Indiana U., Pa., 1980-81. Mem. Internat. Energy Analysts, Gas Processors Assn. (speaker tech. session 1985-86), Nat. Assn. Female Execs. Club: Univ.

CARSON, MARY SILVANO, educator, counselor; b. Mass.; d. Joseph and Alice V. (Sherwood) Silvano; m. Paul E. Carson (dec.); children: Jan Ellen, Jeffrey Paul, Amy Jayne. BS, Simmons Coll., Boston, 1947; MA, U. Chgo., 1961; postgrad., Ctr. Urban Studies, 1970, U. Chgo., 1970, 72, U. Minn., 1977, DePaul U., Chgo., 1980. Cert. sch. and employment counselor, Ill. Mgr. S.W. Youth Opportunity Ctr., Dept. Labor, Chgo., 1966-67; careers' counselor Gordon Tech. High Sch., Chgo., 1971-74; dir. Career and Assessment Ctr., YMCA Community Coll., Chgo., 1974-81; project coord. Career Ctr., Loop Coll., Chgo., 1981-82; adv. bd. City-Wide Coll. Career Ctr. Bd. dirs. Loop YWCA, Chgo., coord. employment project, 1985-87; active Opera Soc., San Francisco, 1988-89. Mem. Women's Share in Pub.

Svc. (v.p.), English Speaking Union, Internat. Counseling Assn., Tchrs. Internat. Inst., Am. Ednl. Rsch. Assn., Am. Counseling and Devel. Assn., Nat. Vocat. Guidance Assn., Bus. and Profl. Women's Club, Pi Lambda Theta (chpt. pres. 1975).

CARSTEN, ARLENE DESMET, financial executive; b. Paterson, N.J., Dec. 5, 1937; d. Albert F. and Ann (Greutert) Desmet; m. Alfred John Carsten, Feb. 11, 1956; children: Christopher Dale, Jonathan Glenn. Student Alfred U., 1955-56. Exec. dir. Inst. for Burn Medicine, San Diego, 1972-81, adv. bd. mem., 1981—; founding trustee, bd. dirs. Nat. Burn Fedn., 1975-83; chief fin. officer A.J. Carsten Co. Inc., San Diego, 1981—. Contbr. articles to profl. jours. Organizer, mem. numerous community groups; chmn. San Diego County Mental Health Adv. Bd., 1972-74, mem., 1971-75; chmn. community relations subcom., mem. exec. com. Emergency Med. Care Com., San Diego, Riverside and Imperial Counties, 1973-75; pub. mem. psychology exam. com. Calif. State Bd. Med. Quality Assurance, 1976-80, chmn., 1977; mem. rep. to Health Services Agy. San Diego County Govt., 1980; mem. Calif. Dem. Cen. Com., 1968-74, exec. com., 1971-72, 73-74; treas. San Diego Dem. County Cen. Com., 1972-74; chmn. edn. for legislation com. women's div. So. Calif. Dem. Com., 1972; dir. Muskie for Pres. Campaign, San Diego, 1972; organizer, dir. numerous local campaigns; councilwoman City of Del Mar, Calif., 1982-86, mayor, 1985-86; bd. dirs. Gentry-Watts Planned Indsl. Devel. Assn., 1986—, pres., 1987—; commencement speaker Alfred U., 1984. Recipient Key Woman award Dem. Party, 1968, 72, 1st Ann. Community award Belles for Mental Health, Mental Health Assn. San Diego, 1974, citation Alfred U. Alumni Assn., 1979. Home: 1415 Via Alta Del Mar CA 92014 Office: 6711 Nancy Ridge Dr San Diego CA 92121

CARSTEN, MARY NASH, nursing educator; b. Omaha, Feb. 1, 1958; d. Kevin C. and Charlotte (Joselyn) Nash; m. Larry Robyn Carsten, Apr. 28, 1984; 1 child, Katheryn Frances. BS in Nursing, Briar Cliff Coll., Sioux City, Iowa, 1982; MS in Nursing, U. Kans., Kansas City, 1990. RN, Mo. Staff nurse Marion Health Ctr., Sioux City, 1979-82; nursing educator St. John's Regional Med. Ctr., Joplin, Mo., 1982, RN refresher coord., 1988—. Mem. Am. Nurses Assn., Mo. Nurses Assn. Home: 1506 N Florida Ave Joplin MO 64801 Office: St John's Regional Med Ctr 2727 McClelland Joplin MO 64804

CARSWELL, CAROL FRANCES, finance director; b. Bklyn., Mar. 5, 1939; d. Jacob S. and Shirley (Brecher) Rubin; m. Howard L. Carswell, Oct. 8, 1972. AAS in Secretarial Skills, Bklyn. Coll., 1959, BA in Econs., 1968; MS in Edn., St. John's U., 1973; postgrad., Queens Coll., 1979-80. Asst. credit mgr., bookkeeper Arista Trading Co., N.Y.C., 1958-59; exec. sec. Lehn and Fink Products Corp., N.Y.C., 1959-61; office mgr., legal sec. Vladeck, Elias, Vladeck, and Engelhard, N.Y.C., 1961-66; tchr. City of N.Y., 1967-72, 1975-76, Farmingdale (N.Y.) High Sch., 1972-73; staff acct. Holtz, Rubenstein & Co., CPA's, Melville, N.Y., 1979-81; pvt. practice acct. Sebastian, Fla., 1982-84; fin. dir. City of Sebastian, 1984—. bd. dirs. Sebastian Area County Library, 1983-84; treas., bd. dirs. ARC, Indian River County, Fla., 1984-85.; bd. dirs. local chpt. Am. Cancer Soc. Mem. Fla. Govt. Fin. Officers Assn., Fla. Mcpl. Treas.'s Assn. (bd. dirs.), Pilot of Sebastian River Club (treas. 1987-88). Office: City of Sebastian PO Box 780127 Sebastian FL 32978

CART, PAULINE HARMON, minister, educator; b. Jamestown, Ky., Nov. 3, 1914; d. Preston L. and Frances L. (Sullivan) Harmon; m. William C. Cart, July 3, 1936; children—Charles W., David N. BS Berea Coll., 1955; MA U. Mich.-Ann Arbor, 1957, postgrad., 1957; postgrad. Ea. Mich. U., 1957, Nanjing Coll. Traditional Medicine, 1987, PhD in Homeopathic Philosophy. Cert. Tuina instr. Mgr., owner Gen. Store, Beattyville, Ky., 1936-41; def. worker GM, Dayton, Ohio, 1941-46; tchr. Ann Arbor Pub. Schs., 1955-83, Leads Sch., Eng., 1963-64 myomassologist Coll. Natureopathic Physicians, St. Louis, 1959-84; minister, counselor Ch. of Universology, Ann Arbor, 1972—; full prof. nutrition and body balancing Inst. Natural Health Scis., Wis. Contbr. poems and short stories to mags. Instr. Touch for Health Found., Pasadena, Calif., 1972—, Ir. dology, Escondido, Calif., 1972—; bd. dir. Music in Trauma Release Touch for Health in Profl. Health Practitioner; mem. Conservative Caucus, Washington, 1973—. Mem. NEA (del. 1959, cons. 1987—), Am. Nutrition Counselors Am., Internat. Myomathetics Fedn. (sec. edn. 1985—), Assn. Mich. Myomassologists Inc. (v.p. 1987—), Federated Organic Garden & Farming of Mich. (v.p. 1985-86), Alumni Assn. U. Mich. (life), Berea Alumni Assn., Delta Kappa Pi. Republican. Avocations: painting, quilting, crafts, writing, traveling. Home: 2564 Hawks Ave Ann Arbor MI 48108 Office: 2450 Hawks Ave Ann Arbor MI 48108

CARTAINO, CAROL ANN, editor; b. N.Y.C., Dec. 7, 1944; d. Pietro Michael and Ann Wanda (Scotch) C. BA, Rutgers U., 1966; postgrad., NYU, 1967-68. Cert. English tchr., N.J. Prodn. editor trade book Prentice-Hall, Inc., Englewood Cliffs, N.J., 1966-68, from asst. to assoc. editor trade book, 1968-72, editor trade book, 1972-77; editor-in-chief Writer's Digest Books, Cin., 1978-86, freelance editor and collaborator, 1986-87; editorial dir. Aslett-Browning, Inc., Pocatello, Idaho, 1987—; assoc. Collier Assoc. Literary Agy., Seaman, Ohio, 1987—; speaker in field; instr. in writing So. State Community Coll., Hillsboro and Wilmington, Ohio, 1989—. Vol. nurses aide Hackensack (N.J.) Hosp. State of N.J. scholar, 1962-66, Emerson (N.J.) PTA scholar, 1962. Roman Catholic. Home and Office: 2000 Flat Run Rd Seaman OH 45679

CARTE, SUZANNE LEWIS, educator; b. S. Charleston, W.Va., Nov. 16, 1943; d. Carson Richard and Thelma Lee (Dew) Lewis; m. John Herman Carte, Sept. 1, 1962; children—John Kevin, Jennifer Kristin, Samuel Jefferson. B.S., W.Va. State Coll., 1973; student W.Va. Coll. Grad. Studies, 1976-86. Tchr., Kanawha County Schs., Charleston, W.Va., 1978, tchr. history, 1979-81, tchr. intensive service unit, 1981, tchr. 6th grade, 1982-86, tchr. social studies, 1986—. Mem. Christian edn. commn. 1st Presbyterian Ch., St. Albans, W.Va., 1978. Mem. Kanawha Fedn. Educators/Am. Fedn. Tchrs., AAUW, Phi Alpha Theta, Kappa Delta Pi, Alpha Delta Kappa. Democrat. Avocations: fishing; reading; traveling. Home: Rt 1 Box 762 Coal River Rd Saint Albans WV 25177 Office: Hayes Jr High Sch 830 Strawberry Rd Saint Albans WV 25177

CARTER, ALDIA SPIERS, legal administrative assistant; b. Boykins, Va., June 13, 1936; d. Roy Roosevelt and Reba Maudine (Swain) Spiers; m. Rupert G. Carter Jr., June 18, 1961; children: John R., Karen, Brian. Grad. high sch., Boykins, 1953. Legal sec. Gilbert W. Francis, Esq., Boykins, 1954-61; administrv. asst. to c/w atty. E. Carter Nettles Jr., Wakefield, Va., 1964—. Mem. Wakefield Town Coun., 1982—, pres., 1986-90. Mem. Wakefield Jr. Woman's Club (pres. 1970-72), Southside Dist. VFWC, Tidewater Patron. Home: 307 Richardson Ave Wakefield VA 23888

CARTER, ANNE COHEN, physician; b. N.Y.C., Nov. 27, 1919; d. Arthur Joseph and Nellie (Zuckerman) Cohen; m. Charles Edward Carter, 1945 (div.); m. William Benjamin Heller, Nov. 4, 1947; children: James Albert, Susan Klee. BA, Wellesley Coll., 1941; MD, Cornell U., 1944. Diplomate Am. Bd. Internal Medicine. Intern Bellevue Hosp., N.Y.C., 1944-45; resident in medicine N.Y. Hosp., N.Y.C., 1945-46; instr. in medicine Cornell U. Med. Coll., N.Y.C., 1948-52, asst. prof. medicine, 1952-55; rsch. fellow Russell Sage Inst. Pathology, N.Y.C., 1951-55; asst. prof. medicine SUNY-Downstate Med. Ctr., Bklyn., 1955-58, assoc. prof. medicine, 1958-68, chief div. endocrinology, 1958-82, prof. medicine, 1968-82, vis. prof. medicine, 1982—; vis. scientist Bronx VA Hosp., Lab. Dr. Solomon A. Berson, Bronx, 1963-64; prof. medicine N.Y. Med. Coll., Valhalla, 1982—; vis. prof. medicine SUNY Health Sci. Ctr., Bklyn., 1982—; asst. attending physician N.Y. Hosp., N.Y.C., 1953-55; asst. vis. physician Kings County Hosp. Ctr., Bklyn., 1955-59, attending physician, 1959-72, active attending physician, 1972-84, cons., 1984—; rsch. assoc. Jewish Chronic Disease Hosp., Bklyn., 1957-67; attending physician State U. Hosp., Bklyn., 1967-84, cons., 1984—; cons. Bklyn. VA Hosp., 1971-84; attending physician Westchester County Med. Ctr., Valhalla, 1982—, dir. ambulatory cancer detection svcs., 1982—. Contbr. chpts. to books, articles to profl. jours. Bd. dirs. Am. Cancer Soc., Inc., N.Y.C., 1977—, Westchester div. Inc., 1985—; trustee Wellesley Coll., 1971-89, trustee emerita, 1989—. Recipient Pub. Edn. award Am. Cancer Soc., Westchester div., 1988, Alumna Achievement award Dana Hall Sch., Wellesley, Mass., 1990. Fellow AAAS, Westchester Acad. Medicine; mem. Am. Soc. Clin. Oncology, Endocrine Soc. (chmn. awards com. 1989-90), Soc. Exptl. Biology and Medicine, Am. Soc. Internal Medicine, Women's Med. Assn. N.Y.C. (v.p. 1990—), Women's Med. Assn. Westchester (pres. 1988-90), AAUP, Am. Diabetes Assn., Am. Fedn. Clin. Research, Am. Med. Women's Assn., Inc., Am. Soc. Bone and Mineral Rsch., Assn. Community Cancer Ctrs., Assn. Women in Sci., Clin. Ligand Assay Soc., Harvey Soc., Internat. Soc. Preventive Oncology, Internat. Soc. Psychoneuroendocrinology, Nat. Hospice Orgn., Inc., N.Y. Acad. Scis., N.Y. Acad. Medicine, N.Y. State Med. Soc., N.Y. State Soc. Internal Medicine, Westchester County Med. Soc., Cosmopolitan Club, Sigma Xi. Democrat. Jewish. Home: 33 E 70th St New York NY 10021 Office: NY Med Coll Dept Medicine Munger Pavilion Valhalla NY 10595

CARTER, BETSY L., magazine editor; b. N.Y.C., June 9, 1945; d. Rudy and Gerda Cohn. BA, U. Mich., 1967. Editorial asst. McGraw Hill, 1967-68; editor co. mag. Am. Security and Trust Co., 1968-69; editorial asst. Atlantic Monthly, 1969-70; researcher Newsweek, N.Y.C., 1971-73, asst. editor, 1973-75, assoc. editor, 1975-80; sr. editor Esquire Mag., N.Y.C., 1980-81, exec. editor, 1981-82, sr. exec. editor, 1982-83, editorial dir., 1983-85; creator, editor-in-chief New York Woman, N.Y.C., 1986—; freelance contbr. to Atlantic, Washington Post, Family Weekly. Mem. Am. Soc. Mag. Editors (exec. com. 1988—). Home: 339 E 18th St New York NY 10003 Office: NY Woman Mag 1120 6th Ave New York NY 10036

CARTER, CARLA CIFELLI, management consultant; b. Chicago Heights, Ill., June 2, 1949; d. John Louis and Irene Frances (Romandine) Cifelli. BA, We. Mich. U., Kalamazoo, 1971; MBA, Ariz. State U., 1985. Tchr. Limestone (Maine) High Sch., 1971-75; mgr. employment and tng. Chubb Life Ins., Concord, N.H., 1975-78; employee relations supr. TRW, Inc., Plainville, Conn., 1978-79; asst. dir. corp. tng. Cigna, Bloomfield, Conn., 1979-82; cons. to human resources dept. Sentry Ins. Co., Scottsdale, Ariz., 1983-84; asst. v.p. Merabank, Phoenix, 1984-87; employee devel. adminstr. City of Phoenix, 1987-90; cons. Am. Productivity and Quality Ctr., Houston, 1990—; regional mgr. Reading & Learning Internat., Mesa, Ariz., 1987—; bd. dirs. Cert. Pub. Mgr. Program, Phoenix, 1988—; nat. presenter Bank Adminstrn. Inst., 1987. Author audio cassette: Understanding the Organization, 1982, The Responsive City, Am. Productivity and Quality Ctr., 1990. Advisor, Literary Vols., Phoenix, 1989. Mem. NAFE., ASTD (govtl. affairs dir. 1988-89), Am. Quality and Participation Soc., Orgn. Devel. Network (nat. presenter 1989), Am. Soc. Personnel Adminstrs., Ariz. Outdoor Club. Home: 4602 E Avalon Phoenix AZ 85018 Office: Am Productivity & Quality Ctr 123 N Post Oak Ln Houston TX 77024

CARTER, CAROLYN HOUCHIN, advertising agency executive; b. Louisville, Nov. 2, 1952; d. Paul Clayton and Georgia Houchin C.; m. Jeffrey Starr, Dec. 8, 1988. B.S.J., Northwestern U., 1974, M.S.J., 1975. Asst. account exec. SSC&B Advt., Inc., N.Y.C., 1975-76, account exec., 1976-77; account exec. Grey Advt., Inc., N.Y.C., 1977-79, account supr., 1979-81, v.p., account supr., 1981-82, v.p., mgmt. supr., 1982-85, v.p., group mgmt. supr., 1985-87, sr. v.p., 1987—; mem. Nat. Advt. Rev. Bd., 1983-87; mem. adv. bd. advt. history Smithsonian Nat. Mus. Am. History, 1988—. Mem. U.S. Council World Communications Yr., 1983. Mem. March of Dimes Media Adv. Council, 1981-84, chmn., 1985-86. Mem. Am. Mktg. Assn., N.Y. Women in Communications (pres. 1982-83, Matrix award in Advt. 1988), Advt. Women of N.Y. (bd. dirs. 1987-88). Office: Grey Advt Inc 777 Third Ave New York NY 10017

CARTER, CAROLYN HOWARD, assistant city manager; b. Danville, Va., Dec. 25, 1950; d. George Rosser and Sarah Elizabeth (Hylton) C.; m. Leonard Glen Green, June 24, 1978; children: Sarah Carter Green, Willis Carter Green. BA, Meredith Coll., 1973; MA in History, Wake Forest U., 1974; MPA, U. N.C., Chapel Hill, 1978. Budget analyst City of Durham, N.C., 1977-79, budget dir., 1979-80, asst. city mgr., 1980-84; asst. city mgr. City of Raleigh, N.C., 1984—. mem. internat. City Mgrs. Assn., N.C. City-County Mgrs. Assn. (2d v.p. 1990-91), Meredith Coll. Alumnae Assn. (Recent Grad. award 1987), U. N.C.-Chapel Hill MPA Alumni Assn. (pres. 1981-82). Methodist. Office: City of Raleigh PO Box 590 Raleigh NC 27602

CARTER, CONNIE BERNICE, small business owner; b. Idaho Falls, Idaho, Jan. 30, 1943; d. James Lazelle Carter and Bernice (Collier) Carter Buttars; m. Welby L. Huffaker, July 4, 1961 (div. 1972); children: Kim Huffaker Walker, Rayna Huffaker Williams. Grad. high sch., Rigby, Idaho. Sales rep. Sta. KUPI, Idaho Falls, 1968-70; sales mgr. Holiday Office Products, Idaho Falls, 1972-77; cons. Snelling & Snelling, Idaho Falls, 1977-81; sales rep. Martin Stationers, Idaho Falls, 1981-84; owner, mgr., counselor Carter Personnel Agy., Idaho Falls, 1984—; cons. Ideal Hardware, Idaho Falls, 1985—, Vo-Tech, Idaho Falls, 1987—. Mem. Idaho Falls C. of C., Achievers Club. Republican. Mormon. Office: Carter Pers Agy 482 Constitution Way Idaho Falls ID 83404

CARTER, CONNIE BEVERLY, teacher, consultant; b. Walla Walla, Wash., Aug. 12, 1926; d. Rowland Averill Yeend and Geraldine (McEvoy) Davis; m. Forest Taylor Carter, 1943 (div. 1984); children: Gordon D., Kathy Jo Altman, Michael J. BA, U. Nev., 1969, M in Curriculum, 1972, postgrad., 1972, M Counseling, 1982. Cert. tchr., Nev. With real estate sales dept. Bartsas Realty, Las Vegas, Nev., 1960; tchr. Clark County Sch. Dist., Las Vegas, 1969—; dir. Edn. Cons. Svcs., Las Vegas, 1987—. Mem. Dem. Cen. Com., Las Vegas, 1985—; advocate ct. apptd. spl. advocate, Las Vegas, 1984—; v.p. United Ch. of Women, Las Vegas, 1959; pres. PTA, Las Vegas, 1958, 62; mem., trustee Nat. Kids Campus, Las Vegas, 1987. Mem. Clark County Classroom Tchrs. Assn. (bd. dirs., serving on negotiations team 1977), Orton Dyslexic Soc., Assn. Children with Learning Disabilities, Assn. Supervision and Curriculum Devel., Am. Assn. for Counseling and Devel. Baptist. Home: 2700 Riley Oaks Ct Las Vegas NV 89108

CARTER, DIANE MASON, banker; b. Lakewood, Ohio, Feb. 5, 1959; d. Charles William and Terry Mason (Brown) Carter. BA, U. Colo., 1981; M Internat. Mgmt., Am. Grad. Sch. Internat. Mgmt., Glendale, Ariz., 1987. Cert. cash mgr. Product mgr. First Interstate Bank of Calif., L.A., 1987-89; calling officer First Interstate Bank Ltd., L.A., 1989—. With USNR 1989—. Recipient Circumnavigators award, Circumnavigators Found., 1986. Mem. Thunderbird Alumni Assn. (pres. 1990), Circumnavigators Club (treas. 1989—), Kappa Kappa Gamma. Republican. Episcopalian. Office: First Interstate Bank Ltd 707 Wilshire Blvd Los Angeles CA 90017

CARTER, EDITH HOUSTON, statistician, educator; b. Charlotte, N.C., Oct. 12, 1936; d. Z. and Ellie (Hartsell) Houston; B.S., Appalachian State U., 1959, M.A., 1960; Ph.D., Va. Poly. Inst. and State U., 1976; m. Fletcher F. Carter, Apr. 2, 1961. Transcript analyst Fla. Dept. Edn., Tallahassee, 1961-65; instr. Radford U., 1969-70; prof. New River Community Coll., Dublin, Va., 1970—, dir. instl. research, 1974-78, asst. dean Coll. Arts and Scis., 1978-79, statistician, 1979-83. Violist Va. Poly. Inst. and State U. Orch., Radford U. Orch., S.W. Va. Opera Soc. Orch. Mem. Am. Ednl. Research Assn., Assn. Instl. Research (exec. bd. 1976-78), Southeastern Assn. Community Coll. Research (exec. bd. 1976-78, Outstanding Service award, Disting. Service award 1981), Nat. Council Research and Planning, Coll. Music Soc., Am. String Tchrs. Assn., Va. Fedn. Women's Clubs (dir. 1968-70). Methodist. Clubs: Radford Garden, Radford Jr. Woman's (pres. 1967-68). Editor Community Coll. Jour. Research and Planning, 1981—, Newsletter Southeastern Assn. Community Coll. Research, 1972—. Home: Box 5781 RU Radford VA 24142 Office: Virginia Tech Blacksburg VA 24061

CARTER, ELEANOR ELIZABETH, corporate professional, social worker; b. Durham, N.C., July 16, 1954; d. Joseph William Jr. and Sheila Dale (Swartz) C. BS in Social Work, N.C. State U., 1977. Field worker family planning Wake County Health Dept., Raleigh, N.C., 1975-76; sales rep. Bristol-Myers Products, N.C., 1977-80; regional adminstn. asst. Bristol-Myers Products, Dallas, Tex., 1980; regional trainer Bristol-Myers Products, Washington, N.C., Va., 1980; sales adminstrn. mgr. corp. hdqrs. Bristol-Myers Products, N.Y.C., 1980-81; dist. supr. Bristol-Myers Products, Cin., 1981-82; account rep. Fuji Photo Film U.S.A., Inc., Cin., 1982-83; spl. account mgr. Fuji Photo Film U.S.A., Inc., Chgo., 1983—. Mem. Nat. Assn. Female Execs., Alpha Kappa Delta. Presbyterian. Office: Fuji Photo Film USA Inc 1285 Hamilton Pkwy Itasca IL 60143-1147

CARTER, ELIZABETH MARIE, corporate financial planner; b. Albany, N.Y., Jan. 7, 1963; d. Betty J. (Moore) C. BA, U. Mass., 1981-85. Corp. fin. planner CIGNA, Springfield, Mass., 1986-88, Kent Moss & Assn., N.Y. Life, Tampa, Fla., 1989; v.p. Reynolds Cons., Inc., Tampa, 1989-90; sales mgr. The New England, Tampa, 1990—. Author: (poems) This is in Memory..., 1983; contbr. articles to profl. jours. Mem. Springfield Assn. Life Underwriters, Tampa Assn. Life Underwriters, Gen. Agts. Mgrs. Assn. Republican. Office: The New England 5510 LaSalle St Tampa FL 33607

CARTER, ELIZABETH NAOMI, speech pathologist; b. Marion, Ill., Jan. 24, 1955; d. Phil and Betty Ruth Trapani; m. Leonard Matthew, Apr. 3, 1982; children: Cassie Anne, Shane Matthew. AS, John A. Logan, Carterville, Ill., 1975; BS, Murray State U., 1978; MS, So. Ill. U., 1981. Cert. Pathologist. Speech pathologist Cloverport Sch., Cloverport, Ky., 1978-80, Tri County Special Ed., Murphysboro, Ill., 1980-81, Galatia Elementary, Ill., 1980-82, Pleasantville Elementary, Fairfield Union Schs., Rushville, 1982—; speech therapist Lancaster Fairfield Hosp., Lancaster, 1983—. Pres. Twig 9 Women's Auxillary, Lancaster, 1985-87, Inter Twig Coun., Lancaster, 1985-88; publicity chmn. Better Speech and Hearing Month, Lancaster, 1988. Mem. Am. Field Svc., Community Concerts, Ohio Speech & Hearing Assn., COSHA. Republican. Methodist.

CARTER, EMILY ANN, physical chemist, educator; b. Los Gatos, Calif., Nov. 28, 1960; d. David and Rebecca (Blumberg) C. BS in Chemistry, U. Calif., Berkeley, 1982; PhD in Chemistry, Calif. Inst. Tech., 1987. Postdoctoral rsch. assoc. U. Colo., Boulder, 1987-88; asst. prof. phys. chemistry UCLA, 1987—. Contbr. articles to tech. jours. Recipient Union Carbide Rsch. Innovation Recognition awards, 1989-90, 90—, New Faculty award Camille and Henry Dreyfus Found., 1988—; Presdl. Young Investigator grantee NSF, 1988—. Mem. Am. Chem. Soc., Am. Phys. Soc., Am. Vacuum Soc., Assn. Women in Sci., Sigma Xi, Phi Beta Kappa. Democrat. Jewish. Office: Chemistry Dept UCLA 405 Hilgard Ave Los Angeles CA 90024-1569

CARTER, GAIL MARIE, advertising executive; b. Chgo., Apr. 4, 1956; d. James Joseph and Muriel (Keaton) C.; m. Bill Leo Herrman, Nov. 16, 1985. BA in Communications, Western Ill. U., 1978; postgrad., Webster U., 1988—. Copywriter, creative coord. Mills, Fife & MacDonald, Des Plaines, Ill., 1978-82; asst. account exec. Ketchum Mandabach & Simms, Chgo., 1982, account exec., 1983-84, account supr., 1984-90, v.p., 1990—. Office: Ketchum Mandabach & Simms 111 N Canal St Chicago IL 60606

CARTER, GINA LEE, microbiologist; b. Scranton, Pa., July 3, 1962; d. Leon Henry Koenig and Carmela Ann (Romolo) Koenigsberg; m. John Henry Carter III, Feb. 11, 1989. BS, Pa. State U., 1984. Rsch. asst. Ctr. for Air Environ. Studies, State College, Pa., 1983-84; fisheries biologist Nat. Marine Fisheries Service, Seattle, 1984-85; rsch. asst. Monterey Mushrooms, Watsonville, Calif., 1985-87; microbiologist Genencor, South San Francisco, 1987—. Mem. Am. Soc. for Microbiology, Soc. for Indsl. Microbiology, Soc. for Cryobiology, U.S. Fedn. of Culture Collections, World Fedn. of Culture Collections, Oceanic Soc., Pa. State Alumni Assn. Democrat. Mem. Christian Ch. Office: Genencor 180 Kimball Way South San Francisco CA 94080

CARTER, JANE FOSTER, agriculture industry executive; b. Stockton, Calif., Jan. 14, 1927; d. Chester William and Bertha Emily Foster; m. Robert Buffington Carter, Feb. 25, 1952; children: Ann Claire Carter Palmer, Benjamin Foster. BA, Stanford U., 1948; MS, NYU, 1949. Pres. Colusa (Calif.) Properties, Inc., 1953—; owner Carter Land and Livestock, Colusa, 1965—; sec.-treas. Carter Farms, Inc., Colusa, 1975—. Author: If the Walls Could Talk, Colusa's Architectural Heritage, 1988; author, editor: Colusa County Survey and Plan for the Arts, 1981, 82, 83, Implementing the Colusa County Arts Plan, 1984, 85, 86. Mem. agrl. adv. com. Yuba Coll., Marysville, Calif., 1976—, Calif. Gov.'s Commn. on Agr., Sacramento, 1979-82; del. Rep. Nat. Conv., Kansas City, Mo., 1976, Detroit, 1980, Dallas, 1984; trustee Calif. Hist. Soc., 1979-89, regional v.p., 1984-89; sec. Calif. Reclamation Bd., 1983—; chmn. heritage preservation com. City of Colusa, 1976-83, vice chmn., 1983—; bd. dirs. Calif. Preservation Found., 1989—. Mem. Sacramento River Water Contractors Assn. (exec. com. 1974—). Episcopalian. Club: Francisca (San Francisco). Home and Office: 909 Oak St Colusa CA 95932

CARTER, JANICE JOENE, telecommunications executive; b. Portland, Oreg., Apr. 17, 1948; d. William George and Charline Betty (Gilbert) P.; m. Ronald Thomas Carter, June 13, 1968; children: Christopher Scott, Jill Suzanne. Student, U. Calif., Berkeley, 1964, U. Portland, 1966-67, U. Colo., Boulder, 1967-68; BA in Math, U. Guam, 1970. Computer programmer Ga.-Pacific Co., Portland, 1972-74; systems analyst ProData, Seattle, 1974-79; systems analyst, mgr. Pacific Northwest Bell, Seattle, 1979-80; data ctr. mgr. Austin Co., Renton, Wash., 1980-83; developer shared tenent svcs. Wright-Runstad, Seattle, 1983-84; system adminstr. Hewlett-Packard, Bellevue, Wash., 1984; telecommunications dir. Nordstrom, Inc., Seattle, 1984—; mem. large customer panel AT&T, Seattle, 1987—. Ski instr. Alpental, Snoqualmie Pass, Wash., 1984-87; bd. dirs. Educationally Gifted Children, Mercer Island, Wash., 1978-80; mem. Sweet Adelines, 1989-90. Mem. Telecommunications Assn., Internat. Communications Assn., System 85/ETN User Group. Office: Nordstrom Inc 1321 2d Ave Seattle WA 98101

CARTER, JENNIFER, engineer; b. Tampa, Fla., Apr. 19, 1963; d. Frank L. and Earnestine (McMillian) C. AA in Pre-Engring., Hillsborough Community Coll., Tampa, 1983; BEE, Fla. A&M U., 1987. Field engr. Ericsson Radio Systems, Richardson, Tex., 1988-89; equipment engr. Cen. Telephone Co. of Fla., Tallahassee, 1989—. Mem. IEEE, NAFE. Baptist. Home: 1198 Copper Creek Dr Tallahassee FL 32301

CARTER, JESSIE ANITA, mathematics educator; b. Ft. Worth, June 3, 1948; d. William Charlie and Ella Marion (Andrews) C. BA in Math., North Tex. State U., 1970; secondary teaching cert., Tex. Christian U., 1975, MA In Edn. Supervision, 1976. Tchr. aide in math. Ft. Worth Ind. Sch. Dist., 1972-73, tchr. math., 1973-85, tchr. computer literacy in gifted and talented program, 1984-88, tchr. math., 1988—. Named Outstanding Math. Tchr. Ft. Worth Independent Sch. Dist., 1973-74, Notable Woman Tex., 1984-85, Outstanding Magnet Tchr., Morningside Middle Sch., 1986-87; Sid Richardson Found. grantee, 1985, 86, 87. Mem. NEA, Internat Council for Computers in Edn., Nat. Council Tchrs. Math., Tex. State Tchr. Assn., Tex. Council Tchrs. Math., Ft. Worth Classroom Tchrs., Ft. Worth Council Tchrs. Math., Assn. for Supervision and Curriculum Devel., Nat. Soc. Tole and Decorative Painters, Ft. Worth Tole and Decorative Painters, Nat. Assn. Female Execs., Beta Sigma Phi. Democrat. Baptist. Home: 7101 Willis Ave Fort Worth TX 76116 Office: Ft Worth Independent Sch Dist 3200 W Lancaster Fort Worth TX 76107

CARTER, JOY EATON, electrical engineer, consultant; b. Comanche, Tex., Feb. 8, 1923; d. Robert Lee and Carrie (Knudson) Eaton; m. Clarence J. Carter, Aug. 22, 1959; 1 child, Kathy Jean. Student, John Tarleton Agrl. Coll., 1939-40; B Music cum laude, N. Tex. State Tchrs. Coll., 1943, postgrad., 1944-45; postgrad., U. Tex., 1945; MSEE, Ohio State U., 1949, PhDEE and Radio Astronomy, 1957. Engr. aide Civil Service Wright Field, Dayton, Ohio, 1945-46; instr. math. Ohio State U., Columbus, 1946-48, research asst., assoc.Research Found., 1947-49, from instr. to asst. prof. elec. engring., 1949-58; research engr. N. Am. Aviation, Columbus, 1955-56; mem. tech. staff Space Tech. Labs. (later TRW Inc.), Redondo Beach, Calif., 1958-68; sect. head, staff engr. electronics research labs. The Aerospace Corp., El Segundo, 1968-72, staff engr. and mgr. system and terminals, USAF Satellite Communications System Program Office, 1972-77, mgr. communications subsystem Def. Satellite Communications System III Program Office, 1978-79; cons. Mayhill, N.Mex., 1979—. Active Mayhill Vol. Fire Dept.; bd. dirs. Mayhill Community Assn., 1988—, sec. bd. dirs. 1988—; co-chair music com. Mayhill Bapt. Ch., 1988—, trustee, 1989—; bd. dirs. Otero County Farm Bur., 1987—. Named Cow Belle of Yr. Otero Cow Belles, 1988. Mem. Am. Astron. Soc., IEEE (sr.), Am. Nat. Cattle Women (sec. Otero CowBelles chpt. 1986-87, 1st v.p. 1988, historian 1989), Sacramento Mountains Hist. Soc. (bd. dirs. 1986—), Sun Country Walking Horse Assn., Calif. Rare Fruit Growers, Native Plant Soc. N.Mex., Sigma Xi (life), Eta Kappa Nu (life), Sigma Alpha Iota (life), Alpha Chi, Kappa Delta Pi, Pi

Mu Epsilon, Sigma Delta Epsilon. Home and Office: PO Box 23 Mayhill NM 88339

CARTER, JUDITH ROCKWELL, real estate broker; b. Belle Plaine, Iowa, Jan. 12, 1939; d. Gilbert Pearl and Marian Alberta (Hoffman) Rockwell; m. John Wesley Carter Jr., Nov. 22, 1959; children: Rebecca Rockwell Carter Stone, Roberta Roxianne Carter Sheda. Student, Coe Coll., 1957-60, St. Lukes Nursing Sch. With reservation dept. United Air Lines, Omaha and Cedar Rapids, Nebr., 1959-66; owner Black Angus Farm, Belle Plaine, 1966-76; salesperson Valley Sales, Belle Plaine, 1976-80; owner Carter Realty, Belle Plaine, 1980—; pres. Iowa Meth. Found., Des Moines, 1990—. Mem. Conf. Coun. Fin. and Adminstrn. Iowa Meth., Des Moines, 1976-84; pres. Belle Plaine Devel. Commn., 1986-88; chmn. Christ United Meth. Adminstrv. Bd., 1989-90; mem. Belle Plaine Improvement Corp., 1986—. Mem. Benton County Bd. Realtors, Belle Plaine C. of C. (exec. bd. dirs. 1990—), Order of Eastern Star, Rotary.

CARTER, KATHY DIANE, tax examiner; b. Dolomite, Ala., Apr. 18, 1957; d. Maggie Carter. BA, Spelman Coll., 1979; JD, Howard U., 1988. Law clk. U.S. Dept. of State, Washington, 1979, 80; law. clk. Gen. Svcs. Adminstrn., Washington, 1981; legal researcher D.C. C. of C., Washington, 1983-84; fed. tax examiner IRS, Atlanta, 1986—. Mem. Neighborhood Watch Com., Atlanta, 1989; precinct capt. polit. campaign, Atlanta, 1989. Mem. Nat. Coun. of Negro Women, Inc., NAFE, Spelman Coll. Alumnae Assn., Delta Theta Phi. Home: PO Box 18808 Atlanta GA 30326

CARTER, LISA JOYCE, paint manufacturing company executive; b. Galveston, Tex., June 1, 1959; d. Carlton and Dorothy Lee (McPeters) Pappas Kelly. Student N. Tex. State U., 1977, Richland Coll., 1978, U. Ark.-Little Rock, 1980, IBM Continuing Edn., 1981-82. Mktg. asst. Membership Services, Irving, Tex., 1978, tech. support asst., 1980; programmer, analyst Mail Mktg. Services, Little Rock, 1980-82; bus. broker VR Bus. Brokers, Longview, Tex., 1982-85; mgr., v.p. Creative Coatings Inc., Kilgore, Tex., 1985—, also bd. dirs. Mem. Mothers Against Drunk Drivers, Longview, Tex., 1985-86, v.p. Gregg County chpt.; sec. East Tex. Area Parkinsonism Soc., 1987—. Mem. Data Processing Mgrs. Assn. Baptist. Avocations: skiing, traveling. Home: #4 Bellingrath Longview TX 75605 Office: Creative Coatings Inc 428 N Longview St Kilgore TX 75662

CARTER, MAE RIEDY, retired college official, consultant; b. Berkeley, Calif., May 20, 1921; d. Carl Joseph and Avis Blanche (Rhodehaver) Riedy; BS, U. Calif., Berkeley, 1943; m. Robert C. Carter, Aug. 19, 1944; children: Catherine, Christin Ann. Ednl. adv., then program specialist div. continuing edn. U. Del., Newark, 1968-78, asst. provost for women's affairs, exec. dir. commn. status women Office Women's Affairs, 1978-86; adv. bd. Rockefeller Family grant project, 1979-83. Regional v.p. Del. PTA, 1960-62; pres. Friends Newark Free Library, 1968-69; mem. fiscal planning com. Newark Spl. Sch. Dist., 1972. Recipient Outstanding Service award Women's Coordinating Council, 1977, 79; Spl. Recognition award, Nat. U. Extension Assn., 1977, award for credit programs, 1971, Creative Programming award, 1971; AAUW grantee, 1968; Fulbright grantee, 1976. Mem. AAUW (past br. pres.), Nat. Assn. Women Deans, Adminstrs. and Counselors, NOW, Women's Legal Def. Fund, Nat. Women's Polit. Caucus. Republican. Author: (with Geis and Butler) Seeing and Evaluating People, 1982, revised, 1986, Research on Seeing and Evaluating People; also papers, reports in field. Home: 604 Dallam Rd Newark DE 19711

CARTER, MARGARET L., legislator; b. La., Dec. 29, 1935; d. Emma Carter; 9 children. BA, Portland State U., 1972; MEd, Oreg. State U., 1973; postgrad., Washington State U. Community organizer, asst. dir. Community Action Agy., Shreveport, La.; tchr. Albina Youth Opportunity Sch., Portland; counselor Portland Community Coll.; mem. Oreg. Ho. of Reps., Salem, 1984—; mem. Joint Trade and Econ. Devel. com., 1985—, co-chair 1989—, Human Resources com., 1985, vice chair, 87, Edn. com., 1985, 87, 89, Conf. com. on Dr. Martin Luther King State Holiday, co-chair, 1985, Joint Health Care com. 1986. Founder, mus. dir. Joyful Sound Singers Piedmont Ch. Christ; vol. counselor various juvenile detention ctrs. and women's prisons, voter registration drives in Portland's black neighborhoods, Project Pride; organizer Oreg. chpt. of Sickle Cell Anemia Found.; founder Oreg. Black Leadership Conf.; mem. Oreg. State Commn. on Post Secondary Edn. and the Oreg. Alliance for Black Sch. Educators, Spl. Commn. for the Parole Bd. on the Matrix System; mem. Gov.'s Task Force on Pregnancy and Substance Abuse, 1989—, Coun. on Alcohol and Drugs, 1989—. Recipient Jeanette Rankin award Oreg. Women's Polit. Caucus, 1985. Mem. Nat. Organ. Black Legis. Elected Women (v.p. 1985), Nat. Black Caucus (exec. com.), Blacks in Gov. (regional pres.), Alpha Kappa Alpha. Democrat. Home: 2948 NE 10th Ave Portland OR 97212 Office: Oreg State Legis H-478 State Capitol Salem OR 97310

CARTER, MARY EDDIE, government adminstrator; b. Americus, Ga., Mar. 14, 1925; d. Walker G. and Esther (Stewart) C. B.A., LaGrange Coll., 1946; M.S., U. Fla., 1949; Ph.D., U. Edinburgh, 1956. Tchr. LaGrange (Ga.) Coll., 1946-47; chemist Callaway Mills, LaGrange, 1947-48; microscopist So. Research Inst., Birmingham, Ala., 1949-51; chemist West Point Mfg. Co., Shawmut, Ala., 1951-53; research assoc. FMC Corp., Am. Viscose div., Marcus Hook, Pa., 1956-71; lab chief textiles and clothing lab. U.S. Dept. Agr., Knoxville, Tenn., 1971-73; dir. So. Regional Research Ctr, 1973-80; asso. adminstr. Agrl. Research Service, Washington, 1980—. Recipient Herty medal Ga. sect. of Am. Chem. Soc., 1979, Meritorious Presdl. Rank award, 1982, 87; Named Fed. Woman of Yr. City Wide Fed. Exec. Bd., 1977. Fellow AAAS; mem. Am. Chem. Soc., Am. Assn. Textile Chemists and Colorists, Inter-Soc. Color Council, Sci. Research Soc. Am., Fiber Soc., Inst. Food Technologists, Am. Assn. Cereal Chemists. Office: US Dept Agr Agrl Rsch Svc 14th & Independence Ave SW Washington DC 20250

CARTER, MARY THOMAS, food service brokerage executive; b. Nashville, July 8, 1956; d. George Edwin and Mary Virginia (Haley) Thomas; m. Theodore Michael Saal, Oct. 10, 1979 (div. 1988); 1 child, Mary Virginia; m. Randy Dean Carter, Nov. 17, 1989. Grad. high sch., Woodbury, Tenn. Office mgr. Penn Mut. Life Ins. Co., Nashville, 1976-77; asst. mgr. Elizabeth Arden, Inc., Nashville, 1977-79, Nashville Trunk and Bag, Nashville, 1979-80; sec. to v.p. Thweatt & Heldman Brokerage Co., Nashville, 1981; sec. to pres. Douglas Food Service Brokerage Co., Nashville, 1982-88; office mgr. Bob Anderson Brokerage Co., Nashville, 1988—. Mem. Nat. Assn. Female Execs. Lutheran. Office: Bob Anderson Brokerage Co 220 Great Circle Rd Ste 108 Nashville TN 37228

CARTER, MEDORA ABBOTT, project administrator; b. Washington, July 18, 1953; d. Jackson Miles and Frances Elizabeth (Dowdle) A.; m. Donald Lynwood Carter, May 14, 1983. Student Chowan Jr. Coll., 1971-72, J. Sargeant Reynolds and Va. Commonwealth U., 1973-76; grad. with honors Am. Inst. Banking, 1981. Asst. cashier, br. mgr. Dominion Nat. Bank, Vienna, Va., 1977-82; fin. analyst MCDonnell Douglas/TYMNET, Inc., Vienna, 1984-87; project adminstr., 1987-89; adminstrv. specialist Def. Communications Agy./DSN, Washington, 1989—. Mem. Colonial chpt. Rep. Women's Club, Alexandria, Va., 1985—; del. to county and state Rep. convs., 1988; mem. membership drive com. Fairfax County C. of C., 1981, 82; treas. Kings Park Shopping Ctr. Mcht.'s Assn., Springfield, Va., 1981; page DAR 1976 Va. State Conv., also active mem.; mem. Alexandria Assn. Recipient Outstanding Achievement award Nat. Assn. Banking Women No. Va., 1981. Episcopalian. Office: DSN/Def Communications Agy Washington DC

CARTER, MILDRED BROWN, administrator; b. Leo, S.C., Feb. 22, 1927; d. Eddie Washington and Hester Lessie Lee (Poston) Brown; m. Richard Bert Carter, Sept. 6, 1952; children: Paul, Mark, Janis, David. Student Pace Seminar, 1977, Dale Carnegie, 1977, Am. Mgmt. Assn., 1977. Various secretarial positions, FBI, Washington, 1943-48, adminstrv. asst., 1948-51; adminstrv. asst., office asso. dir., 1952; with Bellevue (Wash.) Sch. Dist., 1965-75; sec., registrar Hyak Jr. High Sch., 1971-75; asst. to exec. v.p. Bonneville Internat. Corp., Salt Lake City, 1975-83, exec. asst. to pres., 1983—. Mem. PTA Bd., Yakima, Wash., 1963; treas. PTA, Bellevue, 1973. Recipient Hon. Paul Harris Fellow award Rotary Internat., 1985. Mem. Soc. Former FBI Women, Beta Sigma Phi. Mormon. Clubs: Women's Century. Lodge: Soroptimists. Home: 2180 Elaine Dr Bountiful UT 84010 Office: Broadcast House 5 Triad Ctr Salt Lake City UT 84180

CARTER, NANCY YOUNG, nurse; b. Rochester, N.Y., Apr. 4, 1950; d. Frank Albert and Evelyn Mavis (Blake) Young; m. Samuel Dickerson Carter, Aug. 27, 1951; children: Benjamin, Sarah, Andrew. BS in Nursing, Keuka Coll., 1972; BSBA, Auburn U., 1980, MBA, 1981. RN, Ga.; diplomate Am. Bd. Quality Assurance and Utilization Rev. Shift supr. student health ctr. Auburn (Ala.) U., 1978-80; operational auditor Lafayette (La.) Gen. Hosp., 1982-83; dir. utilization and risk mgmt. dept. Emory U. Hosp., Atlanta, 1984—. Author: Physician Handbook for Utilization Management and Prospective Payment, 1987. Maj. U.S. Army, 1970-78, Korea. Named Mgr. of Quarter award Emory U. Hosp., 1988. Republican. Presbyterian. Office: Emory U Hosp 1364 Clifton Rd Atlanta GA 30322

CARTER, PAMELA LYNN, executive assistant to governor; b. South Haven, Mich., Aug. 20, 1949; d. Roscoe Hollis and Dorothy Elizabeth (Hadley) Fanning; m. Michael Anthony Carter, Aug. 26, 1971; children: Michael Anthony Jr., Marcya Alicia. BA cum laude, U. Detroit, 1971; MSW, U. Mich., 1973; JD, Ind. U., 1984. Bar: Ind. 1984. Rsch. analyst, treatment dir. U. Mich. Sch. Pub. Health and UAW, Detroit, 1973-75; exec. dir. Mental Health Ctr. for Women and Children, Detroit, 1975-77; consumer litigation atty. UAW-Gen. Motors Legal Svcs., Indpls., 1983-87; securities atty. Sec. of State, Indpls., 1987-89; Gov.'s exec. asst. for health and human svcs. Gov.'s Office, Indpls., 1989—. Author poems. mem. Cath. Social Svcs., Indpls., Jr. League, Indpls., Dem. Precinct, Indpls. Mem. Nat. Bar Assn., Ind. Bar Assn., Coalition of 100 Black Women. Democrat. Office: Office of Gov 206 State House Rm 206 Indianapolis IN 46204

CARTER, PEGGY WOLFE, artist; b. New Orleans, May 25, 1936; d. Hudson Garland and Kathleen Fearn (Flaspoller) Wolfe; m. William Hodding Carter, III (div. 1978); children: Catherine Ainsworth, Elizebeth Fearn, Wm. Hodding IV, Margaret Lorraine. BA, La. State U., 1957, BS, 1980. Art tchr. Fredericksburg (Va.) Community Ctr., 1957-58; elem. educator Greenville (Miss.) Sch. Dist., 1961-62; reporter womens page The Delta Democrat Times, Greenville; artist freelance. One-woman shows include Pass Christian Art Assn., Pass Christian Library, 1988, Pass Christian, Miss.; The Greater Gulf Coast Arts Council, Biloxi Library/Cultural Ctr. Founder, pres. Greenville (Miss.) Art Assn.; bldg. fund campaign mem. Salvation Army Bd., Greenville; bd. dirs. Twin City Little Theatre, Greenville, PTA, 1966-75; steering com. mem. Delta Arts Festival, Greenville; mem. John F. Kennedy Ctr. Miss. Alliance for Arts Edn., Jackson, Miss., 1973. Mem. Greater Gulf Coast Arts Coun., Pass Christian Art Assn., Greenville Garden Club, Pass Christian Garden Club. Episcopalian. Home: 605 S Washington Ave Greenville MS 38701

CARTER, POLLY SUE, healthcare official; b. Kingsport, Tenn., Mar. 26, 1947; d. Sterlin Herman and Nannie Mae (Herron) Carter; m. James Darwin Carter, Oct. 21, 1968; 1 child, Holly Suzanne. Student, Whitney Bus. Coll., Kingsport, 1966. Supr. ins. dept. Indian Path Hosp.-Health Corp. Am., Kingsport, 1976-82; dept. head, supr. Kingsport Imaging and Breast Ctr., 1983-90; corp. auditor E. Tenn. Ob-Gyn, Kingsport, 1990—. Mem. Am. Assn. Med. Assistance, Am. Assn. Radiology Mgrs., NAFE. Democrat. Baptist. Home: 1000 University Blvd Kingsport TN 37660

CARTER, REBECCA MARIE HUNT, nurse; b. Dayton, Ohio, Feb. 21, 1955; d. Dale Edward and Glenna Lee (Wisecup) Hunt; m. Ronald L. Carter, Jan. 7, 1977; children: Danette, Ronald Jr., Amy Lee Jonathan. AAS, Florence Darlington Tech. Sch., 1975. Staff nurse St. Eugene Community Hosp., Dillon, S.C., head nurse; sch. nurse Dillon Sch. Dist., Latta, S.C. Office: Latta Area Schs Richardson St Latta SC 29565

CARTER, ROBERTA ECCLESTON, educator, therapist; b. Pitts.; d. Robert E. and Emily B. (Bucar) Carter; (div.); children: David Michael, Daniel Michael. Student Edinboro State U., 1962-63; BS, California State U. of Pa., 1966; MEd, U. Pitts., 1969; MA, Rosebridge Grad. Sch., Walnut Creek, Calif., 1987. Tchr., Bethel Park Sch. Dist., Pa., 1966-69; writer, media asst. Field Ednl. Pub., San Francisco, 1969-70; educator, counselor, specialist Alameda Unified Sch. Dist., Calif., 1970—; master trainer Calif. State Dept. Edn., Sacramento, 1984—; personal growth cons., Alameda, 1983—. Author: People, Places and Products, 1970, Teaching/Learning Units, 1969; co-author: Teacher's Manual Let's Read, 1968. Mem. AAUW, Calif. Fedn. Bus. and Profl. Women (legis. chair Alameda br. 1984-85, membership chair 1985), NEA, Calif. Edn. Assn., Alameda Edn. Assn., Charter Planetary Soc., Oakland Mus., Exploratorium, Big Bros. of East Bay, Alameda C. of C. (svc. award 1985). Republican. Club: Commonwealth. Avocations: aerobics, gardening, travel, tennis. Home: 1516 E Shore Dr Alameda CA 94501

CARTER, ROSALYNN SMITH, wife of former President of U.S.; b. Plains, Ga., Aug. 18, 1927; d. Edgar and Allie (Murray) Smith; m. James Earl Carter, Jr., July 7, 1946; children: John William, James Earl III, Donnel Jeffrey, Amy Lynn. Grad., Ga. Southwestern Coll.; DHL (hon.), Morehouse Coll., 1980; LHD (hon.), Winthrop Coll., 1984; D Pub. Service (hon.), Wesleyan Coll., 1986; LLD (hon.), U. Notre Dame, 1987. Disting. centennial lectr. Agnes Scott Coll., Decatur, Ga., 1988—; disting. fellow Emory Univ. Inst. Women's Studies, Atlanta, 1990—. Author: First Lady from Plains, 1984, (with Jimmy Carter) Everything to Gain: Making the Most of the Rest of Your Life, 1987. Mem. Ga. Gov.'s Commn. to Improve Svcs. for the Mentally and Emotionally Handicapped, 1971; hon. chmn. Ga. Spl. Olympics for Retarded Children, 1971-75, Pres.'s Commn. on Mental Health, 1977-78; hon. chmn. bd. trustees John F. Kennedy Center Performing Arts, 1977-80; bd. mem. emeritus Nat. Assn. Mental Health; bd. dirs. Carter Presdl. Ctr., The Friendship Force, The Gannett Co., Crested Butte Physically Challenged Ski Program; bd. advisors Habitat for Humanity; trustee The Menninger Found.; sponsor Nat. Alliance for Research on Schizophrenia and Depression; hon. chair, bd. dirs. Rosalynn Carter Inst. Human Devel., 1987-90; mem. Internat. Commn. on Peace and Food; Kellogg Inst. Adv. Coun. Recipient Vol. of Yr. award Southeastern Assn. Vol. Svcs., 1976, Vincent DeFrancis award for Outstanding Service to Humanity, Am. Humane Assn., 1979, Vol. of Decade award Nat. Mental Health Assn., 1980, Presdl. Citation, Am. Psychol. Assn., 1982, Disting. Christian Woman's award Women's Com. of the So. Bapt. Theol. Sem., 1984, Nathan S. Kline Medal of Merit, Internat. Com. Against Mental Illness, 1984, Disting. Alumnus award. Am. Assn. State Colls. and Univs., 1987, Dorothea Dix award Mental Illness Found., 1988, Centennial award of Distinction Agnes Scott Coll., 1989; disting. fellow Emory U. Inst. Women's Studies, 1990—. Hon. fellow Am. Psychiat. Assn.

CARTER, RUTH B. (MRS. JOSEPH C. CARTER), association executive; b. Charlotte, Vt.; d. Ira E. and Sadie M. (Congdon) Burroughs; m. Joseph C. Carter, June 28, 1935. PhB, U. Vt., 1931. Prin. Newton Acad., Shoreham, Vt., 1931-35; substitute tchr. Spaulding High Sch., Barre, Vt., 1931-35, Woodbury (Vt.) High Sch., 1935-36; tchr. Craftsbury Acad., Craftsbury Common, Vt., 1936-38; sales mgr., buyer Vt. Music Co., Barre, 1939-44; statistician Syracuse U., 1944-46; instr. English Temple U., Phila., 1946-47; records clk. sec. Phila., 1947-56; tchr. English Cen. High Sch., Phila., 1957, Springfield Twp. Sr. High Sch., Montgomery County, Pa., 1964-65; exec. dir. White-Williams Found., 1966-82, trustee, 1982—. Author: (with Joseph C. Carter) Anchors Aweigh Around the World with Ernest Vail Burroughs, 1960, Pilgrimage to the Lovely Lands of our Ancestors, 1984. Recipient Humanitarian award Chapel of Four Chaplains, 1981; city coun. citation City of Phila., 1982. Mem. AAUW (admissions chmn. Phila. chpt. 1959-61, sec. 1961-64, treas. 1965-67), DAR (treas., historian, com. chmn., budget dir., treas., historian, com. chmn., regent Germantown chpt., 1983-86, 89—, registrar 1986-89, pub. rels. chmn. 1986—), Women for Greater Phila., New Eng. Historic Geneal. Soc., Geneal. Soc. Vt., Soc. Mayflower Descs. (bd. dirs. 1983-84, sec. 1985—), Temple U. Faculty Wives Club (rec. sec. 1983-86, pres. Old York group), Temple U. Women's Club, The English Speaking Union, Regent's Club (Phila. chaplain 1986-88). Republican. Methodist. Home: 40 W Mt Carmel Ave Glenside PA 19038

CARTER, SARALEE LESSMAN, immunologist, microbiologist; b. Chgo., Feb. 19, 1951; d. Julius A. and Ida (Oiring) Lessman; B.A., National Coll., 1971; m. John B. Carter, Oct. 7, 1979; children: Robert Oiring, Mollie. Supr. lab. immunology Weiss Meml. Hosp., Chgo., 1973-80; lab. immunology supr. Henrotin Hosp., Chgo., 1980-84; tech. dir. Lexington Med. Labs., West Columbia, S.C., 1984—; mem. nat. workshop faculty Am. Soc. Clin. Pathologists; clin. instr. faculty Med. U. S.C. Mem. Am. Soc. Clin. Pathologists (subspecialty cert. in microbiology and immunology, cert. med. technologist). Researcher Legionnaires Disease and mycoplasma pneumonia World Soc. Pathologists, Jerusalem, Israel, 1980. Contbr. articles to profl. jours.; Mem. Rep. Senoritorial Inner Circle, co-chmn. S.C. Young Profls. for George Bush. Office: 110 E Medical Ln Ste 100 Columbia SC 29169

CARTER, VIRGINIA M., educational consultant; b. St. Louis, Mar. 15, 1946; d. Clark Milton and Ella Mae (Woods) Greenlee; m. Michael L. Carter, Mar. 6, 1965; children: Todd Nelson, Theodore Preston. BA in Elem. Edn., U. Mo., 1968, MA, 1990; postgrad., Cen. Mo. State U., 1986. Cert. tchr., Mo., Kans. Elem. tchr. Ray-Pec Sch. Dist., Raymore, Mo.; prof. U. Mo., Kansas City; cons. Greater Kansas City Writing Project. Choreographer Blue Springs (Mo.) Community Theater; mem. Inst. Children's Lit., Conn., 1989—; beauty cons. Mary Kay Cosmetics; 2d v.p. Raymore Elem. PTA, 1982-84, pres., 1984-85, v.p. Cass County chpt., 1983-84; devotional chmn. Ray-Pec Mid. Sch. PTSA, 1985-87, parliamentarian, 1986-87; den leader Boy Scouts Am., 1976-82, den leader coach, 1981-84, chmn. pack com., 1977-84, dir. cub scout day camp program, 1983, 84, adult leader trainer, 1983-84, v.p. mother's club, 1986-87, pres. mother's club, 1988. Recipient Den Leader's Coach Tng. award Boy Scouts Am., 1982, Den Leader's Tng. award, 1982, Basic Cub Leader Tng. award, 1980. Mem. Internat. Reading Assn., Nat. Coun. Tchrs. of English, Nat. Writing Project, Nat. Trust For Hist. Preservation, Mo. State Tchrs. Assn., Greater Kansas City Assn. Supervision and Curriculum Devel., Network for Women in Sch. Adminstrn. Republican. Presbyterian. Home and Office: Rt 2 Box 309A Peculiar MO 64078

CARTHEL, ANNE FAWVER, educator; b. Floydada, Tex., July 2, 1952; d. Ralph Carlton and Jonnie Louise (Ely) Fawver; m. Hulon Lon Carthel, Aug. 24, 1950; children: Casey Britten, Corey Brock, Cienna Beth. Student, S. Plains Jr. Coll., 1970-71, W. Tex. State U., 1971-75; BS, Wayland Bapt. U., 1979-80; cert. tchr., Tex. Tech. U., 1986-87. Tchr. English and reading Lockney (Tex.) Jr. High Sch., 1980-81; tchr. English Floydada High Sch., 1981, 86-87; tchr. phys. edn. A.B. Duncan Elem. Sch., Floydada, 1986—; coord. Jump Rope for Heart, Floydada, 1986-89; com. mem. Dist. Goals Com., Floydada, 1986-87, Dist. Survey Com., Floydada, 1987-88, Campus Long Range Plan Co., 1987-88. Sec. Floydada Exes Homecoming, 1984-88; neighborhood chmn. Am. Cancer Soc., 1985-88; mem. Punkin' Days Festival Com.; coord. Jump Rope for Heart, Floydada, 1986—; leader 4-H Club. Mem. Assn. Tex. Profl. Educators, Tex. Assn. Health, Phys. Edn., Recreation and Dance, Internat. Platform Assn., Am. Heart Assn., Floydada C. of C. (pres. women's div. 1990-91). Primitive Baptist. Home: 901 W Mississippi Floydada TX 79235

CARTIER, CELINE PAULE, librarian, administrator, consultant; b. Lacolle, Que., Can., May 10, 1930; d. Henri Rodolphe and Irene (Boudreau) Robitaille; m. Georges Cartier, Nov. 29, 1952; children: Nathalie, Guillaume. Diplome superieur en pedagogie, U. Montreal, 1948, certificats en litterature et linguistique, 1952; diplome de bibliothecaire-documentaliste, Inst. Catholique, Paris, 1962; maîtrise en adminstrn. publique, Ecole Nationale d'Adminstrn. Publique, 1976; maîtrise en bibliothéconomie, U. Montreal, 1982. Dir. Bibliotheque Centrale, Commn. des ecoles catholiques, Montreal, 1964-73; dir. spl. collections U. Quebec, 1973-76, dir. sector librs., 1976-77; chief gen. libr. U. Laval, Que., 1977-78; gen. dir. libraries U. Laval, 1978-89; cons. Conseil CRC Cons., 1989—. Contbr. articles to profl. jours. Mem. Corp. des Bibliothecaires Profs. de Quebec.

CARTIER, DENISE MARIE, sales executive; b. Pittsfield, Mass., May 23, 1952; d. Robert E. and Mary S. (Cahill) C. AS in Environ. Studies, Berkshire Community Coll., Pittsfield, 1973; BS in Natural Resources, U. Mass., 1975. Technician GE Plastics, Pittsfield, 1977-81, analytical chemist, 1981-82, product coordinator, 1982-83, mktg. support specialist, 1983-85, tech. sales rep., 1985-86, mgr. tech. sales, 1986—. Office: GE Plastics Rt 295 Canaan Rd Richmond MA 01254

CARTISANO, LINDA ANN, lawyer; b. Phila., Dec. 11, 1953; d. S. James and Anna M. (Morley) C. BA cum laude, Widener U., 1974; JD, Temple U., 1978. Bar: Pa. 1979, U.S. Dist. Ct. (ea. dist.) Pa. 1979. Pvt. practice law Chester, Pa., 1978—; asst. city solicitor City of Chester, 1982—; solicitor Chester Devel. Office, 1985—, Darby Creek Joint Authority, Springfield, Pa., 1987—, Borough Of Upland, Upland, Pa., 1988—; counsel Chester Redevel. Authority, Chester, 1986—; acting exec. dir. Chester Redevel. Authority, 1989. Mem. Widener-PMC Alumni Assn., Chester, 1978, Chester City Health Assn., 1981, Chester-Widener Community Commn. Mem. Pa. Bar Assn., Delaware County Bar Assn., Chester Coun. Republican Women. Roman Catholic. Office: 513 Welsh St Chester PA 19013

CARTWRIGHT, DONNA J., healthcare consultant; b. Morristown, N.J., June 20, 1960; d. Stanley and Sandra Jean (Aldridge) C. BA, York Coll. of Pa. Coder, abstractor Newark Beth Israel Med. Ctr.; data quality mgr. Muhlenberg Regional Med. Ctr., Plainfield, N.J.; asst. dir. med. records Univ. Hosp., Hewark; dir. med. records St. Elizabeth Hosp., Elizabeth, N.J.; dir. hosp. support svcs. N.J. Physicians Rev., Inc., Parsippany. Mem. Am. Med. Record Assn. (pres.-elect), L.I. Med. Record Assn. Home: 120 Littleton Rd Parsippany NJ 07054 Office: 197 Main St Peacock NJ 07977

CARTWRIGHT, FRANCES LYNN, marketing professional; b. Wyandotte, Mich., Jan. 20, 1948; d. Francis W. and Edna May (Bradley) C.; m. George T. Kubicki, Jan. 28, 1966 (div. 1973); children: Keith Allen, Eric Todd; m. Roger L. Moss, Aug. 1983. BS with distinction, U. Mich., Dearborn, 1985. Legal stenographer Conrail, Detroit, 1974-79; v.p. mktg. Elcometer, Troy, Mich., 1981-88; exec. v.p. Distbn. Mgmt. Co., Troy, 1979—; bd. dirs., Tunewell, Inc., Troy, Def. Electronics, Troy. Mem. NAFE. Republican. Home: 1038 Greentree St Bloomfield Hills MI 48013 Office: DMA Inc 335 E Big Beaver St #109 Troy MI 48083

CARTWRIGHT, MARY LOU, laboratory scientist; b. Payette, Idaho, Apr. 5, 1923; d. Ray J. and Nellie Mae (Sherer) Decker; B.S., U. Houston, 1958; M.A., Central Mich. U., 1976; m. Chadwick Louis Cartwright, Sept. 13, 1947. Med. technologist Methodist Hosp., Houston, 1957-59, VA Hosp., Livermore, Calif., 1960-67, Kaiser Permanente Med. Center, Hayward, Calif., 1967-71, United Med. Lab., San Mateo, Calif., 1972-73; sr. med. technologist Oakland (Calif.) Hosp., 1974-86; cons. med. lab. tech. Oakland Public Schs. Chmn., Congressional Dist. 11 steering com. Common Cause, 1974-77; consumer mem. Alameda County (Calif.) Health Systems Agy., 1977-78. Served with USNR, 1945-53. Mem. Calif. Soc. Med. Tech., Calif. Assn. Med. Lab. Tech. (Technologist of Yr. award 1968, 78, Pres.'s award 1977, Service award chpt. 1978, 79), Am. Soc. Med. Tech. (by-laws chmn. 1981-83), Am. Bus. Women's Assn., Nat. Assn. Female Execs. Democrat. Home and Office: 231 Depot St #8 Grass Valley CA 95945

CARTWRIGHT, RHONDA DELRIE, banker, controller; b. Alexandria, La., June 28, 1952; d. Willis and Betty (Holt) Delrie; m. David Owen Cartwright, Jan. 1, 1972; children: Regan Treece, Anthony Holt. BSBA, U. Southwestern La., 1974; MBA, Northwestern State U., Natchitoches, La., 1987. Mgmt. acct. Caterpillar Tractor Co., Peoria, Il., 1974-75; staff acct. Everitt, Knight & Masden CPAs, Alexandria, 1975-76; revenue agt. III La. Dept. Revenue & Taxation, Baton Rouge, 1976-80; internal auditor Rapides Bank & Trust, Alexandria, 1980-83; dept. head acctg. Rapides Bank & Trust, 1983-87, sr. v.p. fin. ops. div., 1987—; tchr. St. Leo Coll., St. Leo, Fla., 1989—. Mem. Am. Inst. Bankers, Bank Adminstrn. Inst., Alexandria-Pineville C. of C., Cath. Daugs., Phi Kappa Phi, Alpha Beta. Roman Catholic. Office: Rapides Bank & Trust 400 Murray St Alexandria LA 71301

CARTY, RITA MARY, educational administrator, nurse; b. Pitts., Dec. 23, 1937; d. Ignatius and Frances (Brisini) Cardillo; m. Wayne Lee Carty, Aug. 20, 1966; 1 child, Gina Marie. Diploma in Nursing, Ohio Valley Gen. Hosp., McKees Rocks, Pa., 1958; BSN, Duquesne U., 1965; MSN, Cath. U., 1966, DNSc, 1977. Sch. nurse South Fayette Twp. Sch. Dist., McDonald, Pa., 1958-60; charge nurse Ohio Valley Gen. Hosp., McKees Rocks, Pa., 1960-62, instr., 1962-65; asst. prof. Cath. U., Washington, 1966-72, lectr., 1974-77; dir. nursing div. univ. affiliated program Georgetown U., Washington, 1972-74; assoc. prof., grad. program coordinator George Mason U., Fairfax, Va., 1978-81, chmn. dept. nursing, 1981-85, dean and prof. sch.

nursing, 1985—. Contbr. articles to profl. jours. Mem. Luxmanor Citizens Assn., Rockville, Md., 1985—; vol. senatorial campaign Citizens for Goldwater, Md., 1987. Recipient Bice Lectureship sch. nursing U. Va., Charlottesville, 1984, Progress of Excellence award region III Nat. U. Continuing Edn., 1985. Fellow Am. Acad. Nursing; mem. Am. Nurses Assn., Va. Soc. Profl. Nursing (bd. dirs. 1985-87), Am. Assn. Coll. Nursing (bd. dirs. 1987—), Nat. League Nursing (exec. com. 1987—), Cath. U. Nurses Alumnae (pres. 1979-81), Sigma Theta Tau (1st v.p. 1970-73). Roman Catholic. Office: George Mason U Sch Nursing 4400 University Dr Fairfax VA 22030

CARUS, MARIANNE, magazine editor; b. Dieringhausen, Rhineland, Germany, June 16, 1928; came to U.S., 1951; d. Gunter Wilhelm Alexander and Elisabeth (Gesell) Sondermann; m. Milton Blouke Carus, Mar. 3, 1951; children—Andre, Christine, Inga. Abitur, Gymnasium, Gummersbach, Germany; M.S., U. Freiburg, Germany; post grad., Sorbonne U., Paris, U. Chgo. Editor Open Court Pub. Co., LaSalle, Ill., 1964-73; editor-in-chief Cricket Mag., LaSalle, 1973—, gen. mgr., 1982—, pub., 1989—; cons. editor for textbooks Open Court Pub. Co., LaSalle, 1975—. Editor, compiler: Cricket's Choice, 1974. Pres. Ill. Valley Garden Club, LaSalle, 1960; dir. Ill. Valley Community Concert Assn., LaSalle, 1960; mem. LaSalle Women's Club, 1960—. Mem. ALA (dir. ALSC div. 1982-85), Mag. Pubs. Assn., Friends of USBBY, Soc. Children's Book Writers, Friends of the CCBC, Inc., Children's Reading Roundtable. Home: 2222 Chartres St Peru IL 61354 Office: Cricket Mag 315 5th St Peru IL 61354

CARUSILLO, JOAN GLORIA, nun; b. Washington, June 10, 1931; d. Louis J. and Anna (Thomas) C. BA, Dunbarton Coll., 1953; MA, Cath. U., Washington, 1965, STB, 1967. Tchr. high sch. English, Latin and theology various high schs., 1957-75; asst. prin. St. Mary's Acad., Alexandria, Va., 1957-77, prin., 1977-81; eastern regional superior Sisters of the Holy Cross, 1981-87; v.p. philosophy and mission Mount Carmel Health, Columbus, Ohio, 1988—; mem. leadership group Sisters of the Holy Cross, Notre Dame, Ind., 1981-87; bd. dirs. Holy Cross Health System, South Bend, Ind., 1981-87; bd. trustees Mount Carmel Health, Columbus, 1981-87; vice-chmn. Leadership Conf. Women Religious, region 4, Pitts., 1983-86. Mem. diocesan sch. bd. Cath. DioceseArlington, 1979-81; mem. hunger seminar adv. coun. Bread for World, Washington, 1983-86; trustee Holy Cross Hosp., Silver Spring, Md., 1989—. Mem. Cath. Health Assn., Franklinton Ministerial Assn. Roman Catholic. Office: Mt Carmel Health 793 W State St Columbus OH 43222

CARUSO, MARIE THERESE, marriage and family therapist, clinical social worker; b. Bklyn., Sept. 26, 1931; d. Cono Louis and Rose Elizabeth (De Lisio) Pecora; m. Fred Theodore Caruso, Sept. 13, 1953; children: Frederick, Rosemarie, Paula, Christopher, Joseph, John. BA magna cum laude, Montclair State Coll., 1979; MSW, Rutgers U., 1981. Lic. marriage counselor, N.J. Kindergarten tchr. Franklin Sch., East Orange, N.J., 1973-78; asst. dir. League for Family Svcs., Bloomfield, N.J., 1978-79; clin. social worker St. Joseph's Hosp., Paterson, N.J., 1979-80, Essex County Guidance Ctr., East Orange, 1980-81, Hosp. Ctr. at Orange, N.J., 1983-85; dir. social svs. Chestnut Hill Convalescent Ctr., Passaic, N.J., 1982-83; adj. prof. Montclair State Coll., Upper Montclair, N.J., 1981-82, dir. counseling program, 1986-89; dir. clin. svcs. Family Svc. Burlington County, Moorestown, N.J., 1989—; pvt. practice; mem. adv. bd. Am. Cancer Soc., East Orange, 1983-85, Paterson Head Start, 1985-86, Youth Consultation Svcs., Moorestown, 1989-90; workshop presenter, mem. program com. N.J. Oncology Social Workers Group, Princeton, N.J., 1984-86. Mem. adv. bd. Big Bros.-Big Sisters, Bloomfield, 1978-79; pres. PTO, East Orange, 1980-82; mem. county com. East Orange Rep. Com., 1982-87; mem. adv. bd. com. on substance abuse Moorestown Bd. Edn., 1989-90. Alumni scholar Montclair State Coll., 1979. Mem. Nat. Assn. Social Workers (diplomate clin. social work), Acad. Cert. Social Workers, Am. Assn. for Marriage and Family Therapy (cert.), N.J. Coun. on Family Rels. (pres. 1980-82), Phi Kappa Phi, Sigma Phi Omega, Omicron Nu. Roman Catholic. Home: 75 Deep Hollow Ln N Columbus NJ 08022

CARUTHERS, BARBARA SUE APGAR, physician, educator; b. Guthrie, Okla., Oct. 4, 1943; d. Wallace Duke and Gloria Jayne (Glover) McMillin; m. Charles George Caruthers, Apr. 1, 1976; 1 child, Larisa Ann. BA in Biology, Loretto Heights Coll., 1965; MS in Anatomy, U. Mich., 1968; MD, Tex. Tech. Med. Sch., 1976. Diplomate Am. Bd. Family Practice, Am. Bd. Med. Examiners. Research asst. Parke Davis, Ann Arbor, Mich., 1965-66, Aerospace Med. Labs Wright-Patterson AFB, Ohio, 1968-70; instr. anatomy dept. Tex. Tech. U. Med. Sch., Lubbock, 1972-74, resident in family practice, 1976-79, clin. asst. prof., 1980-83; physician The Pavilion, Lubbock, 1981-83; sr. physician, dir. gynecology clinic U. Mich., 1983-86, instr. dept. family practice, 1984-89, med. dir. Briarwood Health Ctr., 1986—, also mem. steering com. for ambulatory care, asst. prof. dept. family practice, 1989—, dir. women's health, 1989—; mem. staff Meth. Hosp., St. Mary of the Plains Hosp., U. Mich. Hosp.; mem. med. exec. com. dept. of family practice U. Mich. Mem. adv. bd. Lubbock chpt. March of Dimes, 1972-74. Recipient Upjohn Achievement award, 1976, Psychiatry Achievement award, 1976; Soroptimist Internat. grantee, 1978-79, U. Mich. Dept. Family Practice Resident Teaching award, 1985, 87, 88, 89; fellow Mich. State U., 1989-90. Mem. Am. Acad. Family Practice, Lubbock County Med. Soc., Tex. Med. Assn., Mich. Acad. Family Practice (perinatal com. 1987—), Soc. of Tchrs. of Family Medicine, Am. Soc. Colposcopy and Cervical Pathology, Alpha Omega Alpha. Democrat. Home: 883 Scio Meadow Ann Arbor MI 48103 Office: U Mich Family Practice Dept 1018 Fuller Ann Arbor MI 48109-0708

CARUTHERS, MARILYNN LAIRD, health care consultant; b. Loomis, Calif., Dec. 7, 1922; d. Fenn Warner and Lorena May (Roberts) Laird; m. Ralph Rutland Caruthers, Nov. 16, 1946; children: Robert Lee, Laird David. Degree in nursing, Mt. Zion Hosp., San Francisco, 1944; BS summa cum laude, UCLA, 1960. RN. Nurse U.S. Army, 1944-46; clinic nurse Missionary Clinic, 1954-56, 62-63; sch. nurse San Diego City Schs., 1956-58; supr. sch. health Placer County Schs., Auburn, Calif., 1960-62, supr. nurse head start, 1964-66; sch. nurse Roseville (Calif.) High Sch. Dist., 1967-69; coord. sch. health edn. El Dorado High Sch. Dist., Diamond Springs, Calif., 1969-81, cons. sch. health, health edn., 1981-86; dir. Placer County Sch. Tutorial Program, Auburn, 1966-67; cons. Loomis Basin General Plan, Loomis, Calif., 1975. Mem. AAUW, Calif. Sch. Nurses Orgn., Calif. Coaches Assn., UCLA Alumni Assn., NORCAL Alumni Assn., UCLA Bruin Alumni Assn. (pres. 1959-60), Comstock Club. Democrat.

CARVALHO, ANNA MARIE, entertainer, comedian; b. Kearny, N.J., Apr. 9, 1955; d. Manuel and Mary Frances (Souto) C. AA in Edn., Fla. Jr. Coll., 1975; BS in Edn., Western Carolina U., 1977. Health, physical edn. instr. Duval County Pub. Sch., Jacksonville, Fla., 1977-82; pres. A.Y.S., Inc., Jacksonville, 1983-85; claims svc. rep. Blue Cross/Blue Shield, Jacksonville, 1985, human resource devel. specialist, 1986-87, supr. tng. and devel., 1987—; cons. Duval County Sch. System, Jacksonville, 1983-85, Blue Cross/Blue Shield, Jacksonville, 1986; owner, pres. Unltd. Performance, 1988—. County coordinator Spl. Olympics, Jacksonville, 1983-85, area dir., 1985. Mem. Am. Alliance Health and Physical Edn., Am. Soc. Tng. and Devel., Nat. Assn. Female Execs., Am. Mgmt. Assn., Kappa Delta Pi. Democrat. Roman Catholic. Office: Unlimited Performance PO Box 16431 Jacksonville FL 32216

CARVER, DARLENE T., management consulting educator; b. Washington, July 19, 1954; d. Sara F. Rubin; m. Gary P. Carver, Dec. 27, 1975. BS, U. Md., 1976; postgrad., Frostburg State U. Adminstrv. asst. Nat. Inst. Standards and Tech., Gaithersburg, Md.; instr. Washington Bus. Sch., Rockville, Md., ITT Bus. Inst., Bethesda, Md.; pres., founder Abbie Bus. Inst., Frederick, Md. Mem. JSEC, MBEA, NBEA, AVA, PSI, ProNet, BPW, ASN. Home: 3501 Big Woods Rd Ijamsville MD 21754 Office: 3501 Big Woods Rd Ijamsville MD 21754

CARVER, DOROTHY LEE ESKEW (MRS. JOHN JAMES CARVER), educator; b. Brady, Tex., July 10, 1926; d. Clyde Albert and A. Maurine (Meadows) Eskew; student So. Ore. Coll., 1942-43, Coll. Eastern Utah, 1965-67; B.A., U. Utah, 1968; M.A., Cal. State Coll. at Hayward, 1970; postgrad. Mills Coll., 1971; m. John James Carver, Feb. 26, 1944; children—John James, Sheila Carver Bentley, Chuck, David. Instr., Rutherford Bus. Coll., Dallas, 1944-45; sec. Adolph Coors Co., Golden, Colo., 1945-47; instr. English, Coll. Eastern Utah, Price, 1968-69; instr. speech Modesto (Calif.) Jr. Coll., 1970-71; instr. personal devel. men and women Heald Bus. Colls., Oakland, Calif., 1972-74, dean curricula, Walnut Creek, Calif., 1974-86; instr. Diablo Valley Coll., Pleasant Hill, Calif., 1986—; communications cons. Oakland Army Base, Crocker Bank, U.S. Steel, I. Magnin, Artec Internat. Author: Developing Listening Skills. Mem. Gov.'s Conf. on Higher Edn. in Utah, 1968; mem. finance com. Coll. Eastern Utah, 1967-69; active various community drives. Judge election Republican party, 1960, 64. Bd. dirs. Opportunity Center, Symphony of the Mountain. Mem. AAUW, Bus. and Profl. Womens Club, Nat. Assn. Deans and Women Adminstrs., Delta Kappa Gamma. Episcopalian (supt. Sunday Sch. 1967-69). Clubs: Soroptimist Internat. (pres. Walnut Creek 1979-80 sec., founder region 1978-80); Order Eastern Star. Home: 20 Coronado Ct Walnut Creek CA 94596

CASALASPRO, DEBRA ANN, nurse; b. Barksdale AFB, La., Sept. 30, 1956; d. Joseph Ronald and Pauline Josephine (Bichanich) C. BSN, Molloy Coll., Rockville Centre, N.Y., 1979. Pvt. duty nurse Lynbrook, N.Y., 1979-80; team leader, nurse Med. Meml. Ctr., Ashland, Wis., 1980-81; nurse intern Wilford Hall, USAF, San Antonio, Tex., 1981; commd. USAF, 1981, advanced through grades to capt.; staff nurse USAF Hosp. KI Sawyer AFB, Gwinn, Mich., 1981-84; flight nurse, instr., res. affairs officer 2 AES Rhien Main AFB, Frankfurt, Fed. Republic Germany, 1984-86; staff nurse Air Force Acad. Hosp., Colorado Springs, 1986-87, asst. charge nurse, mem. edn. com., 1987-88, charge nurse, 1988—. Decorated Air Force Commendation medal. Mem. Air Force Assn., Orgn. for Ob-Gyn. and Neonatal Nurses, Aerospace Med. Assn., Co. Grade Officers (adv. coun.), Air Force Acad. Booster. Republican. Roman Catholic. Home: 6890 Deer Bluff Dr Huber Heights OH 45424

CASALE, KAREN A., healthcare facility nursing manager. BS in Nursing, Fairleigh Dickinson U., 1981; MS, Jersey City State Coll., 1990. Staff nurse Riverside Gen. Hosp., Secaucus, N.J., St. Barnabas Med. Ctr., Livingston, N.J.; discharge planning coord., head nurse St. James Hosp., Newark; asst. dir. nursing King David Care Ctr., Atlantic City, N.J.; clin. mgr. Atlantic City Med. Ctr., 1990—; U.S. citizen ambassador nursing del. to People's Rep. China. Mem. NAFE, N.Y. Acad. Scis., Am. Nurses Assn., Sigma Theta Tau, Phi Zeta Kappa. Home: 3507 Tulip Tree Pl Mays Landing NJ 08330

CASALVERI, LAUREN MARY, public relations executive; b. Derby, Conn., Oct. 9, 1960; d. Frank J. and Mary (Boland) C. BS, So. Conn. State U., New Haven, 1982; MBA, Sacred Heart U., Fairfield, 1987. Tchr. Fin. counselor Griffin Hosp., Derby, 1980-83; acct. rep. Physicians Health Svcs., Trumbull, Conn., 1983, asst. to pres., 1984-85, dir. of adminstrn., 1985-89, v.p. corp. and mem. rels., 1989—. Coord. Cardinal Shehan Youth Ctr., Bridgeport, 1983—; bd. dirs. ARC, Ansonia, Conn., 1987—. Mem. N.Y. Assn. of Quality Assurance Profls., Conn. Assn. of Quality Assurance Profls., Soc. of Consumer Affairs Profls. Home: 256 Hawthorne Ave Derby CT 06418 Office: Physicians Health Services 120 Hawley Ln Trumbull CT 06611

CASANO, BRENDA JO, resident director; b. Mt. Holly, N.J., May 23, 1965; d. Joseph Carl and Natalie Theresa (Russo) C. BA, Rider Coll., 1987, postgrad., 1988—. Cert. educator, guidance counselor, N.J. Pub. rels. intern N.J. Dept. Pub. Advocate, Trenton, N.J., 1986; mktg. asst. N.J. Dept. Agriculture, Trenton, 1986; resident advisor Rider Coll. Residence Life, Lawrenceville, N.J., 1986-87; direct mktg. rep. Trump Plaza Hotel & Casino, Atlantic City, 1987-88; resident dir. Rider Coll. Residence Life, Lawrenceville, 1988—; mem. family bus. Russo's Fruit & Vegetable Farm, Tabernacle, N.J., 1978—; mng. editor Rider Coll. Yearbook, Lawrenceville, 1985-87. Republican. Roman Catholic. Home: 19 Chatsworth Rd Tabernacle NJ 08088

CASAZZA, CAROL A., lawyer; b. N.Y.C., Aug. 19, 1957; d. Edward Joseph and Rose Mary Casazza. BA, Rutgers Coll., 1979; JD, Hofstra U., 1984. Bar: N.J. 1985, U.S. Dist. Ct. N.J. 1985, U.S. Dist. Ct. (ea. dist.) N.Y. 1986, U.S. Ct. Appeals (5th cir.) 1986. Rsch. asst. Ctr. for Coastal and Environ. Studies Rutgers U., 1977-79; environ. scientist U.S. EPA, N.Y.C., 1979-81, asst. regional counsel, 1984-87; legal intern Natural Resources Def. Coun., N.Y.C., 1983; environ. atty., assoc. Clapp & Eisenberg, Newark, 1987-89; environ. atty. legal div. environ. affairs Pfizer, Inc., N.Y.C., 1989—. Mem. N.J. Bar Assn. (environ. law sect.). Office: Pfizer Inc Legal Div 235 E 42d St New York NY 10017

CASCINO, MARY DORY, business executive; b. Chgo., Dec. 21, 1949; d. V. Paul and Vada L. (Tuttle) Dory; A.B., Loyola U., Chgo., 1971; M.A., U. Chgo., 1972; m. Anthony E. Cascino, Jr., July 28, 1973; children: Anthony E. III, Christine Anne, Caroline Stephanie. Assoc. planner, local svc. specialist Northeastern Ill. Planning Commn., 1972-76; self-employed park and recreation planner, Highland Park, Ill., 1976-80; owner Mary Anne Products, Glencoe, Ill., 1981-87, Exec. Svcs. Unltd., 1988—. Candidate for alderman City of Chgo., 1971; past sec., v.p., pres. Glencoe PTA; past chairperson Glencoe Village Nominating Com. Mem. Am. Planning Assn. Author: Bicycle Safety Planning Guide.

CASCIO, ANNA THERESA, playwright, screenwriter; b. Arlington, Va., Nov. 7, 1955; d. Morris F. and Blanche Rose (Borzomati) C.; m. W. Patterson Skipper, Jan. 26, 1985. Student, George Mason U., 1973-74; BA, W.Va. U., 1977; MA, Hollins Coll., 1979; MFA, Yale U., 1983. Lit. mgr. Ensemble Studio Theatre, N.Y.C., 1982; playwright Eugene O'Neill Playwrights' Conf., Waterford, Conn., 1983, Fountain Square Players and Am. Ibsen Theatre, Cin. and Pitts., 1983, Carnegie Mellon U., Pitts., 1989; prof. SUNY, Purchase, 1988; prof., playwright-in-residence Ind. State U., Terre Haute, 1988; writer You & Me Kid Prodns., N.Y.C., 1989; screenwriter Sandia Films, N.Y.C., 1989—; writer HBO, L.A., 1990; screenwriter HBO Network, 1990; cons. Manhattan Theatre Club, N.Y.C., 1985-87; writer Another World, N.Y.C., 1987-88, En Garde Arts, N.Y.C., 1988-89. Author: (plays) June 8, 1968, 1988, Bikini Snow, 1989, Minny and The James Boys, 1989, (musical) Birdwatchers, 1990. Rockefeller grantee, 1987. Mem. Writers Guild Am., Sigma Tau Delta. Roman Catholic.

CASE, KAREN ANN, lawyer; b. Milw., Apr. 7, 1944; d. Alfred F. and Hilda M. (Tomich) Case. BS, Marquette U., 1963, JD 1966; LLM, NYU, 1973. Bar: Wis. 1966, U.S. Ct. Claims, 1973, U.S. Tax Ct. 1973. Ptnr. Meldman, Case & Weine, Milw., 1973-85, Meldman, Case & Weine div. Mulcahy & Wherry, S.C., 1985-87; Sec. of Revenue State of Wis., 1987-88; ptnr. Case & Drinka, S.C., Milw., 1989—; lectr. U. Wis., Milw., 1974-78; guest lectr. Marquette U. Law Sch., 1975-78. Mem. gov.'s Commn. on Taliesin, 1988, gov.'s Econ. Adv. Commn., 1989—, pres.'s coun. Alverno Coll., 1988—. Fellow Wis. Bar Found. (dir. 1977-90, treas. 1980-90); mem. ABA, Milw. Assn. Women Lawyers (founding mem., bd. dirs. 1975-78, 81-82), Milw. Bar Assn. (bd. dirs. 1985-87), State Bar Wis. (bd. govs. 1981-85, 87-90, dir. taxation sect. 1981-87, vice chmn. 1986-87, 90-91), Am. Acad. Matrimonial Lawyers (bd. dirs. 1988-90), Nat. Assn. Women Lawyers (Wis. del. 1982-83), Milw. Rose Soc. (pres. 1981, dir. 1981-83), Friends of Boerner Bot. Gardens (founding mem., pres. 1984—), Profl. Dimensions Club (dir. 1985-87), Tempo Club (sec. 1984-85). Contbr. articles to legal jours. Home: 9803 W Meadow Park Dr Hales Corners WI 53130 Office: Case & Drinka 735 N Water St Ste 1220 Milwaukee WI 53202

CASE, MARY ELIZABETH, educator; b. Crawfordsville, Ind., Dec. 10, 1925; d. Ralph Thomas and Leila Luckenbill (Sharar) C. BA, Maryville (Tenn.) Coll., 1947; MS, U. Tenn., 1950; PhD, Yale U., 1957, DSc, 1969. Rsch. asst., lectr. Yale U., New Haven, 1957-72; from assoc. prof. to prof. U. Ga., Athens, 1972—. Office: U Ga Athens GA 30602

CASE, RITA COLEMAN, trade association administrator, consultant; b. Chgo.; d. Harry Arthur and Lorita Marie (Kelly) Coleman; children: John E., Lorita M. BA in English, No. Ill. U., 1982, MA in English, 1986. Tchr.'s aide Elgin Unified Sch. Dist. 46, Streamwood, Ill., 1980-82; teaching intern No. Ill. U., DeKalb, Ill., 1982-83; with Alliance Am. Insurers, Schaumburg, Ill., 1983—, mgr. edn. svcs., 1987-89, dir. edn., 1989—; cons. Rewrites, Schaumburg, 1985—. Contbr. articles to profl. jours. Sec. focus group Harper Community Coll., Palatine, Ill., 1990—; community advisor Northeastern Ill. U., Chgo., 1989—. Mem. Am. Soc. for Tng. and Devel., Soc. for Tech. Communication, Soc. Ins. Trainers and Educators, Chgo. Soc. Assn. Execs. Office: Alliance Am Insurers 1501 Woodfield Rd 400 W Schaumburg IL 60173-4980

CASEI, NEDDA, mezzo-soprano; b. Balt.; d. Howard Thomas and Lyda Marie (Graupman) Casey; m. John A. Wiles, Jr., 1971 (div. 1979); m. Samuel Strasbourger, 1983 (dec. 1987). Student, Mozarteum, Salzburg, Austria, 1959; B in Performing Arts Adminstrn., Fordham U., 1982; studied voice with William P. Herman, N.Y.C.; studied voice with Vittrio Piccinini, Milan, Italy; studied voice with Loretta Corelli, N.Y.C.; also student piano, langs., ballet. Tchr. master classes, lectr. univs. and festivals; judge vocal competitions for Met. Opera, Fulbright Scholarship competition. Operatic debut Theatre Royal de la Monnaie, Brussels, 1960, with La Scala, Milan, Met. Opera, N.Y.C., 1964; operatic performances at Met. Opera, 1964-86, Basel Stadttheater, Gran Liceo, Barcelona, Teatro Carlo Fenice, Genova, San Remo Festival, Trieste Opera, Opera du Rhin, Strasbourg, Salzburg Festspielhaus, Teatro San Carlo, Naples, Chgo. Lyric Opera, Bogota Opera, Caracas Opera, Pitts. Opera, Vancouver Opera, Cape Town Opera, Brno Opera, Bratislava Opera, Kosice Opera, Prague Opera, Miami Opera, Houston Opera, San Diego Opera, Hartford Opera, Phila. Opera, Toledo Opera, Dayton Opera, Memphis Opera, Mobile Opera, Los Angeles Opera, Boston Opera, N.J. Opera, Taipei Opera; performances in numerous mus. festivals, concert tours, also symphonic concerts, oratorios, recitals and operatic guest appearances in Europe, South Africa, Cen. Am., S.Am., Can., U.S., Far East, Middle East and Australia; performed on radio and TV in Holland, Belgium, Leipzig, Japan, U.S., German Dem. Republic, Fed. Republic of Germany, Hong Kong, Singapore; performed at White House, Washington, 1967; made various recs. Supraphon, Everest, Nonesuch, Concert Hall, Vanguard, CETRA, others; contbr. articles to profl. jours.; guest editor Opera Quar. Coord. mus. events and benefits for Internat. Ctr. for the Disabled, Morningside Home, Aging in Am. Gerontol. Acad.; mem. adv. com. Fordham U. at Lincoln Ctr. Recipient New Orleans Opera award, 1959, Rockefeller Found. award, 1962, 64, Community Leaders and Noteworthy Americans, 1975-76, Woman of Achievement award, 1969, Martha Baird Rockefeller awards, 1962, 64, Outstanding Young Singers award, 1959. Mem. AFTRA, Actors Equity, Am. Guild Mus. Artists (bd. govs., nat. pres. 1983—, chmn. relief fund), Am. Coun. for the Arts (bd. dirs.), Nat. Assn. Tchrs. Singing, Nat. Cultural Alliance (bd. dirs.), Theatre for a New Audience (bd. dirs.). Office: Am Guild Mus Artists 1727 Broadway New York NY 10019

CASEL, MARY LYNN, real estate broker; b. Carthage, N.Y., Jan. 16, 1943; d. Floyd Albert and Mary Frances (Schack) Neuroth; m. Ronald Anthony Casel, Nov. 28, 1963 (div. Nov. 1977); children—Mark, Steven, Glen. Grad. Harper Method, Rochester, N.Y., 1961. Lic. real estate broker. Owner M. L. Salon, Rochester, N.Y., 1962-72; specialty tchrs.-aide Broward County, Ft. Lauderdale, Fla., 1973-77; office mgr. Broward County Voter Registration, Margate, Fla., 1977-82; real estate salesperson Pelican Bay, Daytona Beach, Fla., 1982-84, broker, 1984-86, broker, sales mgr., 1986— owner C & F Shakemasters, Inc, 1989—. Mem. adv. bd. Democratic Club, Margate, Fla., 1977-82. Mem. Nat. Assn. Realtors, Fla. Home Builders Assn., Nat. Home Builders Assn., Daytona Beach Home Builders Assn., Daytona Beach Bd. Realtors, Ft. Lauderdale Bd. Realtors, Nat. Assn. Women in Constrn. (v.p. 1988-89, pres.-elect 1989—), NAFE, Sales and Mktg. Council. Avocations: travel, dancing, theater, real estate investments. Democrat. Roman Catholic. Home: 825 Pelican Bay Dr Daytona Beach FL 32019 Office: Churl Corp 138 Sea Hawk Dr Daytona Beach FL 32019

CASEY, BARBARA A. PEREA, state representative, educator; b. Las Vegas, N.Mex., Dec. 21, 1951; d. Joe D. and Julia A. (Armijo) Perea; m. Frank J. Casey, Aug. 5, 1978. BA, N.Mex. U., 1972; MA, Highland U., Las Vegas, N.Mex., 1973. Instr. N.Mex. Highlands U., Las Vegas, 1972-74; tchr. Roswell Ind. Schs., Roswell, N.Mex., 1974—; mem. N.Mex. Ho. of Reps., 1984—; instr. N.Mex. Mil. Inst., Roswell, 1977-82, Roswell Police Acad., 1984. Mem. NEA (Adv. of of Yr.), AAUW, Am. Bus. Women's Assn., N.Mex. Endowment for Humanities. Democrat. Roman Catholic. Home: 1214 E First Roswell NM 88201

CASEY, BEVERLY ANN, postmaster; b. Decaturville, Tenn., Aug. 6, 1949; d. Willie Hugh and Lillian Blanche (Ivy) Tillman; m. John Robert Casey, Jan. 19, 1969 (div. 1982); children—John Gary, Kimberly Jean. Student Jackson State Community Coll., 1982-84. Sec. State of Tenn., Western Institute, 1969-76; post office clk. U.S. Postal Service, Western Institute, 1977-82, postmaster, 1982-84; postmaster U.S. Postal Service, Pickwick Dam, Tenn., 1984—; officer-in-charge U.S. Postal Service, Michie, Tenn., 1984. Bd. dirs. Pickwick Med. Clinic, 1986; vol. Hardeman chpt. Saint Jude, Bolivar, Tenn., 1983; town chmn. Reelfoot council Girl Scouts U.S., 1980-84, activities chmn., 1980-84, recipient Appreciation award, 1983. Named Outstanding 3d Class Postmaster 380 area U.S. Postal Service, 1984; recipient Vol. Service award Cystic Fibrosis Found., Tenn. Chpt., 1982; Vol. Appreciation Cert. Western Mental Health, 1984. Mem. Nat. Assn. Postmasters of U.S., Nat. League of Postmasters (v.p. Tenn. br. 1984-86), 380 Postmasters Assn. (pres. 1983-84), U.S. Postal Service (dir.-at-large women's adv. coun. 1983-88). Baptist. Club: Hardin County Band Boosters. Avocations: walking; tennis. Home: PO Box 363 Pickwick Dam TN 38365 Office: US Postal Service Pickwick Dam TN 38365

CASEY, CATHERINE ELIZABETH, mental health clinic administrator, psychologist; b. Houston, May 14, 1941; d. Robert Randolph and Hazel (Brann) C. BA, Dominican Coll., Houston, 1967; MA, U. Tex., 1973, PhD, 1976. Joined Dominican Order, Roman Cath. Ch. Elem. tchr. St Mary's Sch., Port Arthur, Tex., 1962-65; tchr. St. Piux X High Sch., Houston, 1965-70, Holy Cross High Sch., Austin, Tex., 1970-71; teaching asst. U. Tex., Austin, 1971-73; staff psychologist Counseling Ctr., Georgetown U., Washington, 1976-78; staff psychologist Consultation Ctr., Albany, N.Y., 1978-81; exec. dir. Consultation Ctr., San Antonio, 1981—; cons. to numerous priests, bishops and nun groups throughout U.S. and Can. Contbr. articles to profl. jours. Bd. dirs. San Antonio Free Clinic, 1983; bd. dirs., treas. Las Casas Fund for Cheyennes and Arapahos, Ossining, N.Y., 1986—. Mem. Am. Psychol. Assn., Am. Assn. for Counseling and Devel., Nat. Audubon Soc., Tex. Nature Conservancy. Office: Consultation Ctr 249 W Ligustrum Dr San Antonio TX 78228

CASEY, DENISE MAPES, foundation program director; b. Pontiac, Mich., Nov. 5, 1955; d. Francis Jennings and Ines Evelyn (McReynolds) Mapes; m. Bradford Earl Casey, Aug. 25, 1985; 1 stepchild, Sabrina Isabelle. Cert. in interpretation for hearing impaired, Ohlone Coll., Fremont, Calif., 1984; cert. clin. therapist, Palo Alto Sch. Hypnotherapy, 1990. Asst. project coordinator People First of Calif., San Jose, 1980; pre-vocat. instr. Agnews Devel. Ctr., San Jose, 1980-84; vocat. instr. Community Assn. for the Retarded Inc, Palo Alto, Calif., 1984-85, asst. dir., 1985-86, dir., 1986—; agy. rep. San Jose Spl. Olympics, 1984-85; mem. service providers adv. com. San Andreas Regional Ctr., Campbell, Calif., 1986—; mem. adult services com. San Mateo County Coordinating Council on Devel. Disabilities. Contbr. articles to profl. jours. Organizer Com. to Elect John Anderson for Pres., Fremont, 1980. Mem. Autism Soc. Am., Nat. Assn. Female Execs., Calif. Assn. for Rehabilitatory Facilities, Palo Alto C. of C., Mountain View C. of C. (mentor program), Internat. Assn. Healing Arts. Office: Community Assn for Retarded Inc 2751 Marine Way Ste A Mountain View CA 99043

CASEY, JANICE MARIE, financial analyst; b. Ames, Iowa, July 23, 1954; d. Donald J. and LaDeane (Olser) C. BA, Iowa State U., 1976; postgrad., Ariz. State U., 1984-86, Coll. Fin. Planning, 1987-89. Cert. fin. planner. Sales rep. Vet. Sales Ancom Norden, Smithe-Kline, Phoenix, 1976-77; sales mgr. D.V.M. Inc., Los Angeles, 1977-78; regional cons. mgr. Hospitex, San Jose, Calif., 1978-79; dir. mktg. Incentive Journeys, San Jose, 1979-83; leasing agt., gen. mgr., advt. dir. Granada Mktg. Mgmt., Phoenix, 1983-86; adminstrv. asst. fin. planner McCarthy & Assocs. Anchor Nat. Fin. Services, Inc., Phoenix, 1986-89; mgr. Sun State Fin. Svcs. Corp., Phoenix, 1989; dir. broker, dealer svcs., contractor H.J. Tessier & Co., Phoenix, 1989; investment officer Security Pacific Bank Investments, Phoenix, 1990—. Vocal soloist Maria Goretti Cath. Ch., Scottsdale, Ariz., 1987—. Mem. Internat. Assn. Fin. Planners, Ariz. Vet. Med. Assn. (mem. bus. task force), Nat. Assn. Securities Dealers (registered rep., prin. ins., real estate). Office: Security Pacific Investments Inc 2020 N Central Ave Ste 130 Phoenix AZ 85004

CASEY, JUNE B., investment consultant; b. Waterloo, Ill., July 9, 1924; d. Paul W. and Olivia Katherine (Bessche) Broyles; children: John Jack H. Jr., Paul Jeffrey. Student, Williams Woods Coll., 1943, U. Ill., 1944. Prin. Ind. Investments, Billings, Mont., 1950-67; pvt. practice investment cons. Steilacoom, Wash., 1967—. Mem. NAFE, C. of C., Eastern Star, Marine Corps League Aux. (dept. pres., nat. publicity chmn.), Amaranth. Home: 2596 Madrona Pt Ln Steilacoom WA 98388

CASEY, KAREN ANNE, banker; b. Bklyn., Oct. 5, 1955; d. Stanley Joseph and Helen Katherine (Kosowski) Mozeleski; m. Dennis Joseph Casey, May 14, 1977; 1 child, Christopher Sean. BBA, Baruch Coll., CUNY, 1977. CPA, N.Y., CFP. Jr. acct. Coopers & Lybrand, N.Y.C., 1977-78, sr. acct., 1978-79, supr., 1979-81; asst. fin. contr. Gulf Internat. Bank, N.Y.C., 1981-82, fin. contr., 1982; v.p., fin. contr. Allied Irish Banks plc, N.Y.C., 1982-87, sr. v.p., fin. contr., 1988-89, sr. v.p. mgmt. support svcs., 1989—; bank rep. to Bank Adminstrn. Inst., 1983—, Inst. Fgn. Bankers, 1984—, Com. of Banking Insts. on Taxation, 1984—. Mem. Am. Inst. CPAs. Roman Catholic. Avocations: gardening, golf, tennis, reading. Office: Allied Irish Banks plc 405 Park Ave New York NY 10022

CASEY, KATHLEEN HEIRICH, lawyer, educator; b. Chgo., Mar. 10, 1937; d. Bruneau Ernest and Kathleen Brennan (Grogan) Heirich; m. John M. Casey, Nov. 18, 1959 (div. 1974); children: Sean M., Kyle L., Siobhan C. AB, Radcliffe Coll., 1959; JD, St. John's U., 1974. Bar: N.Y. 1975, U.S. Dist. Ct. (so. and ea. dists.) N.Y. 1975, U.S. Ct. Appeals (2d cir.) 1975, U.S. Supreme Ct. 1976, Calif. 1989, U.S. Dist. Ct. (no. dist.) Calif. 1989, U.S. Ct. Appeals (9th cir.) 1989. Asst. corp. counsel N.Y.C. Law Dept., 1974-76; appellate counsel Div. Criminal Justice, N.Y.C., 1976-77; asst. atty. gen. N.Y. Law Dept., 1977-78; prin. law clk. N.Y. State Supreme Ct., N.Y.C., 1978-81; assoc. Colton, Weissberg, Hartnick, Yamin & Sheresky, N.Y.C., 1981-83, Milbank, Tweed, Hadley & McCloy, N.Y.C., 1983-86; pvt. practice, N.Y.C., 1986—, Orinda, Calif., 1989—; adj. faculty N.Y. Law Sch., N.Y.C., 1983-85; mem. family dispute resolution and comml. panels Am. Arbitration Assn., N.Y.C., 1984—, NASD, 1989—. Contbr. articles to profl. jours. Nassau County committeewoman, 1972-79, 81-87; mem. law com. Nassau County Democratic Party, 1977-81, Navy League of U.S., N.Y. Council, 1980. Fellow Am. Acad. Matrimonial Law; mem. ABA, Calif. Bar Assn., Queen's Bench, N.Y. Women's Bar Assn. (officer 1985—), N.Y. State Bar Assn., Assn. of Bar of City of N.Y., N.Y.C. Lawyers Assn. Office: 120 Village Sq Ste 64 Orinda CA 94563

CASEY, MADELYN BENNETT, marketing professional; b. Marksville, La., Jan. 9, 1951; d. Benjamin Clyde and Mary Frances (Taylor) Bennett; m. Gaynor Paul George, Nov. 29, 1969 (div. 1983); children: Mary, Paul; m. Johnny Carroll Casey, Dec. 21, 1984. Student, La. State U., 1968-70; BA in Journalism, La. Coll., 1988. Owner, operator Hair by George Salon and Boutique, Marksville, 1974-82; exec. acct. Sta. KLAX-TV, Alexandria, La., 1982-83, La. Bus. Jour., Nachitoches, 1983-85; v.p. mktg. Rapides Regional Med. Ctr., 1985-88; Alexandria; pres. MBC & Assoc., Inc., Alexandria, 1988—; pres. MBC & Assocs., Alexandria, 1988—; producer and host of TV health program in Ark., La., Miss., Tenn., N.C., Ga.; cons., speaker in field. Contbr. articles to profl. jours.; contbr. to TV programs. Active United Way, City Park Player. Recipient Bus. Pacesetter award Gov. of La., 1989-90. Mem. NAFE, Am. Assn. Hosp. Pub. Rels., Am. Advt. Fedn., Am. Hosp. Assn., Am. Mgmt. Assn., Alexandria C. of C., Cen. La. C. of C. (chmn. communication), Profl. Womens Exch. Home: 5221 Argonne Alexandria LA 71301 Office: MBC & Assocs 5501 Jackson St Ext Alexandria LA 71303

CASEY, TERRI M., corporate communications specialist; b. Canton, Ohio, June 6, 1954; d. John Thomas and Agnes Delores (Casey) Savasky; m. David Brien Hussey, Oct. 10, 1987. BA in English, Ea. Mont. Coll., 1979. Dir. Writing Improvement Ctr. Ea. Mont. Coll., Billings, 1980; teaching asst. English Dept. Iowa State U., Ames, 1981; reporter Spokesman-Review, Spokane, Wash., 1982-84; features editor News-Herald, Willoughby, Ohio, 1984-86; copy editor Everett (Wash.) Herald, 1987; corp. communications writer Microsoft Corp., Seattle, 1987—. Author: freelance travel articles pub. in Seattle Times, Boston Globe, San Francisco Examiner, 1987-89. Vol. newsletter editor Broadview Emergency Shelter for Women and Children, Seattle, 1990; county coord. Congl. campaignnnnnn of Jeanne Givens, Sandpoint, Idahoa, 1984. Recipient Pacesetter Award, Directory of Profl. Women, Cleve., 1986. Mem. Women in Communications, Internat. Assn. Bus. Communicators, Soc. Tech. Communication. Home: 7465 Corliss Ave N Seattle WA 98103

CASEY, VERONICA ANGELA, service executive; b. Taunton, Mass., Aug. 26, 1952; d. Francis Xavier and Mary Ann (Silvia) C. BA, Am. U., 1974; B in Music Edn., Boston Conservatory, 1977; M in Music, Boston U., 1980. Reservationist Copley Plaza Hotel, Boston, 1980-82, reservation mgr., 1982-85; corp. reservation mgr. Hotels of Distinction, Boston, 1985-88; acct., personnel mgr. Days Inn Middleborough, Mass., 1988—; Soloist 1st Parish Ch., Taunton, Mass., 1983—. Vol. Miss Taunton Scholarship Pagaent Inc., 1974. Recipient Miss Taunton award Miss Taunton Scholarship Pagaent Inc., 1971. Mem. AAUW, Front Office Execs., Music Educators Nat. Conf., Phi Mu, Pi Kappa Lambda, Sigma Alpha Iota (leadership award 1977). Democrat. Roman Catholic. Home: 32 Stevens St East Taunton MA 02718

CASH, ALANA, cultural organization administrator; b. Ft. Worth, June 19, 1950; d. Tolbert Eul and Beryl (Scott) C.; m. Jeffrey Paul, Aug. 4, 1973 (div. Apr. 1978); 1 child, Cameron Alan Cash. BA, UCLA, 1976. Owner Alana Cash Personal Bookkeeping Svc., L.A., 1974-78; prodn. acct. Universal Studios, Universal City, Calif., 1979, New World Pictures, L.A., 1980; staff Irving Paul Lazar Agy., Beverly Hills, Calif., 1981; free-lance acct. L.A., 1981-83, Midland, Tex., 1983-87; pres. Austin (Tex.) Literary Assocs., 1987—; author-reviewer Books and Authors column, The Austin Light, 1990—. Author short stories (Austin Light 1st place award). Named to Oustanding Women of Austin, YWCA, 1989. Mem. Greater Austin C. of C., Women in Communications, Austin Writer's League. Home and Office: Austin Literary Assocs PO Box 5523 Austin TX 78763

CASH, AUDREY SUTTON, educator; b. Ellenton, Ga., Mar. 16, 1926; d. James Young and Martha Anne (Baker) Sutton; m. Thomas Bell, Dec. 24, 1948; children: Thomas M., Martha C. Reubert, Melanie C. Hill, Richard J. Diploma, Baldwin Jr. Coll., 1944; BS, U. Ga., 1947, MS, 1950; postgrad., Richmond Profl. Inst., 1967-68, Fla. State U., 1969. Tchr. Cook High Sch., Adel, Ga., 1950-52, Juliette Law Sch., Savannah, Ga., 1955-57, Terry Parker High Sch., Jacksonville, Fla., 1968-88, Moultrie (Ga.) High Sch., 1947-49; pres. Hope Enterprises of Jacksonville, Fla. Inc. Author: (cookbook) Southern Literary, 1978. Active Jacksonville Rep. Party, 1968-88; tchr. adult Sunday sch. class, 1987-90. Mem. AAUW (v.p. Jacksonville chpt. 1986-87, pres. 1988-89), Phi Kappa Phi, Phi Upsilon Omicron. Baptist. Home: 7210 White Birch Dr Jacksonville FL 32211

CASH, CAROL VIVIAN, sociologist; b. Port Arthur, Tex., Jan. 22, 1929; d. Mano Nathan and Floris Duval (Akin) C.; m. Robert Morrow Welch, Dec. 21, 1951 (div. 1966); children: Catherine Carol, Robert M. III, Candice Claire. AA, Lamar Jr. Coll., 1951; BS in Sociology, U. Houston, 1971. Sec. Port Arthur SS Co., 1948-50; with Gov's Office State of Tex., Austin, 1951-52; legal sec. Wesley M. West, Houston, 1953-55. Author numerous children's books. Active Houston area Boy Scouts Am., Girl Scouts U.S., 1960-76, Port Arthur Hist. Soc.; mem. Tex. Sesquicentennial Com., 1986; active in restoration of Tex. historic homes. Mem. AAUW (chmn. Port Arthur fund raiser 1982), Tex. Artist Mus. Soc., Planetary Soc., Fed. Women's Clubs, Writer's Club (v.p. 1983-84, pres. 1984-85, treas. 1985—), U. Houston Alumni Assn.

CASH, LAVERNE, physicist; b. Statesville, N.C., Oct. 7, 1956; d. William J. and Martha Lee (Stroud) C. BS, Appalachian State U., 1979; MS, Clemson U., 1982; AA, Mitchell Community Coll., 1976; postgrad., Johns Hopkins U. Physicist U.S. Army Material Systems Analysis Activity, Aberdeen Proving Ground, Md.; rsch. physicist U.S. Army Chem. Devel. and Engring. Rsch. Ctr., Aberdeen Proving Ground. Contbr. articles to profl. publs. Mem. Oak Grove Bapt. Ch, Bel Air, Md., singer in choir, sound engr., numerous others. Mem. Am. Phys. Soc., Sigma Phi Sigma, Pi Mu Epsilon, Phi Theta Kappa, Gamma Beta Phi. Baptist. Home: 100 Drexel Dr Bel Air MD 21014

CASH, ROSANNE, singer, songwriter; b. Memphis, May 24, 1955; d. John R. Cash and Vivian (Liberto) Distin; m. Rodney J. Crowell, Apr. 7, 1979; children: Caitlin Rivers, Chelsea Jane. Student, Vol. State Community Coll., 1974, Vanderbilt U., 1976, Lee Strasberg Theatre Inst., 1977. Rec. artist Ariola Records, Europe, 1978-84, CBS Records, worldwide, 1979—. Songwriter Blue Moon with Heartache, 1979, Seven Year Ache, 1980 (Gold Record award Rec. Industry Assn. Am. 1981), I Don't Know Why You Don't Want Me, 1984, Hold On (Robert J. Burton award 1987), King's Record Shop, others; album: Hits 1979-1989, 1989. Bd. advisors Nashvillians for Nuclear Arms Freeze, 1987—. Mem. Nat. Acad. Rec. Arts and Scis. (Grammy award 1985), AFTRA, Am. Fedn. Musicians, Screen Actors Guild, Country Music Assn., Broadcast Music, Inc. (Spl. Achievement awards), Nashville Songwriters Assn. Internat. Democrat. Office: Side One Mgmt 1016 17th Ave S Nashville TN 37212*

CASHELL, JANE GERING, educational technologist, consultant; b. Schenectady, Dec. 20, 1948; d. John Gering Cashell and Sylvia Isobel (England) Naylor; m. Richard Morgan Lent, May 11, 1974 (div. 1984); m. Paul Field Barns, Sept. 1, 1990. BA, Antioch Coll., 197l; MS, Syracuse U., 1973, PhD, 1984. Grad. rsch. asst. Syracuse (N.Y.) U., 1973-76, instrnl. evaluator, 1976-78; rsch. assoc. Devel. and Evaluation Assn., Syracuse, 1978-80, U. Md., College Park, 1980-82; sr. analyst interactive tng. Gen. Physics Corp., Columbia, Md., 1982-83; mgr. computer-based instrn. devel. unit Digital Equipment Corp., Bedford, Mass., 1983-84; edn. mktg. specialist Digital Equipment Corp., Irvine, Calif., 1985-86; computer systems sales rep. Digital Equipment Corp., Costa Mesa, Calif., 1986—; cons. U.S. Army, Syracuse, 1975, State of N.Y., Albany, 1976, Children's TV Workshop, N.Y.C., 1977, Ednl. Radio and TV Iran, Teheran, 1978; speaker, presenter NSF, 198l, Soc. for Coll. Sci. Tchrs., 198l. Contbr. articles to profl. publs.; author tng. manuals U.S. Dept. Commerce, 1982. Democrat. Presbyterian. Home: 4 Greenbriar Irvine CA 92714 Office: Digital Equipment Corp 3390 Harbor Blvd Costa Mesa CA 92626

CASHELL, LOIS D., federal government administrator. Formerly dep. sec. Fed. Energy Regulatory Commn., Dept. of Energy, Washington, sec.,1987—. Office: Dept of Energy Fed Energy Regulatory Commn 825 N Capitol St NE Washington DC 20426*

CASHIN, BONNIE, fashion designer; b. Oakland, Calif., 1915. Designer ballet co.; costume designer Roxy Theatre, N.Y.C., 1934-37; sportswear designer Adler & Adler, N.Y.C., 1937-43; fashion designer Twentieth Century Fox Studios, Calif., 1943-49, Adler & Adler, 1949-52; owner Bonnie Cashin Designs, Inc., N.Y.C., 1952—; major collections for Philip Sills, Inc., N.Y.C.; opened firm The Knittery, 1972; invited by Indian govt. to assist in revitalization program for handloom industry, 1956. Founder Innovative Design Fund. Recipient Nieman Marcus award, N.Y.C. Fashion Critics Winnie, Sports Illus. award, Knitwear Industry award, Phila. Mus. Coll. of Art citation, Woolknit Assn. award, 1961, N.Y. Fashion Critics award, 1961, 68, London Sunday Times Fashion award, 1966, Coty Am. Fashion Critics' Hall of Fame award, 1972; named Woman of Year Lighthouse for Blind, 1961. Office: 860 United Nations Pla New York NY 10017*

CASHMAN, GEORGIA, manufacturing company executive; b. Johnsonburg, Pa., Jan. 15, 1932; d. Ralph Wesley and Gladys M. (Harrington) McClintock; m. Robert Lynn Cashman, Mar. 22, 1956; children: Karen J. Cashman Fowler, Lynn Marie Cashman Paulson, Kim Christine Cashman Standley. BS in Edn., Lock Haven U., 1952. Tchr. physical edn., history, 1953-56; mgr. Laguna Yachts, Calif., 1974-76, Pacific Envelope Co., Calif., 1976-83; chief exec. officer Hallmark Litho, Inc., Anaheim, Calif., 1983—; bd. dirs. Pacific Envelope Co., Delta-Stag Truck Body Co., City Communications Corp. Bd. trustees Anaheim Meml. Hosp. Found., Anaheim Mus., corp. sec.; founding mem. Anaheim Aux. Florence Crittenton Svcs.; active Anaheim Arts Coun., Anaheim Visitors and Convention Bur., Orange YMCA, The Villa Park Women's League. Recipient Profl. and Civic Contribution award Orange County Bd. Suprs. Mem. NAFE, Printing Industries Assn. So. Calif., Nat. Assn. Printers and Lithographers, Am. Bus. Women's Assn. (named one of Top Ten Women of Yr.), Assn. for Corp. Growth (office Orange county chpt.), Anaheim C. of C., Kiwanis. Home: 18482 Park Villa Pl Villa Park CA 92667 Office: Hallmark Litho Inc 1230 S Sherman St Anaheim CA 92805

CASHMORE, PATSY JOY, editor, author, consultant, educator; b. Milw., July 20, 1943; d. Anthony J. and Eva Irene (Arseneau) Peters; m. Gary Roy Cashmore, July 5, 1963 (div. Feb. 1983); children: Jay Allen, Jeffery Scott. Student U. Ill.-Chgo., 1961-62, Inst. Broadcast Arts, Milw., 1966-67, U. Wis.-Milw., 1970, U. Wis.-Madison, 1971-76,labor studies N.Y.C. Grad. Ctr., 1978. Copy writer H. Vincent Allen & Assocs., Chgo., 1961-63; asst. program coord. Sta.-WRIT, Milw., 1967-69; asst. news assignment editor WITI-TV, Milw., 1969-72; pub. rels. asst. Deaconess Hosp., Milw., 1972-73; asst. editor Milw. Labor Press, 1973-81, editor, 1981—; voice talent on radio and TV commls.; instr., mem. faculty adv. com. U. Wis. Extension-Sch. for Workers, Madison; panelist NEH; guest Israeli govt., 1976, Govt. Fed. Republic Germany, 1980, pre-NATO talks Friedrich Ebert Found., 1981, 87, Peoples Republic of China, 1983, All Union Cen. Coun. of Trade Unions of Soviet Union, 1985; studied in East Africa, 1987. Contbr. articles to nat. publs. Chmn. communications com., treas. Milw. Coun. on Drug Abuse, 1981-83, bd. dirs., 1984-87, Milw. Coun. on Alcoholism, 1985-88; mem. community affairs com. United Way, 1983-86; active Variety Club, 1983-87; chmn. community adv. bd. Sta.-WVTV pub. TV, 1982-85; bd. dirs. Goals 2000 Communications Com., 1983; participant U.S. Del. to observe elections in El Salvador, 1989; vol. Earthwatch, Borneo, 1988. Mem. Internat. Labor Communications Assn. (v.p. 1985, 87, Best Signed Column award 1973, Best Feature Story award 1975, award of Merit for best use of art 1982, Best Headline award 1982, First award for gen. excellence newspaper 1982, 83, 87, 88, 1st award Labor History best instl. profile 1986, 87, 88, Best Graphics award 1987, Best Original Cartoon 1987, 88), U.S. Treasury Dept. (Liberty Bell award, 1986), Midwest Labor Press Assn. (pres.), Wis. Labor Press Assn. (treas.), Indsl. Rels. Rsch. Assn. (bd. dirs.), Milw. Jr. Acd. Club (past sec.-treas.). NAFE, Sigma Delta Chi, Wapatule Ski Club (newsletter editor 1984-85), Milw. Press Club, Milw. Pen and Mike Club (Milw.). Avocations: travel, skiing, golf, swimming. Office: Milwaukee County Labor Coun 633 S Hawley Rd Milwaukee WI 53214

CASINO, JOANNE, advertising executive; b. Bklyn., Sept. 5, 1951. BA, L.I. U., 1974. Sales asst. William Morrow & Co., N.Y.C., 1974-76; product mgr. Butterick Pub. Co., N.Y.C., 1976-79; account exec. Calet, Hirsch & Spector, N.Y.C., 1979-82; sr. account exec. D'Arcy, Masius, Benton & Bowles, N.Y.C., 1982-85; v.p., mgmt. supr. Lord Geller Federico Einstein Inc, N.Y.C., 1985-90; acct. dir. Ogilvy & Mather, N.Y.C., 1990—. Edit. cons. So You Want To Be in Advertising, 1988. Pres. Children's All Day Sch. Parents' Assn., 1987-89. Office: Ogilvy & Mather 309 W 49th St New York NY 10019

CASLAVSKA, VERA BARBARA, chemist, researcher; b. Chrudim, Czechoslovakia, Jan. 18, 1934; came to U.S., 1966; d. Vilem and Vera (Kudrnkova) Novak; m. Jaroslav Ladislav Caslavsky, Dec. 25, 1952; 1 child, Veronika. MS, Charles U., Prague, Czechoslovakia, 1957, PhD, 1965. Rsch. assoc. Mining Inst., Prague, 1957-65; chemist Wiener Schwachstrom Werke, Vienna, 1965-66; rsch. assoc. materials rsch. lab. Pa. State U., University Park, 1966-69; asst. staff mem. Forsyth Dental Ctr., Boston, 1969—. Contbr. articles to profl jours. Patentee in field. Recipient Czechoslovak Acad. of Scis. award, 1965. Mem. Am. Assn. for Dental Rsch. (pres. Boston chpt. 1990), Internat. Assn. for Dental Rsch. (pres. mineralized tissue group 1990), Masaryk Club, Sigma Delta Epsilon. Home: 244 East St Lexington MA 02173 Office: Forsyth Dental Ctr 140 The Fenway Boston MA 02115

CASON, ELLEN PEARRE, accountant; b. Memphis, Sept. 12, 1948; d. William Henry and Margaret Emma (Haley) Pearre; m. William Shephard Cason, Dec. 21, 1968; children: William Randall, Jeannine Pearre. Student, Lamar U., 1966-68; BS with highest honors, U. Tex., 1971; MBA with distinction, Pace U., 1983. CPA, N.Y.; cert. tchr. in sci., English, N.Y., Tex. Tchr. chemistry and physics Austin Independent Schs., Austin, Tex., 1971-75; pvt. tutor N.Y.C., 1975-78; owner E.P. Cason Acctg. Svcs., N.Y.C., 1978-83; exec. dir. Nat. Conf. CPA Practitioners, N.Y.C., 1983-84; audit staff M.R. Weiser & Co., CPAs, N.Y.C., 1984-87; owner Ellen Pearre Cason CPA, N.Y.C., 1987—; adj. asst. prof. Pace U., N.Y.C., 1987—; controller Pine Orchard Artists' Festival, Palenville, N.Y., 1981; lectr. entrpreneurial and women's groups. Author: Development of Auditing Standards in Selected Countries, 1985; contbr. articles to Mesa Rsch. Jour., 1979-80. Bd. dirs., asst. treas. Habitat for Humanity-N.Y., N.Y.C., 1988—; chair audit com. N.Y.C. presbytery Presbyn. Ch. USA, 1988—; deacon Fifth Ave Presbyn. Ch., N.Y.C., 1987-88, elder, 1989—; treas., mem. Gifted Children Com., N.Y.C., 1978—. Mem. AAUP, Nat. Conf. CPA Practitioners (com. mem.), Am. Woman's Soc. CPAs (nat. com. chair 1987-89, Nat. Pub. Svc. award 1988), N.Y. State Soc. CPAs (com. mem.), Am. Soc. Women Accts., AICPA, Am. Mensa (treas. N.Y.C. chpt. 1979-80), Manhattan Plaza Assn. (pres., bd. dirs. 1981-82), Phi Kappa Phi, Iota Kappa Lambda, Omicron Delta Epsilon, Delta Mu Delta. Democrat. Presbyterian. Home: 484 W 43d St 14M New York NY 10036 Office: 330 W 42d St New York NY 10036

CASPER, CATHY MOORE, legal assistant; b. Birmingham, Ala., Sept. 20, 1956; d. Willard L. and Violet (Berty) Moore; m. Robert A. Casper, Oct. 31, 1987. BA, U. Ala., 1978; cert., Nat. Ctr. Paralegal Studies, 1979. Legal asst. King and Spalding, Atlanta, Bradley, Arant, Rose and White, Birmingham; freelance legal asst. Raleigh. Mem. NAFE, Raleigh-Wake Paralegal Assn., Alpha Kappa Delta, Chi Delta Phi. Home: 8805 Brandon Station Rd Raleigh NC 27613

CASPER, CHERI LUANN, educator; b. Kansas City, Mo., Jan. 17, 1949; d. Thomas Edmund and Edith Louise (Anderson) Casper; m. Gerald Wayne Hilburn, Feb. 22, 1967 (div. 1967); m. John Joseph Baz-Dresch, June 19, 1976; 1 child Shannon Louise Baz-Casper. BSEd, S.W. Mo. State U., 1971; postgrad., U. Mo., 1977-78, Lewis-Clark State Coll., Lewiston, Ida., 1980-81, N. Idaho Coll., 1982-83. Tchr. Ralls County R-II Sch. Dist., Perry, Mo., 1975-76, Sullivan C-2 Sch. Dist., Sullivan, Mo., 1976-78, Gouverneur (N.Y.) High Sch., 1978-79; with Kirby Co. and Faith Presbyn. Ch., Hayden Lake, Idaho, 1980-82; office mgr. H. James Magnuson, Atty., Coeur d'Alene, Idaho, 1982-85; instr. Trend Colls., Inc., Spokane and Wenatchee, Wash., 1985-87; owner Ghostwriter Pub. Co., Wenatchee, 1987—; instr. Wenatchee Valley Coll., 1989—. Editor newsletter WSS News, 1972-74, Dragon Tales, 1974-75, Bulletin, 1981-82, 83-84, Gem State Bull., 1986-88, Future Quest, 1989—, Habitat for Humanity of Chelan & Douglas Counties, 1990—; prodn. mgr. Ozark Caver jour., 1969-71, Guide to the Caves of Wisconsin, 1972-74, Wis. Speleologist, 1972-74; assoc. editor The News mag., 1976-79, others. Mem. Cen. Am. Peace campaign, Spokane, 1988—; adminstrn. and pub. rels. vol. Wash. Centennial Winter Games, Wenatchee, 1988-89; bd. dirs., exec. bd., sec., newsletter editor Habitat for Humanity of Chelan and Douglas Counties, Wenatchee, 1990—. Mem. AAUW (bd. dirs. 1980-84, bull. editor 1981-82, 83-84, recipient Assn. Bull. award 1987), Gifted Child Advocacy Assn., Future Quest (newsletter editor 1989—), Wenatchee Valley Cat Club. Democrat. Episcopalian. Home: 912 Highland Dr Wenatchee WA 98801 Also: 1200 S Grand #1 Spokane WA 99202 Office: Gonzaga U Coll Law Spokane WA 99258

CASPER, LAURA, health benefits manager; b. Washington, Mar. 20, 1953; d. David and Rosalie Estelle (Jaffe) Markowitz; m. Stewart M. Casper, Oct. 27, 1979; children: Stacey Lynn, Allison Rose. BA in Human Svcs., Northeastern U., Boston, 1976. Personnel rep. Bonwit Teller, N.Y.C., 1976-77; mgr. benefits and rsch. R.H. Macy & Co., Inc., N.Y.C., 1977-81; group ins. specialist Gen. Signal, Stamford, Conn., 1981-83, mgr. health benefits, 1983—; sec., treas. Fairfield (Conn.) Westchester Bus. Group on Health, 1984—. Mem. trustee YWCA, Stamford, 1986-87; mem. pers. com. Shamford Jewish Community Ctr., 1989—. Democrat. Jewish. Home: 55 Old Long Ridge Rd Stamford CT 06903 Office: Gen Signal Corp PO Box 10010 Stamford CT 06904

CASPER, LAURIE KAE, pharmaceutical representative; b. Cleve., Dec. 3, 1965; d. Peter Jon and Janet Arlene (Jones) Casper. BA, U. Ariz., 1988; M. Internat. Mgmt., Am. Grad. Sch. Internat. Mgmt., 1989. Account exec. Phoenix Newspapers Inc., 1987; cons. mktg. Dermatology, Phoenix, 1988-89; mktg. planner Aass Brewery, Drammen, Norway, 1989; rep. pharm. div. Dista products Eli Lilly and Co., Pasadena, Calif., 1990—; cons. assoc. Am. Grad. Sch. Internat. Mgmt., Glendale, Ariz., 1989. Mem. Am. Mktg. Assn., Thunderbird Alumnae Assn., Delta Gamma Alumnae Assn. Home: 1943 Selby Ave #104 Los Angeles CA 90025 Office: Dista Products Company 811 Mutual Savings Bldg 301 E Colorado Blvd Pasadena CA 91101

CASPERS, MARY LOU, biochemistry educator; b. Wyandotte, Mich.; d. Francis T. and Mary Ann (Sabados) C. BS in Chemistry, U. Detroit, 1972; PhD in Biochemistry, Wayne State U., 1977. Asst. prof. biochemistry U. Detroit, 1977-81, assoc. prof. biochemistry, 1981-90, prof. biochemistry, 1990—; guest researcher NIMH, Bethesda, Md., 1984-85; vis. researcher U. Mich., Ann Arbor, 1978. Contbr. articles to sci. jours. Bd. trustees Downriver Recycling Ctr., Trenton, Mich., 1982—; active Am. Health Assistance Found., 1990. Grantee NIH, 1988; Eloise Gerry fellow Sigma Delta Epsilon, 1983. Mem. Am. Soc. Biochemists & Molecular Biologists, Soc. for Neurosci., Am. Chem. Soc. (grantee 1978), AAAS, Mich. Acad. Sci., Sigma Xi. Office: U Detroit Chemistry Dept 4001 W McNichols Detroit MI 48221

CASPERSEN, BARBARA MORRIS, food company executive; b. Phila., Feb. 27, 1945; d. Samuel Wheeler and Eleanor May (Jones) Morris; B.A., Wellesley Coll., 1967, M.A., Drew U., 1983, M.P.H., 1986; m. Finn M.W. Caspersen, June 17, 1967. Treas., dir. Westby Corp., Wilmington, Del., 1971—, Westby Mgmt. Inc., Andover, N.J., 1967—, Tri-Farms, Inc., Andover, 1967—; pres., dir. Clark Hill Sugary Inc., Canaan, N.H., 1971-86. Bd. dirs. v.p. O.W. Caspersen Found., 1967—; trustee Hoosac Sch., 1968-76, Shipley Sch., 1980-84, Peck Sch., 1981—, Community Found. N.J., 1989; bd. dirs. Drew U., 1984—, Groton Sch., 1984—, Gladstone Equestrian Assn.; trustee Hilltop Sch., 1974-83, pres., 1976-80, prin., 1980-81. Mem. English-Speaking Union U.S. (dir. 1972-73, dir. N.Y. chpt. 1970-75). Episcopalian. Club: Colony (N.Y.C.). Office: Westby Corp PO Box 800 Andover NJ 07821

CASSADY, LAURA TAULBEE, public relations professional; b. Atlanta, Nov. 9, 1958; d. Peter Miles and Ann (Grimsley) Taulbee; m. Paul James Cassady, Dec. 9, 1989. BS in Broadcasting, U. Fla., 1979. Producer, anchor WCPX-TV, Orlando, Fla., 1979-83; community rels. asst. Winter Park (Fla.) Meml. Hosp., 1984-85; dir. mktg. HCA West Lake Hosp., Longwood, Fla., 1985-88; dir. pub. rels. Orlando Regional Med. Ctr., 1988—. Mem. Fla. Pub. Rels. Assn. , Am. Coll. Healthcare Execs., Fla. Hosp. Assn. (sec. pub. rels. and mktg. coun. Orlando chpt. 1988-89), Jr. League of Orlando-Winter Park. Republican. Presbyterian. Home: 555 Brookside Cir Maitland FL 32751

CASSANO, PHYLLIS A.M., veterinarian, consultant; b. Jersey City, July 4, 1949; d. Frank and Rose (Fusaro) Cassano. BA, Rutgers U., 1971; MA, Queens Coll., 1973; DVM, U. Bologna, Italy, 1982. In EKG analysis and cardiology Cardiopet, Bklyn., 1983; veterinarian Office of Dr. Phil Frezzo, Bayonne, N.J., 1985-87; vet. cons. Hill's Pet Products, Topeka, 1987—; contbr. vet. medicine advice column, 1989-90. Mem. AVMA, Pa. Vet. Med. Assn., N.J. Vet. Med. Assn., N.J. Shore Vet. Assn., Suburban Vet. Med. Assn. Roman Catholic. Office: Hill's Pet Products PO Box 148 Topeka KS 66601

CASSEL, CHRISTINE KAREN, physician; b. Mpls., Sept. 14, 1945; d. Charles Moore and Virginia Julia (Anderson) C.; AB U. Chgo., 1967; MD U. Mass., 1976. Intern, resident in internal medicine Children's Hosp., San Francisco, 1976-78; fellow in bioethics, Inst. Health Policy Studies, U. Calif., San Francisco, 1978-79; fellow geriatrics Portland (Oreg.) VA Hosp., 1979-81; asst. prof. medicine and public health U. Oreg. Health Scis. U., 1981-83; asst. prof. geriatrics and medicine Mt. Sinai Med. Ctr., N.Y.C., 1983-85; assoc. prof. medicine U. Chgo., 1985—. Woodrow Wilson fellow, 1967; Henry J. Kaiser Family Found. faculty scholar, 1982-85; diplomate Am. Bd. Internal Medicine. Fellow Am. Geriatrics Soc., ACP; mem. Physicians for Social Responsibility (dir. 1983—, pres. 1988—), Soc. Health and Human Values (pres. 1986). Author: Ethical Dimensions in the Health Professions, 1981; Geriatric Medicine: Principles and Practice, 1984; Nuclear Weapons and Nuclear War: A Sourcebook for Health Professionals, 1984. Office: U Chgo Pritzker Sch Medicine Sect Gen Internal Medicine Box 12 Chicago IL 60637

CASSEL, DONA JULIAN, educational consultant; b. Pittsburg, Tex., Jan. 22, 1946; d. Truman Clyde and Rachel Monteze (Morris) Julian; m. Carroll Cassel, June 8, 1968 (div. Dec. 1988); children: John Sterling, Adrian Julian, Autumn Julian. BS, East Tex. State U., 1967, MS, 1971. Cert. tchr., Tex. Tchr. Longview (Tex.) Ind. Sch. Dist., 1967-68, Richardson (Tex.) Ind. Sch. Dist., 1968-71; instr. Tyler (Tex.) Jr. Coll., 1978-84; instr. U. Tex., Tyler, 1984-87, supr. tchr. edn., 1986-87; cons. Region VII Edn. Svc. Ctr., Kilgore, Tex., 1988—. Pres. v.p., pres. PTA, Tyler. Mem. Assn. for Supervision and Curriculum Devel., AAUW, PTA (life), Phi Delta Kappa, Alpha Delta Kappa (program com.). Republican. Methodist. Home: 2031 Woodhaven Tyler TX 75701 Office: Region VII Edn Svc Ctr PO Box 1622 Kilgore TX 75662

CASSEL, SYLVIA ANN, market research company executive; b. Potsdam, N.Y., June 28, 1938; d. Fredrick Mott and Lillian (Walker) C. BS, SUNY, Potsdam, 1960; postgrad., NYU, 1960-61; MBA, CUNY, 1980. Systems engr. IBM, 1961-63; mgr. systems, programming Diners Club, 1963-64; mgr. data processing Katz Agy., 1965-69; mgr. spl. projects Arbitron, N.Y.C., 1970-72; mgr. computer client service Axiom/Simmons Market Research Bur., N.Y.C., 1972-78; sr. v.p. Mediamark Rsch. Inc., N.Y.C., 1978—. SUNY fellow, 1960-61; Alcoa Found. scholar, 1956-60. Mem. Advt. Data Processing Assn. (pres. 1979-80), Am. Mktg. Assn., Advt. Women N.Y., Internat. Advt. Assn. Republican. Club: Advt. of N.Y. Office: Mediamark Rsch Inc 708 3rd Ave New York NY 10017

CASSELL, KAY ANN, librarian; b. Van Wert, Ohio, Sept. 24, 1941; d. Kenneth Miller and Pauline (Zimmerman) C. B.A., Carnegie-Mellon U., 1963; M.L.S., Rutgers U., 1965; M.A., Bklyn. Coll., 1969. Reference librarian Bklyn. Coll. Library, 1965-68; adult svcs. cons. N.J. State Libr., Trenton, 1968-71; libr. cons.-vol. Peace Corps, Rabat, Morocco, 1971-73; adult svcs. cons. Westchester Libr. System, White Plains, N.Y., 1973-75; dir. Bethlehem Pub. Libr., Delmar, N.Y., 1975-81, Huntington (N.Y.) Pub. Libr., 1982-85; exec. dir. Coordinating Coun. Lit. Mags., N.Y.C., 1985-87; univ. libr. New Sch. for Social Rsch., 1987-88; assoc. dir. programs and svcs. br. libs. N.Y. Pub. Libr., 1989—; adj. faculty mem. Grad. Sch. Library Sci., SUNY, Albany, 1976-78, Palmer Sch. of Library and Info. Scis., Long Island U., 1986—; chmn. community adv. com. Capital Dist. Humanities Program, Albany, 1980-81; bd. dirs. Literacy Vols. of Suffolk, Bellport, N.Y., 1981-85. Mem. ALA (pres. reference and adult services div. 1983-84), N.Y. Library Assn. (pres. reference and adult services sect. 1975-76), Beta Phi Mu. Home: 252 E 7th St New York NY 10009 Office: NY Pub Libr Office Programs & Svcs 455 Fifth Ave New York NY 10016

CASSIDY, JOAN KATHRYN, business writing consultant; b. Forest Hills, N.Y., Nov. 21, 1927; d. Joseph Leo and Frances Jean (Rohaly) C. BA in English Lit., Queens Coll., 1949; BA in Journalism, George Washington U., 1956; MA in Journalism, Am. U., 1961. Asst. editor Am. Home Econs. Assn., Washington, 1954-56; dir. pub. relations Page Communications Engrs., Washington, 1956-58; head policy and procedures dept. Naval Security Sta., Washington, 1959-78; pres. Joan K. Cassidy Assocs., Wheaton, Md., 1979—; instr. Grad. Sch. USDA, Washington, 1979-80; lectr. in pub. speaking and bus. writing. Contbr. articles to profl. jours. Commd. ensign USN, 1950, advanced through grades to capt. USNR, ret., 1976. Recipient Silver Tongue award for pub. speaking USN, 1970, Meritorious Service award Naval Security Group, Washington, 1978. Mem. Women Bus. Owners Montgomery County, Nat. Assn. Women Bus. Owners. Democrat.

CASSIDY, MARY CATHERINE, electrical engineer; b. Balt., Aug. 6, 1953; d. Ralph Cleon Wooten and Dolores Ann (Werner) Mozer; m. Louis L. Latimer, Jan. 12, 1980 (div. 1985); m. Richard Albert Cassidy, June 5, 1986; 1 child, Ryan Miles. BSEE, Johns Hopkins U., 1983. Registered profl. engr., Md. Engr. Henry Adams, Inc., Balt., 1978-84; project mgr. Mueller Assocs., Inc., Balt., 1984-87; cons. San Antonio, 1987-88; sr. project engr. KZF, Inc., Cin., 1989—; lighting and advt. cons. Yorklite, Inc., Austin, 1985—. Contbr. articles to profl. jours. Mem. buddy program Cin. C. of C., 1989—. Mem. Illuminating Engring. Soc. (instr., custom fixture designer 1985—, pres. Md. sect. 1984-85, pres. Ohio Valley sect. 1990, com. mem., Sect. Design award 1983, Edwin F. Guth award of merit 1985). Democrat. Unitarian Universalist. Home: 30 Edgewood Rd Edgewood KY 41017 Office: WHB Assocs 3175 Linwood Ave Cincinnati OH 45208

CASSIDY, SUZANNE BLETTERMAN, medical educator; b. N.Y.C., Jan. 12, 1944; d. Maurice and Helene (Soldinger) Bletterman; m. Paul Stark Cassidy, June 25, 1969; 1 child, Joshua Kemp Cassidy; m. Dale Alan Kirshnitz, May 29, 1988. BA, Reed Coll., Portland, Oreg., 1965; MS, Vanderbilt U., Nashville, Tenn., 1973, MD, 1976. Diplomate Am. Bd. Med. Genetics, Am. Bd. Pediatrics. Resident in pediatrics U. Wash., Seattle, 1977-79, fellow in med. genetics, 1979-81; asst. prof. pediatrics U. Conn., Farmington, 1981-87, assoc. prof., 1987-88, asst. prof. ob-gyn., 1986-88, dir. div. med. genetics, dept. pediatrics, 1984-88; assoc. prof. pediatrics U. Ariz., Tucson, 1988—, dir. genetics fellowship tng. program, 1988—; bd. dirs. Prader-Willi Syndrome Assn., St. Louis Park, Minn. Editor newsletter Mountain States Regional Genetics Network, 1988—; contbr. numerous articles to med. jours., chpts. to books. March of Dimes, Birth Defects Found. grantee, 1985, 86, 87. Mem. Am. Soc. Human Genetics, Am. Acad. Pediatrics, Teratology Soc., Western Soc. Human Genetics, Am. Bd. Med. Genetics, Am. Bd. Pediatrics. Democrat. Jewish. Office: U Ariz Health Scis Ctr 1501 N Campbell Ave Dept Pediatrics Tucson AZ 85724

CASSINIS, ELAINE L., architect, consultant; b. Kearny, N.J., Mar. 3, 1957; d. Edward Lawrence and Helen (McCabe) C. BFA with honors, Pratt Inst., 1978. Designer Archisystems Internat., L.A., 1978-79; design dir. Swimmer Cole Martinez Curtis, Marina Del Ray, Calif., 1980-86; design cons. De Polo/Dunbar, N.Y.C., 1986-87; sr. designer Callison Partnership, Seattle, 1987-89; design cons. Baumbgardner Architects, Seattle, 1990—. Designer in field. Home: 201 Galer St #470 Seattle WA 98109 Office: Bumbgardner Architects 101 Stewart St #200 Seattle WA 98109

CAST, ANITA HURSH, small business owner; b. Columbus, Ohio, July 11, 1939; d. Charles Walter and Hulda Marie (Ramsey) Hursh; m. William R. Cast, Apr. 1, 1961; children: Jennifer, Carter, Meghan. BA, DePauw U., 1961. Ptnr. Cast Hursh and Assocs., Ft. Wayne, Ind., 1982; pianist Words and Music, Ft. Wayne, 1983; owner Anita Cast's Wearable Art, Ft. Wayne, 1986—; cons. for bd. tng. Bd. dirs. Am. Symphony Orch. League, vol., v.p., 1985-86; bd. dirs. WBNI Nat. Pub. Radio, Ft. Wayne; commr. Ind. Gov.'s Mansion Commn., 1987, Ind. Arts Commn., 1979-87; chmn., bd. dirs. Fine Arts Found., Ft. Wayne, 1988; pres. Ft. Wayne Philharmonic, 1977-79; mem. leadership adv. bd. Ind. Endowment of the Arts, Ft. Wayne, 1985—; chmn. bd. Arts United of Greater Ft. Wayne, 1988-90; v.p. Met. YMCA, Ft. Wayne, 1986—; active Mayor's Bicentennial Commn. Lily Endowment Leadership fellow. Republican. Episcopalian. Home: 4601 N Washington Rd Fort Wayne IN 46804 Office: Anita Cast Wearable Art 4601 N Washington Rd Fort Wayne IN 46804

CASTAGNARO, SISTER MARIE RENEE, health facility administrator; b. Bklyn., Dec. 23, 1944; d. Anthony and Frances Grace (Sagristano) C. BA in History, English, Nazareth Coll. Rochester, 1971; MS in Edn., Syracuse U., 1976; postgrad., Rochester Inst. Tech., 1983-84; MS in Adminstrn., U. Notre Dame, 1984. Elem. tchr. Guardian Angels Sch., Rochester, N.Y., 1966-74; prin. St. Paul's Elem. Sch., Oswego, N.Y., 1974-79; vice prin. St. Agnes High Sch., Rochester, 1979-82; adminstrv. resident St. Joseph's Hosp., Augusta, Ga., 1984-85; planning asst. St. Joseph's Hosp., Elmira, N.Y., 1985-86, v.p. clin. svcs., 1986-87, exec. v.p., chief oper. officer, 1987-88, pres., chief exec. officer, 1988—; pres. Joint Edn. and Tng. Program, Inc.; bd. dirs. Health Resources, Inc., So. Tier Health Mgmt. Corp. Mem. Channel WXXI Ednl. TV, Commn. on Sisters Edn., Chpt. Govt. Com., Parish Coun. and Sch. Bd., Vocation Core; chair Chpt. Task Force; bd. dirs. St. Joseph's Hosp. Found., United Way, chair Long Range Planning. Mem. Rochester Cath. Diocesan Assn. Secondary Sch. Adminstrs., Rotary. Office: St Joseph's Hosp 555 E Market St Elmira NY 14902

CASTANO, ELVIRA PALMERIO, art gallery director, art historian; b. Cin., July 23, 1929; d. John and Josephine C.; m. Carlo Palmerio, June 1, 1958 (dec.); 1 child, Marina. B. Literary Interpretation, Emerson Coll., Boston, 1950; postgrad., Pius XII Inst., Florence, Italy, 1954-55. Curator Castano Art Gallery, Boston, 1965-78; dir. Castano Art Gallery, Needham, Mass., 1978—; researcher Archives of Am. Art Smithsonian Instn., Boston, 1988-89; Vatican translator; interpreter Italian art, specialist in Macchiaioli art; Italian lang. translator. Mem. Nat. Rep. Congl. Com. presdl. task force Archives of Am. Art. Cardinal Spellman scholar. Mem. Boston Mus. Fine Arts, Brockton (Mass.) Art Mus. (adv. bd.), Fogg Art Mus. of Harvard U., Friends of Needham Library, Needham Hist. Soc., Archives Am. Art Boston, Mass. Fedn. Rep. Women, Rep. Womens Club of Needham. Republican. Romen Catholic. Address: 245 Hunnewell St Needham MA 02194

CASTELLAW, EARLENE JOHNSON, clergywoman; b. Carroll County, Ga., Jan. 11, 1928; d. Earl Clifton and Beulah (Walker) Johnson; m. Chet Lee Castellaw, Mar. 20, 1947 (dec. 1977); children: Gary Lee, Jeffrey, Debra Susan. D Religious Sci., Religious Sci. Inst., Fillmore, Calif., 1975; DD, Religious Sci. Inst., San Diego, 1984. Ordained to ministry, 1964. Asst. minister Ch. of Religious Sci., San Diego, 1961-77, pastor, 1977—; mem. bd. edn. Religious Sci. Inst., Spokane, Wash., 1961—, bd. dirs., 1978—, mem. exec. com., 1980—, chair sponsor program, 1987—; pres. Religious Sci. Inst., San Diego, 1980-84. Home: 3509 Carleton St San Diego CA 92106 Office: Ch Religious Sci Ste 310 1260 Morena Blvd San Diego CA 92110

CASTELLI, DOLORES BENNETT, restaurateur; b. Salamanca, N.Y., Oct. 17, 1932; d. John Albert and Genevieve Ellen (Schwind) Bennett; m. Joseph Castelli, June 27, 1931; children: Deborah Proctor, Lynda CAstelli, John Castelli. A of Arts/Scis. in Bus., Rochester Inst. of Tech., 1953. Asst. buyer Sibley's, Rochester, N.Y., 1953-55; prin., owner Candle House, Rochester, 1960-76; prin. Candle House, Newark, 1976—; v.p., owner Castelli's Village Inn, Newark, N.Y., 1976—. Founding bd. dirs. Wayne County Bus. Coun., Lyons, N.Y., 1979—; bd. dirs. Finger Lakes Assn., 1982—. Mem. Nat. Restaurant Assn., N.Y. State Restaurant Assn., Finger Lakes Women's INterest Network, Newark C. of C. (pres. 1986-87, chmn. employers roundtable, chmn. industry and new bus. com., chmn. Chuck Craig Future Bus. Leader award, editor newsletter 1983—), Roundtable for Women in Food Svc. Republican. Roman Catholic. Home: PO Box 426 Newark NY 14513 Office: Castelli's Village Inn Rte 31 E Newark NY 14513

CASTELLO, JOLI MARION, lawyer; b. San Jose, Calif., May 24, 1963; d. Joseph George and Lia Gloria (Orsi) C. BS cum laude, U. Santa Clara, 1985; JD cum laude, U. Calif., San Francisco, 1988. Bar: Calif. 1988. Crew mem. Channel 48, San Jose, 1983-84; assoc. McCutchen, Doyle, Brown & Enersen, San Jose, 1988—; extern San Francisco Dist. Attys. Office, Youth Guidance Ctr., San Francisco, 1988. Contbr. articles to profl. jours.; exec. bd. mem. Hasting Constitutional Law Quarterly, San Francisco, 1987-88. Vol. Santa Clara County Fairgrounds Assn., 1978-89, Spl. Olympics Program for the Handicapped, Santa Clara, 1985, U. Santa Clara Student Govt., 1981-84. Mem. ABA, Santa Clara County Bar Assn. Republican. Roman Catholic. Home: 1838 Ashmeade Ct San Jose CA 95125 Office: McCutchen Doyle Brown & Enersen 55 S Market St Ste 1500 San Jose CA 95113

CASTELOES, SUSAN CHAMBERS, educator; b. Tucson, Ariz., May 9, 1939; d. Harry Vincent and Edna Louise (Spraggins) Chambers; m. Edward Angelus Casteloes, Sept. 3, 1966; children: Edward Angelus Jr., Stephen Vincent. BS, U. Ariz., 1961. Buyer May Co. of Calif., L.A., 1961-66; tchr. Diocese of New Orleans, 1966-70; buyer Marshall Fields, Cleve., 1970-72; tchr. Manatee County Schs., Bradenton, Fla., 1978-83, Valdosta (Ga.) City Schs., 1983-86; founder, pres. Sit-Safe, Inc., Valdosta, 1987—. Pres. PTA, S.L. Mason Sch., Valdosta, 1985-86; curator Crescent House, Valdosta, 1989—; mem. Lowndes County Tourism Com., Valdosta, 198—; founding mem. Soup Kitchen, Valdosta, 1985, Lowndes Assoc. Ministries to the Poor, Valdosta, 1986, Habitat for Humanity, Valdosta, 1986. Named Family of Yr., Life Underwriters, Washington, 1988, Family of Yr. Fed. Womens Club, 1989, Outstanding Mem., 1989, Woman of Yr. Wymodansis Woman's Club, 1990. Mem. AAUW, Cameilla Garden Club (v.p. 1989—), Beta Sigma Phi (pres. 1986-87). Republican. Presbyterian. Home: 2608 Pebblewood Valdosta GA 31602

CASTIGLIA, PATRICIA ANNE THORSON, nursing school administrator; b. Johnson City, N.Y.; d. Theodore William and Isabelle Alice (Lane) Thorson; children: Karen, Patricia, Joseph. Diploma in Nursing, St. Vincent's Hosp., N.Y.C., 1955; BS in Nursing, U. Buffalo, 1962; MS in Nursing, SUNY, Buffalo, 1965; PhD, SUNY, 1976. RN, N.Y.; cert. sch. nurse tchr., N.Y. Staff nurse Our Lady of Lourdes Hosp., Binghamton, N.Y., 1955-56; asst. head nurse Hosp. of the Good Shepherd, Syracuse, N.Y., 1956; sch. nurse tchr. North Collins Cen. Sch., North Collins, N.Y., 1956-62; clin. instr. SUNY, Buffalo, 1965-73; clin. asst. prof. Niagara U., Niagara U., N.Y., 1976-77; from asst. prof. dir. ind. study to assoc. prof. SUNY, Buffalo, 1977-89, assoc. dean, 1983-89; acting dean Coll. Nursing and Allied Health, U. Tex., El Paso, 1989; dean nursing and allied health U Tex at El Paso Coll Nursing & Allied Health, 1989—; stockholder , treas. Profl. Nurse Consultants P.C., Buffalo; pediatric nurse practitioner Erie County Health Dept., Buffalo, 1982-89. Chair book of yr. awards Pediatric Nursing, 1986-88; manuscript reviewer Pediatric Nursing, Clin. Nurse Specialist, 1985—; editor: Jour. of Pediatric Health Care; contbr. articles to MCN, Pediatric Nursing. Trustee Hamburg Pub. Libr. System, 1985-89; coun. mem. St. Peter & Paul Coun., Hamburg, 1988-89. SUNY Faculty Exchange scholar, Albany, 1985. Mem. Am. Nursing Assn. (cert. pediatric nurse practitioner), N.Y. State Nurse's Assn., N.L.N., Coalition of Nurse Practitioners, WNY Nurse Practitioners Assn., NAPNAP, U. Buffalo Alumni Assn., St. Vincent's Alumni Assn., Sigma Theta Tau. Roman Catholic. Office: U Tex at El Paso Coll Nursing-Allied Health 1101 N Campbell El Paso TX 79902

CASTILLO, KAREN SUE, lawyer services and appraisal company executive; b. Dearborn, Mich., Nov. 18, 1948; d. Florentine and Dorothy Elizabeth (Hand) C.; m. Richard Neil Talbot, Oct. 8, 1966 (div. Nov. 1982); children: Richard Wayne, Terri Lynn. Cert. in bus. adminstrn., La Salle U., Chgo., 1967; diploma in civil svc., Tri-City Adult Coll., 1968; student, Mount San Antonio Coll., 1971-72. Fin. mgr. Hartland Hosp., Baldwin Park, Calif., 1969-74; owner, mgr. Karen's Secretarial Svc., Alta Loma, Calif., 1974-79, Brandy & Beverly's Atty. Svc., Alta Loma, San Bernardino, Calif., 1981-84, Beverly's Atty. Svc., Alta Loma, Cucamonga, Calif., 1982—; social worker II San Bernardino County, Ontario, Calif., 1980-81; adminstrv. asst. Security Mgmt. & Investment, Ontario, 1983, Western Constrn. Co., Montclair, Calif., 1983-84, Gold & Assocs. Realty, Barstow, Calif., 1987-88; v.p. Wilhite Appraisal Svc., Barstow, 1986—; owner, producer Desert Rose Prodns., Daggett, Calif.; owner Comp-U Computer Svcs., Daggett; pub. newsletter The Outreach, 1984—. Polit. cons. to local politicians, 1980-85; chmn. fund raising San Bernardino County Dem. Com., 1980-84; del. So. Calif. Dem. Com., 1981; pres. Victory Jesus Faith Ministries Homeless Shelters, 1983—; active Calico (Calif.) Ghost Town, 1986-89; mem. Rep. Presdl. Task Force, Washington, 1990. Recipient vol. commendation San Bernardino County Bd. Suprs., 1982, outstanding dedication award San Bernardino County Marshall's Office, 1983, dedication award V.J.F.M. Homeless Shelters, 1984-88, cert. for outstanding leadership and accomplishments Nat. Reference Inst., 1990. Mem. NAFE, Smithsonian Assocs., Nat. Audubon Soc., Doris Day Animal League, Assn. for U.S. Army (bd. dirs. Barstow 1987), High Desert Media Assn. (bd. dirs. 1987). Home: PO Box 505 Daggett CA 92327

CASTLE, CONNIE JO, police officer; b. Tyler, Tex., Nov. 10, 1953; d. Joe Edwin Castle and Alice Earl (McCullars) Bowins. Student, Stephen F. Austin Coll., 1974-75; A in Med. Tech., Tyler (Tex.) Jr. Coll., 1977, student, 1986-87; cert. peace officer, East Tex. Police Acad., 1984-87. Lab. technician Pathology Assocs. of Tyler, 1976-78; asst. chief technician Gilmer (Tex.) Hosp., 1978; spl. chemistry technician Pathology Assocs. of Longview, Tex., 1978-79; well site geologist Exploration Services, Inc., Midland, 1979-84; police officer City of Tyler Police Dept., 1984—. Recipient Gold Medal Tex. Police Athletic Fedn., 1986, 87, Gold Medal Internat. Police Olympics, 1986. Mem. NOW, Am. Soc. Clin. Pathologists, Smith County Peace Officer's Assn. Office: Tyler Police Dept 711 W Ferguson Tyler TX 75710

CASTLES, LEONE DEXTER STRICKLAND, county official; b. Columbia, S.C., Apr. 15, 1923; d. Thomas Starling and Ray Livingston (Pou) Strickland; m. Charles Buy Castles, Jr., Dec. 30, 1943; children: Ray Elizabeth, Laura Leone, Charles Guy III. AB in English (magna cum laude), U. S.C., 1943. Secondary educator Chicora High Sch., Charleston, S.C., 1944-47, Dreher High Sch., Columbia, S.C., 1948-50; advisor blue print Dreher High Sch., Columbia, 1948-50; councilman Richland County, Columbia, 1980—; vice-chmn. Richland County Coun., Columbia, 1983-84, 89-90, chmn., 1985-86, chmn. adminstrn. & fin., 1986-87, 90-91, chmn. devel. & svcs., 1989-90. Bd. trustees Erskine Coll., Due West, S.C., 1976, 77; pres. Assoc. Reformed Pres. Synodical, 1976, 77; pres. Columbia Med. Aux., 1978; bd. dirs. S.C. Med. Aux., 1975. Named to Gov.'s Infant Mortality Task Force, 1989-90, Gardener of the Year City Coun., 1965. Mem. Cen. Midlands Hyacinth Garen Club (pres. 1980-81), Silver Elephant Club, Richland County Libr. (bd. dirs. 1983), Lexington-Richland Alcohol & Drug Abuse (bd. dirs. 1990), Columbia Woman's Club, Rep. Women's Club. Republican. Presbyterian. Home: 1331 Adger Rd Columbia SC 29205

CASTOR, ELIZABETH B. (BETTY CASTOR), state education commissioner; b. Glassboro, N.J., May 11, 1941; d. Joseph L. and Gladys (Wright) Bowe; children—Katherine, Karen, Frank. B.A., Glassboro State Coll., 1963; M.A., U. Miami, 1968. Mem. Fla. Senate, Tallahassee, 1976-78, 82-86, pres. pro tem, 1985-86 and formerly; Fla. commr. of edn., Tallahassee, 1987—; Mem. Hillsborough County Bd. Commrs., Fla., 1972-76, chmn., 1975-76; mem. Hillsborough County Environ. Protection Commn., 1972-76, chmn., 1973-74; mem. exec. bd. Tampa Bay Regional Planning Council, 1972-76; mem. U. Fla. Ctr. for Govt. Responsibility, bd. dirs., 1977; mem. Hillsborough Hosp. and Welfare Bd., 1972-76, chmn., 1973-74; mem. council advisers U. South Fla. Recipient Good Govt. award Town 'N Country Jaycees, 1975, Outstanding Legislator of Yr. award FEA, 1977; numerous other awards from state edn. orgns. Mem. LWV, Athena Soc. Democrat. Lutheran. Office: The Capitol PL-08 Tallahassee FL 32399

CASTRO, TERESA HARPER, small business owner; b. Chgo., July 18, 1956; d. Jene Paul and June Edith (Aleff) Harper; m. Oscar Armando Rodriguez (div. 1981); 1 child, Avelina; m. Jorge Castro, Jan. 9, 1988; 1 child, Pablo. AA in Opera, Fleming Coll., Florence, Italy, 1975; BA in Spanish and Portuguese cum laude, U. N.Mex., 1979. Adminstrv. asst. Latin Am. Inst., Albuquerque, 1981-83; law office mgr. Camacho & Hinkle, San Francisco, 1983; owner, founder, pres. Access Word Processing, San Francisco, 1983—; tech. translator, 1983—; free-lance computer and word processing systems analyst, San Francisco and Phoenix, 1985—. State coord. Truth Seekers in Adoption of Calif., San Francisco, 1985—; vol. notary pub. People With AIDS/ARC, 1985—, The AIDS Found./Shanti Project, San Francisco, 1986—; chairperson bilingual adv. bd. Buena Vista Sch., San Francisco, 1986; bd. dirs. Escola Nova de Samba, San Francisco, 1987; vol. working on reunification searches for adoptees and birth parents, Calif., N.Y., Latin Am.; tchr. Spanish law enforcement pers. San Francisco Police Acad., 1988-89, Spanish for med. pers. Kaiser Permanente Med. Ctr., San Francisco, 1988-89. Mem. NAFE, Nat. Notary Assn.

CASWALL, EMILY JANE, buying guide executive; b. Cleve., Apr. 17, 1954; d. Edward L. and Virginia (Reynolds) C.; 1 child, Hannah. BA in English, Ursuline Coll., Cleve., 1979. Group mgr. Halle's Dept. Store, Mentor, Ohio, 1973-81; asst. store mgr. T.J. Maxx, Mentor, 1981-82; store mgr. Lane Bryant, West Palm Beach, Fla., 1983-84; asst. store mgr. J. Bryon's, Miami, Fla., 1984-86; tchr. phys. edn. Laurel Sch., Shaker Heights, Ohio, 1986-89; dir. Mall Network Publs., Beachwood, Ohio, 1989; co-chmn. Cleve. mag., 1988. Chmn. playground fund raising Temple Emmanuel, University Heights, Ohio, 1989-91; mem. Hadassah, Cleve., 1984—. Mem. Fashion Group Cleve., U.S. Field Hockey Assn. (NE Ohio Field Hockey Coach of Yr. 1988). Republican. Office: Mall Network Publs 22035 Chagrin Blvd Beachwood OH 44122 also: Falcon Camp 4251 Delta Rd SW Carrollton OH 44615

CASWELL, DOROTHY ANN COTTRELL, arts administration; b. N.Y.C., Dec. 18, 1938; d. Donald Peery and Eleanor Hildaborg (Westberg) Cottrell; m. Allen Edward Caswell, Oct. 24, 1959; children: David Alan, Bruce Leland. Student, Carleton Coll., Northfield, MN., 1956-59; AB in Psych., George Wash. U., 1960-61; postgrad., SUNY, Oneonta, 1971-76. Sec. U.S. Fgn. Service, Tunis, Tunisia, 1959-61; mng. dir. Glimmerglass Opera, Inc., Cooperstown, N.Y., 1975-78; exec. dir. Upper Catskill Community Council on the Arts, Oneonta, N.Y., 1978-80; devel. officer Catskill Arts Consortium, Oneonta, 1981-83; devel. cons. Otsego Urban Rural Self-Devel. Assocs., Inc., Oneonta, 1982-83; co-founder, pres. Catskill Choral Soc., 1970-76, 81-84; assoc. producer Orpheus Theatre, Inc., Oneonta, 1984-; voice tchr. Oneonta, 1984-; cons., arts adminstr. Dorothy Caswell Assocs., Oneonta, 1981--; pres. Sub-Area Coun. of the Health Systems Agy. N.E. N.Y. Singer/actress with Orpheus Theatre, 1984—; actress WSKG-TV Pub. TV film series Susquehanna Stories, 1990. Vol., mem. chorus Glimmerglass Opera Cooperstown, 1974—. Honored for outstanding performance and svcs. to the community, SUNY, 1975. Mem. Otsego County Health Planning Adv. Coun., Otsego County Tourism Bur. (bd. dirs.), Oneonta Downtown Coalition (bd. dirs. 1982-84), LWV, Ostego County C. of C., Oneonta Profl. Women's Network, Del.-Otsego Mgmt. Assn. Democrat. Protestant.

CATABIA, ELLEN COTY, development officer; b. Albany, N.Y., Aug. 21, 1948; d. Paul E. and Wanda C. (Zegarowski) Coty; m. Ronald G. Catabia, June 27, 1981. BA in English, Elms Coll., 1971; MLS, U. R.I., 1979; MA in English, U. Mass., 1980, MS in Labor Studies, 1984. Cert. secondary tchr., Mass. Tchr. Trinity Sch., Greenfield, Mass., 1969-70, Cathedral High Sch., Springfield, Mass., 1971-73; library supr. Springfield City Library, 1975-81; grants coordinator Springfield Library and Mus., 1981-84, capital campaign coordinator, 1984-85, assoc. dir. devel., 1986-89; dir. devel. The MacDuffie Sch., Springfield, 1989—. Mem. Mass. Arts Advocacy Com., 1987; exec. dir. Kestrel Trust; chmn. Shutesbury Arts Lottery Coun.; mem. steering com. Franklin Coun. Cultural Plan. Mem. New Eng. Mus. Assn. (lectr.), Mass. Libr. Assn. (lectr.), Women in Devel. (treas. 1987, v.p. 1988, pres. 1989). Democrat. Roman Catholic. Home: RFD 3 January Hills Rd Amherst MA 01002 Office: MacDuffie Sch Ames Hill Dr Springfield MA 01105

CATALDO, PATRICIA EDIIN, editor; b. Casper, Wyo.; d. Eric Helio and Clara Burton (Williams) Ediin; m. Fortunato F. Cataldo, Dec. 8, 1956; children: Susan Davis Cataldo Adolf, Lisa Williams Cataldo. AA, Colo. Women's Coll., 1946; BA, U. Colo., 1948. Prodn. mgr. Log Mag., N.Y.C., 1951-53; with Spl. Svcs. Dept. Defense, 1953-56; creative dir. Superior Advt., Ft. Wayne, Ind., 1958-60; editor N.Mex. State U. Alumni Mag., Las Cruces; feature writer, columnist Kwajalein HourGlass, Kwajalein, Marshall Islands, 1966-70; editor SCI, Inc., Huntsville, Ala., 1972-76, Kwajalein HourGlass, 1977-83; freelance writer/editor, 1983-87; editor Intergraph Corp., Huntsville, 1987—. Mem. Soc. Tech. Communications, Huntsville Advt. Fedn. Democrat. Presbyterian. Office: Intergraph Corp 1 Madison Industrial Park Huntsville AL 35807

CATALFAMO, JANICE STELLA, financial consultant; b. Rochester, N.Y., Mar. 21, 1936; d. Anthony R. and Josephine (Di Sano) Barone; m. Carmen J. Catalfamo; children: Jomaine, Kenneth, Anthony, Kevin. Student, Monroe Community Coll. Lic. ins. agt., N.Y.; cert. real estate, N.Y.; notary pub., N.Y. Rep. customer svc. Rochester Community Savs. Bank, 1976-86; dist. rep. Prudential Fin. Svcs., 1988—; owner, ptnr. Richmond Precision Mfg., Inc., 1990—; fin. cons. telecommunications co. start-up, Rochester, 1989—. Active Boy Scouts Am.; former troup leader Girl Scouts U.S.A.; active various polit. campaigns; mem. adv. com. N.Y. State Legislature; coord. family ct. judge campaign; sec., treas. Pop Warner Football League. Mem. NAFE, Life Underwriters Assn., Nat. Assn. Profl. Sales Women, Women of Round Table. Republican. Roman Catholic. Home: 11 Neville Ln Rochester NY 14618 Office: Prudential Fin Svcs 1701 Lac Deville Blvd Rochester NY 14618

CATALFO, BETTY MARIE, health service executive, nutritionist; b. N.Y.C., Nov. 2, 1942; d. Lawrence Santo and Gemma (Patrone) Lorefice; children—Anthony, Philip, Lawrence, Donna. Grad. Newtown High Sch., Elmhurst, N.Y., 1958. Sec., clk. ABC-TV, N.Y.C., 1957-60; lectr., nutritionist Weight Watchers, Manhasset, N.Y., 1976-75; founder, pres. Every-Bodys Diet, Inc. dba Stay Slim, Bronx, N.Y., 1976—; dir. in-home program N.Y. State Dept. Health, N.Y.C., 1985—; lectr. in field. Author: 101 Stay-Slim Recipes, 1983, Get Slim and Stay Slim Diet Cook Book, rev. ed., 1987. Author, dir., producer: (video) Dancersize for Overweight, 1986; author, editor: (video) Eating Right For Life, 1985; author, producer: (video) Eating Habits, 1986—, (video) Isometric Techniques for Weight Reduction, 1986, (video) Patience Is a Virtue When Weight Loss is the Goal, 1986; producer, dir.: (video) Positive and Negative Diet Forces, 1987, (video) Hello It's Me and I'm Thin, 1987, (video) Dance Your Calories A-Weigh, 1987, (video) Positive and Negative Diet Forces, 1987. Sponsor, lectr. St. Pauls Ctr., Bklyn., 1981—, Throgs Neck Assn. Retarded Children, Bronx, 1985—; active ARC, LWV, Am. Italian Assn., United Way Greenwich, Council Chs. and Synagogues, Heart Assn., Meals on Wheels, Health Assn. Fairfield County. Named Woman of Yr., Bayside Womens Club, N.Y., 1983, O, PK Woman of Yr., 1986—, Woman of Yr. Richmond Boys Club, 1987, Woman of Yr. Bronx Press Club Assn., 1987; recipient Merit award for Service Catholic Archdiocese of Bklyn., 1985, Community Service award Sr. Citizens Sacred Heart League Bklyn./Queens Archdiocese. N.Y. State Nutritional Guidance for Children Nat. Assn. Scis. Mem. Nat. C. of C. for Women (Woman of Yr. 1987), Roundtable for Women in Food Service, Bus. and Profl. Women's Club, Pres. Council for Phys. Fitness, Nat. Assn. Female Execs., Assn. for Fitness in Bus. Inc., Nat. Assn. Female Bus. Owners. Democrat. Roman Catholic. Club: Mothers Sacred Heart Sch. (chairperson 1979-82). Avocations: reading; traveling; tennis; spending leisure time with own children. Home: 208-05 15th Rd Bayside NY 11360 also: 58 Riverside Ave Greenwich CT 06878

CATANIA, BARBARA JOSEPHINE, travel industry marketing executive; b. Chgo., Dec. 9, 1939; d. Peter Francis and Florence Katherine (Popo) Caviolo; m. Felice Paul Catania, Dec. 30, 1937 (div. July 1978); children: Brad Alan, Karin Jean, Brian Gerard. Grad. high sch., Oak Park, Ill., 1957. Adminstrv. asst. Radio TV Reps., Chgo., 1957-59; sales mgr. MTI Vacations, Oak Brook, Ill., 1974-75, Prestige Vacations, Oak Brook, 1975-78; cons. Means Career Apparel, Chgo., 1978-81; mktg. mgr. Travel Reps., Chgo., 1981-83; exec. dir. B. J. Catania & Assoc., Westmont, Ill., 1983—. Pres. New Beginnings, Naperville, Ill., 1978; vol. Statesville Prison Art Assn., Joliet, Ill., 1983, Ill. Youth Home, Warrenville, 1984, Lincoln Park Shelter, Chgo., 1986-87, People Educating People, Glen Ellyn, Ill., 1989—. Mem. Am. Soc. Travel Agts. (allied), Pacific Area Travel Assn., Chgo. Women in Travel.

CATANIA, LORRAINE LAURA, psychologist; b. Bklyn., May 2, 1942; d. Harry and Alma (Costarelli) Trempert; m. Frank Catania, July 14, 1963 (div. Apr. 1976); children: Frank Jr., Lori Ann; m. Karl J. Kulczycki, Sept. 8, 1984. BA, Montclair State Coll., 1963, MA, 1976, profl. diploma in sch. psychology, 1977; PhD, Fordham U., 1985. Lic. psychologist, N.J. Dir. residential treatment Straight and Narrow, Inc., Paterson, N.J., 1977-83; coord. outpatient program Family Guidance Ctr., Wash., N.J., 1982-83; cons. employee assistance program Hoffmann La Roche Inc., Nutley, N.J., 1982—; dir. Bergen West Assocs., Ridgewood, N.J., 1985—; cons. Emerson Bd. of Edn., Emerson, N.J., 1981-82; instr. N.J. State Dept. of Health, Trenton, N.J., 1977-83; adv. bd. Family Day Care Project, Warren County, N.J., 1984-85; mem. Local Adv. Coun. on Substance Abuse, Warren County, 1984-86. Mem. woman's aux. Valley Hosp., Ridgewood, 1976, Unity, Neighborly, Integrity, Charity, Opportunity Svc. Orgn., North Haledon, N.J., 1973, Slow on Bottle, Enjoy the Road (S.O.B.E.R.), Hackettstown, N.J., 1984; chmn. D.W.I. Task Force, Hackettstown, 1984-85. Jr. Psychology fellow State of N.J. 1977-78; grad. teaching fellowship Montclair State Coll. 1976. Mem. Am. Psychol. Assn., N.J. Psychol. Assn., N.J. Acad. Psychology, Assn. for Advancement Psychology, Assn. Labor, Mgmt., Adminstrs. and Cons. on Alcoholism, Employee Assistance Profl. Assn., Jr. Women's Club. Republican. Roman Catholic. Home: 25 Stockton Rd North Haledon NJ 07508 Office: Bergen West Assocs 50 W Ridgewood Ave Ridgewood NJ 07450

CATANZARO, KAREN BARBARA, advertising professional; b. Warwick, R.I., Oct. 24, 1960; d. Joseph Anthony and Lorraine Patricia (Manning) C. BS, U. Fla., 1982. From mgmt. trainee to mktg. coord. Peninsula Fed. Savs. and Loan, Miami, Fla., 1984-86; mktg. coord. Savs. of Am., Pompano Beach, Fla., 1986-89; advt. mgr. Dunhill Internat. List Co., Pompano Beach, 1989—. Mem. Fla. Direct Mktg. Assn., Am. Mktg. Assn., Pompano Beach C. of C., Greater Ft. Lauderdale (Fla.) C. of C., Alpha Kappa Psi, Alpha Chi Omega. Roman Catholic. Home: 2845 NE 51st St Fort Lauderdale FL 33308

CATER, ALICE RUTH WALLACE, university educator, real estate broker; b. Kilgore, Tex., June 16, 1935; d. Clarence C. and Mary Alice (Johnson) Wallace; m. Otis Earl Cater, Jr., Aug. 26, 1961 (dec. Sept. 1988); 1 child, Clarence Wallace. BBA, So. Meth. U., 1957; MBA, U. Tex., 1959. Lic. real estate broker, Tex. Instr. McNeese State U., Lake Charles, La., 1959-63; prof. No. Mich. U., Marquette, 1964-65, U. Guam, Agana, 1967-69; broker Cater Real Estate, Beaumont, Tex., 1971—; coord. real estate Lamar U., Beaumont, 1974—, instr. II, 1974-79; instr. III Lamar U., 1979-84, instr. IV, 1984—. Recipient Regents Merit award Lamar U., 1979, President's Leadership award, 1983, Teaching Excellence award, 1985, 87; rsch. grantee Tex. Real Estate Ctr., Tex. A&M U., 1974-79; named one of Outstanding Young Women of Am., 1965. Mem. Am. Fin. Assn., Tex. Real Estate Tchrs. Assn. (charter, state pres. 1978-79, merit award 1982), Real Estate Educators Assn., Tex. Coll. Mgmt. Educators Assn., Tex. Assn. Coll. Tchrs., Sales and Mktg. Execs. Club, Lamar U. Women's Club. Methodist. Home: 795 Howell St Beaumont TX 77706 Office: Lamar U PO Box 10043 Beaumont TX 77710

CATES, JEANETTE SUE, educational administrator; b. Denver, May 2, 1947; d. Harold Willis and Jean (White) Skeen; m. Robert Weldon Cates, Jan. 10, 1970; children: Stephanie, Jennifer, Victoria. BS, Trinity U., 1969; MEd, U. Tex., 1982, PhD, 1988. Auditor Arthur Andersen and Co., Houston, 1969-70; instr. basic skills Army Edn. Ctr., Bad Kissingen, Fed. Republic of Germany, 1971-73, Ton Du Chong, South Korea, 1973-74; instr. office tech. Cen. Tex. Coll., Killeen, 1974-76; dir. adult skills ctr. Cen. Tex. Coll., 1976-78, instr. office tech., 1978-80; curriculum writer Cen. Tex. Manpower Consortium, Killeen, 1980; acctg. instr. Austin Community Coll., Tex., 1981-84; coordinator computer based instrn. Austin Community Coll., 1983—; lectr. U. Tex. at Austin, 1989; cons. Austin Community Coll., 1981-83; owner Balcones Bookkeeping and Tax Svc., Austin, 1981-83, Instrl. Computing Svcs., Austin, 1983-85. Contbr. articles to profl. jours. Bd. dirs. Anderson Mill Swim Team, Austin, 1984-87. Recipient Corvus Nat. award, Corvus Systems, Inc., San Jose, Calif., 1986. Mem. Assn. for Ednl. Communications (copyright com. 1986-89, state host com. 1989, nat. planning com. 1990-91), Tex. Assn. Ednl. Tech. (dir. 1986-88, sec. 1988-89, v.p. 1989-90), Tex. Computer Edn. Assn. (electronic editor 1985-87), Am. Ednl. Rsch. Assn., Assn. Devel. of Computer-Based Instl. Systems, Am. acctg. Assn., Phi Kappa Phi, Kappa Delta Pi. Republican. Club: Mensa. Lodge: P.E.O. Office: Austin Community Coll 1212 Rio Grande Austin TX 78701

CATES, JENNIFER ANN, lawyer, oil company executive; b. Providence, Feb. 22, 1956; d. John Stephen McKnight and Mary Morrison; m. Howard Claran Cates, June 8, 1980. BA in Polit. Sci., Oakland U., 1976; JD, U. Okla., 1980. Bar: Okla. 1980, Tex. 1988, U.S. Ct. Appeals (5th, 10th, 11th and D.C. cirs.) 1981, U.S. Supreme Ct 1983, U.S. Ct. Appeals (8th cir.) 1985, U.S. Dist. Ct. (no. dist.) Okla. 1986. Atty. Phillips Petroleum Co., Bartlesville, Okla., 1980-88; counsel BP Exploration Inc., Houston, 1988-90; v.p., gen. counsel, sec. Tex./Con Oil & Gas Co., Houston, 1990—; apptd. by gov. to Commn. on Oil and Gas Practices, 1990—; mem. legal subcom. Offshore Operators, 1983-87, Commn. on Oil and Gas Practices State of Okla., 1990—. Editor U. Okla. Law Rev., 1978-80. Pres., adv. council Retired Sr. Vol. Program, Bartlesville, 1982-88; bd. dirs. Bluestem Girl Scout Council, Bartlesville, 1982-88, SunFest, Inc., Bartlesville, 1984-88. Named one of Outstanding Young Women in Am., 1984. Mem. ABA (royalty task force 1983), Okla. Bar Assn., Fed. Energy Bar Assn. (commn. on devel. of fed. lands 1989-90), Am. Petroleum Inst. (royalty task force 1983-88), Phi Alpha Delta, Pilot Internat. (coord. 1985-88). Home: 1114 Crossroads Dr Houston TX 77079 Office: Tex/Con Oil & Gas Co 9401 Southwest Frwy Houston TX 77074

CATES, KATHLEEN MARY, elementary educator; b. Prior Lake, Minn., Feb. 27, 1964; d. Richard Anthony and Eileen Mary (Slater) C. BA, Coll. St. Catherine, 1986; AA, Mankato State U., 1984. Cert. elem. tchr., Minn. Tchr. Christ the King Sch., Mpls., 1986-89, Jefferson Elem. Sch., Corona, Calif., 1989—. Vol. Childrens Miracle Network, 1984-90, St. Paul Children's Hosp., 1986-89. Mem. Phi Lambda Theta (v.p., nat. del. biennial coun.), Kappa Delta Pi. Roman Catholic. Home: 2160 High Pointe Dr #209 Corona CA 91719 Office: Jefferson Elem Sch 1040 Vicentia Corona CA 91719

CATES, MARIAN WARD, writer, educator; b. Richmond, Va., Sept. 2, 1947; d. Mitchell Dresner and Marian Granville (Sharwood) C.; m. Carl R. Schilt, Dec. 3, 1970 (div. 1980). BA, Hollins Coll., Roanoke, Va., 1969; MA, Hollins Coll., 1979. Playwright in residence Kalahansa Theatre Co., Asheville, N.C., 1979; theatre reviewer Jour. Newspapers, Arlington, Va., 1981-83, Met. Woman, Richmond, Va., 1985-86; arts column Richmond (Va.) Surroundings Mag.; playwright in residence Green Alley Theatre Co., Richmond, Va., 1986—; instr. Va. Union U., Richmond, 1989—; dir. Kalahansa Theatre Co., Asheville, N.C., 1977-79, Adventure Theatre, Glen Echo, Md., 1982, Source Theatre Co., Wash., 1983, Green Alley Theatre Co., Richmond, Va., 1986. Author: (musical) 27 Blake Street, 1983, (plays) The Fig Leaf, 1985, Cafe Ole, 1986, Trouble in Paradise, 1989; contbr. poetry to various publs., 1980—. Mem. Amnesty Internat., 1986-, on women's bd. Va. Home for Boys, Richmond, 1987--. Home: 812 China St 611 Somerset Ave Richmond VA 23220

CATES, PHYLLIS STORK, educator; b. Phila., Sept. 28, 1921; d. Edwin Gordon and Grace Eleanor (Cummings) Stork; m. Clifton B. Cates, Jr., Apr. 25, 1945; children: Clifton B. III, Phyllis E.B. Cates Beauchamp, Nancy E.B. Cates Burgler. BA, U. Pa., 1942, postgrad., 1943-44; MA, Smith Coll., 1943. Cert. secondary tchr., Pa., tchr. of gifted, Va. Tchr. English, Shipley Sch., Bryn Mawr, Pa., 1943-45, Boys' Cen. High Sch., Phila., 1945-46; pvt. tchr. piano, Fairfax and Alexandria, Va., 1962-68; tchr. gifted Fairfax County Schs., Fairfax, 1968-83; tchr. to would-be tchrs. of gifted Fairfax-Woodson High Sch., 1975—. Choral dir. Newport (R.I.) Navy Wives' Chorus, 1953-58; mem. Fairfax Chorus, 1962-66, Ft. Hunt Chorus, 1967-79, Mt. Vernon Singers, Alexandria, 1979-84, Alexandria Singers, 1984-89. Scholar Phila. Bd. Edn., 1938; Trustee fellow Smith Coll., 1942-43. Mem. Marlan Forest Garden Club (pres. 1985-86, 87-88), Smithsonian Assocs., Mt. Vernon Navy Wives Assn., Bolling Officers Club, Phi Beta Kappa. Episcopalian. Home: 7006 Marlan Dr Alexandria VA 22307

CATHCART, LINDA, art historian. BA in Fine Arts, Calif. State U., Fullerton, 1969; MA in Art History, Hunter Coll., CUNY, 1972. Fulbright fellow Courtauld Art Inst., 1973-74; curator Albright-Knox Art Gallery, Buffalo, 1975-79; prin. Linda Cathcart Gallery; organizer exhbns. in field. Office: 924 Colorado Ave Santa Monica CA 90401

CATHCART, MARTHA KIMBALL, medical researcher, educator; b. Sturgis, Mich., Dec. 3, 1951; d. Leon Squires Kimball and Rolla Marie (Grattan) Cheyne; m. David Blair Cathcart, Aug. 9, 1975; children: Blair Elliot, Grant Alexander. BA magna cum laude, Denison U., 1974; PhD, Case Western Res. U., 1979. Postdoctoral fellow Cleve. Clinic Found., 1979-80, staff scientist, 1980-82, assoc. mem., 1982-85; staff mem. dept. cellular and molecular immunology Rsch. Inst. of the Cleve. Clinic Found., 1985—; adj. asst. prof. Case Western Res. U., Cleve., 1980—, Cleve. State U., 1985—; mem. grant rev. com. Am. Heart Assn., Cleve., 1984—. Contbr. articles to profl. jours.; patentee in field. Vol. YWCA, Cleve.; jr. bd. dirs. Am. Cancer Soc., Cleve., 1990. Recipient N. Paul Hudson rsch. commendation Am. Soc. Microbiology, 1977, William E. Lower award Cleve. Clinic Found., 1980, Career Woman of Achievement award YWCA, 1986; biology fellow Denison U., 1974; grantee NIH, 1982-85, 1989-90. Mem. AAAS, Am. Assn. Immunologists, Am. Coll. Rheumatology, Soc. for Leukocyte Biology, Am. Fedn. Clin. Rsch., N.Y. Acad. Scis. Office: Cleve Clinic Found (NNI) 9500 Euclid Ave Cleveland OH 44195

CATHERMAN, DONNA ELAINE, financial executive; b. Detroit, Sept. 18, 1947; d. Nickolas J. and Mildred (Stamatis) Markas; m. Floyd W. Catherman, Mar. 11, 1969; children: Nickolas W., Sean Michael. Student, U. Mich., 1965-67. Acctg. clk. U. Mich., Ann Arbor, 1965-67; apt. mgr. Boak Constrn., Radcliff, Ky., 1969-70; dept. supr. admitting Elizabethtown (Ky.) Hosp., 1970-72; asst. bookkeeper to hosp. Kings Daus. Hosp., Temple, Tex., 1972-73; apt. complex mgr. Johnson Investments, Temple, 1973-74; v.p. and gen. property mgr. Manor Mgmt. and Invest, Houston, 1974-78; acct. and office mgr. S.J. Kechejian, M.D. & Assocs., K-Med Corp., Dallas, 1978-86; v.p. and co-owner FDC Investments, Inc., Dallas, 1986—. Mem. Dallas Mus. of Art., 1987—. With U.S. Army, 1967-69. Mem. Am. Legion (fin. officer 1986-88, chaplain, 1985-86), Oak Cliff C. of C. Democrat. Roman Catholic. Home: 2334 Deville Circle Dallas TX 75224

CATHEY, M. ELIZABETH, lawyer; b. Syracuse, N.Y., Dec. 19, 1946; d. Phil Franklin Blum and Helen Marie (Yarwood) Drew; children: Denise Anne Beving Harwood, Cynthia Marie Beving; m. Robert Heaton Cathey, July 21, 1988. BA cum laude, (Nat. Merit scholar), U. No. Iowa, 1973; postgrad. Schoitz Hosp. Sch. Med. Tech., 1973-74; JD (rsch. scholar), Washburn U., 1981. Bar: Kans., 1981, U.S. Dist. Ct. Kans. 1981. Quality supr. U.S. Gypsum Co., Ft. Dodge, Iowa, 1974-75, employment supr., 1975-77; realtor assoc. Toothaker Real Estate Co., Manhattan, Kans., 1978, Anderson Realty Agy., Manhattan, 1978-79; rsch. asst. Washburn U. Sch. Law, Topeka, 1979-80; law clk. Kans. Corp. Commn., Topeka, 1980-81; pvt. practice law, Manhattan, 1981-83; mgr. pers. K-State Union, Manhattan, 1981-83; atty. Myers & Pottroff, Manhattan, 1983-89; civilian atty. U.S. Army, Ft. Riley, Kans., 1989—; asst. counselor Riley County, Kans., 1983-89; mem. univ. staff devel. task force, 1981-83, mem. univ. appeal and rev. com., 1982-83. Active LWV, 1977-80; mem. adv. bd. 4-H Club, 1981-84, chmn., 1983-84; solicitor United Way, 1981, 82, bd. dirs., 1984-89, v.p., 1987, pres., 1988, allocations chair, 1986, 87; mem. Local Fed. Coordinating Com., 1990—; solicitor Cancer Crusade, 1975. Mem. ABA (sects. on corps., bus., banking, real property, probate, trust, taxation, econs.), Kans. Bar Assn. (coms. on legal malpractice prevention, continuing legal edn., sects. on corp., bus., banking, real estate, probate, trust, tax), Riley County Bar Assn. (chmn. Law Day 1984, pres. 1987), Am. Trial Lawyers Assn., Kans. Trial Lawyers Assn., North Cen. Iowa Pers. Assn. (sec. 1976-77), Manhattan Pers. Assn., Bus. and Profl. Women, Washburn Women's Legal Forum (v.p. and pres. 1979-80), Manhattan C. of C. (various coms., Leadership award 1983), Manhattan Arts Coun., Am. Legion Aux., Phi Delta Phi. Republican. Methodist. Home: 2030 Hillview Dr Manhattan KS 66502

CATHOU, RENATA EGONE, scientist, consultant; b. Milan, Italy, June 21, 1935; d. Egon and Stella Mary Egone; m. Pierre-Yves Cathou, June 21, 1959. BS, MIT, 1957, PhD, 1963. Postdoctoral fellow, research assoc. in chemistry MIT, Cambridge, 1962-65; research assoc. Harvard U. Med. Sch., Cambridge, 1965-69, instr., 1969-70; research assoc. Mass. Gen. Hosp., 1965-69, instr., 1969-70; asst. prof. dept. biochemistry Sch. Medicine, Tufts U., 1970-73, assoc. prof., 1973-78, prof., 1978-81; pres. Tech. Evaluations, Lexington, Mass., 1983—; sr. cons. SRC Assocs., Park Ridge, N.J., 1984—; sr. investigator Arthritis Found., 1970-75; vis. prof. dept. chemistry UCLA, 1976-77; mem. adv. panel NSF, 1974-75; mem. bd. sci. counselors Nat. Cancer Inst., 1979-83; ind. cons. and writer. Mem. editorial bd. Immunochemistry, 1972-75; contbr. chpts. to books and articles to profl. jours. Mem. council Boston Mus. Fine Arts. NIH predoctoral fellow, 1958-62; grantee Am. Heart Assn., 1969-81, USPHS, 1970-81. Fellow Am. Inst. Chemists; mem. AAAS, Clin. Ligand Assay Soc. (mem. exec. bd. New Eng. chpt. 1987—), Am. Soc. for Biochemistry and Molecular Biology, Am. Assn. Immunologists, N.Y. Acad. Scis. Club: U.S. Power Squadron (Lexington). Office: Tech Evaluations 430 Marrett Rd Lexington MA 02173

CATLIN, B. WESLEY, microbiologist; b. Mt. Vernon, N.Y., June 26, 1917; d. H. Burd and Abby Faber (Dunning) C.; m. Lew S. Cunningham, 1954. AB, U. Calif., L.A., 1941, MS, 1944, PhD, 1947. Med. lab. tech. Pasadena/Long Beach, Calif., 1939-43; teaching asst. in bacteriology UCLA, 1943-47, rsch. assoc. dept. bacteriology, 1947-49; postdoctoral assoc. dept. genetics Carnegie Inst. of Washington, Cold Spring Harbor, N.Y., 1949-50; asst. prof. Marquette U. Sch. Medicine, Milw., 1950-55, assoc. prof., 1955-65; prof. Med. Coll. of Wis., Milw., 1965-87, prof. emeritus, 1987—; guest investigator biophysics group, Carnegie Inst. Washington, 1952; participant Neisseria Rsch. meeting, World Health Orgn., Geneva, 1964; bd. scientific counselors, NIH, Bethesda, Md., 1977-80. Editorial bd. Jour. Bacteriology, 1972-75; adv. com. for Bergey's Manual (8th edit.), Vol. 1, 1968, 79; contbr. articles to profl. jours. and books in field. Recipient rsch. grants Nat. Inst. Allergy and Infectious Diseases, Bethesda, 1955-87, Annual Citation, Nat. Bd. Med. Coll. of Pa., Phila., 1978, Outstanding Achievement in Sci. award YWCA of Milw., 1978, Disting. Svc. award, 1980, Faculty Svc. award, 1982, Med. Coll. Wis., Pasteur award Ill. Soc. Microbiology, Chgo., 1983. Mem. Am. Soc. Microbiology (program com. 1954-56, taxonomy com. 1974-79), Internat. Assn. Biol. Socs. (com. mem. 1963—, sec. 1966-78), Soc. Gen. Microbiology, Genetics Soc. Am., AAAS, Soc. for Study of Evolution.

CATOE, BETTE LORRINA, physician; b. Washington, Apr. 7, 1926; d. John Booker and Laura Beola (Adams) C.; B.S. cum laude, Howard U., 1948, M.D., 1951; m. Warren J. Strudwick, Sept. 17, 1949; children—Laura Christina, Warren J., William J. Intern, Freedmen's Hosp., Washington, 1951-52; pediatric resident Howard U. Freedman's Hosp., 1952-55; practice medicine specializing in pediatrics, Washington, 1956—; instr. bacteriology Howard U., 1955-57; mem. staff Providence Hosp., Cafritz Hosp., Columbia Hosp., Howard U. Hosp., Washington Hosp. Center; sch. health officer Dept. Health, Washington, 1960-64; clin. instr. Howard U., 1956—. Mem. D.C. Health Planning Adv. Council, 1967-77, chmn., 1973-77; chmn. D.C. Devel. Disabilities Adv. Council, 1970-74; mem. D.C. Mayor's Commn. on Food and Nutrition, 1971-72, Mayor's Commn. on Maternal and Child Health. 1978—; mem. D.C. Commn. Jud. Tenure and Disabilities, 1977—, chair, 1984—; bd. dirs. United Way of Nat. Capital Area, 1974-76, chmn. social planning com., 1974-75; bd. govs. St. Alban's Sch., 1978—; bd. dirs. D.C. Health and Welfare Council, 1968-73, pres., 1973-74; del. Democratic Nat. Conv., 1976; bd. dirs. Met. Washington Health and Welfare Council, 1970-72, Parent Council of Washington, 1974-75, Met. Med. Founds., Inc., Silver Spring YMCA, 1977-80. Mem. Am. Acad. Pediatrics, AMA, Nat. Med. Assn., D.C. Chirurg. Soc., D.C. Med. Soc., Am. Med. Women's Assn. (chmn. pediatric com. 1981-83), NAACP, Urban League, Am. Assn. Comprehensive Health Planners (dir. 1975-77), Women's Aux. Medico-Chirurg. Soc., Jack and Jill Am., Century Club of Nat. Assn. Negro Bus. and Profl. Women's Clubs (pres. 1985—), Alpha Kappa Alpha. Baptist. Clubs: Links, Carrousels, Women's Nat. Dem. Home: 1748 Sycamore St NW Washington DC 20012 Office: 5505 5th St Washington DC 20011

CATOE, SANDRA CLYBURN, pediatrician; b. Kershaw, S.C., Apr. 17, 1937; d. William Hampton and Marguerite (Truesdale) Clyburn; m. Earl Ferris Catoe Sr., Mar. 26, 1960; children: Karen, Earl Ferris Jr., Jane, William. BS, U. S.C., 1959; MD, Med. U. S.C., 1963. Diplomate Am. Bd. Pediatrics. Intern Med. U. of S.C., 1963-64, resident in pediatrics, 1964-66; pvt. practice Kershaw, 1966-70; mem. staff dept. mental retardation S.C. Coastal Ctr., Ladson, 1970-72, med. dir., 1972-74; mem. staff Trident Health dist. S.C. Dept. Health Environ. Control, Charleston, 1974-89, asst. health dir., 1989—. Fellow Am. Acad. Pediatrics; mem. Charleston County Med. Soc. (mem. exec. bd. 1990, co-chairperson sch. health com. 1988—). Presbyterian. Office: Trident Health Dist SC DHEC 334 Calhoun St Charleston SC 29401

CATOLINE, PAULINE DESSIE, executive secretary; b. Ft. Worth, Dec. 17, 1937; d. Byron Hillis and Dessie Elizabeth (Plumlee) Doggett; children: Sherry Lou, Brenda Lynn. BA in Labor Relations, Hiram Coll., 1989. Notary public, Ohio. Sec. Gen. Am. Life Ins. Co., Ft. Worth, 1956-57, Kelly Girl Svcs., Youngstown, Ohio, 1965-69; legal sec. Burgstaller, Schwartz & Moore, Youngstown, 1962-65, Green, Schiavoni, Murphy & Haines, Youngstown, 1969-71, Flask & Policy, Youngstown, 1971-83; sec. We. Reserve Care System, Youngstown, 1983-87; exec. sec. We. Reserve Care System, 1987—. Pres. PTA, Cottage Hills, Ill., 1968-69, brownie and scout leader, 1968-69. Mem. Mahoning County Legal Secs. Assn. (v.p. 1973-74, editor monthly booklet 1974-75), Missionary Group Club. Democrat. Methodist. Home: 3961 Cannon Rd Youngstown OH 44515

CATRON, DEBORAH ANN, state agency specialist; b. Wiesbaden, Fed. Republic of Germany, June 23, 1958; came to U.S., 1958; d. Robert William and Barbara Ann (Guminger) C. BA, Rockhurst Coll., Kansas City, Mo., 1979. Intern, caseworker Office Senator John C. Danforth, Kansas City, 1978-79; office mgr. Bond for Gov. Com., Kansas City, 1979-81; mgr. Kansas City Gov.'s Office, 1981; fundraiser Mo. Rep. Party, Kansas City, 1981-82; neighborhood specialist Mo. Dept. Consumer Affairs, Kansas City, 1982-85; community programs specialist Mo. Dept. Econ. Devel., Kansas City, 1985—; mem. rev. com. Ctr. Mgmt. Assistance, Kansas City, 1988; judge Minn. Community Improvement Program, 1988. Editor Neighborhood Assistance Perspective. Co-coordinator 1982 Rep. Gov.'s Conf., Kansas City, 1982; mem. fundraising com. Berkley for Mayor, 1984-86; mem. Friends of Art, 1986-89, Kansas City Concensus, 1987—; organizer Sacred Heart Children's Project, 1989-90. Mem. Internat. Community Devel. Soc. (conf. com. 1988-89, awards com. 1989-90), Nat. Soc. Fundraising Execs., Mo. Community Devel. Soc. (life, Disting. Svc. award 1986, bd. dirs. 1983-86, pres. 1986-88). Roman Catholic. Office: Mo Dept Econ Devel 615 E 13th Ste 516 Kansas City MO 64106

CATTANEO, JACQUELYN ANNETTE KAMMERER, artist, educator; b. Gallup, N.Mex., June 1, 1944; d. Ralph John and Gladys Agnes (O'Sullivan) Kammer; m. John Leo Cattaneo, Apr. 25, 1964; children: John Auro, Paul Anthony. Student Tex. Woman's U., 1962-64. Portrait artist, tchr. Gallup, N. Mex., 1972; coordinator Works Progress Adminstrn. art project renovation McKinley County, Gallup, Octavia Fellin Performing Arts wing dedication, Gallup Pub. Library; formation com. mem. Multi-modal/Multi-Cultural Ctr. for Gallup, N.Mex.; exch. with Soviet Women's Com., USSR Women Artists del., Moscow, Kiev, Leningrad, 1990. One-woman shows include Gallup Pub. Libr., 1963, 66, 77, 78, 81, 87, Gallup Lovelace Med. Clinic, Santa Fe Station Open House, 1981, Gallery 20, Farmington, N.Mex., 1985—, Red Mesa Art Gallery, 1989; group shows include: Navajo Nation Library Invitational, 1978, Santa Fe Festival of the Arts Invitational, 1979, N.Mex. State Fair, 1978, 79, 80, Catharine Lorillard Wolfe, N.Y.C., 1980, 81, 84, 85, 86, 87, 88, 89, 4th ann. exhbn. Salmagundi Club, 1984, 90, 3d ann. Palm Beach Internat., New Orleans, 1984, Fine Arts Ctr. Taos, 1984, The Best and the Brightest O'Brien's Art Emporium, Scottsdale, Ariz., 1986, Gov.'s Gallery, 1989, N.Mex. State Capitol, Santa Fe, 1987, Pastel Soc. West Coast Ann. Exhbn. Sacramento Ctr. for Arts, Calif., 1986—; represented in permanent collections: Zuni Arts and Crafts Ednl. Bldg., U. N.Mex., C.J. Wiemar Collection, McKinley Manor, Gov.'s Office, State Capitol Bldg., Santa Fe, Historic El Rancho Hotel, Gallup, N.Mex., Sunwest Bank. Fine Arts Ctr., En Taos, N.Mex., Armand Hammer Pvt. Collection, Russell Gallery & Studio, Albuquerque, Dallas & Assocs., Ruidoso, N.Mex., Dallas Summers. Mem. Internat. Fine Arts Guild, Am. Portrait Soc. (cert.), Pastel Soc. of W. Coast (cert.), Mus. N.Mex. Found., Mus. Women in the Arts, Fechin Inst., Artists' Co-op. (co-chair), Gallup C. of C., Gallup Area Arts and Crafts Council, Catharine Lorillard Wolfe Art Club of N.Y.C. (oil and pastel juried membership), Chautaugua Art Club. Soroptimists. Address: 210 E Green St Gallup NM 87301

CATTANEO, JO-ANN, electronics company executive; b. Paterson, N.J., Jan. 27, 1950; d. Joseph and Margaret Lena (Phillips) C. BS, Montclair State Coll., 1988. Sec. Balt. Aircoil Co., Ridgewood, N.J., 1968-74; sec. to dir. electronic tech. Singer-Electronic Systems Div., Totowa, N.J., 1974-87; tng. adminstr. Plessey Electronic Systems Corp., Wayne, N.J., 1987—; trainer mgmt. workshops Support Ctr. N.J.; trainer workshop Tribute to Women In Industry Cen. N.J. Tutor Project Literacy, 1988—; mem. Rep. Presdl. Task Force, 1990—. Mem. Am. Soc. Tng. and Devel. (cert. appreciation No. N.J. chpt.), Community Involvement Com., Phi Kappa Phi. Methodist. Home: 8 Richfield Terr Clifton NJ 07012 Office: Plessey Electronic Systems Corp 164 Totowa Rd Wayne NJ 07474

CATTANI, DEBRA, marketing manager; b. N.Y.C., Feb. 20, 1953; d. Frank and Anita (Acciani) C. AA, Nassau Community Coll., 1973; BS, N.Y. Inst. Tech., 1975, MBA, 1981. Tchr. Katharine Gibbs Sec. Sch., N.Y.C., 1975-76; executive asst. Xerox Co., Woodbury, N.Y., 1976-78; systems analyst Xerox Co., Woodbury, 1978-82; systems cons. Aes Data, N.Y.C., 1982-83; nat. customer support tng. mgr. Exxon Office Systems, Stamford, Conn., 1983-84; mgr. customer support Exxon Office Systems, N.Y.C., 1984-85; product mgr. NYNEX Bus. Info. Systems, White Plains, N.Y., 1985-87; customer/sales support mgr. NYNEX Info. Solutions Group, White Plains, 1987-89, nat. account mgr., 1989, dir. strategic mktg., 1989-90; dir. bus. plans and programs NYNEX Network Svcs., White Plains, 1990—. Republican. Roman Catholic. Home: 135 South St New Hyde Park NY 11040 Office: NYNEX Network Svcs 1113 Westchester Ave White Plains NY 10604

CATTANI, MARYELLEN B., lawyer; b. Bakersfield, Calif., Dec. 1, 1943; d. Arnold Theodore and Corinne Marilyn (Kovacevich) C.; m. Frank C. Herringer; 1 child, Sarah. AB, Vassar Coll., Poughkeepsie, N.Y., 1965; JD, U. Calif. (Boalt Hall), 1968. Assoc. Davis Polk & Wardwell, N.Y.C., 1968-69; assoc. Orrick, Herrington & Sutcliffe, San Francisco, 1970-74, ptnr., 1975-81; v.p., gen. counsel TransAmerica Corp., San Francisco, 1981-83, sr. v.p., gen. counsel, 1983-89; ptnr. Morrison & Foerster, San Francisco, 1989—. Author: Calif. Corp. Practice Guide, 1977, Corp. Counselors, 1982. Regent St. Mary's Coll., Calif., Moraga, 1985—, pres., 1990; trustee Vassar Coll., 1985—; bd. dirs. The Exploratorium. 1088—; mem. Ctr. Pub. Resources San Francisco. Mem. ABA, State Bar Calif. (chmn. bus. law sect. 1980-81), Bar Assn. San Francisco (co-chair com. on women 1989—), Calif. Women Lawyers, San Francisco C. of C. (bd. dirs. 1987—, gen. counsel 1990—, sec. 1990—), Am. Corp. Counsel Assn. (bd. dirs. 1982-87), Women's Forum West (bd. dirs. 1984-87), The Exploratorium (bd. dirs. 1988—). Democrat. Roman Catholic. Club: Women's Forum West.

CATTERALL, MARLENE, Canadian legislator; b. Ottawa, Ont., Can., Mar. 1, 1939; d. Paul and Isobel Petzold; m. Ron Catterall, July 14, 1962; children: Karen, Chris, Cheryl. Ed., Carleton U. Alderman, coun. mem. City of Ottawa, 1976-85; mem. from Ottawa West Ho. of Commons, 1988—. Mem. Ont. Residential Standards Bd., Ottawa Coun. for Arts, Coun. of Cans. Mem. Ottawa Women's Network, Bus. and Profl. Women's Inst. Liberal. Roman Catholic. Office: House of Commons, Parliament Bldgs, Ottawa, ON Canada K1A 0A6*

CATTLE, NANCY E., financial consultant; b. Newark, Nov. 11, 1959. BS, Montclair State Coll., 1982. Cert. mgmt. Acct. Sr. acct. Mennen Co., Morristown, N.J.; acct., data processing mgr. In-X Fastener Corp., Fairfield, N.J.; tax preparer State of N.J., Fairlawn; fin. system cons. Computron Tech. Corp., Rutherford, N.J. Mem. Nat. Assn. Accts. (past pres. local chpt.), NAFE, Assn. Women in Computing, ICMA.

CAUCE, ANA MARI, psychology educator; b. Havana, Cuba, Jan. 11, 1956; came to U.S., 1959; d. Vicente and Ana (Vivanco) C. BA summa cum laude, U. Miami, 1979; MS in Psychology, Yale U., 1979, PhD in Psychology, 1984. Asst. prof. psychology U. Del., Newark, 1983-86; assoc. prof. U. Wash., Seattle, 1986—; bd. dirs. CONSEJO Counseling and Referral Svc. for Hispanics, Seattle; mem. minority initiatives com. Alliance for Children, Youth and Families, Seattle; mem com. on cons. and edn. Wash. Coun. for Prevention Child Abuse and Neglect; mem. system analysis adv. com. child and adolescent svc. system project dept. social and health svcs. State of Wash.; speaker and cons. in field; lectr. Quinnipiac Coll., North Haven, Conn., 1979; clin. supr. psychol. svcs. tng. ctr. U. Wash., 1986—. Contbr. numerous chpts. to books and articles to profl. jours.; editorial bd. Am. Jour. Community Psychology; reviewer: Journal of Personality and Social Psychology, Journal of Child Clinical Psychology, Journal of Adolescent Research. The Grant Found. grantee, 1986-87, Grad. Sch. Rsch. Fund U. Wash. grantee, 1987-88, Nat. Inst. Child Health and Human Devel. grantee, 1988—; recipient Silver Knight award Miami Herald, 1974; Yale Bush Ctr. in Child Devel. and Social Policy fellow, 1983; Elizabeth Kay Donor scholar, 1976-77. Fellow (hon.) Am. Psychol. Assn. (clin. psychology div., community psychology div., psychology of women div., soc. for study ethnic minority issues div.); mem. Soc. for Rsch. in Child Devel., Soc. for Rsch. on Adolescence, Am. Psychol. Soc., Phi Kappa Phi, Sigma Xi. Home: 11310 34 NE Seattle WA 98125 Office: U Wash Dept Psychology Seattle WA 98195

CAUDELL, JOY LARAINE, hospital administrator; b. Toccoa, Ga., Aug. 14, 1948; d. Dwain and Nell Marie (Smith) C. BS in Home Econs., U. Ga., 1970; MBA, U. South Ala., 1979. Tng. instr. Davis Bros., Inc., Atlanta, 1970-72; asst. to food svc. dir. West Paces Ferry Hosp., Atlanta, 1972-74; dir. food svcs. Drs. Hosp., Mobile, Ala., 1974-79; adminstrv. asst. Indian Path Hosp., Kingsport, Tenn., 1979-80, asst. adminstr., 1980-82; adminstr. Johnson City (Tenn.) Eye & Ear Hosp., 1982—; food svc. cons., 1974-79; faculty mem. Ctr. for Health Studies, Nashville, 1979-87; bd. dirs. Tenn. Hosp. Assn., exec. com., 1988. Pres., bd. dirs., mem. exec. com. East Tenn. Regional Organ Procurement Agy.; Sunday sch. tchr. Colonial Heights Baptist Ch., 1980-82; adv. Experience Based Career Edn. Program, Murphy High Sch., 1977-79; bd. dirs. United Way Washington County, 1986—, exec. com. 1988, Washington County Am. Heart Assn.; pres. Upper East Tenn. Hosp. Dist., 1986-88; mem. fin., mission coms. Munsey Meml. Meth. Ch. Mem. Am. Coll. Health Execs., Johnson City C. of C. (health svcs. coun., v.p. 1988, bd. dirs.), Leadership 2000, U. Ga. Alumni Assn., U. South Ala. Alumni Assn., AAUW (bd. dirs.), Christian Bus. and Profl. Women (bd. exec. com. 1987-88). Home: 1222 Ridgeway Johnson City TN 37601 Office: Johnson City Eye and Ear Hosp 203 E Watauga Johnson City TN 37601

CAUDILL, MAUREEN, computer consultant; b. Portsmouth, Ohio, July 14, 1951; d. Elmon C. and Harriet L. (Sisler) C. BA, U. Conn., 1973; MA in Teaching, Cornell U., 1974. Customer engr. Raytheon Data Systems, Wellesley, Mass., 1975-78; mem. tech. sales support staff Hewlett-Packard Co., Wallingford, Conn., 1978-81; project programmer Gould Ocean Systems div., Cleve., 1982-83; sr. software engr. Data Systems div. Gen. Dynamics Co., San Diego, 1983-85; computer cons. Rockwell Internat., Hughes Aircraft Corp., Honeywell Corp., other corps., 1985-89; founder, computer cons. Adaptics, San Diego, 1987-89; engrng. specialist space systems div. Gen. Dynamics, San Diego, 1989-90; mgr. tech. and applications support Sci. Applications Internat. Corp., 1990—; organizer ann. meetings on neural networks, San Diego, Boston, Washington, Seattle, 1987—; presenter on neural networks, U.S., Japan, Mex., also others, 1987—. Author: Naturally Intelligent Systems, 1989, Neural Network Primer, 1989. Mem. IEEE (chair publs. Neural Networks Coun.), Internat. Neural Network Soc. (adviser to exec. bd. 1988—), Assn. Computing Machinery.

CAULDER, MARY MEZZANOTTE, bank training officer; b. Phila., Dec. 28, 1953; d. Antonio Joseph and Dora M.; m. Bruce Edward, Oct. 29, 1983; children: Heather, Bruce Jr., Thomas. BS in Labor Relations, LaSalle U., Phila., 1983. Bank clk. Phila. Nat. Bank, 1971-76, tng. specialist, 1976-85; tng. officer Main Line Fed. Savs. Bank, Villanova, Pa., 1986—; instr. Inst. Fin. Edn., Bucks County Community Coll., 1987—. Mem. Am. Soc. for Tng. and Devel., Internat. Assn. Quality Circles (treas. 1983-85), Nat. Assn. Female Execs. Office: Main Line Fed Savs Bank Rt 320 and Lancaster Ave Villanova PA 19085

CAULEY, LINDA NEWBERN, institutional researcher, educator; b. Norfolk, Va., Oct. 20, 1952; d. Willie Milton and Frances Mildred (Royster) Newbern; m. Phil Matthew Cauley, Aug. 16, 1980. BS, Coll. William and Mary, 1974; MS, Va. Poly. Inst. and State U., 1978. Research specialist dept. biology Va. Poly. Inst. and State U., Blacksburg, 1979-80; data analyst planning div. Ministry Agr., Maseru, Lesotho, 1981-84; research assoc. ARAL Project Nat. U., Lesotho, Roma, 1985; extension specialist coop. extension internat. programs Wash. State U., Pullman, 1986; rsch. assoc. Netherlands U. Found. for Internat. Coop. PPIIS Project, Univs., Brawijaya, Malang, Indonesia, 1987-88; program evaluator U.S. AID, Maseru, 1983; cons. editing and writing, 1984; cons. data anlaysis and tng. farming systems research project, 1981-85, land conservation and range devel. project, 1985-86; cons. staff tng. Cath. Relief Svcs., Maseru, 1986; cons. staff tng. Netherland Univs. Found. for Internat. Coop. Project Univs., Brawijaya, Malang, 1988; cons. tng. and programming FSR Project, Wash. State U., Pullman, 1980-86; instnl. assessment and rsch. specialist, adj. asst. prof. biology Dabney S. Lancaster Community Coll., Clifton Forge, Va., 1989—; co-owner, co-mgr. Weltevreden Farm, Millboro, Va. Contbr. articles in field to profl. jours. Mem. Ecol. Soc. Am., Internat. Ecol. Soc., Phi Kappa Phi, Phi Sigma. Republican. Methodist. Home: Rte 1 Box 129 Weltevreden Farm Millboro VA 24460

CAULFIELD, JOAN, educational administrator; b. St. Joseph, Mo., July 17, 1943; d. Joseph A. and Jane (Lisenby) Caulfield; BS in Edn. cum laude, U. Mo., 1963, MA in Spanish, 1965, PhD, 1978; postgrad. (Mexican Govt. scholar) Nat. U. Mexico, 1962-63. TV tchr. Spanish, Kansas City (Mo.) pub. schs., 1963-68; tchr. Spanish, French Bingham Jr. High Schs., Kansas City, 1968-78; asst. prin. S.E. High Sch., Kansas City, 1984; prin. Nowlin Jr. High Sch., Independence, Mo., 1984-86, Lincoln Coll. Preparatory Acad., Kansas City, Mo., 1986-88, asst. supt., Kansas City, 1988-89; part-time instr. U. Mo.-Kansas City; dir. English Inst., Rockhurst Coll., summers, 1972-75, coord. sch. coll. rels., 1989—. Mem. Sister City Commn., Kansas City, 1980—; ofcl. translator to mayor on trip to Seville, Spain, 1969, Historic Kansas City Found. Named Outstanding Secondary Educator, 1973; Delta Kappa Gamma state scholar, 1977-78. Mem. Romance Lang. Assn., Assn. for Supervision and Curriculum Devel., Nat. Assn. Secondary Sch. Prins., Modern Lang. Assn. (contbr. jour.), Am. Assn. Tchrs. Spanish & Portuguese, Friends of Seville, Friends of Art, Friends of the Zoo, Mo. Mid. Sch. Assn. (contbr. jour.), Phi Sigma Iota, Phi Delta Kappa, Delta Kappa Gamma, Phi Kappa Phi, Sigma Delta Pi. Presbyterian. Home: 431 W 70th St Kansas City MO 64113 Office: 5225 Troost Kansas City MO 64110

CAUSEY, ANNETTE DENISE, librarian; b. Macon, Ga., May 20, 1960; d. Tom Wilson Sr. and Betty Mae (Evans) C. BA, Wesleyan Coll., Macon, Ga., 1982; MLS, Atlanta U., 1985. Audio technician Macon (Ga.) Talking Book Ctr., 1982-84; grad. libr. asst. Atlanta U. SLIS, Trevor Arnett Library, Atlanta, 1984-85; libr. technician U.S. Ct. Appeals, Atlanta, 1985-86; libr. Salvation Army SFOT, Atlanta, 1986-87; reference, circulation libr. Life Chiropractic Coll., Ga., 1988—; internship The Bibb County Dept. Family and Children Services, Macon, Ga., 1882, v.p. Student Govt. Assn., 1985, colloquium com. mem. Atlanta U. SLIS, 1985; part-time reference libr. Ga. State U. Big sister Links Wesleyan Coll. Davis Homes, Macon, Ga. Mem. Met. Atlanta Library Assn., American Theo. Library Assn., Nat. Assn. Female Execs., Atlanta Hawks, Booster Club. Democrat. Methodist. Home: 2080 Bent Creek Way SW Atlanta GA 30311 Office: Life Chiropractic Coll 1269 Barclay Cir SE Marietta GA 30311

CAVA, ESTHER L., psychology educator; b. Duluth, Minn., Apr. 3, 1916; d. Jacob and Sarah (Sukov) Laden; m. Michael P. Cava, June 11, 1951; 1 child, John M. JD, Temple U., 1984; BA in Psychology with honors, U. Mich., 1951; MA in Clin. Psychology, Boston U., 1952; PhD in Clin. Psychology, Ohio State U., 1967. Lice. psychologist, Pa. Pediatric and psychiat. nurse U. Mich. Hosp., Ann Arbor, 1939-42; English instr. Ohio State U., Columbus, 1960-63; psychology instr. Temple U., St. Joseph's Coll., Phila., 1970-71; staff psychologist various clinics, Phila., 1971-79; adj. assoc. prof. psychology U. Ala., Tuscaloosa, 1985; cons. to various schs., hosps., and community programs; speaker in workshop leader in field. Author: Complete Question-and-Answer Book of Child Training, 1972, Pediatricians' Guide to Child Behavior Problems, 1979; contbr. chpt. to Textbook of Pediatrics, 1979. Co-chmn. planning com. Commn. on Status of Women, Tuscaloosa, 1987-88. 1st lt. ANC, 1942-45. Mem. Am. Psychol. Assn., Acad. Law and Mental Health, Phi Beta Kappa. Home: 15 Northshore Dr Tuscaloosa AL 35406

CAVACINI, LISA ANN, immunologist, researcher; b. Phila., Apr. 25, 1961; d. John Vincent and Frances Jane (Tilsner) C. BS, U. Scranton, Pa., 1983; PhD, Hahnemann U., 1988. Adminstrv. asst. Grad. Sch. Hahnemann U., Phila., 1984-88; med. technician Hahnemann U. Clin. Lab., Phila., 1984-88; postdoctoral fellow Schering-Plough Rsch., Bloomfield, N.J., 1988-89; rsch. scientist Centocor, Inc., Malvern, Pa., 1989—. Contbr. articles to profl. jours. Mem. Am. Soc. for Microbiology, Am. Assn. Immunology, Columbia Yacht Club. Republican. Roman Catholic. Office: Centocor Inc 244 Great Valley Pkwy Malvern PA 19355

CAVALLARO, MARY CAROLINE, professor of physics; b. Everett, Mass., Feb. 2, 1932; d. Joseph and Domenica Cavallaro. BS, Simmons Coll., 1954, MS, 1956; EdD, Ind. U., 1972; postgrad., Tufts U., 1980-81. Inst. math. and physics Sweet Briar (Va.) Coll., 1955-56; instr. physics Simmons Coll., Boston, 1956-58, Randolph-Macon Woman's Coll., Lynchburg, Va., 1958-59; lectr. Boston U., 1960-61; asst. prof. physics Framingham (Mass.) State Coll., 1961-63; prof. physics Salem (Mass.) State Coll., 1963—, coord. secondary edn., 1990—; cons. Introductory Phys. Scis. group Edn. Devel. Ctr., Newton, 1966; asst. to dean grad. studies Salem State Coll., 1971-78, coord. pre-engring. program, 1980-89, coord. secondary edn. program, 1989—; vis. scholar Harvard U. Grad. Sch. Edn., Cambridge, Mass., 1988-89, 89-90. Grantee NSF, 1962. Mem. NEA, Am. Phys. Soc., Am. Assn. Physics Tchrs., Nat. Sci. Tchrs. Assn., Am. Inst. Physics, Soc. Coll. Sci. Tchrs., Mass. Tchrs. Assn., Simmons Coll. Alumnae Assn., Ind. U. Alumnae Assn., Pi Lambda Theta. Office: Salem State Coll Loring Ave Salem MA 01970

CAVALLON, BETTY GABLER, interior designer; b. Waverly, N.Y., July 17, 1918; d. Wallace Frederick and Harriet (Heaton) Gabler; grad. Parisien Sch. Design, Detroit, 1939; m. Michel Francis Cavollon, Dec. 26, 1946 (dec. 1981); children: Claire, Carol (dec.); stepchildren: Michel, Mary; m. John W. Crist, Nov. 20, 1982. Lic. interior designer, Conn. Fabric coordinator Montgomery Ward, 1940-46; interior designer Betty Cavallon Interiors Ltd., Stamford, Conn., 1946—. Mem. Am. Soc. Interior Designers (corp.). Republican. Episcopalian. Home and Office: 1369 Long Ridge Rd Stamford CT 06903

CAVANAUGH, JEAN, medical secretary; b. Lake City, Iowa, June 27, 1924; d. Orrin Ellsworth and Golda Mae (Howard) VanHorn; m. Clair Joseph Cavanaugh, 1947; children: Thomas Paul, Kathleen Ann Bowman, Michael John, Terrence Joseph, James Clair. BS in Bus. Edn., Ft. Hays State U., Hays, Kans., 1970, MS in Guidance and Counseling, 1971, Edn. Specialist, 1975. Cert. tchr. Clk., fingerprint classifier FBI, Washington, 1942-44; pollster Gallup Polls, Great Bend, Kans., 1974-82; substitute tchr. Great Bend Sch. Dist., 1971-84; med. sec. Cen. Kans. Med. Ctr., Great Bend, 1974—; bd. dirs. First Nat. Bank, Glidden, Iowa. Bd. mem. Unified Sch. Dist. 428, Great Bend, 1979—; exec. sec. Golden Belt Community Concerts, 1979—; sec. Barton County Health Fair Bd., 1983-90; sec. Retired Sr. Volunteer Program, 1985-90). Named Woman of Yr., Bus. and Profl. Women, Great Bend, 1976. Mem. Am. Med. Assn. Aux. (regional v.p. Midwestern region 1985-87), So. Med. Assn. Aux. (councilor 1986-89), C. of C. (edn. com. 1989-90), Pilot Internat. of Great Bend (dir., pres. elect 1989-90). Roman CAtholic. Home: 1320 Cleveland Great Bend KS 67530

CAVASINA, MARY MAGDALENE, surgeon; b. Canonsburg, Pa., Dec. 26, 1927; d. Joseph Edward and Rose (Staffen) C. BS, U. Pitts., 1948; MD, Women's Med. Coll. of Pa., 1952. Diplomate Am. Bd. Surgery. Intern Mercy Hosp., Pitts., 1952-53, resident in gen. surgery, 1953-57; teaching fellow U. Pitts., 1953-57; sr. surg. staff mem. Canonsburg Gen. Hosp., 1957—, chief surgery, 1962-75; cons. gen. surgery Western Ctr., Canonsburg, 1957—. Asst. chief and fire surgeon Canonsburg Vol. Fire Dept. Mem. Cath. Daus. of Am., Bus. and Profl. Women's Club, Pitts. Surg. Soc., Am. Coll. Surgeons. Republican. Roman Catholic. Office: 160 W Pike St Canonsburg PA 15317

CAVE, CATHERINE ANNE N., temporary service branch manager; b. Norwalk, Conn., Dec. 23, 1956; d. John Edward and Rosemary (Nolan) Nelson; m. Dan E. Cave, Sept. 29, 1979; children: Rebecca, Stephanie. BA in Pub. Policy & Govt., Ea. Conn. State U., 1978. Recruiter Robert Half, Greensboro, N.C., 1979-82, Dunhill of Winston-Salem, Kernersville, N.C., 1984-86; branch mgr. Regency Temps., Winston-Salem, N.C., 1986—. Planner St. Paul's Youth Group, Greensboro, 1988-89. Mem. Piedmont Assn. Temp. Svcs. (sec.), Winston-Salem C. of C. (ambassador 1989, bus. after hours com. 1986-89). Democrat. Roman Catholic. Home: 3101 Timmons Ave Greensboro NC 27406 Office: Regency Temps 957 Burke St Winston-Salem NC 27101

CAVERS-HUFF, DASIEA YVONNE, philosopher; b. Cleve., Oct. 24, 1961; d. Lawrence Benjamin and Yvonne (Warner) Cavers; m. Brian Jay Huff, July 26, 1986. BA, Cleve. State U., 1984, MA, 1988; postgrad., U. Md., 1986—. Teaching asst. Cleve. State U., 1983-86; instr. Upward Bound program Case Western Res. U., Cleve., 1986; instr. U. Md., Coll. Park, Md., 1987-89; mem. faculty Charles County Community Coll., 1989—. U. Md. grad. fellow, 1986-87; Ford Found. predoctoral fellow, 1987-89. Mem. Am. Philos. Assn., Minority Grad. Student Assn. (co-chmn. U. Md. 1987-88). Democrat. Home: 16105 Penn Manor Ln Bowie MD 20716 Office: Dept Philosophy U Md 1131 Skinner Bldg College Park MD 20740

CAVNAR, MARGARET MARY (PEGGY CAVNAR), business executive, former state legislator, nurse; b. Buffalo, July 29, 1945; d. James John and Margaret Mary Murtha Nightengale; BS in Nursing, D'Youville Coll., 1967; MBA, Nat. U., 1989; m. Samuel M. Cavnar, 1977; children: Heather Anne, Heide Lynn, Dona Cavnar Hambly, Judy Cavnar Bentrim. Utilization rev. coord. South Nev. Meml. Hosp., Las Vegas, 1975-77; v.p. Ranvac Publs., Las Vegas, 1976—; ptnr. Cavnar & Assocs., Reseda, Calif., 1976—, C & A Mgmt., Las Vegas, 1977—; pres. PS Computer Svc., Las Vegas, 1978—; bd. mem. Nev. Eye Bank, 1987-89, exec. dir., 1990—. Mem. Clark County Republican Cen. Com., 1977-87, Nev. Rep. Cen. Com., 1978-80; mem. Nev. Assembly, 1979-81; Rep. nominee for Nev. Senate, 1980; Rep. nominee for Congress from Nev. 1st dist., 1982, 84; bd. dirs., treas. Nev. Med. Fed. Credit Union; v.p. Community Youth Activities Found., Inc., Civic Assn. Am.; mem. utilization rev. bd. Easter Seals; trustee Nev. Sch. Arts, 1980-87; nat. adviser Project Prayer, 1978—; co-chmn. P.R.I.D.E. Com., 1983—; co-chmn. Tax Limitation Com., 1983, Personal Property Tax Elimination Com., 1979-82, Self-Help Against Food Tax Elimination Denial Com., 1980; mem. nat. bd. dirs., co-chmn. Nev. Pres. Reagan's Citizens for Tax Reform Com., 1985-88; mem. Nev. Profl. Standards Rev. Orgn., 1984; co-chmn. People Against Tax Hikes, 1983-84; bd. dirs. Nev. Eye Bank, 1988—. Mem. Nev. Order Women Legislators (charter, parliamentarian 1980—), Sigma Theta Tau. Club: Cosmopolitanly Hers Info. (pres.). Office: PO Box 26073 Las Vegas NV 89126

CAWRSE, CELESTE POWLUS, insurance company executive; b. Fairborn, Ohio, Aug. 26, 1956; d. Jesse Tilden and Alleen (Gormley) Powlus; m. David Michael Cawrse, Aug. 27, 1977. BS, U. Tenn., 1979; MBA, NYU, 1986. Fin. planner Columbia U., N.Y.C., 1979-81, research asst., 1980-82; internal audit asst. Dean Witter Reynolds, N.Y.C., 1981-82; corp. tax mgr. R. H. Macy and Co., Inc., N.Y.C., 1982-86; investment officer The Guardian Life Ins. Co., N.Y.C., 1987—. Mem. Assn. Real Estate Women, Bklyn. Heights Assn., DAR, Real Estate Bd. N.Y., Urban Land Inst., Internat. Coun. Shopping Ctrs. Republican. Methodist.

CAWS, MARY ANN, educator, critic; b. Wilmington, N.C., Sept. 10, 1933; d. Harmon Chadbourn and Margaret Devereux (Lippitt) Rorison; m. Peter Caws, June 2, 1956 (div. 1987); children: Matthew, Hilary. BA, Bryn Mawr Coll., 1954; MA, Yale U., 1956; PhD, U. Kans., 1962; D.Humane Letters, Union Coll., 1983. Asst. instr. Romance Langs. U. Kans., Lawrence, 1957-62, asst. editor univ. press, 1957-58, vis. asst. prof., spring 1963; lectr. Barnard Coll. Columbia U., N.Y.C., 1962-63; mem. faculty Sarah Lawrence Coll., Bronxville, N.Y., 1963-64; mem. faculty Hunter Coll. CUNY, N.Y.C., 1966—, prof. Hunter Coll., 1969—; exec. officer comparative lit. program CUNY, 1977-79, exec. officer French program, 1979-86, Disting. prof. French and comparative lit., 1983—, prof. English, 1985—, Disting. prof. French, comparative lit., English, 1987—; Phi Beta Kappa vis. scholar, 1982-83; dir. NEH summer seminars for coll. tchrs., 1978, 85; mem. faculty Dartmouth Sch. Criticism and Theory, 1988; co-dir. Peyre Inst. for the Humanities, 1980—. Author: Surrealism and the Literary Imagination, 1966, The Poetry of Dada and Surrealism, 1970, The Inner Theatre of Recent French Poetry, 1972, The Presence of Rene Char, 1976, Rene Char, 1977, The Surrealist Voice of Robert Desnos, 1977, La Main de Pierre Reverdy, 1979, The Eye in the Text, Essays on Perception, Mannerist to Modern, 1981, Andre Breton, 1982, The Metapoetics of the Passage, Architextures in Surrealism and After, 1982, Andre Breton, 1982, Yves Bonnefoy, 1984, Reading Frames in Modern Fiction, 1988, Edmond Jabès, 1988, The Art of INterference: Stressed Readings in Visual and Verbal Texts, 1989; contbr. articles to profl. jours.; editor: Dada-Surrealism, 1972, Le Siecle eclate, 1974, About French Poetry from Dada to Tel Quel, 1974, Selected Poetry Prose of Stephane Mallarme, 1982, Selected Poems of St.-John Perse, 1983, Writing in a Modern Temper, 1984, Textual Analysis, 1986, Perspectives on Perception: Philosophy, Art, and Literature, 1989; translator: Poems of Rene Char, 1976, Approximate Man and other Writings Of Tristan Tzara, 1975, Mad Love, 1987; co-translator: Poems of André Breton, 1984. Decorated officer Palmes Academiques, France; fellow Guggenheim Found., 1972-73, Nat. Endowment Humanities, 1979-80; Fulbright traveling fellow, 1972-73; Getty scholar, 1990. Mem. MLA (exec. coun. 1973-77, v.p. 1982-83, pres. 1983-84), Am. Assn. Tchrs. French, Assn. for Study Dada and Surrealism (pres. 1982-86), Internat. Assn. Philosophy and Lit. (exec. bd. 1982—, chmn. 1984), Acad. Lit. Studies (pres. 1985), Am. Comparative Lit. Assn. (exec. com. 1981—, v.p. 1986—, pres. 1989—). Home: 140 E 81st St New York NY 10028 Office: CUNY Grad Ctr 33 W 42d St New York NY 10036

CAWTHON, ZELMA HARRISON, real estate broker; b. Santa Rosa County, Fla., Dec. 3, 1911; d. Walter Thomas and Ida Ray (Blocker) Harrison; m. Dudley McSwain Cawthon, Apr. 13, 1941; 1 child, Dudley McSwain. BS, Fla. State U., 1936; postgrad., Barry U., Miami Shores, Fla. Home economist FSA, 1937; tchr. English Bonifay (Fla.) sch. bd., 1936-37; home economist Fla. Power & Light Co., Pensacola, 1940-41, U.S. Dept. Agr., Pahokee, Fla., 1941-42; asst. registrar Embry Riddle Sch. Aviation, Miami, Fla., 1942-43; with U.S. Post Office, Miami, 1943-44; real estate broker, pres. Nat. Real Estate Svcs., Inc., Miami Shores, Fla., 1965-87, Tallahassee, Fla., 1987—; v.p. Dudley Cawthon Inc., Miami, Am. Bldrs., Inc., Miami; lectr. on fashion. Contbr. articles to profl. jours. Active in past various civic orgns. Mem. AAUW (past pres.), Fla. State U. Alumni Assn., League Am. Pen Women (auditor), Soc. So. Families (debutante com.), Miami Bd. Realtors. Home and Office: 1112 Lasswade Dr Tallahassee FL 32312

CAYLEFF, SUSAN EVELYN, educator; b. Boston, Mar. 4, 1954; d. Nathan and Frieda (Kates) C. BA, U. Mass., 1976; MA, Sarah Lawrence Coll., 1978, Brown U., 1979; PhD, Brown U., 1983. Teaching fellow Brown U., Providence, 1981-83; asst. prof. Inst. for the Med. Humanities, U. Tex. Med. Br., Galveston, 1983-87; assoc. prof. dept. women's studies San Diego State U., 1987—; mem. adj. faculty Inst. for the Med. Humanities, U. Tex. Med. Br., 1987—; humanities rep. com. for the protection of human subjects San Diego State U., 1988—;. Author: Wash and Healed..., 1987; editorial cons. Tex. Medicine, 1985-87; mem. editorial bd. Med. Humanities Rev., 1986-87; contbr. articles to profl. jours. Vol. pet therapy program Moody State Sch., Galveston, Tex., 1985-86; off-campus interviewer undergrad. admissions Brown U., 1984-87, 88—; faculty advisor Varsity Women's Crew Team, San Diego State U., 1988—; umpire girl's softball Calif. Interscholastic Fedn. San Diego County; vol. Project Wildlife, San Diego, 1989—. Nat. Edowment for the Humanities grantee, 1984, Babe Didrikson Zaharias Meml. Found. grantee, 1986, San Diego State U. Found. grantee, 1988; Kennedy Inst. for Bioethics scholar Georgetown U., 1984, Calif. State U. scholar, 1989—. Mem. Am. Assn. for the History of Medicine, Nat. Women's Studies Assn., Coordinating Group for Women in the Hist. Profession, Western Assn. for Women's Historians, Soc. for Menstrual Cycle Rsch., Brown U. Alumni Assn., Phi Kappa Phi. Democrat. Jewish. Office: San Diego State U Dept Women's Studies San Diego CA 92182

CAYLOR, ANNE MARIE SARA, nurse, army officer, educator; b. Astoria, N.Y., Aug. 25, 1954; d. Harry and Marilyn Theresa (Berta) Sara; m. Nov. 14, 1981; m. Larry Edward Caylor; children: Jason Edward, Ryan Edward, Meghan Marie. BSN, U. Md., Balt., 1976; M Nursing, U. Colo., Denver, 1985. RN, Colo. Commd. 1st lt. U.S. Army, 1976, advanced through grades to maj., 1985; staff nurse Ft. Knox (Ky.) Army Hosp., 1976, head nurse acute respiratory disease ward, 1976-77; adult nurse practitioner Ft. Carson (Colo.) Army Hosp., 1978-83; head nurse, nurse practitioner internal medicine clinic DeWitt Army Hosp., Ft. Belvoir, Va., 1985-89; chief nurse U.S. Army Health Clinic The Pentagon, Washington, 1989—; assoc. clin. prof. nursing George Mason U., Fairfax, Va., 1988-89. Contbg. author: Nursing Care Plans, 1982. Founder, chpt. pres. Am. Diabetes Assn., Colorado Springs, Colo., 1981-84. Mem. Am. Nurses Assn. (cert. adult nurse practitioner), Uniformed Nurse Practitioner Assn., Am. Assn. Diabetes Educators, Sigma Theta Tau. Roman Catholic. Home: 6423 Battle Rock Dr Clifton VA 22024 Office: US Army Health Clinic The Pentagon Attn HSHL-WP Washington DC 20310-5806

CAYLOR, DEE JERLYN, apartment community manager; b. Calhoun, Ga., Dec. 22, 1942; d. George Herbert and Annie Mae (Shirley) Darnell; widowed; children: Mark Gerald, George Alexander, Gregory Wayne. Student, Am. Inst. Banking, 1961, Dalton Jr. Coll., 1979, Continual Learning Inst., Nashville, 1985. Asst. mgr. Holidy Inn, Calhoun, Ga., 1969-72; asst. gen. mgr. Gentry Inn, Nashville, 1973-74; resident mgr. Am. Homes, Nashville, 1975-77; office mgr. Liberty Carpets, Dalton, Ga., 1978-79; owner, operator Age Olde Traditions, Antiques, Calhoun, 1980-83; resident mgr. Allied Mgmt. Co., Nashville, 1984-85; acct. Vawter, Gammon, Norris & Collins, Nashville, 1986, Robert Half & Accountemps, Nashville, 1987-88; resident mgr. Carter Co., Nashville, 1989—. Exec. dir. spl. TV musical Tribute to Women in Country Music, 1990. Mem. Women of Music and Entertainment Network (founder, pres. 1988—), Nashville Apt. Assn. (community svc. com. 1990). Republican. Baptist.

CAZDEN, COURTNEY B(ORDEN), educator; b. Chgo., Nov. 30, 1925; d. John and Courtney (Letts) Borden; m. Norman Cazden (div. 1971); children: Elizabeth, Joanna. BA, Radcliffe Coll., 1946; MEd, U. Ill., 1953; EdD, Harvard U., 1965. Elem. tchr. pub. schs., N.Y., Conn., Calif., 1947-49, 54-61, 74-75; asst. prof. edn. Harvard U., Cambridge, Mass., 1965-68, assoc. prof., 1968-71, prof., 1971—; vis. prof. U. N.Mex. summer 1980, U. Alaska, Fairbanks, summer 1982, U. Auckland, N.Z., spring 1983, Bread Loaf Sch. of English, Vt., 1986—; chairperson bd. trustees Ctr. Applied Linguistics, Washington, 1981-85. Author: Child Language and Education, 1972, Classroom Discourse: The Language of Teaching and Learning, 1987; co-editor: Functions of Language in the Classroom, 1972, English Plus: Issues in Bilingual Education, 1990; editor: Language in Early Childhood Education, rev. edit., 1981. Trustee Highland Ednl. and Research Ctr., New Market, Tenn., 1982-84; bd. dirs. Feminist Press, Old Westbury, N.Y., 1982-84; clk. New Eng. regional office Am. Friends Svc. Com., Cambridge, 1989—. Recipient Alumna Recognition award Radcliffe Coll., 1988; fellow Ctr. Advanced Study in Behavioral Scis., Stanford, Calif., 1978-79; Fulbright research fellow, New Zealand, 1987. Mem. Coun. on Anthropology and Edn. (pres. 1981), Am. Ednl. Rsch. Assn. (exec. com. 1981-84, award for disting. contbns. to ednl. rsch. 1986), Am. Assn. Applied Linguistics (pres. 1985), Nat. Acad. Edn. Quaker. Office: Harvard U Grad Sch Edn Appian Way Cambridge MA 02138

CEASE, JANE HARDY, state senator; b. Columbus, Miss., Jan. 23, 1936; m. Ron Cease, 1960; children—Allison, Abigail. B.F.A., Tulane U. State rep. Oreg. Legislature, Salem, 1979-85, state senator, 1985—. Pres. Portland League Women Voters, 1971-73; chair Portland Area Women's Polit. Caucus, 1977-78, Met. Govts. Subcom. Local Govt. Com., Portland, 1979-83, Portland-Multnomah Commn. Aging Transp. Com., 1983-85; active Nat. Hwy. Safety Adv. Commn., 1980-83, Transp. and Communications Com. of Nat. Coun. State Legislatures, 1983-85, Oreg. Commn. Women, 1985-87, Portland Multnomah Commn. on Aging, 1983-87, Pacific States agreement on radioactive materials transp., 1987-89; chair revenue com. Oreg. Legislature, 1989. Democrat. Home: 2625 NE Hancock St Portland OR 07212 Office: State Capitol Salem OR 97310

CECIL, DORCAS ANN, property management executive; b. Greensboro, N.C., Mar. 31, 1945; d. George Joseph and Marianne Elizabeth (Zimmerman) Ernst; m. Richard Lee Cecil, June 8, 1968; children: Sarah, Matthew. BA, U. Ark., 1967. Pres. B & C Enterprises Property Mgmt., Ltd., O'Fallon, Ill., 1977—. Bd. dirs. O'Fallon Pub. Library, 1983—, v.p., 1986-87, pres., 1987—; sec. St. Vincent de Paul Soc., 1987—. Mem. Inst. Real Estate Mgmt. (cert., v.p. 1987, pres. St. Louis chpt. 1990—, ARM standards com.), Nat. Apt. Assn., St. Louis Multi-Housing Coun., Profl. Housing Mgmt. Assn., Community Assns. Inst., Nat. Assn. Realtors, Belleville Bd. Realtors (chmn. multi-family com. 1990—), O'Fallon C. of C. (bd. dirs. 1987—, v.p. 1988—), So. Ill. Network of Women. Democrat. Roman Catholic. Office: B & C Enterprises 807 W Hwy 50 PO Box 403 O'Fallon IL 62269

CECIL, PAULA BERNICE, writer, management consultant; b. Renwick, Iowa, July 14, 1927; d. Samuel Henry Klassie and Oneida Badgely; m. William J. Cecil, Mar. 27, 1954 (div. 1965); 1 child, Michelle E. BA, State U. Iowa, 1949; MA, U. Redlands, 1979. Systems support rep. IBM Corp., San Jose, Calif., 1965-71; customer support mgr. Trendata Corp., Sunnyvale, Calif., 1971-72; sales tng. analyst Xerox Corp., Rochester, N.Y., 1972-73; writer, cons. Automated Office Resources, Aptos, Calif., 1973—; tchr. San Mateo (Calif.) Sch. Dist., 1975-76, West Valley Coll., Saratoga, Calif., 1975-79, Hartnell Community Coll., Salinas, Calif., 1975-88; guest speaker office automation confs; tchr. Cabrillo Community Coll., Aptos, 1975-76, secretarial adv. com., med. asst. adv. com., 1975—; secretarial adv. com. Foothill Coll., Evergreen Coll. Author: (textbooks) Word Processing in the Modern Office, 1976, 2d ed., 1980, Management of Word Processing, 1980, Office Automation--Careers & Concepts, 1984; publisher, editor: The Observer, 1979—. Asst. campaign mgr. Candidate for Superior Judge, Los Gatos, Calif., 1980. Mem. Aptos C. of C., Calif. Writers' Club, Santa Cruz Symphony Orgn., Casserly Ladies Golf Club, Seascape Seagals (sec., handicap chairperson 1989-90). Republican. Methodist. Home: 812 Via Tornasol Aptos CA 95003

CEDARBAUM, MIRIAM GOLDMAN, federal judge; b. N.Y.C., Sept. 16, 1929; d. Louis Albert and Sarah (Shapiro) Goldman; m. Bernard Cedarbaum, Aug. 25, 1957; children: Daniel Goldman C., Jonathan Goldman C. BA, Barnard Coll., 1950; LLB, Columbia U., 1953. Bar: N.Y. 1954, U.S. Dist. Ct. (so. dist.) N.Y. 1956 U.S. Ct. Appeals (2d cir.) 1956, U.S. Ct. Claims 1958, U.S. Supreme Ct. 1958, U.S. Dist. Ct. (ea. dist.) N.Y. 1980, U.S. Ct. Appeals (5th and 11th cirs.) 1981. Law clk. to judge Edward Jordan Dimock U.S. Dist. Ct. (so. dist.) N.Y., 1953-54, asst. U.S. atty., 1954-57; atty. Dept. Justice, Washington, 1958-59; part-time cons. to law firms in litigation matters, 1959-62; 1st asst. counsel N.Y. State Moreland Act Commn., 1963-64; assoc. counsel Mus. Modern Art, N.Y.C., 1965-79; assoc. litigation dept. Davis, Polk & Wardwell, N.Y.C., 1979-83, sr. atty., 1983-86; acting justice Village of Scarsdale, N.Y., 1978-82, justice, 1982-86; judge U.S. Dist. Ct. (so. dist.) N.Y., 1986—; co-counsel Scarsdale Open Soc. Assn., 1969-86. Mem. adv. com. on labor rels. Scarsdale Bd. Edn., 1976-77; mem. Scarsdale Bd. Archtl. Rev., 1977-79. Mem. Am. Law Inst., ABA (chmn. com. on pictorial graphic sculptural and choreographic works 1979-81), N.Y. State Bar Assn. (chmn. com. on fed. legislation 1978-80), Assn. of Bar of City of N.Y. (com. on copyright and literary property, 1982-84, com. on the Bicentennial), Fed. Bar Coun., Copyright Soc. U.S.A. (trustee, mem. exec. com. 1979-82). Jewish. Office: US Dist Ct US Courthouse 40 Foley Sq New York NY 10007-1581

CEDERSTROM, CAROLE A., financial consultant, accountant; b. Chgo.; d. Philip Robert and Bernadette Cederstrom. BS in Acctg., U. Ill., 1979. CPA, Ill. From acct. to mgr. Arthur Andersen & Co., Chgo., 1977-83; pres., cons. Fin. Controllers, Inc., Chgo., 1983—. Mem. AICPA, Ill. CPAs, Profl. Womens Network, Nat. Assn. Women Bus. Owners. Office: Fin Controllers Inc 155 N Wacker Dr Ste 425 Chicago IL 60606

CEGAN, PATRICIA E., training consultant; b. Miami, Dec. 29, 1943; d. Orville Kenneth Best and Marjorie (McQuien) Jensen; divorced; 1 child, Melony LaRee. AA, Charter Oak State Coll., 1980. Mgr. sales tng. Knoll Pharm. Co., Whippany, N.J., 1972-84; v.p. Surg. Services & Supplies, Inc., Montville, N.J., 1984-85; owner Patricia E. Cegan & Assocs., Morristown, N.J., 1985—. Author sales tng. books; contbr. articles to profl. jours. Emergency med. technician Morristown Ambulance Squad. Mem. Nat. Assn. for Sales Tng. Execs., Nat. Soc. Pharm. Trainers (treas. 1982-83). Home and Office: 17 Edgewood Rd Morristown NJ 07960

CENCI, DEBORAH ANN, company executive; b. Hackensack, N.J., June 4, 1959; d. Armand and Dolors (Palma) C.; m. David Maroldi, Oct. 31, 1956. BA, Fairleigh Dickinson U., 1979. Supr. Hertz Corp., Parsippany, N.J., 1979-81; bus. analyst MDS, Inc., Maywood, N.J., 1981-84; systems cons. Am. Mgmt. Assn., N.Y.C., 1984-85; project leader Meldisco Corp., Mahwah, N.J., 1985-88; dir. Cenci Systems, Paramus, N.J., 1988—. Mem. NAFE (dir. 1983—), N.J. Career Connection (pres. 1983—), Nat. Assn. Accts. (pres. 1989—). Home: 431 Holly Ave Paramus NJ 07652 Office: Cenci Systems 431 Holly Ave Paramus NJ 07652

CEPIELIK, ELIZABETH LINDBERG, educator; b. Syracuse, N.Y., Sept. 18, 1941; d. Herman Elroy and Kathryn Emily (Karl) Lindberg; m. Michael A. Zemel, Apr. 22, 1967 (div. Jan. 1973); 1 child, Molly; m. Martin Joseph Cepielik, Mar. 10, 1973; children: Jeffrey, Kristina, Julie. AA, Stephens Coll., Columbia, Mo., 1961; BA, San Jose State Coll., 1963; postgrad., Calif. State U., L.A., 1963-67. Tchr. Humphreys Ave. Sch., L.A., 1963-71; math. specialist Non-Pub. Schs. Program, L.A., 1971-84; tchr. Sheridan Street Sch., L.A., 1984—; receptionist Weight Watchers, Arcadia, Calif., 1987—. Vol. Sta. KPCC, Pasadena, Calif., 1988—. Mem. DAR, Polish Nat. Alliance (sec. lodge 1980—, sec. coun. 73 1983—), Swedish Am. Cen. Assn. (auditor 1987—, asst. sec. 1990—), Stephens Coll. Alumnae Club (pres. Pasadena chpt. 1967-68), Skandia (auditor asst. sec. Pasadena lodge 1983—). Republican. Presbyterian. Home: PO Box 5925 Pasadena CA 91117-0925

CERAMICOLI, CAROL FRANCES, art director; b. Framingham, Mass., Feb. 17, 1960; d. Mario P. and Theresa L. (Peveri) C. BFA in design, L.I. U., Brookville, N.Y., 1982. Art dir. Studio Henri, Ltd., N.Y.C., 1982-89; pres. Carol C. Design Studio, Inc., N.Y.C., 1989—. Mem. Art Dir's. Club N.Y.C. (chairperson mem. com.), Big Apple Toastmasters. Office: Carol C Design Studio Inc 284 Fifth Ave New York NY 10001

CEREZO, CARMEN CONSUELO, judge; b. 1940. BA, U. P.R., 1963, LLB, 1966. Pvt. practice, 1966-67; law clk. U.S. Dist. Ct., San Juan, 1967-72; judge Superior Ct., P.R., 1972-76, Ct. Intermediate Appeals, 1976-80, U.S. Dist. Ct., P.R., 1980—. Office: PO & Courthouse Bldg Old San Juan Sta PO Box 3671 San Juan PR 00904*

CERINO, ANNE CATHERINE, marketing commuinications manager; b. Bridgeport, Conn., Nov. 22, 1954; d. Anthony Louis and Ann Mary (Cassidy) C. BS in Chemistry, Sacred Heart U., Fairfield, Conn., 1976. Chemist GE, Bridgeport, 1976-79; product specialist Perkin-Elmer, Norwalk, Conn., 1979-85; mktg. mgr. Perkin-Elmer, 1985-86, customer tng. mgr., 1986-87, product mgr., 1987-88, mktg. communications mgr., 1988—. Co-author: Analytical Chemistry Instrumentation, 1986. Pres. bd. dirs. Northridge Condo, Danbury, Conn., 1985; big sister Big Bros./Big Sisters, Danbury, 1982—. Mem. Am. Mktg. Assn., Internat. Exhibitors Assn. Republican. Roman Catholic. Office: Perkin Elmer Corp 761 Main Ave M/S 105 Norwalk CT 06859

CERRA, ROSEANNE, television and radio producer, writer; b. Detroit, Sept. 11, 1950; d. Frank and Catherine (Coschino) C. AA, Macomb Community Coll., Warren, Mich., 1971; BA, Wayne State U., Detroit, 1975. Reporter, announcer, producer Sta. WBRB, Mt. Clemens, Mich., 1972-75; reporter WEYI-TV, Clio, Mich., 1975; anchor, reporter WJRT-TV, Flint, Mich., 1976-78; reporter WDIV-TV, Detroit, 1979, WCAU-TV, Phila., 1980-86, WJBK-TV, Detroit, 1985-89; pres. Roseanne Cerra & Assocs., West Bloomfield, Mich., 1990—; cons. in field. producer, writer documentary Older Americans, 1983. Mem. Internat. TV Assn., AFTRA, Mich. Conservation Club, Archaeol. Inst. Am.

CERRONI, ROSE ELIZABETH, biology educator; b. Weirton, W.Va., Mar. 29, 1930; d. Lawrence R. and Elizabeth K. (Cardille) C. BS in Biology, Coll. of Steubenville, 1952; MA in Biology, Vanderbilt U., 1955, PhD, 1959. Predoctorate fellow USPHS, 1957-59; USPHS postdoctorate fellow Carlsberg Biol. Inst., Copenhagen, 1960-61; rsch. assoc. Temple U., 1961-62; assoc. prof. biology West Liberty State Coll., 1962-66; prof. biology, dir. med. tech. program Franciscan U. Steubenville (Ohio), 1966—; sci. instr. Wheeling Hosp. Sch. Nursing, summers 1952-53, 54-55. Recipient Alumni Svc. to Edn. award Alumni Assn. Franciscan U. Steubenville, 1989. Mem. Am. Inst. Biol. Sci., Sigma Xi (at-large mem.), Alpha Delta Pi (asst. treas. Wheeling Alumni chpt.). Roman Catholic. Office: Franciscan U Franciscan Way Steubenville OH 43952

CERTILMAN, MARTHA ANNE, university administrator; b. Chgo., Mar. 19, 1945; d. Ralph Garrison and Rose Etta (Blumberg) Schwartz; m. Barry A. Adelman (div. Sept. 1985); children: Todd, Lauren; m. Nardy Certilman, June 1990. BS with honors, U. Pa., 1967. Cert. tchr. Elem. sch. tchr. Ypsilanti (Mich.) Pub. Schs. and Rye (N.Y.) Pub. Schs., 1967-70; radio time buyer Robert Eastman & Co., N.Y.C., 1970-71; tchr. English and math. Simmons Sch. Vocat. Arts, White Plains, N.Y., 1983-84; substitute tchr. Scarsdale (N.Y.) Pub. Schs., 1979-84; regional editor Westchester Spotlight mag., Rye, N.Y., 1982-84; dir. spl. events N.Y. Med. Coll., Valhalla, 1985-89; dir. external affairs Poly. U., Hawthorne, N.Y., 1989—; chmn. Westchester secondary sch. com. U. Pa., 1982—. News editor, publicity chmn., program chmn., hospitality chmn. Greenacres PTA, Scarsdale, N.Y., 1976-81. Mem. LWV (dir. pub. rels. 1978-81), Women in Communications. Home: 40 Kingston Rd Scarsdale NY 10583 Office: Poly U 36 Sawmill River Rd Hawthorne NY 10532

CERVENY, KATHRYN M., educational administrator; b. Chgo., May 26, 1939; d. Roland John and Florence Anna (Cooke) Heidenfelder; children: Erick Joseph, Charles George. Student, Milw. Downer Coll. Distbr., county mgr. Vanda Beauty Counselors, Orlando, Fla.; sales assoc., adminstrv. asst. Resource Data Systems, Northbrook, Ill.; dept. asst. Northwestern U., Evanston, Ill.; pvt. piano tchr. Leadership trainer Boy Scouts Am. Recipient Silver Beaver award Boy Scouts Am. Mem. NAFE. Home: PO Box 1617 Evanston IL 60204

CESARIO, MARGARET KANNALY, nurse; b. Boston, Feb. 22, 1937; d. William James and Theresa Margaret (McTague) Kannaly; m. Philip C. Cesario, Mar. 29, 1964 (dec. 1984); children: Philip T., Kimberly T., Jennifer C. Diploma, Mt. Auburn Hosp. Sch. Nursing, 1957; BA, Emmanuel Coll., 1978; EdM, Harvard U., 1979. R.N., Mass.; cert. tchr., Mass. Clin. nurse St. Francis Hosp., Miami Beach, Fla., 1957-61, Mass. Gen. Hosp., Boston, 1961-80; assoc. prof. Aquinas Coll., Milton, Mass., 1980-88; psychiat. nurse Brockton (Mass.) VA Med. Ctr., 1988—; cons. Nursing Career Advance, Boston, 1980-84, Emmanuel Coll., Boston, 1981—. Contbr. articles to various publs. Mem. Mass. Health Educators Assn., New Eng. Coll. Health Assn., Am. Assn. Med. Assts., Mass. Nurses Assn., Phi Delta Kappa (pres. 1983-84), Harvard Club, South Shore Nurses Assn. Home: 43 McCusker Dr Apt #6 Braintree MA 02184 Office: VA Med Ctr 940 Belmont St Brockton MA 02401

CESINGER, JOAN, author; b. Oswego, N.Y., July 2, 1936; d. Guy Wesley and Gladys Matildia (Redlinger) Wagner; m. John Robert Cesinger, July 7, 1956; children: Michael, Richard, Steven. BA in Edn., Northwestern U., 1957. Asst. editor, feature writer Frontier Enterprise, Vernon Town Crier, Mundelein News, Lake Zurich, Ill., 1966-69; editor Lamp of Learning, Lake Zurich, 1967-68; mag. columnist Allen Raymond Inc., Darien, Conn., 1972-77; treas., office mgr., editor Dynamic Resources, La Verne, Calif., 1980—. Author: (with others) Games and Activites for Early Childhood Education, 1967, If I Were . . ., 1975, Kindling Patriotism with Challenging Activties, 1976, Fostering Spelling Achievement with Challenging Games, 1980, American Government: Puzzles, Games, and Individual Activities, 1982, World Cultures: Puzzles, Games, and Individual Activities, 1985, The Plant Kingdom, 1985, Earth and Its Surface, 1985, Air and Weather, 1985, Civics and Citizenship, 1986, World Geography: Puzzles, Games, and Individual Activities, 1985, World History: From the Fall of Rome to Modern Times, 1986, Let's Learn About Dinosaurs, 1987, Holiday Sparklers, 1988. Mem. World Future Soc., Brookfield West Garden (v.p. 1978-79), P.E.O., Kappa Kappa Gamma, P.E.O., San Vicente Country Club. Home and Office: 1200 Industrial Rd Boulder City NV 89005

CETERSKI, DOROTHY, nutritionist; b. Amsterdam, N.Y., Mar. 6, 1950; d. Victor and Esther (Curtis) C. BA, Bemidji State U., 1971; postgrad. in nursing, Hibbing Community Coll., 1978-79; BS, U. Minn., St. Paul, 1983; MS, N.D. State U., 1985. Sec. Marvin Windows, Warroad, Minn., 1971-72; asst. mgr. F.W. Woolworth Co., Dickinson, N.D., 1974-76; field ops. assoc. U.S. Dept. Commerce, Moorhead, Minn., 1980-81; heart researcher U. Minn., Moorhead, 1981-82; cons. nutritionist Fargo, N.D., 1985-88; nutritionist U.S. Peace Corps, Port Antonio, Jamaica, 1988—; mem. vol. adv. coun. Peace Corps, 1988—. County sec. Dem. Farm Labor Party, Moorehad, 1982-84. Baudette High Sch. PTA scholar, 1967. Mem. Jamaica Food and Nutrition Soc., Women in Devel., Ekkeslia. Democrat. Roman Catholic. Home: 3029 16th Ave S Moorhead MN 56560 Office: US Peace Corps, Port Antonio Jamaica

CEYER, SYLVIA, chemistry educator. Grad. summa cum laude, Hope Coll., Holland, Mich.; PhD, U. Calif., Berkeley. Postdoctoral fellow Nat. Bur. Standards; faculty mem. dept. chemistry MIT, Cambridge, Mass., 1981—, now asst. prof. Recipient Recognition award for young scholars AAUW Ednl. Found., 1988. Office: MIT Dept Chemistry Cambridge MA 02139*

CHABOT, GERRI LOUISE, counselor, nurse; b. Detroit, Oct. 2, 1949; d. Henry L. and Betty J. (Hale) Busuttil; m. Robert J. Chabot, Aug. 8, 1970 (div. Aug. 1975); 1 child, Michelle. AS in Arts and Nursing, L.A. Pierce Coll., 1980; B in Psychology cum laude, Calif. State U., Northridge, 1984; M in Counseling Psychology, Pepperdine U., 1986. RN, Calif. Nurse Valley Presbyn. Hosp./Nursery, Van Nuys, Calif., 1978-80; staff nurse Med. Ctr. of Tarzana, Calif., 1980-82; staff nurse renal and surg. units Holy Cross Hosp., Mission Hills, Calif., 1982-84, staff nurse chem. dependency unit, 1984-85, nurse clin. level III oncology dept., 1986—; owner, dir. Santa Clarita (Calif.) Counseling Ctr., 1989—; cons. Holy Cross Med. Ctr., 1988; lectr. in field. Henry Mayo Hosp. Community Health Edn. Com. fellow, 1989—. Fellow Calif. Assn. Marriage and Family Therapists. Roman Catholic. Home: 18142 W American Beauty Dr Apt 1061 Canyon Country CA 91351 Office: Santa Clarita Counseling Ctr 18333 W Dolan Way #206 Canyon County CA 91351

CHABY, DIANE BLOCK, public relations agency executive; b. N.Y.C., Oct. 2, 1935; d. Irving and Tillie Block; m. June 3, 1956 (div.); 1 child, Alan Seth. BA in English, N.Y. U., 1956, MA in English, 1968; postgrad. Yeshiva U., 1972-73, John Clarke Acad., London, 1973. Free-lance columnist Westwood (N.J.) News, 1961-63; tchr., cons., trainer N.Y.C. Bd. Edn., 1966-78; free-lance writer and publicist, 1978; publicist, media specialist Peter Rothholz Assos., N.Y.C., 1979, dir. media rels., 1979-81; account group supr. Van Vechten & Assocs., N.Y.C., 1981-82; founder pres. Chaby Communications, N.Y.C., 1982—; free-lance mag. writer, 1981—; condr. career change workshops; tchr. trainer, lab. mgmt. cons. Right To Read; mem. Right To Read Task Force; cons. ednl. systems. Mem. Women in Communications, Bus. and Profl. Women. Office: 6 Peter Cooper Rd New York NY 10010

CHADWELL, BARBARA SUE, director of prospect research; b. Ft. Bragg, N.C., Oct. 15, 1963; d. John Daniel and Mattie Ruth (Stoudenmire) C. BS, E. Carolina U., Greenville, 1985; MS, U. Ill., Urbana, 1988. Research asst. Appalachian State U., Boone, N.C., 1985-86, U. Ill., Urbana, Ill., 1986-88; dir. prospect research St. Andrews Presbyterian Coll., Laurinburg, N.C., 1988--. Mem. Am. Coun. on Consumer Interests, Am. Prospect Rsch. Assn. Office: St Andrews Presbyn 1700 Dogwood Mile Laurinburg NC 28352

CHADWELL, SUSIE, real estate broker; b. Jellico, Tenn., Aug. 26, 1940; d. Ross James and Irene (Jones) C.; m. Richard Rodriguez, May 30, 1957 (dec. Aug. 1965); children: Susan Denise, Richard. Student in bus., U. Tampa, 1965-67; student, Midland Tech. Coll., 1972-73, Hillsborough Community Coll., 1975-78, Tampa Coll., 1982-83. Ordained to ministry Universal Life Ch.; licensed real estate broker, mortgage broker. Clk. Chad Supply, Tampa, 1977-78, sec., 1978-79; salesperson real estate Chadwell Homes, Seffner, Fla., 1979-82, Thonotossassa, Fla., 1984—; salesperson condominiums Eastfield Slopes, Thonotossassa, 1982-84; pvt. practice mortgage and real estate brokerage Thonotossassa, 1985—; owner Susie Chadwell Assn., Tampa, 1989—; cons., tchr., speaker in field; broker assoc. ERA Joyce Reams Real Estate, Inc., 1990—; broker Chadwell Homes, 1990—; tchr. Mantic Arts. Mem. Wesley Women's Aux., 1957-74, Women's Aux. Phi Delta Kappa, 1967-69, Tampa Lyric Soc., 1967-69, YWCA Ednl. Group, 1971-74; charter mem. Tampa Bay Performing Arts Ctr., 1987—; patron Am. Cnacer So., 1989—. Mem. NAFE, Internat. Platform Assn., Brandon (Fla.) C. of C., Fla. Assn. Mortgage Brokers, Assn. for Rsch. and Enlightenment, 21st Century Women's Club, Gospel Music Assn., Beta Sigma Phi. Home: 9540 Field View Cir Thonotossassa FL 33592 Office: 9540 Field View Cir Thonotosassa FL 33592

CHADWICK, PAIGE PARRISH, marketing professional; b. Waco, Tex., June 1, 1960; d. William E. and Vivian Louis (Norton) Horne; m. Philip Russell Chadwick, Jan. 1, 1988. BS in Advt., U. Tex., 1981. Account exec. DBG&H, Dallas, 1983-85, The Richards Group, Dallas, 1985-86; mgr. advt. and pub. relations Omron Fin. Systems, Dallas, 1986-88; v.p. mktg. Internat. Banking Techs., Atlanta, 1988-90; v.p. Richards/Campbell, Dallas, 1990—. Vol. instr., cons. Jr. Achievement, Atlanta, 1989. Media Sales scholar U. Tex., Austin, 1981. Mem. Atlanta Ad Club, Fin. Instns. Mktg. Assn. Office: Richards/Campbell 7007 Twin Hills Ste 400 Dallas TX 75231

CHADWICK, SARA JANE HAWKS, teacher; b. Clarkedale, Ark., Sept. 14, 1942; d. Roy and Maggie Jane (Elliott) Hawks; m. Jimmy J. Chadwick, Mar. 16, 1967 (div. 1985); children: Dee Anne, Sarah Beth. BA in Bus. Edn., Harding U., Searcy, 1964; MEd, Univ. Ark., Little Rock, 1979. Tchr. Conroe Ind. Sch. Dist., Conroe, Tex., 1964-66, Lonoke Sch. Dist., Lonoke, Ark., 1966-67, Pulaski County Special Sch. Dist., Little Rock, Ark., 1968, UALR Gifted Programs, Little Rock, Ark. Mem. Pulaski Assn. of Classroom Tchrs., Ark. Edn. Assn., Nat. Edn. Assn., Assn. for Supervision Curriculum Devel., Phi Kappa Phi. Ch. of Christ. Home: 109 Tecumseh Trail Jacksonville AR 72076

CHAFEL, JUDITH ANN, educator; b. Rochester, N.Y., Apr. 8, 1945; d. James Arthur and Florence Joan (Santangelo) C. AB, Vassar Coll., 1967; MSEd, Wheelock Coll, 1971; PhD, U. Ill., 1979. Cert. elem. tchr., Mass., N.J., N.Y. Tchr. Spruce St. Sch., Lakewood, N.J., 1972-74, Sodus (N.Y.) Primary Sch., 1974-76; grad. research and teaching asst. U. Ill., Urbana, 1976-79; vis. asst. prof. U. Tex., Austin, 1979-80; asst. prof. dept. curriculum and instrn. Ind. U., Bloomington, 1980-86, assoc. prof., 1986—; reviewer Hist. Publs. and Records Commn., Nat. Archives, Washington, 1979, Little, Brown and Co., Boston, 1982—. Editorial adv. bd. Early Child Devel. and Care, 1985—, Early Childhood Rsch. Quar., 1988—; reviewer and contbr. numerous articles to profl. jours. Proffitt Endowment grantee, Ind. U., 1982, 88; Spencer Found. grantee for young scholars, 1985; Congl. Sci. fellow Soc. for Rsch. in Child Devel., 1989. Mem. Soc. Rsch. in Child Devel.(reviewer conf. proposals 1986), Am. Ednl. Research Assn. (reviewer various conf. proposals 1984, 86, 87, nominations com. 1986, 88), Nat. Assn. for Edn. Young Children (reviewer 1980—), Assn. Childhood Edn. Internat.(publ. com. 1982-84, bull. and pamphlets rev. editor jour., 1982-84, research com. 1984—).

CHAFFEE, SHEILA MARIE, legal secretary; b. Port Jefferson Station, N.Y., Nov. 2, 1966; d. John Roger and Barbara Anna (Grodski) Doscinski; m. Robert Edward Chaffee, Aug. 24, 1985. AAS in Secretarial Sci. w, Suffolk County Community Coll., 1985. Sec. Mac Albert Bank & Co., Riverhead, N.Y., 1982-85; sec. Brookhaven Nat. Lab., Upton, N.Y., 1985-87; legal sec. Blakeney, Alexander & Machen, Charlotte, N.C., 1987—. Recipient scholarship Twin Forks chpt. Profl. Secs. Internat., 1983, acad. scholarship Suffolk County Community Coll., 1983. Mem. Charlotte Legal Secs. Assn. (historian 1988-89, treas. 1989-90), Alpha Beta Gamma, Pi Alpha Sigma. Lutheran. Home: Rt 2 Box 153 Oakboro NC 28129 Office: Blakeney Alexander & Machen 3700 NCNB Plz Charlotte NC 28280

CHAFIN, LYDIA ESTEPP, educator; b. Williamson, W.Va., Apr. 27, 1956; d. Isaac B. and Ella Mae (Chafin) Estepp; m. Claude Simpkins Chafin. Assoc. gen. studies, So. W.Va. Community Coll., 1974; BS, Marshall U., Huntington, W.Va., 1976, MEd, 1980. Tchr. spl. edn. Mino Co. Bd. Edn., Williamson, 1976-77, Red Jacket (W.Va.) Elem. Sch., 1977-80; tchr. spl. edn. Matewan (W.Va.) Jr. High Sch., 1980-89, dean of students, 1989—. Sponsor Nat. Jr. Hon. Soc., Matewan, 1986—, Close-Up Found., 1986—. Mem. Matewan Woman's Club, W.Va. Fedn. Womens Clubs (2d v.p. 1983-84). Democrat. Baptist. Home: PO Box 104 Red Jacket WV 25692 Office: Magnolia High Sch PO Box 535 Matewan WV 25678

CHAFIN, SARA SUSAN, teacher; b. Huntington, W.Va., Mar. 24, 1952; d. William Albert and Margaret Irene (Stigall) C. BA, Coll. William and Mary, 1977. Tchr. The Woods Acad., Bethesda, Md., 1982-83; head tchr. Children's House Washington, 1983, The Vera Gander Montessori Sch., N.Y.C., 1984-85; adminstr., pres. The Manhattan Montessori Sch., 1985-88; tchr. St. Michael's Montessori Sch., N.Y.C., 1988-90, Children's House of Washington, 1990—; instr., speaker Internat. Montessori workshop, N.Y.C., 1986. Active N.Y.C. Friends and Advocates of Mentally Ill, 1985—, also newsletter, legis. coms. Mem. N. Am. Montessori Tchrs. Assn., Assn. Montessori Internat. (cert. adminstr.). Home and Office: 4923 Brandywine St NW Washington DC 20016

CHAGNON, LUCILLE TESSIER, career development and educational consultant; b. Gardner, Mass., June 1, 1936; d. Fred G. Tessier and Alfreda C. (Ross) Noel; m. Richard J. Chagnon, Sept. 16, 1978; children: Daniel, David. B.Mus., Rivier Coll., N.H.; M.Ed., Boston Coll., 1972. Edn. specialist, N.H., 1960-76; internat. cons. Inst. Cultural Affairs, Chgo., 1973-79; staff tng. dir. CO-MHAR, Inc., Phila., 1979-81; pres., owner Chagnon

Assocs., Collingswood, N.J., 1981—; prin. Sacred Heart Sch., 1986-87; founder, dir. Lifeline Literacy Project, Camden, N.J., 1988—; sr. project staff Right Assocs., Phila., 1982—; adj. grad. faculty dept. counseling psychology Temple U. Sch. Edn., Phila., 1985—. Author (with Richard J. Chagnon) The Best Is Yet to Be, 1985. Bd. dirs. Camden County Literacy Vols. of Am., 1987—, Handicapped Advocates for Ind. Living, 1988—; mem. Collingswood Bd. Edn., 1985-89. Mem. Internat. Reading Assn. Brain/Mind Network, Inst. Noetic Scis., Inst. Cultural Affairs, New Horizons for Learning, Earthstewards Network. Home and Office: 1 Courtland Ln Willingboro NJ 08046

CHAGNON, SANDRA TROMBLEY, surgical services administrator; b. St. Albans, Vt., Jan. 24, 1941; d. Harold Lawrence and Claire Catherine (Boyle) T.; m. Ronald Howard, Apr. 28, 1962 (dec. 1970); children: Stephen, Christopher. BA in Human Services Adminstrn., Trinity Coll., Burlington, Vt., 1982. Diploma Jeanne Mance Sch. Nursing. Staff nurse ob.-gyn. Kerbs Meml. Hosp., St Albans, Vt., 1961-63; staff nurse oper. rm. Kerbs Meml. UMC, St Albans, Vt., 1963-87; supr. surg. svc. N.W. Med. Ctr., St Albans, Vt., 1988—; Bd. Dirs. No. Vt. Chap. Assn. Operating Room Nurses Burlington Vt. 1975-77; Chmn. Employee Adv. Com. Northwestern Med. Center St Albans Vt. 1981-82, Wellness Com. Northwestern Med. Center St. Albans 1983--. Prog. dir., chmn. St. Albans City Recreation Com., 1976-81; bd. dirs. Vt. Childrne's Aid Soc., Inc., Burlington, Vt., 1984—; vol. St. Mary's Ch., St. Albans, 1985—, mem. adminstrv. council. Mem. AAUW (pres. Franklin County br.), Bus. and Profl. Women (chmn. young careerist com.), Assn. Operating Rm. Nurses, Vt. Home Extension Group (pres. m1986), Cath. Daus. Am. (treas. 1967-71). Democrat. Roman Catholic. Home: 3 Burnell Terr Saint Albans VT 05478

CHAIKIN, BONNIE PATRICIA, lawyer; b. N.Y.C., Apr. 4, 1953; d. Max and Paula (Blechman) Chaikin. Student Cornell U., 1970-73; B.A., Hofstra U., 1974; J.D., St. John's U., 1977. Law intern Queens Supreme Ct., 1977; admitted to N.Y. bar, 1978, Fla. bar, 1979, U.S. Customs Ct. bar, 1979, U.S. Tax Ct. bar, 1979, U.S. Dist. Ct. bar for Eastern and So. dists. N.Y., 1979, U.S. Ct. Customs and Patent Appeals bar, 1979, U.S. Supreme Ct., 1986; lic. real estate broker. Law asst. firm Weingold & Berman, N.Y.C., 1977-78; assoc. Dollinger, Gonski and Grossman, Carle Place, N.Y., 1978-79; mng. atty. firm Marsha Edelman, N.Y.C., 1979-80; individual practice law, Oceanside, N.Y., 1980—; dep. county atty. Nassau County, 1982—, dep. bur. chief, Mcpl. Affairs, 1986—; profl. fashion model Other Dimensions, N.Y.C., 1980-82. Bd. dirs., counsel South Shore Planning Council, 1982-85. Mem. Fla. Bar Assn., N.Y. State Bar Assn., Nassau County Bar Assn. (sec. immigration law com.), Nassau-Suffolk Womens Bar Assn., Am. Immigration Lawyers, ABA, N.Y. State Juvenile Officers Assn. Office: 1 West St Mineola NY 11572

CHALBERG-PLUNKETT, SHERRI LINELL, construction executive; b. Leavenworth, Kans., Mar. 10, 1960; d. Larry Allen and Esther Louise (Martin) C.; m. James Davidson Plunkett, Oct. 25, 1986. BSBA, William Jewell Coll., 1984; postgrad., Rockhurst Coll., 1985—. Personnel dir. Belger Cartage Service, Kansas City, Mo., 1984-86; v.p. Jim Plunkett, Inc., Kansas City, Kans., 1986—; chief exec. officer Wall Systems Corp., Kansas City, Kans., 1986—. Mem. Home Builders Assn., Assoc. Builders and Contractors, Nat. Assn. Women in Constrn. Republican. Mem. Unity Ch. Home: 13141 W 84th St Lenexa KS 66215 Office: Jim Plunkett Inc 1304 Argentine Kansas City KS 66105

CHALFEN, JUDITH RESNICK, volunteer; b. Boston, June 26, 1925; d. Abram and Rose (Pollen) Resnick; m. Melvin Harold Chalfen, Dec. 18, 1949; children: Robert Noah, Daniel, Andrew David. BA, Smith Coll., Northampton, Mass., 1947. Traffic/music libe Radio Sta. WOR, N.Y.C., 1947-49; announcer, editor Lowell Broadcasting Coun., WGBH-FM, Boston, 1950-52; co-founder, treas. Action for Childrens TV, Newton, Mass., 1968-74; co-founder, dir. Newton Arts Ctr, 1976-78; real estate broker Melvin Cline, Realtors, Newton Highlands, Mass., 1978-87. Co-founder, actress Everyman Theatre, 1959-61. Co-chmn. Cultural Affairs Commn., Newton, 1975-77; pres. Underwood Sch. PTA, Newton, 1963-64; mem. Ward 7 Dem. City Com., Newton, 1957-80; bd. govs. Newton Arts Ctr., 1978—. Mem. Mass. Bd. Realtors. Home: 30 Hyde Ave Newton MA 02158

CHALLIS, NORMA JEAN, educator; b. New Brighton, Pa., Oct. 23, 1934; d. Albert Orm and Elizabeth Freda (Handle) Franklin; m. George Ellery Douds, July 16, 1975 (dec. July 1982); m. Thomas Harold Challis, Mar. 10, 1984; 1 stepchild. BS, Maryville (Tenn.) Coll., 1956; MS, Pa. State U., University Park, 1968. Tchr. elem. edn. Highland Suburban Jointure, Beaver Falls, Pa., 1956-66, tchr. reading, 1966-73; reading specialist Blackhawk Sch. Dist., Beaver Falls, 1973-88; lectr. math. Geneva Coll., Beaver Falls, 1968-75; lectr. reading Community Coll. Beaver County, Monaca, Pa., 1975-77; gifted and talented elem. resource tutorial educator Blackhawk Sch. Dist., Beaver Falls, 1988—; guest lectr. Big Beaver Falls Sch. Dist., Highland Suburban, Beaver Falls, Beaver Valley Intermediate Unit, Monaca, Pattersen PTA, Beaver Falls. Bd. dirs. Greater Beaver Valley Cultural Alliance, 1990; deacon, elder 1st Presbyn. Ch. Beaver Falls. Mem. AAUW (sec. 1981), NEA, Pa. State Edn. Assn., Blackhawk Edn. Assn. (past pres.), Pa. Assn. Gifted Edn., Order Rainbow Girls (grand worthy assoc. advisor 1954), Delta Kappa Gamma (pres. 1982-83). Republican. Home: 1440 River Rd Beaver PA 15009 Office: Blackhawk Sch Dist 402 Shenango Rd Beaver Falls PA 15010

CHALOVICH, PAMELA SUE, rehabilitation administrator; b. Gary, Ind., July 7, 1954; d. John Charles and Dolores Jean (Ozelie) C. BA, St. Mary's Coll., 1976; MA, Loyola Marmount U., 1979. Counselor Clare Found., Los Angeles, 1977; customer service rep. Transam. Title, 1977-78; vocat. rehab. counselor Occupational Support Service, Van Nuys, Calif., 1980-85; vocat. reahb. counselor, gen. ptnr. New Opportunities, Los Angeles, 1985—. Mem. L.A. County Art Mus., L.A. Mus. Contemporary Art. Mem. Am. Psychol. Assn., Calif. Psychol. Assn., Nat. Rehab. Assn., Nat. Assn. Rehab. Profls. in Pvt. Sector, Internat. Platform Assn. Office: New Opportunities 12304 Santa Monica Blvd Los Angeles CA 90405

CHAMBERLAIN, BARBARA GREENE, editor, writer, book and newsletter producer; b. Lewiston, Idaho, Nov. 6, 1962; d. William Arthur and Gladys Marie (Humphrey) Greene; m. Dean Andrew Chamberlain, Sept. 13, 1986. BA in Linguistics and English cum laude, Wash. State U., 1984. Sec. Kelly Svcs., others, Spokane, 1984-86; office mgr. Futurepast: The History Co. and Melior Publs., Spokane, 1986-87, dir. mktg., 1987-88, v.p., 1988-89; owner PageWorks, Post Falls, Idaho, 1989—; vice chmn. bd. Eastern Wash. U. Young Writers Project, 1988-89. Author: North Idaho's Centennial, 1990; co-editor: Washington Songs and Lore, 1988. Mem. Idaho Pro-choice Network, Coeur d'Alene, 1989—; dir. mktg. No. Idaho Centennial Trail Com., Coeur d'Alene, 1989—; bd. dirs. Mus. North Idaho, Coeur d'Alene, 1990—; candidate for Idaho Ho. of Reps., 1990. Mem. Women in Communications Inc., Post Falls C. of C., Coeur d'Alene C. of C., Pacific N.W. Booksellers Assn., AAUW, Am. Mensa Ltd., Coun. for Dem. and Secular Humanism (assoc. charter), NOW, NARAL, Nat. Women's Polit. Caucus, Kappa Delta (alumnae editor). Democrat. Home: E 4555 Ohio Match Ave Post Falls ID 83854-9745

CHAMBERLAIN, BARBARA JEAN, registered nurse; b. Cambridge, May 15, 1949; d. Martin and Geraldine (Gonsalves) M.; m. Michael Hyman Goldberg, June 23, 1968 (dec. 1986); children: Caryn, Sheryl; m. Mark Munroe Chamberlain, Jan. 1, 1988. AAS, Gloucester County Coll., Sewell, N.J., 1981; BA, Glassboro (N.J.) State Coll., 1988, MA, 1989. Cert. in critical care nursing. RN Kennedy Meml. Hosp., Turnersville, N.J., 1981—; preceptor Kennedy Mem. Hosp., 1988; instr. nursing Gloucester County Coll., 1988-89. Mem. Am. Assn. Critical Care Nurses, N.J. State Nurses Assn. (com. mem.), Kappa Delta Pi. Democrat. Episcopalian.

CHAMBERLAIN, DIANE, psychotherapist, clinical social worker, author; b. Plainfield, N.J., Mar. 18, 1950; d. John and Anna Delores (Chamberlain) Lopresti; m. Richard David Chmielewski, Apr. 14, 1973. BSW, San Diego State U., 1975, MSW, 1978. Bd. cert. clin. social worker. Clin. social worker Social Advocates for Youth, San Diego, 1978-80; clin. social worker Sharp Meml. Hosp., San Diego, 1980-83, Children's Hosp. and Nat. Health Ctr., Washington, 1983-85; pvt. practice psychotherapy Alexandria, Va., 1985—. Author: (novels) Private Relations, 1989, Lovers and Strangers, 1990; contbr. nonfiction articles to profl. jours. Mem. Greater Washington Soc. for Clin. Social Workers, Romance Writers Am., Novelists Inc., Washington Romance Writers (bd. mem. 1989-90). Democrat. Office: 1707 Belleview Blvd Ste B-2 Alexandria VA 22307

CHAMBERLAIN, JILL FRANCES, financial services executive; b. Chgo., Mar. 25, 1954; d. Chester Emery and Mary Edythe (Hurd) C. B.A. in Math. with honors, Ill. State U., 1975; M.B.A., U. Chgo., 1981. Programmer Arthur Andersen, Chgo., 1975-76; cons. Laventhol & Horwath, Chgo., 1976-77; fin. systems analyst U. Chgo. Hosp., 1978-80; v.p. CHI/COR Info. Mgmt., Inc., Chgo., 1980-87; systems designer GECC, Stamford, 1987-88; mgr. GE Capital Corp., 1988—; cons. RMS Bus. Systems, Chgo., 1976-77. Mem. Delaware Valley Disaster Recovery Info. Exch. Group, NAFE. Libertarian. Methodist. Avocations: reading, traveling, needlework. Office: GE Capital 3003 Summer St Stamford CT 06927

CHAMBERLAIN, LINDA LEE, psychologist; b. Mpls., Dec. 7, 1951; d. Herbert Arthur and Eunice Josephine (Weisenberger) Welsh; m. Tyrone Alan Chamberlain, Aug. 7, 1976. BA, U. Tex., 1974; MS, Angelo State U., 1980; PsyD, U. Denver, 1989. Emergency svc. dir. S.W. Mental Health Ctr., San Angelo, Tex., 1977-82; program dir. Raleigh Hills Hosp., Dallas, Denver, 1983-86; program coord. Arapahoe House, Denver, 1986-88; intern Denver Gen. Hosp., 1988-89; psychol. asst. Nev. Psychol. Assn., Las Vegas, 1989—; pub. newsletter S.W. Region Psychologists for Social Responsibility, 1987—. Mem. Am. Psychol. Assn., Psychologists for Social Responsibility, Union of Concerned Scientists.

CHAMBERLAIN, THERESA NOWAK, recreational therapist; b. Newark, Oct. 17, 1947; d. William George Jr. and Rita Margaret (Rutherford) Nowak; m. Donald Pierre Chamberlain, July 2, 1983. AA, BS, So. Ill. U., 1977; MA, Nichols State U., 1987. Activity therapist Dwight (Ill.) Correctional Ctr.; recreation therapist Terrebonne Assn. for Retarded Citizens, Thobodauz, La.; adapted phys. edn. tchr. Terrebonne Parish Sch. Bd., Houma, La.; exec. dir. Bayou Area YMCA, Houma; presenter papers in field. Mem. La. Coun. on Child Abuse. Mem. Am. Bus. Women's Assn., Am. Assn. Counseling and Devel., Mental Health Assn. (treas.). Office: PO Box 2415 Houma LA 70361

CHAMBERLIN, CHRISTINE A., advertising agency executive. Former sr. v.p., now exec. v.p. and exec. creative dir. Ingalls, Quinn & Johnson, Boston. Office: Ingalls Quinn & Johnson 855 Boylston St Boston MA 02116*

CHAMBERLIN, ROSETTA E., savings and loan officer; b. Chgo., Aug. 6, 1945; d. Abraham W. and Anna (Paryl) Nelson; m. Laurence Russell Chamberlin, May 26, 1979; children: Lisa, Craig, Kerri, David, Daniel, Kevin, Marena. BA, No. Ill. U. Exec. v.p. Loves Park (Ill.) Fed. Savs. Bank, pres., chief exec. officer, COB; office mgr., asst. sec. Home Fed. Savs. and Loan, Rockford, Ill. Pres. elect Greater Parks Kiwanis Club. Recipient Leadership award YMCA, 1984, 85. Mem. Rockford C. of C., Rockford Home Builders Assn., Loves Park C. of C., NAFE, Fin. Mgrs. Assn., Rockford Bd. Realtors (Saleswoman of Yr.), Million Dollar Club (Old Pen award). Republican. Lutheran. Home: 2238 Dior Dr Rockford IL 61107-1779

CHAMBERLIN, TERRY MCBRIDE, sailmaking company executive; b. San Juan, P.R., Sept. 26; d. Robert Joseph and Sarah J. McBride; m. Donald L. Chamberlin, 1961; children: Karen Leslie, Jeffrey D. BA, Fla. State U., 1961; postgrad., U. So. Fla., 1983. Cert. secondary sch. tchr., Fla. Tchr. Pinellas County Schs., Clearwater, Fla., 1965-81; salesperson Hood Sailmakers, Inc., St. Petersburg, Fla., 1981-85, gen. mgr., 1985—. Chmn. Fla. Edn. Conf., Safety Harbor, 1978; coordinator Campaign to Elect State Senator, Pinellas County, Fla. 1976-80. Mem. Leadership Pinellas (charter mem.), Jr. League of Clearwater (exec. com., corr. sec. 1980), St. Petersburg C. of C. Democrat. Unitarian Universalist. Office: Hood Sailmkers Inc 107 15th Ave SE Saint Petersburg FL 33701

CHAMBERS, IMA LOUISE, secretarial skills educator, secretary; b. Ft. Worth, July 30, 1932; d. Thurman and Pearl (Linehan) Tyson; m. Billy Joe Chambers, Aug. 22, 1954; children: Joseph, Marc, Carol. BS, Tex. Wesleyan Coll., 1953; MEd, U. Mich., 1980. Cert. secondary, vocat. tchr., Mich., Tex., Wis. Travel counselor Am. Automobile Assn., Ft. Worth, 1949-55; stenographer Calif. Dept. Health, Berkeley, 1955-56; elem. tchr. Decoto (Calif.) Pub. Schs., 1956-58; shorthand tchr. Genoa Sch. Dist., Clay Ctr., Ohio, 1964-65; bus. tchr. New Miami High Sch., Hamilton, Ohio, 1966-73, Genesee Area Vocat. Sch., Flint, Mich., 1974-81, Cisco (Tex.) High Sch., 1985-88; sec. Pan Am. Oil Corp., Ft. Worth, 1958-60, Kelly Temp. Svcs., Inc., Milw., 1988—. pastor's wife, ch. tchr. So. Bapt. Ch., Tex., Calif., Ohio, Mich., Minn., Wis., 1956—. Mem. NEA, AAUW (pres. 1988-89), Delta Kappa Gamma, Alpha Chi. Home: 9333 W Congress St Milwaukee WI 53225

CHAMBERS, IMOGENE KLUTTS, school administrator, financial consultant; b. Paden, Okla., Aug. 6, 1928; d. Odes and Lillie (Southard) Klutts; B.A., East Central State U., 1948; M.S., Okla. State U., 1974, Ed.D., 1980; m. Richard Lee Chambers, May 27, 1949. High sch. math. tchr. Marlow (Okla.) Sch. Dist., 1948-49; with Bartlesville (Okla.) Sch. Dist., 1950—, asst. supt. bus. affairs, treas. Ind. Sch. Dist. 30, 1977-87, treas., 1985—; fin. acctg. cons. Okla. State Dept. Edn., 1987—; dir. Plaza Nat. Bank. Bd. dirs. Mutual Girls Club, 1981—. Mem. Am. Assn. Sch. Adminstrs., Okla. Assn. Sch. Bus. Ofcls., Assn. Sch. Bus. Ofcls. Internat., Okla. Assn. Sch. Adminstrs., Okla. State U. Alumni Assn., Rotary, Phi Delta Kappa. Democrat. Methodist. Home: 911 Greystone Place Bartlesville OK 74006 Office: Bartlesville Ind Sch Dist 301100 S Jennings St Bartlesville OK 74005

CHAMBERS, JANET HALDEMAN, lawyer; b. Vancouver, B.C., Can., Oct. 25, 1962; d. Lloyd Herbert and Jeanene (Millard) Haldeman; m. Jeffrey W. Chambers, Apr. 24, 1988. BS in Fgn. Svc. cum laude, Georgetown U., 1984; JD with honors, U. Tex., 1987. Bar: Tex. 1988. Assoc. Baker & Botts, Houston, 1988—. Interviewer, Georgetown Alumni Admissions Program, 1987—. Mem. ABA (internat. sect., customs com., air and space com.), State Bar Tex. (internat. sect.), Houston Young Lawyers Assn. (hunger relief com.), The Houstonian Club, Houston World Trade Assn. Republican. Episcopalian. Office: Baker & Botts 3000 One Shell Plaza Houston TX 77002

CHAMBERS, JOAN LOUISE, university library director; b. Denver, Mar. 22, 1937; d. Joseph Harvey and Clara Elizabeth (Carleton) Baker; m. Donald Ray Chambers, Aug. 17, 1958. B.A. in English Lit., U. No. Colo., Greeley, 1958; M.S. in Library Sci., U. Calif.-Berkeley, 1970; M.S. in Systems Mgmt., U. So. Calif., 1985. Librarian U. Nev., Reno, 1970-79; asst. univ. librarian U. Calif., San Diego, 1979-81; univ. librarian U. Calif., Riverside, 1981-85; dir. libraries Colo. State U., 1985—; mgmt. intern Duke U. Library, Durham, N.C., 1978-79; sr. fellow UCLA, summer 1982; cons. tng. program Assn. of Research Libraries, Washington, 1981; library cons. Calif. State U., Sacramento, 1982-83, U. Wyo., 1985-86. Contbr. articles to profl. jours., chpts. to books. U. Calif. instl. improvement grantee, 1980-81; State of Nev. grantee, 1976, ARL grantee, 1983-84. Mem. ALA, Assn. Coll. and Research Libraries (com. mem. and chmn.), Library Adminstrn. and Mgmt. Assn., Library Info. Tech. Assn., Resources and Tech. Services Assn., Reference and Adult Services Assn., Colo. Library Assn., Internat. Assn. Fin. Planners, United Way, Beta Phi Mu, Phi Lambda Theta, Kappa Delta Phi. Clubs: Sierra, Audubon Soc., Colo. Mountain. Home: 4470 S Lemay #1305 Fort Collins CO 80525 Office: Colo State U Librs Fort Collins CO 80523

CHAMBERS, KAREN JEAN, manufacturing executive; b. Delta, Colo., Nov. 18, 1946; d. Adolf Edward Patterson and Juanita Ann (Pfiel) Mumford; d. Robert LeRoy Chambers, Sept. 4, 1963; children: Ricky Allen, Russell LeRoy. AA in Bus. Mgmt., LaSalle U., 1980. Various factory jobs Samsonite Corp., Denver, 1965-68, teleprocessing oper., 1968-71; dep. sheriff Adams County Sheriff's Dept., Brighton, Colo., 1971-73; analyst computer Samsonite Corp., Denver, 1974-77, analyst finished goods, 1977-79, supr. analysts, 1979-83, supr. analysts scrap depts., 1983-85, supr. inventory control, 1985—; cons. Micro Design Engring., Niwot, Colo., 1980. Mem. Boy Scouts Am., Erie, Colo., 1984—. Mem. Nat. Assn. Female Exec. Republican. Baptist. Office: Samsonite Corp 11200 E 45th Denver CO 80239

CHAMBERS, LESLIE ANN, car rental company executive; b. Rochester, N.Y., May 9, 1963; d. John R. Jr. and Eleanor Gail (Collins) C.; m. Thomas Edward Sciolino; 1 child, Brittany Lee. AS, Monroe Community Coll., Rochester, 1984; student, Boston U., 1985-86. V.p. Dollar Rent a Car, Rochester, 1980—. Mem. N.Y. State Rental Vehicle Assn. (lobbyist 1989—). Republican. Home: 407 Pebbleview Dr Rochester NY 14612 Office: Dollar Rent a Car 1190 Brooks Ave Rochester NY 14624

CHAMBERS, LINDA DIANNE THOMPSON, social worker; b. Mexia, Tex., Apr. 21, 1953; d. Lee and Essie Mae (Hopes) Thompson; m. George Edward Chambers, Nov. 30, 1978; 1 child, Brandon. AS cum laude, Navarro Coll., Tex., 1974; B in Social Work magna cum laude, Tex. Woman's U., 1976; cert. gerontology and Human Svcs. Mgmt., Sam Houston U., 1982; M in Social Work, U. Tex.-Arlington, 1990. Mem. social work staff Dept. Human Resources, Ft. Worth, Tex., 1975, Children's Med. Ctr., Dallas, 1976, Mexia State Sch., Tex., 1976—. Pres., Raven Exquisites, Mexia, 1983-84, sec.-treas., 1984-85; mem. Tex. Hist. Found., Nat. Mus. Women in Arts, 1985—. Recipient numerous awards for scholarship and profl. excellence. Fellow Internat. Biog. Assn. (dep. bd. gov., life); mem. Am. Sociol. Soc. (sec. 1975-76), Univ. Woman's Assn., Am. Childhood Edn. Internat., Nat. Assn. Social Workers, NAFE, Am. Assn. Mental Deficiency, Nat. Assn. Future Women, Am. Soc. Profl. and Exec. Women, Nat. Assn. Negro Bus. and Profl. Women's Clubs, AAUW, Tex. Woman's U. Nat. Alumnae Assn., Mortar Bd. Honor Soc. (sec.-treas. 1975-76), Tex. Soc. Clin. Social Workers, Internat. Platform Assn., Internat. Assn. Bus. and Profl. Women, Tex. Assn. Clin. Social Workers, Am. Biog. Assn. (dep. bd. govs.), Nat. Mus. Women Arts, Los Amigos, Phi Theta Kappa, Alpha Kappa Delta, Alpha Delta Mu, Young Dems. Club. Avocations: reading, gardening, gourmet cooking. Home: 102 Hardin Mexia TX 76667

CHAMBERS, LOIS IRENE, insurance agency executive; b. Omaha, Nov. 24, 1935; d. Edward J. and Evelyn B. (Davidson) Morrison; m. Peter A. Mscichowski, Aug. 16, 1952 (div. 1980); 1 child, Peter Edward; m. Frederick G. Chambers, Apr. 17, 1981. Clk. Gross-Wilson Ins. Agy., Portland, Oreg., 1955-57; sec., bookkeeper Reed-Paulsen Ins. Agy., Portland, 1957-58; office mgr., asst. sec., agt. Don Biggs & Assocs., Vancouver, Wash., 1958-88, v.p. ops., 1988—, automation mgr., 1989—; automation cons. Chambers & Assocs., Tualatin, Oreg., 1985—; chmn. adv. com. Clark Community Coll., Vancouver, 1979—. Mem. citizens com. task force City of Vancouver, 1976-78, mem. Block Grant rev. task force, 1978—. Mem. Ins. Women of S.W. Wash. (pres. 1978, Ins. Woman of Yr. 1979), Nat. Assn. Ins. Women, Nat. Users Agena Systems (charter; pres. 1987-88), Soroptimist Internat. (Vancouver)(pres. 1978-79, Soroptimist of the Year 1979-80, charter pres. 1987—). Democrat. Roman Catholic. Office: Don Biggs & Assocs 916 Main St PO Box 189 Vancouver WA 98666-0189

CHAMBERS, MERLE CATHERINE, oil and gas and transportation company executive; b. Chgo., Dec. 1, 1946; d. Jerry Gamble and Evelyn Macdonald (Hemmings) C.; m. W. Alexander Klikoff, Mar. 12, 1977 (div. 1986); m. Hugh A. Grant, Feb. 6, 1989. BA, U. Calif., Berkeley, 1968; JD, U. Calif., San Francisco, 1977; LLM, U. Denver, 1984. Bar: Calif. 1977, Colo. 1978. Assoc. Weller, Friedrich, Hickisch & Hazlitt, Denver, 1978-80; exec. v.p. Axem Resources Inc., Denver, 1980-86, pres., chief exec. officer, 1986—; chmn. exec. com. Clipper Exxpress Co., Lemont, Ill., 1987—. Mem. Cherry Hills Village (Colo.) City Coun., 1982—; bd. dirs. 1066 Found., Hastings Coll. Law, U. Calif., San Francisco, 1984—, U. Calif.-Berkeley Found., 1986—; bd. dirs., v.p. devel. Women's Found. Colo., Denver, 1987—. Mem. ABA, Colo. Bar Assn., Calif. Bar Assn., Colo. Women's Bar Assn. Office: Axem Resources Inc 7800 E Union Ave Ste 1100 Denver CO 80237

CHAMIS, ALICE YANOSKO, information management consultant; b. Arvida, Quebec, Can.; d. Andy and Anna (Michalcik) Yanosko; m. Christos C. Chamis; children: Chrysanthie Diane, Anna Lisa, Constantinos Andy. BS, McGill U., Montreal, Can., 1959; M.S.L.S., Case Western Res. U., 1962, PhD, 1984. Lit. chemist Alcan, Arvida, 1959-61; libr. mgr. B.F. Goodrich Co., Brecksville, Ohio, 1962-69; asst. dir. Cuyahoga County Pub. Libr., Cleve., 1970-80; project mgr. Case Western Res. U., Cleve., 1985-86; asst. prof. Kent State U., Kent, Ohio, 1986-88; cons. Info. Mgmt. Consultants, Westlake, Ohio, 1980—. Office: Info Mgmt Consultants 24534 Framingham Dr Westlake OH 44145

CHAMPAGNE, ANDRÉE, member Canadian House of Commons; b. 1939. Ed. Inst. Notre-Dame de Lorette, Saint-Hyacinthe. Active for 28 yrs. in communications, including radio, TV, theatre and film in prodn. and distbn., writing and pub. rels. positions; Mem. Ho. of Commons from Saint-Hyacinthe-Bagot, Que., 1984—; minister Ministry of State for Youth, 1984-86, mem. Privy Coun., 1984—; sec. gen. Union des artistes, 1983-84; pres. Chez-nous des artistes, 1983-84; del. Internat. Fedn. Actors Conf., Moscow, 1984. Mem. Institut quebecois du cinema (bd. dirs.). Progressive Conservative. Office: House of Commons, N Centre Block Rm 526, Ottawa, ON Canada K1A 0A6*

CHAMPAGNE, BETTY JUNE, computer analyst, writer; b. Winnsboro, La., June 20, 1949; d. James Levi and June Amanda (Hawthorne) Mahoney; m. Peter Gerald Renz, Apr. 19, 1969 (div. 1977); children: Curtis Alan Renz, Randall Scot Renz; m. Michael Joseph Champagne, Feb. 9, 1979 (dec. 1982). BA in Psychology, N.E. La. U., 1979. Sales, mktg. adminstr. GE Info. Svcs. Co., San Antonio, 1980-82; word processing, documentation specialist, desktop pub. Conoco Inc., Houston, 1982-84; sr. tech. analyst software Transco Energy Co., Houston, 1984-87, documentation and human factors cons., 1986—; exec. reporting tech. publs. mgr. Legent Corp., Vienna, Va., 1987-90; lead tech. writer Landmark Systems Corp., Vienna, 1990—. Vol. Am. Heart Assn., Houston, 1985, 87, Pvt. Sectors Initiative, Houston, 1987, March of Dimes Team Walk, Houston, 1985, 87. Mem. NAFE, Am. Soc. Indexers, Soc. Tech. Communication (judge 1985), Women in Communication, Women's Profl. Assn., ACM. Republican. Lutheran. Home: 129 Summit Hall Rd Gaithersburg MD 20877 Office: Landmark Systems Corp 8000 Towers Crescent Dr Vienna VA 22182-2700

CHAMPAGNE, GAYLE LYNN, advertising executive; b. Detroit, Jan. 24, 1950; d. John Richard and Mary Jeneroux (Howard) C. BS, Western Mich. U., 1971; postgrad., U. Mich., 1973. Tchr. Bur. Indian Affairs, Shonto, Ariz., 1973-76; owner Etcetera Gift Shop, Pinedale, Wyo., 1976-79; sales rep. Cummins Pub., Troy, Mich., 1979-80, Hunter Pub., Des Plaines, Ill., 1979-82, Penthouse Internat., N.Y.C., 1982-84; mgr. Fox Assocs., Detroit, 1984-86; account mgr. U.S. News and World Report, Washington D.C., 1986-88; v.p., dir. advt. sales Aegis Group div. Lintas/Ceco Communications, Troy, 1988-90; mgr. regional sales Travel & Leisure mag., Am. Express Pub., N.Y.C., 1990—. Vol. Mich. Cancer Found., 1979—, Van Patrick Meml. Found., 1986. Mem. Bus. and Profl. Advt. Assn., Detroit Mag. Reps. Assn., Mag. Pubs. Assn., Adcraft Club Detroit, Cleve. Advt. Club, Western Mich. Alumni Assn., U. Mich. Alumni Assn., U.S. Masters Swimmers. Republican. Presbyterian. Office: 401 S Woodward Ste 342 Birmingham MI 48009

CHAMPION, DEBBIE SLOVAK, accountant; b. Dallas, Feb. 11, 1956; d. Walter Louis and Hedy Ann (Zmolik) Slovak; m. Dale B. Champion, Oct. 11, 1986. BBA, So. Meth. U., 1978. CPA, Tex. Sec. Mercantile Nat. Bank, Dallas, 1975-78, trust acct., 1978-80, sr. staff acct., 1980-82; asst. cashier InterFirst Bank Park Cities, Dallas, 1982-85, asst. v.p., 1985-86; chief acct. City of Farmers Branch, Tex., 1987, 88—, acting dir. fin., 1987-88, chief acct., 1988—. Mem. NAFE, Internat. Tng. in Communication (v.p. 1989-90), Am. Bus. Womens Assn. (audit chmn. met. chpt. 1990-91, Woman of Yr., program co-chmn. Dallas area coun. 1988—, treas. nat. conv. 1990), Govt. Fin. Officers Assn., Tex. Soc. CPAs, Mcpl. Treas.'s Assn. Office: City of Farmers Br 13000 William Dodson Pkwy Farmers Branch TX 75234

CHAMPION, MAXINE CHRISTINA, lawyer, business executive; b. N.Y.C.; d. Max and Mini (Ravashiere) Sokol; 1 child, Christina Anne. BA, Pa. State U., 1967; postgrad., U. Wis., 1970; JD, Am. U., 1977. Bar: Pa. 1977, U.S. Ct. Appeals (D.C. cir.) 1977, U.S. Tax Ct. 1977, U.S. Ct. Appeals (fed. cir.) 1978, U.S. Ct. Claims 1978, U.S. Supreme Ct. 1978. Devel. specialist IRS, Washington, 1973-76; atty./advisor to chief judge U.S. Tax

Ct., Washington, 1976-78; trial atty. tax div. Dept. Justice, Washington, 1978-84; tax counsel Ways and Means Com. Ho. Reps., Washington, 1984-88; v.p. LTV Corp., Washington, 1988—; mem. Tax Coalition, Washington, 1984—, chair bd. 1986-89; commr. adv. group Internal Revenue, 1985-89. EEC fellow, 1983. Mem. ABA (tax. and corp. sects. 1977—, editor ann. report 1980), Fed. Bar Assn. (officer 1990—), Capitol Forum. Office: LTV Corp 1025 Thomas Jefferson St NW Ste 511 Washington DC 20007

CHAMPLIN, ELIZABETH ELLEN, international financial markets executive; b. Washington, July 24, 1962; d. William Alfred and Alice Ethel (Parlette) C.; m. David Michael Geske, May 17, 1986. BA, Barnard Coll., 1985; M Internat. Affairs, Columbia U., 1987. Grad. fellow Bus. Execs. for Nat. Security, Washington, 1986; rsch. analyst, mktg. asst. Sci. Applications Internat. Corp., McLean, Va., 1987-88; sr. program mgr., assoc. dir. internat. markets Instnl. Investor, N.Y.C., 1988—. Contbg. author: Frommer's Travel Guide to Eastern Europe, 1986, Black Box: KAL 007 and the Superpowers. Democrat. Episcopalian. Office: Instnl Investor 488 Madison Ave New York NY 10022

CHAMPLIN, GRETA VIRGINIA, education educator; b. Mobile, Ala., Jan. 14, 1947; d. Edward Earl and Wilhelmina X. (Kamphuis) C. MusB, U. Ala., 1974, BME, 1976, postgrad., 1977. Elem. music specialist from Huntsville (Ala.) City Schools to string specialist, 1976-83; secretarial Engring. Firms, Huntsville, Ala., 1983-85; string specialist U. of N. Ala., Florence, Ala., 1985-89; string instr. Huntsville Symphony Orch., Huntsville, Ala.; prin. cellist Schs. Symphony Orch., Florence, Ala., 1985-86; mgr. dir. Huntsville Youth Orchestras, 1986—, conductor Concert and Beginning Strings Orch., Hunstville, 1979—. Mem. AL Orch. Assn., Music Educator Nat. Conf., Huntsville Edn. Assn. Episcopalian. Home: 206 Walker Ave Huntsville AL 35801 Office: Huntsville Youth Orch 206 Walker Ave PO Box 7223 Huntsville AL 35807

CHAMPLIN, MARJORIE WEEDEN, retired educator, writer; b. Newport, R.I., Mar. 26, 1921; d. Lawrence Weeden and Ena (Eddy) C. BA in English, Wheaton Coll., Norton, Mass., 1943; MA in Classics, Brown U., 1959; postgrad., Harvard U., 1961, 65, 67; MA in English, U. R.I., 1974. Cryptographer Signal Corps U.S. Army, Arlington, Va., 1943-45; reporter, copy girl, sec. Washington Post, 1945-46; monitor Christian Sci. Monitor, Boston, 1946-49; tchr. English Cranston (R.I.) High Sch., 1958-59; tchr. Latin and French North Kingston (R.I.) High Sch., 1960-70, debating coach, 1965-70, drama coach, 1968-69. Writer nat. leader in congress. Mem. AAUW, Conn. Island Art Assn. Home: 15 Priscilla Rd Jamestown RI 02835

CHAMSON, SANDRA POTKORONY, psychologist; b. N.Y.C., Nov. 6, 1933; d. Daniel and Rose (Sukenik) Potkorony; m. Allan Chamson, Dec. 25, 1954 (div. 1978); children—Eugene, Amy. B.A. in Psychology, NYU, 1955; M.S. in Sch. Psychology, CCNY, 1957; Ph.D. in Psychology, Fla. Inst. Tech., Melbourne, 1983. Lic. psychologist, N.Y., clin. psychologist, N.Y. Psychologist, Anne Arundel County Schs., Anapolis, Md., 1957-58, Bur. Child Guidance, N.Y.C., 1960-64, Region VI Dist., Bergen County, N.J., 1965-84; sole practice, N.Y.C., 1985—; psychol. cons. Ramaz Sch., N.Y.C., 1974-81. Mem. Am. Psychol. Assn., N.Y. Acad. Sci., Am. Orthopsychiat. Assn. Address: Apt 18-D 200 W 86th St New York NY 10024

CHAN, ELIZA Y., public relations executive, radio and television producer. BA in Journalism and Ethnic Studies, U. Calif., Berkeley, 1977. Reporter/intern Pasadena (Calif.) City Star News, 1974; reporter East/West Jour., San Francisco, 1975-77, Chinese Times, San Francisco, 1977-79; media dir. Chinese for Affirmative Action, San Francisco, 1979-82; pub. rels. dir. San Francisco Bay coun. Girl Scouts U.S., 1982-89; dir. info. and pub. affairs Bay Area Regional Earthquake Preparedness Project, Oakland, 1989—. Bd. dirs. Friends of the Human Rights Commn., San Francisco, 1989—, Asian Women United in Calif., San Francisco, 1990. Recipient Outstanding Svc. award United Way of the Bay Area, 1988, City Focus Prog. fellowship CORO Found., 1989-90. Mem. Am. Women in Radio and TV (v.p. 1990), Women in Communications, Inc. (v.p. 1986-87), Asian-Am. Journalists Assn., Toastmasters Internat. (CTM award 1990), Phi Beta Kappa. Office: Bay Area Regional Earthquake Preparedness 101 8th St Ste 152 Oakland CA 94607

CHAN, SALLY WINGCHONG, physical therapist; b. Hong Kong, Nov. 26, 1962; came to U.S., 1968; d. Bruce Chiu-Lap and Shau King (Lai) C. BS in Kinesiology, UCLA, 1984; MS in Phys. Therapy, U. So. Calif., 1986. Phys. therapist San Gabriel (Calif.) Valley Med. Ctr., 1986-88; outpatient phys. therapist UCLA, 1988—; rsch. asst. Chesapeake Biol. Labs., Balt., 1988—. Contbr. articles to profl. jours. Mem. Am. Phys. Therapy Assn. Republican. Home: 357 S Del Loma Ave San Gabriel CA 91776 Office: UCLA A-7-62 Rehab Ctr 1000 Veteran Ave Los Angeles CA 90024

CHAN, SIU, registered nurse; b. Hong Kong, July 27, 1962; came to U.S., 1962; d. Gee Tong and Siu King (Lee) C.; m. Chung Kong, Sept. 28, 1987. BSN, Hunter Coll., 1984. RN, N.Y.; cert. med. surg. nurse. Staff nurse Meth. Hosp., Bklyn., 1984-87, asst. nursing care coord., 1987-88, coord., 1988—. Hunter Coll. scholars award, 1980-83. Mem. Am. Nurses Assn., N.Y. State Nurses Assn. Office: Meth Hosp 506 6th St Brooklyn NY 11215

CHANDLER, ALICE, university president, educator; b. Bklyn., May 29, 1931; d. Samuel and Jenny (Meller) Kogan; m. Horace Chandler, June 10, 1954; children: Seth, Donald. A.B., Barnard Coll., 1951; M.A., Columbia U., 1953, Ph.D., 1960. Instr. Skidmore Coll., 1953-54; lectr. Barnard Coll., 1954-55, Hunter Coll., 1956-57; from instr. to prof. CCNY, 1961-76, v.p. instl. advancement, 1974-76, v.p. acad. affairs, 1974-76, provost, 1976-79, acting pres., 1979-80; pres. SUNY, New Paltz, 1980—; bd. dirs. Revson Found., 1979. Author: The Prose Spectrum: A Rhetoric and Reader, 1968, The Theme of War, 1969, A Dream of Order, 1970, The Rationale of Rhetoric, 1970, The Rationale of the Essay, 1971, From Smollett to James, 1980, Foreign Student Policy: England, France, and West Germany, 1985. Mem. N.Y. State Council on Humanities. Lizette Fisher fellow. Mem. Am. Assn. State Colls. and Univs. (chairperson), Regional Plan Assn. (bd. dirs. 1987), Lotos, Phi Beta Kappa. Office: SUNY at New Paltz New Paltz NY 12561

CHANDLER, DOROTHY BUFFUM, civic worker; b. Lafayette, Ill.; d. Charles Abel and Fern (Smith) Buffum; m. Norman Chandler, Aug. 30, 1922; children: Camilla (Mrs. F. Daniel Frost), Otis. Student, Stanford U., 1919-22; LHD (hon.), U. Calif., U. Judaism, U. Redlands, Hebrew Union Coll.; LLD (hon.), Occidental Coll., Mt. St. Mary's Coll., U. So. Calif.; DFA (hon.), U. Portland, Pepperdine Coll., Loyola Marymount U.; D of Arts (hon.), Art Inst. Los Angeles County. Hon. life chmn. Los Angeles Philharmonic Assn.; chmn. bd. govs. Performing Arts Council, Music Ctr. Los Angeles County; chmn. The Amazing Blue Ribbon of Music Ctr., Music Ctr. Found.; former regent U. Calif.; hon. life trustee Occidental Coll., Calif. Inst. Tech. Recipient Herbert Hoover medal Stanford Alumni Assn., Humanitarian award Variety Clubs Internat., 1974. Address: Los Angeles Philharm Assn 135 N Grand Avenue Blvd Los Angeles CA 90012*

CHANDLER, ELISABETH GORDON (MRS. LACI DE GERENDAY), sculptor, harpist; b. St. Louis, June 10, 1913; d. Henry Brace and Sara Ellen (Sallee) Gordon; m. Robert Kirkland Chandler, May 27, 1946 (dec.); m. Laci de Gerenday, May 12, 1979. Grad., Lenox Sch., 1931; pvt. study sculpture and harp. Mem. Mildred Dilling Harp Ensemble, 1934-45; instr. portrait sculpture Lyme Acad. Fine Arts, 1976—; dir. Abbott Coin Counter Co., Inc., 1941-55. Exhibited sculpture NAD, Nat. Sculpture Soc., Allied Artists Am., Nat. Arts Club, Pen and Brush, Lyme Art Assn., Mattatuck Mus., Catherine Lorillard Wolfe Art Club, Am. Artists Profl. League, Hudson Valley Art Assn., USIA, 1976-78, Lyme Art Ctr., 1979, retrospective exhbn. Lyme Acad. Fine Arts, 1987, Madison Gallery, 1987, Old State House, Hartford, Conn., 1989, Mellon Art Ctr., Wallingford, Conn., 1989; represented permanent collections, Aircraft Carrier USS Forrestal, Gov. Dummer Acad., James Forrestal Research Ctr. of Princeton U., Lenox Sch., James L. Collins Parochial Sch., Tex., Storm King Art Ctr., Columbia U., Pace U., White Plains, N.Y., St. Patrick's Cathedral, N.Y.C., McAuley Ctr., St. Joseph's Coll., West Hartford, Conn., Forrestal Meml. Medal, Timoschenko Medal for Applied Mechanics, Benjamin Franklin Medal, Albert A. Michelson Medal, Jonathan Edwards Medal, Shafto Broadcasting Award Medal, Woodrow Wilson Sch. of Princeton U., Ga. Pacific Bldg., Atlanta, Messiah Coll., Grantham, Pa., Adlai E. Stevenson High Sch., Ill., Queen Anne's County Courthouse Square, Md., pvt. collections. With mus. therapy div. Am. Theatre Wing, 1942-45; trustee The Lenox Sch., 1953-55; chmn. Associated Taxpayers Old Lyme, 1969-72; mem., trustee Brookgreen Gardens, S.C., 1989—. Recipient 1st prize Bklyn. War Meml. competition, 1945; 1st prize sculpture Catherine Lorillard Wolfe Art Club, 1951, 58, 63, Gold medal, 1969; Founders prize Pen & Brush, 1954, 76, 78, Gold medal, 1957, 61, 63, 69, 74, 76, Am. Heritage award, 1968, Solo Show award, 1961, 69, 75; Thomas R. Proctor prize NAD, 1956, Dessie Geer prize, 1960, 79, 85; Sculpture prize Nat. Arts Club, 1959, 60, 62, Gold medal, 1971; Gold medal Am. Artists Profl. League, 1960, 69, 73, 75, prize, 1981, Anna Hyatt Huntington prize, 1970, 76, Harriet Mayer Meml. prize, 1961; Gold medal Hudson Valley Art Assn., 1956, 69, 74, Mrs. John Newington award, 1976, 78; Lindsey Morris Meml. prize Allied Artists Am., 1973, Gold medal, 1982; sculpture prize Acad. Artists, 1974; Sydney Taylor Meml. prize Knickerbocker Artists, 1975; New Netherlands DAR Bicentennial medal, 1976; Tallix Foundry award, 1979; named Citizen of Yr., Town of Old Lyme, Conn., 1985. Fellow Nat. Sculpture Soc. (council 1976-85, John Spring Founder's award 1986), Am. Artists Profl. League, Internat. Inst. Arts and Letters; mem. Nat. Arts Club, Allied Artists Am., Pen and Brush, Catherine Lorillard Wolf Art Club, Lyme Art Assn. (pres. 1973-75), Council Am. Artists Socs. (dir. 1970-73), Am. Artists Profl. League (dir. 1970-73), NAD, Lyme Acad. Fine Arts (trustee 1976—). Home and Studio: 2 Mill Pond Ln Old Lyme CT 06371

CHANDLER, JEAN KOVER, educator; b. Olney, Ill., Sept. 25, 1939; d. Robert Leslie Blackburn and Nancy Jean (Kover) McKay; m. William Ray Chandler, Sept. 10, 1961; children: Robert Kover, Susan Leslie. BA, Beloit Coll., 1961; postgrad., Ea. Ill. U., 1976, MA, 1988. Substitute tchr. East Richland Schs., Olney, Ill., 1975-83; tchr. English Olney Cen. Coll., 1988—. Contbr. poetry to lit. mags. Vol., Olney Community Concert Assn., hosp. aux. Mem. Olney Tennis Club. Republican. Home: 417 E Monroe St Olney IL 62450 Office: Olney Cen Coll Rte 130 Olney IL 62450

CHANDLER, KARYLN DOROTHY, infosystems specialist; b. Pitts., Mar. 28, 1943; d. Wilbert and Theresa). (McClenny) Scott; m. James R. Chandler, Feb. 17, 1979; 1 child, Tina Marie. AS in Bus. Mgmt., Allegheny Community Coll., 1979. Name processor for city directory R.L. Polk Co., Cleve., 1966; keypunch operator Higbee Co., Cleve., 1968-69; keypunch operator Westinghouse Electric Corp., Forest Hills, Pa., 1970-76, sr. keypunch operator, 1976-80, fin. projects clk., 1980; supr. computer ops. Westinghouse Electric Corp., Pitts., 1980-89, ABB Power Systems, Inc., 1989—. Mem. Assn. Female Execs.

CHANDLER, KATRINA PIPKINS, college official, journalist; b. Montgomery, Ala., Sept. 14, 1955; d. B. Smith and Marjorie E. (Jackson) Pipkins; m. Thomas Clinton Chandler, Jr., Aug. 24, 1975; 1 child, Thomas Clinton III. BA, U. S.C., 1976, M in Mass Communications, 1984. Announcer Sta. WNOK, Columbia, S.C., 1975, Sta. WIS, Columbia, 1975; grad. asst. Coll. Journalism U. S.C., Columbia, 1976; asst. dir. continuity Stas. WONE and WTUE-FM, Dayton, Ohio, 1977-78; advt. sales assoc. Bell Advt., Cin., 1981; counselor student devel. U. S.C., Columbia, 1982-83; mgr. news and info. svcs. Converse Coll., Spartanburg, S.C., 1984—. Mem. adv. bd. Woman Fest, Spartanburg, 1988; bd. dirs. Spartanburg Postal Coun., 1990—; mem. steering com. Women's History Month, 1987-90. Recipient Excellence in Commls. award Dayton Advt. Club, 1978, 79. Mem. AAUW, LWV, Nat. Fedn. Press Women, Media Women S.C. (charter, sec. Piedmont br. 1986-88, chmn. 1990-91, state sec. 1988-89), Coll. News Assn. Carolinas (bd. dirs. 1988-91), S.C. Press Assn. (advisor coll. div. 1988-89), Alpha Epsilon Rho (profl.), Kappa Tau Alpha, Alpha Lambda Delta. Presbyterian. Home: 129 Littlejohn Ct Roebuck SC 29376 Office: Converse Coll 580 E Main St Spartanburg SC 29302-0006

CHANDLER, LINDA CLINE, investment broker, financial consultant; b. Sioux Falls, S.D.; d. Lawrence Alphonse and Wilba Nell (Leatherwood) Dhaemers; m. Terence E. Chandler, Oct. 16, 1976. BS, Iowa State U., 1968, MA, 1972. Registered investment advisor. With Sutro & Co., San Jose, Calif., 1974—, assoc. v.p., 1977-78, v.p. investments, 1978—; pres., founder Chandler Roberts, Inc., Santa Clara, Calif., 1983—, Pacific Integrated Group, 1987—, pres., 1988—; sr. v.p. Morgan, Olmstead, Kennedy & Gardner, 1985—; co-founder, chmn. ElOeste Border, Inc., 1989—; assoc. gen. ptnr. Brichard Properties, Phoenix Portfolio; bd. advisors Rancon Securities; assoc. gen. ptnr. Rancon Pacific, 1988—; co-founder, pres. Uptown Properties of San Diego Inc., First Ptnrs. Corp.; contbg. personal fin. editor Sta. KCSM-TV; fin. commentator Sta. KPEN; speaker No. Calif. Syndication Symposium. Pub. Investment Monitor, 1989; monitor Real Estate Digest, Real Estate Syndicator; publ. essays in investment, 1989; contbr. articles to profl. jours. Bd. dirs. League of Women Friends. Named Fin. Planner of Yr., Am. Home Properties, 1981, 83, one of nations leading brokers Wall Street Transcript, 1982, Nation's Outstanding Fin. Planners, Consol. Capital, 1983, Number One Sales Performance Rancho Cons. Realty, 1983, 85, 86. Fin. Planner of Yr., Brichard & Co., 1985-86, Outstanding Broker of Yr., Brichard & Co., 1986, Fin. Planner of Yr., Rancon Fin., 1986. UN fellow. Mem. Santa Clara County Profl. Brokers Assn., Santa Clara County Profl. Young Women, Internat. Assn. Fin. Planners (keynote conf. speaker, nat. speaker L.A. and Orlando, Fla. 1988), AAUW, Real Estate Securities and Syndications Inst. (nat. conv. speaker 1988), Phi Kappa Phi, Phi Delta Theta, Alpha Delta Pi. Methodist. Clubs: Sutro Century (pres.'s coun. 1978-81), Sutro Second Century, Sutro Pres. Office: 2880 Lakeside Dr Ste 115 Santa Clara CA 95054 also: 2515 Camino Del Rio S Ste 328 San Diego CA 92018

CHANDLER, LOUISE TAYLOR, psychiatric nurse; b. Boston, July 11, 1944; d. Carleton James and Etta (Moore) Batho; m. Arthur B. Chandler, Oct. 20, 1965; children: Mark, Leanne. Diploma in nursing, New Eng. Deaconess Hosp., Boston, 1965; BS in Nursing, Boston U., 1969, MS in Nursing, 1977. RN, Mass. Psychiat. nurse Boston, 1966-67, Medfield (Mass.) State Hosp., 1969-76; psychiat. nurse clinician Human Svcs. S.E. Mass., Attleboro, 1977-90; nursing chairperson Blue Hills Regional Sch. Nursing, Canton, Mass., 1990—. Pres. Ponkapoas Civic Assn., 1990. Mem. Am. Nurses Assn. (cert. psychiat. nurse clinician), Am. Orthopsychiat. Assn., AAUW (sec. 1911187-89), LWV (treas. Canton, Mass. 1981-90). Home: 3 Fairway Dr Canton MA 02021 Office: 800 Randolph St Canton MA 02021

CHANDLER, LYNNE CAROL, non-profit organization administrator, director; b. Nashville, Feb. 21, 1955; d. Dowin and Joyce (Franks) C. BS, U. North Ala., 1977; MSW, U. Tenn., 1981. Lic. social worker, Tenn. Social counselor Tenn. Dept. Human Svcs., Nashville, 1977-82, field supr., 1982-86; program coord. Parents Anonymous of Tenn., Nashville, 1986-88, exec. dir., 1988—. Author: (manual) Hooray For Me, 1988. Mem. Tenn. Leadership, Nashville, 1990—; treas. Nashville Coalition on Child Abuse, 1990—. Mem. Tenn. Conf. on Social Welfare, Tenn. Network for Child Advocacy, Nashville Coalition on Child Abuse (treas. 1989-90), Davidson County Sex Abuse Coun. Methodist. Office: Parents Anonymous of Tenn 3010 Ambrose Ave Nashville TN 37207

CHANDLER, MARCIA SHAW BARNARD, farmer; b. Arlington, Mass., Aug. 22, 1934; d. John Alden and Grace Winifred (Copeland) Barnard; m. Samuel Butler Chandler, Aug. 31, 1952 (dec. 1986); children: Shawn Chandler Seddinger, Mark Thurmond, Matthew Butler. BA, Francis Marion Coll., Florence, S.C., 1976; MEd, U. S.C., 1985. Resource person United Cerebral Palsy of S.C., Dillon, 1976-79; instr. English Horry-Georgetown Tech. Coll., Conway, S.C., 1980-81; farm owner, mgr. Dillon. Cover artist, So. Bell Telephone Directory, 1988, 90. Bd. dirs., publicist, artist Dillon County Theatre, Inc., 1985—; publicist, bd. dirs., artist, MacArthur Ave. Players, Dillon, 1990—; bd. dirs. Friends of Francis Marion Coll., 1985—; pres. Dillon Area Arts Coun., 1980-85, Jr. Charity League of Dillon, 1960-75; nat. poetry judge DAR, 1982. Recipient Honorable Commendation for civic involvement S.C. Ho. Reps., Mar. 22, 1990. Mem. Cousteau Soc., Ctr. Environ. Edn., Internat. Fund Animal Welfare, World Wildlife Fund, Nature Conservancy. Home: 203 Reaves Ave Dillon SC 29536

CHANDLER, MARGARET KUEFFNER, business educator; b. St. Paul, Sept. 30, 1922; d. Otto Carl and Marie (Schaedlich) Kueffner; m. Louis Chandler, Apr. 8, 1943. B.A. in Polit. Sci, U. Chgo., 1942, M.A. in Econs, 1944, Ph.D. in Sociology, 1948. Mem. faculty U. Ill. at Urbana, 1947-62, assoc. prof. sociology and indsl. relations, 1954-62; assoc. prof. sociology U. Ill. at Chgo., 1962-63, prof., 1963-65; prof. bus. Columbia U., 1965—, prof., faculty advisor Police Mgmt. Inst., Grad. Sch. Bus., 1989—, mem. pres.'s arbitration panel, 1977—; Fulbright research prof. econs. Keio U., Tokyo, Japan, 1963-64; lectr. Rutgers U., 1958, McGill U., 1963, Emory U., 1966, Columbia, 1962; labor arbitrator nat. labor panel Am. Arbitration Assn., 1965—, mem. collective bargaining methods study group., 1964—; assoc. mem. Center Advanced Study, U. Ill. Grad. Coll., 1964-65; asso. dir. Program Mng. Complex Techs., 1967—; mem. women's salary rev. bd., also affirmative action Commn. Columbia, 1976—; dir. program for Study Collective Bargaining in Higher Edn., 1975—; mem. N.Y. Gov.'s Panel for Dispute Resolution, 1977—; arbitrator, fact-finder N.J. Pub. Employment Relations Commn., 1975—; adminstrv. bd. Bur. Applied Social Research, 1975—; mem. spl. panel interest arbitrators, State of N.J., 1978—; mem. nat. adv. com. Nat. Center Study of Collective Bargaining in Higher Edn., 1978—; mem. state adv. council Inst. Mgmt. and Labor Relations, Rutgers U., 1982—; mem. Nat. Task Force on Teaching of Alt. Dispute Resolution Methods in Law and Bus. Schs., 1985—. Author: Labor Management Relations in Illini City, vols. 1 and 2, 1953, 54, Management Rights and Union Interests, 1964 (McKinsey Found. book award 1965), Managing Large Systems, 1971 (McKinsey Found. book award 1972); editor-in-chief: Columbia Jour. World Business, 1972—; contbr. articles, monograph to profl. lit. Postdoctoral fellow statistics Yale, 1953-54; Ford Found. Faculty research fellow social sci. and bus. U. Chgo., 1960-61; Ford Found. grantee, 1967—; Fulbright prof. Central U. Planning and Statistics, Warsaw, Poland, 1974; recipient Recognition award Ill. Nurses Assn., 1960. Fellow Am. Sociol. Assn., Soc. Applied Anthropology; mem. Am. Statis. Assn., Am. Econ. Assn., Indsl. Relations Research Assn. (editor research vol. 1960). Office: Columbia U Grad Sch Bus Uris Hall New York NY 10027

CHANDOR, KAREN KAYSER, marketing professional; b. L.A., Feb. 13, 1950; d. Ernest and Kathleen (Adams) Kayser; B.A., Wellesley Coll., 1970; M.B.A., Babson Coll., 1974, also postgrad. V.p. Tech. Steel Corp., Newton, Mass., 1971-73; asst. v.p. Thorndike, Doran, Paine & Lewis, Boston, 1973-76; v.p. Colonial Mgmt. Assos., Boston, 1976-77; v.p. mktg. Gardner and Preston Moss, Inc., Boston, 1977-89, dir. Investment Mgmt. Cons. Assn., 1987-88; v.p., dir. mktg. Standish Ayer & Wood, Inc., Boston, 1989—. Mem. corp. Babson Coll., 1982—; trustee, 1987—; trustee, mem. bd. mgrs. Mass. Eye and Ear Infirmary, 1985—. Cert. employee benefit specialist. Mem. Assn. Investment Mgmt. Sales Execs. (past bd. dirs., past pres.), Internat. Found. Employee Benefits. Home: 9 Village Hill Rd Dover MA 02030 Office: Standish Ayer & Wood Inc 1 Financial Ctr Boston MA 02111

CHANG, DEBORAH SOOK, lawyer, law educator; b. Man, W.Va., Feb. 15, 1960; d. C.H. Joseph and Chung Sook (Chun) C. BA, Kans. U., 1983; JD with honors, Drake U., 1986. Bar: Conn. 1986, U.S. Dist. Ct. Conn. 1987. Law clk. to presiding justice Conn. Appellate Ct., Hartford, 1986-87; assoc. Day, Berry & Howard, Hartford, 1987—; instr. Law Sch. U. Conn., Hartford, 1988—. Speaker, adv. AIDS Project Hartford & Discrimination Forums, 1988—, vol., 1989; active AIDS Legal Network, Hartford, 1989—, vol. Stewart B. McKinney Found. & Scholarship Fund, Hartford, 1989. Mem. Conn. Bar Assn. (young lawyers sect., mem. legal aid com., mem. human rights com.), Hartford Assn. Women Attys. Republican. Methodist. Office: Day Berry & Howard CityPlace 185 Asylum Hartford CT 06103-3499

CHANG, PATRICIA DAVIS, psychiatric nurse; b. Indpls., Oct. 3, 1945; d. Russell Eugene and Mildred Opal (Hayes) Davis; m. Ting-pao Chang; children: Laura Elisabeth, Thomas Evan, Marianne Elaine. BA highest distinction, Purdue U., 1968, AS in Nursing, 1973, MS in Psychology, 1979. RN, Ind. Rsch. nurse med. ctr. radiation oncology Ind. U., Indpls., 1975-77; nursing mgr. rsch. unit Larue Carter Hosp., Indpls., 1977-78; nursing mgr. adult psychiatric unit Valle Vista Hosp., Greenwood, Ind., 1983-84; charge nurse adult psychiatric unit Meth. Hosp., Indpls., 1981-83, 84-85; nurse cons. Ind. Dept. Human Svcs., Indpls., 1987-88; health svcs. coord. group homes Residential Mgmt. Systems, Indpls., 1989; primary care nurse children's psychiatric unit Community Hosp. North, Indpls., 1985-87; supr. Charter Hosp. Lapayette, 1989; primary care nurse CCU St. Vincent Hosp., Indpls., 1979-80; charge nurse adult mental health unit St. Vincent Stress Ctr., Indpls., 1989; clin. nurse specialist St. Vincent Adolescent Stress Ctr., 1989—; psychiat. nurse cons. Child and Adolescent Regional Psychiatric Ctr. Humana Hosp., Indpls., 1988. Co-author Mental Health Assn. Ind. Comprehensive Survey (state-wide) Psychiat. Facilities, 1987. Active in effort to revise state regulations concerning children and adolescents and the admission of minors to adult psychiat. units. Recipient scholarship Ford Found., 1963-67. Mem. Mental Health Assn. Ind. (children and adolescent mental health com. 1984—,subcommittee chairperson 1985-90), Ind. chpt. Prevention Child Abuse, Nat. Audubon Soc., Delta Rho Kappa. Democrat. Roman Catholic. Home: 1133 Stockton St Indianapolis IN 46260 Office: St Vincent Adolescent Stress Ctr 2120 W 86th St Indianapolis IN 46280-0160

CHANG, SUN-YUNG ALICE, mathematics educator; b. Ci-an, China, Mar. 24, 1948; came to U.S., 1970; d. Fann Chang and Li-Ching Chern; m. Paul Chien-Ping Yang, Mar. 24, 1973; children: Ray Yang, Lusann Yang. B.S., Nat. Taiwan U., 1970; Ph.D., U. Calif.-Berkeley, 1974. Asst. prof. math. U. Md., College Park, 1977-79; prof. UCLA, 1981—; speaker Internat. Congress of Math., 1986. Sloan Found. fellow, 1977, 78. Mem. Am. Math. Soc. (v.p. 1989, 90), Am. Women in Math. Office: UCLA Dept Math Los Angeles CA 90024

CHANG, YAU-FUNG OLIVIA, banker; b. Hong Kong, Mar. 31, 1963; came to U.S., 1983; d. Man-Bun and Chiu-Heung (Chow) C. BA in Journalism with high honor, U. Tex., 1986; MBA, U. Tex., Arlington, 1989. Sales supr. Mikura Shirt Co., Hong Kong, 1981-83; sr. sales support U. Tex., 1987-89; br. mgr. NCNB Tex., Dallas, 1989-90; loan prodn. supr., banking officer BCNB Tex., Dallas, 1990—. Acad. scholar U. Tex., 1984-87, Robert Leroy scholar, 1987-88. Mem. Univ. Tex. Communication Honor Soc., Toastmasters, Kappa Tau Alpha. Home: 720 Benge Dr Apt 6 Arlington TX 76013 Office: 1401 Elm St PO Box 830611 Dallas TX 75283-0611

CHANIN, MILDRED MAXINE, editor, educator; b. Cleve., Sept. 23, 1921; d. Abraham and Bessie (Rothenberg) Perelman; m. Abraham S. Chanin; 1 child, Beth Chanin Rudolph. BA, U. Ariz., 1944. Speech instr. U. Ariz., Tucson, 1946, 1947, Cerebral Palsy Found., Tucson, 1951; from tchr. to kindergarten dir. Congregation Anshei Israel, Tucson, 1950-56; tchr. Temple Emanu-El, Tucson, 1979; ptnr., editor Midbar Press, 1979; lectr. Pima Coll., Tucson, 1985; lectr. on pioneer Jewish History, Ariz. Mem. Coalition for the Advancement of Jewish Edn., Jr. Hadassah (Pres. 1941-44). Home: 5536 N Via Entrada Tucson AZ 85718 Office: Midbar Press 5536 N Via Entrada Tucson AZ 85718

CHANNELL, MARY LINCOLN, educational therapist; b. Hartford, Conn., Mar. 24, 1935; d. John Albert and Grace (Morgan) Lincoln; m. Gerald Arthur Channell, Apr. 26, 1956; children: Gerald A. Jr., Catherine Morgan, John Lincoln. Student, Wheaton Coll., Norton, Mass., 1953-56; BS, West Tex. State U., 1965; postgrad., NYU, 1976-80; MA, Fairfield U., 1975. Cert. tchr. spl. edn., ednl. adminstrn. Tchr., tutor Wilton (Conn.) Pub. Schs., 1972-74; resource tchr. Weston (Conn.) Pub. Schs., 1974-78; resource chmn. Darien (Conn.) Pub. Schs., 1978-81; ednl. therapist, cons. Westport, Easton, Conn., 1981—. Editor ednl. film strips, 1978-80. Sec. Libr. Bd. Dirs., Easton, 1989—; mem. Zoning Bd. Appeals, Easton, 1985—; justice of peace Town of Easton, 1985—; mem., sec. Dem. Town Com., Easton, 1985—; pres. Hist. Soc. Easton, 1990—, corr. sec., 1986-90; mem., chmn. Urban Ministry Project, Bridgeport, Conn., 1989—; pres. United Way Wilton (Conn.), 1978-80, chmn. budget com., 1976-78; mem. Wilton Bd. Edn., 1970-71; chmn. bd. stewardship and missions Congregational Ch., Easton, 1986-89, bd. deacons, 1989-90. Mem. Easton Garden Club (chmn., ways and means 1989—), St. Croix Yacht Club. Democrat. Home: 385 Black Rock Rd Easton CT 06612

CHANNING, CAROL, actress; b. Seattle, Jan. 31, 1923; d. George and Adelaide (Glaser) C.; m. Charles F. Lowe, Sept. 5, 1956; 1 son, Channing

George. Student, Bennington Coll. Actress: (Broadway prodns.) No for an Answer, 1941, Let's Face It, 1941, Proof Through the Night, 1942, So Proudly We Hail, Lend an Ear, 1948 (Theatre World award, Critic's Circle award), Show Business, 1959, Show Girl, 1961, George Burns-Carol Channing Musical Revue, 1962, The Millionairess, 1963, Carol Channing with Her Stout-Hearted Men, 1970 (London Critics award), Four on a Garden, 1971, Cabaret, 1972, Festival at Ford's, 1972, Carol Channing and Her Gentlemen Who Prefer Blondes Revue, 1972, (films) First Travelling Saleslady, 1956, Thoroughly Modern Millie, 1967 (Golden Globe award as best supporting actress 1967), Skidoo, 1968, others, (TV prodns.) Svengali and the Blonde, Three Men on a Horse, Crescendo; star: (Broadway prodns.) Gentlemen Prefer Blondes, 1949, 51-53, Wonderful Town, 1953, Pygmalion, 1953, The Vamp, 1955, Hello Dolly, 1964-67, also revival (Tony award for best actress, N.Y. Drama Critics award for best actress), Jerry's Girls, 1984-85, Legends, 1986; toured with play Lorelei, 1973-75. Recipient Best Night Club Act award, 1957, 64, Spl. Tony award, 1968, Theatre World award for Bronze medallion City of N.Y., 1978. Christian Scientist. Office: care William Morris Agy 151 El Camino Blvd Beverly Hills CA 90212*

CHANNING, STOCKARD (SUSAN STOCKARD), actress; b. N.Y.C.. BA cum laude, Harvard U. Performed in exptl. drama with Theatre Co. of Boston, 1967; numerous stage appearances including Two Gentlemen of Verona, N.Y.C., San Francisco, Los Angeles, 1972-73, No Hard Feelings, Martin Beck Theatre, N.Y.C., 1973, Vanities, Mark Taper Forum, L.A., 1976, Ahmanson Theatre, 1977, As You Like It, 1978, They're Playing Our Song, Lady and the Clarinet, 1983, The Golden Age, 1983, The Rink, 1983, Joe Egg, 1985 (Drama Desk nominee, Tony award Best Actress), House of Blue Leaves, Lincoln Ctr.-Vivien Beaumont Theatre (Tony and Drama Desk nominations), 1986, Woman in Mind, 1988 (Drama Desk award Best Actress), Love Letters, 1989, Six Degrees of Separation, 1990; appeared in films including Comforts of Home, 1970, The Fortune, 1975, Sweet Revenge, 1975, The Big Bus, 1976, Grease, 1978 (Peoples's Choice award), Boys Life, 1987, The Cheap Detective, 1978, Without a Trace, 1983, Heartburn, 1986, Men's Club, 1986, Staying Together, 1987, Meet the Applegates, 1988, Married to It, 1990; TV films include The Girl Most Likely To, 1973, Lucan, 1977, Silent Victory: The Kitty O'Neil Story, 1979, Table Settings, 1982, Not My Kid, 1985, The Room Upstairs, 1986, Echoes in the Darkness, 1987 (A.C.E. award Best Actress, Emmy nominee), Tidy Endings, 1988, Perfect Witness, 1989; star of TV series The Stockard Channing Show, 1979-80. Office: Internat Creative Mgmt 8899 Beverly Blvd Los Angeles CA 90048

CHAO, ELAINE L., deputy transportation secretary; d. James S. C. and Ruth M. L. (Chu) C. AB, Mt. Holyoke Coll., 1975; MBA, Harvard U., 1979; LLD (hon.), Villanova U., 1989. Assoc. Gulf Oil Corp., Pitts., summer 1978; sr. lending officer Citicorp, NA, N.Y.C., 1979-83; v.p. capital markets group Bankam., San Francisco, 1984-86; dep. maritime adminstr. U.S. Dept. Transp., Washington, 1986-88; chmn. Fed. Maritime Commn., Washington, 1988; dep. sec. U.S. Dept. of Transp., Washington, 1989—; adj. asst. prof. Grad. Sch. Bus. Adminstrn., St. John's U., 1984. Recipient Young Achiever award Nat. Coun. Women U.S., Inc., 1986; Eisenhower Fellow Assn. fellow, 1984; named. one of 10 Outstanding Women of Am., 1988. Mem. Coun. on Fgn. Rels., Inc., World Affairs Coun., Am. Coun. Young Polit. Leaders (bd. dirs. 1989—), Harvard Bus. Sch. (vis. com. 1989—), Harvard Club (N.Y.C.), Harvard Bus. Sch. Club (greater Washington, bd. dirs.), Phi Tau Phi. Office: US Dept Transp 400 7th St SW Washington DC 20590

CHAO, HELEN, pharmaceutical sales executive; b. Jersey City, N.J., Feb. 8, 1960; d. Carlos Manuel and Fe Esperanza (Hernandez) C. BA, Rutgers U., 1982. Hairdresser, mgr. Hair Guild, West N.Y., N.J., 1978-86; sales rep. N.J. Bus. Systems, Clark, 1986-87; pharm. sales rep. The Upjohn Co., Berwyn, Pa., 1987-90; hosp. sales specialist The Upjohn Co., Berwyn, 1990—. Roman Catholic. Home: 588 65th St West New York NJ 07093

CHAPA, MARIA ESTELA, nurse; b. Rio Grande, Tex., Apr. 17, 1956; d. Ambrosio and Maria (Quintino) Reyna; m. Luis Chapa, Oct. 21, 1978;. BSc., Tex. Woman's U., Denton, 1979. Cert. Child and Adolescent Nurse, Tex. Staff registered nurse Jefferson Davis Hosp., Houston, 1979-80; charge registered nurse, staff registered nurse Meml. Med. Ctr., Corpus Christi, Tex., 198081; head nurse pediatrics Edineburg Gen. Hosp., Tex., 1981-82; head nurse pediatrics Rio Grande Regional Hosp., McAllen, Tex., 1982-83, head nurse orthopedics, 1983-84; charge nurse, prdiatrics-ICU Driscoll Found. Children's, Corpus Christi, Tex., 1984-86, dir. edn., 198688; head nurse, nursery Humana Hosp., Corpus Christi, Tex., 1988-89; dir. nursing edn. Driscoll Hosp., Corpus Christi, 1989—; basic life support instr. Corpus Christi, Tex. 1986-; adjunct prof. Del Mar Coll. Coordinator Continuing Edn. Program, Pedi Code Mgmt. 1987. Mem. Am. Assn. Critical Care Nurses, YMCA Club Corpus Christi Tex., Am. Democratic. Roman Catholic. Home: 3146 China Berry Corpus Christi TX 784;5

CHAPDELAINE, JOAN MURPHY, nursing educator; b. Newport, R.I., July 25, 1936; d. Quentin Leo and Helen (Hamilton) Murphy; m. Armand Joseph Chapdelaine, July 23, 1960. BS in Nursing, Salve Regina Coll., Newport, 1957, MS in Health Svcs. Adminstrn., 1985; MS in Nursing Adminstrn., Boston U., 1972; postgrad,, Walden U., Minn., 1990—. RN, R.I., Mass.; cert. advanced nurse adminstr. Coord. nursing program Newport Hosp. Sch. Nursing, 1957-71; resident in adminstrn. St. Luke's Hosp., New Bedford, Mass., 1971-72; dir. nursing Truesdale Hosp., Fall River, Mass., 1972-77; dir. nursing component R.I. Cancer Control Program, Providence, 1977-79; asst. dir. nursing svcs. St. Luke's Hosp., New Bedford, Mass., 1979-81; asst. prof. nursing Salve Regina Coll., 1981-85, assoc. prof. nursing and health svc. adminstrn., 1985—, dir. grad. program in health svcs. adminstrn., 1985—; cons. nursing dept. St. Luke's Hosp., New Bedford, Mass., 1982-86; cons. Nat. Cancer Inst., 1979; guest speaker on nursing mgmt. and bioethics, 1983—. Mem. evaluation com. United Way, Providence, 1986—; chmn. evaluation task force United Way Southeastern Mass., 1988—; vol. Am. Cancer Soc., Providence, 1986—. Mem. Am. Hosp. Assn., Am. Orgn. Nurse Execs., Salve Regina Coll. Alumni Assn., Boston U. Alumni Assn., Sigma Theta Tau. Roman Catholic. Home: 47 Harrison Ave Newport RI 02840 Office: Salve Regina Coll Ochre Point Ave Newport RI 02840

CHAPELLE, MONIQUE, French diplomat; b. Nantes, France, Apr. 15, 1945; came to U.S., 1988; d. Gustave and Elizabeth (Rabaey) Lor; m. Jean Chapelle (dec. Aug. 198l); children: Ivan, Sebastien. Student, Nat. Inst. Oriental Civilizations and Langs., Paris, 1966, Vienna Acad., Cambridge U., 1965. Asst. dir. French-Russian C. of C., Paris and Moscow, 1967-70; head industrialized countries French Bd. Trade, Paris, 1970-79, head European desk, 1979-82, head energy sector, 1982-84; French trade commr. French Embassy, Pretoria, Republic of South Africa, 1984-88, French Consulate, Atlanta, 1988—. Mem. Chevalier de Tastevin, Commanderie de Bordeaux. Home: 4719 Tall Pines Dr Atlanta GA 30327 Office: French Trade Commn 100 Peathtree St NW 2110 Atlanta GA 30303

CHAPIN, NANCY LOUISE, gourmet sauce company executive; b. N.Y.C., Jan. 29, 1944; d. Merril and Florence (Chapin) Berman; children: Katherine, Julie. BA, U. Colo, 1966; MA, U. Colo, Denver, 1972. Master of Urban and Regional Planning. Econ. devel. trainer Volt Tech. Corp., Denver, 1970-72; prog. dir. Colo. Commn. on Status of Women, Denver, 1972; housing planner City and County of Denver, Denver, 1974; real estate mgmt. restoration Chapin Properties, Denver; chief exec. officer Chapin's Supreme Foods, Denver, 1988—. Dist. Capt. Denver Dem. Party, Denver, 1974; Bd. mem. Colfax on the Hill, Denver, 1986--. Address: Chapin's Supreme Foods 1324A E 17th Ave Denver CO 80218

CHAPIN, SUZANNE PHILLIPS, psychologist; b. Syracuse, N.Y., Aug. 9, 1930; d. Harold Bridge and Charlotte Virginia (Warner) Phillips; m. Richard Hilton Chapin, June 13, 1953 (div. 1964); children: Bruce Phillips Chapin, Linda Chapin Fry. BA, Syracuse U., 1952; MA, Columbia U., 1965. Statis. asst. Syracuse Bd. of Edn., 1952-53; psychol. examiner Stamford (Conn.) Pub. Schs., 1965-68, psychologist Head Start program, 1967-68; psychologist Southbury (Conn.) Tng. Sch., 1968-74, Onondaga Assn. for the Retarded, Syracuse, 1974, Harlem Valley Psychiatric Ctr., Wingdale, N.Y., 1974—. Mem. Danbury Women's Ctr., Nature Conservancy. Democrat. Club: Sierra. Home: 29 Cornell Rd Danbury CT 06811 Office: Harlem Valley Psychiat Ctr Rt 22 Wingdale NY 12594

CHAPLIN, WANDA LOUISE, aviation company executive; b. Plymouth, Wis., Aug. 23, 1950; d. Harry Rial and Carol Imogene (Betts) C. Student, Venezia Isola di Studi, Italy, 1969-70; BFA, Drake U., 1972; MA in Arts Adminstr., U. Wis., 1974. Researcher Mpls. Soc. of Fine Arts, 1972; cons. Exxon Corp., N.Y.C., 1974; community arts coord. W.Va. Arts and Humanities Coun., Charleston, 1975-76; sr. coord. spl. projects Phillip Morris Inc., N.Y.C., 1978-80; owner Du-Most, Des Plaines, Ill., 1980-83; pres. Chaplin Aviation Inc., Sheboygan Falls, Wis., 1983—. Trustee Sheboygan Found. U. Wis., 1985—; gov. appointee aeros. council Wis. Dept. Transp., Madison, 1986—. Mem. Wis. Aviation Trade Assn. (pres. 1985-86), Wis. Aviation Hall of Fame, Nat. Air Transportation Assn., U. Wis. Alumni Club (sec. 1985-86). Republican. Congregationalist.

CHAPMAN, ABIGAIL DIAMOND, artist, calligrapher, illuminator; b. Mpls., Sept. 5, 1937; d. Samuel Joseph and Pauline Vivian (Brill) D.; m. Jerome Chapman, Apr. 16, 1961 (dec. Feb. 1989); children: Amy Roanne, Seth Lance, Lon-Given. BA, U. Minn., 1956; cert., Tobé Coburn Sch. Fashion, 1960, Mpls. Talmu Torah, 1959. Prin. Abigail D. Chapman, Ridgewood, N.J., 1984—; lectr. Hadassah, N.Y.C., 1960—. Exhibited in group shows at Kolbo, Brookline, Mass., In The Spirit, N.Y.C., Gallery Judaica, L.A., Competorary Artifacts 1984, Nat. Mus. Am. Jewish Art, Phila., Harkness Gallery, N.Y.C., 1984, Englewood Libr., N.J., 1984, Master Eagle Gallery, N.Y.C., 1982-84, Newark Libr., Brown U. John D. Rockefeller Jr. Libr., Providence, Balch Inst. for Ethnic Studies, Phila., N.Y. Pub. Libr. Rare Book Collection, N.Y.C., others; numerous pvt. collections. Recipient First Youth award Mpls. Art Inst., 1949, Type Dir. award, N.Y.C., 1979, 83, Met. Printing Assn. award; Profl. Study grant Letter Arts, 1982. Mem. Soc. of Sribes (founding charter mem., workshop conductor). Democrat. Jewish. Home and Studio: 529 Laurel Rd Ridgewood NJ 07450

CHAPMAN, CAROLYN, lawyer; b. Oak Park, Ill., Sept. 8, 1942; d. Edmund Earle Jr. amd Ella Mae (Bryant) C.; m. Gene Paul Cech, July 6, 1963 (div. 1980); children: Geoffrey Paul, Gary Peter, Nancy Carolyn; m. Melvin LeRoy Flood, Apr. 1980 (div. 1982); 1 child, Erik Louis. BS in Music Edn., U. Ill., 1964, MS in Music Edn., 1968; adminstrv. credential, Point Loma Coll., 1983; JD, Western State U., 1988. Bar: Calif. 1989, U.S. Dist. Ct. (so. dist.) Calif. 1989, U.S. Ct. Appeals (9th cir.) 1989. Tchr. music Barrington and Addison (Ill.) Pub. Schs., 1964-67; tchr. history, music, math., English, band, orch., chorus San Diego City Schs., 1971-87; law clk. U.S. Atty.'s Office, San Diego, 1986-87, Law Offices of Eugene G. Iredale, San Diego, 1988-90, Law Offices of Michael Pancer, San Diego, 1990—; curriculum developer moot ct. program Western State U., San Diego, 1985-86; organizer string orch. Dana Jr. High Sch., San Diego, 1972-80. Foster parent; sponsor fgn. student exchange program. Nat. semi-finalist F. Lee Bailey Moot Ct.; Recipient Am. Jury award, Corpus Juris Secundum award; T.J. Smith scholar, 1960-64, McDowell scholar, 1960. Mem. Am. Trial Lawyers Assn., Calif. Women Lawyers, Calif. Assn. Women Lawyers, Lawyers Club San Diego, Courthouse Toastmasters, Delta Theta Phi, Sigma Alpha Iota, Delta Delta Delta. Republican. Home: 10387 Friars Rd #303 San Diego CA 92120-2302 also: 3452 Mission Mesa Way San Diego CA 92120

CHAPMAN, DEBORAH ANN, mortgage loan officer; b. Cheverly, Md., Oct. 11, 1947; d. Mason Howard and Ethel Arlee (Chandler) Cobb; m. Robert Lewis Chapman, Apr. 23, 1966 (div. 1980). Escrow officer Chgo. Title Ins. Co., Washington, 1979-83; settlement sec. Margaretten & Co., Inc., Suitland, Md., 1983-85; loan officer Goldome Realty Credit Corp., Greenbelt, Md., 1985-88; real estate agt. Maximum Referrals, Bowie, Md., 1988—; loan officer Md. Nat. Mortgage Corp., Greenbelt, 1988—. Organist Cen. Bapt. Ch., Bladensberg, Md. Baptist. Home: 1605 Pebble Beach Ct Mitchellville MD 20716 Office: Md Nat Mortgage Corp 7474 Greenway Ctr Dr Greenbelt MD 20770

CHAPMAN, EUGENIA SHELDON, political worker, former state legislator; b. Fairhope, Ala., Jan. 10, 1923; d. Chauncey Bailey and Rose (Donner) Sheldon; B.Ed., Chgo. State U., 1944; m. Gerald M. Chapman, Nov. 24, 1948; children: George, John, Katherine Urgo, Andrew. Tchr. public schs., Cicero, Ill., 1944-47, Chgo., 1947-51; mem. Ill. Ho. of Reps., 1964-83, minority whip, chmn. human resources com., standing com. on appropriations. Mem. Dist. 214 Bd. Edn., Cook County, Ill.; del. Dem. Nat. Nominating Convs., 1972, 80; mem. Cook County Dem. Central Com., 1982—, Ill. Dem. Central Com., 1984—; chief div. sr. citizens' advocacy Office Ill. Atty. Gen., 1983-89. Named Best Legislator Independent Voters. Ill., 1966, 68, 70, 74, 76, 78, 80, 82. Mem. LWV (pres. Arlington Heights 1957-59), Bus. and Profl. Women's Club. Democrat. Address: 16 S Princeton Ct Arlington Heights IL 60005

CHAPMAN, FRANCES ELIZABETH CLAUSEN (MRS. WILLIAM MAMES CHAPMAN), civic worker, writer; b. Atchison, Kans., Feb. 27, 1920; d. Erwin W. and Helen (Hackney) Clausen; BA Wellesley Coll., 1941; m. W. MacLean Johnson, Aug. 31, 1940 (dec. Nov. 1965); children—Stuart MacLean, Duncan Scott, Douglas Hamilton; m. 2d, William James Chapman, Dec. 5, 1970. AA (hon.) St. Louis Community Coll. Project dir. Women in Community Service, Inc., St. Louis, 1965-66; pres. Nursery Found., St. Louis, 1956-58, dir., 1953-59, 65-68; adv. com. Mo. State Children's Day Care, 1963-66; chmn. day care com. Mo. Council Children and Youth, 1961, chmn. foster care sect., 1961-63; spl. asst. to the pres. Webster Coll., 1966-68. Author: Grandmother's House, 1987. Bd. dirs. New City Sch., 1967-69, Mid-County YMCA, 1967-70, St. Louis Conservatory and Sch. Arts, 1978—; mem. Mo. State Coordinating Bd. Higher Edn., 1982-86 ; mem. steering com. Mo. Council on Children and Youth, 1967-69; trustee Jr. Coll. Dist. St. Louis-St. Louis County, 1968-80, pres. bd. trustees, 1971-73, 76-77; trustee John Burroughs Sch., 1973-79, Wellesley Coll., 1976-82; bd. dirs. Assn. Governing Bds. Univs. and Colls., 1970-80, v.p., 1977-78, chmn. bd., 1978-79, hon. dir., 1982-85; bd. commrs. Nat. Commn. on Accrediting, 1971-72; bd. overseers Ctr. for Research on Women in Higher Edn. and Professions, Wellesley, Mass., 1977-82. Recipient Woman of Achievement award, St. Louis Globe-Democrat, 1965, St. Louis Wellesley award, 1971, Golden Palm Laureate award Harris-Stowe St. Coll., 1989. Mem. Nat. Soc. Arts and Letters, Wellesley Coll. Alumnae Assn. (sec., dir. 1958-61). Club: Wellesley Coll. (pres. 1965-67). Home: 10 Overbrook Dr Saint Louis MO 63124

CHAPMAN, KATHLEEN HALLORAN, state legislator, lawyer; b. Estherville, Iowa, Jan. 19, 1937; d. Edward E. and Meryl (McConoughey) Halloran; m. Allen Ray Chapman, Apr. 29, 1961; children: Christopher, Stuart. BA, U. Iowa, 1959, JD, 1974. Bar: Iowa 1974, U.S. Ct. Appeals (8th cir.) 1974. Prin. Booth & Chapman, Cedar Rapids, Iowa, 1974—; mem. Iowa Ho. of Reps., Des Moines, 1983—, vice chmn. judiciary com., 1983-86, vice chmn. ethics com., 1985-88, vice chmn. ways and means com., 1987-88, chmn. rules and adminstrn. com., 1987-88, asst. majority leader, 1989—; legis. Coun. Iowa Gen. Assembly, 1987—; participant Atlantic Exch., 1989. Trustee East Cen. Regional Libr., Cedar Rapids, 1974-80, Children's Home, Cedar Rapids, 1978—. Toll fellow Coun. State Govts., 1988. Mem. Iowa Bar Assn. Democrat. Roman Catholic. Office: 900 The Center Cedar Rapids IA 52401

CHAPMAN, PAULA ANNE, cultural organization administrator; b. Tiffin, Ohio, Sept. 15, 1960; d. Paul Everett and Mary Virginia (Brosious) Young; m. James Nelson Cook, Sept. 16, 1977 (div. Dec. 1981); children: Nichole Adele, Jessica Theresa, Samantha Rebekah; m. Harry N. Chapman, Dec. 10, 1988. BS in Psychology, Heidelberg Coll., 1982; MA in Polit. Sci., Bowling Green (Ohio) State U., 1987. Child therapist Sandusky (Ohio) Youth Referral Svc., 1982-83; parole officer State of Ohio, Columbus, 1983-86; dep. dir. Seneca, Sandusky and Wyandot Commn. Mental Health Bd., Tiffin, 1986-87; program dir. WSOS Community Action Commn., Fremont, Ohio, 1987-88; dir. community devel. Seneca Indsl. and Econ. Devel. Corp., Tiffin, 1988; exec. dir. Tiffin Area C. of C./Seneca Indsl. & Econ. Devel. Corp., Tiffin, 1988—; mem. edn!. adv. bd. Vanguard/Sentinel Vocat. Sch., Fremont, 1989—; chmn. Tiffin Fair Housing Bd., 1985—; bd. dirs. Ohio Indsl. Tng. Program, Sandusky, Pvt. Industry Coun., Fremont, Seneca County Revolving Loan Fund, Tiffin. Mem. Ohio Devel. Assn., Ohio Planning Assn., Am. Econ. Devel. Coun., Bus. and Profl. Women's Assn. (Young Career Woman 1987, 89). Home: 1741 Meadow Lake Dr Tiffin OH 44883 Office: Chapman Community Devel Cons PO Box 676 Tiffin OH 44883

CHAPMAN, SARA SIMMONS, English educator, academic administrator; b. Charleston, W.Va., Apr. 24, 1940; d. Maxwell E. and Billie Morrison Simmons. BA, Morris Harvey Coll., Charleston, W.Va., 1962; MA, Marshall U., Huntington, W.Va., 1966; PhD, Ohio U., 1970; MLS, Ball State U., 1977; D Pedagogy (hon.), U. Charleston, W.Va., 1989. Instr. English Morris Harvey Coll., Charleston, W.Va., 1965-66; instr. English Marshall U., Huntington, W.Va., 1966-67, asst. prof. English, 1969-72, assoc. prof. English, 1972-76, dir. acad. planning, 1975; asst. dean Colls. Arts and Scis., dir. U. Honors Program Kansas State U., Manhattan, 1976-79; assoc. vice chancellor for acad. affairs State U. System Minn., St. Paul, 1979-81; prof. English Newcomb Coll., Tulane U., New Orleans, 1982-86, dean, 1982-86; asst. dir., edn. programs NEH, Washington, 1985-86; vis. prof. dept. English Princeton U., Princeton, N.J., 1987-88; prof. English The Sage Colls., Troy, N.Y., 1988—, pres., 1988—; bd. dirs. N.Y. State Coun. on Econ. Edn., N.Y.C.; nat. cons. Am. Coun. on Edn. Office of Women in Higher Edn. Nat. Forum, Washington, 1989. Author: Henry James's Portrait of the Writer as Hero, 1989. Bd. dirs. Emma Willard Sch., 1988—; hon. adv. com. Ctr. for Disabled, Albany, N.Y., 1989, N.Y. LVW, 1989. Recipient Leadership award Women's Bus. Devel. Ctr., Albany, 1989; Harvard Grad. Sch. Edn. fellow, 1982; Adminstrv. grantee Rockefeller Found., 1974; grantee NEH, 1979-82, Nat. Endowment for Arts, 1984. Mem. Troy (N.Y.) Country Club, University Club (Albany, N.Y.), Ft. Orange Club (Albany). Home: 46 First St Troy NY 12180 Office: The Sage Colls Office of the Pres Troy NY 12180

CHAPMAN, SUSAN KARDEVAN, certified public accountant, real estate developer; b. Phila., May 28, 1953; d. Frank Charles and Mary Catherine (Krewson) Kardevan; m. John G. Chapman, May 10, 1975 (div. 1989). BBA cum laude, U. Miami, Coral Gables, 1975. CPA, Fla. Staff acct. Price Waterhouse & Co., Miami/Ft. Lauderdale, Fla., 1975-78; sr. acct. Price Waterhouse & Co., Ft. Lauderdale, 1979-81; controller Wrono Enterprises, Hallandale, Fla., 1981-83; asst. controller Palm Beach Newspapers, Inc., West Palm Beach, Fla., 1983-84; controller Nat. Subscription TV (subs. Oak Industries, Inc.), Rancho Bernardo, Calif., 1984-85; controller HSW Investments, Inc., Ft. Lauderdale, 1985-87, treas., 1987-89; v.p. Agora Devel., Inc., Newport Beach, Calif., 1989—. Mem. Rep. Nat. Com., Am. Heart Assn. Mem. U. Miami Hurricane Club, U. Miami Alumni Assn., Fla. Inst. CPAs (com.), AICPA, Nat. Assn. Accts., Internat. Coun. Shopping Ctr. Developers, Mortar Bd. (pres. 1974-75), Orange Key Club, Beta Alpha Psi, Delta Delta Delta (treas. 1972-75), Sigma Alpha Epsilon (little sister 1972-75). Office: Agora Devel Inc 1001 Dove St Ste 100 Newport Beach CA 92660

CHAPMAN, TRACY, singer, songwriter; b. Cleve., 1964. BA in Anthropology, Tufts U., 1986. Composer, performer. Albums include Tracy Chapman, 1988, Crossroads, 1989. Recipient Grammy awards for best new artist, best female pop vocal performance and best contemporary folk performance, 1989. Office: care Elektra Records Publicity 9229 Sunset Blvd Ste 718 Los Angeles CA 90069*

CHAPPELEAR, PATSY STALLINGS, chemical engineer; b. Burnet, Tex., Oct. 23, 1931; d. Raymond Dero Stallings and Cora B. Trainer; m. John Emerson Chappelear, Feb. 14, 1955; children: June Keller, Janice Sobieski, Juliet Markovich and Jack. BA, Rice Inst., Houston, 1953, BS, 1954. Engr. Shell Oil, Deer Park, Tex., 1954-55; sr. research assoc. Rice U. Dept. Chem. Engr., Houston, 1955-76; sr. project, process engr. Hudson Engr. Corp., Houston, 1975-86; cons. Houston;, -; editorial review bd. Fluid Phase Equilibria, Elsevier, The Netherlands,1975-87, Gas Processors Assn., Tulsa, 1975-90; bd. dirs. Rice U. Engr. Alumni, Houston, 1978-85. Author: Contbr. Articles to Profl. Mags. Organizer PTA Houston 1961-70; Leader Camp Fire Girls, Girls Scouts Houston 1972-75. Recipient Recognition Award Gas Processors Assn., 1981, Citation for Svc. Gas Processors Assn., 1987. Fellow Am. Inst. Chem. Engrs. (bd. dirs.), R.E.A.D. (Literacy), Sigma Xi, Order Eastern Star. Republican. United Methodist. Office: 9714 S Rice Ave Houston TX 77096

CHAPPELL, BARBARA KELLY, child welfare consultant; b. Columbia, S.C., Oct. 17, 1940; d. Arthur Lee and Katherine (Martin) Kelly; 1 child, Kelly Katherine. BA in English and Edn., U. S.C., 1962, MSW, 1974. Tchr. English, Dept. Edn., Honolulu, 1962-65, Alamo Heights High Sch., San Antonio, 1965-67; caseworker Dept. Social Services, Columbia, S.C., 1969-70; supr. Juvenile Placement and Aftercare, Columbia, 1970-72; child welfare cons. Edna McConnell Clark Found., N.Y.C., 1974-75; dir. Children's Foster Care Rev. Bd. System, Columbia, 1975-85; child welfare cons., 1985—; lectr. in field. Contbr. articles to profl. jours. Coordinator Child's Rights to Parents, Columbia, 1970-75. Epsicopalian. Home and office: 3215 Girardeau Ave Columbia SC 29204

CHAPPLE, ABBY, consumer comunications consultant; b. N.Y.C., Aug. 17, 1939; d. Adolph Emil and Thelma (Pierce) Klueppelberg; m. Ross Victor Chapple (div.); m. Robert Alan Mewhinney (div.); m. Joe David Walker. BA, Am. U., 1961, postgrad., 1961-65. Reporter Washington Star, 1966-81; pres. Chapple/Mewhinney Assocs., Annapolis, Md., 1981-82; spl. asst. to chmn. Consumer Product Safety Commn., Washington, 1982-85; pres. Consumer Communications, Annapolis, 1985—. Recipient Media award Dallas Mkt. Ctr., 1978, Home Furnishngs Hall Fame, 1979, Am. Soc. Interior Designers, 1985, Chmn.'s award Consumer Product Safety Commn., 1984. Mem. Soc. Consumer Affairs Profls., Internat. Furnishings and Design Assn., Nat. Assn. Bus. Women, Pub. Rels. Soc. Am. Republican. Jewish. Home: 1038 Timber Creek Dr Annapolis MD 21403 Office: Consumer Communications Box 4007 Annapolis MD 21403

CHAPPLE, F. COLLEEN, finance, real estate and computer service executive; b. Manhattan, Kans., Sept. 3, 1932; d. Frank Richardson and Mildred (Webster) McKee; m. Gordon R. Chapple, Feb. 19, 1954. Pres. Chapple Fin. Svcs. Inc., Brentwood, Tenn., 1973—, Chapple Computer, Inc., Brentwood, 1983-85; mgr. The Chapple Office Bldg., Brentwood, 1983-90; founding mem. Brentwood Network, 1985—. Mem. charter study com. City of Brentwood, 1986. Recipient Exec. award Nat. Women Execs., Nashville, 1984. Mem. Brentwood C. of C. (bd. dirs. 1984-87, sec. 1986-87). Home: 8110 Patrice Ave Brentwood TN 37027 Office: Chapple Fin Svcs Inc 5200 Maryland Way Ste 103 Brentwood TN 37027

CHAR, CARLENE MAE, technical writer, publisher, editor; b. Honolulu, Oct. 21, 1954; d. Richard Y. and Betty S.M. (Fo) C. BA in Econs., U. Hawaii, 1977; MA in Bus. Adminstrn., Columbia Pacific U., 1984, PhD in Journalism, 1985, Bachelar Gen. Studies in Computer Sci., Roosevelt U., 1986. Freelance writer, Honolulu, 1982—; editor Computer Book Rev., Honolulu, 1983—, tech. writer U.S. Sprint, 1988—.

CHARABATI, VICTORIA FRANCE, publishing executive; b. East Stroudsburg, Pa., Mar. 18, 1954; d. Donald D. and Barbara (Shaffer) France; m. Jihad Charabati, Oct. 13, 1981. BA in French Lang. and Lit. cum laude, N.C. State U., 1975; MA in Linguistics, Oakland U., 1981. Mem. faculty English Lang. Inst. Wayne State U., Detroit, 1981-82; copywriter Percivall Advt. & Mktg. Inc., Raleigh, N.C., 1982-83; acct. rep. Offset Paperback Mfrs., Inc., Dallas, Pa., 1986-87; dir. classes French Alliance, St. Paul, 1984; contbg. editor Newsmakers, Gale Rsch. Co., Detroit, 1985—; prodn. mgr. Bookmakers, Inc., Wilkes-Barre, 1987—. Contbr. articles to Times Leader newspaper. Mem. NAFE, Audubon Soc., Press' Club, Mensa, Intertel. Democrat. Home: 33 Druid Hills Shavertown PA 18708

CHARBONNEAU, RHONA MAE, state legislator; b. Lowell, Mass., Feb. 20, 1928; d. Daniel Francis and Harriette (LaSalle) Shay; m. Claude Maurice Charbonneau, 1950; children: Claudia Charbonneau Dodds, Rhona Charbonneau Wollenhaupt, Richard, Mark, Alida West. Ed., U. Lowell. Pres. Car Develop Corp., 1977—; sec. Continental Acad. Hair Design, Inc., 1981—, also bd. dirs.; pres. Continental Crimping Inc.; mem. N.H. Ho. of Reps., 1982-84; mem. N.H. Senate, 1984—, v.p., 1989-90. Mem. Hudson County Budget Com., N.H., 1983-85; trustee Hudson Libr., 1984-85; chmn. Rep. State Commn.; mem. bd. edn. Mt. Hope Sch.; del. 1984 ConCon; chmn. Rep. State Party, N.H. Named Disting. Woman Leader Nashua (N.H.) YWCA, 1985; recipient Appreciation Svc. award, 1988-89. Mem. Daus. Union Vets. of Civil War (pres. 1949), N.H. Hairdressers and Cosmetologists Assn. (2d v.p. 1982-83, 1st v.p.), Nat. Bd. Cosmetology Assn. (bd. dirs.), Hudson C. of C. (bd. dirs.), Lionesses, Zonta. Republican.

Office: NH State Senate Concord NH 03301 Other: 2 Old Derry Rd Hudson NH 03051

CHARBONNEAU, SHARON MAE, hospital administrator; b. Duluth, Minn., Jan. 31, 1953; d. Sing and Lillian (Raymond) Chinn; m. Gary W. Charbonneau, Aug. 12, 1975. BS magna cum laude, U. Minn., 1975; MS, Ind. U., 1979. Tchr. high sch. English and reading Onamia (Minn.) High Sch., 1975-76; departmental sec. Ind. U., Bloomington, 1976-79, asst. to dir./bus. mgr. div. prof. dev., 1979-82, bus. mgr. adminstrv. computing, 1982-84; asst. dir. for info. svcs. Ind. U. Hosps., Indpls., 1985-89, asst. dir. patient accounts, 1989—; corp. adv. bd. PC Week mag., 1985-89, HFMA, 1990—, AGPAM, 1990—; fin. cons. Cert. Auctioneers' Inst., Bloomington, 1979-81; lic. real estate broker, Ind., 1981-82. Mem. Bloomington Commn. on Status of Women, 1979-81. Mem. Nat. Assn. Female Execs., Data Processing Mgmt. Assn., AAUW (v.p., editor Bloomington newsletter 1980-82), Am. Soc. for Info. Sci., Sierra Club. Republican. Clubs: Indiana U. Womens' Faculty (bd. dirs. 1982-87, pres. 1985-86), Toastmasters. Home: 6785 Lampkins Ridge Rd Bloomington IN 47401 Office: Ind U Hosps 1110 W Michigan St LO-300 Indianapolis IN 46202

CHARDIET, BERNICE KROLL, juvenile books publisher, editor, record and cassette producer; b. N.Y.C., Nov. 12, 1930; d. Saul and Florence Kroll; m. Oscar Chardiet-DeLaTorre, June 23, 1957; children—Simon, Jon Michel. B.A., Queens Coll., N.Y.C., 1950; Ed.M., Hunter Coll., N.Y.C., 1955. Cert. tchr. English, secondary schs. Scriptwriter, composer, jazz pianist, radio, TV, nightclubs, 1950-55; tchr. high sch. English DeWitt Clinton High Sch., N.Y.C., 1955-59; promotion dir. Elem. Mags. Scholastic Inc., N.Y.C., 1964-67, editor See-Saw Book Club, 1967-80, v.p., editorial dir. Scholastic juvenile books, 1980-84, producer, dir. Scholastic records, 1967-84; v.p., ptnr. Parachute Press, N.Y.C., 1984-88; pres. Chardiet Unltd. Inc., 1988—; cons. packager juvenile and adult books various pubs. Author: Cis for Circus, 1971, Juan Bobo and the Pig, 1973, The Monkeys and the Water Monster, 1974, Rapunzel Retold, 1980, The Carrot-Top Mystery ,1984; (recording) Jack and the Beanstalk (ALA Notable 1984). Mem. Authors Guild, ALA, ASCAP Internat., PEN Club, Overseas Press Club, Internat. Reading Assn., Soc. Children's Book Writers. Office: Chardiet Unltd Inc 33 W 17th St New York NY 10011

CHAREN, MONA, syndicated columnist; b. N.Y.C., Feb. 25, 1957; d. George and Claire (Rosenfeld) C.; m. Robert P. Parker. BA, Columbia U., 1979; JD, George Wash. U., 1984. Editorial assoc. Nat. Review Mag., N.Y.C., 1979-81; speechwriter White House, Washington, 1984, assoc. dir., office of pub. liasion, 1985-86; speechwriter Jack Kemp for Pres., Washington, 1986; syndicated columnist Creators Syndicate, L.A., 1987—. Contbr. articles to profl. mags. and publs. Republican. Jewish. Office: Creators Syndicate 5777 Century Blvd Ste 700 Los Angeles CA 90045

CHARLAP, ANNE E., environmental engineer; b. N.Y.C., Mar. 29, 1956; d. Morris I. and Elizabeth Katherine (Sawens) C. BSc, Colo. Sch. Mines, 1988. Asst. to pres. Mitchell Engring., Golden, Colo., Pan Aero, Lakewood, Colo.; environ. engr. Environ. Waste Mgmt. Assocs., Paterson, N.J., Jenny Engring. Corp., Springfield, N.J., Woodward-Clyde Cons., Wayne, N.J.; commr. Ramsey (N.J.) Environ. Commn., 1990—. Mem. Soc. Petroleum Engring. Office: Woodward-Clyde Cons 201 Willowbrook Blvd PO Box 290 Wayne NJ 07470

CHARLES, LISA J., graphics company executive; b. Struthers, Ohio, Dec. 16, 1943; d. Jack Allen and May Ann Cougill. Student, Ind. State U.-Purdue, 1981. Typesetter pasteup Kendallville (Ind.) Printing Co.; office mgr. graphics layout and design Jemco Advt., Inc., Kendallville. Mem. NAFE, Tri Kappa Inc. Home: 525 W Williams Kendallville IN 46755

CHARLES, LYRIA MICHELLE, information systems specialist; b. N.Y.C., Feb. 15, 1957; d. Albert and Loretta (Lilly); m. Jeffrey Charles Jr., Nov. 15, 1979 (div. Feb. 1984). Student, Calif. State U., Long Beach, U. So. Calif., Los Angeles. Math analyst TRW Systems, Redondo Beach, Calif., 1978-85; systems analyst Digital Equipment Corp., Costa Mesa, Calif., 1985-87; systems engr. Sybase, L.A., 1987-88; dir. Dunn Edwards Corp., L.A., 1988—; cons. Image Provider Systems, San Bernardino, Calif., 1987--, TRW Systems Redondo Beach, 1988, ALCOA Aluminum Co., Los Angeles, 1988--. Counselor cub pack Lawndale area Boy Scouts Am., 1988-89. Mem. Data Processing Mgmt. Assn. Office: Dunn Edwards Corp 4885 E 52nd Pl Los Angeles CA 90040

CHARLESWORTH, VELMA LILLIAN, librarian; b. Castile, N.Y., Sept. 30, 1919; d. Sylvanius Frank and Frances Marian (Nichols) Smith; m. George Herbert Charlesworth, Apr. 9, 1944; children: David William, George Herbert, Bonita Beth (dec.). BA, Houghton (N.Y.) Coll., 1941; MSLS, SUNY, Geneseo, 1946; postgrad., U. Md., summer 1959, So. Conn. State Coll., New Haven, summer 1968. Tchr. history/English, librarian Chaumont (N.Y.) Cen. High Sch., 1941-42, Ontario (N.Y.) High Sch., 1942-44; with IBM, Rochester, N.Y., 1944-45; librarian UCLA, 1946-47; asst. prof./librarian U. Md., 1947-53; librarian Nat. Asphalt Inst., College Park, Md., 1957-58, Montgomery County Schs., Silver Spring, Md., 1958-60, Trumbull (Conn.) Sch. Sys., 1965-81; ret.; conductor workshops in field; cons. in field. Author: Two Hundred Years, 1976 (bibliography). Del. to quadrenial United Meth. Women, 1962-86, 90, key woman, 1989—; vol. Literacy Vols. of Am., 1989—; active LWV, 1987-89; recording sec. Bicentennial com., Stratford (Conn.) United Meth. Ch., 1989—, mem. choir; leader Great Decisions, 1983—. Title II grantee, 1973. Mem. AAUW (book reviewer 1967—), Stratford Hist. Soc. (docent 1960—), Needlework Guild Am. Republican. Methodist. Home: 160 Lantern Rd Stratford CT 06497

CHARLETON, MARGARET ANN, child care administrator, consultant; b. Orange, Calif., Aug. 3, 1947; d. Arthur Mitchell and Isabelle Margaret (Esser) C.; (div. Sept. 1985). AA in Liberal Arts, Orange Coast Coll., 1968; BA in Psychology, Chapman Coll., 1984. Head tchr. Presbyn. Ch. of the Master, Mission Viejo, Calif., 1977-81; child care program adminstr. Crystal Stairs, Inc., L.A., 1981—; mem. adv. bd. Children's Home Soc., Santa Ana, Calif., 1982-83; cons. Calif. Sch. Age Consortium, Costa Mesa, 1987, Calif. State Dept. of Edn., 1988. Contbr. articles to profl. jours. Mem. South Orange County Community Svc., Mission Viejo, 1983—; liaison Family Svcs.-Marine Base, El Toro, Calif., 1989—. Recipient Plaque of Recognition, Vietnamese Community of Orange County, 1984. Mem. NAFE. Roman Catholic. Office: Crystal Stairs Inc 5105 W Goldleaf Circle #200 Los Angeles CA 90056

CHARLTON, BETTY JO, state legislator; b. Reno County, Kans., June 15, 1923; d. Joseph and Elma (Johnson) Canning; BA, U. Kans., 1970, MA, 1976; m. Robert Sansom Charlton, Feb. 24, 1946; children: John Robert, Richard Bruce. Asst. instr. polit. sci. and western civiliation U. Kans., Lawrence, 1970-73; legis. adminstrv. svcs. employee State of Kans., Topeka, 1977-78, legis. aide gov's. office, 1979; mem. Kans. Ho. of Reps., 1980—.

CHARMELLO, CATHERINE MARY, language arts educator; b. South Amboy, N.J., Mar. 20, 1942; d. Joseph Andrew and Catherine (Ryan) Smith; m. August John Charmello, Apr. 18, 1964 (dec. June 1989); children: Joseph, Karen. AAS, Middlesex Community Coll., Edison, N.J., 1977; BA, Kean Coll., 1980, postgrad. Cert. elem. tchr., N.J. Sr. bookkeeper Middlesex County Clk., New Brunswick, N.J., 1960-66; tchr. St. Ambrose Sch., Old Bridge, N.J., 1980-81, South Amboy Middle Sch., 1981—. Pres. South Amboy Libr. Bd., 1987—; extraordinary minister St. Mary's Ch., 1977—. Recipient Tchr. Recognition award Gov. N.J., 1986-87. Mem. South Amboy Edn. Assn. (pres. 1987-88, Gov.'s Tchr. Recognition award 1986-87). Democrat. Home: 247 Bordentown Ave South Amboy NJ 08879

CHARNIN, JADE HOBSON, magazine executive; b. N.Y.C., Mar. 12, 1945; d. John Louis Campo and Elizabeth (Anne) Stanton; m. David Alan Hobson, Dec. 30 (div. 1972); m. Martin Charnin, Dec. 18, 1984. BA, NYU, 1967. Asst. editor Glamour mag., N.Y.C., 1970; accessory editor Vogue mag., N.Y.C., 1970-78, fashion editor, 1978-81, fashion dir., 1981-86, creative dir. fashion, 1987-88; v.p., dir. creative svcs. for fashion and design group Revlon, Inc., 1988; exec. creative dir. Mirabella Mag., 1988—; cons. editor Self mag., N.Y.C., 1979-81. Costumer coord. for off broadway shows Laughing Matter, 1989, Martin Charnin, the Hits and the M.S.'s, 1990. Mem. NAFE, Am. Horticultural Soc., Horticultural Soc. N.Y. (bd. dirs.), Humane Soc., Animal Protection Inst. Democrat. Avocations: gardening, opera, ballet, theater, skiing. Office: Mirabella Mag 10 E 53d St New York NY 10022

CHARPENTIER, GAIL WIGUTOW, school director; b. N.Y.C., Mar. 10, 1946; d. Jacob M. and Ethel (Israel) Wigutow; m. Peter Jon Charpentier; children: Elisabeth Marie, Matthew Kyle. BA, CUNY, 1967; MA, New Sch. Social Research, N.Y.C., 1976. Lic. social worker. Tchr. Spl. Service Pub. Sch., Bronx, N.Y., 1967-73; adminstr. Boston City Hosp., 1973-76; dir. Monson Devel. Ctr., Palmer, Mass., 1976; residential dir. Kolburne Sch., New Marlboro, Mass., 1976-79; dir. Berkshire Children's Community, Great Barrington, Mass., 1979—; researcher Nat. Opinion Research Ctr., N.Y.C. and Boston, 1973-76; trainer residential child care, Mass., 1978—; mem. human rights bd. Oakdale Found., Great Barrington, 1980—. Recipient Community Criminal Justice award Justice Resource Inst., 1984. Mem. Mass. Assn. Approved Pvt. Schs. (bd. dirs. 1982-84, ins. trustee 1983-87, Service award 1982), New Eng. Assn. for Child Care, Assn. for Mentally Deficient, Internat. Assn. for Retts Syndrome. Home: Orchard House Tyringham MA 01264 Office: Berkshire Children's Community 41 Taconic Ave Great Barrington MA 01230

CHARREN, PEGGY, consumer activist; b. N.Y.C., Mar. 9, 1928; d. Maxwell and Ruth (Rosenthal) Walzer; m. Stanley Charren, June 17, 1951; children: Deborah, Claudia. BA, Conn. Coll., 1949; LLD (hon.), Regis Coll., 1978; DHL (hon.), Emerson Coll., 1984; EdD (hon.), Bank St. Coll. Edn., 1985; DHL (hon.), Tufts U., 1988; EdD (hon.), Wheelock Coll., 1990. Founder, owner Art Prints, Inc., Providence, 1951-53, Quality Book Fairs, Newton, Mass., 1960-65; dir. Creative Arts Council, Newton, 1966-68; founder, pres. Action for Children's Tel., Inc., Cambridge, Mass., 1968—; mem. Carnegie Commn. on Future of Public Broadcasting, 1977-79; mem. task panel on public attitudes and use of media for promotion of health President's Commn. on Mental Health, 1977-80; mem. Mass. Council on Arts and Humanities, 1980-87; vis. scholar in edn. Harvard Grad. Sch. Edn., 1987—; mem. adv. bd. project on TV advt. and children NSF; mem. adv. bd. project on devel. of programs for children with spl. needs Am. Inst. Research; bd. dirs. Child Devel. Consortium, Media Access Project, Kidsnet. Co-author: Changing Channels: Living Sensibly with Television, 1983, The TV-Smart Book for Kids, 1986; Television, Children and the Constitutional Bicentennial, 1986; contbr. articles to profl. publs. Bd. dirs. Women's Campaign Fund., Young Audiences of Mass.; mem. adv. bd. Am. Repertory Theater. Recipient Disting. Public Info. Service award Am. Acad. Pediatrics, hon. award Motion Picture Assn., Disting. Service award Mass. Radio and TV Assn., 1974, hon. medal Conn. Coll., 1974, Helen Homans Gilbert award Radcliffe Coll., Trustees' award NATAS, 1989; named Humanist of Yr. Ethical Soc. of Boston, 1988. Democrat. Office: Action for Childrens TV 20 University Rd Cambridge MA 02138

CHARTIER, JANELLEN OLSEN, airline inflight service coordinator; b. Chgo., Sept. 12, 1951; d. Roger Carl and Genevieve Ann (McCormick) Olsen; m. Lionel Pierre-Paul Chartier, Nov. 6, 1982; 1 child, Régine Anne. B.A. in French and Home Econs., U. Ill., 1973, M.A. in Teaching French, 1974; student U. Rouen (France), 1971-72. Cert. tchr., Ill. Flight attendant Delta Airlines, Atlanta, 1974—, French qualified, 1974—, Spanish qualified, 1977-82, German qualified, 1980—, in flight service coordinator, 1980—, European in flight service coordinator, 1983—; French examiner In-Flight Service, 1984—; interpreter Formax, Inc., Mokena, Ill., 1976-82. Bd. dirs. One Plus One Dance Co., Champaign, Ill., 1977-78. Mem. Alliance Maison Francaise de Chgo., Phi Delta Kappa, Alpha Lambda Delta. Roman Catholic. Home: 155 N Harbor Dr Apt 3506 Chicago IL 60601

CHARYA, VIJAYALAKSHMI VELAGALETI, city official; b. Mahbubnagar, Andhra, India, Oct. 1, 1956; came to U.S., 1979; d. Krishnama Kidambi and Sheshamma Kidambi (Bukkapatnam) C. BS, Osmania U., Mahbubnagar, 1977; BEd, Dharwad U., Gulbarga, Karnatak, 1979. Tchr. Modern High Sch., Mahbubnagar, 1977-78; water quality asst. City of Wilmington (Del.), 1980—. Mem. Am. Water Works Assn., Am. Ofcl. Analytical Chemists. Home: 506 W 39th St Wilmington DE 19802 Office: City of Wilmington 103 E 16th St Wilmington DE 19802

CHASE, DORIS TOTTEN, sculptor, video artist, filmmaker; b. Seattle, 1923; d. William Phelps and Helen (Feeney) Totten; m. Elmo Chase, Oct. 20, 1943 (div. 1972); children: Gregary Totten, Randall Jarvis Totten. Student, U. Wash., 1941-43. lectr. tours for USIA in S.Am., 1975, Europe, 1978, India, 1972, Australia, 1986, Eastern Europe, 1987. Exhibited in one-woman shows Seligman Gallery, Seattle, 1959, 61, Gallery Numero, Florence, Italy, 1961, Internat. Gallery, Italy, 1962, Hall Coleman Gallery, Seattle, 1962, Formes Gallery, Tokyo, 1963, 70, Bangkok Ctr. Mus., Thailand, 1963, Bolles Gallery, San Francisco, 1964, Suffolk (N.Y.) Mus., 1965, Smolin Gallery, N.Y.C., 1965, Gallery Numero, Rome, 1962, 66, Collectors Gallery, Seattle, 1964, 66, 69, Tacoma Art Mus., 1967, Ruth White Gallery, N.Y.C., 1967, 69, 70, Fountain Gallery, Portland, Oreg., 1970, U. Wash. Henry Gallery, 1971, 77, Wadsworth Atheneum, Hartford, Conn., 1973, Hirshhorn Mus., Washington, 1974, 77, Anthology Film Archives, N.Y.C., 1975, 80, 83, Donnell Library, N.Y.C., 1976, 79, 83, Performing Arts Mus. at Lincoln Ctr., 1976, Mus. Modern Art, N.Y.C., 1978, 80, 87, High Mus., Atlanta, 1978, Herbert Johnson Mus., 1982, A.I.R. Gallery, N.Y.C., 1983-85, Art in Embassies, USIS, 1984-88, Inst. Contemporary Art, London, 1989, Woodside/Braseth Gallery, 1990, John F. Kennedy Ctr., 1990; circulating exhbt., Western Mus. Assn., 1970-71; represented in permanent collections, Finch Coll. Mus., N.Y.C., Mus. Modern Art, N.Y.C., Seattle Art Mus., Ashai Shimbum, Tokyo, Georges Pompidou Ctr., Paris, Battelle Inst., Mus. Fine Arts Boston, Milw. Art Inst., Art Inst. Chgo., Mus. Fine Arts Houston, Frye Art Mus., Seattle, Nat. Collection Fine Arts, Smithsonian Inst., Washington, Wadsworth Atheneum, N.C. Mus. Art, Raleigh, Mus. Modern Art, Kobe, Japan, Pa. Acad. Art, Phila., Portland Art Mus., Vancouver (B.C.) Art Gallery, N.Y.C., Montgomery (Ala.) Mus. Fine Art, Hudson River Mus., N.Y.C., works represented in archival collections Ctr. for Film and Theatre Research, U. Wis., Madison, U. Wash., Seattle, works reproduced in various art mags. and books; executed monumental kinetic sculpture, Kerry Park, Seattle, Anderson, Ind., Expo '70, Osaka, Japan, Sculpture Park, Atlanta, Lake Park, Ind., Met. Mus. Art, N.Y.C., Montgomery Mus. Fine Arts, Seattle Ctr. Theater, multi-media sculpture for 4 ballets, Opera Assn. Seattle; included in, Sculpture in Park program N.Y.C., Playground of Tomorrow ABC-TV, Los Angeles; work in video, TV Exptl. Lab., Sta. WNET; TV prodns. Lies, 1980; Window, 1980, Doris Chase Dance Series produced at Bklyn. Coll., U. Mich., Ann Arbor, Sta. RTSI-TV, Switzerland, Sta. WCET-Cin., Sta. WGBH, Boston, Sta. WNYC, N.Y., NET, producer, Doris Chase Dance Series, 1971-81, Concept Series, 1980-84; prod. By Herself Series: Table for One (with Geraldine Page), 1985, (with Anne Jackson) Dear Papa, 1986, (with Luise Rainer) A Dancer, 1987, (with Priscilla Pointer) Still Frame, 1988, (with Joan Plowright) Sophie, 1989. Recipient honors and awards at numerous festivals in U.S. and fgn. countries; grantee Nat. Endowment for Arts, Am. Film Inst., 1988, N.Y. State Council for Arts, Mich. Arts Council, Jerusalem Film Festival, 1987, Berlin Film Festival, 1985, 87, London Film Festival, 1986, Am. Film Inst. Festival, 1987; subject of documentary Doris Chase: Portrait of the Artist (by Robin Schanzenbach), PBS, 1985. Mem. Actors Studio (writer, dirs. wing 1986, bd. dirs. 911, Art Media Ctr. 1990). Address: Chelsea Hotel 222 W 23d St New York NY 10011

CHASE, HELEN LOUISE, banker; b. Waukegan, Ill., Sept. 29, 1943; d. David William and Ruth Virginia (Sawyer) C. BA, U. Ill., 1965. Sec., exec. sec. Foote, Cone and Belding, Chgo., 1965-66; various positions Continental Bank, Chgo., 1966-73, internat. banking officer, 1973-76, 2nd v.p., 1976-77; Brazil rep. Continental Bank, Sao Paulo, 1977-80; 2nd v.p., sect. head Far East group Continental Bank Internat., N.Y.C., 1980-81; 2nd v.p. internat. div. Continental Bank, Chgo., 1981-83; v.p. N.Am. Union Trust Bank (now Signet Bank), Balt., 1983-84; v.p., mgr. internat. ops. Signet Bank, Balt., 1984-89; v.p. internat. dept. Meridian Bank, Lancaster, Pa., 1989—. Mem. U.S. Coun. on Internat. Banking (nat collections com.), East Bank Club. Office: Meridian Bank 51 S Duke St Lancaster PA 17602

CHASE, JEAN COX, language educator; b. Charlottesville, Va., July 2, 1925; d. Joseph Lee and Wirt (Davidson) Cox; m. John Bryant Chase Jr., June 16, 1951 (wid. June 1978); children: Nancy Davidson Chase, Jean Cox Chase Bagonzi. BA magna cum laude, U. N.C. Woman's Coll., 1946; MA in Eng. and Lit., U. Mich., 1947; postgrad., U. Va., 1950, 53, various univs. Cert. tchr., Va., N.C. Instr. English Carroll Coll., Waukesha, Wis., 1947-49, housemother, 1948-49; teaching asst. English U. Wis., Madison, 1949; editorial proof reader Michie Legal Publs., Charlottesville, Va., 1951; tchr. of English and Latin Lane High Sch., Charlottesville, Va., 1950-53; critic tchr. for sch. edn. in English U. Va., Charlottesville, Va., 1951; tutor Chapel Hill, N.C., 1958-66; teaching English, gifted, remedial Jordan High Sch., Durham, N.C., 1966; tchr. of English Orange County High Sch., Hillsborough, N.C., 1966-67; instr. Cen. Piedmont Community Coll., Charlotte, N.C., 1970-87; co-chmn. fall faculty conf., Cen. Piedmont Community Coll., 1974, vice-chmn. faculty senate, 1976-77, chmn., 1977-78, chmn. writing across the curriculum, 1980-84 and others; judge Charlotte Writers Club Contest, 1984. Co-editor, author: The Communication Course, 1974; contbg. author, The Jane Doe Papers, 1977, Women of Mecklenburg: Making a Difference, 1980. Active N.C. state legis. coun., N.C. Coun. Women's Orgns., World Affairs Conf. Planning Com., Univ. League, Jr. Svc. League, others. Recipient scholarship U. Mich., Ann Arbor, 1946-47, fellowship Nat. Endowment for Humanities, Carnegie Mellon Univ., Pitts., 1981. Mem. Modern Lang. Assn., Nat. Coun. Tchrs. of English, AAUW (various offices, coms.), Phi Beta Kappa, Kappa Delta Pi, Chi Omega (advisor local chpt. 1959-69), others. Democrat. Episcopalian. Home: 300 Woodhaven Rd #3405 Hilton Head Island SC 29928

CHASE, JOYCE ELAINE, accountant, nurse; b. Benton Harbor, Mich., Dec. 4, 1931; d. Richard I. and Evelyn Pauline (Hahn) Winney; m. Ernest Arthur Chase, July 21, 1951; children: Ernest L., Arthur M., Robert J., William R., James R. Student Lake Mich. Coll., 1974-75, Mich. State Ins. Sch., 1974; AA in Nursing, Lake Mich Coll., 1986. Clk. Gillespie's Drug Store, Benton Harbor, 1945, WoolWorth's Store, Benton Harbor, 1946-47; bookkeeper Reeder's Bookkeeping Service, Benton Harbor, 1949; assembler VM Corp., Benton Harbor, 1950; telephone operator Mich. Bell Co., Benton Harbor, 1951; bookkeeper I & M Electric Co., Buchanan, Mich., 1952, Auto Specialties Co., St. Joseph, Mich., 1953; clk. Galien Drug Store, Galien, Mich., 1955; assembler Electro-Voice Corp., Buchanan, Mich., 1958-62; bookkeeper Chase Bookkeeping & Tax Service, Galien, Mich., 1963-78, sr. tax accountant, 1968—; ins. agt. Chase Ins. Service Center, Galien, Mich., 1974-85, registered nurse, Pawating Hosp., Niles, Mich., 1986-89; day supr. Healthwin Hosp., South Bend, Ind., 1989—; emergency med. technician and ambulance driver Galien Vol. Ambulance Service, 1974—. Cub. Scout den mother S.W. Mich. council Cub. Scouts Am., 1963-69; mem. Galien Twp. election bd., 1971-86; mem. Galien Sch. Election Bd., 1971—; pres. Galien Athletic Boosters, 1969; mem. Galien High Sch., PTA, 1966—, adv. com., 1965-68. Mem. Nat. Soc. Pub. Accountants, Mich. Emergency Services Health Council, Am. Legion Aux. Republican. Methodist. Home: US Route 12 East Garwood Lake Galien MI 49113 Office: 112 N Main St Galien MI 49113

CHASE, LIDA GAZLAY, psychology educator; b. Evanston, Ill., May 5, 1938; d. William Loudon and Lida Hampton (Gazlay) Chase. BS, U. Calif., Berkley, 1960, U. Calif., San Francisco, 1963; MS, U. Calif., San Francisco, 1968; PhD, U. Hawaii, 1989. Staff psychiatric nurse Langley Porter Neuro Psychiatric Inst., San Francisco, 1963-65; asst. prof. psychology U. Hawaii-Manoa, Honolulu, 1968—. Contbr. articles to profl. jours.; contbg. author: Sandra Smiths Review of Nursing for State Board Examinations, 1982, Practice Tests for State Board Examinations, 1980; artist etchings: Honolulu Printmakers Ann. Juried shows, 1985, 87. Vol. various charitable orgns. Mem. Honolulu Printmakers, Sigma Theta Tau. Republican. Episcopalian. Home: 3045 Pualei Cir Apt 212 Honolulu HI 69815 Office: U of Hawaii 2528 The Mall Honolulu HI 69822

CHASE, LINDA ARVILLE, musician, writer; b. Cambridge, Mass., Jan. 14, 1953; d. Harold Francis and Irene Bernice (Sakowski) Chase; m. Richard Herbert Adams, July 22, 1974 (div. 1977); m. Michel Phillip Iodice, Apr. 22, 1985. Pvt. student of R. Fitzgerald, New Eng. Conservatory, 1959-68; student, Mass. Coll. Art, 1970, Lesley Coll., 1970-71; pvt. studies, Boston, 1971-78. Writer, pub., performed more than 200 songs; co-writer theme song for movie Once Bitten, 1985, 2 MTV videos, 1985; songwriter movie Rad; writer, producer, performer various TV and radio commercials; songwriter, perfomer movie Savage Streets; with David R. Currier signed with Jim Boyer, 1987. Mem. Am. Fedn. Musicians, Am. Fedn. TV and Radio Artists, Broadcast Music, Inc. Office: Paws Music Inc PO Box 2771 Woburn MA 01888

CHASE, LORIENE ECK, psychologist; b. Sacramento; d. Walter and Genevieve (Bennetts) Eck; m. Leo Goodman-Malauth, 1946 (div. 1951); 1 child, Leo; m. Allen Chase, Mar. 4, 1960 (div.); m. Clifton W. King, 1974. AB, U. So. Calif., 1948, MA, 1949, PhD, 1953. Psychologist Spastic Children's Found., L.A., 1952-55, Inst. Group Psychotherapy, Beverly Hills, Calif., 1957-59; pvt. practice, 1953—; v.p. VSP Exec. Relocation Consultants. Condr., Dr. Loriene Chase Show, ABC-TV, Hollywood, Calif. 1966—; cons. Camarillo State Hosp.; bd. dirs., pres.'s circle U. So. Calif.; founding mem. Achievement Rewards for Coll. Scientists; bd. dirs. Chase-King Personal Devel. Ctr., L.A.; v.p. Chase-King Prodns. Inc., L.A., Shell Beach, Calif.; exec. bd. Cancer Rsch. Ctr., L.A. Author: The Human Mircle; writer syndicated newspaper column Casebook of Dr. Chase; columnist Westways mag. With Waves World War II. Recipient Woman of Yr. in Psychology award Am. Mothers Com. Mem. AFTRA, Diadames, Assn. Media Psychologists, Les Dames de Champagne, Dame de Rotisseur, Nat. Art Assn., Screen Actors Guild, Internat. Platform Assn., Internat. Studies for the Study of Subtle Energies and Energy Medicine, Assn. for the Study of Dreams, Assn. for Past Life Rsch. and Therapy, Regency Club, Lakeside Country Club, Santa Maria Country Club. Home: 375 Palomar Shell Beach CA 93449

CHASE, VICTORIA BYLER, mechanical engineer; b. Dallas, Dec. 19, 1954; d. Edwin Carl Byler Sr. and Annie Orlena Hurlburt; m. Warren Chase, Apr. 9, 1988. BSME, So. Meth. U., 1979; postgrad., U. Tex., Dallas, 1986—. Registered profl. engr., Tex. Design drafter Tex. Instruments, Inc., Dallas, 1973-78, mech. design engr., 1979, lead mech. engr., 1983-85; project engr. Exxon Co., U.S.A., Houston, 1980-81; sr. project engr. Exxon Co., U.S.A., Tyler, Tex., 1981-83; engring. mgr. Tng. Gallery, Inc., Dallas, 1986; lead packaging engr. Boeing Electronics, Inc., Irving, Tex., 1987-88; sr. mech. engr. Sci. Communications, Garland, Tex., 1988-89. Mem. Tex. Soc. Profl. Engrs., Pi Tau Sigma. Presbyterian. Home: 2705 Chariot Ln Garland TX 75044

CHASE-RIBOUD, BARBARA DEWAYNE, sculptor, writer; b. Phila., June 26, 1939; d. Charles Edward and Vivian May (West) C.; m. Marc Eugene Riboud, Dec. 25, 1961(dec. 1981); children: David, Alexis; m. S.G. Tosi, July 4, 1981. M.F.A., Yale U., 1960; hon. doctorate, Temple U., 1981. Exhibited in one-woman shows Berkeley (Calif.) Mus., 1973, Mass. Inst. Tech., 1973, Detroit Art Inst., 1973, Indpls. Art Mus., 1973, Mus. Modern Art, Paris, 1974, Kunstmuseum Dusseldorf, 1974, Bronx Mus., 1979; exhibited in group shows Whitney Mus., N.Y.C., Smithsonian Mus., Washington, Mus. Modern Art, N.Y.C., Carnegie Inst., Pitts., Centre Pompidou, Paris; represented in permanent collections Met. Mus., Mus. Modern Art, Lannan Found., Los Angeles, Centre Pompidou, Nat. Collections, France, others; author: From Memphis and Peking, Poems, 1974, Sally Hemings, A Novel, 1979, Study of a Nude Woman as Cleopatra, Verse Novel 1987, (novel) Valide, 1986, (novel) Echo of Lions, 1989. John Hay Whitney Found. fellow, 1958; Nat. Endowment for Arts fellow, 1973; recipient Kafka prize for best fiction written by an Am. women, 1979, Academic of Italy with Gold medal, 1979, The Carl Sandburg Poetry prize, 1988. Mem. Yale Alumni Assn. also: Palazzo Ricci, Piazza Ricci, Rome 00186, Italy

CHASKELSON, MARSHA INA, neuropsychologist; b. Brookline, Mass., Jan. 6, 1950; d. Hyman and Doris (Sacks) C.; m. Allen Noah Elgart, July 8, 1973; children: Jonah Elgart, Benjamin Elgart, Sarah Elgart. BA in Psychology, U. Mass., 1971; MEd in Spl. Edn., Boston Coll., 1972, PhD Counseling Psychology, 1985. Lic. psychologist; cert. sch. psychologist; cert. provider. Resource room specialist for emotionally disturbed Acton-Boxborough Regional Jr. High Sch., Acton, Mass., 1972-76; faculty mem., on-site facilitator Boston Coll., Chestnut Hill, Mass., 1976-77; in-patient coord., out-patient staff psychologist Kennedy Meml. Hosp., Brighton, Mass., 1977-80; contracted sch. psychologist Beverly Pub. Schs., Beverly,

Mass., 1981; contracted staff psychologist Human Resource Inst., Franklin, Mass., 1980-82; mental retardation coord. Human Resource Inst., 1982-83; clin. specialist Alternatives, Unltd., Whitinsville, Mass., 1981-87; dir. Lexington Psychol. & Ednl. Resources, Lexington, Mass., 1987—; psychology intern psychology dept. Kennedy Meml. Hosp., Brighton, 1976-77, post-doctoral psychologist Children's Hosp. Med. Ctr., Boston, 1984-85; post-doctoral neuropsychologist New Eng. Rehab. Hosp., Woburn, Mass., 1985-86; co-chairperson Lexington A.D.D. Parent Group, 1987-88. Mem. Am. Psychol. Assn., Internat. Neuropsychol. Soc., Mass. Neuropsychol. Soc., Coun. for Exceptional Children, Mass. Psychol. Assn., Mass. Assn. for Children with Learning Disabilities. Democrat. Jewish. Office: Lexington Psychol & Ednl Resources 76 Bedford St Ste 14 Lexington MA 02173

CHASKI, HILDA CECELIA, public health administrator, epidemiologist; b. Balt., Apr. 14, 1951; d. Milton Sylvester and Marylee (Evans) C.; m. Milton George Price, Jr., Oct. 15, 1977 (div. May 1985). BA in Biology, Manhattanville Coll., 1973; MPH, Yale U., 1987. Pub. health sanitarian Del. Dept. Health and Social Svcs., Georgetown, 1974-85; pub. health cons., New Haven, 1987; dep. dir. div. environ. health and epidemiology Mo. Dept. Health, Jefferson City, 1987—, acting div. dir., 1988-90; instr. anatomy and physiology Del. Tech. and Community Coll., Georgetown, 1981-85; presenter in field. Contbr. articles to profl. jours. Pres. Del. Environ. Assn., 1977; mem. Columbia (Mo.) Bd. Plumbing Examiners, 1988-90, Columbia Commn. on Bicycling, 1988-91. Rcipient letter of commendation State of Del., 1981, 84, Young Careerist award DeVries Bus. and Profl. Women's Club, 1980, cert. of appreciation Del. Tech. and Community Coll.-Calif. Coll. Respiratory Therapy, 1981. Mem. APHA, Nat. Environ. Health Assn. (exec. coun. 1977), Mo. Pub. Health Assn. (v.p. Cen. Mo. chpt. 1988-89, pres. 1989-90).

CHASTAIN, DOROTHY STRAUGHAN (JODI CHASTAIN), marketing professional; b. Miami, Fla., May 8, 1950; d. James Lambert and Lena Mae (Trisler) Straughan; children: Shana Jolena, Kara Marlene. BS, U. Fla., 1972. Pers. specialist So. Bell, Gainesville, Fla., 1972-76; pub. rels. sec. Decatur (Ala.) Civic Chorus, 1987-88; mktg. specialist Jay-Jay Assocs. Advt. Agy., Decatur, 1988—. Bd. dirs. Vol. Ctr.; PTA coun. mem. City of Decatur. Mem. NAFE, AAUW, Decatur C. of C., Decatur Women's C. of C., Assn. for Retarded Citizens, Alliance Physically Handicapped, Mental Health Assn. Democrat. Methodist. Home: 1313 Runnymeade Ave Decatur AL 35601 Office: 11 E Moulton St Decatur AL 35601

CHATER, SHIRLEY SEARS, university administrator; b. Shamokin, Pa., July 30, 1932; d. Raymond and Edna (Shamp) Sears; m. Norman Chater, Dec. 5, 1959; children: Cris, Geoffrey. BS, U. Pa., 1956; MS, U. Calif.-San Francisco, 1960; PhD, U. Calif.-Berkeley, 1964. Prof. dept. social and behavioral scis. Sch. Nursing U. Calif., San Francisco, 1973-86, asst. vice chancellor acad. affairs, 1974-77, vice chancellor acad. affairs Sch. Nursing, 1977-82; council assoc. Am. Council Edn., Washington, 1982-84, mem. commn. on women; sr. assoc. Presdl. Search Consultation Svc. Assn. Governing Bds., Washington, 1984-86; pres. Tex. Woman's U., Denton, 1986—; mem. commn. on women, Am. Council on Edn., 1986-90. Mem. adv. com. Robert Wood Johnson Found., Kellogg Nat. Fellows Program, Leadership Am.; bd. dirs. United Educators Ins. Risk Retention Group, Assn. Tex. Colls. and Univs., Assn. for Higher Edn. of North Tex., Denton United Way, Flow Meml. Hosp.; assoc. trustee U. Pa. Mem. Inst. of Medicine, Nat. Acad. of Medicine, Women's Forum West, Denton C. of C. (bd. dirs.), Charter 100, Internat. Alliance. Office: Tex Woman's U Box 23925 TWU Sta Denton TX 76204

CHATFIELD, CHERYL ANN, stock brokerage firm executive, writer; b. King's Park, N.Y., Jan. 24, 1946; d. William David and Mildred Ruth (King) C.; m. Gene Allen Chasser, Feb. 17, 1968 (div. 1979); m. James Bernard Arkebauer, Apr. 16, 1983 (div. 1987). BS, Cen. Conn. Coll., 1968, MS, 1972; PhD, U. Conn., 1976. Cert. gen. prin. securities. Tchr. Bristol East High Sch., Conn., 1968-77; adminstr. New Britain Schs., Conn., 1977-79; prof. Ariz. State U., Phoenix, 1979; stockbroker J. Daniel Bell, Denver, 1980-83, Hyder and Co., Denver, 1983-84; stockbroker; chief exec. officer Chatfield Dean & Co., Denver, 1984—; tchr. investment seminars Front Range Community Coll., Denver, 1984-86; speaker women's groups, Denver, 1983-86. Author: Low-Priced Riches, 1985, Selling Low-Priced Riches, 1986, (newspaper columns) For Women Investors, 1982-84, Commentary, 1985-86; editor, founder (newsletter) Women in Securities . Project bus. cons. Jr. Achievement, Denver, 1986; trustee Orchestra of Santa Fe. Mem. NAFE, Aircraft Owners and Pilots Assn., AAUW, N.Mex. Venture Capital Club (treas.), Kappa Delta Pi. Republican. Roman Catholic. Avocation: flying. Office: Woman Securities Internat 5575 DTC Pkwy Ste 300 Englewood CO 80111

CHATFIELD, RUTH CHRISTINA, nurse, researcher; b. Atlanta, July 9, 1956; d. Gene Hall and Norma Jean (Bryant) C. Diploma in nursing, Ga. Bapt. Med. Ctr., Atlanta, 1979; BS in Nursing, Emory U., 1983. RN, Ga. Staff nurse Windy Hill Hosp., Marietta, Ga., 1979-80; charge nurse Ga. Bapt. Med. Ctr., 1980-83, oncology clinician, 1983-85; clin. educator Humana Women's Hosp., Tampa, Fla., 1985-86; team nurse, coord. nutrition support and pain teams H. Lee Moffit Cancer Ctr. and Rsch., Inst., Tampa, 1986-88; mktg. rep. Am. Home Patient Ctrs., Inc., Franklin, Tenn., 1988-89; mgr. Pharmacia Deltec, Inc., St. Paul, 1989—; presenter in field. Contbr. articles to profl. jours. Vol. Am. Cancer Soc., 1982-84; instr. basic cardiac life support Am. Heart Assn., 1985-86. Mem. Internat. Assn. for Study Pain, Am. Soc. for Parenteral and Enteral Nutrition (Fla. bd. dirs. 1988-90), Oncology Nurses Soc., Fla. Assn. Nutrition Support (nurse counselor 1988, 89, newsletter editor 1989, 90, bd. dirs. 1988-90). Republican. Home: 5106 Bayshore Blvd Tampa FL 33611 Office: Pharmacia Deltec Inc 1265 Grey Fox Rd Saint Paul MN 55112

CHATFIELD-TAYLOR, ADELE, arts administrator, historic preservationist; b. Washington, Jan. 29, 1945; d. Hobart Chatfield-Taylor and Mary Owen (Lyon) C.-T.; m. John Guare, May 20, 1981. BA, Manhattanville Coll., 1966; MS in Historic Preservation, Columbia U., 1974; postgrad. (Loeb fellow), Harvard U., 1978-79. Archtl. historian Historic Am. Bldg. Survey, Washington, 1967; co-founder, dir. Urban Deadline Architects, Inc., 1968-73; landmarks preservation specialist N.Y.C. Landmarks Preservation Commn., 1973-74, asst. to chmn., 1974-79, dir. policy and programs, 1979-80; adj. prof. historic preservation program Grad. Sch. Architecture and Planning, Columbia U., 1976—; exec. dir. N.Y. Landmarks Preservation Found., 1980-84; dir. design arts program Nat. Endowment for Arts, 1984-88; pres. Am. Acad. in Rome, N.Y.C., 1988—; asst. dir. Neighborhood Conservation Conf. Nat. Endowment Arts, 1975; bd. dirs. Preservation ACTION, 1976-84, regional v.p., 1978-83, sec., 1983-84; trustee Ctr. for Bldg. Conservation, 1978-84; mem. U.S. del. to China, Women in Architecture, 1977, 80, U.S. del. to China, Historic Preservationists, 1982; mem. exec. com. U.S./Internat. Coun. on Monuments and Sites, 1979-84; mem. China adv. com. Nat. Endowment Arts, 1980-84, vice chmn. design arts policy panel, 1978-82; bd. dirs. Nat. Alliance of Preservation Commns., 1983-84; trustee Tiber Island History Mus., 1983—; guest lectr. Harvard U., MIT, Columbia U., NYU, U. Va. Contbr. articles to profl. jours. Mem. restoration com. South Street Seaport Mus., 1975-84; mem. Nat. Com. on U.S.-China Relations, 1982—; mem. lawn adv. bd. U. Va., 1982-86; mem. adv. bd. Jeffersonian Restoration, 1989—, Law and the Arts, 1989—; bd. dirs. Greenwich Village Trust for Historic Preservation, 1983-84, Internat. Design Conf. Aspen, 1986—, Nat. Bldg. Mus., 1989—; mem. adv. bd. Jellesonian Restoration, 1989—; mem. Commn. Fine Arts, 1990—. Archtl. fellow Ednl. Facilities Lab Acad. Ednl. Devel., 1982-83; Rome prize Am. Acad. in Rome, 1983-84; fellow N.Y. Inst. Humanities, 1983—. Mem. Nat. Trust Historic Preservation, Friends of Cast Iron Architecture, Preservation League N.Y. State, Met. Mus. Art, Vernacular Architecture Soc., Decorative Arts Soc., Nat. Council of Preservation Execs. Club: Pug Dog of Greater N.Y. Office: Nat Endowment for Arts Design Arts Program 1100 Pennsylvania Ave NW Washington DC 20506

CHATTERJEE, SRABANI, bank officer; b. Calcutta, India; came to U.S., 1979; d. Provashkumar and Arati (Basu) Sinha; m. Samar Chatterjee, Oct. 30, 1969; children: Sanjoy, Sarmistha. BA, Scottish Ch. Coll., Calcutta West Bengal, India, 1966; MA, Univ. Coll., Calcutta West Bengal, India, 1968; cert. in bus., MIT. Clk. Fisons Pharm. Ltd., Loughborough, 1970-71; adminstrv. clk. Scallop Corp., N.Y.C., 1983-85; office aide N.Y.C. Bd. Edn., 1985; clk. typist, data processor State Bank India, N.Y.C., 1985—; tchr. math., gen. sci. and English, Africa, 1977-81. Mem. Rep. Nat. Com.; active various social svcs.; interpreter langs. of Bangladesh and India, U.K. Mem. NAFE. Office: State Bank India 42-08 Main St Flushing NY 11355

CHAUNCEY, SUSAN JOAN, public relations executive; b. Portchester, N.Y., Dec. 20, 1945; d. Arthur L. Annecharico and Julia K. (Campbell) Adamson; children: Julie Ann, Christian Lee. Student, U. Hartford (Conn.). Feature editor, writer The News Examiner, Gallatin, Tenn., 1982-86; pub. rels./mktg. dir. Sumner Meml. Hosp., Gallatin, 1986—; freelance writer, 1982, freelance mktg. cons., Sumner County, Tenn., 1987. Contbr. articles to profl. jours. Bd. mem. Am. Cancer Soc., Sumner County, 1986, ARC, Sumner County, 1982-86, Cumberland Crisis Pregnancy Ctr., Sumner County, 1984-89; mem. allocations com. United Way, Sumner County, 1986. Mem. Bus. and Profl. Women, Gallatin Arts Coun., Gallatin C. of C., Greater Gallatin. Republican. Office: Sumner Meml Hosp PO Box 1558 Gallatin TN 37066

CHAVARRIA, DAWN MARIE, computer operations manager; b. Detroit, Oct. 31, 1960; d. Joseph and Rosemarie (Samuel) Padolski; div.; 1 child, Nicole. Cert., Control Data Inst., Dearborn, Mich., 1979. Computer operator Hughes & Hatcher, Detroit, 1979-82; computer operator Allnet Communications, Birmingham, Mich., 1982-84; lead computer operator Allnet Communications, 1984-86, supr. computer ops., 1986-87, computer ops. mgr., 1987—. Mem. Nat. Assn. for Female Execs. Democrat. Roman Catholic. Office: Allnet Communications 30300 Telegraph Rd Ste 350 Birmingham AL 48010

CHAVARRIA, DOLORES ESPARZA, service executive; b. Levelland, Tex., Nov. 13, 1952; d. Thomas Medina and Hermenejilda (Estrada) Esparza; m. Margarito R. Grimaldo (div. Feb. 1975); children: Maurice Patrick, Margarito; m. Frank Sedillo Chavarria; 1 child, Mecca Esparza. AS, South Plains Community Coll., 1977; student, Tex. Tech U., 1977-78. Supr. cen. supply South Park Med. Ctr., Lubbock, Tex., 1980-84, dir. materials mgmt. dept., 1984—; buyer for city Lubbock, 1990—. Chmn. S.W. Voter's Registration, Lubbock, 1988. Mem. Am. Bus. Women's Assn. Democrat. Roman Catholic. Home: 516 52d St Lubbock TX 79404 Office: 1625 13th St Lubbock TX 79401

CHAVARRIA, ROSEMARY ANN, training professional; b. Amityville, N.Y., Dec. 10, 1954; d. Andrew Anthony and Philomena Rose (Grandinetti) Siniagra; m. Thomas Joseph McCoy, Aug. 14, 1977 (div. 1982); 1 child, Christopher Thomas; m. David Chavarria Jr., Sept. 22, 1985; 1 child, Matthew David; stepchildren: Joey, Rebecca, Albert, Melanie, Sulema. BS in Edn., Hofstra U., 1977. Lic. tchr., N.Y., Tex. Recreation specialist, tchr. arts and crafts Dept. Parks and Recreation Town of Oyster Bay, Massapequa, N.Y., 1972-78; sub. tchr. Massapequa and Farmingdale (N.Y.) Sch. Dists., 1977-78; tchr. fifth grade Roman Catholic Diocese of Houston and Galveston, 1978-79; instr. high sch. equivalency Operation SER/CETA, Galveston, 1980-81, div. continuing edn. Galveston Coll., 1981-82; tchr. arts and crafts, pre-sch. Island Montessori Sch., Galveston, 1981-82; dir. pre-sch. Tex. Parks and Recreation, Texas City, 1982-84; tng. specialist, job developer div. employment and tng. Town of Oyster Bay, Massapequa, N.Y., 1984—. Artist various media. Committeewoman Nassau County Reps., 1985—; committeewoman, v.p. North Massapequa Reps., 1985—. Mem. NAFE, Civil Svc. Employees Assn., Nat. Congress PTA, Hofstra U. Alumni Assn., Delta Chi Delta. Roman Catholic. Home: 222 N Wisconsin Ave North Massapequa NY 11758 Office: Town of Oyster Bay Div Employment and Tng 977 Hicksville Rd Massapequa NY 11758

CHAVEZ, JANIE IGNACIA, educator; b. Monterrey, Mex., July 31, 1946; came to U.S., 1955, naturalized, 1985; d. Guadalupe C. and Josefa (Cuevas) C. Student, Gulf Coast Bus Coll., 1968; BS in Elem. Edn., Tex. So. U., 1984. Cert. tchr., Tex. Typist Concentrated Employment Co., Houston, 1969-71; bookkeeper Phillips 66, Houston, 1971-73; sec. Highlands Ins., Houston, 1974-78; tchr. aide Houston Ind. Sch. Dist., 1978-83, bilingual tchr., 1984-86; substitute tchr. McAllen (Tex.) Ind. Sch. Dist., 1987—; computer cons, CIA Lab., Houston, 1981. Leader, Valley Interfaith, Weslaco-McAllen, 1987; v.p. Roosevelt Elem. PTA, McAllen, 1988-89. Mem. Nat. Tchrs. Assn., Am. Assn. Ret. Persons, Smithsonian Instn., NAFE, Fatima Crusader, Sacred Heart Auto League. Home: 3008 Lucille St McAllen TX 78503

CHAVIS, PEGGY WILKINS, teacher, marketing professional; b. Lumberton, N.C., Mar. 20, 1950; d. Elkins and Sallie (Oxendine) Wilkins; m. Robert Lee Chavis, Sept. 7, 1972; children: Robert Lee Jr., Wendy. AA, Southeastern Community Coll., Whiteville, N.C., 1970; BS, Pembroke (N.C.) State U., 1972; postgrad. in spl. edn., East Carolina U., 1975. Cert. elem. tchr., N.C. Homebound tchr. Columbus County Bd. Edn., Whiteville, N.C., 1972-78; telephone interviewer, Robeson Co. area rep. Trendex, 1978-80, 88—, Research Am., 1980—; telephone interviewer Arbitron TV Ratings, 1980-82; telephone interviewer, N.C. area rep. M/A/R/C Mktg. and Research Co., 1986—; adult high sch. tchr. Robeson Community Coll., Lumberton, 1981-83, 1987—; elem. tchr. Magnolia Sch., Robeson County Bd. Edn., Lumberton, 1978—; math coordinator Magnolia Sch., 1989—; owner Wilkins Cafe and Grocery Store, Jr.'s Mobile Home Park. Candidate NASA Tchr. in Space program, 1985; vol. Magnolia Sch., Lumberton, 1985-87; co-capt. Saddletree Community Crime Prevention, Lumberton, 1983—; lst vice chmn. Robeson County Dems., 1982-84; del. Dist. Congl. Conv., Lumberton and Raleigh, 1983—; treas. Saddletree Precinct, Lumberton, 1983—; chmn. Fairmont (N.C.) Car Show, 1987, 88, 89. Named Tchr. of Yr. Magnolia Sch., 1983-84, Top Vol. Magnolia Sch., 1985-87. Mem. N.C. Assn. Educators (sch. rep.). Mem. Holiness Ch. Home and Office: Rte 10 Box 618 Lumberton NC 28358

CHAVIS-MICKEY, ANGELA YELVERTON, dentist; b. Pembroke, N.C., May 11, 1950; d. Ulysses Preston and Leno (Oxendine) Chavis.; m. Richard Randall Mickey, June 28, 1980; children: Chalena, Candice, Rangley. BS, Pembroke State U., 1971; DDS, U. N.C., 1980. Acctg. clk. E.I. DuPont, Fayetteville, N.C., 1971-73; asst. chemist Kelly Springfield Tire Co., Fayetteville, 1973-76; pvt. practice Rowland, N.C., 1980—. Mem. ADA, N.C. Dental Soc., Southeastern Dental Soc., Rowland C. of C., Com. of 100. Democrat. Baptist. Home: Rt 1 Box 53D Marston NC 28363 Office: 108 S Hickory Rowland NC 28383

CHAVKIN, WENDY, physician; b. N.Y.C., Feb. 17, 1952; d. Samuel and Sylvia (Inzelberg) C.; m. Nicholas Freudenberg; 1 child, Sasha Freudenberg-Chavkin. BA, U. Mich., 1973; MD, SUNY, Stony Brook, 1978; MPH, Columbia U., 1980. Intern in ob-gyn Albert Einstein Coll. Medicine, N.Y.C., 1978-79; Pub. svc. sci. fellow NSF, N.Y.C., 1980; preventive medicine resident N.Y.C. Dept. Health, 1981-84; dir. dept. health Bur. Maternity Svc./Family Planning, N.Y.C., 1984-88; rsch. fellow Rockefeller Found., N.Y.C., 1988—; adj. asst. prof. sch. pub. health Columbia U., N.Y.C., 1985—; cons. Yale U. Med.Ctr.-Occupational Medicine Clinic, New Haven, 1981, coun. on the Humanities, N.Y., 1985—, Suffolk County Health Dept., N.Y., 1988—, Community Family Planning Coun., N.Y.C., 1988—, transition team for incoming county exec., Suffolk County, 1987-88, urban environ. conf. EPA, 1980, A.P.H.A. feasibility study EPA, 1979-80; med. adv. bd. Community Family Planning Coun., N.Y.C., 1988—; presenter in field. Author: Double Exposure: Women's Health Hazards on the Job and at Home, 1984 (Am. Health Mag. Book Award 1985); co-author: Working Women, Trade Unions and State Policy, 1986, The Toxic Crisis: What States Should Do, 1983, Reproductive Hazards in the Workplace--A Curriculum Guide, 1980; contbr. articles to profl. jours. Med. bd. mem. Planned Parenthood N.Y.C., 1986—; project mem. Reproductive Rights for the 1990's, N.Y.C., 1986-88; mem. Nat. Women's Health Network, Washington, 1980—; bd. dirs. Coalition for the Reproductive Rights Workers, Washington, 1980-84; chair task force on perinatal AIDS, N.Y.C. Dept. Health, 1985; mem. pub. policy com. Task Force to Promote Breastfeeding on N.Y.C., 1981-87; adv. bd. mem. Cen. Labor Coun., N.Y.C., 1981-83. Mem. N.Y. Acad. Medicine (subcom. on maternity and family health svcs.), Pub. Health Assn. N.Y.C. (exec. bd. mem. 1982-86, 1988—), Am. Coll. Tchrs. Preventive Medicine, Am. Pub. Health Assn., N.Y. Com. for Occupational Safety and Health (chair reproductive hazards com. 1978-84).

CHAVOOSHIAN, MARGE, artist, educator; b. N.Y.C., Jan. 8, 1925; d. Harry Mesrob and Anna (Tashjian) Kurkjian; m. Barkev Budd Chavooshian, Aug. 11, 1946; children: J. Dean, Nora Ann. Student Art Students League, 1943, Reginald Marsh, N.Y.C., 1943, Mario Cooper, N.Y.C., 1977. Designer Needlework Arts Co., N.Y.C., 1943-44; illustrator John David Men's Store, N.Y.C., 1944-45; illustrator, layout artist Fawcett Publs., N.Y.C., 1945-47; designer, illustrator Pa. State U., University Park, 1947-49; art tchr. Trenton pub. schs., N.J., 1958-68, art cons. Title One Program, 1968-74; painting instr. Princeton Art Assn., N.J., 1974-77, Jewish Community Ctr., Ewing, N.J., 1974-85, Contemporary Club, Trenton, 1974-85, YMCA, YWCA, Trent Ctr., Trenton, 1974—; artist-at-large Alliance For Arts Edn., N.J., 1979-80; adj. asst. prof. art instr. Mercer County Coll., West Windsor, N.J., 1985—. One woman shows include Rider Coll., 1974, Jersey City Mus., 1980, N.J. State Mus., 1981, Trenton City Mus., 1984, 87; exhibited in group shows at Douglas Coll., N.J., 1977, Bergen Mus., Paramus, N.J., 1980, 81, 82, Hunterdon Art Ctr., Clinton, N.J., 1982, Morris Mus., Morristown, N.J., 1984, Oakside Cultural Ctr., Bloomfield, N.J., 1985; represented in permanent collections N.J. State Mus., Jersey City Mus., Trenton City Mus., Morris Mus., Rider Coll., Art Mus. San Lazarre, Italy; mem. Armenian Apostolic Ch. Recipient numerous awards Union Coll., Mercer County Cultural and Heritage Commn., Phillips Mill, Am. Watercolor Soc.; named Woman of Month Woman's Newspaper of Princeton, 1984. N.J. State Council Arts fellow, 1979. Mem. Nat. Assn. Women Artists (two yr. nat. travel award 1985, recipient S. Winston Meml. award 1988), Am. Artists Profl. League (Am. Artists Council award 1973, Winsor Newton award 1980, others), Catherine Lorillard Wolfe Art Club (Bee Paper Co. award 1977, Anna Hyatt Huntington Bronze medal 1979), Allied Artists Am. (elected mem.), N.J. Watercolor Soc. (Newton Art Ctr. award 1972, Helen K. Bermel award 1984, Howard Savs. Bank award 1986-87), Painters and Sculptors Soc. (Medal of Honor, Digby Chandler medal, others), Garden State Watercolor Soc. (Triangle Art Ctr. award 1976, 89, Grumbacher Silver medal 1981, Merit award 1982, Trust Co. award 1987), Midwest Watercolor Soc., Nat. Arts Club (John Elliott award 1988), Phila. Watercolor Club. Democrat. Mem. Apostolic Ch. Avocations: piano, cooking, gardening. Home: 222 Morningside Dr Trenton NJ 08618

CHEAL, MARYLOU, experimental psychologist; b. St. Clair County, Mich.; d. Marion Louis Fast and Leda Eleanor (Shaw) Martin; m. James Cheal, Apr. 13, 1946; children: Thomas James, Catheryn Leda, Robert David. BA in Psychology with honors, Oakland U., 1969; PhD in Psychology, U. Mich., 1973. Rsch.investigator dept. zoology U. Mich., Ann Arbor, 1973-75, rsch. investigator dept. oral biology, 1975-76, lectr. dept. psychology, 1973-76; Charles A. King rsch. fellow Harvard U. Med. Sch., Boston, 1976-77; lectr. on psychology dept. psychiatry Harvard U. Sch. Medicine, Boston, 1977-83; asst. psychologist McLean Hosp., Belmont, Mass., 1977-81, assoc. psychologist, 1981-83; faculty rsch. assoc. dept. psychology Ariz. State U., Tempe, 1983-87, mem. faculty Women's Studies program, 1986; rsch. psychologist U. Dayton Rsch. Inst.-Williams AFB, Higley, Ariz., 1986—; vis. prof. Air Force Systems Command U. Resident Rsch. Program appointment, Williams AFB, Ariz., 1986-88; adj. assoc. prof. psychology Ariz. State U., 1987—; reviewer CUNY, NIMH, NSF, Ont. Mental Health Found., Tufts U. Sch. Medicine. Referee Internat. Jour. Aging and Human Devel., Pharmacology Biochemistry and Behavior, Jour. Experimental Psychology: Animal Behavioral Processes, Jour. Comparative Psychology, Animal Behaviour, Physiology and Behavior, Science, Behavioral Brain Rsch.; contbr. articles to profl. jours. Recipient numerous rsch. awards. Fellow AAAS, APA (program com. 1985, chmn. symposium 1985, fellow physiol. and comparative psychology and psychopharmacology 1986-90, mem. and fellow com. 1986) Am. Psychol. Soc.; mem. Soc. Neurosci., Southwestern Comparative Psychology Assn. (governing bd. 1984-85), Women in Neurosci. (steering com. 1982-85), Psychonomics Soc., Sigma Xi. Office: U Dayton Rsch Inst PO Box 2020 Higley AZ 85236-2020

CHECK, IRENE JOCIUS, educator, researcher; b. Austria, Aug. 2, 1946; came to U.S., 1949; d. Peter and Eleonora (Remeikyte) Jocius; m. William A. Check, June 2, 1973; children: Erika Elizabeth, Martin Peter Casimir. BS, Notre Dame Coll. of Ohio, 1967; PhD, Case Western Res. U., 1972. Diplomate Am. Bd. Med. Lab. Immunology. Rsch. assoc. St. Luke's Hosp., Cleve., 1972-73, U. Chgo., 1974-77; asst. prof. Emory U., Atlanta, 1980-82, assoc. prof., lab. dir. Sch. Medicine, Grad. Sch. Arts & Sci, 1980—; clin. immunology dir. MMSc program Sch. of Medicine Emory U. Hosp., Atlanta, 1985—; cons. CytRx Corp., Norcross, Ga., 1986-89. Contbr. numerous articles to profl. jours. Ortho Pharm. Co. Rsch. grantee, 1981, CytRx Corp. Rsch. grantee, 1986, U.S. Office Naval Rsch. Rsch. grantee, 1986, NIH Rsch. grantee, 1987. Mem. Am. Bd. Med. Lab. Immunology (bd. dirs. 1985—), Am. Soc. Clin. Pathologists (coun. 1989—), Am. Soc. Microbiology (chair elect diagnostic immunology div. 1989—, advisor subcom. on flow cytometry nat. com. for clin. lab. standards 1989—). Office: Emory U Hosp 1364 Clifton Rd Atlanta GA 30322

CHECKOSKY, ANNE CATHERINE, publications administrator; b. Syracuse, N.Y., Mar. 5, 1964; d. Edward A. and Dorothy E. (Williams) C. BA, Temple U., 1985. Prodn. asst. Radnor (Pa.) Cablevision, 1984-86; acctg. clk. Bryn Mawr (Pa.) Hosp., 1986-87; prodn. crewperson Newschannels Cable TV, East Syracuse, N.Y., 1987-88; camera operator Sta. WCNY TV, Liverpool, N.Y., 1987—; communications asst. Le Moyne Coll., Syracuse, 1987-88; editorial prodn. asst. LeMoyne Coll., Syracuse, 1988-89, pubs. coord., 1989—. Mem. Women in Communications, Inc. (bd. dirs. job bank asst. chair 1989-90, bd. dirs. job bank chair 1990-91). Roman Catholic. Home: 103 Worth St #3 East Syracuse NY 13057 Office: LeMoyne Coll Syracuse NY 13214

CHEEK, BARBARA LEE, director reading department, educator; b. Springfield, Mo., Oct. 25, 1935; d. Curtis Earl and Gertrude Helen (Ahonen) Nelson; m. Lee Roy Clyde, June 16, 1961; children: Michael, Paul, Daniel. BA in Edn. cum laude, Pacific Luth. U., 1957; postgrad., U. Wash., Seattle, 1961-62; MA in Elem. Edn., Boise (Idaho) State U., 1982; postgrad., Ea. Oreg. U., 1983, Seattle U., 1989. Cert. elem. and secondary edn. tchr., Wash. Sec. engring. dept. Boeing Aircraft Co., Seattle, 1957; instr. Edmonds (Wash.) Sch. Dist., 1957-61, Clover Pk. Sch. Dist., Tacoma, Wash., 1961-62, Payette (Idaho) Sch. Dist., 1970-74; bookkeeper Cheek Dairy Supply, Payette, 1970-71; instr. Ontario (Oreg.) Sch. Dist., 1975-79; prof. Treasure Valley Community Coll., Ontario, 1979-89; prof. Pierce Coll., Tacoma, 1989—, dir. reading dept., 1989—; sec. Malheur Reading Coun., Ontario, 1986-87, Treasure Valley Community Coll. Faculty, Ontario, 1986-88; mem. Peer Evaluation Oreg. Devel. Edn., Ontario, 1986. Moderator Ont. candidate's fair AAUW, 1985, state sec., Payette, 1972-74, sec. N.W. region, 1974, br. pres., 1970-72, 75-77; bd. dirs. Boy Scouts Am., Oregon, Idaho, 1971-84; deacon, v.p. Luth. Ch., 1986. Mem. AAUW (chpt. pres. 1970-72), Western Coll. Reading Assn., Internat. Reading Assn., Wash. State Community Coll. Faculty Devel. (state com.), Wash. Devel. Edn. Assn., Am. Assn. Women in Community and Jr. Colls., Alpha Delta Kappa (v.p. 1986). Republican. Office: Pierce Coll 9401 Farwest Dr SW Tacoma WA 98498

CHEEKS, DOROTHY ROSS, school system administrator; b. Atlanta, Oct. 19, 1922; d. Ira Eugene and Lillian Beatrice (Wise) Ross; foster d. Jesse and Linnette (Wise) Huguly; m. Walter Franklin Anderson, Dec. 22, 1943 (div. 1962); children: Sandra Anderson Mastin, David Ross Anderson; m. Robert Roy Cheeks Jr., Oct. 18, 1970. BA, Goddard Coll., Plainfield, Vt., 1970; MA, Goddard Coll., 1975. Tchr. Antioch and Community Nursery Sch., Yellow Springs, Ohio, 1952-58; tchr. Bingham Ctr., Cleve., 1958-60; casework reviewer U.S. Govt., Cleve., 1960-61; exec. dir. Cleve. br. YWCA, 1961-65; dir. Day Nursery Assn., Cleve., 1965-69; instr. Cuyahoga Community Coll., Cleve., 1969-70; cons. Head Start and child programs in Ohio, 1970-75; casework supr. Trumble County Childrens Svc., Warren, Ohio, 1975-78; dir. Head Start Coun. Econ. Opportunity in Greater Cleve., 1978—. Author: Learning and Motivation of the Career Mobile Black, 1975; developer recognition program. Bd. dirs. Burton Day Care Ctr.; active in Am. Cancer Soc. Mem. AAUW, LWV, Nat. Assn. for Edn. Young Children, Nat. Black Child Devel. Inst. (pres. Cleve. chpt.), Assn. for Childhood Edn. Internat., Cleve. Assn. for Edn. Young Children, Geauga Community Mental Health Assn., Burton Libr. Friends Assn., Burton C. of C., Burton Clio Club. Democrat. Episcopalian. Home: 14748 Rider Rd Burton OH 44021

CHEESEMAN, VALERIE CHRISTINE, community relations manager; b. Bronx, N.Y., Apr. 6, 1949; d. Frank and Loretta (Kleinklaus) McGowan; m. Raymond Joseph Cheeseman, July 31, 1971. BA, Lehman (Hunter) Coll., Bronx, 1972; MA, U. Denver, 1979. Researcher U.S. Geol. Survey, Flagstaff, Ariz., 1972-75; sr. demographic researcher U.S. Geol. Survey, Denver, 1977-78; agy. liaison environ. dept. State of N.Mex., Roswell, 1974-77; freelance cons., lobbyist Gillette, Wyo., 1980-81; sr. stock analyst, mktg. communications Wall Street West, Inc., Englewood, Colo., 1981-84; investor rels. dir., with analysis of issues Pub. Svc. Co. N.Mex., Albuquerque, 1984-88; mgr. community rels. and issues analysis Westinghouse Savanah River Co., 1990—; strategic planning leader Denver Free U., 1983, 84. Recipient Bronze award Fin. World mag., N.Y.C., 1986, 87, 88, 1st Pl. in Class award Reddy's Communications, Inc., Albuquerque, 1986. Mem. Internat. Assn. Bus. Communicators (bd. dirs., pres. local chpt. 1988-89; Gold Quill award 1987, Silver Quill award 1987), Pub. Rels. Soc. Am. (treas. Albuquerque chpt.), Media Women of S.C., N.Mex. Entrepreneurs' Assn. (chmn. capital com.), Leadership of Aiken County Devel., Aiken Forum (bd. dirs.), Am. Soc. Assn. Execs. (LWV co-chair publicity and lobbying coms.), Internat. Mgmt. Coun. Roman Catholic. Home: 219F Fairway Ridge Aiken SC 29801

CHEEVER, SUSAN LILEY, writer; b. N.Y.C., July 31, 1943; d. John and Mary Watson (Winternitz) C.; m. Robert Cowley, May, 1967 (div. 1975); m. Calvin Tomkins, II, Oct. 1, 1982; m. Warren James Hinkle III, June 10, 1989; children: Sarah Liley Cheever Tomkins, Warren James Hinckle IV. BA, Brown U., 1965. Tchr., Colo. Rocky Mountain Sch., Colo., 1965-67, Scarborough Sch., N.Y., 1968-69; writer Westchester-Rockland Newspapers, N.Y., 1970-72; editor, writer Newsweek Mag., N.Y., 1974-78; free lance writer, N.Y., 1978—. Author: Looking for Work, 1980; A Handsome Man, 1981; The Cage, 1982; Home Before Dark, 1984, Doctors and Women, 1987, Elizabeth Cole, 1989. Guggenheim Found. fellow, 1984. Mem. Pen/Am. Ctr., Authors League. Democrat. Episcopalian.

CHEIFETZ, LORNA GALE, psychologist; b. Phoenix, Mar. 22, 1953; d. Walter and Ruth (Nack) C. BS, Chapman Coll., Orange, Calif., 1975; D of Psychology, Ill. Sch. Profl. Psychology, 1981. Psychology intern Cook County Hosp., Chgo., 1979-80; clin. psychologist City of Chgo., 1980-84, Phoenix Inst. for Psychotherapy, 1984-87; pvt. practice Phoenix, 1987—; cons. to judges, attys., cts., 1984—; adj. faculty Met. U., Phoenix, 1984-88, Ill. Sch. Profl. Psychology, 1982-86. Contbr. chpt. to book Listening and Interpreting, 1984. Cons., vol. Ariz. Bar Assn. Vol. Lawyer Program, 1985—; co-coord. Psychology Info. Referral Svc., Maricopa County, Ariz., 1984—. Named Psychologist of Yr. Ariz. Bar Assn., 1987. Mem. Am. Psychol. Assn. (activist 1989—), Ariz. Psychol. Assn. (activist 1989—), Maricopa Psychol. Soc., Nat. Register Health Svc. Providers in Psychology, Soc. for Psychoanalytic Psychotherapy, Assn. Family and Concilliation Cts., Phoenix Psychoanalytic Study Group. Office: 2211 E Highland Ste 135 Phoenix AZ 85016

CHELL, BEVERLY C., lawyer; b. Phila., Aug. 12, 1942; d. Max M. and Cecelia (Portney) C.; m. Robert M. Chell, June 21, 1964. BA, U. Pa., 1964; JD, N.Y. Law Sch., 1967; LLM, NYU, 1973. Bar: N.Y. 1967. Assoc. Polur & Polur, N.Y.C., 1967-68, Thomas V. Kingham Esq., N.Y.C., 1968-69; v.p., sec., gen. counsel, dir. Athlone Industries Inc., Parsippany, N.J., 1969-81; asst. v.p., asst. sec., assoc. gen. counsel Macmillan Inc., N.Y.C., 1981-85, v.p., sec., gen. counsel, 1985-90; v.p., gen. counsel K-III Holdings, N.Y.C., 1990—. Mem. Assn. of Bar of City of N.Y., Am. Soc. Corp. Secs. Home: 9 Marsh Rd Westport CT 06880 Office: K-III Holdings 599 Lexington Ave New York NY 10022

CHELSTROM, MARILYN ANN, educational institution administrator; b. Mpls., Dec. 5; d. Arthur Rudolph and Signe (Johnson) C. BA, U. Minn., 1950; LHD, Oklahoma City U., 1981. Staff asst. Mpls. Citizens Com. Public Edn., 1950-57; coord. policies and procedures Lithium Corp. Am., Inc., Mpls., N.Y.C., 1957-62; exec. dir. The Robert A. Taft Inst. Govt., N.Y.C., 1962-77, exec. v.p., 1977-78, pres., 1978-89, pres. emeritus, polit. edn. cons., 1990. Editor: Teaching the Excitement of Politics in America, 1984, Political Parties, Two Party Goverment and Democracy in United States, 1988. Active LWV, Mpls., 1950-60, N.Y.C., 1972—; charter mem. Citizens League Greater Mpls., 1952-60; del. White House Conf. on Edn., 1955; vice chmn. Minn. Women for Humphrey, 1954; treas. councilman Luth. Ch. Recipient Cert. of Recognition for Svc. to Mpls. Pub. Schs., Mpls. Citizens Com., 1957; named Town Topper, Mpls. Star, 1958. Mem. Am. Polit. Sci. Assn., Minn. Alumni Assn. (gov. N.Y. 1963—, pres. 1971-73, nat. dir. 1971-75), Minn. Alumni Club (Mpls.). Lutheran. Home: 9600 Portland Ave S Bloomington MN 55420 Office: 155 E 38th St New York NY 10016

CHEN, ALICE TUNG-HUA, computer specialist; b. Taipei, Republic of China, Dec. 3, 1949; d. Kuang Pi and Lee Chiung (Lee) Chen; m. John Tsan, May 27, 1973 (div. Apr. 1985); children: Milly M. Tsan, Maggie M. Tsan. BS, Nat. Taiwan U., Taipei, 1971; MS, SUNY, Stony Brook, 1973, PhD, 1975. Postdoctoral fellow NIH, Bethesda, Md., 1975-77; systems engr. GE Info Svc. Co., Rockville, Md., 1977-81; rsch. specialist Exxon Prodn. Rsch. Co., Houston, 1981-86; computer specialist Lawrence Livermore Nat. Lab., Livermore, Calif., 1986—. V.p. Chinese Am. Assn. LLLRA, Livermore, 1989, bd. dirs., 1990; treas. PTA, Contra Costa Chinese Sch., Walnut Creek, Calif., 1987-90. Mem. IEEE, Chinese Inst. Engrs. USA (life). Home: 3108 Riviera Way San Ramon CA 94583 Office: Lawrence Livermore Nat Lab PO Box 808 Livermore CA 94550

CHEN, ANNE COOPER, journalism educator, researcher; b. Pitts., July 19, 1944; d. George Henry and Dorothy Louise (Pursley) Messerly; m. Charles Chin-tse, July 12, 1986; stepchildren: Diana, Deborah, Derek. AB, Vassar Coll., 1966; MA, U. Mich., 1969; MS, Va. Commonwealth U., 1979; PhD, U. N.C., 1984. Feature writer Daily News, V.I., 1963; writer, editor Asahi Evening News, Tokyo, 1966-68; editor, book pub. John Weatherhill, Inc., Tokyo, 1969-70; writer, columnist Sunday News, York, Pa., 1971-72; writer, editor Commonwealth mag., Richmond, Va., 1974-76; asst. prof. journalism So. Meth. U., Dallas, 1982-83, Mary Baldwin Coll., Staunton, Va., 1983-85; assoc. prof. Ohio U., Athens, 1985—; Author: (with others) Idols, Victims, Pioneers, 1976; contbg. author (chpt.) Global Journalism, Covering Africa; contbr. articles to profl. jours. pres. NOW, Richmond, 1976-77. Mem. Assn. for Edn. in Journalims and Mass Communications (various offices), Women in Communications, Inc. (campus chpt. advisor 1982-83), Kappa Tau Alpha. Office: EW Scripps Sch Journalism Ohio U Athens OH 45701

CHEN, CHING-CHIH, dean, consultant, educator; b. Foochow, Fukien, China, Sept. 3, 1937; came to U.S, 1959; d. Han-chia and May-ying (Liu) Liu; m. Sow-Hsin Chen, Aug. 19, 1961; children: Anne, Catherine, John. A, Nat. Taiwan U., Taipei, 1959; MLS, U. Mich., 1961; PhD, Case Western Res. U., 1974. Asst. Sch. Libr. Sci. U. Mich., Ann Arbor, 1960-61, svc. libr., 1961-62; sci. reference libr. McMaster U., Hamilton, Ont., Can., 1962-63, head sci. libr., 1963-64; sr. sci. libr. U. Waterloo, Ont., Can., 1964-65; head English, math. and sci. libr. U. Waterloo, Can., 1965-68; assoc. sci. libr. MIT, Cambridge, Mass., 1968-71; asst. prof. Sch. Libr. Sci. Simmons Coll., Boston, 19716, asst. dean for acad. affairs Sch. Libr. Sci., 1977-79, assoc. dean, prof. Sch. Libr. Sci., 1979—; mem. faculty home study program Am. Soc. for Info. Sci./Cath. U. of Am., 1976-77; cons. Chung-Shan Inst. Sci. Rsch., Taiwan, 1977-78, Lynn (Mass.) Hosp., Abt Assocs., Inc., 1980, 80-82; cons. Sci. and Tech. Info. Ctr. Nat. Sci. Coun., Taiwan, 1973-77; cons. S.E. Asia region WHO, 1980, 81, Western Pacific region, 1981-82; cons. Engring. Info., Inc., 1982, Berkshire Community Coll., Pittsfield, Mass., 1983, Unesco, Paris, 1984, Nat. Geographic Soc., 1985, Norman Bethuen U. Med. Scis. Libr., 1986. Author: Biomedical, Scientific and Technical Book Reviewing, 1976, Sourcebook on Health Sciences Librarianship, 1977, Quantitative Measurement and Dynamic Library Service, 1978, (with others) Numeric Databases, 1984; contbr. numerous articles to profl. jours. Barbour scholar U. Mich., 1959-61, Case Western Res. U. fellow, 1973-74, NATO fellow, 1975, AAAS fellow, 1985; Emily Hollowell Rsch. grantee, 1972—, Simmons Coll. Fund Rsch. grantee, 1972-81; recipient Disting. Svc. award Chinese-Am. Librs. Assn., 1982, Cert. of Appreciation, Asian-Pacific-Am. Librs. Assn., 1983, Outstanding Svc. award Nat. Cen. Libr., 1986. Mem. AAAS, ALA, Am. Soc. for Info. Sci., Assn. Am. Libr. Schs., Assn. Coll. and Rsch. Librs., AAUP, Libr. Info. Tech. Assn., Mass. Libr. Assn., New Eng. Libr. Assn. Home: 1400 Commonwealth Ave West Newton MA 02165 Office: Simmons Coll 300 The Fenway Boston MA 02115

CHEN, GRACE WEI-YIN, financial analyst, computer specialist; b. Taichung, Taiwan, Aug. 2, 1964; came to U.S., 1972; d. William Wen-Long and Chun-Hwa (Chao) C. Student, Wellesley Coll., 1982-84, Columbia U., 1985; BS in Mgmt., MIT, 1986; MBA in Acctg., Rutgers U., 1990. Software programmer MIT, Cambridge, Mass., 1984-85; fin. underwriter Prudential Ins. Co. Am., Parsipanny, N.J., 1986-88; software cons. Oracle Corp., Iselin, N.J., 1988-89; fin. planning intern, E.F. Hutton & Co., Inc., Boston, 1984; student computer cons. Wellesley Coll., 1983-84. Home: 18 Arden Rd Denville NJ 07834

CHEN, LINDA LI-YUEH HUANG, educator; b. Tokyo, Japan, Mar. 22, 1937; d. Chun-mu and Chiung-tein (Lin) Huang; m. Boris Yuen-jien, Dec. 23, 1961; children: Audrey Huey-wen, Lisa Min-yi. BS in Pharmacy, Nat. Taiwan U., Taipei, Republic of China, 1959; PhD In Biochemistry, U. Louisville, 1964. Rsch. assoc. U. Louisville, 1964-66; asst. prof. U. Ky., Lexington, 1967-72, assoc. prof., 1972-79, prof., 1979—, assoc. dean for rsch. and grad. edn., 1979-81, chmn., 1983-87, dir. multidisciplinary PhD program in nutritional scis., 1989—. Author: Nutritional Biochemistry Laboratory Methods, Expt and Exercises, 1972; Editor: Nutritional Aspects of Aging, Vol I, Vol II, 1986; contbr. articles to profl. jours. Mem. Am. Soc. for Clin. Nutrition, Am. Inst. Nutrition, N.Y. Acad. Sci., Internat. Assn. Vitamins and Nutritional Oncology, Gerontol. Soc. Am., Am. Assn. Home Econs. (Borden award 1990). Home: 531 S Bend Dr Lexington KY 40503 Office: U Ky 212 Funkhouser Bldg Lexington KY 40506

CHEN, MARTHA ALTER, international development, gender and poverty specialist; b. Lebanon, Tenn., Feb. 9, 1944; d. James Payne and Barbara (Beach) Alter; m. Lincoln Chih-Ho Chen, July 1, 1967; children: Gregory, Alexis. BA, Conn. Coll. Women, 1965; PhD, U. Pa., 1989. Co-dir. HELP, cyclone relief orgn., Dhaka, Bangladesh, 1970-71; exec. asst. Bangladesh Rural Advancement Com., Dhaka, 1975-80; project officer Oxfam Am., Boston, 1980-81, field rep., 1982-87; vis. scholar Harvard Inst. Internat. Devel., Cambridge, Mass., 1980-81, rsch. assoc., 1987—; cons. in field. Author: A Quiet Revolution, 1983; co-author: Who Gets What: Why, 1979, Indian Women: Dairying, 1985; contbr. articles to profl. publs. Pres. sch. bd. Am. Embassy Sch., New Delhi, India, 1985-86; mem. sch. bd. Am. Internat. Sch., Dhaka, 1971-72; mem. Friends of Bangladesh, Washington, 1971-72. Grantee Ford Found., 1980-81, 87-89, USAID, World Bank, 1987-89, Oxfam, 1975. Mem. SEEDS Population Coun. Democrat. Office: Harvard Inst Internat Devel 1 Eliot St Cambridge MA 02138

CHENEY, JANICE LOUANNE, educator; b. Toledo, Oct. 16, 1954; d. Irvin Richard and Jeanette Lucille (Bolli) Kohne; m. Christopher John Cheney, Sept. 14, 1974; children: Jessica Hiatt, Taylor Renee, Logan Elizabeth. BEd, U. Toledo, 1976, MEd, 1979, postgrad., 1980-81, 1990—. Elem. tchr. Washington Local Schs., Toledo, 1976—. Mem. Tchrs. Assn. Washington Local Schs., AAUW (group literature leader Toledo 1988-90), U. Toledo Alumni Assn. Democrat. Lutheran. Office: Meadowvale Sch 2755 Edgebrook Dr Toledo OH 43613

CHENEY, LINDA GAIL, business owner; b. Austin, Tex., Aug. 3, 1949; d. Walter D. and Dorothy Mae (Hennig) Haster; m. Daniel Franklin Morgan, May 15, 1971 (div. Nov. 1973); m. John Carl Cheney; children: Edward Austin, Jonathan Travis. BS in Edn., S.W. Tex. State U., San Marcos, 1970. Tchr. English Forest Brook Ind. Sch. Dist., Houston, 1974-75; assoc. editor Outlook mag. Tex. State Tchrs. Assn., Austin, 1972-74; supr. rsch. dept. ROLM Corp., Santa Clara, Calif., 1983-85; pvt. practice quilter, decorator Southlake, Tex., 1985—. Winner 2d Place, Oatlands Needlework Exhibit, 1982, Frederick County Landmarks, 1983, 1st, 2d, 4th and 6th Places, Santa Clara County Fair, 1985. Mem. Dallas Quilt Guild (2d Place 1990, Hon. mention 1990). Home: 1612 Heatherbrook Ct Southlake TX 76092

CHENEY, LYNNE ANN, national cultural organization administrator, writer; b. Casper, Wyo., Aug. 14, 1941; d. Wayne and Edna (Lybyer) Vincent; m. Richard Bruce Cheney, Aug. 29, 1964; children: Elizabeth, Mary. BA, Colo. Coll., 1963; MA, U. Colo., 1964; PhD, U. Wis., 1970. Freelance writer, 1970-83; lectr. George Washington U., Washington, 1972-77, U. Wyo., Casper, 1977-78; researcher, writer Md. Pub. Broadcasting, Owing Mills, 1982-83; sr. editor Washingtonian mag., Washington, 1983-86; chmn. NEH, Washington, 1986—; commr. U.S. Constitution Bicentennial Commn., Washington, 1985—. Author: Executive Privilege, 1978, Sisters, 1981, (with others) Kings of the Hill, 1983, The Body Politic, 1988; contbr. articles to profl. jours. Mem. Women's Forum Washington. Mem. Congl. Club, Phi Beta Kappa, Kappa Alpha Theta. Republican. Methodist. Office: NEH 1100 Pennsylvania Ave NW Washington DC 20506

CHENEY, MEREDITH See BREYMAIER, ANN MEREDITH

CHENEY, RITA MAE, editor, small business owner; b. York, Maine, Apr. 20, 1951; d. Harold Newton and Lillian Dorothy (Kimball) Stevens; m. Charles Leighton Cheney, Sept. 5, 1970; 1 child, Marisa. System control engr., prodn. and inventory control mgr., prodn. drafting/scheduling coord. Hussey Seating Co., Inc., North Berwick, Maine; editor, owner Catalystings, North Berwick. Mem. Am. Prodn. and Inventory Control Soc. (dir. publicity regional level New Eng., past pres. local chpt.). Home and Office: Catalystings PO Box 67 North Berwick ME 03906

CHENG, IRENE TERESA, investment banker; b. Princeton, N.J., June 6, 1954; d. Sin-I and Jean S. C. AB, Harvard U., 1976, MBA, 1980; SM, MIT, 1978. Various positions Exxon Corp., N.Y.C, 1980-87; rsch. analyst Sanford C. Bernstein & Co., Inc., N.Y.C, 1987-90; v.p. The Blackstone Group, N.Y.C., 1990—. Treas. residence coop., N.Y.C., 1982-87. Office: The Blackstone Group 345 Park Ave New York NY 10154

CHENG, YANN-CHIOU WANG, electronics company executive; b. Gi-me, Taiwan, Republic of China, Feb. 13, 1949; d. Hsin-Nan and Huei-Fung (Lee) Wang; m. Hai-Yang Cheng. Assoc., Nat. Taiwan Acad. Arts, Taipei, Republic of China, 1970; B., Chinese Culture U., Taipei, Republic of China, 1975; MA, Chinese Culture U., 1978; MS, Purdue U., 1982. Reporter Daliy News, Taipei, 1969-70; asst. to producer Taiwan TV Corp., Taipei, 1970; instr. Nat. Taiwan Acad. Arts, Taipei, 1970-79, Coll. World Jour., Taipei, 1976-78; instr. prodn. control Little Brown & Co., Waltham, Mass., 1983-85; sales mgr. Hua Hsiah Chinese Broadcasting Inc., Houston, 1987; editor Cen. Daily News., L.I. City, N.Y., 1987, World Jour., Flushing, N.Y., 1987-88; gen. mgr. Super K Electronic Products Inc., Bohemia, N.Y., 1988—. Office: 1633 6 Sycamore Ave Bohemia NY 11716

CHENHALLS, ANNE MARIE, nurse, educator; b. Detroit, May 26, 1929; d. Peter and Beatrice Mary (Elliston) McLeod; m. Horacio Chenhalls, 1953 (dec.); children—Mark, Anne Marie Chenhalls Delamater. Student Detroit Conservatory Music, 1946-47; B. Vocat. Edn., Calif. State U.-Los Angeles, 1967, B.S. in Nursing, 1968; M.A., Calif. State U.-Long Beach, 1985. R.N., Calif. Nurse, Grace Hosp., Detroit, 1951-52; pvt. duty nurse, Mexico City, 1953-54; nurse St. Francis Hosp., Lynwood, Calif., 1957-63; assoc. prof. nursing Compton Coll. (Calif.), 1964-72; health educator, sch. nurse Santa Ana Unified Sch. Dist. (Calif.), 1972-76, 79—; med. coord., internat. health cons. Agape Movement, San Bernardino, Calif., 1976-79; instr. community health, Uganda, 1982; med. evaluator Athletes in Action, 1979. Assoc. staff mem. Campus Crusade for Christ. Solo vocalist, Santa Ana, Orange, Seal Beach, Calif. U.S. govt. grantee, 1968. Mem. Calif. Sch. Nurses Assn., Nat. Educators Assn., Calif. Tchrs. Assn., Internat. Platform Assn. Democrat. Home: 7 Brisa del Lago Rancho Santa Margarita CA 92688 Office: Santa Ana Unified Sch Dist 1405 French St Santa Ana CA 92701

CHENNAULT, ANNA CHAN, aviation executive, author, lecturer; b. Peking, China, June 23, 1925; came to U.S., 1948, naturalized, 1950; d. P.Y. and Isabel (Liao) Chan; m. Claire Lee Chennault, Dec. 21, 1947 (dec. July 1958); children: Claire Anna, Cynthia Louise. BA in Journalism, Lingnan U., Hong Kong, 1944; LittD, Chungang, Seoul, Korea, 1967; LLD (hon.), Lincoln U., 1970; HHD (hon.), Manahath Ednl. Center, 1970, St. Johns U., 1982, Am. U. of Caribbean, 1982; D Bus. Admin. (hon.), John Dewey U. Consortium, 1983. War corr. Central News Agy., 1944-48, spl. Washington corr., 1965—; with Civil Air Transp., Taipei, Taiwan, 1946-57, editor bull., 1946-57, pub. relations officer, 1947-57; chief Chinese Sect. Machine Translation Research, Georgetown U., 1958-63; broadcaster Voice of Am., 1963-66; U.S. corr. Hsin Shen Daily News, Washington, 1958—; v.p. internat. affairs Flying Tiger Line, Inc., Washington, 1968-76; pres. TAC Internat., 1976—; cons. various airlines and aerospace corps.; lectr., writer, fashion designer U.S. and Asia; bd. dirs. Sovran, D.C. Nat. Bank; chmn. bd. dirs. CIC, Inc.; chmn. Nat. Rep. Asian Assembly. Feature writer: Hsin Ming Daily News, Shanghai, 1944-49; Author: Chennault and the Flying Tigers: Way of a Fighter, 1963; best seller A Thousand Springs, 1962; Education of Anna, 1980; also numerous books in Chinese including Song of Yesterday, 1961, M.E.E, 1963, My Two Worlds, 1965, The Other Half, 1966, Letters from U.S.A, 1967, Journey Among Friends and Strangers, Chinese edit, 1978, China Times, Chinese-English Dictionaries. Mem. Pres.'s adv. com. arts John F. Kennedy Center Performing Arts, 1970—; Pres. Nixon's spl. rep. Philippine Aviation Week Celebration, 1973; mem. women's adv. com. on aviation to sec. transp.; v.p. Air and Space Bicentennial Organizing Com.; spl. asst. to chmn. Asian-Pacific council AmChams, mem. spl. com. transp. to sec. transp., 1972, chmn. com. for spl. transp. activities, 1972; mem. U.S. nat. com. for UNESCO, 1970—; mem. adv. council Am. Revolution Bicentennial Adminstrn., 1975-77, also mem. ethnic racial council; advisor Nat. League Families of Am. Prisoners and Missing in S.E. Asia; presdl. appointee Pres.'s Export Council, 1981, vice chmn., 1981-85; pres. Chinese Refugee Relief, Washington, 1962-70, Gen. Claire Chennault Found., 1960—; hon. chmn. Chinese-Am. Nat. Fedn., 1974—; committeewoman Washington Republican Party, 1960—; mem. Nat. Rep. Finance Com., 1969—; cons. heritage groups, nationalites div. Asian affairs Rep. Nat. Com., 1969—; chmn. Nat. Rep. Heritage Council, 1979, 87; bd. govs. Am. Acad. Achievement, Dallas; trustee Center Study Presidency, Library Presdl. Papers, 1970—, Helping Hand Found.; bd. visitors Civil Air Patrol; presdl. appointee Presdl. Scholars Commn., 1985—; bd. dirs. People to People Internat; founder, chmn. Nat. Rep. Asian Assembly. Recipient Woman of Distinction award Tex. Tech U., 1966, Freedom award Order of Lafayette, 1966, Freedom award Free-China Assn., 1966, Lady of Mercy award, 1972, Rep. of Yr. award D.C. Rep. Fedn., 1974, award of honor Chinese-Am. Citizens Alliance, 1972, Mother Gerard Phelan award Marymount Coll., 1985, award Ams. by Choice, 1987, Capital Press Women's award, Women of Achievement Internat. award. Fellow Aerospace Med. Assn. (hon.); mem. Nat. Aero. Assn. (bd. dirs.), Nat. League Am., PEN Women, Writers Assn., Free China Writers Assn., 14th Air Force Assn. (chmn. awards com. 1969—), USAF Wives Club, Flying Tiger Assn., U.S. C. of C. (coun. on trends and perspective), Am. Newspaper Women's Club Washington, Nat. Mil. Families Assn. (founder, chmn.), Theta Sigma Phi, others. Clubs: Overseas Press (N.Y.C.); Pisces, 1925 F Street, International, Capitol Hill, National Press, Aero, George Town, Army-Navy (Washington). Home: 2510 Virginia Ave NW Washington DC 20037 Office: TAC Internat 1511 K St NW Washington DC 20005

CHEPLEN, EVELYN COX, civic worker; b. Etowah, Tenn., Aug. 26, 1923; d. Roy H. and Emma (Hayes) Cox; m. Fred J. Cheplen, Mar. 10, 1947; children: Timothy, Jill, Mark. Student, Milligan (Tenn.) Coll., 1941-42; BS cum laude, Athens (Ala.) State U., 1983; student, Chillicothe (Mo.) Coll., 1944. Lab. tech. Alcoa, Tenn., 1942-44; sec. med. lab., Ft. McPherson, Ga., 1945; office mgr. radio div. Westinghouse, Atlanta, 1946-47; supr. stenographic pool Bur. Reclamation, Denver, 1948-51; broker assoc. Joe Steele, Realty, Huntsville, Ala., 1966-82; lectr.; vol. lectr. art history Huntsville City Sch. System, 1967, 70; vol. tchr. Internat. Sch., Huntsville, 1987, 88. Bd. dirs. Family Counseling Assn., Huntsville, 1962-64; grey lady ARC, Huntsville, 1965; sr. warden St. Stephen's Episcopal Ch., Huntsville, 1979; bd. dirs. Maxwell Place Condominiums, Huntsville, 1990—; mem. Huntsville Mus. Guild, 1967-70. Honor scholar Milligan Coll., 1941-42. Mem. AAUW, Huntsville Womans Club, Sigma Tau Delta, Pi Tau Chi. Republican. Home: 313 Inverness Dr Huntsville AL 35802

CHER (CHERILYN SARKISIAN), singer, actress; b. El Centro, Calif., May 20, 1946; d. Gilbert and Georgia LaPiere; m. Sonny Bono, Oct. 27, 1964 (div.); 1 child, Chastity; m. Gregg Allman, June 1975 (div.); 1 child, Elijah Blue. Student drama coach, Jeff Corey. Singer with husband as team, Sonny and Cher, 1964-74; star TV shows: Cher, 1975-76, The Sonny and Cher Show, 1976-77; concert appearances with husband, 1977, numerous recs., TV, concert and benefit appearances with Sonny Bono; TV appearances, ABC-TV, 1978, appearance with Sonny Bono in motion pictures, Good Times, 1966, Chastity, 1969; film appearances include Silkwood, 1983, Mask, 1985, The Witches of Eastwick, 1987, Suspect, 1987, Moonstruck (Golden Globe award 1988, Acad. award for best actress 1988), 1987; helped form rock band, Black Rose, 1979; recorded albums Black Rose, 1980, Cher, 1987, Heart of Stone, 1989 (Double Platinum and 3 Gold Singles). Office: care Bill Sammeth Orgn 9200 Sunset Blvd Los Angeles CA 90069 also: care Creative Artists Agy 1888 Century Pk E Los Angeles CA 90067

CHERAMIE, SISTER MILDRED, hospital pastoral care director; b. Gretna, La., Nov. 8, 1928; d. Leopold Jules and Edwina Cleona (Borné) C. B., Marillac Coll., 1959; MA in Theology, Marquette U., 1976; postgrad., St. Louis U., 1970-74. RN. Clin. instr. pediatrics Hotel Dieu Hosp., New Orleans, 1951-53; supr. pediatric nursing St. Mary's Hosp., Evansville, Ind., 1955-57; supr. pediatrics DePaul Health Ctr., St. Louis, 1959-64; supr. child psychiatry Child Ctr. Our Lady of Grace, St. Louis, 1965; supr. nursing obstetrics St. Mary's Hosp., Milw., 1966-68; instr. sacred scripture Marillac Coll.-Notre Dame Coll., Normandy, Mo., 1972-77; dir. pastoral care DePaul Health Ctr., Bridgeton, Mo., 1984—; chmn. bd. trustees Hotel Dieu Hosp., New Orleans, 1987—; bd. dirs. Hotel Dieu Hosp., New Orleans; mem. ethics com. DePaul Health Ctr., Bridgeton, 1985—. Named hon. leutenant-forest ranger Shawnee Nat. Forest, Ozark, Ill., 1965-66. Mem. Gateway Catholic Ethics Network, Daughters Charity St. Vincent de Paul (local supr. 1971-84). Home: 7800 Natural Bridge Rd Normandy MO 63121 Office: De Paul Health Ctr 12303 DePaul Dr Bridgeton MO 63044

CHERKIS, LAURA, utility official; b. Balt., Aug. 20, 1944; d. Jack and Pearl (Gantcher) Lipitz; m. Laurence D. Cherkis, Mar. 19, 1966 (div. Aug. 1978); children: Ann Leslie, Nancy Ruth; m. John Katz, May 29, 1988. BA, Queens Coll., 1966. Dir. devel. The Haydn Found., Ardsley, N.Y., 1980-85; v.p. Manor Internatural, Inc., Ardsley, 1985-86; tng. adminstr. N.Y. Power Authority, White Plains, N.Y., 1986-88; tng. specialist N.Y. Power Authority, White Plains, 1988--. Mem. NAFE, Am. Soc. for Tng. and Devel., Phi Beta Kappa. Office: NY Power Authority 123 Main St White Plains NY 10601

CHERNIACK, HELEN WESSEL, professional volunteer, civic worker; b. Nebraska City, Nebr., Mar. 8, 1911; d. Walter Arthur and Constance Esther (Sarbach) Wessel; m. Jay Arthur Cherniack, May 10, 1936 (dec. Mar. 1973); children: Lisbeth C. Stiffel, Wallis C. Klein. BA, Northwestern U., 1933; LHD (hon.), U. Nebr., Omaha, 1982. Mem. adv. com. Adah and Leon Millard Founds., 1977—; bd. dirs. Nebr. Arts Coun., 1987—, Omaha Community Playhouse, 1983—; bd. govs. Boy's Clubs Omaha, 1974—, pres., 1978-79; charter mem. bd. dirs. Nebr. Meth. Hosp. Coll. Nursing, 1988—; chmn. expansion campaign Immanuel Hosp., 1952; chmn. women's div. New Clarkson Sch. Nursing Devel. Fund, 1958; chmn. women's individual gifts com. United Community Svcs., 1964; chmn. women's div NCCJ Brotherhood Dinner, 1969; bd. dirs. Planned Parenthood Omaha and Council Bluffs, 1947-53, Bishop Clarkson hosp. Svc. League, 1953—; pres. bd. dirs. Joslyn Art Mus. Women's Assn., 1962-64, bd. dirs., 1954—; mem. adv. bd. Salvation Army, Omaha, 1977—. Named Outstanding Bd. Mem. of Yr., Family and Child Svc. Omaha, 1969, one of Women of the Midlands, Omaha World-Herald Newspaper, 1974, One of 75 Women of Achievement, Girl Scouts U.S.A, 1987, Woman Distinction YWCA Omaha, 1988; recipient Brotherhood award Nat. Conf. Christians and Jews, 1975, Sta. KMTV TV award, 1978, Strength to Families award Family Svc. Omaha, 1981, B'nai B'rith Am. Citation award, 1983, Others award Salvation Army, 1985, Leon S. McGoogan award Planned Parenthood, 1985, Citizen of the Yr. award United Way of the Midlands, 1988. Mem. Omaha Club, Plaza Club, Highland Country Club, Omicron Delta Kappa. Republican. Jewish.

CHERNOFF, MINDY LEE, business owner; b. Chgo., May 9, 1957; d. Bernard Tatz and Janice (Godfrey) Bendersky; stepfather Alex Bendersky; m. Joel Martin Chernoff, Mar. 17, 1979; children: Sharon Michelle, Aron Michael, Elisha Anna. BS, Stephens Coll., 1978. Horse trainer Carr's Qtr. Horse, Chester Springs, Pa., 1980-87; cake decorator, artist Mindy's Creative Cakes, Phila., 1980-89; head tailor, seamstress Curtain Call Drapes, Phila., 1985—; owner, pres. Word of Mouth Cleaning Svc., Phila., 1987—; judge

Chester County 4-H Club, Malvern, Pa., 1985; judge, Spl. Olympics State Equestrian Event Horse Show, Malvern, 1988, 89. Tchr. phys. edn. Chalutzim Acad., Phila., 1981-84, tchr. Am. sign lang., 1989—; elder's wife Congregation Beth Yeshua, 1970—. 14th runner-up Miss Mo. Pageant, 1978; recipient Appreciation award Spl. Olympics State Equestrian Event Show, 1988, Perceptics award Miss Mo. Pageant, 1978. Mem. Keystone Qtr. Horse Assn., Messianic Jewish Alliance. Home and Office: 7605 Brookhaven Rd Philadelphia PA 19151

CHERNOFF, NANCY ROBIN, advertising company executive; b. New Haven; d. Maxwell B. and Carol D. Chernoff. BA, Simmons Coll. Promotion and graphics asst. Houghton Mifflin Co., Boston; mktg. asst. and project mgr. Can. Dry Internat., N.Y.C.; asst. product mgr. Carter Products, Inc.; product mgr. Boyle Midway, 1980-83; account exec. Darcy MacManus & Masius, 1983-85; sr. account exec. Geers Gross Advt., 1985-87; mgr. advt. accounts Fairchild Publs., 1987—. Recipient Effie award 1986. Mem. Am. Mgmt. Assn. Avocations: running, squash, photography, travel, reading. Home: 131 E 83d St New York NY 10028

CHERNOW, ALLISON, director of production; b. Norwalk, Conn., Feb. 17, 1958; d. Marvin Alexander and Renata Joan (Wells) C.; m., Lloyd Philip Trufelman, June 26, 1988. BA, Brown U., Providence, R.I., 1976-80; MA, N.Y.U., 1982-83. Sr. researcher Mkt. Facts, Inc., Washington, DC, 1980-82; producer WNYC-FM N.Y. Pub. Radio, N.Y.C., 1983-86; exec. producer WNYC Productions, N.Y.C., 1986-89; dir. prodn. WNYC AM & FM, N.Y.C., 1989—. Recipient Armstrong award, Armstrong Found., 1987. mem. American Women in Radio and TV. Democrat. Office: Sta WNYC NY Pub Radio 1 Centre St New York NY 10007

CHERRY, RONA BEATRICE, magazine editor, writer; b. N.Y.C., Apr. 26, 1948; d. Manuel M. and Sylvia Zelda C. B.A., Am. U., 1968; M.S., Columbia U., 1971. Reporter No. Va. Sun, Arlington, 1968; reporter Akron Beacon Jour., Ohio, 1969-70, Wall St. Jour., N.Y.C., 1971-72; assoc. editor Newsweek mag., N.Y.C., 1972-74; reporter N.Y. Times, N.Y.C., 1976-77; exec. editor Glamour mag., N.Y.C., 1977-88; editor-in-chief Longevity mag., v.p., dir. new mag. devel. Gen. Media Internat., N.Y.C., 1988—; lectr. New Sch. Social Research, 1978; lectr. Sch. Continuing Edn., NYU, 1980, faculty Summer Pub. Inst., 1980, 83; faculty Reader's Digest writers' workshops; mem. research com. Internat. Women's Media Conf., 1986; mem. Nat. Mag. Awards screening com., 1980-82, 90; judge Nat. Media awards Am. Speech-Language-Hearing Assn., 1988. Co-author: The World of American Business, 1977; contbg. author: Woman in the Year 2000; contbr. articles to publs. including N.Y. Times Sunday mag., Parade, Ms. mag., Christian Sci. Monitor; contbr. book revs. to Sunday N.Y. Times. Nat. communications council March of Dimes, 1981—. Recipient Media award Nat. Assn. Recycling Industries, 1973, Bus. Journalism award U. Mo., 1977, Am. Coll. Radiology, 1986, Writer's award Am. Soc. Anesthesiologists, 1983, Maggie award Planned Parenthood Fedn. Am., 1985, Media award Am. Coll. Radiology, 1986. Mem. Am. Soc. Mag. Editors (bd. dirs. 1990—), Women in Communications, Newswomen's Club N.Y. (v.p. 1985-87). Home: 140 Riverside Dr #8P New York NY 10024 Office: Longevity Mag 1965 Broadway New York NY 10023

CHERRY, SANDRA WILSON, lawyer; b. Little Rock, Dec. 31, 1941; d. Berlin Alexander and Renna Glen (Barnes) Wilson; m. John Sandefur Cherry, Jr., Sept. 24, 1976; 1 dau., Jane Wilson. BA, U. Ark., 1962; JD, U. Ark. Sch. Law, 1975. Bar: Ark., 1975, U.S. Dist. Ct. (ea. dist.) Ark., 1979, U.S. Supreme Ct. 1979, U.S. Ct. Appeals (8th cir.) 1979. Tchr. social studies Little Rock Sch. Dist., 1966-70; chmn. social studies dept. Horace Mann Jr. High Sch., Little Rock, 1970-72; asst. U.S. atty. Dept. Justice, Little Rock, 1975-81, 83—; commr. Ark. Pub. Service Commn., Little Rock, 1981-83; adj. instr. U. Ark. at Little Rock Sch. Law, Little Rock, 1980. Contbr. case note to Ark. Law Rev., 1975. Pres. bd. dirs. Gaines House, Inc.; pres. U. Ark. at Little Rock Law Sch. Assn., 1980-81, bd. dirs., 1982; bd. dirs. Jr. League Little Rock, 1974. Mem. ABA, Ark. Bar Assn. (Ho. of Del. 1984-86, 89—, sec., treas. 1986-89), Pulaski County Bar Assn. (bd. dirs. 1989-90), Ark. Women Lawyers Assn., Ark. Bar Assn. (com. on the status women and minorities), Little Rock C. of C. (met. coun.), Pi Beta Phi. Republican. Presbyterian. Home: 4100 S Lookout St Little Rock AR 72205 Office: US Atty's Office PO Box 1229 Little Rock AR 72203

CHERRYH, C. J. (CAROLYN JANICE CHERRY), writer; b. St. Louis, Sept. 1, 1942; d. Basil L. and Lois Ruth (Van Deventer) C. B.A. in Latin, U. Okla., 1964; M.A. in Classics, Johns Hopkins U., 1965. Cert. tchr., Okla. Tchr. Oklahoma City Pub. Schs., 1965-77; lectr. in field. Author: novel Gate of Ivrel, 1976, Well of Shiuan, 1978, Brothers of Earth, 1976, Hunter of Worlds, 1976, The Faded Sun: Kutath, 1979, Sunfall, 1981, Star Crusade, 1980, Downbelow Station, 1981 (Hugo award for best novel 1982), The Pride of Chanur, 1982, Merchanter's Luck, 1982, Port Eternity, 1982, The Dreamstone, 1983, The Tree of Swords and Jewels, 1983, Cuckoo's Egg, 1985, Angel with the Sword, 1985, Chanur's Homecoming, 1986, Exile's Gate, 1988, Cyteen, 1988, Smuggler's Gold, 1988, Rimrunners, 1989; ed., Flood Tide, 1990; contbr. short stories to numerous mags. Woodrow Wilson fellow, 1965; recipient Hugo award for best short story, 1979. Mem. Sc. Fiction Writers Assn. (sec.), Nat. Space Soc. (bd. advisors), Phi Beta Kappa. Methodist. *

CHESAK, DONNA, mortgage loan underwriter; b. Mandan, N.D., Nov. 5, 1942; d. Frank Pius and Elizabeth Gertrude (Leingang) Gartner; m. Larry Edward Chesak, June 23, 1972; children: Melissa Jo, Jennifer Lee. BS, U. Mary, Bismarck, N.D., 1984; cert., Inst. Fin. Edn., 1986. Mortgage loan officer Norwest Bank N.D., Mandan, N.D., 1960-68; mortgage loan officer Northwestern Fed. Savs. and Loan, Fargo, N.D., 1968-84; mortgage loan prodn. mgr. Midwest Fed. Savs. Bank, Minot, N.D., 1984-87; acct. exec. Century 21 Mortgage Corp., Bloomington, Minn.; mortgage loan underwriter Bismarck State Bank, 1990—. Mem. NAFE, Nat. Assn. Rev. Appraisers and Mortgage Underwriters. Home: 2416 LaForest Ave Bismarck ND 58501 Office: Bismarck State Bank Bismarck ND 58501

CHESEN, CATHERINE SUE, investigative consumer reporting executive; b. Lancaster, Pa., Aug. 26, 1953; d. Irwin Somberg and Doris Marion (Schimmel) C.; m. Allen Mark Morris, June 18, 1972 (div. Mar. 1977). BS, U. Nebr., 1975; BA in Speech Pathology, MA, U. Kans., Kansas City, 1978. Speech pathologist Joan Davis Sch. Spl. Edn., Kansas City, Mo., 1975-78, Rainbow Mental Health Ctr., Kansas City, 1978-79, Clinicare Home Health Care, Kansas City, 1978-79; prin. Inter-Link of Am., Leawood, Kans., 1980-86; pres. Chesen Communications Ctr., Overland Park, Kans., 1986—. Mem. Am. Bus. Women's Assn., Kansas City Multi-Family Apt. Assn., NOW, Nat. Apt. Assn. Democrat. Jewish. Office: Chesen Communications Ctr Inc PO Box 14551 Lenexa KS 66215

CHESLER, VICTORIA AIMEE, publishing executive, writer; b. N.Y.C., July 8, 1957; d. Bertram Arthur and Naomi (Aronson) C.; m. Matthew Robert Kovner, July 24, 1983; 1 child, Melissa Mae Chesler Kovner. BA cum laude, Conn. Coll., 1979. Editorial asst. Biomedical Info. Corp., N.Y.C., 1979-80; editor Co-op West, N.Y.C., 1980-81; founder, pres. Manhattan Cooperator Publs., Inc., N.Y.C., 1981, mng. editor Manhattan Cooperator, 1981-82, exec. editor, 1982—; exec. editor The Apt. Buyer's Guide, N.Y.C., 1985—; free-lance writer, 1980—. Contbr. articles to Harper's Bazaar, Ski Mag., SAAVY, Redbook mag. Mem. NOW, Real Estate Bd. N.Y., Nat. Assn. Female Execs. Avocations: skiing; sailing; tennis; travel; drawing. Office: Manhattan Cooperator Publs Inc 23 Leonard St 3d Floor New York NY 10013

CHESNEY, PATRICIA SUSAN, financial consultant; b. Balt., Mar. 10, 1951; d. William Andrew and Mildred Catherine (Mazur) C. BBA in Mgmt., Ga. State U., 1979; MAd in Bus., Brenau Coll., 1981. Pres. Nat. Parts Warehouse, Atlanta, 1969-84; owner Fin. Adv. Svc., Atlanta, 1984-87; pres. Curry Mktg. Inc., Atlanta, 1987-89; cons. Fin. Adv. Svcs., 1989—. Editor: The Unnatural Act of Management, 1989. Mem. Women's Commerce Club (bd. dirs. 1987-90).

CHESNEY, SUSAN TALMADGE, human resources specialist; b. N.Y.C., Aug. 12, 1943; d. Morton and Tillie (Talmadge) Chesney; m. Donald Lewis Freitas, Sept. 17, 1967 (div. May 1976); m. Robert Martin Rosenblatt, Apr. 9, 1980. AB, U. Calif., Berkeley, 1967. Placement interviewer U. Calif., Berkeley, 1972-74, program coord., 1974-79; pers. adminstr. Hewlett-Packard Co., Santa Rosa, Calif., 1982-84; pres. Mgmt. Resources, Santa Rosa, 1984—; human resources mgr. BioBottoms Inc., Petaluna, Calif., 1990—; rcons. Kensington Electronics Group, Healdsburg, Calif., 1984-85, Behavioral Medicine Assocs., Santa Rosa, 1985-86, M.C.A.I., Santa Rosa, 1986-87, Bowdon Designs, Santa Rosa, 1987—, Bass & Ingram, Santa Rosa, 1988—. Mem. Sonoma County Arts Council, Nat. Assn. Female Execs. Avocations: Asian cooking, gardening, music.

CHESNICK, JOYCE BAILES, retail executive; b. Memphis, June 6, 1925; d. George W. and Jean (Goldberg) Bailes; m. Joseph Chesnick, Feb. 28, 1945; children: Joan Chesnick Dinerstein, Joseph Jr., Robert G. Student, U. Tex., 1943-45, U. Houston, 1954-56. Co-chmn. Robert Joseph Interiors, Inc., Corpus Christi, Tex., 1981—, Robert Joseph, Inc., Houston, 1982—; prin., co-chmn. Georgetown Manor, Houston, 1968—, San Antonio, 1971—, Beaumont, Tex., 1974—; adv. bd. mem. Ethan Allen, Inc., Danbury, Conn. Bd. govs. Congregation Beth Israel, 1982—; contbg. mem. Mus. Fine Arts, Houston. Mem. Am. Soc. Interior Designers (assoc.), United Daus. Confederacy, S.W. Home Furnishings Assn., Houston Retail Furnishings Assn., Westwood Country Club (gov. 1977-81). Home: 8 Inwood Oaks Houston TX 77024 Office: 8353 Kempwood Houston TX 77055

CHESNUT, CAROL FITTING, economist; b. Pecos, Tex., June 17, 1937; d. Ralph Ulf and Carol (Lowe) Fitting; m. Dwayne A. Chesnut, Dec. 27, 1955; children: Carol Marie, Michelle, Mark Steven. BA magna cum laude, U. Colo., 1971. Research asst. U. Colo., 1972; head quality controller Mathematica, Inc., Denver, 1973-74; cons. Mincome Man., Winnipeg, Can., 1974; cons. economist Energy Cons. Assocs. Inc., Denver, 1974-79; exec. v.p. tng. ECA Intercomp, 1980-81; gen. ptnr. Chestnut Consortium, Las Vegas, 1981—; sec., bd. dirs. Critical Resources, Inc., 1981-83. Rep. Lakehurst Civic Assn., 1968; staff aide Senator Gary Hart, 1978; Dem. precinct capt., 1982-88. Mem. Am. Mgmt. Assn., Soc. Petroleum Engrs., Am. Nuclear Soc. (chmn. conv. space activities for 1989, chair of spouse activities 1989), Am. Geophys. Union, Assn. Women Geoscientists (treas. Denver 1983-85), ACLU, NOW, AAUW (1st v.p. 1989-90), Century Club, Phi Beta Kappa, Phi Chi Theta. Unitarian. Office: 3416 Biscaya Circle Las Vegas NV 89121

CHESS, MURIEL REMES, editor; b. N.Y.C.; d. Nathan R. and Mary (Hurwitz) Remes; m. Irwin W. Chess (div. 1983); children: Karen, Daniel, Nathan. BA, Rutgers U., 1973. Editor Designer Magazine, N.Y.C., 1978-86; editor Profl. Office Design, N.Y.C., 1986—. Recipient Roz Burrows award Design Industry Found. for Aids, N.Y.C., 1988, Outstanding Alumni award High Sch. Music and Art, 1983. Mem. Am. Soc. Internat. Design (bd. dirs. 1985-88; Editorial Excellence award 1980, 1985), Decorator's Club (newsletter editor 1987). Democrat. Jewish. Home: 50 Park Ave New York NY 10016 Office: Profl Office Design 111 8th Ave New York NY 10011

CHESTER, NIA LANE, psychology educator; b. L.A., Dec. 8, 1945; d. Thomas Henry and Virginia (Chalmers) Lane; m. C. Ronald Chester, Aug. 9, 1969 (div. July 1988); children: Caben Paul, Ian Thomas. BA magna cum laude, Smith Coll., 1967; MA, Columbia U., 1968; PhD, Boston U., 1981. Tchr. Elmont (N.Y.) Meml. High Sch., 1967-70; master tchr. Ednl. Collaborative Greater Boston, Cambridge, Mass., 1971-75; teaching fellow Harvard U., Cambridge, 1976-78; rsch. assoc. Boston U., 1981-83, 88—, vis. prof., 1986-88; rsch. scholar Radcliffe Coll., Cambridge, 1983-84; assoc. prof. psychology Pine Manor Coll., Chestnut Hill, Mass., 1983—, Lindsey prof., 1990; reviewer Jour. Personality and Social Psychology, 1985—. Editor: Experience and Meaning of Work in Women's Lives, 1990; contbr. articles to profl. jours., chpts. to books. Bd. dirs. Peabody Aftersch. Program, Cambridge, 1983-85, Tobin Aftersch. Program, Cambridge, 1989—. Fellow NIMH, 1979. Mem. Am. Psychol. Assn., Ea. Psychol. Assn. (program com. 1989—). Office: Pine Manor Coll Dept Psych 400 Heath St Chestnut Hill MA 02168

CHESTER, YVONNE ELIZABETH WONG, lawyer; b. Hong Kong, June 23, 1958. BS, U. Calif., Berkeley, 1979, JD, 1982. Bar: Calif., 1982. Mem. of Troy & Gould, L.A., 1986—. Assoc. editor: Calif. Law Review, 1980-82. Recipient Am. Jurisprudence award. Office: Troy & Gould PC 1801 Century Park E 16th Fl Los Angeles CA 90067

CHESTNUT, ROBERTA, daycare director; b. Conway, S.C., Dec. 16, 1940; d. Fred Jacob Chestnut and Dolly Xereen; m. George Wallace, July 2, 1964; 1 child, S. Dwayne. AAS, Malcolm King Coll., 1974; BA, Adelphi U., 1976, MA, 1980; postgrad. in elem. and early childhood edn., Malcolm King Coll.; degree, Am. Montessori Soc., N.Y.C., 1976. Lic. tchr., N.Y. Tchr. trainer Roberta Montessori Sch., West Chester, N.Y., exec. dir.; asst. dir. Salem Day Care, Westchester, 1986-90; head tchr. West Side Montessori, N.Y.C.; researcher in field. Mem. NAFE, NAACP, Cen. Harlem Assn. Montessori Parents, Am. Mus. Nat. History, Alpha Delta Phi. Roman Catholic.

CHEVERS, WILDA ANITA YARDE, probation officer; b. N.Y.C.,; d. Wilsey Ivan and Herbertlee (Perry) Yarde; m. Kenneth Chevers, May 14, 1950; 1 child, Pamela Anita. BA, CUNY, 1947; MSW, Columbia, 1959; PhD, NYU, 1981. Probation officer, 1947-55; supr. probation officer, 1955-65; br. chief Office Probation for Cts. N.Y.C., 1965-72, asst. dir. probation, 1972-77, dep. commr. dept. probation, 1978-86; prof. pub. adminstrn. John Jay Coll. Criminal Justice CUNY, 1986—; cert. faculty mem. Nat. Council Juvenile and Family Ct. Judges;mem. faculty N.Y.C. Tech. Coll., Nat. Coll. Juvenile Justice; mem. adv. com. Family Ct., First Dept. Sec. Susan E. Wagner Adv. Bd., 1966-70. Sec. bd. dirs. Allen Community Day Care Ctr., 1971-75; bd. dirs. Allen Sr. Citizens Housing, Queensboro Soc. for Prevention Cruelty to Children; chairperson, bd. dir. Allen Christian Sch., 1987—. Named to Hunter Coll. Hall of Fame, 1983. Mem. ABA (assoc.), N.Y. Acad. Pub. Edn., Nat. Council on Crime and Delinquency, Nat. Assn. Social Workers, Acad. Cert. Social Workers. Middle Atlantic States Conf. Correction, Alumni Assn. Columbia Sch. Social Work, NAACP, Am. Soc. Pub. Adminstrn. (mem. council), Counseliers, Hansel and Gretel Club (pres. 1967-69, Queens, N.Y.). Delta Sigma Theta. Home: 105-62 132d St Richmond Hill New York NY 11419 Office: NYC Dept Probation 115 Leonard St New York NY 10013

CHEW, MARY CATHERINE, metaphysical science specialist. Student, Interfaith Metaphys. Ctr., Williamstown, Fla., 1981—. Ordained to ministry Metaphys. Ch., 1982; lic. hypnotherapist, N.J., 1985; cert. tchr. metaphys. field N.J., 1982. Talk show producer/hostess, resident psychic Jones Intercable Co., Turnersville, N.J., 1984—; talk show hostess, WWBZ-AM, Vineland, N.J., 1981-82, WTYO-AM, Hammonton, N.J., 1982-87. Columnist, Courier Post newspaper, Cherry Hill, N.J., 1981-84; contbr. articles to News Weekly newspapers, Riverside, N.J., 1985—, Jersey Woman mag., Bergenfield, 1986—. Mem. Assn. to Advance Parapsychology and Healing Rsch. Republican. Office: PO Box 1304 Blackwood NJ 08012

CHIANESE, CARLA ANN, media executive; b. Trenton, N.J., Sept. 7, 1960; d. Thomas Chester and Teresann (Sansone) C. AS in Liberal Arts, Ocean County Coll., Toms River, N.J., 1980; BS in Bus. Adminstrn., Georgian Ct. Coll., 1982. Expeditor, sales person Bamberger's, Toms River, N.J., 1979-86; media dir. Becker, Jani, Inc., Middletown, N.J., 1984—. Home: 306 Spinnakers Dr Toms River NJ 08753 Office: Becker Jani Inc 113 Tindall Rd Middletown NJ 07748

CHIANG, JULIE JOLEE, province agency administrator; b. Cheng-Du, Peoples Republic of China, Apr. 12, 1947; came to Can., 1967.; d. Charles A.Y. and Kwei-Yu (Mao) C.; children: Michael, Jacqueline. BS, Brandon (Man., Can) U., 1970. Programmer N.Am. Life Assurance, Toronto, Ont., Can., 1970-72; programmer, analyst Govt. Ont., Toronto, 1974-77, Bell Can., Toronto, 1977-81; system analyst Can. Imperial Bank Com., Toronto, 1981-82; project leader-billing system AT&T, Piscataway, N.J., 1984; sr. system analyst Min. Environ., Toronto, 1984—. Recreational dir. Mandarin program Toronto Caths., 1985-86; v.p. Toronto Chinese Opera Group, 1986-87, pres., 1988—. Mem. Chineses Can. Info. Processing Profls., Oversea Chinese Women's Assn. (dir. 1986—), Women in Info. Processing (planning com. 1985—). Home: 5 Kenneth Ave Apt 1005, Willow Dale, ON Canada M2N 6M7 Office: 65 St Clair Ave E, Toronto, ON Canada M4T 2Y3

CHIAPPERINI, PATRICIA BIGNOLI, real estate appraiser, consultant; b. N.Y.C., Jan. 16, 1946; d. Gennaro and Giovanna (Resburgo) Bignoli; m. Joseph M. Chiapperini, Dec. 14, 1968. BS in Acctg. and Econs., St. John's U., 1968; postgrad., U. Ala., 1968, Rutgers U., 1980, Am. Inst. Real Estate Appraisers, 1983. Staff acct. Cleary, During & Co., N.Y.C., 1967-69; chief acct. Montgomery Bapt. Hosp. (Ala.), 1969-70; internal auditor Scottex Corp., N.Y.C., 1970-73; office mgr. Mid-Jersey Realty, East Brunswick, N.J., 1973-79; self-employed real estate appraiser, North Brunswick, N.J., 1979—; guest lect. Middlesex County Coll., 1979—; adj. prof. Jersey City State Coll. Chmn. Arts and Cultural Com., Milltown, N.J., 1979-83; active Am. Legion Aux., Milltown, 1973—. Recipient John Marshall award St. John's U., 1968. Mem. Nat. Assn. Ind. Fee Appraisers, Middlesex County Bd. Realtors, N.J. State Bd. Realtors, Cen. Jersey Ind. Fee Appraisers (treas. 1982-83, v.p. 1984), Am. Soc. Notaries, Monmouth County Bd. Realtors, Soc. Real Estate Appraisers (candidate), Milltown C. of C. (v.p. 1987). Roman Catholic. Office: 735 Georges Rd North Brunswick NJ 08902

CHIAVARIO, NANCY ANNE, business administrator, community relations executive; b. Centralia, Ill., Aug. 17, 1947; d. Victor Jr. and Alma Maria (Arsenault) C. Asst. mgr. rent supplement B.C. Housing Mgmt. Commn., Vancouver, 1975-81, adminstrv. asst., 1981-84, mgr. tenants and ops. svc., 1985—, adminstrv. asst., 1986-87; commr., vice chmn. Vancouver Park Bd., 1986-90. Pres. B.C. Recreation and Pks. Assn., 1989-90; exec. dir. B.C. Sport and Fitness Coun. for the Disabled, 1989-90. Mem. Inst. Housing Mgmt. (cert. adminstr. 1983, cert. finance 1985), West End Commn. Ctr. Assn. (pres. 1985-86), Mt. Pleasant Commn. Ctr. Assn. (pres. 1981-83). Democrat. Home: 1405-1960 Alberni, Vancouver, BC Canada V6G 1B6 Office: Vancouver Bd Parks, and Recreation, 2099 Beach Ave, Vancouver, BC Canada V6G 1Z4

CHICAGO, JUDY, artist; b. Chgo., July 20, 1939; d. Arthur M. and May (Levenson) Cohen. B.A., U. Calif. at Los Angeles, 1962, M.A., 1964. Co-founder Feminist Studio Workshop, Los Angeles, 1973, Through the Flower Corp., 1977. Author: Through the Flower: My Struggle as a Woman Artist, 1975, The Dinner Party: A Symbol of Our Heritage, 1979, Embroidering Our Heritage: The Dinner Party Needlework, 1980, The Birth Project, 1985; one-woman exhbns. include, Pasadena (Calif.) Mus. Art, 1969, Jack Glenn Gallery, Corona del Mar, Calif., 1972, JPL Fine Arts, London, 1975, Quay Ceramics, San Francisco, 1976, San Francisco Mus. Modern Art, 1979, Bklyn. Mus., 1980, Parco Galleries, Japan, 1980, Fine Arts Gallery, Irvine, Calif., 1981, Musee d'Art Contemporain, Montreal, 1982, ACA Galleries, N.Y.C., 1984, 85, 86; group exhbns. include Jewish Mus., N.Y.C., 1966, 67, Whitney Mus., 1972, Winnipeg Art Gallery, 1975; represented in permanent collections Bklyn. Mus., San Francisco Mus. Modern Art, Oakland Mus. Art, Pa. Acad. Fine Arts, L.A. County Mus. Art, also numerous pvt. collections. Office: care ACA Contemporary 41 E 57th St New York NY 10022*

CHICHESTER, SUSAN MARY, counselor; b. Racine, Wis., Oct. 21, 1936; d. Chester Thomas and Mercedes Margaret (Strewler) Organ; m. Norman James Chichester, Aug. 7, 1983. BS, U. Colo., 1965, MA, 1968. Tchr. Jefferson (Colo.) County Pub. Schs., 1965-68; sch. counselor Alameda (Colo.) Jr. High Sch., 1968-87, Arvada (Colo.) Jr. High Sch., 1987—. Sr. v.p. Lakewood (Colo.) on Parade Com., 1981-82; chmn. music scholar exch. com. Lakewood Sister City Program, 1985—; coord. radio communication advisor Mile High chpt. ARC, Denver, 1988—; committeewoman Lakewood Rep. Com., 1972-74, 88—; unit chmn. LWV, 1977-78; pres. UNESCO, Colo. 1982-83; bd. dirs., sec. Rocky Mountain Symphony, 1990. Recipient Disting. Tchr. award Jefferson County chpt., 1985, Outstanding Achievement award Lakewood Sister City, 1986, Humanities award Jefferson County Pub. Schs., 1989. Mem. NEA, Colo. Edn. Assn., Jefferson County Edn. Assn., AAUW (telephone chmn. Lakewood br. 1987-88, roster editor 1988, chmn. home fair workers, 1987, fin. chmn. 1988, ednl. area rep. 1989—, others, co-chmn. Holiday Home Fair), UN Assn. U.S. (Disting. Svc. award 1978), Denver Radio Club (program chmn. 1987-90), Toastmasters (membership chmn. 1988, area gov. 1989, local pres., Able Toastmaster award 1987), Alpha Delta Kappa (pres. Psi chpt. 1983-84), Alpha Delta Kappa (pres. 1983-84, treas. 1989—). Episcopalian. Home: 5822 W Atlantic Pl Lakewood CO 80227 Office: Arvada Jr High Sch 5751 Balsam St Arvada CO 80002

CHICKERING, LAURA LUCILLE, nursing supervisor; b. St. Louis, Mar. 25, 1948; d. Anthony and Lucille (Haarman) Gittemeier; m. Chester R. Chickering, Aug. 19, 1972 (div. July 1981). Nursing diploma, DePaul Hosp. Sch. Nursing, St. Louis, 1969; BA Sociology, Psychology, Simpson Coll., 1974; MA in Health Svcs. Mgmt., Webster U., 1987. RN, Mo. Staff nurse DePaul Hosp., St. Louis, 1969-73; nurse cons. Nursing Homes Madison County, Winterset, 1974-75; staff nurse, utilization rev. coord., inservice coord. Madison County Meml. Hosp., Winterset, Iowa, 1974-80; staff nurse Barnes Hosp., St. Louis, 1981; nursing supr. Mo. Bapt. Med. Ctr., St. Louis, 1981-90; ind. contractor in mgmt. cons., seminar presentations Program for Excellence, 1990—; instr. Des Moines Area Community Coll., Ankeny, Iowa, 1976-80; social svc. cons., RN cons. for local nursing homes, Iowa, 1975-76. Mem. ANA (med./surgical nurse cert. 1981, nursing adminstrn. cert. 1988), NAFE, Nat. League for Nursing, Nat. Nurses in Bus. Assn., Am. Assn. Legal Nurse Cons., Mo. League Nursing.

CHICKEY, REBECCA BUTLER, health care administrator; b. Florence, Ala., Nov. 29, 1959; d. Thomas Oscar and Doris Lynette (Pace) Butler; m. Robert Joseph Chickey, May 18, 1985. BA in Bus. and Psychology, Rhodes Coll., 1982; MPA, Memphis State U., 1988. Rsch. analyst Bapt. Meml. Hosp., Memphis, 1982-84; health planner Rivendell of Am., Memphis, 1984-85, coord. planning, 1985-86, dir. planning, 1986-87; clin. DRG analyst Meth. Hosp. Memphis, 1987-88, sr. clin. DRG analyst, 1988-89; health care adminstr. fellow Rush Presbyn. and Ill. Hosp. Assn., Chgo., 1989-90; sr. staff specialist sect. psychiat. and substance abuse svcs. Am. Hosp. Assn., Chgo., 1990—; cons. AIDS, Regional Med. Ctr., Memphis, 1988-89. Vol. Am. Cancer Soc., Memphis, 1985, Spl. Olympics, Memphis, 1989, Girls Club, Memphis, 1989, Memphis in May, 1988. Mem. Chgo. Health Execs. Forum, Am. Coll. Health Care Execs., Assn. Mental Health Adminstrn., Tenn. Hosp. Assn., Ill. Hosp. Assn., Tenn. Soc. Quality Assurance Profls., Shelby County Mental Health Assn., Phi Beta Kappa, Delta Delta Delta, Phi Kappa Phi, Pi Alpha Alpha. Methodist. Home: 2833 N Burling #2N Chicago IL 60657

CHICOREL, MARIETTA S., publisher; b. Vienna, Austria; came to U.S., 1939, naturalized, 1945; d. Paul and Margaret (Gross) Selby. AB, Wayne State U., 1951; MLS, U. Mich., 1961. Asst. chief library acquisitions div. U. Wash., Seattle, 1962-66; project dir. Macmillan Info. Scis., Inc., N.Y.C., 1968-69; pres. Chicorel Library Pub. Corp., N.Y.C., 1969-79, Am. Library Pub. Co., Inc., 1979—; asst. prof. dept. libr. sci., pub. cons. creative solutions CUNY (Queens Coll.), 1986—, mem. ABPA, 1986; mem. edn. com. Gov.'s Commn. on Status of Women, State of Wash., 1963-65; instr. libr. sci. No. Ariz. U., Flagstaf, 1990; bd. dirs. Skills Devel. Tng. counseling. Chief editor: Ulrich's International Periodicals Directory, 1966-68; editor, pub.: Chicorel Indexes, 1969—; founding editor: Jour. Reading, Writing and Learning Disabilities International, 1985-90; contbr. chpt. on univs. to Library Statistics: A Handbook of Concepts, Definitions and Terminology, 1966. Mem. ALA (exec. bd. tech. services div. 1965-68, chmn. library materials price index com. 1965-68, chmn. serials sect. nominating com. 1968-69, councillor 1969-73), Am. Assn. Profl. Cons., Book League N.Y. (bd. govs. 1975-79), Am. Soc. for Info. Sci., Canadian, Pacific N.W. library assns., New York Library Club, New York Tech. Services Librarians. Home and Office: PO Box 2014 Sedona AZ 86336

CHIERCHIA, MADELINE CARMELLA, management consulting company executive; b. Bklyn., Jan. 30, 1943; d. Lawrence Cataldo Carrozzo and Victoria Angel (Torchio) Carrozzo Petrisic; m. Jerry Chierchia, Oct. 3, 1959 (div. July 1975); children: Gertrude Chierchia Kraljic, Geraldine Rosalie Gorga. Student parochial schs. Bklyn. Pers. mgr. Argyle Pers. Agy., N.Y.C., 1976-77; clk. typist Atlantic Mut. Ins. Co., N.Y.C., 1977-78; sec. ARC, N.Y.C., 1978-82; mgr. D.F. King & Co. Inc. N.Y.C., 1982-89, asst. v.p., 1989—. Mem. Proxy Div. Securities Industry Assn., NAFE, Reorganization Securities Industry Assn., Am. Soc. for Profl. and Exec. Women, Corp. Transfer Agts. Assn. Democrat. Roman Catholic. Avocations: bowling, chess, reading, old movies. Office: DF King & Co 77 Water St New York NY 10005

CHIHARA, CAROL JOYCE, biology educator; b. N.Y.C., Oct. 31, 1941; d. Charles and Elizabeth (Pachtman) Rosen; m. Charles Seiyo Chihara, June 14, 1964; 1 child, Michelle Naomi. BA in Zoology, U. Calif., Berkeley, 1962, PhD in Genetics, 1972; MS in Cell Physiology, San Francisco State U., 1968. Asst. scientist U. Calif., Berkeley, 1974-76; lectr. San Francisco State U., 1974; prof. biology U. San Francisco, 1976—. Fellow NIH, 1970-72; fellow NSF Cambridge (Eng.) U., 1972-73, grantee, 1977-82. Mem. AAAS, Genetics Soc. Am., Soc. for Devel. Biology. Office: U San Francisco Ignatian Heights San Francisco CA 94117

CHILD, JOY CHALLENDER, accountant; b. Newton, Kans., Apr. 23, 1952; d. Willard Alton and Daisy Dolores (Horton) Challender; m. William Chapin Child, June 30, 1979; children: Christopher, Carolyn, Katherine. BBA summa cum laude, Wichita State U., 1978; MBA with honors, Clark U., 1984. CPA, Mass. Budget analyst JI Case, Wichita, 1978-79; bank auditor Shawmut Worcester County Bank, Worcester, Mass., 1979-82; staff acct. Marvin I. Lainer & Co., Worcester, 1982-85, assoc. mgr., 1985-86, ptnr., 1986-89; ptnr., v.p. Lainer, Child and Chambers, P.C., 1990—. Scout leader coun. Girl Scouts U.S., 1990—; v.p. Putnam Bapt. Women's Fellowship, 1987-90, pres., 1990—; asst. treas. Putnam Bapt. Ch., 1986—, fin. chair, 1988—. Mem. Am. Inst. CPAs, Mass. Soc. CPAs. Republican. Office: Lainer Child and Chambers PC 390 Main St Worcester MA 01608

CHILD, JULIA MCWILLIAMS (MRS. PAUL CHILD), cooking expert, television personality, author; b. Pasadena, Calif., Aug. 15, 1912; d. John and Julia Carolyn (Weston) McWilliams; m. Paul Child, Sept. 1, 1945. BA, Smith Coll., 1934. With advt. dept. W.&J. Sloane, N.Y.C., 1939-40; with OSS, Washington, Ceylon, China, 1941-45; co-founder Am. Inst. Wine & Food, 1982. Hostess TV program The French Chef, WGBH-TV, Boston, from 1962, Julia Child & Co., 1978-79, Julia Child & More Co., 1980, Dinner at Julia's, PBS, 1983; occasional cooking segment Good Morning America, ABC-TV, 1980—; video cassettes The Way to Cook, 1982; author: (with Simone Beck and Louisette Bertholle) Mastering the Art of French Cooking, 1961, The French Chef Cookbook, 1968, Mastering the Art of French Cooking, Vol. II, 1970, (with Simone Beck) From Julia Child's Kitchen, 1975, Julia Child & Company, 1978, Julia Child & More Company, 1979, Mastering the Art of French Cooking I & II, 1983, The Way to Cook, 1989; columnist McCall's mag., 1975-82, Parade mag., 1982-86. Recipient Peabody award, 1964, Emmy award, 1966, French Ordre de Merite Agricole, 1967, Ordre National de Merite, 1974. Office: Sta WGBH 125 Western Ave Boston MA 02134 also: care Knopf Inc 201 E 50th St New York NY 10022

CHILD, MARGARET SMILLIE, consultant, former government official; b. Yonkers, N.Y., July 14, 1929; d. Harold Baxter and Marie (Maloney) Smillie; m. James Robert Child, Dec. 30, 1955; children: Peter Truesdale, Elizabeth Baxter, Anne Margaret. B.A., Mount Holyoke Coll., 1951; M.A., Cornell U., 1952; Ph.D., U. Md., 1972. Intelligence officer on Indonesia, CIA, Washington, 1952-61; editor, Monthly Indonesian Press Survey, Joint Publs. Research Service, Dept. Commerce, Washington, 1961-64; teaching asst. U. Md., College Park, 1964-68, instr. history, 1971-74; asst. prof. Am. U., Washington, 1973-75; asst. dir. div. research programs Nat. Endowment for the Humanities, Washington, 1974-82; asst. dir., chief research services Smithsonian Instn. Libraries, Washington, 1982-89; cons. nat. paper preservation program Council on Library Resources, 1984-85; cons. field svc. program N.E. Document Conservation Ctr., 1989—.

CHILDERS, JUDY KAYE, critical care nurse; b. Louisville, Nov. 6, 1946; d. Lyndza Lee and Sallie Mae (Buster) Webb; m. Emmett Childers Jr., Oct. 23, 1965 (div. 1985); children: Deborah Lynn Childers Stone, Dawn Michelle. A.Nursing, Jefferson Community Coll., Louisville, 1975; BN, Bellarmine Coll., Louisville, 1987; postgrad., U. Louisville, 1988—. Critical care staff nurse Meth. Evang. Hosp., Louisville, 1975-78; inservice instr. Meth. Evang. Hosp., 1978-81, critical care educator, 1981-83; critical care educator Humana Hosp. Audubon, 1983-85; critical care nurse rev. educator Wininger Assocs., Louisville and Lexington, 1986-87; critical care educator Humana Hosp. Suburban, Louisville, 1985-87; cardiovascular clinician Cardiovascular Surgery Inc., Evansville, Ind., 1987; nurse mgr. ICU St. Anthony Med. Ctr., Louisville, 1988-89; charge nurse in oncology Humana Hosp. U., Louisville, 1989-90; critical care edn. Jewish Hosp., 1989—; adminstr. Childer's Critical Care Cons., 1989; nursing clin. faculty U. Louisville, 1988; critical care educator VA Med. Ctr., 1990; lectr. critical care; advanced cardiac, life support Ky. affiliate faculty. Contbr. articles to profl. jours. Research com. mem. Bellarmine Coll., 1984-86; adv. bd. Nurses for Christ, Louisville, 1987—; singles council dir. Long Run Bapt. Assn., Louisville, 1986-88; conductor symposium Am. Heart Assn., 1981—. Philip Morris scholar, 1986. Mem. Am. Assn. Critical Care Nurses (cert., chpt. pres. 1989, nat. program com. 1987-88), Am. Nurses Assn., Ky. Nurses Assn., Am. Heart Assn., Ind. Nurses Assn., Bapt. Nurses Assn., Soc. Critical Care Medicine, Kappa Gamma Pi, Sigma Theta Tau. Democrat. Baptist. Home: 3113 Hikes Ln Louisville KY 40220

CHILDERS, SHERI DIANE, pharmacist; b. Dallas, June 15, 1954; d. John Lewis Childers and Dolores Marie (Young) Darnell. AA, El Centro/Richland Coll., 1976; BS in Pharmacy, U. Tex., Austin, 1979. Lic. pharmacist, Tex. Pharmacist, mgr. Eckerd Drug Store, Dallas, 1980—; pharmacist cons. Dallas County Mental Health and Mental Retardation, 1989—. Mem. Tex. Pharm. Assn., Dallas County Pharm. Soc., Am. Bus. Women's Assn. (Woman of Yr. award 1984). Lutheran. Home: 7923 Shining Willow Ln Dallas TX 75230

CHILDERS, SUSAN LYNN, special education educator, human resources specialist; b. Zanesville, Ohio, Mar. 1, 1948; m. Lawrence J. Childers; 1 child, Jeffrey Scott. AA, Ohio U., 1978, BS in Edn. cum laude, 1982. Cert. elem. tchr., Ohio, spl. edn. tchr., Ohio. Educator learning disabilities, developmentally handicapped Maysville Local Sch. Dist., South Zanesville, Ohio, 1982-89; work study coord. Holmes County Office Edn., Millersburg, Ohio, 1990—; mem. Holmes County Spl. Edn. Adv. Coun., Regional Adv. Coun. for Ohio Employability Skills Project; speaker in field; rep. Ohio Developmentally Handicapped Issues Forum. Developer ednl. programs. Mem. Holmes County Adv. Coun. on Litter Prevention; mem. jr. assembly Bethesda Hosp., 1970-78. Recipient award Muskingum County Office Litter Prevention, 1989. Mem. ASCD, Career Edn. Assn., Coun. Exceptional Children, Ohio Assn. Suprs. and Work Study Coords. Home: PO Box 192 Millersburg OH 44654 Office: 2 S Clay St Millersburg OH 44654

CHILDRESS, MARGIE FAYE, accountant; b. Horry County, S.C., July 16, 1954; d. J.C. and Eleanor Louise (Foxworth) Floyd; m. Bernard McElwee Snowden, Sept. 7, 1977 (div. Sept. 1984); m. Gregory Bernard Childress, Sept. 6, 1984; children: Vincent Lorenzo Floyd, Crystal Leilani Childress. BS in Acctg., Am. U., 1976; postgrad., USDA Grad. Sch., 1978. Various positions Washington, 1971-76; acctg. technician U.S. Dept. Treasury BGFO, Washington, 1976-79; tchr. asst. U. Md., Coll. Park, 1981; fin. specialist QUALT EDIT 374th Fin. Sect. U.S. Dept. Army, Ft. Meade, Md., 1978-85; systems acct. Bur. Pub. Debt, Washington, 1979-83; auditor U.S. Govt. Printing Office, Washington, 1983-85; bookkeeper/acct. Maui Linen Supply, Honolulu, 1986-87; sr. pay specialist 411th Engr. Bn.-PSD TM A (Army), Honolulu, 1986-87; USAR unit adminstr. HQ, 411th Engr. Bn., Ft. DeRussy, Honolulu, 1987-88; staff adminstrv. specialist HQ 411th Engr. Bn. Ft. DeRussy, Honolulu, 1988-89; budget analyst HHC, U.S. Army Spl. Ops. Command, Ft. Bragg, N.C., 1990—; tax cons. H & R Block, Honolulu, 1985-89. Mem. NAACP, Fay, N.C., 1989, Mt. Sinai Bapt. Ch., Fay, (musician, choirperson 1990—). Jr. fellow FTC, 1972-76; Model Cities scholar Am. U., 1972, 73; decorated Army Commendation medal USAR, 1982, 86, 88, 89. Mem. NAFE, Treasury Women's Network. Democrat. Home: 4430 Spinel Dr Fayetteville NC 28311-6862

CHILDRESS, PHYLLIS ANN, construction executive; b. Fort Wayne, Ind., Feb. 28, 1937; d. Paschal J. and Pietrina M. (Ceccanese) Pallone; m. Kelly W. Childress, Aug. 24, 1973; children: Patricia, William, Jeffrey. BS in Commerce, Internat. Coll., 1955; postgrad. Pima Community Coll., 1978-80. Cert. constrn. mgr., 1987. Sec. to v.p. trust dept. Lincoln Nat. Bank, Ft. Wayne, Ind., 1955-57; sec. to pres. adminstrn. dept. Internat. Coll., Ft. Wayne, 1957-60; dir., sec. Lightning Homes, Inc., Homebuilders and Developers, Ft. Wayne, 1960-63; sec. to v.p., fin. dept., office mgr. fleet maintenance dept. N.Am. Van Lines, Inc., Ft. Wayne, 1963-71; asst. mktg. dir. ITT Electro-Optical Products, Ft. Wayne, 1972-76; asst. v.p. Empire West Builders, Inc., Tucson, 1977-80; staff constrn. mgmt. Akins Co., Tucson, 1981-82; constrn. mgr. Archtl. Div., City of Tucson, 1982-85; pres. Construction Techniques, Inc., Tucson, 1985—. Block grants advisor Tucson Community Devel. Commn., 1983—. Recipient Appreciation Cert. Nat. Assn. Women Constrn., 1978; named Sec. of Yr. Tawasi chpt. Nat. Secs. Assn., 1967; recipient plaque for outstanding service, 1977. Mem. Cholla Bus. and Profl. Women (past chpt. pres., Woman of Yr. 1986), Nat. Assn. Women Constrn. (past pres.). Democrat. Baptist. Contbr. articles to various publs. Home and Office: 2833 N Laurel Ave Tucson AZ 85712

CHILDS, CAROLE MAI, school administrator; b. Penns Grove, N.J., Dec. 10, 1940; d. William Sawyer and Etta Mai (Clayton) Guest; m. Robert Alan Childs, Aug. 5, 1961; children: Scott William, Melyssa Lea. BS, SUNY, Oswego, 1961; MS, SUNY, Brockport, 1981; Cert. Adv. Study, SUNY, 1981. Tchr. Spencerport Cen. Sch., N.Y., 1961-63, Williamson (N.Y.) Sch., 1963-70; spl. edn. tchr. Monroe I Boces, Fairport, N.Y., 1970-74; spl. edn. prin. Monroe I Boces, 1974-81, dir. personnel, 1981-88; asst. supt. Webster Cen. Sch., N.Y., 1988—. Adv. com. Grow-Council of Aging, Rochester, N.Y., 1984-88. Mem. Ea. Monroe County Personnel Adminstrs., N.Y. State Personnel Adminstrs., Phi Delta Kappa, Delta Kappa Gamma (state personnel chmn. 1987-89). Democrat. Office: Webster Central School 119 South Ave Webster NY 14580

CHILDS, MARJORIE MAY VICTORIA, lawyer; b. N.Y.C., July 13, 1918; d. Charles W. and Eva M. (Tarrant) C. Student Hunter Coll., 1942-46; BA in Econs., U. Calif., Berkeley, 1948; JD, U. San Francisco, 1956; LLD (hon.), Iowa Wesleyan Coll., 1973. Bar: Calif. 1957, U.S. Supreme Ct. 1969. With Office of Regional Counsel, U.S. Navy, Ft. Mason, Calif., 1957-60; asst. county counsel Humboldt County, Calif., 1960-62; pvt. practice, San Francisco, 1962-64, 79—; referee, commr. Juvenile dept. Superior Ct., San Francisco, 1964-79. Contbr. articles to profl. jours. Pres. Diamond Heights Community Assn., 1983-84. Recipient James A. Harlan award Iowa Wesleyan Coll., 1969. Fellow Am. Bar Found.; mem. ABA, Internat. Bar Assn., Lawyers Club San Francisco, Queen's Bench (pres. 1967), Bar Assn. San Francisco, Internat. Fedn. Women Lawyers, Nat. Assn. Women Lawyers (pres. 1974-75), Metropolitan Club. Democrat. Episcopalian. Home: 64 Turquoise Way San Francisco CA 94131 Office: 301 Junipero Serra Blvd #208 San Francisco CA 94127

CHILDS, MARY JANE, account executive yellow page advertising; b. Detroit, Nov. 7, 1936; d. Myron Henry and Helen Jane (Mcclain) Carnahan; m. William Edward Moore, Feb. 2, 1957; children: Jeffrey Kent Moore, Joyce Alison Moore; m. Gerald Blake Childs, Mar. 26, 1967. Student, Purdue U., Ft. Wayne, 1975. From svc. rep. to PR coord. Michigan Bell Telephone Co., Detroit, 1963-66; owner The House of Arden, Dearborn, Mich., 1967-71; instr. in adult edn. 4C-POS, Monroe, 1970-71; with Monroe (Mich.) Community Coll., 1967-71, 1970-71, Dearborn & Edsel Ford High, 1967-71, 1970-71; collector Montgomery Ward, Ill., 1976-82; co-owner ECE Insulation, Decatur, Ill., 1980-81; engring. technician Clinton (Ill.) Power Sta., 1984-86; account exec. Teleconnect, Decatur, 1986—. Vol. Tchr. Project Read, Decatur, 1986. Mem. NAFE, Rotary (charter Machesney Park, Ill.). Lutheran. Home: 2752 E Wallace Decatur IL 62526 Office: 500 2d Ave SE Cedar Rapids IA 52401

CHILDS, SHIRLE MOONE, educational administrator; b. N.Y.C., Aug. 2, 1936; d. Harold McDaniel and Bessie Mary (Batts) Moone; m. William Childs, Sept. 5, 1971; children by previous marriage: Duane Kelby Milner, David Kent Milner. BS, U. Hartford, 1968, MS, 1970; PhD, U. Conn., 1978. Tchr., Hartford (Conn.) Public Schs., 1968-71, vice prin., acting prin. Mark Twain Elem. Sch., 1973-77, early childhood edn. specialist, 1978-84; adminstrv. asst. for instruction Teaneck (N.J.) Pub. Schs., 1984—; lectr., adj. prof., instr. Conn. Coll. for Women, Eastern Conn. State Coll., U. Hartford. Pres. bd. dirs. Women's League Day Care; trustee Hartford ConservatoryTeaneck Libr. Coun., 1987—; mem. Windsor Dem. Club; mem. Commr.'s Task Force on High Sch. Graduation Requirements N.J. Dept. Edn., 1987; assessor Md. and N.J. Assessment Ctrs., 1987; bd. dirs. Assault on Illiteracy, 1980—. Rockefeller Found. fellow, 1977-78; Kettering Found. fellow, 1976-85. Mem. Nat. Assn. Edn. Young Children, Am. Assn. Sch. Adminstrs., Assn. Supervision and Curriculum Devel., Hartford Assn. Edn. Young Children, Conn. Assn. Suprs./Instrs. in Spl. Edn., Urban League, NAACP, Nat. Council Negro Women, Delta Sigma Theta (nat. sec. 1979-83), Phi Delta Kappa, Pi Lambda Theta. Methodist. Lodge: Order Eastern Star. Avocations: Chinese cooking, needlepoint. Home: 26 Regency Dr Windsor CT 06095 Office: 1 Merrison St Teaneck NJ 07666

CHILDS, THEA DOUGLAS WISE, social services administrator, writer; b. Balt., Aug. 1, 1924; d. Hugo Paul and Mildred May (Naas) Wise; m. Richard Donald Childs (dec. 1972); children: Matthew Scott, Abby Margaret Childs Hastings. BA, Denison U., 1947; EdM, Harvard U., 1974; postgrad., several universities. Teacher Robert Coll., Istanbul, Turkey, 1947-62; teacher Caltex-Pacific Oil Co., Sumatra, Indonesia, 1957-62; exec. dir. Girl Scouts, St. Croix Valley, St. Paul, 1975-79, Girl Scouts of Cen. Md., Balt., 1979-82; devel. dir. Washington Coll., Chestertown, Md., 1983; exec. dir. YWCA, Louisville, 1984-86, Mae Volen Sr. Ctr., Boca Raton, Fla., 1986-88; freelance writer and agys. cons. Lehigh Acres, Fla., 1988—. Author: several articles, 1978-79, 1988, annual personal policies; editor: book, Jour. of an Airman, 1989. V.P. AAUW, St. Paul, 1976-77, Agy. Dir. Orgn., St. Paul, 1977-78; Exec. Women's Orgn., Balt., 1980-81; active in Dem. campaign, Alexandria, Va., 1971, Mayor's Com. on Cable, Balt., 1980, Human Rights Commn., St. Paul, 1976, Boy Scouts Manpower, St. Paul, 1977. Recipient Girl Scouts Thanks Badge, Minn., St. Paul, Minn. 1979, Prize for Prose, Denison U., Granville, Ohio, 1974, Mayor's Citation, Mayor Schaefer, Balt., 1979, United Way Com. Svc. Award, Balt., 1981. Mem. Nat. Soc. Fund Raising Execs., Fla. Freelance Writers Assn., Harvard Club of Broward County, Fla., Harvard Club of Palm Beach County, Engring. Soc. of Balt., Harvard Club Ft. Myers., Phi Delta Kappa. Democrat. Episcopalian. Home: 210 Lowery Ave Lehigh Acres FL 33936

CHILSON, NANCY LEE, educator; b. Harrisburg, Pa., July 29, 1944; d. William James and Virginia (Glidewell) C. BA, San Diego U., 1968; postgrad., UCLA, 1969-72, Pepperdine U., 1969-73. Cert. tchr. Calif. Tchr. L.A. Unified Sch. Dist., 1968—. Author: National Teachers Catalog of Creative Program Ideas, 1986. Mem. L.A. Community Action Network, 1987—, South Bay Literacy Council, 1988—, Polit. Action Council for Edn., 1986—. Grantee L.A. Ednl. Ptnrship, in sci., 1986, 88, in math., 1987, in social studies, 1989, in marine biology State of Calif., 1986, Marine Sci. L.A. Ptnrship., 1986. Mem. Am. Biog. Inst. Inc., United Tchrs. of L.A., Calif. Tchrs. Assn., Nat. Edn. Assn., Redondo Beach C. of C., Delta Kappa Gamma (communications chairperson 1988—). Republican. Office: Taper Ave Elem Sch 1824 Taper Ave San Pedro CA 90731

CHILTON, KATHRYN WARD, real estate administrator; b. Sioux Falls, S.D., May 2, 1930; d. Charles David and Juanita Marion (Senecal) Ward; m. Mark Chilton, Aug. 26, 1950; children: Cheryl C. Smith, Carey C. Charyk, Ward William. BA, U. Colo., 1951. Property mgr. Property Mgmt. Svcs., Elko, Nev., 1967—; substitute tchr. Elko County Sch. System, 1957-67. Pres. Elko Gen. Hosp. Aux., 1975, Nev. Hosp. Aux., 1981; bd. dirs., treas. Alcohol and Drug Abuse Ctr., Elko, 1974-77; speaker Elko Gen. Hosp.'s Speaker's Bur., 1980-82. Named Golden Auxillian of Yr. Elko Gen. Aux., 1988. Mem. AAUW (pres. Elko chpt. 1969), PEO (pres. Elko AD chpt. 1988), Navy League U.S. (charter mem. Elko chpt.), Chi Omega. Republican. Presbyterian.

CHILTON, LYNN LOUISE AMBROZ, nursing educator; b. Milw., Oct. 15, 1948; d. Herbert Frank and Marjorie Avis (Holtslander) Ambroz; m. Larry Lane Chilton, Oct. 10, 1970; children: Scott Herbert, Michael Antis. BS in Nursing, Marquette U., 1970; MS in Nursing, Miss. U. Women, 1986. RN, Miss. Supr. East Shore Dist. Nursing, East Providence, R.I., 1971-73; charge nurse Columbus (Miss.) Hosp., 1982-84; dir. skills lab. Miss. U. Women, Columbus, 1984-86, asst. prof. nursing, 1986—. Recipient Geriatric Profl. Devel. award Nat. Disting. Svc. Registry Nursing; faculty rsch. grantee. Mem. Nursing Alumnae Assn. Miss. U. Women (sec., treas.), Sigma Theta Tau (pres., treas. local chpt., Excellence in Nursing Edn. award Zeta Rho chpt. 1990). Home: 117 Sonja Dr Columbus MS 39702

CHILTON, MARY-DELL MATCHETT, chemical company executive; b. Indpls., Feb. 2, 1939; d. William Elliot and Mary Dell (Hayes) Matchett; m. William Scott Chilton, July 9, 1966; children—Andrew Scott, Mark Hayes. B.S. in Chemistry, U. Ill., 1960, Ph.D. in Chemistry, 1967; Dr. honoris causa, U. Louvain, Belgium, 1983. Research asst. prof. U. Wash., Seattle, 1972-77, research assoc. prof., 1977-79; assoc. prof. Washington U., St. Louis, 1979-83; exec. dir. agrl. biotech CIBA-Geigy Corp., Research Triangle Park, N.C., 1983—; adj. prof. genetics N.C. State U., Raleigh, 1983—; adj. prof. biology Washington U., 1983—; Gov. appointee N.C. Bd. Sci. and Tech. Mem. editorial bd. Bio/Tech., Plant Molecular Biology, Proceedings of the Nat. Acad. of Scis.; contbr. articles to profl. jours. Recipient of Rank Prize for Nutrition, 1987. Mem. NAS (coun. 1988—). Office: CIBA-Geigy Biotech Facility PO Box 12257 Research Triangle Park NC 27709

CHIMICK, CLAIRE BESSIE REIFENHEISER, financial analyst; b. College Point, N.Y., Apr. 6, 1933; d. Francis Thomas and Mary Ann (Konzet) Reifenheiser; m. William Michael Chimick, June 20, 1953; children: Christopher Michael, Caren Marie, Gregg William. AA, U. N.H., Durham, 1987; BS, N.H. Coll., Hooksett, 1988. Sec., bookkeeper No. N.H. Mental Health & Devel. Svcs., Conway, 1975—; tutor Community Action Program, No. Conway. Chairperson Mt. Washington Valley Girl Scouts U.S., Conway, 1978; campaign worker Rep. Com., Conway, 1978; mem. adv. coun. Children Unltd., 1988—. Mem. Nat. Assn. Reimbursement Officers, Conway Hist. Soc. (bicentennial com. 1975-77). Roman Catholic. Home: 84 Kennett St Conway NH 03818 Office: No NH Mental Health Washington St Conway NH 03818

CHIN, CECILIA HUI-HSIN, art librarian; b. Tientsin, China; came to U.S., 1961; d. Yu-lin and Ti-yu (Fan) C. B.A., Nat. Taiwan U., Taipei, 1961; M.S.L.S., U. Ill., 1963. Cataloger, reference librarian Roosevelt U., Chgo., 1963; reference librarian, indexer Ryerson & Burnham Libraries, Art Inst. Chgo., 1963-70, head reference dept. indexer,, 1970-75; acting dir. libraries Art Inst. Chgo., 1976-77, assoc. librarian, head reference dept., 1975-82; chief librarian Nat. Mus. Am. Art and Nat. Portrait Gallery, Smithsonian Inst., Washington, 1982—. Compiler: The Art Institute of Chicago Index to Art Periodicals, 1975. Recipient award Nat. Portrait Gallery, Smithsonian Instn., 1984. Mem. ALA, Spl. Libraries Assn., Art Libraries Soc., Coll. Art Assn., Washington Conservation Guild. Office: Nat Mus Am Art & Nat Portrait Gallery Smithsonian Instn Washington DC 20560

CHIN, CINDY LAI, real estate accountant; b. Kowloon, Hong Kong, Dec. 2, 1957; came to U.S., 1964; d. Sau Kuen and Koon On C. BS in Acctg., CUNY, 1980; grad., Real Estate Inst., 1987-90. Real estate acct. Milford Mgmt., Inc., N.Y.C., 1980-82; staff acct. Occidental Petroleum Corp., N.Y.C., 1983-85; portfolio acct. Richard Ellis, Inc., N.Y.C., 1985—; real estate acct. Yarmouth Group Inc., N.Y.C., 1989—; cons. C&M Real Estate Joint Venture, N.Y.C., 1985-89. Mem. China Inst., N.Y.C., 1986. Mem. NAFE, Hunter Coll. Acctg. Alumni Assn. Home: 85-06 Parsons Blvd Jamaica NY 11432 Office: Yarmouth Group Inc 527 Madison Ave New York NY 10022

CHIN, JANET JUE, nurse, secretary; b. Portland, Oreg., Feb. 25, 1930; d. Herbert Sue and Margaret Mai (Lum) Jue; m. George Wai Chin, Mar. 1, 1952; children: Martin, David, Daniel, Cathryn, Cheri, Nancy. BS in Liberal Arts and Nursing, U. Oreg., 1952. RN, Oreg. Sec. Sam Wong & Son, Klamath Falls, Oreg., 1952—; office nurse Dr. J. Robertson, M.D., Merrill, Oreg., 1958-80; charge nurse Oreg. Health Sci. U. Hosp., Portland, 1951-52; staff nurse Merle West Med. Ctr., Klamath Falls, 1988; pub. health nurse Klamath County Health Dept., 1952-53; sch. nurse Klamath County Sch. Dist., Klamath Falls, 1990—. Vol. nurse ARC, 1952—; vol. Klamath County Mental Health Ctr., Klamath Falls, 1979-90; organist 1st Presbyn. Ch., Merrill, 1959-81; bd. dirs. Mental Health Adv. Bd., Klamath Falls, 1979-85, Local Alcohol & Drug Adv. Bd., Klamath Falls, 1984-90. Mem. Oreg. Nurses Assn., AAUW, Lost River Garden Club (pres. 1958-60), Zuleima Temple, Daug. of the Nile. Republican. Home: 17930 Chin Rd Klamath Falls OR 97603 Office: San Wong & Son 17800 Hwy 39 Klamath Falls OR 97603

CHIN, JANET SAU-YING, data processing executive, consultant; b. Hong Kong, July 27, 1949; came to U.S., 1959; d. Arthur Quock-Ming and Jenny (Loo) C. BS in Math, U. Ill., Chgo., 1970; MS in Computer Sci., U. Ill., Urbana, 1972. System programmer Lawrence Livermore (Calif.) Lab., 1972-79; sect. mgr. Tymshare Inc., Cupertino, Calif., 1979-83, Fortune Systems, Redwood City, Calif., 1983-85; div. mgr. Impell Corp, Berkeley, Calif., 1985; pres. Chin Assocs., Oakland, Calif., 1985-88; engring. mgr. Sun Microsystems, Mountain View, Calif., 1988—; Vice-chmn. Am. Nat. Standards Inst. X3H3, N.Y.C., 1979-82, internat. rep. X3H3, 1982-88. Author tech. papers to profl. publs. Mem. Assn. Computing Machinery, Sigma Xi.

CHIN, SUE SOONEMARIAN (SUCHIN CHIN), artist, portraitist, photographer, community affairs activist; b. San Francisco; d. William W. and Soo-Up (Swebe) C. Grad. Calif. Coll. Art, Mpls. Art Inst., (scholar) Schaeffer Design Ctr.; student, Yasuo Kuniyoshi, Louis Hamon, Rico LeBrun. Photojournalist, All Together Now show, 1973, East-West News, Third World Newscasting, 1975-78, Sta. KNBC Sunday Show, L.A., 1975, 76, Live on 4, 1981, Bay Area Scene, 1981; graphics printer, exhbns. include Kaiser Ctr., Zellerbach Pla., Chinese Culture Ctr. Galleries, Capricorn Asunder Art Commn. Gallery (all San Francisco), Newspace Galleries, New Coll. of Calif., L.A. County Mus. Art, Peace Pla. Japan Ctr., Congress Arts Communication, Washington, 1989; SfWA Galleries, 1989, Calif. Mus. Sci. and Industry, Lucien Labaudt Gallery, Salon de Medici, Madrid, Salon Renacimento, Madrid, Sacramento State Fair, AFL-CIO Labor Studies Ctr., Washington, Asian Women Artists (1st prize for conceptual painting, 1st prize photography), 1978; represented in permanent collections L.A. County Fedn. Labor, Calif. Mus. Sci. and Industry, AFL-CIO Labor Studies Ctr., Australian Trades Coun., Hazeland and Co., also pvt. collections. Del. nat., state convs. Nat. Women's Polit. Caucus, 1977-83, San Francisco chpt. affirmative action chairperson, 1978-82, nat. conv. del., 1978-81, Calif. del., 1976-81. Recipient Honorarium AFL-CIO Labor Studies Ctr., Washington, 1975-76; award Centro Studi Ricerche delle Nazioni, Italy, 1985; bd. advisors Psycho Neurology Found. Bicentennial award L.A. County Mus. Art, 1976, 77, 78. Mem. Asian Women Artists (founding v.p., award 1978-79, 1st award in photography of Orient 1978-79), Calif. Chinese Artists (sec.-treas. 1978-81), Japanese Am. Art Coun. (chairperson 1978-84, dir.), San Francisco Women Artists, San Francisco Graphics Guild, Pacific/Asian Women Coalition Bay Area, Chinatown Coun. Performing and Visual Arts. Chmn., Full Moon Products; pres., bd. dir. Aumni Oracle Inc. Featured in Calif. Living Mag., 1981. Address: PO Box 1415 San Francisco CA 94101

CHIN, SYLVIA FUNG, lawyer; b. N.Y.C., June 27, 1949; d. Thomas and Constance (Yao) Fung; m. Edward G.H. Chin, July 10, 1971; children: Arthur F., Benjamin F. BA, NYU, 1971; JD, Fordham U., 1977. Bar: N.Y. 1978, U.S. Dist. Ct. (so. and ea. dists.) N.Y. 1979. Law clk. to dist. judge U.S. Dist. Ct. (so. dist.), N.Y.C., 1977-79; assoc. White & Case, N.Y.C., 1979-86, ptnr., 1986—; adj. prof. law Fordham U., N.Y.C., 1979-81. Co-author (article in book) Negotiating Business Transactions, 1988. Mem. ABA, N.Y. State Bar Assn., N.Y. County Lawyers Assn., Fordham Law Alumni Assn. (bd. dirs., trustee of stichting to promote women's world banking). Office: White & Case 1155 Ave of the Americas New York NY 10036

CHINARD, JEANNE, advertising agency executive. Formerly with Dancer Fitzgerald Sample; with N.W. Ayer, Inc., N.Y.C., 1984—, now sr. v.p., exec. creative dir. Recipient Clio and Andy awards. Office: NW Ayer Inc Worldwide Pla 825 8th Ave New York NY 10019*

CHINEA-VARELA, MIGDIA, scriptwriter; b. Santa Clara, Las Villas, Cuba, Aug. 5, 1952; d. José Antonio Chinea Figueroa and Violeta Eusebia (Suárez) Nicassio; m. Frank C. Varela; 1 child, Frank C. Jr. Grad. high sch., Miami, Fla. Freelance writer TV; dir., producer, story cons. Victory and Romick Prodns.; chmn. Latino Writers Com., Los Angeles, 1979—. Scriptwriter: (TV) Me and Mrs. C., Punky Brewster, What's Happening Now, After Joe, Trapper John, The Facts of Life, Diff'rent Strokes, One Day at a Time, Backalleys, The Incredible Hulk, Phyllis, General Hospital; writer (screenplay) Prisoner of Conscience, 1988. Pub. relations Cuban-Am. Nat. Found., Los Angeles, 1984-87, Latino Writers Council, 1978—; big sister East Los Angeles chpt. Little Sisters. Recipient Nosotros writing award, 1982, Human Relations award, 1988. Mem. Writers Guild Am. (coordinating com., nominating com., fellow), Media Arts and Scis. Club: Century.

CHINITZ, JODY ANNE KOLB, data processing executive; b. Bay City, Mich., July 8, 1953; d. Adam H. and Evelyn I. (Sylvester) Kolb; m. William A. Chinitz, Feb. 11, 1979. Student Saginaw Valley State Coll., 1972, Bklyn. Coll., 1973-76; BA in Russian Lang. and Lit. summa cum laude, CUNY., 1980. With personnel dept. N.Y. Life Ins. Co., N.Y.C., 1972-77, computer programmer, 1977-80; computer systems cons. Soroban Data Systems, Inc., N.Y.C., 1980-82; project leader Midlantic Nat. Bank, West Orange, N.J., 1982-89, asst. v.p., 1989—. Home: 31 Norwood Ave Upper Montclair NJ 07043 Office: 95 Old Short Hills Rd West Orange NJ 07052

CHINN, PEGGY LOIS, nursing educator, editor; b. Columbia, S.C., Feb. 25, 1941; d. Hubert R. and Margaret (Gasteiger) Tatum; m. Philip C. Chinn, June 15, 1964 (div. 1974); children: Kelleth Roger, Jonathan Mark. AA, Mars Hill Coll., 1960; BS, U. Hawaii, 1964; MS, U. Utah, 1970, PhD, 1971. From instr. to asst. prof. U. Utah, Salt Lake City, 1971-74; assoc. dir., prof. Tex. Woman's U., Denton, 1974-78; prof. Wright State U., Dayton, Ohio, 1978-81, SUNY, Buffalo, 1981-90, U. Colo., Denver, 1990—; founder, editor Advances in Nursing Sci., Rockville, Md., 1978—; cons., lectr. in field. Author: Child Health Maintenance, 1974, 2d edit., 1978, Theory in Nursing, 1983, 2d edit., 1987, Peace and Power, 1989; contbr. articles to profl. jours. Co-founder Cassandra: Radical Feminist Nurses Network, nationwide 1982, Margaret Daughters Inc., Buffalo, 1984. Fellow Am. Acad. Nursing (governing coun. 1987-90); mem. Am. Nurses Assn., Nat. League for Nursing, Sigma Theta Tau. Office: U Colo Health Sci Ctr Box C288 4200 E 9th Ave Denver CO 80262

CHINN, PHYLLIS ZWEIG, mathematics educator; b. Rochester, N.Y., Sept. 26, 1941; d. Julian and Gladys Elizabeth (Weinstein) Z.; m. Daryl Ngee Chinn, Dec. 31, 1968; children: Allison Hai-Ting, Wesley Chee. BA, Brandeis U., 1962; MAT, Harvard U., 1963; MS, U. Calif., San Diego, 1966, PhD, Santa Barbara, 1969. Asst. prof. Towson State Coll. Balt., 1969-75; assoc. prof. Humboldt State U., Arcata, Calif., 1975-83, prof., 1984—; exchange prof. U. Central Fla., Orlando, 1983-84. Dir. Redwood Area Math Project, 1988—. Author: (bibliography) Women in Science and Math, 1979, 3rd edit., 1988; also monograph. Contbr. articles to profl. jours. Conf. coordinator Nat. Women's Studies Assn., Arcata, 1982, Expanding Your Horizons in Sci. and Math, Arcata and Orlando, 1980—; dir. Redwood area Math Project, Calif., 1989—. Calif. State U. grantee, 1977. Mem. Assn. for Women in Math., Women and Math., Assn. for Women in Sci., Nat. Council of Tchrs. of Math., Math. Assn. Am., Calif. State U. Task Force on Status of Women in Sci., Engring. and Math., Phi Beta Kappa (elected). Office: Humboldt State U Math Dept Arcata CA 95521

CHINN-HECHTER, MAMIE MAY, state agency administrator; b. Oakland, Calif., Aug. 20, 1951; d. Bing T. and Georgia S. (Ong) C.; m. Marc S. Hechter. BS in Bus., U. Nev., 1974. Loan processor First Fed. Savs. and Loan, Reno, 1974-75, loan processor supr., 1975-76, sr. loan counselor, affirmative action officer, 1977-78; jr. loan officer First Fed. Savs. and Loan, Carson City, Nev., 1976-77; loan officer State of Nev. Housing Div., Carson City, 1978-79, loan adminstr., 1979-83, dep. adminstr., 1983—; mem. exec. com. Housing and Devel. Fin., Ethics Com., Media and Communications Com., Carson City, 1987—. Mem. Carson City Women's Polit. Caucus, Nev. Women's Polit. Caucus. Mem. NAFE Capitol City Club (sec. Carson chpt. 1984-88). Clubs: Capitol City (Carson City) (sec. 1984—), Women's Bowling Assn. (bd. dirs. 1983-84), Nat. 600. Office: State of Nev Housing Div 1050 E William Ste 435 Carson City NV 89710

CHIPMAN, SUSAN ELIZABETH, psychologist; b. St. Paul, Feb. 12, 1946; d. Robert Louis and Margaret Alice (Sjoselius) Fitzgerald; m. Eric George Chipman, Aug. 27, 1966. AB in Math., Harvard U., 1966, MBA, 1967, AM in Psychol., 1969, PhD in Exptl. Psychol., 1973. Asst. prof. U. Mich., Ann Arbor, 1974-75; assoc. Nat. Inst. Edn., Washington, 1976-78, asst. dir., 1979-84; sci. officer U.S. Office Naval Rsch., Arlington, Va., 1984-85, cognitive sci. program mgr., 1985—; mem. adv. bd. James S. McDonnell Found., St. Louis, 1987—. Editor, author: Thinking and Learning Skills, 1985, Women and Mathematics, 1985; contbr. articles to profl. jours. Home: 2606 S Joyce St Arlington VA 22202 Office: Office Naval Rsch 1142CS 800 N Quincy St Arlington VA 22217

CHISHOLM, CAROL LEE, research psychologist; b. Abington, Pa., Mar. 19, 1938; d. Lawrence and Gertrude Evelyn (Macdonald) Christianson; m. Franklin Donald Chisholm, June 10, 1956 (dec. May 1978); children: Jennifer Anne, Stephen Donald. BS in Edn., State Tchrs. Coll., Towson, Md., 1962; MA in Psychology, Towson State U., 1981; PhD in Psychology, U. Del., 1986. Elem. sch. tchr. Balt. County Bd. Edn., 1962-66, tutor, home tchr., 1966-68; instr. Towson State U., 1979-81, U. Del., 1981-85; psychologist, cons. Balt. Gas and Electric Co., 1980-87, computer applications coordinator, 1987-88; rsch. psychologist CIA, Washington, 1988—. Mem. Friends Nat. Zoo, Washington, Smithsonian Resident Assocs., Washington; screening com. Am. Field Svc., Balt.; workshop presenter Lutheran Ch. Named Outstanding Grad. Student in Psychology, Towson State U., 1981, Faculty award, Psychology Dept., 1981. Mem. Am. Psychol. Assn., Ea. Psychol. Assn., Luth. Brotherwood (officer br. 8001), Phi Kappa Phi. Home: 12423 Wolbert Way Bradshaw MO 21021

CHISWICK, NANCY ROSE, psychologist; b. East Orange, N.J., May 8, 1945; d. Haim Hershel and Beatrice May (Levinson) C.; m. Arthur Howard Patterson, Aug. 5, 1973; children: Michael Chiswick-Patterson, Emily Chiswick-Patterson. AB, Smith Coll., 1966; MA, U. Ill., Chgo. Circle, 1970; PhD, U. Ill., 1973. Lic. psychologist, Pa. Intern Northwestern U. Med. Sch., Chgo., 1973; mental retardation specialist The Counseling Svc., Bellefonte, Pa., 1973-75; clin. staff psychologist Pa. State U., 1975-80; dir. clin. psychologist Child, Adult and Family Psychol. Ctr., State College, PA., 1980—; adj. prof. psychology and human devel., Pa. State U., 1974—; mem. allied staff, Ctr. Community Hosp., State College, 1985—; cons. Meadows Psychiat. Hosp., Center Hall, Pa., 1985—. Creator, co-host pub. TV Series About Women, 1979-80. Del. White House Conf. Families, 1980, bd. dirs. Meadows Psychiat. Hosp., 1983-85, Jewish Community Ctr., 1989—. Named Guest in Residence W. Marlin Butts Com. Oberlin (Ohio) Coll., 1978. Fellow Cen. Pa. Psychol. Assn. (sec. 1987-89), mem. APA, Pa. Psychol. Assn. Home: 218 Adams Ave State College PA 16803 Office: Child Adult & Family Psychol Ctr 315 S Allen St #218 State College PA 16801

CHITTY, (MARY) ELIZABETH NICKINSON, university administrator; b. Balt., Apr. 27, 1920; d. Edward Phillips and Em Turner (Merritt) Nickinson; m. Arthur Benjamin Chitty, June 16, 1946; children: Arthur Benjamin, John Abercrombie, Em Turner, Nathan Harsh Brown. BA cum laude, Fla. State U., 1941, MA, 1942; D in Civil Law, U. of South, 1988. Tchr. Fla. Indsl. Sch. for Girls, Ocala, 1942-43; psychometrist neuropsychiat. dept. Sch. Aviation Medicine, Pensacola (Fla.) Naval Air Sta., 1943-46; assoc. editor Sewanee (Tenn.) Alumni News, U. of South, 1946-62; bus. mnr. and mng. editor Sewanee Review, 1962-65, dir. fin. aid and career services, 1970-80, assoc. univ. historiographer, 1980—; freelance editor. Editor: (with H.A. Petry) Sewanee Centennial Alumni Directory, 1954-62; Centennial Report of the Registrar of the University of the South, 1959; (with Arthur Ben Chitty) Too Black, Too White (Ely Green), 1970; author (with Moultrie Guerry and Arthur Ben Chitty) Men Who Made Sewanee, 1981; columnist Sewanee Mountain Messenger, 1985—. Bd. dirs. Sewanee Civic Assn., 1979-80, 86-88; CONTACT-Lifeline of Coffee and Franklin Counties, 1981-84. Mem. Assn. Preservation Tenn. Antiquities (trustee 1985—), AAUW (pres. Sewanee br. 1975-77), Fla. State U. Alumni Assn. (dir. 1941—, permanent pres. Class of 1941), Mortar Bd., Phi Beta Kappa, Phi Kappa Phi, Phi Alpha Theta, Kappa Delta. Democrat. Episcopalian. Club: EQB Faculty (sec. 1975-76, 81-85). Home: 100 SC Ave Sewanee TN 37375 Office: U of the South Sewanee TN 37375

CHITWOOD, PATRICIA MAY, small business co-owner; b. Roseburg, Oreg., June 28, 1958; d. Edward Forrest Blanchard and Jeanine Crystal (Conn) Matthews; m. Randal Scott Chitwood, Sept. 3, 1976; children: Richard Lyle, Andrew James. Grad. high sch., Roseburg. Freight handler Greyhound Lines, Roseburg, 1976-77, ticket sales, scheduling agt., 1977, shift mgr., 1977-79; ch. sec. Westside Christian Ch., Roseburg, 1979-80; dispatcher, bookkeeper Action Salvage & Recovery, Inc., Roseburg, 1980-82; temp. bookkeeper Early & Ritter CPA, Roseburg, 1983; bookkeeper, apprentice locksmith The Svc. Ctr., Roseburg, 1985-87, bookkeeper, full shop locksmith, 1987, co-owner, 1987—; security cons. Neighborhood Watch Program, Douglas County, Oreg., 1987—. Sustaining mem. Boy Scouts Am., 1988, 89; supporting mem. Roseburg Little League Assn., 1989; chair deaconess com. Westside Christian Ch. Roseburg, 1979-80, project chair Women's Fellowship, 1979-80. Mem. Douglas County Locksmiths, Roseburg C. of C.. Republican. Office: The Svc Ctr 1275 NE Stephens Roseburg OR 97470

CHIULLI, E. ANTOINETTE, lawyer; b. Pescara, Italy, Oct. 30, 1950; arrived in U.S., 1955; d. Nino and Maria (Mezzanotte) C.; m. Joseph P. Breig, Sept. 5, 1976; children: Christopher J., Jason A. BA, Marymount Coll., 1972; JD, Rutgers-Camden Sch. Law., 1976. Legal asst. Judge Manuel Greenberg, Atlantic City, N.J., 1976-77; pvt. practice Somerdale, N.J., 1978—; econ. analyst Nat. Econ. Research Assocs., N.Y.C., 1972-73; panelist Matrimonial Settlement Program, 1985. Cons., Alternatives for Women Now, Camden, 1978-80, Women's Counseling Ctr., 1981-83, Glassboro (N.J.) Coll. Together Program, Jaycettes of Camden County; trustee, Haddonfield Child Care, 1989—. Mem. ABA, N.J. State Bar Assn., Tri-County Women Lawyers, Camden County Bar Assn. (family law com., scholarship com.). Office: 10 Grove St Haddonfield NJ 08033-1218

CHIZAUSKAS, CATHLEEN JO, manufacturing company executive; b. Little Rock, Dec. 26, 1954; d. Daniel John and Marilyn (Wolff) Quigley; m. Alan Michael Chizauskas, Nov. 11, 1978; 1 child, Marc Alan. Diploma in Mgmt., Simmons Coll., Boston, 1981. Clk. typist to direct materials buyer Gillette Safety Razor Co., Boston, 1972-79, buyer capital equipment, 1979, mgr. MRO and purchasing svcs., 1979-85, adminstrv. asst. to v.p. mktg., 1985-87, exec. asst. to pres., 1987-88, assoc. brand mgr. shave creams, 1988-89, bus. mgr., 1989—. Mem. Am. Mgmt. Assn., Purchasing Mgmt. Assn., Simmons Coll. Grad. Sch. Alumnae Assn. Roman Catholic. Home: 14 St Lawrence St Braintree MA 02184 Office: Gillette Co Blade/Razor div Gillette NAm Gillette Park Boston MA 02106

CHO, SUNG HEE, mental health counselor; b. Seoul, Republic of Korea, Dec. 18, 1957; came to U.S., 1980; d. Chang Shik and Duk Soo (Hahn) Cho; m. Peter Ungnak Sohn, Aug. 6, 1983; children: Andrew Dongil Sohn, Alan Dongsun Sohn. BA, Yonsei U., Seoul, 1980; PhD, U. Mo., 1988. Lic. profl. counselor. Assoc. psychologist Hannibal Regional Ctr., Hannibal, Mo., 1987-88; counselor, coord. S.W. Ala. Mental Health Ctr., Monroeville, 1989—; instr. Mobile Coll., Mobile, 1989—. Korean Studen scholar U. Mo., 1982, 83. Mem. Am. Psychol. Assn., Ala. Psychol. Assn., Am. Assn. Counseling and Devel. Home: 125 Fran St Jackson AL 36545 Office: SW Ala Mental Health Ctr Monroeville AL 36451

CHOATE, CAROLYN HANNAH, elementary school educator; b. Munday, Tex., Apr. 24, 1930; d. Leland and Ina (Reeves) Hannah; m. Jim K. Choate, Feb. 10, 1952 (div. Feb. 1975); childen: Stefani Choate Ernst, Bryan G. BA magna cum laude, Hardin-Simmons U., 1950; MEd, U. Tex., El Paso, 1985; Counselor, U. Houston, 1976. Cert. tchr., counselor. Tchr. Lubbock, El Paso, Austin (Tex.) Ind. Sch. Dist., 1952-58; counselor County Mental Health Unit, Sherman, Tex., 1975-76; tchr. Ysleta Ind. Sch. Dist., El Paso, 1977—; fellow West Tex. Writing Project, El Paso, 1984—. Mem. Tex. Women's Polit. Caucus, 1987-88. Mem. Assn. Tex. Profl. Educators, AAUW, El Paso Hist. Soc., Internat. Reading Assn. (tchr. of Yr. 1989), Nat. Assn. Tchrs. English. Office: Ysleta Ind Sch Dist 9600 Sims El Paso TX 79925

CHODKOWSKI, BETTYANN, information systems manager; b. Rockville Centre, N.Y., May 23, 1964; d. Leon Michael and Alice Margurite (Gittings) C. BS in Computer Sci., James Madison U., 1986; postgrad. in med. engring., George Washington U., 1988—. Systems programmer Siemens Data Switching Systems, Hauppauge, N.Y., 1986-87; sr. programmer analyst TRT Telecommunications, Washington, 1987-89; programmer, analyst, systems mgr. Nat. Insts. Health/Systex, Bethesda, Md., 1989—. Cardiac vol. Arlington (Va.) Hosp., 1990—. Mem. NAFE, Soc. of Nuclear Medicine (SNM technologist sect., computer and instrumentation coun.). Home: 1607 N Quinn St Apt 101 Arlington VA 22209

CHONTOS, KATHRYN LEE, education programs director, consultant; b. Jacksonville, Fla., Oct. 9, 1951; d. Clifford Wilson and Geneva Kathryn (Jones) Stoner; m. John David Chontos, May 27, 1972; children: Benjamin John, Samuel David. Student, Jacksonville (Fla.) U., 1969-72; BS in Elem. Edn., West Conn. State Coll., 1974, M in Curriculum, 1979; M in Edn. Leadership, Fla. Atlantic U., 1986. Cert. elem. edn. tchr., Fla., N.Y., N.C. Tchr. Carmel (N.Y.) Cen. Schs., 1974-75, homebound tutor, 1975-81; cons. Communications Guideposts, Carmel, 1981-83; cons. tchr. tng., researcher Writing-to-Read, Stuart, Fla., 1982; asst. pub. info. officer Palm Beach County Sch. Bd., West Palm Beach, Fla., 1983; community resource specialist So. Area Alt. Palm Beach County Sch. Bd., West Palm Beach, 1983-85, asst. prin., adminstr., 1985-87, 89-90; asst. prin. Jefferson Davis Middle Sch./Palm Beach County Sch. Bd., 1987-89; edn. programs dir. Wake County Youth Svcs., Raleigh, N.C., 1990—; with middle sch. guidance curriculum Palm Beach County Sch. Bd., 1987-88, with curriculum program rev., 1986-87; cons., editor Gospel Light Pubs., Ventura, Calif., 1988—. Campaign vol. Jimmy Carter for Pres., Peekskill, N.Y., 1975, 76; hostess Dem. Party Conv., N.Y.C., 1976. Mem. Assn. for Supervision and Curriculum Devel., Palm Beach County Asst. Prin. Assn., Fla. Assn. Alt. Schs., Child Adv. of Fla., First Bapt. Ch. Orch., Raleigh Symphony Orch., Phi Delta Kappa. Avocation: violin. Home: 8101 Seaton Ct Raleigh NC 27615 Office: Wake County Youth Svcs 568 Lenoir St Raleigh NC 27610

CHORNEY, THERESA RAND, publishing company executive; b. Richmond, Va., Aug. 18, 1955; d. William Harry and Maria Theresa (McMahon) C. AA in Bus. Adminstrn., Concordia Coll., Bronxville, N.Y., 1973. Sec. to v.p. audio div. Philips Audio Video Systems Corp., Mahwah, N.J., 1973-74, exec. sec. to v.p. video div., 1974-76; sec. flight ops. Gannett Co. Inc., Rochester, N.Y., 1976-77, office mgr., flight ops., 1977-79, exec. sec. to chmn. and chief exec. officer, 1979-85; asst. to chmn. Gannett Co. Inc., Arlington, Va., 1985-86, exec. dir. adminstrn. services, 1986-88, dir. sales devel. USA Today, 1988—. Author various children's poems. Mem. NAFE. Republican. Lutheran. Office: Gannett Co Inc USA Today 1100 Wilson Blvd Arlington VA 22209

CHOROMANSKI, LYNN MARIE, nurse; b. Mpls., June 19, 1954; d. Jerome Jerry and Ursula Agnes (Wagner) Choromanski. BS, U. Minn., 1976, MS, 1981. RN, Minn.; cert. nurse midwife. Staff nurse Golden Valley (Minn.) Health Ctr., 1976, 1979-81; staff cnm Group Health Inc., Mpls., 1981--; mem. adj. faculty U. Minn., 1977—, rsch. asst., 1988—; mem. adj. faculty Yale U., New Haven, 1978; bd. dirs. Crystal Travel Svc.; lobbyist asst. Min. Nurses Assn., St. Paul, 1988. Fundraiser Minn. Pub. TV; mem. Rice Lake North 1st Assn. Capt. USAF, 1976-79. Mem. St. Margaret's Acad. Alumni Assn. Democrat. Home: 9160 Harbor Ln Maple Grove MN 55369 Office: Group Health Inc 1533 Utica Ave S Saint Louis Park MN 55416

CHOSTNER, CHRYSTAL LEA, manufacturing company professional; b. San Diego, Feb. 1, 1963; d. Gilbert E. Chostner and Sheila I. (Preston) Radley. BA, Lindenwood Coll., 1984. Sr. estimator Teledyne Ryan Aero., San Diego, 1985-89; sr. contract pricing adminstr. Sundstrand Power Systems, San Diego, 1989—. Advisor Jr. Achievement, San Diego, 1985. Mem. Inst. Cost Analysis (dir. edn. 1987, 88, v.p. 1989, treas. 1990), Nat. Contract Mgmt. Assn., Nat. Mgmt. Assn. (co-chair scholarship fund 1985). Republican. Seventh-day Adventist. Office: Sundstrand Power Systems 4400 Ruffin Rd San Diego CA 92138-5757

CHOU, LING-TAI LYNNETTE, accountant, educator; b. Taipei, Taiwan, Jan. 11, 1955; came to U.S., 1977; d. Feng-Ho Chou and Ay-Bao Chyou; m. Wellington Yeu-An Liu, 1979. BBA, Nat. Taiwan U., 1977; MSA, U. Houston, 1978, PhD, 1985. CPA. Teaching asst. U. Houston, 1977-78, teaching rsch. asst., 1979-81, asst. prof., 1985—; staff acct. Price Waterhouse & Co., Houston, 1978-79; asst. prof. U. Tex., San Antonio, 1981-82; ptnr. Liu & Liu, CPA's, Houston, 1982-85. Author: A Survey Examination of the Objective of Accounts Receivable Confirmation. Candidate sch. bd. Ft. Bend (Tex.) Ind. Sch. Dist., 1987. Recipient Gold medal award Taipei's First Girls' High Sch. Mem. Am. Acctg. Assn., Chinese Women's Bus. Assn. (bd. dirs. 1986-87). Home: 1434 Sugar Creek Blvd Sugar Land TX 77478 Also: S-2 Alley 3 Lane 770, Ming-Shen E Rd, Taipei Taiwan

CHOVAN, KAREN RYAN, aerospace engineer; b. Lakehurst, N.J., Nov. 26, 1959; d. Robert Charles and Helen Eloise (Hankins) Ryan; m. William Jeffery Chovan, Nov. 19, 1977; 1 child, Shaun Ryan. BS in Engring., U. Ala., 1984, postgrad., 1984—. Registered profl. engr., Ala. Systems engr. Sci. Applications Internat. Corp., Huntsville, Ala., 1984-87; project engr. GE Co., Huntsville, 1987-88; aerospace systems engr. Sci. Applications Internat. Corp., Huntsville, Ala., 1988-90; sr. rsch. engr. Lockheed Missile and Space Co., Huntsville, 1990—. Tech. editor to various publs. in field. Vol. Angels for Children, Huntsville, 1987—. Mem. Nat. Soc. Profl. Engrs., AAUW, AIAA, ASME, Am. Def. Preparedness Assn., Soc. Photo-Optical Instrumentation Engrs., U. Ala. Alumni Assn. (sponsor), Pi Tau Sigma. Republican. Mem. Christian Ch. (Disciples of Christ). Home: 2709 Gaines Rd SE Huntsville AL 35803 Office: Lockheed Missile and Space Agy 4800 Bradford Dr Huntsville AL 35807

CHOW, RITA KATHLEEN, government official; b. San Francisco, Aug. 19, 1926; d. Peter and May (Chan) C. BS, Stanford U., 1950, nursing diploma, 1950; MS, Case Western Res. U., 1955; profl. diploma in nursing edn. adminstrn, Columbia U., 1961, EdD, 1968; B of Individualized Studies, George Mason U., 1983. Asst. in teaching Stanford U., Calif., 1951-52; instr., dir. student health Fresno (Calif.) Gen. Hosp. Sch. Nursing, 1952-54; instr. Wayne State U. Coll. Nursing, Detroit, 1957-58; rsch. assoc., project dir. cardiovascular nursing rsch. Ohio State U., Columbus, 1965-68; commd. officer USPHS, 1968, advanced through grades to nurse dir., 1974; spl. asst. to dep. dir. Nat. Ctr. Health Svcs. Rsch., Health Svcs. and Mental Health Adminstrn., HEW, Rockville, Md., 1969-73; dep. dir. manpower utilization br., 1970-73; dep. dir. Office Long Term Care; dep. chief nurse officer USPHS, Rockville, 1973-77; chief quality assurance br. div. long-term care Office of Standards and Certification, Health Standards and Quality Bur., Health Care Fin. Adminstrn., HHS, 1977-82; supervisory clin. nurse and spl. asst. to health systems adminstr. USPHS Indian Hosp., HRSA, HHS, Rosebud, S.D., 1982-83; dir. patient edn., asst. dir. nursing G.W. Long Hansen's Disease Ctr., USPHS, Carville, La., 1984-89; dir. nursing Fed. Correctional Instn., Ft. Worth, 1989—; dir. nursing Federal Correctional Institution, Fort Worth, Tex., 1989—. Author: Identifying Nursing Action with the Care of Cardiovascular Patients, 1967, Cardiosurgical Nursing Care: Understandings, Concepts, and Principles for Practice, 1975; mem. editorial bd. Nursing and Health Care, 1983—; contbr. to publs. in field. Served with Nurse Corps U.S. Army, 1954-57. AAUW scholar; Nat. League Nursing fellow, 1959-61; recipient research grant Sigma Theta Tau, 1966; recipient Fed. Nursing Service award Assn. Mil. Surgeons U.S., 1969, citation for outstanding contbn. to cardiovascular nursing Am. Heart Assn., 1972, 79, Nursing Edn. Alumni Assn. award for distinguished achievement in nursing research Columbia U. Tchrs. Coll., 1973, Meritorious Service medal USPHS, 1977, Disting. Alumnus award Case Western Res. U. Sch. Nursing, 1979, Disting. Service medal USPHS, 1987, Artist of Life award Internat. Women's Writing Guild, 1987, Women's Honors in Pub. Svcs. award Am. Nurses' Assn. 1988.

CHOYKE, PHYLLIS MAY FORD (MRS. ARTHUR DAVIS CHOYKE, JR.), management executive, editor, poet; b. Buffalo, Oct. 25, 1921; d. Thomas Cecil and Vera (Buchanan) Ford; m. Arthur Davis Choyke Jr., Aug. 18, 1945; children: Christopher Ford, Tyler Van. BS summa cum laude, Northwestern U., 1942. Reporter City News Bur., Chgo., 1942-43, Met. sect. Chgo. Tribune, Chgo., 1943-44; feature writer OWI, N.Y.C., 1944-45; sec. corp. Artcrest Products Co., Inc., Chgo., 1958—, v.p., 1964-88; pres. The Partford Corp., Chgo., 1988—; founder, dir. Harper Sq. Press div., 1966—. Author: (under name Phyllis Ford) (with others) (poetry) Apertures to Anywhere, 1979; editor: Gallery Series One, Poets, 1967, Gallery Series Two, Poets—Poems of the Inner World, 1968, Gallery Series Three Poets: Levitations and Observations, 1970, Gallery Series Four, Poets, I am Talking About Revolution, 1973, Gallery Series Five/Poets—To An Aging Nation (with occult overtones), 1977; (manuscripts and papers in Brown U. Library). Bonbright scholar, 1942. Mem. DAR (Ft. Henry Dearborn chpt.), Soc. Midland Authors (bd. dirs. 1987—, treas. 1988—), Mystery Writers Am. (assoc.), Chgo., Press Vets. Assn., Arts Club (Chgo.), John Evans Club (Northwestern U.), Phi Beta Kappa. Home: 29 E Division St Chicago IL 60610

CHRISCOE, CHRISTINE FAUST, industrial trainer; b. Atlanta, Oct. 29, 1950; d. Henry Charles and Shirley Faye (Birdwell) Faust; B.A., Spring Hill Coll., 1973; postgrad. Ga. State U., 1974—; m. Ralph D. Chriscoe, June 25, 1983. Trainer, Fed. Res. Bank, Atlanta, 1973-77; project mgr., tng. dept. Coca Cola U.S.A., Atlanta, 1977-79, sr. project mgr., 1979-81, mgr. tech. tng., 1981-84, mgr. sales, mgmt. and mktg. tng., 1984-85, mgr. bottler tng., 1984-85; mgr. human resources devel., 1986-88; mgr. tng. and devel., 1988-90; pres. Christine Chriscoe and Assocs., 1990—; speaker Best of Am. Human Resource Conf.. Trustee Ga. Shakespeare Festival. Mem. ASTD, Internat. TV and Video Assn., Soc. for Applied Learning Techs., Tng. Dirs.' Forum (bd. dirs.). Roman Catholic. Office: 9390 Riviera Rd Roswell GA 30075

CHRISMAN, MARLENE SANTIA, special education educator; b. Erie, Pa., Mar. 12, 1946; d. Rudolph Vincent and Angelina Frances (Longo) Santia; m. Alban Edmund Chrisman, Dec. 27, 1971; children: Bree Elizabeth, Bryn Daniels. BA in English, Gannon U., Erie, 1967, MA in English, 1969; MEd in Spl. Edn., Edinboro (Pa.) U., 1981. Cert. spl. edn. tchr., supr., Pa. Instr. Cathedral Prep. Sch., Erie, 1969-70, Opportunities Industrialization Ctr., Erie, 1970-72; program adminstr. Greater Erie Area Community Action Com., 1972-74; asst. dir., counselor Upward Bound, 1974-75; instr. English Gannon U., Erie, 1976-77; instr. spl. edn. Erie Sch. Dist., 1977—, forensics coach, 1988—. Mem. adv. bd. L.I.F.E. House, Inc., Erie, 1989—; mem. bd. Adolescent Parenting Task Force, ERie, 1988—; mem. Ctr. for Study Am. Presidency, N.Y.C., 1987. Recipient John C. Tongren award First Ch. of the Covenant, Erie, 1987. Mem. AAUW (nominating com. 1989-90, chair Holly Trail 1989), Nat. Forensic League, Pa. Speech and Debate Assn., Pa. High Sch. Speech League, Phi Delta Kappa. Democrat. Home: 326 W Arlington Rd Erie PA 16509 Office: Sch Dist City of Erie 1511 Peach St Erie PA 16509

CHRISS, IRENE ADRIENNE, medical management executive; b. Bklyn., Feb. 14, 1944. BA, Ariz. State U., 1963. Adminstr. PPMC Med. Ctr., San Francisco, 1975-80; cons. med. mgmt. Honig and Assoc., San Francisco, 1980-86; practice mgmt. dir. Am. Acad. Ophthalmology, San Francisco, 1986—; adminstr. Nat. Hotline for Ophthalmology, 1986—. Author: Trends in Practice, An Ophthalmic Guide to Practice Management, 1988, 3d edit., 1990. Home: 125 Beau Forest Oakland CA 94611 Office: 655 Beach St San Francisco CA 94120

CHRIST, BETSY ANNE, special educator; b. Buffalo, Aug. 17, 1954; d. Gerald G. and Mary A. (Allen) C. AB in Phys. Edn., Occidental Coll., 1976, MA in Edn., 1977; PhD in Spl. Edn., San Francisco State U. and U. Calif.-Berkeley, 1987. Instr. educationally handicapped Leeway Sch., Glendale, Calif., 1977-78; instr. seriously emotionally disturbed Mid-Valley Sch., West Covina, Calif., 1978-79; resource specialist Glendale Unified Sch., 1979-84; instr. in spl. edn. San Francisco State U.; resource specialist San Juan Unified Sch., Carmichael, Calif., 1987-89; program specialist El Dorado County Office of Edn., Placerville, Calif., 1989-90, prin., 1990—; coord. collaborative consultation project San Juan Unified Sch., 1988-89. Co-author: Collaborative Consultation, 1989, Data-Based Case Study, 1990. Mem. Coun. for Exceptional Children (pres. local chpt. 1990—), Phi Delta Kappa. Office: El Dorado County Office Edn 6767 Green Valley Rd Placerville CA 95667

CHRIST, ELLEN MARIE, marketing professional; b. Chgo., Feb. 29, 1960; d. Christ Theodore and Dolores Marie (Axotis) C. BA in Pub. Rels., Purdue U., 1981. Mktg. communications asst. Gould, Inc., Rolling Meadows, Ill., 1982-84; exhibit coord. Gen. Electric Co., Schenectady, N.Y.,

1984-86; mgr., nat. mktg. svcs. Encyclopaedia Britannica, Chgo., 1986—. Vol. Homework Hotline, Bur. of Vol. Programs, Chgo., 1988; adv. com. Greek Orthodox Young Adult League, Chgo. 1986—. Mem. Women in Communications, Internat. Exhibitors Assn. (Focus award 1986, nat. edn. liaison, 1989—), Purdue Alumni Assn., Alpha Phi Alumni Assn. Greek Orthodox.

CHRIST, SHARON JEANNE, nurse; b. Cleve., Feb. 21, 1958; d. Anthony Chester and Irene Joan (Zielinski) W.; m. James Patrick Christ, May 21, 1983. BS in Nursing, Kent State U., 1980; Student, Flight Nurse Sch., Brooks AFB, 1982; postgrad., Point Park Coll., 1983; Student, U. Pitts. Sch. Nursing, 1986; student, Columbia Union Coll. RN, Md., Pa.; cert. in nursing adminstrn. Am. Nurses Assn. Commd. nurse USAFR, 1982, advanced through grades to capt., 1989; flight nurse 60th AES USAFR, Andrews AFB, Andrews AFB, Md., 1987—. Scholar Hudson Women's Club, 1976, Am. Field Svc., 1976. Mem. Am. Assn. Neurosci. Nurses, Res. Officers Assn. (sec. local chpt., jr. v.p.), NAFE, Am. Orgn. Nurse Execs., Md. Orgn. Mid-Nurse Mgrs. (steering com.), Aerospace Med. Assn. Roman Catholic. Home: 13707 Concord Ave Laurel MD 20707

CHRISTAKOS, SYLVIA, biochemist, educator, researcher; b. N.Y.C., May 19, 1946; d. Constantine and Ethel (Kavisi) Stavropoulos; m. Manny Elias Christakos, Oct. 4, 1970; children: Constantine, Andreas, Athena. BS, Coll. Mt. St. Vincent, 1967; MA, SUNY, Buffalo, 1970, PhD in Biochemistry, 1973. Postdoctoral fellow Roswell Pk. Meml. Inst., Buffalo, 1973-74, Sch. Medicine SUNY, Buffalo, 1974-76; postdoctoral fellow dept. biochemistry U. Calif., Riverside, 1976-80; asst. prof. dept. biochemistry N.J. Med. Sch., Newark, 1980-85, assoc. prof., 1985-90, prof., 1990—; mem. study sect. panel Regulatory Biology NSF, 1985-86. Contbr. chpts. to books, numerous articles to profl. jours. Recipient Rsch. Career Devel. award NIH, 1983-88, Excellence in Teaching award N.J. Med. Sch. Found., 1987, State Wide Faculty Recognition award Chancellor of Edn., N.J., 1988. Mem. AAAS, Am. Soc. Bone and Mineral Rsch. (coun. 1989—), Am. Inst. Nutrition, Am. Soc. Biochemistry and Molecular Biology, The Endocrine Soc., Soc. Neuroscience. Democrat. Greek Orthodox. Office: U Medicine and Dentistry NJ Dept Biochemistry 185 S Orange Ave Newark NJ 07103

CHRISTEN, LYNNE ROBBINS, small business owner, journalist; b. Opp, Ala., Jan. 9, 1946; d. Farrell Gaston and MaryNell (Woodham) R.; m. Johnny David Hughes, July 15, 1971 (div. Feb. 1974); m. Henry Tiffany Christen Jr., Jan. 26, 1975; children: Eric Robbins, Ryan Gallagher. Student, Auburn U., 1964-65; AA, Clayton State U., 1975; interior design cons. designation, ICS Inst., Scranton, Pa., 1981. Flight attendent, supr. Eastern Air Lines, Atlanta, 1965-86; career devel. cons. Careers Plus, Mary Esther, Fla., 1987—; profl. speaker Mary Esther, 1988—. Author: (manual) Be Your Own Decorator, 1984; columnist local periodical, 1988; contbr. bus. related articles to various jours. Mem. adv. bd. Women's Life Ctr., Pensacola, 1989—; chairperson publicity Okaloosa County Environ. Coun., 1988-89; pres. Mary Esther Elem. PTA, 1990. Recipient award of distinction N.W. Fla. Pub. Rels. Assn., 1990. Mem. NAFE, Am. Bus. Women's Assn. (v.p. Emerald Coast chpt. 1989, publicity chairperson 1987, corr. sec. 1988), Ft. Walton Beach C. of C. (editor Coast Lines mag. 1990—, v.p. community rels. 1990, Outstanding Mem. of Yr. 1989), Bldg. Industry Assn., Leadership C. of C. (grad. 1989), Bldg. Industry Assn. (editor Builder's Gambit mag. 1989—), Gayfer's Career Club (rep. 1989-90), Fla. Press Club, N.W. Fla. Press Club. Republican. Methodist. Home and Office: 390 Angela Ln Mary Esther FL 32569

CHRISTENSEN, CAROL ANN, facilities management executive, interior designer; b. Chgo., Aug. 23, 1941; d. Francis A. and Mary C. (Fitzsimmons) Swagler; m. Ronald J. Moody, June 10, 1961 (div. Dec. 1977); children: James, Steven Moody; m. Kenneth P. Christensen, Mar. 21, 1987. Student, U. Ill., 1959-61, Harper Coll., Palatine, Ill., 1973-75. Interior designer DeVries & Co., Dundee, Ill., 1972-74; prin. Carol Moody Designs, Arlington Heights, Ill., 1974-77; office specialist A.B. Dick & Co., Niles, Ill., 1977-81; facilities mgr. Beatrice Foods Co., Chgo., 1981-85; account exec. Henricksen Office Interiors, Itasca, Ill., 1985-87; mgr. facilities and svcs. Am. Brands, Inc., Greenwich, Conn., 1988—, chmn. women and minorities com. task force, 1989—. Contbr. articles to profl. jours. V.p. Svc. League for Handicapped Children N.W. Ill., 1970-71, pres., 1971-72. Mem. NAFE (profl.), Internat. Facility Mgmt. Assn. (profl., pres. Conn. chpt. 1990—), Inst. Bus. Designers (affiliate, mem. membership com. 1984-85). Republican. Roman Catholic. Office: Am Brands Inc 1700 E Putnam Ave Old Greenwich CT 06870

CHRISTENSEN, FERN ELOISE BREAKENRIDGE, university educator; b. Winterset, Iowa, Mar. 26, 1923; d. Raymond Dean Breakenridge and Vera Mabel Bowen; m. Raymond L. Christensen, Feb. 24, 1944; children: R. Lyle Christensen, Christena Christensen Allain. BS in Edn., Drake U., 1959; MS in Edn., So. Ill. U., 1964, postgrad. studies, 1964-66. Tchr. rural schs. Iowa, 1941-46; elem. tchr. Iowa and Ill. schs., 1956-63; library media dir. secondary sch. DuQuoin, Ill., 1963-66; professor, assoc. Coll. Edn. Northwestern State U., Natichitoches, La., 1966—; dir. instr. rsch. ctr., Northwestern State U., Natchitoches, 1985—. Mem. DAR, Daughters Am. Colonists (state historian), United Meth. Nat. History Assn. (v.p. genealogy sect.), Lioness (pres. Natchitoches club 1988-89), Delta Kappa Gamma (pres. 1986-88, state coms. 1987—), Phi Delta Kappa (pres. 1980-81). Home: 1017 Oma St Natchitoches LA 71457-5229 Office: Northwestern State U Dept Edn Natchitoches LA 71497

CHRISTENSEN, KAREN SUE, dietitian, sales executive; b. Minden, Nebr., June 7, 1958; d. Edwin LeRoy and Maxine Carole (Sorenson) C. BS, U. Nebr., 1980; MS, Tex. Woman's U., 1981. Intern Houston VA Med. Ctr., Des Moines, 1980-81; relief dietitian Iowa Meth. Med. Ctr., Des Moines, 1982-83; chief clin. nutritionist Cleveland Meml. Hosp., Shelby, N.C., 1983-85; regional sales mgr. Practorcare, Inc., Denver, 1985-88, sales mgr. western div., 1988—; cons. in field, 1984—; speaker profl. confs., 1985—. Contbr. articles to profl. jours. Mem. Am. Dietetic Assn. (Recognized Young Dietitian of Yr. award 1987), Colo. Dietetic Assn. (exec. com., bd. dirs., sec. 1987-89), Am. Dietic Assn. Found. Republican. Methodist. Office: Practorcare Inc 5770 E Warren Ave Ste #105C Denver CO 80222

CHRISTENSEN, KATHLEEN MARIE, clinical psychologist, health facility administrator; b. St. Peter, Minn., Aug. 25, 1957; d. Val Jean Verdelle and Adeline Mae (Johanson) C. BA, Mankato State U., 1978, MA, 1981; PsyD, Fla. Inst. Tech., Melbourne, 1982. Lic. cons. psychologist, Minn. Doctoral intern VA Med. Ctr., Lyons, N.J., 1981-82; staff psychologist Southwestern Mental Health Ctr., Worthington, Minn., 1983-85, team leader intensive svcs., 1985-86, dir. intensive svcs., 1986-89, clin. dir., 1990—, acting exec. dir., 1990—; cons. psychologist Worthington Regional Hosp., 1986—; adj. faculty Worthington Community Coll., 1986; clin. tng. supr. doctoral students U. S.D., Vermillion, 1986—; psychol. examiner Social Security Disability, St. Paul, 1986—. Mem. Minn. Case Mgmt. Task Force, St. Paul, 1986-87, adv. com. licensure residential facilities adult mentally ill, 1989—; bd. dirs. Nobles Community Hosp., Worthington, 1984—; mem. southwest regional com., chmn. client svcs. com. Minn. AIDS Project. Mem. Nat. Assn. Female Execs., Minn. Assn. Behavior Analysts, Internat. Jugglers Assn., Phi Kappa Phi. Office: Southwestern Mental Health 1024 7th Ave Worthington MN 56187

CHRISTENSEN, MARGARET JANE, interior designer; b. Cedar Falls, Iowa, June 27, 1938; d. Frederick Blaine and Marcele Alice (Fecht) Thompson; m. Guerden Andrew Christensen, Oct. 6, 1963 (div. 1973); children: Ryan Brooks. B of Gen. Studies, State U. Iowa, 1976; one yr. course with honors, Hawkeye Inst. Tech., 1984; student, N.Y. Sch. Interior Design, 1981. Stewardess United Airlines, Chgo., 1961-62; food service supr. Pub. Cafeterias, State U. Iowa Campus, Iowa City, 1962-63; reservation agt. Delta Airlines, St. Louis, 1963-65; interior designer Scruggs-Vandervoorts, St. Louis, 1963-64; free-lance interior designer, weaver Aplington, Iowa, 1965—. Recipient Blue Ribbons Fair Assn., 1987, Legion of Honor medal, 1990; named to Am. Fedn. Chiefs of Police Hall of Fame, The Am. Fedn. Police Hall Fame, 1990. Mem. Am. Soc. Interior Designers, Am. Home Econs. Assn. (cert.), Am. Fedn. Police (merit award 1989), United Air Lines Stewardess Assn. Clipped Wings, Order Eastern Star. Home and Office: 1130 Ellis St Apt 10 Aplington IA 50604

CHRISTENSEN, NORMA SHEPPARD, educator; b. Cherokee, Iowa, Apr. 2, 1924; d. Leslie C. and H. Irene (Green) Sheppard; children: Hedy Reynolds, Tom, Susan Cooper. BA, U. Iowa, 1944; MA, U. Wyo., 1971. Tchr. English Worland (Wyo.) High Sch., 1964-86; part-time English instr. North West Coll., Powell, Wyo., 1980—. State committeewoman Washakie County Dem. Party, Worland, 1985—; diocesan coordinator Edn. for Ministry, U. of South, Sewanee, Tenn., 1989—; Stephen Ministry trainer St. Albans Episcopal Ch., Worland, 1988—. With USN, 1944-46. Mem. NEA, Wyo. Edn. Assn. (pres. 1981-84, Gold Key awd. 1987), Wyo Commn. for Women, Nat. Coun. Accreditation of Tchrs. Edn., Wyo. Adv. Com. to U.S. Civil Rights Commn., AAUW (pres. 1985-87). Democrat. Episcopalian. Home: 820 Park Ave Worland WY 82401

CHRISTENSON, SUSAN ELIZABETH, public relations specialist, journalist; b. East Chicago, Ind., Feb. 10, 1951; d. Raymond Francis and Eleanor Imogene (Dehn) Reis; children: Timothy Andrew Chrstenson, James Patrick Christenson. BS, Ind. State U., 1973. Reporter Reporter Progress Newspapers, Downers Grove, Ill., 1979-84; sect. editor Life Newspapers, Downers Grove, 1984-85; owner PR Creative, Downers Grove, 1985—; reporter Chgo. Tribune, 1986—; pub. rels. specialist Evang. Health Systems, Oak Brook, Ill., 1989—; mem. corp. office activities com. Evang. Health Systems, 1989—. Writer parks and recreation mgmt. script, 1984 (Gold Medal award). Mem. NOW, Women in Communications Inc. (nat. com. on membership 1989—), Greenpeace. Office: Evang Health Systems 2025 Windsor Dr Oak Brook IL 60521

CHRISTI, MARILYN PATRICIA, school superintendent; b. Nashville, Jan. 16, 1950; Div. 1986; children: Christopher Manuel, Christina Marilyn, Catrina Marilyn. Merchandising cert., Bauder Coll., 1969; BS, Tenn. Wesleyan Coll., 1975; MEd., Tenn. Tech., 1979, EdS, 1981. Lic. profl. adminstr. and tchr., Tenn. Head resident/counselor Tenn. Wesleyan Coll., Athens, 1974-75; tchr. Rhea County Dept. Edn., Dayton, Tenn., 1975-81; prin. Rhea County Dept. Edn., 1981, 84-86; adj. coll. instr. Tenn. Tech. U., Cookeville, 1981—; coord. off campus program Tenn. Tech. U., 1981-86; tchr. Rhea County Dept. Edn., Dayton, 1982-83; prin. Rhea County Dept. Edn., 1983-86, supt. schs., 1986—; voting mem. Rhea County Purchase and Fin., Dayton, 1986—. Chairperson Polit. Action Com. for Edn., Dayton, 1978-81; bd. dirs. Battered Women, Inc., Crossville, Tenn., 1987—; chairperson allocations United Way, Dayton, 1987-88; mem. Tenn. Sheriff's Assn., Nashville, 1988—; aide-de-camp Rep. Shirley Duer, Nashville, 1987. Recipient Cert. Appreciation, Am. Legion, 1988, Cert. Participation, Very Spl. Arts, 1989; named Hon. Mem. Staff, Senator Anna Belle O'Brien, Nashville, 1987. Mem. Rhea Dayton Edn. Assn. (faculty rep. 1988—), NEA (past del.), Tenn. Edn. Assn., Tenn. Orgn. Sch. Supts., Alliance for a Drug Free Tenn. (chairperson 1987—), Women Hwy. Safety Leaders Tenn. (county leader 1989), USAF Aux. Aerospace (capt. 1987—), Tenn. Assn. Sch. Bus. Officials, Dayton C. of C., Nat. Police Assn. Republican. Methodist. Home: PO Box 598 Spring City TN 37381 Office: Rhea Count Dept Edn Montague St Dayton TN 37321

CHRISTIAN, BETTY JO, lawyer; b. Temple, Tex., July 27, 1936; d. Joe and Mattie Manor (Brown) Wiest; m. Ernest S. Christian, Jr., Dec. 24, 1960. B.A. summa cum laude, U. Tex., 1957, LL.B. summa cum laude, 1960. Bar: Tex. 1961, U.S. Supreme Ct. 1964, D.C. 1980. Law clk. Supreme Ct. Tex., 1960-61; atty. ICC, 1961-68; asst. gen. counsel ICC, Washington, 1970-72; assoc. gen. counsel ICC, 1972-76, commr., 1976-79; partner firm Steptoe & Johnson, Washington, 1980—; atty. Labor Dept., Dallas, 1968-70. Mem. ABA, Fed. Bar Assn. (Younger Fed. Lawyer award 1964), Tex. Bar Assn., Am. Law Inst., Adminstrv. Conf. U.S., City Tavern Assn. Office: Steptoe & Johnson 1330 Connecticut Ave NW Washington DC 20036

CHRISTIAN, MARY NORDEAN, educator; b. Montgomery, Ala., Oct. 28, 1944; d. Gwyn Thomas and Lillie (Beasley) Wilburn; m. Thurmal Christian, June 1, 1984 (div. Aug. 1981). Student, Tuskegee Inst., 1962-64; BS, Ala. State U., 1967; MA, George Washington U., 1981. Cert. tchr. biology, phys. edn. and English. Tchr. Talladega County Bd. Edn., Talladega, 1967-70; tchr., coach Charles County Bd. Edn., LaPlata, Md., 1970-84, Garvey Sch. Dist., Rosemead, Calif., 1984—; mem. Md. State Track Com., Balt., 1975-84; chmn. So. Md. Athletic Conf. Girls Track Com., 1974-84; mem. Middle States Vis. Coms., 1976, 77, 82, 84. Dir. summer youth program East Washington Heights Bapt. Ch., Washington, 1981; mem. Coun. of Chs. of Greater Washington, 1976-84. Named Coach of Yr., So. Md. Athletic Conf., 1981, 84, Md. Ind. Newspaper, Waldorf, Md., 1984. Mem. NEA, Nat. Congress Parents and Tchrs., Calif. Tchrs. Assn., Garvey Edn. Assn., Alpha Kappa Alpha (parliamentarian 1980-84). Democrat. Baptist. Home: 616 S Glendora Ave Apt A West Covina CA 91790 Office: Temple Intermediate Sch 8470 E Fern Ave Rosemead CA 91770

CHRISTIAN, SUZANNE HALL, financial planner; b. Hollywood, Calif., Apr. 28, 1935; d. Peirson M. and Gertrude (Engel) Hall; children: Colleen, Carolyn, Claudia, Cynthia. BA, UCLA, 1956; Master's, Redlands U., 1979; cert. in fin. planning, U. So. Calif., 1986. Cert. fin. planner. Instr. L.A. City Schs., 1958-59; instr. Claremont (Calif.) Unified Schs., 1972-84, dept. chair, 1981-84; fin. planner Waddell & Reed, Upland, Calif., 1982—, sr. account exec., 1986; corp. mem. Pilgrim Place Found., Claremont; lectr. on fin., estate and tax planning for civic and profl. groups. Author: Steps in Composition, 1979. Mem. legal and estate planning com. Am. Cancer Soc., 1988—; bd. dirs. YWCA-Inland Empire, 1987. Recipient Silver Crest award Torchmark, 1985-87. Mem. Inst. Cert. Fin. Planners, Internat. Assn. Fin. Planners, Planned Giving Roundtable, Internat. Soc. Pre-Retirement Planners, Claremont C. of C. (bd. dirs.), Curtain Raisers Club of Gairison (pres. 1972-75), Kappa Kappa Gamma (pres. 1970-74). Home: PO Box 1237 Claremont CA 91711 Office: Waddell & Reed 545 N Mountain Ste 109 Upland CA 91786

CHRISTIANSEN, LUCILLE, civic worker; b. Gresham, Nebr., Mar. 12, 1918; d. John and Flossie (Harbaugh) Heims; m. Gerald Wallace, June 1, 1941; m. Louis H. Christiansen, Feb. 5, 1985; children: Jeralyn, Dennis, Marcia, Maren. BA, York (Nebr.) Coll., 1938; MA, U. Nebr., 1967. Tchr. English Rising City (Nebr.) High Sch., 1938-40, Battle Creek (Nebr.) High Sch., 1940-41. Exhibited in group show Westmar Coll., 1988. Active Vols. in Mission Svc. Mem. AAUW (chaplain 1988-89), Tex.-Nebr. Assn. (pres. 1984-85), Delta Kappa Gamma. Republican. Methodist.

CHRISTIANSEN, MARJORIE MINER, nutrition educator; b. Canton, Ill., Feb. 28, 1922; d. John Ernest and Margaret Ellen (Wilson) Miner; m. Theodore Leo Christiansen, Aug. 10, 1951; 1 dau., Karen Lee. Student Joliet Jr. Coll., 1939-41, Iowa State U., 1941-42; B.S., U. N.Mex., 1949, M.A., 1955; Ph.D., Utah State U., 1967. Registered dietitian, N.Mex., Va. Instr. sci. and nutrition Regina Sch. Nursing, Albuquerque, 1950-64, project dir., 1966-69; project dir., adj. prof. U. Albuquerque, 1969; prof. home econs. James Madison U., Harrisonburg, Va., 1969-84, prof. emeritus, 1984—; nutrition cons. Mental Devel. Ctr., Albuquerque, 1968-69; project dir. Dietary Mgmt. Seminars, VA Regional Med. Program, 1973-76. Mem. adv. Com. on spl. edn. Harrisonburg (Va.) pub. schs., 1972-84. Utah State U. fellow, 1963-67; grantee Corn Products Co., 1965, Nurse Tng. Act Pub. Health Service, 1966-69. Mem. Am. Dietetic Assn., Va. Dietetic Assn. Methodist. Contbr. articles to profl. jours. Home: 94 Laurel St Harrisonburg VA 22801

CHRISTIANSEN, PAULA SUE, real estate agent; b. Peoria, Ill., June 14, 1956; d. Roy L. and Wilma June (Donath) Richardson; m. William Michael Wilson (div. 1985); m. Thomas Anthony Christiansen, Dec. 17, 1988. AS in Bus. Mgmt., Ill. Cen. Coll., 1987. Sec. Cen. Ill. Light Co., Peoria, 1974-82, real estate agt., 1983—; chairperson Engring. Safety Subcom., Peoria, 1986; mem. Accident Investigation Subcom., Peoria, 1988. Vol. United Way of Cen. Ill., Peoria, 1986-88; project cons. Jr. Achievement of Cen. Ill., Peoria, 1988-89. Mem. Internat. Right Way Assn., Cilco Women's Club (pres. Peoria chpt. 1975-76). Republican. Lutheran. Home: 2102 W Alice Peoria IL 61604 Office: Cen Ill Light Co 300 Liberty St Peoria IL 61602

CHRISTIANSON, ELIN BALLANTYNE, librarian, civic worker; b. Gary, Ind., Nov. 11, 1936; d. Donald B. and Dorothy May (Dunning) Ballantyne; m. Stanley David Christianson, July 26, 1959; children: Erica, David. BA, U. Chgo., 1958, MA, 1961, Cert. advanced studies, 1974. Asst. librarian, then librarian J. Walter Thompson Co., Chgo., 1959-68; library cons., 1968—; part-time lectr. Grad. Library Sch., U. Chgo., 1981-90, Sch. Library and Info. Sci., Ind. U., 1982—, libr., info. svcs. cons., 1968—; editor The Library Quarterly Grad. Library Sch. U. Chgo., 1988-90. Chmn. Hobart Am. Revolution Bicentennial Commn., 1974-76; bd. dirs. Hobart Hist. Soc., 1973—, pres., 1980-90; pres. LWV, Hobart, 1977-79. Recipient Laura Bracken award Hobart Jaycees, 1976, Cert. Achievement Ind. Am. Revolution Bicentennial Commn., 1975; Woman of Yr. award Hobart Bus. and Profl. Women, 1985, Resident Recognition award Northwest Ind. Forum, 1988. Mem. AAUW (pres. Hobart br. 1975-77), ALA, Am. Assn. Info. Sci., Ind. Library Assn., Spl. Libraries Assn. (chmn. advt. and mktg. div. 1967-68), Assn. Library and Info. Sci. Edn., U. Chgo. Grad. Library Sch. Alumni Assn. (v.p. 1971-74, 76-77, pres. 1977-79). Unitarian. Author: Non-Professional and Paraprofessional Staff in Special Libraries, 1973; Directory of Library Resources in Northwest Indiana, 1976; Old Settlers Cemetery, 1976; New Special Libraries: A Summary of Research, 1980; Daniel Nash Handy and the Special Library Movement, 1980; co-author: Subject Headings in Advertising, Marketing and Communications Media, 1964; Special Libraries: A Guide for Management, 1981, rev. 2d edit., 1986; mem. editorial adv. bd. New Standard Encyclopedia, 1986—. Home: 141 Beverly Blvd Hobart IN 46342

CHRISTIANSON, MARCIA LARAYE, educator; b. Austin, Minn., June 14, 1947; d. Arnold Raymond and Rayma Arliene (Peterson) C. AA, Austin Community Coll., 1967; BA, Luther Coll., Decorah, Iowa, 1969; MEd in Ednl. Computing, Cardinal Stritch Coll., Milw., 1986. Cert. tchr., Wis. Tchr. Joint Sch. Dist. 1, West Bend, Wis., 1969—; facilitator, instr. Profl. Improvement Inst., West Bend, 1985-90; co-chair tchr. incentive pilot program, West Bend and Madison, Wis., 1986-88, Dist. Staff Devel. Com., West Bend, 1990—. Mem. NEA, AAUW, Wis. Edn. Assn. Coun., Cedar Lake United Educators (bd. dirs. 1990), West Bend Edn. Assn. (exec. bd., chief negotiator 1982-90), Portside Weavers Guild (past pres.). Lutheran. Home: 125 University Dr Apt 210 West Bend WI 53095 Office: Badger Middle Sch 710 S Main St West Bend WI 53095

CHRISTIE, CAROLE SULLIVAN, advertising agency executive; b. St. Louis; d. John Hinchey and Ann (Houlihan) Sullivan; m. Robert James Christie, Sept. 7, 1974; children: John O'Meara, Kira Ann. BA, Rockhurst Col., 1973. Writer, designer Advt. Assocs., St. Louis, 1975; creative mgrs. mktg. rep. Breckenridge Hotels Corp., St. Louis, 1975-76; sr. writer D'Arcy, MacManus & Masius, St. Louis, 1976-83; v.p., creative dir. Gardner Advt., St. Louis, 1983-85; sr. v.p., group creative dir. D'Arcy, Masius, Benton & Bowles, St. Louis, 1985—; tchr. Principles of Advt. class, St. Louis U., 1982; judge CLIO awards, 1984, Indpls. ADDIs, 1985. Author and numerous dir. numerous film, radio and TV advertisements. Recipient Silver award Internat. Film & TV Festival of N.Y., 1980, award of excellence, 9th dist. ADDIs, 1980, 83, CLIO cert. for creative excellence, 1981, 84, ANDY award Advt. Club of N.Y.,1982, two first place Marconi awards St. Louis Radio Assn., 1983, "honors" Emmy award Nat. Acad. Motion Picture Arts and Scis., 1983 Gold Ring award, cert. of excellence Bus./Profl. Advt. Assn., 1986; others. Mem. Advt. Fed. St. Louis, Nat. Assn. Female Execs. Home: 89 Aberdeen Clayton MO 63105 Office: D'Arcy Masius Benton & Bowles Gateway Tower 1 Memorial Dr Saint Louis MO 63102

CHRISTOFF, BETH GRAVES, women's clothing store executive, artist; b. Galveston, Tex., Jan. 29, 1936; d. James Warren Patterson and Wilna Margaret (Heatherly) Day; m. Lawrence D. Graves, Jr., June 22, 1954 (div. 1975); children: Jacqueline, Keith Alan, Stephen Lee; m. Nicholas Christoff, Nov. 22, 1980; 1 stepchild, Steven Gregory. Student, U. Calif., Tokyo, 1953-54, Blair Bus. Coll., Colorado Springs, Colo., 1969-70; student art, Temple Jr. Coll., 1980-84. Sec. Clear Lake High Sch., Houston, 1973-74; med. sec. Clear Lake Hosp. and Emergency Room, Houston, 1974-75; mgr. dress store Baubles & Beads, Houston, 1975-77; sec. aviation dept. Quintana Petroleum Co., Houston, 1976-78, Trunkline Gas Co., Houston, 1978-80; owner, mgr. Christoff's Fashion Hideaway, Belton, Tex., 1984—. Exhibited in group shows cen. Tex., 1980-85; drawings and poetry Collage Temple Jr. Coll., 1980-84 (Cover awards 1982, 84). Mem. exhibit selection com. Cultural Activities Ctr., Temple, Tex., 1984; mem. pastor-parishh com. 1st United Meth. Ch., Belton, Tex., 1988-90. Democrat. Office: 210 E Central Belton TX 76513

CHRISTOFFERSSON, REA RAIHALA, publishing company executive; b. Astoria, Oreg., June 22, 1945; d. Reno W. and Aili M. (Oja) Raihala; m. John G. Christoffersson, Dec. 12, 1969. BA in Journalism, U. Oreg., 1967; MA in Communications, Stanford U., 1969; MLS, Emory U., 1978. Copywriter Mouton Co., The Hague, The Netherlands, 1968, Acad. Press, London, 1969-70; dep. head promotion Cambridge U. Press, London, 1970-71; assoc. dir. Richard Abel Bookseller, Portland, Oreg., 1972-74; asst. to dir. U. Ga. Librs., Athens, 1974-79; book sales dir. The Mother Earth News, Hendersonville, N.C., 1979-81; dir. advt. Peterson's Guides, Princeton, N.J., 1981-84; dir. mktg. ISI Press, Phila., 1984-86, R.R. Bowker, N.Y.C., 1986-90; direct response mgr. Consumer Reports Books, N.Y.C., 1990—. Ford Found. fellow, 1968-69. Mem. Swedish Am. Hist. Soc. Home: 956 River Rd Washington Crossing PA 18977 Office: R R Bowker 245 W 17th St New York NY 10011

CHRISTOPH, SUSAN CATHERINE, portfolio manager; b. Melrose Park, Ill., Oct. 18, 1960; d. Thomas Elmer and Catherine Annette (Petty) Shoop; m. Ronald Adam Christoph, Aug. 3, 1985. BBA in Fin. and Mgmt. Sci., U. Iowa, 1982; MBA in Fin. with honors, DePaul U., 1988. With Noddings Investment Group, Inc., Oakbrook Terrace, Ill., 1983—, v.p., 1987-90, sr. v.p. portfolio mgmt., 1990—. Mem. DuPage County (Ill.) Young Reps., 1988. Mem. Alpha Xi Delta Alumni Assn., Delta Mu Delta. Home: 113 B Scott Loop Fort Sheridan IL 60037 Office: Noddings Investment Group Inc Two Mid America Pla Ste 920 Oakbrook Terrace IL 60181

CHRISTOPHER, ELISABETH NEAL, industrial management executive; b. Revere, Mass., Aug. 2, 1910; d. Albert Gallatin and Florence Elisabeth (Copeland) Neal; m. Harold William Christopher, Sept. 3, 1932; children: Elisabeth N. Russell, William Neal. BSBA, Boston U., 1931. Exec. sec. New Eng. Power Assn., Boston, 1931-35; from office mgr., acct. to gen. mgr. The Indsl. Plating Co., North Providence, R.I., 1946-70; v.p. BBC Svcs., Laconia, N.H., 1970-80; from acct., computer liaison to v.p., dir. Seven Springs (Fla.) Villas Assn., Inc., 1984—; lectr. Contbr. articles to profl. jours. Mem. R.I. Rep. Cen. Com., Smithfield, 1953; mem. Rep. Nat. Com., 1989, U.S. Congl. Adv. Bd., Washington, 1988; pres. and charter Smithfield Recreational Assn., 1943. Mem. NAFE, AAUW, DAR, Prof. Secs. Internat. (pres. 1963-65, Named Sec. of Yr. 1962), ASME (assoc.), Bus. and Profl. Women (various offices 1952-75, Bus. Woman of Yr. award 1963), Eastern Star, Grand Cross of Color. Republican.

CHRISTOPHER, MAURINE BROOKS, writer, editor; b. Three Springs, Tenn.; d. John Davis and Zula (Pangle) Brooks; m. Milbourne Christopher, June 25, 1949. B.A., Tusculum Coll., 1941. Reporter, feature writer Balt. Sun, 1943-45; TV radio editor Advt. Age, 1947-51, sr. editor, head broadcast dept., 1951-77; dep. exec. editor Advt. Age, N.Y.C., 1977-79, dep. exec. editor, Videotech columnist, 1979-84; producer-moderator Adbeat, syndicated radio show, 1970-78; roving editor, mem. editorial bd. Advt. Age, 1984—, Adbeat, syndicated radio show, 1984—. Author: America's Black Congressmen, 1971, Black Americans in Congress, 1976. Mem. Am. Women in Radio and TV (past pres. N.Y.C. chpt. cert. of merit), Assn. Study Afro-Am. Life and History. Home: 333 Central Park W Apt 25 New York NY 10025 Office: 220 E 42d St New York NY 10017

CHRISTOPHER, SHARON A. BROWN, bishop; b. Corpus Christi, Tex., July 24, 1944; d. Fred L. and Mavis Lorraine (Krueger) Brown; m. Charles Edmond Logsdon Christopher, June 17, 1973. BA, Southwestern U., Georgetown, Tex., 1966; MDiv, Perkins Sch. Theology, 1969; DD, Southwestern U., 1990. Ordained to ministry United Meth. Ch., 1970; elected bishop 1988. Dir. Christian Edn. First United Meth. Ch., Appleton, Wis., 1969-70, assoc. pastor, 1972-73; pastor Calvary United Meth. Ch., Butler and Germantown, Wis., 1972-73, Aldersgate United Meth. Ch., Milw., 1976-80; dist. supt. Ea. Dist. Wis. United Meth. Ch., 1980-85; asst. to bishop Wis. Confs. United Meth. Ch., Sun Prairie, Wis., 1986-88; bishop North Cen. jurisdiction United Meth. Ch., Minn., 1988—. Contbr. articles and papers to religious publs. Bd. dirs. Nat. Coun. Churches of Christ, U.S.A., 1988—, United Meth. Ch. Bd. of Ch. & Soc., 1988—, Walker Meth. Health Ctr., Mpls., 1988—, Meth. Hosp., Mpls., 1988—; trustee Hamline U., St. Paul,

1988—; gen. and jurisdictional conf. del., 1988, 84, 80, 76, chmn. 84; mem. North Cen. Jurisdiction Com. on Episcopacy, 1984-88, Gen. Bd. Global Ministries, 1980-88, chmn. Mission Personnel Resources Program Dept., 1984-88; mem. North Central Jurisdiction Com. on Investgation, 1980—, Nat. United Meth. clergywomen's Consultation, co-chmn. 1983, No. Cen. Juridsdiction Urban Network, 1976-80, United Meth./Roman Cath. Nat. Dialogue on the Eucharist, 1976-79, North Cen. Jurisdiction Leadership Devel. Com., 1970-76; assignments with Gen. Bd. Global Ministries, Jamaica, Zimbabwe, Kenya, Zaire, Brazil, India, Japan, 1980-88; chmn. New Ch. Starts Com. Wis. Conf., 1986—, Task Force to Combat Racism, 1987—, Task Force on Spiritual Formation, 1986—, Conf. Bd. of Global Ministries, 1980-88, Conf. Coun. on Ministries, 1980-86, Commn. on Religion and Race, 1980-85, Commn. on Christian Unity and Inter-religious Concerns, 1980-82, Commn. on Rural and Urban Strategy and Planning, 1975-77, Com. on Conf. Goals and Priorities, 1976-84, chmn. Goals Rsch. Com. 1984. Named one of Eighty for the Eighties, Milw. Jour., 1980. Office: United Meth Ch 122 W Franklin Ave Rm 400 Minneapolis MN 55404

CHRISTOPHER-COLON, MARJORIE ANN, medical services administrator; b. New Roads, La., Feb. 14, 1940; d. Oliver and Hazel (Battley) C.; m. Benny Lyle Colon, July 16, 1939;. AA, La. Met. Coll., 1974; BA, Pepperdine U., 1979. supr. Los Angeles Hosp., 1968-75; supr., coordinator West Adams Med. Ctr., Los Angeles, 1980-85; coordinator, supr. Kaiser, Los Angeles, 1976-82; founder, pres. Concerned Women for a Stronger World, Los Angeles, 1980-; v.p., owner MEDDCO Med. Services, Los Angeles, 1986-. Community activist and leader. Mem. NAFE, Nat. Coun. Black Women, Nat. Women Polit., Nat. Orgn. Women, Nat. Black Survival Fund, Am. Women for Internat. Understanding, L.A. World Affairs Coun. Democrat. Roman Catholic. Home: 5743 Third Ave Los Angeles CA 90043

CHRISTOPHERSON, KARIN AGNES, medical association administrator; b. Moline, Ill., Feb. 19, 1948; d. Peter Ingvald and Mary Patricia (Comnes) C. BS in Edn., Loyola U., 1972; MA in Agency counseling, U. Ala., 1985, MA in Sch. Psychology, 1987. Educator-kindergarten St. Mel's Sch., Chgo., 1972-74; educator-first grade St. Barnabas Sch., Birmingham, Ala., 1974-75; parent educator Birmingham Pub. Schs., Ala., 1975-76, educator-first & second grades, 1976-78; educator-kindergarten & fifth grades Catholic Archdiocese of Birmingham, Ala., 1978-85; dir. of residence life Birmingham Southern Coll., Ala., 1985-86; coord., outpatient Cheaha Mental Health, Lineville, Ala., 1986—; Group leader Weight Watches of North Ala., Orlando, Fla., 1980—; cons. Clay County Schs., Lineville, Ala., 1986—. bd. dirs. Childrens's Trust Fund, 3rd Congl. Dist., 1986—. Named Tchr. of Yr. Newspaper, Birmingham, Ala., 1978. mem. Profls. for Victims Rights, Bus. and Profl. Women. Roman Catholic. Home: RR #2 Box 166 Lineville AL 36266 Office: Cheaha Mental Health Ctr Smith Curve Lineville AL 36266

CHRISTO-SCHLAPP, JOI, marketing professional; b. Elmhurst, N.Y., June 21, 1959; d. James Anastas Jr. and Rosemarie Joan (Cannavina) Christo; m. Steven Thomas Schlapp, July 21, 1984. BS in Communication Arts, St. John's U., 1981. Network sales asst. Eastman Radio, Inc., N.Y.C., 1981-83; nat. sales asst. Hillier, Newmark, Wechsler & Howard, N.Y.C., 1983-84, office mgr., 1984-86, promotion dir., 1986-89, v.p., dir. mktg., 1989—. Mem. Internat. Radio and TV Soc. Home: 60-22 69th Ln Maspeth NY 11378 Office: HNWH-div of Interep Radio Store 100 Park Ave New York NY 10017

CHRISTY, AUDREY MEYER, public relations consultant; b. N.Y.C., Mar. 11, 1933; d. Mathias J. and Harriet Meyer; BA, U. Buffalo, 1967; m. James R. Christy, Apr. 19, 1952; children: James R., III, Kathryn M. Smith, John T., Alysia A. Coleman, William J. Public relations officer Turgeon Bros., Buffalo, 1968-69; mem. pub. rels. staff Sch. Fine Arts, U. Nebr., Omaha, 1972; pub. rels. exec. Mathews & Clark Advt., Sarasota, Fla., 1974-75; profiles editor Tampa Bay mag., Tampa, Fla., 1972; pub. rels. cons. Bildex Corp., 1973-79; owner, operator Christy & Assocs., Venice, Fla., 1976—. Vice chmn. Erie County March of Dimes, 1970; bd. dirs. Sarasota chpt. Am. Cancer Soc., Manasota (Pvt.) Industry Coun., 1987—; mem. S.W. Fla. Ambulance Adv. Com., 1981; pres. Community Health Edn. Coun. Recipient various advt. awards. Mem. Pub. Rels. Soc. Am. (Outstanding Pub. Service award 1984), Fla. Hosp. Assn., Nat. Assn. Women Bus. Owners (charter mem. Sarasota chpt.), Sarasota County C. of C. (v.p., bd. dirs. 1990-91, vice chmn. mktg. 1984-85, 85-86, 86-87, 88-90, 90, vice chmn. 1989-90), Sarasota Manatee Press Club, LWV (editor Sarasota publ. 1978-79). Home: 216 Bayshore Circle Venice FL 33595 Office: Christy & Assoc 100 W Venice Ave #L Venice FL 33595-2240

CHRISTY, CAROLYN THOMAS, development director; b. Columbus, Ohio, 1942; d. David Harris and Virginia Tice (Boring) Thomas; m. H. Richard Wood, May 8, 1965 (div. June 1976); children: Harris Richard, Louisa Lloyd; m. Bruce L. Christy Jan. 2, 1981 (dec.). BA, Conn. Coll., 1964; MA, Ohio State U., 1966. Grad. asst. Ohio State U., Columbus, 1965-66; from tchr. to dir. devel. Columbus Sch. for Girls, 1966-69, 1975; tchr., tutor Hilliud Sch. System, 1966-69, 75—; tchr. Columbus Pub. Schs. Coun. mem., 1973-84; pres. Bexley City Coun., 1982-84. Mem. Ohio Assn. Ind. Schs. of DOD Group, Nat. Assn. Ind. Sch., Impresarios of Opera (pres. 1985-87), Mary Ritter Garden Club (pres. 1988—). Republican. Episcopalian. Home: 212 Ashbourne Rd Columbus OH 43209

CHRISTY, KATHLEEN ANN, nursing educator, consultant, professional development coordinator; b. Cleve., June 13, 1953; d. James J. and Mary Catherine (Coyne) C. BSN magna cum laude, U.Cin., 1979; MSN, Kent (Ohio) State U., 1984. Clin. nurse med. ICU U. Hosps. of Cleve., 1975-81, clin. nurse Hanna Pavillion, 1981-84, profl. devel. coord., 1987—; instr. Frances Payne Bolton Sch. Nursing Case Western Res. U., Cleve., 1984-87, clin. instr. Frances Payne Bolton Sch. Nursing, 1987—; asst. dir. nursing Margaret Wagner House Benjamin Rose Inst., Cleve., 1984-87; mem. speakers bur. U. Hosp. of Cleve., 1987-90, Ohio Citizens League for Nursing, Cleve., 1988-90; presenter Can. Nurses Assn., Halifax, Nova Scotia, 1987, VA Hosp., Cleve., 1989. Mem. Am. Psychiat. Nurses Assn. (charter), Greater Cleve. Nurses Assn., Am. Nurses Assn., Sigma Theta Tau. Home: 955 S Green Rd #3A South Euclid OH 44121 Office: U Hosp of Cleve 2074 Abington Rd Cleveland OH 44106

CHRYSSICAS, VALERIE FOSTER, marketing and advertising executive; b. Newark, June 6, 1955; d. Robert Samuel and Adelaide J. (Nelson) Foster; m. Willie Alton Davis, III, June 14, 1974 (div. 1977); m. John Charles Chryssicas, Jr., Jan. 4, 1980; 1 child, Jason Christopher. Student Randolph-Macon Coll., 1973-75; B.A. in Spanish, Salisbury State Coll., 1977; M.S. in Sociolinguistics, Georgetown U., 1980. Account rep. List Am., Inc., Washington, 1980; account exec. Infomat, Inc., Rolling Hills Estates, Calif., 1981; pres. N.M.C., Inc., Newport Mktg., Newport Beach, Calif., 1982—. Office: NMC Inc and Newport Mktg 1400 Quail St Ste 180 Newport Beach CA 92660

CHRZAN-SEELIG, PATRICIA ANN, corporate professional; b. Springfield, Mass., Mar. 3, 1954; d. Stanley Paul Jr. and Roberta Ann (Casey) Chrzan; m. Harold Cranmer Seelig, Nov. 5, 1977; children: H. Casey, Marguerite Andrea. BS in Human Devel., U. Mass., 1974. Dir. YWCA, Infant Day Care Ctr., Springfield, Mass., 1974-75, Tri-Cities Info. and Referral, Petersburg, Va., 1975-77; policy analyst Office of the Sec. Human Resources, Richmond, Va., 1977-78; data specialist Dept. Mental Health/Retardation, Richmond, Va., 1978-79; programmer Sands Internat., Oakton, Va., 1979-80; programmer analyst Carter Hawley Hale, Richmond, Va., 1980; v.p. Preferred Custom Software, Wilsons, Va., 1980-88; pres. Focused Systems, Inc., Chester, Va., 1988—. Co-chmn. St. Jude's Hosp. (Bikeathon), Blackstone, Va., 1987. Mem. NAFE, Blackstone Woman's Club (v.p. 1985-86), Va., Blackstone Town, Hobby, and Garden Club (pres. 1987-88). Home and Office: 9524 Eagle Cove Circle Matoaca VA 23803 Office: Focused Systems Inc PO Box 1438 Chester VA 23831

CHU, ANN MARIA, radiation oncology educator; came to U.S., 1965; d. Paul Z. and Lai-Chun (Ho) C. ISc, U. Calcutta, 1960; MD, U. Sask., Saskatoon, Can., 1965. Diplomate Am. Bd. Radiology (examiner 1981-85, 87-88). Intern, resident in radiology Med. Coll. Va., Richmond, 1965-69; fellow in radiation oncology M.D. Anderson Hosp. and Tumor Inst., Houston, 1969-71; asst. radiation oncologist, instr. Mass. Gen. Hosp.-Harvard U. Med. Sch., Boston, 1971-78; asst. radation oncologist, asst. prof. Tufts-New Eng. Med. Ctr. Hosp., Boston, 1979-81; dir. clin. radiotherapy, assoc. prof. therapeutic radiology U. Louisville, 1981-83; prof., chmn. dept. radiation oncology Temple U. Hosp., Phila., 1983-89; prof. Hahnemann U., Phila., 1990—; cons. Nat. Cancer Inst., Bethesda, Md., 1980-88; presenter in field; staff depts. medicine and radiology Episcopal Hosp., Phila., 1983—; staff St. Joseph's Hosp., Phila., 1984—, Hahnemann U. Hosp., Wills Eye, 1990—. Contbr. articles to med. jours. Mem. AMA, Am. Coll. Radiology, Am. Soc. Therapeutic Radiologists, Radiol. Soc. N.Am., Am. Radium Soc., Am. Assn. Cancer Edn., Radiation Rsch. Soc., Am. Assn. Cancer Rsch., AAAS, Am. Soc. Clin. Oncology, Am. Med. Womens Assn., Am. Assn. Women Radiologists, Gilbert Fletcher Soc., M.D. Anderson Assocs., Am. Assn. Physicists in Medicine, European Soc. Therapeutic Radiology and Oncology, Pa. Med. Soc., Philadelphia County Med. Soc., Mass. Med. Soc., Phila. Roentgen Ray Soc., Soc. Chairmen Acad. Radiation Oncology Programs. Office: Hahnemann U 230 N Broad St MS 200 Philadelphia PA 19103

CHU, SHIRLEY SHAN-CHI, educator; b. Beijing, Feb. 16, 1929; came to U.S., 1952; d. Ching Tao and Chi Chun (Yao) Yu; m. Ting Li CHu, Sept. 4, 1954; children: Dennis, Dora, Daniel. BS, Nat. Taiwan U., 1951; MS, Duquesne U., 1954; Phd, U. Pitts., 1961. Rsch. assoc. U. Pitts., 1961-67; asst. prof. So. Meth. U., Dallas, 1968-73, assoc. prof., 1973-81, prof., 1981-88; prof. U. South Fla., Tampa, 1988—; cons. Poly Solar Inc., Dallas, 1978-88. Contbr. numerous articles to profl. jours. Panelist NRC, Washington, 1982—; mem. com. Coun. Internat. Exch. of Scholars, Washington, 1986-89. U. Pitts. scholar, 1960. Mem. IEEE, Materials Rsch. Soc., Am. Crystallographic Assn. (publ. com. 1979-82). Office: U South Fla Elec Engring Dept Tampa FL 33620

CHUA, EVELYN BAUTISTA, nurse; b. Manila, May 10, 1950; d. Paulino and Elvira (Lim) Bautista; m. Jose C. Chua Jr., Mar. 21, 1947; children: Jose B., Florence B., Francis B. BSN, U. East Quezon City, Philippines, 1972. RN, Philippines, N.J. Staff nurse U. of the East Hosp., Quezon City, 1972-74, Elizabeth (N.J.) Gen. Med. Ctr., 1974-77, Deehl & Chua, Elizabeth, 1977—. Mem. Cen. Six Jefferson Sch. PTA, Union, N.J., 1988-89; mem. exec. bd. Battlehill Sch. PTA, Union, 1985—; leader Girl Scouts U.S., Union, 1985—. Mem. Battle Hill PTA Bowling League. Roman Catholic. Home: 2530 Poplar St Union NJ 07083

CHUHRAN, LINDA, freelance writer, automotive company executive; b. Ypsilanti, Mich., Aug. 28, 1949; m. Terry Edward Chuhran, Feb. 14, 1970; children: Scott Edward, Stacey Lynn. AAS in Cosmetology Mgmt., Schoolcraft Coll., 1980, AAS in Small Bus. Mgmt., 1983, AAS in Mktg. and Applied Mgmt., 1984, AAS in Gen. Bus., 1986, AAS in Gen. Studies, 1987; BA in Social Sci., Madonna Coll., 1988. Lic. cosmetologist, instr.; cert. model. Sr. clk. Allison div. G.M. Detroit, Redford, Mich., 1969; dir. clerical ops. Canton (Mich.) Township Hall, 1984-88; freelance model, photography cons., 1970—; reporter Community Messenger, 1985-87; disbursement analyst GMC, Canton, 1989—; cons. Photographer and Model Usage Services, Mich., 1976—; del. Southeastern Mich. Councils of Govt., 1984—. Author: Management Study of Michigan General Law Townships and Charter Law Townships, (booklets) 1986 Punch Card Voting System, 1986 Voter Info., Media Relations, 1987, Election Manual for Procedures and Legal Guidelines; creator computer program Absentee Voters, 1986. Adv. bd. Oakwood Hosp., Canton, 1984—; v. chairperson Rep. Forum, Mich., 1986—; mem. Mich. Township Polit. Action Com., Lansing, 1986; advisor Gen. Motors Jr. Achievement, Detroit, 1975-76. Recipient Disting. Advisor award Jr. Achievement of Southeastern Mich., 1975. Mem. NAFE, Schoolcraft Coll. Alumni Bd., Am. Mgmt. Assn., Internat. Records Mgmt. Coun., Bus. and Profl. Women's Orgn., Nat. Hairdressers Assn., Internat. Inst. Mcpl. Clks. Assn. (mem. profl. status com. 1987-88, pub. info. com. 1986-87), Nat. Assn. Govt. Archives and Records Adminstrs., Internat. Platform Assn., Friends Photography, Wayne County Mcpl. and Twp. Clks. Assn. (sec. 1988, treas. 1987-88), Wayne County Realtors Assn., Oakland County Realtors Assn. Home and Office: 44184 Wiclif Ct Canton MI 48187

CHUMLEY, DONNIE ANN, business owner, consultant; b. Nacogdoches, Tex., Mar. 15, 1942; d. Vester Don and J. Erleta (Flowers) Bobo; m. Billy Warren Chumley, Aug. 23, 1958; children: Warren Don, Lanton Dan. Student, Nacogdoches Bus. Coll., 1963. V.p. Stone Ft. Nat. Bank, Nacogdoches, 1963-89; pres. Bobo-Chumley Lumber Co., Inc., Douglass, Tex., 1989—, Donnie Chumley Fin. Svcs., Douglass, 1989—. Chmn. bd. Nacogdoches County Hosp. Dist., 1988—; mem. legis. com. Atty. Gen. Child Support Enforcement, Nacogdoches, 1989—, mem. state bd., Austin, Tex., 1990—; bd. dirs. Nacogdoches County Aging Com., 1988—. mem. Tex. Forestry Assn., Tex. Assn. of Bus. (workers compensation task force 1989). Democrat. Baptist. Home: Rte 1 Box 2975 Douglass TX 75943 Office: Bobo-Chumley Lumber Co Inc Hwy 21 Box 63 Douglass TX 75943

CHUMSKY, SANDRA EVELYN, rehabilitation training administrative chairman; b. Bklyn., June 23, 1934; d. Sidney and Rose (Spilkevitz) Schneider; m. Harold L. Chumsky, Mar. 21, 1931; children: Howard, Alan. BS, Bklyn. Coll., 1954. Pres. North Hills Chpt. Women's Am. Orgn. for Rehab. through Tng., Manhasset Hills, N.Y., 1972-74, North Shore Nassau Region Women's Am. Orgn. for Rehab. Tng., Roslyn, N.Y., 1982-84; fin. sec. N.Y. Dist. Women's Am. Orgn. for Rehab. Tng., N.Y.C., 1989—. Republican. Jewish. Home: 108 Nottingham Rd Manhasset Hills NY 11040 Office: NY Dist Women's Am Ort 29 W 34th St New York NY 10001

CHUN, WENDY SAU WAN, investment company executive; b. China, Oct. 17, 1951; came to U.S., 1975, naturalized, 1988; d. Siu Kee and Lai Ching (Wong) C.; m. Wing Chiu Ng, Aug. 12, 1976. BS, Hong Kong Bapt. Coll., 1973; postgrad. U. Hawaii-Manoa, 1975-77. Real estate saleswoman Tropic Shores Realty Co., Honolulu, 1977-80; pres., prin., broker Advance Realty Investment Co., Honolulu, 1980—; owner Video Fun Centre, Honolulu, 1981-83; pres Asia-Am. Bus Cons., Inc., Canada, 1986—, Money Internat. Ltd., Hong Kong; co-owner, dir. H & N Tax, Honolulu, 1983—; bd. dirs., exec. dir. B.P.D. Internat., Ltd., Hong Kong; exec. dir. Asia-Am. Bus. Cons., Inc., Hong Kong and Taipei brs., 1985—; pres. Asia-Am. Internat., Ltd., Honolulu, 1989. Mem. Nat. Assn. Realtors. Avocations: singing, dancing, swimming, dramatic performances. Home: 2333 Kapiolani Blvd Apt 3302 Honolulu HI 96826

CHUNG, CONSTANCE YU-HWA, broadcast journalist; b. Washington, Aug. 20, 1946; d. William Ling and Margaret (Ma) C.; m. Maurice Richard Povich. B.S., U. Md., 1969; D.J. (hon.), Norwich U., Northfield, Vt., 1974; LHD, Brown U., 1987. TV news reporter WTTG-TV, Metromedia Channel 5, Washington, 1969-71; corr. CBS News, Washington, 1971-76; TV news anchor sta. KNXT-TV, CBS, L.A., 1976-83; anchor NBC News, NBC News at Sunrise, NBC Nightly News (Saturday), NBC News Digests, NBC News, N.Y.C., 1983-86, NBC News Digest, NBC Nightly News (Saturday), NBC News Mag. 1986, 1986-87, NBC News Digests, NBC Nightly News (Saturday), NBC New Spls., 1987-89, Saturday Night With Connie Chung (CBS-TV), CBS Evening News (Sunday ed.), 1989—. Recipient Emmy award for individual achievement Nat. Acad. TV Arts and Scis., 1978, 80, 87; Metro Area Mass Media award AAUW, 1971; cert. of achievement for series of broadcasts which enhanced pub. awareness of cruelties of seal harvesting U.S. Humane Soc., 1969; award Atlanta chpt. Nat. Assn. Media Women, 1973; Outstanding Excellence in News Reporting and Pub. Service award Chinese-Am. Citizens Alliance, 1973; nominated for Woman of Yr. award Ladies Home Jour., 1975; named Outstanding Young Woman of Yr., 1975; recipient award for best TV reporting Los Angeles Press Club, 1977; award for outstanding TV broadcasting Valley Press Club, 1977; Women in Communications award Calif. State U., L.A., 1979; George Foster Peabody award for programs on environment Md. Center Public Broadcasting, 1980; hon. mem. Pepperdine U. Broadcast Club, 1981; Newscaster of Yr. award Temple Emanuel Brotherhood, 1981; Portraits of Excellence award B'nai B'rith, Pacific S.W. Region, 1980; First Amendment award Anti-Defamation League of B'nai B'rith, 1981. Office: CBS 524 W 57th St New York NY 10019

CHUNG, CYNTHIA NORTON, art director; b. Milton, Mass., Apr. 14, 1955; d. Ralph Arnold and Mary Elizabeth (McDonald) N.; m. Chinsoo Chung; 1 child, Sara Jane. BFA in Archtl. and Graphic Design, U. Mass., 1977. Graphic designer Garber Travel, Inc., Brookline, Mass., 1977-78; graphic and exhibit designer Rust Craft, Inc., Dedham, Mass., 1978-80; corp. advt. artist Morse, Inc., Canton, Mass., 1980-83; pvt. practice designer Boston, 1983-84; asst. art dir. Cahners Pub. Co., Newton, Mass., 1984-86, art dir., 1986-87; art dir. Knapp, Inc., Brockton, Mass., 1987—; guest speaker Mt. Ida Jr. Coll., Newton, 1980. Designer graphs and charts for Vols. I and II State Budget Commonwealth of Mass., 1982; art dir. Mini Micro Systems, 1984-87. Mem. Art Dirs. Club Boston, Kappa Kappa Gamma (alumni, pres. 1975-76). Roman Catholic. Home: 13 Connell St Quincy MA 02169 Office: TWA Logan Internat Airport Boston MA

CHUNG, DEBORAH DUEN LING, engineering educator; b. Hong Kong, Sept. 12, 1952; d. Leslie Wah-Leung and Rebecca (Chan) C.; m. Lan Kan Wong, May 29, 1976. BS, Calif. Inst. Tech., 1973, MS, 1973; MS, MIT, 1977, PhD, 1977. Asst. prof. Carnegie Mellon U., Pitts., 1977-82, assoc. prof., 1982-86; prof. SUNY, Buffalo, 1986—; cons. Stewart Lake Resources Inc., Ontario, Can., 1989-90; mem. com. on materials for high density electronic packaging NRC, 1987-90. Contbr. articles to profl. jours. Mem. AIME (Hardy Gold medal 1980), Soc. Automotive Engrs. (Teetor Ednl. award 1987), Am. Carbon Soc. , ASM Internat. (dir. Buffalo chpt. 1987—). Office: SUNY Dept Mech & Aero Engring Buffalo NY 14260

CHUNG, SANDRA L., healthcare facility administrator; b. Cleve., June 2, 1938; d. Gustave and Ruth (Davis) Donner; m. Charles Chung, Apr. 12, 1966. AAS in Nursing, Cuyahoga Community Coll.; postgrad., U. Hawaii. Staff nurse emergency dept. Kaiser Permanente Med. Care Program, Honolulu, supr., grant coord. family practice program, supr. med. subspecialty clinics, clin. supr. Mem. State Health Planning and Devel. Agy. Mem. Hawaii Nurses Assn., Am. Cancer Soc. Home: 2499 Kapiolani Blvd #1803 Honolulu HI 96826 Office: 333 Keahole St Honolulu HI 96825

CHUPACK, LEAH SADOVNICK, educator; b. N.Y.C., Apr. 30, 1921; d. Benjamin and Mollie (Abzug) Sadovnick; m. Henry Chupack, Dec. 18, 1948. BA, Bklyn. Coll., 1941. Cert. tchr., N.Y. Chief rsch. div. textiles and clothing USN, Bklyn., 1942-56; tchr. Great Neck (N.Y.) Pub. Schs., 1962-83; tchr. gifted edn. C.W. Post Coll., Brookville, N.Y., 1981—; cons. various schs. throughout N.Y., travel cons. Inventor leather grading device; contbr. to various publs. Vice pres. fundraising Great Neck Sr. Citizens, 1980—; v.p. membership Great Neck Community Concerts, 1986-88. Mem. AAUW, Mus. for Women in Arts (charter).

CHUPELA, DOLORES CAROLE, children's librarian; b. New Brunswick, N.J., Dec. 25, 1952; d. John Joseph and Cecilia Dolores (Pazdon) C. BS, Douglass Coll., 1975; MLS, Rutgers U., 1984. Cert. tchr., N.J. Libr., Edison Pub. Libr. (N.J.), 1979—. Author: Gates to Lands of Pleasure, 1986; contbg. author 1984 Summer Reading Club Manual. Speaker civic orgns. Recipient Presdl. sports award in figure skating, 1980, Pub. Rels. award, Spl. Recognition award Del. Raritan Girl Scout Coun., 1990; named Tercentennial Citizen-of-Week, Middlesex County, N.J., New Brunswick, 1983, named to Edison High Sch's. Hall of Honor, 1990. Mem. ALA and Assn. Libr. Svc. to Children, N.J. Libr. Assn. (1st place award 1989), Rutgers Alumnae Assn. (speaker radio program), Children's Book Coun., U.S. Figure Skating Assn., Libr. Pub. Rels. Coun. (Share the Wealth award 1990), Princeton Skating Club. Democrat. Roman Catholic. Home: 51 Latonia St Edison NJ 08817 Office: Edison Pub Libr 340 Plainfield Ave Edison NJ 08817

CHURCH, IRENE ZABOLY, personnel services company executive; b. Cleve., Feb. 18, 1947; d. Bela Paul and Irene Elizabeth (Chandas) Zaboly; children: Irene Elizabeth, Elizabeth Anne, Lauren Alexandria Gadd, John Dale Gadd II. Grad. high sch. Pers. cons., recruiter, Cleve., 1965-70; chief exec. officer, pres. Oxford Pers., Pepper Pike, Ohio, 1973-89, Oxford Temporaries, Pepper Pike, 1979—, Oxford Group Ltd., Inc., 1989—; guest lectr. in field, 1974—; expert witness for ct. testimony, 1982—. Troop leader Lake Erie coun. Girl Scouts U.S., 1980-81; mem. Christian action com. Federated Ch., United Ch. Christ, 1981-85, sub-com. to study violence in rels. to women, 1983, creator, presenter programs How Work Affects Family Life and Re-entering the Job Market, 1981, mem. Women's Fellowship Martha-Mary Circle, 1980—, program dir., 1982-84, 87—; chpt. leader Nat. Coalition on TV Violence, 1983—; mem. The Federated Ch., United Ch. of Christ, Chagrin Falls, Ohio, program dir Mary-Martha Circle, 1982—, christian action com. 1981-85, mem. Mary-Martha Circle, Women's fellowship, 1980—; mem Better Bus. Bur., 1973-82. Mem. Nat. Assn. Pers. Cons. (cert., mem. ethics com. 1976-77, co-chairperson ethics com. 1977-78, mem. bus. practices and ethics com. 1980-82, mem. cert. pers. cons. soc. 1980-82, regional leader for membership 1987—, Pres.'s award 1988), Ohio Assn. Pers. Cons. (trustee 1975-80, 85—, sec. 1976-77, 85-87, chairperson bus. practices and ethics com. 1976-77, 81-82, 1st v.p., chairperson resolutions com. 1981-82, chairperson membership com. 1985-89, 2d v.p. 1987—, Outstanding Svc. award 1987, pres. 1988-89), Greater Cleve. Assn. Pers. Cons. (2nd then 1st v.p., 1974-76, state trustee 1975-80, pres. 1976-77, bd. advisor 1977-78, chairperson bus. practices and ethics com. 1974-76, chmn. nominating com., 1983-88, membership com. 1987-87, arbitration com., 1980, 85-87, fundraising, 1980-89, bd. dirs. 1980-89, trustee 1985-89, program chair 1987-89, Vi Pender Outstanding Svc. award 1977), Euclid C. of C. (small bus. com. 1981, chairperson task force com. evaluating funding in social security and vet.'s benefits 1981), Internat. Platform Assn., Am. Bus. Women's Assn., Nat. Assn. Temp. Svcs., Chagrin Valley C. of C. (leader Chagrin Blvd./East chpt. 1987—, Pres.'s award for Outstanding Contbns. 1988), Greater Cleve. Growth Assn. Coun. Small Enterprises, Rotary (vocat. svc. chairperson, program com. 1987—, membership chairperson 1988-89). Home: 8 Ridgecrest Dr Chagrin Falls OH 44022 Office: Oxford Pers 2945 Chagrin Blvd Exec Commons 300 Pepper Pike OH 44122

CHURCH, MARTHA ELEANOR, college president; b. Pitts., Nov. 17, 1930; d. Walter Seward and Eleanor (Boyer) C. BA, Wellesley Coll., 1952; MA, U. Pitts., 1954; PhD, U. Chgo., 1960; DSc (hon.), Lake Erie Coll., 1975; LittD (hon.), Houghton Coll., 1980; LHD (hon.), Queens Coll., 1981, Ursinus Coll., 1981, St. Joseph Coll., 1982, Towson State U., 1983, Dickinson Coll., 1987. Instr. geography Mt. Holyoke Coll., South Hadley, Mass., 1953-57; lectr. geography Ind. U. Gary Center, 1958; instr., then asst. prof. geography Wellesley Coll., 1958-60, 60-65; dean coll., prof. geography Wilson Coll., 1965-71; assoc. exec. sec. Commn. Higher Edn., Middle States Assn. Coll. and Secondary Sch., 1971-75; pres. Hood Coll., Frederick, Md., 1975—; bd. dirs. Farmers and Mechanics Nat. Bank, Montgomery Mut. Ins. Co., 1989-90; cons. for Choice: Books for Coll. Libraries; co-chmn. nat. adv. panel Nat. Ctr. for Research to improve postsecondary teaching and learning, U. Mich., 1985-90; mem. bd. vis. Def. Intelligence Coll., 1988—. Author: The Spatial Organization of Electric Power Territories in Massachusetts, 1960; Co-editor: A Basic Geographical Library: A Selected and Annotated Book List for Am. Colls, 1966; cons. editor, Change mag., 1980—. Bd. dirs. Council for Internat. Exchange of Scholars, 1979-80, Japan Internat. Christian U. Found., 1977—, Nat. Center for Higher Edn. Mgmt. Systems, 1980-83; bd. dirs. Am. Council on Edn., 1976-79, vice chmn., 1978-79, mem. nat. identification panel, 1977—; bd. advisors Fund for Improvement of Postsecondary Edn., HEW, 1976-79; mem. Sec. of Navy's Adv. Bd. on Edn. and Tng., 1976-80; chmn. Md. commn. on Civil Rights, 1981-82; trustee Bradford Coll., Mass., 1982-87, Peddie Sch., N.J., 1982—, Carnegie Found. for the Advancement of Teaching, 1986—, Nat. Geographic Soc., 1989—, Nat. Geographic Soc. Edn. Found., 1989—; mem. pub. adv. com. Bus and Profl. Women's Found., 1982—; chmn. bd. dirs. Medici Found., Princeton, N.J., 1985—; mem. Md. Humanities Council, 1985-86, Md. Jud. Disabilities Commn., 1985—; mem. Edn. Commn. States, 1981—; exec. com. Campus Compact: Project for Pub. and Community Service, 1986-89. Recipient Christian R. and Mary F. Lindback Found., Disting. Teaching award Wilson Coll., 1971. Mem. AAUW, Am. Assn. Advancement of Humanities (dir. 1979-81), Am. Assn. Higher Edn. (chmn. 1980-81, bd. dirs. 1979-83), Nat. Assn. Ind. Colls. and Univs. (bd. dirs. 1983-86), Md. Ind. Colls. and Univs. Assn. (pres. 1979-81, exec. com. 1988-90), Assn. Am. Colls. (adv. com. project on status and edn. of women 1980-85), Women's Coll. Coalition (exec. com. 1976-80, 87-89), Am. Conf. Acad. Deans (sec., editor 1969-71), Council Protestant Colls. and Univs. (bd. dirs. 1969-71), Soc. Coll. and Univ. Planning (editorial bd. 1979—), Inst. Ednl. Leadership (bd. dirs. 1982-87), Sigma Delta Epsilon. Office: Hood Coll Office of Pres Rosemont Ave Frederick MD 21701

CHURCH, SONIA JANE SHUTTER, librarian; b. York, Pa., Dec. 15, 1940; d. Robert Benjamin and Eva Alverta (Horn) Shutter; m. Ernest

Layton Church, May 20, 1966; children: Robert Bruce, Jennifer Grace. B.S. in Edn., Millersville Coll. 1962; M.L.S., U. Pitts., 1978. Playground supr. York City Sch. Dist., Pa., 1961; officer USMC, 1962-66; children's libr. Prunedale br. Monterey County Libr., Calif., 1978-79; youth svcs. coord. Monterey County Libr., 1979-83, 85-88, head libr. Prunedale br., 1983-85; children's svcs. mgr. Ventura (Calif.) County Libr., 1988—; writer Book Beat Column for Fortnighter Newspaper, Salinas 1983-85. Editor pamphlet: What Will we Do with the Baby? a collection of nursery rhymes and finger plays, 1977. Mem. Deferred Comp. Task Force, Monterey County, 1983-88, Mgmt. Coun., Monterey County, 1983-88; chmn. adminstrv. com. Social Svcs. Commn., Monterey County, 1983-85, chmn. ad hoc com., 1983-88; coordinating com. Boy Scouts Am., Salinas, 1983-85; Children's Svcs. Mgmt. Consortium, 1986—; tchr. Sun. Sch., Luth. Ch. Good Shepherd, Salinas, 1982-88; chmn. latchkey com. Child Care Task Force, Ventura County. Served to capt., USMC 1962-66. Sico scholar, 1958-62. Mem. ALA, Assn. Libr. Svc. to Children, Calif. Libr. Assn. (pres. children's svcs. chpt. 1989—), Assn. Children's Librs. of No. Calif., Sch. and Pub. Librs. Assn. Monterey Bay Area (pres. 1979-80, 1985-86, Assn. Childhood Edn. Internat., Storytellers Unltd., Am. Legion (comdr. 1984-85), Women's Internat. Bowling Congress, Women's Bowling Assn., U. Pitts. Alumni Assn., Millersville Tchrs. Coll. Alumni Assn., Beta Phi Mu, Beta Sigma Phi. Democrat. Lutheran. Home: 3505 Ketch Ave Oxnard CA 93035-3132 Office: Ventura County Library 651 E Main St Ventura CA 93001

CHURCHILL, LISA TAYLOR, management consultant; b. Roswell, N.Mex., Apr. 4, 1948; d. James and Monty Taylor; m. Peter Churchill, Apr. 27, 1985; 1 child, Kelly Alisabeth. BS, Minot State U., N.D., 1970; postgrad., Calif. State U., Long Beach, 1978; Cert., Inst. Applied Mgmt., Newport Beach, Calif., 1990. Instr. Orcutt Union Sch. Dis.t, Santa Maria, Calif., 1971-73; dir. personnel Del Webb Hotels, Newport Beach, Calif., 1975-81; employee rels. mgr. Flour Corp., Irvine, Calif., 1981-83; ptnr. The Weaver Co., Huntington Beach, Calif., 1983—. Author workbook: Outplacement Assistance, 1983; author video scripts, 1989. Mem. Am. Mgmt. Assn., Am. Soc. Tng. and Devel., Soc. for Human Resource Mgmt., AAUW, Am. Bus. Women's Assn., Employment Mgmt. Assn., Personnel and Indsl. Rels. Assn. Office: The Weaver Company 9652 Peppertree Dr #H Huntington Beach CA 92646

CHURCHILL, RUTH PIERSON, civic worker; b. Tarrytown, N.Y., Aug. 22, 1896; d. Lincoln and Maria (Noe) P.; m. Arthur Churchill, Aug. 27, 1923 (dec.); children: Emily, Martha, John. BA magna cum laude, Smith Coll. 1919. Joined Overseas Relief Svc., France, 1920; reasearcher Rockefeller Found., N.Y.C., 1921-23. Author: Memories Entwined With Roses, 1984; contbr. hist. vignettes to local publs.; columnist Chatham Courrier, Madison Eagle. 30 yr. mem. Morris County (N.J.) Welfare Bd.; trustee, v.p. N.J. Mental Health Assn.; mem. Rationing Bd. Morris County, W.W. II; mem. Madison Libr. Bd.; active local Smith Coll. Alumnae; 20 yr. Sunday sch. tchr., Community Ch., Summit, N.J., trustee of ch.; former Rep. committeewoman Morris County; researcher histories of families and estates in Madison and Chatham; designated official historian Chatham Twp., 1981. Mem. DAR (nat. Am. history medal 1987 Loantaka chpt.), Smith Coll. Alumnae Assn. (pres. 1946-52), Phi Beta Kappa. Unitarian. Home: 15 Linden Ln Chatham NJ 07928

CHURCHVILLE, LIDA HOLLAND, librarian; b. Dallas, May 5, 1933; d. Norbert R. and Agnes J. (Buckley) Holland; m. Joseph J. Churchville, Oct. 6, 1952 (dec. 1974); children: Lisa, Zoe, Anthony (dec.), Stephen. BA in History, Russell Sage Coll., Troy, N.Y., 1965; MLS, SUNY, Albany, 1967. Libr. Office Legis. Rsch., N.Y. Senate, Albany, 1967-75; chief law libr. U.S. Army Libr., Washington, 1975-78; coord. fed. women's program Dept. Def., The Pentagon, 1976-78; chief libr. Nat. Archives and Records Svcs., 1978-81; reference and spl. project libr. Nat. Archives Libr., 1981-83; spl. project libr. publs. unit Nat. Archives Trust Fund, 1983—, info. specialist Patent & Trademark Office, 1989; active Archives Libr. Info. Ctr., Nat. Archives, 1989—. Mem. Women's Issues Task Force, 1981-83, Women's Nat. Dem. Club, 1981—, Eleanor Roosevelt Dem. Club, Greenbelt, Md.; mem. Paint Branch Unitarian Ch., Adelphi, Md.; docent Greenbelt Mus., 1988—; vol. Arena Stage. Recipient Outstanding Performance award The Pentagon, 1977; mem. Atlantic Regional Archives Conf. Mem. Am. Soc. Info. Sci., D.C. Libr. Assn., Law Librs. Soc. Washington, Soc. Am. Archivists, Nat. Women's Party, DC Online Users Group, Toastmasters. Home: 19Q Ridge Rd Greenbelt MD 20770 Office: ALIC Nat Archives 8th and Pennsylvania Ave NW Rm 200 Washington DC 20408

CHUSID, JUDITH FRANCINE (JUDITH FRANCINE MARKS), school psychologist, psychoanalyst; b. N.Y.C., Dec. 3, 1947; d. Harry and Phyllis A. Chusid; B.A., Queens Coll., 1971; M.A., NYU, 1974, Ph.D. (A.B.D.); P.D., St. John's U., 1978; grad. Manhattan Center for Psychoanalytic Studies, 1981; m. Dec. 12, 1982. Program supr. East N.Y. YM-YWHA, 1970; tchr. Lexington Sch. for Deaf, N.Y.C. Bd. Edn., 1971-76; instr. Adelphi U., Garden City, N.Y., 1976-80; pvt. practice psychoanalytic psychotherapy, Jackson Heights and N.Y.C., 1974—; founder, pres., chmn. bd. Positive Approaches to Sports Success Found., Jackson Heights, 1980-85; faculty Ctr. Modern Psychoanalytic Studies; former mem. teaching faculty, tng. analyst Rockland Inst. for Psychoanalysis and Psychotherapy, Suffern, N.Y.; mem. Joint Council for Mental Health; founder, pres. Positive Approaches to Sports and Performance Success, 1980; lectr. Found. of Thanotology, Columbia U.; lectr. Sara Lawrence Coll.; condr. workshops, lectr. field sports psychology. Bd. dirs. Studio Elem. Sch. Co-founder, Actor's Voice, N.Y.C., 1982. Recipient Otto Klitgord award N.Y., 1967; cert. sch. psychologist, N.Y. State; cert. secondary tchr., physically handicapped tchr., N.Y. Mem. Am. Psychol. Assn., Nat. Accreditation Assn. Psychoanalysis (cert.), N.Y. State Assn. Sch. Psychologists. Contbr. articles to profl. jours.

CHUSMIR, JANET, newspaper editor. Exec. bd. Miami (Fla.) Herald. Office: Miami Herald Pub Co 1 Herald Pla Miami FL 33101*

CHUTE, PEGGY JO, educator; b. Beardstown, Ill., May 14, 1951; d. Calvin Edward and Roselyn Violet (Fair) C. BA, Calif. Bapt. Coll., 1978. Tutor Arlington High Sch., Riverside, Calif., 1979; tchr. elem. sch. Riverside Christian Sch., 1980-87, asst. prin., 1984-87; tchr. Oleander Elem Sch., Fontana, Calif., 1987-89, Almeria Mid. Sch., Fontana, Calif., 1989—; dir. cheerleading, Riverside Christian Sch., 1984-87; sponsor Almeria Travel Club, 1989—. Dir. adult, child choir, Palm Bapt. Ch., Riverside, 1988, youth dir. Rubindoux Bapt. Ch., Riverside, 1972-74. Mem. NEA, Calif. Tchrs. Assn., Fontana Tchrs. Assn. Democrat.

CHUTICH, MARGARET HELEN, lawyer; b. Mpls., June 18, 1958; d. Joseph Daniel and Marlys Chutich. Student, U. Zagreb (Yugoslavia), 1980-81, Stanford U., Palo Alto, Calif., 1976-77; BA, U. Minn., Mpls., 1980; JD cum laude, U. Mich., 1984. Assoc. Tanick & Heins, Mpls., 1986-89; law clk. to presiding justice U.S. Dist. Ct., Minn., 1984-86; assoc. Opperman, Heins & Paquin, Mpls., 1989—; dir. Minn. Dist. Ct. br. 8th Cir. Hist. Soc., Mpls., 1989; dir. Minn. Lawyer's Com. for Internat. Human Rights, Mpls., 1990—. Contbr. Human Rights in Albania, 1990. Dir. Women of Courage, Mpls., 1989; capt. 100 Women's Com., Mpls., 1989-90. Mem. Am. Judicature Soc., Fed. Bar Assn., Minn. Women Lawyers, Minn. State Bar Assn., Hennepin County Bar Assn. Democratic Farmer Labor. Office: Opperman Heins & Paquin 2200 Washington Sq 100 Washington Ave S Minneapolis MN 55401

CHVANY, CATHERINE VAKAR, educator; b. Paris, Apr. 26, 1927; m. 1948; 3 children. B.A., Radcliffe Coll., 1963; Ph.D., Harvard U., 1970. Instr. Russian, Wellesley Coll., 1966-67; instr. MIT, 1967-70, lectr., 1970-71, asst. prof., 1971-74, assoc. prof. Russian, 1974-83, prof., 1983—; fellow Harvard Russian Research Ctr., 1979—. Lilly postdoctoral teaching award fellow MIT, 1975-76. Mem. Am. Assn. Advancement Slavic Studies, Linguistic Soc. Am., Am. Assn. Tchrs. Slavic and Eastern European Langs., Am. Council Teaching of Russian, Bulgarian Studies Assn. Author: On the Syntax of BE-Sentences in Russian, 1975. Co-editor: Slavic Transformational Syntax, 1974, Morphosyntax in Slavic, 1980, Gertruda Vakar. Stikhotvorenija, 1984; New Studies in Russian Language and Literature, 1987 Mem. editorial adv. bd. SEEJ, Folia Slavica, RLJ, Essays in Poetics. Contbr. articles to profl. jours. Address: MIT Bldg 14N Rm 311 77 Massachusetts Ave Cambridge MA 02139

CHWATSKY, ANN (RITA CHWATSKY), photographer, educator; b. Phila., Jan. 11, 1942; d. Jules and Gladys (Coleman) Schneider; m. Robert Schulz, June 23, 1961 (div. 1964); 1 child, Marc; m. Howard Franklin Chwatsky, Nov. 2, 1965; 1 child, Julie. BS in Art Edn., Hofstra U., 1965, MS, 1971; postgrad. L.I. U., 1973-74. Cert. tchr. Photography editor L.I. mag., 1976-80; instr. Internat. Ctr. Photography, N.Y.C., 1979-80, Parrish Art Mus., Southampton, N.Y., 1984—; mem. faculty L.I. U., Greenvale, N.Y., 1982—; coordinator master art workshop Southampton Coll., 1985, 86, 87, 88, dir., 1989. Author, photgrapher The Man In The Street, 1989; photographer The Four Seasons of Shaker Life; photographs featured in Time, Newsweek, Newsday, Manchete, N.Y. Times, MD Medical Times, Photographers Gallery, London, 1985, Shakers, Nassau County Mus. Fine Arts, 1987, Greater Lafayette (Ind.) Mus. Art, 1988; group shows include: The Other, Houston Ctr. Photography, 1988, L.I. Fine Arts Mus., 1984, Women's Interart Ctr., N.Y.C., 1976, 80, Parrish Art Mus., Southampton, 1979, Internat. Ctr. Photography, N.Y.C., 1980, 82, Nassau County Mus. Fine Arts, 1983, Soho 20 Gallery, N.Y.C., 1984, New Orleans World's Fair, 1984, Southampton Gallery, 1988, 89; represented in permanent collections: Forbes N.Y.C. Midtown YWCA, Nassau County Mus. Fine Arts, Susan Rothenberg, others. Author: Four Seasons of Shaker LIfe, 1986; author, photographer: The Man in the Street, 1989. Bd. dirs. Rosa Lee Young Day Care Ctr., Rockville Centre, 1982-85. Recipient Estabrook Disting. Alumni award Hofstra U., 1984; Kodak Profl. Photographers award, 1984; Eastman Found. grantee, 1981-82; Polaroid grantee, 1980. Mem. Assn. Am. Mag. Profls., Picture Profls. Am., Profl. Women Photographers N.Y.C. Democrat. Jewish. Avocations: tennis, gardening. Home: 85 Andover Rd Rockville Centre NY 11570 also: Sag Harbor NY 11963

CIACCIO-CROWLEY, RITAMARIE, hotel sales executive; b. Dover, N.J., Nov. 19, 1966; d. Joseph Edward and Patricia Ann (McKeon) Ciaccio; m. Trevor Joseph Crowley, Oct. 13, 1990. AAS, Mercer County Community Coll., Lawrenceville, N.J., 1988. Sales coord. Compri Hotels/Accor Am., Princeton, N.J., 1988-89; sales mgr. Fresh Ponds Village, Dayton, N.J., 1989-90, dir. sales, 1990—. Mem. Hotel Sales and Mktg. Assocs. Internat., Princeton C. of C., Princeton Bus. and Profl. Women. Office: Fresh Ponds Village 650 Dayton-Jamesburg Rd Dayton NJ 08810

CIAK, BRENDA SUSAN, nurse; b. Springfield, Mass., Jan. 29, 1955; d. Stanley Peter and Jessica Evelyn (Jorkowski) Ciak; divorced, 1989. BS in Pub. Health, U. Mass., 1976, BS in Nursing, 1979; MS in Nursing, Boston U., 1986. RN, Mass.; cert. in infection control. Staff nurse Miriam Hosp., Providence, 1979-80; head nurse Western Mass. Kidney Ctr., Springfield, 1980-85; nurse epidemiologist Providence Hosp., Holyoke, Mass., 1985-86; infection control nurse VA Med. Ctr., Northampton, Mass., 1986—; presenter at profl. confs. Contbr. to profl. publs. Co-founder, co-chair AIDS/HIV Positive Support Group VA Med. Ctr., Northhampton, Mass., 1989—. Mem. NAFE, Assn. Practitioners in Infection Control, Advanced Nursing Practice Group (chmn. 1989—), Zonta Club Internat., Springfield Mus. and Libr. Assn., Sigma Theta Tau (Beta Zeta chpt. archivist 1990—). Home: 102 Wolcott St Springfield MA 01104 Office: VA Med Ctr Rte 9 Northampton MA 01060

CIATTO, DEBI LYNN, educational administrator; b. Ft. Harrison, Ind., Feb. 12, 1956; d. Wendell Holmes and Barbara Ann (Johnson) Overton; div. 1986; 1 child, Theresa Elizabeth. AA, St. Petersburg Jr. Coll., 1976; BA, U. South Fla., 1978. Fin. aid officer Jones Colls., Jacksonville, Fla., 1978-79, Summit Systems Colls. and Schs., Tampa, Fla., 1979-83; cons. J.V. & Assocs., Jacksonville, 1982-85; dir. fin. aid United Schs., Inc., Clearwater, Fla., 1985-88; dir. operational svcs. United Schs., Inc., 1989-90; pres., dir. fin. aid Chgo. State U., 1990—; dir. operational svcs. United Schs., Inc. Clearwater, 1989. Mem. Nat. Assn. Student Fin. Aid Adminstrs., Fla. Assn. Student Fin. Aid Adminstrs., Nat. Home Study Coun., Penn. Assn. Student Fin. Aid Adminstrs., So. Assn. Student Fin. Aid Adminstr., Ill. Assn. Student Fin. Aid Adminstrs. Democrat.

CIAVOLA, LOUISE ARLENE, foundation executive; b. Summit Station, Ohio, July 16, 1933; d. Orus Allen and Marie Elizabeth (White) Helser; m. Rex George Ciavola, May 20, 1961; children: Rex George Jr., Todd Colby, Christina Adelina. BS in Edn. with honors, Ohio U., 1954; postgrad., U. Mich., 1959-60, 84, Western Mich U., 1960, Wayne State U., 1984. Cert. elem. and secondary tcr., Ill., Ohio, Mich. Tchr. pub. schs., Northlake, Ill., 1954-55, Cuyahoga Falls, Ohio, 1955-57, Newark, Ohio, 1957-59, Kalamazoo, 1959-60, Grosse Pointe, Mich., 1960-85; asst. dir. vols. Children's Hosp. Mich., Detroit, 1978-82; assoc. exec. dir. Cystic Fibrosis Found., Grand Rapids, Mich., 1988-89, assoc. exec. dir., Greater Mich. Chpt., 1989—. Bd. dirs., officer Jr. Women's Assn. for Detroit Symphony Orch., 1964-70, Tennis and Crumpets, Inc., Detroit, 1975-82; bd. dirs. Midland (Mich.) Hosp. Ctr., 1985-87, Mother's Club Grosse Pointe South High Sch., 1983-84; co-founder, bd. dirs. Grosse Pointe Found. for Acad. Enrichment, 1970-85; chmn. United Found., Grosse Pointe Park, Mich., 1968; deacon Grosse Pointe Meml. Ch., Grosse Pointe Farms, Mich., 1970. Recipient award for devoted svc. Children's Hosp. Mich., 1982. Mem. Cen. U.S. Ski Assn. (bd. dirs. 1977-81), Spring Lake Country Club, 20th Century Club (Midland), Contemporary Rev. Club (Midland), Otsego Ski Club (Gaylord, Mich.), Chimes, Kappa Delta Pi, Phi Alpha Theta, Tau Beta. Republican. Presbyterian. Home: 16051 Harbor View Dr Spring Lake MI 49456 Office: Cystic Fibrosis Found 404 McKay Tower Grand Rapids MI 49503

CICCONE, ANNE PANEPINTO, artist; b. Bklyn., July 5, 1943; d. Louis and Lucia (Coniglio) Panepinto; m. Francis Anthony Ciccone, Mar. 21, 1971. BA, Queens Coll., 1974. With pub. rels. dept. Hanover Graphics; cons. AFC Assocs., 1979—; instr., cons. Creativity Projects for the Aging, 1979—; creative cons. Commn. for Cultural Affairs, New Hyde Park, N.Y., 1983—; instr. Brooklyn Skills Exch., 1984, Herrick Adult Edn.; exec. asst. to assoc. dir. pub. rels. Hofstra U., 1987—, instr. art and design, 1987—; cons. and instr. in field. Exhibited in group show Morin-Miller Galleries, N.Y.C., (yr.-long represeentation) Ten Preeminent Artists of Wetherhold Galleries, Washington, 1990-91; contbr. articles to various mags.; photographer illustrations for lit. work in Sunday Clothes, Fine Arts mag.; illustrator Bklyn. Skills Exchange Workshop Brochure. Mem. N.Y. Acad. Scis., Inst. for Advancement Health. Roman Catholic.

CICERELLE, CAROLE ANNE, human resources executive; b. Mt. Vernon, N.Y., Jan. 23, 1940; d. Frank James and Antoinette P. (Burolla) Politano; children: Maria, Thomas, Jamie. AAS in Spl. Edn., Middlesex County Coll., 1988; BA in Psychology and Edn., Centenary Coll., 1989. Sr. bookkeeper Arthur Merrill, P.A., Washington, N.J.; owner, mgr. Tody's Deli, Middlesex, N.J.; sr. fin. clk. acct. Johns-Manville Corp., N.J.; ctr. supr. Abilities of N.W. Jersey, Inc., Hackettstown, N.J. Trustee Kresfield. Mem. NAFE, NJARC, COSAC, Mensa. Home: 37 W Church St Washington NJ 07882 Office: 109 Grand Ave Hackettstown NJ 07840

CICHOWSKI, MARYANN EMILY, tool and die executive; b. Deep River, Conn., July 6, 1918; d. Anthony C. and Zofia (Pryga) Wolak; m. Frank A. Cichowski, July 4, 1939; children: Francis A., Ronald J. Diploma in bus., New Britain Secretarial Sch., Conn., 1936; student, St. Joseph Coll., West Hartford, Conn., 1938, Newport (R.I.) Secretarial Sch., 1942. Quality control-office clk. Fafnir Bearing Co., New Britain, 1936-39; clk. typist Naval Torpedo Sta., Newport, 1942-43; office mgr. Fame Tool & Die Co., Plainville, Conn., 1955-77; treas. Fame Tool & Die Co., Inc., Plainville, Conn., 1977-82, pres., 1983—. Treas. St. Paul's Ladies Guild, Kensington, Conn., 1970-71, v.p., 1972-73, pres., 1974-75. Mem. Conn. Bus. and Industry Assn., Polonaise Club, Inc. (treas. New Britain chpt. 1985-90). Home: 28 1/2 Sunset Ln Berlin CT 06037 Office: Fame Tool & Die Co Inc 387 Woodford Ave Ext Plainville CT 06062-0306

CIELINSKI, AUDREY ANN, technical writer, publisher; b. Cleve., Sept. 10, 1957; d. Joseph and Dorothy Antoinette (Hanna) Cielinski. B.J. with high honors, U. Tex., 1979. Reporter, writer Med. World News mag., N.Y.C., 1979, asst. copy chief, Houston, 1983-84; free-lance writer, editor, 1984—; editorial asst. Jour Health and Social Behavior, Houston, 1980-81; sec. dept. psychiatry Baylor Coll. Medicine, Houston, 1980-81; procedures analyst, tech. writer, tech. librarian Harris County Data Processing Dept., Houston, 1981-83; communications specialist III, desktop pub., Wang systems adminstr., desktop pub. Office of Planning and Research, Houston Police Dept., tchr. tech. writing class, 1985-89; tech. writer Chevron Exploration and Prodn. Svcs. Co., Houston, 1990—. Contbr. stories and articles to newspapers and mags. Recipient Commendation award Chief of Police, Houston, Chief's Command Employee of Month award June, 1989. Vol. writer, graphic designer, office religious edn. St. Ambrose Roman Cath. Ch., Houston, 1983—; vol. editor newsletters Greater Houston area Am. Cancer Soc. and VGS, Inc. Mem. NAFE, Assn. for Women in Communications, Women Profls. in Govt., Am. Med. Writers Assn., Soc. for Tech. Communication, Soc. Children's Book Writers (assoc.), Austin Writer's League, Sigma Delta Chi, Phi Kappa Phi, Alpha Lambda Delta. Home: 4250 W 34th St Apt 84 Houston TX 77092 Office: Chevron Exploration & Prodn Svcs Co 2811 Hayes Rd #3224A Houston TX 77042

CIFELLI, BARBARA DORIS, real estate financial accountant; b. Chgo., Dec. 16, 1942; d. Thomas and E. Doris (Jones) C. BA, Mt. Holyoke Coll., 1964. Lic. real estate agt., N.J. Programmer AT&T Co., N.Y.C., 1964-66; systems analyst AT&T Co., Piscataway, N.J., 1967-73; dist. mgr. AT&T Co., Basking Ridge, N.J., 1973-87; pres. Home Equity Enterprises of Warren (N.J.), Inc., 1987—; real estate agt. Weichert Realtors, Bernardsville, N.J., 1987—; mem. Rand Real Estate Corp. Mem. N.J. Orgn. of Women, N.J. Bus. Owners, NJAR Million Dollar Club, Weichert Million Dollar Sales Club. Republican. Roman Catholic. Home: 18 Stockade Rd Warren NJ 07060 Office: Home Equity Enterprises Warren Inc PO Box 4558 Warren NJ 07060-4558

CIHOCKI, TOBIANN, systems programmer; b. E. Chicago, Ind., May 12, 1965; d. Edward Joseph and Wendy (Herbst) C. BS in Systems Engring., U. Pa., 1987, BS in Fin., 1987. Computer cons. Kidder Peabody & Co., Inc., Phila., 1984-87, Smith, Barney, Harris, Upham, Phila., 1986-87; systems programmer J.P. Morgan, N.Y.C., 1987-90; systems analyst Time, Inc. Mags., N.Y.C., 1990—; cons. Howard Johnsons, Juno, Fla., 1988, Janrus & Co., Springfield, Pa., 1985-87. Project. coord. Phila. Coalition for the Homeless, 1986; costume designer Bloomers, Phila., 1985. Mem. Greenwich Masters Swim Team, Phi Sigma Sigma (social chmn. Phila. 1986). Home: 16 Ritch Ave Greenwich CT 06830 Office: Time Inc Mags 1271 Ave of the Americas New York NY 10020

CILETTI, CHRISTINE JOY, marketing professional; b. Bklyn., Sept. 4, 1945; d. John Joseph and Dorothy Frances (LoCicero) Marchese; m. Dominick Emil Ciletti, Oct. 26, 1963; children: Dominick Jr., Christopher. Degree in mktg., U. Bridgeport, Conn., 1979. Prin., pres. Tina Ann Party Plan, Bridgeport, 1968-80; dir. mktg. Tay Mac Corp. McDonalds Restaurants, Woodbridge, Conn., 1980-87; v.p., dir. mktg. Eastern Hospitality Roy Rogers Restaurants, Stamford, Conn., 1987—; grad. asst. Dale Carnegie Pub. Speaking, 1989-90. Project coord. Leukemia Soc., New Haven, Conn., 1988-89, Conn. Spl. Olympics, 1980-87, Easter Seals, Conn., 1988—; bd. dirs. Bridgeport P.A.L., 1983—. Roman Catholic. Home: 55 Sullivan Pl Bridgeport CT 06610 Office: Eastern Hospitality Inc 7 Pearl Ct Allendale NJ 07401

CIMINI, MARIA DOLORES, psychologist; b. White Plains, N.Y., Apr. 30, 1958; d. Elvio and Angelina (Bufalini) C. PhD, SUNY, Albany, 1986. Lic. psychologist, N.Y. Psychology trainee outpatient psychiatry clinic Albany Med. Ctr., 1982-83; behavior specialist Pomenade Hill Day Treatment Ctr., Albany, 1983-84; psychology intern Albany Psychology Internship Consortium, Albany, 1984-85; assoc. psychologist Albany County Mental Health Clinic, Albany, 1985-86; pvt. practice psychologist Albany, 1989—; clin. psychologist St. Anne Inst., Albany, 1986—; staff psychologist univ. counseling ctr. SUNY, Albany, 1989—; adj. clin. prof. assessment and psychol. treatment of adolescents and persons with phys. disabilities dept. psychology SUNY, Albany, 1990—. Community svc. com. mem. SUNY, Albany, 1989—; active Project Access to Broader Learning and Experience, 1975-76. Officer's Discretionary grantee William T. Grant Found., 1983, Sci. Student grantee Found. for Sci. and the Handicapped, 1983, Barnard Coll. grantee, 1978; Assoc. Alumnae of Barnard Coll. Grad. fellow Alumnae Assn. Barnard Coll., 1983; Rudolph Dillman scholar Am. Found. for the Blind, 1983. Mem. Am. Psychol. Assn. (div. 39-psychoanalysis, div. 12-clin. psychology), Psychol. Assn. Northeastern N.Y., Soc. for Pschoanalytic Psychotherapy, AAAS (resource group for opportunities in sci.), Found. for Sci. and the Handicapped. Home: 11 S Lake Ave 306 Albany NY 12203

CIMOCHOWICZ, DIANE MARIE, naval petty officer; b. Jacksonville, Fla., Aug. 13, 1955; d. Richard Clarence and Edith Darlene (Johnson) C. AS in Mgmt., Hawaii Pacific Coll., 1986, BSBA, 1986. Enlisted USN, 1974, advanced through grades to petty officer first class; ops. specialist USN, Naples, Italy, 1975-77; ops. specialist, instr. USN, Dam Neck, Va., 1977-78; resigned USN, 1978, reenlisted, 1980; photographer USN, San Diego, 1980-82, Honolulu, 1982—; owner ICON, Columbia, Md., 1978-79; owner, operator In Other Words, Honolulu, 1988—. Mem. Federally Employed Women, Fleet Res. Assn., Associated Photographers Internat., Hawaii Pacific Coll. Student Bus. Orgn., Nat. Honor Frat. Bus. Adminstrn., Delta Mu Delta. Democrat. Clubs: Lokahi Canoe, Koa Kai (Honolulu). Home: 3110 Woodward SW Wyoming MI 49509 Office: Fleet Intelligence Ctr Pacific Box 500 Pearl Harbor HI 96860

CIMORELL, ALBERTA MAY, retired metal processing company executive; b. Cleve.; d. Victor Albert and Viola (Calandra) Profughi; m. Ray M. Cimorell; children: Randi Cimorell Voelkel and Rayna O'Hara (twins). G-rad. high sch., Cleve. Acctg. dept. Brown Fence & Wire Co., Cleve., 1946-47; office mgr. Royal Machine & Tool Co., Cleve., 1947-49, Cleve. Indsl. Tool Co., Cleve., 1949-53; asst. sec.-treas., corp. sec. Tech. Metal Processing, Inc., Cleve., 1956-84; v.p. fins. Tech. Metal Processing, Inc., 1978-84, retired, 1984; cons. in field; real estate investor. Mem. NAFE, Willoughby Hills Hist. Soc. Roman Catholic. Home: 30401 White Rd Willoughby Hills OH 44092

CINCIOTTA, LINDA ANN, lawyer, administrator; b. Washington, May 18, 1943; d. Nicholas Joseph and Laverne (Oakley) C.; m. John P. Olguin, Aug. 4, 1979. B.S., Georgetown U., 1965; J.D., George Washington U., 1970. Bar: D.C. 1970. Assoc. Arent, Fox, Plotkin & Kahn, Washington, 1970-76, ptnr., 1977-83; dir. Office Atty. Personnel Mgmt., Dept. Justice, Washington, 1983—. Recipient U.S. Law Week award George Washington U. Nat. Law Ctr., 1970. Mem. Fed. Communications Bar Assn. (pres. 1980-81, ABA del. 1977-79), Fed. Bar. Assn., D.C. Bar Assn. Office: US Dept Justice Dir Office Atty Pers Mgmt 10th & Constitution Ave NW Washington DC 20530

CINIGLIO, ADA VIVIAN, marketing executive; b. Monticello, N.Y., June 14, 1935; d. William and Bertha (Schechter) Vapnek; m. Vincent A. Ciniglio, Dec. 24, 1965 (div. Jan. 1983); 1 child, Lorenzo. AB, Skidmore Coll., 1957; MS, SUNY, New Paltz, N.Y., 1963. Asst. prof. SUNY, S. Fallsburg, 1963-75; tng. dir. Met. Museum, N.Y.C., 1973-75; asst. dean. The New Sch. for Social Research, N.Y.C., 1976-78; devel. dir. The Drawing Ctr., N.Y.C., 1978-79; project dir. N.Y. State Urban Devel. Corp., N.Y.C., 1979-81; v.p. The Chase Manhattan Bank, N.Y.C., 1981-90; dir. mktg. Sta. WNET, 1990—; grad. council mem. Empire State Coll., N.Y.C., 1987-89. Bus. vol. and bd. dirs. Deja Vu Dance Theatre, N.Y.C., 1988-89, Inter Media Network, N.Y.C., 1989. Recipient Gold Quill Award Internat. Assn. Bus. Communicators, 1986. Mem. Bank Mktg. Assn. (bd. mem.), Skidmore Coll. Alumni Assn. Democrat. Home: 251 W 71st St New York NY 10023

CIOCCIO, ELLEN LACEY, financial executive; b. Des Moines, Oct. 13, 1935; d. George Albert and Bonita Genevieve (Bradish) L.; m. Nicholas Joseph Cioccio, 1958 (div. 1969); children: Cassandra Lynne Cioccio-Ball, Christopher Albert, Marco David. BA, Drake U., 1958, MS, 1985. Jr. acct. Drake U., Des Moines, 1965-68, acct., 1968-72, asst. controller, 1972-86, dir. fin. svcs., 1986-87, asst. v.p. bus. and fin., 1987—. Sec. Iowa Dem. Conf., Polk County, 1970-72, bd. dirs., 1972-74; precinct com. person, Dem. Party, Des Moines, 1971—; commr. Polk County Condemnation Com., 1975—. Mem. Univ. Risk Mgrs. Assn. (bd. dirs. 1976-79, 89—), Risk Ins. Mgmt. Soc. (v.p. Iowa chpt. 1980-82). Democrat. Unitarian. Home: 4515 Wakonda Pkwy Des Moines IA 50315 Office: Drake U 2507 University Ave Des Moines IA 50311

CIOLLI, ANTOINETTE, librarian, retired educator; b. N.Y.C., Aug. 20, 1915; d. Pietro and Mary (Palumbo) C.; A.B., Bklyn. Coll., 1937, M.A., 1940; B.S. in L.S., Columbia U., 1943. Tchr. history and civics Bklyn. high schs., 1943-44; circulation librarian Bklyn. Coll. Library, 1944-46; instr. history Sch. Gen. Studies, Bklyn. Coll., 1944-50, asst. prof. library dept., 1965-73, assoc. prof., 1973-81, prof. emerita, 1981—; reference librarian Bklyn. Coll. Library, 1947-59, chief sci. librarian, 1959-70, chief spl. collections div., 1970-81, hon. archivist, 1981—. Mem. ALA, Am. Hist. Assn., Spl. Libraries Assn. (museum group chpt. sec. 1950-51, 52-54), N.Y. Library Club, Beta Phi Mu. Author: (with Alexander S. Preminger and Lillian Lester) Urban Educator: Harry D. Gideonse, Brooklyn College and the City University of New York, 1970; contbr. articles to profl. jours. Home: 1129 Bay Ridge Pkwy Brooklyn NY 11228

CIPOLETTI, JOY, management consultant; b. Mt. Lebanon, Pa., Dec. 22, 1959; d. Arthur George and Dolores Shanor (Carroll) C. BS in Acctg., U. Colo., 1981; postgrad. Georgetown U. CPA, Colo. Staff cons. Price Waterhouse, Washington, 1981-83, sr. cons., 1983-85, mgr., 1985-89, sr. mgr., 1989; cons. Am. Mgmt. Systems, Arlington, Va., 1989—. Pres. Little River Sq. Condominium Assn., Annandale, 1984. Mem. AICPAs, Inst. Cert. Data Processors (cert. data processor), Am. Soc. for Tng. and Devel., Am. Assn. for Counseling and Devel., Blessed Sacrament Folk Group. Roman Catholic. Avocations: running, bodybuilding, reading, music (guitar and flute). Office: Am Mgmt Systems 1525 Wilson Blvd 10th Fl Arlington VA 22209

CIPOLLONE, NINA A., bank officer; b. N.Y., May 6, 1953. BA, Queens Coll., 1987. Pers. rep. Hertz Corp., Parsippany, N.J.; spl. projects mgr., adminstrv. mgr. Citibank, N.Y.C., mgr. svc. quality. Mem. NAFE, Am. Soc. Tng. and Devel.

CIPRIANO, GRACE IRENE, estimator, nurse, stables owner; b. Youngstown, Ohio, May 13, 1925; d. Floyd Raymond and Ruth (Walter) Brown; m. Otto Francis Wess, June 11, 1949 (dec. Mar. 1969); children: Raymond Francis, Shannon Grace Wess Morello, Colleen Medody Wess Bloomingdale, Honey Lucile Wess Biondillo, Alyson Rae Wess King, Carol Lynn Wess Sivley; m. James L. Cipriao, June 28, 1987. Student, Bliss Bus. Coll., 1942-43; LLB, LaSalle U., 1952; grad. nurse's tng. Youngstown Hosp. Assn., 1974 . Nurse's aid St. Elizabeth Hosp., Youngstown, 1938-42; traffic clk. B.F. Goodrich Co., Akron, Ohio, 1942-43; rate clk., traffic dept. Gen. Fireproofing Co., Youngstown, 1947-49; pres., co-owner Jewels by Lady Grace, Detroit, 1949-63, Grayce's Treasure Chests, Youngstown, 1949-63, Grayce's Medicine Chests, Youngstown, 1949-63; indsl. and comml. bldg. estimator Ben Rudick & Son, Inc., Youngstown, 1963-71; freelance estimator, North Lima, Ohio, 1971—; newspaper columnist, various newspapers, 1963-68; nurse, 1974—; now staff nurse Drs. Hosp., Lake Worth, Fla.; owner Grace Wess Stables, Inc., Canfield, Ohio, 1949—. Dem. candidate for Mahoning County commr., 1973; bd. dirs. Missing Children Found., Tampa, Fla.; mem. legis. com. Palm Beach County, Mothers Against Drunk Driving. Served with WAVES, 1943-47. Mem. Am. Bus. Women's Assn. (pres. 1969-70, Woman of Yr. award 1970), Youngstown Bus. and Profl. Women's Club, U.S. Trotting Assn., Canfield Harness Horsemen's Assn., Ohio Harness Horsemen's Assn., Am. Legion, VFW, Def. Supply Assn., McGuffey Meml. Assn., Women in Constrn., Constrn. Specifications Inst., Internat. Platform Assn., Home and Sch. Assn., St. Charles Altar and Rosary Soc., Mahoning County Agrl. Soc., Am. German Club of Palm Beaches (Fla.), Youngstown Playhouse, Order Eastern Star (Grand Nurse of Fla. 1986-87, Worthy Matron Lucerne chpt. 1989—), Grange. Democrat. Roman Catholic. Home and Office: 1008 Penn Grove Lake Worth FL 33461

CIPRIANO, MARY LYNN, microbiologist; b. St. Louis, Dec. 8, 1947; d. Lincoln Dominic and Mary (Chappas) C.; m. Thomas Joseph Gimino, Jan. 1981. BS, U. Ill., 1970; MBA, U. Chgo., 1977. Rsch. asst. Coll. Vet. Medicine, U. Ill., Urbana, 1970-72; supr. quality control Lab-Tek div., Miles Labs., Naperville, Ill., 1972-75; specifications editor, hosp. div. Abbott Labs., Abbott Park, Ill., 1975-76; sr. quality engr. Abbott Labs., North Chicago, Ill., 1976; mgr. biol. svcs. Abbott Labs., North Chicago, 1977-80; quality assurance mgr., Murine Co. Abbott Labs., Chgo., 1980-81; mgr. biol. mfg. and devel., chem. div. Abbott Labs., North Chicago, 1981-84; mgr. biosafety, diagnostic div. Abbott Labs., Abbott Park, 1984—. Recipient Walter L. Holms Founders award Northeastern Ill. Section Am. Mem. Am. Biol. Safety Assn. (sec. 1988-90), Am. Soc. for Quality Control (Founders award Northeastern Ill. sect. 1981), U. Chgo. Women's Bus. Group (treas. 1981-83, pres. 1984, Outstanding Svc. award 1987). Republican. Roman Catholic. Home: 1127 Hibbard Rd Wilmette IL 60091 Office: Abbott Labs One Abbott Park Rd Abbott Park IL 60064

CIRICILLO, ROSE CASALE, education educator; b. Newark, June 25, 1922; d. Ralph and Francesca (Di Lorenzo) Casale; m. Samuel Francis Ciricillo, Sept. 29, 1946 (div. Apr. 1959); children: Linda Rose Ciricillo Spock, Michael E. BA, Montclair State Coll., 1942; MA in Student Pers. Svcs., Seton Hall U., 1968; postgrad., Columbia U., 1943-45. Cert. tchr., guidance counselor, supr. fgn. lang., supr. guidance, dir. pupil pers. svcs., N.J. Tchr. French and Spanish, Union (N.J.) High Sch., 1942-50, 51-52, Caldwell (N.J.) High Sch., 1959-62; tchr. French and Spanish, Parsippany (N.J.)-Troy Hills Sch. Dist., 1962-87, counselor, 1969-87; adj. prof. dept. curriculum and teaching Montclair State Coll., Upper Montclair, N.J., 1987—; guest lectr. various colls., schs., profl. orgns. Contbr. articles to profl. jours. Gerald Read travel scholar, People's Republic China, 1985, Ea. Europe, 1988. Mem. NEA, N.J. Edn. Assn., Morris County Edn. Assn., N.J. Counselors Assn. (Counselor of Yr. award 1987), Parisppany-Troy Hills Edn. Assn., N.J. Fgn. Lang. Tchrs. Assn. (pres. 1977-79, career edn. cons., Award Outstanding Contbn. 1981), Morris County Pers. and Guidance Assn. (pres. 1978-79), AAUW (pres. Livingston br. 1987, continuing edn. scholar 1980), Profl. Counselors Morris County (exec. bd.), Cosmopolitan Club Montclair (trustee 1990-91), Phi Delta Kappa (hon. life, Svc. Key 1986), Kappa Delta Pi. Roman Catholic. Home: 7 Clover Ln Livingston NJ 07039

CIRICLIO, SUSAN E., college administrator, photography educator; b. N.Y.C., Nov. 27, 1946; d. Anthony Donald and Janice Ruth (Earl) C. AA with highest distinction, Phoenix Coll., 1969; BFA with distinction, Calif. Coll. Arts & Crafts, Oakland, 1971; MFA, Mills Coll., 1974. Instr. phtography Chabot Coll., Hayward, Calif., 1973-86, San Francisco Art Inst., 1979-85; prof. photography Calif. Coll. Arts & Crafts, 1977—, interim v.p. acad. affairs, 1986-87, v.p. acad. affairs, 1989—; bd. dirs. San Francisco Camerawork Gallery, 1983-86. One-woman shows include U. Nev., 1978, U. Calif., Davis, 1980, U. Hawaii, 1982; exhibited in numerous group shows, 1969—; represented in permanent collections Oakland Mus., San Francisco Mus. Modern Art, Mills. Coll. Jury numerous fine art activities, 1978—. Nat. Endowment for Arts Fellow, 1979. Mem. Soc. Photog. Educators, San Francisco Mus. Modern Art, Coll. Art Assn. Office: Calif Coll Arts & Crafts 5212 Broadway Oakland CA 94618

CIRILLO, VIVIAN LINDA, probation officer; b. Bronx, Sept. 10, 1950; d. Jerome Nathaniel and Renee Marilyn (Cohan) Kaufman; m. Victor Cirillo, Sept. 6, 1970 (div. 1983); children: Robert, Gail. BS, SUNY, Stony Brook, 1971; MS, L.I.U., 1986. Sr. social worker D.C. ARC, Poughkeepsie, N.Y., 1986-87; probation officer D.C. Dept. Probation, Poughkeepsie, 1987—. Regents scholar, 1967. Mem. Am. Assn. Counseling & Devel., Pub. Offenders Counseling Assn.

CIRLOT, KAY CHESHIRE, real estate executive; b. Opelika, Ala., July 27, 1940; d. Howard Clarence Cheshire and Ivy Cliff (Baxley) Weldon; m. R. Patrick Cobb, Feb. 2, 1960 (div. July 1972); m. Neal W. Cirlot Jr., Aug. 4, 1976 (div. Oct. 1979). BS in Secondary Edn., Auburn (Ala.) U., 1962; MA, So. Meth. U., Dallas, 1983; mgmt. cert., U. Ga., 1985; cert., Am. Sch. Real Estate, Montgomery, Ala., 1987. Child welfare worker State of Fla., Pensacola, 1963-68; customer service rep. Gulf Oil Corp., Atlanta, 1969-77; customer service mgr. Arkla Industries, Evansville, Ind., 1977-78; collection mgr. Southland Corp., Dallas, 1979-81; br. mgr. Comdata Inc., Houston, 1981-83; dir. properties Floribec, Internat., Montgomery, 1984-86; fin. analyst Grimmer Realty Co., Inc., Birmingham, Ala., 1987-88; dir. property mgmt. shopping ctr. div. Boothby/Engel Realty, Birmingham, 1989—. Organizer Mother's March on Birth Defects, Snellville, Ga., 1968. Mem. Internat. Coun. Shopping Ctrs. Home: 3119 Melissa Way Birmingham AL 35243

CIRUTI, JOAN ESTELLE, educator; b. Ponchatouia, La., Aug. 8, 1930; d. Joseph Aloysius and Olga (Jordan) C. B.A., Southeastern La. Coll., 1950; M.A., U. Okla, 1954; Ph.D., Tulane U., 1959. Instr. modern langs U. Okla., Norman, 1957-59; asst. prof. U. Okla, Norman, 1959-63; research asst. U.S. Office Edn., Washington, 1959-60; asst. prof. Spanish Mt. Holyoke Coll., South Hadley, Mass., 1963-66; assoc. prof. Mt Holyoke Coll., South Hadley, Mass., 1966-71; chmn. dept. Spanish Mt. Holyoke Coll., South Hadley, Mass., 1965-71; prof. Mt. Holyoke Coll., South Hadley, Mass., 1971-77; Helen Day Gould prof. Spanish Mt. Holyoke Coll., South Hadley, Mass., 1977—, dean studies, 1971-74, chmn. dept, Spanish and Italian, 1975-81, 85-86; cons. Ednl. Testing Service, 1968-79. Co-author: Modern Spanish, 2d edit., 1966, Continuing Spanish, 1967; contbg. editor, Handbook of Latin-American Studies, vol. 28, 1966, Handbook of Latin-American Studies vol. 30, 1968, Handbook of Latin-American Studies, vol. 32, 1970. Named Disting. Alumnus Southeastern La. Coll., 1973. Mem. Am. Council on Teaching Fgn. Langs., MLA (nomination adv. com. 1962-64, nominating com. 1979-80, acad. freedom com. 1980-83), Latin Am. Studies Assn. (mem. steering com. consortium Latin Am. studies programs 1969-72, com. on women 1973-74, nominating com. 1975), New Eng. Council Latin Am. Studies, Am. Assn. Tchrs. Spanish and Portuguese, AAUW. Home: 21 Jewett Ln South Hadley MA 01075 Office: Mt Holyoke Coll Dept Spanish & Italian South Hadley MA 01075

CISEK, CAROL MARIE, image and color consultant, writer; b. Syracuse, N.Y., Aug. 26, 1926; d. Fred Philip and Clara Elizabeth (Raupach) Kies; m. Richard M. Cisek, Sept. 15, 1956 (div. 1972); children—Michael, Melanie, Maria. B.A., Syracuse U., 1948; grad. Med. Technician, Buffalo Gen. Hosp., 1950. Cert. med. technician, Color Me Beautiful cons. Pub. relations dir. Minn. Dance Theatre, Mpls., 1968-71, Sci. Mus. Minn., St. Paul, 1975-76, Employers Overload, Mpls., 1977; ops. mgr. Gem Model and Talent Agy., Mpls., 1979-80; cons., owner Color Me Beautiful, Mpls., 1981—; dir. Wendy Ward program, Montgomery Ward Stores, 1973-75; contbr. fashion and beauty columns publs. Mpls., St. Paul. Editor (newsletter) Image Bazaar. Bd. dirs. Minn. Dance Theatre, 1969-79; founder, bd. mem. Minn. Montessori Found. and Edina Montessori Sch., 1963-71; with pub. relations Democratic Farm Labor Feminist Caucus, Mpls., 1978-80. Mem. Fashion Group, Women in Communications (sec. Mpls. 1978-80), Minn. Press Club. Roman Catholic. Home and Office: Carol Cisek Color 3609 Rhode Island Ave S Minneapolis MN 55426

CISLER, CYNTHIA MARIE, commercial real estate broker; b. Green Bay, Wis., Nov. 3, 1962; d. Alvin George and Rosalyn Elenore (Herlick) C. BA in Psychology/Mgmt., U. Wis., Whitewater, 1985. Cert. nat. task force in leadership & supervisory skills for women. Corp. recruiter Cap Gemini Am., Vienna, Va., 1985-89; comml. real estate broker Speros and Kampa Co., McLean, Va., 1989—. Contbr. computer profl. job guide for the Washington area. Mem. NAFE, Renew Group, Facilities Mgrs. Assn., Arlington and Fairfax Counties C. of C., Internat. Facilities Mgmt. Assn. Roman Catholic. Home: The Carlton 4600 Four Mile Run Dr Unit 416 Arlington VA 22204 Office: Speros & Kampa Co 8180 Greensboro Dr Ste 940 McLean VA 22102

CISLER, THERESA ANN, osteopath; b. Tucson, Dec. 20, 1951; d. William George and Lucille (Seeber) C.; m. Dennis Keith Luttrell, May 1, 1954; 1 child, Daniel Collin. BS in Nursing, U. Ariz., 1974; DO, Kirksville Coll. Osteopathy, 1983. Operating room technician St. Joseph's Hosp., Tucson, 1973-74, operating room nurse, 1974-78, operating room inservice coordinator, 1978-79; intern Tucson Gen. Hosp., 1983-84; family practice and manipulation Assoc. Jane J. Beregi, D.O., Tucson, 1984-87; practice medicine specializing in osteo. manipulation Tucson, 1987—; active med. staff Tucson Gen. Hosp., 1984—, med. records chmn., 1985-87; part time med. staff Westcenter Drug & Rehab., Tucson, 1984-88; vol. med. staff St. Elizabeth Hugary Clinic, 1984-87; mem. substance abuse com. Westcenter - Tucson Gen. Hosp., 1986-88, osteo. concepts com., 1986—, osteo. manipulative cons., 1986—. Eucharistic minister St. Pius X Ch., Tucson, 1984-86, eucharistic minister coordinator, 1987—. Mem. Am. Osteo. Assn., Am. Acad. Osteopathy, Ariz. Osteo. Med. Assn. (mem. at large ho. of dels. 1985—), Kirksville Coll. Osteopathy-Century Club, Cranial Acad., Resources for Women, Am. Bus. Women's Assn. Roman Catholic. Office: 4002 E Grant Rd Ste D Tucson AZ 85712

CISMARU, PAT K., municipal official; b. N.Y.C., Sept. 27, 1933; children: Jay, David. BBA, CCNY, 1958; MEd, CUNY, 1960; MS, Tex. Tech U., 1985, PhD. Cert. social worker, Tex., CEMR, OAMT mgmt. Acad. dir. Park Coll., Lubbock, Tex.; owner Masonry Constrn. Co., Lubbock; owner, dir. respite unit LRMHMR Ctr., Lubbock; programs adminstr. RRIP Lubbock Housing Authority; notary public. Mem. NAFE, AARP, LWV, Goodwill Industries. Home: 5108 79th Dr Lubbock TX 79424 Office: 2812 Weber Dr Lubbock TX 79404

CISNEY, MARCELLA, theater director, administrator; b. Altoona, Pa.; d. Moses J. and Anne (Epstein) Abels; m. Robert C. Schnitzer, June 7, 1953. Student Am. Acad. Dramatic Arts, Bennington Sch. Arts, Neighborhood Playhouse Dirs. Seminar, NYU Radio-TV Workshop. Featured on Broadway in Girls in Uniform, Lady Precious Stream; dir. Off-Broadway and summer theatres; exec. dir. Jacksonville Civic Theatre (Fla.), 1942-45; producer-dir. Pasadena Playhouse (Calif.), 1946-48, Laguna Playhouse (Calif.), Las Palmas Theatre, Hollywood, 1948-49; head coach Warner Bros. Studio, 1948; network dir. for CBS-TV, N.Y., 1950-54; lectr. advanced theatre direction Columbia, 1955; adminstr. Rockefeller Found. project for Hungarian refugee artists, 1956; adminstr., assoc. coordinator U.S. State Dept. Am. Performing Arts Programs, Brussels World's Fair, 1957-58; dir. N.Y.C. Opera, 1957-58; dir. all-star Skin of Our Teeth for Theatre Guild-State Dept. world tour, Latin Am. tour of Glass Menagerie, 1960-61; co-founder, artistic dir. Profl. Theatre Program, U. Mich., Ann Arbor, 1961-73; dir. premieres Child Buyer, 1963, An Evening's Frost, 1964, Wedding Band, 1965, Ivory Tower, 1966, Amazing Grace, 1967, The Castle, 1968, The Conjurer, 1969; dir. nat. tour An Evening's Frost, 1966, ACT West Coast premiere, 1968; producer Siamese Connections, 1971, Last Respects, 1972. Theater chmn. Westport-Weston Arts Council, 1980-86; mem. bd. Westport Arts Ctr., producer Plays-in-Progress Series, 1980-89; arts cons. to pres. U. Bridgeport, 1974-83; moderator seminars White Barn Theatre, 1974-80; 1st v.p. Westport Arts Council, 1978-81; hon. bd. dirs. Nat. Theatre Conf. Recipient Bronze medal Israeli Minister of Culture; Gold medal for Brussels Fair Program, Spl. Pres.'s citation U. Mich., 1972; chosen Outstanding Conn. Woman Gov. of Conn., 1987.

CITROLA, ROSEMARY NICOLINA, music educator; b. Bklyn., Aug. 26, 1958; d. Leo R. and Esther A. (Manzullo) C. BS in Fine Arts, SUNY, Stony Brook, 1980; MS in Secondary Edn., Dowling Coll., Oakdale, N.Y., 1985; D in Music Edn., Columbia Pacific U., San Rafael, Calif., 1990. Lic. tchr., N.Y. Music educator R.C. Acad. Music, Ft. Salonga, N.Y., 1980-84; choral dir. San Remo Elem. Sch., Kings Park, N.Y., 1984-85; music dir. St. Philip Neri Elem., Northport, N.Y., 1984-86; music tchr. Island Trees Sch. dist., Levittown, N.Y., 1986-88; regional coord. Am. Intercultural Student Exch., Wantagh, N.Y., 1986-88; program dir. Student Travel Schs., Ridge, N.Y., 1988-89; music educator William Floyd Sch. Dist., Shirley, N.Y., 1988-89; sta. mgr. Transocean Airways JFK Internat. Airport, Jamaica, N.Y., 1989-90; pres. Legacy, Inc., Commack, N.Y., 1990—; counselor, rep. Cultural Acad. Student Exch., Middletown, N.J., 1988—; advisor R.C. Acad. Music, Elmont, N.Y., 1986—, Island Trees Majorettes, Levittown, 1986-88; festival conductor Diocese Rockville Ctr. Band, Huntington, N.Y., 1985; music dir. Children's Theatre, 1989. Active The Statue of Liberty-Ellis Island Found. N.Y., 1987—. AISE grantee, 1988; recipient scholarship L.I. Orff Schulwerk Assn., 1985. Mem. Am. Orff-Schulwerk Assn., Music Educators Nat. Conf., Suffolk County Music Educators Assn., Suffolk Music Guild, Dowling Coll. Alumni Assn., Stony Brook U. Alumni Assn. Democrat. Roman Catholic. Home: 31 Terry Ln Commack NY 11725 Office: 123 Elzey Ave Elmont NY 11003

CITRON, BEATRICE SALLY, law librarian, library director, educator; b. Phila., May 19, 1929; d. Morris Meyer and Frances (Teplitsky) Levinson; m. Joel P. Citron, Aug. 7, 1955 (dec. Sept. 1977); children: Deborah Ann, Victor Ephraim. BA in Econs. with honors, U. Pa., 1950; MLS, Our Lady of the Lake U., 1978; JD, U. Tex., 1984. Bar: Tex. 1985; cert. secondary level tchr., Tex. Claims examiner Social Security Adminstrn., Pa., Fla. and N.C., 1951-59; head libr. St. Mary's Hall, San Antonio, 1979-80; media, reference and rare book libr., asst. prof. St. Mary's U. Law Libr., San Antonio, 1984-89; asst. dir., head pub. svcs. St. Thomas U. Law Libr., Miami, Fla., 1989—. Mem. ABA, Am. Assn. Law Librs. (pbuls. com. 1987-88), S.W.Assn. Law Librs. (continuing edn. com. 1986-88, fin. com. 1988-89, interlibr. coop. com. 1988-89, chmn. local arrangements 1987-88), S.E. Assn. Law Librs., South Fla. Assn. Law Librs. Office: St Thomas U Law Libr 16400 NW 32d Ave Miami FL 33054

CITRON, ELIZABETH JEAN, software development specialist; b. Haverhill, Mass., Nov. 19, 1961; d. Ted and Maris C. BS in Biology, Fitchburg State Coll., 1983. Quality assurance tech Polymer Technology, Wilmington, Mass., 1983-84; research asst. Human Nutrition Research Ctr., Boston, Mass., 1984-86; Millipore Corp., Milford, Mass., 1986—. Home: 35 Surrey Dr North Andover MA 01845

CIUFFO, CYNTHIA LOUISE (CINDI CIUFFO), nursing sales consultant; b. Kewanee, Ill., Aug. 11, 1946; d. Spencer Eugene and Hazel Elizabeth (Glass) Parker; m. Lawrence Gaspare Ciuffo, July 25, 1970; children: Thomas Lawrence, Spencer Tracy. RN, Meth. Hosp. Sch. Nursing, Peoria, Ill., 1967. Lic. nurse, Calif., Ill. Oper. rm. staff nurse Peoria Meth. Hosp., 1967-69; sr. staff nurse U. Calif. San Diego Hosp., 1969-72; oper. rm. staff nurse Claremont Community Hosp., San Diego, 1972-74, Palomar Meml. Hosp., Escondido, Calif., 1974-77; oper. rm. head nurse Pomerado Hosp., Poway, Calif., 1977-81; oper. rm. supr. Rancho Bernardo Cataract Outpatient Ctr., San Diego, 1982-83; dir., cons. Cinlar-A.S.C. Enterprises, Poway, 1983-86; pres. sales and cons. Cinlar, Ltd., Poway, 1986—; cons., lectr. in field; conductor workshops, seminars in field; chmn. bd. The Gift Seminars, San Diego, 1986-88, Larco Distbrs., San Diego, 1985-88. Contbr. articles to profl. jours.; mem. editorial bd. Perioperative Nursing Quar., 1984-87. Vice chmn. The Hospice Found., San Diego, 1986-88; legis. liaison Assemblyman Bill Bradley, 1985—. Recipient Cert. of Recognition Calif. Legis. Assembly, 1986, Joy Freeman award, 1987; named Outstanding Alumnus, Meth. Hosp. Sch. Nursing, 1987. Mem. Calif. Nurses Assn. (region 2 chpt. pres. 1985-86, 2d v.p. 1986-88, mem. govt. rels. com.), Assn. Operating Room Nurses (pres. 1975-76, parliamentarian 1977—), Nat. Assn. Parliamentarians (v.p. 1983-84). Republican. Methodist. Club: Le Tip Internat. Home: 15010 Pomerado Rd Poway CA 92064

CIULLO, ROSEMARY, psychologist; b. Chgo.. BA, U. Ill., Chgo., 1974; MA, Gov.'s State U., University Park, Ill., 1977; PhD, F.I.P.P., 1986. Psychologist Chgo. Read Mental Health Ctr. Mem. Am. Psychol. Assn., Ill. Psychol. Assn.

CLACK, DOUGLAS MAE, educator, public speaker, lecturer; b. San Antonio, July 10, 1943; d. Douglas Campbell and Ida Mae (Norwood) King; m. Charles Leonard Clack, Aug. 6, 1966 (div. 1973); 1 son, Charles Leonard, Jr. B.A., U. Tex.-San Antonio, 1977; MPIA, St. Mary's U., San Antonio, 1983. Engring. records clk. Southwestern Bell, San Antonio and Houston, 1970-72; clk., sec. Frost Bank, San Antonio, 1972-75; adminstr. San Antonio Independent Sch. Dist., 1977-84; owner, v.p. Diverse Data Systems, Inc., San Antonio, 1984-86 ; cons. various profl. and ednl. agencies, 1980—; instr. Tex. Edn. Agy., Austin, 1980—, Alamo Community Coll. Dist., 1984—; speaker various Tex. sch. dists., nursing orgns., chs., 1980—; trainer Federally Employed Women 21st Nat. Tng. Program, 1990; trustee, tchr. Sunday Sch. Damasus Missionary Bapt. Ch.; task force leader Leadership Group 2-WCC, 1989; presenter workshops, seminars local state orgns.; exec. bd. dirs. Leadership San Antonio, 1987-90, steering com., 1988-89. Bd. dirs. vol. svcs. San Antonio State Chest Hosp.; campaign coord. United Way, 1987, 89; instr. adult continuing edn. courses NE Ind. Sch. Dist., Alamo Community Coll. Dist. Contbr. articles to profl. jours. Sec. PTA, 1975-77, v.p., 1977-78; vol. ARC, 1978, Am. Cancer Soc., 1979; mem. adv. bd. Ella Austin Community Clinic, sec., 1981-84; vol. youth program New Mt. Pleasant Bapt. Ch.; mem. The Women's Coalition; mem. steering com. Women's Fair, 1985. Mem. AAUW (social, awards, scholarship, entertainment coms.), NAACP (youth advisor, exec. bd.), Bus. and Profl. Women (corr. sec. 1983-85), LWV (local chair fin. com.), U. Tex. Alumni Assn., San Antonio Women's C. of C. (1st v.p., chartered), Alamo City C. of C., Bexar County Women's Ctr. Mentor's Program, St. Mary's U. Alumni Assn., Phillis Wheatley Alumni Assn. (charter mem., treas. 1984-85), Gamma Phi Lambda. Democrat. Club: Rising Star Internat. Tng. in Communications (charter mem.), Alamo Ski of San Antonio (v.p.), Dovia. Avocations: swimming; crafts; bicycling; exercising; reading; travel.

CLAGETT, LESLIE PLUMMER, editor; b. Providence, Apr. 30, 1956; d. Robert Eugene and Peg (Hassett) Plummer; m. John Stephen Clagett, June 10, 1982. BA in English, Denison U., 1978. Mng. editor N.Y. Arts Jour., N.Y.C., 1978-81, Arts & Architecture, L.A., 1981-85; assoc. editor architecture Home mag., L.A., 1985—. Mem. Archtl. League, Nat. Trust for Hist. Preservation. Office: Home Mag 5900 Wilshire 15th Fl Los Angeles CA 90036

CLAIBORNE, LIZ (ELISABETH CLAIBORNE ORTENBERG), fashion designer; b. Brussels, Mar. 31, 1929; came to U.S., 1934; d. Omer Villere and Louise Carol (Fenner) C.; m. Arthur Ortenberg, July 5, 1954; 1 son by previous marriage, Alexander G. Schultz. Student, Art Sch., Brussels, 1948-49, Academie, Nice, France, 1950. Asst. Tina Lesser, N.Y.C., 1951-52, Omar Khayam, Ben Reig, Inc., N.Y.C., 1953; designer Juniorite, N.Y.C., 1954-60, Dan Keller, N.Y.C., 1960-76, Youth Guild Inc., N.Y.C., 1976-89; designer, pres., chmn. Liz Claiborne Inc., N.Y.C., 1985—, pres., 1976-89, chmn., chief oper. officer, until 1989; chmn. Liz Claiborne Cosmetics, 1985—; guest lectr. Fashion Inst. Tech., Parsons Sch. Design; bd. dirs. Coun. of Am. Fashion Designers, Fire Island Lighthouse Restoration Com. Recipient Designer of Yr. award Palciode Hierro, Mexico City, 1976, Designer of Yr. award Dayton Co., Mpls., 1978, Ann. Disting. in Design award Marshall Field's 1985, One Co. Makes a Difference award Fashion Inst. Tech., 1985, award Coun. of Fashion Designers, 1986. Mem. Fashion Group. Roman Catholic. Office: Claiborne Inc 1441 Broadway New York NY 10018

CLAING, KAREN SCHAEFER, sales executive; b. Hartford, Conn., Aug. 15, 1952; d. William John and Fern Eloise (Sharrow) Schaefer; m. Richard George Claing, Mar. 18, 1972; 1 child, Caroline Marie. Student, Manchester Community Coll., 1973-75, Cen. Conn. Community Coll., 1985—. Clk. credit dept. Sears Roebuck, Manchester, Conn., 1969-71; clk. Met. Life Ins., Manchester, 1971-75, sr. sales asst., 1975-78; exec. sec. John A. Bailey Assocs., Inc., East Hartford, Conn., 1978-79; sales coord. John A. Bailey Assocs., Inc., East Hartford, 1979-82, asst. sales mgr., 1982-85, mgr. sales, 1985-88, gen. mgr., 1988—. Coach Young Am. Bowling Alliance, East Hartford, 1982-85; mem. Dem. com. Stephen Penny for Mayor, Manchester, 1979-80, 84; advisor assembly #15 Rainbow for Girls Lodge, 1985-87, 88-91. Mem. Women in Communications. Lodge: Order Eastern Star (worthy matron 1980-81). Home: 20 Joan Circle Manchester CT 06040

CLAIR, CAROLYN GREEN, civic worker; b. Boston, Sept. 18, 1909; d. James Maddocks and Marietta Cecelia (Foeley) Green; m. Miles Nelson Clair, June 16, 1928 (div. Jan. 1981); children: Cynthia York Clair Norkin, Valerie DeLuce Clair Stelling, Ardith Monroe Clair Houghton. BS, Boston U., 1930, postgrad., 1933. Clk. of corp., dir. Thompson & Lichtner Co., Inc., 1951-77; treas. MNCC, Inc., 1977—; translator Am. Concrete Inst., Chgo., 1930-37. Regent Mass. Soc. DAR, 1933-35, page, 1932-36; pres. Mass. Soc. Children Am. Revolution, 1936-38, historian, 1937-39; dir., clk. The Thompson & Lichtner Co., Inc., 1951-78; v.p. Mass. chpt. Daus. Colonial Wars, 1969-71; active Salvation Army Aux., 1970-86; assoc. Assn. Country Women World, 1968—, lectr., 1972—, alt. to UN, 1974-80, del. to Conf. U.S. Norway, Kenya, Australia and U.N., 1974-80; bd. dirs., mem. svc. league Boston Hosp. Women, 1966-76, officer, 1969-76; bd. overseers, 1974-82 , chmn. patient care adv. com., 1977—; pres. New Eng. Farm & Garden Assn., 1968-71, chmn. fellowship Woods Hole Oceanographic Instn.; mem. Cataument Civic Assn., Bourne Preservation Open Spaces; assoc. Woods Hole Oceanographic Instn.; trustee Brigham & Women's Hosp. Boston, 1982-87, mem. pathology com.; mem. Women's Rep. Club of N.Y.C., English-Speaking Union; Friend of Libraries of Boston U.; bd. dirs. Boston Morning Musicales, Tufts U., 1966-80; mem. council Boston Symphony Orch., 1969-88; pres. Women's Nat. Farm Assn., 1972-74, chmn. adv. bd., 1974-76; mem. corp. Affiliated Hosps. Ctr., Boston, 1975-76; mem. adv. bd.

Nat. Arboretum, Washington, 1974-78; exec. bd. Country Women's Council, 1972-74; v.p. Mass. Hort. Soc., 1970-79; lectr. environ. concerns. Recipient award Brit. War Relief, 1945. Mem. New Eng. Hist. Soc. (life), Mass. Hist. Soc., Pan Am. Soc., Internat. Platform Assn., People to People (translator S.Am.), Boston Mus. Fine Arts, Internat. Womens Ednl. and Indsl. Union, Assn. Country Women of World (life, council mem.), Audubon Soc., Nat. Wildlife Fedn., Nat. Trust Historic Preservation, Salt Pond Bird Sanctuarires Bourne Conservation Trust, Bostonian Soc., Arnold Arboretum (mem. adv. bd. 1972-78), Buzzards Yacht Club. Republican. Episcopalian. Home: Clair de Loon Box 63 Cataumet MA 02534 also: North Hill 865 Central Ave Apt F401 Needham MA 02192

CLAMAR, APHRODITE J., psychologist; b. Hartford, Conn., Sept. 26, 1933; d. James John and Georgia (Panas) Clamar; m. Richard Cohen, June 24, 1973. BA, CCNY, 1953; MA, Columbia U., 1955; PhD, NYU, 1978. Mgmt. cons., psychologist Milla Alihan Assocs., N.Y.C., 1957-62; rsch. psychologist coord. Inst. Devel. Studies N.Y. Med. Coll., N.Y.C., 1964; intern psychologist Bellevue Psychiat. Hosp., N.Y.C., 1964-66; assoc. prof. Fashion Inst. Tech., N.Y.C., 1966-69; supervising psychologist Lifeline Ctr. Child Devel., N.Y.C., 1966-67; chief psychologist I Spy Health Program Beth Israel Med. Ctr., N.Y.C., 1967-70; dir. community-sch. mental health programs Soundview Community Svcs., Albert Einstein Coll. Medicine Yeshiva U., N.Y.C., 1970-73; dir. treatment program court-related children, dept. child psychiatry Harlem Hosp.; mem. faculty dept. psychiatry Coll. Physicians and Surgeons Columbia U., N.Y.C., 1973-76; pvt. practice psychotherapy N.Y.C., 1976—; cons. to pub. health and mental health agys., N.Y.C., 1976—; mem. faculty Lenox Hill Hosp. Psychoanalytic and Psychotherapy Tng. Program, 1982-88. Author: (with Budd Hopkins) Missing Time, 1981; contbr. articles to profl. jours. Fellow AAAS; mem. Soc. Clin. and Exptl. Hypnosis, Am. Psychol. Assn., Soc. for Psychoanalytic Psychotherapy. Democrat. Greek Orthodox. Home: 162 E 80th St New York NY 10021 Office: 30 E 60th St New York NY 10022

CLAMON, HARLEYNE DIANNE, social service superivsor; b. Camden, Tex., Feb. 12, 1940; d. Harley and Ada Virginia (Handley) C. BA, Sam Houston U., 1961. Cert. social worker, Tex. Tchr. Big Sandy Ind. Sch., Dallardsville, Tex., 1961-62; social worker Tex. Dept. of Human Svcs., Tex. City, 1962-75; social service supr. Tex. Dept. of Human Svcs., Galveston, 1975-79, Tex. City, 1979-80, Livingston, 1980—. Mem. adv. com. Mental Health, Mental Retardation, Livingston, Tex., 1980-87; vol. Polk County Meml. Hosp., 1982-89; adult ladies Sunday sch. tchr. Leggett Bapt. Ch., 1984—. Mem. AAUW (pres. Livingston, Tex. 1984-86), DAR (Indian chmn. 1984—), Bus. and Profl. Women (pres. Livingston 1983-85, Woman of Year 1982-3), Am. Pub. Welfare Assn., Tex. Pub. Employees Assn. (bd. dirs. 1970-75). Democrat. Baptist. Home: 616 W Calhoun Livingston TX 77351 Office: Tex Dept Human Svcs 1102 Holhausen Ste A Livingston TX 77351

CLAMPITT, AMY KATHLEEN, writer, editor; b. New Providence, Iowa, June 15, 1920; d. Roy Justin and Lutie Pauline (Felt) C. B.A. with honors in English, Grinnell Coll., 1941, D.H.L., 1984. Sec., writer Oxford Univ. Press, N.Y.C., 1943-51; reference librarian Nat. Audubon Soc., N.Y.C., 1952-59; free-lance writer, N.Y.C., 1960-77; editor E.P. Dutton, N.Y.C., 1977-82; writer-in-residence Coll. William & Mary, Williamsburg, Va., 1984-85; vis. writer Amherst Coll., 1986-87. Author: (poetry) The Kingfisher, 1983, (poetry) What the Light Was Like, 1985, (poetry) Archaic Figure, 1987, Westward, 1990. Guggenheim fellow, 1982-83; recipient Lit. award Am. Acad. Arts and Letters, 1984; fellow Acad. Am. Poets, 1984; mem. PEN, Authors Guild, Am. Acad. Inst. Arts and Letters. Democrat.

CLAMPITT, MARY O'BRIANT, government official; b. Connehatti, Miss., Feb. 18, 1931; d. Theron Russell and Ola Belle (Thompson) O'Briant; m. William Henry Clampitt, May 7, 1955; children: Russell, Henry, Amy, James. BS, U. Md., 1978, MA, 1982. Editor Chief State Sch. Officers, NEA, Washington, 1976-77; editor NAS, Washington, 1977-78; owner Clampitt Editorial Assocs., Chevy Chase, Md., 1970—; adminstrv. specialist White House Conf. on Aging, Washington, 1980-82; program analyst Office Insp. Gen., Washington, 1982-84; mgmt. analyst Food Safety Inspection Service, Washington, 1984—; mgr. Fed. women's program Food Safety Inspection Service, 1984—; bd. dirs. Am. Fed. Credit Union, 1985—. Bd. dirs. USDA Childcare Found., 1990—; mem. bd. reps. Greentree Home for Children, 1986—; mem. steering com. Forums on Aging, 1987; mem. adv. com. Com. for Ctr. Planning, 1987—. Mem. Federally Employed Women, Interagy. Fed. Women's Program Mgrs., Internat. Platform Assn., Phi Kappa Phi. Republican. Baptist. Clubs: Woman's Action Taskforce (pres.), Bus. and Profl. Women's. Home: 7114 Edgevale St Chevy Chase MD 20815 Office: Food Safety Inspection Svc 14th and Independence Ave Washington DC 20250

CLANCEY, JENNIFER, data processing executive; b. Bethpage, N.Y., July 3, 1958; d. Daniel David and Rita Kathleen (Corcoran) C. Clerical ADP, Melville, N.Y., 1979-81; payroll support ADP, Melville, 1981-83, supr., 1983-86; supr. ADP, Tampa, Fla., 1986-88; regional trainer ADP, Tampa, 1988—. Bd. dirs. Condo Assn., Tampa; vol. for the homeless; tchr. Sunday Sch. Office: Automatic Data Processing 4900 Lemon St Tampa FL 33609

CLANCY, ANITA DOMIGAN, interior designer; b. Houston, Tex., June 26, 1931; d. Horace Wynkoop Domigan and Anita (Vaughan) Kerr; m. Gerald A. Donahue, May 9, 1953 (div. Feb. 1977); children: Anita Vaughan, Gerald Andrew, Jr.; m. William Paul Clancy, Dec. 26, 1978. Student, Columbus Coll. Art & Design, 1947-50, Ohio State U., 1949-53, Scottsdale Community Coll., 1986. Designer Walter Morris Interiors, Columbus, Ohio, 1973-74; buyer Mayfair Interiors, Albany, N.Y., 1974-75; designer Myers Furniture Co., Hyannis, Mass., 1976-80, Anita Clancy Designs, Dennis, Mass., 1980-83, Tasteful Touch, Hyannis, 1983-84, Barrows Furniture, Phoenix, 1984—; v.p., cons. MUR Designs & Photography, Phoenix, 1984—. Columnist Yarmouth Register, 1982-83. Docent Columbus Mus. Art, 1960-70, bd. dirs. 1968-70; mem. women's bd. Columbus Symphony Orch., 1967-69, Phoenix Art Mus., 1984—; mem. Scottsdale (Ariz.) Symphony, 1984—; docent Scottsdale Ctr. Arts, 1984-86. Recipient MAME award for best model home Ariz. Homebuilders Assn., 1987, Most Popular Room award Heard Mus. Showhouse, 1987; named Outstanding Woman of Yr. Columbus Citizen-Jour., 1968. Mem. Am. Soc. Interior Designers (chpt. bd. 1987-89, Svc. award 1988, Merit award 1989), Colonial Dames of XVII Century, Delta Delta Delta Alumnae. Republican. Roman Catholic. Office: Barrows Furniture Co 2301 E Camelback Rd Phoenix AZ 85016

CLANCY, COLLEEN MARIE, university official; b. Chgo., Aug. 23, 1963; d. Robert George and Carol Ann (Haegele) C. BA, DePaul U., 1989. Accounts receivable and inventory control clk. Enesco Imports, Elk Grove, Ill., 1981-83; clk.-typist United Cofee Svc., Elk Grove, 1983-84; payroll clk. Stouffer Oak Brook (Ill.) Hotel, 1986-89; scholarship counselor DePaul U., Chgo., 1989-90, adminstrv. asst., 1986-89; asst. to dir. Zenith Data Systems, Chgo., 1990—. Mem. Internat. Thespian Soc., Ambs. Club. Republican. Roman Catholic. Home: 1339 S Elmwood Ave Berwyn IL 60402

CLANCY, JOAN BENNETT, community health nurse; b. Tunkhannock, Pa., Nov. 19, 1935; d. Julius George and Amilya Nell (Rogers) Bennett; children: Thomas Aquinas, Caroline Julie, Christopher. BS in Nursing, Cath. U. Am., 1957; cert., Barnes Mus. Sch. Art, 1967. RN. Staff nurse NINDB, Bethesda, Md.; sr. nurse Anne Arundal County, State of Md., Annapolis; PRN staff nurse Children's Hosp. Nat. Med. Ctr., Washington; CHN III health ctr. mgr. Anne Arundel County HD, State of Md., Annapolis, 1980—. Bd. dirs., chair nursing and health svcs., mem. health adv. bd. ARC; bd. dirs. Annapolis Chorale, 1987—. Recipient Exceptional Vol. Svc. award ARC; invitational inclusion N.Y. Art Rev. Home: 519 Duckett Ave Fairhaven MD 20754

CLANCY, MARY, member Canadian Parliament; b. Halifax, N.S., Can., Jan. 13, 1948; d. Douglas and Catherine (Casey) C. BA with honors, Mt. St. Vincent U., Halifax, 1970; LLB, Dalhousie U., Halifax, 1974; LLM, U. London. Lawyer, broadcaster, univ. lectr., columnist; mem. Parliament, Ottawa, Ont., Can., 1988—. Bd. govs. Dalhousie U.; bd. govs. Mt. St. Vincent U., pres. nat. bd. alumni; v.p. Atlantic region Nat. Women's Liberal Commn.; pres. St. Joseph's Children's Ctr.; bd. dirs. YWCA, Atlantic Ballet Co., Home of Guardian Angel, Seaweed Theatre. Mem. N.S. Barristers Soc. Liberal. Roman Catholic. Home: 6064 Coburg Rd, Halifax, NS Canada B3H 1Z2 Office: House of Commons, Parliament Bldgs, Ottawa, ON Canada K1A 0A6 also: West End Mall, 6960 Mumford Rd Ste 103-A, Halifax, NS Canada B3L 2H6

CLAPP, MARY ALICE, nurse, educator; b. Beach Haven, N.J., Dec. 1, 1941; d. L. Russell and Alice King (Muir) C. BS in Nursing, Tex. Christian U., 1963. Commd. capt. USAFR, 1969, advanced through grades to col., 1989; staff nurse, head nurse Harris Hosp., Ft. Worth, 1967-74; head nurse plastic surgery operating room Parkland Meml. Hosp., Dallas, 1974-88, operating room nurse educator, 1988—. Outreach coord., mem. vestry St. Christopher's Episcopal Ch., Dallas, 1988-89. Mem. Assn. Oper. Rm. Nurses, Res. Officers Assn. Home: 13518 Waterfall Way Dallas TX 75240 Office: Parkland Meml Hosp 5201 Harry Hines Blvd Dallas TX 75235

CLAPP, MARY STUART, federal agency administrator; b. East Orange, N.J., Oct. 1, 1941; d. William Robinson and Cecil Valentine (Hodgman) C. BA, Drew U., 1963. Import specialist U.S. Customs Svc., N.Y.C., 1963-72; ops. officer U.S. Customs Svc., Washington, 1972-78, supr., 1978-79; supr. U.S. Dept. Commerce, Washington, 1980—. Vestry clk., St. John's in the Village, N.Y.C., 1968-72; sec., Covington Homes Assn., Fairfax, Va., 1976-79. Mem. Internat. Bluegrass Music Assn. Democrat. Episcopalian.

CLAPPER-COOMER, KATHRYN ACCOLA, real estate company official; b. Alton, Ill., July 14, 1942; d. Carl E. and Geraldine (Hendrickson) Accola; m. Larry R. Clapper, Jan. 20, 1963 (div. 1985); children: David Eric, Laura Kay; m. James C. Coomer, May 19, 1990. BA in Edn., Purdue U., 1964. Lic. real estate broker, Mo., Conn., Ill. Tchr. Mountain View (Calif.) Elem. Sch., 1964-66; saleswoman Carl G. Stifel Real Estate, St. Louis, 1972-75, Westledge Assocs., Simsbury, Conn., 1975-77, Ira E. Berry Real Estate, St. Louis, 1977-78, Re/Max Crossroads, Rolling Meadow, Ill., 1984-87; saleswoman Baird & Warner Real Estate, Palatine, Ill., 1979-84, real estate sales mgr., broker, sales assoc., 1987-88, asst. v.p., 1989—. Mem. Nat. Assn. Real Estate Sales Execs. (charter nat. million dollar roundtable), Northwest Suburban Bd. Realtors (bd. dirs. 1984-87), Alpha Chi Omega (pres. Gamma Chi Gamma alumnae chpt. 1986-88, Chgo. area chpt. pres. 1987-88, Outstanding Alumnae award 1988). Republican. Home: 7 Attleboro on Auburn St Rolling Meadows IL 60008 Office: Baird & Warner Real Estate 295 N Northwest Hwy Palatine IL 60067

CLARK, AGI, advertising agency executive; b. Budapest, Hungary, June 21, 1941; came to U.S., 1957; d. Steven and Olga (Altmann) Solti; m. Zsolt Csalog; 1 child from previous marriage, Oren S. BFA, Pratt Inst., 1962. Art dir. Pritchard Wood & Assoc., N.Y.C., 1966-69; creative supr. N.W. Ayer Advt. Agy., N.Y.C., 1969-72, v.p., creative dir., 1972-73, sr. v.p., 1973-79, exec. creative dir., 1979-87, mng. dir. creative svcs., N.Y. bd. dirs., 1987-88; chief creative officer, chmn. bd. dirs. Lord, Geller, Federico, Einstein Inc., N.Y.C., 1988—; pub. svc. activities cons. Impact on Hunger, 1985-86; created advt. UJA Fed., 1986-88, Nat. Coun. Alcoholism (Grand award Internat. Film & TV Festival, others), 1984-87. Translator: Lajos M., Aged 42 (Zsolt Csalog) 1989. Recipient Silver Bell awards for Work on Nat. Coun. on Alcoholism Advt. Coun., 1981-86; Appreciation award Am. Woman's Econ. Devel. Corp., 1982; Merit award for DeBeers Art Dirs. Club, 1980, The Bahamas Ministry of Tourism, 1982, AT&T, 1987; CEBA award Nat. Coun. on Alcoholism, 1987; Silver Effie for AT&T, 1985, JC Penney, 1986, Bronze Effie JC Penney, 1987; HSMA Internat. Grand award, 1982; Internat. Film and TV Festival Grand award 1987 - 'Say Yes To Your Life', for The Nat. Coun. on Alcoholism, 1st Prize award Retail Advt. Conf., 1988; named one of 100 Best and Brightest Women of 1988 Ad Age and Advt. Women of N.Y., 1988. Democrat. Jewish.

CLARK, ALICIA GARCIA, political party official; b. Vera Cruz, Mex.; came to U.S., 1970; d. Rafael Aully and Maria Luisa (Cobos) Garcia; m. Edward E. Clark, Oct. 20, 1970; 1 child, Edward E. MS in Chem. Engring., Nat. U. Mex., Mexico City, 1951. Chemist Celanese Mexicana, Mexico City, 1951-53, lab. mgr., 1951-53, sales promotion mgr., 1958-65, sales promotion and advt. mgr., 1965-70; nat. chmn. Libertarian Party, Houston, 1981-83, coord. coun. state chairs, 1987-90; pres. San Marino (Calif.) Guild of Huntington Hosps., 1981-82, chmn. Celebrity Series, 1989-90. Pres. Multiple Sclerosis Soc., San Gabriel Valley, Calif., 1977-78, San Marino Woman's Club, 1989-90; bd. dirs. L.A. Opera Guild, 1990—; mem. The Club 100 of L.A. Music Ctr., 1990—. Recipient award La Mujer de Hoy mag., 1969. Mem. Fashion Group (treas. 1969-70), Mex. Advt. Assn. (dir. 1969-70, award 1970), San Marino Woman's Club (ways and means chmn. 1987-88).

CLARK, ANDREA TAYLOR, educational consultant; b. Warrenton, Va., Nov. 5, 1952; d. Andrew Earl and Catherine (Dennis) Taylor. BS, Norfolk State U., 1974, MA, 1983; cert., Old Dominion U. Tchr. Fauquier County Schs., Warrenton; child devel. specialist Norfolk (Va.) Pub. Schs., ednl. diagnostician; ednl. cons. Va. State Dept. Edn., Norfolk. Active Lindenwood Civic League, 1987-89, The Urban League of Hampton Roads. Mem. NEA, NAFE, Va. Edn. Assn., Edn. Assn. Norfolk, Coun. Exceptional Children, Delta Sigma Theta. Baptist. Home: 806 Summit Ave Norfolk VA 23504

CLARK, BETTY JEAN, state legislator; b. Kansas City, Kans., Apr. 18, 1920; d. Raymond Carlisle and Mary Priscilla (Hunt) Walker. Student Ft. Hays State U., 1937-38, U. Utah, 1939-40, U. Pacific, 1942-45, Garrett Evang. Sem., 1948; m. Homer Orville Clark, Sept. 3, 1950; children: Peggy, Mark, Paul. Dir. student program Wesley Found., Ames, Iowa, 1948-51; dir. Christian edn. First United Meth. Ch., Mason City, Iowa, 1963-75; mem. Iowa Gen. Assembly, Des Moines, 1977-90. Recipient appreciation River City Kiwanis, 1976, Girl Scouts U.S.A., 1977, Community Achievement award Mason City YWCA, 1978, Recognition of Svc. award Iowa Conf. United Meth. Women, 1978, appreciation High Twelve, 1978, 82, appreciation Community Mental Health Ctrs., 1979, Achievement in Govt. award Mason City Globe Gazette, 1981, Spl. Svc. award Reye's Syndrome Found., 1981, appreciation Nora Springs Kiwanis, 1983, Gov.'s appreciation of svc. to the Commn. on Children, Youth and Families, 1985, Outstanding Svc. award Child Abuse and Neglect Coun., 1985, Pub. Svc. award Iowa Home Econs. Assn., 1987, appreciation of svc. Adult Basic Edn. Adv. Com., 1988, Pub. Health Dept., 1988, recognition of svc. on child support Iowa Supreme Ct., 1989, recognition of outstanding support Iowa Physician's Asst. Soc., others. Mem. Iowa State Bar Assn. (hon.), Rep. Women's Task Force, Bus. and Profl. Women, Women's Polit. Caucus, LWV, Common Cause, Fedn. Rep. Women, P.E.O. Methodist. Clubs: Ch. Women United, Federated Women's Club, Older Women's League, United Meth. Women. Author: (with Harriet Ann Daffron) Nearer to Thee, 1956; columnist So. County News, Rockford Register, Charles City Press, others.

CLARK, BEVERLY JEAN, lawyer; b. Detroit, May 21, 1939; d. Harry and Evelyn Blanche (Mabin) C. BA, U. Mich., 1961, MA, 1963; JD, Wayne State U., 1972. Bar: Mich. 1973, U.S. Dist. Ct. (ea. dist.) Mich. 1973, U.S. Ct. Appeals (6th cir.) 1973. Pvt. practice Detroit, 1973—; bd. dirs. Mich. Indian Legal Services, Traverse City. Co-founder Mich. Women's Campaign Fund, Detroit. Named Ford Scholar, Ford Motor Co., 1957-61. Mem. Mich. Trial Lawyers Assn. (pres. 1983-84), Women Lawyers Assn. (pres. 1978-79, First in Leadership 1987), Nat. Lawyers Guild (bd. dirs.), Mich. Civil Rights Commn. (commr. 1981—). Democrat. Office: 975 E Jefferson Detroit MI 48207

CLARK, CAROL CANDA, art historian, educator; b. N.Y.C., July 21, 1947; d. Henry G. Canda and Dolores C. Adam; m. Jon D. Clark, May 24, 1969 (div. Apr. 1983); m. Charles Parkhurst, July 1986. B.A. with distinction, U. Mich.-Ann Arbor, 1969, M.A., 1971; Ph.D., Case Western Res. U., Cleve., 1981 . Registrar, U. Mich. Mus. Art, Ann Arbor, 1971-72; instr. Tex. Christian U., Ft. Worth, 1975-77; curator Amon Carter Mus. Ft. Worth, 1977-84; exec. prendergast fellow Williams Coll., Williamstown, Mass., 1984-87, lectr. art history, 1984-87; assoc. prof. fine arts Amherst (Mass.) Coll., 1987—; adj. prof. art history So. Methodist U., 1982-83; adj. curator of Am. Art, Clark Art Inst., Williamstown, Mass., 1984-87. Mem. adv. com. Hist. Deerfield. Author: Thomas Moran's Watercolors, 1980; (catalogue) American Impressionist and Realist Paintings, 1978; co-author Maurice and Charles Prendergast, 1990. Mem. art and architecture adv. panel Tex. Commn. on the Arts, 1981-83. Kress Found. fellow, 1972-75, Collections Com. Berkshire Mus. Office: Amherst Coll Fayerweather Hall Amherst MA 01002

CLARK, CAROL LOIS, women's advocate, state government agency administrator, consumer advocate, consultant; b. Salt Lake City, May 23, 1948; d. Norman W. and Lois Amanda (Colt) C. BA in English cum laude, U. Utah, 1970; MEd in Secondary Edn., 1972, PhD in Cultural Founds. of Edn., 1979; postgrad. Columbia U., summer 1980. Cert. profl. tchr., Utah, Mass. Tchr. Jordan Sch. dist., Sandy, Utah, 1972-78, 81-82; curriculum cons. Brigham Young U., Provo, 1978-79, cons., lectr., 1978—; program specialist Utah System Approach to Individualized Learning, Salt Lake City, 1980-81; consumer edn. specialist Utah Atty. Gen.'s Office, Salt Lake City, 1982-84; free-lance editor, curriculum developer Utah Office Edn., Salt Lake City, 1981-82; free-lance editor, cons. Dian Thomas Enterprises, Provo, 1981; gov.'s adminstrv. asst. for edn. and communication, 1984-87; bd. dirs. Communications and Research Utah State Dept. Community and Econ. Devel., 1987-89, dir. Women's Bus. Devel., 1989-90, Deseret Gymnasium, Salt Lake City, 1982—; mem. Fund for Improvement of Post-Secondary Edn., 1986-89; mem. unproven med. practices com. Utah State Med. Assn., 1983-84; mem. Utah Ins. Consumer Action Com., 1983-84; mem. Utah Records Com., 1983-84; mem. Utah Gov.'s Securities Fraud Task Force, 1984; chmn. Utah Atty. Gen.'s Consumer Adv. Com., 1984; state del. U.S. Consumer Product Safety Commn., 1985-87; mem. Utah Higher Edn. Work group for Integrating Women into Work Force, 1985-89; bd. dirs. Salt Lake City Sch. Vols., 1985-88; state chair Initiative for Understanding, 1987-88; arbitrator N.Y. Stock Exch., 1989—, Am. Arbitration Assn., 1989. Author: A Singular Life, 1974; How to Avoid Getting Ripped Off: Essential But Hard-to-Find Consumer Facts for Women, 1985; co-author: Principles of Learning, 1981; contbr.: Consumer's Resource Handbook, 1986; consumer columnist Deseret News, 1982-84, Standard-Examiner, 1983-84, Golden Age, 1983-84, Cache County Citizen, 1984, Park Record, 1984, Sun Advocate, 1984, Richfield Reaper, 1984, Vernal Express, 1984, Color County Spectrum, 1984, Provo Daily Herald, 1984; contbr. articles, poetry to various publs.; editor: The Relief Society Magazine: A Legacy Remembered, 1914-1970, 1982. Mem. gen. bd. Relief Soc., Ch. of Jesus Christ of Latter-day Saints, Salt Lake City, 1973-84, 90—, state del., 1986, adminstrv. asst. to exec. dir., 1990—; acting chmn. Republican Party Voting Dist., Salt Lake City, 1977, dist. vice chmn., 1984; mem. Utah Women's Legis. Council, 1977-79; mem. nomination com. YWCA, 1990—; nat. del.-at-large Rep. Nat. Conv., 1988; mem. Denver region Ford Consumer Appeals Bd., 1983-84; mem. planning com. Utah Ednl. Seminar, 1985-88. Recipient Tchr. of Yr. award Utah State Hist. Soc., 1975, Ann. Achievement award for best consumer publ. Nat. Assn. Consumer Agy. Adminstrs., 1983, Golden Spike award, 1989; named Outstanding Young Woman from Utah, 1982, Young Woman of Achievement, Nat. Council Women, 1984; Ch. of Jesus Christ of Latter-day Saints Historian's Office fellow, 1976. Mem. Salt Lake C. of C. (bus. in edn. com.), Nat. Futures Assn. (edn. adv. com. 1984-86, arbitrator 1989—), Nat. Assn. Consumer Agy. Adminstrs. (Best Consumer Publ. award 1983, Best Book award 1985), Profl. Rep. Women, Utah Women's Forum (founding mem.), Home Econs. Assn. (bd. dirs. 1985-86), Phi Kappa Phi, Alpha Xi Delta, Lambda Delta Sigma. Office: Relief Soc 76 N Main St Salt Lake City UT 84150

CLARK, CAROLYN ARCHER, technologist, scientist; b. Leon County, Tex., Feb. 16, 1944; d. Ray Brooks and Dena Mae (Green) Archer; m. Frank Ray Clark, Nov. 20, 1960 (div. Oct. 1979); children: Frank Ray, Valerie Lynn, Bruce Layne. BA, Sam Houston State U., 1961; MS, Tex. A&M U., 1973, PhD, 1977. Supr., bookkeeper Rep. Sewing Machine Distbrs., Dallas, 1961-65; door-to-door sales Avon Products, Inc., Bryan, Tex., 1965-72; lectr. Tex. A&M U., College Station, Tex., 1977, rsch. assoc., 1977-79; sr. sci. Lockheed Emsco., Houston, 1979-82, prin. scientist, 1983-85; aerospace technologist, phys. scientist NASA Stennis Space Ctr., Miss., 1985-87; staff scientist Lockheed EMSCO, Houston, 1987-88; sr. project mgr., office mgr. Ctr. for Space and Advanced Tech., Houston, 1988—; cons. in field. Contbr. articles to profl. publs. Recipient Commendation for Outstanding Contbns. Lockheed, 1979-80, Commendation for Excellence, 1984; Cert. of Merit U.S. Dept. Agr. 1980; Grad. Rsch. fellow Tex. A&M, 1975-76; NSF co-grantee Tex. A&M, 1976-77. Mem. Am. Soc. Plant Taxonomists, Bot. Soc. Am., Am. Soc. Photogrammetry, Nat. Mgmt. Assn., Sigma Xi, Phi Sigma, Alpha Chi, Kappa Delta Pi. Republican. Office: Ctr for Space and Advanced Tech 2525 Bay Area Blvd Ste 690 Houston TX 77058

CLARK, CAROLYN CHAMBERS, nurse, author; b. Superior, Wis., Mar. 25, 1941; d. John and Phyllis (Olsen) Stark. BS, U. Wis., 1964; MS, Rutgers U., Newark, 1966; EdD, Columbia U., 1976. R.N., N.Y. Instr. Bergen Community Coll., Paramus, N.J., 1972-74; pvt. practice wellness nursing, 1972—; founder, dir. The Wellness Inst., Sloatsburg, 1979-84; assoc. prof., Pace U., Pleasantville, N.Y., 1983-84; prof., wellness coord., U. Tampa, Fla., 1984-86; cons., VA Med. Ctr., Bay Pines, Fla., 1988-89, provider continuing programs for nurses, 1990—. Author: Nursing Concepts and Processes, 1977, The Nurse as Group Leader, 1977, 2d edit., 1987 (also pub. in Swedish, German), Mental Health Aspects of Community Health Nursing, 1978, Classroom Skills for Nurse Educators, 1978, Assertive Skills for Nurses, 1978, Management in Nursing, 1979, The Nurse as Continuing Educator, 1979, Enhancing Wellness: A Guide for Self-Care, 1981, Welness Nursing: Concepts, Theory, Research and Practice, 1986; editor, pub. The Wellness Newsletter, 1980—; contbr. articles to profl. jours.; mem. editorial bd. Am. Jour. Holistic Nursing, 1985-88, Women's Health Care Internat., 1985—. Grantee, N.J. Blue Cross, 1982, Robert Wood Johnson Found., 1983; recipient award, Fla. Free Lance Writers Assn., 1988. Fellow Am. Acad. Nursing. Office: 3451 Central Ave Saint Petersburg FL 33713

CLARK, CONNIE MULLINS, teacher; b. Pound, Va., Mar. 8, 1948; d. Leonard Milton Mullins and Mildred (Cantrell) Rose; m. Marvin William Clark, Apr. 22, 1976. BA in English, Clinch Valley Coll., 1970; BS in Psychology, Va. Poly. Inst. and State U., 1974; MA in Edn., Union Coll., 1975; postgrad. U. R.I., 1978, U. Va., 1984. Sec. State Farm Ins., Pound, 1966-67; tchr. Wise County Sch. Bd., Wise, Va., 1970—; pres. Appalachian Edn. Lab., Charleston, W.Va., 1986-87; salesperson Wise Real Estate, 1989. Precinct worker Democratic Party, Big Stone Gap, 1977—; mem. Dem. state cen. com., 9th dist. com., Wise county com., 1987—; mem. rules com. Va. Dem. Conv., 1988; vice-chmn. Appalachian Traditions, Inc., 1990; legis. asst. Va. Ho. Dels. 2d dist., 1988—. Mem. Va. Bus. and Profl. Women (vice dir. Dist. I 1985-86), Wise County Edn. Assn. (legis. chmn. 1985-87), Bus. and Profl. Women (pres. Wise, Va. 1983-85, pres. elect 1987—, Dock Boggs com. 1986, state legis. com. 1986-87), AAUW (legis. chmn. Big Stone Gap 1985), VEA-PAC (mem. exec. com. 1989), Wise County C. of C. (edn. com. 1988—), Wise County and City Norton Dem. Woman's Club (corr. sec. 1987—). Recipient Appreciation award Va. Edn. Assn., 1985; named One of Outstanding Young Women of Am., 1983. Baptist. Avocations: Reading; music; animals; outdoors. Home and Office: 330 Pearl St Big Stone Gap VA 24219

CLARK, CYNTHIA LYNN, insurance company regional training director; b. Jamaica, N.Y., Apr. 21, 1963; d. Donald Eugene and Karen Lee (Howard) Clark. BS in Fin., U. Md., 1985. Sec. Washington Talent Agy., Rockville, Md., 1980; salesperson T.H. Mandy & Co., Rockville, 1980-82; adminstrv. aide David Taylor Naval Ship Research & Devel. Ctr., Bethesda, Md., 1982-84; loan processor Dominion Mortgage Co., Kensington, Md., 1984-86, Mortgage First/First Atlanta Mgmt., Atlanta, 1986; underwriter Mortgage First/First Atlanta Mgmt., 1986-87, G.E. Mortgage Ins. Co., Atlanta, 1987-88; regional tng. dir. G.E. Mortgage Ins. Co., 1988—; tng. specialist Prudential Home Mortgage, Frederick, Md., 1990—; grad. asst. Dale Carnegie Inst., Atlanta, 1988—. Recipient Summitt Club award G.E. Credit Corp., 1989, Reporting award Dale Carnegie Inst., Atlanta, 1988. Mem. Atlanta Assn. Profl. Mortgage Women, Nat. Assn. for Female Execs., Mortgage Bankers Assn. Ga. (cert. appreciation 1989), Am. Soc. Tng. & Devel. Democrat. Methodist. Office: Prudential Home Mortgage Frederick MD 20901

CLARK, DEBRA FEIOCK, marketing professional; b. Frankfurt, Germany, June 19, 1958; came to U.S., 1960; d. Ray Donald Feiock and Joanne (Hackler) MacNiven; m. Steven D. Clark, Sept. 5, 1981 (div. 1986). BA in Communications, Calif. State U., Fullerton, 1981; cert. in mktg., U. Calif., Berkeley. Mgr. Foto Hall, Inc., Tustin, Calif., 1979-82; copy products sales rep. Kodak Copy Products, Los Angeles, 1982-85; electronic pub. sales Kodak Copy Products, Whittier, Calif., 1985-88; comml. mktg. Kodak Electronic Photography, Fremont, Calif., 1988—; regional account mgr. Thermal Printing Systems Eastman Kodak Co., 1990—; guest speaker Fullerton (Calif.) Community Coll., 1988. Vol. Internat. Spl. Olympics, Reno, 1989,

Girl Scouts U.S., 1989-90. Mem. Sigma Kappa Sorority Alumni Assn. (pres. 1987-88). Office: Eastman Kodak 37741 Madera Ct Fremont CA 94536

CLARK, DENISE LYNN, laboratory executive; b. Norristown, Pa., Oct. 14, 1954; d. James Carl and Rose Ann (DiNofrio) C. BBA, Ursinus Coll., Collegeville, Pa., 1985; postgrad. St. Joe's U., Phila. Customer svc. supr. Upjohn Co., King of Prussia, Pa., 1976-80; mgr. credit and collection SmithKline Clin. Lab., King of Prussia, 1980-85; mgr. nat. credit and collection SmithKline Bio-Sci. Labs., King of Prussia, 1986-87 ; accounts receivable mgr. Internat. Clin. Lab., Nashville, 1987-89; billing project mgr. SmithKline Beecham Labs., King of prussia, 1989—. Notary Pub. Commonwealth Pa. Mem. NAFE, N.J. Assn. Credit Execs. Avocation: travel. Home: 2753 Apple Valley Ln Audubon PA 19403 Office: SmithKline Beecham Labs 600 Park Ave King of Prussia PA 19406

CLARK, DIANNA LEA, broadcast executive; b. Lincoln, Ill., June 27, 1956; d. Raymond Burnell and Patricia JoAnn (Bartle) Kirby; m. Robert Allen Clark, Nov. 25, 1978. AA, Springfield (Ill.) Coll., 1976; BA, Sangamon State U., Springfield, 1979. With broadcast svcs. Sangamon State U., 1977-80; traffic dir. Sta. WIL-FM, St. Louis, 1980-85; ops. dir. Sta. KCLC Lindenwood Coll., St. Charles, Mo., 1985-86; radio sta. mgr. St. Louis Community Coll. at Flo Valley, St. Louis, 1986—. Mem. Am. Bus. Women's Assn. (regional conv. sec. 1990—, Woman of the Yr. 1986), NAFE, W.I.N.O.S. Bowling Club (sec., bd. dirs. 1983—), Am. Legion Aux., Alpha Epsilon Rho (nat. conv. coord. 1987, regional conv. dir. 1989, 90—, nat. project chmn. Tourette Syndrome 1984—, Nat. Outstanding Regional Dir. 1980, Nat. Outstanding Mem. 1986). Office: St Louis Community Coll Sta KCFV 3400 Pershall Rd Saint Louis MO 63135

CLARK, ELEANOR, author; b. Los Angeles; d. Frederick Huntington and Eleanor (Phelps) C.; m. Robert Penn Warren, Dec. 7, 1952; children: Rosanna, Gabriel. B.A., Vassar Coll. Mem. Corp. of Yaddo. Author: novels The Bitter Box, 1946, Baldur's Gate, 1971, Dr. Heart, A Novella, and Other Stories, 1975, Gloria Mundi, 1979, Camping Out, 1986; for children The Song of Roland, 1960; non-fiction Rome and a Villa, 1952, expanded edit., 1975, The Oysters of Locmariaquer, 1964, Eyes, Etc., A Memoir, 1977, Tamrart-13 Days in the Sahara, 1982; translator: Dark Wedding (R. Sender), 1943; contbr. stories, essays and revs. to numerous publs. Served with OSS, 1943-45. Guggenheim fellow, 1946-47, 49-50; recipient Nat. Book Award, 1965. Mem. Nat. Inst. Arts and Letters (award 1946). Address: 2495 Redding Rd Fairfield CT 06430

CLARK, ELIZABETH ANN, nurse; b. Alton, Ill., Dec. 10, 1950; d. Angelo Thomas and Josephine Ann (Lombardo) Alben; grad. St. Joseph's Sch. Nursing, Alton, 1971; BS in Nursing, McKendree Coll., 1985; m. Gary Daniel Clark, Aug. 20, 1970; children: Nicole Leigh, Jason Andrew. Staff nurse obstetrics-gynecology S.W. Tex. Meth. Hosp., San Antonio, 1971; staff nurse operating room Kansas City (Mo.) Gen. Hosp., 1971-73; staff nurse obstetrics, recovery room, med.-surg. Spelman Meml. Hosp., Smithville, Mo., 1974-76; staff nurse operating room Alton Meml. Hosp., 1976-85, head nurse operating room, 1985-86, dir. surgery services, 1986—; sec. Anestat, Inc., 1975-76. Treas. Alton Area Swim Team, 1985—. Mem. Assn. Operating Room Nurses (nominating com. 1985-86, bd. dirs. 1989—, v.p./pres.-elect 1987-88, pres. 1988-89), Phi Theta Kappa. Roman Catholic. Home: 908 Hampton Ct Godfrey IL 62035 Office: Alton Meml Hosp One Memorial Dr Alton IL 62002

CLARK, ELIZABETH ANNETTE, insurance company administrator; b. Mpls., Oct. 6, 1934; d. Walter Burdette and Daveda Marguerite (Hansen) Garver; m. Forrest Halter, May 17, 1958 (div. Feb. 1973); children: Gregory, Linda Halter Balsiger; m. Leslie Matthew Clark, Sept. 28, 1976. AA, Montgomery Coll., 1954; AAS, Greenville (S.C.) Tech. Coll., 1973; B in Gen. Studies, Furman U., 1979; MBA, Clemson (S.C.) U., 1987. CLU. Data processor Liberty Life Ins. Co., Greenville, 1973-84, mgr. quality improvement dept., 1984-88, dir. project mgmt., 1989, asst. v.p. policy forms, 1989—; instr. computer programming part-time Greenville Tech. Coll., 1980-81. Sec. S.C./Piedmont chpt. Nat. Multiple Sclerosis Soc., Greenville, 1974-76; bd. dirs. Greenville Little Theatre, 1974-75; chmn. invitation com. Bicentennial Ball, Greenville, 1976. Fellow Life Mgmt. Inst.; mem. Life Office Mgmt. Assn. (rep. so. systems devel. commn. 1985-90), program chmn. 1987-88, sec. 1988-89, chmn. 1989-90), Mensa, Beta Sigma Phi (pres. Greenville chpt. 1975-76, v.p. coun. 1975-76, Woman of Yr., 1975, 89, 90, Alpha-Omega award 1977). Unitarian. Home: 121 Rockwood Dr Greenville SC 29605 Office: Liberty Life Ins Co PO Box 789 Greenville SC 29602

CLARK, ELOISE ELIZABETH, biologist, university official; b. Grundy, Va., Jan. 20, 1931; d. J. Francis Emmett and Ava Clayton (Harris) C. BA, Mary Washington Coll., 1951; PhD in Zoology, U. N.C., 1958; DSc, King Coll., 1976; postdoctoral rsch., Washington U., St. Louis, 1957-58, U. Calif. at Berkeley, 1958-59. Rsch. asst., then instr. U. N.C., 1952-55; instr. physiology Marine Biol. Lab., Woods Hole, Mass, 1959-69; mem. faculty Columbia U., 1966-69, assoc. prof. biol. sci., 1966-59; with NSF, Washington, 1969-83; head molecular biology NSF, 1971-73, div. dir. biol. and med. scis., 1973-75, dep. asst. dir. biol., behavioral and social scis., 1975-76, asst. dir. biol., behavioral and social scis., 1976-83; v.p. acad. affairs, prof. biol. sci. Bowling Green State U. (Ohio), 1983—. Contbr. articles to profl. jours. Mem. alumnae bd. Mary Washington Coll., U. Va., 1967-70; bd. regents Nat. Libr. of Medicine, 1973-83; mem. policy group competitive grants program U.S. Dept. Agr.; mem. White House interdepartmental task force on women and interagy, 1978-80, task force for conf. on families, 1980, mem. com. on health and medicine, 1976-80, vice chmn. com. on food and renewable resources, 1977-80; mem. selective excellence task force Ohio Bd. Regents, 1984-85; mem. Ohio Adv. Council Coll. Prep. Edn., 1983-84; mem. Ohio Inter-Univ. Council for Provosts, 1983—, chmn., 1984-85, nat. adv. rsch. resources council NIH, 1987-89; mem. informal sci. edn. panel, NSF, 1986-88; program adv. coun. sci., tech. and pub. policy Harvard U., 1988—. Named Disting. Alumnus Mary Washington Coll., 1975; Wilson scholar, 1956; E.C. Drew scholar, 1956; USPHS postdoctoral fellow, 1957-59; recipient Disting. Service award NSF, 1978. Mem. Soc. Gen. Physiology (sec. 1965-67, coun. 1969-71, 89—), AAAS (coun. 1969-71, bd. dirs. 1978-82), Biophys. Soc. (coun. 1975-76), Am. Soc. Cell Biology (coun. 1972-75), Am. Inst. Biol. Scientists, NASULGC (higher edn. and tech. com. 1988—), Ohio Coun. Rsch. and Econ. Devel., Golden Key, Phi Beta Kappa (com. on qualifications 1985—), Sigma Xi, Omicron Delta Kappa. Home: 1222 Brownwood Dr Bowling Green OH 43403 Office: Bowling Green State U McFall Ctr Bowling Green OH 43403

CLARK, ESTHER FRANCES, legal educator; b. Phila., Aug. 29, 1929; d. John and Lucy (Scapula) Giaccio; m. John H. Clark, Jr., June 12, 1954; 1 child, Jacqueline. B.A., Temple U., 1950; J.D., Rutgers U., 1955. Bar: Pa. 1956. Pvt. practice law Chester, 1976; prof. law sch. of law Widener U., Wilmington, 1976—. Assoc. editor: Rutgers U. Law Rev, 1954-55. Bd. dirs. Taylor Hosp., Ridley, Pa., Pa. Bar Inst., Lindsay Law Libr. Fellow Am. Bar Found.; mem. ABA, Pa. Bar Assn. (ho. of dels.), Delaware County Bar Assn. (pres. 1982), Am. Trial Lawyers Assn., Delaware County Legal Assistance Assn. (dir. 1972-77, pres. bd. dirs. 1974-76). Roman Catholic. Home: 207 Knoll Rd Wallingford PA 19086 Office: PO Box 7474 Wilmington DE 19803

CLARK, FAYE LOUISE, drama and speech educator; b. La., Oct. 9, 1936; student Centenary Coll., 1954-55; B.A. with honor, U. Southwestern La., 1962; M.A., U. Ga., 1966; m. Warren James Clark, Aug. 8, 1969; children—Roy, Kay Natalie. Tchr., Nova Exptl. Schs., Fort Lauderdale, Fla., 1963-65; faculty dept. drama and speech DeKalb Community Coll., Atlanta, 1967—, chmn. dept., 1977-81. Pres. Hawthorne Sch. PTA, 1983-84. Mem. Ga. Theatre Conf. (sec. 1968-69, rep. to Southeastern Theatre Conf. 1969), Ga. Psychol. Assn., Ga. Speech Assn., Atlanta Ballet Guild, Friends of the Atlanta Opera, Southeastern Theatre Conf., Atlanta Hist. Soc., Atlanta Artists Club (sec. 1981-83, dir. 1983—), Young Women of Arts, Speech Communication Assn., High Mus. Art, Phi Kappa Phi, Pi Kappa Delta, Sigma Delta Pi, Kappa Delta Pi, Thalian-Blackfriars. Presbyterian. Club: Lake Lanier Sailing. Home: 2521 Melinda Dr NE Atlanta GA 30345 Office: DeKalb Community Coll Humanities div North Campus Dunwoody GA 30338

CLARK, J. JILL, advertising agency executive; b. Griffith, Ind., Nov. 2, 1938; d. John Edward and Millicent Camila (Morin) McClusky; m. Dale Walker Clark, Oct. 8, 1960 (div. Nov. 1963). Student, Northwestern U., Western Mich. U. Asst. buyer SMY, Chgo., 1973-75; buyer CPM, Chgo., 1975-79; media dir. Chase Ehrenberg & Rosene, Chgo., 1979-80; assoc. nat. regional buyer operation dir. Bozell, Jacobs, Kenyon & Eckhardt, Chgo., from 1980; now v.p. Bozell, Inc. (formerly Bozell Ellis Diaz), Tampa, Fla. Office: Bozell Inc 3030 N Rocky Pointe Dr W Ste 280 Tampa FL 33607*

CLARK, JANE ANGELA, educator; b. Linton, Ind., Sept. 18, 1955; d. Frank William and Doris Louise (French) Barlich; m. William H. Clark, June 4, 1977; 1 child, William Daniel. BA, Purdue U., 1976; postgrad., U. Wis., 1978-79, U. Pa., 1985-90. Rsch. asst. Purdue U., West Lafayette, Ind., 1977; pers. specialist Sentry Ins., Stevens Point, Wis., 1977-81; adminstr. Indianhead Med. Group, Rice Lake, Wis., 1981-88, Emergency Room Physicians Group, Rice Lake, 1985—; instr. mgmt. Wis. Indianhead Tech. Coll., Rice Lake, 1985—; cert. instr. Zenger-Miller courses; mem. suprs. mgmt. adv. com. Wis. Indianhead Tech. Coll., 1985-87. Chairperson Am. Heart Assn., Shell Lake, Wis., 1989; bd. dirs. United Way, Rice Lake, 1987-88. Mem. After Five Club (bd. dirs.), Alpha Lambda Delta, Phi Alpha Theta, Kappa Delta Pi, Alpha Lambda. Republican. Baptist. Home: 103 Pederson Dr Shell Lake WI 54871

CLARK, JANE ELIZABETH, kinesiology educator, researcher; b. Niagara Falls, N.Y., Oct. 30, 1946; d. George Douglas and Dorothy Frances (Dibben) C. BEd, SUNY, Brockport, 1968; MEd, U. Wash., 1970; PhD, U. Wis., 1976. Instr. Purdue U., West Lafayette, Ind., 1970-73; asst. prof. U. Iowa, Iowa City, 1976-78, U. Pitts., 1978-81; asst. prof. kinesiology U. Md., College Park, 1981-87, assoc. prof., 1987—. Co-editor: The Development of Movement Control and Coordination, 1978, Advances in Motor Development Research, vols. 1-3, 1987—; contbr. articles on motor devel. to profl. jours. Fellow AAHPER and Dance (pres. rsch. consortium 1989-91); mem. N.Am. Soc. for Psychology Sport and Phys. Activity (publ. dir. 1983-85), Ea. Dist. AAHPER and Dance (Outstanding Tchr. award 1988). Home: 23 Chelsea Ct Annapolis MD 21403 Office: U Md Dept Kinesiology College Park MD 20742

CLARK, JANET EILEEN, political scientist, educator; b. Kansas City, Kans., June 5, 1940; d. Edward Francis and Mildred Lois (Mack) Morrissey; A.A., Kansas City Jr. Coll., 1960; A.B., George Washington U., Washington, 1962, M.A., 1964; Ph.D., U. Ill., 1973; m. Caleb M. Clark, Sept. 28, 1968; children: Emily Claire, Grace Ellen, Evelyn Adair. Staff, U.S. Dept. Labor, Washington, 1962-64; instr. social sci. Kansas City (Kans.) Jr. Coll., 1964-67; instr. polit. sci. Parkland Coll., 1970-71; asst. prof. govt., N.Mex. State U., Las Cruces, 1971-77, assoc. prof., 1977-80; assoc. prof. polit. sci. U. Wyo., 1981-84, prof., 1984—. Co-author: Women, Elections and Representation, 1987, Women in Taiwan Politics: Overcoming Barriers to Women's Participation in a Modernizing Society, 1990. Wolcott fellow, 1963-64, NDEA Title IV fellow, 1967-69. Mem. Internat. Soc. Polit. Psychology Gov. Coun., 1987-89. Mem. NEA (pres. chpt. 1978-79), Am. Polit. Sci. Assn., Western Polit. Sci. Assn. (exec. coun. 1984-87), Western Social Sci. Assn. (exec. coun. 1978-81, v.p. 1982, pres. 1985), Women's Caucus for Polit. Sci. (treas. 1982, pres. 1987), LWV (exec. bd. 1980-83, treas. 1986—), Women's Polit. Caucus, Beta Sigma Phi (v.p. chpt. 1978-79, sec. 1987-88, treas. 1988-89, v.p. 1989-90), Phi Beta Kappa, Chi Omega (prize 1962), Phi Kappa Phi. Democrat. Lutheran. Book rev. editor Social Sci. Jour., 1982-87. Contbr. articles to profl. jours. Home: 519 S 12th St Laramie WY 82070

CLARK, JANET LEE, clinical psychologist; b. Quantico, Va., Aug. 1, 1952; d. Ralph Edward and Mary Jane (Ensalaco) Sullivan; m. James Arthur Clark, Sept. 5, 1981; children: Arthur Lewis, Chelsea Lucille. Student, U. Va., 1970; BS in Elem. Edn. with high honors, St. Cloud (Minn.) State U., 1973; MA in Gen. Psychology, U. N.D., 1979, PhD in Clin. Psychology, 1983. Cert. tchr., Minn.; lic. psychologist, Ohio. Tchr. Wells (Minn.) Ind. Sch. Dist., 1973-75, Red Lake (Minn.) Indian Reservation, 1975-77; small group facilitator U. N.D. Med. Sch., Grand Forks, 1984-86; instr. Columbus (Ohio) State Community Coll., 1989—; supervising psychologist Comprehensive Psychol. Svcs., Columbus, 1990—; team leader chronic pain program Med. Ctr. Rehab. Hosp., Grand Fork, 1983-86; speaker in field; producer films on chronic pain, child abuse, other topics. Contbr. to profl. publs. Mem. Am. Psychol. Assn., Phi Delta Kappa. Unitarian Universalist. Home: 5801 Thompson Rd Columbus OH 43230 Office: 1660 NW Profl Plaza Ste H Columbus OH 43220

CLARK, JOAN FAYE HENRY, teacher, consultant; b. Sharon, Pa., Aug. 30, 1928; d. Victor Holmes and Mabel Joy (Murphy) Henry; m. Donald Eugene Clark, June 9, 1951; children: Mark, Neil, Gary. BA, Westminster Coll., 1950; cert., Edinboro (Pa.) U., 1961. Tchr. Sharon Pub. Schs., 1950-52, Baldwin Twp. Schs., Pitts., 1953, Conneaut Lake (Pa.) Area Schs., 1962; dir. Wee Wisdom Nursery Sch., 1963-64; tchr. Cochranton (Pa.) Pub. Schs., 1965-66, Crawford Cen. Schs., Meadville, Pa., 1967-90; ret. Crawford Cen. Schs.; beauty cons. Mary Kay Cosmetics, Conneaut Lake, Pa., 1990—; alt. instr. Presdl. Classroom, Washington, 1989—. Mem. NEA, Pa. State Edn. Assn., Crawford Cen. Edn. Assn. (faculty rep. 1984), Grottoettes (pres. Meadville chpt. 1988). Republican. Presbyterian. Home and Office: RD 1 Box 743 Conneaut Lake PA 16316

CLARK, JOYCE NAOMI JOHNSON, nurse; b. Corpus Christi, Tex., Oct. 4, 1936; d. Chester Fletcher and Ermal Olita (Bailey) Johnson; m. William Boyd Clark, Jan. 4, 1958; (div. 1967); 1 child, Sherene Joyce. Student, Corpus Christi State U., 1975-77. RN; cert. instrument flight instr. Staff nurse Van Nuys (Calif.) Community Hosp., 1963-64, U.S. Naval Hosp., Corpus Christi, 1964-68; clin. mgr. surgery Meml. Med. Ctr., Corpus Christi, 1968—. Leader Paisano Council Girl Scouts U.S.A., Corpus Christi, 1968-74. Recipient Charles A. Mella award Meml. Med. Ctr., 1981, Paul E. Garber award CAP, 1986, cert. of appreciation in recognition of Support Child Guard Missing Children Edn. Program Nat. Assn. Chiefs of Police, Washington, 1987, Charles E. Yeager Aerospace Edn. Achievement award, 1985, Grover Loenig Aerospace Award, 1986, Cert. of World Leadership Internat. Biographical Ctr., Cambridge, Eng., 1987, Gill Robb Wilson award #1021, 1988, Merit award Drug Free Am. Through Enforcement, Edn., Intelligence Nat. Assn. Chiefs of Police. Mem. Am. Assn. Operating Room Nurses (v.p. 1969), Aircraft Owners and Pilots Assn., USAF Aux. CAP Air Search and Rescue (past comdr. 3d group, wing chief pilot, Sr. Mem. of Yr. 1985), Am. Fed. Police, Smithsonian Instn. Home: 1001 Carmel Pkwy #33 Corpus Christi TX 78411-2152 Office: Meml Med Ctr Oper Rm 4606 Hospital Blvd Corpus Christi TX 78405

CLARK, KAREN ELIZABETH, industrial engineer, consultant; b. Battle Creek, Mich., Feb. 28, 1955; d. Charles Grafton and Thelma Elizabeth (Robertson) C. BS in Indsl. Engring., Purdue U., 1978; MBA, Pepperdine U., 1986. Registered profl. engr., Calif. Ops. analyst Gen. Dynamics Co., Ft. Worth, 1978-80; indsl. engr. assembly div. GM, Arlington, Tex., 1980-82, David Crystal Co., Reading, Pa., 1982; sr. indsl. engr. Emhart Industries, Commerce, Calif., 1983, Northrop Electronics, Hawthorne, Calif., 1983-84; sr. ops. analyst Glendale (Calif.) Fed. Savs. & Loan, 1984-85; sr. mfg. systems engr. Douglas Aircraft Co., Long Beach, Calif., 1985-87; sr. mfg. applications cons. indsl. automation and control div. Honeywell Inc., Phoenix, 1987—; speaker in field. Contbr. articles to profl. publs. Mem. citizens adv. bd., Ft. Worth Planning Coun., 1979-81; treas., Cameo Woods Homeowners Assn., L.A., 1985, 86. Mem. Inst. Indsl. Engrs. (sr., bd. dirs. L.A. chpt. 1984-86, sec. Phoenix chpt. 1988-89, editor newsletter 1984-85), Soc. Mfg. Engrs., Alpha Pi Mu. Republican. Home: 3816 W Carol Ann Way Phoenix AZ 85023 Office: Honeywell Indsl Automation and Control Div 16404 N Black Canyon Frwy Phoenix AZ 85023

CLARK, KAREN HEATH, lawyer; b. Pasadena, Calif., Dec. 17, 1944; d. Wesley Pelton and Lois (Ellenberger) Heath; m. Bruce Robert Clark,Dec. 30, 1967; children: Adam Heath, Andrea Pelton. Student, Pomona Coll., Claremont, Calif., 1962-64; BA, Stanford U., 1964-66; MA in History, U. Washington, Seattle, 1968; JD, U. Mich., 1977. Bar: Calif. 1978. Instr. Henry Ford Community Coll., Dearborn, Mich., 1968-72; assoc. Gibson, Dunn & Crutcher, Newport Beach, 1977-86, ptnr., 1986—. Mem. dean's adv. council Chapman Coll., Orange, Calif., 1986-87, Dem. Found. Orange County, 1988—; bd. dirs. Planned Parenthood of Orange County, Santa Ana, Calif., 1979-82, New Directions for Women, Newport Beach, Calif., 1986-89, Dem. Found. of Orange County, 1989—. Mem. Orange County Bar Assn., Women in Bus. of Orange County (legal counsel 1986-87). Office: Gibson Dunn & Crutcher 800 Newport Center Dr PO Box 2490 Newport Beach CA 92660*

CLARK, KAREN MARIE, public relations executive; b. Chgo., Sept. 1, 1953; d. Robert James and Dolores Marie (Purnell) Scott; m. Ronald Clark, June 1, 1974; children: Darian J., Kyle S., Bryant K., Ariel M. BS in Communications, Ill. State U., 1975; MEd in Journalism, Cen. State U., Edmond Okla., 1986; postgrad., Okla. State U., 1988—. Equal opportunity specialist Human Relations Commn., Bloomington, Ill., 1975-76; job developer Community Action Commn., Madison, Wis., 1976-77; career counselor Madison Area Tech. Coll., Madison, 1977-78; academic specialist U. Wis., Madison, 1978-80; media coord. Urban League, Okla. City, Okla., 1980-81, '86-88; reporter, photographer Black Dispatch Newspaper, Okla. City, 1981-83; coord. of communications Okla. State Dept. Edn., Okla. City, 1988—; cons. Okla. City Northeast, Inc., 1981, Community Action Program, 1982; speaker, presenter One Ch., One Child, Okla. City, 1990—. Author: (rsch. pubs.) The State of Black Oklahoma, 1984, '87; editor (pamphlet) Visitors Guide to Okla. City: A Black Perspective. Mem. Young Adult Coun., Okla. City, 1983-86, Urban League Edn. Task Force, 1986-90; sec. Jack and Jill of Okla. City, 1985-86; press dir. Vicki Miles LaGrange Senate Campaign, Okla. City, 1986; pres. MIllwood Schs. PTA, 1985-88. Recipient 3rd pl. award in photography, McFarland YWCA, Okla. City, 1984, doctoral grant Okla. State U., 1990; named Emerging Black Artist of Okla., Okla. State Arts Coun., 1986. Mem. Women in Communications, Inc. (nat. minority affairs com., 1990-91, treas. Okla. City 1989-90), Black Media Assocs. (pres. 1983-85), Okla. Schs. Pub. Relations Assn. (mktg. officer 1988-90). Democrat. Roman Catholic. Home: 5412 N Stonewall Dr Oklahoma City OK 73111 Office: Okla State Dept Edn 2500 N Lincoln Blvd Oklahoma City OK 73105

CLARK, KRISTA HELEN, lawyer; b. Marshalltown, Ia., Oct. 18, 1951; d. Herbert Eugene and Ruth Elizabeth (Hinkhouse) C. B in Gen Studies, U. Iowa, 1974, MA, 1976; JD, U. Ia., 1979. Staff atty. Dakota Plains Legal Svc., Eagle Butte, S.D., 1979-82; mng. atty. Dakota Plains Legal Svcs., Eagle Butte, S.D., 1983-86; litigation dir. Dakota Plains Legal Svc., Mission, S.D., 1986—; instr. Cheyenne River Community Coll., Eagle Butte, S.D., 1980-85. Mem. Iowa State Bar Assn., S.D. Bar Assn. (chairperson Indian law com. 1988-89). Democrat. Home: Box 1037 Mission SD 57555 Office: Dakota Plains Legal Svcs Box 727 Mission SD 57555

CLARK, LAURIE JANE, lawyer, broker; b. Grosse Point, Mich., Dec. 10, 1951; d. Edward Francis and Doris Henre (Ader) C.; divorced; 1 child, Justin. BA, Mich. State U., 1978; JD, Thomas M. Cooley Sch. Law, 1982; postgrad., Stuoy, Erasmus U., Rotterdam, The Netherlands. Bar: Mich. 1982; lic. real estate broker. Assoc. Rappoart P.C., Lansing, Mich., 1980-82; asst. prosecuting atty. Genessee County Prosecutor, Flint, Mich., 1983-84; pvt. practice law and real estate brokerage Lansing, 1984—; instr. Am. Inst. Paralegals, 1983-85. Primary dir. Iosco County (Mich.) Rep. com., 1978-79. Mem. Mich. Bar Assn., Mich. Trial Lawyers Assn., Mich. Bd. Realtors, Ingam County Bar Assn., Shiawassee County Bar Assn., Mich. News and Video Assn. (pres., exec. dir., counsel). Home: 6330 Lake Dr Haslett MI 48840

CLARK, LEONOR A., social worker; b. Habanai, Cuba, Jan. 26, 1943; came to U.S., 1961; d. Jose and Esther (Lamadriz) Andraca; m. Jose B. Clark, June 27, 1961; children: Leonor, Ana, Jose Jr., Eddie. B Social Work, Fla. Internat. U., 1987, postgrad. Student advisor MDCC, Miami, Fla.; social worker, clinic asst. Epilepsy Found., Miami. William McKnight scholar. Mem. Nat. Assn. Social Workers. Home: 2379 SW 12th St Miami FL 33135

CLARK, LETITIA Z., federal judge; b. 1945. BA, Rice U., 1967; MA, Rutgers U., 1970; JD, Syracuse U., 1973. Atty. EPA, Dallas, 1974-76; asst. U.S. atty. City of Houston, 1982-85; bankruptcy judge U.S. Dist. Ct. (so. dist.) Tex., Houston, 1985—. Office: US Dist Ct 515 Rusk St Houston TX 77208*

CLARK, LINDA ANNE, hospital administrator; b. West Orange, N.J., May 9, 1958; d. Thomas Michael and Kathryn Patricia (Farrell) Clark. BS in Edn., Miami U., Oxford, Ohio, 1980; MBA, Ga. State U., 1984, MHA, 1983. Tchr. Sagamore Hills, Atlanta, 1980-82; restaurant mgr. Dante's Down the Hatch, Atlanta, 1982-84; asst. adminstr. Piedmont Hosp., Atlanta, 1984-90; v.p. ops. Presbyn. Hosp., Charlotte, N.C., 1990—. Pres. bd. dirs. HSI Ventures Home Health Care, Atlanta, 1988-90; bd. dirs. North Atlanta Sr. Svcs., 1987-89; chmn. fundraiser Assn. Retarded Citizens, Atlanta, 1988; mem. Pro Health for Srs., Atlanta, 1986-88. Mem. Am. Coll. Health Care Execs., Women's Health Adminstrs. Network Young Adminstrs. Ga., Ga. State Health Adminstrs. Alumni Assn. (bd. dirs. 1986-88), Atlanta C. of C. (cen. coun. 1987-88), Miami U. Alumni Assn. (steering com. Atlanta chpt. 1987-88), Sports Coun. Steering Com. Ga. Special Olympics. Roman Catholic. Office: Presbyn Hosp 200 Hawthorne Ln PO Box 33549 Charlotte NC 28233-3549

CLARK, LYNDA LEA, secondary school librarian; b. Memphis, Aug. 4, 1944; d. George Creston and Gladys Nola (Artman) C. BE, Memphis State U., 1966, MEd, 1973, postgrad., 1983-85; computer cert., State Tech. Inst., Memphis, 1986-88. Cert. secondary educator, elem. and secondary libr., Tenn. Sch. libr. Memphis City Schs., 1966—. Mem. Memphis Mus. System, 1986—, WKNO/Channel 10 Edn. TV System, Memphis, 1975—, Memphis Humane Soc., 1988—, Memphis Zool. Soc., 1989—. Named Pledge of the Yr. Beta Sigma Phi Women's Sorority, 1970. Mem. Memphis Edn. Assn., Tenn. Edn. Assn., NEA, Greenpeace, World Wildlife Fedn. Republican. Baptist.

CLARK, M. ANNE, publishing executive, author; b. Aurora, Ill., May 19, 1942; d. Henry Bertie and Betty Jane (Furgye) Saunders. AS, Harper Coll., 1972; BS, Loyola U., 1974; MEd, U. Ill., 1975; ABD, Northwestern U., 1980. Registered dental hygienist. Photog. set designer Mel Kaspar Studios, Chgo., 1960-68; kitchen planning cons. Peoples Gas Co., Chgo., 1968-70; pvt. practice as dental hygienist Chgo., 1972-74; asst. dir. edn. Am. Dental Hygienists Assn., Chgo., 1975-76; mem. staff dental edn. council Am. Dental Assn., Chgo., 1976; assoc. dean U. Ill., Chgo., 1978-86; asst. dean Ind. U., Richmond, 1986-88; museum dir. Marie Selby Bot. Gardens, Sarasota, Fla., 1988; entrepreneur Clark Pub., Sarasota, 1988—; chmn. The B.O.A.R.D., Sarasota, 1989. Assoc. editor Internat. Jour. Oral Myology, 1976-80; editor Jour. Am. Dental Hygiene Assn., 1976; columnist Chgo. Dental Soc. Rev., 1975. Bd. dirs. Fla. Studio Theater, Sarasota, 1989-90, Childen's Rehab. Found., Sarasota, 1989, Sarasota Alliance for Hist. Preservation, 1989; mem. Sarasota Opera Guild, Sarasota Arts Council, Humane Soc. Sarasota; chmn. bd. trustees First United Meth. Ch., 1990—. Mem. AAUW, Am. Bus. Women's Assn., Rotary (editor of bulletin), Sarasota County Libr. Bd. Republican. Office: Clark Pub 4030 Maverick Ave Sarasota FL 34233

CLARK, MARGARET, clergywoman; b. Miami, Fla., Feb. 15, 1949; d. George Earle and Margaret (Richards) Owen; m. Gerald Daniel Clark, Sept. 1, 1973. BA with honors, Ind. U., 1970; MA, Columbia U., 1973, Union Theol. Sem., 1973; D in Min., N.Y. Theol. Sem., 1982; DHL (hon.), Chapman Coll. Ordained to ministry Christian Ch. Asst. minister Park Ave. Christian Ch., N.Y.C., 1971-74; asst. to pres. Nikko Ceramics, N.Y.C., 1974-77; assoc. minister Union Meml. Ch., Stamford, Conn., 1977-80; assoc. regional minister Northeast region Christian Ch., N.Y.C., 1980-89, regional minister Pacific S.W. region, 1989—; chmn. Ecumenical Ministries Higher Edn., N.Y.C., 1982-83, Com. Denominational Execs., N.Y.C., 1981-82; pres. So. Calif. Ecumenical Coun.; bd. dirs. Disciples Seminary Found., Church Fin. Coun., Chapman Coll. Author: Voices, 1982; contbr. to book: Go Quickly and Tell, 1966. Recipient Community Leadership Devel. award Stamford Coun. Chs., 1978. Mem. Coun. of Chs. City of N.Y. (bd. dirs.), Religion in Am. Life (bd. dirs.), Tri-State Media Ministry (pres., bd. dirs.), Coun. on Christian Unity (bd. dirs.). Home: 11322 Lull St Sun Valley CA 91352 Office: 3126 Los Feliz Blvd Los Angeles CA 90039

CLARK, MARGARET PRUITT, state legislator; b. Eau Clair, Wis., May 9, 1946; d. Robert Earl and Gladys (Taylor) Pruitt; m. Kenneth Hall Clark, Aug. 14, 1966; children: Deborah Margaret, Robert James (dec.). BA in Sociology, Beloit Coll., 1966; MA in Sociology, U. Ill., Chgo., 1970; PhD in Sociology, U. Tex., 1976. Asst. prof. sociology Bowdoin Coll., Brunswick, Maine, 1980-83; instr. U. Maine, Augusta, 1983; mediator Maine Ct. Mediation Svc., Brunswick, 1985-87; mem. Maine Ho. of Reps., Augusta, 1986—; exec. dir. Adolescent Pregnancy Coalition, 1988—. Vol. coord. steering com. ERA, 1984; coord. Maine chpt. NOW, 1984-86; mem. Gov. Brennen's Task Force on Adolescent Pregnancy and Parenting, 1985-86, Commn. to Study Health Svcs. in Pub. Schs., 1987-88, Blue Ribbon Commn. on Health Care Expenditures, 1987-89, Commn. to Study Status of Nursing and Health Care Professions in Maine, 1988-89; bd. dirs. Family Planning Assn. Maine, 1980-88, chmn. nominating com. 1985-86, v.p., 1987; bd. dirs. pub. policy com. Nat. Coun. on Alcoholism, 1985-88, others. Mem. Northeast Network Progressive Elected Ofcls., Nat. Order Women Legislators, Am. Sociol. Assn., Assn. Clin. Sociologists, Sociologists for Women in Soc., NOW. Office: Maine State Legislature State House Sta #2 Augusta ME 04333

CLARK, MARIA CARIDAD, economic development executive; b. Moron, Cuba, Dec. 21, 1959; came to U.S., 1963; d. Marcelino Evelio and Zonia Maria (Carballo) Alvarez; m. Jack Edward Clark II, Jan. 1, 1983. AA, Hillsborough Community Coll., Tampa, Fla., 1980; BS in Behavioral Sci., U. South Fla., 1982. Leasing cons. Woodlake Village Apts., Palm Bay, Fla., 1983; leasing and mktg. dir. Sutton Properties, Palm Bay, 1983-88; exec. dir. Melbourne (Fla.)/Palm Bay Devel. Coun., 1989—; membership chmn. Spacecoast Info. Network, Melbourne, 1989—. Bd. dirs. Keep Brevard Beautiful, 1986; mem. adv. bd. Equity Outreach, Brevard Community Coll., Melbourne, 1989. Mem. Am. Bus. Women's Assn. (bd. dirs. Melbourne chpt. 1989-90), Fla. Econ. Devel. Coun. (vice chmn. pub. rels. 1989—), Greater South Brevard Area C. of C. (bd. dirs. 1987-88), Palm Bay Area C. of C. (bd. dirs. 1986-87), Leadership Brevard, Fla. Coun. of Internat. Devel. Republican. Roman Catholic. Office: Melbourne Palm Bay Devel Coun 1005 E Strawbridge Ave Melbourne FL 32901

CLARK, MARJORIE MCCUTCHAN, school librarian; b. Charlottesville, Va., June 5, 1938; d. John Wilson and Marjorie Mary (Munn) McCutchan; m. Edward Dale Clark, Apr. 1, 1961; children: Andrew Sutton, Sarah Coleman, Elizabeth Wilson. BA, Swarthmore Coll., 1959. Tchr. Chesterfield (Va.) County Pub. Schs., 1959--63, Richmond (Va.) City Pub. Schs., 1964-67; theme reader Richmond (Va.) County Pub. Schs., 1967-70; librarian Chesterfield County Pub. Schs., 1976—; mem. adv. coun. Thomas Dale High Sch., Chester, Va., 1981—. Sunday sch. tchr. 2d Presbyn. Ch., Richmond, 1966-73, elder, 1973—, chmn. Christian edn. coun., 1989—; troop leader Richmond area Girl Scouts U.S., 1977-79; mem. Chesterfield County Dem. Com., 1988—, co-chmn. Clover Hill Magisterial Dist. campaign, 1989—. Mem. NEA, Va. Edn. Assn., Chesterfield Edn. Assn., Va. Ednl. Media Assn.

CLARK, MARY HIGGINS, author, business executive; b. N.Y.C., Dec. 24, 1931; d. Luke J. and Nora C. (Durkin) Higgins; m. Warren Clark, Dec. 26, 1949 (dec. Sept. 1964); children: Marilyn, Warren, David, Carol, Patricia. BA, Fordham U., 1979; hon. doctorate, Villanova U., 1983, Rider Coll., 1986. Advt. asst. Remington Rand, 1946; stewardess Pan Am., 1949-50; radio scriptwriter, producer Robert G. Jennings, 1965-70; v.p., partner creative dir., producer radio programming Aerial Communications, N.Y.C., 1970-80; chmn. bd., creative dir. D. J. Clark Enterprises, N.Y.C., 1980—. Author: Aspire to the Heavens, A Biography of George Washington, 1969, Where Are the Children, 1976, A Stranger is Watching, 1978, The Cradle Will Fall, 1980, A Cry in the Night, 1982, Stillwatch, 1984, Weep No More, My Lady, 1987, While My Pretty One Sleeps, 1989, The Anastasia Syndrome, 1989. Recipient Grand Prix de Litterature Policiere France, 1980. Mem. Mystery Writers Am. (pres. 1987, dir.), Authors League, Am. Soc. Journalists and Authors, Acad. Arts and Scis. Republican. Roman Catholic.

CLARK, NANCY LEE, legal assistant, paralegal; b. Havre de Grace, Md., Jan. 8, 1948; d. John Harry and Betsy (Evans) Curry; children: Dawn Michelle Greer, Charles T. Greer IV; m. Reamon Roger Clark, Nov. 22, 1979. Exec. sec. The Charter Co., Jacksonville, Fla., 1969-73; legal sec. Bradford, Oswald, Tharp & Fletcher, P.A., Orlando, Fla., 1975-76; legal asst., receptionist, bookkeeper Kenneth F. Oswald, Atty. at Law, Orlando, 1976-78; legal asst., supr. real estate dept. Giles, Hedrick & Robinson, P.A., Orlando, 1978—. Mem. NAFE, Fla. Legal Assts., Orange County Assn. Legal Assts., Greater Orlando C. of C. (com. small bus. profitability). Democrat. Episcopalian.

CLARK, NANCY RANDALL, state legislator; b. Portland, Maine, May 6, 1938; d. Willis Shaw and Marthajane (Lund) Randall; B.S., Husson Coll. with high honors, 1962; M.Ed., U. Maine, 1968. Tchr. bus. edn. Scarborough High Sch., 1962-67, Freeport High Sch. Maine, 1968—; mem. Maine Ho. of Reps., 1972-78; mem. Maine Senate, 1978—. Maine bd. dirs. Arthritis Found., Maine chpt.; trustee Husson Coll., Freeport Conservation Trust. Recipient Vets. Service award Am. Legion Maine, 1978; named Outstanding Legislator, 1977, Woman of Yr., Bus. and Profl. Women's Club, 1982. Mem. NEA, Nat. Order Women Legislators, LWV, AAUW, Maine Tchrs. Assn. (pres. 1974-75), Nat. Bus. Edn. Assn., Bus. Edn. Assn. Maine, New Eng. Bus. Educators Assn., Brunswick Bus. and Profl. Women's Club, Maine Vocat. Assn., Freeport Tchrs. Assn., Freeport Hist. Soc., Tau Epsilon. Democrat. Congregationalist. Lodge: Order Eastern Star. Home: RR 2 Box 37 Freeport ME 04032 Office: Maine State Senate State Capitol Augusta ME 04333

CLARK, PAMELA ANN, educational administrator; b. Bellefontaine, Ohio, Sept. 9, 1955; d. Vance Herbert Bickham and Patricia Ann (Looker) Weisz; m. William Douglas Mercer, Oct. 21, 1978 (div. Oct. 1983); m. Roscelle Clark II; 1 child, Kambria Ann. BS in Edn., Bowling Green State U., 1977; postgrad., Wright State U., 1978-81. Cert. spl. edn., phys. edn. and health tchr., Ohio. Tchr. devel. handicapped Ridgemont High Sch., Ridgeway, Ohio, 1978-84; vocat. spl. edn. coord. Ohio Hi-Point Joint Vocat. Sch., Bellefontaine, 1984—. Recipient spl. person award Regional Spl. Edn. Resource Ctr., 1984-89, transition from sch. to work program award, 1989. Mem. Ohio Assn. Spl. Edn. Coords. (sec. 1989—), Regional Vocat. Assn. for Spl. Edn. Coords. (v.p. 1987-88), Ohio Assn. Work Study Coords. and Suprs. (sect. 1987-88), Ohio Vocat. Assn., Ohio Assn. Spl. Needs Personnel (program presenter 1989), Racquetball Club, Beta Sigma Phi (v.p. Bellefontaine 1982-84). Republican. Home: 428 E High St Bellefontaine OH 43311

CLARK, PATRICIA ANN, federal judge; b. Buffalo, July 26, 1936; d. Andrew A. and Mary (Gardner) Zacher; m. James A. Clark, Mar. 25, 1960; B.A., Goucher Coll., Towson, Md., 1958; postgrad. Duke U., 1958-60; LL.B., U. Colo., 1961. Bar: Colo. 1961, U.S. Dist. Ct. D.C. 1961. With Transamerica Title Ins. Co., 1962-65; assoc. Holme, Roberts and Owen, 1965-70, ptnr., 1970-74; judge U.S. Bankruptcy Ct., Denver, 1974—. Commr., Colo. Civil Rights Commn., 1969-72; trustee Waterman Fund, 1978—; mem. transition adv. com. U.S. Cts., 1980-84, com. jud. resources, 1987—. Recipient Disting. Alumni award U. Colo. Sch. Law, 1984. Mem. Colo. Bar Assn., Denver Bar Assn. Office: US Dist Ct 400 Columbine Bldg 1845 Sherman St Denver CO 80203*

CLARK, PEGGY LYNNE, educator; b. Georgetown, Ill., Feb. 5, 1937; d. Marshall Gilbert and Katherine Marie (Becker) Mahoney; m. Robert Paul Clark, July 10, 1959; children: Robert, Penny, Kerry, Susan. BA, Ea. Mich. U., Ypsilanti, 1959; MA, U. N.Mex., 1980. Tchr. Unit 7 Schs., Philo, Ill., 1959-62; cons. Pa-Wi-Dol Indian Jewelry, Albuquerque, 1974-78; asst. prof. U. N.Mex., Albuquerque, 1980-82; spl. edn. tchr. Albuquerque pub. schs., 1977—; developer curriculum for spl. edn. students, 1980; cons. in field. Sec., MADD, Albuquerque, 1988—; ct. monitor Ct. Appointed Spl. Advocate, Albuquerque. Named Outstanding Vol., Albuquerque Sch. Bd., 1989, Dist. 2 Children's Ct., 1988, MADD, 1988, 89. Mem. Rio Grande Valley Rabbit Assn. (pres. 1988-90), N.Mex. Rabbit Breeders Assn., S.W. Rabbit Assn., Am. Rabbit Breeders, Nat. Angora Rabbit Club, N.Mex. Symphony Guild, P.E.O. Presbyterian. Home: 6504 Arroyo Del Oso NE Albuquerque NM 87109

CLARK, SANDRA HELEN BECKER, geologist; b. Kansas City, Mo., July 27, 1938; d. LuVern John and Mildred (File) Becker; m. Allen LeRoy Clark, Nov. 10, 1955 (div. 1976); children: Ken Allen (dec.), Brett Harlan, Holly Lin. Student, Iowa State U., 1956-60; BS, U. Idaho, 1963, MS, 1964, PhD, 1968. Field asst. Idaho Bur. Mines and Geology, Moscow, summer 1963, 64, Bear Creek Mining Co., Spokane, Wash., 1965; teaching asst. Coll. of Mines U. Idaho, Moscow, 1964-66; geologist Cominco Am., Inc., Spokane, 1966-67; mem. Alaska Gas Pipeline task force U.S. Dept. Interior, Washington, 1974-75, participant depts. mgr. devel. program, 1975-76; geologist Alaskan Mineral Resources br. U.S. Geol. Survey, Menlo Park, Calif., 1967-72; staff geologist Office of Mineral Resources U.S. Geol. Survey, Washington, 1972-74; EEO officer U.S. Geol. Survey, Reston, Va., 1976-80, geologist, commodity specialist Ea. Mineral Resources br., 1980—. Contbr. maps and articles to profl. publs., 1964—. NSF grad. fellow, 1963-64, summer fellow, 1966. Fellow Geol. Soc. Am.; mem. Assn. Women Geologists (v.p. 1989-90), Am. Assn. Petroleum Geologists, Internat. Assn. on Genesis of Ore Deposits, Soc. Econ. Geologists, Soc. Econ. Paleontologists and Mineralogists, Camera Club (pres. 1986). Office: US Geol Survey MS 954 Reston VA 22092

CLARK, SANDRA LEE, health facility administrator; b. Adrian, Mich., Dec. 17, 1949; d. Thomas W. III and Alice J. (Culver) Warren; m. Frank L. Clark, Sept. 1, 1974; children: Casey, Anna, Sarah. BA, Wayne State U., 1978. Social worker Zieger Hosp., Detroit, 1977-78; owner, adminstr. C.F.S. Internat., Benton Harbor, Mich., 1981—; co-owner, adminstr. MEC-1, Benton Harbor, 1983-88; pres. Datasoh's, Benton Harbor, 1987-88; v.p. Americare Med. Assn., Valparaiso, Ind., 1987—; ops. chief Aurora Enterprises, Inc., Benton Harbor, Mich., 1986—; pres. Riverdall Farms, Inc., Benton Harbor, Mich., 1989—, Coastal Air, Inc., Benton Harbor, Mich., 1989—; sec., treas. Regent Products, Inc., Detroit, 1989—; co-owner, sec.-treas. Aurora Corp.; ptnr., chmn. of bd. Aurora Ent., Inc., Benton Harbor. Author: The Brave Brothers; co-author: (with others) Inspection. Fundraiser Twin Cities Symphony, St. Joseph, Mich., 1986, United Way, St. Joseph, 1986. Mem. Nat. Assn. Ambulatory Care (bd. dirs. Mich. chpt. 1985-86), Century Club Wayne State U., In Home Health Care Assn., Phi Beta Kappa. Republican. Home: 544 Onondaga Benton Harbor MI 49022 Office: Aurora Enterprises Inc 872 E Napier Ave Benton Harbor MI 49022

CLARK, SANDRA MARIE, school administrator; b. Hanover, Pa., Feb. 17, 1942; d. Charles Raymond Clark and Mary Josephine (Snyder) Clark Wierman. BS in Elem. Edn., Chestnut Hill Coll., 1980; MS in Curriculum Adminstrn., Nova U., 1985. Cert. elem. tchr., Pa. Tchr. various elem. schs., Pa., 1962-75; asst. vocation directress Mt. St. Joseph Motherhouse, Chestnut Hill, Pa., 1975-76; tchr. St. Catharine's Sch., Spring Lake, N.J., 1976-77; asst. mgr. Jim's Truck Stop, New Oxford, Pa., 1977-81; adminstr. Little People Day Care Sch., Hanover, 1981-88, sec., treas. bd. dirs., 1985-86; coord. regional resource Magic Yrs. Child Care & Learning Ctrs., Inc., Hanover, 1987-88; prin. St. Vincent De Paul Sch., Hanover, Pa., 1988—; presenter Hanover Area Seminar for Day Care Employees, 1983-86. coord. sch. safety patrols St. Vincent's Sch., Hanover, 1969-75, vice-chmn. bd., 1982-84; multi-media instr. first aid ARC, Hanover, 1983-86, bd. dirs., 1984-88; exec. sec. of bd. of dirs. ARC, Hanover, 1988; 1st v.p. Hanover Area Coun. of Chs., 1988, pres., 1989; validator accredidation program Nat. Acad. Early Childhood Programs, Washington, 1987—; bd. dirs. Life Skills Unltd. Handicapped Adults, 1988—; facilitator Harrisburg Diocesan Synod, Hanover, 1985-88, parish del., 1988. Pa. Dept. Pub. Welfare tng. grantee, 1986. Mem. NAFE, Nat. Cath. Ednl. Assn. Democrat. Roman Catholic. Club: Internat. Assn. Turtles (London). Home: 348 Barberry Dr Hanover PA 17331 Office: Saint Vincent De Paul Sch Hanover PA 17331

CLARK, SARA MOTT, teacher; b. Mahaffey, Pa., Sept. 19, 1915; d. William Benjamin and Anna Pearl (Murray) M.; m. Maximilian Steineger, Dec. 13, 1941; children: Max III, Benjamin Alan, Betsy Ann, Kathryn Louise. BS, Juanita Coll., Huntingdon, Pa., 1933-37, Ind. U. Pa., 1940-41. Dietician, Home Econ. Tchr., Internat. Porcelain Art Tchr. Dietician Adrian Hosp., Punxsutawney, Pa., 1937-40; home econs. tchr. Scio High Sch., Ohio., 1941-42, Punxsutawney (Pa.) Area Dist. Sch., 1960-77; artist, tchr. Internat. Porcelain Artist, Bradenton, Fla.; pres. NW Pa. Hosp. Dietetics Orgn., Punxsutawney, 1938-40; chmn. Am. Home Econs. Central We. Dist., Punxsutawney, 1967-68. Vol. Art Display Internat. Porcelain Artist Atlanta Ga. 1986, Art in Action Festival Arts State Coll. 1981-82; Author: Various Porcelain Paintings China and fla. 1986. Den mother Boy Scouts Am., Punxsutawney, 1951-56; Brownie leader Girl Scouts U.S., Punxsutawney, 1959; Sunday Sch. tchr. First Bapt. Ch., Punxsutawney, 1957-60. Recipient Tribute to Porcelain Artist award Punxsutawney Spirit, 1987. Mem. Progressive Study Club (Farewell Luncheon award, pres. 1953-54, 75-76), Treasures of Porcelain Artists, Gulf Coast Porcelain Artist (pres. 1988-90). Republican. Protestant. Home: 4270 B Coquina Circle Bradenton FL 34208

CLARK, SHEREE L., graphic design company executive; b. Saratoga Springs, N.Y., Oct. 10, 1956; d. George R. and Patricia L. (Nestor) C. BS, Rochester Inst. Tech., 1978; MEd, U. Vt., 1980. Coord. Greek life Drake U., Des Moines, 1980-85; co-owner, mgr. Sayles Graphic Design, Inc., Des Moines, 1985—. Author: ETSIS: A History of the Fraternities and Sororities of Drake University (1891-1984), 1984. Named Iowa Up and Comer, Des Moines Register, 1989. Mem. Pub. Rels. Soc. Am., Advt. Profls. Des Moines (pres. 1989-90, Ad Pro of Yr. award 1987, 88), Nat. Assn. Women Bus. Owners, P.E.O. (pres. chpt. HX, 1985-87), Alpha Phi (advisor Gamma Omicron chpt. 1984-86). Office: Sayles Graphic Design Inc 308 8th St Des Moines IA 50309

CLARK, SHERYL MARIE, nurse practitioner; b. Dallas, Nov. 12, 1944; d. William Stanford and Thelma Marie (Johnson) C.; B.S. in Nursing, U. Colo., 1967. Office nurse, supr. Dr. S.E. Wood, Charleston, S.C., 1970-72; staff nurse VA Hosp., Charleston, S.C., VA Hosp., Long Beach, Calif., 1972-73; family nurse practitioner Family Health Program, Long Beach, Calif., 1973-78; research nurse practitioner U. Calif., Irvine, 1978-79; mgr. health services Martin-Marietta Aluminum Corp., Torrance, Calif., 1979-81; mgr. health services TRW, Redondo Beach, Calif., 1981—. Served with USNR, 1967-70. Mem. Calif. Nurses Assn. (past pres. Region 1, past chairperson interregional standing com. nurse practitioners), Am. Nurses Assn. (cert. family nurse practitioner), Am. Public Health Assn., Am. Assn. Occupational Health Nurses (cert. occupational health nurse), Calif. State Assn. Occupational Health Nurses (pres.), Harbor Area Assn. Occupational Health Nurses (pres.). Republican. Home: 2313 Huntington Ln Unit B Redondo Beach CA 90278 Office: One Space Park S/1459 Redondo Beach CA 90278

CLARK, SUSAN (NORA GOULDING), actress; b. Sarnia, Ont., Can., Mar. 8, 1944; d. George Raymond and Eleanor Almond (McNaughton) C. Student, Toronto (Ont.) Children's Players, 1956-59; student (Acad. scholar), Royal Acad. Dramatic Art, London. partner Georgian Bay Prodns. Producer: Jimmy B. and Andre, 1979, Word of Honor, 1980, Maid in America, 1982; star Webster, ABC-TV, 1983-89; appeared in Brit. TV prodns., repertory theatre; appeared in Brit. premiere of play Poor Bitos; appeared in Can. TV prodns., including Heloise and Abelard, Hedda Gabler; starred in Taming of the Shrew; appeared in Sherlock Holmes, Williamstown Theatre Festival, (taped for HBO), 1981, Meeting on the Porch, Canon Theater, Beverly Hills, 1990; appeared in Getting Out, Mark Taper Forum, Los Angeles, 1978, American premiere Meetin's on the Porch; films include The Apple Dumpling Gang, Night Moves, The North Avenue Irregulars, Airport '75, Midnight Man, Porky's, Murder by Decree, Tell Them Willie Boy is Here, Skin Game, City on Fire, Madigan, Coogan's Bluff, Skullduggery, Promises in the Dark, Valdez is Coming, Showdown, Double Negative; appeared in segments of TV series Columbo, Marcus Welby, Barnaby Jones; appeared in Double Solitaire, Pub. Broadcasting System, Babe, MGM-CBS TV spl., 1975 (Emmy award), Amelia Earhart (Emmy nomination), The Choice; 150 episodes of Webster. Mem. ACLU, Am. Film Inst. Office: care Georgian Bay Prodns 3815 W Olive Ave Ste 101 Burbank CA 91505

CLARK, SUSAN JANE, pharmaceutical company executive, sales executive; b. Dalhart, Tex., May 12, 1953; d. Manuel and Isabella (Lindsey) Ramirez; m. Johnny L. Clark, May 11, 1973; children: John Christopher, Courtney Renee. BBA, West Tex. State U., 1981. Sales rep. Merck Sharp and Dohme, Canyon, Tex., 1982-89; sr. profl. sales rep. Merck Sharp and Dohme, Canyon, 1989. Mem. NAFE, Panhandle Infection Control, Amarillo Pharm. Assn.

CLARK, SUSAN MATTHEWS, psychologist; b. Newton, Kans., Aug. 5, 1950; d. Glenn Wesley Matthews and Jane Buckles; m. S. Bruce Clark, Aug. 14, 1971; children: Casandra Jane, Ryan Mathews. BME, Wichita State U., Wichita, 1971, MME, 1975; MA, Wichita, 1982; PhD, N. Tex. State U., Denton, 1985. Tchr. elem. Derby Pub. Sch., Derby, Kans., 1972-74; profl. musician Amarillo Symphony, Amarillo, Tex., 1974-77; psychological cons. Achenbach Ctr., Hardtner, Kans., 1983-85; psychologist Wichita VAMC, Wichita, Kans., 1984-85, St. Francis Homes, Inc., Salina, Kans., 1986-89, The Psychiatric Clinic of Wichita, 1989--; bd. dirs. Salina Coalition for the Prevention of Child Abuse, 1986-87. Author: Grant, 1987. Deacon Plymouth Congl. Ch., Wichita, 1989—. Recipient: Phi Kappa Phi, Mu Phi Epsilon. Mem., Am. Psychol. Assn, Southwestern Psychol. Assn., Kans. Psychol.Assn., Kans. Assn. Profl. Psychologists, Menninger Found., Beta Sigma Phi, Derby, Kans. (v.p.). Republican. Mem. Congregationalist. Office: The Psychiatric Clinic 1148 S Hillside Ste 104 Wichita KS 67211

CLARK, TERESA ELLEN, bank executive; b. Martinsville, Va., Oct. 27, 1959; d. Phillip Lazarus and Ellen Clark. BSc. in Bus. Adminstrn., Coastal Carolina Coll., Conway, S.C., 1982. Loan officer Citizens and So. Nat. Bank, Conway, S.C., 1982-87; asst. v.p. Coastal Federal Savs. Bank, Murrells Inlet, S.C., 1987—. Editor: Award Winning Annual for 1978. Vol. United Way of Horry County, Conway, S.C., 1985—; chmn. South Strand Accomodations, 1989-90. Named one of Outstanding Young Women of Am. 1985, Top Sales Employee of the Month Coastal Federal Savs. Bank Myrtle Beach S.C. 1988. Mem. NAFE, Am. Bus. Women's Assn. (hospitality chmn. 1988-89, recording sec. 1989-90, pres. 1990-91), C. of C. (exec. mem. coun. 1989-90), Coastal Carolina Coll. Alumni Assn. Office: Coastal Fed Savs Bank Inlet Crossing Shopping Ctr Murrells Inlet SC 29576

CLARK-BROOKS, BRONNIE DENISE, auditor, consultant; b. Washington, Dec. 13, 1954; d. Nathaniel Depriest Clark and Kay Frances (Grandy) Clark Joyner; m. John Francis Brooks Jr., May 24, 1975; 1 child, Tynisha Asheba. AA, Strayer Coll., Washington, 1980, BS, 1982, postgrad. computer systems mgmt., U. Md., 1986—; With Riggs Nat. Bank, Washington, 1974-83; sr. EDP audit supr. First Am. Bank, Washington, 1983-85; systems acct. Fed. Home Loan Bank Bd./Fed. Savs. & Loan Ins. Corp./Fin. Assistance Div., Washington, 1985-86; EDP auditor Amtrak, Washington, 1986-88; EDP auditor Columbia First Fed. Savings and Loan Assn., Arlington, Va., 1988. Mem. Apple Grove PTA and Citizens Assn., Fort Washington, Md., 1983, Prince George's County Parent-Tchrs. and Student Assn. Mem. Strayer Coll. Alumni Assn., EDP Auditors Assn., Inst. Internal Auditors, Washington Assn. Urban Bankers (chairperson annual awards banquet 1987-88, treas. 1988-89). Baptist. Avocations: modeling, designing, reading, dancing. Office: Columbia First Fed Savings and Loan 1560 Wilson Blvd Arlington VA 22211

CLARK-CAMERON, BONNIE, construction executive; b. Sharon, Pa., Oct. 17, 1946; d. William George and Nellie Marie (Maloy) Bowman; m. Charles C. Clark, Oct. 22, 1965 (div. May 1982); children: Tonya, Paul, LaVonne; m. Ralph Lee Cameron, Aug. 22, 1986. Grad., Dave Buster Sch. Constrn., 1985. Realtor, salesman Metroplex, Inc., Gainesville, Fla., 1979-81; v.p. Kirkpatrick Builders, Gainesville, 1981-83, Countryside Homes of Gainesville, 1983-87; pres. Paramount Mktg. Assocs., Inc., Gainesville, 1987-90; with Paramount Builders and Developers, Inc., 1989-90; v.p. M.M. Parrish-Coldwell Banker, 1990—; pres. Home Owners Warranty Corp, Gainesville, 1986-87. Chmn. Crime Trac, Gainesville, 1986, bd. dirs., 1981-87; pres. Mercer, Pa. PTA, 1976, 77; bd. dirs. Big Bros./Big Sisters, Gainesville, 1980-84. Mem. Fla. Assn. Realtors, Gainesville Home Builders Assn. (pres. elect 1987, pres. 1988, bd. dirs. 1984—, Assoc. of the Yr. 1984), Gainesville Bd. Realtors (d. dirs. 1984—, Assoc. of the Yr. 1980, pres. 1990—), Gainesville C. of C. (bd. dirs. 1987), Swimming Boosters (pres. 1987). Home: 6030 NW 53re Terr Gainesville FL 32606

CLARKE, GRETA FIELDS, dermatologist; b. Detroit; d. George William and Willa (Wright) Fields; B.S., U. Mich., 1962; 1 child, Richard Clement Clarke. MD, Howard U., 1967. Resident in dermatology NYU, 1969-72, clin. instr., 1972-77; practice medicine specializing in dermatology, N.Y.C., 1972-77; dermatologist Arlington Med. Group, Oakland, Calif., 1977-79; practice medicine specializing in dermatology, Berkeley, Calif., 1979—. Bd. dirs. Bay Area Black United Fund. Diplomate Am. Bd. Dermatology. Mem. Nat. Med. Assn. (chmn. council on concerns of women physicians 1983-88, chmn. region VI, jud. coun. 1988—), Golden State Med. Assn., Am. Acad. Dermatology, San Francisco Dermatol., Jack and Jill Club Am. (chpt. pres. 1984-85), Alameda-Contra Costa Links Club. Office: 2500 Milvia St Berkeley CA 94704

CLARKE, KAREN ELISABETH, business owner; b. Pawtucket, R.I., Nov. 6, 1946; d. Milton H. and Elizabeth Ann (Auble) Combs; m. Richard F. Clarke, Nov., 1973 (div. Sept. 1979); m. Martin H. Rogol, Feb. 4, 1989; 1 child, Chad Clarke. BS, Ohio U., 1969; MEd, Fla. Atlantic U., 1975, postgrad., 1977-80. Classroom tchr. Martin County Schs., Stuart, Fla., 1969-73, circulation coord., 1973-76; exec. dir. Fla. Consumers Fedn., West Palm Beach, Fla., 1979-88; prin. Strategic Perspectives, North Palm Beach, Fla., 1990—; cons. in field. Editor: (booklet) Fla. Lemon-Aid Manual, 1980. Rep. staff dir. Citizen Action Com., Washington, 1982-88; bd. dirs. Urban League, West Palm Beach, 1986-88, Campaign for Human Devel., Palm Beach, Fla., 1988-90; active Planned Parenthood Inc.; del. Nat. Dem. Conv., 1984, 88. Mem. Fla. Consumers Fedn. Democrat.

CLARKE, KIT HANSEN, radiologist; b. Louisville, May 24, 1944; d. Hans Peter and Katie (Jones) Hansen; A.B., Randolph-Macon Woman's Coll., 1966; M.D., U. Louisville, 1969; m. Dr. John M. Clarke, Feb. 14, 1976; children: Brett Bonnett, Blair Hansen, Brandon Chamberlain; stepchildren: Gray Campbell, Jeffrey William John M. Intern, Louisville Gen. Hosp., 1969-70; resident in internal medicine and radiology U. Tenn., Knoxville, 1970-73; resident in radiology U.S. Fla., Tampa, 1973-74; staff radiologist, chief spl. procedures Palms of Pasadena, St. Petersburg, Fla., 1974—. Active Fla. Competitive Swim Assn. of AAU. Diplomate Am. Bd. Radiology. Fellow Am. Coll. Radiology; mem. Fla. West Coast Radiology Soc., Radiol. Soc. N.Am., AMA, Fla. Med. Assn., Pinellas County Med. Soc., Fla. Radiology Soc. Episcopalian. Home: 7171 9th St S Saint Petersburg FL 33705 Office: 1609 Pasadena Ave S Saint Petersburg FL 33707

CLARKE, LINDA LOUISE See HERNÁNDEZ, LINDA LOUISE

CLARKE, MARTHA, choreographer; b. Balt., June 3, 1944. Student, Conn. Coll., Juilliard Sch., N.Y.C. Formerly with modern dance co. Anna Sokolow; mem. Pilobolus Dance Theatre, until 1979; co-founder Crowsnest Co., 1979—. Collaborator (with Linda Hunt) Portraits, 1977, A Metamorphosis in Miniature (Obie award 1982); choreographer The Garden of Earthly Delights, 1984, Vienna: Lusthaus, 1986, The Hunger Artist, 1987, Miracolo d'Amore, Spoleto Festival U.S.A., Charleston, 1988; creator solo dances. Grantee Nat. Endowment for Arts, Rockefeller Found., Guggenheim Found., MacArthur Found., 1990. Office: Crowsnest care Sheldon Soffer Mgmt Inc 130 W 56th St New York NY 10019*

CLARKE, MARY ELIZABETH, retired army officer; b. Rochester, N.Y., Dec. 3, 1924; d. James M. and Lillian E. (Young) Kennedy. Student U. Md., 1962; D.Mil.Sci., Norwich U., Northfield, Vt., 1978. Joined U.S. Army as pvt., 1945, advanced through grades to maj. gen., 1978; exec. asst. to Chief of Plans and Policies, Office of Econ. Opportunity, 1966-67; comdr. WAC Tng. Bn., 1967-68; office dep. chief of staff for pers., 1968-71; WAC staff adviser 6th Army, 1971-72; comdr., comdt. U.S. Women's Army Corps Ctr. and Sch., 1972-74; chief WAC Adv. Office, U.S. Army Mil. Pers. Ctr., Washington, 1974-75, dir. Women's Army Corps, Washington, 1975-78; comdr. U.S. Army Mil. Police and Chem. Sch. Tng. Ctr., Ft. McClellan, Ala., 1978-80; dir. human resources devel. Office of Dep. Chief of Staff for Personnel, Washington, 1980-81, ret., 1981; hon. prof. mil. sci. Jacksonville (Ala.) State U. Mem. Def. Adv. Com. on Women in the Svcs., 1984—, vice chmn., 1986—; mem. adv. com. Women Veterans, 1989. Decorated D.S.M.; recipient Toastmasters Internat. award, 1984. Mem. Assn. of U.S. Army (coun. trustees), United States Automobile Assn. (bd. dirs. 1978—), WAC Assn., WAC Mus. Found., Bus. and Profl. Women's Club. Address: 514 Fairway Dr SW Jacksonville AL 36265

CLARKE, ROSEMARY, musician, composer, educator; b. Daytona Beach, Fla.; d. Silas H. and Violet (McCoy) C. MusB, Stetson U., 1940; MusM, Phila. Mus. Acad., 1941, organ diploma, 1942; PhD, Eastman Sch. Music, 1950. Mem. faculty Stetson U., 1942-57, head organ dept., 1942-46, assoc. prof. piano and theory, 1947-57; founder Rosemary Clark Conservatory Music, Deland, 1949; assoc. prof. music, artist-in-residence U. Dubuque, Iowa, 1957-62; dir. music 1st Congl. Ch., Dubuque, 1960-62; assoc. prof. music Wis. State Coll., Platteville, 1962-63, prof., 1963-84; prof. Wis. State U. Music, Platteville. Works include Symphony in E Flat, 1946, 2d Piano Concerto, 1947, Piano Trio, 1947, Passion for soli, chorus and orch., 1950, Fantasy for band and piano solo, 1964, Wrath for soprano and orch., 1971, A Canticle of Praise for chorus, organ, piano and 2 trumpets, 1984, numerous other works for solo and duo piano, violin, violincello, organ, songs, madrigals, anthems, and piano and string teaching material. Organist Westminster Presbyn. Ch., Dubuque, 1962-65; organist, dir. Community Meth. Ch., Daytona Beach, 1943, St. Barnabas Episcopal Ch., Deland, 1951-57, St. John's Ch., Dubuque, 1977-82, St. Thomas Ch., Dubuque, 1983-87, Trinity Ch., Platteville, 1987-90. Fellow Am. Guild Organists; mem. Fla. Composers League (past pres.), Southeastern Composers League, Univ. Composers Exch., Music Tchrs. Nat. Assn., Am. Malocological Union, Wis. Music Tchrs. Assn., Iowa Music Tchrs. Assn., Am. Women Composers, Iowa Composers Forum, Phi Beta.

CLARKE, URANA, musician, writer, educator; b. Wickliffe-on-the-Lake, Ohio, Sept. 8, 1902; d. Graham Warren and Grace Urana (Olsaver) C.; artists and tchrs. diploma Mannes Music Sch., N.Y.C., 1925; cert. Dalcroze Sch. Music, N.Y.C., 1950; student Pembroke Coll., Brown U.; BS, Mont. State U., 1967, M of Applied Sci., 1970. Mem. faculty Mannes Music Sch., 1922-49, Dalcroze Sch. Music, 1949-54; adv. editor in music The Book of Knowledge, 1949-65; v.p., dir. Saugatuck Circle Housing Devel.; guest lectr. Hayden Planetarium, 1945; guest lectr., bd. dirs. Roger Williams Park Planetarium, Providence; radio show New Eng. Skies, Providence, 1961-64, Skies Over the Big Sky Country, Livingston, Mont., 1964-79, Birds of the Big Sky Country, 1972-79, Great Music of Religion, 1974-79; mem. adv. com. Nat. Rivers and Harbors Congress, 1947-58; instr. continuing edn. Mont. State U. Chmn. Park County chpt. ARC, 1967—, co-chmn. county blood program, first aid instr. trainer, 1941—; instr. ARC cardio-pulmonary resuscitation, 1976-84; mem. Mont. Commn. Nursing and Nursing Edn., 1974-76; mem. Park County Local Govt. Study Commn., 1974-76, chmn., 1984-86; mem. Greater Yellowstone Coalition. Mem. Am. Acad. Polit. Sci., Am. Musicol. Soc., Royal Astron. Soc. Can., Inst. Nav., Maria Mitchell Soc. Nantucket, N.Am. Yacht Racing Union, AAAS, Meteoritical Soc., Internat. Soc. Mus. Research, Skyscrapers (sec.-treas. 1960-63), Am. Guild Organists, Park County Wilderness Assn. (treas.), Trout Unlimited, Nature Conservancy, Big Sky Astron. Soc. (dir. 1965—), Sierra Club. Lutheran. Club: Cedar Point Yacht. Author: The Heavens are Telling (astronomy), 1951; Skies Over the Big Sky Country, 1965; also astron. news-letter, View It Yourself, weekly column Big Skies; contbr. to mags. on music, nav. and astronomy. Pub. Five Chorale Preludes for Organ, 1975; also elem. two-piano pieces. Inventor, builder of Clarke Adjustable Piano Stool. Address: Log-A-Rhythm 9th St Island Livingston MT 59047

CLARK-EDGE, VIRGINIA LEE, director of nursing; b. Bklyn., Oct. 20, 1945; d. Willie and Ganell P. (Johnson) Harrison; m. Alphonso Clark Sr., May 22, 1965 (dec. 1970); children: Alphonso Clark Jr. (dec. 1989), Wendolyn L. Clark-Marshall; m. Theron James Edge. LPN, Boces, Lindenhurst, N.Y., 1971; RN, SUNY, Farmingdale, 1974; BS in Health Adminstrn., St. Joseph's Coll., Patchogne, N.Y., 1985. Cert. gerontology. Staff LPN Suffolk State Sch. for Disturbed and Retarded Children, Melville, N.Y., 1966-72; asst. head nurse N. Shore U. Hosp., Manhassette, N.Y., 1974-81; nursing dir. Quality Care, Smithtown, N.Y., 1985-87; supr. Fairhaven Nursing Home, Lowell, Mass., 1987-89; dir. nursing Countryview Nursing Home, N. Bellerica, Mass., 1989; RN Tewksbury (Mass.) State Hosp., 1990—. Mem. Eastern Star. Home: 21 Lynne Ave Tyngsboro MA 01879

CLARKSON, CAROLE LAWRENCE, insurance company executive; b. Fredericksburg, Va., Dec. 18, 1942; d. Jerry Allen and Gladys Mae (Eubank) Lawrence; m. David Wendell Morris, Aug. 14, 1965 (div. 1977); 1 child, Peyton Lawrence; m. Lawrence Herbert Clarkson, Aug. 14, 1982. BA, Purdue U., 1965; postgrad., Ind. U., Indpls., 1970, U. Ill., 1971-73, U. Louisville Sch. of Bus., 1980-82. Pub. sch. tchr. various, Ind., Okla., Ill., N.C., Italy, 1965-75; librarian documentation U. Louisville Computing Ctr., 1980-82, IBM Corp., Austin, Tex., 1983-85; ins. mgr. Ohio State Life Ins. Co., Columbus, 1985-88, Community Life Ins. Co., Columbus, 1988—; supervisory mgr. Ins. Inst. of Am., 1987—. Mem. Internat. Claims Assn. (assoc. life and health claims 1987), Nat. Assn. Female Execs., Purdue U. Alumni Assn. Home: 8348 Waco Ln Powell OH 43065

CLARKSON, ELISABETH ANN HUDNUT, civic worker; b. Youngstown, Ohio, Apr. 20, 1925; d. Herbert Beecher and Edith (Schaaf) Hudnut; A.B., Wilson Coll., 1947; M.A., State U. N.Y., 1973, also postgrad.; L.H.D. (hon.), Wilson Coll., 1985; m. William M.E. Clarkson, Sept. 23, 1950; children—Alison H., David B., Andrew E. With J.L. Hudson Co., Detroit, 1947-50; writer The Minute Parade, daily Sta. WGR, Detroit, 1948-50; trustee Wilson Coll., Chambersburg, Pa., 1970-83, chmn. bd. trustees, 1979-82; bd. dirs. Buffalo Mus. Sci., 1972-87, 90—; bd. dirs., companion in charge Soc. Companion of the Holy Cross, 1986-90; past chmn. jr. group Alright Knox Art Gallery; collector, curator Graphic Controls Corp. collection art, 1976-83; dir. Bischoff Clarkson Hudnut Corp., North Creek, N.Y., 1973-83; mem. Buffalo Art Commn., 1983—, chmn. 1990— ; mem. exec. bd. arts adv. council SUNY at Buffalo, 1985—; bd. dirs. N.Y. State Mus. Assoc., Albany. Recipient Trustee award for disting. svc. Wilson Coll., 1983, trustee emeritus. Episcopalian. Clubs: Garret, Buffalo Tennis and Squash. Author: You Can Always Tell a Freshman, 1949; also articles, dramatic presentations, archival materials Adirondack Mus., 1950-77. Home: 156 Bryant St Buffalo NY 14222 also: Windover North Creek NY 12853

CLARKSON, JOCELYN ADRENE, medical technologist; b. Bennettsville, S.C., July 9, 1952; d. Henry Louis and Frankie Allene (Carter) C. BA in Biology, Columbia Coll., 1973; cert. medical technology, Presbyterian Hosp., Charlotte, N.C., 1975. Coll. tutor of Germanic language Columbia Coll., S.C., 1970-73, switchboard operator, 1972-73; lab aide Richland Memorial Hosp., Columbia, S.C., 1974, medical technologist. Author: poems, Compilation, short stories, Messages from Hijac, lyrics, Untitled, 1989. mem. Am. Soc. of Clinical Pathologists. Roman Catholic. Home: 201 HL Clarkson Rd Hopkins SC 29061

CLARKSTON, RONNÉ, surgical center official; b. Spokane, Wash., Mar. 20, 1941; d. Lyle and Trudy (Cunningham) C.; m. June 14, 1963 (div. Dec. 1968); 1 child, Whitney Dosh. Student, Pierce Coll., Tacoma, 1966-68. Bus. mgr. Tacoma Neurol. Assocs., 1983-88, Green River Surg. Ctr., Auburn, Wash., 1988—; owner, mgr. NW Strategic Insights, Mercer Island, Wash., 1989—. Sec. Am. Cancer Soc., Kent, Wash., 1989; mem. steering com. Bur. Indian Affairs, Auburn. Mem. NAFE, Federated Ambulatory Surgery Assn., Med. Group Mgmt. Assn., Auburn C. of C., Rotary. Republican. Home: 10430 Gravelly Lake Dr SW Apt 44 Tacoma WA 98499 Office: Green River Surg Ctr 126 Auburn Ave Ste 200 Auburn WA 98002

CLARY, ALEXIA BARBARA, manufacturing representative; b. Waterbury, Conn., Sept. 17, 1954; d. John Joseph and Veza (Mandzik) Zurlis; m. Craig Farrell Clary, Feb. 2, 1980; 1 child, Jason Farrell. BBA, U. Miami, Coral Gables, Fla., 1976; postgrad., U. New Haven, 1978-80, Mercer U., 1988-89. Buyer Hewlett Packard, Cupeztino, Calif., 1981-83; sr. buyer Mannesman Tally, Seattle, 1983; purchase mgr. ICI, Redmond, Wash., 1983-84; commodity mgr. No. Telecom, St. Mountain, Ga., 1985-88; mfg. rep. Montgomery Mktg., Norcross, Ga., 1988—. Named U. Miami scholar, 1973. Mem. Women in Electronics (v.p. sponsors 1989-90, guest speaker 1989), Nat. Assn. Female Execs., Nat. Assn. Purchasing Mgrs. Republican. Methodist. Home: 3824 Jettie Ct Lilburn GA 30247

CLARY, ELSIE RAY, transportation design engineer; b. Millville, N.J., June 18, 1948; d. Godfrey and Margaret Edith (Graham) Slimmer; m. Warren George Clary, Mar. 19, 1971. BS in Astronomy, Ohio State U., 1970; MA in Astronomy, U. S. Fla., 1973. Registered profl. engr., Fla. Statistician Fla. Dept. Transp., Tallahassee, 1973-77, engr., 1979-84, profl. engr., 1984-85, 87—; rsch. asst. Fla. Hwy. Safety Commn., Tallahassee, 1977-79; analyst Mizar Graphics, Inc., Denver, 1985-86; engring. analyst Mizar Graphics, Inc., Newark, 1986-87; adj. instr. Tallahassee Community Coll., 1988; cons. in field. Mem. Assn. Computing Machinery, Shell Point Sailboard Club. Republican. Methodist. Home: 1125 Seminole Dr Tallahassee FL 32301 Office: Fla Dept Transp 605 Suwannee St MS 69 Tallahassee FL 32399

CLARY, ROSALIE BRANDON STANTON, timber farm executive, civic worker; b. Evanston, Ill., Aug. 3, 1928; d. Frederick Charles Hite-Smith and Rose Cecile (Liebich) Stanton; BS, Northwestern U., 1950, MA, 1954; m. Virgil Vincent Clary, Oct. 17, 1959; children: Rosalie Marian Hawley, Frederick Stanton, Virgil Vincent, Kathleen Elizabeth. Tchr., Chgo. Public Schs., 1951-55, adjustment tchr., 1956-61; faculty Loyola U., Chgo., 1963; v.p. Stanton Enterprises, Inc., Adams County, Miss., 1971-89; author Family History Record, genealogy record book, Kenilworth, Ill., 1977—. also lectr. Leader Girl Scouts U.S., Winnetka, Ill., 1969-71, 78-86, Cub Scouts, 1972-77; badge counselor Boy Scouts Am., 1978-87 ; election judge Rep. Com., 1977—. Mem. Nat. Soc. DAR (Ill. rec. sec. 1979-81, nat. vice chmn. program com. 1980-83, state vice regent 1986-88, state regent 1989—), Am. Forestry Assn., Forest Farmers Assn., North Suburban Geneal. Soc. (governing bd. 1979-86), Winnetka Hist. Soc. (governing bd. 1978—), Internat. Platform Assn., Delta Gamma (mem. nat. cabinet 1985-89). Roman Catholic. Home: 509 Elder Ln Winnetka IL 60093 Office: PO Box 401 Kenilworth IL 60043

CLASTER, JILL NADELL, university administrator, history educator; d. Harry K. and Edith Lillian Nadell; m. Millard L. Midonick, May 24, 1979; 1 child from previous marriage, Elizabeth Claster (dec.). B.A., NYU, 1952, M.A., 1954; Ph.D., U. Pa., 1959. Instr. history U. Pa., 1956-58; instr. ancient and medieval history U. Ky., Lexington, 1959-61; asst. prof. U. Ky., 1961-64; adj. asst. prof. classics NYU, N.Y.C., 1964-65; asst. prof. history NYU, 1965-68, assoc. prof., 1968-84, prof., 1984—, acting undergrad. chmn. history, 1972-73, dir. M.A. in liberal studies program, 1976-78; asso. dean Washington Sq. and Univ. Coll., 1978, acting dean, 1978-79, dean, 1979-86; bd. dirs. Hebrew Immigrant Aid Soc., Turtle Bay Music Sch. Author: Athenian Democracy: Triumph or Travesty, 1967, The Medieval Experience, 1982; Contbr. articles to profl. jours. Danforth grantee, 1966-68; Fulbright grantee, 1958-59. Mem. Am. Hist. Assn., Medieval Acad. Am., Archaeol. Inst. Am., Medieval Club N.Y., Women's Forum. Home: 32 Washington Sq W New York NY 10011 Office: NYU Dept History 19 University Pl New York NY 10003

CLAUS, CAROL JEAN, computer software company executive; b. Uniondale, N.Y., Dec. 17, 1959; d. Charles Joseph and Frances Meta (Fichter) C.; m. Armand Joseph Gasperetti, Jr., July 7, 1985. Student pub. schs., Uniondale. Asst. mgr. Record World, L.I., N.Y., 1977-82, mgr. Info. Builders Inc., N.Y.C., 1982—. Mem. NAFE, Nat. Organization for Women. Democrat. Roman Catholic.

CLAUS, KIMBERLY KAY, manufacturing company administrator; b. Long Beach, Calif., Apr. 26, 1965; d. Cornelis H. and Grace (Siegers) C. BA in Comunications, U. So. Calif., 1988. Archtl. rep., with pub. rels. dept. Pacific Polymers, Inc., Garden Grove, Calif., 1987—. Mem. Constrn. Specificiations Inst. (sec. 1989—), AIA, Pi Beta Phi. Republican. Office: Pacific Polymers Inc 12271 Monarch St Garden Grove CA 92641

CLAUSEN, BETTY JANE HANSEN, retired social services administrator; b. Brooklyn, Wis., Oct. 25, 1925; d. Arthur John and Kathryn (Hefty) Hansen; B.A., Beloit Coll., 1947; m. Henry Albert Clausen, Jan. 31, 1948 (div. 1976); 1 son, Scott Alyn. Psychometric sec., Vocat. Counseling Bur., Rockford (Ill.) Coll., 1947-48; classified ad-taker Beloit (Wis.) Daily News, 1948-49; copy-writer WROK, Rockford, 1955-60; tchr. elementary schs., Rockford, Elmhurst, Ill., 1960-61; exec. mgr. Melrose Park (Ill.) C. of C., 1961-67; mng. dir. S.W. Sr. Center, Parma Heights, Ohio, 1967-77; exec. dir. Sr. Citizens, Inc., Hamilton, Ohio, 1977-90, ret. 1990. Founder, pres. Easter Seal Parents Group Rockford, 1957-60, project chmn. Villa Park, Ill., 1963-65; treas. Easter Seal Aux., 1965-66; treas. United Cerebral Palsy, Rockford, 1959-60, bd. dirs. Ill. Soc., 1959-60; co-chmn. 53-Minute March, Elmhurst, 1963; pres. Freeman Sch. PTA., Rockford, 1959-60; chmn. exceptional child PTA, Elmhurst, 1962-66; hon. life mem. Ill. PTA.; mem. S.W. Community Resource Council, 1968-77, Butler County Council on Aging, 1977-83; bd. dirs. Council Exceptional Children, New Neighbors League, S.W. Ceveland chpt., 1967; mem. council on aging Cin. Area Adv. Council, 1979-83, coun. task force on aging Butler County Human Svcs. Named Citizen of Week, Elmhurst Press, 1966. Mem. Ill. C. of C., Ill. Assn. C. of C. Execs., West Suburban Council Chambers, Ohio Assn. Sr. Citizens Ctrs., Delta Delta Delta. Club: Altrusa. Methodist. Home: 1224 Beissinger Rd Hamilton OH 45013

CLAUSEN, JUDITH H., environmental, occupational health consultant. AB, Mount Holyoke Coll.; PhD, Pa. State U. Cert. indsl. hygienist; diplomate Am. Acad. Indsl. Hygiene. Mem. Mass. Asbestos Commn., 1976-80. Recipient Sequicentennial award Mount Holyoke Coll., 1988. Mem. Am. Chem. Soc.,Am. Indsl. Hygiene Assn.

CLAUSEN, SALLY ILENE, school system administrator, academic dean; b. New Orleans, July 4, 1945; d. Everette and Nell (Wilkes) C.; m. Bob Brumberger, June 4, 1967 (div.); children: Rebecca, David. BS, La. State U., 1967, MEd, 1971, EdD, 1980. Tchr. East Baton Rouge Parish Sch. Bd., Baton Rouge, 1968-70, coord. evaluation and psychol. svc., 1981-84; coord. in-svc. tng., edn. cons. La. State U., Baton Rouge, 1975-78, asst. prof., 1981-84; fed. auditor, cons. U.S. Dist. Ct. La., Baton Rouge, 1980; dep. commr. adminstrn. State of La., Baton Rouge, 1984-88; commr. State of La. Bd. Regents, Baton Rouge, 1988—; asst. dean students, legis. and community liason Southeastern La. U.; chairperson adv. com. La. Quality Support Fund, Baton Rouge, 1988—; coord. Student Govt. Pres.'s Human Rels. Com., 1988—. Cons., vol. Kennedy Found., Washington, 1983-87; campaign coord. Supt. of Edn., Baton Rouge, 1982-83; chairperson, specialist State and Internat. Olympics, Baton Rouge, 1983-84; mem. Gov.'s task force on Minority Participation in State Procurement, 1988—. Mem. State Higher Edn. Officers, Edn. Commn. of the States, Am. Mgmt. Assn., Young Women's Bus. Assn., Phi Delta Kappa. Democrat. Home: 1481 S Elaine Dr Baton Rouge LA 70815

CLAWSON, CAROL A., communications executive; b. N.Y.C., Nov. 13, 1946; d. Lester P. and Helen (Nathan) David; m. Ken W. Clawson, Mar. 16, 1969;. BA, Ohio Wesleyan U., 1967. Staff writer, reporter Toledo Blade, 1967-68; staff writer Congl. Quarterly, Washington, 1968-69; Washington correspondent Newhouse News Svc., 1969-75; press sec. com. adminstrn. U.S. Ho. Reps., Washington, 1975-77, press sec. com. sci. and tech., 1977-78, press sec. com. small bus., 1978-82; mgr. corp. com. L. I. Lighting Co., Hicksville, N.Y., 1982-85; v.p. communication GPU Nuclear Corp., Parsippany, N.J., 1985—. Mem. Nat. Press Club, Inst. Nuclear Power Ops. (mem. communications com., 1989—). Republican. Jewish. Home: 6 Blaier Ct Towaco NJ 07082 Office: GPU Nuclear Corp One Upper Pond Rd Parsippany NJ 07054

CLAWSON, ROXANN ELOISE, college administrator, computer company executive; b. Dallas, Oct. 15, 1945; d. Robert Wellington Clawson and Jeannette Irene (Rodenhauser) Clawson Clayton. BFA, Mich. State U., 1968. Library asst. Cooper Union, N.Y.C., 1970-75, asst. librarian, 1976-82, asst. to dean, 1985—; pres. Standing By Wordprocessing, N.Y.C., 1982—; v.p. Word Group, N.Y.C., 1984—; computer cons., 1986—. Acting appearance in The Dragon's Nest, La MaMa Theatre, 1989. Mem. Nat. Assn. Female Execs., N.Y. Personal Computer Group. Democrat. Lutheran. Avocation: administration.

CLAX, FREDA MARIE, publication designer; b. Red Bank, N.J., Nov. 19, 1959; d. Joseph and Anita (Desbordes) C. Assoc. Specialized Tech., Art Inst. Pitts., 1981; BFA, Sch. Visual Arts, N.Y.C., 1987. Freelance graphics designer and illustrator various cos., N.Y.C., 1981-85; freelance designer Self Mag., Conde Nast Publs., N.Y.C., 1981; freelance designer communications design dept. Citicorp, N.Y.C., 1987, Weight Watchers Mag., N.Y.C., 1987; jr. designer Prima Mag., Gruner and Jahr Publs., N.Y.C., 1987-88; freelance designer In Fashion and Internat. Sportswear, Murdoch Publs., N.Y.C., 1988; asst. art dir. Footwear News, Fairchild Publs., N.Y.C., 1988-89; sr. designer Essence Mag., N.Y.C., 1989—; freelance cons. Mademoiselle mag. Mem. Am. Inst. Graphic Arts. Democrat. Roman Catholic. Home: 34-C Arcadia Rd Hackensack NJ 07610

CLAXTON, HARRIETT MAROY JONES, retired English educator; b. Dublin, Ga., Aug. 27, 1930; d. Paul Jackson and Maroy Athalia (Chappell) Jones; m. Edward B. Claxton, Jr., May 27, 1953; children—E. B. III, Paula Jones. AA, Bethel Woman's Coll., 1949; AB magna cum laude, Mercer U., 1951; MEd, Ga. Coll., 1965. Social worker Laurens County Welfare Bd., Dublin, 1951-56; high sch. tchr., Dublin, 1961-66; instr. Middle Ga. Coll., Cochran, 1966-71, asst. prof. English, lit. and speech, 1971-85, assoc. prof. 1985-86; research tchr. Trinity Christian Sch., 1986, sr. English tchr., 1986-87; part-time tchr., Ga. Coll., 1987, Emanuel County Jr. Coll., 1988. Contbr. articles to profl. jours. and newspapers; editor Laurens County History, II, 1987. Pres. bd. Dublin Assn. Fine Arts, 1974-76, 82-84, Dublin Hist. Soc., 1976-78; mem. Laurens County Library Bd., 1960-68; chmn. Dublin Hist. Rev. Bd., 1980-85. Named Woman of Yr., St. Patrick's Festival, Dublin, 1979; recipient Outstanding Service award Cancer Soc., Dublin, 1985. Mem. DAR (regent, state, dist. and nat. awards), Sigma Mu, Alpha Delta Pi, Phi Theta Kappa, Chi Delta Phi, Delta Kappa Gamma. Democrat. Baptist. Clubs: Woman's Study (pres.), Erin Garden (pres.) (Dublin). Home: 101 Rosewood Dr Dublin GA 31021

CLAY, CAROLYNE, metallurgist; b. Chgo., Apr. 30, 1952; d. Calvin and Leanet (May) C. B.S., Rensselaer Poly. Inst., 1974; M.S., MIT, 1976, Metall. Engr., 1978. Research asst. MIT, Cambridge, 1975-77; research metallurgist Ford Motor Co. Sci. Research Lab., Dearborn, Mich., 1977-79; sr. metallurgist Kaiser Aluminum & Chem. Co.-Trentwood Works, Spokane, Wash., 1979-85; staff metallurgist Kaiser Aluminum & Chem. Co.-Trentwood Works, 1985-87, prodn. gen. foreman, 1988—; vis. com. MIT Material Sci. and Engring. Corp., 1978. Recipient Karl T. Compton award, 1977; recipient Scott MacKay award, 1974. Mem. Am. Soc. Metals, AIME, Nat. Soc. Profl. Engrs., NAACP, Sigma Xi, Delta Sigma Theta. Congregationalist. Office: Trentwood Works PO Box 15108 Spokane WA 99215

CLAY, DONNA JEAN, barrister; b. Fresno, Calif., June 21, 1958; d. Gustav and Leona (Brown) P.; married. BA, Fresno Pacific, 1982. Auditor Sears, Sacramento, Calif., 1976-78; floral designer Hieberts Vista Flowers, Fresno, Calif., 1978-82; librarian asst. Fresno Pacific Coll., 1978-82; bookkeeper Halls Disbributing, Fresno, Calif.; communications op. Fresno Police Dept., 1983--; reserve police officer Fresno Police Dept., 1988; consulting mem. Fresno Police/Fire Dept., 1988. Recipient Scholarship March of Dimes, Sacramento, 1976, Scholarship Music Drama Fresno Pacific Coll., 1978-82. Democrat. Mennonite. Home: 5125 E Ln #114 Fresno CA 93727

CLAY, TOMMIE SENIOR, elementary school principal; b. Huntsville, Tex.; d. Tom L. and LuBerta (Dickey) Shackelford; m. Donald Eugene Clay, Oct. 2, 1948 (dec. July 1983); 1 child, Donna Paulette Clay-Conti. BS, Prairie View U., 1949; MA, Tex. So. U., 1955, San Francisco State U., 1974; EdD, Nova U., 1980. Tchr. Jack Yates High Sch., Houston, 1955-60; elem. tchr. Oakland (Calif.) Unified Sch. Dist., 1961-72, resource reading tchr., 1972-74, dist. math tch. special assignment, 1974-77, asst. prin., 1977-82, prin., 1982—; dist. elem. monitor and review team, Oakland Unified Sch., Calif., 1974-77, 86-87, presenter math workshops, 1974-77, elem. edn. master tchr., 1964-68, dist. textbook selection mem., 1980-81, 83-84, dist. attendance task force, 1986-87, dist. mentor tchr. interview comm., 1987-88. Author: Kitchen Metrics for Children, 1976. Mem. Prairie View U. Alumni Bd. Dirs., 1959-60. Mem. Phi Delta Kappa, Alpha Kappa Alpha, Alpha Nu Omega (standards com. chmn. 1988—). Democrat. Home: 7968 Phaeton Dr Oakland CA 94605

CLAYTON, CYNTHIA CARLSON, physician; b. Boston, Feb. 25, 1943; d. Harry and Anita (Pearl) Carlson; m. William Frank Clayton, July 4, 1965; children—William Justin, Austin Buck. B.A., Smith Coll., 1964; M.D., NYU, 1967. Intern and resident in pediatrics Buffalo Children's Hosp., 1967-71; pvt. practice medicine, specializing in pediatrics and adolescent medicine, East Aurora, N.Y., 1974—; clin. asst. prof. pediatrics SUNY-Buffalo, 1973—; sch. physician Iroquois Central Schs., Elma, N.Y., 1980—. Fellow Am. Acad. Pediatrics; mem. N.Y. Med. Soc., Erie County Med. Soc., Sigma Xi. Avocations: writing; running; karate. Home: 29 Braunview Way Orchard Park NY 14127 Office: 100 Riley St East Aurora NY 14052

CLAYTON, ELLEN WRIGHT, law educator, pediatrician; b. Houston, June 22, 1952; d. James Thomas and Maidel Reta (Wright) Wright; m. John Bunyan Clayton IV, June 19, 1982; 2 children. BS, Duke U., 1974; MS, Stanford U., 1976; JD, Yale U., 1979; MD, Harvard U., 1985. Bar: Tex. 1980. Diplomate Am. Bd. Pediatrics. Law clk. Hon. John C. Godbold, Montgomery, Ala., 1979-80; atty. Vinson & Elkins, Houston, 1980-81; vis. asst. prof. law U. Wis., Madison, 1985; resident U. Wis. Hosp., Madison, 1985-88; asst. prof. law, asst. prof. pediatrics Vanderbilt U., Nashville, 1988—. Contbr. articles to profl. jours. Recipient Costello award for best intern U. Wis. Hosp., 1986. Mem. Am. Acad. Pediatrics (bioethics com. 1989—), Am. Soc. Law and Medicine, State Bar of Tex.

CLAYTON, EVELYN WILLIAMS, company executive; b. Durham, N.C., Feb. 11, 1951; d. Virge and Inez Florence (Jordan) Williams; m. Archie L. Clayton, Mar. 1, 1972 (div. May 1975); 1 child, Dorel. Student Durham Tech. Inst., 1969-71, Durham Bus. Coll., 1971-72, U. N.C.-Chapel Hill, 1977-81; A.B.A., Durham Tech. Inst., 1971. Fiscal officer Durham County Health Dept. (N.C.), 1974-82; dir. fin. MedVisit Inc., Butner, N.C., 1982—; exec. dir., pres. EC & Assocs., fin. mgmt. and cons. firm, Durham, 1982—. Mem. Durham Com. on Affairs of Black People; cubmaster, Pack 442, Boy Scouts Am.; mem. Durham County Women's Commn.; active congl. campaign Kenneth B. Spaulding, 1985. Mem. N.C. Assn. Home Care (treas. 1980-83), N.C. Public Health Assn., NAACP. Democrat. Baptist. Home: 36 Burgess Ln Durham NC 27707 Office: EC & Assocs 3510 University Dr Durham NC 27707

CLAYTON, FRANCES ELIZABETH, educator; b. Texarkana, Tex., Nov. 6, 1922; d. Carl C. and Louise (Heath) C. A.A., Texarkana Coll., 1942; B.A., Tex. Womens U., 1944; M.A., U. Tex., 1947, Ph.D., 1951. Instr. U. Ark., Fayetteville, 1950-51, mem. faculty, 1954—, prof. zoology, 1961-87, prof. emeritus, 1987—; instr. U. Tex., Austin, 1951-52; Rosalie B. Hite Postdoctoral fellow U. Tex., 1952-53, research scientist, 1953-54; vis. colleague in genetics U. Hawaii, 1963-64; researcher cytology species of Drosophila. Contbr. articles to tech. jours. Fellow AAAS; mem. Am. Genetic Assn., Evolution Soc., Soc. Am. Naturalists. Home: 1923 E Joyce St Apt 362 Fayetteville AR 72703 Office: U Ark Dept Zool SE 632 Fayetteville AR 72701

CLAYTON, JOY MAY, tourism industry executive; b. Mobile, Ala., Nov. 23, 1947; d. Allen Clark and Catherine (Finch) May. BS In English, U. So. Miss., 1970, MEd, 1971. Asst. dir. communications and devel. St. Mary's Hosp., Galveston, Tex., 1980-81; dir. communications and pub. rels. Galveston C. of C., 1981-82; dir. pub. relations and sales Galveston Arts!, 1982-83; exec. dir., v.p. Col. Paddlewheel Boat, Galveston, 1985—, also bd. dirs.; reserve faculty Galveston Coll., 1978—. Author: Journal of Creative Behavior, 1978. Bd. dirs. Col. Mus., Inc., Moody Found.; founder, bd. dirs. Galveston Acad. Booster Club, 1977; bd. dirs. Clean Galveston, 1981, 87, Jr. League Galveston County, 1981—, Mental Health Assn., 1983; bd. dirs. Galveston Attractions Assn., 1986—, pres., 1990; chmn., founder Galveston Island Jazz Festival; trustee Galveston Park Bd., 1987—, sec., treas. Named one of Outstanding Young Women Am., 1975, Outstanding Tchr. Evening Optimists Galveston Ind. Sch. Dist., 1978. Mem. Nat. Tour Assn., Tex. Soc. Asst. Execs., Rotary, Delta Kappa Gamma. Episcopalian. Home: 5222 Denver Dr Galveston TX 77551 Office: Col Paddlewheel Boat 111 Tremont Galveston TX 77550

CLAYTON, PEGGY L., administrative assistant, human resources professional; b. Chisholm, Minn., May 28, 1953; d. Henry Joseph and Carolyn Jean (Zaitz) Falcone; m. Richard J. Clayton Jr., Mar. 23, 1985; children: Bradley, Lindsay. Student, Orlando Sch. Cashiers, 1973. Cert. aerobic instr. Legal sec. Henry H. Bank, Atty., Mpls.; office mgr. S.H. Press & Co.,

Orlando, Fla.; exec. sec. No. Ductile Castings, Hibbing, Minn., Ryan Constrn Co., Hibbing; adminstrv. asst., human resources officer Itasca Courthouse, Grand Rapids, Minn. Salesperson Maroon and Gold All Star Hockey, U.S. Hockey Hall of Fame Golf Classic. Mem. Profl. Secs. Internat. (past pres.), Grand Rapids Amateur Hockey Assn. (sec.). Home: 4500 Wendigo Park Rd Grand Rapids MN 55744

CLEARY, BEVERLY ATLEE (MRS. CLARENCE T. CLEARY), author; b. McMinnville, Oreg.; d. Chester Lloyd and Mable (Atlee) Bunn; m. Clarence T. Cleary, Oct. 6, 1940; children: Marianne Elisabeth, Malcolm James. BA, U. Calif., 1938; BA in Librarianship, U. Wash., 1939. Children's librarian Yakima, Wash., 1939-40; post librarian Regional Hosp., Oakland, Calif., 1942-45. Author: Henry Huggins, 1950, Ellen Tebbits, 1951, Henry and Beezus, 1952, Otis Spofford, 1953, Henry and Ribsy, 1954, Beezus and Ramona, 1955, Fifteen, 1956, Henry and the Paper Route, 1957, The Luckiest Girl, 1958, Jean and Johnny, 1959, Hullabaloo ABC, 1960, Emily's Runaway Imagination, 1961, Henry and the Clubhouse, 1962, Sister of the Bride, 1963, Ribsy, 1964, The Mouse and the Motorcycle, 1965, Mitch and Amy, 1967, Ramona the Pest, 1968, Runaway Ralph, 1970, Socks, 1973, Ramona the Brave, 1975, Ramona and her Father, 1977 (Honor Book for U.S., Internat. Bd. and Books for Young People), Ramona and Her Mother, 1979, Ramona Quimby, Age 8, 1981, Ralph S. Mouse, 1982, Dear Mr. Henshaw, 1983, Ramona Forever, 1984, Lucky Chuck, 1984, The Ramona Quimby Diary, 1984, Two Dog Biscuits, 1985, The Real Hole, 1985, Beezus and Ramona Diary, 1986, Janet's Thingamajigs, 1987, The Growing Up Feet, 1987, A Girl from Yamhill, 1988, Muggie Maggie, 1990, Strider, 1991. Recipient Laura Ingalls Wilder award Children's Services div. ALA 1975, Newbery Honor Book award 1978, 82, Regina medal Cath. Library Assn. 1980, Am. Book award, 1981, Golden Kite award Soc. Children's Book Writers, 1983, Christopher award, 1983, George C. Stone award Claremont Colls., 1983, Calif. Tchrs. English award, 1983, Newbery medal, 1984, Hans Christian Andersen medal nominee, 1984, Everychild award Children's Book Council, 1985, Ludington award Ednl. Paperback Assn., 1987. Am. Book award, 1981, George C. Stone award Claremont Colls., 1983. Mem. Authors Guild of Authors League Am. Address: care William Morrow 105 Madison Ave New York NY 10016

CLEARY, LYNDA WOODS, insurance and business consultant; b. Birmingham, Ala., June 18, 1950; d. Eugene and Elizabeth (Wright) Woods; m. George Cassius Riley, Nov. 29, 1975 (div. 1979); m. Richard Charles Cleary, Dec. 12, 1987. Student, Dartmouth Coll., 1970-71; BA, Tougaloo (Miss.) Coll., 1972; postgrad., N.Y. Inst. Tech., 1985-86. Comml. underwriter Continental Ins. Co., N.Y.C., 1973-74; lectr. John Ericson Sch., Ostersund, Sweden, 1974; asst. underwriting cons. Prudential Property and Casualty, Holmdel, N.J., 1975-80; market rsch. analyst Continental Ins. Co., Piscataway, N.J., 1981-86; bus. systems analyst Am. Internat. Group, N.Y.C., 1986-87; ins. agt. Equitable Fin. Cos., N.Y.C., 1988; spl. agt. Northwestern Mut. Life, Princeton, N.J., 1988-89; cons. Cleary Woods Cons., Princeton, 1989—; cons. Nat. Torque Tech. Labs., Piscataway, 1989—. Com. mem. Princeton Walk Homeowners Assn., 1988—; fundraiser Crossroads Theatre, New Brunswick, N.J., 1988—. Recipient Cert. of Appreciation Concerned Community Women of Jersey City, Inc., 1990. Mem. Women Life Underwriters Confedn., Am. Mgmt. Assn., NAFE, Nat. Assn. Life Underwriters. Democrat. Baptist. Home: 22 Springwood Ct Princeton NJ 08540

CLEARY, MANON CATHERINE, artist, educator; b. St. Louis, Nov. 14, 1942; d. Frank and Crystal (Maret) C. BFA, Washington U., St. Louis, 1964; MFA, Tyler Sch. Art, Temple U., 1968. Instr. fine arts SUNY, Oswego, 1968-70; from instr. to assoc. prof. D.C. Tchrs. Coll., Washington, 1970-78; from assoc. prof. to prof. art U. D.C., Washington, 1978-90, acting chmn. dept. art, 1985-86. One woman shows include Mus. Modern Art Gulbenkian Found., Lisbon, Portugal, 1985, Iolas/Jackson Gallery, N.Y.C., 1982, Osuna Gallery, Washington, 1974, 77, 80, 84, 89, Univ. D.C., 1987, Tyler Gallery SUNY at Oswego, 1987, others; group exhibits include Twenthieth Century Am. Drawings: The Figure in Context, Traveled Nat. Acad. Design, 1984-85, others. Artist-in-residence Herning Hojskole, Denmark, 1980, Ucross Found., Wyo., 1984. Recipient Faculty Rsch. award, U. D.C., 1983, 89. Mem. NEA, Coll. Art Assn., Pi Beta Phi. Democrat. Presbyterian. Home: 1736 Columbia Rd NW NW Apt 402 Washington DC 20009 Office: U DC Art Dept 916 G St NW Washington DC 20001

CLEAVE, MARY L., environmental engineer, astronaut; b. Southampton, N.Y., Feb. 5, 1947. BS in Biol. Scis., Colo. State U., 1969; MS in Microbiol. Ecology, Utah State U., 1975, PhD in Civil and Environ. Engring., 1979. Mem. rsch. staff Utah State U., 1971-80; astronaut NASA, Lyndon B. Johnson Space Ctr., Houston, 1980—, mission specialist STS 61-B, 1985, mission specialist STS-30, 1989. Mem. Tex. Soc. Profl. Engrs., Water Pollution Control Fedn., Sigma Xi, Tau Beta Pi. Office: NASA Johnson Space Ctr Astronaut Office Houston TX 77058*

CLEIN, CHERYL LEE, mathematician, analyst; b. Seattle, Mar. 18, 1948; d. Merle and Elaine Edith (Skersies) Hottenstein; m. Richard Thomas Larson, Mar. 24, 1972 (div. Jan. 1989). BS, Seattle Pacific U., 1970. Computer aide R.W. Beck and Assocs., Seattle, 1970-71, sr. computer aide, 1971-72, jr. technician, 1972-73, engring. technician, 1973-76, sr. technician, 1976-78, sr. analyst, 1978—; v.p. the Network of R.W. Beck and Assocs., 1982-85. Vol. reach to recovery Am. Cancer Soc. Mem. NAFE, Am. Poetry Assn. (Poet of Merit 1989), Am. Guild Organists. Office: RW Beck and Assocs 2101 4th Ave Ste 600 Seattle WA 98121-2375

CLELAND, GLADYS LEE, university administrator; b. Schenectady, Feb. 27, 1959; d. Anthony John and Anna Mae (Feight) Campana; m. Michael Joseph Cleland, Aug. 4, 1984. BA in Communications and Edn. cum laude, SUNY, Plattsburgh, 1981; MA summa cum laude, U. Fla., 1986. Asst. instr. communications SUNY, Plattsburgh, 1982-83, admissions/media rels. advisor, 1987-88; asst. instr. communications U. Fla., Gainesville, 1985-86; instr. English and communications Clinton Community Coll., Plattsburgh, 1986-87; news cons., acad. liaison Sta. WCFE-TV, Plattsburgh, 1987-88; pub. info. dir. Syracuse (N.Y.) U., 1989—; news cons. Sta. WCFE-TV 57, Plattsburgh, 1987-88; producer, researcher CVPH Med. Ctr., Plattsburgh, 1982-87; media rels. cons. Sta. WIXT-TV9, Syracuse, 1988—; press steward Winter Olympic Games, Lake Placid, N.Y., 1980; radio announcer, news reporter, sales rep. Sta. WIRY-AM, Plattsburgh, 1980-83; producer, news reporter Sta. WPBT-TV, Miami, Fla., 1983-84. Author: Satellite News Gathering, 1986. Recipient broadcast awards N.Y. State Broadcast Assn., Plattsburgh, 1982-84, Outstanding Talent award Internat. TV Assn., Gainesville, 1986. Mem. Women in Communications, Inc., Internat. TV Assn., League Women Voters (publs. coord. 1986—), Friends Historic Onondaga Lake, SUNY Coll. Admissions Personnel, Omicron Delta Kappa, Alpha Epsilon Rho, Phi Kappa Chi. Roman Catholic. Home: 4239 Mill Run Rd Liverpool NY 13090 Office: Syracuse U 270 Huntington Hall Syracuse NY 13244-2340

CLEM, ELIZABETH ANN STUMPF, music educator; b. San Antonio, July 9, 1945; d. David Joseph and Elizabeth Burch (Wathen) Stumpf; m. D. Bruce Clem, June 17, 1972; children: Sean David, Jeremy Andrew. BA in Music Edn., St. Mary-of-the-Woods (Ind.) Coll., 1970; MEd, Drury Coll., Springfield, Mo., 1979. Elem. tchr. St. Christopher Sch., Speedway, Ind., 1970-71; elem. and jr. high sch. tchr. Indpls. Sch. System, 1971-72; elem. tchr. Augusta (Ga.) Sch. System, 1972-73; Wabash (Ind.) Sch. System, 1976-77; pvt. practice piano tchr. Wabash, Ind., 1975-77, Honolulu, 1983-86, Burke, Va., 1986—. Dist. fund raiser rep. Wabash chpt. Am. Cancer Soc., 1975; leadership coordinator Wabash council Girl Scouts Am., 1976; music coordinator Ft. Shafter Sacred Heart Chapel, Honolulu, 1985-86. Mem. Nat. Guild Piano Tchrs., No. Va. Music Tchrs. Assn., Springfield Music Club. Republican. Roman Catholic. Home and Office: 6316 Wilmington Dr Burke VA 22015

CLEMENS, TAMMY L., geriatrics nurse; b. Roaring Spring, Pa., Apr. 2, 1958; d. Ronald Robert and Doris Marie (Ott) Ferry; m. Richard S. Clemens III, Feb. 9, 1980; 1 child, Jamie Marie. Diploma, Altoona Hosp. Sch. Nursing, 1979. RN, Pa. Charge nurse, staff nurse Nason Hosp., Roaring Spring, 1979-83; nursing supr. Morrisons Cove Home for Aged, Martinsburg, Pa., 1983—. Substitute ch. organist Trinity United Meth. Ch., Roaing Spring, Pa., 1974-79, ch. sch. pianist, 1974-79; asst. leader troop #640 Girl Scouts U.S., 1988—. Mem. Friendship Fire Co. #1, Inc. Republican. Home: 430 Locust St Roaring Spring PA 16673 Office: Morrisons Cove Home for Aged 429 S Market St Martinsburg PA 16662

CLEMENT, BETSY KAY, computer company executive; b. Columbus, Ohio, Oct. 12, 1952; d. Harold Francis and Carley June (Davidson) Snider; m. Laurence Peter Clement, July 10, 1981. B in Music, U. Fla., 1975; M in Music, New Eng. Conservatory, 1979. Singer Musicana Enterprises, Inc., Vero Beach, Fla., 1975-77; opera singer N.Y.C., 1979-83; asst. to programming dir. Showtime/The Movie Channel, N.Y.C., 1983-84; asst. to program guide dir. United Satellite Communications, N.Y.C., 1984; founding ptnr. Mobile Word Assocs., N.Y.C. and Tampa, Fla., 1985-90; microcomputer tng. and support specialist City of Clearwater, Fla., 1990—; cons. Time, Inc., N.Y.C., CBS TV Rsch., N.Y.C., Cosmopolitan Personnel, N.Y.C., Computerlands of Tampa Bay, Anheuser-Busch Inc., Fla. Power Corp., Fla. Fed. Savs. and Loan. Developer computer tng. courses, workbooks, reference manuals, programs. Mem. Tampa Master Chorale. Mem. NAFE, Ind. Computer Cons. Assn., NOW (v.p. East Hillsborough chpt.), Sigma Alpha Iota, Sigma Kappa. Home: 306 Greenview Dr Brandon FL 33510 Office: City of Clearwater Dept Adminstrv Svcs DIS PO Box 4748 Clearwater FL 34618-4748

CLEMENT, HOPE ELIZABETH ANNA, librarian; b. North Sydney, N.S., Can., Dec. 29, 1930; d. Harry Wells and Lana (Perkins) C. BA, U. of King's Coll., 1951; MA, Dalhousie U., 1953; BLS, U. Toronto, 1955. With Nat. Library of Can., Ottawa, Ont., 1955—; chief nat. bibliography div. Nat. Library of Can., 1966-70, asst. dir. research and planning br., 1970-73, dir. research and planning br., 1973-77, assoc. nat. librarian, 1977—. Editor: Canadiana, 1966-69. Mem. Can. Libr. Assn., Iinternat. Fedn. Libr. Assns., Profl. Bd. (chmn.). Office: Nat Library Can, 395 Wellington St, Ottawa, ON Canada K1A 0N4

CLEMENT, JANICE FAYE, nursing adminstrator; b. Norfolk, Nebr., Aug. 19, 1946; d. Allen Edward and Hilda Bernice (Stange) Reeves; m. Roger Allen Clement, Oct. 6, 1968 (dec. July 1974).; m. August H. Allen, Sept. 17, 1988. RN, Meth. Sch. Nursing, Omaha, 1967; BS in Nursing, magna cum laude, Creighton U., 1978; MS in Nursing, U. Nebr., 1981; cert. in nursing adminstrn. With Meth. Hosp., 1967-68, 70-83, asst. head nurse, 1974-77, staff devel. nurse, 1977-81, dir. staff adminstrv. services, 1981-83; pub. health nurse Wichita-Sedgwick County Health Dept., Wichita, Kans., 1970-72; dir. nursing Meth. Med. Ctr., St. Joseph, Mo., 1983-84, Broadlawns Med. Ctr., Des Moines, 1984—; adj. clin. faculty nursing Drake U. Nursing, Des Moines, 1986—, mem. adv. bd., 1984—, Cen. Campus Practical Nursing, 1984—; mem. adv. bd. Des Moines Area Community Coll. Dist., 1987—, Des Moines Area Community Coll. Nursing Bd., 1987—, Grandview Coll., 1988—; bd. dirs. Vis. Nurse Svcs., 1988—. Mem. Am. Nurses Assn., Iowa Nurses Assn., Nat. League Nursing, Am. Orgn. Nurse Execs., (Iowa chpt.), Cen. Iowa Nursing Leadership Conf. (pres. 1985—), Colloquium Nursing Leaders Cen. Iowa, Iowa League for Nursing (treas. 1987-89, pres. 1989), Iowa Orgn. Nurse Execs. (treas. 1987, sec. 1989), Iowa Hosp. Assn. Council on Patient Services, 1988—, Am. Mgmt. Assn., Sigma Theta Tau. Republican. Methodist. Avocations: flying, sewing, golfing, walking, reading. Home: 764 Knolls Ct West Des Moines IA 50265 Office: Broadlawns Med Ctr 18th and Hickman Rd Des Moines IA 50314

CLEMENT, SHIRLEY GEORGE, educational services executive; b. El Paso, Tex., Feb. 14, 1926; d. Claude Samuel and Elizabeth Estelle (Mattice) Gillett; m. Paul Vincent Clement, Mar. 23, 1946; children: Brian Frank, Robert Vincent, Carol Elizabeth, Rosemary Adele. BA in English, Tex. Western Coll., 1963; postgrad. U. Tex., El Paso, N.Mex. State U.; MEd in Reading, Sul Ross State U., 1987. Tchr. lang. arts Ysleta Ind. Schs., El Paso, 1960-62; tchr. adult edn., 1962-64, tchr. reading/lang. arts, 1964-77; owner, dir. Crestline Learning Systems, Inc., El Paso, 1980—; dir. tutorial for sports teams U. Tex., El Paso, 1984; dir. continuing edn. program El Paso Community Coll., 1985; mem. curriculum com. Ysleta Ind. Schs., El Paso, 1974; mem. Right to Read Task Force, 1975-77; mem. Bi-Centennial Steering Com., El Paso, 1975-76; lectr. on reading in 4 states. Author: Beginning the Search, 1979; contbr. poems to Behold Texas, 1983. Treas. El Paso Rep. Women, 1956; facilitator Goals for El Paso, 1975; mem. hospitality com. Sun Carnival, 1974, Cotton Festival, 1975. Mem. Internat. Reading Assn. (pres. El Paso County council 1973-74, presentor 1987-89), Assn. Children with Learning Disabilities (tchr. 1980), Poetry Soc. Tex. (Panhandle Penwomen's first place award 1981), Nat. Fedn. State Poetry Soc. (1st place award ann. contest 1988), Chi Omega Alumnae (pres. 1952-53). Home: 114 Casas Bellas Ln PO Box 1645 Santa Teresa NM 88008-1645 Office: Crestline Secondary Sch and Tutor House 481 N Resler St D & E El Paso TX 79912

CLEMENTE, ALICE RODRIGUES, language educator; b. Pawtucket, R.I., July 28, 1934; d. Alipio Rodrigues and Maria (Joaquim) C. AB, Brown Univ., 1956, MA, 1959, PhD, 1967. Instr. Randolph-Macon Woman's Coll., Lynchburg, Va., 1959-61, Wheaton Coll., Norton, Mass., 1964; prof. Spanish and Portuguese Smith Coll., Northampton, Mass., 1964—. Contbr. articles to profl. jours. Former pres. League of Women Voters. Mem. Assn. Internat. Hispanistas, Northeast Modern Language Assn., Northeast Assn. Brazilianists, Medieval Soc. Am. Home: 523 Kennedy Rd Leeds MA 01053 Office: Smith Coll Northampton MA 01063

CLEMENTS, EMILIA GONZÁLEZ, anthropologist, consultant; b. Palacios, Tex., Jan. 13, 1944; d. Petronilo and Lidia (Teran) Gonzalez; m. Louis Elias Cohen, Jr., Apr. 1, 1965 (div. 1983); children: Samantha, Rebecca; m. Luther Davis Clements, Jr., June 11, 1983. AA, Alvin Jr. Coll., 1964; BA, Niagara U., Lewiston, N.Y., 1973; MA, Tex. Tech. U., 1981. Social worker Buckner Children's Home, Lubbock, Tex., 1981; instr. Tex. Tech. U., Lubbock, 1982; ethnic outreach coord. Lubbock Regional MH/MR Ctr., Lubbock, 1982-84; pres. Devel. Systems and Applications, Lincoln, 1985—; exec. dir. Lincoln (Nebr.) Commn. Status of Women, 1986-87; regional coord. Unitarian Universalist Svc. Commn. Prairie Star Dist., 1987—; lectr. Creighton U., Omaha, 1988, cons., 1988—; cons. Iowa State U., Ames, 1989, Nebr. State Health Dept., 1989, City of Lexington, Nebr., Lincoln Pub. Sch. System, Omaha Pub. Sch. System, U. Nebr., Lincoln. Compiler (directory) Nebraska Women of Color, 1989. Active exec. com. Lancaster County Dems., Lincoln, 1987; pres. Internat. Ctr., Lincoln, 1987—, UN Assn., 1988, mem. state bd., 1988—; coord. com. city planning project StarVentrue, Lincoln, 1987-88. Field Rsch. grantee Tex. Tech. U., 1980, field work grantee Guerra Contra El Hambre, Dominican Republic, 1989, Guatemala Rural Health Workers grantee USAID, U. Nebr., 1989, 90. Fellow Soc. for Applied Anthropology; mem. Am. Anthrop. Assn., High Plains Soc. for Applied Anthropology, Soc. for Visual Anthropolgy, Assn. Women in Devel., LWV (Nebr., intern. rels. chpt. 1987-88), Assn. Latinos Anthropology. Democrat. Unitarian. Home and Office: 8010 Lillibridge St Lincoln NE 68506

CLEMENTS, JOYE ARLINE, health care administrator; b. Boston, July 23, 1936; d. Raymond Eugene and Arline M. (Olson) Moreau; m. Richard A. Meuse, July 11, 1953 (div. 1972); children: Darlene Trombly, Thomas, Richard; m. Walter E. Clements, Aug. 15, 1975 (dec.); 1 child, Douglas. Student, No. Essex Coll., 1971-80; BS in Nursing, Northeastern U., 1980. Cert. Am. Coll. Health Care Adminstrs. Dir. nursing Winthrop House, Medford, Mass., 1980-82; exec. dir. Elder Care Services Inc., Rowley, Mass., 1982-84; pres., chief exec. officer Briarcliff Inc., Gloucester, Mass., 1984—; mem. state regulators com. Mass. Fedn. Nursing Homes, 1986—, Blueprint 2000 com. Commonwealth of Mass., 1987-88, adv. com. nursing home and rest home regulations Mass. Dept. Pub. Health, 1988. Author: (manual) Quality Assurance, 1983. Mem. Rest Home Orgn. Mass. (pres. 1987-88), Nat. Bus. and Profl. Women (chpt. v.p. f1980-81, chpt. pres. 1981-82, Woman Yr. 1984), Gloucester C. of C., Cape Ann C. of C. (steering com. bus. women 1987-88). Roman Catholic. Home: 46 Summer St Gloucester MA 01930 Office: Briarcliff Inc PO Box 1151 Gloucester MA 01930

CLEMENTS, JULIA ANNE, infosystems specialist; b. Atlanta, Nov. 9, 1953; d. James Luther and Margaret Anita (Cannon) C.; BS, Ga. State U., 1979, MBA, 1985, M Bus. Info. Systems, 1987. Tax examiner bus. div. IRS, Atlanta, 1983-84; co-ordinator nat. response ctr. Honeywell Info. Systems, Atlanta, 1984-85; office mgr. Ronald L. Hilley, Attorney At Law, Atlanta, 1985-86; appren. systems analyst Bell So. Services: Info. Systems Services, Atlanta, 1986-87; programmer, analyst mgmt. info. services Contel Texocom Co., Atlanta, 1987-88; systems support rep. Software AG, Atlanta, 1988—. Mem. Crawford W. Long Hosp. Aux., Atlanta, Putnam County Hist. Soc., Eatonton, Ga. Mem. AAUW, Assn. Computing Machinery, IEEE. Office: Software AG 100 Ashford Ctr N Ste 350 Atlanta GA 30338

CLEMENTS, LYNNE FLEMING, family therapist, programmer; b. Bklyn., Aug. 8, 1945; d. Daniel Gillies and Dorthy Frances (Zitzmann) Fleming; m. Louis Myrick Clements, Feb. 19, 1972; children: Ryan Louis, Glenn Fleming. BA in Sociology, Bradley U., 1967; MSW, Fordham U., 1973; postgrad. studies, Columbia U., 1970-71; family theapy cert., Inst. for Mental Health Edn., 1990. Computer programmer Employer's Comml. Union Group of Insur. Cos., Boston, 1967-69, Harvard Bus. Sch., Cambridge, Mass., 1969-70, Volkswagon of Am., Englewood Cliffs, N.J., 1971; psychiatric social worker Associated Catholic Charities Family and Children's Svcs., Paramus, N.J., 1973-74, Christian Health Ctr., Wyckoff, N.J., 1976; owner, mgr. Wicker Wagon, Bergenfield, N.J., 1977-85; psychotherapist The Psychotherapy Counseling Ctr., Bergenfield, N.J., 1982-89; programmer, analyst Atlas Computing Svcs., Secaucus, N.J., 1984-86; program coord., family therapist Div. of Family Guidance, Hackensack, N.J., 1986—; admnstv. dir. Corp. Family Resources, Ridgewood, N.J., 1989—; part-time family therapist N.J. Ctr. for Psychotherapy Inc., Ridgefield Park, N.J., 1990—. Sunday Sch. Tchr. All Saints Ch., 1982-89; mem. Twin-Boro Youth Ministry Coun., 1989—, Bergen County Family Day Care Coalition, 1989—. Recipient 1st and 2d pl. awards Bergenfield (N.J.) 1980 Art Contest; NIMH grantee 1973. Mem. AAUW, Gifted Child Soc. (parent workshop coord. 1989—), Nat. Assn. Social Workers, Acad. Cert. Social Workers, Am. Orthopsychiat. Assn., Fordham U. Alumni Assn. Episcopalian. Home: 148 Harcourt Ave Bergenfield NJ 07621 Office: Corp Family Resources 201 E Ridgewood Ave Ridgewood NJ 07450

CLEMINSHAW, HELEN K. MARIE, psychologist, educator; b. Elizabeth, N.J., May 16, 1938; d. Fred A. and Helen W. (Bittner) Kronseder; m. John G. Cleminshaw, June 24, 1960; children: John David, Suzanne Christine. BS, Rutgers U., 1960; MA, Kent (Ohio) State U., 1972, PhD, 1977. Lic. psychologist, Ohio. Sch. psychologist Maple Heights (Ohio) Schs., 1972-75; assoc. prof. psychology U. Akron, Ohio, 1976-88, prof., 1988—; psychologist Hudson (Ohio) Psychol. Assocs., 1980—; dir. Child Life Specialist Tng. Program, Akron, 1979—, Ctr. Family Studies, Akron, 1981—. Co-editor: Alcoholism: New Perspectives, 1983; contbr. articles to profl. jours. U. Akron Faculty Rsch. grantee, 1978-79, 87-88; grantee NIMH, 1979-84, Ednl. Found., AAUW, 1986-87, Ohio Dept. Mental Health, 1987-90. Mem. Am. Psychol. Assn., Nat. Coun. Family Rels., Assn. for Care of Children's Health. Office: U Akron Schrank Hall S 215 Akron OH 44325

CLEMMONS, FRANCES ANNE MANSELL, insurance company official; b. Camden, Miss., Dec. 21, 1915; d. Otho Franklin and Pearl (Dunlap) Mansell; m. Rowe Sanders Crowder, Dec. 17, 1938 (div. Mar. 1954); children—Rowe Sanders, Frances Elizabeth; m. Slaton Clemmons, Nov. 21, 1965. BS Belhaven Coll., 1937, MusB, 1937. Owner, operator Crowder Art Gallery, Jackson, Miss., 1946-50; dept. mgr., buyer Valley Dry Goods Co., Vicksburg, 1954-56; with Social Security Adminstrn., 1956-84, asst. dist. mgr., Rome, Ga., 1962-84; MEDICARE hearing officer, 1984—; cons. Polly Clemmons Health Ins., 1989—. Charter mem., bd. dirs. Citizens Adv. Coun. on Energy, 1986—; mem. Rome Little Theatre. Salvation Army Aux. Mem. Rome Community Concert Assn., Rome Symphony Heritage Soc., Rome Area C. of C. Democrat. Presbyterian. Club: Quota Internat. Inc. (pres. Rome 1974-76, dist. 8 lt. gov. 1979-80, gov. 1980-82, bd. dirs. 1984-86). Home: 412 E 3d Ave Rome GA 30161

CLEMMONS, JANE GOODRICH, religious organization administrator; b. Casper, Wyo., Apr. 10, 1934; d. Leon Chauncey and Grace (Austin) Goodrich; m. Thomas Powell Clemmons; 1 child, Bradley Powell. AA, Casper Coll., 1954; BA, U. Wash., 1976. Tchr. Stitchin' Time Sewing Sch., Bellevue, Wash., 1966-73, dir. sch., 1970-73; chmn. Bishops Commn. Edn., Seattle, 1981-84, 86-89; mem. N.W. Episc. educators Diocese of Olympia, Episc. Ch., Seattle, 1983—, pres. overlake convocation, 1983-85, mem. bishop's adv. com. on admission to the ministry, 1985—, mem. sch. of theology bd., 1983-84, 86—, sec., 1987-88, pres., 1988-90; sec. diocesan coun. Diocese of Olympia, Episc. Ch., 1987, v.p. diocesan coun., 1988—; mem. Tng. and Cons. Svcs., Seattle, 1984—. cons. Girl Scouts USA, Totem Coun., 1989; publicity chmn. League of Women Voters, Colo., 1961-62. Recipient Bishops Cross award for vol. svcs., 1989. Mem. Omicron Nu, Phi Theta Kappa (nat. historian 1953-54). Episcopalian. Home: 15650 Main Bellevue WA 98008

CLEMO, POLLY GRETCHEN HOWE, marketing director; b. Cleve., Apr. 3, 1941; d. Edwin James and Gertrude Irene (Boedicker) Howe; m. James A. Clemo, Aug. 24, 1963 (div. May 1989); children: James Edwin, Julie Anne. BA, Albion (Mich.) Coll., 1963. Dir. devel. New Directions, Glen Willow, Ohio, 1984-86; dir. communications Kenston Local Schs., Bainbridge, Ohio, 1984-86; pres. Polly Clemo & Co., Bainbridge, 1984-86; dir. mktg. and communications Ostendorf-Morris Co., Cleve., 1986—; mem. adv. bd. Mktg. Cleve. to Clevelanders, 1989—. Mem. Mayor's Award Com. for Volunteerism, Cleve., 1982-84; mem. pub. rels. adv. com. City of Cleve., 1982-84, 86—; mem. hon. bd. Bellflower Ctr., Cleve., 1984—; exec. com. ARC, Cleve., 1984—; pres. Jr. League of Cleve., 1982-84. Mem. Cleve. Advt. Club, Downtown Bus. Coun. (vice chmn. communications coun. 1989—). Republican. Office: Ostendorf Morris 1100 Superior Cleveland OH 44022

CLEMONS, JULIE PAYNE, telephone company executive; b. Attleboro, Mass., June 13, 1948; d. John Gordon and Claire (Paquin) P.; m. W. Richard Johnson, Oct. 10, 1970 (div. Oct. 1980); m. E.L. Clemons, Apr. 23, 1988. BBA, U. R.I., 1970. Svc. rep. New England Telephone, East Greenwich, R.I., 1970-71; svc. rep. So. Bell, Jacksonville, Fla., 1971-73, bus. office supr., 1973-77, bus. office mgr., 1978-84, staff mgr. assessment, 1984-86, mgr. assessment ctr., 1987-89, mgr. customer svcs. Revenue Recovery Ctr., 1989—; dir. human resources assessment State of Fla., 1987—. Vol. Learn to Read; bd. dirs. Duval Assn. of Retarded Citizens, Jacksonville, 1981-86, treas. 1983-84. Mem. NAFE, Am. Mgmt. Assn., Pioneers of Am. Roman Catholic. Office: So Bell Tower 301 W Bay St 4DD1 Jacksonville FL 32202

CLERC, JEANNE MARIE, educator; b. Midland, Mich., Aug. 29, 1954; d. Eugene Henry and Janet Ruth (Christiansen) C. BS, Saginaw Valley State U., 1974; MA, Cen. Mich. U., 1977; EdD, U. Houston, 1983. Registered med. technologist. Med. technologist Midland (Mich.) Hosp., 1975-77; instr. Delta Community Coll., Univ. Ctr., Mich., 1977-79; asst. prof. Okla. U. Health Ctr., Oklahoma City, 1979-80; med. technologist Meth. Hosp., Houston, 1980-81, U. Houston Health Ctr., 1981-82, Hermann Hosp., Houston, 1982-83; assoc. prof. Ea. Mich. U., Ypsilanti, Mich., 1983—. Contbr. articles to profl. jours. Mem. Am. Soc. Med. Technologists, Am. Soc. for Allied Health Profls. Home: 4561 Meadowview Ct Apt 2C Ypsilanti MI 48197

CLEVELAND, PEGGY ROSE RICHEY, cytotechnologist; b. Cannelton, Ind., Dec. 9, 1929; d. "Pat" Clarence Francis and Alice Marie (Hall) Richey; cert. U. Louisville, 1956; B. Health Sci., U. Louisville, 1984; m. Peter Leslie Cleveland, Nov. 25, 1948 (dec. 1973); children: Pamela Cleveland Litch, Paula Cleveland Bertloff, Peter L. Registered cytotechnologist, N.Y., 1989. Cytotechnologist cancer survey project NIH, Louisville, 1956-59; chief cytotechnologist Parker Cytology Lab., Inc., Louisville, 1959-75; mgr. cytology dept. Am. Biomed. Corp., 1976-78, Nat. Health Labs., Inc., Louisville, 1978-89; clin. instr. cytology Sch. Allied Health U. Louisville, 1980—, cytology adv. com., 1980-81, chair, 1982-89, ednl. coord. Nat. Health Labs., Inc. with cytology program U. Louisville; chair Am. cytotechnologist del. to People's Republic of China, 1986; ptnr. Sham Star Stable thoroughbred horse breeding and racing. Mem. Am. Soc. Clin. Pathologist (cert. cytotechnologist), Internat. Acad. Cytology (cert. cytotechnologist), Am. Soc. Cytology (pilot program continuing edn. certification), Horseman's Benevolent and Protective Assn. Democrat. Roman Catholic. Home: Rte 1 Box 393 Lanesville IN 47136

CLEVELAND, SUSAN ELIZABETH, library administrator, researcher; b. Plainfield, N.J., Mar. 14, 1946; d. Robert Astbury and Grace Ann (Long) Williamson; m. Stuart Craig Cleveland, Aug. 21, 1971; children—Heather Elizabeth, Catherine Elisa. B.A., Douglass Coll., Rutgers U., 1968; M.L.S., Rutgers U., 1969. Acquisitions librarian Jefferson U., Phila., 1970-71; biomed. librarian VA Hosp., Hines, Ill., 1972; med. cataloger U. Ariz., Tucson, 1973-74; dir. U. Pa. Hosps. Library, Phila., 1974-87; exec. dir. C.L.U. Assocs., 1987-89; libr. dir. Mt. Sinai Hosp., Phila., 1989, West Jersey Health System, Voorhees, N.J., 1990—; cons. in field, Phila. USPHS fellow, Detroit, 1969-70; recipient Chapel of 4 Chaplains Legion of Honor. Mem. Med. Libr. Assn. (Phila. chpt.), Spl. Libr. Assn., Caravan Club. Home: 612 N Hobart Dr Laurel Springs NJ 08021

CLEVEN, CAROL CHAPMAN, state legislator; b. Hanover, Ill., Nov. 2, 1928; d. Edward William and Vivian (Stausser) Chapman; m. Walter Arnold Cleven, children: Kern W., Jeffrey P. BS, U. Ill., 1950, postgrad., 1950-56. Elem. sch. tchr. Derinda Ctr., Ill., 1946-47; with rsch. staff U. Ill., Urbana, 1950-56; exec. dir. Crittenton Hasting House, Brighton, Mass., 1975-86; mem. Ho. of Reps. of Mass. Great and Gen. Ct., Boston, 1987—, edn. com., HUD com., fed. fin. assistance com., Commn. on Indoor Air Pollution; mem. Rep. Task Force on AIDS, Mass. Caucus of Women Legislators, Spl. Commn. on Worker Availablity in Human Svcs. Professions, Commn. on Indoor Air Pollution, Commn. on Mobile Home Parks. Mem. Chelmsford (Mass.) Sch. Com., 1969-87, mem. elem. needs com., 1969-71, sch. bldg. com., 1971-76; mem. adv. bd. Camp Paul for Exceptional Children, 1987; past pres. Lowell (Mass.) YWCA, Lowell Coll. Club.; mem. Merrimack River Watershed Council, Mass. Coalition for Pregnant and Parenting Teens, Alliance for Young Families; 1st v.p. Boston Ctr. Blind Children; bd. dirs. Chelmsford Ednl. Found. Mem. Mass. Assn. Sch. Coms., Friends of the Library, Chelmsford Hist. Soc., Chelmsford LWV, Florence Crittenton League of Lowell, Phi Sigma, Sigma Delta Epsilon. Congregationalist. Home: 4 Arbutus Ave Chelmsford MA 01824 Office: State House Rm 36 Boston MA 02133

CLEVENGER, PENELOPE, association executive; b. Denver, Dec. 6, 1940; d. Harold Friedland and Charlotte (Glatt) Friedland Beskin; m. Willie K. Clevenger, Oct. 15, 1961 (div.). A.A., Stephens Coll., 1960. Office mgr. Malcolm S. Gerald, Chgo., 1977-79; pers. mgr. Rolm/Midwest, Chgo., 1979-82; office adminstr. Nutech Engrs., Chgo., 1982-83; office mgr. Am. Acad. Orthopaedic Surgeons, Chgo., 1983-85; dir. adminstrn. Telecommunications Industry Assn. (formerly U.S. Telecommunications Suppliers Assn.), Chgo., 1985-88; pres. Inter World Svcs., Ltd., 1988—. Bd. dirs. Ctr. Tng. and Rehab. of Disabled, Chgo., 1981-84; vol. Northwestern Meml. Hosp., 1985—. Mem. Am. Soc. Assn. Execs., Am. Soc. Personnel Adminstrn., Internat. Meeting Planner Assn., Women in Internat. Trade, Ill. World Trade Commn., Japanese Am. Soc. Chgo. Democrat. Jewish. Home: 233 E Wacker Dr Apt 3913 Chicago IL 60601 Office: 233 E Wacker Dr Suite 3913 Chicago IL 60601

CLEVER, LINDA HAWES, physician; b. Seattle; d. Nathan Harrison and Evelyn Lorraine (Johnson) Hawes; m. James Alexander Clever, Aug. 20, 1960; 1 child, Sarah Lou. AB with distinction, Stanford U., 1962, MD, 1965. Diplomate Am. Bd. Internal Medicine, Am. Bd. Preventive Medicine in Occupational Medicine. Intern Stanford U. Hosp., Palo Alto, Calif., 1965-66; resident Stanford U. Hosp., Palo Alto, 1966-67, fellow in infectious disease, 1967-68; fellow in community medicine U. Calif., San Francisco, 1968-69, resident, 1969-70; med. dir. Sister Mary Philippa Diagonostic and Treatment Ctr. St. Mary's Hosp., San Francisco, 1970-77; chmn. dept. occupational health Pacific Presbyn. Med. Ctr., San Francisco, 1977—; clin. prof. medicine Med. Sch., U. Calif., San Francisco; NIH rsch. fellow Sch. Medicine, Stanford U., 1967-68; mem. San Francisco Comprehensive Health Planning Coun., 1971-76, bd. dir.; mem. Calif.-OSHA Adv. Com. on Hazard Evaluation System and Info. Svc., 1979-85, Calif. Statewide Profl. Standards Rev. Coun., 1977-81, San Francisco Regional Commn. on White House Fellows, 1978-81, 83-89, chmn., 1979-81. Contbr. articles to profl. jours. Trustee Stanford U., 1972-76, 81—, v.p., 1985—; trustee Marin Country Day Sch., 1978-85; bd. dirs. Sta. KQED, 1976-83, chmn., 1979-81; bd. dirs. Independent Sector, 1980-86, vice chmn., 1985-86; bd. dirs. San Francisco U. High Sch., 1983-90, chmn. 1987-88. Fellow ACP (gov. No. Calif. region 1985-89, chmn. bd. govs. 1989-90, regent 1990—), Am. Coll. Occupational Medicine; mem. Inst. Medicine NAS, Calif. Med. Assn., Calif. Acad. Medicine, Am. Pub. Health Assn., Western Occupational Medicine Assn., Chi Omega, Stanford U. Women's Club (bd. dirs. 1971-80). Office: 2351 Clay St San Francisco CA 94115

CLEWIS, CHARLOTTE WRIGHT STAUB, teacher; b. Pitts., Aug. 20, 1935; d. Schirmer Chalfant and Charlotte Wright (Rodgers) Staub; student Memphis State Coll., 1953-54, U. Wis., 1957-59; BA, Newark State Coll., 1963; MAT, Loyola Marymount U., 1974; m. John Edward Clewis, Aug. 11, 1954; 1 dau., Charlotte Wright. Asst. to dir., housemother Leota Sch. and Camp, Evansville, Wis., 1957-59; tchr. math. Rahway Jr. High Sch. (N.J.), 1963-70; tchr. math. Torrance (Calif.) Unified Sch. Dist., 1970—, coord. math. dept., 1977—, mem. math. steering com., 1978-83, 86—, mem. proficiency exam writing com., 1977—; mem. instructional materials rev. panel State of Calif., 1986. Sec., pres. Larga Vista Property Owners Assn., 1975-84; mem. Rolling Hills Estates City Celebration Com., 1975-81; treas. adult leaders YMCA, Metuchen, N.J., 1967-69; bd. dirs. Peninsula Symphony Assn., 1978-84; commr. Rolling Hills Estates Parks and Activities, 1981—, chmn., 1985, 90. Named Tchr. of Yr., Rahway Jr. High Sch., 1966; recipient Appreciation award PTA, 1984, Hon. Service award PTA, 1986. Mem. Nat. Coun. Tchrs. Math., Calif. Math. Coun. Club: Phidippides Track (sec. 1980-82, pres. 1982-83) (L.A.). Avocations: marathon running, camping, reading, computers. Home: 1 Gaucho Dr Rolling Hills Estates CA 90274 Office: Calle Mayor Mid Sch 4800 Calle Mayor Torrance CA 90505

CLIFF, JOHNNIE MARIE, mathematics and chemistry educator; b. Lamkin, Miss., May 10, 1935; d. John and Modest Alma (Lewis) Walton; m. William Henry Cliff, Apr. 1, 1961 (dec. 1983); 1 child, Karen Marie. BA in Chemistry, Math., U. Indpls., 1956; postgrad., NSF Inst., Butler U., 1960; MA in Chemistry, Ind. U., 1964; MS in Math., U. Notre Dame, 1980. Cert. tchr., Ind. Rsch. chemist Ind. U. Med. Ctr., Indpls., 1956-59; tchr. sci. and math. Indpls. Pub. Schs., 1960-88; tchr. chemistry, math. Martin Ctr. Coll., Indpls., 1989—, chmn. math. dept., 1990—. Contbr. rsch. papers to sci. jours. Grantee NSF, 1961-64, 73-76, 78-79, Woodrow Wilson Found., 1987-88; scholarship U. Indpls., 1952-56, NSF Inst. Reed Coll., 1961, C. of C., 1963. Mem. AAUW, NAACP, NEA, Assn. Women in Sci., Neal-Marshall-Ind. U. Alumni Assn., U. Indpls. Alumni Assn., Urban League, N.Y. Acad. Sci., Am. Chem. Soc., Nat. Coun. Math. Tchrs., Am. Assn. Physics Tchrs., Nat. Sci. Tchrs. Assn., Am. Assn. Ret. Persons, Ind. U. Chemist Assn., Delta Sigma Theta. Democrat. Baptist. Home: 405 Golf Ln Indianapolis IN 46260 Office: Martin Ctr Coll 2171 Avondale Pl Indianapolis IN 46218

CLIFF, JUDITH ANITA, author and lecturer on Biblical studies; b. Chgo., July 13, 1941; d. Howard Allen and Anita Caroline (Bell) Cliff. Student, Whittier Coll., 1961-64. Lectr. Bibl. studies Santa Rosa, Calif., 1971-74; author, lectr. Bibl. studies Jerusalem, Israel, 1974-78, Santa Rosa, St. Helena, Napa and San Francisco, 1978-89; author Bibl. studies La Jolla, Calif., 1989—. Author: Jesus: A Gospel Guide to His Life, 1976; Land of the Bible, 1978; The Christmas Journey, 1984; The Leaves of the Tree, 1984; The Healing Teachings of Jesus, 1985; author, pub. newsletter The Bibl. Rev., 1978, 89; author/narrator numerous lecture cassettes.

CLIFF, LINDA A., economics professional; b. Cape May Court House, N.J., June 25, 1951; d. Paul Otto and Verna (Schellinger) Schuster; m. Edward H. Cliff, May 21, 1977. BS, U. Del., 1973; MBA, Monmouth Coll., 1980. Mgr. prodn. econs. Atlantic Electric Co., Pleasantville, N.J., 1985-86, mgr. prodn. adminstrn., 1986-89, gen. mgr. power econs., 1990—. Office: 1199 Black Horse Pike PO Box 1500 Pleasantville NJ 08232

CLIFFORD, FRANCESCA BISHOP, media relations and public relations specialist; b. London, May 6, 1959; came to U.S., 1962;; d. Gabriel Anthony Patrick and Philomena Christina (O'Meara) Bishop; m. Gordon Brian Clifford, Oct. 16, 1982; children: Kennedy Francis Jude, Alexandra Christina Mary. BA in English and Social Svc., U. Portland, 1981. Prodn. coordinator Encore Arts in Performance mag., Portland, Oreg., 1981-83, editor-in-chief, 1983-85; media liaison Portland YWCA, 1983-85; media relations dir. U. Portland, 1985—. Newsletter editor Portland Ad-2 Advt. Fedn., 1985-86; author articles. Mem. Women in Communications Inc. (v.p. 1990—), Council for Advancement and Support of Edn. (Bronze award for newswriting 1990), Internat. Assn. Bus. Communicators (Pacesetter 1990). Roman Catholic. Office: U Portland 5000 N Willamette Blvd Portland OR 97203

CLIFFORD, GARRY CARROLL, publishing executive; b. Washington, May 25, 1934; d. Thomas Patrick and Agnes (McGarry) Carroll; m. George Clifford, Jr. (dec. Aug. 1985); children: George III, Thomas Carroll, Eamon M. Reporter Ottawa Jour., 1956-59; press officer Kennedy Campaign, Washington, 1960; freelance writer Chevy Chase, Md., 1961-74; corr. Time, Inc., Washington, 1974-80; bur. chief People mag., Washington, 1980—; nat. polit. corr., 1989—. Bd. trustees Lab. Sch. Washington, 1984—. Roman Catholic. Home: 146 Grafton St Chevy Chase MD 20815 Office: People Mag 1050 Connecticut Ave NW Washington DC 20036

CLIFFORD, GERALDINE MARIE JONCICH (MRS. WILLIAM F. CLIFFORD), educator; b. San Pedro, Calif., Apr. 17, 1931; d. Marion and Geraldine (Mustacich) Joncich; m. William F. Clifford, July 12, 1969. A.B., UCLA, 1954, M.Ed., 1957; Ed.D., Columbia U., 1961. Tchr. San Lorenzo, Calif., 1954-56, Maracaibo, Venezuela, 1957-58; researcher Inst. Lang. Arts, Tchrs. Coll., Columbia, 1958-61; asst. prof. edn. U. Calif. at Berkeley, 1962-67, asso. prof., 1967-74, prof., 1974—, asso. dean, 1976-78, chmn. dept. edn., 1978-81, acting dean Sch. Edn., 1980-81, 82-83; dir. edn. abroad program U. Calif., Australia, New Zealand, 1988, 89. Author: The Sane Positivist: A Biography of Edward L. Thorndike, 1968, The Shape of American Education, 1975, Ed Sch: A Brief for Professional Education, 1988, Lone Voyagers: Academic Women in Coeducational Universities, 1870-1937, 1989. Macmillan fellow, 1958-59; Guggenheim fellow, 1965-66; Rockefeller fellow, 1977-78. Mem. History Edn. Soc., Am. Ednl. Studies Assn., Phi Beta Kappa, Pi Lambda Theta. Home: 2428 Prince St Berkeley CA 94705

CLIFFORD, MARGARET CORT, writer; b. Cin., Sept. 20, 1929; d. George Edward and Margaret Barrington (Mackoy) C. BA, Chatham Coll., 1951. Reporter Pitts. Sun Telegraph, 1950; copywriter various agys., Pitts. and N.Y.C., 1951-53; reporter, editor Aspen (Colo.) Flyer/Aspen Times, 1953-59; freelance journalist and writer Santa Monica, Calif., 1959—; story analyst, editor NBC-TV, Burbank, Calif., 1984-87; screenwriter NBC Prodns., N. Hollywood, Calif., 1987-88; archive Santa Monica Pier, 1989. Author: Elliott, 1968, Gnu and Guru, 1970, Dreams and Dilemmas, 1970, To Aspen and Back, 1980. Recipient Parkhurst Community Svc. award Colo. Press Assn., 1959. Mem. Writers Guild of Am. Democrat.

CLIFFORD, MARGARET LOUISE, psychologist; b. Lakeland, Fla., Dec. 13, 1920; d. Thomas Saxon and Beatrice (Tillie) C.; m. Charles Robert Davis, Apr. 4, 1950. BA in Edn., Chapman Coll., Orange, Calif., 1950; MS in Cons. & Sch. Psycho, San Diego State U., Calif., 1972; PhD Psychology, Union Graduate Sch., Cin., 1976. Tchr. Elem. schs., Blythe, San Diego., Calif., 1950-68; columnist Daily Midway Driller, Taft, Calif., 1955; owner, operator Marge Davis Sch. Dance, Blythe, Calif., 1961-64; psychologist U.S. Peace Corps, Kingston, Jamaica, 1973-76, Apalachee Community Mental Health Ctr., Talahassee, Fla., 1977-80; coordinator of elderly services Beth Johnson Community Mental Health Ctr., Orlando, Fla., 1980-83; crisis support counselor Mental Health Services of Orange County, Orlando, 1983-88; supr. therapist Peace River Ctr. for Personal Devel., Bartow, Fla., 1988-89; therapist pvt. practice, Winter Garden, Fla., 1989—; guest speaker Fla. So. Coll., Orlando, 1981-82, Rollins Coll., Winter Park, Fla. Organized, bd. pres. widowed Person Svc. of Orange County, Orlando; bd. dirs. Co un. on Aging, sec. 1982-85. Mem. Fla. Coun. Community Mental Health (pres. 1978-81), Am. Psychol. Assn. Home: 223 N Central St Winter Garden FL 34787

CLIFTON, ANNE RUTENBER, psychotherapist; b. New Haven, Dec. 11, 1938; d. Ralph Dudley and Cleminette (Downing) Rutenber; m. Roger Lambert Clifton, Sept. 9, 1961; 1 dau., Dawn Anne. BA, Smith Coll., 1960, MSW, 1962. Diplomate in Clin. Social Work. Psychiat. case worker adult psychiatry unit Tufts-New Eng. Med. Ctr., Boston, 1962-68, supr. students, 1967-68; pvt. practice psychotherapy, Cambridge, Mass., 1966—; supr. med. students, staff social workers out-patient psychiatry Tufts New Eng. Med. Ctr., 1973—, also mem. exec. bd. Women's Resource Ctr., interim co-dir., 1986-88. Lic. clin. social worker, Mass. asst. clin. prof. psychiatry Tufts U. Med. Sch., 1974—, research dept. psychiatry, 1966-68, 73, 77—. Mem. Acad. Cert. Social Workers, Nat. Assn. Social Workers, Phi Beta Kappa, Sigma Xi. Clubs: Cambridge Tennis, Mt. Auburn Tennis. Contbr. articles to profl. jours. Home: 126 Homer St Newton Center MA 02159 Office: 20 University Rd Cambridge MA 02138

CLIFTON, JUDY RAELENE, association administrator; b. Safford, Ariz., Nov. 8, 1946; d. Ralph Newton and Fayrene (Goodner) Johnson; student Biola Coll., 1964-65; BA in Christian Edn., Southwestern Coll., 1970; married. Editorial asst. Accent Publications, Denver, 1970-73; expediter Phelps Dodge Corp., Douglas, Ariz., 1974-78; exec. asst. So. Ariz. Internat. Livestock Assn., Inc., Tucson, 1978-81; supt.'s sec. Phelps Dodge Corp., 1981—; sec. exec. bd. PAC, Phelps Dodge, 1985—. Mem. adv. bd. Ariz. Lung Assn.; mem. Silver City Arts Coun., 1986—; mem. Am. Security Council, 1979—; leader 4-H, Douglas; mem. Rep. Nat. Com., 1978—, Conservative Caucus, 1979—. Recipient Am. Legion Good Citizen award, 1964, DAR award, 1964. Mem. DAR, Nat. Assn. Evangelicals, U.S. Tennis Assn., Nat. Assn. Female Execs., Inc., So. Ariz. Internat. Livestock Assn., AAUW, Eagle Forum, Freedon Found., N.Mex. Eagle Forum, Mus. N.Mex. Found., Lordsburg/Hidalgo County C. of C. (bd. dirs. 1990—), Sigma Lambda Delta. Baptist. Clubs: Trunk & Tusk, Pima County Republican, Centre Ct., Westerners Internat., So. Ariz. Depression Glass, Tucson Tennis, Rep. Senatorial. Home: Drawer M Playas NM 88009

CLIFTON, LUCILLE THELMA, author; b. Depew, N.Y., June 27, 1936; d. Samuel Louis and Thelma (Moore) Sayles; m. Fred James Clifton, May 10, 1958 (dec. Nov. 1984); children—Sidney, Fredrica, Channing, Gillian, Graham, Alexia. Student, Howard U., 1953-55, Fredonia (N.Y.) State Tchrs. Coll., 1955. Prof. literature and creative writing U. Calif., Santa Cruz, 1985—. Poet-in-residence, Coppin State Coll., Balt., 1972-76, Jenny Moore vis. writer, George Washington U., 1982-83. Author: Good Times, 1969, Good News About The Earth, 1972, An Ordinary Woman, 1974, Generations, 1976, Two-Headed Woman, 1980, Sonora Beautiful, 1981, Next, 1987, Good Woman, 1987; Everett Anderson books and other books for children; co-author: Free to Be You and Me, 1974 (Emmy award), Free To Be A Family. Named Poet Laureate, State of Md., 1979; Recipient Discovery award Poetry Center, 1969; YMHA grantee, 1969; Nat. Endowment Arts grantee, 1970, 72. Mem. Authors League, Author Guild, P.E.N.

CLIFTON, ROBIN MARY, data processing consultant; b. Rochester, Minn., Sept. 23, 1962; d. Robert Henry and Genene Pauline (Smith) Gordish; m. Jerry Lynn Clifton, Oct. 14, 1984; 1 child, Jacinth. Student, Red Wing Cen. high, Minn., 1980, Naval Sch. Music, Norfolk, Va., 1981, Red Wing Tech. Inst., Minn., 1985-87. Musician U.S. Marine Corps, Quantico, Va., 1980-84; programmer Transport Am., Mpls., Minn., 1987--; data processing cons. L.P.S. Inc., Mpls., 1988--; wood wind quintet U.S. Marine Corps, Quantito Va., 1983-84; student com. Oboist, English horn various local concerts, Southeastern Minn., 1984-87. Recipient Several awards in Music MMEA U. Minn. 1980, Several Letters of. Mem. Data Processing Mgrs. Assn. Home: 455 Longfellow Fridley MN 55432

CLINE, CAROLYN JOAN, plastic and reconstructive surgeon; b. Boston; d. Paul S. and Elizabeth (Flom) Cline. BA, Wellesley Coll., 1962; MA, U. Cin., 1966; PhD, Washington U., 1970; diploma Washington Sch. Psychiatry, 1972; MD, U. Miami (Fla.) 1975. Diplomate Am. Bd. Plastic and Reconstructive Surgery. Rsch. asst. Harvard Dental Sch., Boston, 1962-64; rsch. asst. physiology Laser Lab., Children's Hosp. Research Found., Cin., 1964, psychology dept. U. Cin., 1964-65; intern in clin. psychology St. Elizabeth's Hosp., Washington, 1966-67; psychologist Alexandria (Va.) Community Mental Health Ctr., 1967-68; research fellow NIH, Washington, 1968-69; chief psychologist Kingsbury Ctr. for Children, Washington, 1969-73; sole practice clin. psychology, Washington, 1970-73; intern internal medicine U. Wis. Hosps., Ctr. for Health Sci., Madison, 1975-76; resident in surgery Stanford U. Med. Ctr., 1976-78; fellow microvascular surgery dept. surgery U. Calif.-San Francisco, 1978-79; resident in plastic surgery St. Francis Hosp., San Francisco, 1979-82; practice medicine, specializing in plastic and reconstructive surgery, San Francisco, 1982—. Contbr. chpt. to plastic surgery textbook, articles to profl. jours. Mem. Am. Bd. Plastic and Reconstructive Surgery (cert. 1986). Address: 450 Sutter St Ste 2433 San Francisco CA 94108

CLINE, EILEEN MARIE, data processing executive; b. East St. Louis, Ill., June 3, 1947; d. John Francis and Elizabeth Bridget (Cobb) Rauth; m. Jerry K. Cline, Jan. 26, 1974 (div. 1987); 1 child, Steven. BA in Math., St. Mary Coll., Leavenworth, Kans., 1969. Supr. McDonnell Douglas Corp., St. Louis, 1976-78; sect. mgr. McDonnell Douglas Corp., 1978-80, sr. sect. mgr., 1980-82, mgr. mfg. and engring. bus. programming, 1982-86, dir. engring./sci. programming, 1986-89, dir. bus. computing svcs., 1989—; co-facilitator/cons. Weinberg & Weinberg, Lincoln, Nebr., 1988; lectr. in field; co-author/designer and trainer seminar, The Human Side of Change, 1989. Com. mem. cub scouts Boy Scouts Am., St. Louis, 1986-89; pub. speaker match prog. Pattonville Sch. Dist., Bridgeton, Mo., 1987-88. Recipient Valuable People award, McDonnell Douglas, 1983, 84, others. Mem. Aerospace Ind. Assn. (sub-com. chmn. on software devel. 1988-89), Women in Bus. (founding mem.), Am. Contract Bridge League. Roman Catholic. Home: 634 Stablestone Dr Chesterfield MO 63017

CLINE, LINDA CAROL, computer specialist, consultant; b. Newgulf, Tex.; d. Ernest Delbert and Hazle (Collins) C. BS summa cum laude, U. Tex., 1975; MBA, St. Edward's U., Austin, Tex., 1982; PhD, Pacific Western U., 1990. Cert. Purchasing Mgr. Buyer Westinghouse Corp., Round Rock, Tex., 1980-83; purchasing sec. mgr. Tex. Instruments Corp., Austin, Tex., 1983-86; purchasing mgr. Eagle Signal Controls, Austin, 1986-87; mgr. procurement, planning and strategy dept. Dell Computer Corp., Austin, 1987-89; mgr., mfg. ops., 1989-90; dir. of material P.C. Brand, Inc., Chgo., 1990; pres., chief exec. officer U.S. Data Logic, 1990—; cons. in field. Judge Jr. Achievement, Austin, 1984, 85. Mem. Austin Purchasing Mgmt. Assn. (bd. dirs. 1981-83, v.p. 1983-84, pres. 1984-85, dir. for nat. affairs 1985-86, trade show coord. 1985, Outstanding Mem. 1988), Am. Prodn. and Inventory Control Soc. Office: PC Brand Inc 954 W Washington St Chicago IL 60607

CLINE, LUCILLE GLASSER, management company executive; b. Boston, Nov. 23, 1927; d. Abraham Albert and Ruth (Stoleski) Glasser; m. Penneth Melvin Cline, Mar. 10, 1946 (dec. Apr. 1976); children: Steven, Joni, Hope. Student, Boston U., 1943-46. Asst. property mgr. Payne Assocs., Inc., Newton, Mass., 1976-80, property mgr., 1980-83, pres., chief exec. officer, 1983—. Mem. Temple Emanuel, Brandeis U., Beth Israel Hosp., Children's Hosp., Dana-Farber Cancer Ctr., Am. Jewish Com., Am. Jewish Cong., Am. Friends Hebrew U., Multiple Sclerosis Found., Muscular Dystrophy Found. Recipient Good Works award Am. Cancer Soc., 1982, 86. Mem. Internat. Coun. Shopping Ctrs., Newton-Needham C. of C., Spring Valley Country Club, NOEML. Jewish. Office: Payne Assocs Inc 51 Winchester St Newton MA 02161

CLINE, PAULINE M., educational administrator; b. Seattle, Aug. 25, 1947; d. Paul A. and Margaret V. (Reinhart) C. BA in Edn., Seattle U., 1969, MEd, 1975, EdD, 1983. Cert. tchr., prin., supt., Wash. Tchr., Marysville High Sch., Wash., 1969-70; tchr./adminstr. Blanchet High Sch., Seattle, 1970-78; asst. prin. Edmonds High Sch., Wash., 1978-84; prin. College Place Middle Sch., Edmonds, 1984-85, Mountlake Terrace High Sch., Wash., 1985—; cons. Mem. Mountlake Terrace Centennial Commn., 1985-87; chair Assumption Sch. Bd., Seattle, 1977. IDEA Kettering fellow, 1984, 86, 87. Mem. South Snohomish County C. of C., Nat. Assn. Secondary Sch. Prins., Assn. Wash. Sch. Prins., Edmonds Prins. Assn., Assn. Supervision and Curriculum Devel., Phi Delta Kappa. Roman Catholic. Club: Women's University (Seattle). Lodge: Rotary (charter, v.p.. Alderwood club). Avocations: skiing; kayaking; backpacking. Office: Mountlake Terr High Sch 21801 44th Ave W Mountlake Terrace WA 98043

CLINE, RUTH ELEANOR HARWOOD, translator; b. Middletown, Conn., Oct. 31, 1946; d. Burton Henry and Eleanor May (Cash) Harwood; A.B., Smith Coll., 1968; M.A., Rutgers U., 1969; cert. translation from French, Georgetown U., 1978; m. William R. Cline, June 10, 1967; children—Alison, Marian. Reviewer, U.S. Dept. State, Washington, 1975—. V.p. Smith Coll. Class of 1968. Mem. Am. Translators Assn. (cert. in French, Spanish and Portuguese), MLA, Internat. Arthurian Soc. Episcopalian. Translator English verse: Yvain; or the Knight with the Lion (Chretien de Troyes), 1975; Perceval; or the Story of the Grail (Chretien de Troyes), 1983, Lancelot or the Knight of the Cart (Chretien de Troyes), 1990. Home: 5315 Oakland Rd Chevy Chase MD 20815

CLINE, SHELIA RHONDA See FIELDS, SHELIA RHONDA

CLINK-PUBALOWSKI, LORI LEE, preschool and elementary teacher; b. Sandusky, Mich., Aug. 21, 1965; d. Roy Robert and Diane Loretta (Messing) Clink. BS in Early Childhood and Elem. Edn., Mich. State U., 1988. Speech and lang. asst. Roose-Valley Spl. Edn. Coop., Poplar, Mont., 1988-89; presch. tchr. Jewish Community Ctr., Springfield, Mass., 1989—. Roman Catholic. Home: 4496 Atwater Rd Box 204 Harbor Beach MI 48441

CLINKSCALES, ANNA LEE JAMES, civic leader, public relations consultant; b. Balt., Aug. 8, 1931; d. Jesse and Margaret James; children—Alfred Jr., Angela, Antonio Jose. B.A., U. Md., 1973. Pres., Am. White House, Balt.; pres., founder Abraham Lincoln Reading and Tutoring Group, Balt.; founder, dir. Community Services Info Ctr., Balt.; owner Original Design by Anna (Swedish embroidery), Balt., 1976-77. Writer pilot program Stay In Sch. (Youth Opportunity award Pres. Lyndon B. Johnson, 1967). Convenor First Job Corps for Girls, Balt. (cited by OEC for outstanding service); chmn. first coordinating council Women in Community Service; former mem. steering com. Interracial and Interreligious Council W. Balt.; former bd. dirs. Balt. chpt. NAACP, Balt. Neighborhoods Inc., Greater Balt. Com., Allendale-Lynhurst Neighborhood Assn.; pres. Md., Nat. Council Negro Women. Recipient award Nat. Council Negro Women, 1967; honored by Pres. U.S., 1972, 73. Mem. Colonial and Indian Am. Cultures Internat. (coordinator, founder, dir. 1983), Colonial and Indian Am. Crafts Internat. (coordinator, founder, dir. 1983), Cultural Relations Internat. (coordinator 1983), Hobbies and Crafts Assn. (founder, dir.). Democrat. Roman Catholic.

CLOAR, PATRICIA ANN SANDSTEAD, artist, illustrator; b. Harrison, Ark., Sept. 22, 1932; d. Ronald Dennis and Eva Jewell (Pumphrey) Sandstead; m. Vincent M. Harrington III, Oct. 7, 1951 (div. Jan. 1973); children: Barbara Ann, Eve Elisabeth; m. Carroll Cloar. Student, Cottey Coll., 1948-49, U. Ark., 1949-51; B in Secondary Edn., Ark. State U., 1959. Prin. Pat Cloar, Inc., Memphis, 1976—; cons. in lace and antique textiles Memphis Brooks Mus. Art, 1976—, Memphis State U., 1985—, Fontaine House: curator various exhbns. Memphis Brooks Mus. ARt, 1982, 85; lectr. in field. Illustrator: The Caring Woman, 1985; one-woman shows include Oates Gallery, Memphis, 1982, McCarty Gallery, Monteagle, Tenn., 1983, Leu Gallery, Nashville, 1985, 86, Memphis Brooks Mus. Art, 1986, The Round Table, Memphis, 1986, 87, Albers Fine Art Gallery, Memphis, 1987. Recipient award Tombigbee Women Miss., 1984. Mem. ASCAP. Democrat. Presbyterian. Home and Office: 235 S Greer St Memphis TN 38111

CLODFELTER, CATHERINE JOY, clinical psychologist; b. Winston-Salem, N.C., Dec. 17, 1955; d. Robert Lee and Margaret Jean (Shermer) C. BA, Wake Forest U., 1978; M in Edn., Georgia State U., 1982; MA, U. So. Miss., 1986, PhD, 1988. Edn. specialist Surry-Yadkin Mental Health, Yadkinville, N.C., 1978-80; mental health assoc. West Paces Ferry Hosp., Atlanta, 1980-83; staff psychologist Miss. State Hosp., Whitfield, 1986-87; psychology intern Med. Coll. of Ga., Augusta, 1987-88; staff psychologist Forsyth Hosp., Winston-Salem, 1988—. Fellow NIMH, 1984-86. Mem. Am. Psychol. Assn., Internat. Neuropsychol. Soc. Democrat. Mem. Moravian Ch. Home: 612 Gales Ave Winston-Salem NC 27103 Office: Forsyth Hosp-Whitaker Ctr 3333 Silas Creek Pkwy Winston-Salem NC 27103

CLODIUS, JULIA MARIE, business owner, ceramist; b. Laramie, Wyo., Mar. 27, 1958; d. Fredric Cordes and Shirley (Forbes) C. AS, J. Sargeant Reynolds Coll., 1978. Dental technician Chemodent, Charlottesville, Va., 1978-84; dental ceramist Boyadjian Dental Lab., Charlottesville, 1984-87; owner, ceramist Skyline Dental Lab., Charlottesville, 1987—. Emergency med. technician Lake Monticello Rescue, Palmyra, Va., 1986—. Mem. Nat. Cert. Dental Technicians. Home: 22 Wildwood Dr Palmyra VA 22963 Office: Skyline Dental Lab 2776 Hydraulic Rd #9 Charlottesville VA 22901

CLOPINE, MARJORIE SHOWERS, librarian; b. N.Y.C., June 25, 1914; d. Ralph Walter and Angelina (Jackson) Showers; m. John Junior Clopine, June 19, 1948 (div.); m. Frank Mason Storck, Sept. 14, 1985. BA, Pa. State U., 1935; MS, Drexel U., 1936; MS, Columbia U., 1949. Gen. asst. Libr., Drexel U., Phila., 1937-42; asst. libr. Gen. Chem. Div., Allied Chem. Corp., Morristown, N.J., 1943-46; bibliographer U.S. Office Tech. Svcs., Washington, 1946; med. libr. VA Hosp., Washington, 1946-49; asst. libr. U.S. Naval Obs., Washington, 1949-52, libr., 1952-63; assoc. libr. Bethany (W.Va.) Coll., 1967-69; assoc. libr. Marine Rsch. Lab. Fla. Dept. Natural Resources, St. Petersburg, 1971-73; cons. in astronomy Dewey Decimal Classification Editorial Office, Library of Congress, Washington, 1956. Chmn., Community Improvement program, Fla. Dist. 14, Gen. Fedn. Women's Clubs, 1980-82; libr. cons. Garden Ctr., Oglebay Park, Wheeling, W.Va., 1965-69. Alice B. Kroeger Meml. scholar, 1935-36. Mem. AAUW, LWV, NOW, Inst. Retired Execs. and Profls., Women's Resource Ctr. of Sarasota, Friends of the Arts and Scis., Nat. Assn. Ret. Fed. Employees, Spl. Libraries Assn., Beta Phi Mu. Clubs: Woman's of Sarasota. Contbr. articles to profl. jours. Home and Office: 8400 Vamo Rd Apt 540 Sarasota FL 34231

CLOPINE, SANDRA LOU, religious organization administrator; b. Ft. Wayne, Ind., May 12, 1936; d. Clarence Melvin and Gwendola Louise (Copp) Burry; m. Sidney Ray Goodwin, July 12, 1957 (dec. 1963); 1 child, Gwenda Lynn Goodwin Stewart; m. Myron Stanley Clopine, Aug 7, 1982; stepchildren: Charles, Dan, Linda Clopine Palser, Lynnette Clopine Blackstone. BA, Southwestern Assemblies of God, Waxahachie, Tex., 1958; BS, West Tex. State U., 1968; MA, Assemblies of God Theol. Sem., Springfield, Mo., 1979. Ordained to ministry West Tex. Assemblies of God, 1971. Fgn. missionary Assemblies of God Ch., Ghana, West Africa, 1961-65; social worker Tex. Ctr. Human Devel., Amarillo, 1968-69, dir. vol. svcs., 1969-70; instr. Arusha Bible Sch., Tanzania, East Africa, 1970-80; instr. sociology Evang. Coll. Assemblies of God, Springfield, 1979-80; office of info. coord. Internat. Corr. Inst., Brussels, 1980-82; state dir. Women's Ministries, Nebr., 1984-85; nat. sec., dept. head for denomination Assemblies of God Women's Ministries, Springfield, Mo., 1986—; speaker women's convs., leadership seminars, other orgns. Recipient Outstanding Contbn. award Internat. Corr. Inst., 1983, Leadership Friend of Yr. award Highland Child Placement Ctr., Kansas City, Mo., 1989; named Disting. Alumnus Southwestern Assemblies of God Coll., 1989. Mem. Nat. Assn. Evangs. Women's Commn. (exec. bd., 1st vice-chmn. 1989—), Evang. Press Assn., Nat. Women's Leadership Task Force (steering com. 1990—), Internat. Pentecostal Press Assn., Delta Epsilon Chi. Republican. Office: Assemblies of God 1445 Boonville Ave Springfield MO 65802

CLOSE, ELIZABETH SCHEU, architect; b. Vienna, Austria, June 4, 1912; came to U.S., 1932, naturalized, 1938; d. Gustav and Helene (Riesz) C.; m. Winston A. Close, 1938; children—Anne Miriam (Mrs. Milton Ulmer), Roy Michel, Robert Arthur. Student, Technische Hochschule, Vienna, 1931-32; B.Arch., Mass. Inst. Tech., 1934, M.Arch., 1935. Draftsman Oscar Stonorov, Architect, Phila., 1935-36; designer Magney & Tusler, Mpls., 1936-38; partner, architect Elizabeth and Winston Close (changed to Close Assos., Inc., 1969), Mpls., 1938—; instr. Mpls. Sch. Art, 1936-37; instr. design U. Minn. Sch. Architecture, 1938-39. Prin. works include Garden City Devel, Brooklyn Center, Minn., 1957, Duff House, variety structures Met. Med. Center Complex, 1960-75, Golden Age Homes, 1960, Peavey Tech. Center, Chaska, Minn., 1970, Gray Freshwater Biol. Inst., Orono, Minn., 1974, U. Minn. Music Bldg., Mpls., 1985, Internat. Sch. Minn., Eden Prairie, 1988. Bd. dirs. Civic Orch. Mpls., 1951-68; bd. dirs. Minn. Opera Co.; past pres. New Friends Chamber Music; mem. Commn. on Minn.'s Future. Recipient Honor award Pub. Housing Adminstrn., 1964; hon. mention F.D. Roosevelt Meml. competion, 1960, 25 Yr. award MSAIA, 1988; named Outstanding Woman of Yr., YWCA, 1983. Fellow AIA (dir. Mpls. chpt. 1964-69, jury of Fellows 1986-87); mem. Minn. Soc. Architects (pres., Honor award 1975), Minn. Hist. Soc. (jury bldg. competition 1986). Home: 1588 Fulham St Saint Paul MN 55108 Office: Close Assocs Inc 3101 E Franklin Ave Minneapolis MN 55406

CLOSE, GLENN, actress; b. Greenwich, Conn., Mar. 19, 1947; d. William and Bettine Close; m. Cabot Wade (div.); m. James Marlas, 1984 (div.); 1 child, Annie Maude Starke. B.A., Coll. William and Mary, 1974. Joined New Phoenix Repertory Co., 1974; made Broadway debut in Love for Love, also appeared in The Rules of the Game, The Member of the Wedding, 1974-75 season; other repertory and regional theater appearances; appeared in Broadway musicals Rex, Barnum, 1980-81 (nominated Tony award); other theater roles include The Singular Life of Albert Nobbs, off-Broadway, 1982 (Obie award), Childhood, 1985, one performance oratorio Joan of Arc at the Stake, 1985; Broadway appearances in the Real Thing, 1984-85 (Tony award for best actress in drama), Benefactors, 1986; films include The World According to Garp, 1982 (nominated for an Oscar), The Big Chill, 1983 (nominated for an Oscar), The Natural, 1984 (nominated for an Oscar), The Stone Boy, 1984, Maxie, 1985, Jagged Edge, 1985, Fatal Attraction, 1987, Dangerous Liaisons, 1988, Immediate Family, 1989, Orders, Reversal of Fortune, 1990, The White Crow; TV films include Too Far To Go, 1979, Orphan Train, 1979, Something about Amelia, 1984 (nominated for an Emmy), Stones for Ibarra, 1988. Recipient Woman of Yr. award Hasty Pudding Theatricals, 1990, Dartmouth Film Soc. award, 1990. Mem. Phi Beta Kappa. Office: care Creative Artists Agy Inc Ste 1400 1888 Century Park E Los Angeles CA 90067*

CLOSE, KAREN ELIZABETH, marketing executive, educator; b. Chgo., Oct. 5, 1951; d. Gordon Ralph and Ruth (Kernwein) C. BFA cum laude, U. Ariz., 1973. Creative dir. Progressive Communications, Colorado Springs, Colo., 1976-78; art dir. PRACO Advt., Colorado Springs, 1978-80; creative dir. Erickson-Fuller Advt., Aspen, Colo., 1980-81; pres., owner Close Communications, Inc., Denver, 1982—; exec. distbr. Nuskin Internat., 1987—; instr. evenings Colo. Inst. Art, Denver, 1984-87. Design corp. identity packages, 1987—. Active Big Sisters/Little Sisters, United Way, Denver, 1986; v.p. mktg. Jr. Golf Acad., Colo. 1987—. Mem. Nat. Safety Council, Denver C. of C. (spl. olympics com.), Kappa Alpha Theta (scholarship chmn.). Episcopalian. Club: Denver Athetic (medalist). Avocations: painting, playing piano and guitar, skiing, tennis. Office: Close Communications 2561 S Jersey Denver CO 80222

CLOUD, DOLORES ONA, educator; b. Ponemah, Minn., Aug. 6, 1941. Diploma in bus. tng., Haskell Inst., Lawrence, Kans., 1962; student, U. Minn., Bemidji (Minn.) State U. Tchr., coordinator ojibwe lang. program An. Indian S, U. Minn., 1969-74; tchr., coordinator ojibwe tchrs., tng. and linguistic workshop Bemidji State U., 1974—; cons. South St. Paul Schs., 1973-74, Interstate Research Assocs., Indian Day Care Project, Washington, 1973, Bur. Indian Affairs, 1972, Nat. Indian Edn. Assn., 1971; chmn. adv. council St. Paul Arts and Scis. Mus., 1973-74, panel speaker Nat. Indian Edn. Conf., Seattle, 1975; mem. Red Lake Edn. Task Force, tng. for Title IV staff Minn. Dept. Edn., also tng. for curriculum devel., coordinator Indian adult basic edn. program. Bd. Dirs. Ams. for Indian Opportunity, 1970-73; mem. Red Lake Band Chippewa Indians, Red Lake (Minn.) Indian Reservation; chairpersonSenate Dist. #4 Dems., Minn., 1982-83, treas. 1983, del. 1980, 82, 84, 86. Co-recipient Showcase Program award U.S. Dept. Edn. Indian Edn. Program, 1989. Mem. Nat. Indian Edn. Assn., Am. Indian Student Assn. (pres. U. Minn. chpt., 1970-71, dir. 73-74, co-recipient FICRES Exemplary award 1988). Mailing address: 2824 Timberlane Way SW Bemidji MN 56601

CLOUD, LINDA BEAL, retired educator; b. Jay, Fla., Dec. 4, 1937; d. Charles Rockwood and Agnes (Diamond) Beal; m. Robert Vincent Cloud (Aug. 15, 1959 (dec. 1985). BA, Miss. Coll., 1959; MEd, U. So. Fla., 1976; EdS, Nova U., 1982; postgrad., Walden U., 1983. Cert. tchr., Fla. Tchr. Ft. Meade (Fla.) Jr.-Sr. High Sch., 1959-67, 80-89, Lake Wales (Fla.) High Sch., 1967-80; part-time tchr. Spanish, English Polk County Adult Schs., 1960-76; instr. in Spanish Warner So. Coll., Lake Wales, 1974; cons., pvt. tutor in field. Contbr. articles to profl. publs.; author, dir. numerous pageants for schs. Mem. Lake Wales Little Theatre, Inc., 1976; dir. Four Sq. swing choir; entertainer for various local orgns.; ring announcer Fla. State Fair, 1987-88; judge poetry and essay contests. Recipient Best Actress award Lake Wales Little Theatre, Inc., 1978-79. Mem. AAUW, Nat. Coun. Tchrs. of English, Fla. Coun. Tchrs. of English, Polk Coun. of Tchrs. of English, Polk Fgn. Lang. Assn., Ye Mystic Krewe de Perú, Southeastern Peruvian Horse Club (life). Republican. Mem. United Ch. of Christ. Home: 1654 Seminole Rd Babson Park FL 33827

CLOUGH, NADINE DOERR, school psychologist, psychotherapist; b. Chgo., Mar. 28, 1942; d. Edward L. and Alma S. (Youngstrum) Doerr; children: Kristen S., Meighan E. BA, Northwestern U., 1964; MA, U. Colo., 1971, PhD, 1983. Cert. sch. psychologist, Colo. Tchr. St. Vrain Valley Sch. Dist., Longmont, Colo., 1965-71, tchr. spl. edn., 1971-73; co-dir. Boulder (Colo.) Children's Ctr., 1974-81; sch. psychologist Boulder Valley Sch. Dist., 1980-85, Jefferson County Schs., Lakewood, Colo., 1985—; pvt. practice psychotherapy, Lakewood, 1981—. Mem. APA, NEA, Colo. Soc. Sch. Psychologists, Colo. Edn. Assn., Phi Delta Kappa. Democrat. Lutheran. Home: 8795 W Cornell Ave Apt 5 Lakewood CO 80227 Office: 7125 W Jefferson Ave Ste 300 Lakewood CO 80235

CLOUGHLY, CECILIA LOUISE, college administrator; b. Albuquerque, Feb. 18, 1943; d. Cecil Pershing and Mary Louise (Bezemek) C.; m. Frank R. Stott; children: Heidi Louise, Charles Edward. BA magna cum laude, Oberlin Coll., 1965; Fulbright scholar U. Munich, Fed. Republic Germany, 1965-66; MA, Northwestern U., 1967, PhD, 1970; MBA Claremont Grad. Sch., 1989. French hornist Graunke Orch., Munich, 1965-66; assoc. prof. German, chmn. dept. Elmhurst Coll., Ill., 1968-73; Fulbright and study abroad adviser Inst. Internat. Edn., Chgo., 1973-74; dir. Oldenborg Ctr. for Modern Langs. and Internat. Rels., Pomona Coll., Calif., 1974-84, Internat. Edn. dir. Pomona Coll., 1984-90; French hornist community orchs., 1966—. Author: Advisor's Guide to Study Abroad, 1975; Wilhelm Mueller, The Poet of the Schubert Song Cycles: His Life and Works, 1981. Translator: A Pictorial History of the Horn, 1975. Assoc. editor Schatzkammer der deutschen Sprachlehre, Dichtung und Geschichte, 1978—. Contbr. articles to profl. jours. Recipient Merit cert. Goethe House N.Y. and Am. Assn. Tchrs. German, 1978; sr. Fulbright fellow, Fed. Republic Germany, 1979. Mem. MLA, Am. Assn. Tchrs. German (co-founder, co-dir. placement info. ctrs. 1973-77), Nat. Assn. Fgn. Students Affairs, Council on Internat. Edn. Exchange (bd. dirs., 1985-89), Phi Beta Kappa.

CLOUTIER, ANNE O'ROURKE, clinical nurse specialist, manager; b. Providence, Jan. 21, 1955; d. James Henry and Florence Gertrude (Langford) O'Rourke; m. Paul Eugene Cloutier, Sept. 24, 1988. BA, R.I. Coll., 1977, BSN, 1977; MSN, Yale U., 1984. Clin. nurse Day Kimball Hosp., Putnam, Conn., 1977-78, St. Joseph's Hosp., North Providence, R.I., 1978-80, Hospice Care R.I., Rumford, 1980-82, R.I. Hosp., Providence, 1980-84; clin. nurse specialist Beth Israel Hosp., Boston, 1987-88; clin. nurse specialist Roger Williams Gen. Hosp., Providence, 1984-87, 88-89, nurse mgr., 1989-90; clin. nurse specialist Broward Gen. Med. Ctr., Ft. Lauderdale, Fla., 1990—. Contbr. chpt. to book, articles to profl. jours. Mem., vol. Am. Cancer Soc., Pawtucket, R.I., 1987—; sec. bd. trustees R.I. chpt. Leukemia Soc. Am., Cranston, 1989—, vol., 1985—, chmn. planning com., 1986-90; vol. Hospice Care R.I., Rumford, 1982-85. Mem. Oncology Nursing Soc., R.I. Oncology Nursing Soc., Internat. Assn. Nurses in Cancer Care, R.I. Nurses Assn., Sigma Theta Tau. Roman Catholic. Home: Po Box 273636 Boca Raton FL 33427 Office: Broward Gen Med Ctr 1600 S Andrews Ave Fort Lauderdale FL 33316

CLOUTIER, PATRICIA AYOTTE, business owner; b. Franklin, N.H., Mar. 9, 1938; d. Antonio D. Ayotte and Cecile (Bourque) Flanders; divorced; children: Michael, David, Scott, Donald. A in Court Reporting, Johnson & Wales Coll., 1975; BS in Bus. Studies magna cum laude, N.H. Coll., 1989. Co-owner franchise Montgomery Ward Catalogue Store, Concord, N.H., 1968-70, Laconia, N.H., 1969-70; court reporter Jordan and Connelly, Manchester, N.H., 1975-76; co-owner Apartment House, Cape Canaveral, Fla., 1977-79; sec., med. staff coordinator Wuesthoff Meml. Hosp., Rockledge, Fla., 1978-85; human resource adminstr. Sheaffer Eaton, Pittsfield, Mass., 1986-89; real estate agent Sunshine Realty, Titusville, Fla., 1980-84. Canvasser Heart Fund Dr., Concord, 1969; chair ARC, Rockledge, 1985. Mem. NAFE. Republican. Roman Catholic. Club: Hilton Hotel 9-5. Home: 117 Horne Rd Laconia NH 03246

CLOWRY, SUZANNE KATHLEEN, small business owner; b. Bridgeport, Conn., June 29, 1943; d. Peter Joseph Jr. and Gertrude Emma (Lockwood) C. AA, Cape Cod Community Coll., 1963; BA in Psychology, Russell Sage Coll., 1965; MEd in Elem. Edn., Bridgewater State Coll., 1971; postgrad., Worcester (Mass.) State Coll., 1979-81. Cert. elem. librarian. Tchr. Webutuck Cen. Schs., Amenia, N.Y., 1965-67, Orleans (Mass.) Elem. Sch., 1967-86; pres., owner Bearly in Bus., Brewster, Mass., 1986—; mgr. Cape Cod Melody Tent, Hyannis, 1967-69, Allegro Theatre, Orleans, 1984-85. Mem. Brewster Fin. Com., 1978-9. Mem. DAR, Mass. Tchrs. Assn., NEA, Acad. Performing Arts. Republican. Baptist. Home and Office: 3811 Main St Brewster MA 02631

CLUTE, KAREN LESLIE, lawyer, musician; b. Ithaca, N.Y., July 9, 1956; d. DeHart Bindman and Norma Jean (Reuther) C. BA in Music, SUNY, Binghamton, 1977, MusM in Performance, 1981; JD, NYU, 1986. Bar: Conn. 1986, U.S. Dist. Ct. Conn. 1987. Dir. music Ross Meml. Presbyn. Ch., Binghamton, 1980-83; organist, dir. choir 1st Congl. Ch. in Fair Haven, New Haven, Conn., 1986-89, Spring Glen Ch., Hamden, Conn., 1989—; law clk. to presiding justice U.S. Dist. Ct. Conn., New Haven, 1986-87; assoc. Wiggin & Dana, New Haven, 1987—; bd. dirs. and chmn. legal com. Conn. Women's Edn. and Legal Fund, Hartford, 1987—. Mem. Conn. Bar Assn. (com. arts and the law 1988—), Am. Guild Organists. Home: 227 Highland St New Haven CT 06511 Office: Wiggin & Dana 195 Church St PO Box 1832 New Haven CT 06508

CLUTTER, MARY ELIZABETH, national foundation administrator; b. Charleroi, Pa.; BS, Allegheny Coll., 1953, DSc., 1986, MS, U. Pitts., 1957, PhD in Botany, 1960; Rsch. assoc. Yale U., 1961-73, lectr. biology, 1965-78, sr. rsch. assoc., 1973-78; program dir. NSF, Washington, 1976-81, sect. head, 1981-84, div. dir., 1984-85, 87-88, asst. dir., 1989—, sr. sci. adviser, 1985-87. Mem. AAAS (bd. dirs. Washington), Internat. Soc. Plant Molecular Biology, Am. Soc. Cell Biology, Am. Soc. Plant Physiologists, Soc. Devel. Biology, Assn. Women in Sci. Office: NSF 1800 G St NW Washington DC 20550

CLYDE, GLENDA ESTELLE, speech educator; b. Phillipsburg, Mo., Apr. 18, 1937; d. Victor and Jewel (Howerton) Clyde. BA, Colo. State Coll., 1958; MA, U. Denver, 1962; PhD, So. Ill. U., 1966. Tchr. Herculaneum (Mo.) High Sch., 1959-60, N.W. High Sch., House Springs, Mo., 1960-62; instr. Wayne State Coll., Nebr., 1962-63; grad. asst. So. Ill. U., Carbondale, 1964-65; assoc. prof. speech N.E. Mo. State Coll., Kirksville, 1965-69; prof. speech N.E. Mo. State U., 1969—; cons. in field. Mem. Cen. States Communication Assn., Speech Communication Assn., Internat. Soc. Gen. Semantics, Inst. Gen. Semantics, Speech and Theatre Assn. of Mo., Alpha Sigma Tau. Home: 27 Town & Country Kirksville MO 63501 Office: Northeast Mo State U Kirksville MO 63501

CLYMORE, SUE ALLISON, accountant; b. Portsmouth, Va., Apr. 19, 1959; d. Robert Stetson Perry and Shirley Carole (York) Dickter; m. Ray Allen Clymore Jr., June 12, 1982. BS in Acctg., Loyola Marymount U., 1981. CPA, Calif. Sr. auditor Touche Ross and Co., Los Angeles, 1981-85; fin. rep. mgr. Thrifty Corp., Los Angeles, 1985-86; sr. fin. analyst Toyota Motor Credit Corp., Torrance, Calif., 1987-88, adminstr. systems devel., 1988-89, adminstr. sr. systems devel., 1989—. Mem. AICPA, NAFE, Calif. Soc. CPA's, Am. Soc. Women Accts. Republican. Methodist. Office: Toyota Motor Credit Corp 1515 W 190th St Torrance CA 90509-2958

CLYNE, ROSEMARIE BLACKSTONE, technical services librarian; b. Utica, N.Y., May 16, 1926; d. Arthur C. and Mary C. (Hofsass) Blackstone; m. Robert F. Clyne, Sr., Aug. 6, 1947; children: Robert Jr., Judi, James, Jeanne, Richard, Jeffrey, Cynthia, Debra, Lisa. AA, AS with honors, Polk Community Coll., 1970; BA magna cum laude, U. South Fla., 1972, MA magna cum laude, 1978. Cert. librarian. Ins. clk. Utica Mut. Ins. Co., 1943-46; clk. libr. Polk Community Coll., Winter Haven, Fla., 1971-73, libr. asst., 1973-78, libr. tech. svcs., 1978—, libr. coord., 1989—; sec. collection devel. com. U. South Fla. and related librs., 1990. Mem. Fla. Assn. Community Colls. (2nd v.p., chair learning resources com. 1990). Office: Polk Community Coll 999 Ave H NE Winter Haven FL 33881

CMAR, JANICE BUTKO, education educator; b. Pitts., Nov. 10, 1954; d. Edward Michael and Ruth Lillian (Pickard) Butko; m. Dennis Paul Cmar. BS, Mansfield U., 1976; MS, Duquesne U., 1990. Cert. home economist; vocational cert. quantity foods, food mgmt. prodn. and svc. Home econ. tchr. Duquesne (Pa.) Sch. Dist., 1978-83; special edn. tchr. Allegheny Intermediate Unit, Pitts., 1985--; sponsor, Duquesne High Sch., YúTeens & Future Homemakers Am., 1979-83, Pathfinder Student Coun., Bethel Park, Pa., Mon-Valley Secondary Yearbook, West Mifflin, Pa. Vol. Allegheny County Dept. Community Services, Pitts., 1986--, Catherine Baker Knoll for State Treas. Campaign, Pitts., 1987-88. Mem. Am. Fed. Tchrs., Am. Home Econs. Assn., Pa. Home Econs. Assn., Alpha Sigma Tau. Democrat. Home: 1067 Huston Ave West Mifflin PA 15122 Office: 200 Commerce Ct Pittsburgh PA 15219

COAKLEY, MRS. CHARLES E. See NOVINA, TRUDI

COAN, PAMELA ELAINE, educator, supervisor; b. Teaneck, N.J., Aug. 19, 1959; d. George Pruitt and Marjorie Elaine (Martin) C. AA, Brevard Coll., 1979; BA, U. N.C., Asheville, 1982; MEd in Adminstrn. and Supervision, George Mason U., 1988. Cert. secondary tchr., prin., supr., Va. Tchr. Prince William County Schs., Woodbridge, Va., 1982-83, 85-89, tchr., supr., 1989—; tchr. Aquinas Sch., Woodbridge, 1983-85; corp. ops. Nat. Technology, Arlington, Va., 1985; asst. prin. Prince William County Summer Sch., Dumphies, 1988; dir. drill team Prince William County Schs., 1985—. Lead Emergency Med. Technician O.W.L. Vol. Fire and Rescue, Woodbridge, 1988—; charter mem. Community Task Force, Woodbridge, 1988—; mem. Prince William County Youth Assessment, Woodbridge, 1988—, Woodbridge Community Choir, Prince William County Commn. on Women; vol. counselor for children's program Action Through Community Svc., 1983; head usher St. Paul's Meth. Ch., Sunday sch. tchr., acolyte chairperson; started first women's history month ceremonies in Prince William County. Mem. AAUW (v.p. Woodbridge chpt. 1984-90), Emmaus, Ski Club of Washington, Phi Alpha Theta. Home: 13009 Smoketown Rd Woodbridge VA 22192 Office: Woodbridge Sr High Sch 3001 Old Bridge Rd Woodbridge VA 22192

COATES, DIANNE KAY, social worker; b. Adrian, Mich., Jan. 4, 1945; d. John Milton Yaw and Margaret Esther (Skinner) Yaw-Carpenter; widow; 1 child, Cindi Kae McCarty. Student Jackson Bus. U., Mich., 1962-63; AA with honors, Macomb Community Coll., Warren, Mich., 1977; BA with high distinction, Madonna Coll., Livonia, Mich., 1979; MSW, Wayne State U., 1982; postgrad. Internat. Grad. Sch., St. Louis, 1984, Eastern Mich. U., 1989. Cert. social worker, Mich. Nat. service officer Mil. Order of the Purple Heart, Detroit, 1973-80; psychology technician VA Med. Ctr., Allen Park, Mich., 1980-84; clin. cons. HOMEBASE, Detroit, 1983-85; clin. social worker Community Counseling Assocs., Adrian, Mich., 1983, Roseville, Mich., 1983-87; clin social worker Ypsilanti (Mich.) Regional Psychiat. Hosp., Mich., 1987—; field instr. Wayne State U., 1988—; internat. exch. counselor Edn. Found. Fgn. Study, 1987—; ind. contract therapist Renaissance West Community Mental Health Services Clinic, Detroit, 1988-89; Caknipe-Kovach Assocs., 1988—; vol. HAVEN, Pontiac, Mich., 1986-87; group counselor Survivors of Homicide Detroit, 1981-82. Mem. Nat. Assn. Social Workers (bd. cert. diplomate), Nat. Acad. Cert. Social Workers, Mich. Mental Health Assn., Social Work Assn. Madonna Coll. (co-founder), Mich. Alcohol and Addiction Assn., Wayne State U. Alumni Assn., Vietnam Vets. Am. (hon. life assoc. mem.). Lodges: Ladies Aux. Mil. Order of Purple Heart (region 2 v.p. 1985-86), Ladies Aux. VFW, Ladies Aux., DAV. Home: 1502 Elias Westland MI 48185

COATS, LINDA TUGGLES, education educator; b. Holly Springs, Miss., Nov. 5, 1958; d. Joe L. and Mary Ellen (Falkner) Tuggles; m. Billie Anthtony Coats;. BA, Miss. State U., 1979; MA, Jackson (Miss.) State U., 1982. Tchr. Holly Springs (Miss.) High Sch., 1979-80; sec. Rust Coll., Holly Springs, 1980-81; graduate asst. Jackson State U., 1981-82; lectr. Miss. State U., 1982-83; asst. prof. Mary Holmes Coll., West Point, Miss., 1984--. Author: Sex Discrimination on the Job, 1982, Poem: My Prayer, 1976; participant leadership Starkville, Miss., 1989; talk show host Sta. WVSB-TV, 1989—. Mem. Sudduth PTA Club, Overstreet PTA, Alpha Kappa Alpha (pres. 1977-78). Democratic. Baptist. Home: 104A Park Circle Starkville MS 39759

COBB, CAROLYN JANE, graphic design executive; b. Harrisburg, Pa., Aug. 20, 1943; d. Edward John and Doris May (Magel) Swerk; m. Don Rickey Hall, June 1, 1961 (div. Dec. 1979); m. Phil Allison Cobb, July 10, 1981; children: Jon David, Allison C. Weaver. BFA cum laude, U. Tex., 1964. Tchr. NE Ind. Sch. Dist., San Antonio, 1964-66, Austin (Tex.) Ind. Sch. Dist., 1966-68; illustrator Tex. Employment Commn., Austin, 1968-77, instructional media technician, 1977-78, staff services asst., 1978-80, mgr. design/graphics, 1980—; v.p. Cruise Line Assocs., Inc., Austin, 1985—. Works adopted by Am. Greetings card co., 1981. Mem. Nat. Assn. Cruise Only Agencies (founding), Internat. Assn. Personnel in Employment Security (State award 1974), Nat. Assn. Female Execs., So. Watercolor Soc. (award 1983), Alpha Lambda Delta. Home: 2610 Chowan Way Round Rock TX 78681 Office: Tex Employment Commn TEC Bldg Rm 272 101 E 15th St Austin TX 78778-0001

COBB, DONNA DEANNE HILL, physical therapist; b. Albany, Calif., May 6, 1943; d. Clifford Odell and Dorothy Vera (Smith) Hill; m. Milton Lawrence Cobb, June 25, 1966; children: Laura Janine Cobb Carder, Katrina Alicia. BS, Baylor U., 1966. Lic. phys. therapist, Mo.; registered Am. Registry Phys. Therapists. Phys. therapist, arthritis team leader Parkland Meml. Hosp., Dallas, 1966-67; phys. therapist NW R.R. Hosp., Tacoma, summer 1966; phys. therapist, mem. and team leader of scoliosis and amputee clinic team Scottish Rite Crippled Children's Hosp., Dallas, 1967-68; phys. therapist Rehab. Ctr., Albuquerque, 1968-69; contract phys. therapist Dallas, 1969-71, various hosps., Bossier City, Shreveport, La., 1972-74; owner, pres. Cons. Phys. Therapy, St. Louis, 1978-83; owner, pres., adminstrv. dir. Therapy Finders, Inc., St. Louis, 1984—; cons. Easter Seal Soc., Albuquerque, 1968-69. Leader, organizer Girl Scouts Am., St. Louis, 1974-84; pres. Baylor U. Parents League, St. Louis, 1988—; mem. devel. coun. Baylor U., Waco, Tex., 1988—; deacon Kirkwood (Mo.) Bapt. Ch., 1979—; active Arthritis Found. Funding, 1966-67, Habitat for Humanity, St. Louis, 1990—. Recipient Woman Entrepreneur award St. Louis Community Coll., 1989; Alumni scholar Kans. State Coll. of Pitts., 1961-62, scholar Nat. Found., 1961-65. Mem. Am. Phys. Therapy Assn., Mo. Phys. Therapy Assn. (refresher course com. ea. dist., co-chmn. pub. rels. edn. 1988-90, bd. dirs., chmn. student liaison com. 1990—), Nat. Assn. Health Adminstrs., Nat. Assn. Women Bus. Owners (Woman in Charge award 1989, membership com. 1990—), Aux. St. Anthony's Hosp., Windsor Forest Garden Club (historian 1985—). Baptist. Home: 1425 Forest Ave Saint Louis MO 63122 Office: Therapy Finders Inc 135 W Adams St Ste 305 Saint Louis MO 63122

COBB, JEWEL PLUMMER, retired college president; b. Chgo., Jan. 17, 1924; divorced; 1 child. A.B., Talladega Coll., 1944; M.S., N.Y. U., 1947, Ph.D. in Biology, 1950. Fellow Nat. Cancer Inst., 1950-52; instr. anatomy U. Ill. Coll. Medicine, 1952-54; research surgery Postgrad. Med. Coll., N.Y. U., 1955, asst. prof., 1955-60; Cancer Research Found. prof. biology Sarah Lawrence Coll., 1960-69; prof. zoology, dean Conn. Coll., 1969-76; prof. biology, dean Douglass Coll., Rutgers U., 1976-81; pres. Calif. State U., Fullerton, 1981-90; condr. research on tissue culture, studies human neoplasm, changes produced by promising chemotherapeutic agents, normal and abnormal pigment cell metabolism; dir. Travelers Ins. Co.; Former mem. commn. on acad. affairs Am. Council on Edn.; Bd. dirs. 21st Century Found., Nat. Center Resource Recovery, Nat. Sci. Bd., 1974-80, Nat. Inst. Medicine, CPC Internat., Inc., Allied/Signal Corp., First Interstate Bancorp. Recipient Alumnae Woman of Yr. award N.Y. U., 1979. Fellow N.Y. Acad. Scis., Tissue Culture Assn.; mem. AAUW, Sigma Xi. Office: Calif State U-Fullerton Office of Pres Fullerton CA 92634*

COBB, RUTH, artist; b. Boston, Feb. 20, 1914; d. Charles Edward and Bessie (Cohen) C.; m. Lawrence Kupferman, Apr. 29, 1937; children: Nancy Rose, David. Diploma, Mass. Coll. Art, 1935. One-woman shows, Shore Gallery, Boston, 1958, 60, 63, 65, 70, DeCordova Mus., Lincoln, Mass., 1955, Art Unlimited Gallery, San Francisco, 1961, Cober Gallery, N.Y.C., 1962, 65, 67, McNay Mus., San Antonio, 1966, Phila. Art Alliance, 1962, Galerie Moos, Montreal, Que., Can., 1969, Witte Mus., San Antonio, 1967, Harold Ernst Gallery, Boston, 1974, 75, 76, Midtown Gallery, N.Y.C., 1981, 82, Foster Harmon Gallery, Sarasota, 1984, Francesca Anderson Gallery, Boston, 1984, 87, Cen. Pl. Galleries, Bangor, Maine, 1988; represented in permanent collections, Boston Mus. Fine Arts, Brandeis U., Butler Inst. Am. Art, Munson-Williams-Proctor Inst., Addison Gallery Am. Art, Va. Mus. Fine Arts, DeCordova Mus., Tufts U.; featured in TV program Artist At Work, 1981; work featured in Am. Artist mag., 1979. Recipient awards Pa. Acad. Fine Arts, 1967, awards Allied Artists N.Y.C., 1966. Mem. Am. Watercolor Soc. (award), New Eng. Watercolor Soc., Allied Artists Am. (award), NAD (award).

COBB, SHIRLEY ANN, public relations specialist, journalist; b. Oklahoma City, Jan. 1, 1936; d. William Ray and Irene (Fewell) Dodson; m. Roy Lampkin Cobb, Jr., June 21, 1958; children: Kendra Leigh, Cary William, Paul Alan. BA in Journalism with distinction, U. Okla., 1958, postgrad., 1972; postgrad., Jacksonville U., 1962. Info. specialist Pacific Missle Test Ctr., Pt. Mugu, Calif., 1975-76; corr. Religious News Service, N.Y.C., 1979-81; splty. editor fashion and religion Thousand Oaks (Calif.) News Chronicle, 1977-81; pub. relations cons., Camarillo, Calif., 1977—; media mgr. pub. info City of Thousand Oaks, 1983—. Contbr. articles to profl. jours. Trustee Ocean View Sch. Bd., 1976-79; pres. Pt. Mugu Officers' Wives Club, 1975-76, 90—, Calif. Assn. Pub. Rels. Officials, 1989-90; bd. dirs. Camarillo Hospice, 1983-85. Recipient Spot News award San Fernando Valley Press Club, 1979. Mem. Pub. Rels. Soc. Am., Sigma Delta Chi, Phi Beta Kappa, Chi Omega. Republican. Clubs: Las Posas Country, Town Hall of Calif. Home: 2481 Brookhill Dr Camarillo CA 93010 Office: 2150 W Hillcrest Dr Thousand Oaks CA 91320

COBES, MADELINE JOYCE, physical education educator; b. Blairsville, Pa., May 30, 1941; d. John Wayne and Ruby Emilie (Bricker) C. BS, U. Pitts., 1963; MA, NYU, 1967. Cert. elem. tchr., N.Y. Phys. edn. tchr. East Meadow (N.Y.) Pub. Schs., 1963-69, Bellmore-Merrick Cen. High Sch. Dist., North Merrick, N.Y., 1969-81, Merrick (N.Y.) Unified Free Sch. Dist., 1981—. Life mem. Chatterton PTA, Merrick, 1989—. Mem. Assn. Women in Phys. Edn. (state pres. 1981-82, state svc. award 1983), N.Y. State Pub. High Sch. Athletic Assn. (chairperson jr. high sch. girls' soccer 1977-80), Nassau Area Assn. Women in Phys. Edn. N.Y. (cert. of recognition 1975). Republican. Methodist. Home: 1134 Logan Rd Wantagh NY 11793 Office: Chatterton Elem Sch 108 N Merrick Ave Merrick NY 11566

COBLE, M(ARY) SUSAN, insurance broker executive; b. Decatur, Ill., May 14, 1949; d. Robert B. and Alice Virginia (Davern) C. AB, U. Calif., Riverside, 1971; postgrad., Golden Gate U., 1981-83. Claims examiner, asst. claims mgr. State Compensation Ins. Fund, San Francisco, 1971-79; workers' compensation mgr. Transamerica Corp., San Francisco, 1979-83; v.p. claims mgmt. services Sedgwick James, Inc., Chgo., 1983-85, sr. v.p. CMS, 1986—; bd. dirs. Workers' Compensation Research Inst., Boston. Mem. Nat. Coun. Self-Insurers, Calif. Self-Insurers Assn., Internat. Assn. Indsl. Accidents Bds. and Commns., Nat. Hist. Trust, Chgo. Hist. Soc., Chgo. Archtl. Found., Friends of the River, Mensa.

COBLENTZ, JANE CUDLIP, volunteer educator; b. Iron Mountain, Mich., May 4, 1922; d. William Stacey and Mary Elva (Martin) Cudlip; m. George Samuel Coblentz, June 8, 1942 (dec. June 1989); children: Bruce Harper, Keith George, Nancy Allison Coblentz Healy. BA, Mills Coll., 1942. Mem. Sch. Resource and Career Guidance Vols., Inc., Atherton, Calif., 1965-69, pres., chief exec. officer, 1969—. Proofreader, contbr. Mills Coll. Quarterly mag. Life gov. Royal Children's Hosp., Melbourne, Australia, 1963—; v.p. United Menlo Park (Calif.) Homeowner's Assn.; nat. pres. Mills Coll. Alumnae Assn., 1969-73, bd. trustees 1975-83. Named Vol. of the Yr., Sequoia Union High Sch. Dist., 1988. Mem. AAUW, Atherlons, Palo Alto (Calif.) Area Mills Coll. Club (pres. 1986), Phi Beta Kappa. Republican. Episcopalian. Home: 1109 Valparaiso Ave Menlo Park CA 94025

COBURN, FRANCES GULLETT, educator; b. Princess, Ky., Apr. 20, 1919; d. Gilbert G. and Lula (Kitchen) Gullett; m. Ralph L. Coburn, Dec. 20, 1941 (dec. Feb. 1966). BS cum laude, Morris Harvey Coll., 1950; MA in Adminstrn., Marshall U., 1952. Tchr. Braeholm (W.Va.) Elem. Sch., 1938-49; tchr. Amherstdale (W.Va.) Elem. Sch., 1949-51; prin. King Fuel Elem. Sch., Emmett, W.Va., 1951-53; tchr. Peyton Elem. Sch., Huntington, W.Va., 1953-78; supervising tchr. Marshall U., Huntington, 1953-78. Contbr. articles to profl. jours. Vol. Huntington Mus. Art; assistant with crafts at 2 Huntington nursing homes; sec. adminstrv. bd. Johnson Meml. Ch., 1981-90, sec. coun. on ministries, 1990, mem. circle 7; donor rm. asst. ARC (recipient 30 yr. pin); mem. Logan County coun. Girl Scouts U.S., Logan, W.Va. Mem. AAUW, Woman's Club Huntington, Huntington Garden Club, Panhellenic, Delta Kappa Gamma, Kappa Delta Phi, Phi Mu. Methodist. Home: 1034 12th Ave Huntington WV 25701

COBURN, KATHRYN, academic administrator; b. Atlanta, Dec. 17, 1943; d. Leslie Leonce and Isabelle (McMurray) Charbonnet; m. Richard Gardner Coburn, June 26, 1975 (div. Nov. 1984); children: Colleen Marie, Rachel Mary. AB, U. S. Fla., 1970. Tchr. Hudson (Fla.) Sr. High Sch., 1969-75; adminstr. Baylor Coll. Medicine, Houston, 1975—; cons. Coburn Cons., Houston, 1986—; lic. mentor for self-esteem enhancement course, 1989. Vol. The Life Tng., Houston, 1983; lay minister Christ Ch. Cathedral, Houston, 1984-87; grants writer Omega House Hospice, Houston, 1986—; coord. adv. bd. The Peace Project, Houston, 1986—. Served with USAF, 1962-64. Fla. State scholar, 1967. Mem. Am. Mgmt. Assn., Am. Assn. Female Execs., Nat. Council of Univ. Research Adminstrs., Soc. Research Adminstrs. Democrat. Episcopalian. Office: Baylor Coll Medicine Ctr Biotech 4000 Research Forest Dr The Woodlands TX 77381

COBURN, MARJORIE FOSTER, psychologist, educator; b. Salt Lake City, Feb. 28, 1939; d. Harlan A. and Alma (Ballinger) Polk; m. Robert Byron Coburn, July 2, 1977; children: Polly Klea Foster, Matthew Byron Foster, Robert Scott Coburn, Kelly Anne Coburn. B.A. in Sociology, UCLA, 1960; Montessori Internat. Diploma honor grad. Washington Montessori Inst., 1968; M.A. in Psychology, U. No. Colo., 1979; Ph.D. in Counseling Psychology, U. Denver, 1983. Licensed clin. psychologist. Probation officer Alameda County (Calif.), Oakland, 1960-62, Contra Costa County (Calif.), El Cerrito, 1966, Fairfax County (Va.), Fairfax, 1967; dir. Friendship Club, Orlando, Fla., 1963-65; tchr. Va. Montessori Sch., Fairfax, 1968-70; spl. edn. tchr. Leary Sch., Falls Church, Va., 1970-72, sch. adminstr., 1973-76; tchr. Aseltine Sch., San Diego, 1976-77, Coburn Montessori Sch., Colorado Springs, Colo., 1977-79; pvt. practice psychotherapy, Colorado Springs, 1979-82, San Diego, 1982—; cons. spl. edn., agoraphobia, women in transition. Mem. Am. Psychol. Assn., Am. Orthopsychiat. Assn., Phobia Soc., Council Exceptional Children, Calif. Psychol. Assn., Acad. San Diego Psychologists, AAUW, NOW, Mensa. Episcopalian. Lodge: Rotary. Contbr. articles to profl. jours.; author: (with R.C. Orem) Montessori: Prescription for Children with Learning Disabilities, 1977. Office: 826 Prospect Ste 201 La Jolla CA 92037

COBURN, PEGGY ANN, staff assistant; b. Dayton, Ohio, Dec. 7, 1946; d. Hager Wilford and Edna Lorraine (Williams) Stamper; m. Chester Coburn Jr. (dec.); 1 child, Cristi. Grad.high sch., Camargo, Ky., 1964. Cert. class III water distbn. system operator, Ky. Mgr. water system City of Jeffersonville, Ky., 1970—, city clk., 1970—; staff asst. Gateway Area Devel. Dist., Owingsville, Ky., 1988—. Contbr. columns to local newspapers, 1984—. Precinct chmn. Young Dems. of Ky., Jeffersonville, 1970-75, Jeffersonville Dems., 1978—; sec. Camargo PTO, 1978-80; mem. Wilderness Road Girl Scout Council, Camargo, 1978-83, Am. Cancer Soc., 1980—; bd. dirs. Gateway Health Assn., 1986-87, Montgomery County Sch. Heritage Commn., 1985-87; sec. Jeffersonville HomeMakers, 1986—; vol. Gateway Early Childhood Devel. Ctr.; chairperson Com. for Montgomery County Sch. Mus. Named Ky. Col., 1976. Mem. Ky. City Clks. Assn., Ky. Rural Water Assn. Home: 210 Compton Rd Jeffersonville KY 40337 Office: Gateway Area Devel Dist PO Box 1070 Owingsville KY 40360

COBUZZI, BARBARA J., printing company executive; b. Phila., Jan. 25, 1955; d. Daniel R. and Norma (Shockman) Compaine; m. Robert R. Cobuzzi, Apr. 16, 1983; 1 child, Jennifer Leah. BS, Rensselaer Poly. Inst., 1977; MBA, NYU, 1982. Packaging mgr. Lederle Labs., Pearl River, N.Y., project mgr.; mfg. systems cons. Coopers & Lybrand, N.Y.C.; mgr. prodn. planning Barr Labs., Pomona, N.Y.; account rep. Met. Life Ins. Co., Rochelle Park, N.J., Challenge Printing, Wallington, N.J. Mem. Am. Prodn. and Inventory Control Soc., Epsilon Delta Sigma, Beta Gamma Sigma (Sterling award). Home: 3 Running Brook Dr Tinton Falls NJ 07724

COCANOWER, LIANA CHERYL, lawyer; b. Salt Lake City, June 19, 1953; d. Elbert Ernest and Dorothy June (Smith) Miller; m. Michael A. Thiessen, Aug., 1973 (div. 1975); m. Michael Andrew Maher, Oct. 15, 1975 (div. Feb. 1981); m. David Lehman Cocanower, Sept. 21, 1983; children: Michael Whitten, Joseph Charles, Emily Elizabeth. B.E., Western Wash. State Coll., 1973; J.D., McGeorge Sch. Law, U. Pacific, 1979; LL.M. in Taxation, NYU, 1980. Bar: Calif. 1979, Ariz. 1980. Assoc. Lewis and Roca, Phoenix, 1980-85, ptnr., 1985-87; assoc. Storey & Ross, 1987-89; assoc. Squire, Sanders & Dempsey, 1989—. Served with USAF, 1975-76. Mem. ABA (tax sect., com. small bus., chmn. subcom. on publs.. real property, probate and trust div., vice chmn. com on spl. problems of bus. owners), Calif. State Bar, Ariz. State Bar (cert. tax specialist, tax sect.), Phi Delta Phi. Republican. Presbyterian. Home: 202 E McLellan Blvd Phoenix AZ 85012 Office: Squire Sanders & Dempsey 201 N Central # 2200 Phoenix AZ 85073

COCCARO, SHIRLEY LORRAINE, security officer; b. Uffington, W.Va., Sept. 1, 1943; d. John Albert and Mable Virginia (Arnold) Darnell; m. Anthony E. Coccaro (div. Aug. 1986), m. Lawrence T. Gilbert. Paralegal, Md. U., 1980, BBA, 1985; AA, Prince Georges Community Coll., Largo, Md., 1983. Adminstrv. asst. ADT Protection Svcs., Washington, 1965-74; police technician Prince George's County Police Dept., Forestville, Md., 1974-76; sec. IV Wash. Suburban Sanitary Commn., Hyattsville, Md., 1978-86; adminstrv. asst. Ocean Tech., Burbank, Calif., 1987-88; contractor spl. security officer Jet Propulsion Lab., Pasadena, Calif., 1987—. Mem. NAFE, Am. Soc. Indsl. Security, Nat. Profl. Bus. Women's Assn., Nat. Notary Assn. Home: 2029 E Ave R-10 Palmdale CA 93550 Office: Jet Propulsion Lab 4800 Oak Grove Dr Pasadena CA 91109

COCHIN, RITA R., nurse; b. Chgo., Feb. 13, 1936; d. Louis and Mary (Nims) Gang; m. Alan Cochin, Dec. 31, 1960; 1 child, Gayle Lynn. Diploma in Nursing, Michael Reese Hosp., Chgo., 1961; diploma in employee rels., Cornell U., Ithaca, N.Y., 1963. RN, Ill., N.Y. Asst. head nurse oper. rm. Michael Reese Hosp., 1961; head nurse labor & delivery Brookdale Hosp., Bklyn., 1962-63; staff nurse labor & delivery Michael Reese Hosp., 1963-64, phlebotomist-blood bank, 1965-69; staff nurse labor & delivery Luth. Gen. Hosp., Park Ridge, Ill., 1973-77, NST/OCT testing program, 1977-86, staff nurse perinatal unit, 1986—. active Immunization Clinic, Health Dept., Hoffman Estates, Ill., 1978. Mem. Nurses Assn. Ob-Gyn. Democrat. Jewish. Home: 1595 W Oakmont Rd Hoffman Estates IL 60194 Office: Luth Gen Hosp 1775 Dempster St 2 E Perinatal Park Ridge IL 60068

COCHRAN, CAROLYN, librarian; b. Tyler, Tex., July 13, 1934; d. Sidney Allen and Eudelle (Frazier) C.; m. Guy Milford Eley, June 1, 1963 (div.). BA, Beaver Coll., 1956; MA, U. Tex., 1960; MLS, Tex. Woman's U., 1970. Libr., Canadian (Tex.) High Sch., 1970-71; rep. United Food Co., Amarillo, Tex., 1971-72; libr. Bishop Coll., Dallas, 1972-74; interviewer Tex. Employment Commn., Dallas, 1975-76; libr. St. Mary's Dominican, New Orleans, 1976-77, DeVry Inst. Tech., Irving, Tex., 1978—; with Database Searching Handicapped Individuals, Irving, 1983—; vol. bibliographer Assn. Individuals with Disabilities, Dallas, 1982-85. Mem. Am. Coalition of Citizens with Disabilities, 1982—, Assn. Individuals with Disabilities, 1982-86, Vols. in Tech. Assistance, 1985—, Radio Amateur Satellite Corp., 1985-86; sponsor 500, Inc., 1988—. HEW fellow, 1967; honored Black History Collection, Dallas Morning News, Bishop Coll., Dallas, 1973. Mem. ALA, Spl. Libr. Assn. Club: Toastmistress (pres. 1982-83) (Irving). Reviewer Library Jour., 1974, Dallas Morning News, 1972-74, Amarillo Globe-News, 1970-71. Office: DeVry Inst Tech 4250 N Beltline Rd Irving TX 75038-4299

COCHRAN, ELEANOR BETTS, military career officer, retired; b. Hannibal, Mo., Oct. 24, 1914; d. William E. and Sarah Ada (Gould) Betts. BS in Nursing, Cath. U. Am., 1961. RN, Tex. Oper. room nurse Hines (Ill.) VA Hosp., 1938-43, U.S. Army, Ft. Riley, Kans., 1943-46; ship duty nurse U.S. Army Transp. Corps., 1946-49; oper. room nurse Hunter AFB, Savannah, Ga., 1949-52; flight nurse Travis AFB, Calif., 1952-55; recruiting officer USAF, Phila., 1955-59; flight nurse Rhein-Main AFB, Fed. Republic Germany, 1961-64; asst. chmn. dept. nursing Wilford Hall Air Force Med. Ctr., San Antonio, Tex., 1964-68; vis. nurse United Svcs. Auto Assn., San Antonio, 1968-77; pres. San Antonio Indsl. Nurses, 1969-72, San Antonio Unit Women's Overseas Svc. League, 1980-81. Mem. AAUW, Women's Overseas Svc. League (nat. officer, area bd. dirs. 1986—), Bus. and Profl. Women (coun. pres.'s), Retired Officers Assn., San Antonio C. of C. (red carpet com.). Democrat. Roman Catholic. Home: 123 Brackenridge #328 San Antonio TX 78209

COCHRAN, HELEN HEGE, publisher; b. Coral Gables, Fla., July 26, 1953; d. John Roy and Dorothy White (Huff) Hege. Student, Baylor U., 1971, So. State Coll., 1972-74; BA in Journalism, U. Ga., 1976. Gen. mgr. Thomasville (Ga.) Courier, 1976-78; mktg. dir. The Mountain Press, Gatlinburg, Tenn., 1978-80, mng. editor, 1980; gen. mgr. Brazos County Rev., Bryan, Tex., 1980-81; classified mgr. Bryan Coll. Sta. Eagle, 1981-84; classified mgr. Caller-Times Pub. Co., Corpus Christi, Tex., 1984-85, retail advt. dir., 1985-86; v.p. Harte-Hanks Community Newspapers, Carrollton, Tex., 1986-88; pub. Carrollton (Tex.) Chronicle, Farmers Br. Times, 1986-88, Transcript Newspapers-Harte Hanks, Deham, Mass., 1989—; bd. dirs. regional adv. bd. Am. Press Inst., Reston, Va. Mem. Newspaper Advt. Bur. (future advt. com.), Assn. Newspaper Classified Advt. Mgrs., Soc. Profl. Journalists.

COCHRAN, JACQUELINE LOUISE, general management executive; b. Franklin, Ind., Mar. 12, 1953; d. Charles Morris and Marjorie Elizabeth (Rohrbaugh) C. BA, DePauw U., 1975; MBA, U. Chgo., 1977. Fin. analyst Pan Am World Airways, N.Y.C., 1977-79, Gen. Bus. Group W. R. Grace & Co., N.Y.C., 1979-80; sr. fin. analyst Gen. Bus. Group div. W. R. Grace & Co., N.Y.C., 1980-81, mgr. fin. analysis, 1981-82, dir. fin. planning and analysis, 1982-85; v.p. fin. Am. Breeders Service div. W. R. Grace & Co., DeForest, Wis., 1985-87; v.p. feed ops. Grace Animal Svc. div. W. R. Grace & Co., DeForest, Wis., 1987-89; gen. mgr., chief ops. officer Soft Kat div. W.R. Grace & Co., Chatsworth, Calif., 1990; pres. W.R. Grace & Co., Chatsworth, 1990—. Recipient Women of Distinction award Madison (Wis.) YWCA, 1987; named to Acad. Women Achievers YWCA N.Y., 1984. Mem. Am. Soc. Profl. & Exec. Women, U. Chgo. Women's Bus. Group, Dane County United Way Key Club, Mortor Bd., Rotary, Madison Tempo, Phi Beta Kappa, Alpha Lambda Delta, Delta Delta Delta (advisor scholarship com. madison chpt. 1985-89, treas. 1986-89, house corp. bd. 1986-89, fin. advisor 1989-90). Republican. Methodist. Office: SoftKat div W R Grace & Co 20630 Nordhoff St Chatsworth CA 91311

COCHRAN, RUTH ELAINE BEARDSLEY, nurse, ethicist, philosopher, instructor; b. El Paso, Tex., June 14, 1936; d. David Albert and Theona Elaine (Lambert) Beardsley; m. Thomas Crowther Cochran Jr., Sept. 17, 1958; children: Thomas David, Laura Elaine. BS in Nursing, U. Utah, 1958; MA, U. Colo., 1975, PhD, 1985. RN, Utah, Colo. Staff and asst. head nurse Bernalillo County Indian Hosp., Albuquerque, 1958-59; instr. nursing Columbus Hosp. and Sch. Nursing, Great Falls, Mont., 1960-61, St. Margaret's Hosp. and Sch. Nursing, Montgomery, Ala., 1967-68; instr. philosophy Pikes Peak Community Coll., Colorado Springs, Colo., 1980—, U. So. Colo., Pueblo, 1986—; cons. private clients and institutions, 1985—; leader discussion groups Penrose Pub. Library, Colorado Springs, 1970-75. Writer, producer ednl. film Language Distortion and Propaganda Techniques, 1983-84. Editorial bd. Dialectics and Humanism. Grantee NEH, 1982. Mem. Pikes Peak Weavers' Guild (pres. 1983-84). Democrat. Unitarian. Home: 18060 E Forest Dr Monument CO 80132 Office: Pikes Peak Community Coll 5675 S Academy Blvd Colorado Springs CO 80906

COCHRAN, SACHIKO TOMIE, radiologist; b. Heart Mountain, Wyo., Feb. 17, 1945; d. Kageaki and Emiko Tomie. BA, UCLA, 1967; MD, U. Md. Sch. Medicine, 1971. Intern LAC/USC Med. Ctr., L.A., 1971-72; resident Kaiser Permanente Hosp., L.A., 1972-75; fellowship UCLA Med. Ctr., 1975-76; asst. prof. UCLA Sch. Medicine, L.A., 1976-84, assoc. prof., 1984—. consulting editor Investigative Radiology Jour., 1989—; consulting reviewer Radiology Jour., 1979-82, 85—; contbr. articles to profl. jours., chpts. to books. Grantee Mallinkrodt Inst., 1981, Cancer Rsch. Coord. Com., 1984, E.R. Squibbs, 1985, Johnson Computer Career Ctr., 1985, Cook Imaging, 1990. Mem. Soc. Uroradiology, Radiol. Soc. N.A., Assn. Acad. Radiologists, Am. Roentgen Ray Soc., Calif. Radiol. Soc., Am. Coll. Radiology, L.A. Radiol. Soc. (Jonsson Career Ctr., Assn. Acad. Women (treas. 1989—). Office: Dept Radiology UCLA 10833 Le Conte Ave Los Angeles CA 90024

COCHRANE, BETSY LANE, state legislator; b. Asheboro, N.C.; d. William Jennings and Bobbie (Campbell) Lane; m. Joe Kenneth Cochrane, 1958; children: Lisa, Craig. BA, Meredith Coll., 1958. Co-founder, sec. Consol. Wholesale Corp., 1953-56; owner, operator Village Super Market, 1953-56; chmn. bd. Bunker Hill Packing Corp., Bedford, Va., Assoc. Brokers, Inc., State Bank of Raleigh; state rep. State of N.C., 1980-88, state senator, 1988—; mem. Nat. Rep. Platform Com. Bd. dirs. Raleigh Community Hosp. Baptist. Office: PO Box 517 BR Advance NC 27006*

COCKER, BARBARA JOAN, marine artist, interior designer; b. Uxbridge, Mass.; A.A., Becker Jr. Coll., 1943; student Mt. St. Mary Coll., 1944-45, Clark U., 1945, N.Y. Sch. Interior Design, 1965-67. Owner, operator Barbara J. Cocker, Interior Design, Rumson, N.J., 1966—; owner Barbara J. Cocker Paintings of the Sea Gallery, Nantucket, Mass., 1975-86; tchr. adult edn. courses in interior design, 1965-68; artist, pvt. instr. marine art; pres. Maximus Praetorius Corp., Nantucket, Mass., 1979—; one-man shows marine paintings: Little Gallery, Barbizon, N.Y., 1971, Old Mill Assn., 1971, Pacem en Terris Gallery, N.Y.C., 1972, Central Jersey Bank & Trust Co., Rumson, 1971, 72, 74, 77, 79, Little Gallery, Nantucket Art Assn., 1975, 77, 79, 81, 84, 87, Caravan House Galleries, N.Y.C., 1975, 79, Guild of Creative Art, Shrewsbury, N.J., 1976, 81, 85, 88, IBM Corp., N.J., 1977, South St. Seaport Mus., N.Y., 1977, 80, Provident Nat. Bank, Phila., 1978, Gallery 100, Princeton, 1978, Bell Telephone Research Labs., 1982, 86, AT&T, 87, Midlantic Bank, N.J., 1988, Art Alliance N.J., 1983, Gilpin House Gallery (Va.), Swain Art Gallery, N.J., 1984, Oceanic Libr., N.J., 1989, Red Bank Libr., N.J, 1989; group shows include: Burr Artists N.Y., Guild Creative Art N.J., Composers, Authors and Artists Am. NAD, Salmagundi Club N.Y.C., Monmouth Coll. Festival of Arts, Caravan House Galleries, Pen and Brush Club, N.Y.C., N.Y.C., Lever House Galleries, N.Y.C., Nat. Arts Club, N.Y.C., Ocean County Artists Guild, N.J. Named Woman of Yr. Zonta Internat., 1986. Mem. Catharine Lorillard Wolfe Arts Club, Am. Artists Profl. League, N.Y. Guild Creative Arts, Nantucket Art Assn., Composers, Authors and Artists Am., Allied Artists Am., Monmouth Arts Found. (N.J.), So. Vt. Artists Inc., Pen and Brush Club (N.Y.C.). Address: 3 Rumson Rd Rumson NJ 07760 Also: Paintings Of Sea Studio Old South Wharf Box 574 Nantucket MA 02554

COCKRELL, DEBRA ANN, real estate professional, consultant; b. Rantoul, Ill., July 13, 1950; d. Veryl Clayton and Geraldine Marie (McConnell) Hewitt; m. John C. Sherrard, June 5, 1971 (div. July 1976); m. Franklin D. Cockrell, June 6, 1981; children: Matthew Franklin, Michael Allen. AAS, Parkland Coll., Champaign, Ill., 1970. Advt. asst. Needham, Harper & Steers, Inc., Chgo., 1970-71; ins. dept. head Citizens Bldg. Assn., Urbana, Ill., 1975-77; mem. staff Joint Cruise Missiles Project, Chrystal City, 1978; project head Vitro Labs., Silver Spring, Md., 1978-81; sr. system analyst Advanced Tech. Co., Reston, Va., 1981-86; realtor Jackson-Temple, Inc. Realtors, Vienna, Va., 1987—; owner, cons. Computer Profl. Mgmt., Inc., Vienna, 1983—; owner Glamour Shots store Equipose Devel. Corp., 1990—. Co-editor: (software manual) The Property Manager, 1984. Mem. Nat. Assn. Realtors, Nat. Exec. Females, Va. Assn. Realtors. Methodist. Home and Office: 408 Ridge Rd SW Vienna VA 22180 Office: CPMI 8600 Dellway Ln Vienna VA 22180

COCKRELL, LILA MAY BANKS, mayor; b. Ft. Worth, Jan. 19, 1922; d. Bruce and Velma (Tompkins) Banks; m. Sidney Earl Cockrell Jr., June 20, 1942 (dec. 1983); children: Carol Ann Cockrell Gulley, Cathy Lynn Cockrell Carmen. Student, Ward-Belmont Coll., 1938-39; BA, So. Meth. U., 1942. City councilwoman San Antonio, 1963-70, 73-75; mayor of San Antonio, 1975-81, 89—; mem. community devel. com. Nat. League of Cities, 1967-68, bd. dirs., 1975-76, adv. coun., from 1977, mem. task force on arts, from 1977; pres. region 7 Tex. Mcpl. League, 1965-66, bd. dirs., from 1973, 2d v.p., 1973, 1st v.p., 1974, pres., from 1976; mem. exec. com. Alamo Area Coun. Govts., 1970, vice chmn., 1971; vice chmn. Gov.'s Commn. Status of Women, 1970-72, sec. charter revision com., San Antonio, 1971; chmn. River Corridor Com., Mayor's Econ. Devel. Com.; chmn. bd. trustees Fire and Police Pension Fund; mem. Tex. Adv. Commn. Intergovtl. rels.; mem. S.W. regional adv. com. Pres.'s Commn. White Ho. Fellowships; mem. mayor's econ. adv. bd. U.S. Conf. Mayors, vice chmn. human resources com., from 1977, mem. task force on arts, from 1977, chmn. ERA ratification task force, from 1977; mem. ofl. del. to Taiwan, 1978, to People's Republic China, 1979. Trustee McAllister Scholarship Fund, 1962-63. Ensign WAVES, 1943-44. Recipient Headliner of Yr. award Theta Sigma Phi, 1964, Women of Achievement award So. Meth. U., 1967, Woman of Achievement award San Antonio Bus. and Profl. Women's Club, 1969; named Outstanding Citizen of Yr. League United Latin Am. Citizens Coun., 1972. Office: City Hall Office of Mayor 100 Military Pla San Antonio TX 78205*

COCUZZI, KATHLEEN JOAN, homemaker; b. Cleve., Nov. 26, 1951; d. Frank Steve and Agnes Helen (Hiznay) Pollack; m. David Anthony Cocuzzi, Aug. 31, 1974; children: Matthew, Elizabeth, Joanna. BA in Speech Pathology and Psychology, Cleve. State U., 1974. With retail mktg. dept. NCR Corp., Cleve., 1974-82; pvt. practice cons. Columbus, Ohio, 1982-83; homemaker Westerville, Ohio, 1982—; with retail sales dept. Longaberger Baskets, Dresden, Ohio, 1985-87; participant back to sch. for a day Westerville Pub. Schs., 1989; mem., trustee, bd. trustees Westerville Pub. Libr., 1990—. Leader Girl Scouts U.S. Cleve. and Westerville, 1977-85; mem. long range planning com. West Pub. Libr., Waterville, 1990—; v.p. McVay PTA, Westerville, 1990—; pres. Friends of Westerville Pub. Libr., 1986-90; mem., trustee Westerville Libr. Bd. Dirs., 1990—; Sun. sch. tchr. St. Paul's Ch., 1989—. Recipient Lifetime Membership Svc. award Friends of Westerville Pub. Libr., 1990. Mem. AAUW (sec. 1986-88, scholarship chmn. 1988—), Westerville C. of C., Newcomers (v.p. 1983-84, pub. newsletter 1984-85). Republican. Home: 1029 Bluesail Dr Westerville OH 43081

CODY, VIVIAN, crystallographer, research scientist; b. San Diego, Jan. 28, 1943; d. Leo N. and Florida M. (Polanco) C. BS, U. Mich., 1965; PhD, U. Cin., 1969. NSF trainee U. Cin., 1967-69; postdoctoral fellow U. Mo., St. Louis, 1969-70; postdoctoral trainee Med. Found. Buffalo, Inc., 1970-72, rsch. assoc., 1972-79, rsch. scientist, 1979-87, sr. rsch. scientist, 1987—; rsch. asst. prof. Sch. Pharmacy SUNY, Buffalo, 1988—, rsch. assoc. prof. Sch. Medicine, 1979—; cons. U. N.C. Computer Graphics, Chapel Hill, 1990—. Editor Jour. Molecular Graphics, 1988—; assoc. editor Endocrine Rsch., 1987—. Am. Cancer Soc. Rsch. grantee, 1985-90. Mem. Am. Crystallographic Assn. (sec. 1988—), Am. Chem. Soc. (treas. sect. 1988-90), Assn. Women in Sci. (treas. chpt. 1980—), Zonta Internat. (pres. Buffalo club 1990), Sigma Xi (pres. Buffalo chpt. 1988-90). Office: Med Found Buffalo 73 High St Buffalo NY 14203

COE, ILSE G., lawyer; b. Koenigsberg, Germany, May 28, 1911; came to U.S., 1938, naturalized, 1946. Referendar, U. Koenigsberg, 1935, JSD, 1936; LLB, Bklyn. Law Sch., 1946. Bar: N.Y. 1946. Dir. econ. research Internat. Gen. Electric Co., Berlin, 1936-38; asst. to sales promotion and advt. mgr. Ralph C. Coxhead Corp., N.Y.C., 1940-44; law clk. Mendes & Mount, N.Y.C., 1944-46; assoc. Hill, Rivkins & Middleton, N.Y.C., 1946-50, McNutt, Longcope & Proctor, N.Y.C., 1950-52, Chadbourne, Hunt, Jaeckel & Brown, N.Y.C., 1952-54; asst. v.p., asst. trust officer Schroder Trust Co. and J. Henry Schroder Banking Corp., N.Y.C., 1954-76; dir., sec., editor Fgn. Tax Law Assn., Inc., L.I., 1945-55; tchr. Drakes Bus. Sch., N.Y.C.,

1946-49; lectr. on estate planning to ch., women's and bar assn. groups, 1947—; tutor literacy vols., 1977-79; lectr. wills trusts and estates and photography Pace U., St. Francis Coll. Mem. exec. bd. Active Retirement Ctr., Pace U., 1977-79, v.p., 1980-81, pres., 1982-85, life mem. exec. bd., 1986—; Rep. county com. woman, 1948-50; former deacon, now ruling elder, chmn. investment com. 1st Presbyn. Ch., Bklyn.; v.p., chair house com. Florence Ct. Corp. Coop., 1985-88. Recipient Human Relations award NCCJ, 1979. Mem. Bklyn. Women's Bar Assn. (past treas., sec., bd. dirs. 1960—), Protestant Lawyers Assn. of N.Y. Inc. (sec. 1960-75, 1st v.p. 1976-77, pres. 1978-88, lifetime pres. emeritus 1988—), Internat. Fedn. Women Lawyers, Bklyn. Heights Assn., Bklyn. Hist. Soc. (former mem. investment com.), N.Y. Color Slide Club (by-laws chmn. 1983—, bd. dirs. 1973-74), Bklyn. Mus., Bklyn. Botanic Garden, others. Home: 187 Hicks St Brooklyn Heights NY 11201

COE, JUDITH LYNN, automobile manufacturing company administrator; b. Washington, Oct. 4, 1945; d. Raymond G. and Lynn (Pulliam) Coe. BA in Math.,, Converse Coll., 1967; Exec. Sec. cert., Washington Sch. for Secs., 1968. Sec. to v.p. and sec. Nonprescription Drug Mfrs. Assn., Washington, 1968-72; sec. to regional mgr. Electro-Motive div. GM Corp., Atlanta, 1972-83; sec. to asst. zone mgrs. Pontiac div. GM Corp., Atlanta, 1983-87; zone mgr.'s sec. Pontiac div. GM Corp., Washington, 1987—; bd. dirs., corp. sec. Lynn Properties, Washington, 1989—. Mem. Converse Coll. Alumnae Assn. Republican. Methodist. Home: 4803 Jamestown Rd Bethesda MD 20816 Office: Pontiac Div Gen Motors 1395 Piccard Dr Rockville MD 20850

COE, LINDA MARLENE WOLFE, small business owner, photographer; b. Logan, Ohio, Apr. 5, 1941; d. Kenneth William and Mary Martha (Eddy) Wolfe; m. Frederic Morrow Coe, Sept. 15, 1962; children: Christopher, Jennifer, Peter, Michael. BFA, Columbus Coll. of Art and Design, 1978. Freelance photographer Columbus, 1978—; sec., receptionist Plaza Dental, Columbus, 1983; sec. Worthington (Ohio) Dental Group, 1983-85; owner Custom Corp. Gift Svc., Worthington, 1985—; trustees Met. Women's Ctr., Columbus, 1986-87. Docent trainee Columbus Mus. Art, 1982-83; mem. Worthington Arts Coun., 1982, 83, 85, 87, 89. Mem. Specialty Advt. Assn. Internat., Specialty Advt. Assn. Cent. Ohio, Nat. Assn. Profl. Saleswomen, Women's Bus. Bd., Columbus Bus. and Profl. Women, Columbus C. of C., Columbus Sales Exec. Club, Worthington C. of C. (com. mem. 1985—). Republican. Roman Catholic. Home: 320 E South St Worthington OH 43085 Office: Giftshopper 867 High St Worthington OH 43085

COE, MARGARET LOUISE SHAW, community service volunteer; b. Cody, Wyo., Dec. 25, 1917; d. Ernest Francis and Effie Victoria (Abrahamson) Shaw; m. Henry Huttleston Rogers Coe, Oct. 8, 1943 (dec. Aug. 1966); children: Anne Rogers Hayes, Henry H.R., Jr., Robert Douglas II. AA, Stephens Coll., 1937; BA, U. Wyo., 1939. Asst. to editor The Cody Enterprise, 1939-42, editor, 1968-71. Chmn. bd. trustees Buffalo Bill Hist. Ctr., Cody, 1966—, Cody Med. Found., 1964—; bd. dirs. Shoshone First Nat. Bank, Cody, 1967—; commr. Wyo. Centennial Commn., Cheyenne, 1986—. Recipient The Westerner award Old West Trails Found., 1980, Gold Medallion award Nat. Assn. Sec. of State, 1982, Disting. Alumni award U. Wyo, 1984, Govs. award for Arts, 1988; inducted Hall of Fame Nat. Cowgirl Hall of Fame, 1983. Mem. P.E.O., Delta Delta Delta. Republican. Episcopalian. Home: 1400 Eleventh St Cody WY 82414

COELLO, ELENA COROMOTO, psychologist; b. Caracas, Venezuela, Apr. 9, 1952; came to U.S., 1977; d. Hermes and Cira (Adrianza) C.; m. Hilario V. Guanipa (div. Nov. 1984); 1 child, Hilario; m. Julio Brener, July 14, 1986. BA in Psychology, U. Calif., Davis, 1981; MS in Psychology, Nova U., 1983, Caribbean Ctr Advanced Studies, 1987; PhD in Clin. Neuropsychology, Caribbean Ctr Advanced Studies, 1989. Lic. mental health counselor. Psychotherapist stress unit Inst. Bricmont, Caracas, 1983-84; team leader South Shore Hosp., Miami, Fla., 1984-87; psychoedn. cons., doctoral intern Miami Children's Hosp., 1988-89; psychology assoc. Bon Secours Hosp., Miami, 1989—; pvt. practice psychologist Sunset Mental Health Assocs., Miami, 1989—; assoc. prof. Miami Inst. of Pyschology, Miami, 1989—; day counselor Diogenesis Shelter for Runaways, Davis, Calif., 1981; lectr. South Shore Hosp., Miami Beach, Fla., 1986, 87, Bricmont Inst., Caracas, 1984, Miami Mental Health Ednl. Ctr., 1986.. Mem. Am. Psychol. Assn. (assoc.), Internat. Neuropsychology Soc. (assoc.), Am. Assn. Counseling & Devel. (assoc.), Biofeedback Assn. Fla. (assoc.), Nat. Honor Soc. Fla. (assoc.). Home: 1925 Brickell Ave D 1811 Miami FL 33129 Office: Bon Secours Hosp 1050 NE 125th St North Miami FL 33161

COEN, VICTORIA LYNN, psychotherapist, group and private consultant, psychology educator; b. Seattle, Jan. 8, 1954; d. Thomas Judson and Janet (Dunn) C. BA, Wagner Coll., Bregenz, Austria, 1975, Western Wash. U., 1976; MSW, U. Wash., Seattle, 1981. Cert. social worker, Wash. Med. social worker Children's Hosp., Seattle, 1976; psychiat. social worker St. John's Hosp., Longview, Wash., 1976-77, mental health profl., 1977-79; Adminstr. King County div. Human Svcs., Seattle, 1979-80; med. social worker Harborview Hosp., Seattle, 1980; instr., researcher U. Wash., Wash. Dept. Licensing, Seattle, 1980-81; psychotherapist Eastside Mental Health, Bellevue, Wash., 1980-85, Divorce Lifeline, Seattle, 1986-88; pvt. practice psychotherapist Seattle, 1982—; group cons. Parents Anonymous, Longview, 1976-78; co-founder ADAPT: Battered Women's shelter, Longview, 1978-79; media interviewee Seattle Times, KING, KIRO Radio stas., KING-TV, KOMO-TV, 1984—. Author numerous pub. poems. Mem. Seattle Art Mus., 1987. Mortar Bd. scholar U. Wash., 1980. Mem. Nat. Assn. Social Workers, Phobia Soc. Am., Am. Assn. Behavioral Therapists, Jungian Soc., Green Peace (vol.), Sierra Club (vol.). Home: 737 N 71st St Seattle WA 98103 Office: 2808 II E Madison Ste 200 Seattle WA 98112

COFFEE, VIRGINIA CLAIRE, civic worker, former mayor; b. Alliance, Nebr., Dec. 8, 1920; d. James Maddigan and Adelaide Mary (Forde) Kennedy; BS, Chadron State Coll., 1942; m. Bill Brown Coffee, June 21, 1942; children: Claire, Sara, Virginia Anne, Sue. High sch. prin., Whitman, Nebr., 1942; bookkeeper Coffee & Son, Inc., Harrison, Nebr., 1965—, officer, 1967—, pres., 1987—; dir. Friends of Agate Fossil BEOS, Inc., 1988, v.p. 1989—; mayor City of Harrison, 1978-80. Leader, Girl Scouts U.S.A., 1953-63; mem. Harrison Elem. Sch. bd., 1958-64; mem. liaison com. Chadron State Coll., 1975; pub. rels. chmn. Nebr. Cowbelles, 1968; sec. NW Stock Growers, 1971-73; corp. officer Ft. Robinson Centennial, 1973-88; officer Gov.'s Ft. Robinson Centennial Commn., 1973-75; hon. gov. Nebr. Centennial, 1967; chmn. Sioux County Bicentennial, 1973-77; trustee Nebr. State Hist. Soc. Found., 1975—, Village of Harrison, 1973-80; bd. dirs. Harrison Community Club, Inc., 1983-86, officer, 1984-86; apptd. Sioux County Vis. com. 1989—. Mem. Nebr. State Hist. Soc. (life, dir. 1979-85, 2d v.p. 1982-84, 1st v.p. 1984-85, com. for marker to honor Harrison centennial 1985-86), Wyo. State Hist. Soc. (cardinal key honor frat.), Sioux County Hist. Soc. (bd. dirs. 1975-81, 83-84, 87, pres. 1988—, past pres., co-pres., sec., v.p.) Sioux county history book com. 1985-86, contbr. articles. Roman Catholic. Clubs: Sioux County Cowbelles, Nebr. Cowbells, Ladies Community, Harrison Community Inc. Contbr. articles to area newspapers; chmn. compilation com. book Sioux County Memoirs of Its Pioneers, 1967; coordinator Harrison sect. book Nebraska Our Towns, 1988. Address: PO Box 336 Harrison NE 69346

COFFEY, HELEN ERNESTINE, nursing consultant; b. Erick, Okla., May 4, 1934; d. Clyde Raymond Ambrose and Mary Ellen (Holland) Brindle; m. Curtis L. Coffey, Jan. 1, 1966; children: Aveta, Kimberly. Diploma, Okla. Bapt. Hosp. Sch. Nsg., 1960. RN, Okla., Tex.; I.V. therapist. Charge nurse, gen. duty Sayre (Okla.) Meml. Hosp.; nursing home cons. Grand Place Nursing Ctr., Sayre, 1983-90. Active ARC. Mem. CONE. Mem. Nazarene Ch.

COFFEY, KATHRYN R(OBINSON) (KAY COFFEY), civic worker; m. Clarence W. Coffey; children: Clarence William, Kathryn Ann. BS in Govt., West Tex. State U., 1937; HHD (hon.), Northwestern State U., Natchitoches, La., 1987. Active Lakeview Presbyn. Ch., New Orleans, 1944—, deacon, 1968-71, bd. dirs. kindergarten and nursery sch., 1965-68; mem. com. on home and family nurture Presbytery South La., 1967-69; mem. exec. com., chmn. dept. relation to pub. schs. Greater New Orleans Fedn. Chs., 1970-76; mem. Presbyn. campus life com. Presbytery New Orleans, 1978-82; mem. various coms. Orleans Parish (La.) Sch. Bd., 1953-77; active PTA, including bd. dirs. New Orleans Council, 1956-75, pres., 1965-67, v.p., chmn. legis. services and pres. Dist One La., 1967-72, mem. legis. com. Nat. Congress, 1969-72; mem. New Orleans Pub. Library Bd., 1956-62; v.p., chmn. membership com. Civic Council New Orleans, 1952-75; organizer, exec. sec. New Orleans Citizens for Support of Pub. Schs., 1968-76; bd. dirs., mem. coms. La. Assn. Mental Health, 1968-71; mem. La. Commn. Law Enforcement and Adminstrn. Criminal Justice, 1968-70; pres. La. Orgns. for State Legis., 1972-76; com. mem., bd. dirs. regional adv. group La. Regional Med. Program Inc., 1970-76; numerous activites for gifted edn. and spl. edn., including: founder, v.p., legis. chmn. Greater New Orleans Spl. Edn. PTA, 1971-77; mem. exec. com. La. Adv. Council for Learning Disabilities, 1972-76; co-chmn. Speak Out for Spl. Children, New Orleans, 1972-77; mem. Task Force for Implementation of Act 368 of 1972, La., 1972-76; spl. hearing officer Fed. Dist. Ct., New Orleans, 1973-77; chmn. La. Adv. Com. for Gifted and Talented, 1973-76; pres., organizer Assn. Gifted and Talented Students Inc., 1973-86; editor newsletter, 1973-81, contbg. editor, 1981-87; com. mem., chmn. nomination com. La. Gov.'s 4-C Policy Bd., 1974-77; project reader Office Gifted and Talented, Office Edn., 1975-76; mem. La. Coalition on Handicapped, 1975-88; mem. U. New Orleans Task Force on Gifted and Talented, 1976-82; regional rep. La. Gov.'s White House Conf. on Handicapped, 1977; bd. dirs. Nat. Assn. Gifted Children, 1977-86; mem. La. Gov.'s Adv. Com. on Edn. of Handicapped, 1978-81; mem. adv. bd. Gifted Advocacy Info. Network, 1979-83; mem. adv. bd. Inst. Gifted and Talented Edn., N.J. Dept. Edn., 1978-81; rev. editor Jour. Edn. of Gifted, Assn. for Gifted, 1980-82; vice-chmn. bd. dirs. La. Sch. for Math., Sci. and the Arts, Natchitoches, 1981-85, chmn. bd., 1985-87; mem. adv. bd. Gifted Children's Newsletter, 1981—; mem. Gov.'s Adv. Com. Ednl. Block Grants. Recipient Life Membership in La. PTA, Edward Hynes PTA, 1954; cert. of merit Mayor New Orleans, 1969; life Membership of Nat. Congress Parents and Tchrs., New Orleans Council PTA's, 1970; award for outstanding service Gov.'s Commn. on Law Enforcement and Adminstrn. Criminal Juvenile Deliquency Com., 1970; Outstanding Scouter award Greater New Orleans Fedn. Chs., 1972, Outstanding Citizen award Council Exceptional Children, 1974; award for outstanding service Dir. Office Gifted and Talented, Office Edn., 1976; award of appreciation Assn. Gifted and Talented Students, 1980, award for outstanding service Isnt. Gifted and Talented Edn., N.J. Dept. Edn., 1980; named Hon. Senator, Lt. Gov. and Pres. of La. Senate, 1975; award for outstanding service Inst. Arts and Humanities Inc., Kansas City, Mo., 1982; Conv. Parent of Yr., Nat. Assn. Gifted Children, 1982; award for service to bd. dirs. Nat. Assn. Gifted Children, 1987; Spl. Edn. Pioneer award for outstanding contbn. to edn. for children La. Dept. Edn., 1987; Kathryn Robinson Day declared by Mayor of Natchitoches, Nov. 19, 1987; awarded "hon. student" status, 1987; awarded 9th degree award Northwestern State U. La., Natchitoches, 1987; U. New Orleans Library designated Kay Coffey Archives, 1987; Kay Coffey Libr. of Benjamin Franklin High Sch., New Orleans, named in her honor, 1987. Home: 59 Oceanaire Dr Rancho Palos Verdes CA 90274

COFFEY, NANCY ANN, real estate broker; b. Palm Springs, Calif.; d. Arthur Johnson and Joan (Hunter) C. BA, Stanford U., MS in Engring. Indsl. real estate broker Coldwell Banker, Houston, 1977-79; comml. broker Coldwell Banker, San Francisco, 1980-87, Cushman & Wakefield, N.Y.C., 1987—. Active Jr. League, San Francisco, 1981-87, N.Y.C., 1987—. Office: Cushman & Wakefield 500 Fifth Ave New York NY 10110

COFFEY, ROSEMARY KLINEBERG, educator; b. N.Y.C., Jan. 5, 1937; d. Otto and Selma Ruth (Gintzler) Klineberg; m. Joseph I. Coffey, June 28, 1963 (div. 1977); children: Megan Forbes, Susan Fox, James Odell; m. Zigmund L. Dermer, Apr. 7, 1990. BA, Vassar Coll., Poughkeepsie, N.Y., 1953-57; MA, Tufts U., Medford, Mass., 1958-59. Clk. typist United Nations Secretariat, N.Y.C., 1956, 1957; asst. editor, assoc. editor World Peace Found., Boston, 1959-61; research asst., assoc. Inst. for Defense Analyses, Washington, D.C., 1961-63; researcher Ctr. for Research on Conflict Resol, U. Mich., Ann Arbor, Mich., 1963-64; tchr. Pitts. Bd. Pub. Edn., 1975-78, tchr., editor, 1979—; researcher, writer Brandegee Assocs., Pitts., 1978-79; co-chair joint Bd. Union Coms. on Profl. Edn., Pitts., 1987, 1989. Author: The Story of Pittsburgh, 1986, co-author: America as Story, 1988. Com. chair Pitts. Friends Meeting, 1978—, sec. Renaissance and Baroque Soc., 1983-85, Renaissance City Wind Music Soc., Pitts., 1987-90, class pres. Vassar Coll., Class 1957, Poughkeepsie, 1987—. Mem. Educators for Social Responsibility, Pitts. Vassar Club (treas., newsletter editor), World Federalist of Pitts. Assn. (bd. dirs. 1990—). Democrat. Home: 916 Bellefonte St Pittsburgh PA 15232

COFFILL, MARJORIE LOUISE, civic leader; b. Sonora, Calif., June 11, 1917; d. Eric J. and Pearl (Needham) Segerstrom; A.B. with distinction in Social Sci., Stanford U., 1938, M.A. in Edn., 1941; m. William Charles Coffill, Jan. 25, 1948, (dec.); children: William James, Eric John. Asst. mgr. Sonora Abstract & Title Co. (Calif.), 1938-39; mem. dean of women's staff Stanford, 1939-41; social dir. women's campus Pomona Coll., 1941-43, instr. psychology, 1941-43; asst. to field dir. ARC, Lee Moore AFB, Calif., 1944-46; partner Riverbank Water Co., Riverbank and Hughson, Calif., 1950-68. Mem. Tuolumne County Mental Health Adv. Com., 1963-70; mem. central advisory council Supplementary Edn. Center, Stockton, Calif., 1966-70; mem. advisory com. Columbia Jr. Coll., 1972-89, pres., 1980—; pres. Columbia Found., 1972-74, bd. dirs., 1974-77; mem. Tuolumne County Bicentennial Com., 1974—; active PTA, ARC. Pres., Tuolumne County Rep. Women, 1952—, assoc. mem. Calif. Rep. Central Com., 1950. Trustee Sonora Union High Sch., 1969-73, Salvation Army Tuolumne County, 1973—; bd. dirs. Lung Assn. Valley Lode Counties, 1974—(life 1986—). Recipient Pi Lambda Theta award, 1940; Outstanding Citizen award C. of C., 1974, Citizen of Yr. award, 1987. Mem. AAUW (charter mem. Tuolumne County br., pres. Sonora br. 1965-66). Episcopalian (mem. vestry 1968, 75). Home: 376 E Summit Ave Sonora CA 95370

COFFIN, BERTHA LOUISE, management; b. Atlanta, Aug. 19, 1919; d. William Wesley and Bertha Louise (Marsh) Mendenhall; m. J. Donald Coffin, Feb. 14, 1943 (dec. Sept. 1978). BA, U. Kans., 1940. Med. technologist Midwest Research Lab., Emporia, Kans., 1940-43; ins. agt. Coffin Ins. Agy., Council Grove, Kans., 1943-, sole owner, mgr., 1978-82; treas. Council Grove Telephone Co., 1947-50, sec.-treas., 1950-78, pres., gen. mgr., chmn. bd., 1978—; del. legis. confs. Nat. Telephone Coop. Assn., 1986, 88. Copy preparation, The Story of the Santa Fe Trail, 1982, Tel. Directory. Pres. various lit. clubs, Council Grove, 1945-72; speaker various civic, polit. and religious groups, 1962—; mem. adv. coun. Manhattan Christian Coll., 1983-86, trustee, 1986—. Mem. Independent Tel. Pioneers (dir. 1984--). Democrat. Office: Council Grove Tel Co PO Box 272 Council Grove KS 66846

COFFMAN, CHRISTINE ROBERTA, retired secretary; b. Bradford, Ark., Sept. 14, 1914; d. John Franklin and Martha Vannetta (Eubank) C. AA, Cen. Bapt. Coll., Conway, Ark., 1933; BS, U. Cen. Ark., 1935; postgrad., U. Ark., Fayetteville. Elem. tchr. Washington Sch., Fayetteville, Ark., 1935-37, Cleveland Ave. Sch., Camden, Ark., 1937-42; teller First Comml. (formerly Comml. Nat. Bank), Little Rock, 1942-44; stenographer FBI, Little Rock, 1944-54, sec. to asst. agt. in charge for Ark., 1954-69; sec. to spl. agt. in charge for Ark. FBI, 1969-88. Active membership drives Community Concert assn., Little Rock, 1970s, 1980s; mem. AAUW, Little Rock, 1970s, 1980s, Am. Assn. Retired Persons, Little Rock, 1989, Nat. Assn. Retired Fed. Employees, Little Rock, 1989; pres. Ark. Bapt. Bus. Women, 1950s; pres., other offices Pulaski County Fedn. Bapt. Women, 1960s, 70s, 80s, Baptist Women, Immanuel Bapt. Ch., 1960s, 70s, 80s; Sunday sch. tchr. Bapt. Ch., Camden, Little Rock, 1940s-80s; tchr. conversational English, Friendship Internat., 1988. Mem. Fine Arts Club of Ark. Art Ctr., PEO Sisterhood (pres., other offices). Republican. Home: 705 N Cedar Apt 2B Little Rock AR 72205

COFFMAN, DIANE SHARON, computer systems manager; b. Alexandria, Va., Mar. 25, 1952; d. Thornton Decatur Wilt and Ann Cecelia (Mazetis) Sozonoff; m. John Russell Forbes, (div.); children: Allison Leigh, Lesley Dianne; m. Stephen Leslie Coffman, Dec. 18, 1987. Student, No. Va. Community Coll., Alexandria, 1979, U. New Orleans, 1978—. Computer programmer Dept. of Justice, Washington, 1977-79, computer system analyst, 1979-81; office mgr. Internat. Marine Casualty, Metairie, La., 1986-88; computer systems mgr. Dept. of Justice, New Orleans, 1988—; mem. Tech. Assistance Group for the Exec. Office of the U.S. Trustees, Washington, 1988—. Copy-editor: (quarterly systems newsletter) U.S.T. Data News, 1989—. Mem. Assn. Women in Computing, IBM Users Group, Federally Employed Women, Cross Gates Racquetball Club. Republican. Roman Catholic. Home: 103 Camborne Ln Slidell LA 70461 Office: Dept of Justice 400 Poydras St Ste 1820 New Orleans LA 70130

COFFMAN, ORENE BURTON, hotel executive; b. Fluvanna, Va., Mar. 13, 1938; d. John C. and Adele (Melton) Burton; m. John H. Emerson, Aug. 5, 1955 (div. 1972); 1 child, Norman Jay; m. Mack H. Coffman, Oct. 26, 1986. Degree in hotel and motel mgmt., Michigan State U., 1966-70. Cert. hotel mgr., Mich. State U., 1970. Telephone operator Colonial Williamsburg (Va.) Hotel, 1962-64; room clk. Colonial Williamsburg (Va.) Hotel, 1964-68; mgr. front office Colonial Williamsburg (Va.) Hotel, 1968-83; asst. mgr. Williamsburg Inn, 1983—; pres. Colonial Williamsburg Employees Fed. Credit Union, 1980-85. Mem. Am. Hotel Motel Assn. (nat. acctg. award 1970). Democrat. Baptist. Office: Williamsburg Inn PO Box B Williamsburg VA 23187

COFFMAN, RENAE K., data processing security official; b. Horton, Kans., Oct. 1, 1957; d. Delbert R. and Thelma L. (Coonse) Clark; m. Jerry L. Coffman, May 30, 1981. AB in Computer Sci., U. Mo., 1984, BS in Acctg., 1984. CPA. Auditor Mo. State Auditor's Office, Jefferson City, 1985-88; data processing security officer Mo. State Lottery, Jefferson City, 1988—. Mem. NAFE, Assn. Govt. Accts., Mo. Soc. CPA's, Nat. Assn. Accts., Am. Women's Soc. CPAs, Computer Security Inst., EDP Auditor's Assn., Inc., Info. Systems Security Assn., Inc. Home: 917 Jason Rd Jefferson City MO 65109

COFFMAN, SANDRA JEANNE, psychologist; b. San Antonio, May 31, 1945; d. Frederick and Dorothy Jane (Rothenbech) C.; m. David W. Hutchinson, Apr. 8, 1977; children: Kevin, Sean. BA in English & French, Purdue U., 1967; MA in Internat. Studies, The Am. U., 1969; PhD in Ednl. Psychology, U. Wash., 1978. Licensed psychologist, Wash. Counselor Femal Offender Project, Seattle, 1973-74; counseling intern U. Wash. Counseling Ctr., Seattle, 1975-76; dir. SCCC Women's Programs, Seattle, 1977-78; post doctoral intern U. Wash. Counseling Ctr., Women's Inst., Seattle, 1982; coord., counselor New Directions in Work, Highline Community Coll., Seattle, 1979-81; group leader YWCA Abused Womens Groups, Seattle, 1981-82; clin. supr., psychologist U. Wash., Dept. Psychology, NIMH, Seattle, 1984-87, clin. asst. prof., 1988—; clin. cons. Eastside Domestic Violence Project, Bellevue, W.Va., 1987—; co-dir. Women's Counseling Group, Seattle, 1981—. Co-author: Talking It Out, 1984. Recipient Fellowship For Travel U. Wash., 1976, Mortarboard Scholarship Purdue U., 1967, Scholarship U. Wash., 1973. Mem. Am. Psychol. Assn., Assn. Women in Psychology, Feminist Therapy Inst., Nat. Coalition Against Domestic Violence, Assn. Advancement Behavior Therapy, Am. Orthopsychiat. Assn. Office: 2001 Western Ave #340 Seattle WA 98121

COFFMAN, VIRGINIA SUE, traffic administrator; b. Bermuda, May 20, 1954; d. Thomas L. and Margaret A. (Jumper) Distel; m. John J. Coffman, Apr. 27, 1973; children: Jeremy Michael, Janel Marie. With Nat. Machinery Co., Tiffin, Ohio, 1972—, traffic sec., 1978-84, traffic adminstr., 1984—. Advisor 4-H Club, Tiffin, 1980—, sec. advisor coun., 1988—. Republican. Roman Catholic. Office: Nat Machinery Co 161 Greenfield St Tiffin OH 44883

COGGER, BARBARA SUE, corporate professional; b. Mount Holly, N.J., Apr. 19, 1965; d. John W. and Jennie L. (Pengelski) C. BA in Psychology, Thomas Edison State Coll., 1990. Personal care attendant to handicapped children Matheny Sch., Peapack, N.J., 1983-85; office mgr. Werner Adam Corp., Basking Ridge, N.J., 1985-90; v.p. Werner Adam Corp., Telluride, Colo., 1990—. Presbyterian. Home and Office: PO Box 2136 Telluride CO 81435

COGGESHALL, JANICE R., city mayor; b. Trenton, N.J., June 27, 1935; d. James Clendenin and Geraldine (Badenoch) Reddig; m. Richard Edwin Coggeshall, Nov. 29, 1958; children: John, Heidi, James, Joshua. BA, Wellesley Coll., 1957. Mem. council City of Galveston, Tex., 1979—, mayor, 1984—; chmn. women mayors subcom. to U.S. Conf. Mayors, 1986-89. Presbyterian. Office: City Galveston City Hall Box 779 Galveston TX 77553

COGGIN, CHARLOTTE JOAN, cardiologist, educator; b. Takoma Park, Md., Aug. 6, 1928; d. Charles Benjamin and Nanette (McDonald) Coggin; BA, Columbia Union Coll., 1948; MD, Loma Linda U., 1952, MPH, 1987; Intern, Los Angeles County Gen. Hosp., Los Angeles, 1952-53, resident in medicine, 1953-55; fellow in cardiology Children's Hosp., Los Angeles, 1955-56, White Meml. Hosp., Los Angeles., 1955-56; research assoc. in cardiology, house physician Hammersmith Hosp., London, 1956-57; resident in pediatrics and pediatric cardiology Hosp. for Sick Children, Toronto, Ont., Can., 1965-67; cardiologist, co-dir. heart surgery team Loma Linda (Calif.) U., asst. prof. medicine , 1961-73, asso. prof., 1973—, asst. dean Sch. Medicine Internat. Programs, 1973-75, assoc. dean, 1975—, co-dir., cardiologist heart surgery team missions to Pakistan and Asia, 1963, Greece, 67, 69, Saigon, Vietnam, 1974, 75, to Saudi Arabia, 1976-87, China, 1984, Hong Kong, 1985, Zimbabwe, 1988, Kenya, 1988; mem. Pres's. Advisory Panel on Heart Disease, 1972—. Apptd. Med. Quality Rev. Com.-Dist. 12, 1976-80. Recipient award for service to people of Pakistan City of Karachi, 1963, Medallion award Evangelismos Hosp., Athens, Greece, 1967, Gold medal of health South Vietnam Ministry of Health, 1974, Charles Elliott Weinger award for excellence, 1976, Wall Street Jour. Achievement award, 1987; named Honored Alumnus Loma Linda U. Sch. Medicine, 1973, Outstanding Women in Gen. Conf. Seventh-day Adventists, 1975, Alumnus of Yr., Columbia Union Coll., 1984. Diplomate Am. Bd. Pediatrics. Mem. Am. Coll. Cardiology, AMA (physicians adv. com. 1969—) Calif. Med. Assn. (com. on med. schs., com. on member services), San Bernardino County Med. Soc. (chmn. communications com. 1975-77, mem. communications com. 1987-88, editor bull. 1975-76), Am. Heart Assn., AAUP, Med. Research Assn. Calif., Calif. Heart Assn., AAUW, Am. Acad. Pediatrics, World Affairs Council, Internat. Platform Assn., Calif. Museum Sci. and Industry MUSES (Outstanding Woman of Year in Sci. 1969), Am. Med. Women's Assn., Loma Linda Sch. Medicine Alumni Assn. (pres. 1978), Alpha Omega Alpha, Delta Omega. Author: Atrial Septal Defects, motion picture (Golden Eagle Cine award and 1st prize Venice Film Festival 1964); contbr. articles to med. jours. Democrat. Home: 11495 Benton St Loma Linda CA 92354 Office: Loma Linda U Med Ctr Loma Linda CA 92354

COGGINS, CYNTHIA ANNE, school administrator; b. Greenville, S.C., Apr. 29, 1954; d. Harry Edwin and Hazel Leonia (Edwards) C. BA, Furman U., 1976, MA, 1980. Cert. tchr., S.C. Tchr. emotionally handicapped Athens Elem. Sch., Travelers Rest, S.C., 1976-77; tchr. emotionally handicapped Arrington Elem. Sch., Greenville, 1977-80, tchr. learning disabilities, 1980-88; asst. prin. Brushy Creek Elem. Sch., Taylors, S.C., 1988—. Mem. Greenville Civic Chorale, 1980-81; deacon First Bapt. Ch., Greenville, 1984-87; bd. dirs. North Greenville Mental Health Clinic, 1977-78. Named one of Outstanding Young Women of Am., 1983, 85, 87, Outstanding Young Woman of S.C., 1987, Arrington Elem. Tchr. Yr., 1986-87, Greenville County Tchr. Yr., Greenville Coun. for Exceptional Children, 1986-87. Mem. S.C. Coun. for Exceptional Children (S.C. Tchr. Yr. 1987, sec. 1980-82, treas. 1983-86, v.p. 1986-87, pres.-elect 1987—, pres. 1988-89), Delta Kappa Gamma. Home: 14 Batesview Dr Greenville SC 29607 Office: Brushy Creek Elem Sch 1344 Brushy Creek Rd Taylors SC 29687

COGHLAN, MARY ELLEN, commercial real estate appraiser; b. Jersey City, June 18, 1954; d. James Joseph and Mary Dolores (Rotar) C. BA, Ramap Coll., 1976. Assoc. appraiser Coghlan Appraisal Co., Ramsey, N.J., 1976-81; appraiser Mfrs. Hanover Trust, N.Y.C., 1982-83; sr. appraiser Cushman & Wakefield, East Rutherford, N.J., 1983—. Supporter Greenpeace, Washington, 1988—. Recipient N.Y. Soc. Real Estate Appraisers scholar, 1983. Mem. Assoc. Meadowlands Bd. Realtors, Am. Soc. for Prevention of Cruelty to Animals, Am. Inst. Real Estate Appraisers, Titanic Hist. Soc., Am. Inst. of Real Estate Appaisers. Roman Catholic. Home: 19 Spanktown Rd Warwick NY 10990 Office: Cushman & Wakefield NJ One Medowlands Pla Ste 1100 East Rutherford NJ 07073

COHAN, CAROLE, advertising agency executive. Former v.p. and exec. v.p. Saatchi & Saatchi Compton, Inc., N.Y.C.; now sr. v.p. and dir. broadcast prodn. McCann-Erickson N.Y., N.Y.C. Office: McCann-Erickson NY 750 3d Ave New York NY 10017*

COHANE, HEATHER CHRISTINA, magazine publisher; b. Camberley, Surrey, Eng., May 27, 1934; came to U.S., 1982; d. William Willoughby and Naomi Mary (Winder) Fausset; m. John Philip Cohane, May 13, 1961 (dec. Dec. 1981); children: Alexander, Candida, Ondine; m. Ossian Kare Berga, Nov. 2, 1985. Student pvt. schs., Isle of Wight, Eng. and Neuchatel, Switzerland. Pub. Quest mag., N.Y.C., 1987—. Office: Quest Mags Inc 152 E 79th St New York NY 10021

COHEN, ALYSIA, tour operator; b. N.Y.C., Sept. 15, 1952; d. Jack and Anna (Wolfman) Garzick. BA in Comm., Queens Coll., N.Y.C., 1972; MBA in Mktg., NYU, 1980. Comm. instr. Queens Coll., CUNY, 1972-73; tech. writer St. John's Episc. Hosp., N.Y.C., 1973-75; cons. Stone & Webster Mgmt. Cons., N.Y.C., 1976-78; mgr. new product devel. Philip Morris USA, N.Y.C., 1979-83, Coca Cola USA, Atlanta, 1984-86; v.p. mktg. The Seagram Beverage Co., N.Y.C., 1987-89; pres., tour operator Gallivanting, Inc., N.Y.C., 1989—. Mem. Phi Beta Kappa, Beta Gamma Sigma, Kappa Delta Pi. Jewish. Home: 515 E 79th St New York NY 10021

COHEN, AUDREY C., college president; b. May 14; d. Abe Cohen and Esther Cohen Morgan; children—Dawn Jennifer, Winifred Alisa. B.A. magna cum laude, U. Pitts., 1953; postgrad. in polit. sci. and edn. George Washington U., 1957-58. Founder, pres. Coll. Human Services, N.Y.C., 1964—, Am. Council Human Service, 1974—; exec. dir. Women's Talent Corps., 1964-68; founder, pres. Part-Time Research Assocs., 1958-64; lectr. in field; cons. Commn. Occupational Status Women in Nat. Vocat. Guidance Assn. Contbr. articles to profl. jours. Active subcom. higher edn. N.Y.C. Partnership; chmn. Com. on Yr. 2000, N.Y. World Future Soc.; nat. adv. com. Horizons-Bicentennial Commn.; mem. planning com. Hemispheric Congress Women, Miami, Fla., 1975-76; chmn. Nat. Task Force on Women, Edn. and Work, 1975; active Manhattan Borough Pres.'s Adv. Com. on Health Careers for Disadvantaged, Pub. Edn. Assn. Project for Restructured Edn. System N.Y.C. Recipient Stanley M. Isaacs award Am. Jewish Com., 1969; George Champion award Chase Manhattan Bank, 1970; Disting. Vis. prof. award U. Mass., 1975; Ednl. Devel. Cert. of Achievement award Atlantic Richfield Co., 1979; Otty award Our Town newspaper, 1981; Mina Shaughnessy scholarship award U.S. Office Edn., 1983; Empire State award, 1984-85; Outstanding Leadership in Higher Edn. award Commn. Ind. Colls. and Univs., 1984-85. Mem. Support Services Alliance, Inc. (bd. dirs.), Fin. Women's Assn., Am. Jewish Com. (exec. com., bd. dirs.), council Higher Ednl. Instns. Clubs: Economic, Harvard, Lotos, Women's Forum. Home: 37 E 67th St New York NY 10014 Office: Coll Human Svcs 345 Hudson St New York NY 10014*

COHEN, BEVERLY SINGER, environmental health researcher, educator; b. N.Y.C., Jan. 2, 1933; d. Abraham C. and Charlotte (Scher) Singer; m. Murray Leon Cohen, Mar. 27, 1955; children—Mark L., David E., Steven M. B.A., Bryn Mawr Coll., 1953; M.A., Cornell U., 1961; Ph.D., NYU, 1979. Cert. in radiol. physics. Research asst. dept. radiol. physics Coll. Physicians and Surgeons, N.Y.C., 1953-56; instr. physics Mt. St. Mary Coll., Newburgh, N.Y., 1968-73; asst. research scientist Inst. Environ. Medicine, NYU Med. Ctr., N.Y.C., 1976-79, assoc. research scientist, 1979-80, research asst. prof., 1980-85, research assoc. prof., 1985-89, rsch. prof., 1989—; deputy program dir. in occupational hygiene NYU, 1986—; dir. rsch. tng. NIOSH Region II Ednl. Resource Ctr., 1987—; cons. Contbr. articles to profl. jours. Bd. dirs. Temple Beth Jacob, Newburgh, N.Y., 1977-81. Recipient cert. of merit Am. Roentgen Ray Soc., 1956; fellow Sloan Kettering Inst. for Cancer Research, 1956-57, Nat. Ctr. for Radiol. Health, 1974, Nat. Inst. Environ. Health Scis., 1975; NSF grantee, 1972-73; Nat. Inst. Occupational Safety and Health research career awardee, 1984. Mem. Am. Phys. Soc., Am. Phys. Soc. (div. biol. physics), Health Physics Soc., N.Y. Acad. Scis., Am. Conf. Govtl. Indsl. Hygienists, Am. Indsl. Hygiene Assn., Am. Assn. for Aerosol Research, Gesellschaft für Aerosolforschung eV, Sigma Xi. Democrat. Avocations: skiing; sailing; swimming. Office: NYU Med Ctr Inst Environ Medicine 550 1st Ave New York NY 10006

COHEN, CARLA LYNN, publisher; b. N.Y.C., Feb. 27, 1937; d. Barnet and Florence (Skolnick) Ellowis; children—Beth Diane, Jeffrey. Student Clark U., Adelphi U. Editor, Oceanside (N.Y.) Beacon, 1975-77; adminstrv. asst. pub. relations Bd. Suprs. Nassau County, 1977-78; pres. Carla Cohen Communications, Oceanside, N.Y., pres. Cotar Publs., Nassau Borders Papers, Floral Park, N.Y., 1981—; editor Voters Guide, Lawrence, N.Y., 1979-80. Grand Marshall Meml. Day parade, 1986. Recipient Patriotic Service award VFW, 1976; Outstanding Achievement award Am. Cancer Soc., 1976-77; Pub. Service award USAF, 1983; named Woman of Yr., B'nai B'rith, 1985, Sons of Italy, 1985. Mem. C. of C. (v.p. 1982—), LWV (v.p. 1979), Internat. Platform Assn. Republican. Jewish. Office: PO Box 155 Franklin Square NY 11010

COHEN, CARYN LEE, temporary employment agency official; b. Bronx, N.Y., Feb. 26, 1957; d. Bernhard Cohen and Sylvia Moskovitz-Cohen; m. Effraim Rahamin; m. Caine Alan (div. Apr. 1982); 1 child. AAS, Rockland Community Coll., Suffern, N.Y., 1976. Dept. mgr., merchandiser Caldors Dept. Stores, Suffern, Nanuet, N.Y., 1974; merchandiser Bradlees Dept. Stores, Ramsey, N.J., 1980-82; showroom sales mgr. Kranfeurs Everwarm, N.Y., 1982-85; office mgr., account supr. New Dimensions in Temps, Hackensack, N.J. Author: Pauses in Time, Impressions, Foundation Anthology. Home: 288 Waterside Dr Little Ferry NJ 07643 Office: New Dimensions in Temps 10 E Camden St Hackensack NJ 07601

COHEN, CATHI, program coordinator; b. Boston, June 11, 1960; d. Melvin George and Paula Joy (Rosenbaum) O. BA summa cum laude, Tufts U., 1982; MSW, Columbia U., 1986. Staff worker, intern St. Mark's Psychiatric Ctr., London, 1981; staff psychotherapist Montague Sch., Bklyn., 1984-85, Jewish Bd. Family & Childrens Svcs., Bklyn., 1985-87; coord. svcs. ctr. for family violence Jewish Bd. Family & Childrens Svcs., 1987-89; adult day program supr. Fairfax County Govt., Reston, Va., 1989—; cons. in field. Co-chair Bklyn. com. N.Y.C. Task Force Against Sexual Assault, 1988-89. Mem. Nat. Assn. Social Workers, Am. Group Psychotherapy Assn. Office: Fairfax County Govt Northwest Ctr 1850 Cameron Glen Dr Reston VA 22090

COHEN, CHERYL DIANE DURDA, communications executive; b. Mpls., Jan. 26, 1947; d. Joseph and Dolores Catherine (Monahan) Durda; m. Miles Jon Cohen, June 24, 1967; children: Christopher, Michael, Brian, Katherine Kelly. BA, U. Minn., 1978; postgrad., Harvard U., 1990—. Writer Aeration Industries Internat. Inc., Chaska, Minn., 1982-85, communications asst., 1985-86, communications mgr., 1986-88, v.p. pub. rels., 1988—. Editor AIRE-02 News, 1985—, AQUA-02 News, 1988—; contbr. articles on water restoration and aquaculture to U.S. and internat. profl. jours., also conf. proc.; film editor, producer, 1986—. Bd. dirs. Minn. Assn. Retarded Citizens, Mpls., 1984-85, Joseph Durda Found., St. David's Sch. for Exceptional Children, Minnetonka, 1980-85; mem. adv. bd. Minnetonka Schs. CARE, Minn., 1982—; dir. communications Minnetonka Football Assn., 1986—, founding mem., 1986; founding mem. Minnetonka Basketball Club, 1984; bd. dirs. St. David's Sch. Exceptional Children, Minnetonka, 1980-85; bd. dirs. The Joseph Durda Found., 1990—; active legis. testimony, lobbying, pub. speaking Adv. for Severely Disabled, 1981—; mem. U. Minn. Gopher Football Team's Parent Club, 1988—; co-facilitator Devel. Capable Young People series for Minnetoka community, 1983-84. Mem. Water Pollution Control Fedn., World Aquaculture Soc., Asian Fisheries Soc., U. Minn Alumni Assn., U. Minn. Pres. Club, Women's Athletics Club (chpt. mem., adv. coun. women's intercoll. athletics), Minn. Press Club, Booster Club (producer cable TV sports show 1988—, co-chair publicity 1988—). Office: Aeration Industries Internat Inc 4100 Peavey Rd Chaska MN 55318

COHEN, CORA, artist; b. N.Y.C., Oct. 19, 1943; d. George and Anne (Lenarsky) C. BA, Bennington Coll., 1964, MA, 1972. One person show Everson Mus. Art, Syracuse, N.Y.C., 1974, Max Hutchinson Gallery, N.Y.C., 1979-84; painter Baxter Art Gallery, Pasadena, Calif., 1985, Am. Acad. & Inst. Arts & Letters, N.Y.C., Barbara Krakow Gallery, Boston, Mass., 1987; vis. artist Art Inst. Chgo., U. Chgo., 1983-85, Boston Mus. Sch. Fine Arts, 1985, Vt. Studio Sch., 1990, Tyler Sch. Art, 1990. one person show Wolff Gallery, 1988, Holly Solomon Gallery, 1990; contbr. articles to profl. jours. Recipient Painting Fellowship award Nat. Endowment for the Arts, N.Y. Found. for the Arts., Gottlieb Found. award, 1990; Yaddo Residence grantee. Mem. Simon Wiesenthal Ctr., Coll. Art Assn. Jewish. Home: 287 Broadway New York NY 10007

COHEN, CYNTHIA MARYLYN, lawyer; b. Bklyn., Sept. 5, 1945. AB, Cornell U., 1967; JD cum laude, NYU, 1970. Bar: N.Y. 1971, U.S. Ct. Appeals (2d cir.) 1972, (9th cir.) 1980, U.S. Dist. Ct. (so. and ea. dists.) N.Y. 1972, (cen. and no. dists.) Calif. 1980, U.S. Supreme Ct. 1975, U.S. Dist. Ct. (so. dist.) Calif. 1981, U.S. Dist. Ct. (ea. dist.) 1986. Assoc. Simpson Thacher & Bartlett, N.Y.C., 1970-76, Kaye, Scholer, Fierman, Hayes & Handler, N.Y.C., 1976-80; assoc. Stutman, Treister & Glatt, P.C., L.A., 1980-81, ptnr., 1981-87; ptnr. Hughes, Hubbard & Reed, N.Y.C. and L.A., 1987—. Bd. dirs. N.Y. chpt. Am. Cancer Soc., 1977-80. Recipient Am. Jurisprudence award for evidence, torts and legal instns., 1968-69; John Norton Pomeroy scholar NYU, 1968-70, Founders Day Cert., 1969. Mem. ABA (antitrust & litigation sect.), Assn. Bar City N.Y. (trade regulations com. 1976-79), L.A. County Bar Assn. (antitrust & comml. law & banking sects.), Assn. Bus. Trial Lawyers, Fin. Lawyers Conf., N.Y. State Bar Assn. (chmn. class-action com. 1979), State Bar Calif. (antitrust & bus. law sects.), Delta Gamma, Order of Coif. Home: 4818 Bonvue Ave Los Angeles CA 90027 Office: Hughes Hubbard & Reed 555 S Flower St Los Angeles CA 90071

COHEN, DENISE JODI, athletic director; b. N.Y.C., Mar. 14, 1961; d. Howard Leonard and Shirley (Alpert) C. BA, Bucknell U., 1983; MA, Adelphi U., 1987. Asst. coach basketball Molloy Coll., Rockville Centre, N.Y., 1983-84; dir. athletics Molloy Coll., Rockville Centre, 1984—; asst. mgr. tickets, media cons. U.S. Tennis Assn., N.Y.C., 1983-84; dir. athletics Molloy Coll., Rockville Ctr., N.Y., 1984-90; media cons. U.S. Tennis Assn., N.Y.C., 1985-90; asst. athletic dir. U. Hartford, West Hartford, Conn., 1990—; dir. athletics Whitestone (N.Y.) Youth Ctr., 1986—; asst. to dir. ops. World Championship Tennis, 1985—, commr. Empire State Conf., 1985—; founder, organizer Molloy Coll. Women's Basketball League, 1988; mem. eligibility com. Ea. Colls. Athletics Conf., 1988—; mem. conf. com. Ea. Colls. Athletics, 1989—. Mem. Nat. Assn. Coll. Dirs. Athletics, Coll. Sports Info. Dirs. Am., Met. Colls. Athletic Dirs. Assn. (treas. 1988), NAFE, N.Y. Collegiate Athletic Conf. (chmn. volleyball and tennis), Met. Collegiate Athletic Dirs. (v.p.). Office: U Hartford 200 Bloomfield Ave West Hartford CT 06117

COHEN, DIANE BERKOWITZ, lawyer; b. Vineland, N.J., June 11, 1938; d. Myer and Ida Mae (Subin) Berkowitz; m. Robert H. Cohen, June 11, 1958 (div. Dec. 1980); children: Ronald Jay, Stuart Daniel, Amy Suzanne; m. Samuel Gerstein, Aug. 5, 1984. AA magna cum laude, Fairleigh Dickinson U., 1958; BA summa cum laude, Glassboro State Coll., 1976; JD, Temple U., 1979. Bar: Pa. 1979, N.J. 1980, U.S. Ct. Appeals (3d cir.) 1981. Assoc. Lewis Katz, Cherry Hill, N.J., 1979-81, Steven D. Weinstein, Cherry Hill, 1981-83; sole practice Collingswood, N.J., 1983-85; ptnr. Gerstein, Cohen & Spevak, PA, Haddonfield, N.J., 1985—; active ethics com. N.J. Supreme Ct. Vice chmn. Allied Jewish Appeal, Cherry Hill, 1968-72; v.p. Nat. Council Jewish Women, Haddonfield, 1969-71; bd. dirs. Planned Parenthood Assn. Camden County, N.J., 1982—. Mem. ABA, N.J. Bar Assn., Camden County Bar Assn. (chmn. women lawyers com., mem. jud. appointment com., budget and fin. com., trustee 1986-89, sec. 1989—), Assn. Trial Lawyers Am. Office: Gerstein Cohen & Spevak PA 20 Kings Hwy W Haddonfield NJ 08033

COHEN, DONNA EDEN, lawyer; b. Harlingen, Tex., Oct. 23, 1956; d. Gerald Myer and Annette Rose (Rodman) C. Student, U. Hawaii, 1976-77; BA, U. Mass., 1978; JD, Suffolk U., 1981. Bar: Mass. 1981, U.S. Dist. Ct. Mass. 1982, U.S. Ct. Appeals (1st cir.) 1982, U.S. Supreme Ct. 1988. Assoc. Gilman, McLaughlin & Hanrahan, Boston, 1981-89, ptnr., 1989—; of counsel Gerald M. Cohen, Andover, Mass., 1986—; counsel Commonwealth Mass. Purchasing Agt., Boston, 1982. Contbg. editor: Landlord/Tenant Law, Mass. Practice Libr., Lawyers Coop. Mem. Mass. Gov.'s Prepaid Legal Svcs. Com., Boston, 1982—; bd. dirs. Am. Heart Assn., Needham, Mass., 1983-87; trustee Fisher Hill Estates Condominium, 1989—. Mem. ABA, Mass. Bar Assn., Boston Bar Assn., Assn. Trial Lawyers Am. (v.p. Suffolk chpt. 1979-81), Mass. Acad. Trial Attys. (lectr. continuing legal edn. seminar 1982—), New Eng. Women in Real Estate, Phi Delta Phi. Democrat. Jewish. Office: Gilman McLaughlin & Hanrahan 470 Atlantic Ave Boston MA 02210

COHEN, ESTHER RHEA, business executive, civic leader; b. Chgo., Sept. 13, 1937; d. Max and Dora (Feldman) Wolf; m. Melvyn M. Kupetz, Aug. 21, 1956 (div. July 1973); children: Debra Lynn Ehr, Sandra Kupetz; m. Melvin Aaron Cohen, Oct. 23, 1973; stepchildren: Nisa Levy, Devra H., Justin D. Student, U. Colo. Pres., gen. mgr. A.K. Glass Co., Denver, 1973-79; pres., gen. mgr., also bd. dirs. ABC Glass Co., Denver, 1980—, A.K. Car Co., Denver, 1977—; sec., bd. dirs. Generic Water Co., Denver, 1981—, T.A.D. Co. Inc., Denver, 1981—. Founder, pres., bd. dirs. Golda Meir Meml. Assn., Denver, 1981—; sec., bd. dirs. Com. to Save Golda's Home, Denver, 1984—; founder, sec., bd. dirs. Safe Cars and Trucks Now Inc., Denver, 1981—; ex-officio mem. Auraria Higher Edn. Ctr. Golda Meir House Rev. Panel, Denver, 1987—. Mem. Ind. Auto Dealers Assn., Glass Dealers Assn., Women's Bus. Owners Assn. Democrat. Jewish. Lodge: B'Nai B'rith. Office: Golda Meir Meml Assn PO Box 9693 Denver CO 80209

COHEN, GERALDINE M., association executive; b. Pitts., Mar. 6, 1919; d. Jacob Howard and Sara (Tolochko) Marcus; m. Abraham S. Cantor, Dec. 24, 1939 (dec. 1952); children: Charles Cantor Cohen, Henry Cantor Cohen; m. N. Hart Cohen, May 15, 1953 (dec. 1982). BA, U. Pitts., 1939. Office asst./writer U. Pitts., Grad. Sch. Pub. Health, 1949-52; acct. exec. Radio WEIR, Weirton, W.Va., 1959-62; interim dir. pub. svc. City of Steubenville, Ohio, 1962; dir. budget and purchasing City of Steubenville, 1962-63; buyer The Hub of Steubenville, 1966-68, personnel dir., 1968-75; exec. sec. Jefferson County Taxpayers Assn., Steubenville, 1978—. Columnist Steubenville Herald Star, 1978—; contbr. articles to profl. jours. Exec. com., bd. advs. U. Steubenville, 1980-83; bd. dirs. Ohio Pub. Expenditure Council, Columbus, 1987—; steering com. Old Fort Steuben Project, Steubenville, 1987—; bd. trustees St. John's Med. Ctr., 1985—. Mem. Rotary (1st woman mem. Steubenville chpt.). Republican. Jewish. Home: 209 Braebarton Steubenville OH 43952 Office: Jefferson County Taxpayers 916 Sinclair Bldg Steubenville OH 43952

COHEN, GLORIA ERNESTINE, educator; b. Bklyn., July 6, 1942; d. Victor George and Marion Theodosia (Roberts) C. BS in Edn., Wilberforce U., 1965; MA in Elem. Edn., Adelphi U., 1975; Profl. Diploma in Ednl. Adminstrn., L.I. U., 1984; MS in Edn., Bklyn. Coll., 1986. Tchr. Bd. Edn., Bklyn., 1965—; case worker Dept. Welfare, Bklyn., 1965—; mem. comprehensive sch. improvement program Pub. Sch. 149, mem. open corridor planning com., mem. consultation com. Mem. Northwest Civic Assn., Freeport, N.Y., 1973—. Mem. NAFE, Assn. for Supervision and Curriculum Devel., Nat. Alliance of Black Sch. Educators, Inc., Bklyn. Reading Coun. of Internat. Reading Assn., N.Y. State Reading Assn., Assn. Black Educators of N.Y., FSO Internat. Club, Freeport Indoor Tennis Club, Zeta Phi Beta, Kappa Delta Pi. Democrat. Roman Catholic. Home: 4 Sterling Pl Freeport NY 11520 Office: Bd Edn PS 149 700 Sutter Ave Brooklyn NY 11207

COHEN, HARRIET NEWMAN, lawyer; b. Providence, Dec. 8, 1932; d. Morris and Marion Newman; B.A. in Latin and Greek, Barnard Coll., 1952; M.A. in Latin and Greek (Tuition scholar), Bryn Mawr Coll., 1953; J.D. cum laude, Bklyn. Law Sch., 1974; 4 daus. Bar: N.Y. 1975, Fed. Ct. 1975, U.S. Supreme Ct. 1982. Assoc. Squadron, Gartenberg, Ellenoff & Plesent, N.Y.C., 1974-76, Phillips, Nizer, Benjamin, Krim & Ballon, N.Y.C., 1976-80, Golenbock & Barell, N.Y.C., 1980-83; ptnr. Golenbock and Barell, 1984-86, Solin & Breindel, 1986—; tchr. domestic relations law Continuing Edn. div. CUNY, 1980—, adv. bd., 1982—; lectr. Assn. Bar City N.Y., 1982, N.Y. Women's Bar Assn., 1981, 82, N.Y. State Trial Lawyers Assn., 1981, 82, ABA, 1986; apptd. to N.Y. Child Support Commn., 1984—; mem. jud. screening bd. Ct. Appeals, 1985, 86. Author: The Equitable Distribution Law in Divorce: The New York Experience. Mem. N.Y. Women's Bar Assn., (v.p. 1983-84, pres. 1985-86), Assn. Bar City N.Y., N.Y. State Bar Assn., Bklyn. Law Rev. Alumni Assn. (trustee 1981—), Women's Bar Assn. State of N.Y. (dir. 1983-86), Coalition on Women's Legis. Issues (co-chair 1986—). Office: Solin & Breindel 100 E 42nd St 22nd Fl New York NY 10017

COHEN, IDA BOGIN (MRS. SAVIN COHEN), export/import executive; b. Bklyn.; d. Joseph and Yetta (Harris) Bogin; student St. Johns U.; B.S., N.Y.U.; m. Barnet Gaster, June 26, 1941 (div. May 1955); m. 2d, Savin Cohen, Aug. 30, 1964. Sec.-treas. J. Gerber & Co., Inc., N.Y.C., 1942-54, v.p., dir., 1954-73; pres., dir. Austracan U.S.A., Inc., N.Y.C., 1960-73; v.p. Parts Warehouse, Inc., Woodside, N.Y., 1970-72, sec.-treas., 1972-83; also engaged in pvt. investments. Contbr. articles to South African Outspan, newspapers. Home: 12 Shorewood Dr Sands Point NY 11050

COHEN, JERI FRIED, recruiting service executive; b. Passaic, N.J., July 22, 1956; d. Jules Robert and Arlyne (Levinson) Fried; m. Jeffrey Arnold Cohen, Oct. 23, 1983; 1 child, Diana Leigh. BS in Econs., Rutgers U., 1978; postgrad., Fordham U., 1982-83. Registered sales asst. Merrill Lynch Pierce Fenner & Smith, Inc., N.Y.C., 1978-80; trust officer Citibank, N.Y.C., 1980-83; sr. v.p., dir. trust and investment, executive recruiter A-L Assocs., Inc., N.Y.C., 1983-90; pres. J. Cohen Assocs., Inc., N.Y.C., 1990—; guest lectr. Rutgers U., 1982-83; cons. in field. Mem. NAFE, Nat. Assn. Bank Women, Am. Mgmt. Assn., Alpha Zeta, Nat. Orgn. of Women, Nat. Assn. Working Women.

COHEN, JOYCE E., state senator, investment executive; b. McIntosh, S.D., Mar. 27, 1937; d. Joseph and Evelyn (Sampson) Petik; children: Julia Jo, Aaron J. Grad., Coll. Med. Tech., Minn., 1955; student, UCLA, Minn., 1957-78, Santa Ana Coll., Minn., 1961-62. Med. rsch. technician dept. surgery U. Minn., 1955-58; dept. tech. U. Calif., 1958-59, dept. bacteriology, 1959-61; med. rsch. scientist Allergan Pharms., Santa Ana, Calif., 1961-70; ptnr. Co-Fo Investments, Lake Oswego, Oreg., 1978—; mem. Oreg. Ho. of Reps., from 1979, now state senator. Mem. Jud. Com., Ho. of Reps. and Senate, 1979—, chmn. 1989—; mem. banking and pub. fin. com., Ho. of Reps. and Senate, 1981—; co-chmn. Joint Trade and Econ. Devel. coms., 1985-87; mem. hazardous waste com., agr. and nat. resources coms., environ. and energy coms., housing and urban devel. coms., ins. and arson coms. task force on ethics; chmn. Vet.'s Task Force; chmn. jud. com.; vice chmn. trade and econ. devel. and health ins. and biologic coms.; mem. Oreg. Criminal Justice Coun.; mem. Jud. Br. State Energy Policy Rev. Com., 1979; mem. Gov.'s Commn on Child Support. Woodrow Wilson Lecture series fellow, 1988. Mem. Assn. Family Conciliation Cts., Citizens Coun. of Cts., LWV, Oreg. Environ. Coun., Oreg. Women's Polit. Caucus. Democrat. Office: Oreg State Senate State Capitol Salem OR 97310*

COHEN, JUDITH ANN, child psychiatrist, educator; b. Knoxville, Tenn., Dec. 7, 1953; d. Bernard L. and Anna (Foner) C.; m. Michael J. Rogal; children: Shari, Aren, Lauren. BA, Bowdoin Coll., 1974; MD, U. Pitts., 1978. Diplomate Am. Bd. Psychiatry and Neurology, Am. Bd. Gen. and Child Psychiatry. Pediatric intern Mercy Hosp., Pitts., 1978-79; resident and fellow in psychiatry and child psychiatry Western Psychiat. Inst., Pitts., 1979-83, med. dir. Ctr. for Children and Families, 1986-88, med. dir. Child and Adolescent Sexual Abuse Clinic, 1988—; asst. prof. child psychiatry U. Pitts. Sch. Medicine, 1983—, cons. student health svc., 1986—; cons. Karma House Drug and Alcohol Ctr., Pitts., 1981-82, Asklepieion Juvenile Offenders Program, Pitts., 1983, Alternatives Drug and Alcohol Ctr., Pitts., 1983-85. Contbr. articles to med. jours., chpts. to books. Cons. Allegheny County Task Force on Child Sexual Abuse, Pitts., 1983-84. NIMH grantee, 1986—. Mem. AMA, Am. Psychiat. Assn., Am. Acad. Child and Adolescent Psychiatry, Pitts. Regional Orgn. Child and Adolescent Psychiatry. Office: Western Psychiat Inst 3811 O'Hara St Pittsburgh PA 15213

COHEN, JUDITH RACHAEL, marketing professional; b. Phila., Sept. 3, 1954; d. Jack and Ethel (Shuman) C.; m. Jerry Cohen, Aug. 4, 1974; children: Stefan, Beth. B Social Welfare cum laude, Temple U., 1976; AAS in Bus. Mgmt., Delaware County Community Coll, 1988. Head tchr. Downtown Children's Ctr., Phila., 1976-79; search coord. Adoption Forum Phila., 1980-83; beauty cons. Mary Kay Cosmetics, Downingtown, Pa., 1982-83; fitness instr. Aqua-Terra Fitness Systems, Glenolden, Pa., 1983-86; owner, dir. Nat. Scholarship Rsch. Group, Media, Pa., 1986-88; mktg. mgr. Bertholon-Rowland, Media, 1988—. Mem. AFTRA, Phila. Direct Mktg. Assn. (Benny award 1989). Office: Bertholon Rowland Box 77 Media PA 19063

COHEN, LAJLA JANE, teacher; b. Fergus Falls, Minn., Feb. 26, 1928; d. Charles Gerlinger and Lajla Marie Dale; m. Irvine Cohen, Oct. 7, 1951 (div. 1970); children: Mary Ann, Emily, Lajla. MA, L.I. U., N.Y.C., 1969; BA, Macalester Coll., St. Paul, 1950. Prog. asst. sec. Sloane House YMCA, N.Y.C., 1950-51; rsch. writing Inst. Internat. Edn., N.Y.C., 1951-56; tchr. Shepaug Valley Regional Sch. Dist., Wash., 1969-89. Author: Cat and Dog Series, 1980, The Other Dance, 1988. Pres., Washington-Warren VNA, 1974-78; mem. Litchfield Hist. Soc., Conn., 1987—, Common Cause Nat. Orgn., 1986—, Wilderness Soc., Nat. Orgn., 1985—. Mem. Conn. Edn. Assn., Shepaug Valley Edn. Assn. Democrat.

COHEN, LAUREN ANN, psychologist; b. Albany, N.Y., Mar. 23, 1949; d. David and Sylvia (Bernstein) Cohen; m. Irving A. Cohen, May 29, 1983; children: David, Benjamin. BA, U. Rochester, 1971; MA, U. Md., 1975, PhD, 1977. Lic. psychologist, Md., N.Y. Psychologist Kennedy Inst., Balt., 1978-85, Children's Hosp. of Buffalo, N.Y., 1985-89; chief psychologist Children's Hosp. Rehab. Ctr., Buffalo, 1989—; psychologist Sunrise Mental Health Assn., West Seneca, N.Y., 1987—; cons. Parents Anonymous, Buffalo, 1989—. Mem. Am. Psychol. Assn., Am. Orthopsychiatric Assn. Home: 101 Cadman Dr Williamsville NY 14221 Office: Childrens Hosp of Buffalo Delaware Ave Buffalo NY 14205

COHEN, MARGARET ANN, corporate art consultant, artist; b. Ridgewood, N.J., Nov. 13, 1953; d. Ralph B. and Madeline (Krug) Tompkins; m. Ian Phillip Cohen, Apr. 28, 1985; children: Andrew Michael, Matthew Scott. Student, U. Tours, France, 1975; BA in Studio Art, Rutgers U., 1976. Libr. asst. Rutgers U., New Brunswick, N.J., 1977-78; asst. art buyer Brentano's, N.Y.C., 1978-80; West Coast regional mgr. Brentano's, Beverly Hills, Calif., 1980-81; saleswoman Wally Findlay Galleries, Beverly Hills, 1981-82; corp. art cons. dir. Creative Galleries, L.A., 1983-90; art cons. Gen. Telephone Calif. Hdqrs., Thousand Oaks, 1986-88, Transam. Ins. Hdqrs., L.A., 1987-89, Princess Cruises, L.A., 1988-90. Mem. adv. coun. Middlesex County (N.J.) Cultural and Heritage Commn., 1977. Mem. Los Angeles County Mus. Art. Home: 14829 Yukon Ave Hawthorne CA 90250

COHEN, MARJORIE K., nursing educator; b. N.Y.C., Nov. 27, 1953; d. Meyer and Marion (Garrick) Weisberg; m. Bruce A. Cohen, Aug. 24, 1980; children: Melissa, Samantha, Marlo. BS, SUNY, Bklyn., 1974; MA, NYU, 1979. RN. Nurse Boston Hosp. for Women, 1974-75; nurse N.Y. Hosp., N.Y.C., 1975-78; instr. Downstate Coll. Nursing SUNY, Bklyn., 1979-81, Alvernia Coll., Reading, Pa., 1982-84, Reading Area Community Coll., 1988—; cons. Avalon Nurses Registry, N.Y.C., 1980-81. Bd. dirs. Berks County chpt. ARC, Reading, 1985—; mem. Jr. League, Reading, 1988—. Mem. AAUW, Sigma Theta Tau. Home: 321 Limekiln Rd Reading PA 19606 Office: Reading Area Community Coll 10 S 2nd St Box 1706 Reading PA 19603

COHEN, MARLENE L., pharmacologist; b. New Haven, May 5, 1945; d. Abraham David and Jeanette (Bader) C.; m. Jerome H. Fleisch, Aug. 11, 1976; children: Abby, Sheryl. BS, U. Conn., 1968; PhD, U. Calif., San Francisco, 1973. Registered pharmacist, Calif. Postdoctoral fellow Roche Inst. of Molecular Biology, Nutley, N.J., 1973-75; sr. pharmacologist Eli Lilly & Co., Indpls., 1975-80, rsch. scientist, 1980-85, sr. rsch. scientist, 1985-89, rsch. advisor, 1989—; adj. asst. prof. dept. pharmacology and toxicology Ind. U. Sch. Medicine, Indpls., 1976-82, adj. assoc. prof., 1982-86, adj. prof., 1987—; rsch. asst. Pfizer Labs., Groton, Conn., 1967; cons. Drug Dependence Inst., Yale U., New Haven, 1974. Editorial bd. Jour. Clin. and Exptl. Hypertension, 1978—, Proceedings of the Soc. for Exptl. Biology and Medicine, 1979-84, Life Scis., 1984—, Jour. Pharmacology and Exptl. Therapeutics, 1987—; ad hoc reviewer for profl. jours.; author: (with others) Principles of Medicinal Chemistry, 1974, 3d edit., 1989, New Antihypertensive Drugs, 1976, Principles of Chemistry, 2d edit., 1981, The Serotonin Receptors, 1988, The Peripheral Actions of 5-Hydroxytryptamine, 1989; contbr. articles to profl. jours. Recipient grad. div. traineeship NSF, 1969-72; NIH fellow, 1972-73; recipient Pharm. Chemistry award, 1966, Pharmacognosy award and Bristol Labs. Activity award, 1967, Pharmacology award, 1968, Nat. Lundsford Richardson Undergrad. Rsch. award, 1968; named one of Outstanding Young Women of Am., 1979. Mem. Soc. for Exptl. Biology and Medicine, Am. Soc. for Pharmacology and Exptl. Therapeutics (chairperson subcom. on women in pharmacology 1984-89, chairperson nominating com. 1984, com. on profl. affairs 1984-89, membership com. 1989-92, bd. publs. trustees 1989-92), Serotonin Club (councilor 1987-90, nomenclature com. 1988—), Alpha Lambda Delta, Phi Kappa Phi, Rho Chi. Office: Lilly Rsch Labs Lilly Corp Ctr Indianapolis IN 46285

COHEN, MARY ANN, judge; b. Albuquerque, July 16, 1943; d. Gus R. and Mary Carolyn (Avriette) C. BS, UCLA, 1964; JD, U. So. Calif., 1967. Bar: Calif. 1967. Ptnr. Abbott & Cohen, P.C. and predecessors, Los Angeles, 1967-82; judge U.S. Tax Ct., Washington 1982—. Mem. ABA (sect. taxation), Legion Lex. Republican. Office: US Tax Ct 400 2nd St NW Washington DC 20217

COHEN, NINA, advertising agency executive. Pres. BBDO Miami (formerly CAK, Inc.). Office: BBDO Miami 7200 Corporate Center Dr Miami FL 33126*

COHEN, NOREEN MARIE, dietitian; b. Holyoke, Colo., July 30, 1955; d. Chester Charles and Sibyl Norreen (Jackson) Krueger; m. Randy Scott Cohen, Sept. 24, 1978; 1 child, Brian. BA, U. No. Colo., 1977; MS summa cum laude, Incarnate Word Coll., San Antonio, 1985. Registered dietitian, Tex. Intern Brooke Army Med. Ctr., Ft. Sam Houston, Tex., 1977-78; with nutrition clinic Darnall Army Community Hosp., Ft. Hood, Tex., 1978-79, prodn. and svc. staff mem., 1979-80; clin. dietitian Walter Reed Army Med. Ctr., Washington, 1980-82; instr. Acad. Health Scis., Ft. Sam Houston, 1982-84; clin. nutritionist Tripler Army Med. Ctr., Honolulu, 1985-87, asst. chief clin. nutrition, 1987-89; chief nutrition care div. Irwin Army Community Hosp., Ft. Riley, Kans., 1989—; commd. lt. U.S. Army, 1977, advanced through grades to maj., 1989. Mem. Am. Dietetic Assn. Lutheran. Office: Nutrition Care Div Bld 600 Fort Riley KS 66442

COHEN, PAULA BETH, company executive, financial consultant; b. Cin., Dec. 24, 1963; d. Bert H. and Sandra G. (Shuster) C. BA in Econs., Loyola Coll., Balt., 1985, MBA, 1987. Rsch. assoc. Roberts Ryan & Bentley, Balt., 1985-87; project acct. Continental Ins. Co., Piscataway, N.J., 1987-88; sr. fin. analyst Pepsi-Cola Co., Balt., 1988; contr. Ebert Enterprises, Balt., 1988—; with Curry Copy Ctr., Balt. Mem. Nat. Assn. Women Bus. Owners, Nat. Assn. MBA Execs., Nat. Jesuit Honor Soc. Republican. Jewish. Office: Curry Copy Ctr 310 N Charles St Baltimore MD 21201

COHEN, PHYLLIS CLAIRE, marketing professional; b. Mexico City, Apr. 25, 1960; came to U.S., 1981; d. Donald William and Mary (Greenstein) Koppel; m. Paul Howard Cohen, Aug. 8, 1982. Student, U. Autonoma, Mexico City, 1980, U. Calif., San Diego, 1985. Docent educator Museo de Antropologia, Mexico City, 1981-84; dir. customer svcs. Dan Demetriad Inc., N.Y.C., 1985-88; market rsch. coord. Internat. Thompson Retail Press, N.Y.C., 1988-89; sr. mgr. rsch. and devel. AFS Intercultural Programs, N.Y.C., 1989—; dir. Hispanic div. Analysis/Rsch. Ltd., Mexico City, 1981-83. One-man shows include Art for Alternative Spaces, San Diego, 1985, Annex Gallery, Mandeville Gallery, La Jolla, Calif., 1986, Queensborough Community Coll., 1989; exhibited in group shows at UCSD Gallery, San Diego, 1984-85, Bohen Gallery, San Carlos, Calif., 1985, Art for Alternative Spaces, 1986, Mandeville Gallery, 1986, Painted Bride Arts Ctr., Phila., 1987, Oakside/Bloomfield (N.J.) Cultural Ctr., 1990. Activist Coalition for the Homeless, N.Y.C., 1988-90; photographer Niños de la Calle, Tijuana, Mexico, 1981-86; vol. Am. Field Svc. (club pres. 1981-85). Pres.' undegrad. fellow U. Calif., 1985, grantee for the arts, 1983, 84. Mem. NAFE. Democrat. Jewish. Home: 240 E 27th St #18F New York NY 10016 Office: AFS Intercultural Programs 313 E 43d St New York NY 10017

COHEN, RACHELLE SHARON, journalist; b. Phila., Oct. 21, 1946; d. Hyman and Diane Doris (Schultz) Goldberg; m. Stanley Martin Cohen, June 22, 1968; 1 dau., Avril Heather. B.S., Temple U., Phila., 1968. Editor, Somerville Jour. (Mass.), 1968-70; reporter Lowell Sun (Mass.), 1970-72, AP, Boston, 1972-79; state house bur. chief Boston Herald Am., 1979-80, editorial page editor, 1980-82; editorial page editor Boston Herald, 1982—. Office: Boston Herald 1 Herald Sq Boston MA 02106*

COHEN, RUTH SCHIFF, lawyer; b. N.Y.C., Nov. 19, 1957; d. Elliott Schiff and Gladys (Gelfman) C. BA, Princeton (N.J.) U., 1979; JD, Duke U., 1983. Bar: N.C. 1984. Assoc. Fletcher, Maggiolo & Chaney, Durham, N.C., 1984-85, Maggiolo & Chaney, Durham, 1985, Law Offices Robert Maggiolo, Durham, 1985-86; asst. atty. Durham County, 1986-87; sr. litigation assoc. McPherson & Maggiolo, Durham, 1987-88, Law Offices of William V. McPherson, Jr., Durham, 1988—; legal counsel Durham Jaycees, 1989—. Mem. N.C. Bar Assn., Durham County Bar Assn. (bd. dirs., treas. young lawyers div. 1987-89). Home: Rt 6 Box 251 Kepley Rd Chapel Hill NC 27514 Office: Law Offices W McPherson Jr PO Box 2729 Durham NC 27705

COHEN, SALLY ANN, university official; b. Zanesville, Ohio, Mar. 20, 1942; d. Walter W. and Helen Jean (Bateman) Seifert; m. Donald B. Cohen, Sept. 16, 1967. BS, Miami U., Oxford, Ohio, 1964; MA in with honors, Loyola Marymount U., L.A., 1976. High sch. tchr. Columbus (Ohio) Pub. Schs., 1964-66, Bexley (Ohio) Pub. Schs., 1967-69; hosp. adminstr. Hollywood Community Hosp., L.A., 1969-71; office mgr. Loyola Marymount U., 1971-75; exec. officer UCLA, 1976-86, fund mgr., 1986—. Organizer, fund raiser L.A. Rep. Com., 1988—. Recipient outstanding performance award UCLA, 1979, 81, 89. Mem. NAFE (chmn. L.A. network 1989—), UCLA Staff Assn. (leader career devel. 1976—). Unitarian. Office: UCLA Dept Pub Affairs 405 Hilgard Ave Los Angeles CA 90024

COHEN, SELMA, reference librarian, researcher; b. N.Y.C., Mar. 14, 1930; d. George and Rose (Cohen) Unger; m. Irwin H. Cohen, Nov. 19, 1950; children: Barbara Katzeff, Joel. Grad. high sch., William Howard Taft High Sch., 1948. Asst. bookkeeper acctg. dept. Severud, Perrone et al, N.Y.C., 1970-75; asst. bookkeeper acctg. dept. Russell Reynolds Assocs., Inc., N.Y.C., 1976-77, rsch. asst., 1977—, reference libr., 1985—. Chairwoman Scott Tower Charity Com., Bronx, 1976-84, Scott Tower Property Improvement Com., Bronx, 1983-84. Home: 3400 J Paul Ave New York NY 10468 Office: Russell Reynolds Assocs 200 Park Ave New York NY 10166

COHEN, SHARON ANNE, travel agency executive; b. Marion, Ind., May 1; d. Rollie and Esther (Bowman) Lendman; m. Allan R. Cohen, Nov. 10; 1 child, Gregory S. Student, Long Beach State U., Indiana U. Systems and procedure cons. Shaw-Walker Co., Indpls., 1974-77; procedure analyst Blue Cross-Blue Shield, Indpls., 1977-79; personnel mgr. Jewel Co., Chgo., 1979-81; travel cons. Cobb Travel, Birmingham, Ala., 1981-83, Hilton Green Travel, Marietta, Ga., 1983-84; co-owner, pres. Travel Corner Inc., Marietta, 1984-85; pres./owner Uniglobe First In Travel, Marietta, 1985—. Mem. Am. Soc. Travel Agts., Inst. Cert. Travel Agts., Travel Industry Assn. Ga., Atlanta C. of C. Office: Uniglobe First in Travel 1165 Northchase Pkwy 175 Marietta GA 30067

COHEN, SHERA, municipal official; b. Springfield, Mass.; d. Robert Cohen and Helen Cohen Tenanbaum. BA in English and History, Cen. Conn. State U., 1972; postgrad., U. Mass., 1974; MPA, Am. Internat. U., Springfield, 1990. Community affairs dir. Mayor's Office Cultural Affairs, Springfield, 1977-86; dir. devel. Vis. Nurse Assn., Springfield, 1986-88; devel. asst. Springfield Tech. Community Coll., 1988; exec. dir. Chicopee (Mass.) Centennial, 1988—. Contbr. articles to popular publs. Newsletter editor Com. to Elect Kateri Walsh, Springfield; issues com. Com. to Elect Bill Bennett, Springfield, 1990; parade asst. Basketball Hall of Fame, Springfield, 1985; chmn. celebration month Springfield's 350th Anniversary, 1984-86; bd. dirs. Am. Cancer Soc.; chmn. pub. rels. com. Peach Basket Festival. Mem. Readers and Playwrights Theatre (pres.), Community Theatre Assn. (bd. dirs.), Springfield Film Soc. (bd. dirs.), NAFE, Women in Devel. (bd. dirs.). Democrat. Jewish. Home: 235 State St Springfield MA 01103 Office: Chicopee Centennial PO Box 1990 Chicopee MA 01021

COHEN, SUSAN BERK, professional association administrator; b. Queens, N.Y., June 24, 1942; d. Murray Adrian Berk and Barbara Hortense (Garfunkel) Berk Gordon; m. Samuel Jay Cohen, June 12, 1965 (div. June 1979); children: Jennifer Elise, Jessica Amelia. Student, Brandeis U., 1960-62, UCLA, 1962-63; BA cum laude, Brandeis U., 1964; MA, U. Calif., Irvine, 1967. Instr. English U. Calif., Irvine, 1966-68, co-dir. English program, 1968; paralegal, investigator Pub. Defender's Office Santa Clara County, 1972-75; planner delinquency prevention Mexican-Am. Community Svc. Agy., San Jose, 1975-77; coord. correctional tng. Cañada Coll., Redwood City, Calif., 1981-82; cons. Calif. Bd. Corrections, Sacramento, 1977-82; exec. asst. to dir. Dept. Corrections State Of Calif., Sacramento, 1982-83; exec. dir. Calif. Probation, Parole and Correctional Assn., Sacramento, 1983—; cons. corrections Nat. Inst. Corrections, 1978—. Author, editor: Guidelines to Minimum Jail Standards, 1980; editor: The Power of Public Support, 1985. Bd. dirs. Friends Outside, 1987—; chmn. ad hoc com. on female prisoner needs County of Santa Clara, Calif., 1976-77. Mem. Am. Probation and Parole Assn., Am. Correctional Assn., Calif. Probation, Parole and Correctional Assn., Am. Jail Assn., Nat. Assn. Women in Criminal Justice. Democrat. Office: CPPCA 211 Lathrop Way Ste M Sacramento CA 95815-4242

COHL, CLAUDIA HOPE, editor; b. Detroit, Nov. 23, 1939; d. Isaac and Jennie (Mellinoff) C. B.A., Wayne State U., 1961. Tchr. Detroit Bd. Edn., 1961-62; asst. then assoc. editor New Book Knowledge, Grolier Inc., N.Y.C., 1962-66; editor social studies Franklin Watts Inc., div. Grolier, N.Y.C., 1966-74; editor Tchr. Mag., Macmillan Inc., Greenwich, Conn., 1974-75; editor, dir. elem. dept. sch. div. Scholastic Inc., N.Y.C., 1975-77, editor-in-chief classroom mags., 1977-83; editor-in-chief Family Computing mag., from 1983; editor-in-chief, corp. v.p. Home Office Computing mag., Scholastic Inc., N.Y.C., 1983—. Office: Home Office Computing 730 Broadway New York NY 10003*

COHN, JANE SHAPIRO, public relations executive; b. N.Y.C., May 19, 1935; d. Harry I. and Ann (Safanie) Shapiro; m. Albert M. Cohn, June 30, 1957 (div. 1972); children: Theodore David, William Alan. BA, Brandeis U., 1956; postgrad., Coll. of New Rochelle, 1974-76. Dir. pub. rels. Hudson River Mus., Yonkers, N.Y., 1976-79; account exec. Dudley-Anderson Yutzy Pub. Rels. Agy. subs. Ogilvy Mather, N.Y.C., 1979-81; dir. communications Haines Lundberg Waehler, N.Y.C., 1981—; cons. Inst. Contemporary Art, Phila., 1983; speaker, mktg. promotion strategies conf., 1989. Contbr. articles to profl. jours. Mem. AIA (assoc. 1988, speaker annual conv.), Pub. Relations Soc. Am., Internat. Assn. Bus. Communicators, Art Table, Soc. for Mktg. Profl. Svcs. (bd. dirs. N.Y. chpt. 1988-89), Am. Mktg. Assn. (panelist ann. conv. 1987, moderator profl. services sect. ann. conv. 1988, exec. mem.), Practice Mgmt. Assn. (speaker promotion strategies conf. 1989). Democrat. Jewish.

COHN, MARIANNE WINTER MILLER, civic activist; b. Denver, Jan. 15, 1928; d. Henry Abraham II and Esther (Sheflan) Winter; m. Benjamin K. Miller, Dec. 29, 1948 (dec. Dec. 1972); children: Judy Ellen, Philip Henry; m. Isidore Cohn Jr., Jan. 3, 1976; children: Ian Jeffrey, Lauren Kerry. Student, Colo. U., 1946-47. Mem. exec. bd. Greater New Orleans Tourist and Conv. Commn., 1985; chmn. Am. Coll. Surgeons arrangement in La., 1985; mem. exec. bd. Nat. Conf. Christians and Jews, New Orleans, 1987—; bd. dirs. Jewish Endowment Found., New Orleans, 1987-88; mem. Arts Council of New Orleans, 1988—; pres. La. Mus. Found. of La. State Museum, 1989-90; mem. Sisterhood of Temple Emanuel (pres. 1957-60); bd. dirs. Nat. Jewish Hosp. at Denver, 1951-80, pres., 1986-69, sec., 1974-75; s, bd. dirs. New Orleans Symphony Aux., 1980; mem. nat. bd. Nat. Jewish Ctr., 1976—. Recipient Woman of Fashion award, 1989. Republican.

COHN, MILDRED, biochemist, educator; b. N.Y.C., July 12, 1913; d. Isidore M. and Bertha (Klein) Cohn; m. Henry Primakoff, May 31, 1938; children: Nina, Paul, Laura. BA, Hunter Coll., 1931, ScD (hon.), 1984; MA, Columbia U., 1932, PhD, 1938; ScD (hon.), Women's Med. Coll., 1966, Radcliffe Coll., 1978, Washington U., St. Louis, 1981, Brandeis U., 1984, U. Pa., Phila., 1984, U. N.C., 1985; PhD (hon.), Weizmann Inst. Sci., Israel, 1988; ScD (hon.), U. Miami, 1990. Research asst. biochemistry George Washington U. Sch. Medicine, 1937-38; research assoc. Cornell U., 1938-46; research assoc. Washington U., 1946-50, 51-58, assoc. prof. biol. chemistry, 1958-60; assoc. prof. biophysics and phys. biochemistry U. Pa. Med. Sch., 1960-61, prof., 1961-78, emeritus, 1982—, Benjamin Rush prof. physiol. chemistry, 1978-82; sr. mem. Inst. Cancer Research, Phila., 1982-85; Chancellor's disting. prof. biophysics U. Calif., Berkeley, spring 1981; vis. prof. biol. chemistry Johns Hopkins U. Med. Sch., 1985—; research assoc. Harvard U., 1950-51; established investigator Am. Heart Assn., 1953-59, career investigator, 1964-78. Editorial bd. jour. Biol. Chemistry, 1958-63, 67-72. Recipient Cresson medal Franklin Inst., 1976, award Internat. Assn. Women Biochemists, 1979, Nat. Medal Sci., 1982, Chandler medal Columbia U., 1986, Disting. Service award Coll. Physicians, Phila., 1987. Mem. Am. Philos. Soc., NAS, Am. Chem. Soc. (Garvan medal 1963, Remsen award Md. sect. 1988), Harvey Soc., Am. Soc. Biol. Chemists (pres. 1978-79), Am. Biophys. Soc., Am. Acad. Arts and Scis., Phi Beta Kappa, Sigma Xi, Iota Sigma Pi (hon. nat. mem. 1988). Office: U Pa Med Sch Dept Biochemistry & Biophysics Philadelphia PA 19104-6089

COHN, ROBIN JEAN, public relations executive; b. Portsmith, Va., Oct. 18, 1952; d. Murry and Mildred (Shachtman) Cohn. BA magna cum laude (Pres.'s scholar), Temple U., 1974. Dir., David Gary Ltd., Ft. Lauderdale, Fla., 1974-75; advt. mgr. Tamarac Topic (Fla.), 1975-76; dir. pub. rels. Biscayne Med. Ctr., Miami, Fla., 1976-78; staff v.p. Air Fla., Miami, 1978-84, Alamo Rent A Car, 1984-86; dir. pub. rels. N.Y. Air, 1986-87; dir. pub. rels. MacAndrews & Forbes, 1987-88; pres. Romann & Tannenholz Pub. Rels., N.Y.C., 1989—; guest lectr. U. Miami; cons. in field. Dir. Miami City Ballet, 1985-88; adj. prof. MA Program in Corp. and Orgnl. Communications Fairleigh Dickinson U., 1990—; guest lectr., mem. Am. Woman's Econ. Devel. Corp., 1989—. Mem. pub. rels. com. Miami's For Me, 1982, 83, host com., 1983; active Leadership Miami, 1982-85, Miami Forum, 1981-86, Fla. Tourism Adv. Coun., 1983-86; bd. dirs. Miami City Ballet, 1985-88, Project Horizon, 1986; mem. pub. rels. com., Broward Arts Coun., 1984-86, YMCA Acad. Women Achievers, 1989—. Named to YWCA's Acad. Women Achievers, 1986, One of Outstanding Young Women Am., 1981.

COHOON, CHRISTEN ANN, elementary educator; b. Greenwich, Conn., Oct. 8, 1964; d. Wiley Lee III and Patricia Ann (Brzoska) Bradford; m. Paul Tosh Cohoon, III, June 24, 1989. BA in Psychology, Mary Washington U., 1986; postgrad., Old Dominion U., 1987-89. Cert. tchr. emotionally disturbed children, Va. Camp counselor/asst. Shalom Children's Ctr. Jewish Community Ctr., Norfolk, Va., 1986-87; asst. tchr. Norfolk Pub. Schs., 1987-88, 89; tchr. emotionally disturbed Virginia Beach (Va.) Pub. Schs., 1989—. Active Cape Story Civic Assn., Virginia Beach, 1976—. Mem. NEA, Assn. Supervision and Curriculum Devel., Coun. for Exceptional Children. Home: 2263 Walke St Virginia Beach VA 23451 Office: Point o View Elem Sch 5400 S Parliament Dr Virginia Beach VA 23464

COHOWICZ, LUCY ANN, construction executive; b. N.Y.C., Mar. 11, 1950; d. Albert LaGrutta and Ruth Mae (Stanke) Porcelli; m. Michael C. Cohowicz, May 10, 1986; children: Christina-Lee Queler, Adam Eliot Queler, Robert Michael. Grad. high sch., L.I., N.Y., 1979. V.p. sales div. J&L Plastics Corp., Bklyn., 1971-72; pres. Plachem Plastics Corp., College Point, N.Y., 1972-74; owner, pres. Spunky's Boutique, Inc., Floral Park, N.Y., 1974-77, Six Love, Inc., L.I., 1974-75, Lucy and Co., Inc., Floral Park, N.Y., 1975-78; owner, v.p. Coler Custom Homes, Inc., Stroudsburg, Pa., 1983—. Fundraiser Coma Recovery Assn., Floral Park, 1980. Mem. Floral Park C. of C. (pres. 1975-76), Pocono Mt. C. of C. (mem. bldg. com. 1984—), Am. Builders' Assn. (Pocono Chpt.), Wedgewood Soc. Republican. Roman Catholic. Home: 62 Penn Estates East Stroudsburg PA 18301 Office: Coler Custom Houses Inc 729 Sarah St Stroudsburg PA 18360

COIN, SHEILA REGAN, management consultant; b. Columbus, Ohio, Feb. 17, 1942; d. James Daniel and Jean (Hodgson) Cook; m. Tasso H. Coin, Sept. 17, 1967 (div.); children: Tasso, Alison Regan; m. Robert James Hall, Feb. 28, 1987. BS, U. Iowa, 1964. RN Staff nurse VA Hosp., Boston, 1964-66; field rep. ARC, Chgo., 1966-67, adminstr., 1967; asst. div. dir. Am. Hosp. Assn., sec. Am. Soc. Hosp. Dirs. Nursing, Chgo., 1967-69; owner Coin & Assocs., Chgo., 1975-77; ptnr. Coin, Newell & Assocs., Chgo., 1977—; instr. dept. continuing edn. Loyola U., Chgo., 1975-77, Rock Valley Coll. Mgmt. Inst., Rockford, Ill., 1978-80, Ill. Central Coll. Inst. Personal and Profl. Devel., Peoria, 1979—, Triton Coll. Continuing Edn., River Grove, Ill., 1983-86, No. Ill. U. Continuing Edn., DeKalb, 1983—. Vol. Art Inst., Chgo., 1968-69; mem. Chgo. Beautiful Com., 1968-73; chmn. Mayor Daley's Chgo. Beautiful Awards Project, 1972; mem. jr. bd. Girl Scouts Assn., Chgo., 1975-76; mem. jr. governing bd. Chgo. Symphony Orch., 1971—, pres., 1977-78; governing mem. Orchestral Assn., Chgo., 1977-81; bd. dirs. Mid-Am. chpt. ARC, Chgo., 1979-81, vice chmn. 1986-89; Bd. dirs., mem. Survive Alive House Found., 1989—; bd. dirs. Chgo. dist., 1981-89, chmn. fin. devel. com., 1982-85, vice chmn. dist. bd., 1986-89; dir. Com. for Thalossemia Chgo. Bd., 1981-82; mem. Women's bd. Nat. Com. Prevention Child Abuse, Chgo., 1981-82; mem. State of Ill. Disabled Persons Advocacy Div. Consumers Task Force, 1988—. Mem. Am. Mgmt. Assn., Am. Soc. Tng. and Devel., Ill. Tng. and Devel. Assn. Democrat. Roman Catholic. Avocations: piano, tennis, national and international travel, spectator sports, family activities. Home: 1037 W North Shore Ave Chicago IL 60626 Office: Coin Newell & Assocs 919 N Michigan Ave Chicago IL 60611

COIT, MICHELE VIVIAN, radio station executive; b. Oakland, Calif., Jan. 8, 1954; d. Vivian (Williams) C. BA in Radio and TV, San Jose State U., 1978. Fire rater Calif. Farms Ins. Co., 1976-77; radio continuity dir. Sta. KYA, 1978-79; radio traffic mgr. Sta. KQAK, 1979-82; continuity dir. Sta. KBLX, Berkeley, Calif., 1984-85; sales asst. Sta. KLOK, San Francisco, 1985-86; traffic dir. Sta. KFRC, San Francisco, 1986—. Mem. Jubilee West, Oakland, 1988; past pres. Young adults Beebe Meml. Christian Meth. Episc. Ch., Oakland, lay leader 1st women's conf. San Jose State U., , 1976; sec. Mattie E. Coleman Youth Worker; mem., sec. lay dept. No. Calif. Ann. Conf., 1989—. Beebe Meml. Christian Meth. Episc. Ch. scholar, 1972. Mem. NAFE, Sigma Gamma Rho. Democrat. Home: 10944 San Pablo Ave Apt 322 El Cerrito CA 94530 Office: Sta KFRC 500 Washington St San Francisco CA 94111

COKER, CLAUDIA GERMAINE, savings and loan executive; b. Walnut Ridge, Ark., Jan. 6, 1953; d. Zack Tiley and Germaine Marie (Piantoni) C. BS, Ark. State U., 1975. Cashier Harps Supermarket, Walnut Ridge, 1972-73, Rorex Supermarket Hoxie, Ark., 1973-74; office mgr. Higginbotham Burial Ins., Walnut Ridge, 1975; clk. typist Crane Co., Jonesboro, Ark., 1975-76; savs. and loan examiner Fed. Home Loan Bank Bd., Little Rock, 1976-85, Fed. Home Loan Bank, Dallas, 1985-87; v.p., regulatory compliance officer, pers. officer United Fed. Savs. and Loan, Jonesboro, Ark., 1987—. Mem. Leadership Jonesboro 1988. Recipient Civil Svcs. Beta award Fed. Home Loan Bank Bd., 1978. Bd. dirs. United Way, Jonesboro; trustee United Way Craighead County. Mem. Assn. Bus. Profl. Women (1st v.p. Downtown Jonesboro chpt. 1988-89), Fin. Mgrs. Soc., NAFE. Baptist. Clubs: Altrusa (Jonesboro), Confederate Air Force (security detachment) (Harlingen, Tex.); Razorback Wing (security detachment)(Pine Bluff, Ark.). Avocations: counted cross stitch, knitting, needlepoint, reading, collecting depression-era glass. Home: 2106 Wind Cove Jonesboro AR 72401 Office: United Fed Savs and Loan 515 West Washington Jonesboro AR 72401

COKER, ELIZABETH BOATWRIGHT (MRS. JAMES LIDE COKER), writer; b. Darlington, S.C., Apr. 21, 1909; d. Purves Jenkins and Bessie (Heard) Boatwright; m. James Lide Coker, Sept. 27, 1930; children: Penelope, James Lide. A.B., Converse Coll., 1929; postgrad., Middlebury Coll., 1938. Asso. prof. English Appalachian State U., Boone, N.C., 1971-72. Author: Daughter of Strangers, 1950, The Day of the Peacock, 1952, India Allan, 1953, The Big Drum, 1957, La Belle, 1959, Lady Rich, 1963, The Bees, 1968, Blood Red Roses, 1977, The Grasshopper King, 1981; Contbr. mag. articles, poems. Mem. Hartsville Sch. Bd., 1939-49; sec., dir. Blowing Rock Horse Show Assn., 1943-49; dir. United Cerebral Palsy of S.C.; mem. nat. bd. Med. Coll. Pa.; trustee Converse Coll.; nat. adv. council I.S.S. Mem. Poetry Soc. Ga., AAUW, P.E.N., S.C. Poetry Soc., Authors Guild, Acad. Am. Poets, S.C. Hist. Soc., Garden Club Am., Caroliniana Soc. (exec. council 1983—). Republican. Episcopalian. Clubs: Springdale Hall (Camden, S.C.); Hound Ears (Blowing Rock, N.C.).

COKER, LINDA LOU, registered nurse; b. Ft. Wayne, Ind., Sept. 23, 1940; d. Clifton Eugene and Marlowe Maxine (Copeland) C. BSN, Coll. Saint Teresa, 1980; MA, Saint Mary's Coll., 1988. RN, Minn. Lic. practical nurse Parkview Hosp., Ft. Wayne, 1966-73, Saint Marys Hosp., Rochester, Minn., 1973-80; staff nurse Saint Marys Hosp., Rochester, 1980-82; supr. orientation and continuing edn. Saint Mary's Hosp., Rochester, 1982—, coord. perioperative nursing program, 1984—. Mem. Reformed Ch. Women, Rochester, 1988, Rochester Symphony, 1976-89. Mem. Assn. Operating Room Nurses (pres. 1988-89). Home: 4545 Fourth St NW Rochester MN 55901 Office: Saint Mary's Hosp 1216 Second St SW Rochester MN 55901

COLAGUORI, JUNE CAROL, cosmetics marketing executive; b. Pitts., Oct. 17, 1955; d. Julius Ceasar and Margaret (Hauerlesko) Bilecky. Student, U. Pitts, Wheeler Bus. Sch., Pitts., Forbes Tech. Sch., Pitts. Account exec. Jhirmack, Inc., Pitts., 1980; mktg. asst. Gen. Nutrition Corp., Pitts., 1981, mgr. mktg., 1982-83, mgr. promotions, 1984, new product buyer, 1985, mgr. new bus. and new product devel., 1986; dir. mktg. Moxie Industries div. ICN Pharms. Corp., Anaheim, Calif., 1986-87; mgr. mktg. div. skincare, haircare and fragrance products Merle Norman Cosmetics, Los Angeles, 1988—. Mem. Nat. Assn. Female Execs., Personal Dynamics Inst. (cert.). Episcopalian. Office: 9130 Bellanca Ave at Arbor Vitae Los Angeles CA 90045

COLAMARINO, KATRIN BELENKY, lawyer; b. N.Y.C., Apr. 29, 1951; d. Allen Abram and Selma (Burwasser) Belenky Lang; m. Leonard J. Colamarino, Mar. 20, 1982; m. Barry E. Brenner, June 1, 1974 (div. June 1979); 1 dau., Rachel Erin. B.A., Vassar Coll., 1972; J.D., U. Richmond, 1976. Bar: Ohio 1976, U.S. Ct. Apls. (Fed. cir.), 1982. Staff atty. AM Internat. Inc., Cleve., 1976-78; atty. Lipkowitz & Plaut, N.Y.C., 1980-81; atty. Docutel Olivetti Corp., Tarrytown, N.Y., 1981-84; atty. NYNEX Bus. Info. Systems, White Plains, N.Y., 1984-85; corp. counsel, sec. Logica Data Architects, Inc., N.Y.C., 1986—. Class agt. Fieldston Sch., N.Y.C., 1980—, exec. bd. Ethical Fieldston Alumni Assn., 1980—, v.p. 1987—; alumnae council rep. Vassar Coll., 1982-86. Mem. Assn. of Bar of City of N.Y., Westchester Fairfield Corp. Counsel Assn. Office: Logica Data Architects Inc 5 Penn Pla New York NY 10001

COLASANTI, BRENDA KAREN, educator; b. Charleston, W.Va., Dec. 5, 1945; d. Harry Gordon and Mary Louise (Moore) Frame. AB, W.Va. U., 1966, PhD, 1970. Postdoctoral fellow Mt. Sinai Sch. Medicine CUNY, N.Y.C., 1970-72; asst. prof. ophthalmology and pharmacology W.Va. U., Morgantown, 1972-76, assoc. prof., 1976-80, prof. ophthalmology and pharmacology, 1980—. Contbr. chpts. in books. Recipient Benedum Disting. Scholar award W.Va. U., 1989. Mem. Am. Soc. for Pharmacology and Exptl. Therapeutics, Am. Soc. for Neurochemistry, Assn. for Rsch. in Vision and Ophthalmology, Sleep Rsch. Soc., Sigma Xi (pres. local chpt. 1986-87). Office: WVa U Health Sci Ctr N Morgantown WV 26506

COLBERT, HEATHER, microcomputer analyst; b. Scituate, Mass., Sept. 12, 1950; d. Thomas Edward and Jeanne Louise (Eisenhauer) Brown; m. Walter Thomas Colbert, Sept. 10, 1989. AS in Bus. Adminstrn. with highest honors, Massasoit Community Coll., 1979; BS in Acctg., Bentley Coll., 1981, MBA, 1987. Claims clk. CNA Ins., Boston, 1970-71; export clk. Cabot Corp., Boston, 1971-76, fin. sec., 1977, acct., 1978-81; fin. analyst Cabot Corp., Waltham, Mass., 1981-86, microcomputer analyst, 1987—, dir. credit union, 1978—; geology lab asst. Bentley Coll., Waltham, 1980-83. Contbr. articles to Bentley Newspaper, 1980-82, Cabot Corp. Newspaper, 1979-80; editor Cabot Corp. PC Network Newsletter, 1987—. Mem. Nat. Assn. Female Execs. Roman Catholic. Office: Cabot Corp 950 Winter St Waltham MA 02254

COLBERT-KELLY, JUDITH ANN, systems accountant; b. Annapolis, Md., Feb. 20, 1956; d. Hillary and Ruth (Smith) Colbert; m. Anthony Sean Kelly Sr., July 5, 1987; children: Juanita Patrice, Sean Ahmád, Amy Rasheedah, Catherine Ann, Anthony S. II. BS, Morgan State U., 1979.

Bus. analyst Dun and Bradstreet Corp., N.Y.C.; operation acct. USN, Washington; systems acct. U.S. Gen. Svcs. Adminstrn., Washington. Mem. Ardmore Ardwick Civic Assn., 1985—. Mem. Am. Soc. Mil. Comptrollers, NAFE, Fed. Women's Program Com. Mem. AME Ch. Home: 3534 Edwards St Landover MD 20785 Office: Gen Services Adminstrn Office of Comptroller 18th and F Sts NW Washington DC 20405

COLBORN, PATRICIA HARRISON, nurse; b. Annapolis, Md., Oct. 30, 1952; d. William Carlton and Marjorie Louise (Stillwagon) Harrison; m. Eugene Walter Colborn Jr., Nov. 8, 1975; 1 child, Sabrina Marie. BS in Nursing, U. Tenn., 1974; MNursing, La. State U., 1984. RN, Va., La., Md., Tenn., Fla. Staff nurse Meth. Hosp., Memphis, 1974-75, Riverside Hosp., Newport News, Va., 1978-79; charge nurse Montgomery Gen. Hosp., Olney, Md., 1976-78; head nurse Parkland Hosp., Baton Rouge, La., 1980-82, asst. dir. nursing, 1982; instr. Our Lady of the Lake Sch. Nursing, Baton Rouge, 1982-89; mem. staff Anclote Manor Hosp., Tarpon Springs, Fla., 1909—; mem. staff Parkland Hosp., 1986-89; researcher in field. Mem. Nat. League Nursing, Southwestern La. Psychiat. Nurses Assn., Am. Bus. Women's Assn. (v.p. local chpt. 1987-88), Western Pa. Conservancy, Nat. Trust for Hist. Preservation, Sigma Theta Tau. Republican. Methodist. Office: Anclote Manor Hosp 1527 Riverside Dr Tarpon Springs FL 34689

COLBORN, THEO E., environmentalist; b. Plainfield, N.J., Mar. 28, 1927; d. Theodore and Margaret L. (DeForge) Decker; m. Harry R. Colborn, Jan. 20,1949 (dec. Aug. 1983); children: Harry R. III, Christine M., Susan T., Mark D. BS, Rutgers U., 1947; MA, Western State Coll., 1981; PhD, U. Wis., 1985. Pharmacist various pharmacies, N.J., Colo, 1948-85; from congl. fellow to analyst Office Tech. assessment, Washington, 1985-87; from assoc. to sr. fellow The Conservation Found., Washington, 1987—; sr. fellow The Conservation Found.; adj. faculty Western State Coll. Colo., 1979-81,George Mason U., 1988—; dir. water workshops, U. Wis., Madison, 1980-85; teaching asst. U. Wis., Madison, 1982-85; cons. Environment Canada, Ottawa, 1988, Health Welfare Canada, Ottawa, 1988-89, Internat. Forest Commn.(subcom. The Earth Effects), Windsor, Ontario, 1988-90. Contbr. books and papers in field. Mem. Newton (N.J.) Sch. Bd., 1954-63, Colo. Natural Areas Program, 1978-87, Fairfax (Va.) Audubon Soc., 1987-89; leader 4H, Hotchkiss, Colo., 1964-87. Mem. Am. Water Resources Assn., Soc. Environ. Toxicology and Chemistry, Rocky Mountain Biol. Lab., Colo. Field Ornithologists. Office: World Wildlife Fund 1250 24th St NW Washington DC 20037

COLBURN, JULIA KATHERINE LEE, educator; b. Columbus, Ohio, Feb. 8, 1927; d. Fred Merritt and Lillian May (Getrost) Lee; m. Joseph Linn Colburn, Sept. 5, 1947; children—Joseph Linn, Jr., David Laird, Andrew Lee, Julia LeeAnne. B.S. in Edn., Ohio State U., 1948. Library asst. Columbus Pub. Library, 1945-48, Ohio State U. Library, Columbus, 1945-47; life ins. acct. Nationwide Ins., Columbus, 1949-50; substitute tchr. Columbus Pub. Schs., 1965-69, 79-81; vol. resource person Columbus Pub. Schs., 1979—. Author: The Six Who Signed, Christmas at Valley Forge; editor, compiler (state pub.) Ohio Daughters of 1812, Star and Anchor, 1983-85 (nat. first award, 1984, 85). Presiding judge Franklin County Bd. Elections, Columbus, 1959—; pres. Linden Jr. Civic Club, Columbus, 1953, Rhapsody Unit, Columbus Symphony, 1975-77, Arlington Park PTA, Columbus, 1963-64, Linden-McKinley Jr.-Sr. High PTA, Columbus, 1964-66, Northland High PTA, Columbus, 1972-73; organizing pres. Lazarus Cancer Ray, Columbus, 1953; leader Northland council Girl Scouts U.S., 1968-70; vol. Vision Ctr., Columbus, 1969-72 (Named Vol. of Yr. 1971); v.p. Linden United Meth. Women, Columbus, 1965-66, pres. 1966-68, various coms. 1963—; pres. Meth. Youth Fellowship, Columbus, 1944-45; adminstrv. bd. Linden United Meth. Ch., Columbus, 1944-45, 52—, choir soloist, mem., 1945—, Sun. sch. tchr., 1959—, spl. membership awards 1971, 77; dist. chmn. Christian Global Concerns Columbus North Dist. United Meth. Women, 1973-77. Recipient Silver Good Citizenship medal Ohio Soc. SAR, 1978, Medal of Appreciation, Benjamin Franklin chpt. SAR, 1978, Martha Washington meda. Ohio SAR, 1989. Mem. Ohio Geneal. Soc. (speakers staff 1978—), First Families of Ohio, DAR (Good Citizenship cert. 1945, state rec. sec. 1983-86, state vice regent 1986-89, state regent 1989—, various offices and coms. 1976—), NSDAR (speakers staff 1983—), Children of Am. Revolution (sr. pres. state 1976-78, sr. nat. rec. sec. 1982-84, various coms. 1974—, Ohio Service award, 1979, maj. benefactor 1986, nat. vice chmn. 1980-83), U.S. Daus. of 1812 (parliamentarian, chmn. nat. membership 1985-88, state pres. 1983-85, treas. Nat. Hdqrs. Endowment Trust Fund, 1988—), Colonial Dames XVII Century (state first v.p. 1985-87), Daus. Colonial Wars (state historian 1984-86, nat. vice chmn. 1983-89, state rec. sec. 1989—), Women Desc. Ancient and Honorable Arty. Co. (state rec. sec. 1983-86, state pres. 1986-89, nat. parliamentarian 1989—), Daus. Am. Colonists (Old Trails chpt. treas. 1981-85, vice regent 1985-87, regent 1987-89), New Eng. Women (pres. Columbus colony 1984-87, nat. chmn. 1987—), Colonial Daus. Seventeenth Century, Daus. Union Vets., Zeta Phi Eta. Republican. Club: Ohio Fedn. Women's (trustee, chmn. 1974-83). Lodges: Order of Eastern Star (star point 1961-62), Linden Lawanis (Kiwanis Aux. pres. 1964). Avocations: genealogy; music; writing. Home: 1887 Northcliff Dr Columbus OH 43229

COLBY, ANNE, psychologist; b. Galveston, Tex., Feb. 10, 1946; d. Malcolm Young and Emily Jane (Armacost) C.; m. William V.B. Damon; 1 dau., Caroline Colby. B.A., McGill U., 1968; Ph.D., Columbia U., 1972. Research assoc., lectr. Harvard U., Cambridge, Mass., 1972-80; dir. Henry A. Murray Research Center of Radcliffe Coll., Cambridge, 1980—; dir. research Clin. Devel. Inst. Lic. psychologist, Mass. Mem. Nat. Council for Research on Women (dir.). Author: The Measurement of Moral Judgment, 1987. Office: Radcliff Coll H A Murray Research Ctr 10 Garden St Cambridge MA 02138

COLBY, KAREN LYNN See WEINER, KAREN LYNN

COLBY, MARVELLE SEITMAN, educator, administrator; b. N.Y.C., Oct. 31, 1932; d. Charles Edward and Lily (Zimmerman) Seitman; m. Robert S. Colby, Apr. 11, 1954 (div. Apr. 1979); children: Lisa, Eric; m. Selig J. Alkon, Dec. 6, 1986. BA, Hunter Coll., 1954; MA, U. N.Colo., 1973; PhD in Pub. Adminstrn., Nova U., 1977; cert., Harvard Grad. Sch. Bus., 1979. V.p. SE Region URC Mgmt. Services Corp., Washington, 1972-77; dir. devel. Hunter Coll. Woman's Ctr. Community Leadership, N.Y.C., 1977-78; dir. tng. and career devel. Girl Scouts U.S., N.Y.C., 1978-79; dir. Overseas Tour Ops. Am. Jewish Congress, N.Y.C., 1979-81; chief exec. officer Girl Scout Council Greater N.Y.C., 1981-82; adminstr., assoc. prof. bus. mgmt., chmn. bus. mgmt. and acctg. div. Marymount Manhattan Coll., N.Y.C., 1982-90; adj. prof. N.Y.U., 1986—; mem. exec. com. Assn. Recreation Mgmt., N.Y.C., 1981; cons. Rockport Mgmt., Washington, 1974-78. Author: Test Your Management IQ, 1984; co-author: Lovejoy's Four Year College Guide for the Learning Disabled, 1985; contbr. articles to profl. jours. Chmn. Met. Dade County Commn. Status Women, Miami, 1975-77; chief planner Met. Dade County U.S. SBA 1st annual conf. Future Women Bus., 1977. Named to Hunter Coll. Hall of Fame, 1986. Mem. Acad. Mgmt., Hunter Coll. Alumni Assn. (bd. dirs. 1978-79), Phi Delta Kappa. Club: Lotos (mem. literary com. 1983-89). Home: 242 E 72d St New York NY 10021 Office: Marymount Manhattan Coll 221 E 71st St New York NY 10021

COLBY, PATRICIA FARLEY, political consultant; b. Ashland, Ky., Mar. 28, 1958; d. Donald B. and Esta (Picklesimer) Farley; m. Richard Bradley Colby, Jr., May 28, 1988. BA in English, U. Cin., 1980; postgrad., U. Pa., 1989—. Dir. spl. events Assembly Majority Office, Trenton, N.J., 1986-87; pub. affairs rep., lobbyist Jersey Cen. Power & Light Co., Morristown, N.J., 1987-89; v.p. Colby Communications, Palmyra, N.J., 1986—; cons. Chuck Shrout for City Coun., Cin., 1985, Len Kaiser for Freeholder, North Arlington, N.J., 1986, Art Jones for Congress, Hackensack, N.J., 1986, Don Farley for State Rep., Ashland, Ky., 1988—. Chmn. Young Profls. for Reagan/Bush, Cin., 1984; mem. steering com. Reagen/Bush, Cin., 1984; mgr. DiGaetano/Donovan for Assembly, Lyndhurst, N.J., 1985, DiGaetano for State Senate, Lyndhurst, 1987. Mem. Prevent Bindness N.J., Phila. Leadership Coun. Republican. Home: 4044 Harbour Dr Palmyra NJ 08065

COLBY, VIRGINIA LITTLE, lay worker; b. Saugus, Mass., May 1, 1917; d. Guy L. and Alberta M. (Chadwick) Little; m. Robert G. Colby, Dec. 25, 1951. AB, U. Mass., 1940. Svc. rep. N.E.T. and T. Co. Bus. Office, Concord, N.H., 1940-67; tchr. Shaker Regional Sch. Dist., Belmont, N.H., 1967-77. Contbr. articles to profl. publs. Mem. AAUW (past pres. Concord br.), Lakes Region Retired Tchrs. Assn. (past pres.), No. N.H. Telephone Pioneers Am. (past pres.), Boscawen Hist. Soc., Inc. (sec., libr.), Concord Ch. Women United (past pres., v.p.), N.H. State Ch. Women United (v.p.), Delta Kappa Gamma (hon. mem. Beta chpt.). Home: 134 Mountain Rd Rte 11 Concord NH 03301

COLBY-HALL, ALICE MARY, Romance studies educator; b. Portland, Maine, Feb. 25, 1932; d. Frederick Eugene and Angie Fraser (Drown) C.; m. Robert A. Hall, Jr., May 8, 1976; stepchildren: Philip, Diana Hall Goodall, Carol Hall Erickson. B.A., Colby Coll., 1953; M.A., Middlebury Coll., 1954; Ph.D., Columbia U., 1962. Tchr. French, Latin Orono (Maine) High Sch., 1954-55; tchr. French Gould Acad., Bethel, Maine, 1955-57; lectr. French Columbia U., 1959-60; instr. romance lit. Cornell U., Ithaca, N.Y., 1962-63; asst. prof. Cornell U., 1963-66, assoc. prof., 1966-75, prof. romance studies, 1975—. Author: The Portrait in Twelfth Century French Literature: An Example of the Stylistic Originality of Chrétien de Troyes, 1965; mem. editorial bd.: Speculum, 1976-79, Olifant, 1974—. Fulbright grantee, 1953-54; NEH fellow, 1984-85; recipient Médaille des Amis d'Orange, 1985. Mem. Modern Lang. Assn., Medieval Acad. Am. (councillor 1983-86), Internat. Arthurian Soc., Société Rencesvals, Académie de Vaucluse, Phi Beta Kappa. Republican. Conglist. Home: 308 Cayuga Heights Rd Ithaca NY 14850 Office: Cornell U Dept Romance Studies Ithaca NY 14853

COLDREN, DIANE, educator; b. Portland, Ind., Sept. 18, 1945; d. Mark and Florence (Fudge) Wiley; m. John Edward Coldren, May 30, 1965; children: Jade Everett, Eric David, Julie Donell. BS, Ball State U., Muncie, Ind., 1981; student, Manchester Coll., N. Manchester, Ind., 1963-65, Ind. U., Bloomington, 1967. Substitute tchr. Jay County Sch. Corp., Portland, 1970—. Former mem. Jay County Hosp. Aux.; former mem. bd. dirs. Whitewater Opera Co.; pres. Jay County Rep. Women, 1973-75; mem. handbell choir Meth. Ch. Mem. Ind. Assembly Woman's Assn., Portland Women's Golf Assn. (past pres.), Jay-Portland Abstract Bowling League (past pres.), AAUW, Plant Hoe and Hope Club (past pres.), Beta Gamma Sigma, Kappa Kappa Kappa (past pres.). Republican. Methodist. Home: 520 E High St Portland IN 47371

COLE, BARBARA RUTH, pediatrician, nephrologist; b. Hope, Kans., May 14, 1941; d. John E. and Ruth I. (Klingberg) C. BA, Doane Coll., 1963; MD, U. Kans., 1967. Diplomate Am. Bd. Pediatric Medicine, Am. Bd. Pediatric Nephrology. Intern and resident U. Kans. Med. Ctr.; fellow in pediatric nephrology Washington U., St. Louis, instr. pediatrics, 1972-73, asst. prof. pediatrics, 1973-81, assoc. prof. pediatrics, 1981—, dir. div. pediatric nephrology, 1988—; med. dir. pediatric dialysis and transplantation St. Louis Children's Hosp., 1974—; sci. adviser Nat. Kidney Found., N.Y.C., 1984-89; chair Mo. Kidney Program, Columbia, 1985-87. Contbr. chpts. to books, articles to med. jours. Mem. Am. Soc. Pediatric Nephrology (pres. 1989-90), Polycystic Kidney Rsch. Found. (sci. adviser 1984—), Am. Soc. Nephrology, Am. Fedn. Clin. Rsch., Am. Physiol. Soc., Soc. Pediatric Rsch., Am. Pediatric Soc. Mem. United Ch. of Christ. Office: Washington U Dept Pediatrics 400 S Kingshighway Saint Louis MO 63110

COLE, BETTY LOU MCDONEL SHELTON (MRS. DEWEY G. COLE, JR.), judge; b. Elwood, Ind., June 5, 1926; d. Bernard Miller and Vee Marie (Robertson) McDonel; m. Elbert Shelton, Dec. 13, 1944; children: Steven Elbert, Jeanette Louise; m. 2d, Dewey G. Cole, Jr., Dec. 24, 1975. Student, Ind. U., 1947-50, LLB, 1969; postgrad., Ball State U., 1964-65. Bar: Ind. 1969, Fed. Cts., 1969. Pvt. practice, Muncie, Ind., 1969—, Betty L. Shelton Law Office, 1970-78; sr. ptnr. firm Dunnuck, Cole, Rankin and Wyrick, Muncie, 1978-80; judge Delaware County Superior Ct., 1980—. Mem. ABA, Ind. Bar Assn., Muncie Bar Assn., Ind. Judges Assn., Am. Trial Lawyers, Ind. U. Law Alumni Assn., Nat. Assn. Women Judges, LWV (league pres. 1963-64), Altrusa Internat. Club, Bus. and Profl. Women., Riley-Jones Club, Columbia Club. Office: Del County Courthouse 100 W Main St Muncie IN 47305

COLE, DAWN VROEGOP, corporate banking analyst; b. Kalamazoo, Mich., Oct. 3, 1966; d. Peter and Evelyn A. (Tuinier) V. BBA, U. Mich., 1988. Rsch. asst. Bus. Sch. U. Mich., Ann Arbor, 1986-88; sales cons. Jacobson, Kalamazoo, 1987; corp. banking analyst 1st Nat. Bank of Chgo., 1988—. Mem. Women's Nat. Rep. Club, Fin. Women Internat., U. Mich. Alumni Assn. (candidate chartered fin. analyst). Home: 245 E 44th St #25B New York NY 10017 Office: 1st Nat Bank Chgo 153 W 51st St New York NY 10019

COLE, DIANE JACKSON, textile manufacturing company executive; b. Amesbury, Mass., Sept. 14, 1952; d. Robert Keith and Lois Elizabeth (Fogg) Jackson. B.F.A. cum laude, U. N.H., 1974; student U. London, Sir John Cass Coll. Art, London, Richmond Coll., Surrey, Eng. Owner Diane Jackson Cole Handweaving, Kennebunk, Maine, 1974—; pres. Kennebunk Weavers, Inc., 1981—. Contbr. articles to profl. jours., mags. Exhbns. include: Fiber Invitational, Milw., 1977, Currier Gallery Art, N.H., 1981, League N.H. Craftsmen, 1983. Mem. Profl. Crafts Orgn. Maine (newsletter editor 1978, sec. 1979, v.p. 1980), League N.H. Craftsmen, Nat. Bath, Bed and Linen Assn. Republican. Avocations: swimming, sailing, skiing, reading. Office: Kennebunk Weavers Inc Box A Canal St Suncook NH 03275

COLE, DORTHY GATLIN, state legislator, nurse anesthestist, farmer, rancher; b. Laurel, Miss., Apr. 14, 1933; d. Louis M. and Minerva (Evans) Gatlin; m. Edwin H. Cole; children: Martha Rachel, Lewis Bond, Stephen Curtiss, John Burt. AA, Jones Jr. Coll., 1953; RN degree, South Miss. Charity Hosp., 1955; BS Nursing, William Carey Coll., 1981. Oper. rm. supr. South Miss. Charity Hosp., Laurel, 1955-58, nursing instr., 1959-63, dir. nursing, 1963-66; mem. staff anesthesia Perry County Gen. Hosp., Richton, Miss., 1966-87; mem. Miss. Ho. of Reps., Jackson, 1988—. Mem. Perry County Farm Bur. Women (chair 1976-89), Perry County Cattle Assn., Richton Rotary, Richton Women's Club. Democrat. Methodist. Home: PO Drawer 2 Richton MS 39476

COLE, ELMA PHILLIPSON (MRS. JOHN STRICKLER COLE), social welfare executive; b. Piqua, Ohio, Aug. 9, 1909; d. Brice Leroy and Mabel (Gale) Phillipson; m. John Strickler Cole, Oct. 3, 1959. AB, Berea Coll., 1930; MA, U. Chgo., 1938. Various positions in social work, 1930-42; dir. dept. social svc. Children's Hosp. D.C., Washington, 1942-49; cons. pub. coop. Midcentury White House Conf. on Children and Youth, Washington, 1949-51; exec. sec. Nat. Midcentury Com. on Children and Youth, Washington, 1951-53; cons. recruitment Am. Assn. Med. Social Workers, 1953; assoc. dir. Nat. Legal Aid and Defender Assn., 1953-56; exec. sec. Marshall Field Awards, Inc., 1956-57; dir. assoc. orgns. Nat. Assembly Social Policy and Devel., 1957-73; assoc. exec. dir. Nat. Assembly Nat. Vol. Health and Social Welfare Orgns., 1974; dir. edn. parenthood project Salvation Army, 1974-76, asst. sec. dept. women's and children's social svcs., 1976-78, dir. rsch. project devel. bur., 1978—; mem. Manhattan adv. bd., 1975—, sec., 1984—, mem. hist. commn., 1978—, mem. exec. com., 1988—; cons. nat. orgns. Golden Anniversary White House Conf. on Children and Youth, 1959-60; mem. adv. coun. pub. svc. Nat. Assn. Life Underwriters & Inst. Life Ins.; mem. judges com. Louis I. Dublin Pub. Svc. awards, 1961-74; v.p. Blue Ridge Inst. So. Community Svc. Execs., 1977-79, mem. exec. com., 1979-81; mem. awards jury Girls Clubs of Am., 1981—; mem. adv. bd. Nat. Family Life Edn. Network, 1982—. Mem. com. pub. rels. and fund raising Am. Found. for Blind Commn. on Accreditation, 1964-67; mem. task force on vol. accreditation Coun. Nat. Orgns. for Adult Edn., 1974-78; mem. adv. bd. sexuality edn. project Ctr. for Population Options, 1977-86; sec., bd. dirs. James Lenox House and James Lenox House Assn., 1985-89, pres., 1989—; bd. dirs. Values and Human Sexuality Inst., 1980—. Mem. Pub. Rels. Soc. Am. (cert.), Nat. Assn. Social Workers (cert.), Nat. Conf. Social Welfare (mem. pub. rels. com. 1961-66, 69-82, chair adminstrn. sect. 1966-67), Jr. League N.Y., Women's Club of N.Y., Pi Gamma Mu, Phi Kappa Phi. Home: 19 Washington Sq N New York NY 10011 Office: 440 W Nyack Rd West Nyack NY 10994-0635

COLE, ELSA KIRCHER, lawyer; b. Dec. 5, 1949; d. Paul and Hester Marie (Pellegrom) Kircher; m. Roland J. Cole, Aug. 16, 1975; children: Isabel Ashley, Madeline Aldis. AB in History with distinction, Stanford U., 1971; JD, Boston U., 1974. Bar: Wash. 1974, U.S. Supreme Ct. 1980, Mich. 1989. Asst. atty gen., rep. dept. motor vehicles State of Wash., Seattle, 1974-75, asst. atty. gen., rep. dept. social and health svcs., 1975-76, asst. atty. gen., rep. U. Wash., 1976-89; gen. counsel U. Mich., Ann Arbor, 1989—; presenter ednl. issues various confs. and workshops. Contbr. articles to profl. jours. Mem. Nat. Assn. Coll. and Univ. Attys. (nominations and site selection coms. 1987-88, program, fin., articles and by-law coms. 1988-89, co-chair student affairs sect. 1987-88, 88-89, bd. dirs. 1988—), Wash. State Bar Assn. (chair law sch. liaison com. 1988-89), Wash. Women Lawyers (pres. Seattle-King County chpt. 1986, v.p. membership, state bd. 1987, 88, state chair candidate endorsement com. 1987, 88), Seattle-King County Bar Assn. Congregationalist. Office: U Mich Office of the Gen Counsel 4020 Fleming Bldg Ann Arbor MI 48109

COLE, GRETCHEN BORNOR, distribution and service executive; b. Detroit, Nov. 12, 1927; d. Maurice Frank and Dora Levina (Richardson) Bornor; m. Ernest James Cole, Mar. 31, 1951; (div. May, 1981); children: Cynthia, Sara Ann. BA, DePauw U., 1949; MSW, Wayne State U., 1980. Cert. social worker. Regional sec. Kenyon and Eckhardt, Detroit, 1951-52; office mgr. W.O. Earl Assocs., Detroit, 1952-54; v.p. Detroit Air Compressor and Pump Co., Ferndale, Mich., 1963-82; pres. Detroit Air Compressor and Pump Co., Ferndale, 1984—; social worker St. Joseph Mercy Hosp., Pontiac, Mich., 1980-82; regional dir., v.p. Atlas Copco Distributor Assn., 1987-90. Named one of Top 50 Woman Bus. Owners State of Mich., 1986. Mem. Women's Econ. Club, Nat. Assn. of Women Bus. Owners, Nat. Distbrs. Assn. (bd. dirs.), Econ. Club of Detroit, Alpha Chi Omega. Republican. Episcopalian. Office: Detroit Air Compressor and Pump Co 3205 Bermuda Ferndale MI 48220

COLE, JANE BAGBY, librarian; b. Tulsa, May 23, 1931; d. Walter James and Mary Frances (Eakin) Bagby; m. Bruce Herman Cole, June 7, 1953; children—Rosemary Neilsen, Dorothy Domrzalski, Robert Bagby, Frances. B.A., Grinnell Coll., 1953; M.A., U. Chgo., 1977. Library asst. Elem. Dist. 101, Western Springs, Ill., 1961-71, library aide, 1973-75; librarian Elem. Dist. 102, La Grange, Ill., 1975-77, River Forest Jr. High Sch., Ill., 1977-79; audio-visual dir. Elem. Dist. 7, Phoenix, 1980-83; library dir., curator Desert Bot. Garden, Phoenix, 1983—; discussion leader Gt. Books Found., Chgo., 1965-79, Phoenix, 1981—. Editor Saguaroland Bull., 1984-86. Precinct worker senatorial campaign, Cook County, Ill., 1966-67, Maricopa County, Ariz., 1980. Mem. ALA, Spl. Libraries Assn., Ariz. Paper and Photograph Conservation Group, Council Bot. and Hort. Libraries. Office: Desert Bot Garden 1201 N Galvin Pkwy Phoenix AZ 85008

COLE, JANET See HUNTER, KIM

COLE, JOAN HAYS, social worker, clinical psychologist; b. Pitts., Sept. 4, 1929; d. Frank L. Wertheimer and Edith H. Einstein; BA, Western Res. U., 1951; MSSA in Social Work, Case Western Res. U., 1962; PhD, Wright Inst., 1975; m. Robert M. Wendlinger, June 1984; children: Geoffrey F. Cole, Douglas R. Cole, Peter Hays Cole. Social group worker Alta House Settlement House, Cleve., 1958-59; housing dir. Cleve. Urban League, 1961-62; dir. Citizens for Safe Housing, Cleve., 1963; housing dir. United Planning Orgn., Washington, 1963-68; asst. prof. community orgn. U. Md., Balt., 1968-72; asso. prof. Lone Mountain Coll., San Francisco, 1975-78; psychotherapist, supr., organizational cons., Berkeley, Calif., 1977—; cons. various public and vol. social welfare, health and housing agys., 1969-85; mem. adj. faculty Union Grad. Sch. and Antioch West Coll., 1978-80; lectr. U. Calif. Sch. Social Welfare, Berkeley, 1980-84; mem. faculty Berkeley Psychotherapy Inst., 1981—, pres., 1983-85. NIMH grantee, 1971-72, Sr. Social Work Career Devel. grantee, 1973-75. Fellow Soc. Clin. Social Work, Am. Orthopsychiat. Assn.; mem. Nat. Assn. Social Workers, Soc. Study of Social Issues, ACLU, NOW, Acad. Cert. Social Workers, Nat. Conf. on social Welfare and Psychotherapists for Social Responsibility. Home: 20 Treasure Hill Oakland CA 94618 Office: 6239 College Ave Oakland CA 94618

COLE, JOHNNETTA BETSCH, academic administrator; b. Jacksonville, Fla., Oct. 19, 1936; d. John Thomas and Mary Frances (Lewis) Betsch; m. Robert Eugene Cole (div. 1982); children: David, Aaron, Ethan; m. Arthur Robinson, Jr., 1988. Student, Fisk U., 1953; BA in Sociology, Oberlin Coll., 1957; MA in Anthropology, Northwestern U., Evanston, Ill., 1959, PhD, 1967. Instr. U. Calif., Los Angeles, 1964; dir. black studies Wash. State U., Pullman, 1969-70; prof. anthropology U. Mass., Amherst, 1970-83, assoc. provost undergrad. edn., 1981-83; vis. prof. Hunter Coll., N.Y.C., 1983-84, prof. anthropology, 1983-87, dir. Inter-Am. Affairs Program, 1984-87; pres. Spelman Coll., Atlanta, 1987—; pres. Internat. Women's Anthropology Conf.; bd. dirs. Am. Coun. on Edn., The Feminist Press. Author, editor: Anthropology for the Eighties, 1982, All American Women, 1986, Anthropology for the Nineties, 1988; mem. editorial bd. The Blackscholar. Fellow Am. Anthrop. Assn.; mem. Assn. Black Anthropologists (past pres.). Baptist. Office: Spelman Coll 350 Spelman Ln SW Atlanta GA 30314

COLE, JULIA PATRICIA, healthcare facility administrator; b. Altoona, Pa., Apr. 6, 1952; d. Dale Thomas and Norma Rae (Thomas) Shaffer; m. Charles R. Cole, Nov. 28, 1984; children: Victor, Candace. AS in Nursing, Community Coll. Allegheny Co., 1972; BS in Edn. and Pub. Health, California (Pa.) State U., 1976; M Health Adminstrn., St. Thomas U., Miami, Fla., 1989. Dir. nursing Hanover House, Miami; head nurse North Miami (Fla.) Med. Ctr.; adminstrv. dir., med.-psychiat. head nurse Hialeah (Fla.) Hosp.; asst. adminstr. Calderwood Lodge-ACLF, Homestead, Fla.; instr., leader workshops in field. Recipient Exceptionally Able Youth award Allegheny County. Mem. Psychiat. Nursing Network. Home: 4955 NW 199 St #115 Miami FL 33055

COLE, JUNE ROBERTSON, psychotherapist; b. Dothan, Ala., Sept. 29, 1931; d. C. Pete and Mary (Danzey) Robertson; m. Robert Walker Cole, Jr., Feb. 11, 1956; children: Robert Pete, Mary Cathlyn. AA, Del Mar Coll., 1974; BA, Tex. A&I U., 1976; MA, Corpus Christi State U., 1978; postgrad Fielding Inst., Santa Barbara, 1985—. Actress, singer, radio, films, TV, stage, 1933-55; rec. artist Gold Label Records, 1951-55; pres. Coastal Bend Security Co., Corpus Christi, 1969-71; dir. Reality Therapy Ctr., Corpus Christi, 1975—; co dir. Counseling and Psychology Resource Ctr., Corpus Christi, 1984—; pvt. practice psychotherapy, 1976—; mem. mental health staff Bayview Psychiatric Hosp., Corpus Christi, 1986—, Southside Community Hosp., Corpus Christi, 1989—, Charter Psychiart. Hosp., Corpus Christi, 1990. Presenter major papers to field faculty on compatiability of reality therapy as psychol. modiality with self-help groups in addictions Park Coll., Naval Air Sta., Corpus Christi, 1988-89. Bd. dirs. Coastal Bend Jazz Soc., 1978-79. Mem. Am. Assn. for Counseling and Devel., Am. Assn. for Mental Health Counselors, Am. Assn. Behavior Therapists, Am. Psychol. Assn., Tex. Psychol. Assn., Internat. Assn. for Group Psychotherapists, Corpus Christi Council Women, NOW, Nueces County Psychol. Assn., Tex. Assn. Counseling and Devel., Gulf Coast Assn. Counseling and Devel., Tex. Mental Health Counselors Assn., Coastal Bend Marriage and Family Therapists Assn., Internat. Inst. Reality Therapists Office: 5934 S Staples #216 Ste 2 Corpus Christi TX 78413-3842

COLE, KELLIE BIRDGETT ARNDT, interior designer; b. Detroit, Sept. 15, 1964; d. Glenn Earl and Phyllis Karen (Paulson) Arndt; m. Robert Preston Cole, June 11, 1988. Student, Stetson U., 1982-83, Internat. Acad. Merchandising and Design, 1983-86, Oakland Community Coll., 1989—. Interior designer Roberts' Interior Design, Inc., Largo, Fla., 1984-88, 90—; with Dickinson, Wright, Moon, Van Dusen & Freeman, counselors at law, Royal Oaks, Mich., 1988-89; cons. in field. Mem. Tampa Bay Interior Design Assn., Am. Soc. for Prevention of Cruelty to Animals, People for Ethical Treatment of Animals, Humane Soc. U.S., Greenpeace. Republican. Lutheran. Home: 523 S Vermont Royal Oak MI 48067

COLE, MARGARET ELIZABETH, food scientist; b. Newport News, Va., Aug. 7, 1960; d. Ronald and Jacquelyn Ann (Lanz) Kolenkiewicz; m. Russell William Cole, Mar. 3, 1989. BS summa cum laude, U. Md., College Park, 1982; MS, U. Md., 1985; PhD, Kans. State U., Manhattan, 1988; cert., U. Calif., Berkeley, 1990. Computer operator Computer Scis./Technicolor Assocs., Greenbelt, Md., 1979; lab. technician USDA, Beltsville, Md., 1979-82; rsch. asst. Pa. State U., University Park, 1982-83; rsch. assoc. U. Md., College Park, 1983-85; USDA nat. needs rsch. fellow Kans. State U., Manhattan, 1985-88; rsch. food technologist USDA, Albany, Calif., 1988—. Safeway Stores scholar, 1982, U. Md. scholar, 1983-84. Mem. Inst. Food

Techs., ASTM, Am. Assn. Cereal Chemists, Soc. Chem. Industry, Am. Soc. for Quality Control, European Chemoreception Rsch. Orgn., Soc. for Consumer Psychology, Assn. for Chemoreception Scis., Sigma Xi, Phi Kappa Phi, Phi Sigma, Gamma Sigma Delta, Omicron Nu, Phi Tau Sigma, Alpha Lambda Delta, Phi Upsilon Omicron. Office: USDA 800 Buchanan St Albany CA 94710

COLE, MICHELLE, author, social anthropologist, consultant; b. Los Angeles, Aug. 21, 1940; d. Henry and Joyce (Raskin) Goldman; m. Laurence S. Cole, Aug. 30, 1959; 1 child, Jarett Evan. BA, U. Calif.-Santa Barbara, 1960; postgrad. Sophie Newcomb U., 1961, Columbia U., 1961-64; EdD, Franconia Coll., 1970. Asst. fashion editor Playboy Mag., N.Y.C., 1962-64; exec. dir. Lower Eastside Action Project, Inc., N.Y.C., 1964-75; dir. Inst. Juvenile Justice, N.Y.C., 1970-78; editorial cons.; childrens programming cons. Lamico Co., Los Angeles, 1976—. Author: Checking it Out, 1970; Violent Sheep, 1980; (with others) Anthology, 1972. Contbr. articles to profl. publs. Bd. dirs. E. Harlem Tenants Council, N.Y.C., 1964-73, Escuela Montessori Sch., N.Y.C., 1968-70; mem. Lower Eastside Coordinating Council, N.Y.C., 1964-78, Commn. for Sane Nuclear Policy, N.Y.C., 1970—, Human Factors Soc., 1975—. Norman Found. fellow, 1974; grantee Astor Found., 1972. Mem. Author's Guild. Jewish. Avocations: Computer applications to education, children's films, architecture, media archives. Office: 16260 Ventura Blvd Ste 825 Encino CA 91436

COLE, NYLA JESSAMINE, psychiatrist; b. Wasco, Calif., Dec. 5, 1925; d. Rolland Tisdale and Emily Evangeline (Moisling) C.; m. Albert Hulbert Kelson, Dec. 14, 1955 (dec.). BA, U. Calif., Berkeley, 1947; MD, U. Rochester, 1951. Diplomate Am. Bd. Psychiatry and Neurology. Intern, 1951-52, resident in psychiatry, 1952-55; asst. prof. U. Utah, Salt Lake City, 1960-68, assoc. prof., 1968-85, assoc. prof. emerita, 1986—; psychiat. cons. Hill Air Force Base, Utah, 1967-83. Contbr. articles to profl. jours. Chmn. Pres.'s Com. on the Mentally Handicapped, Washington, 1972-73. Fellow Am. Psychiat. Assn. (life, chmn. com. on rehab. 1969-73). Office: U Utah Health Sci Ctr 50 N Medical Dr Salt Lake City UT 84112

COLE, PATRICIA ANN ELIZABETH, law office manager; b. Phila., Feb. 14, 1958; d. John Robert and Mary Ellen (Youse) Blechl; m. William S. Cole, Apr. 16, 1977 (div. Jan. 1980). Grad. high sch., Phila., 1976; student, Court Reporting Inst., Phila., 1990—. Sec. internat. div. Electric Storage Battery Ray-O-Vac, Phila., 1976-78; exec. sec. Automatic Retailers Am. Svcs., Phila., 1978-79; asst. office mgr. John Erickson Co., Real Estate Mgmt., Phila., 1979-80; exec. sec. pub. rels. J. Gross & Bro. Real Estate, Upper Darby, Pa., 1980-82; office mgr. Shuster and Marvin, Law Firm, Bala-Cynwyd, Pa., 1982—. Pres. LWV Upper Darby Area, 1985-90, 1st v.p., 1990—; mem. Greater Lansdowne Civic Assn., 1990. Democrat. Roman Catholic. Home: 110 Aldan Ave Aldan PA 19018 Office: Shuster and Marvin 3 Bala Pla W Ste 100 Bala Ste 100 Bala-Cynwyd PA 19004

COLE, ROSALIE M., property management executive; b. Winterset, Iowa, May 4, 1926; d. Charles P. and Nellie M. (Fry) Peterson; m. Lynn H. Cole, Apr. 21, 1945; children: Rosalyn, Janet, Steven. Diploma practical nurse, N. Iowa Area Community Coll., 1973; student in real estate sales, Am. Inst. Bus., 1972. Lic. practical nurse, Iowa, real estate assoc., Iowa. Program dir. KRIB Radio Sta., Mason City, Iowa; owner Manage Rentals, Gordonville, Pa. Publicity chmn., hosp. vol. Iowa chpt. ARC, YWCA; mem. Sr. Citizen's Program Planning Bd.; mem. Nat. Rep. Senatorial Com.; registered speaker UN of Iowa; publicity chmn. North Cen. Iowa Area Activity Dirs. Mem. LWV, C. of C. (hostess), Mason City Country Club, Gamma Beta Phi. Republican. Home and Office: 2939 Lincoln Hwy E Gordonville PA 17529

COLE, SHARON F., school principal; b. Mexico, Mo., May 21, 1941; d. Cubert C. and Ruby Bunch (Chappell) Moore; m. Verlon R. Cole, Oct. 14, 1978; 1 child, Melinda. BS, Cen. Mo. State U., 1971; MS, Cen. State U., Edmond, Okla., 1975. Reading specialist Corona-Norco Sch. Dist., Corona, Calif., Jackson (Mo.) Sch. Dist.; vice prin. Delano (Calif.) Union Sch. Dist.; prin. Etiwanda (Calif.) Sch. Dist. Mem. Assn. Calif. Sch. Adminstrs., AAUW, Assn. Curriculum Suprs., Phi Delta Kappa. Home: 16372 Montgomery Ave Fontana CA 92336 Office: PO Box 248 Etiwanda CA 91739

COLE, SONYA KRESSLER, educational administrator; b. Fountain Hill, Pa., Aug. 15, 1941; d. Paul and Elba (Jennings) Kressler; m. Horace Samuel Cole, Oct. 17, 1975; children: Kevin Thomas, Kelly Richard, Christopher Gayle, Brandon Kennard. BS, East Stroudsburg (Pa.) U., 1963, MEd, 1974; Elem. Adminstrn. Cert., Pa. State U., 1980; Cert., U. Scranton, 1989. Tchr. Easton (Pa.) Area Sch. Dist., 1963, Belvidere (N.J.) Sch. Dist., 1963-64, Pocono Mountain Sch. Dist., Swiftwater, Pa., 1965-68, East Stroudsburg Sch. Dist., 1968-86; elem. prin. Delaware Valley Sch. Dist., Milford, Pa., 1986—. Player agt. East Stroudsburg Little League, 1979—, aux. chmn., 1982—; elder East Stroudsburg Presbyn. Ch., 1985—. Mem. ASCD, NAESP, Pa. Assn. for Supervision and Curriculum Devel., Pa. Assn. Elem. Sch. Prins., Intermediate Unit 20 Elem. Prins. Group (pres. 1990—), AAUW (v.p. 1986-89), Antique Auto. Club Am., Austin Healey Sports and Touring Club. Republican. Home: 288 Marguerite St East Stroudsburg PA 18301 Office: Delaware Valley Sch Dist SR Box 379 D Milford PA 18337

COLE, SUSIE CLEORA, government employee relations official; b. Bloomsburg, Pa.; d. Harry E. and Chloe Ann (McKinstry) Cole; m. Richard Edward Miller, July 31, 1959 (div. Aug. 1977); 1 child, Terri Lee Miller; m. Gerald Edward Nelson, Feb. 18, 1978 (div. June 1982). Student in history No. Va. Community Coll., 1982; also govt. courses. With Dept. Navy, Washington, 1957-74, clk., technician U.S. Dept. Navy, Washington, 1957-67, Navy mil. pay regulations specialist, 1962-71; mgr. error detection and reduction program for mil. pay, allowances and travel, 1967-71, fiscal acct. 1971-74, fiscal clk. Dept. State, Washington, 1975-77, sr. retirement claims examiner, 1977-83, employee rels. officer, 1983—, also mgr. fed. health benefits program and mgr. fed. life ins. program, 1983—. Active Citizen's Band Radio Club, Fairfax, Va., 1974-82, Retarded Children's Ctr., Fairfax, 1981-82. Recipient various govt. awards, including Sustained Exceptional Achievement award Dept. State, 1983, 84, 85, 86, 87, 88. Democrat. Avocations: reading, travel, history, music, art. Home: 4605 John Tyler Ct Apt 104 Annandale VA 22003 Office: US Dept State Bur Personnel Office Employee Relations 2201 C St NW Washington DC 20520

COLE, VIRGINIA STARR, substance abuse and family counselor; b. N.Y.C., July 26, 1953; d. Benjamin S. and Virginia (Norment) C.; m. Stephen Corsaro, Oct. 20, 1974 (div. 1977); m. Roger L. Ford, June 19, 1982; children: Cole Conrad, Charles Lee. BA cum laude, U. Mass., Boston, 1977. Studio mgr. Singer Co., Brookline, Mass., 1976-78; asst. mgr. Calliope, Brookline, 1978-80; bus. mgr. Dada Corp., Boston, 1980-81; mktg. dir., personnel asst. Cleary Cleaners, Dover, N.H., 1980-82; group facilitator Navy Alcohol & Drug Safety Action Program U. Ariz., Portsmouth, N.H., 1988-89; substance abuse counselor Frisbee Meml. Hosp., Rochester, N.H., 1989—; mgmt. assoc., layout artist Val-Pak of the Seacoast, Dover, N.H., 1983—. Co-founder Informed Choice, Stratham, N.H., 1986—, Informed Birth, 1987; hotline vol. Alcoholics Anonymous, Dover, 1987. Mem. Seacoast Women's Network (program com.), Triangle Club. Democrat. Home: 169 Blackwater Rd Somersworth NH 03878

COLEBROOK, ELIZABETH POSS, retired psychologist; b. Cleve., Jan. 5, 1923; d. Louis Oliver and Flora Amelia (Gedecke) Poss; m. Jack Leonard Colebrook, June 12, 1943; children: Michael. Susan, Deborah, Kristina. BA, Vassar Coll., 1944; MEd, Kent State U., 1972, PhD, 1981. Ret., 1989; pvt. practice Ctr. for Better Living, Aurora and Chagrin Falls, Ohio. Founder kindergarten Aurora (Ohio) Pub. Schs., 1950, Aurora Summer Recreation Program, 1955, Aurora Adult Edn., 1960, Aurora Community Theatre, 1974, Ctr. for Better Living, 1974. Democrat. Home: 850 Old Mill Rd Aurora CO 44202

COLEHUCKEBA, PAULA JILL, banker; b. Manhattan Beach, Calif., Nov. 30, 1948; d. Paul Burk and Ruth Marie (Seifried) Cole; m. Charles Merritt Huckeba, Aug. 10, 1968; children: Maia Merritt, Ghislaine Soliel. AA, Antelope Valley Coll., 1968; student, U. So. Calif., L.A., 1968-69; BA, U. Calif., Santa Barbara, 1970; cert. in mgmt. tng., Bank of Am., 1985; postgrad., Antioch U. With Bank of Am., 1972-87; preferred banking officer Bank of Am., Santa Barbara, 1985, mgr. Motecito office, 1985-87; dist. mgr., 2d v.p. Chase Manhattan, Santa Barbara, 1987-88, v.p., 1988—. Mem. corp. cup relay team Bank of Am., So. Calif., 1984; bd. dirs. March of Dimes, Coastal div., Calif., 1985-88, Klein Bottle Social Advocates for Youth, Santa Barbara, 1985—. Recipient Cert. of Appreciation, Klein Bottle Social Advocates for Youth, 1989, Cert. of Appreciation March of Dimes Found., 1988. Mem. NAFE, Santa Barbara Assocs., Montecito Mchts. Assn. (sec. exec. bd. Santa Barbara chpt. 1985-87), Leads Club of Santa Barbara (chpt. bd. dirs. 1986-88), Univ. Club of Santa Barbara. Democrat. Office: Chase Manhattan Calif 1525 State St Ste 100 Santa Barbara CA 93101

COLEMAN, ANGELA MARIE, data processing specialist; b. San Angelo, Tex., Apr. 19, 1960; d. Ronnie E. and L. Pauline (Barton) Lawler; m. Rickey Joe Coleman, Mar. 6, 1981; 1 child, Jeremy Michael. Ordained elder Presbyn. Ch. Computer programmer Datasmith, Inc., Odessa, Tex., 1979-85; data processing mgr. EnClean, Inc., Odessa, 1986—. Sunday sch. supt. St. Matthew Cumberland Presbyn. Ch., Burleson, Tex., 1990. Republican. Home and Office: 937 Springhill St Burleson TX 76028

COLEMAN, ANGELLA COBB, college program administrator; b. Kinston, N.C., May 30, 1962; d. Ervin Ray and Shirley (Simmons) Cobb; m. Dwain Edward Coleman, Sept. 5, 1987. AAS in Mktg. Retail, Lenoir Community Coll., 1982; BA in Pub. Adminstrn., N.C. Cen. U., 1985. Computer operator Kinston City Schs., 1986-87; accounts payable clk. Brame Splty. Co., Durham, N.C., 1987-88; student accounts mgr. Rutledge Coll., Durham, 1988-89, placement dir., 1989—. Mem. NAFE, Pub. Adminstrn. Club (sec. 1984-85). Democrat. Baptist. Home: 1125 Elmo St Apt C Durham NC 27701 Office: Rutledge Coll 410 W Chapel Hill St Durham NC 27701

COLEMAN, ANNETTE WILBOIS, biology educator; b. Des Moines, Feb. 28, 1934; d. Fred J. and Agnes D. Wilbois; m. John R. Coleman, July 26, 1958; children: Alan, Benjamin, Suzanne. B.A., Columbia U., 1955; Ph.D., U. Ind., 1958. Postdoctoral fellow Johns Hopkins U., Balt., 1958-61; rsch. assoc. U. Conn., 1961-63; rsch. assoc. Brown U., Providence, 1964-72, asst. prof. biology rsch., 1972-76, asst. prof., 1976-80, assoc. prof., 1980-84, prof., 1984—, Stephen T. Olney prof. natural history, 1984—. NSF postdoctoral fellow, 1955-58, 58-60; Guggenheim fellow, 1983-84, recipient Provasoli award, 1985, Darbaker award, 1986. Fellow N.Y. Acad. Scis.; mem. Bot. Soc. Am., Soc. Protozoologists, Phcol. Soc. Am. (pres. 1981-82). Office: Brown U Dept Biology Providence RI 02912

COLEMAN, BARBARA LEE WEINSTEIN, city official; b. L.A., Apr. 2, 1948; d. Merrill Franklin and Vivian Berniece (Koller) Hale; m. Carl Weinstein, July 9, 1976 (div. Dec. 1988); 1 child, Dena Lynn; m. Basil Bruce Coleman, May 1, 1989. AA in Sociology, East L.A. Coll., 1969; BS in Recreation Edn., Calif. State U., L.A., 1972. Tchr. arts and crafts East L.A. YWCA, 1967-68; resident and day camp counselor West San Gabriel Valley YMCA, Alhambra, Calif., 1967-68; counselor Happy Day Nursery and Day Camp, Monterey Park, Calif., 1968-72; playground leader City of Las Vegas (Nev.), 1973-76, summer dist. coord., 1977, recreation leader, 1978-79, community sch. coord., 1979—; bus driver Clark County Sch. Dist., Las Vegas, 1973-78. Editor Checkered Flag newsletter, 1984-86. Advisor Tri-Hi-Y, West San Gabriel YMCA, 1966-68; asst. leader Sierra Madre coun. Girl Scouts U.S.A., 1967-68, leader Frontier coun., 1976-77, 85-86. Mem. Nat. Recreation and Park Assn. (sec. Pacific Southwest regional coun. 1989-90), Nev. Recreation and Park Soc. (hist. chmn. 1981-84, sec. 1981-83, mem.-at-large 1983-84, 87-88, chmmn. bylaws 1983-89, v.p. South 1985-86, pres. 1989-90, past pres. 1990—, citation 1985, program excellence award 1988), Nev. Assn. for Community Edn. (sec.-treas. 1984—), Sports Car Club Am. (asst. regional exec. Las Vegas region 1984-86, membership com. 1985-88), Calif. Sports Car Club. Office: Brinley Community Sch 6200 Smoke Ranch Rd Las Vegas NV 89108

COLEMAN, BETHANY BALDWIN, insurance executive; b. Miami, Fla., Dec. 4, 1950; d. C. Jackson and Mary Susanne (Bonner) Baldwin; m. Carl Randolph Coleman, May 27, 1983 (div.); 1 child, Carole Jacqueline. Student U. Ala., 1969-72. Lic. property and casualty ins. agt., life ins. agt., claims adjuster, Fla. Claims adjuster Liberty Mut. Ins. Co., Miami, 1973-75, Kemper Ins. Co., Miami, 1975-76; asst. to pres. Baldwin Ins. Agy., Miami, 1976—, also bd. dirs. Trustee Expo 500: 1992 Columbus Exposition, 1982—; Miami chairperson Nat. Family Bus. Council, 1983-84, bd. dirs., 1983; mem. citizens adv. bd. Bloomingdale's So. Fla., 1984—; mem. Orange Bowl Com., Miami, 1985—; mem. new tequestians com. Hist. Mus. of So. Fla., 1985—; chairwoman dinner com. Big Brothers/Big Sisters Greater Miami, 1986-87; mem. devel. adv. bd. Doctors Hosp. Coral Gables, 1987-90; chairperson Ann. Fla. Art Show Riviera Country Club, 1989—. Mem. Fla. Assn. Ind. Agts., Nat. Assn. Security Dealers, Ind. Ins. Agts. of Dade County, Greater Miami C. of C. (com. for United Way 1985), U. Ala. Alumni Assn., Phi Beta Phi. Clubs: Generation of Miami (pres. 1983-84, chmn. 1984-85), Riviera Country (Coral Gables, Fla.); Palm Bay, New World Ctr., U. Miami Hurricane (bd. dirs.), Bankers, (Miami). Home: 1532 Dorado Ave Coral Gables FL 33146 Office: Baldwin Ins Agy Inc 840 Biscayne Blvd Miami FL 33132

COLEMAN, DEBORAH ANN, computer company executive; b. Central Falls, R.I., Jan. 22, 1953; d. John Austin and Joan Mary Coleman. BA, Brown U., 1974; MBA, Stanford U., 1978; PhD in Engrng. (hon.), Worcester (Mass.) Poly., 1987. Prodn. supr. metals and controls Tex. Instruments, Attleboro, Mass., 1974; fin. mgmt. tng. program Gen. Electric, Providence, 1974-76; gen. acctg. supr., fin. system analyst components group Hewlett-Packard, Cupertino, Calif., 1978-79, cost acctg. supr. instrument group, 1980, fin. mgr. tech. computer group, 1981; controller Macintosh project Apple Computer, Cupertino, 1981-82, div. controller Macintosh project, 1982-83, sr. fin. controller Apple 32 product group, 1983-84, ops. mgr. Macintosh div., 1984, dir. ops. Macintosh div., 1985, v.p. ops., 1986-87, chief fin. officer, v.p. fin., 1987-89, v.p. corp. Macintosh div., 1989—; bd. dirs. Claris Software, Santa Clara, Calif. Advisor Harvard U. Bus. Sch.; bd. dirs. Resource Ctr,. for Women, Palo Alto, Calif., 1986—; mem. Def. Mfg. Bd., 1988—; trustee SCV Children's Shelter, 1989—, San Jose/Cleve. Ballet, 1989—. Mem. Stanford Inst. Mfg. and Automation (indsl. advisor 1985-87), Com. 200, APICS. Democrat. Roman Catholic. Office: Apple Computer Inc 20525 Marian Ave Cupertino CA 95014

COLEMAN, DONNA ANN, former state legislator; b. Sao Paulo, Brazil, Mar. 11, 1949; d. John M. and Donna (Hendricks) C.; BS, U. Utah, 1974; MBA, Washington U., St. Louis, 1985; corp. sec.-treas., dir., fin. officer Engineered Fire Protection, Inc., St. Louis, 1977—, bd. dirs., trustee employee profit sharing trust. Mem. Mo. Ho. of Reps., 1981-82, 83-84; dir. speakers bur. Mo. Citizens Council, 1979-80; del. Mo. Rep. Conv., 1980, 84; mem. Mo. Rep. Platform Com., 1984; chmn. Mo. Ho. of Reps. Rep. Caucus Campaign Com., 1983-84; appointed 2 yr. term 1986-87, reappointed 3 yr. term , 1988 vice chmn. Mo. Council Women's Econ. Devel. and Tng. Mormon. Home: 2449 Baxton Way Chesterfield MO 63017

COLEMAN, ELIZABETH, college president; b. N.Y.C., Nov. 23, 1937; d. Lewis and Sophie (Brantman) Ginsburg; m. Aaron Coleman, June 14, 1959; children: Daniel, David. B.A., U. Chgo., 1958; M.A., Cornell U., 1959; Ph.D., Columbia U., 1965. Instr. humanities SUNY, N.Y.C., 1960-65; assoc. dean faculty New Sch. Social Research, N.Y.C., 1966-76, dean Coll. Arts and Scis., 1977-84; prof. literature and humanities New Sch. Social Research, 1984-87; pres. Bennington (Vt.) Coll., 1987—; vis. lectr. Hebrew U., 1972, SUNY-Stony Brook, 1975; curriculum cons. Howard U., 1973; chmn. outside evaluating com. CUNY, 1976. Contbr. articles to profl. pubs. Mem. nat. adv. coun. Woodrow Wilson Found., 1990; bd. dirs. Cen. Vt. Pub. Svc. Corp., 1990. Fellow Ford Found., 1954-58; Woodrow Wilson fellow, 1958-59; F.J.E. Woodbridge fellow Columbia U., 1963-64; Pres.'s fellow Columbia U., 1964-65. Mem. MLA, Nat. Assn. Acad. Deans, Nat. Assn. Women Deans, Am. Assn. Colls. Home & Office: Bennington Coll Office of Pres Bennington VT 05201

COLEMAN, FRANCES ALINE, executive, owner of service business; b. Frankfurt, Fed. Republic of Germany, June 29, 1955; (parents Am. citizens); d. Philip Dan and Marjorie Aline (Taylor) C. BA, Cath. U., Washington, 1977; MA in Religion, Yale U., 1985. Counselor supr. Desert Willow Ranch, Tucson, 1978-80; counselor Big Bros. and Big Sisters, Tucson, 1980-82, Tucson Pre-Release Ctr., 1985-86; exec. dir., owner Elder In-Home Svcs., Tucson, 1987—. Sec. and co-founder Dunbar Neighborhood Assn., 1986-88; exec. com. Community devel. Adv. com., 1989. Mem. NAFE. Democrat. Unitarian.

COLEMAN, IVORY CLAUDETTE, nurse; b. Phila., Dec. 10, 1947; d. Louis and Ivory Lucille (Aikens) C. BS in Nursing, Hampton U., 1970; MS in Nursing, Pa. State U., 1979. Staff nurse John Hopkins Hosp., Balt., 1970-71; staff nurse Phila. Gen. Hosp., 1971-74, head nurse, 1974-75; staff nurse, icu Episcopal Hosp., Phila., 1979-80; eductor Community Coll. Phila., 1980--. Mem. Pa. Nurse Assn., Black Nurse Assn., Pa. League for Nurses, Chi Eta Phi. Democrat. Baptist. Home: 3834 N 15th St Philadelphia PA 19140 Office: Community Coll Phila 1700 Spring Garden Philadelphia PA 19130

COLEMAN, JEAN BLACK, nurse, physician assistant; b. Sharon, Pa., Jan. 11, 1925; d. Charles B. and Sue E. (Dougherty) Black; m. Donald A. Coleman, July 3, 1946; children: Sue Ann Coleman Lynn, Donald Ashley. RN, Spencer Hosp. Sch. Nursing, Meadville, Pa., 1945; student Vanderbilt U., 1952-54. Nurse, dir. nursing Bulloch Meml. Hosp., Statesboro, Ga., 1948-51, nurse supr. surgery, 1954-67, dir. nursing, 1967-71; physicians asst., nurse anesthetist to Robert H. Swint, Statesboro, 1971—; mem. physician assts. adv. com. Bd. Med. Examiners Ga., 1987-89, 90—. Named Woman of Yr. in Med. Field, Bus. and Profl. Women, 1980. Mem. Am. Nurses Assn., Ga. Nurses Assn., Am. Acad. Physicians Assts., Ga. Assn. Physicians Assts. (bd. dirs. 1975-79, v.p. 1979-80, pres. 1980-81). Democrat. Roman Catholic.

COLEMAN, K(ATHERINE) ANN, educator; b. Plattsburg, N.Y.; d. John and Anna C. BS, Elms Coll., 1963; MS, Springfield Coll., 1964; PhD, Boston Coll., 1971; MPH, Harvard U., 1977. Psychologist Exec. Office of the Pres., Washington, 1964-66; research assoc. Harvard U., Cambridge, Mass., 1970-71; asst. prof. SUNY, Stony Brook, 1971-75, assoc. prof., 1975-78; assoc. prof. Boston U., 1978—; owner, pres. La Di Da Properties, Cambridge, 1986—. Contbr. numerous articles to profl. jours. Mem. New Eng. Ednl. Rsch. Orgn. (bd. dirs. 1974-86, v.p. 1985-86, pres. 1986-87), Ea. Ednl. Rsch. Orgn. (div. chmn. 1979—, bd. dirs. 1985—). Home: 32 Shepard St Cambridge MA 02138 Office: Boston U Psychology Dept 64 Cummington St Boston MA 02215

COLEMAN, LILLIAN SIMONS, editor, writer; b. Atlanta, Jan. 26, 1955; d. Henry Mazyck and Martha Jane (Mack) Simons; m. John Dozier Coleman III, Nov. 29, 1975; children: Keating Simons, Lillian Marshall, John Dozier IV. BA in English, Columbia (S.C.) Coll., 1977; M in Mass Communications, U. S.C., 1980. Instr. journalism U. S.C., Sumter, 1979-82; communications mgr. Assn. for Edn. in Journalism and Mass Communications, Columbia, 1982-84, asst. editor, 1984-87, editor AEJMC News and Journalism and Mass Communications Directory, 1987—; freelance writer, photographer Sandlapper mag., Columbia, 1980-82, Carolina Lifestyle mag., Columbia, 1983. Republican. Home: 629 Springlake Rd Columbia SC 29206 Office: Assn for Edn in Journalism and Mass Communication 1621 College St Columbia SC 29208-0251

COLEMAN, LINDA R., financial executive. BA, U. Md., 1970; MBA, Seton Hall U. Various positions Johnson & Johnson, 1972-77; sr. product mgr. toiletry products div. Richardson-Vick, 1978-79; sr. products mgr. Chesebrough-Ponds Inc., 1980-82, mgr. mktg., 1982-84; v.p. product planning and mktg. N.Y. Stock Exch., N.Y.C., 1984-86, v.p. corp. mktg., 1986-87, v.p. strategic planning, mktg. and bus. devel., 1987-88; exec. v.p. planning and devel. Boston Stock Exch., 1988-89. Home: 71 Aiken St #Q-14 Norwalk CT 06851

COLEMAN, MARCIA LEPRI, laboratory manager. AB in Chemistry, Mount Holyoke Coll., 1969; PhD in Chem. Physics, MIT, 1973. Various rsch. mgmt. and rsch. positions E.I. DuPont de Nemours & Co., Wilmington, Del., 1973-84, product mgr., 1984-86, planning mgr., 1986-88, lab. mgr., 1988—.

COLEMAN, MARGARET ANN, accountant; b. Oak Hill, W.Va., Nov. 15, 1959; d. Carl Edward and Ollie Myrtle (Hess) Ayersman; m. Jackie Ray Coleman, Jan. 6, 1979. BS in Acctg., W.Va. Inst. Tech., 1980. CPA, W.Va. Asst. auditor Raleigh County Nat. Bank, Beckley, W.Va., 1980-81; controller and treas. W.Va. Belt Sales and Repairs, Inc., Mount Hope, W.Va., 1981-90; treas., bd. dirs. Beckley Child Care Ctr., Inc., 1989-90; owner CPA firm Beckley, 1989—. Home: Rte 1 Box 44-A Oak Hill WV 25901 Office: One White Oak Trace Beckley WV 25801

COLEMAN, MARY CATHERINE, educator; b. Buffalo, N.Y., May 16, 1929; d. Leo Walter and Anne Grace (Klemach) C. BS in Foods/Nutrition, Mich. State U., 1951; MS in Nutrition, U. Iowa, 1953; PhD in Food Sci., Mich. State U., 1966. Therapeutic dietitian U. Mich. Med. Ctr., Ann Arbor, 1952-54; head therapeutic dietitian Mt. Sinai Hosp., Cleve., 1954-55; instr. food and nutrition Mich. State U., East Lansing, 1955-66, asst. prof. food and nutrition, 1966-68; assoc. prof. exptl. foods Pa. State U., University Park, 1968-74, prof. exptl. foods, 1974-89, prof. emerita, 1989—; cons. recipe testing div. Gen. Foods Corp., White Plains, N.Y., 1968; academic work in China to study Foodways, 1982. Author textbook for cultural foods courses, lab. manuals. active local food bank Friends of Palmer Art Mus. Recipient fellowship, Gen. Foods Corp., White Plains, 1963-65. Home: 339 Oakley Dr State College PA 16803 Office: Pa State U Coll Health/Human Devel University Park PA 16802

COLEMAN, NANCY PEES, environmental toxicologist; b. Yoder, Kans., Oct. 5, 1955; d. James Walter and Barbara Jeanne (Robbins) Pees; m. Ronald L. Coleman, Oct. 7, 1985. BS in Environ. Health, Old Dominion U., 1976; MPH in Environ. Health, U. Okla., 1978, PhD in Environ. Health, 1985. Registered sanitarian, Okla. Sanitarian USPHS, Albuquerque, 1977; environ. toxicologist Environ. Cons., Oklahoma City, 1978-85, Okla. State Dept. Health, Oklahoma City, 1985—. Contbr. articles to profl. publs. Mem. Am. Acad. Sanitarians (bd. dirs. 1989—, diplomate), AAAS, Am. Indsl. Hygiene Assn., Nat. Environ. Health Assn., Am. Conf. Govtl. Indsl. Hygienists.

COLEMAN, PATRICIA ANNE, engineering management firm executive, contractor; b. Washington, Sept. 21, 1943; d. Lee and Annie (Birch) Suey; m. Jimmy Wayne Coleman, Feb. 11, 1961; children: J. Wesley, Karen L., Kimberly M., Katherine R. Exec. sec. Value Engring. Lab., Alexandria, Va., 1973-75; dir. spl. projects Columbia Rsch. Corp., Arlington, Va., 1975-87; program dir., co-owner Global Assocs., Ltd., Arlington, Va., 1987—. Office: Global Assocs Ltd 2300 Clarendon Blvd Arlington VA 22201

COLEMAN, SHERI LYNN, television producer; b. Union City, Tenn., June 30, 1960; d. Kenneth Caleb and Carolyn (Lebo) C. BA in Communications, U. Tenn., Martin, 1985. Master control switcher Sta. WJWT-TV, Jackson, Tenn., 1985-86; producer, dir. Sta. WLJT-TV, Martin, 1986—. Videographer, editor: Special Olympics video, 1988, 89, United Way tng. tape, 1987. Named one of Outstanding Young Women Am., 1989; recipient Broadcasting award Tenn. Assn. Broadcasters, 1985, Sta. WENK-Radio, 1985. Mem. Aerho Broadcast Frat. (hon.). Democrat. Baptist. Home: 311 Oxford Apt 4 Martin TN 38237 Office: Sta WLJT-TV PO Box 966 Martin TN 38237

COLEMAN, WINIFRED ELLEN, management; b. Syracuse, N.Y., Oct. 3, 1932; d. Peter Andrew and Josephine (Fahey) C. BA, Lemoyne Coll., Syracuse, N.Y., 1954; MA, Marquette U., 1956. Dean of students Cazenovia (N.Y.) Coll., 1957-71; dean of students Trinity Coll., Washington, 1971-81; exec. dir. Nat. Coun. Catholic Women, Washington, 1981-85; pres. Cashel House, Syracuse, N.Y., 1985—; bd. trustees, Lemoyne Coll., Syracuse, 1980-86, Loretto Geriatric Ctr, Syracuse, 1987—, St. Vincent DePaul Soc., Syracuse; mem. Nat. Assn. Women Deans, Washington, 1957-81. Vice chmn. Syracuse Commn. for Women, Syracuse, 1986—; commr. Metro. Commn. for Aging, Syracuse, 1987—. Hon. Trinity Coll. Alumnae, Washington, 1978, Cazenovia (N.Y.) Coll. Alumnae, 1968, Naming of Winifred E. Coleman Student Union, Cazenovia Coll., 1961; recipient Chantal Award, Catholic Daughters of the Am. 1963. Bd. dirs. Cen. N.Y. Girl Scout Coun., Alpha Sigma Nu (nat. bd. dirs. 1980-82). Roman Catholic. Home: 103 S Lowell Ave Syracuse NY 13204 Office: Cashel House 224 Tompkins St Syracuse NY 13204

COLEMAN-JOHNSON, DEBRA LYNN, electrical engineer; b. Mobile, Ala., Apr. 7, 1966; d. Fred and Mattie Lois (Carter) C.; married, June 2, 1990. BSEE, Boston U., 1988. Test engr. Raytheon Corp., Andover, Mass., 1987-88; liaison design engr. Boeing Corp., Everett, Wash., 1988-89; software engr. Boeing Corp., Seattle, 1989—; lectr. Math., Engring., Sci. Achievement orgn., 1989—; v.p. Seattle City Tours Inc., 1990—. Tutor Mt. Zion Ethnic Sch., Seattle, 1988—. Mem. Nat. Soc. Black Engrs., Puget Sound Coun. Black Profl. Engrs. Home: PO Box 88571 Seattle WA 98138-2571 Office: Boeing Corp PO Box 3707 MS 4E 77 Seattle WA 98124

COLEMAN WOOD, KRISTA ANN, physical therapy educator; b. Decatur, Ill., July 28, 1956; d. Wayne Dudley and Shirley Margaret (Doner) Coleman; m. Earl Andrew Wood, Mar. 21, 1987. BS, Eastern Ill. U., Charleston, 1978; BS in Phys. Therapy, U. Ill., Peoria, 1980; MSc in Bioengring., U. Strathclyde, Glasgow, Scotland, 1986; MS in Phys. Therapy, U. Minn., Mpls., 1988. Lic. phys. therapist, Minn., Wis. Staff phys. therapist Bellin Meml. Hosp., Green Bay, Wis., 1980-82, Rehab. Specialists, Anoka, Minn., 1982-83, Fairview Hosp., Mpls., 1983-85; grad. rsch. and teaching asst. U. Minn., Mpls., 1984-85, 86-89, instr. phys. therapy curriculum, dept. phys. medicine, 1989—; cons. Recreational Opportunities for Physically Disabled, Green Bay, Wis., 1980-82; mem. survey team Green Bay Area Accessibility Guide, 1982. Mem. Robbinsdale (Minn.) Crime Prevention Assn., 1989. Rotary Found. grad. fellow, 1985-86, Charles and Constance Murcott Found. scholar Found. Phys. Therapy, 1988-89. Mem. Am. Phys. Therapy Assn., Am. Coll. Sports Medicine, Rehab. Engring. Soc. N.Am., Internat. Soc. Biomechanics, Soc. Orthopedic Medicine, Orthopedic Phys. Therapy Study Group, Phi Sigma. Methodist. Office: U Minn Minneapolis MN 55455

COLES, ANNA LOUISE BAILEY, nursing administrator, college dean; b. Kansas City, Kans., Jan. 16, 1925; d. Gordon Alonzo and Lillie Mai (Buchanan) Bailey; children—Margot, Michelle, Gina. Diploma, Freedmen's Hosp. Sch. Nursing, 1948; B.S. in Nursing, Avila Coll., Kansas City, Mo., 1958; M.S. in Nursing, Cath. U. Am., 1960, Ph.D. in Higher Edn., 1967. Instr. VA Hosp., Topeka, 1950-52; supr. VA Hosp., Kansas City, Mo., 1952-58; asst. dir. in-service edn. Freedmen's Hosp., Washington, 1960-61; adminstrv. asst. to dir. nursing Freedmen's Hosp., 1961-66, assoc. dir. nursing services, 1966-67, dir. nursing, 1967-69; dean Coll. Nursing, Howard U., Washington, 1968-86, dean emeritus, 1986—; cons. pvt. practice, Kansas City, Kans.; cons. Gen. Research Support Program, NIH, 1972-76, VA health care com. NRC-Nat. Acad. Scis., 1975-76, VA Central Office continuing edn. com., 1976—; pres. Nurses Examining Bd., 1967-68; mem. Inst. Medicine, Nat. Acad. Scis., 1974—; Mem. D.C. Health Planning Adv. Com., 1968-71, Tri-State Regional Planning Com. for Nursing Edn., 1969, Health Adv. Council, Nat. Urban Coalition, 1971-73. Contbr. articles to profl. jours. Bd. dirs. Iona Whipper Home for Unwed Mothers, 1970-72; bd. dirs. Nursing Edn. Opportunities, 1970-72; trustee Community Group Health Found., 1976-77, cons., 1977—; bd. regents State Univ. System Fla., 1977; adv. bd. Am. Assn. Med. Vols., 1970-72. Recipient Sustained Superior Performance award HEW, 1962; Meritorious Public Service award Govt. of D.C., 1968; Avila Coll. medal of honor, 1969. Mem. Nat. League Nursing (dir.), Am. Nurses Assn., Freedmen's Hosp. Nursing Alumni Assn., Am. Congress Rehab. Medicine, Am. Assn. Colls. of Nursing (sec. 1975-76), Sigma Theta Tau, Alpha Kappa Alpha. Home: 6841 Garfield Dr Kansas City KS 66102

COLES, JANE ELLEN, development company executive, career consultant; b. Lynn, Mass., Sept. 12, 1952; d. Felix Thomas and Joan Marie (Callahan) D'Agnese; m. Brian S. Coles Sept. 22, 1983 (div. 1986). BA in Liberal Arts, St. John's Coll., 1975. Mgr. prodn. control Erewhon, Inc., Cambridge, Mass., 1976-82; analyst computer systems Gen. Electric Corp., Lynn, 1982-87; sr. analyst fin. systems Polaroid Corp., Cambridge, 1987-88; mgr. tech. support Lotus Devel. Corp., Cambridge, 1988—. Office: Lotus Devel Corp 55 Cambridge Pkwy Cambridge MA 02141

COLES, LORRAINE MCCLELLAN, vehicle maintenance analyst; b. Chgo., Nov. 1, 1929; d. Wiley and Cornelia (Robinson) Packnett; m. Sam Taylor, Feb. 10, 1947 (div. 1962); children: Diana, Arvetta Lorraine, Samuel Joseph, Conella Elizabeth; m. Earskin G. Coles, Jan. 3, 1982. Student, Truman Coll., Chgo., 1980, Loop Coll., 1982-84, U. Okla. Postal Acad., Norman, 1981-83, City-Wide Coll., 1988. Asst. forelady Diana Sportswear, Chgo., 1951-52; sr. balancer Spiegel's, Inc., Chgo., 1959-60; intermittent claims examiner Ill. Dept. of Labor, 1963-72; with U.S. Postal Service, Chgo., 1960—; acting fleet mgr. Gary, Ind., 1981; supt. delivery and vehicle maintenance U.S. Postal Service, Chgo., 1986-89, acting mgr. delivery and retail programs, 1989—. Mem. Scheme Rev. Com., Chgo., 1986—. Mem. Nat. Assn. Female Execs., Nat. Geographic Soc., Black Bus. and Profl. Women Assn., League Women Voters, Presbyn. Women's Assn. (sec. 1986—). Home: 233 E Wacker Dr #1405 Chicago IL 60601

COLE-SCHIRALDI, MARILYN BUSH, occupational therapy educator; b. N.Y.C., Jan. 29, 1945; d. George Lyman and Theis Odette (Maurer) Bush; m. Carl E. Cole, Aug. 31, 1968 (div. June 1981); children: Charlot E. Cole, Bradley Eric Cole; m. Martin M. Schiraldi Sr., July 3, 1982. BA, U. Conn., 1966; grad. cert., U. Pa., 1969; MS, U. Bridgeport, 1982. Registered occupational therapist, Conn. Staff occupational therapy Ea. Pa. Psychiat. Inst., Phila., 1968-69; dir. occupational therapy Middlesex Meml. Hosp., Middletown, Conn., 1973-76; supervising occupational therapist Lawrence & Meml. Hosps. Day Treatment Ctr., New London, Conn., 1976-79; staff occupational therapist Newington Children's Hosp., Newington, Conn., 1980-82; asst. prof. occupational therapy Quinnipiac Coll., Hamden, Conn., 1982—; cons. psychiat. svcs. VA Med Ctr., West Haven, Conn., 1983—; cons. Fairfield Hills Hosp., Newtown, Conn., 1989—. Co-author: Structured Group Experiences, 1982, Group Process and Structure, 1988; Contbr. articles to profl. jours. Grantee Quinnipiac Coll, 1986. Mem. Am. Occupational Therapy Assn. (Communications award 1976, cert.), Conn. Occupational Therapy Assn. (sec. 1978, nominations chair 1982—), AAUW (cultural chair 1972, publicity chair 1973-76, edn. chair 1989—), Ctr. for Study Sensory Integrative Dysfunction (certification 1979). Republican. Episcopalian. Office: Quinnipiac Coll Occupational Therapy Dept Mount Carmel Ave Hamden CT 06518

COLEY, CAROL ANN, hospital administrator; b. St. Joseph, Mo., Oct. 25, 1947; d. Charles Edward and Elizabeth A. (Wilkerson) Roster; m. James Scott Coley, Aug. 17, 1974. AA, Mo. Western U., St. Joseph, 1967; BS, U. Mo., 1970; MS, Cen. Mo. U., Warrensburg, 1974. Clin. psychologist Fulton (Mo.) State Hosp., 1974-75, supr. psychology dept., 1975-84, asst. quality assurance adminstr., 1985-1986; quality assurance adminstr. PHP Healthcare SEH, Washington, clin. svcs. adminstr., 1989-90; pub. health svc. lt. comdr. refugee mental health program Nat. Inst. Mental Health, Rockville, Md., 1990—. Pres. Callaway Co. LWV, Fulton, 1981; bd. mem. Mo. Assn. of Social Welfare, Jefferson City, 1975; treas. Concerned Citizens for Callaway Co., Fulton, 1985, vol. Gephardt for Pres. Nat. Hdqrs., Washington, 1988. Recipient Work Study award State of Mo., Jefferson City, 1972. Democrat. Presbyterian. Office: Refugee Mental Health Program Parklawn Bldg Rockville MD

COLEY, CAROLINE RITA, producer; b. Syracuse, N.Y., Mar. 3, 1962; d. Daniel Edward and Jacqueline Rita (Langan) C. BA, SUNY, Oswego, 1984. Prodn. asst. Syracuse Newschannels, 1984-89; reporter, producer Sta. WTVH-TV, Syracuse, 1985-88; reporter WHEN Radio, Syracuse, 1986; dir. mktg. Syracuse Sports Corp., 1989; producer Sta. WCNY-TV, Syracuse, 1989—, producer, host CNY Close Up: Profile, 1990. CNY Close-Up winner, best pub. affairs series, N.Y. State Broadcasters Assn., 1990, Emmy award Acad. TV Arts and Scis., 1990. Mem. Women in Communications, Inc., Syracuse Press Club. Roman Catholic. Office: Sta WCNY-TV 506 Old Liverpool Rd PO Box 2400 Syracuse NY 13220-2400

COLEY, EVA MARIE, government agency official; b. Evanston, Ill., Sept. 21, 1943; d. Charles and Jimmie (Wells) McCain; m. John E. Coley, Aug. 18, 1964; children: Christopher, Joel. BA, Northeastern Ill. U., 1973, postgrad., 1974-79. Girls prog. dir. YWCA of Chgo., 1969-73; personnel clk. Northeastern Ill. U., Chgo., 1973-74; admissions office mgr. Northeastern Ill. U., 1974-81; with Dept. of Navy, Vallejo, Calif., 1982-83; purchasing agt. Dept. of Navy, 1984, dep. equal employment opportunity officer, 1984—. Council mem. Uptown Model Cities Planning Council, Chgo., 1971-73. Mem. Ladies of Le Club. Democrat. Baptist. Home: 214-12th St Vallejo CA 94590 Office: Naval Electronic System Eng Vallejo CA 94590

COLGATE, DORIS ELEANOR, retailer, sailing school administrator; b. Washington, May 12, 1941; d. Bernard Leonard and Frances Lillian (Goldstein) Horecker; m. Richard G. Buchanan, Sept. 6, 1959 (div. Aug. 1967); m. Stephen Colgate, Dec. 17, 1969. Student Antioch Coll., 1958-60, NYU, 1960-62. Rsch. supr. Geyer Moyer Ballard, N.Y.C., 1962-64; adminstrv. asst. Yachting Mag., N.Y.C., 1964-68; v.p. Offshore Sailing Sch. Ltd., Inc., N.Y.C., 1968-78, pres., Ft. Myers, Fla., 1978—; chief exec. officer On and Offshore, Inc., Ft. Myers, 1984—; v.p. Offshore Travel, Inc., City Island, 1978-88. Author: The Bareboat Gourmet, 1983; contbr. articles to profl. jours. Mem. Royal Ocean Racing Club (London chpt., chair nat. women's adv. bd. on sailing 1990—), Am. Women's Econ. Devel. Corp. (adv. bd. 1980-86), Doubles Club (N.Y.C.). Avocations: sailing, photography, writing, cooking. Home: 1555 San Carlos Bay Dr Sanibel FL 33957 Office: Offshore Sailing Sch Ltd Inc 16731 McGregor Blvd Fort Myers FL 33908

COLIN, GEORGIA TALMEY, interior designer; b. Boston; d. George Nathan and Rose (Broad) Talmey; m. Ralph Frederick Colin, June 2, 1931 (dec.); children—Ralph Frederick, Pamela Talmey Colin Harlech. Student Smith Coll., 1928, U. Genoble (France), 1927. Co-ptnr., Talmey Inc., Interior Designers, N.Y.C., 1928-54, pres., 1954-88. Sec. Young Peoples Concert Com. of N.Y. Philharmonic Soc., 1940-49; mem. vis. com. Smith Coll. Mus. Art, 1951-70, chmn., 1954-57; bd. counselors Smith Coll., 1954-57. Mem. Am. Inst. Interior Designers, Decorators Club, Nat. Soc. Interior Designers, Am. Soc. Interior Designers. Home and Office: 941 Park Ave New York NY 10028

COLLETT, JOAN, librarian; b. St. Louis; d. Robert and Mary (Hoolan) C.; m. John E. Dustin, Nov. 19, 1983. B.A. magna cum laude, Maryville Coll., 1947; M.A., Washington U., St. Louis, 1950; M.S. in L.S, U. Ill., Urbana, 1954. Regional cons. W.Va. Libr. Commn., Spencer, W.Va., 1954-56; instr. Rosary Coll., River Forest, Ill., 1956-57; head extension dept. Gary (Ind.) Pub. Libr., 1957-64; libr. Grailville Libr., 1965; regional libr. USIA, Latin Am., Africa, 1966-78; exec. dir. libr. St. Louis Pub. Libr., 1978-86; libr. dir. Great Neck (N.Y.) Libr., 1986-87, CUNY Grad. Ctr. Mina Rees Libr., N.Y.C., 1988, St. John's U. Libr., Jamaica, N.Y., 1988—. Mem. ALA (councilor 1986—). Office: St John's U Libr Jamaica NY 11439

COLLETTA, PATRICIA R., pediatrician; b. N.Y.C., Mar. 29, 1954; d. John Michael Sr. and Grace (Durso) C.; m. Steven G. Ross, Oct. 29, 1989. BA, Rivier Coll., 1976; MD, U. Autonoma de Guadalajara, Guadalajara, Mex., 1980; postgrad., N.Y. Med. Coll., Valhalla, 1982-83. Intern and resident pediatrics Long Island Coll. Hosp., Bklyn., 1983-86; pvt. attending Community Hosp. at Glen Cove (N.Y.), 1986—, with div. pediatric emergency rm., 1986-89; pediatrics attending ER Trauma Com. Protocol, East Meadow, N.Y., 1989—; chmn. child abuse com. Community Hosp. at Glen Cove, 1986—. Office: 8 Medical Plaza Glen Cove NY 11542

COLLETTE, CAROLYN PENNEY, English language educator; b. Boston, Aug. 2, 1945; d. George Kenneth and Mary (Takessian) Penney; m. David Raymond Collette, July 9, 1967; children—Matthew, Andrew. A.B., Mt. Holyoke Coll., 1967; M.A., U. Mass., 1969, Ph.D., 1971. With Mt. Holyoke Coll., South Hadley, Mass., 1970—, asst. prof., 1972-77, assoc. prof., 1977—; prof. 1986—, dir. freshman English, 1986-87. Contbr. articles to profl. jours. Woodrow Wilson fellow, 1967; NDEA fellow, 1969; NEH summer fellow, 1976. Mem. MLA, Medieval Acad. Am., William Morris Soc., Modern Humanities Research Assn., Phi Beta Kappa, Phi Kappa Phi. Episcopalian. Office: Mount Holyoke Coll Dept English South Hadley MA 01075

COLLETTE, FRANCES MADELYN, tax consultant, lawyer; b. Yonkers, N.Y., Aug. 5, 1947; d. Morris Aaron and Esther (Gang) Volbert; m. Roger Warren Collette, Dec. 25, 1971; children: Darren Roger, Bonnie Frances. B.Ed. summa cum laude, SUNY-Buffalo, 1969; J.D., cum laude, U. Miami, 1980. Bar: Fla. 1980. Employment counselor Fla. Bur. Employment Security, Miami, 1969-73; unemployment claims adjudicator Fla. Bur. Unemployment Claims, Miami, 1973-77; Fla. unemployment tax and personnel cons.; pres. Unemployment Svcs. Fla., Inc., Miami, 1977—; lectr. in field. Mem. Printing Industry S. Fla., Fla. Pest Control Assn., Better Bus. Bur. S. Fla. (1st v.p. 1980-81, bd. govs., 1079—, 2d vice chmn. 1981-82), Greater Miami C. of C. (trustee). Jewish. Office: Unemployment Services Fla Inc 7220 SW 39th Terr Miami FL 33155

COLLETTE, SUSAN HARTER, transportation engineer; b. Portsmouth, Va., Mar. 2, 1948; d. Richard Lee and Elizabeth Wilson (Sellers) Harter; m. Martin John Collette, June 1, 1980. BA, U. Calif., San Diego, 1970; MS, U. Calif., Berkeley, 1985. Sci. editor CRM, Del Mar, Calif., 1971-75; tech. editor Harcourt Brace Jovanovich, San Diego, 1977-81; mgr. documentation dept. White Data Systems, San Diego, 1981-83; airports analyst Peat, Marwick, Mitchell, San Mateo, Calif., 1985; sr. indsl. engr. Flying Tiger Line, L.A., 1986-89; transp. planner City of L.A., 1989—. Editor: Physical Geography Today, 1974, Biology Today, 1975, Fundamentals of Chemistry, 1979, Basic Statistics, 1979. Fund raiser Del Mar C. of C., 1971. Mem. Ops. Rsch. Soc. Am., Inst. Traffic Engrs., Assn. Airport Employees (co-chmn. budget com., mem. spl. events com.), Women's Transp. Seminar. Office: City of LA Dept Airports 1 World Way Los Angeles CA 90045

COLLETT-SUTTON, FAYE, school system administrator, consultant; b. Pineville, Ky., Mar. 8, 1944; d. Evelyn Howard; m. Robert T. Sutton, Jan. 2, 1988. BA, Berea (Ky.) Coll., 1965; MA, Ea. Ky. U., 1968. Sr. publicity specialist Gov. L.B. Nunn, Frankfort, Ky., 1968; tchr. Sierra Jr. High Sch., Bakersfield, Calif., 1969-73, Ballard/Westport High Sch., Louisville, 1973-74; admissions and fin. aid dir. Ky. State Dept. of Edn., Louisville, 1974-77; prof. U. Louisville, 1977-87; tng. and employment coord. Exxon Chem. Americas, Baton Rouge, 1988-89; adminstr. Exxon Chem. Americas, 1990—; program chairperson So. Coll. Placement Assn., 1985. Author: Supervisor's Manual, 1981. Speaker U. Louisville, 1977-90; coord. White House Office Pres.'s Debate, Louisville, 1984; cons., commr. candidate for U.S. Senate, Louisville, 1989-90; cons. in field; faculty sponsor So. Coll. Placement Assn., 1985. Named Tchr. of the Yr., Red Bird Mission, 1966; NSF scholar, 1974. Mem. Am. Soc. Tng. and Devel., Bus. and Profl. Women, Coun. for Advance and Support of Edn., Am. Soc. for Engring. Edn., Ky. Coll. Placement Assn. (pres. 1984-85), NAFE. Home: 2532 Ashbrook Ave Louisville KY 40220 Office: U Louisville JB Speed Sci Sch Louisville KY 40292

COLLIAS, ELSIE COLE, zoologist; b. Tiffin, Ohio, Mar. 24, 1920; d. Heath Kirk and Dora Della (Dunn) Cole; m. Nicholas Elias Collias, Dec. 21, 1948; 1 child, Karen Joyce. BA, Heidelberg Coll., Tiffin, Ohio, 1942; MS, U. Wis., 1944, PhD, 1948. Teaching asst. Heidelberg Coll., Tiffin, 1941-42, U. Wis., Madison, 1942-46; entomologist CDC, Savannah, Ga., 1946-47; rsch. asst. U. Wis. Dept. entomology, 1947-48; asst. prof. Heidelberg Coll., 1948-49; instr. zoology U. Wis., 1950; assoc. prof. biology Ill. Coll., Jacksonville, 1952-56; rsch. assoc. L.A. County Mus. Natural History, 1963—, UCLA, 1960—. Co-author: Nest Building and Bird Behavior, 1984, Evolution of Nest Building in the Weaverbirds, 1964; contbr. articles to profl. jours. Recipient World First Breeding award Am. Fedn. Agriculture, 1977, Elliott Coues award Am. Ornithologists Union, 1980, Jack Ward Film prize Animal Behavior Soc., 1989. Fellow Am. Ornithologists Union; mem. Animal Behavior Soc. (founder). Office: Univ of Calif Biology Dept Los Angeles CA 90024

COLLIER, BARBARA LEE, public relations executive; b. Tacoma, Sept. 20, 1959; d. Frank Gene and Alice Beverly (Fardis) C. B in Communications/Advt., Wash. State U., 1981. Spl. events coord. Nordstrom, Inc., Seattle, 1981-84; advt. coord. Nordstrom, Inc., San Mateo, Calif., 1984; admissions rep. The Art Inst. Seattle, 1984-86, asst. dir. admissions, 1987-89, dir. pub. rels., 1989—. Mem. Women in Communications Inc., Pub. Rels. Soc. Am., Bus. Mktg. Communications Assn. Presbyterian. Office: The Art Inst Seattle 2323 Elliot Ave Seattle WA 98121

COLLIER, CHARLOTTE MAE MEIER, publishing company executive; b. Wooster, Ohio, Sept. 24, 1947; d. Ferris Thorld and Sarah Edith (Johnson) Meier; m. John Edward Collier, Dec. 27, 1971; children: Elda Mae, John Icel. Student Case Western Res. U.; 1965-67; BA, U. Mass., 1969, MA, 1971, PhD, 1978. Project mgr. Chilton Research Services, Radnor, Pa., 1980-81; research mgr. Springhouse Corp., Pa., 1981-84, dir. research, 1984—; chair research com. Assn. Bus. Pubs., N.Y.C., 1985-86. Contbr. articles and papers to profl. lit. Mem. Montgomery County Task Force on Older Adults, Pa., 1971-78, sec., 1977; cons. on aging programs Southeastern Pa. Lutheran Synod, Phila., 1980. Univ. fellow U. Mass., 1969-72; Gerontol. Soc. fellow, 1979-80. Mem. Am. Mktg. Assn., Am. Hosp. Assn., Nat. Assn. Home Care, Phi Beta Kappa. Democrat. Lutheran. Avocation: bicycling. Office: Springhouse Corp 1111 Bethlehem Pike Spring House PA 19477

COLLIER, ELLEN CLODFELTER, foreign policy specialist; b. Lawrence, Kans., Oct. 19, 1927; d. Harve Malone and Martha June (Lambert) Clodfelter; m. Edwin Collier, May 25, 1951; children: Stephen Harve, Martha Lambert Collier Riva, Sarah Reiner Munsey, John Reiner, Catherine Fiorello. BA cum laude with high distinction, Ohio State U., 1949; MA, Am. U., 1951; grad., Nat. War Coll., 1978. Analyst U.S. fgn. policy fgn. affairs div. Congl. Rsch. Svc., Libr. of Congress, Washington, 1949-55, analyst U.S. fgn. policy, 1960-69, specialist, 1969—; head spl. project sect., 1972-75, head fgn. issues and nat. policy sect., 1975-76, head global issues sect., 1976-77; mem. staff subcom. on disarmament U.S. Senate Fgn. Rels. Com., 1955-59. Author govt. reports; editor: Congress and Fgn. Policy, 1979-88. Mem. Internat. Studies Assn., Am. Soc. Internat. Law, Exec. Women in Govt., Phi Beta Kappa, Pi Sigma Alpha, Potomac Pedalers Pedalers Club. Home: 9905 Holmhurst Rd Bethesda MD 20817 Office: Libr Congress Congl Rsch Svc Washington DC 20540

COLLIER, JEANNINE HENDERSON, chemist; b. Chgo., Oct. 1, 1956; d. Talley Henderson and Lillian (Lewis) Sledge. BS in Chemistry, Ill. Inst. Tech., 1978. Chemist DeSoto Inc., Mt. Prospect, Ill., 1979, chemist II, 1979, chemist I, 1982, sr. chemist, 1988—. Mem. Fed. Socs. for Coatings Tech.-Chgo. Soc., Kappa Phi Delta (Chgo. chpt. 1986—, reunion chmn., v.p.). Office: DeSoto Inc 1700 S Mt Prospect Rd #5030 Chicago IL 60017

COLLIER, JUNE, automotive parts company executive; m. Bobby Greenwood (div.); m. Ben Collier (div. 1985); m. Roy Mason, Jan. 1, 1987 (div.); 5 children. Grad. high sch., East Prairie, Mo. Receptionist, then bookkeeper Mid-South Elec. Fabricators (name changed to Nat. Industries Inc.), Miss., from 1961; pres., chief exec. officer Nat. Industries Inc., Montgomery, Ala., 1964—. Founder Citizens Against Fgn. Control of Am., 1982. Named to Working Woman mag. Hall of Fame, 1987. Office: Nat Industries Inc PO Box 3528 Montgomery AL 36109*

COLLIER, NORMA JEAN, public relations executive, advertising executive; b. Yankton, S.D.; d. Guy L. and Elizabeth J. (Donegan) C. Student George Washington U., L.A. City Coll., U. Md.-Seoul, Korea. Exec. sec. Universal Studios, Universal City, Calif., 1955-58, Leo Burnett Advt. Co., Hollywood, Calif., 1958-60; adminstrv. asst. Survey & Research Co., Seoul, 1960-63; exec. asst. John E. Horton Assocs., Washington, 1963-72; exec. asst. Doremus & Co., Washington, 1972-74; account exec. Doremus/West, L.A., 1974-79, v.p., 1979-85; v.p., acting mgr. Doremus/L.A. Advt., 1985-87; sr. v.p., gen. mgr. Doremus & Co. Adv. and Pub. Rels., 1987—. Recipient Letter of Appreciation, Republic of Korea, 1963. Mem. L.A. Advt. Club, Women in Communications (dir. chpt.), Town Hall. Republican. Roman Catholic. Club: Hollywood Studio (pres. 1957-58, house council). Home: 11147 Huston St N Hollywood CA 91601 Office: Doremus/Co Adv and Pub Rels 11755 Wilshire Blvd Los Angeles CA 90025

COLLIER-EVANS, DEMETRA FRANCES, veterans' benefits counselor; b. Nashville, Dec. 18, 1937; d. Oscar Collier and Earllee Elizabeth (Williams) Collier-Sheffield; m. George Perry Evans, Dec. 21, 1966; 1 child, Richard Edward. AA in Social Sci., Solano Community Coll., Suisun City, Calif., 1974; BA in Social Sci., Chapman Coll., Orange, Calif., 1981. Cert. tchr., Calif. Specialist placement, case responsible person employment devel. dept. City of San Diego, 1975-82; vocat. tchr. San Diego Community Coll., 1982-83; specialist placement N.J. Job Service, Camden, 1984-86, mgr. job bank, 1985; specialist placement Abilities Ctr., Westville, N.J., 1987-88; veteran's benifits counselor VA, Phila. 1988—; cons. Bumble Bee Canning Co., San Diego, 1982. Developer women's seminar Women's Opportunity Week, City of San Diego, 1982, network seminar Fed. Women's Week, City of Phila., 1986. Bd. dirs. Welfare Rights Orgn., San Diego, 1982; mem. Internat. YWCA. Served with USAF, 1956-59. Recipient Excellence cert. San Diego Employer Adv. Bd., 1981, Leadership cert. Nat. U., San Diego, 1981. Mem. Black Advs. State Service (charter, corr. sec. San Diego chpt. 1981-82), Nat. Assn. Female Execs., AAUW, NAACP (life, rec. sec. San Diego 1982), Chapman Coll. Alumni Assn., Alpha Gamma Sigma. Democrat. Avocation: calligraphy. Office: VA 5000 Wissahickon Ave Philadelphia PA 19144

COLLINGS, LORI JO, insurance agent; b. Gibson City, Ill., Mar. 25, 1959; d. Benjamin Jacob Jr. and Jeanne Ann (Herbert) C.; m. Larry Rance Williams, Jr., Oct. 18, 1980 (div. 1984). Grad. high sch., Buckley, Ill. Unit leader underwriting dept. Dun & Bradstreet Plan Svcs., Inc., Tampa, Fla., 1981-83; regional office mgr. Dun & Bradstreet Plan Svcs., Inc., Rosemont, Ill., 1984-85; health ins. underwriter United Fire Ins. Co., Des Plaines, Ill., 1985-88; asst. mgr. underwriting dept. Strategic Health Care, Des Plaines, 1988-90, sr. tech. cons., 1990—. Mem. Health Ins. Assn. Am., Chgo. Home Office Life Underwriters Assn. Republican. Methodist. Office: Strategic Health Care 2250 E Devon Ave Des Plaines IL 60018

COLLINS, ANITA MARGUERITE, research geneticist; b. Allentown, Pa., Nov. 8, 1947; d. Edmund III and Virginia (Hunsicker) C. BSc in Zoology, Pa. State U., 1969; MSc in Genetics, Ohio State U., 1972, PhD in Genetics, 1976. Instr. biology Mercyhurst Coll., Erie, Pa., 1975-76; rsch. geneticist Honey Bee Breeding Lab., Agrl. Rsch. Svc., USDA, Baton Rouge, 1976-88; rsch. leader Honey Bee Breeding Lab., Agrl. Rsch. Svc., USDA, Weslaco, Tex., 1988—. Co-author: Bee Genetics & Breeding, 1986; contbr. articles to profl. jours. Mem. Entomological Soc. Am. (pres. elect, sec. Sect. Cb 1990), Assn. for Women in Sci. (pres. Baton Rouge chpt. 1982), Am. Beekeeping Fedn. (rsch. com. 1990), Am. Genetics Assn., Animal Behavior Soc., Internat. Union for the Study Social Insects, Sigma Xi. Office: USDA ARS Honey Bee Rsch 2413 East Hwy 83 Weslaco TX 78596

COLLINS, ANN ELIZABETH AVERITT (MRS. GALEN FRANKLIN COLLINS), civic leader; b. Peru, Ind., July 28, 1934; d. Robert Chancellor and Cleo (Hite) Averitt; m. Galen Franklin Collins, Sept. 30, 1956; children: Galen Robert, Amelia Lynn, Scott Franklin, Daniel Chancellor. BA, Fla. Internat. U. Free-lance writer, 1972—. Co-editor: (soc. page) Elkhart (Ind.) Truth, 1955-56; musical compositions include Why Am I Old?, Little Boy, My Dear Son, Color, Willows, Soldier Boy, Is That Your Voice I Hear?. Mem. Elkhart Civic Theatre, 1957-60, Chenango County (N.Y.) Community Players, 1960-63; co-founder Dogwood Playhouse, Bristol, Va.-Tenn., 1964, bd. dirs., 1964-69; co-founder Collero Puppets, Bristol, 1967; coordinator, specialist sr. citizen ctr. recreation program div. parks and recreation City of Lynchburg, Va., 1983—; dir. Christian edn. United Ch. Christ, Miami, 1978-82. Home: 1431 Club Dr Lynchburg VA 24503

COLLINS, ARLENE R(YCOMBEL), virology educator, researcher; b. Buffalo, Jan. 2, 1940; d. Alex and Jean (Krzyzaniak) R.; m. Charles R. J. Collins, Oct. 11, 1965; children: Heather, Charles, James. BA cum laude, D'Youville Coll., 1961; MA, SUNY, Buffalo, 1964, PhD, 1967. Postdoctoral researcher Med. Coll. Wis., Milw., 1968-70; NIH postdoctoral fellow, researcher SUNY, Buffalo, 1967-68, asst. prof. virology, 1971-78, assoc. prof., 1978—; vis. researcher Scripps Clinic and Rsch. Found., La Jolla, Calif., 1980-81; peer rev. cons. Nat. Heart, Lung and Blood Inst., 1985—; mem. med.-sci. adv. bd. ARC, Buffalo, 1986—. Contbr. article to World Book Ency. Mem. Am. Soc. for Virology (charter), Am. Soc. for Microbiology (councillor 1987-89), Ernest Witebsky Ctr. for Immunology. Home: 24 Hendricks Blvd Amherst NY 14226 Office: SUNY Dept Microbiology Buffalo NY 14214

COLLINS, BARBARA GERAGHTY, administrator; b. Bklyn, June 3, 1948; d. John Joseph and Sarah Shirls (Williston) Geraghty; m. Richard Snyder Collins, Aug. 19, 1974; children: Emily Banks, Oliver Williston, Zachary Snyder. Student, U. De Caen, France, 1967-68; BA, Nasson Coll., 1970. Asst. to dep. mayor for intergovernmental affairs City of N.Y., Mayor's Office, 1972-75; asst. to dep. mayor for fin. City of N.Y., 1975-77;

dir. office of contract mgmt. City of N.Y., OMB, 1977; sec. to the fin. control bd. N.Y. State Fin. Control Bd., assoc. dir., 1987—. Mem. Jr. League, Greenwich, Conn., 1974--, Local PTA, Greenwich, 1987--. Office: NYS Fin Control Bd 270 Broadway New York NY 10007

COLLINS, BARBARA JO, college program director; b. Waverly, Iowa, Aug. 20, 1958; d. Norman Dale and Jeanette Esther (Kosbau) Fintel; m. William Gregory Collins, Dec. 26, 1987; children: Nora Marie, Jeanette Lee. BA, U. Minn., 1980. Resident mgr. Warm Heart Retirement Community, Blacksburg, Va., 1981-84; dir. devel. William Mitchell Coll. Law, St. Paul, 1984-87; dir. prospect rsch. St. Norbert Coll., DePere, Wis., 1988—. Active stewardship commn. Hope Luth. Ch., Mpls., 1986-87; vol. Calvary Luth. Ch., Green Bay, Wis., 1987—; bd. dirs. local YWCA, 1989—. Nat. Soc. Fund Raising Execs. scholar, Mpls., 1986. Mem. Coun. for Support and Advancement of Edn. Home: 4670 Creek Valley Ln Oneida WI 54155

COLLINS, BARBARA-ROSE, congresswoman; b. Detroit, Apr. 13, 1939; d. Lamar N. Sr. and Versa (Jones) R.; widowed; children: Cynthia Lynn, Christopher Loren. Student, Wayne State U. Commr. Human Rights Commn., Detroit, 1974-75; Mich. state rep., 1975-81; councilwoman City of Detroit, from 1982; elected to Congress from Mich. dist. 13, 1990; regional coord. Nat. Black Caucus of Local Elected Officials, 1984. Chmn. Detroit City Coun. Task Force on Teenage Violence, 1985. Recipient Dist. Community Svc. award Shrines of the Black Madonna Pan African Orthodox Christian Ch., 1981, Devoted Svc. award Metro Boy Scouts Am., 1984, Invaluable Svc. award Pershing High Sch., Detroit, 1985. Address: Offices of House Members care The Postmaster Washington DC 20515*

COLLINS, BETTYE FINE, real estate executive; b. Hanceville, Ala., Oct. 11, 1936; d. Joseph Lloyd and Bertha Evora (Thompson) Fine; m. Bill R. Collins, Sept. 5, 1954; children: David Brian, Kimberly Dee. Realtor assoc. Chambers Realty, Birmingham, Ala., 1977-79, Lowder Realty, Birmingham, 1979-81, Johnson, Rast & Hays, Birmingham, 1981-84; assoc. broker Re/Max Realty, Birmingham, 1984—. Mem. Birmingham City Council, 1981-87, Nat. League Cities FAIR Com., Washington, 1986-88; state del. White House Conf. on Libraries, Washington, 1980; bd. mem. Birmingham City Sch. System, 1974-81; bd. dirs. So. Mus. Flight, Birmingham, 1986-88, Community Affairs Com., Birmingham, 1987-88, Birmingham Festival of Arts Com., 1987-88, Operation New Birmingham, 1987-88. Mem. Birmingham Area Bd. Realtors Million Dollar Club (life), Ea. Area C. of C. (pres. 1989-90), Ala. Pub. Libr. Svc. (bd. dirs. 1988—). Republican. Baptist. Home: 504 Red Bud Dr Birmingham AL 35206 Office: Re/Max Realty East Inc 623 Red Lane Rd Birmingham AL 35215

COLLINS, CANDACE BROWN, photographer, poet; b. London, Ont., Can., Jan. 20, 1950; came to U.S., 1952; d. Garfield Norman and Regina Mary (Fejes) Brown; m. Paul Collins, Dec. 30, 1978; 1 child, Chauvon. BFA, U. Mich., 1971. Photog. model Detroit and N.Y.C., 1965-71; freelance still photographer and TV producer, 1971—; media coord. Grand Rapids (Mich.) Pub. Schs., 1974-80; photographer, writer Martin Luther King, Jr. Ctr. for Non-Violent Social Change, Atlanta, 1978-80; photographer Joseph P. Kennedy Found. Spl. Olympics, Washington, 1977-83. Photographer, designer, editor: Gerald R. Ford-A Man in Perspective, 1976; documentary photographer Grand Canyon, 1974, Wounded Knee, Pine Ridge and Rose Bud Reservations, 1976-78, Working Americans, 1979-83, Egypt, 1988, Israel, Uncommon Ground, 1986-89, Kenya, Triumph and Tribulation, 1990; editor, photographer: Great Beautiful Black Women, 1978; contbr. photographs, articles and poetry to various publs. Fundraiser, event co-chmn. Kendall Sch. Art, Grand Rapids, 1985; rep. coord. United Negro Coll. Fund, 1989-90. Mem. NAFE, Jr. League Grand Rapids. Office: 615 Kent Hills Rd NE Grand Rapids MI 49505

COLLINS, CARDISS, congresswoman; b. St. Louis, Sept. 24, 1931; m. George W. Collins (dec.); 1 child, Kevin. Ed., Northwestern U.; hon. degree, Winston-Salem State U., Spelman Coll. Barber Scotia Coll.; sec. Ill. Dept. Revenue, then acct., revenue auditor; mem. 93d-102nd Congresses from 7th Ill. Dist., 1973—, mem. Govt. Ops. com., Energy and Commerce com. oversight and investigation com., select com. on narcotics and substance abuse, subcom. health and fin.; chmn. govt. active and transp. subcom., former majority whip-at-large; past chmn. Congl. Black Caucus, sec.; former chmn. Mems. of Congress for Peace through Law. Mem. NAACP, The Chgo. Network, The Links. Mem. Nat. Coun. Negro Women, Chgo. Urban League, Black Women's Agenda, Alpha Gamma Pi, Alpha Kappa Alpha. Democrat. Baptist. Office: US Ho of Reps 2264 Rayburn Washington DC 20515

COLLINS, CATHERINE FRENCH, marketing executive; b. Charleston, W.Va., Sept. 9, 1955; d. John F. and S. Patricia (Moore) C. BS, Va. Tech., 1981. Dir. mem. govt. and pub. rels. Equicor Health Plan, Richmond, Va., 1984-88; mgr. mail order div. Best Products, Inc., Richmond, 1988—. Mem. NAFE, Dir. Mktg. Assn., Am. Mktg. Assn. Home: 506 Smoketree Pl Richmond VA 23236 Office: PO Box 25031 Richmond VA 23260

COLLINS, CHRISSIE WOOLCOCK, retired music teacher; b. Douglas, Great Britain, July 30, 1906; came to U.S., 1912; d. Thomas Herbert and Wilhelmina Jane (Milne) Woolcock; m. Marion Carter Collins, June 19, 1929 (dec. Aug. 1977); children: Michael Bruce, Margaret, Linda, Thomas Peter. BMusic, Coll. of Pacific, 1928. Cert. tchr., Calif. Supr. music in elem. schs. Turlock, Calif., 1928-29; choral dir. Turlock High Sch. Adult Edn., 1932-34. Bd. dirs. Community Concert Assn., Turlock, 1953—, pres., 1958-62; co-founder Medic Alert Found., 1956, bd. dirs., Turlock, 1960-88; bd. dirs., pres. AFS Intercultural Programs, Turlock, 1962-86; bd. dirs., pres. Muir Trail council Girl Scouts U.S., 1965-71, troop leader Turlock council, 1942-50. Named Woman of Achievement Soroptimist Club, Turlock, 1975, Citizen of Yr., C. of C. and City Council of Turlock, 1983; recipient Peggy Mensinger award Muir Trail council Girl Scouts U.S., 1989, other honors. Mem. Mu Phi Epsilon, Pi Kappa Lambda. Republican. Episcopalian. Home: 1030 Sierra Dr Turlock CA 95380

COLLINS, DEBORAH RUSSELL, security management; b. Sagamihara, Japan, May 21, 1958; came to U.S., 1959; d. Arthur Stanley and Joan Alma (Grady) Russell; m. Harold H. Collins, Nov. 3, 1984. BS in Bus. Adminstrn., Radford U., 1980; MS/Human Resource Mgmt., Chapman Coll., 1987. Mgr., security adminstrn. and tng., corp. security staff ESL, Sunnyvale, Calif., 1980—; owner, cons. Collins Cons. Group Mgmt. and Indsl. Security Cons., Monterey, Calif., 1988—; dir. Special Security Svcs., L.A. Pres. USS Enterprise Officers Wives Club, Alameda, Calif., 1988-89. Named to Outstanding Young Women of Am., 1983, 86. Mem. Nat. Classification Mgmt. Soc. (bd. dirs. 1984—, nat. pres. 1989-90), AAUW (v.p. 1986-87). Republican. Methodist. Office: ESL/TRW 495 Java Dr PO Box 3510 Sunnyvale CA 94088-3510

COLLINS, DIANA JOSEPHINE, psychologist; b. Potsdam, N.Y., Apr. 27, 1944; d. Philip Joseph and Janet Dorothy (Lynke) C.; grad. with high honors, SUNY; Psy.D., Mass. Sch. Profl. Psychology, 1981. Psychologist, N.H. Hosp., Concord, 1974-79; asst. dir. forensic unit, 1979-80; founder, dir. Victim/Witness Service County of Hillsborough, Manchester, N.H., 1980-84; pvt. practice, North Chelmsford, Mass.; adj. assoc. prof. U. N.H., 1974; adj. assoc. prof. Antioch Coll. of New Eng. Mem. AAUW, N.H. Psychol. Assn., Mass. Psychol. Assn., Eastern Psychol. Assn., Internat. Assn. Psychotherapists and Counselors, Internat. Platform Assn., Am. Assn. Female Execs., Roman Catholic. Home: RFD 2 Contoocook NH 03229 Office: 85 Tyngsboro Rd Box 2036 North Chelmsford MA 01863

COLLINS, DIANA MARIE, telecommunications manager; b. Roslyn, N.Y., Mar. 3, 1958; d. John Arthur and Patricia Agnes (Baumgartner) C.; m. Joseph J. Bilello, May 26, (div. 1988). Regents grad. high sch., Lindenhurst, N.Y. Area supr. Semoran Mgmt. Corp., Orlando, Fla., 1982-88; team mgr. Nat. Telephone Svc., Orlando, 1988—. Mem. Nat. Antivivi Section Soc., Nat. Assn. Female Execs. Office: Nat Telephone Svc Orlando FL 32806

COLLINS, DIANE ELIZABETH, director information systems; b. Des Moines, May 18, 1948; d. James Francis Collins and Pearl Maurine (Sevde) Price. MBA, U. Minn.; BS, Iowa State U., 1968-71. Cert. Systems Profl. Programmer First Nat. Bank, Chgo., 1974-75; analyst Ministers Life Ins. Co., Mpls., 1975-78; mgr. Price Waterhouse, Mpls., 1978-82, CENEX, St. Paul, 1982-85; dir. Northwest Airlines, St. Paul, 1988-89; pres. Artemis, Inc., Mpls., 1989—; dir. fin. mgmt. systems U. Minn., St. Paul, 1990—; mem. Twin Cities Computer Tng. Program for the Disabled, Mpls. 1986-88. Mem. Profl. Assn. for Systems Mgmt. (sec. 1984-85, treas. 1985-86, v.p. 1986-87, pres. 1987-88). Office: U Minn 1885 University Ave Ste 50 Saint Paul MN 55104

COLLINS, EARLEAN, state legislator; b. Rolling Fork, Miss.; m. John Grant, July 31, 1978; 1 child, Dwarrye. BA in Sociology, U. Ill., Chgo. Social service adminstr. State of Ill., Chgo., 1972-76, elected state senator, 1977—, asst. majority leader; bd. dirs. Nat. Caucus of Black Legislators, Westside Bus. Assn. of Chgo., Nat. Conf. State Legislators. Sponsor Unwed Mothers United, Chgo., 1977—, Collins Queenettes, Chgo., 1977—, Westside Progressive Women's Orgn., Chgo., 1980—. Numerous best legislator & recognition awards from profl. & civic groups. Mem. Intergovtl. Coop. Council, Operation PUSH, Ill. Job Tng. Council, NAACP, Conf. Women Legislators. Democrat. Baptist. Office: 5943 W Madison Chicago IL 60644*

COLLINS, EILEEN LOUISE, economist; b. Chillicothe, Ohio, Dec. 15, 1942; d. Theodore Milton and Louise Alma (Suess) C. BA (regional scholar), Bryn Mawr Coll., 1964; MA, U. Wis., 1967, PhD, 1975. Lectr. dept. econs. U. Waterloo, Ont., Can., 1971-73; asst. prof. dept. econs. Barnard Coll., N.Y.C., 1975-76; asst. prof. dept. econs. Fordham U., N.Y.C., 1976-78; economist NSF, Washington, 1978-86, sr. economist, 1986—. Editor: American Jobs and the Changing Industrial Base, 1984, The Economics of American Universities: Management, Operations, and Fiscal Environment, 1990; contbr. papers and reports in field. Recipient NSF Outstanding Performance award, 1979, 81, 83, 84; NIMH fellow, 1969-71; Nat. Inst. Public Affairs fellow, 1966-67. Mem. AAAS, Am. Econ. Assn., Soc. Govt. Economists, Nat. Assn. Bus. Economists, Washington Philos. Soc., Nat. Economists Club (v.p. seminars 1986). Office: NSF 1800 G St NW Room L-611 Washington DC 20550

COLLINS, GWENDOLYN BETH, educational administrator; b. Akron, Ohio, Dec. 28, 1943; d. Emmert Samuel and Lillice Elizabeth (Matthews) Shaffer; m. Charles F. Collins, Feb. 10, 1969 (div. 1976); 1 child, Holly Marie. BA, Case Western Res. U., 1971. Social worker Ohio Div. Pub. Welfare, Akron, Cleve., 1970-72; social services dir. Smithville-Western Care Ctr., Wooster, Ohio, 1975-76, social work cons., 1976; social worker Edwin Shaw Hosp., Akron, 1976-78; clin. treatment services coordinator The Blick Clinic for Devel. Disabilities, Tallmadge, Ohio, 1978; co-adminstr. The Sun Ctr. Inc., Akron, 1979-81; exec. dir. Canton Area Regional Health Edn. Network, 1981-88; project dir. Region VII Cancer Registry, Canton, Ohio, 1984-88; health program devel. cons., 1986—; mem. continuing med. edn. com. Aultman Hosp., 1983-88. Mem. adv. com. Camp Y-Noah, 1985-86. HHS grantee, Canton, 1986-88. Mem. Cancer Control Consortium Ohio (mem. cancer incidence mgmt. com. 1986-87). Republican. Home: 13013 89th Ave N Seminole FL 34646

COLLINS, HELEN JOHNSON, insurance company executive; b. 1911. Chmn. bd. Atlanta Life Ins. Co., Atlanta. Office: Atlanta Life Ins Co 100 Auburn Ave NE Atlanta GA 30303*

COLLINS, JACQUELINE WIGHT, educator; b. New Rochelle, N.Y., July 17, 1930; d. Alvin D. and Cora A. (Gunthorpe) Wight; m. LeRoy M. Collins, July 26, 1952; children: LeRoy Wight, Laurie Ann. MusB., Syracuse U., 1952; MS in Edn., Hoftra U., 1971. Cert. guidance counselor. Case worker Westchester County Dept. Social Svcs., White Plains, N.Y., 1952-54; tchr. Meml. Jr. High Sch., 1954-59, 68-70; edn. coord. Summer Sch. E.O.C. Corrdinated Program, Inwood, N.Y., 1967-68; guidance counselor Roosevelt Pub. Schs., Roosevelt, N.Y., 1970—; piano tchr., Nassau County, 1954-85. Treas., Am. Field Svc., N.Y.; pres. PTA, Inwood, 1967-68; v.p. Five Towns Child Care Ctr., Inwood, 1987-88, bd. dirs., 1986-90. Recipient Jenkins award N.Y. PTA. Mem. L.I. Counselors Assn., N.Y. Personnel Assn., L.I. Black Educators and Counselors Assn., Suburban League, Jack and Jill Am. Assocs., Alpha Kappa Alpha. Episcopalian.

COLLINS, JAVA L., secretary; b. Coffeyville, Kans., Sept. 28, 1960; d. Elmore Wiley Jr. and Norma Jean (Collins) Anderson; m. Milton S. Ramos, July 3, 1979 (div. Aug. 1981); 1 child, Milton S. Jr. Student, U. Md., Stuttgart, Fed. Republic Germany, 1979-80; cert. in civil/geol. drafting, Platt Coll., 1981-82; BBA, Golden State U., 1983, MA in Counseling and Therapy, 1986; cert. med. asst., Tulsa Area Vocat. Tech. Sch., 1978, cert. nursing asst., 1987. Various positions TAMA/TRI-CETA, 1974-78; draftsperson, mapping clk. Petroleum Info., 1982-84; sales assoc. Sanger Harris, 1984-85; bookkeeper, office mgr. Cen. Parking System, 1985-87; sec., acctg. clk. Riddle & Brown, P.C., Dallas, 1988—. Mem. Smithsonian Inst., 1988—. With U.S. Army, 1978-80. Named one of 2,000 Most Notable Am. Women, 1989, 90. Democrat. Baptist.

COLLINS, JILL HARRISON, corporate manager, small business owner; b. Boise, Idaho, Aug. 18, 1957; d. Robert Maurice Harrison and Elsie Louise (Otto) C. Student, Contra Costa Jr. Coll., 1975-77, Diablo Valley Jr. Coll., 1977-80; cert., L.B.'s Sch. Bartending, 1980. Mgr., trainer Foodmaker, Inc., Hayward, Calif., 1974-80; co-owner,operator T.J.'s Catering, Pleasant Hill, Calif., 1978-80; mgr. Am. Recreation Ctrs., Pinole, Calif., 1980-81; asst. ops. mgr. Dobb's Houses Inc., Oakland, Calif., 1982-82; fin. mgr. Richmond (Calif.) Kawasaki, 1983-85, Dexter Enterprises, San Rafael, Calif., 1985-87; owner, operator Jill Collins Ins. Agy., El Sobrante, Calif., 1984-88; corp. office mgr. Studio 96 Ltd., Las Vegas, Nev., 1989—; cons. Home Improvement Unltd., Union City, Calif., 1987; rep. Gt. Am. Motorcycle Show, San Francisco, 1978-80; speaker Foodmaker Inc., 1983-84; creator various TV, radio and newspaper advertisements, 1980-85. Co-designer software program Motorcycle Finance, Ins., 1984. Mem. Ams. for Legal Reform, U.S. Olympic Com., 1987—. Mem. Nat. Assn. for Female Execs., Nat. C. of C. for Women, Am. Mgmt. Assn., Women on Wheels; Modified Motorcycle Assn. (gold card, guest speaker 1984,86). Home: 1921 Elm Ave Las Vegas NV 89101 Office: Studio 96 Ltd 3896 S Swenson St Las Vegas NV 89119

COLLINS, JOAN HENRIETTA, actress; b. London, May 23, 1933; came to U.S., 1954; d. Joseph William and Elsa (Bessant) C.; m. Ronald S. Kass, Mar. 1972 (div.); 1 child, Katie; m. Anthony Newley (div.); children: Tara, Sacha; m. Peter Holm, 1985 (div.). Films include: I Believe in You, 1952, Girl in the Red Velvet Swing, Rally Round the Flag Boys, Island in the Sun, Seven Thieves, Road to Hong Kong, Sunburn, The Stud, Game for Vultures, The Bitch, The Big Sleep, The Good Die Young, 1954, Land of the Pharoahs, 1955, The Bravados, 1958, Esther and the King, 1960, Warning Shot, 1967, The Executioner, 1970, Tales from the Crypt, The Bawdy Adventures of Tom Jones, 1975; theater appearance in The Last of Mrs. Cheyney; TV films include: Drive Hard, Drive Fast, 1973, The Man Who Came to Dinner, Paper Dolls, 1982, The Wild Women of Chastity Gulch, 1982, The Cartier Affair, The Making of a Male Model, 1983, Her Life as a Man, 1984; miniseries: The Moneychangers, 1976, Sins, 1986, Monte Carlo, 1986; appeared in Faerie Tale Theater, Showtime TV, 1982; star TV series: Dynasty, 1981-89; author: Past Imperfect (autobiography), 1978, Katy, A Fight for Life, Joan Collins Beauty Book, novel Prime Time, 1988. Recipient Emmy nomination, Golden Glove award.

COLLINS, KATHLEEN ELIZABETH, pharmaceutical company official; b. Rock Island, Ill., Jan. 14, 1951; d. A. Phillip and Henrietta (Zeis) C.; m. David Mark Hasenmiller, June 23, 1973 (div. June 1975). Fgn. student, U. Grenoble, 1970; student, Barat Coll., 1968-70, U. Wis., 1970-71; BA in French and English, St. Ambrose Coll., Davenport, Iowa, 1972; postgrad. secondary edn., Augustana Coll., Rock Island, 1975, U. Iowa, 1979, 84. Sales clk. Scharff's Dept. Store, Bettendorf, Iowa, 1970-72; teller Moline (Ill.) Nat. Bank, 1972-73; mgr. Music Box, Rock Island, 1973-74, Disc Records, Moline, 1974-75; with quality assurance dept. U.S. Army, Savanna, Ill., 1975-76; sales rep. Burroughs Wellcome Co., Rsch. Triangle Park, N.C., 1976-81; vol. nutritionist Peace Corps, Niger, 1981-82; sales rep. Phil Collins Co., Rock Island, 1982-85; med. rep. Lederle Labs., Overland Park, Kans., 1985-88; sales rep. Summit (N.J.) Pharms. Co. div. Ciba-Geigy, 1988—. vol. Big Bros./Big Sisters, Moline, 1984-85, Pathway Hospice, Luth. Hosp., Moline, 1984-86, 88. Mem. Quad Cities Pharm. Assn. (treas. 1978, 86, v.p. 1979, sec. 1987, sec./treas. 1988), Jr. League Quad Cities. Roman Catholic. Clubs: Davenport, Outing (Davenport). Home: 3649 Cedarview Ct Bettendorf IA 52722 Office: Summit Pharms care Ciba Geigy 556 Morris Ave Summit NJ 07901

COLLINS, LENA VESTAL, school system administrator, director; b. Russellville, Ark., Dec. 31, 1933; d. Vester B. and Lena Lillian (Lasater) Lemley; m. E.T. Collins, Aug. 18, 1950; 1 child, Cheryl L. Beall. Student, UCLA, 1975, Ctr. for Early Edn., 1975, Berean Sch. of the Bible, 1982. Exec. sec. S.W. Hotels, Inc., Hot Springs, Ark., 1952-54, C.F. Braun & Co., Engring., Alhambra, Calif., 1954-55; pers. and ins. sec. Universal Rundle Corp., Redlands, Calif., 1955-56; data processer, sec. Real Gold Juice Co., Redlands, 1958-61; data processing mgr. Diamond A. Cattle Industry, Thermal, Calif., 1966-68; data processer Data Processing Ctr., Indio, Calif., 1968-69; acct. Nat. Lumber, National City, Calif., 1972; pre-sch. dir., adminstr. Tiny Farmer Preschool & Gardena Assembly Christian Elem., Gardena, Calif., 1972—; sci. chairperson Calif. State U., Dominguez, 1979—; cons. 1st Assembly of God Ch. of Gardena, 1972—. Mem. Christian Sch. Adminstrs., Assembly God Pvt. Schs., Ch. Music Dir., Ch. Organist Assn., Ladies Aux. (pres. Gardena chpt. 1980—). Republican. Address: Klassic Travel Svcs Gardena CA 92390

COLLINS, LISA (ANNA ELIZABETH COLLINS), accountant, fiduciary; b. Riedenburg, Bavaria, Germany, Dec. 3, 1920; came to U.S., 1950; d. Henrich Andreas and Anna Maria (Eichinger) Lauterbach; m. Paul Collins, Aug. 21, 1947 (div. 1985); children: Annelise, Andrew, Stephen. BS, Hindenburg U., 1943; postgrad., NYU, 1975, 77, 79. Exec. sec. Ernst Heinkel Fluqzeugwerke, Jenbach, Austria, 1943-44; asst. to pres. Industrie & Handelskammer, Nuremberg, Fed. Republic of Germany, 1944-45; product mgr. Bayer Wirtschaftsministerium Zweigstelle Nuremberg, 1945-47; office mgr. Nabors Ins. Agy., Waco, Tex., 1947-51; acct. Reader's Digest Assn., Inc., Chappaqua, N.Y., 1970-85; chief acct.- DeWitt and Lila Wallace Reader's Digest Fund, N.Y.C., 1985—; asst. treas. Wallace Funds, N.Y.C., 1971—; co-trustee preferred stock trusts DeWitt and Lila Wallace, N.Y.C., 1980—. Office: DeWitt Wallace Reader's Digest Fund 261 Madison Ave New York NY 10016

COLLINS, MARTHA LAYNE, college president, former governor; b. Shelby County, Ky., Dec. 7, 1936; d. Everett Larkin and Mary Lorena (Taylor) Hall; m. Bill Collins, July 3, 1959; children: Stephen Louis, Marla Ann. Student, Lindenwood Coll.; B.S., U. Ky., 1959. Former tchr. Fairdale High Sch., Louisville, Seneca High Sch., Louisville, Woodford County Jr. High Sch., Versailles; lt. gov. State of Ky., 1979-83, gov., 1983-87; exec. in residence U. Louisville Sch. of Bus., from 1988; pres. St. Catherine Coll., St. Catherine, Ky., 1990—; pres. Martha Layne Collins & Assocs., Lexington, 1988—; sec. Ky. Edn. and Humanities Cabinet, 1984-87; chmn. Nat. Conf. Lt. Govs., 1982-83, So. Growth Policies Bd., 1986-87, So. Regional Edn. Bd., 1986, Nat. Gov.'s Task Force on Drug ans Substance Abuse, 1987, So. Growth Policies Bd., 1986; bd. dirs. Eastman-Kodak Co., Inc., Rochester, N.Y., R.R. Donnelley & Sons, Chgo., Bank of Louisville. Mem. Woodford County (Ky.) Democratic Exec. Com.; mem. Dem. Nat. Com., 1972-76; chmn. Dem. Nat. Conv., San Francisco, 1984; former coordinator Women's Activities for State Dem. Hdqrs.; del. Dem. Nat. Conv., Miami, 1972, Midterm charter Conf., Kansas City, 1974; mem. credentials com. Dem. Nat. Com. Vice Presdl. Selection Process Commn., co-chair credentials com. Dem. Nat. Conv., Atlanta, 1988; Ky. chairwoman 51.3 Com. for Carter, 1976; mem. Ky. Dem. Central Exec. Com.; sec. Ky. Dem. Party; elected clk. Ct. of Appeals, 1975; clk. Supreme Ct. Ky., 1975; past tchr. Sunday sch.; mem. Ky. Commn. on Women; exec. dir. Ky. Friendship Force; mem. Dem. Nat. Com. Policy Commn. and Fairness Commn.; hon. chmn. bd. USO of Ky. Inc.; hon. co-chmn. Parents Against Child Exploitation; mem. adv. bd. Lexington Child Abuse Council; bd. govs. Dream Factory; organized first Woodford County Jr. Miss Pageant. Fellow Harvard U. Inst.; mem. So. Gov.'s Assn. (chmn. 1987), Woodford County Jaycee-ettes (past pres.), U. Ky. Alumni Assn., Women's Missionary Union (past pres.), Nat. Conf. Appellate Ct. Clks., Leukemia Soc. Am. (hon. chairperson), Young Writer's Contest Found. (hon. bd. advs.), Ky. Alliance for Arts Edn. (hon. bd. dirs.), Leadership Ky. (bd. dirs.) Japan Am. Soc. Ky., Internat. Women's Forum, Hope for Drug-Free Am. (statesmen com.), Psi Omega Dental Aux. (past pres.). Baptist. Clubs: Bus. and Profl, Women's, Order Eastern Star. Office: St Catharine Coll Pres's Office Saint Catherine KY 40061*

COLLINS, MARVA DELOISE NETTLES, educator; b. Monroeville, Ala., Aug. 31, 1936; d. Alex L. and Bessie Maye (Knight) Nettles; m. Clarence Collins, Sept. 2, 1960; children: Patrick, Eric, Cynthia. B.A., Clark Coll., 1957; B.A. (hon.), Howard U., 1980; D.H.L. (hon.), Wilberforce U., 1980, Chgo. State U., 1981; D.Hum. (hon.), Dartmouth Coll., 1981. Founder, tchr. Westside Prep. Sch., Chgo., 1975—. Subject of numerous publs. including Marva Collins' Way, 1982; subject of feature film Welcome to Success: The Marva Collins Story, 1981. Mem. Pres.'s Commn. on White House Fellowships, from 1981. Recipient numerous awards including: Reading Found. Am. award, 1979; Sojourner Truth Nat. award, 1980; Tchr. of Yr. award Phi Delta Kappa, 1980; Am. Public Service award Am. Inst. for Public Service, 1981; Endow a Dream award, 1980; Educator of Yr. award Chgo. Urban League, 1980; Jefferson Nat. award, 1981. Mem. Alpha Kappa Alpha. Baptist. Club: Executive. Office: Westside Prep Sch 4146 Chicago Ave Chicago IL 60641*

COLLINS, MARY, Canadian legislator; b. Vancouver, B.C., Can., Sept. 26, 1940; d. Fredrick Claude and Isabel Margaret (Copp) Wilkins; children: David, Robert, Sarah. Student, U. B.C., Queen's U., Kingston, Ont., Can. Mem. Can. Ho. of Commons, 1984—; Mem. fed. cabinet of Can.; assoc. minister of nat. def., 1989—. Active Can. House of Commons for Capilano-Howe Sound. Mem. Progressive Conservative Party. Home: 540 Besserer Ave, Ottawa, ON Canada K1N 6C7 Office: House of Commons, Parliament Bldgs, Ottawa, ON Canada K1A 0A6

COLLINS, MARY ALICE, psychiatric social worker, educator; b. Everett, Wash., Apr. 20, 1937; d. Harry Edward and Mary (Yates) Caton; B.A. in Sociology, Seattle Pacific Coll., 1959; M.S.W., U. Mich., 1966; Ph.D., Mich. State U., 1974; m. Gerald C. Brocker, Mar. 24, 1980. Diplomate Am. Bd. Social Workers, Am. Bd. Health Care Workers. Dir. teenage, adult and counseling depts. YWCA, Flint, Mich., 1959-64, 66-68; social worker Catholic Social Services, Flint, 1969-71, Ingham Med. Mental Health Center, Lansing, Mich., 1971-73; clin. social worker Genesee Psychiat. Center, Flint, 1974-82, Psychol. Evaluation and Treatment Ctr., East Lansing, Mich., 1982-84; pvt. practice, East Lansing, 1984—; instr. social work Lansing Community Coll. and Mich. State U., 1974, Mich. State U., 1987—; vis. prof. Hurley Med. Center, 1979-84; cons. Ingham County Dept. Social Services, 1971-73; instr. Mich. State U., 1987. Advisor human relations Youth League, Flint Council Chs., 1964-65; sec. Genesee County Young Democrats, 1960-61, pres. Round Lake Improvement Assn., 1984-87. Mem. Nat. Assn. Social Workers, Acad. Cert. Social Workers, Phi Kappa Phi, Alpha Kappa Sigma. Contbr. articles to profl. jours. Home: 5945 Round Lake Rd Laingsburg MI 48848 also: Lansing MI 48823

COLLINS, MARY BETH, association executive; b. Detroit, Jan. 3, 1925; d. James Edward and Mildred Ina (Barding) Hughes; B.A., Manhattanville Coll. Sacred Heart, 1947; M.A., Ariz. State U., 1970; m. Taber Loree Collins, Aug. 7, 1947; children—Louise Collins Lindsay, James, Suzanne, Mary Beth Collins Brenner, Mildred Collins Hittner, Marguerite Collins Zeller, Miriam Collins Huston, Frank, Jesse, Kathleen Collins Cheo, Martha DeVault. Community services coordinator Alcohol and Drug Abuse div. Ariz. Health Dept., Phoenix, 1967-68, acting dir., 1968-70; coordinator City of Phoenix Drug Control, 1970-73; exec. dir. Drug Action Coalition, Montgomery County, Md., 1973-74; exec. dir. Community Orgn. for Drug Abuse Control, 1974-76; adminstr. Office Substance Abuse Services, Mich. Dept. Pub. Health, Lansing, 1977-78; chmn. N.Y. State Commn. Prevention and Edn. of Alcohol and Substance Abuse, Albany, 1978-79; exec. dir. Internat. Assn. Prevention Programs, 1974—. Pres. Ariz. Family, Inc., 1970-71; bd. dirs. Community Orgn. for Drug Abuse Control, 1969-73; mem. adv. bd. Good Samaritan Hosp., Mental Health Services; mem. bd. Nat. Coordinating Council on Drug Edn., 1974-76. Mem. Internat. Council on Alcoholism and Addictions, Drugs, Alcohol and Women's Health Coalition (regional chmn.), Ariz. Alumnae of Sacred Heart (founding pres. 1963-64), Pi Lambda Theta. Home: PO Box 1825 Cave Creek AZ 85331 Office: PO Box 812 Carefree AZ 85377

COLLINS, MARY ELIZABETH, soil scientist, educator; b. Jersey City, N.J., July 19, 1953; d. Edward Peter and Mary Elizabeth (McCarthy) C.; m. Ronald John Kuehl, Feb. 10, 1990. AAS, SUNY, Cobleskill, 1973; BS, Cornell U., 1975; MS, Iowa State U., 1977, PhD, 1980. Lectr. Cornell U., Ithaca, N.Y., 1979; soil scientist USDA Soil Conservation Svc., Iowa, N.Y., 1977-80; rsch. asst. Iowa State U., Ames, 1975-77, rsch. assoc., 1977-81; asst. prof. U. Fla., Gainesville, 1981-86, assoc. prof., 1986—; speaker in field; vis. scientist Nat. Acad. Sci., People's Republic of China, 1988; vis. prof. Universidad de Extremadura, Spain, 1988-89. Contbr. chapters to several books and articles to numerous profl. jours. Recipient Appreciation Plaque Agronomy Soils Club, 1984. Mem. Am. Soc. Agronomy, Soil Sci. Soc. Am., Internat. Soc. Soil Sci., Soil and Crop Sci. Soc. Fla., Assn. So. Agrl. Scientists, Profl. Soil Classifiers, Sigma Xi (Appreciation plaque 1984), Gamma Sigma Delta. Office: U Fla Soil Sci Dept 2171 McCarty Hall Gainesville FL 32611

COLLINS, NANCY ELIZABETH, public relations executive; b. Caribou, Maine, Oct. 7, 1954; d. Donald Frederick and Patricia Roseleen (McGuigan) Collins. AB cum laude, Bowdoin Coll., Brunswick, Maine, 1976; postgrad., New Eng. Conservatory of Music, Boston, 1978-80. Editor Mass. Health Research Inst., Boston, 1979-81; pub. relations generalist The Children's Hosp., Boston, 1982-84; media relations coord. The Children's Hosp., 1984-87; dir. pub. affairs Dartmouth-Hitchcock Med. Ctr., Hanover, N.H., 1987-88; dir. pub. relations The Children's Hosp. of Phila., 1988—. Mem. Pub. Relations Soc. Am., Am. Assn. Med. Colls. (group on pub. affairs), Am. Soc. Hosp. Mktg. and Pub. Relations, Del. Valley Hosp. Pub. Relations and Mktg. Assn., Phila. Pub. Relations Assn. Office: Children's Hosp of Phila 34th St and Civic Ctr Blvd Philadelphia PA 19104

COLLINS, NATALIE A., small business owner, consultant; b. Vancouver, B.C., Can.; d. Walter P. and Jenny (Ferley) Koohtow. BS, McGill U., 1949. Internat. clearance officer Gillette Co., Boston; mgr. internat. ops., chemist program mgr. Chemist-Blood Bank, Can. Red Cross Blood Transfusion Svc.; rsch. asst. in neurophysiology Allen Meml. Inst., Montreal; owner, sole propr. SUMIDAR, North Easton, Mass.; cons. Damon Biotech, 1988-89. Co-author rsch. publs. in field. Bd. dirs. Children's Mus. in Easton, 1989—. Mem. NAFE, Internat. Congress Physiology, Am. Chem. Soc., Soc. Cosmetic Chemists (cert., nat. bd. dirs., U.S. rep. to exec. bd. Internat. Fedn.), New Eng. Women Bus. Owners, Kappa Alpha Theta (life). Office: SUMIDAR PO Box 275 Easton MA 02334

COLLINS, PAULINE, actress; b. Exmouth, Devon, Eng., Sept. 3, 1940; d. William Henry and Mary Honora (Callanan) C.; m. John Alderton; 3 children. Student, Cen. Sch. Speech and Drama. Made 1st appearence in A Gazelle in Park Lane, Theatre Royal, Windsor, Eng., 1962, 1st London appearance in Passion Flower Hotel, Prince of Wales, 1965; appeared in The Erpingham Camp, 1967, The Happy Apple, 1967, 70, Importance of Being Earnest, 1968, Come As Your Are, 1970, Judies, 1974, Engaged, 1976, Confusions, 1976, Rattle of a Simple Man, 1980, Romantic Comdey, 1983, Shirley Valentine, 1988, 89; TV actress, 1962—, shows include No Honestly; appearances include Upstairs Downstairs, Thomas and Sarah; also plays. Recipient Best Actress award Brit. Acad. Film and TV Arts, 1989, Tony award for best actress in Shirley Valentine, 1989. Office: care James Sharkey Assocs, 15 Golden Sq, London W1R 3AG, England*

COLLINS, SALLY MAE, academic administrator; b. Rome, Ga., Aug. 21, 1956; d. B. Ray and Willie Mae (Saturday) C. BS in Sociology and Psychology, Ga. So. U., 1978; MS in Higher Edn., Fla. State U., 1980. Dir. student devel. Fla. State U., Tallahassee, 1978-80; dir. student activities Rutgers U., New Brunswick, N.J., 1980-82; dean of students Westminster Choir Coll., Princeton, N.J., 1982-88; coord. student affairs Columbia U., N.Y.C., 1988—; chmn. dean of students div. Ind. Colls. N.J., Summit, 1986-88. Mem. Nat. Assn. Student Pers. Adminstrs., Nat. Assn. Women Deans, Adminstrs., & Counselors, Am. Assn. Higher Edn., Am. Sociol. Assn. Home: 438 W 116th St #55B New York NY 10027 Office: Columbia U 116th & Broadway New York NY 10027

COLLINS, SAXON LYNN, educator; b. Cheyenne, Wyo., Feb. 25, 1963; d. Harry Goodgame and Elizabeth Lorraine (Jones) C. BS in Psychology, Old Dominion U., 1985; postgrad. in spl. edn., U. Ala., Birmingham; 1985—. Tchr. Pioneer Playsch., Birmingham, 1979-81. active MADD, Atlanta chpt., 1989. Mem. Soc. for Autistic Adults and Children, Coun. for Children with Behavioral Disorders (legislator), Ala. Coun. for Exceptional Children, Omicron Delta Kappa, Phi Kappa Phi, Kappa Delta Pi, Alpha Chi, Psi Chi. Republican. Episcopalian. Home: 3044 Cahaba Cliff Dr Birmingham AL 35243

COLLINS, SHIRLEY JEAN, legislator; b. Hamilton, Ont., Can., Oct. 7, 1952; d. John and Dorothy (Quilliam) C.; m. George Culp (div.); children: Chad, Candace; m. Robert Rankin, July 30, 1988. Student, McMaster U., Hamilton, Queens U., Kingston. Spl. asst. Minister of Indian Affairs and No. Devel., Can., 1979-81; constituency asst. Sheila Copps MPP, Ont., 1981-82; regional councillor Region of Hamilton-Wentworth, Ont., 1982-87; alderman City of Hamilton(Ont.), 1982-87; mem. Provincial Parliament Province of Ont.-Riding of Wentworth East, 1987—; parliamentary asst. Minister of Labour and Women's Issues, Toronto, Ont., 1987-88; minister without portfolio responsible for disabled persons, 1989; chmn. regional health and social svcs. com., region Hamilton-Wentworth Dist. Mem. East Hamilton-Stoney Creek Health Assn. (founding co-chmn.), Hamilton East Provincial Liberal Assn. (candidate 1985), Wentworth East Provincial Liberal Assn. (candidate 1987). Office: Ont Parliament, Parliament Bldgs, Toronto, ON Canada M7A 1A2

COLLINS, SUSAN BALLANTYNE, health educator, consultant; b. Mineola, N.Y., Oct. 12, 1938; d. Howard Samuel and Bessie Eleanor (MacFarlane) Ballantyne; m. Richard J. Collins, July 12, 1962 (div. July 1978); children: Mark Richard, Matthew Howard. Diploma, Roosevelt Hosp. Sch. Nursing, N.Y.C., 1959; BS, Columbia U., 1963; MEd, U. Md., 1972. M Sci. Nursing, 1988; cert. pub. health nurse, Calif. Staff nurse Roosevelt Hosp., N.Y.C., 1959-62, War Meml. Hosp., Saulte Ste. Marie, Mich., 1962; faculty Joseph Lawrence Sch. Nursing, New London, Conn., 1964-66; dir., founder Prince William County Sch. Practical Nursing, Manassas, Va., 1969-72; guest lectr. learning disabilities U. Va., Reston, 1970-73; counselor, educator Woodbridge, Va., 1972-74; nurse counselor Golden Gate Regional Ctr., San Francisco, 1974-76; cons., Novato, Calif., 1976-77; dir. nurses Pacific Rehab. Ctr., Oakland, Calif., 1977-78; faculty continuing edn. dept. Sch. Nursing, U. Calif.-San Francisco, 1977-80, adult edn. dept. Coll. of Marin, Kentfield, Calif., 1981; instr., asst. dir. student services Samuel Merritt Hosp. Coll. Nursing, Oakland, 1978-81; adminstrv. nursing supr. Marin Gen. Hosp., San Rafael, Calif., 1980-84; faculty life long learning Dominican Coll., San Rafael, 1980-84; pres. Sue Collins & Assocs., Petaluma, Calif., 1985-90; adminstrv. coord., nurse educator Petaluma Valley Hosp., 1989—; family nurse practitioner Bullhead Med. Ctr., Bullhead City, AZ, 1989—; faculty extended edn. dept. Sonoma State U. Vestryperson, St. Francis Ch., Novato, 1977-80; commr., chair Commn. Status of Women, Sonoma County, Calif., 1979-83; mem. adv. bd. Dominican Coll. Mem. ANA (cert. family practitioner 1988) Calif. Nurses Assn. (bd. dirs.), Marin Aid Retarded Citizens, Redwood Empire Soc. Health Educators and Trainers, Am. Soc. Health Educators and Trainers, Redwood Empire Soc. Health Educators and Trainers, Calif. Health Resources, Inc. (pres. bd. dirs.), Bus. and Profl. Womnes Assn. (v.p. Colo. River chpt. 1989-90), Sigma Theta Tau. Republican. Episcopalian. Avocations: gardening, photography, herbs. Home: HCR Box 6265 Bullhead City AZ 86430 Office: Bullhead Med Ctr Bullhead City AZ 86442

COLLINS, SUZANNE MALLORY, fashion accesories company executive; b. Memphis, Oct. 4, 1956; d. Edwin Paxson and Susan (Hayward) C. AB, Sweet Briar Coll., 1978. Psychometrist dept. neuropsychology U. Va., Charlottesville, 1978-80; pres., chief exec officer, designer, sales mgr. Briar Patch Designs, Inc., Greenville, S.C., 1980—. Mem. Greenville Jr. League, 1984—; vol. Rape Crisis Coun., Greenville, 1987—, bd. dirs. 1988—; vol. Women in Crisis Shelter, Greenville, 1988—. Mem. Greenville C. of C., Sweet Briar Coll. Alumni Club (Greenville, pres. 1985—). Office: Briar Patch Designs Inc 2114-B Augusta Rd Greenville SC 29605

COLLINS, WINIFRED QUICK (MRS. HOWARD LYMAN COLLINS), organizational executive, retired navy officer; b. Great Falls, Mont.; m. Howard Lyman Collins (dec.). B.S., U. So. Calif., 1935; grad. Harvard-Radcliffe Program in Bus. Adminstrn., 1938; M.A., Stanford U., 1952. Commd. ensign U.S. Navy, 1942, advanced through grades to capt. 1957; personnel dir. Midshipman's Sch., Smith Coll., 1942-43; asst. chief Naval Personnel for Women, 1957-62; ret.; nat. v.p. U.S. Navy League, 1964-70, nat. dir. and chmn. nat. awards com., 1964—; nat. dir. Ret. Officers Assn.; former cons. HEW; former trustee Helping Hand Found.; former mem. Sec. Navy's Bd. Advs. and Tng. of Naval Personnel; dir. CPC Internat., Inc., 1977-84, chmn. employee investment com., mem. audit, exec. compensation and exec. coms.; bd. dirs. Interseas Fast Craft Co., Leadership Found.; trustee U.S. Naval Acad. Found., 1977—. First v.p. Republican Women of D.C. Decorated Legion of Merit, Bronze Star; recipient Navy's Disting. Civilian Pub. Service award, 1971, Disting. Service award Navy League of U.S., 1973; named to Hall of Fame Nat. Navy League, 1990. Mem. Harvard Grad. Bus. Sch. Washington Club (past dir.), Army Navy Town Club, Army Navy Country Club, Chevy Chase Club. Home: Harbour Sq 540 N St SW Washington DC 20024

COLLINS-EILAND, KAREN WISLER, psychologist; b. Oklahoma City, Mar. 25, 1949; d. Charles C. and Frances Joan (Higgins) Wisler; BA with honors, Stephen F. Austin State U., Nacogdoches, Tex., 1973; MA, Tex. Christian U., 1978, PhD, 1979; m. David C. Eiland. Asst. prof. Dickinson (N.D.) State Coll., 1979-80; rsch. asst. prof. psychiatry U. Tex. Med. Br., Galveston, 1980-81, asst. prof. dept. ob-gyn and sr. asso. Office Ednl. Devel., 1981-85; dir. acad. counseling, 1986-89; asst. prof. dept. psychiatry and behavirol scis., 1986—; cons. Med. Educators and Galveston Ind. Sch. Dist., 1981—. Contbr. articles to prolf. jours. Mem. Am. Psychol. Assn., Am. Ednl. Research Assn., Sigma Xi, Psi Chi, Alpha Kappa Delta, Alpha Chi, Delta Zeta. Methodist.

COLLISON, DIANE WITTROCK, communications executive; b. Carroll, Iowa, May 11, 1939; d. Michael August and Alberta Ernestine (Marcucci) Wittrock; m. David Michael Collison, Nov. 28, 1959 (div.); children: Christopher, Lucia, Charles, Nicholas, Paul, Michael. BA, Iowa State U., 1979, postgrad., 1979-80. Dir. communications and orgn. Rep. State Cen. Com, state, gubernatorial, nat., presdl. polit. campaigns Rep. Party Iowa, 1979-85; arts mgmt. Denver Symphony Orch., 1985-87, Boulder Philharm. Orch., Boulder, Colo., 1985-87; bus. communications specialist US West Communications, Denver, 1987-89; dir. pub. rels. Internat. Guide Acad., Denver, 1989—; coord. career edn. program Regis Coll., Denver; presenter in field; pub. speaker, 1983—. Author numerous sales and motivation seminars. Pres. Am. Field Service Foreign Exchange Program, Iowa, 1977; regional rep. Ames Internat. Orch. Fest. Assn., 1977-78; mem. Colo. steering com. Dole Presdl. Campaign, 1987-88; mem. Rep. Nat. Com., 1980—; bd. dirs. Am. Lung Assn. of Iowa, 1978-79, 89—, Centennial Philharmonic Orch., Denver. Recipient Music award Arion Found. Mem. Internat. Platform Assn., Journalism Soc. Roman Catholic. Office: Internat Guide Acad 3003 Arapahoe St Ste 101 Denver CO 80205

COLLISTER, DONNA MARIE, communications specialist; b. Newark, Mar. 9, 1959; d. Donald Alfred Berg and Dolores May (Piceno) Woolley; m. Robertwayne Charles Collister, Aug. 27, 1983; 1 child, Bobbywayne Charles. Student, U. Ariz., 1977-79; cert., Pima Community Coll., Tucson, 1980, Pima Community Coll., Tucson, 1981; Assoc. of Gen. Studies, Pima Community Coll., Tucson, 1990. Basic emergency med. technician S. Tucson Fire Dept., 1980-82, intermediate emergency med. technician, 1982-83; basic emergency med. technician Ariz. Med. Transport, Tucson, 1980-82; intermediate emergency med. technician Ariz. Med. Transport, 1982-84; emergency telecommunications operator Rural/Metro Corp., Tucson, 1984-85, emergency communications shift supr., 1985—; instr. CPR Am. Heart Assn., Tucson; instr. emergency med. dispatching Rural/Metro Corp., Tucson; mem. Pima County Critical Incident Debriefing Team. Mem. Associated Pub. Safety Communications Officers (Ariz. chpt.). Home: 1111 E Limberlost #28 Tucson AZ 85719 Office: Rural/Metro Corp 4151 W El Camino Del Cerro Tucson AZ 85745

COLLURA, NATALIE, psychologist; b. Easton, Pa., May 23, 1962; d. Joseph Collura and Georgia Pulizzano; m. Harold Plasterer, Apr. 7, 1990. BA, Gettysburg Coll., 1984; MA, West Chester (Pa.) U., 1987. Psychol. intern West Chester (Pa.) U. Counseling Ctr., 1986-87; psychiat. technician Mahlenberg Hosp. Ctr., Bethlehem, Pa., 1987-89; casework specialist Assn. of the Blind and Visually Impaired, Allentown, Pa., 1987-88; drug and alcohol treatment specialist Graterford (Pa.) Prison, 1988-89; rehab. psychologist Mechanicsburg (Pa.) Rehab. Hosp., Harrisburg, Pa., 1990—. Contbr. poetry to jours. Mem. Am. Psychol. Assn. (assoc.), Pa. Psychol. Assn.

COLMAN, WENDY, psychoanalytic psychotherapist; b. Flushing, N.Y., July 6, 1950; d. Leo M. and Ray (Fine) C. BS, Tufts U., 1972; MA, NYU, 1977, PhD, 1984; postgrad., Phila. Sch. for Psychoanalysis, 1988—. Occupational therapist Extended Family Ctr., San Francisco, 1973-74; cons. child abuse San Francisco, 1974-75; sr. occupational therapist Roosevelt Hosp., N.Y.C., 1975-77; adj. instr. occupational therapy dept. NYU, N.Y.C., 1977-80; asst. prof. occupational therapy dept. Boston U., 1980-83; dir. grad. edn. occupational therapy, dept. assoc. prof. Temple U., Phila., 1984-87; cons. curriculum design Kean Coll. N.J., Union, 1985-88; cons. spl. projects, vice provost for rsch.- grad. studies Temple U., Phila., 1987-88; evaluation rsch. coord. Nat. Inst. Adolescent Pregnancy, Phila., 1986-90; pvt. practice psychotherapy, 1989—. Contbr. articles to profl. jours. and texts. Mem. Am. Occupational Therapy Assn., World Fedn. Occupational Therapy, Pa. Occupational Therapy Assn., Am. Assn. for Counseling and Devel., Nat. Assn. for Advancement Psychoanalysis. Office: The Benson East 100 Old York Rd Ste 1208 Jenkintown PA 19046

COLMUS, MARY ANNE, sales executive; b. Carson City, Mich., Dec. 1, 1946; d. Henry and Katheryn (Spohn) Brink; m. Jacob Lorenzo Colmus Jr., July 16, 1966 (div. Jan. 1970); 1 child, Martin Andrew. Grad., McBain Rural Agr. Sch., 1964. Seamstress Fashion Industries, Cadillac, Mich., 1965-66; proofreader R.L. Polk, Traverse City, Mich., 1966-68; clk., sec. H.L. Green, Cadillac, 1969-70, asst. mgr., 1970-72; receptionist Dr. Mosberg & Moriarty, Cadillac, 1973-76; direct sales accessory specialist Home Interiors & Gifts Inc., Dallas, 1977—, unit mgr., 1981—. Home and Office: 3773 W M-55 Cadillac MI 49601

COLODNE, ANGELA, clothing manufacturing company executive; b. Guayaquil, Ecuador, Feb. 12, 1956; came to U.S., 1965; d. Victor Hugo and Yolanda (Ramos) Espinoza; m. Mark Ralph Colodne, Feb. 6, 1975; children: Jeyme, Chiara. BA in Polit. Sci., Fordham U., 1983. Pres. Magikal Childwear, Inc., N.Y.C., 1984—.

COLÔN, LYDIA M., investment banker, import/export broker; b. Santurce, P.R., June 2, 1947; d. Angel Luis and Lydia Maria (Pagán) Colón. BA magna cum laude, Marymount Manhattan Coll., 1978. Admissions office supr. NYU, N.Y.C., 1965-70; asst. v.p. Chem. Bank, N.Y.C., 1971-85; sr. assoc. First Washington Assocs., Arlington, Va., 1985-87; owner LMC Internat., N.Y.C., 1987—. Co-author: Innovations in Industrial Competitiveness at the State Level, 1985, Guide to State Capital Formation, 1984; contbr. articles to profl. jours. Vice chmn. N.Y. State Adv. Council for Minority and Women-Owned Bus. Enterprise, 1984-87; mem. ARC Minorities Initiative Task Force, 1985-87, N.Y. Bus. Devel. Corp. Gov.'s Task Force N.Y., 1985; trustee Community Service Soc., N.Y., 1985-87; mem. Gov.'s Task Force on Work and the Family, 1988-89; co-founder Nat. P.R. Women's Caucus, Inc. Recipient Woman of the 80's award U.S. Dept. of Housing and Urban Devel., 1985, Polit. Sci. Gold medal Marymount Manhattan Coll., N.Y., 1978, Achievement/Leadership award Pres. of City Coun., 1989. Mem. U.S. Hispanic Women's C. of C. (bd. dirs., sec. 1989—), Nat. Assn. Bank Women, Nat. Conf. Puerto Rican Women, 100 Hispanic Women. Office: LMC Internat 342 Madison Ave Ste 1223 New York NY 10173

COLON, PHYLLIS JANET, school system administrator; b. Taylor, Tex., Sept. 1, 1938; d. Jack and Lydia Windmeyer; m. Henry J. Colon, Feb. 12, 1977; children: Walter N. Barnes III, Bradley H. Barnes, Mark A. Barnes. AA in Pub. Adminstrn., Del Mar Coll.; postgrad. in Acctg., Durham Jr. Coll.; BAAS in Pub. Adminstrn., Tex. A&I U., 1987; postgrad., Art Inst. Dayton. Registered profl. appraiser, Tex., assessor, Tex.; cert. tax adminstr., sch. tax adminstr., Tex.; lec. real estate broker, Tex. Mgr. info. Med. Arts Lab., Dayton, Ohio, 1970-73; appraiser Nueces County Appraisal Dist., Corpus Christi, 1973-82; assessor, collector Flour Bluff Ind. Sch. Dist., Corpus Christi, 1982—. Mem. Southside Kiwanis, 1987—, treas., 1989-90, pres. 1990—; C. of C., 1985—; Art Mus. South Tex., 1974—. Recipient achievement award State of Tex., Hero award City of Corpus Christi. Mem. NAFE, AAUW (bd. dirs.), Tex. Assn. Assessing Officers, Tex. Sch. Assessor Assn., Inst. Tax Adminstrs., Inst. Cert. Tax Adminstrs., Am. Soc. Notaries, Corpus Christi Libr. Advance Planning Bd., DelMar Coll. Ad Hoc Planning Com. (chmn. 1989—), Bd. Profl. Tax Examiners. Republican. Lutheran. Home: 1301 Aswan Dr Corpus Christi TX 78412 Office: PO Box 181029 Corpus Christi TX 78480

COLONEL, SHERI LYNN, advertising agency executive; b. Bklyn., Sept. 3, 1955; d. Irwin Murray Glaser and Rosalind (Mendelson) Krasik; m. Peter T. Colonel, Sept. 20, 1981. B.A. in Psychology, SUNY-Cortland, 1977. Account exec. Ted Bates Co., N.Y.C., 1978-80; account exec. SSC&B Advt. (name now LINTAS), Inc., N.Y.C., 1980-82, v.p. account supr., 1982-83, v.p. mgmt. supr., 1983-84, sr. v.p. mgmt. supr., 1984-88, exec. v.p., 1988—, bd. dirs. 1990—. Mem. Advt. Women N.Y., NAFE. Home: 280 Park Ave S New York NY 10010 Office: Lintas 1 Dag Hammarskjold Pla New York NY 10017

COLONY-COKELY, PAMELA CAMERON, medical researcher; b. Boston, Apr. 18, 1947; d. Donald Gifford Colony and Priscilla (Adams) Pratley; m. E. Paul Cokely Jr., Apr. 26, 1986. BA, Wellesley (Mass.) Coll., 1969; PhD, Boston U., 1976. Research asst. Peter Bent Brigham Hosp., Boston, 1973-75, assoc. staff in medicine, 1977-79; research asst. Harvard Med. Sch., Boston, 1975-77, sr. fellow, instr., 1979-81; asst. prof. anatomy and medicine Pa. State Coll. Medicine, Hershey, Pa., 1981-88; adj. assoc. prof., pre-health advisor Franklin and Marshall Coll., Lancaster, Pa., 1988—; ind. assessor Nat. Health & Med. Research Council, Australia, 1985—; ad-hoc reviewer NIH, Nat. Cancer Inst., Bethesda, Md., 1986. Contbr. articles to profl. jours. Fellow Nat. Fedn. Ileitis & Colitis, 1979-81; grantee Fed. Republic Germany, 1978, Cancer Research Ctr., 1982-83, NIH, 1982—. Mem. AAAS, Am. Soc. Cell Biology, N.Y. Acad. Sci., Am. Gastroent. Assn., Nat. Assn. Advisors Health Profls. Home: Shamrock Farm RD 2 Box 1760 Lebanon PA 17042 Office: Franklin and Marshall Coll Dept Biology PO Box 3003 Lancaster PA 17604

COLOT, ROSEANN MARIE, company executive; b. Point Pleasant, N.J., Oct. 6, 1957; d. Robert Richard and Joann Marie (Redeker) C. BSBA, Boston U., 1980, MBA, 1987. Internat. supr. Arthur D. Little, Inc., Cambridge, Mass., 1980-82, cost acctg. mgr., 1982-84, sr. fin. analyst, 1984-87, mgr. treasury adminstrn. and benefits, 1987—; sec. Back Bay Investors, Boston, 1989—; cons. Colot Assocs., Boston, 1987—. Mem. schs. com. Boston U. Alumni, 1986—. Recipient Scarlet Key Alumni award Boston U. Scarlet Key Alumni Assn., 1980. Mem. Neighbor Assn. Back Bay, Boston, 1986—. Republican. Home: 153 Beacon St Apt 7 Boston MA 02116 Office: Arthur D Little Acorn Park Cambridge MA 02140

COLSON, ARDANNA ORAN, entertainment company executive and accountant; b. Beaumont, Tex., Mar. 31, 1953; d. Sippy Wallace and Mildred (Griffin) Long; 1 child, Miguel Joseph Colson Jr. Student, Marymount Palos Verdes Coll., 1970-71, Calif. State U., Long Beach, 1971, 73-75, Calif. State U., Los Angeles, 1986; BS in Bus. Adminstrn., U. Redlands, 1988. Asst. bookkeeper Valet Parking Service, Inc., Los Angeles, 1976-80; supr. bus. mgmt. Jamner, Pariser & Meschures, Los Angeles, 1980-87, Stevland Morris, Burbank, Calif., 1987—. Mem. Nat. Notary Assn., Nat. Assn. for Female Execs. Democrat. Office: Stevland Morris 4616 Magnola Blvd Burbank CA 91505

COLSON, CHERRILL WILCOX, nurse; b. Galesburg, Ill., Sept. 14, 1941; d. Thomas Glade and Minnie (Nelson) Wilcox; m. C. David Colson, Sept. 11, 1964; children: Christopher, Katherine. BSN, U. Mich., 1963; MA, NYU, 1974; postgrad., Columbia U., 1982—. RN, N.Y., Mich., Fla. Stewardess TWA, N.Y.C., 1963-64; charge nurse Sparrow Hosp., Lansing, Mich., 1964-65; child psychiat. nurse Langley Porter Neuropsychiat. Inst., San Francisco, 1965-66; charge nurse Meml. Hosp., Sarasota, Fla., 1966-69; psychiat. nurse Maimonides Community Mental Health, Bklyn., 1969-74; staff devel. specialist Westchester Med. Ctr., Valhalla, N.Y., 1974-81; assoc. in nursing Columbia U. Sch. Nursing, N.Y.C., 1981-88; asst. prof. Lehman Coll. Sch. Nursing, Bronx, N.Y., 1988-89; home care mental health nurse United Hosp., Port Chester, N.Y., 1989—; reviewer psychiat. nursing textbooks Mosby Co.; coord. nurse continuing edn. workshops. Leader Cub Scouts Am., Harrison, N.Y., 1975-77, Girl Scouts U.S.A., Port Chester, 1984—; chmn. Merriewold Youth Com., Forestburgh, N.Y., 1983-87. Upjohn Co. scholar, 1960; NIMH grantee, 1972-74. Fellow Am. Orthopsychiat. Assn.; mem. Am. Nurses Assn. (cert. clin. specialist child and adolescent psychiat. nursing), Advs. for Child Psychiat. Nursing (nat. chmn. 1981-84), Columbia Clin. Specialists, Sigma Theta Tau. Presbyterian. Home: 8 Berkeley Dr Rye Brook NY 10573

COLSON, ELIZABETH FLORENCE, anthropologist; b. Hewitt, Minn., June 15, 1917; d. Louis H. and Metta (Damon) C. BA, U. Minn., 1938, MA, 1940; MA, Radcliffe Coll., 1941, PhD, 1945; PhD (hon.), Brown U., 1978, D of Sociology, 1979; D.Sc., U. Rochester, 1985. Asst. social sci. analyst War Relocation Authority, 1942-43; research asst. Harvard, 1944-45; research officer Rhodes-Livingstone Inst., 1946-47, dir., 1948-51; sr. lectr. Manchester U., 1951-53; assoc. prof. Goucher Coll., 1954-55; research assoc., assoc. prof. African Research Program, Boston U., 1955-59, part-time, 1959-63; prof. anthropology Brandeis U., 1959-63; prof. anthropology U. Calif.-Berkeley, 1964-84, prof. emeritus, 1984—; vis. prof. U. Zambia, 1987; Lewis Henry Morgan lectr. U. Rochester, 1973; vis. rsch. assoc. refugee studies program Queen Elizabeth House, Oxford, 1988-89. Author: The Makah, 1953, Marriage and the Family Among The Plateau Tonga, 1958, Social Organization of the Gwembe Tonga, 1960, The Plateau Tonga, 1962, The Social Consequences of Resettlement, 1971, Tradition and Contract, 1974; jr. author Secondary Education and the Formation of an Elite, 1980, Voluntary Efforts in Decentralized Management, 1983, sr. author For Prayer and Profit, 1988; sr. editor: Seven Tribes of British Central Africa, 1951; jr. editor People in Upheaval, 1987. AAUW travelling fellow, 1941-42, fellow Ctr. Advanced Study Behavioral Scis., 1967-68, Fairchild fellow Calif. Inst. Tech., 1975-76. Fellow Am. Anthrop. Assn., Brit. Assn. Social Anthropologists, Royal Anthrop. Inst. (hon.); mem. Nat. Acad. Sci., Am. Acad. Arts and Scis., Am. Assn. African Studies (Disting. Africanist award 1988), Soc. Woman. Geographers, Phi Beta Kappa. Office: U Calif Dept Anthropology Berkeley CA 94720

COLTOFF, BETH JAMIE, psychologist; b. Phila., Mar. 19, 1955; d. Sheldon and Phyllis Irene (Brenner) C. BFA in Arch., Carnegie-Mellon U., 1978; MA in Clin. Psychology, West Chester U., 1983; cert., Inst. Comp. Family Therapy, 1988. Lic. psychologist. Adminstrv. asst., intake coord., staff therapist Inst. for Comprehensive Family Therapy, Spring House, Pa., 1982-88, adminstrv. dir., 1989-90, instr., 1989—; pvt. practice individual, marital and family therapy Spring House and Phila., 1987—. Bd. dirs., chmn. friends Inst. Comprehensive Family Therapy, 1989-90. Named one of Outstanding Young Women Am., 1986. Mem. Am. Assn. Marriage and Family Therapy, Pa. Psychol. Assn. Jewish. Office: 1018 Bethlehem Pike Ste 200-B Spring House PA 19477

COLVETT, CARON ELAINE, stunt woman; b. San Jose, Calif., Jan. 25, 1962; d. Herbert William and Katherene (Homage) C. AA, El Camino Coll., 1984; X-Ray License, Harbor-UCLA Med. Ctr., 1984. X-ray technician Radiol. Profl. Svcs., Ft. Lauderdale, Fla., 1985—; stunt woman Paramount, Universal, 20th Century Fox Studios, Miami, 1986—. Mem. Screen Actors Guild, Am. Registry Radiol. Technology.

COLVIN, AMELIA E., sales management executive; b. Freeport, Tex., July 20, 1957; d. Frances (Barton) Colvin. Student, U. Tex., Austin, 1974-77; Degree in fashion design with honors, Fashion Inst. Design, 1980. Account exec. Video Sytems, L.A., 1980-81; mktg. dir. Third and Palm Prodns., L.A., 1981-83; account exec. Sta. WPIX TV, N.Y.C., 1983-84; mktg. cons. Allen Cohen & Assocs., N.Y.C., 1984-86; account exec. Midwest Chgo. D.L.

Taffner, Chgo., 1986-87; v.p. Midwest region Peregrine Film Distbn., Chgo., 1987-89; pres. Media Svcs. Internat., L.A., 1989—. Counselor Richstone Ctr., United Way, L.A., 1989. Recipient Peacock award Bob Mackie, L.A. Republican. Presbyterian.

COLVIN, SHARON KAY, graphic arts administrator; b. Kansas City, Mo., June 24, 1947; d. Sidney Robert Colvin and J. Ruth (Smith) Russell. BA, St. Mary Coll., Leavenworth, Kans., 1984; MBA, Websters U., Kansas City, Mo., 1990. Pres., owner Circle C Tng. Stables, Inc., Leavenworth, 1968-79; v.p. Bacon and Jeffries Title Co., Leavenworth, 1972-77; asst. mgr. McCaffree Short Title Co., Leavenworth, 1978-80; sect. mgr. Hallmark Cards, Inc., Leavenworth, 1980-86, mgr. quality assurance dept., 1986-90. Active Community Cultural coun. St. Mary Coll., 1982—. Mem. Assn. Quality and Participation (Heart of Am. chpt.), Am. Soc. for Quality Control, St. Mary Coll. Alumni Assn. (bd. dirs. 1987—). Republican. Methodist. Home: RR 5 Box 390 Leavenworth KS 66048 Office: Hallmark Cards Inc 2501 Mcgee Kansas City MO 64141-6580

COLWELL, GRETCHEN FRANCES, educator; b. Mpls., Nov. 19, 1946; d. Aloysius Theodore and Frances (O'Connor) Kranz; m. John Vincel Colwell, May 25, 1968 (div. 1979); children: Adam John, Amy Margaret. BS, Coll. St. Teresa, Winona, Minn., 1968; MS, U. Wis., River Falls, 1981; postgrad., U. Minn., 1987—. Tchr. 2nd grade Burnsville (Minn.) pub. schs., 1968-69; substitute tchr. Hastings (Minn.) pub. schs., 1970-75, tchr. 3rd grade, 1975-76, tchr. 2nd grade, 1978-85, kindergarden tchr., 1985—; tchr. 4th grade Warwick pub. schs., Lititz, Pa., 1978; active crisis intervention team, K-12 math evaluation team, K-12 sci. evaluation com., gifted edn. com., early childhood issues com., dist. 200 reading task force, Hastings pub. schs; lectr. in field. Block capt. United Way, Hastings, 1986—; host family Nacel Cultural Exchange Prog., St. Paul, 1988; Stephen minister St. Elizabeth Ann Seaton Parish, Hastings; coop. tchr. U. Wis. Student Tchrs.; mem. ednl. adv. bd. Nature Ctr. Named Hastings Tchr. of the Yr., Hastings, Edn. Assn., 1988, Educator of the Yr., Hastings C. of C., 1988; finalist Minn. Tchr. of Yr., 1988, Ashland Oil Tchr. Achievement award, 1989. Mem. Hastings Edn. Assn. (bldg. rep. 1986-88), Minn. Kindergarten Assn., Minn. Assn. for Edn. Young Children, Kerlan Friend, AAUW (bd. dirs. 1988—). Roman Catholic. Home: 539 W 2d St Hastings MN 55033

COLWELL, RITA ROSSI, research scientist, microbiologist, educator; b. Beverly, Mass., Nov. 23, 1934; d. Louis and Louise (Di Palma) Rossi; m. Jack H. Colwell, May 31, 1956; children: Alison E.L., Stacie A. BS with distinction, Purdue U., 1956, MS, 1958; PhD, U. Wash., 1961; DSc (hon.), Heriot-Watt U., Edinburgh, Scotland, 1987, U. Queensland, Australia, 1988. Asst. rsch. prof. U. Wash., Seattle, 1961-64; guest scientist div. applied biology NRC of Can., 1961-63; vis. asst. prof. biology Georgetown U., Washington, 1963-64, asst. prof. biology, 1964-66, assoc. prof., 1966-72; prof. microbiology U. Md., College Park, 1972—, dir. sea grant program, 1977-83, acting dir. Ctr. for Environ. and Estuarine Studies, 1980-81; v.p. acad. affairs U. Md. System, 1983-87; dir. Md. Biotech. Inst., 1987—, Ctr. Marine Biotechnology, 1987—; hon. prof. U. Queensland, Brisbane, Australia, 1988; cons., adviser to Washington area communications media, Congressman and legislators, 1978—; external examiner various univs. abroad, 1964—; mem. coastal resources adv. com. dept. natural resources State of Md., 1979—; mem. numerical data adv. bd. NCR, 1973-76, ocean scis. bd., 1977-80; mem. Nat. Sci. Bd., 1984-90; mem. sci. adv. bd. Oak Ridge Nat. Labs., 1988-90, adv. com. FDA, 1990—. Author 14 books including (manual numerical taxonomy) Collecting the Data, 1970, (with M. Zambruski) Rodina-Methods in Aquatic Microbiology, 1972, (with L.H. Stevenson) Estuarine Microbiology Ecology, 1973, (with R.Y. Morita) Effect of the Ocean Environment on Microbial Activities, 1974, (with A. Sinsky and N. Pariser) Marine Biotechnology, 1983, Vibrios in the Environment, 1985; mem. editorial bd.: Microbial Ecology, 1972-90, Applied and Environ. Microbiology, 1969-81, Johns Hopkins U. Oceanographic Series, 1981-83, Revue de la Found. Oceanographique Ricard, 1981-88, Oil and Petrochem. Pollution, 1980—; assoc. editor: Can. Jour. Microbiology, 1972-75; editor-in-chief: Marine Tech. Soc. Jour., 1981-90; contbr. numerous articles on marine microbiology, biotechnology and ecology to sci jours. Mem. Gov.'s Sci. Adv. Council, State of Md., 1979—. Recipient Outstanding Woman on Campus award U. Md., 1979. Fellow AAAS, Grad. Women in Sci., Can. Coll. of Microbiologists, Am. Acad. Microbiology (chmn. bd. govs. 1989—), Washington Acad. Scis. (bd. mgrs. 1976-79), Marine Tech. Soc. (exec. coun. 1982-88), Sigma Delta Epsilon; mem. Am. Soc. Microbiology (mem. various sci. coms. 1961—, pres. 1984-85, chmn. program com. REGEM-1 1988; Fisher award 1985), World Fedn. Culture Collections, Internat. Union Microbiol. Soc. (v.p. 1986-90), U.S. Fedn. Culture Collections (governing bd. 1978-88), Am. Inst. Biol. Scis. (bd. govs. 1976-82), Am. Soc. Limnology and Oceanography, Soc. for Indsl. Microbiology (bd. govs. 1976-79), Classification Research Group of Eng. (charter), Soc. for Gen. Microbiology, Phi Beta Kappa, Sigma Xi (Ann. Achievement award 1981, Research award 1984, nat. pres.-elect 1989-90, pres. 1990—). Home: 5010 River Hill Rd Bethesda MD 20816 Office: U Md Md Biotech Inst Campus Dr Biotech Bldg College Park MD 20742

COLY, LISETTE, foundation executive; b. N.Y.C., Apr. 6, 1950; d. Robert Raymond and Eileen (Lyttle-Garrett) C.; children: George Robert Damalas, Anastasia Eileen Damalas. BA cum laude, Hunter Coll., 1973. Sec. Parapsychology Found., Inc., N.Y.C., 1972-75, assoc. editor, 1975—, v.p., 1978—. Assoc. editor Parapsychology Rev. and Procs. Ann. Internat. Parapsychology Found. Confs., 1978—. Office: 1 Parapsychology Found Inc 228 E 71st St New York NY 10021

COLYER, SHERYL LYNN, psychologist; b. Portsmouth, Va., Dec. 20, 1959; d. Joshua Clark and Lubertha (Alexander) C. BS, Howard U., 1981; MA, Columbia U., N.Y.C., 1983. Pers. psychologist, employee devel. specialist IRS, Washington, 1983-84; human resource devel. cons. Tech. Applications, Falls Church, Va., 1984-85; human resource devel. specialist GM, Ft. Wayne, Ind., 1985-88; tng. and devel. cons. Freddie Mac, Reston, Va., 1988-90; div. tng. mgr. PepsiCo, Hanover, Md., 1990—. Mem. ASTD, Soc. for Indsl. and Orgnl. Psychology, Inc. chpt. APA, Pers. Testing Coun. Met. Wash., Delta Sigma Theta (pres. 1981-81). Home: 507 E Indian Spring Dr Silver Spring MD 20901 Office: PepsiCo 7250 Parkway Dr Ste 200 Hanover MD 21076

COMBS, JO KAREN KOBECK, artist, writer; b. Lawrenceburg, Tenn., Apr. 10, 1944; d. William Horatio and Ethel Marie (Hendrix) Kobeck; m. James R. Benson, May 10, 1963 (div. May 1974); children: Pamela Jo Benson Powers, Anita Marie Benson Bosaw; m. Johnny Ray Lothar Combs, Mar. 9, 1980. Cert. drafting, Miss. Gulf Coast Jr. Coll., 1974, Mountain Empire Community Coll, 1980; cert. engring. graphics, U. Tenn., 1975. Advt. asst. Rogers, Inc., Florence, Ala., 1966-67; drafter Litton Industries, Pascagoula, Miss., 1972-74; drafter, artist Cities Svc. Co., Cooperhill, Tenn., 1974-78; drafter Westmoreland Coal Co., Big Stone Gap, Va., 1978-88; drafter, neon designer and illustrator Designs by Jo, East Stone Gap, Va., 1983—. Lectr. Take Off Pounds Sensibly, Appalachia, Va., 1985-87; active Friends of the Libr., Big Stone Gap, 1988, pres., 1989; registrant SHARE, Big Stone Gap, 1988; bd. dirs. H.E.L.P. Ctr., Big Stone Gap. Mem. Christian Ch. Home: Rt 683 East Stone Gap VA 24246 Office: Designs by Jo State Rt 683 Box 187 East Stone Gap VA 24246

COMBS, LINDA JONES, educator, researcher; b. Jonesboro, Ark., Apr. 12, 1948; d. Dale Jones and Neva Mae (Craig) Green; m. Nathan Lewis Combs, Jan. 13, 1968; 1 child, Nathan Issac. BSBA, U. Ark., 1971, MBA, 1972, PhD in Bus. Adminstrn., 1983. Assoc. economist Bur. Bus. and Econ. Rsch., Fayetteville, Ark., 1973-76; pres. Combs Mgmt. Co., Springdale, Ark., 1976-83; asst. prof. fin. U. Ark., Fayetteville, 1983-87; asst. prof. fin. and mktg. Western Ill. U., Macomb, 1987-88; asst. prof. bus. adminstrn. Cen. Mo. State U., Warrensburg, 1988-89; assoc. prof. bus. adminstrn. N.E. State U., Tahlequah, Okla., 1989-90; cons. Sears Roebuck, Chgo., 1973-74, Fayetteville Adv. Coun., 1975-76, King Pizza, Fayetteville, 1985—; cons. in fin. and banking, Fayetteville, 1973-76. Contbr. articles to profl. jours. Mem. gov.'s inaugural com. State of Ark., Little Rock, 1985; county co-chmn. Clinton for Gov., Washington County, Ark., 1984, 90; bd. dirs. Shiloh Mus., Am. Cancer Soc., North Ark. Symphony Soc., Children's Hosp. Aux.; active many polit. campaigns for candidates and issues. Mem. Am. Mktg. Assn., S.W. Mktg. Assn., Transp. Rsch. Forum, Am. Assn. Pub. Adminstrn., Coun. Logistics Mgmt., Maple Hill Garden Club, Beta Sigma Phi. Office: Combs Mgmt Co PO Box 1452 Fayetteville AR 72701

COMBS-JORDAN, VALDA JEAN, lawyer; b. Cleburne, Tex., Sept. 8, 1956; d. Willie Booker and Talmadge (Boothe) C. BA, U. Houston, 1980; JD, South Tex. Coll. of Law, 1985. Bar: U.S. Dist. Ct. (so. dist.) Tex. 1987. Pvt. practice Hempstead, Tex., 1985—; adj. prof. Prairie View (Tex.) A&M U., 1987-88, South Tex. Coll. Law, Houston, 1988-89. Editor: Full Disclosure, 1989. Mem. Mt. Corinth Bapt. Ch., Hempstead, 1987, Extension Home Econs. Com., Hempstead, 1987, Community Outreach, Hempstead, 1987—, Waller County Dem. Club; elected atty. Waller County, 1989—. Mem. ABA (exec. com. pre law counseling com. 1987—, vice chmn. young lawyers div. govt. lawyers com. 1989—), Assn. Trial Lawyers Am., Tex. Bar Assn., Waller County Bar Assn., Tex. Dist. and County Attys. Assn. Office: County of Waller 836 Austin St Rm 109 Hempstead TX 77445

COMDEN, BETTY, writer, dramatist, lyricist, performer; b. Bklyn., May 3, 1919; d. Leo and Rebecca (Sadvoransky) C.; m. Steven Kyle, Jan. 4, 1942; children: Susanna, Alan. Student, Bklyn. Ethical Culture Sch., Erasmus Hall High Sch.; B.S., N.Y. U. Writer, performer nightclub act, Revuers; writer: (with Adolph Green) book and lyrics Broadway shows On The Town, 1944-45, Billion Dollar Baby, Two on the Aisle, Bells are Ringing, Fade-Out-Fade-In, Subways are for Sleeping, On the Twentiewth Century, A Doll's Life, 1982 (Tony award), (with Adolph Green) lyrics for Hallelujah, Baby!; screenplays Auntie Mame, Good News, The Barkleys of Broadway, Singin' in the Rain, The Bard Wagon, others; screenplay and lyrics for On the Town, Bells are Ringing, Fade-Out-Fade-In, Subways are for Sleeping, A Doll's Life, 1982 (Tony award); with Adloph Green) lyrics for Hallelujah, Baby!; screenplays Auntie Mame, Good News, The Barkleys of Broadway, Singin' in the Rain, The Bard Wagon, others; screenplay and lyrics for On the Town, Bell Are Ringing, Its Alsyas Fair Weather, What a Way to Go; co-author: Book for Applause, 1970; lyricist, dir.: (with Adolph Green) book for "Lorelei". 1973; book and lyrics On the 20th Century, 1978; appeared in: On the Town, 1944; performed wtih Adolph Green, 1959, 77; also appeared in play Isn't it Romantic, 1983, in movie Garbor Talks, 1985, the Bandwagon. Recipient Donaldson award and Tony award for Wonderful Town, as co-lyricist best score 1983; Tony award for Hallelujah, Baby, as co-writer best score 1968; Tony award for Applause 1970; Tony award for lyrics and book On the 20th Century, A Doll's Life; Woman of Achievement award NYU Alumnae Assn. 1978; N.Y.C. Mayor's award Art and Culture 1978; named to Songwriters Hall of Fame 1980, Theatre Hall of Fame. Mem. Dramatists Guild (council, v.p. Dramatists Guild Fund). Office: care The Dramatists Guild 234 W 44th St New York NY 10036

COMEAU, LORENE ANITA EMERSON, real estate developer; b. Haverhill, Mass., Sept. 6, 1952; d. Russell Paul and Jeannette (La Course) Emerson; m. Peter Robert Comeau, May 6, 1950; children: Stephen David, Michelle Patricia. BA with honors, Northeastern U., 1975. Lic. real estate broker. Housing rep., pub. liaison U.S. Dept. HUD, Boston, 1975-78; devel. mgr. John M. Corcoran & Co., Milton, Mass., 1978-84, v.p., 1984—; v.p. Merrimack Valley Housing Partnership, Lowell, Mass., 1986-89. Treas. Andover (Mass.) br. Merrimack Valley YMCA, 1982—, pres. 1990—; assoc. mem. Andover Zoning Bd. Appeals, 1984-87; mem. Andover Fair Housing Com., 1982-87, Andover Master Plan Com., 1982-84, Andover Housing Partnership Com., 1990—; fin. com., corp. bd. mem. Merrimack Valley YMCA, Lawrence, Mass., 1984—; mem., chmn. Andover Master Plan Com. Housing Update Component, chmn. com. to develop Andover Housing Action Plan, 1989—. Mem. LWV (fin. chair Andover chpt. 1982-83, budget chair 1983-84, 86-87), New Eng. Women in Real Estate (mem. seminars com.), Developers Coun.-Builders Assn. Greater Boston, Nat. Leased Housing Assn. Washington, Urban Land Inst. (assoc.), Internat. Coun. Shopping Ctrs., Nat. Assn. Indsl. and and Office Pks. Republican. Episcopalian. Home: PO Box 4108BV Andover MA 01810 Office: John M Corcoran & Co 500 Granite Ave Milton MA 02186

COMEFORO, JEAN ELIZABETH, special education educator; b. Urbana, Ill., June 2, 1947; d. Jay E. and Jean Carolyn (Raff) Comeforo. BS in Biology, Coll. St. Elizabeth, 1969; M Edn. of Deaf, Smith Coll., 1972; MEd, Cheyney State Coll., 1982. Cert. tchr. of deaf, N.J., Pa., oral interpreter for deaf. Houseparent Katazenbach Sch. for Deaf, West Trenton, N.J., 1969-70; math. and sci. tchr. Western Pa. Sch. for Deaf, Edgewood, 1971-76; tchr. of deaf Delaware County Intermediate Unit, Media, Pa., 1976—, itinerant hearing therapist; presenter papers in field. Leader coun. Girl Scouts U.S.; chaperone Miss Deaf Pa., 1087-89; pres. Alexander G. Bell Assn. for the Deaf of Marion Quick chpt., 1989—. Recipient citation for inspirational teaching of sci. subjects Buhl Planetarium, Annie Sullivan award; named Best Producer Community Svc. TV Program, Am. Cablevision Pa. Mem. Quota Internat., Alexander G. Bell Assn. for Deaf (pres. Marion Quick chpt.), Delaware Valley Assn. for Oral Hearing Impaired, Quota Clubs (gov. dist. II 1985-87), Beta Beta Beta. Home: 616 N Lemon St Media PA 19063

COMELLA, PATRICIA ANN EGAN, government official, lawyer, consultant; b. N.Y.C., Jan. 26, 1941; d. John J. and Helen (Courtois) Egan; m. August John Comella, May 30, 1964; 1 son, Christopher. BA, Hofstra U., 1962, JD, Georgetown U., 1987. Mathematician, NASA Goddard Space Flight Ctr., Greenbelt, Md., 1962-75; policy analyst Office of Policy Evaluation, U.S. Nuclear Regulatory Commn., Washington, 1975-79, br. chief Office of Standards Devel., 1979-81, dep. div. dir. Office Nuclear Regulatory Research, 1981-84; sr. regulatory assurance specialist Battelle Meml. Inst., Washington, 1984-86; licensing mgr. Roy F. Weston, Inc., Washington, 1986-87; atty. Newman & Holtzinger, Washington, 1987—.

COMER, CARLA A., high school principal; b. Colquitt, Ga., Oct. 14, 1949; d. William Carlye and Anne Sue (Smith) Bryan; m. Robert Wade Comer, July 19, 1981. BS, U. Ga., 1973; postgrad. in edn., Ga. So. Coll., 1982; MEd, Valdosta State Coll., 1981, Ga. Southwestern U., 1974. Asst. adminstr. Liberty County Bd. Edn., Hinesville, Ga.; tchr. Dougherty County Bd. Edn., Albany, Ga.; prin. Tattnal County Bd. Edn., Reidsville, Ga. Mem. NAFE, Ga. Assn. Ednl. Leaders, Ga. Assn. Secondary Sch. Prins., Assn. Supervision and Curriculum. Office: 721 E Barnard St Glennville GA 30427

COMER, DEBRA RUTH, management educator; b. Phila., Apr. 11, 1960; d. Nathan Lawrence and Rita (Ellis) C. BA, Swarthmore (Pa.) Coll., 1982; MA, Yale U., 1984, M in Philosophy, 1985, PhD, 1986. Instr. Yale U., New Haven, 1984; orgnl. devel. cons. Port Authority of N.Y. & N.J., N.Y.C., 1984-87; asst. prof. mgmt. Hofstra U., Hempstead, N.Y., 1987—. Contbr. articles to profl. jours. Yale U. fellow, 1982-86, Joshua B. Lippincott fellow Swarthmore Coll., 1982; Hofstra U. grantee, 1988, 89, 90. Mem. Am. Psychol. Assn., Assn. of Mgmt., Acad. of Mgmt. Jewish. Office: Hofstra U Dept of Mgmt Hempstead NY 11550

COMER, KELVIE CURETON, college dean; b. Santa Cruz, Calif., Oct. 4, 1946; d. West MacKelvie and Eula Felton (Council) Cureton; m. Lee Comer, Aug. 8, 1968 (div. 1979); 1 child, Ross Ward. BS in Edn., Pa. State U., University Park, 1968; EdM, Temple U., 1973, EdD, 1978. Bilingual advisor Coll. Edn. Temple U., Phila., 1973-74, ombudsman Coll. Edn., 1974-76, staff asst., exec. dir. faculty senate, 1976-78; asst. to and asst. dean U. Akron, Ohio, 1978-85, acting dean Coll. Fine and Applied Arts, 1986-87, assoc. dean Coll. Fine and Applied Arts, 1985-88; dean Sch Profl. Studies Eastern Conn. State U., Willimantic, 1988—; cons. U.S. Dept. Edn., Washington, 1985—, Rsch. for Better Schs., Phila., 1974-75. Co-author: Curriculum and Instruction: A Guide to Alternatives, 1976; contbr. articles to profl. jours. Named Summit County Woman of Yr. in Edn., Woman's History Week Project, Akron, 1988. Mem. AAUW (nat. membership com. 1984-86, state membership v.p. 1983-85, nat. program award 1983, Ednl. Found. Award for Individual Project Grant 1984, state topics chair 1989—, nat. coll./univ. rels. com. 1990—), Am. Assn. Higher Edn., Am. Assn. Colls. Tchr. Edn., Nat. Assn. Acad. Affairs Adminstrs., Nat. Network Ednl. Women's Adv. Group. Republican. Episcopalian. Home: 21 Oakwood Dr Storrs CT 06268 Office: Eastern Conn State U 83 Windham St Willimantic CT 06226

COMES, JENNIFER LYNN, journalist; b. Ft. Dix, N.J., May 1, 1955; d. John Edward Comes and Peggy Joyce (Cummings) Ipson. Student, U. Colo., 1980-82; BA, Wichita State U., 1987; studying fellow, Atlantik Brukke/Bosch Found., Berlin, 1989. Editorial writer The Wichita (Kans.) Eagle, 1986-89, staff writer, 1989—. Mem. Nat. Conf. Editorial Writers, Soc. Profl. Journalists, Women in Communications (v.p. Wichita chpt. 1987—). Office: The Wichita Eagle 825 E Douglas Wichita KS 67201

COMET, CATHERINE, conductor; m. Michael Aiken; 1 child, Caroline. MusM in Orch. Conducting, Juilliard Sch. Music; studied with Pierre Boulez, Nadia Boulanger, Igor Markevich. Former music dir. and conductor U. Wis. Symphony & Chamber Orch.; EXXON-Arts Ednowment condr. St. Louis Symphony Orch., 1981-84; music dir. St. Louis Youth Orch.; assoc. condr. Balt. Symphony Orch., 1984-86; music dir. Grand Rapids (Mich.) Symphony Orch., 1986-90, Am. Symphony Orch., N.Y.C., 1990—; guest condr. Pasadena Symphony, Buffalo Philharm., Ala. Symphony, Nat. Symphony, others. Recipient 1st prize Internat. Young Condrs.' Competition, France, 1966, Dmitri Mitropoulos Internat. Contest prize, 1968. Office: Am Symphony Orch Inc 161 W 54th St Ste 1202 New York NY 10019*

COMET-EPSTEIN, SHARON, educator, management consultant; b. Cleve., Oct. 25, 1950; d. Sol S. and Fay (Shochet) Comet; m. Robert E. Epstein, Sept. 1, 1974; children: Adam Scott, Rachel. BS cum laude, Ohio State U., 1972; MS, Case Western Res. U., 1974, PhD, 1985, postgrad. Instr. Columbus Jr. Theatre Arts, 1971; instr., designer allied health scis. Ohio State U., Columbus, 1971-72; ednl. project dir. Sch. Dentistry Case Western Res. U., Cleve., 1972-76, dir. ednl. resources and pub. affairs, 1976-85, asst. prof., 1986—; ednl. dir. Western Res. Geriatric Ctr., 1986-87; mgmt. cons., 1982—; asst. dean for ednl. devel., 1989. Contbr. articles to profl. jours; editor Focus, 1975-77, Off the Cusp, 1976-78; nat. speaker in field. Mem. Jewish Nat. Fund New Gen., Hadassah, Orgn. Rehab. through Tng. Recipient 40 Under Forty award Cleve. Jewish News, 1987-88, 2d pl. award Health Scis. Communications Assn., 1974. Mem. Women in Communications, Health Scis. Communications Assn., Profl. Ethics Dentistry Network, Am. Soc. Tng. and Devel., Am. Assn. Dental Schs. Jewish. Office: 2123 Abington Rd Cleveland OH 44106

COMFORT, PRISCILLA MARIA, human resources executive; b. Ft. Dix, N.J., Feb. 20, 1947; d. Jennie Rita (Manes) McGuire; children: James, Aimee. BS, Montclair State Coll., 1969; MEd, Trenton State Coll., 1980. Cert. tchr., N.J., guidance counselor, secondary guidance counselor, pub. mgr., N.J. Tchr. Burlington (N.J.) Twp. and City Schs., 1969-72; employment svc. interviewer N.J. Dept. Labor and Industry, Trenton, 1972-74; prin. career devel. specialist N.J. Dept. Civil Svc., Trenton, 1974-76, prin. pers. technician, 1976-79; dir. pers. svcs. Stockton State Coll., Pomona, N.J., 1979-89; asst. v.p. human resources Stockton State Coll., Pomona, 1989—. Tchr. CCD Assumption Ch., Pomona, 1981-84, mem. CCD adv. bd., 1983-84; active Little League, PTO, 1977-84; mem. pers. com. Big Bros., Big Sisters Adv. Com., 1988. Recipient Tribute to Women in Industry award YWCA, 1987, Mgmt. Merit award, 1986, Sun award Chapel of the Four Chaplains, 1988. Mem. Am. Soc. Pub. Adminstrs., Cert. Pub. Mgrs. Assn. N.J., Atlantic County Pers. Assn., N.J. Assn. Affirmative Action in Higher Edn. (panelist), N.J. Coll. and Univ. Pers. Assn. (chair 1988), N.J. Pers. Coun., Atlantic Cty C. of C. (mem. adv. bd., mem. pers. task force 1985), Coll. and Univ. Pers. Assn. (nat. legis. com. 1989-90, chairwoman membership com. N.J. chpt. 1989—). Roman Catholic. Office: Stockton State Coll Jim Leeds Rd Pomona NJ 08240

COMINSKY, LYNN RUTH, physics and astronomy educator; b. Buffalo, Nov. 19, 1953; d. Martyn Francis Cominsky and Lois Mona (Joseph) Klein; m. Jesse Garrett Jernigan, Jr., June 1, 1980. BA, Brandeis U., 1975; PhD, MIT, 1981. Sci. ops. and data analysis adminstr. U. Calif. Space Scis. Lab., Berkeley, 1984-85, systems devel. mgr., 1985-86; assoc. prof. Sonoma State U., Rohnert Park, Calif., 1986—. Author numerous rsch. papers. Mem. Am. Astron. Soc., Am. Phys. Soc., Am. Assn. of Physics Tchrs., Assn. Women in Sci., Sigma Xi. Office: Dept Physics and Astronomy Sonoma State U Rohnert Park CA 94928

COMLEY, NANCY RICH, academic administrator; b. Mt. Vernon, N.Y., Apr. 29, 1935; d. Walter Wheaton and Ruth Irene (Wilkinson) Rich; m. John Munson Comley, Jr., May 1, 1954 (dec. Dec. 1974); children: Heath Stewart, Ann Noyes, Ellen Munson. BA, Brown U., Providence, 1971, PhD, 1977. Lectr. Brown U., Providence, 1977-78; vis. asst. prof. of English Trinity Coll., Hartford, Conn., 1978-79; instr. U. Okla., Norman, 1979-80, asst. prof., 1980-82; asst. prof. Queens Coll., CUNY, Flushing, 1982-87; assoc. prof. Queens Coll., CUNY, 1987—. Contbr. articles to profl. jours. Mem. MLA, N.E. MLA, Nat. Coun. Tchrs. of English, Coun. of Writing Program Adminstrs., James Joyce Soc., Phi Beta Kappa. Office: Queens Coll CUNY Dept of English Flushing NY 11367

COMMANDER, SHARI L., business owner; b. Port Arthur, Tex., Mar. 24, 1950; d. Marvin Vallery and Dorthy Marie (Gunn) Louvier; m. Carey C. Commander, Feb. 10, 1977 (div. Mar.1983); 1 child, Clint Commander. BS in Elem. Edn., Lamar U., 1973, M. in Mid-Mgmt., 1977, cert. in supervision and prin., 1979. English as second lang. tchr. DeQueen Elem., Port Arthur, 1976, elem. tchr., 1973-76; part-time prin. Wheatley Elem., Port Arthur, 1983-89; owner, dir. Fashion Showcase Sch. and Agy., Beaumont, Tex., 1983-89, Commander Acad., Houston, 1990—. Editor, contbr. Talent Showcase Internat., 1988. Casting dir. Beaumont Sesquicentennial, 1987; sponsor Sunday in the Park Project, Beaumont, 1987-88; mem. Leadership Beaumont, 1988. Named one of Outstanding Young Women of Am., Outstanding Prof. Pub. Speaker. Home: 2750 Wallingford 1709 Houston TX 77042 Office: Commander Acad 4801 Woodway Dr Ste 300E Houston TX 77056

COMMERFORD, KATHLEEN ANNE, psychologist; b. Mpls., July 6, 1951; d. Joseph Dennis and Emily (Assad) C.; m. Scott Andrew Greer, August 1, 1986; 1 child, Alexander James Greer. PhD, U. Ariz., 1984; MA, U. Ore., 1978; BA, St. Louis U., 1973. Lic. psychologist, Ore.; Cert. school psychologist. Tchr. Tex. and Iowa Pub. Schs., Tex. and Iowa, 1973-76; sch. psychologist Oreg. and Ariz. Pub. Schs., 1978-81; coord. Health Scis. Ariz. U., Tucson, 1981-85; psych. resident Clackamas County Mental Health Ctr., Portland, Oreg., 1985-86; dir. Behavioral Sci. Oreg. U. Health Scis., Portland, 1986-89; psychologist Portland, 1990—. Contbr. articles to profl. jours. Mem. APA, Soc. of Tchrs. of Family Med. (mem. com.), Oreg. Psych. Assn., Psi Chi, Phi Beta Kappa. Office: Providence Medical Building 545 NE 47th Ave ste 206 Portland OR 97213

COMNINOU, MARIA, engineering educator; b. Athens, Greece, Aug. 12, 1947; came to U.S., 1970; BSCE, Nat. Tech. U., Athens, 1970; MS in Applied Mechanics, Northwestern U., Evanston, Ill., 1971, PhD in Applied Mechanics, 1973. Instr. MIT, Cambridge, 1973-74; asst. prof. U. Mich., Ann Arbor, 1974-79, assoc. prof., 1979-85, prof. of engring., 1985—. Author numerous tech. papers. Recipient Alfred Noble prize, 1978, Faculty Recognition award, U. Mich., 1981, Alumnae award, Northwestern U., 1984. Mem. Soc. Engring. Sci. (exec. bd. 1986-89, pres. 1990, editor newsletter, 1981—), ASCE (editor and chmn. engring. mechanics div. 1979-81, exec. bd. tech. and soc. div. 1989). Office: U Mich Dept Mech Engring Ann Arbor MI 48109-2125

COMPAIN, RITA, librarian; b. N.Y.C., Dec. 4, 1926; d. Benjamin and Sara (Modell) Romer; m. Ernest A. Compain, Apr. 17, 1948 (div. 1987); children: Michael, Daniel, Andrew. BS, CUNY, 1947; MLS, L.I. U., 1963; Profl. Dipl., St. John's U., N.Y.C., 1975; postgrad., Columbia U., 1969-70. Children's librarian Bklyn. Pub. Library, 1947-49; library coordinator Oceanside (N.Y.) pub. schs., 1959-61; librarian Franklin Sq. (N.Y.) pub. schs., 1961-71; staff developer BOCES Nassau, Jericho, N.Y., 1974-76; serials librarian Am. Mus. Natural History, N.Y.C., 1977-79; library cons. Rita Compain Agy., N.Y.C., 1980-85; project dir. "Open Sesame" Am. Reading Council, N.Y.C., 1985-88; staff developer library media Kingston (N.Y.) pub. schs., 1988—; asst. prof. L.I. U., Greenvale, 1969-75; library cons. Great Neck pub. schs., 1975-76; adj. prof. SUNY, New Paltz, 1988—; ednl. cons.; lectr. in field; mem. com. Nassau County Jail Library Pilot Prog., E. Meadow, 1979. Contbg. author: Open Sesame Guide to Implementation, 1987; contbg. author/dir. video: Teacher Training Film, 1986. Mem. Internat. Reading Assn., N.Y. State Reading Assn., Nassau-Suffolk Sch. Library Assn. (pres. 1969-70), N.Y. State Library Assn., ALA, Amnesty Internat., Old Westbury Club, Delta Kappa Gamma. Home: 89 Yerry Hill Rd Woodstock NY 12498

COMPEL, DEBORAH CATHERINE, critical care pediatrics nurse; b. Miami, Fla., Apr. 10, 1955; d. Joseph and Lorraine Marie (Oleszkiewicz) C. BS in Nursing, Barry Coll., 1977; postgrad., U. Miami, 1979; M

Nursing, UCLA, 1985. Head nurse neonatal ICU Mt. Sinai Med. Ctr., Miami Beach, Fla.; PNP Hemophilia Ctr. U. Miami; staff nurse pediatric emergency room Variety Childrens Hosp., Miami; clin. nurse specialist Childrens Hosp. L.A.; researcher in field. Fellow NAPNAP (exec. bd. L.A. chpt.); mem. AHP-SC (pres.), AJAO, Sigma Theta Tau. Office: Children's Hosp of LA 4650 Sunset Blvd Los Angeles CA 90027

COMPTON, ANN WOODRUFF, news correspondent; b. Chgo., Jan. 19, 1947; d. Charles Edward and Barbara (Ortlund) C.; m. William Stevenson Hughes, Nov. 25, 1978; children: William Compton, Edward Opie, Ann Woodruff, Michael Stevenson. B.A., Hollins (Va.) Coll., 1969. Reporter, anchorwoman WDBJ-TV (CBS), Roanoke, Va., 1969-70; polit. reporter, state capitol bur. chief WDBJ-TV (CBS), Richmond, Va., 1971-73; fellow Washington Journalism Center, 1970, trustee, 1978—; network radio anchorwoman ABC News, N.Y.C., 1973-74; White House corr. ABC News, Washington, 1974-79, 81-84, congl. corr., 1979-81, 84—, chief Ho. of Reps. corr., 1987—; mem. adv. bd. Gannett Found. Ctr. for Media Studies, Columbia U., 1984—. Trustee Hollins Coll., 1987—. Named Mother of Yr., Nat. Mother's Day Com., 1987. Mem. White House Corrs. Assn. (dir. 1977-79), Radio-TV Corrs. Bd. (chmn. 1987). Office: ABC News 1717 DeSales St NW Washington DC 20036*

COMPTON, MARY BEATRICE BROWN (MRS. RALPH THEODORE COMPTON), public relations executive, writer; b. Washington, May 25, 1923; d. Robert James and Abia Eliza (Stone) Brown. Grad. Thayer Acad., Chandler Sch., Leland Powers Sch. Radio, TV and Theatre, Boston, 1942; m. Ralph Theodore Compton, Mar. 18, 1961, step-children—Ralph Theodore, Patricia (Mrs. William R. Schnitzler). Radio program dir. Converse Co., Malden, Mass., 1942-45; head radio continuity dept. Sta. WAAB, Yankee Network, Worcester, Mass., 1945-46; asst. dir. radio Leland Powers Sch. Radio, TV and Theatre, Boston, 1946-49, dir., 1949-51; program asst. Sta. KNBH, Hollywood, Calif., 1951-52; v.p. Acorn Film Co., Boston, 1953-54; dir. women's communications, editor Program Notes, radio interviewer NAM, N.Y.C., 1954-61. Celebrities pub. rels. Nat. Citizens for Nixon, 1968, Kennedy Ctr. Pub. Info., 1985—. Mem. Soc. Old Plymouth Colony Descs., Magna Carta Dames, Nat. Trust for Hist. Preservation. Clubs: Congl. Country (Bethesda, Md.), Brooke Manor Country (Rockville, Md.). Home: 15300 Wallbrook Ct 3F Silver Spring MD 20906

COMPTON, NORMA HAYNES, retired university dean; b. Washington, Nov. 16, 1924; d. Thomas N. and Lillian (Laffin) Haynes; m. William Randall Compton, Mar. 27, 1946; children: William Randall, Anne Elizabeth. AB, George Washington U., 1950; MS, U. Md., 1957, Ph.D., 1962. Researcher Julius Garfinckel & Co., Washington, 1955; tchr. Montgomery Blair High Sch., Silver Spring, Md., 1955-57; instr. U. Md., 1957-60, teaching and research fellow Inst. Child Study, 1960-61, assoc. prof., 1962-63; psychology extern St. Elizabeths Hosp., Washington, 1962-63; assoc. prof. Utah State U., 1963-64, prof., 1964-68, head dept. clothing and textiles, 1963-68; dir. Utah State U. (Inst. for Research on Man and His Personal Environment), 1967-68; dean Sch. Home Econs. Auburn (Ala.) U., 1968-73; dean Sch. Consumer and Family Scis. Purdue U., 1973-87, prof. family studies, 1987-90; bd. dirs. Armour and Co., Phoenix, 1976-82, Home Hosp., Lafayette, Ind., 1983-89; cons. Burgess Publishing Co., Minneapolis, 1975-81, Nat. Advt. Review Bd., N.Y.C., 1978-82;. Author: (with Olive Hall) Foundations of Home Economics Research, 1972, (with John Tuliatos) Approaches to Child Study, 1983, Research Methods in Human Ecology/ Home Economics, 1988; contbr. articles to profl. jours. Mem. Am. Home Econs. Assn., Am. Psychol. Assn., Phi Beta Kappa, Sigma Xi, Phi Kappa Phi, Omicron Nu, Psi Chi. Presbyterian.

COMPTON, SHANNON LEIGH, optometrist; b. Statesville, N.C., Apr. 28, 1953; d. Charles Muncy and Helen Elrose (Hale) C.; m. Fredrick Paul Reynolds, Aug. 16, 1986. BA, Milligan College (Tenn.), 1975; BS, U. Ala., Birmingham, 1977, OD, 1979. Optometrist Martinsville, Va., 1979-82, Salem, Va., 1982—, Amherst, Va., 1986—. Mem. Am. Optometric Assn., Va. Optometric Assn., Va. Fedn. Bus. and Profl. Women, Southwestern Va. Optometric Soc. (pres. 1987-88), Roanoke Bus. and Profl. Women (pres. 1986-88, Woman of Yr. 1988). Democrat. Ch. of Christ. Home: 402 Woodland Circle Lynchburg VA 24502 Office: 115 Boulevard Salem VA 24153

COMPTON, SUSAN LANELL, retired librarian; b. Batesville, Ark., Aug. 20, 1917; d. Thomas Smith and Susan (Whitlow) Compton. BS in Edn., Ark. State Tchrs. Coll., 1939; BS in Libr. Sci., Peabody Coll. Tchrs., 1948. Asst. cataloger U. Ark. Gen. Libr., Fayetteville, 1948-49; head catalog dept. Ark. Libr. Commn., Little Rock, 1949-77, chief cataloger, bibliographer, indexer, 1977-79; free-lance writer. Mem. Nat. League Am. Pen Women (v.p., program chmn. Ark. Pioneer br. 1972-74, pres. 1974-76), AAUW, Am. Libr. Assn. (life), Ark. Hist. Assn., Ark. Fedn. Women's Clubs. Author: Beauty Transient & Other Poems, 1969, Looking Forward to a New Day, 1984, Ozark Sketches: A Family Chronicle, 1990; contbr. to Collier's Ency., 1970-76; editor quar. libr. bull. Ark. Librs., 1949-74. Christadelphian. Home: 620 N Oak St Little Rock AR 72205

COMRIE, SANDRA MELTON, human resource executive; b. Plant City, Fla., Sept. 15, 1940; d. Finis and Estelle (Black) Melton; m. Allan Crecelius; children: Shannon Melissa, Colleen Megan. BA, UCLA, 1962, grad. exec. program, 1984. Div. mgr. City of L.A., 1973-77, asst. pers. dir., 1977-84; v.p. Transam. Life Cos., L.A., 1984-89; chief operating officer Treacy & Rhodes Consultants, Solana Beach, Calif., 1989—; bd. dirs. Found. for Employment and Disability, Sacramento, Clif.; mem. Asian Pacific Employment Task Force, Los Angeles, 1986-89. Bd. dirs. L.A. Urban League, 1985—, Vols. of Am.-L.A., 1985-89; active United Way Downtown Bus. Consortium, Child Care Task Force, L.A., 1985-86; mem. adv. bd. L.A. City Child Care, 1987-89. Recipient Young Woman of Achievement award Soroptimists of Los Angeles, 1979. Mem. Internat. Personnel Mgmt. Assn. (mem. assessment council, co-chair program com. for 1982 nat. conf., chair human rights com. 1983, pres. 1985), So. Calif. Personnel Mgmt. Assn., Personnel Testing Council, Personnel and Indsl. Rels., Inc., Los Angeles C. of C. (human resources com. 1986-89). Democrat. Office: 462 Stevens Ave Solana Beach CA

COMSTOCK, DONNA LEE, publishing company executive; b. Buffalo, Sept. 16, 1929; d. James William Comstock and Mary Margaret (Honaker) Campbell; m. William A. Forrest Jr., Dec. 29, 1952 (div.); m. Walter J. Maytham III, Oct. 15, 1983. BA in English and Dance, Randolph-Macon Women's Coll., 1953; MA in Ednl. Adminstrn., NYU, 1968; MBA, Fordham U., 1980. Sr. editor, basal reading CBS-Holt Rhinehart, 1971-73, dir. field cons., 1973-76; mgmt. devel. exec. CBS Pub. Group, 1976-78; sr. mktg. mgr. McGraw-Hill Inc., N.Y.C., 1978-80, mgr. bus. devel., 1980-81, dir. planning, 1981-83, editorial dir., 1983-86, v.p. editorial and prodn., 1986—. Office: McGraw-Hill Inc 1221 Ave of the Americas New York NY 10020

CONAGHAN, DOROTHY DELL, state legislator; b. Oklahoma City, Sept. 24, 1930; d. John Joseph and Wilhelmina Elizabeth (Boyer) Miller; student U. Okla., 1949-51; m. Brian Francis Conaghan, June 10, 1951 (dec. Apr. 1973); children: Joseph Lee, Charles Alan, Roger Lloyd; m. Robert K. Chiles, Aug. 15, 1986. Mem. Okla. Ho. of Reps., 1973-86, minority caucus sec., 1977-82, asst. minority leader, 1983-86. Bd. dirs. Alpha II, 1973-86, Community Liaison Council Juvenile Services, Ponca City, Okla., 1983-84, Alcohol, Drug Abuse and Community Mental Health Planning and Coordinating Bd., 1984-86, Okla. Christian Found., 1984-89; trustee Okla. chpt. Leukemia Soc. Am., 1985-87; pres. Washington Sch. PTA, Tonkawa, 1965, Okla. Christian Found., 1988; vice chmn. Kay County Republican Com., 1960-64, 6th Dist. Congl. Rep. Com., 1967; del. Rep. Nat. Conv., 1968; 3d vice moderator Christian Ch. (Disciples of Christ), 1986-88; lay mem. Okla. Health Planning Commn., 1988—. Recipient Women Helping Women award Ponca City Soroptimist Club, 1975, hon. mem., 1978. Mem. Nat. Order Women Legislators, Am. Legis. Exchange Council (state dir.), Tonkawa C. of C., Am. Legion Aux., P.E.O., Okla. Alliance for Artisans (v.p., bd. dirs.), Beta Sigma Phi (hon.). Clubs: Delphi Study, Order Eastern Star (past matron), Soroptimists Internat. of Ams. (hon.).

CONANT, COLLEEN CHRISTNER, newspaper editor; b. Oklahoma City, Dec. 17, 1947; d. John Frederick and Mary Louise (Holloway) Christner; m. Terry Morse Conant, Jan. 20, 1973; children: Andrew John, David Ryan. MusB, Oklahoma City U., 1970. Reporter The Stuart (Fla.) News, 1970-75, city editor, 1975-80, mng. editor, 1980-85; mng. editor The Comml. Appeal, Memphis, 1985—. Mem. editorial bd. Ch. News, Tenn. Episc. Diocese, Memphis, 1989; mem. pres.'s coun. Rhodes Coll., Mmephis, 1987-89, LeMoyne-Owen Coll., Memphis, 1989; juror Pulitzer Prize, 1987, 89. Mem. AP Mng. Editors Assn. (bd. dirs. 1989—), Tenn. AP Mng. Editors Assn. (pres. 1987-87), Scripps Howard Mng. Editors Assn., Rotary. Democrat. Home: 7260 Stamford Dr Germantown TN 38138 Office: The Comml Appeal 495 Union Ave Memphis TN 38103

CONANT, SHARI, insurance company executive; b. Cleve., Nov. 12, 1947; d. Rudy Louis and Christine Barbara (Testman) Jaros; m. Donald Richard Conant, Dec. 23, 1967; children: Donald R. II, Amy Dawn. AA in Underwriting, Ins. Inst. Am., 1981; postgrad., Life Office Mgmt. Inst., 1983, Am. Coll., 1986. Cert. profl. ins. woman, 1981; CLU. Claims clk. CNA Ins. Co., Cleve., 1966-67; underwriter Fireman's Fund Ins. Co., Cleve., 1967-70, Beacon Mut. Ins. Co., Columbus, Ohio, 1976-79; sales mgr. Avon Co., Columbus, 1972-76; underwriter for farm owners Country Mut. Ins. Co., Bloomington, Ill., 1979, property tng. coordinator, 1979-80; coordinator agy. tng. info. Country Cos., Bloomington, 1980-81, agt. tng. specialist, 1981-88, agt. tng. design specialist, 1989—. Sec., treas. McLean Soccer Referees Assn., Normal, Ill., 1984—, Cen. Ill. Soccer Ofcls. Assn., Springfield, 1988—; mem. Twin City Civic Newcomers, Normal, 1979—. Named one of Outstanding Young Woman of Am., 1983. Mem. Bloomington-Normal Ins. Assn. (sec. 1979-81, treas. 1981-84, v.p. 1984-85, pres. 1985-86, Assoc. of Yr. award 1986), Nat. Assn. Ins., Women Internat., Bloomington-Normal Life Underwriters, Nat. Assn. Life Underwriters, Am. Soc. Chartered Life Underwriters. Democrat. Lutheran. Home: 1203 Valentine Dr Normal IL 61761 Office: Country Cos 1701 Towanda Ave Bloomington IL 61701

CONANT-LAWER, MARCIE LEE, professional singer, actress; b. Englewood, N.J., Nov. 16, 1960; d. John Edward and Michelle Angel (Paradise) Conant; m. Robert Alton Lawer, June 25, 1989. BA, Westminster Coll., 1982, Jersey City State Coll., 1984. Juvenile detention officer Bergen County Juvenile Detention Ctr., Paramus, N.J., 1982; subs. tchr. Bergen County Sch. Dist., 1982-84; soloist Amato Opera, N.Y.C., 1982-86; tchr. Passaic (N.J.) Cath. Regional, 1986-; soloist Westside Presbyn. Ch., Englewood, 1984-86; chorister, soloist Oakland Opera, 1988—; chorister San Francisco Opera, 1986-. Mem. Am. Guild Musical Artists. Office: San Francisco Opera War Meml Opera House San Francisco CA 94107

CONARD, DIANE JOY, architect; b. Princeton, N.J., Sept. 5, 1959; d. Charles Lefferts and Fay (Duvall) C. BS, Rensselaer Poly. Inst., 1981, BArch, 1982; MS, U. Vt., Burlington, 1985. Registered architect, N.Y. Asst. rehab. specialist West Hill Improvement Corp., Albany, N.Y., 1981-82; cons. Historic Albany Found., 1980-84; engr. technician Keegan Assocs., Albany, 1982-84; rehab. specialist South End Improvement Corp., Albany, 1984; teaching asst. U. Vt., Burlington, 1984-85; architect, mgr. Stracher-Roth-Gilmore, Schenectady, N.Y., 1986-90; asst. dir. Hudson Housing Svcs. Corp., Hudson, N.Y., 1990—; prin. D.J. Conard RA, AIA, Scotia, N.Y., 1990—; cons. in field; career cons. Hudson Valley Community Coll., Troy, N.Y., 1982-85. Author, coord. booklet, slide tape on rural preservation, 1986. Mem. AIA, NAFE, Nat. Trust Historic Preservation, Assn. Preservation Tech. Office: Hudson Housing Svcs 444 Warren St Hudson NY 12534

CONAWAY, JANE ELLEN, educator; b. Fostoria, Ohio, July 9, 1941; d. Robert and Virginia Conaway; B.A. in Elem. Edn., Mary Manse Coll., Toledo, 1966; M.Ed. in Elem. Edn., U. Ariz., 1969; postgrad. in reading, U. Toledo, 1975-77; postgrad. U. Wis., 1987—. Tchr. Sandusky pub. schs., Ohio, 1966-67, Bellevue City Schs., Ohio, 1969-70; coord. 1st grade small group instrn. program St. Mary's Grade Sch., Sandusky, 1970-71; tchr. Chpt. I remedial reading Eastwood Local schs., Pemberville, Ohio, 1971-87, also dist. dir. Right to Read program; reading specialist Middleton-Cross Plains (Wis.) Area Sch. Dist., 1987—. Mem. NEA, Wis. Edn. Assn., Middleton Edn. Assn., Madison Area Reading Coun., Delta Kappa Gamma. Cert. as reading specialist in diagnostic and remedial reading, Wis. Home: 1302 Wexford Dr Waunakee WI 53597 Office: Middleton Cross Plains Sch Dist 6701 Woodgate Rd Middleton WI 53562

CONCHERI, KATHLEEN ELSIE, soft drink company representative; b. Methuen, Mass., Oct. 10, 1963; d. Richard Lee and May (Bistany) C. BS, Boston Coll., 1985. Ter. sales mgr. Coca-Cola USA, Mt. Laurel, N.J., 1985-86, ter. sales mgr. II, 1986-87; area account exec. Coca-Cola USA, Boston, 1987—, area trainer, coll. recruiter, 1988—. Mem. NAFE, New Eng. Health and Racquet Club. Roman Catholic. Office: Coca-Cola USA Reservoir Pl 1601 Trapelo Rd Waltham MA 02154

CONDE, ALICE, association executive; b. Havana, Cuba, Jan. 4, 1946; came to U.S. 1961; d. Augusto F. and Catalina deSena (Ramos) Conde; m. Jose L. Martinez, Sept. 3, 1966 (div.). B.A., George Washington U., 1968, postgrad., 1968-70. Registrar univ. div. George Washington U., Washington, 1968-69; programs coordinator Am. Psychiat. Assn., Washington, 1969-83; exec. dir. Am. Coll. Psychiatrists, Greenbelt, Md., 1983—; cons. Group for Advancement of Psychiatry, 1980-88, Am. Acad. Psychiatrists in Alcoholism and Addictions, 1985—, Am. Assn. Geriatric Psychiatry, 1987—, Am. Psychiat. Assn. Aux., 1989—. Vol. Greenbelt Mus. Com. Recipient Fellowship Appreciation, Mead Johnson Pharm. Div. and Am. Psychiat. Assn., 1983. Mem. Meeting Planners Internat., Greater Washington Soc. Assn. Execs., Profl. Conv. Mgmt. Assn., Nat. Assn. Female Execs., Pan Am. Soc., Nat. Assn. Cuban-Am. Women in U.S.A. Republican. Roman Catholic. Home: 4 Olivewood Ct Greenbelt MD 20770 Office: Am Coll Psychiatrists PO Box 365 Greenbelt MD 20768

CONDIE, CAROL JOY, anthropologist, research facility administrator; b. Provo, Utah, Dec. 28, 1931; d. LeRoy and Thelma (Graff) C.; m. M. Kent Stout, June 18, 1954; children: Carla Ann, Erik Roy, Paula Jane. BA in Anthropology, U. Utah, 1953; MEd in Elem. Edn., Cornell U., 1954; PhD in Anthropology, U. N.Mex., 1973. Edn. coordinator Maxwell Mus. Anthropology, U. N.Mex., Albuquerque, 1973, interpretation dir., 1974-77; asst. prof. anthropology U. N.Mex., 1975-77; cons. Albuquerque, 1977-78; pres. Quivira Research Ctr., Albuquerque, 1978—; cons. anthropologist U.S. Congl. Office Tech. Assessment, chair Archeol. Resources Planning Adv. Com., Albuquerque, 1985-86; leader Crow Canyon Archeol. Ctr. field seminars, 1986—; appointee Albuquerque dist. adv. coun., bur. land mgmt. U.S. Dept. Interior, 1989. Author: The Nighthawk Site (LA 5685), a Pithouse Site on Sandia Pueblo Land, Bernalillo County, New Mexico, 1982, Five Sites on the Pecos River Road, 1985; co-editor: Anthropology of the Desert West, 1985; also articles. Mem. Downtown Core Area Schs. Com., Albuquerque, 1982. Ford Found. fellow, 1953-54; recipient Am. Planning Assn. award, 1985-86, Gov.'s award, 1986. Fellow Am. Anthropol. Assn., mem. Soc. Am. Anthropology (chmn. Native Am. Relations com. 1983-85), N.M. Archeol. Council (pres. 1982-83, Hist. Preservation, 1988), Maxwell Mus. Assn. (bd. dirs.), Las Arañas Spinners and Weavers Guild (pres. 1972). Democrat. Home and Office: Quivira Research Ctr 1809 Notre Dame NE Albuquerque NM 87106

CONDIT, MADELEINE KAY BRYANT, executive search specialist; b. Indpls., May 1, 1941; d. H. Herschel and Helen L. (McDaniel) Bryant; m. Philip Murray Condit, Jan. 25, 1963 (div. 198l); children: Nicole Lynn, Megan Anne. BA, U. Calif., Berkeley, 1963; MBA, U. Colo., 1983. Exec. fellow Sloan Sch., MIT, Cambridge, 1975; seminar coord. ID Ctr., Seattle, 1975-78; editor Puget Soundings mag., Seattle, 1981-83; v.p. Boettcher & Co., Denver, 1983-85; prin. Korn-Ferry Internat., Chgo., 1985—. Bd. dirs. Heads Up, Bellevue, Wash., 1972-74, A Contemporary Theatre, Seattle, 1976-81, Jr. League Seattle, 1976, 78, 80, Mercer Island (Wash.) Youth Svcs., 1980-81, Big Sisters Colo., Denver, 1983-87, mem. adv. coun., 1988-90; bd. dirs. Kent Denver Sch., 1985-90, AMC Cancer Rsch. Ctr.; chmn. Wash. Commn. on Community Affairs and Continuing Edn., Olympia, 1977-81; mem. nat. evaluation task force Girl Scouts U.S.A., 1980; mem. Colo. Efficiency and Mgmt. Com., 1986; found. mem. Pacific Sci. Ctr., Seattle, 1980—; chmn. bus. adv. coun. U. Denver, 1988-90, mem. bd. fellows, 1987—; mem. adv. coun. Colo. Advanced Tech. Inst., 1986-90, AMC Cancer Rsch. Ctr., 1989—. Mem. Securities Industry Assn., Investment Assn. N.Y., Women in Syndicate, Syndicate Round Table, River Club. Episcopalian. Home: Korn-Ferry Internat 120 S Riverside Pla #918 Chicago IL 60606

CONDOS, BARBARA SEALE, real estate investment consultant, broker; b. Kenedy, Tex., Feb. 24, 1925; d. John Edgar and Bess Rochelle (Ainsworth) Seale; m. George James Condos, Dec. 24, 1955 (dec.); 1 child, James Alexander. MusB magna cum laude, Incarnate Word Coll., San Antonio, 1946. Lic. real estate broker, Tex. Ptnr., chief exec. officer Mountain Top-V.I. Devel. Properties, V.I., 1977-85; ptnr. Condos & Rhame, San Antonio, 1976—, Investment Realty Co., San Antonio, 1978—; pres. Hallmark Realty, Inc., San Antonio, 1978—. Choreographer, dancer San Antonio Symphony's Youth Concerts and Opera Festival; actress San Antonio Little Theatre-Patio-Players 1948—. Trustee San Antonio Little Theatre, 1953-76; trustee Incarnate Word Coll., 1977-89, vice chair, 1980-82, trustee emerita, 1989—; mem. coun. McNay Mus., 1986—, chair coun., 1987—; chair coun. McNay Art Inst., 1988—; trustee McNay Art Mus., 1989—; bd. dirs. San Antonio Performing Arts Assn., 1978—. Mem. Internat. Real Estate Fedn., Internat. Inst. of Valuers, Real Estate Securities and Syndication Inst., Nat. Assn. Realtors, Tex. Assn. Realtors, San Antonio Bd. Realtors, The Argyle Club. Avocation: painting. Home: 217 Geneseo Rd San Antonio TX 78209 Office: Investment Realty Co 1635 NE Loop 410 San Antonio TX 78209

CONDRA, FRANCES RIFE, real estate broker, investor, genealogist; b. San Antonio, July 28, 1929; d. Thadeus D. and Jean (Templeton) Rife; m. Lee R. Condra, Sept. 26, 1950; children: Russell L., Roger C., Richard N. BA, Our Lady of the Lake U., 1983, MBA, 1985; postgrad, Lincoln Graduate Ctr., 1987. Cert. master sr. appraiser. Owner Condra Real Estate, San Antonio, 1970—. First woman to file for county commr., Bexar County, Tex. Mem. San Antonio Hist. and Geneal. Soc., Hist. and Geneal. Soc. of Caldwell County, Tex. State Hist. Soc., Wilson County Hist. Commn., San Antonio Conservation Soc. (assoc. mem.), San Antonio Bd. of Realtors, Tex. Assn. of Realtors, Nat. Assn. of Realtors, German Heritage Soc. of Tex., Nat. Assn. of Master Appraisers (cert. residential, farm and land appraiser 1987), German Tex. Heritage Soc., San Antonio Women's C. of C., Southside C. of C., Tex. State Geneal. Soc., Am. Assn. U. Women, Bexar County Hist. Commn., The U. Tex. Inst. Texan Cultures, Dau. Rep. of Tex. (Alamo chpt.), Nat. Soc. of Dau. Am. Revolution (James McHenry chpt.), United Daus. of Confederacy (Albert Sidney Johnston chpt.), Castle Hills Woman's Club, U. Women's Garden Club. Republican. Methodist. Home: 204 Glentower Dr San Antonio TX 78213 Office: Condra Real Estate 2161 NW Military Hwy San Antonio TX 78213

CONDRA, NORMA LEE, newspaper publisher; b. Russell, Ky.; d. Pem Burton and Lottie Lee (Edleman) Kuhn; children: David, Cynthia Condra Snyder. Student U. Tenn. Pub. Country Hot Line News, Nashville, 1977-79, Wilson World, Lebanon, Tenn., 1979-80; founder, pub. Town & Country Courier, Nashville, 1981—, Hendersonville (Tenn.) Free Press, 1975—; pub. Goodlettsville Free Press, Madison Free Press, White House Free Press; bd. dirs. Dominion City Bank. Chmn. Hendersonville Arts Council, 1978-79; mem. Sumner County Literacy Bd.; community bd. dirs. Vol. State Community Coll. Mem. Nat. Fedn. Ind. Bus. (Tenn. adv. bd.), White House Conf. Small Bus. (Tenn. del.), Suburban Newspapers of Am. (bd. dirs. 1981-85), Hendersonville C. of C. (bd. dirs., pres.-elect 1982). Republican. Methodist. Club: Tenn. Women's Golf Assn. (pres. 1980-82), Hillwood Country, Bluegrass Country (Hendersonville). Home: 106 Christopher St Nashville TN 37205 Office: Hendersonville Free Press 131 Sanders Ferry Rd Hendersonville TN 37075

CONDRAN, CYNTHIA MARIE, gospel musician; b. Avon Pk., Fla., Apr. 29, 1953; d. Kenneth Dale and Ruth Mae (Garber) Grubb; m. Lee Light Condran, July 3, 1971. Student, Lebanon Valley Coll., 1970-72. Piano tchr. Sebring, Fla., 1968-70, Annville, Pa., 1971-90; gospel musician, writer, arranger Condran Music Co., Annville, Pa., 1972-90, also recording engr.; writer comml. jingles. Sang by spl. invitation at the Elipse of The White House, 1982; composer The Only Thing Holding You Back, 1977, Just A Few More Rivers, 1975, The Patchwork Quilt, 1978, Freedom, 1976, The Little Things, 1980, We're America, Heavens Fiesta, He's the Lord of Everyday, 1989, I've Never Known Such Love, 1990, I Just Want To Talk To You, 1990, Sweep Our Sins, 1990. Mem. Gospel Music Assn., Broadcast Music Inc., Christian Bus. and Profl. Women (music chmn.). Republican. Home: RD 3 Box 602 Annville PA 17003

CONDRAVY, JOAN CAROL, English language educator; b. Allentown, Pa., June 13, 1952; d. John William and Hilda (Wunderley) Condravy; m Timothy Douglas Chase, Jan. 8, 1983. BA in English, Gettysburg Coll., 1974; MS in Counseling, Shippensburg U., 1977. Cert. tchr., Pa. Tchr. English Gettysburg (Pa.) Area Sch. Dist., 1974-81; assoc. prof. Slippery Rock (Pa.) U., 1981—, chmn. women's studies program, 1985—, also tutorial svcs. coordinator. Author articles on writing process; poet. Mem. AAUW, Nat. Women's Studies Assn., Nat. Council Tchrs. English, Coll. Composition and Communication Assn., Nat. Assn. for Devel. Educators. Office: Slippery Rock U B106 Bailey Library Slippery Rock PA 16057

CONDRILL, JO ELLARESA, logistician, speaker; b. Hull, Tex., Oct. 25, 1935; d. Freddie and Ida (Donatto) Founteno; m. Edwin Leon Ellis, Jan. 9, 1955 (div. 1979); children—Michael Edwin, James Alcia, Resa Ann, Thomas Matthew; m. Donald Richard Condrill, Sept. 21, 1980 (div. 1985). BS in Bus. Adminstrn., Our Lady of the Lake U., 1982; grad. Logistics Exec. Devel. Course, Army Logistics Mgmt. Ctr., 1985; MS in Pub. Adminstrn., Cen. Mich. U., 1987; grad. Program Mgmt. Course, Def. Systems Mgmt. Coll., 1989. Cert. seminar coord. Sec. USAF, Wiesbaden, Fed. Republic Germany, 1968-73; sec. mil. tng. ctr. USAF, San Antonio, 1973-77; editorial asst. Airman Mag., San Antonio, 1978; mgmt. analyst San Antonio Air Logistics Ctr., San Antonio, 1979-82; inventory mgr. ground fuels Detachment 29, Alexandria, Va., 1982-83; logistics plans officer Mil. Dist. Washington, 1983-85, chief logistics plans ops. and mgmt., 1985-88, hdqrs. dept. of the army staff Office of the Dep. Chief of Staff for Logistics, 1988—; owner Seminars by Jo, Alexandria, Va., 1984-86; field instr. Golden State U., L.A., 1985-86; instr. Fairfax County Adult Edn., Springfield, Va., 1984; vol. aide ARC Wilford Hall Hosp., San Antonio, 1978; constn. drafter KC Women's Aux., San Antonio, 1977; den mother Boy Scouts Am., San Antonio, 1967; docent Nat. Mus. Am. History, 1988. Recipient Cert. of Achievement, Dept. Army, 1984; Best Speaker award Def. Logistics Agy. Mem. Soc. Logistics Engrs., Federally Employed Women (Pentagon I chpt. treas. 1987-88), Internat. Platform Assn., Am. Soc. Pub. Adminstrn., Toastmasters (area gov. 1984-85, div. lt. gov. 1988-89, adminstrv. lt. gov. 1989-90, dist. 27 ednl. lt. gov. 1990—). Republican. Roman Catholic. Home: 5904 Mount Eagle Dr #317 Alexandria VA 22303

CONE, BONNIE ETHEL, university administrator; b. Lodge, S.C., June 22, 1907; d. Charles Jefferson and Addie Lavinia (Harter) C. BS, Coker Coll., 1928; AM, Duke U., 1941; DLitt (hon.), Coker Coll., 1961; LLD (hon.), Davidson Coll., 1961. Various teaching positions, 1928-47; tchr. math. Charlotte Ctr., U. N.C., 1947-49; dir., tchr. math. Charlotte Coll., 1949-61; asst. sec., treas. Charlotte Community Coll. System, 1958-63; pres. Charlotte Coll., Charlotte Community Coll. System, 1961-63; pres. state-supported sr. coll. Charlotte Coll., 1963-65; acting chancellor U. N.C., Charlotte, 1965-66, vice chancellor for student affairs and community rels., 1966-73; liaison officer Found. of the U. N.C., Charlotte, 1973-77; vice chancellor emerita U. N.C., Charlotte, 1973—. Author: Personalities of the South, 1970, North Carolina Lives, 1962, Outstanding Educators of America, 1972; contbr. articles to profl. jours. Bd. trustees Coker Coll., 1954-72, 74-79, chairperson, 1974-76; bd. dirs. Charlotte YWCA, 1958-61, rsch. and svc. coun. So. Assn. Colls. and Schs., 1959, United Arts Coun., 1964, Scholarship Fund of the Southeastern Fair, 1964, Consumer Credit Counseling Svc., 1968, Hezekiah Alexander Restoration Fund, 1969-73, Mecklenburg Inner City, Inc., 1973-74, Charlotte Opera Assn., 1977-80, Habitat for Humanity, 1984-86; bd. Christian edn. Myers Park Bapt. Ch., 1959; bd. visitors Davidson Coll., 1961. Recipient Sta. WBT Radio Woman of Yr. award, 1956, Sta. WSOC Broadcasting Corp. Pub. Svc. Achievement award, 1958, Silver Medallion award Mecklenburg chpt. NCCJ, 1962, Disting. Citizens award Charlotte Civitan Club, 1964-65, Disting. Citizenship award N.C. Dist. Civitan Internat., 1965, Liberty Bell award Law Day USA, 26th Jud. Dist. Bar Assn., 1966, Disting. Svc. award Royal Soc. of Knights of the Carrousel, 1967, Elaine Nichols award UNCC Black Studies Ctr., 1975, many other awards. Mem. Am. Assn. Jr. Colls. (chairperson editorial bd. Jr. Coll. Jour. 1958-61), N.C. Edn. Assn., NEA, AAUW, Delta Kappa Gamma, Pi Mu Epsilon. Home: 9234 Sandburg Ave Charlotte NC 28213

CONE, FERNE GELLER, author, designer; b. Portland, Oreg., Oct. 9, 1921; d. Borus and Sadie Gertrude (Cohen) Geller; m. J. Morton Cone, Mar. 21, 1948; children: Carol Ann Cone Gulan, Wendy Lee Cone Dore. Student, U. Wash., 1960-61. Sec. Oreg. Welfare Commn., Portland, 1941-42; adminstrv. asst. Office of Price Adminstrn., Portland, 1942-44; publicity asst. RWR, San Francisco, 1944-46; with White Stag Mfg. Co., Portland, 1946-48; owner The Yarn Boutique, Seattle, 1963-68; freelance designer Seattle, 1960—; community devel. specialist Office Community Devel., U. Wash., Seattle, 1980; cons. in field. Author: Knit Art, 1975, Knutty Knitting for Kids, 1977, Knit with Style, 1979, Crazy Crocheting, 1981, Classy Knitting, 1984, Knitting for Real People, 1990; contbr. articles to profl. jours. Coord. writers conf. Pacific N.W., 1982-84; bd. dirs. Sr. League of Seattle, KUOW Pub. Radio, 1976-85; solicitor Rep Party. Mem. The Fashion Group (edn. chmn. 1970-72), Sml. Bus. Assn., Soc. Children's Book Writers, Seattle Art Mus., Am. Crafts Coun., Seattle Freelances (pres. 1982-84). Home and Office: 6401 Sand Point Way NE Seattle WA 98115

CONE, FRANCES MCFADDEN, data processing consultant; b. Columbia, S.C., Oct. 20, 1938; d. Joseph Means and Francis (Graham) McFadden; m. Charles Cone Jr., May 1962 (div. Sept. 1964); 1 child, Deborah Ann Cone Craytor. BS, U. S.C., 1960, MEd, 1973, M Math., 1977. Systems svc. rep. IBM, 1960-62; programmer/analyst Ga. Power Co., Atlanta, 1964-68, S.C. Fin. and Data Processing, Columbia, 1968-69; instr., head dept. Midlands Tech. Coll., Columbia, 1969-75; tng. coord. S.C. Nat. Bank, Columbia, 1975-79; systems analyst S.C. Dept. Health and Environ. Control, Columbia, 1979-80; project analyst So. Co. Svcs., Atlanta, 1980-89; cons. George Martin Assocs., Atlanta, 1989—; adj. prof. Golden Gate U., Sumter, S.C., 1976-80. Mem. Nat. Mgmt. Assn. (sec., treas., awards chmn. 1981-89). Republican. Episcopalian. Office: George Martin Assocs 12 Executive Park Dr NE Atlanta GA 30329

CONE, KAREN ELIZABETH, management analyst; b. Quitman, Ga., Apr. 19, 1961; d. Arnold and Willie Elizabeth (Cook) Croft; m. John H. Cone Jr., Sept. 28, 1988; 1 child, Kasey Elizabeth. BA in Polit Sci. with honors, Valdosta State Coll., 1984; postgrad., Tex. A&M U., 1984, South Tex. Coll., 1985-86; MPA with honors, Valdosta State Coll., 1987. Grad. asst. Tex. A&M U., College Station, 1984; sr. staff cons. Keypeople Resources, Houston, 1985; coord. assn. Tall Timbers Rsch. Sta., Tallahassee, Fla., 1986-87; program auditor office auditor gen. State of Fla., Tallahassee, 1987-88; sr. mgmt. analyst office inspector gen. dept. natural resour State of Fla., 1988—. Participant fund drive United Way, Moultrie, Ga., 1982, blood drive ARC, 1982; judge Sci. Fair Leon County Sch. System, Tallahassee, 1987; speaker Ga. Pol. Sci. Conv., Savannah, 1987, del. Model UN, N.Y.C., 1983; active Tallahassee Community Chorus. Ty Cobb scholar, 1982-84. Mem. AAUW (newsletter editor 1988-89), NAFE, Pi Gamma Mu (pres. 1983-84), Omicron Delta Kappa (v.p. 1983-84), Sigma Alpha Chi. Methodist. Home: 5016 Stoneler Rd Tallahassee FL 32303

CONE, MARY, English educator; b. Doddsville, Miss., Mar. 13, 1923; d. John Edmon and Sally Elsie (Morris) C. BA, Miss. U. for Women, 1945; MA, U. Miss., 1953, PhD, 1970. English tchr. Glen Allan (Miss.) High Sch., 1945-48, Bay High Sch., Bay St. Louis, Miss., 1948-49, Minter City (Miss.) High Sch., 1949-51, Morgan City (Miss.) High Sch., 1951-53; English instr. N.W. Miss. Jr. Coll., Senatobia, 1953-58; part-time English instr. U. Miss., Oxford, 1958-65; asst. prof. English Miss. U. for Women, Columbus, 1965-70, assoc. prof. English, 1970-86, assoc. prof. emeritus, 1986—. Author: Fletcher Without Beaumont: A Study of the Independent Plays of John Fletcher, 1976. Mem. AAUW, Phi Kappa Phi, Sigma Tau Delta. Democrat. Methodist. Home: 901 Second Ave N Apt 1 Columbus MS 39701

CONE, VIRGIE HORNE HYMAN, former educator, civic worker; b. Brooksville, Fla.; d. George G. and Virgie (Horne) Hyman; m. Edward Elbert Cone, Dec. 20, 1930 (dec. Feb. 1962); children: Molly Gentile (dec. Jan. 1989), Edward Elbert. BS, Fla. State Coll. Women; MEd, U. Fla., 1956. Tchr., Meml. Jr. High Sch., Hillsborough County, 1929-31; tchr. Duval County Robert E. Lee Sr. High Sch., Jacksonville, Fla., 1943-55, dean, 1955-70; prin. Lee High Sch. (1st woman secondary sch. prin. in county), 1971-74; owner Cone's Antiques. Chmn., ARC night vols. St. Vincent's Hosp., 1969-71; mem. task force Mayor's Community Planning Coun., 1969; pres. Hamilton County unit Am. Cancer Soc., 1974-76; v.p. Hamilton County Meml. Hosp. Aux., 1975-76; mem. adv. coun. Health and Rehab. Svcs., Dist. 3, Fla.; dir. Area Agy. on Aging, 1977-82, bd. dirs., 1982—; del. White House Conf. on Aging, 1981; mem. adv. coun. Social Security; mem. state legis. com. Am. Assn. Retired Persons, 1983-87, chmn., 1986-87; mem. State Longterm Care Ombudsman Coun., 1983-87, chmn. 1985-87 mem. adv. coun. State Civil Rights Commn.; pres. North Fla. Mental Health Bd., 1978-80; mem. Hamilton County Planning Coun., Gov.'s Commn. on Status Women, 1978-80; mem. exec. bd. North Central Fla. Health Planning Coun., 1979-80; bd. dirs. Mid. Fla. Area Agy. on Aging, State Comprehensive Health Assn.; mem. pub. issues com. Am. Cancer Soc.; mem. Banking Sunset Task Force, Fla., 1990—. Mem. Fla. Coun. Tchrs. Math. (curriculum chmn. 1952, sec. 1949), AAUW (Jacksonville v.p. 1953), Duval Tchrs. Assn. (chmn. profl. rights and responsibilities com. 1965-66), Jacksonville Panhellenic Assn. (pres. 1959-60, mem. scholarship com. 1963-68), Duval Personnel and Guidance Assn. (organizing chmn. 1966-69), Nat., Fla. assns. secondary prins., Hamilton Ret. Tchrs., Fla. Assn. Area Agy. Dirs. (pres.), Am. Assn. Ret. Persons (capitol city task force, state legis. com.), Delta Kappa Gamma (chpt. pres. 1959-61), Sigma Kappa (nat. scholarship chmn. 1963-77). Clubs: Pilot of Jacksonville, Suwannee Valley Country (dir. 1978-80). Home: NW 3d St Jasper FL 32052

CONE, VIRGINIA WILLIAMS, retired history educator; b. Noble, Ill.; d. George Washington and Ella (Maddox) Williams; m. Elmer Newton Searls, Nov. 27, 1933 (div. 1948); children: Leslie, Janice; m. Leon Winston Cone, Mar. 25, 1948; children: Henrietta Maria, Winston George. BA in History summa cum laude, U. Ill., 1943, MA, 1946; student, Blackburn Coll., 1930-32. Educator U. Ill., Champaign, 1943-48, Purdue U., LaFayette, Ind., 1948-62, U. Ghana, Accra, 1958-59, U. Dar es Salaam, Tanzania, 1962-64, Kenya Inst. Adminstrn., Nairobi, 1964-66; assoc. prof. African history So. Conn. State U., New Haven, 1967-82, adj. prof. of women in U.S. history, 1982—. Author: Africa: A World in Progress, 1961, Kenya Women Look Ahead, 1965. Mem. AAUW (del. to Forum '85), Pnenex Soc. (pres.), Phi Beta Kappa. Republican. Congregationalist. Home: 9 Cedar Rd Woodbridge CT 06525

CONERLY, ERLENE BRINSON, chemist; b. Jackson, Miss., Nov. 16, 1938; d. Alvin Bryan and Erlene (Brinson) C. BS, Millsaps Coll., 1959; MS in Tech. Mgmt., Am. U., 1978. Chemist NIH, Bethesda, Md., 1962-78; research biologist Dynamac, Rockville, Md., 1979-80; chemist U.S. EPA, Washington, 1980—. Democrat. Episcopalian. Office: US Environ Protection Agy 401 M St SW TS 769 C Washington DC 20460

CONEY, CAROLE ANNE, accountant; b. Berkeley, Calif., Aug. 11, 1944; d. Martin James and Ida Constance (Ditora) Skuce; m. David Michael Coney, June 20, 1964; children: Kristine Marie, Kenneth Michael. BS cum laude, Calif. State Poly. U., 1985, MBA, 1988; MBA, Calif. State Poly. U., Pomona, 1989. Tax cons., instr. H&R Block, Portland, Oreg., 1969-71; acct., asst. sec.-treas. Surety Ins. Co., La Habra, Calif., 1973-76; bookkeeper Homemakers Furniture, Downers Grove, Ill., 1976-79; office mgr., acct. Helen's Pl. Printing, Upland, 1979-80; bookkeeper Vanguard Cos., Upland, 1980-82; dir. acctg. Coll. Osteopathic Medicine of Pacific, Pomona, Calif., 1982-89; acctg. mgr. City of Ontario, Calif., 1989—. Pres. Brea/La Habra Newcomers, 1975; treas. Alta Loma (Calif.) Com. to Elect Robert Neufeld, 1981. Mem. NAFE, Nat. Assn. Coll. and Univ. Bus. Officers, Assn. Coll. and Univ. Auditors, CSMFO, GFOA, Coun. Fiscal Officers, Soroptomists, Delta Mu Delta, Alpha Iota. Democrat. Roman Catholic. Lodge: Soroptimists. Home: 9521 Konocti St Cucamonga CA 91730 Office: City of Ontario 303 East B St Ontario CA 91764

CONFORTI, JOANNE, advertising executive; b. N.Y.C., Apr. 17, 1944; d. Ralph and Josephine (Amico) C. Student, Bklyn. Coll., 1961-63. Trainee, Gen. Motors, N.Y.C., 1960-62, adminstrv. asst., 1962-66, personnel asst., 1966-70; staff asst. Bozell & Jacobs, Inc., N.Y.C., 1973-75, personnel and office mgr., 1975-77, personnel and office v.p., 1977-79, human resources dir., v.p., 1979-81, corp. human resources dir., sr. v.p., from 1981, now exec. v.p. corp. human resources. Mem. Advt. Women of N.Y. Home: 252 E 61st St New York NY 10021 Office: Bozell Inc 40 W 23d St New York NY 10010

CONGDON, SARAH-BRAEME, medical equipment company executive; b. East Orange, N.J., Aug. 10, 1952; d. Alfred Bird Jr. and Barbara-Anne (Jones) Stewart; m. James Boote Congdon, Feb. 21, 1976; children: Arthur Edward, James Westbrook. Student, U. N.C., Greensboro, 1971; AA, Katherine Gibbs Sch., Montclair, N.J., 1973; BBA, U. Pa., 1989. With CIA, Washington, 1973-75; asst. to pres. and chmn. bd. Affiliated Mfrs., Inc., North Branch, N.J., 1975-76; bus. adminstr. U. Pa., Phila., 1976-82; project mgr. Inst. for Structural and Functional Studies, Phila., 1982-86, mng. dir., 1986—; v.p. ops. Phospho-Energetics, Inc., Havertown, Pa., 1978-86, dir. rsch. adminstrn., 1986-88; v.p. NIM, Inc., Phila., 1987-88, pres., 1988—; cons. Phospho-Energetics, Inc., Havertown, Pa., 1988—; v.p. Synchrotronics, Inc., Phila., 1988—. Mem. Spruce Hill Community Assn., Phila., 1979. Mem. NAFE, Soc. Rsch. Adminstrs., Licensing Execs. Soc., Nat. Trust for Hist. Preservation, University City Hist. Soc. Home: 4100 Spruce St Philadelphia PA 19104 Office: NIM Inc 3401 Market St Ste 100 Philadelphia PA 19104

CONGER, VIRGINIA LEE, ceramics designer; b. Atlanta, Oct. 3, 1961; d. Ledlie William Conger and Virginia (Lee) Kirby. BS in Home Econs., U. Ga., 1983; cert., Sch. of Design, 1988. Color and design selector Gulf Tile Dist., Tampa, Fla., 1985-87; kitchen and bath specialist Dal Tile Dist., Tampa, 1988—. Painter Paint Your Heart out Tampa, 1989. Mem. Am. Soc. Interior Designers (assoc.), Builders Assn. Greater Tampa (assoc.). Republican. Episcopalian.

CONGER, VIRGINIA LOUISE (GINGER CONGER), personnel director; b. Borger, Tex., July 27, 1945; d. Roy Virgil and Mary Louise (Boynton) Keeth; children: Ronald Lee, Jr., Matthew Keeth. BS in Bus., Okla. State U., Stillwater, 1966. Mktg. sec. Cities Svc. Oil Co., Tulsa, 1966-69; human resources adminstr. EG & G Chandler Engring., Tulsa, 1980—. Mem. Indsl. Rels. Assn., Tulsa Pers. Assn., Profl. Secs. Internat. Republican. Methodist. Office: EG&G Chandler Engring 7707 E 38th St Tulsa OK 74145

CONGLETON, LAURA HELEN, multimedia consultant; b. Stamford, Conn., Jan. 14, 1962; d. Edward Blackburn and Lois Helen (Foster) C. BA, Mt. Holyoke Coll., S. Hadley, Mass., 1984. Mgr. svc. stds. Chase Manhattan Bank, N.Y.C., 1984-87; mng. editor Sci. DataLink, N.Y.C., 1987-89; multimedia cons. N.Y.C., 1989—. Asst. producer Videowall installation, 1990; free-lance writer; computer software instr. Vol. The Pearl Theatre Co., N.Y.C., 1988—, InTouch Networks, N.Y.C., 1990. Mem. Women in Communications, N.Y. Acad. TV Arts and Scis.

CONIBEAR, SHIRLEY A., occupational health consultant, physician; b. Amboy, Ill., Aug. 20, 1946; d. Herbert Louis and Margaret (Cenkar) C.; m. Bertram Carnow, Oct. 31, 1975; children: Rebecca, Kalinka, Tina. BA, Shimer Coll., 1968; MD, U. Ill., 1973, MPH, 1976. Diplomate Am. Bd. Preventive Medicine, Am. Bd. Family Practice. Dir. health and hazard evaluation Cook County Hosp., Chgo., 1977-78; dir. programs in medicine, occupational medicine residency U. Ill. Coll. Medicine, Chgo., 1978-79, assoc. prof. occupational medicine, 1982-88; v.p. Carnow, Conibear & Assocs., Chgo., 1977-88, pres., 1988—; epidemiologist Argonne Nat. Lab., Lemont, Ill., 1979-81; chief med. officer Milw. RR, Chgo., 1982-86; cons. to Dept. Energy, Washington, 1986—. Author: Medical Surveillance of Hazardous Waste Workers, 1990; editor: First Aid Manual for Chemical Accidents, 1989; contbr. chpts. to books; editorial adviser Occupational Health and Safety Jour. Fellow Am. Coll. Preventive Medicine; mem. Am. Coll. Epidemiology, Am. Coll. Toxicology, Am. Med. Women's Assn., Am. Indsl. Hygiene Assn., Am. Coll. Occupational Medicine, Am. Pub. Health Assn. Office: Carnow Conibear & Assocs 333 W Wacker Dr Ste 1400 Chicago IL 60606

CONKLIN, ANNA IMMACULATA G., mathematics teacher, treasurer; b. N.Y.C., Aug. 9, 1951; d. Cosimo Phillip and Josephine Anna (D'Andra) Zotti; m. Joseph Dennis Conklin. BA in Early Childhood Edn, Jersey City State U., 1973; MA in ESL, Kean Coll., Union, N.J., 1984; postgrad., Rutgers U., 1984—. Tchr. sci. and math. St. Michael's, Jersey City, 1973-74; tchr. math. and lang. arts Union City (N.J.) Bd. Edn., 1974—; box office mgr. Pk. Players Theater Orgn., Union City, 1984—; active Passion Play, Union City, 1974—. Vol. ARC, Am. Cancer Soc. Mem. N.J. Edn. Assn., World Wildlife Fedn., Am. Cetacean Soc., Phi Delta Kappa. Democrat. Roman Catholic.

CONKLIN, FRANCES PHILLIPS, retired radiologist, educator; b. Port Jervis, N.Y., July 8, 1924; d. Robert Conkling and Marion (Rice) Phillips; m. J. Wallace Conklin, July 31, 1949 (div. 1983); children: Jonathan, Jennifer, Elizabeth, Suzanne. BA, U. Wis., 1945; MD cum laude, U. Vt., 1951. Diplomate Am. Bd. Radiology, Nat. Bd. Med. Examiners. Rotating intern Santa Barbara (Calif.) Coll. Hosp., 1951-52; resident in radiology U. Minn. and U. Minn. Hosps., Mpls., 1952-55; staff radiologist Temple U. Hosp., Phila., 1955-56; radiologist in-charge radiation therapy R.I. Hosp., Providence, 1958-72; pvt. practice, Providence, 1972-89; ret., 1989; clin. asst. prof. radiation medicine Brown U., Providence, 1984-90; mem. bd. med. discipline and licensure State of R.I., Providence, 1987-90; corp. mem. Blue Cross & Blue Shield R.I. Author: (with Coleman and Olfelt) Manual of Radiation Therapy, 1957; contbr. articles to med. jours. Med. dir. reach to recovery, past chmn. svc. and rehab. com. R.I. div. Am. Cancer Soc.; trustee Episcopal Housing Found. R.I.; bd. mgrs. Hallworth House; mem. med. adv. com. Hospice Care R.I., Inc.; bd. dirs. R.I. Lung Assn. Recipient Therese Lasser award Am. Cancer Soc., 1980, Woman Physician of Yr. award R.I. Med. Women's Assn., 1989, Charles L. Hill award R.I. Med. Soc., 1990. Fellow Am. Coll. Radiology; mem. R.I. Med. Soc. (treas. 1986-90, recipient Charles L. Hill award, 1990), Providence Med. Assn. (pres. 1984-85, exec. com. 1989), Save the Bay, Seaport '76, Am. Assn. Ret. Persons. Republican. Home: 54 Hybrid Dr Cranston RI 02920

CONKLIN, SUSAN JOAN, psychotherapist; b. Bklyn., Feb. 7, 1950; d. Joseph Thomas Hallek and Stella Joan (Kubis) Kuceluk; m. John Lariviere Conklin, July 25, 1981; children: Genevieve Therese, Michelle Therese. BA, CCNY, 1972; MSW, CUNY, 1975. Lic. ind. clin. social worker; cert. diplomat. Shop counselor Assn. for Help of Retarded Citizens, N.y.C., 1971-75; dir. social svcs., acting exec. dir. North Berkshire Assn. for Retarded Citizens, North Adams, Mass., 1975-77; project dir. Title XX tng. grant State of Mass., North Adams, 1978-79; pvt. practice psychotherapy Williamstown, Mass., 1979—; asst. prof., North Adams State Coll., 1977-85, Berkshire Community Coll., Pittsfield, Mass., 1985-86. Mem. Nat. Assn. Social Workers (bd. dirs. 1981-83, regional coun. mem. 1980-85), Nurse Healers-Profl. Assn., Inc. (editor-in-chief Cooperative Connection newsletter 1983-88). Democrat. Episcopalian. Home and Office: 85 Hawthorne Rd Williamstown MA 01267

CONLEY, BARBARA BERNADETTE, freelance writer; b. Mass.; d. Manuel and Georgiana (Costa) Vieira; m. Douglas J. Salter, July 19, 1958 (div. 1971); children: Cheryl-ann, Sandra Gail, Douglas J. Jr.; m. David D. Conley, Nov. 23, 1984. Student, Los Altos High Sch., 1967-68; grad., Writer's Digest Sch., Cin., 1987. Data processing clk. Bank of Am., San Francisco, 1961-64; circulation mgr. The Poultry Times, Gainesville, Ga., 1968-71; full-charge bookkeeper Ditch Witch of Colo., Commerce City, 1972-74; asst. mgr. Avco Fin. Svcs., Thornton, Colo., 1974-79; loan officer Security Ind. Bank, Denver, 1979-80; exec. br. mgr. TransAmerica Fin. Svcs., Colo., 1980-87; freelance writer Commerce City, 1988—; loan originator Teller Fin. Svcs., Lakewood, Colo., 1988; reporter Commerce City Beacon, 1989—. Vol. Literacy Program for Adams County, Commerce City, Colo., 1988—. Home and Office: 6110 E 61st Ave Commerce City CO 80022

CONLEY, MARIITA AROSEMENA, municipal government official; b. Spokane, Wash., Mar. 23, 1951; d. John G. and Doris Elida (Arosemena) C. BA, Purdue U., 1973; MA in Econs., U. Tex., Austin, 1976; postgrad., U. Chgo., 1978. Mgr. strategic planning Beatrice Co., Chgo., 1978-81, mgr. pub. affairs, 1981-86; exec. dir. Beatrice Found., Chgo., 1986-88; dep. commr. Mayor's Office of Employment and Tng., Chgo., 1989—; pres. Corp. Responsibility Group Greater Chgo., 1989-90. Bd. dirs. Chgo. Latinos in Philanthropy, 1988-89, Greater Chgo. Food Depository, 1989-90; mem. adv. bd. Make-A-Wish Found., Chgo., 1989-91. Mem. Am. Soc. Tng. and Devel., Hispanics in Philanthropy, Ind. Sector. Democrat. Roman Catholic. Office: Mayors Office Employment and Tng 510 Peshtigo Ct Chicago IL 60611

CONLIN, JOANNE, infosystems specialist, writer; b. Mt. Holly, N.J., July 11, 1955; d. George Albert and Margaret Laura (Rainier) C.; m. Dennis Charles Haller, Apr. 2, 1982 (div. Dec. 1987). Degree with honors, Blair Sch. for Journalism, 1972; AA in Journalism, Burlington County Coll., 1977; BA in Journalism/Communications, Temple U., 1981; postgrad., Monmouth Coll., 1988—. Reporter, writer Tampa (Fla.) Tribune Newspaper, 1973-74; asst. mgr. customer svc. govt. systems div. Western Union, 1974-80; sr. tech. writer GTE Info. Systems, 1980; from sr. tech. writer to mgr. advt. and promotion Threshold Tech. Inc., 1980-81; specialist mgmt. info. systems documentation Datamedia Corp., 1981; from writer assoc. to programs adminstr. Okidata, Mt. Laurel, N.J., 1982-87; project mgr., writer AT&T, Middletown, N.J., 1987—. Contbr. articles to profl. jours. Vol. Monmouth County; mem. Clean Ocean Action; pres. Redford Corners Condominium Assn. Mem. NAFE (bd. dirs.), Nat. Soc. for Tech. Communications (sr. mem., Excellence award 1987, 88, Merit award 1988, 89, Distinction award 1989). Episcopalian. Home: 2501 Municipal Ct Wall Township NJ 07719 Office: AT&T 200 Laurel Ave Middletown NJ 07748

CONLIN, NANCY MARIE, professional counselor; b. Dallas, May 25, 1949; d. William Wayne and Lela Marie (Robinson) Kidd; m. Miller Frederick Jr., May 24, 1975; children: Randy, Shannon, Kelly. Student, Okla. Baptist U., 1969; BS in Elem. Edn., Southeast Mo. State Coll., 1971; postgrad., U. Houston, 1976. Lic. profl. counselor. Kindergarten tchr. Houston Independent Sch. Dist., 1971-76, early childhood handicapped coord., 1976-78; ch. staff profl. counselor First Baptist Ch., Tulsa, Okla., 1985-. vol. counselor S. Main Baptist ch., Houston, 1978-80, First Baptist ch., Tulsa, 1983-85. mem. Christian Assn. Psychological Studies. Republican. Home: 1514 S 76th E Ave Tulsa OK 74112 Office: First Bapt Church 403 S Cincinnati Tulsa OK 74103

CONLIN, OLIVE WESTBERRY, educator; b. Savannah, Ga., Sept. 2, 1943; d. James R. and Ann (Dixon) Westberry; m. George F. Conlin, Dec. 30, 1966; children: George F. Jr., Karen, Lisa, Joseph. BS, Stetson U., 1964; MEd, Armstrong-Savannah State Coll., 1979; EdD, U. Ga., 1989. Programmer IBM, Houston, 1965-66; tchr. various pvt. schs., Savannah, 1972-80; instr. Armstrong State Coll., Savannah, 1981-85; computer resource tchr. Chatham County Bd. Edn., Savannah, 1985—; conf. presenter Mid-South Assn. Computer Educators, Baton Rouge, 1988, Ga. Instnl. Tech. Conf., Columbus, Ga., 1989. Leader Girl Scouts U.S.A., Savannah, 1983-85. Ford Found. fellow, 1964. Mem. Internat. Assn. Computer Edn., Assn. for Supervision and Curriculum Devel., Phi Delta Kappa. Baptist. Office: Chatham County Bd Edn 208 Bull St Savannah GA 31401

CONLIN, ROXANNE BARTON, lawyer; b. Huron, S.D., June 30, 1944; d. Marion William and Alyce Muraine (Madden) Barton; m. James Clyde Conlin, Mar. 21, 1964; children: Jacalyn Rae, James Barton, Deborah Ann, Douglas Benton. B.A., Drake U., 1964, J.D., 1966, M.P.A., 1979; LL.D. (hon.), U. Dubuque, 1975. Bar: Iowa 1966. Assoc. firm Davis, Huebner, Johnson & Burt, Des Moines, 1966-67; dep. indsl. commr. State of Iowa, 1967-68, asst. atty. gen., 1969-76; U.S. atty. So. Dist. Iowa, 1977-81; ptnr. Galligan & Conlin, P.C., 1983—; gen. counsel Legal Def. and Edn. Fund, NOW, 1985-88, pres., 1986-88; adj. prof. law U. Iowa, 1977-79; guest lectr. numerous univs. Chmn. Iowa Women's Polit. Caucus, 1973-75, del. nat. steering com., 1973-77; cons. U.S. Commn. on Internat. Women's Year, 1976-77. Contbr. articles to profl. publs. Nat. committeewoman Iowa Young Democrats; also pres. Polk County Young Dems., 1965-66; del. Iowa Presdl. Conv., 1972; Dem. candidate for gov. of Iowa, 1982; bd. dirs. Riverhills Day Care Center, YWCA; chmn. Drake U. Law Sch. Endowment Trust, 1985-86; bd. counselors Drake U., 1982-86; pres. Civil Justice Found., 1986-88. Recipient award Iowa ACLU, 1974, Iowa Citizen's Action Network, 1987, Alumnus of Yr. award Drake U. Law Sch., 1989, also others; named to Iowa Women's Hall of Fame, 1981; scholar Reader's Digest, 1963-64, Fischer Found., 1965-66. Mem. ABA, Iowa Bar Assn., Assn. Trial Lawyers Iowa (bd. dirs.), Assn. Trial Lawyers Am. (chmn. consumer and victims coalition com. 1985-87, chmn. edn. dept. 1987-88, parliamentarian 1988-89, sec. 1989-90), ACLU, Common Cause, Women's Equity Action League, NOW (bd. dirs. 1986-88), Higher Edn. Comm. Iowa (co-chmn. 1988-90), Phi Beta Kappa, Alpha Lambda Delta, Chi Omega (Social Svc. award). Office: 300 Walnut Pla Ste 5 Des Moines IA 50309-3790

CONLON, APRIL HARRINGTON, creative services executive; b. Orchard Pk., N.Y., Mar. 9, 1958; d. John William and Anna (Szarowski) Harrington; m. Kevin John Conlon, May 3, 1985. BA in Communication, SUNY, Buffalo, 1980. Asst. promotion mgr. WGRZ-TV2, Buffalo, 1980-87, creative svcs. dir., 1987-89; ind. broadcast cons., 1989—. Mktg. cons. Muscular Dystrophy Assn., Alcohol Svcs. Erie County Adolescent Bldg. Campaign, 1987-89; pub. rels., bd. dirs. ARC, Buffalo, 1988—. Recipient Gold Medallion Broadcast Promotion and Mktg. Execs., 1985, Cert. of Meit, 1985, N.Y. State Broadcasters award, 1985, Broadcast Journalism award Pat Weaver-Muscular Dystrophy Assn., 1987, Am. Lung Assn. award Buffalo Chpt., 1988, Multiple Sclerosis Appreciation award Western N.Y. Soc., 1988. Mem. Broadcast Promotion and Mktg. Execs., Profl. Communicators Western N.Y. (Silver award 1990). Roman Catholic. Home: 151 Crownview Hamburg NY 14075

CONLON, KATHRYN ANN, county official; b. Mankato, Minn., July 30, 1958; d. Ralph Raymond and Joan Margaret (Meyer) Walter; m. James Alan Conlon, Oct. 1, 1977; children: Jessica Marie, Brian Michael. Student, Mankato Vocat. Sch. Teller Mankato Credit Union, 1977; clk. Nicollet County Credit Bur., Minn., 1977-78; abstracter Lorna Holmquist, St. Peter, Minn., 1978-82; dep. recorder, abstracter Nicollet County, 1982-84, county recorder, abstracter, 1984—, sec. to dept. heads, 1985, chmn. dept. heads, 1986. Mem. Spina Bifida Assn. Minn., 1981—, Spina Bifida Assn. S.W. Minn., 1983—; bd. dirs. Children's Cen. Child Care, 1985-87. Mem. Minn. Assn. County Recorders, VFW Aux., Am. Legion Aux., St. Peter Area C. of C. Avocations: handcrafting, camping, volleyball. Home: Rte 3 Box 116 Saint Peter MN 56082 Office: Nicollet County Recorder PO Box 493 Saint Peter MN 56082

CONLON, SUZANNE B., federal judge; b. 1939. AB, Mundelein Coll., 1963; JD, Loyola U., Chgo., 1968; postgrad., U. London, 1971. Law clk. to judge U.S. Dist. Ct. No. Dist. Ill., 1968-71, asst. U.S. atty., 1976-77, 82-86, judge, 1988—; assoc. Pattishall, McAuliffe & Hostetter, 1972-73, Schiff Hardin & Waite, 1973-75; asst. U.S. atty. U.S. Dist. Ct. Cen. Dist. Calif., 1978-82; exec. dir. U.S. Sentencing Commn., 1986-88; asst. prof. law De Paul U., Chgo., 1972-73, lectr., 1973-75. Mem. ABA, Fed. Bar Assn., Calif. Bar Assn., L.A. County Bar Assn., Chgo. Bar Assn., Nat. Assn. Women Judges. Office: US Dist Ct 219 S Dearborn St Chicago IL 60604*

CONN, ADINA, association executive; b. Bklyn., Aug. 7, 1962; d. Leo and Marion (Feingold) C. BA in Theatre Arts magna cum laude, Brandeis U., 1984; MA in Mass Communications, U. Fla., 1986. Pub. info. cons. Hillel Found., Gainesville, Fla., 1984-85; editor dept. pediatrics U. Fla., Gainesville, 1984-86, survey specialist, 1986; asst. account coord. Ehrlich Manes & Assocs., Washington, 1985; editor, creative dir., advt. mgr. Am. Land Title Assn., Washington, 1987—; celebrity personality interviewer, Washington, 1987—; asst. rep. for fine artists and illustrators Adina Conn and Assocs., Washington, 1989—; cons., researcher Palm Beach Post, Gainesville, 1986; mem. faculty Folio mag. Hansen Pub. Group, N.Y.C., 1989. Author: (play) Ethel: The Song Unsung, 1984. Pres. ALS Chpt. Greater Washington, 1989—. Reicpient This Is My Best award U. Fla. Sch. Mass. Communications, 1989-90. Mem. Soc. Nat. Assn. Publs. (sec.-treas. 1988-89, v.p. 1989-90, pres.-elect 1990-91, speaker 1988-90, cons., researcher 1988), Am. Soc. Assn. Execs., Brandeis U. Alumni Assn. (steering com 1988-89), U. Fla. Alumni Assn., NIH R:W Theatre Group, U.S. Holocaust Meml. Mus. (cons., researcher, writer 1990), Phi Rho Sigma. Jewish. Office: Adina Conn & Assocs 3130 Wisconsin Ave NW Ste 413 Washington DC 20016 Office: Adina Conn & Assocs 3130 Wisconsin Ave NW Ste 413 Washington DC 20016

CONN, EUNICE MARIE JANICKI, vending machine company executive; b. Jan. 2, 1938; m. Donald F. Conn, May 10, 1958; 4 children. Student, U. Ill., 1956, Wright Jr. Coll., 1957. Sec., bookkeeper Strom Constrn. Co., Chgo., 1954-58; v.p., gen. contractor Variety Home Builders, 1956-58; saleswoman Studio Girl Cosmetics, Hollywood, Calif., 1963-65, regional mgr., 1965-68; regional mgr. Fashion Frocks, Ohio, 1968-70; officer, office mgr. E.B. Conn Vending, Inc., Niles, Ill., 1970—; pres., mgr. Playhouse Prodns., Inc., Niles, 1983—; mem. region 5 small bus. adv. coun., SBA, 1984—; mem. Ill. Small Bus. Conf., 1984, Govt. Assisted Industry Network, 1985-86, No. Cook County Pvt. Industry Coun., 1986; del. White House Conf. on Small Bus., 1980, 86; bd. dirs. Chgo. Entrepreneur Inst., 1986-88; former mem. small bus. adv. coun. Oakton Community Coll.; mem. Ill. Conf. on Small Bus. Exports, 1988. Active numerous civic orgns., 1970—, including Sr. Girl Scouts U.S.A., 1977-78; fund raising chmn. Boy Scouts Am., 1970-72; bd. dirs. St. Isaac Jogues Women's Club, 1970-81, pres., 1972-73; dist. pres. Archdiocese of Chgo. Cath. Women's Club, 1974-75; mem. Niles Twp. Task Force on Drug Abuse, 1981-82; bd. dirs. Ill. Coun. on Tourism, 1985—; mem. Chgo. Crime Commn., 1988—; mem. nat. exec. bd. Small Bus. People for Reagan, 1980; committeewoman 9th Congl. Dist. Rep. Cen. Com., 1984-86; Rep. candidate for state representative, 1990. Recipient President's Meritorious Svc. award Nat. Assn. Postage Stamp Vendors, 1982, Co-Vendor of Yr. award, 1984; co-Ill. Small Bus. Media Adv. of Yr. award SBA, 1985. Mem. Ind. Bus. Assn. Ill. (co-founder, bd. dirs. 1981-88, pres. 1985-86, treas. 1987-88), Chgo. Assn. Commerce and Industry (exec. bd. 1985-87, v.p. small bus. coun. 1985-87, Outstanding Contbns. to Small Bus. Community award 1985, Vol. Leadership award 1988). Home: 9245 Maple Ct Morton Grove IL 60053 Office: 8565 W Dempster Rd Ste 200 Niles IL 60648

CONN, VIRGINIA LOUISE STARBUCK, volunteer; b. Youngstown, Ohio, Nov. 9, 1916; d. Daniel Karl and Louise Gilette (Mills) Starbuck; m. James J. Conn, June 27, 1940; children: James R., Steven, Christopher, Kathleen. BA and BS in Edn., Ohio State U., 1938, MA, 1942. High sch. tchr. Worthington, Ohio, 1938-40; rsch. asst. Coll. Edn. Ohio State U., Columbus, 1943-44; pers. asst. State of Ind., Indpls., 1944-45. Dir. Ohio State Alumni Assn., Columbus, 1966-71, Ohio State Devel. Fund Bd., Columbus, 1971-76; past pres. Ohio State Alumnae Coun., 1962-64. Recipient 25 Yr. Svc. award Franklin County Heart Assn., 1983, 25 Yr. award Columbus Symphony Orchestra, 1985, Centennial award Ohio State Univ., 1970, Disting. Svc. award Ohio State Univ., 1986, Josephine Failer Svc. award Alumni Assn. Ohio State Univ., 1990. mem. AAUW (chair to book group, 1954-56), Alumnae Scholarship House Bd. (chair, 1957—), Starling Ohio Women's Club (past pres.), Woman's Aux. to Columbus Acad. Medicine (past pres.).

CONNELL, ELIZABETH BISHOP, obstetrician/gynecologist, educator; b. Springfield, Mass., Oct. 17, 1925; d. Homer Guy and Margaret (Kincaid) Bishop; m. John Thomas Connell, June 11, 1949 (div. Dec. 1975); children: Robert, Thomas, Richard, David, James, Patricia; m. Howard J. Tatum, June 28, 1980. AB, U. Pa., 1947, MD, 1951. Diplomate Am. Bd. Ob-Gyn. Intern, resident in pathology, anesthesia Lankenau Hosp., Phila., 1951-53; assoc. prof. dept. ob-gyn. N.Y. Med. Coll., N.Y.C., 1964-69; resident in gynecology Grad. Hosp. U. Pa., Phila., 1958-60; resident in obstetrics Mt. Sinai Hosp., N.Y.C., 1960-61; Am. Cancer fellow Kings County Hosp. SUNY, Bklyn., 1961-62; pvt. practice Blue Hill, Maine, 1953-58; assoc. prof. Coll. Physicians, Surgeons Columbia U., N.Y.C., 1970-73; assoc. dir. Health Scis. Rockefeller Found., N.Y.C., 1973-78; assoc. prof., lectr. Northwestern U., Chgo., 1978-85; prof. Sch. Med. Emory U., Atlanta, 1981—; dir. Family Planning Ctr. N.Y. Med. Coll., 1964-69, Family Planning Program Internat. Inst. for Study Human Reproduction Columbia U., 1970-73; active adv. com. and panels FDA, 1970—; rsch. adv. com. Agy. Internat. Devel. U.S. Dept. State, 1973-82, cons. Health Scis., 1982—; rsch. project devel. coord. Program Applied Rsch. on Fertility Regulation Northwestern U., 1978-80; guest researcher Ctr. Health Promotion and Edn. Ctrs. for Disease Control, Atlanta, 1981—; cons. Emory Med. TV Network, 1986—. Active numerous coms., assns. and bd. dirs. Planned Parenthood Fedn. Am., 1964—;exec. com. Assn. Voluntary Sterilization, 1969-76, v.p., 1974-76, 78-80, bd. dirs., 1980-83; mem. Population Crisis Com., 1970-74; v.p. Population Resource Ctr., 1976-77, chair bd. advisors, 1976-79; mem. Gov.'s Spl. Coun. Family Planning, 1989—. Mem. Internat. Soc. Advancement Humanistic Studies in Gynecology, Am. Coll. Obstetricians and Gynecologists, Am. Fertility Soc., Assn. Reproductive Health Profls., N.Y. Obstet. Soc. Home: 3159 Marne Dr NW Atlanta GA 30305 Office: Emory U Sch Med 69 Butler St SE Atlanta GA 30303

CONNELL, KATHLEEN SULLIVAN, state government official; b. Newport, R.I., May 24, 1937; d. Lawrence Francis and Margaret (Byrnes) Sullivan; m. Gerald Connell, June 11, 1960; children: Lawrence, Margaret, Kathleen. BS in Nursing magna cum laude, Salve Regina Coll., 1958; postgrad., Boston Coll., U. R.I., R.I. Coll. Registered nurse Newport Vis. Nurses Assn., 1958-61; health educator Newport Sch. Dept., 1970-86; sec. of state State of R.I., Providence, 1987—; pres., bd. dirs. Shake-a-Leg, Inc. Mem. Middletown Sch. Com. 1965-76, chmn. 1972-76; mem. Middletown Town Council 1977-83, vice-chmn. 1981-83; active Save the Bay, Aquidneck (R.I.) Goals Group, Aquidneck Ecology; mem. council nominating com. Newport Girl Scouts of U.S.; bd. dirs. Vis. Nurse Service of Newport County; vice-chmn. R.I. Dem. Com.; mem. Dem. Women's Caucus, Middletown Charter Rev. Commn.; mem. Dem. Nat. Com. Recipient awards R.I. Library Assn., Vol. Services for Animals, John F. Kennedy Ctr. for Performing Arts, Very Spl. Arts Assn.; named Alumnus of Yr. Salve Regina Coll., 1987. Mem. Am. Nurses Assn., R.I. State Nurses Assn., R.I. Sch. Nurses Assn., NEA, R.I. Edn. Assn., LWV, Women's Network, Vietnam Vets. of Am. (assoc.), Newport Irish Heritage Soc. (bd. dirs.), Nat. Conf. State Legislatures (com. labor and edn.), Delta Kappa Gamma. Home: 233 Tuckerman Ave Middletown RI 02840 Office: Office Sec of State 217 State House Smith St Providence RI 02903*

CONNELL, LINDA MARIE, dietitian; b. Williamsport, Pa., Jan. 30, 1957; d. Gerald Thomas and Marlot Wilma (Klein) C. BS in Dietetics, U. Ariz., 1980, MS in Dietetics, 1983. Dietician Tucson Med. Ctr., 1982-83; dietician Canyon Ranch Resort, Tucson, 1983-86, dir. nutrition svcs., 1986-89; dietitian Houstonian Club, Houston, 1989—; nutrition cons., Tucson, 1982-89. Author (column) Restaurant Revealing, 1986; contbr. articles to profl. jours. Mem. Am. Dietetic Assn., Nat. Council Against Health Fraud, Ctr. for Sci. in Pub. Interest, Am. Running and Fitness Assn., Sports and Cardiovascular Nutritionists. Home: 8027 Oakwood Forest Dr Houston TX 77040 Office: Houstonian Club 111 N Post Oak Ln Houston TX 77024

CONNELL, SHIRLEY HUDGINS, public relations professional; b. Washington, Oct. 5, 1946; d. Orville Thomas and Mary (Beran) H.; m. David Day Connell, Dec. 13, 1980 (div. 1985). BA, U. R.I., 1968, MA, 1970. Clk., editor MGM Studios, Culver City, Calif., 1970-72; scriptor, talent Monarch Records, Studio City, 1972-73; communications specialist U. So. Calif., L.A., 1973-81; dir. pub. rels. Six Flags Movieland, Buena Park, Calif., 1981-82, Donald J. Fager & Assocs., N.Y.C., 1982—; cons. Children's TV Workshop, N.Y.C., 1978. Contbr. articles to profl. jours.; contbg. editor Greater N.Y. Doctor's Shopper mag., 1987—. Pres. bd. trustees Oaks at North Brunswick Condominium Assn., 1987—; founding mem. Mcpl. Svcs. Com., North Brunswick; mgr. Animal Rescue Force, North Brunswick, 1988—; apptd. mem. environ. com. Twp. of North Brunswick, chmn., 1990. Mem. NAFE, Marine Tech. Soc. (vice chmn. 1980-81), Mensa (pub. rels. adv. com. 1989—), Oceanic Soc. (bd. dirs. 1979-81, instr. Princeton rev. 1990)), L.A. Press Club.

CONNELLY, BECKY LOU, retail buyer; b. Cheyenne, Wyo., Oct. 11, 1940; d. Newcomb B. Bennett and Thelma L. (Saunders) Heidke; m. Robert M. Connelly, Oct. 28, 1960 (div. 1975);1 children: Candace L., Robert M. Student, U. Md., 1958-60. Buyer Jacobson's, Winter Park, Fla., 1975—. Mem. NAFE, PEO, Adult Literacy League, Nat. Abortion Rights Action League, Gamma Phi Beta. Republican. Home: 372 Shadow Bay Blvd N Longwood FL 32779 Office: Jacobsons 245 Driggs Dr Winter Park FL 32792

CONNELLY, CAROLYN THOMAS, chemistry educator; b. Brownville, Maine, Feb. 25, 1941; d. Adna Moulton and Lillian (Davis) Thomas; m. Edwin Russell Connelly, Aug. 11, 1984. BA in Chemistry, U. Maine, Orono, 1963; PhD in Chemistry, Northeastern U., 1968. Cert. secondary sch. tchr. in chemistry, Pa. Lectr. Lincoln Coll., Northeastern U., Boston, 1967-68; rsch. chemist U.S. Army Natick (Mass.) Labs., 1967-68; asst. prof. chemistry Waynesburg (Pa.) Coll., 1968-73, assoc. prof. chemistry, 1973-77, prof. chemistry, 1977—. Mem. Warrior Trail Hiking. NSF fellow, Boston, 1965; rsch. grantee faculty rsch. Waynesburg Coll., 1969-70. Mem. Am. Chem. Soc., Sigma Xi. Office: Waynesburg Coll Waynesburg PA 15370

CONNELLY, EILEEN BERNADETTE, art director; b. N.Y.C., Jan. 26, 1965; d. Paul and Marion Theresa (O'Donahue) C. Student, Parsons Sch. Design, N.Y.C., 1983-85; BFA, Sch. Visual Arts, N.Y.C., 1988. Layout artist Village Voice, N.Y.C., 1987-89; designer PolyGram Records, N.Y.C., 1988-89; art dir. ARISTA Records, N.Y.C., 1989—. Office: ARISTA Records 6 W 57th St New York NY 10019

CONNELLY, PATRICIA LORRAINE, travel executive; b. Phila., Mar. 29, 1948; d. Robert H. and Helen (Kinsley) Nickerson; m. Joseph J. Connelly, Jan. 10, 1986. BA, Western State U., 1987; postgrad., Holy Family Coll., 1988. Mgr. Trainseair Travel Inc., Phila.; assn. tax acct. Gen. Refractories Co., Phila.; travel mgr. Morgan, Lewis, Bockius, Phila.; adv. bd. Four Seasons Hotel. Mem. Nat. Passenger Traffic Assn. (past v.p.), Delaware Valley Corp. Travel Mgrs. Assn. (past v.p.), Am. Soc. Travel Agts. (cert.), Meeting Planners Internat., Internat. Soc. Meeting Planners (cert. meeting planner), Torresdale Civic Assn., Penn Ctr. House Civic Assn.

CONNER, COLLEEN COLGAN, staff training consultant; b. Kewanee, Ill., Jan. 1, 1949; d. Joseph Patrick and Majella Catherine (Harty) Colgan; m. John L. Conner, Aug. 21, 1971 (div. Mar. 1986); children: Sarah, Jeffrey. Student, U. Fribourg, Switzerland, 1969-70; BA in French, Rosary Coll., 1971; MEd, U. Nev., 1989. Cert. elem. and secondary edn. tchr., Nev., Ill. Counselor 4H Camp Assn. at U. Ill., Champaign, 1968-71; tchr. Washoe County Sch. Dist., Reno, 1971-78, 85-90; mem. No. Nev. writing project Washoe County Sch. Dist., 1985—, staff tng. cons., 1990—; reader of writing proficiency exams Nev. Dept. Edn., Carson City, 1988-89, participant urban-rural tchr. exch., 1989; participant Lang. Pract-Inn, Calif. Fgn. Lang. Tchrs. Assn., Lake Tahoe, Nev., 1988. Active Holy Cross Ch. Bazaar, Sparks, Nev., chmn., 1981; vol. instr. Reno Jr. Ski Program. French Lang. Immersion Inst. grantee Nev. Dept. Edn., U. Calif., Berkeley, 1989. Mem. AAUW, Am. Assn. Tchrs. of French (local v.p. 1989—), Am. Coun. Tchrs. Fgn. Lang., Washoe County Tchrs. Assn., ESL (cert.), Assn. Supervision and Curriculum Devel. Democrat. Roman Catholic. Home: 2964 Lida Ln Sparks NV 89434 Office: Profl Devel Ctr Washoe County Sch Dist 425 Ninth St Reno NV 89520

CONNER, GAY ARTERBURN, public relations associate; b. Oklahoma City, Aug. 2, 1962; d. David Craig and Elizabeth Anna (Broach) Wright; m. Christopher Noel Conner, Oct. 14, 1990; 1 child, Danielle Marie Arterburn. BA in English, Oklahoma City U., 1984. Prodn. asst. C.L. Davis & Assocs., Oklahoma City, 1984-85; brochure devel. coord. Okla. Tourism and Recreation Dept., Oklahoma City, 1985-87; communications editor Am. Fidelity Cos., Oklahoma City, 1987-89; pub. rels. assoc. Bapt. Med. Ctr. Okla., Oklahoma City, 1989—; pub. rels. cons. Casa Bonita Restaurants, Inc., 1985-87, Oklahoma City profl. chpt. Soc. Profl. Earth Scientists, 1986. Chmn. in-house editors subcom. United Way of Cen. Okla., 1988, chmn. spl. events com., 1990—; v.p. publicity Friends of Met. Libr., Oklahoma City, 1989; newsletter art dir. Freedom of Info. Okla. Inc., 1990-91; mem. com. Okla. Bar Media Rels., 1990—. Recipient B.L. Semtner award United Way of Cen. Okla., 1987, 88, 89; Bronze Derrick award Pub. Rels. Soc. Am., 1987, 88; cert. of recognition Friends of Met. Libr., Oklahoma City, 1989, others. Mem. Women in Communications Inc. (newsletter editor 1986-87, treas. 1987-88, v.p. programs 1988-89, Byliner's chair 1989-90, pres. 1990-91), Okla. Hosp. Assn. (hosp. pub. rels., mktg. soc.), Phi Eta Sigma. Home: 5016 NW 62d St Oklahoma City OK 73122 Office: Bapt Med Ctr Okla Pub Rels Dept 3300 NW Expressway Oklahoma City OK 73112

CONNER, JANET AUSTIN, foundation administrator; b. Chgo., Sept. 14, 1946; d. Jess and Lillie (Clay) Austin; m. Robert Anthony Conner, July 10, 1966; 1 child, Robyn Jani. BS, Chgo. State U., 1973, MS, 1975. Social svc. coordinator Chgo. Assn. for Retarded Citizens, 1974-75, adminstr., 1975-89, cons., 1989—; pres. Events Unltd., Chgo., 1986—; cons. in field. Pres.-elect Roseland Community Hosp. Aux., 1985-87, pres., 1987—; chmn. Sickle Cell Anemia Vol. Enterprise, Michael Reese Hosp., 1986-89, pres., 1989—. Mem. Am. Assn. Mental Deficiency, Am. Healthcare Assn., Nat. Soc. Fundraising Exec., Meeting Planners Internat., Meeting Cons. Network, Ill. C. of C., Toastmasters Internat. Office: 25 E Washington St Ste 1101 Chicago IL 60602

CONNER, JANET CHESTELYNN, financial broker; b. Albany, Ky., Nov. 24, 1953; d. Kathleen (Stearns) C. Student, Purdue U. V.p. mktg. Brandon Polo Club, Fla., 1981-82; asst. Puller Mortgage, Indpls., 1982-83; pres., owner Excalibur Fin., New Castle, Ind., 1983—. Appointed mem. Ind. Venture Capital Conf., Indpls., 1983. Named Hon. Lt. Gov., Lt. Gov. Mutz of Ind., 1983. Mem. Nat. Assn. Women Bus. Owners, Network Women in Bus., Nat. Assn. Sec. Services, Internat. Entrepreneurs Assn., Delta Sigma Pi. Republican. Methodist. Clubs: Brandon (Fla.) Polo; Ind. Sanyo Users (Indpls.) (chmn.). Avocations: polo, business, fox-hunting, computers, airplanes. Home: 9180 Whitestown Rd Zionsville IN 46077

CONNER, JEANETTE JONES, educator; b. St. Charles, Va., Nov. 29, 1934; d. Luster and Georgia (Jessee) Jones; m. Samuel Barton Conner, Aug. 3, 1966. BS in Edn., Campbellsville Coll., 1979; MA in Edn., Western Ky. U., 1980, cert. sch. psychometrist, 1980, cert. in exceptional edn. K-12, 1981, cert. reading specialist, 1984, cert. elem. sch. supr., 1985, Edn. Specialist degree, 1986. Lic. tchr., Ky. Factory worker Lee Co. Garment Factory, Pennington Gap, Va., 1956-58; receptionist Harlan (Ky.) Appalachian Hosp., 1959-67; sec. Kemper & Assocs., Louisville, 1967-69, Murray (Ky.) State U., 1970-71, Greer & Assoc., Louisville, 1971-73, Cambellsville (Ky.) Coll., 1974-76; tchr. Taylor Co. Bd. Edn., Campbellsville, 1980—. Commd. Kentucky Col. Mem. AAUW (pres. 1989-90), South Cen. Reading Coun. of the Internat. Reading Assn. (Pres. 1989-90, v.p. 1990-91), Ky. State Coun. of the Internat. Reading Assn. (bd. dirs. 1988-91), Taylor County Edn. Assn. (v.p. 1989-90), Ky. State Reading Council (chair com. on parents and reading 1990-91, svc. awards for promoting reading 1989-90), Ky. Edn. Assn., NEA, Taylor County Bus. and Profl. Women, Phi Delta Kappa. Republican. Baptist. Home: 619 Shawnee Dr Campbellsville KY 42718 Office: Taylor County Elem Sch Old Lebanon Rd Campbellsville KY 42718

CONNER, JUDY SUE, accountant; b. Toppenish, Wash., Dec. 11, 1947; d. Lee M. and Susie (Boersma) Lappier; m. Irwin G. Conner, Nov. 30, 1969. BA, Cen. Wash. U., 1969. CPA, Wash. Ptnr. Cordell, Neher & Co., Wenatchee, Wash.; profl. speaker on estate planning, 1985—; treas. WAsh. State Senator, Olympia, 1976—. Pres. bd. dirs. Wenatchee Valley Coll. Found., 1985, sec.-treas. 1987-90; co-founder The Guild House, Wenatchee, 1986. Named Young Career Woman, Wash. Fedn. Bus. Profl. Women, 1975. Mem. AICPA, Wash. Soc. CPAs (state bd. dirs. 1981, pres. Wenatchee chpt. 1980, PAC com. 1988—), Rotary. Lutheran. Home: 1707 Canyon Crest Dr Wenatchee WA 98801

CONNER, KAREN JEAN, health services administrator; b. Clinton, Ind., Sept. 21, 1941; d. Charles A. and Lola M. (Jackson) Williams; m. Charles L. Conner, Sept. 21, 1962; 1 child, Kella Renee Conner-Lucas. Student, Ind. State U.; diploma, Union Hosp. Sch. Nursing. RN, Ind. Office nurse Dr. E.M. Johnson, Terre Haute, Ind., Dr. Robert Rourke, Terre Haute; dir. nursing svc. Williams Home Health Svcs., Terre Haute; dir. nursing svcs. Hooper Holmes DBA Nurses' Unltd., Vero Beach, Fla., The Isles of Vero Beach. Mem. Fla. State Nurses Assn. (home health aide com., adv. bd. nursing asst.), Soc. Nursing Profls. Home: 6516 5th Pl Vero Beach FL 32968

CONNER, VIRGINIA LEA, clinical neuropsychologist; b. Balt., Mar. 18, 1935; d. Robert Lee and Edith Margaret (Mallonee) Heubeck; m. Herbert Conner, July 11, 1955 (div. July 1985); children: Mark Clay, Reta Lynn, Julie Rae Martin. BA in Mgmt., Communications, Prescott Coll., 1974; MA in Psychology, No. Ariz. U., 1978, EdD in Ednl. Psychology, 1982. Cert. psychologist. Cowgirl Boquillas Cattle Co., Seligman, Ariz., 1955-71; sec. Prescott Coll., Prescott, Ariz., 1971-74; registrar Prescott Coll., 1974-78, dir. student svcs., 1978-79, from adj. prof. to prof. psychology, 1978—, chmn. human devel. program, 1980-85; from asst. prof. to assoc. prof. No. Ariz. U., Flagstaff, 1982—; postdoctoral fellowship clin. neuropsychology Braintree Hosp., 1985-86; clin. neuropsychologist Prescott Neurol. Inst., Prescott, 1986—; cons. Dept. Econ. Security-Vocat. Rehab., Prescott, 1986—; med. staff Yavapai Regional Med. Ctr., Prescott, 1987—, Ariz. Children's Rehab. Svcs., Phoenix, 1989. Vice mayor Town of Chino Valley, Ariz., 1977-79; mem. Planning Zoning Commn., Chino Valley, 1972-75, Chino Valley City Coun., 1975-77. Named Rodeo Queen Prescott Rodeo Assn., 1955, All Around Cowgirl Prescott Profl. Rodeo Cowboy Assn. Mem. Internat. Neuropsychology Soc., Am. Psychol. Assn., Ariz. State Psychol. Assn. Democrat. Home: 309 Bloom Pl Prescott AZ 86303 Office: Prescott Neurol Inst 1000 Willow Creek Rd Ste K Prescott AZ 86301

CONNERLY, DIANNA JEAN, business official; b. Urbana, Ill., June 7, 1947; d. Ellsworth Wayne and Imogene (Sundermeyer) Connerly; student Ill. Comml. Coll., 1967. Bookkeeper, Jerry Earl Pontiac, 1968-72; officer mgr. Jack Nicklaus Pontiac, 1972-76; office mgr. Simon Motors Inc., Palm Springs, Calif., 1977-83; bus. mgr., 1983—. Mem. Am. Bus. Women's Assn. (pub. relations dir. Trendsetter chpt. 1983—). Office: 78611 Highway 111 LaQuinta CA 92253

CONNERY, CAROL JEAN, marketing executive; b. Amarillo, Tex., Oct. 22, 1948; d. William Wayne and Joyce Jean (Forney) Connery. AA, Christian Coll., 1969; BJ, U. Tex., Austin, 1971. Cert. neuro-linguistic practitioner. Asst. dir. admissions Columbia (Mo.) Coll., 1971-80; exec. dir. nat. office Teenworld Scholarship Program, Overland Park, Kan., 1980-82; account exec. Mktg. Communications, Inc., Lenexa, Kans., 1983-86; account supr. Krupp/Taylor USA, Dallas, 1986—; cons. in field. Trustee Columbia Coll. Mem. Mid-Am. Soc. Assn. Execs., Direct Mktg. Assn. of Tex., Zeta Tau Alpha, Phi Theta Kappa (past nat. v.p.). Methodist. Home: 9002 Cumberland Dr Irving TX 75063 Office: Krupp/Taylor USA 545 E Carpenter Frwy Ste 1400 Irving TX 75062

CONNOLLY, ELIZABETH ANNE, market professional; b. Hackensack, N.J., Nov. 16, 1957; d. Richard Thomas and Helen Pauline (Jurik) C. BA, William Patterson, 1979; MA, NYU, 1981, PhD, 1986. Sr. rsch. analyst The Prudential, Newark, N.J., 1985—; sr. research analyst The Prudential, Newark. Mem. Sociologists in Bus. Home: 10 Brewster Ave Ridgefield Park NJ 07660 Office: The Equitable 155 Prospect Ave West Orange NJ 07052

CONNOLLY, ELMA TROUTMAN, contractor; b. Middleburg, Pa., May 10, 1931; d. Benjamin F. and Eva Ellen (DeLong) Hollenback; m. Jerome P. Connolly, Apr. 15, 1973; children: Kenneth Troutman, Linda Troutman, Robert Troutman. Student, Lock Haven State Tchrs. Coll., 1949. Cons. for exceptions unit Pa. Tax Bur., Harrisburg; pres. Arts ETC Co., Sunbury, Pa.; artist South Am. hall Smithsonian Mus. Natural History, 1974, Govt. of Taipei (Taiwan); contractor artist, designer George C. Page, Mus. of La Brea, L.A.; bus. cons. Cohen, Danville, 1970-72. Grantee U.S. Govt. Mem. Sunbury Merchants Coun. (pres.), C. of C. (govt. affairs com.), NAFE, Susquehanna Art League. Republican. Home: 102 South U S 11-15 Selinsgrove PA 17870

CONNOLLY, JANE TERRELL, newsletter publishing company executive; b. Washington, Aug. 15, 1942; d. Daniel Starr and Martha Jane (Skidmore) Terrell; m. Raymond Joseph Connolly, Feb. 10, 1979; stepchildren: Brion, Evan. BA, Drew U., 1964. Exec. sec. Avon Internat. Inc., N.Y.C., 1965-68; asst. publicist, office mgr. Metro-Goldwyn-Mayer, Inc., London, 1968-72; compt. King Pub. Group, Washington, 1973—. Mem. NAFE, Newsletter Assn., Nat. Press Club, Am. Mgmt. Assn. Home: 618 4th Pl SW Washington DC 20024 Office: King Pub Group 627 Nat Press Bldg Washington DC 20045

CONNOLLY, JANET E., criminal justice educator; b. New Rochelle, N.Y., June 28, 1929; d. Michael A. and Vincentia (Bonitatibus) Dandry; m. Edward C. Connolly, June 7, 1952; children: Michael, Matthew, Christopher, Benedict, Andrew. BA, Chestnut Hill Coll., Phila., 1951; MA, Temple U., Phila., 1970, PHD, 1975. Intelligence clk. CIA, Washington, 1951-52; tchr. Prince George's County Bd. Edn., Hyattsville, Md., 1952-53; rsch. assoc. Pa. Prison Soc., Phila., 1974-76; field dir. rsch. Georgetown U. Law Sch., Washington, 1976-77; rsch. dir. Phila. Commn. for Effective Criminal Justice, 1977-78; mem. faculty dept. criminal justice Temple U., Phila., 1980—; cons. Bucks County Correctional Facility, Doylestown, Pa., 1987—; evaluator Phila. Prison System, 1973. Campaign chairperson, Doylestown, Pa., 1980, 82, 84, 86, 90; pres. Bucks County Assn. for Corrections and Rehab., Doylestown, 1988—; trustee Bucks County Community Coll., Newtown, Pa., 1989—; bd. dirs. ARC, Bucks County chpt., Doylestown, 1980-82; mem. New Hope (Pa.) Civil Svc. Commn., 1986—; bd. dirs. Planned Parenthood, 1986-88. U.S. Justice Dept. dissertation grantee, Washington, 1972. Mem. ACLU, League Women Voters, Law and Soc. Assn., Am. Correctional Assn. Republican. Home: 130 N Main St New Hope PA 18938 Office: Temple U 223 Widener Hall Ambler PA 19002

CONNOLLY, MARGARET THERESA, real estate broker; b. County Monaghan, Ireland, Aug. 31, 1942; came to U.S., 1959, naturalized, 1966; d. Terrence and Elizabeth (McGivney) Clarke; m. Thady J. Connolly, Apr. 24, 1965; children—Francis J., Christine M. Grad. Diakin Sch. Real Estate, N.Y., 1976; cert. Empire Sch. Real Estate, 1983. Pres., Connolly Realty Co. doing bus. as Active Realty, Washingtonville, N.Y., 1976—. Mem. Internat. Assn. Real Estate Appraisers, Nat. Assn. Female Execs. Democrat. Roman Catholic. Avocations: painting; gardening. Home: MD 1-Rt 208 Washingtonville NY 10992 Office: Active Realty RD 2 Rt 208 Washingtonville NY 10992

CONNOLLY, MAUREEN ANN, editor; b. St. Louis, Feb. 21, 1958; d. James and Ellen Catherine (Wangler) C. Postgrad., Webster U., 1988-89; BS in Secondary Edn. and English, S.E. Mo. State U., 1980. Cert. tchr., Mo. Tchr. English Rockwood Sch. Dist., St. Louis, 1980-81; customer svc. rep. Hickey-Mitchell Ins., St. Louis, 1983-85; legal asst. Bryan, Cave, McPheeters & McRoberts, St. Louis, 1985-90; intern Sta. KSDK-TV, St. Louis, 1989; copy editor Laryngoscope Jour., St. Louis, 1989—. Vol., bd. dirs. St. Louis Crisis Nursery, 1987—. Recipient Kid's award St. Louis Crisis Nursery, 1988. Mem. Internat. Assn. Bus. Communicators, Nat. Coun. Tchrs. of English, Women in Communications, Inc. Home: 8717 Watson Rd #8 Saint Louis MO 63119

CONNOLLY, PEGGY, educator; b. Fargo, N.D., Mar. 10, 1951; d. James Burke and Mildred Katherine (Higgins) C.; m. Christopher Pooley Sandvig, July 9, 1977; children: Erica Sandvig, Cailin Sandvig. BS, U. N.D., 1973, MA, 1976; EdD, Portland State U., Oreg. State U., U. Oreg., 1989. Dir. testing, community svc. coord. Jesuit High Sch., Portland, Oreg., 1978-80; counselor, coord. Mt. Hood Community Coll., Gresham, Oreg., 1981. Trustee Coll. of DuPage, Glen Ellyn, Ill., 1989—; math. mentoring coord. AAUW, Wheaton, Ill., Glen Ellyn, 1989—, bd. dirs., 1985—. Mem. Ill. Community Coll. Trustee Assn. (fed. rels. com., state rels. com.). Office: Coll of DuPage 22nd & Lambert Rd Glen Ellyn IL 60137

CONNOLLY, ROBERTA SUE, banker, business owner; b. Evanston, Ill., Oct. 13, 1947; d. Robert Joel and Margaret J. (Castor) Berndtson; m. Peter E. Connolly, 1970 (div. 1978); 1 child, J. Erik. BA in Econs., Wittenberg U., 1969; MBA in Fin., Loyola U., Chgo., 1977. Examiner FDIC, Chgo., 1969-73; with No. Trust Bank Corp., Chgo., 1976—, v.p., sr. loan rev. officer; pres., owner R.S.C. Group, catering svc., Elk Grove, Ill., 1984—; pres., co-owner HQ/Hamilton Lakes, Inc., restaurant, Itasca, Ill., 1987—; chairperson internat. com. Robert Morris Assocs., Chgo., 1985-86, mem. loan rev. round table, 1987—, 2nd v.p., 1989—. Bd. dirs. Elk Grove Grenadiers Booster Club, Elk Grove Village, Ill., 1988—, career counseling com. Elk Grove High Sch., 1989—. Mem. Nat. Assn. Bank Women. Republican. Episcopalian. Home: 29 Grange Pl Elk Grove Village IL 60007 Office: No Trust Bank 50 S LaSalle St Chicago IL 60675

CONNOLLY-O'NEILL, BARRIE JANE, interior designer; b. San Francisco, Dec. 22, 1943; d. Harry Jr. and Jane Isabelle (Barr) Wallach; m.

Peter Smith O'Neill, Nov. 27, 1983. Cert. of design, N.Y. Sch. Interior Design, 1975; BAF in Environ. Design, Calif. Coll. Arts and Crafts, 1978. Profl. model Brebner Agy., San Francisco, 1963-72; TV personality KGO TV, San Francisco, 1969-72; interior designer Barrie Connolly & Assocs., Boise, Idaho, 1978—. Recipient Best Interior Design award Mktg. and Merchandising Excellence, 1981, 84, Best Interior Design award Sales and Mktg. Coun., 1985, 86, Best Residential Design award Boise Design Revue Com., 1983, Grand award Best in Am. Living Nat. Assn. Home Builders, 1986, 89, 2 Gold Nugget Merit awards, 1990. Mem. Nat. Assn. Home Builders, Am. Soc. Interior Designers (affiliate), Inst. Residential Mktg. Home and Office: Barrie Connolly and Assocs 2188 Bluestem Ln Boise ID 83706

CONNOR, CONSTANCE GIBSON WEHRMAN, trade official, publisher, writer, consultant; b. Harrisburg, Pa., May 7, 1935; d. William and Lucile Elisabeth (Phillips) Gibson; m. Philip William Wehrman, Nov. 1955 (div. 1978); children: William Thomas, Holly Elizabeth Miller, Philip Gibson; m. Robert T. Connor, Nov. 1978 (div. 1985). AA, Centenary Coll., 1956; student, Baptist Coll., Charleston, S.C., 1970, U. Va., Naples, Italy, 1974, U. Md., 1975, No. Va. Community Coll., 1978. Tchr. Bangkok, Thailand, Key West, Fla. and Fairfax County, Va., 1966-70; art importer Gibson Wehrman Imports, Charleston, S.C. and Falls Church, Va., 1972-75; protocol officer Dept. of State and White House, Washington, 1981-83; owner ind. pub. co. Falls Church, 1970—; social sec. Embassy of Can., Washington, 1983-89; founder, publisher Mil. Travel News, also Travel News, Oakton, Va., 1970—; comml. officer tourism Embassy of Canada, Washington, 1989, comml. officer trade and investment/environ., 1989—; instr. English, Rabot, Morocco, 1975-76; model, 1948-56; movie extra, Italy, 1974-75. Author: World Travel Guide, 1970, Join the Jet Set on Military and Retirement Pay, 1973-81, Space Available (Free Flights) 1986, 87, 88, 89, 90. Wardrobe mistress Bob Hope Vietnam Christmas Show, 1967; swimming instr. ARC, 1958-75; com. mem. Reagan/Bush Presdl. Inauguration, 1980-81, 84-85, Bush/Quayle Presdl. Inauguration, 1988-89; vol. Pres.'s Adv. Com. on Arts, John F. Kennedy Ctr. for Performing Arts, 1987; active Nutmeg Players, Madison, Conn., 1952-56, Key West Players, 1965-66, CARE, ARC, Salvation Army, Spl. Projects, Willard Intercontinental Hotel, 1989—. Mem. Washington Internat. Trade Assn. Home: The Atrium 1530 N Key Blvd Apt 230 Arlington VA 22209 Office: Mil Travel News Box 9 Oakton VA 22124

CONNOR, LAURA LOUISE, manufacturing company executive; b. Bartlesville, Okla., July 19, 1962; d. James William and Louise (Rucker) C. BSBA in Mktg., U. Tulsa, 1984, MBA, 1988. Account mgr. NCR Corp., Tulsa, 1985-87; asst. dir. ops. Allen Chapman Activity Ctr., U. Tulsa, 1987-89; sales rep. Eastman Kodak Co., Oklahoma City, 1989-90; systems and solutions account mgr. Eastman Kodak Co., Houston, 1990—. Vol. Tulsa Speech and Hearing Assn., 1985-87, Houston Sch. for the Deaf, 1990. Fellowship U. Tulsa Grad. Sch., 1988; recipient Outstanding Young Women of Am. award, 1988. Mem. PEO, Chi Omega (pres. 1984). Republican. Roman Catholic. Home: 2701 Revere Apt 281 Houston TX 77098 Office: Eastman Kodak Co 16945 Northchase Dr Ste 1800 Houston TX 77060

CONNOR, MARGO (MARGARET BIGGS CONNOR), sales executive, consultant; b. Washington, June 23, 1943; d. Herbert Stetser and Margaret Johnson (Biggs) Murphy; m. James Robert Connor, July 12, 1969; 1 child, Meredith Lauren. BA in Chemistry, U. N.C., 1965. Research assoc. Harvard Med. Sch., Boston, 1965-66; assoc. scientist Polaroid Corp., Cambridge, Mass., 1966-74; pres., owner Margo Connor Interiors, Wellesley, Mass., 1972—; promotional cons. Ultima II Inc., N.Y.C., 1975-77; mktg. mgr. Ionomet Co. Inc., Brighton, Mass., 1978-79; co-mgr. documentation Computer Identics Inc., Canton, Mass., 1982-84; sr. communications specialist Prime Computer Inc., Natick, Mass., 1984-86, sales mgmt. tng. mgr., 1986-89, regional ednl. cons., 1986-89; pvt. practice industry cons. Wellesley, Mass., 1989—; account exec. Boston 128 Fin. Group, 1990—; bd. dirs., broker, cons. Charterhouse Devel. Corp., Wellesley, 1985—. Troop leader Girl Scouts U.S.A., Wellesley, 1980-90; bd. dirs. Youth Pro Musica, Natick, 1988—, pres. bd. dirs., 1989—; bd. dirs. John Oliver Chorale, Boston, 1988—; mem. Tanglewood Festival Chorus, Boston Symphony Orch., 1972—, Jr. League Boston, 1973—. Congregationalist. Home: 12 Brook St Wellesley MA 02181 Office: Boston 128 Fin Group Federal Reserve Pla 30th Fl 600 Atlantic Ave Boston MA 02210-2254

CONNOR, MARIE STELLA, psychotherapist, medical-psychiatric social worker; b. Chgo., Mar. 7, 1918; d. Charles Dean and Stella (McHale) C. BS, Northwestern U., 1940; AM, U. Chgo., 1943. Diplomate Am. Bd. Social Work; lic. social worker, Ill. Social worker Michael Reese Hosp., Chgo., 1943-47, St. Louis U. Hosps., 1948-49; family therapist Cath. Charities of Archdiocese of N.Y., 1949-50; child welfare worker and supr. Ill. Dept. Pub. Welfare, Chgo., 1950-61; med. social cons. U. Ill., Chgo., 1961-66; dir. social work Angel Guardian Home for Children, Chgo., 1969; psychiat. social worker and preceptor VA Med. Ctr., North Chicago, Ill., 1971—. Recipient letter of appreciation VA Med. Ctr., 1975, commendation, 1976, 77, Superior Performance award, 1986, Spl. Contbr. award for pet therapy, 1989. Mem. Nat. Assn. Social Workers, Acad. Cert. Social Workers, Lake Shore Animal Found., Therapy Dog Internat., Registered Clin. Social Workers, Pullman Civic Assn., Hist. Pullman Assn., South Shore Country Club, Alumni Club, Red Carpet Club United, Yorkshire Terrior Club Am., Delta Soc. Home: 11222 Champlain Chicago IL 60628 Office: Social Work Svc VA Med Ctr North Chicago IL 60064

CONNOR, SUSAN, psychologist; b. N.Y.C., Feb. 2, 1958; d. Raymond John and Ann Marie (Black) C.; m. David Andrew Payne, Feb. 14, 1987. BA in Psychology with honors, Denison U., Granville, Ohio, 1980; MA in Psychology, Duquesne U., 1981, PhD in Psychology, 1986. Dir. admissions Dominion Psychiat. Hosp., Falls Church, Va., 1984-89; therapist Sleepy Hollow Psychol. Ctr., Falls Church, 1986-89; dir. ednl. outreach Dominion Psychiat. Hosp., Falls Church, Va., 1990—; cons. in field; guest on TV and radio talk shows. Contbr. articles to various publs. Mem. Am. Psychol. Assn., Va. Psychol. Assn., Nat. Assn. Admitting Mgrs., No. Va. Youth Coalition, Epilepsy Found. (bd. dirs. 1986—, mental health cons., educator, speaker 1986—). Home: 5510 Ridgeton Hill Ct Fairfax VA 22032 Office: Dominion Hosp 2960 Sleepy Hollow Rd Falls Church VA 22044

CONNOR, WILDA, state agency administrator; b. Pleasantville, N.J., Apr. 9, 1947; d. Herman Smith and Rubina (Miraglilo) Cooney; m. James J. Connor Jr., Nov. 5, 1966; 1 child, James J. III. BSBA cum laude, Glassboro (N.J.) State Coll., 1985; postgrad., U. Pa., 1988—. Employee services coord. Turning Point Drug Outpatient Program, Collingswood, N.J., 1976-78; mgmt. specialist Camden County Ctr. Addictive Diseases, Lakeland, N.J., 1978-87; adminstr. Family Practice Ctrs. Camden (N.J.) County Health Dept., 1988—. Com. fund raiser Camden County Dem. Congl. Campaign, Stratford, N.J., 1986; mem. Solid Waste Adv. Coun., Camden County; mem. Coastal Resources Adv. Commn. Dept. Environ. Protection. Mem. N.J. Assn. Alcoholism Counselors, N.J. Substance Abuse Cert. Bd. (cert. 1987, 89 MSA), LWV, Solid Waste Adv. Council. Roman Catholic. Home: 228 E Vasey Ave PO Box 226 Lindenwold NJ 08021 Office: Camden County Dept Health Family Practice Ctrs 2631 Federal St Camden NJ 08705

CONNORS, CATHERINE LOUISE, accountant; b. South Bend, Ind., Nov. 19, 1960; d. James Joseph and Louise Helen (Zawierucha) C. BSBA, Ind. U., South Bend, 1986. Clk. Liberty Mut. Ins. Co., South Bend, 1979-82, group health claims rep., 1982-87; sr. assoc. Coopers & Lybrand, South Bend, 1987—. Mem. AICPA (assoc.), Ind. CPA Soc. (assoc.), Ind. Women's CPA Soc. (assoc.). Office: Coopers & Lybrand 211 W Washington South Bend IN 46634-4157

CONNORS, DORSEY, television and radio commentator, newspaper columnist; b. Chgo.; d. William J. and Sarah (MacLain) C.; m. John E. Forbes; 1 dau., Stephanie. B.A. cum laude, U. Ill. Floor reporter WGN-TV Republican Nat. Conv., Chgo., Democratic Nat. Conv., Los Angeles, 1960. Appeared on: Personality Profiles, WGN-TV, Chgo., 1948, Dorsey Connors Show, WMAQ-TV, Chgo., 1949-58, 61-63, Armchair Travels, WMAQ-TV, 1952-55, Homeshow, NBC, 1954-57, NBC Today Show, Dorsey Connors program, WGN, 1958-61, Tempo Nine, WGN-TV, 1961, Society in Chgo, WMAQ-TV, 1964; writer: column Hi! I'm Dorsey Connors, Chgo. Sun Times, 1965—; Author: Gadgets Galore, 1953, Save Time, Save Money, Save Yourself, 1972, Helpful Hints for Hurried Homemakers, 1988. Founder Ill. Epilepsy League; mem. woman's bd. Children's Home and Aid Soc., mem. women's bd. USO. Mem. AFTRA, Screen Actor's Guild, NATAS, Mus. Broadcast Communications (founding mem.), Soc. Midland Authors, Chgo. Hist. Soc. (guild com., costume com.), Chi Omega. Roman Catholic. Office: Chgo Sun Times 401 N Wabash Chicago IL 60611

CONNORS, KATHRYN DUGHI, human resources executive; b. Newark, May 7, 1947; d. Charles Anthony and Katherine (Ephron) Dughi. BA in Edn., Seton Hall U., 1969, JD, 1977, MBA in Human Resources, 1986. Bar: N.J., 1977. Tchr. Harding Twp. Sch., New Vernon, N.J., 1969-77; atty., mgr., dir. human resources Allied Signal Corp., N.Y.C. and Morristown, N.J., 1977-83; v.p. human resources Liz Claiborne Inc., N.Y.C., 1983—; pres. Harmony Early Learning Ctr., Secaucus, N.J., 1987—, also bd. dirs. Mem. ABA. Republican. Roman Catholic. Home: 68-A Troy Dr Springfield NJ 07081 Office: Liz Claiborne Inc 1441 Broadway New York NY 10018

CONNORS, MARY EILEEN, psychologist; b. Springfield, Mass., Sept. 15, 1953; d. John Joseph and Mary Ellen (Teahan) Connors; m. Roger F. Thomson, Nov. 10, 1984. BA, New Coll., Sarasota, Fla., 1975; MA, DePaul U., Chgo., 1980; PhD, DePaul U., 1983. Lic. clin. psychologist, 1985. Psychol. intern Michael Reese Hosp., Chgo., 1980-81; staff psychologist DePaul U. Counseling Ctr., Chgo., 1981-83; rsch. assoc. Northwestern U., Chgo., 1984-86; faculty Northwestern U., 1984—; core faculty mem. Ill. Sch. Profl. Psychology, Chgo., 1989—; pvt. practice psychology Chgo., 1983—; cons. Michael Reese Hosp., 1984—. Co-author: Etiology and Treatment of Bulimic Nervosa: A Biopsychosocial Perspective, 1987; contbr. articles to profl. jours. Schmitt fellow, DePaul U., 1979, Phalin fellow, 1980. Mem. Am. Psychol. Assn., Ill. Psychol. Assn., Chgo. Assn. for Psychoanalytic Psychology. Home: 7549 N Oakley Chicago IL 60645 Office: 55 E Washington #2007 Chicago IL 60602

CONOLEY, JOANN SHIPMAN, educational administrator; b. Bartlesville, Okla., July 19, 1931; d. Joe and Frances Loomis (Wall) Shipman; m. Travis A. Conoley, Oct. 29, 1976; children by previous marriage: James F. Lane, Joe Scott Lane, Kimberly Diane Lane. BS in English and Edn., Midwestern State U., Wichita Falls, Tex., 1968, MS in English and Edn., 1971, postgrad. Tex. A&M U., 1978—. Cert. elem. and high sch. tchr., reading/language arts coord., reading cons., adminstr., supt., Tex. Tchr. 3d grade Queen of Peace Sch., Wichita Falls, 1968-69; lang. arts team leader, jr. high sch. Wichita Falls Public Schs., 1969-74; fed. programs dir., reading coordinator Rockdale (Tex.) Public Schs., 1974-78, adminstrv. asst. to supt., 1978-79, asst. supt. adminstrn. and instrn., 1979—; reading cons. ALCOA, 1977—; site cons. U.S. Dept. Edn. Secondary Sch. Recognition Program, 1987, 89; mem. secondary sch. selection panel Tex. Edn. Agy., 1989. Bd. dirs. Rockdale Public Library, 1975-79, pres., 1976-77; bd. dirs. Am. Cancer Soc. Named Yellow Rose Tex. Gov. of Tex. Mem. NEA, Tex. State Tchrs. Assn., Nat. Council Tchrs. English, Internat. Reading Assn., Assn. Compensatory Edn. Tex. (exec. bd. 1977-83), Assn. Supervision and Curriculum Devel., Alpha Chi, Delta Kappa Gamma, Kappa Delta Pi. Home: 405 Bounds St Rockdale TX 76567 Office: Box 632 Rockdale TX 76567

CONOVER, CAROLE ANN, small business owner; b. Hackensack, N.J., Jan. 28, 1941; d. Harry Sayles Conover and Gloria Belle (Dalton) Reed; m. Henry Meursinge Duys Jr., May 30, 1964 (div. 1969); children: Henry M. III, Lizabeth Conover, Noah Ogden. BA in Lit. and Journalism, Smith Coll., 1963. Pres. Carole Conover Pub. Relations, N.Y.C., 1972-79; assoc. Carl Byoir and Assocs., N.Y.C., 1979-81; pub. affairs specialist MasterCard Internat., N.Y.C., 1981-82; pres. Conover Assocs., N.Y.C., 1981—; chmn. Conover Models and Talent Internat., N.Y.C., 1985—. Author: (book and play) Cover Girls: A Biography of Harry Conover, 1978; writer 10th and 11th Daytime Emmies Award Show for NATAS, 1982-83. Adoption chmn. Wilton (Conn.) Animals in Distress, 1965-68. Named Best Young Writer Winter Park (Fla.) Bulletin, 1952. Mem. NAFE, Authors and Writers League, Dramatists Guild, Wilton Riding Club. Democrat. Roman Catholic. Office: care Kennedy 8 E 48th St Ste 3C New York NY 10017

CONOVER, CATHERINE, academic administrator; b. Meadville, Pa., July 9, 1949; d. George Robert and Faye (Bowman) Conover; m. James Charles Albisetti, July 14, 1973 (div.); m. Christopher William Covert, July 27, 1980. AB, Mt. Holyoke Coll., 1971; MA, Columbia U., 1973. Editorial asst. Barnard Coll., N.Y.C., 1971-73; staff asst. employee communications dept. Yale U., New Haven, Conn., 1973-76, grants mgr., 1976-78; asst. dir. communications and devel. Hamilton Coll., Clinton, N.Y., 1978-80; dir. ann. giving Wheaton Coll., Norton, Mass., 1980-83, dir. reunion giving, 1983-84, assoc. campaign dir., 1984-86, dir. devel., 1986-88; v.p. for devel. RISD, Providence, 1988—. Bd. dirs. R.I. Arts Advs., 1989—, Planned Parenthood of R.I., 1990—. Mem. Coun. for Advancement and Support of Edn., Women in Devel. of Greater Boston (job network chair 1987-89, bd. dirs. 1987-89), Planned Giving Group New Eng., R.I. Women's Network, Providence Art Club, Stone House Club, Crater Club. Office: RISD 2 College St Providence RI 02903

CONOVER, NELLIE COBURN, retail furniture company executive; b. Lebanon, Ohio, Dec. 21, 1921; d. Frank C. and Isabel (Murphy) Coburn; student public schs.; m. Lawrence E. Conover, Jan. 11, 1941; children—Lawrence R., Carol, David C., Constance, Christina. Co-founder, 1949, since exec. sec.-treas. Larry Conover Furniture & Appliance, Inc., and predecessor, Milford, Ohio, also trustee co. pension fund. Mem. Milford C. of C., Cin. Hist. Soc., Milford Hist. Soc., DAR. Democrat. Roman Catholic. Address: 438 Main St Milford OH 45150

CONOVER, SARAH MILLER, physical therapist; b. Valparaiso, Ind., Oct. 16, 1965; d. Lloyd H. and Margie (Evans) Miller; m. David M. Conover, July 11, 1987. BS in Phys. Therapy, U. Evansville, 1987. Lic. phys. therapist, Va., Ohio. Staff phys. therapist Sentara Norfolk (Va.) Gen. Hosp., 1987-89; clin. supr. phys. therapy Stouder Meml. Hosp., Troy, Ohio, 1989—; mem. profl. adv. com. Multiple Sclerosis Soc., Norfolk, 1988-89, cons., vol., Dayton, Ohio, 1989—; cons. Muscular Dystrophy Assn., Norfolk, 1988-89. Youth advisor Presbyn. Ch., Norfolk, 1987-89; mem. Welcome Wagon, Troy, 1989—. Recipient Outstanding Svc. award Sentara Norfolk Gen. Hosp., 1980. Mem. Am. Phys. Therapy Assn., NAFE. Office: Stouder Meml Hosp 4th Fl 920 Summit Ave Troy OH 45373

CONOVER, VAL VAGTS, historian, artist; b. Red Wing, Minn., Oct. 15, 1930; d. Jost and Madge Hazel (Merrell) Vagts; m. Hugh Dickson Conover, Feb. 9, 1952; children: Reeve Merrell, Charles Shaw, Robert Hugh. Student, Cleve. Inst. Art., 1950-51. Exhibits, exhibit backdrop and graphic artist Gregory Mus., Hicksville, N.Y., 1973-89, Vanderbilt Mus., Centerport, N.Y., 1983-86. Editor: The Cupola Jour., 1983—; contbr. hist. articles to mags. Trustee Gregory Mus., 1969—. Mem. L.I. Shell Club. also: Vanderbilt Mus 180 Little Neck Rd Centerport NY 11721

CONRAD, BARBARA KAY, data processing consultant; b. Erwin, N.C., Nov. 22, 1946; d. James Walter and Gaynelle (Sealey) Allen. BS, Pembroke (N.C.) State U., 1968. Tchr. Cumberland County Schs., Hope Mills, N.C., 1968-69, Lumberton (N.C.) City Schs., 1970-7l; programmer, analyst West Point Pepperell, Lumberton, 1971-74, Pfizer Inc., Sanford, N.C., 1974-77, Rockwell Internat., Raleigh, N.C., 1977-78, Salem Carpet Mills, Winston-Salem, N.C., 1978-8l; cons. Computer Task Group, Buffalo, 1981—. Mem. NAFE. Democrat. Baptist. Home: PO Box 5l172 Raleigh NC 27609 Office: 5540 Centerview Dr Ste 308 Raleigh NC 27606

CONRAD, HELEN BOTT, organization executive; b. Triadelphia, W.Va., Dec. 21, 1918; d. Carl J. and Catherine (Wagner) Bott; widow; children: Carol Conrad Stickel, Joan Conrad Wildpret, Cinday Conrad Peters. Student, Elliot Sch. Bus., Wheeling, W.Va., 1937-38. Sec. Wheeling Steel and Wheeling Pitts. Steel Corp., 1940-7l; ret., 197l; membership sec. Brooks Bird Club, Inc., Wheeling, 1973—, hon. mem., 1978, reservationist, 1982—, adminstr., 1986—. Office: Brooks Bird Club Inc 707 Warwood Ave Wheeling WV 26003

CONRAD, KATHRYN JO, cancer institute administrator, nursing educator; b. Punxsutawney, Pa., July 7, 1956; d. Paul Edward and Mary Margaret (Wood) C. Diploma, Indiana Hosp. Sch. Nursing, Pa., 1977; BSN, U. Pitts., 1981, MS in Nursing, 1985. RN, Pa. Staff nurse Presbyn.-Univ. Hosp., Pitts., 1977-79, staff nurse II, 1979-81, head nurse, 1981-85, clin. instr., 1985-87, liaison nurse with Pitts. Cancer Inst., 1987-89; clin. dir. ednl. resources and svcs. Pitts. Cancer Inst., 1989—; adj. instr. U. Pitts. Sch. Nursing, 1988—; chpts. editor Springhouse Skill Book, 1988—. Author: Getting Your Questions Answered, 1985. Bd. dirs. Am. Cancer Soc., Pitts., 1983-88, sec., 1988—, chmn. svcs. and rehab. com., 1989—. Named Vol. of Yr. Am. Cancer Soc., 1990, Nurse of Hope, 1981, scholar, 1983-85; Bessie Li Sze Found. scholar, 1985. Mem. Oncology Nursing Soc. (cert., editor Pitts. chpt. 1986-87, pres. 1987-88, nat. clin. practice com. 1989—, Most Improved Newsletter award 1987). Office: Pitts Cancer Inst 367 Victoria Bldg Pittsburgh PA 15261

CONRAD, KAY ANN, reference librarian; b. Wabash, Ind., Mar. 18, 1945; d. Frank Robert and Helen A. (Little) C. BA, Manchester Coll., North Manchester, Ind., 1967; MLS, Ind. U., 1968. Cert. permanent grade I pub. libr., Wis. Asst. prof. Valley City (N.D.) State Coll., 1968-72; head reference libr. Fond du Lac (Wis.) Pub. Libr., 1972—. Compiler: Index of 1854 History of Fond du Lac County, Wisconsin, 1988. Mem. Fond du Lac Sesquicentennial Com., 1986. Mem. ALA, Wis. Libr. Assn. (bd. dirs. reference and adult svcs. sect. 1985—), AAUW, Fond du Lac County Hist. Soc., Fond du Lac Community Theatre Assn. Office: Fond du Lac Pub Libr 32 Sheboygan St Fond du Lac WI 54935

CONRAD, NATALIE TERESA, psychologist; b. San Francisco, May 2, 1953; d. David Matthew and Gladys Pearl (Krause) C.; m. Craig Kenji Goishi, Aug. 9, 1985. BA in English, Calif. State U., Fullerton, 1976, BS in Human Svcs., 1976, MS in Counseling, 1978; PhD in Clin. Psychology, Calif. Sch. Profl. Psychology, San Diego, 1982. Lic. psychologist, Calif. Legal svcs. coord., psychol. intern Battered Women's Svcs., YWCA, San Diego, 1979; psychol. intern McAllister Inst. for Treatment and Edn., San Diego, 1980-81; mental health specialist San Diego County Mental Health, 1981-82; postdoctoral fellow Shasta County Mental Health, Redding, Calif., 1982-83; clin. psychologist Casa Colina Hosp. for Rehab. Medicine, Pomona, Calif., 1984; dir. tng., clin. psychologist Orange County Health Care Agy. Mental Health, Children and Youth Svcs., Westminster, Calif., 1984-89, svc. chief II, 1988-89; pvt. practice clin. psychology Santa Rosa, Calif., 1989—; clin. psychologist Family Life Ctr., Petaluma, Calif., 1989—; cons. Head Start Programs, Westminster, Garden Grove, sch. dists., Garden Grove Unified, Huntington Beach, West Orange County Consortium for Spl. Edn., 1984-89; conducted various presentations and seminars. Mem. Am. Psychol. Assn. Democrat. Office: Family Life Ctr 365 Kuck Ln Petaluma CA 95442

CONRAD, SALLY Y., state legislator; b. Palmer, Mass., Mar. 1, 1941; m. David Conrad; 1 child. B.A., Boston U., 1963, M.Ed., Northeastern U., 1967. Former exec. dir. ret. sr. vol. program County of Chittenden; mem. Vt. Senate, 1985—; mem. Champlain Valley Women's Polit. Caucus. Unitarian Universalist. Office: Vt State Senate Montpelier VT 05602 Home: 35 Wilson St Burlington VT 05401*

CONRAD, SUSAN LYNNE, nursing educator; b. Washington, Apr. 12, 1948; d. Charles W. and Thordis A. (Johansen) DeBaun; m. Frederick H. Conrad, Dec. 24, 1973; children: Matthew, Kathryn. BS in Nursing, U. Evansville, 1970; MS, Tex. Women's U., 1973; PhD, U. Tex., 1982. Instr. Tex. Women's U., Dallas; asst. prof. U. Tex., Arlington; assoc. prof. Framingham (Mass.) State Coll. Contbr. articles to profl. publs. Mem. needs assessment/data collection com. United Way, 1988-90; camp fire leader, 1987—; child adv. Grantee in field; recipient Vol. Appreciation award ARC, 1988, Disting. Svc. award, 1987-88. Mem. Mass./R.I. League Nursing Baccalaureate and Higher Degree Coun. (v.p.), S. Middlesex Coun. for Children (chair). Home: 31 Bogastow Brook Rd Sherborn MA 01770

CONROY, GEORGETTA ANN, sales and marketing executive; b. Pitts., Sept. 7, 1946; d. Aldo Delfino and Catherine Marie (Chiatello) Conti; children: Thomas Christopher,Gina Marie. Student, Community Coll. Allegheny, Pitts., 1984, U. Pitts., 1989. Cert. med. asst. Sec. Blackburn's Physicians Pharmacy Inc., Tarentum, Pa., 1978-82, rehab. sales rep., 1982-85, supr. rehab. sales dept., 1985-89, dir. sales and mktg. div., 1989—; cons. Rehab. Tech. Terms, Rehab. Inst. Pitts., D.T. Watson Rehab. Hosp., 1985—; Dale Carnegie teaching asst. Inst. Human Resources, Pitts., 1984, 85, 86, 87. Pres. Am. Cancer Soc., 4 Corners, Pa., 1985-86. Mem. Assn. Rehab. Nurses, Rehab. Engrs. Soc. N.Am. Democrat. Roman Catholic. Home: 1015 California Ave Natrona Heights PA 15065 Office: Blackburns Physicians 301 Corbet St Tarentum PA 15084

CONROY, ROSE MAUREEN, firefighter; b. Nevada City, Calif., Oct. 5, 1953; d. David Kearin and Catherine Cecila (Dalton) C. BA in Phys. Edu., U. Calif. Davis, 1975. Cert. tchr., Calif. Firefighter City of Davis, 1979-85, fire capt., 1985—. Democrat. Roman Catholic. Home: PO Box 1605 Davis CA 95617

CONS, JEAN MARIE ABELE, anatomist, educator; b. Lancaster, Pa., Dec. 23, 1934; d. John Israel and Blanche Esther (Henry) Abele; m. Rafel Cons, Jr., May 16, 1955; children: Rafel John, Patricia Anne. AA, Oakland (Calif.) Community, 1957; BA in Biol. Sci., Calif. State U., San Francisco, 1960; MA in Anatomy, U. Calif., San Francisco, 1963, PhD in Endocrinology, 1972. Cert. tchr., Calif. Rsch. asst. U. Calif., San Francisco, 1960-64, rsch. anatomist, 1964-68, assoc. in anatomy, physiology, 1966-72; postdoctoral fellow U. Calif., Berkeley, 1972-74, lectr. anatomy, physiology, 1972-75, asst. rsch. physiologist, 1974-75; assoc. prof. anatomy, physiology Coll. of Notre Dame, Belmont, Calif., 1975-77; prof. anatomy, physiology Coll. of San Mateo (Calif.), 1976—. Editor: (newsletter) Health Update, 1985-89; contbg. author: Fetal and Maternal Hormones, 1983. Mem. No. Calif. Soc. Anatomists, Inst. Anat. Scis. Office: College of San Mateo 1700 W Hillsdale Blvd San Mateo CA 94044

CONSER, GERALDINE M., photographer; b. Detroit; d. Clyde William and Dorothy May (Odell) Love; m. John C. Conser; children: Anne, Kari, Christi. BA, Long Beach State U., 1965. Owner Aerial Yacht Photographer, Costa Mesa, Calif., 1978—. Exhibited in group show at the La Jolla Museum of Contemporary Art, 1986; one woman show includes "Neiman Marcus salutes Geri Conser", 1987. Home and Office: Aerial Yacht Photography 1995 Irvine Ave Costa Mesa CA 92627

CONSIDINE, ANN-MARIE GWIAZDOWSKI, construction consultant; b. Norwich, Conn., Feb. 7, 1962; d. Peter Paul and Helen Carol (Bujnowski) Gwiazdowski; m. Matthew Andrew Considine, Aug. 8, 1986. BA cum laude, Conn. Coll., 1984; postgrad., N.Y. Inst. Fin., 1984, U. Conn., 1986. Jr. analyst Bear, Stearns & Co., N.Y.C., 1984-85; account exec. Data Resources div. McGraw Hill, Stamford, Conn., 1985-87; chem. cons. Data Resources div. McGraw Hill, Phila., 1987-88; sr. account cons. constrn. industry F.W. Dodge div. McGraw Hill, Phila., 1988—. Vol. ARC, 1988—. Mem. Nat. Assn. Bus. Economists, Conn. Coll. Alumni Assn. (interviewer 1984—). Republican. Roman Catholic. Home: 331 S 18th St Philadelphia PA 19103 Office: FW Dodge div McGraw Hill 1234 Market St Philadelphia PA 19107

CONSIDINE, SUSAN MARY, manufacturing executive; b. Queens, N.Y., Jan. 21, 1958; d. Richard Thomas and Mary Michael (Zappulo) C.; 1 child, Shane Anthony. Diploma in Nursing, Samaritan Hosp., Troy, N.Y., 1979; BS, SUNY, Utica, 1981; MBA, Rensselaer Poly. Inst., 1989. RN. Nurse St. Elizabeth Hosp., Utica, 1980-81, Marcy Psychiat. Ctr., Utica, 1981-84; sales mgr. Lincoln Logs Ltd., Chestertown, N.Y., 1984-86, v.p. dealer devel., 1986-87, v.p. customer svc., 1987-90; exec. v.p. Lincoln Logs Ltd., 1990—; also bd. dirs. Lincoln Logs Ltd., Chestertown, N.Y. Mem. NAFE. Home: RR 1 Box 485A Chestertown NY 12817 Office: Lincoln Logs Ltd 1 Riverside Dr Chestertown NY 12817

CONSILIO, BARBARA ANN, court administrator; b. Cleve., June 22, 1938; d. Joseph B. and Anna E. (Ford) C. BS, Kent State U., 1962; MA, U. Detroit, 1973. Cert. social worker, Mich. Tchr. Chagrin Falls (Ohio) High Sch., 1962-64; probation officer Macomb County Juvenile Ct., Mt. Clemens, Mich., 1965-68, asst. casework supr., 1968-74; dir. children's svcs. Macomb County Juvenile Ct., Mt. Clemens, 1974-79; mgr. foster care and instns.

Oakland County Juvenile Ct., Pontiac, Mich., 1979-83; ct. adminstr. Oakland County Probate Ct., Pontiac, 1983—. Bd. dirs. Children's Charter Cts. of Mich., Lansing, 1984—, Statewide Adv. Bd. on Sexual Abuse, Lansing, 1986—, Havenwyck Hosp., Auburn Hills, 1986—, Orchards Children's Svcs., Southfield, 1987, Oakland County Coun. Children at Risk, Pontiac, 1987—, pres.; mem. Nat. Women's Polit. Caucus, N.Y.C.; bd. dirs., vice chairperson Inter Agy. Coun. on Youth, 1989; bd. dirs. Care House, Pontiac. Mem. Nat. Coun. Juvenile and Family Ct. Adminstrs. Group, Mich. Probate and Juvenile Register's Assn., Mich. Juvenile Ct. Adminstrs. Assn., Nat. Assn. Ct. Mgrs., Supreme Ct. Task Force on Racial and Ethnic Bias 1988-89, Office of Children and Youth Svcs. (state foster care system review com.). Home: 4045 Chestnut Hill Troy MI 48098

CONSTABLE, ELINOR GREER, diplomat; b. San Diego, Feb. 8, 1934; d. Marshall Raymond and Katherine (French) Greer; m. Peter Dalton Constable, Mar. 8, 1958; children: Robert, Philip, Julia. B.A., Wellesley Coll., 1955. Mem. staff Dept. Interior, 1955-71, Dept. State, 1955-71, OEO, 1955-71; sr. assoc. Transcentury Corp., Washington, 1971-72; with Dept. State, Washington, 1973-80, 83—, dir. investment affairs, 1978-80; dep. asst. sec. Internat. Fin. and Devel., 1980-83; dep. asst. sec. for econ. and bus. affairs Dept. State, from 1983; Ambassador to Kenya, 1986-89; now with Am. Embassy, Georgetown, Guyana; capital devel. officer US AID, Pakistan, 1977-78. *

CONSTANTINE, JAN FRIEDMAN, lawyer; b. N.Y.C., Jan. 22, 1948; d. Howard J. and Elayne (Sercus) Friedman; m. Lawrence Levien, Oct. 11, 1970 (div. Sept. 1974); m. Lloyd E. Constantine, June 22, 1975; children: Isaac, Sarah, Elizabeth. BA, Smith Coll., Northampton, Mass., 1970; JD, George Washington U., 1973. Bar: N.Y. 1974, U.S. Dist. Ct. (so. and ea. dists.) N.Y. 1975, U.S. Ct. Appeals (2d cir.) 1975. Staff atty. div. spl. projects FTC, Washington, 1973-75; staff atty. N.Y. office FTC, N.Y.C., 1975-77; asst. atty. U.S. Dist. Ct. (ea. dist.) N.Y., Bklyn., 1977-82; litigation counsel Macmillan, Inc., N.Y.C., 1982-84, assoc. gen. counsel, 1985—; vis. asst. prof. George Washington U. Law Sch., Washington, 1974. Mem. Bar Assn. of City of N.Y. (mem. consumer protection com. 1981-84, corp. law com. 1987—). Home: 10 W 66th St New York NY 10023 Office: Macmillan Inc 866 3rd Ave 10th Fl New York NY 10022*

CONSTANTINI, JOANN M., records and information management consultant; b. Danbury, Conn., July 30, 1948; d. William J. and Mathilda J. (Ressler) C. BA, Coll. White Plains, N.Y., 1970; student Central Conn. State Coll., 1977-78, U. Hartford, 1985-88 . Cert. records mgr., 1987. Psychiat. social worker N.Y. State Dept. Mental Hygiene, Wassaic, 1970-73; with Northeast Utilities, Hartford, Conn., 1973-88, methods analyst, 1979-82, records and procedures mgmt. adminstr., 1982-88, cert. records mgr., 1987—, N.C. real estate lic., 1988; dir. Meridan (Conn.) YWCA, 1976-77, My Sisters Place, 1984-87; mem. faculty Cen. Piedmont Community Coll., 1989-90. Bd. dirs. Meriden YWCA, Conn., 1978-79; vol., 1984—, Queen City Friends, Charlotte, 1988-89; nat. chair Industry Action Com., 1989—; mem. Greater Charlotte Bd. Realtors. Mem. Assn. Record Mgmt. and Adminstrs. (sec. 1984-85, bd. dirs., 1984-86, internat. chair industry action program 1989—, chair industry action com. for pub. utilities, 1986-89), Assn. Image and Info. Mgmt. (dir. 1984-86), Electric Council New Eng. (chair records mgmt. com. 1985-87), Coll. White Plains Alumnae Assn., Nat. Trust for Hist. Preservation, Inst. Cert. Records Mgrs., Charlotte Bd. Realtors. Democrat. Roman Catholic. Club: Northeast Utilities Women's Forum. (treas. 1983-88). Avocations: antiques; gardening; traveling; collecting cookbooks. Home: 13600 Portpatrick Ln Matthews NC 28105

CONSTANTINO-BANA, ROSE EVA, nursing educator, researcher; b. Labangan Zamboanga del Sur, Philippines, Dec. 25, 1940; came to U.S., 1964; naturalized, 1982; d. Norberto C. and Rosalia (Torres) Bana; m. Abraham Antonio Constantino, Jr., Dec. 13, 1964; children: Charles Edward, Kenneth Richard, Abraham Anthony III. B.S. in Nursing, Philippine Union Coll., Manila, 1962; M.Nursing, U. Pitts., 1971, Ph.D., 1979; J.D., Duquesne U., Pitts., 1984. Lic. clin. specialist in psychiatric-mental health nursing; registered nurse. Instr. Philippine Union Co., 1963-65, Spring Grove State Hosp., Balt., 1965-67, Montefiore Sch. Nursing, Pitts., 1967-70; instr. U. Pitts., 1971-74, asst. prof., 1974-83, assoc. prof., 1983—, chmn. Senate Athletic Com., 1985-86, 89—; project dir. grant div. of nursing HHS, Washington, 1983-85; bd. dirs. Internat. Council on Women's Health Issues, 1986—. Author: (with others) Principles and Practice of Psychiatric Nursing, 1982; contbr. chpts. to books and articles to profl. jours. Mem. Republican Presdl. Task Force, Washington, 1980, Rep. Senatorial Com., Washington, 1980. Mem. ABA, Am. Nurses Assn., Pa. Nurses Assn., Nat. League Nursing, Pa. League Nursing (chairperson area 6), U. Pitts. Sch. Nursing Alumni Assn., U. Duquesne Law Alumni Assn., Sigma Theta Tau, Phi Alpha Delta. Seventh-Day Adventist. Avocations: cooking, playing the piano. Home: 6 Carmel Ct Pittsburgh PA 15221 Office: U Pitts Sch Nursing 467 Victoria Bldg Pittsburgh PA 15261

CONTE, ANDREA, retail executive, health care consultant; b. Great Barrington, Mass., Feb. 13, 1941; d. Louis William and Rosalie (Salvini) C.; m. Philip Norman Bredesen, Nov. 22, 1974; 1 child, Benjamin Conte. BS in Nursing, U. Wash., 1968; MBA, Tenn. State U., 1983. RN. Nurse various hosps. and med. ctrs., Mass. and Calif., 1961-68, Vis. Nurse Service, Boston, 1968-70; clin. coordinator RMP Boston City Hosp., 1970-72; trainer computer systems Searle Medidata, Lexington, Mass., 1973-75; dir. nursing mgmt. services Hosp. Corp. Am., Nashville, 1975-78; cons. various health care cos., Nashville, 1978-81; mgr. Ernst and Whinney, Nashville, 1981-83; pres. Conte Philips, Nashville, 1983—. Bd. dirs. Family and Children Svcs., 1988—, Cumberland Sci. Mus., 1988—, Shepherd's Ctr. of West Edn, 1989—, Cable, 1989—, Tenn. Performing Arts Ctr., Nat. Conf. Christians and Jews; mem. assoc. bd. St. Thomas Hosp. Mem. Internat. Assn. Cooking Profls., Nat. Assn. Splty. Food Trade. Republican. Roman Catholic.

CONTE, MARYANNE MICCHELLI, radio station executive; b. Newark, June 15, 1959; d. Mario R. and Lucy C. (Attanasio) Micchelli, m. Andrew Conte, June 28, 1987. B.A., Rutgers U., 1981. Sales asst. Sta.-WNBC, N.Y.C., 1981-84, account exec., 1985-88; account exec. Sta. WFAN Sportsradio, N.Y.C., 1988—; account exec. Sta.-WHN, N.Y.C., 1984-85; speaker Fairleigh Dickenson U., Teaneck, N.J., 1985-86, career seminars YWCA, N.Y.C., 1985-86. Mem. Advt. Club North Jersey, NAFE, Internat. Radio and TV Soc., Radio Club Am., N.Y. Market Radio Broadcasters Assn., Rutgers U. Alumnae Assn., Rutgers Club of N.Y. (N.Y.C.). Roman Catholic. Avocations: photography, tennis, travel, music. Home: 113 Mapes Ave Nutley NJ 07110 Office: Sta WFAN Sportsradio 1372 Broadway New York NY 10018

CONTI, ISABELLA, psychologist, consultant; b. Torino, Italy, Jan. 1, 1942; came to U.S., 1964; d. Giuseppe and Zaira (Melis) Ferro; m. Ugo Conti, Sept. 5, 1964; 1 child, Maurice. J.D., U. Rome, 1966; Ph.D. in Psychology, U. Calif.-Berkeley, 1975. Lic. psychologist. Sr. analyst Research Inst. for Study of Man, Berkeley, Calif., 1967-68; postgrad. research psychologist Personality Assessment and Research Inst., U. Calif.-Berkeley, 1968-71; intern U. Calif.-Berkeley and VA Hosp., San Francisco, 1969-75; asst. prof. St. Mary's Coll., Moraga, Calif., 1978-84; cons. psychologist Conti Resources, Berkeley, Calif., 1977-85; v.p. Barnes & Conti Assocs., Inc., Berkeley, 1985-89; pres. Lisardco, Albany, Calif., 1989—; v.p. ElectroMagnetic Instruments, Inc., El Cerrito, Calif., 1985—. Contbr. articles on creativity and mgmt. cons. to profl. jours. Regents fellow U. Calif.-Berkeley, 1972; NIMH predoctoral research fellow, 1972-73. Mem. Am. Psychol. Assn. Office: Lisardco 835 Pomona Ave Albany CA 94706

CONTI, LAURIE ANN, optometrist; b. Erie, Pa., Dec. 28, 1961; d. Theodore S. and Ann E. (Kweder) C. BS, Ind. U. of Pa., 1984; DO, Pa. Coll. Optometry, 1987; O.D. Cert. optometrist, Pa., Va. Optometrist Erie (Pa.) Eye Clinic, Inc., 1987-88, Dr. May & Hettler, O.D., P.C., Manassas, Alexandria, Va., 1988—, Kaiser Permanente, Springfield, Va., 1990—. Assoc. Wolf Trap Assoc., Vienna, Va., 1990. Mem. No. Va. Optometric Soc., Am. Optometric Assn. Roman Catholic.

CONTICCHIO, LINDA ANNE, marketing executive; b. New Brunswick, N.J., June 3, 1953; d. Thomas V. and Saveria (Malinconico) C. BA, Douglass Coll., New Brunswick, N.J., 1976; MBA in Mktg., Fairleigh Dickinson U., Teaneck, N.J., 1985. Fin. acct. PPC, Milltown, N.J., 1978-81, cost acct., 1981-83; sr. mktg. acct. personal products Johnson & Johnson, Milltown, 1983-86; sr. auditor Johnson & Johnson, New Brunswick, 1986-88, sr. audit specialist, 1988—. Author, trainer advt. and sales promotions, 1990. Mem. Nat. Assn. Accts., Am. Soc. Indsl. Security, Upward Mobility of Women (co-chairperson 1989—). Home: 305 Merrywood Dr Edison NJ 08817 Office: Johnson & Johnson George St Kilmer House 302 New Brunswick NJ 08933

CONWAY, BETTY ANN, rehabilitation consultant; b. Kansas City, Mo., Nov. 13, 1930; d. Ernest and Anna Marie (Schekorra) Alborn; m. John Steven Kolodey, Feb. 17, 1951 (dec. July 1952); m. Joseph Patrick Conway, Aug. 30, 1958; children: Cheryl, Michael, Lynn. BS in Edn., Cleve. State U., 1971; MS in Edn., Ind. U., 1980. Cert. tchr., Ind., Ohio. Sec. Ohio Turnpike Commn., Berea, 1956-59; elem. tchr. North Olmsted (Ohio) Schs., 1971-74; substitute tchr. Troy (Ohio) Schs., 1974-76, Kokomo (Ind.) Ctr. Twp. Schs., 1977-78; with Kokomo Opportunities Industrialization Ctr., 1978-82, youth employment and tng. dir., 1980, adminstr., 1980-82; rehab. cons. indsl. commn. Ohio Rehab. Div., Cleve., 1982—. Mem. AAUW (sec. 1977-78, historian 1978-79, bd. dirs. 1979-80). Home: 18848 Canyon Rd Fairview Park OH 44126 Office: Cleve Rehab Div Bur Workers Compensation 10524 Euclid Ave Cleveland OH 44106

CONWAY, JILL KATHRYN KER, former college president; b. Hillston, New South Wales, Australia, Oct. 9, 1934; d. William Innis and Evelyn Mary (Adames) Ker; m. John James Conway, Dec. 22, 1962. B.A., U. Sydney, Australia, 1958; Ph.D., Harvard U., 1969; hon. degrees, St. Thomas (N.B.) U., 1974, Mt. Holyoke Coll., 1975, Amherst Coll., 1976, York U., Toronto, 1977, U. N.H., 1977, Westfield State Coll., 1979, Mt. St. Vincent U., Halifax, N.S., 1980, Wesleyan U., 1980, U. Mass., 1981, Williams Coll., 1982, Queen's U., 1983, U. Toronto, 1984, McGill U., 1984, Potsdam Coll., SUNY, 1986, Providence Coll., 1987, Smith Coll., 1988, Miami U., 1989. Lectr. history U. Toronto, Ont., Can., 1964-68, asst. prof., 1968-70, assoc. prof., 1970-75, v.p., 1973-75; pres. Smith Coll., Northampton, Mass., 1975-85, Sophia Smith prof., 1975-85; vis. scholar MIT, Boston, 1985—; bd. dirs. Merrill Lynch Co., Arthur D. Little, Inc., Colgate-Palmolive Co., Brascan, Nike, Inc., Allen Group Inc.; adv. bd. IBM Asia Pacific, 1986. Author: The Female Experience in Eighteenth-and Nineteenth-Century America: A Guide to the History of American Women, 1982, Women Reformers and American Culture, 1987, The Road from Coorain, 1989; editor: (with Joan Scott and Susan Bourque) Learning About Women, 1989; researcher numerous publs. on Am. social and intellectual history, history of family life and sex roles, and history of edn. Trustee Hampshire Coll., Northfield Mt. Hermon Sch., New England Med. Ctr.; former trustee Clarke Sch. for Deaf, Coll. Retirement Equities Fund, Acad. of Music, Northampton; bd. dirs. Ctr. Communications. Mem. Am. Hist. Assn., Can. Hist. Assn., Am. Antiquarian Soc. (chair). Home: 125 Canton Ave Milton MA 02186 Office: MIT Program Sci Tech & Soc Cambridge MA 02139

CONWAY, LYNN ANN, computer scientist, educator; b. Mount Vernon, N.Y., Jan. 2, 1938. B.S., Columbia U., 1962, M.S. in Elec. Engring., 1963. Mem. research staff IBM Corp., Yorktown Heights, N.Y., 1964-68; sr. staff engr. Memorex Corp., Santa Clara, Calif., 1969-73; mem. research staff Xerox Corp., Palo Alto, Calif., 1973-78, research fellow, mgr. VLSI systems area, 1978-82, research fellow, mgr. knowledge systems area, 1982-83; asst. dir. for strategic computing Def. Advanced Research Projects Agy., Arlington, Va., 1983-85; prof. elec. engring. and computer sci., assoc. dean Coll. Engring. U. Mich., Ann Arbor, Mich., 1985—; vis. assoc. prof. elec. engring. and computer sci. MIT, Cambridge, Mass., 1978-79; mem. sci. adv. bd. USAF, 1987—. Co-author: textbook Introduction to VLSI Systems, 1980. Recipient Ann. Achievement award Electronics mag., 1981, Harold Pender award U. Pa., 1984, Wetherill Medal Franklin Inst., 1985, Sec. of Def. Meritorious Civilian Service award, 1985; sr. fellow U. Mich. Soc. Fellows, 1987—. Fellow IEEE; mem. AAAS, NAE, Am. Assn. for Artificial Intelligence, Soc. Women Engrs. (Ann. Achievement award 1990). Office: U Mich 2307 EECS Bldg Ann Arbor MI 48109

CONWAY, MARY ELIZABETH, retired university dean, nursing educator; b. Albany, N.Y., Nov. 4, 1923; d. Paul H. and Elizabeth J. (Miller) C. Student, Syracuse U., 1941-43; B.S. in Nursing, Columbia U., 1947; M.Nursing Adminstrn., U. Minn., 1958; Ph.D. in Sociology, Boston U., 1972. Supr. surg. services Mass. Gen. Hosp., Boston, 1953-57; asst. dir. nursing Albany (N.Y.) Med. Center, 1958-63; dir. nursing Monroe Community Hosp., Rochester, N.Y., 1963-65; cons. nurse Bur. Hosp. Nursing, N.Y. State Health Dept., Albany, 1965-68; assoc. prof. Boston U. Sch. Nursing, 1972-76; chmn. Boston U. Sch. Nursing (D.Nursing Sci. program), 1972-76; dean Sch. Nursing, U. Wis., Milw., 1976-80; dean Med. Coll. Ga., Augusta, 1980-90, dean emeritus, 1990—, prof. emeritus, 1990—; cons. Sch. Nursing, SUNY, Albany, 1975-76, Russell Sage Coll., Troy, N.Y., 1973-77; chmn. nurse adv. council to SSS, N.Y. State, 1966-68; dir. study of nursing Republic of China 1985; chair nursing sci. rev. com. NIH, 1986-90. Editorial bd.: Jour. Research in Nursing and Health, 1977. Mem. N.Y. Gov.'s Adv. Coun. on Vocat. Rehab., 1966-68; bd. dirs. Health Svcs. Rensselaer Area, Troy, 1966-68; mem. allocations bd. United Way Greater Milw., 1976-80; founder SAFE Homes Augusta, Inc.; mem. exec. bd. Am. Bur. for Med. Advancement in China, 1989—. Recipient citation Pres. U.S., 1965-68; HEW grantee, 1979-80; Disting. Alumnus award Columbia U., Presbyn. Hosp., Sch. Nursing, 1987. Fellow Am. Acad. Nursing (pres. 1980-81); mem. Sigma Xi, Sigma Theta Tau (Mary Tolle Wright award 1985). Home: 1308 Jamaica Ct Augusta GA 30909 Office: Med Coll Ga Sch Nursing Augusta GA 30912

CONWAY, MAUREEN ANN, program manager; b. Hoboken, N.J., July 25, 1945; d. Michael A. and Margaret (Spiegel) C.; B.A., William Paterson Coll., 1966; M.A., Montclair State Coll., 1971; M.B.A., Temple U., 1980. Tchr. math. high sch., Palisade Park, N.J., 1966-68; mem. tech. staff Bell Tel. Labs., Whippany, N.J., 1968-75; dir. info. systems IUIMC, Phila., 1975-83; dir. ops. CCA, Boston, 1983-88; program mgr. Apollo Computer IMC, Chelmsford, Mass., Inc., 1988-89, HP/Apollo Computer div, 1989—. Bd. dirs. Penns Landing Sq. Condominium, 1977-83. Mem. IEEE, Assn. Computing Machinery, Am. Mgmt. Assn., Beta Gamma Sigma. Office: Apoll Computer 330 Billerica Rd Chelmsford MA 01824

CONWAY CAREY, ALLISON BRANDES, banker; b. N.Y.C., May 4, 1957; d. Edmund Virgil and Audrey (Oehler) Conway; m. Richard Brian Carey, Mar. 7, 1987. BA, Bowdoin Coll., 1979; MBA, Columbia U., 1983. Credit analyst, asst. sec. Mfrs. Hanover Trust Co., N.Y.C., 1979-81, asst. v.p., 1983-85, v.p., investment banking, 1985—. Active Friends of Sta. WNET-13, N.Y.C., 1983—. Mem. Jr. League N.Y. Republican. Home: 240 E 76th St New York NY 10021 Office: Mfrs Hanover Trust 270 Park Ave New York NY 10017

CONWELL, ESTHER MARLY, physicist; b. N.Y.C., May 23, 1922; d. Charles and Ida (Korn) C.; m. Abraham A. Rothberg, Sept. 30, 1945; 1 son, Lewis J. B.A., Bklyn. Coll., 1942; M.S., U. Rochester, N.Y., 1945; Ph.D., U. Chgo., 1948. Lectr. Bklyn. Coll., 1946-51; mem. tech. staff Bell Telephone Labs., 1951-52; physicist GTE Labs., Bayside, N.Y., 1952-61; mgr. physics dept. GTE Labs., 1961-72; vis. prof. U. Paris, 1962-63; Abby Rockefeller Mauze prof. M.I.T., 1972; prin. scientist Xerox Corp., Webster, N.Y., 1972-80; research fellow Xerox Corp., 1981—; cons., mem. adv. com. engring. NSF, 1978-81. Author: High Field Transport in Semiconductors, 1967, also research papers; mem. editorial bd. Jour. Applied Physics; Proc. of IEEE; patentee in field. Fellow IEEE, Am. Phys. Soc. (sec.-treas. div. condensed matter physics 1977-82); mem. NAS, Soc. Women Engrs. (Achievement award 1960), Nat. Acad. Engring. Office: 800 Phillips Rd Webster NY 14580

CONWELL, THERESA GALLO, insurance company executive; b. Utica, N.Y., Mar. 6, 1947; d. Ernest and Anna (Caiazzo) Gallo; m. Charles Ray Conwell, Aug. 19, 1978. B.S.Ed., SUNY-Potsdam, 1968; M.A.Ed., SUNY-Cortland, 1978; Cert. tchr., N.Y.; C.L.U.; chartered fin. cons., registered rep. Tchr. pub. schs., Clinton, N.Y., 1969-78, Portland, Conn., 1978-80; supr. mktg. services Phoenix Mut. Life Ins. Co., Hartford, Conn., 1980-82, assoc. mgr. agt. tng., 1982-84, mgr. agt. tng., 1984-85, dir. agt./mgmt. devel., 1985-88, fin. svcs. rep., 1988—; speaker to small bus. orgns., women's groups, N.Y., New Eng., 1986—. Mem. New Eng. Tng. Dir.'s Assn., Nat. Assn. Life Underwriters, Internat. Assn. Fin. Planners, Women's Life Underwriters Coun. (sec./treas.), NAFE, Nat. Assn. Securities Dealers, Nat. Assn. Profl. Saleswomen, Bus. and Profl. Women of Glastonbury, NOW. Democrat. Avocations: tennis; golf; swimming; aerobics; reading. Home: 191 Knollwood Dr Glastonbury CT 06033 Office: Phoenix Mut Life Ins Co One American Row Hartford CT 06115

COOGAN, ALICE, educational association administrator, writer; b. Sao Paulo, Brazil, Mar. 27, 1944; came to U.S., 1947; d. James Alan and Helen (Townsley) C. BA, Stanford (Calif.) U., 1965. Designer Interior Design Collaborative, San Francisco, 1971-75; dep. dir. travel/study programs Stanford Alumni Assn., 1975—. Writer (travel column) Stanford mag., 1984—. Office: Stanford Alumni Assn Bowman Alumni House Stanford CA 94305-4005

COOGAN, ROBYN KAY ANKNEY, teacher; b. Pitts., Aug. 1, 1951; d. Ralph Albert and Gertrude Irene (Stenzel) Ankney; m. James Francis Coogan, Aug. 7, 1976 (div. Apr. 1985); children: James Kevin, Rachel Ann. MusB, U. Mich., 1973; M in Elem. Edn., Ea. Mich. U., 1977; M in Secondary Math., U. Detroit, 1990. Substitute tchr. Beecher (Mich.) Sch. Dist., 1973-74; substitute tchr. Taylor (Mich.) Sch. Dist., 1974-75, tchr., 1975-79, 84—; cons. Bloomfield Hills (Mich.) Sch. Dist., 1988; mem. Taylor's Gifted and Talented Com., 1987-90. Mem. Am. Diabetic Assn., Southfield, Mich., 1981—, MADD, Ctr. for Sci. in the Pub. Interest Nutrition Health Letter, Washington, 1988-90, Planned Parenthood, N.Y.C., 1988-90. Recipient grant for devel. math. Taylor (Mich.) Categorical Grants, 1989-90. Mem. Mich. Reading Assn. Home: 24444 Heritage Dr Woodhaven MI 48183

COOK, ANDA SUNA, civil rights advocate; b. Riga, Latvia, Mar. 15, 1935; came to U.S., 1952.; d. Janis Suna and Erna Alexandra (Kletnieks) Sirmais; m. William E. Cook, May 27, 1961; children: Lisa Inara Hamilton, Inta Marie Mitterbach, John William. Student, Augustana Coll., Sioux Falls, S.D., 1954-55, Cleve. State U., 1970-85; MS, Case Western Res. U., 1989. Lic. real estate agt. Mgr. housing dept. Cuyahoga Plan of Ohio, Inc., Cleve., 1976-88, dir. resource devel., 1988—; v.p. regional div. U.S. Orgn. Internat. Trade, Inc., Cleve., 1989—; price analyst U.S. Steel Corp., Cleve., 1955-62; stringer The Cleve. Press, 1974-76; pres. ASC Cons.-Orgn. Devel., Cleve., 1988—. Writer 60 Years of League of Women Voters, 1980; writer, producer Vama in Action, 1989. Bd. mem. Dept. Human Svcs., Cuayhoga County, 1984—, Citizens League, 1989—; trustee Friends of Cleve. Met. Housing Authority, Cleve., 1986—; mem. bd. Cudell Sr. Adv. Coun., 1980-85; mem. Cuyahoga Community Coll. Adv. Bd., 1980—; bd. trustees Citizens League, Cleve., 1989—; chair Young Audiences Vols., 1972-75; legis. chair Cleve. PTA, 1972-73; pres. PTA, Louisa May Alcott Elem. Sch., Cleve., 1971-72; pres. LWV, Cleve., 1975-77. Recipient Dedicated Svc. award The Cuyahoga Plan, Cleve., 1985, Cleve. Leadership award United Way, 1976. Mem. Am. Soc. Tng. and Devel., Nat. Soc. for Fund Raising Execs. Democrat. Lutheran. Home: 9801 Lake Ave Cleveland OH 44102 Office: US Orgn Internat Trade Inc 777 Statler Office Tower Cleveland OH 44115

COOK, ANN JENNALIE, English language educator; b. Wewoka, Okla., Oct. 19, 1934; d. Arthur Holly and Bertha Mabelle (Stafford) C.; children: Lee Ann Merrick, Amy Ceil Leonard; m. John Donelson Whalley, Sept. 10, 1975. BA, U. Okla., 1956, MA, 1959; PhD, Vanderbilt U., 1972. Instr. English U. Okla., 1956-57; tchr. English N.C. and Conn., 1958-61; instr. So. Conn. State Coll., 1962-64; asst. prof. U. S.C., 1972-74; adj. asst. prof. Vanderbilt U., 1977-82, assoc. prof., 1982-89, prof., 1990—; exec. sec. Shakespeare Assn. Am., 1975-87; chmn. Internat. Shakespeare Assn., 1988—. Author: Privileged Playgoers of Shakespeare's London, 1981, Making a Match: Courtship in Shakespeare and His Society, 1990; assoc. editor: Shakespeare Studies, 1973-80; mem. editorial bd.: Medieval and Renaissance Drama in Eng., Shakespeare Quar., Shakespeare Studies; contbr. articles to profl. publs. Trustee Folger Shakespeare Libr., Assn. Creative Theatre, Edn. Rsch. Recipient Letseizer award, 1956, Nat. Leadership award Delta Delta Delta, 1956; Danforth fellow, 1968-72, Folger summer fellow, 1973, Donelson fellow, 1974-75; Rockefeller Found. fellow, 1984, Guggenheim Found. fellow, 1984-85. Mem. Shakespeare Assn. Am., MLA, AAUP, Shakespeare Inst., Soc. Values in Higher Edn., Renaissance Soc. Am. (bd. dirs.), Southeastern Renaissance Soc., Phi Beta Kappa. Episcopalian. Home: 91 Valley Forge Nashville TN 37205 Office: Vanderbilt U Dept English Nashville TN 37235

COOK, BERNADINE HLADIK, physics educator; b. Gloversville, N.Y., Mar. 31, 1949; d. Paul Peter and Rose (Sefcovic) Hladik; m. Keith Walker Cook, Dec. 26, 1970 (div. June 1973); 1 child, Heather Ammons. Postgrad., U. Rochester, 1980; BS in Physics, Clarkson U., 1971; MS in Physics Edn., SUNY, Oneonta, 1982; postgrad., Union Coll., Schenectady, 1988, Rensselaer Poly. Inst., 1988. Cert. physics, chemistry, earth sci., and math. tchr., N.Y. Tchr. physics Greater Johnstown (N.Y.) Sch. Dist., 1974—, chmn. sci. dept., 1988—; physics cons. N.Y. State Bur. Sci. Edn., Albany, 1978—; project dir. NSF, Union Coll., 1988—; proposal evaluator NSF, 1989. Author: Brief Review in Physics, 1990. Sec., mem. exec. bd. swim team YMCA, Johnstown, 1983-86. NSF grantee, 1988—. Mem. Am. Assn. Physics Tchrs., Sci. Tchrs. N.Y. State, N.Y. State United Tchrs. Assn., Johnstown Tchrs. Assn. Republican. Roman Catholic. Home: 347 W Main St Johnstown NY 12095 Office: Johnstown High Sch 2 Wright Dr Johnstown NY 12095

COOK, BETH MARIE, author, poet, software executive; b. Electra, Tex., Jan. 4, 1933; d. Charles Bolivar Allen and Ida Marie (Nelson) Burton; m. William H. Cook, May 30, 1955 (div. Nov. 1981); children: David M., Dianne M. Gleason. Student, Rockmont Coll., 1951-54; BA, Antioch U. West, 1981. County coord. office econ. opportunity Upper Arkansas Council, Salida, Colo., 1974-76; dir. area agy. on aging Upper Arkansas Council/Dept. Social Services div. State of Colo., 1976-80; specialist community devel. Mountain Plains Congress Sr. Orgns., Denver, 1980-82; sr. adminstrv. asst. Digital Research Inc., Monterey, Calif., 1983-85; asst. to pres. Digital Research Inc., Monterey, 1985-87, retail rep., 1987-88; co-owner, ptnr. Scotia Gallery, Monterey, 1983-86; chief operating officer MiniSoft, Inc., Phoenix, 1988-89; exec. asst. Ft. Collins (Colo.) Housing Authority, 1989—; hostess Sr. Sound-Off show Sta. KVRH, Salida, 1978-80; cons. Devel. Assocs. Inc., Denver, 1982. Author: (poem) Jessie, 1989-90. Exec. asst. Fort Collins Housing Authority, 1989—; coord. crisis intervention line Chaffee County Community Crisis Ctr., Salida, 1976-80; committeewoman Chaffee County Dem. Cen. Com., Salida, 1979-80; speaker, program com. Colo. Gov.'s Conf. on Aging, Denver, 1980. Recipient Human Devel. Svc. award HHS, 1980, Golden Poet award, 1989; named Woman of Yr. Chaffee County Bus. and Profl. Women's Club, 1978. Mem. Am. Assn. Ret. Persons, Colo. Gerontol. Soc., Summit Profl. Orgn., Inc., NAFE, World Soc. Poetry. Presbyterian.

COOK, BETTE WALKER PHILPOTT, investment company executive; b. Loma Linda, Calif., Mar. 6, 1941; d. Reed Clemems and Edna (Pace) Walker; m. Donald M. Cook, Dec. 30, 1982; children: Jane, Anne, James, Daniel. BA in Psychology, UCLA, 1964. Personnel testing specialist N.Am. Aviation, El Segundo, Calif., 1964; kindergarten tchr. Am.-Nicaraguan Sch., Managua, Nicaragua, 1975-76; real estate sales person Ackerman Real Estate Services, Washington, 1976-78; v.p. Internat. Investment Counsel, Los Angeles, 1978-83, Sundance Homes Calif., Inc., Los Angeles, 1983-85, Internat. Capital Mgmt., Beverly Hills, 1985-88, WSGP Fin. Mgmt. Co., Century City, Calif., 1988—. Mem. Pasadena Playhouse Guild. Mem. AAUW, NOW, LWV. Home: 2714 Fleur Dr San Marino CA 91108 Office: WSGP Fin Mgmt Co 1800 Century Park East #1000 Los Angeles CA 90067

COOK, BLANCHE MCLANE, artist; b. Moulton, Iowa, July 1, 1901; d. Alva Randolph and Eva (Wynn) Mclane; m. Harry Christian Cook, Feb. 19, 1938 (dec. 1983); m. Rankin A. Nebinger, May 4, 1984. Grad. with high honors, Moore Coll. Art, 1929; BA, Cen. Wash. U., 1959, MA, 1965. Tchr. Moore Coll. Art and Baldwin Sch., Phila., 1928-30; free-lance comml. artist, 1928—; irrigation dep. Yakima County Treas., Wash., 1930-34, chief dep. treas., 1934-40; pvt. instr. art, 1930—; art instr. Yakima Valley Jr. Coll., Wash., 1933-48, 57-58; portrait painter, 1928—; art instr., counselor Moxee Elem. Sch., Yakima, 1959-60; art instr. Wilson Jr. High Sch., Yakima, 1961-66, chmn. art dept., 1962-66; founder art dept. Yakima Valley Jr. Coll., 1933. Works exhibited at Larson Gallery, Yakima, 1954-63, Seattle Art Mus., Woessner Gallery, Seattle, Studio Gallery, Seattle, Palace Legion of Honor,

San Francisco, Spokane (Wash.) Art Gallery, others; represented in permanent collections Seattle Art Mus., Frye Mus., Yakima Valley Jr. Coll.; organized Yakima Valley Artists Exhibit, 1937-41, Larson Gallery Guild, 1957. Organizer, founder Yakima Valley Art Coun., 1945; mem. Seattle Art Mus., 1948—; organizer Larson Gallery Guild, 1957. Recipient award Northwest Exhibit, Spokane Art Gallery Guild, 1957, named One of 41 Women in History Yakima Valley, 1986; Pemberton Morris fellow Moore Coll. Art; Blanche McLane Cook Art Libr. named in her honor Bleyhl Communityh Libr., 1977; named to 100 Years-100 Women 1889-89 of Yakima County, 1989. Mem. Women Painters of Wash., Yakima allied Art Coun. (founder), Yakima Valley Soc. Artists (charter), Moore Coll. Art Alumni Assn., Cen. Wash. U. Alumni (life), Order of Eastern Star (life), Women's Century Club (life), PEO Internat. (Wash., Conn. chpts.), Wash. State Ret. Assn., PEN Women Internat., Rosicrucians, Delta Kappa Gamma (res.), Alpha Sigma (reserve). Home: 207 23nd Ave Yakima WA 98902

COOK, BLANCHE WIESEN, history educator, journalist; b. N.Y.C., Apr. 20, 1941; d. David Theodore and Sadonia (Ecker) Wiesen. B.A., Hunter Coll., 1962; M.A., Johns Hopkins U., 1964, Ph.D., 1970. Instr. Hampton Inst., Va., 1963; instr. Stern Coll. for Women, Yeshiva U., N.Y.C., 1964-67; prof. history John Jay Coll., Grad. Faculty CUNY, 1968—; producer, broadcaster program stas. WBAI and KPFK, N.Y.C. and Los Angeles, 1978—; vis. prof. UCLA, 1982-83; syndicated journalist; bd. dirs. Women's Fgn. Policy Adv. Coun., Inst. for Media Analysis; bd. dirs., v.p., co-chair Fund for Open Info. and Accountability; mem. freedom to write com. PEN. Author: Crystal Eastman on Women and Revolution, 1978, Declassified Eisenhower, 1981, Biography of Eleanor Roosevelt, 1990; sr. editor: The Garland Library of War and Peace, 360 vols., 1970-80; contbr. articles to various publs. Appointed to com. on documents for fgn. relations U.S. Dept. State, 1986—. Faculty fellow CUNY, 1978-84. Mem. Orgn. Am. Historians (co-chair freedom of info. com.), Am. Hist. Assn., Coordinating Com. Women in Hist. Profession (pres. N.Y.C. chpt. 1969-71), Berkshire Women Historians, Soc. Historians Am. Fgn. Relations, Conf. on Peace Research in History (bd. dirs., v.p.), Women's Internat. League for Peace and Freedom, Pi Sigma Alpha, Phi Alpha Theta. Office: CUNY John Jay Coll Dept History 445 W 59th St New York NY 10019

COOK, CINDY KAYE, pharmaceutical company clinical researcher; b. Milw., Aug. 7, 1952; d. Harold Frederick and Ruth Marion (Kassulke) Hasse; m. Thomas Judd Cook, Oct. 10, 1987. BS in Biology, U. Wis., Oshkosh, 1974, MS in Biology, 1982. Quality control chemist Seven-Up Bottling Co., Oshkosh, 1975-76; research analyst U. Wis/Fox Valley Water Quality Planning Agy., Oshkosh, 1980-81; electronic microscopy asst. U. Wis., Oshkosh, 1980-81; instr. biology and chemistry Mt. Senario Coll., Ladysmith, Wis., 1982-84, asst. prof., 1984-85; clin. trial analyst Boehringer Ingelheim Pharmaceuticals, Ridgefield, Conn., 1986-87, med. research assoc., 1987-89; clin. rsch. scientist Glaxo Inc, Research Triangle Park, N.C., 1990—; disting. lectr. Lake Superior Assn. Colls. and Univs., 1984-85. Mem. grants review panel Charles A. Lindbergh Fund, Summit, N.J., 1984—. Grantee Charles A. Lindberg Fund, 1983. Mem. Assocs. Clin. Pharmacology, Sigma Xi. Office: Glaxo Inc 5 Moore Dr Research Triangle Park NC 27709

COOK, DIANE G(REFE), management executive, consultant; b. Ft. Bragg, N.C., Aug. 13, 1943; d. Richard William and Marjorie Louise (Sine) G.; m. Gary M. Cook, Sept. 3, 1966; children: Christian M., Lauren S. B.A., Smith Coll., 1965. Program dir. N.Y.C. Commn. to UN and Consular Corps, 1968-70; exec. dir. Internat. Visitors Info. Svc., Washington, 1971-74; v.p. Nat. Coun. for Internat. Vistors, Washington, 1981-83, pres. 1983-84; pres. Diane Cook Assocs., Golden, Colo.; sr. v.p. Mktg. World News Digest, Denver; bd. dirs. Telecommunications Coop. Network, N.Y.C.; founder, officer of bd. Tulsa Coun. for Internat. Visitors, 1976-83; mem. exec. com. Meridian House Internat., Washington, 1983-84; nat. adv. coun. Experiment in Internat. Living, Brattleboro, Vt., 1979—. Author speaker in field. Pres. Assn. of Seven Colls. of Tulsa, 1978-80; chmn. Tulsa Humanities Com., 1980-82; mem. pub. sector Okla. Found. for Humanities, Oklahoma City, 1981-83; mem. Mayor's Com. on Internat. Visistors, Washington, 1972-74. Community internat. fellow USIA, 1981; recipient Commendation award, U.S. Dept. State, 1974, Mayor's award, Washington, 1974. Mem. Am. Soc. Tng. and Devel., Am. Mgmt. Assn., Denver Com. on Fgn. Rels., Inst. Internat. Edn. Republican. Club: Smith Coll. (pres. Tulsa 1977-83). Office: World News Digest 999 18th St Denver CO 80202 also: Diane Cook Assocs 25298 Foothills Dr North Golden CO 80401

COOK, DORIS MARIE, accountant, educator; b. Fayetteville, Ark., June 11, 1924; d. Ira and Mettie Jewel (Dorman) C. BS in Bus. Adminstrn., U. Ark., 1946, MS, 1949; PhD, U. Tex., 1969. CPA, Okla., Ark. Jr. acct. Haskins & Sells, Tulsa, 1946-47; instr. acctg. U. Ark., Fayetteville, 1947-52, asst. prof., 1952-62, assoc. prof., 1962-69, prof., 1969-88, Univ. prof. and Nolan E. Williams lectr. in acctg., 1988—; mem. Ark. State Bd. Pub. Accountancy, 1987—, treas., 1989—; appointed Nolan E. Williams lectureship in acctg., 1988—. Mem. rev. bd. Ark. Bus. Rev., Jour. Managerial Issues; contbr. articles to profl. jours. Mem. Ark. Bus. Assn. (editor newsletter 1982-85), Am. Acctg. Assn. (chair nat. membership 1982-83, chair Arthur Carter Scholarship com. 1984-85, chair membership Ark. 1985-87), Am. Inst. CPA's, Am. Women's Soc. CPA's, Ark. Soc. CPA's (v.p. 1975-76, pres. NW Ark. chpt. 1980-81, sec. Student Loan Found. 1981-84, treas. Student Loan Found. 1984—, chair pub. relations 1984-88), Acad. Acctg. Historians (trustee 1985-87, mem. rev. bd. of Working Papers Series 1984—), Ark. Fedn. Bus. and Profl. Women's Clubs (treas. 1979-80), Mortar Bd., Beta Gamma Sigma, Beta Alpha Psi (editor nat. newsletter 1973-77, nat. pres. 1977-78), Phi Gamma Nu, Alpha Lambda Delta, Delta Kappa Gamma (sec. 1976-78, pres. 1978-80), Phi Kappa Phi. Club: Fayetteville Bus. and Profl. Women's (pres. 1973-74, 75-76, Woman of Yr. 1977). Home: 1115 Leverett St Fayetteville AR 72703 Office: U Ark Dept Acctg Fayetteville AR 72701

COOK, ELLEN ANN DE CORTE, management consultant; b. Grosse Pointe, Mich., Nov. 18, 1943; d. Thomas Joseph and Margaret (Carnaghi) DeCorte; m. David Yeats Cook, Oct. 28, 1966; children: Christopher, Timothy. BA maxima cum laude, St. Mary's Coll., Orchard Lake, Mich., 1982; MA, Oakland U., Rochester, Mich., 1984. Tng. cons. Gen. Motors Edn. & Tng., Warren, Mich., 1984—, The Tng. Support Group, Fenton, Mich., 1988—; organizational devel. cons. Saturn Corp., Troy, Mich., 1988—. Mem. AAUW, Am. Soc. Tng. & Devel. Home and Office: 54294 Horizon Dr Shelby Twp MI 48316

COOK, ELSA ESTELLE, writer; b. Belleville, Ill., Jan. 29, 1932; d. Walter Eugene and Elsa Caroline (Adler) Ogle; m. Rodney Lee Pitts, Apr. 5, 1954 (div. 1972); children: Patricia Sue Grant, Barbara Lynn Larson; m. Frank Shelley Cook, July 5, 1974. BJ, U. Mo., 1955; MA, St. Louis U., 1969. Cert. tchr., Mo. Copywriter Sears, Roebuck & Co., St. Louis, 1961; tchr. McCluer High Sch., Florissant, Mo., 1963-88; freelance writer St. Louis, 1980—. Author: novel Satin Dolls, 1987. Fulbright scholar, 1980; Nat. Endowment for Humanities grantee, 1986. Mem. Writer's Guild, Romance Writers Am., Nat. Coun. for Social Studies. Democrat. Mem. Ethical Soc. Home: 8112 Pershing Saint Louis MO 63105

COOK, FRANCES D., diplomat; b. Charleston, W.Va., Sept. 7, 1945; d. Nash and Vivian Cook. B.A., Mary Washington Coll. of U. Va., 1967; M.P.A., Harvard U., 1978. Certificats d'Etudes, Université d'Aix-Marseille (France), 1966. Commd. fgn. svc. officer Dept. State, 1967; spl. asst. to R.S. Shriver amb. to France, Paris, 1968-69; mem. U.S. Del. Paris Peace Talks on Viet-Nam, 1970-71; cultural affairs officer, consul Am. Consul Gen., Sydney, Australia, 1971-73; cultural affairs officer, first sec. Am. Embassy, Dakar, Senegal, 1973-75; personnel officer for Africa USIA, Washington, 1975-77; dir. office public affairs African Bur. Dept. State, Washington, 1978-80; amb. to Republic of Burundi Dept. State, Bujumbura, 1980-83; consul gen. Dept. State, Alexandria, Egypt, 1983-86; dep. asst. sec. of state Dept. State, Washington, 1986-87, dir. Office of West African Affairs, 1987-89; amb. to Cameroon Dept. State, Yaoundé, 1989—. mem. policy coun. Una Chapman Cox Found. Recipient various honor awards Dept. State. Mem. Am. Fgn. Service Assn., Am. Polit. Sci. Assn., Coun. on Fgn. Rels., Washington Alumni Coun. Kennedy Sch. Harvard U., Harvard Club of N.Y.C.

COOK, GLORIA HOUSTON, civic leader; b. Portland, Maine, Aug. 22, 1933; d. Ellwyn Kenelm and May Elvera (Delay) Houston; m. James Thomas Cook Jr., Jan. 28, 1952; children: Victoria Cook Leonhardt, Sheryl Ann. Student, U. Fla., 1950-52. Invitee, White House Conf. on Food, Nutrition and Health, 1969, cons. to Fla. conf., 1970; Gen. Synod del. from Fla., United Ch. of Christ, 1975-77; dir. pub. rels., trustee, chmn. nominating com., mem. pulpit com., tchr. Sunday sch., mem. stewardship bd., Seabreeze United Ch.; legis. appointee, sec. exec. bd., Volusia County Charter Rev. Commn., 1975-77; mem. Volusia County Personnel and Merit Bd., 1974-85, chmn., 1980-83; bd. counselors, Bethune-Cookman Coll., 1977-84; bd. dirs., Atlantic Ctr. for Arts, New Smyrna Beach, Fla.; pres., bd. dirs., exec. com. Meml. Hosp., Ormond Beach, Fla., 1980—, mem. hosp. estate planning com., chmn., treas. personnel com., chmn. fin. com., v.p., chief exec. officer search, evaluation and compensation com.; hon. life dir., Volusia/Flagler Easter Seal Soc., 1955—; past pres., v.p., sec. Fla. Easter Seal Soc., Nat. Easter Seal Soc., chair, mem. rels.; vice chmn. Ho. of Dels. Nat. Easter Seal Soc.; mem. nat. adv. child health and human devel. Coun. Nat. Insts. Health, 1990—; past pres. Jr. League Daytona Beach. Recipient Meritorious Service and Outstanding Vol. Service awards Nat. Easter Seal Soc.; named Layman of Yr., Fla. Med. Soc., 1985. Mem. Oceanside Country Club, Highlands Country Club (N.C.). Republican. Home: 1239 Ocean Shore Blvd Apt 9D Ormond Beach FL 32176

COOK, JUANITA, library director; b. Pine Bluff, Ark., Aug. 25, 1948; d. Andrew Jackson and Queen Esther (Day) Kimbell; m. Curtis Lee Cook, Nov. 28. 1970; children: Melanie LaJune, Reginald, Cheryl Nicole. BS, U. Ark., Pine Bluff, 1970; MLS, Ball State U., 1972. Reference libr. Colorado Coll./Pennrose Pub., Colorado Springs, 1971, Longview Community, Lee's Summit, Mo., 1973-77; dir. IMC, instr. U. Ark., Pine Bluff, 1977-80; libr. Russellville Pub. Schs., Russellville, Ark., 1981-85, Arkadelphia Pub. Schs., Arkadelphia, Ark., 1985-87; head libr., asst. prof. So. Ark. U. TECH, Camden, 1987—. Pres. Ouachita-Calhoun County Literacy, Camden, 1988-89. Danforth Found. fellow, 1970, Nat. Black Studies Ins. fellow, 1989. Mem. ALA, Ark. Libr. Assn. , Nat. Assn. Female Execs., Zeta Phi Beta. Democrat. Apostolic. Office: So Ark U Tech 100 Carr Rd Camden AR 71701

COOK, KAREN SUE, accountant; b. Middletown, Ohio, Mar. 28, 1960; d. Carl Franklin Cook and Wanda June (Harris) Miller. BS, Miami U., Oxford, Ohio, 1982; postgrad., Cen. Conn. State U., 1987-89, U. Hartford, 1990—. Bookkeeper, receptionist Guardian Assocs., Columbus, Ohio, 1982-83; acct., clk. Victors Temprares, Columbus, 1983-84; tax auditor The Ltd., Columbus, 1984-86; sr. acctg. analyst Phoenix Mut. Life Ins., Hartford, Conn., 1987-89, sr. re-ins. fin. acct., 1989—. Author poetry. Recruiter Jr. Achievement, Hartford, 1988; vol. Conn. Child and Family Svcs., Farmington, Conn., 1988-89. Mem. Nat. Assn. Accts., Am. Bus. Women's Assn. (scholar 1978), Alpha Phi Omega, Conn. Sports Club. Republican. Home: 27 Brandywine Ln Suffield CT 06078 Office: Phoenix Mut Life Ins Bright Meadow Blvd Enfield CT 06115

COOK, KATHRYN ANN, executive fashion director; b. Muncie, Ind., Mar. 22, 1965; . John William and Lisabeth Ann (Randall) Dawson; m. Thomas Darrell Cook, Sept. 24, 1988. BS in Indsl. Distribution, Clarkson U., 1987. Evening mgr. Corner Stop, New Harbor, Maine, 1986; asst. mgr. Thompson Cottages, New Harbor, 1985-86; asst. athletic trainer Clarkson U., Potsdam, N.Y., 1983-87; sales engr. Eaton Corp., Milw., 1987; cosmetic mgr. Clinique Cosmetics, N.Y.C., 1987-88; account mgr. Office Bus. Systems and Xerox, Pine Brook, N.J., 1988-89; exec. fashion dir. Macy's, Livingston, N.J., 1988—, account exec. corp. gift svcs., 1988—; balloon handler Macy's Thanksgiving Day Parade, 1989, capt. Warner Bros. float, 1990. Mem. Smithsonian Inst. Named Clarkson U. Trustee scholar, 1983-87. Mem. Am. Prodn. and Inventory Control Soc., Nat. Athletic Soc., Indsl. Distribution Soc., Order of Rainbow, Order of Eastern Star, Fitness Club, Ski Club, Delta Zeta. Lutheran. Home: 46 Irving Ave Livingston NJ 07039 Office: Macy's Exec Offices Walnut & South Orange Ave Livingston NJ 07039

COOK, KATHRYN ELLA, special education administrator, private consultant; b. Rumford, Maine, Sept. 19, 1945; d. Rupert Rowe and Doris Phillips (Kidder) Huntoon; m. Edward Thomas Cook, July 30, 1966 (div. Apr. 1971); 1 child, Edward Thomas Jr. BS, U. Maine, 1967; MA, Oakland U., Rochester, Mich., 1981. Tchr. remedial reading Livermore Falls (Maine) Pub. Schs., 1967; elem. resource tchr. Bd. Coop. Ednl. Svcs., Fairport, N.Y., 1967-68; secondary resource tchr. Winslow (Maine) Pub. Schs., 1971; coord. spl. edn. curriculum Waterville (Maine) Sr. High Sch., 1971-73; spl. edn. tchr. cons. Bloomfield Hills (Mich.) Pub. Schs., 1974-85; diagnostic-prescriptive cons. Kennett Sr. High Sch., Conway, N.H., 1985-87; cons. Ednl. Devel. Svcs., Mich., N.H., Tex., 1983-88; mgr. quality assurance Maine Bur. Mental Retardation, Augusta, 1989-90; dir. spl. edn. Sch. Union #30, Lisbon Falls, Maine, 1990—; ednl. cons. Oakland Community Coll., Farmington, Mich. 1983-85, North Country Ednl. Svcs., Lancaster, N.H., 1986-87, Winston Sch., San Antonio, 1988, David Mandt & Assocs. Behavior Mgmt. Group, Richardson, Tex., 1990; photog. and style show model. Author: Winner's Manual for High School Survival, 1985; developer vocat. assessment test. Actress, dir. community theatre. Mem. Coun. for Exceptional Children, Assn. for Persons with Severe Handicaps, Maine Assn. Spl. Edn. Dirs., Nat. Assn. of Spl. Edn. Dirs., Coun. on Transition (bd. dirs.), New England Coun. for Ednl. Leaders. Republican. Home: 37 Munroe Ln Topsham ME 04086 Office: Sch Union #30 Spl Edn Office Rte 196 Lisbon Falls ME 04252

COOK, LEANN CECILIA, paralegal; b. Wheeling, W.Va., Oct. 14, 1950; d. Leo Elbin Cook and Phyllis Marie (Bargiel) Cook-Allen. Cert. in computers and computer programming, Contemporary Inst., Pitts., 1971; student, Ohio U., 1979-81; Paralegal Cert., Am. Inst. Paralegal Studies, Inc., North Canton, Ohio, 1986. Computer operator Riechart's Furniture Co., Wheeling, 1971-72, Wheeling Machine Products Co., 1972-74; data technician Belmont Tech. Coll., St. Clairsville, Ohio, 1974-76; adminstrv. asst. Belmont County Treas. Office, St. Clairsville, 1977-87; paralegal specialist Office of Dist. Counsel VA, Lexington, Ohio, 1987-88; fin. litigation agt. U.S. Atty.'s Office, Columbus, 1988-90; with Streski Reporting Svc., Martins Ferry, 1990—; data processing instr. adult edn. Belmont Joint Vocat Sch., St. Clairsville, 1974-79. Mem. pub. rels. com., Tri-County Task Force for Sexual Abuse, St. Clairsville, 1985-86; mem. Women's Crisis Ctr., St. Clairsville, 1986, St. Clairsville's Bus. and Profl. Women, 1986-87; coord. fed. women's program So. Dist. Ohio, Columbus, 1989; vol. amb. Chinese Imperial Arts Program, Columbus, 1989. Mem. NAFE, Legal Assts. Cen. Ohio, St. Clairsville Law Library Assn., Female Execs., Inc., Fed. Employed Women Assn., Columbus Bar Assn., Pitts. Paralegal Assn. (assoc.), Northeastern Ohio Paralegal Assn. Democrat. Roman Catholic. Home: PO Box 156 Saint Clairsville OH 43950 Office: US Atty's Office Dept Justice Rm 200 85 Marconi Blvd Columbus OH 43215

COOK, MARIAN ALICE, musician; b. Louisville, Aug. 4, 1928; d. Clarence Frederick and Aline (Swisher) C. MusB, Ohio Wesleyan U., Delaware, 1950; MEd, Miami U., Oxford, Ohio, 1955. Organist Lindenwald Meth. Ch., Hamilton, Ohio, 1955-58; music tchr. Hamilton Pub. Sch., 1951-58; music specialist Pinellas County Schs., Clearater, Fla., 1958-81; organist First United Meth. Ch., St. Petersburg, Fla., 1987—. Sec. Pinellas Youth Symphony Bd., 1976-80; docent chmn. Mus. Fine Arts, 1989-90. Recipient Recognition award West Coast Profl. Panhellenic, 1967, Recognition award St. Petersburg Boychoir, 1968. Mem. Fellowship of United Meths. in Music Worship and other Arts, Am. Guild of Organists, Stuart Soc., Zonta, Tiger Bay Club, Delta Kappa Gamma (pres. 1972-74), Mu Phi Epsilon. United Meth. Home: 4210 24th Ave N Saint Petersburg FL 33713

COOK, MARJORIE ELLEN, nursing administrator; b. Logansport, Ind., Oct. 31, 1942; d. Frank A. and Florence M. (Weiand) Lind; m. Rudolph W. Cook, Oct. 30, 1970 (dec. July 1978); 1 child, Franklin R. BS in Nursing, Ind. U., 1964, MS in Nursing, 1969. Lic. nurse, Fla., RN, Ind. Staff RN VA Med. Ctr., Indpls., 1964-67; staff RN, instr. Community Mental Health Ctr., Indpls., 1968-69; dir. nursing St. Mary's Hosp., West Palm Beach, Fla., 1969-70; supr. nursing Arden Hill Hosp., Community Mental Health Ctr., Goshen, N.Y., 1971-72; instr. Mt. St. Mary's Coll., Newburg, N.Y., 1973-76; head nurse VA Med. Ctr., Bay Pine, Fla., 1976-78; asst. chief nurse VA Med. Ctr., Poplar Bluff, Mo., 1978-81, Danville, Ill., 1981-83; chief VA Med. Ctr., Ft. Wayne, Ind., 1983-86, Topeka, 1986—; adv. coun. to coll. RN program, Poplar Bluff, Danville, Ft. Wayne; mentor new students, VA Med. Ctr., Topeka, 1989. NIH scholar, 1968. Mem. Am. Nurses Assn., Am. Orgn. Nurse Execs., AAUW (pres. 1980-81), Bus. and Profl. Women, Sigma Theta Tau (com.), Pi Lambda Theta. Methodist. Home: 2655 SW Ashworth Pl Topeka KS 66614 Office: VA Med Ctr 2200 Gage Blvd Topeka KS 66605

COOK, MARY FRANCES, university official; b. Whiteivlle, N.C., June 20, 1962; d. David Cotten and Mary Frances (Powell) C. BS, Ariz. State U., 1984. Credentials evaluator Ariz. State U., Tempe, 1985-87, acad. advisor, 1987—. Recipient award of merit Ariz. State U., 1990. Mem. Nat. Assn. Acad. Advisors, Univ. Career Women. Home: 3639 W Lisbon Ln Phoenix AZ 85023 Office: Ariz State U W Cronkite Sch Journalism-Telecommun Tempe AZ 85287-1305

COOK, MARY JOENE, accountant; b. Marlow, Okla., Dec. 30, 1943; d. Woodrow and Joan (Jones) Lambert; m. Sidney Wayne Cook, Aug. 2, 1963; children: Shawn, Cindy, Amy. BBA in Acctg., Midwestern State U., Wichita Falls, Tex., 1979. CPA, Tex. Asst. v.p., acctg. mgr. 1st Wichita Nat. Bank, Wichita Falls, Tex., 1979-83; sr. v.p., treas. Ind. Am. Savs. Assn., Irving, Tex., 1983-85; pres. Ind. Am. Fin. Mgmt., Irving, 1985-86; co-owner Genesis Mktg. Group, Arlington, Tex., 1986—. Tchr. Sunday sch. Grace Luth. Ch., Arlington; mem. Arlington PTA. Mem. Am. Inst. CPA's, Tex. Soc. CPA's, Alpha Chi. Republican. Lutheran. Club: Officer's Wives (Carswell AFB, Ft. Worth).

COOK, MARY LYNN B., counselor; b. Portales, N.Mex., June 3, 1934; d. C.D. and Mary Ann (Wilhite) Bostick; m. Curtis Clifton Cook; children: Glen André, Cheryl Lynn. Student, So. Meth. U. Sec. City Dallas, Alameda County, Am. Airlines, various cities, 1951-58; dept. head Froug's, Tulsa, 1965-71; with Tulsa Area Safety Council, 1972, dir. driver improvement, 1972-79, tng. mgr., 1979-80; founder, pres. Okla. Tng. Systems Inst., Owasso, 1980—; instr. defensive driving, 1973—, alcohol/drug abuse, 1980—, driver improvement, 1980—, community CPR, 1989—; instr., trainer DDC, 1975-80. Author: Driver Improvement, 1980 (ann. revisions), Substance Abuse, 1980 (ann. revisions); contbr. articles to local newspapers. Lectr. defensive driving course and alcohol/drug substance abuse to schs., civic orgns., pvt. industry; den mother Cub Scouts, 1964-65; vol. Speakers Bur. Tulsa Pub. Schs., 1977-80, ARC Blood Svcs., 1988—, ARC Disaster Svcs., 1989—; founder youth drug abuse orgn., 1983; instr. CPR. Recipient 6 telemarketing awards Am. Red Cross, 3 instr. achievement awards Nat. Safety Coun. Mem. NAFE, Okla. Assn. DUI Sch. Adminstr., Okla. Cage Bird Soc., Am. Budgerigar Soc. Office: Okla Tng Systems Inst 9999 N 112th E Ave (Rear) Owasso OK 74055

COOK, MARY MARGARET, steamfitter; b. Royal Oak, Mich., Apr. 28, 1944; d. John Patrick and Agnes Hannah (Anderson) McM.; m. Barney Albert Cahill, Aug. 19, 1967 (div. Apr. 1971); m. Frank Melvin Cook, Jan. 26, 1974. BA in Elem. Edn., Ariz. State U., 1971; Cert., Ariz. Community Coll. Cert. elem. tchr., Ohio, Ariz.; lic. mech. journeyman. Tchr. St. Agnes Elem. Sch., Phoenix, 1967-71, Bevis Elem. Sch., Cin., 1971-73, Yavapai Adult Learning Ctr., Scottsdale, Ariz., 1975-78; steamfitter United Assn. Local 469, Phoenix, 1978—; instr. piping math. Rio Salado Community Coll., Phoenix, 1985—; cons. Math. Improvement Unit State of Ariz., 1988—; state dir. AFL-CIO Apprenticeship Awareness Program. Editor Internat. Tng. in Communication Newsletter, 1988-89. Speaker Ctr. for Ednl. Devel., Tucson, 1988. Mem. Ariz. Apple Users Group, Ariz. Tchrs. Math., Mensa, Ariz. State U. Alumni Assn. (life), Internat. Tng. in Communication Club (sec. 1988-89, pres. 1989-90, del. to coun. 1990-91). Home: 15827 N 23d Dr Phoenix AZ 85023

COOK, MARY ROZELLA, psychophysiologist; b. Ardmore, Okla., Sept. 30, 1936; d. Fred Roy and Ada Ruth (Chappell) Mouck; children: Steven Michael, Sheri Jo, Nathan Andrew. BA, U. Okla., 1961; PhD, U. Okla., Oklahoma City, 1970. Rsch. assoc. unit for exptl. psychiatry Inst. of the Pa. Hosp., Phila., 1970-74; sr. psychophysiologist Midwest Rsch. Inst., Kansas City, Mo., 1974-77, prin. pyschophysiologist, 1977-78, sect. head, 1978—. Editor Biofeedback & Self-Regulation, 1985—; contbr. articles in sci. jours. Rsch. grantee Nat. Cancer Inst., 1975, Nat. Heart, Lung & Blood Inst., 1975, Ctr. for Nursing Rsch., Bethesda, Md., 1987, Sch. Aerospace Medicine, San Antonio, USAF. Mem. Biofeedback Soc. Am. (bd. dirs. 1986-89), Soc. for Psychophysiological Rsch. (nominating com. 1973, 79, 82), Reversal Theory Soc., Zonta Internat. (chpt. pres. 1985-87), Phi Beta Kappa, Sigma Xi (chpt. pres. 1982-83). Office: Midwest Rsch Inst 425 Volker Blvd Kansas City MO 64110

COOK, NANCY W., state legislator; b. May 11, 1936. Ed. U. Del. Mem. Del. Senate from 15th Dist.; mem. Kent County Dem. Com. Democrat. Home: PO Box 127 Kenton DE 19955 Office: Del State Senate Dover DE 19901*

COOK, PAT MOFFITT, composer, teacher; b. Mpls., Apr. 24, 1956; d. David Andrew and Phyllis June (Frisk) Moffitt; m. Daniel H. Cook, Jan. 1, 1983; 1 child, Sarah. BA, Sarah Lawrence Coll., 1978; MA, So. Meth. U., 1987; postgrad., U. Wash. Musical dir., composer Global Concepts, Inc., N.Y.C.; composer music prodn. Media Group, Inc., Weston, Conn., 1978-83; co-owner, mgr. Rudi South, Inc., Art Gallery, Dallas, 1983-90; music, medicine and health tchr. White Crane Sch., Bogor, Indonesia, 1981; presenter workshops in field. Composer for films and TV. Meadows Composition Endowed Chair Grad. fellow So. Meth. U.; grantee Meet the Composers. Mem. Broadcast Music, Inc., Composers Forum. Home: 6717 NE Marshall Rd Bainbridge Island WA 98110

COOK, PEGGY LOU, produce company executive; b. Iantha, Mo., Apr. 29, 1935; d. Burson Clare and Amy (Phillips) Fast; m. Richard Daniel Cook, July 14, 1957; children: Randall R., Marilyn Sue Cook Joyce. Student, Pittsburg State Coll., 1953-55. With Bess Hotel, Pittsburg, Kans., 1951-52; sales rep. S.H. Kress, Pittsburg, 1952-53; opr. Pittsburg Cleaners, 1953-55; sales rep. F.W. Woolworth Co., Pittsburg, 1955-57; sales mgr. TG&Y, Wichita, Kans., 1959; asst. mgr. Cook Produce, Wichita, 1959-83, sec., 1959—, co-owner, mgr., 1969—. Mem. Fresh Fruit and Vegetable Assn., Downtown Farm and Art Market Assn., Nat. Audubon Soc., Am. Assn. Ret. Persons, Kans. Far Bur. Assn., Minden High Sch. Alumni Assn., Nat. Com. To Preserve Social Security. Office: 2452 N Hoover St Wichita KS 67205

COOK, REBECCA JOHNSON, lawyer, educator; A.B., Columbia U., 1970; M.A., Tufts U., 1972; M.P.A., Harvard U., 1973; J.D., Georgetown U., 1982; LLM Columbia U. 1987. Bar: D.C. 1982. Dir. law program Internat. Planned Parenthood Fedn., London, 1973-78; assoc. firm Beveridge, Fairbanks and Diamond, 1980; cons. U.S. Congress, 1978-81; mem. legal counsel office The Upjohn Co., 1981-82; asst. prof. faculty of law, faculty of medicine, dir. Internat. Human Rights Program, U. Toronto, 1987—; asst. prof. clin. pub. health Columbia U., N.Y.C., 1983-87, staff atty. devel. law and policy program Ctr. for Population and Family Health, 1983-87, adj. asst. prof., 1987—; adj. faculty Humphrey Inst. Pub. Affairs, U. Minn., 1985-87; dep. dir. Internat. Women's Rights Action Watch, 1986-87. Contbr. articles to profl. jours. Bd. dirs. Operation Crossroads Africa, 1972-74, Pathfinder Fund, 1978—, Assn. for Vol. Surg. Contraception, 1982-87, Internat. Projects Assistance Service, 1982—; mem. adv. com. on depo provera AID, 1978-80; adv. bd. Program for Intro. and Adaptation of Contraceptive Tech., 1982—, standing com. study of ethical aspects of human reproduction Internat. Fedn. Gynecology and Obstetrics, 1986—; expert adv. panel on human reproduction WHO, 1988—; U.S. del. 2d World Conf. on Nat. Parks, 1972; mem. Mass. Citizens Com. for Environ. Affairs 1972. Office: U Toronto, Faculty of Law, Toronto, ON Canada M5S 2C5

COOK, RUTH ELLEN, utilities commissioner, former state legislator; b. Berlin, Nov. 11, 1929; came to U.S., 1943; d. Samuel and Ilse (Meyer) Mohr; student N.Y. U.; m. John Oliver Cook, Oct. 31, 1954 (dec.); children—Roger Mohr, Judith Ellen. Exec. dir. State Council for Social Legis.; mem. N.C. Ho. of Reps., 1974-83, mem., chmn. appropriations base budget com. on human resources, vice-chmn. appropriations base budget com., vice-chmn. appropriations expansion budget com., vice-chmn. human resources com., vice-chmn. mental health com.; chmn. N.C. Housing Programs Study Commn., 1981-82; mem. Gov's Task Force on Sci. and Tech.; commr. N.C. Utilities Commn. 1983—. Bd. dirs. N.C. Housing Finance Agy., Women's Center Raleigh; chmn. N.C. Council for Hearing Impaired; exec. dir. State

Council Social Legislation, 1966-74; charter mem. Raleigh Interch. Housing Corp., 1966-69. Mem N.C. Consumers Council (pres. 1977), Raleigh Wake LWV (past pres.), Women Execs. in State Govt., Arts Advocates N.C. (bd. dirs.), N.C. Ctr. Pub. Policy Research (bd. dirs.).

COOK, SUSAN FARWELL, director of alumni relations; b. Boston, Apr. 28, 1953; d. Benjamin and Beverly (Brooks) Conant; m. James Samuel Cook Jr., Aug. 17, 1985; 1 child, Emily Farwell. AB, Colby Coll., 1975. Bank teller Boston 5 Cent Savs. Bank, 1975-76; asst. technician plan cost John Hancock Mut. Life Ins. Co., Boston, 1976-77, technician plan cost, 1977-78, sr. technician plan cost, 1978-79, asst. mgr. group pension plan cost, 1979-81; assoc. dir. alumni rels. Colby Coll., Waterville, Maine, 1981-86; dir. alumni rels. Colby Coll., Waterville, 1986—; co-dir. adv. bd. women's studies Colby Coll., 1987-89, adv. women's group, 1987-89. Bd. dirs., newsletter sec. Literacy Vols. Maine, Waterville, 1986-89; bd. dirs. Congress Lake Assns., Yarmouth, Maine, 1988—. Mem. Coun. Advancement and Support Edn. Home: RFD 1 Box 446 Albion ME 04910 Office: Colby Coll Mayflower Hill Waterville ME 04901

COOKE, BARBARA AYRES, non-profit executive; b. Mpls., Dec. 4, 1936; d. Paul Revere and Mildred (Davidson) Ayres; m. Ralph F. Montgomery, Aug. 17, 1958 (div. 1969); m. James F. Cooke, May 14, 1975. BS, Ind. U., 1959. Tchr., Indpls. Pub. Sch. System, 1959-61; found. exec. Continental Ill. Nat. Bank and Trust of Chgo., 1969-74; exec. dir. ARC, Berrien County, St. Joseph, Mich., 1975-77, Mid. Am. ARC, Chgo., 1977-87; exec. dir. Washtenaw County Am. Cancer Soc., Ann Arbor, Mich., 1988; dir. fund devel. Oaklawn Hosp., Marshall, Mich, 1989—; adj. prof. Aurora U., Ill., 1985-86. Author: Leadership Portfolio, 1977. Mem. women's bd. Muncie Symphony, Ind., 1968; pres. Women's Aux. Ball Meml. Hosp., Muncie, 1968; bd. dirs. Thresholds, Chgo., 1973, Reading Is Fundamental, Chgo., 1973. Recipient Pelican award (2), Mid. Am. ARC, 1984, 85. Mem. NAFE, Nat. Soc. Fund Raising Execs., Nat. Assn. Hosp. Devel., Altrusa. Home: 1147 Arms St Marshall MI 49068 Office: Oaklawn Hosp 200 N Madison St Marshall MI 49068

COOKE, BETTE LOUISE, library director, academic administrator; b. Emporia, Kans., Oct. 26, 1929; d. Oscar Oliver and Ada Luella (Williams) C. Student, Grinnell (Iowa) Coll., 1947-49; BS in Edn., U. Mo., 1951; MA in Libr. Sci., Vanderbilt U., 1964; EdD, Ind. U., 1971. Tchr. pub. schs. Mo. & ILL, 1951-63; instr. in libr. sci. N.E. Mo. State U., Kirksville, 1964-66; asst. prof. libr. sci. Western Ill. U., Macomb, 1966-72; assoc. prof., chair dept. libr. sci. and instructional tech. Cen. Mo. State U., Warrensburg, 1972-80; prof. libr. sci., dir. libr. St. Mary of the Plains Coll., Dodge City, 1983—; cons. sch. librs., Ill. and Mo., 1971-79; judge S.W. Kans. Project Fair Project, Dodge City, 1987—; grant evaluator Nat. Endowment for the Humanites, 1979; chair Dodge City Libr. Consortium, Dodge City, 1985. Mem. Dodge City Friends of Pub. Libr., 1987—; bd. dirs. Homeowners Assn., Dodge City, 1989k—. Ind. U. scholar, 1971; NEH/ACRL grantee, 1987. Mem. ALA, Kans. Libr. Assn., Kans. Coll. and Rsch. Librs. (program com.), Kans. Pvt. Acad. Librs., AAUW. Republican. Presbyterian. Home: 1408 Circle Kake Dr Dodge City KS 67801

COOKE, CONSTANCE BLANDY, librarian; b. Woodbury, N.J., Mar. 7, 1935; d. John Chase and Josephine Spond (Black) Blandy; m. Len B. Cooke Jr., Jan. 7, 1978 (div. Nov. 1987). B.A., U. Pa., 1956; M.A., U. Denver, 1957. Adult cons. Onondaga Library System, Syracuse, N.Y., 1965-66; asst. dir. Mt. Vernon (N.Y.) Public Library, 1966-75; dep. dir. Queens Borough Public Library, Jamaica, N.Y., 1975-79; dir. Queens Borough Public Library, 1980—; founder pres. Literacy Vols. Mt. Vernon, 1972-74. Trustee METRO, 1980—, v.p., 1985-88, pres. 1988—; dir. Queens C. of C., 1982—, v.p., 1985—; mem. adv. council LSCA, 1982-88, chmn., 1986-87; mem. bd. Queens Council on the Arts, 1988—; mem. bd. Queens Mus., 1988—. Mem. ALA, Am. Mgmt. Assn., N.Y. Libr. Assn. Democrat. Episcopalian. Home: 209-20 18th Ave Bayside NY 11360 Office: Queens Borough Pub Libr 89-11 Merrick Blvd Jamaica NY 11432

COOKE, DOROTHY HELENA COSBY, mathematics educator, counselor; b. Gloucester, Va., Jan. 8, 1941; d. Calvert Luchal and Pagie Florene (Dedmon) Cosby; m. Nathaniel Randolph Cooke, Sept. 2, 1961; 1 child, Nathaniel Randolph, Jr. B.S. in Math. Edn., Va. Union U., 1963; M.A. in Math. Edn., Hampton Inst., Va., 1970, M.A. in Guidance and Counseling, 1976; cert. Advanced Grad. Studies in Counselor Edn., Va. Poly. Inst. and State U., Blacksburg, 1981; D. Edn. in Counselor Edn. and Student Personnel Svcs., 1982. Secondary math. tchr. Va. pub. schs. 1963-71; instr. math. Rappahannock Community Coll., Glenns, Va., 1971-75, asst. prof. math. and counseling 1975-77, assoc. prof. math. and counseling, dir. student spl. svcs., 1977-82, prof. math. and counseling, dir. student spl. svcs., 1982-86, dir. student personnel svcs., 1986—, cons., lectr., 1971—, oucester County Pub. Sch. System, Va.; bd. dirs. Gloucester chpt. ARC; mem. NAACP, non-resident mem. Lancaster and Northumberland Counties Devel. Svcs. (Lands, Inc.), Kilmarnock, Va., past mem. local, state and nat. PTAs; past dir. Christian Edn. Bethel Bapt. Ch., Sassafras, Va.; mem. Gloucester County Sch. Bd. Selection Commn. Recipient Grad. Asst. for Minority Virginians Va. State Council Higher Edn. Mem. Am. Assn. Counseling and Devel., Va. Assn. Ednl. Opportunity Personnel, Mid-Eastern Assn. Ednl. Opportunity Personnel, Minority Affairs Coalition Va., Va. Counselors' Assn., Va. Assn. Non-White Concerns, So. Regional Council Black Am. Affairs, Assn. Community and Jr. Colls., Eastern Regional Counselors Adv. Council, Rappahannock Community Coll. Instl. Reps., Bd. Nat. Council Black Affairs, Am. Assn. Community and Jr. Colls., Kappa Delta Pi, Delta Psi Omega. Democrat. Avocations: singing, dramatic activities. Home: Rt 6 Box 4525 Gloucester VA 23061 Office: Rappahannock Community Coll Glenns VA 23149

COOKE, GILLIAN LEWIS, social worker, consultant; b. Birmingham, Eng., Nov. 9, 1935; came to U.S, 1957; d. Fred Stuart Lewis and Irene Lillian (Turner) Tonks; m. Thomas Wayne Cooke, Sept. 4, 1954; children: Roberta Louise Prater, Rebecca, Russell Lewis. Student, U. Md., Fed. Republic of Germany, 1960-63; cert. in advanced mgmt. tng., Miss. U., 1983; student, U. Houston, 1984-85; cert. in social work, Tex. Dept. Human Svcs., Austin, 1985. Social work counselor ARC, 1959-67; in-svc. tng. dir. MacGregor Med. Assn., Houston, 1971-84; tng. dir. Children's Resource & Info. Svc., Houston, 1984-85; pres. Anderson & Cooke Inc., Houston, 1985-87; pvt. practice human devel. cons. Houston, 1987—; rsch. interviewer Baylor & Temple U., Houston, 1988—; cons., dir. med. rsch. labs., Houston, Ariz. and N.Y., 1987—; cons., dir. Group II Mktg., Houston, 1987-89; tchr., social worker People on the Sts., South Main Bapt. Ch., Houston, 1988—. Lectr. agys. and hosps. dealing with child abuse, Houston, 1985—, Baylor Coll. of Medicine, Houston, 1987-88, U. Houston, 1988, Child Abuse Prevention Coun., Houston, 1989-90. Mem. Am. Soc. for Quality Control, Am. Corrections Health Orgn. Assn., Med. Group Mgmt. Assn. Home: 507 S Belknap Sugar Land TX 77478 Office: 6910 Fannin Ste 323N Houston TX 77030

COOKE, MARY A., hospice director; b. Hoboken, N.J., Sept. 22, 1944; d. John F. and Mary A. (Schmidt) C. RN, St. Joseph Sch. Nursing, Syracuse, N.Y., 1966; BS, Seton Hall U., South Orange, N.J., 1968; MA, NYU, 1972. Staff nurse St. Mary's Hosp., Hoboken, N.J., 1966, Holy Name Hosp., Teaneck, N.J., 1967-68, St. Barnabas Med. Ctr., Livingston, N.J., 1969; instr. Elizabeth (N.J.) Gen. Hosp., 1969-72, clin. nurse specialist, 1972-74; nursing care coordinator Cabrini Med. Ctr., N.Y.C., 1974-82; nursing dir. Cabrini Hospice, N.Y.C., 1982-83; dir. Cabrini Hospice, 1983—; ptnr., prog. dir. Ahmed, Gordon & Mancino, N.Y.C., 1981-83; lectr. in field. Contbr. articles to profl. jours. Mem. Am. Nurses Assn., N.Y. State Nurses Assn., N.J. Nurses Assn. (v.p. 1971, bd. dirs. 1972-76), Sigma Theta Tau. Democrat. Roman Catholic. Home: 160 E 27th St New York NY 10016 Office: Cabrini Hospice 227 E 19th St New York NY 10003

COOKE, NOREEN ANN, educator, consultant; b. Waltham, Mass., Oct. 14, 1943; d. Warren William and Alice Noreen (Van Wart) C.; m. Dennis A. McCluggage, Dec. 19, 1970 (div. Jan. 1978). BS in Edn., Mass. State Coll., Framingham, 1965. Cert. elem. tchr., Mass., Alaska. Tchr. 3d grade Juneau (Alaska) Borough Sch. Dist., 1965-66, tchr. 1st grade, 1966-68, tchr. 2d grade, 1970-87; tchr. 1st grade Lake Washington Sch. Dist., Kirkland, Wash., 1968-70; rep. dist. Alaska State Writing Consortium, Juneau, 1986—, cons., 1987—. Author: My Juneau Adventure, 1984; editor Alaska State Writing Consortium jour. Shaping the Landscape, 1988. Mem. Dem. Nat. Com., Washington, 1984, Juneau Arts and Humanities Coun., 1985—, Big Bros./Big Sisters of Juneau, Inc., 1986—. Mem. NEA (bd. dirs. Alaska chpt. 1981-83), Juneau Edn. Assn. (pres. 1980-81, Tchr. of Yr. 1986-87), Belleek Collector's Soc., Soc. of Children's Book Writers, Juneau Ret. Tchrs. Assn. Democrat. Roman Catholic. Home and Office: 1558 Penn Rd Mount Vernon WA 98273

COOKE, SARA GRAFF, fundraiser; b. Phila., Dec. 29, 1935; d. Charles Henry and Elizabeth (Mullin) Brandt; m. Peter Fischer Cooke, June 29, 1963 (div. July 1984); children: Anna, Peter Jr., Frances Elizabeth, Sara Reynolds, Laina Koerting. AA, Bennett Coll., 1955; BE in Child Edn., Westchester State Tchrs. Coll., 1956. Asst. to tchr. 1st grade The Woodlyn Sch., 1956-58; tchr. Sara Bircher's Kindergarten, Germantown, Pa., 1958-62, Chestnut Hill (Pa.) Acad., 1962-63, Tarleton Sch., Devon, Pa., 1963-64; with F.C.I. Mktg. Co-ordinators Inc., N.Y.C., New Canaan, Conn., 1980-86; fundraiser Daisy Day, Children's Hosp. Phila., 1989—. Mem. bd. auxiliary Children's Hosp. Phila., 1970-76, mem. women's bd., 1977-87; mem. commonwealth bd. Med. Coll. Pa., 1984-87. Mem. Pa. Assn. Hosp. Auxiliaries (health rep.), Nat. Soc. Colonial Dames, Women's Assn. (past pres.). Republican. Episcopalian. Office: 529 E Gravers Ln Springfield PA 19118

COOKE, SARAH BELLE, health care facility professional, farmer; b. Murfreesboro, Tenn., Sept. 14, 1910; d. Robert Jesse and Mattie (Neal) C. BS, Middle Tenn. State U., 1961. Cert. tchr., Tenn. Patient funds clk. VA Med. Ctr., Murfreesboro, 1943; voucher auditor VA Med. Supply Svc., Murfreesboro, 1945-46, purchasing agt., 1946-83, contracting officer, 1984-89; now ret. Pres. VA Fed. Employees Credit Union, Murfreesboro, 1965-86. Mem. AAUW (pres. Murfreesboro chpt. 1977-79), Tenn. Credit Union League (br. pres. 1973-79). Democrat. Mem. Church of Christ. Home: 5078 Sulphur Spring Rd Murfreesboro TN 37129

COOK-KOLLARS, KAYE V., clinical psychologist, educator; b. Augusta, Ga., Sept. 1, 1950; d. James Edward and Jennie Louise (Rivers) Cook; m. Charles D. Cook-Kollars, May 27, 1989. BA, Georgia Coll., 1971; MA, U. N.C., 1977, PhD, 1978. Staff clinician Children's Hosp., Boston, 1985-89; lic. clinician Feeding/Eating Specialists, Brookline, Mass., 1989—; prof. Gordon Coll., Wenham, Mass., 1978—; cons. Beverly (Mass.) Preschool, 1980-82. Contbr. articles profl. jours. Mem. Am. Psychol. Assn., Soc. for Rsch. in Child Devel. Office: Gordon Coll 255 Grapevine Rd Wenham MA 01984

COOKSON, GRACE ELIZABETH, nurse; b. Peabody, Mass., Apr. 7, 1948; d. Earl R. and Virginia M. Cookson. Degree, Beverly Hosp. Sch. Nursing, 1969; BS in Nursing cum laude, Cath. U., 1979. RN, Tex. Nursing cons. Aetna Life and Casualty, San Antonio, 1986-87; head nurse Med. Ctr. Hosp., San Antonio, 1987—. Maj. USAF, 1986. Mem. Am. Assn. Critical Care Nurses, Oncology Nurses Soc., AHA, NAFE. Home: 9810 Big Geronimo San Antonio TX 78254 Office: Med Ctr Hosp 4502 Medical Dr San Antonio TX 78229

COOKSON, JANE, investment counselor; b. Phila., Mar. 11, 1939; d. Frank Walter and Josephine (Hunter) Potter; m. Donald Howland Cookson II, June 22, 1963. BS in Chemistry cum laude, Carnegie Mellon U., 1961. Cert. fin. planner. Organic rsch. chemist Gulf Oil, Pitts., 1961-66; investment advisor, sr. v.p., dir. C.S. McKee, Pitts., 1966-83; pres. Cookson Assocs., Pitts., 1983-84, Cookson, Peirce & Co., Pitts., 1984—; bd. dirs. Dollar Bank, Pitts. Trustee Eye and Ear Inst., Pitts., 1981—; bd. dirs. World Affairs Coun. Pitts., 1988—. Mem. Econ. Club Pitts. (dir. 1972-78, pres. 1973), Greater Pitts. C. of C. (dir. 1976-82), Duquesne Club, Rolling Rock Club. Republican. Presbyterian. Office: Cookson Peirce & Co Inc 535 Smithfield St Pittsburgh PA 15222

COOL, KIM PATMORE, retail executive, needlework consultant; b. Cleve., Feb. 1, 1940; d. Herman Chester Earl and Eva (Geneau) Patmore; m. Kenneth Adams Cool Jr., Mar. 12, 1963; 1 child, Heidi Adams. BA in Econs., Sweet Briar Coll., 1962; postgrad., Case Western Reserve U., 1962-63. Test adminstr. Pradco, Cleve., 1962-63; pvt. needlework cons. Cleve., 1970-72; retail v.p., treas., custom designer And Sew On, Inc., Cleve., 1973—, exec. v.p., treas., 1982—; tchr. Wellesley Coll. Continuing Edn. Program, 1986; pub. Fredericktown Press, Md. Artist collector quality custom hand-painted canvases; co-author: How to Market Needlepoint-The Definitive Manual, 1988, Easy Macrame, 1990, Basic Macrame, 1990, Wearable Macrame, 1990. Rep. committeeman Cuyahoga County, Shaker Heights, Ohio, 1964-72. Regional Curling champion, 1987-88. Mem. Nat. Needlework Assn. (lectr. seminar on mktg. needlepoint, charter assoc. retail, conductor of senimars on buying and merchandising 1988—), Embroiderers Guild of Cleve. (bd. dirs. 1980-82), Am. Profl. Needlework Retailers, S.E. Yarncrafters Guild (conductor merchandising seminars 1989—), Nat. Standards Coun. Am. Embroiderers, U.S. Figure Skating Assn. (nat. judge gold and senior competitions 1967—, sect. precision judge), Sweet Briar Coll. Alumnae Assn. (nat. bd. dirs. upper Midwest region 1965-66, class sec. 1988-89), Cleve. Skating Club, Mayfield Country Club. Baptist. Home: 14500 Washington Blvd University Heights OH 44118 Office: And Sew On Inc 2243 Warrensville Ctr University Heights OH 44118

COOLEY, ELSIE MARIE ENDRESS, small business owner; b. Leroy, Ohio, July 24, 1932; d. John K. and Ann (Gartman) Endress; m. Roger Martin Cooley, Feb. 6, 1931; children: R. Scott, Lisa Ann, Karen Susan. Grad. high sch., Westlake, Ohio; student, Miami U., Oxford, Ohio, 1950-51. Sec. Luth. Med. Ctr., Cleve., 1976-78, Glenbrook High Sch., Glenview, Ill., 1978-79; owner, operator Brass Tack Shoppe, Westerville, Ohio, 1981-82, 1820 Gift Co., Westlake, Ohio, 1984—. Pres. Am. Field Svc., Westlake, Ohio, 1966-68, host family, 1973-74, 1979-80; pres. PTA Parkside Jr. High, Westlake, 1970-71; trustee Westlake (Ohio) Porter Libr., 1974-78, Westlake Arts Coun., 1986—; founder Christmas boutique, 1970-75, Mrs. Claus Closet; mem. devel. bd. St. John's West Shore Hosp., 1985—, co-chmn. Zoofari Benefit sub-com., 1986—; mem. coun. Dover Congl. Ch., Westlake, 1988-90. Republican. Mem. United Ch. of Christ. Home: 2952 Southwood Dr Westlake OH 44145 Office: 1820 Gift Co 27748 Ctr Ridge Rd Westlake OH 44145

COOLEY, GLADYS CECILIA, recruitment coordinator, translator; b. Panama, Panama, Feb. 13, 1954; came to U.S., 1982; d. J.B. and Gladys C. (Conliffe) Planes; m. Stanley B. Cooley, Dec. 14, 1985; 1 child, Christopher, Michael. BBA, U. Panama, 1982; MA, Ohio U., 1984. Offl. translator and interpreter. Adminstrv. asst. Lawrence Johnson & Assocs., Washington, 1984-85; recruitment coord. Covington & Burling, Washington, 1985—; translator ABL Assocs., Washington, 1990—; asst. to v.p. Internat. United Distbrs., Panama br., 1980; office mgr. Singer Sewing Machine Co., Panama br., 1977. Republican. Roman Catholic. Office: Covington & Burling 1201 Pennsylvania Ave NW Washington DC 20044

COOLEY, HILARY ELIZABETH, business manager; b. Leesburg, Va., May 8, 1953; d. Thomas McIntyre and Helen Strong (Stringham) C. BA in Econs., U. Pitts., 1976; postgrad. in bus. adminstrn., Hood Coll., Frederick, Md., 1985—. Mgr. Montgomery Ward, Frederick, 1976-80, merchandiser, 1980-82; asst. bus. mgr. Arundel Communications, Leesburg, 1982-84; bus. mgr. Loudoun Country Day Sch., Leesburg, 1984-85, bd. trustees, 1987—, sec. bd. trustees, 1989—; contr. Foxcroft Sch., Middleburg, Va., 1985-87; corr. Loudoun Times Mirror, Leesburg, 1985-87; estate mgr. Delta Farm Inc., Leesburg, 1988—. Area chair, Keep Loudoun Beautiful, Middleburg, 1983—; mem. Piedmont Environ. Coun.; pres. Waterford (Va.) Citizen's Assn., 1985-86, Waterford Players, 1986-88; hon. bd. dirs. Waterford Found., Inc., 1980—, Loudoun Hist. Soc., Leesburg, 1987. Mem. Penn Hall Alumnae Ann. (pres. 1987-90). Democrat. Episcopalian. Home and Office: Delta Farm Rte 1 Box 97 Middleburg VA 22117

COOLEY, KATHLEEN SHANNON, speech-language pathologist; b. Wilmington, Del., Aug. 3, 1939; d. Thomas Joseph and Anne C. (Whalen) Shannon; m. John A. Cooley, Oct. 20, 1962 (div. 1980). Postgrad., Neumann Coll., Aston, Pa., 1980-81; BS, Westchester U., 1982-85; MS, Loyola Coll., Balt., 1985-86. Asst. sec. Colonial Mortgage Svc., Wilmington, Del., 1965-70; sales support Conn. Gen. Life, Wilmington, Del., 1975-80; speech-lang. pathologist Charleston (S.C.) County Schs., 1986-88, Trident Therapy Svcs., Summerville, S.C., 1988-89; pvt. practice home care provider Mt. Pleasant, S.C., 1989—. Author: book-manual, Toward Effective Parish Visitation to the Sick, 1980. Supporter Christian Broadcasting Network, Virginia Beach, 1975—, Ednl. TV Endowment, Charleston Art Guild, 1989; mem. Christ Our King RC. Ch., Mt. Pleasant, 1988—. Mem. American Speech Hearing Assn., Nat. Student Speech Hearing. Republican. Home and Office: 857B Liriope Ln Mount Pleasant SC 29464

COOLEY, MARIE SZPIRUK, financial company executive; b. Gnezno, Poland, Dec. 20, 1935; came to U.S., 1950; d. Pavlo and Taisia (Bohdaniw) Szpiruk; m. Victor Cooley, Sept. 19, 1954; children: George, Oleg, Paul. Student, CUNY, 1955-56, Montgomery Coll., 1975, Am. U., 1975-77; BS, U. Md., 1982. Purchase clk. Am. U., Washington, 1975-77; asst. internal auditor Citizens Savs. Bank, Silver Spring, Md., 1977-83; asst. v.p., sec., treas. First Citizens Mortgage Corp., Silver Spring, 1984—; pres. Ukrainian Washington Fed. Credit Union, 1984-86, treas., 1986—. Mem. Dumka Choir, N.Y.C., 1953-55; v.p. St. Olga's Sisterhood, Washington, 1970; instr. Ukrainian Easter Eggs White House Exhibits, 1975-80; mem. com. painting inside St. Andrew's Ukrainian Orthodox Cathedral, Washington. Mem. Ukrainian Assn. of Washington, Smithsonian Assn. Ukranian. Office: First Citizens Mortgage Corp 12501 Prosperity Dr Ste 200 Silver Spring MD 20904

COOL-FOLEY, ALICIA ANN, internist; b. Balt., June 22, 1956; d. John E. and Marjorie Alicia (Dehn) Cool; m. Thomas Andrew Foley, July 29, 1978; 1 child, Marjorie Alicia. BA, Johns Hopkins U., 1977; MD, U. Md., Balt., 1982. Diplomate Am. Bd. Internal Medicine. Internal medicine intern South Balt. Gen. Hosp., 1981-82; resident in internal medicine Union Meml. Hosp., Balt., 1982-84, mem. clin. faculty, 1984—, med. dir. extended care facility, 1988—; pvt. practice Balt., 1984—. Mem. AMA, ACP (assoc.). Republican. Episcopalian. Office: 201 E University Pkwy Baltimore MD 21218

COOLIDGE, MARTHA, film director; b. New Haven, Aug. 17, 1946; m. Michael Backes. Ed. RISD, Columbia U. Dir. films: Valley Girl, 1983, The City Girl, 1983, Joy of Sex, 1984, Real Genius, 1985, Plain Clothes, 1988, documentary David: Off and On, 1972, More Than a School, 1973, Old Fashioned Woman, 1974, Not A Pretty Picture, 1976 (all 3 won Am. Film Festival awards); dir. TV shows Sledge Hammer pilot episode, 3 episodes The Twilight Zone, CBS miniseries The Winners. Address: care The Gersh Agy Inc PO Box 5617 Beverly Hills CA 90210*

COOLIDGE, MARTHA HENDERSON, volunteer environmental specialist; b. Cambridge, Mass., Jan. 26, 1925; d. Robert Graham and Lucy (Gregory) Henderson; m. Harold Jefferson Coolidge, May 26, 1972 (dec. Feb. 1985). Student, Smith Coll., 1942-43; BA, Radcliffe Coll., 1946; MA, Harvard U., 1956, postgrad., 1956-57, 58-60. Asst. sec. China Program Harvard U., Cambridge, Mass., 1948; adminstr. Fulbright Program Inst. Internat. Edn., N.Y.C., 1949-50; assoc. dir. GARIOA program GARIOA Program Inst. Internat. Edn., N.Y.C., 1950-51; staff mem. Ctr. for Internat. Studies at MIT, Cambridge, 1953-54; exec. sec. The Japan Soc. of Boston, 1958-62; asst. to mng. dir., dir. film services Ednl. Devel. Inc., Watertown, Mass., 1963-65; program dir. for internat. exchanges Smithsonian Instn., Washington, 1965-66; edn. assoc. Cen. Atlantic Regional Edn. Labs., Washington, 1966-68; sr. assoc. for edn. The Conservation Found., Washington, 1968-70; ednl. assoc. Pub. Broadcasting Environ. Ctr., Washington, 1970-71; vol., bd. dirs. Coolidge Ctr. for Environ. Leadership, Cambridge, 1983—, vice chmn., 1983-85; rsch. asst. to Prof. John K. Fairbank Harvard U., Cambridge, 1989—; mem. temp. staff student adaption study MIT, 1962-63; cons. social studies curriculum project Harvard Grad. Sch. Edn., Cambridge, 1964-65; mem. adv. com. INFORM, N.Y.C. Author articles in field. Bd. dirs. Lincoln Filene Ctr. for Citizenship and Pub. Affairs Tufts U., Medford, Mass.; affiliate Dudley House, Harvard U.; council mem. New Eng. Aquarium, Boston. Grantee Yenching Inst., 1958; Fulbright scholar Tokyo U., 1957-58. Mem. Fragment Soc., Cosmos Club, Somerset Club, Women's Travel Club, Harvard Travellers' Club. Episcopalian. Home: 19 Brewster St Cambridge MA 02138 Office: The Coolidge Ctr for Environ Leadership 1675 Massachusetts Ave Cambridge MA 02138

COOMBS, C'CEAL PHELPS (MRS. BRUCE AVERY COOMBS), air company executive, civic worker; b. nr. Portland, Oreg.; d. Perry Edwin and Flora (Gowey) Phelps m. Bruce Avery Coombs, Nov. 28, 1929; children: Keith Avery, Glinda C'Ceal (Mrs. Nick E. Mason). BS, U. Idaho, 1929; postgrad., Wash. State Coll., 1941. Tchr. pub schs., Idaho, 1929-30; adminstrv. asst. Coombs West-Air Co. and Coombs Flying C Ranches, Yakima, Wash., 1945—; lobbyist for civic activities Wash. Legislature, 1947—; genealogist, notary pub., Wash., 1960—. Del. White House Conf. on Children and Youth, 1960, Wash. State White House Conf. on Edn., 1955; mem. Wash. Citizens Coun., Nat. Coun. Crime & Delinquency, 1956—; bd. dirs., mem. exec. com. Wash. State Coun. Crime & Delinquency, 1956—, chmn., 1970-71, recipient Spl. State award, 1972, 76; mem. Allied Sch. Coun. Wash. 1951-53; mem. Western regional scholarship com. Ford Found., 1955-57; chmn. regional dist. Wash. Cities Legislation, 1960; chmn. Yakima County Sch. Bd., 1957-59; mem. Yakima County Health Dept., 1959-60; city councilwoman Yakima, 1959-61, asst. mayor, 1960; mem. Wash. Libr. Commn., 1960, 64-68, 72—, vice chmn., 1965-70, 75-76, recipient gov's. citation, 1976; del. UNESCO Conf. Crime & Delinquency, Kyoto, Japan, 1970, Caracus, Venezuela, 1980; del. to Internat. Libr. Assn., Toronto, 1968, Washington, 1975, del. to worldwide seminar, Seoul, 1976, London, Brussels, 1977; del. Internat. Fedn. Librs., Manila, 1980; trustee Wash. 4-H Found., 1960-79, chmn., 1969—, hon. trustee, 1979—; bd. mem. Wash. State Friends of Librs., 1976, pres., 1977; mem. bd. Yakima County Law and Justice; mem. Gov.'s Mansion Found., Washington. Recipient Outstanding Citizen award Western Correctional Assn., 1974, Lobbyist Honor award Third House Orgn. of the Washington State Legislature, 1988; named one of 100 women in Centennial Wash. state publ. Mem. Am. Libr. Trustee Assn. (regional dir. 1962—, pres. 1967-68), C. of C., Oreg. Hist. Soc., Idaho Hist. Soc., Elmore County Hist. Soc., Washington County Hist. Soc., Calif. Hist. Soc., Windsor (Conn.) Hist. Assn. (life), Friends of Tewkesbury Abbey Eng. (life), Daus. Am. Colonists, Founders and Patriots, New Eng. Hist. Geneal. Soc., Conn. Hist. Soc., Dorchester (Mass.) Antiquarian and Hist. Soc., Conn. Soc. Genealogists, Ft. Simcoe Restoration Soc. (life), ALA (internat. trustee citation 1966, mem. bd. 1972—, coun. 1967-68, 71-72), Pacific N.W. Libr. Assn. (chmn. trustee sect. 1962-63), Wash. Libr. Assn. (chmn. 1960, trustee award 1967), Nat. Soc. Crown of Charlemagne, LWV, Allied Arts Coun., Broadway Theatre League, Nat. Aviation Assn., Am. Aviation Assn., P.E.O., Federated Women, Colonial Dames (state rec. sec., pres. local chpt., XVII Century award for outstanding contbn. 1988), Altrusa, Nat. Soc. Magna Charta Dames, Descs. of Conqueror and His Companions, Friends of N.Y.C. Libr., Order of the Crown of Charlemagne, Friends of the Washginton Libr. (life). Home: 11430 Mieras Rd Yakima WA 98901

COOMBS, VICKI J., registered nurse, exercise physiologist; b. Leesville, L.A., Apr. 9, 1956; d. William Joseph and JoAnn (Jewell) C. ADN, Miami U., 1976, BSN, 1986, MS, 1988. Asst. head nurse Reid Memorial Hosp., Richmond, Ind., 1976-79; head nurse Internist Inc., Richmond, Ind., 1979-83; charge nurse McCullough Hyde Mem. Hosp., Oxford, Ohio, 1983-85; cardiac rehab. coord. McCullough Hyde Meml. Hosp., Oxford, Ohio, 1985-88; rsch. nurse coord., sr. exercise physiologist Johns Hopkins Medical Inst., Baltimore, Md., 1988--. Volunteer, Baltimore Zoo, 1988--, advisor, 4H, Ohio, 1974-86, mem. Miami Univ. Alumni Assn., 1976--, Save the Whales Internat., Hawaii, 1988--. Mme. Am. Assn. Critical Care Nurses, Am. Coll. Sports Medicine, Am. Heart Assn., Chesapeake Bay chpt. Am. Assn. Critical Care Nurses, John Hopkins Nursing Rsch. Interest Group, Am. Lung Assn., Am. Nurses Assn., Nat. Disting. Svc. Registry in Nursing, Coun. Cardiovascular Nursing, Am. Assn. Cardiopulmonary Rehab. Methodist. Home: 5K Shelby's Path Baltimore MD 21152 Office: Johns Hopkins Medical Inst 530 Blalock 600 N Wolfe St Baltimore MD 21205

COONEY, BARBARA, illustrator, author; b. Bklyn., Aug. 6, 1917; d. Russell Schenck and Mae Evelyn (Bossert) C.; m. Guy Murchie, Dec. 1942 (div. Mar. 1947); children: Gretel, Barnaby; m. Charles T. Porter, July 16, 1949; children: Charles Talbot, Phoebe. B.A., Smith Coll., 1938; student, Art Students League, 1940; PhD (hon.), Fitchburg State Coll., 1988. Author, illustrator: Miss Rumphius, 1982, The Little Juggler, 1961, Little Prayer, 1967, Christmas, 1967, Little Brother and Little Sister, 1982, Island Boy,

1988; illustrator numerous children's books. 2d lt. Women's Army Corps, World War II. Recipient Caldecott medal for Chanticleer and the Fox, 1958, U. So. Miss. medal, 1975, Smith Coll. medal, 1976. Caldecott medal for Ox-Cart Man, 1980, Am. Book award, 1983, Keene State Coll. award, 1989, Globe-Horn Book honor award, 1989.

COONEY, CHRISTINE JOYCE, management recruiter; b. Darby, Pa., Dec. 24, 1954; d. Charles Thomas and Joyce (Skillman) Pennacchio. BA in Home Econs., Coll. Notre Dame, Belmont, Calif., 1976; postgrad., Golden Gate U., 1988—. Recruiter personnel Bakers Square Restaurants, Fremont, Calif., 1982—. Named for Outstanding Contributions in the Interests of People with Disabilities Dept. Rehab. Health & Welfare Agy., State of Calif., 1988. Home: 219 Marvilla Creek Pacifica CA 94004 Office: Bakers Square Restaurants 39175 Liberty St 211 Fremont CA 94538

COONEY, DIANE, advertising agency executive. Sr. v.p., then exec. v.p., creative dir. Suddler & Hennessey. Office: Sudler & Hennessey 1633 Broadway New York NY 10019*

COONEY, JOAN GANZ, broadcasting executive; b. Phoenix, Nov. 30, 1929; d. Sylvan C. and Pauline (Reardan) Ganz; m. Timothy J. Cooney, 1964 (div. 1975); m. Peter G. Peterson, 1980. BA, U. Ariz., 1951; hon. degrees, Boston Coll., 1970, Hofstra U., Oberlin Coll., Ohio Wesleyan U., 1971, Princeton U., 1973, Russell Sage Coll., 1974, U. Ariz., Harvard U., 1975, Allegheny Coll., 1976, Georgetown U., 1978, U. Notre Dame, 1982, Smith Coll., 1986, Brown U., 1987. Reporter Ariz. Republic, Phoenix, 1953-54; publicist NBC, 1954-55, U.S. Steel Hour, 1955-62; producer Sta. WNET, Channel 13; pub. affairs documentaries Sta. WNET, Channel 13, N.Y.C., 1962-67; TV cons. Carnegie Corp. N.Y., N.Y.C., 1967-68; exec. dir. Children's TV Workshop (producers Sesame Street, Electric Company, others), N.Y.C., 1968-70, pres., trustee, 1970—; trustee Channel 13/Ednl. Broadcasting Corp.; dir. Xerox Corp., Johnson & Johnson, Chase Manhattan Corp., Chase Manhattan Bank N.A., Met. Life Ins. Co. Mem. Pres.'s Commn. on Marijuana and Drug Abuse, 1971-73, Nat. News Council, 1973-81, Council Fgn. Relations, 1974—, Pres.'s Commn. for Agenda for 80's, 1980-81, Adv. Com. for Trade Negotiations, 1978-80; mem. Gov.'s Commn. on Internat. Yr. of the Child, 1979, Carnegie Found. Nat. Panel on High Sch., 1980-82. Recipient numerous awards for Sesame Street and other TV programs including Nat. Sch. Pub. Relations Assn. Gold Key 1971; Disting. Service medal Columbia Tchrs. Coll., 1971; Soc. Family Man award, 1971; Nat. Inst. Social Scis. Gold medal, 1971; Frederick Douglass award N.Y. Urban League, 1972; Silver Satellite award Am. Women in Radio and TV; Woman of Yr. in Edn. award Ladies Home Jour., 1975; Woman of Decade award, 1979; NEA Friends of Edn. award; Kiwanis Decency award; NAEB Disting. Service award; 5th Women's Achiever award Girl Scouts U.S.A.; Stephen S. Wise award, 1981; Harris Found. award, 1982; Ednl. Achievement award AAUW, 1984; Disting. Service to Children award Nat. Assn. Elem. Sch. Prins., 1985; DeWitt Carter Reddick award Coll. Communications, U. Tex.-Austin, 1986; named to Hall of Fame Acad. TV Arts and Scis., 1990. Mem. NOW, Nat. Acad. TV Arts and Scis., Nat. Inst. Social Scis., Internat. Radio and TV Soc., Am. Women in Radio and TV. Office: Children's TV Workshop 1 Lincoln Pla New York NY 10023

COONEY, LENORE, public relations executive. V.p., then exec. v.p. D-A-Y Pub. Rels., N.Y.C.; now pres. Ogilvy & Mather Pub. Rels., N.Y.C. Office: Ogilvy & Mather Pub Rels 450 Park Ave S New York NY 10019*

COONEY, MIRIAM P., professor of mathematics; b. South Bend, Ind., May 6, 1925; d. Walter James and Catherine (McGuiness) C. BS, Saint Mary's Coll., 1951; MS, U. Notre Dame, 1953; PhD, U. Chgo., 1969. V.p., pub. rels. and devel. Saint Mary's Coll., Notre Dame, Ind., 1958-61, prof. of math., 1950—, dept. chair, 1967—; tchr. math., sci. Maria Goretti Sch., Fort Portal, Uganda, East Africa, 1971 (summer); lectr. Colegio Santa Maria, Sao Paulo, Brazil, 1974 (summer), N.E. Normal U., Changchun, China, 1985 (summer); vis. prof. St Patrick's Coll., Maynooth, Ireland, 1980. Mem. Math. Assn. Am. (com. on women 1989—). Roman Catholic. Home and Office: Saint Mary's Coll Dept Math Notre Dame IN 46556

COONEY, PATRICIA RUTH, civic worker; b. Englewood, N.J.; d. Charles Aloysius and Ruth Jeannette (Foster) McEwen; m. J. Gordon Cooney, June 8, 1957; 1 child, J. Gordon, Jr. Student, Fordham U., 1950-51. Blood bank chmn. Strafford Village Civic Assn., 1968-69, sec., 1970-71; vice chmn. Spl. Gifts Com. Cath. Charities Appeal of Archdiocese of Phila., 1980—, chmn., 1985. Mem. Coun. of Mgrs. Archdiocese of Phila., 1982-88, sec., exec. com., 1983-88; bd. dirs. Cath. Charities of Archdiocese of Phila., 1984—, sec., exec. com., 1988—; bd. dirs. Village of Divine Providence, Phila., 1982—, sec., 1983-85, v.p. exec. com., 1990—; bd. dirs. St. Edmond's Home for Crippled Children, Phila., 1984—, v.p. exec. com., 1990—; bd. dirs. Don Guanella Village of Archdiocese of Phila., 1984—, v.p. exec. com., 1990— ; mem. Women's Com. Wills Eye Hosp., 1973—, mem.-at-large, 1st v.p.; mem. Women's Aux. St. Francis Country House, Darby, Pa., 1976—, treas., 1978-82; exec. com. United Way of Southeastern Pa., 1984-90, sec., 1986-88; bd. dirs. Chapel of Four Chaplains, 1984-89, Phila. Criminal Justice Task Force, 1989-90. Decorated Cross Pro Ecclesia et Pontifice, 1982. Republican. Home: 320 Gatcombe Ln Bryn Mawr PA 19010

COONROD, ANNE TAYLOR, small business owner; b. Austin, Tex., July 15, 1944; d. Charles Smith and Anne (Finch) Taylor; m. David Kelly Coonrod, Dec. 21, 1967,(div. Dec. 1984); children: Katherine Anne, David Kelly, Jr. BA, U. Tex., 1967. Owner, mgr. Atlantic Seafood, Bait and Tackle, Fernandina, Fla., 1974—, Amelia Island Crab Plant, Fernandina, 1982-85; originator, bd. dirs. First Coast Savs. Bank, Fernandina, 1985—; ptnr. The Boat House, Fernandina, 1984—; mng. ptnr. Fernandina Harbor Marina, 1987—; pres. First Coast Savs. Bank Amelia Island Br., 1990. Chmn. Nassau County Planning and Zoning Bd., Fernandina, 1973-89; bd. dir. govt. affairs com. of 100, 1983-89. Recipient Outstanding Svc. award Optimists Club, 1985, 86, Nassau County Commn., 1986. Mem. Amelia Island, Fernandina C. of C. (pres. 1987-88), Magnolia Garden (treas. 1978-79). Democrat. Episcopalian. Home: 1900 Highland Dr Fernandina FL 32034

COOPER, ANN EISENBERG, writer, consultant; b. N.Y.C., Dec. 12, 1936; d. Arthur A. and Helen Adelaide (Gantz) Eisenberg; m. Michael A. Cooper, Apr. 29, 1962 (div. Aug. 1988); children: Jeffrey, Sarah, Paul. BA, Wellesley (Mass.) Coll., 1958; MA, Columbia U., N.Y.C., 1961. Tchr. history Calhoun Sch., N.Y.C., 1958-59; editor N.Y. Hist. Soc., N.Y.C., 1962-65; freelance writer, editor N.J. and N.Y., 1965—; pvt. practice search cons. Essex County N.J., 1979—; N.J. dir. Hands Across America, 1986; English as second lang. tchr. Am. Cultural Ctr., Taipei, Taiwan, 1987-88; sec. North Country Sch., Lake Placid, N.Y., 1977-83, Garden State Ballet, Newark, 1979-82, N.J. Shakespeare Festival, Madison, N.J., 1982-87; vice chair bd. dirs. Essex County Coll., Newark, 1980-87. Editor: (editorial page, sports, culture page) The China News, 1987-88. Elected mem. Millburn (N.J.) Twp. Governing Body, 1974-77, Essex County Charter Study Commn., N.J., 1987; mem. Citizens Adv. Panel Tri-State Regional Planning, 1980; mem. Millburn Planning Bd., 1975-77, 79-81; fire commr., Millburn Twp., 1974-77; founder, tchr. Fgn. Lang. Program, Millburn, 1969-77; bd. dirs. Marlboro Music Sch. and Festival, 1980—. Recipient N.J. Federation of Democratic Women award, 1977; named Woman of the Yr., Millburn-Short Hills Bus. and Profl. Women, 1983, Woman of the Yr., N.J. Bus. and Profl. Women, 1986. Mem. Nat. Housing Inst. (bd. dirs. 1988—). Democrat. Home and Office: 36 Sullivan Dr West Orange NJ 07052

COOPER, CAMILLE SUTRO, lawyer; b. Belleville, N.J., May 23, 1946; d. David Paul and Lotte (Weil) C. AB, Smith Coll., 1968; MS, Boston U., 1971; JD, Bklyn. Law Sch., 1982. Bar: N.Y. 1983, U.S. Dist Ct. (so. dist.) N.Y. Assoc. S.N. Solomon, Esq., N.Y.C., 1980-83; assoc. counsel Swissre Holding (N.A.) Inc., N.Y.C., 1983—; bd. dirs. Switzerland Ins. Holding USA, Inc., Del., 1986—, Switzerland Ins. Svcs. Inc., 1987—. Mem. ABA, Assn. of Bar of City of N.Y. Office: Swissre Holding (NA) Inc 237 Park Ave New York NY 10017

COOPER, CAROL ANN, physical education and recreation educator; b. Berkeley, Calif., Sept. 10, 1940; d. Joseph David and Nell Phyllis (Aiken) C. BS, Oreg. State U., 1961; MS, Smith Coll., 1966; EdD, U. N.C., 1975. Instr. Mapleton (Oreg.) Pub. Schs., 1961-64; camp dir. Camp Fire Girls, Yakima, Wash., 1967-68; swim coach, instr. So. Ill. U., Carbondale, 1967-72; assoc. prof. U. No. Iowa, Cedar Falls, 1972—. Contbr. articles to profl. publs. Mem. dist. bd. dirs. Camp Fire Girls. ARC spl. arts grantee. Mem. Am. Camping Assn., Am. Assn. Leisure and Recreation (past pres., Outstanding Achievement award 1988), Am. Alliance HPERD. Republican. Presbyterian. Home: 912 W 16th Cedar Falls IA 50613 Office: U No Iowa Cedar Falls IA 50614

COOPER, CAROLINE ANN, health science facility administrator; b. Gardner, Mass., Oct. 16, 1943; d. Frank D. and Florence M. (O'Neil) Toohey; m. Paul Geoffrey Cooper, Apr. 16, 1973; children: Geoffrey Paul, Heather Ann. BS, Russell Sage Coll., 1966; MBA, Bryant Coll., 1983. Adminstrv. dietitian Mass. Gen. Hosp., Boston, 1967-68; with rsrch., devel., mktg. Mkt. Forge Co., Everett, Mass., 1968-71; food svc. administrv. Jane Brown R.I. Hosp., Providence, 1971-74; self-employed pres., cons. pvt. practice, Attleboro, Mass.; from instr. to asst. prof. Johnson and Wales U., Providence, 1978-86, acad. coord., 1984-86, dept. chair HRI, Hospitality, Food Svc. Mgmt., 1986—. Vol. Parent Orgn. for Sch., 1978—, Pub. Sch. System, 1981-84, Community Sports Program, 1989—. Named Pacesetter Nat. Roundtable for Women, 1988. Mem. Am. Dietetic Assn., Am. Hotel Motel Assn. (Outstanding Educator award Ednl. Inst.), Computer Application Food Svc. Edn. (pres. 1987-89). Office: Johnson and Wales U Abbott Park Pl Providence RI 02903

COOPER, CAROLYN HELEN, education consultant; b. St. Louis; m. Stanley Cooper, Jan. 25, 1947; children: Pamela Lee, Douglas Alan. BA, U. Md., 1965, MEd, 1982. Elem. tchr. Bd. of Edn., Prince George's, Md., 1965-81; exec. dir. Literacy Coun. of Prince George's, 1982-89; cons. Prince George's, 1989—; exec. dir. Nat. Coalition for Pub. Edn., Washington, 1986-88; cons. Prince George's Libr. System, Md., 1989—; mem. State Adv. Coun. on Literacy, 1987. Unit chair mem. League of Women Voters, Prince George's County, 1986; founding mem. Henson Valley Montessori Sch., 1966—. Mem. AAUW (life), Md. State Coalition for Literacy (v.p. 1989, pres. 1986-88). Home: 12324 Arrow Park Dr Fort Washington MD 20744

COOPER, CHARLOTTE WYNN, printing company executive; b. New Castle, Pa., July 14, 1941; d. Theodore Edwin and Marian Evelyn (Jackson) Benson; m. Donald Matz. BS in Edn., Ind. U., 1963. Tchr. North Hills Sch. Dist., Pitts., 1963-64, Perris (Calif.) Union Sch. Dist., 1964, Elkhart (Ind.) Inst. Tech., 1965-66; bank officer Hamilton Bank, Lancaster, 1978-82; sales analyst Kiwi Polish Co., Douglassville, Pa., 1982-83; pres. Standard Offset Printing Co., Reading, Pa., 1983--. Bd. dirs. Planned Parenthood Berks County, Hawk Mountain Coun., Leadership Berks. Mem. Susquehanna Litho Club, Berks Women's Network, Berks County C. of C. Republican. Presbyterian. Office: Standard Offset Printing Co 426 Pearl St Reading PA 19602

COOPER, CLARE DUNLAP, civic worker, writer; b. Berkeley, Calif., Nov. 1, 1938; d. Claude and Mathilda (Egger) D.; m. William Secord Cooper, July 22, 1964; children: Constance, Edwin, Emily. AA, Cottey Coll., Nevada, Mo., 1958; BA, U. Calif., Berkeley, 1960; MA, San Francisco State U., 1981. Tchr. drama and English Istanbul, Turkey, 1960-63; pipe organist in concert and in svc. to various chs. 1989; writer for local newspapers, Orinda and Lafayette, Calif. Author: (play) Good and Perfect Gifts, 1988; author poems, adaptations and short plays related to teaching. Tchr. music, drama and English as second lang. local schs. and community ctrs.; gen. coord. benefit auction party Coll. Prep. Sch. Parents Assn., 1989-90. Mem. AAUW (gen. coord. fundraising Ednl. Found. 1989). Home: 84 La Espiral Rd Orinda CA 94563

COOPER, CYNTHIA LEE, public relations administrator, director; b. Wellsboro, Pa., Aug. 28, 1964; d. Charles Larue and Karen Lynn (Whitaker) C. Student, Internat. Inst. French Studies, 1985; BA, Juniata Coll., 1986. From reporter to bur. chief Star Gazette Newspaper, Corning, N.Y., 1986-87; pub. rels. dir. North Penn Comprehensive Health Svcs., Blossburg, Pa., 1987-88, Keuka Coll., Keuka Park, N.Y., 1988—; freelance writer Corning Glass Works, 1988. Mem. Steuben County Local Emergency Planning Com., Bath, N.Y., 1988-90. Mem. Women in Communications, Inc., Penn Yan Area C. of C. (bd. dirs. 1988—, Dir. of the Yr.). Office: Keuka Coll Keuka Park NY 14478

COOPER, DOLORES ANN, real estate professional, consultant, small business owner; b. Phila., Feb. 12, 1935; d. Daniel Mellor and Anne (Howard) C. BSBA, Widener U., 1983. Sec., travel coordinator Westinghouse Elec. Corp., Lester, Pa., 1953-86; owner, pres. DC Relocation Assistance Co., Bookhaven, Pa., 1986—; real estate sales assoc. Coldwell Banker Real Estate. Contbr. articles to profl. jours. Mem. NAFE, Soc. Cert. Profl. Secs., Nat. Writers Club, Delaware County Bd. Realtors, Tri-County Bd. Realtors, Phi Kappa Phi, Alpha Sigma Lambda. Republican. Roman Catholic. Office: DC Relocation Assistance Co Wayne PA 19087 also: Coldwell Banker Real Estate 314 E Lancaster Ave Wayne PA 19087

COOPER, DOLORES G., state legislator; b. Balt., Nov. 2, 1922; m. David Cooper (dec. Aug. 1986); 2 children. Student, Johns Hopkins U. Coll. for Tchrs., 1939-41, Bard Avon Bus. Sch., 1941-42, YMCA Bus. Coll., 1942-43, Stockton State Coll., 1972-74. Clk. typist adminstr. Edgewood Arsenal, Md., 1942-44; cryptographer U.S. War Dept., Ft. Richardson, Alaska, 1944-47; dir. pub. info. Fedn. Jewish Agys. Atlantic County, 1974-82; mem. 2d dist. N.J. Gen. Assembly, Trenton, 1982—, asst. majority whip, vice chmn. vets. select com., mem. sr. citizens, higher edn. and regulated professions coms., Commn. to Study Hunger in N.J., mem. Alzheimer's Commn., Monorail Commn. Mem. Alaska for Statehood Assn., 1945-47, Atlantic County Water Supply Adv. Com., 1986; vice chmn., historian Atlantic County Optional Charter Commn., 1973; freeholder-at-large Atlantic County, 1979-82; mem. exec. bd. Atlantic Area council Boy Scouts Am., 1987. Recipient award Spl. Theatre Arts and Recreation, 1984, Human Services award Jewish War Vets., 1985, cert. of appreciation Internat. Toastmistress Club, 1985, Community Relations award N.J. State Jewish War Vets., 1987; named Woman of Valor Sisterhood of Temple Emeth Shalom, 1980, Outstanding Co-legislator of 1980, Citizen of Yr. CARING, Inc., 1982, Most Outstanding Jewish Woman in Atlantic County Women's Am. O.R.T., 1983; named a Woman of Achievement Israel Inst. Tech., 1984. Mem. Hadassah (pres. Atlantic chpt. women's league 1956-58, pres. women's Zionist Orgn. 1965-67, Mother of Yr. 1984), N.J. Fedn. Bus. and Profl. Women (one of Top 10 Women in N.J. honor 1984). Clubs: Exchange, Avoda. Lodge: Lions. Office: 2430 Atlantic Ave Atlantic City NJ 08401

COOPER, DONA HANKS, network televison executive, consultant; b. Oklahoma City, Nov. 5, 1950; d. Charles William and Betty Hopkins (Cragen) C. B.A., Am. U., 1972; postgrad. U. Minn., 1972-73. Caseworker U.S. Senator Marlow W. Cook, Washington, 1973-74, U.S. Congressman Benjamin A. Gilman, Washington, 1974-75; artistic dir. Am. Soc. Theatre Arts, Washington, 1975-79; mng. dir. Ensemble Studio Theatre, L.A., 1979-81; story analyst Metro Media, Hollywood, Calif., 1981-82, NBC, Burbank, Calif., 1982-87; dir. story dept. NBC, 1987—, HBO, L.A., 1984-85; dir. Oliver Hailey's Playwrighting Group, L.A., 1982-85; radio drama cons. Radio Am., Washington, 1986; cons. Edgar Scherick Assocs., L.A., 1985; instr. Am. Film Inst., L.A., 1989—. Author plays: The Works of Lizzie Borden, 1981, California Calico, 1982, The Lone Star State, 1983, Rules of the House, 1984, Bosom Buddies, 1986. Mem. Nat. Assn. Female Execs., Dramatist Guild (assoc.), Phi Beta Phi. Democrat. Avocations: quilting; researching women's roles in Am. history. Home: PO Box 1798 Frazier Park CA 93225 Office: NBC 3000 W Alameda #C108 Burbank CA 91523

COOPER, DORIS JEAN, market research executive; b. N.Y.C., Dec. 17, 1934; d. James N. and Georgina N. (Cassidy) Breslin; student Sch. of Commerce, N.Y. U., 1953-55, Hunter Coll., 1956-57; m. S. James Cooper, June 17, 1956; 1 son, David Austin. Asst. coding supr. Crossley S-D Surveys, N.Y.C., 1955-57; asst. field supr. Trendex, Inc., N.Y.C., 1957-59; coding dir. J. Walter Thompson Co., N.Y.C., 1960-63, Audits & Surveys, N.Y.C., 1964-65; pvt. practice cons., N.Y.C., 1965-73; pres. Cooper Svcs., Hastings-on-Hudson, N.Y., 1973—; pres., chief exec. officer, computer tabulation and lang. manipulation Doris J. Cooper Assocs., Hastings, N.Y., 1989—; cons. market rsch. Mem. Am. Mktg. Assn. (N.Y. chpt.), Nat. Bus. Women Owners Assn., Am. Assn. Pub. Opinion Researchers (N.Y. chpt.), Hastings C. of C. Republican. Episcopalian. Office: Cooper Services 419 Warburton Ave Hastings-on-Hudson NY 10706 also: 419 Warbunton Ave Hastings NY 10706

COOPER, DOROTHY W., construction executive; b. Dublin, Ga., Sept. 21, 1955; d. Frank Watkins and Sammie Lee (Sinclair) Watkins; m. Edgar Cooper Jr., Jan. 21, 1977; children: Dione, Eric. BS, Tuskegee U., 1977. Tchr. Bibb County Bd. Edn., Macon, Ga.; pres. Lee and Denise, Macon. Mem. Macon YDC, adv. bd. Springdale PTC Exec. Bd. Mem. NAFE, Alpha Kappa Mu. Home and Office: 5840 Kentucky Downs Dr Macon GA 31210

COOPER, ELIZABETH M., business consultant, trainer; b. Northridge, Calif., June 6, 1954; d. John Joseph and Mildred Marie (Holschlag) Panasuk; m. Jeffrey D. Cooper, Oct. 17, 1981; children: Christopher, Jeremy. BS, LaVerne U., 1989, postgrad.; student, Art Instrn. Sch., 1972. Dir. staff devel. and edn. Magnolia Gardens, 1979-81; mgr. tng. and edn. Pacesetter Systems, Inc., Sylmar, Calif., 1982-90; exec. dir. Sylvan Learning Ctr., Valencia, Calif., 1990—; pres. E.J.C. Bus. Advisors, Inc., Valencia, 1990—; speaker in field. Recipient Achievement award Bank of Am., 1972. Mem. Am. Soc. Tng. and Devel., Am. Heart Assn. Home: 27616 Glasser Canyon Country CA 91351 Office: 27201 Tourney Rd #121 Valencia CA 91355

COOPER, FRIEDA LOUISE, bank officer; b. Ft. Worth, Nov. 20, 1944; d. Orville Adell and Myrtle Frances (Lewis) Burns; m. Robert Joe Cooper, Feb. 15, 1964. AA in Banking and Fin., Tarrant County Jr. Coll., 1989; cert., Tex. Tech. Sch. of Banking, 1989. Asst. v.p. Bank of N. Tex., Hurst, 1977-87, Am. Bank-Haltom City, Ft. Worth, 1987-89, Bedford (Tex.) Nat. Bank, 1989—. Named Mem. of Yr., Ft. Worth Greater Group, 1987. Mem. Fin. Women Internat. (pres. state coun. 1990—), Toastmasters (sec.-treas. Northeast Early Birds chpt. 1989-89), Profl. Women Con. (vice chair 1989-90), Fin. Expl. Investment Club (v.p. 1988-89). Office: Bedford Nat Bank 3005 Hwy 121N Bedford TX 76021

COOPER, GLORIA, human resources development company executive; b. Highland Park, Mich., Sept. 11, 1937; d. Willie Ward Cooper and Mildred Martha (Huell) Vines; m. Floyd Victor Bell, Sept. 1, 1956 (div. 1968); children: Laura Diane, Gloria Michelle; m. Leon H. Atchison, June 7, 1969 (div. May 1982); 1 child, Erika Dawn. BA, Wayne State U., 1968. Teller City Nat. Bank, Detroit, 1962-66; jr. clk. Mich. Nat. Bank, Detroit, 1966-67; sec. Community Legal Counsel, Detroit, 1967-68; social worker Neighborhood Legal Svc., Detroit, 1968-70; family counselor Community Svr. Ctr., Highland Park, 1970; adoption caseworker Homes for Black children, Detroit, 1970-74; community rels. adminstr. Detroit Bd. Edn., 1977-79; pres. Renaissance Careers Assocs., Detroit, 1979—; cons., fundraiser Detroit Parks and Recreation, 1982-84. Author: (career manual) Twelve Keys, 1986; contbr. articles to local newspapers. Chmn. fin. com. Wayne County Substance Abuse Commn., Detroit, 1974; Hilberry Theatre fundraiser Wayne State U., Detroit, 1977—; v.p. Cotillion Wives Aux., Detroit, 1971-73; bd. dirs. Homes for Black children, 1978-88. Recipient Spirit of Detroit award Detroit City Coun., 1982-85, mayor's cert. of merit City of Detroit, 1985, resolution Mich. Ho. of Reps., 1985. Mem. Greater Detroit C of C. (chmn. small bus. adv. com. 1983-85), Optimist (bd. dirs. Detroit 1988). Democrat. Baptist. Office: Renaissance Career Assocs 11000 W McNichols Ste 100 Detroit MI 48221

COOPER, JANE ELIZABETH, biology educator; b. Bethlehem, Pa., June 2, 1937; d. Frank Edward and Emma Alice (Lockhuff) C. AB summa cum laude, Lindenwood Coll, 1959; PhD, U. Pa., Phila., 1965. Instr. biology Drexel Inst. Tech., Phila., 1964-66, asst. prof. biology, 1966-67; asst. prof. biology Pa. State U., Media, 1967-72, assoc. prof. biology, 1972—; cons. quality assurance in nursing homes Southeastern Pa. Synod, Phila., ELCA, 1987—. Coord. Tim Mark Endowment fund, Pa. State U., 1990—. Fellow Woodrow Wilson Found., 1959-60, NSF, 1960-61. Mem. AAAS, Genetics Soc. Am., Hastings Ctr., Sigma Xi (assoc. mem.). Lutheran. Office: Pa State U Delaware County Campus Media PA 19063

COOPER, JANE TODD, poet, writer, educator; b. Bklyn., Dec. 24, 1943; d. John Curtis and Margaret E. (Johnston) C.; m. William Hudson Shoff; children: Donald Charles Taylor, Eamon Robert Taylor, Savannah Elizabeth Cooper-Ramsey. Student U. Pitts., 1965-68; BA in Lit., Duquesne U., 1965. Research asst. U. Pitts., 1966; instr. high sch., Pitts., 1967-73; ednl. dir. drug and alcohol treatment facility Pa. Dept. Corrections, Camp Hill, 1974-78; project trainer domiciliary care, dept. behavioral sci. Pa. State Coll. Medicine, Hershey, 1979-80; dir. primary health care projct Elizabethtown Hosp., Pa., 1980-81; mgr. personal care boarding home provider tng. project, dept. family and community medicine Pa. State Coll. Medicine, Hershey, 1982; cons. Pa. Dept. Aging, Pa. Dept. Pub. Welfare, Pa. Council on Arts, 1979—, others; coordinator Fellow in Arts Mgmt. Program, 1985-87; free lance writer, Harrisburg (Pa.) and Phila., 1979—; mem. steering com. Women in the Arts, Harrisburg, 1979-83; coordinator Eye Poets Reading Series, Lancaster, Pa., 1985-87, Manchester Craftsmen's Guild Reading Series, Pitts., 1988-89. Author: (poetry) Entering Pisces, 1985; editor: AR-TREACH, 1984, Home Management for Personal Care Boarding Home Providers, 1982; edit. bd. Shooting Star Rev., 1987—; poetry and prose pub. in lit. jours. and anthologies; poet, poetry adv. bd., Geraldine R. Dodge Found., Madison, N.J., 1987—. Artist in residence N.J. State Arts Council, Pa. Council on the Arts, 1982—; Carroll scholar, 1964-65; Warner Lambert/Nat. Merit scholar, 1961-65. Mem. Poets and Writers, Acad. Am. Poets. Home: 339 S 4th St Philadelphia PA 19106

COOPER, JOSEPHINE SMITH, public relations executive; b. Raleigh, N.C., Aug. 2, 1945; d. Joseph W. and Marie (Peele) S. BA in bus. and econs., Meredith Coll., Raleigh, 1967; MS in mgmt., Duke U., 1977. Program analyst Office of Air & Quality Planning and Standards EPA, Rsch., Triangle Park, N.C., 1968-78; environ. prot. specialist Office of Rsch. and Devel., Washington, 1978-80; mem. profl. staff majority leader Howard H. Baker, Jr., U.S. Senate Com. on Environ. and Public Works, Washington, 1980-83; asst. adminstr. for external affairs EPA, Washington, 1983-85; asst. v.p. for environ. and health program Am. Paper Inst., Washington, 1985-86; sr. v.p. for policy Synthetic Organic Chem. Mfrs. Assn., Washington, 1986-88; sr. v.p., dir. environmental policy Hill & Knowlton, Inc., Washington, 1988—; treas. RTP Fed. Credit Union, 1969-72, pres., 1975; pres. Women's Coun. on Energy and Environment, 1986-88, Nat. Coun. on Clean Indoor Air, 1988—. Congl. fellow, 1979-80. Mem. Federally Employed Women (treas., pres. 1972-77), Women in Govt. Rels., Tenley Sport and Health Club. Mem. Disciples of Christ. Office: Hill & Knowlton Inc 901 31st St NW Washington DC 20007

COOPER, KRISTINA MARIE, psychologist; b. Burlington, Iowa, Jan. 18, 1955; d. Joseph Edward and Agnes Catherine (Moehn) Braun; children: Sara, Michael. BS with honors and high distinction, U. Iowa, 1976; MA, Ariz. State U., 1982, PhD, 1983. Cert. psychologist. Asst. dir. Good Samaritan Med. Ctr., Phoenix, 1984—; adj. asst. prof. Ariz. State U., Tempe, 1990—; presenter profl. meetings and orgn. chpts., Ariz., 1983—. Contbr. articles to profl. jours. Bd. mem. Juvenile Diabetes Found., Phoenix, 1987-88; co-facilitator New Horizons Support Group, Phoenix, 1986—. Mem. Am. Psychol. Assn., Coun. for Nat. Register of Health Svc. Providers in Psychology. Office: Good Samaritan Med Ctr 925 E McDowell Phoenix AZ 85062

COOPER, LINDA FRANCES, genetic counselor; b. Queens, N.Y., Jan. 18, 1961; d. Justin Lehman and Judith (Beethoven) C. BA, U. Pa., 1982; MS in Genetic Counseling, U. Calif., Berkeley, 1984. Diplomate Am. Bd. Med. Genetics. Instr. dept. pediatrics Johns Hopkins U. Sch. Medicine, Balt., 1990—, genetic counselor, 1984—. Vol. Children's Hosp. of Phila., 1980-82, Children's Ctr., Johns Hopkins Hosp., Balt., 1990. Newhouse Found grantee U. Calif., 1982. Mem. Am. Soc. Human Genetics, Nat. Soc. Genetic Counselors. Office: Johns Hopkins Hosp Ctr for Med Genetics 600 N Wolfe St Baltimore MD 21205

COOPER, LISA IVY, lawyer; b. Port Jervis, N.Y., July 26, 1961; d. Jerome Sanford and Zelda (Paymer) Cohen; m. Lyndon F. Cooper, June 14, 1987. BS, Syracuse U., 1983, JD, 1985. Bar: N.Y. 1985. Assoc. Nixon,

Hargrave, Devans & Doyle, Rochester, N.Y., 1985—. Chmn. Brighton (N.Y.) Beautification Com., 1987-88; co-leader law explorers Boy Scouts Am., Webster, N.Y., 1985-86; participant Jefferson Mid. Sch. Partnership, Rochester, 1989. Mem. N.Y. State Bar Assn., Water Pollution Control Assn. (chmn. N.Y. State legis. forum 1988—), Water Pollution Control Fedn. (rsch. com.). Office: Nixon Hargrave Devans & Doyle Clinton Square Rochester NY 14603

COOPER, MARGERY WILKENS, investment company executive; b. Glen Cove, N.Y., May 14, 1947; d. Robert George and Caroline L. (Jones) Wilkens; m. Daniel S. Cooper, May 6, 1967; 1 child, Christopher S. AA, Mt. Vernon Jr. Coll., 1967; BS, Russell Sage Coll., 1976. Registered securities rep. Chief fin. officer D.S. Cooper and Co., Troy, N.Y., 1981-87. Bd. dirs. Albany Boys' Club, Investment Soc. N.E. N.Y., St. Peter's Women's Assn., Parsons Assn.; past pres. Albany Jr. League. Republican. Episcopal.

COOPER, MARY ADRIENNE, publishing executive; b. Bklyn., Jan. 27, 1927; d. James H. and Helen (Hofeditz) C. BSBA, SUNY, Albany, 1948; postgrad. in bus., NYU, 1949-50, Columbia U., 1976. With McGraw Hill, Inc., N.Y.C., 1953—, asst. v.p. corp. fin. ops., 1973-75, v.p. corp. fin. ops., 1975-76, v.p. adminstrv. services, 1976-84, v.p. fin. services, 1984-85, sr. v.p. adminstrv. services, 1985-86, sr. v.p. corp. affairs, exec. asst. to chief exec. officer, chmn., 1986—. Mem. Fin. Execs. Inst. (com. on govt. liaison N.Y.C. chpt., bd. dirs. 1986—). Roman Catholic. Avocations: golf, biking, reading, travel. Office: McGraw-Hill Inc 1221 Ave of the Americas New York NY 10020

COOPER, MERRI-ANN, psychologist; b. N.Y.C., Dec. 22, 1946; d. Isidore and Florence (Koplick) C.; m. Stephan Kessler, Aug. 23, 1965 (div. 1971). BA in Psychology cum laude, Bklyn. Coll., 1967; PhD, U. Chgo., 1974; postdoctoral student, U. Minn., 1976-78. Rsch. asst. U. Chgo., 1969-71; asst. prof. Ill. State U., Bloomington, 1972-76; personnel researcher Hennepin County Dept. Personnel, Mpls., 1977-78; rsch. scientist Advanced Rsch. Resources Orgn., Bethesda, Md., 1979-81, sr. rsch. scientist, 1981-85, program mgr., 1985-87; project dir. Univ. Rsch. Corp., Bethesda, Md., 1988-90, prin. rsch. scientist, 1990—; adj. assoc. prof. U. Md., College Park, 1985-86; expert witness litigation support-selection/promotion, 1986, 89; presenter in field; co-chair conf. on employment testing Bur. Nat. Affairs, 1988. Developer selection/promotion tests FBI spl. agts., RR engrs., etc.; contbr. articles to profl. jours. Recipient USPHS traineeship U. Chgo. Mem. Personnel Testing Coun. (recorder 1986-87, sec. 1985-86, pres. 1988-89), Soc. for Indsl./Organizational Psychology (edn. and tng. com. 1983-84, program com. 1985), Am. Psychology. Home: 4515 Willard Ave Chevy Chase MD 20815 Office: Univ Rsch Corp 7200 Wisconsin Ave Bethesda MD 20814

COOPER, PATRICIA DAWKINS, foundation administrator; b. Houston, Feb. 5, 1944; d. Austin Eli and Sarah Lorraine (Rountree) Dawkins; children from previous marriage: Catherine Sloane, Sarah Riley, Patricia Daily. BA, Columbia Coll., 1965. Appointments sec. to Congressman Tom Gettys, Washington, 1965; tchr. Lugoff (S.C.) Elem. Sch., 1967-68, Camden (S.C.) Elem. Sch., 1969-70; ombudsman State of S.C., 1970-73; asst. dir. Carolina Cup and Colonial Cup Internat., Camden, 1973-87; adminstr. Camden Feed Co., 1973-87; office mgr. Camden Tng. Ctr., thoroughbreds, 1973-87; asst. sec. Mulberry Resources, Inc., 1980-82; sec.-treas. Equistar Products Co., 1980-87; mktg. dir. Holiday Inn of Lugoff-Camden, Holiday Inn of Sumter, S.C., 1987-88; dir. Devel. Bapt. Med. Ctr. Found., 1988-89; exec. v.p. S.C. State Mus. Fedn., Columbia, 1989—. Bd. dirs. Kershaw County Fine Arts Ctr.; sustaining mem. Camden Jr. Welfare League; mem. Inaugural Class, Leadership Kershaw County, 1986-87, participant Statewide Program, 1987-88; adv. com. Charleston Steeplechase; mem. Santee-Lynches Coun. Govts., 1987-88; bd. dirs. Kershaw County unit Am. Cancer Soc., 1980—, S.C. chpt. Leukemia Soc. Am., 1987—; chmn. bd. dirs. Kershaw unit Am. Heart Assn., 1984-86; bd. dirs. Palmetto Balloon Classic, 1983-86; mem. Bd. Appeals, City of Camden, 1985-87; vice chmn. Kershaw County Tourism Adv. Com., 1987-88; adminstrv. bd. Lyttleton St. United Meth. Ch., Camden, 1986-88; chmn. leadership com. Kershaw County, 1988—; mem. Columbia Action Coun., 1988—, Columbia Forum, 1988—; adv. com. S.C. Joint Legis. Com. on Cultural Affairs, 1989—; active Assembly on the Future of S.C., 1989, Columbai Forum, 1988—; trustee S.C. bd. Leukemia Soc. of Am., 1987—. Mem. Greater Kershaw County C. of C. (v.p. pub. affairs 1983-86, William F. Nettles award 1988), Thoroughbred Assn. S.C. (sec.-treas. 1986-88), Leadership S.C. Alumni (bd. dirs. 1988—), Greater Columbia C. of C., S.C. Alumni Assn. (bd. dirs. leadership 1988—), Camden Country Club, Sprindale Hall Club, Univ. Assocs. Club, Rotary. Democrat. Methodist. Home: 409 Laurens Ct Camden SC 29020 Office: SC State Mus Found PO Box 100107 Columbia SC 29202-3107

COOPER, PAULETTE MARCIA, writer; b. Antwerp, Belgium, July 26, 1942; came to U.S., 1948; naturalized, 1951; d. Ted S. and Stella R. (Toepfer) C.; B.A. with honors, Brandeis U., 1964; M.A., CUNY, 1968. Free-lance writer, 1968—. Recipient Edgar Allan Poe spl. award Mystery Writers Am., 1975, Spl. award Am. Soc. Journalists and Authors, 1988. Mem. Am. Soc. Journalists and Authors, Nat. Acad. TV Arts & Scis., Travel Journalists Guild. Author 6 books including: The Scandal of Scientology; The Medical Detectives; also 500 articles. Address: 401 E 74th St New York NY 10021

COOPER, REBECCA, art dealer; b. Phila., July 11, 1957; d. Frank N. Cooper and Bernice (Silverstein) Lewis; m. Michael J. Waldman, June 27, 1982. BA NYU, 1969, MA 1971, postgrad. Owner Gallery Rebecca Cooper, Washington, 1970s; pres. Rebecca Cooper, Inc., N.Y.C., 1980s; sec. bd. assocs. Am. Craft Mus., lectr. Collectors Circle, 1985, 86; nat. patron Am. Fed. Art., Ind. Creators; assoc. Mus. Modern Art, Met. Mus. Mem. Whitney Circle of Friends (exhbn. com.), Assocs. of Guggenheim Mus.

COOPER, ROCHELLA, president sailing school; b. Bloemfontein, Republic South Africa, July 14, 1933; came to U.S., 1961; d. Lester Julius and Dolfanna (Rose) Brown; children: Charles, Andrew, Jonathan. MusB, U. Cape Town, Republic South Africa, 1954. Lst flutist Haifa (Israel) Symphony, 1958; tchr. music London Sch. System, 1959-61; dir. Sch. of Woods Montessori Sch., Houston, 1963-70; pres. Cooper & Co., archtl. fiberworks, Houston, 1972-78; exec. dir. Houston Internat. Festival, 1979-86; pres. Women at The Helm Sailing Sch., Houston, 1987—; cons. Greenway Plaza Children's House, Houston, 1970-72, Clear Lake Econ. Devel. Found., Houston, 1986-87. Panelist United Way, Houston, 1987—; singer Houston Oratorio Soc., 1987—. Mem. Boating Trades Assn., Clear Lake C. of C. Office: At the Helm Inc FM 2094 Kemah/Houston TX 77565

COOPER, SHARON MARSHA, marketing, advertising executive; b. Chgo., Feb. 6, 1944; d. Ralph and Esther Lepack; m. Steven Jon Cooper; children: Robin Eve, Erik Scott. BA, Northeastern Ill. U., Chgo., 1974; MEd, Loyola U., Chgo., 1977. Adj. asst. prof. Chgo. Med. Sch., North Chicago, Ill., 1974-79; edn./media coordinator Humana Hosp., Aurora, Colo., 1980-82; v.p. Healthcare Mktg. Corp., Denver, 1982-84; pres. Sharon Cooper Assocs., Ltd., Englewood, Colo., 1984—; cons./speaker Jason Pharms., Balt., 1988—; cons. Am. Soc. Bariatric Physicians; lectr. in field; guest lectr. U. Denver, 1988—. Illustrator: A Manual of Radiographic Positioning, 1973; contbr. articles to profl. jours. Bd. dirs., v.p. The Barre Assn./Colo. Ballet, Denver, 1989—; bd. dirs. Am. Diabetes Assn., Denver, 1983—, Am. Cancer Soc., Denver, 1988—, Hospice of St. John, Denver, 1986-90. Named Co-Woman of the Yr., Lerner Newspapers, Chgo., 1973, Silver Microphone award, 1988, Golden Leaflet award, Colo. Hosp. Assn., 1981, 84. Mem. Am. Hosp. Assn., Assn. Healthcare Pub. Rels. and Mktg. (reg. rep. 1987—), Colo. Soc. Health Care Pub. Rels., Pub. Rels. Soc. Am., Zonta, Toastmasters (sec. 1972-84). Home: 8522 E Dry Creek Pl Englewood CO 80112 Office: Sharon Cooper Assocs Ltd 9085 E Mineral Cir #160 Englewood CO 80112

COOPER, SYLVIA JANE, librarian; b. Columbia, Mo., June 10, 1936; d. George B. and Jessie Merle (Turner) Edmondson; m. Richard Grant, Jan. 31, 1970. BS, U. Mo., Columbia, 1958; MEd, U. Mo., 1962, M.A. in Libr. Sci., 1972. Vocat. home econ. tchr. Paris High Sch., Paris, Mo., 1958-61, Macon High Sch., Macon, Mo., 1962-67; libr. and student asst. U. Mo. Libr., Columbia, Mo., 1967-69; reader service librarian St. Louis County Libr., 1969-70; librarian U.S.D.I. Fish Pesticide Research Lab., Columbia, Mo., 1970-71; libr. dir. Okla. Osteopathic Hosp., 1976—. Recipient Scholarship Mo. C. of C. Edn. Found., 1965. Mem. ALA, South Cen. Regional Group of Med. Libr. Assn., Hosp. Sect. of South Cen. Regional Group of Med. Libr. Assn. (chmn. 1989-90), Spl. Libr. Assn., Okla. Health Soc. Libr. Assn. (past pres.), Sungate Garden Club, Beta Sigma Phi. Office: Tulsa Regional Med Ctr Libr 744 W Ninth Tulsa OK 74127

COOPER, WENDY FEIN, lawyer; b. Irvington, N.J., May 10, 1946; d. Jacob and Rose (Rothman) Fein; m. James C. Faltot, Apr. 4, 1971 (div. 1982); m. Leonard J. Cooper, June 19, 1983; children: Jennifer Regan, Ian Joshua. AB cum laude, Bryn Mawr Coll., 1968; JD, Temple U., 1973, LLM in Taxation, 1983. Assoc. Beitch & Block, Phila., 1973-76, ptnr., 1976-79; assoc. Narin & Chait, Phila., 1980-83, ptnr., 1983-85; assoc. Griffith & Burr P.C., Phila., 1985; shareholder Dolchin, Slotkin & Todd, P.C., Phila., 1987—. Bd. dirs., sec. Phila. Festival Theatre for New Plays, 1981—. Mem. ABA, Phila. Bar Assn. Home: 1603 Harris Rd Laverock PA 19118 Office: Dolchin Slotkin & Todd PC 1234 Market St Ste 2000 Philadelphia PA 19107

COOPER-LEWTER, MARCIA JEAN, educator, administrative assistant; b. Petersburg, Va., Nov. 2, 1959; d. Andrew Ezekiel and Lillian (Bonner) Wyatt; m. Nicholas Charles Cooper-Lewter, Nov. 29, 1986. BS in Elem. Edn., Va. State U., Ettrick, 1984. Lic. minister, 1987; ordained to clergy, 1990. Tchr. Marion (Ind.) Community Schs., 1985-86, Inglewood (Calif.) Unified Schs., 1986-87; office mgr. C.R.A.V.E. Christ Counseling, Tustin, Calif., 1986—; asst. minister New Garden of Gethsemane B.C., L.A., 1987-90; assoc. pastor New Garden of Gethsemane B.C., L.A., 1990—; pres. C.R.A.V.E. Christ Singers, L.A., 1987-90; adminstr. asst. Eldorado Bank, Orange, Calif., 1988-90; tchr. Mpls. Sch. Dist., 1990—; advisor Am. Biog. Inst., N.C., 1990—. Named one of Outstanding Young Women of Am., 1987. Mem. NAFE, C.R.A.V.E. Christ Ministries, Inc., Alpha Kappa Alpha. Office: Wyatt Cooper-Lewter Cons 2473 W 7th St Ste 225 Saint Paul MN 55116

COOPER-SCOTT, NEDRA DENISE, judicial administrator; b. Detroit, May 5, 1953; d. William Eldredge and Jeri (Weaver) Cooper; m. Feb. 10, 1973 (div. May 1982); children: Morenike Rene, Moneer Abdullah. BA in Psychology, Internat. Coll., 1977; BSW, U. Las Vegas, 1982; MBA, MA in Mgmt., Nat. U., 1986. Lic. social worker. Youth counselor aide Clark County Juvenile Cts., Las Vegas, 1974, youth counselor I, 1974-76, youth counselor II, 1976-77, supr. Child Haven, 1977-86, supr. intake, 1986—; coordinator parenting project Clark County Juvenile Ct. System. Appointed to gov. commn. on King Holiday, Las Vegas, 1987; hon. consul to Haiti, Pres.' Commn. on Martin Luther King Holiday, Washington, 1987; mem. Dem. Caucus, Las Vegas, 1987. Mem. NAACP (life), AAUW, Nat. Assn. Female Execs., Dr. Martin Luther King Jr. Com. (Las Vegas chpt.), Delta Sigma Theta (2nd v.p. Las Vegas alumnae chpt.). Club: Am. Topical (Milw.). Office: Clark County Juvenile Cts 3401 E Bonanza Rd Las Vegas NV 89101

COOPERSMITH, SHIRLEY ANN, data processing management consultant; b. Kansas City, Mo., Feb. 4, 1944; d. Louis and Yetta (Swartz) Agronin, m. Henry Joseph Coopersmith, Sept. 3, 1970 (div. 1978); m. James Edward Reischman, Apr. 16, 1988; children: Marc Daniel, Stacy Janine. AAS, Kans. City Jr. Coll., 1963; student, U. Alberta, 1964. Project mgr. Optigan Inc., Compton, Calif., 1971-72; cons. Tustin, Calif., 1972-78; sr. mktg. analyst Basic Four Corp., Irvine, Calif., 1978-80; regional mgr. Data Solutions Inc., Santa Ana, Calif., 1980-82; info. resources mgr. Pacific Nat. Ins. Co., Fullerton, Calif., 1982-88. Pres. Tustin Village II, 1984-85, bd. dirs. 1985-86. Mem. Data Processing Mgmt. Assn. (legis. com. 1985-86), Calif. State Homeopathic Med. Soc., Internat. Found. Homeopathy. Libertarian.

COOVER, PAULA LOUISE, association executive; b. White Plains, N.Y., Mar. 5, 1947; d. Raymond Francis and Carolyn Louise (Landis) Henry; m. John David Coover, Nov. 18, 1967; children: Jeffrey Darren, Robert Benson, Jennifer Danielle (dec.). AA in Psychology, Monmouth Coll., 1967; student, Pace U., 1976. Chair gifted and talented com., then pres. Hunterdon County (N.J.) Coun. PTAs, 1980-86; chmn. county pres. group, nat. conv. del., gen. conv. chmn. N.J. Congress Parents & Tchrs., Trenton, 1985-87, field svc. chmn., 1985-89, pres., 1989—. Mem. sch. bd., Union Twp. Bd. Edn. Hampton, N.J., 1983-87, del. to assembly, 1984-87, legis. chmn., 1984-87, policy chmn., 1986-87, edn. chmn. 1984-85; trustee Jennie M. Hauer Scholarship Fund, 1984-89; mem. Hunterdon County Edn. Coalition, 1984-88, Child Abuse and Missing Children Com. Hunterdon, 1987—, Hunterdon County Youth Svcs. Commn., Fleminton, 1988—; treas. Fannie B. Abbott Student Loan Found., 1985-90; v.p. Hunterdon County Child Assault Protection Program, Flemington, 1986-90. Republican. Methodist. Home: 679 Deerfield Ln Asbury NJ 08802 Office: NJ Congress Parents Tchrs 900 Berkeley Ave Trenton NJ 08618

COOVER-CLARK, CAROL, architect; b. Tulsa, Dec. 31, 1955; d. Theodore Wilbur and Helen Harriet (Crawford) C.; m. Charles David Clark, Jr.; children: Amanda, Faye. BArch, U. Okla., 1979. Registered profl. architect, Okla., Colo. Intern architect Holleyman Assocs., Oklahoma City, 1978-80, Thomas Roberts & Assocs., Oklahoma City, 1980-83, John M. Eggner Architect, Norman, Okla., 1983-84; project architect Remy McKinney Assocs., Norman, 1984-85; architect FKW, Inc., Oklahoma City, 1985-87; architect Badgett & Coover-Clark Architects, Oklahoma City, 1987—, Denver, 1989—. Pres., historian Santa Fe Depot Restoration Com., Norman, 1987-89; archtl. advisor Canadian County Historic Commn., El Reno, Okla., 1986—. Named one of Outstanding Young Women Am., 1984. Mem. AAUW, AIA (publicity and pub. awareness chmn. 1987—, chmn. Capitol Hill Design Competition 1986-87, honor awards juror 1983, regional dir. cen. states 1983-84, bd. dirs. Okla. chpt. 1983—, Outstanding Assoc. Okla. chpt. 1985), Nat. Council Archtl. Registration Bds. (cert.). Democrat. Methodist. Office: Badgett & Coover-Clark Arch 2718 NW 39th St Oklahoma City OK 73112 also: Badgett & Coover-Clark 2382 S Carr Ct Denver CO 80227

COPA, KATHLEEN THERESE, physical therapist, health education specialist; b. Little Falls, Minn., July 18, 1955; d. Wilfred Walter and Adrienne Anne (Knoll) C.; m. Donald Paul Hertel, July 18, 1973; m. Jesse Neil Gellis, Nov. 30, 1985. BS magna cum laude, Calif. State U., Northridge, 1978, postgrad. Cert. phys. therapist, Calif. Phys. therapist Holy Cross Hosp., Mission Hills, Calif., 1980-84, Facey Med. Group, Mission Hills, 1984-90; phys. therapist, sports injuries specialist Granada Phys. Therapy, Granada Hills, Calif., 1990—. Vol. UCLA Ctr. Health Scis., 1977. Mem. Am. Phys. Therapy Assn., Calif. Phys. Therapy Assn., Nat. Wildlife Fedn., Sierra Club, Alpha Lambda Delta, Eta Sigma Gamma.

COPE, BRENDA LOUISE, writer, speaker, public relations specialist; b. Denver, Apr. 25, 1956; d. Virgil Glenn Moseley and Trese Ann (Nutting) Millington; m. David Bruce Cope, Sept. 7, 1973; children: Jessica Christine, David Jeremiah. Adminstrv. asst. grad., Barnes Bus. Coll., Denver, 1987-88. Retail clk. Safeway Stores, Inc., Denver, 1974-82; accounts receivable Wymodak, Inc., Aurora, Colo., 1982-83; accounts payable Info. Solutions, Englewood, Colo., 1983-84; admissions rep. Colo. Coll. Med. and Dental Careers, Denver, 1984-85; merchandising rep. Scripto, Aurora, 1985-86; ter. mgr. Rocky Mountain Mktg. Svcs., Denver, 1986-88; regional merchandising mgr. A.H. Robins Consumer Products, Richmond, Va., 1989-90; chief exec. officer Internal Affairs, Aurora, 1989—; dir. pub. rels. Asthma Ski Found. Pres. Home Owners Assn., Aurora, 1988, 89; Rep. precinct committeeperson, Arapahoe County, 1988, 89. Mem. NAFE, Nat. Writers Club. Home: 4121 S Andes Way Aurora CO 80013 Office: Internal Affairs 4121 S Andes Way Aurora CO 80013

COPE, ESTHER SIDNEY, history educator; b. West Chester, Pa., Sept. 10, 1942; d. Robert Wellington and Jane Davis (Stanton) C. BA, Wilson Coll., 1964; MA, U. Wis.-Madison, 1965; PhD, Bryn Mawr Coll., 1969. Instr. history Ursinus Coll., Collegeville, Pa., 1968-70, asst. prof. history, 1970-75; asst. prof. history U. Nebr., Lincoln, 1975-76, assoc. prof., 1976-81, prof., 1981—, chmn. dept. history, from 1982; bd. dirs. Yale Ctr. Parliamentary History, New Haven, 1981—. Mem. Nebr. Com. for Humanities, 1987. Author: Life of a Public Man, 1981, Politics Without Parliaments, 1986; Editor: Procs. of Short Parliament 1640, 1977. Fellow Royal Hist. Soc.; mem. Am. Hist. Assn., Conf. Brit. Studies (rec. sec. 1975-81), Internat. Commn. on Hist. Rep. and Parliamentary Instns., Berkshire Conf. Women Historians, Phi Beta Kappa. Mem. Soc. of Friends. Office: U Nebr Dept History Lincoln NE 68588

COPE, HESTER LEE, volunteer; b. Louisville, Nov. 18, 1940; d. William and Hester Lee (Hines) Black; m. David Delano Cope, Aug. 31, 1963; 1 child, Katherine Lee. BS, U. Houston, 1963. Tchr. Cleve. Pub. Schs., 1963-65; tchr. New Orleans Pub. Schs., 1965-66, Huntsville Pub. Schs., Huntsville, Ala., 1967-68, Tuscaloosa Pub. Schs., Tuscaloosa, Ala., 1968-69. Organizer 1st mcpl. curbside recycling in Ala., Florence, 1988-89, campaign mgr. 1st woman to be elected to city coun., Florence, 1988; mem. textbook selection com., city schs., Florence, 1986-87; organizer Sheffield, Ala. curbside recycling, 1989—. Mem. Ala. Conservancy (state bd. 1988-89), AAUW (treas. Shoals, Ala. br. 1987-89), LWV (pres. Shoals chpt. 1989—), Ala. Renaissance Faire (bd. dirs. 1988-89), Keep Am. Beautiful (bd. dirs. Shoals chpt. 1989—). Presbyterian. Home: 1750 Eunice Ave Florence AL 35630

COPE, NANCY ELIZABETH, television news producer; b. Woodbury, N.J., Dec. 4, 1952; d. William Fox and Kathryn Florence (Pime) C. B.S., U. Tenn., 1974. News reporter, editor Houston News Svc., 1975-78; news assignment editor Sta. KHOU-TV, Houston, 1978-79; news producer Sta. KTRK-TV, Houston, 1979-86, exec. producer, 1986-89, Sta. KGO-TV, San Francisco, 1989—. Mem. Soc. Profl. Journalists, NOW, Internat. Platform Assn., Radio-TV News Dirs. Assn. Office: Sta KGO-TV 900 Front St San Francisco CA 94111

COPELAND, ANNE PITCAIRN, psychologist; b. Pitts., Sept. 3, 1951; d. James Dudley and Barbara (Findley) C.; m. James Potter Womack, Dec. 15, 1984; children: Caroline Copeland, Katherine Copeland. BA, Eckerd Coll., St. Petersburg, Fla., 1973; PhD, Am. U., 1977. Lic. psychologist, Mass. Med. psychology intern child devel. and rehab. ctr. Oreg. Health Scis. U., Portland, 1976-77; asst. prof. psychology Kent (Ohio) State U., 1977-79; asst. prof. psychology Boston U., 1979-85, assoc. prof. psychology, 1985—; acad. advisor, acting dir. British programmes Boston U., London, Oxford, 1988-89. Contbr. articles to profl. jours. Recipient Alumni Achievement award Eckerd Coll., 1988. Mem. Am. Psychol. Assn., New England Psychol. Assn. (pres. 1985), Soc. for Rsch. in Child and Adolescent Psychopathology, Soc. for Rsch. in Child Devel., AAUP, Sigma Xi, Phi Beta Delta Soc. Internat. Scholars. Office: Boston U Psychology Dept 64 Cummington St Boston MA 02215

COPELAND, CAROLYN ABIGAIL, university dean; b. White Plains, N.Y., May 5, 1931; d. Robert Erford and Mary Terwilliger; B.A. (CEW scholar), U. Mich., 1973, M.A. (Rackham Grad. Student scholar), 1979; m. William E. Copeland, Aug. 16, 1964; children—Rob Cameron, Diana Elizabeth Bosworth. With dean's office Coll. Lit., Sci. and Arts, U. Mich., Ann Arbor, 1967—, asst. dean, 1980-84, assoc. dean, 1984—. Mem. Mortar Bd., Phi Beta Kappa (v.p. Alpha chpt. 1984-86, pres. Alpha chpt. 1986-88). Author: Tankas from the Koelz Collection, 1980; Walter Norman Koelz, A Biography, in progress. Research in Buddhist art history. Home: 520 Darwin Rd Pinckney MI 48169 Office: U Mich Ann Arbor MI 48109

COPELAND, ELAINE WILSON, data processing analyst; b. Ft. Worth, Sept. 16, 1944; d. Phillip Loren and Artie Inez (Neel) Wilson; m. Robert J. Copeland, Aug. 17, 1963 (div. 1983); children: Karen Kay Prince, Donna Lynn Copeland-Nay. BS in Bus., Info. Systems, U. Colo., Denver, 1984. Sec. Hartford Life Ins. Co., Dallas, 1964-66, St. George's Episcopal Ch., Dallas, 1976-77; technician data processing Manville Corp., Denver, 1980-81, assoc. analyst, 1984-85, analyst data processing, 1985—; fin. technician 1st Interstate Bank, Denver, 1982-84. Chmn. precinct Rep. Party Tex., Dallas, 1970-76. Recipient Silver Spark award Camp Fire Girls, Denver, 1982. Mem. Soc. Info. Mgmt., Data Processing Mgmt. Assn. (v.p. publicity 1986-88, sec. 1989—, asst. editor newsletter 1985-86), Jaycee-Ettes (hon. lifetime), Grand Prairie (Tex.) C. of C. (Newcomer of Yr. 1971), St. Paul's Ultreya Club (lay leader 1987-88). Episcopalian. Office: Manville Corp PO Box 5108 Denver CO 80217-5108

COPELAND, JANE CONYERS, not-for-profit organization executive; b. Elyria, Ohio, Sept. 1, 1941; d. David Kepler and Frances Elizabeth (Ertel) Conyers; m. Jack L. Copeland (div. 1977); children: Robin Janette, William Baugh. BS summa cum laude, Ohio State U., 1962; MA with honors, So. Meth. U., 1970; cert. Neurodevelopmental Treatment, U. Conn., 1986; cert. Hippotherapy, Kuratorium, Wildbad, Germany, 1987. Phys. therapist Easter Seal Soc., Daytona Beach, Fla., 1962-65; instr. Ohio State U., Columbus, Ohio, 1966-68; dir. therapy/recreation Silver Hill Psychiatric Hosp., New Canaan, Conn., 1971-72; cons./direct svc. Copeland Phys. Therapy, Darien, Conn., 1974-90; Exec. dir. Pegasus Therapeutic Riding, Inc., Darien, Conn., 1984-90; bd. dirs. Delta Soc.(chmn. nominating, devel. dr. cabinet), Renton, Wash.; mem. Dirs. Vol. in Agcys.(v.p. 1987-89), Internat. Delta Soc. (del., presenter, Monaco, France, 1989). Patentee: Peggy the Teaching Horse; author, co-author: articles and books in field. Active Darien (Conn.) Arts Coun. 1985—, Rep. Town Meeting, Darien, Conn., 1972-76, (Darien) Conn. Choraliers (social chmn., 1983-89), Maritime Ctr., Norwalk, Conn., 1988-90. Recipient fellowship Veterans Rehab. Assn., 1968-69, Alumnae scholarship Pi Beta Phi Frat., 1989. Mem. N.Am. Riding for the Handicapped (conf. presentation chmn. 1988-90), Am. Phys. Therapy Assn. (state rep. for sch.-based therapy, 1968-90), P. C. Users Club, Pi Beta Phi, Fairfield County Alumni Club (pres. 1976-78, treas. 1973-75, nat. officer 1974-77), Met. Golf Assn., Country Club Darien. Republican. Roman Catholic. Home: 17 Middlesex Rd Darien CT 06820

COPELAND, MAXINE, systems analyst, consultant; b. Jackson, Tenn., Aug. 5, 1956; d. Emma Louise (Randolph) Copeland. BBA in Fin., U. Wis., Milw., 1979. Sr. programmer analyst So. Co. Services, Atlanta, 1980-85; software systems cons. Am. Software, Inc., Atlanta, 1985-86; systems analyst RFC Intemediaries, Inc., Atlanta, 1986—; v.p. fin. Another Wear, Atlanta, 1986-88; cons. CAP Gemini Am., Atlanta, 1988; pres. Copeland Data Processing Solutions, Atlanta, 1988-89; sr. cons. Gen. Electric Consulting Svcs., Inc., Atlanta, 1989—. Mem. Black Data Processing Assocs. (treas. 1987-88). Home: 1192 Winston Dr Atlanta GA 30032

COPELAND, SUZANNE JOHNSON, real estate executive; b. Chgo., Aug. 1, 1943; d. John Berger and Eleanor (Dreger) Johnson; m. John Robert Copeland, Aug. 1, 1971 (div. June 1976). Assoc. French Lang. and Culture, Richland Coll., Dallas, 1974; BFA, Ill. Wesleyan U., Bloomington, 1965. Commercial artist Barney Donley Studio, Inc., Chgo., 1966-69; art dir. Levines Dept. Store, Dallas, 1970-74; creative dir. Titche-Goettinger, Inc., Dallas, 1974-78; catering mgr. Dunfey Hotel, Dallas, 1978-82; regional dir. corp. sales Lakeway/World of Tennis Resort, Austin, Tex., 1982-84; real estate sales assoc. Henry S. Miller, Dallas, 1984-86; v.p. Exclusive Properties Internat., Inc., Dallas, 1986—; cons. North Tex. Commn., Dallas, 1988. Acquisitions editor: Unser, An American Family Portrait, 1988. Mem. The Rep. Forum, Dallas, 1983-90; vol. Stars for Children, Dallas, 1988, Soc. for Prevention of Cruelty to Animals, Dallas, 1973-90. Mem. Nat. Assn. Realtors, Tex. Assn. Realtors, Greater Dallas Assn. Realtors (com. chmn., Summit award 1984, 85), North Tex. Arabian Horse Club (bd. dirs. 1975-76, Pres. award 1978), Tex. Horse Racing Assn., Dallas Zool. Soc., Humane Soc. Dallas County (v.p. 1973-74), Dallas Mus. Art League, Delta Phi Delta. Lutheran. Office: Exclusive Properties 5025 Capitol Ave Dallas TX 75206

COPELAND, TATIANA BRANDT, accountant, tax executive; b. Dresden, Germany; came to U.S., 1959, naturalized, 1967; d. Cyril Alexander and Maria (von Satin) Brandt; m. Gerret van Sweringen Copeland, May 12, 1979. BS summa cum laude, UCLA, 1964; MBA, U. Calif.-Berkeley, 1966. Sr. tax cons. Price Waterhouse & Co., Los Angeles, 1966-72; asst. tax mgr. Whittaker Corp., L.A., 1972-75; mgr. internat. dept. E. I. Du Pont de Nemours, Wilmington, Del., 1975-80; pres. Tebec Assocs. Ltd., Wilmington, 1980—; chief fin. officer Bouchaine Vineyards, Inc., Napa, Calif.; pres. The Wine & Spirit Co., Greenville, Del.; v.p. Rokeby Realty Co., Wilmington. Bd. dirs. Del. Symphony, Grand Opera House, Nat. Symphony Orch., Washington; presdl. appointee Adv. Com. for Trade Negotiations, 1982-87. Mem. Am. Inst. CPAs, Del. Soc. CPAs, Am. Woman's Soc. CPA's, Am. Soc. Women Accts., Internat. Fiscal Assn., Rodney Square Club (dir.), Phi Beta Kappa. Home: 175 Brecks Ln Wilmington DE 19807 Office: PO Box 3662 Wilmington DE 19807

COPELAND, TERRILYN DENISE, speech pathologist; b. Toledo, May 2, 1954. BS, Kent State U., 1976; MA, Bowling Green State U., 1980. Lic. speech pathologist, Ohio. Instr. Lucas County Bd. Mental Retardation, Toledo, 1977-78, speech pathologist, 1978-81; speech pathologist cons. Lucas County Children's Svcs. Bd., Toledo, 1985-86; speech pathologist Speech Lang. Svcs. Inc., Toledo, 1981-86, Upjohn Healthcare Svcs., Toledo, 1983-86, Toledo Mental Health Ctr., 1986-89, St. Francis Rehab. Hosp., Green Springs, Ohio, 1986-88, Flower Meml. Healthplex, Sylvania, Ohio, 1988-89; dir. speech pathology and audiology St. Francis Rehab. Hosp., Green Springs, Ohio, 1989—; mem. edn. subcom. St. Francis Rehab. Hosp., 1987. Mem. Jr. League, Toledo, 1989—. Mem. LWV (bd. dirs. 1990—), Am. Speech and Hearing Assn., Ohio Speech and Hearing Assn., Nat. Head Injury Found., Jr. Leauge, Aphasiology Assn. Ohio (N.W. rep. 1987—), Toledo Mus. Art, Delta Sigma Theta. Democrat. Methodist. Office: St Francis Rehab Hosp 401 N Broadway Green Springs OH 44836

COPELAND, WILMA T., teacher; b. Newton, Mass., Dec. 8, 1940; d. Willie Clifford and Lillie (Johnson) Thompson; m. James William Copeland, Sept. 14, 1963 (div. Oct. 1983); 1 child, James Kevin. BS, Alcorn State, 1963; MA, U. Cin., 1970. Tchr. Yalobusha County Schs., Coffeeville, Miss., 1963-65, Cin. Pub. Schs., 1965—. Membership capt. Cin. Art Mus., 1988-89; campaign chmn. Cin. Fine Arts Fund, Cin., 1990. Mem. Chums, Inc. (pres. Cin. chpt. 1982-86), Delta Kappa Gamma (corresponding sec. 1984-86), Delta Sigma Theta (chaplain 1987-89). Baptist. Home: 11651 Norbourne Dr #205 Cincinnati OH 45240 Office: Roselawn Condon Sch 7735 Greenland Pl Cincinnati OH 45237

COPESS, JOYCE TRAVIS, association executive; b. Lamar, Colo., Jan. 29, 1947; d. Morris Eugene and Mildred Marie (Neary) T.; m. Richard Dee Copess, Sept. 19, 1970. B.A., Colo. State U., 1969; postgrad. U. No. Colo., 1970-73, Ill. State U., 1976-81. Staff asst. in mgmt. communications State Farm Ins., Bloomington, Ill., 1969-81; staff v.p. edn. and communications Inst. Real Estate Mgmt. of Nat. Assn. Realtors, Chgo., 1981—; cons., lectr. in field. Mem. Pub. Relations Soc. Am., Internat. Bus. Communications, Women in Communications. Office: Inst Real Estate Mgmt 430 N Michigan Ave Chicago IL 60611

COPLAND, ELIZABETH ANN, radiologist, nuclear medicine specialist; b. Norman, Okla., Oct. 29, 1951; d. George Victor and Martha Rosalee (Shock) C. BS, Okla. State U., 1973; MD, U. Okla., 1977. Diplomate Am. Bd. Radiology, Am. Bd. Nuclear Medicine. Intern U. Okla. Health Scis. Ctr., Oklahoma City, 1977-78; resident in radiology Bapt. Med. Ctr., Oklahoma City, 1978-81; radiologist Okmulgee (Okla.) Meml. Hosp., 1981-83, Wichita Gen. Hosp., Wichita Falls, Tex., 1983-85; fellow in computed tomography and ultrasound William Beaumont Hosp., Royal Oak, Mich., 1985-86, resident in nuclear medicine, 1986-87; dir. nuclear medicine, radiologist St. Joseph Mercy Hosp., Ann Arbor, Mich., 1987—. Mem. Soc. Nuclear Medicine, Radiol. Soc. N.Am., Am. Coll. Radiology, Am. Assn. Women Radiologists. Presbyterian. Home: 3971 Waldenwood Ann Arbor MI 48105 Office: St Joseph Mercy Hosp 5301 E Huron River Dr Ann Arbor MI 48106

COPLAR, NANCY LOCKHART, banker, lawyer; b. Port Chester, N.Y., Mar. 21, 1958; d. Stephen Anthony and Hope Lockhart (Godde) C.; m. Leonard Recchione; 1 child, Lauren Anne. BS in Psychology, Fordham U., 1980; JD, U. Conn., 1983. Bar: N.Y. 1984. Corp. trust adminstr. Bank of Tokyo Trust Co., N.Y.C., 1984-85, trust officer, 1986-87, asst. v.p., 1987—. Office: Bank of Tokyo Trust Co 100 Broadway 3d Fl New York NY 10005

COPLEY, HELEN KINNEY, newspaper publisher; b. Cedar Rapids, Iowa, Nov. 28, 1922; d. Fred Everett and Margaret (Casey) Kinney; m. James S. Copley, Aug. 16, 1965 (dec.); 1 child, David Casey. Attended, Hunter Coll., N.Y.C., 1945. Assoc. The Copley Press, Inc., 1952—, chmn. exec. com., chmn. corp., dir., 1973—, chief exec. officer, sr. mgmt. bd., 1974—; chmn. bd. Copley News Svc., San Diego, 1973—; chmn. editorial bd. Union-Tribune Pub. Co., 1976—; pub. The San Diego Union and San Diego Tribune, 1973—. Chmn. bd., trustee James S. Copley Found., 1973—; life mem. Friends of Internat. Center, La Jolla, San Diego Hall of Sci., Scripps Meml. Hosp. Aux., Star of India Aux., Zool. Soc. San Diego; mem. San Diego Mus. Contemporary Art, La Jolla Town Coun. Inc., San Diego Soc. Natural History, YWCA; life patroness Makua Aux.; mem. YWCA; hon. chmn., bd. dirs. Washington Crossing Found.; trustee, mem. audit and compensation com. Howard Hughes Med. Inst.; chmn. San Diego Coun. Literacy. Mem. Inter Am. Press Assn., Am. Newspapers Pubs. Assn., Calif. Press Assn., Am. Soc. Newspaper Editors, Am. Press Inst., Calif. Newspaper Pubs. Assn. Greater L.A., Newspaper Advt. Bur. (bd. dirs.), Soc. Profl. Journalists, San Francisco Press Club, Sigma Delta Chi. Republican. Roman Catholic. Clubs: Aurora (Ill.) Country; Army and Navy (D.C.); San Diego Yacht, Univ., La Jolla Beach and Tennis, La Jolla Country, Kona Kai (San Diego). Office: Copley Press Inc 350 Camino de la Reina San Diego CA 92108

COPLON, DEE ANNE, controller; b. Silver Spring, Md., Oct. 18, 1963; d. Sidney and Doris (Diamond) C. BS, U. Md., 1985. CPA, Mo. Acct. Hillman, Glorioso & Co., Silver Spring, Md., 1985-87; CPA Lagrone, Taksey & Co., Rockville, Md., 1987-88; controller JTE, Inc., Cabin John, Md., 1988—. Mem. Constrn. Fin. Mgmt. Assn., Md. Assn. CPAs, Am. Inst. CPAs.

COPP, LAUREL ARCHER, nursing educator, administrator; b. Sioux Falls, S.D., 1931; m. John Dixon Copp. BS in Nursing Edn., Dakota Wesleyan U., 1956; M.Nursing, U. Pitts., 1960, Ph.D., 1967; P.H.S.M. cert., Harvard U. Bus. Sch., 1973. Assoc. prof. nursing Pa. State U., 1966-72, acting head nursing dept., 1971-72; chief nursing research VA Central Office, Washington, 1972-75; prof., dean Sch. of Nursing U. N.C., Chapel Hill, 1975—; vis. prof. Georgetown U., Washington, 1974-75, U. Tex.-Arlington, summer 1982; lectr. in field. Editor: The Patient Experiencing Pain, 2d edit., 1981, Recent Advances in Nursing: Care of the Aging, 1981, Recent Advanced in Nursing: Perspectives in Pain, 1985; editorial bd. Nursing and Health Care; overseas adviser Jour. Advanced Nursing; editor Jour. Profl. Nursing, 1988—; contbr. articles to profl. jours., chpts. to books. Recipient commendation VA, 1975, Disting. Alumni award Dakota Wesleyan U., 1982, U. Pitts., 1982. Fellow Am. Acad. Nursing; mem. Am. Assn. Colls. Nursing, Am. Nurses Assn., Nat. League for Nursing, Va./Carolinas Doctoral Consortium, N.C. Council Baccalaureate Deans. Home: 107 Ledge Ln Chapel Hill NC 27514 Office: U NC Chapel Hill Sch Nursing CB# 7460 107 Carrington Hall Chapel Hill NC 27599

COPPEDGE, CHRISTY, hotel manager; b. Columbia, Tenn., Oct. 26, 1955; d. John Fletcher and Frances Allen (Anderson) C. BS in Food Adminstrn., U. Tenn., 1977. Front desk clk. Opryland Hotel, Nashville, 1977-78; asst. mgr. Capt. D's Seafood, Kingsport, Tenn., 1978-80, Clinton Seafood, Knoxville, Tenn., 1980-84; mgr. concourse ops. Dobbs Houses-Hartsfield, Atlanta, 1984-85; mgr. Courtyard by Marriott, Atlanta, 1985—. Active Epilepsy Found. Am., Knoxville, Atlanta, 1980—, Alliance Theater, Atlanta, 1988—. Mem. Nat. Assn. Female Execs., Planetary Soc., NOW. Republican. Methodist. Home: 3109 Woodlands Dr Smyrna GA 30080

COPPOLA, ALLISON MARIE, information resources company official; b. Yonkers, N.Y., Feb. 20, 1965; d. Frank James and Mary Lou (Balling) C. BA, Boston Coll., 1986; MBA, Babson Coll., 1989. Mktg. prodn. asst. Krupp Securities, Boston, 1986-87; mktg. rsch. asst. Chadwick Martin Bailey, Boston, 1985-86; indsl. liaison asst. MIT, Cambridge, 1987-88; assoc. project dir. Info. Resources, Inc., Darien, Conn., 1989—; psychology and social work cons., Stamford, Conn., 1989—. Vol. Lawrence Hosp., Bronxville, N.Y., 1980-82. Mem. Advt. Rsch. Found. Home: 421-D Hope St Stamford CT 06906 Office: Info Resources Inc 30 Old Kings Hwy S Darien CT 06820

COPPOLA, LENORA ELAINE DAVIS, civic worker; b. Miami Beach, Fla., Feb. 24, 1948; d. John Seymour Weston and Celia Borghild (Ronningen) Davis; m. Henry Nicholas Coppola, May 22, 1970. AA, U. Fla., 1967, BA in Math., 1969. Cert. math. and sci. tchr., Fla. Tchr. math. Palm Beach County Sch. Bd., West Palm Beach, Fla., 1975-83, math. tutor, 1974—; substitute tchr., Fla., Miss., Okla., Calif., 1969-74. 2d v.p. Palms West Hosp. Aux., Loxahatchee, Fla., 1986-87, 1st v.p., 1987-90, coord. charity fashion shows, 1988-90; corr. sec. Wellington (Fla.) Women's Club, 1986-87, pres., 1988-89, advisor, 1989-90; mem. fin. com. St. Peter's Meth. Ch., 1986—. Recipient cert. of appreciation Palms West Hosp. Aux., 1987, 89. Mem. AAUW, Mensa, Fla. Aero Club. Lutheran. Home: 12466 Quercus Ln Wellington West Palm Beach FL 33414

COPPOLA, NANCY WALTERS, writing consultant; b. Bridgeport, Conn., July 31, 1945; d. Harold and Doris Madelaine (Daine) Walters; m. Nicholas Frank Coppola, Sept. 8, 1973; children: Daine Nicholas, Katherine Ann. AAS, Fashion Inst. Tech., N.Y.C., 1965; BA, Simmons Coll., 1977; MA, Syracuse U., 1980, ArtsD, 1982. Mng. editor Parents' Mag. Enterprises, N.Y.C., 1968-72; account exec. William G. Hetherington, Newark, 1972-74; pvt. practice writing, 1974-78; instr. Syracuse (N.Y.) U., 1978-82; assoc. prof. N.J. Inst. Tech., Newark, 1982-87; writing cons., owner Nancy Walters Coppola Assocs., Mountain Lakes, N.J., 1987—; lectr. Seton Hall U. Tech. Writing Inst. for Coll. Eng. Tchrs., West Orange, N.J., 1984, coord., 1985. Author short stories appearing in various publs.; contbr. more than 100 articles to consumer, trade and specialty mags., 1974-87. Bd. dirs. Friends of Mountain Lakes Libr., 1987—; mem. Home and Sch. Assn., Recreation Commn. Named Outstanding Student Writer Boston Mag., 1977. Mem. LWV (chmn. membership Mountain Lakes chpt. 1989), Sigma Tau Delta. Republican. Roman Catholic.

COPPOLECHIA, YILLIAN CASTRO, college educator; b. Cuba, July 26, 1948; came to U.S., 1961.; AA, Miami-Dade Community Coll., 1968; BA in French and German Lang. and Lit., cum laude, U. Miami, Coral Gables, Fla., 1971, MA in French Lang. and Lit., 1973, EdD in Adminstn. Higher Edn., 1984; postgrad., Fla. Atlantic U., U. Miami, Barry U., 1976-79. Adj. instr. Wolfson Campus, Miami-Dade Community Coll., 1972-75, coordinator bilingual program, 1975-78, chmn. bilingual dept., 1978-79, founding assoc. dean Div. Bilingual Studies, now Interam. Ctr., 1979-84, acting dean adminstrn., 1984-85, dean for community and bus. relations, North Campus, 1985-86, exec. dir. Miami Book Fair Internat., Wolfson Campus, 1986-88; full prof. French and Spanish Miami-Dade Community Coll., 1988—; evaluator various colls. for Higher Edn. Commn. Middle States Assn. Colls. and Schs., 1980—; testifier on bilingual edn. State of Fla. Postsecondary Edn. Planning Commn, 1984; mem. planning coms., coordinator symposium various ednl. confs.; keynote speaker seminar Hispanic Orgn. Pvt. Entrepreneurs (Project HOPE), April, 1987; participant Leadership Miami, 1986. Mem. dropout prevention adv. council, participant bus. and industry subcom. Dade County Pub. Schs., 1984-86; appointed Hialeah Community Leaders Colloquia, 1985—; vol., mem. elderly services rev. panel, United Way Dade County, 1986-87. Named one of top ten Women of Yr. for 1978 Cuban Women's Club, Inc., 1978, one of Outstanding Miami-Dade Community Coll. adminstrs. U. Tex. Austin Community Coll. Leadership Program, 1985; recipient Cert. of Honor Student Congress Miami-Dade Community Coll., 1975-76, 78-79, Civic Leadership Cert. Miami Lions Club, 1978, Cert. of Honor Women's Com. of 100, 1978, commendation awards for ednl contbns. Mayor Met. Dade County, 1977, Mayor of City of Miami, 1977, plaque for dedicated service Miami-Dade Community Coll., 1985; grantee Fund for Improvement Postsecondary Edn., 1984-85. Mem. Am. Council for the Arts, Latin Bus. and Profl. Women's Club (bd. dirs., bus. sec. 1987-88), Coalition of Hispanic Am. Women (bd. dirs., mem. various coms 1987-88, plaque award 1987), Fla. Assn. Community Colls., Nat. Council Instructional Adminstrs., Nat. Assn. Bilingual Edn., Fla. Coalition Hispanic Educators, Latin Bus. and Profl. Women (pres. 1989-90). Office: Miami-Dade Community Coll 300 NE 2 Ave Miami FL 33132

COPPOTELLI, H. CATHERINA, psychologist, consultant; b. Goslar, Fed. Republic Germany, Oct. 15, 1944; came to U.S., 1956; d. Otto H. and Paula A. (Kullmann) Arndt; m. Frederic Coppotelli, Aug. 21, 1965 (div. 1988); 1 child, Constantine. BA, New Coll., 1975; MA, Duke U., 1981, PhD, 1983. Lic. psychologist. Asst. prof. New Coll., Sarasota, Fla., 1979; resident in psychology VA, Tampa, Fla., 1983-84; psychologist Byron, Harless, Reid & Assocs., Jacksonville, Fla., 1984-86; pvt. practice Jacksonville, Fla., 1986—; adj. prof. Jacksonville (Fla.) U., 1987, U. North Fla., Jacksonville, 1987-90; nat. speaker for AMA, Pub. Rels. Soc. Am., Vol. The Nat. Orgn., Jacksonville, 1985—; clin. dir. Critical Incident Stress Debriefing Program of N.E. Fla., Jacksonville, Fla., 1989—. Author: Negotiating for Public Relations Professionals, 1990; contbr. articles to profl. jours. Named finalist Vol. of Yr., Vol. Jacksonville, 1990. Mem. Am. Psychol. Assn., Fla. Psychol. Assn. (exec. coun. mem., mktg. chairperson). Office: 9432 Baymeadows Rd Ste 110 Jacksonville FL 32256

COPPS, SHEILA MAUREEN, Canadian legislator; b. Hamilton, Ont., Can., Nov. 27, 1952; d. Victor Kennedy and Geraldine (Guthro) C.; m. Richard Dennis Marrero, July 6, 1985; 1 child, Danelle Lauran Copps Marrero. BA in French, English with hons., U. Western Ont., London, 1970-74; postgrad., Université de Rouen, France, 1972-73, McMaster U., Hamilton, 1976-77. Reporter Ottawa Citizen, 1974-76, Hamilton Spectator, 1977; asst. Liberal Leader Stuart Smith, Hamilton, 1977-81; mem. legislative assembly Ont. Toronto, 1981-84; mem. House of Commons Ottawa, 1984—. Author: Nobody's Baby, 1986. Liberal. Roman Catholic. Office: House of Commons, Room 440C, Ottawa, ON Canada L8M 2P7*

COQUILLA, BEATRIZ HORDISTA, dermatologist, army officer; b. Antequera, Bohol, The Philippines, May 9, 1948; came to U.S., 1955; d. Agapito Morgia and Alfonsa (Hordista) C. BS, U. Santo Tomas, Manila, 1970, MD, 1974. Diplomate Am. Bd. Dermatology. Commd. lt. col. U.S. Army, 1979; intern Fitzsimons Army Med. Ctr., Aurora, Colo., 1979-80; gen. med. officer 125th Med. Detachment, Korea, 1980-81; gen. med. officer, phys. asst. preceptor, brigade surgeon Evans Army Hosp., Ft. Carson, Colo., 1981-82; resident in dermatology Brooke Army Med. Ctr., Ft. Sam Houston, Tex., 1982-85; chief dermatology Womack Army Community Hosp., Fayetteville, N.C., 1985-87, Gen. Leonard Wood Hosp., Ft. Leonard Wood, Mo., 1988; grad. Advanced Officers Course Acad. Health Scis., Ft. Sam Houston, 1987-88; assigned to U.S. Army-Baylor Health Adminstrn. Program, San Antonio, 1988—. Contbr. articles to med. jours. Fellow Am. Acad. Dermatology; mem. Am. Coll. Health Care Execs., Assn. Mil. Dermatologists, Tex. Dermatologic Soc., San Antonio Dermatologic Soc., Women's Dermatologic Soc., Tex. Hosp. Assn., Assn. U.S. Army, Assn. Mil. Surgeons, Fayetteville Bus. and Profl. Women, U.S. Army-Baylor U. Alumni Club, Sierra Club. Roman Catholic. Home: 8715 Carrington San Antonio TX 78239

CORAH, DEBORAH JEAN, respiratory therapist; b. Los Angeles, May 27, 1960; d. Ronald Bruce and Dorothy Jean (Meier) Dahlstrom; m. Paul Frank Corah, June 26, 1982. Student, Oreg. State U., 1978-81; Assocs. of Respiratory Therapy, Mt. Hood Community Coll., 1986. Registered Respiratory Therapist, Oreg. Respiratory therapy asst. St. Vincent Med. Ctr., Portland, Oreg., 1981-83, respiratory therapy technician, 1983-86, cert. respiratory therapy technician, 1986-88; registered respiratory therapist St. Vincent Med. Ctr., Portland, 1988—; cert. respiratory therapy technician Portland Adventist Med. Ctr., Portland, 1986-88; respiratory therapy clin. instr. Mt. Hood Community Coll., Portland, 1987—. Mem. Am. Assn. Respiratory Care, Oreg. Edn. Assn. Republican. Roman Catholic.

CORATO, WENDI CHERYL, advertising and public relations executive; b. Irvington, N.J., Oct. 16, 1958; d. William Wallace and Barbara Jayne (Moore) Friberger; m. Louis C. Corato, Oct. 5, 1986. Sales training asst. CIBA Geigy Corp., Summit, N.J., 1977-80; pub. affairs specialist Westinghouse Broadcasting Co., N.Y.C., 1980-85, mgr., corp. communication, 1985-87; dir., advt., pub. rels. Degnan Boyle Realtors, Livingston, N.J. Office: Degnan Boyle Realtors 50 E Mt Pleasant Ave Livingston NJ 07039

CORAY, STEPHANIE MARY, nurse, career development officer; b. Crosby, Eng., May 17, 1938; d. Harold Joseph and Joan Hilda (Beer) McCann; m. Stephen A. Coray, (div. 1976); 1 child, Patrick Kael. RN, Queen of Angels Sch. of Nursing, 1959; BA, Calif. State U., Northridge, 1966; MBA, Pepperdine U., 1973. RN, Calif. Nurse pvt. physician, Oxnard, Calif., 1959-63, Oxnard Elem. Sch. Dist., 1963-71; employee devel. specialist Pacific Missile Test Ctr., Point Mugu, Calif., 1973-82, head career devel. div., 1982-87, orgn. devel. program mgr., 1987-89; dep. dir. regional tng. ctr. U.S. Office of Personnel Mgmt., San Francisco, 1989—; gen. ptnr. Achievement Inst. for Women, Oxnard, 1976-79; exec. chair Ventura County Combined Fed. Campaign, Point Mugu, 1985-87. Named Outstanding Woman of Yr., Bus. and Profl. Womens Club, 1977; recipient Chairperson's and Leadership awards Combined Fed. Campaign, 1985, 86. Mem. Am. Soc. Tng. and Devel., Am. Mgmt. Assn., Internat. Personnel Mgmt. Assn.

CORBETT, CAROLYN SUSANNE, hospital administrator, nurse; b. Springfield, Mass., July 3, 1951; d. Harold John and Shirley Jean (Clark) C. Diploma in nursing, Jewish Hosp. Sch. Nursing, 1976; BSN, St. Louis U., 1979, MSN, 1986; Cert. in Nursing Adminstrn. Advanced. RN, Mo., Pa. Staff nurse St. Louis Children's Hosp., 1976-78, patient care mgr., 1978-85, staff specialist psychiatry dept., 1985-86; spl. projects profl., nursing dept. Jewish Hosp., 1986-87; asst. v.p. nursing Robert Packer Hosp., Sayre, Pa., 1987-89, v.p. hosp., 1989—. Mem. task force N.Y. AIDS Policy Group, Binghampton, N.Y., 1988-89; bd. dirs. ARC, Waverly, N.Y., 1989—; mem. adv. coun. bd. for nursing edn. Elmira (N.Y.) Coll., 1990; mem. adv. coun. Broome Community Coll., N.Y., 1990—. Mem. Am. Orgn. Nurse Execs. (co-chair VHA-Pa. task force), Am. Nurses Assn., Nat. League for Nursing, Pa. League for Nursing (chmn. area III, mem. nominating com.), Sigma Theta Tau. Office: Robert Packer Hosp Guthrie Med Ctr Sayre PA 18840

CORBETT, IDNA MARITZA, university program director; b. San Pedro Sula, Honduras, Oct. 26, 1960; arrived in U.S., 1986; d. Samuel and Adaljitza Julieta (Rivera) Castellon; m. Robert James Corbett, June 17, 1986. BA, Goshen Coll., 1980; MA, Mich. State U., 1983; postgrad., Temple U., 1988—. Cons. Mktg. Ctr., San Pedro Sula, Honduras, 1982; tchr. Summer Hill Sch., Tegucigalpa, Honduras, 1982-83; prof., dept. head U. Pedagógica Nat., Tegucigalpa, Honduras, 1982-86; guidance counselor Escuela Internat. Sampedrana, San Pedra Sula, Honduras, 1983-86; tchr. Westtown (Pa.) Sch., 1986-87; instr. Messiah Coll., Phila., 1987-89; counseling coord. Temple U., Phila., 1988-89, program dir., 1989—. Youth communications coord. Ptnrs. of the Ams., San Pedro Sula, 1985-86. Mem. Pa. Assn. Ednl. Opportunities Program (sec. 1990—), Assn. Supervision and Curriculum Devel., Am. Assn. Counseling & Devel., Mid-Ea. Assn. Ednl. Opportunity Program Pers. Methodist. Home: Westtown Sch Westtown Rd Westtown PA 19395

CORBETT, JOAN DUFNER, insurance company executive; b. St. Louis, Feb. 4, 1928; d. Arthur Edmond and Cecelia (Higgins) Dufner; m. Jerome Corbett, Feb. 13, 1955; children: Kelly Corbett Danis, Dufner. BS, Webster Coll., 1950; postgrad., St. Louis U., 1950. Ins. producer, v.p. Dufner Corbett, Inc., 1990—. Home: One French St Hardin IL 62047

CORBETT, LORRAINE T., economic research executive; b. N.Y.C., Mar. 12, 1954; d. Walter George and Margaret Mary (O'Leary) C. AA, Bronx Community Coll., 1975; BA in Art, Lehman Coll., 1977; postgrad., Mercy, 1986—. Graphic artist Smilen & Safian Inc., N.Y.C., 1976—, statistical clk., 1977—, research asst., 1978—, research supr., 1979—, mgr., 1982; v.p. Safian Investment Research, N.Y.C., 1985—. Democrat. Roman Catholic. Home: 67 Kincaid Dr Yonkers NY 10710 Office: Safian Investment Rsch 709 Westchester Ave White Plains NY 10604

CORBETT, SUZANNE ELAINE, small business owner, marketing executive, food professional; b. St. Louis, Jan. 23, 1953; d. George Edward and Opal Laverne (Duncan) Traxel; m. James Joseph Corbett, Jr., July 17, 1970; 1 child, James J. III. Student, St. Louis Community Coll., 1970-71; cert., U. Mo., 1983. Cert. culinary profl., Nat. Inst. Food Svc. Industry, 1984, Internat. Assn. Culinary Profls., 1988; cert. tchr. vocat. home econs., food svc., Mo. Tchr. Inst. Continuing Edn. St. Louis Community Coll., 1976—; tchr. community edn. Lindbergh Sch. Dist. Pub. Schs., St. Louis, 1983-89; confectioner/caterer Suzanne Corbett Seasonal Confections, St. Louis, 1977-84; test baker Fleishman's Yeast, St. Louis, 1983; food stylist St. Louis, 1980—; rsch. cons./food mktg. and rsch. food/product history Suzanne Corbett/Culinary Concepts Inc., St. Louis, 1988—; food historian/folk lorist St. Louis County Parks and Recreation, Mo. Hist. Soc., 1978—, St. Louis Art Mus., 1988—, Colonial Dames Am., 1989—; food media trainer Internat. Assn. Culinary Profls., 1990; lectr. in field. food writer/cook book editor 1980—; contbg. author: Bread Winners, Breadwinners Too!; editor: Blue Owl Cookbook, 1989; author: Cowpuncher's Provision, 1988, River Fare, 1990. Folklife grantee, Ralston Purina, 1989. Mem. Mo. Press Women (v.p. 1990—, communication award 1989), Women in Communications (bd. dirs. 1988—, communication award 1989), Women's Commerce Assn. (bd. dirs. 1990—), St. Louis Regional Commerce & Growth Assn. (exec. com., event chmn. 1989-90), Victorian Soc. Am., James Beard Found. (charter mem.), Food Mktg. Communicators (charter mem.), Am. Inst. Wine and Food (Chgo. chpt.), Internat. Assn. Culinary Profls. (cert., culinary hist. Boston and Ann Arbor), Press Club St. Louis, Nat. Fedn. Press Women (Communication and Writing awards), Nat. Assn. Women Bus. Owners, Nat. Trust for Hist. Preservation, St. Louis Culinary Soc. (foodways com.) Order Eastern Star. Republican. Roman Catholic. Home: 5850 Pebble Oak Saint Louis MO 63128 Office: 5850 Pebble Oak Saint Louis MO 63128

CORBIN, CHRISTINE MARIE, health facility human resources administrator; b. St. Louis, Oct. 10, 1947; d. Norbert and Berenice (Openlander) Ortwerth; 1 child, Myles. Diploma, St. John's Mercy Sch. Nursing, St. Louis, 1968; BA, Webster U., 1981, postgrad., 1982—. Cert. in ACLS. Instr. insvc. edn. Jewish Hosp., St. Louis, 1972-73; coord. emergency med. svcs. St. Anthony's Med. Ctr., St. Louis, 1975-79; head nurse Barnes St. Peter's (Mo.) Hosp., St. Louis, 1980; dir. employment and recruitment Barnes Hosp., St. Louis, 1980-90; dir. pers. St. Joseph Hosp., Kirkwood, Mo., 1990—. Editorial cons. RN Mag., 1982-83; poetry pub. Great Poems of the Western World, 1989, American Poetry Anthology. Mem. Nat. Assn. Health Care Recruiters (rep. State of Mo.), Employment Mgmt. Assn., Soc. for Human Resource Mgmt., Human Resources Mgmt. Assn., Am. Soc. for Healthcare Human Resources Adminstrn., Soc. Nursing Profls. Home: 2410 Hidden Meadow Ln Ballwin MO 63021

CORBIN, KRESTINE MARGARET, manufacturing company executive, fashion designer, columnist; b. Reno, Apr. 24, 1937; d. Lawrence Albert and Judie Ellen (Johnston) Dickinson; m. Lee D. Corbin, May 16, 1959 (div. 1982); children: Michelle Marie, Sheri Karin. BS, U. Calif., Davis, 1958. Asst. prof. Bauder Coll., Sacramento, 1974—; columnist Sacramento Bee, 1976-81; owner Creative Sewing Co., Sacramento, 1976—; pres., chief exec. officer Sierra Machinery Inc., Sparks, Nev., 1984, also bd. dirs.; nat. sales and promotion mgr. Westwood Retail Fabrics, N.Y.C., 1985—; bd. dirs. F.S.C. Mgmt. Svcs. Ltd., Sierra Pacific Resources, Land of Sierras, NEWTRAC, Falcon Air Cargo Svcs., No. Internat. Bank, England, Exim Factors, Ltd.; mem. Meadow Community Coll. Found. Bd.; cons. in field. Author: Suede Fabric Sewing Guide, 1973, Creative Sewing Book, 1978, (audio-visual) Fashions in the Making, 1974; producer: (nat. buyers show) Cream of the Cream Collections, 1978—, Style is What You Make It!, 1978-83. Mem. found. bd. TrucKee M. Community Coll. Named Exporter of Yr. State of Nev., 1989. Mem. Crocker Art Gallery Assn., 1960-78, Rep. Election Com., Sacramento, 1964, 68; apptd. by Gov. of Nev. to Internat. Program Adv. Com. Mem. Home Economists in Bus., Am. Home Econs. Assn., Internat. Fashion Group, Women's Fashion Fabrics Assn., Nat. Machine Tool Builders Assn. (mem. internat. export com.), Nat. Fluid Power Assn., Nev. World Trade Coun. (bd. dir.), Omicron Nu. Office: Sierra Machinery Inc 1651 Glendale Rd Sparks NV 89431 also: PO Box 435 Reno NV 89504

CORBIN, RORI COOPER, therapeutic recreation specialist, educator, consultant; b. N.Y.C., July 30, 1951; d. Charles Kneeland and Rose Elizabeth (Maggio) Cooper; m. William Ogden Corbin Jr., Apr. 19, 1980; children: Drew Cooper, Laurel Foxworth, Joannah, J. Hope. BA, SUNY, Purchase, 1973; MA, NYU, 1980. Cert. therapeutic recreation specialist. Sr. recreation therapist N.Y. State Letchworth, Thiells, 1975-86; cons. Corbin & Corbin Cons., Monroe, N.Y., 1986-88; dir. optifast program Our Lady Mercy Med. Ctr., Bronx, N.Y., 1988—; cons. behaviorist Optifast program Nyack (N.Y.) Hosp.; cons. behaviorist, researcher joint obesity study U. Pa. and Sandoz Pharms.; mem. guest faculty Keane Coll., N.J., 1981; instr., trainer N.Y. Office Mental Retardation/Devel. Disabilities, 1981-82. Writer, editor newsletter: The Fourth "r", 1983-85; contbr. weekly column The Tree of Life Bronx Times Reporter, 1990—. N.Y. State grantee, 1979-80. Mem. NAFE, Nat. Recreation and Parks Assn., N.Y. State Recreation and Parks Soc., Internat. Platform Assn. Republican. Roman Catholic. Avocations: gardening, bicycling, reading, camping. Home and Office: 61 Pine Tree Rd Monroe NY 10950

CORBIN, ROSEMARY MAC GOWAN, councilmember; b. Santa Cruz, Calif., Apr. 3, 1940; d. Frederick Patrick and Lorena Maude (Parr) MacGowan; m. Douglas Tenny Corbin, Apr. 6, 1968; children: Jeffrey, Diana. BA, San Francisco State U., 1961; MLS, U. Calif., Berkeley, 1966. Libr. Stanford (Calif.) U., 1966-68, Richmond (Calif.) Pub. Libr., 1968-69, Kaiser Found. Health Plan, Oakland, Calif., 1976-81, San Francisco Pub. Libr., 1981-82, U. Calif., Berkeley, 1982-83; elected mem. coun. City of Richmond, 1985—, vice mayor, 1986-87; mem. Solid Waste Mgmt. Authority, 1985—, Contra Costa Hazardous Materials Commn., Martinez, Calif., 1987—, San Francisco Bay Conservation and Devel. Commn., 1987—. Contbr. articles to profl. publs. Pres. Richmond PTA, 1979-80; dist. mgr. fundraising event KQED-TV, San Francisco, 1975-77; pres. Bancroft Nursery Sch., Berkeley, 1974-76. Mem. Calif. Libr. Assn., Local Govt. Commn., League Calif. Cities, Nat. League Cities, LWV,, Women's Forum West Contra Costa County, Nat. Women's Polit. Caucus. Democrat. Home: 114 Crest Ave Richmond CA 94801 Office: Richmond City Hall 2600 Barrett Ave Richmond CA 94804

CORBOY, MICHELE LARUE, publishing executive; b. Shreveport, La., May 6, 1952; d. Robert Gerald and Gail (Burke) LaRue; m. Robert Philip Corboy, June 20, 1988; children: Michael, Monica, Richard, Wendy. Studied with Patricia Stevens, Honolulu. Model Wild Wahine Swimwear, Honolulu; mgr. Memory Lane Computers, Honolulu, Tech. Svcs., Inc., Honolulu; desktop pub. Profl. Image, Inc., Honolulu. Mem. NAFE, Profl. Women's Network. Address: 125 Merchant St Honolulu HI 96813

CORCORAN, CLARE MARY, college dean; b. Cambridge, Mass., Dec. 5, 1929; d. Theodald Splaine and Anna Theresa (Donovan) C. B.S. in Edn., Framingham State Tchrs. Coll., 1951; Ed.M., Boston U., 1955, Ed.D., 1961; postgrad. Oxford U., 1973. Tchr. pub. schs., Lexington, Mass., 1951-55; tchr. pub. schs., Winchester, Mass., 1955-56, reading cons., 1956-61, personnel dir., 1977-79, prin., 1961-85; asst. dean Grad. Sch., Lesley Coll., Cambridge, Mass., 1985—, coord. ednl. certification, 1985, prof., 1988—; lectr. Tufts U., Medford, Mass., 1963-68, Regis Coll., Weston, Mass., 1971; asst. prof. Boston Coll., 1968-69, co dir. reading clinic, 1966, 68, 69. Trustee scholarship com. Vinson Owen Sch., Winchester, 1979—. Recipient Outstanding Alumni award State Tchrs. Coll. Framingham, 1961; Clare M. Corcoran scholar Vinson Owen Sch., 1985—. Mem. Internat. Reading Assn., New Eng. Reading Assn. (bd. dirs., sec. 1959-62), Pi Lambda Theta, Delta Kappa Gamma. Roman Catholic. Home: 35 Richardson Rd Belmont MA 02178 Office: Lesley Coll 29 Everett St Cambridge MA 02138

CORCORAN, MARY BARBARA, language educator; b. Pasadena, Calif., May 22, 1924; d. George Ernest Morrison and Ina Pearl (Thomas) Phippen; m. James Leonard Corcoran, Dec. 22, 1956; children: Ann Morrison, Elizabeth Phippen DedGroodt. BA, Wellesley Coll., 1946; MA, Radcliffe Coll., 1949; postgrad., U. Munich, 1949-50; PhD, Bryn Mawr Coll., 1958. Translator U.S. War Dept., Nuremberg, Fed. Republic of Germany, 1946-47; prof. German Vassar Coll., Poughkeepsie, N.Y., from 1953, 1977-90; part-time instr. Wellesley (Mass.) Coll., 1947-48. Translator: The Romantic Fairy Tale, 1964. Mem. Am. Assn. Tchrs. German, AAUP, MLA. Mem. United Ch. of Christ. Home: 11 Overlook Rd Poughkeepsie NY 12603

CORCORAN, MAUREEN ELIZABETH, lawyer; b. Iowa City, Feb. 4, 1944; d. Joseph and Velma (Tobin) C. BA in English with honors, U. Iowa, 1966, MA in English, 1967; JD, U. Calif., San Francisco, 1979. Bar: Calif. 1979, D.C. 1988, U.S. Ct. Appeals (9th cir.), 1979, U.S. Dist. Ct. (no. dist.) Calif., 1979, U.S. Dist. Ct. (cen. dist.) Calif., 1979, U.S. Ct. Appeals (D.C. cir.) 1983. Assoc. Hassard Bonnington Rogers & Huber, San Francisco, 1979-81; spl. asst. to gen. counsel HHS, Washington, 1981-83; assoc. Weissburg & Aronson, San Francisco, 1983-84; gen. counsel U.S. Dept. Edn., Washington, 1984-86; of counsel Pillsbury, Madison & Sutro, San Francisco, 1987—; chair Managed Health Care Conf., 1989; mem. AIDS adv. com. Ctrs. for Disease Control, 1989—; speaker health law mtgs. Editorial adv. bd.: Jour. of Compensation and Benefits; contbr. articles on health law to profl. jours. Mem. U.S. delegation to 1985 World Conf. to Review and Appraise Achievements of UN Decade for Women, Nairobi, Kenya, 1985; mem. Adminstrv. Conf. U.S., Washington, 1985. Mem. ABA (Forum on Healthcare Law), Calif. State Bar Assn., Nat. Health Lawyers Assn., Calif. Soc. Healthcare Attys. Office: Pillsbury Madison & Sutro 225 Bush St San Francisco CA 94104

CORCORAN-GADSBY, BARBARA ANN, financial planner, small business owner, consultant; b. Springfield, Mass., Dec. 24, 1945; d. Edward F. and Margaret E. (Price) Corcoran; m. Thomas F. Tiedgen, Apr. 27, 1968 (div. June 1975); m. G. Lawrence Gadsby Jr., May 5, 1978. AA, Vt. Coll., Montpelier, 1965. CLU; chartered fin. cons. Adminstrv. asst. Mass. Mut. Life Co., Springfield and Hartford, Conn., 1965-75; office mgr. Am. Nat. Life Ins. Co., Springfield, 1976; traveling trainee Conn. Gen. Life Ins. Co., Bloomfield, 1976; sales rep. Conn. Gen. Life Ins. Co., Springfield, 1976-77; dir. mktg. NN Life Ins. Services, Johnston, R.I., 1978-80; sales rep. New Eng. Mut. Life Co., Providence, 1980-82; pvt. practice fin. planner Southeastern New Eng. Fin. Group, Newport, R.I., 1982—; pres., founder Heritage Prodns., Ltd., Newport, R.I., 1988—; cons. Northwestern Mut. Life Ins. Co., Providence, 1986-87; co-founder, bd. dirs. Career Connections Inc. Bd. dirs. YWCA of Greater R.I. Mem. Am. Soc. of CLU's and Chartered Fin. Cons. (pres. 1989—), Nat. Assn. Life Underwriters, R.I. Life Underwriters, Newport County Women's Network (co-founder), R.I. Women's Career Network. Republican. Episcopalian. Home: 33 Bonniefield Dr Tiverton RI 02878 Office: Southeastern New Eng Fin Group 1341 W Main Rd Middletown RI 02840

CORDANO, VIRA ELDA, freelance writer; b. Eugene, Oreg., Sept. 21, 1918; d. Charles A. Brown and Mary Berthina (Wood) Brown; m. Ceasar Anthony Cordano, Apr. 15, 1944; 1 child, Joan Frances. AA, American River Coll., 1979; BA, Calif. State U., Sacramento, 1981; Masters, Calif. State U., 1981. Legal asst., legis. liason Calif. State Tchrs. Assn., Sacramento, 1964-73, notary pub., Italian translator, 1970-73; self employed freelance writer Shingle Springs, Calif., 1973--; mem. contbr. Oreg. Historical Soc., Sons and Daughters Oreg. Pioneers. Regent DAR, 1986, 87, librarian El Dorado chpt., 1987-89. Mem. Nat. League Am. Penwomen, Sacramento Symphony League, El Dorado Arts Coun. Roman Catholic. Home: 3150 Ponderosa Rd Shingle Springs CA 95682

CORDAY, BARBARA, television producer and executive; b. N.Y.C., Oct. 15, 1944; m. Barney Rozenzweig. V.p. for comedy series devel. ABC-TV, 1982-84; pres. Columbia Pictures TV, Burbank, Calif., 1984-87; exec. v.p. for prime-time programs CBS Entertainment, L.A., 1988-90. Co-creator TV series Cagney and Lacey. *

CORDEIRO, MARGARET C., office manager; b. Fall River, Mass., Oct. 22, 1945; d. Frank and Noella M. (Cavanaugh) C.; div. Diploma with top honors, Conn. Bus. Inst., 1984; student, Sacred Heart U., Bridgeport, Conn., 1988-89. Sec. C & C Fence Co., Derby, Conn., 1964-70; sec., bookkeeper Mark Hardware Store, Ansonia, Conn., 1970-72; bookkeeper Valley Work Ctr., Ansonia, 1984-86; office mgr., instr. clerical skills Valley Mental Health Ctr., Ansonia, 1986-90, mgmt. info. systems asst., 1990—. Outreach vol. VITA, Literacy Vols. Am. Mem. NAFE. Jehovah's Witness. Office: Valley Mental Health Ctr 435 E Main St Ansonia CT 06401

CORDER, BILLIE FARMER, clinical psychologist, artist; b. Dundee, Miss., Sept. 12, 1934; d. Lee Kennith and Jimmy Louise (Hawkins) Farmer; B.S., Memphis State U., 1957; M.A., Vanderbilt U., 1959; Ed.D., U. Ky., 1966; student Memphis Acad. Art, 1959, Sch. Design, N.C. State U., 1971-75; m. Robert Floyd Corder, July 11, 1961. Intern, U. Tenn. Sch. Medicine, Memphis, 1959; staff psychologist Eastern State Hosp., Lexington, Ky., 1960-65, Child Guidance Clinic, Lexington, 1965-67; asst. prof. psychology Inter-Am. U., P.R., 1967-68; dir. psychology adolescent day care Area Community Mental Health Center, Washington, 1968-70; dir. psychol. services Alcoholic Rehab. Center, Butner, N.C., 1970-71; co-dir. psychol. services in child psychiatry Dix Hosp., Raleigh, N.C., 1971—; mem. adv. bd. Raleigh Developmental Evaluation Clinic, 1976—; adj. faculty psychology dept. N.C. State U., Raleigh, 1975—, U. N.C. Sch. Medicine, 1975—. Mem. Wake County Youth Adv. Bd., 1979-80; mem. adv. com. Raleigh Arts Commn.; bd. dirs. Haven House for Children, Nazareth House for Children. Recipient best research award N.C. Dept. Mental Health, 1965, cert. of appreciation Washington Tchrs. Assn., 1969; numerous awards for art, including Purchase award N.C. Mus. Art, 1976, awards N.C. Watercolor Soc., 1978, 79; numerous research grants. Mem. Am. Psychol. Assn., Southeastern Psychol. Assn., N.C. Psychol. Assn., Am. Assn. Psychiat. Services for Children (program chmn. 1976-77), Raleigh Artists Guild, Raleigh Fine Arts Soc., N.C. Art Soc., Women's Equity Action League. N.C. Women's Polit. Caucus, Durham Artists Guild, N.C. Watercolor Soc. (v.p.), AAUW. Democrat. Baptist. Club: Raleigh Racquet. Contbr. articles to profl. jours.; dir. editorial bd. N.C. Jour. Mental Health, 1974—; adj. editorial rev. bd. Hosp. and Community Psychiatry, Quar. Jour. Studies on Alcohol. Office: Child Psychiatry Clinic Dix Hospital Raleigh NC 27611

CORDERY, SARA BROWN, educator; b. Chester, S.C., Feb. 4, 1920; d. William and Fannie (Halsey) Brown; m. Albert Theodore Cordery, Mar. 30, 1947. BS, S.C. State U., 1942; MA, Columbia U., 1946, EdD, 1957. Statis. analyst Quartermaster Corps, U.S. Army, Washington, 1942-45; tchr., div. chairperson, prof., registrar, dir. alumni affairs, dir. Centennial Celebration, dir. instnl. self-study, assoc. dir. instnl. devel., spl. asst. to pres. Barber-Scotia Coll., Concord, N.C., 1947-73; prof. Sch. Bus. and Mgmt., Morgan State U., Balt., assoc. dean, 1976-85, acting dean, 1980-82; cons. Walkers and Monroe, Inc. Mem. youth motivation task force Nat. Alliance of Bus.; chair nat. com. of self-devel. United Presbyn. Ch., U.S., 1979-84; pres. Balt. Presbyterial, 1985-88; moderator presbytery of Balt. Presbyn. Ch. Mem. Am. Bus. Communication Assn., Assn. Tchr. Educators, Assn. Supervision and Curriculum Devel., AAUP, Nat. Bus. Edn. Assn., Eastern Bus. Tchrs. Assn., Fedn. Negro Women (pres. Concord, N.C.), United Presbyn. Women, Delta Sigma Theta, Sponsors Club (Balt.). Home: 2718 Meredith Rd White Hall MD 21161

CORDES, DORIS KAISER, volunteer, educator; b. Freeport, Ill., Jan. 21, 1934; d. Clyde C. and Kathryn (Folgate) Kaiser; m. A. Wallace Cordes, June 9, 1956; children: David W., Janet L., Karen L., Roger D. BS, No. Ill. U., 1956; MEd, U. Ill., Urbana, 1959. Cert. tchr., adult edn., Ill. Elem. tchr. St. Joseph (Ill.) Grade Sch., 1956-58; tchr. Ogden (Ill.) High Sch., 1958-59; advisor U. Ark. Mortar Bd., Fayetteville, 1984—. Vol. Sr. Ctr., local health clinic, Fayetteville, 1988—; devel. child care assoc. Head Start, Fayetteville, 1968-78; mem. various offices LWV. Mem. AAUW, Univ. Women's Club (v.p. Fayetteville chpt. 1986, 1987-89). Methodist.

CORDES, MARY KENRICK, psychologist; b. Flint, Mich., Aug. 6, 1933; d. Charles Fay and Margaret Lydia (Mitchell) Kenrick; m. John Cordes, July 30, 1955 (dec. 1970); children: James Charles, Mari Kenrick Cordes. BA, Denison U., 1955; MA, Oakland U., 1969. Lic. psychologist, Mich. Rsch. asst. Lafayette Clinic, Detroit, 1968; sch. psychologist Roseville (Mich.) Community Schs., 1968—; assoc. Rochester (Mich.) Psychol. Clinic, 1970-82; mem. State Licensure Bd. of Psychology, Lansing, Mich., 1978-81, Spl. Edn. Adv. Com., Lansing, 1984-88. Vol. counselor Crossroads-St. Paul's Cathedral, Detroit, 1982—; singer Rochester Community Chorus, 1986—. Mem. Am. Psychol. Assn. (assoc.), Nat. Assn. Sch. Psychologists, Mich. Assn. Sch. Psychologists (regional bd. dirs. 1973-77, Outstanding State Psychologist 1979), Macomb County Psychol. Assocs. (pres. 1972-73). Home: 2452 Blockton Rochester MI 48306 Office: Roseville Schs 18975 Church St Roseville MI 48066

CORDINGLEY, MARY JEANETTE BOWLES (MRS. WILLIAM ANDREW CORDINGLEY), social worker, psychologist, artist; b. Des Moines, Jan. 1, 1918; d. William David and Florence (Spurrier) Bowles; m. William Andrew Cordingley, Mar. 17, 1942; children: Willima Andrew, Thomas Kent, Constance Louise. Student, Stephens Coll., 1936; BA, Carleton Coll., 1939; postgrad. U. Denver, 1944-45; MA in Psychiat. Social Work, U. Minn., 1948; grad. art student, 1963; MA in Counseling Psychology Pepperdine U. Co-pub. Univ. News, 1939-40; with U.S.O. Travelers Aid Service, 1942-44; mem. Jr. League, Des Moines, 1943, bd. dirs., sec. Mpls., 1951-56; clinic psychiat. social worker U. Minn. Hosp., 1947-48; social worker community service project neuropediatrics U. Minn., 1964-65; med. dir. med. sch. svc. Mont. Deaconess Hosp., 1970-74; instigator, pres. Original Pioneer Prints Notepaper Co.; paintings in variety of galleries and traveling shows; exhibited in numerous one man shows include Chas. Russell Gallery, Mont., Student Union U. Minn., Nat. Biennial League Am. Pen Women, 1968, 70, U. Mont., 1974, Mont. Traveling Exhibit, 1966-67, Mus. of the Rockies hist. show, 1976, Bergen Art Guild, 1976-78, U.S. Traveling Show, 1987-89, Russell Auction, 1977, Kessel Long Gallery, Scottsdale, Mon. Artist Exhibit-Gov.'s Mansion, 1990; graphic artist in metal etchings; therapist Mental Health Center, 1977-82. Organizer, Hazeltine Nat. Golf Club Womens Assn., 1962-64, I. & R. Ctr., 1967; pres. adv. bd. Mont. State U.; past mem. bd. dirs. United Way, Youth Guidance Home. Recipient various awards. Mem. Nat. Assn. Social Workers, State Arts Coun., Acad. Cert. Social Workers (art instr., traveling exhibit 1987-88), Ariz. Authors Assn., Ariz. Artists League, Ariz. Artists Guile. Co-author: Series on Mont. Instns. Home (winter): 7525 Gainey Ranch Rd #133 Scottsdale AZ 85258 Address (summer): 545 Lakeshore Dr Incline Village NV 89450

CORDOVA, KAREN SUE, fastener industry professional; b. Walsenburg, Colo., Nov. 1, 1951; d. Moses Efren and Rachel Linda (Martinez) C.; 1 child, Elizabeth Kathleen Riley. BA summa cum laude, U. Calif., Irvine, 1975, MBA, 1984. Dir. undergraduate scholarship program U. Calif., Irvine, 1975-77; salesperson Cordova Bolt, Buena Park, Calif., 1978-81; account rep. Unisys Corp., Irvine, 1984-88, Cordova Bolt, 1987—. Troop leader Girl Scouts U.S., Irvine, 1982-84; active Irvine Coordinating Com. for the Arts, 1984, Young Reps., Orange County, Calif., 1986-87. Mem. Los Angeles Fastener Assn., Assn. Computing Machinery, U. Calif. Irvine Grad. Sch. Mgmt. Alumni (bd. dirs. 1986-87), Phi Beta Kappa. Club: Contemporary (Newport Harbor Art Mus., Newport Beach, Calif.). Home: 5 Robinsong Irvine CA 92714 Office: Cordova Bolt 5601 Dolly Buena Park CA 90621

CORDOVA-SALINAS, MARIA ASUNCION, dentist; b. Punta Arenas, Magallanes, Chile, May 14, 1941; came to U.S., 1972; d. Miguel Cordova and Maria Asuncion Requena; m. Carlos F. Salinas, July 27, 1965; children: Carlos M., Claudio A., Lola. DDS, U. Chile, Santiago, 1965; DMD, U. S.C., 1986. From instr. to assoc. prof. medicine U. Chile Dept. Physiology, Valparaiso, 1965-72; postdoctoral fellow Johns Hopkins U., Balt., 1972-75; from instr. to asst. prof. medicine U. S.C. Dept. Physiology, Charleston, 1975-86; pvt. practice Charleston, 1987—; vis. scientist N.Y. Med. Coll., 1975. Contbr. articles to profl. jours. Coord. Amnesty Internat., U.S.A., Piccolo Spoleto, Neighborday, Charleston, S.C.; bd. dirs. Ptnrs. of Ams. Named Citizen of Honor, City of Mayaquez, P.R., 1984. Mem. Charleston Women's Network (pres. 1989—), S.C. Law Country Women's Coalition. Roman Catholic. Office: Maria A Cordova DMD 159 Wentworth St Charleston SC 29401

CORE, MARY CAROLYN W. PARSONS, radiologic technologist; b. Valparaiso, Fla., Dec. 8, 1949; d. Levi and Mary Etta (Elliott) Willey; m. Joel Kent Core, Aug. 3, 1979; 1 child, Candace W. Parsons. Student, Peninsula Gen. Hosp. Sch. Radiologic Tech., Salisbury, Md., 1969; student, U. Del., 1969-73, Del. Tech. Community Coll., 1973-79, St. Joseph's Coll., 1983-86; BSBA, St. Joseph's Coll., 1987. Technologist Peninsula Gen. Hosp., Salisbury, 1967-72; tech. dir. edn. Sch. Radiologic Tech., Salisbury, 1973-75; technologist Johns Hopkins Hosp., Salisbury, 1972-73, Nanticoke Meml. Hosp., Seaford, Del., 1975-79; adminstrv. chief technologist, imaging depts. Shady Grove Adventist Hosp., Rockville, Md., 1979-81; dir. dept. radiol. scis. Anne Arundel Diagnostics, Inc., Rockville, 1981—; chief ops. officer Anne Arundel MRI (Magnetic Resonance Imaging, Annapolis, Md., 1981—; chief exec. officer Anne Arundel Diagnostics, Inc. and Anne Arundel MRI, Annapolis, Md., 1981—. Mem. Cen. Md. coun. Girl Scouts U.S., Pres.'s award svc. team, 1989. Recipient twin awards YWCA, 1988. Mem. NAFE, Md. Soc. Radiologic Technologists (pres. 1980-81, sr. bd. mem. 1982-83, various awards including 1st Pl. Essay awards 1974, 76, 84, 87), Am. Hosp. Radiology Adminstrs. (v.p. 1984-85, chmn. by-laws com. 1984-85, statis. resources com. 1985-86), Am. Mgmt. Assn., Radiology Bus. Mgrs. Assn., Ea. Shore Dist. Radiologic Technologists (pres. 1976-78). Republican. Methodist. Home: 1907 Harcourt Ave Crofton MD 21114 Office: Franklin and Cathedral Sts Annapolis MD 21401

CORELL, BELLE OLIVER, civic worker, writer; b. Suffolk, Va., July 30, 1902; d. Samuel Columbus and Eureka (Ashburn) Oliver; m. James Wesley Simmons, Apr. 27, 1926 (div. Apr. 1929); children—Belle Oliver (Mrs. Wm. E. Traver II), John Oliver; m. Harold Clifford Hart, Oct. 15, 1934 (dec. July 1937); m. Archibald Gerald Corell, Nov. 2, 1974 (dec. Aug. 1980). Student Mary Washington Coll., Fredericksburg, Va., 1920-22; A.B., George Washington U., 1944. Tchr., Martha Washington Coll., Abingdon, Va., 1922-23, Harpers Ferry (W.Va.) High Sch., 1923-24, Hopewell (Va.) High Sch., 1924-26, 28-29; asst. prin., Tenacre and Wellesley, Mass., 1938-39; asst. state service officer Dept. Public Welfare, Richmond, Va., 1929-31; adminstrv. asst. Dept. Justice, Washington, 1931-33; sec. NRA, Fed. Emergency Relief Adminstrn., U.S. Govt., 1933-34; nat. def. WPB, Washington, 1940-44; exec. sec. woman's aux. Episcopal Diocese Mass., Boston, 1945-48; asso. John M. Hancock, Lehman Bros., N.Y.C., 1948-54. Pres. Boston chpt. U.D.C., 1945-47, 58-59, rec. sec. gen., 1955-57, mil. meml. awards com., 1959-62; pres., Wellesley Council Ch. Women, 1958-60; mem. bd. Northfield League, 1955-64; bd. dirs. Mass. N.E. Grenfell Assn.; sec. Belleair Beach Property Owners Assn., 1965-68, bd. dirs., 1981—; dir. Bellaire Beach Park Bd., 1978-79, bd. dirs., 1981—; dir. altar guild Calvary Episcopal Ch. Mem. DAR (regent Amos Mills chpt. Wellesley 1961-63), Mary Washington Coll. Alumnae Assn. (pres. 1941-44), AAUW, Belleair Beach Garden Club (pres. 1967-69), Federated Hills Garden Club (rec. sec. 1956, pres. 1961-62, sustaining mem.), Power Squadron of CAP. Episcopalian. Clubs: Bath (St. Petersburg Beach, Fla.); No. Lake George Yacht. Author: Footprints (history of the establishing in 1959 the United Daughters of the Confederacy award at the U.S. Air Force Acad. honoring and memorializing Lt. Gen. Claire L. Chennault for his exceptional contribution toward developing and strengthening the air power of the U.S.--awarded annually to a graduate cadet ranking in basic scis.). Address: 117 5th St Belleair Beach FL 34635

COREY, MELINDA ANN, writer, business owner; b. Balt., Apr. 18, 1957; d. John and Dorothy Marie (Malarik) C.; m. George Ochoa, Aug. 22, 1987. BA, U. Chgo., 1979, MA, 1982. Assoc. editor Macmillan Pub. Co., N.Y.C., 1983-86; editor Blue Cliff Editions, N.Y.C., 1986-88; sr. editor Media Projects, Inc., N.Y.C., 1988-89; instr. in writing, researcher N.Y. Pub. Libr., N.Y.C., 1988-89; co-owner Corey & Ochoa, Bklyn., 1988—; cons. Literacy Vols. of N.Y.C., 1987—, The Coll. Bd., N.Y.C., 1990—. Author: (with others) Official Couch Potato Cookbook, 1988, The Man in Lincoln's Nose, 1990, The Book of Answers, 1990, The Official Model Railroader's Catalogue, 1991; author, editor: The Thanksgiving Book, 1987. Democrat. Roman Catholic. Home and Office: 167 Nelson St Brooklyn NY 11231

COREY ARCHER, PAMELA, diplomat; b. L.A., May 2, 1940; d. George Raymond Corey Jr. and Katherine Elizabeth (Barnard) de la Chesnaye; children: Christopher Warren Archer, Jonathan Clark Archer. BA, Scripps Coll., 1962. Journalist Bangkok World Sunday Mag., 1969-70, Diplomatist Mag., Vientiane, Laos, 1971-73; advt. copywriter McCann-Erickson, Panama City, Panama, 1974-76; freelance film producer Buenos Aires, 1976-79; publicist Nat. Pub. Radio, Washington, 1980; internat. broadcaster U.S. Info. Agy., Washington, 1980-81, fgn. svc. officer, 1981—. Mem. Am. Fgn. Svc. Assn., NOW. Episcopalian.

CORK, LINDA KATHERINE, veterinary pathologist, educator; b. Texarkana, Tex., Dec. 14, 1936; d. Albert James and Martine Sessions (Buntyn) Collins; m. P.S. Cork Jr., Mar. 1955 (div. 1965); children: Robin E., Jerald W. BS, Tex. A&M U., 1969, DVM, 1970; PhD, Wash. State U., 1974. Diplomate Am. Coll. Vet. Pathologists. Fellow Wash. State U., Pullman, 1970-74; asst. prof. U. Ga., Athens, 1974-76; asst. prof. Johns Hopkins U., Balt., 1976-82, assoc. prof., 1982-88, assoc. dir. rsch. Alzheimer's Disease Rsch. Ctr., 1985—, prof., 1988—; coun. mem. NIH div. Rsch. Resources, Bethesda, Md., 1985-89; adv. bd. Registry Comparative Pathology, Bethesda. Grantee Nat. Inst. on Aging, 1985-89, Nat. Inst. Health, 1986-91, 86-93, 87-92. Mem. Inst. Medicine, Am. Assn. Neuropathologists (chmn. June 1988), Am. Assn. Pathology, U.S.-Can. Acad. Pathology. Methodist. Office: Johns Hopkins Hosp Div Comparative Medicine 720 Rutland Ave Baltimore MD 21205

CORLEY, GEORGIA BUCKNER, educator; b. Chgo., Aug. 9, 1923; d. Albert Nelsona nd Amanda (Crabtree) Buckner; m. William Corley (dec.); children: Tomacenna, William, Cheryl; m. Roosevelt McNair, Feb. 8, 1961; children: Monica, Melvin. BS in Math., Tenn. A & I U., 1942; MS, Bradley U., Peoria, Ill., 1974; EdS, Western Ill. U., 1982. Tchr. Chgo. Spl. Summer Sch., 1956-67; math instr. GED Prog., Ill. Cen. Coll., East Peoria, Ill., 1973-74; reading tchr. Phila. pub. schs., 1946-54; tchr. Chgo. pub. schs., 1955-78; blackk studies dir. Bradley U., Peoria, 1974-75; reading specialist Crete (Ill.) High Sch., 1979-89; ret.; cons. in field; prin. (part-time) Holy Family Luth. Sch., Chgo., 1987-88; tour dir. Chgo. Pub. Schs. Shoop Sch., 1961-68. Author: Recreation in Mathematics, 1942, An Alternative School, 1982; contbr. articles to profl. jours. Named Most Creative Tchr., Chgo. Pub. Schs., Most Outstanding Tchr., Chgo. Bd. Edn., Dist. 16; Human rels. fellow, 1950. Mem. AAUW, Ill. Reading Coun., Assn. for Supervision and Curriculum Devel., Ill. Edn. Assn., Kiwanis, Toastmasters. Democrat. Methodist. Address: 14802 Clark St Dolton IL 60419

CORLEY, JOYCE, personnel executive; b. Schenectady, Jan. 10; d. J. Edmund and Jean (Hausman) C. Assoc. Sci., Harcum Jr. Coll., 1962; postgrad. Temple U. Cert. human resources profl. Med. asst. Bryn Mawr Med. & Diagnostic Clinic Ltd. (Pa.), 1962-66; sec. Calif. Computer Products, Bala Cynwya, Pa., 1966-70, Drexel Firestone, Phila., 1970-71; exec. sec. IU International, Phila., 1972-76; adminstrv. asst. KPMG Peat Marwick, 1976-81, mgr. personnel services, 1981—. Mem. central allocations com. United Way, 1983-85, mem. sr. services rev. com., 1984-85, com. corp. edn. Am. Cancer Soc., 1988-90. Mem. Nat. Assn. Female Execs., Human Resources Profl. Assn. (bd. dirs. 1985-90, treas. 1986-88 v.p. adminstrv. services 1988—), Am. Soc. Personnel Adminstrs., Delaware Valley Corp. Travel Mgrs. Assn. Republican. Office: Peat Marwick Main & Co 1600 Market St Philadelphia PA 19103

CORMAN, KAREN MARIE, insurance company executive; b. Pasaic, N.J., Mar. 27, 1962; d. Joseph Rudolph and Sophie Marie (Gebarowski) Cinzio; m. Warren Stephen, Sept. 6, 1986. BA in Math. cum laude, SUNY, Potsdam. Methods analyst Prentice Hall Pubs., Old Tappan, N.J., 1984-85; sr. staff claim rep. Allstate Ins. Co., Whippany, N.J., 1985—, chmn. customer svc. com., co. editor Echo newspaper, 1989. Mem. Garfield Cadets Drum & Bugle Corps., MICA League; Jack La Lanne Health Club. Office: Allstate Ins Co Valley Forge Park MCO 1018 W 9th St King of Prussia PA 19406

CORN, LESLIE JOAN, producer, director, writer, programming executive; b. N.Y.C., Mar. 30, 1949; d. Peter and Jacqueline (DuVal) C. Student Northwestern U., 1966-68; B.A. in English, Finch Coll., 1970; M.A. in Psychology, New Sch. for Social Research, 1976. Radio interviewer Australian Broadcasting Commn., Sydney, 1970; asst. to writers Tonight Show, NBC-TV, N.Y.C., 1971, Burbank, Calif., 1971; assoc. producer Parent's Mag. Films, N.Y.C., 1972; asst. nationally syndicated show Living Easy with Dr. Joyce Brothers, N.Y.C., 1973; assoc. producer various TV commls., N.Y.C., 1974, RKO-TV documentary Inflation: A Few Answers, 1974; producer CARE's Internat. Children's Party, 1974; prodn. assoc. Money Maze, ABC-TV, N.Y.C., 1974-75; producer, dir. Miller-Brody Prodns., N.Y.C., 1975-78; dir. program and pub. services ABC Radio Network, N.Y.C., 1979-80, dir. program prodn., 1980-81; dir. programming CBS Radio Networks, 1981-83; pres., chief exec. officer Arielle Prodns. Internat., Ltd., N.Y.C., 1984—; producer, dir., writer Love Notes radio spl., 1984; producer, dir. Erma Bombeck in Motherhood: The Second Oldest Profession radio feature series, 1984-86, Leo Buscaglia in Loving Each Other radio feature series, 1985; dir., adapter books on tape for Warner Audio Publishing, including Rebecca (du Maurier), I the Jury (Spillane), Reflex (Francis), Brain (Cook), also dir. To Your Scattered Bodies Go (Farmer), Mosby's Memoirs (Bellow); producer, dir. adapter books on tape for Bantam Audio Pub. including Changing (Liv Ullmann), Yeager: An Autobiography, Mission: Success! The Greatest Salesman in the World Part Two (Og Mandino), And So It Goes (Linda Ellerbee), Suspects, (Caunitz), (A Christmas Carol, (Sir John Gielgud, Grammy nominee awards 1989), Sun Signs, Living through Personal Crisis, Over the Edge, (Kellerman), Butcher's Theater (Ben Kingsley), Blood Test, When the Bough Breaks, Soulmates (Stearn), The Shell Seekers (Pilcher), Newman Communications including The New! Improved! Bob and Ray Boon (Bob Elliott and Ray Goulding), Smart Cookies Don't Crumble (Sonya Friedman), Listen for Pleasure including The Magician of Lublin (Isaac Bashevis Singer), Wiley Sound Business including Getting New Clients (Connors and Davidson), McGraw-Hill

Audio including Motherhood: The Second Oldest Profession (Erma Bombeck, Grammy award nominee 1990), Harper Audio including I Want to Grow Hair...I Want to Grow Up...I Want to Go to Boise (Erma Bombeck, Grammy award nominee 1990), Random House Audio Pub. including G is for Guidance, F is for Fugitive, G is for Gumshoe (Sud Grafton), Listening Libr. including Ramona & Her Mother (Beverly Clearly, Parents Choice Honor award 1989); programming cons. Warner Communications, N.Y.C. and Columbus, Ohio, 1976-78; panelist Nat. Emmy awards, 1974-77, nominations panelist children's programming, 1977; vis. lectr. NYU Sr. Seminar, 1980, Spiritual Frontiers Fellowship, 1984, 85, Folio, 1987. Mem. Internat. Radio and TV Soc. (bd. govs. 1977-81), Nat. Acad. Rec. Arts and Scis., Mensa, Spiritual Frontiers Fellowship (programming com. 1984—), Delta Delta Delta. Office: Arielle Prodns Internat Ltd 242 E 72nd St Suite 5A New York NY 10021

CORN, WANDA M., fine arts educator; b. New Haven, Nov. 13, 1940; d. Keith M. and Lydia M. (Fox) Jones; m. Joseph J. Corn, July 27, 1963. B.A., NYU, 1963, M.A., 1965, Ph.D., 1974. Instr. art history Washington Sq. Coll., NYU, 1965-66; lectr. U. Calif.-Berkeley, 1970, vis. asst. prof., 1976; lectr. Mills Coll., Oakland, Calif., 1970, vis. asst. prof., 1971, asst. prof., 1972-77, assoc. prof., 1977-80; assoc. prof. Stanford U., Calif., 1980-89, prof., 1989—, chair dept. of art, 1989—; acting dir. Standford Mus., 1989—; vis. curator Fine Arts Mus., San Francisco, 1972, 73, 76; vis. curator Mpls. Inst. Arts, 1983-84, Grant Wood travelling exhbn. to Whitney Mus. Am. Art, N.Y.C., Art Inst. Chgo., Fine Arts Mus. San Francisco. Author: The Color of Mood, American Tonalism, 1880-1910, 1972; The Art of Andrew Wyeth, 1973; Grant Wood: The Regionalist Vision, 1983; contbr. articles to profl. jours. Commr. Nat. Mus. Am. Art, 1988—. Ford Found. fellow, 1966-70; recipient Graves award 1974-75; Smithsonian fellow, 1978-79; Woodrow Wilson fellow, 1979-80; Stanford Humanities Ctr. fellow, 1982-83, Regents fellow Smithsonian Inst., 1987; Am. Coun. Learned Socs. grantee, 1982, 86; rsch. assoc. Smithsonian Instn., 1983—; Phi Beta Kappa scholar, 1984-85. Mem. Coll. Art Assn. (bd. dirs. 1970-73, 1980-84, program chmn. ann. meeting, 1981, mem. numerous coms.), Women's Caucus for Art, Am. Studies Assn. (nat. coun. 1986-89), Assn. Historians of Am. Art. Office: Stanford U Dept of Art Stanford CA 94305

CORNELIUS, CATHERINE PETREY, college president; b. Lakeland, Fla., May 3, 1941; d. Thomas Burch and Carolyn (Petrey) C. BA, Rollins Coll., 1963, MA in Teaching, 1966; EdS, U. Fla., 1976, EdD, 1978. Cert. educator/adminstr., Fla. Tchr. Spanish, history Orange County Pub. Schs., Orlando, Fla., 1963-67; instr. fgn. lang. Seminole Community Coll., Sanford, Fla., 1967-73, dir. coop. and career edn., 1973-78; dir. arts and scis. Daytona Beach (Fla.) Community Coll., 1978-79, v.p. acad. affairs, 1979-84; pres. South Fla. Community Coll., Avon Park, 1984—. Author: (with others) Experiential Education, 1983. Bd. dirs. Highlands Art League, Sebring, Fla., 1985-87, Fla. Endowment Fund for Higher Edn., Tampa, 1985—, Walker Meml. Hosp., Avon Park, 1986—. Named Educator of the Yr., Sebring C. of C., 1987; recipient Disting. Alumni Svc. award Rollins Coll., 1988, Nat. Pacesetter award Nat. Coun. for Community Rels., 1988, Nat. Presdl. Leadership award U. Tex., 1989. Mem. Am. Assn. Higher Edn., Am. Assn. Community/Jr. Colls., Fla. Assn. Community Colls. (pres. 1986, Service award 1986), Fla. Council Pres. (chmn. 1987-88), Highlands Council of 100 (pres. 1986-88), Phi Delta Kappa (pres. 1983-84, Service award 1984). Methodist. Lodge: Rotary (Avon Park Breakfast Club). Office: South Fla Community Coll 600 W College Dr Avon Park FL 33825

CORNELIUS, LINDA LOUISE, advertising executive; b. Buffalo, Mar. 7, 1953; d. Adam Edward, Jr. and Virginia Elizabeth (Becker) Cornelius. B.A. summa cum laude, U. Pa., 1975, M.B.A., 1979; m. Andrew Neiser, Sept., 1989. Asst. account exec. Ogilvy & Mather Advt., N.Y.C., 1979-80, account exec., 1980-82, account supr., 1982, v.p., account supr., 1983-84, v.p., mgmt. supr., 1984-87, sr. v.p., 1987-89. Mem. Phi Beta Kappa. Office: Ogilvy & Mather Advt 2 E 48th St New York NY 10017

CORNELL, MRS. DOUGLAS B. See **THOMAS, HELEN A.**

CORNELL, TANIS JILL, communications company official; b. Tulsa, May 19, 1953; d. Winston Leon and Joy Gail (Petty) Lugar; m. Jimmy Lee Williams, July 28, 1973 (div. Feb. 1978); m. Donald Phillip Cornell, Aug. 8, 1987; stepchildren: Jennifer, Jay; 1 child, Christopher. BA, North Tex. State U., 1975, postgrad., 1976-78. Tchr. Mesquite (Tex.) Ind. Sch. Dist., 1976-77, Grand Prairie (Tex.) Ind. Sch. Dist., 1978; sales rep. Knoll Pharm., Whippany, N.J., 1979, Communications Corp. Am., Dallas, 1980; sales mgr. Communications Corp. Am., Waco, Tex., 1981-82; sales mgr., br. mgr. Communications Corp. Am., Oklahoma City, 1983-86; sales mgr. Centel Communications Systems, Oklahoma City, 1987, dist. sales mgr., 1988, major account mgr., 1989—; cons. on coll. textbook, 1989. Vol. Big Bros.-Bis Sisters, Oklahoma City, 1987-88. Mem. Sales and Mktg. Execs., Okla. Communications Mgrs. Assn. (treas. 1988), Successful Businesswomens Assn. (treas. 1986, pres. 1987), Waterford Bus. Club. Republican. Mem. Ch. of Christ. Home: 13400 Fox Creek Dr Oklahoma City OK 73131 Office: Centel Communications Sys 100 W Wilshire C-4 Oklahoma City OK 73116

CORNETT, LAUREEN ELIZABETH, small business owner, photographer; b. San Diego, Nov. 14, 1946; d. Clarence Alex and Barbara Ann (Mesku) Lane; m. Bruce Walter Cornett, Oct. 17, 1981; children: Cherie Ann, Robert Michael, John David. Student, San Diego State U., 1964-70. Exec. sec. Boyle Engring., San Diego, 1964-69, Design Cons., San Diego, 1969-71; owner Laureen's Secretarial Svc., San Diego, 1979-83; exec. sec. Covi Corp., San Diego, 1979-83; owner Laureen Cornett Word Processing, San Diego, 1982—; owner, photographer Panoramix, San Diego, 1984—; owner Laureen Cornett Med. Transcription Co., 1984—; prof. Mesa Jr. Coll., 1989—. Photographer for brochures, newspaper ads. Mem. Am. Assn. for Med. Transcription. Office: Panoramix PO Box 15323 San Diego CA 92115

CORNING, JOY COLE, state legislator; b. Bridgewater, Iowa, Sept. 7, 1932; d. Perry Aaron and Ethel Marie (Sullivan) Cole; m. Burton Eugene Corning, June 19, 1955; children: Carol, Claudia, Ann. BA, U. No. Iowa, 1954. Cert. elem. tchr., Iowa. Tchr. elem. sch. Greenfield (Iowa) Sch. Dist., 1951-53, Waterloo (Iowa) Community Sch. Dist., 1954-55; mem. Iowa Senate, Des Moines, 1984—, asst. Rep. leader, 1989—; bd. dirs. Iowa Nat. Bankshares, Midway Bank & Trust. Pres. Cedar Falls (Iowa) Sch. Bd., 1975-83; state pres. Iowa Talented and Gifted, 1975-77; mem. adv. bd. Waterloo Theatre, Cedar Arts Forum; bd. dirs. Iowa Housing Fin. Authority, Des Moines, 1981-84, Iowa Assn. Sch. Bds., Des Moines, 1983-84, Iowa Peace Inst., 1987—; mem. Edn. Commn. of States, 1987—. Named Citizen of Yr., Cedar Falls C. of C., 1984; recipient Alumni Achievement award U. No. Iowa, 1985. Mem. AAUW, LWV, PEO, Delta Kappa Gamma. Republican. Mem. United Ch. of Christ. Office: 1017 Oak Park Blvd Cedar Falls IA 50613

CORNISH, ELIZABETH TURVEREY, stockbroker; b. Ionia, N.Y., Dec. 31, 1919; d. Clifford Dwight and Mildred Althea (Spicer) T.; m. Louis Joseph Cornish, June 21, 1941 (div. June 1955); 1 child, Carol Cornish Reeves. BS, Cornell U., 1941. Lic. stockbroker N.Y. Stock Exch., Prin. Reg. Options Prin., Commodity prin., Insur. prin. Teletype operator, sec. to mgr. Carl M. Loeb Rhoades & Co., Ithaca, N.Y., 1955-65; reg. rep. Carl M. Loeb Rhoades & Co., Ithaca, 1962-75; branch mgr. Loeb, Rhoades & Co., Ithaca, 1975-82; registered rep. Shearson Loeb Rhoades, Shearson Am. Express, Ithaca, 1982-86, Hutton, Shearson, Ithaca, 1986-88, First Albany Corp., Ithaca, 1988—; charter mem. Nuveen Adv. Coun. 1984, 85, 86. Mem. Planning Com. Downtown Mall, Ithaca, N.Y., 1972-75; chmn. campaign United Way Tompkins County, Ithaca, 1983, dir., 1983-89; bd. dirs. Ithaca Neighborhood Housing, Leadership Tompkins, 1986-88; pres. Friends of Ithaca Coll., 1985-86. Mem. Downtown Bus. Women (pres. 1971-72), Tompkins County C. of C. (bd. dirs. 1974-77, 83-86, v.p. 1980-81, pres.-elect 1989, pres. 1990), Ithaca Yacht Club (bd. dirs. 1988—). Republican. Episcopalian. Office: 1st Albany Corp 171 The Commons PO Box 130 Ithaca NY 14851

CORNISH, MARIE ANGELA, television company executive; b. Phila., July 8, 1960; d. Thomas James and Susan Dolores (Massanova) Egitto; m. C. Daniel Cornish, Jr., Oct. 29, 1983. BA Arts and Scis., Temple U., 1982. Sales exec. Alcare Communications, Phila., 1981-82, Ind. Radio Network, Greenwich, Conn., 1982-86; cons. Malcolm Smith Advt., Smithtown, N.Y., 1982-86; pres., founder Cornish Communications, Inc., N.Y.C., 1986—; v.p., producer Yale Roe Films, N.Y.C., 1989—. Producer, writer nat. TV programs and commercials, 1986-88. Mem. Nat. Assn. TV Arts and Scis., Nat. Assn. TV Program Execs. Republican. Roman Catholic. Office: Yale Roe Films 90 Park Ave New York NY 10012

CORNSWEET, CAROL, clinical child psychologist, researcher; b. New Haven, June 2, 1958; d. Tom Normand Cornsweet and Janet (Crum) Vandre. BA with distinction in Psychology, Swarthmore Coll., 1980; PhD in Clin. Psychology, Vanderbilt U., 1984. Lic. psychologist, Calif., Kans. Postdoctoral fellow U. Calif., San Francisco, 1985-86; asst. clin. prof. U. Calif., Irvine, 1987-88; staff psychologist children's div. Menninger Clinic, Topeka, 1988—. Contbr. articles to profl. jours. Fellow Mellon Found., 1979; Harold Stirling Vanderbilt scholar, 1980-84. Mem. APA, Am. Orthopsychiat. Assn., Phi Beta Kappa, Sigma Xi. Mem. Soc. of Friends. Office: Menninger Clinic Children's Div Box 829 Topeka KS 66601

CORNWALL, DEBORAH JOYCE, consulting firm executive, management consultant; b. Wilmington, Del., Dec. 9, 1946; d. Samuel and Norma (Bram) Handloff; m. Barry Newland Cornwall, June 22, 1968; 1 child, Deborah Leigh. BA, Mount Holyoke, 1967; MBA, Boston U., 1975. Editor Houghton Mifflin Co., Boston, 1967-69; editor Harbridge House, Inc., Boston, 1969-73, cons., 1973-74, assoc., 1974-75, sr. assoc., 1975-77, prin., 1977-79, v.p., 1979-81, v.p., div. mgr., 1981-83, sr. v.p., div. mgr., 1983—; mem. mid. mgmt. excellence com. City of Boston, 1986. Mem. Phi Beta Kappa, Beta Gamma Sigma. Office: Harbridge House Inc 11 Arlington St Boston MA 02116

CORNWELL, ILENE JONES, writer, editor, small business owner. Student, Tenn. State U., 1987-89, Cumberland U., 1990—. Pub. info. officer Tenn. Hist. Commn., Nashville, 1974-78; publs. editor, pub. info. officer Vanderbilt U. Med. Ctr., Nashville, 1978-81; writer, editor, owner So. Resources Unlimited, Nashville, 1981—. Author: Footsteps Along the Harpeth, 1970, 76, Travel Guide to the Natchez Trace Parkway, 1984, Biographical Directory of the Tennessee General Assembly, (4 vols.) 1987, 88, 89, 90, Ruskin!, 1972, (with Jim Leeson) The Old Trace in Tennessee, 1972 (2 screenplays) Early Travels on the Natchez Trace, 1974, Natchez Trace: Pathway to Parkway, 1986 (nominated Nashville's Emmy 1988); editor various publs.; contbr. to publs. Charter mem. West Nashville Founders' Mus., Nashville, 1987, bd. dirs., 1989; chmn. Richland Creek Campaign, West Nashville Community Coun., 1989, 90; founder Bellevue-Harpeth Hist. Soc., 1970, 3-term pres.; program presenter Internat. Conf. on Pwkys., Riverways, and Greenways Asheville, N.C., 1989; chair Natchez Trace Adv. Com. Tenn., 1990—. Recipient Outstanding Svc. and Leadership award, West Nashville Community Coun., 1989, Pres. award Natchez Trace Pkwy. Assn., 1989, Vintage award Internat. Assn. Bus. Communicators, 1980, MacEachern award Am. Hosp. Assn., 1981, Tenn. Outstanding Young Woman, 1975. Mem. National League of Am. Pen Women (Nashville br., former pres., v.p. , state conv. chairwoman), Tenn. Woman's Press and Authors Club (affiliate of Nat. Fedn. of Press Women, pres. 1978, former v.p. and chairwoman of state conv.), NAFE, Tenn. Screenwriting Assn., White Bridge Neighborhood Assn., Tenn. Environ. Coun., NOW, CABLE, Am. Biog. Inst. Rsch. Assn. (selected assoc. and mem. adv. bd. 1990). Home and Office: 5632 Meadowcrest Ln Nashville TN 37209

CORPORON, NANCY ANN, marketing executive; b. Independence, Kans., Nov. 11, 1949; d. Lewis Leonard and Helen Maxine (Church) Corporon. BM in Music Performance, Oklahoma City U., 1971; MBA, NYU, 1985. French hornist, 1970-85; mgr. mktg. Am. Express Co., 1987—; assoc. Mgmt. Practice Cons. Ptnrs., 1985-87; cons. Urban Bus. Assistance Corp., N.Y.C., 1981-83, v.p., 1983-84; artistic dir. San Francisco Winds Freedom, 1990—; music dir. N.Y Community Marching Band, N.Y.C., 1979-81; founder, pres. Trimusicangle, Inc., N.Y.C., 1979-82. Recipient Cardinal Key, Oklahoma City U., 1971, Sword of Honor Sigma Alpha Iota, 1971. Mem. Pi Kappa Lambda. Home: 72 Elm Ave San Anselmo CA 94960

CORPREW-BEVERLY, THERESA LOUISE, secretary; b. Portsmouth, Va., Feb. 16, 1958; d. Ossia Sylvester and Annie Delores (Jones) Corprew; m. Claude Bernard Beverly, Feb. 23, 1985; 1 child, Kristina Renee. Student, Norfolk (Va.) State U., 1976-78, Kee Bus. Coll., Newport News, Va., 1986-87. Personnel records specialist 546th Personnel Svc. Co., U.S. Army, Ft. Hood, Tex., 1979-80; officer, records clk. 569th Personnel Svc. Co., U.S. Army, Neu Ulm, Fed. Republic of Germany, 1980-82; enlisted U.S. Army, 1982; records clk. mil. personnel office HC USATCFE, Ft. Eustis, Va., 1982-88; sec. def. subsistence region EUROPE Def. Logistics Agy., Bremerhaven, Fed. Republic of Germany, 1988—. Mem. NAFE. Home: 1817 E Burson Dr Chesapeake VA 23323

CORPUZ, TERESA AGRIFINA, school principal; b. San Francisco, Apr. 4, 1951; d. Faustino Ceria and Virginia (Baltazar) C. BA in English, San Francisco State U., 1972; MS in Counseling, Calif State U., Hayward, 1981. Cert. secondary tchr., Calif. Tchr. Mendota (Calif.) Sch. Dist., 1973-75, Tracy (Calif.) Sch. Dist., 1975-82; counselor Livermore (Calif.) Sch. Dist., 1982-83; vice-prin. Albany (Calif.) Unified Sch. Dist., 1983-85, prin., 1987—; prin. Sunnyvale (Calif.) Elem. Sch. Dist., 1985-87; cons. sch. edn. U. Calif., Berkeley, 1987-88. Bd. dirs. Albany-Berkeley YMCA, 1987-89. Recipient Calif. Educator award Calif. State Dept. Edn. and Milken Family Found., 1987. Mem. Assn. Calif. Sch. Adminstrs., Assn. Supervision and Curriculum Devel., Phi Delta Kappa, Delta Kappa Gamma. Democrat. Roman Catholic. Office: Albany Mid Sch 1000 Jackson St Albany CA 94706

CORRE', NITA LEVY, healthcare executive; b. Gibraltar, Mar. 11, 1938; came to U.S., 1957; d. Isaac Solomon and Rachel (Hassan) Levy; m. Alan David Corre; children: Jacob, Giselle, Raquel, Isaac. BS, U. Wis., Milw., 1970, MS, 1973. Diplomate Am. Bd. Clin. Social Work. Social worker Milw. Jewish Home, 1972-74, casework supr., dir. social svcs., 1974-77, asst. adminstr., dir. social svcs., 1977-78, exec. v.p., 1978-84, pres., 1984—. V.p., sec., bd. dirs. Porspect Congregate Housing; v.p., bd. dirs. Conf. Jewish Communal Svc., Nat. Assn. Jewish Homes and Housing for the Aged; bd. dirs. Wis. Assn. Homes and Svcs. for the Aging, Hillel House, Lake Park Synagogue, Milw. Community High Sch. Mem. Gerontol. Soc., Nat. Assn. Social Workers, Phi Kappa Phi. Office: Milw Jewish Home 1414 N Prospect Ave Milwaukee WI 53202

CORREIA, SISTER CLARISSE ANN, academic administrator; b. New Bedford, Mass., Jan. 18, 1943; d. Manuel Lawrence and Clarisse (Mello) C. RN, St. Luke's Sch. Nursing, New Bedford, 1963; BS, St. Joseph's Coll., Emmitsburg, Md., 1968; MS, U. Rochester, 1976. Joined Daughters of Charity of St. Vincent de Paul. Staff nurse St. Luke's Hosp., 1963-64; head nurse, in-service instr., coordinator continuing edn. St. Mary's Hosp., Rochester, 1969-76; adminstr. St. Louise House, Albany, N.Y., 1976-82; pres. St. John of God Hosp., Brighton, Mass., 1982-89, Laboure Coll., Boston, 1989—; bd. dirs. Carney Hosp., Dorchester, Mass., St. Vincent's Med.Ctr., Bridgeport, Conn., Good Samaritan Hosp., Brighton, Laboure Coll., Dorchester. Chmn. elder task force, Archdiocese of Boston, 1986—, active AIDS task force, 1987—, mem. pastoral coun. Mem. Am. Coll. Healthcare Execs., Am. Hosp. Assn. (governing coun. aging and long term sect.), Archdiocese of Boston Synod, Am. Soc. Aging. Office: Laboure Coll 2120 Dorchester Ave Boston MA 02124

CORRELL, HELEN BUTTS, botanist, researcher; b. Providence, R.I., Apr. 24, 1907; d. George Lyman and Albertine Louise (Christiansen) B.; m. Donovan Stewart Correll (dec. 1983); children: Louise, Stewart, Selena, Charles. AB, Brown U., 1928, AM, 1929; PhD, Duke U., 1934. Instr. Smith Coll., Northampton, Mass., 1929-31, Wellesly (Mass.) Coll., 1934-39; assoc. prof. U. Md., Towson, 1956; research assoc. Tex. Research Found., Renner, 1959-65, co-investigator aquatic plant research, 1966-71; collaborator, adjunct staff Fairchild Tropical Garden, Miami, Fla., 1973—. Co-author: Aquatic and Wetland Plants of the Southwestern United States, 1972, 2dn. ed. 1975, Flora of the Bahama Archipelago, 1982; editor: Wrightia Botanical Jour., 1959-63; contbr. articles to profl. jours. Chmn., Library Bd., Richardson, Tex., 1965-70. Recipient disting. alumna citation Brown U., 1983, Marjory Stoneman Douglas award Fla. Native Plant Soc., 1985. Mem. Nat. Arboretum (adv. coun. 1974-79), Bahama Trust, So. Appalachian Bot. Club, Soc. for Econ. Botany, Soc. Woman Geographers, Friends of Fairchild (v.p. 1986-87, pres. 1987-89), Altrusa Club (officer 1964-71), Sigma Xi, Phi Beta Kappa. Congregationalist. Home: 216 E Ridge Village Dr Miami FL 33157 Office: Fairchild Tropical Garden 10901 Old Cutler Rd Miami FL 33156

CORRIGAN, LYNDA DYANN, banker; b. Selmer, Tenn., Nov. 24, 1949; d. A. Sammuel and Eunice (Burks) Davis. BBA, Mid. Tenn. State U., 1978; MBA, U. Tenn., 1979; JD, Nashville Sch. Law, 1984. CPA, Tenn.; bar: Tenn. 1985. Sr. v.p. First Am. Corp., Nashville, 1980—; faculty Am. Inst. Banking, Nashville, 1982—; mem. Nat. Panel Consumer Arbitrators, Nashville, 1985-87. Pres. Buddies of Nashville, 1985; treas. Mid.-East Tenn. Arthritis Found., Nashville, 1982-85, Floyd Cramer Celebrity Golf Tournament, Nashville, 1981-84; bd. dirs. Nashville Br. Arthritis Found., 1980-87. Recipient Leadership award Mid.-East Tenn. Arthritis Found, 1985, Gold award Jr. Chamber, 1981. Mem. ABA (mem. tax com. 1987—), Nashville Bar Assn. (mem. tax com. 1986—, vice chmn. tax sect. 1989, chair tax sect. 1990—), Tenn. Taxpayers and Mfrs. Assn. (mem. tax com. 1986—), Tenn. Soc. CPA's. Home: 806 Fountainhead Ct Brentwood TN 37027

CORRIGAN, MAURA DENISE, lawyer; b. Cleve., June 14, 1948; d. Peter James and Mae Ardell (McCrone) C.; m. Joseph Dante Grano, July 11, 1976; children: Megan Elizabeth, Daniel Corrigan. BA with honors, Marygrove Coll., 1969; JD with honors, U. Detroit, 1973. Bar: Mich., 1974. Jud. clk. Mich. Ct. Appeals, Detroit, 1973-74; asst. prosecutor Wayne County, Mich., Detroit, 1974-79; asst. U.S. atty., Detroit, 1979-89, chief appellate div., 1979-86; chief asst. U.S. atty., 1986-89; assoc. Plunkett & Cooney, P.C., Detroit, 1989—; vice chmn. Mich. Com. To Formulate Rules of Criminal Procedure, Mich. Supreme Ct., 1982—; mem. com. on standard jury instrns. State Bar Mich., 1978-82; lectr. Mich. Jud. Inst. sixth cir. Judicial Workshop, Inst. Continuing Legal Edn., ABA-Cin. Bar Litigation Sects., Dept. Justice Advocacy Inst. Contbr. chpt. to book, articles to legal rev. Vice chmn. Project Transition, Detroit, 1976—; mem. Citizens Adv. Council Lafayette Clinic, Detroit, 1979-87; bd. dirs. Detroit Wayne County Criminal Advocacy Program, 1983-86. Recipient award of merit Detroit Commn. on Human Relations, 1974, Dir.'s award Dept. Justice, 1985, Outstanding Practitioner of Criminal Law award Fed. Bar Assn., 1989. Mem. ABA, Women Lawyers Assn., Mich. Bar. Detroit Bar, Fed. Bar Assn. (pres.-elect Detroit chpt.). Republican. Home: 721 Balfour Rd Grosse Pointe Park MI 48230 Office: Plunkett & Cooney PC 900 Marquette Bldg Detroit MI 48226-3260

CORROTHERS, HELEN GLADYS, government criminal justice official; b. Montrose, Ark., Mar. 19, 1937; d. Thomas and Christene (Farley) Curl; m. Edward Corrothers, Dec. 17, 1968 (div. Sept. 1983); 1 child, Michael Edward. AA in Liberal Arts magna cum laude, Ark. Bapt. Coll., 1955; BS in Bus. Adminstrn. Mgmt., Roosevelt U., 1965; grad. officer leadership sch., WAC Sch., 1965; grad, Inst. Criminal Justice, Exec. Ctr. Continuing Edn., U. Chgo., 1973; postgrad., Calif. Coast U., 1981—. Enlisted U.S. Army, 1956, advanced through grades to capt., 1969; chief mil. pers. U.S. Army, Ft. Meyer, Va., 1965-67; dir. for housing Giessen Support Ctr., Fed. Republic Germany, 1967-69; resigned, 1969; social interviewer Ark. Dept. Corrections, Grady, 1970-71; supt. women's unit Ark. Dept. Corrections, Pine Bluff, 1971-83; commr. U.S. Parole Commn., Burlingame, Calif., 1983-85, U.S. Sentencing Commn., Washington, 1985—; instr. corrections U.Ark.-Pine Bluff, 1976-79; mem. bd. visitation Jefferson County Juvenile Ct., Pine Bluff, 1978-81; bd. dirs. Vols. in Cts., 1979-84, Vols. Am., 1985-88; mem. Am./Can. study team, Mexican penal system Am. Correctional Assn., Islas Marias, Mex., summer 1981; mem. Ark. Commn. on Crimes and Law Enforcement, 1975-78. Mem. Ark. Commn. on Status of Women, 1976-78; bd. dirs. Com. Against Spouse Abuse, 1982-84. Recipient Ark. Woman of Achievement award Ark. Press Women's Assn., 1980, Human Relations award Ark. Edn. Assn., 1980, Outstanding Woman of Achievement award Sta.-KATV-TV, Little Rock, 1981, Correctional Service award Vols. Am., 1984, William H. Hastie award Nat. Assn. Blacks in Criminal Justice, 1986. Mem. Am. Correctional Assn. (treas. 1980-86, v.p. 1986-88, pres.-elect 1988-90, pres. 1990—), U.S. Attorney Gen.'s Correctional Policy Study Team, 1987, N.Am. Assn. Wardens and Supts., Ark. Law Enforcement Assn., Nat. Assn. Female Execs., Nat. Council on Crime and Delinquency, Am. Soc. Criminology, Ark. Sheriff's Assn. (hon.), Delta Sigma Theta (local sec. 1976-79, local parliamentarian 1983-84). Baptist. Office: US Sentencing Commn 1331 Pennsylvania Ave NW Washington DC 20004

CORT, DIANA, social worker; b. N.Y.C., Oct. 27, 1934; d. Arthur and Augusta Deutsch; B.S., N.Y.U., 1955; M.S.W., Columbia U., 1957; m. Leonard Van Arsdale, Sept. 17, 1978; children by previous marriage—Hayley, Daniel. Clinician, Payne Whitney Clinic, N.Y. Hosp., N.Y.C., 1957-59, psychiat. clinic Jewish Bd. Guardians, N.Y.C., 1959-61; founder, pres. Big Six Towers Nursery Sch., N.Y.C., 1962-67; dir. intake and social service L.I. Consultation Center, Forest Hills, N.Y., 1966-84, clin. dir., coordinator clin. services, 1984-86; supr., faculty mem. L.I. Inst. Mental Health, 1973-86; adminstr. Bleuler Psychotherapy Ctr., Forest Hills, 1986-87; cons. in social work Bergen Ctr. for Child Devel., 1981—; dir. Seniors Option Service, Allendale, N.J., 1980—. Mem. Nat. Assn. Social Workers, N.Y. Soc. Clin. Social Workers. Address: 97 17 64th Rd Forest Hills NY 11374

CORT, WINIFRED MITCHELL, microbiologist, biochemist; b. Cleve., Dec. 9, 1917; d. Walter James and Winifred Jane (Chenoweth) Mitchell; m. Nicholas Cort, Mar. 21, 1947; children: Peter C., Alison C. Thurau. BS cum laude, U. Ill., 1941, MS, 1943, PhD, 1946. Rsch. microbiologist Comml. Solvents, Terre Haute, Ind., 1943-45; rsch. biochemist Pfizer, Bklyn., 1946-47; sect. leader Nat. Dairy, Oakdale, N.Y., 1951-59, Evans Rsch. and Devel., N.Y.C., 1959-65; assoc. dir. product devel. Hoffmann LaRoche, Nutley, N.J., 1965-85; cons. Cort Assocs., Sarasota, Fla., 1985—; sec.-treas. Biochem. Discussion Group, N.Y.C., 1959; lectr. Adelphi U., Garden City, N.Y., 1959-60. Contbr. numerous chpts. to books and articles to profl. jours. Recipient Bond award Am. Oil Chem. Soc., 1974. Mem. Am. Chem. Soc. (emeritus, chmn. N.Y.C. program com. 1961), Am. Soc. Microbiology (emeritus), N.Y. Chem. Soc., Inst. Food Tech. (Food Scientist award 1973-76), Sigma Xi. Home and Office: 4395 Brandywine Dr Sarasota FL 34241

CORTA, NANCY RUTH, nurse; b. Gorman, Tex., Feb. 15, 1957; d. Dale Newton and Perelene Ruth (Wright) Johnson; m. Peter Joseph Corta. BSN, Tex. Woman's U., Denton, 1980. Staff nurse Baylor U. Med. Ctr., Dallas, 1980-81; charge nurse ICU/CCU DeLeon Hosp., Tex., 1981-82; staff nurse MICU/CCU VA Med. Ctr., Phoenix, 1982-83; staff nurse Harris Hosp. Meth., Ft. Worth, 1983-84, Tex. Dept. Health, Stephenville, 1984—. Mem. Tex. Women's U. Alumni Assn., Epsilon Sigma Alpha. Lodge: Order Eastern Star. Home: Rt 2 Box 192 DeLeon TX 76444 Office: Texas Dept Health PHR-5 2301 Northwest Loop Suite B Stephenville TX 76401

CORWIN, JOYCE ELIZABETH STEDMAN, construction company executive; b. Chgo.; d. Cresswell Edward and Elizabeth Josephine (Kimbell) Stedman; student Fla. State U., U. Miami; m. William Corwin, May 1, 1965; children: Robert Edmund Newman, Jillanne Elizabeth Newman. Pres. Am. Properties, Inc., Miami, Fla., 1966-72; v.p. Stedman Constrn. Co., Miami, 1971—; owner Joy-Win Horses, Gray lady ARC, 1969-70. Guidance worker Youth Hall, 1969-70; sponsor Para Med. Group of Coral Park High Sch., 1969-70; hostess, Rep. presdl. campaign, 1968; aide Rep. Nat. Conv., 1972. Mem. Dade County Med. Aux. (chmn. directory com. 1970), Marion County Med. Aux., Fla. Psychiat. Soc. Aux., Fla. Morgan Horse Assn., Fla. Thoroughbred Breeders Assn. Clubs: Coral Gables Jr. Women's (chmn. casework com.), Golden Hills Golf and Turf, Heritage, Royal Dames of Ocala. Home: Windrift Farm 8500 NW 120th St Reddick FL 32686

CORWIN, KIM HENSON, gas company executive; b. Niles, Mich., Jan. 20, 1957; d. David W. and Patricia Ann (Snyder) Henson; m. Austin Walden Corwin, Oct. 5, 1985. BS, MIT, 1980. V.p. Robert Bell & Co., Severna Park, Md.; mgr. performance improvement Bay State Gas Co., Canton, Mass. Mem. Inst. Indsl. Engrs., Jr. Achievement Alumni (named Outstanding Young Bus. Woman). Address: 34 Tedesco St Marblehead MA 01945

CORWIN, VERA-ANNE VERSFELT, small business owner, consultant; b. Montclair, NJ; d. Porter LaRoy and Vera Anna (Price) Versfelt; m. John M. Corwin, Apr. 9, 1955; children: Gail Elizabeth Corwin Bayne, Gregory John, Lynn B. Corwin Byers. BS, Upsala Coll., 1954; MEd, Wayne State U.,

1972, PhD, 1977; PhD, Wayne State U., 1977. Instr. Wayne (N.J.) Sch. Dist., 1954-55; engr., spec., analyst Chrysler Corp., Highland Park, Mich., 1955-56, 78-85; instr. Royal Oak (Mich.) Sch. Dist., 1968-78; sr. systems engr. Electronic Data Systems, Troy, Mich., 1985-87; pres. Unique Solutions, Inc., Royal Oak, 1987—; tech. cons. Teltech, Inc., 1990—; adj. prof. U. Mich., Dearborn, Mich., 1989—, Wayne State U., 1989—; trainer Soc. Mfg. Engrs., Dearborn, 1987—. Pres. Arlington Park Homeowners Assn., Royal Oak, 1984-85, road commr., 1984-90. Mem. Soc. Automotive Engrs. (chmn. design experiments joint subcom.), Automotive Industry Action Group, Am. Soc. Quality Control (sr.), Soc. Mfg. Engrs. (sr.). Office: Unique Solutions Inc PO Box 1711 Royal Oak MI 48068

CORY, MARGARET F., retired nursing educator; b. Colorado Spgs., Colo., Nov. 4, 1911; d. Rudolph William and Mary Amelia (Farr) Heyse; m. Philip Braden Cory, June 5, 1976 (dec. 1986). BA, Colo. Coll., 1933; MS, U. Rochester, N.Y., 1934; RN, Mass. Gen. Hosp., Boston, 1937. Instr. U. Colo. Sch. Nursing, Denver, 1937-40, Yale U., New Haven, 1940-41; instr. to asst. prof. U. Minn., Mpls., 1941-46; asst. to assoc. prof. nursing Wayne State U., Detroit, 1946-54; prof. nursing U. Ark., Little Rock, 1954-57; prof. and dean sch. nursing U. N.D., Grand Forks, 1958-77; dean emeritus nursing U. N.D., 1977—; cons. in field. Bd. dirs. United Hosp., Grand Forks, N.D., 1977—. Recipient Disting. Svc. award, U. N.D. Alumni Assn., 1974. Mem. Am. Nurses Assn., N.D. Nurses Assn., Ret. Tchrs. Assn. (v.p. 1987-89). Democrat. United Ch. of Christ. Home: 749 S 30th St #232 Grand Forks ND 58201

COSBY, JAE TRAINA, administrative assistant; b. Atlanta, Sept. 13, 1960; d. Paul J. and Mary Ann (Delehanty) Traina; m. Stephen Jay Cosby, Oct. 12, 1985; 1 child, John Paul Stephen. BA in Journalism, Ga. State U. Adminstrv. asst. Fulton County Info. and Pub. Affairs, Atlanta. Mem. Women in Communicatons, AAUW, Mortar Board. Democrat. Roman Catholic. Home: 6547 Sevenoaks Dr Tucker GA 30084 Office: Fulton Co Info/Pub Affairs 141 Pryor St Ste 10063 Atlanta GA 30303

COSGROVE, BEATRICE MARY, retired executive secretary; b. Salt Lake City, July 27, 1917; d. David DAvis and Gladys Zillah (Sorrick) Connell; m. Frank Bailey Cosgrove Jr., Apr. 20, 1940 (div.); children: Frank Bailey III, Michael King. BA in Bus. Adminstrn., San Jose State U., 1938. Exec. sec. Lockheed Missiles & Space Co., Sunnyvale, Calif., 1956-81; exec. sec. to pres. DIALOG Info. Svcs., subsidiary of Lockheed Corp., Palo Alto, Calif., 1981-88; ret. Mem. Stanford Alumni Assn. (life), AAUW (chair. world affairs com. 1968-71), Stanford Club of Palo Alto. Republican. Christian Science.

COSSMAN, JOANNE PATRICIA TULLY, health facility administrator; b. Ventnor, N.J., Dec. 14, 1949; d. Joseph William and Gertrude (Herr) Tully; m. John W. Cossman, Sept. 23, 1982 (div. 1989); 1 child, Michael. BSN, Villanova U., 1971; MPH, U. N.C., 1976. RN Conn., N.J., Ohio, Del. Staff nurse Children's Seashore House, Atlantic City, N.J., 1971; pub. health nurse Atlantic County Health Dept., Mays Landing, N.J., 1971-74; clin. instr. sch. nursing Bryn Mawr (Pa.) Hosp., 1974-75; sr. nurse coord. Del. Cancer Network, Wilmington, 1976-79; dir. nursing Emily P. Bissell Hosp., Wilmington, 1979; asst. prof., oncology coord. Med. Coll. Ohio, Toledo, 1979-83; asst. exec. dir. Vis. Nurse Assn., New Haven, Conn., 1983-86; adminstr. Community Health Care Plan, New Haven, 1986—; asst. prof. U. Del., Newark, 1978-79; asst. dir. nursing Riverside Hosp., Toledo, 1981-83; asst. prof. Yale U. Sch. Nursing, New Haven, 1984—; cons. Fox Chase Cancer Ctr., Phila., 1983-84, The HMO Group, N.J., 1988; dir. Hamden (Conn.) Regional Adult Day Ctr., 1989—. Author, editor: Helping Cancer Patients Effectively, 1977; contbr. author: Home Health Administration, 1988; editor: Core Curriculum for Oncology, 1987. Mem. Rotary, Sigma Theta Tau. Roman Catholic. Home: 99 Mowry St North Haven CT 06473 Office: Community Health Care Plan 97 Barnes Rd Wallingford CT 06472

COSTA, CATHERINE AURORA, state senator; b. Bklyn., Mar. 21, 1926; d. Salvatore and Matilde (Giumporcaro) Bravo; m. Joseph F. Costa, Sept. 7, 1946; children: Nicholas, Theodore, Nadine. Freeholder, Burlington County (N.J.), 1972-83; mem. N.J. Gen. Assembly, 1982-83; mem. N.J. Senate, 1984—; asst. majority leader. Founder, Willingboro Library (N.J.), 1959, trustee, 1962-66; bd. dirs., chmn. Willingboro Zoning Bd. Adjustment, 1969-73; soil conservation dist. supr., 1971—. Named N.J. Mother of Yr., 1976, Citizen of Yr., VFW, Willingboro, 1982; recipient Soil Conservation Supr. award N.J. Assn. Natural Resource Dists., 1973, Appreciation award N.J. Coalition for Sch. Age Child Care, Outstanding Svc. award Jewish War Vets. U.S.A., Pres.' award N.J. Assn. Rehab. Facilities, Legis. Leadership award So. N.J. Pa. State, Woman of Achievement award Bus. and Profl. Women. Democrat. Roman Catholic. Home: 32 Twig Ln Willingboro NJ 08046 Office: NJ State Senate 11 W Broad St Burlington NJ 08016

COSTA, DONNA MARIE, secondary education educator; b. Peabody, Mass., Dec. 5, 1955; d. Antonio Sariva Costa and Lulu Rose (Silva) Costa-Smith; m. Brian Michael Phelan, Oct. 27, 1972 (div. 1982); children: Dawne Marie Phelan, Brian Michael Phelan II. AS, N. Shore Community Coll., Beverly, Mass., 1982; BA, U. Mass. at Boston, 1986; MEd in Sch. Adminstrn., Salem (Mass.) State Coll., 1988; postgrad., Harvard U., 1989-91. Cert. occupational tchr., Mass. Electronic technician P/M Instrument Co., Dedham, Mass., 1974-80; instr./dept. head Peabody Sch. Dept., 1981—; mem. Faculty Adv., Vocat. Adv., Electronics Adv., Ednl. Tech., Extended After Sch. Program bds., Peabody Sch. Dept., ednl. tech. com. Author, editor: 4 yr. electronics curriculum, 1990. Vol. ARC. Recipient Horace Mann grants, 1988, 89. Mem. NAFE, Assn. Supervision and Curriculum Devel., Smithsonian Instn., Phi Delta Kappa. Roman Catholic. Home: 63 Tracey St Peabody MA 01960

COSTA, MARY, soprano; b. Knoxville, Tenn.; student Los Angeles Conservatory of Music. Film voice of Sleeping Beauty by Walt Disney; appeared TV commls., 1955-57; debut Los Angeles Opera, 1958, in La Boheme, San Francisco Opera, 1959, as Violetta in La Traviata at Met. Opera, N.Y.C., 1964; appeared Glyndebourne Opera House, Royal Opera House Covent Garden, Teatro Nacional de San Carlos, Grand Theatre de Geneve, Vancouver, Lisbon, Kiev, Leningrad, Tbilisi, Boston, Cin., Hartford, Newark, Phila., San Antonio, Seattle; toured U.S. with Bernstein's Candide; appeared English prodn. Candide; revival Bernstein's Candide at John F. Kennedy Center for Performing Arts, 1971; tour Soviet Union, 1970; Bolshoi debut in La Traviatta, 1970; starring role motion picture The Great Waltz, 1972; appeared internat. recitals, orchs.; v.p. Hawaiian Fragrances, Honolulu, 1972. Vice pres. Calif. Inst. Arts. Named Woman of yr., Los Angeles, 1959; recipient DAR Honor medal, 1974, Tenn. Hall of Fame award, 1987; Mary Costa Scholarship established at U. Tenn., 1979. Address: care Calif Artists Mgmt 1182 Market St Suite 418 San Francisco CA 94102

COSTA, MARYANNE SUGARMAN, editor; b. Washington, Mar. 1, 1959; d. Jule Meyer and Sheila (Shanley) Sugarman; m. Anthony Eugene Costa, Sept. 19, 1987. BA in Psychology, Vanderbilt U., 1980. Asst. editor Academe: Bull. of the AAUP, Washington, 1982-87; editor Nat. Bus. Woman, Washington, 1988—. Contbr. features and nonfiction articles to profl. jours. Mem. Bus. & Profl. Women USA, Washington Independent Writers, Women in Communications. Office: Bus & Profl Women USA 2012 Massachusetts Ave NW Washington DC 20036

COSTANTINO, LORINE PROTZMAN, woodworking co. exec.; b. Chattanooga, Feb. 8, 1921; d. John Edgar and Rosa Jane (Ellis) McClelland; student U. Balt., U. Ill.; m. Conrad Protzman, 1937 (dec. 1958); children—Rosa Lorine, Charles Conrad, James Paul, Sharon Lee; m. 2d, Anthony A. Costantino, Feb. 27, 1960. With Conrad Protzman, Inc., Balt., 1954—, pres., chief exec., 1958—; developer apprenticeship programs for woodworking industry. Mem. Archtl. Woodworking Inst. (dir.), Bldg. Congress and Exchange Balt., Am. Sub-Contractors Assn., Nat. Assn. Women Bus. Owners, Iota Lambda Sigma (hon. mem. Nu chpt.). Republican. Roman Catholic. Club: Hillendale Country. Office: Conrad Protzman Inc 2325 Banger St Baltimore MD 21230

COSTANZO, HILDA ALBA, retired banker; b. Newark, Feb. 4; d. Smeraldo Louis and Giovanna Marianna (Mancuso) C. Pub. rels. cert., Princeton U., N.J. Bankers Assn. Sch., 1965; pre-standard cert., Am. Inst. Banking, 1967, standard cert., 1972; now student, Caldwell Coll. Various positions Howard Savs. Bank, Newark, 1943-66, asst. sec., 1966-74, asst. to pres., 1974-76, corp. sec., 1976-80, v.p., corp. sec., 1980-87, ret., 1987. Mem. Nat. Assn. Bank Women, Zonta Internat. (v.p. 1973-74). Republican. Presbyterian. Home: 3-H Nob Hill Roseland NJ 07068

COSTELLO, CHRISTINE ANN, chemist, polymer; b. Pitts., Feb. 5, 1958; d. Angela C. (Tedeslo) Costello. BS Chemistry, Carnegie Mellon U., 1980; PhD, U. Mass., 1987. Chemist Calgon Corp., Pitts., 1980-82; prin. rsch. chemist Air Products & Chems. Inc., Allentown, Pa., 1987-89; sr. chemist Exxon Rsch. & Engring. Co., Clinton, N.J., 1989—. Patentee in field. contbr. articles to profl. jours. Mem. Am. Chem. Soc.(Polmer Chemistry Div., Polymeric Materials Section.). Office: Exxon Rsch and Engring Co Rte 22 E Annandale NJ 08801

COSTELLO, CHRISTINE CLAIRE, company executive; b. Berwyn, Ill., May 14, 1968; d. William Thomas and Gloria Jean (Reich) Costello. BS in Acctg., DePaul U., Chgo., 1990. Adminstrv. mgr. Focus Group Ltd., Chgo., 1988-90; fin. analyst CCC Info. Svcs., Chgo., 1990—. Mem. Am. Soc. Women Accts., Golden Key, Theta Phi Alpha, Delta Mu Delta, Alpha Lambda Delta, Phi Alpha Delta. Republican. Roman Catholic. Home: 1215 S Clarence Ave Berwyn IL 60402 Office: CCC Info Svcs 640 N LaSalle Chicago IL 60610

COSTELLO, CLAUDIA J., automobile manufacturing company executive; b. Utica, N.Y., June 18, 1954; d. Wilbur Dean Yockey and Alice (Pettigrew) Spence; m. Joseph Francis Costello; children: Jessica, Corinne, Ashley. Student, Mohawk Valley Community Coll., Utica, 1972-73. Clk. Equitable Life Assurance Co., Syracuse, N.Y., 1974-75, mgr., 1975-83; mgr. Equitable Life Assurance Co., Columbus, Ohio, 1983-87; adminstrv. mgr. Toyota Motor Mfg., USA, Inc., Georgetown, Ky., 1987—. Mem. Internat. Facility Mgmt. Assn. Presbyterian. Office: Toyota Motor Mfg USA Inc 1001 Cherry Blossom Way Georgetown KY 40324

COSTELLO, DAWN ELIZABETH BARNES, nurse, hospital administrator; b. Allentown, Pa., Dec. 7, 1940; d. Earl O. and Thelma (Walp) Barnes; m. Robert G. Costello, May 12, 1962; children: Michael R., Kelly L. BS in Nursing, U. Pa., 1962, postgrad., 1987—; MEd, Temple U., 1967; EdD in Adminstrn., Lehigh U., 1973. Nurse Allentown Sch. Dists., 1963-67; dir. rsch. and records Lehigh County Community Coll., Schnecksville, Pa., 1972-74; assoc. dir. nursing Lehigh Valley Hosp., Allentown, 1974-78; assoc. dir. personal health svc. City of Allentown, 1979-81; dir. nursing Coaldale State Gen. (Pa.) Hosp., 1981—, dir. profl. svcs., 1989—; 1st bd. dir. pub. health nursing Bi-City Health Bur., Allentown and Bethlehem, Pa., 1979; adv. bd. Assoc. Nursing Degree Lehigh County Community Coll., 1987—, sec., 1988—, LPN program, 1984, Carbon County Vocat.-Tech. Inst., Jim Thorpe, Pa., 1981-84; cons. Northwestern Ctr., Schnecksville, 1978—. Mem. adv. bd. Am. Heart Assn. Bethlehem, 1974-78; sec., bd. dirs. Vols. in Am. Day Care, Allentown, 1972-78. Mem. Pa. Orgn. Nurse Execs. (pres. Eastern region 1988—), Lehigh Valley Assn. for Learning Disabilities (pres. 1981-83), Sigma Tau (nursing honor soc.), Sigma Theta Tau. Republican. Roman Catholic. Home: RD #1 Box 240-A Schnecksville PA 18078 Office: Coaldale Gen Hosp 7th St Coaldale PA 18218

COSTELLO, MARY, consulting company executive; b. Omaha, Oct. 25, 1940; d. Patrick Francis and Margaret Helen (Costello) Henry; m. Donald F. Costello, Sept. 2, 1961; children—Maureen, Rick, Dan, Peter, Tom, Ben, Meg. B.A. in Sociology, Duchesne Coll., 1964. Vice pres. Costello & Assocs., Lincoln, Nebr., 1970—; reporter, editor Sun Papers, Lincoln, 1970-80; editor Tafelspitz Mag., Vienna, Austria, 1981—. Author: The Mary Costello How to Get a Job Book, 1988; weekly column Over the Coffee Cup (1st place award Nat. Suburban Newspaper Assn., 1985, Nat. Fedn. Press Women 1975—). Bd. dirs. Cedars Found. Children's Home, Lincoln, 1984—; pres. Alzheimer's Disease and Related Disorders Assn., Lincoln, 1988—. Mem. Nebr. Press Women, Nat. Press Women. Office: Costello & Assocs 4210 S 33d St Lincoln NE 68506

COSTELLO, SHAWN RANDOLPH, agromomist; b. Arlington, Va., July 14, 1960; d. George William and Barbara (Stelle) C. BS, Va. Poly. Inst. and State U., 1982; MS, U. Fla., 1984. Biologist Dupont Co., Newark, 1985—. Contbr. articles to profl. jours. Office: Dupont Co Stine Haskell Lab PO Box 30 Newark DE 19711

COSTENBADER, CYNTHIA LOU, pediatrics educator; b. Denver, Aug. 15, 1956; d. Carl Willard and Mary Ruth (Simmons) C.; m. Frederick Albert McGrath, Sept. 17, 1988. BS, U. Md., 1978, MD, 1982. Diplomate Am. Bd. Pediatrics. Intern Children's Nat. Med. Ctr., Washington, 1982-83, resident in pediatrics, 1983-85; pvt. practice Alexandria, Va., 1985-86; clin. instr. pediatrics George Washington U. Sch. Medicine, Washington, 1986-89, asst. prof., 1989—. Contbr. articles to profl. jours. Fellow Am. Acad. Pediatrics; mem. Va. Pediatric Soc. Republican. Methodist. Office: George Washington U Health Plan 6303 Little River Turnpike Alexandria VA 22312

COSTER, NANCY L., financial advisor; b. N.Y.C., Apr. 17, 1941; d. Robert Louis and Frances (Rozran) Boehm; m. Paul Greenfield, June 15, 1965 (div. Sept. 1970); m. Charles Stuart Coster, June 26, 1977. BA, U. Wis., 1963; MA, New Sch. for Social Rsch., 1968; postgrad., Boston Coll., 1986-87. Researcher Dr. Max Wolff, Sociologist, N.Y.C., 1964; researcher, organizer of press confs. Am. Com. on Africa, N.Y.C., 1967-68; exec. dir. Boehm Found., N.Y.C., 1980-86; fin. advisor Boehm Enterprises, N.Y.C., 1989—; trustee Boehm Found., N.Y.C., 1986—. Exhibited in photography show, Boston, 1984. Intern, Congressman Barney Frank, Newton, Mass., 1988. Mem. Women & Founds. Corp. Philanthropy, Coun. on Founds., Nat. Network of Grant Makers, Boston Network for Women in Govt. Politics. Home: 4 Sparks Pl Cambridge MA 02138

COSTLEY, JENNIFER L., technology planner; b. Monterrey, Tenn., May 26, 1956; d. Cleve C. and Twila P. (Raber) Costley. Student, Lehigh U., Bethlehem, Pa., 1974-75; BA, Brandeis U., Waltham, Mass., 1978; MA, Columbia U., N.Y.C., 1980, PhD, 1983. Mem. tech. staff Bell Labs-Bus. Analysis Ctr., Murray Hill, N.J., 1982-86, supr., 1986-88; v.p. Fin., Planning, Adminstrn. Bankers Trust, N.Y.C., 1988--. Treas. Personal Liberty Fund, New Brunswick N.J. 1984--. Recipient Chemistry Honors award Chemistry Dept. Brandeis U., 1978. Mem. Phi Beta Kappa. Home: 1021 Grand St Apt 3D Hoboken NJ 07030

COSTON, NEEOMA LEE, medical center administrator; b. Stilwell, Okla., Sept. 17, 1935; d. George R. and Dessie D. (Burnett) Mathews; m. Theodore J. Coston, Jan. 22, 1960; childern: Scott Theodore, Julie Ann. AA in Pub. Rels., Arapahoe Community Coll., Littleton, Colo., 1973; BA in Communication, Loretto Heights Coll., Denver, 1974. Lic. real estate agt., cosmetologist, Colo. Personnel security clk. Martin Marietta Co., Denver, 1959-60; news reporter Littleton Ind., 1964-70; state advisor March of Dimes, Denver, 1965-75; dir. devel. and communication Arthritis Found., Denver, 1977-84; exec. dir. Leukemia Soc., Denver, 1984-86; cons. Coston & Assocs., Denver, 1986-88; nat. dir. auxs. Nat. Jewish Ctr. for Immunology and Respiratory Medicine, Denver, 1988—. Contbr. articles to profl. jours. Bd. dirs., vols. St. Anthony Hosp., Denver, 1972; del. Colo. Rep. Conv., 1986. Mem. Colo. Assn. Fund Raisers, Colo. Health Assn. (bd. dirs. 1986-88), Phi Theta Kappa, Epsilon Sigma Alpha (chpt. pres. 1974-75, mem. state coun. 1978-87, state pres. 1984, Woman of Yr. award Epsilon coun. 1984), Phi Theta Kappa, Epsilon Sigma Alpha. Lutheran. Home: 8253 S St Paul Way Littleton CO 80122 Office: Nat Jewish Ctr Immunology 1400 Jackson Denver CO 80206

COTA, KAREN L., newspaper editor; b. Lima, Ohio, Feb. 7, 1957; d. Robert Frederick and Dorothy (Riepenhoff) Nadler; m. Daniel M. Cota, Oct. 25, 1980; children: Caroline, Danielle. BS in Journalism, Bowling Green (Ohio) State U., 1979. Pub. rels. intern Bowling Green State U. Office Pubs., 1978-79; news reporter The Lima (Ohio) News, 1979-80; news reporter, lifestyle editor The Sentinel-Tribune, Bowling Green, 1980—; editor Little People of Am., Inc., 1983-84. Fin. com. chmn. St. Thomas More Ch., 1990—, Eucharistic minister, 1986—. Mem. AaUW (nominating com.), Little People of Am. Democrat. Roman Catholic. Home: 19170 Mercer Rd Bowling Green OH 43402

COTANT, MARILYN JEAN, vocational evaluator, administrator; b. Scottsbluff, Nebr., May 18, 1950; d. Charles Alexander and Betty May (Locker) Lee; m. Patrick Wayne Cotant, Dec. 27, 1968; children: Casey Lee, Brian Jerome. AS, Nebr. Western Coll., 1974; BA, Chadron State Coll., 1984. Cert. vocat. evaluator, Nebr., Wyo. Coord. Scotts Bluff County Child Abuse Coun., Scottsbluff, 1978; counselor-aide N.E. div. Rehab., Scottsbluff, 1974-80, acting rehab. counselor, 1980-81; vocat. evaluator career assessment ctr. N.E. Western Coll., Scottsbluff, 1981-85, dir. career assessment ctr., 1985-86; dir. S.E. Wyo. Vocat. Assessment and Evaluation Ctr. Ea. Wyo. Coll., Torrington, 1986—; tech. asst. Wyo. Schs. and Agys., 1986—. Mem. Foster Care Rev. Bd., Scottsbluff, 1984; sec. Band Adv. Coun. United Parents, Torrington, 1988-89, Meth. Ch. Adminstrv. Coun., Gering, Nebr., 1983. Mem. An. Vocat. Assn., Nat. Assn. Vocat. Evaluation In Edn., Ea. Wyo. Higher Edn. Profl. Assn. (social chair), Regional and County Transitional Svcs. Team, Goshen County Human Svc. Providers Assn. Democrat. Office: Ea Wyo Coll 3200 West C St Torrington WY 82240

COTE, LOUISE ROSEANN, art director, designer; b. Quincy, Mass., Sept. 16, 1959; d. John Anthony and Theresa Janet (Oriola) Burke; m. Robert Andrew Cote, Aug. 6, 1983. BA, Bridgewater State Coll., 1981. Advt. asst. Dunnington Super Drug, Brockton, Mass., 1978-81; forms and graphics designer Shawmut Bank of Boston, N.A., 1981-86; artist aftermarket div. Allied-Signal Inc., East Providence, R.I., 1986-89; creative svcs. adminstr. aftermarket electronics div. Allied-Signal Inc., 1989—. Mem. Women's Advt. Club R.I. Roman Catholic. Office: Allied-Signal Inc Aftermarket Electronics Div 105 Pawtucket Ave East Providence RI 02916

COTE, SALLY SPILKER, infosystems manager; b. Huntington, W.Va., Nov. 16, 1946; d. Norman David and Nancy Ann (Gracie) S; m. Francis (Frank) Loyal Cote, Mar. 14, 1980. BS in Math., U. Ky., 1968; MBA, U. Detroit, 1983. Systems programmer analyst, supr. Ford Motor Credit Co., Dearborn, Mich., 1968-84, systems planning and devel. mgr., 1984-86, systems sect. supr. fin. staff, 1986-87, systems office mgr. office gen. counsel, 1987—. Active Dearborn Hills Civic Assn., 1983—; animal rights activist and environmentalist. Presbyterian. Office: Ford Motor Co Office Gen Counsel Parklane Towers West Ste 820 Dearborn MI 48126

COTE-BEAUPRE, CAMILLE YVETTE, artist, educator; b. Worcester, Mass., May 21, 1926; d. Harvey and Blanche (Trahan) Cote; B.A. cum laude, Am. Internat. Coll., 1949; cert. in fine arts, Walker Studio Group, 1952; M.S., U. Bridgeport, 1967. Dir. arts and crafts South End Community Center, Springfield, Mass., 1955-58; art tchr. YWCA, Springfield, 1958-61; dir. workshops Hall Neighborhood House, Bridgeport, Conn., 1961-64, Jewish Community Center, Bridgeport, 1964-69; tchr., chmn. art dept. Notre Dame High Sch., Fairfield, Conn., 1970—; one-woman shows: Bridgeport Cath. Center, 1978, Creative Mind Gallery, Stratford, Conn., 1978, Burroughs Library, Bridgeport, 1979, Trumbull (Conn.) Library, 1981, St. Vincent's Hosp., Bridgeport, 1981, St. Joseph Manor, Trumbull, 1981; group shows include: Stamford (Conn.) Mus., 1977, Slade Mus., Norwich, Conn., 1975, Mus. Sci. and Industry, Bridgeport, 1974, Sacred Heart U., Bridgeport, 1979, Fairfield (Conn.) U., 1979, 56th grand nat. Am. Artists Profl. League, others; represented in permanent collections: Eastern Conn. State Coll., Trumbull Library Assn., St. Vincent's Hosp., St. Joseph's Manor. Mem. Conn. Classic Artists, Diocesan Bridgeport Edn. Assn., Newtown Soc. for Creative Arts, Am. Portrait Soc., Acad. Artists Assn., Nat. Arts Club, Conn. Pastel Soc. Home: 12 Melon Patch Ln Monroe CT 06468 Office: Notre Dame High Sch 220 Jefferson St Fairfield CT 06430

COTHORNE, ROBIN J., medical/surgical nurse; b. Balt., Dec. 6, 1961; d. Ernest Lee and Ida Mae (Lockett) Williams; m. Roland Clifton Cothorne II, Feb. 22, 1986. BSN, Coppin State Coll., 1985. RN; cert. in advanced trauma life support. Charge nurse minor care emergency rm. and med. surg. fl. Comanche County Meml. Hosp., Lawton, Okla., 1986-89; primary nurse adult emergency rm. U. Md.Med. System, Balt., 1989-90; utilization rev. coord., case mgr. Homewood Hosp. Ctr., Balt., 1990. With Med. Svc. Corps, 1986-88; 1st lt. Mil. Police, U.S. Army, 1988-90. ROTC scholar, 1983-85. Mem. Emergency Nurses Assn., Md. Nurses Assn., Nat. Black Nurses Assn., State Assn. Quality Assn. Profls., Iota Phi Lamda. Home: 4 Crooked Willow Ct Baltimore MD 21228 Office: Homewood Hosp Ctr 3100 Wyman Park Dr Baltimore MD 21211

COTMAN, SHIRLEY ANN, secretary; b. Birmingham, Ala.; d. Carl Thomas and Nora (Mitchell) C. Student, Wheeler Bus. Sch. Former diagnostic X-ray file clk., now sec. U. Ala., Birmingham; sec. Stonewall Ins., Birmingham. Vol. Univ. Hosp. Aux. Dance Ptnrs., ARC, Birminghan Humane Soc. Mem. NAFE, Profl. Secs. Internat. Republican. Methodist. Home: 1573 Berry Rd Birmingham AL 35226

COTNER, C(AROL) BETH, financial services company executive; b. Bremerton, Wash., Dec. 20, 1952; d. Robert Arthur and Doris (Kerns) C.; m. James D. Leatherberry, Dec. 14, 1974 (div. Aug. 1982); m. John M. Alogna, 1984. BA, Ohio State U., 1974; MBA, George Washington U., 1976. Cert. fin. analyst. Investment analyst Am. Security Bank, Washington, 1975-77; portfolio mgr. Sears Investment Mgmt., Chgo., 1979-84; investment analyst Kemper Fin. Svcs., Chgo., 1977-79, portfolio mgr., 1984—. Bd. dirs. Body Politic Theatre, Chgo., 1988—. Mem. Investment Analysts Soc. Chgo. (sec. 1984, bd. dirs. 1985-89), Consumer Analysts Soc. Chgo. (chmn. 1980-81), Phi Beta Kappa. Republican. Episcopalian. Office: Kemper Fin Svcs 120 S La Salle St Chicago IL 60603

COTTEN, CATHERYN DEON, medical center international advisor; b. Erwin, N.C., Apr. 13, 1952; d. Ben Hur and Minnie Lee (Smith) C. BS in Anthropology, Duke U., 1975. Asst. internat. advisor Med. Ctr. Duke U., Durham, N.C., 1975-76; internat. advisor Med. Ctr. Duke U., Durham, 1976—. Mem., bd. dirs., tutor Durham Lit. Coun., 1985—; mem. internat. com. Durham County ARC, 1987—. Recipient Cert. Recognition So. Regional Coun. Black Am. Affairs, Atlanta, 1985. Mem. Assn. Internat. Educators (govt. regulations adv. com. 1985—, chair Southeastern region 1989-90, dep. chair 1990-91), Altrusa Club (pres. Durham chpt. 1987-89, presentor internat. conf. 1989). Office: Duke U Med Ctr Box 3882 Durham NC 27710

COTTER, LUCY ANN, animal research technician; b. Pitts., Aug. 4, 1957; d. William John and Elizabeth Louise (Crozier) C. BA in Animal and Vet. Sci., W.Va. U., 1979. Lic. animal health technician, Pa. Lab. asst. W.Va. U., Morgantown, 1975-79; asst. mgr. Greengrocer, Pitts., 1980; vet. asst. Pitts. Animal Hosp., 1980-87; rsch. technician II, Eye and Ear Hosp., Pitts., 1986-88, Eye and Ear Inst. Pitts., 1988—. Mem. Am. Assn. Lab. Animal Sci. (registered lab. animal technologist),, Vet. Technicians Asst. Assn. Office: Eye and Ear Inst Pitts 203 Lothrop St Pittsburgh PA 15213

COTTER, SHIRLEY ANN, financial planner; b. Slim River, Malaysia; came to U.S., 1974; naturalized, 1987; d. Isaac V. and Ivy (D'Cruez) Pereira; m. Gary W. Cotter, Dec. 11, 1982. RN, Queen Mary's Hosp., Sidcup, Kent, Eng., 1965; postgrad., Sussex Maternity Hosp., Brighton, Eng., 1965, Dartford Hosp., Kent, Eng., 1966, McGill U., Montreal, Que., 1974. Med. adminstr. U.S. Peace Corps., Kuala Lumpur, Malaysia, 1969-73; RN intensive care unit Meml. Med. Ctr., Corpus Christi, Tex., 1974-76, Spohn Hosp., Corpus Christi, 1976-78; registered rep. Investors Diversified Services, Inc., Mpls., 1979-83; branch mgr. WZW Fin. Services, Inc., Shawnee Mission, Kans., 1983-84; registered rep. The Planner's Securities Group, Inc., Atlanta, 1985-89; v.p. Cotter & Cotter Fin. Group, Corpus Christi, 1984—, Cotter & Cotter Risk Mgmt. Corp., Corpus Christi, 1985—, Cotter & Cotter Fin. Cons., Inc., Corpus Christi, 1984—. Mem. Internat. Assn. Fin. Planning (dir. 1986—), Inst. for Cert. Fin. Planners (provisional mem. 1983-85). Office: Cotter & Cotter Fin Group 705 MBank Center North Corpus Christi TX 78471-0801

COTTER, VERONICA IRENE, hotel executive; b. Altoona, Pa., June 2, 1949; d. William John and Joan Elmyra (Pennington) C.; m. Kenneth Brown, Sept. 12, 1971 (div. Mar. 1977); 1 child, Jennifer Alena. BS, Northeastern U., Boston, 1978. With nat. group sales office The Sheraton Corp., Boston, 1978-79; with sales tng. program The Sheraton Boston, 1980; account exec. Billings (Mont.) Sheraton, 1980; corp. sales mgr., account exec. Sheraton Columbus, Ohio, 1980-82; sr. account exec. Sheraton Steamboat

Springs, Colo., 1982-83; mgr. sales Sheraton Charleston, S.C., 1983-84; dir. sales Sheraton Denver Airport Hotel, 1985-86; sr. account mgr. Sheraton Grande Hotel, Los Angeles, 1986-88; nat. acct. mgr. Walt Disney World Dolphin Hotel, Lake Buena Vista, Fla., 1988—; instr. mktg. Am. Coll. Hotel Restaurant Mgmt. Area advisor Jr. Achievement, Nashville, 1985; vol. Buddy at AIDS Project, Los Angeles. Mem. Am. Soc. Assn. Execs., Meeting Planners Internat., Hotel Sales and Mktg. Assn. (pres. 1988-89), Greater Washington Soc. Assn. Execs. Democrat. Roman Catholic. Home: 2058 Country Side Circle S Orlando FL 32804 Office: Walt Disney World Dolphin 1500 EPCOT Resort Blvd Lake Buena Vista FL 32830

COTTERILL, NANCY ANN, publisher; b. Waukegan, Ill., Sept. 25, 1950; d. Elmore Arthur and Lucile Elizabeth (Legge) Heppner; m. James Robert Cotterill, Aug. 14, 1970; children: Christopher Ward, Theodore Coates. Student, Butler U., 1972. Assoc. editor Indpls. Monthly, 1978-80; editor Indpls. Bus. Jour., 1980-87, pub., 1987-90; editorial dir. Bus. Jour. Pub. Co., Indpls., 1984-87; pub. Indpls. C.E.O. Mag., 1990—; reporter bus. news local CBS Affiliate, Sta. WISH-TV, Indpls., 1984-90; co-anchor PBS Ind. Bus., Indpls., 1982-87. Mem. exec. com. Start with Art Week, Indpls., 1989, 90, Indpls. Charity Horse Show, 1990; bd. dirs. Ronald McDonald House, Indpls., 1990—. Recipient Francis Wright award Women in Communications, Inc., 1987, Thomas Keating Excellence award, 1990, SBA Ind. Medice award, 1990. Mem. Ind. Small Bus. Coun. (charter bd. dirs. Indpls. chpt. 1984-86), Network of Women in Bus., Rotary Internat.

COTTINGTON, LINDA RENEÉ, communications executive; b. Des Moines, Sept. 12, 1948; d. Richard G. and Janet (Halverson) C.; m. Thomas J. Miller, Jan. 10, 1981; 1 child, Matthew. BS, Iowa State U., 1970; MBA, Drake U., 1977. Dir. Dept. Social Svcs., Des Moines, 1977-80; v.p. Preferred Risk, Des Moines, 1980-82; ptnr. McGladrey & Pullen, Des Moines, 1982-89; chmn. Cara Communications, Des Moines, 1989—. Pres. YWCA, Des Moines, 1989; bd. dirs. Iowa Group-Econ. Devel., 1990, Mayor's Drug Task Force, 1990. Named Outstanding Alumnus Iowa State U., 1983, Iowa's Up and Comer, 1986, Most Powerful Woman, 1990 Des Moines Register. Bd. dirs. Iowa State Alumni Assn., Des Moines Chamber (exec. com. 1985—), Iowa Group for Econ. Devel. Home: 213 28th St Des Moines IA 50312

COTTON, ANNE, college registrar; b. Columbus, Ohio, June 19, 1933; d. James Harry and Luella Faye (Goodhart) C. AB, Smith Coll., 1955; EdM, Harvard U., 1972, EdD, 1982. Sec. Doubleday Pub. Co., N.Y.C., 1956-57, Met. Opera Assn., N.Y.C., 1957-62; staff asst. Health Svcs. Harvard U., Cambridge, Mass., 1962-67, asst. registrar, then registrar Grad. Sch. Edn., 1967-87; registrar Mount Holyoke Coll., South Hadley, Mass., 1987—. Recording sec. Reform Independent Dems., N.Y.C., 1961-62; vol. various causes, 1962—. Mem. Am. Assn. Collegiate Registrars and Admissions Officers, New England Assn. Collegiate Registrars and Admissions Officers, Friends of Irene Adler. Democrat. Congregationalist. Office: Mount Holyoke Coll South Hadley MA 01075

COTTON, LORI LEE, computer engineer; b. Houston, Tex., Sept. 19, 1956; d. Louis H. and Stella Lou (Todd) C.; m. Aldo Carrera, Aug. 15, 1980; (div. Sept. 1983). BS CS, SIUE, Edwardsville, 1983. Computer operator MICC, Edwardsville, 1978-82; application programmer GTE, Chgo., 1983-87; software engr. Emerson Electric Co., St. Louis, 1987—; cons. in field. Author: (Database Program), 1986, (Laser Printer Preprocessor), 1988. Mem. Pro-Choice, Hazelwood Racquettball Club. Home: 765 Pebble Florissant MO 63033 Office: Emerson Electric Co 8100 W Florissant Saint Louis MO 63136

COTTON, PATRICIA ALICE, psychology educator, counselor; b. N.Y.C., June 5, 1940; d. Earnest Patrick and Mary Amelia (Toich) Cotton; m. Frederick Lawton Cox, Nov. 7, 1959 (div. 1974); 1 child, Constance Saige Cox McDonald. BA in Art Edn., English, U. Tex., El Paso, 1973, M. in Counseling Guidance, 1974; EdD in Psychology, U. Houston, 1985. Lic. profl. counselor; cert. tchr., nat. cert. clin. mental health counselor. Vocat. counselor, coord. group program U. Tex., El Paso, 1971-74; asst. dir. Cath. Counseling Svcs., El Paso, 1974-79; personnel rsch. specialist City of Houston, 1981-82; pvt. practice counselor Houston, 1983-88; teaching asst. U. Houston, 1979-85; instr. Houston Community Coll., 1980-88; asst. program dir., counselor Houston N.W. Med. Ctr., 1985-88; pvt. practice counselor Alamo Mental Health Group, San Antonio, 1989—; instr. psychology St. Mary's U., San Antonio, 1990—; counseling cons. Dr. M.J. Chojnacki, Houston, 1985-87. Artist sculpture "Rinocessoris", 1965 (Nat. Army Art/Craft award); contbr. articles to profl. jours. Active outreach seminars for jobless Exec.-Blue Collar North West Med. Ctr., Houston, 1986. Recipient Scholastic Achievement award Kappa Delta Pi, 1972; 2-yr. grantee outreach for work with elderly City of El Paso, 1975-77. Mem. Am. Psychol. Assn., Tex. Assn. for Counseling & Devel. Roman Catholic. Home: 14215 Parksite Woods San Antonio TX 78249 Office: Alamo Mental Health Group 4242 Medical Dr San Antonio TX 78229

COTTONE, LINDA MARIE, bank executive; b. Lawrence, Mass., Jan. 29, 1945; d. Salvatore Joseph and Mary Dolores (Rizzotti) Laudani; m. Vincent Paul Cottone, May 31, 1964; children: Dina L., Lauren A. Cert., Wash. Sch. for Secs., 1961; student, No. Essex Community Coll., Haverhill, Mass., 1980—, U. Lowell, 1980—; cert., Fairfield U., 1984. With Lawrence Savs. Bank, 1973-86, asst. br. mgr., 1979-80, br. mgr., 1980-86; asst. treas., br. mgr. Andover (Mass.) Savs. Bank, 1986—; chairperson Bankers Ednl. Forum, Essex, Merrimack, Mass. and Andover, 1988-89; mem. Ladies of Merrimack Coll., North Andover, Mass., 1986—; notary pub. Commonwealth of Mass., Boston, 1980—; registered savs. bank and life ins. agent Savs. Bank Life Ins., Woburn, Mass., 1977—. Vol. Am. Heart Assn., North Andover, 1987—, Read-A-Loud program Tarbox Sch., Lawrence, 1988—. Mem. Andover C. of C., Exch. Club Greater Lawrence (pres. 1977-78). Roman Catholic. Home: 7 Bonny Ln North Andover MA 01845 Office: Andover Savs Bank 159 River Rd Andover MA 01810

COTTRELL, JANET ANN, retail executive; b. Berea, Ohio, Dec. 2, 1943; d. Carmen and Hazel (French) Volpe; m. Melvin M. Cottrell, Mar. 2, 1963; children: Lori A., Gregory C. Student, Los Angeles State Coll., 1961-63. Lic. ins. agt., Calif. Loan processing Eastern Lenders, Covina, 1962-64; asst. bookkeeper Golden Rule Discount Stores, Rosemead, Calif., 1964-66; acctg. supr. Walter Carpet Mills, Industry, Calif., 1967-69; co-owner Motorcycle Specialties Co., Industry, 1969-78, Covina (Calif.) Kawasaki, 1978-84; v.p., contr. M.C. Specialties Inc., Covina, 1984—; active various coms. relating to promotion, safety and advancement of the recreational vehicle and auto industry, So. Calif., 1981—. Mem. com. Miss Covina Pageant, 1986—, presdl. task force, nat., 1982—, Rep. nat. com., 1986—. Mem. Covina C. of C., Calif. Motorcycle Dealers Assn., Nat. Auto Dealers Assn., Internat. Jet Ski Boating Assn. Republican. Office: MC Specialties Inc 1017 W San Bernardino Rd Covina CA 91722

COTTRELL, MARY-PATRICIA TROSS, banker; b. Seattle, Apr. 24, 1934; d. Alfred Carl and Alice-Grace (O'Neal) Tross; m. Richard Smith Cottrell, May 17, 1969. BBA, U. Wash., 1955. Systems service rep. IBM, Seattle, also Endicott, N.Y., 1955-58, customer edn. instr., Endicott, 1958-60, 62-65, edn. planning rep., San Jose, Calif. and Endicott, N.Y., 1960-62; cons. data processing, Stamford, Conn., 1965-66; asst. treas. Union Trust Co., Stamford, 1967-68, asst. v.p., 1969-76, v.p., 1976-78, v.p., head corp. services, 1978-83; v.p. corp. fin. services Citytrust, Bridgeport, Conn., 1983—. Bd. dirs. Family and Children's Aid of Greater Norwalk (Conn.), chmn. 1986-87, Gaylord Hosp., 1986—, Bridgeport Housing Services, New Eng. Network, Inc., Bank Mktg. Assn., 1988—. Mem. Electronic Funds Transfer Assn. (vice chmn., bd. dirs., chmn. bd. dirs. 1983-84), Fairfield County Bankers Assn. (dir., pres. 1984-85), West Norwalk Assn. (bd. dirs.), Phi Beta Kappa, Beta Gamma Sigma. Republican. Roman Catholic. Club: Grad. Office: Citytrust 961 Main St Bridgeport CT 06601

COUCH, B. JOYCE, management career consultant; b. Mobile, Ala., Apr. 26, 1954; d. Robert Chesley and Barbara Allen (Joyce) C. BS, Auburn U., 1976; MS, U. Ala., Birmingham, 1980; EdD, Memphis State U., 1984. Pers. adjustment specialist Delgado Jr. Coll., New Orleans, 1976-77; vocat. evaluation specialist Ala. Inst. for the Deaf & Blind, Talladega, Ala., 1977-80; pvt. practice career planning cons. Memphis, 1980-90; mgr., human resources planning First Tenn. Bank, Memphis. Author: Job Match: A Process for Hiring Qualified Handicapped, 1984; contbr. articles to profl. jours. Mem. World Future Soc., Am. Soc. for Tng.Devel., Nat. Rehab. Assn., Sierra Club, Cousteau Soc. Episcopalian. Office: Cons Service 752 Crossover Ln Memphis TN 38117

COUCH, MARGARET WHELAND, research chemist; b. Chgo., Aug. 27, 1941; d. George Willard and Elizabeth (Clayton) Wheland; m. Leon Worthington Couch II, Aug. 15, 1964; children: Leon III, Jonathan, Rebecca. BS, Duke U., 1963; MS, U. Fla., 1966, PhD, 1969. Rsch. assoc. in radiology U. Fla. Coll. Medicine, Gainesville, 1970-71, asst. rsch. prof. dept. radiology, 1971—; rsch. chemist VA Med. Ctr., Gainesville, 1971—. Methodist. Office: VA Med Ctr Nuclear Medicine Svc Gainesville FL 32602

COUCHMAN, MARY CATHERINE, administrative assistant; b. Centerville, Iowa, Aug. 24, 1945; d. George Richard and Genevieve Catherine (Rash) Mincks; m. Gary Joe Couchman, Nov. 7, 1965; children: Duane Lee, Troy Dean. Student, N.E. Mo. State U., 1963-65, Indian Hills Community Coll., 1965, Parsons Coll., Mt. Pleasant, Iowa, 1971. Sec. various orgns., 1962-66, 75-77, 77-82; sch. tchr. substitute R 3, Unionville, Mo., 1974-77; adminstrv. asst. Rathbun Area Mental Ctr., Centerville, 1982—, support staff coordinator, 1983—. Mem. Community Betterment Com., Seymour, Iowa, Extension Council Wayne County, Corydon, Iowa, 1984-86; pres. United Meth. Women, Seymour, fin. chmn. United Meth. Ch., Seymour, 1985-87. Named one of Outstanding Young Women of Am., 1971. Mem. Nat. Assn. Female Execs., Beta Tau Delta. Republican. Club: Rainbow (Seymour) (worthy advisor 1962-63). Home: RR #1 Box 77 Seymour IA 52590 Office: Rathbun Area Mental Health Ctr 211 E State Centerville IA 52544

COUGHLIN, ELIZABETH ANN, union official, consultant; b. Americus, Ga., Oct. 1, 1945; d. Sammie Raymond and Ruth Willie (Missledine) Simmons; m. Richard Paul Coughlin, Aug. 21, 1965. BA in Social Sci., St. Mary's Coll., 1978. Cert. employed assistance profl. Sr. med. abstractor Kaiser Hosp., Oakland, Calif., 1965-74; union rep. Office and Profl. Employees Union 29, Emeryville, Calif., 1974-76; cons. Nat. Council on Alcoholism, San Francisco, 1976-80, Simmons Coughlin Ltd., Oakland, 1980-88, sec.-treas., 1988—. Office and Profl. Employees Union 29, Emeryville, 1982—; mem. wage bd. State Calif. Indsl. Welfare Commn., Sacramento, 1976; co-chair Calif. Women's Commn. on Alcoholism, San Francisco, 1976-79; lectr., faculty mem. U. San Francisco, Duke U., U. Utah, Vista Coll., 1977-83; cons. State Calif., Sacramento, 1978-79. Prin. co-author: You Know You're a Peace Officer's Wife When, 1978. Editor The 29er, 1982-83. Mem. Friendship Force Internat., San Francisco, 1984—. Recipient Past Pres. award Past Pres. Com. of Peace Officers' Wives' Club Affiliated Calif., 1978, Resolution of Spl. Pub. Honor and Highest Commendation, Calif. Legislature, 1980, Disting. Service award Nat. Council on Alcoholism, San Francisco, 1981; named Unionist of Yr., Alameda County Labor Council, Oakland, Calif., 1980. Mem. Assn. Labor/Mgmt. Adminstrs. and Cons. on Alcoholism, Problems of Alcoholism in Labor and Mgmt. (bd. dirs. 1984—). Avocations: world travel; reading. Home: 6121 Buenaventura Oakland CA 94605 Office: Office and Profl Employees Union 29 1475 Powell St Emeryville CA 94608

COUGHLIN, SISTER KATHLEEN, hospital administrator; b. St. Louis, July 10, 1941; d. Thomas Carlyle and Lucille Marie (Baumker) C. B.S. in Nursing, Incarnate Word Coll., San Antonio, 1967; M.H.A., St. Louis U., 1972. Joined Sisters of Charity of Incarnate Word, 1960; dir. nurses St. Joseph's Hosp., Paris, Tex., 1967-70; adminstrv. resident Mercy Hosp., Denver, 1971-72; asst. adminstr. St. Anthony's Hosp., Amarillo, Tex., 1972-73, adminstr., 1973-79; dir. Community and Apostolic Ministry-Provincial Council, St. Louis, 1978-81; pres. Spohn Hosp., Corpus Christi, Tex., 1981—. Trustee Incarnate Word Hosp., St. Louis, 1973—, chmn., 1985; trustee Tex. Conf. Catholic Health Facilities, 1978-84, pres., 1983; trustee Mary, Queen and Mother Nursing Home, 1979-81, Midtown Med. Ctr. Redevel. Corp., 1979-81, Sisters of Charity Health System, 1984—. Recipient Woman of Yr. award, Amarillo, Tex., 1976; Women in Careers award YWCA, Corpus Christi, 1984. Fellow Am. Coll. Hosp. Adminstrs.; mem. Cath. Health Assn. (trustee 1978-84), Corpus Christi C. of C. (trustee 1983—), Tex. Conf. Catholic Heatlh Facilities, Tex. Hosp. Assn. (trustee 1984—).

COUGHLIN, MARGARET ANN, communications executive; b. Muncie, Ind., Oct. 14, 1955; d. Thomas Francis and Mary Alice (Guffigan) C.; m. John M. Riley III, Mar. 24, 1984; 1 child, Meaghan Coughlin. BA, Skidmore Coll., 1977; MBA, Babson Coll., 1984. Sales mgr. Procter & Gamble, Cin., 1977-79; account exec. Hill Holiday Advt., Boston, 1979-81; account supr. HBM Advt., Boston, 1982-84; dir. bus. devel., mgmt. supr. Ingalls Quinn & Johnson, Boston, 1984—, now v.p. Bd. dirs. Boston Children's Svc. Assn., 1988—. Mem. Women in Communications (pres. 1988—). Office: Ingalls Quinn & Johnson 855 Boylston St Boston MA 02116*

COULSON, ARLENE ANN, educator; b. Chgo., Aug. 27, 1935; d. Arthur C. and Pearl M. (Witt) Albrecht; m. Donald L. Coulson, Sept. 1, 1956; children: Carl S., Kurth C., Heidi B. BA, Trinity U., Deerfield, Ill., 1975; MA, Northfield U., DeKalb, Ill., 1985. Cert. tchr. Tchr. Sch. Dist. So., Libertyville, Ill., 1975—; v.p. ops. Coulson and Assocs. Ltd., Libertyville, Ill., 1958--. Mem. L.E.A., AAUW, Eastern Star. Republican. Presbyterian. Home: 600 Wrightwood Libertyville IL 60048

COULSON, CAROLYN LU, bridal retail owner; b. Brush, Colo., Dec. 25, 1937; d. Doyle Grover and Lucille Delois (McNeill) Clark; m. Richard Lee Coulson, Apr. 9, 1955; children: Kenneth Lee, Kay Luanne, William Alan. Student, Colo. State U., 1972. Water safety instr. City of Loveland, 1956-59; teaching R2J Sch. Dist., Loveland, 1972-76; sr. order adminstrn. Hewlett Packard Co., Loveland, 1976-84; retail owner Satin Rose Bridal Salon Ltd., Loveland, 1984—; bd. dirs. Meals on Wheel, Loveland, 1972-74, Loveland Econ. Devel. Council, 1987—, Valley Nat. Bank, Loveland, 1987--. Council woman Loveland City Coun., 1974-80, mayor pro tem, 1980-82; resdl. chairwoman United Way, Loveland, 1967. Mem. Loveland C. of C., Friends of Hosp., Fire Dept. Aux. Republican. Office: Satin Rose Bridal Salon 103 E 42nd St Loveland CO 80538

COULSON, PATRICIA BUNKER, endocrinologist; b. Kankakee, Ill., Apr. 27, 1942; d. Francis Marian and Wilhamine (Kammann) Bunker; m. James Coulson, Jan. 31, 1965 (div. 1985); children: Christina Louise, Pamela Crabel Coulson. BS, U. Ill., 1964, MS, 1966, PhD, 1970; postgrad., U. Tenn., 1970-72. Tchr. asst. dept. physiology U. Ill., Urbana, 1965-67, rsch. asst., USPHR trainee dept. physiology, 1967-70; asst. prof. dept. zoology U. Tenn., Knoxville, 1970-78, asst. rsch. prof. dept. med. biology, 1977-78, assoc. prof. ob-gyn, Coll. of Medicine, 1981-85; assoc. prof. dept. physiology, Coll. of Medicine East Tenn. State U., Johnson City, 1978-81, assoc. rsch. prof. ob-gyn, Coll. of Medicine, 1987—; pres. Tenn. Endocrine Reference Lab., Knoxville, 1985—; bd. dirs. endocrine sect., Blount Meml. Hosp./Pathology, Maryville, Tenn., endocrine lab. East Tenn. State U. Coll. Medicine, Ob-Gyn; co-dir., tumor marker lab., Thompson Cancer Surgery Ctr., Knoxville, 1989—. Contbr. articles to profl. jours. Mem. Soc. for Study of Reproduction, Endocrine Soc., Clin. Ligand Assay Soc., Am. Fertility Soc., Am. Assn. Clin. Chemists. Home: 7417 Sheffield Dr Knoxville TN 37919-2418 Office: TERL/Pathology Dept Blount Meml Hosp 907 East Lamar Alex Pkwy Maryville TN 37801

COULSON, ZOE ELIZABETH, food processing executive; b. Sullivan, Ind., Sept. 22, 1932; d. Marion Allan and Mary Anne (Thompson) C. B.S., Purdue U., 1954; A.M.P., Harvard Bus. Sch., 1983. asst. dir. home econs. Am. Meat Inst., Chgo., 1954-57; account exec. J. Walter Thompson Co., Chgo., 1957-60; creative consumer dir. Leo Burnett Co., Chgo., 1960-64; mag. editor-in-chief Donnelley-Dun & Bradstreet, N.Y.C., 1964-68; food editor Good Housekeeping Inst., N.Y.C., 1968-76, dir., 1976-81; v.p. Campbell Soup Co., Camden, N.J., 1981—; bd. dirs. Rubbermaid Inc., Campbell Sales Co. Author: Good Housekeeping Illustrated Cookbook, 1981; Good Housekeeping Cookbook, 1972. Trustee Cooper Hosp./Univ. Med. Ctr., 1982—. Named Disting. Alumnae, Purdue U., 1971. Mem. Women's Econ. Bus. Alliance (bd. govs.), Food and Drug Law Inst. (bd. dirs. 1979-81), Kappa Alpha Theta Alumnae Assn. Republican. Presbyterian. Avocation: meso-Am. archaeology. Office: Campbell Soup Co Campbell Pl Camden NJ 08103-1799

COULTER, ELIZABETH JACKSON, biostatistician; b. Balt., Nov. 2, 1919; d. Waddie Pennington and Bessie (Gills) Jackson; m. Norman Arthur Coulter Jr., June 23, 1951; 1 child, Robert Jackson. A.B., Swarthmore Coll., 1941; A.M., Radcliffe Coll., 1946, Ph.D., 1948. Asst. dir. health study Bur. Labor Stats., San Juan, P.R., 1946; research asst. Milbank Meml. Fund, N.Y.C., 1948-51; economist Office Def. Prodn., 1951-52; research analyst Children's Bur.-HEW, 1952-53; statistician, then chief statistician Ohio Dept. Health, 1954-65; lectr. econs., then clin. asst. prof. preventive medicine Ohio State U., 1954-65; asst. clin. prof. biostats. U. Pitts. Sch. Pub. Health, 1958-62; assoc. prof. biostats. U. N.C., Chapel Hill, 1965-72, prof., 1972-90, prof. emerita, 1990—, assoc. dean undergrad. pub. health studies, 1979-86, assoc. prof. econs., 1965-78; adj. assoc. prof.. hosp. adminstrn. Duke U., 1972-79. Contbr. articles to profl. jours. Mem. Am. Pub. Health Assn. (governing coun. 1970-72), Am. Econ. Assn., Am. Statis. Assn., Am. Acad. Polit. and Social Sci., AAAS, Biometric Soc., AAUP, Am. Evaluation Soc., Assn. for Health Svcs. Rsch., Sigma Xi, Delta Omega. Methodist. Home: 1825 North Lake Shore Dr Chapel Hill NC 27514 Office: U NC Sch Pub Health Chapel Hill NC 27599

COULTER, KYLE JANE, federal administrator; b. Brownwood, Tex., Oct. 1, 1937; d. Pat and Opal (Mitchell) Cagle; m. Gene Edward Coulter, Apr. 18, 1957 (div. 1967); children—Kimberly Shannon, Patrick Eugene, Katherine Venet. Student Iowa State U., 1955-57; B.S., Tex. Tech U., 1960, M.S., 1968, Ed.D., 1971; postgrad. Colo. State U., 1970, Mich. State U., 1971. Asst. prof. home econs. Tex. Tech U., Lubbock, 1972-76, assoc. prof., assoc. dean home econs., 1976-80; dep. dir. Office of Higher Edn., Dept. Agr., Washington, 1980-82, dir., 1982—. Contbg. author to tech. publs., profl. jours. Recipient New Faculty Excellence in Teaching award Tex. Tech U., 1973; Dir.'s award Dept. Agr., 1980. Mem. Am. Council Consumer Interests (dissertation research award 1972), Am. Home Econs. Assn., Va. Home Econs. Assn., Sigma Xi, Phi Kappa Phi, Phi Upsilon Omicron. Methodist. Office: Dept Agriculture Higher Edn Programs 14th & Independence Ave Washington DC 20250*

COULTON, MARTHA JEAN GLASSCOE (MRS. MARTIN J. COULTON), librarian; b. Dayton, Ohio, Dec. 11, 1927; d. Lafayette Pierre and Gertrude Blanche (Miller) Glasscoe; m. Martin J. Coulton, Sept. 6, 1947; children: Perry Jean, Martin John. student Dayton Art Inst., 1946-47. Dir., Milton (Ohio) Union Pub. Libr., 1968-89; libr. cons., Centerville, Ohio, 1989—. Active, West Milton (Ohio) Cable TV Com. Named Outstanding Woman Jaycees, 1978-1979; recipient Spl. Recognition award Ohio Ho. Reps., 1989. Mem. ALA, Ohio Library Assn., Miami Valley Library Orgn. (sec. 1981, v.p. 1982, pres. 1983), Internat. Platform Assn., Puppeteers of Am., West Milton C. of C., DAR, Union Internat. Marionnette, Amnesty Internat., Pub. Citizen Health. Home and Office: 6029 Buggywhip Ln Centerville OH 45459

COUNIHAN, DARLYN JOYCE, mathematics educator; b. Cumberland, Md., May 1, 1948; d. Joseph Paul and Clara Kathryn (Miller) C.; m. Mark W. Chambré, Jan. 20, 1979. AB, Hood Coll., 1970, MA, 1982; postgrad., U. Md., 1971-73. Tchr. math. Cabin John Jr. High Sch., Montgomery County, Md., 1970-75, coach girls volleyball team, 1975; math. resource tchr. Takoma Park (Md.) Jr. High Sch., 1975-77, Ridgeview Jr. High Sch., Gaithersburg, Md., 1977-81; math. tchr. Kennedy High Sch., Silver Spring, Md., 1982-84; magnet math. tchr. Takoma Park Intermediate Sch., 1984—, also math. team coach; mem. area 3 adv. coun. Montgomery County Pub. Schs., 1972-73; coach boys basketball team Montgomery County Recreation Assn., 1971; mem. Mathcounts Adv. Group, Md. Mathalon Com. Co-author geometry textbook. Recipient various acad., athletic awards in high sch., coll.; NSF grantee, 1971-72. Mem. Am. Fedn. Tchrs., Assn. for Supervision and Curriculum Devel., Women in Edn., Montgomery County Math. Tchrs. Assn., Nat. Coun. Tchrs. Math., Capts. Cove Golf and Yacht Club, Lake Holiday Country Club, Phi Kappa Phi. Home: 13900 Zeigler Way Silver Spring MD 20904 Office: Takoma Park Intermediate Sch 7611 Piney Branch Rd Silver Spring MD 20910

COUNSELMAN, ELIZABETH BURKE, consultant; b. New Haven, Conn., Sept. 23, 1954; d. Theodore Benton Counselman and Elizabeth (Cass) Strong. BS, William Smith Coll., 1977; MBA, U. N.C., Chapel Hill, 1986. Staff cons. Anistics, Inc., N.Y.C., 1977-80; sr. analyst Aetna Life & Casualty, Hartford, Conn., 1981-84; cons. Sibson & Co., Princeton, N.J., 1987-88, Princeton U., 1988—. Bd. dirs. Singles Helping Others. Mem. AAUW, Assn. Women in Computing, Mensa. Office: Princeton U CIT-87 Prospect Ave Princeton NJ 08544

COUNTEE, SANDRA FLOWERS, rehabilitation services administrator; b. Oklahoma City, Feb. 15, 1943; d. LeRoy and Minnie Ola Flowers; m. Harry J. McNeill. BS, Kans. U., 1965. MS, Columbia U., 1975; MPA, NYU, 1979, PhD, 1988. Cert. social worker, N.Y.; lic. occupational therapist, N.Y. Staff occupational therapist D.C. Gen. Hosp. Community Mental Health, 1965-68; supr. occupational therapy Columbia U.-Harlem Hosp. Ctr. N.Y.C., 1968-76, chief occupational therapy, 1976-78; asst. prof., dir. field work edn. Temple U., Phila., 1978-81; dist. mgr. N.Y. Commn. Blind and Visually Handicapped, N.Y. State Dept. Social Services, N.Y.C., 1981-82; dist. mgr. Office of Vocat. Rehab., N.Y. State Dept. Edn., White Plains, 1982—; clin. instr. rehab. medicine Columbia U., 1977-78; cons. Trinity Ch. and St. Margaret's House Devel., N.Y.C., 1979; adj. prof. L.I. U., 1988—. Adv. bd. Community Home Health Services of Phila., 1980-81; mem. Westchester County Pvt. Industry Council, 1983—, Westchester County Council Disabled, 1983—; mem. bd. mgrs. Nyack YMCA, 1985-87. Mem. Am. Pub. Health Assn., Am. Soc. Pub. Adminstrn., Am. Occupational Therapy Assn. Home: 107 S Highland Ave South Nyack NY 10960

COUNTERMAN, SHARON ANN, police communications supervisor; b. Milw.; m. Richard J. Fredrickson, 1966 (div. 1976); children: Brian, Christopher; m. Michael E. Counterman; 1 stepchild, Melyssa. Student, U. Nev., Las Vegas, 1989—. Key punch operator Clark County Ct. House, Las Vegas, 1975-76; communications specialist Las Vegas Met. Police Dept., 1976-79, communications supr., 1979—; 911 transition coord. N000, 1985-86, local area network mgr., 1988—. Mem. Nat. Emergency Number Assn., Assn. Pub. Safety Communications Officers, NAFE. Office: Las Vegas Met Police Dept 400 Stewart Ave Las Vegas NV 89101

COUNTS, CATHERINE ANN, non-commissioned air force officer; b. Big Spring, Tex., Nov. 9, 1962; d. Roger Lowell and Margaret Ann (Day) C.; 1 child, Shari Shannon. Assoc. in Instructional Tech., Community Coll. of Air Force, Austin, Tex., 1989. Enlisted USAF, 1981, staff sgt., 1988; various assignments USAF, San Angelo, Tex., 1984-88; instructional systems developer USAF, Austin, 1988—; ind. preparer income taxes Austin, 1986—. Vol. Spl. Olympics. Mem. NAFE, Non-commissioned Officers Club, Non-commissioned Officers Acad. Grads. Assn. Home: 401 Kornegy Austin TX 78719

COURAUD, KATHERINE SEAMAN, management executive; b. Bklyn., Nov. 13, 1955; d. John Edward and Ruth Martha (Bottom) Seaman; m. Andreas Couraud, Apr. 7, 1979 (div. Jan. 1988); 1 child, Nicolas Yves. BA in French, SUNY, Oswego, 1977; MBA in Fin. Mgmt., Pace U., 1984. English teaching asst. Lycee D'Etat Rabelais, Paris, 1977-78; asst. to sec. Pacific/Indian Ocean maritime shipping conf. La Compagnie Generale Maritime, Paris, La Defense, France, 1979-80; treasury clk. The Penn Cen. Corp., N.Y.C., 1980, sr. treasury clk., 1981, assoc. treasury analyst, 1982-83; sr. fin. analyst, corp. cash The Hertz Corp., N.Y.C., 1985-86, sr. fin. analyst, fin. ops., 1986-88; mgr., treasury ops. The Hertz Corp., Park Ridge, N.J., 1989—. Mem. ProArte Chorale, Ridgewood, N.J., 1988, Goodman Chamber Singers, N.Y.C., 1986-87. Mem. Nat. Assn. Female Execs., Occasional Music Soc. (various offices). Republican. Episcopalian. Office: The Hertz Corp 225 Brae Blvd Park Ridge NJ 07656-0713

COURRIER-CARPENTER, ELAINE F., nursing home consultant; b. Smith Center, Kans., Mar. 17, 1919; d. Roy Elmo and Celia Frances Lattin; m. Ray Lester Carpenter, June 3, 1941 (dec. 1984); foster children: Carolyn Ann Knight, Zelma Warren. BSBA, Ft. Hays State U., MBA; PhD, Kans. State U., 1982. Tchr. various pub. sch. systems, Kans., 1936-42, 45-48; bookkeeper J.M. McDonald Co., Smith Center, 1947-57; owner, bookkeeper Carpenter Concrete Co., Smith Center, 1958-64; owner, adminstr. Carpenter Manor Nursing Home, Smith Center, 1965-79; cons. to nursing homes,

1979—; prof. Barton Community Coll., Great Bend, Kans., 1977-79; program. coord. Kans. state Coll., Manhattan, 1974-75; chair confs. on aging; cons. Kans. Bur. Nursing Homes, 1978-79, mem. coms. Mem. Kans Adult Day Care Assn., Citizens Coun. Aginmg, Nat. Inst. Rural Aging, Nat. Inst. Adult Day Care, Phi Delta Kappa. Home: 8001 E Broadway Apt 7154 Mesa AZ 85208

COURSHON, CAROL BIEL, civic worker; b. Cleve., Sept. 5, 1923; d. Maurice and Rita (Glueck) Biel; student Wesleyan Coll., Macon, Ga., 1941-42; m. Arthur Howard Courshon, Feb. 20, 1943; children: Barbara Mills, Deanne. With Washington Savs. & Loan Assn., Miami Beach, Fla., 1979-80, chmn. adv. bd., 1979-80, dir., 1980-82. Chmn. hotel-motel div. Mothers March Dimes, 1948-53; co-chmn. bus. div. Greater Miami Heart Fund campaign, 1977-78; bd. dirs. Children's Svc. Bur. of Dade County, 1960-70, Family Svc. Assn. Am., 1977-84, United Family and Children's Svc. (now Family Counseling Svcs.), Dade County, 1970—; mem. adv. com. U. Miami-Jackson Meml. Children's Hosp. Ctr., 1983—; vol. tchrs. aide handicapped Dade County (Fla.) pub. schs., 1956-81; del. Democratic Nat. Conv., 1968; adv. bd. Jefferson Nat. Bank, Miami Beach, 1981—. Mem. Nat. Savs. and Loan League (exec. women's group 1979-83), Nat. Coun. Jewish Women (v.p. Bay div. 1953-55), Hadassah. Office: 301 41st St Miami FL 33140

COURSON, MARNA B. P., public relations executive; b. Waynesboro, Pa., Feb. 22, 1951; d. Eugene Perry and Charlotte Mae (Sherman) Roschli; m. Sydney E. Courson, May 24, 1982; 1 child, Sydney Alexandra. BA, Franklin and Marshall Coll., 1973; postgrad., U. Kans., Kansas City. Reporter Beach Haven Times/The Beacon, Manahawkin, N.J., 1973-74, Dailey Observer Newspaper, Toms River, N.J., 1974-76; communications mgr. Frick India Ltd., New Delhi, 1976-77; reporter, dictationist UPI, Washington, 1978-80; reporter UPI, Richmond, Va.; reporter, editor AP, Balt., 1980-84; communications coord. St. Luke's Hosp. Found., Kansas City, Mo., 1986-88; exec. v.p. pub. rels. Spaw and Assocs., Inc., Overland Park, Kans., 1988-89; exec. v.p. CCI, Shawnee Mission, Kans., 1990—. Recipient Prism award for fund raising, numerous awards and honors for reporting, 1973-80. Mem. NAFE, Pub. Rels. Soc. Am. (Pres.'s award Kansas City chpt. 1988), Internat. Assn. Bus. Communicators, Silicon Prairie Tech. Assn., C. of C. Home: 13404 W 66th Terr Shawnee KS 66216 Office: PO Box 16153 Shawnee Mission KS 66203

COURT, KATHRYN DIANA, editor; b. London, Dec. 23, 1948; came to U.S., 1976; d. Ian Howard and Elizabeth Irene (Freeman) Onslow; m. David Court, Mar. 25, 1972; m. Jonathan Coleman, July 8, 1978. BA in English with honors, U. Leicester, 1970. Editor William Heinemann Ltd., London, 1971-76, Penguin Books, N.Y.C., 1977-79; editorial dir. Penguin Books, 1979-83; editor-in-chief Viking Penguin Inc., 1984-87, v.p., sr. exec. editor, 1987—. Mem. Assn. Am. Pubs. (mem. freedom to publish com.). Office: Penguin USA 375 Hudson St New York NY 10014

COURTENAY, IRENE DORIS, nursing consultant; b. Regina, Sask., Can., July 1, 1920; d. Thomas Greer and May Elizabeth (York) C. BS in Nursing, U. Western Ont., 1956, MPH, U. Mich., 1957. RN. Occupation health nurse Chrysler of Can., 1948-50, 52-55; cons. occupational health nursing N.C. Bd. Health, 1958-61; occupational health nursing specialist Nat. League for Nursing, 1961-64; cons. occupational health nursing Dept. Nat. Health and Welfare, Ottawa, Ont., 1966-69; asst. prof., dir. grad. program occupational health nursing U. N.C., Chapel Hill, 1971-75; assoc. prof. occupational health N.Y. U., 1975-78; pvt. practice cons. occupational health nursing, 1978—. Author several publs. Mem. Am. Nurses Assn., Nat. League Nursing, Am. Assn. Occupational Health Nurses, Am. Bd. Occupational Health Nurses (bd. dirs.), Am. Indsl. Hygiene Assn. (assoc.), Permanent Commn. and Internat. Assn. Occupational Health, AAUP, Am. Pub. Health Assn., Can. Council Occupational Health Nurses (bd. dirs., chmn. exam. com.). Mem. Anglican Ch. Home: 5110 Wyandotte St E, #X14, Windsor, ON Canada N8S 1L2

COURTER, AMY S., information systems specialist; b. Flint, Mich., Nov. 11, 1961; d. Guy Ray and Erma Louise (Ketchum) C. BA, Kalamazoo Coll., 1983. Systems programmer Kalamazoo Coll.; software specialist Digital Equipment Corp., Novi, Mich.; dir. MIS Valassis Inserts, Livonia, Mich. Squad comdr. Civil Air Patrol. Named Hon. Capt. Civil Air Patrol. Mem. NAFE, AMA. Address: 27623 Kingsgate Farmington Hills MI 48334

COURTNEY, PATTI LYNN, banker; b. Fredricksburg, Va., Dec. 29, 1957; d. Edward Spencer and Blanche J. (Jett) C.; m. David Andrew Nufrio, Aug. 6, 1983. BA, U. Richmond, Va., 1980; cert. paralegal, Upsala Coll., 1981. With Carteret Savs. Bank, F.A., Morristown, N.J., 1980—, asst. v.p., 1985-88; v.p. Carteret Savs. Bank, F.A., Parsippany, N.J., 1989—. Mem. NAFE. Roman Catholic. Office: Carteret Savs Bank FA 10 Waterview Blvd Parsippany NJ 07054

COURTS, BARBARA JANE, educator; b. Mpls., Nov. 5, 1931; d. Oral Robert and Mary Gladys (Alexander) Neal; m. Robert James Donley, June 15, 1951 (div. 1965); children: Steven Courts, Douglas Courts; m. Robert Eugene Courts, June 16, 1968; 1 child, Robin Courts Best. Student, Macalester Coll., 1949-51; BS, U. Minn., 1954, postgrad., 1955-56, 65, 70; postgrad., U. Calif., 1972, U. Minn., Mankato, 1974-75, St. Thomas U., 1990. Cert. tchr., Minn. Elem. tchr. Hopkins (Minn.) Sch. Dist., 1954-58, St. Louis Park (Minn.) Sch. Dist., 1963—; mem. Supts. Adv. Coun., 1976-78, Math Scope and Sequence, 1985-90, Contract Preparation Com., 1985, 87, Faculty Action Com., 1990. Mem. supt. adv. coun. St. Louis Park Sch. Dist., 1976-78, math scope and sequence, 1985-89. Mem. AAUW, NEA, U. Minn. Edn. Alumni Assn., Park Assn. Tchrs. (bldg. rep. 1972-73, 76-77, 78-82, 85-87), Minn. Edn. Assn. Republican. Office: Peter Hobart Sch 6500 W 26d St Saint Louis Park MN 55426

COURY, BEVERLY SUE, government official; b. Cin., Dec. 17, 1945; d. Wilbur H. and Ellen B. (Jones) Duescher; m. Gary K. Coury, June 18, 1966; 1 child, Korin E. AS, U. Cin., 1965. Field agt. Bur. Labor Stats. U.S. Dept. Labor, Cin., 1978-90, econ. asst., 1990—. Field agt. Bur. Labor Stat. U.S. Dept. Labor, Cin., 1978—; 2d v.p. Mt. Washington Ea. Hills Jr. Woman's Club, 1987, 1st v.p., 1988, pres., 1989, raffle chmn., 1986. Recipient Clover award Ohio Fedn. of Women's Club, 1989. Mem. Alpha Gamma Delta (sec. 1964-65). Roman Catholic. Home: 3744 Fallen Tree Way Amelia OH 45102

COUSIN, MARIBETH ANNE, food microbiologist, educator; b. Beloit, Wis., Jan. 26, 1949; d. John Raymond and Roberta Margaret (Stanton) C. BS, U. Wis., 1971, MS, 1972, PhD, 1976. Rsch. asst. U. Wis., Madison, 1971-76; mgr. coffee/dairy rsch. and devel. Great Atlantic and Pacific Tea Co., Horseheads, N.Y., 1977-78; asst. prof. Purdue U., West Lafayette, Ind., 1978-84, assoc. prof., 1984-90, prof., 1990—. Mem. editorial bd. Jour. Dairy Sci., 1984-90, Applied Environ. Microbiology, 1986-89; contbr. articles to profl. publs., chpts. to books. Active with neighborhood activities, 1980—; vol. Vietnamese Resettlement, West Lafayette, 1985-86. Rsch. grantee various govt. and industry founds., 1972—. Mem. Inst. Food Technologists (exec. com. food microbiology div. 1983-85), Am. Soc. Microbiology (chair food microbiology edn. com. 1987-88, Richard M. Hoyt Meml. award 1977), Am. Dairy Sci. Assn., Soc. for Indsl. Microbiology, Phi Tau Sigma (pres. Ind. chpt. 1981, 85). Office: Purdue U Dept Food Sci Smith Hall West Lafayette IN 47907

COUSIN, REBECCA ELIZABETH, city official; b. Murfreesboro, Tenn., Oct. 30, 1932; d. Richard Taylor Clark and Mildred Lee (Petway) Armstrong; m. Marvin Lee Cousin, Jr., Oct. 14, 1951 (div. Jan. 1961). Student, Northwestern U., 1975-78. Clk. typist USMC, Camp LeJeune, N.C., 1952-53, Cherry Pt., N.C., 1953-54; legal sec. Looby & Williams, Nashville, 1954-58, Wilkins, Wilkins & Wilkins, Chgo., 1958-59; from clk. typist to exec. office adminstr. Chgo. Transit Authority, 1959—; bd. dirs. Chgo. Transit Authority/Regional Transit Authority Fed. Credit Union, mem. credit com, 1984, sec. bd. dirs., 1987. Recipient Superior Pub. Service award, City of Chgo., 1988. Democrat. Roman Catholic. Home: 1130 S Michigan 4201 Chicago IL 60605-2325

COUSINS, BERNICE BRIGANDO, educator, consultant; b. Flushing, N.Y., Nov. 2, 1937; d. August and Olympia (Tortora) Brigando; BFA in Interior Design, Pratt Inst., 1955, postgrad. 1959; postgrad. City U. N.Y., 1966; children—David Bruce, Jason Bruce. Asst. to dir., tchr., Mus. Modern Art, Dept. Edn., N.Y.C., 1963-72; tchr. N.Y.C. Bd. Edn., 1966-73; with Am. Map Corp., N.Y.C., 1975-84, dir cartographic services, dir. mktg. services, also dir., 1979-81; co-dir. CW Assocs., Flushing, N.Y., 1982—; mgr. ops. support svcs. Consol. Appraisal Co., Inc., N.Y.C., 1987—; tchr. Adminstrv. Directorate Actualism Ctr., N.Y.C., 1980—; lectr. in field. Curriculum Adv. Com., Pub. Sch. 85Q, 1976-77. Mem. NAFE, Assn. for Research and Enlightment, News Women Bus. Owners N.Y., Am. Space Found., High Frontier Soc., Am. Fedn. Astrologers. Contbr. articles to profl. jours.; researcher, compiler, editor: Nutritive Value of Common Foods, 1978; researcher, editor: Art Work: Schick-Colorprint Anatomy Charts, 1976-84. Office: 41-19 23d Ave Astoria NY 11105

COUTURE, ANDREA MARIE, writer, editor, communications executive; b. May 26, 1943. AB in English, Emmanuel Coll., 1965; cert., MIT, 1979. Writer-editor John Hancock Mut. Life Ins., Boston, 1965-66; reporter-editor Nowels Publs., Menlo Park, Calif., 1967-69; news editor North Shore Weeklies, Ipswich, Mass., 1969-71; dir. communications Unitarian Universalist Svc. Com., Boston, 1972-76; writer-cons. Boston, N.Y.C., 1978-88; mng. editor, dir. communications Am. Soc. Mag. Photographers, N.Y.C., 1988-89; mng. editor The Jour. of Art, N.Y.C., 1989. Author: For the People; For a Change, 1978; newsletter editor Citizens for Participation in Politics, 1971-76; photography exhbn., 1976, 78, 79. Active Dem. Ward 5 Com., Boston, 1971-76;. Recipient 1st prize best news story, second prize best feature story, spl. award series reporting New Eng. Press Assn., 1970, silver medals Boston Art Dirs. Club Boston, 1973, 74; grantee Nat. Endowment Humanities, 1979. Home and Office: 1812 2nd Ave #1RN New York NY 10128

COVARRUBIAS, PATRICIA OLIVIA, speech instructor, small business owner, consultant, author; b. Mexico, Mex., Sept. 17, 1951; came to U.S., 1959; d. Alfredo Izaguirre and Carmen (Baillet) C.; m. Robert Elvin Smith, Sept. 11, 1982. BA in French, Calif. State U., Sacramento, 1973, MA in French, 1978. Léctrice d'anglais High Sch., Albi, France, 1973-74; instr. French Calif. State U., Sacramento, 1974-75; videotape editor Sta. KCRA-TV, Sacramento, 1977, news asst. assignment editor, 1978, news reporter, 1978-82; founder, exec. dir., instr. OCELOTL, Stockton, Calif., 1984—; guest speaker OCELOTL Speakers Bur., 1984—, Stockton Speakers Bur., 1985—; instr. lifelong learning program U. Pacific, Stockton, 1985—; instr. community edn. San Joaquin Delta Coll., 1989—; instr. Nat. U., 1990—; cert. tutor Laubach Literacy Program, Stockton, 1984—. Author: (workbooks) Speaking Up with Style, 1985, Marketing Your Professional Self, 1986, The Speech Planner - 10 steps to Successful Speaking, 1990, (video programs) Gear Up For Speaking English, 1987, Conversational English Made Easy, 1988; contbr. articles to profl. jours.; editor (newsletter) IV's Forum, 1985-86. Child sponsor Feed the Children, Oklahoma City, 1986—; bd. dirs. San Joaquin County Arts Council, Stockton, 1985—. Mem. Exec. Female, Internat. Tng. in Communication (instr. communication dynamics 1985—, Florence Van Gilder award 1985), AAUW, Lodi Writers Assn., Calif. Reading Assn., Pacific Delta Area Trainers, Greater Stockton C. of C. (liaison com. 1989—), Calif. State U. Alumni Assn. (bd. dirs. 1988—), Nat. Speakers Assn., Pi Delta Phi, Phi Kappa Phi. Home: 3144 Sea Gull Ln Stockton CA 95209 Office: OCELOTL PO Box 7521 Stockton CA 95267

COVE, LINDSAY SUZANNE, office manager; b. St. Paul, Dec. 13, 1940; d. Lindsay Sleeper and Jane (Henderson) Smith; m. Louis Spencer Cove, June 15, 1969 (div. Aug. 1979); 1 child, Marc Lindsay. Student, Monroe High Sch., St. Paul, 1958. Exec. sec. 3M Co., St. Paul, 1962-70; office mgr. Schumacher Chiropractic Clinic, St. Paul, 1977--; legal asst. Victor B. Anderson Law Office, St. Paul, 1977--; cons. Rawlings Chiropractic Clinic, St. Paul, 1980--, Napoli Chiropractic Clinic, Fridley, Minn., 1982--. Mem. St. Paul Grand Slam Club (sec. 1985-88), American Contract Bridge League. Republican. Jewish. Home: 26 W 10th St #1910 Saint Paul MN 55102 Office: Schumacher Chiropractic Cli 1201 Payne Ave Saint Paul MN 55101

COVELLI, JOY ALLENE, sales executive; b. Milw., May 29, 1941; d. Robert Henry and Carolyn Mary (Guinn) Hanke; m. Nicholas Joseph Covelli, Aug. 18, 1962; children: Joseph Robert, Nicholas Joseph Jr., Jeffrey Scott. BEd, U. Wis., 1963, MS, 1978; MS, U. Ill., 1968. Cert. tchr. Bus. edn. tchr. Wilmot (Wis.) High Sch., 1970-81, guidance counselor, bus. edn. tchr., 1981-83; consumer info. coord. SC Johnson Wax, Racine, Wis., 1983-85, sales office mgr. U.S. consumer products, 1985-90, customer svc. supr. splty. chems., 1990—; adv. bd. chairperson Gateway Tech. Coll., Racine, Wis., 1988--. Hospice vol. St. Mary Ch., Burlington, Wis., Burlington Meml. Hosp. Mem. Internat. Customer Svc. Assn., Nat. Customer Assn., Ill. Customer Svc. Assn., Wis. Customer Svc. Assn., Johnson Mutual Assn., Wis. Bus. Edn. Assn., Nat. Bus. Edn. Assn. Home: 3013 S Browns Lake Dr Burlington WI 53105 Office: SC Johnson Wax 1525 Howe St Racine WI 53403

COVEN, BERDEEN, psychotherapist; b. Portland, Oreg., July 24, 1941; d. Sylvan and Helen (Woffman) Saperstein; m. Lee Coven, May 25, 1962; children: Cynthia, Andrew. BA, San Jose State U., 1965; MA, Santa Clara U., 1976. Cert. tchr. counselor, Calif. Human resource mgr., psychotherapist Cupertino, Calif. Mem. Am. Assn. Marriage and Family Therapists, Calif. Assn. Marriage and Family Therapists, Am. Assn. for Counseling and Devel.

COVER, EVA NAST TIMRUD, communications director, association executive; b. Kansas City, Mo., Apr. 7, 1946; d. Philip V. Nasti and Katherine Hall (Evans) Timrud; m. Thomas James Riley, Nov. 30, 1968 (div.); m. Jehu Fell Cover, May 23, 1982. BJ in Advt., U. Mo., 1968. Editor, Waddell & Reed Inc., Kansas City, Mo., 1968-70; copywriter Berry World Travel, Kansas City, 1970-71, Western Auto, Kansas City, 1971-72; editor Nat. Sch. Supply and Equipment Assn., Arlington, Va., 1973-78, dir. communications, 1978-80; dir. communications Internat. Bus. Forms Industries, Inc., Arlington, 1980-87, v.p. communications, 1987—. Author: The World of Business Forms, 1983; exec. editor, pub. Forms Mfg. mag., 1987—. Pub. rels. dir. Univ. Theatre U. Mo., Columbia, 1966-67. Roy A. Roberts scholar Kansas City Star, 1964-68, Curator's scholar U. Mo., 1964-66, honors cert., 1966. Mem. Women in Communications, Inc. (bd. dirs. Washington profl. chpt. 1983-85), Am. Soc. Assn. Execs. (assn. mgmt. cert. 1989), Greater Washington Sco. Assn. Execs., Internat. Assn. Bus. Communicators, Alpha Gamma Delta (1st v.p. 1966-67), Sigma Alpha Iota. Republican. Office: Internat Bus Forms Industries Inc 2111 Wilson Blvd Ste 350 Arlington VA 22201

COVERMAN, FRANYE JILL, clinical social worker; b. N.Y.C., Jan. 19, 1949; d. Bernard Cohen and Mollie (Katz) Sacks; (div. Sept. 1978); 1 child, Jana; m. Sdney M. Coverman, June 20, 1982; children: Nathan, Sheri. BSW, Barry U., 1978, MSW, 1979. Lic. social worker, Fla., Calif.; cert. hypnotherapist, Fla. Group Counselor Women's Detention Ctr., Miami, Fla., 1976-78; social worker State of Fla., 1977-79; therapist Domestic Intervention, 1979-82, Contemporary Family Consultants, Coral Gables, Fla., 1977-80, 84-85; liason Bread & Roses and San Quentin Prison, Mill Valley, Calif., 1980-81; social worker Conservatorship Investigator, San Rafael, Calif., 1981-83, Home Health Orgns., West Palm Beach, Fla., 1983-87; therapist Counseling & Psychotherapy, 1987-90. Mem. Nat. Assn. Social Workers, NOW (status of women com.). Democrat. Jewish. Office: 470 Columbia Dr Ste 201 West Palm Beach FL 33409

COVERT, ROBERTA MARSHA, nurse; b. Detroit, Dec. 11, 1950; d. William Thompson and Eilene Mary (Brown) Covert. Diploma in Nursing, Sacred Heart Hosp. Sch., 1972; student, Allentown (Pa.) Coll. St., 1989; BSN, St. Francis DeSalle Coll. RN, Pa.; cert. post-anesthesia nurse. Staff nurse CCU, Sacred Heart Hosp., Allentown, 1972-78, staff operating rm. nurse, 1978-85; clin. instr. Allentown Hosp., 1987; staff post anesthesia care unit Sacred Heart Hosp., Allentown, 1986—; instr. Am. Heart Assn., 1976—. Mem. Am. Assn. Operating Room Nurses, Am. Soc. Post Anesthesia Nurses, Nat. Assn. Orthopaedic Nurses. Democrat. Roman Catholic. Office: Sacred Heart Hosp 421 Chew St Allentown PA 18102

COVEY, NORMA SCOTT, travel service executive; b. Cambridge, Mass., Feb. 16, 1924; d. Irving Osgood and Leah (Crowell) Scott; m. Myles Edward Covey, July 8, 1950; children: Chrisann and Cynthia (twins). BE, Boston U., 1947. Tchr. East Hartford (Conn.) Schs., 1947-57; mgr., owner, pres. Myles Travel, Glastonbury, Conn., 1975—; bd. dirs. C&W Mfg., Glastonbury; computer instr. Conlin-Hallissey Travel Sch., Glastonbury, 1984-86. Columnist for 3 local newspapers. Vol. Foster Parents Plan Outreach Group, 1984—. Mem. Am. Soc. Travel Agts., Internat. Airlines Travel Agts. Assn., Cruise Lines Internat. Assn., Pacific Area Travel Assn., Bus. and Profl. Women, Nat. Assn. Female Execs. Republican. Congregationalist. Club: Boston U. Alumni. Home: 174 Carriage Dr Glastonbury CT 06033 Office: Myles Travel Agy 13 Welles St Glastonbury CT 06033

COVINGTON, ANN K., judge; b. Fairmont, W.Va., Mar. 5, 1942; d. James R. and Elizabeth Ann (Hornor) Kettering; m. James E. Waddell, Aug. 17, 1963 (div. Aug. 1976); children: Mary Elizabeth Waddell, Paul Kettering Waddell; m. Joe E. Covington, May 14, 1977. B.A., Duke U., 1963; J.D., U. Mo., 1977. Bar: Mo. 1977, U.S. Dist. Ct. (we. dist.) Mo. 1977. Asst. atty. gen. State of Mo., Jefferson City, 1977-79; ptnr. Covington & Maier, Columbia, Mo., 1979-81, Butcher, Cline, Mallory & Covington, Columbia, Mo., 1981-87; justice Mo. Ct. Appeals (we. dist.), Kansas City, 1987-89, Mo. Supreme Ct., 1989—; bd. dirs. Mid Mo. Legal Services Corp., Columbia, 1983-87; chmn. Juvenile Justice Adv. Bd., Columbia, 1984-87. Bd. dirs. Ellis Fischel State Cancer Hosp., Columbia, 1982-83; chmn. Columbia Indsl. Revenue Bond Authority, 1984-87; trustee United Meth. Ch., Columbia, 1983-86. Mem. Boone County Bar Assn. (sec. 1981-82), ABA (family law sect.), Mo. Bar. Assn. Home: 1109 Falcon Dr Columbia MO 65201 Office: Mo Supreme Ct Box 150 Jefferson City MO 65102*

COVINGTON, B(ATHILD) JUNE, business owner, advocate; b. Butte, Mont., June 21, 1950; d. Joe Talmage Covington Sr. and Betty Lou (Jones) Tomlinson; m. Mark Halsey Stephens, Aug. 2, 1969 (div. 1982); children; Mark Halsey Jr., Kimm Covington Stephens; m. James Bradford Hams, Feb. 20, 1987; 1 stepchild, Brent Keir Mulvaney. Student, So. Utah State U., 1968-69, Indian Valley Colls., 1981-83. Advt. asst. McPhail's, Inc., San Rafael, Calif., 1973-75; mgr. Clothes Factory, San Francisco, 1976; graphic designer Press Rm. Printing, Redding, Calif., 1977; co-owner Player's Choice Retail Store, Redding, 1978-80; with advt. and in-house display dept. Indian Valley Colls. Book Store, Novato, Calif., 1981-82; advt. mgr. part-time Heritage Homes Realty, Novato, 1983-87; interior design asst., graphic designer, project coord. Ruth Livingston Interior Design, Tiburon, Calif., 1983-85, 87; project mgr., spl. needs design div. head Potter & Co. Builders, Richmond, Calif., 1987-88; owner, prin. CDT Assocs., Novato, 1988—; master's candidate advisor Acad. Art Coll., San Francisco, 1989—; pvt. practice cons. sexual abuse, No. Calif., 1982—. Co-producer video documentary Victims of Incest: The Price They Pay, 1983, Surviving Incest: A Path to the Future, 1988; producer video pilot program Straight From the Lip, 1985, We Are 68, 1988. Mem. maj. gifts com. Novato Human Needs Ctr., 1988; foster parent Marin County Social Svcs., San Rafael, 1983-84; pub. speaker Ind. and Parents United, Calif., 1982—; sponsor Sexual Abuse Survivors, Marin County, 1988-89. Coll. of Marin Found. scholar, 1983; Marin Community Colls. grantee, 1983, 88. Mem. Hospitality Industry Assn. (co-chair philanthropy com. San Francisco chpt. 1988-89, chair, fundraiser San Francisco chpt. 1988-89), Parents United of Marin County (chair interior design com. 1987-89, bd. dirs., v.p., chair edn. com. 1989—). Democrat. Home: 27 Arrowhead Ln Novato CA 94949 Office: CDT Assocs PO Box 1721 Novato CA 94948

COVINGTON, GAIL LYNN, clinical educator, practice consultant; b. N.J., Apr. 4, 1950; d. George and Ina May (Smith) Poole; m. Alexander Palmer Covington, May 20, 1972 (div. June 1979). BS in Nursing, East Carolina U., 1972; MS in Nursing, U. N.C., 1977. Cert. color analyst, beauty cons., 1983, childbirth educator. Instr. Stuart Circle Hosp. Sch. Nursing, Richmond, Va., 1972-73; instr. Richmond Meml. Hosp. Sch. Nursing, 1973-74, relief staff nurse, 1973-74; staff nurse Rex Hosp., Raleigh, N.C., 1974-76; coordinator pediatric nursing Watts Hosp. Sch. Nursing, Durham, N.C., 1977-78; dir. clin. edn. Wake Med. Ctr., Raleigh, 1978-90; practice cons. N.C. Bd. of Nursing, Raleigh, 1990—; cons. in field. Editor: Pregnancy, 1976. Author: Post-Partum Exercises, 1977, 86. Coordinator med. vols. Wake County Olympic Sports Festival, 1987; charge nurse Am. Red Cross, N.C. State Fair, 1985—. Mem. Nurses Assn. Am. Coll. Obstetrics & Gynecology (v.chair 1980-82, sec.-treas. 1984-87). Home: 1421 Sitterson Dr Raleigh NC 27603 Office: NC Bd of Nursing PO Box 2129 Raleigh NC 27602

COVINGTON, PAMELA JEAN, government official; b. Long Beach, Calif., July 30, 1956; d. James Milton and Mary Louise (Dodge) C. Student, Austro Am. Inst. Edn., Vienna, Austria, 1976; BS in Polit. Sci., U. So. Calif., 1978; MBA, So. Meth. U., 1979. Lic. real estate agt., Tex. Gen. ptnr. J.P. Leasing Co., Whittier, Calif., 1977—; dir. scheduling Tom Loeffler for Gov., Austin, Tex., 1985-86, Proposition 19, Super Conducting Super Collider Bond Campaign, Austin, 1987; surrogate scheduling coord. Bill Clements for Gov., Austin, 1986; day events chmn. 1987 Tex. Inaugural Com., Austin, 1987; del. mgmt. and tracking phone bank dir. George Bush for Pres., Washington, 1988; surrogate lead scheduler Bush/Quayle for Pres. Campaign, Washington, 1988; asst. dir. adminstrn. Office of Presdl. Pers., Washington, 1988-89, dir. adminstrn. and spl. placement, 1989-90; dep. asst. sec. for passport svcs. Dept. of State, Washington, 1990—; chairwoman immigration com., citizen rep. Health and Human Svcs. Coordinating Coun., Austin, 1987-88. Active Rep. Nat. Com. Mem. Tex. Women's Alliance, Senatorial Inner Circle, Dallas Producers Club, Ctr. for Strategic and Internat. Studies. Episcopalian. Home: 1001 N Wilson Blvd #808 Arlington VA 22209 Office: Dept of State 2201 C St NW Room 6831 Washington DC 20520

COVINGTON, PATRICIA ANN, educator, university administrator, director, artist; b. Mount Vernon, Ill., June 21, 1946; d. Charles J. and Lois Ellen (Combs) C.; m. Burl Vance Beene, Aug. 10, 1968 (div. 1981). BA, U. N.Mex., 1968; MS in Ed., So. Ill. U., 1974, PhD, 1981. Lab dir. Anasazi Origins Project, Albuquerque, 1969; tchr. pub. schs., Albuquerque, 1969-70; teaching asst. So. Ill. U., Carbondale, 1971-74, prof. art, 1974-88, adminstr. in admissions, 1988—; bd. dir. Artist of the Month for U.S. rep. Paul Simon, Washington, 1974-81; vis. curator Mitchell Mus., Mt. Vernon, Ill., 1977-83, judge Mitchell Mus., Dept. Conservation; panel mem. Ill. Arts Coun., Chgo., 1982; faculty advisor European Bus. Seminar, London, 1983; edn. cons. Ill. Dept. Aging, Springfield, 1978-81, Apple Computer, Cupertino, Calif., 1982-83; mem. Adminstrv. Profl. Coun. So. Ill. U., 1989—. Exhibited papercastings in nat. and internat. shows in Chgo., Fla., Calif., Tenn., N.Y. and others, 1974—; author: Diary of a Workshop, 1979, History of the School of Art at Southern Illinois University at Carbondale, 1981; reviewer Mayfield Pub., Random House, (with William C. Brown) Holt, Reinhart & Winston. Bd. dirs. Humanities Coun. John A. Logan Coll., Carterville, Ill., 1982-88; mem. Ill. Higher Edn. Art Assn. (chmn. bd. dirs. 1978-88), Post-Doctoral Acad., 1981—; sec. adminstrv. profl. coun., 1989-90. Grantee Kresge Found., 1978, Nat. Endowment for the Arts, 1977, 81; named Outstanding Young Woman of Yr. for Ill., 1981. Fellow Ill. Ozarks Craft Guild (bd. dirs. 1976-83); mem. NOW, Am. Assn. Coll. Registrars and Admissions Officers, Ill. Am. Assn. Coll. Registrars and Admissions Officers, Sphinx (hon.), Phi Kappa Phi. Presbyterian. Home: 352 Lake Dr Rte 6 Murphysboro IL 62966 Office: So Ill U Admissions and Records Carbondale IL 62901

COWAN, GENI, human services executive; b. Carson City, Nev., Feb. 6, 1955; d. Leon D. and Cora M. (Smith) C. BA, Biola U., 1977; MA, Profession Sch for Psychol. Studies, San Diego, 1985; postgrad., U. Calif., Santa Barbara. Cert. HIV counselor. Exec. dir. The Resource Ctr., 1983-90; dir. tech. assistance svcs. Calif. Assn. AIDS Agys. Regional co-chair Nat. March on Washington for Lesbian and Gay Rights; co-chair Nat. Gay and Lesbian Task Force, 1989, 90; sec. Calif. Assn. AIDS Agys., 1989, bd. dirs., 1988-89. Named Local Hero Santa Barbara Ind., 1987, Woman of Yr., 1985, 87; Community Svc. award So. Calif. Women for Understanding, 1988. Mem. Nat. Gay and Lesbian Task Force (bd. dirs.), Calif. Assn. AIDS Agys. (sec.). Office: 926 J St Ste 803 Sacramento CA 95814

COWDEN, JULIANAN, steel company executive; craftsman; b. Midland, Tex.; d. Robert Edwin and Jett (Baker) Cowden; student Hockaday Jr. Coll., 1940-41; B.A., U. Tex., 1944. Rancher, oil investments JAL Co., Alvarado, Tex., 1950—, chmn. bd., 1970—; treas. J & M Steel Co., Inc., Ft. Worth, 1971—. Instr. jewelry and silversmith Ft. Worth Art Center, 1963-66; exhibited jewelry and sculpture in one-man shows at Simpson Gallery, Amarillo, 1969, Sq. House Mus., Panhandle, 1971; exhibited in group shows at Ft.

Worth Art Center, Carlin Gallery, Mus. Internat. Folk Art, Santa Fe, Wichita Falls (Tex.) Art Mus., Tex. Tech U. Mus., Lubbock, Artist's Jamboree, San Antonio. Trustee, past pres. Tex. Sch. Bd. Assn.; mem. adv. com., mem. tech. and telecommunications systems adv. com. Tex State Bd. Edn.; mem. Fed. Relations Network; pres. Alvarado Ind. Sch. Dist. Bd., 1966-86; mem. Nat. Fedn. Republican Women; sustaining mem. Rep. Party, 1979—; mem. Rep. Senatorial Inner Circle; mem. Task Force Com. on Sch./Coll. Articulation; trustee Hockaday Sch., 1971-73; bd. dirs. Christian Heritage Found.; Mem. Nat. Sch. Bd. Assn., Tex. Designer Craftsmen, U. Tex. Ex-Students Assn. (life), Tex. Artists Craftsmen Guild (pres. 1970-72), S. W. Cattleraisers Assn., Ranch Heritage Assn., West Tex. C. of C. (dir.), Zeta Tau Alpha, Phi Delta Kappa. Episcopalian. Clubs: Amarillo, Fort Worth. Home: PO Box 305-308 Alvarado TX 76009

COWDERY, JOY RISE, educator; b. Marietta, Ohio, Jan. 16, 1954; d. J. Kermit Gatten and Betty L. (Barnard) Leonard; m. R. Joe Cowdery, June 17, 1972; children: Aaron Joseph, Benjamin Charles, Dylan Kyle. BA, Marietta Coll., 1976; postgrad., W.Va. U., 1989. With Ohio Hist. Soc., Marietta, 1972-75; instr. Washington Tech. Coll., Marietta, 1976-77; tchr. Warren High Sch., Vincent, Ohio, 1977—; mem. Warren local Drug and Alcohol Prevention Com., 1985-89, Speaker's Assn. for Preventing Teenage Pregnancy, Wash. County, 1988-89. Bd. dirs. E. Muskingum Civic Assn., Marietta, 1986-88; mem. Bantam League Baseball, Marietta, 1980-89, Marlin's Swimteam, 1986-89, City League Soccer, 1987-89. Recipient Ashland Oil Golden Apple award Ashland Oil, 1989. Mem. S.E. Coun. Tchrs. English, NEA, Ohio Edn. Assn. (bldg. rep. 1988-89), AAUW, Delta Kappa Gamma (profl. affairs 1988—). Democrat. Home: 133 Seneca Dr Marietta OH 45750 Office: Warren High Sch Rte 1 Vincent OH 45712

COWIE, CATHERINE CHRISTINE, epidemiologist; b. Detroit, Aug. 22, 1953; d. George Durno and Elsie Elizabeth (Swan) C.; m. Keith Foster Rust, Mar. 22, 1986. BS, Mich. State U., E. Lansing, 1976; MPH, U. Mich., 1979, PhD, 1988. Office asst. Mich. State Clin. Ctr., East Lansing, 1977; rsch. asst. U. Mich., Ann Arbor, 1978-79; assoc. epidemiologist I The UpJohn Co., Kalamazoo, 1979-81; epidemiologic cons. Internat. Health Awareness Ctr., Kalamazoo, 1981-83, The UpJohn Co., 1982; rsch. asst. dept. epidemiology U. Mich., 1982-84, grad. teaching asst., 1983; sr. rsch. epidemiologist Social and Scientific Systems, Inc. NIH, Bethesda, Md., 1988—; mem. epidemiology coordinating com. Nat. Inst. Diabetes, Digestive and Kidney Diseases NIH, Bethesda, 1988-; participant Office of Minority Health Resource Ctr., Resource Persons Network, Washington; lectr. in field. Contbr. articles to profl. jours. Mem. Montgomery County Humane Soc., Rockville, Md., 1988—. Grantee, NIH, 1977-79, 83-88, Health Care Fin. Adminstrn., 1986-87. Mem. Soc. for Epidemiologic Research, Am. Diabetes Assn., Am. Pub. Health Assn., Wilderness Soc., Sierra Club. Office: Social & Sci Systems Inc 7101 Wisconsin Ave #610 Bethesda MD 20814

COWLES, MILLY, educator; b. Ramer, Ala., May 29, 1932; d. Russell Fail and Sara (Mills) C. B.S., Troy State U., 1952; M.A., U. Ala., 1958, Ph.D. (grad. fellow), 1962. Tchr. pub. schs. Montgomery, Ala., 1952-59; asst., then assoc. prof. Grad. Sch. Edn. Rutgers U., 1962-66; assoc. prof. U. Ga., 1966-67; prof., dir. early childhood devel. and edn. Sch. Edn., U. S.C., Columbia, 1967-73; assoc. dean, prof. Sch. Edn., U. Ala., Birmingham, 1973-80; dean, prof. Sch. Edn., U. Ala., 1980-87, Disting. Prof. edn., 1987—; Dir. Williamsburg County Schs. Career Opportunity Program, 1970-73; cons. So. Edn. Found., Atlanta, Ga. Inst. Higher Edn. U. Ga., also numerous sch. systems throughout Northeast and South. Editor, contbg. author: Perspectives in the Education of Disadvantaged Children, 1967; co-author: Taming the Young Savage, Developmental Discipline; mem. editorial bd. Dimensions, 1987—, The Professional Educator, 1986—; researcher, author numerous publs. on psycholinguistic behaviors of rural children. Bd. dirs. S.C. Assn. on Children Under Six, 1969-73. Recipient Outstanding Public Educator award Capstone Coll. Edn. Soc. U. Ala., 1977, Outstanding Alumna award Troy State U., 1984. Mem. Am. Ednl. Research Assn., Soc. for Research Child Devel., AAAS, AAUP, Nat. Council Tchrs. English, Internat. Reading Assn., Assn. for Supervision and Curriculum Devel. (mem. council on early childhood edn. 1969—, dir. 1978-82), Nat. Assn. for Edn. Young Children, Assn. for Childhood Devel. Internat., So. Assn. Children Under Six (bd. dirs. 1985-87), Ala. Assn. Young Children (pres. 1984-85), Ala. Assn. for Colls. for Tchr. Edn. (pres. 1986-88), Ala. Assn. Supervision and Curriculum Devel. (pres. 1985-86), N.Y. Acad. Scis., Kappa Delta Pi (chpt. treas. 1964-66), Kelta Kappa Gamma. Home: 60 Springwater Chase Newnan GA 30263

COWLISHAW, MARY LOU, state legislator; b. Rockford, Ill., Feb. 20, 1932; d. Donald George and Mildred Corinne (Hayes) Miller; m. Wayne Arnold Cowlishaw, July 24, 1954; children: Beth Cowlishaw McDaniel, John, Paula. BS in Journalism, U. Ill., 1954. Mem. editorial staff Naperville (Ill.) Sun newspaper, 1977-83; mem. Ill. Ho. of Reps., Springfield, 1983—, minority spokesman elem. and secondary edn. com., mem. joint Ho.-Senate edn. reform oversight com., 1985—. Author: This Band's Been Here Quite a Spell, 1983. Mem. Naperville Dist. 203 Bd. Edn., 1972-83, Ill. Citizens Council on Sch. Problems, Springfield, 1985—. Recipient 1st pl. award Ill. Press Assn., 1981, commendation Naperville Jaycees, 1986; named Best Legislator Ill. Citizens for Better Care, 1985, Woman of Yr. Naperville AAUW, 1987. Mem. Am. Legis. Exchange Council, Conf. Women Legislators, Nat. Fedn. Rep. Women, DAR. Methodist. Home: 924 Merrimac Circle Naperville IL 60540 Office: Ho Reps 552 S Washington St #119 Naperville IL 60540

COX, ANN BRUGER, biological scientist, editor, researcher; b. Salinas, Calif.; d. Albert Matthews and Adrienne (Bruger) C. SB, U. Chgo.; MA in Biology, Boston U., PhD, 1976. Rsch. technician U. Chgo. Clinics, 1965-69, Mass. Gen. Hosp., Boston, 1970; rsch. asst. Harvard Sch. Pub. Health, Boston, 1975; rsch. assoc. Colo. State U., Ft. Collins, 1979-86; rsch. physiologist Sch. Aerospace Medicine USAF, San Antonio, 1987—; adj. asst. prof. Health Sci. Ctr. U. Tex., San Antonio, 1990—. Assoc. editor Academic Press, San Diego, 1982—. Singer Brooks (AFB) Chorus Unlimited, Tex., 1987—; bd. dirs. High Plains Arts Ctr., Ft. Collins, 1980-84. Recipient predoctoral fellowship NIH, post doctoral fellowship, summer fellowships NASA-Am. Soc. for Engring. Edn., 1983, 84. Mem. Am. Soc. Cell Biology, Aerospace Med. Assn., Radiation Rsch. Soc., Com. on Space Rsch. (exec. com. 1988—), Sigma Xi. Home: PO Box 35506 San Antonio TX 78235 Office: USAF Sch Aerospace Med USAFSAM/RZB Brooks AFB TX 78235-5301

COX, ANNA LEE, retired administrative assistant; b. Knoxville, Tenn., Feb. 18, 1931; d. Carter Calloway and Fairy Belle (Byers) Bayless; m. William Smith Cox, Sept. 4, 1952; 1 child, Catherine Anne Cox Faust. Grad. high sch., Knoxville. Sec. Am. Mut. Liability Ins. Co., Knoxville, 1948-53; flight procedures clk. FAA, Atlanta, 1963-66; legal sec., paralegal U.S. Atty.'s Office for Dist. S.C., Greenville, 1972-79; sec. criminal investigation div. IRS, Knoxville, 1981-84; sec., adminstrv. asst. CIA, Knoxville, 1984-88; adminstrv. asst. U.S. Dept. Def., Knoxville, 1988-91, ret., 1991. Tutor Greenville Literacy Assn., 1977-79; founder-dir. NATO Women's Chorus, Izmir, Turkey, 1969-7l; choir dir., pres. United Meth. Women, Stephenson Meml. Meth. Ch., Greenville, 1972-79; bd. dirs. Fountainhead Conservatory Music, Knoxville, 1983-85. Republican. Home: 6724 Arapahoe Trail Knoxville TN 37918

COX, BARBARA ROOSE, public relations executive; b. Houston, Mar. 15, 1951; d. Kenneth E. and Patsy L. (Hinsley) Roose; m. John B. Goss Jr. (div. Apr. 1979); children: Benjamin Jason, Christopher John; m. James O. Cox III, Sept. 28, 1979. Student, U. Houston, 1969-75. Claims rep. State Farm Ins., Houston, 1969-73; adminstrv. asst. S.W. Bancshares Inc., Houston, 1973-77; account exec. Mel Anderson Communications, Houston, 1978-79; v.p. James Cox Inc., Houston, 1979-82, also bd. dirs.; pres. Barbara Cox Pub. Relations, Houston, 1982-83; account supr. Daniel J. Edelman Inc., Houston, 1983-85, v.p., 1985-86, sr. v.p., 1986-88. Advisor to pres. Houston Jaycees, 1987; bd. dirs. First United Meth. Ch., Houston, 1985-86; chmn. pub. relations com. Houston Ballet Nutcracker Market, 1986; publicity chair Mayor's Ball/Houston Internat. Festival, 1985. Mem. Pub. Relations Soc. Am. (Silver Anvil 1988, Excalibur awards Houston chpt. 1985, 87). Clubs: Houston City, Gov.'s, Forum (Houston); Quail Valley (Missour City, Tex.). Office: Edelman Pub Rels One Greenway Plaza Ste 700 Houston TX 77046

COX, BEVERLEY LENORE, biology professor; b. Huntingdon, Pa., Jan. 11, 1929; d. Elwood Beck and Orlee Arcola (Davis) C. BS, Pa. State U., 1951, MS, 1953; PhD, U. Okla., 1960. Instr. physiology U. Okla., Norman, 1959-60; rsch. assoc., NIH fellow U. Oreg., Eugene, 1960-61; from asst. prof. to prof. Biology Cen. State U., Edmond, Okla., 1961—; vis. lectr. U. Okla., Norman, Okla., 1967, 1968, 1969, 1974. Contbr. articles to profl. jours. Recipient fellow NIH, U. Okla. Sch. Medicine, 1963, NSF, U. Okla., Norman, Okla., 1963, 1964, 1965. Mem. AAAS, Am. Soc. Zool., Okla. Soc. Physiologists (sec.-treas. 1985-87, pres. elect 1988-89, pres. 1989-90), Sigma Xi. Democrat. Methodist. Home: Rte 1 Box 184 Oklahoma City OK 73131

COX, BEVERLY ELAINE See HOLT, BEVERLY ELAINE

COX, CAROL ANN, transportation executive; b. Shenandoah, Pa., Sept. 29, 1950; d. Stanley Joseph and Julia (Whitecavage) Wozniewicz; 1 child, Michelle Lynn; m. Robert Earl Cox, July 26, 1980. Diploma, TLC Travel Inst., Pennsburg, Pa., 1986. Lab. technician Philco-Ford, Inc., Spring City, Pa., 1969-71; parking enforcement officer Pottstown (Pa.) Police Dept., 1973-75; sec., billing clk. Cates Ford, Inc., Pottstown, 1975-77; corrections mail insp. Graterford (Pa.) Correctional Inst., 1977-83; decorator cons. Princess House, Inc., Reading, Pa., 1983-86; asst. mgr. Avante Apts., Gilbertsville, Pa., 1985-86; travel agt. Village Travel, Montgomeryville, Pa., 1986, Chadwick Travel Ltd., Pottstown, 1986-88; travel coord. Hewlett-Packard Corp., Valley Forge, Pa., 1988; customer rels. coord. Rosenbluth Travel, Wayne, Pa., 1988—, supr. customer svc.; cruise escort Chadwick Travel Ltd., Pottstown, 1987-88. Mem. NAFE, Internat. Assn. Travel Agts. Roman Catholic. Home: 950 Jackson St Pottstown PA 19464

COX, CATHLEEN RUTH, zoologist, educator; b. Vallejo, Calif., Oct. 20, 1948; d. Charles W. and Betty B. (Born) Cox; BA, U. Calif., San Diego, 1970, PhD, Stanford U., 1976; m. William S. Bain, Dec. 14, 1985. Postdoctoral fellow Am. Mus. Natural History, N.Y.C., 1976-78; rsch. assoc. Barnard Coll., N.Y.C., 1978-79; rsch. zoologist UCLA, 1979-82; asst. prof. Calif. State U., Northridge, 1980-84; dir. rsch. L.A. Zoo, 1981—. Recipient W.C. Allee award Animal Behavior Soc., 1976; NSF rsch. grantee, 1978. Mem. Am. Assn. Zool. Parks and Aquaria, Am. Ornithol. Union, Animal Behavior Soc., Am. Primatol. Soc. Contbr. articles to profl. jours. Office: 5333 Zoo Dr Los Angeles CA 90027

COX, DOROTHY DEASY, facility management consultant; b. Bronx, N.Y., June 11, 1937; d. Jack and Bianca (Iorio) Federico; m. Logan O. Cox; children: Theresa Deasy Stanton, Dorothy Deasy. Student, Bklyn. Coll., 1955. Adminstrv. mgr., acct. Price Waterhouse, Chgo., 1972-81; facility mgr. Beatrice Foods U.S., Chgo., 1981-88; facility cons. Tropicana Products, Bradenton, Fla., 1988; adminstrv. mgr. Kemper Lesnik Orgn., Northbrook, Ill., 1988—. Mem: Internat. Faculity Mgrs. Assn., N. Glen Bus. and Profl. Women, Loop Chap. Women in Mgmt. Office: Kemper Lesnik Orgn 500 Skokie Blvd Northbrook IL 60062

COX, EILEEN FRANCES HINSHAW, foundation and business executive; b. Washington, Oct. 24, 1935; d. Max O. and Marguerite Mary (Wootton) Hinshaw; m. Robert Gene Cox, July 10, 1953; children: Ann Rebecca Cox Taylor, Allan Robert. BA with honors, U. Md., 1967; MA, Rutgers U., 1971, Columbia U., 1973. Staff asst. to dir. U.S./Mex. Border Devel. Commn., Exec. Office of Pres., Washington, 1967-68; asst. to Am. ambassador Conf. on Mex. Border Devel., San Diego, 1968; office mgr. Am. Acad. Cons., N.Y.C., 1971; devel. assoc. Found. Center, Inc., N.Y.C. and Cleve., 1975-78, cons., 1979; pres. Sloane & Hinshaw, Inc., N.Y.C., 1979-80, All Souls Music Soc., 1981-85; cons. to bd. dirs. LeRoy Industries, Inc., 1985-86; mem. U.S. del. U.S.-Mex. Trade Conf., Washington, 1967; Mem. N.Y.C. area council Unitarian Universalist Assn., 1979-80, mem. service com., 1979—; bd. dirs. Neighborhood Coalition for Shelter, Inc., 1983—, Neighborhood Ctr. for Homeless People, Inc., 1988—; bd. mgrs. Soc. for Assistance of the Aging, 1985—. Mem. Met. Opera Guild, Center Inter-Am. Relations, Women's Econ. Round Table, Legal Aid Soc. N.Y., Pi Sigma Alpha, Phi Kappa Phi. Democrat. Home: 225 Central Park W Suite 1207 New York NY 10024

COX, GERALDINE VANG, association executive; b. Phila., Jan. 10, 1944; d. Karl Earling and Geraldine Florence (Oldroyd) Vang; m. Walter George Cox, Sept. 10, 1965. BS, Drexel Inst. Tech., 1966, MS, Drexel U., 1967, PhD, 1970. Environ. scientist submarine signal div. Raytheon Corp., Portsmouth, R.I., 1970-76; White House fellow, spl. asst. to Sec. Labor, Washington, 1976-77; environ. scientist Am. Petroleum Inst., Washington, 1977-79; v.p., tech. dir. Chem. Mfrs. Assn., Washington, 1979—; v.p. planning Bus. Ptnrs., 1986-87, pres., 1987. Mem. D.C. adv. group Internat. Rescue Com., 1981-84; bd. govs. N.J. Inst. Tech., 1984—; D.C. fund raising chmn. Drexel U., 1977, alumnae adviser 1976-88; mem. chem. transp. adv. com. USCG, 1980—; chmn. Marine Occupational Safety and Health Subcom., 1987—. Recipient R.I. Gov.'s citation, 1975, Sci. and Engring. award Drexel U., 1987; named Harriet E. Worrell Outstanding Alumna, Drexel U., 1977. Mem. ASTM, Am. Assn. of Engring. Socs. (vice chmn. engring. affairs coun. 1990—) Am. Chem. Soc. (com. on sci., bd. coun. com. on environ. sci. 1987—), Water Pollution Control Fedn., Soc. Women Engrs. (Engring. Achievement award 1984), Fedn. Orgns. for Profl. Women (bd. govs. 1980-82, pres. 1983-85), Conservation Found. Environ. Dialogue Group, White House Fellows Found., Phi Kappa Phi, Alpha Sigma Alpha (province dir. 1970-73, exec. v.p. 1972-76, recognition of eminence award 1986). Republican. Author: Marine Bioassays, 1975; editor: Oil Spill Studies-Strategies and Techniques, 1977; contbr. articles to profl. jours. Office: Chem Mfrs Assn 2501 M St NW Washington DC 20037

COX, GERRY MCMILLIAN, federal agency administrator; b. Atmore, Ala., Nov. 6, 1949; d. Willie Lewis and Bessie (Abney) McMillian; m. Charles Thomas Cox, Jan. 11, 1967 (div. 1986); children: Alvin Thomas, Calvin Frederick, Charles Thomas Jr. AS, Pensacola Jr. Coll., 1975; student, U. West Fla., 1975-79, Troy State U., 1977, U. Ala., 1976-79. Clk. typist USN, Bainbridge, Md., 1971-72, mil. personnel tech., 1972-74; ed. tech. USN, Pensacola, Fla., 1974-78, mgmt. analyst, 1978-80; mgmt. analyst USN, Norfolk, Va., 1980-87, program analysis officer, 1987-88; project mgmt. officer USN, Chesapeake, Va., 1988—; mgmt. engr. USN, Norfolk, 1979-80, data base mgr., Portsmouth, Va., 1982-84. Editor: Fleet Bulletin, 1985-87. Panel mem. United Way Allocation Com., Norfolk, 1982-84; active Las Fidelas, Va. Beach, Va., 1985-87. Mem. Tidewater Women's Network, Am. Bus. Women Assn. Democrat. Home: 1133 Evert Dr Virginia Beach VA 23464 Office: Navy Mgmt Systems Support Office 1441 Crossways Blvd Chesapeake VA 23320

COX, HELEN RUTH, teacher; b. Missouri, Sept. 14, 1939; d. Clarence L. and Edna A. (Wetherell) P.; m. James M Cox, March 21, 1964; children: Denise K., Michael J. BS, BA, U. Denver, 1961; MA, U. Colo., 1974. Tchr., counselor Horace Mann Jr. High, Denver, 1961-69; tchr. Kepner Jr. High, Denver, 1974-75; tchr. West High Sch., Denver, 1975-79, Boe Coordinator; Boe coord., adviser FBLA Denver, 1979-89. Recipient Citation for Success award Denver Fedn. Exec. Bd., Master Tchr. award Am. Legion, 1988. mem. Audio Visual Com. State of Colo. 1989, I-Team Co. Bus. Edn. Denver 1989, Phi Gamma Nu (Honorary award), Delta Pi Epsilon (teaching award). Protestant. Home: 6922 W Walden Pl Littleton CO 80123

COX, JOY DEAN, business executive; b. Oklahoma City, Sept. 13, 1940; d. Wordy John Neely and Ethel (Russell) Neely Biggs; m. Sidney Lee Johnson, Sept. 10, 1958 (div. 1963); m. Ronald Gene Cox, Sept. 22, 1964; children: Beverly Kay, Jeffrey Wilson; 1 stepchild, Ronald D. Student pub. schs., Oklahoma City. Long-distance operator S.W. Bell Tel. Co., Oklahoma City, 1958-59, L.A., 1959-60; clk. John Pilling Shoes Oklahoma City, 1960-62; cashier Dial Fin. Co., Houston, 1966; file clk., typist N. Am. Ins. Co., Oklahoma City, 1966-67; bookkeeper, co-owner farm and ranch op., Dewey County, Okla., 1969-78, Panola, Okla., 1978—; co-owner/operator Apco Service Sta. and Bulk Fuel Plant, Taloga, Okla., 1972-75, D&R Svc. & Supply Co., Panola, 1979-89, Eufaula, Okla., 1989—; co-owner, operator Panola Store, 1980-85; dealer/co-owner Cox Chevrolet, Wilburton, Okla., 1985. Pres. Taloga Extension Homemakers, 1971-73, sec.-treas., 1973-75; entertainer Latimer County Rest Homes, Wilburton, 1978-89, County of McIntosh, Eufaula, 1990—; leader, contbr. funds to drug abuse program Latimer County 4-H, Wilburton, 1979-89; active ARC, Am. Heart Assn., Girl Scouts U.S., Panola PTA, Drug Abuse Program, Panola, Salvation Army, Pittsburg County, 1968-89, Am. Cancer Soc., 1968-69, Nat. Help Hospitalized Vets.; contbr. funds to drug abuse program Wilburton, Quinton and Okla. Police Detp. Contbr. articles to newspapers and jours. Recipient Leadership award Latimer County 4-H, 1983. Mem. Lake Eufaula Assn. (bd. dirs., entertainer ann. fund raiser 1989), Friendly Lake Eufaula Area Supporters, Lake Eufaula Area Flying Coun. (pub. rels. rep.), Internat. Platform Assn., Heritage Found. Democrat. Avocations: water skiing, swimming, walking, bowling, reading. Office: D&R Svc and Supply 2000 Binkes Rd Eufaula OK 74432 also: Ranch Box 55 Panola OK 74559

COX, KAREN SUE, insurance executive; b. Ft. Leonard Wood, Mo., Oct. 14, 1953; d. Edward Earl and Alice Esther (Cowan) Stahl; m. Stanley Huebert Arnoldy, Oct. 20, 1973 (div. 1976); m. Michael Duane Cox, Aug. 18, 1978; children: Zachary, Kendal. Student, Kans. State U., 1971-73; BBA, Wichita State U., 1976. Dist rep. Blue Cross & Blue Shield, Wichita, Kans., 1976-83, group rep., 1983-85, regional mgr., 1985—; mem. Sedgwick County Health Care Cost Containment Roundtable, Wichita, 1987—. Mem. Cen. Kans. Assn. Health Underwriters, Wichita Chamber (bd. dirs. 1989—), Wichita/Sedgwick County Partnership for Growth (pub. rels.-mktg. com.). Democrat. Lutheran. Home: 2606 N Pershing St Wichita KS 67220 Office: Blue Cross Blue Shield 257 N Broadway Wichita KS 67201

COX, LEE ANN, therapist, social service administrator; b. Litchfield, Ill., Nov. 12, 1956; d. Nelson Carrol Hoffman and Wanda Jane (Blackwelder) Hoffman Barringer; m. Kim Eugene Cox, Sept. 22, 1984; 1 child, Katherine Rebecca. BS, Ill. State U., 1978, MS, 1980. Lic. mental health counselor, Fla. Counselor McLean County Mental Health, Bloomington, Ill., 1980-84, Lighthouse Residential Substance Abuse Program, Bloomington, 1984-86; clinician Am. Med. Internat. Employee Assn., Dallas, 1986-88; counselor Ctr. for Women, Tampa, Fla., 1988-89, asst. dir., 1989—; bd. dirs. Hillsborough Community College Pay Equity, Tampa, 1989—, Hillsborough Community Coll. Displaced Homemakers, Tampa, 1989—, Erwin Vo-Tech Displaced Homemakers, Tampa, 1989—. Mem. Employee Assistance Program Assn., Bay Area Consortium for Women (bd. dirs.), Displaced Homemaker Nat. Network, Mental Health Assn. (community concerns com., chair legis. reception 1990). Democrat. Home: 12612 Forest Hills Dr Tampa FL 33612 Office: Ctr for Women 305 S Hyde Park Ave Tampa FL 33606

COX, LINDA BLANKENSHIP, educator; b. Princeton, W.Va., Feb. 26, 1952; d. Watt Jr. and Willie Beatrice (Steele) Blankenship; m. Roger Dale Cox, Aug. 4, 1973; children: Joshua Dale, Jamie Lynn. BS, Concord Coll., Athens, W.Va., 1972; MA, W.Va. Coll. Grad. Studies, 1975; postgrad., W.Va. U., 1976-85, Marshall U., 1976-85. Cert. tchr., W.Va. Bus. tchr. Park Ungraded High Sch., Bluefield, W.Va., 1972-79, coordinator media ctr., job placement, 1979-80; resource specialist acting coordinator Mercer County Vocat. Tech. Ctr., Princeton, 1980-87, seminar ctr. tchr., coordinator, 1987—; bus. computer cons. Computers Plus, Charleston, W.Va., 1985—; coordinator VICA state skills State Dept. Edn., Charleston, 1986-87; tchr. bus. adult program Vocat. Tech. Ctr., Prinecton, 1972-77; coordinator seminars in field. Citizen ambassador to China, People to People Internat., Spokane, Wash., 1987; bd. dirs. Princeton Towne Fair Beauty Pageant, 1987-88; dir. Awana, Johnston Chapel Bapt. Ch., Princeton, 1987. Recipient Dedication and Svc. plaque W.Va. County Bd. Edn., 1987. Mem. Am. Vocat. Assn., Acad. Boosters Club, Phi Delta Kappa. Home: 1156 Old Athens Rd Princeton WV 24740 Office: Mercer County Vocat Tech Ct 105 Old Bluefield Rd Princeton WV 24740

COX, LISA CZIRJAK, marketing executive; b. New Kensington, Pa., Mar. 6, 1958; d. Rose (Czirjak) Stuczynski; m. Courtney James Cox, June 6, 1987; 1 child, Jeffrey Donald. Student, Pa. State U., 1976-77; BFA, Carnegie-Mellon U., 198l; MBA, Loyola Coll., Balt., 1987. Graphic designer Applied Sci. Assocs., Denver, 198l; mgr. trade show Nurad, Inc., Balt., 1981-83, dir. communications and advt., 1985-87, dir. def. mktg., 1987-89, dir. program mgmt., 1989—; graphic design cons. Motorcycle Safety Found., Elkridge, Md., 1981-82; cons. Applied Sci. Assn., Landover, Md., 1986-88. Recipient best read advt. award BM/E mag., 1984, 85, best advt. award Broadcast Communications, 1986. Mem. Contract Mgmt. Assn., Am. Inst. Graphic Artists, Armed Forces Communications and Electronics Assn., Assn. Old Crows, Delta Gamma. Republican. Episcopalian. Home: 15413 Empress Way Bowie MD 20716 Office: Nurad Inc 2165 Druid Park Dr Baltimore MD 21211

COX, MARILYN ARLENE, nurse; b. Olney, Ill., Mar. 28, 1960; d. Jerry Eugene and Carolyn Irene (Brooks) Cowman; m. John Orval Cox, Aug. 14, 1981; 1child, Sharilyn. A in Nursing, Olney Cen. Coll., 1980. RN, Ill. Nurses aide Burgin Nursing Manor, Olney; staff nurse LPN Richland Meml. Hosp., Olney; staff nurse Good Samaritan Hosp., Vincennes, Ind., nurse supr. Ch. worker. Mem. AACCN. Republican. Home: 1000 S East St Olney IL 62450

COX, MARTHA JEAN, sales executive; b. Rochester, N.Y., Sept. 19, 1956; d. Thomas Elwood and Diane (Martin) C. BSChemE, Purdue U., 1978. Process engr. UOP, Inc., Des Plaines, Ill., 1979-81, sales engr., 1981-85; dist. sales mgr. Ingold Electrodes, Inc., Wilmington, Mass., 1986-89, nat. sales mgr., 1989—; flutist Elmhurst (Ill.) Symphony, 1982-84. Author: Dissolved Oxygen Measurement in the Soft Drink Production Process. Mem. Am. Inst. Chem. Engrs. (student v.p. 1977-78), Soc. Soft Drink Technologists (asst. communications chmn. 1988-89), Instrument Soc. Am., Am. Soc. Microbiologists. Office: Ingold Electrodes Inc 261 Ballardvale St Wilmington MA 01887

COX, MARY E., physics and engineering educator, consultant; b. Detroit, Nov. 11, 1937; d. Willis H. and Dorothy E. (Nicholls) Buckles; m. Kendall B. Cox, July 1, 1961; 1 child, Kendall M. AB, Albion Coll., 1959; MA, U. Mich., 1961; PhD, UCLA, 1984. Tutor in physics Sommerville Coll. U. Oxford, Eng., 1977-78, demonstrator Clarendon Lab., 1977-78; instr. physics U. Mich., Flint, 1966-71, asst. prof. physics, 1971-76, assoc. prof., 1976-84, chmn. dept. physics and astronomy, 1976-77, acting dean for curriculum and program devel. Coll. Arts and Scis., 1981-82; rsch. assoc. The Crump Inst. for Med. Engring., 1982-84, rsch. scientist, 1984-87; assoc. prof. physics and engring. U. Mich., Flint, 1984-88, prof., 1988—, chmn. dept. physics and engring. sci., 1987-89. Contbr. articles to profl. jours. Recipient Ralph and Marjorie Crump prize for excellence in med. engring., 1984; NSF grantee, 1977-78. Mem. Optical Soc. Am., Am. Assn. Physics Tchrs. (pres. Mich. sect. 1975), Am. Phys. Soc., Soc. Photo-Instrumentation Engrs. Office: U Mich-Flint Flint MI 48502-2186

COX, MARY LINDA, paper distribution company executive; b. Alton, Ill., July 3, 1946; d. William M. and Helen (Winters) C. B.A., McKendree Coll., 1970; M.B.A., So. Ill. U., 1977; postgrad. date St. Louis U., 1984—. Exec. dir. Girl Scouts U.S., 1969-76; instr. So. Ill. U., Edwardsville, 1976-80; mgr. Smith-Scharff, St. Louis, 1980-81; account exec. AT&T, Tulsa, 1981-82; pres. Mo. Disposable Products, St. Louis, 1982—. Media specialist Tenn. Rep. Party, 1974; bd. dirs., pub. rels. chmn. YWCA, Alton; mem. fin. com. Greater St. Louis council Girl Scouts U.S.; mem. youth panel United Way St. Louis; mem. City of Wood River planning commn. Mem. Central Bus. Assn. (v.p. 1985), Beta Gamma Sigma (chpt. pres. 1978-79). Office: Mo Disposable Products 2649 Washington St Saint Louis MO 63103

COX, PAMELA L., pediatrician; b. Highland Park, Mich., Dec. 19, 1957; d. Richard Alfred and Norma Mae (Veck) C. BS, Wayne State U., 1980, MD, 1984. Pvt. practice Rochester, Mich. Recipient Abstract Competition award MCAAP. Mem. AMA, Am. Acad. Pediatrics, Wayne State U. Alumni Assn. Address: 492 Buttercup Rochester MI 48307

COX, SAMMIE TYREE, college administrator; b. Hope, Ark., Mar. 12, 1943; d. William McKinley and Reggie Marene (Winfield) Tyee; m. Roosevelt Cox, July 12, 1963; 1 child, Vona Rae Cox. BS, U. Ark., Pine Bluff, 1965; MS, U. Toledo, 1972; EdD, Nova U., 1986. Rsch. asst. Case Western Res. U., Cleve., 1965-68; High sch. sci. tchr. Cleve. Bd. Edn., 1968-70; high sch. counselor Toledo Bd. Edn., 1971-72; various adminstrv. positions Cuyahoga Community Coll., Cleve., 1972—, exec. asst. to the provost/v.p., 1988-90, asst. dean evening & weekend office & events scheduling dept,

1985-88, asst. dean admissions ctr., 1990—; cons. stress mgmt. workshops Time Mgmt. Profl. Life Planning, Nat. Adult Learners Conf., U.S.C., Columbia, others. Bd. trustees Urban League Greater Cleve., 1985—; treas. Karamu Women's Com., 1985—; selected as a Leader of the 80's, 1985, Christians' Women Aux. Marion B. Anderson Cir., 1981—, Shaker Hts. Community Cn., 1981—; past pres. Women of Metro; v.p. Shaker Hts. Interest Group, 1984—; bd. mgmt. YWCA, 1981—; v.p. Ohio Soc. Allied Health Profls., Columbus, 1979. Recipient Cert. of Recognition, Leaders of the 80's, 1985, Cert. Vol. Svc. YWCA, 1985, Cert. of Recognition, Warrensville Heights (Ohio) Sr. High Sch., 1982, Cert. Appreciatin for Vol. Svc., Cuyahoga County Welfare Dept., Cleve., 1981, Outstanding Young Woman in Am. award, 1978, 80, Cert. of Recognition, House Dist. 9, Ohio Ho. of Reps., 1980, Cert. of Appreciation, North Cen. Regional Coun. on Black Am. Affairs, 1979; named Outstanding Cleveland Heights Resident, Sun Press Newspaper, 1981. Mem. Black Profl. Assn., Nat. Coun. Negro Women, Am. Assn. Community and Jr. Colls. (instr. for Leadership League of Innovations), Women in Nat. Svc. Assn., Local Attys. Wives Club (historian), Delta Sigma Theta (membership com.). Home: 3363 Chelsea Dr Cleveland Heights OH 44118 Office: Cuyahoga Community Coll 2900 Community College Ave Cleveland OH 44115

COX, THELMA BANKS, educational consultant; b. Cambridge, Md., July 21, 1928; d. Charles Monroe and Ida Mae (Slacum) Banks; BS, Morgan State U., 1948, MS, 1972; PhD, Union Grad. Sch., Cin., 1980; m. Leonard Cox, June 25, 1949. Social caseworker Phila. Dept. Public Assistance, 1948-49; sci. tchr., Annapolis, Md., 1949-50; English tchr., Balt., 1950-65, reading tchr., 1965-66, dept. head, 1966-67, coordinator community schs., 1967-68, spl. projects coordinator, 1968-72, project mgr., 1972-73, regional supt., 1973-79, asst. supt. intergovtl. relations, 1980-83; mem. Md. Council Higher Edn., 1970-76, State Bd. Higher Edn., 1976-86. Pres., Girl Scouts of Cen. Md., 1982-86; bd. dirs. Girl Scouts of U.S., 1985-87; founder Cox Edn. Fund, 1983. Named Woman of Yr. Greyhound Bus Co., 1972. Mem. Am. Assn. Sch. Adminstrs., Nat. Assn. Black Sch. Educators, African-Am. Heritage Soc. (founder 1988), Delta Sigma Theta. Democrat. Editor: The Heritage of the Baltimore Chapter of Delta Sigma Theta, 1979. Home: 3344 Dolfield Ave Baltimore MD 21215

COY, PATRICIA ANN, special educational programs director, consultant; b. Beardstown, Ill., Apr. 2, 1952; d. Ben L. and Dorothy Lee (Hubbell) C. BS in Elem. and Spl. Edn., No. Ill. U., 1974; MS in Spl. Edn., Northeastern Ill. U., 1976, MA in Spl. Edn., 1978; postgrad., No. Ill. U., 1987—. Cert. elem. and spl. edn. tchr.; cert. counselor. Mental health supr. Waukegan (Ill.) Devel. Ctr., 1974-77; ednl. therapist Grove Sch. and Residential Program, Lake Forest, Ill., 1977-78; dir. residential svcs. N.W. Suburban Aid for the Retarded, Park Ridge, Ill., 1978-83; exec. dir. The Learning Tree, Des Plaines, Ill., 1983—; dir. residential svcs. Augustana Ctr., Luth. Social Svcs. of Ill., Chgo., 1984-86, dir. planning and evaluation, 1986—; behavior advisor Habilitative Systems, Inc., Chgo., 1985-88; program coord. Human Resource Devel. Inst., Chgo., 1986-89; project dir. Support Svcs. Ill., Inc., Chgo., 1987—. Contbr. articles to profl. jours. Mem. Coun. for Exceptional Children, Am. Assn. Mental Deficiency, Chgo. Assn. Behavioral Analysis, Behavior Analysis Soc. Ill., Assn. for Supervision and Curriculum Devel., Nat. Rehab. Assn., Coun. for Disability Rights, Assn. for Learning Disability, Grand Prix Ski Club, Cwens, Echoes, Mortar Bd., Kappa Delta Pi. Democrat. Mem. United Ch. of Christ. Home: 8936 Parkside #118 Des Plaines IL 60016 Office: Augustana Ctr Luth Social Svcs 7464 N Sheridan Rd Chicago IL 60626

COYLE, DEBORAH KNOTT, educator; b. Ithaca, N.Y., Feb. 19, 1932; d. James Edward and Deborah (Cummings) Knott; m. Harry Boies Coyle; children: David, Deborah, Jennifer, Kathleen. BS, Cornell U., 1953; MA, Holy Names Coll., 1973. Life early childhood edn. credential. Dir., tchr. Creative Play Ctr., Pleasant Hill, Calif., 1965—; owner Mooley Cow Prodns., Lafayette, Calif., 1985—; instr. part-time Diablo Valley Coll., Pleasant Hill, 1973—; adv. bd. home econs. dept. Ygnacio Valley High Sch., Walnut Creek, Calif., 1986-90, regional occupational program Mt. Diablo High Sch., Concord, Calif., 1989—. Compiler (songbook) Everybody Sings!, 1985; co-author: (booklet) A Time To Grow, 1984. Mem. Task Force on Child Care, Pleasant Hill, Calif., 1971; bd. dirs. Recreation and Park Dist., Pleasant Hill, 1975-76; camp dir. San Francisco Bay Girl Scouts U.S., Two Sentinels, Calif., 1973-78; dist. rep. Am. Field Svc., Diablo Valley, 1980-83; elder Presbyn. ch. Recipient Life Membership award Calif. Coun. Parent Participation Pre-Sch., 1973, Kiddie award Contra Costa Child Care Coun., 1988; named nominee Citizen of Yr., Pleasant Hill, 1978. Mem. Nat. Assn. for the Edn. of Young Children, Diablo Valley Dir.'s Coun. Parent Participation Nursery Schs. (organizer), Cornell Human Ecology Alumnae Assn., Cornell Alumni, Delta Gamma (mem. alumnae). Republican. Office: Creative Play Ctr 2323 Pleasant Hill Rd Pleasant Hill CA 94523

COYLE, KATHERINE GALLAGHER, lawyer; b. Tulsa, Feb. 8, 1947; d. James William and Katherine (Quinlan) Gallagher; m. John F. Coyle II, June 22, 1974; children: John Francis, Ryan Christopher, David Tyler. BA, Hollins Coll., 1969; JD, U. Tulsa, 1973; LLM in Taxation, NYU, 1975. Bar: U.S. Tax. Ct., U.S. Ct. Appeals (10th and 9th cirs.). Law clk. to presiding justice U.S. Ct. Appeals (10th cir.), Oklahoma City, 1972-73; assoc. Pepper, Hamilton & Scheetz, Phila., 1974-76, Ray Quinney & Webeker, Salt Lake City, 1976-78, Conner & Winters, Tulsa, 1980—. Pres., mem. bd. trustees Holland Hall Sch., Tulsa, 1989—. Mem. ABA, Okla. Bar Assn., Tulsa County Bar Assn., Tulsa Women Lawyers Assn. (trustee ednl. fund 1988—), LWV (trustee ednl. fund Tulsa chpt. 1988—). Republican. Roman Catholic. Office: Conner & Winters 2400 First Nat Tower Tulsa OK 74114

COYLE, MARIE, financial planner; b. Bklyn., June 20, 1935; d. John J. and Katherine (Ditrani) Magrino; m. Sept. 12, 1964; children: Catherine, Edward, Patricia, Christopher, Warren. AAS, Fashion Inst. Tech., N.Y.C., 1955; cert. in fin. planning, Adelphi U., 1984. Sole propr. Marie Coyle, Cert. Fin. Planner, Glen Cove, N.Y., 1984—; registered rep., mktg. mgr. Life Planning, Inc., Garden City, N.Y., 1984-88; registered rep. Global Capital Securities, Garden City, 1987-90, Commonwealth Equity Svc., Newton, Mass., 1990—; host Moneytalk program WGBB-FM, Merrick, N.Y., 1987; tchr. fin. planning O/E Learning, Inc., Troy, Mich., 1989. Contbr. articles to various publs. Mem. fin. commn. St. Boniface Ch., Sea Cliff, N.J., 1985—; mem. investment adv. bd. Nassau County Girl Scouts U.S., Garden City, 1987—. Mem. Internat. Assn. Fin. Planning, Nat. Assn. for Self Employed, Glen Cove C. of C. Office: 51 Hammond Rd Glen Cove NY 11542

COYLE, MARIE BRIDGET, microbiologist, laboratory director; b. Chgo., May 13, 1935; d. John and Bridget Veronica (Fitzpatrick) C. BA, Mundelein Coll., 1957; MS, St. Louis U., 1963; PhD, Kans. State U., 1965. Diplomate Am. Bd. Med. Microbiology. Sci. instr. Sch. Nursing Columbus Hosp., Chgo., 1957-59; research assoc. U. Chgo., 1967-70; instr. U. Ill., Chgo., 1970-71; asst. prof. U. Wash., Seattle, 1973-80, assoc. prof., 1980—; assoc. dir. microbiology labs Univ. Hosp., Seattle, 1973-76; dir. microbiology labs Harborview Med. Ctr., Univ. Wash., 1976—; co-dir. Postdoc Training Clinic Microbiology, Univ. Wash., 1978—. Contbr. articles to profl. jours. Fellow Am. Acad. Microbiology; mem. Acad. Clin. Lab. Physicians and Scientists (sec.-treas. 1980-83, exec. com. 1985—), Am. Soc. Microbiology (chmn. clin. microbiology div. 1984-85), Kappa Gamma Pi. Democrat. Roman Catholic. Office: Harborview Med Ctr 325 9th Ave Seattle WA 98104

COYNE, ELIZABETH ANN, bank examiner; b. Youngstown, Ohio, May 19, 1962; d. Richard Thomas and Betty (Erwin) C. BA, Barat Coll., 1984. Mgmt. trainee First Bank & Trust Co. of Palatine, Ill., 1984-85; customer svc. rep. Bank & Trust Co. of Arlington Heights, Ill., 1985-86; bank examiner FDIC, San Francisco, 1986—. Recipient Sister Anne Madden Svc. award Barat Coll., 1980. Mem. NAFE. Home: 2749 Golden Gate Ave #2 San Francisco CA 94118 Office: FDIC 25 Ecker St Ste 2300 San Francisco CA 94105

COYNE, M. COLLEEN, editor; b. Cleve., Oct. 18, 1958; d. James Francis and Lois May (Margo) Walsh; m. Douglas James Coyne, May 20, 1989; 1 child, Aidan Thomas. BA in Journalism, U. Ga., 1982. Reporter The Augusta (Ga.) Chronicle, 1982-83; copywriter Cox, Bryant & Blair Advt., Columbia, S.C., 1983-84; pub. info. specialist Sea Grant Consortium, Charleston, S.C., 1984-86; editor BP Am. Inc., Cleve., 1986—. Vol. Vis. Nurse Assn. Hospice, Cleve., 1987-88, BP America Mentors Program, 1989—. Mem. Internat. Assn. Bus. Communicators (Silver Quill award of excellence 1989), Cleve. Desk and Derrick Club (bd. dirs. 1988-89). Roman Catholic. Home: 4117 Ridgeview Rd Cleveland OH 44144 Office: BP Am Inc 200 Pub Sq 36-M Cleveland OH 44114

COYNE, M. JEANNE, state supreme court justice; b. Mpls., Dec. 7, 1926; d. Vincent Mathias and Mae Lucille (Steinmetz) C. B.S. in Law, U. Minn., 1955, J.D., 1957. Bar: Minn. 1957, U.S. Dist. Ct. Minn. 1957, U.S. Ct. Appeals (8th cir.) 1958, U.S. Supreme Ct. 1964. Law clk. Minn. Supreme Ct., St. Paul, 1956-57; assoc. Meagher, Geer & Markham, Mpls., 1957-70, ptnr., 1970-82; assoc. justice Minn. Supreme Ct., St. Paul, 1982—; mem. Am. Arbitration Assn., 1967-82; mem. bd. conciliation Archdiocese St. Paul and Mpls., 1981-82; instr. U. Minn. Law Sch., Mpls.; 1964-68; mem. Lawyers Profl. Responsibility Bd., St. Paul, 1982; chmn. com. rules of civil appellate procedure Minn. Supreme Ct., St. Paul, 1982—. Editor: Women Lawyers Jour., 1971-72. Mem. ABA, Minn. State Bar Assn., Nat. Assn. Women Lawyers, Nat. Assn. Women Judges, Minn. Women Lawyers Assn., U. Minn. Law Alumni Assn. (bd. dirs.). Office: Minn Supreme Ct 230 State Capitol Saint Paul MN 55155*

COZZARELLI, ISABELLE MARY, hydrologist; b. Jersey City, July 12, 1961; d. Francis Anthony and Kathleen (Burke) C.; m. Bruce Scott Friedman, Aug. 1985. BS in Geomechanics, U. Rochester, 1983; MS in Environ. Scis., U. Va., 1986, postgrad., 1986—. Engring. technician Office Environ. and Energy, FAA, Washington, 1983; teaching and rsch. asst. in hydrology and environ. geology U. Va., Charlottesville, 1983-85; hydrologist nat. rsch. program water resources div. U.S. Geol. Survey, Reston, Va., 1985—; presenter, condr. seminars at sci. meetings and univs., 1985—; speaker Internat. Geologic Congress, Washington, 1989. Contbr. articles and abstracts on environ. geochemistry to profl. jours. Mem. Am. Geophys. Union, Am. Assn. Ground Water Scientists and Engrs. Office: US Geol Survey 431 National Ctr Reston VA 22092

COZZOLINO, DOROTHY ARAMINI, law librarian; b. Flushing, N.Y., Jan. 9, 1938; d. William George and Anna Amelia (Brignole) Aramini; student U. Conn., 1955-58; m. Joseph M. Cozzolino, Nov. 30, 1957; children: Suzan, Alison, Matthew. BS in Geography, Trenton State Coll., 1973; MS, Drexel U., 1975. Asst. librarian U.S. Ct. Appeals (3d Cir.), Phila., 1975-79, chief librarian, 1979-88; cons., 1988—. Trustee, Morrisville (Pa.) Vis. Nurse Assn., 1972-75; fin. chairperson, treas. Morrisville Jr. Women's Club, 1970-74. Mem. Am. Assn. Law Libraries, Greater Phila. Law Library Assn. (treas. 1979-81, dir. 1978).

CRABB, BARBARA BRANDRIFF, federal judge; b. Green Bay, Wis., Mar. 17, 1939; d. Charles Edward and Mary (Forrest) Brandriff; m. Theodore E. Crabb, Jr., Aug. 29, 1959; children: Julia Forrest, Philip Elliott. A.B., U. Wis., 1960, J.D., 1962. Bar: Wis. 1963. Assoc. Roberts, Boardman, Suhr and Curry, Madison, 1968-70; research asst. Law Sch. U. Wis., 1968-70; research asst. Am. Bar Assn., Madison, 1970-71; U.S. magistrate Madison, 1971-79; judge U.S. Dist. Ct. (we. dist.) Wis., Madison, 1979—, chief judge, 1980—; mem. Gov. Wis. Task Force Prison Reform, 1971-73. Membership chmn., v.p. Milw. LWV, 1966-68; mem. Milw. Jr. League, 1967-68. Mem. ABA, Nat. Assn. Women Judges, State Bar Wis., Dane County Bar Assn., U. Wis. Law Alumni Assn.(defender svcs. com. jud. conf.). Home: 741 Seneca Pl Madison WI 53711 Office: US Dist Ct PO Box 591 Madison WI 53701*

CRABTREE, JEAN LOUISE, systems analyst; b. Racine, Wis., Nov. 22, 1958; d. William Roderick and Katherine Marie (Umnus) C. BBA, U. Wis., Oshkosh, 1980. Programmer Aid Assn. for Luths., Appleton, Wis., 1980-83; systems analyst Northwestern Mut. Life Ins. Co., Milw., 1983—. Fellow Life Office Mgmt. Assn.; mem. Women's Exchange of Milw. Roman Catholic.

CRAFT, BRIGETTA DITOMASO, military officer; b. Cleve., June 8, 1954; d. James and Brigetta (Lencl) DiTomaso; m. Emmette Bryce Craft, Feb. 26, 1977; children: England Michael-Lee, Bryce Holland. BS in Nursing, U. Cin, 1976; MS in Nursing, U. Texas, 1987. RN, Ohio. Commd. 2d lt. USAF, advanced through grades to maj., 1987; staff nurse obstetrics ward The Jew. Hosp. Cin., 1976-78, USAF, Tampa, Fla., 1978-83; charge nurse nursery USAF, Austin, Tex., 1983-84, charge nurse obstetric/gynecology clinic, 1984-86, charge nurse obstetrics ward, 1986-87; clin. nurse coord. USAF, Edwards, Calif., 1987-88, dir. ambulatory svcs., 1988—; instr. child birth edn. Air Force Hosp., Edwards, 1987—; cons. maternal child health USAF, Andrews AFB, 1989—. Vol. Rosemond (Calif) Community Health Fair, 1988, Lancaster (Calif.) Community Health Fair, 1989. Named Outstanding Young Women Am., 1989. Mem. Am. Nurses Assn., Nurses Assn. Am. Coll. Ob-gyn., Tex. Nurses Assn., Sigma Theta Tau. Democrat. Office: USAF AFSC Hosp Edwards/SGHZ Edwards AFB CA 93523-5300

CRAFT, JOYCE PRESSLEY, government official; b. Asheville, N.C., Nov. 30, 1942; d. Columbus Manley and Martha Reba (Hampton) Pressley; m. Neil Lewis Goode, Aug. 28, 1965 (div. 1981); children: Mark Allen, Keith Lewis; m. Robert Lee Craft, Jan. 14, 1989. ABA, Catawba Valley Community Coll., Hickory, N.C., 1987. Cashier/bookkeeper Winn-Dixie, Asheville, N.C., 1960-63; sec. Boy Scouts Am., Asheville, 1963-65; clk.-typist Farmers Home Adminstrn., U.S. Dept. Agr., Asheville, 1965-80; loan tech. Farmers Home Adminstrn., Hickory, N.C., 1980-87; loan specialist U.S. Dept. HUD, Greensboro, N.C., 1987—; beauty cons. Mary Kay Cosmetics, High Point, N.C., 1987—. Mem. Clerical Assn. of Farmers Home Adminstrn. (reg. coordinator 1985-87). Republican. Baptist. Home: 438 Chesterwoods Ct High Point NC 27260

CRAFTS, MARY ELIZABETH, education administrator; b. N.Y.C., Sept. 4, 1941; d. Edward Robert and Kathryn Mary (Quinlan) Amend; m. Walter Crafts, Aug. 18, 1973; children: Walter Michael, Susan Elizabeth. BA in Hist. and Polit. Sci., The Coll. of St. Rose, 1963; postgrad., U. Md., 1977-79. Claims rep. HHS, Flushing, N.Y., 1963-68; budget analyst HHS, Balt., 1968-74; exec. dir. Advocates for Children & Youth, Inc., Balt., 1987-88; adminstrv. asst. St. William of York Sch., Balt., 1989—; sch. rep. St. William of York Parish Coun., Activities Com., Balt., 1989—; sec. St. William of York Fin. Com., Balt., 1989—. Sec. Westside Dem. Club, Balt., 1984-85, newsletter editor, 1985-87, pres., 1987-89, bd. dirs., 1989—; coord. of vols. Com to Elect the Seven Sitting Judges, Balt., 1986; mem. St. William of York Activities Com., Balt., 1979—, exec. com., 1980-82, 1987-89; sec. St. William of York Parish Coun., Balt., 1985-86, pres., 1986-88; lector St. William of York Parish, 1988—. Mem. AAUW (Balt. br. bd. dirs. 1977-79, program v.p. 1979-81, legislative chmn. 1981-82, 1986-87, pres. 1982-84; Md. div. convention chair 1984-85, resolutions chair 1985-86, by-laws chair 1990—), Ten Hills Garden Club (sec. 1983-84, v.p. 1984-85, pres. 1985-87, adviser to pres. 1987-89), Tenn Hills Assn. (bd. dirs. 1979-83), Hunting Hills Swimming Club, Inc. (sec. 1984-87). Home: 503 N Chapel Gate Ln Baltimore MD 21229 Office: St William of York Sch 600 Cooks Ln Baltimore MD 21229

CRAIG, GAIL HEIDBREDER, architect, educator; b. Balt., Jan. 20, 1941; d. Gerald August and Ora Henderson (Longley) Heidbreder; m. Val Dean Craig, Jan. 19, 1985; children: Laura Temple, John Temple. BA, Stanford U., 1966, postgrad., 1975-78. Registered architect, Calif. With various firms, 1969-85; owner Gail Craig, AIA, Porterville, Calif, 1985—; instr. various constrn. and drafting courses Calif. Community Colls., Tulare County, 1985—. Mem. AIA, Internat. Conf. Bldg. Offcls., Main St. Inc. (pres.). Office: 639A N Main St Porterville CA 93257

CRAIG, JEAN (JEAN CRAIG MCNEILLY), advertising executive; b. Cin., June 1, 1937; d. Carl George and Loretta Rose (Meis) Westerman; m. Christopher Kevin Craig, Dec. 28, 1960 (dec. Oct. 1977); children: Deirdre, Christopher, Erin, Maureen; m. Edward R. McNeilly, Nov. 25, 1983 (dec. Mar. 1988). BA, Benedictine Heights Coll., Tulsa, 1959. Copywriter The Lansdale Co., L.A., 1961-62, Guild, Bascom, Bonfigli, L.A., 1963-65; assoc. creative dir. Foote, Cone & Belding, L.A., 1965-77; pres., creative dir. Cunningham, Root & Craig, L.A., 1977-85, Kresser/Craig, L.A., 1985—; mem. faculty UCLA Extension, L.A., 1980-83. Bd. dirs. Am. Heart Assn., L.A., 1980-83. Recipient Clio award, 1985, 87, Athena award Newspaper Advt. Bur., 1983, 84, 85, 15 Internat. Broadcasting awards, 1965-88, Agy. of Yr. award Am. Advt. Fedn., 1984, London Film Festival award, 1985, 87, numerous others; named Outstanding Communicator, L.A. Advt. Women, 1984, One of Top 100 Ad Women in U.S., Advt. Age Mag., 1988. Mem. L.A. Advt. Club (bd. dirs. 1979-84, 12 Belding Bowls 1965-88), L.A. Art Dirs. (mem. adv. bd.), Western States Advt. Agys. Assn. (bd. dirs. 1983-87), L.A. Creative Club (founder, 1st pres. 1979-80, 81). Roman Catholic. Home: 21446 Rambla Vista Malibu CA 90265 Office: Kresser-Craig 2029 Century Park E 5th Fl Los Angeles CA 90067

CRAIG, JUANITA MOOSE, personnel placement company executive; b. Charlotte, N.C., Nov. 10, 1941; d. John Franklin and Anne Arlene (Stout) Moose; m. Burlin Thomas Craig Jr., Nov. 21, 1959; children: Burlin Thomas III, Kurt DeWayne, Jonathan Shane. BBA summa cum laude, U. N.C., 1984, postgrad., 1986. Lic. real estate broker, N.C. Stock position reporter Southeastern Securities, Charlotte, 1960-62; office mgr. Withers, Price & Co., Charlotte, 1962-66; account exec. asst. Hornblower & Weeks, Charlotte, 1966-70; investor coord. The Ervin Co., Charlotte, 1970-73; office mgr. Cannon & Blair, Charlotte, 1973-74; cash mgr. Korf Industries Inc., Charlotte, 1974-84; v.p. personnel and adminstrn. Cogentrix Inc., Charlotte, 1984-88; pres. Staff Additions Inc., Charlotte, 1988—. Mem. Westchester Polit. Action Group, Charlotte, 1986—; pres. Western Pony League, Charlotte, 1973-76. Mem. NAFE, Charlotte Area Personnel Assn., The Employers Assn. (program com. 1987—), Am. Mgmt. Assn., Am. Soc. Personnel Adminstrs., Nat. Assn. Temp. Svcs., N.C. Assn. Temp. Svcs. (membership com. 1988—), South Park Exec. Club, Westchester Garden Club (v.p. 1986-87, pres. 1987—). Republican. Lutheran. Home: 4607 Westridge Dr Charlotte NC 28208 Office: Staff Additions Inc 6100 Fairview Rd Ste 550 Charlotte NC 28210

CRAIG, JUDITH, clergywoman; b. Lexington, Mo., June 5, 1937; d. Raymond Luther and Edna Amelia (Forsha) C. BA, William Jewell Coll., 1959; MA in Christian Edn., Eden Theol. Sem., 1961; MDiv, Union Theol. Sem., 1968; DD, Baldwin Wallace Coll., 1981; DHL, Adrian Coll., 1985. Youth dir. Bellefontaine United Meth. Ch., St. Louis, 1959-61; intern children's work Nat. Coun. of Chs. of Christ, N.Y.C., 1961-62; dir. Christian edn. 1st United Meth. Ch., Stamford, Ct., 1962-66; inst. adult basic edn. N.Y.C. Schs., 1967; dir. Christian edn. Epworth Euclid United Meth. Ch., Cleve., 1969-72, assoc. pastor, 1972-76; pastor Pleasant Hills United Meth. Ch., Middleburg Heights, Ohio, 1976-80; conf. council dir. East Ohio Conf. United Meth. Ch., Canton, 1980-84; bishop United Meth. Ch., Detroit, 1984—; mem. Nat. Task Force on Itineracy, 1977-80; responder to World Coun. of Chs. (document on Baptism, Eucharest and Ministry 1975); gen. conf. del., 1980, 84. Contbr. articles to ministry mags. Bd. dirs. YWCA, Middleburg Heights, 1976-80. Recipient Citation of Achievement William Jewell Coll., 1985. Mem. Internat. Women Minister's Assn. Office: The United Meth Ch 155 W Congress Ste 200 Detroit MI 48226*

CRAIG, KAREN LYNN, accountant; b. Detroit, Mar. 17, 1959; d. John and Corinne (Legel) C.; m. Robert A. Steshetz, May 3, 1986. A. in Commerce, Henry Ford Community Coll., 1980; BS in Bus. and Acctg., Wayne State U., 1982. CPA, Mich., Calif. Cost and staff acct. Wilson Dairy Co., Detroit, 1982-83, sr. acct., 1983-84, acting contr., 1984; staff acct. Coopers & Lybrand, Detroit, 1984-85, sr. acct., 1986-87, supr. acct., Newport Beach, Calif., 1987-89; asst. corp. contr. J.F. Shea Co., Inc., Walnut, Calif., 1989—. Mem. Mich. Assn. CPA's, NAFE. Avocations: music, photography, baseball. Office: JF Shea Co Inc 655 Brea Canyon Rd Walnut CA 91789

CRAIG, LAURA J., accounting manager; b. Milw., July 19, 1958; d. Kenneth Leo and Audrey Anita (Zimmermann) Mischker; m. Kevin J. Craig, Apr. 2, 1987. AA, Fox Valley Tech., Fond du Lac, Wis., 1978. Accounts payable supr. Miles Kimball Co., Oshkosh, Wis.; accounting-credit mgr. Nelson Mktg., Oshkosh. Vol. Big Bros./Big Sisters, 1979-81. Mem. NAFE, Am. Mgmt. Assn. Republican. Home: W8336 Lincoln Ave Oakfield WI 53065 Office: 210 Commerce St Oshkosh WI 54901

CRAIG, LEXIE FERRELL, career development specialist and guidance counselor; b. Halls, Tenn., Dec. 12, 1921; d. Monroe Stancil and Hester May (Martin) Ferrell; m. Philip L. Craig, May 19, 1951; children: Douglas H., Laurie K., Barbara J. BS magna cum laude, George Peabody Coll., Vanderbilt U., 1944; MA with honors, Denver U., 1965; postgrad. Colo. U., 1972—, Colo. State U., 1964—, U. No. Colo., 1964—. Cert. local vocat. adminstr., vocat. guidance specialist, vocat. bus. specialist, vocat. home econs. specialist, reading specialist, nat. recreation dir. specialist. Danforth grad. fellow, counselor Mich. State U., East Lansing, 1944-46; nat. student counselor, field dir. dept. of univ. pastor and student work in the dept. of higher r edn. Am. Bapt. Conv., summer svc. career projects dir. U.S. and Europe, 1946-51; coord. religious and career activities counselor, Colo. U., 1951-52; tchr. home econs., phys. edn., counseling, dist. 96, Riverside, Ill., 1952-54; substitute tchr., psychometrist, reading specialist part time, Deerfield, Ill., 1956-59; substitute tchr. Littleton (Colo.) Dist. VI, 1961-63, guidance and career counselor Littleton Pub. Schs., 1963-67, 68-86, career devel. specialist, guidance counselor spl. assignments state and nat., Gov.'s Youth 2000 Task Force Com., 1988—, also mem. vocat. needs and assessment com., 1988—; chmn. leadership team AARP Works, Teane, Colo.; dir., counselor YWCA Extension Program, Job Corps, Denver, 1967-68; tchr. adult edn. home econs. evenings, 1963-66; mem. Colo. State Career Task Force, 1973-77; cons. vol. home econ. cons. Colo. State U extension office, 1988-89. Lay conf. rep. Meth. Ch. Pastor/Parish Commn.; vol. sr. citizens programs United Meth. Ch., Littleton Community Ctr., mem. nominating and personnel work area com.; chmn. membership com. St. Andrew United Meth. Ch., Colo. Ch. Women United; mem. Greater Denver Frienship Force; bd. dirs. Career Awareness Council Boy Scouts Am., Metro Denver; also mem. Colo. Career Awareness Council; mem. So. Suburban Recreation, Littleton Community Arts Ctr.; adv. council Powell PTO, 1981-84; adv. council SEMBCS area vocat. schs.; mem. local caucus com. Republican Party; mem. Dist. Environ. Sci. Council. Didcott scholar, 1942; mem. AVS adv. council Early Childhood Edn., Health Occupation, Restaurant Arts and Coop Career Devel., 1970—; pres. Colo. Assn. Adult Devel. & Aging, 1989-91. Danforth home econs. and leadership scholar, 1943; Am. Leadership Camp Found. scholar, Shelby, Mich., 1942-45; Hildegarde Sweet Scholar, 1983; recipient Sullivan award and grant, named outstanding grad., 1944; named Littleton Mother of Year, 1977, Colo. Vocat. Counselor of Yr., 1978, Colo. Vocat. Guidance Assoc. Counselor of Yr., 1984; recipient plaque for recruiting and career guidance Navy and Air Force, 1980, Clifford G. Houston Colo. Counselor award, 1985, Outstanding award Boy Scouts of Am. Career Awareness Council, 1986, Recognition Gold Pin award United Meth. Ch. Women, 1988. Mem. NEA, AAUW, Colo. Religious Values Assn. (mem. chmn. 1989) Arapohoe County Ret. Tchr. Assn. (v.p. 1989-90), Colo. Edn. Assn., Littleton Edn. Assn., Am. Vocat. Assn., Colo. Vocat. Assn., Am. Assn. Counseling and Devel., Colo. Assn. for Counseling and Devel. (exec. bd.), Nat. Career Devel. Assn. (membership chmn.), Colo. Career Devel. Assn. (past pres., membership chmn.), Nat. Vocat. Guidance Assn. (Colo. rep.), Am. Assn. Retired Persons (v.p.), Colo. Retired Sch. Employees Assn., Arapahoe County Retired Tchrs. Assn., Colo. Sch. Counselors Assn., Am. Field Service (pres. Littleton chpt.), Lit. Book Club Littleton Arts Ctr., Home Economists in Homemaking (Littleton and Bega, Australia clubs), Phi Delta Kappa, Delta Kappa Gamma Alpha Delta (past chpt. pres., Omega State DKG, state com. chmn. personal growth and svcs.), Order EAstern Star, Countryn Western Dance Club, Delta Pi Epsilon (past pres.), Pi Omega Pi (past pres.), Pi Gamma Mu (past pres.), Kappa Delta Pi (past pres.). Editor, pub. Join in a 1949; editor The Church Follows Its Youth, 1950, curriculum units in consumer edn., home econs., careers, parenting classes. Office: 2655 S Sheridan Ct Lakewood CO 80227

CRAIG, MARGARET WILCOX, education educator; b. Hackensack, N.J., Jan. 3, 1934; d. John A. and Ethel M. (Furry) Wilcox; m. Robert B. Craig, Oct. 29, 1966; children: John R., Scott W., Todd A., James W. BSc., Ohio State U., 1956; MA, Wm. Paterson Coll., Wayne, N.J., 1979. Tchr. Newark Pub. Schs., 1956-57, Dade Co. Pub. Schs., Fla., 1957-58; bus. sch. tchr. Ridgewood (N.J.) Secretarial Sch., 1958-60, co-owner, dir., 1960-67; adminstrn. asst. to pres. Bergen Community Coll., Paramus, N.J., 1967-68; mem. sch. bd. Wyckoff Pub. Schs., N.J., 1980-90. Chmn. Cub Pack 198 Boy Scouts Am., Wyckoff, 1977-87; treas. Economy Shop, Wyckoff, 1982-90; pres. Ramapo Apts., Franklin Lakes, N.J., 1985-87, 1989—; pres., v.p.

Wyckoff Sch. Bd., 1985-89. Named Woman of Yr. Wyckoff YMCA, 1988. Mem. Mensa, Pi Lambda Theta. Republican. Episcopalian. Home: 647 Wishing Well Rd Wyckoff NJ 07481

CRAIG, MARTHA ANN, retail store owner; b. Evansville, Ind., Oct. 31, 1952; d. Leonard Vincent and Bernice Gertrude (Deuser) Stratman; m. Gary Myron Craig, June 7, 1975; children: Grant, Adam. BEd, Ind. U., 1974; MEd, Ind. State U., 1976. Pharmacy technician Med. Arts Pharmacy, Evansville, Ind., 1969-71; tchr. Catholic Diocese of Evansville, 1974-79; owner, mgr. Classroom Paraphernalia, Evansville, 1978—; substitute tchr. Catholic Diocese Evansville, 1979-86; presenter workshops in field. Active Boy Scouts Am., Evansville, 1988—; mem. Westside Cath. Consol. Sch. Bd., Evansville, 1988—, v.p., 1989, 90—. Mem. Nat. Sch. Supply Equipment Assn., Ednl. Dealers Suppliers Assn., Ind. U. Alumni Assn., VFW Auxiliary, Evansville C. of C., Kennel Club. Roman Catholic. Office: Classroom Paraphernalia 2258 E Morgan Ave Evansville IN 47711

CRAIK, EVA LEE, science educator; b. Gatesville, Tex., Aug. 12, 1919; d. Clarence J. and Leona B. (Blair) Young; m. David Warren Craik, Aug. 3, 1941 (dec. Dec. 1963); children: David D., Robert A., Gary C., Philip L. BS, Tex. Women's U., 1940; MEd, Hardin-Simmons U., 1960; EdD, North Tex. State U., Denton, 1966. Cert. tchr., Tex. Tchr. home econs. Ranger (Tex.) High Sch. & Jr. Coll., 1940-43; tchr. sci. Pinckney Elem. Sch., Lawrence, Kans., 1943-44; tchr. home econs. Novice (Tex.) High Sch., 1959-60, Hawyley (Tex.) High Sch., 1960-61; tchr. biology and sci. edn. Hardin-Simmons U., Abilene, Tex., 1962-84, ret., 1984. Vol. tchr. Fgn. Mission Bd., Monrovia, Tex. and Liberia, W. Africa, 1984—, English as a Second Lang., Abilene, 1987-90; vol. hosp. aux. Hendrick Med. Ctr., Abilene, 1986-90. Tex. Acad. Sci. fellow. Mem. AAUW (edn. found. chair 1986-90). Baptist. Home: 1802 N 11th Abilene TX 79603

CRAIN, GERTRUDE RAMSAY, publishing company executive; m. G.D. Crain Jr. (dec. Dec. 1973); children: Keith, Rance. D in Journalism (hon.), DePauw U., 1987; LHD (hon.), U. Detroit, 1988. Asst. treas. Crain Communications Inc., Chgo., 1942, sec., asst. treas., 1943-62, sec., treas., 1962-74, chmn. bd., 1974—; bd. dirs. Internat. Advt. Assn., Mag. Pubs. Am., Execs. Club of Chgo., The Nat. Press Found. of Wash., Advt. Coun. of N.Y. Trustee Lincoln Acad. of Ill., James Webb Young Scholarship U. of Ill.; founding mem. Com. of 200, 1982; bd. dirs. Mus. of Broadcast Communications in Chgo., Northwestern Meml. Hosp. Corp.-Chgo., Mus.of Sci. and Industry. Named to Working Woman Hall of Fame, 1987; named Chicagoan of Yr. Boys and Girls Club of Chgo., 1987, One of Top 60 Women Bus. Owners Saavy Mag., 1987, One of Top 50 Businesswomen Mich. Womans Mag., 1987; recipient Magnificat medal Mundelein Coll., Chgo., 1988. Mem. Internat. Advt. Assn. (bd. dirs.), Mag. Pubs. Am. (bd. dirs.), Nat. Press Found. Washington, Advt. Club N.Y., Execs. Club Chgo. Office: Crain Communications Inc 740 N Rush St Chicago IL 60611

CRAIN, NANCY L., trade association executive; b. Waco, Tex., Feb. 5, 1953; d. Kenneth H. and Alberta H. (Trosen) Hubbard; m. Michael W. Crain; children: Joy, Wendy, Tara. Student, U. Ark., 1971-75. Coord. OPCMIA JATC, Peoria, Ill.; adminstr. Combined Cen. Ill. Constrn. Industry Fund, Peoria; exec. mgr. Greater Peoria Contractors and Suppliers Assn., Inc. Active Downtown and Riverfront Devel. Com., 1987—; co-chmn. All America CIty Peoria Proud Parade, 1990. Named Outstanding Fundraiser for Peoria City Am. Heart Assn. Mem. Internat. Builders Exch. Execs. (chair North Cen. region), Nat. Assn. Women in Constrn. (past pres. Peoria chpt., named Women in Constrn. of Yr. 1982), Ill. Soc. Assn. Execs. Office: 512 W Main Peoria IL 61606

CRAMER, MARJORIE, plastic surgeon; b. London, Apr. 26, 1941; came to U.S., 1957; d. Thomas and Mary Mullen; m. Philip Cramer, Feb. 1964; children: Jennifer, Heather. AB, Barnard Coll., 1964; MD, SUNY, Bklyn., 1968. Intern in surgery Kings County Downstate Med. Ctr., Bklyn., 1968-69, resident in gen. surgery, 1969-72, resident in plastic surgery, 1972-74; pvt. practice N.Y.C., 1974—. Fellow Am. Coll. Surgeons; mem. Am. Soc. Plastic and Reconstructive Surgeons, Regional Soc. Plastic and Reconstructive Surgeons. Office: 800A Fifth Ave Ste 101 New York NY 10021

CRAMER, ROXANNE HERRICK, educator; b. Albion, Mich., Apr. 24; d. Donald F. and Kathryn L. (Beery) Herrick; m. James Loveday Hofford, Jan. 29, 1955 (div.); children: William Herrick, Dana Webster, Paul Christopher; m. Harold Leslie Cramer, Apr. 20, 1967. Student, U. Mich., 1952-55; BA, U. Toledo, 1956; EdM, Harvard U., 1967; EdD, Va. Poly. Inst. and State U., 1990. Tchr. Wayland (Mass.) Pub. Schs., 1966-70, Fairfax County (Va.) Pub. Schs., 1970—; tchr./team leader Gifted/Talented program, 1975—; coordinating instr. Trinity Coll., Washington, 1978; nat. coord. gifted children programs Am. Mensa, Ltd., 1981-84. Editor newsletter Va. Assn. for the Edn. of Gifted; contbr. articles to profl. jours. Mem. NEA, Nat. Assn. Gifted Children, Am. Assn. Gifted Children, Coalition for Advancement Gifted Edn. (bd. dirs. 1982-84), World Coun. Gifted and Talented Children, Intertel Found., Inc. (bd. dirs.), chmn. Hollingworth award com. 1984—), Fairfax County Assn. Gifted, Va. Edn. Assn., Fairfax Edn. Assn., Mensa, Phi Delta Kappa. Club: Harvard (Washington). Home: 4300 Sideburn Rd Fairfax VA 22030 Office: Louise Archer Gifted Ctr 324 Nutley St NW Vienna VA 22180

CRANAGE, KATHLEEN LYNN, executive vice president finance; b. Deming, N.M., Aug. 30, 1952; d. Everett Matthew and Marie Louise (Jonas) C.;p m. James Edward Stephey, June 17, 1979. BA, Eastern N.M. U., 1975, MBA, 1977. Client service agent III N.M. Health and Social Service Dept., Hobbs, N.M., 1975; assoc. natl. bank. exam. Off. Compt. Curr. US Treas. Grd., Junction, Colo., 1978-83; internal auditor N.M. Educator's FCU, Albuq., N.M., 1983-84, controller, exec. v.p. finance, 1989--. Mem. Paradise Hills Civic Assn. Albuquerque, 1988-89, N.Mex. Right to Choose, 1987-89, ACLU, 1986, 89, Am. Cancer Rsch. Inst., 1986-88. Mem. NAFE. Democrat. Office: NMex Educators Federa 6501 Indian Sch NE Albuquerque NM 87198

CRANDALL, ARLENE BERNADETTE, school psychologist; b. Bklyn., Feb. 22, 1956; d. Walter Brooks and Agnes (Fink) C. BA, Marywood Coll., 1978; MEd, St. John's U., Jamaica, N.Y., 1981, MS, 1983; PD in Ednl. Adminstrn., Long Island U., 1988. Cert. Sch. Psychologist. Instr. Holy Trinity High Sch., Hicksville, N.Y., 1978-82; instr. psychology Marywood Coll., Scranton, Pa., 1982; sch. psychologist Shield Inst. for Mentally Retarded, Flushing, N.Y., 1983-85, Smithtown (N.Y.) Cen. Sch. Dist., 1985-90; coord. spl. edn. Mid. Country Cen. Sch. Dist., 1990—; presenter N.Y. State conventions, Nat. Sch. Psychologists conventions on suicide prevention, 1985—. Pres. coun. Pupil Svc. Orgn. N.Y. State, 1989—. Mem. N.Y. Assn. Sch. Psychologists (pres. 1988-90), Nat. Assn. Sch. Psychologists, Nassau County Psychol. Assn., Am. Assn. Suicidology, NOW, Am. Assn. Univ. Women, Nat. Assn. Female Execs., Mensa. Democrat. Home: 26 Smith St Glen Cove NY 11542 Office: Unity Drive Sch Mid Country Cen Sch Dist Centereach NY 11720

CRANDALL, NANCY LEE, state legislator, nurse; b. Gary, Ind., Sept. 28, 1940; d. Lawson E. and Lela A. (Bartley) Cox; m. Donald K. Crandall; children: D. Kenneth, Keith A., Bradley D. BS in Nursing, Ind. U., 1961. RN. With ob-gyn. dept. George Ade Hosp., Brook, Ind., 1961; with pediatrics dept. Univ. Hosp., Ann Arbor, Mich., 1961-62; instr. psychiat. nursing Mercywood Hosp., Ann Arbor, 1962-63; owner, operator Lakeshore Tennis Shop, Spring Lake, Mich., 1978-81; with community rels. dept. Hackley Hosp., Muskegon, Mich., 1983-86; with community svc. dept. Muskegon Community Coll., 1987-88; mem. Mich. Ho. of Reps., 1988—. Past pres. Mich. State Med. Soc. Aux., East Lansing, Muskegon County Med. Soc. Aux.; commr. West Mich. Regional Shoreline Com., Muskegon, 1983-86; mem. Mich. Export Devel. Authority, Lansing, 1987—; fitness tchr. local YFCA; vol. S.W. Outward Bound Sch., 1980, Earthwatch Rsch. Team, 1985, Muskegon Community Leadership Acad.; mem. Norton Shores (Mich.) City Coun., 1981-86; mem. Muskegon County Rep. Exec. Com., 1986—; mem. adminstrv. bd. Cen. United Meth. Ch.; bd. dirs. Muskegon YFCA, others. Mem. AAUW, PEO, LWV (bd. dirs. Muskegon chpt.), Zonta. Home: 3981 Norton Hills Muskegon MI 49441 Office: Mich Ho of Reps State Capitol Lansing MI 48913

CRANDALL, SONIA JANE, educator; b. Quincy, Ill., Sept. 2, 1952; d. Gerald Madison and Roselma Louise (Zeiger) Syrcle; m. Edward Young Crandall, June 28, 1975. Diploma, Michael Reese Med. Ctr., Chgo., 1974; BS, Western Ill. U., 1974; MED, U. Ill., 1980; PhD, U. Okla., 1989. Med. tech. U. Mo. Med. Ctr., Columbia, 1974-75; med. tech., clin. instr. St. Johns Hosp., Springfield, Ill., 1976-81; med. tech., supr. Okla. Teaching Hosp., 1982-85, tng. officer, 1986; Kellog fellow Univ. of Okla., 1987-89, asst. prof., asst. dir. edn. div. dept. family medicine, 1989—. Contbr. articles to prof jours. Named Outstanding Young Woman in Am. Mem. Am. Edn. Rsch. Assn., Am. Assn. for Adult and Continuing Edn., Am. Soc. Clin. Pathology, Soc. Tchrs. Family Medicine, Nat. Cert. Agy. Med. Lab. Pers., Phi Delta Kappa, Phi Kappa Phi. Home: 8440 NW 85th St Oklahoma City OK 73132 Office: U Okla Health Sci Ctr Dept Family Med 800 NE 15th St Ste 503 Oklahoma City OK 73190

CRANDALL, SUZANNE, adult day care centers executive; b. Rockford, Ill., Sept. 4, 1934; d. I. Milo and Una Belle (Allen) Smallwood; m. John Chapman Crandall, Mar. 27, 1954; children: Michael John, Julie Sue. BS in Anthropology and Sociology, Rockford Coll., 1983. Cert. activity cons. Dir. Bright Side Adult Day Care Ctrs./Protestant Community Svc., Rockford, 1973—, Protestant Community Svcs., Rockford, 1987-89; teaching assoc. U. Ill. Med. Sch., Rockford; planner, conf. presenter Ill. Dept. on Aging. Com. mem. Rockford Twp. Sr. Citizens Commn. Recipient Profl. Woman award YWCA, 1986. Mem. AAUW, LWV, Ill. Assn. Adult Day Care Providers (past bd. dirs.), Nat. Council on Aging. Home: 2234 Humboldt Dr Rockford IL 61101

CRANE, DEBRA OHNMACHT, architectural drafter; b. Sedan, Kans., Aug. 19, 1956; d. Alvin Eugene and Foye Lorrain (Sears) Ohnmacht; m. Roger James Crane, July 7, 1979; 1 child, Turner Leigh. BS in Architecture, Calif. Poly., San Luis Obispo, 1979. Draftsman Bates & Pekarek, Irvine, Calif., 1979-81; freelance draftsman, Irvine, 1982-84; dir. forward planning Barbuto Bldg. & Devel., San Dimas, Calif., 1984-85; owner, mgr. Debra Crane Archtl. Drafting Svcs., Mission Viejo, Calif., 1985—. Mem. AAUW, Calif. Poly. Alumni Assn. Democrat. Office: 24852 Lirio Mission Viejo CA 92692

CRANE, EILEEN CUNNINGHAM, foundation educational consultant; b. N.Y.C., Apr. 27, 1935; d. Daniel and Ella (Gavigan) Cunningham; m. Donald Charles Crane, Apt. 12, 1958; children: Kathryn Crane Rodimer, Ellen Crane Williams, Mary. BS in Foods and Nutrition, Hunter Coll., 1956; teaching cert., Montclair State Coll., 1971; postgrad. in edn., Lehman Coll., 1970-74. Cert. home economist. Staff dietitian Columbia-Presbyn. Hosp., N.Y.C., 1956-58; tchr. home econs. No. Valley Regional High Sch. Dist., Demarest and Old Tappan, N.J., 1970-88; cons. in values edn. Joseph P. Kennedy Jr. Found., Washington, 1988—; cons. in edn. Wakefern Corp., Elizabeth, N.J., 1980-86; text reviewer Prentice-Hall Inc., 1983. text reviewer Prentice Hall, Inc., 1983, Glencoe Pubs., 1989; author tchrs. and students guides, 1986. Participant White House Conf. on Families, 1980, White House Conf. on Children, 1982; vol. Morris County Consumer Affairs Commn., Morristown, N.J., 1982-84. Recipient award for excellence in edn. Gov. State of N.J., 1988; N.J. Dept. Edn. grantee, 1980, 86, 88. Mem. Am. Home Econs. Assn., N.J. Edn. Assn., N.J. Home Econs. Assn. (treas. 1982-86, Home Econs. Tchr. of Yr. award 1980), AAUW (chpt. chmn. family life com. 1987-88). Republican. Roman Catholic. Home and Office: 17 Diane Ln Ortley Beach NJ 08751

CRANE, GLENDA PAULETTE, educator; b. Orlando, Fla., June 29, 1946; d. James Author and Elizabeth Lorine (Johnson) C. AA in Edn., Orlando Jr. Coll., 1966; BA in Elem. Edn., U. S. Fla., 1967; postgrad. So. Bapt. Theol. Sem., 1970; MEd, Rollins Coll., 1985. Tchr., Orange County Schs., Orlando, 1967-70, 79-80, Lake Highland Prep. Sch., Orlando, 1981—; tchr. Belle Glade (Fla.) Christian Sch., 1970-79, asst. prin., 1970-74, prin., 1975-79. State treas. Fla. Rainbow Girls., 1964. Mem. NEA, Fla. Edn. Assn., Fla. Council Tchrs. English, Orange County Tchrs. Assn., Assn. Supervision and Curriculum Devel., Internat. Reading Assn., Orange County Reading Council of Internat. Reading Assn., Fla. Reading Assn., Nat. Council for the Social Studies, Alumni Assn. U. South Fla., Alumni Assn. So. Bapt. Theol. Sem., Fla. Coun. Tchrs. of Math, Kappa Delta Pi. Democrat. Baptist. Clubs: Winter Park Pilot, Eastern Star, Winter Park Rainbow Girls. Home: 2406 S Bumby St Orlando FL 32806 Office: 901 N Highland Ave Orlando FL 32803

CRANE, MARGARET ANN, real estate appraiser; b. Evansville, Ind., May 27, 1940; d. Robert Lindell and Margaret (Pearson) Wulff; m. Arvel Lee Crane, Dec. 26, 1956; children: LeAnn Crane Powell, Steven Lynn, Thomas Glen. Student, U. Evansville, 1977—. Lic. real estate broker, Ind. Real estate sales person Citizens, Jarrett Realty, Huber Realtors, Evansville, 1968-77; staff appraiser Citizens Realty & Ins., Evansville, 1977-79, David Matthews Assocs., Evansville, 1981-86; pres. Margaret A. Crane Appraisal Co., Evansville, 1986—. Mem. Am. Inst. Real Estate Appraisers (residential mem.), Ind. Assn. Realtors, Nat. Assn. Realtors, Evansville Bd. Realtors, Women's Coun. Realtors, Women's Bus. Initiative. Office: Margaret A Crane Appraisal 1714 Bayard Park Dr Evansville IN 47714

CRANE, REGINA ANN, technical writer; b. Pine Bluff, Ark., Jan. 13, 1961; d. Lois Lynell and Lois Virginia (Martin) C. BA in Profl. & Tech. Writing, U. Ark. at Little Rock, 1983. Researcher, writer Ark. Women's History Inst., Little Rock, 1984; tech. writer UNISYS Corp., Nat. Ctr. for Toxicological Rsch., Jefferson, Ark., 1984-87; tech. editor CAE Link Corp., Link Tng. Svcs. Div., Jacksonville, Ark., 1988—. Recipient Acad. Scholarship U. Ark. at Little Rock, 1979-80, Journalism Scholarship, 1982. Mem. Women in Communications, Inc., U. Ark. at Little Rock Alumni Assn. Democrat. Baptist. Office: CAE Link Corp PO Box 1282 Jacksonville AR 72076

CRANEY, MYRNA, accountant; b. Brackenridge, Pa., Feb. 24, 1936; d. Ralph I. Howells and Margaret E. (Bavetz) Mivec; m. Patrick M. Craney, June 19, 1954; children: Michael P., T. Bryan, Kathleen E. BS, U. So. Ind., 1980. CPA, Ind. Acct. Geo. S. Olive & Co., Evansville, Ind., 1976-81; accountant Harding & Shymanski, Evansville, Ind., 1981-83; ptnr. Craney & Wilson, Evansville, 1983-86, Brown, Smith & Settle, Evansville, 1986—; lectr. U. So. Ind., Evansville, 1981-84. Mem. AICPA, Ind. CPA Soc., Women's Bus. Initiative, Petroleum Club. Office: Brown Smith & Settle 777 Oak Hill Rd Evansville IN 47711

CRANFILL, LINDA WILLIAMSON, health facility specialist; b. Wilkes-Barre, Pa., Aug. 8, 1949; d. William Benedict and Florence Mary (Dombroski) Williamson; m. Robert Sidney Cranfill, Oct. 4, 1975; 1 child, Katherine Best. BA, U. Ky., 1971. Mgmt. asst. VA Med. Ctr., Lexington, Ky., 1971-78, quality assurance coord., 1978-86, staff asst. to dir., 1986—. Office: VA Med Ctr Lexington KY 40511

CRANIN, MARILYN SUNNERS, landscape designer; b. N.Y.C., Aug. 1, 1932; d. William And Rebecca (Yates) Sunners; m. A. Norman Cranin, June 14, 1953; children: Jonathan Blake, Andrew Ross, Elizabeth S., June 14, 1953. BA, Beaver Coll., Glenside, Pa., 1954; student, Harvard U., 1981-82. Landscape designer N.Y. Bot. Gardens, N.Y.C., 1974-76; hort. therapist Beth Abraham Hosp., 1975-85, N.Y. Bot. Gardens, N.Y.C., 1976-78; master gardener Nassau County Coop Extension Service, N.Y.C., 1976-80; landscape designer London Landscape, Massapequa, N.Y., 1984—. Columnist South Shore Record, 1980-82. V.p., bd.dirs. 5 Towns Music and Art Found., Woodmere, N.Y., 1962—; trustee, dep. mayor Village Hewlett Bay Park, N.Y., 1974-84; trustee Hewlett-Woodmere Pub. Library, 1977—, Nassau Library System, Uniondale, N.Y., 1980-86, Waldorf Sch., Garden City, N.Y., 1985—, Am. Chamber Ensemble, 1981—, Beaver Coll. Alumni Bd., 1979-86, Beaver Coll., 1987—. Mem. Am. Hort. Soc., Nassau County Coop Extension Service, N.Y. Bot. Garden, Wave Hill Hort. Soc. Clubs: Woodmere Bay Yacht, The Woodmere.

CRANK, RUTH ELIZABETH, financial planning executive, life insurance executive, manufacturing company executive, employment agency executive; b. Sidney, Ohio, Aug. 18, 1938; d. Charles Max Stephenson and Mildred Katherine (Hoover) Stephenson Foresythe; m. Robert G. Crank, Dec. 2, 1978; children—Rochelle, Roxanne, Troy, Juliana, Trent, Dominique. Dir. sch. project and ctr. U. Dayton, Father Phillip Hoelle, Ohio, 1971; field mgr. Avon Co., Cin., 1972-74; life ins. agt. N.Y. Life Ins. Co., Dayton, 1974—; pres., chmn. bd. Am. Fin. Concepts, Inc., Dayton, 1982—; owner Acad. Am. Fin. Concepts; speaker in field; cons. in field. Co-editor new sales industry manual The Crank Formula. Leader Buckeye Trails council Girl Scouts U.S. lead Drill Team, Cheerleading Camps., 1964-74; founder Woodman Play Sch.; mem. Better Bus. Bur. Named Ace of Yr., N.Y. Life, 1975, Star & Exec. council, 1974-84, Centurim, 1974-1984; recipient Golden Eagle award Am. Mut. Life Ins. Co., 1989; mem. Women's Million Dollar Round Table; first woman ins. agt. recognized by Dayton Gen. Mgmt. and Mgrs. Life Assn. for outstanding work, 1976. Mem. Dayton C. of C. Republican. Roman Catholic. Avocations: camping, swimming. Home and Office: Crank & Crank 4837 Kentfield Dr Dayton OH 45426

CRANSTON, CAROLINE WOOD, educator; b. Fredonia, N.Y., Nov. 4, 1925; d. Fred Jacob and Mary (Hall) Wood; m. Melvin Claude Cranston, Dec. 23, 1978. BA in Sci., Cornell U., 1947; BS in Edn., SUNY, Fredonia, 1948, MS in Edn., 1952. Cert. secondary edn. tchr., N.Y. Tchr. elem. S.G. Love Sch., Jamestown, N.Y., 1948-59; tchr. elem. Fredonia Cen. Schs., 1959-82, ret., 1982. Mem. Nat. Grape Coop, N.Y. State Ret. Tchrs. Assn., Am. Dairy-Goat Assn., Farm Bur., Affenpinsher Dog Club, German Shepherd Dog Club, AAUW, Order of Eastern Star, Rebekah Lodge, Am. Assn. Ret. Persons, Fredonia Grange #1. Republican. Methodist. Home: 3624 E Main Rd Fredonia NY 14063

CRANSTON, MARY B., lawyer; b. Palo alto, Calif., Dec. 29, 1947; d. James Alfred and Bettye (Luhnow) Bailey; m. Harold David Cranston, Aug. 15, 1970; children: Susan Anne, John David. AB in Polit. Sci., Stanford U., 1969, JD, 1975; MA in Psychology, UCLA, 1970. Bar: Calif. 1975. Assoc. atty. Pillsbury, Madison & Sutro, San Francisco, 1975-82, ptnr., 1983—; faculty Nat. Inst. Trial Advocacy, San Francisco, 1986—, Calif. Continuing Edn. of the Bar, 1985—, The Rutter Group, 1984—. Contbr. articles to profl. jours. Mem. Calif. Com. on Women in Law, San Francisco and Los Angeles, 1985-86; bd. dirs. Legal Services for Children, San Francisco, 1983-87. Fellow ABA (chmn. Sherman Act Com. of antitrust sect. 1986-89, Found. fellow); mem. Calif. Bar Assn., San Francisco Bar Assn., Stanford U. Alumni Assn. (bd. dirs. 1986—, pres. 1989). Club: Cap & Gown (Stanford) (treas. 1974-75). Office: Pillsbury Madison & Sutro 225 Bush St San Francisco CA 94104

CRAPO, SHEILA ANNE, telecommunications company professional, artist; b. Elko, Nev., June 11, 1951; d. John Lewis and June Florene (Lani) C. BA, U. Nev., 1974. Various svc. positions CP Nat. Corp. subs. Alltel, Elko, 1974-78, svc. rep., 1978-84, bus. office supr., 1984-87, bus. supr. Nev. office, 1987—; speaker in field; writer, artist, 1974—. Officer, organizer Freedom Com., Elko, 1984. Mem. Credit Women Internat., AAUW (editor newsletter Elko 1980-82), Northeastern Nev. Hist. Soc., Animal Relief Found., Ducks Unltd., Bookworms. Office: CP Nat Corp Ill W Front St Elko NV 89801

CRASWELL, ELLEN, state senator; b. Seattle, May 25, 1932; m. Bruce A. Craswell, 1953; children—Richard Bruce, James Arthur, Patricia Louise Craswell Johnson, Jill Ellen Craswell Solano. Student U. Wash. Mem. Wash. State Senate, pres. task force to sec. edn. Am. Legis. Exchange Council; dir. Gt. N.W. Fed. Savs. and Loan. Bd. dirs. Seattle Hearing and Speech Clinic. Republican. Baptist. Club: Altrusa. Home: 8066 Chico Way NW Bremerton WA 98312*

CRAUN BROWN, TAMMY LEE, pharmacist; b. Winchester, Va., Apr. 4, 1963; d. Charles Rimel and Lois Rebecca (Himelright) Craun; m. Gerald James Brown, Sept. 20, 1986. BS in Pharmacy, Med. Coll. of Va., Richmond, 1986. Pharmacist People Drug Store, Alexandria, Va., 1986-87; pharmacist, asst. mgr. Revco Drug Store, Front Royal, Va., 1984—, Haymarket Pharmacy, 1989—. Active Am. Cancer Soc. Mem. Va. Pharm. Assn., Am. Pharm. Assn. Home: 1958 Kathy Ct Winchester VA 22601 Office: Revco Drug Store 324 W Bobcawen St Winchester VA 22601 also: 6611 Jefferson St Haymarket VA 22069

CRAWFORD, ANN MACCOLLOM, journalist; b. Sterling, Mass., Apr. 8, 1927; d. Donald Bingham and Marjorie (Stiles) MacCollom; m. H. Vance Crawford, Jan. 24, 1948; children: Joel, Peter. BA, Wellesley Coll., 1947. Corr. Sta. WAGM, Presque Isle, Maine, 1953-55; script writer Impcomation, Sterling Forest, N.Y., 1960-63; reporter Rockland Jour. News, Nyack, N.Y., 1965-67; reporter, editorial writer, columnist Bergen Record, Hackensack, N.J., 1963-65, 67-81, asst. editor, 1981—. Recipient Deadline Writing award Soc. of Silurians, N.Y.C., 1973. Mem. Beta Beta Beta. Office: Bergen Record 150 River St Hackensack NJ 07601

CRAWFORD, CAREN, quality systems specialist, quality engineer; b. Maywood, Calif., Sept. 1, 1954; d. Charles Earl and Wilma May (Flom) Hillhouse; m. Jimmie Crawford, Aug. 6, 1983. BA, Adams State Coll., 1976; AA, Western Nev. Community Coll., 1980. CRP planner Bently Nev. Corp., Minden; MRB and source inspection coord. Apple Computer, Cupertino, Calif., 1981-83; quality assurance specialist Convergent Tech., San Jose, Calif., 1983-88; sr. project coord. Sun Microsystems, Mt. View, Calif., 1988-90; quality engr. Sun Microsystems, 1990. Mem. APICS, Am. Soc. Quality Control (cert.), Order Eastern Star, White Shine Jeruselum (worth shepardess 1981).

CRAWFORD, CARMELA RACANELLI, management consultant; b. N.Y.C., Apr. 17, 1954; d. Domenico and Marie (DiMaggio) Racanelli; m. Tom Stewart Crawford, Sept. 20, 1980. BA, CUNY-Queens Coll., 1976. With Bloomingdale's, N.Y.C., 1976—, project leader, 1984-86, project coordinator, 1986-88, payroll mgr., 1988-89; dir. payroll systems Bloomingdale's, 1989-90; mgmt. cons. Coopers & Lybrand, N.Y.C., 1990—. Mem. Am. Payroll Assn., Nat. Assn. Female Execs., Cyborg User Assn. (author bulletin 1987—). Republican. Roman Catholic. Home: Scarsdale County Estates Scarsdale NY 10583

CRAWFORD, DEBRA FOSSETT, education educator; b. Scottsboro, Ala., May 9, 1959; d. Quiniss Ladue and Annie (Brooks) Fossett; m. Thomas Edward Crawford,. Student, Auburn U., Ala., 1977-80; BA, U. Ala., 1980-82; M, Ala. U., 1984-88. Tchr. Scottsboro City Schs., Ala., 1982—. Mem. Scottsboro Art League, 1983; mem. steering com. 1st Bapt. Learning Ctr., Scottsboro. Mem. NEA, Ala. Edn. Assn., Scottsboro Edn. Assn. (faculty rep.), AAUW (chmn. pub. info. bd. Scottsboro). Democrat. Home: RR 6 Box 37 Scottsboro AL 35768 Office: Brownwood Elem Sch 305 Bingham Scottsboro AL 35768

CRAWFORD, DIANA JEAN, advertising executive; b. Portland, Maine, July 2, 1945; d. Howard Odell and Bertha Amelia (Munch) Bollinger; m. L. David Crawford, Feb. 13, 1965 (div. Dec. 1975); children: Kimberly Anne Crawford Arrington, Erin Beth. Student, Lynchburg Coll., 1964; student, Moseley Flint Sch. Real Estate, Richmond, Va., 1978. Lic. real estate. Adminstrv. asst. to pres. Pet Mgmt. Svcs., Pet Luv Stores, Richmond, Va., 1975-78; with real estate sales Roy B. Amason & Assocs., Richmond, 1979-81; dir. fin. The Martin Agy., Richmond, 1981-86; v.p. Deady Advt., Richmond, 1986—; v.p. Talley Sports Prodns., Richmond, 1990—. Creator ad copy for various brochures, ads, press releases, etc.; editor, author (newsletter) Pet Luv News, 1976. Supporting mem. The Nature Conservancy, Arlington, Va., 1988—; registration com. Young Republicans, Virginia Beach, Va., 1965-66. Coll. scholar Amelia (Va.) Woman's Club, 1963. Mem. NAFE (founder and bd. dirs. Richmond chpt. 1989—), Ad Club Richmond (membership com. 1986—), Japan-Va. Soc., Tips Club. Home: 10812 Sebring Dr Richmond VA 23233 Office: Deady Advt 17 E Cary St Richmond VA 23219

CRAWFORD, ELOUISE S., quality control, auditing and servicing company executive; b. San Francisco, Sept. 18, 1949; d. Everett George and Orissa Minchey (Haymond) Goodrick; 1 child from previous marriage, Patricia. Grad., Moseley Flint Sch. Real Estate, Charlottesville, Va., 1985. Lic. real estate assoc., Calif. Asst. to acct., office mgr. Schoonmaker, Susalito, Calif.; asst. to pres. Brooks Monroe & Co., Charlottesville; realtor assoc. Clover Realty, Charlottesville; asst. designer Flower Nook Florist, San Rafael, Calif.; loan processor Am. Savs. Bank, San Rafael, Allied Savings Bank, Santa Rosa. Mem. Luth. Ch. Women Parents and Tchrs. Mem. NAFE, ABWA. Address: 1318 Gaspar Ct Rohnert Park CA 94928

CRAWFORD, JEAN ANDRE, counselor; b. Chgo., Apr. 12, 1941; d. William Moses and Geneva Mae (Lacy) Jones; student Shimer Coll., 1959-60; BA, Carthage Coll., 1966; MEd, Loyola U., Chgo., 1971; postgrad. Nat. Coll. Edn., Evanston, Ill., 1971-77, Northwestern U., 1976-83; m. John N. Crawford, Jr., June 28, 1969; cert. counselor Nat. Bd. Cert. Counselors, elem. edn., spl. edn. and pupil personnel services, Ill. Med. technologist, Chgo., 1960-62; primary and spl. edn. tchr. Chgo. Pub. Schs., 1966-71, counselor maladjusted children and their families, 1971-88; counselor juvenile first-offenders, 1968-88; post-secondary vocat. counselor, 1988—. Vol. Sta. WTTW-TV; vol. counselor deaf children and their families; counselor post-secondary students. Mem. Ill. Assn. Counseling and Devel., Am., Ill. sch. counselors assns., Council Exceptional Children, Am. Assn. Counseling Devel., Coordinating Council Handicapped Children, Shimer Coll. Alumni Assn. (sec. 1982-84), Phi Delta Kappa. Home: 601 E 32d St Chicago IL 60616 Office: 3233 W 31st St Chicago IL 60623

CRAWFORD, JUDITH ANN, public relations executive; b. Indpls., Mar. 26, 1952; d. William and Beth Aileen (Hammill) C.; m. Jon Alan Krieger, Oct. 13, 1984. Student, Miami U., Oxford, Ohio, 1970-73; BA in Journalism, U. Wyo., 1974. Pub. info. asst. Wyo. Hwy. Dept., Cheyenne, 1974-77; promotion specialist Drake U., Des Moines, 1978-79; info. specialist Iowa Energy Policy Coun., Des Moines, 1979; assoc. travel editor Better Homes & Gardens, Des Moines, 1979-83; nat. advt. mgr. Better Homes & Gardens Real Estate Svc., Des Moines, 1983-86; staff writer Phoenix Bus. Jour., 1986-87; dir. pub. rels. Ramada Internat. Hotels and Resorts, Phoenix, 1987—. Mem. publicity com. Wyo. Heart Assn., 1977-78; chmn. vol. week United Way, Des Moines, 1986. Mem. Pub. Rels. Soc. Am., Travel Industry Assn. Am. (press and pub. rels. com. 1989—), Am. Hotel and Motel Assn. (communications com. 1989—), Sigma Delta Chi. Presbyterian. Office: Ramada Internat. Hotels and Resorts 3838 E Van Buren Phoenix AZ 85038

CRAWFORD, LINDA CAROLE, insurance executive; b. Wichita, Kans., July 14, 1944; d. Rodney Gene and Anna Lee (Rosenberger) Armour; m. Gary James Crawford, Oct. 14, 1966; children: Cheryl Lynn, Jennie Elizabeth. BS in Secondary Edn., Emporia State U., 1966; BBA, Washburn U., 1981. CPA, Kans.; master fellow Life Mgmt. Inst. Math. tchr. Unified Sch. Dist. 501, Topeka, 1966-69, substitute tchr., 1978-79; income tax asst. Sue Brandenburg, CPA, Topeka, 1982; acct. Victory Life Ins. Co., Topeka, 1982-83, mgr. fin. reporting, 1983-84, asst. contr., 1984-87, v.p., treas., 1987—. Mem. Nat. Assn. Accts. (bd. dirs. 1989—), Kans. Soc. CPAs (cert.). Republican. Office: Victory Life Ins Co 300 SW 8th Ave Topeka KS 66603

CRAWFORD, LINDA LOUISE, secretary; b. Owensboro, Ky., Jan. 26, 1949; d. John L. Jr. and Mariam Gladys (Kasey) Oberst; m. David Mark Crawford, Nov. 1, 1984; children: Shannon Reneé Hill, Timothy Hill. Grad., Owensboro (Ky.) Bus. Coll., 1977. Long distance tel. operator So. Bell. Tel. Co., Owensboro, 1968; sec. Collignon & Nunley Architects, Owensboro, 1977, Tex. Gas Transmission Corp., Owensboro, 1977—. Mem. NAFE, Profl. Secs. Internat. Office: PO Box 1160 Owensboro KY 42302

CRAWFORD, LINDA SIBERY, lawyer, educator; b. Ann Arbor, Mich., Apr. 27, 1947; d. Donald Eugene and Verla Lillian (Schneck) Sibery; m. Leland Allardice Crawford, Apr. 4, 1970; children: Christina, Lillian, Leland. Student, Keele U., 1969; BA, U. Mich., 1969; postgrad., SUNY, Potsdam, 1971; JD, U. Maine, 1977. Bar: Maine 1977, U.S. Dist. Ct. Maine 1982, U.S. Ct. Appeals (1st cir.) 1983. Tchr. Pub. Sch., Tupper Lake, N.Y., 1970-71; asst. dist. atty. State of Maine, Farmington, 1977-79; asst. atty. gen. State of Maine, Augusta, Maine, 1979—; ptnr. The Forensic Cons. Group, Lexington, Mass., 1988—; legal advisor U. Maine, Farmington, 1975; legal counsel Fire Marshall's Office, Maine, 1980-83, Warden Svc., Maine, 1981-83, Dept. Mental Health, 1983-89, litigation div., 1989—; teaching team trial advocacy Law Sch. Harvard U., Cambridge, Mass., 1987—; legal counsel for litigation div., U.S. Atty. Gen. Mem. Natural Resources Coun., Maine, 1985—; bd. dirs. Diocesan Human Rels.ns Coun., Maine, 1977-78, Arthritis Found., Maine, 1983-88. Named one of Outstanding Young Women of Yr. Jaycees, 1981. Mem. ABA, Maine Bar Assn., Kennebec County Bar Assn., Assn. Trial Lawyers Am., Maine Trial Lawyers Assn., Nat. Assn. State Mental Health Attys. (treas. 1984-86, vice chmn. 1987-89, chmn. 1989—). Home: 25 Winthrop St Hallowell ME 04347 Office: State of Maine Dept of Atty Gen State House Sta #6 Augusta ME 04333

CRAWFORD, LINNEA RUTH, automotive parts manager; b. Springfield, Mass., Oct. 31, 1952; d. Hale Edmund and Thyra Linnea (Wallin) Roberts; m. Bruce W. Crawford, Sept. 7, 1974 (div. 1980); 1 child, Justin Bruce. Parts mgr. City Motors, Springfield, Mass., 1971-80, Enfield (Conn.) Motors, 1980-81; asst. parts mgr. DePalma Motor Sales, Feeding Hills, Mass., 1981-83; store mgr. Motomart, Agawam, Mass., 1983-85; parts mgr. Lipman AMC/Jeep/Renault, Hartford, Conn., 1986, Michael's Jeep/Eagle, Springfield, Mass., 1986-89, Suburban Chevrolet, Southwick, Mass., 1989—. Mem. Springfield Libr. Assn. Baptist. Home: 12 Cosgrove Ave Agawam MA 01001

CRAWFORD, MARIAN SCHUMACHER, librarian; b. Dansville, N.Y., May 13, 1929; d. Nicholas John and Agnes Louise (Neu) Schumacher; m. Bert Greenleaf Crawford, June 23, 1951 (dec. Dec. 1984); 1 child, Suzanne. BS in and LS, SUNY, Geneseo, 1950, MS in Edn., 1960, postgrad., 1964; postgrad., UU. Rochester, 1964. Cert. elem. tchr., libr., in supervision, N.Y. High sch. libr. Warsaw (N.Y.) Cen. Sch., 1950-52; elem. tchr. Nunda (N.Y.) Cen. Sch., 1955-58; elem. tchr Dansville (N.Y.) Cen. Sch., 1958-60, elem. libr., 1960—, dir. gifted program, 1980—, dir. media svcs., 1983—; instr. SUNY, Geneseo, 1965—; cons. to elem. media specialists and adminstrs., N.Y., 1980—; v.p. libr. coun. Bd. Coop. Ednl. Svcs., Mt. Morris, N.Y., 1989—; reviewer media evaluation, 1965—. Author: (handbook) Study Skills, 1965; contbr. articles to profl. publs. Mem. Women's Civic Club, Dansville, 1950—, Nicholas Noyes Hosp. Aux., Dansville, 1975—; bd. dirs. Genesee Valley Coun. on Arts, Geneseo, 1986-88. Named Tchr. of Yr., Genesee Valley Tchrs. Assn., 1979. Mem. ALA, N.Y. Libr. Assn. (chmn. awards com. 1980-84), Sch. Libr. Media Specialists (sec. 1970), N.Y. United Tchrs. (com. chmn. 1968-72), Dansville Tchrs. Assn. (bd. edn. rep. 1963-83), Greater Rochester Area Media Specialists (liaison officer 1983-86), Genesee Valley Devel. Learning Group, Kiwanis (sec. Dansville 1986—, 1st Woman of Kiwanis award Genesee div. 1986). Republican. Roman Catholic. Home: 1867 Rte 63 Wayland NY 14572 Office: Ellis B Hyde Elem Sch Libr 85 N Main St Dansville NY 14437

CRAWFORD, MARY ANNE, naval officer; b. Lafayette, Ind., Sept. 24, 1952; d. William Curtis and Lorene (Koch) C.; m. John Byron Hunt, July 4, 1986. BS in Math., U. Wash., 1980; MS in Ops. Rsch., Naval Postgrad. Sch., 1988. Commd. ensign USN, 1980, advanced through grades to lt. comdr., 1989; polar transport navigator, Antarctic Devel. Squadron USN, Point Mugu, Calif., 1981-84; instr., naval flight officer USN, Jacksonville, Fla., 1986-89; aircraft handling officer USN, USS Lexington, Pensacola, Fla., 1989—. Mem. Ops. Rsch. Soc., Mil. Ops. Rsch. Soc., 99s Club. Republican.

CRAWFORD, MARY B., small business owner; b. Indpls., May 21, 1949; d. Charles R. Sr. and Fredonia D. Wright.; m. Oliver W. Crawford III; children: Kathleen, Gloria, Karla, Gloria. Student, Roosevelt U., Tenn. State U. Pub. health adminstr. Chgo. Bd. Health; adminstrv. asst. Office of Mayor, Chgo.; founder, pres. Albertina Walker Found., Chgo.; prin. Air Fresh Oxygen & Equipment Co., Gary, Ind. Named Woman of Yr. New Second Hope Ch. Mem. NAFE, Assn. Women Execs., Megmt. Assn. (pres.), Aux. Cook Physicians Assn. (named Woman of Yr.). Address: 3290 Grant St Gary IN 46408

CRAWFORD, MARY LOUISE PERRI, naval officer; b. Grand Haven, Mich.; d. Louis and Helen Marie (Buckley) Perri; m. Keith Eugene Crawford, Feb. 23, 1974 (dec. Oct. 1986); children: Matthew Perri, Michael Kirk. AA, Muskegon County Community Coll., 1969; BA, U. Mich., 1971. Commd. ensign U.S. Navy, 1972, advanced through grades to comdr., 1987; pub. affairs officer Naval Air Sta., Key West, Fla., 1974-77, adminstrv., personnel officer Naval Air Res. Detachment, Patuxent River, Md., 1977-78, adminstrn. br. head Strike Aircraft Test Directorate, Naval Air Test Ctr., Patuxent River, 1978-80, ops. watch officer Command Ctr., Comdr.-in-Chief Naval Forces Europe Staff, London, 1980-84, officer-in-charge Personnel Support Activity Detachment, Patuxent River, 1984-86; engring. officer Chief Test and Evaluation Div., Strategic C3 Systems Directorate, Ctr. for Command, Control, and Communications, Def. Communications Agy., Washington, 1986-89; mgr. ultra high frequency Joint Satellite Communications Ctr., Joints Chiefs Staff, Pentagon, Washington, 1989—. Mem. AAUW, Women's Overseas Svc. League, U. Mich. Alumni Assn. Roman Catholic. Avocations: painting, ballet. Office: Joint Staff/J6Z Pentagon Rm 2B913 Washington DC 20318-6000

CRAWFORD, MURIEL LAURA, lawyer, author, educator; d. Mason Leland and Pauline Marie (DesIlets) Henderson; m. Barrett Matson Crawford, May 10, 1959; children: Laura Joanne, Janet Muriel, Barbara Elizabeth. Student, U. Calif., Berkeley, 1958-60, 67-69; B.A. with honors, U. Ill., 1973; J.D. with honors, Ill. Inst. Tech., 1977; cert. employee benefit specialist U. Pa., 1989. Bar: Ill. 1977, U.S. Dist. Ct. (no. dist.) Ill. 1977, U.S. Ct. Appeals (7th cir.) 1977; CLU Chartered fin. cons. Atty., Washington Nat. Ins. Co., Evanston, Ill., 1977-80, sr. atty., 1980-81, asst. counsel, 1982-83, asst. gen. counsel, 1984-87, assoc. gen. counsel, sec., 1987-89, cons., employee benefit specialist, 1989—, . Author: (with Beadles) Law and the Life Insurance Contract, 1989; co-author Legal Aspects of AIDS, 1990; contbr. articles to profl. jours. Recipient Am. Jurisprudence award Lawyer's Coop. Pub. Co., 1975, 2nd prize Internat. LeTourneau Student Med.-Legal Article contest, 1976, Bar and Gavel Soc. award Ill. Inst. Tech./Chgo.-Kent Student Bar Assn., 1977. Fellow Life Mgmt. Inst.; mem. ABA, Ill. Inst. Tech./Chgo.-Kent Alumni Assn. (bd. dir. 1983-89). Democrat. Congregationalist.

CRAWFORD, NORMA VIVIAN, nurse; b. Cleveland, Tex., Dec. 29, 1936; d. Ira Wesley and Lizzie Augusta (Godejohn) C.; m. Arthur B. Crawford, Sept. 20, 1956 (dec.); children: Pamela, Desiree. Lic. vis. nurse, Lee Jr. Coll., 1971-72; RN, Cumberland County Coll., 1977; BSN, U. Mary-Hardin Baylor, 1986. Charge nurse Patrick Henry Hosp., Newport News, Va., 1972-73; staff nurse Salem (N.J.) County Nursing Home, 1975-77, Nicholson Nursing Home, Penns Grove, N.J., 1977; nurse ICU, Metroplex Hosp., Killeen, Tex., 1977-79; dir. nurses Wind Crest Nursing Ctr., Copperas Cove, Tex., 1979-82; staff nurse supr., unit mgr. med./surg. unit, supr., home health nurse, dir. home health Metroplex Hosp., Killeen, Tex., 1979-87; dir. Metroplex Home Health Svcs., Killeen, Tex., 1988—. Mem. Order of Eastern Star. Baptist. Home: 604 Yucca Dr Copperas Cove TX 76522 Office: PO Box 10219 Killeen TX 76547-0219

CRAWFORD, PAMELA E., management; b. Aurora, Ill., Oct. 8, 1950; d. Marvin Marshall Brown and Lorraine Lillian (Natzke) Brown Silvernail; m. Gibson Lovell Crawford II, 1971. BA, U. of the Pacific, 1971; MSc., Golden Gate U., 1986. Cert. tchr., Calif. Tchr. India, Calif., Okla., 1969-76; affirmative action rep. Safeway Stores, Inc., Oklahoma City, 1977-78; employment rep. Safeway Stores, Inc., Sacramento, 1978; equal ops. rep. Safeway Stores, Inc., Oakland, Calif., 1978-84; human resource supr. Safeway Stores, Inc., Sacramento, 1984-86; pers. mgr. Denny's Inc., Sacramento, 1986-88; instr. Golden Gate U., Sacramento, 1988; pers. rep. Am. River Hosp., Carmichael, Calif., 1988; adj. prof. Montana State U., Bozeman, 1988—; tchr. Adult Community Edn.; pvt. cons. Vol. Project Ptnrship., Oakland, 1981-84, Bay Area Crisis Nursery, Concord Calif., 1982-84; bd. dirs. REACH, Inc., Bozeman, 1990. Recipient White Ho. awards for employment of the handicapped and earthquake preparedness campaign. Mem. Pers. Assn. (local chpt., program chair 1989, v.p., pres. elect 1990), Assn. of Bus. Communications, Soc. Human Resources Mgmt., Western Acad. of Mgmt.

CRAWFORD, SALLY SUE, health care administrator; b. LaGrange, Ga., Nov. 7, 1944; children from previous marriage: Patricia Anne, Elizabeth Sue, James Burton Jr. AA, DeKalb Coll. Nursing, 1973; BA, Ga. State U., Atlanta, 1971, MEd, 1978; EDS, U. Ga., 1987. RN. Sr. health educator Ga. Dept. Human Resources, Lawrenceville, 1975-88; asst. dir. staff devel. ARC, Atlanta, 1988; with Atlanta Eye Screening, 1988-89; outreach coord. Cataract Inst., Atlanta, 1989-90; tng. coord. S.E. Regional Ctr. For Drug-Free Schs. & Communities, 1990—. Contbr. articles to various jours. Lt. Ga. Army Nat. Guard. Mem. NAFE, Ga. Fedn. Profl. Health Educators, Am. Soc. for Tng. and Devel., Am. Alliance for Health, Physical Edn., Recreation and Dance, UDC (state chmn. 1988-90, nat. chmn. of pages 1989), Daus. of 1812 (1st v.p. chpt. 1989—), Continental Soc., Daus. of Indian Wars (state chmn. 1990), DAR (organizer regent chpt. 1982-84, nat. speakers staff 1986-88), Daus. Am. Colonists (chpt. regent 1988—, state chmn. 1988—), Colonial Dames of XVII Century (local registrar), Ga. Soc. Magna Charta Dames (state officer 1986-90), First Families of Ga., Lions (1st female mem. Atlanta club, chmn. sight and vision 1989-90, 3d v.p. 1990—). Episcopalian. Home: H-12 Christian Dr Newnan GA 30263

CRAWFORD, SARAH CARTER (SALLY CRAWFORD), broadcast executive; b. Glen Ridge, N.J., Oct. 3, 1938; d. Raymond Hitchings and Katherine Latta (Gribbel) Carter; m. Joseph Paul Crawford III, Sept. 10, 1960 (div. 1966). BA, Smith Coll., 1960. Media dir. Kampmann & Bright, Phila., 1961-64; sr. media buyer Foote, Cone & Belding, N.Y.C., 1964-69; assoc. media dir. Grey Advt., Los Angeles, 1969-75; account exec., research dir. Sta. KHJ-TV, Los Angeles, 1975-76; mgr. local sales Sta. KCOP-TV, Los Angeles, 1977-82; gen. sales mgr. Sta. KTVF-TV, Fairbanks, Alaska, 1982—; bd. dirs. Vista Travel, Fairbanks; mem. adv. com. Golden Valley Electric Corp., Fairbanks, 1984-86;mem. steering com. UAF-Sch. of Career Continuing Edn. Mem. UAF Sch. of Career Continuing Edn. Coun., 1989—; vice chmn. Fairbanks Health and Social Svc. Commn., 1986—; pres. Fairbanks Meml. Hosp. Aux., 1988-90, creator trust fund; bd. dirs. Fairbanks Downtown Assn., 1984-87; mem. needs assessment update com. United Way. Mem. Fairbanks Womens Hockey Assn., Fairbanks Womens Softball Assn. Republican. Episcopalian. Home: 518 Juneau Fairbanks AK 99701 Office: Sta KTVF-TV Box 70950 Fairbanks AK 99707

CRAWFORD, SHEILA SIMMONS, bank executive; b. Chgo., May 23, 1948; d. Harold Sr. and Alice (Petermon) Simmons; m. James W. Crawford; children: Angela Norman, Kevin Johnson, Michelle Johnson. BS in Bus. Mgmt., Bentley Coll., 1988. Systems analyst Sears, Chgo., 1971-78; project leader Internat. Harvester Co., Chgo., 1978-82; project mgr. Marshall's, Inc., Woburn, Mass., 1982-87; asst. v.p. The Boston Co., Boston, 1987—. Advo. women's rights. Mem. NAFE, Data Processing Mgmt. Assn., Boston Urban Bankers, Nat. Assn. Negro Bus. and Profl. Women. Office: Boston Co One Cabot Rd WTO2B Bedford MA 02155

CRAWFORD, SUSAN JEAN, lawyer, federal government official; b. Pitts., Apr. 22, 1947; d. William Elmer Jr. and Joan Ruth (Bielau) C.; m. Roger W. Higgins; 1 child, Kelley S. BA, Bucknell U., 1969; JD, New Eng. Sch. Law, 1977. Bar: Md. 1977, D.C. 1980. History tchr., coach Radnor (Pa.) High Sch., 1969-74; assoc. Burnett & Eiswert, Oakland, Md., 1977-79; ptnr. Burnett, Eiswert and Crawford, Oakland, 1979-81; prin. dep. gen. counsel U.S. Dept. Army, Washington, 1981-83, gen. counsel, 1983-89; asst. states atty. Garrett County, Md., 1978-79; inspector gen. U.S. Dept. Def., Arlington, Va., 1989—; instr. Garrett County Community Coll., 1979-81. Del. Md. Forestry Adv. Commn., Garrett County, 1978-81, Md. Commn. for Women, Garrett County, 1980-83; chair Rep. State Cen. Com., Garrett County, 1978-81; trustee Bucknell U., 1988, New Eng. Sch. of Law, 1989. Mem. ABA, Md. Bar Assn., D.C. Bar Assn., Fed. Bar Assn., Am. Arbitration Assn., Bus. & Profl. Women. Presbyterian. Office: US Dept Def 400 Army Navy Dr The Pentagon Arlington VA 22202-2884

CRAWFORD-KUMMER, SONDRA, printing/fund-raising company executive, consultant; b. Balt., July 12, 1950; d. Donald Revere and Phyllis Edna (Finck) Crawford; m. Charles A. Kummer III, Mar. 17, 1979. Student Edinboro State U. Sec. RT&A Assocs., Balt., 1977-78; sec. Barton-Cotton, Inc., Balt., 1978-79, adminstrv. asst., 1979-81, mem. sales service staff, 1981-82, v.p. sales, 1982—, fund-raising cons., 1982—, v.p. in Balt. Mem. Nat. Assn. Female Execs., Nat. Cath. Devel. Council, Nat. Soc. Fund-Raising Execs. Republican. Presbyterian. Avocations: snow skiing, water skiing, basketball, yoga, meditation. Home: 6229 Gilston Park Rd Baltimore MD 21228 Office: Barton-Cotton Inc 1405 Parker Rd Baltimore MD 21227

CRAWLEY, JACQUELINE NINA, neuroscientist; b. Phila., June 14, 1950; d. Samuel and Miriam (Schultz) Lerner; m. Carl B. Crawley, Sept. 1971 (div. 1979); m. Barry B. Wolfe, May 4, 1986; 1 child, Andrew Lerner. BA, Univ. Pa., Phila., 1971; MS, U. Md., 1973, PhD, 1976. Instr. U. Md., College Park, 1975-76, Prince Georges Community Coll., Largo, Md., 1976, Yale U., New Haven, Conn., 1978; postdoctoral fellow Yale U., New Haven, 1976-79; pharmacology rsch. assoc. NIMH, Bethesda, Md., 1979-81; sr. neurobiologist E.I. DuPont de Nemours & Co., Wilmington, Del., 1981-83; chief unit behavioral neuropharmacology NIMH, Bethesda, 1983—; co-organizer 1st Internat. Conf. Neuronal Cholecystokinin, Brussels, 1984; fin. chairperson Winter Neuropeptide Conf., Breckenridge, Colo., 1984-89; internat. rsch. collaborations, Stockholm, Paris, Tubingen, Fed. Republic of Germany; guest lectr. George Washington U., Washington, 1987—, U. Md., College Park, 1987—, U. Pa., Phila., 1986—, Found. for Advancement Edn. Scis., Bethesda, 1984—. Editor: Neuronal Cholecystokinin, 1985; editorial bd. Jour. Neuroendocrinology, Pharmacology, Biochemistry and Behavior, Topics in Exptl. Psychopharmacology; contbr. over 120 articles to profl. jours.; appearances on TV documentaries on neurosci. and brain rsch.. Recipient Nat. Rsch. Scientist award NIH, Bethesda, 1985-88, NSF Vis. Scientist award, 1988-89; grantee A.H. Robins Co., Richmond, Va., Pfizer Co., Groton, Conn., 1986-90. Mem. Soc. Neurosci. (pres. Potomac chpt. 1986-87), Am. Coll. Neuropsychopharmacology, AAAS, Am. Psychol. Assn., Washington Eating Disorders Soc., N.Y. Acad. Scis., Animal Behavior Soc., NSF (mem. panel on neural mechanisms of behavior 1989—). Office: NIMH Bldg 10 Rm 4N214 Bethesda MD 20892

CREAGER, JOAN GUYNN, biology educator; b. Austin, Ind., Dec. 8, 1932; d. Hubert Rider Wiley and Mary (Royce) Guynn; m. John A. Creager, June 28, 1952; children: Richard, Diane, Edward, Mark. BS, Trinity U., 1955, MS, 1958; PhD, George Washington U., 1964. Rsch. assoc. Nat. Acad. Scis., Washington, 1966-69; assoc. prof. biology Nova Community Coll., Alexandria, Va., 1969-72, 74-80; prof. Marymount U., Arlington, Va., 1980—. Author: Human Anatomy and Physiology, 1983, Microbiology: Principles and Applications, 1990; editor: Am. Biology Tchr., 1974-81; contbr. numerous articles to profl. jours. NSF fellow George Washington U., 1962-64. Mem. AAAS, Nat. Assn. Biology Tchrs., Va. Assn. for Biology Edn., Textbook Authors Assn., Sigma Xi. Office: Marymount U Glebe & Old Dominion Arlington VA 22207

CREAMER, LINDA EDITH, rehabilitation center administrator; b. San Diego, Jan. 8, 1954; d. William Gene and Betty Jean (Barrington) C. Student, S.W. Tex. State U., 1972-73. Cert. med. staff coordinator. Tax examiner, taxpayer delinquency investigator IRS, Austin, Tex., 1973-76; legal sec. Jerry Loftin, atty. at law, Ft. Worth, 1978; administrv. sec. Bowling Proprietors Assn. Am., Arlington, Tex., 1978-80, Clark Ins. Co., Arlington, 1980-81, Tex. Assn. Retarded Citizens, Austin, 1982-83; med. transcriptionist Brown Schs. Ranch Treatment Ctr., Austin, 1983—; med. staff coordinator Healthcare Rehab. Ctr., Austin, 1985—; mem. communications task force Healthcare Rehab. Ctr., 1985-86; sec. med./profl. staff, Austin, 1985—; chmn. Staff appreciation Com., Austin, 1985—. Vol. LBJ Library and Mus., Austin, 1982—, Spl. Olympics, Austin, 1988. Recipient Spl. Recognition award LBJ Library and Mus., 1987. Mem. Am. Assn. Med. Transcriptionists, Nat. Assn. Med. Staff Svcs., Tex. Soc. Med. Staff Svcs., Tex. Hosp. Assn., Beta Sigma Phi (sec. 1980-81). Democrat. Baptist. Home: 4500 Norwood Ln Austin TX 78744 Office: Healthcare Rehab Ctr 1106 W Dittmar Austin TX 78745

CREDLE, CONSTANCE CLOVER, nurse; b. Clearfield, Pa., June 6, 1934; d. James Edward and Kathryn Jury (Stiffler) Clover; children from previous marriage: Sharon Elizabeth, Laura Lynn. RN, U. Pa. Presbyn. Med. Ctr., 1955; BSN, Coll. William and Mary, Norfolk, Va., 1959. Staff nurse rsch. NIH, Bethesda, Md., 1956-57; head nurse USPHS Hosp., Norfolk, 1957-64, Roanoke (Va.) Meml. Hosp., 1964-65; charge staff nurse VA Med. Ctr., Salem, Va., 1965-67, Roanoke, 1970-90. Mem. ANA (cert.), NAFE. Republican. Episcopalian. Home: 2015 Maiden Ln SW Roanoke VA 24015

CREGER, CAROLYN SUE, educator; b. Waterloo, Iowa, Sept. 18, 1939; d. Howard Fred and Sylvia A. (Bennett) Barnett; m. John D. Creger; children: Daniel D., Douglas D., David J. AS, U. No. Iowa, 1959; BS, Drake U., 1969. Cert. tchr., Wyo., Iowa. Tchr. West Des Moines (Iowa) Sch. Dist., 1960-66, Des Moines Pub. Schs., 1969-70, Natrona County Sch. Dist., Casper, Wyo., 1972—. Mem. adv. bd. Rocky Mt. Easter Seals, Great Falls, Mont., 1989—; mem. gov.'s com. for the employment of the handicapped State of Wyo., 1972-76. Mem. NEA, ASCD (Ft. Caspar assn.), AAUW (v.p. membership com. Wyo. div. 1989-91), Natrona County Edn. Assn., Internat. Reading Assn., Nat. Fedn. Rep. Women, Delta Kappa Gamma (chpt. pres. 1989—), Phi Delta Kappa.

CREIGHTON, HARRIET BALDWIN, retired botany educator; b. Delavan, Ill., June 27, 1909; d. Cyrus Murray and Bertha (Baldwin) C. BA, Wellesley, 1929; PhD, Cornell U., 1933. Lab. asst. Cornell U., Ithaca, N.Y., 1929-33, instr. botany, 1933-34; instr. botany Conn. Coll., New London, 1934-39, asst. prof. botany, 1939-40; assoc. prof. botany Wellesley (Mass.) Coll., 1940-52, prof. botany, 1952-74, prof. emerita, 1974—; Fulbright lectr. in genetics U. Western Australia, Perth, 1952-53, U. Cuzco (Peru), 1959-60; genetics cons. NSF, Osmania U., Hyderabad, India, NSF, U. Allahabad (India). Contbr. articles to profl. jours. Fellow AAAS (v.p. sect. G 1964), Bot. Soc. Am. (pres. 1956), Phi Beta Kappa, Sigma Xi, Phi Kappa Phi. Home: PO Box 64 Wellesley MA 02181

CREMER, MABELLE A., obstetrician, gynecologist; b. N.Y.C., Dec. 26, 1927; d. Charles M. and Alfriede (Mommsen) C.; m. Martin Elliot Silverstein, Dec. 10, 1962. BA, Smith Coll., 1948; MD, N.Y. Med. Coll., 1953. Diplomate Am. Bd. Obstetrics and Gynecology, Am. Bd. Med. Examiners. Asst. attending physicians Flushing Hosp. and Dispensary, N.Y.C., 1957-63; dir. rsch. facilities Menorah Med. Ctr., Kansas City, Mo., 1963-66; asst. to dir. Strang Cancer Detection Ctr., N.Y.C., 1968-69; asst. attending physician N.Y. Infirmary, N.Y.C., 1968-69, assoc. attending physician, 1969; ob-gyn. Group Health Assn., Inc., Washington, 1972-75, mem. med. council, 1974-75; clin. instr., ob-gyn. George Washington U. Sch. Med., Washington, 1972-75; ob-gyn. specialist Group Health Med. Assocs., Tucson, 1975—; chmn. quality assurance and chart rev. Tucson Med. Ctr., 1982-85, mem. quality assurance com., 1986-88, chmn. dept. ob-gyn., 1990—. Treas., trustee Claudia Gips Found., Inc., N.Y.C., 1967—. Mem. AMA, Ariz. Med. Soc., Pima County Med. Soc., Tucson Gynecol. Soc. (pres. 1988-89); fellow Am. Coll. Surgeons. Home: 7041 N Corrida de Venado Tucson AZ 85718 Office: Group Health Med Assocs 6565 E Carondelet Tucson AZ 85710

CREMIN, SUSAN E., lawyer; b. Chgo., July 2, 1947. AB cum laude, Vassar Coll., 1969; JD, Northwestern U., Chgo., 1976. Assoc. Winston & Strawn, Chgo., 1976-83, ptnr., 1983—. Office: Winston & Strawn 35 W Wacker Dr Chicago IL 60601

CRENNA, KAREN KATHLEEN, personnel executive; b. Evergreen Park, Ill., Apr. 17, 1959; d. Albert William and Dorothy Mae (Agnos) Keaton; m. Joseph Richard Crenna, July 17, 1982; children: Ryan Joseph, Lauren Michelle. BS, Western Ill. U., 1981. With Amoco Container Co., West Chgo., 1981-83; prodn. processor Aurora (Ill.) Pump, 1983-84; personnel adminstr. Lord & Taylor, Aurora, 1984-85; personnel mgr. Crystals Internat., Inc., Plant City, Fla., 1986—. Mem. Soc. for Human Resource Mgmt., Personnel Adminstrn. Assn. Greater Tampa. Republican. Methodist. Office: Crystals International Inc 1111 W Haines St Plant City FL 33566

CRENSHAW, CLAUDIA REGAN, psychotherapist; b. Rosedale, N.Y., Feb. 12, 1951; d. Edward Joseph and Claire Marie (Rioux) Regan; m. Rice Fitzpatrick Crenshaw, Oct. 10, 1981; children: Catherine, Diane, Janet. BS in Biology, Emory U., Atlanta, 1972; BSN, Emory U., 1977, MSN, 1979. Cert. chem. dependence nurse; cert. eating disorder therapist. Chemist DeKalb Co., Decatur, Ga., 1972-75; staff nurse med. emergency Grady Hosp., Atlanta, 1977-78; charge nurse in psychiatry Ga. Bapt. Hosp., Atlanta, 1978-80; dir. therapeutic svcs. Anneewakee Found., Rockmart, Ga., 1980; psychiatric clin. specialist Cen. Fulton Community Health Ctr., Atlanta, 1980-84; prog. dir. substance abuse treatment unit/eating disorder Decatur Hosp., Atlanta, 1984-88; asst. dir. nursing, dir. psychiatry and neuropsychiatry Wesley Woods Geriatric Hosp., Atlanta, 1988-89; pvt. practice psychotherapy and orgnl. cons. Decatur, 1989—; instr. Nell Hodgson Woodruff Sch. Nursing, Emory U., 1980—; clin. asst. prof. Sch. Nursing, Ga. State U., Atlanta, 1986—; clin. supr. M Community Counseling, 1984-88; condr. workshops, lectr. and cons. in field. Contbr. articles to profl. jours. Bd. dirs. Community Friendship, Inc., 1985—, sec. bd. dirs., 1987—; vol. Dem. Nat. Conv., Atlanta, 1988; chmn. Com. to Endow the Rose C. Dilday Scholarship Fund, 1985-86. NIMH grantee, 1978-79. Mem. Am. Nurses Assn., Ga. Nurses Assn., Ga. Assn. Marriage and Family Therapy, Internat. Assn. Eating Disorders Profls., Metro Atlanta Advanced Practice Psychiatric Nurse Group, Nat. Consortium ofr Chem. Dependency Nurses Inc., Nat. Nurses Soc. on Addictions, Emory U. Alumni Assn. (pres.1988—), Sigma Theta Tau. Democrat. Roman Catholic. Office: 150 E Ponce Deleon #180 Decatur GA 30030

CRENSHAW, MARVA LOUISE, lawyer; b. DeFuniak Springs, Fla., Sept. 21, 1951; d. Lewis and Helen (Anderson) Crenshaw; m. Norman P. Campbell, Dec. 30, 1977; children: Kalinda I., Kamaria A. BS in Polit. Sci. with honors, Tuskegee Inst., Ala., 1973; JD, U. Fla., Gainesville, 1975. Bar: U.S. Dist. Ct. (mid. dist.) Fla., 1978, U.S. Ct. Appeals (11th cir.) 1978. Asst. state's atty. Dade County State's Atty. (Fla.), Miami, 1976-78; mng. atty. Bay Area Legal Services, Tampa, Fla., 1978-84, dep. dir., 1984-89; cons. tng. adv. com. Fla. Legal Service, Tallahassee, 1982-84; judge Hillsborough County Ct., 1989—. Vice pres. bd. dirs. Suicide and Crises Ctr., Tampa, 1983-84, pres., 1984-85, also mem. Aux. Mem. ABA, Hillsborough County Bar Assn. (chmn. county ct. civil rules com. 1984-85, mem. mock trial com. 1987-88, bulletin com. 1988-89), Fla. Bar Assn., George Edgecomb Bar Assn., Nat. Inst. Trial Advocacy, Delta Sigma Theta (legal advisor local chpt. 1988-89). Democrat. Baptist. Home: 14522 Wessex St Tampa FL 33625

CRENSHAW, PATRICIA SHRYACK, manfacturing executive, consultant; b. Kansas City, Mo., Oct. 7, 1941; d. George Randolf and Velma Irene (Carroll) Shryack; m. Paul Burton, Mar. 24, 1961 (div. 1971); m. Peter Frederick Schmidt, Jan. 21, 1989. Student, William Jewell Coll., 1959-60, S.W. Mo. State U., 1960-61; BEd, U. Mo., 1967; postgrad., Cen. Mo. State U., 1971-73. Cert. tchr. secondary edn. and history, Mo. Tchr. Lillis High Sch., Kansas City, 1967-69, Park Hill High Sch., Kansas City, 1969-73; terr. mgr. Hollister, Inc., Kansas City, 1973-75, field trainer, 1974-75; sales edn. mgr. Hollister, Inc., Chgo., 1975; dist. sales mgr. Detroit Mich., 1976-81; regional sales mgr. Chgo., 1981-84; dir. contract sales Chgo. Serta, Inc., 1984-86, nat. dir. contract sales div., 1987-89, v.p. nat. contract sales, 1989-90; area v.p. B G Industries, Northridge, Calif., 1990—. Mem. women's com. Young Reps., Kansas City, 1962. Mem. NOW, NAFE, U.S. Golf Assn., Lake Barrington Shores (Ill.) Golf Club. Republican. Home: 275 B Hickory Ln Barrington IL 60010 Office: B G Industries 8550 Balboa Blvd Ste 214 Northridge CA 91325

CREPPEL, CLAIRE BINET, hotel owner; b. New Orleans, Nov. 30, 1936; d. Albert Leo and Leocadie (Dominique) Binet; m. Jacques Jules Creppel, Feb. 2, 1957; children: INgrid, Foster, Collette and Gregg (twins), Lisa, Morgan. BA in English, U. Southwestern La., 1971; MEd in Guidance/ Counseling Psychology, U. New Orlenas, 1975; postgrad., Tulane U., New Orleans, 1978. Instr. English and Spanish Booker T. Washington Sr. High Sch., 1972-74, instr. English and reading, 1974-76, guidance counselor, 1976-77; intervention counselor Sophie B. Wright Middle Sch., 1977-79; owner, gen. mgr. Columns Hotel, New Orleans, 1980—. New Orleans regional dir. La. Coun. on Child Abuse, 1985-87; mem. citizens adv. bd. Jo Ellen Smith Hosp.; mem. task force Ct. Appointed Spl. Advocate; bd. dirs. So. Repretory Theatre of New Orleans, Overture to the Cultural Season, New Orleans. Named one of Top Exec. Women New Orleans, 1990. Mem. Am. Personnel and Guidance Assn., AAUW, La. Personnel and Guidance Assn., Orleans Sch. Counselors Assn., St. Charles Ave. Bus. Assn., Street Car Inns, Kappa Delta Pi, Sigma Delta Pi. Republican. Roman Catholic. Home: 7927 Saint Gharles Ave New Orleans LA 70118 Office: Columns Hotel 3811 St Charles Ave New Orleans LA 70115

CRESAP, THEDA BEATTY, educator; b. Murrysville, Pa., Apr. 27, 1943; d. Harry Earl and Virginia Grace Beatty; m. Robert W. Cresap, June 30, 1969; children: Amy, Michael. BS, Ind. U., 1965; postgrad., Colo. U., 1965, U. Pitts., 1967. Tchr. Franklin Regional Sch. Dist., Murrysville, Pa., 1965-69, Eatontown (N.J.) Sch. Dist., 1969-71; rsch. interviewer Starch, Inra, and Hooper, Murrysville, 1987-88; ch. directory cons. United Ch. Directories, Murrysville, 1987—. Republican. Lutheran. Home: PO Box 131 Murrysville PA 15668

CRESPIN, REGINE, soprano; b. Marseilles, France; d. Henri and Margherite (DiMeirone) C. Student, Lycée Français, Conservatoire de Paris. Appeared in numerous operas including Lohengrin, Mulhouse, France, 1950, Paris, 1951, N.Y.C., 1964, Tosca, Il Trovatore, Otello, Die Walkuere, Oberon, Fidelio, Der Rosenkavalier, Marseilles, Le Nozze di Figaro, Paris, 1956, Dialogues of the Carmelites, 1957, Parsifal, 1958, Ballo in Maschera, 1958, Fedra, Milan, Italy, 1959, Die Walkuere, Vienna, 1959, Der Rosenkavalier, Berlin, 1960, as the Marshallin, London, 1961, Les Troyens, Paris, 1961, Penelope, Buenos Aires, 1961, Otello, Ballo in Maschera, Die Walkuere, Der Rosenkavalier, Vienna, also Rosenkavalier, N.Y.C., 1962, Flying Dutchman, N.Y.C., 1962, Ballo in Maschera, N.Y.C., 1962, La Vestale, N.Y.C., 1962, Herodiade, N.Y.C., 1963, Fidelio, Ballo in Maschera, Tannhauser, Fidelio, Chgo., 1963, Carnegie Hall, 1973, Met. Opera, 1973, Carmen, Met. Opera, 1975, Cavalleria Rusticana, San Francisco Opera, 1976, Dialogues of the Carmelites, Met. Opera, 1977, 78, soloist, N.Y. Philharmonic, 1964-65, appeared in recital, Hunter Coll., 1965. Office: Herbert H Breslin 119 W 57th St New York NY 10019

CRESWELL, DOROTHY ANNE, computer consultant; b. Burlington, Iowa, Feb. 6, 1943; d. Robert Emerson and Agnes Imogene (Gardner) Mefford; m. John Lewis Creswell, Aug. 28, 1965. AA, Burlington Community Coll., 1963; BA in Math., U. Iowa, 1965; MS in Math., Western Ill. U., 1970; postgrad., Iowa State U., 1974—. Computer programmer Mason & Hanger, Silas Mason Co., Inc., Burlington, Iowa, 1965-74; systems programmer Contractor's Hotline, Ft. Dodge, Iowa, 1974; dir. data processing Iowa Cen. Community Coll., Ft. Dodge, 1975-80; systems programming mgr. Norand Corp., Cedar Rapids, Iowa, 1980-82; spl. svcs. mgr. Pioneer Hi-Bred Internat., Inc., Cedar Rapids, 1982-87; owner, pres. D.C. Cons., Ankeny, Iowa, 1987—; computers-in-edn. del. to People's Rep. China, People to People Internat., Kansas City, Mo., 1987. Contbr. articles, papers to profl. publs. Mem. Data Processing Mgmt. Assn. (bd. dirs. 1986-87, v.p. 1988), Adminstrv. Mgmt. Soc. (sec. 1985-86, v.p. 1986-90, merit award 1987), Assn. Computing Machinery, Hawkeye Personal Computer Users, DEC Users Group (v.p. eastern Iowa chpt. 1981-82) Ind. Computer Cons. Assn. (editorial bd. 1989). Democrat. Methodist. Office: DC Cons PO Box 195 Ankeny IA 50021

CRETIN, SHAN, business executive; b. New Orleans, Dec. 5, 1946; d. Theodore David and Rosemary Mamie (Lombardino) C.; m. Burns Woodward, June 15, 1968 (div. July 1976); 1 child: Mikala Marie; m. Emmett Brown Keeler, Sept. 26, 1976; children: Lauren Shan, Alexis Marie. SBME, MIT, 1968; MPH, Yale U., 1970; PhD in Ops. Rsch., MIT, 1975. Rsch. assoc. Yale U., New Haven, Conn., 1970-71; asst. prof. Harvard U., Cambridge, Mass., 1974-76; asst. prof. UCLA, 1976-81, assoc. prof., 1981-88, prof., 1988-90; pres. Shan Cretin and Assoc., Santa Monica, Calif., 1990—; cons. Rand Corp., Santa Monica, Calif., 1977 —, Nat. Ctr. Health Svcs. Rsch., Bethesda, Md., 1980 --, World Bank, Washington, D.C., 1984 --. Author: Cholesterol, Children, and Heart Disease, 1980; contbr. articles to profl. jours. Mem. Ops. Rsch. soc. Am., Am. Soc. for Quality Control, APHA, Sigma Xi, Pi Tau Sigma, Delta Omega. Democrat. Mem. Soc. of Friends. Office: Shan Cretin and Associates 402 15th St Santa Monica CA 90402

CREVOISERAT, PATRICIA JILL, special education teacher; b. Freeport, N.Y., Dec. 11, 1955; d. Russell Ritchie and Dorothy A. (Gallinagh) C. BS in Edn., SUNY, Geneseo, N.Y., 1978; MS, Adelphi U., 1981, L.I. Univ., 1986; postgrad., Hofstra U., 1987—. Cert. in spl. edn., reading, math., nursery, and elem. edn., N.Y. Freelance tutor, 1979—; learning disabilities therapist Adelphi U. L.D. Clinic, Garden City, N.Y., 1979-81; field supr. Adelphi U., Garden City, N.Y., 1980; spl. edn. tchr. Brentwood Pub. Schs., 1980, in-svc. instr., 1982-83, resource room tchr., 1980—; freelance computer programmer, 1980—; club advisor Brentwood Pub. Schs., 1982-84, swim team timer and scorekeeper, 1982-88. Contbr. writer Study Skills Pack--Jr. Coll. Level, 1978-79; line editor Basal reading series, 1980-81. Sponsor Spl. Olympics, Washington, 1986—, U.S. Olympic Com., Colorado Springs, Colo., 1986—; mem. Cousteau Soc., Norfolk, Va., 1982—, World Wildlife Fund, Washington, 1983—, Nat. Wildlife Found., Vienna, Va., 1983—, Nat. Audubon Soc., N.Y.C., 1987—, Nature Conservancy, Balt., 1988—; sponsor Geneseo Found., Geneseo, N.Y., 1980—, Adelphi U. Fund, Garden City, N.Y., 1982—, Human Resources Ctr., Albertson, N.Y., 1987—, Am. Printing House for the Blind, Pleasantville, N.Y., 1986—. Mem. Coun. for Exceptional Children, N.Y. Assn. for Learning Disabled, Assn. for Children with Learning Disabilities, Internat. Reading Assn., Nassau/Suffolk Reading Coun., Kappa Delta Pi. Republican. Office: NW Ctr Leahy Ave Brentwood NY 11717

CREWS, RUTHELLEN, education educator; b. McCaysville, Ga., July 3, 1927; d. Robert Harvey and Della P. (Mason) C. B.A., Maryville Coll., 1949; M.S., U. Tenn., 1959; Ed.D., Columbia U., 1966. Tchr. English and speech Cradock High Sch., Portsmouth, Va., 1949-50; elem. tchr. Rose Sch., Morristown, Tenn., 1951-54; tchr. English and speech Morristown High Sch., 1954-58; elem. sch. librarian Knox County Schs. Materials Ctr., Knoxville, Tenn., 1958-60; supr. instrn. Knox County Schs., Knoxville, 1960-65; prof. edn. U. Fla., Gainesville, 1966—; cons. curriculum devel. in pub. schs., lectr. in field. Author: (with others) The World of Language textbook series, 1970, rev. edit., 1973; (with others) Pathfinder textbook series, 1978; contbr. articles in field of edn. to profl. jours. Mem. Nat. Council Tchrs. English, Assn. for Supervision and Curriculum Devel., Internat. Reading Assn., Delta Kappa Gamma. Home: 1719-4B NW 23d Ave Gainesville FL 32605 Office: U Fla Coll of Edn Gainesville FL 32611

CRICCO-LIZZA, ROBERTA, nursing educator; b. Hoboken, N.J., Nov. 11, 1952; d. Carl F. and Mary (McDonough) Cricco; m. Eli F. Lizza, June 15, 1974; children: Carla, Gianna, Marcello. RN, Misericordia Hosp. Sch. Nursing, 1972; BSN summa cum laude, Dominican Coll. Blauvelt, 1979; MSN, MPH, Columbia U., 1981. RN, N.J. Staff nurse St. Vincent's Hosp., N.Y.C.; home care nurse Rome; nursing supr. Riverside Gen. Hosp., Secaucus, N.J.; dir. nursing svc. Uniontown (Pa.) Hosp.; mem. nursing faculty St. Peter's Coll., Jersey City. Mem. ANA, N.J. State Nurses Assn., Sigma Theta Tau. Home: 182 Vreeland Ave Rutherford NJ 07070

CRIDER, CORA ELIZABETH, accountant, financial executive; b. Greencastle, Pa., Mar. 4, 1927; d. Russell Benjamin and Mary Julia (Frush) Trumpower; m. Floyd Donald Crider, Apr. 19, 1946; 1 child, David Rowland. Grad. high sch., Greencastle. Sec. Allstate Life Ins. Co., Hagerstown, Md., 1945-53; exec. sec. Fairchild Aircraft Co., Hagerstown, 1953-61; sec., acct. Fox Buick, Greencastle, 1961-77; fin. mgr. Greencastle Metal Works, Inc., 1977—. Mem. Am. Bus. Women's Assn. (past officer, Woman of Yr. 1974, 78, mem. inner circle, Diamond Star award), Lioness (past officer, Lioness of Yr. 1983), Order Eastern Star. Home: 118 E Madison St Greencastle PA 17225

CRIDER, IRENE PERRITT, educator, consultant; b. Chatfield, Ark., Apr. 29, 1921; d. Dolphus France and Eula Allan (Springer) Perritt; m. Willis Jewel Crider, Aug. 3, 1945; 1 child, Larry Willis. BA, Bethel Coll., 1944; MA, Memphis State U., 1957; EdD, Fla. State U., 1977. Cert. elem., secondary tchr., administr., Tenn. Tchr. various schs., Tenn., 1941-57; dean girls Lake Worth (Fla.) Jr. High, 1957-65; dean women Lake Worth High Sch., 1965-73; gen. instructional supr. Palm Beach (Fla.) County Pub. Schs., 1973-75; asst. prin. Jupiter (Fla.) High Sch., 1975-76; supr. interns Fla. Atlantic U., Boca Raton, 1977-83, Palm Beach Atlantic Coll., West Palm Beach, Fla., 1982-84; cons. Paris, Tenn., 1984-87; founding dir. Ultrime Success Network, Tallahassee; instr. edn. Bethel Coll., McKenzie, Tenn., 1987, prof. MEd Grad. Program; cons. in field. Contbr. articles to profl. jours. Bd. dirs., founder, charter mem. Palm Beach County Kidney Assn., 1973-86; chairperson citizens action com. Fla. Ch. Women United, 1982-84. Mem. Zonta (Lake Worth, pres. 1969-70), Order Ea. Star, Delta Kappa Gamma (charter pres. Beta Xi-Mu 1968-70, chmn. state com., scholarship), Phi Delta Kappa. Democrat. Methodist. Home and Office: 1606 N Meridian Rd Tallahassee FL 32303

CRIGER, NANCY S., banker; b. Ypsilanti, Mich., Apr. 16, 1951; d. Douglas D. and Edith (Nicoll) Smith; m. Dane Criger, July 9, 1982; children: Amanda L. Denomme, William G. Denomme, Jr. Student, Mich. State U., 1969-71; BS in Elem. Edn., Wayne State U., 1973. Asst. v.p. Nat. Bank of Detroit, 1978-87, Comerica Bank, Detroit, 1987-88; v.p. employee benefits Comerica Bank, 1988—. Asst. treas. Jr. League of Detroit, 1985-86, treas., 1986-87; treas. women's assn. Detroit Symphony Orch., 1987-89; mem. Assistance League N.E. Guidance Ctr. Detroit Symphony League, past bd. dirs.; mem. Friends of Greenfield Village, Detroit Inst. Arts, Detroit Sci. Ctr., Smithsonian Instn., Archives of Am. Art. Mem. Detroit Hist. Soc., Chi Omega. Office: Comerica Bank 211 W Fort St Detroit MI 48275-1034

CRILE, SUSAN, artist; b. Cleve., Aug. 12, 1942; d. George Jr. and Jane (Halle) C.; m. Joseph S. Murphy, May 18, 1984. Student, NYU; BA, Bennington Coll., 1965. Mem. faculty Fordham U., N.Y.C., 1972-76, Princeton (N.J.) U., 1974-76, Sarah Lawrence Coll., Bronxville, N.Y., 1976-79, Sch. Visual Arts, N.Y.C., 1976-82, Barnard Coll., N.Y.C., 1983—, Hunter Coll., N.Y.C., 1983—; travelling rep. to Hungary and Portugal with exhbn. Am. Paintings in the Eighties, Internat. Communication Agy., Washington, 1981; mem. Yaddo Corp. One-woman shows include Kornblee Gallery, N.Y.C., 1971, 72, 73, Fischbach Gallery, N.Y.C., 1974, 75, 77, Brooke Alexander Gallery, N.Y.C., 1975, Phillips Collection, Washington, 1975, New Gallery, Cleve., 1977, Ctr. Gallery Bucknell U., Lewisburg, Pa., 1978, Droll Kolbert Gallery, N.Y.C., 1978, 80, Ivory Kimpton Gallery, San Francisco, 1981, 84, 88, Van Straten Gallery, Chgo., 1983, Lincoln Ctr. Gallery, N.Y.C., 1983, Cleve. Ctr. for Contemporary Art, 1984, Nina Freundenheim Gallery, Buffalo, N.Y., 1980, 84, Graham Modern, N.Y.C., 1985, 87, 88, 90, Adams Middleton Gallery, Dallas, 1986, Gloria Luria, Bay Harbor Island, Fla., 1987, 88, 90; exhibited in group shows at Whitney Mus. Art, N.Y.C., 1972, 82, Indpls. Mus. Art, 1972, 74, Kent State U., 1972, Art Inst. Chgo., 1972, Corcoran Gallery Art, Washington, 1973, Va. Mus. Fine Arts, 1975, U.S.I.A., 1979, Grey Art Gallery, N.Y.C., 1979, 83, Janie C. Lee Gallery, Houston, 1979, Meml. Art Gallery, U. Rochester, 1980, Bklyn. Mus., 1980, 81, 83, Carnegie Inst., Pitts., 1981, Inst. Contemporary Art, 1981, Am. Acad. Arts and Letters, 1983, Weatherspoon Gallery, Greensboro, N.C., 1984, Columbus (Ga.) Mus. Arts and Sci., 1985, Queens Mus., 1986, Portland (Maine) Mus. Art, 1986, Mus. Fine Arts, Boston, 1986, Cleve. Mus. Art, 1987, Mt. Holyoke Coll. Art Mus., South Hadley, Mass., 1987, Hudson River Mus., 1988; poster commn.: Live from Lincoln Ctr., N.Y.C., 1980, Mostly Mozart, 1985, IBM Gallery Aci. & Art, N.Y.C., 1989, Nat. Gallery Art, Washington, 1989; represented in permanent collections Albright-Knox Art Gallery, Buffalo, Bklyn. Mus., Mus. Art Carnegie Inst., Pitts., Guggenheim Mus., N.Y.C., Hirshhorn Mus., Washington, Met. Mus. Art, N.Y.C., Phillips Collection, Washington, Cleve. Mus. Art, Nat. Gallery Art, The Smithsonian, Washingaton.; residence in painting Am. Acad. in Rome, 1990. Trustee Bennington Coll., 1979-81; bd. dirs. Hand Hollow Found., 1983-85; mem. corp. Yaddo, 1985—. Recipient resident grant Yaddo, 1970, 71, 74-75, 78, Acad. in Rome, 1990, Ingram Mertill Found. grant, 1972, MacDowell Colony resident grant, 1972; NEA fellow, 1982, 89. Home: 168 W 86th St New York NY 10024

CRILLY, KAREN ANN, registered nurse; b. Union, N.J., Aug. 27, 1963; d. John Cornell and Nancy Alice (Wallace) C. BSN, Seton Hall U., 1986. RN, N.J., critical care RN. EKG tech. John F. Kennedy Med. Ctr., Edison, N.J., 1984, nursing unit asst., 1984-86, RN critical care unit, 1986-89, asst. nursing care coord., 1989-90, RN surg. intensive care unit coronary care unit, 1990—. Mem. Am. Assn. Critical Care Nurses. Office: John F Kennedy Med Ctr James St Edison NJ 08817

CRINER, KATY LYNN, equipment company executive; b. Detroit, Dec. 20, 1960; d. Donald Robert and Johne M. (Ruks) C. B. in Bus., U. Mich., 1983. Mfrs. rep. Chartpak, Leeds, Mass., 1983-84; sales rep. DMI Industries, Madison Heights, Mich., 1984-86; graphic engr. Hydramatic div. Gen. Motors, Ypsilanti, Mich., 1986-87; ter. mgr. Varitronic Systems Inc., Mpls., 1987-89; major accounts visual systems cons. Comml. Equipment Co., Southfield, Mich., 1989—. Home: 2200 Fuller Rd #902B Ann Arbor MI 48105

CRINO, MARJANNE HELEN, anesthesiologist; b. Rochester, N.Y., Aug. 18, 1933; d. Michael Jay and Helen Barbara (Kennedy) Crino; m. Michael Anthony La Iuppa, Nov. 12, 1960; children: James Michael, Barbara Anne, John Christopher. BS, Coll. St. Teresa, 1955; MD, Med. Coll. Wis., 1959; postgrad. in theology, St. Bernard's Inst., 1986—. Diplomate Nat. Bd. Med. Examiners. House staff Genesee Hosp., Rochester, 1959-61; perinatal mortality rsch., resident in anesthesiology Jackson Meml Hosp.-U. Miami, 1962-65; attending staff in anesthesiology Genesee Hosp., Rochester, N.Y., 1969—, acting chmn. dept. anesthesiology, 1989, chmn. pain control com., 1989—; clin. instr. anesthesiology U. Rochester Sch. Medicine, 1983—; cons. anesthesiology Rochester Psychiat. Ctr., 1975-85; instr. anesthesiology U. Miami Sch. medicine, 1966, 67; attending staff anesthesiology Jackson Meml. Hosp., Miami, 1966, 67. Mem. com. Pittsford (N.Y.) Republican Party, 1970s-80s. Mem. N.Y. State Soc. Anesthesiologists (bd. dirs., vice speaker 1983-86), Am. Soc. Anesthesiologists (del. 1979-86), AMA, N.Y. State Med.Soc., Med. Soc. County of Monroe, Rochester Acad. Medicine, Cath. Physicians Guild Rochester (pres. 1988-89), Margaret Roper Guild (pres. 1975-76). Roman Catholic. Office: Genesee Hosp Dept Anesthesiology 224 Alexander St Rochester NY 14607

CRISCO, KELLY REID, public relations executive; b. Charlotte, N.C., Oct. 3, 1963; d. Elmer Reid and Sarah (Jackson) Crisco. BA in English, Appalachian State U., Boone, N.C., 1984; BS magna cum laude in Textile Mgmt. and Tech., N.C. State U. Copywriter Belk Stores Svcs., Charlotte, 1984-86; dir. pub. rels. The Daly Group, Winston-Salem, N.C., 1987-89, Burris Creech, Inc., High Point, N.C., 1989—. Contbr. articles to local and profl. publs. Mem. NAFE. Home: 2124-L Crossing Way High Point NC 27262

CRISCUOLO, WENDY LAURA, lawyer, interior design consultant; b. N.Y.C., Dec. 17, 1949; d. Joseph Andrew and Betty Jane (Jackson) C.; m. John Howard Price, Jr., Sept. 5, 1970 (div. Apr. 1981); m. Ross J. Turner, July 23, 1988. AB with honors in Design, U. Calif., Berkeley, 1973; JD, U. San Francisco, 1982. Space planner GSA, San Francisco, 1973-79; sr. interior designer E. Lew & Assocs., San Francisco, 1979-80; design dir. Beier & Gunderson, Inc., Oakland, Calif., 1980-81; sr. interior designer Environ. Planning and Rsch., San Francisco, 1981-82; interior design cons. Hillsborough, Calif., 1982—; law clk. to Judge Spencer Williams U.S. Dist. Ct., San Francisco, 1983-84; atty. Ciros Investments, Hillsborough, 1985—. Author: (with others) Guide to the Laws of Charitable Giving, 3d rev. edit., 1983; mem. editorial bd. U. San Francisco Law Rev., 1983. Bd. dirs., v.p. and treas. Marin Citizens for Energy Planning, 1986-89; bd. dirs., pres. The Wildlife Ctr., 1987-90; bd. dirs. Coyote Point Mus. Environ. Edn.; trustee Cayote Point Mus. For Environ. Edn. Mem. ABA, State Bar Calif., Queen's Bench (San Francisco), Calif. Women Lawyers, Nat. Environ. Leadership Coun., Commonwealth Club. Republican. Episcopalian.

CRISP, ELIZABETH AMANDA, physician; b. Uvalde, Tex., Dec. 17, 1922; d. David Hardee and Mary Gazelle (Poynor) C. BS, Tex. Women's U., Denton, 1943; MD, La. State U., New Orleans, 1951. Diplomate Am. Bd. of Obstetrics/Gynecology. Internship Garfield Meml. Hosp., Washington, 1950-51; residency gen. surgery Long Beach Meml. Hosp., 1954-55, residency Ob/Gyn, 1954-56; residency Ob/Gyn Columbia Hosp. for Women, Washington, 1957-60; pvt. practice medicine specializing Obstetrics and Gynecology, Wash., 1960—; chief gynecology service Columbia Hosp. Women, 1971-73; v. chief of med. staff Columbia Hosp. Women, Wash., 1974-76, chief med. staff, 1976-78; asst. clin. prof. George Wash. U. Sch. Medicine, Wash., 1976-80; clin. assoc. prof. Georgetown U. Sch. Medicine, Wash., 1980—; mem. exec. bd. Med. Soc. D.C. Wash., 1985-87; mem. bd. dir. Nat. Women's Health Resource Ctr. Wash., 1988—. Lt. USNR, 1950-54. Recipient Distinguished Alumnae Award Tex. Women's U. Denton, 1977. Fellow Am. Coll. Surgeons, Am. Coll. Obstetrics and Gynecology; Am. Fertility and Sterility Soc., Wash. Gynecologic Soc., Med. Soc. D.C., Am. Med. Soc. Christian. Office: Women Physicians Assn 16220 Frederick Rd Gaithersburg MD 20877

CRISP, POLLY LENORE, psychologist; b. Atlanta, May 20, 1952; d. John Pershing and Dorotha Amelia (Hogan) C. BA, U. Tenn., 1976; MA, Mich. State U., 1981, PhD, 1984. Psychotherapist Arbours Ctr., London, 1983-85; clin. psychologist Kennebec Valley Mental Health Ctr., Augusta, Maine, 1987—. Contbr. articles to profl. publs. Mem. Brit. Psychol. Soc., Am. Psychol. Assn. (membership com. 1990—), Soc. Psychotherapy Rsch., N.Y. Acad. Scis., Phi Beta Kappa, Phi Kappa Phi, Alpha Lambda Delta. Office: Kennebec Valley Mental Hlt 66 Stone St Augusta ME 04330

CRISP, SHELLEY JEAN, English and women's studies educator; b. Asheboro, N.C., Nov. 8, 1951; d. William Thomas and Helen Elizabeth (Eyster) C.; m. Myles Erwin Standish, June 6, 1981; children: Edward Reid, Alice Starr. BA, U. N.C., 1972; MA, N.C. State U., 1980; PhD, U. Mass., 1987. Teaching assoc. English dept. N.C. State U., Raleigh, 1976-80, U. Mass., Amherst, 1980-81; lectr. English dept. U. N.C., Charlotte, 1982-87, coord. women's studies, 1987-89, vis. asst. prof. English, 1989—. Named Faculty Woman of Yr., U. N.C., Charlotte, 1988. Mem. Nat. Women's Studies Assn. (regional program chmn. 1987-88), S.E. Women's Studies Assn. (editor News, Charlotte, 1982-83, program chmn. 1989—), South Atlantic MLA, S.E. 19th Century Assn., Carolinas Brit. Symposium, Philol. Assn. Carolinas, AAUW (campus rep. 1988-89). Democrat. Home: 168 Huntley Pl Charlotte NC 28207 Office: U NC English Dept Charlotte NC 28223

CRISPIN, MILDRED SWIFT (MRS. FREDERICK EATON CRISPIN), civic worker, writer; b. Branson, Mo.; d. Albert Duane and Anna (Harlan) Swift; m. Herbert William Kochs, Dec. 1, 1928 (div. Mar. 1955); children: Susan Kochs Gudevine (dec.), Herbert William Jr., Judith Ann (Mrs. Nelson Shaw); m. Geroge Walter King Snyder, Oct. 6, 1962 (dec. 1969); m. Frederick Eaton Crispin, May 20, 1972. Student, Galloway Woman's Coll., 1922-24. Bd. dirs. Travelers Aid Soc., Chgo., 1936-68, nat. dir., 1948-71; founding mem. U.S.O., Chgo., 1944-65, nat. dir., 1951-57; bd. dirs. John Howard Assn., 1958-67, Community Fund Chgo., 1950-56, Welfare Coun. Met. Chgo., 1950-56; chmn. woman's div. Crusade of Mercy, Chgo., 1964. Mem. U.S. Women's Curling Assn. (co-founder 1947, pres. 1950, founder Indian Hill Women's Curling Club, Winnetka, Ill., 1945, chmn. 1945-46), DAR, Daus. Am. Colonists, Saddle and Cycle Club, Town and Country Arts Club (pres. 1957-58, Chgo., Everglades Club (Palm Beach, Fla.), Venice (Fla.) Yacht Club, Coral Ridge Yacht Club (Ft. Lauderdale, Fla.), Bird Key Yacht Club (Sarasota, Fla.). Republican. Methodist. Home: Box 1098 Osprey FL 34229 also: 560 N Casey Key Rd Osprey FL 34229

CRISS, DARLENE JUNE, educator; b. Potwin, Kans., Feb. 4, 1931; d. Leroy Eckard and Sarah Caroline (Weber) Edwards; m. James Harold Criss, July 18, 1948; children: Melissa Colleen, Melinda Collette, James Anthony, Michael Jordan, Troy Mitchell, Shayne Lee. BA, Wichita State U., 1976, MEd., 1979. Cert. tchr., Kans. Tchr. English Unit Sch. Dist. 265, Goddard (Kans.) High Sch., 1976—, chmn. dept. lang. arts, 1979—; lectr. on creativity, 1977—; adviser yearbook and creative arts mag. Prism, 1976—. Editor (newsletter) Sunflower Seeds, 1974-84; contbr. poetry to English Jour. Leader Camp Fire Girls, Wichita, dist. program leader, Wichita 1960-65; area chair Am. Heart Assn., Wichita 1958-73; pres. South High PTA, Wichita, 1969-71. Recipient Wakan award Camp Fire Girls, Wichita, 1968; named one of 5 state finalists Tchr. in Space Program, 1985. Mem. NEA, Kans. Edn. Assn., Goddard Edn. Assn. (chief negotiator 1981-84), Nat. Assn. Tchrs. English, Kans. Assn. Tchrs. English, Mensa (life; nat. rep. internat. bd. dirs. 1987—, nat. sec. 1988—, editor nat. bull. 1982-84, editor Isolated M newsletter 1984—, pub. agt. Internat. Mensa Jour. 1985—, Disting. Svc. award 1986). Democrat. Presbyterian. Home: 2311 S Santa Fe Wichita KS 67211 Office: Goddard High Sch 501 S Main Goddard KS 67052

CRISSINGER, KAREN DENISE, pediatric gastroenterologist, physiologist; b. Birmingham, Ala., Feb. 18, 1956; d. Lloyd Charles Jr. and Ella Ruth (Hester) C. BS summa cum laude, U. Ala., 1977; MD, Johns Hopkins U., 1981; PhD, La. State U., 1988. Diplomate Am. Bd. Pediatrics. Resident in pediatrics Johns Hopkins Hosp., Balt., 1981-84; fellow in pediatric gastroenterology Children's Hosp. Med. Ctr., Cin., 1984-86; rsch. fellow La. State U. Med. Ctr., Shreveport, 1986-88, asst. prof. pediatrics, 1989—, asst. prof. physiology, 1989—. Active Am. Heart Assn., 1989-90, Stiles Trust Fund, 1989-90, Biomed. Rsch. Support, 1989-90. Grantee NIH, 1990—. Mem. Am. Gastroent. Assn. Home: 509 Elmwood St Shreveport LA 71104

Office: La State U Med Ctr Dept Pediatrics PO Box 33932 Shreveport LA 71130

CRIST, JUDITH KLEIN, film and drama critic; b. N.Y.C., May 22, 1922; d. Solomon and Helen (Schoenberg) Klein; m. William B. Crist, July 3, 1947; 1 son, Steven Gordon. A.B., Hunter Coll., 1941; teaching fellow, State Coll. Wash., 1942-43; M.Sc. in Journalism, Columbia, 1945. Civilian instr. 3091st Army Air Forces Base Unit, 1943-44; reporter N.Y. Herald Tribune, 1945-60, editor arts, 1960-63, assoc. theater critic, 1957-63, film critic, 1963-66; film, theater critic NBC-TV Today Show, 1963-73; film critic World Jour. Tribune, 1966-67; critic-at-large Ladies Home Jour., 1966-67; contbg. editor and film critic TV Guide, 1966-88; film critic N.Y. mag., 1968-75, The Washingtonian, 1970-72, Palm Springs Life, 1971-75; contbg. editor, film critic Saturday Rev., 1975-77, 80-84, N.Y. Post, 1977-78, MD/Mrs., 1977—, 50 Plus, 1978-83, L'Officiel/USA, 1979-80; arts critic Sta. WWOR-TV Channel 9 News, 1981-87; critical columnist on Coming Attractions, 1985—; instr. journalism Hunter Coll., 1947, Sarah Lawrence Coll., 1958-59; assoc. journalism Columbia Grad. Sch. Journalism, 1959-62, lectr. journalism, 1962-64, adj. prof., 1964—. Author: The Private Eye, The Cowboy and the Very Naked Girl, 1968, Judith Crist's TV Guide to the Movies, 1974, Take 22: Moviemakers on Moviemaking, 1984. Contbr. articles to nat. mags. Trustee Anne O'Hare McCormick Scholarship Fund. Recipient Page One award N.Y. Newspaper Guild, 1955; George Polk award, 1961; N.Y. Newspaper Women's Club award, 1955, 59, 63, 65, 67; Edn. Writers Assn. award, 1952; Columbia Grad. Sch. Journalism Alumni award, 1961; named to 50th Anniversary Honors List, 1963; Centennial Pres.'s medal Hunter Coll., 1970; named to Hunter Alumni Hall of Fame, 1973. Mem. Columbia Journalism Alumni (pres. 1967-70), N.Y. Film Critics Circle, Nat. Soc. Film Critics, Sigma Tau Delta. Office: 180 Riverside Dr New York NY 10024

CRIST, MARY JANE, fundraising executive; b. Hobbs, N.Mex., Sept. 19, 1946; d. Robert Elliott and Jane Elizabeth (Murray) Jackson; m. Warren Anderson Crist, Sept. 28, 1973. BS, U. Ariz., 1968; MS, Ind. U., 1969. Asst. fgn. student advisor U. Ariz., Tucson, 1969-71, asst. dean of students, 1971-79, asst. dir. admissions, 1979-85; v.p. pub. affairs Tempe (Ariz.) St. Luke's Hosp., 1985-89; exec. dir. St. Luke's Found., Phoenix, 1989—. Mem. Valley Leadership, Phoenix, 1981—; bd. dirs. East Valley Cancer Resource Network, Mesa, Ariz., 1988—; pres. Tempe Leadership, 1990—. Mem. Nat. Assn. for Hosp. Devel., Nat. Soc. Fund Raising Execs., Kappa Kappa Gamma (devel. com.). Republican. Presbyterian. Office: St Lukes Found 1800 E Van Buren Phoenix AZ 85006

CRISTINA, DONNA MARIE, public relations, advertising executive; b. N.Y.C., June 27, 1948; d. Anthony R. and Marie (Greco) C. AS, Fashion Inst. Tech., N.Y.C., 1968; postgrad., CUNY, 1968-69. Asst. fashion coordinator Ind. Retailors Syndicate, N.Y.C., 1968-70; fashion coordinator Frederick Atkins, Inc., N.Y.C., 1970-75; assoc. fashion dir. Bergdorf Goodman, N.Y.C., 1975-79; v.p. fashion merchandising I.M. Internat., N.Y.C., 1979-81; account exec., creative dir. Jody Donohue Assocs., N.Y.C., 1981-82; v.p., ptnr. Cristina, Gottfried and Loving, Inc., N.Y.C., 1982-84; pres. Cristina & Shafer, Inc., N.Y.C., 1984-87; v.p. sales promotion, advt., visual merchandising Adrienne Vittadini Inc., N.Y.C., 1987—. Elected to Creative Achievements in Fashion Merchandising Hall of Fame Fashion Inst. Tech., N.Y.C., 1979-80. Mem. The Fashion Group (various coms.). Democrat. Roman Catholic. Office: Adrienne Vittadini Inc 575 Seventh Ave New York NY 10018 also: 261 Broadway #7D New York NY 10007

CRISTINI, ANGELA LOUISE, biology educator; b. Englewood, N.J., Oct. 2, 1948; d. Joseph and Florence (Desideratti) C.; m. Robert John Lazell, Sept. 18, 1983; 1 child, Jeffrey. BA, Northeastern U., 1971; PhD, CUNY, 1977. Asst. prof. Ramapo Coll. of N.J., Mahwah, 1978-84, assoc. prof., 1984-88, prof., 1988—; asst. dir. environ. rsch. N.J. Dept. Environ. Protection, Trenton, 1987-88. Contbr. articles to profl. publs. Mem. Soc. Environ. Toxicology and Chemistry (pres. Hudson/Delaware chpt. 1989—), Am. Soc. Zoology, Assn. Women in Sci., Estuarine Rsch. Fedn., AAAS. Office: Ramapo Coll of NJ 505 Ramapo Valley Rd Mahwah NJ 07430

CRISWELL, ARTHURINE, social services administrator; b. Memphis, Tenn., Jan. 30, 1953; d. Arthur and Celia (Hambrick) Denton; m. Gordon Maxwell Criswell, May 11, 1981; 1 child, Joshua Michael. BA, Park Coll., 1973; M Social Svcs., U. Kans., 1981. Income maintenance worker Kans. Dept. Social & Rehab. Services, 1976-77, 1977-79; grad. research asst. Univ. Kans., Lawrence, 1979-81; income maintenance supr. Kans Dept. Social & Rehab. Services, Leavenworth, 1981-84; area dir. Kans. Dept. Social & Rehab. Services, Osawatomie, 1984-87, kans. Dept. Social & Rehab. Services, 1987-89; project dir. Project Eagle, U. Kans. Med. Ctr., Kansas City, 1989—. Bd. dirs. Pvt. Industry Coun., Kansas City, 1988; bd. dirs. Wyandotte County United Way. Mem. Assn. Couples for Marriage Enrichment, Nat. Forum Black Pub. Adminstrs. Office: Project Eagle PO Box 172382 Kansas City KS 66117

CRISWELL, KATHLEEN JEAN, insurance agent; b. Junction City, Kans., Nov. 7, 1949; d. Herman and Julia (Jones) Borkert; m. Fred Lee Criswell, June 17, 1967 (div. July 1988); children: Carl Dean, Sheila Louise. Grad. high sch., Kansas City, Kans. Sec. W.R. Grace, Kansas City, Mo., 1967-69, Shawne Mission (Kans.) Park and Recreation, 1971-73; day care owner Kansas City, Kans., 1973-75; ins. agt. Bill McKinney Ins., Memphis, Tenn., 1975—. Pres. PTA, Whitehaven Elem., 1979-83; asst. Girl Scouts Am., 1981, Boy Scouts Am., 1980-85. Home: 6320 Ashton Rd Memphis TN 38134

CRISWELL, KIMBERLY ANN, public relations executive, dancer; b. L.A., Dec. 6, 1957; d. Robert Burton and Carolyn Joyce (Semko) C. BA with honors, U. Calif.-Santa Cruz, 1980. Instr., English Lang. Services, Oakland, Calif., 1980-81; freelance writer Gambit mag., New Orleans, 1981; instr. Tulane U., New Orleans, 1981; instr., editor Haitian-English Lang. Program, New Orleans, 1981-82; instr. Delgado Coll., New Orleans, 1982-83; instr., program coord. Vietnamese Youth Ctr., San Francisco, 1984; dancer Khadra Internat. Folk Ballet, San Francisco, 1984-89; dir. mktg. communications Centram Systems West, Inc., Berkeley, Calif., 1984-87; communications coord. Safeway Stores, Inc., Oakland, 1985; dir. corp. communications TOPS, div. Sun Microsystems, Inc, 1987-88; pres. Criswell Communications, 1988—. Vol. coord. Friends of Haitians, 1981, editor, writer newsletter, 1981; dancer Komenka Ethnic Dance Ensemble, New Orleans, 1983; mem. Contemp. Art Ctr.'s Krewe of Clones, New Orleans, 1983, Americans for Nonsmokers Rights, Berkeley, 1985. Mem. Internat. Assn. Bus. Communicators, Sci. Meets the Arts Soc. (founding), NAFE, Dance Action, Bay Area Dance Coalition, Oakland Mus. Assn., Mus. Soc. Democrat. Avocations: visual arts, travel, creative writing. Office: 2560 9th St #315A Berkeley CA 94710

CRITCHLOW, SUSAN MELISSA, public relations executive, advertising and printing consultant; b. Gainesville, Fla., Dec. 24, 1950; d. James Carlton and Mildred Estelle (Pringle) Barley; m. Warren Hartzell Critchlow, Jr., Aug. 18, 1973. BA, U. South Fla., 1972, MA in Speech Communication with honors, 1973. Asst. dir. pub. relations Goodwill Industries of N. Fla., Inc., 1973-74; dir. pub. relations St. Luke's Hosp., Jacksonville, Fla., 1974; dir. informational services Greater Orange Park Community Hosp., Orange Park, Fla., 1974-82; pres. Susan Critchlow & Assocs., SC&A Pub. Co., Inc., Orange Park, 1976—. Mem. bd. dirs. Children's Haven. Named N.E. Fla. Bus. Communicator of Month, 1975, 78. Mem. Fla. Hosp. Assn. (bd. dirs. pub. relations council 1976-78, Gold award 1975, Silver award 1976, 78), Jacksonville Hosp. Pub. Relations Council (chmn. 1975-77), Fla. Pub. Relations Assn. (Golden Image award 1975-83), Pub. Relations Soc. Am., Jacksonville Advt. Fedn. (Addy award 1982-86). Democrat. Episcopalian. Office: 1580 Wells Rd Ste 15 Orange Park FL 32073

CRITTENDEN, SOPHIE MARIE, communications executive; b. Mansfield, Ohio, Apr. 14, 1926; d. Joseph S. and Mary Ellen (Hagerman) Wojcik; m. Robert Eugene Crittenden, Aug. 24, 1946 (dec. 1987); children: Robert J., Mark A., Christopher E., Laura Ann. Student, Coll. St. Francis, 1944-45, Ohio U., 1945-46, North Cen. Tech. Coll., 1976-78. Substitute tchr. Mansfield City Schs., 1956-62; lab. technician The Ohio Brass Co., Mansfield, 1962-68, draftsman, 1968, mgr. internal publs., 1969-78, mgr. advt., 1978-83, mgr. communications, 1983-88; cons. communications EFE N.Am., Inc., Mansfield, 1989-90; account coord. D & S Creative Advt., Inc., Mansfield, 1990—. Creator and shower of quilts. Com. chmn. United Way Campaign, Mansfield and Richland, Ohio, 1978; pub. relations chmn. Tribute to Women and Industry Project, Mansfield, 1986 (award 1985). Named Mrs. Mansfield Mrs. Am. Contest, 1961. Mem. Mktg. Club of North Cen. Ohio (dir., sec. 1987-90), Altrusa (pres. 1976). Republican. Roman Catholic. Home: 84 Wildwood Dr Mansfield OH 44907 Office: 140 Park Ave E Mansfield OH 44902

CRITTENDEN, VICTORIA LYNN, assistant educator; b. Newport, Ark., Aug. 30, 1956; d. Orval Andrew and Ester Lee (Caldwell) Scritchfield; m. William Frederick Crittenden, Aug. 2, 1980; 1 child, Carl Ambrose II. BA, Ark. Coll., 1978; MBA, U. of Ark., 1979; student, Fla. State U., 1983-84; D of Bus. Adminstrn., Harvard U., 1989. Grad. asst. U. Ark., Fayetteville, 1978-79; instr. Ark. Tech. U., Russellville, 1979-81; teaching asst. Fla. State U., Tallahassee, 1982-83; rsch. asst. Harvard Bus. Sch., Boston, 1985-86; asst. prof. Boston Coll., Chestnut Hill, Mass., 1988—; bd. dirs. Intronics, Inc., Canton, Mass.; adj. instr. Tallahassee Community Coll. 1982-83; cons. various U.S. South Am. and Mexican companies. contbr. articles to profl. jours. AAUW Edn. Found. fellow, 1987-88, Stephen X. Doyle Doctoral fellow, 1987-88, Am. Mktg. Assn. Doctoral Consortium fellow, 1986. Mem. AAUW (dissertation proposal reviewer, 1990—), Am. Mktg. Assn. (manuscript reviewer, 1990), Prod. and Oper. Mgmt. Soc., Assn. for Consumer Rsch. The Inst. of Mgmt. Sciences, The Acad. of Mktg. Sciences Inst. (manuscript reviewer, 1989), Strategic Mgmt. Soc., Assn. of Voluntary Action Scholars, Phi Beta Lambda. Home: 564 Concord Ave Lexington MA 02173 Office: Boston College Fulton 301A Chestnut Hill MA 02167

CRNIC, LINDA SMITH, psychobiologist, educator; b. Ft. Wayne, Ind., Mar. 29, 1948; d. Herman Edward and Patricia Ellen (Leeth) Smith; m. David Michael Crnic, June 21, 1969 (div. June 1976); m. Stanley Loyd Wilks, May 3, 1986. AB, U. Chgo., 1970; MA, U. Ill., Chgo., 1972, PhD, 1975. Postdoctoral fellow U. Colo. Sch. Medicine, Denver, 1975-77, instr. pediatrics and psychiatry, 1977-78, asst. prof., 1979-85, assoc. prof., 1985—. Contbr. articles to profl. jours. NIH grantee, 1975—; recipient research career devel. award NIMH, 1987—. Mem. Internat. Soc. Devel. Psychobiology (sec./treas. 1983-86), Internat. Soc. Devel. Neurosci., Soc. Neurosci.(chmn. Rocky Mountain region group 1983-86), Western Soc. Pediatric Research, Animal Behavior Soc. Office: U Colo Sch Med 4200 E 9th Ave Box C233 Denver CO 80262

CROCE, ARLENE LOUISE, critic; b. Providence, May 5, 1934; d. Michael Daniel and Louise Natalie (Pensa) C. Student, Women's Coll., U. N.C., 1951-53; BA, Barnard Coll., 1955. Founder, editor Ballet Rev., 1965-78; dance critic New Yorker mag., 1973—; dance panelist Nat. Endowment for Arts, 1977-80. Author: The Fred Astaire & Ginger Rogers Book, 1972, Afterimages, 1977, Going to the Dance, 1982, Sight Lines, 1987. Recipient AAAL award, 1979, Award of Honor for arts and culture Mayor N.Y.C., 1979, Janeway prize Barnard Coll., 1955; Hodder fellow Princeton U., 1971; Guggenheim fellow, 1972, 86. Office: New Yorker Mag 25 W 43d St New York NY 10036

CROCKER, SAONE BARON, lawyer; b. Bulawayo, Zimbabwe, Jan. 11, 1943; came to U.S., 1963; d. Benjamin and Rachel (Joffe) Baron; m. Chester Arthur Crocker, Dec. 18, 1965; children: Bathsheba Nell, Karena Wynne, Rebecca Masten. BA, U. Cape Town, 1961, BA with honors, 1962; MA, Johns Hopkins U., 1966; JD cum laude, Georgetown U., 1983. Bar: D.C. 1983, U.S. Ct. Appeals (D.C. cir.) 1985, U.S. Dist. Ct. D.C. 1990, U.S. Supreme Ct. 1990. Adminstr. Guinea program African Am. Inst., Washington, 1965-66, author Africa Report, 1966; writer fgn. affairs div. Am. U., Washington, 1967-68; freelance writer Washington, 1968-80; atty. firm Wilmer, Cutler & Pickering, Washington, 1983-84; clk. to judge U.S. Ct. Appeals for D.C. Circuit, 1984-85; atty. firm O'Melveny & Myers, Washington, 1985—. Contbg. author: Zambia Handbook, 1967. AAUW fellow, 1963-65; Fulbright fellow, 1963; Johns Hopkins U. fellow, 1964-65; recipient Lawyers Coop. Pub. Co. awards, 1980. Mem. ABA, U.S. Friends of Hague Acad. Internat. Law (sec.-treas. 1990—). Office: O'Melveny & Myers 555 13th St NW Suite 500W Washington DC 20004

CROCKETT, MAVIS, academic adminstrator. Instr. Profl. Bus. Sch., St. Louis, 1978-79; dir. info. systems Anderson, Preuss Bachman Co., St. Louis, 1978-81; mgmt. cons. APC Skills, Inc., Chgo., 1981-82; pub. relations dir. Perry Mgmt. Co., St. Louis, 1982-83; bookkeeper, office mgr. spl. edn. dept. Jones County Sch., Ellisville, Miss., 1986-87; edn. fin. specialist So. Corp./Miss. Power Co., Hattiesburg, Miss., 1987-89; v.p. bus. and fin. Bay Ridge Christian Coll., Kendleton, Tex., 1989—; ptnr., founder Walton Group Redevel. Co., St. Louis, 1981—; founder Creative Images, Laurel, Miss., 1986—. Bd. dirs. Pearl River Valley Opportunities Inc., Laurel; judge Miss. Hairdresser Assn., Laurel, 1985; del. select United Negro Coll. Fund, 1984-87; mem. Laurel Little Theatre, 1988; mem. exec. bd. Dem. Party, Laurel, 1988; bd. dirs. St. Louis Assn. Community Orgn., 1987. Mem. Am. Soc. Profl. Women, Am. Mgmt. Soc., Direct Selling Assn. Mem. Ch. of God. Office: Bay Ridge Christian Coll East Bernard TX 77435

CROCKETT, PHYLLIS DARLENE, reporter; b. Chgo., July 14, 1950; d. Leo F. Crockett and Mae (Corbin) Williams; divorced; 1 child, Adina Darlene Gittens. BA, U. Ill., Chgo., 1972; MS in Journalism, Northwestern U., 1978. Free-lance reporter AP and UPI, Raleigh and Durham, N.C., 1978-80; news writer Sta. WTTG-TV, Washington, 1981-82; free-lance writer Pacific News Svc., San Francisco, 1984; producer, reporter, anchorperson Sta. WSOC, Charlotte, N.C., 1978-79, Stas. WFNC/WQSM, Fayetteville, N.C., 1979-80; exec. editor, talk show moderator Sheridan Broadcasting Network, Washington, 1980-81; reporter gen. assignments Nat. Pub. Radio, Washington, 1981-89, White House corr., 1989—; panelist Am.'s Black Forum, Washington, 1980-83; analyst C-Span Cable TV Network, Black Entertainment TV, Washington and Sta. WHMM-TV, Washington, 1987—; cons. Clark-Atlanta U., others, 1982—; vis. instr. Fayetteville State U., 1980, Johnson C. Smith U., Charlotte, 1979; guest lectr. Howard U., U. D.C., Fairfax (Va.) Pub. Schs., 1980—. Contbr. book revs. to N.Y. Times, 1988, L.A. Times, 1989. Recipient NEA award, 1988, Robert F. Kennedy award, 1990. Mem. Nat. Assn. Black Journalists (Frederick Douglass award 1984), Washington Assn. Black Journalists (v.p. 1982), Sigma Delta Chi. Baptist. Office: Nat Pub Radio 2025 M St NW Washington DC 20036

CROFFORD, HELEN LOIS, accountant; b. Mesa, Ariz., Sept. 1, 1932; d. Elmer Earl and Lillian Irene (Williams) C.; grad. Lamson Bus. Coll., Phoenix, 1952. Acct., Bob Fisher Enterprises, Inc., Holbrook, Ariz., 1964-78; office mgr. for physician, Holbrook, 1978-79; office mgr. Trans Western Services, Inc., Holbrook, 1979; acct., Northland Pioneer Coll., Holbrook, 1980—. Squadron comdr. CAP, 1965-67, mission coordinator, 1970-79, group comdr., 1972-77, mem. regional staff, 1977-79, wing. historian, 1984—; mem. Navajo Fair Commn., 1966-75; mem. Navajo County Natural Resource Conservation Dist., 1970—, sec.-treas., 1971-81, chairperson, 1981-88; chmn. Navajo County Emergency Service Council, 1984-87; co-chmn. Navajo County Local Emergency Planning Com., 1987-88; troop com. sec. Boy Scouts Am., 1989. Mem. Ariz. Assn. Conservation Dists. (exec. bd. 1977-78, sec., 1979-80, v.p. 1981-82, pres. 1983-84, past pres. 1985), Nat. Assn. Conservation Dists. (past pres., edn. com. 1981-84), DAR, Nat. Assn. Search and Rescue. Democrat. Home: Box 36 Woodruff AZ 85942 Office: 1200 E Hermosa Dr Holbrook AZ 86025

CROFT, BARBARA YODER, medical educator; b. Port Chester, N.Y., Aug. 11, 1940; d. Paul Henry Yoder and Harriet French (Postle) McBride; m. Joseph Edward Croft, Dec. 15, 1977 (dec. 1988); m. Jerry Porter, Oct. 15, 1989. BS, Swarthmore Coll., 1962; MS, Johns Hopkins U., 1964, PhD, 1967. Sr. scientist Johnston Labs., Inc., Balt., 1967-68; programmer U. Va., Charlottesville, 1968, instr. dept. radiology, 1969-72, asst. prof. dept. radiology, 1972-87, assoc. prof. dept. radiology, 1987—; rsch. assoc. Oak Ridge (Tenn.) Associated Univs., 1972; vis. scholar U. N.Mex., Albuquerque, 1975. Co-author: Basics of Radiopharmacy, 1974; author: Single Photon Emission Computed Tomography, 1986. Fellow Am. Coll. Nuclear Physicians; mem. AAAS, AAUP (pres. 1978-79), Am. Chem. Soc., Soc. Nuclear Medicine (pres. 1988-89). Democrat. Episcopalian. Office: U Va Dept Radiology Box 170 Charlottesville VA 22908

CROFT, KATHERINE MAY-ING, educational administrator; b. Bluefield, W.Va., May 28, 1939; d. Edward Mung Yok and Ruby (Hsia) Tsoi; m. Stephen W. Croft (div. Oct. 1987); children: Dawn Ai-Ming, Lisa May-Ling. BS, U. Wis., 1961; MS, Butler U., 1967. Cert. city parish supr., prin., supr. student teaching, supr. child welfare, La. Tchr. Orchard Park and Hoyt Schs., Madison, Wis., 1961-64, Alice Birney Sch., Metairie, La., 1970-74; curriculum coord. Alice Birney Sch., Metairie, 1974-77; adminstrv. asst. Alice Birney, Bissonet, Schneckenburger, Metairie, 1977-84; prin. Greenlawn Terr. Sch., Kenner, La., 1985—; mem. state com. La. Dept. Edn., Baton Rouge, 1983-84; textbook reviewer, cons. Laidlaw Pub. Co., Chgo., 1985. Mem. La. Assn. Prins., La. Assn. Sch. Execs., La. Coun. for Social Studies, La. Reading Assn., Jamacia, Krewe of Argus (Metairie), Jamacia Dance Club. Presbyterian. Home: 4704 Bissoner Dr Metairie LA 70003 Office: Greenlawn Terr Sch 1500 38th St Kenner LA 70065

CROFTS, LISA CHRISTINE, foundation administrator, educator; b. Bryn Mawr, Pa., Sept. 16, 1955; d. Frederick and Jane C.; m. Brian E. McNutt; children: Rebecca, Melissa. BS in Natural Scis., Mich. State U.; postgrad., Western Mich. U. Registered sanitarian, Mich.; cert. pesticide operator, sewage enforcement officer, food handler. Environ., vector sanitarian Chester County Health Dept., West Chester, Pa., 1978-80; dir. Livingston County Lakewater Assessment Project Livingston County Health Dept., Howell, Mich., 1980-84; mgr. regional svcs. Nat. Sanitation Found., Ann Arbor, Mich., 1984—. Author various environ. surveys. Mem. Friends of Fenner Arboretum, Recyclers. Oakland-Livingston Human Svcs. grantee. Mem. NAFE, ASTM, Nat. Environ. Health Assn., Mich. Environ. Health Assn. (chmn. continuing edn. com., mem. food svc. and profl. devel. coms.), Minn. Environ. Health Assn., Internat. Assn. Milk, Food and Environ. Sanitarians, Am. Pub. Health Assn. Office: Nat Sanitation Found 3475 Plymouth Rd Ann Arbor MI 48106

CROMACK, MARGOT SCHLEGEL, health care administrator; b. Phila., Nov. 25, 1952; d. Richard Arthur and Margot Ward (Wheelock) Schlegel; m. Douglas T. Cromack, Aug. 2, 1986; children: Margot Anne, Phillip Douglas. BSN, Syracuse U., 1975; MSHA in Health Svcs., George Washington U., 1988. Cert. critical care nurse. Staff nurse Mt. Sinai Hosp., N.Y.C.; various positions in critical care, 1975-88; adminstrv. fellow Christian Health System, St. Louis, 1989—. Mem. Am. Assn. Critical Care Nurses, Am. Coll. Health Care Execs. Mem. Soc. of Friends. Home: 7606 Gannon Saint Louis MO 63130

CROMER, JENNY LU, marketing executive; b. Freeburn, Ky., Nov. 14, 1954; d. John Henry and Jenny Jacquline (Bodenheimer) Cromer; m. James Robert Logan IV, Oct. 12, 1985; 1 child, David Cromer. AB, Centre Coll. Ky., Danville, 1976; MBA, Tulane U., 1981. News reporter WTRE-AM/FM, Greensburg, Ind., 1976-77; news dir. WLBJ-AM/FM, Bowling Green, Ky., 1977-78; trainee J.C. Penney Co., Frankfort, Ky., 1978-79; v.p. mktg. First Miss. Nat. Bank, Hattiesburg, 1981-83, Howard, Weil, Labouisse, Freidrichs, Inc., New Orleans, 1983-89; v.p., mktg. mgr. First Commerce Corp., New Orleans, 1989—; conductor workshops in field. Allocations com. United Way, New Orleans, 1989; subcom. Met. Area Com. Partnerships in Edn. Recipient Honor award, Nat. Sch. Pub. Relations, 1989, Silver Anvil, Pub. Relation Soc., New Orleans, 1988. Mem. Tulane Assn. Bus. Alumni, Securities Industry Assn., Mktg. & Advt. Roundtable. Republican. Presbyterian. Office: First Commerce Corp 925 Common St New Orleans LA 70160

CROMWELL, FLORENCE STEVENS, occupational therapist; b. Lewistown, Pa., May 14, 1922; d. William Andrew and Florence (Stevens) C. BS in Edn., Miami U., Oxford, Ohio, 1943; BS in Occupational Therapy, Washington U., St. Louis, 1949; MA, U. So. Calif., 1952; cert. in health facility adminstrn., UCLA, 1978. Mem. staff, then supervising therapist Los Angeles County Gen. Hosp., 1949-53; occupational therapist Goodwill Industries, Los Angeles, 1954-55; staff therapist Vis. Nurse Assn., Phila., 1955-56; research therapist United Cerebral Palsy Assn., Los Angeles, 1956-60; dir. occupational therapy Orthopaedic Hosp., Los Angeles, 1961-67; coordinator occupational therapy Research and Tng. Ctr. U. So. Calif., Los Angeles, 1967-70, assoc. prof., 1970-76, acting chmn. dept. occupational therapy, 1973-76, mem. adv. bd. project SEARCH, Sch. Medicine, 1969-72; founding editor Occupational Therapy in Health Care jour., 1984-88, editor emerita, 1988—; assoc. dir. Los Angeles Job Corps Ctr., 1977-78, cons. in edn. and program devel., 1976—. Author: Manual for Basic Skills Assessment, 1960; also articles. Mem. scholarship com. Los Angeles March of Dimes, 1963-70; Bd. dirs. Am. Occupational Therapy Found., 1965-69, v.p., 1966-69; bd. dirs. Nat. Health Council, 1975-78. Served to lt. (j.g.) WAVES, 1943-46. Recipient Disting. Alumni award Washington U., 1978, Disting. Lectr. Calif. Occupational Therapy Found., 1986. Fellow Am. Occupational Therapy Assn. (pres. 1967-73); mem. Inst. Medicine of Nat. Acad. Scis. (sr. 1989—), So. Calif. Occupational Therapy Assn. (pres. 1950-51, 75-76), Coalition Ind. Health Professions (chmn. 1973-74), Assn. Schs. Allied Health Professions (dir. 1973-74), World Fedn. Occupational Therapists, Cwen, Mortar Bd., Kappa Delta Pi, Kappa Kappa Gamma. Address: 1179 Yocum St Pasadena CA 91103

CRONAU, REBECCA LYNN, business analyst; b. Tokyo, Aug. 9, 1962; came to U.S., 1968; d. Jackie Don Baize and Hisako (Ogawa) Ishimoto; m. Stephen Leslie Cronau, Apr. 21, 1982; children: Tanya Lynn, Andrew James. Student, U. Pitts., 1982-87, U. Tex., 1980-82. Coordinator data mgmt. and outreach, liaison to Ctr. Continuing Edn. Health Scis. U. Pitts., 1983-87; cons. TRW-Fla. Ops. Def. Systems Group, Cape Canaveral Air Force Sta., 1987, bus. analyst, 1987—. Democrat. Roman Catholic. Office: TRW Def Systems Group PO Box 903 Cape Canaveral FL 32920

CRONE, CHRISTINE HESS, civic volunteer; b. Cleve., Jan. 6, 1917. BA, Case Western Res. U., 1938. Chmn. book dept. Gardens Ctr. Elephant White Sale, Cleve., 1955—; chmn. fundraising com. ARC, Euclid, 1940-42; trustee, officer Euclid Pub. Library, 1963-75; trustee Euclid Opportunity Sch., 1969—. Mem. Flora Stone Mather Coll. Alumni Assn. (bd. dirs. 1949-52, pres. 1951-52), Lake Shore Garden Club (pres., bd. dirs. Euclid, Ohio chpt. 1939—), AAUW (officer 1953—). Republican.

CRONHOLM, LOIS S., biology educator; b. St. Louis, Aug. 15, 1930; d. Fred and Emma (Tobias) Kisslinger; m. James Cronholm, Sept. 15, 1965 (div. 1974); children: Judith Frances, Peter Foster; m. Stuart E. Neff, Apr. 11, 1975. BA, U. Louisville, 1962, PhD, 1966. Asst. prof. biology dept. U. Louisville, 1973-76, assoc. prof., 1976-80, dean arts and scis., 1979-85; prof. U. Louisville, 1980—; dean arts and scis., prof. Temple U., Phila., 1985—. Contbr. articles to profl. jours. Chmn. Human Relations Commn., Louisville, 1976-79; group capt. Dems., Valley Station, Ky., 1975-78; sec. Grass Roots Dem. Club, Valley Station, 1975; chmn. Southwestern Jefferson County Econ. Devel. Com., Valley Station, 1983-84. Recipient Pre-Doctoral fellowship NIH, 1963-66, Post-Doctoral fellowship NIH, 1967-70; named Prin. Investigator Dept. Interior, 1978-79. Mem. Nat. Assn. Land Grant and Urban Univs. (chmn. com. arts and scis. 1987-89, bd. dirs. div. urban affairs 1988-90), Council Colls. Arts and Scis. (bd. dirs. 1987-90, pres.-elect 1989-90), Am. Assn. Colls. Democrat. Jewish. Office: Temple Univ Anderson Hall Berks Mall Philadelphia PA 19122

CRONIN, PATTI ADRIENNE WRIGHT, state agency administrator; b. Chgo., May 25, 1943; d. Rodney Adrian and Dorothy Louise (Thiele) Wright; m. Kevin Brian Cronin, May 1, 1971; 1 child, Kevin. BA, Beloit (Wis.) Coll., 1965; JD, U. Wis., 1983. Vol. Peace Corps, Turkey, 1965-67; recruiter Peace Corps, Washington, 1967-68; tchr. English Kamehameha III Sch., Lahaina, Hawaii, 1968-70, Evansville (Wis.) High Sch., 1972-77; tchr. math. and history Killian Sch., Hartford, Wis., 1977-78; tchr. English Kaiser High Sch., Honolulu, 1979-80; intern Wis. Ct. Appeals, Madison, 1983; exec. dir. waste facility siting bd. State of Wis., Madison, 1983—; founder, v.p., bd. dirs. Justice Ctr. Honolulu, 1979-82; sec., treas. Cronin Constrn. Co., Inc., Madison, 1986—. Editor: Internat. Law Jour., 1982. Bd. dirs. Neighborhood Bd., Honolulu, 1979-82. Recipient Mayor's award of outstanding achievement, City of Honolulu, 1980. Mem. Soc. Profls. in Dispute Resoultion, ABA, State Bar Wis. Office: Waste Facility Siting Bd 132 E Wilson St #201 Madison WI 53702

CRONN, DAGMAR RAIS, atmospheric chemistry educator; b. Vicksburg, Miss., Nov. 9, 1946; d. Wesley Edward and Sarah Margaret (Courtney) Rais; m. Robert Stuart Cronn, June 22, 1968. BS, U. Wash., 1969, MS, 1972, PhD, 1975. Teaching asst. U. Wash., Seattle, 1969-71, research asst., 1971-

75; asst. research chemist Wash. State U., Pullman, 1975-79, asst. prof., 1977-79, assoc. prof., 1979-86, prof. atmospheric chemistry, 1986-89, asst. program dir., 1985-86, chair environ. sci. and regional planning program, 1986-88; dean Coll. of Sci. U. Maine, Orono, 1989—; cons. Am. Plywood Assn., Tacoma, 1977, EPA, Research Triangle Park, N.C., 1979-81, Meteorology Research Inc., Santa Rosa, Calif., 1981, Environ. Research and Tech., Inc., Westlake Village, Calif., 1981, W.K. Kellogg Found., Battle Creek, Mich., 1985, NSF, Washington, 1986. Contbr. numerous articles to profl. jours. Kellogg Found. fellow, 1981-84, Am. Council Edn. fellow, 1988-89; Welsh Fund scholar, 1965-69. Air Pollution Control Assn. (chair regional meeting 1982), Soc. Women Engrs. (nat. keynote speaker 1983), Antarctican Soc. (speaker 1986), Sigma Xi. Home: 166 Main Orono ME 04473 Office: U Maine Coll of Sci Aubert Hall Portland ME 04469 also: U Calif Office of Chancellor 4148 Adminstrn Bldg Riverside CA 92521

CROOK, TRESSA HELEN, clinical psychologist; b. Balt., Jan. 21, 1956; d. John Fahey and Elizabeth Helen (Cecil) C. BA, Towson (Md.) State U., 1979; PsyD, Fla. Inst. Tech., 1985. Lic. clin. psychologist, Ill. Counselor Community and Family Health Ctr., Greater Balt. Med. Ctr., 1977-78; therapist, teaching assst. Forbush Children's Ctr., Sheppard and Enoch Pratt Hosp., Towson, 1979; psychometrist Md. Sch. for Blind, Balt., 1980-81; psychotherapist Brevard County Health Ctr., Melbourne, Fla., 1982-83; psychotherapist, grad. teaching asst., adj. instr. Fla. Inst. Tech., Melbourne, 1982-83; asst. prof. Norwestern State U. La., Natchitoches, 1984-85; clin. dir. Ctr. for Childen's Svcs., Danville, Ill., 1985—; teaching asst. Towson State U., 1979; conf. presenter, 1987. Mem. APA, Execs. Club Danville, Psi Chi. Home: 2200 N Vermilion St Apt 105 Danville IL 61832 Office: Ctr for Children's Svcs 702 N Logan Danville IL 61832

CROOKE, ROSANNE MUZYKA, pharmacologist; b. Pittsfield, Mass., Oct. 30, 1955; d. Myron Michael and Marian Geneva (Russell) Muzyka; m. Stanley T. Crooke, Sept. 5, 1986; 1 child, Evan C. BA, Williams Coll., 1978; PhD, U. Pa., 1986. Rsch. asst. endocrine sec. dept. medicine U. Pa., Phila., 1978-81; fellow Wistar Inst. Anatomy and Biology, Phila., 1986-89; scientist ISIS Pharms., Carlsbad, Calif., 1989—. Contbr. articles to profl. jours. Mem. AAAS. Home: 3211 Piragua St Carlsbad CA 92009 Office: ISIS Pharms 2280 Faraday Carlsbad CA 92008

CROOKSHANKS, BARBARA MALONE, magazine editor; b. South Charleston, W.Va., Nov. 16, 1928; d. Joseph William and Lucy (Caldwell) Malone; m. Robert Vincent Crookshanks, Dec. 29, 1951; children: Lee Pelham Crookshanks Cotton, Virginia Anne Crookshanks Johnson. BS in Journalism, W.Va. U., 1950; postgrad. in English, U. Pa., 1954-56. Asst. to make-up editor Ladies' Home Jour., Phila., 1952-56; reporter Free Lance Star newspaper, Fredericksburg, Va., 1956-61; editor Fredericksburg Tideland Times mag., 1974—; copy editor Personal Selling Power mag., Fredericksburg, 1981—. Editor: Fredericksburg Tideland Times Cook Book, 1989 (1st pl. Va. Press Women 1989-90, Nat. award 1989-90 Nat. Press Women 1989-90); contbr. articles on antiques to profl. jours. Bd. dirs. Thomas Jefferson Inst., Fredericksburg. Mem. Nat. Press Women, Va. Press Women, DAR (corr. sec. Washington-Lewis chpt.), United Daus. of Confederacy, Kappa Tau Alpha. Home: 1300 Washington Ave Fredericksburg VA 22401

CROOKSHANKS, BETTY DORSEY, radio station executive, state legislator; b. Rainelle, W.Va., Oct. 27, 1944; d. Talmage Lee and Gilda Marie (Sovine) Dorsey; BA, W.Va. Inst. Tech., 1968; MA, W.Va. U., 1973; m. Donald Eugene Crookshanks, Sept. 1, 1972. Sec., NIH, 1965-66; tchr., coach Fayette County Bd. Edn., Meadow Bridge, W.Va., 1968-78; life underwriter Farm Family Life Ins. Co., 1979-82; tchr. Greenbrier (W.Va.) West High Sch., 1981-84; mgr. Sta. WYKM, 1984—; mem. W.Va. Ho. of Dels., 1977-89, chmn. coal mine health and safety interior com., 1987-89. Mem. adv. bd. W.Va. Woman's Commn., 1977—, Greenbrier Valley Domestic Violence Com.; treas. Rupert Community Libr., 1977—; bd. dirs. Seneca Mental Health/Mental Retardation Coun.,1978-82, treas., 1979-80, pres., 1980-82; bd. dirs. W.Va. Health Systems Agy., 1980-82; bd. dirs. W.Va. div. Am. Cancer Soc., 1981-83; pres. Greenbrier County Cancer Soc., 1981-82; treas. Big Clear Creek Baptist Ch., 1982-85. Recipient meritorious award W.Va. div. Isaac Walton League of Am., 1978; Disting. Service award W.Va. Osteo. Sch. Medicine, 1982; named Outstanding Young Woman of W.Va., 1980, Outstanding Citizen Rupert Rotary. Mem. Order of Women Legislators, Rainelle Bus. and Profl. Women's Club (treas. 1984-86, pres. 1986-88, chmn. dist. 5 1986), Delta Kappa Gamma (sec. 1980-82, 1st v.p. 1982-85). Democrat. Clubs: Quota (bd. dirs. 1981-83), Rupert Woman's (pres. 1979-80). Lodges: Order of Eastern Star, White Shrine, Rebekah. Office: Mountain State Bd Corp Rupert WV 25984

CROOM, HENRIETTA BROWN, biology educator; b. Burlington, N.C., Sept. 23, 1940; d. Grady Anderson and Emma Mabel (Cheek) Brown; m. Frederick Hailey Croom, Aug. 17, 1963; children: Elizabeth Bonner, Frederick H. Jr. AB in Chemistry, U. N.C., 1962, PhD in Biochemistry, 1968. Rsch. assoc. U. Ky., Lexington, 1969-70; asst. prof. U. of the South, Sewanee, Tenn., 1972-82, assoc. prof., 1982-88, prof. biology, 1988—; vis. prof. microbiology La. State U., Baton Rouge, 1977-78; vis. scholar Vanderbilt U., Nashville, 1981-82, U. Hawaii-Manoa, Honolulu, 1989-90, U. Ky., Lexington. County dist. commr. U.S. Pony Clubs, Sewanee, 1973-76; bd. dirs. St. Andrews-Sewanee Sch., Sewanee, 1986—; leader Girl Scouts U.S., Sewanee, 1971-72. Recipient STP award NSF, 1973-77, Faculty Devel. award Mellon Found., 1981-82, Rsch. Opportunity award NSF, 1989; rsch. grantee Bishop Rsch. Inst., Honolulu, 1990; Pew fellow Faculty Scholars Program, Lexington, 1988, 90. Mem. Am. Soc. for Cell Biology, Phi Beta Kappa, Sigma Xi. Democrat. Episcopalian. Home: Tennessee Ave Sewanee TN 37375 Office: U of the South Dept of Biology Sewanee TN 37375

CROPPER, SUSAN PEGGY, veterinarian; b. N.Y.C., Feb. 11, 1941; d. Eli and Ruth (Rader) Abrahams; divorced; 1 child, Tracy Lynn. BS, Kans. State U., 1962, DVM, 1964. Assoc. veterinarian Asbury Park (N.J.) Animal Hosp., 1964-65; instr. in Vet. Sci. Kans. State U., Manhattan, 1965-66; owner, veterinarian Markle (Ind.) Vet. Clinic, 1966-71, Meisels Animal Hosp. Clinic, Elmwood Park, N.J., 1971-73, Ridgewood (N.J.) Animal Hosp., 1973-75, Cropper House Call Practice, Wyckoff, N.J., 1975—; editor Nat. Assn. Women Vets., 1966-68; mem. Audibon Soc. Mus. Natural History. Editor WJMA Jour., 1973; photographer: Best Diving Spots in Western Hemisphere, 1987. Leader Brownie troop Girl Scouts of Am., Glen Rock, N.J., 1976-77, Wyckoff, 1977-83; chair No. Jersey Tridents, Ridgefield, N.J., 1985-86. Mem. AVMA, Soc. Aquatic Vet. Medicine, Northern N.J. Vet. Med. Assn. (pres. 1972-73), Met. Vet. Med. Assn., N.Y. Zool. Soc., Van Saun Zool. Soc., N.J. Acad. Clubs: Ski & Scuba (Westwood, N.J.); North Jersey Tridents (Ridgefield) (chair 1985-86). Office: 310 Newtown Rd Wyckoff NJ 07481

CROSBY, SUSAN, mental heath services executive; b. Muncie, Ind., Oct. 16, 1945; d. Thomas and Patricia (Roberts) Ray; m. Joseph E. Crosby, Jan. 19, 1968; children: Todd, Thomas. BA in Psychology, Purdue U., 1979; postgrad., Ind. State U. Asst. dir. devel. Depauw U., Greencastle, Ind.; exec. dir., chief exec. officer Associated Patient Svcs., Indpls. Recipient Jefferson award, Jane award State of Ind. Active Nat. Com. Mental Health Needs in Rural Am.; mem. Select Adv. Com. for Pub. Welfare, Com. on Dirs. Mental Health. Mem. Nat. Mental Health Assn. (v.p. tng.), Nat. Alliance for Rsch. on Schizophrenia and Depression (bd. dirs.), Mental Health Assn. Ind. (past pres.). Democrat. Presbyterian. Home: RR1 Box 134 Roachdale IN 46172 Office: 1433 N Meridian Indianapolis IN 46202

CROSHAL, KATHLEEN KLOTZ See HEARN, KATHLEEN K.

CROSS, BETTY FELT, small business owner; b. Newcastle, Ind., Jan. 8, 1920; d. Frank Ernest and Olive (Shock) Felt; m. Paris O. Cross, July 14, 1939 (div.); children—Ernest, Betty J., Robert D., Paris, Toni, Frank; m. John B. Gatlin, 1976. Owner, mgr. Salon D'Or, Indpls., 1956-74; owner Bejon, Madison, Ind., 1974-78, Brass & Things, Madison, 1978—; pres. Silver City USA I, Madison, Felts Mfg., Inc., 1966—. Mem. Nashville C. of C. Avocation: collecting dolls, gold and silver coins, art objects, antique jewelry, silver sterling flat ware. Office: Silver City USA Olde Towne Village Madison TN 37115

CROSS, DOLORES E., university administrator, educator; b. Newark, Aug. 29, 1936; d. Charles and Ozie (Johnson) Tucker; children: Thomas E., Jane E. BS, Seton Hall U., 1963; MS, Hofstra U. 1968; PhD, U. Mich. 1971. Asst. prof. edn. Northwestern U., Evanston, Ill. 1971-74; assoc. prof. Claremont Grad. Sch., Calif., 1974-78; vice chancellor CUNY, 1978-81; prof. Brooklyn Coll., 1978—; pres. N.Y. State Higher Edn. Service Corp., Albany, 1981-88; assoc. provost, assoc. v.p. academic affairs U. Minn., Mpls., 1988—. Bd. dirs. 100 Black Women, Albany, 1983-88; bd. dirs. Nat. Council Higher Edn. Loan Program, Washington, 1982—. Editor: Teaching in a Multicultural Society, 1978. Mem. NAACP (life), Am. Edn. Research Assn., Am. Council on Edn., Women Execs. in State Govt. (adv. bd.). Avocations: running, hiking, bicycling, theater, writing. Office: Chicago State Univ Office of Pres 95th St at King Dr Chicago IL 60628

CROSS, DOROTHY ABIGAIL, librarian; b. Bangor, Mich., Sept. 9, 1924; d. John Laird and Alice Estelle (Wilcox) C.; B.A., Wayne State U., 1956; M.A. in Library Sci., U. Mich., 1957. Jr. librarian Detroit Public Library, 1957-59; adminstrv. librarian U.S. Army, Braconne, France, 1959-61, Poitiers, France, 1961-63; area library supr., 1963, asst. command librarian, Kaiserslautern, Germany, 1963-67, acquisitions librarian, Aschaffenburg, Germany, 1967, Munich, Germany, 1967-69, sr. staff library specialist, Munich, 1969-72, command librarian, Stuttgart, Germany, 1972-75, dep. staff librarian, Heidelberg, Germany, 1975-77; chief librarian 18th Airborne Corps and Ft. Bragg (N.C.), 1977-79; chief ADP sect. Pentagon Library, Washington, 1979-80, chief readers services br., 1980-83, dir., 1983—. Mem. ALA, U. Mich. Alumni assn., Delta Omicron. Methodist. Home: 6511 Delia Dr Alexandria VA 22310 Office: Pentagon Libr Rm 1A526 Pentagon Washington DC 20310-6000

CROSS, JANICE EILEEN, hospital controller and executive; b. Ripley, Miss., May 4, 1944; d. Thomas Leland and Martha Juanita (Moore) Wigington; m. Frederick Neil Cross, Nov. 29, 1969; children: Steven Edward, Cynthia Juanita, Ginger Wigington. AA, N.E. Miss. Jr. Coll., Booneville, 1964; BS, Miss. State Coll. for Women, 1966; postgrad., Miss. State U., 1966-69, U. Miss., 1989—. Tchr. Amory (Miss.) Pub. Schs., 1966-68, Tippah County Schs., Walnut, Miss., 1970; specialist curriculum coordinating unit Miss. State U., Starkville, 1968-69; asst. v.p. Bank of Falkner, Miss., 1971-72, 76-82; note clk. Peoples Bank, Ripley, 1982-83; adminstrv. sec. Tippah County Hosp., Ripley, 1970-71, bus. office dir., contr., 1983—. Mem. Ripley Heritage Soc., 1980-88; active Tippah County Leadership Group. Mem. Miss. chpt. Healthcare Fin. Mgmt. Assn. (area coun. chmn. 1986-89, state coun. chmn. 1989—, Outstanding Area Chmn. 1987-88, 88-89), Jaycettes (pres. Ripley chpt. 1972, Jaycette of Yr. 1974), Pi Omega Pi. Baptist. Home: 501 Forest Gate Ripley MS 38663

CROSS, JAYNE ROBERTA, chimney sweep; b. Streator, Ill., Oct. 17, 1953; d. John Richard and Evelyn Mary (Reiuf) Skinner; m. Daniel John Cross, May 17, 1975; children: Jamie Lynn, Jonathan, Benjamin. Diploma, Charron William Bus. Coll., Miami, Fla., 1971; student, Widener U., 1982, Delaware County Community, 1982-83. Exec. sec. Dept. Navy, Alexandria, Va., 1972-74; graphic artist intermediate unit Montgomery County, Blue Bell, Pa., 1976-78; owner, mgr. Chim Chimney Sweeps, Media, Pa., 1981-90; v.p., chief exec. officer D.J Cross, Inc., Media, 1990—. Recipient Disting. Svc. award Dept. Navy, 1974, Golden Top Hat award, 1987, 88, 89. Mem. Nat. Chimney Sweep Guild (best newspaper advt. award 1985), Delaware County C. of C., Phila. C. of C. Republican. Presbyterian. Home: 266 S Old Middletown Rd Media PA 19063 Office: 2 Old Pennell Rd Media PA 19063

CROSS, LAURA ELIZABETH, lawyer; b. Lathrop, Mo.; d. Pross T. and Nina (Peel) C.; A.B., Lindenwood Coll., 1923; B.Litt., Columbia Sch. Journalism, 1925; J.D., George Washington U., 1939. Bar: D.C. 1940. Bibliog. rsch. Libr. of Congress, Washington, 1931-42; atty. Office Chief of Engrs., U.S. Army, 1942-73; practiced in Washington, 1973—. Mem. ABA, Fed. Bar Assn., D.C. bar assns., Am. Judicature Soc., Women in Communications, Kappa Beta Pi, Theta Sigma Phi. Home: 2500 Wisconsin Ave NW Apt 709 Washington DC 20007

CROSS, SUSAN LEE, consulting actuary; b. Abington, Pa., Mar. 10, 1960; d. James Robert and Mary Elizabeth (Schleiden) Garris; m. Kevin Michael Cross, July 15, 1979. BS in Math., U. Md., 1981. Actuarial asst. The Wyatt Co., Washington, 1981-83; actuarial asst. Tillinghast a Towers Perrin Co. (formerly Tillinghast), Hamilton, Bermuda, 1984-85, asst. v.p., 1985-86; cons. acturary Tillinghast a Towers Perrin Co. (formerly Tillinghast), Vienna, Va., 1987—. Fellow Casualty Actuarial Soc.; mem. Am. Acad. Actuaries, Soc. of Actuaries (assoc.). Republican. Home: 12041 Lake Newport Rd Reston VA 22070 Office: Tillinghast 4601 N Fairfax Dr Ste #1100 Arlington VA 22203

CROSS, VIRGINIA ROSE, research chemist; b. Portland, Oreg., May 15, 1950; d. Remi Joseph and Rose Matilda (Schallberger) Coussens; m. John Parson Cross, Aug. 17, 1974; children: Richard, Robert, David. BS, Oreg. State U., 1972; PhD in Chemistry, MIT, 1976; MBA, U. Houston, 1986. Rsch. chemist Celanese Corp., Greer, S.C., 1976-79; sr. rsch. chemist Am. Hoechst, Greer, 1979-80; sr. research chemist Exxon Chem. Co., Baytown, Tex., 1980-85, staff chemist, 1985—. Patentee in field. Republican. Roman Catholic. Home: 3419 Ledgestone Dr Houston TX 77059 Office: Exxon Chem Co 5200 Bayway Dr Baytown TX 77520

CROSSLAND, HARRIET KENT, artist; b. Cleve., Sept. 8, 1902; d. Carl and Harriet Emily (Bacon) Dueringer; studies with Margaret McDonald Phillips; m. Paul Marion Crossland, Sept. 20, 1959. Portrait painter, 1952—; freelance editor med. papers, 1953-70; represented in permanent collection John F. Kennedy Libr., Boston. Mem. art mus. com. Luther Burbank Ctr. for the Arts, Santa Rosa, 1982—. Recipient award of merit Am. Cancer Soc., 1979, 84. Mem. Sonoma County Med. Assn. Aux., Am. Med. Women's Assn. (friend), DAR, Stanford U. Alumni Assn., Ret. Officers Wives Club, Sat. Afternoon Club (Santa Rosa). Editor, illustrator: X-Rays and Radium in Treatment of Diseases of the Skin, 1967; included in The Fifty American Artists by Margaret McDonald Phillips, 1969. Prin. donor Crossland Lab. for Audiovisual Learning in Dermatology, Stanford U. Sch. Medicine. Address: 2247 Sunrise Dr Santa Rosa CA 95405

CROSSLEY, KAY FRANCES, affirmative action coordinator; b. Kansas City, Kans., Sept. 10, 1946; d. John LeRoy and Frances Esther (Karriger) Bradford; m. Michael Aaron Crossley, Apr. 8, 1966; children: John Thomas, Philip Creighton. AA, Kansas City Community Coll., 1966. With Continental Elec. Co., Kansas City, Mo., 1964-66, Fairbanks-Morse Corp., Kansas City, Kans., 1966-68, Electra-Midland Corp., Kansas City, 1968-69, Gustin Bacon/St. Gobain Corp., Kansas City, 1969, Providence-St. Margaret Health Ctr., Kansas City, 1969-73, Bulk Mail Ctr. U.S. Postal Service, Kansas City, 1974-79; account rep. Main Post Office, Kansas City, 1979-85; coord. womens' programs Mid-Am. Dist., Shawnee Mission, Kans., 1985-86; affirmative action/equal employment opportunity coord. State of Mo., Kansas City, 1986—. Mem. Federally Employed Women, Am. Bus. Women's Assn., Nat. Assn. Female Execs., Nat. Assn. Postal Suprs., U. Kans. Alumni Assn. Mem. Christian Church. Home: 1823 N 78th Pl Kansas City KS 66112-2052

CROSSLEY, LINDA SUSAN, university alumni association executive; b. New Brunswick, N.J., July 21, 1950; d. Richard Lawrence and Mary Vee (Adams) C. BA in Journalism, Ohio State U., 1972; MBA, Ball State U., 1984. Adminstrv. asst. for news and info. svcs. Ohio State U., Newark, 1972-77, Cen. Ohio Tech. Coll., Newark, 1971-77; dir. pub. info. svcs. Olivet (Mich.) Coll., 1977-80; asst. dir. News Bur., Ball State U., Muncie, Ind., 1980-84; communications dir. Ohio State U. Alumni Assn., Columbus, 1984-88, asst. dir. alumni affairs, 1988-90, assoc. dir. alumni affairs, 1990—. Elder Berlin Presbyn. Ch., 1987-90; bd. mgrs., treas. Hillside Condomium Assn., Columbus, 1987-90, v.p., 1989-90. Named Outstanding Adminstr., Olivet Coll., 1980. Mem. Coun. for Advancement and Support Edn. (bd. dirs. dist. 5, 1990—, dist. trustee 1989-91, Jr. League Columbus, Kappa Tau Alpha, Sigma Iota Epsilon, Beta Gamma Sigma. Office: Ohio State U Alumni Assn 2400 Olentangy River Rd Columbus OH 43210-1061

CROSSMAN, ANNE E., computer company executive, director; b. Riverside, Calif., Feb. 25, 1957; d. John Bruce and Mary Anne (Kennedy) Paterson; m. Calvin Raley Crossman, Oct. 29, 1983; 1 child, Samuel Kyle. BA, Cath. U. Am., 1979; cert., Computer Learning Ctr., Springfield, Va., 1980. Programmer analyst PEPCO, Washington; project leader Tymshare/McDonnell Douglas, Vienna, Va.; dir. Microcmputer's Info. Analysis, Inc., Dunn Loring, Va. Mem. NAFE. Office: 2222 Gallows Rd #300 Washington DC 22027

CROSSWELL, LAURIE ELLEN, legal assocation administration; b. Dallas, Mar. 19, 1956; d. Lowell Edward and Margaret Louise (Rudy) Dushman; m. Joe David (div.). Student, U. Tex., 1977, Tex. Christian U., 1978; BS, Tarleton State U., 1979; postgrad., Tex. A&M U., 1981. Field biologist Brothers Farm & Ranch Cons., Stepenville, Tex., 1980; salesperson Marvin Tate Realty, Coll. Station, Tex., 1983-84; broker Phyllis Young & Assocs., Bryan, 1985; rsch. analyst Dushman & Friedman, P.C., Ft. Worth, 1986--. Mem. Tex. Real Estate Pol. Action Com., Bryan, 1983-84. Mem. Tex. Reining Horse Assn., Southwest Reining Horse Assn., Nat. Reining Horse Assn., Nat. Assn. Female Exec.

CROSSWHITE, BEVERLY ANN, small business service company executive; b. Florence, Ala., Dec. 25, 1953; d. Hubert Lee and Shirley Ann (Williams) C. BS Secondary Music Edn., Auburn U., 1976; postgrad., Inst. Bibl. Studies, San Bernardino, Calif., 1976-77. Substitute tchr. Decatur (Ala.) City Sch. System, 1976-77; internat. coord. Campus Crusade for Christ, San Bernardino, 1977-80; asst. v.p. fin. Diaconate Group, Pompano Beach, Fla., 1980-83; corp. sec. Anuc, Inc., Pompano Beach, 1980-83; mgmt. trainee Parisians, Decatur, 1984-85; freelance youth, emotional and substance abuse units Charter Hosp., Decatur, 1985-86; ops. dir. Fin. Express, Dallas, 1986—; corp. sec. Fin. Express Systems Inc., Dallas, 1986—; bus. planning cons., Dallas, 1986—. Contbr. photographs to various publs. Counselor substance abuse programs, Decatur, 1985-86, Dallas, 1986—; conv. worker Eagle Forum, Dallas, 1986, mem. ann. com., 1988; precinct worker Dallas County Rep. Com., 1988-89. Mem. Bus. and Profl. Women, Dallas Women's Club, Delta Omicron. Presbyterian. Home: 16000 Bent Tree Forest Circle Apt 1123 Dallas TX 75248 Office: Fin Express Systems Inc 14679 Midway Ste 101 Dallas TX 75244

CROSSWHITE, JESSIE SOWERS, register of deeds; b. Statesville, N.C., Aug. 9, 1934; d. Neil Sharpe and Jessie Sherrill (Swanson) Sowers; m. William Eugene Crosswhite, June 2, 1956; children: Joseph Neil, Robert Neil, Rebekah c. Perdue. BA, U. N.C., Greensboro, 1953; MA, Wakeforest U., 1961. Loan officer NCNB formerly Merchant & Farmers Bank, Statesville, 1954-58; placement dir. Wake Forest U., Winston-Salem, N.C., 1958-61; acct. exec. High Country Broadcasting, Statesville, 1984-86; county commr. Iredell County, Statesville, 1984-90, register of deeds, 1990—; mem. fin. com. N.C. Assn. County Commrs., Raleigh, 1986-90, mem. Nat. Assn. Counties Fin. Coms., Washington, 1988-90, N.C. govs. adv. com. on devel. disabilities, Raleigh, 1990—. Artist (oil paintings) Snow Bound, 1967, Alaskan Winter, 1968, Autumn in Blue Ridge, 1969, Bass Lake, 1975. Art coun. Statesville & Iredell County, 1975-80; elected ofcl. Iredell County, Statesville, 1984—, bd. health 1984-90; civil svc. bd. City of Statesville, 1981-84; task force on transp. Carolinas Coallition, Charlotte, N.C., 1987—. Mem. N.C. Registers Deeds Assn. (fin. com. 1990—), Nat. Assn. Registers Deeds, Exec. Women's Assn. Republican. Home: 564 Stoney Brook Rd Statesville NC 28677

CROTHERS, JOAN HELSEL, librarian; b. Columbus, Ohio, Feb. 11, 1946; d. Kenneth Drake and Virginia Jane (Rush) Helsel; m. James Swift, Mar. 9, 1968; children: Joshua, Seth. BA in English, U. R.I., 1968, MLS, 1976. Cert. tchr. libr. sci., R.I. Scouting rep. Girls Scouts of R.I., Providence, 1968-70; paraprofl. U. R.I. Libr., Kingston, 1974-77; media specialist Warwick (R.I.) Sch. Dept., 1977-79, Westerly (R.I.) Sch. Dept., Scituate (R.I.) Sch. Dept., 1981--. Dept. dir., adminstr., leader LaLeche League Internat., Franklin Park, Ill., 1973-87, bd. dirs., 1987—; active State Adv. Coun. on Librs., Providence, 1987—; mem. sch. com. South Kingston (R.I.) Sch. Dept., 1985-89, chmn. sch. com., 1989—. Mem. R.I. Assn. Sch. Coms. Home: 953 Tuckertown Rd Wakefield RI 02879 Office: North Scituate School 46 Institute Ln North Scituate RI 02857

CROUCH, BARBARA LEE, human resources management consultant; b. Sebring, Fla., Oct. 8, 1936; d. Elmer Nichols and Emily (Dreiss) Butler; m. Ralph Dean Crouch, Dec. 4, 1931; children: Ralph Dean, Barbara Lee, Clair Christopher, Kelly Andrew. Student, Long Beach City Coll., 1975, Cerritos (Calif.) Coll., 1976; cert. personnel mgmt., UCLA, 1978. Asst. to cons. Merchants and Mfrs. Assn., L.A., 1975-78, library mgr., 1978-80; personnel mgr. TAD Avanti, Inc., Compton, Calif., 1980-82, Ole's Home Ctrs., Pasadena, Calif., 1982-84; staff cons. Merchants and Mfrs. Assn., Tustin, Calif., 1984-85; mgr. inland empire Merchants and Mfrs. Assn., Riverside, Calif., 1986—; lectr., trainer human resource; coord. Inland Empire Legis. Task Force, San Bernardino, Riverside Counties, Calif., 1986; mem. adv. bd. Employer Adv. Coun., Ontario and Riverside, 1985—, Dept. Fair Employment Housing Commn. Regional Round Table, San Bernardino, Riverside Counties, 1985—. Contbr. articles to newsletters and profl. jours. Mem. Inland Empire Liaison Group Inc., San Bernardino, Riverside counties, 1985—. Winner Gold medal Amateur Roller Skating Assn. Am., 1971, 72, 73. Mem. Indsl. Rels. Rsch. Assn. (conf. coord. 1986—, mem. planning bd. 1986—, bd. dirs. 1986—, v.p. 1990), Personnel Indsl. Rels. Assn. (treas. 1981, program chair 1981, 82), Soc. Human Resource Mgmt., Assn. Labor-Mgmt. Adminstrs. and Cons. on Alcoholism, Pomona Valley Personnel Adminstrn. Democrat. Baptist. Home: 24490 Via Del Sol St Moreno Valley CA 92388 Office: Merchants and Mfrs Assn 3600 Lime St Ste 326 Riverside CA 92501

CROUCH, CONSTANCE W., real estate professional; b. Portsmouth, Ohio, May 19, 1941; d. Ellsworth Fremont and Ethel Thelma (Kidd) Waite; m. Harry Randall Crouch, Sept. 12, 1959 (div. 1979); children: Alan Fremont, Jana Katherine. AB, Brown U., 1962, M, 1963; student, U. R.I., 1966, Stetson U., 1973-75. Cert. tchr., Fla. Tchr. Lincoln Sch., Providence, 1963-66, Brevard Community Coll., Cocoa, Fla., 1981, Phillips Jr. Coll., Melbourne, Fla., 1989; mktg. dir. Byrd Pla., Cocoa, 1976; mgr. mktg. Brownell Assocs., Inc., Sarasota, Fla., 1977-88; dir. pub. rels. Easter Seal Ctr., Melbourne, 1988-89; pvt. practice Melbourne, 1990—. Contbr. chpt. to book. Recipient Mktg. and Sales Coord. Yr., SEE mag., 1978-79, Outstanding Mktg. Campaign, 1984. Mem. AAUW (recording sec. 1966-67), Jr. League South Brevard, Melbourne C. of C., Cocoa Beach C. of C., Space Coast Pub. Rels. Assn.

CROUCH, FLORELLA G., quality control professional; b. Dothan, Ala., Oct. 14, 1953; d. Walter Dozier and Shirley Marie (Fussell) C. Labs. supr. Grumman Aircraft Systems, Milledgeville, Ga. Mem. Am. Soc. Nondestructive Testing. Address: 186 Blackcreek Rd Gordon GA 31031

CROUCH, HELEN OLIVE, microbiologist; b. Norwood, N.Y., Nov. 25, 1925; d. William Nelson and Ethel Grace (Austin) C. BS, U. Bridgeport, 1981, MS, 1983. Med. technologist St. Agnes Hosp., White Plains, N.Y., 1958-62, Burke Rehab. Ctr., White Plains, N.Y., 1962-66; technician dept. labs. and research County of Westchester, Valhalla, N.Y., 1966-69, sr. technician, 1969-78, microbiologist II, 1978-84, chief microbiologist, 1984-86, sr. microbiologist, 1986—. Mem. Am. Soc. Clin. Pathologists (assoc., registered med. technologist), Am. Soc. for Microbiology. Office: Westchester County Dept Labs Hammond House Rd Valhalla NY 10595

CROUCH, JENNIFER ELAINE, hospitality management educator; b. Gt. Barrington, Mass., Jan. 1, 1952; d. Donald Wayne and Christine Elizabeth (Wisser) C. BA in Philosophy, U. Minn., 1977; MBA HRI, Mich. State U., 1982; postgrad., Cornell U., 1989—. Baker Bernie's Restaurant & Deli, Mpls., 1978-79; brewery apprentice The James Paine Brewery, Ltd., St. Neots, England, 1981; grad. asst. Mich. State U., E. Lansing, 1980-82; advt. mgr. The F.X. Matt Brewing Co., Utica, N.Y., 1982-84; Choice brand mgr. The F.X. Matt Brewing Co., 1984; freelance writer Utica, Seattle, 1984-86; sales/mktg. coord. Mangetout Catering, Seattle, 1985-86; vis. instr. Schiller Internat. U., Strasbourg, France, 1988; asst. prof. Niagara U., Niagara Falls, N.Y., 1986—; freelance copywriter Restaurant Svc., inc., Seattle, 1986; program author Northwest Cooking & Kitchen Show, Seattle, 1986; seminar speaker/coord. Northwest Culinary Alliance, Seattle, 1985; panelist Annual Nat. Homebrew & Microbrewery Conf., Denver, 1984. Guest editor Northwest Gourmet, 1986; contbr. articles to Modern Brewery Age, 1985-86; columnist The New Brewer, 1984-85. Grad. fellow Mich. State U., 1979-

82, Cornell U., 1989—; Mich. Restaurant Assn. scholar, 1981. Mem. Nat. Restaurant Assn., N.Y. State Restaurant Assn., Zonta. Democrat. Mem. Religious Soc. of Friends. Home: 1805 Slaterville Rd Ithaca NY 14850

CROUCH, JOYCE GREER, educator; b. Jamestown, Tenn., Dec. 25, 1925; d. Porter A. Greer and Cassie L. Hull; m. Dennis A. Crouch (dec. 1961); children: Paul A., Linda K. Crouch Walton. BS, Tenn. Tech. U., Cookeville, 1954; MA, Tenn. Tech. U., Cookesville, 1959; EdD, U. Tenn., Knoxville, 1968. Elem. sch. tchr. Fentress County Sch., Jamestown, Tenn., 1954-59; high sch. English tchr. York Agr. Inst., Jamestown, 1959-66; asst. prof. psychology Appalachian State U., Boone, N.C., 1967-68, assoc. prof., 1969-73, prof., 1974-75, prof. chair dept. psychologist, 1975-87, prof. psychology, 1987--. Author: Perceptual and Motor Skill, 1987, Adolescence, 1988; contbr. articles to profl. jours. Mem. Am. Psychol. Assn., Soc. for Rsch. Child Devel., Delta Kappa Gamma, Phi Kappa Phi. Democrat. Methodist. Home: PO Box 1578 Boone NC 28607

CROUCH, MARGARET ANN, philosophy educator; b. L.A., Apr. 22, 1956; d. Glenn Leroy and Norma Jeanne (Gabehart) C. BA, Colo. State U., 1978; PhD, U. Minn., 1985. Asst. prof. philosophy Villanova (Pa.) U., 1985-87; asst. prof. philosophy Ea. Mich. U., Ypsilanti, 1987—, dir. women's studies, 1990—. Mem. Soc. for Women in Philosophy, Am. Philos. Assn. Office: Eastern Michigan Univ Dept History and Philosophy Ypsilanti MI 48197

CROUCH, MARILEE S., small business owner; b. Tyler, Tex., Mar. 2, 1951; d. John Luther Jr. and Margaret Evelyn (Reynolds) Dove; m. Randy Douglas Crouch, Sept. 21, 1977; children: Andy Douglas, Lori Shannon, Rands Michell. AAS, Eastfield Coll., cert. in mgmt., 1989. Prin. Resource Mgmt. Co., Fate, Tex.; cons. Marilee's Meticulous Moppery, Rockwell, Tex., Penny & Assocs., Rockwell; graphics asst. Eastfield Coll., Mesquite, Tex., computer specialist placement ctr. Campaign chmn. Charles Pitman for Sch. Bd., Mesquite; active Tex. State PTA. Mem. Mesquite C. of C., Eastfield Mgmt. Alumni Assn., Data Processing Mgmt. Assn., Phi Theta Kappa. Home and Office: PO Box 161 Fate TX 75032

CROUCH, MICHELLE ELAINE, advertising executive; b. Indpls., Apr. 24, 1964; d. Robert Andrew and Myrna Ruth (Sailor) O'Neal; m. Larry Paul Crouch, Nov. 12, 1988. BS, U. Indpls., 1987. Prodn. coord. Goldsmith Mktg. Group, Inc., Indpls., 1987—, account coord., 1989—, dir. agy. svc., 1990—. Co-author AIDS Campaign, TV, Just Say No., 1988, Rehab. Campaign, TV, Walk a Mile in My Shoes, 1988. Advt., pub. relations implementations Marion County Reps., Indpls., 1987—; co-chmn. Pan Am. Games Pub. Info. Com., Indpls., summer 1987; com. mem. Leukemia Soc. Indpls., 1989—. Mem. Advt. Club Indpls., Literacy Soc. Indpls. (tutor). Republican. Roman Catholic. Office: Goldsmith Mktg Group 47 S Meridian St Ste 202 Indianapolis IN 46204

CROUSE, LINDSAY, actress; b. N.Y.C., May 12, 1948; d. Russel and Anna (Erskine) C.; m. David Mamet, Dec. 21, 1977. BA, Radcliffe Coll., 1970. Films include Slapshot, Between-the-Lines, All the President's Men, Prince of the City, The Verdict, Daniel, Iceman, Places in the Heart (Acad. award nomination 1985), House of Games, Communion, Desperate Hours, 1990; author: (with David Mamet) The Owl, 1987. Recipient Village Voice Obie award for Acting in Reunion, 1980. Mem. Circle Repertory Co., Atlantic Theater Co. (bd. dirs. 1984—).

CROUT, ELIZABETH ROOP, retired educator; b. Linwood, Md., Aug. 25, 1925; d. John Daniel and Edith Elizabeth (Pfoutz) Roop; m. Alan Lee Crout, Mar. 31, 1951; children: J. Daniel, Peter A., John W., Ruth Ann. BS in Gen. Edn., Manchester Coll., North Manchester, Ind., 1948; postgrad., Miami U., Oxford, Ohio, 1963-87. Med. technologist State of Md., Sykesville, 1945-46, Ch. of Brethren, Castañer, P.R., 1946-47, Middletown (Ohio) Hosp., 1949-53, Hughes Hosp., Hamilton, Ohio, 1956-63; tchr. Middletown Bd. Edn., 1964-87; ret., 1987. Prayer warrior Living Word Ch., 1980—; chmn. Aglow Outreach, 1988—; tutor, Trenton, Ohio, 1987—. Mem. AAUW. Mem. Full Gospel Ch. Home: 5389 Wayne Madison Rd Trenton OH 45067

CROW, CECILE MARIE, sales executive; b. Wichita Falls, Tex., Apr. 21, 1938; d. Edward Patrick and Frances Beatrice (Bruckner) Hopkins. BS in Psychology, North Tex. U., 1971, MS in Social Sci., 1972; postgrad., Columbia U., 1980. Tchr. Eastfield Coll., Dallas, 1972-73; rep. sales Am. Can Co., Dallas, 1973-75; exec. nat. accounts Am. Can Co., Miami, 1975-77; mgr. dist. sales Am. Can Co., Boston, 1977-78; mgr. foodservice mktg. develop. Am. Can Co., Greenwich, Conn., 1978-81; dir. sales devel. James River Corp., Norwalk, Conn., 1981-87; dir. nat. accounts James River Corp., Norwalk, 1987—. Grantee North Tex. U., 1971. Mem. Internat. Foodsvc. Mfrs. Assn., Platform Speakers of Am. (bd. dirs.). Office: James River Corp 800 Conn Ave PO Box 6000 River Park Norwalk CT 06856

CROW, ELIZABETH SMITH, publishing company executive; b. N.Y.C.; d. Harrison Venture and Marlis (deGreve) Smith; m. Charles P. Crow, Mar. 2, 1974; children: Samuel Harrison, Rachel Venture, Sarah Gibson. B.A., Mills Coll., 1968; postgrad., Brown U., 1969-70. Editorial asst. New Yorker mag., N.Y.C., 1968-69; editorial asst., exec. editor New York mag., N.Y.C., 1970-78; pres., editorial dir. Parents mag., N.Y.C., 1978-88; pres. Gruner & Jahr USA Pub., 1988—; free-lance book reviewer N.Y. Times Book Rev. and Washington Post Book World; v.p. Editors' Organizing Com., 1982—; screener, judge Nat. Mag. Awards, 1984—. Mem. media adv. coun. March of Dimes; mem. mng. com. Alternative Def. Project; mem. bd. advisors The Giraffe Project; trustee Mills Coll., 1986—; bd. dirs. YWCA of N.Y., Met. Opera Guild. Mem. Am. Soc. Mag. Editors (exec. bd.), Mag. Pubs. of Am. (bd. dirs.). Democrat. Club: Cosmopolitan. Office: Gruner & Jahr USA Pub 685 3rd Ave New York NY 10017

CROW, LESLIE ELLEN, public historian; b. Kenosha, Wis., Apr. 11, 1954; d. Robert Findlay and Dorothy Virginia (Taylor) Crow; m. Thomas Peter Hora, Sept. 20, 1980. BA with honors, U. of the Pacific, 1978. Archival asst. Holt-Atherton Pacific Ctr. for Western Studies, Stockton, Calif., 1978-79; hist. inventory coord. City of Vacaville (Calif.), 1979-80; hist. preservation specialist Cen. Sierra Planning Coun., San Andreas, Calif., 1980-82; reader San Joaquin Delta Coll., Stockton, Calif., 1981—; docent vol. San Joaquin County Hist. Soc., Lodi, Calif., 1987—; photographer Locher tool collection project San Joaquin County Hist. Soc., Lodi, 1990; hist. preservation cons. Barnett-Range Developers, Stockton, 1980, Grupe Devel. Co., Stockton, 1980, Woodbridge (Calif.) lodge 131 Masons, 1988; hist. researcher Yosemite Natural History Assn., Yosemite Valley, Calif., 1984. Author: Preston School of Industry Pacific Historian, 1979; editor (newsletter) San Joaquin County Hist. Soc. & Mus., 1985—, (index) Pacific Historian, 1986, 87. Chair Stockton Cultural Heritage Bd., 1990—; tutor Stockton Libr. Literacy Project, 1985-89. Alumni fellow U. of the Pacific, 1980. Mem. AAUW, San Joaquin County Hist. Soc. and Mus., U. of the Pacific Soc. of Alumni Fellows, Phi Kappa Phi. Home and Office: 9364 Kirkby Circle Stockton CA 95210

CROW, LYNNE CAMPBELL SMITH, insurance company executive; b. Buffalo, Oct. 13, 1942; d. Stephen Smith and Jean Campbell (Ruggles) Hall; m. William David Crow II, Apr. 16, 1966 (div. Dec. 1989); children: William David III, Alexander Fairbairn, Margaret Campbell. BA, Sweet Briar (Va.) Coll., 1964; postgrad., Am. Coll., 1986. CLU. Claims rep. Liberty Mut. Ins. Co., Bklyn. and N.Y.C., 1964-66; with McGraw-Hill Corp., N.Y.C., 1966-67; claims rep. Liberty Mut. Ins. Co., East Orange, N.J., 1967-68; sales assoc. Realty World/Allsopp Realtors, Millburn, N.J., 1981-82; field rep. Guardian Life Ins. Co., Millburn, 1982—. Bd. dirs. Jr. League of the Oranges and Short Hills, Millburn, 1979-80, Millburn LWV, 1979-80; campaign chair, bus. chair, bd. dirs. United Way of Millburn/Short Hills, 1981-88, 90—. Mem. Assn. Chartered Life Underwriters and Chartered Fin. Cons., Newark Assn. Life Underwriters (bd. dirs. 1986—, sec. 1987-88, treas. 1988-89, 3d v.p. 1989-90, 2nd v.p. 1990-91), Million Dollar Round Table (qualifying mem.), Women's Life Underwriters Confedn., Jr. League the Oranges and Short Hills, Internat. Platform Assn. (Nat. Quality award, Nat. Health award). Republican. Episcopalian. Home: 22 The Crescent Short Hills NJ 07078 Office: Ferrara Assocs 181 Millburn Ave Millburn NJ 07041

CROW, MARY LYNN, educator, psychologist; b. Denton, Tex., Aug. 30, 1934; d. Herman G. and Harriett (Copeland) Cox; m. Charles H. Farmer; 1 child, Karl F. Student, Monticello Coll., Alton, Ill., 1952-53; BA, Tex. Christian U., 1956, MEd, 1967; PhD, U. North Tex., 1970. Cert. tchr., Tex.; lic. psychologist, Tex., Mass. Tchr. Ft. Worth and Tyler (Tex.) pub. schs., 1956-59, Romper Room Internat. TV Kindergarten, Dallas, Ft. Worth, 1961-67; counselor Hurst-Euless-Bedford (Tex.) pub. schs., 1967-68; adj. prof. counselor edn. U. N. Tex., Denton, 1970-76; asst. prof. edn. U. Tex., Arlington, 1970-72, assoc. prof., 1973-77, prof., 1978—, dir. faculty devel. resource ctr., 1973-85; pvt. practive psychology Ft. Worth, 1973—. Author: Teaching on Television, 1977; co-author: Faculty Development in Southern Universities, 1976; contbr. articles to acad. publs. bd. dirs., past pres. Dispute Resolution Svcs. of Tarrant County, 1984—; bd. dirs., chmn. scholarship com. Tarrant County Mental Health Assn., 1986—. Named Outstanding Tchr., Amoco Found., 1972, Piper Prof. of Tex., 1975, Face of Arlington, Arlington Daily News, 1976, Female Newsmaker of Yr., Arlington Citizen Jour., 1975, Woman of Yr., Bus. and Profl. Women's Club, 1988. Mem. Tarrant Psychol. Assn., Tex. Psychol. Assn., Am. Psychol. Assn., Profl. and Orgnl. Devel. Network in High Edn. (pres. 1977-78). Office: U Tex Ctr Profl Tchr Edn Box 19227 Arlington TX 76019

CROWDER, ANITA PAULINE, pottery executive; b. Springfield, Mo., Dec. 5, 1933; d. Robert P. and Mildred E. (Goodnight) Henry; m. William M. Crowder, Dec. 5, 1952; 1 child, Michael Lee. Student, S.W. Mo. State U., 1951-52, Drury Coll., 1980. Typesetter Ind. Printing Co., Springfield, 1950-74; sales person R.L. Polk, Springfield, 1979; art instr. Springfield City Park Bd., 1980-82; artist Springfield News, Springfield Leader, 1983; owner, tchr. Studio South Art Coop., Springfield, 1982-84; owner Terra Cotta Creations, Springfield and Nixa, Mo., 1984—; chmn. state conv. Mo. State China Painters Assn., Springfield, 1979. Author: Springfield Coloring Book, Sesquicentennial edit. (recognition award). Decor designer Dem. Com. Reception for First Lady Carter, Springfield, 1980, Dem. Com. Reception for Pres. Carter, Springfield, 1980. Republican. Baptist. Office: Terra Cotta Creations Rte 2 Box 160-5 Nixa MO 65714

CROWDER, BARBARA LYNN, lawyer; b. Mattoon, Ill., Feb. 3, 1956; d. Robert Dale and Martha Elizabeth (Harrison) C.; m. Lawrence Owen Taliana, Apr. 17, 1982; children: Paul Joseph, Robert Lawrence. BA, U. Ill., 1978, JD, 1981. Bar: Ill. 1981. Assoc. Louis E. Olivero, Peru, Ill., 1981-82; asst. state's atty. Madison County, Edwardsville, Ill., 1982-84; ptnr. Robbins & Crowder, Edwardsville, 1985-87, Robbins, Crowder & Bader, Edwardsville, 1987-88, Crowder & Taliana, 1988—. Chmn. City of Edwardsville Zoning Bd. Appeals, 1986-87; committee woman. Edwardsville Dem. Precinct 15, 1986—; mem. City of Edwardsville Planning Commn., 1985-87. Named Best Oral Advocate, Moot Ct. Bd., 1979, Outstanding Young Career Woman, Dist. XIV. Ill. Bus. and Profl. Women, 1986; recipient Alice Paul award Alton-Edwardsville NOW, 1987; named Outstanding Working Woman of Ill. Ill. Fed. of Bus. and Profl. Women, 1988-89. Mem. ABA, Ill. Bar Assn., Assn. Trial Lawyers Am., Women Lawyers Assn. Met. East (v.p. 1985, pres. 1986), LWV, Edwardsville Bus. and Profl. Women's Club (Woman of Achievement 1985, Jr. Service award 1987, pres. 1988-89, treas. 1989—), U. Ill. Alumni Assn. (bd. dirs. Metro East chpt. 1989-90), Phi Alpha Delta. Democrat. Home: 982 Surrey Dr Edwardsville IL 62025 Office: Crowder & Taliana 216 N Main Edwardsville IL 62025

CROWDER, ELIZABETH See WADDINGTON, BETTE HOPE

CROWELL, CAROL ANN, communications company infosystems specialist; b. St. Petersburg, Fla., Aug. 19, 1958; d. John Richard and Dolores (Pavick) C. BA in English, Western Carolina U., 1980, MA in English, 1982. Graduate asst. Western Carolina U., Cullowhee, N.C., 1980-82; editorial asst. Creative Computing Ziff-Davis, N.Y.C., 1984-85; assoc. editor Yourdon Press, N.Y.C., 1985-86; editor production Simon and Schuster Brady Books, N.Y.C., 1986-87; mng. editor Software Div. Simon and Schuster, N.Y.C., 1987-88; mng. editor software Harper & Row, N.Y.C., 1988—. Contbr. articles to jours. Mem. Women's Nat. Book Assn., Software Profl. Developers Assn., Boston Computer Soc. Office: Harper and Row Inc 10 E 53d St New York NY 10022

CROWELL, ROSEMARY ELAINE, criminal justice professional; b. Monroe, N.C., Sept. 14, 1942; d. Frederick Perry and Berthenia (Alexander) C. AA, Clinton Jr. Coll., 1961. Mem. staff Betty Bacharach Home Afflicted Children, Atlantic City, 1964-66, Murdoch Ctr., Butner, N.C., 1964-66; cottage parent N.C. Dept. Human Resources, Butner, 1966-68, cottage parent, then cottage mgr. C.A. Dillon Sch. div. youth svcs., 1968-82; asst. unit adminstr. N.C. Dept. Human Resources, 1982—. Del. to Dem. Nat. Conv., Atlanta, 1988; Dem. precinct chmn., Butner, 1989; active Dem. presdl. candidate campaigns, 1988. Mem. Nat. Abortion Rights Action League, Elks. Episcopalian. Home: 1004 East F St Butner NC 27509

CROWFOOT, BARBARA LYNNE, educational consultant; b. Hammond, Ind., Nov. 17, 1945; d. Donald Leo and Helen Frances (Spurrier) Frick; m. John Christopher Crowfoot, June 14, 1979; children: Adrian John, Amy Lynne. BS, Colo. State U., 1967; MA, U. Colo., 1974. Cert. tchr., Colo. Tchr. Sch. Dist. 11, Colorado Springs, Colo., 1967-73, substitute tchr., 1976-78; adult adviser State Student Coun. Leadership Camp, Ft. Collins, Colo., 1980-88; substitute tchr. Poudre R-1 Sch. Dist., Ft. Collins, 1985-89, enrichment aide, 1989—; spokesperson Edn. Quality for Able Learners, Ft. Collins, 1986—; appointee Colo. Commn. Jud. Discipline, Denver, 1987-91, Ft. Collins Liquor Licensing Authority, 1989-93. Dem. precinct coord., Larimer County, 1979-84, house dist. dir., 1984-87; county coord. govs. race, 1985-86, 89-90; campaign coord. city coun. races, 1987, 89. Named Vol. of Yr., Gov. of Colo., 1986. Mem. AAUW (program chair 1989-91, edn. chmn. 1988-91), Colo. Assn. Gifted and Talented (Parent of Yr. award 1987). Roman Catholic. Home: 1733 Concord Dr Fort Collins CO 80526

CROWL, MARTHA JEAN, nurse; b. Cleve., June 13, 1941; d. Thomas Laird and Bernice (Pugh) C. Diploma in Nursing, M.B. Johnson Sch. Nursing, Elyria, Ohio, 1962; postgrad., Baldwin Wallace Coll., Berea, Ohio, Cuyahoga Community Coll., Parma, Ohio. RN, Ohio, N.C.; cert. quality assurance profl. Asst. head nurse, instr. Lakewood (Ohio) Hosp., 1963-71; corp. quality assurance dir. Carolina Eye Assocs., Southern Pines, N.C., Va., 1971-76; operating room supr. Luth. Hosp., Cleve., 1976-80; assoc. dir. surgery services Moore Meml. Hosp., Pinehurst, N.C., 1981-83; asst. dir. nursing Community Med. Ctr., Marion, Ohio, 1983-84; adminstr. and project coordinator Dr. John Marquardt Eye Clinic, Mansfield, Ohio, 1984-85; nat. quality assurance dir. MediVision, Inc., Boston, 1985-86; nurse cons., quality assurance dir. Carolina Eye Assocs., Southern Pines, N.C., 1981-88; corp. quality risk mgr. Eye Am., N.C. and Va., 1988—; surgical asst. adv. bd. Cuyahoga Community Coll., 1967-72; dir. operating room tech. program Fairview Gen. Hosp., 1971-76; faculty mem. Ambulatory Surgical Ctr. lecture series Carolina Eye Assocs., 1983-85; chairperson Sandhills Multi-Inst. Rev. Bd.; lectr. in field. Contbr. articles to profl. jours. Mem. Cleve. Orch. Womens Com., 1976-81; 1983; exec. bd. Great Lakes Festival Women's Com., 1976-81; bd. dirs. Health Fair, Marion, 1983. Mem. Assn. Operating Room Nurses, Assn. Opthalmic RNs, Am. Assn. Allied Health Personnel in Opthalmology, We. Res. Hist. Soc., Am. Soc. Health Care Risk Mgmt., Nat. Assn. Quality Assurance Profls. Democrat. Office: Carolina Eye Assocs 2170 Midland Rd PO Box 250 Southern Pines NC 28387

CROWLEY, ELIZABETH MARLENE, management consultant; b. LeCenter, Minn., Dec. 30, 1940; d. Roman Aloysius and Elizabeth Winifred (Cummings) Malinski; m. John Patrick Crowley, Aug. 3, 1963; children: Elizabeth J., John S., Ann B. BS in English, History, Mankato State U., 1960; MS in Orgn. Devel., U. Wis., Green Bay, 1985. English instr. various schs., Minn., Calif., Wis., 1960-69; communications instr. Northeast Wis. Tech. Coll., Green Bay, 1973-74, human resources devel. cons., coordinator, 1974-83; pres. Human Resources Devel. Cons., Green Bay, 1979-83; exec. dir. Fin. Mgmt. Concepts, Green Bay, 1983-85; asst. to pres. Univ. Bank, Green Bay, 1983-85; pres. Crowley, Lautenbach & Assocs., Green Bay, 1985—. Contbr. articles to profl. jours. Dir. Brown County Hist. Soc., Green Bay, 1978-85, YMCA, Green Bay, 1978. Mem. Assn. Mgmt. Cons. (v.p. 1987—), Am. Assn. Univ. Women (v.p. 1969-83), Am. Soc. Tng. and Devel., Ind. Bus. Assn. Wis. Roman Catholic. Office: Crowley Lautenbach & Assocs PO Box 24032 Green Bay WI 54324-4032

CROWLEY-LONG, KATHLEEN, psychology educator; b. Troy, N.Y., Sept. 18, 1958; d. Martin Joseph and Katherine Anna (Saur) Crowley; m. Kenneth Joseph Long, Aug. 30, 1980; 1 child, Samuel Frederick Long. BA, Syracuse U., 1980; MS, SUNY, Albany, 1983, PhD, 1987. Asst. prof. psychology Coll. of St. Rose, Albany, N.Y., 1986—; presenter Internat. Conv. on Teaching Psychology, 1990. Contbr. articles to profl. jours. Rsch. mini-grantee Coll. of St. Rose, 1989. Mem. Am. Psychol. Assn. (presenter nat. conv. 1989), Northeast Ednl. Rsch. Assn. Office: Coll of Saint Rose 432 Western Ave Albany NY 12203

CROWN, NANCY ELIZABETH, retail executive; b. Bronx, Mar. 27, 1955; d. Paul and Joanne Barbara (Newman) C.; children: Rebecca, Adam. BA, Barnard Coll., 1977, MA, 1978, MEd, 1983; postgrad., Nova Law Sch., 1989—. Cert. tchrs. Tchr. Sachem Sch. Dist., Holbrook, N.Y., 1978-82; dir. mail order dept. Haber-Klein, Inc., Hicksville, N.Y., 1984-86; mgr. mdse., dir. ops. Sure Card Inc., Pompano Beach, Fla., 1988-89. Mem. Fla. Assn. Women Lawyer's (adminstrv. asst.), Phi Alpha Delta. Democrat. Jewish. Club: Barnard of L.I.

CROWTHER, CHRISTY LYNN, nurse, trauma consultant; b. Ogden, Utah, Jan. 4, 1958; d. Kenneth Bert and Barbara Joyce (Thornblad) C. AS, Weber State Coll., Ogden, Utah, 1977; BSN, U. Utah, 1981; MS, U. Md., 1987. RN, Utah, Md.; cert. critical care nurse, adult nurse practitioner. Nurse III, Johns Hopkins Hosp., Balt., 1977-81; nurse McKay-Dee Hosp., Ogden, 1980-81; nurse, unit tchr., critical care recovery unit Md. Inst. Emergency Med. System, Balt., 1981-87, lectr. trauma prevention program, 1983-87; nurse practitioner infectious diseases Shock Trauma Assocs., P.A., Balt., 1987—; nurse practitioner in infectious disease U. Md. Hosp., B, 1987—. Contbg. author: Case Studies in Trauma Nursing, 1989. Pub. communications dir. Ch. of Jesus Christ of Latter-day Saints, Annapolis, Md., 1984-89; merit badge counselor Boy Scouts Am., Balt., 1987—. Mem. Sigma Theta Tau, Phi Kappa Phi. Home: 10 Brenda Ct Severna Park MD 21146-3604 Office: U Md Hosp Infectious Dis 22 S Greene St Baltimore MD 21201

CROXFORD, LYNNE LOUISE, social services administrator; b. Schenectady, N.Y., Nov. 9, 1947; d. Frederick William and Elizabeth Elger (Irish) C.; BA, Kalamazoo Coll., 1969; MPA, Wayne State U., 1975; m. Daniel Roderick Talhelm; 2 children, Alan Frederick, Thomas Arthur. Caseworker dept. social svc. County of Calhoun, Battle Creek, Mich., 1969-70; caseworker, supr. County of Oakland, Pontiac, Mich., 1970-76; program specialist Mich. Dept. Social Svcs., Lansing, 1976-78; exec. coord. for programming Mich. State Planning Coun. for Devel. Disabilities, 1978-79; staff coord. Gov. Com. on Unification of Pub. Mental Health System, Lansing, 1979-80; dir. dept. social svc. County of Ingham, Lansing, 1980-90; dir. fin. control Mich. Dept. Social Svcs., 1990—; adv. Mich. Assn. Non-Profit Residential Facilities, 1976-78. Trustee, Unitarian Universalist Ch. of Greater Lansing, 1979-82, v.p., 1980-82; bd. dirs. Coun. for Prevention Child Abuse and Neglect, 1980-83; mem. Lansing Tri-County Pvt. Industry Coun., 1980-90; chair Pvt. Industry Coun. Steering Com., 1987-90. Mem. Am. Soc. Pub. Adminstrn. (nat. coun. 1986—), Am. Pub. Welfare Assn., Michigan County Social Svcs. Assn. Club: Zonta (charter Mich. Capitol area). Recipient Disting. Alumnus award Wayne State U. Grad. Program in Pub. Adminstrn., 1988. Contbr. in field. Home: 531 Gainsborough Dr East Lansing MI 48823 Office: 235 S Grand PO Box 30037 Lansing MI 48909

CROZAZ, GHISLAINE, earth and planetary sciences educator; b. Brussels, Aug. 31, 1939; came to U.S., 1969; m. Robert M. Walker, Aug. 24, 1973. PhD, Free U. Brussels, 1967. Charge' rsch. Fonds Nat. Recherche Scientifique, Belgium, 1967-71; rsch. assoc. Washington U., St. Louis, 1969-73, asst. prof. earth and planetary scis., 1973-76, assoc. prof., 1976-82, prof., 1982—; mem. lunar and planetary sci. rev. panel NASA, 1977-79; mem. meteorite working group NSF, 1981-85. Assoc. editor Proc. Lunar Planetary Sci. Conf., 1974, 77, 80, Jour. Geophys. Rsch., 1983-86; contbr. numerous articles to sci. jours. Recipient Stas-Spring award Royal Acad. and Chem. Soc., Belgium, 1967, Antarctic Svc. medal NSF, 1982. Fellow Meteoritical Soc. (coun. 1978-82); mem. Geochem. Soc., Am. Geophys. Union. Office: Washington U Box 1169 One Brookings Dr Saint Louis MO 63130

CROZIER, LUCILLE BREEDING, civic worker; b. Springfield, Ill., June 7, 1907; m. Alfred Crozier (dec.); 2 children. AB, U. Pitts., 1934, MLitt, 1946. Contbr. articles to med. aux. publs. Pres. Pa. Med. Aux., 1956-57; parliamentarian AMA Med. Aux., 1970-71; trustee U. Pitts., 1971-77. Recipient medal of distinction U. Pitts., 1987. Mem. AAUW (pres. Pa. 1958-60), Disting. Daus. Pa. (pres. 1975-76, medal of distinction 1963), Coll. Club (pres. 1960-62), 20th Century Club (lecture chmn. 1985-87), Pi Kappa Delta. Home: 4601 5th Ave Apt 820 Pittsburgh PA 15213

CROZIER, PRUDENCE SLITOR, economist; b. Boston, Oct. 27, 1940; d. Richard Eaton and Louise (Bean) S.; m. William Marshall Crozier, Jr., June 20, 1964; children: Matthew Eaton, Abigail Parsons, Patience Wells. B.A. with honors, Wellesley Coll., 1962; M.A. in Econs., Yale U., 1963; Ph.D. in Econs., Harvard U., 1971. Research asst. Fed. Reserve Bank, Boston, 1963-64; teaching fellow-tutor Harvard U., Cambridge, Mass., 1966-69; instr. Wellesley Coll., Mass., 1969-70; sr. economist Data Resources Inc., Lexington, Mass., 1973-74; bd. dirs. Mass. Health and Ednl. Facilities Authority, 1985—, Omega Fund, 1984-87. Contbr. article to profl. jour. Trustee Newton Wellesley Hosp., Mass., 1978—; overseer Center Research on Women, Wellesley, 1982-83; trustee Wellesley Coll., 1980—. Mem. Am. Econ. Assn., Boston Econ. Club, Phi Beta Kappa. Home: Ridge Hill Farm Rd Wellesley MA 02181

CRUDEN, JOAN PATRICIA, marketing representative; b. Bklyn., Aug. 18, 1951; d. Vincent Julius and Josephine (Mietla) Dudar; m. Walter Cruden, Sept. 1971 (div. 1984). BA cum laude, U. Houston, 1979. Sales sec. E.F. Hutton, N.Y.C., 1969-70, CBS, N.Y.C., 1970-75; sales asst. Physio Control, Ft. Worth, 1976-78; mktg. rep. IBM Corp., Houston, 1979—. Republican. Home: 1669 S Voss #145 Houston TX 77057 Office: IBM Corp 2 Riverway Houston TX 77056

CRUICKSHANK, SHEILA ETHEL, farmer; b. Ilford, Essex, Eng., June 26, 1937; came to U.S., 1956; d. Lesley Edward Richard and Ethel Maud (Davage) Bradley; m. Alfred William Cruickshank, May 26, 1956 (dec. 1984); children: Carol Ann Cruickshank Hoffman, William Alfred. Student, St. Mary's Convent, South Woodford, Essex. Bookkeeper Swiss Travel Service, London, 1954-56; co-owner Al Cruickshank Farming, Woodland, Calif., 1964-84; owner Cruickshank Farms, Woodland, 1984—. Coordinator, tchr. religious edn. St. Paul's Parish, Knights Landing, Calif., 1985—, pres. Altar Soc., 1986—. Democrat. Roman Catholic. Clubs: Priscilla (pres. 1978-79), Yolo Thursday (pres. 1978-79).

CRULL, LINDA BEFELD, library director; b. Beaumont, Tex., July 23, 1947; d. Rudolph Frank and Lillian (Moore) B.; m. R. Jerald Crull, Aug. 3, 1985. BA, Baylor U., 1968; MEd in Librarianship, Bridgewater U., 1973; Cert. in Early Childhood Edn., U. Denver, 1979. Cert. tchr., Tex., Fla. Ga. Tchr. Latin Travis High Sch., Austin, Tex., 1968-69, Valdosta (Ga.) Christian Sch., 1969-70; tchr. Latin and English Port St. Joe (Fla.) High Sch., 1970-71; head spl. collections Sturgis Libr., Barnstable, Mass., 1971-79; children's libr. Arvada (Colo.) Pub. Libr., 1979-80, Mt. Carmel Sch., Houston, 1983-86; publishers rep. Grolier (Colo.) Ednl. Corp., 1980-83; children's libr., head youth svcs. Mobile (Ala.) Pub. Libr., 1986-89; dir. libr. Foley (Ala.) Pub. Libr., 1989—; cons. in field. Author: (short story) Once Upon A Time, 1988; storyteller Cherokee Rose Festival, 1987, 89, Bayside Yarnspinner, 1988, Nat. Congress, 1989, Nat. Storytelling Festival, 1990, Optimist Clubs, Rotarians, Foley Civic League, numerous others. Mem. ALA (conv. com. and reading com. 1987—), Nat. Assn. for Preservation and Perpetuation of Storytelling (founder, chair So. chpt.), Nat. Story League (founder Mobile chpt. 1986), Jubilee Story League (founder), Assn. Records Mgrs. (exec. com. 1979-80), Colo. Media Assn. (pres. 1982-83). Mem. Ch. of Religious Sci. Home: PO Box 1514 Fairhope AL 36533 Office: Foley Pub Libr 319 E Laurel Ave Foley AL 36525

CRUMBO, MINISA, artist; b. Tulsa, Sept. 2, 1942: d. Woodrow and Lillian (Hogue) C.; student Tex. Western U., El Paso, 1961-62, U. Colo., Boulder, 1970-71, Taos (N.Mex.) Acad. Fine Arts, 1972-74, Sch. Visual Arts, N.Y.C.,

1974-75, Wasatch (Utah) Acad.; children—Woody Carter, Cris Carter. One-woman shows: Gilcrease Inst. Am. History and Art, Tulsa, 1976, Tulsey Town Gallery, Tulsa, 1975, USSR, 1978-79, Roy Clark Ranch Party-TV Spl., 1976, Pottawatomie Agrl. and Cultural Center, Shawnee, Okla., 1977, Okla. Gov.'s Spl. Showing, 1976, Adobe Gallery, Las Vegas, 1977; traveling exhbn. Indian Art Show, U. Oreg., 1977; other exhbns.; Pushkin Mus., Moscow, Montreux (Switzerland) Jazz Festival, 1979, Harwelden, Tulsa, 1979, Oklahoma City U., 1981, Independence (Kans.) Community Coll., 1981, Native Am. Women in Art, Kans. Mus. History, 1984, Native Am. Women Show, Indian Ter. Gallery, Sapulpa, Okla., 1985, Exhbn. Mus. Ethnography, Budapest, Hungary, 1988; represented in permanent collections at Heard Mus., Phoenix, Gilcrease Inst. Am. History and Art, Philbrook Art Center, Tulsa, U. Tulsa Art Center, Pushkin Mus., Moscow, Wasatch Acad., Oklahoma City U., Baker U., Baldwin, Kans., Independence (Kans.) Community Coll., also pvt. collections in U.S. and Europe; guest artist instr. Taos Pueblo Day Sch. Center; designer, instr. Native Am. Studies program Wasatch Acad., Utah. Recipient Graphics award for pencil drawing Creek Woman, 29th Am. Indian Exhbn. at Philbrook Art Center; Disting. Alumni award Wasatch Acad., 1980; Disting. Service award Baker U., 1982. Home: 17351 Sunset Blvd #403 Pacific Palisades CA 90272-4198 Office: PO Box 4003 Beverly Hills CA 90213

CRUMB-WOLFE, BRENDA JEAN, chemical engineer; b. Colorado Springs, Colo., May 10, 1962; d. DeWayne William and Candace (Hertneky) Crumb; m. Paul Hamilton Wolfe, Aug. 2, 1986; 1 child, Jeffrey L. BS in Chem. Engring., Colo. Sch. Mines, 1984. Sales engr. Nalco Chem. Co., Vernal, Utah, 1985-86; applications engr. Nalco Chem. Co., Midland, Tex., 1986-88; project engr. Eagle-Picher Industries, Colorado Springs, 1988-89, program mgr., 1989—. Judge Colo. Youth awards. Mem. AAUW (bd. dirs. 1989—), Am. Inst. Chem. Engrs., U.S. Volleyball Assn. (team rep.), Colo. Volleyball Ofcls. Assn. Democrat. Office: Eagle Picher Industries 3820 S Hancock Expwy Colorado Springs CO 80911

CRUMP, CONSTANCE A., journalist; b. Detroit, Aug. 20, 1948; d. William B. and Marion A. (Wass) C. BA, U. Mich., 1969. Pers. asst. Detroit Free Press, 1970; gen. mgr. Kitchen Port Inc., Ann Arbor, Mich., 1970; acct. Carty's Music Co., Ypsilanti, Mich., 1971, U. Cellar Inc., Ann Arbor, 1972-80; freelance writer Ypsilanti, 1980-82; sr. feature writer Ann Arbor News, 1982-89; fin. reporter Crain's Detroit Bus., 1989—. Contbr. articles to local newspapers and nat. mags. including Billboard, Weightwatchers, Art and Antiques Weekly, Ohio Antiques Rev., Detroit Free Press, Detroit Mo.; restaurant reviewer Detroit Mo. Mag. Mem. Culinary Historians of Am., Detroit Area Art Deco Assn., Preservatoin Wayne, Mich. Theater Found., The Ark Coffeehouse, Ann Arbor Art Assn. (dir.), Am. Inst. Wine and Food, Les Amis Du Vin, Ypsilanti Heritage Found. Office: Crain Communications Inc 1400 Woodbridge Detroit MI 48207

CRUMPACKER, CAROL A., advertising executive; b. Springdale, Ark., Dec. 6, 1958; d. Ralph Crumpacker and Mozelle R. Knoll. BS, U. Ark., 1982. Mktg. rep. Jones Truck Lines, Springdale; customer rels. specialist ATC Long Distance, Fayetteville, Ark.; br. mgr. Comtel Systems, Inc., Fayetteville, Ark.; ptnr., co-owner The Advantage Group Advt. Agy., Inc., Springdale. Mem. Univ. Baptist Ch. Mem. Beta Sigma Phi. Home: 304 S Gutensohn Springdale AR 72764

CRUSE, EMILY E., data processing executive; b. Gainesville, Fla., June 18, 1952; d. Lemmie C. and Gladys Jones C. Tech. support/system operator MCI, Dallas; night ops. Omega Optical, Dallas; internal/remote systems operator Nat. FSI, Dallas; system adminstr. Hartford Inc. Co., Dallas. Home: 2912 White Oak Dr Plano TX 75074

CRUSE, IRMA BELLE RUSSELL, writer; b. Hackneyville, Ala., May 3, 1911; d. Charles Henry and Nellie Dunn (Ledbetter) Russell; m. Jesse Clyde Cruse, Dec. 22, 1931; children: Allan Baird, Howard Russell. Student, Birmingham So. Coll., 1927-28; corr. student, U. Chgo., U. Wis., U. Minn., intermittently 1958-68; AB, U. Ala., 1976; MA in English, Samford U., MA in History, 1984. With So. Bell and successor South Cen. Bell, Birmingham, Ala., 1928-44, 54-76, pub. rels. supr., 1965-68, rate supr., 1968-76; free lance writer, 1956—. Editor: The Ala. Bapt. Historian, 1986-89; contbr. articles to various publs. Bd. dirs. Festival of Arts, Birmingham, 1970-73, Birmingham Council Christian Edn.; v.p. Birmingham Council Clubs, 1973-74; pres. Jefferson County Radio and TV Council, 1971-72; mem. Gov.'s Commn. Employment of Handicapped; chmn. oral history program Ala. Bapt. Hist. Commn., 1985-89; clk. Mt. Brook Bapt. Ch., 1986-88. Recipient numerous awards including Freedoms Found., 1967-69, Silver Bowl for Lit. award Birmingham Festival of Arts, 1988; named Beautiful Activist, 1972; named to Ala. Voter Hall of Fame, 1986, Ala. Bapt. Historian of Yr., 1990. Mem. AAUW (chmn. women's work/women's worth Birmingham chpt. 1987-89), Birmingham Bus. Communicators, Ala. Writers' Conclave (pres. 1973-74), Met. Bus. and Profl. Women (pres. 1970-71, woman of achievement 1970-71), Women in Communications (pres. 1970-71), Birmingham Bus. Communicators (pres. 1968-69), Telephone Pioneers Am. (editor newsletter 1970-74, pres. Birmingham South Life Mem. Club 1986-87, historian Ala. chpt. 1987-90), Ala. State Poetry Soc. (program chmn. 1972-74, editor newsletter 1976-78), Women's C. of C. (2d v.p. 1978-79), Ala. Bapt. Hist. Commn., Freedoms Found. of Valley Forge, Birmingham Geneal. Soc., Salvation Army Women's Aux. (chaplain 1988-89), Women's C. of C., Nat. Soc. Am. Pen Women (1st v.p. programs 1988-90), Arlington Hist. Assn., Quota Club of Birmingham (pres. 1976-77), Sigma Tau Delta, Phi Kappa Phi, Phi Alpha Theta. Home: 136 Memory Ct Birmingham AL 35213

CRUVER, SUZANNE LEE, director resource development; b. Indpls., Mar. 24, 1942; d. William Edward and Margaret Rosetta (McArtor) Ozzard; m. Donald Richard Cruver, June 9, 1963 (div. Feb. 1989); children: Donald Scott, Kimberly Sue, Brian Richard. BA in English, Rutgers U., 1964; postgrad., Rice U., 1990—. Asst. dir. pub. rels. dept. Upsala Coll., East Orange, N.J., 1964-65; asst. planner, pub. editor N.J. Div. State & Regional Planning, Trenton, 1967-68; realtor Vonnie Cobb Realtors, Houston, 1979-81; exec. v.p., mktg. mgr. Photoflight Aviation Corp., Sugar Land, Tex., 1982; exec. v.p., artist mgr. H. McMillan Orgn., Inc., Sugar Land, 1983-85; account exec. Mel Anderson Communications, Inc., Houston, 1986; exec. dir. Ft. Bend Arts Coun., Sugar Land, 1986-87; dir. resource devel. vol. svcs., pub. info. Richmond (Tex.) State Sch. Mental Health/Mental Retardation, 1987—; mem. adv. bd. Ft. Bend Regional Coun. on Alcoholism and Drug Abuse, Rosenburg, Tex., 1989—. Writer, editor: PATCH Handbook: A Parent to Parent Guide to Texas Children's Hospital, 1983, Ft. Bend mag., 1985-86. Pres. Ft. Bend Arts Coun., Ft. Bend County, Tex., 1987-89; founding dir. PATCH, Tex. Children's Hosp., Houston, 1982. Mem. Nat. Soc. Fundraising Execs., Women in Communications, Inc., Ft. Bend Profl. Women, NAFE, Pub. Rels. Soc. Am., Houston World Trade Assn., Ft. Bend C.of C., Rosenberg/Rich C. of C., Leadership Tex. Alumni Assn. Republican. Methodist. Office: Richmond State Sch 2100 Preston Richmond TX 77469

CRUZ, CATHERINE STANNIE, apparel designer; b. Houston, Sept. 22, 1960; d. Lauro and Clarice (Sebesta) C. BS in Home Econs., U. Tex., 1983. Asst. designer Tobria, Dallas, 1984-86; pattern maker Sunny-South, Dallas, 1986-89; asst. designer Hairston-Roberson, Dallas, 1989—. Recipient Designer award Natural Fibers Commn., 1984. Mem. BBNC Club. Home: 6024 Lewis Dallas TX 75206 Office: Hairston-Roberson 5106 Redfield Dallas TX 75235

CRUZ, NORMA OROPESA, microscopic module processor; b. Bangued, The Philippines, July 9, 1943; came to U.S., 1966; d. Cresencio O. Oropesa and Gertrudis B. Valeros; m. Roberto F. Cruz Jr., May 14, 1969; children: Roberto C. III, Robert Alexander, Robert Jeremy. Cert. phys. therapy tech., Anderson Sch. Sci. Massage, Princeton, Ill., 1976; AA, R.I. Jr. Coll., Warwick, 1980; BA, Salve Regina Coll., 1983, MA, 1986. Phys. therapy technician Our Lady of Lourdes Hosp., Manila, 1961-65; supr. dept. phys. therapy Flagstaff-Beaver Aux. Hosp., Killam, Alta., 1966-69; cen. supply technician Newport Hosp., R.I., 1969-79; asst. to prof. Salve Regina Coll., Newport, 1981-86; caseworker Martin Luther King Ctr., Newport, 1986; module processor Raytheon Submarine Signal Div., Portsmouth, R.I., 1987—. Mem. Filipino Am. Assn. (v.p. 1983-87). Home: 1 D Rolling Green Rd Newport RI 02840

CRUZ, SHERRY LARAINE See ANGELINI, SHERRY LARAINE

CRYAN, ALLISON FOIL, management consultant; b. Homer, La., Dec. 29, 1961; d. Robert Rodney and Patti Sue (Thomas) Foil; m. James Nixon Cryan, June 18, 1987. BA, Rice U., 1983. System engr. Electronic Data Systems, Dallas, 1983-85; technical staff Software Design Assocs., N.Y.C., 1985-86; sr. cons. Price Waterhouse, N.Y.C., 1986-88, mgr., 1988-90, sr. mgr., 1990—. Home: 109 S Main St Yardley PA 19067

CSAPOSS, JEAN FOX, English and religion educator; b. N.Y.C., Mar. 13, 1931; d. John Edward and Elizabeth Marie (Lynch) Fox; m. James Csaposs, Apr. 25, 1981. BA, Manhattanville Coll., 1953, MA, 1971; MA, Columbia U., 1954. Tchr. English, history Acad. of the Holy Angels, Ft. Lee, N.J., 1954-57; asst. in pub. info. Manhattanville Coll., Purchase, N.J., 1958-66, dir. pub. rels., 1966-69, dir. devel. svcs., 1969-72; editor, mgr. publs. AAUW, Washington, 1972-77; spl. asst. to asst. sec. for pub. affairs U.S. Dept. HHS, Washington, 1977-82; lectr. English, religion Bergen Community Coll., Paramus, N.J., 1985—; cons. Bergen County (N.J.) Spl. Svcs. Sch. Dist., 1989—. Editor, contbr. mag. and newspaper of AAUW (annual awards from Ednl. Press Assn., 1973-77). Bd. trustees Manhattanville Coll., Purchase, 1987-90; bd. dirs. Bergen County coun. Girl Scouts U.S., 1989—. Recipient Disting. Alumni award Manhattanville Coll., 1978. Mem. Nat. Coun. Tchrs. English, N.J. Coll. English Assn., Reading Reform Found., Heightened Independence and Progress (bd. dirs. 1988—, v.p. 1989—, pres. 1990—), Nat. Soc. Fund Raising Execs., Columbia U. Alumni Club Bergen-Passaic Counties (v.p. 1989—). Democrat. Roman Catholic. Home: 644 Wyoming Ave Maywood NJ 07607 Office: Bergen Community Coll 400 Paramus Rd Paramus NJ 07652

CUBINE, MARGARET VIRGINIA, retired educator; b. Flinstone, Ga., Mar. 28, 1919; d. Ralph Darrell and Anna Lou-Genia (Morgan) C. AB, LaGrange Coll., 1939; MA in English, U. N.C., 1944; MA in Religion, Northwestern U., 1947; BD, Garrett Theol. Sem., 1949; PhD, Northwestern U., 1955. Tchr. English Chattanooga Valley High Sch., 1939-42; tchr. English Bethany High Sch., Reidsville, N.C., 1942-43; instr. English Reinhardt Coll., Waleska, Ga., 1943-45; instr. English, religion Ward-Belmont, Nashville, 1947-50; instr. English Martin Coll., Pulaski, Tenn., 1947; asst. prof. religion Aurora (Ill.) Coll., 1952-53, Huntingdon Coll., Montgomery, Ala., 1953-55; prof. English, religion LaGrange (Ga.) Coll., 1955-61; prof. religion Erskine Coll., Due West, S.C., 1961-89. Mem. Amnesty Internat. Mem. AAUW (various local offices 1965—), Am. Acad. Religion (regional pres. 1976), Assn. for Clin. Pastoral Edn. (clin.), Mental Health Assn. (pres. 1984). Democrat. Presbyterian. Home: 18 Depot St PO417 Due West SC 29639

CUDDEHE, JUDITH LINK, quality assurance engineer; b. Reading, Pa., June 28, 1961; d. Carl Walter and Miriam Ruth (Kline) Link; m. John Gerard Cuddehe, Feb. 18, 1989. BA in Orgn. Behavioral Sci. with honors, Nat. Coll. Edn., 1988; postgrad., Strayer Coll., 1989—. Cert. in cryptographic tech. USAF. Communications electronics officer, fgn. svc. U.S. Dept. State, Washington, 1986-87, engring. project mgr., 1987-90; sect. chief engring. testing, quality assurance U.S. State Dept., 1990—. Vol. counselor Spl. Friends, Cheyenne, Wyo., 1982, rape crisis ctr. YWCA, Cheyenne, 1982-85, YWCA Unwed Mothers' Home, Cheyenne, 1984-85. Sgt. USAF, 1981-85. Decorated Air Force Longevity Svc. medal, Good Conduct medal, Small Arms Expert Marksmanship medal. Mem. NAFE, Woodbridge Art Guild. Lutheran.

CUDLIPP, ALICE VERNER, healthcare executive; b. Richmond, Va., Nov. 1, 1941; d. Joseph Henry and Mary Irene (Mills) C. BA, Bridgewater (Va.) Coll., 1962; MA, U. Richmond, 1968; postgrad. U. Va., Nova U. Tchr., dept. head Chesterfield (Va.) County Pub. Schs., 1967-71, Nansemond County Pub. Schs., Va., 1962-67; instr. Va. Commonwealth U., 1968-71; lectr. in residence, U. Va., 1973-74; v.p. Smithdeal-Massey Coll., Richmond, 1975-78; instr. J. Sargeant Reynolds Coll., Richmond, 1982-84; asst. to v.p. patient services Columbia Hosp., Milw., 1982-84; pres., chief exec. officer Med. Placement Services Inc., Milw., 1984—; pres. Cons. Resources, Inc., Richmond, 1974-81; gen. ptnr. Courtland Ltd., Richmond, 1981—; pres., chief exec. officer Shafer Rand Assocs., Inc., Glendale, Wis., 1987—; dir. David A. Linney, Inc., Milwaukee, 1987—; cons. and lectr. in field. Dir. Interfaith Programs, Milw.; v.p., bd. dirs. Shoreline Interfaith Outreach To The Elderly, Shorewood, 1988—. Mem. Clovernook Homeowners Assn.; ruling elder North Shore Presbyn. Ch., Shorewood, Wis., 1988—. Named one of Outstanding Young Women of Am., U.S. Jaycees, 1974; Nat. Sci. Found. fellow Longwood Coll., 1964; DuPont fellow U. Va., 1972. Mem. Columbia Coll. Nursing Alumni Assn. (chmn. 1984-85), Nat. League Nursing, Southeastern Wis. Home Health Assn., Assn. Profl. Saleswomen, Am. Mgmt. Assn., Nat. Assn. for Home Care, Wis. Home Care Orgn., NAFE, Am. Pub. Health Assn., Wis. Women Entrepreneurs, Wis. Assn. of Healthcare Staffing (pres. 1989), Rotary, Phi Delta Epsilon, Alpha Psi Omega, Delta Kappa Gamma. Office: Med Placement Services Inc 710 N Plankinton Ave Milwaukee WI 53203

CULBERSON, CHICITA FRANCES, botany educator, chemist; b. Phila., Nov. 1, 1931; d. Alfred Gilbert and Frances Eva (Cieman) Forman; m. William Louis Culberson, Aug. 24, 1953. BS, U. Cin., 1953; MS, U. Wis., 1954; PhD, Duke U., 1959. Rsch. assoc. in chemistry Duke U., Durham, N.C., 1959-61, sr. rsch. assoc. in botany, 1961-80, lectr., 1971-80, adj. prof., 1980—. Author: Chemical and Botanical Guide to Lichen Products, 1969, (with others) 2d supplement Chemical and Botanical Guide to Lichen Products, 1977. Mem. AAAS, Am. Chem. Soc., Bot. Soc. Am., Phi Beta Kappa, Sigma Xi. Office: Duke U Dept Botany Durham NC 27706

CULBERT, JOYCE LAURA, securities analyst, accountant; b. Cornwall, Ont., Can., Apr. 1, 1945; came to U.S., 1947, naturalized, 1980; d. Aubrey Kennedy Culbert and Denise Isabel (Moreland) White; m. Robert William Salmon, Dec. 16, 1967 (div. 1971). BS in Anthropology, Hunter Coll., 1972; MBA in Fin., NYU, 1977. CPA, Ill.; chartered fin. analyst. With Blyth Eastman Dilloan, 1972-74, Mfrs. Hanover Bank, 1974-76, Prudential Ins. Co., Newark, 1976-78, No. Trust Bank, Chgo., 1978-80, Kemper Fin. Co., Chgo., 1980-85; securities analyst S.G. Warburg Securities, Inc., N.Y.C., 1986—. Mem. AICPA, Soc. Chartered Fin. Analysts. Republican. Methodist. Office: SG Warburg Securities Inc 787 7th Ave New York NY 10019

CULBRETH, LUANN JANINE, educational consultant; b. Chattanooga, Sept. 26, 1961; d. Richard M. and Dorothy I. (Jones) Carter; m. Stephen A. Culbreth, Mar. 20, 1982. AS, Chattanooga State Coll., 1981; B Med. Sci., Emory U., 1984; MEd, Ga. State U., 1986. Registered radiologic technologist. Staff radiol. technologist Emory U. Hosp., Atlanta, 1981-84; instr. Sch. Radiology Grady Meml. Hosp., Atlanta, 1984-87; instr. Magnetic Resonance Imaging Magnetic Resonance Edn. Ctr., 1987—; mem adv. bd. Chattanooga State Coll., 1988—. Judge Ga. Occupational Award of Leadership, Atlanta, 1985-86. Mem. NAFE, Am. Soc. Radiologic Technologists, Ga. Soc. Radiologic Technologists (faculty speaker student and grad. technologists' seminar 1988, 90), Soc. for Magnetic Resonance Imaging, Atlanta Soc. Radiologic Technologists, Assn. Educators in Radiol. Scis. Republican. Baptist. Home: 1376 Oakengate Dr Stone Mountain GA 30083 Office: Magnetic Resonance Edn Ctr Emory U PO Box 23853 Atlanta GA 30322

CULLEN, HELEN FRANCES, mathematician, educator; b. Boston, Jan. 4, 1919; d. James Francis and Letitia Ellen (Johnson) C.; AB, Radcliffe Coll., 1940; MA, U. Mich., 1944, PhD, 1950. Asst. engr. Gen. Electric Co., Lynn, Mass., 1940-43; teaching fellow U. Mich., 1946-49; asst. prof. math. U. Mass., Amherst, 1949-56, assoc. prof., 1956-71, prof., 1971—. Sec. Hadley (Mass.) Dem. Town Com., 1976-84. Mem. Am. Math. Soc., Am. Phys. Soc., Math. Assn. Am., Sigma Xi. Unitarian. Author: Introduction to General Topology, 1968; contbr. articles to math. jours. Home: 92 Rocky Hill Rd PO Box 321 Hadley MA 01035 Office: U Mass Math Stats Dept Lederle Towers Amherst MA 01003

CULLEN, KATHLEEN CHRISTINA, parking consultant; b. Detroit, Mich.; d. James Patrick and Catherine C. (Moffatt) C.;m. Gerald R. Heinrich, July 10, 1954; (div. 1975); children: Catherine, Bridget, Deirdre, Maureen, Kurt. BA, Detroit Found. Sch. Music, 1957. V.p. D. J. Babcock, Inc., St. Clair Shores, Mich., 1965-76; mktg. mgr. Rich & Associates, Inc., Southfield, Mich., 1977-79; consumer rsch. mgr. Volkswagen of Am., Englewood Cliffs, N.J., 1980-83; v.p. Babcock/Frank & Assocs., Santa Monica, Calif., 1983-88; regional mgr. Rich & Associates, Inc., Marina del Rey, Calif., 1988--. Mem. Inst. Mcpl. Parking Congress, Soc. for Mktg. Profl. Svcs., Calif. Public Parking Assn.; Calif. Yacht Club. Office: Rich & Assocs 310 Washington St #103P Marina del Rey CA 90292

CULLEN, LINDA JO KROZSER, marketing executive; b. Cleve., May 29, 1955; d. Joseph James and Elsie Ruth (Boros) K. BA in Psychology, Marietta Coll., 1977; MBA, Ohio State U., 1980. Sales rep. Procter & Gamble, Akron, Ohio, 1977-79; market research asst. Gen. Mills, Inc., Mpls., 1981-82, market research asst. mgr., 1982-85; market research mgr. Tropicana Products, Inc., Bradenton, Fla., 1985; market research mgr. Pillsbury Co., Mpls., 1985-88, assoc. dir., 1988—. Chmn. com. bd. mgmt. Downtown YMCA, Mpls., 1983—. Mem. Am. Mktg. Assn., MBA Assn. (pres. 1980). Roman Catholic. Home: 5355 East St White Bear Lake MN 55110 Office: Pillsbury Ctr MS 29U9 Minneapolis MN 55402

CULLEN, MARYGAEL, tourism administrator; b. Springfield, Ill., Sept. 30, 1951; d. Loren Matthew and Mary Kathryn (Daley) Cullen; m. James Michael Veselenak, Sept. 3, 1983; 1 child, Devin Michael. AA, Springfield Coll., 1971; BA in Mgmt., Sangamon State U., 1980. Asst. coordinator for spl. events Ill. Dept. Conservation, Springfield, 1980-83; chief pub. info. officer Ill. Hist. Preservation Agy., Springfield, 1983-90; dir. tourism Springfield Conv. and Visitors Bur., 1990—. Recipient managerial competency and achievement award Wall St. Jour., 1980. Mem. Women in Communications Inc. (pres. 1988-89, v.p. communication 1987-88), Women in Govt., Pub. Relations Soc. Am. Roman Catholic. Office: Springfield Conv/Visitors 109 N 7th St Springfield IL 62701

CULLER, CHERYLE FAYE LEACH, civil engineer; b. Jamestown, Ohio, June 15, 1955; d. Charles Ritenour and Garnet Faye (Arnold) Leach; m. Lawrence Robert Culler, Aug. 25, 1979; children: Christen Faye, Kevin Robert. BS in Civil Engring., U. Dayton, 1977. Registered profl. engr., Ohio, Ind. Project engr. Cen. Foundry div. Gen. Motors Corp., Defiance, Ohio, 1977-80; resident engr. Amax Coal-Minnehaha Mine, Sullivan, Ind., 1980-85; mgr. Ace Equipment Co., Antwerp, Ohio, 1985-87; asst. chief engr. City of Ft. Wayne (Ind.), 1987-90; dir. ops. Ace Equipment Co., Antwerp, Ohio, 1990—. Mem. Nat. Soc. Profl. Engrs., Ohio Soc. Profl. Engrs., Am. Water Works Assn., Nat. Assn. Female Execs. Republican. Office: Ace Equipment Co Route 1 Box 30 Antwerp OH 45813

CULLER-PENNEY, ANNETTE LORENA, writer, public relations executive; b. Cordele, Ga., July 1, 1916; d. Jake Phillip Haynes Culler Sr. and Maude Burke; m. Robert A. Penney. BBA, So. Ga. Coll., 1942, George Wash. U., 1956; postgrad., Am. U., 1961-62; diploma, Lewis Hotel Sch., 1978. News reporter Fairchild Publ., Washington, 1946-61; pres. Internat. Mktg. Communications, Inc., Upperville, Va., 1966—. Author: Dirksen, The Golden Voice of the Senate, 1978; co-author: Private Lives In Public Wars. Mem. Internat. Home Fashions League (pres. 1952-53, v.p. 1961-62), Piedmont Rep. Women (v.p. 1984-85, pres. 1986-87), Women's Nat. Press Club (3rd v.p. 1954), Am. Newswomen's Club (v.p. 1960). Baptist. Home and Office: Internat Mktg & Communications Inc Rte #1 Box 1 Upperville VA 22176

CULLINGFORD, HATICE S., chemical engineer; b. Konya, Turkey, June 10, 1945; came to U.S., 1966; d. Ahmet and Emine (Kadayifcioglu) Harmanci. Student, Mid. East Tech. U., 1962-66; BS in Engring. with honors, N.C. State U., 1969, PhD, 1974. Registered profl. engr., Tex.; cert. mgr. Statis. clk. Rsch. Triangle Park Inst., 1966; reactor engr. AEC, Washington, 1973-75; spl. asst. ERDA, Washington, 1975; mech. engr. Dept. Energy, Washington, 1975-78; staff mem. Los Alamos Nat. Lab., 1978-82; sci. cons. Houston, 1982-84; ECLSS test bed mgr. Johnson Space Ctr., NASA, Houston, 1984-85, sr. project engr. advanced tech. dept., 1985-86, sr. staff engr. div. solar system exploration, 1986-88, asst. div. advanced devel., 1988—; mem. internal adv. com. Ctr. for Nonlinear Studies Los Alamos Nat. Lab., 1981; organizer tech. workshops, sessions at soc. meetings; lectr. in field. Editor, author tech. reports; contbr. articles to profl. jours.; patentee in field. Mem. curriculum rev. com. U. N.Mex., Los Alamos, 1980. Recipient Woman's badge Tau Beta Pi, 1968, ERDA Spl. Achievement award, 1976, Inventor award Los Alamos Nat. Lab., 1982, Group Achievement award Johnson Space Ctr., NASA, 1987; Cities Svc. fellow, 1969-72. Mem. AIAA (organizer, 1st chmn. in-space life support com. Houston chpt. 1988—), Am. Nuclear Soc. (sec.-treas. fusion energy div. 1982-84, vice chmn. South Tex. sect. 1984-86, mem. local sects. com. 1986-88), Am. Inst. Chem. Engrs. (organizer, 1st chmn. No. N.Mex. club 1980-81, chmn. low-pressure processes and tech. 1981-89), Am. Chem. Soc., Fusion Power Assocs., Soc. for Risk Analysis (organizer, sec. Lone Star chpt. 1986-88, chmn. soc. publicity 1990—), No. N.Mex. Chem. Engrs. Club, Engrs. Coun. Houston (councilor, sec. energy com.), Sierra Club, Houston Orienteering Club, Phi Kappa Phi, Pi Mu Epsilon. Office: NASA Lyndon B Johnson Space Ctr Mail Code SN11 Houston TX 77058

CULLUM, GAY NELLE, government executive; b. Belton, Tex., Mar. 10, 1952; d. Thomas Clarence Brewster and Lillian Robertina (Howell) Stoker. AA in Acctg., Danville (Ill.) Area Community Coll., 1979; BA in Mgmt., Sangamon State U., 1985. Aviation machinist mate, airman USN, Cecil Field, Fla., 1973-75; voucher auditor/fiscal accounts clk. VA Med. Ctr., Danville, 1977-79, air condition ops. mechanic, 1979-84; mgr., co-owner Field Constrn., Danville, 1984-86; dir. victim assistance program Vermilion County State's Atty. Office, Danville, 1986-88; pricing specialist Valmont Electric Co., Danville, 1988-90; regional mgr.Champaign region div. of child support State of Ill., 1990—. Paraprofl. counselor/cons. for incest survivors, founder, coord., facilitator and speaker incest self-help group YWCA, Danville; Ensign USN, 1973-75. Named Outstanding Young Am. Woman, 1986. Home: 3127 Golf Cir Danville IL 61832

CULMER, CARA LEE, internist; b. Mpls., Nov. 22, 1949; d. William J.A. and Doris (Pitula) C. BA, U. Minn., 1971; MD, U. Ill., Chgo., 1983. Internist Ill. Masonic Med. Ctr., Chgo., 1986—. Office: Women's Health Resources 1003 W Wellington Chicago IL 60657

CULOTTA, DENISE FERN, owner public relations firm, consultant, writer; b. Jersey City, June 1, 1958; d. Robert Redler and Barbara P. (Rosenberg) Telymonde; m. Joseph V. Culotta Jr., Nov. 22, 1980; 1 child, Brittany Michelle. BA in Speech, Theatre, Communications, Monmouth Coll., West Long Branch, N.J., 1980. Communications mgr. The Bloom Cos., Dallas, 1980-85; account exec. Freda Gail Stern Pub. Rels., Dallas, 1985-86; dir. pub. rels. Homsey Advt. and Pub. Rels., Dallas, 1986-87; owner DFC Communications, Dallas, 1987—. Contbr. poetry Monmouth Lit. Rev., 1979. 5th v.p. pub. rels. Dallas Children's Advocacy League, 1990—. Mem. Pi Kappa Delta. Office: DFC Communications 14275 Midway #220 Dallas TX 75244

CULP, MILDRED LOUISE, corporate executive, expert on living and the work-place; b. Ft. Monroe, Va., Jan. 13, 1949; d. William W. and Winifred (Stilwell) C. BA in English, Knox Coll., 1971; AM in religion and literature, U. Chgo., 1974, PhD The Com. on History of Culture, 1976. Coll. faculty, adminstr., 1976-81; dir. Exec. Résumés, Seattle, 1981—; pres. Exec. Directions Internat., Inc., Seattle, 1985—. Columnist, Seattle Daily Jour. Commerce, 1982-88, featured on TV and radio; contbr. articles and book revs. to profl. jours.; syndicated radio program WorkWise, 1990—. Admissions advisor U. Chgo., 1981—; mem. Knox Coll. Alumni Network, 1990—; mem. Nat. Alliance Mentally Ill of Hamilton County, 1984—, bd. dirs., 1987, adv. bd. 1988; mem. A.M.I. Hamilton county, 1984—; founding mem. People Against Telephone Terrorism & Harassment, 1990—. Recipient Knox Coll. Alumni Achievement award, 1990. Mem. Network Exec. Women, U. Chgo. Puget Sound Alumni Club. Office: Exec Directions Internat Inc 3313 39th Ave W Seattle WA 98199

CULPEPPER, JERRI LEA, periodical editor; b. Tulsa, Sept. 20, 1958; d. William Franklin and Betty Joene (Winnard) C. BA in Journalism, U. Okla., 1983. Reporter, columnist The Norman (Okla.) Transcript, 1980-88; writer, editor News Svcs. U. Okla., Norman, 1988—. Editor U. Okla. newsletter, 1988— (exceptional achievement award Coun. Advancement and

Support Edn. 1988-89). Recipient cert. of merit Norman Arts and Humanities Coun., 1989. Mem. AAUW (pub. info. officer 1989-90), Galaxy Fedn. Writers. Democrat. Home: 1228 Camden Way Norman OK 73069-5302 Office: Univ Okla 900 Asp Ave Norman OK 73019-0401

CULVER, FLORENCE MORROW, volunteer; b. Central Lake, Mich., Nov. 27, 1915; d. Robert Edmund Morrow and Roxana Grace Wilkinson; m. Charles Beach Culver, Oct. 1935 (dec. Sept. 1967); children: Sara Roxana, Eric Charles; m. Clair Lawrence Magoon, July 23, 1977. Student, Detroit (Mich.) Bus. Sch. Vol. group leader Recovery, Inc., Bloomfield Hills, Mich., 1964—; producer United Cable TV, Channel 52 for Rochester Symphony Concerts. Vol. pres. Huntington Woods (Mich.) Study Club, 1967-69; vol. pres., founder Rochester (Mich.) Symphony Guild, 1978-80, publicity chmn. currently; vol. pres. Rochester (Mich.) Symphony Bd., 1982-84, corr. sec. currently. Recipient Spl. Tribute, Mich. State Legislature, 1986. Democrat. Unitarian. Home: 719 Apple Hill Ln Rochester Hills MI 48064

CULVERHOUSE, RENEE DANIEL, management educator, university official; b. Tuskegee, Ala., Nov. 10, 1950; d. Gerald Lee and Janelle (Dyson) Daniel; m. Charles E. Culverhouse III, May 27, 1978; 1 child, Danielle Renee. BA in Fgn. Langs., Auburn U., 1972, postgrad., 1972-73; JD, Cumberland Sch. Law, 1978. Bar: Ala., 1979. Assoc. Dinsmore, Waites & Stovall, Birmingham, Ala., 1978-81; asst. prof. mgmt. Auburn U., Montgomery, Ala., 1981-86, assoc. prof., 1986—, undergrad. coord., 1985-88, asst. vice chancellor for acad. affairs, 1989—; cons. EEOC. Montgomery, 1983-84. Abstract editor Jour. Direct Mkgt.; contbr. numerous articles on employment law to profl. jours. Mem. adv. bd. Montgomery AIDS Outreach. Mem. Atlantic Mktg. Assn., Am. Bus. Law Assn., Ala. Acad. Scis., So. Bus. Law Assn., Southeastern Bus. Law Assn., Southwestern Social Scis. Assn., Pi Sigma Epsilon. Home: 651 Carol Villa Dr Montgomery AL 36109 Office: Auburn U Acad Affairs Office Montgomery AL 36117

CULVERWELL, ROSEMARY JEAN, educator, principal; b. Chgo., Jan. 15, 1934; d. August John and Marie Josephine (Westermeyer) Flashing; m. Paul Jerome Culverwell, Apr. 26, 1958; children: Joanne, Mary Frances, Janet, Nancy, Amy. BEd, Chgo. State U., 1955, MEd in Library Sci., 1958; postgrad., DePaul U., 1973. Cert. supr., tchr. Tchr. Otis Sch., Chgo., 1955-59; tchr., libr. Yates Sch., Chgo., 1960-61, Nash Sch., Chgo., 1962-63, Boys Chgo. Parental, 1969-72, Edgebrook and Reilly Schs., Chgo., 1965-67; counselor, libr. Reilly Sch., Chgo., 1968, tchr., libr., asst. prin., 1973, prin., 1974—. Pres. Infant Jesus Guild, Park Ridge, Ill., 1969-70; troup leader Girl Scouts U.S., Park Ridge, 1967-69; sec. Home-Sch. Assn., Park Ridge, 1969, v.p. spl. projects, 1970. Recipient Outstanding Prin. award Citizens Schs. Com., Chgo., 1987, For Character award, 1984-85, Whitman Award for Excellence in Edn. Mgmt., 1990. Mem. AAUW, LWV (chmn. speakers bur. 1969), Delta Kappa Gamma, Phi Delta Kappa. Home: 1929 S Ashland Ave Park Ridge IL 60068 Office: FW Reilly Sch 3650 W School St Chicago IL 60618

CUMMINGS, BETTY ELLEN, manager; b. Tecumseh, Mich., Oct. 31, 1940; d. Merle Leroy and Emily Patricia (Smith) C. BA, Siena Heights Coll., 1982. Cert. profl. sec. Sec. Gruner Corp., Jackson, Mich., 1959-60; office mgr. Autohaus-Jackson, Inc., Jackson, 1960-66; sr. sec. The Univ. Mich., Ann Arbor, 1966-68, prin. sec., 1968-75, exec. sec., 1975-82, adminstrv. assoc., 1982-86, adminstrv. mgr., 1986—. Author: Wellness and Working, 1981, What Does CPS Really Mean, 1979. Sec. Manchester (Mich.) Area Hist. Soc., 1985—. Named Sec. of the Year Jackson/Albion Chpt., 1973. Mem. Profl. Secs. Internat. (div. pres. 1978-79, div. v.p. 1977-78, div. recording sec. 1976-77), CPS Acad., Irish/Am. (treas. 1985—). Home: 8220 Grossman Rd Manchester MI 48158 Office: The Univ Michigan 1301 Beal Ave Ann Arbor MI 48109-2122

CUMMINGS, CONSTANCE, actress; b. Seattle; d. Dallas Vernon and Kate Logan (Cummings) Halverstadt; m. Benn Wolfe Levy, 1933; children: Jonathan, Jemina. Chmn. Young People's Theatre Panel; mem. Arts Council, 1963-69. Broadway debut Treasure Girl, 1928; London debut Sour Grapes, Repertory Players, 1934; film debut Movie Crazy, 1932; appeared on radio, TV, films, theatre; joined Nat. Theatre Co., 1971; appeared in London stage prodns.: Madame Bovary, 1937; Romeo and Juliet, 1939, Saint Joan, 1939, The Petrified Forest, 1942, Return to Tyass, 1950, Lysistrata, 1957, The Rape of the Belt, 1957, Who's Afraid of Virginia Woolf?, 1964, Justice is a Woman, 1966, Fallen Angel, 1967, Nat. Theatre Co., A Long Day's Journey Into Night, 1972, The Cherry Orchard, 1973, The Circle, 1975, Mrs. Warren's Profession, Vienna, 1976, Wings, U.S., 1978, London, 1979 (Tony award 1979), Hay Fever, 1980, The Golden Age, 1981, The Chalk Garden, N.Y.C., 1982, The Glass Menagerie, N.Y.C., London, 1984, The Glass Menagerie, 1985, (one woman show) Fanny Kemble, 1986, Crown Matrimonial, 1987, others; performed in Claudel-Honnegar oratorio St. Joan at the Stake, Albert Hall, London, 1949, Peter and the Wolf, Albert Hall, 1955, Wings on Am. pub. TV; dir. Royal Ct. Theatre. Recipient Obie award, 1979, Drama Desk award, 1979; decorated Comdr. Brit. Empire. Mem. Brit. Actors Equity (mem. council), Royal Soc. for Encouragement of Arts and Commerce. Mem. Labour Party. Club: Chelsea Arts.

CUMMINGS, DIANA K., financial investment executive; b. Battle Creek, Mich., Jan. 17, 1943; d. James Harry and Frances Virginia (Garrett) Prill; m. Robert George Pershing, Sept. 16, 1961 (div. Jan. 1989); m. Martin John Cummings, Aug. 12, 1989; children: Carolyn Frances, Robert James Lester. Student, Kent (Ohio) State U., 1967. Real estate sec. Village Realty, Glen Ellyn, Ill., 1975-76, rep. real estate, 1976-77; real estate sales Crown Realty, Glen Ellyn, 1977-79; corp. sec. Teltrend Inc., St. Charles, Ill., 1979-88; also bd. dirs. Teltrend Inc.; pres. Teltrend Inc., Villa Park, Ill., 1985—; also bd. dirs. DKP Prodns. Inc., Villa Park, Ill. Mem. NAFE, NARAS, Nat. Assn. Ind. Record Distbrs. Office: DKP Prodns 739 N Harvard Villa Park IL 60181

CUMMINGS, ELIZABETH VERONICA, travel consultant; b. Northampton, Mass., Feb. 4, 1962; d. George Francis and Elizabeth Anne (LaValle) Cummings. AS in Travel Mgmt., Daniel Webster Coll., Nashua, N.H., 1983. With Carroll Travel Bur., Amherst, Mass., 1983-85, Council Travel Svcs., Amherst, 1985-87, Magicworld Travel, Springfield, Mass., 1987; travel cons. Global Travel Agy., Westfield, Mass., 1987-89; asst. mgr. Village Travel Ctr., South Hadley, Mass., 1989—. Chmn. City of Northampton Rep. Com., 1985-89, treas. 1989—; asst. registrar Northampton, 1989—; mem. Rep. Nat. Com., 1984—. Mem. Mass. Fedn. Young Rep. Roman Catholic. Home: 16 Dewey Ct Northampton MA 01060 Office: Village Travel Ctr 29 College St South Hadley MA 01075

CUMMINGS, ERIKA HELGA, personal financial planner; b. Offenbach, Fed. Republic Germany; came to U.S., 1978; d. Erwin and Edith (Trunski) Maier; m. Robert H. Cummings, Dec. 1970; 1 child, Marisa Anne. BSBA, Calif. State U., Bakersfield, Calif.; M in Internat. Mgmt., Am. Grad. Sch. Internat. Mgmt., Glendale, Ariz., 1983. Inflight supr. TWA, Paris; internat. ops. mgr. Cooper LaserSonics, Santa Clara, Calif.; sales mgr. Oaks Club, Osprey, Fla.; personal fin. planner IDS Fin. Svcs., Sarasota, Fla. Mem. NAFE, Toastmasters, Beta Gamma Sigma. Office: IDS Fin Svcs One Sarasota Tower Ste 604 2 N Tamiami Trail Sarasota FL 34236

CUMMINGS, JANIS MARIE STAHL, educator; b. San Angelo, Tex., May 16, 1936; d. Linus Adolph and Olivia Margaret (Nesbitt) Stahl; m. Billy Murl Cummings, Feb. 3, 1961. AA, San Angelo Coll., 1963; diploma, Inst. Childrens' Lit., 1975; BS in Elem. Edn., Angelo State U., 1977, educable mentally retarded cert., 1977. Tchr. day care ctrs. Community Action Coun., San Angelo, 1973-75; tchr.'s aide, active various ednl. programs San Angelo Ind. Sch. Dist., 1963-73, resource rm. tchr., 1977—. Author: (poetry) The Thought of Things, 1975; writer song lyrics. Past mem. Ronald Reagan Congl. Victory Fund, Ronald Reagan Rep. Ctr., Ronald Reagan Presdl. Found., Rep. Nat. Com.; life mem. Rep. Task Force. Mem. NEA, Tex. State Tchr.'s Assn. faculty rep. 1987-88, 88-89), Classroom Tchr.'s Assn., Assn. for Supervision and Curriculum Devel. Roman Catholic. Home: 1826 Wyoming Ave San Angelo TX 76904 Office: San Angelo Ind Sch Dist 1621 University San Angelo TX 76904

CUMMINGS, JOSEPHINE ANNA, advertising executive; b. Gainesville, Fla., July 12, 1949; d. Robert Jay and Marcella Dee (Mount) Cummings; m. David Allan Pitts, June 9, 1975 (div. Sept., 1988). A.B.J./Design cum laude, U. Ga., Athens, 1971. Copywriter William Cook, Jacksonville, Fla., 1971-73; creative dir. Leo Burnett, Chgo., 1973-76; sr. v.p., group creative dir. Needham Harper & Steers, Chgo., 1976-84, Saatchi-Saatchi Compton, N.Y.C., 1984; exec. creative dir. Ted Bates, N.Y.C., 1984; exec. v.p., chief creative officer Tracy-Locke, Dallas, 1985-87; exec. creative dir. Bozell, Chgo, 1989; mem. Y&R, N.Y.C., 1990—. Author: (play) Azaleas, 1988, (short story collection) Crimes of Passion, 1988, (childrens' book) The Hospital is a Funny Place, 1988, (novel) Pulling The Plug, 1988, (short film) Night Magic, 1989. Named as creator One of Hundred Best TV Commls. Advt. Age, 1978-79, one of Advt. 100 Best Advt. Age, 1986, one of People to Watch Fortune mag., 1986, one of Best and Brightest Advt. Age, 1985; recipient Andy award of Excellence Advt. Club N.Y., 1981, Merit award Art Dirs. Club, 1982. Mem. Dallas Communications Coun., Ninety Niners Club. Office: Y&R 285 Madison Ave New York NY 10017

CUMMINGS, MARIE ELLEN, product development supervisor; b. Phila.; d. Joseph Alvord and Thelma May (Schlosser) Lirio; m. Daniel Edward Cummings, Sept. 13, 1986. BS in Food Sci., U. Del., 1984. Food technician Tastykake, Inc., Phila., 1982-83; food technologist Gen. Foods, Dover, Del., 1984, Theresa Friedman & Sons, Inc., Phila., 1984-87; product devel. supr. Sanofi Bio-Industries, Inc., Phila., 1987-90. Patentee in field. Mem. Inst. Food Techologists (profl.), Nat. Women Execs. Republican. Roman Catholic. Home: 524 Old Elm St Conshohocken PA 19428

CUMMINGS, MARY DAPPERT, communications executive, business owner, teacher; b. Carbondale, Ill., Sept. 22, 1922; d. Anselmo Fulton and Edith (Spates) Dappert; m. Robert Louis Cummings, Apr. 28, 1968 (dec. Sept. 1978). AB, Cornell U., 1943, M in Indsl. Labor Rels., 1950; MEd, SUNY, Albany, 1948. Cert. English tchr., N.Y. Copywriter Gen. Electric Co., Schenectady, N.Y., 1945-47; editor co. newspaper Winthrop-Stearns Pharm. Co., Rensselaer, N.Y., 1948-49; indsl. rels. asst. E.R. Squibb & Sons, New Brunswick, N.J., 1950-52; personnel mgr. Milliken & Co., N.Y.C., 1952-55; asst. dir. personnel rsch., supr. written communications Equitable Life Assurance Soc. of U.S., N.Y.C., 1955-68; owner, cons. Cummings Communications, Delmar, N.Y., 1988—; mem. adv. coun. Blue Cross/Blue Shield, Albany, 1983—. Mem. Albany Inst. History and Art (women's coun.), Assn. for Bus. Communications, Assn. Profl. Writing Cons., Albany Country Club, Univ. Club. Republican. Presbyterian. Home and Office: PO Box 297 Delmar NY 12054

CUMMINGS, MERILYN LLOY, nutritionist; b. St. Paul, Sept. 25, 1939; d. Earl Russell and Vinette Murial (Abrahamson) Stenberg; m. James Walter Cummings, Jan. 3, 1958 (div. June 1974); children: James Walter Jr., Catherine Cummings Bonse; m. Don David Kirby, Oct. 3, 1981; 1 child, Michael William. BS in Dietetics with high distinction, U. Minn., 1974, MPH, 1989. Registered dietitian. Dietetic trainee Hennepin County Med. Ctr., Mpls., 1974-75; liaison dietitian U. Minn. and ARA Foods Co., Mpls., 1976; dir. nutrition Eitel Hosp., Mpls., 1977-84, Lakeview Hosp., Stillwater, Minn., 1984-86; pres. The M C Corp., Stillwater, 1986—; sec. Minn. Ind. Pubs., Mpls., 1987-88. Author/creator: (nutrition books, tapes and games) Diet to Lose & Win, 1985, The Good Food Game, 1989. Chairperson nutrition com. Am. Heart Assn., Mpls., 1986, mem., 1986-89; sec. Stillwater PTA, 1971; chairperson environ. com. LWV, Mahtomedi, Minn., 1971. Named Dietetic Trainee of Yr., Mead Johnson Co., Mpls., 1976. Mem. Am. Dietetic Assn. (registered), Minn. Dietetic Assn., Minn. Nutrition Coun. (communicator chmn. 1987-89, newsletter editor 1987-89), Pubs. Mktg. Assn., Rotary. Lutheran.

CUMMINGS, NANCY BOUCOT, nephrologist; b. Phila., Feb. 21, 1927; d. Arthur B. Guest and Katharine (Rosenbaum) Sturgis; m. Milton Curtis Cummings Jr., July 1959 (div. 1985); children: Christopher Ronald, Jonathan Benton, Susan Sturgis. BA, Oberlin Coll., 1947; postgrad., Radcliffe Coll., 1947; MD, U. Pa., 1951. Rotating intern Pa. Hosp., Phila., 1951-52; resident in internal medicine Hosp. of the U. Pa., Phila., 1952-54; rsch. and clin. asst. Royal Hosp. St. Bartholomew, London, 1954-55, Manchester (Eng.) Royal Infirmary, 1955; rsch. fellow in internal medicine, nephrology Harvard Med. Sch., Boston, 1955-58; medicine asst. Peter Bent-Brigham Hosp., Boston, 1955-58; rsch. fellow in biochemistry Harvard Med. Sch., Boston, 1958-59; guest worker Lab. Intermediary Metabolism Nat. Inst. Arthritis and Metabolic Diseases, Bethesda, 1959-62; rsch. med. officer Walter Reed Army Inst., Washington, 1962-66; exptl. medicine researcher USN Med. Rsch. Inst., Bethesda, Md., 1966-72; clin. instr. medicine Georgetown U., Washington, 1960-70, clin. asst. prof. medicine, 1970-81, clin. assoc. prof. medicine, 1981-88, clin. prof. medicine, 1988—; officer Kidney Disease Collaborative Program Nat. Inst. for Arthritis, Metabolism and Digestive Diseases (now Nat. Inst. of Diabetes, Digestive and Kidney Diseases)/NIH, Bethesda, 1972-73, asst. to dir., 1973-74, acting assoc. dir. for kidney, urologic and blood diseases, 1974-76, assoc. dir. for kidney, urologic, and blood diseases, 1976-84, assoc. dir. for research and assessment, 1984—; nephrological cons. NIH, 1972—, USN Hosp., Bethesda, 1966-72. Editor: Prevention of Kidney and Urinary Tract Diseases, 1978, Immune Mechanisms in Renal Disease, 1982, Chronic Renal Failure, 1985. Lay reader Cathedral of St. Peter and Paul, Washington, 1976—; vestry St. Albans Ch., Washington, 1975-79, 89—; chmn. St. Albans Sunday Forum, 1986-89; chmn. com. med. ethics Diocese (Episcopal) of Washington. Recipient Jacob Ehrenzeller award Pa. Hosp., 1986, Hall of Fame award Cheltenham High Sch. Alumni Assn., 1984. Mem. Am. Soc. Nephrology, Internat. Soc. Nephrology, Am. Fedn. for Clin. Rsch., Nat. Kidney Found. (sci. adv. bd. 1973-79, Disting. Svc. award 1981), Washington Acad. Medicine (bd. dirs. 1989—), European Dialysis and Transplant Assn., Exec. Women in Govt. (treas. 1978-79), Women in Nephrology (program chmn. 1987—), Cosmos Club. Episcopalian. Home: 3900 Connecticut Ave NW Apt 501-F Washington DC 20008 Office: NIH Nat Inst Diabetes Digestive & Kidney Diseases Bethesda MD 20892

CUMMINGS, ROSE BEHELER, county official; b. Welch, W.Va., Apr. 4, 1959; d. Robert Macon and Geraldine (Roberts) Beheler; m. R. Lee Reed (div. Sept. 1988); 1 child, Stefanie Rose; m. William Douglas Cummings, Apr. 1, 1989; 1 child, Hannah Elizabeth. BS cum laude, Western Carolina U., 1981. Reporter Welch Daily News, 1976-77; news director Sta. WRGC, Sylva, N.C., 1981; news reporter Sta. WLOS-TV, Asheville, N.C., 1981-84, producer PM Mag., 1984-86; dir. community affairs Sta. WHNS-TV, Asheville, 1986-87; field dir. Pisgah coun. Ahseville, 1987-88; pub. info. specialist Mecklenburg County, Charlotte, N.C., 1986-88, pub. info. dir., 1988—. Contbr. articles to various publs. Walk chmn. March of Dimes, Asheville, 1986; mem., chmn. subcom. Charlotte Pride Com., 1988—; mem. communicaitons bd. United Way, Charlotte, 1988—; mem. Leadership Charlotte, Urban Inst., 1989; mem. coun. Girl Scouts U.S. Mem. Nat. Assn. County Info. Officers (so. bd. dirs. 1987—, treas. 1990, writing excellence award 1988), Charlotte Pub. Rels. Soc. Home: 2524 Haybrook Ln Charlotte NC 28213 Office: Mecklenburg County 600 E 4th St 2d Fl Charlotte NC 28202

CUMMINGS, SANDRA BIELAWA, writer, editor; b. Phila., Pa, June 8, 1961; d. Henry Walter and Claire Marcella (Riley) Bielawa. BA, Amherst Coll., 1983. Sr. editor Quinlan Press, Boston, Mass., 1984-88; med. editor Shriners Burn Inst., Boston, 1988-89; prodn. mgr. Total Learning Concepts, Boston, 1989—. Author: All Booked Up, 1988; editor: We Will Be Heard, 1987, Dukakis and The Reform Impulse, 1988, My Dad, The Babe, 1988. Mem. NAFE, Coun. of Biology Editors, Am. Med. Writers Assn. Office: Total Learning Concepts 30 The Fenway Boston MA 02215

CUMMINGS, SUE CAROL, professor of chemistry; b. Dayton, Ohio, Apr. 24, 1941; d. Carl L. and Kathryn I. (Hurlow) C.; m. H. Glynn Marsh, June 15, 1979. BA, Northwestern U., 1963; MS, Ohio State U., 1965, PhD, 1968. Chemist The Dow Chem. Co., Midland, Mich., 1965-66; vis. rsch. assoc. Aerospace Rsch. Labs., Wright-Patterson AFB, Ohio, 1968-69; asst. to assoc. prof. Wright State U., Dayton, 1969-77, acting assoc. dean sch. grad. studies, 1976-77, prof., 1977—, chair of chemistry, 1988—; vis. rsch. assoc. C.F. Kettering Rsch. Lab., Yellow Springs, Ohio, 1981-82; cons. Diconix Eastman Kodak, Dayton, 1985-86; coun. mem. Marietta Coll. Adv. Coun., 1988—; panel mem. NSF/NRC Panel on Grad. Fellowships, Washington, 1989-92. Contbr. articles to profl. jours. Named Outstanding Engr. and Scientist award Engring. Found. and Affiliate Socs. Coun., 1976; numerous grants, 1969—. Office: Dept Chemistry Wright State U Dayton OH 45435

CUMMINGS, VIRGINIA J., real estate company executive; b. Greenwood, S.C., June 24; d. Samuel Barksdale and Alma Virginia (Davis) Jones; m. John W. Cummings, Nov. 7, 1938; children: John W., Martha Jean Wells. Student, U. Miami; PhD (hon.), Colo. State Christian Coll., 1973. Sec. Pine Crest Pvt. Sch., Ft. Lauderdale, Fla., 1956-59; real estate broker Am. Realty, Ft. Lauderdale, 1959-62; pres., founder Cummings Realty Inc., Ft. Lauderdale, 1962-85, chmn. bd. dirs., 1985—; v.p. Magic Carpet Travel, Ft. Lauderdale, 1975-89. Feature writer Fla. Living Mag., 1969-74; contbr. articles to profl. jours. Mem. Women's Council of Realtors (pres. 1962), Ft. Lauderdale Area Bd. Realtors, Nat. Bd. Realtors, DAR. Democrat. Home: 4300 N Ocean Blvd #19 AB Fort Lauderdale FL 33308

CUMMINS, KAREN MUIR, social worker; b. Nashville, Sept. 17, 1959; e. Duane Manson Muir and Nancy Perkins Jordan. AD, Martin Meth. Coll., 1979; BS, U. Tenn., 1981, MSW, 1987. Case worker, exec. dir. Travelers Aid Nashville; dir. travelers aid program Nashville Union Mission; coord. wedding receptions, photographer's asst. Vol. Mountain Tenn. Outreach Project; bd. dirs. Community Enhancement Advocacy. Named one of Outstanding Young Women of Am., U.S. Jaycees. Mem. NASW, N.Am. Assn. Christian Social Workers, Tenn. Conf. Social Welfare, Nashville Coalition for Homeless.

CUMMINS, KATHRYN LEWIS, museum director; b. Chgo., Oct. 14, 1908; d. Floyd Watson and Ina Catherine (Steckert) Lewis; m. Glen James Cummins (dec.); 1 child, David Lewis. BS, Cen. Mich. U., 1950; postgrad., U. Mich., 1952. Tchr. Pub. Schs., Midland, Mich., 1928-32, 42-52; social worker Midland County Red Cross, 1936-39; chem. analyst Dow Chem. Co., Midland, 1939-42; exec. sec. Midland County Hist. Mus., 1952-70, dir., 1970—. Editor, contbr. Midland Log mag., 1921-70. Tchr. 1st Bapt. Ch., Midland. Named Citizen of Yr. Civitan Club, 1976; honoree Mich. State Hist. Soc., 1974, Mich. State Sen., 1976. Mem. Am. Assn. Mus., Am. Assn. State and Local History, AAUW (honors with named gift 1987), Mich. Mus. Assn., Mich. Edn. Assn., Mich. Cen. U. Alumnus, Am. Bus. Women (pres. 1989-90, Woman of Yr. 1981).

CUMMINS, NANCYELLEN HECKEROTH, electronics executive; b. Long Beach, Calif., May 22, 1948; d. George and Ruth May (Anderson) Heckeroth; m. Weldon Jay, Sept. 15, 1987; stepchildren: Tracy Lynn, John Scott, Darren Elliott. Student avionics, USMC, Memphis, 1966-67. Tech. publ. engr. Lockheed Missile and Space Div., Sunnyvale, Calif., 1973-76, engring. instr., 1977; test engr. Gen. Dynamics, Pomona, Calif., 1980-83; quality assurance test engr. Interstate Electronics Co., Anaheim, Calif., 1983-84; quality engr., certification engr. Rockwell Internat., Anaheim, 1985-86; sr. quality assurance programmer Point 4 Data, Tustin, Calif., 1986-87; software quality assurance specialist Lawrence Livermore Nat. Lab., Yucca Mountain Project, Livermore, Calif., 1987-89, software quality mgr., 1989-90; with EG&G Rocky Flats, Golden, Colo., 1990—; customer engr. IBM Gen. Systems, Orange, Calif., 1979; electronics engr. LDS Ch. Exhibits Div., Salt Lake City, 1978; electronics repair specialist Weber State Coll., 1977-78. Author: Package Area Test Set, 6 vols., 1975, Software Quality Assurance Plan, 1989. Instr. emergency preparedness and survival, Modesto, Calif., 1989, Clairmont, Calif., 1982-84, Living History Pre-1840's, Calif. 1984—; sec. Livermore Lab. Armed Forces VA, 1987-90. With USMC, 1966-67, USMCR, 1981-85. Mem. NAFE, NRA, Nat. Muzzle Loading Rifle Assn., Am. Soc. Quality Control, Job's Daus. (majority mem.). Republican. Mem. LDS Ch. Home: 9057 Ute Hwy Longmont CO 80503 Office: EG&G Rocky Flats PO Box 464 T-130H Golden CO 80402-0464

CUMMINS, SHIRLEY JEAN, psychologist; b. Seminole, Tex., May 14, 1948; d. Shirley Vern and Ina Jean (Teague) C. BA, Tex. Tech. U., Lubbock, 1970; MA, U. Tulsa, 1973; PhD, U. North Tex., Denton, 1983. Lic. psychologist, Okla., Tex. Assoc. sch. psychologist PESO region SVI Edn. Svc. Ctr., Amarillo, Tex., 1973-76; teaching asst. psychology dept. U. North Tex., Denton, 1977-79; psychology intern VA Med. Ctr., North Chicago (Ill.) Ctr., 1980-81; psychologist Green Country Mental Health Ctr., Muskogee, Okla., 1983-86, Kaiser Rehab. Ct.r, Hillcrest Med. Ctr., Tulsa, 1986-88, Wichita Falls (Tex.) State Hosp., 1988—. Bd. mem. Hospice, Muskogee, Okla., 1984-86. Mem. Am. Psychol. Assn. Democrat. Methodist. Office: Wichita Falls State Hosp PO Box 300 Wichita Falls TX 76307

CUMMINS-HOXSEY, PATRICIA ANN, real estate specialist, educator; b. Portland, Maine, Sept. 29, 1945; d. Arther M. and Eunice G. (Swan) Peterson Griggs; m. Gerald D. Cummins, July 4, 1964 (div. 1971); children: Mark David, Christine Diane, Scott David; m. Michael Hoxsey, Dec. 1988. AA, San Diego City, 1967; BA, Nat. U., 1977, MBA, 1977; D in Bus. Adminstn., U.S. Internat. U., 1980. Real estate broker Carlton Oaks Realty and Investment, Santee, Calif., 1967-86, Century 21 Teamwork, Santee, Calif., 1987-90; tax acct. Larson CPA, San Diego, 1966-86, asset mgr. Mesa Mortgage, San Diego, 1970-80; bus. prof. U.S. Internat. U., San Diego, 1980-82; instr. Grossmont Coll., El Cajon, Calif., 1982. Author: (with others) Inside Secrets IRS, 1981, Tax Dictionary, 1981; producer broadway mus., San Diego, 1980. Active Boy Scouts Am., Pop Warner youth softball league, Santee, 1972-80; dir. Calif. Performing Arts, San Diego, 1980—; reader 1st Ch. Christ Scientist, Lakeside, Calif. Mem. Nat. Assn. Realtors, Calif. Assn. Realtors, NRA, Planned Parenthood, Santee C. of C., Calif. Performing Arts (dir. 1980—), Flying Club, Loa Ancianos Club. Republican. Home: PO Box 710187 Santee CA 92072

CUNINGGIM, WHITTY DANIEL, educator; b. Oxford, N.C., Aug. 18, 1918; d. Ethrel Jenkins and Annie Penelope (Whitty) Daniel; m. Merrimon Cuninggim, June 10, 1939; children: Lee C. Neff, Penny, Terry (dec.). BA, Duke U., 1938. Founder, chmn. Reading Is Fun-damental, St. Louis, 1970-76; bd. of edn. Spl. Sch. Dist. St. Louis County, St. Louis, 1970-75; pres. Spl. Sch. Dist. St. Louis County, 1975-76; chmn. Adv. Coun. for Exceptional Children, Winston Salem, N.C., 1976-82; Bd. dirs. Nat. Citizens' Com. for Support of Pub. Schs., 1970-76, Nat. Sch. Vol. Program, Alexandria, Va., 1976-83, White House Conference on Edn. Co-founder Catalyst Assocs., St. Louis, 1974; chmn. Forsyth County N.C. "2000", 1982; pres. Women's Forum, N.C., 1985-86, Arts Coun., Winston-Salem, N.C., 1982-83; mem. N.C. Pub. Edn. Policy Coun., 1983-84; bd. assocs. N.C. Child Advocacy Inst., 1987-89, Met. Edn. Coalition, Balt., 1989—; exec. com. N.C. Dems., 1980-84. Recipient Duke U. Alumni award, Duke U. Alumni Assn., Winston Salem, 1982, award for Community Svc., League of Women Voters, N.C., 1989; named Woman of Achievment, St. Louis Globe-Democrat, 1968, Nat. Sch. Vol of Year, Nat. Sch. Vol. Program, 1979. Mem. AAUW, Atlantic Coun. of U.S., Nat. Women's Dem. Club, LWV (bd. dirs.), Phi Beta Kappa, Phi Delta Kappa. Democrat. Home: 13801 York Rd #E9 Cockeysville MD 21030

CUNNANE, PATRICIA S., medical facility administrator; b. Clinton, Iowa, Sept. 7, 1946; d. Cyril J. and Corinne Spain; m. Edward J. Cunnane, June 19, 1971. AA, Mt. St. Clare Coll., Clinton, Iowa, 1966. Mgr. Eye Med. Clinic of Santa Clara Valley, San Jose, Calif. Mem. Med. Adminstrs. Calif. Polit. Action Com., San Francisco, 1987. Mem. Med. Group Mgmt. Assn., Am. Coll. Med. Group Adminstrs. (nominee), Nat. Notary Assn., Resource Ctr. for Women, NAFE, Exec. Women Internat. (v.p. 1986-87, pres. 1987—), Profl. Secs. Internat. (sec. 1979-80), Am. Soc. Ophthalmic Adminstrs., Women Health Care Execs., Healthcare Human Resource Mgmt. Assn. Calif. Roman Catholic. Home: 232 Tolin Ct San Jose CA 95139 Office: Eye Med Clinic of Santa Clara Valley 220 Meridian Ave San Jose CA 95126

CUNNIFF, NELDA NORENE, physician; b. Ackerly, Tex., Oct. 18, 1935; d. Elmo Milton Brown; and Hazel Orel (Gregston) Cobern; m. Vaughn H. Cunniff, June 9, 1951 (div. Aug. 1985); children: Sheron, Allen, Jerry. Postgrad., John Peter Smith Sch. Nursing, Ft. Worth, 1963; BS, Tex. Wesleyan, 1968; postgrad., Tex. Coll. Osteopathic Medicine, 1974. RN, Tex. Rn Blvd. Hosp., Ft. Worth, 1963-70; Hurst (Tex.) Gen. Hosp., 1970; pvt. practice in gen. and family medicine and obstetrics Family Clinic, Burleson, Tex., 1975—; pvt. practice Alvarado (Tex.) Family Clinic, 1975—; clin. preceptor Tex. Coll. Osteopathic Med., Ft. Worth, 1977—. Bd. mem. Tex. Coll. Osteopathic Med. Found., Ft. Worth, 1988—. Mem. Am. Osteopathic Assn., Tex. Osteopathic Medicine Assn. (pres. dist. II 1983, sec. 1981), Am. Coll. Osteo. and Gen. Practitioners, Tex. State Soc. Am. Coll. Osteo. and Gen. Practitioners (program chmn. 1986-87, pres. 1988-89). Republican. Home: Rte 7 Burleson TX 76028 Office: Family Clinic 200 E Ellison Burleson TX 76028

CUNNING, JAN ELIZABETH, social work administrator; b. Sharon, Pa., Jan. 20, 1944; d. Edward Leroy and Phyllis Naomi (Huber) C. BA, Edinboro State Coll., 1967; MS, W. Va. U., Morgantown, 1973; MSW, Rutgers U., New Brunswick, 1978. Social Worker. Child welfare caseworker Children's Services of Erie County, Erie, Pa., 1967-69; field intake worker Dauphin Country Bd. of Assistance, Harrisburg, Pa., 1969-70; field coordinator Fayette County Bd. of Assistance, Uniontown, Pa., 1970-72; med. social worker Children's Seashore House, Atlantic City, N.J., dir. social work, 1974-78; dir. social work John F. Kennedy Med. Ctr. Johnson Inst., Edison, N.J., 1978-81, Hunterdon Med. Ctr., Flemington, N.J., 1981-84, St. Peters Med. Ctr., New Brunswick, N.J., 1984-88; dir. admissions, asst. adminstr., social worker Edison Estates Rehab. & Conv. Ctr., Edison, N.J., 1988-89, adminstr., 1989—; adv. com. mem. Woodbridge Visiting Nurse Assn., 1980-81, Visiting Homemakers Soc., Hunterdon, 1982-84; rehab. bd. mem. Am. Cancer Soc., Middlesex County, 1980-81; bd. dir. Home Health Assembly, Princeton, N.J. State Home Care Accreditation. Contbr. articles to profl. jours. Tutor N.J. Bell Tutoring Program for Learning Disabilities, 1971-72; chairperson Com. on Barrier Free Designs, Cumberland County, 1974-75. Mem. Gov. Task Force on Child Abuse, Nat. Assn. of Social Workers, Soc. for Hosp. Work Dirs. Office: Edison Estates Rehabs & Con 465 Plainfield Ave Edison NJ 08817

CUNNINGHAM, SISTER AGNES, patristic theology educator, author; b. Middlesborough, Yorkshire, Eng., May 26, 1923; came to U.S., 1926; d. Michael Steven and Monica Gertrude (Burns) C. BS, St. Louis U., 1954; MA, Marquette U., 1963; STL, Facultes CAtholiques, Lyon, France, 1964, STD, 1968. Tchr. Holy Family Acad., Beaverville, Ill., 1943-52; prin., tchr. St. Mary Magdalene Elem. Sch., Joliet, Ill., 1954-57; prin. St. Gall Elem. Sch., Chgo., 1957-60; instr. Mundelein Coll. for Women, Chgo., 1960-63; dir., asst. prof. Newman Found. at the U. Ill., Champaign, 1967-69; prof. patristic theology and early christianity Mundelein (Ill.) Sem., U. of St. Mary of the Lake, 1967—; mem. com. on Role of Women in Soc. and Ch., Washington, 1971-89; exec. sec. Chgo. Theol. Inst., 1981—; bd. dirs. Sacred Heart Sch. Theology, Hales Corners, Wis. Author: Prayer: Personal & Liturgical, 1985, The Significance of Mary, 1988; translator, editor: The Early Church and the State, 1982; assoc. editor: Chicago Studies, 1985—; contbr. articles to profl. jours. ATS grantee, 1980. Mem. Am. Theol. Soc., Cath. Theol. Soc. Am. (pres. 1977-78), Internat. Assn. Patristic Scholars. Roman Catholic. Home: 717 N Batavia Batavia IL 60510 Office: Mundelein Sem U St Mary of the Lake Mundelein IL 60060

CUNNINGHAM, DOROTHY RUTH, real estate investment officer; b. Ashland, Ky., Nov. 23, 1951; d. Clayton Allen and Jamie Sue (Rogers) C. BS in Acctg. magna cum laude, U. Balt., 1981, postgrad., 1985—. CPA, Md. Word processing supr. R.M. Towill Corp., Honolulu, 1971-73; real estate reviewer Prudential Ins. Co., Balt., 1973-78; real estate investment analyst Equitable Life Assurance Soc. U.S., Balt., Washington, 1978-83; v.p. Chevy Chase Savs. Bank, Md., 1983-89; investment officer Wellington Real Estate, Washington, 1989—; instr. Am. Inst. Banking, 1988-89. Vol. Nat. Aquarium in Balt., 1982-85. Mem. Comml. Real Estate Women (pres. and founder Balt. chpt. 1985-86, nat. steering com. 1986-87, nat. bd. dirs. 1987-89), Mortgage Bankers Assn. Wash. and Md., Nat. Assn. Indsl. and Office Parks, Urban Land Inst., Am. Inst. Real Estate Appraisers. Avocations: home renovation; racquetball; reading; computers. Home: 14 E Churchill St Baltimore MD 21230 Office: Wellington Real Estate 1608 New Hampshire Ave NW Washington DC 20009

CUNNINGHAM, ELLEN, mathematics and computer science educator; b. Chgo., June 20, 1940; d. Michael and Catherine (O'Connor) C. BA, St. Mary of the Woods Coll., 1963; MA, Cath. U. Am., 1970; PhD, U. Md., 1974; MS, U. Evansville, Ind., 1985. Joined Sisters of Providence, 1959. Mem. faculty Cen. Cath. High Sch., Ft. Wayne, Ind., 1964-66, St. John High Sch., Loogootee, Ind., 1966-67, St. Mary-of-the-Woods (Ind.) Coll., 1974—; chair dept. sci. and math. St. Mary of the Woods (Ind.) Coll., 1981—; programmer/analyst McCord and Assocs., Chgo., 1982-83; bd. dirs. Kovalevskaia Fund for Women in Sci., Seattle, 1988—. Author articles and presentations. Mem. coms. on conciliation, sanctuary, nuclear weaponry Sisters of Providence, 1974-88; mem. adv. com. on sex discrimination, Ind. Civil Rights Commn., 1975-80; adv. com. on justice edn. Assn. Cath. Colls. and Univs., 1977-81. Mem. Math. Assn. Am., Assn. for Women in Math., Computer Profls. for Social Responsibility. Home: 429 Washington Ave Terre Haute IN 47802 Office: St Mary-of-the-Woods Coll Saint Mary-of-the-Woods IN 47876

CUNNINGHAM, GAIL BLAIR, educational association administrator; b. Harrisonburg, Va., Oct. 21, 1950; d. Francis Tappey Cunningham and Brownie Elizabeth Miller. BS, Madison Coll., 1973; MEd, James Madison U., 1977. Kindergarten tchr. Rockbridge Pub. Schs., Lexington, Va., 1973-76, Harrisonburg (Va.) City Pub. Schs., 1976-84; with UniServ N.C. Assn. Educators, Fayetteville, 1984-87; UniServ dir. Va. Edn. Assn., Richmond, 1987—. Del. 1984 Dem. Conv.; regional lobbyist Va. Educators Assn., Va. Gen. Assembly, other. Mem. Va. Educators Assn. (bd. dirs., PAC exec. com.), Va. Profl. Staff Assn. (exec. com.). Home: 114 Idlewood Ave Portsmouth VA 23704 Office: 100 7th St Ste 102 Portsmouth VA 23704

CUNNINGHAM, JACQUELINE LEMMÉ, developmental disabilities fellow; b. Biddeford, Maine, Apr. 22, 1941; d. S. James and Alice (Fréchette) Lemmé; m. Seymour II Cunningham, Dec. 16, 1960 (dec. 1987); children: Macklin Todd, Danielle, Alyssa. BA in Psychology, U. Maine, Orono, 1963; MS in Psychology, U. South Ala., 1983; student, U. Tex., 1990. Tchr. Mobile (Ala.) Pub. Schs., 1976-81; doctoral candidate U. Tex., 1984-90; clinician Devereux Found., Devon, Pa., 1988-89; fellow devel. disabilities Harvard Med. Sch., Cambridge, Mass., 1990—; cons. in field. Contbr. articles to profl. jours. Mem. Am. Psychol. Assn., Internat. Neuropsychol. Soc., Soc. History Behavioral Scis., Phi Kappa Phi.

CUNNINGHAM, JEAN DIGIORGIO, newspaper official; b. Schenectady, N.Y., Mar. 31, 1961; d. Ralph and Carmela (Morra) DiGiorgio; m. James LeRoy Cunningham. Student, Oswego State U., 1979-83. Account exec. WKLI, WABY, Albany, N.Y., 1983-86; regional account exec. Omaha World Herald, 1987—. Recipient Silver award, Best 4-Color Mag. Ad., Sunday Mag. Advt. Conf., 1989. Mem. Ad Clubs. Democrat. Roman Catholic. Home: 639 Chapel Hill Dr Elkhorn NE 68022 Office: Omaha World Herald World Herald Square Omaha NE 68102

CUNNINGHAM, KARIN OLSEN, public relations executive; b. Dallas, Oct. 15, 1959; d. Kenneth Bruce and Marilyn (Jennings) Olsen; m. Donald M. Cunningham, Dec. 12, 1987. Grad., Okla. State U., 1981. Editor, sales rep. Country Club Publs., Oklahoma City, 1981-88; dir. communications United Way Cen. Okla., Oklahoma City, 1988-89; dir. pub. rels. Multimedia Cablevision, Edmond, Okla., 1990—. Contbr. articles to profl. jours. Active Big Bros.-Big Sisters, Oklahoma City, 1984-85; mem. Citizens Adv. Coun. Am. Inst. Cancer Rsch., Washington, 1984. Mem. Women in Communications (pres. 1980-81, chmn. membership com. 1989-90), Oklahoma City Advt. Club (co-chmn. Addy Awards gala 1990), Am. Women in Radio and TV (chmn. publicity com. 1989-90), Pi Beta Phi. Republican. Unitarian. Home: 11550 N Maly #107 Oklahoma City OK 73120 Office: Multimedia Cablevision PO Box 1899 Edmond OK 73083

CUNNINGHAM, LORINNE MITCHELL, civic worker; b. Tupelo, Miss., Mar. 8, 1909; d. Guy William and Rosa Lavelle (Rogers) Mitchell; m. William Jefferson Cunningham, Nov. 18, 1932; children: Rose Rogers Cunningham Trigg, Nine Lorinne Cunningham Redding, Sarah Mitchell Cunningham Gay. BA, Rhodes Coll., 1931. Writer youth publs. United Meth. Ch., Memphis, 1961-63; tchr. Schs. Mission, Bd. Missions, United Meth. Ch., 1968-79. Contbr. articles to various publs. Organizer, chmn. bd. dirs. Transitional Ctrs. for Men and Women Coming Out of Prison, Memphis, 1972-82, Police and Community Together Pact, Memphis, 1976-79; mem., chmn. Police Adv. Commn., Memphis, 1978-88; organizer, chmn. Econ. Justice for Women Coalition, Memphis, 1983—; community rep. Com. To Study Need and Future County Pub. Hosp., Shelby County, Tenn., 1979; pres. Ch. Women United local unit, 1973-75, chmn. citizen action com., 1975-83. Recipient Community Svc. award NCCJ, 1979, Bill of Rights award West Tenn. regional chpt. ACLU, 1984, Women of Achievement award, 1986. Mem. LWV, AAUW (named gift award to fellowship endowment 1976), Amnesty Internat., Women's Polit. Caucus. Democrat. Home: 5127 Mason Rd Memphis TN 38117

CUNNINGHAM, MARY ELIZABETH, venture capital company executive; b. Portland, Maine, Sept. 1, 1951; d. Shirley (Sears) C.; m. William Joseph Agee, June 5, 1982; children: Mary Alana, William Nolan. BA, Wellesley Coll., 1973; MBA, Harvard U., 1979; postgrad. Trinity Coll., Dublin, 1972; DHL (hon.), Franklin Pierce Coll., 1983, Loyola U., 1990. Asst. treas. Chase Manhattan Bank, N.Y.C., 1974-77; corp. v.p. strategic planning Bendix Corp., Southfield, Mich., 1979-80; exec. v.p. planning, corp. v.p. strategic planning Joseph Seagram & Sons, N.Y.C., 1981-84; pres., chief operating officer Semper Enterprises, Inc., Osterville, Mass., 1982—; exec. dir. The Nurturing Network, Inc.; vice chmn. Lojack Corp., 1983-90. Author: Powerplay, 1984; contbr. articles to profl. jours. Bd. dirs. Franklin Pierce Coll., Rindge, N.H., 1983—, Marymount Manhattan Coll., N.Y.C., 1983-88, Alternatives to Abortion Internat., Dartmouth Aquinas House; bd. advisors council Collegiate Research Services, Inc., Jour. Bus. Strategy; mem. strategic planning com. The Conf. Bd.; mem. United Negro Coll. Fund, Women's Equity Action League; mem. women's forum, nat. corp. adv. bd. NOW Legal Def. and Edn. Fund; mem. adv. com. Com. for Nat. Security; chmn.'s advisor U.S. Congl. Adv. Bd. Recipient Econ. Equity award Women's Equity Action League, N.Y.C., 1982; named to YWCA's Acad. Women Achievers, 1980. Mem. Am. Mgmt. Assn., Phi Beta Kappa. Roman Catholic. Clubs: Commonwealth of Calif. (San Francisco); Economic (N.Y.C.); Women's Economic (Detroit). Home: Oyster Harbors Osterville MA 02655 Office: The Nurturing Network Ste 360 Box 2050 910 Main St Boise ID 83701

CUNNINGHAM, MARY ELIZABETH, physician; b. Newark, Apr. 21, 1931; d. William Rutherford and Mary Agnes (Harvey) C. AB, Mt. Holyoke Coll., 1953; MS, U. Ill., 1957; PhD, U. Oreg., 1964; MD, U. Conn., 1982. Diplomate Am. Bd. Emergency Med., 1988. Grad. asst. dept. physics U. Oreg., Eugene, 1957-64; sr. physicist Lawrence Livermore (Calif.) Nat. Lab., 1964-78, cons. Earth scis. div., 1978-80; instr., resident Mich. State. U. Affiliated Hosps., Lansing, 1982-85; chief resident emergency medicine Mich. State U. Affiliated Hosps., Lansing, 1985; assoc. staff mem. dept. emergency Ingham Med. Ctr., Lansing, Mich., 1984-85; med. staff Hayes Green Beach Hosp., Charlotte, Mich., 1984-85; physician The Permanente Med. Group, Sacramento, 1985-88, sr. physician, 1988—. Contbr. articles to profl. jours. Fellow Am. Coll. Emergency Physicians; mem. AMA, Am. Phys. Soc., N.Y. Acad. Scis., Sacramento-El Dorado County Med. Soc., Phi Beta Kappa, Sigma Xi (rsch. grantee 1963-64), Pi Mu Epsilon. Republican. Roman Catholic. Office: Kaiser-Permanente Med Ctr 6600 Bruceville Rd Sacramento CA 95823

CUNNINGHAM, MARY LOUISE, nurse; b. Lake Charles, La., Aug. 30, 1954; d. William Michael and Dale (Weyand) C. BS in Nursing, U. Mo., 1976; MS, Tex. Woman's U., 1988. RN, Mo., Iowa, Tex.; cert. oncology nurse. Sch. nurse Ames (Iowa) Sch. System, 1977-79; staff nurse VA Hosp., Columbia, Mo., 1976-77; staff nurse M.D. Anderson Cancer Ctr., Houston, 1979-88, clin. nurse specialist, 1988—. Contbr. Core Curforons Certification, 1987. Chairperson Patient Aid Com., Houston, 1981-84; bd. dirs. Leukemia Soc., Houston, 1982—. Mem. Oncology Nursing Soc. (clin. practice com. 1984-86, congress com. 1987-89, Schering-ONS Excellence in Clin. Practice award 1989), Sigma Theta Tau. Presbyterian.

CUNNINGHAM, NINA STRICKLER, researcher, educator; b. Chgo., Dec. 24, 1947; d. Sidney and Betty (Rosmarin) Strickler; m. H. Stuart Cunningham, Apr. 17, 1975; children: Gwyneth, Anna. Ph.D. in Philosophy, DePaul U., 1973; M.A. in Library Sci., Rosary Coll., 1980. Teaching asst. DePaul U., 1970; pres., owner Quidlibet Research, Inc., Oak Park, Ill., 1977—; adminstr. U.S. Dist. Cts., Chgo., 1973-83, cons., 1983; cons. Rosenthal and Schanfield, Chgo., 1983, DePaul U., Chgo., 1984, Neal, Gerber & Eisenberg, 1987—. Editor: Ethics & Advocacy newsletter. Founder, bd. dirs. Ctr. for Legal Ethics, Edn. and Research, Chgo., 1984. Fellow DePaul U., 1970, Inst. for Humane Studies, 1976; Marsden Found. grantee, 1972. Mem. Am. Legal Studies Assn., Am. Soc. Study of Law and Legal Philosophy, Royal Inst. Philosophy, Soc. Study of History of Philosophy, Am. Federalist Soc. Jewish. Avocations: creative writing, bookselling, genealogy. Home and Office: Quidlibet Rsch Inc 643 N Elmwood Ave Oak Park IL 60302

CUNNINGHAM, SUE CAROL, educational program coordinator; b. River Falls, Wis., Oct. 4, 1940; d. Kenneth Robert and Ida Jane (Dawson) Dorgan; m. Frank Joseph Cunningham, Sept. 5, 1964; children: Chip, Stephanie, Kenneth R., Sally. Student, U. Wis., 1958-61; BA, U. Guam, Mangilao, 1973; MEd, U. Guam, 1975. Phys. edn. tchr. J.F.K. High Sch., Tumon, Guam, 1973-76; resettlement counselor U.S. Catholic Conf., South Bend, Ind., 1980-83; experiential learning program coordinator U. Notre Dame, Ind., 1985—; Chmn. Literacy Task Force St. Joseph County, South Bend, 1983-85, United Nations Day, South Bend, 1987. Vol. coordinator City of South Bend, 1983-85, East Race Kayaking Activities, South Bend, 1983-86; bd. dirs. English Second Language Sch., South Bend, 1980-83. Roman Catholic. Office: Ctr for Social Concerns Box F Univ Notre Dame Notre Dame IN 46556

CUNNINGHAM, VICKI FRANCES, publishing executive; b. Houma, La., Aug. 27, 1963; d. Charles and Joyce Rita (Guidry) C. Student, Nicholls State U., 1981-87, Spring Hill Coll., 1983; student Profl. Pub. Program, Stanford U., 1989. Pub. Gulf Oil Field Service Co., Inc., Houma, 1978-87, sec., treas., 1987—; real estate assoc. Century 21, Houma, 1982; instr. Nicholls State u., Thibodaux, La., 1984; pvt. practice law clk., abstractor, La., 1984-86; pub., pres. Faces South Pubs., Inc., Kenner, La., 1986—; cons. small pubs., New Orleans, 1987—. Contbr. articles to profl. jours. Active dept. econ. devel. U. New Orleans, 1988—, small bus. devel. ctr., 1988—. Mem. NAFE, Doris Day Animal League. Roman Catholic. Home: 310 Estate Dr Houma LA 70364

CUOMO, ANA-MARIE PATRICIA, educator; b. N.Y.C., Sept. 7, 1960; d. Anthony Jr. and Mary Theresa (O'Connor) C. BS, East Carolina U., 1982, MA in Edn., 1986; postgrad., N.C. State U., 1988—. Cert. tchr., N.C. Tchr. Harnett County Schs., Dunn, N.C., 1983-84, Greenville (N.C.) City Extended Day Sch., 1984-85, Kinston (N.C.) City Schs., 1985-87; composition instr. Wake Tech. Community Coll., Raleigh, N.C., 1987-88; writing specialist, tchr. trainer N.C. Dept. Community Colls., Raleigh, 1988—; instr., writing lab. tutor, East Carolina U., Greenville, 1984-87; adj. prof., Shaw U., Raleigh, 1988—. Coord. Community Coun. for Arts, Kinston, 1986, tchr. adventures in art program, 1986, 87; bd. dirs. Wake Health Svcs., Raleigh, 1989—. Mem. N.C. Community Coll. and Adult Edn. Assn., N.C. Assn. Educators (chair communications com., newsletter editor), Nat. Coun. Tchrs. English (lit. judge), Kappa Delta Pi. Republican. Roman Catholic. Office: NC Dept Community Colls 200 W Jones St Raleigh NC 27603

CUPP, LUCY PASCHALL, elementary school educator; b. Portsmouth, Va., Sept. 18, 1949; d. John Robert Paschall and Frances Wright Pridgen; m. Daniel Lee Cupp, Aug. 17, 1968; children: Jeannie Kay, Paul Daniel. BS in Elem. Edn., Old Dominion U., 1970, MS in Edn. Adminstrn./Supervision, 1980; MA in Counseling, Liberty U., 1987; postgrad., various instns. Cert. elem. tchr., 1-7, elem. prin., elem. supr., elem. counselor, Va. Counselor and edn. diagnostic cons. for exceptional children Psycho-Ednl. Diagnostic Svcs.; tchr. spiral classes, regular elem. edn. Norfolk (Va.) Pub. Schs.; educator Ingleside Bapt. Ch., Norfolk, Va. Recipient Sch. Bell award, Norfolk Pub. Schs., Honor Citation, AWANA Clubs Internat., Meritorious Achievement award. Mem. Norfolk Fedn. Tchrs., Am. Fedn. Tchrs., Am. Assn. Counseling and Devel. Am. Assn. Elem. Sch. Guidance Counselors, Am. Sch. Counselor Assn. Office: Psycho-Ednl Diagnostic Svcs 5821 Hartwick Dr Norfolk VA 23518

CUPPLES, JANET CUMMINGS, business executive; b. Burnsville, Miss., Dec. 22, 1942; d. James E. and Juanita (Hale) Cummings; m. David C. Linton, May 21, 1961 (div. 1984); 1 child, Jeffory Mark; m. Thomas Gilbert Cupples, Mar. 5, 1984. Student, NE Miss. Jr. Coll., 1960-61, Memphis State U., 1975-76, Sheffield Tech. Ctr., Memphis, 1984-85. Property owner, Burnsville, 1974—; mem. bus. adv. com. Sheffield Tech. Ctr., 1987; mem. bus. dept. Parkwood Hosp., Olive Branch, Miss., 1989-90. Co-editor Internat. Heritage Bull./Newsletter. Vol. Memphis Brooks Mus. Art, 1980—; mem. exec. com., pub. info. officer Bldg. Bridges for A Better Memphis, 1985—; pres. Eagle Watch Assn.; founder Janet C. Cupples Citizenship awards, Memphis City Inter-City Sch., Student Leadership award, Memphis City Schs.; founder, chair women's com. on crime, City of Memphis, 1985—, chair Heritage-City of Memphis, chair internat. heritage program, 1987, 88—, Ethnic Outreach Neighborfest, 1988; hon. mem. city council, 1987; donor, exec. com. Women of Achievement, Inc., Memphis, 1986; mem. speakers bur. United Way of Greater Memphis, Friends of Shelby County Library, 1986—, YWCA; chair ethnic outreach com. Neighborfest, Memphis, 1987, chairperson exec. com. 1988; amb. Memphis Internat. Heritage Commn., 1988; youth mentor Memphis Youth Leadership Devel. Inst.; internat. coordinator Neighborfest '88; chairperson Internat. Heritage City of Memphis, 1987, Ethnic Outreach Neighborfest, 1988. Contbr. articles to newspapers. Mem. community coun. Memphis City Schs., Memphis Cablevision Edn. Task Force; appointed col. aide de camp to staff of Gov. Ned McWherter of Tenn., 1988. Recipient 6 certs. of recognition Memphis City Council, 1986-89, Outstanding Service to Pub. Edn. award, 1986, merit award City of Memphis, 1987; named Outstanding Female Participant, Neighborhood, Inc., 1987; named Woman of Achievement 1988; honored by Pres. George Bush as Outstanding Vol., 1989; featured one of top 1000 Vols. in Mid-South, 1989. Mem. NAFE, NOW (2d v.p. Memphis chpt. 1987, del. nat. conf. 1987, 2d v.p.), Network Profl. Women's Orgn., NCCJ, Rep. Career Women, Memphis Peace and Justice Ctr., Women's Polit. Caucus Tenn. Methodist. Avocations: community service, writing, teaching. Office: 3021 Eagle Dr Memphis TN 38115

CURA, ALICE MILLER, financial analyst; b. Cambridge, Mass., May 11, 1959; d. Richard Pearson and Elinor (Kellogg) Miller; m. Peter Joseph Cura, Oct. 12, 1985. BS in Acctg., Babson Coll., 1981. Acct. PruCapital, Inc., Newark, 1981-85; supr. fin. GTE Sylvania, Danvers, Mass., 1985-86; gen. acctg. mgr. Medi-tech. Inc., Watertown, Mass., 1986-89; sr. fin. analyst Remanco Systems, Inc., Danvers, Mass., 1989—. Pres. Bd. Trustees Winchester Green Condo Assn., Winchester, Mass., 1986-89. Office: Remanco Systems Inc 300 Rosewood Dr Danvers MA 01923

CURCIE, BONNIE E., financial services executive; b. Pa., Nov. 20, 1952; d. Ivan L. Book and Mary R. Sulivan; 1 child, Douglas. Student, Bucks County Community Coll., Antioch U. Cert. D-A counselor, Pa. Family and intake counselor Today, Inc., Newtown; pvt. practice home decorating Levittown, Pa.; supr. billing accounts receivable Honeywell, Inc., Fort Washington, Pa. Mem. NAFE, NOW. Home: 42 Idolstone Rd Levittown PA 19057

CURCIO, BARBARA ANN, insurance executive; b. New York, Jan. 19, 1951; d. Thomas Louis and Margaret Rose (Tasca) Curcio. BS, St. John's U., 1973. Lic. ins. broker. Asst. v.p., account exec. Fred S. James & Co. of N.Y., N.Y.C., 1977-84; v.p., producer, account exec. Rollins Burdick Hunter, N.Y.C., 1984-89, Corroon & Black of N.Y., Inc., N.Y.C., 1989—. Mem. Assn. Profl. Ins. Women. Republican. Roman Catholic. Office: Corroon & Black of NY Inc 7 Hanover Sq New York NY 10004

CURCIO, FRANCES RENA, mathematics education educator; b. S.I., N.Y., Aug. 22, 1951; d. Raffaele John and Margaret Marie (Cipolaro) C. BS, St. Francis Coll., 1973; MA, NYU, 1975, PhD, 1981. High sch. math. tchr. St. John Villa Acad., S.I., N.Y., 1973-77; intern asst. prin. Pub. Sch. 104K, Bklyn., 1979-80; prof. edn. St. Francis Coll., Bklyn., 1977-85, coord. secondary edn. tchr. tng. program, 1977-85, chmn. dept. edn., 1982-85; asst. prof. math. edn. Queens Coll., CUNY, 1985-90, assoc. prof., 1991—; cons. N.Y.C. Bd. Edn., 1981-84. Nat. Inst. Edn. grantee, 1980, St. Francis Coll. faculty research grantee, 1980, enrichment program grantee, 1983, N.Y. State Mini-Project Program grantee, 1979, 80, PSC-CUNY grantee, 1989. Mem. Nat. Coun. Tchrs. Math. (bd. dirs. 1990—, editor Teaching and Learning: A Problem Solving Focus 1987), Math. Assn. Am., Assn. Supervision and Curriculum Devel., Am. Ednl. Research Assn., Internat. Reading Assn., Coun. Basic Edn., Internat. Soc. for Tech. in Edn., Soc. for Tech. in Edn., Assn. Math. Tchrs. N.Y. State, S.I. Guild Math. Assocs., Assn. Tchrs. Math. N.Y.C., Phi Delta Kappa (Henry Meissner Rsch. award 1981), Kappa Delta Pi, Kappa Mu Epsilon. Roman Catholic. Author: Supplemental Tests, Real Math Program, 1982, Soviet Politics and Education, 1986, Developing Graph Comprehension: Elementary and Middle Activities, 1989; editor: Teaching and Learning: A Problem-Solving Focus, 1987, N.Y. State Math. Tchrs. Jour., 1982-87, Middle Grades Addenda to the Curriculum and Evaluation Standards for School Mathematics, 1990-91. Home: 1111 Tompkins Ave Staten Island NY 10305 Office: Queens Coll Dept Elem & Early Childhood Edn 65-30 Kissena Blvd Flushing NY 11367-0904

CURE, CAROL CAMPBELL, lawyer; b. Phoenix, Dec. 16, 1944; d. Richard Converse Nowell and Nancy (Newcomb) Olson; m. Robert Norman Campbell, Jan. 2, 1965 (div. 1968); 1 child, Kelly Christine; m. Harding Briggs Cure, June 28, 1984. BA, Ariz. State U.-Tempe, 1972, JD, 1978. Bar: Ariz. 1979, Calif. 1979, U.S. Dist. Ct. Ariz. 1979, U.S. Ct. Appeals (9th cir.) 1981, U.S. Dist. Ct. (cen. dist.) Calif. 1984. Ptnr. O'Connor, Cavanagh, Anderson, Westover, Killingsworth & Beshears, Phoenix, 1978—; faculty mem. Pacific regional chpt. Nat. Inst. Trial Advocacy, 1985-86; faculty mem. Ariz. Trial Coll., 1988, Ariz. MCBA NITA Trial Advocacy Program, 1986, 87. Bd. dirs. Ariz. Coun. of the Blind, Social Svcs. and Rehab. Inc., 1980-85, sec., 1980-82, v.p. ops. 1983-84; bd. dirs. Phoenix Childrens Theatre, 1981-83, v.p. ops., 1982-83; bd. dirs. Ariz. Cen. Credit Union, 1985-87; judge pro tem Ariz. Ct. Appeals, 1985; judge pro tem Maricope County Superior Ct., 1988-90; mem. steering com. Pro Bono Juvenile Project, 1989-90; mem. Camelback East Village Planning Com., 1987-90. Mem. ABA (vice-chair rules and procedures com. 1983-87, chair-elect, 1987, chair, 1988-89, co-chair long range planning subcom. 1984-85, sr. vice chair tort ins. practice sect. 1989-90, chair ann. mktg. arrangements rules and procedures com. 1986-87, publ. subcom. for The Brief 1987, mem. professionalism com. 1989-90, chair policy com. 1989-90, chair use of expert witness subcom. of com. trial practice 1982-90, ABA litigation sect.), State Bar Ariz. (com. on rules of civil practice and procedure, chmn. publs. subcom. trial practice sect., exec. com. trail practice sect.), Maricopa County Bar Assn. (bd. dirs. 1983-88, chair med./legal liaison com., 1987-89), Maricopa County Bar Found. (trustee 1984-88, sec. 1986-88, treas. 1988—), Nucleus (chair membership com. 1984-85, chair 1986-87, bd. dirs. 1988—), AAUW (parliamentarian, bd. dirs. Ariz. State div. 1980-82), Ariz. State U. Alumni Assn. (bd. dirs. 1980-83), Kappa Delta Pi, Assn. Trial Lawyers Am., Phoenix Assn. Def. Counsel, Ariz. Women Lawyers Assn., Def. Rsch. Inst. (practice and procedure com.). Democrat. Episcopalian. Office: O'Connor Cavanagh Anderson Westover Killingsworth & Beshears 1 E Camelback Rd Phoenix AZ 85012

CURIE, EVE, author, lecturer; b. Paris, Dec. 6, 1904; d. Pierre (Nobel prize winner for work in radium 1903) and Marie (Sklodowska) (Nobel prize winner in radio-active substances, 1903, in chemistry 1911) Curie; B.S., Ph.B., Sevigne Coll.; D.H.L. (hon.), Mills Coll., 1939, Russell Sage Coll., 1941; Litt.D. (hon.), U. Rochester, 1941; Hartwick Coll., 1983; m. Henry Richardson Labouisse, Nov. 19, 1954. Took up study of music and gave first concert as pianist, Paris, 1925; later concerts in France and Belgium; mus. critic for Candide (weekly jour.) for several years; also wrote articles on motion pictures and the theater; made first visit to U.S. with mother, 1921; on 2d visit lectured in 10 U.S. cities (speaks English, French and Polish), 1939; witnessed fall of France, 1940, went to London to work for cause of Free France; came to U.S., 1941, lectured on war in France and Eng.; because of pro-ally activities deprived of French citizenship by Vichy Govt., 1941. Served in Europe with Fighting French as officer in Women's div. of army; one of pubs. Paris Presse (daily), resigned to return to ind. writing, 1949. Spl. adviser Sec. Gen., NATO, 1952-54. Decorated Chevalier Legion of Honor (France), 1939; Polonia Restituta (Poland), 1939; Croix de Guerre (France), 1944. Author: Madame Curie (selection of Lit. Guild, Jr. Guild, Book-of-the-Month Club, Scientific Book of the month; Nat. book award for non-fiction), 1937; Journey Among Warriors (Lit. Guild Selection), 1943. Home: 1 Sutton Pl S New York NY 10022

CURKENDALL, BRENDA IRENE, business owner, consultant; b. Mesa, Ariz., Dec. 20, 1954; d. Arthur Blatt and Dorothy June (Goodnight) Dalton; m. James Patrick Monagle (div.); m. Christopher Lee Curkendall; 1 child, Chad Michael. Student, Edison Jr. Coll., 1971-72; BS in History, Fla. State U., 1976. Registered investment advisor. Realtor Harold A. Allen Co. Realtors, Tacoma, 1983; salesperson Computerland, Bellevue, Wash., 1983-

84; systems analyst for contract labor Boeing Computer Svcs., Tukwila, Wash., 1985; stock broker Shearson Lehman Bros., Tacoma, 1985-87; fin. planner Curkendall Fin. Programs, Inc., Puyallup, Wash., 1988—; instr. Pierce Coll., Tacoma. Contbr. articles to profl. jours. Capt. U.S. Army, 1976-82, Korea. Mem. Apt. Assn. Pierce County (pres. 1988), Ft. Hood Flying Club (pres. 1980), Rotary Internat. Office: Curkendall Fin Programs Inc 12012 98th Ave E Ste B Puyallup WA 98373

CURLE, ROBIN LEA, computer software industry executive; b. Denver, Feb. 23, 1950; d. Fred Warren and Claudia Jean (Harding) C.; m. Lucien Ray Reed, Feb. 23, 1981 (div. Oct. 1984). BS, U. Ky., 1972. Systems analyst 1st Nat. BAnk, Lexington, Ky., 1972-73, SW BancShares, Houston, 1973-77; sales rep. Software Internat., Houston, 1977-80; dist. mgr. Uccell, Dallas, 1980-82; v.p. Info. Sci., Atlanta, 1982-83; v.p. sales TesserAct, San Francisco, 1983-85, Foothill Research, San Francisco, 1986-87; v.p. sales and field ops. Natural Lang., Inc., Berkeley, Calif., 1987-89; pres., founder Curle Cons. Group, San Francisco, 1987-89; mgr. strategic mktg. MCC, Austin, Tex., 1989—. Mem. U. Ky. Alumni Assn., Delta Gamma (pres. 1969). Republican. Home: 10601 San Souci Pl Austin TX 78759

CURLEY, CLARE MARY, municipal bond analyst; b. Glen Cove, N.Y., May 25, 1961; d. Arthur James and Mary Elizabeth (Gavin) C. Student, Dartmouth Coll., 1982; BA, Wheaton Coll., Norton, Mass., 1983; MBA, Columbia U., 1990. Assoc. Fin. Guaranty Ins. Co., N.Y.C., 1983-87; sr. analyst Mcpl. Bond Investors Assurance Corp., Armonk, N.Y., 1987-89; asst. v.p. Capital Reinsurance Mgmt. Corp., N.Y.C., 1989—. Active St. Bartholomew's Community Club, N.Y.C. Mem. Mcpl. Analyst's Group of N.Y., Women's Mcpl. Bond Club of N.Y., Fin. Women's Assn., The Nature Conservancy, Wheaton Coll. Alumnae Assn. (bd. dirs., dir.-at-large 1983-86). Office: Capital Reinsurance Mgmt Corp 787 Seventh Ave New York NY 10019

CURLEY, EILEEN SARA, oil services executive, investment analyst; b. Milw., Apr. 18, 1936; d. Thomas Bernard and Florence E. Curley. BS, Marquette U., Milw., 1958. With WITI-TV, Milw., 1958-62; copywriter Shear Advt., Milw., 1962-63; research asst. Frederick and Co., Inc., Milw., 1963-68; investment analyst Robert W. Baird & Co. The Gaspar Report, Milw., 1968—, asst. v.p. oil, svcs. investment analyst. Mem. Nat. Assn. Petroleum Analysts, Milw. Investment Analyst Soc., Assn. for Investement Mgmt. and Rsch., St. Mary's Hosp. Guild, Milw. Athletic Club, Vagabonds, Options, Laumiere League. Republican. Roman Catholic. Office: Robert W Baird and Co 777 E Wisconsin Ave Milwaukee WI 53202

CURLEY, MARY KAY O'BRIEN, marketing coordinator; b. Binghamton, N.Y., Dec. 27, 1959; d. James Ralph and Mary Alexia (Luchansky) O'Brien; m. Michael Joseph Curley, Mar. 19, 1983; children: Michele B., Andrea E. BS, Utica Coll. of Syracuse U., 1982. Mktg. specialist Chase Lincoln First Bank, Binghamton, 1982-85; mktg./advt. specialist Crowley Foods, Inc., Binghamton, 1986-87; cons. mktg./writing Binghamton, 1987-88; sales/mktg. specialist Keith Clark, Inc., Sidney, N.Y., 1988—, sr. mktg. coord., 1990—; Bd. dirs. Sunrise Terr. Assn. Pub. rels. dir. Jr. League, Binghamton, 1987—; mem. pub. rels. com. United Way, Binghamton, 1983—, Children's Dicovery Ctr., Binghamton, 1985—; vol. Emergency Children's Shelter, Binghamton, 1989; active PTO, St. Catherines Sch. Mem. Pub. Relations Soc. Democrat. Roman Catholic. Home: 3 Rosedale Dr Binghamton NY 13905

CURLEY, SARAH SHARER, bankruptcy judge; b. Oak Park, Ill.; d. Robert F. Sharer and Marian Elizabeth (White) Fitzgerald; m. Roger D. Curley; 1 child. AB, Mount Holyoke Coll., 1971; JD cum laude, N.Y. Law Sch., 1977. Bar: N.Y. 1978, Wis. 1983, Ariz. 1986, U.S. Dist. Ct. (so., ea. dists.) N.Y., U.S. Dist. Ct. Ariz., U.S. Ct. Appeals (2nd cir.). Law clk. U.S. Dist. Ct., N.Y.C., 1977; atty. Fogelson, Fogelson & Collins, N.Y.C., 1978, Otterbourg, Steindler, Houston & Rosen, N.Y.C., 1979-82; asst. counsel First Wisconsin Corp., Milw., 1982-86; atty. Ayers & Graham, Phoenix, 1986; bankruptcy judge Fed. Gov., Phoenix, 1986—. Contbr. articles to profl. jours.; exec. editor: Bankruptcy Bar Bulletin, 1978. Fellow Ariz. Bar Found., Nat. Assn. Women Judges; mem. Nat. Conf. Bankruptcy Judges, Ariz. State Bar, Maricopa County Bar Assn., Ariz. Women's Lawyers Assn., State Bar of Wis., Am. Bar Assn., Soroptimists, Mount Holyoke Club (v.p.). Office: US Bankruptcy Ct 230 N 1st Ave Rm 5208 Phoenix AZ 85025

CURNS, EILEEN BOHAN, stress counselor, writer; b. Chgo., May 22, 1927; d. Alvin Joseph and Lorraine Kathleen (White) Bohan; m. John R. Curns, July 1, 1950 (div. 1975); children: James Richard, Barbara Curns Obrokta. BA in Sociology, DePaul U., Chgo.; MEd in Psychology and Edn., Loyola U., Chgo.; postgrad., U. Wis. Cert. Gestalt therapist. Prin. ACCORD, Deerfield, Ill.; designer, presenter speeches, worshops, seminars on teamwork, communication, people and mgmt. skills, stress mgmt. and wellness; researcher, implementer tng. program for orgns., med. facilities; negotiator corps. and community action groups. Author: (workbooks) Pathways to People, From Stress to Balance, Negatives to Positives; author self-scored tests, First Aid for Stress poster. Recipient Golden Deeds award Exchange Club, 1965, commendation Queen Mary Vets. Hosp., Montreal, 1975. Mem. Am. Bd. Med. Psychotherapists (cert.), Nat. Wellness Assn., Am. Soc. Counseling and Devel., Internat. Human Learning Resource Network, Midwest Soc. Profl. Cons. Home: 825 Waterview Circle Vernon Hills IL 60061 Office: Accord Box 393 Deerfield IL 60015

CURRAN, CAITLIN TAVENNER, lawyer; b. Pottsville, Pa., June 30, 1963; d. James Joseph Jr. and Carolyn Lucille (Tavenner) C. BS in Fgn. Svc., Georgetown U., 1985, JD, 1988. Bar: Pa. 1988. Assoc. Baskin Flaherty Elliott & Mannino, P.C., Phila., 1988-90, Elliot Mannino & Flaherty, P.C., Phila., 1990—; tchr. Hill Sch., Pottstown, Pa., summers 1989-90. Mem. Union League Phila., Racquet Club Phila. (devel. com. 1988-90). Republican. Roman Catholic. Home: 1520 Spruce St Apt 1008 Philadelphia PA 19102

CURRAN, CONNIE, health care executive; b. Berlin, Wis., Sept. 16, 1947; d. Patrick J. and Kathleen (Ottoway) C.; m. Donovan W. Riley, Aug. 28, 1983; 1 child, Melissa Curran. BS, U. Wis., 1969; MS, DePaul U., 1972; EdD, No. Ill. U., 1974; postgrad., U. San Francisco, 1978-80. Nurse, instr. Mt. Sinai Hosp., Chgo., 1969-72; instr. Chgo. City Coll., Chgo., 1972-73; dept. chmn. Loyola U., Chgo., 1974-77; assoc. dean, prof. U. San Francisco, 1977-81; dean of Coll. Nursing Med. Coll. Wis., Milw., 1980-83; prof. CUNY, 1983-85; chmn. nursing Montefiore Med. Ctr., N.Y.C., 1983-85; v.p. Am. Hosp. Assn., Chgo., 1985-88; sr. v.p. Medicus Systems, Evanston, Ill., 1987-89; pres. The Curran Group, Chgo., 1988—; bd. dirs. Alverno Coll.; cons. various hosps. and colls., 1980—; mem. faculty Columbia U., N.Y.C., 1987—. Author: Preparation for Practice, 1981; anchor numerous TV segments, 1983—; contbr. article to profl. jour. Grantee Commonwealth Fund, 1987, Pew Charitable Trust, 1988. Mem. Am. Acad. Nursing (bd. dirs. 1987—), Nat. Commn. Nursing (bd. dirs. 1985-88), Sigma Theta Tau (Media award 1982).

CURRAN, DONNA RAE, bank officer; b. Bristol, Pa., Mar. 15, 1955; d. Donald Raymond and Isabel (Garcia) C. Student, Indiana U. Pa., 1973-75; BA in Econs., Duquesne U., 1978; postgrad., Allegheny Community Coll., 1987-88. Notary pub., Pa. Escrow analysis adminstr., then supr. escrow Ryan Fin. Svcs., Inc., Pitts., 1979-82; asst. v.p., mgr. investor acctg. RFS/NVR Mortgage L.P., Pitts., 1982-88; asst. v.p., mgr. investor acctg. and computer svcs. Ryan Fin. Svcs. Inc./NVR Mortgage L.P., Pitts., 1988-89; asst. v.p., asst. servicing mgr. RFS/NVR Mortgage L.P., Pitts., 1989-90; v.p. mortgage ops. EquiBank, Pitts., 1990—; committeeperson savs. and loan com. Computer Power, Inc., Jacksonville, Fla. Mem. Vectors/Pitts., 1987-89. Mem. NAFE, Mortgage Bankers Assn., MidAtlantic CPI User Group, Women in Mgmt., Pa. Assn. Notaries. Office: EquiBank 2 Oliver Plaza Pittsburgh PA 15230

CURRAN, ELEANOR GAVIGAN, personnel executive; b. West Haven, Conn., Sept. 30, 1924; d. Edward Joseph and Mary Catherine (Dickinson) Gavigan; m. Vincent John Curran, Nov. 8, 1947; children: Robert Joseph, Laura Marie, Vincent John. Grad. high sch. Bookkeeper New Haven R.R., 1942-47, Talon, Inc., Hamden, Conn., 1947-52, Eli Moore, Hamden, 1965-70; pers. dir. Johnny Barton, Inc., North Haven, Conn., 1970—; bd. dirs. Conn. Fed. Credit Union, North Haven, 1980—. Vice-chariperson Hamden Dem. Town Com., 1965-69, asst. registrar of voters, 1969-77. Democrat. Roman Catholic. Home: 75 Cumpstone Dr Hamden CT 06518

CURRAN, HILDA PATRICIA, social worker; b. Patterson, N.J., Jan. 15, 1938; d. James Patrick and Hilda Lucille (Walsh) C.; m. Robert S. Kennon, Nov. 1980. AB, Hiram Coll., 1959; MSW, Ohio State U., 1963. Tchr. Cin. Bd. Edn., 1960; caseworker Franklin County Welfare Dept., Columbus, Ohio, 1960-61; mem. relocation staff Springfield (Mass.) Redevel. Authority, 1963-64; neighborhood organizer Community Council Greater Springfield, 1964-65; mem. program devel. staff United Community Ctrs., Bklyn., 1965-67; facilities devel. specialist in vocat. rehab. Mich. Dept. Edn., Lansing, 1967-70; program devel. specialist Bur. Community Services, Mich. Dept. Labor, Lansing, 1970-78, dir. Office Women and Work, 1978—. Mem. Ingham County Housing Commn., 1977-79, Ingham County Social Services Bd., 1979-82; bd. dirs., officer Big Bros.-Big Sisters Greater Lansing, 1968-82; charter mem. bd., officer Big Bros.-Big Sisters Am., 1977-89, Big Sisters Internat., 1973-77, pres. 1976-77; trustee Hiram Coll., 1985—; mem. adv. bd. Salvation Army, 1986—; mem. zoning bd. appeals City of Lansing, 1986—; pres. Greater Lansing Food Bank, 1988—. Recipient Diana award in govt. YWCA, 1977, ann. award for outstanding achievement Hiram Coll., 1980. Mem. Nat. Assn. Social Workers (mem. del. assembly 1977, 81, 84, 87, fin. com. 1985—, pres. Lansing-Jackson chpt. 1978-80, Lansing-Jackson Social Worker of Yr. 1977), Acad. Cert. Social Workers, AAUW (pres. East Lansing br. 1989—), Women as Agt. of Change award 1981), Phi Kappa Phi (life). Club: Torch (pres. 1979-80) (Lansing). Lodge: Zonta. Home: 415 McPherson Lansing MI 48915 Office: 309 N Washington St Lansing MI 48909

CURRAN, JERRY LYNNE, critical care nurse administrator, consultant; b. L.A., Aug. 14; d. George Lynn Mallow and Sybil Jane (Bates) Harmeier; m. Thomas Charles Curran, Oct. 29, 1955 (div. Mar. 1978); children: Dennis Patrick, Michael Thomas. ADAS, Grayson Coll., 1972; BS in Nursing Mgmt., Midwestern State, 1984; BS in Health Care Scis., U. Tex., 1988. RN, Tex.; cert. health adminstrn., nursing adminstrn. Supr. Bethania Regional Med. Ctr., Wichita Falls, Tex., 1972-76; clinic mgr. Bell Helicopter Internat., Esfahan, Iran, 1976-78; nursing supr. Bethania Regional Med. Ctr., Wichita Falls, Tex., 1978-81; head nurse U. Tex. Med. Br., Galveston, Tex., 1981-83, nursing coord., 1983-84; dir. critical care svcs. St. Mary's Hosp., Galveston, Tex., 1984-87, dir. mktg. ambulatory care, 1987-88; quality assurance coord. U. Tex. Med. Br., Galveston, 1988-89; RN critical care Houston, 1989-90; regional mgr. analytical Med. Enterprises, Houston, 1990—; CPR instr. Am. Heart Assn., 1973—; critical care instr. St. Mary's Hosp., Galveston, 1987-88; computer instr. U. Tex. Med. Br., Galveston, 1982-84; infectious disease instr. St. Mary's Hosp., Galveston, 1988. Bd. dirs. The 1894 Grand Opera House, Galveston, 1989—; vol. chair Galveston Hist. Found., 1985—; vol. Galveston Dem. League, 1990. Mem. Am. Nurses Assn., Tex. Nurses Assn. (sec. 1986-88), Am. Mgmt. Assn., Health Svcs. Mktg. Soc., Sigma Theta Tau. Methodist. Home: 1900 Back Bay Dr Galveston TX 77551

CURRAN, KRISTINE CHARNOWSKI, marketing executive; b. Winona, Minn., Dec. 10, 1954; d. H.J. and Louise (Golt) C.; m. Mark A. Curran, June 1, 1985. BA in Sociology, Loyola U., Chgo., 1977; MA in Sociology, U. Chgo., 1979, PhD in Sociology, 1982. Research analyst U. Chgo., 1977-81; cons. demographics City Bond Cons., Oakland, Calif., 1981-82; sr. research analyst Allstate Ins. Co., Menlo Park, Calif., 1982-84; cons. mktg. Bank Am., San Francisco, 1984-86; mgr. mktg. Pacific Bell Corp., San Francisco, 1986—. Coordinator Ogle County McGovern for Pres., Rochelle, Ill., 1972; bd. dirs. East Bay chpt. Big Bros./Big Sisters, 1988—. Mem. Am. Mktg. Assn., Am. Population Assn., Am. Sociol. Assn., U. Chgo. Alumni Assn. (bd. dirs. No. Calif. chpt. 1986—), Alpha Sigma Nu. Democrat. Roman Catholic. Club: Oakland Athletic. Home: 5882 Ascot Dr Oakland CA 94611 Office: Pacific Bell Corp 2600 Camino Ramon Rm 4 S 700C San Ramon CA 94583

CURRENT, JORETTA LOUISE, medical record administrator; b. Lancaster, Pa., Jan. 11, 1960; d. Joseph Eugene and JoAnn Loree (Comfort) C. AS, Oxford (Ga.) Coll., 1979; BS, U. Cen. Fla., 1982. Registered record administr. Asst. dir. med. records St. Francis Community Hosp., Greenville, S.C., 1982-85; dir. med. records and utilization mgmt. Jupiter (Fla.) Hosp., Inc., 1985-90; med. records cons. Care Communications, Inc., Chgo., 1990—. Mem. Am. Med. Record Assn., Fla. Med. Record Assn., Nat. Mgmt. Assn., Suncoast Med. Record Assn. (pres. 1988). Republican. Baptist.

CURRID, CHERYL CLARKE, information systems executive, technical writer; b. Newark, July 21, 1950; d. Charles McAleer and Evelyn (Agusta) Clarke; m. Raymond E. Currid Jr., Nov. 17, 1979; children: Raymond E. III, Justin Clarke. BA in Psychology, George Mason U., 1972, postgrad. in systems, 1976-77. Sales rep. R.J. Reynolds Co., Annandale, Va., 1975-78; sales mgr. M&M Mars Co., Annandale, 1978-82; systems mgr. Coca-Cola Foods, Houston, 1983—; bd. dirs. Connectivity Solutions 88 Personal Computer expo, Englewood Cliffs, N.J., 1987—; bd. advisors Networld, Dallas, 1989—, Comdex, Needham, Mass., 1989—. Author: The Power User Guide to R: Base, 1989, Mastering Novell Netware, 1990; columnist weekly Risky Business PC Week mag., 1989—; contbr. articles to profl. jours. Mem. Software Assocs. Group (pres. 1979-82), Capital Personal Computer Users Group, Houston Area League of Personal Computer Users, Netware In Common., Microcomputer Mgrs. Assn. Republican. Home: 818 Herdsman Houston TX 77079 Office: Coca-Cola Foods 2000 St James Pl Houston TX 77056

CURRIE, BARBARA FLYNN, state legislator; b. LaCrosse, Wis., May 3, 1940; d. Frank T. and Elsie R. (Gobel) Flynn; AB cum laude, U. Chgo., 1968, AM, 1973; m. David P. Currie, Dec. 29, 1959; children: Stephen Francis, Margaret Rose. Asst. study dir. Nat. Opinion Rsch. Ctr., Chgo., 1973-77; part time instr. polit. sci. DePaul U., Chgo., 1973-74; mem. Ill. Ho. of Reps., 1979—, chmn. House Dem. Study Group, 1981-83; chair House Revenue Com.; vice chair House Appropriations II Com.; co-chair Ill. Citizens Assembly, Ill. Coun. on Women; mem. House Energy, Environ. and Natural Resources, Human Svcs., Pub. Utilities Coms. Mem. adv. bd. Harriet Harris YWCA; v.p. Chgo. LWV, 1965-69; mem. ACLU, Hyde Park-Kenwood Community Conf., South Shore Commn., South Shore Hist. Soc., Ind. Voters of Ill.-Ind. Precinct Orgn., Hyde Park Coop. Soc., Ams. for Dem. Action. Named best legislator Ind. Voters of Ill., 1980, 82, 84, 86, 88, Ethel Parker award, 1982, 86, 88, best legislator Ill. Credit Union League; recipient Ill. Environ. Coun. award, Ill. Community Action Agys. award, Ill. Women's Polit. Caucus Lottie Holman O'Neill award; Outstanding Legislator Ill. Hosp. Assn., 1987; Susan B. Anthony award, honor award Nat. Trust Historic Preservation; awards Welfare Rights Coalition of Orgns., Ill. Pub. Action Coun., Chgo. Heart Assn.; named Legislator of Yr., Ill. Nurses Assn., 1984, Nat. Assn. Social Workers, 1984, Ill. Women's Substance Abuse Coalition, 1984; recipient BEST BETS award Nat. Ctr. Policy Alternatives, 1988, Svc. award Nat. Ctr. For Freedom of Info. Studies, 1989, Cert. of Appreciation SEIU Local 880, 1989, March of Dimes, 1988. Mem. ACLU, DAV, Ill. Conf. Women Legislators, Nat. Order Women Legislators, Delta Kappa Gamma. Contbr. article to publ. Office: 2107 Stratton Office Bldg Springfield IL 62706

CURRIE, SISTER EILEEN, college president; BA in Psychology, Cabrini Coll., 1966; MA in Religious Edn., LaSalle Coll., 1976; postgrad. Bryn Mawr Coll./HERS Summer Inst., 1982, Inst. for Ednl. Mgmt./Harvard U., 1983. Tchr. religion/English, coordinator Confraternity Christian Doctrine programs, mem. vicariate religious edn. bd. Sacred Hearts of Jesus and Mary Sch., Bklyn., 1970-73, mem. parish council, 1971-77, prin., 1973-77, chairperson area cluster schs. for consol., 1975-77; tchr. Mother Cabrini High Sch., N.Y.C., 1977-81, acting prin., 1978-79, coll. advisor, 1979-80, moderator student body assn., 1979-81; dean student affairs Cabrini Coll., Radnor, Pa., 1981-82, pres., 1982—, past trustee; chairperson Apostolic Evaluation Team U.S. Provinces, Missionary Sisters of Sacred Heart, 1975-76, mem. provincial council ea. province, 1978-81; trustee St. Clare's Health Ctr., N.Y., 1981-82; mem. bd. adminstrn. Santa Cabrini Hosp., Montreal, Can., 1983—. Office: Cabrini Coll Eagle and King of Prussia Rds Radnor PA 19087*

CURRIE, MADELINE ASHBURN, business administration educator; b. Rankin, Tex., Sept. 28; d. Herman and Ivan G. Vinson; BS, Tex. Woman's U., 1962; MA, Calif. State U., 1967; EdD, UCLA, 1974; m. Gail G. Currie; children: Robb Ashburn, Mark Ashburn, Michael Ashburn. Tchr., Edgewood High Sch., West Covina, Calif., 1962-69 ; instr. Rio Hondo Coll., Whittier, Calif., 1968-69; prof., grad. dir. Coll. Bus. Adminstrn., Calif. State Poly. U., Pomona, 1969-88, prof. emerita, 1988—. Recipient award Alpha Lambda Delta, Prof. Emerita award 1988, Exceptional Merit award, Meritorious Service awards Calif. State Poly. U., 1984. Mem. Grad. Sch. Edn., UCLA. Mem. Calif. Bus. Edn. Assn. (Recognition award), Tex. Woman's U. Alumnae Assn., Women in Mgmt., Rotary Internat. (Upland club, bd. mem.) Delta Pi Epsilon, Pi Lambda Theta, Delta Kappa Gamma (chpt. pres.), Delta Mu Delta.

CURRIER, SUSAN ANNE, computer software company executive; b. Melbourne, Victoria, Australia, Nov. 20, 1949; d. David Eric and Irene Hazel (Baker) Bruce-Smith; m. Kenneth Palmer Currier, Feb. 16, 1974. Student, Melbourne U., 1967-70. Fashion model Eileen Ford Model Agy., N.Y.C., 1971-74, Wilhelmina Models, N.Y.C., 1974-82; owner Softsync Inc., N.Y.C., 1981-90; pres. Expert Software div. Bloc Devel., Coral Gables, Fla., 1990—. Home: 201 Crandon Blvd #1102 Key Biscayne FL 33149 Office: Bloc Devel Expert Software Div 800 SW 37th Ave Ste 765 Coral Gables FL 33134

CURRIN, MARGARET PERSON, prosecutor; b. 1950. AB, Meredith Coll., 1972; JD, Campbell U., 1979. Bar: N.C. 1979. Legis. asst.to U.S. Senator John Tower, 1979-80; asst. dean, asst. prof. Campbell U., Buies Creek, N.C., from 1981; U.S. atty. U.S. Dist. Ct. Ea. Dist. N.C., Raleigh, 1988—; gen. counsel N.C. Rep. Party, 1981-83; mem. Wake County Bd. Elections, 1983-87, chmn., 1985-87. Mem. Phi Kappa Phi. Office: PO Box 26897 Raleigh NC 27611*

CURRY, BEATRICE CHESROWN, English educator; b. Lakefork, Ohio, Jan. 14, 1932; d. Tod Shields and Sadie Irene (Springer) C.; m. Elton Wheeler Curry, Sept. 9, 1967 (div. 1988); 1 child, James Christopher. BA, Ashland (Ohio) Coll., 1954; MA, Western Res. U., 1965. English tchr. Hamilton Jr. High Sch., Houston, 1954-58, Alexander Hamilton Jr. High Sch., Cleve., 1958-59, Glenville High Sch., Cleve., 1959-60; tchr. English, head dept. Fonville Jr. High Sch., Houston, 1960-66; prof. English, Columbia (Tenn.) State Community Coll., 1967—. Bd. dirs. Child Care Svc. Columbia, 1973-76. Nea grantee, 1979, Mellon grantee, 1981, 82. Mem. Maury County Creative Arts Guild (literary chmn. 1984-86), Alpha Delta Kappa (Beta Alpha chpt. pres. 1990). Home: 810 Barrow Ct Columbia TN 38401 Office: Columbia State Comm Coll Hampshire Pike Columbia TN 38401

CURRY, DENISE, federal agency investigator; b. River Rouge, Mich., Aug. 15, 1952; d. Ben and Lillie (Frazier) Curry. BA in Psychology, Mercy Coll. of Detroit, 1974; MA in Pub. Adminstrn., U. Detroit, 1980; postgrad., Detroit Coll. Law, 1985, Whittier Coll., 1987—. Compliance investigator Drug Enforcement Adminstrn., Detroit, 1974-85; supervisory investigator Drug Enforcement Adminstrn., L.A., 1986—; fed. women's program coordinator Drug Enforcement Adminstrn., Detroit, 1975-84, mem. regional EEO adv. coun., 1979-81. Mem. Am. Soc. Pub. Adminstrs. (L.A. met. chpt.), The Chem. People (Southeastern Mich. Substance Abuse Svcs. orgn., cert. of recognition 1983). Democrat. Baptist. Office: Drug Enforcement Adminstrn 350 S Fiqueroa Ste 800 Los Angeles CA 90071

CURRY, KATHLEEN BRIDGET, librarian; b. Parnell, Iowa, May 19, 1931; d. John Michael and Ellen Theresa (Clear) C. BS in Libr. Sci., Marycrest Coll., 1953. Head libr. Moline (Ill.) Sr. High Sch., 1953—; part-time libr. Moline Pub. Hosp. Sch. of Nursing, 1957-66; mem. sch. nursing libr. St. Anthony's Hosp., Rock Island, Ill., 1955; hit. libr. Rock Island Hist. Libr., Moline, 1956-59; libr. Black Hawk Coll., Moline, 1958-59. Exec. bd. Miss Iowa Pageant, Davenport, Iowa, 1987—; bd. dirs. Miss Black Hawk Valley Pageant, Moline, 1986—, Quad City Arts Coun., Davenport, 1990; guild mem. Quad City Symphony Orch., Davenport, 1972—. Recipient Disting. Svc. award Marycrest Coll., 1987, Disting. Svc. award Moline High Sch. PTA, 1983. Mem. Ill. Edn. Assn., NEA, Ill. Sch. Libr. Assn., AAUW, Moline Edn. Assn., Ilowa Libr. Assn., Zonta Internat., Delta Kappa Gamma. Democrat. Roman Catholic. Home: 1851 18th Ave Moline IL 61265 Office: Moline Sr High Sch 3600 23rd Ave Moline IL 61265

CURRY, LEYLA CAMBEL, legal services administrator; b. Evanston, Ill., Nov. 18, 1953; d. Ali Bulent Cambel and Marion R.A. dePaar; m. Ronald C. Curry, Sr., Oct. 1, 1983; 1 child, Brian. Student, U. So. Calif. Exec. asst. Kaye, Scholer, Fierman, Hays & Handler, L.A., 1987-88, Debevoise & Plimpton, L.A., 1988-89; mng. adminstr. Law Offices Robert K. Pollak, L.A., 1989—; pres. LCC Assocs., LaPuente, Calif.; cons. law office initiation and mgmt.; provider mgmt. tng. programs for office personnel. Mem. NAFE, Legal Assts. Assn. Mem. Soc. of Friends. Home and Office: 15833 Loukelton St La Puente CA 91744

CURRY, MARY GRACE, environmental impact officer; b. New Orleans, June 16, 1947; d. Clyde Lalio and Gladys Ruth (Ehret) C. BS in Biology, U. New Orleans, 1969, MS in Biology, 1971; PhD in Botany, La. State U., 1973. Cert. environ. profl. La. Environ. scientist VTN La., Inc., Metairie, 1974-79; environ. impact officer The Parish of Jefferson, Harahan, La., 1979—; cons. La., 1979—. Author: Gretna-A Sesquicen, 1986; editor jour. The Louisiana Environmental Professional, 1984—; contbr. articles to hist. and profl. jours. Chmn. City of Gretna (La.) Sesquicentennial, 1985-86; pres. Gretna (La.) Hist. Soc., 1986-88; founder Friends of the La. St. Fire Mus., 1987; charter mem. Jefferson Hist. Soc. La. Mary Grace Curry Day named in her honor, City of Gretna, 1985. Mem. DAR (historian), La. Acad. Scis. (chmn. environ. scis. sect.), La. Environ. Profls. Assn. (founder, pres. 1979, 88, 89, v.p. 1990), UDC (pres. New Orleans 1984—, Jefferson Davis award 1986), German Heritage, Cultural and Geneal. Soc. of La. (charter, v.p. 1987—). Democrat. Roman Catholic. Home: 3404 Tolmas Dr Metairie LA 70002 Office: The Parish of Jefferson 1221 Elmwood Park Blvd Harahan LA 71023

CURRY, NANCY ELLEN, education educator; b. Brockway, Pa., Jan. 26, 1931; d. George R. and Mary F. (Covert) C. BA, Grove City Coll., 1952; MEd, U. Pitts., 1956, PhD, 1972; grad., Pitts. Psychoanalytic Inst., 1988. Lic. psychologist, Pa. Tchr. public schs. East Brady and Oakmont, Pa., 1952-55; presch. demonstration tchr. Arsenal Family and Children's Center, U. Pitts., 1955-79, assoc. dir., 1971-79; from instr. in psychiatry to prof. child devel., program dir. child devel. Sch. Social Work, U. Pitts., 1972-88; also mem. faculty U. Pitts Sch. Medicine, Sch. Edn., Sch. Health Related Professions.; Fulbright exchange tchr. North Oxford Nursery Sch., Oxford, Eng., 1957-58; vis. prof. Oreg. State U., summer, 1964, Ariz. State U., summer, 1969; assoc. dir. early childhood project Edn. Professions Devel. Act, U.S. Office of Edn., 1970-74; cons. in field. Co-producer 12 films on children's play; author numerous articles on child devel. Mem. AAUP, Assn. for Care of Children in Hosps., Nat. Assn. for Edn. of Young Children, Am. Psychol. Assn., Am. Psychoanalytic Assn. Office: U Pitts 1717 CL Pittsburgh PA 15260

CURRY, RUBY COTTON, community service volunteer; b. Bardstown, Ky., Mar. 7, 1907; d. William McCagha and Leona (Ashby) C.; m. D.P. Curry, Nov. 22, 1930 (widowed); children: Ralph, Leonard. AB, Bowling Green (Ky.) State U., 1928; MA, Western Ky. U., 1959; MLS, Spalding Coll., 1969. Cert. English tchr., Ky. Tchr. English Cave City (Ky.) High Sch., 1928-43, Elkton (Ky.) Todd County High Sch., 1943-47; tchr. English and Latin langs. Campbellsville (Ky.) High Sch., 1947-67; tchr. in English and library sci. Cambpellsville Coll., 1967-73, tchr., librarian, 1973-74; with communication media Taylor County Bank, Campbellsville, 1980-88; ret., 1989; sponsor of future tchrs. Campbellsville High Sch., 1961-67; coord. library sci. program Campbellsville Coll., 1970-74. Co-sponsor gift shop Taylor County Hosp., Campbellsville, 1974-84; mem. com. Campbellsville and Taylor Counties July 4th Celebration, 1978; sec. Friends of the Library, Campbellsville, 1978—; v.p. Bus. and Profl. Women's Club, 1976-77; pres. AAUW, Campbellsville, 1979-81. Recipient Woman of Achievement award Bus. and Profl. Women's Club, 1977, named Woman of the Yr., 1979. Democrat. Baptist. Home: 320 Sharon Dr Campbellsville KY 42718

CURTIN, CATHERINE MARIE, foreign trade consultant, product market research and analysis consultant; b. Portland, Oreg., July 3, 1951; d. Edmond and Olive Joan (Schrantz) C. BA, U. Portland, 1973; BA, Univ. Coll., Cork, Ireland, 1976, MA, 1976. Historian Archdiocese of Portland, 1976-78; market research devel. Property Mgmt. Services Inc., Vancouver, Wash., 1978-80; adj. instr. history U. Portland, 1981—; dir. contbns. Nike, Inc., Beaverton, Oreg., 1981-84, research asst. to chmn., 1984-87; pres. CMC Research Internat. , 1987—. Contbr. articles to hist. and profl. jours. Vol., Oreg. Hist. Soc., 1980, Spl. Olympics, Portland, 1981—; pres. bd. dirs. Oreg. Spl. Olympics. Mem. Am. Com. on Irish Studies, All Ireland Cultural Soc., U.S.-China Peoples Friendship Assn., N.W. China Council, Soc. Competitor Intelligence Profls. Democrat. Club: Oreg. Road Runners (Portland). Avocations: early 20th century Chinese history, Chinese lang./writing, running. Office: PO Box 10932 Portland OR 97210-0932

CURTIN, JANE THERESE, actress, writer; b. Cambridge, Mass., Sept. 6, 1947; d. John Joseph and Mary Constance (Farrell) C.; m. Patrick F. Lynch, Apr. 31, 1975. A.A., Elizabeth Seton Jr. Coll., 1967; student, Northeastern U., 1967-68. Appeared in plays The Proposition, Cambridge and N.Y.C., 1968-72, Last of the Red Hot Lovers touring co., 1973; Broadway debut in Candida, 1981; author, actress Off-Broadway mus. rev. Pretzels, 1974-75; star TV series NBC Saturday Night Live, 1975-79, Kate & Allie, 1984-88, Working It Out, 1990—; appeared in films including Mr. Mike's Mondo Video, 1979, How to Beat the High Cost of Living, 1980, O.C. and Stiggs, 1987; TV films include Divorce Wars-A Love Story, 1982, Suspicion, 1988, Maybe Baby, 1988, Common Ground, 1990. Recipient Emmy nomination, 1977; Emmy awards for outstanding actress in comedy series, 1984, 85. Mem. Screen Actors Guild, Actors Equity, AFTRA. Office: care Creative Artists Agy 9830 Wilshire Blvd Beverly Hills CA 90212*

CURTIN, VIRGINIA MARIE, nurse; b. Needham, Mass., June 26, 1958; d. David John and Eileen Mary (Foley) C. BS, Simmons Coll., 1980; MS, U. Calif., San Francisco, 1986. Cert. RN, Pediatric Nurse Practitioner. Student nursing asst., clin. nurse specialist Children's Hosp. Med. Ctr., Boston, 1978-80, patient activities dept., 1979-80; staff nurse surgical unit Children's Hosp. Nat. Med. Ctr., Washington, 1980-81, staff nurse pediatric med. unit, 1981-84; staff nurse med. respiratory unit Children's Hosp., Oakland, Calif., 1985-86; coord. cord blood screening program hemoglobinopathies Children's Hosp., Oakland, 1986-87, craniofacial clin. nurse specialist, 1986—; research asst. Pediatric Pain Study Univ. Calif., San Francisco, 1985-86. Recipient Commendation for Outstanding Primary Nursing Children's Hosp. Nat. Med. Ctr., 1984, Donna Pruzansky Meml. Fund Scholarship Am. Cleft Palate Conf., 1988. Mem. Assn. for the Care of Children's Health, Calif. Nurse's Assn., Am. Cleft Palate Craniofacial Assn., Clin. Nurse Specialists No. Calif., Sigma Theta Tau. Democrat. Roman Catholic. Home: 491 Twenty Third Ave San Francisco CA 94121 Office: Craniofacial Clinic Children's Hosp 747 52d St Oakland CA 94609

CURTIS, ALVA MARSH, artist; b. N.Y.C., June 15, 1911; d. Charles Johan and Elizabeth (Hagstrom) Berg; student Art Students League, N.Y.C., 1928-29, Grand Central Art Sch., 1934-36, N.Y. Sch. Fine Arts, 1930-31, Nat. Acad., N.Y.C., 1934-35, Columbia U., 1943-44, Yale U., 1969-70; m. Terrill Belknap Marsh, Nov. 3, 1932; children: Owen Thayer, Charles Ames, Ronald Belknap; m. Russell G. Curtis, Aug. 11, 1979; children—Russell G. Jr., William E. One woman shows: Scranton Meml. Library, Madison, Conn., 1969, Phippsburg (Maine) Library, 1964, Town and County Club, Hartford, Conn., 1976, Conn. Bank & Trust Co., Madison, 1977, 1st Fed. Savs. & Loan, Madison, 1977; group shows include: The Mariner's Mus., Newport News, Va., Va. Salmagundi Club, N.Y.C., Smithsonian Inst., Washington, 1964, 66, Internat. Maritime Art Award Show (Sculpture award), 1981, Nat. League Am. Penwomen Art Show (Sculpture award), Atlanta, 1982, Arnold Gallery, Newport, R.I., 1984, Copley Gallery, Boston, 1986, Candlewood Gallery (Sculpture award 1986), New Milford, Conn., 1986; represented in permanent collections: Swedish Club, Chgo., Conn. Bank & Trust Co., Windsor, Phippsburg Library, also pvt. collections; ptnr., art dir. Terrill Belknap Marsh, Assos., N.Y.C., 1934-69; lectr. in field. Vice chmn. Madison Inland Wetlands Agy., 1974-84. Mem. Am. Soc. Marine Artists, New Eng. Sculpture Assn., Nat. Arts Club, Nat. League Am. Penwomen (pres. 1978—, Greenwich br. 1958). Republican. Episcopalian. Clubs: Lyme Art Assn., Madison Winter, Garden Madison. Home: 319 Essex Meadows Essex CT 06426

CURTIS, GLENDA MORRIS, management consultant, state training specialist; b. Plant City, Fla., Jan. 22, 1939; d. James F. and Gladys I. (Bledsoe) Dedmon; m. James K. Morris, Nov. 22, 1958 (div.); children: Jennifer, Jan, Mark, Bryan; m. Richard Perry Curtis, May 14, 1988 (div. 1990). BS, U. Tenn., 1961; MEd., Vanderbilt U., 1986. Supr. Social Security Adminstrn., Melbourne, Fla., 1962-87; mgmt. trainer and cons. Nashville, 1982—; tng. specialist State of Tenn. Human Svcs., Nashville, 1987—; vol. cons. N.W. Tenn. Regional Health Office, Union City, 1986. Contbr. articles to several newspapers. Pres. Jaycettes, Dyersburg, Tenn., 1965, Freed-Hardeman Women's Soc., Paris, Tenn, 1973, Union City Bus. and Profl. Women, 1985, Union City Civic Chorus, 1986. Mem. Am. Soc. Tng. and Devel. (Tenn. Trainer award 1985), Assn. for Quality and Participation, NAFE, Tenn. State Employees' Assn. Republican. Home: 756A McPherson Dr Nashville TN 37221 Office: State of Tenn Human Svcs 400 Deaderick 4th Fl SDU Nashville TN 37219

CURTIS, MARY PACIFICO, advertising agency executive; b. Chgo., Feb. 22, 1953; d. Louis Enrico Pacifico and Margaret (Geneva) Peterson; m. Douglas Reid Curtis, Jan. 2, 1982. BS, Northwestern U., 1973. Assoc. producer Panorama Prodns., Santa Clara, Calif., 1975-76; copy chief Moorhead Mktg., San Francisco, 1976-77; pres. Pacifico & Assocs. Inc., San Jose, Calif., 1977—; founder Silicon Valley Bank, San Jose, 1984—. Bd. dirs. Childrens Counseling Ctr., Santa Clara, 1980—, pres.; bd. dirs. San Jose Symphony Assn., 1984—. Recipient San Francisco Cable Car award San Francisco Ad Club, 1978; Best in the West awards of merit, 1979, 80; Maggie award, 1980; Addy award, 1984; Joey award, 1984; Murphy award, 1984, 85, 86, 88, BPAA Award of Merit, 1987, 89. Mem. San Jose Ad Club, Peninsula Women in Advt., San Jose Women in Advt., Western States Ad Agys. Assn., Am. Mktg. Assn. Roman Catholic. Avocations: photography; tennis; skiing. Office: Pacifico & Assocs Inc 2145 The Alameda Suite 101 San Jose CA 95126

CURTIS, NANCY RUTH, elementary school educator; b. Mpls., Nov. 3, 1937; d. James Arthur and Helen Ruth (Street) Harris; m. John Harold Curtis, Aug. 26, 1960; 1 child, Nancy Elizabeth. AB, MacMurray Coll., 1959; MEd, Valdosta (Ga.) State Coll., 1976, EdS, 1981. Cert. early childhood edn. Tchr. Pembroke (Mass.) Sch. Dist., 1959-60, Norwell (Mass.) Sch. Dist., 1960-62, Kewanee (Ill.) Sch. Dist., 1963, Toulon (Ill.) Sch. Dist., 1964-65, Danville (Ill.) Sch. Dist., 1967-69, Leon County Sch. Dist., Tallahassee, 1969-71, Lowndes County, Valdosta, 1971—. Mrm. AAUW (treas. Valdosta br. 1978-80, sec. 1983-85), NEA, Delta Kappa Gamma, Sigma Alpha Iota (patroness). Democrat. Episcopalian. Office: Lake Park Sch Lake Park GA 31636

CURTIS, PATRICIA ELLEN, consultant, educator; b. Buffalo, Nov. 14, 1930; d. Alfred John and Irene (Doll) C. BA in Music, Rosary Hill Coll., Amherst, N.Y., 1952; BS in Piano Performance, Julliard Sch. Music, 1955; MA in Musicology, Columbia U., 1957. V.p., sec. Economy Reduction Corp., Buffalo, 1957-67; prof. and chmn. dept. music Daemen Coll., Amherst, N.Y., 1958-75; v.p. acad. affairs, dean Daemen Coll., 1975-84; sr. assoc. McManis Assocs., Inc., Washington, 1984—; pres. Curtis Cons. Assocs., Inc., Buffalo, 1987—; trustee, treas. Community Music Sch., Buffalo, 1984-88, pres., 1988—; cons. ORS Arts Found., Buffalo Zoo, numerous other orgns., 1984—; lectr. arts and mgmt. topics to civic, profl. and ednl. orgns. Author program notes Buffalo Philharm. Orch., 1958-65. Mem. Amherst Community Edn. Adv. Council, 1985—, community adv. coun. SUNY, Buffalo, 1988—; div. chmn. United Way, Buffalo, 1986-87. Mem. Am. Assn. Higher Edn., Am. Council on Edn., Buffalo C. of C. Office: Curtis Cons Assocs Inc Olympic Towers 300 Pearl St Buffalo NY 14202

CURTIS, VERNA P., elementary school educator; b. Jackson, Miss., Mar. 20, 1940; d. William Grady Polk and Mary Ann Gray; m. Edward L. Curtis, Apr. 12, 1968; 1 child, Vera. BS cum laude, Jackson State U., 1962; MEd, Boston U., 1968; EdS, Jackson State U., 1987; postgrad., Cornell U. Reading specialist/reading facilitator Jackson Pub. Schs., tchr.; reading instr. Jackson State U. Recipient fellowship. Mem. Assn. for Supervision and Curriculum Devel., Jackson Area Reading, IRA, MSCD, Miss. Reading Assn. Home: 114 Waylawn Ct Jackson MS 39206

CURTS, CONSTANCE ELAINE, communications specialist; b. Babylon, N.Y., Dec. 8, 1957; d. Calvin Aldrich and June Ione (Cornwell) S.; m. John M. Curts, Feb. 6, 1976. BS in Electronics, Mo. Inst. Tech., Kansas City, 1978; Post. Grad., U. Mo., 1989—. Field svc. engr. Telegraphic Bus. Systems, Mission, Kans., 1976-78; communications tech. AT&T, Kansas City, 1978-89; asst. prof. De Vry Inst., Kansas City, Mo., 1989—; staffwriter AT&T, Kansas City, 1984-89; cons. Advanced Computer Techs. Independence, Mo., 1988; staff writer Am. Tel. & Tel., K.C., 1984-89, customer rels. spokesman, Am. Tel. & Tel., K.C., 1983-89. Editor: Mo. Inst. Tech. K.C. 1976-78, (contbg.) Communications Workers Am., through 1989, (chmn. 1987); author: (short story) Charlie's Perspective, 1989, (game clues for board game) Clever Endeavor, 1989; contbr. articles to profl. jours. Fundraiser Kans. Sch. for the Deaf, Olathe, 1981—, Friends-Indian Aid, Riverside, Mo., 1988-89; vol. pub. TV, KCPT-19, K.C., 1988—. Mem. Telephone Pioneers Am. (chmn. 1985-89), DeVry Alumni Assn. Home: 9121 Riggs Ln Overland Park KS 66212

CUSACK, MARY JOSEPHINE, lawyer; b. Canton, Ohio, Mar. 3, 1935; d. Edward Thomas and Mary (O'Meara) Cusack; AB, Marquette U., 1957; JD, Ohio State U., 1959. Bar: Ohio 1959, U.S. Supreme Ct. 1962. Atty., Indsl. Commn. Ohio, Columbus, 1960-61, Ohio Dept. Taxation, Columbus, 1961-65; adj. prof. family and probate law Capital U., Columbus, 1971-82; spl. counsel to Ohio Atty. Gen., 1971-82; ptnr. Cotruvo & Cusack, Columbus, 1961-79; pvt. practice Columbus, 1979—. Mem. Ohio Commn. on Status of Women; councilperson Village of Riverlea. Fellow Ohio State Bar Found., Columbus Bar Found. (charter), ABA (mem. house of dels.), Am. Bar Found., Ohio Bar Assn. (past chmn. workmen's compensation com., mem. council dels.), Columbus Bar Assn. (profl. ethics com., adv. com. fees, workmen's compensation; mem. Women Lawyers Club Columbus (past pres.), Ohio Acad. Trial Lawyers (workmen's compensation com.), Franklin County Trial Lawyers (sec., past pres.), Nat. Assn. Women Lawyers (rec. sec., past pres.), Ohio Assn. Attys. Gen. (past pres.), Nat. Bd. trial Advocacy, Am. Arbitration Assn. (nat. panel arbitrators), Thomas More Soc., Toastmasters (past pres. Columbus), Columbus Met. Club, Pilot of Columbus Inc., Press Club of Ohio, Kappa Beta Pi (past internat. pres., del. Profl. Frat. Assn.), Theta Phi Alpha. Office: 50 W Broad St Columbus OH 43215

CUSHING, KAY SMITH, public relations executive; b. Pitts., Feb. 21, 1944; d. George Byron and Margaret Elizabeth (Smith) C.; m. Kenneth Neuhausen, May 16, 1981. BA, Lindenwood Coll., 1965. Gen. mgr. Pitts. Ballet Theatre, 1975-78; account supr. Ketchum Pub. Relations, Pitts., 1978-79, v.p., 1979-82, group mgr., 1982—, sr. v.p., 1984—. Mem. strategic planning com. United Way of Allegheny County; trustee Am. Fed. Aging Research; bd. dirs. Gateway to Music, Pitts. Pub. Theater, Winchester-Thurston Sch. Recipient Matrix award Women in Communications, Pitts., 1983-84. Mem. Pub. Relations Soc. Am. (pres. Pitts. chpt. 1986-87; Vic Barkman award 1984), Fedn. Girls Sch. Socs. Republican. Roman Catholic. Clubs: Carnegie 100, Rivers, Concordia (Pitts.). Office: Ketchum Pub Rels 6 PPG Pl Pittsburgh PA 15222

CUSHING, MARGARET CHANNING, travel agent; b. Boston, Aug. 12, 1941; d. George Marston Jr. and Mary Margaret (Loring) Cushing. AA, Pine Manor Jr. Coll., Wellesley, Mass., 1961; BSBA, Boston U., 1978. Cert. travel counselor. Travel coordinator Fed. Travel Svc., Boston, 1974-77; travel coordinator Raymond & Whitcomb Co., Boston, 1978-79, N.Y.C., 1979-83; commn. agt. Inverness Travel Inc., N.Y.C., 1983—. Mem. Inst. Cert Travel Agts. (life), 41-74 Club for Women in Travel, Nat. Soc. Colonial Dames. Episcopalian. Office: Inverness Travel Inc 770 Lexington Ave New York NY 10021

CUSHING, PAMELA HIGLEY, municipal development executive; b. Elgin, Ill., Dec. 16, 1943; d. Philip Isidro and Helen Leonore (Bettis) Higley; m. Victor Merchant Cushing, July 8, 1967 (div. 1981); 1 child, Jason Philip. BS in Retailing, Mich. State U., 1966. Supr. Bridgeport (Conn.) Hosp., 1969-71; owner, mgr. Cushing Dressage Ctr., Neenah, Wis., 1983-85; exec. dir. Future Neenah Devel. Corp., 1985-87, Downtown Neenah Action Com., Inc., 1986-87, City Ctr. Devel. Authority, Bellingham, Wash., 1987—; cons. Internat. Downtown Assn., Washington, 1986—, Internat. Coun. Shopping Ctrs., 1987—, Urban Land Inst., 1987—. Contbr. articles to profl. jours. Mem. Horizon's PTA, Appleton, Wis., 1986-87, Happy Valley PTA, Bellingham, 1987-88, Silver Beach PTA, 1988—, Washington State Downtown Coun. Home: 2832 Pullman St Bellingham WA 98226 Office: City Ctr Devel Authority PO Box 5785 Bellingham WA 98227

CUSHMAN, ANN LOUISE, education educator; b. Boulder, Colo., July 1, 1961; d. James Otis and Beverly Ann (Barrett) Moore; m. Mark Andrew Cushman, Nov. 27, 1981. BA, U. Colo., 1986, MS, 1989. Instr. U. Colo., Colorado Springs, 1986-89, U. So. Colo., Pueblo, 1989—. Mem. Am. Math. Soc. Office: U So Colo 2200 Bonforte Blvd Pueblo CO 81001

CUSHMAN, LAURA ANN, orthopaedics rehabilitation professor; b. Rochester, N.Y., May 11, 1958; d. Eugene S. Cushman and Rita Norene (Ames) Nordquist; m. Alan K. Stetler, Sept. 19, 1987. BA, Wheaton (Ill.) Coll., 1979; PhD, Wayne State U., 1984. Lic. psychologist N.Y. Assoc. prof. U. Rochester (N.Y.), Sch. of Medicine and Dentistry, 1984—. Contbr. articles to profl. jours. Bd. dirs. Mental Health Assn., Rochester, 1985—. Recipient Thomas G. Rumble fellowship Wayne State U., Detroit, 1979. Mem. Internat. Neuropsychological Soc., Am. Psychol. Assn., Nat. Acad. Neuropsychologists, Am. Assn. Spinal Cord Injury Psychologists and Social Workers. Democrat. Episcopalian. Office: U Rochester Med Ctr 601 Elmwood Ave Box 664 Rochester NY 14642

CUSHMAN, MARGARET JANE, home care executive, nurse; b. Pahokee, Fla., Nov. 17, 1948; d. Edmund Francis and Mary Margaret (Adams) C. Diploma in nursing, Johns Hopkins Hosp., 1969; BSN, U. Pa., 1972; MSN, Yale U., 1976. Asst. dir. nursing St. Joseph's Hosp., Phila., 1972-74; asst. dir. Regional Vis. Nurse Agy., North Haven, Conn., 1976-78; exec. dir. Waterbury (Conn.) Vis. Nurse Assn., 1978-82; exec. v.p. Vis. Nurse and Home Care, Inc., Plainville, Conn., 1982-86, pres. VNA Group Inc. subs., 1986—; asst. clin. prof., Yale U. Sch. Nursing, New Haven, 1978—; cons. U. S.C. Sch. Nursing, 1987—, U. Tex., San Antonio, Sch. of Nursing, 1989—. Contbrg. author: chpt. Home Health Administration, 1988; contbr. articles to profl. jours. Mem. Gov.'s Blue Ribbon Com. to Investigate the Nursing Home Industry in Conn., Hartford, 1975-77. Robert Wood Johnson/Nat. League for Nursing summer fellow, 1975; recipient Andrew Veckerelli prize Yale U. Sch. of Nursing, 1976, Disting. Alumni award, 1986, Creative Thinking Tribute award Creative Thinking Assn. of Am., 1990. Mem. Am. Nurses Assn., Conn. Assn. for Home Care (sec. 1981-85), Nat. League for Nursing, Nat. Assn. for Home Care (chmn. 1986-88, Mem. of Yr. award 1984), Sigma Theta Tau. Republican. Home: 170B Brittany Farms Rd New Britain CT 06053 Office: VNA Group inc 146 New Britain Ave Plainville CT 06062

CUSHMAN, PAULETTE BESSIRE, museum volunteer; b. London, United Kingdom, Feb. 14, 1931; d. Paul Frederic and Antoinette Louise (Schupbach) B.; m. Paul Cushman Jr., Feb. 4, 1930; children: Paul, Clare Hepburn. Student, Putney, England, 1948. Dep. asst. Andre Cie, Switzerland, 1951-52, Bank for Internat. Settlements, Switzerland, 1952-54; mgr. La Chatelainie, Switzerland, 1954-56, City Display, London, UK; founder, owner First Impressions USA, Richmond, Va., 1985-87; U.S. mgr. Roger Lascelles Clocks of London, 1986—. Pres., sec. Bandwagon, N.Y.C., 1975-76.

CUSSON-COBB, JODY MARIE, lawyer; b. Peoria, Ill., Jan. 2, 1957; d. Joseph Richard and Fern Margaret (De Giovanni) Cusson; m. Grant Sutherland Cobb, Sept. 27, 1980; 1 child, Sara Elizabeth. BSW, Ind. U., Indpls., 1981, JD, 1985. Bar: Ind., 1985, U.S. Dist. Ct. (no. and so. dists.) Ind., 1985. Rsch. asst. Office Ind. Atty. Gen., Indpls., 1983-85, dep. atty. gen., 1985-86; staff counsel Ind. Utility Regulatory Commn., Indpls., 1986-87, gen. counsel, 1988-89; dist. prosecuting atty. U.S. Ct. Appeals (8th cir.), 1989—; staff atty. The Associated Group, Indpls., 1990—. Mem. bd. edn. Our Lady of the Greenwood (Ind.) Cath. Ch., 1989—; mem. devel. com., chair membership com. Ind. chpt. for Prevention Child Abuse, Indpls., 1989—. Mem. Ind. State Bar Assn., Phi Alpha Delta, Kappa Kappa Kappa (treas. 1989—). Roman Catholic.

CUSTURERI, MARY CATHERINE FOCA, teacher; b. Jersey City, Dec. 28, 1929; d. Joseph and Rosa (Scala) Foca; m. Domenick Custureri, July 31, 1948; children: Frank, Richard. BS, Fla. Atlantic U., 1969, MEd, 1972, EdS, 1986, EdD, 1989. English and reading tchr., basic program coord. Cardinal Newman High Sch., West Palm Beach, Fla., 1969—; ednl. cons., cons. at risk students Inservice Insts.; speaker at confs. in field. Contbr. articles to profl. jours. Bd. dirs. Respect Life, Palm Beach County, 1989—. Recipient cert. of appreciation Am. Cancer Soc., 1984; grantee Palm Beach County Edn. Found., 1985, Fla. Atlantic U., 1980. Mem. Internat. Reading Assn. (speaker 1988), Nat. Cath. Edn. Assn., Fla. Reading Assn., Palm Beach County Reading Assn., Nat. Coun. Tchrs. English (speaker 1988), Palm Beach County Tchrs. English (bd. dirs. 1988—), AAUW, Internat. Computer Club, Delta Kappa Gamma (v.p. North Palm Beach chpt. 1988—). Roman Catholic.

CUTLER, BEVERLY WINSLOW, judge; b. Washington, Sept. 10, 1949; d. Lloyd Norton and Louise Winslow (Howe) Cutler; m. Mark Andrew Weaver, Sept. 22, 1977; children: Lucia Mary, Andrew Thaddeus, Rebecca Howe. BA, Stanford U., 1971; J.D., Yale U., 1974. Bar: Alaska 1975. Research atty. Alaska Jud. Council, Anchorage, 1974-75; atty. Alaska Pub. Defender Agy., Anchorage, 1975-77; judge Alaska Dist. Ct., Anchorage, 1977-82, Alaska Superior Ct., Palmer, 1982—. Fellow ABA, Alaska Bar Assn., Anchorage Assn. Women Lawyers, Nat. Assn. Women Judges, Nat. Assn. Women in Criminal Justice. Office: Alaska Ct System 435 S Denali St Palmer AK 99645

CUTLER, CYNTHIA ANN, operations executive; b. Pitts., Aug. 15, 1953; d. William David and Margaret Thresa (Neu) Lockhart; m. Raymond W. Cutler, May 15, 1976; children: Russell Ray, Gina Marie. Grad. high sch., McMurray, Pa. Bookkeeper Phillip S. Weiner, Pitts., 1971-73; asst. controller Vibroflotation Found. Co., Pitts., 1973-75; gen. mgr. Vault Am., Pitts., 1983-88; v.p. Data Mgmt., Inc., Pitts., 1988—. Mem. Assn. Records Mgrs. & Adminstrs., Inc. (treas. 1987-88, v.p. 1988-89, pres. 1989—, sec. 1988—). Office: Data Mgmt Inc 20 Parkway View Dr Pittsburgh PA 15205

CUTLER, LAUREL, advertising agency executive; b. N.Y.C., Dec. 8, 1926; d. A. Smith and Dorothy (Glaser) C.; m. Stanley Bernstein, July 3, 1952 (div. 1983); children—Jon Cutler, Amy Sarah, Seth Perry. B.A., Wellesley Coll., 1946. Reporter Washington Post, 1946-48; copywriter J. Walter Thompson, N.Y.C., 1947-50; copy chief Wesley Assocs., 1950-56; v.p. Fletcher, Richard, Calkins & Holden, N.Y.C., 1956-63; sr. v.p., creative dir. McCann Erickson, N.Y.C., 1963-72; sr. v.p. Leber Katz Ptnrs., N.Y.C., 1972-80, exec. v.p., dir. mktg. planning, 1980-84, vice chmn., 1984—; vice chmn. FCB/Leber Katz Ptnrs., N.Y.C., 1986—; v.p. consumer affairs Chrysler Corp., Highland Park, Mich., 1988—; speaker to orgns. including Assn. Nat. Advertisers, Am. Mktg. Assn., Produce Mktg. Assn., Grocery Mfrs. Am., Conf. Bd. Recipient Matrix award Women in Communications, 1985, Achievment award Wellesley Alumni Assn., 1990. Mem. Fashion Group. Home: 15 W 53d St New York NY 10028 Office: Chrysler Corp 12000 Chrysler Dr Highland Park MI 48288

CUTLER, LAUREN ELIZABETH SAVAGE, sales executive; b. Syracuse, N.Y., July 10, 1961; d. William Edward and Patricia Noreen (Anable) Savage; m. Robert Lee Cutler, Aug. 30, 1986. BS, Clarkson U., 1983. Sales rep. Tab Products of Cen. N.Y., Cazenovia, 1983-84, Satellite Bus. Systems (div. IBM), Mpls., 1984-85; market researcher Tompkins Bros. Co., Inc., Syracuse, 1985-86; ter. mgr. Monarch Marking, Fairfield, N.J., 1986—; mem. bd. dirs., corp. sec. Cutler Indsl. Sales, Bayshore, N.Y., 1986—. Mem. NAFE, Am. Prodn. and Inventory Control Soc. (speaker, bd. dirs., v.p. programs). Republican. Roman Catholic. Home: 105 Country Village Ln East Islip NY 11730

CUTLER, LYNN GERMAIN, political worker; b. Chgo., Oct. 15, 1938; d. Charles T. and Berniece F. (Feldman) Germain; m. Henry Cutler, June 10, 1963 (dec.); children: Megan, Jennifer, Allison, Allan. B.A., U. No. Iowa, 1962, M.A., 1967. Tchr. pub. schs. Cedar Falls, Iowa, 1962-65; grad. asst. U. No. Iowa, 1965-67; adminstr. Head Start, 1967-71; dir. Vol. Bur., Black Hawk County, Iowa, 1971-75; supr. Black Hawk County, 1975—; now vice chmn. Dem. Nat. Com., 1975-82; vice chmn. Dem. Nat. Com.; mem. Adv. Commn. on Intergovtl. Rels., Washington, 1977-82, vice chmn., 1978—. Active Iowa Commn. Children and Youth, 1963-69; chmn. Iowa State Manpower Coun., 1977—; Dem. candidate for Congress, 1980, 82; adv. com. Nat. Women's Edn. Fund. Mem. LWV, Nat. Assn. Counties (bd. dirs.), Nat. Assn. Regional Councils (bd. dirs.), Iowa Women's Polit. Caucus. Jewish. Office: Dem Nat Com 430 S Capitol St SE Washington DC 20003

CUTLER, MORENE PARTEN, civic worker; b. Waxahachie, Tex., July 27, 1911; d. Bedford Taylor and Lofie Mae (Stockton) Parten; m. Robert Ward Cutler, Apr. 27, 1954. Student, Trinity U., 1929, U. Okla., 1931, U. Tex., 1933. Asst. to dir. N.Y. Sch. for Interior Decoration, N.Y.C., 1938; chief cons. Hilton Hotels Corp., Chgo., 1946-48; free-lance interior designer, 1948-54. Author: Stagecoach Inn--Iron Skillet and Velvet Potholder, 1981. 1st. pres., chmn. bd. dirs. Salado (Tex.) Bicentennial Com., 1974—, chmn. Salado Sesquitennial Com., 1984—; bd. dirs. Cen. Tex. Bicentennial Com., 1974; mem. Internat. Debutante Ball, N.Y.C., 1956—, Beautify Tex. Coun., 1976—; chmn. Beutify Salado Com., 1979-80; founder Tex. Bluebonnet Com., 1961; trustee Cen. Tex. Area Mus., Salado, 1968-75; hon. mem. Ellis County Mus., Waxahachie, 1967—. Recipient Tex Good Will awards, 1960—, Outstanding Dist. Gov. award Beautify Tex. Coun., 1984. Mem. AIA (founder N.Y. aux. chpt. 1958, citation 1966), Chautauqua Preservation Soc. (bd. dirs. Waxahachie chpt. 1975), Preservation Soc. Newport County, Salado C. of C. (bd. dirs. aux. chpt. 1974-75), Tex. Soc. Washington. Episcopalian. Club: Met. (N.Y.C.). Home: PO Box 26 Salado TX 76571

CUTLER, RHODA, psychologist; b. N.Y.C.; d. Samuel and Sophia (Petrushinsky) C. AB in Physiology/Psychology, Hunter Coll.; AM in Psychology, NYU; postgrad., Yeshiva U.; PhD, NYU. Lic. psychologist, N.Y. Counseling psychologist N.Y. Assn. for New Ams., N.Y.C., 1947-60; asst. instr. psychiatry N.Y. Med. Coll., N.Y.C., 1961-65; sch. psychologist Bur. of Child Guidance, N.Y.C., 1964-65; psychol. cons. Bur. Child Welfare, Div. Adoption Svcs., N.Y.C., 1965—; psychotherapist Mental Health Cons. Ctr., N.Y.C., 1967-70; rsch. assoc. prof. Inst. for Developmental Studies, NYU, 1966-68, vis. assoc. prof., 1969; asst. prof. psychiatry N.Y. Med. Coll., N.Y.C., 1968-69; rsch. psychologist Child Devel. Ctr., N.Y.C., 1969-70; asst. clin. prof. Mt. Sinai Coll. Medicine/Beth Israel Med. Ctr., N.Y.C., 1970—. Contbr. articles to profl. jours. Mem. Am. Psychol. Assn., N.Y. Psychol. Assn., N.Y. Soc. Clin. Psychologists, N.Y. Acad. Sci., Soc. of Clin. and Exptl. Hypnosis. Home: 230 E 88th St New York NY 10128

CUTLER, RUTH ELLEN LEMON, aircraft company executive; b. York, Nebr., Feb. 26, 1928; d. Harry Oliver and Ruby Elizabeth (Hartgrave) Lemon; m. Hal Max Cutler, Nov. 17, 1944 (div. 1971); children: Sheryl, Harold Max, Pamela. Student Latter-day Saints Bus. Coll., 1946. Sec., photostat operator IRS, Salt Lake City, 1951-54; sec. Purdue U. Sch. Civil Engring., West Lafayette, Ind. and engring. firms, 1954-59; sec. to the fin. commn. State of Utah., 1959-60; exec. sec. Rico Argentine Mining Co., Salt Lake City and Rico, Colo., 1960-63; exec., legal sec. Manpower, Inc., Salt Lake City, 1959-71; owner, operator Mountain View Motel and Country Club Motel, Salt Lake City, 1963-64; exec. sec., adminstrv. asst. to clin. psychologist in pvt. practice, Salt Lake City, 1964-70; legal sec., head office staff Watkins & Faber, attys., Salt Lake City, 1971-73; adminstrv. sec. F-15 Radar div. Hughes Aircraft Co., El Segundo, Calif., 1973—; dir., v.p., sec. Cutler Enterprises, Inc., Salt Lake City, 1963-71; founder, pres., pub., bd. dirs. Gallant House Inc., Sandy, Utah, 1983—. Utah Rep. del., 1967-69; active various community drives; Rep. del. Utah, 1967-69, 90-92. Mem. League Utah Writers.

CUTLER, WINNIFRED BERG, biologist; b. Phila., Oct. 13, 1944; d. Adolph and Eleanor Berg; m. Stephen William Cutler, Dec. 18, 1962 (div. 1982); children: Jodie Elizabeth, Evan Karl; m. Thomas E. Quay, May. 13, 1989. PhD, U. Pa., Phila., 1979; BSc., Ursinus Coll., Collegeville, Pa. Asst. prof. biology Beaver Coll., Glenside, Pa., 1982-83; research assoc. Gynecology Dept. U. Pa. Hosp., 1981-84; co-founder, scientific dir. Woman's Wellness Program U. Pa. Hosp., Phila., 1984-86; dir., pres. Athena Inst. for Women's Wellness Research, Haverford, Pa., 1986—; founder Stanford Menopause Study, Calif., 1980-81. Author: Hysterectomy: Before and After, 1988; co-author: A Guide for Women and the Men Who Love Them, 1983, The Medical Management of Menopause, 1984; co-inventor pheromones; author numerous sci. papers. Mem. Outreach Coun. Bryn Mawr Presbyterian Ch., Pa., 1984-90. Mem. Internat. Soc. for Study of Time, Internat. Acad. Sex Rsch., Am. Fertility Soc., Conf. on Reproductive Behavior, Human Biology Coun. Republican. Presbyterian.

CUTRIE, SHERRI ANN, social services administrator; b. Trenton, N.J., June 21, 1948; d. Joseph Cutry and Ruth P. Gonzalez. Cert. surg. tech., St. Francis Med. Ctr., 1967; student, Mercer County Community Coll. Adminstrv. supr. Dept. Human Svcs.-Adult Mentally Retarded, Trenton, 1970-80; owner, adminstr. Lic. Skill Devel. Home-Mentally Retarded, Trenton, 1981—; program cons. for homeless woman House of Ruth Shelters, Washington, 1985-86, asst. dir., 1986-87, interim exec. dir., 1987; v.p. Deep Programming Assoc., Inc., Trenton, 1988—; co-owner S & R Music, Trenton, N.J., 1989—; cons. various local human svc. agencies, Trenton, 1981-85, Echo Elderly, Trenton, 1982, Opportunities for Older Ams., Washington, 1987, Dept. Devel. Disabilities (sponsorship recognition 1988), Trenton, 1980—; bd. dirs. D.P.A., Inc., Delaware, Trenton, 1988—. Mem. West Trenton Fire Co. Ladies Auxillary, 1969; vol. United Way, Trenton, 1982, Community Food Svc. to Elderly, Trenton, 1982-83. Mem. NAFE, NOW, N.J. Bd. Realtors, N.J. Mentally Retarded Assn. Democrat. Home and Office: 239 Chestnut Ave Trenton NJ 08609

CUTRUBUS, CHRISTINA N., publisher; b. Ogden, Utah, Feb. 8, 1934; d. Gus James and Athanasia (Gogoras) C. Student, Weber St. Coll., 1952-54, U. Utah, 1954-56. Publicist Metro Goldwyn Mayer; owner Phonic Arts Agy., Univ. Svcs. Corp., 1971; owner, pubr./editor Utah Preservation/Restoration Mag.; personal rep., press agt. His Eminence Archbishop Iakovos, primate of Greek Orthodox Archidocese of N. and S. Am.; advisor, cons. Goya Nat. Conf. Editor/pubr. Utah Ballet West Mag.; compiler, editor, pubr. book: The Salt Lake Temple: A Monument to a People; compiler, author book: D. Alt: Impressions of an Impressionist (1989 Award of Merit, Rounce & Coffin Club). Recipient Power of the Pen honor award Nat. Trust For Hist. Preservations in U.S. Mem. Salt Lake Advt. Club, Salt Lake C. of C., Zeta Phi Eta. Address: 1159 2nd Ave Salt Lake City UT 84103

CUTTER, PORTIA LYNETTE, mathematics educator; b. N.Y.C., Dec. 28, 1938; d. JeRoyd Wiley and Portia Mae (Russell) Greene; m. James Allen Cutter Sr., Mar. 3, 1962; children: James Allen Jr., Michelle Denise. Student, Long Beach State Coll., 1962-63, Morgan State Coll., 1955-57; BA, CUNY, 1961; MS in Teaching, Memphis State U., 1972, postgrad., 1980-83. cert. math. educator, Tenn. Tchr. 7th grade Del Norte Elem. Sch., West Covina, Calif., 1961-62; tchr. algebra Vanguard Jr. High Sch., Compton, Calif., 1963-64; tchr. 7th grade math Klondike Elem. Sch., Memphis, 1965; tchr. 7th grade sci. Humboldt (Tenn.) Jr. High Sch., 1966-68; tchr. 7th and 8th grade math Georgian Hills Jr. High Sch., Memphis, 1968-71; tchr. algebra Kingsbury Jr. High Sch., Memphis, 1971—, chair math dept., 1982—. Fin. sec. Greater Faith Baptist Ch., 1975—. Office: Kingsbury Jr High Sch 1276 N Graham Memphis TN 38122

CUZZONE, MARY JO, banker; b. Chgo., Nov. 12, 1953; d. Dominic Tony and Rose Marie (Raucci) Cuzzone. With Nat. Bank Commerce, Berkeley, Ill., 1972—, v.p., 1985—. Office: Nat Bank Commerce 5500 St Charles Rd Berkeley IL 60163

CVELJO, KATHERINE, education educator, retired; b. Farrell, Pa.; d. Peter and Angela (Ikica) C. Diplomed Econ., U. Zagreb, Yugoslavia, 1951; MSLS, Case Western Res. U., 1959, MS in Slavic Lang., Lit., 1967, PhD in Information Sci., 1975. Reference libr. Detroit Pub. Libr., 1959-61; libr. Ohio State U., Columbus, 1961-65; bus./sci./tech. reference libr. Cleve. Pub. Libr., 1965-67; bibliographer/reference libr. Case Western Res. U., Cleve., 1967-69; assoc. prof. U. S.C., Columbia, 1970-74, U. Ky., Lexington, 1974-77; prof. U. N. Tex., Denton, 1977-88, prof. emerita, 1988—. Editorial bd.: Informatologia Yugoslavica, Zagreb, 1979—; contbr. articles to profl. jours., encyclopedias, reviews, 1959—. Recipient Fulbright Scholar award, Council for Internat. Exchange of Scholars, Washington, 1989-90, Tng. award, U.S. Dept. HEW, U. S.C., 1972-73, Harold Lancour Scholarship, Beta Phi Mu Honor Soc., Pitts., 1978, HEA Title IIB Fellowship, Health Edn. Act Title IIB, Washington, 1970-71, Disting. Mem. award, Special Librs. Assn., Washington, 1989. Mem. (hon.) ALA, Tex. Libr. Assn., Special Librs. Assn. (com. on standards 1986-88), Internat. Fedn. Libr. Assns. (sci. and tech. com. 1983-85), Altrusa (coms. 1988—), AAUW (v.p. 1985-87, corp. rep. 1983-88). Democrat. Roman Catholic. Home: 2329 Windsor Dr Denton TX 76201 Office: Univ North Tex Sch Libr and Info Scis Denton TX 76203

CWIRKO, TRACEY ALICE, restaurant owner; b. Englewood, N.J., Aug. 18, 1963; d. Roy Arnold Jr. and Joyce Alice (Wolff) Askling; m. Arnold Anthony Cwirko, Oct. 25, 1986; 1 child, Anthony Edwin. Assocs. in Liberal Arts, Fairleigh Dickinson U., 1985, BS, 1987. Owner Zacchino Inc., Milton, N.J., 1985—. Mem. Admisty Internat. & Christian Children's Fund. Mem. Amnestry Internat., Omicron Nu Epsilon. Republican. Home: 51 Liberty Ln Franklin NJ 07416 Office: Zacchino Inc 5531 Berkshire Valley Rd Milton NJ 07438

CYMERMAN, SANDRA RAE, educational administrator, consultant; b. Valparaiso, Ind., Feb. 8, 1942; d. Oscar and Dorothy E. (Magid) Rosenberg; m. Allen Cymerman, July 3, 1966; children: Ami L., David O. BS in Edn., Ind. U., 1964; MS in Counselor Edn., Boston U., 1972. Cert. elem. tchr., Mass., Ill., Pa., guidance counselor, elem. prin. Tchr. Wilmette (Ill.) Pub. Schs., 1964-66, Radnor (Pa.) Twp. Pub. Schs., 1966-68, Wellesley (Mass.) Pub. Schs., 1968-70; lectr., supr. Lesley Coll., Cambridge, Mass., 1970-85; supr. student tchrs. Assumption Coll., Worcester, 1973; lectr., supr. Framingham (Mass.) State Coll., 1980-87; cons. gifted and talented edn. Mass. Dept. Edn., 1984—; dir. project diffusion Sage Program via Nat. Diffusion Network Nat. Diffusion Network Framingham Pub. Schs., 1985—; assoc. producer Kable Kids, Channel 23 Community Cablevision, Framingham, 1981-83; tchr. Coll. Gate, Natick, Mass., 1984-85, Summer Sage, Framingham, 1987-88; fed. project adminstr. Nat. Diffusion Network, U.S. Dept. Edn., Washington. Mem. creative arts coun. Framingham Pub. Schs., 1976-86; vol. vocat. counselor YMCA Women's Resource Ctr., Framingham, 1979-81; bd. dirs. South Middlesex County Office for Children, Framingham, 1984-86; mem. exec. bd. Metro West ARC, Framingham, 1989—. Nike award Bus. and Profl. Women's Assn., 1984; U.S. Dept. Edn. grantee, 1985-88. Mem. Mass. Assn. for Advancement Individual Potential (v.p. 1986-87), Nat. Assn. for Gifted Children (creativity com.), ASTD, Assn. for Supervision and Curriculum Devel., Coun. for Exceptional Children, Mortar Bd., Brandeis Women's Com. (pres. 1973-74, sec. 1974-75, nat. fin. sec. 1975-76). Home: 78 Delmar Ave Framingham MA 01701 Office: Framingham Pub Schs 454 Water St Framingham MA 01701

CYN, T. G., writer; b. Hollywood, Calif., Feb. 29, 1948; d. Edwin Whitfield and Virginia Lou (Newcomb) McKinley; m. Gerald J. Harvey, June 26, 1970 (div. 1976); m. Stanley John Maleski Jr., Oct. 21, 1979 (div. 1984); m. Bruce B. McCulloch, Sept. 13, 1986. Student, Riverside City Coll., 1965-67; student, Orange Coast Coll., 1967-68. Editor Al Buraag mag., 1979; freelance writer, editor, profl. horseman, equine practitioner, small animal practitioner The Cons., Arabian Horse Mktg. and Bus. Rev., Washington, 1980-82; dir. publs. Am. Horse Council, Washington, 1982-84; cons. Haifa Arabians, Diamond Bar, Calif., 1983-86, Khemosabi Syndicate, Diamond Bar, 1983-85; pres. T.G. Cyn & Co., Gainsville, Va., 1986—; owner Ancient Promise Arabians. Author: Tangled Mane, 1983, Gardner Bloodstock Consultant, 1980, Resilient Heart, 1985, Cowards, 1985, Tangled Mane, Vol. II, 1986, The Lonesome Pony, 1986, A New Wrinkle, 1988, National Champion, 1989. Mem. Internat. Arabian Horse Assn., Arabian Horse Registry Am., Am. Horse Shows Assn., Arabian Horse Trust Bedouin Club.

CYNAR, SANDRA JEAN, electrical engineering educator; b. Chgo., Aug. 7, 1941; d. Lionel Thomas and Dorothy Adeline (Swain) Bowers; m. Raymond John Cynar, Mar. 6, 1965; 1 child, Mark Jon. BSEE, Long Beach (Calif.) State U., 1963; MSEE, Calif. State U., Long Beach, 1978; PhD in Engring., U. Calif., Irvine, 1986. Controls engr. Gen. Dynamics, Pomona, Calif., 1963-64; mgmt. trainee Pacific Telephone, Alhambra, Calif., 1964-65; sci. programmer N. Am. Rockwell, Downey, Calif., 1965-68, McDonnell Douglas, Long Beach, 1968-70; prof. engring./computer sci. Calif. State U., Long Beach, 1977—; faculty advisor Calif. State U. Computer Soc., 1988—, Soc. of Women Engrs., 1988—; prog. chmn. Simulation & Engring. Edn., San Diego, 1988-89, conf. chmn., 1989-90. Contbr. articles to profl. jours.; creator animated films: Tuned Pendulum, 1988, Solution of Ode's, 1989. Mem. IEEE (sr. mem.), Soc. Computer Simulation, Nat. Computer Graphics Assn., Am. Soc. Engring. Edn., ACM. Republican. Methodist. Office: Calif State Univ 1250 Bellflower Blvd Long Beach CA 90840

CYR, ELLIE R., geologist, educator; b. Cambridge, Mass., Jan. 21, 1942; d. Philip and Pauline (Nemser) Raab; m. Guy A. Cyr, Sept. 1, 1968 (div. June 1980); children: Barry, Gary. BA in Philosophy cum laude, Clark U., 1963; postgrad., U. Mass., 1965; MS in Geology, Lehigh U., 1967. Cert. geolog. scientist, sewage enforcement officer; reg. profl. geologist, S.C. City geologist Dept. Pub. Works, Bethlehem, Pa., 1966-68; geologist Rosdor Constrn., Ardsley, N.Y., 1968-69; tchr. Jewish Day Sch., Allentown, Pa., 1970-74; owner, v.p. M&E Sewerage Specialists, Inc., Nazareth, Pa., 1974-78; geologist R&G Engring. Co., Inc., Bethlehem, Pa., 1977-78; cons. geologist Macungie Pa. and Durham N.C., 1979—. Zoning officer Bushkill Township, Nazareth, 1974-76; planner Bushkill Planning Commn., 1975-78; vol. firefighter Macungie Fire Dept., 1980-86. Recipient Cert. of Merit, Nat. Assn. Home Builders, 1982; Chester Kingsley fellow, 1965. Mem. Geol. Soc. Am., Am. Inst. Profl. Geologists, Phi Beta Kappa, Sigma Gamma Epsilon, Fireman's Relief Assn. (treas. 1981-85), Carolina Geologic Soc. Democrat. Jewish. Home and Office: 529 Woodwinds Dr Durham NC 27713

CYRUS, TERIECE DYER, educational adminstrator; b. West Monroe, La., Feb. 17, 1912; d. Virge Lee and Nora (Green) Ivey; m. Isaac S. Dyer, Oct. 7, 1930; (dec.); children: Virgie Lee, Gwendolyn Marie, Nora Jean; m. Wiliam Cyrus, Dec. 29, 1960. BS, Grambling State U., 1951. Tchr. Quachita Parish Sch. Bd., Monroe, La., 1930-32, 61-71, Webster Parish Sch. Bd., Minden, La., 1940-60; dir. Westside Devel. Ctr., West Monroe, 1973—; summer dir. Headstart Program, Monroe, 1962-74. Bd. dirs. Quchita Parish Girl Scouts U.S., 1966-73, Sr. Citizen's Ctr., West Monroe, 1979-83; v.p. Mayor's Commn. on Needs of Women, Monroe, 1986—, pres., 1988-89; bd. dirs. Interchurch Conf., State of La., 1988—. Recipient Merit Service award Christian Meth. Ch., 1980. Mem. NEA, LWV (pres. 1980-82), Delta Sigma Theta (treas. 1978-80). Democrat.

CZAJA, MARY FOREST MCLEAN, purchasing director; b. East St. Louis, Ill., Oct. 25, 1928; d. Malcolm William and Clara Leona (Forest) McLean; m. Thomas Robert Czaja, Oct. 7, 1950 (dec.); children: Thomas, Julie, Nancy. AA, Elgin Community Coll., 1972; BA, Nat. Coll. of Educ., 1986. File clerk, typist Haynes and Koenig, Patent Lawyers, St. Louis, Mo., 1946-49; sales clerk, dept. mgr. Carson Pirie Scott & Co., Carpentersville, Ill., 1959-64; sec. Algonquin (Ill.) Jr. High Sch., 1964-66, Am. Can Co., Barrington, Ill., 1966-67; sec. to bus. mgr. Elgin (Ill.) Community Coll., 1967-70, coord. institutional studies, 1970-72, purchasing agent, 1972-73, dir. purchasing, 1973—. Mem. Nat. Assn. Edn. Buyers (sec., treas. Ill.-Wis. area group 1987—), Kiwanis (sec., treas. Elgin-Fox Valley chpt. 1988—), Gamma Phi Beta, Alpha Delta Gamma. Office: Elgin Community Coll 1700 Spartan Dr Elgin IL 60123

CZAJKOWSKI, EVA ANNA, engineer; b. New Britain, Conn., Sept. 4, 1961; d. Jan Wiktor and Weronika Janina (Nadolny) C. Student Yale U., 1978; BS cum laude in Aero. Engring., Rensselaer Poly. Inst., 1983, MEngring. in Aero. Engring., 1983; MS in Aeronautics and Astronautics MIT, 1985; PhD in Aerospace Engring. Va. Poly. Inst. and State U., 1988. Registered profl. engr., N.Y. Student trainee U.S. Govt., Washington, 1981-82; intern N.Y. State Assembly, Albany, 1983; teaching asst. Rensselaer Poly. Inst., Troy, N.Y., 1983; rsch. asst. U.S. Army Rsch. Office Ctr. Excellence, Rensselaer Poly. Inst., 1982-83; engring. analyst Pratt & Whitney Aircraft, West Palm Beach, Fla., 1984; rsch. asst. Gas Turbine and Plasma Dynamics Lab., Cambridge, 1984-85; rsch. asst., teaching asst. Dept. of Aerospace and Ocean Engring, Va. Poly. Inst. and State U., Blacksburg, 1985—77-79. Contbr. papers to confs., articles to profl. jours. and ency. Vol. New Britain Gen. Hosp., 1977-79. Assoc. mem. Nat. Air and Space Mus., Am. Mus. Natural History. Recipient Commemorative Medal of Honor, 1987; named Woman of Yr., 1990; Amelia Earhart fellow Zonta Internat., 1983-84, 84-85; scholar Am. Helicopter Soc. Vertical Flight Found., 1983, Unico Nat., 1979-80; fellow Prat Presdl. Engring. Program, 1985-88. Mem. N.Y. Acad. Scis., AIAA, Am. Astronautical Soc., AAAS, Am. Helicopter Soc., The Planetary Soc., Internat. Platform Assn., Nat. Assn. Female Execs., Nat. Space Soc., Confederation Chivalry, Sigma Xi, Sigma Gamma Tau, Tau Beta Pi, Phi Kappa Phi, Gamma Beta Phi. Avocations: art, horseback riding, piano, flying private plane, skiing, swimming, tennis. Home: 170 Carlton St New Britain CT 06053

CZEKALSKI, LONI RAVEN, air transportation systems executive; b. Atlantic City, Aug. 24, 1948; d. Zigman Stanley Czekalski and Eleanor Frieda (Schnegelberger) Raven. BA in Math., Glassboro State Coll., 1970; M in Aviation Mgmt., Embry Riddle U., 1984. Mathematician data processing div. FAA Dept. Transp., Atlantic City, 1970-71, mathematician enroute systems div., 1971-74, mathematician terminal sect., 1974-76, mathematician systems sect., 1976-78, computer specialist, 1978-81, supr. mathematician, tech. program mgr., 1981-83, 1983-84, spl. asst. for programs Office of Dir., 1984-85, operations research analyst Office Sci. and Advanced Tech., 1985-88, asst. mgr. ind. operational test and evaluation div., mgmt. and control svc., 1988—. Contbr. articles to profl. jours. Jehovah's Witness. Office: FAA Atlantic City NJ 08405

CZIN, FELICIA TEDESCHI, language/literature educator, small business owner; b. Vallata, Avellino, Italy, Jan. 20, 1950; came to U.S., 1958; d. Pasquale Aurelio and Maria (Branca) Tedeschi; m. Peter Czin, Oct. 19, 1972; children: Jonathan, Michael. BA, Douglass Coll., Rutgers U., 1972; MA, NYU, 1978, ABD, 1981, postgrad. Assoc. producer RAI Corp. Italian TV, N.Y.C., 1973-77; teaching asst. dept. Italian NYU, 1977-79, adj. instr. dept. English, 1979-81; asst. prof. Vassar Coll., Poughkeepsie, N.Y., 1981-84; co-owner Czin Opticians, Teaneck, N.J., 1984—; coordinator Symposium on Italian Poetry, N.Y.C., 1978. Editor Out of London Press, N.Y.C., 1977-82, dir. pub. relations, 1977-82; editor jour. Yale Italian Studies, 1979-82; translator for jours.

CZIRR, RUTH PATRICE, mental health administrator; b. Turlock, Calif., July 5, 1954; d. Raymond W. and Rose Willa (Rathbun) C.; m. Paul Robert Willenborg, Aug. 21, 1976. AB in Psychology with honors, Ind. U., 1976; MS in Psychology, Vanderbilt U., Nashville, 1981, PhD in Clin. and Community Psychology, 1984. Lic. psychologist. Rsch. psychologist Ctr. for Study Psychotherapy and Aging, Menlo Park, Calif., 1982-85; clin. psychologist Profl. Counseling Assocs., Little Rock, 1986-87, dir. quality control, 1987—. Author: The Pastoral Counselor's Psychiatric Deskbook, 1989; contbr. articles to profl. jours., chpts. to books. Grad. fellow George Peabody Coll. Mem. Am. Psychol. Assn. Quaker. Office: Profl Counseling Assocs PO Drawer 24210 Little Rock AR 72221

CZUSZAK, JANIS MARIE, underwriter, researcher; b. Greensburg, Pa., Aug. 3, 1956; d. Charles Clyde and Olga (Plica) C. BS, Indiana U. of Pa., 1978; MBA, U. Pitts., 1985, postgrad., 1987—. Supervising sr. acct., computer audit specialist KPMG Peat Marwick, Pitts., 1979-81; with Westinghouse Credit Corp., Pitts., 1981—, real estate financing rep., 1986-88, assoc. investment mgr., 1988—. Mem. Greater Pitts. Commn. for Women, 1989—. Mem. Nat. Comml. Fin. Assn., NAFE. Democrat. Lutheran. Office: Westinghouse Credit Corp One Oxford Centre Pittsburgh PA 15219

DAANE, MARY ANN, psychiatric social worker; b. Ann Arbor, Mich., Feb. 8, 1932; d. Thomas Marion and Alice (Wuerfel) Pryor; m. Roderick Kaye Daane; children: Mark, Jennifer, Thomas, Alison. BA, U. Mich., 1976, MSW, 1978. Lic. social worker, Mich. Foster care worker Ozone House, Ann Arbor, 1973-74; psychotherapist Cath. Social Svcs., Ann Arbor, 1976-77; psychotherapist, psychol. clinic U. Mich., Ann Arbor, 1977-79; pvt. practice Ann Arbor, 1979—. Bd. mem. Cath. Social Service, Ann Arbor, 1974-76. Mem. Nat. Assn. Social Workers, U. Mich. Alumni Assn. (rep. 1986-87), U. Mich. Sch. Social Work Alumni Soc. (pres. 1985—, bd. dirs. 1985-90). Office: Huron Twrs 2200 Fuller Rd Ste 608B Ann Arbor MI 48104

D'ABATE, JANINA MONICA, library administrator; b. Providence, June 20, 1921; d. John Lawrence and Marya Ann (Swiatlowski) Barlowski; m. John D'Abate, Apr. 10, 1943; children: Marya Ann, John G., Janina V. BA, Brown U., 1943; MLS, U. R.I., 1977. Br. libr. Cranston (R.I.) Pub. Libr., 1966-70; dir. North Scituate (R.I.) Pub. Libr., 1974—; mem. steering com. Gov. Conf. on Libr. and Info. Sci., 1977-79. Pres. bd. trustees Mohr Meml. Libr., Johnston, R.I., 1964-69; bd. dirs. R.I. Philharm., chmn. childrens concert com., 1976-78; bd. dirs. Nickerson House, Providence, 1947—, sec., 1952-72; bd. dirs. Camp Fire Inc. R.I., 1980—, sec., 1980-86, pres., 1987. Mem. R.I. Libr. Assn., Beta Phi Mu. Home: 28 Reservoir Ave Johnston RI 02919 Office: Greenville Rd North Scituate RI 02857

DABICH, DANICA, biochemist, educator; b. Detroit, Aug. 6, 1930; d. Milan and Mildred D. BS in Chemistry, U. Mich., 1952; MS, Ohio State U., 1955; PhD, U. Ill., 1960. Analytical chemist Phillips Petroleum Co., Bartlesville, Okla., 1952-53; rsch. asst. E.B. Ford Rsch. Inst. for Med. Rsch., Detroit, 1955-56; postdoctoral fellow U. Freiburg, Fed. Republic Germany, 1960-61; rsch. assoc. Wayne State U. Med. Sch., Detroit, 1961-63, instr., 1963-65, asst. prof., 1966-70, assoc. prof. biochemistry, 1970—. Contbr. numerous articles to profl. publs. Mem. AAAS, Am. Chem. Soc., Am. Soc. Biol. Chemistry and Molecular Biology, Sigma Xi, Sigma Delta Epsilon, Iota Sigma Pi. Serbian Orthodox. Avocations: sports, gardening, music. Office: Wayne State U Sch Medicine Dept Biochemistry 540 E Canfield St Detroit MI 48201

DABNEY, ANITA ELIZABETH, real estate specialist; b. Belleville, Ill., July 27, 1951; d. Oliver Junious and Lois (Blayton) D. BS cum laude, Spelman Coll., 1973; MS, Cornell U., 1976. Mgr. neighborhood revitalization City of Buffalo Dept. Community Devel., 1978-79; community devel. rep. N.Y. Div. Housing and Community Renewal, Buffalo, 1979-81; with real estate investment dept. The Travelers Ins. Co., Houston, 1981-87, Dallas, 1987-89; pres. Real Estate Ventures Plus, Dallas, 1989—. Bd. mem., chmn. fin. com. YWCA Erie County, Buffalo, 1977-80; bd. mem., mem. housing com. Buffalo Urban League, 1979-81; mem. adv. com. Houston Met. Ministries, 1986-87, Friends Dallas Opportunities Industrialization Ctrs. Am., 1988—; mem., coordinator polit. forums Nat. Coalition 100 Black Women, Houston, 1985-87; mem. fin. com. new sanctuary devel. Windsor Village Meth. Ch., Houston, 1986-87; founding mem. Christia Adair Soc. Polit. Action com., 1987—. Recipient Felicitations award City of Buffalo Common Council, 1981. Mem. Urban Bankers Assn., Comml. Real Estate Women Dallas (outstanding new mem. 1989). Democrat. Methodist. Club: Girl Friends, Inc. (Houston) (rec. sec. 1984-86). Office: Price Appraisal Svcs Inc 14875 Landmark Blvd Suite 202 Dallas TX 75240

DABNEY, MICHELLE SHEILA, administrative assistant; b. Newark, NJ, Oct. 19, 1959; d. Charlie Louis and Agatha Cecelia Talley; m. James Charles Dabney, Oct. 3, 1981; children: Jameel Charles, Nadiyah Aliyah. Student, Del. State Coll., 1977-79, Union County Coll., 1979-83; certificate, Taylor Bus. Inst, Bridgewater, N.J., 1985; student, Raritan Valley Coll., 1984—. Sec., adminstrv. asst. Newark Beth Israel Med. Ctr., 1978-85; sec. AT&T Info. Svcs., Piscataway, N.J., 1985-87; legal sec. Timins & Lesniak, Esq., Elizabeth, N.J., 1987; adminstrv. asst. AT&T Communications, Piscataway, N.J., 1987—. Mem. IDE Alliance of Black Telecommunications Employees, Coalition of 100 Black Women N.J. Democrat. Home: 30 Leland AVe Plainfield NJ 07062 Office: AT&T Communications 290 Davidson Ave Somerset NJ 08873

DACEY, EILEEN M., lawyer; b. N.Y.C., Dec. 15, 1948; d. Gabriel A. and Mary (Breen) D.; m. Kinchen C. Bizzell, Jan. 1, 1984 B.A. in Sociology, SUNY-Stony Brook, 1970; J.D., St. John's U., 1975. Assoc. Mendes & Mount, N.Y.C., 1976-80, jr. ptnr., 1980-88; ptnr. Adams, Duque & Hazeltine, N.Y.C., 1988—. Sec. Woodbury Hist. Soc. Mem. Vol. Lawyers for the Arts. Mem. ABA, Assn. Bar City N.Y. Republican. Home: 208 E 35th St New York NY 10016 also: 19 Maple Rd Central Valley NY 10917 Office: Adams Duque & Hazeltine 551 Madison Ave New York NY 10022

DACEY, KATHLEEN RYAN, judge; b. Boston; m. William A. Dacey (dec. Aug. 1986); 1 child, Mary Dacey White. A.B. with honors, Emmanuel Coll., 1941; M.S. in L.S., Simmons Coll., 1942; J.D., Northeastern U., 1945; postgrad., Boston U. Law Sch., 1945-46. Bar: Mass. 1945, U.S. Supreme Ct. 1957. Practiced in Boston, 1947-75; asst. atty. gen., chief civil bur. Mass. Dept. Atty. Gen., Boston, 1975-77; law clk. to justices Mass. Supreme Jud. Ct., 1945-47; U.S. adminstrv. law judge Boston, 1977—; auditor, master Commonwealth of Mass., 1972-75, Suffolk and Norfolk Counties, Mass., 1972-75; asst. dist. atty. Suffolk County, Mass., 1971-72; mem. panel def. counsel for indigent persons U.S. Dist. Ct. Dist. Mass.; lectr., speaker in field. Contbr. articles to profl. jours. Bd. dirs. Mission United Neighborhood Improvement Team, Boston; mem. Boston Sch. Com., 1945-46, chmn., 1946-47. Recipient Silver Shingle award Boston U. Sch. Law, 1980; named Alumnae Woman of Yr., Northeastern U. Law Sch. Assn., 1976. Mem. ABA (ho. of dels. 1982—, exec. com. conf. of adminstrv. law judges jud. adminstrn. div. 1987—), Internat. Bar Assn., Mass. Bar Assn., Boston Bar Assn., Norfolk Bar Lawyers Assn., Nat. Assn. Women Lawyers (pres.), Mass. Assn. Women Lawyers, Internat. Fedn. Women Lawyers, Boston U. Law Sch. Alumni Assn. (corr. sec. 1974-76), Boston U. Nat. Alumni Council. Office: SSA-OHA 10 Causeway St Room 417 Boston MA 02221-0091

DACHOWSKI, MARJORIE MCCORMICK, clinical psychologist; b. Chgo., Sept. 26, 1932; d. Harold Elmo and Irene Lillian (Fenn) McCormick; m. Lawrence W. Dachowski, Aug. 20, 1960; children: Elizabeth, David, Kathleen, Anne. Student Drury Coll., 1950-52; BA in Sociology, U. Ill., 1954, MA in Sociology, 1956, PhD in Clin. Psychology, 1961. Counselor, Counseling Ctr. U. Ill., Urbana, 1959-62; psychologist Charity Hosp. Sch. Nursing, New Orleans, 1964-66; asst. prof. Dillard U., New Orleans, 1966-67, prof., 1968-74; dir. counseling Career Devel. and Placement Ctr., Loyola U., New Orleans, 1974-87, dir. admissions, 1987-88, instl. rsch., 1988—, chair women's studies, 1990; cons. Tulane Counseling Ctr., 1979-80, Our Lady of the Cross, 1981-82, Charity Hosp. Sch. Nursing, 1966-70; vis. lectr. Tulane U. Mem. Am. Psychol. Assn., Am. Assn. Counseling and Devel., Assn. Univ. and Coll. Counseling Ctr. Dirs. (steering com. 1983-84), Democrat. Unitarian. Home: 1809 S Carrollton Ave New Orleans LA 70118 Office: Loyola U Box 089 New Orleans LA 70118

DACHTLER, JILENE RAE, medical sales; b. Quinn, S.D., Apr. 4, 1961; d. Lee Robert Gore and Marcia Rae (Rhynard) Gorton; m. Apr. 1, 1977 (div. Apr. 1979); 1 child, Kelly Ray. BS, U. S.D., 1984. Sales rep. Combined Ins. Co., Rapid City, S.D., 1978-79, McNeil Pharma., Sioux Falls, S.D., 1984-88, Squibb Diagnostics, Los Angeles, 1988—. Mem. Women in Healthcare. Democrat. Home: 227 24th St Hermosa Beach CA 90254 Office: Squibb Diagnostics PO Box 4500 Princeton NJ 08540-4500

DACK, JERILYN, advertising agency executive. Former v.p. and sr. v.p. D'Arcy Masius Benton & Bowles, Inc., N.Y.C.; sr. v.p., dir. media & consumer planning Altschiller Reitzfeld Davis/Tracy-Locke, N.Y.C., 1989—. Office: Altschiller Reitzfeld Davis Tracy-Locke 1740 Broadway 21st Fl New York NY 10019*

DA COSTA, ANA M., controller, accountant; b. Porto, Portugal, Feb. 13, 1957; d. Jose M. and Idalina (Guiomar) Correia; m. Antonio S. Da Costa, July 2, 1977; children: Eunice C., Caroline C. BS, Jersey City Coll., 1980. Bookkeeper, file clk. Balk, Goldberger, Mandell, Seligsohn & O'Connor PA, Newark, 1974—; staff acct. Adolph B. Frenchman, CPA, Randolph, N.J., 1980—; acct. Balk & Mandell, P.A., Newark, 1983—; contr. Leber Funeral Home, Inc., Union City, N.J., 1984—. Mem. Nat. Assn. Pub. Accts. Home: 947 Jefferson Ave Elizabeth NJ 07201

DACOSTA, JACQUELINE, advertising company executive; b. N.Y.C., Jan. 21, 1927; d. Joachim and Tirsa (Olmeda) DaC. BA in Bus. Adminstrn., Hunter Coll., 1952. Asst. exporter mgr. Morse Internat., N.Y.C., 1946-52; supr. media research Biow, Beirn, Toigo, Inc., N.Y.C., 1952-55; media research analyst Ted Bates & Co., N.Y.C., 1955-63, asst. v.p. media research, 1963-65, coordinator internat. media, 1965—, v.p., dir. media info. and analysis, 1965-78, sr. v.p., 1977-86, media dir., 1978-86, ret., 1986; pres. JDC Communications Marketing Cons., N.Y.C., 1986—; exec. v.p. AC&R-Rossi Hispanic div. Ted Bates Worldwide, 1984-85; cons. media, research, mktg., govt. and pvt. orgns.; internat. lectr. Contbr. articles to trade jours. Mem. adv. bd. Nat. Urban Coalition; bd. govs. Nat. Conf. P.R. Women, 1975-77; active P.R. Family Inst., 1977-87, 88, Hamilton Madison Settlement House, 1977—, pres., 1981, 87, chmn., 1989—; bd. dirs. Bus. Council for UN Decade for Women, pres., 1979; bd. dirs. Broadcast Pioneers Found. Mem. Am. Advt. Fedn. (dir., named Advt. Woman of Yr. 1974), Advt. Research Found. (bd. dirs.), Advt. Women N.Y. (pres. 1973-74), Internat. Radio TV Soc., Internat. Radio TV Found., Hispanics in Communications (founder, pres. 1980-87). Home: 6403 Greenvale Ln Houston TX 77066 Office: JDC Communications Mktg Cons 340 E 64th St New York NY 10021

DADLEY, ARLENE JEANNE, sleep therapist; b. Cleve., Sept. 13, 1941; d. Bernard and Bernice Anne (Selleck) Davis; m. Charles George Dadley, Sept. 15, 1967 (div. Oct. 1977); children: Anitra, Charles. BA in Bus., Ursuline Coll., 1980; postgrad., Cuyahoga Community Coll., Cleve., 1981-82, Case Western Res. U., 1983-85, Stanford U., 1988. Registered polysomnographic technologist. Jr. fund acct. Am. Univ., Washington, 1967-70; v.p. Shenandoah Stables, Inc., Front Royal, Va., 1970-75; freelance bookkeeper/acct. Front Royal, 1970-75; editor, publisher Trojan Horse Newspaper, Front Royal, 1972-74; biol. rsch. asst. Case Western Res. U., Cleve., 1976-87, gastroent. rsch. assoc., 1984, sleep rsch. assoc., 1985-87; clin. sleep technologist Metrohealth Med. Ctr., Cleve., 1987—; tchr./trainer Metrohealth Med. Ctr., 1987—; judge regional and state sci. fairs., 1984-86. Exhbited in group shows at Cleve. Mus. Art, 1965 (1st prize graphics award), Butler Inst. Art, 1966, Corcoran Gallery Art, Washington, 1967, Internat. Traveling Am. Artists Exhibit, Cleve., 1965-66; contbr. articles to profl. jours., 1983, 85-87. Co-chairperson Ohio-Chgo. Art Project, Cleve., 1981; cons., resource person LWV, Cleve., 1977-79; pres., state rep. NOW, Cleve., 1976-78. Pell grantee, 1976-80; Ohio Instructional grantee, 1976-80; scholarship recipient Case Western Res. U., 1976-80, Yale U., 1982, Respironics, Inc., 1988; recipient presdl. lit. achievement citation League of Am. Pen Women, 1974, econs. award Ursuline Coll., 1980. Mem. AAAS, Assn. Bus. and Profl. Women, Assn. Polysomnographic Technologists. Office: Metrohealth Med Ctr 3395 Scranton Rd Hamann Bldg #323 Cleveland OH 44109

DAFFER, STEPHANIE LEE, bankcard executive; b. Albuquerque, Sept. 30, 1952; d. Peter Gilbertson and Lee (Zito) D.; m. Robert Lee Michels, Nov. 21, 1984. BA in Spanish, U. N.Mex., 1973; MA in Spanish, U. Tex., El Paso, 1975; MBA in Mgmt., Pepperdine U., 1980. Systems engr. Electronic Data Systems, Dallas, 1977-78; sr. systems analyst Kaiser Aluminum, Oakland, Calif., 1978-80; mgr. systems and programming Computer Scis. Corp., El Segundo, Calif., 1980-84; v.p. strategic planning VISA Internat., San Mateo, Calif., 1984—. Republican. Roman Catholic. Office: VISA Internat PO Box 8999 San Francisco CA 94128

DAFFERN, SHARI LYNN, auditor; b. Victoria, Tex., May 27, 1949; d. Arthur Edward and Dorothy Aline (Pels) Walkowiak; m. Eddie Earl Daffern, May 30, 1970. BBA, Texas Tech U, 1971. CPA, Tex. Acct., office mgr. Western Assocs., Inc., Lubbock, Tex., 1971-73; acct. Rodman Oil Co., Odessa, Tex., 1973-74; acct. Tex. Tech U., Lubbock, 1974-78, internal auditor, 1980-88; acct. Mason, Nickels & Warner, CPA's, Lubbock, 1978-79; acct., bus. mgr. La Fonda del Sol, Lubbock, 1979-80; dir. internal audit West Tex. State U., Canyon, 1988—. Mem. Tex. Assn. Coll. and U. Auditors (sec. 1989), Inst. Internal Auditors (cert.), Daus. of Nile. Roman Catholic. Home: WT Box 518 Canyon TX 79016

DAFFRON, MARY ELIZABETH FOLEY, computer specialist, industrial engineer; b. Williamsburg, Va., Feb. 17, 1965; d. Charles Sherwood and Donna Mae (Somers) F. BS in Indsl. Engring. & Ops. Rsch., Va. Poly. Inst. & State U., 1988. Customer rels. rep. Quantum Compute Svcs., Vienna, Va., 1988-89, tng. specialist, 1989—. Recipient Honorable Mention, No. Va. Photography Show, 1989; named Qualified Artist, An Occasion for the Arts Show, 1989. Mem. NAFE, Concerned Women Am., Outstanding Coll. Students Am., Phi Mu (v.p. 1986-87). Office: Quantum Computer Svcs Inc 8619 Westwood Center Dr Vienna VA 22182

DAFFRON, MARYELLEN, librarian; b. Richmond, Va., Nov. 12, 1946; d. William Charles and Ellen (Ahern) D. BA, Coll. Mt. St. Joseph on Ohio, Cin., 1968; MLS, Drexel U., 1970. Libr. Richmond Pub. Libr., 1969-73, FMC, Washington, 1973—. Vol. No. Va. Hotline, Arlington, 1974-79. City of Richmond fellow, 1968. Mem. Law Libr. Soc. Washington, Beta Phi Mu. Roman Catholic. Office: FMC 1100 L St NW Washington DC 20573

DAGENAIS, SANDRA LEE, human resources director, consultant; b. Chgo., Mar. 15, 1958; d. Robert Joseph and Joan Edith (Bechtel) D.; m. James J. Kukuczka, Sept. 5, 1981 (div. June 1988). AAS, Moraine Valley Coll., 1982; BA, Nat. Coll. Edn., 1986. Corr. N.Am. Co., Chgo., 1975-76; paralegal James Wilton, Atty., Chgo., 1977-78; asst. mgr. E&E, Inc., Worth, Ill., 1978; text processing mgr. Pullman Trailmobile, Chgo., 1978-80; dir. pers. Ill. Cancer Coun., Chgo., 1980-89, dir. human resources, 1990—; owner, mgr. Resumes, Etc., Frankfort, Ill., 1989—; v.p. The Mgmt. Team, Inc., Highland Park, Ill., 1989—. Mem. NAFE, Soc. Human Resource Mgmt., Soc. Human Resource Profls., Women Employed, Profl. Info. Exchange. Lutheran. Office: Ill Cancer Coun 36 S Wabash Ste 700 Chicago IL 60603

DAGGETT, BEVERLY CLARK, state legislator; b. Florence, S.C., Sept. 9, 1945; d. John and Beth Clark; m. Thomas A. Daggett, May 8, 1971; children: John, Page, Paul. BS in Biology, Hillsdale Coll., 1967. Mem. Maine Ho. of Reps., Augusta, 1987—. Coun. State Govts. Toll fellow, 1990. Democrat. Home: 10 Pine St Augusta ME 04330

DAGIRMANJIAN, ROSE, pharmacology and toxicology educator; b. Whitinsville, Mass., July 4, 1930; d. Roupen and Esther (Arakelian) D. BA magna cum laude, Clark U., 1952; MS, U. Rochester, 1954, PhD, 1960. Postdoctoral fellow A.R.C. Inst. Animal Physiology, Babraham, Cambridge, Eng., 1960-62, U. Rochester, N.Y., 1962-63; asst. prof. Ohio State U. Coll. Medicine, Columbus, 1963-69; assoc. prof. pharmacology and toxicology U. Louisville Sch. Medicine, 1969-75, prof., 1975—. Mem. Am. Soc. Pharmacology and Exptl. Therapeutics, Am. Chem. Soc., Assn. Women in Sci. (charter mem.), Soc. for Neurosci. (charter mem.), AAUP (pres. U. Louisville chpt. 1977-78, pres. conf. 1986-88), Sigma Delta Epsilon. Office: U Louisville Dept Pharmacology-Toxicology Louisville KY 40292

D'AGNESE, HELEN JEAN, artist; b. N.Y.C.; d. Leonardo and Rose (Redavid) De Santis; m. John J. D'Agnese, Oct. 29, 1942; children—John, Linda, Diane, Michele, Helen, Gina, Paul. Student CUNY, 1940-42; student Atlanta Coll. Art, 1972-76. One-man shows: Maude Sullivan Gallery, El Paso, 1964, John Wanamaker Gallery, Phila., 1966, U. N.Mex., 1967, Karo Manducci Gallery, San Francisco, 1968, Tuskegee Inst. Carver Mus., 1968, Lord & Taylor Gallery, N.Y.C., 1969, Harmon Gallery, Naples, Fla., 1970, Fountainbleau, Miami, 1970, Reflections Gallery, Atlanta, 1972, Williams Gallery, Atlanta, 1973, Atlanta Coll. of Art, 1976-80, Americana Gallery, Mineola, Tex., 1977, E. M. Howard Gallery, Amelia Island, Fla., 1978, Haitian Primitives Gallery, 1981, Highland Gallery, Atlanta, 1987, others; group shows: Musseo des Artes, Juárez, México, 1968, Benedictine Art Show, N.Y.C., 1967, Southeast Contemporary Art Show, Atlanta, 1968, Atlanta U., 1969, Red Piano Gallery, Hilton Head, S.C., Terrace Gallery, Atlanta, Ann. Bible Heritage Art Exhibit, Marietta, Ga., 1976, Nat. Judaic Theme Exhbn., Atlanta, 1976, Crystal Britton Gallery, Atlanta, Odyssey Collection Gallery, Mich., 1988; represented in permanent collections: Carter Libr. Mus., Atlanta, Juarez (Mexico) Art Mus., Vatican Mus., Rome, Nassau (Fla.) County Pub. Library. Judge art show Mt. Loretto Acad., El Paso, 1967; commd. sculptor of Bob Marley in Limestone, 1985; art demonstration and lectr. Margaret Harris Sch., Atlanta, 1970; artist-in-residence Montessori Sch., Atlanta, 1978-79. Recipient Gold medal Accademia Italia delle Arti, Italy, 1979, Calvatone, 1982, Golden Flame award, 1986; 1st place sculpture award Tybee Island Art Festival, 1982, Golden Flame award Parliamento U.S.A., 1987, Golden Palette award Academia Europea, 1986, 87, Gold medal Internat. Parliament for the Arts, 1982. Mem. Nat. Mus. of Women in the Arts (chartered), Arts Alliance Amelia Island, Nat. Mus. Women in Arts (chartered). Address: 3240 S Fletcher Ave Fernandina Beach FL 32034 Office: D'Agnese Studio & Fine Art Gallery 14 1/2 N 4th St Fernandina Beach FL 32034

DAHL, ARLENE, actress, author, designer, cosmetic executive; b. Mpls., Aug. 11, 1928; d. Rudolph and Idelle (Swan) D.; m. Marc A. Rosen; children: Lorenzo Lamas, Carole Christine Holmes, Stephen Andreas Schaum. Student, U. Minn., 1943-44, Mpls. Inst. Art, 1945, Minn. Coll. Music, Minn. Bus. Coll. Pres. Arlene Dahl Enterprises, 1952-77; v.p. Kenyon & Eckhart, 1967-72, pres. Woman's World div., 1967-72; nat. beauty advisor Sears Roebuck Co., 1970-75; internat. dir. Sales and Mktg. Execs. Internat., 1972-75; fashion dir. O.M.A., 1975-78; pres. Dahlia Parfums, Inc., 1975-80, Dahlia Prodns., Inc., 1978-81, Dahlmark Prodns., 1981—, Scandia Cosmetics, Ltd., 1978-80; pres., chmn. Lasting Beauty Ltd., 1986—. Author: Always Ask a Man, 1965, 12 Beautyscope books, 1968, rev. edit., 1978, Arlene Dahl's Secrets of Hair Care, 1970, Arlene Dahl's Secrets of Skin Care, 1972, Beyond Beauty, 1980, Arlene Dahl's Lovescopes, 1983, Arlene Dahl's 1991 Astro Forecast; actress: (Broadway plays) including Mr. Strauss Goes to Boston, Questionable Ladies, Cyrano de Bergerac, Applause (Tony award musical), (films) including (debut) My Wild Irish Rose, The Bride Goes Wild, Reign of Terror, A Southern Yankee, Ambush, The Outriders, Three Little Words, Watch the Birdie, Scene of the Crime, Inside Straight, No Questions Asked, Desert Legion, Slightly Scarlet, Sangaree, Caribbean Gold, Jamaica Run, Diamond Queen, Here Come the Girls, Bengal Brigade, Kisses for My President, Woman's World, Journey to the Center of the Earth, Wicked as They Come, She Played with Fire, Les Poneyettes, Du Blé Enliases, The Land Raiders, The Way to Kathmandu, Fortune is a Woman, The Big Bank Roll, Who Killed Maxwell Thorn?, Midnight Warriors, 1990 (TV shows) Lux Video Theatre, 1952-53; guest starring appearances on The Love Boat, Fantasy Island, Love American Style, One Life to Live, 1981-84, Night of 100 Stars, 1983, Happy Birthday Hollywood, 1987; hostess (TV series): Pepsi-Cola Theatre, 1954, Opening Night, 1958, Arlene Dahl's Beauty Spot, 1966, Arlene Dahl's Starscope, 1979-80, Arlene Dahl's Lovescope, 1980-82; played throughout U.S. in One Touch of Venus, The Camel Bell, Blithe Spirit, Liliom, The King and I, Roman Candle, I Married an Angel, Bell, Book and Candle, Applause, Marriage Go Round, Pal Joey, A Little Night Music, Forty Carats, Life With Father, Murder Among Friends; (nightclub acts) Flamingo Hotel, Las Vegas, Latin Quarter, N.Y.C.; internat. syndicated beauty columnist, Chgo. Tribune/ N.Y. News Syndicate, 1950-70, Arlene Dahl's Lucky Stars Column, Globe Communications, 1988-90; designer sleepwear for A.N. Saab & Co., 1952-57, In Vogue with Arlene Dahl (Patterns), 1980-85; Arlene Dahl Pvt. Collection Jewelry, 1989—. Hon. life mem. Father Flannagan's Boys Town; internat. chair Pearl Buck Found.; bd. dirs. Hollywood Mus. Recipient 8 Laurel awards Box Office mag., Hollywood Walk of Fame Star, Coup de Chapeau Deaville Film Festival award, 1982; named Best Coiffed, Heads of Fame awards 1967-72, 80, Woman of the Yr., Adv. Club of N.Y.C., 1969, Mother of the Yr., 1979. Mem. NATAS, UNIFEM, Author's Guild, Acad. Motion Picture Arts and Scis., Commanderie des Bontemps du Medoc et Graves, Internat. Platform Assn., Am. Acad. TV Arts and Scis., Sierra Club, Nat. Trust Hist. Preservation, The Film Soc., Smithsonian Instn. Office: Dahlmark Prodns PO Box 116 Sparkill NY 10976

DAHL, BREN BENNINGTON, screenwriter; b. Gary, Ind., Nov. 15, 1954; d. Paul Wayland and Shirley Ann (Havard) Bennington; 1 child, Austin Brooks. Student Principia Coll., Elsah, Ill., 1972-74, Sch. of Art Inst. of Chgo., 1983; BA in English with honors, U. Hawaii, 1977. Tchr. English, Peace Corps, Mbuji-Mayi, Zaire, 1977-79, Asahi Cultural Ctr., Osaka, Japan, 1981-82, Osaka Inst. Fgn. Trade, Osaka, 1981-82, Kansai U. of Fgn. Studies, Osaka, 1980-82, Matsushita Electric, Osaka, 1982; pres., owner Video Enterprises, North Palm Beach, Fla., 1983-87; producer's asst. Casady Entertainment, Hollywood, Calif., 1989. Mem. Palm Beach Opera Chorus, 1984-85. Fred Waring Scholar, 1972. Mem. Exec. Women of Palm Beaches, Fla. Motion Picture and TV Assn., Am. Film Inst., No. Palm Beach County C. of C. (co-chmn. spl. events 1985-86), Better Bus. Bur. Republican. Avocation: song recording.

DAHL, NANCY MARIE, marketing professional; b. Gaylord, Minn., Sept. 27, 1960; d. John Lloyd and Dorothy Mae (Rylander) Johnson; m. Brian Donald Dahl, Sept. 7, 1985. BA in Bus., BA in Communications, Gustavus Adolphus Coll., 1983; M of Bus., St. Thomas Coll., St. Paul, 1990. Mgmt. analyst Minn. Mut. Life Ins., St. Paul, 1983-84, promotion svcs. supr., 1984-85; asst. mktg. mgr. Nordicware Corp., Mpls., 1985-86, mktg. mgr., 1986-88, spl. accounts nat. sales mgr., 1987-88; dir. mktg. Lifetouch Inc., Mpls., 1988—; cons. mktg., Mpls., 1985—. Bd. dirs. Minn. Women's Network, Mpls., 1985-86. Mem. Am. Mktg. Assn. (officer bd. dirs 1985-87). Office: Lifetouch Inc 7831 Glenroy Rd Ste 445 Minneapolis MN 55439

DAHLE, KAREN, actress, announcer; b. Paterson, N.J., Oct. 24, 1945; d. Walter R. and Marjorie L. (van Rossum) Rosendale. B.A., SUNY-Oswego, 1967; postgrad. Utica Coll. Syracuse U., 1968; cert. The Neighborhood Playhouse Sch. of Theatre, 1969-71. Tchr. English, theater and speech New Hartford Central Sch., N.Y., 1967-69; actress, announcer, N.Y.C., 1969-82; staff announcer NBC, N.Y.C., 1982—. Actress various TV series and spls.; narrator, commentator, announcer various documentary and indsl. films, radio, TV commls.; actress off Broadway, regional and stock theatres. Mem. Actors Equity Assn., AFTRA, Screen Actors Guild (nat. bd. dirs. 1978-84, exec. com. 1980-84, various coms.), Alpha Psi Omega, Alpha Delta Eta. Democrat. Unitarian. Avocations: bicycling; crafts; cooking; backgammon. Home: 330 E 80th St New York NY 10021 Office: NBC 30 Rockefeller Plaza New York NY 10020

DAHLGREN, CHRISTINE KENYON, secondary education educator; b. South Kingstown, R.I., Oct. 14, 1949; d. Bradford Howell and Patricia Emma (Dunklee) Kenyon; m. Eric Sven Joseph Dahlgren, Sept. 25, 1982. BA in Home Econs. Edn., Linfield Coll., 1972. Cert. tchr., Oreg. Tchr. Reynolds High Sch., Troutdale, Oreg., 1972-77; tchr., dept. head Columbia High Sch., Troutdale, 1977-82; tchr. St. Helens (Oreg.) Jr. High, 1984—. Chmn. event Am. Cancer Soc., St. Helens, 1989, com. chmn., 1990; com. chmn. Toy and Joy, St. Helens, 1989. Mem. AAUW (program v.p. 1985-87, pres. 1987-89), NEA, Tchrs. of Home Econs. in Oreg.

DAHLINGER, KATHLEEN GAYLE, probation officer; b. Denver, Colo., July 29, 1942; d. Spencer Charles and Helen Freida (Schall) G.; children: Heather A., Sean G. BA, U. Denver, Denver, 1964; Postgrad., U. Colo., 1966-67. Probation officer 18th Jud. Dist., Littleton, Colo., 1964-72; teaching asst. Aurora Pub. Sch., Aurora, Colo., 1980-82; probation officer City of Aurora, Aurora, 1983—; bd. dirs. Chins Group Homes, Littleton, Colo., 1972-76, founder. Div Chmn.: Colo Children's Code, Procedure Manual, 1970-71. Sate parliamentarian Colo. Legal Sec., Colo., 1967; founder, pres. Aurora Arts & Humanities Coun., 1979-86; sec. Fox Theatre Renovation Bd., 1982-84. Recipient Mayor's Vol. to Community award, 1985. Mem. Met. Area Probation Officers Assn., Colo. Arabian Horse Club (chmn. 1989-90), Beta Sigma (pres.). Dem. Roman Catholic.

DAHMER, ANN, appliance manufacturer executive; b. Battle Creek, Mich., June 22, 1956; d. Roy S. and Marguerite W. (Weese) D.; m. Kevin Joseph Geiser. BA, Kalamazoo Coll., 1978; MBA, Boston U., 1983. Cons. Data Resources, Inc., McGraw-Hill, Chgo., 1978-80; auditor, sr. auditor Whirlpool Corp., Benton Harbor, Mich., 1983-84; supr. internal audit Whirlpool Corp., Benton Harbor, 1984-85, market analyst, 1985-86, mgr. forecasting and market analyst, 1986-87, mgr. strategic planning, 1987-88, product devel. mgr. laundry, 1988-89, dir. product devel. kitchens and laundry products, 1989—. Bd. dirs. Emergency Shelter Svcs., Benton Harbor, 1989—; mem. Krasl Art Mus. Mem. AAUW. Office: Whirlpool Corp US 63 North Benton Harbor MI 49022

DAI, JING LING, medical writer, researcher, consultant; b. Tacoma; d. Yunan and Yet Sze Ling; m. Shenyu Dai (div.); children: Alexander M., Benjamin M. Student Temple U., 1960-63; BA in Journalism, Calif. State U., Long Beach, 1968; MPH, UCLA, 1977; CME, U. So. Calif., 1984. Exec. editor Bearing & Transmission Specialist, 1971-72; dir. publs. City of Hope Nat. Med. Ctr., Duarte, Calif., 1972-74; sr. proposal engr., writer, subcontractor for aerospace cos., 1965-66, 79-82, 86—; med. affairs rsch. cons., Gravity Guidance, Inc., Pasadena, Calif., 1982-84; freelance writer, cons.; rsch. cons. Musculo-Skeletal Clinic, Pasadena, 1982-84. Condr. study on premarital rubella antibody tests, 1977; contbr. articles to profl. jours. Bd. dirs., v.p. Bouggless-White Scholarship Found., Long Beach, 1967-71; publicity adviser Am. Cancer Soc., L.A., 1975; adv. Metric Cert. Specialist Bd., U.S. Metric Assn., 1981—. USPHS grantee, UCLA, 1975-77. Mem. Women in Communications (chmn. careers conf., L.A., 1975, award 1975), Am. Med. Writers Assn., Am. Pub. Health Assn., Nat. Assn. Female Execs., Assn. Health Svc. Rsch., Soc. Tech. Communication (chmn. ways/means, internat. tech. com. conf. 1978), Coun. Biology Editors, U.S. Metric Assn. (planning com. ann. conf. 1987). Home: 320 S Gramercy Place Los Angeles CA 90020

DAIE, JALEH, science administrator, educator, researcher; b. Broojerd, Iran, July 17, 1948; came to U.S., 1973; d. Mohammad Ali Daie and Dordaneh Zahiroleslam Zadeh; m. Roger E. Wyse, Dec. 27, 1986. BS, U. Jondi-Shapur, Ahwaz, Iran, 1970; MS, U. Calif., Davis, 1975; PhD, Utah State U., 1981. Soil chemist Safiabad Agrl. Rsch. Ctr., 1970-73, citrus specialist, 1975-76; postdoctoral fellow Agrl. Rsch. Svc. U.S. Dept. Agr., Logan, Utah, 1980-82; rsch. asst. prof. Utah State U., Logan, 1982-85; assoc. prof. Rutgers U., New Brunswick, N.J., 1985-89, prof. dept. crop sci., 1989—, dir. plant biology grad. program, 1987—, acting chmn. crop sci. dept., 1989—, also chmn. George H. Cook Honors, 1988-90. Editor quar. Plant Growth Regulator Sci. Am., 1989; contbr. articles to profl. jours. Grantee NSF, others. Mem. Am. Soc. for Horticulture Sci. (com. chmn. 1988—), Sigma Xi (pres. 1989-90). Office: Rutgers U Dept Crop Sci Lipman Hall New Brunswick NJ 08903-0231

DAIGLE, JANICE B., internal charge auditor; b. Worcester, Mass., Apr. 11, 1955; d. Albert Vezina and Doris Evelyn St. Martin; m. Joseph C. Daigle, June 12, 1982; children: Jason Allan Bercume, J. Christopher Daigle, Jr. Stock analyst, adminstrv. asst. Paine Webber Jackson & Curtis, Inc., Worcester; sr. buyer med. ctr. U. Mass., Worcester. Mem. NAFE, Mass. Rehab. Commn. Home: 8 Suzanne Dr North Oxford MA 01537 Office: U Mass Med Ctr Mgmt Systems Engring 55 Lake Ave N Rm H1-773 Worcester MA 01655

DAIGNEAULT, DIANE SUE, school director; b. Washington, May 18, 1955; d. Harold Barnett Parks and Rebecca (Haithcock) Klick; m. Gary Frank Choy, July 21, 1973 (div. Sept. 1984); 1 child, Edward Raymond Choy; m. Michael George Daigneault, Nov. 4, 1987; 1 child, Jacqueline Marie Daigneault. Student, Montgomery Coll., Takoma Park, Md., 1973; student, Montgomery Coll., Rockville, Md., 1984, Delta Coll., 1985; grad., St. Luke's Hosp., Milw., 1986. Lic. practical nurse. Pvt. duty psychiat. nurse Advanced Placement Svc., Inc., Bethesda, Md., 1986-89; pres., owner Queen of Kleen, Inc., Germantown, Md., 1986-89; admissions dir. Image Makers Beauty Acad., Washington, 1988-89; founder, admission dir., v.p., co-owner FAME Sch. of Nail Design, Rockville, Md., 1989—. Mem. NAFE. Home: 11313 Corinthian Ct Germantown MD 20874 Office: FAME Sch of Nail Design 12730 Twinbrook Pkwy Rockville MD 20852

DAIGNEAULT, MARILYN YVONNE, meeting planner, consultant, association executive; b. Atlanta, Apr. 18, 1935; d. Charles Frederick and Gaynell Edith (Teem) Eichwurtzle; m. William Lawrence Stephenson, June 17, 1955 (div. 1960); children: Beverly, Mark, Douglas; m. George Arthur Daigneault, Jan. 21, 1962; children: Ruth, Susan, Joseph, David; stepchildren: Rachelle, Michael. BA in Journalism, Maine U., 1957. Adminstrv. asst. H.B. Atkinson Co., Washington, 1963-66; free lance proofreader, Washington, 1970-75; meeting and incentive planner, corps. and assns., Washington, 1975—; dir. D&D Assocs., Rockville, 1982—; exec. dir. Assn. Ind. Meeting Planners, 1986—; editor-in-chief The Ind. Meeting Planner, 1986-88; exec. dir., founder emeritus Ind. Meeting Planners Assn., 1988—; v.p. Daigneault Communications, Inc., 1990. Active Nat. Fedn. Republican Women, 1983-86; sponsor GOP Victory Fund, 1984-87; mem. Rep. Presdl. Citizen's Adv. Commn., 1989; sustaining mem. Rep. Nat. Com., 1989; charter founder Ronald Reagan Rep. Ctr., 1990; mem. Nat. Audubon Soc., 1989, The Nature Conservancy, 1989, N.A. Bluebird Soc., 1989, Nat. Wildlife Fedn., 1989. Mem. Nat. Assn. Female Execs. (network dir. 1985-87), Am. Soc. Assn. Execs., Am. Soc. Writers, Nat. Assn. Women Bus. Owners, Am. Assn. Profl. Cons., The Cons. League, Epsilon Delta Chi. Republican. Avocations: writing, research, teaching meeting planning, traveling.

DAIL, HILDA LEE, psychotherapist; b. Franklin Spgs., Ga., Aug. 23, 1920; d. Ransom Harvey and Mattie (Gray) Lee; m. Francis Roderick Dail, Dec. 27, 1941; children: Janice Sylvia, Roderick Lee. BA, Piedmont Coll., 1941; PhD, Union of Exp. Coll and U., 1979. Cert. experiential psychotherapist, 1979. Tchr. pub. schs. N.C., Tenn. and Ga., 1939-54; assoc. sec. Bd. of Missions, Methodist Ch., New York, 1954-60; dir. pub. rels. and tchr. Leonard Theol. Coll., Jabalpur, India, 1960-64; editor lit. Bd. of Missions, United Meth. Ch., N.Y.C.; exec. dir. Int. Found. Ewha Women's Univ., Seoul, Republic of Korea, 1970-71; dir. develop. Ch. Women United., 1971-73; dir. resources cen. nat. bd. YWCA, 1973-75; pres. Hilda Lee Dail & Assoc. Internat., N.Y.C., 1975-83, Myrtle Beach, S.C., 1983—; adj. faculty, Coastal Carolina Coll., Conway, 1981-89, Webster U., Myrtle Beach, 1981-89, dir. Enablement Inc., Boston, Mass., 1975-89, Assoc. of Coop. Agys. Asian Women's Coll., 1971-85. Author: Decision and Destiny, 1957, Encounters Extraordinary, 1969, Let's Try a Workshop With Teen Women, 1974, The Lotus and the Pool, 1983, How to Create Your Own Career, 1989. Dir. Citizens Against Spouse Abuse, Myrtle Beach, 1982-88, pres. Gotham Bus. and Prof. Women's Club, N.Y., 1978, dir. Green Chimney Sch., N.Y., 1978-83, v.p., Zonta Internat., N.Y., 1976-84. Fellow Am. Assn. of Artist-Therapists, (speaker 1983-89); mem. Costal Advt. Fedn., Am. Assn. for Tng. and Develop. (bd. dir. 1972-89), Mental Health Assn. (dir., pres., 1988-89), Am. Assn. for Couns. and Devel., 1987-89. Democrat. United Methodist. Home: 154 Pine Tree Ln Briarcliffe Acres Myrtle Beach SC 29572 Office: 1807 Legion St Myrtle Beach SC 29577

DAILEY, COLEEN HALL, lawyer; b. East Liverpool, Ohio, Aug. 10, 1955; d. David Lawrence and Deloris Mae (Rosensteel) Hall; m. Donald W. Dailey Jr., Aug. 16, 1980; children: Erin Elizabeth, Daniel Lester. Student, Wittenberg U., 1973-75; BA, Youngstown State U., 1977; JD, U. Cin., 1980. Bar: Ohio 1981, U.S. Dist. Ct. (no. dist.) Ohio 1981. Sr. library assoc. Marx Law Library, Cin., 1979-80; law clk. Kapp Law Office, East Liverpool, 1979, 1980-81, assoc., 1981-85; sole practice East Liverpool, 1985—; spl. counsel Atty. Gen. Ohio, 1985—. Pres. Columbiana County (Ohio) Young Dems., 1985-87; bd. dirs. Big Bros. Big Sisters Columbiana County, Inc., Lisbon, Ohio, 1984-87. Mem. ABA, Ohio Bar Assn., Columbiana County Bar Assn., Assn. Trial Lawyers Am., Ohio Trial Lawyers Assn., St. Clair Bus. and Profl. Women Assn. (pres. 1985-87). Democrat. Lutheran. Office: 16687 St Clair Ave PO Box 2519 East Liverpool OH 43920

DAILEY, IRENE ELEANOR, hospital volunteer services professional; b. Pitts., May 13, 1952; d. Russell Ford and Betty (Andra) D. BS in Secondary Edn., Slippery Rock U., 1974. Personnel cons. Liken Svcs., Inc., Pitts., 1974-76; asst. to regional campaign coord. John Heinz for Senate Com., Pitts., 1976; staff asst. community rels. H. John Heinz, U.S. Senate, Pitts., 1977-82; asst. dir. community and vol. svcs. Forbes Regional Health Ctr., Monroeville, Pa., 1983-86; dir. vol. svcs. Sewickley (Pa.) Valley Hosp., 1986—. Mem. Women's Polit. Caucus, Pitts., 1980, Minority Bus. Devel. Com., Pitts., 1982; bd. trainer United Way, Pitts., 1988—. Mem. NAFE, Soc. Dirs. Vol. Svcs. (legis. chair Pitts. unit 1984-85, membership chair 1990), Zonta Club Pitts., Zonta Three Rivers Pitts. East (bd. dirs. 1984-85, v.p. 1986-88, pres. 1988-89, del. to internat. conv. 1988). Republican. Roman Catholic. Home: 1815 Kleber St Pittsburgh PA 15212 Office: Sewickley Valley Hosp Blackburn Rd Sewickley PA 15143

DAILEY, JANET, romance novelist; b. Storm Lake, Iowa, May 21, 1944; m. William Dailey; 2 stepchildren. Student pub. schs., Independence, Iowa. Sec. Omaha, 1963-74. Author: No Quarter Asked, 1974, After the Storm, 1975, Sweet Promise, 1976, The Widow and the Wastrel, 1977, Giant of Mesabi, 1978, The Bride of the Delta Queen, 1979, Lord of the High Lonesome, 1980, Night Way, 1981, This Calder Sky, 1981, This Calder Range, 1982, Stands a Calder Man, 1982, Lancaster Men, 1981, Terms of

Surrender, 1982, With a Little Luck, 1982, Wildcatter's Woman, 1982, Silver Wings, Santiago Blue, 1984, The Pride of Hannah Wade, 1985, The Glory Game, 1985, The Great Alone, 1986, Calder Born, Calder Bred, 1983, Heiress, 1987, Rivals, 1989, numerous other novels. Recipient Golden Heart award Romance Writers Am., 1981, Romantic Times Contemporary award, 1983.

DAILEY, KATHLEEN HUMPHREYS, construction company executive; b. Bennington, Vt., Dec. 16, 1956; d. Donald Walter and Gloria Ann (Bashaw) Humphreys; m. Terrance Patrick Dailey, May 10, 1980; children: Michelle Lee, Jessica Lynn, Christine Marie. BS in Rsch., U. Vt. Precious metals buyer Internat. Coins & Currency, Montpelier, Vt., 1978-81; demographics researcher Shelbourne Technologies, Burlington, Vt., 1981-83; electronics buyer Environ. Technologies, Largo, Fla., 1983-85; v.p. Dailey Constrn., Inc., Indian Shores, Fla., 1985—. Republican. Roman Catholic. Office: Dailey Constrn Co Inc 19217 Whispering Pines Dr Indian Shores FL 34635

DAILY, ELLEN WILMOTH MATTHEWS, technical writer, training analyst; b. Marfa, Tex., Aug. 13, 1949; d. Lynn Henry Sr. and Wilmoth Hamilton (Cox) Matthews; m. John Scott Daily Sr., Mar. 21, 1970; children: John Scott Jr., Kristen Michelle. BS in Physics, U. Tex., El Paso, 1971; postgrad., George Mason U., Fairfax, Va., 1980. House dir., activity counselor Southwestern Children's Home, El Paso, Tex., 1965-68; analyst Schellenger Research Found. Labs, El Paso, 1968-70; computer operator, supr. keypunch El Paso Nat. Bank, 1970-73; supr., progam analyst El Paso Sand Products, 1973-74; tech. rep. Xerox Corp., Jackson, Miss., 1975-77; product tech. specialist Xerox Corp., Jackson, 1977-79; tech. trainer Xerox Corp., Leesburg, Va., 1979-82; sr. tech. writer, tng. analyst Xerox Corp., Lewisville, Tex., 1982—; group rep. Xerox Corp., various cities, 1975—; owner Daily Delight Cattery, Chantilly, Va. and Carrollton, Tex., 1979—; co-owner J & M Answering Service, Dallas, 1983-84. Co-author: (electronic Bible verse) Verse of the Day, 1987—. Team and div. mgr. Chantilly Youth Assn., 1980-82; bd. dirs., swim team dir. Brookfield Swim Club, Chantilly, 1980-82; vol. Metrocrest Svc. Ctr., Carrollton, 1986—; elder Nor'Kirk Presbyn. Ch., Carrollton, 1989—. Mem. U. Tex. El Paso Cannoneers Club (sec.-treas. 1967-71), Xerox Bowling League (pres. 1988-89), Sigma Pi Sigma, Kappa Delta (social service dir. 1969-70). Home: 3701 Grasmere Carrollton TX 75007 Office: Xerox Corp 1301 Ridgeview Dr MS181 Lewisville TX 75067

DAILY, FAY KENOYER, botany educator; b. Indpls., Feb. 17, 1911; d. Fredrick and Camellia Thea (Neal) Kenoyer; A.B., Butler U., 1935, M.S., 1952; m. William Allen Daily, June 24, 1937. Lab. technician Eli Lilly & Co., Indpls., 1935-37, Abbott Labs., North Chicago, Ill., 1939, William S. Merrell & Co., Ohio, 1940-41; lubrication chemist Indpls. Propellor div. Curtiss-Wright Corp., 1945; lectr. botany Butler U., Indpls., 1947-49, instr. immunology and microbiology, 1957-58, lectr. microbiology, 1962-63, mem. herbarium staff, 1949-87, curator cryptogamic herbarium, 1987—. Grantee Ind. Acad. Sci., 1961-62. Mem. Am. Inst. Biol. Sci., Bot. Soc. Am., Phycol. Soc. Am., Internat. Phycol. Soc., Ind. Acad. Sci., Torrey Bot. Club, Sigma Xi, Phi Kappa Phi, Sigma Delta Epsilon. Republican. Methodist. Co-author book on sci. history. Contbr. articles on fossil and extant charophytes (algae) to profl. jours. Home: 5884 Compton St Indianapolis IN 46220

DAILY, JEANETTE MARIE, sales representative; b. Indpls., July 20, 1965; d. Roy M. Jr. and Donna Marie (Scherer) D. BS in Journalism, Ball State U., Muncie, Ind., 1988. Asst. sales rep. Forest Lawn Memory Gardens, Greenwood, Ind., 1984-86; advt. dir. Expo mag., Muncie, Ind., 1986-87; adminstrv. asst. Student Found. Ball State U., Muncie, 1986-87; ad rev. dept. mgr. Better Bus. Bur., Muncie, 1987-88; admissions asst. Ind. Bus. Coll., Indpls., 1988—; communications asst. Am. Heart Assn., Indpls., 1988—; account rep. AT&T Info. Systems, Indpls., 1988—. Home: 1412 Chipmunk Circle Greenwood IN 46142

DAINS, MARY KATHLEEN, association executive; b. Glasgow, Ill., July 14, 1936; d. James Everett and Lela Francis (Wilson) Hester; m. Jay Dee Dains, Sept. 9, 1956; children: Everett Michael, Stephen Bert. BS in Edn., U. Mo., 1958, MA in Am. History, 1964. Rsch. asst. State Hist. Soc. Mo., Columbia, 1963-72, assoc. editor, 1972—, asst. dir., 1986-90, assoc. dir., 1990—; hist. co-cons. Hearne Bros. Map, Detroit, 1980; humanities cons. Bethel Community History, Boone County, Mo., 1986-87; hist. cons. Childrens Press, Chgo., 1989. Author: Partners with God, 1982; editor: Show Me Missouri Women, 1989; co-editor: Thomas Hart Benton: Artist, Writer, Intellectual, 1989; contbr. articles to profl. jours. Librarian First Christian Ch., Columbia, 1984—. Mem. AAUW (br. v.p. 1987-89, br. pres. 1989—), Am. Bus. Women's Assn. (chpt. pres. 1978-79, Chpt. Woman of Yr. 1979, 90), Mo. Writers' Guild (co-editor newsletter 1987—), State Hist. Soc. Mo., Disciples of Christ Hist. Soc. Democrat. Disciple of Christ. Home: 700 E High Point Ln Columbia MO 65203 Office: State Hist Soc Mo 1020 Lowry St Columbia MO 65201

DAISAK, BARBARA NINA, training and support consultant; b. Staten Island, N.Y., Feb. 3, 1961; d. Stephen and Jennie Josephine (Horbachewski) Daisak. BS, St. John's U., 1983; postgrad. Methods analyst and trainer Royal Ins. Co., N.Y.C., 1983-84; systems tng. and devel. specialist Irving Trust Co., N.Y.C., 1984-88; tng. and support cons. Conti Constrn. Co., South Plainfield, N.J., 1988—. Mem. Am. Soc. for Tng. and Devel.

DAITCH, JACQUELINE SHIRLEY, marketing professional; b. Boston, Dec. 29, 1935; d. Harry V. and Eve (Finkelstein) Cohen; m. Burton Daitch; children: Bryan S., Barry K., Jennifer S. Tech. sales Millipore Corp., Bedford, Mass., 1974-76, tech. service adminstr., 1976-79, product specialist, 1979-81, adminstr. govt. contracts, 1981-82, nat. account mgr., 1983-84, application specialist, 1984-85, sr. application specialist, 1985-88, mgr. mktg., 1986-89, application specialist, 1989-; bd. dirs. Ace Muffler Clinic Inc., Lowell, Mass. Mem. Nat. Assn. for Female Execs., Nat. Asbestos Council, Am. Standards Testing Materials, Mass. Environ. Health Assn., Internat. Food Tech., Nat. Soft Drink Assn. Jewish. Home: 100 Indian Ridge Rd Sudbury MA 01776 Office: Millipore Corp Ashby Rd Bedford MA 01730

DAITCH, PEGGY, magazine executive; b. Detroit, Aug. 20, 1946; d. Stanley B. and Miriam L. Friedman; m. Marvin C. Daitch; children: Joshua, Karen. Degree, Universite de Grenoble (France), 1966; BA, U. Mich., 1967. Producer Sta.-WTAK, Detroit, 1968-70; pub. rels. mgr. Sta. WTVS-TV, Pub. Broadcasting System, Detroit, 1970-72; broadcast producer/writer Loren/Snyder Advt., Detroit, 1976-78; broadcast producer/writer D'Arcy MacManus & Masius, Bloomfield Hills, Mich., 1978-79, account exec., 1979-84, account supr., 1984-86, v.p. 1985-86; mgr. Vogue Mag. and 16Q Mag., Detroit, 1986—; br. mgr. Conde Nast, 1990—. Adv. Bd. dirs. Founders Jr. Coun., Detroit Inst. Arts, 1976—, sec., 1978, v.p., 1980; bd. trustees Arts Found. of Mich., 1988—. Mem. Adcraft Club Detroit, Women's Advt. Club Detroit, Women's Econ. Club, The Fashion Group, Detroit Zool. Soc., Detroit Artists Market, Franklin Hill Country Club, The Renaissance Club. Jewish. Home: 8621 Hendrie Blvd Huntington Woods MI 48070 Office: Vogue Mag 3250 W Big Beaver Rd Ste 233 Troy MI 48084

DAKIN, MARY MEIER, small business owner, consultant; b. Macon, Ga., Sept. 15, 1956; d. John Lawrence Meier and Sally Ellen (Dunn) Page; m. Charles Loftis Dakin, Dec. 27, 1948; children: Charles Robert, Ross Loftis. BA in Interior Design, Mich. State U., 1978. Interior designer Contract Interiors, 1978-79; project mgr., sr. analyst, sr. interior designer Nat. Bank of Detroit, 1979-83; mktg. dir. Arnold Mfg., Ltd., Louisville, 1983-87, Catallo Assocs., Inc., Birmingham, Mich., 1987-89; owner, pres. Dakin Design, Inc., Birmingham, 1989—; mktg. cons. various architecture, interior design, comml. interior design, and automotive firms, fin. instns., and hospitality markets, Vancouver, B.C., Chgo., Mich., 1989—. Treas. Thornwood Subdiv., Troy, Mich., 1986-88. Mem. Am. Soc. Interior Designers (profl. mem.), Jr. League Birmingham, Kappa Kappa Gamma. Republican. Roman Catholic. Home and Office: Dakin Design Inc 625 Wimbleton Birmingham MI 48009

D'ALBERGARIA, NANCY KECK, marketing educator; b. Gillette, Wyo., Dec. 22, 1956; d. James Cletus and Mary Viola (Fulkerson) Keck; m. Thomas Gregory D'Albergaria, June 28, 1986. BA, U. Wyo., 1979, MBA, 1981. Mgmt. trainee Wyo. Bancorp., Cheyenne, 1982; sr. acct. Mitchell & Co., Ft. Collins, Colo., 1982-83; asst. prof. mktg. Adams State Coll., Alamosa, Colo., 1983-89; instr. mktg. U. No. Colo., Greeley, 1989—. Mem. Am. Mktg. Assn., Western Mktg. Educators Assn. Democrat. Home: 3328 W 34th St Greeley CO 80634 Office: U No Colo Dept Mktg Coll Bus Greeley CO 80639

DALE, BRENDA STEPHENS, educator; b. Hickory, N.C., Sept. 24, 1942; d. John Doyle and Bertha (Hahn) Stephens; m. James Darrell Dale, June 13, 1964; children: Ginger Leigh, Jami Lynne. BS in English, Appalachian State U., 1964, MA in Reading Edn., 1977; cert. edn. academically gifted, Lenoir Rhyne, Hickory, N.C., 1982. High. sch. tchr. Moore County Schs., Carthage, N.C., 1964; high sch. tchr. Asheboro (N.C.) City Schs., 1964-65; 8th grade tchr. Davidson County Schs., Thomasville, N.C., 1967-68; reading specialist Randolph County Schs., Trinity, N.C., 1970-72; reading specialist Wilkes N.C. Schs., Wilkesboro, 1972-82, tchr. acad. gifted, 1982—; part-time tchr. Davidson County Community Coll., Lexington, N.C., 1965-68, Wilkes Community Coll., Wilkesboro, 1982-87, adult literary tutor. Edn. chmn., bd. dirs. Am. Cancer Soc., North Wilkesboro, N.C., 1985—; mem. YMCA. Tchr. Scholar fellow N.C. Ctr. for the Advancement of Teaching, Western Carolina U., 1990. Mem. Nat. Assn. Educators, N.C. Assn. Educators, Internat. Reading Assn. (sec. 1985-86), AAUW (fundraising 1977-78), Mary Hemphill Svc. Group, Lynnwoode Recreation Club, Alpha Delta Kappa. Methodist. Home: 202 Laurel Mountain Rd North Wilkesboro NC 28659 Office: Wilkes County Schs Main St Wilkesboro NC 28697

DALE, JUDY RIES, religious organization administrator, educational consultant; b. Memphis, Dec. 13, 1944; d. James Lorigan and Julia Marie (Schwinn) Ries; m. Eddie Melvin Ashmore, July 12, 1969 (div. Dec. 1983). BA, Rhodes Coll., 1966; M in Religious Edn., So. Bapt. Theol. Sem., 1969, Grad. Specialist in Religious Edn., 1969. Cert. tchr. educable mentally handicapped, secondary English adminstrn. and supervision in spl. edn. EMH tchr., curriculum writer, tchr. trainer Jefferson County Bd. Edn., Louisville, 1969-88, ednl. cons., 1988-90; dist. coord. Great Lakes Dist. Universal Fellowship Met. Community Chs., Louisville, 1990—; lectr. Jefferson Community Coll., Louisville, 1987—, U. Louisville, 1976-77, 1987—; mem. program advisory com. Internat. Conf. Spl. Edn., Bejing, 1987-88, gen. coun. Universal Fellowship Met. Community Chs. Editor, writer: (handbook) Handbook for Beginning Teachers, 1989, A Manual of Instructional Strategies, 1985; author: (kit) Math Activities Cards, 1978. Bd. sec. Comm. Ten, Inc., Louisville, 1987—; active Greater Louisville Human Rights Commn., 1985—, Ky. Civil Liberties Union, 1986—; v.p. GLUE, 1988—. Recipient Honorable Order of Ky. Cols., 1976; named Outstanding Elem. Tchr. Am., 1975. Mem. NOW, The Council for Exceptional Children (keynote speaker, 1984-88, internat. pres. 1986-87, exec. com. 1984-88, bd. govs. 1981-88), Ky. Coun. Exceptional Children (bd. 1976—, Mem. of Yr. 1987), Colonelettes (bd. dirs. 1972-80), Women's Alliance, Phi Delta Kappa. Democrat. Universal Fellowship of Metro. Community Chs. Home and Office: 1300 Ambridge Dr Louisville KY 40207-2410

DALE, LORRAINE HENDERSON, educational administrator; b. Phila., Aug. 30, 1942; d. Samuel and Dorothy (Polite) Henderson; children: Kevin, Matthew. BA, U. Guam, 1975, MEd, 1977; postgrad., U. Hawaii, 1977-85, U. S.C., 1988. Tchr. pub. schs. Kaiser High Sch., Honolulu, 1975-79; curriculum coord., tchr. Nanakuli (Hawaii) High Sch., 1979-83; lang. arts resource tchr. Leeward Dist., 1983-85; v.p. Waianae (Hawaii) Intermediate Sch., 1985-87; actg. prin. Lehoku (Hawaii) Elem. Sch., 1987; v.p. Aliamanu (Hawaii) Intermediate Sch., 1987-88; vice prin. Kaimuki High Sch., Honolulu, 1988—; validator Nat. Tchr. Examinations, 1985; bd. dirs. summer sch. program, acad. summer camp Waianae High Sch., 1987. Staff writer Afro Hawaii News. Mem. Nat. Assn. Secondary Sch. Prins., Hawaii Assn. Secondary Sch. Adminstrs. (sec.), Assn. Supervision and Curriculum Devel., Hawaii Edn. Assn., Hawaii Community Edn. Assn., Hawaii SState Tchrs. Assn., Hawaii Govt. Employees Assn., Alpha Delta Kappa. Office: Kaimuki High Sch 2705 Kaimuki Ave Honolulu HI 96825

DALE, NAN A., child welfare agency executive; b. N.Y.C., Jan. 27, 1942; d. Charles H. and Lois (Schermer) Whitebrook; m. Harvey P. Dale, Apr. 8, 1965; children: Lisa, Oliver. BA, NYU, 1963; MA, Yeshiva U., 1965. Child care worker, tchr. Wiltwyck Sch. for Boys, N.Y.C., 1964-66; tchr. Mobilization for Youth, N.Y.C., 1966-67; tchr., tchr. trainer Jr. High Sch. Dist. 71, N.Y.C., 1967-68; tchr. trainer, supr. Two Bridges Model Sch. Dist., N.Y.C., 1968; project dir. Vols. of the Shelters, Inc., N.Y.C., 1969-70; mem. faculty BOCES, N.Y.C., 1972-75; exec. dir. Wiltwyck Sch. for Boys, Yorktown, N.Y., 1980-81, Children's Village, Dobbs Ferry, N.Y., 1981—; bd. dirs., past v.p., sec. Coun. Family & Child Care Agys., N.Y.C., 1984—; bd. dirs., pres. Wiltwyck Sch. for Boys. Mem. Child Welfare League of Am. (bd. dirs. 1985—), Nat. Adv. Comm. to Child Welfare League of Am. (chmn.). Office: The Childrens Village Dobbs Ferry NY 10522

DALE, VIRGINIA HOUSE, ecologist, educator; b. Rochester, N.Y., Sept. 9, 1951; d. William Andrew and Corinne (Howell) D.; m. Alan B. Adams, June 11, 1971 (div. 1984); 1 child, Wendy Mae; m. Leonard Charles Hensley, May 2, 1987; 1 child, William Bradley. BA, U. Tenn., 1974, MS, 1975; PhD, U. Wash., 1980. Rsch. asst. Oak Ridge (Tenn.) Nat. Lab., 1975, U. Wash., Seattle, 1977-79; rsch. assoc. Oreg. State U., Corvallis, 1981, U. Wash., Seattle, 1981-83; instr. U. Puget Sound, Tacoma, Wash., 1982-83; asst. prof. Pacific Luth. U., Tacoma, 1981-82; rsch. scientist Oak Ridge (Tenn.) Nat. Lab., 1984—. Contbr. articles, reports to profl. jours., chpts. to books; editor spl. issue Landscape Ecology, 1989. Chair conservation com. Wash. Native Plant Soc., Seattle, 1982-83; chair Environ. Quality Adv. Bd., Oak Ridge, 1986-89, Citizens for Quality Growth, Oak Ridge, 1989-90. Recipient award Northwest Sci. Assn., 1979, Rsch. Corp., 1982, Earthwatch, 1982-83, NSF, 1988, Nat. Geog. Soc., 1989. Mem. Ecol. Soc. Am., Internat. Assn. for Landscape Ecology, AAAS. Office: Oak Ridge Nat Lab MS 6038 PO Box 2008 Oak Ridge TN 37831-6038

D'ALENE, ALIXANDRIA FRANCES, management consultant; b. Buffalo, Oct. 21, 1951; d. Fern (Hill) D'A.; B.A., Canisius Coll., Buffalo, 1973, M.S., 1975, M.B.A., 1980. Tchr., Buffalo public schs., 1973-76; pers. cons. Sanford Rose Assos., Williamsville, N.Y., 1976-78; mgr. benefits adminstrn. Svc. Systems Corp., Clarence, N.Y., 1978-80; mgr. employee rels. Del Monte Corp., Walnut Creek, Calif., 1980-82; human resource mgmt. cons. H.R.S., Inc., Winston-Salem, N.C., 1982-87; corp. pers. specialist Advance Stores Co., Inc., Roanoke, Va., 1987-88; pers. dir. Alfred (N.Y.) U., 1988—; adj. prof. bus., 1988—. Mem. Assn. Pers. Adminstrs., Indsl. Pers. Soc., Coll. and U. Pers. Assn., Phi Alpha Theta. Episcopalian.

DALESSANDRO, ANGELA, bank official; b. Ft. Dix, N.J., Mar. 23, 1956; d. Lugino Danial and Janet Eugenia (Garnand) Dalessandro; m. Kenneth Szyndel, Oct. 25, 1986. BBA summa cum laude, U. Okla., 1984. Commd. examiner FRS. Credit analyst Union Bank & Trust Co., Oklahoma City, 1984-85; enforcement examiner Fed. Res. Bank, Dallas, 1985-88, coord. surveillance, 1989—; ptnr. Whim-Z Comml. Photography, Dallas, 1988—. Sgt. USMC, 1975-79. Recipient commendation FRS, 1986. Mem. Mensa, Dallas-Ft. Worth Basenji Club, Phi Lambda Alpha. Republican. Home: ll03 Seminole Trail E Carrollton TX 75007-6204 Office: Fed Res Bank 400 S Akard Dallas TX 75222

DALESSANDRRI, KATHIE MARIE, surgeon, educator; b. Stambaugh, Mich., May 4, 1947; d. Paris H. and Kathryn (Macuga) D.; m. Gordon William Frost, 1986. BS, Mich. Technol. U., 1969; MS, Purdue U., 1971; MD, U. Mich., 1976. Diplomate Am. Bd. Surgery. Intern Martinez VA Hosp., 1976-77; resident U. Calif., Davis, 1977-81; gen. surgeon Martinez (Calif.) VA Hosp., 1982—; asst. prof. surgery U. Calif., Davis, 1983—; gen. surgeon Project Hope, Grenada, 1984, 89, Hosp. Albert Sweitzer, Haiti, 1986. Contbr. articles to med. jours. VA grantee, 1983. Fellow ACS, Internat. Coll. Surgeons; mem. Am. Med. Women's Assn., Nat. Coun. Internat. Health, S.W. Surg. Soc. Office: Martinez VA Hosp 150 Muir Rd Martinez CA 94553

D'ALESSIO, JACQUELINE ANN, English educator; b. Morristown, N.J., Jan. 26, 1943; d. Clifford Corbet and Helen Ann (Chrenko) Compton; m. Harold F. D'Alessio, Oct. 28, 1967. BA English, Coll. New Rochelle, 1964; MA English, Seton Hall U., 1969. Tchr. Bridgewater (N.J.)-Raritan Regional Sch. Dist., 1964—; advisor, student coun., newspaper, dramatics, Hillside Sch., Bridgewater, N.J., 1966—. Chmn. pub. rels. Mount St. Mary Devel. Office., 1985—. Named Outstanding Elem. Tchr. U.S., 1971; Recipient Gov. Tchr. Recognition, N.J. Dept. Edn., Trenton, 1989. Mem. AAUW (N.J. Div. pres., 1990-92, program v.p., 1988-90, rep. Women's Agenda, 1989-92). Roman Catholic. Home: 30 Putnam St Somerville NJ 08876

D'ALESSIO, KITTY, cosmetic and clothing co. exec.; b. Sea Girt, N.J., 1929; B.A., Upsala Coll., 1948; Formerly with B. Altman and Co., N.Y.C.; fashion cons. NBC/TV, N.Y.C.; sr. v.p., dir. Norman, Craig, and Kummel, until 1979; pres. Chanel, Inc., N.Y.C., 1979-88, vice chmn. new ventures and spl. projects, 1988—. Office: Chanel Inc 9 W 57th St New York NY 10019

DALEY, LAVERNE DOYLE, writer; b. Memphis; d. Eugene and Lorine (Kramer) Doyle; m. Richard Daley, Dec. 27, 1945; children: Sharon, Richard, David, Lisa, Denise. BA in Journalism, Memphis State U., 1984. Staff writer Memphis Bus. Jour., 1984-87; editor alumni publs. Memphis State U., 1987-89; free lance writer, editor Memphis, 1973—; corr. S.E. region Adweek Mag., Atlanta, 1986—. Contbr. articles to profl. jours. and mags. Mem. Women in Communications (sec. 1988-90, publicity chair 1990-91), Soc. Profl. Journalists (sec. 1987-89), Memphis State U. Journalism Alumni (bd. mem. 1986-90). Roman Catholic.

D'ALISA, ROSE, biochemist; b. Savona, Italy, Mar. 14, 1948; came to U.S., 1957; d. Giovanni and Guiseppina (Fico) D'Alisa. AB, Lehman Coll., 1969; PhD, Columbia U., 1975. Grad. fellow Columbia U., N.Y.C., 1969-75; postdoctoral fellow Rockefeller U., N.Y.C., 1975-78; rsrch. assoc. Columbia U., N.Y.C., 1978-81; sr. rsch. scientist Revlon Health Care Group, Tuckahoe, N.Y., 1981-84, assoc. rsrch. fellow, 1984-85; prin. scientist Meloy Labs., Springfield, Va., 1985-88; sr. rsch. scientist Rorer Biotech. Inc., King of Prussia, Pa., 1988-89, rsch. fellow, 1989—, sect. mgr., 1988—. Contbr. articles to profl. jours. Mem. N.Y. Acad. Scis., Am. Assn. Immunologists, Sigma Xi, Iota Sigma Pi. Democrat. Roman Catholic. Office: Rorer Biotech Inc 680 Allendale Rd King of Prussia PA 19406

DALKE, CONSTANCE OLIVIA LOGAN, education educator; b. Denver, Oct. 21, 1950; d. Phillip George and Anna Evelina (Carlson) Logan. BA, U. Colo., 1972; MA, U. Denver, 1974, PhD, 1984. Tchr. spl. edn. Farmington (N.Mex.) Schs., 1974-78, 80-81, Aztec (N.Mex.) Schs., 1978-80; prof. edn., dir. learning disabilities support program U. Wis., Whitewater, 1984—; assoc. prof. support programs in higher edn. for students with disabilities, Access for All. Contbr. articles to profl. jours. Recipient award Assn. Handicapped Student Svc. Programs in Postsecondary Edn., 1988, outstanding rsch. award Coll. Edn., U. Wis., Whitewater, 1989; grantee State of Wis., 1985-86, 87-88, 89-90, U.S. Dept. Edn., 1985-90. Mem. ASCD, Coun. for Exceptional Children, Coun. for Learning Disabilities, Internat. Assn. Spl. Edn., Midwest Ednl. Rsch. Assn. Home: 522-A W Main St Whitewater WI 53190 Office: U Wis Roseman 2019 Whitewater WI 53190

DALLAL KHALILI, MARYLOUISE, management and marketing educator; b. Harlingen, Tex., Sept. 13, 1937; d. Tewfik Gabrial and Minerva (Laham) Dallal. BS in Bus., Central State U., 1961; MS in Bus., Calif. State U., Long Beach, 1971; PhD in Bus., U. Okla., 1990; cert. in communications, U. Hawaii, 1972. High sch. tchr. Okla., Calif. and Kans., 1961-71; dir. family planning Govt. of Iran, Tehran, 1972-76; prof. Oklahoma City U., 1976—; cons. Shifting Gears Unltd., Oklahoma City, 1985—; realtor ERA Bob Linn & Assocs., Oklahoma City, 1985—. Author: Sign of the Times, 1975. Vol. Planned Parenthood Am., Oklahoma City, 1976—, United Cerebral Palsy, Oklahoma City, 1989—, Mar. of Dimes, Oklahoma City, 1976-81; organizer Ptnrs. for Excellence in Edn., Okla., 1985—; campaigner Okla. Dems., 1987-88; vol. Salvation Army, Jesus Ho., Meals on Wheels. Mem. various mgmt. orgns., Delta Pi Epsilon (v.p. 1979-81, pres. 1981-82). Home: 2304 NW 28th Oklahoma City OK 73107 Office: Shifting Gears Unltd PO Box 12426 Oklahoma City OK 73157

DALLAS, NOELLE MARIE, senior financial analyst; b. Louisville, Sept. 24, 1959; d. Glenn Hoyle and Micheline Alice (Boudrias) Madison; m. Stephen Stavros Dallas Jr., Nov. 4, 1989. Student, Benjamin Franklin U., 1978-80; BS in Biology, George Mason U., 1984, postgrad, 1988; postgrad, Montgomery Coll., 1986-88. Mgr. Holly Enterprises, Alexandria, Va., 1975-81; gov. rels. intern TRW, Rosslyn, Va., 1984-85; med. asst. Cardiology and Internal Medicine, P.A., Chevy Chase, Md., 1985-86; sr. cons. Ernst & Young, Washington, 1986-90; sr. fin. analyst Community Energy Alternatives, Ridgewood, N.J., 1990—. Mem. NAFE, Coun. Econ. Priorities, Nat. Resources Defense Coun., N.J. Environ. Group, Friends of the Earth, Bound Brook Land Preservation Soc., Chi Omega Alumni Assn. Roman Catholic. Home: 103 W 2d St Bound Brook NJ 08805 Office: Community Energy Alternatives 1200 E Ridgewood Ave Ridgewood NJ 07450

DALLMANN-SCHAPER, MARY LOUISE, banker; b. Duluth, Minn., July 4, 1951; d. Norbert Henry and Lahja Mildred (Mykra) D. BA in Bus. Adminstrn., U. Minn., 1974; M in Mgmt. Adminstrn., Met. State U., 1987. With Norwest Info. Svcs., Inc., 1971-85; tech. contingency planner First Bank Systems, Inc., 1985-87, tech. support supr., 1987-88, client mgr. human resource info. systems, 1988-89, sr. ops. project leader/officer, 1989—. Mem. NAFE, Data Processing Mgmt. Assn., Minn. Women's Network. Home: 1500 76th Ct Brooklyn Park MN 55444 Office: First Bank System Inc 1200 First Bank Pl Minneapolis MN 55480

DALLMEYER, DOROTHY MARIE See UTESCH, DOROTHY MARIE

DALLMEYER, MARY DORINDA GILMORE, lawyer; b. Macon, Ga., Sept. 11, 1952; d. Hubert Respess and Betty (Kennedy) Gilmore; m. R. David Dallmeyer, Mar. 15, 1975. BS in Geology, U. Ga., 1973, MS in Geology, 1977, JD, 1984. Bar: Ga. 1984. Rsch. technician dept. zoology U. Ga., Athens, 1978-81, rsch. dir. Dean Rusk Ctr. Internat. and Comparative Law, 1984—. Editor: Strategic Defense Initiative, 1986, U.S.-Japan Trade Relations, 1986, Chinese Economic Law, 1988, Rights to Oceanic Resources, 1989. Vol., Recording for the Blind, Athens, 1988—. Grantee U.S. Sea Grant Prog., 1986, Can. Embassy, 1988, 90, John D. and Catherine T. MacArthur Found., 1989, Ford Found., 1990, Hewlett Found., 1990. Mem. Coun. Fgn. Rels., ABA, Am. Soc. Internat. Law, State Bar Ga., Lawyers Alliance for Nuclear Arms Control. Democrat. Methodist. Office: U Ga Dean Rusk Ctr Law Athens GA 30602

DALLONS, BERNA LOU WRIGHT, manufacturing executive, director, business owner; b. Belleville, Ill., Feb. 7, 1928; d. Robert E. and Alice (Mason) Wright; m. B.J. Horton, Feb. 4, 1947 (div. 1974); 1 child, Kathryn Elizabeth Horton Galati; m. John A. Dallons, July 1, 1978. BA, Calif. State U., L.A., 1963; MA, Calif. Poly. U., San Luis Obispo, 1967. Tchr. Belvedere Jr. High Sch., L.A., 1963-64; tchr. Morro Bay (Calif.) High Sch., 1964-67, counselor, 1967-74, 77-79; dir. guidance Internat. Sch. of Kenya, Nairobi, 1974-77; owner, mfr. Western Quartz Products, Paso Robles, Calif., 1979—; bd. dirs. Citizens Bank of Paso Robles. Fellow Radio Club of Paso Robles (pres. 1985-86, treas. 1987-89), AAUW (pres. 1989-91). Republican. Home: 9985 Santa Rosa Creek Rd Templeton CA 93465

D'ALOISIO, VIRGINIA MARIE, teacher; b. Bklyn., Sept. 2, 1951; d. Ralph and Erminia Mamie (Venuto) D'A. AA, Queensborough Community Coll., 1972; BS, Bklyn. Coll., 1974; MA, U. No. Colo., 1977; postgrad., Bklyn. Coll., 1989—. Cert. tchr., N.Y., N.J. Switchboard operator, bookkeeper Answerphone, Rego Park, N.Y., 1974-75; mem. inter-libr. loans staff U. No. Colo., Greeley, 1976-77; substitute tchr. various schs., N.H. and N.Y., 1974-81; tchr. Glen Cove (N.Y.) Pub. Schs., 1981-82, St. Kevin's Elem. Sch., Bayside, N.Y., 1982-85, Van Wyck Jr. High Sch., Jamaica, N.Y., 1985-87, Shellbank Jr. High Sch., Sheepshead Bay, N.Y., 1987—; tchr. trainer Diocese of Bklyn., 1984-85, N.Y.C. Bd. Edn., 1990—; cons. in writing of N.Y. State Cath. sch. phys. edn. curriculum, 1984-85. Builder miniature working models of athletic cts. and gymnastic equipment. Emergency med. technician N.Y. State Dept. Health, Woodhaven/Richmond Hill Vol. Ambulance. Mem. N.Y. State Assn. Health, Phys. Edn., Recreation and Dance (newsletter editor), AAHPRD. Republican. Roman Catholic. Home: 87-24 108th St Richmond Hill NY 11418 Office: Shellbank Jr High Sch 2424 Batchelder St Sheepshead Bay NY 11235

DALPES, LINDA FRANCES, management executive; b. New Orleans, Jan. 3, 1938; d. Walter James and Frances Katherine (Jordan) Fountain. AA, Stephens Coll., 1957; BA, U. Hawaii, 1959. Cert. dental asst. Sr. claims analyst Am. Gen. Life Inc. Co., Houston, 1960-64; mgr. claims Southwest region Calif. Western States Life Ins. Co., Houston, 1964-68; mgmt. cons. Met. Agy., Houston, 1968-70; clinic adminstr. Harris & Adams, Inc., Houston, 1970-75; founder, pres. Team Coordinators, Houston, 1975—; clinician major dental meetings; internat. lectr., cons. south, southwest univs.; exec. sec. Tex. Dental Hygienists Assn., 1972-75. Mem. LWV, Am. Mgmt. Assn., AAUW, Nat. Assn. Women Bus. Owners, Nat. Assn. Female Execs. Republican. Episcopalian. Office: PO Box 1181 Cleveland TX 77327

DALRYMPLE, JEAN VAN KIRK, theatrical producer, publicist, author; b. Morristown, N.J., Sept. 2, 1902; d. George Hull and Elizabeth Van Kirk (Collins) D.; m. Ward Morehouse, Mar. 31, 1932 (div. 1937); m. Philip De Witt Ginder, Nov. 1, 1951 (dec. Nov. 1968). Ed. pvt. tutors; DFA (hon.), Wheaton Coll., 1959. Bd. dirs. N.Y.C. Ctr. Music and Drama, Soldiers, Sailors and Airmen's Club, N.Y.C., Profl. Children's Sch., N.Y.C., N.Y. World's Fair, 1964-65; cons. Performing Arts Program, N.Y. World's Fair; dir. U.S. Performing Arts Program, Fed. Pavilion, N.Y. World's Fair; mem. adv. bd. N.C. Sch. Arts; bd. dirs. Am. Theatre Wing, 1940—, co-moderator Working in the Theatre Am. Theatre Wing seminar 1973—, Tony Awards nominator, voter; currently pres. Light Opera of Manhattan; on Manhattan Cable TV CUNY Program, 1977—. bd. dirs. N.Y.C. Ctr. Music and Drama, 1943-69, Soldiers, Sailors and Airmens Club, N.Y.C., Am. Theatre Wing, ANTA, N.Y. World's Fair, 1964-65; cons. Performing Arts Program Fed. Pavillion, N.Y. Worlds Fair; mem. adv. bd. N.C. Sch. Arts; Actress, writer, 1926-29; writer, producer, dir. (with Daniel Jarrett) one act plays for Orpheum and Keith-Albee vaudeville circuits, two featuring first appearances of Jimmy Cagney and Cary Grant; publicist for Broadway producer John Golden, 1929-33, publicist, mgr. for artists including Grace Moore, Lily Pons, Bidu Sayoa, Glinka Milanov, Nathan Milstein, Leopold Stokowski, William Steinberg, Anton Dorati, Andre Kostelanetz, 1933-54, Jose Iturbi, 1933-81, permanent dir., N.Y. City Ctr. Theatre and Light Opera Cos., 1943-69; Broadway press agt. for plays starring Tallulah Bankhead, Mary Martin, Margaret Sullivan, Ballet Russe de Monte Carlo; vol. publicity dir. N.Y.C. Ctr., 1943-68, Lewisohn Stadium concerts, New Opera Co., 1941-42, Marques de Quevas Ballet, 1941-42; Broadway producer Hope For The Best (Franchot Tone), 1944, Brighten the Corner (Charles Butterworth, Franchot Tone), 1945, Burlesque (Bert Lahr), 1946-48, Red Gloves (Charles Boyer), 1948-49; prod., dir. summer cir. The Second Man (Franchot Tone), Harvey (Burgess Meredith), Voice of the Turtle (Ella Raines and George Englund), Petrified Forest (Franchot Tone and Betsy von Furstenberg), 1950-53; permanent dir. Drama Co. N.Y. City Ctr.; producer 4 plays, Cyrano de Bergerac, The Shrike, Richard III, Charlie's Aunt (all with Jose Ferrer), 1953-54, What Every Woman Knows (Helen Hayes), The Fourposter (Hume Cronin and Jessica Tandy), Time of Your Life (Franchot Tone), Wisteria Trees (Helen Hayes), 1955, King Lear (Orson Welles), Marcel Marceau, Streetcar Named Desire, 1957 (Tallulah Bankhead), Light Opera Co. N.Y. City Ctr.; producer Carousel (spl. Christmas show); dir., producer over 30 others; producer numerous TV programs and films; assoc. producer film Children of Theatre Street (Princess Grace of Naratov), 1976; producer La Casa de Te de la Luna de Agosta, U.S. Dept. State, Mex. and S.Am., 1956-57, Variations on the Same Theme by Ionesco, Guggenheim Mus., N.Y.C., 1980; coordinator U.S. Performing Arts Program, Brussels World's Fair, 1958 including Carousel, Wonderful Town, world premier Marie Golovin by Gian Carlo Menotti, Time of Your Life, Ballet USA by Jerome Robbins, Van Cliburn Piano Concerto with Phila. Orch., many solo stars including Jose Iturbi, Benny Goodman, Harry Belafonte, others; coordinator Am. program Berlin Arts Festival, 1951, Internat. Festival of Entertainment; Author: September Child, 1963, Careers and Opportunities in the Theatre, 1969, Jean Dalrymple's Pinafore Farm Cookbook, 1971, (with Fay Lavan) The Folklore and Facts of Natural Nutrition, 1973, From the Last Row, 1975, The Complete Handbook for Community Theatre, 1977, also articles, sketches, plays; mem. Nat. Council on Arts, 1968-74, NEA Opera Panel, 1975-76, Theatre Panel, 1977-78; pioneered in TV prodn. operas, drama for Paramount Pictures. Decorated Knight Order Crown for Brussels World's Fair work, Belgium; recipient 6 citations for City Ctr. work from mayors of N.. Mem. Nat. Council on Arts, ANTA (bd. dirs., treas.), New Dramatists. Home: 150 W 55th St New York NY 10019

DAL SANTO, DIANE, judge; b. East Chicago, Ind., Sept. 20, 1949; d. John Quentin Dal Santo and Helen (Koval) D.; m. Fred O'Cheskey, June 29, 1985. BA, U. N. Mex., 1971; cert. Inst. Internat. and Comparative Law, Guadalajara, Mex., 1978; JD, U. San Diego, 1980. Bar: N.Mex. 1980, U.S. Dist. Ct. N.Mex. 1980. Ct. planner Met. Criminal Justice Coordinating Coun., Albuquerque, 1973-75; planning coord. Dist. Atty.'s Office, Albuquerque, 1975-76, exec. asst. to dist. atty., 1976-77, asst dist. atty. for violent crimes, 1980-82; chief dep. city atty. City of Albuquerque, 1983; assoc. firm T.B. Keleher & Assocs., 1983-84; judge Met. Ct., 1985-89, chief judge, 1988-89; judge Dist. Ct., 1989—. Bd. dirs. Nat. Coun. Alcoholism, 1984, S.W. Ballet Co., Albuquerque, 1982-83; mem. Mayor's Task Force on Alcoholism and Crime. Recipient Woman of Yr. award Duke City Bus. and Profl. Women, 1985, YWCA Women on the Move award, 1989; U. San Diego scholar, 1978-79. Mem, ABA, N.Mex. Bar Assn., Albuquerque Bar Assn., Nat. Assn. Women Judges, Greater Albuquerque C. of C. (steering com. 1989), LWV, N.Mex. Coun. on Crime and Delinquency, N.Mex. Magistrate Judges Assn. (v.p. 1985-89), Dist. Judges Assn. Democrat. Home: 4139 Coe Dr NE Albuquerque NM 87110 Office: Dist Ct 415 Tijeras NW Albuquerque NM 87103

DAL SANTO, PAULA, architect; d. John Quentin and Helen (Koval) Dal S.; m. Edward Anlian Jr., June 6, 1981; children: Whitney, Kendall. BArch, U. N.Mex., 1981, MArch, 1986. Lic. architect, N.Mex. Prin. Dal Santo Constrn., Albuquerque, 1979—; project architect Vogt & Byrnes, Architects, Albuquerque, 1986-87; prin. Techline Studio, Albuquerque, 1987—, Paula Dal Santo, Architect, Albuquerque, 1988—. Com. chmn. Jr. League Albuquerque, 1987-90; mem. steering com. judicial race, Albuquerque, 1990. Mem. AIA. Office: Paula Dal Santo Architect 4100 Menaul Blvd NE Albuquerque NM 87110

DALTON, CARYL, school psychologist; b. Mineral Wells, Tex., Aug. 8, 1949; d. Pat Francis Dalton and Yvonne (Ridings) Erwin. BA, U. Tex., 1970, MEd, 1977, PhD, 1987. Tchr. Brown Schs., Austin, San Marcos, Tex., 1971-73; homebound tchr. Rochester (N.Y.) City Schs., 1974-75; asst. dir. Big Buddies, Austin, Tex., 1975-77; ednl. cons. Edn. Svc. Ctr. XIII, Austin, Tex., 1978-79, pvt. practice, Austin, Tex., 1979-84; asst. instr. U. Tex., Austin, Tex., 1983-86; from doctoral intern to sch. psychologist Balcones Special Svcs. Coop., Austin, Tex., 1986—; psychologist Associated Psychological Svcs., Austin, Tex., 1989—, cons. Edn. Svc. Ctr. XIII, Austin, Tex., adj. prof. U. Tex., Austin, 1990. Mem. YMCA, Austin, Tex., bd. dirs. Austin (Tex.) Rape Crisis Ctr. Mem. Am. Psychological Assn. Office: Balcones Special Svcs Coop 601 Westbank Dr Austin TX 78746

DALTON, CLAUDETTE ELLIS HARLOE, physician, medical school administrator; b. Roanoke, Va., Jan. 18, 1947; d. John Pinckney and Dorothy Anne (Ellis) Harloe; m. Henry Tucker Dalton, May 17, 1973 (div. 1979); 1 child, Gordon Tucker. BA, Sweet Briar Coll., 1969; MD, U. Va., 1974. Resident in anesthesiology U. N.C., Chapel Hill, 1974-77; med. edn. Lenoir County Meml Hosp./East Carolina U., Kinston, N.C., 1978-80; med. edn. in intensive care Presbyn Hosp., Charlotte, N.C., 1981-82; practice anesthesiology Charlotte Eye, Ear, Nose and Throat Hosp., 1982-85, Medivision of Charlotte and Orthopedic Hosp. of Charlotte, 1985-89; asst. dean U. Va. Health Scis. Ctr., Charlottesville, 1989—, also asst. prof. internal medicine; bd. dirs. Dept. Health, Kinston, 1979-81; chmn. com. on Tel-Med System, Mecklenburg County Med. Soc. Author developer patient edn. materials for illiterate patients, 1979—, emergency med. svc. tng. program, 1981. Exec. dir. Community Involvement Council Lenoir County, Kinston, 1979; county coordinator Internat. Yr. of the Child, Kinston, 1979; bd. dirs. Council on Aging, Lenoir County Community Coll., Cancer Soc., others. Recipient Gov.'s award State of N.C., 1980; cert. of merit for svc. to children N.C. Dept. Human Resources. Mem. Va. Med. Soc., Albemarle County Med. Soc., Va. Soc. Anesthesiology, Women's Faculty and Profl. Assn., U. Va. Med. Sch. Women's Task Force, Greencroft Club, Colonnade Club. Office: U Va Med Sch Box 324 Charlottesville VA 22908

DALTON, DEBBIE JO, public relations executive; b. Victoria, Tex., Oct. 4, 1966; d. Martine Joseph and Almeda Frances (Tesh) D. BS in Advt., U. Tex., 1988. Pub. info. coord. Am. Diabetes Assn., Austin, Tex., 1988-89; pub. rels. coord. Motivators, Inc., Houston, 1989—; cons. Personal Touch Communications, Houston, 1989—, Bus. Vols. for the Arts, Houston, 1989—; communications coord. Houston Animal Rights Team, 1989—. contbr. articles to mags. and newspapers. Recipient Excalibur for Excellence Pub. Rels. Soc. Am., Houston, 1989, Mercury award Nat. Media Conf., 1989, Excellence in Advt. scholarship Bus. Profl. Advt. Assn., 1987. Mem. Women in Communications, Inc. (bd. dirs., hosp. chair 1990—, chpt. pres. 1987-88), Ad2 Houston (bd. dirs., fundraising chmn. 1990-91), World Wildlife Fund, Environ. Def. Fund, Amnesty Internat., NOW. Home: 7243 Augustine Houston TX 77036

DALTON, EDWINA P., state legislator; b. Cin., June 12, 1936. BA, Radford U. Mem. Va. State Senate. Trustee U. Richmond; chmn. bd. Va. sect. Am. Cancer Soc. Mem. Women's Club Richmond, Tuckahoe Woman's Club. Republican. Baptist. *

DALTON, PHYLLIS IRENE, library consultant; b. Marietta, Kans., Sept. 25, 1909; d. Benjamin Reuben and Pearl (Travelute) Bull; m. Jack Mason Dalton, Feb. 13, 1950. B.S., U. Nebr., 1931, M.A., 1941; M.A., U. Denver, 1942. Tchr. city schs., Marysville, Kans., 1931-40; reference librarian Lincoln Pub. Library, Nebr.; librarian U. Nebr., Lincoln, 1941-48; librarian Calif. State Library, Sacramento, 1948-57, asst. state librarian, 1957-72; pvt. library cons., Scottsdale, Ariz., 1972—. Author: Library Service to the Deaf and Hearing Impaired, 1985 (Pres.' Com. Employment of Handicapped award 1985). Contbr. chpt., articles, reports to books and publs. in field. Mem. exec. bd. So. Nev. Hist. Soc., Las Vegas, 1983-84; mem. So. Nev. Com. on Employment of Handicapped, 1980-89, chairperson, 1988-89; mem. adv. com. Nat. Orgn. on Disability, 1982—; mem., sec. resident coun. Forum Pueblo Norte Retirement Village, 1990—; bd. dirs. Friends of So. Nev. Libraries; trustee Univ. Library Soc., U. Nev.-Las Vegas; mem. Allied Arts Council, Pres.' Com. on Employment of People with Disabilities, mem. emeritus 1989—. Recipient Libraria Sodalitas, U. So. Calif., 1972, Alumni Achievement award U. Denver, 1977, Alumni Achievement award U. Nebr., Lincoln, 1983. Mem. LWV, ALA (councilor 1963-64, exceptional service award 1981), Assn. State Libraries (pres. 1964-65), Calif. Library Assn. (pres. 1969), Nev. Library Assn. (hon.), Internat. Fedn. Library Assns. and Instns. (chair working group on library service to prisons, mem. standing com. Sect. Libraries Serving Disadvantaged Persons 1987—), Nat. League Am. Pen Women (Las Vegas chpt. 1988—, parliamentarian Scottsdale chpt. 1989—), Pilot Internat. (mem.-at-large). Republican. Presbyterian. Home: 7090 E Mescal St Apt 261 Scottsdale AZ 85254

DALY, JANET MORGAN, trade publishing editor; b. White Plains, N.Y., Jan. 14, 1937; d. William George and Laura Elizabeth (Josten) Russell; m. Hugh Thomas Morgan Jr., June 27, 1959 (div. Oct. 1976); 1 child, Hugh Thomas; m. Alan Frederic Daly, Oct. 5, 1985. Student, Washington Sq. Coll., N.Y.C., 1954-55. Ops. mgr. WISH-TV, Indpls., 1967-68; freelance writer various trade books and periodicals, 1969-72; assoc. pub. Earnshaw's Rev. and Small World, N.Y.C., 1972-75; sr. editor Men's Wear mag., N.Y.C., 1975-79, Chain Store Age, N.Y.C., 1979-80, HFD and Home Fashions Textiles, N.Y.C., 1980-84; v.p. Dan River Co., N.Y.C., 1984, Gear, Inc., N.Y.C., 1985; editor Floor Covering Weekly, N.Y.C., 1985—; tchr. Parsons Buying Interior Furnishings, N.Y.C., 1986-87. Vol. fin. com. ARC, Westchester County, N.Y., 1988—. Mem. Internat. Furnishings and Design Assn. (pres. N.Y. chpt. 1986, mem. career day com. 1987—). Office: Floor Covering Weekly 555 W 57th St New York NY 10019

DALY, JUDITH MARIE, retail executive; b. Cedar Rapids, Iowa, Dec. 2, 1950; d. Elmer Frederick and Lucille Magdalen (Bousek) Vorhies; m. James Francis Daly, Sept. 3, 1970 (div. 1979); children: Jonathan W., Jaime B. Student, U. No. Iowa, 1970, Ind. U. N.W., 1988—. Head cashier Home Hardware Co., St. Charles, Ill., 1972-73, dept. mgr., 1973-74, buyer, merchandiser, 1974-79; head buyer Home Hardware Co., West Chicago, Ill., 1979-81, v.p. purchasing, 1982-86; sr. v.p. Home Hardware Co., Portage, Ind., 1987—; also bd. dirs. Home Hardware Co., Marengo, Ill.; pres. Nationwide Wholesale Supply, Portage, Ind., 1984—. Mem. Nat. Assn. Female Execs. Avocation: golf. Home: 156 Southport Dr Valparaiso IN 46383 Office: Nationwide Wholesale Supply 6044 Central Ave Portage IN 46368

DALY, MARY F., feminist philosopher; A.B., Coll. of St. Rose, Albany, N.Y.; A.M., Cath. U.; S.T.L., S.T.D., Ph.D., U. Fribourg; Ph.D. in Religion, U. Notre Dame. Assoc. prof. dept. theology Boston Coll. Author: The Church and the Second Sex, 1968, 3d rev. ed., 1985; Beyond God the Father, 1973, 2nd edit. rev. 1985; Gyn/Ecology, 1979, Pure Lust, 1984. Address: Boston College Dept Theology Chestnut Hill MA 02167*

DALY, NANCY JANE, retail and manufacturing company executive; b. Mpls., May 30, 1932; d. John Vivien and Willis Faye (Parks) Crisp; m. Niler Alan Lewis, Jan. 13, 1952 (div.); children: Brenda Lynette, Brad Alan; m. Richard Alan Daly, May 11, 1967. AA in Bus. summa cum laude, L.A. Valley Coll., 1951; student, UCLA, 1951; cert. real estate, Murphy's Bus. Coll., No. Hollywood, Calif., 1965. Admissions sec. Art Ctr. Coll. of Design, West L.A., Calif., 1965-66; v.p. Western Precision Bolt, Van Nuys, Calif., 1967-70; bonding, suretyship Agent's Bonding Service, Van Nuys, 1970-72; supr., steno pool Coachella Valley County Water Dist., Coachella, Calif., 1972-74; v.p. Slumberline Sleep Products, Inc., Phoenix, 1974-76; sec., treas. Customline, Inc., Lake Havasu City, Ariz., 1976-81, Newport Pacific, Inc., Hilo, Hawaii, 1981—, Royal Heir of Hawaii, Inc., Honolulu, 1985-89; owner Sleepcraft of Calif., 1989—; dir. Tropical Sleep Ctrs., Hawaii, 1983—; sales tng. Marsh Cos., Hawaii, 1985—. Supporter, Hilo Boy's Club, 1987-88; hon. mem. adv. bd. ABI Rsch., 1990. Mem. Internat. Platform Assn., NWRA, NBWA, Hawaii Hotel Assn., Coast Guard Aux., Eastern Star, Beta Tau Epsilon. Republican. Home: PO Box 1265 Pahoa HI 96778 Office: Tropical Sleep Ctrs 58 Kinoole St Hilo HI 96720

DALY, PATRICIA MARIE, accountant; b. Paterson, N.J., May 10, 1963; d. Joseph James and Kathleen Lillian (Doran) D. BS in Acctg., Fairfield U., 1985; postgrad., Marquette U., 1988—. CPA, N.J. Tax cons. Deloitte, Haskins & Sells, Hackensack, N.J., 1985-87; sr. tax cons. Deloitte, Haskins & Sells, Hackensack, 1987-88; dir. taxes Sybron Corp., Milwaukee, Wis., 1988—; adj. prof. Taxation Montclair (N.J.) State Coll., 1987-88. Mem. Am. Inst. CPA's, N.J. Inst. CPA's. Roman Catholic. Office: Sybron Corp 411 E Wisconsin Ave Milwaukee WI 53202

DALY, SUSAN CAROL CAMPBELL, psychiatry educator; b. New London, Conn., Jan. 7, 1948; d. Donald Durant and Alma (Whitman) Campbell; m. Douglas Chapman Daly, Feb. 1975; children: Daniel, Diana, Erik, Amanda. BA, Mt. Holyoke Coll., 1970; MD, U. Conn., Farmington, 1977. Diplomate Am. Bd. Psychiatry and Neurology. Intern in pediatrics U. Conn. Health Ctr., 1977-79, resident in psychiatry, 1979-82, asst. prof., 1988-89; fellow in consultation psychiatry Yale U. Sch. Medicine, New Haven, 1983-84, asst. dir. neuropsychiatry assessment unit, 1984; asst. clin. prof. psychiatry Yale U. Sch. Medicine, 1985—; staff psychiatrist Mt. Sinai Hosp., Hartford, Conn., 1985-88. Leader Girl Scouts U.S.A., Cub Scouts Am., Glastonbury, Conn. Mem. AMA, Am. Psychiat. Assn., Am. Group Psychotherapy Assn. Congregationalist. Home: 48 Ridgecrest Rd Glastonbury CT 06033

DALY, SUSAN S., psychologist; b. Dumont, N.J., Sept. 1, 1939; d. William Curtis and Sarah Elizabeth (Hennion) Singleton; m. John Groom Daly, June 8, 1963 (div. 1980); children: Timothy, Mark, Aries. BS, Hartwick Coll., 1961; PhD, SUNY, Albany, 1984. Lic. psychologist, N.Y. Clin. cons. psychiat. nursing svc. Albany Med. Ctr., 1981-82; intern in psychology Albany Psychol. Consortium, 1982-83; staff psychologist Albany VA Med. Ctr., 1984-89, asst. chief psychology svc., 1989—; adj. clin. asst. prof. dept. counseling and psychology SUNY, Albany, 1985—; clin. asst. prof. dept. psychiatry Albany Med. Coll., 1988—; psychol. cons. N.E. Parent & Child Soc., Schenectady, N.Y., 1983-84; cons. N.Y. State Psychology Licensing Bd., Albany, 1989. Contbr. numerous articles to profl. jours. Recipient Faculty Rsch. award SUNY-Albany, 1989-90, Disting. Tchr. award Albany Med. Coll., 1989. Mem. Am. Psychol. Assn., Psychol. Assn. of Northern N.Y. (chair ethics com. 1985-87)., Vis. Nurses Assn. (chair future dirs. com. Albany chpt. 1988—, sec. bd. dirs. 1990—). Home: 20 Northgate Dr Albany NY 12203 Office: VA Med Ctr 113 Holland Ave Albany NY 12208

DALY, TYNE, actress; b. N.Y.C., 1947; d. James Daly and Hope Newell; m. Georg Stanford Brown; children: Alisabeth, Kathryne, Alexandra. Student, Brandeis U., Am. Music and Dramatic Acad. Performed at Am. Shakespeare Festival, Stratford, Conn.; appeared on Broadway in Gypsy, 1988 revival; films include The Enforcer, 1976, Telefon, 1977, Zoot Suite, 1982, The Aviator, 1985, Movers and Shakers, 1985; made TV debut in series The Virginian; guest appearances in various TV series, starring role in Cagney and Lacey, 1982-88 (Emmy awards 1983, 84, 88); TV films include In Search of America, 1971, A Howling in the Woods, 1971, Heat of Anger, 1972, The Man Who Could Talk to Kids, 1973, Larry, 1974, The Entertainer, 1976, Intimate Strangers, 1977, Better Late Than Never, 1979, The Women's Room, 1980, A Matter of Life and Death, 1981, Your Place or Mine, 1983, Kids Like These, 1987, Stuck With Each Other, 1989. Office: care Camden Artists Ltd 2121 Ave of the Stars Ste 410 Los Angeles CA 90067*

DALZELL, GRACE ROSALIE, office manager; b. Mexico City, Dec. 2, 1936; naturalized U.S. citizen, 1978; d. Robert M. Dalzell and Anita Fernandez Dalzell Daniel, H. Morgan Daniel (stepfather); m. Joseph J. Matz, Apr. 11, 1955 (div. 1973); children: Anna Matz Bennett, Elizabeth G., Amelia Matz Reed, Adrienne Matz Carter, Eva E.; m. Emmet O. Whitaker, Jr., Nov. 7, 1974; 1 stepchild, John L. Whitaker. Student, Tex. Tech. U., 1960, Del Mar Coll., Corpus Christi, Tex., 1961, San Antonio Coll., 1975, St. Mary's U., 1976. Office mgr. Law Office Carl R. Crites, San Antonio, 1973-75; adminstr. U. Tex. Health Sci. Ctr., San Antonio, 1975-85; mgr. and adminstr. S. Tex. Orthopaedic & Spinal Surgery Assocs., San Antonio, 1986—, Ray Vista, Inc., San Antonio, 1987—. Author poetry. Participant office edn. prog. Clark High Sch., San Antonio, 1980—; rep. United Way Fund Dr., San Antonio, 1979-81, co-rep., 1985; mem. Valley St. light com. City of Leon, 1977-78; vol. San Antonio Crisis Intervention Telephone Ctr., 1975-76. Recipient Recognition award Clark High Sch., 1988-89, Recognition cert. San Antonio Crisis Intervention Ctr., 1976. Mem. San Antonio Med. Mgrs., NAFE, Tex. Soc. Med. Assts., NOW. Home: 6910 Forest Crest N San Antonio TX 78240 Office: 7940 Floyd Curl Dr #400 San Antonio TX 78229-3900

DALZELL, JAN, artist; b. Glen Ridge, N.J., Apr. 16, 1938; d. Stewart and Jeannette (Johnson) D. BA, Mt. Holyoke Coll., South Hadley, Mass., 1968. cons. Ellarslie, Trenton, N.J., 1988, commn. Chapel, St. Lawrence Rehab. Ctr., 1986. Exhibited in shows at Back Door Gallery, U. League, Nassau Presbyn. Ch., Trenton City Museum, Coll. Morris, Jersey City State Coll., Trenton State Coll., Ctr. Health Affairs, Printmaking Couns. N.J., Mt. Holyoke Coll. and others. Mem. Mt. Holyoke Club Princeton, Artworks, Edn. Ministry. Episcopalian. Home: 810 Blue Spring Rd Princeton NJ 08540

D'AMATO, JEAN MARIE, educator; b. Boston, July 20, 1945; d. Hector Loreto and Frances Lydia (Trotta) D'A.; m. Fleming A. Thomas, Mar. 12, 1989. AB, Tufts U., 1967; MA, Middlebury Coll., 1969; PhD, The Johns Hopkins U., 1975. Teaching asst. Intercollegiate Ctr. for Classical Studies, Rome, 1973-74; lectr. Williams Coll., 1975-76; asst. prof. classics U. So. Calif., 1976-81; prof. in charge, dir. Intercollegiate Ctr. for Classical Studies Northwestern State U., Natchitoches, 1981-82, assoc. prof. La. Scholars' Coll., 1981—; humanities adminstr. NEH; dir. Vergilian Soc. Am. Rome and Cumae, summer 1978; co-dir. U. So. Calif., summer 1979. Author: A New Fragment of Eustathius of Matera, Mediaeval Studies, Vol. 46, 1984. Fellow Am. Assn. Univ. Coun. of Learned Socs., 1977; named an Outstanding Woman of Am., 1981. Mem. AAUW (dissertation fellow 1972), Am. Philol. Assn., La. Classical Assn. Roman Catholic. Home: 332 Henry Ave Natchitoches LA 71457 Office: Northwestern State U La Scholars' Coll Natchitoches LA 71457

D'AMBROSIO, BLANCHE FADA GRAWE, hotel executive; b. Baton Rouge, Mar. 18, 1926; d. Walter Theodore and Blanche Laura (Causey) Bozant; m. Arthur Nolan Grawe, June 5, 1949; children: Cary Nolan, Geoffrey Allan; m. Anthony Francis D'Ambrosio, Feb. 18, 1978. Student La. State U., 1943-45, U. So. Calif., 1945-47. Society editor Herald Am. newspaper, Compton, Calif., 1957-61; asst. editor Host mag., Oreg. Restaurant and Beverage Assn., Portland, 1962-66; agt. Oreg. Liquor Control Commn., Portland, 1966-69; dir. sales and catering Cosmopolitan El Mirador, Sacramento, Calif., 1969-71; mgr. Umpqua Hotel, Roseburg, Oreg., 1971-74; gen. mgr. Inn at Spanish Head, Lincoln City, Oreg., 1974—. Mem. Lincoln City Advt. Com.; mem. job service employers com. Dept. Human Resources of Lincoln County. Mem. Nat. Restaurant Assn., Oreg. Hotel and Motel Assn. (past pres., chmn. bd.), Am. Hotel and Motel Assn. (bd. dirs., mem. condominium com.), Oreg. Motor Hotel Assn. (bd. dirs.), Restaurants of Oreg. Assn., Lincoln City Motel Assn. (dir.), Women's Assn. of Allied Beverage Industry (past pres. Portland chpt), Oreg. Lodging Assn. (pres. hotels). Club: Norwalk (Calif.) Jr. Women's (life, past pres.). Office: Inn at Spanish Head 4009 S Hwy 101 Lincoln City OR 97367

DAMEROW, MAE WRIGHT, retail executive; b. Northampton, Mass., Nov. 14, 1956; d. Lawrence Sheperd and Caroline Mary (La Rose) Wright; m. Robert Frederick Haley, June 10, 1978 (div. 1980); m. Frederick Wright Damerow, Aug. 7, 1981. BS in Mech. Engring., Worcester (Mass.) Poly., 1980. Assoc. engr. nuclear safety Westinghouse Electric Corp., Monroeville, Pa., 1978-80, engr. nuclear safety, 1980, shift tech. advisor Salem nuclear plant, 1980-81, engr. info. program, 1981-84, sr. engr. info. program, 1984, mgr. info. program, 1984-86, mgr. bus. relations, 1987-88; mgr. community rels. West Valley (N.Y.) Demonstration Project, 1988—; mgr. community rels. and total quality West Valley Demonstration Project, 1990—; speaker Campus Am., nationwide, 1979-81; bd. dirs. Energy Source Edn. Council, Washington, 1987, bd. pres., 1988—; mem. mgmt. com. Electric Info. Council, N.D., 1987-89; mem. program com. U.S. Com. for Energy Awareness, Washington, 1987-89, publications subcom. U.S. Council for Energy Awareness, 1988-89. Mem. Nat. Assn. of Female Execs. Office: West Valley Demonstrative Project Rock Springs Rd West Valley NY 14171

DAMERST, LISA YVONNE, art director; b. Denver, Nov. 21, 1958; d. Thomas Dent and Frances Grace (Scott) Street; m. Richard Lee Silva, Aug. 30, 1980 (div. Apr. 1983); m. Douglas Harry Damerst, Oct. 12, 1986. AS, Colo. Inst. Art, 1978. Designer Speedcraft Printing, Denver, 1978; art dir. Gart Bros. Sporting Goods, Denver, 1978-80, Knight Ridder-Adams Div., Denver, 1980, AAA Auto Club of Colo., Denver, 1980-87; sr. designer Am. Chem. Soc., Washington, 1987-88; art dir. Nat. Jour., Inc., Govt. Exec. mag., Washington, 1988-89; pres. Lisa Damerst Design, 1989—. VA scholar, 1976. Mem. Art Dirs. Club of Washington. Episcopalian.

DAMICO, DEBRA LYNN, reading specialist, educator; b. Passaic, N.J., Apr. 15, 1956; d. Nicholas Biagio and Eleanore Lorraine (Hugle) D. BA, Montclair State Coll., 1978, MA, 1989; MA, 1989. Cert. tchr., N.J, reading specialist. Tchr. St. Francis Sch., Hackensack, N.J., 1978-79, Saddle Brook (N.J.) High Sch., 1979-80, St. Dominic Acad., Jersey City, 1980-84; adult basic edn./gen. edn devel. and ESL instr. Adult Learning Ctr. Montclair (N.J.) State Coll., 1974—; internat. student advisor Manhattan Coll., Bronx, N.Y., 1984—, ESL instr., 1986—; instr. Writing Inst. Adult Edn. Resource Ctr., Jersey City State Coll., 1987—; Outstanding Internat. Student advisor, 1989—. Mem. Dist. Wide Curriculum Council, Lodi, N.J., 1977-78; ch. cantor and musician. Nat. Assn. for Foreign Student Affairs grantee, 1985-86; named Outstanding Young Woman Am., 1986. Mem. Nat. Assn. Tchrs. of Eng. as a Fgn. Lang., N.Y. Tchrs. of ESL, Nat. Assn. Fgn. Student Affairs, Metro-Internat., Am. Assn. Tchrs. French, YMCA Internat. Student Svc., Kappa Delta Pi, Pi Delta Phi. Democrat. Roman Catholic. Office: Manhattan Coll 4513 Manhattan Coll Pkwy Bronx NY 10471

DAMISCH, HARRIET DARLEY, farm manager; b. Balt., Dec. 28, 1927; d. John Wilmerton and Alberta Whiton (Roller) Darley; m. John William Damisch, June 16, 1952; children: Peter Whiton, Mark William. BS, U. Ariz., 1949; MS, Northwestern U., 1951. Sec. Am. Auto. Assn., Chgo., 1942, Wash. Nat. Ins.Co., Evanston, Ill., 1943; seminar mgr. Inst. Human Sci., Winnetka, Ill., 1951-52; asst. nat. conv. mgr. Kappa Alpha Theta, Indpls., 1963-72; nat. conv. mgr. Kappa Alpha Theta, 1972-82; farm mgr. family farms, Northfield, Ill., 1959—; investment mgr. family investments,

Northfield, 1977—. Trustee/sec. Kappa Alpha Theta Found., Indpls., 1982-88. Mem. The Chgo. Farmers, Bette Locke Soc., Chgo. Coun. Fgn. Rels., Mensa, Sheridan Shore Yacht Club, John Evans Club, Phi Beta Kappa, Phi Kappa Phi, Pi Mu Epsilon, Kappa Alpha Theta. Republican. Address: 186 Coach Rd Northfield IL 60093

DAMJANOV, ANDREA, researcher developmental biologist; b. Zagreb, Yugoslavia, Dec. 18, 1940; came to U.S.A., 1967; d. Teodor and Andjelka (Mihaljevic) Zivanovic; m. Ivan Damjanov, Mar. 31, 1941; children: Nevena, Ivana, Milena. BA, U. Zagreb, 1960, MS, 1973. Research assoc. Hahnemann U., Phila., 1983-86, Thomas Jefferson U., Phila., 1986--. Contbr. articles to profl. jours. Home: 129 Edgewood Rd Ardmore PA 19003 Office: Thomas Jefferson U 1020 Locust St Philadelphia PA 19107

DAMON, GENE See GRIER, BARBARA G.

DAMON, LAURA PROVOST, English educator; b. Buffalo, Apr. 26, 1938; d. Mason Orne and Louise (Provost) D.; children: Lisa Damon Martin, Sarah Allen Martin. BA, Smith Coll., Northampton, Mass., 1960; MA, Yale U., 1964. Tchr. English Opoku Ware Secondary Sch., Kumasi, Ghana, 1961-63, J.A. Hillhouse High Sch., New Haven, 1964-66; field advisor Girl Scouts Am., Savannah, Ga., 1966-67; instr. U. Ga., Athens, 1967-68; tchr. English Niagara County Community Coll., Sanborn, N.Y., 1980—. Bd. mem. Planned Parenthood of Niagara County, Niagara Falls, N.Y., 1972-78, 86—, fund dr. chair, 1989—; bd. mem. Lewiston Porter Bd. Edn., Youngstown, N.Y. Mem. AAUW (bd. mem.), Community Coll. Humanities Assn., N.Y. State English Coun. Home: 916 Oneida St Lewiston NY 14092 Office: Niagara County Community 3111 Saunders Settlement Rd Sanborn NY 14132

DAMOS, DIANE LYNN, education educator; b. Waukegan, Ill., May 29, 1949; d. Thomas Samuel and Virginia Ruth (Whitson); m. Bryan Coolican, Feb. 8, 1949. BS, U. Ill., 1970, MA, 1973; PhD, 1977. Asst. prof. indsl. engring. SUNY, Buffalo, 1977-81; asst. prof. psychology Ariz. State U., Tempe, 1981-85; assoc. prof. human factors U. So. Calif., La., 1985--. Contbr. articles to profl. jours. Mem. Human Factors Soc., Aerospace Med. Assn., Psychonomics, Assn. of Aviation Psycholgists, Western European Assn. of Aviation Psycholgists, Phi Beta Kappa, Phi Kappa Phi, Sigma Xi. Republican. Office: U So Calif Inst Safety and Systems Mgmt Dept of Human Factors Los Angeles CA 90089

D'AMOUR, CLAIRE MARIE, marketing professional; b. Holyoke, Mass., Aug. 13, 1956; d. Gerald Emil and Jeanne Eva (Fontaine) D'A. BA, U. Mass., 1978. Dir. advt. Big Y Foods, Inc., Springfield, Mass., 1978-85, v.p. advt. and media ops., 1981—, v.p. advt. and pub. rels., 1985-89, v.p. mktg., 1989—; bd. dirs. Multibank Nat. Western Mass., Springfield. Bd. dirs. United Way Pioneer Valley, Springfield, 1988—, Pvt. Industry Coun., Springfield, 1988—, ARC, Springfield, 1989—, Springfield Coll., 1990—; corporator MacDuffie Sch., Springfield, 1986—, Mercy Hosp., Springfield, 1987—; chmn. Easter Seals Telethon, Western Mass., 1990. Mem. Advt. Club Western Mass., Greater Hartford Ad Club, Rotary Club Springfield, Greater Springfield C. of C. Office: Big Y Foods Inc 280 Chestnut St PO Box 7840 Springfield MA 01102-7840

DAMRON, VIRGINIA LEE, retirement home administrative assistant; b. Tampa, Fla., Aug. 10, 1937; d. Lawton and Thelma (Langdale) Johnson; m. Howard Willis Damron, May 3, 1956; children: Gary K., Gerald W. Student, U. Alaska, Fairbanks, 1979-85, U. Alaska, Anchorage, 1985-89, U. Alaska S.E., Juneau, 1986-90, SUNY Off Campus Program, 1986-88. Recreation aide USAF, Eielson AFB, Alaska, 1974-78, recreation specialist, 1978-82; adminstrv. asst. Pioneers' Benefits, State of Alaska, Fairbanks, 1983—. Founding bd. dirs. Fairbanks Youth Sports, 1976-83; agy. dir. United Way of Alaska, 1974-82; facilitator/v.p. Beginning Experience, Fairbanks, 1982—; mem. Breast Cancer Detection Ctr.; charter mem. Nat. Com. for Prevention of Elder Abuse. Recipient Cert. of Recognition, Fairbanks North Star Borough, 1982; Disting. Pub. Svc. award State of Alaska, 1989. Mem. Alaska Pub. Health Assn., Nat. Assn. Female Execs. Democrat. Home: 9228 Richardson Hwy Salcha AK 99714

DAMROSCH, BARBARA, landscape designer; b. N.Y.C., July 28, 1942; d. Douglas Stanton and Eleanor (Southern) D.; 1 child, Christopher. BA, Wheaton Coll., 1964; MA, Columbia U., 1967. Prin. Barbara Damrosch Landscape Design, Washington Depot, Conn., 1979—. Author: Theme Gardens, 1982, The Garden Primer, 1988, gen. cons. Taylor's Guide To Garden Design, 1988. Mem. Garden Writers of Am. Assn. Democrat. Office: Barbara Damrosch Landscape Design Washington Depot CT 06794

DAMSBO, ANN MARIE, psychologist; b. Cortland, N.Y., July 7, 1931; d. Jorgen Einer and Agatha Irene (Schenck) D. B.S., San Diego State Coll., 1952; M.A., U.S. Internat. U., 1974, Ph.D., 1975. Diplomate Am. Acad. Pain Mgmt. Commd. 2d lt. U.S. Army, 1952, advanced through grades to capt., 1957; staff therapist Letterman Army Hosp., San Francisco, 1953-54, 56-58, 61-62, Ft. Devers, Mass., 1955-56, Walter Reed Army Hosp., Washington, 1958-59, Tripler Army Hosp., Hawaii, 1959-61, Ft. Benning, Ga., 1962-64; chief therapist U.S. Army Hosp., Ft. McPherson, Ga., 1964-67; ret. U.S. Army, 1967; med. missionary So. Presbyterian Ch., Taiwan, 1968-70; psychology intern Naval Regional Med. Ctr., San Diego, 1975, pre-doctoral intern, 1975-76, postdoctoral intern, 1976-77, chief, founder pain clinic, 1977-86; adj. tchr. U. Calif. Med. Sch., San Diego; lectr., U.S., Can., Eng., France, Australia, cons. forensic hypnosis to law enforcement agys. Contbr. articles to profl. publs., chpt. to book. Tchr. Sunday sch. Methodist Ch., 1945—; mem. Republican Presdl. Adv. Com. Fellow Am. Soc. Clin. Hypnosis (psychology mem. at large, exec. bd. 1989—); mem. San Diego Soc. Clin. Hypnosis (pres. 1980), Am. Phys. Therapy Assn., Calif. Soc. Clin. and Hypnosis (bd. govs.), Internat. Soc. Clin. and Exptl. Hypnosis, Am. Soc. Clin. Hypnosis (exec. com. 1989), AAUW, Internat. Platform Assn., Am. Soc. Clin. Hypnosis (exec. bd.), Ret. Officers Am., Toastmasters (local pres.), Job's Daus. Club, Zonta. Republican. Home and Office: 1062 W 5th Ave Escondido CA 92025

DAMSEY, JOAN, medical management consultant; b. Jamestown, N.Y., Sept. 12, 1931; d. Frederick Vincent and Sara (Caccamise) Landy; m. Lloyd Damsey, June 12, 1955 (dec. Oct. 1985); children: Eve, Laurie, Lloyd Jr., J. Landy. BA, Coll. St. Elizabeth, 1953; MA, Cath. U. Am., 1981. Founder, bd. dirs. First Nat. Bank Fla. Keys, Marathon, 1974-83; pres. Damsey & Assocs. Ltd., Portsmouth, Va., 1980—; dir. practice mgmt. Eastern Va. Med. Sch., Norfolk, 1982—; founder, bd. dirs. Resource Bank, Virginia Beach, Va., 1987—. Author: Joan Damsey Mgmt. Seminars, 1986; contbr. articles to mgmt. jours. Vice-chmn. Dem. State Com., Fla., 1964-68; del. Dem. Nat. Conv., Atlantic City, 1964. Fellow Am. Coll. Med. Group Adminstrs.; mem. Med. Group Mgmt. Assn., Tidewater Med. Group Mgmt. Assn., Soc. Med.-Dental Cons., Va. Med. Group Mgmt. Assn. Roman Catholic.

DANBURG, DEBRA, state legislator; b. Houston, Sept. 25, 1951; d. Stanley and Barbara Jean (Walker) D. BA, U. Houston, 1974, JD, 1979. Asst. dir., lobbyist Texans for ERA, 1974-75; atty. pvt. practice, Houston, 1979—; mem. Tex. Ho. of Reps., 1981—; mem. Appropriations Com.; chair Budget & Oversight for Cultural and Hist. Resources Com., Appropriations Subcom. on AIDS; mem. Appropriations Subcom. on the State Employee Classification System; Speaker's appointments Tex. Adv. Commn. on Intergov. Rels. and Tex. Health & Human Svcs. Coord. Coun.; del. Dem. Nat. Convention, 1984; Tex. rep. Am. Coun. of Young Polit. Leaders, 1982; mem. bilateral adv. com. Cultural Exchange The Netherlands-USA, 1986; mem. adv. bd. Omega House, 1989—. Named Outstanding feminist Now, 1975, best legislator Houston mag., 1981, Vol. of Yr. KS/AIDS Found., 1984, Outstanding Houston Profl. Woman by Fedn. of Houston Profl. Women, 1988, Tex. Recreation and Park Soc. Legislator of Yr., 1987; recipient Spl. Presdl. award Houston Apt. Assn., 1985, Environ. Def. award Sierra Club, 1987, Outstanding Legislator award Tex. Assn. of Symphony Orchs., 1990, Good Brick award Greater Houston Preservation Alliance, 1990. Mem. Harris County Criminal Lawyers Assn. (bd. dirs. 1982-83). Office: Tex Ho Reps PO Box 2910 Austin TX 78768-2910

DANCHAK, ANNE MARIE ROSE, pharmacist; b. Hillside, N.J., Dec. 16, 1964; d. Gerald and Caroline Catherine (Nazar) D. BS in Pharmacy, Rutgers U., 1987. Registered pharmacist, Va. Relief pharmacist Peoples Drug Store, Alexandria, Va., 1987; investigational supplies pharmacist Boehringer Pharm. Corp., Rockville, Md., 1988—. Mem. Va. Pharm. Assn., N.J. Pharm. Assn., Found. Biomed. Rsch., Rutgers Alumni Assn., Smithsonian Instn., Lambda Kappa Sigma. Home: 263 Congressional Ln #314 Rockville MD 20852 Office: Boehringer Mannheim Pharm Corp 15204 Omega Dr Rockville MD 20850

DANCO, LINDA MARIE, environmental engineer, consultant; b. Tampa, Fla., June 13, 1961; d. William Richard and Rosemarie (Christ) D.; m. James David MacGregor. B in Environ. and Water Resources Engring., Vanderbilt U., 1983. Registered profl. engr., Ga. Engr. Knepper & Willard, Inc., Tampa, 1983-86; sr. engr. Brown and Caldwell, Atlanta, 1986—. Cultural amb. Friendship Force, Inc., Tbilisi, Ga., USSR, 1990—. Mme. Am. Soc. Civil Engrs., Am. Water Resources Assn., Am. Pub. Works Assn. (gen. sec. Atlanta chpt. 1989), NAFE, Water Pollution Control Fedn., Soc. Women Engrs. Home: 1900 Noble Forest Dr Norcross GA 30092 Office: Brown and Caldwell 32 Perimeter Ctr E Ste 120 Atlanta GA 30346

DANDOY, SUZANNE EGGLESTON, physician, educator; b. Los Angeles, Jan. 2, 1935; d. Leonard Lester and Catherine (Wheelwright) Eggleston; m. Jeremiah Richard Dandoy, June 14, 1958; children: Kevin, Bret, Jolyn. BA, U. Calif., Los Angeles, 1956; MD, UCLA, 1960, MPH, 1963. Diplomate: Am. Bd. Preventive Medicine. Intern, Los Angeles Harbor Gen. Hosp., Torrance, Calif., 1960-61; resident Los Angeles Health Dept., 1961-62, 63-64; epidemiologist San Diego Dept. Pub. Health, 1967-68; bur. chief Ariz. Dept. Health Service, Phoenix, 1970-73; asst. commr. Ariz. Dept. Health Service, 1973-74, asst. dir., 1974-75, dir., 1975-80; prof. health adminstrn. Ariz. State U., Tempe, 1981-85; exec. dir. Utah Dept. Health, Salt Lake City, 1985—; adj. prof. U. Utah; bd. dirs. Pub. Health Found. Chair editorial bd. Am. Jour. Pub. Health; contbr. articles to profl. jours. Chair Nat. Vaccine Adv. Com., HHS; adv. com. on immunization practices HEW; pres. Utah Women's Forum. Recipient award Ariz. Dietetic Assn., 1976; award Maricopa County Med. Soc., 1980. Fellow Am. Pub. Health Assn., Am. Coll. Preventive Medicine (pres. 1991—); mem. AMA, Utah Med. Assn., Utah Pub. Health Assn., Assn. State Health Officers (pres. 1990-91), Phi Beta Kappa, Delta Omega. Democrat. Mormon. Home: 990 S Oak Hills Way Salt Lake City UT 84108 Office: Utah Health Dept PO Box 16700 Salt Lake City UT 84116-0700

D'ANDREA, DENISE MARIE, physician; b. Glenridge, N.J., Mar. 11, 1961; d. Fred and Carmela (Ridolfo) D'A. BS magna cum laude, U. Scranton, Pa., 1983; MD, Georgetown U., 1987. Diplomate Nat. Bd. Med. Examiners. Resident in internal medicine UMDNJ Robert Wood Johnson Med. Sch., New Brunswick, N.J., 1987-90; Krön Med. Corp., Chapel Hill, N.C. Vol. Mt. Carmel Guild for the Blind, Newark, 1975—. Named one of Outstanding Young Women in Am., 1983, 87, 88. Mem. ACP (assoc.), AMA, Alpha Epsilon Delta, Alpha Mu Gamma. Home: 6 Appleton Pl Upper Montclair NJ 07043

DANE, LEILA FINLAY, psychologist; b. N.Y.C., Dec. 13, 1936; d. Luke William and Anne Sue (Tucker) Finlay; m. Francis Pierre Bohin, June 15, 1957 (div. Jan. 1968); children: Christopher Scott, Patrick Charles; m. Ernest Blaney Dane III, Nov. 16, 1968; 1 child, Leila Ann. BA, Am. U., 1975; MA, Cath. U. Am., 1978; PhD, Fla. Inst. Tech., 1986. Lic. psychologist, D.C. Translator, researcher Porter Internat. Mgmt. Cons. Co., Washington, 1968-69; editor orientation publs. Am. Assn. Fgn. Svc. Women, Madras, India, 1970-71; mental health liaison Am. Assn. Fgn. Svc. Women, Washington, 1974-78; co-chair Fgn. Svc. Community Mental Health Com., Washington, 1979-81; various positions, 1970-71, 77-86; founding dir. Inst. for Victims of Trauma, McLean, Va., 1987—; crisis cons. Assn. Am. Fgn. Svc. Women, Washington, 1975—, Am. Fgn. Svc. Assn., Washington, 1986—; cons. in field. Mem. Am. Psychol. Assn., D.C. Psychol. Assn., Internat. Soc. Polit. Psychology, Nat. Orgn. for Victim Assistance, Psychologists for Social Responsibility, Soc. for the Psychol. Study of Social Issues, Soc. Traumatic Stress Studies, World Fedn. for Mental Health, World Future Soc., World Affairs Coun. Democrat. Episcopalian. Office: Inst for Victims of Trauma 6801 Market Sq Dr McLean VA 22101

DANEY, TAMARA KAY, lawyer; b. Denver, Oct. 8, 1957; d. William C. and Barbara J. (Packan) D. BA, U. Calif. Berkeley, 1980; JD, Hastings Law Sch., 1986. Bar: Calif. 1987, U.S. Ct. Appeals (9th cir.) 1990, U.S. Dist. Ct. (no. dist.) Calif. 1990. Researcher European U. Inst., Florence, Italy, 1986-87, U. Florence Law Sch., 1987-89; assoc. Law Offices of Charles Bond, Berkeley, Calif., 1989—. ABA, World Affairs Coun., Calif. Bar Assn., Nat. Lawyers Guild, Sierra Club. Home: 5343 Broadway Terr #206 Oakland CA 94618

DANFORTH, FRANCES MUELLER (MRS. WILLIAM PAUL DANFORTH), civic worker; b. Austin, Tex., Mar. 23, 1914; d. Rudolph George and Laura Emma (Von Boeckmann) Mueller; B.J., U. Tex., 1935, B.A., 1936; M.S., Columbia U., 1938; m. William Paul Danforth, Aug. 16, 1942; children—William Paul, Douglas Mueller, Donald Lee. Grader dept. journalism U. Tex., Austin, 1934; asst. dir. Interscholastic League Press Bur., U. Tex., 1936-37; asst. editor Alcade, monthly alumni mag., 1936-37, 38-42; editor Star Points, nat. papers Delta Delta Delta Chgo., 1968-70; now buyer, bookkeeper Danforth's Antiques and Gifts, Austin. Pres., Austin Symphony League, 1967-68; state v.p. Tex. Women's Assn. Symphony Orchs.,, 1970; pres. Austin Vol. Bur., 1966-68; bd. dirs., sec. USO, 1971-72; bd. dirs. Symphony Orch. Soc.; bd. dirs., sec. Cen-Tex. chpt. ARC, pres. Altenheim, 1961-62. Mem. Women in Communications, Mortar Board (Austin alumna pres. 1978—) Delta Delta Delta, Lutheran (pres. ch. women 1972-74). Clubs: Settlement, Lawyers Wives (mem. bd., sec. 1973-74), Woman's (sec. 1972-74, v.p. 1977-79) (all Austin). Home: 1400 West Ave Austin TX 78701

DANFORTH, LINDA MANGOLD, human resources development consulting company executive; b. Buffalo, May 7, 1944; d. Sylvester Peter and Elizabeth Ann (Noble) Mangold; m. Thomas J. Zawislak, Oct. 14, 1961 (div. 1981); children: Lynn Zawislak Rojek, John, Peter; m. Ronald A. Danforth, Jan. 16, 1988. Student, Niagara Community Coll., 1975-76, SUNY, Buffalo, 1981. Lic. real estate broker, N.Y. Relocation coord. Realty World-Hettman, Inc., Tonawanda, N.Y., 1975-79; property mgr., comptr. Lamplighter Mgmt. Co., Buffalo, 1979-84; property mgr. Buffalo Mgmt. Co., 1984-85; v.p. sales Austin, Brooks & Chase, Indialantic, Fla., 1988-90; ptnr. Danforth Assocs., Indialantic, 1988—. Instr., Niagara County Spl. Edn., 1970-76; instr., counselor, Friendship House, Niagara Falls, 1971-73; home vol., Niagara County Runaway Program, North Tonawanda, N.Y., 1981-82; founding trustee, Ensemble Theatre Fla., Melbourne, 1987. Mem. ASTD, Greater South Brevard C. of C., Brevard Profl. Women's Network. Republican. Home: 100 Uranus Ct Indialantic FL 32903 Office: Danforth Assocs 100 Uranus Ct Indialantic FL 32903

D'ANGELO, FRANCES BONACORSA, educator; b. N.Y.C., May 30, 1914; d. Vito and Francesca Paula (DeLuca) Bonacorsa; m. Carmine John D'Angelo, Aug. 30, 1936. BA, CUNY, 1937, MA, 1942; cert. supr. and prin., NYU, 1963, postgrad., 1950. Cert. tchr., supr. and prin., N.Y. Tchr. St. Joan of Arc Sch., Jackson Heights, N.Y., 1941-43; tchr. Union Free Sch. Dist., Franklin Square, N.Y., 1943-60, curriculum coord., asst. prin., 1960-65, reading specialist, 1966-76, prin. summer sch., 1966-74; asst. prin. South Shore Christian Sch., Seaford, N.Y., 1978-81; supr. student tchr. St. John's U., Jamaica, N.Y., 1983—; reading specialist Evangel Christian Sch., L.I., N.Y., 1987—. Chmn. March Dimes, 1970-75, bd. dirs. 1968-75; bd. dirs. Glen Cove Scholarship Fund, 1972—. Recipient Community Svc. award, 1975, Outstanding Svc. award March of Dimes, 1975, Disting. Svc. award Arthritus Found., 1978, Outstanding Contbr. award Am. Com. Italian Migration, 1982. Mem. AAUP, Am. Assn. Retired Persons (v.p. 1980-84), N.Y. State Retired Tchrs., Nat. Italian Am. Found., L.I. Fedn. Women's Clubs, Nassau Fedn. Rep. Women, Lioness Club (2d v.p., Glen Cove chpt. 1989), Ladies Aux. Elks (chaplain 1987-90), Dante Cultural Soc. (pres. 1969-74), Women's Club Glen Cove, Order Sons Italy in Am. (pres. 1981-83). Roman Catholic. Home: 57 St Andrews Ln Glen Cove NY 11542

DANGLADE, RUTH ELLEN, special education administrator; b. Marion, Ind., Jan. 27, 1940; d. Harold Davis and Elizabeth (Lake) Neel; m. James K. Danglade, Sept. 2, 1961 (div. Nov. 1979); children: Annette, John. BS, Ball State U., 1961, MA, 1964. Cert. elem., secondary bus., spl. edn. and speech pathology tchr., Ind. Tchr. orthopedically handicapped Muncie (Ind.) Community Schs., 1961-67, tchr. of multiply handicapped, 1969-74, tchr. learning disabled, 1976-79; spl. edn. instr. Ball State U., Muncie, 1974-79; asst. dir. spl. edn. Delaware County Spl. Edn. Coop., Muncie, 1979—; sci. curriculum cons. NSF, Muncie, 1976-78; learning disabilities cons. Ball State U., 1974-80. Bd. dirs. Del. County Easter Seal Soc., 1967—; chairperson, adv. coun. Ball State U. Coll. Bus., 1985—; adminstrv. bd. High St. United Meth. Ch., Muncie, 1984-88, youth coord., 1985-88; bd. dirs. Minnetrista Cultural Found., Inc., 1989—. Mem. Assn. for Children with Learning Disabilities, Ind. Council Adminstrs. in Spl. Edn., Council for Exceptional Children (pres. Delaware County chpt. 1977-78), Phi Delta Kappa, Pi Beta Phi. Methodist. Office: Delaware County Spl Edn Coop 2501 N Oakwood Ave Muncie IN 47304

DANGREMOND, DALE JOAN, non profit organization administrator; b. Seneca Falls, N.Y., Dec. 31, 1957; d. James Leroy and Joan Ottellie (Kross) Dangremond; m. Mark J. Myers, Apr. 28, 1984; 1 child, Zachary James. B of Social Work, Rochester Inst. Tech., 1979; cert., Nat. Tech. Inst. for the Deaf, Rochester, N.Y., 1980; MBA, U. Phoenix, 1990. Ind. interpreter Rochester, 1980-81; social worker Rochester Rehab. Ctr., 1981-82; coord. deaf svcs. The Workshop, Inc., Albany, N.Y., 1982-84; interpreter tng./human svcs. Cen. Piedmont Community Coll., Charlotte, N.C., 1984-85; exec. dir. Ctr. on Deafness, Denver, 1985-88; asst. exec. dir. Seneca ARC, Waterloo, N.Y., 1988-90; cons. Labor Rels. Alternatives, Albany, N.Y., 1990—; adj. instr. interpreter tng. SUNY, Albany, 1982-84; dir. adv. com. on deafness State of Colo., Denver, 1985-88. Sec. Colo. Ind. Living Network, Denver, 1985-88. Mem. Am. Deafness and Rehab. Assn., Registry of Interpreters for the Deaf. Democrat. Methodist. Home: 2809 Coniston Rd Schenectady NY 12304

DANIEL, BETH, professional golfer; b. Charleston, S.C., Oct. 14, 1956; d. Robert and Lucia D. Grad., Furman U., 1978. Profl. golfer Ladies Profl. Golf Assn. tour, 1979—; Winner U.S. Amateur Title, 1975, 77; youngest mem. S.C. Hall of Fame, 1979. Recipient 1st pl. awards: Patty Berg Classic, 1979, World Ladies, Japan, 1979, World Series Women's Golf, 1980, 81, Columbia Savs. Classic, 1980, Patty Berg Classic, 1980, Golden Lights, 1980, J.C. Penney Classic, 1981, Lady Citurs, 1981, Bent Tree Classic, 1982, Sun City Classic, 1982, Birmingham Classic, 1982, Columbia Savs. Classic, 1982, WUI Classic, 1982, McDonald's Kids Classic, 1983, Kyocera Inamori Classic, 1985, Rail Charity Classic, 1989, Konica San Jose Classic, 1989, Greater Washington Open, 1989, Safeco Classic, 1989, J & B Putting Championship, 1982, 85, LPGA Championship, 1990; Mazda Series winner, 1982; named Rookie of Yr., Ladies Profl. Golf Assn., 1979, Player of Yr., 1980, Golfer of Yr. Seagrams Seven Crown Royal, 1981. Office: care Pros Inc PO Box 673 Richmond VA 23206

DANIEL, CECILE MARGARET, township official; b. New Bedford, Mass., Mar. 28, 1956; d. Romeo Alfred and Leona Blanch (Lemiuex) D.; m. George Walter Waterman III, Aug. 4, 1984; 1 child, Nathan Daniel. B.A. in Polit. Sci., U. Mass., 1978; M.A. in Pub. Adminstrn., Pa. State U., 1981. Mgr. Towamencin Twp., Pa., 1981-87, Perkiomen Twp., Pa., 1987. Chairperson Task Force on Ednl. Curriculum Mgr./Council; appropriations com. United Way, 1984-86; mem. North Penn Solid Waste Commn. Mem. Pa. Assn. Mcpl. Mgrs., Southeast Pa. Mgrs. Assn., Montgomery Assn. Twp. Ofcls. (sec. 1983-85, program chair 1986), Pa. Mgr's. Ednl. Com. (chairperson 1985-86), Pa. Mcpl. Mgrs. Inst. Republican. Roman Catholic. Avocations: reading, running, tennis. Home: 20 Aspen Ln Gilbertsville PA 19525 Office: Perkiomen Twp 467 Gravel Park Collegeville PA 19426

DANIEL, ELEANOR A., academic administrator; b. Milton, Ill., Feb. 28, 1940; d. Donal W. Daniel and Bernice Hillig. BA summa cum laude, Lincoln Christian Coll., 1962; MA, Lincoln Christian Seminary, Ill., 1965; EdM, U. Ill., 1969, PhD, 1975. Cons. Standard Pub., Cin.; dean grad. studies Cin. Bible Coll. and Seminary. Author: Introduction to Christian Education , 1980, rev., 1987, What the Bible Says About Sexual Identity, 1982, The ABC's of VBS, 1983; contbr. articles to profl. jours. Active several bds. and coms. of religious orgns. and ednl. task forces. Recipient Restoration Award for Outstanding Svc. in Edn., Lincoln Christian Col. and Seminary Alumni Assn., 1974; named Runnerup for Educator of the Yr., Logan City, Ill., 1974. Mem. Am. Edn. Rsch. Assn., Nat. Assn. Profs. of Christian Edn., Nat. Assn. Dirs. of Christian Edn., Assn. Tchr. Educators, Assn. Profs. and Researchers in Religious Edn., Delta Kappa Gamma Soc., Delta Aleph Tau, Delta Epsilon Chi, Gamma Alpha Chi. Mem. Christian Ch. Office: 2700 Glenway Cincinnati OH 45204

DANIEL, ELEANOR SAUER, economist, real estate executive; b. N.Y.C., Feb. 8, 1917; d. Charles Peter and Elsie Edna (Dommer) Sauer; m. John Carl Daniel, Dec. 31, 1952; children: Victoria Ann, Charles Timothy. BA magna cum laude (Bardwell fellow), Mt. Holyoke Coll., 1936; MA (Perkins fellow), Columbia U., 1937. Economist, U.S. Steel Co., N.Y.C., 1938; lectr. econs. Bklyn. Coll., 1939-40; with Mut. Life Ins. Co. N.Y., N.Y.C., 1940-74, asst. v.p., 1972-74, sr. econ. adviser, 1972-74; economist Fed. Home Loan Bank, N.Y.C., 1974-75; v.p., dir. Daniel Realty Cos., N.Y.C., 1975—; pres. Midtown Daniel, 1986—; former dir., chmn. fin. com. Atlantic City Electric Co.; past chmn. fin. com. Atlantic Energy, Inc.; former mem. bd. mgrs. U.S. Savs. Bank Newark; mem. Pres's. Task Force Fed. Credit Programs, 1968-69; mem. N.J. Gov's. Econ. Recovery Com., 1975-76; mem. econ. adv. bd. U.S. Sec. Commerce, 1971-73; mem. bus. research adv. council U.S. Bur. Labor Statistics, 1966-86. Author: (with J.J. O'Leary and S.F. Foster) Our National Debt and Our Savings; contbr. articles to profl. jours. Former trustee Blue Shield of N.J., trustee fellow Mt. Holyoke Coll., also past vice chmn., mem. fin. com., trustee. Mem. Am. Econ. Assn., Am. Fin. Assn. (past dir.), Phi Beta Kappa. Home and Office: 34 North Dr East Brunswick NJ 08816

DANIEL, EVELYN HOPE, university dean; b. Whitefield, Maine, Nov. 23, 1933; d. George Snowdeal and Evelyn Lura (Cole) Cunningham; m. Alfred Eugene Foulkes, Mar. 30, 1951 (div. 1956); children: Nancy Karen, George Warren; m. Harold Clifford Daniel, Jan. 1, 1957 (div. 1974); children: Jeffrey Martin, Dawn Hope. AB magna cum laude, U. N.C., Wilmington, 1968; MLS, U. Md., 1969, Ph.D., 1974. Asst. prof. Coll. Library Sci. U. Ky., 1972-74; asst. prof. Grad. Sch. Library U. R.I., 1974-76; assoc. prof., asst. dean Sch. Info. Studies Syracuse (N.Y.) U., 1976-81, dean and prof., 1981-85; dean, prof. U. N.C., Chapel Hill, 1985—; cons. ednl. radio and TV, Tehran, Iran, 1976-77, Millersville State Coll., Pa., 1983, Fgn. Service Inst., U.S. Dept. State, Washington, 1983-85, Rutgers U., 1985, Case Western Res. U., Cleve., 1985, U. So. Fla., 1986, McGill U., 1986, U. Ky., 1986, U. Iowa, 1987, Nat. Library Medicine, 1987, Emporia (Kans.) U., 1987, Ohio State U., 1988. Co-author: Reader in Library and Information Sciences, 1974, Media and Microcomputers in the Library, 1983; mem. editorial bd.: Library and Info. Sci. Research jour., 1979—; contbr. articles to profl. jours. NDEA fellow, 1968-69; recipient Sch. Library Media award, 1984—. Mem. ALA (chmn. standing com. on edn. 1980-83, coordinator Library Edn. Assembly 1980-83), N.Y. Statewide Continuing Library Edn. Adv. Com. (vice chmn. 1982-84), Assn. for Library and Edn. Sci. Educators (chmn. 1983-84). Office: U NC Sch Info & Libr Sci 100 Manning Hall CB# 3360 Chapel Hill NC 27599-3360

DANIEL, MARVA JEANE, principal, home relations consultant; b. Buffalo, Oct. 8, 1943; d. Edmund and Beatrice Lessie (Jones) Howell; m. Marvin Lawrence Daniel, Dec. 23, 1976; children: Marcia Marie, Marion Darcel. BS, SUNY, Buffalo, 1968, MS, 1970. Cert. elem. tchr., N.Y. Instr. elem. Buffalo Bd. Edn., 1968-73, home sch. coord., 1973-76, human relations specialist, 1976-83, asst. prin., 1984-85, prin., 1985—; adminstrv. asst. Buffalo Sch. of Performing Arts, 1983-84; lectr. SUNY Coop. Coll. Ctr., Buffalo, 1970-73; desegregation cons. U.S. Dept. Justice Community Relations, Cherry Hill, N.J., 1977; cons. youth conf. Community Action Orgn. of Erie County, Buffalo, 1984, 85; test cons. Ednl. Testing Service, Princeton, N.J., 1985, 86, 87; facilitator trainer Effective Parenting Info. for Children, Buffalo, 1982—. Author: U.S. proposal on literacy, Linking with Literacy, 1986; co-author: U.S. Justice Dept.'s Conf. Jour., 1977. V.p. B.U.I.L.D. Orgn., Buffalo, 1975; facilitator vol. Western N.Y. Assn. for Learning Disabled, Buffalo, 1983, Parent Anonymous, Buffalo, 1985; tutor vol. Literacy Vols. of Am., Buffalo, 1986-87. Mem. Black Educator Assn., N.Y. State Fedn. of Sch. Adminstrs., Buffalo Suprs. and Cen. Office Adminstrs., Assn. for Supervision and Curriculum Devel., Smithsonian Inst., Afro-Am. Hist.

Assn. Democrat. Club: Links (Erie County). Office: Buffalo Futures Acad 295 Carlton St Buffalo NY 14204

DANIEL, REBECCA SUSAN, engineer, military officer; b. South Charleston, W.Va., Sept. 17, 1959; d. Charles David and Juliet Sue (Summers) D.; m. Joey Lee McCoy, July 10, 1978 (div. June 1983); m. Gregory Scott Williams, Jan. 2, 1987 (div. May 1989). BS in Electrical and Electronic Engring., Calif. State U., Sacramento, 1985; MBA, Embry-Riddle Aero. U., 1988; Grad., Squadron Officer Sch., 1988. Radio systems technician USAF, George AFB, Calif., 1978-80; radio systems instr. USAF, Keeler AFB, Miss., 1980-82; commd. 2d lt. USAF, 1985; program mgr. USAF, McClellan AFB, Calif., 1985-86, project engr., 1986-89; project mgr. USAF, L.A. AFB, 1989—; report survey officer Sacramento Air Logistics Ctr., 1985-87. Math. and English tutor Dyer-Kelly Elem. Sch., Sacramento, 1985-87. Mem. Co. Grade Officers' Council (Officer Quarter 1987), Air Force Assn., Armed Forces Communications-Electronics Assn. Democrat. Home: 1808 Vanderbilt Ln #4 Redondo Beach CA 90278

DANIEL, YVETTE FELICE, municipal official; b. Hammond, Ind., Nov. 18, 1959; d. Donald Fredrick and Dorothy Daniel. BA, U. Denver, 1983. Asst. supr. Goodwill Rehab., Denver, 1980-82; lab. aide Kaiser Permanente, Denver, 1983; rep. mktg. Nat. Home Health Care, Houston, 1983-84, also bd. dirs.; environ. technician City of Houston, 1984-87; architect, engr. rep. Am. Standard, Inc., Houston, 1987-90; sales rep. Am. Standard, Inc., Oklahoma City, 1990—. Officer Dorothy Smith Ednl. Found., Houston, 1979—; alumni admissions counselor U. Denver Alumni Assn., 1984—; vol. March Dimes Walk-A-Thon, 1989; mem. rsch. bd. advisors Am. Biog. Inst., 1989. Recipient Gov. Vol. award State of Tex., 1978; Katrina McCormick Barnes scholar U. Denver, 1978; named one of Outstanding Young Women of Am., 1987. Mem. NAFE, Am. Inst. of Architects (affiliate Houston Chpt.). Club: Links (Houston).

DANIEL-DREYFUS, SUSAN B. RUSSE, civic worker; b. St. Louis, May 30, 1940; d. Frederick William and Suzanne (Mackay) Russe; m. Don B. Faerber, Nov. 27, 1962 (div. Nov. 1968); 1 child, Suzanne Mackay; m. Marc Andre Daniel-Dreyfus, Aug. 9, 1969; 1 child, Cable Dunster. Student, Smith Coll., 1958-60, Corcoran Sch. Fine Arts, 1960-61, Washington U., St. Louis, 1961-62. Mng. ptnr. Communications, Inc., 1980-82; asst. dir. Harvard Bus. Sch. Fund, Cambridge, 1982-86; pres. SCR Assocs. Corp., Cambridge, 1986—; mem. bd. advisors Odysseum, Inc.; bd. dirs. Future Mgmt. Systems. Mem. St. Louis-St. Louis County White House Conf. on Edn., 1966-68; mem. Mo. 1st Gov.'s Conf. on Edn., 1966, 2d Conf., 1968; bd. dirs. Tunbridge Sch., 1973-78, St. Louis Smith Coll.; hon. bd. dirs. New Music Circle; mem. woman's bd. dirs. Washington U., New Music Circle, 1963-67; mem. woman's bd. Mo. Hist. Soc.; bd. dirs. Non-Partisan Ct. Plan for Mo., Young Audiences Inc., 1967-69; bd. dirs. Childrens Art Bazaar, 1968-70; founder St. Louis Opera Theater; chmn. Art. Mus. Bond Issue election St. Louis, 1966; jr. bd. dirs. St. Louis Symphony, 1966-68, Opportunities Indsl. Center, Boston; legis. chmn. bd. dirs. Boston LWV, 1969-72; mem. council, bd. dirs. Jr. League Boston, 1970-72, 74-76, v.p. Bd. of Family Counseling Services-Region West, Boston, 1979—; pres. Family Counseling Bd., Brookline, Mass.; bd. govs. Tunbridge Sch.; trustee Chestnut Hill Sch., Boston, Brookline Friendly Soc.; mem. steering com. ann. fund Boston Children's Hosp. Med. Center, 1980-84; v.p. Nat. Friends Bd., Joslin Diabetes Found., 1980-83; mem. corp. bd. Joslin Diabetes Ctr.; v.p. bd. dirs. Boston Ctr. Internat. Visitors, 1979-82; Boston bd. dirs. Mass. Soc. Prevention of Cruelty to Children, 1980-84; exec. v.p. Ctr. for Middle East Bus., 1978-82; pres. bd. Brookline Community Fund, 1984—; overseer Old Sturbridge Village, 1987—. Mem. Colonial Dames, Soc. Art Historians. Clubs: Women's City (dir.) (Boston); Vincent (dir.). Home: 120 Middlesex Rd Chestnut Hill MA 02167

DANIELS, ALRIE MCNIFF, cancer society marketing communication director; b. Yonkers, N.Y., Sept. 5, 1962; d. Robert Bellarmine and Elaine (Curtis) McNiff; m. Steven John Danielczyk, Oct. 7, 1984. BA, Cath. U. Am., 1984. Editorial asst. United Brotherhood Carpenters, Washington, 1984-87; editor Calif. Nurses Assn., San Francisco, 1988-89; mktg. communication dir. Alameda County unit Am. Cancer Soc., Oakland, Calif., 1990—. Editor: Cardinal, 1984. Promotions vol. Oakland (Calif.) Athletics, 1987—; vol. Am. Cancer Soc., Oakland, 1987—; vice chmn. Ballena Bay Homeowners Assn., Alameda, Calif., 1989—. Mem. Pub. Rels. Soc. Am. Democrat. Roman Catholic. Home: 420-D Cola Ballena Alameda CA 94501 Office: 3100 Summit #5-B Oakland CA 94609

DANIELS, CAROLYN ELIZABETH, lawyer; b. Trenton, N.J., Nov. 22, 1946; d. Marion Penfield and Edith Lucille (Blackwell) D. AB, Mt. Holyoke Coll., 1969; AM, U. Pa., 1970; JD, Harvard U., 1975. Bar: Mass. 1975, Colo. 1975. Clk. to judge U.S. Ct. Appeals for 10th Cir., Denver, 1975-76; assoc. Holme Roberts & Owen, Denver, 1976—; mem. law com. Colo. Bd. Law Examiners, 1978—. Mem. adv. com. Denver Found., 1986—; bd. dirs. Colo. Endowment for Humanities, 1988—. Fellow Colo. Bar Found. (trustee 1988—); mem. ABA, Colo. Bar Assn. (bd. govs. 1983-85, coun. tax sect. 1986—, sec.-treas. 1988-89, chmn. 1990-91), Denver Bar Assn. Office: Holme Roberts & Owen 1700 Lincoln St Ste 4100 Denver CO 80203

DANIELS, CINDY LOU, electronics engineer; b. Moline, Ill., Sept. 24, 1959; d. Ronald McCrae and Mary Lou (McLaughlin) Guthrie; m. Charles Burton Daniels, June 19, 1982. Student, Augustana Coll., Rock Island, Ill., 1977-78; BS cum laude, No. Mich. U., 1981. Field engr. Ford Aerospace, Houston, 1982-83; engr. flight ops. McDonnell Douglas Corp., Houston, 1983-85; electronics engr. Johnson Space Ctr. NASA, Houston, 1985-89, project mgr., 1989—, mission control ctr. upgrade project mgr., 1990—; dynamics controller, NASA-Johnson Space Ctr., 1982-83; payload data engr., NASA, 1983-84, earth radiation budget sattelite joint ops. integration plan mgr., 1984; payload assist module team mem., NASA-McDonnell Douglas Corp., 1984-85; project mgr. multiple program control ctr. NASA. Home: 3703 Pine Trail LaPorte TX 77571 Office: Mission Ops Directorate DC3 Johnson Space Ctr Houston TX 77058

DANIELS, DEBORAH J., U.S. attorney. BA, De Pauw U., 1973; JD, Ind. U. Bar: Ind., U.S. Dist. Ct. (so. dist.) Ind., U.S. Ct. Appeals (7th cir.), U.S. Supreme Ct. 1987. U.S. attorney U.S. Dist. Ct. So. Dist. Ind., 1988—. Office: US Courthouse 46 E Ohio St 5th Fl Indianapolis IN 46204*

DANIELS, DEE ARLANE, coordinator special hospital programs; b. Middletown, Ohio, Jan. 10, 1955; d. Neal Tait Kurfiss and Goldie May Bell; m. Stephen Robert Daniels, Jan. 2, 1982; children: Zachary, Barret, Carlen. BS in Nursing, Ohio State U., 1977; MS in Nursing, U. Cin., 1982; postgrad., Wright State U., 1976. Cert. Red Cross instr. parenting and preparation for parenting. Staff nurse/discharge planning coord. Children's Hosp., Cin.; staff nurse pediatrics Duke Hosp. Med. Ctr., Durham, N.C.; instr. obstetrics and pediatrics Sch. of Nursing Good Samaritan Hosp., coord. spl. programs. Recipient Greek Honor award, Good Samaritan Hosp. Guild Funding for Cons. Svc., 1988. Mem. Assn. for Care of Children's Health (chmn. faculty devel. com.), Am. Red Cross, Nurses Assn. of Am. Coll. Ob-Gyn, Kindervelt of Cin., Adoption Option, Sigma Theta Tau. Methodist. Home: 3159 Lookout Circle Cincinnati OH 45208

DANIELS, DORIA LYNN, manufacturing executive; b. Kent, Ohio, Apr. 22, 1951; d. Eli and Henrietta (Johnson) D. BBA, Kent State U., 1973; postgrad., Old Dominion U., 1975-76, Akron U., 1984-86. Mgmt. trainee Cardinal Fed. Savs., Cleve., 1973-74; acctg. mgr. People Savs. and Loan, Hampton, Va., 1974-77; ins. agt. John Hancock Mut. Life Ins., Hampton, 1977-79; prodn. planner Little Tikes Mfg., Hudson, Ohio, 1979—; pres., co-founder Thomas Anderson Devel. Corp., 1986. Mem. Kent (Ohio) Bd. Edn., 1987, Shade Tree Commn. Kent City Council, 1987; candidate ward 3 council seat Rep. Party, Kent, 1969, co-founder and chmn. Thomas-Anderson Devel. Corp. Kent, 1986—; mem. bd. advisors Portage County Human Services Dept., 1988. City of Kent scholar, 1969; recipient Gov.'s Recognition award Gov. of Ohio, 1986, commendation from Ohio Ho. of Reps., 1987, Ohio House of Reps. State Commendation for record service to the Kent community, 1987, Kent Edn. Assn. awards, 1988. Mem. NAACP (life, polit. advisor), Am. Prodn. Inventory Control Soc., Nat. Assn. Female Execs., Internat. Platform Assn., Nat. Council Negro Women. Baptist. Home: 234 Dodge St Kent OH 44240 Office: Little Tikes Mfg 2180 Barlow Rd Hudson OH 44236

DANIELS, LAURA KIDD, management consultant; b. Detroit, May 21, 1957; d. A. Duncan and Jean (Hyde) Kidd; m. Ray Daniels, Nov. 26, 1983. BA in Econs., Yale U., 1979; MBA, Harvard U., 1983. Intern assoc. Kidder, Peabody & Co., N.Y.C., 1979-81; assoc. McKinsey & Co., Inc., Chgo., 1983-89, dir. of assoc. devel., 1989—. Trustee Lourdes High Sch., Chgo., 1987—. Mem. Chgo. United. Democrat. Roman Catholic. Home: 2847 N Racine Ave Chicago IL 60657 Office: McKinsey & Co Inc 2 First National Pla Chicago IL 60603

DANIELS, MARILYN SNELL, real estate broker; b. Painseville, Ohio, June 17, 1925; d. Roy Addison and Mabelle Irene (Denning) Snell; m. Lyle Franklin Daniels Jr., Oct. 14, 1950; children: Mitchell D., Nancy L., Ted G. BA, Kent State U., 1946. Asst. to account exec. Foster & Davies, Inc., Cleve., 1947-53; broker Wyman Assn., Inc., Painesville, 1975-84, Launders & Assocs., Inc., Painesville, 1984—. Mem. Old Mentor Found., Lake County Hist. Soc. Republican. Methodist. Home: 7493 Cadle Ave Mentor OH 44060

DANIELS, NORMA, state legislator; m. Robert M. Daniels. Mem. state senate from dist. 31 State of Kans. Democrat. Office: PO Box 128 Valley Center KS 67147*

DANIELS, PHYLLIS HYDER, apartment property manager; b. Hendersonville, N.C., Feb. 21, 1951; d. Otis Samuel and Pearl Faye (McCombs) Hyder; m. William L. Odom, Aug. 28, 1970 (div. June 1983); children: Angela, Jason; m. John M. Daniels, Apr. 26, 1986. Student, Florence-Darling Tech. Coll., 1988—. Cert. occupancy specialist HUD. Loan processor Aiken Loan & Security, Florence, 1969-70; bookkeeper, sec. Guardian Fedelity, Florence, 1970-73; steno sec. Manpower Temp. Employer, Florence, 1973-75; receptionist SCN Bank, Florence, 1975-76; tchrs. aide Greenwood Bapt. Ch., Florence, 1977-81; sec. Housing Authority of Florence, 1981-83; apt. mgr. Village Creek Apts., 1983—; cons. Southland Devel. Corp., Florence, 1987—. Active Florence Just Say No Program, 1989. Mary Staat Meml. scholar, 1989—, Florence Jr. Welfare scholar, 1990. Mem. Nat. Ctr. Housing Mgmt., Nat. Assn. Housing Redevel. Ofcls. (nat. peer svcs. program), S.C. Real Estate Commn., Florence Apt. Assn. Republican. Baptist. Home and Office: 2212 Pamplico Hwy B-7 Florence SC 29501

DANIELSKI, LINDA SHARON, insurance company official; b. Portage, Wis., Nov. 26, 1955; d. Lyle William and Sharon June (McCarthy) Hayes; m. Randolph Michael Danielski, Aug. 25, 1979. BS, U. Wis., Stevens Point, 1979. Office adminstr. Allendale Mut. Ins. Co., Milw., 1980-87, adminstr. field accounts, 1987—. Office: Allendale Mut Ins Co 900l N 76th St Ste 307 Milwaukee WI 53223

DANIELSON, PATRICIA ROCHELLE FRANK, urban planner; b. Manhattan, N.Y., Dec. 22, 1941; d. Maxwell and Theresa (Kleckner) Frank; m. Michael Nils Danielson, Sept. 8, 1979 (div. Oct. 1989); m. Seymour B. Fingerhood, Sept. 15, 1963 (div. Dec. 1978); children: Karl John, Louisa Laura. A.A., Thomas Edison State Coll., 1973; M.U.P., Princeton U., 1976. policy planner Gov's Office, Trenton, 1978-80; program devel. specialist N.J. Dept. Community Affairs, Trenton, 1980-82; sr. planner Eggers Group, N.Y.C., 1982-85; pvt. rsch. cons., Princeton, N.J., 1985-87; dir. mktg. and membership svcs. N.J. Retail Mcht.'s Assn., 1987-88; spl. cons. Ednl. Testing Svc., 1989—. Mem. bd. trustees Thomas A. Edison State Coll., Trenton, 1978—, chmn., 1984-87. Mem. Princeton Research Forum, N.J. State Coll. Gov. Bd. Assn., Am. Soc. Public Adminstrs. Avocations: creative writing; folk music.

DANIELSON, PHYLLIS I., art school administrator, tapestry artist, management consultant; b. Marion, Ind. BA in Art, Ball State U., 1953; MA, Mich. State U., 1960, EdS, 1966; EdD, Ind. U., 1968; DFA (hon.) Kendall Coll. Art and Design, 1989. One-person shows include Jewish Community Ctr., Indpls., 1972, Eye-Opener Gallery, Cin., 1972, Mint Mus. Art, 1974, Herron Art Gallery, Indpls., 1974, Sloane O'Stickey Gallery, Cleve., 1974, Women in Art, West Bend, Wis., 1976; group exhbns. include Weatherspoon Gallery, Greensboro, N.C., 1969, 70, Stichery, Pa., 1971, Iowa, 1975; Matrix Gallery, Bloomington, Ind., 1972; pres. Kendall Coll. Art and Design, Grand Rapids, Mich., 1976—, Danielson & Kayser, Inc., 1990—, Mgmt. Cons.; asst. prof. art Ball State U., Muncie, Ind., 1966-67; asst. prof. art edn. U. N.C., Greensboro, 1968-70; assoc. prof. edn. and art Herron Sch. Art, Indpls., 1970-76. Contbr. articles to profl. jours. Mem. Nat. Coun. Art Adminstrs., Nat. Assn. Schs. Art and Design, Coll. Art Assn. Office: Danielson & Kayser Inc 6137 Chamonix Ct SE Grand Rapids MI 49546

DANIELSON, STACY ANN, real estate professional; b. Mpls., Mar. 5, 1963; d. Richard Warren and Jean Arlette (Almgren) K. BS in Mech. Engring., U. Minn., 1987. Work mgmt. engr. IDS Fin. Svcs., Inc., Mpls., 1987-88, svcs. quality engr., 1988-89, supr. field real estate ops., 1989—. Counselor Cassia Counseling Ctr., Mpls., 1987—. Mem. Inst. Indsl. Engr. (pres.-elect 1990—, sec. 1989-90, chpt. devel. chmn. 1988-89).

DANITZ, MARILYNN PATRICIA, choreographer; b. Buffalo. BS in Chemistry, Le Moyne Coll.; MS in Chem. Engring., Columbia U. Artistic dir. High Frequency Wavelengths/Danitz Dances, worldwide, 1976—; assoc. prof. Tainan Cheng Chuan Coll., Taiwan, 1984; profl. dancer Ballet Mcpl. Strasbourg, France, Ballet Mcpl. Geneva, Switzerland; choreography commns. include The 11th Internat. Ballet Comp. Varna, Bulgaria, 1983, Tbilisi Ballet Co., USSR, Nat. Ballet of Colombia, Nat. Cheng Kung Dance Group, Taiwan, Cheng Chuan Dancers, Taiwan, others internationally; master choreography workshops include The Cen. Ballet, Beijing, Chinese Cultural U., Taipei, Taiwan Ballet, Philippines, Manila, New South Wales Coll. Dance, Sydney, Australia, The Ballet Sch., Bogota, Colombia, others internationally; video prodn. resident NEA, 1990. TV prodns. of works include Nat. Broadcasting, Venezuela, Nat. Broadcasting, Colombia, Pub. Broadcasting, Albany, N.Y.C., Mpls; works performed by Nat. Philharm. Orch. of Colombia Gala Performance, 1984; contbr. articles to Jour. Colloidal Chemistry, Jour. Clinical Pathology, others. Active Performance Project. Recipient Gold medal Conservatoire de Geneve, N.Y. State Regents award, one of 3 Outstanding Dance-Theater Works of 1986 award Dance Brew-ATV Cable Manhattan; NIH Fellow; N.Y. State Regents scholar, Le Moyne Coll. Chemistry scholar, Finnerty Sch. Dance scholar, Immaculata Acad. scholar, others; chosen for Bessie Schonberg Lab. for Experienced Choreographers, Dance Theater Workshop. Mem. Nat. Assn. for Regional Ballet (Distinction award, mem. choreography conf.), Performance Project, Dance Theater Workshop, Am. Dance Guild (nat. conf. planning com., seminars for choreographers com.), Albany League of Arts, Rensselaer League of Arts. Address: 560 Riverside Dr New York NY 10027 also: PO Box 216 Sand Lake NY 12153

DANKO, BARBARA DALY, controller; b. Washington, July 9, 1953; d. Joseph Aloysius and Dorothy Louise (Morris) D.; m. George Michael Danko, Dec. 27, 1980; children: Michael Joseph, Elizabeth Grace, Stephen Daly. BA in Econs., St. Joseph U., Phila., 1975; MPA, U. Tex., 1981. Staff aide U.S. Sen. J.B. Johnston, Washington, 1975-76; research asst. Library of Congress, Washington, 1976-78; info. coordinator Nat. Gov.'s Assn., Washington, 1978-79; prog. analyst State of Tex., legis. Budget Office, Austin, 1981-84; sr. budget analyst City of Austin, Fin. Svcs. Dept., 1984-85, City of Pitts., 1985-88; controller Pitts. Water and Sewer Authority, 1988—. Mem. Govt. Fin. Officers Assn., Am. Soc. Pub. Adminstrn., Internat. City Mgmt. Assn. Democrat. Roman Catholic. Home: 1140 Lancaster Ave Pittsburgh PA 15218 Office: Pitts Water & Sewer Author 601 Grant St Pittsburgh PA 15218

DANKO, PATRICIA ST. JOHN, visual artist, writer; b. Orange, Tex., Aug. 7, 1944; d. George Milton and Rebecca Alice (McCoppin) Solomon; m. Jim Danko, Aug. 19, 1973 (dec. 1983). BA, Dominican Coll., Houston, 1965; postgrad. U. Ibero-Americana, Mexico, 1965, Mich. State U., 1965, Mus. Fine Arts Sch., Houston, 1972; BFA, U. Houston, 1979. Teaching asst. Mich. State U., East Lansing, 1965; vol. Peace Corps, Chile, 1965-68; silk-screen apprentice, printer Atelier Zárate, Buenos Aires, 1969; tchr. high sch. Orange Ind. Sch. Dist. (Tex.), 1971, Houston Ind. Sch. Dist., 1973; instr. English, English Lang. Svcs., Houston, 1973-75; instr. English, Spanish, Inlingua Lang. Schs., 1976; instr. Art League Houston, 1978-81; performance art writer Houston Art Scene, 1979-84, editor, 1981-84, mng. editor, 1982-83, exec. editor, 1983-84; acting Tex. editor New Art Examiner, 1985-86; contbg. editor Tex. New Art Examiner, 1986-88; ind. art hist. researcher, writer; freelance writer; visual artist, pub. collections: Nat. Mus. Women in Arts, Washington, Libr. and Rsch. Archives, Washington, N.Y. Feminist Art Inst., Equinox Theatre, Houston, Chomo Uri Collective, U. Mass., Memphis-Brooks Mus. Art, Several Dancers Core Sch., Atlanta, McGlothlin Ins. Agy., Houston, Cameron Petroleum Co., Houston, Emdyne, Inc. Designer numerous artistic and theatrical performances; exhbns. of artistic work to numerous museums and cultural instns. throughout U.S. and Mex. Jesse H. Jones Found. scholar, 1961-65; recipient Presdl. Commendation by Pres. Johnson for Service to U.S. and Chile, 1968; named Outstanding Young Woman of Am., OYWA Press, Chgo., 1970; Sum Arts grantee for sculpture The Matriarch as Phoenix, 1981; Shell Found. grantee for performance of Thanatopsis, 1983, grantee Ruth Chevon Found., Inc., 1987, Change, Inc., N.Y.C., 1987, Adolph and Esther Gottlieb Found., 1988; Lamar Found. grantee, 1989; Impact II Developer grantee, 1990—. Mem. Artists Equity Assn., Contemporary Arts Mus. (Houston). Roman Catholic. Address: 2112 Dunlavy Houston TX 77006

DANKWORTH, CLEMENTINA DINAH See LAINE, CLEO

DANN, EMILY, chemical company executive; b. Albany, Ga., July 26, 1932; d. Jesse Lyman and Evelyn (Calhoun) Dann; m. Christian A. Hansen, June 7, 1977; children: Leslie Montgomery Eagan, Ann Montgomery, Robin Hansen, Randall Hansen, Rhonda Hansen McHeavey, Rheta Hansen. BA, Huntingdon Coll., 1954; MS in Math., U. Houston, 1964; EdD, Rutgers U., 1976. Instr., Lee Coll., Baytown, Tex., 1965-67; prof. Middlesex County Coll., Edison, N.J., 1967-81; dir. human resources LCP Chem. & Plastics Co., Edison, 1981-84, systems analyst, 1986-89; dir. MIS Hanlin Group, Inc., Edison, 1989—; vis. assoc. prof. Drew U., 1984-86; cons. Title I math. program Bedminster (N.J.) Pub. Sch., 1976-77; mem. co-adj. faculty Grad. Sch. Edn., Rutgers U., 1976-81, Kean Coll., 1980-81. Contbr. articles to profl. jours. Mem. Acad. Mgmt., Orgn. Devel. Network, Am. Soc. Tng. and Devel., Am. Math. Assn., Jean Piaget Soc. Home: 1 Scenic Dr Highlands NJ 07732 Office: LCP Chem & Plastics Co Raritan Plaza II Edison NJ 08837

DANNA, JO J., publisher, author, anthropologist; b. N.Y.C.; d. Lucy (Macaluso) D.; m. David Pender (div. 1961). BA, Hunter Coll., 1948; MA, Columbia U., 1964, PhD, 1974. Elem. sch. tchr. N.Y.C. Bd. Edn., 1956-65; asst. dir., cons. Villaggio Del Superdotato, Sicily, Italy, 1967-70; asst. prof. anthropology Baldwin Wallace Coll., Berea, Ohio, 1971-73; dir., writer ethnic studies curriculum edn. dept. NYU, Albany, 1975-76; asst. prof. La Trobe U., Melbourne, Australia, 1976-79; freelance writer, 1982—; pub. Palomino Press, N.Y.C., 1983—; founder Network Ind. Pubs. Greater N.Y. Contbr. articles to profl. jours. Mem. Pubs. Mktg. Assn., Com. Small Mag. Editors and Pubs. Home and Office: 86-07 144th St Briarwood NY 11435

DANNA, MARGARET ANN, oil executive; b. Abilene, Tex., Jan. 16, 1942; d. S.E. Boyd and Margaret Mac Gillivary (Withington) Smith; m. Frank Paul Danna, June 28, 1971; 1 child, Elizabeth Ann. BS in Elem. Edn., Hardin-Simmons U., 1964; postgrad., Claremont (Calif.) Coll.; MEd, U. Southwestern La., 1973. Tchr. Lafayette (La.) Parish Sch. Bd., 1965-71; instr. geography U. Southwestern La., Lafayette, 1970-71; owner, mgr. Queen's Cabinet, Ltd., Lafayette, 1982-84; v.p. Danna Oil Corp., Lafayette, 1984—; speaker in field. Bd. dirs. Acadiana Symphony Assn., 1983-86, Acadiana Symphony Womens League, 1987—, La. Epilepsy Assn., 1984—, mem. exec. com., 1989—; bd. dirs. Epilepsy Task Force of Lafayette, 1985—, v.p., 1989—; mem. AIDS Task Force; mem. pub. rels. com. Job Starter Coun.; mem. profl. adv. bd. Performing Arts Soc.; mem. Mayor's Task Force on Human Svcs. Mem. Jr. League of Lafayette (pub. rels. com., Acdian Village chair, tng. com. sustaining advisor 1989—), Avec Souci Womens Club (past pres., charitable works chmn., ways and means chair, treas., sec. and publicity chairperson). Home: 151 Southlawn Dr Lafayette LA 70503 Office: Danna Oil Corp 1126 Coolidge Lafayette LA 70505

DANNEHL, MARY ZEITLER, pharmaceutical sales specialist; b. Nashville, Aug. 28, 1959; d. John Ransom and Carol (Miller) Zeitler; m. Karl Niels Dannehl, Aug. 1, 1987. BA, Salem Coll., 1982. In pharm. sales E.R. Squibb & Sons, Inc., Louisville, 1982-84, Miles Pharm., Atlanta, 1984—. Mem. Atlanta Jr. League (advisor 1988—), Piedmont Garden Club (sec. 1989-90, pres. computer com. 1990—), Kappa Kappa Gamma Alumnae. Presbyterian.

DANNER, PATSY ANN (MRS. C. M. MEYER), businesswoman, state legislator; b. Louisville, Jan. 13, 1934; d. Henry J. and Catherine M. (Shaheen) Berrer; m. Lavon Danner, Feb. 12, 1951 (div.); children: Stephen, Stephanie, Shane, Shavonne.; m. C.M. Meyer, Dec. 30, 1982. Student, Hannibal-LaGrange Coll., 1952; B.A. in Polit. Sci. cum laude, N.E. Mo. State U., 1972. Dist. asst. to Congressman Jerry Litton, Kansas City, Mo., 1973-76; fed. co-chmn. Ozarks Regional Commn., Washington, 1977-81; owner, prin. Danner & Assocs., 1981—; mem. Mo. State Senate, 1983—. Mem. Bus. and Profl. Women, AAUW, Beta Sigma Phi. Roman Catholic. Home: 6 Nantucket Court Smithville MO 64089

D'ANNIBALLE, PRISCILLA LUCILLE, contracting company executive, consultant; b. Martins Ferry, Ohio, Oct. 28, 1950; d. James Louis and Smyrna Isabell (Prieto) D'A. BE, U. Toledo, 1973. Credit mgr. Kabat Distbg. Co., Toledo, 1973-80; comml. ops. officer Ohio Citizens Bank, Toledo, 1980-81, credit officer, 1981-82, mktg. officer, 1982-83, mortgage banking officer, 1983-85; owner, pres. D'Ann Enterprises, Inc., Holland, Ohio, 1985—. Mem. fund drive United Way, Toledo, 1982, Jr. Achievement, Toledo, 1983; bd. dirs. Voluntary Action Ctr., Toledo, 1981-82. Mem. Nat. Assn. Credit Mgmt. (bd. dirs. 1981-87, Credit Exec. Yr. 1987), Nat. Assn. Credit Mgmt. Ednl. Forum (bd. dirs. 1976-82, Credit Person of Yr. 1982). Roman Catholic. Home: 704 Oak Park Dr Toledo OH 43617 Office: D'Ann Enterprises Inc 1049 S McCord Holland OH 43528

DANNIS-APPLEGATE, FERN SUE, urban planner, housing consultant; b. Cleve., Nov. 16, 1953; d. Mark Libman and Doris Louise (Haimsohn) D.; m. John Worley Applegate, May 17, 1987; 1 child, Rebecca Marie. BA, Miami U., Oxford, Ohio, 1975; M in Planning, U. Va., 1977. Planner Johnson, Johnson & Roy, Ann Arbor, Mich., 1977-78, City of Alexandria, Va., 1978-80; project mgr. Nat. Assn. Housing Coops., Washington, 1980-81; devel. asst., trainer Multi-Family Housing Svcs., Inc., Balt., 1981-83, pvt. practice cons., 1983-84; exec. dir. Community Investment Inst., Balt., Md., 1984-85; housing devel. officer Community Devel. Adminstrn., Annapolis, Md., 1985-86; program officer Devel. Tng. Inst., Balt., 1986-87; trainer, housing cons. Dannis and Assocs., Balt., 1987—. Democrat.

DANOFF-KRAUS, PAMELA SUE, shopping center development executive; b. Gallup, N.Mex., Aug. 29, 1946; d. Isadore Harry and Armida Catherine (Ceccardi) Danoff; m. Milo Joseph Warner III, Dec. 28, 1968 (div. 1974); m. Robert Warren Kraus, Nov. 30, 1985; 1 child, Jillian Amaris. BA, U. N.Mex., 1968. Lic. in real estate, Calif. Real estate rep. Kaiser Aetna, Newport Beach, Calif., 1975-76; leasing agt. Alexander Haagen Co., Rolling Hills, Calif., 1976-77; dir. leasing Warren Kellogg & Assocs., Newport Beach, 1977-81, Center Devel. Co., Newport Beach, 1981-84; exec. v.p., ptnr. The Von Der Ahe Co., Newport Beach, 1984-86; ptnr. Marketplace Properties, Tustin, Calif., 1986—; lectr. in field; panelist various convs., univs.; conductor seminars in field. Contbr. articles to profl. jours. Sponsor Californians Working Together to End Hunger and Homelessness, Los Angeles, 1988; mem. Orange County Performing Arts Ctr., 1983-85. Mem. Internat. Coun. Shopping Ctrs. (program chmn. 1987-89, small ctr. devel. com., state chmn. for pub. rels. and community affairs for Calif. 1990—), Calif. Bus. Properties Assn., Women in Retail Real Estate, Calif. Redevel. Assn., Chi Omega. Republican. Roman Catholic. Home: 10182 Brier Ln Santa Ana CA 92705-1531 Office: Marketplace Properties 13522 Newport Ave Ste 100 Tustin CA 92680

DANSER, BONITA KAY, legal administrator, consultant; b. Altadena, Calif., Mar. 26, 1949; d. Earl Peters and Sara Grace (Myer) Nissley; m. Robin Danser, Aug. 26, 1971 (div. Feb. 1978); m. John Hullett, June 3, 1989. AA, Pasadena City Coll., 1969; student, San Diego State U., 1970-76;

BSBA, U. Redlands, 1988. Legal adminstr. Rhodes, Kendall & Harrington, Newport Beach, Calif., 1978-86, Gardner and Martin, Newport Beach, 1986, Martin and Wilson, Santa Ana, Calif., 1987-89; freelance contract legal adminstr. Irvine, Calif., 1986-88; legal administrator, cons. Parilla, Hubbard & Militzok, Irvine, 1989—. Citizen ambassador to China, People-to-People Internat., 1988. Mem. Assn. Legal Adminstrs. (treas. 1983, 85, sec. 1984, 2d v.p. 1990), Theta Chi Epsilon (nat. bd. dirs. 1984-90, Achievement award 1979). Office: Parilla Hubbard & Militzok 18400 Von Karman Ave Ste 600 Irvine CA 92715-1509

DANSER, MARY HELEN, pharmacist; b. Dawson Springs, Ky., Mar. 8, 1940; d. Maurice and Emma Louise (Thorn) Lisanby; m. Richard Allen Danser, June 8, 1963 (dec. Apr. 1976); 1 child, Richard Allen Jr. AA, Lindsey Wilson Jr. Coll., 1961; BS in Pharmacy, U. Ky., 1965. cons. in field; instr. Coll. Law Enforcement Dept. Traffic Safety, Eastern Ky. U., 1968-84, vis. lectr.; instr. Jefferson County Police Dept., Louisville, Ky., 1985—. Intern U. Ky. Med. Ctr., 1965; intern, pharmacist Hubbard & Curry Druggists, Lexington, Ky., 1965-66; chief pharmacist Ky. Dept. Mental Health, Frankfort, Ky., 1966-73, Ky. Bur. Health Services, Frankfort, Ky., 1973-84; pharmacy services program mgr. Ky. Dept. Mental Health Cabinet for Human Resources, Frankfort, Ky., 1984—. Mem. pastor/parish com. 1st Meth. Ch., Lexington, 1971-77, adminstrv. bd., 1972-74; chmn. com. Troop 276, Boy Scouts Am., Lexington, 1984—; youth counselor Antioch Christian Ch., 1984-86. Named to Hon. Order Ky. Cols., 1988, Order of the Arrow, Boy Scout Honor Campers, 1989. Mem. Bluegrass Pharm. Assn. (chair peer rev. com. 1986-87), Ky. Soc. Hosp. Pharmacists (sec. 1970), Am. Soc. Hosp. Pharmacists (panelist 1975-77). Democrat. Mem. Christian Ch. (Disciples of Christ). Office: Dept Mental Health 275 E Main St Frankfort KY 40621

DANZIG, LISA, financial analyst; b. Savannah, Ga., Sept. 8, 1958; d. Lamont Earl Danzig and Suzanne (Feidelson) Mendonsa; m. Richard Mark Schetman, June 9, 1985 (div. Oct. 1988); m. Franklin Minerva, Oct. 7, 1989. BA in Human Biology, Brown U., 1980; MBA in Fin., NYU, 1985. Mortgage analyst Loyola Fed. Savs. & Loan Assn., Bethesda, Md., 1981-82; customer svc. rep. Phila. Saving Fund Soc., 1982-83; rating analyst Standard & Poor's Corp., N.Y.C., 1985-86, rating specialist, 1986-87, rating officer, 1987-88, asst. v.p., 1989-90, v.p., 1990—. Active Assn. for a Better N.Y. Mem. Mcpl. Analysts Group of N.Y. Democrat. Jewish. Office: Standard & Poors Corp 25 Broadway New York NY 10025

DANZIG, SHEILA RING, marketing and direct mail executive; b. N.Y.C., Mar. 18, 1948; d. David and Yetta Ring; m. William Harold Danzig, Aug. 11, 1968; children: David Scott, Gregory Charles. BS, CUNY, 1968. Tchr. N.Y.C. Bd. Edn., 1968-71; treas. Nat. Success Mktg. Inc., Sunrise, Fla., 1969—; pres. Innovative Communications Market Cons., Plantation, Fla., 1984-87; cons. Crush Softball Team, Hollywood, Fla., 1986-87, The Eye Ctr., Sunrise, 1986-87, Bus. Expo., Plantation, 1987. Author: You Deserve to be Rich, 1972, A Free Press, 1990, A Better Medical Practice, 1986; contbr. articles to profl. jours. Coordinator Day Out program Mills Boys' Shelter, Ft. Lauderdale, Fla., 1985, 87, Put Seat Belts on Sch. Buses program Broward County Sch. Bd., 1986; vol. Miami Children's Hosp.; campaign dir. Help the Handicapped Keep Their Parking Spots, 1987. Mem. Mail Order Bus. Bd., Am. Med. Writers Assn., Plantation Bus. and Profl. Women's Assn., MADD, Speechcrafters. Office: Nat Success Mktg 2574 N University Dr Sunrise FL 33322

DANZIGER, DEBRA ROSENBLUM, bank marketer; b. Cleve., Apr. 5, 1954; d. R. Donald and Harriet (Biber) Rosenblum; m. Stephen F. Danziger. BA, Ohio State U., 1976. Personal banker Huntington Nat. Bank, Columbus, Ohio, 1977-79; mgr. No. Trust Co., Chgo., 1979-81, office. customer service and mktg. mgr., 1981-83, v.p., product mgr., v.p., mktg., 1987—. Contbg. author: (book) Cash Flow and Treasury Mgmt, 1987; contbr. articles to profl. jours. Office: No Trust Co 50 S LaSalle St Chicago IL 60675

DANZIGER, GERTRUDE SEELIG, metal fabricating executive; b. Chgo., Oct. 24, 1919; d. Isidor and Clara (Fuchs) Seelig; widowed; children: Robert, James. Student, Northwestern U., U. Wis. Treas. Homak Mfg. Co., Inc., Chgo., 1966-79; pres. Homak Mfg. Co., Inc., 1979—. Patentee in field.

DANZIGER, JOAN, sculptor; b. N.Y.C., June 17, 1934; d. Emanuel and Martha (Kaplan) Schwartz; m. Martin Danziger, June 17, 1958. B.F.A., Cornell U., 1954; B.F.A. (hon.), Acad. Fine Art, Rome, 1958. One woman exhbns. include: Corcoran Gallery, Washington, 1975, Calif. Mus. Sci. and Industry, Los Angeles, 1977, Muckenthal Cultural Ctr., Los Angeles, 1977, SUNY-Albany, 1978, Jacksonville Mus. Art and Sci. (Fla.), 1979, Fendrick Gallery, Washington, 1979, Terry Dintenfass Gallery, N.Y.C., 1980, Joy Horwich Gallery, Chgo., N.J. State Mus., Trenton, 1982, Benjamin Mangel Gallery, Phila., Louisiana World Expn., New Orleans, 1984, Textile Mus., Washington, 1985, Nat. Mus. Women in Arts, 1987. Vis. artist, lectr. Smithsonian Instn., 1980-82; artist-in-residence AFL-CIO Labor Studies Ctr., 1975; visual arts panelist D.C. Commn. Arts and Humanities, 1974-79, 84-85; sculpture panelist N.J. State Council Arts, 1982. Commd. by Nat. Mus. Am. Art, Jacksonville Mus. Arts and Scis., Columbia Hosp., Washington, Frostburg State Coll. (Md.), George Meany Labor Studies Ctr., New Orleans Mus. Art, D.C. Conv. Ctr., Nat. Mus. Women in Arts, N.J. State Mus., Nat. Endowment Arts grantee, 1975, grantee Internat. des Arts, Paris, 1986. Mem. Artists Equity, Washington Sculptors Group (bd. dirs.), Internat. Sculpture Ctr., Sculpture Source. Home: 2909 Brandywine St NW Washington DC 20008

DANZIS, JO-ANN FINE, tennis club executive; b. N.Y.C., Feb. 26, 1941; d. H. Sanford Fine and Mildred (Deerson) Skidell; m. Colin Michael, Nov. 16, 1963; children: Mitchell, Nicholas. BA, Mt. Holyoke Coll., South Hadley, 1961; MA, Columbia U., N.Y.C., 1964. Biochemical rsch. Rockefeller Inst., N.Y.C., 1961-63; teaching fellow Columbia U., N.Y.C., 1962-63; chemistry tchr. Irvington High Sch., 1964-65; chemistry instr. Middlesex County Coll., Edison, 1965-69; asst. prof. chemistry County Coll. of Morris, Randolf, 1971-79; mng. rep. for creditors Livingston Racketball & Health Club, 1980-81; ptnr., exec. West Orange Tennis Club, 1982—. Mem. AAUP, Am. Chem. Soc., Newark Acad. Parents Assn. Bd., Jockey Club. Office: West Orange Tennis Club 1448 Pleasant Valley Way West Orange NJ 07052

D'ARCY, ADELYSE MARIE, foundation president; b. London, England, Feb. 2, 1934; came to U.S., 1959; d. Norman Wilfred and Aliette (de Tournemire) D.; m. Paul J. Bohannan, Feb. 28, 1981. RN, Guy's Hosp., London, England, 1956; BA, Calif. State U., 1972, MA, 1976. Nurse House of Lords, London, England, 1957-59; charge nurse Peter Bent Brigham Hosp., Boston, 1959-61, Bay Med. Group, San Diego, 1961-63, Mercy Hosp., San Diego, 1963-66; nurse freelance, San Diego, 1966-74; tchr. English as a Second Lang. San Diego Community Coll., Santa Barbara Community Coll., 1971-76, 76-82; anthrop. research Western Behavioral Sci. Inst., La Jolla, Calif., 1974-78; sr. sales rep. Merrill Lynch Realty, San Marino, Calif., 1985-88; pres. Three Rivers (Calif.) Anthrop. Found., 1989—. Mem. Phi Kappa Phi, AAUW (v.p. membership 1986-88). Office: Three Rivers Anthrop Found PO Box 877 Three Rivers CA 93271

D'ARCY, ROSEMARY V., academic administrator; b. N.Y.C., Nov. 16, 1944; d. Justin Emard and Theresa (Andrews) Collins; m. Herbert J. D'Arcy, May 21, 1966; children: Mark Ian, Keith Thomas. BA, Merrimack Coll., 1966; MLS, U. R.I., 1973. Libr. Sperry Gyroscope Corp., Great Neck, N.Y., 1967-68, Mansfield (Conn.) Pub. Libr., 1971-72, E.O. Smith High Sch., Mansfield, 1972-73, Bishop Keough High Sch., Pawtucket, R.I., 1975-78, Town of Coventry (R.I.) Schs., 1978-79; asst. dir. fin. aid Bryant Coll., Smithfield, R.I., 1980-83, mktg. coord. Ctr. for Mgmt. Devel., 1983-84; asst. and assoc. dir. Ctr. for mgmt. devel. Bryant Coll., Smithfield, 1984-88; dir. ctr. for mgmt. devel. Bryant Coll., Smithfield, R.I., 1988—; chairperson Mgmt. Devel. Dirs., Tarpon Springs, Fla., 1989—; nominating chair ACHE Region I. Contbr. articles to profl. jours. Bd. dirs. Greenville (R.I.) Pub. Libr., 1986-88. Named one of Outstanding Young Women in Am., 1971. Mem. Assn. Continuing Higher Edn. (nominating chair 1988-89), Nat. Univ. Continuing Edn. Assn., NOW, NAFE. Office: Bryant Coll Ctr Mgmt Devel 450 Douglas Pike Smithfield RI 02917-1283

DARDEN, DAWN L., company executive; b. Maury County, Tenn., Apr. 5, 1963; d. James Allen Darden and Carla Mae Scheiwiller. BS, Bethel Coll., McKenzie, Tenn., 1985. Contracts specialist IBM Corp., Gaithersburg, Md., assoc. buyer; prodn. analyzer Kelly Svcs., Columbia, Tenn.; fin. asst. Dialogic Communications Crop., Franklin, Tenn.; subcontracts adminstr. IBM Corp., Gaithersburg, Md.; instr. in fin. Mem. NAFE. Home: 13223 Whitechurch Circle Germantown MD 20874

DARKEN, TERESA JOAN JOYCE, publicity executive; b. Buffalo, May 11, 1961; d. John Joseph and Noel Carol (Kraynik) J.; m. Kevin J. Darken, May 1990. BA cum laude, Kenyon Coll., 1983. Asst. editor Harcourt Brace Jovanovich, Washington, 1984-87; dir. Newsmakers, Inc., Washington, 1987-89; publicity dir. Nat. Acad. Press, Washington, 1989—; publicist NEH, Washington, 1987. Democrat. Roman Catholic. Home: 2950 Van Ness St NW #304 Washington DC 20008

DARKOVICH, SHARON MARIE, nurse; b. Ft. Wayne, Ind., Dec. 10, 1949; d. Gerald Antone LaCanne and Ida Eileen (Bowman) LaCanne Cutler; m. Robert Eliot Ness, July 17, 1971 (dec. Aug. 1976); m. Paul Darkovich, Jan. 23, 1981; 1 child, Amy Elizabeth. B.S. in Nursing, Case Western Res. U., 1973, B.A. in Psychology, 1978. R.N., Ohio. Staff nurse Univ. Hosps., Cleve., 1973, asst. head nurse, 1973-76; quality assurance coordinator St. Luke's Hosp., Cleve., 1976-83, 84—, dir. nursing, 1983-84. cons. to long-term care facilities, 1986—, pressure ulcer dressing devel. B.F. Goodrich Co., 1988—. Mem. Am. Nurses Assn., Greater Cleve. Nurses Assn. (mem. dist. council on practice, 1982-84), Sigma Theta Tau. Avocations: reading; needlework; sewing; camping.

DARLING, ALBERTA STATKUS, state representative, marketing executive, former art museum executive; b. Hammond, Ind., Apr. 28, 1944; d. Albert William and Helen Anne (Vaicunas) Statkus; m. William Anthony Darling, Aug. 12, 1967; children—Elizabeth Suzanne, William Anthony. BS, U. Wis., 1967. English tchr. Nathan Hale High Sch., West Allis, Wis., 1967-69, Castle Rock High Sch., West Allis, Colo., 1969-71; community vol. worker Castle Rock High Sch., West Allis, Milw., 1971—; cons. orgn. devel., Milw., 1982—; dir. mktg. and communications Milw. Art Mus., 1981-88; exec. dir. mktg. architectural firm, 1988-90; State Rep. Wis., 1990—, mem. urban edn. com., children and human svcs. com., tourism com., homelessness com., teeenage pregnancy com., vice chmn. gov.'s housing policy commn., assembly coms. Pres. Community Action Seminar for Women, 1979-80; a founder Goals for Greater Milw. 2000, 1980-84; co-chair Action 2000, 1984-86; co-chmn. Icebreaker Am. Winterfestival; chmn. Community Action Seminar for Women, 1988; bd. dirs., exec. com. United Way, Milw., 1982—, chair project 1985, 1984-85, chmn. policy com. 1988; founder Today's Girls/Tomorrow's Women, Milw., 1982—; pres. Jr. League Milw., 1980-82, Planned Parenthood Milw., 1982-84, Future Milw., 1983-85; vice chmn. State of Wis. Strategic Planning Council, 1988—, chmn. small bus./entrpreneur com.; mem. Greater Milw. Com.'s Mktg. Task Force, 1987-88; chmn. United Way Policy Com., 1987-88; participant Bus. Ptnrs. White House Conf., 1987; mem. summerfest adv. com. on Winter Festivals, 1989; founder Women's Fund of Milw. Found. Recipient Vol. Action award Milw. Civic Alliance, 1984, Community Service award United Way, 1984, Leader of Future award Milw. Mag., 1988, Nat. Assn. Community Leadership Orgn. award, 1986, Today's Girls/Tomorrow's Women Leadership award, 1987, Future Milw. Community Leadership award, 1988. Mem. Greater Milw. Com., TEMPO Profl. Women, Am. Mktg. Assn. (Marketer of Yr. 1984), Pub. Relations Soc. Am., Ctr. for Pub. Representation (state bd. 1988), ARC (bd. dirs., exec. fin. coms. 1987—), Women's Fund (steering com. 1988), Internat. Assn. Bus. Communicators, Greater Milw. Com. Republican. Home: 1325 W Dean Rd Milwaukee WI 53217 Office: State Capitol PO Box 8952 Madison WI 53708

DARLING, DEBRA BETH, banker; b. Hartford, Conn., June 5, 1953; d. Harry and Leah (Katzen) D. BA, So. Conn. State U., 1975; MBA, Simmons Coll., 1984. Cons. Care About Now, Chelsea, Mass., 1978-80; purchasing mgr. Spectrowax Corp., Brighton, Mass., 1981-83; cons. Ogden Corp., N.Y.C., 1985; asst. v.p. Bank of Boston, 1986—. Mem. Brookline (Mass.) Town Meeting, 1987-89; vol. Vista, 1976-77. Mem. Simmons Coll. Alumnae Assn., Mus. Fine Arts, PBS, NOW. Democrat. Jewish. Home: 160 St Paul St Apt 2A Brookline MA 02146 Office: Bank of Boston 100 Federal St Boston MA 02110

DARLING, MARIE C, publications official; b. Windsor, Vt., July 15, 1963; d. Melvin Cross and Mary C. (Castellini) D. AS, Trinity Coll., 1989. Receptionist U.S. Army Cold Regions Rsch. & Engring. Lab., Hanover, N.H., 1983-86, editorial clk., 1986-90, tech. publs. technician, 1990—. Home: RR 1 Box 50 Hartland VT 05048

DARLING, SHARON KATHLEEN, communications specialist, consultant, designer; b. Ft. Benning, Ga., Jan. 12, 1959; d. Harold Francis and Helen Inez (Swearingen) D. BA in Journalism, U. N.C., 1981. Reporter King (N.C.) Times-News, 1981, Register Pub. Co., Danville, Va., 1982-84; rsch. asst., asst. editor Compute! Publs., Greensboro, N.C., 1984-85; freelance writer Pace mag., Greensboro, 1985-86; coord. news and info. Greensboro Pub. Schs., 1986-89; communications specialist Goodyear Tire & Rubber Co., Randleman, N.C., 1989—. Contbr. articles to mags., chpts. to books; designer brochures, books, 1986—. Treas. N.C. Bicentennial on Constn., Greensboro, 1989—. Named Outstanding 1st Yr. Mem., Danville Jaycettes, 1982; recipient Blue Ribbon award N.C. Sch. Pub. Rels. Assn., 1988, 89. Mem. Internat. Mgmt. Coun., Kappa Alpha Theta (sec., Panhellenic del. alumnae chpt. Greensboro 1987-88). Democrat. Presbyterian. Home: 4326-D Edith Ln Greensboro NC 27409 Office: Goodyear Tire & Rubber Co 800 Pineview St Randleman NC 27317

DARLINGTON, JUDITH MABEL, social worker; b. Deckerville, Mich., Nov. 29, 1942; d. Wallace and Mabel Lillian (Rich) Cole; m. Clare Robert Darlington, Dec. 15, 1962; children: Debra Lynn, Dawn Elizabeth. BA, Mich. State U., 1962; MSW, U. Mich., 1983. Tchr. Limestone (Maine) Presque Isle Schs., 1963-64; substitute tchr. Crestwood Sch. Dist., Dearborn Heights, Mich., 1971-74; monitor, tchr. Renewing Life Ministries, Annandale, Va., 1976-82; clin. social worker Westland (Mich.) Counseling Svc., 1983-84; family therapist, counselor Family Svc. of Detroit and Wayne County, Wyandotte, Mich., 1984-86; specialist substance abuse Plymouth (Mich.) Family Svc., 1986-87; exec. dir. Christian Conciliation Svc. of S.E. Mich., Detroit, 1987—; speaker in field. Mem. Nat. Assn. Social Workers (cert.), Christian Women's Club (chmn. Livonia, Mich. chpt. 1981-82), Kappa Delta Pi. Presbyterian. Home: 12211 Cherrywood Ct Plymouth MI 48170 Office: Christian Conciliation Svc SE Mich 27350 W Chicago Detroit MI 48239

DARLOW, JULIA DONOVAN, lawyer; b. Detroit, Sept. 18, 1941; d. Frank William Donovan and Helen Adele Turner; m. George Anthony Gratton Darlow (div.); 1 child, Gillian; m. John Corbett O'Meara. A.B., Vassar Coll., 1963; postgrad., Columbia U. Law Sch., 1964-65; J.D. cum laude, Wayne State U., 1971. Bar: Mich. 1971, U.S. Dist. Ct. (ea. dist.) Mich. 1971. Assoc. Dickinson, Wright, McKean, Cudlip & Moon, Detroit, 1971-78; ptnr. Dickinson, Wright, Moon, Van Dusen & Freeman, Detroit, 1978—; adj. prof. Wayne State U. Law Sch., 1974-75; commr. State Bar Mich., 1977-87, mem. exec. com., 1979-83, 84-87, sec. 1980-81, v.p. 1984-85, pres.-elect 1985-86, pres. 1986-87, council corp. fin. and bus. law sect. 1980-86, council computer law sect. 1985-88; chair Mich. Supreme Ct. Task Force on Gender Issues in the Cts., 1987-89. Reporter: Mich. Nonprofit Corp. Act, 1977-82. Bd. dirs. Hutzel Hosp., 1984—, Mich. Opera Theater, 1985—, Mich. Women's Found., 1986—; trustee Internat. Inst. Met. Detroit, 1986—, Mich. Met. coun. Girl Scouts U.S., 1988—, Detroit area coun. Boy Scouts Am., 1988—, Mich. Coun. for the Humanities, 1988—; mem. Blue Cross-Blue Shield Prospective Reimbursement Com., Detroit, 1979-81; v.p., exec. com. United Found., 1988—. Fellow Am. Bar Found.; mem. Detroit Bar Assn. Found. (treas. 1984-85, trustee 1982-85), Mich. Bar Found. (trustee 1987—), Am. Judicature Soc. (bd. dirs. 1985-88), Internat. Women's Forum, Women Lawyers Assn. (pres. 1977-78), Mich. Women's Campaign Fund (charter). Democrat. Club: Renaissance (Detroit). Office: Dickinson Wright Moon & Van Dusen & Freeman 800 First Nat Bldg Detroit MI 48226

DARNELL, BETTY JEAN (B. J. DARNELL), small animal consultant, association executive; b. Augusta, Ga., Sept. 6, 1942; d. Rufus Eugene Randall and Martha Lee (Payne) Darnell-Bush. AS in Vet Medicine. Technician emergency room Lee County Hosp., Sanford, N.C., 1965-67; supr. vet. technicians Durham (N.C.) Animal Hosp., 1967-68; vet. technician Vine Vet. Hosp., Chapel Hill, N.C., 1968; supr. vet. technicians Rossville Vet Clinic, Chattanooga, 1968-71; owner Profl. Kennels, Ft. Oglethorpe, Ga., 1971—; stockholder Our Gang, Inc., Chattanooga, 1972-75; co-owner Us Girls, Inc., Chattanooga, 1972-74; cons. Groom & Bd. mag., Chgo., 1984-87; pub. speaker Pet Industry, 1981—. Author: mag. Jour. AVMA, 1971; author, editor: mag. Chattanoogan, 1974-76; editor mag. Clipperblade, 1979-80. Mem. Nat. Fedn. Idn. Bus., Am. Boarding Kennels (regional dir. 1984-87, v.p. 1986-87, pres.-elect 1987—, pres. 1987—, Svc. award 1981, 82, 83, Nat. award 1982, 88, 89), Ga. Profl. Dog Groomers (pres. 1982-83), Am. Inst. Parliamentarians, Catoosa County C. of C., Better Bus. Bur., Civitan (parliamentarian 1988-89, dir. 1989-90), Ladies Oriental Shrine of N.Am. (High Priestess 1987-88, Bhakti Ct. #25 Atlanta, Grand Page 1988, Hon. Grand Page 1988-89). Democrat. Home: 1811 Old Lafayette Rd Fort Oglethorpe GA 30742 Office: Profl Grooming & Boarding Kennels 1813 Old Lafayette Rd Fort Oglethorpe GA 30742

DA ROZA, VICTORIA CECILIA, human resource administrator; b. East Orange, N.J., Aug. 30, 1945; d. Victor and Cynthia Helen (Krupa) Hawkins; m. Thomas Howard Kaminski, Aug. 28, 1971 (div. 1977); 1 child, Sarah Hawkins; m. Robert Anthony da Roza, Nov. 25, 1983. BA, U. Mich., 1967; MA, U. Mo., 1968. Contract compliance mgr. City of San Diego, 1972-75; v.p. personnel Bank of Calif., San Francisco, 1975-77; with human resources Lawrence Livermore (Calif.) Nat. Lab., 1978-86; pvt. cons. Victoria Kaminski-da Roza & Assocs., 1986—; lectr. in field; videotape workshop program on mid-career planning used by IEEE. Contbr. numerous articles to profl. jours. Mem. social policy com. City of Livermore, 1982. Mem. Am. Soc. Tng. and Devel., Western Gerontol. Soc. (planning com. Older Worker Track 1983), Gerontol. Soc. Am. Home and Office: 385 Borica Dr Danville CA 94526

DARPHIN, SARAH WINIFRED, flight attendant; b. Jennings, La., Aug. 24, 1949; d. Robert Douglas and Sarah Winifred (Gulley) D. BA, NW State U. of La., 1971. Sec. First Nat. Bank, Dallas, 1971-72, Sun Oil Co., Dallas, 1972-73; flight attendant Am. Airlines, N.Y.C., 1973-76, flight service supr., 1976-82, flight attendant, 1982—; com. chairperson quality of work life Am. Airlines, N.Y.C., 1984-86; developed and coordinated flight attendant SabreComputer Tng., 1985, and Life Enhancement Sems., 1986. Creator fundraiser, co-chairperson World Hunger Yr., Harvest for Hunger Benefit, N.Y.C., 1985, Save the Children, Am. Harvest Benefit, N.Y.C., 1986, The Starlight Found., Am. Harvest Benefit, N.Y.C., 1987, 88, Am. Airlines Flight Attendants and Friends for Hands Across Am., N.Y.C., 1986; vol. Union Settlement Games Day, N.Y.C., 1990, Birds of a Feather Ball, N.Y.C., 1990. Recipient Profl. Flight Attendant award Am. Airlines, 1976, 83, 85, Vol. award Starlight Found., 1987. Democrat. Presbyterian. Home: 408 E 65th St #4E New York NY 10021 Office: Am Airlines Internat Flight Svc John F Kennedy Airport Jamaica NY 11431

DARR, BARBARA HARMAN, engineering technician; b. Washington, June 14, 1927; d. William Kenneth Harman and Mabel (Christena) Swab; m. Ralph Eugene Darr, July 17, 1948 (div. Aug. 1978); children: Victoria Regina, Michael Christopher. Student, LA City Coll., 1945-46, UCLA, 1945; cert., Anne Arundel Community Coll., Arnold, Md., 1982, U. Md., 1980. Dispatcher C&P Telephone Co., Washington, 1947-52; engring. technician C&P Telephone Co., Wheaton, Md., 1964-71; computer analyst David Taylor Naval Rsch. & Devel. Ctr., Annapolis, Md., 1971-73; engring. technician U.S. Naval Acad., Annapolis, 1973-90; legal researcher Richard C. Goodwin, atty., Annapolis, 1988—; cartographer Annapolis, 1965—; mem. Gov.'s Task Force Long Term Care of Handicapped, Balt., 1988—; chief exec. officer Barbara & Assocs., Annapolis, 1990—, cons. firm, Annapolis, 1985—. Bd. dirs. Beverley Beach Civic Assn., Mayo, Md., 1970-78, Annapolis Head Injury Support Group, Annapolis, 1983-85; cons., chair March of Dimes, 1988—. Mem. Nat. Wildlife Found., Md. Head Injury Found., Arthritis Found., Hi Friends (chief exec. officer 1985—), Women of the Moose. Home: 125 Orchard Rd Box 234 Riva MD 21140 Office: Richard C Goodwin Atty 59 Franklin St Annapolis MD 21401

DARRAH, KATHERINE SIMPSON, foundation executive; b. L.A., 1937; d. Robert O. and Ida (Bell) Simpson; m. Jack Lee Darrah (dec.); children: James E., Susan Lynn Keating. Student, Spokane Community Coll., 1983-89. Bank teller, 1975-76; with J.C. Penny, 1980, Key-Tronics, 1987-88, Westco Corp., 1988—; charter founder Ronald Reagan Rep. Ctr., Washington; mem. Presdl. Task Force, Washington, 1989—. Designer infant car seat program, 1981. Vol. Lilac Festival Parade Com., Spokane, Wash., 1981-89, Spokane Inland N.W. Community Found., 1966-88; bd. dirs. Carta, Spokane, 1982-86; sustaining mem. Rep. Nat. Com., 1987—, presiding mem. 1990; past mem. Manito Presbyn. Ch. Recipient Medal of Merit, Pres. Bush, 1990. Mem. Nat. Law Enforcement Ofcls., NAFE, Smithsonian Assocs., Moose, Order of Eastern Star, Rainbow Broad. Presbyterian. Home: E 1940 Tilsley Pl 7 Spokane WA 99207

DARRELL, EVELYN BOYDEN, psychologist, educator; b. Spring Lake, N.J.; d. John and Ethel (Notis) Boyden; m. Thomas E. Darrell, Sept. 4, 1954 (div. Oct. 1972); 1 child, Michele Ann (dec.). AB, NYU, 1959, MA, PhD, 1961; hon. degree, Hamilton State Coll., 1970. Lic. psychologist, N.Y., N.J.; cert. tchr. psychology, N.J. Supr. testing Testing and Advisement Ctr., NYU, 1960-63, psychometrist, 1960-61; intern psychologist Bellevue Psychiat. Hosp., 1963-64; teaching asst. psychology dept. Grad. Sch. Edn. NYU, 1964-65; clin. psychologist charge adolescent girls svc. Bellvue Hosp., 1964—; rsch. assoc. charge testing NYU, 1966—; supervising clin. psychologist, clin. instr. dept. psychiatry NYU Med. Sch., 1968—; clin. therapist, cons. St. Barnabas House, N.Y.C., 1974-75; cons. N.Y. State Office Vocat. Rehab., 1980-82, N.Y. Med. Coll.-Cornell U.; mem. child placement rev. bd. Superior Ct. N.J., 1981—. Contbr. articles to profl. jours. Del. Cen. Labor Coun., Dist. Coun. 37 AFL-CIO, mem. exec. bd. city psychologists local; bd. dirs. Montclair-N. Essex YWCA, 1973-88. Recipient Role Model award Coalition of 100 Black Women N.J., 1983, Cert. of Merit Superior Ct. Essex County, 1984. Mem. NAACP (sec. 1955-56, bicentennial chair 1963, Am. Psychol. Assn., Assn. Black Psyhcologists (treas. N.J. chpt. 1967-70), Iota Phi Lambda (pres. Phi chpt. 1966-69, Ea. region journalist 1972-74). Presbyterian. Home: 36 Hawthorne Pl Montclair NJ 07042 Office: NYU Bellevue Med Ctr 1st Ave and 27th St New York NY 10016

DARROW, KATHERINE PRAGER, lawyer, publishing executive; b. Chgo., Dec. 26, 1943; d. Frank D. and Herta Prager; m. Peter H. Darrow, June 29, 1968; children: Alexander, Jessica, James. AB, U. Chgo., 1965; JD, Columbia U., 1969. Bar: N.Y. 1970. Assoc. N.Y. Times Co., N.Y.C., 1968, staff atty., 1970-71, 73-76, asst. gen. atty., 1976-80, gen. atty., 1980-81, gen. counsel, from 1981, v.p., from 1988, now v.p. broadcasting, info. svcs. and corp. devel.; assoc. Gottesman, Evans & Van Merkeanstein, 1971-73. Trustee U. Chgo., from 1982. Mem. ABA, Am. Newspaper Pubs. Assn. (mem. press/bar rels. com.), ABA/Am. Newspaper Pubs. Assn. Joint Task Force, Assn. of Bar of City of N.Y. Office: NY Times Co 229 W 43d St New York NY 10036*

DARSEY, BETTY JEAN, health facility administrator; b. Rayville, La., Apr. 21, 1931; d. Josie Waldo Darsey and Effie Mae Rogers. BS, La. Tech. U., 1952. Med. lab. technologist E.A. Conway Meml. Hosp., Monroe, La., Arcadia, La.; supr.-coord. Green Clinic-Phy-Cor, Inc., Ruston, La. Recipient Green Clinic Administrator and Med. Dir.'s award, 1986. Fellow Am. Med. Technologists, Am. Coll. Med. Technologists; mem. Nat. Cert. Agy. for Lab. Personnel (clin. lab. scientist), Am. Soc. Med. Technologists (mem. technologist), NAFE, La. Sheriffs Assn. (hon. mem.). Home: 501 Second St PO Box 9712 Arcadia LA 71001

DARTING, EDITH ANNE, pharmaceutical company executive; b. Hillsboro, Kans., Jan. 1, 1945; d. Sammuel E. and Carrie (Swehla) Jewett; m. John Ronald Darting, Aug. 8, 1979; children—Theresa Michelle, Lloyd L. Grad., Emporia State Tchrs. Coll., 1963-65. Materials insp. Sterling Drug Inc., McPherson, Kans., 1977-78, auditor, 1978-82, coordinator, 1982—. Mem. Nat. Assn. Female Execs., Am. Soc. Quality Control. Republican. Methodist. Home: 320 N Birch St Hillsboro KS 67063 Office: Sterling Drug Inc Box 1048 McPherson KS 67460

DARWIN, REBECCA WESSON, magazine publishing executive; b. Chattanooga, July 5, 1953; d. William Hinton and Louise Christine (Yeattes) Wesson; m. Cress Darwin, May 24, 1980. BA, U. N.C., 1975; A of Occupational Studies, Tobe-Coburn Sch. for Fashion Careers, N.Y.C., 1977. Dir. mktg. GQ Mag., N.Y.C., 1977-85; corp. mktg. dir. The New Yorker Mag., N.Y.C., 1985-86, v.p., assoc. pub., 1986-87, v.p., pub., 1988; pub. Woman mag., 1988—. Mem. Advt. Women of N.Y., The Fashion Group. Presbyterian. Home: 110 W 86th St #10E New York NY 10024 Office: Woman Mag 360 Madison Ave New York NY 10017

DAS, MANJUSRI, biochemist; b. Bengal, India, Dec. 27, 1946; came to U.S., 1974; d. Kshirode Behari Das and Kamala Dutta; Ph.D., Christian Med. Coll. Hosp., Vellore, India, 1974; m. Subal Bishayee, July 23, 1975. Research asso. Albert Einstein Coll. Medicine, Bronx, N.Y., 1974-76; postdoctoral asso. Molecular Biology Inst., UCLA, 1976-78; asst. prof. biochemistry and biophysics U. Pa. Sch. Medicine, Phila., 1978-84, assoc. prof., 1984-88, prof., 1988—. NIH Research Career Devel. awardee, 1980-84; NIH research grantee, 1979—. Fellow AAAS; mem. Am. Soc. Biol. Chemists, Am. Soc. Cell Biology, N.Y. Acad. Scis., Sigma Xi. Contbr. articles to profl. jours. Office: U Pa Dept Biochemistry and Biophysics Philadelphia PA 19104-6059

DASH, TRACY, marketing professional; b. Glendale, Calif., Jan. 18, 1958; d. Gerald B. MacDonald and Marilyn Lawler; m. Mark Dash, June 22, 1986; children: Lauren, Kelsey. Student, Calif. State U., Northridge. V.p. grocery sales Billings-Horn, Cerritos, Calif. Mem. NAFE. Republican. Jewish. Home: 6255 Sunset Blvd #2100 Hollywood CA 90078 Office: Billings-Horn 13030 Alondra Blvd Cerritos CA 90701

DATA, JOANN LUCILLE, pharmaceutical company executive, physician; b. N.Y.C., Apr. 20, 1944; d. John Batiste and Grace Emma (Karr) D.; m. Herman Aquilla Cantrell, Nov. 13, 1976. BS with highest honors, Purdue U., 1966; MD, Washington U., 1970; PhD, Vanderbilt U., 1977. Intern SUNY, Buffalo, 1970-71, resident, 1971-73; fellow div. Clin. Pharmacology Vanderbilt U., Nashville, 1973-75, instr. medicine/pharmacology, 1975-76; clin. research physician Bronson Clin. Investigational Unit Upjohn Co., Kalamazoo, 1976-80; med./teaching staff Southwestern Mich. Area Health Edn. Ctr., Bronson Meth. Hosp., Kalamazoo, 1976-80; asst. clin. prof. Dept. Medicine Mich. State U., East Lansing, 1978-80; sr. clin. research scientist I Burroughs Wellcome Co., Research Triangle Park, N.C., 1980-82; adj. asst. prof. pharmacology Duke U. Med. Ctr., Durham, N.C., 1982—; dir. Dept. Clin. Pharmacology Hoffmann-LaRoche, Inc., Nutley, N.J., 1982-85, v.p., dir. clin. rsch. and devel., 1985-89, v.p., dir. clin. rsch., 1989—; adj. asst. prof. pharmacology, medicine Cornell U., N.Y.C., 1987—; lectr. in field; conductor seminars in field. Contbr. articles to profl. jours. Trustee, chmn. bd. dirs. N.J. Organ and Tissue Sharing Network Inc., 1987-89, bd. dirs., 1989—. Mortar Bd. scholar, 1966. Mem. AMA, Am. Soc. Pharmacology and Exptl. Therapeutics, Am. Fedn. Clin. Rsch., Am. Med. Women's Assn., Am. Soc. Clin. Pharmacology and Therapeutics (v.p. 1988-90). Republican. Office: The Upjohn Co Bldg 24-1 Kalamazoo MI 49001

DATE, ELAINE S., physician; b. San Jose, Calif., Feb. 19, 1957. BS, Stanford U., 1978; MD, Med. Coll. Pa., 1982. Diplomate of Nat. Bd. Med. Examainers. Diplomate Am. Bd. Phys. Medicine and Rehab. Dir. phys. medicine and rehab. Stanford (Calif.) U. Sch. Medicine, 1985-88, rehab. medicine sect. chief, 1988—; rehab. medicine chief Palo Alto (Calif.) VA Med. Ctr., 1988—. Fellow Am. Acad. Phys. Medicine and Rehab., Am. Assn. Electromyography & Electrodiagnosis. Office: VA Med Ctr 3801 Miranda Ave Palo Alto CA 94304

DATRI, TAMARA JO, systems analyst and designer; b. New Kensington, Pa., Nov. 23, 1960; d. Frank T. and Esther L. (Summers) D. BS in Math., Computer Sci., Slippery Rock State Coll., 1982; MS in Info. Sci., U. Pitts., 1988; postgrad., 1989—. Programmer, statis. clk. Allegheny Ludlum Steel Corp., Brackenridge, Pa., 1983-87, programmer "A", 1987-88, systems programmer, 1988-89, project leader, systems programmer, 1989-90, systems analyst, 1990—. Systems cons. Mt. St. Peter Ch., New Kensington, 1985—. Roman Catholic. Office: Allegheny Ludlum Steel Corp 130 Lincoln Ave Vandergrift PA 15690

DAUBENAS, JEAN DOROTHY TENBRINCK, librarian; b. N.Y.C., Apr. 4; d. Eduard J.A. and Margaret Dorothy (Schaffner) Tenbrinck; m. Joseph Anthony Daubenas, May 29, 1965. AB, Barnard Coll., 1962; grad. Am. Acad. Dramatic Arts, 1963; MA, N.Y. U., 1965; MLS, U. Ariz., 1972; PhD, U. Utah, 1986. Tchr., Beth Jacob Tchrs. Sem. Am., Bronx, 1965-66; caseworker, Dept. Social Services, N.Y.C., 1966-67; actress Boothbay (Maine) Playhouse, others, 1967-70; reference librarian Ariz. State U., Tempe, 1972-75; asst. librarian, asst. prof. library sci. Avila Coll., Kansas City, Mo., 1979-83; assoc. prof./librarian St. John's U., Jamaica, N.Y., 1983—; grad. asst. U. Utah, 1976-77. N.Y. State Regents scholar, 1958-62, U. Ariz. scholar, 1971-72. Mem. ALA, Actors Equity Assn., AAUP, Theatre Libr. Assn., Assn. Theatre in Higher Edn., Beta Phi Mu, Phi Kappa Phi. Roman Catholic. Office: Library St Johns U Grand Central and Utopia Pkwys Jamaica NY 11439

DAUBENSPECK, NORA JANE, teacher; b. Oil City, Pa., May 11, 1950; d. Ralph Clinton and Emily Jeanette (Mehaffey) D. BA, Westminster Coll., 1972. Tchr. 3d grade Warren (Pa.) County Sch. Dist., 1972—; artist in field. Mem. Warren County PTA, 1972—, United Meth. Ch., Warren, 1974, Art League, Warren, 1974—, Friends of the Library Theatre, Warren, 1979, Hospice, Warren, 1988, Act 178 Com., Warren, 1988-89. Mem. Internat. Reading Assn. (Erie coun.), Pa. Soc. Edn. Assn., NEA, Delta Kappa Gamma (recording sec. 1975-78). Republican. Office: Warren CountySchs Jefferson 200 Conewango Ave Warren PA 16365

DAUFIN, EVIE-KAIULANI, journalism educator; b. Jersey City, Mar. 24, 1960; 1 child, Queue D. BA in Theatre Arts and French, Morgan State U., Balt., 1980; cert. completion, Ctr. Overseas Undergrad. Study, Paris, 1978; MA in Mass Communications, Ohio State U., 1985, PhD in Mass Communications, 1985. Prodn. asst. Eyewitness News, Sta. WJZ-TV, Balt., 1976; teaching assoc. Ohio State U., Columbus, 1981-84; rsch. assoc. Ohio Bd. Regents, Columbus, 1984; journalism adviser Xavier U. La., New Orleans, 1985-87; assoc. prof. journalism, advisor journalism program Calif. State U., L.A., 1987—; cons. on pub. rels. Nat. Forest Svc., Portland, Oreg., 1989-90; rsch. asst. Kewalo Basin Marine Mammal Lab., Honolulu, 1989; workshop leader and facilitator; host TV miniseries The Bandung Files, 1988. Author, producer: (ednl. video) The Right Way To Use PC-Write, 1988; contbr. articles, poems and short stories to various publs. Mem. steering com. SW Young Thinking Adults of Unity, L.A., 1989—; vol. Rosa Parks Sexual Assault Ctr., L.A., 1990; workshop facilitator Alcoholism Ctr. for Women, L.A., 1990. Recipient merit award World of Poetry, 1987, 88, Stars of Eagles Spirit award Sisters of African Star, 1988; grantee Calif. State U., L.A., 1987-90, Calif. State U. System, 1990; fellow Poynter Inst., 1988. Mem. Women in Communications (scholar 1988), Assn. for Edn. in Journalism and Mass Communications (grantee 1990), Nat. Assn. Black Journalists, Coll. Media Advisors (minorities co-chmn. 1987—), Sigma Delta Chi-Soc. Profl. Journalism (mentor L.A. 1988-89). Office: Calif State U Communication Studies 5151 State University Dr Los Angeles CA 90032-8113

DAUGHERTY, BETTY JANE, librarian; b. Muncie, Ind., Mar. 6, 1920; d. Clyde E. and Mary E. (Hummer) Shaffer; m. Earl M. Lewis, Feb. 27, 19--, (div. 1963; children: William E., Linda L.; m. Keith L., May 28, 19-- . Student, Ind. Bus. Coll., Muncie, 1939, Ball State U., Muncie, 1974. Dir. of library services Ball Meml. Hosp., Muncie, Ind., 1966-89. Named Woman of the Year Sears Roebuck & Co., 1985-86. Mem. Med. Library Assn., Ind. On Line Users Group, Ind. Health Sci. Library Assn., Midwest Health Sci. Library, Ind. Cooperative Library Services Authority. Republican. Home: 2004 N Maddox Dr Muncie IN 47304 Office: Ball Meml Hosp 2401 University Ave Muncie IN 47303

DAUGHERTY, BETTYE DILLINGHAM, hospital corporation administrator; b. Kingston Spring, Tenn., Oct. 9, 1936; d. Buford W. and Elizabeth (Taylor) Dillingham; m. John B. Daugherty, Sept. 15, 1956 (div. 1982). Student, U. Tenn., 1970-73; cert., Nat. Ctr. Paralegal Tng., Atlanta, 1977; student, Belmont Coll., Nashville, 1989—. Cert. paralegal. Statis. clk. S. Central Bell Telephone Co., Nashville, 1954-67; legal sec. Warfield, Entrekin & Jones, Nashville, 1967-70; asst. to pres. Nashville Bridge Co., 1970-73; paralegal Butler, Tune & Entrekin, Nashville, 1973-77; owner, operator Dillingham Gallery, Nashville, 1977-79; asst. corp. sec., dir. alternative dispute resolution Hosp. Corp. Am., Nashville, 1979—; dir. Southeastern Paralegal Inst., Nashville, 1981—; corp. sec. Trimediation Svcs. Inc., Nashville, 1987—. Bd. dirs., v.p. Rape and Sexual Abuse Ctr., Nashville. Recipient Donald J. MacNaughton award The HCA Found., Nashville, 1988. Mem. Am. Soc. Corp. Secs., Assn. Law Office Adminstrs., ABA (assoc.), LWV (dir., v.p.). Republican. Mem. Ch. of Christ. Office: Hosp Corp Am 1 Park Plaza Nashville TN 37203

DAUGHERTY, JEAN M. (BUNNY DAUGHERTY), educator; b. Louisville, Feb. 5, 1931; d. William S. Daugherty and Marietta (Dugan) Daugherty McDevitt. AB, Ursuline Coll., Louisville, 1953; MA, Ind. U., 1956, Dir.'s degree in Physical Edn., 1960. Tchr., coach Holy Rosary Acad., Louisville, 1949-53; tchr., coach, athletic dir. Loretto High Sch., Louisville, 1953-73, Sacred Heart Acad., Louisville, 1973—; instr., coach Spalding Coll., Louisville, 1971-73. Named Tchr. of Yr., Cath. Schs., Louisville, 1970, 1960's Coach of Yr., State of Ky., 1975-76, Wilson Nation Coach of Field Hockey, 1990. Mem. Nat. Athletic Dirs. Assn., Nat. Coaches Assn., NEA, U.S. Field Hockey Assn., Ky. Coaches Assn. (life), Ky. Athletic Dirs. Assn. Roman Catholic. Home: 4120 Stoneview Dr Apt 4 Louisville KY 40207 Office: Sacred Heart Acad 3175 Lexington Rd Louisville KY 40206

DAUGHTRY, LEAH DENYATTA, political organization worker; b. Bklyn., Aug. 27, 1963; d. Herbert Daniel and Karen Ann (Smith) D. BA, Dartmouth Coll., 1984. Exec. asst. House of the Lord Chs., Bklyn., 1984-85; staff asst. to congressman Edolphus Towns, Washington, 1985, legis. corr., 1985-87, legis. asst., 1987-89; exec. asst. Dem. Nat. Conv. Comm., Washington, 1989—; bd. dirs. Randolph Evans Meml. Found., Bklyn. Trustee House of the Lord Chs., Inc., Bklyn., 1986—. Recipient Marcus Heiman Achievement award Dartmouth Coll., 1983. Mem. Dartmouth Coll. Class of 1984 (treas. Hanover, N.H. chpt. 1989—), Dartmouth Coll. Class Officers Assn. Pentecostal. Home: 808 Fourth St NE Washington DC 20002 Office: Dem Nat Com 430 S Capitol St SE Washington DC 20003

DAUGHTRY, PAMELA, healthcare executive; b. Bklyn., Nov. 7, 1961; d. Lamar and Betty Mildred (Johnson) D. AAS, N.Y.C. Tech. Coll., 1982; BBA, Baruch Coll., 1985. Asst. to v.p. SUNY Health Sci. Ctr., Bklyn., 1985-87, exec. asst. to sr. v.p., 1987—. Kindergarten tchr. Mt. Carmel Bapt. Ch., Bklyn., 1973—; mem. adv. commn. N.Y.C. Tech. Coll., 1987—; active The Recreated Woman. Named to Outstanding Young Women Am., 1987. Mem. NAFE, Coalition of 100 Black Women, Beta Gamma Sigma, Tau Phi Sigma. Democrat. Office: SUNY Health Sci Ctr 450 Clarkson Ave Brooklyn NY 11203

DAUME, DAPHNE MARIE, editor; b. Grand Rapids, Mich., June 17, 1924; d. Selden Bennett and Elizabeth Marie (Hixson) D. BS, Northwestern U., 1945; MA, Columbia U., 1948. Copy editor Ency. Britannica, Chgo., 1948-59, asst. editor, 1959-64, assoc. editor, 1964-73, editor, Book of Yr., 1973—. Bd. dirs. LWV, Chgo., 1970. Mem. Women in Communications, Inc., Coun. on Fgn. Rels. (Chgo.). Democrat. Episcopalian. Home: 1545 W Chase #205 Chicago IL 60626 Office: Ency Britannica 310 S Michigan Ave Chicago IL 60604

DAUN, MARY AGNES, information systems specialist; b. Jersey City, Oct. 9, 1945; d. John Patrick and Juliana Elizabeth (Schaefer) Larney; m. James Archie Curtiss, Oct. 22, 1966 (div. 1976); m. Dennis Emil Daun, Nov. 17, 1979; 1 adopted child, Timothy Curtiss; legal guardian of Jeffrey Anderson; stepchildren: Timothy, Brian, Andrew. BS, East Stroudsburg (Pa.) State Coll., 1966; MS, Cardinal Stritch Coll., 1984. Programmer analyst Am. Motors Corp., Kenosha, Wis., 1966-69, freelance contract programmer, 1969-76, sr. analyst, 1976-77, supr. mgmt. info. systems, 1977-80; mgr. ops. Am. Motors Corp., Milw., 1980-81, mgr. systems programming, 1981-84, mgr. info. systems, 1984-87; dir. corp. info. services Am. Motors Corp., Detroit, 1987; mgr. application systems, svc. part systems Chrysler Motors Corp., Centerline, Mich., 1987-89; mgr. Can. infosytems Chrysler Corp., 1989-90; mgr. fin. procurement and pers. systems Chrysler Motors Corp., Centerldne, Mich., 1990—; instr. math Gateway Tech. Inst., Kenosha, 1975-76. Recipient Silver Knight Mgmt. award Nat. Mgmt. Assn., 1984. Mem. Detroit Women's Econ. Club. Office: Chrysler Motors Corp 25999 Lawrence Ave Centerline MI 48015

DAUS, ANITA DACPANO, dean; b. La Union, Philippines, Jan. 16, 1935; came to U.S., 1967; d. Gabriel R. and Felicidad (Baltazar) Dacpano; m. Cayetano D. Daus, Dec. 18, 1960; children: Patrick, Cliff, Liza. BS in Nursing, Santo Tomas U., Philippines, 1956; MS in Nursing, Wayne State U., 1974; PhD, Mich. State U., 1985. RN, Mich. Instr., nurse Baguio Gen. Hosp., Philippines, 1956-67; instr. Hurley Sch. Nursing, Flint, Mich., 1967-72; mem. faculty Mott Community Coll., Flint, 1974-79; div. chair Mott Community Coll., 1979-88, dean, 1988—. Mem., Nat. Coun. State Bd. Nursing Examination Com., 1986-88; apptd. mem. Mich. Bd. Nursing, 1984-92. Ctr. for Creative Leadership scholar, 1973-74; Helene Fuld Trust grantee, 1987. Mem. Flint Nurses Assn. (Nurse of Yr. award 1987), Toastmasters (Pres. of Yr. award 1987, pres. 1986—). Home: 6467 W Cimarron Tr Flint MI 48504 Office: Mott Community Coll 1401 E Court Rd Flint MI 48502

DAUSER, KIMBERLY ANN, physician assistant; b. Detroit, Nov. 20, 1947; d. George Leonard and Jeanne (Austin) Wilkie; m. Steven Kent Dauser, Nov. 10, 1983; 1 child, Aaron Thomas. AA, Pensacola Jr. Coll., 1971; BS in Medicine, physician's asst. cert. in medicine, U. Ala., Birmingham, 1976; cert. in mgmt., Am. Mgmt. Assn., 1989. Cert. physician's asst. Asst. mgr. Christo's, Gulf Breeze, Fla., 1966-67; teller, bookkeeper loan dept. Bank Gulf Breeze, 1967-72; med. tech. aide USN Hosp., Pensacola, 1972, physician's asst., 1972-73; physician's asst. John Kingsley, MD, Pensacola, 1976, Mountain Comprehensive Health Corp., Whitesburg, Ky., 1976-78; physician's asst. N.W. Fla. Nephrology, Pensacola, 1978, med. adminstr., 1984—; asst. adminstr. Nephrology Ctr. of Pensacola, Fla., 1987-89, med. adminstr., 1989-90; v.p. med. affairs Nephrology Ctr. of Pensacola, 1990—; 1978-89; physician's asst. N.W. Fla. Artificial Kidney Ctr., Pensacola, 1980-87; med. adminstr. Nephrology Ctr. Pensacola, 1987—. Fellow Am. Acad. Physician's Assts. (del. nat. mtg. 1979), Nat. Commn. on Cert. Physician's Assts., Fla. Acad. Physician's Assts. (mem. jud. com. 1979-80), Natural Wildlife Assn. Republican. Roman Catholic. Office: NW Fla Nephrology 1717 North E St Ste 501 Pensacola FL 32501

DAUST, MARY FRANCES, administrative assistant, director; b. Bay City, Mich., May 28, 1964; d. James Earl and Karen Marie (Kotila) D.; m. Philip Leigh Oberst, Feb. 22, 1985 (div. Jan. 1987); 1 child, Jennifer Marie. Student, Davenport Bus. Coll., 1985-86, 87-89. Cert. nurses aide. Payroll clk., sec. Whitehills Healthcare Ctr., Lansing, Mich., 1983-84; adminstrv. asst. Mich. Press Assn., Lansing, 1986-87; office coord. Mich. Pharmacist Assn., Lansing, 1987; exec. sec. Mich. Dairy Assn., Lansing, 1988, 1st Centrum Corp., East Lansing, Mich., 1988-89; exec. asst., dir. membership Mich. Occupational Edn. Assn., Lansing, 1989-90; adminstrv. asst. Mich. Soc. Assn. Execs., Lansing, 1990—. Tutor Capital Area Literacy Coalition, Lansing, 1990—. Mem. Profl. Secs. Internat. (fin. dir. 1990—), NAFE. Democrat. Roman Catholic. Home: 6138 Hermandad East Lansing MI 48823 Office: Michigan Soc Assn Execs 523 W Ionia Lansing MI 58933

DAVANCAZE, ROSALIE KATHERINE, computer executive; b. San Francisco, Sept. 11, 1964; d. Joseph John and Marlene Ann (Olmo) D. BSBA, San Francisco State U., 1986; AA in Bus., San Francisco City Coll., 1984. Computer operator trainee PLM Railcar Maintenance, San Francisco, 1985-86; data processing coord. Fist Deposit Nat. Bank, San Francisco, 1986-87, Pacific Stock Exch., San Francisco, 1987-90; computer adminstr. PacTel Properties, San Francisco, 1990—. Roman Catholic. Home: 673 15th Ave San Francisco CA 94118 Office: PacTel Properties 111 Pine St Ste 1700 San Francisco CA 94111

DAVENPORT, ANN ADELE MAYFIELD, college official; b. New Orleans, Nov. 12, 1941; d. Henry Louis and Myrtie Iola (Cason) Mayfield; m. John Wayne, June 18, 1966; children: Steven Lyle, Daniel Ryan, Elaine Adele. BA, Southeasten La. Coll., 1963; MA in Edn., George Peabody C., 1965; MA in Sociology, Tex. Tech. U., 1971. Tchr. various schs., 1963-70; instr. of sociology Tex. Tech. U., Lubbock, 1970-74, James Madison U., Harrisonburg, Va., 1981-82, Ga. So. Coll., Statesboro; 5th grade tchr. Bulloch county Schs., Statesboro, Ga., 1985-87; gerontology project coord. Dept. of Nursing Ga. So. Coll., 1987-88; project dir. Sr. Campanion Program Ctr. for Rural Health Ga. Southern U., Statesboro, 1988—. Bd. dirs. Citizens Against Violence, Statesboro, 1987-88, Ogeechee Home Health Agy., 1989—, Habitat for Humanity, 1990—; pres. Coun. on Children and Parents, Statesboro, 1988-89; mem. steering com. Bulloch County Commn. on Human Svcs., 1989—. Mem. Ga. Rural Health Assn. (sec. 1988-89, editor state newsletter 1989—), So. Sociol. Soc., Ga. Gerontol. Assn., Ga. Sociol. Assn., AAUW (newsletter editor Statesboro 1987-89), Am. Soc. on Aging. Home: 1 Greenwood Ave Statesboro GA 30458 Office: Ga So U GSC Area Sr Companion Program Ctr Rural Health Ga Statesboro GA 30458

DAVENPORT, BETTY JOAN, communications specialist; b. Boise, Idaho, Sept. 26, 1954; d. Delmer Clyde and Mary Elizabeth (Petrie) D.; children: Phillip, Steven, Laura. Grad. high sch., Henderson, Nev. With social svcs. dept. Econ. Opportunity Bd., Las Vegas, Nev., 1974-76; communications specialist Met. Police Dept., Las Vegas, 1981—. Contbr. poetry to various publs. Mem. Writer's Group Nev. (co-founder).

DAVENPORT, PAMELA BEAVER, rancher, small business owner; b. Big Spring, Tex., Nov. 18, 1948; d. Frank Jones and Doris Glynn (Wills) Beaver; m. Robert Sampson Davenport, Feb. 2, 1982; 1 child, Danielle. BS in mktg. and textiles, Tex. Tech U., 1969, MS, 1970; cert. in spinal orthotics, Northwestern U., 1976. Adminstrv. asst. Tex-Togs, Inc., El Paso, Tex., 1971-75; dir. edn. Camp Internat., Jackson, Mich., 1975-79; realtor Tom Carpenter, Realtor, San Angelo, Tex., 1979-83; retailer Davenport Barber & Beauty, San Angelo, 1985—; rancher Gail, Tex., 1970—. Contr. articles to profl. journals. Vice chmn. San Angelo Recreation Dept. Adv. Bd., 1987—; chmn. adv. bd. Recreation Dept. River Stage, 1989—; chmn. Tom Green Co. Adult Literacy Coun., 1989—; publicity chmn. San Angelo Cultural Affairs Coun., 1986; treas. Angelo Community Hosp. Aux., 1980-82; publicity chmn. Christmas at Old Fort Condio, 1986; mem. Leadership San Angelo. Mem. AAUW (cultural chmn. Tex. bd. 1988—, pres. 1986-88, chmn. conv. 1984-86). Methodist. Home: 3234 Palo Duro Dr San Angelo TX 76904 Office: Davenport Barber & Beauty Supplies 22 W Twobig San Angelo TX 76901

DAVENPORT, PATRICIA JENNINGS, business analyst; b. Richmond, Va., Nov. 29, 1959; d. Alvin Pritchett and JoAllen (Baptist) Jennings; m. Raymond William Davenport, Oct. 5, 1985. BS, James Madison U., 1982; MBA, Marymount U., 1986. System analyst Computing Analysis Corp., Arlington, Va., 1983-84; system analyst Am. Mgmt. Systems, Arlington, 1984-86, sr. system analyst, 1990—; tech. contract mgr. Logicon, Inc., Arlington, 1986-88; project mgr. MCI Telecommunications, Arlington, 1988-89; bus. analyst Am. Mgmt. Systems, Arlington, Va., 1990—. Mem. NAFE, Arlington Jaycees (state dir., pres. 1990—). Office: Am Mgmt Systems 1777 N Kent St Arlington VA 22209

DAVEY, JANET CHRISTOPHERSON, state official; b. Salt Lake City, Apr. 18, 1928; d. Alvin Roy and Ada (Stringham) Christopherson; m. Ronald H. Davey, June 14, 1957; children: Carolyn, Christine. BS in English, Brigham Young U., 1949. Sec. to dean Coll. Mines, U. Utah, Salt Lake City, 1949-54, to dean Grad. Sch., 1956-57; legal sec. Romney & Nelson, Salt Lake City, 1967-73; sec. Office Atty. Gen., Salt Lake City, 1973-77; adminstrv. asst. Office Lt. Gov. State of Utah, Salt Lake City, 1977—. Del. voting dist. Salt Lake City Rep. Com. Mem. LDS Ch. Office: Lt Gov's Office 203 State Capitol Bldg Salt Lake City UT 84114

DAVID, CATHERINE ANNE, national account executive; b. N.Y.C., Sept. 18, 1963; d. James Hayes and Patricia Kathleen (Lombard) D. BBA, U. Notre Dame, 1985. Mgr. Irish Gardens Flower Shop, Notre Dame, Ind., 1983-85; sales rep. Gallo Wine Co., L.A., 1985-86; sales trainer Gallo Wine Co., 1986-87, mgr. tng., 1987; mktg. mgr. E.&J. Gallo Winery, Modesto, Calif., 1987-89; systems cons. E&J Gallo Winery, Lisle, Ill., 1989-90, nat. acct. exec., 1990—; mem. adv. coun. Univ. of Notre Dame Coll. of Bus. Adminstrn. Bd. dirs. Notre Dame Club Orange County, Calif., 1986-87. Recipient Rev. Lester E. Collins award, 1985; LILCO Athlete scholar, Little League scholar Plainview Little League, N.Y., 1981. Mem. NAFE, Notre Dame Club Chgo. Roman Catholic. Home: 1624 W Fullerton 3F Chicago IL 60614

DAVID, JUDY BREINER, advertising and promotion consultant, writer, producer; b. Milw., May 26, 1938; d. James Mirko and Fannie (Apple) Breiner; divorced; children—Rod Alan, Donna Lyn. Student Washington U., St. Louis, 1956-58. Dir./producer amateur theatricals Empire Producing Co., Kansas City, Mo., 1959; supr. pub. relations, tours, producer and host interview show Sta. KETC-TV, St. Louis, 1959-60; freelance pub. relations writer, St. Louis, 1966-69; copywriter George Johnson Advt., Inc., St. Louis, 1968, Ridgeway Advt., St. Louis, 1969; copywriter, producer Gardner/Wells, Rich, Greene, Inc., St. Louis, 1970-74; sr. writer, producer McCann-Erickson, Inc., Atlanta, 1974-77; freelance writer, producer, promotions, cons., doing bus. as A Functional Literate, Atlanta, 1977—; judge CLIO Awards, 1982, 84, 86, 87, ADDY Awards, 1980, 81, 83, 84, 86, Hollywood Radio and TV Internat. Broadcast awards, 1984; panelist, lectr. Ga. State U., DeKalb Coll., Portfolio Ctr., various seminars and workshops; amateur performer, cartoonist, comedy writer, product designer. Author: Moonlighter's Guide to Success, 1978. Vol., Atlanta Soc. for Blind, 1975, 76, 77, Ga. Press Assn. Gridiron, 1978, 79, 80, 81, Jewish Vocat. Services, 1982, others; bd. dirs. Camp Fire Boys and Girls, Inc., 1987; mem. communications adv. bd. Atlanta Jewish Fedn., 1985, 86, 87, 88, Interfaith Shelters for Homeless, 1984, 85, 86, 87, 88, 89. Named Top Writer, Atlanta Bus. Chronical Profl. Poll, 1986, hon. mention, 1987, 88, ADWEEK All Am. Creative Team, 1982; recipient Addy awards, 1974, 75, 77, 80-85, Phoenix award, 1974, 75, 76, 78, 81, 82, Andy awards, 1976, 78, 80-83, CLIO, 1975, 81, 85, Maxi award, 1982, 83, Cable Mktg. award, 1983, Telly award, 1985, Hollywood Radio & TV Internat. Broadcast award, 1983, Internat. TV and Radio Festival of N.Y. award, 1985, 88, Silver Microphone awards, 1984, 86, Silver award Health Services Mktg., 1987. Mem. Atlanta Soc. Communication Artists (dir. 1974-75), Art Dirs. Club (bd. dirs. Atlanta chpt. 1986, 87, 88, 89), Portfolio Ctr. (bd. advs. 1986, 87), Women Bus. Owners, High Mus. Soc., Greenpeace, Zool. Soc., Bot. Soc. Address: 1073 Lanier Blvd Atlanta GA 30306

DAVID, MARTHA LENA HUFFAKER, educator, real estate agent; b. Susie, Ky., Feb. 7, 1925; d. Andrew Michael and Nora Marie (Cook) Huffaker; m. William Edward David, June 24, 1952 (div. Jan. 1986); children: Edward Garry, William Andrew, Carolyn Ann, Robert Cook. AB in Music magna cum laude, Georgetown (Ky.) Coll., 1947; postgrad., Vanderbilt U., 1957-58; Spanish cert., Lang. Sch., Costa Rica, 1959; MEd, U. Ga., 1972. Elem. tchr. Wayne County Bd. Edn., Spann, Ky., 1944-45; music tchr. Mason County, Mayslick, Ky., 1947-49, Hikes Grade Sch., Buechel, Ky., 1949-53; English and Spanish tchr. Jefferson (Ga.) High Sch., 1961-63; music and English tchr. Athens (Ga.) Acad., 1967-71; music tchr. Barrow County Bd. Edn., Winder, Ga., 1971-88; real estate agt. South Best Realty, Athens, 1986—; data collector Regional Ednl. Svcs. Agy., Athens and Winder, 19176-78; tchr. music Union Theol. Sem., Buenos Aires, 1957-60. Author: (poems) Parcels of Love, 1980; composer (music plays) The B.B.'s, The Missing Tune, A Dream Come True, The Stars Who Creep Out of Orbit, 1976-86. Active cultural affairs orgns., Athens, 1962—; entertainer nursing homes and civic orgns., Athens, 1962; chmn. cancer drives, heart fund drive United Way, March of Dimes, Athens, 1962—; elder, pianist Christian Ch. Winner regional piano competition Ky. Philharm. Orch., 1946; nominated Tchrs. Hall of Fame, Barrow County, 1981. Mem. Ret. Tchrs. Assn., Writer's Group, Ga. Music Tchrs., Nat. Music Tchrs. Assn., Athens Music Tchrs. Assn. (pres., recital chmn.), Touchdown Club, Band Boosters, Alpha Delta Kappa, Delta Omicron (life, scholar 1944). Republican. Mem. Christian Ch. Home: 1151 Clairmont Pl Watkinsville GA 30677

DAVID, MILDRED, principal; b. Bklyn., Nov. 21, 1935; d. Isaac and Molly (Michelson) Cohen; m. Arthur David, Apr. 29, 1956; children: Miriam David Gray, Jonathan. BA, Bklyn. Coll., 1956; MA, Hofstra U., 1968, profl. diploma, 1972, EdD, 1977. Tchr. Pub. Sch. 139, Bklyn., 1963-65, Franklin Elem. Sch., Hewlett, N.Y., 1965-68; instructional asst. Hewlett-Woodmere Pub. Schs., 1968-72; prin. Hewlett Elem. Sch., 1972—; adj. prof. Hofstra U., Hempstead, N.Y., 1972-78; vis. prof. C.W. Post Coll., Greenvale, N.Y., 1985-88, Adelphi U., Garden City, N.Y., 1989. Mem. Nat. Elem. Prin.'s Assn., Assn. for Supervision and Curriculum Devel., South Shore Adminstrs. Assn., Phi Delta Kappa. Home: 369 Eastwood Rd Woodmere NY 11598 Office: Hewlett Elem Sch Broadway Hewlett NY 11557

DAVID, MIRIAM LANG, physician; b. Chgo., June 8, 1945; d. Gerhard Paul and Elsie Caroline (Reese) Lang; div.; children: Heidi Katherine, Christopher Kent. BS in Nursing, U. Mich., 1967; MS in Pub. Health, U. Mo., 1973; postgrad., U. Md., 1976-77; D of Medicine, U. Ky., 1983. Nursing positions Mo. hosps., 1967-71; instr. nursing Cen. Mo. State U., Fayette, 1973-74; ind. childbirth educator Columbia, Mo., 1973-74; ind. parent educator Lexington, Ky., 1978—; intern Chandler Med. Ctr., Lexington, 1983-84, resident in family practice medicine, 1984-85, resident in occupational medicine, 1987-88; pvt. practice Lexington, 1988—. Co-contbr. articles to profl. publs. Mem. Nat. Conf. of Christians and Jews, Lexington, 1988—; bd. dirs. Ky. div. Am. Cancer Soc., 1988—. Rsch. grantee NIH, Bethesda, Md., 1987. Mem. AMA, Am. Coll. Preventive Medicine, Am. Occupational Med. Assn., Ky. Occupational Med. Assn., U. Mich. Alumni Club of the Bluegrass (bd. dirs. 1983—), Sigma Theta Tau, Alpha Omega Alpha, Alpha Lambda Delta, Phi Kappa Phi, Mortar Board. Lutheran. Home and Office: 3415 Brookhaven Dr Lexington KY 40502

DAVID, THERESA (TERRI DAVID), communications executive; b. Detroit, Feb. 7, 1959; d. George A. and Marie K. D. BA, Mich. State U., 1980; MBA, Grand Valley State U., Allendale, Mich., 1987. Forecasting asst. GTE Mich., Muskegon, 1981; network access asst. GTE Ind., Fort Wayne, 1981-83; primary svcs. analyst GTE North, Inc., Muskegon, 1983-89; sr. adminstr. GTE Telephone Ops., 1989—. Bd. Mem. GTE Tel. Employees Assn., Muskegon, 1985-86, GTE North Community Affairs Team, Muskegon, 1986—; Explorer Post advisor Boy Scouts Am., Grand Rapids, Mich. 1986. Recipient Outstanding Dist. Dir. award Mich. Jaycees-Lansing, 1987, named Outstanding Chpt. Pres., 1989; recipient State Program award U.S. Jaycees, 1988; named Outstanding Young Woman of Am., City of Montgomery (Ala.), 1987, 88, Outstanding State Chmn., Mich. Jaycees, 1988. Mem. NAFE, Am. Mgmt. Assn. Home: 435 Alex Coppell TX 75019

DAVIDOVICH, BELLA, pianist; b. Baku, Azerbaijan, USSR, July 16, 1928; arrived in U.S., 1978; naturalized, 1984; d. Mikhail and Lyusya; m. Yulian Sitkovetsky (dec.); 1 child, Demitri. Studies with C. Igumnov, Y. Flier; grad, Moscow Conservatory, 1951. Mem. faculty Moscow Conservatory, from 1962, Juilliard Sch. Music, N.Y.C., from 1982. Concert pianist touring Russia, Japan, Israel, Europe; performed with Leningrad Philharmonic, 28 seasons; U.S. debut Newport Music Festival, 1979, Carnegie Hall, N.Y.C., 1979; numerous recs. for Philips and Orfeo. Recipient 1st prize Chopin Competition, Warsaw, 1949; named Deserving Artist of USSR. Office: care Columbia Artists Mgmt 165 W 57th St New York NY 10019*

DAVIDSON, ANNE STOWELL, lawyer; b. Rye, N.Y., Feb. 24, 1949; d. Robert Harold and Anne (Breeding) Davidson. B.A. magna cum laude, Smith Coll., 1971; J.D. cum laude, George Washington U., 1974. Bar: D.C. 1975, U.S. Dist. Ct. D.C. 1975, U.S. Ct. Appeals (D.C. cir.) 1975, U.S. Supreme Ct. 1980. Asst. gen. counsel FDA, Rockville, Md., 1974-78; counsel Abbott Labs., North Chicago, Ill., 1978-79; counsel U.S. Pharm. Ops. Schering-Plough Corp., Kenilworth, N.J., 1979-83; sr. counsel Sandoz Pharms. Corp., Inc., East Hanover, N.J., 1983-86, v.p., assoc. gen. counsel, 1987—. Trustee, N.J. Pops Orch. Recipient Dawes Prize Smith Coll., 1971. Mem. ABA, Pharm. Mfrs. Assn., Food and Drug Law Inst., Proprietary Assn. (govt. affairs com.). Republican. Presbyterian. Club: Smith Coll. (pres. 1981-82). Contbr. articles to profl. jours. Office: Sandoz Pharms Corp 59 Rt 10 East Hanover NJ 07936

DAVIDSON, BARBARA TAYLOR, retired real estate agent; b. Ames, Iowa, Jan. 30, 1920; d. Harvey Nelson and Ruby (Britten) Taylor; m. Donald Thomas Davidson Sr., May 22, 1942 (dec. Oct. 1962); children: Donald Thomas Jr., John Taylor, Ann Elizabeth Davidson Costanzo. BS in Home Econs. Sci., Iowa State U., 1943. Assoc. tchr. Ames (Iowa) Pub. Schs., 1970-73; retail mgr. Gen. Nutrition Ctr., Ames, 1974-77; sales assoc. Century 21 Real Estate, Ames, 1978-82, Friedrich Realty, Ames, 1982-89; cons. Delta Zeta Corp.; chmn. adv. bd. Delta Zeta Corp., Ames, 1956-62. Pres. Ames City PTA Council, 1950; leader, advisor Boy Scouts Am., Ames, 1952-58; chmn. Campfire Leaders' Assn., Ames, 1959-61; sec. bd. dirs. Campfire Girls, Ames, 1964-66; property com. United Meth. Ch., Ames, 1964-67; mem. Octagon for the Arts, Brunier Gallery, Med. Ctr. Auxiliary. Mem. Nat. Assn. Realtors, Iowa Assn. Realtors, Nat. Home Econs. in Homemaking (chmn. fgn. student relations com.), Internat. Orch. Assn., Iowa State U. Meml. Union (life), Iowa State U. Alumni Assn. (life). Republican. Home: 1416 Harding Ave Ames IA 50010 Office: Friedrich Realty Sixth at Duff Ave Ames IA 50010

DAVIDSON, DEBORAH, utilities company executive, electrical engineer; b. Nashville, Mar. 23, 1951; d. Tuyl Kenneth and Therese (Hanley) Davidson; m. Gerald Michael Ground, July 14, 1969 (div. 1976); m. Bobby Glenn Pate, Aug. 7, 1978 (div. 1986); foster children: Lorie Ellen Lewis, Randy James Lewis. B.S. in Engring., U. Tenn., 1981. Registered profl. engr., Tenn. Audit cler, Tenn. Dept. Rev., Nashville, 1974-75; account clk. Blair, Follen, Allen, & Walker, Nashville, 1975-76; freelance wallpaper hanger, decorator, Nashville, 1976-81; materials engr. Nashville Electric Service, 1982-87, asst. mgr. purchasing, stores, 1987—. Recipient Andrew Holt scholarship U. Tenn. Alumnae, 1976-81. Mem. Internat. Assn. Quality Circle, (leader), Mensa. Republican. Roman Catholic. Club: Toastmasters Internat. Avocations: horticulture; needlework; bluegrass music. Home: 106 Jackstaff Dr Hendersonville TN 37075 Office: Nashville Electric Service 1214 Church St Nashville TN 37203

DAVIDSON, GRACE EVELYN, nursing administrator, educator; b. Wabash, Ind., Aug. 2, 1920; d. William Alexander and Jennie Lavinia (Baker) Davidson. Diploma, Columbia Presbyn. Sch. Nursing, 1942; BS, U. Minn., 1948; MA in Teaching, Columbia U., 1954, postgrad. 1961, 63-64. Instr. Sch. Nursing, Columbia U., N.Y.C., 1948-51; assoc. prof. Skidmore Coll., Saratoga Springs, N.Y., 1954-66; asst. adminstr., dir. nursing Univ. Hosp., NYU Med. Ctr., 1966-79, assoc. prof., 1977-79, prof. 1979—; cons. nursing svc. adminstrn., N.Y.C., 1980—. Contbr. articles to profl. jours. With to maj. Army Nurse Corps, 1943-46, World War II, 51-53, Korea, Res., 53-60, Ret. Recipient Alumni Fedn. medal Columbia U., 1981, Plaque for leadership in nursing NYU Med. Ctr., 1983. Mem. Nursing Edn. Alumnae Assn. Tchrs. Coll. Columbia U. (achievement award 1977), Am. Nurses Assn., Nat. League Nursing, Soc. Nursing History Coun., Columbia U.-Presbyn. Hosp. Sch. Nursing Alumnae Assn. (pres. 1970-76, edn. bd. 1985—, Disting. Alumnae award 1981), Fedn. Alumni Assn. Columbia U., Ret. Officers Assn., Women Club of Dumont. Republican. Presbyterian. Home: 67 Chestnut St Dumont NJ 07628

DAVIDSON, HONEY IRIS, account executive; b. Queens, N.Y., May 18, 1959; d. Leslie Martin and Paula Gloria (Katzman) D. BA in Communications, Glassboro State (N.J.) Coll., 1981. Promotion asst. Family Media, Inc., N.Y.C., 1983; asst. dept. mgr. Hahne's Dept. Store, Livingston, N.J., 1981-82; asst. promotion mgr. Home mag., N.Y.C., 1983-86; collectors club adminstr. Royal Doulton Internat., Somerset, N.J., 1986-87; product mgr. DMS, Inc., Greenwich, Conn., 1986-87; account exec. Merritt Group, Inc., Norwalk, Conn., 1988—. Mem. Advt. Club N.Y. Home: 87 Glenbrook Rd #6B Stamford CT 06902

DAVIDSON, JILL ELAINE, ballet dancer; b. Hollywood, Fla., Sept. 1, 1962; d. Arnold Simon and Cora Lee (Killian) D. Grad. high sch., Marlton, N.J., 1980; student, Fred Astaire Dance Studios, N.Y.C., 1987-90. Dancer Boston Ballet Ensemble, 1980-81; dancer Joffrey II Dancers, N.Y.C., 1981-82, Joffrey Ballet, N.Y.C., 1982-90, Oreg. Ballet Theater, Portland, 1990—. Office: Oreg Ballet Theatre 1119 SW Park Ave Portland OR 97205-2445

DAVIDSON, JULI, medical word processor, artist; b. Houston, Aug. 23, 1960; d. Martin J. Davidson and Ruth Carol Rosenberg. Diploma, Park Sch., Brooklandville, Md., 1978; Cert., Richmond Coll., Surrey, Eng., 1981; student, Austin Coll., U. N.Mex, others, 1978-84. Cert. med. terminology and transcription, 1981. Mail order owner, artist Surrenderings, Albuquerque; owner, artist Juli Davidson Studio Gallery, Albuquerque, 1987-89; freelance writer, editor, photographer Albuquerque, 1985-89; word processor Lovelace Med. Ctr., Albuquerque. Contbr. articles to profl. jours. Co-sec. Zuni Smokefree Club, Albuquerque, 1990. Recipient 2d and 3d place photography awards, Churches, N.Mex. exhibit, 4th place Colorfest Human Interest Category, Colo. Mem. Am. Med. Record Assn., Albuquerque Art Bus. Assn. (exec. adminstr. 1989), Albuquerque United Artists (bd. dirs., sec.), Wingspread Collector's Guide, NAFE. Home: PO Box 21 669 Surrenderings Albuquerque NM 87154

DAVIDSON, KAREN SUE, computer software designer; b. Chgo., July 24, 1950; d. Woodrow Wilson and Velma Louise (Dickinson) D. BS in Communications, U. Ill., 1972; MBA, De Paul U., 1977. News producer Sta. WIND, Westinghouse Broadcasting Co., Chgo., 1973-75; mktg. rep. div. data processing IBM, Chgo., 1977-80, process industry specialist, 1980; industry applications specialist IBM, White Plains, N.Y., 1981-83; sr. sales rep. Wang Labs., Chgo., 1983-84; ptnr. KDA-K Davidson & Assocs., Centralia, Ill., 1984—; pres. KDA Software Inc., Centralia, 1988—; cons. desktop pub. Greater Centralia C. of C., 1987-88. Author/designer software programs; contbr. articles to profl. pubs. State of Ill. Small Bus. Adv. Bd., Internat. Trade/ Export Rep., 1990. Named Outstanding Working Woman of Ill. Fedn. Bus. & Profl. Women's Clubs, 1990. Mem. Soc. Profl. Journalists, Ind. Computer Cons. Assn., Ill. Software Assn., Chgo. High Tech. Assn. Assn. St. Louis Info. Systems Trainers (v.p. 1988), Centralia Cultural Soc., Inventors' Assn. St. Louis, Greater Centralia C. of C. (bd. dirs. 1990-93, good will amb. 1990), Rotary, Zeta Tau Alpha. Democrat. Methodist. Office: KDA Software Inc 315 E Third St PO Box 1163 Centralia IL 62801

DAVIDSON, LACINDA SUSAN, materials engineer, chemist; b. Terre Haute, Ind., Jan. 6, 1958; d. John Robert and Patricia Ann (Ophoff) Spencer; m. James Robert Davidson, Dec. 28, 1982. BS, Eastern Ill. U., 1980. Chem. tchr. Peoria (Ill.) High Sch., 1980-81, Metamora (Ill.) Twp. High Sch., 1981-82, Suffolk Hills High Sch., Tucson, Ariz., 1982-83, Walden Sch., Anaheim, Calif., 1983-84; engr. Rohr Industries, Riverside, Calif., 1987-88, McDonnell-Douglas Aircraft Corp., Mesa, Ariz., 1985 --. Mem. NAFE, Am. Electroplaters and Surface Finishers Soc., Soc. Advancement of Materials and Process Engrs. Republican. Roman Catholic. Office: McDonnell Douglas 5000 E McDowell Dept 7219 M/S 403-G46 Mesa AZ 85205

DAVIDSON, M. BERNICE, secretarial service executive; b. Pickering, Ontario, Canada, July 7, 1935; d. George Franklin and Annie Muriel (Dunn) Duncan; m. Frederick William DeCaire, May 23, 1953 (div. 1982); children: Lance, Rhonda, Dale, Annette. Grad. high sch., Pickering, Ont., Canada. Personnel asst. McCulloch of Canada Ltd., Toronto, Ont., 1965-70; personnel supr. Zellers Inc., Sarnia, Ont., 1970-74; adminstrv. asst. Des Parker Town Planner, Prince George, B.C., Canada, 1974-75; v.p. Beneath the Sea, Revelstoke, B.C., 1975-80; v.p. Tri-C Secretarial Services Inc., Vancouver, B.C., 1980-84, pres., 1984—. Gov. YMCA, Vancouver, B.C., 1986—. Mem. Sales and Mktg. Execs., (exec. dir. 1984—), Western Bus. Women's Assoc., Nat. Assoc Secretarial Services, Canadian Office Services Assoc. United Church. Club: Canadian (Vancouver) (sec. 1982—). Office: Tri-C Secretarial Services, 1250 Homer St, Vancouver, BC Canada V6B2Y5

DAVIDSON, MARCELLA SCHOOLS, food products executive; b. St. Petersburg, Fla., Mar. 27, 1952; d. James Askew and Elizabeth Marie (Preston) Schools; divorced; children: James Matthew, Ashley Elizabeth. BS, Va. Poly. Inst., 1974. Dir. compliance and quality Eberwine Bros., Inc., Suffolk, Va., 1974-76; supr. quality control Planters Nuts, Suffolk, 1976-78, mgr. packaging specifications div., 1978-79, mgr. audits div., 1979-81, mgr. material evaluation div., 1981; mgr. quality assurance and environ. affairs Hershey Chocolate Co., Stuarts Draft, Va., 1981-87; asst. to v.p. mfg. Luden's div. Hershey (Pa.) Chocolate Co., 1987-89; mgr. mfg. H.B. Reese div. Hershey Chocolate USA, 1989-90, plant mgr., 1990—; mem. food sci. adv. com. U. Ill., 1989—; mem. strategy com. Va. Poly. Inst., 1989. Bd. dirs., 2d v.p. Jr. Achievement Waynesboro (Va.)/Augusta County, 1982-87; mem. Shenandoah River Basin Com., 1985-87, Future Agr. Study, Va., 1986-87; bd. dirs. Hershey Youth Football Assn., 1988—. Recipient Disting. Svc. award of merit Gamma Sigma Delta, 1985, Disting. Alumni award dept. food sci. and tech. Va. Poly. Inst., 1988. Mem. Inst. Food Technologists, Va. Food Processors Assn. (bd. dirs., pres. 1980-81), Am. Soc. Quality Control, Cen. Atlantic States Assn. Food and Drug Ofcls. (assoc. membership chmn.), Va. Mfg. Assn. (environ. affairs com. 1983-87), Va. Poly. Inst. Agr. Alumni Orgn. (bd. dirs. 1980-87, 88—, v.p. 1982-83, pres. 1983-84), Nat. Agr. Alumni and Devel. Assn. (bd. dirs. 1985—, sec.-treas. 1990—). Office: H B Reese Candy Co Rt 422 W Hershey PA 17033

DAVIDSON, MARIE DIANE, publisher; b. Los Angeles, Mar. 6, 1924; d. Charles Casper and Stella Ruth (Bateman) Winnia; divorced, 1953; children: David William, Ronald Mark. AB, U. Calif., Berkeley, 1943; MA, Calif. State U., Sacramento, 1959. cert. secondary tchr., 1944. Tchr. Campbell (Calif.) High Sch., 1944-45; actress Pasadena (Calif.) Playhouse, 1945, U.S.O. Camp Shows, N.Y.C., 1946-47, El Camino High Sch., Sacramento, 1954-85; publisher, editor Swan Books, Fair Oaks, Calif., 1979—; actress, cons. Valley Inst. TV Assn, Sacramento, 1971; writer Crown Pubs., N.Y.C., 1969. Author: Feversham, 1969; illustrator, editor (book series) Shakespeare on Stage, 1979, Shakespeare for Young People, 1986. Mem. Author's Guild, Calif. Writer's Club, NEA, Calif. Tchrs. Assn., Pi Lambda Theta, Phi Beta Kappa. Democrat. Episcopalian. Office: Swan Books PO Box 2498 Fair Oaks CA 95628

DAVIDSON, MARY FRANCES LOGUE, protective services official; b. Balt., Aug. 26, 1958; d. Thomas Hemler and Ruth Marie (Zulauf) Logue; m. James D. Davidson, Oct. 7, 1984; 1 child, Chelsea Estelle; stepchildren: Heather, Dax. BA, U. Md., 1980; cert. European Criminal Justice, U. Copenhagen, 1979. Spl. agt. U.S. Secret Svc., Balt., 1980—; instr. USSS-MCI Computer System U.S. Secret Svc., L.A., 1984-86. Leader Girl Scouts U.S., Hacienda Heights, Calif., 1986-87; foster mother Chino Hills, Calif., 1986-87. Mem. NAFE. Republican. Office: US Secret Svc US Courthouse Rm 7100 101 W Lombard St Baltimore MD 21201

DAVIE, AUDREY NELSENE, financial analyst; b. Moscow, Idaho, Jan. 30, 1961; d. Dale Everette Davie and Holly Jean (McCown) Miles. BSBA, Coll. of Gt. Falls, Mont., 1986. Asst. mgr. Pied Piper, Inc., Idaho Falls, Idaho, 1987-89; fin. analyst Rockwell-INEL, Idaho Falls, 1989—. Advisor Jr. Achievement Bonniville County, Idaho Falls, 1989-90. Mem. AAUW (treas. Idaho Falls br. 1989-90, pres. 1990-91), Kappa Pi Lambda. Office: Rockwell-INEL PO Box 1469 MS 0110 Idaho Falls ID 83403

DAVIES, CATHERINE THERESE, sales professional, industrial engineer; b. Mankato, Minn., Oct. 21, 1955; d. George William Jr. and Dorothy Cecelia (Novotny) D.; m. Olav Nevin Johnson, Apr. 21, 1979 (div. Mar. 1987). BA, Coll. of St. Catherine, St. Paul, 1977; MBA, Western New Eng. Coll., Springfield, Mass., 1988. Substitute tchr. Mpls. Pub. Schs., 1977; engring. technologist magnetic audio video products 3M Co., Hutchinson, Minn., 1977-80, advanced indsl. engr., 1980-81; advanced mfg. engr. staff mfg. div. 3M Co., St. Paul, 1981-84; advanced process and indsl. engr. Dynacolor div. 3M Co., Springfield, 1984-85, sr. engr., maintenance supr., 1985-86, account rep., 1986-87; tech. sales rep. printing and pub. systems div. 3M Co., Atlanta, 1987—. Contbr. articles to various publs. Named state champion Wool Producers N.Y., 1986. Mem. Inst. Indsl. Engrs., Mensa, Women on Wheels (bd. dirs. Atlanta chpt. 1988-89, Ga. bd. dirs. 1989-80, Most Active Mem. award Atlanta chpt. 1989, High Miles award 1989), Pi Mu Epsilon. Lutheran. Home: 125 Amethyst Cove Alpharetta GA 30201 Office: 3M Co 2860 Bankers Industrial Dr Atlanta GA 30360

DAVIES, JANE B(ADGER) (MRS. LYN DAVIES), architectural historian; b. Amboy, Ill., Sept. 9, 1913; d. Henry Harold and Clara May (Heermans) Badger; m. Lyn Davies, July 18, 1942. BA, Wellesley Coll., 1935; MA, Columbia U., 1942, BS in L.S. with high honors, 1944; postgrad., U. Mich., 1936, U. Wis., 1937, 38. Tchr. Monticello Prep. Sch., Godfrey, Ill., 1935-37, Kent Sch. Girls, Denver, 1937-41; reference libr. Columbia Univ. Librs., 1944-50, rare book cataloger, 1951-77; cons. Nat. Trust for Hist. Preservation, 1965, 87-88, Smithsonian Inst., 1967, Greensboro (N.C.) Preservation Soc., 1967-70, Historic Green Springs, 1970-73, 82, Llewellyn Park Hist. Dist., 1982-84, Hist. Hudson Valley , 1986-88; guest curator, author catalog A.J. Davis and Am. Classicism, Fed. Hall Mus., N.Y.C., 1989; lectr. on Am. archtl. history. Author: intro. Houston Mus. Fine Arts: The Gothic Revival Style in America, 1830-1870, 1976; Alexander Jackson Davis; Rural Residences (1837), 1980; editorial asst. Jour. Soc. Archtl. Historians, 1964-65; contbr. articles on Am. archtl. history to mags., jours. and reference books. Am. Coun. Learned Socs. grantee, 1970, Am. Philos. Soc. grantee, 1970-71; NEH fellow, 1978. Mem. Soc. Archtl. Historians (sec.-treas. N.Y. chpt. 1959-67), Victorian Soc. Am. (adv. com. 1966-76), Nat. Trust Historic Preservation, Friends of Lyndhurst, N.Y. Hist. Soc., Preservation League N.Y. State, Greensboro Preservation Soc. (hon.), Phi Beta Kappa, Beta Phi Mu. Presbyterian. Home: 549 W 123d St New York NY 10027

DAVIES, S. CONNALLY, bank marketing consultant; b. Chattanooga, Sept. 12, 1961; d. Richard Blair and Janet (Keese) D. BA with high distinction, U. Va., 1983. Mgmt. trainee S.C. Nat. Bank, Columbia, 1983-84, merger specialist, 1984; dir. mktg. William Puryear & Co., Nashville, 1984-85; project coord. FISI-Madison Fin. Corp. (formerly Madison Fin. Corp.), Nashville, 1985-86, mgr. product adminstrn., 1986-88, mgr. product support, 1988-89; v.p., nat. accounts exec. FISI-Madison Fin. Corp. (formerly Madison Fin. Corp), Nashville, 1989-90, v.p. new product devel., 1990—. Office: FISI-Madison Fin Corp Box 40726 Nashville TN 37204

DAVIES, VONDA SINES, financial analyst; b. Findlay, Ohio, Nov. 30, 1947; d. Harold Lawrence and Lucille Evelyn (Marquart) Sines; m. John Severy Davies, Jr., Feb. 11, 1978, (div. 1984); 1 child, Elizabeth Anne. BS in Journalism, Northwestern U., Evanston, Ill., 1970. Editorial, advt. positions various, 1970-85; contract cost analyst Mil. Traffic Mgmt. Command, Falls Church, Va., 1985—; pres. Chicagoland Women's Fed. Credit Union, Chgo., 1977-78. Contbr. articles to Family Circle mag., newspaper. Vice-pres. Nat. Found. for Ileitis and Colitis. Recipient Marathon Oil Scholarship, Finlay, Ohio, 1966-70, Scripps-Howard Journalism Grants, Cin., 1969-70. Mem. Nat. Contract Mgmt. Assn., Women in Communications, Inc., Zeta Tau Alpha. Republican. Episcopalian. Home: 2112 Mager Dr Herndon VA 22070

DAVILA, ELISA, Spanish language & literature teacher; b. Libano, Tolima, Colombia, May 29, 1944; came to U.S., 1974; d. Rafael Antonio Davila and Amalia Parra; m. Bruce Roger Smith, Oct. 17, 1977 (div. 1981). BA, U. Pedagogica Nat., Bogota, Colombia, 1966; MA, U. Pacific, 1972; PhD, U. Calif., Santa Barbara, 1983. Asst. prof. U. Valle, Cali, Colombia, 1968-73; researcher Inst. Colombiano de Pedagogia, Bogota, 1973-73; assoc. U. Calif., Santa Barbara, 1974-78, 78-80; instr. W. Tex. State U., Canyon, Tex., 1978-80, Def. Lang. Inst., Calif., 1981-82; visiting lectr. U. Calif., Santa Cruz, 1982-84; asst. prof. SUNY, New Paltz, 1984—; bilingual cons., Carpinteria (Calif.) Unified Sch. Dist., 1980-81; reader, evaluator, N.J. Dept. Higher Edn., Princeton, 1987-89; reader, Ednl. Testing Svc., Princeton, 1987-89; acad. dir. Spanish Immersion Inst., Bd. Edn. and Office Mental Health, N.Y.C. and Albany, 1987-89. Fellow Ulster County & YWCA, 1987, Poetry Reading Cen. Am. Week, 1988; The Heloise Brainer scholar, 1964, LASPAU scholar, 1968. Mem. MLA, Am. Assn. Tchr. Spanish & Portuguese, Assn. Para la Ensenanza del Espanol, Latin-Am. Studies Assn. Home: 37 River Rd New Paltz NY 12561

DAVILA-JOHNSTON, RUTH MARIE, computer programmer and analyst; b. Honolulu, Oct. 11, 1960; d. Daniel and Sally (Yunson) Davila; m. Johnnie Dean Johnston, Sept. 15, 1984; children: Jacob Harrison, Travis Daniel. BS, Southwest Mo. State U., Springfield, 1982. Computer programmer/analyst Marine Corps Fin. Ctr., Kansas City, Mo., 1983—. Mem. Nat. Assn. Female Execs., Southwest Mo. State U. Alumni Assn., Delta Sigma Pi. Roman Catholic. Avocations: shopping craft shows, swimming, dancing, reading. Home: 7 Belmo St Belton MO 64012 Office: Marine Corps Fin Ctr 1500 E 95th St Kansas City MO 64197

DAVION, ETHEL JOHNSON, educational administrator, workshop facilitator; b. Raleigh, N.C., July 21, 1948; d. John Arthur and Ethel Mae (Morgan) Johnson; m. Joel Davion, Aug. 6, 1988, 1 child, Laura Christal. BA, Livingstone Coll., 1971; MA, Glassboro (N.J.) State U., 1983. Cert. tchr. English, supr. and principal. Sr. English tchr. Camden (N.J.) Bd. Edn., 1977-81; tchr. of English Westfield (N.J.) Bd. Edn., 1982-85, Union County Regional Dist. 1, Berkeley Heights, N.J., 1981-82, Hillside (N.J.) Bd. Edn., 1985-87; supr. language arts Irvington (N.J.) Bd. Edn., 1987—; writer, researcher Collegiate Rsch. Systems, Camden, 1976-77; participant Inst. on Writing, Reading and Civic Edn., Harvard U., 1989. Contbr. articles to jours. Former mem. bd. dirs., sec. Emmanuel Tabernacle, Linden, N.J. Fellow N.J. Edn. Assn., Nat. Coun. Tchrs. English; mem. Linden Scholarship Guild (sec. 1985—), Assn. for Supervision and Curriculum Devel., Prin. and Suprs. Assn., Irvington Adminstrs. Assn., Internat. Platform Assn., Good Samaritans Club, Obsidian Civic Club (Westfield, historian 1985—). Democrat. Pentecostal. Home: 610 E Blancke St Linden NJ 07036

DAVIS, ALICE J., municipal employee; b. Galveston, Tex., Aug. 4, 1929; d. Joseph Edward Reagan and Gertrude Bertha Zeller Reagan; m. Bob J. Davis, Oct. 22, 1948; 1 child, Paula Lynn Davis Baughman. AA, San Jacinto Coll., 1966; BS, Western Ill. U., 1976. With office staff various automobile dealerships, Houston, 1951-68, Yeast Printing Co., Macomb, Ill., 1974-77; clk. Office of City Clk., City of Macomb, 1977-86. Youth program leader 1st Meth. Ch., Pasadena, Tex., 1960-63; mem. choir Wesley United Meth. Ch., Macomb, 1968—, worship com., 1987-88, 89, chmn. Alter Guild, 1987-89, 90; area chmn. Macomb United Way, 1970-71, program chmn., 1984-85. Mem. Univ. Faculty Women, Macomb Home Econs. Assn. (pres. 1981-82, treas. 1987-89, 90), Kappa Omicron Phi, Phi Kappa Phi, Beta Sigma Phi (treas. 1987-89, 90), Xi Epsilon Rho (pres. 1981-82, 86-87). Lodges: Eastern Star, White Shrine, Deer. Office: Office of City Clerk Macomb IL 61455

DAVIS, ANDREA DENISE, educator; b. Rocky Mount, N.C., Sept. 19, 1964; d. Willie Lee and Vivian Marie (Shaw) Porter; m. Ronald Davis, June 2, 1987. Cert., Edgecombe Tech., Rocky Mount, 1987. Tchr. Kindercare Learning Ctr., Alexandria, Va., 1988—. Home: 3701 4th St SE 202 Washington DC 20032

DAVIS, ANN JANETTE, personnel director; b. Detroit, Dec. 8, 1942; d. Curtis Woodrow and Thelma Irene (Gettelfinger) Lewis; m. Gary William Davis, July 9, 1960 (div. May 1981); children: Amy, Karen, Kathleen. Grad. high sch., Ann Arbor, Mich., 1960. Clk. typist U. Mich. Rsch. Personnel, Ann Arbor, 1960; sec., receptionist Drury, Lacy, Ferguson Advt., Ann Arbor, 1961; sec. to owner, pub. The Ypsilanti (Mich.) Press, 1962; sec., bookkeeper, mgr. of temporary personnel Personnel Systems Inc., Ann Arbor, 1976-78; adminstrv. sec. Great Lakes Basin Commn., Ann Arbor, 1978-81; adminstrv. asst. Applied Dynamics Internat., Ann Arbor, 1981-86, personnel mgr., 1986—. Active Leadership Ann Arbor, 1990. Mem. Ann Arbor Hi-Tech Personnel Assn. (sec. 1984-85, treas. 1988-89, pres. 1989-90), Am. Soc. Personnel Adminstrn., Mich. Tech. Coun., Sci. and Tech. Quest, Ann Arbor Area Personnel Assn., Ea. Mich. U. Human Resource Com., Ann Arbor C. of C. (mem. govt. rels. com. 1988-89). Office: Applied Dynamics Internat 3800 Stone School Rd Ann Arbor MI 48108

DAVIS, ANNA MARIE, engineer; b. Cleve., July 18, 1946; d. John Joseph and Mary Barbara (Mancos) Spirnak; m. Richard Lee Davis Jr., Jan. 2, 1975; 1 child, Courtney Marie. Cert., Whiting Bus. Coll., 1968. Bookkeeper Union Commerce Bank, Cleve., 1964; with Ohio Bell Telephone, Cleve., 1964-73, records supr., 1970-72, engr., 1972-73; engr. Pacific Bell Corp., Sacramento, 1973-79, sr. engr., 1979—. Contbr. Blue Ribbon Recipies, 1987; featured in Country Am. mag. Vol. United Way, Sacramento, 1979-80; leader Girl Scouts U.S., Sacramento, 1985—; master food preserver U. Calif. Coop. Extension, Sacramento, 1984—; v.p. Sacramento Master Food Preserver Group, 1989-90; vice chmn. Fair Oaks (Calif.) Planning Coun., 1976-79. Finalist, Pillsbury Corp. Bake-Off, 1971; recipient recognition award Tel. Pioneers of Am., 1990. Mem. Pacific Bell Project Mgmt. Assn. Democrat. Roman Catholic. Home: 7704 Palmyra Dr Fair Oaks CA 95628

DAVIS, BARBARA JEAN, educational consultant; b. Manistee, Mich., Jan. 28, 1942; d. Hugo Brynnolf and Martha Matilda (Kiuimaa) Troppi; m. James Stephen Davis, Mar. 21, 1964; Children: Katherine Ruth, James Harold. BA in Edn., Mich. State U., 1963, MA in Journalism, 1974; postgrad., U. Chgo., 1987—. High sch. eng. tchr. Bullock Creek Pub. Schs., Midland, Mich., 1963-64, Charlotte (Mich.) Pub. Schs., 1964-67; coord. programs for talented Eaton Intermediate Sch. Dist., Charlotte, 1974—; cons. in field. Co-author: MSALG: A Better Way to Measure, 1988. Vol. Mich. Alliance for Gifted Edn., 1983—, Charlotte Mobile Meals, Inc., 1965—; Sun. sch. tchr. Peace Lutheran Ch., 1964—, choir mem., 1967—; bd. dirs. Eaton County Child Abuse & Neglect Prevention Coun., 1978-83. Recipient Award of Excellence The Assn. for Gifted, 1986; Century scholar U. Chgo. Edn. Found., 1987-88, Project Renew scholar AAUW Edn. Found., 1987. Mem. Mich. Assn. of Edn. for Gifted, Talented and Creative (founder and pres., 1983, Excellence award 1990), Am. Ednl. Rsch. Assn., Assn. for Supervision & Curriculum Devel.,. Democrat. Home: 1700 W Kalamo Rte 2 Charlotte MI 48813

DAVIS, BARBARA JEAN SIEMENS, service company executive; b. Louisville, Nov. 12, 1931; d. Gustav Adolph Siemens and Alberta Jeanette (McAdams) Simon; m. Donald Elmore Davis, Aug. 4, 1950; children—Dale Montgomery, Gale Sue Davis Beaty. Mktg. and personnel mgr. Kelly Services, Louisville, 1962-65; tchr. asst. TV English, Jefferson County Schs., Louisville, 1960-70; wedding and floral designer Wedding Ring, Louisville, 1971-73; owner, designer Nook Flowers and Gifts, Memphis, 1973-75; cons. pub. relations Dixie Rents, Memphis, 1975-79; div. mgr. pres. Party Concepts, Inc., Memphis, 1980-88; pres. Siemens-Davis Assoc., Cordova, Tenn., 1989—. Author: Wedding Workshop Brides Work Book, 1984. Mem. Sales and Mktg. Execs., Am. Rental Assn. (mem. party council 1985—), Nat. Assn. Wedding Cons. (pres. 1983-87); NAFE(dir. Memphis Network, mem. Internat. Platform Assn.). Republican. Presbyterian. Home: 2414 Old Orrville Rd Selma AL 36701

DAVIS, BARBARA M(AE), librarian; b. Cranston, R.I., Dec. 23, 1926; d. Harrie S. and Marguerite M. (Cameron) D.; SB in Chemistry, Brown U., 1948; MS in Library Sci., Simmons Coll., 1956. Asst. research librarian research and devel. dept. Cabot Corp., Cambridge, Mass., 1948-57, research librarian, 1957-61, research librarian Billerica (Mass.) Research Center, 1961-68, head tech. info. services, 1968-81, mgr. tech. info. center, 1981-87 . Dir. Cabot Boston Credit Union, 1956-59, 61-64, 72-78, clk., 1961-64, 72-77, v.p., 1977-78; chmn. research com. Greater Boston Young Rep.Club, 1959-61; treas. Women's Rep. Club Lexington, 1988—. Mem. Am. Chem. Soc. (sec. div. chem. lit. 1961-65), Spl. Libraries Assn. (chmn. Boston chpt. 1965-66, chmn. chemistry div. 1971-72), Simmons Coll. Library Sch. Alumni (v.p. 1965-66). Home: 37 Drummer Boy Way Lexington MA 02173

DAVIS, BERTHA G., artist; b. Vilno, Lithuania, 1911; came to U.S., 1940, naturalized, 1941; d. Abraham and Dvora Germaize; student Stewart Van Orden, Pan Am. Coll., 1960-61, Fred Samualson and James Pinco, Art Inst. of San Migual Allende, Mex., 1965, Harold Phenix, 1972-73, Ed Whitney, 1973-74, Bud, 1976, Zoltan Stabo, 1977, Morris Shubin, 1977; children: Sylvia Caplan Rawley, Doryn Davis Chervin. Owner, operator art gallery, Houston, 1969-72; asst. mgr. Art Internat., Houston, 1972-75; asst. mgr. Kirt Niven Gallery, Dallas, 1977-78; one woman shows: Pan Am. Coll., 1960, Jewish Community Ctr., Houston, McAllen State Bank, 1974, La Ciuldadela, Monterey, Mex., Houston Pub. Libr., U. Tex. Health Sci. Ctr., Dallas, 1979, Gallery of Discovery, Dallas, 1981, Channel 13 TV Gallery, Dallas, 1981, Sol Del Rio Gallery, San Antonio, 1982, Wichita Falls, Tex., 1985, Jewish Community Ctr., 1986, Barens, Blackman, Houston, 1988, O'Kane Gallery, U. Houston, 1988, Artcetera Showing, 1988, First City Bank, Houston, 1988, also others; group shows include: Watercolor Soc. Houston, S.W. Watercolor Soc., Am. Painters in Paris, Cooperstown Art Exhibit, Issac Delgado Mus. Art, New Orleans, Corpus Christi Art Found., Salmagundi Club Art Show, N.Y.C., 1979, Dallas, Laguna Gloria Mus., Austin, Tex., 1979, 84, Catharine Lorillard Wolfe Art Club, N.Y.C., 1980, Houshangs Gallery, Dallas, 1980, Nimbus Gallery, Dallas, Highland Park Bank, 1989; showings in Marsha London Gallery, N.Y.C., Nat. Design Center, N.Y.C., Fonteinbleau Gallery of N.Y., Deportive Israelita de México, Paige Gallery, 1984, Dallas S.L. Gallery, 1984; represented in permanent collection: Shell Oil Co., Houston, Transco Tower, Arthur Anderson Acctg. Co. Mem. Tex. Fine Art Assn., S.W. Watercolor Assn., S.W. Watercolor Assn., Richardson Civic Art Assn., Artist Sculptors Contemporary Assn., Art League Houston, Houston Art Assn., Watercolor Art Soc. Houston, La Revue Moderne De Paris, Repetorium Artis Monte Carlo. Prin. illustrator: Open Dallas, 1976; works reproduced in various publs. Home: 8803 Jackwood St Houston TX 77036

DAVIS, BETTY HARRINGTON, entrepreneur; b. Longview, Tex., July 11, 1936; d. William Henry Byrd and Minnie Lee Tidwell; 1 child, Randy Lee Harrington. AA, Cedar Valley DCCCD, Dallas, 1988. Adminstrv. asst. Conf. Coun. on Ministries United Meth. Ch., Dallas, 1983-86; pres., actress, model, entertainer Kathy King Entertainment Agy., DeSoto, Tex., 1956—; pres. Bi-Weekly Mortgage Reduction Svc./Career Planning Svc., DeSoto, Tex., 1987—. Author: The Dallas Dazzler. Mem. AFTRA, AGVA, Bi-Weekly Mortgage Assn., Greater Dallas C. of C. Republican. Methodist. Home: 1338 E Parkerville Rd DeSoto TX 75115

DAVIS, BETTY JEAN BOURBONIA, real estate investment executive; b. Ft. Bayard, N.Mex., Mar. 12, 1931; d. John Alexander and Ora M. (Caudill) Bourbonia; BS in Elem. Edn., U. N.Mex., 1954; children: Janice Ann Cox Plagge, Elizabeth Ora Cox. Gen. partner BJD Realty Co., Albuquerque, 1977—. Bd. dirs. Albuquerque Opera Guild, 1977-79, 81-83, 85-86, 86-87, membership co-chmn., 1977-79; mem. Friends of Art, 1978-85, Friends of Little Theatre, 1973-85, Mus. N.Mex. Found.; mem. grand exec. com. N.Mex. Internat. Order of Rainbow for Girls. Recipient Matrix award for journalism Jr. League. Mem. Albuquerque Mus. Assn., N.M. Hist. Soc., N.Mex. Symphony Guild, Jr. League Albuquerque, Alumni Assn. U. N.Mex. (dir. 1973-76), Mus. N.Mex. Found., Alpha Chi Omega (Beta Gamma Beta chpt., adv., bldg. corp. 1962-77), Tanoan Country Club, Order Eastern Star, Order Rainbow for Girls (past grand worthy adv. N.Mex., past mother adv. Friendship Assembly 50, grand exec. com. 1989). Republican. Methodist. Home: 9505 Augusta NE Albuquerque NM 87111

DAVIS, BILLIE JOHNSTON, school counselor; b. Charleston, W.Va., Sept. 24, 1933; d. William Andrew, Jr. and Garnet Macil (Johnston) D.; B.S., Morris Harvey Coll., Charleston, W.Va., 1954; M.A., W.Va. U., 1959. Tchr. math. Kanawha County schs., Charleston, 1954-59, counselor, 1959—; mem. public edn. study commn. W.Va. Legislature, 1980. Mem. W.Va. Commn. on Juvenile Law, 1982—; bd. dirs. W.Va. Com. for Prevention Child Abuse, W.Va. Sch. Health Adv. Com.; appointed W.Va. rep. at Tchr.'s Inaugural Experience for Inauguration of Pres. George Bush by Gov. of W.Va., 1989. Recipient Anne Maynard award W.Va. Sch. Counselor Assn., 1986; named Am. mid./jr. high Sch. Counselor of Yr. Am. Sch. Counselors Assn., 1987, Citizen of the Yr., Dunbar Lions Club. Mem. Am. Assn. Counseling and Devel., W.Va. Assn. Counseling and Devel. (pres. 1964-66, legis. chmn., 1974—; spl. award legis. svcs. 1981), W.Va. Edn. Assn. (past legis. chmn.), Kanawha County Sch. Counselors Assn. (pres., legis. chmn. 1974—), W.Va. Sch. Counselors Assn. (chmn. gov. rels., parliamentarian), Alpha Delta Kappa (past chpt. pres.), Phi Delta Kappa. Democrat. Baptist. Home: 12 Warren Pl Charleston WV 25302 Office: Ben Franklin Career and Tech Edn Ctr 500 28th St Dunbar WV 25064

DAVIS, CAROL LYN, research consultant; b. West Palm Beach, Fla., Oct. 22, 1953; d. Robert Lee and Barbara Jean (Collett) D. B.F.A., Tex. Christian U., Ft. Worth, 1975, M.A. in Am. Studies, 1977. Research and devel. product line designer Am. Handicrafts/Merribee Needlearts, Ft. Worth, 1977-81; ceramics/china sales cons. Dillard's, Ft. Worth, 1981-82, dept. mgr., 1981; dept. mgr. Stripling-Cox, Ft. Worth, 1982-83; freelance ceramic and string art designer, 1982-83; with phase III, IV, V hist.sites inventory of Tarrant County for Hist. Preservation Coun. for Tarrant County (Tex.) and Page, Anderson & Turnbull, Inc., San Francisco, 1983-86; Tarrant County rep. Greater Ft. Worth Housing Starts, Texas Update, Inc., 1987—, MPF Rsch., Inc., Dallas, 1989—; mem. mgmt. adv. panel Chem. Week, 1981. Mem. Nat. Trust Hist. Preservation, Ft. Worth Opera Assn., Royal Oak Found., Daus. Brit. Empire in the USA. Democrat. Episcopalian. Author pamphlets in field. Home: 7800 Garza Ave Fort Worth TX 76116 Office: Tex Update Inc 1221 W Campbell Rd Suite 291 Richardson TX 75080

DAVIS, CAROL LYNN, accountant; b. Orange, Calif., Mar. 8, 1963; d. Robert Stanley Davis and Patricia (Geiger) Griffo. BA, Calif. State U., Fullerton, 1988. Computer operator Graybar Electric, Los Angeles, 1981-82; clk. Tam's Stationers, Inc., Whitier, Calif., 1982-84; asst. dir. of tng. Tam's Books, Inc., Paramount, Calif., 1985, with promotions/advt., 1985-86; accounts receivable analyst McDonnell Douglas Fin. Corp., Long Beach, Calif., 1987-88; acct. Lance, Soll & Lunghard, Whittier, 1988—. Co-author: Tam's Beginning Employee's Training Manual, 1985. Mem. Nat. Assn. Accts., Alpha Delta Pi. Republican. Presbyterian. Lodge: Job's Daus. (pres. 1978-79, honored queen). Home: 10006 Melgar Dr Whittier CA 90603

DAVIS, CAROLE JOAN, psychologist; b. Norristown, Pa., Aug. 15, 1942; d. John Morgan and Eva (Pierson) D.; children: Kevin Jae, Kara Megan. AB in English Lit., U. Pa., 1964; MA in Psychology, Temple U., 1967; PhD in Child Devel. and Clin. Evaluation, Bryn Mawr (Pa.) Coll., 1973. Lic. psychologist Pa. Sr. clin. psychologist Camden County Psychiat. Hosp., Lakeland, N.J., 1967-76; psychologist counselling ctr. staff Chestnut Hill Coll., Phila., 1976-89; psychologist hearing impaired programs Phila. (Pa.) Sch. Dist., 1984-85; pvt. practice Phila., 1974-89, New Britain, Pa., 1989—; cons. psychologist Pa. Sch. for the Deaf, Phila., 1970-84, Lutheran Children & Family Svc., Phila., 1974-80, Willis & Elizabeth Martin Sch., Phila., 1975-84, Overbrook Sch. for the Blind, Phila., 1978—; lectr. in psychology Chestnut Hill Coll., Phila., 1974—; adj. prof. Chestnut Hill Coll. Grad. Div., Phila., 1980—. Mem. Am. Psychol. Assn., Pa. Psychol. Assn., Phila. Soc. Clin. Psychologists (exec. bd. 1981-83), Nat. Register of Health Svc. Providers in Psychology, Psychologists for the Ethical Treatment Animals. Home: 62 Shady Grove Circle Doylestown PA 18901 Office: 39 Iron Hill Rd New Britain PA 18901

DAVIS, CAROLYN KAHLE, health care consultant; b. Penn Yan, N.Y., Jan. 31, 1932; d. Paul Frederick Kahle and Alice Edgerton (Kahle) Cargill; m. Ott Howard Davis, June 28, 1953; 1 son, Richard Ott. BS in Nursing, Johns Hopkins U., 1954; MS in Nursing, Syracuse U., 1965, PhD, 1972; LittD (hon.), Georgetown U., 1982; DSc (hon.), U. Evansville, 1982, U. Medicine & Dentistry N.J., 1984; LLD (hon.), Adelphi U., 1985; LHD (hon.), U. S.C. Med. Sch., 1986, Eastern Mich. U., 1989. Chmn. baccalaureate nursing program Syracuse U., 1969-73; dean sch. nursing U. Mich., Ann Arbor, 1973-75, prof. nursing and edn., 1973-81, assoc. v.p. acad. affairs, 1975-81; adminstr. Health Care Fin. Adminstrn. HHS, Washington, 1981-85; cons. Ernst & Whinney, Washington, 1985-89, Ernst & Young, Washington, 1989—; bd. dirs. Beverly Enterprises, Pasadena, Calif., Beckman Inst., Irvine, Calif., Prudential Ins. Co. of Am., Newark, Merck, Rahway, N.J. Mem. editorial bd. Modern Health Care, Nursing Economics, Chgo.; contbr. more than 100 articles to profl. jours. Bd. govs. ARC, 1988-89; bd. dirs. Nat. Mus. Health and Medicine; devel. collegiate athletics, Washington, 1977-80; assoc. trustee U. Pa. Med. Ctr., Phila., 1987—. Recipient Disting. Alumnus award Johns Hopkins U., 1981, Spl. Recognition award Assn. Am. Med. Colls., 1986; named one of the Top Young Leaders in Am. Acad. Change Mag., 1978. Mem. Nat. League for Nursing (dir. 1979-81, chmn. community health accreditation program 1988—), Sigma Theta Tau, Phi Delta Kappa. Republican. Office: Ernst & Young 1200 19th St NW Washington DC 20036

DAVIS, CHERYL ANN, human resources vice-president; b. Brighton, Mass., Jan. 3, 1962; d. Roy Wayland and Jean (Porras) D. BS, Northeastern U., 1984. Mgmt. trainee TAD Tech. Svcs., Cambridge, Mass., 1984; weekend supr. Greater Boston Conv./Visitors Bur., Boston, 1985, supr. visitor svcs., 1985-86, housing coord., 1986; personnel asst. Carney Hosp., Boston, 1986-87; human resources asst. Hahnemann Hosp., Boston, 1987-88, dir. human resources, 1988-89, v.p. human resources, 1989—. Mem. Boston Assn. Female Exec., Mass. Healthcare Human Resources Assn., AAIM. Office: Hahnemann Hosp 1515 Commonwealth Ave Boston MA 02135

DAVIS, COLEEN COCKERILL, teacher; b. Pampa, Tex., Sept. 20, 1930; d. Charles Clifford and Myrtle Edith (Harris) Cockerill; m. Richard Harding Davis, June 22, 1952 (div. Dec. 1984); children: David Christopher, Denis Benjamin (dec. 1979). BS, U. Okla., 1951; MS, UCLA, 1952; postgrad. U. So. Calif., Whittier Coll., UCLA. Cert. tchr., Calif. Chmn, dept. home econs., tchr. Whittier Union High Sch. Dist., Calif., 1952-85; substitute tchr., 1985—; home tchr., 1985—, cons. 1986—; co-host Am.'s Bed & Breakfast, Whittier, 1983—, also founder, pres., exec. dir. Contbr. articles to newspapers. Founder Children of Murdered Parents, Whittier, 1984, chpt. leader; founder Parents of Muredered CHildren, Whittier, 1984, chpt. leader; founder Coalition of Orgns. and People, Whittier, 1984, Whistle, Ltd., Whittier, 1984; mem. citizens' adv. bd. Fred C. Nelles Sch. Mem. Calif. Tchrs. Assn., NEA, Internat. Tour Mgmt. Inst., Whittier C. of C. (ambassador). Republican. Episcopalian. Avocation: volunteer worker. Office: Am's Bed & Breakfast PO Box 9302 Whittier CA 90608

DAVIS, CYNTHIA JEANNE, academic administrator; b. Wheeling, W.Va., Feb. 27, 1948; d. Albert and Lois (Munn) Shriver; m. Charles B. Davis, Oct. 21, 1969 (dec. Aug. 1989); 1 child, Katya. BS in Biology, U. Ala., 1978. Adminstr. learning mus. program Carnegie Mus. Natural History, Pitts., 1978-79; adminstr. Pitts. NMR Ctr. for biomed. rsch. Carnegie Mellon U., Pitts., 1979—. Mem. Soc. for Rsch. Adminstrs., NAFE, West Pa. Bot. Soc., World Wildlife Found., Greenpeace, Amnesty Internat. Democrat. Home: 44 Courtney St Pittsburgh PA 15202 Office: Carnegie Mellon U 4400 Fifth Ave Pittsburgh PA 15213

DAVIS, DAISY SIDNEY, educator; b. Bay City, Tex., Nov. 7, 1944; d. Alex. C. and Alice M. (Edison) Sidney; m. John Dee Davis, Apr. 17, 1968; children: Anaca Michelle, Lowell Kent. BS, Bishop Coll., 1966; MS, East Tex. State U., 1971; MEd, Prairie View A&M and Mech., 1980. Cert. profl. lifetime secondary tchr., Tex.; mid-mgmt. adminstr. Tchr., Dallas pub. schs., 1966—. Coord. Get Out the Vote campaign, Dallas, 1972, 80, 84, 88. Recipient Outstanding Tchr. award Dallas pub. schs., 1980, Jack Lowe award for ednl. excellence, 1982; Free Enterprise scholar So. Meth. U., 1987; Constitutionalism fellow U. Dallas, 1988; named to Hall of Fame, Holmes Acad., 1979. Mem. NEA, Tex. State Tchrs. Assn., Classroom Tchrs. Dallas (faculty rep. 1971-77), Dallas County History Tchrs., Afro-Am. Daus. Republic of Tex. (founder), Zeta Phi Beta. Democrat. Baptist. Club: Jack & Jill, (Dallas) (rec. sec., v.p., chair Beautillion Ball). Home: 1302 Mill Stream Dr Dallas TX 75232 Office: 9339 S Polk St Dallas TX 75232

DAVIS, DEBORAH HANSON, executive administrator; b. Chgo., Mar. 2, 1945; d. Charles William and Mary Elizabeth Parker; m. Casey B. Davis, Aug. 8, 1988. BS, Columbia U., 1973. Exec. adminstr. Wildrick and Miller, Inc. Advt. Agy., N.Y.C., 1976-78; adminstrv. asst. Leo Press, Inc., Pub. Co., Hoboken, N.J., 1978-79; exec. adminstr. Wettstein/Bolchalk Advt. Pub. Rels., Inc., Tucson, Ariz., 1979-83; exec. adminstr., sr. account mgr. Allan Anderson & Assocs., Ft. Collins, Colo., 1984-88, Weltstein Bolchelle, Tucson, Ariz., 1988—. Mem. NAFE, Tucson C. of C., Am. Mgmt. Assn.

DAVIS, DONNA RAE, protective services official; b. Monett, Mo., Dec. 13, 1942; d. Bertram Woodrow and Mildred June (Eddingfield) Wilson; m. Michael Lee Davis, Sept. 3, 1960; children: Michael Bryan, Carmen Annette. AA, Longview Community Coll., Kansas City, Mo., 1974; BA, U. Mo., Kansas City, 1976; MS, Cen. Mo. State U., 1983. Profl. adminstr. juvenile justice. Dep. juvenile officer Cass County Juvenile Ct., Harrisonville, Mo., 1978-82; chief dep. juvenile officer Cass County Juvenile Ct., Harrisonville, 1982-86, chief juvenile officer, 1986—. Author: Highlights of Harrisonville in Verse, 1979. Bd. dirs. West Cen. Mo. Mental Health Ctr., 1987-88; mem. CAPS com. Vocat. Tech. Sch., 1988—, Harrisonville Alcohol and Drug Task Force, 1989—. Mem. AAUW (pres. local chpt. 1984-86), Nat. Juvenile Ct. Svcs. Assn., Nat. Juvenile Dentention Assn., Mo. Juvenile Justice Assn. (bd. mem. 1985-88, com. mem. 1987—), Bus. and Profl. Women (legis. chmn. local chpt. 1989—), Phi Theta Kappa. Methodist. Office: Cass County Juvenile Office 2000 E Mechanic Harrisonville MO 64701

DAVIS, DORINNE SUE TAYLOR LOVAS, audiologist; b. East Orange, N.J., Mar. 29, 1949; d. William Henry and Evelyn Doris (Thorp) Taylor; BA, Montclair State Coll., 1971, MA, 1973; m. Warren B. Davis, Jr., Aug. 10, 1985; children: Larissa Louise, Peter Alexander. Ednl. audiologist Kinnelon (N.J.) Bd. Edn., 1972—, Inst. for Career Advancement, Inc., 1980-82, Dover Gen. Hosp., 1984-86; pres. HEAR YOU ARE, INC., 1987—. Cert. tchr. of hearing impaired, speech correctionist, tchr. speech and drama N.J. Dept. Edn.; supr. nursery sch. endorsement. Mem. NEA, Internat. Orgn. Educators Hearing Impaired, Am. Speech and Hearing Assn. (cert. of clin. competence in audiology), Alexander Graham Bell Assn., N.J. Speech and Hearing Assn., Morris County Speech and Hearing Assn., N.J. Edn. Assn., Morris County Edn. Assn., Kinnelon Edn. Assn., Self Help for the Hard of Hearing, Ednl. Audiology Assn. (past pres.). Methodist. Home: 4 Musconetcong Ave Stanhope NJ 07874 Office: Kinnelon Bd Edn Spl Services Kiel Ave Kinnelon NJ 07405 also: HEAR YOU ARE INC 4 Musconetcong Ave Stanhope NJ 07874

DAVIS, DOROTHY SALISBURY, author; b. Chgo., Apr. 26, 1916; d. Alfred Joseph and Margaret Jane (Greer) Salisbury; m. Harry Davis, Apr. 25, 1946. A.B., Barat Coll., Lake Forest, Ill., 1938. Mystery and hist. novelist, short story writer. Author: A Gentle Murderer, 1951, A Town of Masks, 1952, Men of No Property, 1956, Death of an Old Sinner, 1957, A Gentleman Called, 1958, The Evening of the Good Samaritan, 1961, Black Sheep, White Lamb, 1963, The Pale Betrayer, 1965, Enemy and Brother, 1967, God Speed The Night, 1968, Where the Dark Streets Go, 1969, Shock Wave, 1972, The Little Brothers, 1973, A Death in the Life, 1976, Scarlet Night, 1980, A Lullaby of Murder, 1984, Tales for a Stormy Night, 1985, The Habit of Fear, 1987. Recipient Life Achievement award Bouchereon, 1989. Mem. Authors Guild, Mystery Writers of Am. (former pres., recipient Grand Master award 1985). Home: Palisades NY 10964

DAVIS, ELEANOR LAURIA, educator, volunteer, lecturer; b. Pitts., Aug. 29, 1923; d. Anthony Francis and Antonia Jennie (Bove) Lauria; m. Earle Richard Davis, May 7, 1946; children: Susan Davis Hickerson, Janice Davis Johnston, Lisa Davis Kulp, Elena Davis Smoulder, Amy Davis Gordon, Kent Earle, Eric J. BS, U. Pitts., 1944, M Letters in Biology, 1950. Grad. teaching asst. in physiology dept. biology U. Pitts., 1944-46; instr. in biology Pa. Coll. for Women (now Chatham Coll.), Pitts., 1946-53; libr. Carnegie Libr., Pitts., 1947-50. Co-author: Lab. Manual for Biology, 1948; contbr. editorials to profl. newsletter. Pres. St. Joseph's Hosp. Aux., Pitts., 1977-78, Allegheny County Med. Soc. Aux., 1981-83, Pa. Med. Soc. Aux., Harrisburg, 1988-89; mem. Coun. on Govt. Rels. and Pa. Med. Polit. Action Com., Harrisburg, 1987—, Pa. Atty. Gens. Task Force Drugs, 1989-90, Pa. Task Force on Aging, 1988-90, Pa. Task Force on AIDS, 1988-90, Pa. Task Force on the Impaired Physician, 1988-90; Dem. vice chairperson O'Hara Twp., 1983—, by-laws com., Allegheny County, 1986-88; bd. dirs. Parental Stress Ctr., 1977—, Bright Beginnings, 1979—, Am. Cancer Soc. Aux., 1984-86, Vocat. Rehab. Ctr., 1986-88, Self Help Group Network, 1989; Rx Coun., 1986—, S.W. region Pa. Assn. Hosp. Auxs., 1990—; pub. policy chmn. Alzheimers Disease and Related Disorders, 1987—; mem. parish coun. St. Scholastica Ch., 1988-90, Grass Roots Intelligence Team, South Hills Health System, 1989—. Recipient honor scholarship U. Pitts., 1941-44, Benjamin Rush award Allegheny County Med. Soc., 1987, Person of Yr. award South Hills Health System and Found., Pitts., 1989. Mem. AAUW, Women's Agenda, Nat. Inst. Adult Day Care (standards com.), Nat. Coun. Aging (task force for day care standards 1989-90), Allegheny County Med. Soc. (legis. com. 1989—), Pa. Med. Soc. (fed. key contact com. 1990), Allegheny County Fedn. Women's Clubs, Stanton Heights Garden Club (pres. 1974-85), Piccadilly Herb Club, Chapel Area Women's Club (bd. dirs. 1980—). Home: 109 Woodshire Dr Pittsburgh PA 15215

DAVIS, ELISE MILLER (MRS. LEO M. DAVIS), author; b. Corsicana, Tex., Oct. 12, 1915; d. Moses Myre and Rachelle (Daniels) Miller; student U. Tex., 1930-31; m. Jay Albert Davis, June 27, 1937 (dec. June 1973); 1 dau., Rayna Miller (Mrs. Michael Edwin Loeb); m. 2d, Leo M. Davis, Aug. 23, 1974. Freelance writer, 1945—; merchandiser and dir. Jay Davis, Inc., Amarillo, Tex., 1956-73; instr. mag. writing U. Tex., Dallas, 1978; lectr. creative writing Baylor U., Waco, Tex., 1980, 81, 83. Mem. Am. Soc. Journalists and Authors (bd. dirs. 1985—). Author: The Answer Is God, 1955; articles to periodicals including Reader's Digest, Woman's Day, Nation's Business, others. Home: 3906 Old Mill Rd Waco TX 76710

DAVIS, ELIZABETH ANN, city official; b. Kansas City, Mo., Jan. 16, 1941; d. Samuel Wyatt Jr. and Maurita Bell (Irick) Driggers; m. Roy Edward Davis Jr., July 1, 1957; children: Scott Edward, Catherine Elizabeth, Christopher Kelly, Sean Wyatt. Cert. mcpl. clk., Tex. Sec. First Nat. Bank, Ft. Worth, 1966-69; office mgr. City of Luling, Tex., 1972-73; adminstrv. sec. State of Tex., Austin, 1973-74; office coordinator City of Arlington, Tex., 1974-77; city sec. City of Granbury, Tex., 1977-83, city sec., ct. adminstr., records officer City of Bedford, Tex., 1983—; mem. legis policy com. fin. and adminstrn. Tex. Mcpl. League, 1990—; adv. mem. mcpl. records project Tex. State Library, Austin, 1984, adv. mem. local govt. records project, 1989. V.p. Greater Green Valley Home Owners Assn., 1987-88. Bd. dirs. Tarrant County Crimestoppers, 1988-89, N.E. Tarrant Coun. on Alcoholism and Drug Abuse, 1989—. Mem. Tex. Assn. of Elections Adminstrs., Assn. City Clks. and Secs. of Tex. (chair resolutions com. 1984, mem. retirement com. 1985, mem. legis. com. 1987, mem. resolutions com. 1989, chair scholarship com. 1990), Internat. Inst. Mcpl. Clks. (cert. Advanced Acad., state mem. chmn. 1986, conf. com. 1987-88, profl. status com., 1984, fed. legis. com., 1985, chair membership com. 1987, internat. study tour com. 1989—), North Tex. City Secs. Assn. (sec.-treas. 1985, v.p. 1986, pres. 1987, chair membership com. 1989), Nat. Assn. for Court Mgmt., Assn. for Info. and Image Mgmt. (treas. Dallas/Ft. Worth chpt. 1989—), Assn. Records Mgrs. and Adminstrs., Digital Image Applications Group, Bus. and Profl. Women, Hurst-Euless-Bedford C. of C. (crime prevention com. 1987—, legis. com. 1989—, community rels. com. 1989—). Methodist. Avocations: music, travel, reading, cooking, arts. Home: 7720 Aubrey Ln North Richland Hills TX 76180 Office: City of Bedford PO Box 157 Bedford TX 76095

DAVIS, EMMA R., horticulturist; b. Balt., Nov. 22, 1944. BA in Urban Planning, Morgan State U., 1979; BA, Towson State U. Tchr. Dept. Edn., Balt.; caseworker Balt. Pub. Welfare Social Svcs.; supr. Westinghouse, Cockeysville, Md.; proprietor Davis Plants and Landscaping, Balt. Mem. Big Sisters, Girl Scouts U.S.; active First Apostolic Faith Ch. Home: PO Box 66195 Baltimore MD 21239

DAVIS, EVELYN CADENHEAD, human resource executive; b. Commerce, Tex., July 29, 1948; d. Orville Lavern and Mary Kathryn (Rogers) C.; m. John Maynard Davis, Feb. 9, 1973; children: Lauren Mary, Megan Elizabeth. BA, Mary Hardin-Baylor U., 1969; MA, North Tex. State U., 1972; MBA, U. Dallas, 1983. From flight attendant to mgr. centralized tng. Am. Airlines, Dallas, N.Y.C. and Chgo., 1972-80; co-owner Patt Walker Assoc., Dallas, 1980-81; mgr. mgmt. tng. Surgikos, Arlington, Tex., 1981-82; in-flight dir. Continental Airlines, Houston, 1982-83; dir. compensation and benefits Sky Chefs, Inc., Arlington, 1983-87; dir. corp. office human resources Volume Shoe Corp., Topeka, 1987-89, dir. human resources planning, 1989—; benefits cons. Child Care Dallas, 1987. Mem. Am. Soc. Personnel Assocs., Am. Compensation Assn. Office: Volume Shoe Corp 3231 E 6th St Topeka KS 66601

DAVIS, FRANCES KAY, lawyer; b. Phila., Apr. 1, 1952; d. Francis Kaye and Ida May (Lamplugh) D. BA, Mount Holyoke Coll., 1974; MA, Duke U., 1976; JD, Villanova U., 1983-86. Legal asst. Cozen, Begier & O'Connor, Phila., 1982-83; summer assoc. Montgomery, McCracken, Walker & Roads, Phila., 1985, assoc., 1986-89; assoc. Cozen & O'Connor, 1989—. Served to capt. USAF, 1977-82. Mem. Phila. Bar Assn., Assn. Trial Lawyers Am. (Trial Advocacy award Phila. chpt. 1986), Welsh Soc. Phila. (bd. stewards 1990—, scholar 1984-85).

DAVIS, FRANCES M., lawyer, corporate executive; b. 1925. Grad., UCLA, 1946; JD, U. Calif., Berkeley, 1953. Bar: Calif. 1954. Ptnr. LeProhn & LeProhn, 1960-67; asst. dean Earl Warren Legal Ctr. Calif. Coll. Trial Judges, 1968-72; assoc. Pillsbury, Madison & Sutro, 1972-75; v.p., gen. counsel Potlach Corp., San Francisco, 1975—; mem. Pvt. Industry Council of San Francisco. Bd. overseers U. Calif., San Francisco; mem. adv. bd. Sta. KOIT, San Francisco. Office: Potlatch Corp 1 Maritime Pla PO Box 3591 San Francisco CA 94111

DAVIS, GEENA, actress; m. Jeff Goldblum. Student, Boston U.; mem., Mt. Washington (N.H.) Repertory Theatre Co. Motion picture appearances include Tootsie, 1982, Fletch, 1985, Transylvania 6-5000, 1985,The Fly, 1986, Beetlejuice, 1988, The Accidental Tourist, 1988 (Academy award Best Supporting Actress, 1989), Earth Girls Are Easy, 1989; TV series: Buffalo Bill, 1983-84, Sara, 1985; appeared in TV film Secret Weapons, 1985, episodes series Family Ties, 1984. Address: care ICM 8899 Beverly Blvd Los Angeles CA 90048*

DAVIS, GEORGEANN L., educator; b. Chgo., Mar. 30, 1954; d. Carl Davis and Patricia E. (Kelsey) Johnson. BS, Mo. Valley Coll., 1976; MS in Edn., Purdue U., 1981. Educator South Met. Assn., Flossmoor, Ill., 1981—. Bd. dirs. Girl Scouts of the Calumet Council, Highland, Ind., 1985-89, first v.p., 1989. Mem. Council for Exceptional Children, Sierra, Greenpeace, Nat. Wildlife Fedn., Nature Conservancy, NOW, Amnesty Internat. Office: S Metropolitan Assn 800 Governor's Hwy Flossmoor IL 60422

DAVIS, GLORIA (KING), educational association administrator; b. Grand Saline, Tex., Aug. 22, 1940; d. Needom Leroy and Roxie Belle (Stevens) King; m. Perry N. Davis, Sept. 9, 1961; children: Steven P., Kenneth P., S. Suzanne. AA magna cum laude, Tyler (Tex.) Jr. Coll., 1978; BA, U. Tex., Tyler, 1979, MA, 1982. Sales coord. Dearborn Brass, Tyler, 1979-81; tchr. English T.K. Gorman High Sch., Tyler, 1981-82; div. exec. Tejas Girl Scout Coun., Dallas, 1982—; instr. part-time Tyler Jr. Coll., 1982—; mem. steering com. DOVIA of Tyler, 1987-88; mem. Tyler Human Svc. Providers, 1985—. Mem. Assn. Girl Scout Exec. Staff, East Tex. Women's Resource Coun., AAUW, U. Tex. at Tyler Alumni Assn. (sec. 1984-85, v.p. 1985-86, pres. 1986-87), Zonta (bd. dirs. Tyler). Republican. Baptist. Office: Tejas Girl Scout Coun Inc 1901 Rickety Ln #107 Tyler TX 75703

DAVIS, HELEN GORDON, state senator; b. N.Y.C., Dec. 25; d. Harry Gordon and Doree Gordon; m. Gene Davis; children: Stephanie, Karen, Gordon. BA, Bklyn. Coll.; postgrad., U. South Fla., 1967-70. Tchr., High Sch. Commerce, N.Y.C., Hillsborough High Sch., Tampa, Fla.; grad. asst. U. South Fla., 1968; mem. Fla. Ho. of Reps., 1974-88, state senator, 1988—. Jud. chmn. Local Govt. Study Commn. Hillsborough County (Fla.), 1964; mem. Tampa Commn. on Juvenile Delinquency, 1966-69, Mayor's Citizens Adv. Com., 1966-69, Quality Edn. Commn., 1966-68, Gov.'s Citizen Com. for Ct. Reform, 1972, Hillsborough County Planning Commn., 1973-74; mem. Gov.'s Commn. on Jud. Reform, 1976; mem. employment com. Commn. Community Relations, 1966-69; by-laws chmn. Arts Coun. Tampa, 1971-74; 1st v.p. Tampa Symphony Guild, 1974; bd. dirs. U. South Fla. Found., 1968-74, Stop Rape, 1973-74; founder Ctr. for Women, Tampa, 1978; past pres. PTA; active adv. commn. campaign Nat. Child Care Action, Nat. Ctr. for Crime and Delinquency. Recipient U. South Fla. Young Democrats Humanitarian award, 1974, Diana award NOW, 1975, Woman of Achievement in Arts award Tampa, 1975, Tampa Human Rels. award, 1976, Hannah G. Solomon Citizen of Yr. award, 1980, St. Petersburg Times/Fla. Civil Liberties award, 1980, Friend of Edn. award, 1981, Fla. Alliance for Responsible Parenting award, 1981, Humanitarian award Judeo-Christian Clinic, 1984, Fla. Network of Runaway Youth award, 1985, Ctr. for Women Leader-advocate Friend award, 1985, Nat. Assn. Juvenile Ct. Judges Appreciation award 1986, Legis. Leadership appreciation Centre for Woemn, 1986, Children's Crisis Ctr. Leadership award, 1987, AAUW leadership award, 1987, Hillsborough County Halfway House appreciation, 1988, Martin Luther King award City of Tampa, 1988, Nat. Fedn. Dem. Women appreciation, 1989, Dept. Legal Affairs appreciation, 1990, Superwoman award Mus. Sci. and Industry, 1990; named. Fla. Motion Picture and TV Outstanding Legislator, 1990, others. Mem. LWV (pres. Hillsborough County 1966-69, lobbyist, Fla. adminstrn. of justice chmn. 1969-74), Temple Guild Sisterhood (past pres.), Am. Arbitration Assn. Home: 45 Adalia Ave Tampa FL 33606 also: 178 E Davis Blvd Tampa FL 33606

DAVIS, HELEN NANCY MATSON (MRS. CHAUNCEY D. DAVIS), real estate broker, civic worker; b. Zanesville, Ohio, Nov. 18, 1905; d. Austin F. and Georgianna (Hale) Matson; grad. high sch.; m. Chauncey D. Davis, May 1, 1924; children—James Harvey, Robert Lee. Real estate broker, South Bend, Wash., 1964—. Chmn. Park Bd., South Bend, 1955—; ofcl. Pacific County Bicentennial Pageant, Dedication Ft. Columbia, 1959; trustee Pacific County Hist. Soc. Named Woman of Yr. Pacific County C. of C., 1949, 61. Mem. Nat. League Am. Pen Women, Dramatists Guild Inc., Propaelaeum Study Club, Chinook Indian Tribe (hon.), The Dramatist Guild N.Y., Delta Kappa Gamma (hon.). Republican. Methodist. Rebekah. Club: Garden (South Bend). Composer: Washington, My Home (ofcl. state song Wash.), 1959; Eliza and the Lumberjack (mus. play) (ofcl. territorial centennial play Wash.), 1954. Home: 606 W 2d St South Bend WA 98586 Office: 705 Robert Bush Dr South Bend WA 98586

DAVIS, HOLLY, academic administrator; b. N.Y.C., Aug. 9, 1951; d. Bernard and Trudy D.; m. George Kovac, Oct. 9, 1977; children: Michael, Justin Alexander. BA, Mich. State U., 1973; JD, U. Chgo., 1976. Bar: Ill. 1977. Atty. Continental Bank, Chgo., 1976-79; asst. dean Law Sch. U. Chgo., 1979—. Office: Univ Chgo Law Sch 1111 E 60th St Chicago IL 60603

DAVIS, INGER PEDERSEN, social work educator; b. Holstebro, Denmark, Oct. 16, 1927; came to U.S., 1961; naturalized, 1970; d. Niels Aage and Ansine Wilhelmine (Larsen) Pedersen; m. Kenneth Culp Davis, 1962. BS, Statens Kursus, Copenhagen, 1948; MSW, Copenhagen Sch. Social Work, 1952; MA (U.N. fellow), U. Chgo., 1962, PhD, 1972. Dir. reference library dept. Social Affairs, Copenhagen, 1954-59; lectr. Copenhagen Sch. Social Work, 1959-61, research asst., textbook writer, 1962-64; parent counselor, caseworker Chgo. Child Care Soc., 1965-67; lectr. then asst. prof. sch. social service adminstrn. U. Chgo., 1971-76; mem. faculty sch. social work San Diego State U., 1977—, prof. social work, 1981—, also bd. dirs. found.; mem. regional steering com. Child Welfare Tng. Ctr., UCLA, 1979-82; mem. San Diego County Commn. Children and Youth, 1987—; co-investigator NIMH Foster Care Rsch. Project, 1989—. Author: Adolescents Theoretical and Helping Perspectives, 1985; contbr. rsch. and clin. practice articles to profl. jours. Fulbright fellow, 1956, 61-62; Fed. Child Welfare Teaching grantee, 1977-82. Mem. Internat. Assn. Schs. Social Work, Coun. Social Work Edn., Nat. Assn. Social Workers, Nat. Coun. of Family Rels. Office: San Diego State U San Diego CA 92182

DAVIS, JAN, small business owner, artisan, former secondary school educator; b. Corpus Christi, Tex., June 29, 1943; d. Reuben T. and Ruby (Englert) Pattillo; AA, Del Mar Coll., 1963; BA, U. Houston, 1965; teaching cert. S.W. Tex. State U., 1971; children: William A., Wade. Tchr., Edna (Tex.) Jr. High Sch., 1966-67, counselor, 1967-68; tchr. Pleasanton (Tex.) High Sch., 1972-85; mem. supt.'s com. Pleasanton Pub. Schs., 1975-77, 78-79; chmn. social studies dept., 1976-85; owner Crystal Rose Enterprises, 1988—. Leader 4-H, 1978-89, 4-H youth coord. County of Atascosa, Tex., 1986-89. Recipient Meritorious Svc. award Vol. Leaders Assn. Tex., Mem. Tex. Classroom Tchrs. Assn. (Tchr. of Year 1979), Pleasanton Classroom Tchrs. Assn., Nat. Speakers Assn., South Tex. Profl. Speakers Assn., Lay Preaching Guild, 4-H Vol. Leaders Assn. (pres. Dist. 13 1987-88), Pleasanton Jr. Woman's Club (1st v.p. 1976, pres. 1977), A&M Women's Club of Atascosa County (pres. 1978-80), Toastmasters. Roman Catholic.

DAVIS, JANE STRAUSS, banker; b. Chgo., July 3, 1944; d. Joseph Loeb and Leonore (Purvin) Strauss; m. Muller Davis, Dec. 28, 1963; children: Melissa Jane Smith, Muller Jr., Joseph. BA with honors in Am. Culture, Northwestern U., 1981. Residential saleswoman Kenneth Friend Realty, Winnetka, Ill., 1971-74, J.H. Kahn Realty, Glencoe, Ill., 1974-77; v.p. personal trust dept. Harris Trust & Savs. Bank, Chgo., 1983-89; v.p. Bankers Trust Co. Pvt. Bank, Chgo., 1989—. Mem. women's bd. Rush-Presbyn.-St. Luke's Med. Ctr., Chgo., 1971—; bd. dirs. United Charities Chgo., 1978—; co-chmn. med. rsch. campaign Michael Reese Med. Ctr., Chgo., 1982; mem. costume com. Chgo. Hist. Soc., 1980-90; mem. campaign for gt. tchrs. Northwestern U., Evanston, Ill., 1988-90, vis. com., 1990—; mem. Chgo. Symphony Orch. Woman's Assn., 1990—.

DAVIS, JANICE ANN, marketing professional; b. Honolulu, Hawaii, Oct. 26, 1953; d. Patricia Ann (Jarcki) Pardee; m. Alfred Ross Davis, June 12, 1976, (div. Jan. 1978); child: Megan Patricia. BA, San Diego State U., 1975, MA, 1977-79; AB, Kent State U., 1979-81. Promotion dir. Los Altos Shopping Center, Long Beach, Calif., 1976-77; grad. teaching asst. San Diego State U., 1977-79; univ. fellow Kent (Ohio) State U., 1979-81; asst. prof. N.D. State U., Fargo, dir. grad. studies, 1983-84; pres. Davis and Assocs., 1984-86; sr. tng. cons. The Evans Group, Dallas, 1986-87; dir. devel. Morehead and Co., Los Angeles, 1987-; cons. No. Telecom, Ericsson Inc., IBM, Xerox, Deloitte, Haskins & Sells. Mem. Am. Soc. Tng. Devel., Am. Mgmt. Assn., Internat. Communication Assn., Speech Communication Assn. Republican. Home: 1809 Camden Blvd #1 Los Angeles CA 90025 Office: Morehead and Co 2029 Century Park E Suite 820 Los Angeles CA 90067

DAVIS, JARITA DELORES, airline executive; b. Pitts., Jan. 8, 1958; d. John Robert Sr. and Julia Diggs; m. Tony Lamar Davis, May 13, 1989. BA, Hampton U., 1979. Cert. realtor, ins. agt. Quality control supr., prodn. supr. Procter & Gamble, Co., Chgo., 1979-82, prodn. staff mgr., 1982-83; gen. plant supr. Pepsi Co., Inc., Detroit, 1983-85; airport ops. mgmt. assoc. United Airlines, Chgo., 1985-86; supr. ramp svcs. United Airlines - O'Hare, Chgo., 1986-88; gen. mgr. ops. United Airlines - O'Hare, Peoria, 1988; staff exec. svcs. planning div. United Airlines - O'Hare, Elk Grove, Ill., 1989—; owner, pres. Europea Auto Imports, Inc., Schaumburg, Ill., 1986-89, Europea Mktg. Group, Schaumburg, Ill., 1989—. Author: (booklets) Luxury Motorcar Opportunity Report, 1986; author company newsletter "Pacific News" 1990, co. tng. materials. Mem. Urban League, Chgo., 1987—; dir. accommodations Corinthian Bus. and Profl. Guild, Chgo., 1985-89; co. coord. Jr. Achievement, Chgo., 1980-82, Youth Motivation Program/Chgo. Assn. Commerce and Industry, 1980-82; mem. Evangel Assembly of God Ch., Schaumburg. Recipient music award Corinthian Temple Radio Choir, Chgo., 1979-82; named to Outstanding Young Women of Am., 1981, 83, 85, 88. Mem. Am. Mgmt. Assn., NAFE, Black Profl. United Orgn., Women United. Office: United Airlines PO Box 66100 Chicago IL 60666

DAVIS, JEANINE MARIE, horticulturist, educator; b. Oak Park, Ill., Jan. 21, 1955; d. Clayton Joseph and Annamarie (Henneberg) Schwartz; m. Glen Richard Davis, May 27, 1981; 1 child, Shannon Jeanine Davis. AA in Fine Art, Montgomery County Cmmnty Coll., 1975; BS in Horticulture, Del. Valley Coll., 1980; MS in Horticulture, Washington State U., 1983, PhD in Horticulture, 1987. Teaching asst. Washington State U., Pullman, 1981-82, rsch. asst., 1981-87, teaching asst., 1987-88; asst. prof. Mountain Hort. Crops Rsch. & Extension Ctr. N.C. State U., Fletcher, 1988—; advisor N.C. Herb Assn., 1990—, N.C. Tomato Growers Assn., 1988—. Contbr. articles to profl. jours. Mem. City Coun. City of Albion, Washington, 1987. Recipient Outstanding Woman in Grad. Studies award Washington State U. Assn. for Faculty Women, 1986; Frances Premo scholar Washington State U., 1984, 85, Lindahl Meml. scholar Washington State U., 1983, 86; Arnold & Julia Greenwell fellow Washington State U., 1981. Mem. Am. Soc. for Hort. Sci. (nat. and so. region), Am. Soc. of Plant Physiologists, Sigma Xi (Student Rsch. Paper award 1987). Office: NC State Univ Mountain Hort Crops Rsch & Extension Ctr 2016 Fanning Bridge Rd Fletcher NC 28732

DAVIS, JILL RENEA, jeweler; b. Houston, Mar. 16, 1966; d. Lowell Key and Francys (Joyce) D. Student, S.W. Tex. State U., San Marcos, 1990—. Salesperson Dillard's, Austin, Tex., 1982-84; office mgr. Corrigans-Zale Corp., Austin, 1985—. Contbr. articles to profl. jours. Mem. Am. Mktg. Assn., Soc. Profl. Journalists, Pub. Rels. Student Soc. Am., NAFE, Phi Chi Theta. Home: 112 West Ave #163 San Marcos TX 78666-6674

DAVIS, JOAN, land developer, consultant, tax preparer; b. Anderson, Ind., Nov. 24, 1947; d. Harold Brewer and Alice Marie (Doll) Hall; m. L.R. Collier Sr., May 19, 1967 (div. 1980); children: Missy JoAn Collier Basham, L.R. Jr.; m. Timothy G. Davis, Oct. 10, 1982; stepchildren: Geraldine Marie, Eugene Francis. Grad. high sch., Riverside, Calif. Sec. Svc. Electric, Inc., Riverside, 1966-68; pres. Power Electric, Inc., Norco, Calif., 1972-76; office mgr. Cutter Electric, Inc., Rialto, Calif., 1976-77; exec. asst., controller, corp. sec. Home & Country, Inc., Riverside, 1977—; owner, tax preparer Davis Bus. Svc., Riverside, 1978—. Mem. Rubidoux Falcon Football Boosters (sec. publicity com. Riverside chpt. 1983-88). Republican. Home: 6981 Pacheco Ct Riverside CA 92504 Office: Home & Country Inc 7265 Jurupa Ave Riverside CA 92504

DAVIS, JOANNE KING HERRING, foreign service officer, consultant, television personality; b. San Antonio; d. W. Dunlap and Maelan McGill (Johnson); m. Robert R. Herring (dec.); children—Beau S. King, Robin D. King; m. Lloyd K. Davis. Ed., U. Tex. TV talk show hostess, editor Sta. KHOU TV, Houston, 1963-72, Sta. KPRC-TV, Houston, 1973-75; hon. consul of Morocco, Houston, 1973—; cons. LTV, WEDTECH, CONTRAVES; bd. dirs. First Bank Houston, Coronado Oil Co., Kittinger Furniture, Internat. Films Prodns. Inc.; hostess numerous fgn. ministers, princes, ambassadors including Kings of Sweden, Jordan, Morocco, Pres. of Egypt, Pres. of Pakistan, Shah of Iran, Prime Minister of Belgium, Houston. Knighted, King of Belgium; Decorated, Pres. Pakistan. Bd. dirs. Lindbergh Fund, Moroccan Am. Found., Houston Ballet, Houston Youth Symphony. Republican. Presbyterian. Clubs: Lyford Cay; Met. (N.Y.C.); Rivers Oaks Country, Ramada, Houston.

DAVIS, JODI A., copy editor, page designer; b. Point Pleasant, N.J., Aug. 5, 1964; d. Richard M. and Joanne L. (Newman) D. BS magna cum laude, Syracuse U., 1985. Editing intern Syracuse (N.Y.) Newspapers, 1985; rsch. asst. Syracuse U., 1985; copy editor The Register, Shrewsbury, N.J., 1985-86, Asbury Park Press, Neptune, N.J., 1987—; adj. prof. Monmouth Coll., West Long Branch, N.J., 1987-88; coordinator sch. journalism workshops, Monmouth County, N.J., 1986—. Active Greenpeace, 1989. Mem. Aircraft Owners and Pilots Assn. Republican. Home: 3431 Bridge Ave #2 Point Pleasant NJ 08742 Office: Asbury Park Press 3601 Hwy 66 Neptune NJ 07754

DAVIS, JOLENE BRYANT, publisher, editor; b. Lehigh, Iowa, Dec. 11, 1942; d. Joseph Albert and Joyce (Olson) Bryant; m. Richard Alan Alper, Feb. 2, 1967 (dec. July 1975); m. Steven Andrew Davis, Apr. 16, 1979; children: Bryant David, Suzanne Joyce. BA, U. Iowa, 1964; MA, Calif. State U., San Jose, 1972. Registered dietitian, Ind. Home economist The Oregonian, newspaper, Portland, 1965-67; dietitian Ind. U. Sch. Medicine, Indpls., 1973-74; clin. dietitian U. Calif. Hosps. and Clins., San Francisco, 1974-75, chief clin. dietitian, 1975-78, chief rsch. dietitian Clin. Study Ctr., 1979-83; pub., editor-in-chief Our Kids mag. Branford Pub., Inc., San Antonio, 1984—, v.p., 1988—, also bd. dirs.; sec., bd. govs. Parenting Publs. Am., San Antonio, 1988-89. Mem. San Antonio Conservation Soc., 1985—; bd. dirs. Jewish Family Svc. Assn., San Antonio, 1986-88, Family Resource Ctr., San Antonio; chmn. cultural arts PTA, San Antonio, 1988—. Mem. Women in Communications (editor mag. column and Best mag. 1988, Best Column award 1988), Am. Dietetic Assn., Soc. Nutrition Edn., San Antonio Dist. Dietetic Assn., Pi Beta Phi. Home: 102 Wisteria Dr San Antonio TX 78213 Office: Our Kids Mag 6804 West Ave San Antonio TX 78213

DAVIS, JOY LEE, English educator; b. N.Y.C., Apr. 3, 1931; d. William Henry and Genevieve (Rhein) Belknap; m. Peter John King, Aug. 26, 1955 (div. Feb. 1985); children: William Belknap King, Russell Stuart King; m. John Bradford Davis, Jr., July 5, 1986. AB, Wellesley Coll., 1952, AM, 1953; PhD, Rutgers U., 1968; postgrad., Oxford (Eng.) U., 1978. Tchr. English Dana Hall Sch. for Girls, Wellesley, Mass., 1953-54; instr. English U. Mo., Columbia, 1954-55, Boston U., 1955-56; tchr. English Brookline (Mass.) High Sch., Spartanburg (S.C.) High Sch., 1956-60; prof. English Ohio Wesleyan U., Delaware, 1966-71, Hamline U., St. Paul, 1972-74, U. Minn., Mpls., 1974-77, Coll. St. Thomas, St. Paul, 1977-88; lectr., tutor Joy Davis Seminars, North Oaks, Minn., 1988—. Pub. poetry in New World Writing and Crisp Pine Anthology. Bd. trustees Ramsey County Arts and Sci. Coun., St. Paul, 1974-80. Wellesley Coll. scholar, 1952. Mem. AAUW (bd. dirs., chair cultural com. 1986—, Svc. award St. Paul br. 1983), Midwest MLA, Mpls. Inst. Fine Arts, Minn. Club (bd. dirs. 1982-88), New Century Club (bd. dirs., spl. subjects chmn.), Schubert Club (bd. dirs., chmn. mus. com.), Wellesley Coll. Club (regional campaign com.), Delta Kappa Gamma. Republican. Presbyterian. Home and Office: 18 E Pleasant Lake Rd North Oaks MN 55127

DAVIS, JOY LYNN EDWARDS, educator; b. Speedwell, Tenn., Apr. 5, 1945; d. Arnold Vergil and Mary Jane (Maddox) Edwards; m. Joe Mac Davis, 1969. BA, Lincoln Meml. U., 1967; postgrad., Berea (Ky.) Coll., 1972, U. Tenn., 1969-73; MA, Union Coll., Barbourville, Ky., 1974. Classroom tchr. Montegomery Co. Bd. Edn., Dayton, Ohio, 1967, Campbell County Bd. Edn., Jacksboro, Tenn., 1967—; cons. Appalachian studies, various groups in Ea. Tenn., 1972—. Contbg. author: Immigrants and First Families of America, 1988, More Seedwell Families, 1988; poetry included in The American Poetry Anthology, The World of Poetry. Active Internat. Wildlife Fund, Washington, 1987—, Nature Conservancy; inductee Lincoln Meml. U. Literary Hall of Fame, 1985. Recipient Stokley Fellowship award Stokely Inst. for Liberal Arts. Mem. NEA, Campbell County Edn. Assn., Tenn. Ednl. Assn., Nat. Wildlife Fedn., Smithsonian Assn., Nat. Coun. Tchrs. English, Delta Kappa Gamma. Home and Office: Rte 2 Box 302 LaFollette TN 37766

DAVIS, JOYCE NANNETTE, pharmaceutical executive; b. Rocky Mount, N.C., Feb. 5, 1958; d. William Roy Davis, Jr. and Joyce Carter; m. Stuart William Davis, July 8, 1979. Grad., U. N.C., 1978. Cert. CPR instr., EMT. Infirmary RN U.N.C./Wilmington Health Assocs., Wilmington, N.C.; staff RN, relief charge nurse emergency dept. New Hanover Meml. Hosp., Wilmington; pub. health RN New Hanover County Health Dept.; clin. rsch. assoc. Pharm. Prodn. Devel. Home: 806 Fitzgerald Dr Wilmington NC 28405

DAVIS, JUDY ANN, nurse; b. Hastings, Nebr., Mar. 3, 1942; d. Creighton Russell and Esther Maysie (Light) Marymee; m. Dale Arlen Davis, Nov. 22, 1969; children: Melissa Ann, Jennifer Ruth. RN with honors, Immanuel Hosp. Sch. Nursing, Omaha, 1964; AAS in Data Processing with dean's honors, City Coll. Chgo., 1985. Lic. nurse, Ind., Nebr. Sec. dept. medicine U. Nebr. Med. Ctr., Omaha, 1960-61; evening charge nurse Children's Meml. Hosp., Omaha, 1964-65; head nurse pediatrics Bapt. Meml. Hosp., Kansas City, Mo., 1965-69; nurse technician U. Nebr. Med. Ctr., Omaha, 1969-71; staff nurse Stormont Vail Hosp., Topeka, 1978-79; staff devel. coord. Hillhaven of Topeka, 1979; afterhours caseworker ARC, Landstahl, Fed. Republic Germany, 1981-82; clin. team leader info. systems St. Vincent Hosp. and Healthcare Ctr., Indpls., 1985-89; project mgr., team leader mainframe applications info. systems Immanuel Med. Ctr., Omaha, 1989—. Editor newsletter U.S. Army Ordnance Ctr. and Sch. Wives Club, 1972. Bd. mem. Topeka Artist's Associated, 1979-81; mem. Mayor's Disaster Adv. Coun., Topeka, 1979-81; bd. mem. Anchorage Concert Assn., 1976-78; chmn. jr. youth program ARC, Ft. Richardson, Alaska, 1976. Mem. NAFE. Republican. Baptist. Home: 13431 Lake St Omaha NE 68164 Office: Immanuel Med Ctr 6901 N 72d St Omaha NE 68122

DAVIS, JULIA MCBROOM, speech pathology and audiology educator; b. Alexandria, La., Sept. 29, 1930; d. Guy Clarence and Addie (McElroy) McBroom; m. Cecil Ponder Davis, Aug. 25, 1951 (div. 1981); children: Mark Holden, Paul Houston, Anne Hamilton; m. David G. Reynolds, Aug. 26, 1987. BA, Northwestern State U., Natchitoches, La., 1951; MS, U. So. Miss., 1965, PhD, 1966. Cert. in clin. competence in audiology. Asst. prof. U. So. Miss., Hattiesburg, 1966-69, assoc., 1969-71; assoc. prof. Southwestern State U., Hammond, 1971; faculty U. Iowa, Iowa City, 1971-87; prof., chmn. dept. speech pathology and audiology U. Iowa, 1980-85, assoc. dean Coll. Liberal Arts, 1985-87, dir. Speech and Hearing Ctr., 1979-80; dean Coll. Social and Behavioral Scis. U. South Fla., Tampa, 1987—. Author: (with Edward J. Hardick) Rehabilitative Audiology for Children and Adults, 1981; editor: Our Forgotten Children, 1977; assoc. editor Jour. Speech Hearing Research, 1975-77, Jour. Speech Hearing Disorders, 1982-83. Fellow Am. Speech-Hearing-Lang. Assn. (chmn. program com. 1980-81), Iowa Speech and Hearing Assn. (v.p.-liaison 1972-73, honors 1985); mem. Acad. Rehabilitative Audiology (pres. 1979-80), Iowa Conf. for Hearing Impaired (pres. 1975-76), Sigma Xi. Democrat. Methodist. Office: U South Fla Coll Social and Behavioral Scis Tampa FL 33620

DAVIS, JULIE MANN, public relations and marketing firm executive; b. Atlanta, Oct. 5, 1960; d. Hunter M. and Paula (Elliott) Mann. AA, Emory U. Oxford College, 1980; BA in Journalism, Ga. State U., 1983. Researcher, prod. asst. NBC News, S.E. Bureau, Atlanta, 1980-84; pub. rels. account exec. Burton Campbell, Atlanta, 1984-87; prin. Kimble-Davis Mktg., Atlanta, 1987-89; pres. Julie Davis Assocs., Atlanta, 1989—. Vol. pub. rels High Mus., Cancer Soc., Hunger Walk, Kidney Found. Bot. Garden, Arts Alive; bd. dirs. Combined Health Appeal; vol. Dukakis for Pres. of U.S. campaign; media and image cons. Atlanta Jour.-Constitution polit. coverage. Named to All Star Team, Atlanta Bus. Chronicle, 1988, named one of Women to Watch, 1990, named to Atlanta Agy. Dream Team, AdWeek Mag. 1989. Mem. Women In Communication (Atlanta chpt.), bd. dirs. Atlanta Ad Club. Presbyterian. Office: 3565 Piedmont Rd Bldg 3 Ste 515 Atlanta GA 30305

DAVIS, KAREN PADGETT, economist, educator; b. Blackwell, Okla., Nov. 14, 1942; d. Walter Dwight and Thelma Louise (Kohler) Padgett; 1 child, Kelly Denise. BA, Rice U., 1965, PhD, 1969. Asst. prof. econs. Rice U., 1969-70; econ. policy fellow Social Security Adminstrn. Brookings Instn., Washington, 1970-71, rsch. assoc., 1971-74, sr. fellow, 1974-77; dep. asst. sec. for planning and evaluation, health HEW, Washington, 1977-80; adminstr. health resources adminstrn. USPHS, Washington, 1980-81; prof. Johns Hopkins U., Washington, 1981—, chmn. dept. health policy and mgmt., 1983—; dir. The Commonwealth Fund Commn. on Elderly People Living Alone, 1985—; vis. lectr. Harvard U., 1974-75. Author: National Health Insurance: Benefits, Costs and Consequences, 1975, Health and the War on Poverty, 1978, Medicare Policy: New Directions for Health and Long-Term Care, 1986; assoc. editor Milbank Meml. Fund Quar., Health and Soc., 1972-77; regional editor Health Policy, 1985—; mem. Physician Payment Rev. Commn., 1986—. Mem. Inst. Medicine, Am. Econs. Assn., Phi Beta Kappa. Democrat. Methodist. Home: 414 New Jersey Ave SE Washington DC 20003 Office: Johns Hopkins U Sch Hygiene Dept Health Policy & Mgmt 624 N Broadway Baltimore MD 21205

DAVIS, KATHARINE CLELAND, retired law librarian, information specialist, researcher; b. Ft. Myers, Va., Oct. 15, 1907; d. Cleland and Mabel Tillou (Young) D.; m. Alfred Stuart, May 1936 (div.). BA, Wells Coll., Aurora, N.Y., 1930; MFA, Yale U., 1933. Tech. dir. Shubert Corp. Theater, N.Y.C., 1933-34; info. specialist USDA, Washington, 1951-53; asst. to ASTIA after process U.S. Libr. of Congress, 1954-56; asst. law libr. U. Miami, Coral Gables, Fla., 1957-74, 88—, Nova U., Ft. Lauderdale, Fla., 1974-76; exec. asst. Loebe Rhodes Investment Co., South Miami, Fla., 1977-81; libr. asst. Drexel, Burnham, Lambert & Sochet, South Miami, Fla., 1981-88; libr. asst. Sochet & Co., South Miami, 1988-90, ret., 1990. Contbr. articles to profl. jours. Charter mem. Rep. Presdl. Task Force, Washington, 1981—; mem. High Frontier, Washington, 1983—; reader Recording for the Blind, 1958-78. Lt. comdr. USN, 1942-46. Mem. Yale U. Alumni Assn., Actors Equity Assn., Mil. Order Wars (comdr. 1988-89), Coun. for Inter-Am. Security, State Dept. Watch, Security and Intelligence, Moral Rearmament Breakthroughs, Accuracy in Media, Yale Club Miami, Wells Club Fla. Home: 4045 Malaga Ave Coconut Grove FL 33133

DAVIS, KATHLEEN ANN, journalist; b. Lubbock, Tex., Oct. 5, 1955; d. Richard Arlen and Jacqueline A. (Anderson) Harris; m. Kenneth Don Harris, June 19, 1976 (div. Nov. 1981); children: Spring Dawn, Nathan Don. BS, Tex. Tech U., 1978, M of Agriculture, 1987. Instr. journalism Tex. Tech U., Lubbock, 1986-87; freelance writer, 1978—; editor The Adventure, Episcopal Diocese N.W. Tex., Lubbock, 1988-89; farm editor Lubbock Avalanche Jour., 1978-89; sci. writer Tex. A&M U., Coll. Sta., 1990—. Author: Such are the Trials, 1990; contbr. over 120 articles to mags. Recipient 3 First Place and 1 Third Place awards Tex. Press Women, 1990, 2nd Place award Nat. Assn. Agriculture Journalists, 1990, Pub. Svc. award AP Tex., 1989. Mem. Nat. Assn. Agriculture Journalists (pres. 1989), Women In Communications, Inc. (freedom of info. chair 1989, Communicator of Yr. award 1989), Tex. Press Women (Lubbock area v.p. 1989). Episcopalian. Home: 212 Rustic Oaks Dr Bryan TX 77802

DAVIS, KATHRYN LEOLA, labor union administrator; b. Muskogee, Okla., Apr. 23, 1954; d. Hershall Alvin and Jwell Juanita (Hale) Brown; m. Larry Dewayne Workman, Aug. 7, 1970 (div. Oct. 1978); 1 child, Tracy L. AS in Quality Control Tech., U. Tulsa; BS in Indsl. Technology, Northeastern State U., 1985, M in Indsl. Technology, 1987; postgrad., Tulsa U. Coll. Law, 1988. Cert. union counselor United Way Labor Community Services, 1979; lic. in airframe and powerplant, FAA. Machine operator Swan Hose Co., Stillwater, Okla., 1972-73; quality control inspector Dorsett

Electronics/Labarge, Inc., Tulsa, Okla., 1973-74; mechanic Cessna Aircraft Co., Wichita, Kans., 1974-75; quality control lab. technician Red Devil, Pryor, Okla., 1975; mechanic McDonnell Douglas Corp., Tulsa, 1975-78, inspector, 1978-80, quality control analyst, 1980-86, structures and installations planner, 1986—; Mem. exec. bd., recording sec. UAW Local 1093, Tulsa, 1978-84, chair women's com., 1978-86, voting del. polit. action com., 1978—, voting del. community action com., 1978—, fin. sec., 1986—. Mem. community service com. Camp Fire Girls, Tulsa, 1978—, Claremore, Okla., 1980-82, Claremore Christian Fellowship Ch. Mem. Am. Soc. for Quality Control, Coalition of Labor Union Women (del. convention 1982-86, 88), Local Union Press Assn., Epsilon Pi Tau, Phi Alpha Delta. Democrat. Lodge: Eastern Star. Home: 201 W 20th St Owasso OK 74055 Office: UAW Local 1093 1414 N Memorial Tulsa OK 74112

DAVIS, KATHRYN WASSERMAN, foundation executive, writer, lecturer; b. Phila., Feb. 25, 1907; d. Joseph and Edith (Stix) Wasserman; m. Shelby Cullom Davis, Jan. 4, 1932; children: Shelby M. Cullom, Diana Davis Spencer, Priscella Alden (dec.). BA, Wellesley Coll., 1928; MA, Columbia U., 1931; D Es Polit. Sci., U. Geneva, 1934. Researcher Coun. on Fgn. Rels., N.Y.C., 1934-36, State of Pa., Phila., 1936-37; writer and lectr. on fgn. affairs N.Y., 1937—; ptnr. Shelby Cullom Davis & Co., N.Y.C., 1985—; pres. Shelby Cullom Davis Found., N.Y.C., 1985—; lectr. in field. Author: Soviets at Geneva, 1934. Trustee Wellesley Coll., 1983—; v.p. Women's Nat. Rep. Club, 1976—, chmn. internat. affairs com.; bd. govs. Harvard U., mem. vis. com. Russian studies, 1986—; pres. LWV. Mem. Cosmopolitan Club (N.Y.C., com. fgn. visitors), Sleepy Hollow Club Scarborough, N.Y. Harbor Club, Seal Harbor Club (Maine). Home: 193 Wilson Park Dr Tarrytown NY 10591 Office: Shelby Cullom Davis & Co 70 Pine St New York NY 10270

DAVIS, KIM MCALISTER, retail executive; b. Woodruff, S.C., Dec. 30, 1958; d. James Calhoun and Nancy (Caldwell) McAlister; m. Robert James Godfrey; 1 child, Lindsey Paige; m. Don Brigham Davis. BA in Elem. Edn., U. S.C., 1982, MBA, 1983—. Cert. tchr., S.C.; lic. real estate, Fla. Adminstrv. asst. Dr. G.R. Shanbhag and Assocs., Woodruff, 1977-78; sales rep. Reimer's Dept. Store, Woodruff, 1978-80; tchr. Spartanburg County Sch. Dist., Woodruff, 1981-82; pres., owner Godfrey Carpets, Inc., Woodruff, 1983-88; pharm. sales rep. Parke-Davis Pharm. Co., Ponte Vedra Beach, Fla., 1989—. Mem. decorating com. 1st Bapt. Ch., Woodruff, 1984-87, now mem. music com.; chmn. bd. dirs. Small Towns Program, Woodruff, 1987—; Rep. candidate for Spartanburg County Coun., 1987; mem. S.C. Rep. Com.; chmn. Nat. Bus. Women's Week, 1984; bd. dirs. Ponte Vedra-Palm Valley Elem. Sch. Named Young Careerist of the Yr., Nat. Bus. and Profl. Women, 1984. Mem. NAFE, Nat. Fedn. Ind. Bus., Greater Woodruff Area C. of C. (pub. speaker, bd. dirs. 1985-87, pres. 1986), Bus. and Profl. Women (v.p. 1985), Woodruff Jr. Women's Club, Oak Bridge Women's Club. Home and Office: 4401 Cypress Creek Dr Ponte Vedra Beach FL 32082

DAVIS, KRISTIN WOODFORD, banker; b. Palo Alto, Calif., June 20, 1944; d. William Woodford and Meredith Gene (Wilber) D.; children: Jillian Barry Davis-Leavens. Student, Oreg. State U., 1962-64, Drew U., Madison, N.J., 1966; BA, U. Redlands, 1968. Social worker County Welfare Dept., San Bernardino, Calif., 1968-69, Bur. Children's Svcs., Morristown, N.J., 1969-70; program dir. Human Resources Inst., Brussels, Belgium, 1974-76; sales agt. Prudential Ins. Co., West Orange, N.J., 1981-82; underwriter Chubb Group Ins. Cos., Warren, N.J., 1982-85; v.p. Carteret Savs. Bank, Morristown, N.J., 1985-88, Nat. Westminster Bank, U.S.A., N.Y.C., 1988—; bd. dirs. Bankers Ins. Co., Ltd., Bermuda; mem. adv. bd. Coll. Ins., N.Y.C., 1987—. Bd. dirs. Internat. Youth Ctr., Brussels, 1973-76. Mem. Risk and Ins. Mgmt. Soc. (v.p., sec. 1986-88), Am. Womens Club Brussels (dir. 1972-76). Office: Nat Westminster Bank 175 Water St New York NY 10038

DAVIS, LAURA ANN, marketing manager; b. Wilmington, Del., Dec. 30, 1959; d. James W. and Jean E. (Sachtjen) D. BA in Sociology with high honors, U. Del., 1981; MBA in Mktg., Emory U., 1985. Credit-collection analyst Chase Manhattan Bank, Wilmington, 1982-84; retail store supr. Exxon Co., Dallas, 1985-86; project and product mgr., sr. rsch. analyst Equifax Inc., Atlanta, 1986-89, project dir. new product devel., 1989—; adj. prof. Mercer Univ., 1988—; participant numerous seminars and profl. tng. courses in field. Mem. Save the Children. Recipient MBA Merit scholarship, Emory U., 1983-85, Sociology Award for Excellence, Alpha Kappa Delta, 1981. Mem. NAFE, Am. Mktg. Assn., World Future Soc., Amnesty Internat. (literacy tutor), Planning Forum, Toastmasters, Sierra Club. Republican. Episcopalian. Home: 1101 Collier Rd NW Apt U-5 Atlanta GA 30318

DAVIS, LAURA ARLENE, foundation administrator; b. Battle Creek, Mich., Apr. 14, 1935; d. Paul Bennett and Daisy E. (Coston) Borgard; m. John R. Davis, Aug. 7, 1955; children—Scott Judson, Cynthia Ann Davis Welker. B.S., Central Mich. U., 1986. Sec., Mich. Loan Co., Battle Creek, 1952-56; legal sec. Ryan, Sullivan & Hamilton, Battle Creek, 1957-64; exec. sec. W.K. Kellogg Found., Battle Creek, 1965-76, adminstrn./program asst., 1976, fellowship dir., 1977, asst. v.p. adminstrn., asst. corp. sec., 1978-84; v.p. corp. affairs, corp. sec., 1984—. Mem. word processing adv. com. Kellogg Community Coll., Battle Creek, 1982—; v.p. bd. dirs. State Tech. Inst. and Rehab. Ctr., Delton, Mich., 1983-84; pres. bd. dirs. Charitable Union, Battle Creek, 1983-85; mem. allocations panel United Way of Battle Creek, 1983, v.p. community rels., 1990—; bd. dirs. Battle Creek Gas Co., 1990—; trustee Binder Park Zoo; mem. adv. coun. Argubright Bus. Coll., 1990; mem. Visionquest 5000, 1989. Mem. Adminstrv. Mgmt. Soc. (pres. chpt. 1982-83), Soc. Office Automation Profls., Am. Mgmt. Assn. Home: 131 Hanson Dr Battle Creek MI 49017 Office: W K Kellogg Found 400 North Ave Battle Creek MI 49017

DAVIS, LILA ROSS, public health officer; b. Balt., June 16, 1941; d. Robert P. and Lila (Norfleet) D. BA in Psychology, Mary Washington Coll., 1963; cert. in med. record adminstrn., USPHS Sch. for Med. Record Adminstrs., 1964. Chief med. record dept. DePaul Hosp., Norfolk, Va., 1964-66, Kings Daughters Children's Hosp., Norfolk, 1966-69; research analyst Norfolk Gen. Hosp., 1969-73; commd. officer USPHS, 1973, advanced through grades to capt., 1983; dep. chief med. record dept. USPHS Hosp., Norfolk, 1973-74; chief USPHS Hosp., 1974-79; chief med. record dept. USPHS Hosp., San Francisco, 1979-81; dep. dir. USPHS Health Data Ctr., Lanham, Md., 1981-83, dir., 1983-86; dir. USPHS Health Data Ctr., GWL Hansen's Disease Ctr., Carville, La., 1986—; cons. Fed. Bur. Prisons, Springfield, Mo., 1982; participant, cons. disaster med. assistance program Bur. Health Care and Delivery, Rockville, Md., 1983-86. Mem. Am. Med. Record Assn., La. Med. Record Assn., Commd. Officer Assn. USPHS, Assn. Mil. Surgeons U.S. Presbyterian. Lodge: Zonta. Home and Office: GWL Hansens Disease Ctr Carville LA 70721

DAVIS, LINDA JACOBS, small business owner; b. Miami, July 10, 1955; d. Martin Jacque and Doris Harriet (Stucker) Jacobs; m. John Joseph Mantos, Jan. 1, 1984 (dec. 1988); m. Perry Davis, June 4, 1989; 1 child, Aaron. Student, U. South Fla., 1977. Mgr., cons. Werner Erhard & Assocs., San Francisco, 1978-82, program leader, 1979—; asst. exec. dir. The Breakthrough Found., San Francisco, 1982-88; owner MantagarisGalleries, San Francisco, 1988—; profl. fund-raiser. Vol. The Hunger Project, Fla., 1977-78. Recipient Outstanding Young Women Am. Democrat. Jewish. Homw: 75 Milland Dr Mill Valley CA 94941 Office: Mantagaris Galleries 77 Geary San Francisco CA 94108

DAVIS, LINDA ROONEY, health care administrator; b. Pittston, Pa., Sept. 4, 1953; d. Leo G. and Genevieve (Szychowski) Rooney; m. Craig A. Davis, Oct. 1, 1983. Diploma in Nursing, Pittston Hosp. Sch. Nursing, 1974; BBA, Pa. State U., 1977, postgrad., 1987—. RN. Asst. instr. Pittston Hosp. Sch. Nursing, 1974-75; staff nurse M.S. Hershey (Pa.) Med. Ctr., 1975-77; resident care coord. Children's Care Ctr., Hummelstown, Pa., 1977-79; dir. edn. Emergency Health Svcs. Fedn. S. Cen. Pa., Lemoyne, 1979-80; asst. dir. Emergency Health Svcs. Fedn. S. Cen. Pa., 1980-81; dir. emergency/trauma edn. Harrisburg Hosp., Harrisburg, Pa., 1981-84; dir. primary care mgmt. Capital Health System, Harrisburg, 1984-90; adj. faculty Harrisburg Area Community Coll., 1981—, Harrisburg Inst. of Emergency Med. Svcs.; bd. dirs. Middletown (Pa.) Emergency Med. Svcs.; Mem. Med. Group Mgmt. Assn., Am. Group Practice Assn. Republican. Presbyterian. Home: 830 Ridgewood Dr Mechanicsburg PA 17055

DAVIS, LOIS ANN, computer software specialist, educator; b. Thermopolis, Wyo., Nov. 29, 1945; d. Hester Oliver and Ruth Louise (Baker) Davis; m. Harold W. Wright, Dec. 22, 1969 (div. 1988); children: Geraldine Ann, Harold W. III. BS in Bus. Edn. cum laude, U. Wyo., 1968, MS in Bus. Edn., 1988. Cert. office automation profl., Wyo. Instr. Lander (Wyo.) Valley High Sch., 1968-70, Cath. Sch., Chandler, Ariz., 1970-71; part-time instr. Casper (Wyo.) Coll., 1981-83, instr. bus. div., 1983—; textbook reviewer Prentice-Hall, Englewood, N.J., 1989—. Mem. NAFE, Office Automation Soc. Internat. (nominating com. 1990), Small Bus. Inst. Dirs. Assn. Home: PO Box 4358 Casper WY 82604 Office: Casper Coll Bus Div 125 College Dr Casper WY 82601

DAVIS, LORRAINE JENSEN, book editor; b. Omaha, Apr. 2, 1924; d. Theron R. and L. Mildred (Henkel) Jensen; m. Richard Morris Davis, Apr. 4, 1959 (dec.); 1 child, Laura Jensen. B.A., U. Denver, 1946. Copywriter Glamour mag., N.Y.C., 1946-54, prodn. editor, 1954-61; prodn. editor Vogue Children mag., N.Y.C., 1963-66. Writer, assoc. features editor, Vogue mag., N.Y.C., 1966-77; mng. editor, writer women's news column, 1977-88; editorial dir. Conde Nast Books, 1988—; editor: Vogue Living and Food Guide, 1975; editorial cons.: Vogue Beauty and Health Guide, 1979-82; editor: Cooking with Colette (by Colette Rossant), 1975, Fairchild Dictionary of Fashion (by Charlotte Calasibetta), 1975, English translation Paul Bocuse's French Cooking, 1977. Recipient Disting. Citizen award Alpha Gamma Delta, 1981. Mem. NOW. Democrat. Episcopalian. Club: Cosmopolitan. Home: 425 E 63d St W3J New York NY 10021 Office: Condé Nast Bldg 350 Madison Ave New York NY 10017

DAVIS, LOUISE SPIERS, educator; b. Malden, Mass., Jan. 11, 1911; d. Thomas H. and Elizabeth (Sullivan) Spiers; m. Frank L. Davis, June 24, 1939 (dec. Oct. 1952); children: Elizabeth Davis Littleton, Jane F. Davis-Gavin. AB, Boston U., 1932, MA, 1965; EdM, Tufts U., 1962; student U. London, 1966, Goldsmith Coll. London, 1966. Cert. secondary tchr., Mass. Tchr., Malden Pub. Schs., 1932-39; with Bedford Pub. Schs., 1953-73, program adminstr. social studies, 1960-73, tchr. emeritus, cons., 1973—; tchr. adult edn. program Hanscom AFB, Bedford, Mass., 1973-84; critic tchr. B.U. Tufts U., U. Mass., Boston Coll., Suffolk U.; lectr., cons. in field; mem. Mass. Dept. Edn. Nat. Coun. Social Studies, 1960-73; Mass. rep. Nat. Educators Conf. on Fgn. Policy, Dept. of State, Washington, 1967; Author pamplet; contbr. articles to profl. jours. Editor: Mass. Industry, 1966-67. Demonstration tchr., lectr. Newsweek Mag., 1970-73. Co-chmn. Bedford Dem. Town Com., 1976-78, coord., 1972-84, assoc. mem., 1984.; elected mem. Barnstable Dem. Town Com., 1986—, program chmn.; advisor Human Rels. Coun., 1962-63; del. Dem. State Conv., Springfield, Mass., 1982; class agt. ann. fund raising Boston U., Tufts U. Recipient Disting. Svc. Tchrs. medal Freedoms Found., 1970; State Citation, Dept. Edn., 1962, 63, 64, State Citation in field of human rels., Mass., 1962, 63; Coe fellow; Louise S. Davis Ann. Citizenship scholar. Mem. Mem. NEA, Mass. Tchrs. Assn., Nat. Coun. Social Studies, New Eng. History Tchrs. Assn., AAUW (pres. Housatonic Br. 1947-49, del. to Issue Conv. of Dem. Party of Mass. 1989), Tufts Alumni Assn., Boston U. Alumni Assn. Roman Catholic. Clubs: Hyannisport Yacht, Hyannis Yacht (assoc.); Boston U. of Cape Cod, Tufts U. of Cape Cod; Bedfords Woman's Community (com. chmn. 1965-70), Bedford Hist. Assn., Theta Phi Alpha (class agt. and corr. for CLA class of 1932 1982—), Delta Sigma Rho. Home: 36 Craigville Beach Rd PO Box 171 Hyannis Port MA 02647 also: 1410 Playa Azul III Luquillo PR 00673

DAVIS, LOURIE IRENE BELL, computer education specialist; b. Las Vegas, N.Mex., Apr. 8, 1930; d. Currie Oscar and Minnie I. (Rodgers) Bell; m. Robert Eugene Davis, Aug. 21, 1950; children: Judith Anne, Robert Patrick, (adopted) Jaime Alleyn, Flint Christopher. BS, West Tex. U., 1959; student Ea. N.Mex. U., 1947-49. Cert. systems profl.; cert. data processing profl. Programmer/analyst Blue Cross/Blue Shield Okla., Tulsa, 1972-75, mgr. systems, 1977-81, dir. info. systems, 1981-82, mgr. project control, 1982-83, mgr. info. ctr., 1984-85, mgr. profl. cons. and tng., 1985-87; ind. profl. cons., Tulsa, 1987; faculty devel. coord. tech. br. CAID Okla. State U., Okmulgee, 1987—; systems curriculum coord. Tulsa Jr. Coll., 1975-76, mem. computer sci. adv. bd., 1976-83; mem. steering com. U.S. Senate Bus. Adv. Bd., 1981; lectr. computer assisted instruction success League of Innovation Conf., St. Louis, 1989, Music Users Group Conf., U. Tenn., Chattanooga, 1989. Mem. budget panel United Way Tulsa, 1981-87, Allocations Exec. Com. Appreciation award, 1987; mem. U.S. Presdl. Task Force, 1982—. Winner League of Innovation for Community Colls. Competition, IBM, 1989. Mem. Assn. Systems Mgmt. (regional dir. 1985-86, chpt. membership chair 1982-84; internat. awards 1980, 84), NAFE, AAUW, Tulsa Area Systems Edn. Assn. (recorder 1980-81), Higher Edn. Acad. Coun. of Okla., Alpha Chi, Mensa, Intertel (nat. acceptance com. chair 1978, dir. region VIII 1987—). Republican. Mem. Unity Ch. of Christianity. Home: 2403 W Oklahoma Tulsa OK 74127 Office: OSU Tech 1801 E 4th Okmulgee OK 74447

DAVIS, LYDIA JOANNA, publishing executive; b. Kokomo, Ind., May 4, 1958; d. Henderson Sheridan and Ruth Vinita (Patterson) D. BA magna cum laude, Howard U., 1980. Reporter trainee Sta. WRTV-TV, Indpls., 1980-81; writer, researcher Johnson Pub. Co., Chgo., 1981-82, asst. dir. pub. relations, 1983, assoc. producer Ebony/Jet Celebrity Showcase, 1983, dir. promotion, 1983-85, v.p. promotion, 1985—. Recipient cert. Merit Circulation Direct Mail awards, 1984, Communications Excellence to Black Audiences, 1986, 88, 89. Mem. Chgo. Assn. Direct Mktg., League Black Women, Women's Advt. Club Chgo., Nat. Women of Achievement. Mem. African Methodist Episcopal Ch. Office: Johnson Pub Co 820 S Michigan Ave Chicago IL 60605

DAVIS, MARCIA WELCH, interior designer; b. Atlanta, Sept. 29, 1949; d. Edward Douglas and Annie Laurie (Smith) Welch; m. James J. Davis, Oct. 23, 1971 (div. Sept. 1982). B in Visual Arts, Ga. State U., 1971. With sales, unit control depts. J.P. Allen, Atlanta, 1968-71; draftsman U.S. Exchange System, Frankfurt, Fed. Republic Germany, 1972-74; leasing mgr. Post Properties, Atlanta, 1975; interior designer Alan L. Ferry Designers, Atlanta, 1976-81; pres. Davis-Kloss Interior Design and Space Planning, Atlanta, 1981-88, Marcia Davis & Assocs., Atlanta, 1988—. Contbr. articles to profl. jours. Trustee High Mus. Decorative Art, 1986-87. Mem. Am. Soc. of Interior Designers (bd. dirs. 1986—, v.p., 1982, chair coms. 1979-83), Women C. of C. (chmn. com. 1981, 87, bd. dirs. 1982-84, Named Outstanding Chmn. 1981), Atlanta C. of C., Midtown Bus. Assn., Buckhead Bus. Assn. Republican. Episcopalian. Home: 1421 Peachtree St #212 Atlanta GA 30309 Office: Marcia Davis & Assocs One Piedmont Ctr 3565 Piedmont Rd Ste 22 Atlanta GA 30305

DAVIS, MARGARET BRYAN, paleoecology researcher, educator; b. Boston, Oct. 23, 1931. AB, Radcliffe Coll., 1953; PhD in Biology, Harvard U., 1957. NSF fellow dept. biology Harvard U., Cambridge, Mass., 1957-58, dept. geosci. Calif. Inst. Tech., Pasadena, 1959-60; research fellow dept. zoology Yale U., New Haven, 1960-61, prof. biology, 1973-76; research assoc. dept. botany U. Mich., Ann Arbor, 1961-64, assoc. research biologist Great Lakes Research div., 1964-70, research biologist, assoc. prof. dept. zoology, 1966-70, research biologist, prof. zoology, 1970-73; head dept. ecology and behavioral biology U. Minn., Mpls., 1976-81, prof. ecology, 1976-82, Regents prof., 1982—; vis. prof. Quaternary Research Ctr., U. Wash., 1973; vis. investigator environ. studies program U. Calif., Santa Barbara, 1981-82; mem. adv. panel for ecology, NSF, 1976-79, mem. sci. adv. com. for biology, behavior and social scis., 1989—; mem. planetary biology com. Nat. Rsch. Coun., 1981-82, mem. global change com., 1987—, mem. screening com. in plant scis., mem. internat. exch. of persons com. 1972-75, mem. sci. and tech. edn. com., 1984-86; vis. rsch. scientist scholarly exch. com. NAS/Nat. Rsch. Coun., People's Republic of China; mem. U.S. nat. com. Internat. Union Quarternary Rsch., 1966-74. Mem. editorial bd. Quaternary Research, 1969-82, Trends in Ecology and Evolution, 1986—. Recipient Sci. Achievement award Sci. Mus. Minn., 1988, Alumnae Recognition award Radcliffe Coll., 1988. Fellow AAAS, Geol. Soc. Am.; mem. NAS (nominations com. 1988), Ecol. Soc. Am. (pres. 1987-88), Am. Quaternary Assn. (councillor 1969-70, 72-76, pres. 1978-80), Am. Soc. Limnology and Oceanography, Internat. Assn. for Great Lakes Research (bd. dirs. 1970-73), Nature Conservancy (bd. dirs. Minn. chpt. 1979-85), Phi Beta Kappa, Sigma Xi. Office: U Minn 107 Zool Bldg 318 Church St Minneapolis MN 55455

DAVIS, MARIE HENRIETTA, vocalist; b. Casper, Wyo., Aug. 13, 1929; d. James Otto and Bessie (Williams) Minor; m. Ernest Oliver Davis, Nov. 26, 1950; children: Beverly, Ernest Oliver Jr., Garrick, Teresa. AA, Casper Community Coll., 1950; BS in Music and Polit. Sci., Coll. of Notre Dame, 1980. Steno clk. prodn. acctg. Mobil Oil, Casper, 1962-64; ch. sec. Scott Meth. Ch., Denver, 1964-66; office clk. Dr. John Bookhardt, Denver, 1966-68; playground supr. San Mateo (Calif.) Elem. Sch. Dist., 1975-76; pvt. practice soprano soloist Foster City, Calif., 1950—; sec. Wyo. adv. com. to pres. Nat. Commn. on Civil Rights, 1961-64; remedy temp. San Mateo Temp. Assignments, 1990—. Del. alt. Dem. Nat. Conv., Calif., 1988; sec. Dem. Cen. Com., San Mateo, 1983-86; trustee, bd. dirs. Peninsula Assn. Retarded Children & Adults, San Mateo, 1984-89; bd. dirs. San Mateo County Arts Assn., 1987—. Mem. Am. Bus. Women's Assn. (charter), No. Calif. Assn. Cartoonists, NAACP (bd. dirs. San Mateo chpt. 1981—), Masterworks Chorale, AAUW, Order of Eastern Star (worthy matron 1956—). Methodist. Home: 317 Menhaden Ct Foster City CA 94404

DAVIS, MARION PEASE (MRS. PAUL DAVIS), social work administrator, therapist; b. Derby, Conn., Oct. 9, 1918; d. John Wood and Myrtle Stowe (Humphrey) Pease; m. Paul Davis, Oct. 15, 1938; children: Linda Davis Payne, Robert, Richard. BA in Psychology, U. Bridgeport, 1964; MSW, U. Conn., 1969. Cert. Ind. social worker, Conn.; cert. hypnotherapist, past life therapist. Caseworker dept. welfare State of Conn., Bridgeport, 1964-65, social worker dept. protective svcs., 1965-67, supr. protective svcs. unit, 1969-73, sr. psychiat. social worker, 1973-75, supervisory psychiat. social worker, 1975-78; dir. psychiat. social workers Greater Bridgeport Community Mental Health Ctr., 1973-82, chmn. housing com., 1974-78, mem. accreditation com., 1974-78, chmn., 1978-81, chief psychiat. social work, 1978-82; pvt. practice psychiatric social worker, 1982—; owner Winning Combinations, 1983-86. Contbg. author: The Courage to Grow Old. Mem. profl. adv. com. Vis. Nurses Assn., 1987—; mem. Sr. Citizens Needs Assessment Com., 1987-89; sec., co-chair by-laws com. Washington Sr. Citizens Ctr. Coun., 1987-89; vice-chair Washington Srs. Coun., 1987-88; mem. profl. adv. bd. Rainbow Nursery Sch. Co-editor: Washington Sr. Ctr. News, 1987-89. Mem. Nat. Assn. Social Workers (diplomate, registered clin. social worker, mem. exec. com. 1974-75, editorial com. 1975-77), Am. Assn. Marriage Family Counsellors (assoc. 1978-80), Logos World Univ. Bd. (chair curriculum com. 1986-88), Huxley Inst. Biosocial Rsch. (v.p., bd. dirs. 1978-81), Conn. Assn. Human Svcs., Mental Health Svcs. Coordinating Com. (rec. sec., exec. com. 1975-82, corr. sec. 1978-82), Assn. for Rsch. and Enlightenment (rep. study group 1963-79, 84—), Conn. Assn. Rsch. and Enlightenment (sec. 1986-88, v.p. 1987-88, chair Conn. coun. 1989—, editorial com. 1989—), Assn. for Past Life Rsch. and Therapy (accreditation 1988), Soc. for Clin. and Exptl. Hypnosis, Internat. Soc. Hypnosis, Nat. Guild Hypnotists (cert. 1988), Assn. for Study Dreams, LWV (bd. dirs. 1985—, pres. 1986-88, chair agrl. study com. 1986-88, co-chmn. mem. com. 1988—), Acad. of Certified Social Workers. Home: 47 Sunset Ln Washington Depot CT 06794

DAVIS, MARSHA ROSS, educator; b. Paducah, Ky., Jan. 4, 1952; d. William Elliot and Lillian Maxine (Moores) Ross; m. B. Owen Davis Jr., Dec. 29, 1977; 1 child, William Jacob. AA, Henderson (Ky.) Community Coll., 1972; BS, Western Ky. U., 1974, MS, 1977; postgrad. Murray State U., 1980. Tchr. Smith Mills (Ky.) Elem., 1974-84, East Heights Elem., Henderson, Ky., 1984—; mem. faculty adv. council Henderson County Schs. Mem. Spottsville (Ky.) Vol. Fire Dept., 1982—. Recipient Presdl. scholarship, Western Ky. U., 1974. Mem. NEA, Ky. Edn. Assn., Internat. Council for Computers in Edn. Democrat. Methodist. Hom: 8621 Old US 60 Spottsville KY 42458 Office: East Heights Elem Sch 1776 Adams Ln Henderson KY 42420

DAVIS, M(ARSHA) SUE, dietitian; b. Reedley, Calif., Apr. 18, 1948; d. Julius Virgil and June Adeen (Root) Toews; m. Robert Cary Davis, Sept. 1964 (div. Dec. 1978); children: Tami, Robbie, Shelley. BS, Loma Linda U., 1981, MS, 1985. Computer dietitian Loma Linda (Calif.) U. Med. Ctr., 1982-89; dir. Nutritional Svcs. Feather River Hosp., Paradise, Calif., 1989—; speaker in field. Recipient scholarship Am. Dietary Products, 1981-82. Mem. NAFE, Am. Dietetic Assn., Electronic Computing Health Oriented. Republican. Office: Feather River Hosp The Nutri-Group Inc 5974 Pentz Rd Paradise CA 95969

DAVIS, MARTHA DEMETER, assistant principal, educator; b. Uniontown, Pa., Oct. 31, 1949; d. Michael Edward and Virginia Iris (Groover) Demeter; m. Gareth Andrew Davis, Dec. 19, 1970 (div. May 1990); children: Gary, Elaine, Joy. BS in Edn., California (Pa.) State Coll., 1970; MEd, W.Va. U., 1975; postgrad., Loyola Coll., Balt., 1987—. Cert. elem. and middle sch. tchr., reading specialist, elem. and middle sch. prin.-supr. Tchr. Connellsville (Pa.) Area Sch. Dist., 1970-74; tchr. Harford County Bd. Edn., Bel Air, Md., 1974-89, asst. prin., 1989—. Mem. Nat. Assn. Elem. Sch. Prins., Md. Assn. for Supervision and Curriculum Devel., State of Md. Internat. Reading Coun., Alpha Delta Kappa. Democrat. Roman Catholic.

DAVIS, MARY HELEN, psychiatrist, educator; b. Kingsville, Tex., Dec. 2, 1949; d. Garnett Stant and Emogene (Campbell) D. BA, U. Tex., 1970; MD, U. Tex., Galveston, 1975. Cert. Nat. Bd. Med. Examiners, Am. Bd. Psychiatry and Neurology, Child and Adolescent Psychiatry. Intern, then resident in psychiatry SUNY, Buffalo, 1975-78; fellow in child psychiatry U. Cin., 1978-80; asst. prof. Med. Coll. Wis., Milw., 1980-89, clin. assoc. prof., 1989—; med. dir. adolescent treatment unit Milw. Psychiat. Hosp., 1981-86, Schroeder Child Ctr., 1986-89; pvt. practice, 1989—; cons. Milw. Mental Health Cons., 1980—, Children's Svc. Soc., Milw., 1982—. Bd. dirs. Next Generation Theater, Milw., 1988—. Named one of Outstanding Young Women of Am., 1985. Mem. Am. Psychiat. Assn., Am. Soc. Adolescent Psychiatry, Am. Acad. Child and Adolescent Psychiatry, Am. Med. Women's Assn. Baptist. Club: Univ. (Milw.). Office: 1055 N Mayfair Rd Wauwatosa WI 53226

DAVIS, MARY IONE, systems analyst; b. Missoula, Mont., Mar. 19, 1942; d. Eugene Charles and Alice Ione (Raben) D. Student, U. Mont., 1960-64; cert., Animal Control Acad., Billings, Mont., 1986. Tech. asst. Booz, Allen Applied Research, Bethesda, Md., 1967-72; research asst. Booz, Allen Systems, Washington, 1970-71; assoc. scientist Booz, Allen Applied Research, Bethesda, 1972-77, Transp. Consulting Div., Bethesda, 1977; systems analyst Great Falls (Mont.) Police Dept., 1977-78, Blue Cross & Blue Shield of Mont., Great Falls, 1979-87, Agrl. Stabilization and Conservation Svc., USDA, Great Falls, 1989—; cons. Internat. Bus. Svcs., Inc., Washington, 1978, Wilbur Smith and Assocs., Denver, 1978. Author: various manuals, 1970-87. Past mem. Nat. Space Club, Washington, 1973-77, Am. Astronautical Soc., Washington, 1970-77, Mont. State Soc., Washington, 1960-77. Mem. NAFE, Electric City Kennel Club (Great Falls, pres. 1984, 85), Action for Animals (Great Falls, pres. 1988). Office: 7725 Brookeville Rd Chevy Chase MD 20815

DAVIS, MARY JANE, lawyer; b. Omaha, May 21, 1951; d. Edwin and Jane Elizabeth (Young) D.; m. Joseph A. Meo, Aug. 30, 1971 (div. Feb. 1985). BA, Beaver Coll., 1978; JD, Temple U., 1986. Bar: Pa. 1987. Tchr., tutor Colonial and Springfield Sch. Dists., Montgomery County, Pa., 1978-81; assoc. Meredith & Cohen, Phila., 1986-88, Margolis, Edelstein, Scherlis, Sarowitz and Kraemer, Phila., 1988—. Chmn. legis. action League of Women Voters, Montgomery County, 1982-83; mem. adv. com. Spl. Olympics, Bucks and Montgomery County, 1980-84. Mem. Phila. Bar Assn. (co-chair problems of homeless com., 1986—, mem. mental disabilities com., 1986—; bd. dirs. disabilities law project), Pa. Mental Health Assn. (govt. rels. com.). Democrat. Office: Margolis Edelstein Scherlis Sarowitz & Kraemer/Curtis Ctr 4th Fl/Independence Square W Philadelphia PA 19106

DAVIS, MARY JOSEPHINE, executive assistant; b. Newark, Ohio, Mar. 24, 1947; d. Jacob George Spillman and Alice Caroline (Mintier) Toothman; 1 child, Jeffrey Dale Davis. Student in pub. rels., Juliet Gibson Career Coll., Columbus, Ohio, 1966. Lic. real estate agt., Fla. Owner/operator Four Pines Ctr, Utica, Ohio, 1968-75; real estate salesperson Carroll Biggs Realty, Utica, Ohio, 1975-79; sec. to the pres. Tequesta (Fla.) Properties, Inc., 1979-81; office mgr. Huntzinger Constrn. Corp., Jupiter, Fla., 1981-83; exec. asst. to the pres. U.S. Sports, Inc., Lake Worth, Fla., 1983—; Mem. Jupiter/Tequesta Bd. Realtors, 1981—. Fund raiser Licking County Dem. Party, Newark, 1970-72; mem. Two/Ten Nat. Found. Charity Trust, Watertown,

Mass., 1986—. Recipient Lion of Judah award women's div., Jewish Fedn., Palm Beach, Fla., 1983. Mem. Notary Pub. Assn. of Fla., NRA, NAFE, Nat. Assn. Realtors, Fla. Assn. Realtors. Home: 1144 11th Court Jupiter FL 33477 Office: US Sports Inc 2601 Tenth Ave North Lake Worth FL 33461

DAVIS, MONIQUE (DEON DAVIS), state legislator; b. Chgo., Aug. 19, 1936; d. James and Constance (Dutton) McKay; divorced; children: Robert Jr., Monique C. Conway. BS in Edn., Chgo. State U., 1967, MS in Guidance and Counseling, 1976. Tchr. Chgo. Bd. Edn., 1967-86, coordinator, 1986—; rep. 36th dist. Ill. Ho. of Reps., 1987—. Mem. legis. com. Chgo. Area Alliance Black Sch. Edn., 1982-84, Independent Voters of Ill.-Independent Precinct Orgns., Chgo., 1982-83; coordinator 21st ward, Citizens for Mayor Washington, 1985, 87. Recipient GRIT award Roseland Womens Orgn., 1987; named a Tchr. Who Makes a Difference PTA, 1978, 85. Mem. Chgo. Area Tchrs. Alliance (chmn.), Christian Bd. Edn. (bd. dirs. 1978-82), Phi Delta Kappa. Mem. United Ch. of Christ. Office: 9449 S Ashland Chicago IL 60820

DAVIS, NATALIE ZEMON, history educator; b. Detroit, Nov. 8, 1928; d. Julian Leon and Helen (Lamport) Zemon; m. H. Chandler Davis, Aug. 16, 1948; children: Aaron Bancroft, Hannah Penrose, Simone Weil. BA, Smith Coll., 1949, DHL (hon.), 1977; MA, Radcliffe Coll., 1950; PhD, U. Mich., 1959; D hon., Universite Lyon II (France), 1983; DHL (hon.), Northwestern U., 1983, U. Rochester, 1986, Lawrence U., 1984, George Washington U., 1987; LLD (hon.), Tufts U., 1987; DHL (hon.), Reed Coll., 1988, Muhlenberg Coll., 1989, New Sch. for Social Rsch., 1989; LLD (hon.), Williams Coll., 1987; LLD, Goucher Coll., 1989; LLD (hon.), Muhlenberg Coll., 1989, New Sch. for Social Rsch., 1989. Lectr. to asst. prof. Brown U., 1959-63; asst. prof. to assoc. prof. U. Toronto, 1963-71; prof. history U. Calif.-Berkeley, 1971-77; Henry Charles Lea prof. history Princeton U., 1978—. Author: Society and Culture in Early Modern France, 1975 (Berkeshire Conf. spl. award 1976), The Return of Martin Guerre, 1983, Fiction in the Archives: Pardon Tales and Their Tellers in Sixteenth-Century France, 1987. Recipient teaching citation U. Calif.-Berkeley, 1974, Outstanding Achievement award U. Mich., 1975, New Eng. Hist. Assn. Media award, 1985; decorated Chevalier Ordre des Palmes Academiques France, 1976. Fellow Am. Acad. Arts and Scis.; mem. Renaissance Soc. Am., Soc. French Hist. Studies (pres. 1976-77), Am. Hist. Assn. (council 1972-75, pres. modern history sect. 1980, pres. 1987), Soc. Reformation Research, Am. Antiquarian Soc. (selected mem. 1987). Democrat. Jewish. Home: 78 Alexander St Princeton NJ 08540 Office: Princeton U Dept History Princeton NJ 08544

DAVIS, PAMELA BOWES, physician; b. Jamaica, N.Y., July 20, 1949; d. Elmer George and Florence (Welsch) Bowes; m. Glenn C. Davis, June 28, 1970 (div. Mar. 1987); children: Jason, Galen. AB, Smith Coll., 1968; PhD, Duke U., 1973, MD, 1974. Intern in internal medicine Duke Hosp., 1973-74, resident in internal medicine, 1974-75; sr. investigator Nat. Inst. of Arthritis, Metabolism & Digestive Diseases/NIH, Bethesda, Md., 1977-79; asst. prof. U. Tenn. Coll. Medicine, Memphis, 1979-81; asst. prof. Case Western Res. U. Sch. Medicine, Cleve., 1981-85, assoc. prof., 1985-89, prof., 1989—, chief, pediatric pulmonary div., 1985—; pres. Am. Fedn. for Clin. Rsch., Thorpofare, N.J., 1989-90; bd. trustees Rsch! Am., Arlington, Va., 1989-90. Contbr. articles to profl. jours. Chmn., med. adv. coun. Cystic Fibrosis Found., Bethesda, 1988-90. Fellow Am. Coll. Physicians; mem. Am. Physiol. Soc., Am. Thoracic Soc., Soc. for Pediatric Rsch., Phi Beta Kappa, Sigma Xi. Office: Rainbow Babies/Child Hosp 2101 Adelbert Rd Cleveland OH 44106

DAVIS, PAMELA EILEEN, banker; b. Johnstown, Pa., Feb. 29, 1956; d. William Ashley and Dorothy Eileen D. BA in Econs. cum laude, Dickinson Coll., 1978; postgrad., Pa. Sch. Banking, Bucknell U., 1981-82; postgrad, Stonier Grad. Sch. Banking. Officer loan dept. Am. Bank, 1980-82, asst. v.p. SBA loan dept., 1982-83; v.p., mgr. SBA loan dept. Meridian Bank, Reading, Pa., 1984—. Mem. adv. com. Kutztown U. Coll. of Bus.; treas. Berks Women's Council; bd. dirs. Berks County YWCA, chmn. long range planning com., 1986-88, mem. fin. com. 1990—' chmn. City of Reading Enterprize Zone loan com. Recipient Berks County YWCA Trendsetter Yr. award, 1986. Mem. Nat. Assn. Accts. (pres. Reading chpt. 1984-85, rep. Mid-Atlantic Council 1986-89), SBA (Region III Phila. Adv. Council 1988—, Adv. of Yr. award 1986), Robert Morris Assocs., Berks Women's Network (1st v.p. and chmn. membership com. 1987-88), Berks County C. of C. (chmn. Program for Women com., Small Bus. com.), WAFER (co-founder). Republican. Presbyterian. Office: Meridian Bank PO Box 1102 Reading PA 19603

DAVIS, PAULETTE JEAN TURNER, educator, editor, consultant; b. Racine, Wis., Apr. 9, 1946; d. Thomas Elmer and Lorraine Lucille (McClure) Turner; m. Wesley Kent Davis, June 1, 1968; children: Rebecca Lynn, Rachel Marie, Shannon Ruth. BS cum laude, U. Wis., Whitewater, 1968. Cert. secondary edn. and English tchr., Wis. Tchr. Ft. Atkinson (Wis.) Schs., 1968-69, Janesville (Wis.) Sch. Dist., 1969-74, 88—, Beloit (Wis.) Pub. Schs., 1984, Blackhawk Tech. Inst., Janesville, 1984, U. Wis.-Rock Ctr., Janesville, 1985; editor joint project for Janesville Found., Janesville Pub. Sch. Dist. and Janesville Pub. Libr., 1983-85; del. White House Conf. on Domestic and Fgn. Affairs, 1980. Mem. com. Dem. Party of Wis., Janesville, 1983-85; edn. dir. St. Mark's Luth. Ch., Janesville, 1984-86; co-chair many local and state campaigns, Wis., 1983—; vice chair 1st Congl. Dist. Dem. Party of Wis., 1989—; mem. Nat. Women's Polit. Caucus, YMCA, YWCA. Mem. NEA, Wis. Edn. Assn., Janesville Edn. Assn., Rock Valley United Tchrs. Assn. (bd. dirs. 1973-74), PTA, AAUW (women's chair Janesville chpt. 1980-82, bd. dirs. 1980—), Ch. Women United (bd. dirs. Janesville chpt. 1980—, vice chair). Home: 2441 Kenwood Ave Janesville WI 53545

DAVIS, PEGGY COOPER, law educator; b. Hamilton, Ohio, Feb. 19, 1943; d. George Clinton and Margaret (Gillespie) Cooper; m. Gordon Jamison Davis, Aug. 24, 1968; 1 child, Elizabeth Cooper. BA, Western Coll. for Women, 1963; student, Barnard Coll., 1963-64; JD, Harvard U., 1968; student, N.Y. Soc. for Freudian Psychologists, 1972-73. Bar: N.Y., 1969, U.S. Supreme Ct., 1976. Law clk. to judge U.S. Dist. Ct., N.Y.C., 1972-73; asst. counsel capital punishment project NAACP Legal Def., N.Y.C., 1973-77; assoc. prof. law Rutgers U., N.J., 1977-78; assoc. prof., NYU, 1983-86, prof. 1987—; dep. criminal justice coordinator City of N.Y., 1979-80; judge Family Ct. State of N.Y., 1980-83. Contbr. articles to profl. jours. Bd. dirs. Vera Inst., N.Y.C., Com. for Modern Cts., Fund for City of N.Y. Fellow N.Y. Inst. for Humanities. Office: NYU Sch Law 40 Washington Sq New York NY 10012*

DAVIS, RAYTHEA GALE, counselor, writer; b. Poteau, Okla., Nov. 12, 1943; d. Arnold Dean Davis and Anne Leora (Weaver) Page; m. James R. Pickle, May 21, 1959 (div. Aug. 1987); children: Vickie Pickle Davis, Silvan Wayne, Kimberley Pickle Maio, Sami Gale. AS in Psychology, N.Mex. State U., Grants, 1981; BA in Psychology, U. N.Mex., 1984, MA in Counselor Edn., 1986. Career counselor Grants campus N.Mex. State U., 1982—; v.p. N.Mex. Placement Coun., 1986-87, pres., 1987-88. Writer (newspaper) Career Talk, 1987—, View From My Window, 1989—; pub., editor: West Wind mag., 1990—; author: Jour. for Adult Career Devel., 1987. Vice pres. United Way of Cibola County, Grants, 1987—; chair edn. com. Grants C. of C., 1988. Recipient Cibola County Woman of Achievement award N.Mex. State U. Women's Resource Conf., 1990. Mem. AAUW (sec. Grants chpt. 1987-88), Rotary. Democrat. Home: 705 Flagstaff Grants NM 87020 Office: NMex State U 1500 N Third St Grants NM 87020

DAVIS, RUTH C., pharmacy educator; b. Wilkes-Barre, Pa., Oct. 27, 1943; d. Morris David Davis and Helen Jane Gillis. BS, Phila. Coll. Pharmacy and Sci., 1967. Cert. pharmacist, Pa., Md. Mgr., pharmacist Neighborcare Pharmacy, Balt.; tchr., pharmacist Boothwyn Pharmacy, Phila. Republican. Baptist. Home and Office: 90 Lion Dr Hanover PA 17331

DAVIS, RUTH LENORE, college president; b. Toledo, Ohio, Mar. 24, 1910; d. Thurber Phillips and Ila L. (Andrews) D. BSBA, U. Ariz., 1932, postgrad., 1932-34; postgrad., U. Mich., 1941-42; DEd, Johnson and Wales Coll., R.I., 1983. Sec. to supt. schs. Tucson Pub. Schs., 1934-35; tchr. Tucson Sr. High Sch., 1935-41; supervising and sr. acct. Jeep Corp., Toledo, 1942-45; v.p. Davis Coll., Toledo, 1941-42, 45-56; pres. Davis Coll., 1956-85, pres. emeritus, 1985—. Trustee Epworth United Meth. Ch., Toledo, 1986-89; mem. Com. of 100, Toledo, 1985-88; fin. com. YWCA, Toledo, 1982. Recipient Outstanding Citizenship award, Internat. Inst. Phi Theta Phi, 1987, Outstanding Bus. Educator, 1973, Svc. award Mid-Am. Bank, 1980. Mem. Adminstrv. Mgmt. Soc. (pres. 1973-74, 300 Club award), Ohio Bus. Sch. Assn. (pres. 1946-49), Davis Jr. Coll. Bd. (v.p., trustee 1983—), Toledo Zonta Club (pres. 1984-49), Internat. Personnel Women Toledo (pres. 1975-76). Republican. Methodist. Home: 2720 Inwood Dr Toledo OH 43606

DAVIS, RUTH MARGARET (MRS. BENJAMIN FRANKLIN LOHR), former government official, computer executive; b. Sharpsville, Pa., Oct. 19, 1928; d. W. George and Mary Anna (Ackermann) D.; m. Benjamin F. Lohr, Apr. 29, 1961. BA, Am. U., 1950; MA, U. Md., 1952, PhD, 1955. Statistician FAO, UN, Washington, 1946-49; mathematician Nat. Bur. Standards, 1950-51; head ops. rsch. div. David Taylor Model Basin, 1955-61; staff asst. Office Dir. Def. Rsch. and Engring. Dept. Def., 1961-67; asso. dir. rsch. and devel. Nat. Libr. Medicine, 1967-68; dir. Lister Hill Nat. Center for Biomed. Communications, 1968-70; dir. Inst. for Computer Scis. and Tech. Nat. Bur. Standards, 1970-77; dep. undersec. def. for rsch. and engring., 1977-79; asst. sec. resource applications U.S. Dept. Energy, 1979-81; pres. Pymatuning Group Inc., 1981—; bd. dirs. Control Data Corp., United Telecommunications Inc., Air Products and Chems., Varian Assocs., BTG, Inc., Premark Internat., Inc., Prin. Fin. Group Inc.; trustee Consol. Edison Co. of N.Y., Aerospace Corp.; lectr. U. Md., 1955-57, Am. U., 1957-58; vis. prof. computer sci. U. Pa., 1969-72; adj. prof. U. Pitts.; cons. Office Naval Rsch., Washington, 1957-58; mem. Md. Gov.'s Sci. Adv. Coun., 1971-77; chmn. nat. adv. coun. Electric Power Rsch. Inst., 1975-76. Contbr. articles to profl. jours. Trustee Inst. Def. Analysis; bd. visitors Cath. U. Am. Recipient Rockefeller Tech. Mgmt. award 1973, Fed. Woman of the Yr. award, 1973, Systems Profl. of Yr. award, 1979, Disting. Svc. medal U.S. Dept. Def., 1979, Disting. Svc. medal U.S. Dept. Energy, 1981, Gold medal, 1981, Ada A. Lovelace award, 1984; inducted into Computer News Hall of Fame, 1988. Fellow AIAA, Soc. for Info. Display; mem. AAAS, Am. Math Soc., Math Assn. Am., Nat. Acad. Engring., Nat. Acad. Pub. Adminstrn., Washington Philos. Soc., Phi Kappa Phi, Sigma Pi Sigma. Office: Pymatuning Group Inc 2000 N 15th St Ste 707 Arlington VA 22201

DAVIS, SARA A., librarian; b. Beaver, Pa., Sept. 27, 1956; d. Eugene H. and Blanche (Pogemiller) D. BS in Edn. and LS, Edinboro U. Pa., 1978; MLS, Tex. Woman's U., 1981. High sch. libr. Houston Ind. Sch. Dist., 1978-80; resident asst. Tex. Woman's U., Denton, 1980-81; libr. Jacobs Engring. Group, Houston, 1981—. Choir dir. Woodhaven Bapt. Deaf Ch., Houston, 1987-90; interpreter Houston Community Coll., 1987-89; researcher Dukakis Campaign, Houston, 1988. Mem. Spl. Librs. Assn. (student liaison person, nominations chmn., editor newsletter Houston LPG 1980-85, chmn. consultation 1988-90), AAUW, Greater Houston Interpreters for Deaf, Sweet Adelines. Office: Jacobs Engring Group 4848 Loop Central Dr Houston TX 77081

DAVIS, SARA LEA, pharmacist; b. Knoxville, Tenn., Aug. 1, 1951; d. Horace William and Margaret Jewel (Hill) D. BS in Liberal Arts, U. Tenn., 1973; BS in Pharmacy, U. Tenn., Memphis, 1976, PharmD, 1977. Asst. mgr. Pharmaco Nuclear, Inc., Chgo., 1977-79; nuclear pharmacist Kansas City, Mo., 1979, Bapt. Meml. Hosp., Memphis, 1979-83; asst. mgr. Syncor, Inc., Washington, 1983-84; staff pharmacist Rite Aid Corp., Knoxville, 1984-87, pharmacist-in-charge, 1987—; rep. 3d High Country Nuclear Medicine Conf., Vail, Colo., 1983; mem. adv. bd. V.I.P. Home Nursing & Rehab., Knoxville, 1985-86. Active Leconte Exec. Women's Coun. Mem. Am. Pharm. Assn., Acad. Pharm. Sci. (sect. nuclear pharmacy), Soc. Nuclear Medicine, Memphis Bus. and Profl. Women's Assn. (bd. dirs. 1982-83), Mortar Bd., Phi Beta Kappa, Phi Kappa Phi, Rho Chi, Alpha Lambda Delta. Baptist. Club: Club Leconte, U. Tenn. Century Club. Office: Rite Aid Pharmacy 824 Tri-County Blvd Oliver Springs TN 37840

DAVIS, SHARLA JANE, court official; b. Sacramento, Oct. 24, 1963; d. Eddie Wayne and Lillie Louise (Little) Hash; m. David Russell Davis, Nov. 22, 1986. Student, Shasta Coll., 1982-83, 87—, Chico State U., 1990—. Legal sec. David L. Morrow, Redding, Calif., 1982-86; legal sec., ct. clk. to U.S. magistrate U.S. Dist. Ct. for Ea. Dist. Calif., Redding, 1986—. Mem. NAFE. Republican. Mem. Christian and Missionary Alliance Ch. Office: US Magistrate J Ross Carter 1736 Tehama St Redding CA 96001

DAVIS, SHARRON KAY, credit reporting company executive; b. Lubbock, Tex., Mar. 27, 1953; d. Cleon Elmer and Wilma (Dawson) D.; m. (div. Sept. 1977). Diploma in fashion merchandising and bus. Bauder Fashion Coll., Arlington, Tex., 1972. Dist. sec. Gen. Electric Credit Corp., Lubbock, 1973-77; asst. to mgr. Equico Lessors, Lubbock, 1977-78; loan processor Nat. Mortgage Co., San Antonio, 1978-79; gen. mgr. Chilton Credit Reporting (merged with TRW Inc.), Lubbock, 1979-89, br. sales mgr. TRW Credit Data, Lubbock, 1989—. Local vol. worker Am. Cancer Soc., 1982—, March of Dimes, 1985; 2nd v.p. ICA of South Plains, 1990. Named Mgr. of Yr., Chilton Credit Reporting, 1983. Mem. Credit Women Internat. (Boss of Yr. award 1985). Republican. Home: 4609 62d St Lubbock TX 79414 Office: TRW Credit Data 5502 58th St #300 Lubbock TX 79414

DAVIS, SHEREE RENEE, personnel specialist; b. Kansas City, Kans., Oct. 7, 1965; d. Theodore and Willie Earlene (Bolden) Shade; m. Reginald O. Davis, Aug. 29, 1987; 1 child, Brianna Sheree. BA in Personnel Adminstrn., U. Kans., 1987. Teller Capitol Fed. Savs. & Loan, Topeka, 1987-88; sec. Shawnee County Courthouse, Topeka, 1988; asst. mgr. Kay-Bee Toy Store, Topeka, 1988-89; personnel specialist Topeka Capital-Jour., 1989—. Mem. Project Redirectory Com., Topeka, 1990—. U. Kans. scholar, 1983-84. Mem. Job Svc. Employer's Com. Democrat. Home: 967 SW Lindenwood Topeka KS 66606 Office: Topeka Capital Jour 616 SE Jefferson St Topeka KS 66607

DAVIS, SUSAN ELIZABETH, physical therapist; b. Oklahoma City, Okla., July 26, 1955; d. Fred Allison and Beverly Ann (Ralph) Farmer; m. Mark Edward Davis, May 19, 1978. BS/Cert. Physical Therapy, Northwestern U., Chgo., 1977. Physical therapist Christian Hosp., St. Louis, 1977-78, Monmouth Med. Ctr., Long Branch, N.J., 1978-81; asst. chief physical therapist Somerset Med. Ctr., Somerville, N.J., 1981-82, chief physical therapist, 1982-84; dir. rehab. Jersey Shore Med. Ctr., Neptune, N.J., 1984-86; pres. Marlboro Physical Therapy, PA, Morganville, N.J., 1986—, 1986—; instr. Union County Coll., Scotch Plains, N.J., 1981-82, adv. com. Physical Therapist Asst. Program, 1982-83. Mem. First Baptist Ch., Red Bank, N.J., 1978—, bd. fin., 1989. Mem. Am. Physical Therapy Assn. (sec. N.J. chpt. 1983-85, N.J. del. 1981-84), N.J. Assn. Woman Bus. Owners, North Jersey Shore, Alumnae Club Kappa Kappa Gamma. Office: Marlboro Physical Therapy Ste 104 100 Campus Dr Morganville NJ 07751

DAVIS, SUSAN FRANCES, international real estate broker; b. Chgo., Mar. 5, 1939; d. John S. Wysocke and Patricia (Dyess) Roberts; m. George Davis, Jan. 27, 1973; 1 child, Lisa. A. BS, So. Ill. U., 1962; postgrad., San Diego State Grad. Sch., 1963-64. Elem. sch. tchr. Elk Grove Sch. Dist., Arlington Heights, Ill., 1968-74; realtor Livable Forest, Kingwood, Tex., 1977-82; v.p. Corp. Investment Bus. Brokers, Houston, 1985-86; owner, broker Investments Internat., Kingwood, 1983—; pres., owner Reunions with Class, Kingwood, 1987—. Mem. AAUW, Internat. Real Estate Fedn. (v.p. Houston chpt.), Internat. Realtors Assn. Roman Catholic. Club: Republican Woman's (Kingwood). Home and Office: 1726 Chestnut-Ridge Kingwood TX 77339

DAVIS, SUSAN GLORIA, sales representative, consultant; b. St. Louis, Oct. 5, 1957; d. Victor Henry and Vivian Norma (Stille) D. BS, Maryville Coll., 1982; MBA, Oklahoma City U., 1983. Mktg. coord. HBE Bank Facilities, St. Louis, 1979-82; sales rep. NCR Corp., St. Louis, 1983-85; sr. sales rep. UNISYS, St. Louis, 1985-88; account exec. Gould Electronics, St. Louis, 1988-89; sales rep. Tandem Computers, Inc., St. Louis, 1989—. Mem. NAFE. Republican. Congregationalist. Office: Tandem Computers Inc One City Pl Dr Saint Louis MO 63141

DAVIS, SUZANNE GOULD, small business owner; b. N.Y.C., Apr. 22, 1947; d. Lawrence Robert and Diana (Klotz) Gould; 2 children. Diploma in French Civilization Studies with honors, Sorbonne U., Paris, 1967; BA in French magna cum laude, Tufts U., 1968; MA in ESL Edn., Columbia U., 1975, MLS, 1984. Prodn. asst. James Garrett and Ptnrs., N.Y.C., 1969-70; adminstrv. asst. Alvin Toffler, N.Y.C., 1970-71; dir. mktg. Econ. Models Ltd., London, 1971; mgr. John Player Info. Bur., London, 1972-73; mgr. mktg. Berkey Film Processing, N.Y.C., 1974-75; free-lance editor, translator N.Y.C., 1975-82; gen. mgr. Rosemary Scott Temps. Inc., N.Y.C., 1983-86; pres. Suzanne Davis Temps. Inc., N.Y.C., 1986—. Editor-translator: La Méthode Orange: Teacher's Manual, 1977. Mem. Arts and Bus. Council, N.Y.C., 1984—. Mem. NAFE, Nat. Assn. Women Bus. Owners, Spl. Librs. Assn., N.Y. Assn. Temp. Svcs. (bd. dirs. 1986-87, co-chmn. program com.), Murray Hill Bus. and Profl. Women's Orgn. (bd. dirs. chmn. scholarship com. 1985, young careerist award 1886-90), Beta Phi Mu. Office: Suzanne Davis Temps Inc 20 E 46th St Ste 302 New York NY 10017

DAVIS, SYBIL ALICIA, physician; b. New Haven, Feb. 24, 1954; d. Ezra Davis and Gladys Isabel (Friedland) Gabrielson; m. Jeremy Nathan Williams, Aug. 7, 1974; children: Meredith Davis-Williams, Emily Davis-Williams. BA, Boston U., 1974; life sci. teaching credential, Calif. State U., Northridge, 1976; MS in Biology, Calif. State U., L.A., 1982; MD, U. So. Calif., 1986. Diplomate Nat. Bd. Med. Examiners. Biology instr. L.A. Unified Schs., 1976; sci., math. instr. Santa Monica-Malibu (Calif.) Unified Schs., 1976-80; lectr. botany, zoology Calif. State U., L.A., 1981-82; intern, resident Kaiser Permanente Med. Found., L.A., 1986-90, staff physician dept. ob-gyn., 1990—. vol. tchr. Operation Headstart, Cambridge, 1973, Northridge Hosp. Emergency Rm., 1980-82, Sherman Oaks Luth. Children's Ctr., 1982, 84. Recipient citation for Meritorious Svc. to Pub. Edn. Masonic Lodges, 1977, Svc. Award Sherman Oaks Luth. Children's Ctr., 1982, 84. Fellow Am. Coll. Ob-Gyn. (jr.); mem. AMA, Calif. Med. Assn. (biomedical ethics com. L.A. County chpt. 1983-85). Office: Kaiser Sunset Dept Ob-Gyn 4900 Sunset Blvd Los Angeles CA 90027

DAVIS, T. ELEANOR, realtor, consultant, financial advisor; b. Atlanta, Aug. 25, 1960; d. Charles L. and Thora (Gwinn) D. AA with honors, Emory U., Oxford, Ga., 1980; BBA in Internat. Bus., U. Ga., 1982. Lic. stockbroker, real estate agt., Ga.; cert. comml. investment mem., investment real estate coun. Stockbroker Merrill Lynch, Atlanta, 1983-84; fin. advisor for stocks and real estate investors, Atlanta, 1984—, realtor, cons. on site analyzation retail developers, users, 1986—; realtor Remax of Atlanta, Tucker, Ga., 1986-89, Metro Brokers, Atlanta, 1989—. Social chmn. singles dept. Rainbow Park Bapt. Ch., Decatur, Ga., 1980—; mem. adv. bd. March of Dimes, Atlanta, 1982-87; chmn. comml. coun. DeKalb Bd. Realtors, 1988-89. Mem. Ga. Indsl. Developers Assn., Assn. Ga. Real Estate Exchangers, DeKalb Bd. Realtors (chmn. comml. coun. 1988-90, bd. dirs., pres. soc. comml. realtors 1990—, Gem of Month award 1990), Atlanta Bd. Realtors, So. Ctr. for Internat. Studies. Republican. Home: 2697 Union Church Rd SW Stockbridge GA 30281 Office: Metro Brokers 750 Hammond Dr Bldg 1 Atlanta GA 30328

DAVIS, TAMRA KATHLEEN, medical management professional; b. Chgo., Apr. 15, 1958; d. Bernard B. and Lynda Kathleen Huss; m. Jeffrey B. Anderson. BS in Bus., Long Beach State U., 1983. Adminstr. San Juan Family Med. Group, San Juan Capistrano, Calif., 1982-86, Los Alamitos (Calif.) Med. Group, 1986-88; ops. mgr. Health Care Physician Svcs. Corp., Tustin, Calif., 1989, dir. physician and office svcs., 1989-90; adminstr. Drs. of Women Health Ctr. Inc., Irvine, Calif., 1990—; med. mgmt. cons., Anaheim (Calif.) Hills Med. Group, 1988, Brea (Calif.) Med. Group, 1988. Mem. Med. Group Mgmt. Assn., Orange County Med. Group Adminstrs. (treas. 1987, v.p. 1988, pres. 1990-91), Newport Area Profl. Soc., San Juan Capistrano C. of C. (pres. 1989-90). Office: Drs of Women Health Ctr Inc 4050 Barranca #160 Irvine CA 92714

DAVIS, TERRI M., pastoral counselor; b. Binghampton, N.Y., Dec. 2, 1947; d. Michael Sr. and Patricia Ann (Bentz) Maslak; m. Thomas Leon Davis, Dec. 20, 1969; children: Eric, Annette. BS in Dietetics, Okla. State U., 1970; MA in Pastoral Care and Counseling, Phillips Grad. Sem., 1988; postgrad., Coll. for Fin. Planning, 1984-86. Pub. relations cons. TMD Enterprises, Tulsa, 1984-85, proprietor, cons., 1985-86; systems analyst Arrow Specialty Co. div. Masco Corp., Tulsa, 1986; dir. communication services Arrow Specialty Co. div. Masco Industries, Tulsa, 1986-87, inventory control mgr., 1987-89; cons. computer systems Resonance for Women, Tulsa, 1983-86, pastoral counselor, 1989—; cons. Cascia Hall Prep Sch., Tulsa, 1986-87. Editor (newsletters) Arrow Update, Arrow News. Cabinet advisor Camp Fire, Tulsa, 1986-87, advisor, 1984—, discovery treas., 1987-89; active Mothers Against Drunk Driving. Elks Found. scholar, Endicott, 1965. Mem. NAFE, Nat. Math Scholarship Assn., Holland Hall Parents Assn. (treas. 1982-83). Republican. Episcopalian. Home: 1810 E 43d St Tulsa OK 74105 Office: Resonance for Women 2524 E 41st St Tulsa OK 74105

DAVIS, VERONICA A., management executive; b. Henderson, Tenn., June 10, 1959; d. Hiawatha Daniel and Laura Mae (Green) Thompson; 1 child, Shemenya A. Davis. Cert. stenographer, Miller-Hawkins B. Coll., 1979; Cert. data transcriber, IRS, Memphis, Tenn., 1981; Cert. computer operator, U.S. Army, Newport News, Va., 1985, Cert. computer programmer, 1987. Stenographer Memphis & Shelby County Health Dept., Memphis, 1979-80; cash clk./data transcriber IRS, Memphis, 1980-82; data transcriber U.S. Army, Fort Sheridan, Ill., 1982-83; work order clk. U.S. Army, Fort Sheridan, 1984-85, quality control clk., 1985-89, mgmt. asst., 1989—; data transcriber Selective Svc., North Chicago, Ill., 1983-84; telemarketer Allstate Ins. Co., Northbrook, Ill., 1986-88; unit supr. Allstate Ins. Co., Glenview, Ill., 1988—; chmn. task force Allstate, Glenview, 1990. Mem. NAFE, Am. Cancer Soc. Baptist. Home: 1601 Berwick Blvd 1-D Waukegan IL 60085 Office: Allstate Ins Co 3701 W Lake Glenview IL 60025

DAVIS, VICKIE BEENE, pharmacist, educator; b. Atlanta, Tex., Apr. 6, 1951; d. Leonard D. and Grace Evelyn (Dial) B.; m. Paul Gaylon Davis, Nov. 27, 1971. Student, Texarkana (Tex.) Jr. Coll., 1969-70, Northwestern State U., Natchitoches, La., 1970-71; BS in Pharmacy, U. Houston, 1974, postgrad. in engring., 1987—. Registered pharmacist, Tex. Pharmacist intern Hillcroft Pharmacy, Houston, 1974-75; staff pharmacist K-Mart, Inc., Houston, 1975-76, Bissonnet Pharmacy, Houston, 1976-79; asst. dir. pharmacy HCA Woman's Hosp. Tex., Houston, 1979—. Recipient Appreciation award HCA Info. Svcs., Inc., Nashville, 1987; named Hosp. Pharmacy Preceptor of Yr., U. Houston Coll. Pharmacy, 1989. Mem. Am. Soc. Hosp. Pharmacists, Tex. Soc. Hosp. Pharmacists, Aircraft Owners and Pilots Assn., Exptl. Aircraft Assn., Phi Kappa Phi, Rho Chi, Kappa Epsilon, Eta Kappa Nu. Home: 11830 S Little John Circle Houston TX 77071 Office: HCA Womans Hosp Tex 7600 Fannin Houston TX 77054

DAVIS, VIKKI ANN, janitorial supply company executive; b. Troy, N.C., Apr. 17, 1952; d. Melwood L. and Ann (Norris) D.; 1 child, William Corwin McKinney II. BS in Sociology, Edgecliff Coll., Cin., 1974; MBA, Xavier U., Cin., 1985. Sales mgr. Ross Labs., Cin., 1975-80, Johnson & Johnson, Cin., 1980-83, Ayerst Labs., Cin., 1983-85; pres. Multi-Devel. Janitorial Supply Co., Cin., 1985—. Mem. Legal Def. and Edn. Fund, Am. Mgmt. Assn., NAFE, Nat. Assn. Minority Contractors, Internat. Platform Assn. (bd. dirs.). Republican. Presbyterian. Office: Multi-Devel Janitorial Supply 956 Wareham Dr Cincinnati OH 45202

DAVIS, VIRGINIA MARIE, financial analyst, consultant; b. Chgo., Mar. 17, 1947; d. Robert Frank and Verne J. (Van Cata) Davis; divorced; children: Jack R. R. Barnette, Christopher D. M. Barnette, David T. J. Neuburger. Student Moorpark Coll., Calif., 1984-86. Ins. lic., Calif.; ordained to ministry Temple of Light, 1977. Sales mgr. Grand Plaza Hotel, Rosemont, Ill., 1975-77; pastor, founder God's House, Evanston, Ill., 1977-80; athletics bus. mgr. Pepperdine U., Malibu, Calif., 1980-82, budget and planning analyst, 1984-87; mktg. rep. GNA, Long Beach, Calif., 1987—; field underwriter N.Y. Life Ins. and Annuity Corp. Cons., Calif., 1984-87; founder budget control assistance co. My Manager, 1986; mgmt. cons. Checkbook, Thousand Oaks, Calif., 1984—; dir., founder Ins.. Seminars, Ventura County, Calif., 1984-85; cons. Farmers Ins., Simi Valley, Calif., 1985-86; dir., lectr. Alternative Med. Treatment, 1977-78. Author: Herbology, 1976. Com. chairperson Ventura council Boy Scouts Am., 1982-84; pres., founder Pepperdine Hiker's Club, 1985-86; affirmative action adv. com. Pepperdine U., 1985-87, sec., 1987, officer, 1986-87. Recipient Vol. of

Yr. award Boy Scouts Am. Troop 799, 1982-84; State of Ill. scholar, 1965; Swedish Covenant Hosp., 1965. Mem. Nat. Assn. Life Underwriters. Republican. Club: Toastmasters (Malibu, Calif.)(adminstv. v.p. 1987). Lodge: Zonta (asst. treas. and budget chairperson local club 1984). Avocations: cross country hiking; herbology; geology.

DAVIS, WANDA ROSE, lawyer; b. Lampasas, Tex., Oct. 4, 1937; d. Ellis DeWitt and Julia Doris (Rose) Cockrell; m. Richard Andrew Fulcher, May 9, 1959 (div. 1969); 1 child, Greg Ellis; m. Edwin Leon Davis, Jan. 14, 1973 (div. 1985). BBA, U. Tex., 1959, JD, 1971. Bar: Tex. 1971, Colo. 1981, U.S. Dist. Ct. (no. dist.) Tex. 1972, U.S. Dist. Ct. Colo. 1981, U.S. Ct. Appeals (10th cir. 1981, U.S. Supreme Ct. 1976. Atty. Atlantic Richfield Co., Dallas, 1971; assoc. firm Crocker & Murphy, Dallas, 1971-72; prin. Wanda Davis, Atty. at Law, Dallas, 1972-73; ptnr. firm Davis & Davis Inc., Dallas, 1973-75; atty. adviser HUD, Dallas, 1974-75, Air Force Acctg. and Fin. Ctr., Denver, 1976—; co-chmn. regional Profl. Devel. Inst., Am. Soc. Mil. Comptrollers, Colorado Springs, Colo., 1982; chmn. Lowry AFB Noontime Edn. Program, Exercise Program, Denver, 1977-83; mem. speakers bur. Colo. Women's Bar, 1982-83, Lowry AFB, 1981-83; mem. fed. ct. liaison com. U.S. Dist. Ct. Colo., 1983; mem. Leaders of the Fed. Bar Assn. People to People Del. to China, USSR and Finland, 1986. Contbr. numerous articles to profl. jours. Bd. dirs. Pres.'s Coun. Met. Denver, 1981-83; mem. Lowry AFB Alcohol Abuse Exec. Com., 1981-84. Recipient Spl. Achievement award USAF, 1978; Upward Mobility award Fed. Profl. and Adminstrv. Women, Denver, 1979. Mem. Fed. Bar Assn. (pres. Colo. 1982-83, mem. nat. coun. 1984—, Earl W. Kintner Disting. Svc. award 1983, 1st v.p. 10th cir. 1986—), Colo. Trial Lawyers Assn., Bus. and Profl. Women's Club (dist. IV East dir. 1983-84, Colo. pres. 1988-89), Am. Soc. Mil. Comptrollers (pres. 1984-85), Denver South Met. Bus. and Profl. Women's Club (pres. 1982-83), Denver Silver Spruce Am. Bus. Women's Assn. (pres. 1981-82; Woman of Yr. award 1982), Colo. Jud. Inst., Colo. Concerned Lawyers, Profl. Mgrs. Assn., Fed. Women's Program (v.p. Denver 1980), Colo. Woman News Community adv. bd., 1988—, Dallas Bar Assn., Tex. Bar Assn., Denver Bar Assn., Altrusa, Zonta, Denver Nancy Langhorn Federally Employed Women. (pres. 1979-80). Christian. Office: Air Force Acctg and Fin Ctr AFAFC/JAL Denver CO 80279-5000

DAVIS, YVONNE DOLORES, civil servant; b. Orange, N.J., Sept. 21, 1947; d. William J. and Alice-Ruth (Eubanks) Patterson; m. Royce Davis; children: Shannon K., Sarah K. BA in Spanish, Montclair State Coll., Upper Montclair, N.J., 1975; cert. pub. mgmt., Kean Coll., Union, N.J., 1982; cert. equal employment, Rutgers U., 1984. Bilingual family svc. worker Essex County Div. Welfare, Dept. Citizen Svcs., Newark, 1971-78, family svc. supr., 1978-81, adminstrv. analyst, 1981-83, prin. personnel technician, 1983-86; personnel mgmt. specialist, supr. prin. personnel technician Essex County Dept. Citizen Svcs., East Orange, N.J., 1984—. Mem. exec. bd. Essex County Minority Employees Assn., Newark, 1984-85; active Epilepsy Found. Am., Trenton. Recipient Excellence in Personnel Mgmt. award Essex County Minority Employees Assn., 1986, Excellence in Spanish award Nat. Assn. Tchrs. Spanish, 1964, 65, Excellence in French award Nat. Assn. Tchrs. French, 1965, Recognition award United Way, 1984-88; cert. of appreciation U.S. Dept. Treas., 1984, tng. cert. N.J. Div. Civil Rights, 1988. Mem. Am. Assn. Affirmative Action, Nat. Assn. Pub. Sector Equal Opportunity officers, Mcpl. Career Women Newark Inc., NAFE. Democrat. Baptist. Office: County Essex Dept Citizen Svcs 15 S Munn Ave East Orange NJ 07018

DAVIS, YVONNE SINGLETON, college administrator; b. N.Y.C., Dec. 18, 1952; d. Robert Delaney and Anna Aramentha (Love) S.; m. Wesley Davis. BA, CCNY, 1973. Adminstrv. asst. Fordham U., Bronx, N.Y., 1976-79; sec. legal dept. Marvel Comics Group, N.Y.C., 1979-81; adminstrv. sec. United Ch. of Christ, N.Y.C., 1981-83; rsch. sec. Ogilvy & Mather Direct Response, N.Y.C., 1983-86; personal asst. H.L. Hunt, N.Y., Tex., 1986-88; asst. to dir. CCNY, 1988—. Mem. NAFE, Black Women of Achievement (pres. 1987), NAACP, Nat. Assn. Black Bus. and Profl. Women's Clubs (recording sec. 1984), Young Adult Club N.Y.C., Eastern Star. Methodist. Office: JHS 164M 401 W 164 St New York NY 10032

DAVISON, BARBARA, small business owner; b. Palmerton, Pa., Jan. 3, 1936; d. David and Lillian (Roth) Seiden; m. Maxwell E. Davison, Aug. 25, 1957; children: Mark, Andrew, Douglas. Student, Simmons Coll., 1953-55, MBA, 1984; student, Cedar Crest Coll., 1973. Travel cons. Group Travel Assocs., Allentown, Pa., 1974-80; campaign dir. State of Pa., 1980-81; stockbroker Warren York and Co., Inc., Allentown, 1981-83; v.p. ops. GTA Travel, Allentown, 1984-86; owner Resumes, etc., Allentown, 1986—; lectr. Lehigh County Community Coll., Allentown, 1987—. Bd. dirs. Pa. Sinfonia Orch., 1988-89. Mem. Nat. Assn. Profl. Saleswomen, Womens Health Ctr., Exec. Womens Council, Allentown C. of C. Home: 2535 Brunner Rd Emmaus PA 18049

DAVISON, HELEN IRENE, teacher, counselor; b. Oskaloosa, Iowa, Dec. 19, 1926; d. Grover C. and Beulah (Williams) Hawk; m. Walter Francis Davison, June 20, 1953 (div.); 1 child, Linda Ellen. BS in Zoology, Iowa State U., 1948; MS in Biol. Sci., U. Chgo., 1951; MA in Ednl. Psychology and Counseling, Calif. State U., Northridge, 1985. Med. rsch. technician U. Chgo. Med. Sch., 1951-53; tchr. sci. Lane High Sch., Charlottesville, Va., 1953-55; med. rsch. asst. U. Va. Med. Sch., Charlottesville, 1955-56, U. Mich., Ann Arbor, 1956-60; tchr. sci. Monroe High Sch., Sepulveda, Calif., 1966—, chmn. sci. dept., 1990—; chmn. sci. dept. Monroe High Sch., 1990—; rsch. technician Los Alamos Sci. Labs., summer 1954; part-time counselor psychotherapy Forte Found., Van Nuys, Calif., 1987—. V.p. San Fernando Valley chpt. Am. Field Svc., 1980-81; vol. counselor Planned Parenthood Am., L.A., 1982-88. NSF fellow, 1985-86. Mem. Calif. Tchrs. Assn., Calif. Assn. Marriage and Family Therapists, Iowa Acad. Sci. (assoc.), AAUW. Home: 17425 Vintage St Northridge CA 91325 Office: James Monroe High Sch 9229 Haskell Ave Sepulveda CA 91343

DAVISON, IMOGENE See GLOVER, IMOGENE

DAVISON, NANCY REYNOLDS, artist; b. Hastings, Neb., June 30, 1944; d. David F. and Mildred L. (Marsh) Reynolds; m. Ralph M. Davison, June 6, 1966. BA, Smith Coll., 1966; MA, U. Mich., 1973, PhD, 1980. Asst. to keeper of prints Boston Pub. Libr., 1967-72; cons., print catalogue W.L. Clements Library, Ann Arbor, 1972-74; artist, printmaker various cities, 1970—; owner operator BlueStocking Studio, York Beach, Maine, 1985—; presenter print confs., Winterthur, Libr. of Congress, Colonial Williamsburg, Syracuse U., N.Y. Hist. Soc., 1970—. Numerous one-woman shows, U.S., Sweden; represented in permanent collections mus. and corps. Bd. dirs. art orgns., various cities, 1970—. Fred Harris Daniels fellow Am. Antiquarian Soc., 1977. Mem. Ogunquit Art Assn. (pres.), Assoc. Artists Pitts., Boston Printmakers, Smith Coll. Club. Office: BlueStocking Studio PO Box 1257 York Beach ME 03910

DAVISON-MCLANE, DENISE ROSETTA, social worker; b. Chgo., May 7, 1963; d. James Roosevelt and Janet (Arnold) McL.; m. Jimmie Davison; children: Jasmine, Jessica. BS, Ill. State U., 1985; AM, U. Chgo., 1987; postgrad., Nat. Coll. of Edn., 1988—. Social worker intern St. Joseph's Hosp., Bloomington, Ill., 1984; social worker S. Suburban Sr. Svcs., Cath. Charities, Harvey, Ill., 1985; social worker intern Human Resource Devel. Inst., Chgo., 1985-86, Chgo. Pub. Schs., 1986-87; sch. social worker Harvey Pub. Schs. Dist. 152, 1987-89, Chgo. Pub. Schs., 1989—; cons. Corp. Child Care, Chgo., 1989—. Mem. Nat. Assn. Social Workers, Nat. Assn. Black Social Workers, Chgo. Assn. for Edn. Young Children, Ill. Assn. Sch. Social Workers. Home: 19517 Lake Shore Dr Lynwood IL 60411

DAVISSON, SHARON RYAN, county official, accountant; b. St. Louis, Aug. 13, 1940; d. Tom E. and Eleanor (Rudolph) Ryan; m. Walter F. Davisson, 1963; children: Patricia, Valerie, Ann. BS, St. Louis U., 1962. CPA, Mo. Computer programmer McDonnell Douglas, St. Louis, 1962-64; computer programmer biomed lab. Washington U., St. Louis, 1964-66; pvt. practice acctg. Jefferson City, Mo., 1983—; auditor Cole County, Jefferson City, 1984-86, presiding commr., 1987-90; chmn. Cole County Emergency Planning Bd., Jefferson City, 1988-90. Treas. Heart of Mo. coun. Girl Scouts U.S., Jefferson City, 1984-87; bd. regents St. Mary's Health Ctr., Jefferson City, 1987—; div. chair United Way, Jefferson City, 1989. Mem. AICPA, Mo. Soc. CPAs, Govtl. Acctng. Assn., Mo. Assn. Counties (bd. dirs. 1987-90), Jefferson City C. of C., Mo. Assn. of County Commrs. (sec. 1988, v.p. 1989, pres. 1990), Cole County Med. Aux., Cole County Women's Rep. Club, Pachyderms Club (v.p. 1988), Rotary. Roman Catholic. Home: 3730 Schott Rd Jefferson City MO 65101 Office: Cole County Courthouse 301 E High St Jefferson City MO 65101

DAW, LENORE E., elementary school teacher; b. Pitts.; d. James E. Owens and Lillian E. Gregory; m. Matthew L. Daw, July 27, 1947 (dec.); children: Andrea, Matthew Jr., Alan. BA, Calif. State U., 1968; MA, San Francisco U., 1977; postgrad., Pacific Coll., 1979. Cert. tchr., libr., adminstr., Calif. Elem. tchr. 3d and 4th grades Alvina Sch. Dist., Caruthers, Calif.; elem. libr., secondary libr./career edn. coord. Fresno (Calif.) Unified Sch. Dist., dist. libr. K-12. Min. of music, soloist Second Bapt. Ch. Recipient G.W. Hayden award Second Bapt. Ch., 1990, Gold Apple award United Black Men Fresno, 1990, cert. of recognition Calif. Legis. Assembly, 1990, cert. of honor City of Fresno, 1990. Mem. Assn. for Supervision and Curriculum Devel., Assn. Calif. Sch. Adminstr., ALA, Am. Assn. Sch. Librs. Calif., Calif. Reading Assn., Reading Initiative Coordinating Coun., Internat. Reading Assn., NEA, Fresno Boys and Girls Club (exec. bd.), Calif. Media and Libr. Assn., Inst. Materials Evaluation Panel, Alpha Kappa Alpha (Mildred L. Robinson Alumna Basileus award 1975, Outstanding Svc. award Iota Omicron Omega chpt.. 1990), Phi Delta Kappa, Iota Phi Lambda. Office: IMC Fresno Unified Sch Dist 3132 E Fairmont Ave Fresno CA 93727

DAWDY, FAYE MARIE CATANIA, photographer, lecturer; b. San Mateo, Calif., Sept. 15, 1954; d. Frank Benjamin and Melba Rita (Arata) Catania; m. John Thomas Dawdy, May 5, 1974. AA, Coll. San Mateo, 1979; student, San Francisco State U., 1979—. With Proctor & Gamble Distbg. Co., San Mateo, 1973-78; ptnr. Dawdy Photography, Millbrae, Calif., 1978—; dir., sec.-treas. Millbrae Stamp Co., 1980—; lectr. Mills High Sch., Millbrae, Millbrae Women's Club, Portola Camera Club, Fla. State Photography Conv., Nev. State Photography Conv., Profl. Photographers Am. Contbr. articles to profl. jours. Area chmn. Millbrae Am. Heart Assn. Ann. Fund Dr., 1977-82; mem. fund raising and nutrition coms. San Mateo County chpt. Am. Heart Assn., 1980-88; co-chmn. Miss Millbrae Pageant, 1981, Queen Isabella Columbus Day Festival, 1981; judge arts and crafts exhbns. Millbrae Art and Wine Festival; judge photography competition Marin County Fair Photography Exhibit; trustee Golden Gate Sch. Profl. Photographers, 1985—. Recipient awards No. Calif. Coun. Camera Clubs, 1979, 81, Mktg. Contest award Mktg. Today mag., 1988. Mem. Millbrae C. of C. (sec. women's div. 1979), Wedding Photographers Internat., Millbrae Art Assn. (pres. 1979-80), Portola Camera Club (nature chmn. 1978—), Friends of Millbrae Libr., Italian Cath. Fedn., Nat. Assn. Female Execs., Photog. Soc. Am., Calif. Women in Profl. Photography, Profl. Photographers Calif., Fedn. Ind. Bus., Soroptomists (sec. Millbrae-San Bruno chpt. 1981-82), St. Dunstan Women's Club. Democrat. Roman Catholic. Office: 1653 El Camino Real Millbrae CA 94030

DAWKINS, JACQUELINN HAWKINS, infosystems specialist; b. Sacramento, Sept. 10, 1938; d. Jack Alfred Hawkins and Gladys Lynn (Shipp) Schmeckenbecher; m. Michael Stuart Dawkins, Apr. 12, 1970; children from previous marriage: Cherly Lynn Myers (dec.), Tamara Annette Mercer. BA in Pub. Adminstrn. summa cum laude, Upper Iowa U., 1982; MBA in Mgmt., Calif. Coast U., 1989. Computer operator 437th hdqrs. squadron USAF, Charleston AFB, S.C., 1967-71; computer operator Keesler (AFB) Tech. Tng. Ctr. USAF, Miss., 1971; computer aid base suppley computer facility USAF, Keesler AFB, Miss., 1971-75, computer specialist, 1975-78, supply mgmt. analyst, 1978-79, cost and mgmt. program analyst, 1979-83, program analyst, 1983—. Vol. income tax assistance program Keesler AFB, 1982—. Mem. Am. Soc. Mil. Comptrollers, Inst. Cost Analysis (cert.). Republican. Home: 6349 Chaucer Dr Ocean Springs MS 39564

DAWKINS, MARVA PHYLLIS, psychologist; b. Jacksonville, Fla., Apr. 12, 1948; d. Ralph and Altamese (Padgett) D.; student U. Freiburg (W.Ger.), 1969-70; B.S., Stetson U., 1971; M.S., Fla. State U., 1972, Ph.D., 1975. Research asst. Fla. State U., Tallahassee, 1970-72; clin. intern, psychology dept. Presbyn.-St. Luke's Med. Ctr. and mental health dept. Mile Square Health Ctr., Chgo., 1973-74; staff psychologist, dir. aftercare treatment program, mental health dept. Mile Square Health Ctr., Chgo., 1974-75, staff psychologist, coordinator devel. disabilities program, 1976-79; asst. prof. psychology U. North Fla., Jacksonville, 1975-76, Rush U.-Presbyn. St. Luke's Med. Ctr., Chgo., 1976—; pvt. practice clin. psychology, 1977—; exec. dir. Inst. for Community Mental Health, 1979—; cons. safety evaluation program Isaac Ray Ctr., 1986—; psychology cons. Disability Policy Br. Social Security Adminstrn., Chgo, 1980—. Registered psychologist, Ill. Mem. Am. Psychol. Assn., Assn. Black Psychologists.

DAWSON, ANNA MAE HARNE, music educator; b. Ottawa, Ill., Aug. 17, 1931; d. Fletcher Brigham Harne and Ethel Kathrine (Feuerbach) Rupley; m. Donald Gene Dawson, Aug. 11, 1962 (div. 1979); children: Arthur Fletcher (dec.), Michael Gene, David Christopher, Lynne Ann. B in Music Edn., Ill. Wesleyan U , 1953; MusM, So. Ill. U., 1976; studied with, Ruth Slenczynska, St. Louis and N.Y.C., 1974-89; postgrad., Hochshule fur Music, Vienna, Austria, summer 1980, 81. Cert. music tchr., Ill. Pvt. tchr. piano Moline, Ill., 1953—; tchr. music Silvis (Ill.) Schs., 1953-57; tchr. music and social studies Moline (Ill.) Pub. Schs., 1957-69; prof. piano Blackhawk Coll., Moline, 1977-84; tchr. music St. Mary Cath. Sch., East Moline, 1979-89; choral dir. Union Congl. Ch., Moline, 1987-90; recitalist in field. Mem. Fedn. Tchrs. and Counselors (chmn. student recitals 1987-90), AAUW (arts advisor 1989-90), Fine Arts Club (pres. 1976-78, program chair 1972-76), Delta Omicron Alumni Assn. Home: 1509 41st St Moline IL 61265

DAWSON, CAROL GENE, federal official; b. Indpls., Sept. 8, 1937; d. Ernest Eugene (dec.) and Hilda Lou (Carroll) D.; m. Robert Edmund Bauman, Nov. 19, 1960 (div. 1982); children: Edward Carroll, Eugenie Marie, Victoria Anne, James Shields; m. Franklin Dean Smith, Aug. 2, 1986. BA, Dunbarton Coll., Washington, 1959, Cath. U., Washington, 1960. Staff asst. Senator Kenneth B. Keating, Washington, 1959; exec. asst. Americans for Constl. Action, Washington, 1959; exec. sec. Youth for Nixon Lodge, Washington, 1959-60; legis. asst. Rep. Donald C. Bruce, Washington, 1961-63; dep. dir., pub. info. Goldwater for Pres. Campaign and Rep. Nat. Com., Washington, 1963-64; editor, assoc. editor The New Guard Mag., Washington, 1965-66; dir. info. Am. Conservative Union, Washington, 1966-67; publs. and news analyst White House, Washington, 1969—; staff reporter Easton (Md.) Star-Democrat, 1971-72; freelance writer Easton, 1972-77; real estate salesperson Latham Realtors, Easton, 1977-80; sr. staff asst. presdl. transition U.S. Office of Personnel Mgmt., Washington, 1980-81; dep. press sec. U.S. Dept. Energy, Washington, 1981-82, dep. spl. asst. to sec., 1982-84; commr. U.S. Consumer Product Safety Commn., Washington, 1984—; editor Cath. Currents newsletter, Washington, 1969-70. Bd. visitors Inst. Polit. Journalism, Georgetown U., 1985-89; active in past various polit. activities. Recipient Award of Merit Young Americans for Freedom, 1970. Mem. Exec. Women in Govt., Reagan Appointees Alumni, Capitol Hill Club, The Fairfax Hunt Club (bd. govs.). Roman Catholic. Home: 320 Canterwood Ln Great Falls VA 22066 Office: Consumer Product Safety Commn 5401 Westbard Ave Bethesda MD 20816

DAWSON, DAWN PAIGE, publisher; b. Paradise, Calif., Nov. 10, 1956; d. Wayne Paul and Donna Jean (Peckham) D.; m. Justin Keith Anderson, Mar. 12, 1989. AB, Occidental Coll., 1979. Editorial asst. Salem Press Inc., Pasadena, Calif., 1979-80, copy editor, 1980-81, sr. editor, 1982-83, mgr. editor, 1984-87, v.p. editing and prodn., 1987—. Mem. Customer's Guild West. Mem. Soc. Scholarly Pub., Nat. Assn. Female Execs. Office: Salem Press Inc 150 S Los Robles Ste 720 Pasadena CA 91101

DAWSON, DIANE, travel service executive; b. Berkeley, Calif., June 23, 1954; d. John Victor and Joan (Merritt) D.; m. Gerald F. Verhasselt, Oct. 9, 1987; 1 child, Chelsea Diane. BS, U. Santa Clara, Calif., 1976. Pres. Exec. Travel, Mountain View, Calif., 1978—. Bd. dirs. U. Santa Clara Alumni Assn., 1986-89. Republican. Office: Exec Travel Svc 1890 N Shoreline Blvd Mountain View CA 94043

DAWSON, SISTER JOAN HELEN, superintendent of Catholic Schools; b. Rochester, N.Y., Feb. 13, 1941; d. Daniel William and Mary Christine (Van de Castle) D. BA in English, St. Bonaventure U., 1963; MA in English, U. Notre Dame, 1968; EdD, Wayne State U., 1975. Cert. secondary educator and adminstr., Fla. Tchr., libr. St. Mary of the Angels Acad., Haddonfield, N.J., 1963-67, Bishop Verot High Sch., Ft. Meyers, Fla., 1967-68, St. Paul High Sch., St. Petersburg, Fla., 1968-69; instr. St. Elizabeth Tchr. Coll., Allegany, N.Y., 1967-69; tchr., dept. chair Archbishop Walsh High Sch., Olean, N.Y., 1969-72; tchr. St. John the Baptist High Sch., West Islip, N.Y., 1975-76; asst. prin. Bishop Verot High Sch., Ft. Myers, Fla., 1976-79; asst. supt. Office Cath. Schs. Diocese of St. Petersburg, 1979-84, supt. Office Cath. Schs., 1984—; dir. Allegany Health System, St. Petersburg, 1984—; trustee Jr. Achievement, St. Petersburg, 1985—; mem. FCC Accreditation Com., Tallahassee, Fla., 1984—. Recipient Gen. Excellence-Arts award St. Bonaventure U., 1963, Star Tchr. award St. Petersburg Times, 1969, Grad. Fellowship Wayne State U., 1972-74, Grad. Profl. Scholarship Wayne State U., 1974. Mem. Phi Delta Kappa, Nat. Cath. Ednl. Assn., Chief Adminstrs. Cath. Edn., Nat. Assn. Secondary Sch. Principals, Fla. Assn. Acad. Nonpublic Schs., Notre Dame Alumni Assn., Wayne State U. Alumni Assn. Democrat. Roman Catholic. Office: Office Cath. Schs. 6533 Ninth Ave N Saint Petersburg FL 33710

DAWSON, JOANN OVERTON, chemist; b. Tazewell, Tenn., Apr. 2, 1934; d. Henley Floyd and Ida Grace (Surgener) Overton; m. Thomas Larry Dawson, Aug. 4, 1957 (div. Dec. 1982); children; Katherine Ann, Thomas Larry. BA, Berea Coll., 1956; postgrad., Morris Harvey Coll., 1976-77, W.Va. State Coll., 1978-79. Asst. chemist Koppers Co., Verona, Pa., 1956; sci. educator Emma Willard Sch., Troy, N.Y., 1956-57; analytical chemist Agrl. Experiment Station, Lexington, Ky., 1957-60; substitute tchr. Kanawha County Schs., Charleston, W.Va., 1972-78; lab. technician Union Carbide Corp., South Charleston, 1978-85, chemist, 1985—. Leader Camp Fire Girls, Charleston, 1968-72; Sunday sch. tchr. 1st United Meth. Ch., South Charleston, 1973-78; mem. W.Va. State Coll., Bus., Industry and Edn. Rels. Cluster. Mem. Am. Chem. Soc., Assn. Standard Testing Methods, Forest Hills Garden Club, Kanawha Valley Road Runners Club (treas. 1983-85). Republican. Methodist. Home: 731 Churchill Dr Charleston WV 25314 Office: Union Carbide Corp PO Box 2831 Charleston WV 25330

DAWSON, MARY ELIZABETH, paralegal, consultant; b. Seattle, Nov. 6, 1961; d. Robert Ward and Cecilia Ann (Becker) Freedman; m. H. Michael Dawson, July 19, 1986. BA in Bus. Adminstrn., Coll. of Idaho, 1985. Legal sec. Robert Ward Freedman, Seattle, 1982, 83; paralegal Davis Wright Tremaine, Portland, 1988—. J.R. Simplot scholar, 1983-85, Judge C.C. Chavelle scholar, 1983-85, Women and Bus. Conf. scholar, 1987. Mem. AAUW (bd. dirs. Seattle 1985-86, Lake Oswego, Oreg. 1987-89). Roman Catholic. Home: 5322 SW Charleton Ct Lake Oswego OR 97035 Office: Davis Wright Tremaine 1300 SW 5th Ave Portland OR 97201

DAWSON, MIMI (MIMI WEYFORTH), government official; b. St. Louis, Aug. 31, 1944; d. Francis Griffin and Jeanne (Gething) Weyforth; m. Rhett Brewer Dawson, Jan. 15, 1976; 2 children: Elizabeth Stuart, Andrew Brewer. AB, Washington U., St. Louis, 1966. Legis. asst. Rep. Richard Ichord, Mo. Dist., 1969-72, 73; press sec., legis. asst. to Rep. James Symington, Mo. Dist., 1973; pres. sec., adminstrv. asst., chief staff, legis. dir. Sen. Bob Packwood, Oreg., 1973-81; commr. FCC, Washington, 1981-87; dep. sec. U.S. Dept. of Transportation, Washington, DC, 1987-89; govt. affairs specialist Wiley, Rein and Fielding, Washington, 1989—; pres. Am. Coun. Young Polit. Leaders. Republican. Roman Catholic. Office: Wiley Rein and Fielding 1776 K St NW Washington DC 20006

DAWSON, SUE ELLEN, publishing executive; b. Jefferson City, Mo., Dec. 19, 1955; d. Dale William and Margaret Mary (Nuernberger) Warren; m. Monty Paul Meyer (div. Sept. 1978); m. Joseph Charles Dawson Jr., Apr. 15, 1983 (div. Aug. 1988); 1 child, Meghan Lee. Grad. high sch., Bloomington, Ill. Sec. A&P Transp., Louisville, 1977-78; graphic art dir. Copy Boy Printing Co., Louisville, 1978-86; v.p. On-Line Copy & Pub. Svcs., Louisville, 1986—. Recipient Pub. Speaking award Dale Carnegie, 1986, Human Relations award, 1987. Mem. Entrepreneur Soc. Republican. Home: 4116 Wheeler Ave Louisville KY 40215

DAY, ALI MAE, artist; b. Berea, Ohio, May 1, 1959; d. Andrew Thomas and Melissa Jane (Burrows) Kukulka; m. Edward Francis Day, July 2, 1976 (div. Mar. 1979); 1 child, Angela Jeneen; m. Leonard John Brittelli, Feb. 19, 1981. BA, Cooper Sch. Art, Cleve., 1979. Cons. Mgmt. Insights Inc., Dallas, 1983-85; dark room mgr., med. photographer Dallas, 1985-88; owner, operator Originals by Ali, Euless, Tex., 1988—. Home: 300 Springridge Ln Euless TX 76039

DAY, ANNE GLENDENNING WHITE PARKER, nurse; b. Cin., July 9, 1926; d. Pinkney McGilla nd Anna Pearl (Glendenning) White; m. Raymond Eric Parker, Mar. 6, 1948 (div. 1969); children: Douglas McGill, Stephanie Morse. Diploma, Christ Hosp. Sch. Nursing, Cin., 1947. RN, cert. chem. dependency nurse. Staff nurse to asst. head nurse Holmes div. U. Cin., 1948-84; nursing supr. Villa Hope Extended Care Facility, Cin., 1970-72; staff nurse Hillenbrand Nursing Home, Cin., 1980-82, Emerson A. North Hosp., Cin., 1982—. Vol. Group Against Smoke Pollution, Cin., 1989; donor Zoo, Cin., 1989, Voters for Choice, Ohio, 1989, Ams. for Non-Smokers Rights, Calif., 1989, Action on Smoking or Health, 1989. Episcopalian.

DAY, BRIGITTE KAPITAEN, corporate executive; b. Bad Ischl, Austria, May 8, 1951; came to U.S., 1951; d. Joseph and Rose (Steigerwald) Kapitaen. BA, West Chester U., 1973; MBA in Fin., Drexel U., 1989. Cert. elem. edn. tchr., Pa. Program coord. MOT Community Action Ctr., Middletown, Del., 1974; engring. asst. Burroughs Corp., Downingtown, Pa., 1975-76; with Oxford (Pa.) Intermediate Sch., 1977-78; caseworker Kelsch Assocs., Lionville, Pa., 1977-78; mgr. tng. SEI Corp., Wayne, Pa., 1978—. Vol. patient rep. Brandywine Hosp., Coatesville, Pa., 1987, counselor Open Door, West Chester, Pa., 1972-73, archeology Valley Forge Nat. Park, 1987. Recipient Charles S. Swope award First Nat. Bank of West Chester, 1970. Mem. Am. Soc. Tng. and Devel. Roman Catholic. Clubs: Congrega (Coatesville); Women's (Brandywine) (pres. 1988). Home: Rd 2 Box 374D Coatesville PA 19320 Office: SEI Corp 680 E Swedesford Rd Wayne PA 19087

DAY, JENNIE D., state legislator; b. Madera, Pa., Dec. 13, 1921; m. Marvin Day. Ed. Temple U. City councilwoman, Coventry, R.I., 1978-84; realtor; mem. R.I. Senate, 1985—. Mem. Coventry Hist. Soc. Democrat. Roman Catholic. Office: RI State Senate State Capitol Providence RI 02903 Other: 19 Beachwood St Coventry RI 02816*

DAY, LUCILLE ELIZABETH, educator, author; b. Oakland, Calif., Dec. 5, 1947; d. Richard Allen and Evelyn Marietta (Hazard) Lang; m. Frank Lawrence Day, Nov. 6, 1965; 1 child, Liana Sherrine; m. 2nd. Theodore Herman Fleischman, June 23, 1974; 1 child, Tamarind Channah. AB, U. Calif., Berkeley, 1971, MA, 1973, PhD, 1979. Teaching asst. U. Calif., Berkeley, 1971-72, 75-76, research asst., 1975, 77-78; tchr. sci. Magic Mountain Sch., Berkeley, 1977; specialist math. and sci. Novato (Calif.) Unified Sch. Dist., 1979-81; instr. sci. Project Bridge, Laney Coll., Oakland, Calif., 1984-86; sci. writer and dir. edn. planning and evaluation, Lawrence Berkeley (Calif.) Lab., 1986-90, life scis. staff coord., 1990—. Author numerous poems, articles and book reviews; author: (with Joan Skolnick and Carol Langbort) How to Encourage Girls in Math and Science: Strategies for Parents and Educators, 1982; Self-Portrait with Hand Microscope (poetry collection), 1982. NSF Grad. fellow, 1972-75; recipient Joseph Henry Jackson award in lit. San Francisco Found., 1982. Mem. AAAS, No. Calif. Sci. Writers Assn., Nat. Assn. Sci. Writers, Women in Communications, Phi Beta Kappa, Iota Sigma Pi. Home: 1057 Walker Ave Oakland CA 94610 Office: Lawrence Berkeley Lab 466 Donner Lab Berkeley CA 94720

DAY, MARY JANE THOMAS, cartographer; b. Connors, New Brunswick, Can., Oct. 12, 1927; d. Angus (dec.) and Delina (dec.) (Michaud) Thomas; m. Howard M. Day, Jan. 17, 1923; children: Laurie Anne Day Greene, Angus Howard. BS in Geography, U. Md., 1974, BS in Bus. & Mgmt., 1977. Meteorol. aide Hangar 8 Eastern Airlines, N.Y.C., 1946-47, U.S. Weather Bur., Washington, 1948-50; cartographic aide U.S. Navy Hydrographic Office, Suitland, Md., 1950-57, cartographer, 1957-62; cartographer U.S. Navy Oceanographic Office, Suitland, 1962-72, Def. Mapping Agy., Suitland, 1972—; cartographer USNS Harkness, 1978, Indonesian Naval Personnel, Jakarta, Indonesia, 1981-82. Compiled, wrote and published: The Descendants of John Thomas of Connors, N.B., 1988. Mem. Nat. Aeronautic Assn., Am. Soc. Photogrammetry & Remote Sensing. Club: Andrews Officers (Md.). Home: 3532 28th Pkwy Temple Hills MD 20748

DAY, MARYLOUISE MULDOON (MRS. RICHARD DAYTON DAY), appraiser; b. St. Louis; d. Joseph A. and Dorothy (Lang) Muldoon; A.B., Washington U., St. Louis, 1940; postgrad. Air U., 1958, George Washington U., 1963-64; grad. Real Estate Inst. Md., 1972; m. Richard Dayton Day, Aug. 15, 1959. Intelligence specialist U.S. Air Force, Washington, 1947-60; program officer, spl. asst. to dir. project devel. VISTA, OEO, 1965-67; with Joint Intelligence Bur., London, Eng., 1953; appraiser, cons. on antiques, fine arts, 1969—; pres. Agts. For Sales Ltd., 1974—, Marylouise M. Day, Inc., 1978—. Recipient citation U.S. Air Force, 1960. Fellow Inc. Soc. Valuers and Auctioneers (London), Am. Soc. Appraisers (chpt. 1st v.p. 1977-78, pres. 1978-79, chmn. fine arts forum 1976-78, gov. Region 3 1980-82, internat. sec. 1982-84, treas. ednl. found. 1986—); mem. Appraisers Assn. Am., Irish Georgian Soc., Winterthur Guild, Assn. Former Intelligence Officers, Decorative Arts Trust, Delta Gamma. Club: Kenwood Golf and Country (Washington). Home: 4928 Sentinel Dr Bethesda MD 20816

DAY, PEGGY JEAN, school system administrator, special education consultant; b. Nixon, Tex., July 3, 1946; d. Eugene Estle and S. Mildred (Wishert) D.; divorced; children: Jason Edmonson, Courtney Edmonson. BS, Tex. A&I U., 1968; MEd, U. Houston, 1982. Migrant ednl. liaison Edinburg (Tex.) Ind. Sch. Dist., 1974-78; ednl. cons. Tex. Rehab., Gonzales, 1978, Devereaux Found., Victoria, Tex., 1983; ednl. diagnostician Harlandale Ind. Sch. Dist., San Antonio, 1985-89; adminstr. spl. edn. Victoria Ind. Sch. Dist., 1989—; ednl. cons., 1982—; cons. spl. edn., 1990—. Contbr. articles on emotional disturbances and learning disabilities to profl. jours. Leader Girl Scouts Am., Victoria, 1983; chairperson Dem. Party, Victoria, 1985; activist, spokesperson Human Soc.-Man and Beast Assn., San Antonio, 1986—. Recipient Vol. award Gov. of Tex., 1983, 84. Mem. NAFE, Victoria Fedn. Tchrs., Tex. Coun. Adminstrs. Spl. Edn., NOW, Am. Fedn. Tchrs., Tex. Ednl. Diagnostician Assn., Tex. Suprs. Assn., Coun. Exceptional Assn. Mem. Unity Ch. Office: Lamar Consol Ind Sch Dist 3911 Ave I Rosenberg TX 77471

DAY, SUZANNE MARIE, art school owner, educator, illustrator; b. Beaufort, S.C., Sept. 20, 1953; d. Arthur George and Patricia Ann (Koperski) Proulx; m. Joseph John Day, July 7, 1979; children: Jason Thomas, Jayme Elizabeth.. AA, Beaufort Coll., 1973, U. Ariz., 1982; BS, Sacred Heart U., Fairfield, Conn., 1986; MFA, Syracuse U., 1991. Devel. officer The Unquowa Sch., Fairfield, 1983-86; owner, tchr. Avante Guard Art Sch., Southbury, Conn., 1986—; outplacement counselor Nat. Coun. for Aging, Westport, Conn., 1984-86; mem. show com. Soc. Illustrators, N.Y.C., 1984-86; free-lance illustrator, 1986—. Exhibited in Regional Hospice Show, Ridgefield, Conn., 1986—, won Best in Show award, 1987 (2), 88, 89. Recipient scholarship Syracuse U., 1989-90. Mem. Am. Acad. Psychoanalysis, Nat. Art Edn. Assn., Graphic Artist Guild, Hospice Artists, Westport Artists (assoc.), Greenpeace. Roman Catholic. Home: 933 Georges Hill Rd Southbury CT 06488

DAY, TERRY LEE, real estate development executive; b. Dania, Fla., Dec. 16, 1955; d. Robert S. and Rachel I. (Dykes) D.; m. Mark G. Minnick, Sept. 14, 1974 (div. June 1976). Student, Valencia Community Coll., 1976, 79, 81. Lic. real estate broker, Fla.; lic. mortgage broker, Fla. Credit specialist Credithrift of Am., Inc., Orlando, Fla., 1976-77; loan officer Nationwide Acceptance, Orlando, 1977-79; asst. dist. credit mgr. Gen. Tire and Rubber Co., Orlando, 1979-80; leasing assoc. J.S. Karlton Mgmt., Inc., Wilmington, Del., 1980-82; v.p. fin. Complete Interiors, Inc., Altamonte Springs, Fla., 1982-87; pres. T.L. Day Properties, Orlando, Fla., 1987—. Editor UHURU mag., 1972. Active fund raiser Am. Heart Assn., Orlando, 1986; chmn. Altamonte Springs Water Quality Adv. Bd. Mem. Internat. Platform Assn. Republican. Office: 1337 W Colonial Dr Orlando FL 32804

DAYHARSH, VIRGINIA FIENGO, educator; b. New Haven, Dec. 2, 1942; d. Edward Arthur and Rose (Giaquinto) Fiengo; m. George R. Dayharsh, Dec. 31, 1966 (div. Nov. 1983; children: Regina Lynn, Jennifer Allison. BA, Coll. of New Rochelle, N.Y., 1964; MA, So. Conn. State U., 1974, cert. advanced study, 1985. Cert. social studies tchr., Conn. Tchr. Troup Jr. High Sch., New Haven, 1964-65, East Haven (Conn.) Jr. High Sch., 1965-69; tchr., dept. chairperson Lauralton Hall, Milford, Conn., 1979-81; tchr. Nathan Hale Ray High Sch., East Haddam, Conn., 1981-85, Naugatuck (Conn.) High Sch., 1985—. Mem. Rep. Town Com., East Haven, 1968-72, Library Bd., East Haven, 1968-81, Bd. of Edn., East Haven, 1986-87. Mem. Conn. Coun. Social Studies, Conn. Edn. Assn., Naugatuck Tchrs.' League, Coun. Social Studies Leadership Coun., NEA, Coun. Cath. Women. Home: 578 Thompson Ave East Haven CT 06512

DAYTON, NANCY ELIZABETH, nursing educator; b. Towanda, Pa., May 30, 1945; d. L. Lang and Jean (MacLaren) D.; m. Charles B. Herron, June 24, 1967 (div. Jan. 31, 1988); children: Mark Dayton Herron, Deborah Jean Herron. BS in Nursing, Duke U., 1967; MS in Nursing, U. Tenn., 1982; MS, Memphis State U., 1986, EdD candidate, 1989. RN, Tenn., N.C. Staff nurse Pa. Dept. Health, Towanda, 1967, Forest Hills VA Hosp., Augusta, Ga., 1968-69; inservice dir. U. Hosp., Augusta, 1969-70; instr. Union U., Jackson, Tenn., 1978-85; asst. prof. Union U., Jackson, 1985-90; assoc. prof. Union U., Memphis, 1990—; charge nurse cons. Jackson Psychiat. Hosp., 1987-88. Prin. works include Safe Harbor, 1986, Winterhaven, 1988. Mem. Ch. Choir, Jackson, 1988-89, Host Home, Jackson, 1988-89. Mem. Santa Filomena, Am. Nursing Assn., Tenn. Nursing Assn., Dist. #6 Tenn. Nurses Assn. (v.p. 1984-86), Phi Delta Kappa, Sigma Theta Tau. Prebyterian. Home: 1941 Innsbruck Dr Germantown TN 38138

DEA, MARGARET MARY, wholesale school supplies company executive; b. St. Albans, Vt., Feb. 8, 1946; s. Ralph Homer and Irene Mae (Trombly) Wilson; m. Eugene Michael Dea, Aug. 26, 1967 (dec.); children: Francesca Meredith, Vanessa Laurel. BA, U. Vt., 1967; postgrad., Art Students League, 1972-77, Sch. Visual Arts, 1975-77. Tchr. French, Hun Sch., Princeton, N.J., 1968-70; tchr. French, Spanish, Newark Acad., Short Hills, N.J., 1970-71; dir. reading, rsch. and edn. Park Sch., Indpls., 1968-71; exec. tng. pers. Bloomingdale's, N.Y.C., 1972-74; commn. portrait artist, Englewood, N.J., Lake Forest, Ill., 1974-79; pres. Svc. Plus, Inc., Fort Myers, Fla., 1979—, United So., Inc., 1983—; art designer E.M. Dea & Assocs., Inc., Fort Myers, 1984—; pres. Margaret Dea Graphics Studio, Fort Myers, 1986—. Editor, author Bloomingdale's employee mag. Faces, 1972-74. Mem. NAFE, Womens Network, Lee County Alliance Arts, Art Students League of N.Y., Mensa (chpt. South by S.W.), Jr. League Bergen County Club. Republican. Roman Catholic. Avocations: piano, needlework, drawing, photography. Office: Svc Plus Inc 30 Mildred Dr Fort Myers FL 33901

DEA, PHOEBE KIN-KIN, chemistry educator; b. Canton, Kwong-Tung, People's Republic of China, June 17, 1946; came to U.S., 1964; d. Kwok-Hung and Hon-Kuan (Lau) Wong; m. Frank J. Dea, Dec. 23, 1967; children: Denise, Melvin. BS, UCLA, 1967; PhD, Calif. Inst. Tech., 1972. Research fellow ICN Nucleic Acid Research Inst., Irvine, Calif., 1972-74; head dept. ICN Pharm., Irvine, 1974-76; asst. prof. chemistry Calif. State U., L.A., 1976-79, assoc. prof., 1979-82, prof., 1982—. Author: Practical Introductory Quantitative Analysis, 1983; contbr. articles to profl. jours. Grantee NSF, NIH, Am. Chem. Soc. Petroleum Research Fund. Mem. So. Calif. Thermal Analysis Group (treas. 1985-88, bd. dirs. 1985—), Phi Kappa Phi (bd. dirs. 1985—, pres. 1989-90). Home: 1155 Sherwood Rd San Marino CA 91108 Office: Calif State U 5151 State University Dr Los Angeles CA 90032-8202

DEAL, JANET JEAN, printing company executive; b. Champaign, Ill., July 8, 1936; d. Mervin Mark and Mary Allison (Grimes) Hughes; m. Alfred John Gemrich, June 19, 1957 (div. 1973); children: Alexander, Anna, Andrew; m. John Lawrence Deal, Oct. 18, 1973 (dec. 1980). BA in Edn., Western Mich. U., 1958; postgrad., U. De Los Andes, Bogotá, Colombia, 1959; BA in Printing Mgmt., Western Mich. U., 1978. Cert. tchr., Mich. Tchr. Kalamazoo (Mich.) Pub. Schs., 1958-60, Orange (Conn.) Pub. Schs., 1960-63; tutor Woodbridge (Conn.) Pub. Schs., 1961-63; substitute tchr. Delton (Mich.) Pub. Schs., 1971-72; office mgr., sales staff Ihling Bros., Everand Co., Kalamazoo, 1979-81, printing sales mgr., 1981-87, mgr. printing div., 1987—; speaker, panelist ednl. and profl. orgns.; presenter workshops. Bd. dirs. Lakeside Boys and Girls Residence, Kalamazoo, 1974—; mem. communications staff Greater Kalamazoo United Way, 1980-84; chmn. bd. dirs. Arts Coun. Greater Kalamazoo, 1988-90; mem. steering com. Kalamazoo Bd. Edn., 1990-92. Mem. Women in Communications (fin. chair 1984, v.p. programs 1990), Profl. Fraternity Assn. (membership svc. com. 1990), Coll. Fraterinty Editor Assn. (workshop presenter), Kalamazoo Women's Network. Office: Ihling Bros Everand Co 2022 Fulford St Kalamazoo MI 49001

DEALMEIDA, MARCELLA J., banker; d. Floyd Francis and Ruth Elma (Cox) Craig; grad. Sch. Consumer Banking, U. Va., 1973; children—Steven Craig and Victor James (twins). Fashion model, 1941-42; tchr. of voice, piano and organ, 1943-53; with First Nat. Bank & Trust Co., Joplin, Mo., 1953-81, v.p., 1976-81; sr. v.p. Centerre Bank of Springfield (Mo.), 1981—; condr. TV program on banking and fin., 1974-75, workshops for Am. Bankers Assn., 1974-75; speaker in field. Bd. dirs. S.W. Mo. Health Systems Agy., 1975-79; mem. Gov. Mo. Adv. Council, 1971-74; exec. com. Jasper County Devel. Assn., 1969-72; vice chmn. Mo. Health Planning Council, 1976; mem. adv. council U. Mo. Health Services Research Center, U. Mo. Spl. Emphasis Health Care Tech. Center. Named to Hall of Honor, Joplin Ann. Celebration Commn., 1973. Mem. Nat. Assn. Bank Women (past chmn. Ozark group), Mo. (past chmn., dir. women's div.), Am. (adv. bd. installment loan div. 1973-79) bankers assns., Am. Inst. Banking (div. dir., bd. govs.), Joplin C. of C. (chmn. red carpet com. 1970-79). Baptist. Clubs: Briarbrook Golf and Country, Mid-Am. Press (dir. 1975—). Home: Route 2 Fair Grove MO 65648 Office: 300 S Jefferson St PO Box 1745SSS Springfield MO 65806

DEAN, ANNA ROSE, hospital administrator; b. Boston, Mar. 22, 1940; d. Thomas and Anna Rose (Mulcahy) Donnelly; m. David Doonan, Sept. 21, 1958 (div. June 1968); children: Kathleen, Dennis, Christopher. AS, Cape Cod Community Coll., 1982; BS, Lesley Coll., 1986; MS, Lesley Coll. Grad. Sch. Mgmt., 1988. Computer programmer United Concrete Pipe Corp., Baldwin Park, Calif., 1968-71; data processing operator FMC Corp., Pomona, Calif., 1971-75; with admissions dept. Falmouth (Mass.) Hosp., 1975-79, personnel asst., 1979-81, dir. personnel, 1981-87, dir. human resources, 1987; outreach adminstr. grad. outreach div. Lesley Coll., Cambridge, Mass., 1987-89; bd. trustees Rita Kendall Day Care Ctr., Falmouth, Mass., 1987—. Mem. Falmouth Personnel Bd., 1987; vol. Am. Cancer Soc., Hyannis, Mass., 1986, United Way Hyannis, 1987, 88. Mem. Vis. Nurses Assn. (chair personnel com. Falmouth 1985—, trustee), Am. Soc. Hosp. Human Resources, Mass. Soc. Hosp. Human Resources, Am. Soc. Personnel, Cape Cod Personnel Assn., Southeastern Hosp. Personnel Dirs. Assn. Republican. Roman Catholic. Home: 176 Palmer Ave Apt #2 Falmouth MA 02540

DEAN, ANNE FREY, health care consultant; b. Piketon, Ohio, Sept. 9, 1942; d. Robert Frederick and Margaret Anne (Wynn) F.; m. Michael Russell Fox Dean, Dec. 16, 1961 (div. 1978); children: Heather, Elizabeth, Michael Bruce, Stephanie Lara Anne. Assoc. Nursing, San Antonio Community Coll., 1974; BSN, U. Tex., San Antonio, 1979. Staff nurse SICU Med. Ctr. Hosp., San Antonio, 1974-75; recovery charge nurse Med. Ctr. Hosp., 1975-77, operating rm. supr., 1977-79; exec. dir. S.W. Tex. Meth. Hosp., San Antonio, 1979-83; freelance cons. in health care DeLand, Fla., 1983-84; pres., cons. Anne Dean Assocs., DeLand, 1985—; cons. S.W. Tex. Meth. Hosp., 1981-83; lectr. in field. Contbr. articles to profl. jours., chpts. in books. Mem. Assn. Operating Rm. Nurses (membership co-chmn. 1981-83, pres. 1980-83), Deland Hist. Soc., Soc. for Hist. Preservation, Sierra Club. Republican. Episcopalian. Home: 911 E Minnesota Ave DeLand FL 32724

DEAN, BETTY MARLENE, community college administrator; b. Alpena, Mich., July 31, 1941; d. Paul Harvey and Marietta Marlene (Wright) D. Student, Santa Ana Coll., 1965-66; BS, Calif. State U., 1969; MS, U. Calif., San Francisco, 1970; EdD, Brigham Young U., 1976. RN, Calif., N.Y.; Calif. community coll. chief administr. credential, Calif. community coll. supervisory credential; pub. health nursing credential, Calif., coll. teaching credential, Calif. Staff, supr. nursing, med.-surg.-critical nurse nursing Ithaca, N.Y., Orange, Calif., 1962-69; tchr., coord. ednl. planning and curriculum Santa Barbara City Coll., Santa Barbara, Calif., 1975-77; instr. assoc. degree nursing program/EMT Santa Barbara City Coll., 1970-78, asst. dir. health occupations, 1971-78; dir. health professions, assoc. dean sci., health Golden West Coll., Huntington Beach, Calif., 1978-81; assoc. dean bus. tech., pub. svcs. and vocat. edn. Golden West Coll., 1981-82, assoc. dean. community svcs., 1982-83, dean community svcs. and continuing edn., 1983-85; pres. Mission Coll., Santa Clara, Calif., 1985-90; supr., pres. Butte Coll., Oroville, Calif., 1990—; pres. Mgmt. Assn., Coast Community Coll. Dist., Costa Mesa, Calif., 1983-84; treas. Mission-West Valley Ednl. Found., Santa Clara, 1986-87, sec., 1986—; mem. exec. com. Calif. Community Coll. Occupational Edn. Coalition, Sacramento, 1987-88. Cons. editor: Nursing Perspectives & Issues, 1977, Nursing Concepts & Processes, 1977, Patient-Care Studies, 1978, Pharmacological Aspects of Nursing Care, 1983. Mem. Santa Barbara County Health Commn., 1976-78; bd. dirs. Pilgrim Haven Retirement Ctr., Los Altos, Calif., 1985—; bd. dirs. cen. area chpt. United Way, Santa Clara County, 1988—, Butte Coll. Found., 1990—; mem. Chico Youth Commn., 1990—. Recipient Status of Women award League of Friends, Santa Clara County, 1987; named Regional Person of Yr. Calif. Community Coll. Coun. on Community Svcs./Continuing Edn., 1988. Mem. Chief Exec. Officers Calif. Community Colls., AAUW, Soroptimists (Woman of Yr. award 1986), Sigma Theta Tau, Phi Delta Kappa. Office: Butte Coll 3536 Butte Campus Dr Oroville CA 95965

DEAN, CATHERINE JEAN, rehabilitation facility administrator; b. Oshkosh, Wis., July 4, 1950; d. Peter Walter and Ruth Anna (Rasmussen) Kersztyn; m. Jeffrey Willis Dean; children: Christopher Peter, Casey Catherine. Student, St. Norbert Coll., 1968-69, Ohio State U., 1969-70; BS in Rehab. Counseling, U. Wis., 1972, MS in Rehab. Counseling, 1973. Work fl. supr. Rock County Rehab., Inc., Janesville, Wis., 1973-74, program supr., 1974-75; adminstrv. asst. Lakeland Counseling Ctr., Elkhorn, Wis., 1975-84; adminstr. Parkside Lodge of Wis., Inc., Janesville, 1984—. Leader Cub Scouts Pack 234, Walworth, Wis., 1987—; vol. Literacy Coun., Janesville, 1988—. Office: Parkside Lodge Wis 320 Lincoln St Walworth WI 53545

DEAN, DEAREST (LORENE GLOSUP), songwriter; b. Volin, S.D., Oct. 4, 1911; d. John Henry and Bessie Marie Donnelly Peterson; m. Eddie Dean, Sept. 11, 1931; children: Donna Lee Knorr, Edgar Glosup II. Grad. high sch., Yankton, S.D. Bd. dirs. Acad. Country Music, Hollywood, 1960-62. Composer songs including: One Has My Name, 1948, The Lonely Hours, 1970, 1501 Miles of Heaven, 1970, Walk Beside Me, 1980. Sec. ARC, Burbank, Calif., 1943. Mem. ASCAP. Republican. Roman Catholic. Avocation: golf.

DEAN, DEBORAH GORE, consultant, public relations executive; b. N.Y.C., Nov. 30, 1954; d. Gordon Evans and Mary (Gore) D. B.S., Georgetown U., 1980. Mng. editor Encore Mag., Washington, 1978-79; pub. City Life Mag., Washington, 1979-81; dir. pub. relations Global Research Internat., Washington, 1981; spl. asst. to asst. sec. Congl. Intergovtl. and Pub. Affairs, Washington, 1981-82; spl. asst. to sec. U.S. Dept. Housing and Urban Devel., Washington, 1982-84; exec. asst. to sec. HUD, 1984-87; pres. Dean & Assocs. Cons., Washington, 1988—. Editor mag. The Georgetowner, 1978, mng. editor Encore Mag., 1979; pub. City Life Mag., 1980. Speechwriter Leadership Found., Washington, 1972, 73, Gore for Gov. Campaigns, Rockville, Md., 1974, 78; vol. Reagan-Bush, Rockville, 1979-80; fundraiser The Textile Mus., Washington DC, 1984; mem. Fund Am.'s Future, Rep. Women's Fed. Forum; mem. Women's Com. for Nat. Mus. of Women in Arts. Recipient W. "Bill" Calloway Pub. Service award, Nat. Assn. Real Estate Brokers, 1986, Key to City, Providence, 1984, Key to City, Rockford, Ill., 1986, Key to City, Manchester, N.H., 1986, Key to City, Greenville, S.C., 1986, Key to City, Cleve., 1986. Mem. Nat. Press Club, Nat. Strategy Info. Ctr., Rep. Women of Capitol Hill, Nat. Assn. Female Execs. Roman Catholic.

DEAN, DONNA JOYCE, health scientist administrator; b. Danville, Ky., Apr. 22, 1947; d. Joe Harvey and Anna Mae (Jarvis) D. AB in Chemistry, Berea (Ky.) Coll., 1969; PhD in Biochemistry, Duke U., 1974. Rsch. faculty Princeton (N.J.) U., 1974-77; consumer safety officer FDA, Washington, 1979-82; research biochemist NIH, Bethesda, Md., 1977-79, scientist adminstr., chmn. tng. com., 1982—; cons. numerous profl. assns. Contbr. articles to profl. jours., 1971-85. Recipient post-doctoral fellowship Nat. Cancer Inst., 1974-77. Mem. AAAS, Am. Assn. Pathologists, Am. Inst. Nutrition, Am. Chem. Soc., Sci. Fair Assn. (mem. exec. bd. 1986—), Berea Coll. Alumni Assn. (mem. com. 1987—). Office: NIH Westwood 340 Bethesda MD 20892

DEAN, FRANCES CHILDERS, librarian; b. Parker County, Tex., Apr. 20, 1930; d. John and Audrey (Ribble) Childers; divorced; 1 dau., Deborah Jane. B.S., Tex. Woman's U., Denton, 1959, M.L.S., 1962; postgrad., U. Md. Libr. pub. schs. Dallas and Fairfax, Va., 1959-63; libr., then coord. evaluation and selection Montgomery County (Md.) Pub. Schs., 1963-76, dir. div. instructional materials, 1976-80, dir. dept. instructional resources, 1980—. Recipient Intellectual Freedom award Am. Assn. Sch. Librarians. Mem. ALA (trustee Freedom to Read Found. 1974-76), Ednl. Film Library Assn. (dir. 1980—), Children's Book Guild Washington, Assn. Supervision and Curriculum, Soc. for Sch. Librarians Internat. (pres. 1987-88), Beta Phi Mu, Delta Kappa Gamma. Democrat. Home: 528 Meadow Hall Rockville MD 20851 Office: Montgomery County Pub Schs 850 Hungerford Dr Rockville MD 20850

DEAN, HELEN BARBARA, sales executive; b. Roanoke, Va., Apr. 10, 1945; d. George William and Hestenia B. (Motley) Ferguson; m. Robert L. Dean, June 1972. BS, Knoxville Coll., 1967. Tchr. Hart Jr. High Sch., Washington, 1967-69; system analyst IBM, Indpls., 1969-72; administv. aide Ind. U., Bloomington, 1972-74; with sales mktg. dept. Redactron, Indpls., 1974-75; trainer Xerox, Chgo., 1975-77, mgr. branch support, 1977-79; mgr. nat. support Xerox, Dallas, 1979-82; mgr. regional sales Xerox, Chgo., 1982-85; sr. v.p. Thomson Fin. Networks, Inc., Newton, Mass., 1985—. Democrat. Presbyterian. Home: 236 Congress St Milford MA 01757 Office: Thomson Fin Networks 85 Wells Ave Newton MA 02159

DEAN, HELEN HENRIETTA, volunteer; b. Pasadena, Calif., Mar. 25, 1905; d. Edward Merrill and Hannah (Damasche) Burnell; m. Frederic Percival Dean, Dec. 31, 1930 (dec. Aug. 1986); children: James Frederic, Gordon Burnell, Carolyn. Student, San Diego State Coll., 1925; BE, Cen. Wash. State U., 1960, postgrad., 1962. Instr. Chula Vista (Calif.) Grammar Sch., 1925, Lincoln Sch., Ontario, Calif., 1925-30, Broadway Elem. Sch., Yakima, Wash., 1958-70; with vocat. testing div. Detention Home, Yakima, 1970-76. Vol. Congl. Christian Ch., Yakima, 1960—, Friends in Svc. for Humanity YWCA, Yakima, 1971-74; vision examiner Wash. Soc. to Prevent Blindness, Yakima, 1969-87; chmn. UNICEF sales Ch. Women United, Yakima, 1970—; scrap book chmn. Home Base Sch. Program, Yakima, 1975—; docent Yakima Valley Mus., 1972—; lectr. Yakima Schs.and others on Beatrix Potter, 1960—. Named Wash. State Outstanding Vol., 1975, Community Svc. award Woman of Achievement, 1977, Woman in History, 1985, Runner-up in YWCA award, 1990; Helen Dean Circle named in her honor, 1989. Mem. AAUW (ednl. grantee 1989), Ret. Tchrs. Yakima, Allied Arts Club, Century Club (mem. 2 depts.), Agenda Club, Knife and Fork Club, Alpha Delta Kappa. Republican. Home: 214 N 33d Ave Yakima WA 98902

DEAN, JACLYNN LEE, health care investigator; b. Eau Calire, Wis., Mar. 14, 1947; d. Raymond Henry and Delores (Fjelstad) Forcier; m. Robert Zich, Oct. 1969 (div. 1973); 1 child, Kurt; m. Douglas Justin Dean, Mar. 31, 1990. RN, St. Mary's Sch. Nursing, Rochester, Minn., 1968. Staff surg. nurse Luther Hosp., Eau Claire, 1968-69; staff nurse Lorenz Inst., Eau Claire, 1969-71, Sacred Heart Hosp., Eau Claire, 1971-73; staff psychiatric nurse Sacred Heart Hosp., 1973-74, head nurse psychiatry, 1974-77; nurse coordinator Med. Edn. Prog. Planner, St. Paul, 1977-79; staff nurse Health & Wellness Clinic, St. Paul, 1982-83; nurse coordiantor Brown County Mental Health Ctr., Green Bay, Wis., 1983-85; owner Jaclu, Mpls., 1985-87; health care investigator State of Minn., St. Paul, 1987—; cons. in field. Named Employee of Yr., Brown County Mental Health Ctr., 1984, Achievement award, State of Minn., 1988, 90.

DEAN, JACQUELYN MARIE, federal agency administrator; b. Jersey City, Feb. 26, 1954; d. Justin Caswell Dean and Hazel Virginia (Jimerson) Dean-John. BA in English, SUNY, Fredonia, 1976; MEd, Harvard U., 1978, cert. of advanced study in human devel., 1981. Adminstrv. asst., bookkeeper Seneca Nation of Indians, Salamanca, N.Y., 1976-77, head start tchr., adminstr., 1979; head tchr. Boston Indian Council, Jamaica Plain, Mass., 1980, coordinator Wabanaki Curriculum Project, 1981-83, dir. edn. dept., 1983-84; dir. pub. info. Presdl. Commn. on Indian Reservation Econs., Washington, 1984; tng. specialist Native Am. Cons., Inc., Washington, 1984-85, tech. specialist, 1985-86; spl. asst. to Dep. to Asst. Sec. on Indian Affairs, Office of Trust and Econ. Devel. of Bur. of Indian Affairs, Washington, 1987-88; program analyst, Office of Sec. Office of Constrn. Mgmt., Washington, 1988; cons. ORBIS, Washington, 1981—, Indian edn. Boston schs., 1980-84; speaker curriculum devel. State of Maine Dept. Indian Edn., Augusta, 1987. Book reviewer Interracial Books for Children, 1986. Mem. community adv. bd. Sta. WGBH-TV, Boston, 1983-85. Recipient Spl. Achievement award U.S. Dept. Interior, 1985, Superior Accomplishment award, 1989. Mem. Nat. Assn. Female Execs., Nat. Indian Council on Aging, Native Am. Pub. Broadcasting Consortium, Am. Indian Sci. and Engring. Soc. Mem. Ch. Longhouse Traditional Senecas. Home: 5543 Columbia Pike #309 Arlington VA 22204

DEAN, LAURA, choreographer, composer; b. S.I., N.Y., Dec. 3, 1945; d. Arthur Douglas and Esther Dorothy (Sweedler) D. Student public schs. Pres. Dean Dance and Music Found.; Mem. N.Y. State Council on the Arts Dance Panel, 1974, 75, Nat. Endowment Arts Dance and Inter-Arts Panels. With 1st co. of dancers, Laura Dean and Dance Co., 1971-75; created Stamping Dance, 1971, Circle Dance, 1972, Jumping Dance, Changing Pattern, Steady Pulse, Walking Dance, Sq. Dance, 1973, Spinning Dance, Response Dance, 1974, Drumming, 1975; choreographer/composer, Laura Dean Dancers and Musicians, 1976—, Song, Dance, 1976, Spiral, 1977, Music, 1979, (for Joffrey Ballet) Night, 1980, Tympani, 1980, Sky Light, 1982, (for Joffrey Ballet) Fire, 1982, Inner Circle, 1983, Burn (for John Curry Skaters), 1983, Enochian, 1983, Trio, 1984, Tehillim (with music by Steve Reich for BAT-DOR Co. of Israel), 1984, Impact (with music by Steve Reich), 1985, Transformer (with music by Anthony Davis), 1985, Patterns of Change (with music by Philip Glass for Ohio Ballet), 1985, Force Field (with music by Steve Reich), 1986, For Two (with music by Jean-Baptiste Breval), 1987, Magnetic, 1987, Dream Collector (with music by Terry Riley), 1988, Space (with music by Steve Reich), 1988, Equator, 1988; appeared, PBS Dance in America series, 1980; contbr. articles to: Contemporary Dance, Drama Rev., Dance Scope. Creative Artist Public Service fellow, 1976; Guggenheim fellow, 1977, 82; grantee Jerome Found., 1978-80, Mobil Found., 1979-85, Rockefeller Found., 1980, N.Y. State Council on Arts, 1973-85, Nat. Endowment Arts, 1977-85, Chem. Bank, 1982-84, Con Edison, 1983, Exxon Corp., 1980-84, Philip Morris Corp., 1983-85, numerous others; challenge grantee, 1980; recognition by N.Y.C. Commn. on Status of Women, 1985. Office: Dean Dance & Music Found Inc 552 Broadway New York NY 10012*

DEAN, LYDIA MARGARET CARTER (MRS. HALSEY ALBERT DEAN), author, nutrition coordinator, consultant; b. Bedford, Va., July 11, 1919; d. Christopher C. and Hettie (Gross) Carter; m. Halsey Albert Jr., John Carter, Lydia Margerae. Grad., Averett Coll.; BS, Madison Coll., 1941; MS, Va. Poly. Inst. and State U., 1951; postgrad., U. Va., Mich. State U.; PhD, DSc, UCLA Med. Sch., 1985. Dietetic intern, therapeutic dietitian St. Vincent de Paul Hosp., Norfolk, Va., 1942; physicist U.S. Naval Op. Base, Norfolk, 1943-45; clin. dietitian Roanoke Meml. Hosps., 1946-51; assoc. prof. Va. Poly. Inst. and State U., 1946-53; community nutritionist Roanoke, Va., 1953-60; dir. dept. nutrition and dietetics Southwestern Va. Med. Ctr., Roanoke, 1960-67; food and nutrition cons. Nat. Hdqrs. ARC, Washington, 1967—; staff and vol. Nat. Hdqrs. ARC, 1973—; nutrition scientist, cons. Dept. Army, Washington, 1973—, Dept. Agr., 1973—; pres. Dean Assocs.; cons., assoc. dir. Am. Dietetic Assn., 1975—; coord. new degree program U. Hawaii, 1974-75; dir., nutrition coord. programs HHS, Washington, 1973—; mem. task force White House Conf. Food and Nutrition, 1969—; chmn. fed. com. Interagy. Com. on Nutrition Edn., 1970-71; tech. rep. to AID and State Dept.; chmn. Crusade for Nutrition Edn.,

Washington, 1970—; participant, cons. Nat. Nutrition Policy Conf., 1974. Author: (with Virginia McMasters) Community Emergency Feeding, 1972, Help My Child How to Eat Right, 1973, rev. edit., 1978, The Complete Gourmet Nutrition Cookbook: The Joy of Eating Well and Right, 1978, rev. edit., 1982, The Stress Foodbook, 1980, rev. edit., 1990; contbr. articles to profl. jours. Trustee World U., 1987—; apptd. rsch. bd. advisors Am. Biog. Inst., 1990. Fellow Am. Pub. Health Assn., Internat. Inst. Community Service; mem. AAUW, Am. Dietetic Assn., Bus. and Profl. Women's Clubs (cons. 1970—, pres. 1981-82), Am. Home Econs. Assn. (rep. and treas. joint congl. com.), Inst. Food Technologists, Blue Ribbon (speaker 1972). Home: 7816 Birnam Wood Dr McLean VA 22102

DEAN, MARGARET MAHLER (MRS. J. SIMPSON DEAN, JR.), civic worker; b. Wilmington, Del., July 3, 1944; d. John Anthony and Maggie Naomi (Davis) Mahler; m. James Hoge Tyler McConnell, Apr. 25, 1973 (dec.) ; m. J. Simpson Dean, Jr. AA, Marjorie Webster Coll., 1964. Sec. CIA, Washington, 1964-65, Hercules, Inc., Wilmington, 1965-66; with Delaware Trust Co., Wilmington, 1966-73, asst. corp. sec., 1969-72, asst. v.p., 1972-73. Bd. dirs., corp. sec. Del. Mus. Natural History, Wilmington, 1969-79; asst. sec., treas. Cecil County (Md.) Breeders' Fair, 1969-75; sec., mem. exec. com. Fair Hill (Md.) Races, 1969-75; bd. dirs. Wilmington Vis. Nurse Assn., 1974—, sec., 1982-86; bd. dirs. Brandywine YMCA, Wilmington, 1977-82, Del. Art Mus., 1983-88, Soc. Four Arts, 1985—. Mem. Nat. Assn. Bank Women, Del. Assn. Bank Women, Nat. Steeplechase & Hunt Assn., Del. Soc. Fine Arts, Farmington (Va.) Country Club, River Club (N.Y.C.), Vicmead Hunt Club, Everglades Club (Palm Beach, Fla.), Bath and Tennis Club, Wilmington Country, Rehoboth Beach, Greenville Country Club. Democrat. Episcopalian. Home: 179 Via Del Lago Palm Beach FL 33480 also: 2255 Creek Rd Rt 82 Greenville DE 19807

DEAN, MARGO, artistic director; b. Ft. Worth, Dec. 9, 1930; d. Arthur Augustus and Margaret (Holliday) Webster; m. Beale Dean, Sept. 3, 1948; children: Webster Beale, Giselle Liseanne. BFA, Ward-Belmont Coll., 1947; postgrad., Tex. Christian U., 1948. Ballet appearances, Louisville, 1948, Dallas, 1947; prin. dancer, choreographer Ft. Worth Opera Ballet, 1955-60; dir. Ft. Worth Ballet Assn., 1961; artistic dir. Ballet Concerto, Ft. Worth, 1969—. Bd. dirs. Ft. Worth Symphony Orch.; mem. dance panel Tex. Commn. on the Arts, 1990—. Mem. Southwestern Regional Ballet Assn. (pres. 1985-86, bd. dirs. 1985-88), Nat. Assn. Regional Ballet. Republican. Presbyterian. Clubs: Ft. Worth, Ft. Worth Boat, Ridglea Country. Office: Ballet Concerto 3803 Camp Bowie Blvd Fort Worth TX 76107

DEAN, MARY ANN, theater manager; b. Nashville, Sept. 21, 1941; d. Clifton and Mary Elizabeth (Lee) Gregory; m. Patrick Donovan Dean, Apr. 27, 1964; children: Patrick Donovan Jr., Gregory Lee. BA, Agnes Scott Coll., Decatur, Ga., 1963. Flight attendant Pan Am. Airlines, N.Y.C., 1963-64; bus. mgr. Civic Theatre of Central Fla., Orlando, 1976-81, gen. mgr., 1981—; mem. ad hoc com. Fla. State Theatre Bd., Tallahassee, 1988—; cons. Tallahassee Little Theatre, Ocala Civic Theatre; grants rev. panelist Div. Cultural Affairs, Tallahassee, 1989—; speaker in field. Bd. dirs. WMFE-TV and Radio PBS, Orlando, 1988—, Fla. Sch. of Arts; theatre workshop leader Army Entertainment in Germany, 1990. Mem. Fla. Theatre Conf., Am. Assn. Community Theatres, Cen. Fla. Alumnae Assn. Agnes Scott Coll. (pres. 1979), Civic Theatre Guild, Rotary. Republican. Roman Catholic. Home: 1907 Lakeside Dr Orlando FL 32803 Office: Civic Theatre of Central Fl 1001 E Princeton St Orlando FL 32803

DEAN, NANCY ANN, financial executive; b. Newark, Mar. 30, 1959; d. Herbert and Jennie (Zaborowski) Dean; m. Bernard L. Dieguez, Apr. 26, 1986. BS, Seton Hall U., South Orange, N.J., 1981. Research asst. Seton Hall U., South Orange, 1978-81; fin. analyst Prudential Property & Casualty Ins. Co., Holmdel, N.J., 1981-82, Robert Wood Johnson U. Hosp., New Brunswick, N.J., 1982-84; mgr. reimbursement Robert Wood Johnson U. Hosp., 1984-86; sr. cons. Network, Inc., Randolph, N.J., 1986; corp. v.p. budgets and reimbursement Cathedral Healthcare System, Inc., Newark, 1986—; adj. faculty Kean Coll., Union, N.J. 1984—; cons. in field. Contbr. articles to profl. jours. Mem. Healthcare Fin. Mgmt. Assn., Beta Gamma Sigma. Democrat. Roman Catholic. Home: 261 Rudolph Ave Rahway NJ 07065 Office: Cathedral Healthcare Sys 1 Gateway Ctr Suite 2600 Newark NJ 07102

DEAN, ROXANE, inventory control specialist; b. Farmerville, La., Sept. 23, 1956; d. Gladden Everett Dean and Elva Gray Nolan. BA, La. Tech. U., 1978, MA, 1986. Material control coord. Inland Fisher Guide Div. of GM, Monroe, La., Design Force Interiors, Monroe, La. Mem. YWCA. Mem. NAFE, DAR. Home: RT 3 Box 980 Rayville LA 71269

DEAN, THELMA J., audit manager; b. Pitts., Feb. 4, 1944; d. William Clark Widdowson and Mabel L. Burkhart; m. Walter R. Dean, Feb. 5, 1967. BSBA, Duquesne U., 1977, postgrad. Cert. CPA, Pa. System analyst Westinghouse Electric, Pitts., 1963-73; mgmt. cons. Grant Thorton, Pitts., 1977-83; audit mgr. EDP, CNG Svc. Co. Inc., Pitts., 1984—. Mem. AICPA, EDP Auditors Assn., Am. Women's Soc. CPAs (treas. 1988-90), Pa. Inst. CPAs, Beta Gamma Sigma, Beta Alpha Phi. Home: 4940 Third St Verona PA 15174 Office: CNG Svc Co Inc CNG Tower Pittsburgh PA 15222

DEANE, SALLY JAN, health services administrator, consultant; b. Downey, Calif., Sept. 24, 1948; d. Virgil Eldred and Pearl Jan (Kettell) D. BA, Whittier Coll., 1970; MEd, Boston U., 1971, MPH, 1988. Mgr. community health Peter Bent Brigham Hosp., Boston, 1974-76; coord. WIC program Martha Eliot Health Ctr., 1976-78; dir. S.W. Boston WIC program Shattock Hosp. Corp., 1978-80; exec. dir. Fenway Community Health Ctr., 1980-84; exec. asst. commr. Boston Dept. Health & Hosps., 1984-86; assoc. dir. spl. projects Health Policy Inst. Boston U., 1986-87; dir. ambulatory reimbursement Mass. Medicaid, 1987-88; assoc. Cambridge (Mass.) Mgmt. Group, 1989—; cons. Mass. Dept. Pub. Health, Boston, 1978-80, Citicorp Corp. Hdqrs., N.Y.C., 1986, Digital Equipment Corp., Maynard, Mass., 1987. Mem. Mayor's Task Force on AIDS, Boston, 1983-86; v.p. Trustees Charitable Donations, Boston, 1984-86; bd. dirs. Bay Windows Community Newspaper, Boston, 1984-88. Mem. Mass. Pub. Health Assn., Am. Pub. Health Assn., Women in Health Care Mgmt. Presbyterian. Home: 115 University Rd Brookline MA 02146-4532 Office: Deane & Assocs 185 Alewife Brook Pkwy Ste 4200 Cambridge MA 02138

DE ANGELIS, DEBORAH ANN AYARS, university athletics official; b. San Diego, July 2, 1948; d. Charles Orvil and Janet Isabel (Glithero) Ayars; m. David C. De Angelis, Sept. 29, 1984. B.A., U. Calif.-Santa Barbara, 1970, Certificate in Social Services, 1972; M.S., U. Mass., 1979. Eligibility worker County Welfare Dept., Santa Barbara, Calif., 1970-73; women's crew coach, U. Mass., 1978-79, Northeastern U., Boston, 1979-83, bus. mgr. women's athletics, 1983-87, asst. dir. bus., 1987-89; mgr. athletics bus. Calif. State U., Northridge, 1989—; com. mem. Women's Olympic Rowing Com., 1976-84; life trustee Nat. Rowing Found., 1984; life mem. selection com. Rowing Found. Hall of Fame, 1984—; rowing mgr. Women's Olympic Team, 1976, 80; head mgr. U.S. Olympic Festival, Syracuse, N.Y., 1981, coach, Indpls., 1982, Colorado Springs, Colo., 1983; mem. alcohol and drug awareness com. Northeastern U., 1983. Mem. Nat. Women's Rowing Assn. (Woman of Yr. award 1983), Fedn. Sociétés d'Aviron (women's commn. 1978—, U.S. del. to ann. congress 1978, 80-88), U.S. Rowing Assn. (del. 1988, bd. dirs. 1975-80, 85-89, co-chmn. internat. div., co-chmn. events div. 1985-86, chmn. internat. div. 1986-88, women's v.p. 1985-88, mem. exec. com. 1985-89, exec. v.p. 1988-89). Club: ZLAC Rowing. Home: 18300 Napa St Apt M Northridge CA 91325

DEANGELIS, MARGARET SCALZA, publishing executive; b. Jersey City, May 27, 1936; d. Louis Patrick and Josephine M. (Cleary) Scalza; m. David Jenkins, Sept. 30, 1951 (div. 1962); children: Alison Brittain, Cynthia Higgins, Ann Marie; m. Henry DeAngelis, Aug. 28, 1977; children: Valerie, Brenda DeAngelis Falato, Louise DeAngelis Brine, Henry Jr. Owner Towne House Restaurant, Hackettstown, N.J., 1963-65; pres. Kinsley Assocs., Inc., Florham Park, N.J., 1966—, Kinsley Publs., Inc., Florham Park, 1972—; pub. purchasing guides, sch. directories, N.J., N.Y., Ohio, Mass., Calif. Co-chmn. Northwestern N.J. div. U.S. Postal Customer Council, 1978—. Mem. Nat. Assn. Sch. Bus. Ofcls., Morris County Bd. Realtors, Nat. Assn. Female Execs., Hackettstown Trade Assn. (sec.-treas., bd. dirs. 1963). Republican. Roman Catholic. Home: 20 E Madison Ave Florham Park NJ 07932 Office: 300 Mine Hill Farm Schooleys Mountain NJ 07870

DEANGELIS, SUSAN PENNY, jewelry manufacturing executive; b. N.Y.C., Nov. 20, 1950; s. Milton Abraham and Anne Pearl (Fleischer) Zwilling; m. Ivo DeAngelis, July 25, 1971 (div. Feb. 1982); m. Benjamin H. Pfeffer, May 17, 1985. BA cum laude, Bklyn. Coll., 1971. Spl. projects coordinator, customer service rep. N.Y. Property Ins. Underwriting Assocs., N.Y.C., 1971-72; office mgr. Pyramid Personnel Agy., N.Y.C., 1972-73; v.p. human resources Feature Enterprises Inc., N.Y.C., 1973—; cons. JWJ Enterprises, Inc., N.Y.C., 1984-85. N.Y. State Bd. Regents scholar, 1967. Mem. N.Y. Assn. New Ams. (chairperson pvt. sector adv. com. 1985-88). Jewish. Avocations: photography, calligraphy, painting. Home: 2258 E 27th St Brooklyn NY 11229 Office: Feature Enterprises Inc 130 W 46th St New York NY 10036

DEANS, ANGELA VICK, hospital financial official; b. Wilson, N.C., Sept. 14, 1957; d. Arthur Lee and Eleanor (Boykin) Vick; m. Thomas Elmer Deans, Jr., Jan. 14, 1979; children: Thomas Elmer III, Courtney Leigh. BSBA, Atlantic Christian U., Wilson, 1979. Sec. emergency room Wilson Meml. Hosp., Inc., 1975-78, cashier, 1976-78, staff asst. bus. office, 1978-83, asst. mgr. bus. office, 1983-85, mgr. patient accts., 1985—. Mem. stewardship, budget and nominating coms. Nobles Chapel Bapt. Ch., Sims, N.C., 1987—; speaker to sr. citizens groups, Optimist Club, Wilson, 1989. Named Employee of Month, Wilson Meml. Hosp., 1985. Mem. Healthcare Fin. Mgmt. Assn. (advanced mem., edn. coun. N.C. 1987—, patient acctg. com. 1987—). Office: Wilson Meml Hosp Inc 1705 S Tarboro St Wilson NC 27893

DEAN-ZUBRITSKY, CYNTHIA MARIAN, psychologist, reseacher; b. Urbana, Ill., Oct. 27, 1950; d. William Bonaparte and Lois (Doran) Dean; m. John Jay Zubritsky , Sept. 15, 1979; 1 child, Grant Doran. BA, Ind. U., 1972; M in Psychology, Pa. State U., 1978; PhD, Temple U., 1989. Counselor New Castle (Pa.) Youth Devel. Ctr., 1972-76; dir. Ill. Family Edn. Ctr., Danville, 1976-77; researcher Pa. State U., University Park, 1977-78, 89—; film cons. Ill. Devel. Disabilities Council, Springfield, 1978; psychologist Atkins House, York, Pa., 1978-82; quality assurance specialist Pa. Office Mental Retardation, Harrisburg, 1982-84; dir. tng. and staff devel. Pa. Office Mental Health, Harrisburg, 1984-89; pvt. practice psychology Harrisburg, 1989—; bd. dir. children and youth services Vermilion County Mental Health Program, Danville, 1975-77; psychologist Loysville (Pa.) Youth Devel. Ctr., 1981-82; tchr. Danville Community Coll., 1975; cons. U. Ill., Urbana, 1976, Danville Sch. System, 1975-76; faculty U. Pa. dept. Psychiatry, 1989—; rsch. alliance for mentally ill Pa., 1989—. Vol. ARC, 1967-87, YWCA, 1970-89; mem. Pa. Task Force on Mental Health: Women, Harrisburg, 1986-87. Human Resource Devel. grantee NIMH, 1985-87. Mem. Internat. Psychogeriatric Assn., Nat. Assn. State Mental Health Program Dirs., Am. Horticulture Soc., Phi Delta Kappa, Phi Mu. Republican. Presbyterian. Office: U Pa Dept Psychiatry Philadelphia PA 19104

DEARBORN, LAURA, advertising agency executive. Former sr. v.p. Dancer Fitzgerald & Sample (now Saatchi & Saatchi DFS), San Francisco; now exec. v.p. Saatchi & Saatchi DFS/Pacific, San Francisco. Office: Saatchi & Saatchi DFS/Pacific 1010 Battery St PO Box 7166 San Francisco CA 94120*

DEARBORN, MAUREEN MARKT, speech and language clinician; b. Brockton, Mass., Jan. 19, 1948; d. Francis Joseph and Marjorie Agnes (White) M.; m. James Clement Bovin, Nov. 6, 1970 (div. June 1973); m. David C. Dearborn, Jan. 14, 1989. BA in Speech Pathology and Audiology, U. Mass., 1970; MA in Ednl. Psychology, Am. Internat. Coll., Springfield, Mass. Speech and lang. clinician Holyoke (Mass.) Pub. Schs., 1970—. Chmn. Holyoke Cancer Crusade, 1985; voter registration chmn. Holyoke Dem. Com., 1987; mem. Hist. Deerfield (Mass.); chmn. deaconesses 2d Congregational Ch. Holyoke. Mem. Hampden County Tchrs. Assn. (pres. 1981, sec. 1982, v.p. 1984-86, treas. 1988-90), Holyoke Tchrs. Assn. (treas. 1989, DAR historian), Am. Speech, Hearing and Langs. Assn. (continuing edn. adv. bd. 1988-90, congl. action contact continuing edn. adv. bd. 1988-90), Mass. Tchrs. Assn., Mass. Speech, Hearing and Langs. Assn., New England Hist. and Geneal. Soc., Western Geneal. Soc., Mass. Genealogical Soc., Assn. for Gravestone Studies, DAR (historian Eunice Day 1984-90). Congregationalist. Club: Friends Quadrangle. Home: 257 Franklin St Holyoke MA 01040 Office: Holyoke Pub Schs 98 Suffolk St Holyoke MA 01040

DE ARMOND, ANNA JANNEY, English educator; b. Phila., Feb. 10, 1910; d. James Keyser and Emily (Janney) De A. AB with highest honors, Swarthmore Coll., 1932; postgrad., Bryn Mawr Coll., 1932-33, 34-35; MA, Columbia U., 1934; PhD, U. Pa., 1947. From instr. English to prof. English U. Del., Newark, 1935-75, prof. emeritus English, 1975—; vis. prof. Sheffield (Eng.) U., 1967, New Eng. U., Armidalw, NSW, Australia, 1974, Ocean U. Qingdao (People's Republic China), 1988; Fulbright prof. U. Munich, 1956-57; mem. coms. Del. Humanities Forum; mem. commn. on English, Harvard U., 1965; dir. NDEA English Inst., 1966; adviser Am. studies Conf. Bd. Associated Rsch. Couns., Washington, 1957-58; presenter radio and TV; lectr. in field; cons. office edn. HEW, 1967, Del. Coun. on Tchr. Edn., 1965-74, Del. Coun. on English, Salem County, N.J., 1960-61. Author: Andrew Bradford, 1949, reprint, 1969; contbr. articles and book revs. to profl. jours. Mem. Phila. Zoo. Mem. AAUW, ACLU, Women's Internat. League, UN Assn., Nat. Trust Hist. Preservation, Pa. Hist. Soc., Phi Beta Kappa (founding mem. U. Del. chpt.). Home: 119 Manns Ave Newark DE 19711

DEASY, THERESA, accountant, financial executive; b. N.Y.C., May 19, 1958; d. Thomas Edward Deasy and Dorothy Beatrice (Federico) Deasy Cox; m. Dennis James Stanton, May 29, 1983. BS in Commerce, DePaul U., 1981; postgrad. Keller Grad. Sch. Bus. Acctg. clk. Kirkland & Ellis, Chgo., 1977-80; fin. div. clk. Talman Home Fed. Savs. & Loan, Chgo., 1980-81; with acctg. staff Sachnoff Weaver & Rubenstien, Chgo., 1981-83, asst. contr., 1984-86, contr., 1987-88; specialist emerging bus. svcs. Coopers & Lybrand, CPA, Chgo., 1989—. Vol. dir., treas. The Commons of Evanston, 1985-87; leader Ravenswood Hosp. Mental Health Ctr., Chgo., 1984. Mem. Am. Soc. Women Accts., Digital Equipment Corp. Users Soc., NAFE, Chgo. Council Fgn. Rels., Ill. Notaries Assn., Assn. Legal Adminstrn., Law Office Mgrs. Assn. Avocations: traveling, photography, skiing, racquetball. Home: 1408 W Norwood Chicago IL 60660 Office: Coopers & Lybrand CPA 203 N LaSalle St Chicago IL 60601

DEATON, TERESA PRESSLEY, consulting company executive; b. Charlotte, N.C., Aug. 12, 1951; d. Robert Perry and Flozelia (Price) Pressley; m. R.W. Deaton, 1972 (div. 1976). Student, Cen. Piedmont Community Coll., Charlotte, 1970. Sec. ABC Southeastern Theatres, Charlotte, 1969-73; v.p. Risk Cons., Inc., Charlotte, 1973—; corp. sec.-treas. Ins. Mgmt. Bur., Charlotte, 1981—; v.p. Quorum Exec. Stes., Charlotte, 1986—. Dir. pub. rels. Park Sharon Athletic Assn., 1977-81; sec. Tarheel Youth Soccer League, 1979-81; corp. sec. Carmel Bapt. Ch., 1983—, personnel chmn., 1988-90. Republican. Home: 8123 Tremaine Ct Charlotte NC 28227 Office: Risk Cons Inc 7506 E Independence Blvd Charlotte NC 28227

DE BARBIERI, MARY ANN, performing company executive; b. Winston-Salem, N.C., May 1, 1945; d. Robert Carroll and Annie Louise (Neal) Hutcherson; m. Alfredo Emanuelle De B.; children: Maria Luisa, Riccardo Roberto. BA in Theatre Arts, Mary Washington Coll., 1967; student, Herbert Berghof Studio, 1967-69. With J. Walter Thompson, N.Y.C., 1967-68; asst. to producer Norman Twain Prodns., N.Y.C., 1968-69, Contemporary Theatre Co., N.Y.C., 1971-74; co. mgr. Folger Theatre Group, Washington, 1974-77, bus. mgr., 1977-80; mng. dir. Shakespeare Theatre at the Folger, Washington, 1980—; treas. League of Washington Theatres, 1983-86, bd. dirs., 1983-89. Bd. dirs. Washington Area Lawyers for Arts, 1984—, Cultural Alliance Greater Washington, 1986—; chair Performing Arts Coun., Alexandria, Va., 1981-84; chair Alexandria Commn. for Arts, 1984-88, theatre commr., 1984—; contbr. to study of downtown stages for new theatre in Washington, 1985. Recipient Outstanding Svc. to Theatre Community award League of Washington Theatres, 1990. Home: 3812 Fort Worth Ave Alexandria VA 22304 Office: Shakespeare Theatre at the Folger 301 E Capitol St Washington DC 20003

DEBARDELEBEN, MARIAN ZALIS, industrial librarian; b. New Brunswick, N.J., Sept. 30, 1946; d. Albert Anthony and Anita (Karch) Zalis; m. John F. DeBardeleben (div.). BA in Spanish and Eng. Lit., U. N.H., 1968; MS in Info. Sci., SUNY, Albany, 1969. Asst. libr. Philip Morris USA, Research Ctr., Richmond, 1969-73; assoc. libr. Philip Morris USA, Researh Ctr., Richmond, 1973-74; info. analyst, tech. writer Philip Morris USA, Research Ctr., Richmond, 1974-78, research scientist, 1978-85, assoc. sr. scientist, info. ctr. leader, 1985—; cons. Bus. Govt. Editor: Dictionary of Tobacco Terminology, 1978, 2d edit., 1986. Mem. Spl. Librs. Assn., Am. Chem. Soc., Soc. Competitive Intelligence Profls. Home: 2106 Rocky Point Pkwy Richmond VA 23233 Office: Philip Morris Rsch Ctr 4201 Commerce Rd Richmond VA 23234

DEBIAGI, ANNA LILLIAN, retired educator; b. N.Y.C., July 21, 1930; d. Giovanni-Battista and Michelina (Caramanna) Pollara; m. Giovanni DeBiagi, Nov. 19, 1955; children: Gianni Deo, Maria-Michelina Cologera. BA, CUNY, 1952; MA, Columbia U., 1957; postgrad., L.I. U., 1977. Tchr. Massapequa (N.Y.) Pub. Schs., 1953-87. Tchr. Ch. St. John the Bapt., Bronx, 1952-54, supt. 1954-56; instr. CPR, Am. Heart Assn., 1976-78; tchr. rep. PTA. Mem. AAUW (chmn. 1964-65, pres. 1977-79, chmn. 1981—, Commendation award 1982, Eleanor Roosevelt Found. name grant 1990), Am. Italian Hist. Soc., Hist. Soc. Massapequas, Massapequa Fedn. Ret. Tchrs., Lang. Club. Home: 80 Avoca Ave Massapequa Park NY 11762

DEBLASIS, DONNA MARIA, development executive; b. N.Y.C., July 6, 1946; d. John and Antoinette (Caldiero) Iraci; 1 child, Thomas John. BS in Edn., Duquesne U., 1968; postgrad., Carlow Coll., 1987-88. Cert. tchr., Pa. Tchr. North Allegheny Schs., Pitts., 1968-69, St. Teresa Sch., Pitts., 1977-86; dir. devel. Goodwill Industries Pitts., 1986-88, Hist. Soc. Western Pa., Pitts., 1988—; writing cons., Pa. Dept. Edn., Harrisburg, 1983-86. Mem. ad hoc com. on women, Community Coll. Allegheny County, Pitts., 1972-77. Mem. AAUW, Women in Communication, Nat. Soc. Fund Raising Execs. (com. chair 1989-91; Bronze award 1989), NAFE, Pitts. Planned Giving Coun. Republican. Roman Catholic. Home: 119 Inverness Dr Pittsburgh PA 15237 Office: Hist Soc Western Pa 4338 Bigelow Blvd Pittsburgh PA 15237

DEBLINGER, MICHELLE SUZANNE PORTELL, manager; b. Detroit, Sept. 23, 1955; d. Walter Lewis and Carmen (Britton) Portell; m. Ronald Arthur Deblinger, Aug. 2, 1987; 1 child. BS, U. Mich., 1977. English conversation instr. YBU English Ctr., Kyoto, Japan, 1978-79; from flight attendant to sr. flight attendant Air Fla., Miami, 1980-83, part-time flight attendant, 1984; from account exec. to dir. mktg., v.p. S.W. region Audiocom, Inc., Miami Lakes, Fla.; v.p. Interludes Prodns. Corp. (subs. Audiocom Inc.), Miami Lakes, Fla., 1987—; mem. Profit, Inc., Miami, Fla. Mem. Zonta Club of Miami Lakes (bd. dirs.), Japan-Am. Soc. South Fla. (former bd. dirs.). Republican. Office: Audiocom Inc 8100 Oak Ln #401 Miami Lakes FL 33016

DEBOFSKY, GRETA M., cosmetics executive; b. Chgo., Apr. 28, 1928; d. Edward A. and Dorothy (Brotman) Morgan; m. Arthur DeBofsky, Jan. 27, 1952; 1 child, Mark. BS, U. Ill., 1949. V.p. Ruder and Finn, Chgo., 1970-79; exec. v.p. M. Korshak Assocs., Inc., Chgo., 1979-85; v.p. Beecham Cosmetics Inc., Chgo., 1985-88, Quintessence Inc., Chgo., 1988—. Mem. Pub. Relations Soc. Am. (nat. exec. com., corp. sec. 1987—), Cosmetics, Toiletries and Fragrance Assn. (pub. relations com. 1986—), Mus. Broadcast Communications (bd. dirs. 1979-86), Women in Communications (Clarion award), Publicity Club Chgo. (Golden Trumpet awards), Internat. Assn. Bus. Communicators (Spectra award).

DEBOLT, JOANNA LAWRENCE, property management company executive; b. Richmond, Va., Aug. 28, 1937; d. John Henry and Helen Margaret (Clark) Lawrence; 1 child, Douglas Lyn Conti. Student, Southwestern Coll., Chula Vista, Calif., Fla. State U., Panama City, Ringling Art, Sarasota, Fla. Exec. dir. Am. Cancer Soc., Panama City, Fla.; instr. career devel. employability skills Gulf Coast Community Coll., Panama City; dir. ops. Oliver Assocs., Richmond; co-owner Chula Bus. Svcs., Chula Vista. Home: 8918 Turnbull Ave Richmond VA 23229

DEBORD, MARILYN ANNE, educator; b. Nampa, Idaho, Dec. 14, 1936; d. Stanley Bryce and Pauline (Shirk) Keim; m. Robert Franklin DeBord, July 16, 1959; children: Christopher James, Eric Richard. BS, McPherson Coll., 1958. Cert. secondary tchr. Tchr. Boise Independent Dist., Boise, Idaho, 1958-62; tchr. Bishop Kelly High Sch., Boise, 1965, Payette High Sch., Payette, Idaho, 1968—. Reporter CBS, NBC, Payette, 1985-89. Mem. Idaho Coun. Tchrs. English, Payette Edn. Assn. (pres.), Idaho Edn. Assn. (regional rep.), AAUW (pres. Payette chpt. 1987-89). Republican. Methodist. Office: Payette High Sch 1500 6th Ave S Payette ID 83661

DE BRUN, SHAUNA DOYLE, investment banker; b. Boston, June 3, 1956; d. John Justin and Marie Therese (Carey) Doyle; m. Seamus Christopher de Brun, July 24, 1982; 1 child, Brendan Joseph. Student U. Salzburg, 1974-75; BA, Mt. Holyoke Coll., 1978; postgrad. Harvard U., 1981-82; M in Internat. Affairs Columbia U., 1984. Cert. fin. analyst. Assoc., Salomon Brothers, N.Y.C., 1978; research assoc. Kennedy Sch. Govt., Cambridge, Mass., 1979-80; faculty assoc. Harvard Bus. Sch., 1980-81; fgn. expert Beijing Normal U., Peoples Republic China, 1981-82; assoc. dir. N.Y. Capital Resources, N.Y.C., 1984-85; ptnr. Eppler & Co., Denver, 1985-87, pres., Teaneck, N.J., 1987-88; v.p. fin. Patten Corp., Stamford, Vt., 1988—, Contract cons. Booz, Allen & Hamilton, N.Y.C., 1981-82. Columbia U. Internat. fellow, 1982; Sarah Williston scholar Mt. Holyoke Coll., 1975. Mem. N.Y. Soc. Security Analysts, Soc. Internat. Devel., Phi Beta Kappa. Club: Harvard. Avocations: piano; horseback riding. Office: Patten Corp 646 Main Rd Stamford VT 05352

DEBSKI, JO ANN, auditor, accountant; b. Concord, N.H., Apr. 13, 1959; d. Norman Honore and Patricia Olive (Browning) Bonenfant. AS, N.H. Coll., 1982, BS magna cum laude, 1990. Staff auditor Bank N.H., N.A., Manchester, 1986-88; acctg. mgr. IDSC Rental Co., Manchester, 1988-89; examiner II, Numerica Fin. Corp., Manchester, 1989-90; staff auditor III audit div. N.H. Office Legis. Budget Asst., Concord, 1990—. Mem. NAFE, Delta Mu Delta. Office: NH Office Legis Budget Asst State House Rm 102 Concord NH 03301

DEBUS, ELEANOR VIOLA, business management company executive; b. Buffalo, May 19, 1920; d. Arthur Adam and Viola Charlotte (Pohl) D.; student Chown Bus. Sch., 1939. Sec., Buffalo Wire Works, 1939-45; home talent producer Empire Producing Co., Kansas City, Mo., sec. Owens Corning Fiberglass, Buffalo; public relations and publicity Niagara Falls Theatre, Ont., Can.; pub. rels. dir. Woman's Internat. Bowling Congress, Columbus, Ohio, 1957-59; publicist, sec. Ice Capades, Hollywood, Calif., 1961-63; sec. to contr. Rexall Drug Co., L.A., 1963-67; bus. mgmt. acct. Samuel Berke & Co., Beverly Hills, Calif., 1967-75; Gadbois Mgmt. Co., Beverly Hills, 1975-76; sec., treas. Sasha Corp., L.A., 1976—; bus. mgr. Dean Martin; pres. Tempo Co., L.A., 1976—. Mem. NAFE, Nat. Notary Assn., Am. Film Inst. Republican. Lodge: Order Ea. Star. Contbr. articles to various mags. Office: Tempo Co 1900 Ave of Stars #1230 Los Angeles CA 90067

DECESARE, JEANNE ANNE, physical therapist, consultant; b. Providence, Nov. 30, 1949; d. Nicholas Sr. and Jeanne (DeSimone) DeC.; m. Peter William Zimmermann, Apr. 29, 1978; children: Andrew, Catherine. BS in Phys. Therapy, U. Conn., 1971; MS in Phys. Therapy, Boston U., 1976. Staff phys. therapist Easter SEal of East Fairfield County, Bridgeport, Conn., 1971-72, John's Hopkins Hosp., Balt., 1973-75; asst. supr. phys. therapy dept. Children's Hosp., Boston, 1976-80, rsch. phys. therapist, 1981-84; pvt. practice Milton, Mass., 1984—; ednl. cons. Chest Phys. Therapy Svcs., Arlington, Mass., 1980—; phys. therapy cons. Weymouth (Mass.) Manor Nursing Home, 1984-86, Boston Home, Inc., 1986—, William B. Rice Eventide Home, Quincy, Mass., 1988—; mem. intraspecialty med. adv. bd. Blue Cross/Blue Shield, Boston, 1989—. Mem. Com. to Override Proposition 2 1/2, Milton, 1988, 89; co-pres parent tchr. orgn. Tucker Sch., Milton, 1990-91. Mem. Am. Phys. Therapy Assn., Mass. chpt. of Am. Phys. Therapy Assn. (cardio-pulmonary sect., rsch. com. 1985—), AAUW. Democrat. Roman Catholic. Home and Office: 64 Hudson St Milton MA 02186

DECESARE, PAULA DOREEN, small business owner; b. Berlin, N.H., June 29, 1936; d. William Briry and Mildred Victoria (Sloan) Raymond; m. William Joseph DeCesare, Feb. 16, 1957; children: Jay Raymond, Mark William, Brett Patrick. Student, Jackson Coll., 1954; AA in Communication, Leland Powers Sch. Broadcasting and Speech, 1955-57. Copy writer, salesperson Sta. WHVW Radio, Hyde Park, N.Y., 1963-67; mgr. real estate Mobile Home Park, Hudson, N.Y., 1967—; pres., sole incorporator Alice in Videoland Ltd., Kingston, N.Y., 1983—; mgr. real estate numerous comml. holdings, 1967—; sales agt. Equitable Life Assurance, N.Y.C., 1975-77; account exec. sales Sta. WKIP Radio, Poughkeepsie, N.Y., 1977-83. Episcopalian. Home: 36 Roosevelt Rd Hyde Park NY 12538

DE CHAMPLAIN, VERA CHOPAK, artist, painter; b. Kulmbach, Fed. Republic Germany, Jan. 26, 1928; Am. citizen; d. Nathaniel and Selma (Stiefel) Florsheim; m. Albert Chopak de Champlain, 1948. Student, Art Students League, N.Y.C., 1950-60; spl. studies with Edwin Dickinson, 1962-64. Art dir., tchr. Emanuel Ctr., N.Y.C., 1967—. One person show Consulate Fed. Republic of Germany, N.Y.C., 1986, Fusco Gallery, N.Y.C., 1969-70, B. Altman Gallery, N.Y.C., 1982; exhibited group shows including Munich, Fed. Republic of Germany, 1966, Rudolph Gallery, Woodstock, N.Y., 1967, Artists Equity Gallery, N.Y.C., 1970-77, Lever House, N.Y.C., 1974, 80, 85, 88; Avery Fisher Hall-Cork Gallery, N.Y.C., 1970, 82, 83, 84, 87, 89, Fontainebleau Gallery, N.Y.C., 1972, 73, 74, NYU, 1978, Met. Mus., 1979, Muriel Karasik Gallery, Westhampton Beach, N.Y., 1980; represented in permanent collections Butler Inst. Am. Art, Youngstown, Ohio, Ga. Mus. Art, Athens, Slater Mus., Norwich, Conn., Webster Coll., St. Louis, Evansville Mus. Arts and Sci. (Ind.), Smithsonian Instn., Archives Am. Art, Washington, Jacob Javits Fed. Bldg., N.Y.; traveling exhbn. in U.S, 1988-89. Recipient award in portrait painting, Hainesfalls, N.Y., 1965, First Prize-World award, Acad. Italia, Parma, 1985, 87; subject of TV interview, 1984. Fellow Royal Soc. Arts (London); mem. Artists Equity Assn. N.Y., Arts Students League (life), Nat. Soc. Arts and Letters (art chmn. 1969—), Kappa Pi (life). Clubs: Woman Pays, Liederkranz City of N.Y. (trustee 1979—). Home: 230 Riverside Dr New York NY 10025

DECHARY, JENET LYNN, broadcaster; b. Plaquemine, La., Feb. 14, 1946; d. Paul Luke and Mary Poynter (Schwing) D.; divorced; 1 child, Paul Joseph. BA, U. Southwestern La., 1968. Script asst. Sta. WRC-TV, Washington, 1969-71, mem. on-air promotion staff, 1971-72, license coord., 1972-74, reports analyst, 1980-86, analyst, standards coord., 1986-88, adminstr. reports and broadcast standards, 1988—; mem. comml. standards staff Stas. WRC-TV, WKYS-FM, WRC-AM, Washington, 1974-80. Author: (play) Souvenirs, 1984. Mem. Women in Communications, Am. Film Inst., The Writer's Ctr., Washington Ind. Writers. Unitarian Universalist.

DECICCO, ANNE LOMMEL, association executive; b. N.Y.C., Sept. 27, 1950; d. Richard Arthur and Nancy (Robertson) Lommel; m. Bruce A. Hydo; children: Geoffrey Lommel DeCicco, Melanie Paige DeCicco, Benjamin Bruce Hydo, Wynne Meredith Hydo. Cert. assn. exec., meeting profl. V.p. N.J. Hosp. Assn., Princeton, 1981-84, v.p. corp. and strategic planning, 1984; corp. v.p. Ctr. Health Affairs, Inc., 1985—; bd. dirs. Somerset (N.J.) Med. Ctr., Healthcare Employees Fed. Credit Union, LBI Group Co., Inc., Trans Ocean Post, Inc., Somerset HealthCare Enterprises; apptd. women's bus. adv. coun. N.J. Dept. Commerce. Mem. European Soc. Assn. Execs., Internat. Hosp. Fedn., Am. Soc. Assn. Execs. (internat. sect. coun., planning com.), N.J. Soc. of Assn. Execs. Home: 37 Highmont Dr West Windsor NJ 08691 Office: Ctr Health Affairs 760 Alexander Rd Princeton NJ 08543-0001

DECKER, BARBARA BODINE, publisher, writer; b. Pasadena, Calif., Apr. 23, 1929; d. Roger Campbell and Mable Gregory (Hill) Bodine; m. John W. Henneberger, May 22, 1952 (div. 1975); children: Diane, Sally Henneberger Mervin, Roger C.; m. Robert W. Decker, 1975. BA, U. Calif., 1951. Freelance writer Mariposa, Calif., 1958—; pres. Double Decker Press, Mariposa, 1985--. Author: Volcano Watching, 1980, Volcanoes, 1981, revised edit. 1989; author pub. nat. park rd. guides. Mem. No. Calif. Sci. Writers Assn. Home: 4087 Silver Bar Rd Mariposa CA 95338 Office: Double Decker Press 4087 Silver Bar Rd Mariposa CA 95338

DECKER, DEBRA ELNORA, librarian; b. Williamsport, Pa., Oct. 25, 1946; d. Herman Thomas and Harriett Lucina (Mullen) Palmer; B.S., Lock Haven State Coll., 1968; M.Ed., West Chester State Coll., 1971; M.S. in Library Sci., Clarion State Coll., 1981; m. Sept. 7, 1969; 1 dau., Moana Kai. Tchr., Owen J. Roberts Sch. Dist., Pottstown, Pa., 1968-73; instr., Becker Research Learning Center, Clarion (Pa.) State Coll., 1976-80, librarian instr., Instructional Materials Center, 1980-84, serials coordinator Carlson Library, 1984—. Neighborhood chmn. Brookville Council Girls Scouts U.S., 1976-82; bd. dirs. Brookville Area United Fund, 1980-83; officer Zion United Methodist Ch., 1977—. Mem. NEA, ALA, Pa. Library Assn., Pa. Edn. Assn., Assn. Pa. State Coll. and Univ. Faculties, Phi Delta Kappa. Democrat. Home: RD 4 Box 250 Brookville PA 15825 Office: Carlson Library Clarion State Coll Clarion PA 16214

DECKER, ELIZABETH ANNE, educator; b. Hilo, Hawaii, Feb. 16, 1952; d. Floyd Edward Jr. and Dorothy (Wilson) D. BA in English, U. Hawaii, 1974, BA in Polit. Sci., 1989. Cert. secondary tchr., Hawaii. Feature writer Coalfield Progress newspaper, Norton, Va., 1974-75; tchr. St. Joseph High Sch., Hilo, 1975-78, Hilo High Sch., 1979-80, 81-82, Mountain View (Hawaii) Elem.-Intermediate Sch., 1980-81, Waiakea Intermediate Sch., Hilo, 1982—; tchr.-coord. econs. program Project Bus., Hilo, 1984—; student tchr. trainer U. Hawaii-Chaminade U., Hilo, 1985-89; tchr. Upward Bound Summer Program, Hilo, 1989. Layreader Holy Apostles Ch., Hilo, 1986—. Mem. NEA, Nat. Coun. Tchrs. English, Internat. Reading Assn. (v.p. 1983-84, pres. 1984-85, exec. bd. 1985-86), Hawaii Tchrs. Assn. Republican. Episcopalian. Office: Waiakea Intermediate Sch 200 W Puainako St Hilo HI 96720

DECKER, JOSEPHINE I., clinic administrator; b. Barling, Ark., May 24, 1933; d. Ralph and Ada A. (Claborn) Snider; BS in Health Mgmt., Kennedy Western U., 1986, MS in Bus. Adminstrn., 1987; m. William Arlen Decker, Feb. 4, 1952; 1 son, Peter A. With Southwestern Bell Telephone Co., Ft. Smith, Ark., 1951-52; with Holt Krock Clinic, Ft. Smith, 1952—, bus. adminstr., 1970—. Bd. dirs. Sparks Credit Union, Adv. Council Northside and Southside high schs., Ft. Smith, Ft. Smith Girls Shelter, Ft. Smith Credit Bur. Mem. Credit Women Internat., Soc. Cert. Consumer Credit Execs. Office: Holt Krock Clinic 1500 Dodson Ave Fort Smith AR 72901

DECKER, JUDITH ELAINE, land development company executive; b. Derry, N.H., Nov. 2, 1940; d. Clayton Kent and Ariel Almina (Palmer) Gillis; m. Marshall Norman Decker, Nov. 2, 1965; children: Timothy, Jennifer, James, Wesley. Diploma, McIntosh Bus. Sch., 1958-59; BS magna cum laude, Franklin Pierce Coll., 1986. Treas. N.H. Electric, Inc., Salem, 1974-77; treas. J.E.D. Assocs., Inc., Danville, N.H., 1978-86, pres., chief exec. officer, 1986—; bd. dirs. J.E.D. Assocs., Inc., Danville, MarDec, Inc., Salem, Shalles Corp., Salem. Chmn. Thompson for Gov., Salem, 1970, Heart Fund, Salem, 1969, 70, 71; troop leader Girl Scouts of Am., Salem, 1969-72. Mem. Nat. Assn. Female Execs., Greater Haverhill C. of C., Nat. Assn. Self Employed. Republican. Home: 82 Lake St Salem NH 03079 Office: MarDec Inc 82 Lake St Salem NH 03079

DECKER, KARRIE LYNN, health facility administrator, therapist; b. San Francisco, July 24, 1956; d. Gilbert Paul and Beverly Diane (Phillips) D. BS in Occupational Therapy and Psychology, San Jose (Calif.) State U., 1978; M in Health Sci., Whitworth Coll., 1983. Sr. occupational therapist Sacred Heart Med. Ctr., Spokane, Wash., 1980-84; dir. phys. medicine and rehab. St. Luke's Meml. Hosp., Spokane, 1984-87; dir. rehab. svcs. Douglas Community Hosp., Roseburg, Oreg., 1987-88; program dir. Neurocare Inc., Portland, Oreg., 1988-90; pres. Med. Rehab. Cons. Svcs., Beaverton, Oreg., 1990—; advisor Spokane Head Injury Support Group, 1983-87; med. advisor Arthritis Club, Spokane, 1984-87, Oreg. Head Injury Found., Portland, 1988—. Mem. N.W. Assn. Rehab. Facilities (pres. 1988), Acad. Phys. Medicine and Rehab., Occupational Therapy Assn., Nat. Assn. Rehab. Facilities, Rotary. Office: Med Rehab Cons Svcs 7668 S W Cresmoor Dr Beaverton OR 97205

DECKER, MARTHA ILENE, photojournalist, retail store executive; b. Dearborn, Mich., Aug. 4, 1954; d. Robert Gene and Suzanne Charlotte (Smith) Hazzard; children: Robert John Wells, Jason Allen Wells; m. Kenneth Lowell Decker, Sept. 12, 1986. Cert. in TV, Eastfield Coll., Mesquite, Tex., 1979. Freelance photojournalist Gun Barrel City, Tex., 1972—; photo editor Mesquite (Tex.) News, 1982, various newspapers, Mesquito, 1982-84; asst. editor Lakeside Record Am., Rowlett, Tex., 1984-85; reporter Tri-County News, Mabank, Tex., 1985; owner, mgr., buyer Martha's Discount Fragrances, Gun Barrel City, 1987—; photo editor Univ. Dallas, 1989—; res. police officer City of Seven Points (Tex.), 1985-86; patrol lt. Network Security Corp., Carrollton, 1986-87; columnist Wilderness Way, Village Press, Mabank, 1987—; editor Mabank Banner, 1989—; speaker in field. Author: photographer East Tex. Vignettes, 1989. Bd. dirs. Athens (Tex.) Creative Ctr., 1987—; rescue diver Gun Barrel City Vol. Fire Depts., 1988-89; rescue diver Res. Underwater Specialist Team, Cedar Creek Lake, Tex., 1988—; mem. Gun Barrel City bd. adjustment, 1989—; mem. census team City of Gun Barrel City, 1989; candidate for Gun Barrel City Coun., 1989. Mem. Nat. Press Photographers Assn., Tex. Photographic Soc., Cedar Creek C. of C. (cert. of appreciation 1979). Republican. Roman Catholic. Home: 128 Garrett Ln Gun Barrel City TX 75147 Office: Rte 8 Box 272 Kemp TX 75143

DECKER SLANEY, MARY TERESA, athlete; b. Bunnvale, N.J., Aug. 4, 1958; d. John and Jacqueline Decker; m. Ron Tabb (div. 1983); m. Richard Slaney, June 1, 1985; 1 child, Ashley Lynn. Student, U. Colo., 1977-78. Amateur runner, 1969—, holder several world track and field records, 1980—; winner 2 gold medals at 1500 and 3000 meters World Track and Field Championship, Helsinki, Finland, 1983; mem. U.S. Olympic teams, 1980, 84; cons. to CBS Records, Timex, Eastman Kodak. Recipient Jesse Owens Internat. Amateur Athlete award, 1982, Sullivan award AAU, 1982; named Amateur Sportswoman of the Yr., Women's Sports Found., 1982, 83, Top Sportswoman A.P. Europe, 1985. Address: 2923 Flintlock St Eugene OR 97401-4660*

DECKERT, DONNA KAY, human resources specialist; b. Lubbock, Tex., Nov. 3, 1963; d. Ronald Lloyd and Sara Evelyn (Mills) Wartes; m. Edward Phillip Deckert III, Dec. 31, 1983; 1 child, Sara Ann. BBA in Human Resources, U. Tex., San Antonio, 1985. Compensation coord. Nat. Bancshares Corp. Tex., San Antonio, 1985—; pres. Resume Resources, San Antonio, 1987—; cons., San Antonio Country Club, 1986, Project Bus., San Antonio Jr. Achievement, 1986—. Contbr. articles to various publs. Mem. NAFE, Am. Soc. Personnel Adminstrs., San Antonio Personnel and Mgrs. Assn.

DECKERT, MYRNA JEAN, social service executive; b. McPherson, Kans., Nov. 4, 1936; d. Francis J. and Grace (Killion) George; m. Ray A. Deckert, Sept. 29, 1957; children: Rachelle, Kimberly, Charles, Michael. AA, Coll. of Sequoilas, 1956; BBA, U. Beverly Hills, 1983, MBA, 1984. Youth dir. Asbury Meth. Ch., El Paso, Tex., 1960-63; teen program dir. YWCA of El Paso, 1963-69, assoc. exec. dir., 1969-70, exec. dir., 1970—; mem. contrn. com. and trainer YWCA of the U.S.A., N.Y.C.; bd. dirs. InterFirst Bank-Chelmont, El Paso; vice chmn. El Paso Commn. for Women, 1985-86. Mem. state dept Human Resources D.C. Task Force, Austin, Tex., exec. forum bd.; adv. dir. NCNB-Tex. at El Paso; chmn. Tex. State Title XX Day Care Providers, 1987-89; commr. Housing Authority City of El Paso, 1989—. Recipient Hannah Soloman Community Svc. award Nat. Coun. Jewish Women, Sertoma Club award Svc. to Mankind, 1974, Merit award Adalante Mujer, 1986, Social Svc. award KVIA/Sunturians, 1986, Excellence award Nat. Assn. YWCA Execs., 1990; inducted to El Paso Women's Hall of Fame, 1990. Mem. Coun. of Agy. Execs., UTEP Profl. Network, Rotary (bd. dirs. Club of El Paso 1990—). Methodist. Home: 4276 Canterbury Dr El Paso TX 79902

DECOTIS, DEBORAH ANNE, investment banker; b. Salem, Mass., Nov. 13, 1952; d. John and Marie (Mahoney) DeC. B.A., Smith Coll., 1974; M.B.A. (Miller scholar), Stanford U., 1978. Analyst, Morgan Stanley & Co., Inc., N.Y.C., 1974-76, assoc., 1978-81, v.p., London, 1982-84, prin., N.Y.C., 1985—. Home: 211 Central Park W New York NY 10024 Office: Morgan Stanley & Co Inc 1251 Avenue of the Americas New York NY 10020

DE CRESCENZO-RIVARD, SARAH CAROLE, controller; b. Fall River, Mass., Sept. 10, 1941; d. Anthony Joseph and Sarah (Pinheiro) De Crescenzo; m. Joseph R. Cirillo, Sept. 3, 1963 (div. Aug. 1974); children: Janice M. Cirillo, Joseph T. Cirillo, Karen A. Cirillo; m. John M. Rivard, Oct. 7, 1984. B.S.S. cum laude, Bryant Coll., 1961; BS cum laude Fin. Acctg., Roger Williams Coll., 1985; postgrad., U. R.I., 1987—. Asst. controller Guild Drilling Co., E. Providence, R.I., 1972-75; acct. R.L. Abedon Co., Providence, 1976-78; acct., office mgr. Flair Display Inc., Providence, 1978-80, Pease & Curren, Warwick, R.I., 1980-86; controller, office mgr. Ashaway Line & Twine, Ashaway, R.I., 1986-88; controller, bus. mgr. Rainbow Power & Equipment Corp., Warwick, 1989—; v.p. Mfrs. Assn. So. Conn. & R.I., Ashaway, 1986-88. Mem. Nat. Assn. Female Execs., N.Y.C., 1982. Mem. E. Greenwich Bus. Profl. Women. Roman Catholic. Home: 82 Linwood Dr North Kingstown RI 02852 Office: Rainbow Power & Equipment 17 OKeefe Ln Warwick RI 02888

DECROSTA, SUSAN ELYSE, graphic artist; b. Cambridge, Mass., Aug. 28, 1956; d. Joseph Mario and Gertrude Ermelinda (Galligani) DeC. BFA, Mass. Coll. Art, 1980. certified art tchr., supr. Graphic artist Nixdorf Computer Corp., Burlington, Mass., 1981-86; lead artist, illustrator Raytheon Co., Andover, Mass., 1986—; illustrator Rivers, Trainor, Doyle, Providence, R.I., 1987; freelance graphic artist, 1980—. Recipient Excellence award Soc. Tech. Communications & Art Direction, 1986. Mem. Arlington Ctr. Arts, Mass. Art Alumni Assn., Creative Club Boston. Democrat. Roman Catholic. Home: 15 Old Colony Ln Arlington MA 02174 Office: Raytheon Co 350 Lowell St Andover MA 01810

DE CROW, KAREN, lawyer, author, lecturer; b. Chgo., Dec. 18, 1937; d. Samuel Meyer and Juliette (Abt) Lipschultz; m. Alexander Allen Kolben, 1960 (div. 1965); m. Roger Edward DeCrow, 1965 (div. 1972). B.S., Northwestern U., 1959; J.D., Syracuse U., 1972. Bar: N.Y., U.S. Dist. Ct. (no. dist.) N.Y. Resorts editor Golf Digest mag., Evanston, Ill., 1959-60; editor Am. Soc. Planning Ofcls., Chgo., 1960-61; writer Center for Study Liberal Edn. for Adults, Chgo., 1961-64; editor Holt, Rinehart, Winston, Inc., N.Y.C., 1965; textbook editor L.W. Singer, Syracuse, N.Y., 1965-66; writer Eastern Regional Inst. for Edn., Syracuse, 1967-69, Pub. Broadcasting System, 1977; tchr. women and law, 1972-74; nat. bd. mem. NOW, 1968-77, nat. pres., 1974-77, also nat. politics task force chmn.; cons. affirmative action; lectr. corps., polit. groups, colls. and univs. U.S., Canada, Finland, Peoples Republic of China, Greece, USSR; nat. coordinator Women's Strike for Equality, 1970; N.Y. State del. Internat. Women's Year, 1977; candidate for mayor, Syracuse, 1969; originated Schs. for Candidates; bd. advisors Working Women's Inst.; participant DeCrow-Schlafly ERA Debates, from 1975; co-founder World Woman Watch, 1988; lectr. for univs. and corps. various topics including law, gender, internat. feminism in U.S., Can., Mexico, Greece, Finland and USSR. Author: (with Roger DeCrow) University Adult Education: A Selected Bibliography, 1967, The Young Woman's Guide to Liberation, 1971, Sexist Justice, 1974, First Women's State of the Union Message, 1977; (with Robert Seidenberg) Women Who Marry Houses: Panic and Protest in Agoraphobia, 1983, Turkish edit., 1988, 2d Turkist edit., 1989; editor: The Pregnant Teenager (Howard Osofsky), 1968, Corporate Wives, Corporate Casualties (Robert Seidenberg), 1973; contbr. articles to USA Today, N.Y. Times, Los Angeles Times, Boston Globe, Vogue, Mademoiselle, Newsday, Chgo. Sun Times, Penthouse, Washington Post, Los Angeles Times Mag., Policy Review, Miami Herald, Internat. Herald Tribune, Social Problems, Houston Chronicle, San Francisco Chronicle, Civil Rights Quar., other newspapers, mags.; columnist: Syracuse New Times; recording: Opening Up Marriage, 1980. Hon. trustee Elizabeth Cady Stanton Found.; co-founder (with Robert Seidenberg) World Woman Watch, 1988; Liberal party candidate for mayor of Syracuse, N.Y., 1969; life mem. Art Inst. Chgo.; bd. advisors Workimng Women's Inst. Recipient Profl. Recognition award for best newspaper column Syracuse Press Club, 1990. Mem. Am. Arbitration Assn., Dist. Attys. Adv. Council, ACLU (Ralph E. Kharas award N.Y. chpt. 1985), N.Y. State Women's Bar Assn. (Cen. N.Y. chpt. pres. 1989-90, task force on gender bias, specialization com.), N.Y. State Bar Assn., Onondaga County Bar Assn. (profl. ethics com.) Atlantic States Legal Found., Nat. Women's Polit. Causus, Nat. Congress for Men (gender issues advisor), The Nature Conservancy, The Wilderness Soc., Syracuse Friends Chamber Music (bd. dirs.), Yale Polit. Union (hon. life), NOW (nat. pres. 1974-77, nat. bd. dirs. 1968-74), The Nature Conservancy, The Wilderness Soc., Northwestern U. Alumni Assn., Theta Sigma Pi. Address: 7 Fir Tree Ln Jamesville NY 13078

DECYK, ROXANNE JEAN, manufacturing company executive lawyer; b. Chgo., Nov. 5, 1952; d. Walter and Tillie (Kuzma) D.; m. John F. Chlewbowski, June 27, 1987. AB, U. Ill., 1973; JD, Marquette U., 1977. Bar: Wis. 1977, Ill. 1981. Pres. Penta Advt., Champaign, Ill., 1972-73; staff journalist Coll. Medicine U. Ill., 1973-74; assoc. Foley & Lardner, Milw., 1977-79; pres. Corp. Legal Communications, Milw., 1980-81; v.p., sec., asst. to chmn. Internat. Harvester Co., Chgo., 1981-83, v.p. adminstrn., sec., 1983-84, sr. v.p. corp. relations, 1984-86, sr. v.p. adminstrn., 1986-89, sr. v.p. dealer planning and devel., 1989—; bd. dirs. Lincoln Nat. Pension, Ft. Wayne, Ind., Material Scis. Corp., Elk Grove Village, Ill., Northwestern Meml. Corp., Chgo. Mem. Voices for Ill. Children, The Chgo. Network, Hubbard St. Dance Co. Recipient Nat. Merit Scholar award Outboard Marine Corp., 1970. Mem. Econ. Club Chgo., ABA, State Bar Wis., Ill. State Bar Assn., Chgo. Network, Phi Beta Kappa. Home: 1540 Lake Shore Dr Chicago IL 60610 Office: Navistar Internat Transp Corp 401 N Michigan Ave Chicago IL 60611

DEDINSKY, MARY LEE, newspaper editor; b. Milw., June 2, 1948; d. Joseph Stephen and Lois Edna (Lee) D. BS in Journalism, Northwestern U., 1969, MS, 1970. Intern reporter Lansing (Mich.) State Jour., 1969; chief edn. writer Chgo. Today, 1970; formerly met. editor, now mng. editor Chgo. Sun-Times. Office: Chgo Sun-Times Inc 401 N Wabash Rm 110 Chicago IL 60611*

DEDO, DOROTHY JUNELL TURNER, civic worker; b. Norway, Mich., Oct. 17, 1920; d. Raymond and Esther Elvira (Junell) Turner; m. Lewis Joseph Dedo, Dec. 24, 1945; children: Craig Turner, Drew Jonathan. Student, U. So. Calif., 1939-40; AB with honors, U. Mich., 1942; postgrad., U. N.D., 1942, Marquette U., 1942-43. Cert. tchr., Wis. Safety person Kearney & Trecker Corp., Milw., 1942-43; supr. Town of Shelby, La Crosse, Wis., 1973-77, clk., 1977-8l, chmn., 1981-85; pres. Turner Lands, Inc., Milw., 1985—; supr. County of LaCrosse, 1990—. Contbr. numerous articles to La Crosse Tribune. Producer, dir. actor La Crosse Children's Theater, 1959-65; sales mgr., actor LaCrosse Community Theatre, 1965-69; sec. Western Wis. Health Planning Orgn., 1964-68; chmn. Christian edn., mem. coun. English Luth. Ch., 1969-72; nominations chmn. bd. advisors Viterbo Coll., 1971—; bd. dirs. Luth Hosp. Found., 1978—, Winding Rivers Libr. System, 1990—; sec. Wis. Towns Assn., 1973-85; v.p. LaCrosse Area Devel. Corp., 1981-85; mem. LaCrosse Area Planning Com., 1981-85; pres. LaCrosse County Rep. Women., 1976-78. Lt. comdr. USNR, 1943-52. Recipient Dionysos award in bus. La Crosse Community Theatre, 1965, Women of Yr. award La Crosse Bus. and Profl. Women, 1982, Tribute to Outstanding Woman award YWCA, La Crosse, 1983. Mem. AAUW (pres. LaCrosse 1974-76, Wis. 1981-83, named grant honoree 1977), Am. Assn. Ret. Persons, Viterbo Coll. President's Club, Heritage Club, LaCrosse Country Club, Pearl Investment Club (pres. 1988—), Earthwatch, Alpha Kappa Delta, Alpha Lambda Delta, Alpha Chi Omega. Home: l06l Cedar Rd La Crosse WI 54601

DEE, VIVIEN, nurse, hospital administrator; b. Manila, Nov. 12, 1944; came to U.S., 1962; d. David Hawkins and Ivy Marie (Woo) D.; m. John Robert Smith, Sept. 30, 1984. BSN, Loma Linda U., 1966; MN, UCLA, 1974; D in Nursing Sci., U. Calif., San Francisco, 1986. Staff nurse White Meml. Med. Ctr., L.A., 1966; pub. health nurse Los Angeles County Health Dept., L.A., 1966-69; program nurse specialist Child Devel. and Mental Retardation ctr. U. Wash., Seattle, 1969-72; asst. prof. nursing Calif. State U., L.A., 1974-75; nursing cons. Western Regional Ctr. for the Developmentally Disabled, Santa Monica, Calif., 1974-75; clin. nurse coordinator child ambulatory svcs. UCLA, 1975-76; asst. dir. nursing Neuropsychiat. Inst. and Hosp. UCLA, L.A., 1977-87, assoc. hosp. adminstr., dir. nursing, 1987—; cons. Dee & Smith Assocs., Rolling Hills Estates, Calif., 1985—; pres. Am. Nursing Seminars, Rolling Hills Estates, 1989—. Contbg. author: The Nurse and the Developmentally Disabled Adolescent, 1977; contbr. articles to profl. jours. Mem. Am. Nurses Assn., Am. Orgn. Nurse Execs., Calif. Soc. Nursing Svc. Adminstrs., Sigma Theta Tau. Home: 1509 Via Fernandez Palos Verdes Estates CA 90274

DEEL, FRANCES QUINN, librarian; b. Pottsville, Pa., Mar. 9, 1939; d. Charles Joseph and Carrie Miriam (Ketner) Q.; m. Ronald Eugene Deel, Feb. 5, 1983. B.S., Millersville State Coll., 1960; M.L.S., Rutgers U., 1964; M.P.A., U. West Fla., 1981. Post librarian U.S. Army Armor (Desert Tng. Ctr.), Ft. Irwin, Calif., 1964-66; staff librarian Mil. Dist. of Washington, 1966-67; supervisory librarian 1st Logistical Command, APO San Francisco, 1967-68; tech. process specialist Naval Edn. and Tng. Supervisory Command, Washington, 1968-77, Pensacola, Fla., 1968-77; chief tech. library USAF Armament Lab., Eglin AFB, Fla., 1977-81; dir. command libraries Air Force Systems Command (Andrews AFB), Washington, 1981—; mem. exec. adv. council Fed. Library and Info. Network, Washington, 1983-86. Mem. ALA (dir.-at-large armed forces libraries sect. Chgo. 1983-86), Spl. Libraries Assn., D.C. Library Assn. Roman Catholic. Home: 9225 Forest Haven Dr Alexandria VA 22309 Office: Air Force Systems Command/DPSL Libr Div Andrews AFB Washington DC 20334-5000

DEEMER, CANDY KAELIN, advertising executive; b. Burbank, Calif., May 31, 1954; d. Louis David and Arlene Marie (McCammon) Kaelin; m. Kenneth McKeon Deemer, Sept. 21, 1985; 1 child, Kevin. BS, Northwestern U., 1976, MS, 1977. Asst. account exec. Needham Harper & Steers, Chgo., 1977-78, account exec., 1978-79; account exec. Botsford Ketchum, San Francisco, 1979-80; account exec. Doyle Dane Bernbach, L.A., 1980-81, account supr., 1982-84, v.p., 1983, mgmt. supr., 1984—, sr. v.p., 1986—. Republican. Roman Catholic. Office: DDB Needham Worldwide 5900 Wilshire Blvd Los Angeles CA 90036

DEEN, EDITH ALDERMAN, author; b. Weatherford, Tex., Feb. 28, 1905; d. James Harris and Sara (Scheuber) Alderman; m. Edgar Deen, Dec. 30, 1945 (dec.). Student, Tex. U., 1922-23, Columbia U., 1926; student, Tex. Christian U., 1923-24, LittD, 1972; BA, Tex. Woman's U., 1953, LittD, 1959, MA, 1960; LittD (hon.), Pepperdine U., 1987. Woman's editor, daily columnist Ft. Worth Evening Press, 1924-54. Mem. Fort Worth City Council, 1965-67; mem. bd. regents Tex. Woman's Univ., 1951-63. Author: All of the Women of the Bible, 1955, Great Women of the Christian Faith, 1959, Family Living in the Bible, 1963, The Bibl's Legacy for Womanhood, 1970, All the Bible's Men of Hope, 1974, Wisdom from Women in the Bible, 1978. Named Exec. Woman of Year, Zonta Club, 1983; recipient First Lady award Altrusa Club, 1949, Disting. Sr. Citizen award Women's Civic Club, 1974, medal of honor Mary Isham Keith chpt. Nat. Soc. Am. Revolution, 1987. Mem. Tex. Inst. Letters, Women in Communications (Headliner award 1963). Home and Office: 2420 Refugio St Fort Worth TX 76106

DEES, LYNNE, artist; b. Ft. Worth, Jan. 1, 1954; d. Eddie John and Jatis Lael (Perryman) D.; m. W.R. Jr. Crawford, Mar. 2, 1987. BFA magna cum laude, North Tex. State U., 1975, MFA magna cum laude, 1980. Dir. fine arts Lake County Acad., Ft. Worth, 1976-81; art instr. Purnell Sch., Pottersville, N.J., 1981-83, Tarrant County Jr. Coll., Ft. Worth, 1984—, Bauder Coll., Arlington, Tex., 1985-89, Tarleton State U., Stephenville, Tex., 1983-90, Colo. Mountain Coll., Vail, 1990—; lectr. in field. One woman shows include Tex. Schemes, N.Y.C. Dreams, Ft. Worth, 1985, Spring Fever, Dallas, 1988; exhibited in group shows at Critics Choice Exhbn., Bethlehem, Pa., 1983, Am. Craft Coun. Fair, Dallas, 1984, Tex. Realism 1985, 1985, Art in the Metroplex, Ft. Worth, 1985, 86, Person, Place, Thing, Somerville, N.J., 1985, Women Artists of 3 States, Dallas, 1987, Dallas Invitational, 1988, Color Statements, Denton, 1989. Recipient Merit awards Allentown (Pa.) Art Mus., 1983, Hunterdon Art Ctr., Clinton, N.J., 1983, State Fair at Disneyland, Anaheim Calif., 1988, Excellence in Drawing award Internat. Art Competition, 1984, Achievement award, Dallas Women's Caucus, 1987. Mem. Am. Crafts Coun., Handweavers Guild Am. (Best of Show award 1985, 87), Tex. Designer-Craftsmen Assn., Tex. Fine Arts Assn., Women's Caucus of Art. Office: Dept Fine Arts and Speech Box T-39 Tarleton State U Stephenville TX 76402

DEES, SANDRA KAY MARTIN, psychologist; b. Omaha, Apr. 18, 1944; d. Leslie B. and Ruth Lillian (May) Martin; m. Doyce B. Dees; BA magna cum laude, Tex. Christian U., 1965, MA, 1972, PhD, 1989. Adminstrv. asst./rsch. coord. Hosp. Improvement Project, Wichita Falls (Tex.) State Hosp., 1968-69; caseworker adoptions Edna Gladney Home, Ft. Worth, Tex., 1970-71; psychologist Mexia (Tex.) State Sch., 1971-72; sch. psychologist Ft. Worth Ind. Sch. Dist., 1971-78, program evaluator, 1978-86; pvt. counselor, 1986-88; rsch. assoc. Tex. Christian U., 1989—; project mgr. Growth Center Project, 1975-77. Founder Alateen Group, Wichita Falls, 1969; bd. dirs Because We Care, Ft. Worth, 1988—. Dallas TCU Women's Club creative writing scholar, 1962-64, Virginia Alpha scholar, 1963; NASA research asst., 1965-67; USPHS trainee, 1967-68; cert. Am. Montessori Soc., 1977. Mem. Am. Ednl. Rsch. Assn., Mental Health Assn., Mortar Bd., Mensa, Alpha Chi, Phi Alpha Theta, Psi Chi, Phi Delta Kappa. Contbr. articles to profl. publs. Home: 29 Bounty Rd W Fort Worth TX 76132 Office: Tex Christian U Dept Psychology Fort Worth TX 76129

DEESE, SEBELLE KYLE GATES, educational consultant; b. Natchez, Miss., Oct. 17, 1944; d. Sam Wess and Sadie Louise (Moran) G.; m. Walter Eugene Deese, Sept. 12, 1970 (dec. Sept. 1985). AS in Legal Sec. Sci., Valencia Community Coll., Orlando, Fla., 1972; BS in Bus. Edn., U. Hawaii, Honolulu, 1975; MS in Bus. Edn., Utah State U., 1979. Adj. instr. Palomar Community Coll., San Marcos, Calif., 1976-78; instr. Am. Inst. Bus., Des Moines, 1978-81; asst. prof. Mt. Wachusett Community Coll., Gardner, Mass., 1982-85; agt., registered rep. N.Y. Life Ins. Co., Gardner, 1985-88; owner Creative Ednl. Cons., Gardner, 1988—; coord. Sr. Days at the Mount, Gardner, 1989-90; Zenger-Miller Frontline leader facilitator Simplex Time Recorder Co., Gardner, 1989—; coord. Diversity on Common Ground Conf., Gardner, 1989-90. Mem. exhibit com. The Gardner Mus., 1989—; v.p. Gardner-Athol unit Am. Cancer Soc., 1988-89, 89-90. Mem. Greater Gardner Bus. and Profl. Women's Club (treas. 1985-86, corr. sec. 1988-89, 89-90), Rotary Internat. Democrat. Home: 25 E Jonathan St Gardner MA 01440 Office: Creative Ednl Cons 25 E Jonathan St Gardner MA 01440

DEETER, ELIZABETH JEAN, hospital executive; b. Harrisburg, Pa., Nov. 18, 1918; d. Edmund Mather and Martha Ann (Foltz) D. Diploma in nursing, Pa. Hosp.-Sch. Nursing, 1943; BS in Nursing Edn., U. Pa., 1955. RN, Pa. Gen. staff nurse Pa. Hosp., Phila., 1943-44, staff nurse, asst. instr., asst. dir., assoc. dir. nursing, 1950-63; gen. staff nurse Harrisburg (Pa.) Hosp., 1944-45, head nurse, 1946-50, dir. nursing, asst. adminstr., asst. v.p., 1963-69, patient rep./risk mgr., 1979-87, patient rep., dept. dir., 1987—; lectr. on ethics in patient care variouso orgns., 1981-83; pres. Susquehanna Ctr. Aux., Harrisburg, 1984-86. Tchr. home nursing ARC, Phila., 1956-57; sec. Westminster Found., Phila., 1960-63; bd. dirs. Pa. Health Planning Coun., Harrisburg, 1973-75; past bd. dirs. So. Cen. Pa. Lung Assn., Carlisle; past preceptor Pa. State U., Elizabethtown Coll.; past mem. Harrisburg Choral Soc.-Mendelsohn Club Phila.; mem. Pine St. Presbyn. Ch. Chancel Choir, ruling elder, 1972—. Recipient Innovation award Hosp. Assn. of Pa., Camp Hill, 1983. Mem. Nat. Soc. Patient Reps. and Consumer Affairs, Pa. Soc. Patient Reps. (pres. 1988-89), WomanCare (mem. adv. bd. 1987—), Women's Club of Mechanicsburg (Pa.). Republican. Home: 634 Allenview Mechanicsburg PA 17055 Office: Harrisburg Hosp S Front St Harrisburg PA 17101

DEFAZIO, LYNETTE STEVENS, dancer, choreographer, educator, chiropractor; b. Berkeley, Calif., Sept. 29; d. Honore and Mabel J. (Estavan) Stevens; student U. Calif., Berkeley, 1950-55, San Francisco State Coll., 1950-51; D. Chiropractic, Life-West Chiropractic Coll., San Lorenzo, Calif., 1983, BA in Humanities, New Coll. Calif., 1986; children—Joey H. Panganiban, Joanna Pang. Diplomate Nat. Sci. Bd.; eminence in dance edn., Calif. Community Colls. dance specialist, standard services, childrens ctrs. credentials Calif. Dept. Edn. Contract child dancer Monogram Movie Studio, Hollywood, Calif., 1938-40; dance instr. San Francisco Ballet, 1953-64; performer San Francisco Opera Ring, 1960-67; performer, choreographer Oakland (Calif.) Civic Light Opera, 1963-70; fgn. exchange dance dir. Academie de Danses-Salle Pleyel, Paris, France, 1966; dir. Ballet Arts Studio, Oakland, 1960—; teaching specialist Oakland Unified Sch. Dist.-Childrens Ctrs., 1968-80; instr. Peralta Community Coll. Dist., Oakland, 1971—, chmn. dance dept., 1985—; cons., instr. extension courses UCLA, Dirs. and Suprs. Assn., Pittsburg Unified Sch. Dist., Tulare (Calif.) Sch. Dist., 1971-73; researcher Ednl. Testing Services, HEW, Berkeley, 1974; resident choreographer San Francisco Childrens Opera, 1970—, Oakland Civic Theater; ballet mistress Dimensions Dance Theater, Oakland, 1977-80; cons. Gianchetta Sch. Dance, San Francisco, Robicheau Boston Ballet, TV series Patchwork Family, CBS, N.Y.C.; choreographer Ravel's Valses Nobles et Sentimentales, 1976. Author: The Opera Ballets; A Choreographic Manual, Vols. I-V, 1986. Recipient Foremost Women of 20th Century, 1985, Merit award San Francisco Children's Opera, 1985. Mem. Profl. Dance Tchrs. Assn. Am. Author: Basic Music Outlines for Dance Classes, 1960, rev., 1968; Teaching Techniques and Choreography for Advanced Dancers, 1965; Basic Music Outlines for Dance Classes, 1965; Goals and Objectives in Improving Physical Capabilities, 1970; A Teacher's Guide for Ballet Techniques, 1970; Principle Procedures in Basic Curriculum, 1974; Objectives and Standards of Performance for Physical Development, 1975. Assoc. music arranger Le Ballet du Cirque, 1964, Techniques of a Ballet School, 1970, rev., 1974; assoc. composer, lyricist The Ballet of Mother Goose, 1968; choreographer: Valses Nobles Et Sentimentales (Ravel); Cannon in D for Strings and Continuo (Pachelbel), 1979. Home and Office: 4923 Harbord Dr Oakland CA 94618

DEFELICE, KIMBERLE LEVIN, business owner, consultant; b. Phila., Aug. 21, 1963; d. Herbert and Mary Virginia (Wallace) Levin; divorced; 1 child, Jessika Anne. AS, Bradford Sch., 1982. Exec. sec. Arthur Andersen & Co., Phila., 1981-85; corp. sec. Asbestec Industries, Inc., Pennsauken, N.J., 1985-88; co-owner JVC Techs., Inc., Wayne, Pa., 1987—, also bd. dirs.; cons. Excel Group, Inc., Hockessin, Del., 1988—. Mem. NAFE. Office: JVC Techs Inc 996 Old Eagle Sch Rd Wayne PA 19087

DEFRANCES, LISA KRUL, interior designer; b. Painesville, Ohio, Feb. 27, 1957; d. Rollin Paul and Elizabeth Ann (Balla) Krul; m. Alan Quirino Defrances, Dec. 3, 1983. BA in Interior Design, Kent (Ohio) State U., 1979. Lic. interior desigbner, Fla. Interior designer Monarch Interiors, Inc., Beachwood, Ohio, 1979-81, The Cabinet Shoppes, Chagrin Falls, Ohio, 1981-82; sr. designer Meehans Bus. Interiors, Melbourne, Fla., 1982-85; interior designer/owner, v.p. Interiorworks, Inc., Palm Bay, Fla., 1985—. Peer counselor South Brevard Women's Ctr., Melbourne, 1988—. Mem. Am. Soc. Interior Designers, Toastmasters (pres. 1989-90). Lutheran. Office: Interiorworks Inc 1317 Prum Ave NW Palm Bay FL 32907

DE FRANCESCO, JOSEPHINE CATHERINE, retired anesthesiologist; b. Phila., June 26, 1923; d. Nicholas Antonio and Santa (Vitullo) DeF.; m. Hernando Trujillo,. BA, Temple U., 1944, postgrad., 1948. Diplomate Am. Bd. Anesthesiologists. Intern Albert Einstein Med. Ctr., Phila., 1948-50; resident Columbia Presbyn. Med. Ctr., N.Y.C., 1951-53; anesthesiologist St. Christopher's Hosp., Phila., 1953-54, Crozer Chester (Pa.) Med. Ctr., 1954-64, Taylor Hosp., Ridley Park, Pa., 1956-64, Sacred Heart Hosp., Chester, Pa., 1959-64; anesthesiologist St. Francis Med. Ctr., Trenton, 1964-88, ret., 1988. Fellow Am. Coll. Anesthesiologists; mem. Am. Med. Assn., Mercer. Republican. Roman Catholic. Home: 103 Sutphin Pines Yardley PA 19067

DEFRANCIS, SUELLEN MARIA, interior architect; b. Bklyn., Sept. 21, 1946; d. Joseph Agustino and Mary (Moran) DeF.; m. James D. Block, Apr. 23, 1965 (div. 1981); children: Melissa, Louis, Maximillian. BS, CCNY, 1982; BArch, CUNY, 1982, M. Urban Design, 1983. Designer, dir. interiors Peter Gisolfi Architects, Hastings-on-Hudson, N.Y., 1983-85; designer John Burgee Architects, N.Y.C., 1985-86; prin., owner Suellen DeFrancis Archtl. Interiors, Scarsdale, 1986—. Prin. works include features in Asset Housing mag., Mitsubishi Home mag. Recipient Del Guadio award N.Y. Soc. Architects, 1982; AIA scholar, 1982. Mem. AIA (assoc.), Am. Soc. Interior Designers, Internat. House of Japan, Ardsley Country Club, Nippon Club. Office: 155 Garth Rd Scarsdale NY 10583

DEFURIO, SUSAN SNELLING, teacher; b. Atlanta, Aug. 22, 1948; d. Charles Mercer III and Elisabeth Belle (Acree) Snelling; m. Robert Allen deFurio, Aug. 30,1969; children: David Acree, Roger Duvall. Student, Ga. State U., 1967, 68; BA in History, Agnes Scott Coll., 1970; postgrad., Calif. State U., Turlock, 1983-86, Bowling Green State U., 1987. Cert. tchr., Ohio. Substitute tchr. Maumee (Ohio) Sch. Dist., 1971-72, Ottawa Hills Sch. Dist., Toledo, 1971-73, 76-77, Springfield Local Sch. Dist., Holland, Ohio, 1987-88, Sylvania (Ohio) Sch. Dist., 1988-89; speech therapist Signal Ctrs. for Spl. Children, Cleve. and Chattanooga, Tenn., 1989—. Active, Girl Scouts U.S., various locations, 1970-72, 82-85; Sunday sch. tchr., United Meth. Ch., Toledo and Modesto, Calif., 1975—; officer, Welcome Wagon Clubs, Toledo and Sylvania, 1971-74, 78-82, 86-88; vol. fundraiser, Toledo Mus. Art, 1981-82, 86-87; vol. hearing screener, Cheers for Ears program, 1987—. Mem. AAUW (recording sec. 1985-86, ehmn., editor membership directory, Toledo chpt. 1987-88), Nat. Students Speech, Lang. and Hearing Assn. Democrat. Office: Signal Ctrs for Spl Children 509 20th St Cleveland TN 37311

DEGENHART, PEARL C., artist, educator; b. Phillipsburg, Mont., Feb. 25; d. L.C. and Ellen (O'Neill) Degenhart; A.B., U. Mont., 1923; A.M., Columbia, 1928. Instr. art Arcata (Calif.) Union High Sch., 1928—, chmn. art dept., 1930-65; one-man shows Stafford Inn, Scotia, Calif., 1954, Humboldt State Coll., 1951; exhibited group shows San Francisco Art Assn., 1932, 37, 40; Contemporary Arts Gallery, N.Y.C., 1939; Denver, 1938; Humboldt State Coll., 1935, 45, 54; Spokane Wash., 1948; Oakland Art Gallery, 1948; Humboldt Fed. Gallery, 1966; Eureka Courthouse, 1968, Redwood Art Assn., Eureka, 1976-80, Old Town Art Guild, Eureka, 1977, San Rafael, Calif., 1978-79. Mem. Nat. League Am. Pen Women, Alpha Xi Delta, Delta Phi Delta. Contbr. to art, juvenile mags.; author children's story book. Address: Box 142 Trinidad CA 95570

DE GERENDAY, MRS. LACI See CHANDLER, ELISABETH GORDON

DEGNAN, ELIZABETH J., psychologist, educator; b. East Newark, N.J., June 19, 1927; d. James A. and Elizabeth J. (Berkise) D. BA, Montclair State Coll., 1949; MA, Cath. U., 1961; EdD, Rutgers U., 1971. Lic. psychologist; diplomate Sch. Psychology. Tchr. Sparta, Wayne, Oceanport, N.J., 1949-56, USAF Dependent Schs., Morocco, Eng., Rep. Germany, 1956-59; student activities coord. Cath. U., Washington, 1959-60, asst. dean of women, dir. women's residences, 1960-61; math. tchr. Farmingdale (N.Y.) High Sch., 1961-62; guidance counselor Shore Regional High Sch., West Long Branch, N.J., 1962-68; psychologist Middletown (N.J.) Twp. Bd. Edn., 1970-89; pvt. practice psychologist Oceanport, N.J., 1976—; supr. psychol. cons. Family and Community Svcs., Red Bank, N.J., 1987—, Family Life Bur.-Diocese, Trenton, West Long Branch, 1989—; speaker confs. in field. Mem. Monmouth County (N.J.) Right-to-Life, 1987—; advocate Children and Adults with Learning Disabilities, Oceanport, 1970—; task force substance abuse, Borough of Oceanport, 1988-89; ministry bd. Cath. Women of Zion, Middletown, 1989—. Recipient Psychol. Recognition award N.J. Acad. Psychologists, 1980-83, 84-86. Mem. Am. Psychol. Assn., N.J. Psychol. Assn. (exec. bd. 1976-79), Monmouth-Ocean County Psychol. Assn. (Outstanding Contbrn. award 1977-78, 74-89), NEA, N.J. Edn. Assn., Monmouth County Edn. Assn., Middletown Twp. Edn. Assn. (exec. bd. 1972-84). Office: 12 Horicon Ave Oceanport NJ 07757

DEGNAN, KIM E., communications executive; b. Lakewood, Ohio, June 18, 1956; d. Richard Patrick and K.C. (Morrison) D. Student, Bryn Mawr Coll., 1973-75; BA, U. Calif. Berkeley, 1976, MA in Pub. Policy, 1978; MS in Telecommunications Engring., George Washington U., 1980. Cert. spectrum engr., fin. mgr. Analyst, telecommunications Aspen (Colo.) Inst., 1977; presdl. mgmt. intern Nat. Telecom and Info. Agy., Washington, 1978-80, dir. spectrum econs. program, 1980-81; chief editor Satellite Communications mag., Denver, 1981-83; fin. cons. various clients, orgns. including Warner Communications, MCI, 1981-83; exec. asst. to dir. gen. Intelsat, Washington, 1983-85, dir. pub. and media rels., 1983-85; dir. bus. devel. TRT Internat., Washington, 1986-89; exec. v.p. Pacific Satellite, Inc., Washington, 1987—; chmn. Satellite Communications Users Conf., 1981-83; lectr. Satellite Fundamentals seminar, 1982-84, Econs. of Comml. Satellite Industry seminar, 1988-90, Internat. Telecommunications Regulation seminar, 1988-90. Editor, author: Communications For Tomorrow, 1978; author monthly column High Definition TV, 1989—; contbr. articles to profl. jours.; speechwriter in field. Vol. D.C. Women's Shelter, Animal Rescue League. Named Presdl. Mgmt. Intern Exec. Br. White House Program, 1978-80, Exxon Young Leadership scholar, Exxon Corp., 1977, Nat. Merit finalist, L.A., 1973, Calif. State Champion original oratory, L.A., 1971-73, finalist Nat. Forensics and Debate Tournament, 1973. Mem. Soc. Satellite Profls. (founding bd. dirs. 1982-84), Internat. Teleconf. Assn. (charter mem.), Am. Women in Radio and TV, NAFE, Soc. Profl. Journalists, Internat. Assn. Bus. Communications, Am. Mgmt. Assn. Home: 2920 McKinley St NW Washington DC 20015

DEGONIA, MARY ELISE, government, community relations executive; b. St. Louis, Sept. 23, 1954; d. Joseph Milton and Janice Doris (Walls) DeG.; m. Kenneth Michael Quinn, June 26, 1976. Student, Riverside Community Coll., 1971-73, Calif. State U., 1973-76. Dir., youth svcs. Los Pandrinos, San Bernardino, Calif., 1975-78; chief, planning and evaluation Mayor's Office of Employment and Tng., San Bernardino, 1978-79; program mgr. V.P. Mondale Task Force on Youth, Washington, 1979-80; sr. policy analyst Nat. Youth Work Alliance, Washington, 1979-81; v.p., govt. relations 70001 Youth Employment Co., Washington, 1981-88; pres. Capitol Perspectives, Washington, 1988—; dir., pub. policy and legis. Nat. Youth Employment Ctr., N.Y.C., 1979-89; founding mem. Nat. Assn. for Community Based Orgn., Washington, 1979-83. Co-author: State Coordination Guide, 1987, Food for Thought, 1988, Stalking the Large Green Grant, 1979, Fund Diversification Guide, 1988. Founding chmn. Calif. Child, Youth and Family Coalition, Sacramento, 1976-78. Recipient Outstanding Performance award, U.S. Dept. Labor, Washington, 1980, Disting. Achievement award, U.S. Basics, Alexandria, Va., 1988. Mem. Nat. Youth Employment Coalition, State Issues Forum (exec. mem., bd. dirs.), Nat. Job. Tng. Partnership. Home: 1915 17th St NW #100 Washington DC 20009 Office: Capitol Perspectives 1915 17th St NW #200 Washington DC 20009

DEGRAFFENREID, BRENDA JEAN, procurement analyst, consultant; b. Spartanburg, S.C., Sept. 21, 1947; d. Willie and Vencie DeGraffenreid. BS, Morgan U., 1970, MBA, 1976; postgrad., U. So. Calif., Washington, 1990. Part-time, temp. and substitute tchr. Balt. City Pub. Schs., 1971; bus. specialist State of Md., Balt., 1973-75; bus. enterprise analyst Entrepreneurial Devel. Project, Balt., 1975-76; risk analyst trainee Comml. Credit Corp., Balt., 1976; contract specialist Energy Rsch. & Devel. Adminstrn., Washington, 1976-78; small bus. specialist U.S. Dept. Energy, Washington, 1978-83; minority bus. specialist USCG, Washington, 1983-84; small bus. specialist VA, 1984-87; procurement analyst Dept. Energy, Washington, 1987—; acct. Robert's Food Stores, Balt., 1974-84, Saltor's Mechanic Shop, Balt., 1986-87; real estate agt. Mitchell, Balt., from 1985; cons. Metar Corp., Balt., also several small local cos., 1982-84. Big sister Big Bros./Big Sisters, Balt., 1984—. Mem. Nat. Bus. League, Am. Assn. MBA Execs. Republican. Methodist. Home: 2505 W Forest Pk Ave Baltimore MD 21215 Office: US Dept Energy 1000 Independence Ave SW Washington DC 20585

DE GRAFFENRIED, VELDA MAE CAMP (MRS. THOMAS P. DE GRAFFENRIED), clinical laboratory executive; b. Kirwin, Kans.; d. George Robert and Laura (Woodward) Camp; student No. Ill. U., 1959-60; m. Thomas P. deGraffenried, May 23, 1942; children—Donna Rae McCaffrey, Albert Lawrence II, Nicholas Thomas. Office mgr. deGraffenried & Fisher Clin. Labs., DeKalb, Ill., 1957-64, exec. sec., 1964—, dir. pub. affairs until 1985; dir. public affairs deGraffenried Med. Cons. Service, Inc. Vice pres. Haish Sch. PTA, DeKalb, 1958-59; den mother cub scouts Chief Shabbona council Boy Scouts Am., 1957-60; supr. Teen Age Club, Louisville, 1949-50; county crusade chmn. Am. Cancer Soc. (recipient commendation, 1987), 1965, mem. exec. bd. DeKalb County, 1964—, dir. public affairs, 1970—, chmn. bd., 1978-80, chmn. Radiothon, 1972-82, 83-87, sec. DeKalb County Soc., 1969—, mem. state bd. Ill. div., 1985—. Recipient commendations Am. Cancer Soc., 1965, 74, Boy Scouts Am., 1955. Mem. DeKalb County Med. Soc. Aux. (sec. 1959-60, 76—, pres. 1973-74), DeKalb Hosp. Aux. Methodist. Home: 1208 Sunnymeade Trail DeKalb IL 60115

DE GRAZIA, LORETTA THERESA, oil company executive; b. Boston, May 17, 1955; d. Gaetano T.P. and Nancy R. (Serino) De G. A in Mgmt./Mktg. magna cum laude, Newbury Coll., 1986. V.p. mktg. and sales Grimes Oil Co., Boston, 1977-85; pres. East Coast Petroleum, Boston, 1985—. Fellow New Eng. Women Bus. Owners, Nat. Assn. Women in Constrn., Greater Boston Women's Network, NAFE. Office: East Coast Petroleum Corp 320 Adams St Boston MA 02122-3538

DEGROAT, GAIL BARBARA, advertising executive; b. Phila., Oct. 21, 1937; d. Harold George and Irene (Brown) Glenn; m. John Albert DeGroat, July 23, 1976. BS, Pa. State U., 1960; postgrad., Temple U., 1963-66. Pers. asst. Reuben H. Donnelly Tel. Directory Co., 1963-66; indsl. rels. asst. Action Mfg. Co., 1966-67; supr. benefits GTE Info. Systems, Inc., Stamford, Conn., 1967-72; plant pers. supr. GTE Info. Systems, Inc., Stamford, 1972, mgr. benefits and svcs., 1972-74, mgr. benefits and compensation, 1974-76; v.p. mgr. benefits and pers. adminstrn. B&B, Inc., N.Y.C., 1976-85; corp. v.p. dir. benefits and pers. adminstrn. D'Arcy Masius Benton & Bowles, Inc., N.Y.C., 1985—. Mem. Am. Soc. Pers. Adminstrs., N.Y. Pers. Mgmt. Assn., Internat. Found. Employee Benefits, Am. Compensation Assn. Office: D'Arcy Masius Benton & Bowles 1675 Broadway New York NY 10019

DEGROAT, JOANNE E., computer engineering educator, researcher; b. Ridgway, Pa., June 15, 1951; d. Joseph Henry and Lucille Marie (Giordano) DeG. BS in Engring. Sci., Pa. State U., 1973; MSEE, Syracuse U., 1978; PhD, U. Ill., 1990. Devel. engr. Eastman Kodak Co., Rochester, N.Y., 1973-74; commd. 2d lt. USAF, 1974, advanced through grades to maj., 1986; br. officer-in-charge, wing job control officer 416th Bomg Wing, Griffiss AFB, 1974-78; devel. engr. Rome Air Devel. Ctr., Griffiss AFB, 1978-80; instr. elec. engring. Air Force Inst. Tech., Wright-Patterson AFB, Ohio, 1985-89; hon. discharge, 1989; asst. prof. elec. engring. Ohio State U., Columbus, 1990—. Mem. IEEE (sr., steering com. design automation standards subcom. 1988—, fin. chmn. 1989—), Assn. for Computer Machinery, VHDL Users Group (steering com. 1989—). Roman Catholic. Home: 8225 Snowhill Ct Westerville OH 43081 Office: Ohio State U 2015 Neil Ave Columbus OH 43210

DEGUZMAN, BETTY FREEHILL, educator; b. Urbana, Ill., Dec. 20, 1959; d. Louis Anthony and Crescentia (Rock) Freehill; m. Bernard Zachacy DeGuzman, Aug. 25, 1962; children: Diane Elizabeth, David Bernard, Darryl Louis, Doyle William, Daniel Zachary. BA, Rosary Coll., River Forest, Ill., 1961; MA, Kean Coll., 1985. Tchr. Spanish, Willowbrook Sch. Dist., Villa Park, Ill., 1961-63; music dir. Ch. of Resurrection, Memphis, 1970-79; tchr. Spanish and ESL, Summit (N.J.) Bd. Edn., 1979—; speaker, panelist Nat. Gov.'s Conf., New Brunswick, N.J., 1989; presenter N.E. Conf. Fgn. Langs., N.Y.C., 1985, 87, 89. Trustee Summit Ednl. Found., 1987—, Summit Symphony, 1989—. Recipient Gov.'s Recognition award State of N.J., 1989; Juan Carlos I Quincentennial fellow, Madrid, 1989, 90. Mem. Am. Assn. Tchrs. Spanish and Portuguese, Am. Coun. on Teaching Fgn. Langs. (presenter 1988, 90), N.J. Tchrs. English to Speakers Other Langs., N.J. Fgn. Lang. Educators, AAUW, Summit Coll. Club (chmn. yearbook 1987-89), Internat. Club (moderator 1986—), Phi Delta Kappa. Republican. Roman Catholic. Home: 7 Webster Ave Summit NJ 07901 Office: Summit Bd Edn 292 Morris Ave Summit NJ 07901

DE HAAN-PULS, JOYCE ELAINE, sales account representative; b. Grand Rapids, Mich., Dec. 22, 1941; d. Harry Herman and Dorothy Elaine (Kikstra) DeHaan; student Calvin Coll., 1960-61; BS with honors, Grand Valley State Colls., 1978; postgrad. U. Sarajevo, Yugoslavia, 1978, Grad. Inst., Siedman Grad. Coll., 1979—; M in Speech Communications Wayne State U., 1986 ; children: Bruce Todd, Daniel Lane, Cristy-Ann Sara Elizabeth Puls. Owner, operator Joyce Elaine's Beauty Parlor, Grandville, Mich., 1960-64; asst. assessor City of Hudsonville, Mich., 1978; dir. displaced homemaker program Women's Resource Ctr., Grand Rapids, 1979-81; visual products rep. 3M Corp., Grand Rapids, 1982-85, sr. account rep., Detroit, 1985-89, regional sales mgr. S.E. Mich., 1989—; mem. Ottawa County (Mich.) CETA Adv. Bd. Bd. dirs. Downtown Day Care Ctr., Grand Rapids, 1972. Recipient Cert. of Appreciation Bishop of Saigon, Vietnam, 1969; Top Sales rep. 3M/US, 1983, VIP, 1983, 84, 85, 86, 87, 88, 89; Phillip Morris scholar, 1975. Mem. Preservation Wayne, Detroit Internat. Vis. Coun. Mem. NAFE, Internat. Visitors Coun., Nat. Assn. Fgn. Students, Grand Rapids Coun. on World Affairs, Am. Soc. Pub. Adminstrn, Hist. Indian Village Assn. Republican. Home: 2141 Seminole Detroit MI 48214 Office: 2225 Oak Industrial Dr Grand Rapids MI 49505

DEHN, LETHA ARLENE See FIGGINS, LETHA ARLENE

DEHN, PAULA FAYE, biology educator; b. Richmond, Ind., Feb. 15, 1951; d. Leonard Franklin and Joyce Alyadean (Murphy) D. AB in Zoology, DePauw U., 1973, MA in Zoology, 1974; PhD in Biology, U. South Fla., 1980. Vis. fellow Nat. Sci.-Engring. Rsch. Coun. Can., 1980-82; asst. prof. U. Tex., San Antonio, 1982-89; assoc. prof. biology, chmn. dept. Canisius Coll., Buffalo, 1989—; rsch. asst. EPA and U. South Fla., Tampa, 1974-76; cons. minority access to rsch. careers program Nat. Inst. Gen. Med. Scis.-NIH, 1984-88, finfish mariculture program U. Tex. Marine Sci. Inst., Port Aransas, 1987-88; collaborator Agrl. Rsch. Svc., USDA, 1985-87; faculty advisor Alpha Phi Omega, 1983; chmn., organizer Expanding Your Horizons in Sci. and Math. Consortium, San Antonio, 1985-88; participant San Antonio Target 90 Scientist-Sci. Tchrs. Coop., 1987-88. Contbr. articles to profl. jours. Pres. bd. dirs. Unity Ch. San Antonio, 1987-89. Named Sunday's Woman, San Antonio Light, 1988; Ind. State scholar, 1969; grantee NIH, 1985-90. Fellow Tex. Acad. Scis. (pres. 1990); mem. AAS, Am. Fisheries Soc., Tissue Culture Assn., Am. Soc. Zoologists, Sigma Xi. Democrat. Office: Canisius Coll Biology Dept 2001 Main St Buffalo NY 14208

DEIBLER, BARBARA ELLEN, librarian; b. Pottsville, Pa., Aug. 11, 1943; d. Samuel Elwood and Miriam Elizabeth (Houser) D. BA, Pa. State U., 1965; MS, Drexel U., 1966. Cataloger State Libr. Pa., Harrisburg, 1966-82, head cataloger, 1972-82, rare book librarian, 1980—, asst. coordinator collection mgmt., 1982—; librarian Hist. Soc. Schuylkill County, 1971-77. Author: Pennsylvania German Barn Signs: For Protection or Just for Nice, 1978, Simplified Cataloging for Libraries, 1978, The State Library of Pennsylvania: The Philadelphia Years, 1982, Books of State: A Peripatetic Collection, 1983, A Treasure Trove of Books, 1986, How Libraries Stack Up With Authors, 1987, Anne Royall's Visit to Carlisle in 1828, 1987, Anne Newport Royall: Indomitable Eccentric, 1987, The Bookish Aurands, 1988, The Aurands in Print, 1989, The Aurands of Beaver Springs and Harrisburg, 1990. Mem. Am. Acad. Polit. and Social Scis., Acad. Polit. Sci., Soc. Polit. Enquiries (sec. 1987—), Schuylkill County Allied Artists (dir. 1976-77), Pa. Library Assn., Hist. Soc. Pa., Descendants Schwenkfeldian Exiles, Pa. German Soc. Baptist. Clubs: Pilot of Pottsville (rec. sec. 1974-75, dir. 1975-77), Pilot of Harrisburg (pres. 1979-81, 87-88, treas. 1978-79, dir. 1981-83, 88-89, sec. 1983-85, v.p. 1985-87). Home: 2285 W Norwegian St Pottsville PA 17901 Office: State Libr Pa Box 1601 Harrisburg PA 17105

DEIBLER, MARIE PHILLIPS, university media relations specialist, political activist; b. Gary, W. Va., May 20; d. George Monroe and Lura (Watson) Phillips; m. William Dan Deibler, Apr. 10, 1944 (dec.); 1 child, Deborah Deibler Steele. BA Marshall U., 1943; postgrad. George Washington U., U. South Fla. Writer Washington Post, Washington, 1940-41, 43-44; staff writer/reporter A.P., Jacksonville, Fla., 1944-47; editor Que Pasa in Puerto Rico, San Juan, 1951-54; asst. editor U.S. Lady mag., Washington, 1961-65; editor U. Tampa mag. (Fla.), 1966-71; writer/media rels. specialist U. South Fla., Tampa, 1972—. Author: What Every Military Kid Should Know, 1969; contbr. articles to mags. and newspapers. Bd. dirs. Hillsborough Polit. Caucus, Tampa, 1983—, mem. Dem. exec. com., 1988—; bd. dirs., v.p. Friends of Temple Terrace Library (Fla.), 1978-85; mem. citizens adv. com. Met. Planning, Orgn., Tampa, 1986-88; mem. USF Lecture Series com.; bd. dirs. Fla. Suncoast Writers Conf. Mem. Am. News Women Club (Washington), Women in Communications, Tiger Bay Club (Tampa). Democrat. Episcopalian. Office: U South Fla Office Pub Affairs Tampa FL 33620

DEICHERT, ANNE VAN NUYS See SINCLAIR, ANNE VAN NUYS

DEILER, DEANA DAVIS, educator; b. Marion, Ala., Oct. 19, 1959; d. Joe Edward and Dorothy Dean (Marsh) Davis; m. Michael Kevin Deiler, Aug. 11, 1984; children: Sean Michael, Robert Patrick. BA in Elem. Edn., Judson Coll., Marion, 1982; cert. in math., U. Ala., Tuscaloosa, 1985. Cert. math., Spanish and elem. tchr., Ala., Fla. Tchr. math. Greensboro (Ala.) High

Sch., 1982-84; tchr. Spanish, Choctawhatchee High Sch., Ft. Walton Beach, Fla., 1986—. Grantee U. Ala., Yucatan, Mex., 1981, Ala. Dept. Edn., 1982. Mem. NEA, Fla. Fgn. Lang. Assn., AAUW, Am. Assn. Tchrs. of Spanish and Protuguese. Home: 3012 Blue Pine Ln Niceville FL 32578 Office: Choctawhatchee High Sch 110 Racetrack Rd Fort Walton Beach FL 32578

DEILY, LINNET FRAZIER, banker; b. Dallas, June 20, 1945; d. William Harold and Ruth (White) Frazier; m. Myron Bonham Deily, Apr. 18, 1981. B.A., U. Tex.-Austin, 1967; M.A., U. Tex-Dallas, 1976. Banking officer, asst. v.p., then v.p. Republic Bank Dallas, N.A., 1975-80, sr. v.p., 1980-81; v.p. First Interstate Bancorp, Los Angeles, 1981-83; sr. v.p., div. mgr. First Interstate Bank Calif., 1983-84; past sr. v.p., chief fin. officer, now pres. First Interstate Bank Ltd.; bd. dirs. First Interstate Inst., Los Angeles. Club: Univ. (mem. fin. com.) (Los Angeles). Office: 1st Interstate Bank Tex 1000 Louisiana 7th Fl Houston TX 77002*

DEIOTTE, MARGARET TUKEY, software consulting firm executive; b. Lafayette, Ind., Mar. 6, 1952; d. Ronald B. and Elizabeth A. (Williams) Tukey; m. Charles E. Deiotte, Sept. 11, 1971; children: Raymond, Karl, Ronald. Student, U. Wash., 1969-72, 77-79. V.p., treas. Logical Systems, Inc., Colorado Springs, 1982-86; v.p. CEDSYS, Inc., Colorado Springs, 1987—; pres. Penrose Enrichment Program Found., Colorado Springs, Colo., 1988-89. Mem. adv. bd. Gifted and Talented, Sch. Dist. 11, 1989—; pres. Penrose Elem. PTA, 1989—; 1st v.p. El Paso coun. PTA, 1990-91; mem. grants commn. Colo. State PTA, 1990-91; coach Odyssey of the Mind, 1990. Mem. NAFE. Home and Office: 2973 Fascination Circle Colorado Springs CO 80917

DEITCH, ARLINE DOUGLIS, research scientist; b. N.Y.C., Mar. 12, 1922. BA cum laude, CUNY, 1944; MA in Zoology, Columbia U., 1946, PhD in Zoology, 1954. Postdoctoral fellow Neurology and Blindness div. NIH, 1955-56; research assoc. Columbia U., N.Y.C., 1956-62, asst. prof. microbiology, 1962-68, asst. prof. pathology, 1968-73, assoc. prof. clin. pathology, 1973-81, assoc. prof. clin. pathology and urology in anatomy, 1981-84; adj. prof. urology U. Calif. Davis Sch. Medicine, Sacramento, 1984—; researcher various projects NIH, 1967-77, 83—, Nat. Cancer Inst. 1985—; dir. NIH cancer research grant, 1977-81; local chmn. Third Internat. Congress Histochemistry and Cytochemistry, N.Y.C., 1968. Contbr. articles to profl. jours. Mem. Soc. for Analytical Cytology, Am. Soc. Cell Biology, Histochem. Soc. (program chmn. 1964-68, council mem. 1964-68, 1973-77), Tissue Culture Assn. (organizer symposium on flow cytometry Meml. Sloan-Kettering Cancer Ctr. 1982), Sigma Xi. Office: U Calif Davis Med Sch Dept Urology Ste 2220 4301 X St Profl Bldg Sacramento CA 95817

DEITCH, DONNA MARIE, health care and retirement company executive; d. Raymond P. and Lorraine M. (Stewart) Douillet; m. Barry N. Deitch, Nov. 4, 1984.; children: Daniel Terrill, Paul Terrill, Wendy. BS, Quinnipiac Coll., Hamden, Conn., 1987; MS, Hartford (Conn.) Grad. Ctr., 1991. Lic. nursing home adminstr. Asst. adminstr. Mediplex of Danbury (Conn.), 1986-87; adminstr. Health Care and Retirement Corp., Toledo, 1987—. Mem. Am. Coll. Health Care Adminstrs., Phi Theta Kappa, Alpha Beta Gamma. Home: 101 Madeline Ave Apt 46 Waterbury CT 06708

DEITCH, IRENE M., psychology educator; b. N.Y.C., July 10, 1930; d. Michael and Dora (Marder) Danzker; m. Jack Deitch, July 2, 1955; children: Michele Yve, Jonathan Scott. BA, Bklyn. Coll., 1952; MA, Columbia U., 1953, profl. diploma, 1955; PhD, Yeshiva U., 1981. Lic. psychologist, N.Y.; cert. sch. psychologist, N.Y., cert. Head Start psychologist, edn./vocat. guidance counselor. Prof. psychology Coll. Staten Island (N.Y.), 1964—; clin. cons. Camelot Counseling Ctr., Staten Island, 1985—; ind. clin. psychologist cons., Staten Island, 1982—; chairperson OPTIONS, Coll. Study for Older Adults, Coll. Staten Island, 1988—; host, producer radio show, 1987—. Co-author: Women Therapists Helping Women. Bd. dirs. Staten Island Coun. on Arts, 1983-89, Staten Island Cancer Soc., 1984—, Staten Island Jewish Community Ctr., 1987—, Staten Island Interagency Coun. on Aging. Recipient Soroptimist award Women Helping Women, Staten Island, 1982, Compeer award, 1985. Mem. N.Y. State Psychol. Soc. (pres. social psychology div. 1989-90, pres. acad. div. 1987-88, Am. Psychol. Assn. (chair com. on aging and ageism 1987—, pres. running psychologists), Internat. Coun. Psychologists, Assn. for Death Edn. & Counseling, Richmond County Psychol. Assn. (pres. 1981-83). Home: 59 Butterworth Ave Staten Island NY 10301 Office: Coll Staten Island Psychology 715 Ocean Terr Staten Island NY 10301

DEITERS, SISTER JOAN ADELE, nun, chemistry educator; b. Cin., Apr. 28, 1934; d. Alfred Harry and Rose Catherine (Rusche) D. B.A., Coll. Mt. St. Joseph, Cin., 1963; M. Christian Spirituality, Creighton U., Omaha, 1985; Ph.D., U. Cin., 1967. Joined Sisters of Charity, Roman Cath. Ch., 1952; prof. chemistry Coll. Mt. St. Joseph, Cin., 1968-78; prof. chemistry, Vassar Coll., Poughkeepsie, N.Y., 1978—. Contbr. articles to profl. jours. Mem. Am. Chem. Soc., Sisters of Charity, Sigma Xi. Democrat. Home and Office: Vassar Coll Dept Chemistry Box 143 Poughkeepsie NY 12601

DEITSCH, MARIAN MIMI, writer, editor; b. Scranton, Pa., Apr. 9, 1933; d. David T. and Florence V. (Chait) Rubin; m. Thomas A. Deitsch, Oct. 16, 1955 (dec. Nov. 1983); children: Lisa Ellen, Thomas Alan. AB, Barnard Coll., 1954; postgrad. NYU, 1956-57, William Paterson Coll., Wayne, N.J., 1982-83. Writer, Scranton Times, 1954; asst. economist Fed. Res. Bank N.Y., N.Y.C., 1955-60; mktg. rep. Welcome Wagon Internat., Memphis, 1974-79; writer Jewish News, East Orange, N.J., 1979; editor C.H. Kline & Co., Inc., Fairfield, N.J., 1979-84, sr. cons., 1984-88 ; pub. relations mgr. Fin. Execs. Inst., Morristown, N.J., 1988—. Author: (with others) Guide to Energy, 198 editor: Guide to Plastics Industry, 1982; Guide to Packaging Industry, 1980; Entering Livingston, 1963; contbr. articles to profl. jours. Bd. dirs. Hemlock Farms Community Assn., Lords Valley, Pa., 1977-78, 83-85; mem. various coms., 1977-86; pres. Livingston (N.J.) LWV, 1969-71; chmn. Livingston Ednl. Liaison Com., 1968-69. Mem. Women in Communications, Chem. Mktg. and Econs. Group N.Y. of Am. Chem. Soc. (bd. dirs. 1986-88). Home: 21 Coddington Terr Livingston NJ 07039 Office: Fin Execs Inst 10 Madison Ave Morristown NJ 07960

DEITZ, SUSAN ROSE, newspaper advice columnist; b. Far Rockaway, N.Y., Mar. 21, 1934; d. Emanuel and Florence Jean (Goodstein) Davis; m. Morris J. Mandelker, Nov. 29, 1975; 1 son, Scott Richard; m. Richard Alan Deitz, Dec. 22, 1958 (dec. 1967). Student Smith Coll., Barnard Coll., N.Y.C., Art Students League, N.Y.C., Stella Adler Theater Studio. Syndicated advice columnist L.A. Times Syndicate, 1975—; mem. faculty New Sch., N.Y.C., 1977-79; radio personality, 1979; columnist Prodigy Svcs., White Plains, N.Y., 1987—; speaker satellite conf. NAFE, 1990. Author: (novel) Valency Girl, 1976, Single File, 1989, paperback edit., 1990. Mem. Women in Communications (Outstanding Mem. award 1984), Authors Guild, Overseas Press Club (elect), Smith Coll. Club.

DEJMEK, LINDA MARIE, optometrist; b. Memphis, June 2, 1953. BS in Optometry, Ind. U., 1975, OD, 1977. Owner, operator Appleton (Wis.) Eye Clinic, 1977—. Med. illustrator System for Ophthalmic Dispensing, 1979; illustrator Diver Mag., 1985, Skin Diver mag., 1985; exhibited in group shows at Appleton Gallery Arts, 1979—. Recipient Harold Bailey Award Am. Optometric Found., 1977; named Hon. Citizen, City of Clarksville, Tenn., 1976. Mem. Am. Optometric Assn., Wis. Optometric Assn. (bd. dirs. 1988-89), Fox Cities Optometric Soc. (pres. 1984-86), Wis. Fedn. Bus. and Profl. Women (chmn. state membership com. 1985-86, state 1st v.p. 1986-87, pres. elect 1987-88, pres. 1988-89), Wis. Optometric Assn. (bd. dirs. 1987-88), State of Wis. Optometry Examining Bd., Mid-Day Bus. and Profl. Women (treas. 1980-81, founding chmn. 1981-84, pres. 1984-86), Fox Cities C. of C. (govtl. rels. com. 1986-87), Appleton Jr. Womens Club (illustrator 1981-82). Office: Appleton Eye Clinic 509 Chain Dr Appleton WI 54915

DEKKER, HARRIETT GROMB, psychologist; b. Bklyn., Mar. 1, 1942; d. Jack and Rachel (Bershinsky) Gromb; m. Marcel Dekker, July 22, 1967; children: Russell, David, Jacqueline. BA, Queens Coll., 1964; MA, NYU, 1967; postgrad. in spl. edn., Coll. of New Rochelle, 1974; cert. in handwriting, New Sch. for Social Rsch., 1988. Cert. elem. tchr. Tchr. grades 5 and 6 Pub. Sch. 152, Woodside, N.Y., 1964-66; tchr. grade 3 Flower Hill Sch., Huntington, N.Y., 1965-67; tchr. lang. arts Hallen Ctr. Maximum Edn., White Plains, N.Y., 1974-76; pvt. practice Greenwich, Conn., 1976-78; counselor, coord., dir. Support Svcs.-Aid for Retarded, Stamford, Conn., 1978-84; dir. Profl. Insight, Inc., Greenwich, Conn., 1985—. Bd. dirs. Gateway Communities, Inc., Greenwich, 1988—. Mem. Am. Psychol. Assn. (assoc.), Am. Soc. Profl. Graphologists, Nat. Graphological Soc. Home: 41 Londonderry Dr Greenwich CT 06830 Office: Profl Insight Inc PO Box 7854 Greenwich CT 06836

DELABARRE, GINGER ANN, nurse manager; b. New Haven, Conn., Aug. 28, 1954; d. Everett Merrill and Zora Lou (Ezzell) D. AA in Liberal Arts, Greenfield Community Coll., Greenfield, Mass., 1978, AS in Nursing, 1983; LPN, Thompson Sch. Practical Nurses, Brattleboro, Vt., 1981. RN, Mass. Practical nurse Farren Meml. Hosp., Montague, Mass., 1981-83, RN, 1983-88; RN clinic mgr. U. Health Svcs. U. Mass., Amherst, 1988—; EMT, Conway Fire Dept. Ambulance, Conway, Mass., 1976—; charge nurse Beacon Detoxification Unit, Greenfield, Mass., 1981-85; charge nurse U. Health Svcs., U. Mass., Amherst, 1986-88; guest lectr. various EMT & nurses' orgns. Author: poetry, 1979-80. Vol. Alternative Energy Coalition, Greenfield, 1976-78, pediatric unit Northampton (Mass.) Nursing Home, 1978, Franklin County Health Fair, Greenfield, 1982; instr. CPR, ARC, Greenfield, 1977-83, First Aid, 1978-84; worthy advisor Order of Rainbow for Girls, Greenfield, 1970. Mem. Emergency Nurses Assn., Am. Diabetes Assn., Franklin County EMT Assn., Am. Mensa. Home: Whately Rd Conway MA 01341 Office: Univ Health Svcs Infirmary Way U Mass Amherst MA 01002

DELABARRE POWERS, NANCY MAY, management analyst; b. Fargo, N.D., Aug. 17, 1941; d. Marvin Stanley Ness and Lila Mae (Mohagen) Weldon; m. Delbert Melvin DelaBarre, Apr. 1, 1961 (div. 1967); children: Garret Scott, Eric Allen; m. William Rhodes Powers, Feb. 28, 1988. Student, U. N.D., 1959-60, U. Nev., 1977, 83, 84. Legal sec. B.L. Spears, Atty., San Bernardino, Calif., 1967; asst. to pres. A & B Enterprises, Yucaipa, Calif., 1967-72; escrow agt., adminstrv. asst. Title Ins. and Trust, San Bernardino, 1972-75; customer svc. rep. Lewis Homes of Nev., Las Vegas, 1975-77; mgmt. analyst, asst. right of way agt. City of Las Vegas, 1977-84; dir. emergency mgmt., handicap compliance coord., mgmt. analyst, grant adminstr., registered lobbyist City of North Las Vegas, 1984—. Mem. So. Nev. Women's Polit. Caucus, Clark County, 1988-89, polit. action com. chmn., 1990. Recipient Valley of Heros award Clark County Boys & Girls Club, 1988, Cert. of Appreciation ARC, 1986. Mem. Am. Pub. Works Assn. (chmn. 1989-90, vice chair 1988-89, sec., treas. 1987-88, exec. bd. 1986), Am. Soc. Pub. Adminstrs., Nat. C. of C. Emergency Mgrs., Toastmasters. Office: City of North Las Vegas 2200 Civic Ctr Dr North Las Vegas NV 89030

DELACEY, DEBORAH HARTWELL, dairy industry executive; b. Mobile, Alabama, June 19, 1952; d. Charles Kent and Joan Louise (Merriwether) Hartwell; m. Robert Floyd. BS in Home Econs., Auburn U., 1974. Pub. info. specialist Alabama Commn. on Aging, Montgomery, 1974-75; extension home economist U. Ky., Lexington, 1975-78; home economist Kettering (Ohio) Convalescent Ctr., 1978-79; area dir. Dairy & Nutrition Council MidEasst, Cin., 1979-88; dir. nutrition edn. MidEast United Dairy Ind. Assn., Columbus, 1988—; bd. dirs. Ohio Nutrition Edn. Adv. Program, Columbus; cons. Kahn's. Contbr. articles to local mag. Pres., v.p. Queensgate Civic Assn., Cin., 1983-87; bd. dirs. Butler Co. Mem. Am. Home Econs. Ass., Home Econ. Bus. (sec. 1987--), Am. Pub. Health Assn. (chmn. 1984-88), Ohio Nutrition Council (fin. chmn. 1985-87),. Office: MidEast United Dairy Ind 3592 Corporate Dr Columbus OH 43231

DELACY, SARAH ROSALEE, administrative assistant; b. Sacramento, Calif., Oct. 5, 1941; d. Victor Lee and Grace Alla (Griggs) Argo; m. Wayne Lyle Morrison, Dec. 2, 1962 (div. 1982); children: Michael Jeffrey, Sherri Elaine Myers, Maria Denise; m. William Edward DeLacy Jr., Nov. 6, 1982. Personnel adminstrv. asst. Aerojet Liquid Rocket Co., Sacramento, 1964-75; adminstrv. asst. McClatchy Newspapers, Sacramento, 1975—. Mem. Rocklin-Roseville Bus. and Profl. Women (pres. 1989-90), Sacramento Area Literacy Coalition, Lions (pres. 1989-90). Methodist. Home: 6343 Indian Springs Rd Loomis CA 95650

DELAGE, CAROL ANNE, quality assurance consultant; b. St. Paul, Jan. 28, 1958; d. Donald Duane and Delores Anne (Mercil) D. BA, Coll. St. Catherine, St. Paul, 1980; MS, U. Minn., 1988. Nurse United Hosp., St. Paul, 1980-87, nurse educator, 1987-90; quality assurance cons. Prudential Insurance Co. America, Mpls., 1990—; lectr. Lakewood Community Coll., White Bear Lake, Minn., 1986—, Met. State U., St. Paul, 1986—. Author self-learning packet, 1987-88. Tchr. St. Pius X Ch., White Bear Lake, 1986-88. Mem. Am. Nurses Assn., North Am. Nursing Diagnosis Assn., Minn. Nursing Diagnosis Interest Group (pres. 1988—), Coll. of St. Catherine Alumnae Assn. (class rep. 1982-84, fundraiser 1984-88), Sigma Theta Tau. Office: Prudential Ins Co PO Box 1143 Minneapolis MN 55440

DE LAGUNA, FREDERICA, anthropology educator emeritus, consultant; b. Ann Arbor, Mich., Oct. 3, 1906; d. Theodore and Grace Mead (Andrus) de L. A.B., Bryn Mawr Coll., 1927; Ph.D., Columbia U., 1933; L.H.D. (hon.), U. Alaska, 1982. Asst., field dir. U. Pa. Mus., Phila., 1931-35; lectr. anthropology Bryn Mawr Coll., Pa., 1938-41, asst. prof., 1941-42, 46-49, assoc. prof., 1949-55, prof. anthropology, 1955-75, prof. emeritus, 1975—; vis. lectr. or vis. prof. U. Pa., U. Calif.-Berkeley, Bryn Mawr Coll. Author: The Thousand March: Adventures of an American Boy with Garibaldi, 1930, The Archaeology of Cook Inlet, Alaska, 1934, reprinted, 1975, The Arrow Points to Murder, 1937, Fog on the Mountain, 1938, (with Kaj Birket-Smith) The Eyak Indians of the Copper River Delta, Alaska, 1938, Prehistory of Northern America as Seen from the Yukon, 1947, Chugach Prehistory: The Archaeology of Prince William Sound, 1956, reprinted 1967, The Story of a Tlingit Community, 1960, (with others) The Archeology of the Yakutat Bay Area, Alaska, 1964, Under Mount Saint Elias, 3 vols., 1972, Voyage to Greenland: A Personal Initiation into Anthropology, 1977; editor: Selected Papers from the American Anthropologist, 1888-1920, 1960, reprinted 1976. Recipient Lindback award for Disting. Teaching, Bryn Mawr Coll., 1975, Rochester Mus. award and fellowship, 1941, numerous fellowships including: Columbia U., 1930-31, NRC, 1936-37, Rockefeller Found., 1945-46, Wenner-Gren Found., 1949-50, Social Sci. Research Council, 1962-63; grantee Am. Philos. Soc., Arctic Inst. of N.Am., Bryn Mawr Coll., NEH, NSF, U. Pa. Mus., Wenner-Gren Found. for Anthrop. Rsch. Fellow AAAS, Am. Anthrop. Assn. (pres.-elect, pres. 1965-67, Disting. Service award 1986), Arctic Inst. of N.Am. (hon. life); mem. Nat. Acad. Scis., Soc. for Am. Archaeology (1st v.p. 1949-50, 50th Ann. award 1986), Phila. Anthropology Soc. (pres. 1939-40), Alaska Anthrop. Assn. (hon. life), Homer (Alaska) Natural History Soc. (hon. life). Democrat. Home: 1830 Montgomery Ave Apt 510 Apt 510 Bryn Mawr PA 19010

DELAHANTY, LINDA MICHELE, dietitian; b. Boston, Feb. 8, 1957; d. John Joseph and Helen Mary (Salami) D.; m. Paul Joseph Gorski, June 14, 1987. BS summa cum laude, U. Mass., 1978; MS summa cum laude, Boston U., 1980. Adminstrv. dietitian Joslin Diabetic Camp, Charlton, Mass., 1978; nutritional research asst. Lemuel Shattuck Hosp., Jamaica Plain, Mass., 1979; nutrition educator Home Med. Service-Univ. Hosps., Boston, 1980, Boston City Hosp., 1980-81; clin. dietitian Mass. Gen. Hosp., Boston, 1981—; researcher Diabetes Ctr. Mass. Gen. Hosp., Boston, 1983—; nutrition coord. Diabetes Control and Complications Trial, NIH, 1987—; cons. New Eng. Diabetes and Endocrinology Ctr., Brookline, Mass., 1985-86; panelist NIH Consensus Devel. Conf., Bethesda, Md., 1986; assoc. lectr. Harvard U. Geriatric Edn. Ctr., 1984—. Contbr. articles to profl. jours. Named Young Dietitian of Yr. Am. Dietetic Assn., 1984. Mem. Mass. Area Rehab. Dietitians (co-chair 1983-84), Diabetes Care and Edn. Practice Group (sec. 1985-87), Mass. Gerontol. Nutrition Practice Group (chair 1984-85), Mass. Dietetic Assn. (chair community dietetics div. 1983-84, coun. on practices), Am. Dietetic Assn. (area coord. gerontol. nutrition and dietetic practice group 1988—). Roman Catholic. Home: 18 Saybrook Rd Framingham MA 01701 Office: Mass Gen Hosp Dept Dietetics Fruit St Boston MA 02114

DELALIC, ZDENKA JOAN, electrical engineering educator; came to U.S., 1972; d. Martin and Ana (Nemetz) D.; m. Glenn Boseman; children; Eric Marvin, Rachael Dorothy. BSEE, U. Zagreb, Yugoslavia, 1970; MSEE, U. Zagreb, 1971; MS in Systems, U. Pa., 1974, PhD, 1981. Elec. engr. GE, Phila., 1971-81, RCA, Moorestown, 1981-84; assoc. prof. Temple U., Phila., 1984—. Contbg. author: VLSI Handbook, 1989; contbr. articles to profl. jours. Recipient scholarship GE, 1975. Mem. IEEE (sect. chair chpt. 21 1985—), Internat. Soc. Hybrid Microelectronics (student chpt. advisor), Am. Soc. Elec. Engrs. Home: 202 Lone Oak Dr Bryn Mawr PA 19010 Office: Temple U Coll Engring 12th & Norris Sts Philadelphia PA 19122

DELAMATTER, DONNA ANNE, computer company executive; b. Lakewood, Ohio, Apr. 12, 1942; d. W. Richard and Martha Caroline (Jahnke) Hoecker; m. Thomas C. DeLamatter, Dec. 12, 1976. Cert. bus., Baldwin Wallace Coll., 1965. Exec. sec. World Pub. Co., Cleve., 1965-67, Mayor of Lakewood, 1968-72; adminstrv. asst. Saul N. Davidson & Assocs., Denver, 1973-76; adminstrv. asst. Telxon Corp., Akron, Ohio, 1977-79, asst. to v.p. sales, 1979-80, asst. sec., 1979-83, dir. personnel and adminstrn., 1980-83, v.p., 1983—, sec., 1983-84. Mem. Akron YWCA, bd. trustees, 1988—. Named one of Greater Cleve.'s Enterprising Women, 1986. Mem. Sales and Mktg. Execs. Akron, Catawba Island Club. Republican. Home: 273 Treetop Spur Akron OH 44321 Office: Telxon Corp 3330 W Market St Akron OH 44313

DELANEY, KATHERINE CARROLL, educational organization official; b. Leona, Kans., May 11, 1941; d. Dick and Ann M. (Meara) D. BA in Piano, Mt. St. Scholastica Coll., Atchison, Kans., 1969; MA in Philosophy, Laval U., Quebec City, Que., Can., 1973, PhD in Philosophy, 1978. Asst. prof. philosophy Benedictine Coll., Atchison, 1974-78, v.p. acad. affairs, 1978-87; acting pres. Benedictine Coll., Atchison, 1987-88; lectr. Creighton U., Omaha, 1988-89; vis. staff assoc. North Cen. Assn. Commn. on Instns. Higher Edn., Chgo., 1989-90; v.p. acad. affairs Nat. Louis U., Evanston, Ill., 1990—. Bd. dirs. Mt. St. Scholastica Coll., 1978-88. Named Adminstr. of Yr., Benedictine Coll., 1984. Democrat. Roman Catholic. Office: Nat-Louis U 2840 Sheridan Rd Evanston IL 60201

DELANEY, KATHLEEN HANLEY, broadcasting executive; b. N.Y.C., Oct. 31, 1938; d. Robert Emmett and Noreen (Broderick) Hanley; m. Paul C. Delaney, Apr. 8, 1962 (div. 1973); children: Noreen, Robert, Sheila. BA cum laude, Marymount Coll., Tarrytown, N.Y., 1960. Pres. Videoway Corp., Manhassest, N.Y., 1972-80; account exec. Turner Broadcasting, Atlanta, 1980-84; v.p. nat. sales Turner Broadcasting Inc., N.Y.C., 1984—. Mem. Better World Soc., Washington, 1985—; speaker YWCA, N.Y.C., 1983—; patron Mus. of Broadcasting, N.Y.C., 1987—, Tennis Hall of Fame, Newport, R.I., 1986—. Named Woman of Yr. YWCA, 1986. Mem. Nat. Acad. TV Arts and Scis., Nat. Assn. Broadcasters, Cousteau Soc., Mus. Broadcasting, Internat. Radio & TV Soc., Detroit Adcrafter Club. Home: 9 Barry Rd Scarsdale NY 10583 Office: Turner Broadcasting Inc 6 E 43d St New York NY 10017

DELANEY, MARION PATRICIA, advertising agency executive; b. Hartford, Conn., May 20, 1952; d. William Pride Delaney and Marian Patricia (Utley) Murphy. BA, Union Coll., Schenectady, N.Y., 1973. Adminstrv. asst. N.Y. State Assembly, Albany, 1973-74; account exec. Foote, Cone & Belding, N.Y.C., 1974-78; sr. account exec. Dailey & Assocs., Los Angeles, 1978-81; pub. relations com. NOW, Washington, 1981-83; account supr. BBDO/West, Los Angeles, 1983-85; v.p. Grey Advt., Los Angeles, 1985-87, San Francisco, 1987-89; v.p. McCann-Erickson, San Francisco, 1989—. Del. Dem. Nat. Conv., San Francisco, 1984; v.p. NOW, L.A., 1980-83, pres., 1984, advisor, 1985-87. Mem. Commonwealth Club. Congregationalist. Home: 3682 Fillmore St San Francisco CA 94123

DELANEY, MARY MARGARET, design consultant; b. Syracuse, NY, Apr. 15, 1950; d. Arthur William and Jean Louise (Dolan) D. BA, D'Youville Coll., 1972; MBA, Keller Grad. Sch., 1980. Assoc. buyer Sears Roebuck and Co., Buffalo, Calif., 1966-77, Chgo., 1977-85; design cons. Colonial Group, N.Y., 1989; sales mgr. RVL Packaging, Van Nuys, Calif., 1989—; fashion design cons. Curtis Corp. Sydney, 1988—. Roman Catholic.

DELANEY, NANCY JO, statistician, consultant; b. Buffalo, N.Y., Sept. 15, 1941; d. Howard Joseph and Josephine Laura (Garguiolo) Klein; m. Thomas James Delaney; 1 child, Kathleen Grace Delaney. BS in Math., SUNY, 1962, MS in Math., 1963; MS in Stats., Rensselaer Poly. Inst., 1975, PhD in Stats., 1979. Math. tchr. various high schs. and jr. coll., Albany, Schenectady, N.Y., 1966-74; data analyst Space Astronomy Lab., Albany, 1974-76; asst. prof. Union Coll. Inst. Adminstrn. and Mgmt., Schenectady, 1978-82, Northeastern U. Coll. Bus., Boston, 1982-88; statis. advisor Mobil Solar Energy Corp., Billerica, Mass., 1988—; cons. Gen. Foods, Inc., Tarrytown, N.Y., 1978, Sterling Drugs, Albany, 1981, Bard Cardiosurgery, Billerica, 1985-86. Contbr. articles to profl. jours. Mem. Am. Soc. for Quality Control, Ops. Rsch. Soc. Am., Am. Statis. Assn. (Boston chpt., program chmn. 1984-85, treas. 1986—), Epsilon Delta Sigma. Office: Mobil Solar Energy Corp 4 Suburban Park Dr Billerica MA 01821

DELANO, MARCIA PATRICIA, sales executive; b. N.Y.C., Mar. 17, 1939; d. Joseph and Mildred (Simkin) Getelman; m. Philip Delano, Aug. 27, 1983; children: Russell, Daryl, Dana, Lauri, Robin, Kristin. BA, SUNY, New Paltz, 1960. Pres. MD Design Co., Pompton Lakes, N.J., 1985—, Delta Force Temporary Svc., Inc., Totowa, N.J., 1990—. Mem. Women in Cable, C. of C. Home: 41 Van Ness Ave Pompton Lakes NJ 07442 Office: 41 Vreeland Ave Totowa NJ 07512

DELANY, DANA, actress; b. N.Y.C.. Student, Wesleyan U. Appeared in TV series Love of Life, As the World Turns, Magnum PI, 1986-88, China Beach, 1988— (Emmy award for best actress in a drama series 1989), in TV films Threesome, 1984, Liberty, 1986, A Winner Never Quits, 1986, in films Almost You, 1985, Where the River Runs Black, 1986, Masquerade, 1988, Moon over Parador, 1988. Office: care Triad Artists Inc 10100 Santa Monica Blvd 16th Fl Los Angeles CA 90067*

DELANY, IRENE BEISSNER, obstetrician-gynecologist; b. San Antonio, Dec. 7, 1945; d. Emmet A. and Agnes A. (Lamm) Beissner; m. Stephen Delany, May 29, 1966 (div. 1981); children: Tiffany, Cynthia; m. Thomas Steckel, May 2, 1987. BS, St. Mary's U., San Antonio, 1967; MD, U. Tex. Health Sci. Ctr., San Antonio, 1980. Diplomate Am. Bd. Ob.-Gyn. Computer programmer 1st Nat. Bank Chgo., 1967-69; efficiency analyst 1st Nat. Bank, San Antonio, 1972-75; intern U. Tex. Health Sci. Ctr., Med. Ctr. Hosp., San Antonio, 1980-81, resident, 1981-84; pvt. practice physician San Antonio, 1984-87; physician Family Dr. Med. Group, Benicia, Calif., 1987—; vice-chmn. dept. ob-gyn., chmn. quality rev. com. Mt. Diablo Hosp., Concord, Calif., 1990—. Fellow Am. Coll. Ob.-Gyn.; mem. Calif. Med. Assn., Solano, Alpha Omega Alpha. Roman Catholic. Office: Family Dr Med Group 160 East N St Benicia CA 94510

DELAROSA, DENISE MARIA, legal administrator; b. Oakland, Calif., Dec. 30, 1954; d. David and Doris Elizabeth (Cantrell) Eirich; m. Robert Joseph Turocy, Dec. 30, 1972 (div. Dec. 1976); children: Robert Justin, Shannon James; m. Oscar Quiroga DeLaRosa, May 1, 1983. AAS, Truman Coll., 1983; BABA, DePaul U., 1987. Legal adminstr. Taylor, Miller, Sprowl, Hoffnagle & Merletti, Chgo., 1985—; ESL tutor Literacy Vols., Chgo., 1985-86; mem. Lincoln Park Zool. Soc., Chgo. Mem. ABA (assoc.), Ill. Bar Assn., Women Employed, Law Office Mgrs. Assn. of Chgo., Assn. Legal Adminstrs., Chgo. Pub. Schs. Alumni Assn. Democrat. Methodist. Office: Taylor Miller Sprowl Hoffnagle & Merletti 33 N LaSalle Ste 2222 Chicago IL 60602

DE LARROCHA, ALICIA, concert pianist; b. Barcelona, Spain, May 23, 1923; d. Eduardo and Teresa (De La Calle) de L.; m. Juan Torra, June 21, 1950; children: Juan, Alicia. Grad. (prize extraordinary, Gold medal), Acad. Marshall, Barcelona; MusD (hon.), U. Ann Arbor, 1979, Middlebury Coll., 1981, Carnegie-Mellon, 1985. Debut, Barcelona, 1929, solo recitalist, concert pianist maj. orchs. in, Europe, U.S., Can., Cen. and S.Am., South Africa, New Zealand, Australia, Japan; dir. Acad. Marshall, 1959—; rec. artist: Hispavox, CBS, Decca-London; records; (Grammy award 1974, 75, 78, 79, 1st Gold medal Merito a la Vocacion 1972). Recipient Harriet Cohen Internat. Music award, 1968; Paderewski Meml. medal, 1961; Grand prix du Disque Acad. Charles Cros, 1960, 74; Edison award, 1968; decorated Order Civil Merit Order Isabel la Catolica, Spain). Mem. Musica en Compostela (dir.), Hispanic Soc. Am. (corr.), Internat. Piano Archives (hon. pres.). Office: Farmaceutic Carbonell, 46-48 Atic, Barcelona 34, Spain Office:

Columbia Artists Mgmt Inc care Wilford Div 165 W 57th St New York NY 10019

DELAURO, ROSA, congresswoman. Student, London Sch. Econs. & Polit. Sci., 1962-63; BA in History and Polit Sci. cum laude, Marymount Coll., 1964; MA in Internat. Politics, Columbia U., 1966. Tng. assoc. Community Progress Inc., New Haven, Conn., 1967-69; instr. in internat. rels. Albertus Magnus Coll., 1967-68; adminstrv. asst. Nat. Urban Fellows, 1969-72, asst. dir., dir., 1972-75; city coord. Carter-Mondale Presdl. Campaign, New Haven, 1976; exec. asst. Mayor Frank Logue, New Haven, 1976-77, campaign mgr., 1977; exec. asst., devel. adminstr. City of New Haven, 1977-79; campaign mgr. Chris Dodd for U.S. Senate, 1979-80, 86; adminstrv. asst. U.S. Senator Christopher J. Dodd, Washington, 1981-87; state dir. Mondale-Ferraro Presdl. Campaign, N.J., 1986; ptnr. DeLauro-Geller, 1987-88; regional dir. Dukakis for Pres. Campaign, N.Y., N.J., Con.., 1988; exec. dir. EMILY's List, 1989; elected to U.S. Ho. of Reps., 1990; del. to Dem. Nat. Conv., 1984; bd. dirs. Pax Ams. Bd. dirs. Shubert Theater for Performing Arts, New Haven; past pres. New Haven Arts Coun. Assoc. fellow Timothy Dwight Coll., Yale U.; recipient Leadership award Am. Com. on Italian Migration. Mem. Nat. Italian-Am. Found., Dem. Women for Progress. Office: Offices of House Members care The Postmaster Washington DC 20515*

DE LA VEGA, DIANNE WINIFRED DEMARINIS (MRS. JORGE DE LA VEGA), government official; b. Cleve.; d. Gerald M. and Dorothy (Philp) DeMarinis; student Case Western Res. U., 1948-50, MA, 1969; BA, U. Am., 1952; PhD in Psychology, Internat. Coll., Los Angeles, 1977; MA, Goddard Coll., 1978; m. Jorge Alejandro de la Vega, July 19, 1952; children: Constance, Francisco Javier, Alexandra. Faculty, Western Res. U., Cleve., 1961-62; instr. Instituto Mexicano-Norteamericano de Relaciones Culturales, Mexico, 1967; supr. fgn. press Mexican Olympic Organizing Com., Mexico, 1968; asst. to producer Producciones Ojo, Canal 8 TV, Mexico, 1969; exec. asst. Internat. Exec. Service Corps, Mexico City, 1969-70; asst. to dir. U.S. Internat. U. Mexico, Mexico City, 1970-75; family planning evaluator for Latin Am., AID, 1976; with dept. spl. edn. region IX Nat. Ctr. on Child Abuse and Neglect, Children's Bur., Office Child Devel., HEW, Calif. State U., 1977—. Chmn. Puppet's Jr. League, Mexico City, 1967, chmn. ways and means, 1968; sec. Tlaxcala-Okla. Partner's of Alliance for Progress, 1967—; pres. acculturating hispanic refugee children Los Angeles Unified Sch. Dist.; bd. dirs. Hot Line of Mexico City; mem. Los Angeles adv. com. 1984 Olympics. Lic. marriage and family counselor. Mem. Los Angeles chpt. Calif. Marriage and Family Therapists Assn., Flying Samaritans, Pro Salud Maternal, Transactional Analysis Assn. Club: Jr. League (Los Angeles). Home: 130 Alta Ave D Santa Monica CA 90402

DELAY, DOROTHY (MRS. EDWARD NEWHOUSE), violinist, educator; b. Medicine Lodge, Kans., Mar. 31, 1917; d. Glenn Adney and Cecile (Osborn) DeLay; m. Edward Newhouse, Mar. 5, 1941; children: Jeffrey H., Alison Dinsmore. Student, Oberlin Coll., 1933-34, MusD (hon.), 1981; BA, Mich. State U., 1937; Artists diploma, Juilliard Grad. Sch. Music, 1941. Prof. violin The Juilliard Sch., N.Y.C., 1947—, Starling prof. violin, 1987—; mem. faculty Sarah Lawrence Coll., 1948-87, Meadowmount Summer Sch. Music, Westport, N.Y., 1948-70, Aspen Summer Music Sch., 1971—; Starling prof. violin U. Cin., 1974—; vis. prof. violin Phila. Coll. Performing Arts, 1977-83, New Eng. Conservatory, 1978-87, Royal Coll. Music, Eng., 1987—; condr. Master classes univs. and conservatories in U.S., Europe, Asia, Africa, Near East. Solo, chamber music performances in, U.S., Can., S.Am., 1937-46, violinist, founder, Stuyvesant Trio, 1940-42; Contbr. articles on violins, violinists to various encys. Recipient Outstanding Artist-Tchr. award Am. String Tchrs. Assn., 1975, Highest honor citation Fedn. of Music Clubs, 1983, Gov.'s award State of Kans., 1982, Alumni Accomplishment award Mich. State U., 1984, King Solomon award America-Israel Cultural Found., 1985. Fellow Royal Coll. Music, Gt. Brit.; mem. Mu Phi Epsilon (award of merit 1989). Home: 349 N Broadway Upper Nyack NY 10960 Office: Juilliard Sch Lincoln Center Pla New York NY 10023

DELBONO, ELIZABETH ANNE, researcher; b. Brighton, Mass., Sept. 8, 1951; d. Adam Alfred and Victoria Anne (Simons) D. BA, Emmanuel Coll., Boston, 1973; MPH, Boston U., Sch. Pub. Health, 1982. Rsch. assoc. Faulkner & Lemuel Shattuck Hosp., Boston, 1973-90; epidemiology studies rsch. assoc., epidemiology unit Mass. Eye and Ear Infirmary, Boston, 1990—. Author: Contbr. articles to profl. jours., 1978--. Recipient Psi Chi award Nat. Honor Soc. in Psychology, 1973, Sigma Chi Nat. Honor Soc., 1973. Mem. Mass. Thoracic Soc., Am. Pub. Health Assn., N.Y. Acad. Sci., Internat. Lung Sounds Assn. Roman Catholic. Home: 1662 Commonwealth Ave Brighton MA 02135 Office: Mass Eye and Ear Infirmary Epidemiology Unit 243 Charles St Boston MA 02114

DEL CARMEN, REBECCA, psychologist; b. San Diego, Oct. 18, 1957; d. Alberto Ong and Amelia (Touma) Del C. BA, Cath. U., Fredericksburg, Va., 1979; MA, Cath. U. Am., 1981; PhD, Ohio State U., Columbus, 1987. Asst. prof. Am. U., Washington, 1987-89; rsch. fellow NIH, Bethesda, Md., 1989—. Author: (book chpt.) Asian-American Family Assessment, 1990, Prenatal Stress, 1990. Psychologist Project Cope and Hope (mental health for homeless), Washington, 1990—. NIH Rsch. grantee, 1989. Mem. Am. Psychol. Assn., Soc. for Rsch. in Child Devel. Democrat. Roman Catholic. Office: NIH 9000 Rockville Pike Bldg 31 B2B15 Bethesda MD 20892

DEL CASTILLO, JEANNE LOUISE TAILLAC, oil industry executive; b. New Orleans, May 15, 1933; d. Roland Jean and Louise (Schwall) Taillac; m. Roberto Eduardo del Castillo (div.); children: Esther, Jeanne, Roberto, Eduardo, Tammy. Nursing student, Charity Hosp., New Orleans, 1951-52; student, various bus. mgmt. courses, 1952-86. Asst. office mgr. Ray Merc. Co., New Orleans, 1958-64; consul, maritime comml. officer Consulate Gen. Panama, New Orleans, 1964-72; mgr. McDermott Internat., Inc., New Orleans, 1972—; pres., owner Kiddie Kare Train'n Sta.; cons. Consulates of Panama, Houston, New Orleans, 1972—; coordinator Panama Maritime Licensing, 1985—. Co-chmn. Jerry Lewis Telethon, New Orleans, 1977; fundraising co-chair Annual Handicapped Children's Easter Parade, bd. dirs. La. Sch. for Deaf, Baton Rouge, 1985—, Sta. WNNR-Radio, 1972-74, New Orleans Soccer Assn., 1969-73; pres. Costa Rica Soccer Assn., 1969-72; fundraiser Bayside Vol. Fire Dept., Bay St. Louis, Miss., 1986—; co-chmn. State Sex Edn. Handicapped Children Comn., Baton Rouge, 1986—; chmn. Handicapped Children Christmas Program; coord. various Christmas programs for sick, elderly and needy; mem. Hancock County Humane Soc. Recipient merit award Bayside Fire Dept., Bay St. Louis, 1987, New Orleans Soccer Leagues merit award, 1971. Mem. Panama Maritime Adv. Com., Panama C. of C. and Industry, U.S. C. of C. in Panama, Miss. C. of C. Republican. Roman Catholic. Home: 4413 Senac Dr Metairie LA 70003

DELCOTTO, PAMELA MARIE, therapist; b. Angola, Ind., Jan. 20, 1956; d. Jack George and Wanda Lee (Townson) Danford; children: Adrianne Marie, Aaron Alexander. BS in Edn., Ohio U., 1978, MEd, 1979. Cert. art tchr. Substance abuse counselor Residential Treatment Program, Athens, Ohio, 1978-80; substitute tchr. Athens County Schs, 1979-86; pre sch. tchr. Athens (Ohio) Recreation Dept., 1986-87; instr. activity therapy Hocking Tech. Coll., Nelsonville, Ohio; art therapist, clin. supr. activity therapy Athens (Ohio) Mental Health Ctr., 1987--. Jr. ch. coord., tchr. Richland United Meth. Ch., Athens, 1986-88; Brownie leader Black Diamond coun., Girl Scouts U.S.A., 1986-88. Mem. Buckeye Art Theraphy Assn. Home: 28 United Apts Athens OH 45701 Office: Athens Mental Health Ctr Richland Ave Athens OH 43701

DELEHANTY, MARY JOAN, association executive; b. Rutland, Vt., July 26, 1936; d. Joseph Nicholas and Madeline (McCarthy) D. BS, Mary Washington Coll., Fredericksburg, Va., 1957; MS, Boston U., 1968; PhD, SUNY, Albany, 1989. Lic. phys. therapist. Phys. therapist Coolidge Hill Sch., Pittsfield, Mass., 1957-59, Vt. Rehab. Ctr., Burlington, 1959-61; clin. coordinator Cerebral Palsy Ctr., Albany, N.Y., 1961-67; dir. tng. in phys. therapy Shriver Ctr., Waltham, Mass., 1968-74; coordinator grad. prog. Sargent Coll., Boston, 1974-76; lectr., cons. U. Vt., Burlington, 1976-84; assoc. dir. edn. Am. Phys. Therapy Assn., Alexandria, Va., 1988—; cons. in field. Pres. Forest Park Assn., South Burlington, 1984. Presdl. fellow, SUNY, Albany, 1984-88. Mem. Am. Phys. Therapy Assn., Am. Sociol. Assn., Am. Assn. for Adult Edn. Roman Catholic. Home: 1341 Chetworth Ct Alexandria VA 22314 Office: Am Phys Therapy Assn 1111 N Fairfax St Alexandria VA 22314

DE LEMOS, SHEILA VICTORIA, photographer; b. Bklyn., Feb. 12, 1949; d. William and Gussie (Herman) Herman; m. Richard Alan de Lemos, June 18, 1969; 1 child, Brian. BFA, U. Miami, Coral Gables, Fla., 1985, MFA in Photography, 1987. Pvt. practice Coconut Grove, Fla., 1978—; teaching asst. U. Miami, Coral Gables, 1983-87, adj. prof., 1985-86, 89, Barry U., Miami Shores, Fla., 1986; photography instr. Ransom Everdades Day Sch., Coconut Grove. Photographer: University of Miami Art Department Catalog, 1985, Picture South Florida, 1988; designer, photographer: Innerspace, 1987; exhibited in group shows, including Impact: Women of South Florida Hist. Mus. So. Fla., 1989. Pres. Riviera Day Sch. Parents Orgn., Coral Gables, 1983-84. Recipient Photo awards Lowe Art Mus., Coral Gables, 1982, 83, 84, 85, Photographic Services award, Miami, Fla., 1985. Mem. Photogroup Miami (photography award 1984), Am. Soc. Mag. Photographers, Inc. (asst. editor bull. 1987-88), Coll. Art Assn., South Miami Bus. Network. Republican. Jewish.

DELEO, MARYANN, journalist, television producer; b. N.Y.C., Aug. 13, 1952; d. Dominic Anthony and Dorothy (Terranova) DeL. BA, SUNY, Old Westbury, 1978. Reporter, producer Downtown Community TV Ctr., N.Y.C., 1980—; photographer SIPA Press, N.Y.C., 1985—; reporter, producer NBC, 1985—; producer, directorof documentary HBO, 1990—. Recipient grand prize Tokyo Video Festival, 1985, Nat. Emmy award NATAS, 1986, Cine Eagle award, 1989; fellow N.Y. Found. for Arts, N.Y. State Coun. on Arts, 1989. Mem. Nat. Press Photographers' Assn.

DE LEON, LIDIA MARIA, magazine editor; b. Havana, Cuba, Sept. 10, 1957; d. Leon J. and Lydia (Diaz Cruz) de L. B.A. in Communications cum laude, U. Miami, Coral Gables, Fla., 1979. Staff writer Miami Herald, Fla., 1978-79; editorial asst. Halsey Pub. Co., Miami, 1980-81, assoc. editor, 1981, editor, 1981—, editor Delta Sky mag., 1983—. Mem. Fla. Mag. Assn., Am. Soc. Mag. Editors, Golden Key Nat. Honor Soc., Am. Assn. Travel Editors, Sigma Delta Chi. Democrat. Roman Catholic. Clubs: Jockey, Cricket (Miami). Office: Delta Sky 12955 Biscayne Blvd North Miami FL 33181

DELEON, PATRICIA ANASTASIA, human geneticist, educator; b. Port Maria, Jamaica, W.I., July 13, 1944; came to U.S., 1976; d. Leonard Percival and Louise Monica (Green) Martin; m. Winston Emanuel DeLeon, Dec. 16, 1971; children: Ruth, Jeffrey. BSc, U. W.I., Kingston, 1967, MSc in Med. Genetics, 1969; PhD in Microscopic Anatomy, U. Western Ont., 1972. Postdoctoral fellow McGill U., Montreal, Que., Can., 1972-75, sessional lectr., 1975-76; asst. prof. sch. life scis. U. Del., 1976-81; assoc. prof. biology dept., U. Del., Newark, 1981—; vis. scientist Sch. Medicine, Johns Hopkins U., Balt., 1983-84; vis. scientist, speaker Franklin Inst., Phila., 1990—; genetic counselor; cons. Tektagen, Malvern, Pa., 1990—. Bd. dirs. local chpt. March of Dimes. Jamaica Tchrs. scholar, 1964-67; NIH rsch. grantee, 1980-88. Mem. Am. Soc. Human Genetics, Del. Tchrs. Sci., Sigma Xi (sec. Del. chpt. 1981-82, v.p. 1982-83, 85). Presbyterian. Contbr. book chpts., articles to sci. jours. Avocations: cooking, gardening, theatre. Office: U Del Sch Life and Health Scis Newark DE 19716

DELESSIO-NEUBAUER, ELIZABETH MARY, school psychologist; b. Queens, N.Y., July 20, 1950; d. James William and Elizabeth Fay (Pell) DeLessio; m. John Daniel Neubauer, Nov. 14, 1982; children: Mary Elizabeth Teicher, Kathryn. BA, SUNY, 1977; MS, Coll. New Rochelle, 1982; PhD in Psychology, Yeshiva U., Bronx, N.Y., 1990. Sch. psychologist Wappingers (N.Y.) Cen. Schools, 1982--; cons. Early Edn. Ctr., Highland, N.Y., 1982--. Mem. Nat. Assn. of Sch. Psychologists, N.Y. Assn. of Sch. Psychologist, Phi Theta Kappa. Home: 330 Beekman Rd Hopewell Junction NY 12533 Office: Wappingers Schs 26 Old Rte 9 Wappingers Falls NY 12590

DELGADO, LENORE R., bilingual editor, educator; b. N.Y.C., Oct. 31, 1948; d. Irving and Ruth (Horngrad) Reisman; m. G. Delgado, Jan. 25, 1976 (div. July 1982). BA, Bklyn. Coll., 1969; MA, Stanford U., 1972, AB, 1974. Prof. English Nat. Autonomous U. of Mex., Mexico City, 1977-83; nat. ESL cons. McGraw-Hill Internat., Mexico City, 1983-85; freelance ESL writer Prentice Hall/Regents, Englewood Cliffs, N.J., 1986-88; ESL instr. Bronx (N.Y.) Community Coll., 1988; acting asst. prof. Spanish L.I. U., Bklyn., 1988; Spanish instr. Chabot Coll., Haywood, Calif., 1989-90, DeAnza Coll., Cupertino, Calif., 1989—; bilingual editor Addison-Wesley Publ. Co., Menlo Park, Calif., 1989-90, Microlytics Corp., Rochester, N.Y., 1990—. Author: Diálogo cortado, 1985, (with others) Reading Comprehension for Psychology, 1980; editor: Mathematics (Spanish ed.), 1990, (software) Spanish WordFinder, 1990. Mem. Am. Assn. of Tchrs. of Spanish and Portuguese, Tchrs. of English to Speakers of Other Langs., Phi Beta Kappa.

DELGADO, LUCIA DE LA CARIDAD, physical therapist; b. Havana, Cuba, Aug. 11, 1964; came to U.S., 1968; d. Francisco and Elena (De La Vega) D. AA, Miami-Dade Community Coll., 1986; BS in Phys. Therapy, Fla. Internat. U., 1988. Registered phys. therapist, Fla. Phys. therapy aide Palmetto Gen. Hosp., Miami, 1985-87, Parkway Regional Med. Ctr., Miami, 1987-88; staff phys. therapist Mount Sinai Med. Ctr., Miami, 1988—. Mem. Am. Phys. Therapy Assn., NAFE, Women's Internat. Tennis Assn., U.S. Tennis Assn., Fla. Internat. U. Alumni Assn. Home: 528 E 33rd St Hialeah FL 33013

DEL GALDO, BICE, human resource professional; b. Gioi, Italy; d. Giovanni and Anna (Ferra) Del G.; children: Jeannette, Lori Santora. BSBA, Montclair (N.J.) State Coll., 1980; MBA, Fairleigh Dickinson U., 1985. Adminstrv. asst. Tri-Chem, Inc., Harrison, N.J., 1975-77, employee rels. adminstr., 1977-81; employee rels. mgr. Prescolite U.S.I., Inc., San Leandro, Calif., 1981-84, Purolator Courier Corp., Basking Ridge, N.J., 1984-86; personnel mgr. Brevel Motors, Inc. subs. Vernitron Corp., 1986-88; sr. assoc. Mgmt. Cons. Firm, N.J., 1988-89; human resource mgr. Ames, Inc., Secaucus, N.J., 1989—. Mem. Soc. of Human Resource Mgmt. Office: Ames Inc 125 Castle Rd Secaucus NJ 07094

DELGORIO, FRANCES ANN, real estate executive; b. S.I., N.Y., Feb. 10, 1954; d. Benjamin and Josephine (DeGrace) Rabito; m. Michael Delgorio, May 17, 1975. BS summa cum laude, N.Y. Inst. Tech., 1981; real estate diploma, NYU, 1987. Legal adminstr., paralegal Warner & Stackpole, Boston, 1982-85; real estate portfolio mgr. Sibag Investments, Inc., N.Y.C., 1985—. Mem., vol. Make a Wish Found., Westchester, N.Y., 1989—. Mem. Am. Legion Aux. : 3 Georgia Ln Croton on Hudson NY 10520 Office: Sibag Investments Inc 767 Fifth Ave New York NY 10153

DELIA, SYLVIA, television distribution company executive; b. N.Y.C., May 7, 1954; d. Arthur Lester and Melinda Norris (Kennedy) Talkington; m. Joseph Francis Delia, June 26, 1976. BA, Sarah Lawrence Coll., 1976. Freelance prodn. asst., stylist N.Y.C., 1976-78; asst. producer N. Bonet Enterprises, Ltd., N.Y.C., 1978-80; exec. dir. Victorian Video, N.Y.C., 1981-83; dir. programming Wometco Home Theatre, Fairfield, N.J., 1983-84; v.p. sales WW Entertainment, N.Y.C., 1984-88; dir. acquisitions and mktg. 4D TV, Paris, 1988-89; v.p. cable sales BBC Lionheart TV, N.Y.C., 1989—. Mem. Nat. Acad. Cable Programming, N.Y. Women in Film (co-chmn. programming com. 1987-89, v.p. bd. dirs.). Democrat. Home: 53 Hickory Hill Rd Tappan NY 10983 Office: BBC Lionheart TV 630 Fifth Ave Ste 2220 New York NY 10111

DELIBERO, MARY SMELLIE, insurance; b. Hartford, Conn., Nov. 6, 1950; d. Robert Henderson and Dorothy Lee (Jones) Smellie; m. Philip Lee DeLibero, Dec. 18, 1976 (div. 1987); children: Anthony Philip, Mark Edward. MusB, Queens Coll., Charlotte, N.C., 1972; MusM, Hartt Coll. of Mus., W. Hartford, Conn., 1975; student, Inst. European Studies, Vienna, Austria, 1971. Instr. Piano Westfield (Mass.) State Coll., 1974-83; instr. piano Hartt Sch. of Mus., W. Hartford, Conn., 1974-78; underwriter CIGNA Corp., Group Pension Div., Hartford, Conn., 1984-88, trainer/tech. writer, 1988—; solo and chamber recitalist, Conn., Mass., N.Y. 1974-83. Events Coord. United Way (CIGNA Campaign), Hartford, 1986 (solicitor 1988), com. mem. CARE SHARE, Hartford, 1987. Presser Found Mus. scholar, Charlotte, N.C. 1970; recipient Charlotte Mus. Club Award, 1971, 76. Mem. Delta Omicron (pres. 1971-72). Congregational. Home: 14 Randal Ave West Hartford CT 06110

DELIBES, CLAUDE BLANCHE, communications company executive; b. Paris, Sept. 20, 1932; came to U.S., 1940; naturalized, 1954; d. Andre Jean and Simone (Barou) Seligmann; m. Maurice Delibes, Dec. 31, 1961; 1 child by previous marriage, Roger Schwartz; 1 child, Jacqueline Delibes, 1954. B.A., Sorbonne U., Paris, 1953 . Editor Fairchild Publications, N.Y.C., 1961-65; dir. pub. rels. West Point Pepperell Corp., N.Y.C., 1968-72; sr. account supr. The Siesel Co., N.Y.C., 1972-75; pres. Delibes Communications, Ltd., N.Y.C., 1975—. Mem. Women Execs. in Pub. Rels., Fashion Group, Internat. Furnishings and Design Assn., Euro-Am. Club. Home: 1601 Third Ave New York NY 10028 Office: 200 W 57th St New York NY 10019

DELIZASOAIN, PATRICIA MARIA, data processing executive, accountant; b. Washington D.C., July 3, 1962; d. Gabriel V. and Barbara Joan (Swift) DeL. BS in Acctg., Fla. Atlantic U., 1984, MBA, 1985. CPA, Fla.; lic. real estate and mortgage broker, pilot. Acct. Peat Marwick Main (KPMG), Ft. Lauderdale, Fla., 1986-87; pres. and programmer Cee Concepts, Inc., Boca Raton, Fla., 1982—; v.p. Cee Peripherals, Inc., Boca Raton, 1982-88; real estate salesman Realteck of Caldwell Bankers, Miami Lakes, Fla., 1984—; prof. Palm Beach Community Coll., Boca Raton, 1988—; comptroller and mgmt. cons. Brown Mgmt. Group, Deerfield Beach, Fla., 1989—; network dir. Nat. Assn. of Female Execs., Boca Raton. Mem. Aircraft Owners & Pilots Assn., Fla., 1987—. Recipient U.S. All Am. Swimming, U.S. Masters Swimming, 1987. Mem. Am. Inst. of CPAs, Fla. Inst. of CPAs, Mission Bay Club. Republican. Roman Catholic.

DELL, DIANA LYNN, obstetrician, gynecologist; b. Kirksville, Mo., Sept. 20, 1948; d. Leonard E. and Ruby (Davidson) D. BA in Psychology, U. New Orleans, 1971; BS in Nursing, William Carey Coll., 1976; MD, La. State U., 1982. Diplomate Am. Bd. Ob-Gyn. Intern and resident Charity Hosp. of New Orleans, 1982-86; pvt. practice Baton Rouge, 1986—. Fellow Am. Coll. Ob-Gyn; mem. AMA, Am. Med. Women's Assn. (pres. local br. 1988, regional gov.). Republican. Office: 8304 O'Hara Ct Baton Rouge LA 70806

DELL, RUTH HARTMAN, psychologist, educator; b. Wauseon, Ohio, Jan. 18, 1918; d. Carl Floyd and Pearl Viola (Reynolds) Hartmann; m. Charles E. Dell, Feb. 4, 1950; children: John C., James. R. AB, U. Mich., 1939, MS, 1947, MClinPsychology, 1948. Intern, counselor Bur. Psychol. Svcs. U. Mich., Ann Arbor, 1947-49, counselor Mental Health Svc., 1949-51. Mem. Fairfax County Sch. Bd., Fairfax, Va., 1974-80, Human Rights Com. No. Va. Tng. Ctr., Fairfax, 1987—, Va. PTA (life); pres. Fairfax County PTA, 1968-70; pres. Hollin Hills Community Assn., 1982-84; bd. dirs. Mt. Vernon Health Ctr., 1982-87. Recipient Community Svc. award No. Va. br. Urban League, 1980; named Life Mem. Va. PTA. Mem. AAUW, Mental Health Assn. No. Va., U. Mich. Alumni Assn., Fairfax Com. of 100 (treas. 1988—), LWV (chmn. Fairfax unit 1988—), Delta Kappa Gamma (hon.). Democrat. Unitarian. Home: 1819 Drury Ln Alexandria VA 22307

DELLACATO, CHRISTINE LISA, financial analyst; b. N.Y.C., May 18, 1965; d. Michael Joseph and Florence (Opesso) D. BS in Econs., Boston U., 1987. Account rep. Grove Savs. Bank, Boston, 1987-88; account adminstr., sr. account adminstr., sales rep. Bond Timing Svcs., Waltham, Mass., 1988-89; sales rep. Bond Timing Securities, Waltham, 1989; fin. cons. Merrill Lynch, San Diego, 1989—. Mem. NAFE, Boston U. Alumni Assn., Jaycees, San Diego Athletic Club. Republican. Roman Catholic. Home: 12837 Cijon St San Diego CA 92129 Office: Merrill Lynch 701 B St Ste 2400 San Diego CA 92101

DELLAFERA, MARY ANN, neuroscientist, veterinarian, educator; b. Wilmington, Del., Mar. 29, 1954; d. Vincent William and Mary (Rickel) DellaFera. BA in Biology, U. Del., 1975; VMD, U. Pa., 1979, PhD in neuroscience, 1980. Rsch. asst. prof. Univ. Pa., Phila., 1982; rsch. specialist Monsanto Co., St. Louis, 1982-84, rsch. group leader, 1984-86; rsch. asst. prof. Washington U. Sch. Medicine, St. Louis, 1986-89; resident in lab. animal medicine, rsch. asst. prof. U. Pa., Phila., 1989—; adj. asst. prof. U. Mo., 1987-89, 90—. Contbr. articles to profl. jours. Mem. Soc. for Neuroscience, Am. Physiol. Soc., Am. Vet. Med. Assn., Mo. Office: U Pa Univ Lab Animal Resources 100 Blockley Hall Philadelphia PA 19104-6021

DELLAGNENA, GAIL LYNN, computer specialist; b. Akron, Ohio, Oct. 19, 1956; d. George McInnes and Iva Gena (Ridgeway) Massie. BA in Polit. Sci., Kent (Ohio) State U., 1977. Programmer Soc. Nat. Bank, Cleve., 1982-84; programmer, analyst Ohio Savs. and Loan, Cleve., 1984-86, Coulter Electronics Inc., Hialeah, Fla., 1986-89; with Paccar Inc., Renton, Wash., 1990—. Served with U.S. Army, 1978-82. Mem. NOW, Am. Mgmt. Assn. Democrat. Presbyterian. Home: 13305 NE 171 St Apt D-227 Woodenville WA 98072 Office: Paccar Mgmt Info. Systems 480 Houser Way North Renton WA 98055

DELLA PAOLERA, ELISABETH, educator; b. Newton, Mass., Dec. 20, 1950; d. Henry Jerome and Alma Elizabeth (Lungren) Della P. BA cum laude, Curry Coll., 1973; MEd, Boston U., 1980. Cert. tchr., Mass. Tchr. Cambridge (Mass.) Pub. Schs., 1976—; cons., IBM Corp., Atlanta, 1988—; speaker on computer-use in edn., various profl. confs. Co-designer, editorial developer ednl. software and manuals; contbr. articles to edn. publs. Mem. Boston U. Women Grad. Club. Home: Apt 76 10 Williams St Watertown MA 02172 Office: Sch of Future Tobin Sch 197 Vassal Ln Cambridge MA 02138

DELLOMO, PATRICIA TURVEY, real estate executive; b. S.I., N.Y., Apr. 19, 1938; d. Samuel Aloysius and Alice (Cosgrove) Turvey; m. Frank Dellomo, Oct. 28, 1961; children: Tracy, Alysen. BA, Chestnut Hill Coll., 1959. Real estate sales person The Turvey Agency, Staten Island, N.Y., 1959-64; real estate appraiser & broker The Turvey Agency, Staten Island, 1964, sr. real estate appraiser, 1968, pres., sr. broker and appraiser, 1970—. Founder and pres. Jr. Vis. Nurse Assn., S.I., 1965; treas. Vis. Nurse Assn., S.I., 1968; pres. Vis. Nurse Assn., S.I., 1972-76. Mem. Soc. of Real Estate Appraisers (sr. mem.), N.Y. State Soc. Real Estate Appraisers, Staten Island Bd. of Realtors, L.I. Bd. of Realtors. Home: Pound Hollow Rd Old Brookville NY 11545 Office: The Turvey Agy 513 Bement Ave Staten Island NY 10310

DELOHERY, HOLLY, social worker; b. White Plains, N.Y., Dec. 8, 1952; d. Michael Frances III and Madeline (W.) D. AB in Psychology, Roger Williams Coll., 1975; student, Fordham U., 11975-78, Columbia U., 1985. Mental health worker in psychiat. nursing dept. N.Y. Hosp. Cornell Med. Ctr., Westchester Div., White Plains, 1976-84; social svcs. Westchester County, White Plains, 1984—. Active Jr. League of Greenwich (Conn.), 1988, Girl Scouts U.S. Mem. Roger Williams Alumni Assn., Child Welfare League Am., Old Greenwich Yacht Club. Home: 35 Putnam Green A Greenwich CT 06830 Office: Westchester County 112 E Post Rd 4th Fl White Plains NY 10601-4201

DE LONG, ERIKA VENTA, psychiatrist; b. Riga, Latvia, Oct. 14, 1925; came to U.S., 1949; d. Janis and Zinaida (v. Weseler) Cielens; m. Mark Eldridge De Long, Apr. 12, 1952; 1 child, Ruth Ellen De Long Pearce. Cand Med, U. Goettingen, 1949; MD, U. Vienna, 1957. Diplomate Am. Bd. Psychiatry and Neurology. Fellow in cardiovascular rsch. Mt. Zion Hosp., San Francisco, 1957-58; intern Trumbull Meml. and Hosp., Warren, Ohio, 1958-59; resident in psychiatry Cleve. Psychiat. Inst. and Hosp., 1959-63; pvt. practice Cleve., 1963—; chmn. psychiat. dept. Fairview Gen. Hosp., Cleve., 1981—. Mem. Rep. Task Force, Washington, 1981. Mem. AMA, Ohio Med Assn., Cleve. Acad. Medicine, Cleve. Psychiat. Soc., Ohio Trotting Assn., Cleve. Playhouse. Lutheran. Home: 4495 Valley Forge Dr Fairview Park OH 44126 Office: 20800 Westgate Pla Fairview Park OH 44126

DE LONG, KATHARINE, retired secondary teacher; b. Germantown, Pa., Aug. 31, 1927; d. Melvin Clinton and Katherine Frances (Brunner) Barr; m. Alfred Alvin De Long, June 21, 1947; children: Renée, Claudia, Jane. AA, Mesa Jr. Coll., Grand Junction, Colo., 1962; BA, Western State Coll., Gunnison, Colo., 1964; MA, Colo. State U., 1972. Tchr. Mesa County Valley Sch. Dist. #51, Grand Junction, 1964-84; ret., 1984; substitute tchr. Mesa

Coll., 1986-90. Bd. dirs. Chipeta Girl Scout Coun., Grand Junction, 1960-66; pct. committeewoman Mesa County Dem. Party; mem., vice-chmn. Profl. Rights and Responsibilities Commn. for Dist. #51 Schs., Grand Junction, 1978-84; trustee Western Colo. Ctr. for the Arts, Grand Junction, 1987-88; mem. Mesa County Hist. Soc. Mem. AAUW (pres. local chpt. 1979-81, chmn. state cultural interest), Am. Assn. Ret. Persons (Colo. legis. com. Area I, asst. state dir., mem. transp. task force), Pub. Employers Retirement Assn. (legis. adv. com. 1990-91), Colo. Ret. Sch. Employees Assn., Sierra Club, Phi Theta Kappa. Congregationalist.

DELONG, LOIS ANNE, editor, writer; b. Bklyn., Aug. 13, 1955; d. George Edmund and Elizabeth Martha (Behrens) DeL. BA, NYU, 1977. With Am. Inst. Chem. Engrs., N.Y.C., 1978—, asst. mgr. communications dept., 1987—, editor Chapter One, 1987—; pub. rels. coord. Brentwood (N.Y.) Fine Arts Festival, 1978-82; editor The Spark newsletter, Flushing, N.Y., 1988—; producer, publicist The ADD Co., Brentwood, 1988—. Mem. Alumni Assn. Scholarship Winners (v.p. 1988—). Democrat. Presbyterian. Office: Am Inst Chem Engrs 345 E 47th St New York NY 10017

DELONG, ROBERTA KAY, real estate company officer, accountant; b. Elkhorn, Wis., June 25, 1946; d. Robert E. and Evelyn M. (Lees) DeL.; m. Kenneth M. Kramer, Nov. 11, 1967 (div. 1985); 1 child Jeffery M. Kramer. BA in Bus. Mgmt., Nat. Louis U., 1990. Sr. acct. Pvt. Tele-Communications, Chgo., 1969-77; contr. Murdoch, Coll and Lillibridge Inc., Chgo., 1977 --; cons. Housekeeping Unlimited, Glenview, Ill., 1987-88. Dem. staff mem., Chgo., 1974-75; bd. dirs. PTA, Arlington Heights, Ill., 1976; pres. Boy Scouts pack, Arlington Heights, 1976-77; vol. ERA, Arlington Heights, 1978. Mem. NOW, Bldg. and Owners Mgmt. Assn. Chgo.

DELOUGHERY, GRACE LEONA, nursing educator; b. Allison, Iowa, Jan. 17, 1933; d. Ed F. and Alma K. (Kampman) Meinen; B.S., U. Minn., 1955, M.P.H., 1960; Ph.D., Claremont Grad. Sch., 1966; m. Henry O. Deloughery, Nov. 30, 1962; children—Paul Edward, Michael, Kathleen. Staff nurse Mpls. Dept. Pub. Health, 1955-59; research fellow U. Minn. Sch. Pub. Health, 1960-63; sch. nurse Val Verde Sch. Dist., Perris, Calif., part-time 1963-66; community coord., nurse in Title I pilot project in San Jacinto, Riverside (Calif.) County Schs., 1966, cons. Title I, 1966-67; assoc. prof. U. N.C. Coll. Nursing, 1967-68; asst. prof. U. Calif. Sch. Nursing, L.A., 1968-72; dean Center Nursing Edn., Spokane, 1972-74; assoc. prof., head dept. nursing Winona (Minn.) State U., 1975-77; adminstr. Deloughery Home Sr. Adults, 1977-84; assoc. prof. Ind. U., New Albany, 1984—, Bellarmine Coll., Louisville, 1987—, U. Louisville Hosp.; nurse practitioner Nursing Resources and Svcs., Geogertown, Ind., 1988—; participant seminars, condr. workshops, cons. in field. Recipient award for research Calif. Edn. Research and Guidance Assn., 1967. Fellow Am. Pub. Health Assn., Am. Assn. Social Psychiatry (treas. 1974-78); mem. Am. Nurses Assn., Nat. League Nursing, Am. Sch. Health Assn., Internat. Mental Health Fedn., Wash. Pub. Health Assn., Acad. Polit. and Social Sci., Acad. Polit. Sci., Pi Lambda Theta, Sigma Theta Tau. Lutheran. Club: Winona Country. Contbr. to profl. jours.

DEL PAPA, FRANKIE SUE, state official; b. 1949. BA, U. Nev.; JD, George Washington U., 1974. Bar: Nev. 1974. Staff asst. U.S. Senator Alan Bible, Washington, 1971-74; assoc. Law Office of Leslie B. Grey, Reno, Nev., 1975-78; legis. asst. to U.S. Senator Howard Cannon, Washington, 1978-79; ptnr. Thornton & Del Papa, 1979-84; pvt. practice Reno, 1984-87; sec. of state State of Nev., Carson City, 1987-91; atty. gen. State of Nev., 1991—. Mem. Sierra Arts Found. (bd. dirs.), Trust for Pub. Land (adv. com.), Nev. Women's Fund. Democrat. Office: Office of Atty Gen Heroes Meml Bldg Carson City NV 89710

DEL PIZZO, NANCY ANN, magazine editor; b. Paterson, N.J., Oct. 10, 1962; d. Dante Francis and Rose Mary (La Mastra) Del P. AA, U. Fla., 1983; BS in Communications, William Paterson Coll., 1986. Prodn. asst. Dell Pub. Co., N.Y.C., 1986; sr. assoc. editor, recruiter Gralla Publs., N.Y.C., 1986-89; sr. editor 20/20 mag. Jobson Pub. Co., N.Y.C., 1989—. Author: (play) Moving On, 1985 (hon. mention Playwriting Festival); contbr. articles to mags. Fundraiser AIDS walk Gay Men's Health Crisis, N.Y.C., 1988-90. Mem. Women in Communications, N.Y. Bus. Press Editors (bd. dirs. 1990—, planning com.). Home: 340 Undercliff Ave Apt 4A Edgewater NJ 07020 Office: Jobson Pub Co 20/20 Mag 352 Park Ave S New York NY 10010

DEL RIO DIAZ, ESTYNE, psychologist; b. Chgo., July 30, 1945; d. Sal Ernest and Evelyn Sandea (Del Rio) Bernhardt; m. Raul Diaz, Nov. 21, 1987. PhD, Jackson State U., 1974; postgrad., U. Pa., 1975, Robbins Research Inst., 1985. Pres. Psychelogistics Inc., N.Y.C., 1960-80; TV talk show personality various shows, N.Y.C., 1971; practicing psychologist, 1974—; psychologist Ghana, 1975; v.p. Jo-Del Consol. Ltd., 1976; columnist Health and Diet Times, N.Y.C., 1980; exec. producer, host Encounters, N.Y.C., 1986—. Mem. Assn. Nat. Christian Counselors, Am. Bd. Christian Psychology, Assn. Humanistic Psychology. Democrat. Clubs: N.Y. Health and Racquet, Century 21.

DEL SARDO, HELEN ANN, financial analyst; b. Boston, Jan. 5, 1954; d. Nick James and Mary Florence (Marino) Falce; m. Anthony Robert Del Sardo, June 25, 1982. BA in Polit. Sci., Duquesne U., 1976. Lic. securities dealer, ins. salesperson, Pa. Sr. budget analyst Allegheny County Controller's Office, Pitts., 1979-84; rep. Equitable Life Assurance Soc., Pitts., 1985-86; registered rep. Lincoln Investment Planning, Inc., Pitts., 1986-87, Renaissance Fin. Group, Pitts., 1987—; budget analyst U. Surg. Assocs., Inc. Med. and Health Care div. U. Pitts., 1988—. Vol. Frank J. Lucchino for State Auditor Gen., Pitts., 1984; mem. YWCA Greater Pitts. Mem. Nat. Assn. Life Underwriters, Nat. Assn. Female Execs., Duquesne U. Alumni Assn. Democrat. Roman Catholic. Home: 2711 Brentwood Ave Pittsburgh PA 15227 Office: U Surg Assoc Inc 3471 5th Ave Ste 302 Pittsburgh PA 15213

DELUCA, BARBARA H., director continuing education; b. Boston; m. Albert J. DeLuca, Dec. 26, 1959; children: Jay, Janice, David, Diane, Michael. BS, Boston U., 1959, MEd, 1973; postgrad., U. Mass., 1976, Lesley Coll., 1978. Mass. Teaching cert. Tchr. Escambia County Schs., Pensacola, Fla., 1959-60; instr. Aquinas Coll. at Milton, Milton, Mass., 1970-74; chairperson Garland Jr. Coll., Boston, 1975-78; tchr. Quincy (Mass.) Pub. Schs., 1978-83; dir. alumnae Aquinas Coll. at Milton, Milton, 1983-84, dir. continuing edn., 1985—; facilitator Women in Mgmt. Seminars, 1974; Wang Word Processing Trainer, 1977; lectr. Putnam Cos., Braintree, Mass., current. Vol. John Flood for Gov. Com., Braintree, 1989—, VIA, 1987—, Flatley Nursing Home, 1985—; lector St. Agatha Ch., Milton, 1982—. Recipient grant Lily Found., 1973. Mem. AAUW (hospitality program, pub. rels. coms.), Mass. Adult and Continuing Edn., Mass. Bus. Edn. Assn., Profl. Secs. Assn., Delta Pi Epsilon. Roman Catholic. Office: Aquinas Coll at Milton 303 Adams St Milton MA 02186

DELUCA, DIANE LYNELLE, advertising executive; b. Erie, Pa., Aug. 7, 1955; d. Vincent F. and Delores E. (Snyder) DeL. Student, Gen. McLane, Edinboro, Pa., 1973. Cert. home improvement, life and disability ins., Calif.; cert. real estate, Pa. Sales designer Capri Pools and Spas, Vista, Calif., 1977-80; pre-need counselor Internat. Funeral Svcs. Inc., San Diego, 1980-82; exec. adminstr. World Energy Leasing, San Diego, 1982-84; gen. mgr., ptnr. Accents & Elegance, Solana Beach, Calif., 1984-85; mgr. spl. projects CareAm./Great Lakes Health, Erie, 1985-87; account exec. Donn Advt. Assocs., Erie, 1985—. Mem. NAFE, Internat. Assn. Bus. Communicators (past pres. Erie chpt.), Sales and Mktg. Execs. Erie, Am. Bus. Women's Assn., Erie Toastmasters Club. Office: 901 W 12th St Erie PA 16501

DE LUCA, GRACE MARY, financial executive; b. Bermuda, Sept. 7, 1947; d. Douglas Kepler and Rena Louise (Benney) Campbell; m. David John De Luca, Jan. 14, 1978. BS, U. San Francisco, 1981; MBA, Golden Gate U., 1987. Fin. analyst Castle & Cooke, San Francisco, 1969-76; budget dir. St. Francis Meml. Hosp., San Francisco, 1976-77; mgr. planning Heublein, San Francisco, 1977-78; mgr. clinics St. Francis Meml. Hosp., San Francisco, 1978-82; v.p., chief fin. officer ISC Wines of Calif., San Francisco, 1983-87, Fritzi of Calif., San Francisco, 1987—; cons. Li'l Rascals, Mill Valley, Calif., 1982-83. Advisor Jr. Achievement, San Jose, Calif., 1971-74; mem. Citizens for a Better Environment, Nat. Pub. Radio. Mem. Nat. Assn. Accts. Home: 1820 Clemens Rd Oakland CA 94602 Office: Fritzi of Calif 199 1st St San Francisco CA 94105

DE LUCE, VIRGINIA, entertainer; b. San Francisco, Mar. 25, 1921. Student, Bishop-Lee Sch. of Theatre, Beacon Hill, Mass. Lic. real estate broker, Mass. Model John Roberts Powers, Harry Conover; dir. New Wrinkle Theatre; actress 20th Century Fox Film Corp., Columbia Pictures, Paramount Pictures; actress commls.; pres. Soc. Prodns., Cosmic Sci. Inst., Earth Jazz, Texloid Products, Blue Dove Enterprises, Contessa Spring Prodns. Actress: (musicals and plays) including Kiss Me Kate, Brigadoon, Can Can, Pal Joey, Will Success Spoil Rock Hunter, Twelfth Night, Emperor Jones, Pygmalion and Galatea, White Iris, Leave It To Psmith, The Sacrifice, Bonanza, The Beggars' Opera, (Broadway play) Who Was That Lady at Martin Beck Theatre, (musical revues) Vaudeville at Palace Theatre, New Faces at Royale Theatre, Chic at Orpheum Theatre, Billy Barnes' Review at Carnegie Hall, Have A Heart at Madison Sq. Garden; producer: (concert) Blue Dove's Many Feathers; appeared in hotel shows and cabarets including Ritz Carlton Hotel, Montreal, Can., Le Cabaret, Toronto, Can., Copacobana Palace, Rio De Janeiro, Brazil, Copacobana, N.Y.C., Comedy Club, N.Y.C., Twelfth Night Club, N.Y.C., Waldorf Astoria, N.Y.C., Biltmore Bowl, L.A., Golden Horseshoe, Disneyland, Calif., Hotel Roosevelt, New Orleans, Scotch and Sirloin, L.A., #1 Fifth Avenue, N.Y.C., Di Maggio's Yacht Club, San Francisco, Leon & Eddie's, N.Y.C., The Ballroom, N.Y.C., Mayfair, Boston, Pirates' Den, Hollywood, Calif., Trocadero, Hollywood, House of Vienna, N.Y.C., Blue Angel, N.Y.C., Lambs' Club, N.Y.C., Hollywood (Calif.) Canteen, Stage Door Canteen, N.Y.C.; advance "man" for Spike Jones Orch., Coast to Coast Tour; appearances in TV shows including Play of the Week (NTA), Repetoire Workshop, Tonight Show, Sgt. Bilko series, others, also radio shows, local and network telethons; appeared in rodeos Leo Carillo, Roy Rogers Rodeos, Coliseum, L.A.; author, composer: The Boston Nod, (scripts, songs and poetry) Dallas Sal, Spider, Give All His Love to Her, Great Sun, Victory, Making Up-Silent Song, Pow Wow Smile, Saga of Jini, When Love is Near, The Thorns of Summer; author: Your Own Voice, My Learning Path, Crystal Gazing Lessons, Your Heart's Desire, Lucky Break; creator: Wood Spirits, also astrological paintings, datascope, delineations, Dog-O-Scope, Cat-O-Scope; creator documentary series for Four Winds Prodn., Hello Again, 1971; also painter, fashion designer and songwriter. Sec. Rep. Town Com., Charlemont, Mass., 1989, 90; mem. Rep. Town Com., Weston, Mass., Girl Scouts U.S., 5 Civilized Tribes-Choctaw, Chickasaw, Cherokee, Creek, Seminole; alt. Senator Silver Haired Legis., Mass.; asst. to mgr. Eisenhower-Nixon Bandwagon Hdqtrs., N.Y.C.; creator theme, chmn. entertainment Inaugural Ball Pres. Nixon; asst. coord., bd. dir. pub. rels. Mass. Satellite Inaugural Ball for Pres. Reagan, 1980; precinct dir. Re-elect Pres. Reagan, 1984; coord. Dr. Richard A. Jones for Senator campaign, Weston; speaker, writer LWV Candidate Night; apptd. election officer Town of Weston, also apptd. Fence Viewer; author Mass. Legis. House bills; bd. dirs. Arts and Crafts Assn.; mem. Environment Task Force, Mass., Rep. Nat. Com., USCG Res., 1943-44, seaman first class, 1944-45; aux. police woman Office of Civil Def., City of N.Y.; co-chairperson, sec. Rep. Town Com.; past mem. numerous other civic orgns., bds.; vol. worker, performer for charities. Named to Times Square Hall of Fame; recipient Theatre World award, Yale U. Drama Salute. Mem. Am. Guild Variety Artists, Screen Actors' Guild, Actor's Equity Assn., AFTRA, Franklin County C. of C., Am. Legion, Mass. Fedn. Rep. Women (bd. dirs.), Nat. Rifle Assn., Am. Fedn. Astrologers, Gun Owners' Action League, Am. Indian Movement (former treas. L.A. chpt.). Office: care William Morris Agy 1350 Ave of the Americas New York NY 10019

DE LUCIA, DIANE MARIE, systems analyst; b. Huntington, N.Y., Apr. 29, 1964; d. Salvatore Joseph and Margaret Ann (Baker) De L. BA in Econs. and Spanish, Clemson U., 1986. Cons. O.I.T., Inc., Huntington, 1986-87; systems analyst Blackbaud Micro Systems, Huntington, 1987-88, Datability Software Systems, N.Y.C., 1988-89, Aetna Life & Casualty Co., Lake Success, N.Y., 1989—; owner Lazer Tech., 1990—. Mem. Dem. Com. Town of Huntington. Mem. Am. Mgmt. Assn., NAFE. Office: Aetna Life & Casualty Co 1981 Marcus Ave Lake Success NY 11042

DELYS, CHANTAL, executive education director of graduate school; b. France, Oct. 5, 1953; came to U.S., 1975; d. Jules Louis Emile and Jacqueline (Despret) Delys; m. Thomas R. Vessely; 1 child, Yann. BA with honors and MA, Pau (France) U., 1975; MA in French, Ind. U., 1977, MBA, 1979. Teaching asst. Kirkcaldy (Scotland) High Sch., 1973-74; instr. Ind. U., Bloomington, 1975-79; program coord. Grad. Sch. Bus. U. Tex., Austin, 1981-83, assoc. dir. mgmt. devel. programs Grad. Sch. Bus., 1983-84, dir. exec. edn. Grad. Sch. Bus., 1984—; guest speaker women in mgmt. Sta. KUT, 1983. Recipient Extra Mile award Southland Corp. Mktg. Div., 1986. Mem. Human Resource Planning Soc., Consortium for Univ. Exec. Program Dirs., Internat. Directory Univ. Exec. Programs (adb. bd.), Nat. Univ. Continuing Edn. Assn, Women in Mgmt. Office: U Tex Grad Sch Bus PO Box 7337 Austin TX 78713

DEMAAR, NATALIE, federal agency administrator; b. Balt., July 8, 1950; d. Paul and Vera Rebecca (Abrams) Rosenbaum; m. Verrell Leon Dethloff Jr., June 2, 1974 (div. 1987); children: Daniel, Joseph; m. Michael Henry deMaar, June 4, 1988; 1 child, Michael Henry deMaar Jr.; stepchildren: Alexander, Peter, Andrew. BA, Simmons Coll., 1972; JD with honors, U. Md., Balt., 1976. Bar: Md. 1976, U.S. Ct. Appeals (4th, 5th, 10th cirs.), U.S. Dist. Ct. Md., U.S. Supreme Ct. With HHS, Seattle, 1976—, regional adminstr. family support adminstrn. div., 1987—; speaker in field. Contbr. articles to profl. jours. Mem. Wash. Commn. for Humanities, Alliance for Children, Youth & Families, Nat. Child Support Advocacy Coalition. Mem. Md. Bar Assn., Northwest Women's Bar Assn., Seattle-King County Bar Assn., Am. Assn. Pub. Welfare Attys., NAFE, Am. Pub. Welfare Assn., Campfire, City Club. Office: Family Support Adminstrn 2201 6th Ave M/S RX-70 Seattle WA 98121

DEMAIO, DOROTHY J., nurse, educator; b. Jersey City, Jan. 12, 1927; d. John Joseph and Agnes (McEnroe) Jengo; m. Laurence R. DeMaio, Oct. 15, 1950; children: Maureen, Michele, Laurence J., Diane, James. BS, Jersey City State Coll., 1948; MA, NYU, 1970; postgrad., Rutgers U., 1970—. Supr. pediatrics svc. and edn. Jersey City Med. Ctr., 1964-65; instr. nursing Charles E. Gregory Sch. Nursing, Perth Amboy, N.J., 1965-68; instr. Rutgers U., Newark, 1970-75, dir. pediatric nurse practitioner program, from 1972, coord. nurse practitioner programs, from 1974, assoc. prof. nursing, 1975-76, assoc. prof. grad. program parent-child nursing, from 1976, now dean Coll. of Nursing; sec., treas. N.J. Bd. Nursing, from 1975; chmn. Ad Hoc Com. to Redefine Nursing, 1973-74. Bd. dirs. Crossroads Girl Scouts U.S., 1963-69; active Colonia Sch. 17 PTO, 1959-72. Recipient Outstanding Alumnae award Jersey State Coll., 1956, Thanks badge Girl Scouts U.S., 1969. Office: Rutgers-State U Coll Nursing Ackerson Hall 180 Univ Ave Newark NJ 07102*

DEMANCHE, SISTER EDNA LOUISE, parochial school administrator; b. Marionville, Mo., Jan. 1, 1915; d. Alfred Campbell and Katherine Lena (Koller) D. BS in Biology, Mount St. Vincent, 1940; MS in Biology, U. Notre Dame, 1964, PhD, 1969. Tchr. various Cath. Schs., Hawaii, 1940-60; curriculum writer, researcher and tchr. trainer U. Hawaii, Honolulu, 1967-80; curriculum rsch. and devel resource to Cath. Schs. Cath. Sch. Dept. of Hawaii, 1960-67, 83—; exec. sec. Hawaiian Acad. Sci., Honolulu, 1980-83; univ. courses for tchrs. Schs. in Micronesia, Marshall Island, Sch. in Am. Samoa, 1984, Mil. Schs. of Far East, 1969. Author five books. organizer Conservation Coun. of Hawaii, 1960—, Environ. Assn. Hawaii, 1960—, and various ednl. groups, 1960—. Recipient Environ. award Hawaii Assn. Conservation, 1974; fellowship NSF, 1962-63. Mem. Hawaiian Acad. Sci. (exec. coun., exec. sec. 1980-83, Pres. Svcs. 1989), Hawaii Sci. Tchrs. Assn. (exec. coun., Outstanding Sci. Tchr. 1975, 86), Environ. Edn. Assn. (founder, 1st pres. 1973), Nat. Cath. Edn. Assn. (pres. Hawaii chpt.), Assn. for Supervision and Curriculum Devel., Conservation Coun. for Hawaii. Roman Catholic. Office: Cath Sch Dept 6301 Pali Hwy Kaneohe HI 96744

D'EMANUELE, MAY ANN, consulting company executive; b. Lawrence, Mass., June 21, 1934; d. Michael and Ann (Catanese) D'E. BA, Merrimack Coll., 1956. Chief ops. Alexander Proudfoot Co., Chgo., 1972-82; account exec. Inst. Mgmt. Resources, Westlake Village, Calif., 1982-85; v.p. ops. The Princeton (N.J.) Group, 1985-88; asst. bus. group mgr. Sci. Mgmt. Corp., Basking Ridge, N.J., 1988—. Mem. NAFE, Am. Mgmt. Assn. Office: Sci Mgmt Corp PO Box 0600 Basking Ridge NJ 07920

DE MAR, LEODA MILLER, fabric and wallcovering designer; b. N.Y.C., May 26, 1929; d. Benjamin and Malvina (Altman) Miller; m. Robert Mathis de Mar, Dec. 30, 1955 (div. Jan. 1985); children: Victoria, Miller Mathis, Charles David. Diploma, Parson's Sch. of Design, N.Y.C., 1946-49; postgrad., Parson's Sch. of Design, Eng., France, Italy, 1949, NYU, 1950-53. Designer Joseph B. Platt, Indsl. Design, N.Y.C., 1950-53; instr. textiles Parson's Sch. Design, N.Y.C., 1953-55; freelance designer various companies, N.Y.C., 1956-62; designer Leoda de Mar, Inc., N.Y.C., 1962-74; designer, advt. cons. Woodson Wallpapers, N.Y.C., 1975-85, Richard E. Thibaut, Inc., Irvington, N.J., 1985—. Designer 1st wallpaper collection Pippin Papers, N.Y.C., 1954, 1st wallpaper collection Woodson Wallpapers, 1955, own collections Richard E. Thibaut, Inc., 1985—, fabric and wallcovering designs featured in various popular mags.; contbr. articles to mags. Recipient Creativity award Art Direction mag., 1981. Home and Office: 350 Riversville Rd Greenwich CT 06831

DEMARCO, ANITA JOYCE, elementary educator; b. New Castle, Pa., Feb. 9, 1933; d. Alex Durgam and Emma (Hasson) Durgam; m. Pat S. DeMarco, Oct. 18, 1952; children: Donald, Gerald, David. BS in Edn., Slippery Rock U., 1972, M.Ed, 1975, MEd in Supervision of Reading, 1978. Cluster II tchr. Franklin (Pa.) Schs.-Polk, 1973-75, tchr. 2d grade, 1982-90; reading specialist Title I ESEA, 1975-82; tchr. grad. courses I.U. IV Grove City, 1980—. Author: Title I Helpbook, Helping Energetic Learning Parents in Readiness, 1979. Mem. Delta Kappa Gamma (2d v.p. 1990). Home: 508 Oakland Ave Grove City PA 16127

DEMARCO, DIANE LYNN, contractor; b. Fort Worth, June 4, 1958; d. Ronald Charles and Rita Bernice (Davis) DeM. BS, U. Fla., 1981. Cert. gen. contractor, Fla. Vice pres. DeMarco Homes, Boca Raton, Fla., 1981-86, pres., 1986—. Project coordiantor Boca Raton Hist. Soc., 1983-85; cons. historic Palm Beach County Preservation bd., 1984-85; pres. DeMarco Constrn., Inc., Boca Raton, 1986—; bd. dirs. St. Joan of Arc Catholic Ch. Constrn. Bd., Boca Raton, 1985; restorationist Old Town Hall, 1983-85, Raulerson House, 1986; bd. dirs. City Boca Raton Preservation Bd., 1984—, Boca Raton Bd. Realtors, 1987—; vice-chmn. preservation bd. City of Delray Beach Historic, 1989—; fundraiser staging chmn. Jr. League of Boca Raton, 1987—; con. preservation fundraiser Children's Mus. of Boca Raton at Sing Pine, 1988—; restorer Tarrimore an old sch. squ. historic dist., Delray Beach, 1989; mem. Delray Beach Visions 2000 Com., 1989; chmn. preservation Delray Beach Hist. Soc., 1988—. Recipient Spl. Achievement award Fa. Trust for Historic Preservation, 1985, Fed. Restoration grant Fla. Dept. Ste, 1984, Leadership 84 award Boca Raton C. of C., 1984. Mem. Boca Raton C. of C. (com. chmn. 1985), Boca Raton Hist. Soc., Nat. Assn. Home Builders, Fla. Atlantic Builders Assn., Nat. Assn. Women in Constrn., Nat. Bldg. Mus., Fellowship Single Profls. (pres. 1984-85), Nat. Assn. Miniature Enthusiasts, Fla. Atlantic Builders Assn. (mem. remodeler's council 1985-87), Boca Raton Bd. Realtors, Nat. Assn. Homebuilders, Jr. League, Sigma Lambda Chi. Republican. Avocations: doll and miniature collecting, camping, quilting. Office: DeMarco Homes Inc 290 SW 2d Ave Boca Raton FL 33432

DE MARCO, NATALIE ANNE, personnel executive; b. Easton, Pa., Feb. 9, 1961; d. Lawrence Adriano and Donna Louise (Gordon) De M. Student, Indiana U. Pa., 1979-81, Northampton Community Coll., 1982, Broward Community Coll., 1986. Mgr. Louise's Contourella, Easton, 1982-83; sales rep. Wainwright's Travel, Bethlehem, Pa., 1983-84; sec. Benthor-Sanijura Inc., North Miami Beach, Fla., 1984, pres., treas., corp. officer, 1984-89; br. mgr. ADIA Pers. Svcs., Miami, Fla., 1989—. Roman Catholic.

DE MARNEFFE, BARBARA ROWE, small business owner; b. Boston, June 2, 1929; d. H.S. Payson and Florence Van Arnhem (Cassard) Rowe; m. James Hopkins, Oct. 9, 1954 (div. 1969); m. Francis de Marneffe; stepchildren: Peter, Daphne, Colette. BA, Vassar Coll., 1952; postgrad., Boston U., 1959. Tchr. Chapin Sch., N.Y.C., 1952-54; adminstrv. asst. to dean Sch. of Indsl. Mgmt. MIT, Cambridge, Mass., 1959-60; asst. pub. rels. dir. Peter Bent Brigham Hosp., Boston, 1960-61, pub. rels. dir., 1961-63; pub. rels. cons. Diabetes Found. and Joslin Clinic, Boston, 1963-64; pub. rels. dir. McLean Hosp., Belmont, Mass., 1964-68; pres. de Marneffe Selections, Cambridge, 1978—. Contbr. articles to profl. jours. Trustee, v.p. Archives of Am. Art of the Smithsonian Inst., Washington, D.C., 1983—; com. mem. Ellis Meml. Settlement House Antiques Show, 1968-89; bd. dirs. Friends of McLean Hosp., Belmont, Mass., 1967-89; officer, bd. dirs. Family Counseling Svc. of Cambridge, 1969-78; Mass. Rep. State Committeewoman, 1977-80; exec. sec. Cambridge Rep. City Com., 1956-57; pub. rels. dir. Peabody for Congress Campaign, Newton, Mass., 1968; bd. dirs. Nat. Com. on the Treatment of Intractable Pain, Washington D.C., 1980—; trustee Peterborough Players, N.H., 1983-89. Mem. Jewelers of Am., Inc., Cambridge C. of C. (pub. affairs dir. 1975-78), Vassar Club (pres. Boston chpt. 1989). Home and Office: 308 Cambridge Woods Way Raleigh NC 27608

DE MARR, MARY JEAN, English language educator; b. Champaign, Ill., Sept. 20, 1932; d. William Fleming and Laura Alice (Shauman) Bailey. B.A., Lawrence Coll., 1954; M.A., U. Ill., 1957, Ph.D., 1963; postgrad., Universitaet Tuebingen, 1954-55, Moscow State U., 1961-62. Asst. prof. English Willamette U., 1964-65; asst. prof. English Ind. State U., 1965-70, asso. prof., 1970-75, prof., 1975—. Co-author: Adolescent Female Portraits in the American Novel, 1961-81: An Annotated Bibliography, 1983, The Adolescent in The American Novel Since 1960, 1986; Am. editor: Annual Bibliography of English Language and Literature, 1979—. Recipient Fulbright assistantship, 1954-55. Mem. MLA, Modern Humanities Research Assn., AAUP, Nat. Council Tchrs. English, ACLU, Phi Beta Kappa, Phi Kappa Phi. Home: 594 Woodbine Dr Terre Haute IN 47803 Office: Ind State U Dept English Terre Haute IN 47809

DE MARS, CARON EMERSON, property claims manager; b. Rock Springs, Wyo., Oct. 18, 1955; d. Eugene Reynders and Mildred Evelyn (Bohmont) E.; m. Bruce David DeMars, Aug. 11, 1984. BS, U. Wyo., 1978; Assoc. in Mgmt., 1990. Chartered property and casualty underwriter, 1987; casualty claims law assoc., 1982. Claims adjuster Crawford and Co. Ins. Adjusters, Great Falls, Mont., 1978-79; adjuster-in-charge Rawlins, Wyo., 1979-80; field claim rep. State Farm Ins., Sheridan, Wyo., 1980, sr. field claim rep., 1981-82; specialist arson State Farm Ins., Casper, Wyo., 1982-85; reinsp., trainer State Farm Ins., Colorado Springs, Colo., 1985-87; property claims mgr. United Svcs. Automobile Assn., Colorado Springs, 1987-89; claims trainer United Svcs. Automobile Assn., San Antonio, 1989-90, property loss mgr., 1990—. Bd. dirs. Wyo. Girl Scout Coun., Green River, 1974, Crimestoppers Cen. Wyo., Casper, 1982-85; chair publicity Sheridan County Reps., 1980-82, Jr. League, 1988—; campaigner United Way Corp., 1989; docent San Antonio Zoo., 1990—. Mem. Western Ins. Info. Svc. (Wyo. coordinator level III 1987), Bus. and Profl. Women (chair young careerist com. 1985, state Outstanding Young Career Woman 1984), Nat. Assn. for Female Execs., VFW (aux.), Toastmasters (sec. dist. 26, 1988-89, Toastmaster of Yr. Rocky Mountain Eagles 1989), Soc. of Chartered Property Casualty Underwriters, Kappa Delta Alumnae Assn. (editor 1988-89). Republican. Mem. Unity Ch. Club: Toastmasters (pres. Casper chpt. 1984-85, ednl. v.p. Colorado Springs chpt. 1987, Competent Toastmaster 1983, pres. Colo. Springs chpt. 1988-89, sec. 1988-89, Disting. Toastmaster 1989). Home: 8554 Echo Creek Ln San Antonio TX 78240 Office: United Svcs Automobile Assn USAA Bldg San Antonio TX 78288

DE MASSA, JESSIE G., media specialist. BJ, Temple U.; MLS, San Jose State U., 1967; postgrad., U. Okla., U. So. Calif. Tchr. Palo Alto (Calif.) Unified Sch. Dist., 1966; librarian Antelope Valley Joint Union High Sch. Dist., Lancaster, Calif., 1966-68, ABC Unified Sch. Dist., Artesia, Calif., 1968-72; dist. librarian Tehachapi (Calif.) Unified Sch. Dist., 1972-81; also media specialist, free lance writer, 1981—. Contbr. articles to profl. jours. Mem. Statue of Liberty Ellis Island Found., Inc. Fellow Internat. Biog. Assn.; mem. Calif. Media and Library Educators Assn., Calif. Assn. Sch. Librarians (exec. council), AAUW (bull. editor, assoc. editor state bull., chmn. publicity 1955-68), Nat. Mus. Women in Arts (charter), Hon. Fellows John F. Kennedy Library (founding mem.), The Nat. Writers Club. Home: 9951 Garrett Circle Huntington Beach CA 92646

DEMASTUS, MELODYE ROSE, treasurer; b. Akron, Ohio, Feb. 11, 1958; d. Robert Glen Demastus and Marjorie Lea (Steele) Sowers. BA in Bus. Mgmt., Franklin U., 1985. Youth counselor Portage County Ohio CETA, Ravenna, 1976-78; asst. portfolio mgr. Bank One Trust Co., N.A., Columbus, Ohio, 1979-83; mgr. short term investments Midland Mut. Life Ins., Columbus, 1983-84, dir. fixed income investments, 1984-86; asst. treas. Accel Internat. Corp., Dublin, Ohio, 1986—, treas., 1989—. Co-chairperson co. campaign United Way of Franklin County, Columbus, 1985. Mem. Nat. Assn. Corp. Cash Mgmt., Columbus Cash Mgmt. Assn., Columbus Stock & Bond Club. Republican. Office: Accel Internat Corp 475 Metro Pl N Dublin OH 43017

DEMATTEO, GLORIA JEAN, insurance saleswoman; b. Perth Amboy, N.J., May 23, 1943; d. John J. and Helena (Elias) Kancz; m. Ronald D. DeMatteo, Feb. 20, 1965 (div. Nov. 1987); children: Douglas J., Keith G. Student, Berkeley Sch., 1961. Exec. sec. Rhodia Inc., New Brunswick, N.J., 1961-65; real estate saleswomen Mid-Jersey Realty, East Brunswick, N.J., 1974-79; pntr. Realty World Garden of Homes, East Brunswick, 1979-81; spl. agt. Prudential Ins. Co., Woodbridge, N.J., 1981—. V.p. Belcourt Condo Assn., North Brunswick, N.J., 1987-88. Mem. Nat. Assn. Life Underwriters (nat. sales achievement award 1988, nat. quality award 1987), Prudential Leaders Club. Home: 1144 Schmidt Ln North Brunswick NJ 08902 Office: Prudential Ins Co 1 Woodridge Ctr Woodbridge NJ 07095

DEMBECK, MARY GRACE, artist, writer; b. N.Y.C., Oct. 29, 1931; d. August and Lucia Louisa (De Sanctis) Menghini; m. John Francis Dembeck, June 14, 1958; children: Christine Elizabeth, John Francis Jr. Student, St. John's U., N.Y.C., 1950-51, Fordham U., 1951-52, Fairfield U., 1982-83; studies with, Charles Reid, Daniel Green, John Mc Clelland, Leonard Everett Fisher, John C. Pellew and Mary Ann Hoberman, Conn., N.Y., 1974-82. Artist, pres. Pinafore, Ltd., Westport, Conn., 1987—. works exhibited at Eagle Tower Gallery, Stamford, Conn., 1979, 80, Nat. Acad. Design, N.Y.C., 1981, Westport Nature Ctr., Westport Ctr. Arts, 1983-85, Rowayton (Conn.) Arts Ctr., 1983-87 (acrylic award 1983, 89), Trumbull (Conn.) Library, 1985-87, Gallery Four, Norwalk, 1986, Norfield Art Show, Weston, Conn., 1987, Fairfield (Conn.) U., St. Vincent, Bridgeport Gallery, 1987, Portland Pl. Gallery, South Norwalk, Conn., Gallery 53, Meriden Ct. (art award Conn. Classic Arts 1990); one woman shows include St. Vincent's Bridgeport, Conn., 1989; contbr. light verse, humor and poetry to mags., newspapers including Nat. Wildlife Fedn's. Ranger Rick Mag., Westport News, 1979-83, Banker's Newsletter, 1985, Wall Street Jour., 1985—, Reader's Digest, 1988, NBC News, Steve Allen Radio Program, 1988, Garrison Keillor's Am. Radio Co. of The Air, 1990; creator cartoon character "Harriet"; mng. editor, staff artist Carousel Mag., 1988-89; panelist local radio, cable TV arts/humor discussions. Designer Mass book cover St. Patrick's Cathedral, N.Y.C., 1977—; judge children's poetry and short story Trumbull Arts Festival, 1986-89; mem. Westport Hist. Soc., Westport Women's Club (awards for acrylics 1985, 86, 87); artist mem. Italian Apostolate Archdiocese N.Y.C. Recipient Nat. Pub. Radio award, 1987. Mem. Rowayton Arts Ctr., Westport Ctr. for the Arts, So. Vt. Arts Ctr., Conn. Classic Arts, Trumbull (award 1987), Nat. League of Pen Women (poetry award 1983, best humorous poem 1984) Nat. Soc. Painters in Acrylic & Casein (assoc.), Brontë Soc. (life). Roman Catholic.

DE MENESES, MARY ROADES, nursing educator, researcher, consultant, writer; b. Alton, Ill., Apr. 16, 1939; d. Charles Franklin and Eunice Lorea (Nolan) Roades; m. William C. Meneses, May 31, 1973; children: Luis Alberto, Daniel William. Diploma, St. Luke's Sch. Nursing, St. Louis, 1960; BS in Nursing, DePaul U., 1970, MA, 1973, MS in Nursing, 1975; EdD in Leadership and Ednl. Policy Studies, No. Ill. U., 1982. RN, Mo. Staff nurse St. Lukes Hosp., St. Louis, 1960-61, Our Lady of Lourdes Hosp., Binghampton, N.Y, 1961-64; supr., head nurse St. Joseph's Hosp., Alton, Ill., 1964-66; head nurse St. Joseph's Hosp., Chgo., 1966-69; head instr. nursing Michael Reese Med. Ctr., Chgo., 1969-74; from instr. to assoc. prof. dept. nursing DePaul U., Chgo., 1974-82; prof. nursing So. Ill. U., Edwardsville, 1982—, coord. grad. nursing program, 1985—; legal cons. Regional Law Firm, Ill., 1983—; med. cons. VA, St. Louis, 1986—; item writer C.V. Mosby/N Y Regents, St. Louis, 1986-87. Author: (book) Nursing Process, 1986; mem. editorial bd. Focus on Critical Care/AJN, 1988; contbr. articles to profl. jours. Recipient Teaching Excellence award So. Ill. U., 1990. Mem. Am. Nurses Assn. (dist. v.p. 1983-86), Coun. Nurse Researchers, Am. Heart Assn. (bd. dirs. Edwardsville unit 1982—), Am. Assn. Critical Care Nurses (treas. So. Ill. chpt. 1983-85), Ill. Nurses Assn. (med. cons. 1982—, v.p. local dist. 1985-87), Ill. Legis. Rsch. Network, Am. Cancer Soc., DePaul U. Nursing Alumni (pres. 1980-81), Kappa Delta Pi, Sigma Theta Tau, Phi Kappa Phi, Phi Delta Kappa. Republican. Roman Catholic. Home: 4710 Fantasy Ln Alton IL 62002 Office: So Ill U Sch Nursing Box 1066 Edwardsville IL 62026

DE MERE-DWYER, LEONA, medical artist; b. Memphis, May 1, 1928; d. Clifton and Leona (McCarthy) De M. BA, Rhodes Coll., Memphis, 1949; MSc, Memphis State U., 1984; PhD, Kennedy-Western U., 1990. Lic. embalmer, funeral dir.; m. John Thomas Dwyer, May 10, 1952; children: John, DeMere, Patrice, Brian, Anne-Clifton DeMere Dwyer, McCarthy-DeMere Dwyer. Med. artist for McCarthy DeMere, Memphis, 1950-80; pres. Aesthetic Med. & Forensic Art, 1984—; speech therapist, Memphis, 1950-82; lectr. on med. art univs., conf., assns.; cons. in prostheses Vocat. Rehab. Svcs.; elected expert witness in funeralization Nat. Forensic Ctr. Bereavement counselor Organizer Ladies of St. Jude, Memphis, 1960; active Brooks Art Gallery League of Memphis; leader Confraternity of Christian Doctrine, St. Louis Cath. Ch., 1966-67; vice dir. Tellico Hist. Found., 1980-80; mem. exec. bd. Chickasaw council Boy Scouts Am.; active Rep. campaign coms. Recipient Disting. Svc. award Gupton-Jones Coll. Mortuary Sci., 1981, Silver medal Sons of the Am. Revolution medal, 1985, Martha Washington medal. Mem. Fedn. Internat. de'Automobile (internat. car racing 1972, lic.), Assn. Med. Illustrators, Am. Assn. Med. Assts., Emergency Dept. Nurses Assn., Am. Physicians Nurses Assn., Am. Soc. Plastic and Reconstructive Surgeons Found. (guest mem., cons.), Women in Law (chmn. assocs.), Exec. Women Am., Brandeis U. Women, DAR (1st v.p. regent 1980), UDC (pres. Nathan Bedford Forrest chpt.), Cotton Carnival Assn. (chairperson children's ct. 1968-70), Pi Sigma Eta, Kappa Delta (adv.), Kappa Delta Pi. Clubs: Tenn., Royal Matron Amaranth (Faith Ct.), Sertoma (1st female mem. Memphis, 1st female life mem., elected pres. 1989-90) (Memphis). Contbr. articles to profl. jours. Home: 660 W Suggs Dr Memphis TN 38119

DEMEREE, GLORIA See LENNOX, GLORIA

DEMERS, JUDY LEE, university dean, state legislator; b. Grand Forks, N.D., June 27, 1944; d. Robert L. and V. Margaret (Harming) Prosser; m. Donald E. DeMers, Oct. 3, 1964 (div. Oct. 1971); 1 child, Robert M.; m. Joseph M. Murphy, Mar. 5, 1977 (div. Oct. 1983). BS in Nursing, U. N.D., 1966; MEd, U. Wash., 1973, postgrad., 1973-75. Pub. health nurse Govt. D.C., 1966-68, Combined Nursing Service, Mpls., 1968-69; instr. pub. health nursing U. N.D., Grand Forks, 1969-71, assoc. dir. Medex program, 1970-72, dir., family nurse practitioner program, 1977-82, assoc. dir. rural health, 1982-85 , dir. undergrad. med. edn., 1982-83, assoc. dean, 1983—; research assoc. U. Wash., Seattle, 1973-76; cons. Health Manpower Devel. Staff, Honolulu, 1975-81, Assn. Physician Asst. Programs, Washington, 1979-82; site visitor, cons. AMA-Com. Allied Health Edn. Accreditation, Chgo., 1979-81. Author: Educating New Health Practitioners, 1976; mem. editorial bd.: P.A. Jour., 1976-78; contbr. articles to profl. jours. Sec., bd. dirs. Valley Family Planning and Edn. Ctr., Grand Forks, N.D., 1982—; exec. com., bd. dirs. Agassiz Health Systems Agy., Grand Forks, 1982-86; mem. N.D. Ho. of Reps., 1982—, N.D. State Daycare Adv. Com., 1983—, Mayor's Adv. Com. on Police Policy, Grand Forks, 1983-85, N.D. State Foster Care Adv. Com., 1985-87, N.D. State Hypertension Adv. Com., 1983-85, Gov.'s Com. on DUI and Traffic Safety, 1985—, Statewide Adv. Com. on AIDS, 1985—; bd. dirs. Casey Found. Families First Initiative, 1988—; adv. com. Ruth Meiers Adolescent Ctr., Grand Forks, 1988—; mem. Commn. on Future of VA Health Care, 1990—. Recipient award Alpha Lambda Delta, 1963, Pub. Citizen of Yr. award N.D. chpt. Nat. Assn. Social Workers, 1986, Golden Grain award N.D. Dietitics Assn., 1988, Person of Yr. award U. N.D. Law Women Caucus, 1990, Legislator of Yr. award Northern Valley Labor Coun., 1990; U. Wash. regional med. program service fellow, 1972-73; Toll fellow, 1989, U. Wash. Kellogg Allied health fellow, 1972. Mem. Am. Nurses Assn., N.D. Nurses Assn. (mem. cabinet on edn. and practice 1982-86, Nurse of Yr. 1983), Am. Pub. Health Assn., Am. Ednl. Research Assn., N.D. Pub. Health Assn., N.D. Mental Health Assn., Assn. for Retarded Citizens, NOW, ACLU, LWV, Pi Lambda Theta, Sigma Theta Tau. Democrat. Home: 1826 Lewis Blvd Grand Forks ND 58203 Office: U ND Sch Medicine 501 Columbia Rd Grand Forks ND 58203

DEMERY, BARBARA BELL, interior designer; b. Cleve., Jan. 8, 1947; d. Andrew and Ruth M. (Morrison) Bell; m. Luther E. Demery, Aug. 10, 1968; children: Tiffany, David. AB, Cuyahoga Community Coll., Cleve., 1988. Interior design asst. Helen M. Moran Inc., Cleveland Heights, Ohio; adminstrv. sec. LaFeminique Inc., Cleve.; sec. Approaches Inc., Cleve.; interior designer Dept. Vets. Affairs, Brecksville, Ohio. Recipient Superior Performance award Dept. Vets. Affairs. Mem. NAFE, AIA, Coun. Fed. Interior Designers. Home: 4296 Larkspur Ln Warrensville Heights OH 44128

DEMET, MARGADETTE MOFFATT, lawyer; b. Pontiac, Ill., Aug. 20, 1927; d. Thomas Henry and Margaret Veronica (Maher) Moffatt; m. Francis Joseph Demet, Nov. 27, 1954; children: Donal Moffatt, Maura Megan, Kerry Denise, Michael Brendan, Barry Brendan, Kevin John, Brigid Honora, Deirdre Dianthe. BA summa cum laude, Coll. of St. Francis, Joliet, Ill., 1947; LLB, Marquette U., 1950. Bar: Wis. 1950, U.S. Dist. Ct. (ea. dist.) Wis. 1950, U.S. Dist. Ct. (no. dist.) Ill. 1956, U.S. Ct. Appeals (7th cir.) 1955, U.S. Supreme Ct. 1966. Asst. to pres. Milw. Gas Light Co., 1950-55; ptnr. Demet & Demet, S.C., Milw., 1954-75, v.p., treas., ptnr., 1975—; assoc. dir. Milw. Plan for Legal Svcs., 1966-69; bd. dirs. Client Security Fund. Editor Wis. Continuing Legal Edn.; mem. Marquette Law Rev., 1949-50. Mem., past chmn. Milw. Ethics Bd., 1974—; mem. Archdiocesan Due Process Bd., Milw., 1975—; bd. dirs., mem. exec. com. Milwaukee County Hist. Soc., 1978—; bd. dirs., past pres. Milw. Cath. Home, 1983—; bd. dirs., past officer St. Catherine's Residence for Women, Milw., 1984—; bd. dirs. Marquette High Sch. Found., Milw., 1985—, Villa Clement, Milw., 1986—; bd. dirs., mem. exec. com. Sacred Heart Sch. Theology. Recipient svc. award U. Wis. Law Sch., Madison, 1984, 88, Milw. Ethics Bd., 1987, Marquette High Sch. Found., 1989; profl. achievement award Coll. of St. Francis, 1986, Mary Neville Bielefeld award Marquette U., 1988. Mem. ABA (coms. 1954—), State Bar Wis. (sec. 1984-86, bd. dirs. 1986-90, Pro Bono Publico award 1980), 7th Cir. Bar Assn. (Civil Practitioner of Yr. award 1988), Milw. Bar Assn. (exec. editor, bd. dirs., editor Gavel 1960-66, Meritorious Svc. to Bar award 1960, 66), St. Thomas More Soc. (past bd. dirs.), Tempo, Women's Club Wis., Coll. Women's Club. Office: 815 N Cass St Milwaukee WI 53202

DEMETRY-JEYNES, MARY KAY, college dean; b. Miami, Fla., Oct. 31, 1941; d. Nasrallah and Martha (Jabaly) Demetry; m. Paul Jeynes, Sept. 30, 1978. BS, Fla. State U., 1963. Program dir. Orange County YMCA, Orlando, Fla., 1964-69, Ea. Queens YMCA, Belrose, N.Y., 1970-73; regional coord. N.Y. State Park and Recreation Commn., N.Y.C., 1974-77; dir. health, fitness and recreation YWCA of N.Y.C., 1978-79; dean courses for adults Marymount Manhattan Coll., N.Y.C., 1980—. Office: Marymount Manhattan Coll 221 E 71st St New York NY 10021

DEMIK, ANITA LORRAINE, executive secretary; b. Aurora, Ill., Oct. 11, 1945; d. Thorston Oscar and Emily Kristine (Sorensen) Ostergren; m. Robert A. DeMik, Sept. 11, 1965; children: Thor Arnold, Michael James, Todd Arthur. Cert. profl. sec. Legal sec. McDermott, Will & Emery, Chgo., 1977-81; adminstrv. asst. Sch. Social Svc., U. Chgo., 1981-82; legal sec., dept. coord. Kirkland & Ellis, Chgo., 1982-84; legal sec., legal asst. Bell, Boyd & Lloyd, Chgo., 1984—; v.p., sec. Atina, Inc., Park Forest, Ill., 1984-86; exec. sec. Morgan Stanley & Co., Chgo., 1986-88, exec. sec. Barbara Oil, 1988—. Author papers on secretarial professionalism and ethics. Guest speaker EPA, Chgo., 1984-85; guest instr. Catherine Bus. Coll., Chgo., 1985; speaker Archdiocese Carousel of Learning, Chgo., 1985. Mem. Profl. Secs. Internat. (sec. 1982-83, v.p. 1983-84, pres. 1984-85, membership chmn. 1985-86, Chgo. chpt.; chmn. retirement ctrs. trust ctr., Ill. div., 1986—; del. internat. conv. Toronto 1964, alt. internat. conv. Louisville 1965), Nat. Assn. for Exec. Women. Democrat. Lutheran. Club: Will County Extension (pres. 1972-73) (Beecher, Ill.). Avocations: computers, writing. Home: 3 Wheaton Center Wheaton IL 60187 Office: Barbara Oil Co One First Nat Pla Chicago IL 60603

DE MILLE, AGNES, choreographer; d. William Churchill and Anna (George) de M.; m. Walter F. Prude, June 14, 1943; 1 child, Jonathan. A.B. cum laude, U. Calif.; Litt.D. (hon.), Mills Coll., 1952, Russell Sage Coll., 1953, Smith Coll., 1954, Western Coll., 1955, Hood Coll., 1957, Northwestern U., 1960, Goucher Coll., 1961, Clark U., 1962, UCLA, 1964, Franklin and Marshall, 1965, Western Mich. U., 1967, Nasson Coll., 1971; L.H.D., Dartmouth Coll., 1974, Duke U., 1975, U. N.C., 1980, NYU, 1981. Dance recitalist U.S., Eng., France, Denmark, 1928-42; choreographer and dancer The Black Crook, 1929; choreographer (film) Romeo and Juliet, 1936; (musicals) Nymph Errant, 1933, Hooray for What, 1937, Oklahoma, 1943, One Touch of Venus, 1943, Bloomer Girl, 1944, Carousel, 1945, Brigadoon, 1947, Gentlemen Prefer Blondes, 1949, Paint Your Wagon, 1951, The Girl in Pink Tights, 1954, Goldilocks, 1958, Juno, 1959, Kwamina, 1961; (ballets) OBeah Black Ritual, 1940, Three Virgins and a Devil, 1942, Drums Sound in Hackensack, 1941, Rodeo, 1942, Tally-Ho, 1944, Fall River Legend, 1948, The Harvest According, 1952, Oklahoma (film), 1955, The Wind in the Mountains, 1965, The Four Mary's, 1965, The Informer, 1988; choreographer, dir. Allegro, 1947; dir. Rape of Lucrecia, 1949, Out of this World, 1950, Come Summer, 1969; choreographer (musical) 110 In the Shade, 1963; head Agnes de Mille Dance Theatre, presented by S. Hurok, 6 mos. tour, 126 cities, 1953-54, Agnes de Mille Heritage Dance Theater, 1973, 74, Conversations About the Dance, 1974, 75, Omnibus lectrs. and ballets, 1956-57; choreographer for Ballet Russe de Monte Carlo, 1942, Royal Winnipeg Ballet, 1972; author: Dance to the Piper, 1952, And Promenade Home, 1958, To A Young Dancer, 1962, The Book of the Dance, 1963, Lizzie Borden Dance of Death, 1968, Dance in America, 1970, Russian Journals, 1970, Speak to Me, Dance with Me, 1974, Where the Wings Grow, 1978, America Dances, 1980, Reprieve, 1981. Contbr. to McCalls, Atlantic Monthly, N.Y. Times mag., Vogue, Good Housekeeping, Esquire, Horizon mags. Recipient N.Y. Cirtics prize, 1942-46, Donaldson award, 1943-47, Madamoiselle Merit award, 1944, Antoinette Perry award, 1947, 62, Lord and Taylor award, 1947, Dancing Masters award of merit, 1950, Dance Mag. award, 1957, Capezio award, 1966, Handel award Mayor N.Y.C., 1975, Kennedy award Pres. U.S., 1980, Commonwealth award in dramatic arts, 1980, Nat. Medal of Arts, 1986; named Woman of Yr. Am. Newspaper Woman's Guild, 1946, named to Theatre Hall of Fame, 1973; Agnes de Mille Theatre, N.C. Sch. Arts, Winston-Salem named in her honor, 1975. Mem. Soc. Stage Dirs. and Choreographers (pres. 1965-66). Office: Harold Ober Assocs 40 E 49th St New York NY 10017

DEMILLE, DARCY See JACKSON, WILMA

DEMILLION, JULIANNE, health/fitness specialist and personal trainer, rehabilitation consultant; b. Monessen, Pa., Dec. 20, 1955; d. William Vincent and Enise Mary (Tocci) DeM. BA, BS, U. Pitts., 1977; cert. massage therapist Phoenix Therapeutic Massage Coll., 1985. Mgr. program devel. Exclusively Women Spas, Scottsdale, 1977-81; pvt. exercise therapist, Scottsdale, 1981-83, pvt. personal trainer, Scottsdale, 1983—; cons. City of Phoenix, 1981—; instr. advanced techniques Phoenix Therapeutic Massage Coll., 1986—. Mem. NAFE, Am. Massage Therapy Assn. (State Meritorious award 1989), Ariz. Massage Therapy Assn. (sec.-treas. 1986—), Internat. Dance and Exercise Assn., Circulo-Systems Ltd., Am. Coll. Sports Medicine.

DEMING, ANNE LOUISE, counseling administrator; b. Pottsville, Pa., Feb. 23, 1939; d. James J. and Anne V. (Kelly) Bruggy; m. Robert H. Deming, Mar. 3, 1962; children: Michael, Maura, Sean. AB in French, Coll. Notre Dame of Md., 1961; MA in French, Miami U., Oxford, Ohio, 1969; MEd in Counseling, SUNY, Buffalo, 1974, PhD, 1977. Asst. prof. psychology SUNY, Fredonia, 1977-79, counseling psychologist, 1978-83, asst. to pres. devel./alumni affairs, exec. dir. Found., 1983-88; v.p. advancement West Chester (Pa.) U., 1988—; mem. adj. faculty, mentor Empire State Coll., Fredonia, 1978-88; cons. Employee Assistance Program, Perrysville, N.Y., 1979-82, Inmate Coll. Adv. Project, Albany, N.Y., 1977-78. Contbr. articles to profl. jours., translator articles from Frech, review books Choice mag. Mem. exec. com., adv. bd. Chester County Coun. Aging, West Chester, 1989—; pres. Fredonia Citizens Adv. Com., 1986-87; chmn. Chautauqua County Community Svcs. Bd., Maryville, N.Y., 1983-85. Recipient Calista Jones award for advancing rights women Lakeshore Women's Svcs. Coalition, Chautauqua County, N.Y., 1988. Mem. Am. Assn. Profl. Hypnotherapists, Nat. Soc. Fund Raising Execs., Coun. Advancement and Support of Edn., Western N.Y. Com. Am. Coun. Edn's. Nat. Identification Program for Advancement Women in Higher Edn. Adminstrn., Pi Delta Phi, Phi Lambda Theata. Roman Catholic. Office: West Chester U Smith House Rm 102 West Chester PA 19383

DEMITCHELL, TERRI ANN, lawyer; b. San Diego, Apr. 10, 1953; d. William Edward and Rose Annette (Carreras) Wheeler; m. Todd Allan DeMitchell, Aug. 14, 1982. AB in English with honors, San Diego State U., 1975; JD, U. San Diego, 1984; MA in Edn., U. Calif., Davis, 1990; doctoral study, Harvard U., 1989—. Bar: Calif. 1985, U.S. Dist. Ct. (so. dist.) Calif. 1985; cert. elem. tchr., Calif. Assoc. Biddle and Hamilton, Sacramento, 1986—; teaching asst. U. Calif., Davis, 1987. Author: The California Teacher and the Law, 1985, The Law in Relation to Teacher, Out of School Behavior. Mem. ABA, Calif. Bar Assn., Sacramento County Bar Assn., Women Lawyers Sacramento Assn., Nat. Orgn. Legal Problems in Edn., Pi Lambda Theta.

DEMLER, LINDA KASS, corporate executive; b. Pocatello, Idaho, Feb. 17, 1954; d. Theodore Edwin and Pauline Therese (Gaudreau) Kass; m. Frederick Russel Demler, Aug. 26, 1976; children: Todd Frederick, Scott Frederick. B.S. cum laude in Psychology, Pa. State U., 1976. Dining mgr. Holiday Inn, State College, Pa., 1976-77; restaurant mgr. Corner Room, State College, 1977-78; acctg. mgr. Heim, Heckendorn & Bruce, State College, 1978-80; div. mgr. N.Y. Life Ins. Co., N.Y.C., 1980—. Active Republican Nat. Com., Washington, 1985—. Mem. NAFE, Am. Mgmt. Assn., Chi Omega, Psi Chi, Alpha Lambda Delta. Home: 4 Effingham Rd Yardley PA 19067

DEMOND, JOAN, marine biologist; b. L.A.; d. Earle Frank and Lucile (Long) Demond. BA with highest honors, UCLA; MA summa cum laude, Mills Coll.; postgrad., U. Hawaii, Stanford U. Fishery aide NOAA-Nat. Fisheries Svc., Honolulu; sci.asst. Inter-Am. Tropical Tuna Commn.; rsch. biologist Scripps Inst. Oceanography, U. Calif.; marine zoologist div. mollusks U.S. Nat. Mus.; rsch. assoc., mus. scientist, instr. phys. sci. UCLA; marine biologist. NSF grantee. Mem. Underwater Photog. Soc., Western Soc. Naturalists, Western Soc. Malacologists, Am. Malacological Union, Phi Beta Kappa. Office: PO Box 5064 Santa Monica CA 90405-0064

DEMONTIER, PAULETTE LAPOINTE, chemist; b. Milw., Jan. 12, 1948; d. Paul Wilfred and Gladys Marie (Graf) LaPointe; m. Roger Heber DeMontier, June 9, 1969 (dec. June 1986). BS, U. Miami, Coral Gables, Fla., 1970; MS, U. Miami, 1972, PhD, 1987; postgrad., Kennedy-Western U., 1987-88. Lic. clin. chemist, Fla. Lab. asst. TLC Corp. subs. Eastman Kodak, Miami, Fla., 1969-71; lab. supr. Tocci Labs., Inc., Miami, 1971-72; asst. organic chemist Coulter Electronics, Hialeah, Fla., 1972-75; analytical chemist Coulter Diagnostics, Hialeah, 1976-80; research scientist Dade Baxter Travenol, Miami, 1981-86, sr. analytical chemist, 1986—; pres., chief chemist, cons. Indsl. Assocs., Miami, 1980—. Patentee chems.; contbr. articles to sci. jours. Task force mem. NOW, Miami, 1986. Recipient Dade Sci. Contbn. Citation Am. Dade County, 1985. Mem. Am. Chem. Soc. (mem. analytical div. 1974—, women chemists com. 1985—), Am. Assn. for Clin. Chemistry (chmn. Fla. sect. 1985-86, membership chmn. 1987-89), S. Fla. Chromatography Discussion Group. Office: Dade Baxter Travenol PO Box 520672 Miami FL 33152

DEMOOR, BARBARA JEAN, investment management company executive; b. Kalamazoo, Mich., Mar. 6, 1956; d. Isaac Marcus and Berendiena (DeHaan) D. Master of Mgmt., Aquinas Coll., Grand Rapids, 1980-83; BA, Western Mich. U., Kalamazoo, 1974-78. Asst. treas. McNamara Motor Express, Kalamazoo, Mich., 1978-79; fin. analyst Old Kent Bank & Trust Co., Grand Rapids, Mich., 1979-81; trust operations officer Old Kent Bank & Trust Co., Grand Rapids, 1981-83, corp. trust officer, 1983-84, v.p. trust investments, 1984-87; v.p. Ambs Investment Counsel, Inc., Grand Rapids, 1988—; fin. instructor, Aquinas Coll., Grand Rapids, 1988. Vol. United Way Kent County, Grand Rapids, 19181-84; bd. dirs., pres. HELP Pregnancy Crisis Aid, 1982-88. Recipient: Alumni vol. Excellence, Western Mich. U., Kalamazoo, 1987. Mme. Fin. Analysts Fedn. Western Mich. (assoc.), Western Mich. U. Alumni Assn. (treas. Grand Rapids chpt. 1989). Independent Universalist. Home: 706 Hoyt SE Grand Rapids MI 49507 Office: Ambs Investment Counsel Inc 1501 McKay Tower Grand Rapids MI 49503

DEMORE, JANE ELYSE, nurse, psychotherapist; b. Waterbury, Conn., Dec. 8, 1950; d. George Lawrence and Mae (Carlin) DeM; m. Richard A. Holcomb, Nov. 2, 1974 (div. 1978). BSN, Emory U., 1972, MS in Nursing, 1979. RN, Ga. ICU staff nurse Grady Meml. Hosp., Atlanta, 1972-74; nurse epidemiologist Ctr. for Disease Control, Atlanta, 1974-75; pub. health nurse Fulton County Health Dept., Atlanta, 1975-78; unit dir. Hamilton Meml. Hosp., Dalton, Ga., 1979-81; head nurse VA Med. Ctr., Decatur, Ga., 1981-83, clin. nurse specialist, 1983-87; nurse psychotherapist Ansley Therapy Assocs., Atlanta, 1983—; dir. nursing CPC Parkwood Hosp., Atlanta, 1987—. Author: Parameters of Mental Health, 1979. Mem. Am. Nurses Assn. (cert. clin. specialist in psychiat. nursing), Sigma Theta Tau. Home: 1466 Kay Ln Atlanta GA 30306 Office: CPC Parkwood Hosp 1999Cliff Valley Rd NE Atlanta GA 30329

DEMOS, VICTORIA CAMILLE, psychologist; b. St. Albans, N.Y., Feb. 25, 1959; d. Nicholas John and Camille Victoria (Grydyk) D.; d. Nichols John and Camille Victoria (Grydyk) D. BA in Psychology, Bucknell U., 1981; PhD in Clin. Psychology, Hahnemann U., 1987. Mental health worker Fair Oaks Hosp., Summit, N.J., 1981-82; intern psychology Irving Schwartz Inst., Phila., 1982-83; addiction counselor Fair Oaks Hosp. Cocaine Hotline, Summit, 1983; intern psychology Phila. Mental Health Ctr., 1983-84, Albert Einstein Med. Ctr., Phila., 1984-86, The Devereux Found., Devon, Pa., 1986-87; psychologist Crozer Chester (Pa.) Med. Ctr., Hahnemann U., 1987-89, Hahnemann U. Student Counseling Ctr., Phila., 1989-90; acting coord. tng. univ. counseling svc. U. Pa., Phila., 1990—; cons. Grad. Hosp. Health & Fitness Weight Loss Program, Phila., 1988—. Vol. Preservation Techniques, Phila., 1987-88. Mem. Am. Psychol. Assn., Pa. Psychol. Assn., Phila. Soc. Clin. Psychologists, Phila. Soc. For Psychoanalytic Psychology, Study Group for Contemporary Psychoanalytic Process. Office: Hahnemann U Student Coun Ct MS 515 Broad & Vine Sts Philadelphia PA 19102-1192

DEMPSEY, GAIL ROLADER, retail company executive; b. Monroe, Ga., May 5, 1949; d. Ezra Thomas and Flora Myrtle (Lipham) Rolader; m. Douglas Dempsey, July 3, 1969; children: Stephen Douglas, Richard David. AA, DeKalb Coll., Atlanta, 1969. Sec. G.B. Sawyer Co., Inc., Atlanta, 1967-79; pres., owner Dempsey Demonstration Svcs., Inc., Atlanta, 1979—. Contbr. articles to newspapers. Mem. NAFE, Nat. Frozen Food Assn. (Silver Penguin award 1989, Golden Penguin award 1989), Frozen Food Coun. Ga. (1st female pres. 1989), Female Execs. North Atlanta (sec. 1989, 90), Atlanta Food Brokers Assn., Women's Internat. Bowling Congress 500 Club. Home and Office: 431 Oakland Rd Lawrenceville GA 30244

DEMPSTER, LAURAMAY TINSLEY, botanist; b. El Paso, Tex., May 11, 1905; d. Clayton Rollins and Lucy Whiting (Burgess) Tinsley; m. Everett Ross Dempster, Oct. 8, 1927; children: Iris Dempster Green, Philip Tinsley Dempster. BA, U. Calif., Berkeley, 1925, MA, 1927. Tchr. Cora Williams Jr. Coll., Berkeley, 1928-29; rsch. asst. U. Calif., Berkeley, 1933-35, herbarium botanist, rsch. geneticist, 1951-67, rsch. assoc., 1967—. Author: Rubiaceae in Jepson Flora, 1979, Galium in S.A. (4 parts), 1980-89; contbr. papers to sci. publs. Fellow Calif. Acad. Scis.; mem. Am. Soc. Plant Taxonomists, Calif. Botan. Soc. Office: U Calif Jepson Herbarium Berkeley CA 94720

DEMSEY, BARBARA BLACKSTONE, secondary teacher; b. Caribou, Maine, Sept. 24, 1921; d. Milford Hollis and Reubena (Long) Blackstone; m. Norton Eugene Demsey, Jr., July 26, 1952; 1 child, David Blackstone. BS, U. Maine, 1943; MEd, Harvard U., 1946. Tchr., home econ. Pub. Sch., Cape Elizabeth, Maine, 1943-45; dean girls Maine Cen. Inst., Pittsfield,

Maine, 1946-50; asst. dean, dir. vocat. guidance Colby Jr. Coll., New London, N.H., 1950-51; dean girls Winchester (Mass.) High School, 1951-52; asst. organist, organist Unitarian Ch., Winchester, Mass., Caribou, Maine, 1956—; accompanist U. Maine, Presque Isle Theater, Caribou Choral Soc., Presque Isle Community Players. Active Rep.; vol. Winchester (Mass.) Schs.; mem. Washburn (Maine) Planning Bd. Mem. AAUW (pres. 1984-85), Salmon Br. Hist. Soc. Home: 16 Hines St P O Box 236 Washburn ME 04786

DEMUS, LEE ANNE, aircraft executive; b. Fairmont, Wv., Aug. 29, 1959; d. Walter Leroy and Eleanor Kay (Bosley) Smouse; m. Nick Demus III, Sept. 29, 1984; children: Nick Demus, Lauren Nicole, Alyssa Marie. AS, Fairmont State Coll., 1979. Office mgr. Gulf Mineral Resources, Inc., 1983; gen. mgr. TNG, Inc., Morgantown, W.Va., 1983—. Named One of Ams. 2000 Most Notable Women, Am. Biog. Inst., 1989. Mem. NAFE. Home: 127 Rosewood Ave Fairmont WV 26554

DEMYAN, JEANNE RAUCH, veterinarian; b. Columbia, S.C., Nov. 1, 1951; d. Jacob Elton and Edna Mae (Long) Rauch; divorced; m. Don Fowler, June 15, 1989. BS with honors, Clemson U., 1972; DVM, U. Ga., 1976. Assoc. veterinarian Johnson McKee Animal Hosp., Salisbury, Md., 1976; zoo veterinarian Riverbanks Zoo, Columbia, S.C., 1976; research assoc. Squibb Inst. Med. Research, New Brunswick, N.J., 1976-78, dir. lab. animal medicine, Princeton, N.J., 1978; owner Travelers Rest (S.C.) Animal Hosp., 1979—; mem. adv. council North Greenville Hosp., Travelers Rest, 1981-83; dancer Greenville Concert Ballet, 1983-84. Mem. AVMA, NOW (convenor 1st S.C. chpt. 1971, pres. 1972), S.C. Veterinary Med. Assn. (upstate legis. del. 1990), Greenville Vet. Med. Assn., Blue Ridge Vet. Med. Assn. (v.p., pres. 1990), Am. Holistic Veterinary Med. Assn., Internat. Veterinary Acupuncture Soc. (cert. 1989), Target Investment Club (pres. Greenville chpt. 1989, v.p. 1990). Episcopalian. Office: Travelers Rest Animal Hosp 409 Old Buncombe Rd Travelers Rest SC 29690

DENATALE, CAROLE EGAN, lawyer; b. Buffalo, Dec. 10, 1954; d. John Lloyd and Dorothy (Nigro) Egan; m. Richard Grimes DeNatale, Aug. 18, 1979. B.A. magna cum laude, Mt. Holyoke Coll., 1976; J.D., SUNY-Buffalo, 1979. Bar: N.Y. 1980, Ariz. 1980, U.S. Dist. Ct. (so. and ea. dists.) N.Y. 1985. Law clk. Diebold & Millonzi, Buffalo, 1978-79; assoc. John Lloyd Egan, Buffalo, 1979-80, Cates & Roediger, Phoenix, 1980-81, Kuhn, Muller & Bazerman, N.Y.C., 1982-84, Kane, Dalsimer, Sullivan, Kurucz, Levy, Eisele & Richard, N.Y.C., 1984—. Sarah Williston scholar, Mt. Holyoke Coll., 1973; Mary Lyon Scholar, 1976. Recipient Jessie Goodwin Spaulding Prize, Mt. Holyoke Coll., 1974, Cornelia Catlin Coulter Prize, 1975, Jean Renneisen Toub Prize, 1976. Mem. ABA, N.Y. State Bar Assn., State Bar Ariz., N.Y. Patent, Trademark and Copyright Law Assn., Jr. League, Phi Beta Kappa. Office: Kane Dalsimer Sullivan Kurucz Levy Eisele & Richard 711 3d Ave 20th Fl New York NY 10017

DENATALE, REGINA ANN, physical education teacher; b. N.Y.C., Oct. 1, 1958; d. Ralph and Rose Marie (DiMarsico) DeN. BS in Phys. Edn., U. N.H., 1980; MA in Exercise Physiology, Adelphi U., 1985. Cert. elem. tchr., N.Y., kindergarten through 12th grade phys. edn. tchr., N.Y. Tchr. sci., phys. edn. St. Patrick Sch., Bedford, N.Y., 1980-83; tchr. phys. edn., coach Irvington (N.Y.) Sch. Dist., 1984-85, New Rochelle (N.Y.) Sch. Dist., 1985-86, Edgemont Sch. Dist., Scarsdale, N.Y., 1986—; coach high sch. Mamaroneck (N.Y.) Sch. Dist., 1980-88. Vol. internat. coach Sport for Understanding, Washington, 1987-89 (Internat. Coach of Yr. award 1988); active on selection com. Empire State Games Hudson Valley Region, N.Y., 1988-90. Mem. AAHPER and Dance, N.Y. State Assn. Health, Phys. Edn., Recreation and Dance (v.p. elem. phys. edn. SE zone 1989—), Am. Assn. for Leisure and Recreation, Am. Running and Fitness Assn., Nat. Assn. for Sport and Phys. Edn., U.S. Field Hockey Assn., Field Hockey Coaches Assn. (pres. 1987-89), Rye Golf Club. Roman Catholic. Home: 44 Wetmore Pl Rye NY 10580 Office: Edgemont Sch Dist Glendale Rd Scarsdale NY 10583

DENDE-GALLIO, LUSIA MARIE, city planner; b. Detroit, Oct. 20, 1953; d. Edward Anthony and Cornelia Louise (Szubka) Dende; m. Christon Thomas Gallio, June 4, 1977. BS in Polit. Sci., U. Detroit, 1974; M Urban Planning, U. Pitts., 1976; cert. econs. and trade, Adam Micklewicz U., Poznan, Poland, 1984. Planning intern Green Internat., Sewickley, Pa., 1976; housing and land use planner Genesee, Lapeer, Shiawasee/Region V Planning & Devel. Commn., Flint, Mich., 1978-79; transp. planner Southeast Mich. Transp. Authority, Detroit, 1979-82; assoc. transp. planner Broward County Office Planning, Ft. Lauderdale, Fla., 1982-85; city planner City of Coconut Creek, Fla., 1985-86, City of Sunrise, Fla., 1986-88; dir. planning City of Pompano Beach, Fla., 1988—; chmn. tech. adv.com., Transp. for Disadvantaged, Broward County, 1983-85; vice-chmn. Broward County Tech. Adv. Com., 1986-88, chmn., 1989—. Mem. Am. Planning Assn., Fla. Planning Assn., Broward County Planning Assn., Am. Inst. Cert. Planners, Met. Planning Orgn. (tech. coord. com. 1986-89). Republican. Roman Catholic. Office: City of Pompano Beach PO Drawer 1300 Pompano Beach FL 33061

DENERO, NANCY STURDY, management consultant; b. Los Angeles, Dec. 1, 1946; d. Herbert Francis Sturdy and Jane Adeline (Kellogg) Ochsner; m. Henry Thomas DeNero, Dec. 27, 1968; children: Karen Frances, John Sturdy. BA, Smith Coll., Northampton, Mass., 1968; MBA, Stanford U., Calif., 1974. Mktg. Avery Internat., Azusa, Calif., 1974-78; dir. corporate strategy Dart Industries, L.A., 1979-80; spl. assignment, reporting to chmn. Dart & Kraft, Chgo., 1980-82; ptnr. Lineberger, Kidd, Kamm, Beverly Hills, Calif., 1985-86; prin. Svcs. to Threshold Co., San Marino, Calif., 1986—. Trustee Westridge Sch., Pasadena; bd. dirs. Armory Ctr. for Arts, Pasadena. Named First woman in mgmt. at Avery Pasadena Calif. 1974, Highest Ranking Exec. at Dart L.A., 1980, One of Two Sr. Women Execs. at Dart & Kraft 1981. Mem. Am. Mgmt. Assn., Orgn. Women Execs. (founder, past pres.). Office: Services for Threshold Comp 1613 Chelsea Rd #348 San Marino CA 91108

DENES, MAGDA, psychologist; came to U.S., 1950; d. Gyula and Margaret (Indig) D.; m. Michel Radomisli, May 1963 (div. Jan. 1976); children: Gregory John, Timothy Evan. BA, CCNY, 1956; MA, Boston U., 1958; PhD, Yeshiva U., 1961; cert. psychoanalysis, psychotherapy, NYU, 1967. Lic. psychologist, N.Y. Pvt. practice psychoanalysis, psychotherapy N.Y.C., 1961—; clin. prof. supr. tng. analyst Inst. Psychol. Studies Adelphi U., Garden City, 1969—, Inst. Advanced Psychol. Studies, 1970—; sr. cons. VA, N.Y.C., 1971-73; assoc. clin. prof. supr. and tng. analyst NYU, N.Y.C., 1972—; cons. ABC-TV FYI Pub. Service program, 1980-84; mem. faculty, supr. dept. psychiatry Mt. Sinai Sch. Medicine, N.Y.C., 1981—. Author: In Necessity and Sorrow: Life and Death in an Abortion Hospital, 1976; contbr. articles to profl. jours., newspapers and mags. Fellow Am. Psychol. Assn. (various coms.); mem. N.Y. Soc. Clin. Psychologists (pres. 1978-79), N.Y. State Psychol. Assn. (pres. 1986-87). Club: Williams Coll. Home: 40 E 84th St New York NY 10028 Office: 125 E 87th St New York NY 10128

DENGLER, JANA ELIZABETH, construction executive; b. York, Pa., Feb. 5, 1956; d. George L. and Marjory (Wolf) D. Student, Albright Coll., 1974-77; BA in Bus. Adminstrn., Pa. State U., 1979. V.p. pub. mkgt. Common Health, Inc., Reading, Pa., 1977-80; carpenter, foreman M&S Constrn., Reading, 1980-85; property mgr. Property Resources Inc., Boston, 1985-88; project coordinator Bankoh Corp. Bank of Hawaii, Honolulu, 1989-90; owner, pres. Dengler Constrn., Camp Hill, Pa., furniture design, constrn., hist. restoration, 1985—. Mem. Pi Alpha Tau (v.-. 1972, 73). Home and Office: 393 Maiden Ln King of Prussia PA 19406 Office: Bankoh Corp Bank of Hawaii PO Box 2900 Honolulu HI 96846

DENGROVE, IDA LIBBY, artist; b. Phila., Sept. 12, 1918; d. Harry and Lillian (Chan) Leibovitz; m. Edward Dengrove, oct. 4, 1941; children: Richard, Robert, Lois. BFA, Moore Coll., Phila., 1940. Cert. artist. Art tchr. Phila. Bd. of Edn., 1941-43, Monmouth County (N.J.) Adult, 1958=71; courtroom illstr. NBC-TV, N.Y., 1972-86; illstr. Sports Illustrated, N.Y.; portrait painter N.J. Studio, 1986-88; prof. of art Monmouth Coll., N.J., 1987--; lecturer many coll. and orgn., 1980--. Writer: William Morrow, 1989. Recipient N.Y. Press Club award, 1983, N.Y. Chpt. Nat. Assn. TV Arts and Scis. Emmy award for Son of Sam, 1977-78, for Craig Crimmins Murder at Met, 1980-81. Mem. Natas, N.Y. Chpt. Republican. Home: 541 N Edgemere Dr West Allenhurst NJ 07711

DENHAM, MARY WASHKO, development director; b. Springfeld, Ill., May 29, 1957; d. George Joseph and Betty Jean (Downen) Washko; m. William A. Denham III, Oct. 6, 1984. AA, Sprinfield Coll. in Ill., 1977; BA, Blackburn Coll., 1979; MA in Psychology, Sangamon State U., 1981. Sec. LincolnFest, Springfield, Ill., 1982-83; mgr. spl. events Perfect Impressions, Springfield, 1983-88; devel. dir. Springfield Coll., 1988—. Interpreter Dana-Thomas State Hist. Site, Springfield, 1981—. Recipient Named Gift Endowment AAUW, 1986, Volunteer of the Year award Dana-Thomas Found., 1985. Mem. AAUW (pres. 1988-90), Soc. for Tng. & Devel., AAUW (pres. 1988—, treas. 1984-86). Democrat. Lutheran. Home: 40 Westwood Terrace Springfield IL 62702 Office: Springfield Coll 1500 N Fifth Springfield IL 62702

DENHAM, PATRICIA EILEEN KELLER, law librarian; b. Columbus, Ohio, Mar. 1, 1952; d. William Waite and Eileen Catherine (Miller) Keller; m. Richard Whitley Denham, Oct. 10, 1981 (div. Mar. 1986); 1 child, Michael Richard. BS, Findlay Coll., 1974; MSLS, U. Ky., 1978. Acquisitions librarian Supreme Ct. Ohio Law Library, Columbus, 1974-76; acquisitions librarian Robert S. Marx Law Library U. Cin., 1978-88, head preservation and archives, 1988—; librarian Rendigs, Fry, Kiely & Dennis, Cin., 1979-85. Mem. AAUW, NOW, Assn. Women Faculty, AAUP, Am. Assn. Law Librs. (travel grantee 1984), Ohio Regional Assn. Law Librs., Midwest Archives Conf., Soc. Ohio Archivists. Republican. Episcopalian. Office: U Cin Robert S Marx Law Libr Location 142 Cincinnati OH 45221

DENHART, GUN, direct mail order company executive; b. Lund, Sweden, July 14, 1945; came to U.S., 1975; d. Gunnar Arnold and Elsa (Bjôrklund) Brime; m. Thomas E. Denhart, Aug. 29, 1975; children: Philip, Christian. MBA, Lund U., Sweden, 1967. Tchr. Swedish Pub. Sch., Landskrona, Sweden, 1972-73; asst. to sec. gen., bus. and industry adv. com. OECD, Paris, 1973-75; fin. mgr. EF Colls. Ltd., Greenwich, Conn., 1978-84; chief exec. officer Hanna Andersson Corp., Portland, Oreg., 1984—. Mem. Young Pres. Orgn. Office: Hanna Andersson Corp 327 NW 10th Portland OR 97209

DENINNIS, MICHELE, personnel specialist; b. Rochester, N.Y., Apr. 15, 1962; d. Antonio and Mary (Amato) DeN. A in Secretarial Studies, Bryant & Stratton Bus. Inst., 1982. Pers. specialist in employee devel. and tng. AC Rochester (N.Y.) div. GM, 1981—. Democrat. Roman Catholic. Home: 9 Wyndover Rd Rochester NY 14616

DENMAN, CATHERINE CHERYL, nuclear quality control specialist; b. Phoenix, Oct. 29, 1958; d. Irving Lloyd and Yvonne Catherine (Price) D. Student, Tarleton State U., Stephenville, Tex., 1976-77. Nuclear insp. Comanche Peak Nuclear Sta., Brown & Root, Houston, 1979-89; quality specialist Gilbert Commonwealth, Reading, Pa., 1989—.

DENMAN, MARY ELIZABETH, advertising and marketing firm executive; b. Power, W.Va., June 28, 1922; d. Thomas Joseph and Rose Anna (Care) Williams; m. Richard H. Denman, Jan. 29, 1944; children: Daryl Ann, Deborah, Richard T. BS in Edn., Miami U., Oxford, Ohio, 1943. Tchr. Corpus Christi Ind. Sch. Dist., 1960-64; host, producer Our Town KENS-TV, San Antonio, 1966-73, news co-anchor Noon News, 1974; host Morning Mag. WOAI, San Antonio, 1976-86; host, producer Mary Denman Show KRNN, San Antonio, 1987; dir. mktg. Geriatric Svcs., Inc., San Antonio, 1990—; owner, pres. Mary Denman, Inc., Advt., San Antonio, 1987—. Pres., San Antonio Little Theatre, 1990—; trustee Our Lady of the Lake U., San Antonio, 1972-73; vice chmn. Def. Adv. Com. on Women in the Svcs., 1972-74; bd. dirs. San Antonio Arts Council, 1972-75, pres., 1974-75; bd. dirs. Goodwill Industries, 1984—. Recipient Woman of Achievement award Joske's of Tex., 1982; Top Communicators award Women's Hall of Fame, 1984; named Disting. Alumna, Miami U. of Ohio, 1973. Mem. Internat. Women's Forum, Women in Communications Inc. (Headliner award 1989), Am. Women in Radio and TV (nat. bd. dirs., area v.p. 1969-73, chmn. nat. conv. 1980, Broadcaster of Yr. 1972). Methodist. Home and office: 1734 Donerail San Antonio TX 78248

DENMEAD, DORIS LOUISE, medical facility administrator; b. N.Y.C., Feb. 17, 1933; d. Robert William and Florence Mary (Hunt) Tobin; m. James Gordon, Oct. 19, 1958; 1 child, Linda Mary. BBA, St. John's U., N.Y.C., 1954; MBA, Columbia U., 1975. Sr. pub. acct. Harris, Kerr, Foster and Co., N.Y.C., 1959-63; asst. controller John Hay Whitney, N.Y.C., 1963-71; instr. acctg. Drake Coll., Plainfield, N.J., 1971-75; fin. analyst Gen. Learning Corp., Morristown, N.J., 1975-76; internal fiscal auditor Seton Hall U., South Orange, N.J., 1976-77; controller Am. Cancer Soc., Union, N.J., 1978-80, Bonnie Brae Sch. for Spl. Boys, Millington, N.J., 1980-82; fiscal coordinator U. Medicine and Dentistry of N.J., Piscataway, N.J., 1982—. Nat. Assn. Female Execs., Accts. for Pub. Interest, Soc. Bus. and Profl. Women (pres. Somerset N.J. chpt. 1974-75, 77-78) Am. Legion Aux. (v.p. Warren, N.J. club 1986-87). Democrat. Roman Catholic. Home: 33 Mountain Ave Warren NJ 07060 Office: U Medicine and Dentistry Robert Wood Johnson Med Sch 675 Hoes Ln Piscataway NJ 08854

DENMON, MELANIE PATRICIA, insurance executive; b. Springhill, La., Jan. 22, 1954; d. Thomas Winton and Marjorie Loyce (Crisp) D. BA in Speech Pathology and Audiology, U. Southwestern La., 1976. Mgr. ins. brokerage, cons., agy. supr. Charles D. Bernard Agy., Ltd./Transamerica Life Ins. Services, Lafayette, La., 1979—. Col. Staff of Gov. David C. Treen, Baton Rouge, 1980; mem. Acadiana Arts Council, Lafayette Ballet Co. Mem. Nat. Assn. Female Exec., Nat. Assn. Life Underwriters (mem. women life underwriters conf.), Acadiana Assn. Life Underwriters of Nat. Assn. Life Underwriters, Lafayette Fine Arts Assn.. Republican. Methodist. Home: 200 Lodge Dr Unit #110 Lafayette LA 70506 Office: Charles D Bernard Agy Ltd 102 Jomela Dr Lafayette LA 70503

DENNARD, PEGGY ETHERIDGE, educational administrator; b. Baker County, Fla., Nov. 12, 1937; d. Herschel Virgil and Lillie Virginia (Burnsed) Etheridge; m. William Irvin Dennard Jr.; children: Margaret Leslie, William Irvin III. Student, Stetson U., 1955-57; BA in Edn., U. Fla., 1959; MEd with honors, U. North Fla., 1975. Tchr. Duval County Schs., Jacksonville, Fla., 1959-64; media specialist Nassau County Schs., Fernandina Beach, Fla., 1965-73, dir. instructional support svcs., 1973—; edn. coord. County Bicentennial Com., Nassau, Fla., 1975-76; inservice instr. Nassau County Schs., Fernandina Beach, 1973-88; area rep. Fla. Govs. Conf., 1977. Contbr. articles to profl. jours. Bd. dirs. Hist. Mus., Fernandina Beach, 1975-77; tchr. adult Bible class local Bapt. ch., 1976—, treas. 1980—. Named Outstanding Young Educator, Jaycees, Nassau County, 1968. Mem. AAUW (v.p. 1973-77), Fla. Assn. Media in Edn. (scholarship chmn. 1978-79), Fla. Assn. Suprs. Media, Fla. Assn. Computer Supervision, Alpha Delta Kappa (treas. 1976-78, pres. elect 1988-90, pres. 1990—), Theta Alpha Phi. Democrat. Baptist. Office: Sch Bd Nassau County 1201 Atlantic Ave Fernandina Beach FL 32034

DENNETT, ELLEN LOUGHRIN, manufacturing company executive; b. Grand Rapids, Mich., Dec. 24, 1960; d. Richard Norbert and Mary Ruth (Dark) Loughrin; m. William Frank. Student, Mich. Tech. U., 1979-81; BA in Journalism, Mich. State U., 1983. Staff reporter Mich. Tech. Lode Newspaper, Houghton, Mich., 1979-80; editor-in-chief Mich. Tech. Lode, Houghton, 1980-81; photo staff asst. Mich. State Instructional Media Ctr., East Lansing, 1981-83; staff asst. to research Mich. Tech. U., Houghton, 1983-84; process engr., brand mgr. Procter & Gamble Paper Co., Green Bay, Wis., 1984-87; quality mgr., tng. mgr. Boise Cascade, Wallula, Wash., 1987--; statistical process control mgr. Boise Cascade, Wallula, 1988—, vice chmn., chair elect, 1989—. Mem. Am. Soc. Quality Control. Home: 7808 Harbor Blvd Pasco WA 99301 Office: Boise Cascade Box 500 Walla Walla WA 99363

DENNIE, DEBORAH THOMAS, minister; b. Memphis, Sept. 20, 1939; d. Willie Timothy and Beatrice (Bell) Thomas; m. Thurman Paul Dennie, Sept. 30, 1965; children: Deirdre Beatrice, Thurman Phillip. BA, Cen. State U., Wilberforce, Ohio, 1961; MA, Memphis State U., 1967; postgrad., Vanderbilt U., 1969-70. Lic. marriage and family therapist, profl. counselor, Tenn. Tchr. Memphis City Schs., 1962-65; instr. S.A. Owen Jr. Coll., Memphis, 1965-68, Lemoyne-Owen Coll., Memphis, 1968-69; assoc. editor Tri-State Defender Newspaper, Memphis, 1970-76; radio host WLOK Radio, Memphis, 1976-78; counselor Shelby County Sheriff's Dept., Memphis, 1978-87; chief hearing officer Shelby County Sheriff's Dept., 1987-89, asst. to chief jailer, 1989—; dir. Crisis & Stress Mgmt. Inst., Memphis, 1982-86; psychotherapist in pvt. practice Memphis, 1982—; pastor African Meth. Episcopal Ch., Memphis, 1983—. Author: Sing Sweet Orpheus, Sing, 1976; editor-in-chief newspaper, Ministers' Alliance of W. Tennessee, 1990. Bd. dirs. N. Memphis Health Clinic, 1978-83. Named Outstanding Citizen Seventh Day Adventists, 1985; Rev. Deborah Thomas Dennie Day named in honor by Sheriff of Shelby County, 1990. Mem. AAUW, Tenn. Corrections Assn. Shelby County (treas. 1989), AME Ministers Alliance of W. Tenn. (pres. 1990), Phi Delta Kappa. Republican. Home: 3294 Harris Ave Memphis TN 38111

DENNIES, SANDRA LEE, city administrator; b. Buffalo, Dec. 26, 1951; d. Norman John and Shirley Edith (Dils) D.; m. Robert Francis Gilbane, Sept. 21, 1974 (div. Apr. 1987); children: Brandon Michael, Gianpatrick. AS in Dental Hygiene, U. Bridgeport, Conn., 1972, BS in Dental Hygiene Edn., 1973; MS in Health Scis., So. Conn. State U., 1979. Dental hygienist various orgns., New Haven, 1972-73, Leonard B. Zaslow, DDS, Westport, Conn., 1973-81; lectr. U. Bridgeport, 1973-76; planner City of Bridgeport, 1977-79, planning asst., 1979-81; grants dir. City of Stamford, Conn., 1981—; sec. Com. on Emergency Med. Disaster Planning, Bridgeport, 1978-79; dep. dir. Stamford Coliseum Authority, 1982-88, Stamford Film Commn., 1986-88. Editor, chief: Hy-Light Jour., 1973-76. Mem. Stamford Youth Planning and Adv., 1981—, United Way Corp., Stamford, 1986—; pres., sec. The Alcohol and Drug Abuse Coun., 1987—; mem. NSCC bd. Christian Outreach, Stamford, 1988—, Coun. of Chs. and Synagogues Assembly, Stamford, 1989—. Mem. NAFE, Nat. Soc. Fund Raising Execs. Democrat. Congregationalist. Home: 171 Shadow Ridge Rd Stamford CT 06905 Office: City of Stamford 888 Washington Blvd Stamford CT 06904-2152

DENNING, BRENDA FAY, nursing executive; b. Coaldale, Pa., Mar. 15, 1949; d. Wayne Allen and Ruth Annabelle (Kriner) Hartung; m. Joseph Cliff Denning, July 30, 1971; children: Joseph Cliff III, Jereme Wayne. RN diploma, Pottsville Hosp. Sch. Nursing, Pottsville, Pa., 1969; BS in Nursing, Kutztown U., 1987. Cert. in nursing adminstrn. Am. Nurse's Assn. Staff nurse Pottsville Hosp. & Warne Clinic, Pottsville, Pa., 1969-78; day adminstrv. supr. Pottsville Hosp. & Warne Clinic, 1978-83, asst. dir. patient care, 1983-84, assoc. dir. patient care, 1984-88; dep. coroner Schuylkill County Coroner's Office, Pottsville, 1985-88; acting dir. patient care Pottsville Hosp. & Warne Clinic, 1986, 88, v.p. patient care svcs., 1988—; adv. com. dept. nursing Kutztown U. Mem. Ch. Coun. and Support Coms., 1986—; chmn. witness com. Trinity Luth. Ch., Pottsville, 1987—, chmn. 1987-89, mem. witness com., 1986—; mem. Pottsville Hosp. Aux. Mem. Nursing Svc. Adminstrn. of Hosp. Assn. Pa., Pa.Ea. Region Orgn. Nurse Execs., Pottsville Hosp. Alumni Assn., Kutztown U. Alumni Assn. Republican. Home: Box 382 Mary D PA 17952 Office: Pottsville Hosp & Warne Clinic 420 S Jackson St Pottsville PA 17901

DENNING, DOROTHY ELIZABETH ROBLING, computer scientist; b. Grand Rapids, Mich., Aug. 12, 1945; d. C. Lowell and Helen Dorothy (Watson) R.; m. Peter James Denning, Jan. 24, 1974. BA in Math., U. Mich., 1967, MA in Math., 1969; PhD in Computer Sci., Purdue U., 1975. Systems programmer, instr. U. Rochester, N.Y., 1968-72; asst. prof. Purdue U., West Lafayette, Ind., 1975-81, assoc. prof., 1981-83; computer scientist, sr. staff scientist SRI Internat., Menlo Park, Calif., 1983-87; computer scientist, researcher Digital Equipment Corp., Palo Alto, Calif., 1987—. Author: Cryptography and Data Security, 1982. Mem. Trails adv. com., San Mateo (Calif.) County, 1988—. Mem. Internat. Assn. Cryptologic Rsch. (pres. 1983-86), Assn. for Computing Machinery (svc. award 1985), Computer Soc. of IEEE (Best Paper award tech. com. on security and privacy, 1987), Sigma Xi. Office: Digital Equipment Corp 130 Lytton Ave Palo Alto CA 94301 Home: 30 Bear Gulch Dr Portola Valley CA 94028

DENNING, EILEEN BONAR, management consultant; b. Chester, Pa., June 24, 1944; d. Michael Bonar and Lucille J. Denbroeder. Pres. Denning and Co., Castro Valley, Calif., 1975—; mem. adv. bd. Diablo Valley Coll. bus. div.; faculty adv. bd. Am. Inst. Banking. Coord. Castro Valley Earthquake Preparedness, 1980—; fundraiser Castro Valley Schs., 1976—. Mem. Nat. Women's Polit. Caucus. Home and Office: 3446 Brookdale Castro Valley CA 94546

DENNING, HAZEL MAY, research foundation administrator, consultant; b. Woodstock, Ill., Mar. 1, 1907; d. William Frederick O'Connor and Cora May (Anderson) Dale; m. Burl Roy Denning, Mar. 1, 1931 (dec.); adopted children: Dora May Stormon, Burl Warren, Ray Allison (dec.). BA, U. Calif., Riverside, 1956; MA, Claremont (Calif.) Grad. Sch., 1962, Redlands (Calif.) U., 1981; PhD, Internat. Coll., 1984. From sec. to office mgr. Cen. Jr. High Sch., Riverside, 1927-30; with 1st Meth. Ch., Riverside, 1933-72, staff youth dir., 1957-61, dir., choreographer for dance troup, 1966-69; founder, pres. Parapsychology Assn. of Riverside, Inc., 1971-85; producer-dir. drama program 1st Meth. Ch., Riverside, 1937-72; adminstr. pks. rsch. and edn. project Parapsychology Assn. of Riverside, Inc., 1979—; exec. dir. Assn. for Past Life Rsch. & Therapies, Riverside, 1983-89; dir. emeritus, ambassador-at-large, 1990—; freelance lectr., 1926—; pvt. practice metaphys. counselor, Riverside, 1945—; instr. tng. workshop Assn. for Past Life Rsch. & Therapies, Inc., 1984—. Contbr. articles to profl. jours. Mem. Riverside YWCA, 1957—, tchr., 1970-71; active mem. Riverside PTA, 1940-49; charter mem. Riverside Mental Health Assn., 1949—, v.p., 1952-53. Recipient 1st award Tri-County Press Writer's Contest, 1972; named Best Female Performer, Riverside Community Players, 1973, 74; Park's Electronics grantee, 1979. Mem. AAUW (pres. local br. 1968-70), Nat. League for Am. Penwomen (pres. local chpt. 1976-80, Woman of Achievement award 1976), Rocky Mountain Rsch. Inst. (internat. adv. bd. 1988-89), Inst. for Noetic Scis., Am. Soc. for Psychic Rsch., Assn. for Transpersonal Psychology, Riverside Writer's Club, Teen Girl's Assts. (pres. Riverside chpt. 1967-68). Republican. Methodist. Office: Alternative Healthcare 7111 Magnolia Ave Ste G Riverside CA 92504

DENNING, LESLIE BARBARA, accountant; b. Phila., Feb. 3, 1952; d. Ernest and Patricia Nancy Denning. BA in Polit. Sci., Pa. State U., 1973; cert. in purchasing and inventory control mgmt., Mercyhurst Coll., 1983; postgrad., Nova U., 1976; student, Gannon Coll., 1978. Inventory taker Retail Grocer's Inventory Specialists, Erie, Pa., 1973-75; acct. The Warren Co., Erie, 1973-86; bookkeeper Rodeway Inn South, Orlando, Fla., 1986; staff acct. Empire of Am. Relocation Svcs., Orlando, 1986—. Sec. Mid. Brook Pines Condominium Assn., Orlando, 1987—, editor newsletter, 1988—. Mem. AAUW, Penn. State Alumni Assn., Cen. Fla. Penn. State Club, Sigma Delta Chi. Republican. Home: 5260 Middle Ct Orlando FL 32811 Office: Empire of Am Relocation Svc 201 S Orange Ave Orlando FL 32801

DENNIS, BETTY JO, interior designer; b. Erin, Tenn., June 29, 1935; d. James Alvin and Icie Evelyn (Warfield) Greene; m. Thomas H. Dennis, Apr. 11, 1953; (dec. Mar. 3, 1984); 1 child, Janet Elaine Dennis Philpot. Grad. high sch., Granite City, Ill.; student, Am. Inst. Banking, 1960-62, Postal Svc. Tng., Norman, Okla., 1970-74, Internat. Correspondence Sch., 1982-84, U. Ky., 1982-83, U. Ind., Bloomington, 1984. Teller State Bank, Havana, Ill., 1958-59; bookkeeper Havana (Ill.) Nat Bank, 1959-62; traffic mgr. Ashby Corp., Benton, Ky., 1963-66; bookkeeper Empire Fin. Co., London, Ky., 1966-70; clk. U.S. Postal Svc., London, 1970-80; postmaster U.S. Postal Svc., Bradfordsville, Ky., 1980-84; owner, operator Den-Mark Decorating, Corbin, Middlesboro, Ky., 1984—; postmaster trainer U.S. Postal Svc., Louisville, 1983-84, promotion bd. mem., 1984. Author: (video tape series) You Can Do It, 1989; contbr. articles to mags. Mother advisor Order of Rainbow for Girls, London, Ky., 1977-78; chmn. mem. com. Nat. Assn. Postmasters, 1981-84, Marion Co., Ky., dir. meml. svcs, 1984. Named Ky. Col. Gov. of Ky., 1985. Mem. Nat. Decorating Dealers Assn., Bus. & Profl. Women's Club, Middlesboro (Ky.) C. of C., Merchants Assn., Middlesboro, Order of Eastern Star. Democrat. Baptist. Home: 411 College St London KY 40741 Office: Den-Mark Decorating 2131 Cumberland Ave Middlesboro KY 40965

DENNIS, CANDY S., real estate developer; b. Kansas City, Mo., Feb. 26, 1952; d. Joseph Woodruff and Lucy Christina (Thompson) D. Student, Fort Osage high sch., Independence, Mo., 1966-70, Ft. Osage Osage Vo-Tech., Independence, Mo., 1969-70, Cen. Mo. State, Warrensburg, 1970-71, Avila Coll., Kansas City, Mo., 1977-78. Asst. to chief of police Independence Polic*e Dept., Mo., 1970-78; asst. chmn. Milgram Food Stores, Kansas City, Mo., 1978-80; v.p., mktg. The Hoyt Group, Ltd., Mission, Kansas, 1980--. Pres. Profl. Sec. Internat., Kansas City Mo., 1980-81. Recipient Outstanding Citizen award Independence Police Dept., Mo. 1974; Presentation awards Dale Carnegie Courses, Mission Kansas 1979; Named Product Rep. Yr. Am. Capital Equit., St. Louis 1986. Mem. Nat. Assn. Securities Dealers. Republican. Presbyterian. Office: The Hoyt Group Ltd 5453 W 61st Place Mission KS 66205

DENNIS, DARIENNE LEIGH, journalist; b. Ridgewood, N.J., Jan. 5, 1956; d. John Michael and Betty Fayerweather (Armstrong) D. BA, Mt. Holyoke Coll., 1978; MA in Law and Diplomacy, Tufts U., 1981. Intern US State Dept., Gabon, West Africa, 1980; reporter Fortune mag. Time Inc., N.Y.C., 1982—. Contbr. articles to local mag. Trustee Mt. Holyoke Coll., South Hadley, Mass., 1979-82, trustee fellow, 1988—. Mem. Mt. Holyoke Alumnae Assn. (nominating com. 1985-88). Office: Fortune Time Life Bldg 1261 6th Ave New York NY 10020

DENNIS, DIANE LIPTON, childcare facility executive; b. Phila., July 11, 1950; d. Leonard S. and Ruth Lipton; m. Warren L. Dennis, Dec. 28, 1968; children—Joanna, Seth. B.S., Temple U., 1970; M.S., George Mason U., 1975. Tchr., Phila. pub. schs., 1970; reading specialist Greenhedges Sch., Vienna, Va., 1975-77; from dir. to dist. mgr. Kindercare Learning Ctrs., 1977-81, dir. personnel and mgmt. tng. Eastern seaboard, Reston, Va., 1981-83, regional mgr. Mid-Eastern states, 1983-88; founder, pres. Lipton Corp. Childcare Ctrs., Washington, 1988—; gov.'s task force day care licensing, Va., 1985-86. Mem. Kindercare Execs. of Roundtable, LWV (chmn. Reston chpt. 1975-77). Home: 7113 Holyrood Dr McLean VA 22101

DENNIS, DONNA, sculptor; b. Springfield, Ohio, 1942. One-person exhbns. include: Hotels, West Broadway Gallery, N.Y.C., 1973, Donna Dennis, Wilcox Gallery, Swarthmore Coll., Pa., 1974, Subway Stations and Tourist Cabins, Holly Solomon Gallery, N.Y.C., 1976, City Station and Country Stops, JFK Ctr. Performing Arts, Washington, 1977, Maquettes and Drawings, Adler Gallery, Los Angeles, 1978, Donna Dennis, Holly Solomon Gallery, N.Y.C., 1978, Three Sculptures by Donna Dennis, Contemporary Arts Ctr., Cin., 1979, Donna Dennis, Sullivant Gallery, Ohio State U., Columbus, 1980, Drawings and Maquettes, Holly Solomon Gallery, N.Y.C., 1980, N.Y. and N.J., Holly Solomon Gallery, 1980, Maquettes and Drawings, Locus Solus Gallery, Genoa, Italy, 1981, Mad River Tunnel, Entrance and Exit, Dayton, 1981, Holly Solomon Gallery, N.Y.C., 1983, Abe Adler Gallery, Los Angeles, 1983, Moccasin Creek Cabins, Outdoor Installation, Moccasin Creek, Aberdeen, S.D., 1983, Night Stops, Neuberger Mus. SUNY-Purchase, 1985, Deep Stas., U. Mass.-Amherst, 1985, Deep Sta., Bklyn. Mus., 1987, 26 Bars, Richard Green Gallery, N.Y.C., 1987, Del. Art Mus., Wilmington, 1988, Muhlenberg Coll., Allentown, Pa., 1988, Madison (Wis.) Art Ctr., 1989; group exhbns. include: Venice Beienale, Italy, 1984, numerous museums and galleries, U.S. and Europe, 1972-75, others; set designer: Midsummer's Night Dream, 1973; TV Interviews: Gulliver's Travels series, 1979, CBS Cable Network, 1981, Manhattan Cable TV, 1986; permanent commns. Dreaming of Faraway Places: The Ships Come to Washington Market, Decorative st. fence for P.S. 234, N.Y.C., 1988. Bd. govs. N.Y. Found. Arts, 1988—. Recipient Excellence in Design award Art Commn. of City of N.Y., 1987, Alumni award Carleton Coll., 1989, Community Svc. award Parks Coun. of N.Y., 1989, Bard Merit award City Club of N.Y., 1989; pub. svc. grantee N.Y. State Creative Artists, 1975, 81, Am. Acad. and Inst. Arts and Letters grantee, 1984; N.Y. Found. Arts, 1985; fellow NEA, 1977, 80, 86, Guggenheim Found., 1979. Address: 131 Duane St New York NY 10013

DENNIS, GAIL, lead management analyst; b. Phila., Nov. 26, 1943; d. Albert Eugene and Ruth Kathryn (Gruber) D. BA in Art History and Theory, George Washington U., 1966. Documents methods specialist, mgmt. analyst U.S. Govt. Printing Office, Washington, 1966-72; mgmt. analyst I and dir., mgmt. systems and review office Fed. City Coll., Washington, 1972-74; mgmt. analyst, lead analyst GSA Info. Resources Mgmt. Svc., Washington, 1974—. Mem. Nat. Assn. for Miniature Enthusiasts, Am. Trust Historic Preservation, The Smithsonian Instn., Friends of Corcoran Gallery of Art, Friends of Kennedy Ctr., Friends of Nat. Symphony Orch., Nat. Mus. for Women in Arts, Gourmet Group. Episcopalian. Office: GSA IRMS KMPS Washington DC 20405

DENNIS, LYNETTE COLLEEN, contract administrator; b. Des Moines, Aug. 27, 1946; d. Benjamin W. and Vernette L. (Ronnenberg) D.; children: Eric Marshall, Jason Robert. B.S., N.W. Mo. State U., 1968; M.A., Antioch Sch. Law, Washington, 1985. Notary public. Ct. services Fairfax County sheriff, Va., 1978-80; adminstrv. mgr. Tech. Applications, Falls Church, Va., 1980-81; contract adminstr. Advanced Tech., Reston, Va., 1981-83; sr. contract analyst Maxfield Assocs. Ltd., Arlington, Va., 1983-85; sr. contract planner Wheeler Industries, Arlington, 1985-86; program mgr., Integrated Systems Analysts, 1986—. Adminstr., Glenside Counseling Ctr., Glendale Heights, Ill., 1976-77; proprietress Red Bank Farm, Charlottesville, Va. Mem. Profl. Women's Network, AAUW. Avocations: furniture and house restoration (owner, restorer Red Bank Farm, Fork Union, Va.), investments. Home: 5912 Pocol Dr Clifton VA 22024

DENNIS, PATRICIA DIAZ, government official, lawyer; b. Santa Rita, N.Mex., Oct. 2, 1946; d. Porfirio Madrid and Mary (Romero) Diaz; m. Michael John Dennis, Aug. 3, 1968; children: Ashley Elizabeth, Geoffrey Diaz, Alicia Sarah Diaz. A.B. in English, UCLA, 1970; J.D., Loyola U., Los Angeles, 1973. Bar: Calif. 1973, D.C. 1984. Law clk. Calif. Rural Legal Asst., McFarland, Calif., 1971; assoc. Paul, Hastings, Janofsky & Walker, Los Angeles, 1973-76; atty. Pacific Lighting Corp., Los Angeles, 1976-78; atty., asst. gen. atty. ABC, Hollywood, Calif., 1978-83; mem. NLRB, Washington, 1983-86; commr. FCC, Washington, 1986-89; mem. law firm Jones, Day, Reavis & Pogue, Washington, 1989—; chmn. U.S. del. ITU Region 2 Broadcasting Conf., Rio de Janeiro, 1988. Exec. editor: Loyola Law Rev., 1972-73. Com. mem. Coro Found. Hispanic Leadership Program, Los Angeles, 1981-82; U.S. del. UN Commn. on Status Women, 30th session Econ. and Social Council, Vienna, Austria, 1984, World Conf. UN Decade for Women, Nairobi, Kenya, 1985; bd. dirs. Resources for Infant Educarers, 1981-83, Nat. Network Hispanic Women, Los Angeles, 1983—; mem. exec. com., nat. adv. bd. Leadership Am., Found. for Women's Resources, 1987—. Recipient cert. of achievement YWCA, Los Angeles, 1979, Woman of Yr. award of merit Mex. Am. Opportunity Found., 1984, Recognition for Outstanding Achievements award Nat. Council Hispanic Women, 1986, Woman of Achievement award City Club of Cleve., 1986, Friend of the Family award The Family Place, 1987, Woman of Yr. award Hispanic Women's Coun., Inc., 1989; named one of 100 Influentials, Hispanic Bus. mag., 1987. Mem. Mex.-Am. Bar Assn. (sec. 1980-81, trustee 1979-80, 81-82), Los Angeles County Bar Assn. (child abuse subcom. chmn. barristers sect. 1980-81, exec. com. barristers sect. 1980-82), Hispanic Bar Assn. D.C., ABA (com. labor arbitration and the law of collective bargaining agreements, labor law sect. 1979-82), Women's Forum Washington. Democrat. Roman Catholic. Office: Jones Day Reavis & Pogue Met Sq 1450 G St NW Washington DC 20005*

DENNIS, (MARY) RUTH, retired librarian; b. Bloomfield, Iowa, July 16, 1907; d. Claude Charles and Nora Jane (Townsend) Atwood; m. Donald A. Dennis, Sept. 11, 1932 (div. Dec. 1955); children: Larry, Mary Jo Bousek. Student, Ottumwa Heights Jr. Coll., Ottumwa, Iowa, 1927-28; cert. in libr. sci., USDA Grad. Sch., 1964. Libr. asst. Ottumwa Pub. Libr., 1929-31; agt. Met. Life Ins. Co., Marshalltown, Iowa, 1943-45; continuity writer Sta. KFJB, Marshalltown, 1953-56; housemother Signa Alpha Epsilon, Iowa City, 1956-57; libr. asst. U. Iowa, Iowa City, 1957-59; cataloging asst. U.S. Bur. Census, Andrews AFB, Md., 1959-64; reference libr. U.S. Weather Bur. Libr., Washington, 1959-64; asst. libr. USDA, Peoria, Ill., 1964-66; libr. Herbert Hoover Presdl. Libr., West Brandh, Iowa, 1966-72; ret., 1972. Author: Homes of the Hoovers, 1986. Bd. dirs. Cedar County chpt. Am. Cancer Soc., Tipton, Iowa, 1987—; past pres. West Branch Heritage; v.p. Friends Eniow Pub. Libr., West Branch. Mem. Herbert Hoover Presdl. Libr. Assn., Questers (historian Red Cedar chpt., past pres.), Order Ea. Star (worthy matron, 1971, 81). Republican. Mem. Christian Ch. (Disciples of Christ). Home: 330 1/2 W Main St Box 144 West Branch IA 52358

DENNIS, SHARINA MARIE, systems analyst, income tax consultant; b. Dearborn, Mich., Apr. 26, 1963; d. Carol Alvin and Dorothy Marie (Phy) D. AS in Computer Info. Systems summa cum laude, Henry Ford Community Coll., Dearborn, 1985; BA in Computer Sci. summa cum laude, Wayne State U., 1987. Lead programmer, asst. systems mgr. The Board Room, Detroit, 1986; sr. user systems analyst AAA Mich., Livonia, 1987—. Co-capt. March of Dimes Walkathon/AAA, Farmington Hills, Mich., 1990. Mem. NAFE, Founders Soc. Detroit Inst. Arts, Golden Key (life), Phi Beta Kappa. Republican. Baptist. Home: 20130 Koths St Taylor MI 48180-3836 Office: AAA Mich 17380 Laurel Park Dr N Livonia MI 48152

DENNIS-HOLLIS, ROBBIE SMAGULA, sales promotion and advertising executive; b. Dover, Del., Oct. 15, 1957; d. Thomas David and Billie Jo (Talkington) Smagula; m. Mark Steven Dennis, May 26, 1979 (div. May 1982); 1 child, Gregory Steven; m. Stuart D. B. Hollis, Nov. 18, 1989. BS in Marine Biology, Tex. A&M U., 1978. Tech. writer Tex. Trans. Inst., College Station, Tex., 1978-80; documentation coord. Genentech, Inc., South San Francisco, Calif., 1980-82; sr. tech. writer Cen. & South West Svcs., Inc., Dallas, 1982-88; sales promotion mgr. Computer Assocs. (formerly UCCEL Corp.), Dallas, 1984-88; with corp. communications J. Driscoll & Assocs., Dallas, 1988-89; mgr. advt. and sales promotion ANTRIM Corp., Plano, Tex., 1989—. Mem. Soc. Tech. Communication (Best of Show and Excellence Achievement award 1985, 86), Internat. Assn. Bus. Communicators, NAFE. Home: 875A Dublin Dr Richardson TX 75080 Office: ANTRIM Corp 101 E Park Blvd 12th Fl Plano TX 75074

DENNISON, THERESA MARIE, cable television network administrator, writer; b. Bristol, Pa., June 9, 1965; d. Timothy Joseph Jr. and Dolores Marie (Hemmerle) Coyne; m. Edward L. Dennison, Oct. 26, 1985; children: Christopher P., Joseph T. BA, Trenton State Coll., 1987. Writer Advance of Bucks County, Newtown, Pa., 1986-87, Levittown (Pa.) Express, 1989; control operator Cable TV Network, Trenton, N.J., 1987-89, promotion mgr., 1989—; writer Advt. Community Times, Phila., 1989—. Judge of election Penndel (Pa.) Dem. Assn., 1990. Mem. Nat. Assn. for Female Execs., Broadcast Promotion and Mktg. Execs. (assoc.). Democrat. Roman Catholic. Home: 344 W Woodland Ave Penndel PA 19047 Office: Cable TV Network 124 W State St Trenton NJ 08608

DENNISTON, MARJORIE MCGEORGE, educator; b. Coraopolis, Pa., Mar. 21, 1913; d. Chauncey Kirk and Elsie (George) McGeorge; m. Delbert Dicks Denniston, Dec. 25, 1942 (dec. 1973); 1 child, Robert Bruce. Student, Ohio U., 1931-33; BA, Westminster Coll., 1936; postgrad., U. Kans., 1959, Western Ill. U., 1962, 64. Elem. tchr. county schs. West Pittsburg, Pa., 1936-42, New Castle Sch. System, Pa., 1942, 51-78. Vol. aid Pa. Assn. Retarded Children, Jameson Hosp., Law County Home, 1983—; trustee Presbyn. Ch., New Castle, 1986—. Named First Lady of New Castle, 1989. Mem. AAUW, LWV (sec. New Castle chpt. 1986—), Coll. Club (v.p. 1987—), Woman's Club (parliamentarian Lawrence County fedn. 1984—, sec. 1986—), Delta Kappa Gamma. Republican. Home: 331 Laurel Blvd New Castle PA 16101

DENNISTON, PAMELA BOGGS, organizational development consultant; b. San Diego, Feb. 15, 1948; d. Warren Leo and Edna Mae (Hippensteel) Boggs; m. John Henry Cynkar, July 26, 1969 (div. 1973); m. Warren Kent Denniston Jr., Mar. 20, 1980; step children—Julie, Warren, Edward, Scott. AA, Coll. DuPage, 1984; BA in Applied Behavioral Sci., Nat. Coll. Edn., 1985; MA, Loyola U., 1987. Sales cons. ARA Services, Des Plaines, Ill., 1977-78; regional sales mgr. Canteen Corp., Chgo., 1978-79; nat. mktg. mgr. Borg-Warner Leasing, Schaumburg, Ill., 1979-81; owner, cons. Adv. Mgmt. Systems, Downers Grove, Ill., 1981-86; ptnr. Eating Disorders Treatment Ctr., 1986-87; pres. Aretê, Inc, Naperville, Ill., 1987—; owner, mgr. Boggs Homemade Ice Cream Shoppe, Downers Grove, 1980-86; cons. Downers Grove C. of C., 1981-87; mem. planning Commn. Village of Downers Grove, 1984-86; bd. dirs. Indian Boundary YMCA, Downers Grove, 1981—. Mem. Soroptimist (pres. DuPage County chpt.). Avocations: travel, sailing, camping, hiking, art. Home: 805 Biltmore Naperville IL 60563 Office: Aretê Inc 1755 Park St Ste 260 Naperville IL 60563

DENNO, ZETTA LEE, social services administrator; b. Pueblo, Colo., Apr. 22, 1943; d. Clarence Loyd P. and Myrtle Louise (McFerren) Bewley; m. Robert E. Everhart, Feb. 13, 1965 (div. 1975); children—Tod Alan, Shelly Anne, Karen Marie; m. Roy Joseph Denno, Aug. 12, 1977; stepchildren—Roy Scott, Randy Michael. Student Columbia Pacific U. Youth dir. Rochester YWCA, N.Y., 1972-81; pres. Parents Without Ptnrs., chpt., 1975-76; program coordinator Regional Parents Without Ptnrs., 1976-77; youth employment specialist Genesee Settlement House, Rochester, 1981-82, family services coordinator, 1982—. Bd. dirs. Twelve Corners Day Care Ctr., Rochester, 1978—, Parents Anonymous of Rochester, 1978-86; co-chmn. adv. com. Monroe County Blue Cross, 1986-87, vol. counselor Health Assn., 1987—. Mem. Nat. Assn. Female Execs., Nat. Assn. Edn. Young Children, Internat. Platform Assn. Methodist. Club: Altrusa. Home: 930 Garden Ln Webster NY 14580 Office: Genesee Settlement House Inc 10 Dake St Rochester NY 14605

DENNY, JUDITH ANN, lawyer; b. Lamar, Mo., Sept. 18, 1946; d. Lee Livingston and Genevieve Adelpha (Falke) D.; m. Thomas M. Lenard, May 29, 1976; children: Julia Lee, Michael William. BA, La. Tech. U., 1968; JD, George Washington U., 1972. Bar: D.C. 1973. Asst. spl. prosecutor Watergate Spl. Prosecution Office, Washington, 1973-75; pros. atty. U.S. Dept. Justice, Washington, 1975-78; dir. div. compliance U.S. Office Edn. HEW, Washington, 1978-80; acting asst. insp. gen. for investigations U.S. Dept. Edn., Washington, 1980; dep. dir. policy and compliance, office of revenue sharing U.S. Dept. Treasury, Washington, 1980-83, counselor to gen. counsel, 1983-89; insp. gen. ACTION, Washington, 1989—. Mem. D.C. Bar Assn. Home: 3214 Porter St NW Washington DC 20008 Office: 1100 Vermont Ave NW Washington DC 20525

DENNY, MARY LU MAGASANO, foundation executive; b. Pitts., May 3, 1949; d. Dominick and Rose Rith (Profeta) Magasano; m. James Clarence Denny, June 26, 1971. BA, U. Pitts., 1975. Clk. Beechview Hardware, Pitts., 1963-71; br. ops. asst. Pitts. Nat. Bank, 1971-82; asst. cashier City Nat. Bank, Beverly Hills, Calif., 1982-83; exec. asst., bd. dirs. Station Sq. Transp. Mus., Pitts., 1990—; dir. membership svcs. Pitts. History and Landmarks Found., 1984—. Treas. Am. Women's Assn. Singapore, 1978-79, v.p., 1979-80, pres., 1980-81. Mem. Soc. Station Sq. Transp. Mus. (sec. 1988—), Brookside Women's Club (pres. 1987), Upper St. Clair Women's Club, Greater Pitts.Mus. Council. Republican. Home: 212 Cherokee Rd Upper St Clair PA 15241-1516 Office: Pitts History/Landmarks Fdn 450 Landmarks Bldg Station Sq Pittsburgh PA 15219-1170

DENOMME, SHARON LYNN, data processing executive; b. Detroit, Feb. 27, 1958; d. Philippe Leon and Geraldine (Hensley) D. BS in Computer Sci., Wayne State U., 1980. Sr. systems analyst Burroughs Corp. (UNISYS), Detroit, 1980-86; data processing mgr. Utley James Constrn. Co., Auburn, 1986-87; data processing mgr. Sch. Medicine Wayne State U., Detroit, 1987—; cons. Affiliated Buying Group, Birmingham, 1986—. Editor Questings, 1986. Tchr. of elderly Highland Park Bapt. Ch., Southfield, Mich., 1986-88. Mem. Mich. Focus Users Group, N.W. Ohio Focus Users Group (sec. 1987-88, pres. 1988—). Republican. Office: Wayne State U Sch Medicine 1211 Scott Hall Detroit MI 48201

DENOYER, GEORGIA ANN, human resource executive; b. Trenton, Mich., July 17, 1948; d. Lloyd George and Vera Eunice (Lawrence) Robertson; m. Thomas James DeNoyer, Sept. 7, 1968; 1 child, Matthew. AA, Oakland Community Coll., 1981, AAS, 1982; BS in Liberal Arts, USNY, Albany, 1986; AAS in Nursing, 1989. Cert. Electrocardiographic Technician; cert. Phlebotomy Technician; cert. Med. Asst. with Clin. Specialty. Med. asst. Davis-Smith Med.-Dental Employment Svc., Southfield, Mich., 1982-84; phlebotomist Nat. Health Labs., Oak Park, Mich., 1984-86; pres., owner Affirmative Mgmt. Group, Inc., Canton, Mich., 1986—; phlebotomist Oakwood Hosp., Dearborn, Mich., 1988, emergency rm. nurse Canton Ctr., 1990—; nurse emergency rm. Sinai Hosp., Detroit, 1989-90; instr. med. assisting Nat. Edn. Ctr., Detroit, 1988-89; med. assisting instr. South Lyons Pub. Schs./Ross Career Schs., 1990—. Vol., Oakwood Hosp., 1984-88, Catherine McAuley Health Ctr., Ann Arbor, Mich., 1984-89. Mem. Am. Assn. Med. Assts. (treas. Western Wayne chpt. 1987-88), Am. Soc. Profl. and Exec. Women, Nat. Assn. Women Cons., NAFE, Mich. League Nursing, Mensa, Intertel, Internat. Platform Assn., Emergency Nurses Assn., Am. Assn. Critical Care Nurses. Roman Catholic. Home: 46744 Maidstone Rd Canton MI 48187-1454 Office: Affirmative Mgmt Group Inc 46744 Maidstone Rd Canton MI 48187

DENSLOW, DEBORAH PIERSON, educator; b. Phila., May 2, 1947; d. Merrill Tracy Jr. and Margaret (Aiman) D.; m. James Tracy Grey III, Nov. 24, 1972 (div. Dec. 1980); 1 child, Sarah Elizabeth. BS, Gwynedd Mercy Coll., 1971. Tchr. Willingboro (N.J.) Bd. Edn., 1971—; union rep. Burlington County Edn. Assn., Willingboro, 1981-82. Committeewoman 1st ward Morrisville (Pa.) Rep. Com., 1986—; mem. borough coun., Morrisville, 1988—; Rep. candidate for borough coun., 1985; borough chmn. Am. Cancer Soc., 1986-87; sec. bd. dirs. Morrisville Free Libr., 1988-90, mem. bd. dirs., 1988—. Mem. NEA, N.J. Edn. Assn., Willngboro Edn. Assn. (union rep. 1981-82, alt. union rep. 1988-89), Parents without Ptnrs. (bd. dirs. Mercer County chpt. 1981-82, sec. 1982-84), Bucks County Boroughs Assn. (bd. dirs. 1989—, v.p. 1990—). Presbyterian. Home: 1206 Ohio Ave Morrisville PA 19067

DENSMORE, ANN, writer, speech pathologist, audiologist; b. L.A., Nov. 24, 1941; d. Ray B. and Margaret M. (Walsh) D.; BS cum laude, UCLA, 1963; MA in Communicative Disorders, Calif. State U., 1975; student Cape Cod Conservatory of Arts, 1977-79, Harvard U. graphics-architecture program, 1980—; children—Kristin Ann, Jennifer Ann. Tchr., Santa Monica (Calif.) Unified Sch. Dist., 1973-74; speech pathologist Kennedy Child Study Center, 1975-76; audiologist VA Hosp. Sepulveda, Calif., 1976-77, New Eng. Rehab. Hosp., Woburn, Mass., 1978; audiology cons. Wellesley (Mass.) Public Schs., 1979; speech pathologist Framingham (Mass.) Public Schs., 1979; speech pathologist and audiologist The Learning Center for Deaf Children, Framingham, 1978-80; dir. ann. fund Babson Coll., 1981-83; asst. dir. devel. Lakey Clinic Med. Ctr., 1984-86; assoc. dir. corp. devel. Harvard Med. Sch., 1986—; career counselor corp. execs. Mackenna/Jandl Assoc., Inc., 1983—; rsch. asst. Presch. Learning Lab, Harvard U., 1989; free-lance photographer, 1979—; v.p. U.S. sales Boston Corp.; exhibited photographs Copley Soc. of Boston, 1979-80. Contbr. articles to Boston Globe, 1986—. Lic. speech pathologist and audiologist Calif. Mem. Am. Speech and Hearing Assn. (cert. clin. competence, speech pathologist-audiologist), Artists Assn. of Nantucket, Nat. Assn. Security Dealers. Copley Soc. of Boston. Episcopalian. Home: 9 Roanoke Wellesley MA 02181 also: 40 Salem St Lynnfield MA 01940

DENTON, BETTY LOU, magazine editor; b. Fort Scott, Kans., July 7, 1925; d. Walter Earl and Mary Pearl (Hall) Collins; m. Leland Granville Denton, Jan. 27, 1946; children: Deborah Lynne Wilson, Randall Lee. Diploma, Ft. Scott (Kans.) Jr. Coll., 1945; BS in Home Econs., Kans. State U., 1947. Cert. home economist. Cashier-clk. S.H. Kress & Co., Ft. Scott, 1942; acctg. clk. Western Ins. Co., Ft. Scott, 1942-45; elem. tchr. Cleveland Dist., Riley County, Kans., 1947-48; home svc. dir. Kans. Power & Light Co., Topeka, 1948-50; supt. foods Topeka Free Fair, Mid Am. Fair, 1955-76; food svc. dir. First Presbyn. Ch., Topeka, 1956-60; foods editor The Topeka Capital-Jour., 1958-64; night sch. tchr. home mgmt. Topeka High Sch., 1957-58, 73-76; rural living editor Kans. Farmer Mag., Topeka, 1964—; color food editor Pa. Farm, Ohio Farmer, Mo. Ruralist, Mich. Farmer, Harrisburg and Columbus, 1986—; coord. women's activity ctr. Western Farm Show, Kansas City, Mo., 1965—; advisor Future Homemakers Am., Kans. Editor, revision author: Kansas Farmer Cookbook, 1964; contbr. articles to profl. jours. Mem. Shawnee County 4-H Fair Bd., Topeka; mem. steering com. Kans. Master 4-H Club Alumni, 1985—. Recipient 4-H Alumni awards Kans. 4-H Found., 1970, Nat. 4-H Found. and Olin Corp., Chgo., 1971. Mem. Am. Home Econs. Assn., Kans. Home Econs. Assn. (pres. 1983), Topeka Home Econs. Assn. (pres., treas.), Am. Agrl. Editors Assn. (pres. 1980), Greater Kansas City Home Economists in Bus. (com. chmn.), Women in Communications Inc. (pres. Topeka chpt.), Nat. Fedn. Press Women (awards), Kans. Fedn. Press Women (v.p.), Topeka Fedn. Press Women, Kans. Nutrition Coun. (chmn.), Kans. Youthpower Food and Careers Com. (pub. rels. chmn.), Nat. Farm Home Editors Assn., Kans. State U. Alumni Assn. Republican. Presbyterian. Home: 2300 Sw Brookhaven Ln Topeka KS 66614-4427

DENTON, EMMA MANEY, landscape design appraiser, bank executive; b. Hiawassee, Ga., Nov. 25, 1905; d. Milton M. and Missouri (Eller) Maney; student pvt. schs., Hiawassee; m. James Young Denton, May 20, 1920 (dec. Jan. 1982); children: J.C., Evelyn Isabel Denton Groves, Ruth Elois Denton Anderson, J. William, Emma Jean Denton Anderson. Assoc. cashier Bank of Hiawassee, 1936-70, cashier, 1970—, dir., 1950—. Chmn. county drive Am. Cancer Soc., 1944-60; adult Sunday sch. tchr. various locations, 1934—; flower show judge; mem. Atlanta Flower Show. Recipient Svc. award Am. Cancer Soc., 1977; Emma Denton Day named in honor Bank of Hiawassee, 1979; cert. appreciation Bankers in Ga.; nat. awards flower shows. Mem. DAR, Am. Bankers Assn. (citation), Friendship Community Club, Hiawassee Garden Club (charter mem., pres. 1960—), State Garden Club Ga. (hon. life), Nat. Coun. Garden Clubs (life). Baptist. Address: Bank of Hiawassee Main St Hiawassee GA 30546

DENTON, GISELE ANN, advertising executive; b. Italy, Oct. 21, 1937; d. Erasmus R. and Amelia Claire (Finamore) P.; m. L. Karl Denton, Aug. 26, 1961; children: Lewis K. II, Lance Kip. BSBA in Stats., U. Denver, 1961. Media liaison Saturday Evening Post mag., div. Curtis Pub. Co., Phila., 1955-58; mgr. merchandising Valspar Corp., Denver, 1961-66; v.p., media dir. Henderson, Bucknum, Denver, 1967-72, Barickman Advt., Denver, 1972-80, Doyle Dane Bernbach Advt., Denver, 1980-86, DDB Needham Worldwide, Denver, 1986-89; pres. Denton Media/Mktg. Svcs., Inc., Englewood, Colo., 1989—. Del. Arapahoe County Reps., Aurora, Colo., 1976-86, Douglas County Reps., Castle Rock, Colo., 1984-88; vol. Colo. Heart Assn., Colfax Project, Excelsior House, Denver, 1970-87; chmn. publicity com. Mother Cabrini Shrine, Golden, 1986-87. Mem. Nat. Acad. TV Arts and Scis. (treas. 1986-88), Denver Advt. Fedn. (sec. centennial com. 1988), Colo. Broadcasters Assn. (assoc.), AAUW (treas. local chpt. 1978-80), Il Circolo Italiano (v.p. 1980-87). Republican. Roman Catholic. Home: 4910 Hwy 67 Sedalia CO 80135 Office: 7430 E Caley Ste 200 Englewood CO 80111

DENTON, LOUISE W., educator, consultant; b. Grenada, Miss., Sept. 30, 1940; d. Byrd and Lorraine (Graham) Willis; m. Charles Gary Denton, June 1, 1961; children: Fanesta Gail, Charles Gary Jr. BS, Jackson (Miss.) State U., 1961; MA, Concordia Coll., 1980. Cert. tchr., Miss., Ill. Tchr. Broad St. Sch., Shelby, Miss., 1961-62, Mason Primary Sch., Chgo., 1963-68; adj. tchr. Triton Coll., River Grove, Ill., 1982-84; tchr. Irving Elem. Sch., Maywood, Ill., 1968—; dir. after sch. tutoring program, Maywood, 1984-86; asst. dir. summer sch. programs, Maywood, 1988; judge sci. fair Concordia Coll., Maywood, 1983-85; lab. asst. U. Ill., Chgo., 1980. Mem. budget and fin. com. United Way, 1985—, mem., 1984—, Maywood Beautification Commn., Maywood, 1982-88; voter registrar Dem. Party, Maywood, 1987-88. Recipient Dedicated Svc. award Maywood Youth Commn., 1982, Devotion to Children award Irving Student Coun., 1985-86, Cert. of Appreciation, Maywood United Way, 1986, Cert. of merit Second Bapt. Ch., 1987, Cert. of Appreciation, Village of Maywood, 1988. Mem. Ill. Math. League, Delta Sigma Theta (sec. 1982-84). Home: 1237 S 15th Ave Maywood IL 60153 Office: Irving Sch 805 S 17th Ave Maywood IL 60153

DENTON, REBECCA LIEGH, lawyer; b. New Orleans, Nov. 4, 1958; d. Frank Marion and Elizabeth Ann (Colvin) D. BFA in Theater cum laude, Tex. Christian U., 1980; JD, Loyola U., New Orleans, 1988. Bar: U.S. Dist. Ct. (we. and mid. dist.) La. 1989, U.S. Dist. Ct. (ea. dist.) La. 1990, U.S. Ct. Appeals (5th cir.) 1989. Jud. law clk. 16th Jud. Dist. Ct., Franklin, La., spring 1988; assoc. Bergstedt & Mount, Lake Charles, La., 1990—. Mem. ABA, La. Bar Assn., Bus. and Profl. Women (1st v.p.). Democrat. Office: Bergstedt & Mount PO Box 3004 Lake Charles LA 70602

DENUNZIO, SHARON KISTLER, investment banker; b. Pitts., May 17, 1959; d. R. Drew and Mary Virginia (Simpson) Kistler; m. Peter Dwight DeNunzio, May 30, 1986. BS in Engring. magna cum laude, Princeton U., 1981; MBA, Columbia U., 1986. Mgmt. cons. Arthur Andersen & Co., Boston, N.Y.C., 1981-83; market rsch. analyst Bristol-Myers Co., N.Y.C., 1983-84; assoc. corp. fin. Bankers Trust, N.Y.C., 1986-88, v.p. Employee Stock Ownership Plan fin. and pvt. placements, 1989—. Vol. N.Y. Jr. League, N.Y.C., 1983-87. Fellow profs.' com. Columbia U. Bus. Sch., 1984-86. Mem. Stanwich Club, Beta Gamma Sigma. Republican. Roman Catholic. Office: Bankers Trust Co 130 Liberty St New York NY 10006

DENVER, EILEEN ANN, magazine editor; b. N.Y.C., Nov. 16, 1942; d. Daniel Joseph and Katherine Agnes (Boland) D.; m. Duncan C. Stephens, July 2, 1988. B.A., Coll. New Rochelle, 1964; certificate, Radcliffe Sch. Pub., 1964; M.A., Ind. U., 1967. Editorial asst. Mass. Inst. Tech. Tech. Review, Boston, 1965-66; instr. English St. Peter's Coll., Jersey City, 1967-70; assoc. editor, writer Am. Home mag., N.Y.C., 1971-75; asst. editor Consumer Reports, Mt. Vernon, N.Y., 1975-77, asst. mng. editor, 1977-79, mng. editor, 1979—. Office: Consumer Reports 256 Washington St Mount Vernon NY 10553

DEOL, SHARON ROSE, computer company executive; b. Bay Shore, N.Y., Nov. 30, 1962; d. Ben and Yetta (Cohen) Eskenazi; m. Jasvinder Singh Deol, Oct. 10, 1986. BA in Econs., SUNY, Stony Brook, 1984; MS in mgmt., Purdue U., West Lafayette, Ind., 1986. Princing analyst U.S. group NCR Corp., Dayton, Ohio, 1986-88, self-svc. product mgr., 1988-90, customer svcs. div. mgr., 1990—. Home: 121-D N Village Dr Centerville OH 45459

DEOLA, LINDA LEE, nursing consultant; children: Martha, Chris, Bryan, Sarah. Student, James Madison U., 1964-70; BA in Sociology, Mary Washington Coll., 1974; BS in Nursing, George Mason U., 1979; MS in Health Scis., James Madison U., 1988. RN, Va; cert. chem. dependency nurse, Nat. Consortium Chem. Dependency Nurses, 1988, Nat. Chem. Dependency Nurse Certification Bd., 1988, alcoholism specialist, 1989. Staff nurse Radford (Va.) Community Hosp. Pediatrics, 1964-65, Fredericksburg (Va.) Nursing Home, 1976; office nurse Dr. Richard H. Smith, Harrisonburg, Va., 1967-68; clin. instr. Rockingham Meml. Hosp. Sch. Nursing, Harrisonburg, 1969-71; insvc. instr. Mary Washington Hosp., Fredericksburg, Va., 1976-78; vocat. rehab. nurse Vocat. Placement Svcs., 1978-79; nurse coordinator Staunton Correctional Ctr., 1979-86; program dir. Arlington Treatment Ctr., Harrisonberg, 1986—; cons. Bensinger, DuPont & Assocs., Chgo., 1988—. Mem. Am. Nurses Assn., Va. Nurses Assn., Am. Correctional Assn., Community Health Nurses Assn., Va. Assn. Alcoholism and Drug Abuse Counselors, Va. Correctional Nurses Assn., Harrisonburg-Rockingham Mental Health Assn., LWV. Home: 920 S Dogwood Dr Harrisonburg VA 22801

DEPAOLI, GERI MARY, artist; b. June 8, 1941; m. Alexander DePaoli, July 4, 1961; children: Alexander Mark, Michael Alexander. BA, U. Md., 1974, MA, 1978; student, U. Calif., Davis, 1965-68. Art history educator, artist, curator slides and photos Nat. Mus., Bangkok, Thailand, 1968-71; art prof. Montgomery Coll., Rockville, Md., 1978-82; cons. oriental slide and photo collection Princeton U., 1983-84; lectr. Princeton Sch. Visual Arts, 1986—; curator The Mus. Art, Ft. Lauderdale, Fla., 1986; dir. Coun. for Creative Projects, N.Y.C., 1989—; faculty artworks Princeton Sch. Visual Arts, 1984—; cons. in field. Artist/exhibitor Dawson Gallery, Rockville, Md., Washington, 1972-78, East/West Gallery, Bethesda, Md., 1972-78; editor/co-curator Exhbn. Catalog, Transcending Abstraction, 1986; author/curator The Transparent Thread: Asian Philosophy in Am. Art 1950-1990; contbr. articles to profl. jours.; one-man shows include E.W. Gallery, Bethesda, Md., 1978, Dawson Gallery, 1979-80, Upstairs gallery, Kingston, N.J., 1982, Gallery at The Purple Barge, N.Y.C., 1984, The Art Gallery, Kingston, N.J., 1985, Back Door Gallery, Princeton, 1986, Campion Gallery of Art, 1987 Princeton, 1986, AT&T Corp. Gallery, Princeton, 1989, Rider Coll. Gallery, Lawrenceville, N.J., 1990; group shows include Mercer Med. Ctr. Gallery, Trenton, N.J., 1988, Princeton Visual Arts sch., 1986, 87, 88, 89, 90, Princeton Artist Alliance, Forrestal Vallage, Princeton, 1989, Trenton Artworks Gallery, 1989; premanent collections Squibb Corp., New Brunskwick, N.J., Perfect Solutions Corp., Woodland, Calif., Janes Collection, Bethesda, Md., Rider Coll. Gallery, Designers Two, Inc., Seattle. Councilor Nat. Abortion Rights Action League, 1989—. Recipient award for excellence in pub., Office of Pres. of U.S., 1969. Fellow Soc. for Arts Religion and Contemporary Culture, 1989; mem. Assn. Ind. Historians of Art (v.p. 1988—), Coll. Art Assn., Princeton Rsch. Forum, Nat. Coalition of Ind. Scholars, Sierra Club, Green Peace, Newcomers Club. Buddhist. Office: Coun for Creative Projects 45 Herrontown Ln Princeton NJ 08540

DE PAPP, ELISE WACHENFELD, physician; b. Orange, N.J., Sept. 26, 1933; d. William Arnold and Anne G. (Weir) Wachenfeld; m. Zsolt G. de Papp, Mar. 26, 1959 (div. 1976); children: Anne E., John W., Erika D. BA, Sweet Briar (Va.) Coll., 1955; MD, U. Rochester, N.Y., 1960. Intern Strong Meml. Hosp., Rochester, 1960-61, assoc. resident in pediatrics, 1966-67, asst. resident in pathology, 1967-68, chief resident in pathology, 1968-69; asst. prof. pathology Strong Meml. Hosp. U. Rochester, Rochester, 1969-86, asst. prof. ob.-gyn., nursing, 1975-76; clin. assoc. prof. pathology Strong Meml. Hosp. Strong Meml. Hosp., Rochester, 1986—; sr. attending pathologist Genesee Hosp., Rochester, 1976—; assoc. pathologist Lakeside Meml. Hosp., Brockport, N.Y., 1976—. Contbr. articles to profl. jours. Fellow Coll. Am. Pathologists; mem. Internat. Acad. Pathology, Internat. Soc. Gynecologic Pathologists, Phi Beta Kappa. Office: Genesee Hosp 224 Alexander St Rochester NY 14607

DE PASSE, SUZANNE, record company executive; m. Paul Le Mat. Student, Manhattan Community Coll. Former talent coordinator Cheetah Disco, N.Y.C.; creative asst. to pres. Motown Prodns., Los Angeles, 1968-81, pres., 1981—. Acts signed and developed for Motown include The Commodores, The Jackson Five, Frankie Valli and the Four Seasons, Lionel Richie, Thelma Houston, Billy Preston, Teena Marie, Rick James, Stephanie Mills; co-author screenplay for film Lady Sings the Blues (Acad. award nomination); exec. producer: (TV miniseries) Lonesome Dove, (TV series) Motown on Showtime, Nightlife starring David Brenner, Motown Revue starring Smokey Robinson, Motown Returns to the Apollo (Emmy award, NAACP Image award), (TV spl.) Motown 25: Yesterday, Today, Forever (Emmy award, NAACP Image award); writer: (TV spls.) Happy Endings, Jackson 5 Goin' Back to Indiana, Diana; creative cons: Git on Broadway-Diana Ross & The Supremes & Temptations, TCB-Diana Ross & The Supremes & Temptations. Office: Motown Prodns 6255 W Sunset Blvd Los Angeles CA 90028*

DE PAUW, LINDA GRANT, history educator; b. N.Y.C., Jan. 19, 1940; d. Phillip and Ruth (Marks) Grant. BA, Swarthmore Coll., 1961; PhD, Johns Hopkins U., 1964. Asst. prof. history George Mason Coll.-U. Va., Fairfax, 1964-65; spl. asst. to archivist U.S. Nat. Archives, Washington, 1965-66; asst. prof. history George Washington U., Washington, 1966-69, assoc. prof., 1969-75, prof. Am. history, 1975—. Editor-in-chief, project dir. Documentary History of the First Fed. COngress, 1966-84; author: The Eleventh Pillar: New York State and the Federal Constitution, 1966, Founding Mothers: Women of America in the Revolutionary Era, 1975, Remember the Ladies, 1976, Seafaring Women, 1982; editor, pub. Minerva: Quar. Report in Women and the Mil., 1983—, Minerva's Bulletin Bd., 1987—; writer/producer Minerva on the Air (armed forces radio), 1987-89. Founder, pres. The Minerva Ctr., 1983—. Woodrow Wilson fellow, 1961. Mem. Am. Hist. Assn. (Beveridge award 1964), Am. Mil. Inst., Coordinating Com. on Women in Hist. Profession, Inter-Univ. Seminar on Armed Forces and Soc., Women in Internat. Security, Orgn. Am. Historians, So. Hist. Assn. Home: 1101 S Arlington Ridge Rd Arlington VA 22202 Office: George Washington U Dept History Washington DC 20052

DEPEW, MARIE KATHRYN, retired educator; b. Sterling, Colo., Dec. 1, 1928; d. Amos Carl and Dorothy Emelyn (Whiteley) Mehl; m. Emil Carlton DePew, Aug. 30, 1952 (dec. 1973). BA, U. Colo., 1950, MA, 1953. Post grad. Harvard U., Cambridge, Mass., 1962; tchr. Jefferson County Pub. Schs., Arvada, 1953-73; mgr. Colo. Accountability Program, Denver, 1973-83; sr. cons. Colo. Dept. Edn., Denver, 1973-85, ret., 1985. Author: (pamphlet) History of Hammil, Georgetown, Colorado, 1967; contbr. articles to profl. jours. Chmn. Colo. State Accountability Com., Denver, 1971-75. Fellow IDEA Programs, 1976-77, 79-81. Mem. Colo. Hist. Assn., Jefferson County Edn. Assn. (pres. 1963-64), Colo. Edn. Assn. (bd. dirs. 1965-70), Ky. Colonels (hon. mem.), Phi Beta Kappa. Republican. Methodist. Home: 920 Pennsylvania Denver CO 80203

DE PONTE, VELMA ALANA, health care executive; b. Los Angeles, Jan. 13, 1949; d. Clell Millard and Virginia Yvonne (Roberts) Thomas; 1 child, Deris Jermaine Flenoil (dec.). BA magna cum laude, U. So. Calif., 1969; MA in Pub. Adminstrn. with honors, Calif. State U., Long Beach, 1978. Social worker Los Angeles County Dept. Pub. Social Svcs., 1969-71, eligibility worker, 1971-74, supr. eligibility worker, 1974-76, children's treatment cons., 1976-79; pers. analyst Los Angeles County Dept. Pers., 1979-81; adminstrv. analyst Los Angeles County Chief Adminstrv. Office, 1981-83; exec. asst. to exec. dir. Los Angeles County Human Rels. Commn., 1983-87; spl. asst. to dep. dir. Los Angeles County Health Svcs. Adminstrn., 1987—. Mem. Am. Massage Therapy Assn., Am. Soc. Pub. Adminstrn., Calif. Women in Govt., Assn. Black Women Mgrs., Nat. Assn. Female Execs. Seventh Day Adventist.

DEPPE, VICTORIA LYNN, software development professional; b. Omaha, Oct. 17, 1963; d. Robert Ellery and Judy Lee (Solomon) Andreasen; m. James Gerard Deppe, Sept. 28, 1985. BS in Computer Sci., U. Ill., 1985; postgrad., No. Ill. U. Programmer Kuck & Assocs., Inc., Champaign, Ill., 1984; grader/cons. U. Ill., Urbana, 1985; programmer Learned-Mahn, Inc., Boise, Idaho, 1985-86; cons. Computer Dimensions Inc., Lombard, Ill., 1986-87, St. Anne's Reg. Med. Assn., Chgo., 1987; programmer, analyst AT&T Communications, Lisle, Ill., 1987-89; sr. assoc. Coopers & Lybrand, Chgo., 1989—. Badge ldr. Calvary Temple Missionettes, Naperville, Ill. 1988; mem. AT&T Affirmative Action com. Mem. Nat. Assn. Female Execs. Office: Coopers & Lybrand 203 N LaSalle St Chicago IL 60601

DEPREZ, CLAUDIA, real estate broker, mortgage company executive; b. Miami, Fla., Dec. 17, 1948; m. Carl R. Addlesberger, Aug. 5, 1968 (div. 1978); children: Scott A., Jeny Lyn. AA in Psychology, Miami Dade Jr. Coll., 1971; student, Fla. Atlantic U., 1967, Barry U., 1982—. Cert. residential specialist. Sales assoc. Keyes Co. Realtors, Miami, 1974-76; v.p. Midtown Realty, Inc., Miami, 1976-80; v.p., gen. sales mgr. Wilcox Realtors, N. Palm Beach, Fla., 1980-81; sales assoc. Marian Lewis Realtors, N. Palm Beach, 1982-84; pres. Fla. Singles Real Estate, Inc., N. Palm Beach, 1984—. Mem. Northwood Neighborhood Assn., W. Palm Beach, Fla., 1986—. Mem. No. Palm Beach County Assn. Realtors (bd. dirs. 1985-86, chmn. Rookie Club 1989—, chmn. Realtors Grievance Com. 1989-90), Fla. Assn. Mortgage Brokers (bd. dirs. No. Palm Beach chpt. 1985), Nat. Assn. Realtors, Nat. Assn. Mortgage Brokers, Nat. Assn. Rev. Appraisers and Underwriters, No. Palm Beach County Bd. Realtors Honor Soc., Real Estate Leaders of Am., Nat. Speakers Assn. Office: Fla Singles Real Estate Inc 11436 US Hwy #1 North Palm Beach FL 33408

DEPRIEST, DESIREE LYNNE, business and writing services executive; b. Kansas City, Kans., Nov. 26, 1956; d. Ottie Swan and Delores Mary (Mabion) DeP. BS, Howard U., Washington, 1978; postgrad., Scientology Inst., Arlington, Va., 1982. Cert. child care worker. Residential supr. Hillcrest Children's Ctr., Washington, 1977-80; psychiat. technician Psychiat. Inst., Washington, 1980-82; lease holder Profl. Resume Svcs., Inc., Hyattsville, Md., 1982-83; owner PATH Bus. and Writing Svcs., Hyattsville, 1983—. Mem. NAFE, Nat. Theosphical Soc. Office: 7515 Annapolis Rd #410 Hyattsville MD 20784

DE PRIEST, MARY, accountant; b. Laurel, Md., Aug. 18, 1945; d. Albert Carl and Mary Katherine (Richards) De P.; m. Harry R. Phelps, Apr. 29, 1978 (div. 1986); children: Alan L., Shirley D., Jennie E., Pamela K. Valente. AA summa cum laude, Prince Georges Comm. Coll., 1987; BS summa cum laude, Strayer Coll., 1989. Bookkeeper So. Ry. Co., Washington, 1970-83, Organic Farms, Inc., Beltsville, Md., 1983-85; jr. acct. Fresh, Inc., Washington, 1985—; pvt. practice, fin. cons. income taxes Greenbelt, Md., 1986—. Mem. St. Phillips Episc. Ch., Laurel, 1978—, christian educator, 1983-86, bookkeeper, 1983-85. Mem. NAFE, Md. Soc. Accts., Alphi Chi Hon. Soc., (treas. 1988-89). Democrat. Protestant. Home and Office: 1-H Plateau Pl Greenbelt MD 20770

DEPRIEST, REAH, bank executive. Sr. v.p. Seafirst Bank, Seattle. Office: Seafirst Bank 701 5th Ave Fl 16 Seattle WA 98104*

DEPUE, JOSEPHINE HELEN, teacher; b. Amesville, Ohio, June 15, 1948; d. Leonard Simmons and Josephine Helen (Carr) DeP. BS in Edn., Ohio U., Athens, 1972; MSS, Ohio U., 1984. Cert. secondary edn. tchr., Ohio. Tchr. Logan (Ohio) City Schs., 1969-71, Zanesville (Ohio) City Schs., 1972--. Adv. Roosevelt Remembered, school history of Roosevelt Jr. High Sch., Zanesville, 1988. Sec. Bd. of Christian Edn., First Baptist Ch., Zanesville, 1988—, club comdr. Awana Clubs youth program. Mem. AAUW, NEA, Pioneer and Hist. Soc., Ohio Acad. of History, Ohio Hist. Soc., Ohio Edn. Assn., Eastern Ohio Edn. Assn. Democrat. Baptist. Home: 1219 Hazel Ave Zanesville OH 43701 Office: Roosevelt Jr High Sch 1275 Roosevelt Ave Zanesville OH 43701

DE RAN, SUSAN LOUISE, financial analyst; b. Dayton, Ohio, Feb. 20, 1952; d. Robert G. and D. Louise (Johnson) Deis. BBA, U. Toledo, 1982, MBA, 1989. Sec. Hayes Albion Corp., Tiffin, Ohio, 1973-76, Owens-Ill. Inc., Toledo, Ohio, 1976-79; cashier Owens-Ill. Inc., Toledo, 1979-80, act. control asst., acct., 1983-84; cost and budget supr. Owens-Ill. Inc., 1984-88; sr. fin. bus. analyst Owens-Ill. Inc., Toledo, 1988-89; sr. fin. analyst Libbey-Owens-Ford Co., Toledo, 1989—. Mem. Natl. Assn. Female Exec. Office: Libbey-Owens-Ford Co 811 Madison Ave Toledo OH 43695

DERBER, DANA M., advertising executive; b. Beaver Dam, Wis., Oct. 23, 1955; d. Paul Oscar and Virginia May (Linck) Derber; m. Kevin Andre' Sullivan, Sept. 4, 1988. BS in Art, U. Wis., 1977. Graphic designer Storyboard, Inc., Madison, Wis., 1982-85; dir. advt. C. G. Rein Co., Mpls., 1985—. Vol. art dir. Madcity Music Sheet, Madison, Wis., 1977-81. Lutheran.

DERBY, CHERYL ANN, insurance company writer; b. Paterson, N.J., Jan. 19, 1946; d. Elles Mayo and Sarah Emma (Steele) D. BA, Elmira Coll., 1967; MBA, NYU, 1982. Tchr. Ramsey (N.J.) High Sch., 1967-70; contbns. analyst Met. Life Ins. Co., N.Y.C., 1970-83, fin. writer investments dept., 1983—; editor MetLife Investments mag., 1983—. Vice-pres., bd. trustees United Meth. Ch. of Waldwick (N.J.), 1989—. Fellow Nat. Orchestral Assn. (aux. com. 1989—), Life Mgmt. Inst. (bd. dirs. Greater N.Y. chpt. 1984—, pres. 1986, nat. adminstrv. com., mktg. subcom. 1985-88); mem. Elmira Coll. Alumni Club of N.J. (exec. bd. 1982-87). Methodist. Office: Met Life 1 Madison Ave New York NY 10010

DER MANUELIAN, LUCY, Armenian art and architecture educator; b. Arlington, Mass. AB in English lit., Radcliffe Coll.; MA in Art History, Boston U., 1975, PhD in Art History, 1980. Head teaching fellow Boston U., 1975-76; vist. lectr. Framingham State Coll., 1979-80; archivist, Armenian Archtl. Archives Project, 1979-84; lectr. Armenian art and architecture Tufts U., Medford, Mass., 1984—, Arthur H. Dadlan and Aza Oztemel chair, 1989—; mus. cons. Darmouth Coll.; acad. lectr. univs. and colls. including Poly. Inst., U. Erevan, USSR, U. Aarhus, Denmark, Courtauld Inst., Eng., McGill U., U. Mich., U. Pa., Harvard U., Brown U., Chgo. U., Columbia U., Northeastern U., UCLA, Dartmouth Coll., Wellesley Coll., Mt. Holyoke Coll., Queens Coll.; lectr. mus., cultural and community orgns. U.S. and abroad; author/narrator 4 TV documentaries on Armenian art. Author: Armenian Architecture, 4 vols., 1981-88; Dictionary of the Middle Ages, 1982—, Dictionary of Art, The Gregorian Collection-Armenian Rugs, 1983, Weavers, Merchants and Kings: The Inscribed Rugs of Armenia, 1984, contbr. to publs. in field including: Dictionary of the Middle Ages, Classical Armenian Culture, 1982, Medieval Armenian Culture, 1984, others. Exchange fellow to USSR, 1977-78; fellow Bunting Inst., Radcliffe Coll., 1971-73; Samuel H. Kress grantee, Boston U., 1975, 78; rsch. grantee Nat. Assn. for Armenian Studies and Rsch. to USSR, 1972, 78; sr. scholar grantee Am. Coun. Learned Socs./Soviet Acad. Scis., 1983; recipient Jack H. Kolligian award Nat. Assn. Armenian Studies and Rsch., 1981, Boyan award Armenian Students Assn.; named to Boston U. Acad. Disting. Alumni, 1986; Accademia Tiberina of Rome, 1987.

DERNULC, LESLIE ANN, reporter, writer; b. Hammond, Ind., May 2, 1965; d. Edward Charles and Julie Regina (Danculovich) D. BS in Telecommunications, Purdue U., 1988. Reporter Sta. WJOB-AM, Hammond, 1988-89; reporter, rewrite City News Bur. of Chgo., 1989-90; freelance reporter and writer The Times, Hammond, 1989, Chgo. Tribune, 1989, Chgo. Sun-Times, 1990—. Vol. White House Press Advance Office, West Lafayette, Ind., 1987. Mem. Women in Communications (publicity com. 1987), Sigma Delta Chi.

DE ROE DEVON, THE MARCHIONESS See **GERRINGER-BUSENBARK, ELIZABETH JACQUELINE**

DEROSA, MARY CATHERINE, obstetrician, gynecologist; b. Utica, N.Y., Dec. 13, 1952; d. Humbert Francis Jr. and Anne Theresa (Cavallo) DeR.; m. John Michael Ellsworth, Dec. 22, 1979 (div. Sept. 1985); m. Paul Francis Hanrahan, Aug. 18, 1990. BA, Western Md. Coll., 1974; MD, SUNY, Syracuse, 1978. Diplomate Am. Bd. Ob-Gyn. Intern and resident program in ob-gyn. U. Rochester (N.Y.), 1978-82; pvt. practice, Rochester, N.Y., 1982-89, Warwick, R.I., 1989—. Fellow Am. Coll. Ob-Gyn; mem. Am. Fertility Soc., Am. Med. Women's Assn., Physicians for Social Responsibility, Save the Bay, Sierra Club, Greenpeace. Roman Catholic. Office: RI Group Health Assn 400 Baldhill Rd Warwick RI 02800

DEROSA, PATTI JEAN, educational administrator; b. Cleve., June 23, 1946; d. Angelo John and Agnes Anna(Anderson) DeRosa. BSEd., Kent State U., 1976; MBA in Mktg., Miami U., Oxford, Ohio, 1983. Specialist Community Info. Svc., Cleve., 1970-72; asst. to pres. William Dorsky & Assocs., Beachwood, Ohio, 1972-76, Agrl. Equipment, Inc., Mission, Kans., 1977; mktg. analyst Standard Havens, Inc., Kansas City, Mo., 1977-78; distributive edn. coord. Washington High Sch., Kansas City, Kans., 1978-82; dir. small bus. resource ctr. Cuyahoga Community Coll., Cleve., 1984—; cons. Kansas City, Mo., 1977-80, Cleve., 1984—; instr. Cuyahoga Community Coll., Cleve., 1985—; pub. speaker mktg. and small bus. topics, 1984—; vis. prof. bus. adminstrn. John Cabot Internat. U., Rome, 1990. Com. chair Cleve. Waterfront Coalition, 1985-88; vol. coun. Big Bros./Big Sisters, Cleve., Kansas City, 1977—; adv. bd. Am. Lung Assn., Cleve., 1988—; mem. Cleveland Heights (Ohio) Local Devel. Corp., 1985—. Recipient SBI Dist. award SBA, 1983. Mem. Am. Mktg. Assn. (com. chair 1984-86, SBIR adv. com. 1984— , v.p. 1986-88, pres. 1988-89), Miami Alumni Assn. (adv. com.), Cuyahoga Community Coll. Mktg. (adv. com. 1988—). Roman Catholic. Office: Cuyahoga Community Coll 2415 Woodland Ave Cleveland OH 44115

DEROSBIL, ANDREA MARIE, bank teller; b. Grosse Point Park, Mich., Apr. 9, 1965; d. Andrew Phillip and Johanna Karen (Rinne) Barych. Student, Macomb Community Coll., Warren, Mich. Teller Standard Fed. Bank, Sterling Heights, Mich., 1987-88; head cashier Dunham's Athleisure, Roseville, Mich., 1985-87; head teller First of Am. Bank-S.E. Mich., West Bloomfield, Mich., 1988—. Recipient Scholastic art award The Art Ctr. Mount Clemens. mem. Founders Soc. Detroit Inst. Arts. Democrat. Lutheran. Home: 23348 Teppert Ave East Detroit MI 48021-4412 Office: First Am Bank-SW Mich 6230 Orchard Lake Rd Ste 290 West Bloomfield MI 48322

DEROSE, KATHERINE ANNE, television production coordinator; b. Astoria, N.Y., Nov. 1, 1957; d. Joseph John and Katherine (LaVecchia) DeR. BA in Communications, Coll. of Mt. St. Vincent, Riverdale, N.Y., 1979. Adminstrv. asst. Major League Baseball, N.Y.C., 1980-85; coord. prodn. Major League Baseball Prodns., Stamford, Conn., 1985—. Roman Catholic.

DE ROSE, MARY FRANCES, producer, designer; b. Denver, Apr. 28, 1957; d. Francis and Eileen Joan (McGovern) De R. AAS, Fashion Inst. Tech., 1978; BA, U. Colo., 1981, MPA, 1985, MArch in Urban Design, 1987; LHD (hon.), SUNY, N.Y.C., 1986. Mgr. Abraham and Straus, Bklyn., 1977; jr. exec. Neusteters, Denver, 1978-79; prodn. coord. CINE Collaborative, Denver, 1980-82; dir. spl. projects Commn. Cultural Affairs, Denver, 1983-85; exec. dir. Metta Fund, San Francisco, 1986; sr. v.p. Compton Group, Chgo., 1987-89; prin., chief exec. officer Perisphere Creative, Denver, 1989—; ptnr. CDR Design, Chgo., 1988—; bd. dirs. Metta Internat., N.Y.C. Author: Making Places, 1987; editor jour. Interdisciplinary Design, 1986; mng. editor jour. Urban Design and Preservation, 1987. Bd. dirs. Urban Design Forum, Denver, 1988-89. Nat. Endowment for Arts fellow, 1985, Janus Found. for Interdisciplinary Studies fellow, 1990; Williams MacLaughlin Genius Fund grantee, 1988-90; Beyond 20th Century Fund scholar, 1989—. Fellow Mcpl. Art Soc.; mem. Am. Soc. for Pub. Adminstrn., Mensa. Home: 6630 W 84th Way Arvada CO 80003

DE ROSE, SANDRA MICHELE, psychotherapist, teacher, administrator; b. Beacon, N.Y.; d. Michael Joseph Borrell and Mabel Adelaide Edic Sloane; m. James Joseph De Rose, June 28, 1964 (div. 1977); 1 child, Stacey Marie. Diploma in nursing, St. Luke's Hosp., 1964; BA in Child Psychology, Albertus Magnus Coll., 1983; MS in Counseling Psychology, Century U., 1986, PhD in Counseling Psychology with honors, 1987. Gen. duty float nurse St. Luke's Hosp., Newburgh, N.Y., 1964-65; supr. nurses Craig House Hosp., Beacon, N.Y., 1965-70; team leader, dir. staff devel. div. of outpatient svcs. Conn. Mental Health Ctr., New Haven, 1970—; clin. instr. Sch. Nursing Yale U., New Haven, 1979—, clin. instr. dept. psychiatry, 1989—; pvt. practice, 1976—. Mem. Am. Nurses Assn. (cert.), Conn. Nurses Assn., Sigma Theta Tau, Delta Mu, Alpha Sigma Lambda. Office: Conn Mental Health Ctr 34 Park St New Haven CT 06511 also: 210 Prospect St New Haven CT 06511

DERR, JOY REESE, director communications, writer; b. Crookston, Minn., Oct. 1, 1941; d. Llewellyn Alfred and Evelyn (Funnell) Reese; m. John Witt Derr, Aug. 1, 1964; children: David, Elizabeth, Andrew, Amy. AA, Itasca Community Coll., Grand Rapids, Minn., 1961; BS, Iowa State U., Ames, 1963; postgrad., Hood Grad. Sch., 1990—. Writer Scholastic Mags., Inc., N.Y.C., 1963-64; women's editor Frederick (Md.) News-Post, 1964-66; dir. pub. info. Hood Coll., Frederick, 1966-68; freelance writer Frederick, 1968-78; pres. Image Bldg., Frederick, 1980-85, sr. assoc. dir. communications, editor Hood mag., 1978—; cons. Frederick County Tourism Coun., 1989, mem. publ rels. com., 1990—; chair community rels. com., bd. dirs. United Way, Frederick, 1990—; mem. pub. rels. com. Econ. & Devel. Commn. Frederick County, 1988—; mem. Frederick Meml. Hosp. Aux., 1964—; charter mem. Frederick County Family Life Ctr.; past mem. Am. Heart Assn., Frederick, March of Dimes, Frederick, Jaycee Wives, Frederick. Recipient Appreciation award Rose Hill Children's Mus., 1978, Md. 350th Celebration of Frederick County, 1984, Frederick Heart Assn., 1983. Mem. Coun. for Advancement and Support of Edn., Pub. Rels. Officers. Md. Republican. Lutheran. Home: 4601 Deer Spring Rd Braddock Heights MD 21714 Office: Hood Coll Rosemont Ave Frederick MD 21701

DERR, TERESA MARIE, chaplain; b. Jamaica, N.Y., Nov. 26, 1953; d. Emmanuel Henry and Catherine Elizabeth (Junker) D. BA magna cum laude, Georgian Ct. Coll., Lakewood, N.J., 1975; MDiv, Princeton Theol. Sem., 1980; therapist in tngs. Dynamics of Psycho., Washington Sch. Psychiatry, 1989—. Tchr. religion Notre Dame High Sch., Lawrenceville, N.J., 1975-76; tchr. religion, campus minister Stuart Country Day Sch., Princeton, N.J., 1977-78; chaplain AMI Presbyn.-St. Luke's Med. Ctr., Denver, 1978, 84-85, supr., 1984-85; chaplain Bethesda PsycHealth System, Denver, 1978-79; alcohol counselor Rescue Mission Trenton (N.J.), Inc., 1979-80; chaplain St. Peter's Med. ctr., New Brunswick, N.J., 1980-83, Children's Hosp., Denver, 1983-84; assoc. dir. pastoral care Luth. Med. Ctr., Bklyn., 1985-88; assoc. dir. pastoral care, dir. clin. pastoral edn. Washington Hosp. Ctr., 1988-90; dep. dir. devel. Women in Mil. Svc. for Am., Meml. Found., Washington, 1990—; therapist Eugene Meyer II Treatment Ctr., 1990—; lay minister St. Francis Ch., Brant Beach, N.J., summer 1977; dir. children's summer prog. St. Michael's Episcopal Ch., Trenton, summer 1979; workshop leader Ctr. for Humanizing Healthcare, Washington, 1988-90; mem. employee and physician devel. com. Ctr. for Humanizing Healthcare. Choral singer various groups incl. Oratorio Soc. of N.Y. Mem. Bread for World; co-leader, organizer support group for people with cancer, Bklyn., 1985-86; rep. Trenton Diocesan Pastoral Coun., 1976. Mem. AAUW, Assn. Clin. Pastoral Edn. (assoc. supr., com. mem. 1986—), Am. Orthopsychiat. Assn., Pastoral Care Network for Social Responsibility, Washington Psychologists for Study of Psychoanalysis, Women's Ordination Conf., Cath. Alumni Club, Sigma Phi Sigma, Phi Delta Phi. Democrat. Roman Catholic. Office: Women in Mil Svc for Am Meml Found Inc Dept 560 Washington DC 20042-0560

DERRICK-WHITE, ELIZABETH, marketing consultant, chaplain; b. Atlanta, Dec. 11, 1940; d. Andrew O. and J. Elizabeth (Rawlins) Derrick; m. Oct. 1958 (dec.); 1 child, Deborah Helene. LLB, U. New South Wales, Australia, 1974. Pres. Edmund Strange Assocs. Ltd., Atlanta, 1958-62; gen. mgr. Associated Brokerage Corp., Atlanta, 1962-66; trust officer Stewart Title Co. Ga., Atlanta, 1964-66; mgr. advt. Barkers Inc., N.Y.C., 1967-68; pres. White, Hufham and Young Ltd., Atlanta, 1978-82; creative dir. Effective Letters Party Ltd., Johannesburg, Rep. South Africa, 1982-83; mktg./creative dir. J. Walter Thompson, Lintas, Ogilvey & Mather Direct, Johannesburg, 1983-84; dir. Vineyard Christian Ctr. for Singles, Johannesburg, 1984-85; dir. mktg. Design Co., Atlanta, 1985-86; seminarian Candler Sch. Theology Emory U., Atlanta; counselor Genesis Christian Ctr., Johannesburg, 1983-84; mktg. dir. Response Products, Atlanta, 1988, D & G Research and Mktg., 1988. Author: Home Care for the Long Term Patient, 1979. Founding mem. Individual Rights Party, Australia, 1978; mem. nat. congl. Rep. com., 1980; mem. Am. Security Council, 1979-86, Caritas Ministry Team, Johannesburg, 1984-88, Team Ministeries, St. Pat's Episcopal Ch., Atlanta, 1988, Women's Caucus, Emory U., 1988; mem. Friends of St. Benedict Ch. Eng. Mem. Direct Mktg. Assn. Australia (dir. mktg. group 1974-76), Cons. Assn. (founder, pres.), Direct Mktg. Assn. S.E. (organizer), Commonwealth Journalists Assn. , Bridge to Africa (ops. officer), Am. Assn. Clin. Pastoral Edn., Assn. Counter-Terrorism Officers. Republican. Anglican. Home: 1785 N Decatur Rd Atlanta GA 30307 Office: 1785 N Decatur Rd #5 Atlanta GA 30307

DERRIG, LESLIE ANNE, civic volunteer; b. Oneonta, N.Y., Nov. 8, 1951; d. Harry Edwin and Joan Hazel (Ullmann) Dorr; m. William Joseph Derrig III, July 7, 1979; children: Danielle, Gabrielle. AA, Mohawk Valley Community Coll., Utica, N.Y., 1970. Flight attendant United Airlines, Inc., Chgo., 1972-84; sales rep. class A farm team N.Y. Yankees, Oneonta, 1975-78; pres. The Derrig Corp. dba Mr. Bulky's. Author: (children's book series) Working Mommy, 1984. Civic project chairwoman Kansas City (Mo.) Young Matrons, 1987—; vol. Ronald McDonald Ho., Kansas City, 1988—; bd. dirs. The Dream Factory, Kansas City, 1986—, Kansas City Art Inst. Palatteers, 1988-89. Republican. Presbyterian. Home: 12612 Cambridge Leawood KS 66209

DERSH, RHODA E., management consultant, business executive; b. Phila., Sept. 10, 1934; d. Maurice S. and Kay (Wiener) Eisman; m. Jerome Dersh, Dec. 23, 1956; children: Debra Lori, Jeffrey Jonathan. BA, U. Pa., 1955; MA, Tufts U., 1956; MBA, Manhattan Coll., 1980. Interpreter Consul of Chile, 1954-57; various teaching and staff positions Albright Coll., Mt. Holyoke Coll., Amherst Coll., Marple Newtown Sch., 1957-64; systems designer Systems Inc., Reading, Pa., 1964-67; pres., chief exec. officer Profl. Practice Mgmt. Assocs., Reading, 1976—, Pace Inst., Reading, 1981—, Pace Mgmt., Inc., 1983—; chief exec. officer Pace Microcomputers Internat., 1986—; pres. Wordserv, 1984—. Author: The School Budget is Your Business, 1976, Business Management for Professional Offices, 1977, The School Budget: It's Your Money, It's Your Business, 1979, Improving Public School Management Practices, 1979, Part-Time Professional and Managerial Personnel: The Employers View, 1979; contbr. articles to profl. jours. Pa. State Bd. Pvt. Lic. Schs., 1987—; cons. dir. pub. sch. budget study project City of Reading, 1967-78, chmn. comprehensive community plan task force, 1973-75, chmn. pub. svc. cons. project, 1980—; panel chmn. budget allocations United Way, 1974-76; del. White House Conf. on Children Youth, 1970; co-founder World Affairs Coun., Reading and Berks County, 1963-65; chmn. Berks County Com. for Children Youth, 1968-72; commr. Trial Ct. Nominating Commn. of Berks County (Pa.), 1982-84; bd. dirs. United Way of Berks County, 1984-89; chmn. programs Leadership Berks, 1986-87. Recipient Outstanding Womens award Jr. League Reading, Trendsetter award YWCA, 1985. Mem. AAUW (ednl. found. grant.), NAFE, LWV, Inst. Community Affairs (exec. com. 1975-79), Pa. Assn. Pvt. Sch. Bus. Adminstrs. (bd. dirs. 1985-89), Berks County C. of C. (bd. dirs. 1983-86, chmn. edn. com. 1983-85), Pa. Chamber of Bus. and Industry (edn. com.), Am. Mgmt. Assn., Am. Acad. Ind. Cons. (pres. 1978-80), Nat. Com. Citizens in Edn., Am. Acad. Polit. Social Sci., Reading and Berks C. of C (bd. dirs., chmn. edn. com., Entrepreneur of Yr. 1985), Rotary (bd. dirs. Reading, Pa., chpt. 1989-90). Office: 606 Court St Reading PA 19601

DERUBERTIS, PATRICIA SANDRA, software company executive; b. Bayonne, N.J., July 10, 1950; d. George Joseph and Veronica (Lukaszewich) Uhl; m. Michael DeRubertis, 1986. BS, U. Md., 1972. Account rep. Gen. Electric Co., San Francisco, 1975-77; tech. rep. Computer Scis. Corp., San Francisco, 1977-78; cons., pres. Uhl Assocs., Tiburon, Calif., 1978-81; cons. mgr. Ross Systems, Palo Alto, Calif., 1981-83; exec. v.p., chief operating officer Distributed Planning Systems, Calabasas, Calif., 1983—. Troop leader San Francisco council Girl Scouts U.S., 1974; participant Women On Water, Marina Del Rey, Calif., 1983. Mem. NAFE, Delta Delta Delta. Democrat. Office: Distributed Planning Systems 23501 Park Sorrento Ste 106 Calabasas CA 91302

DERUS, PATRICIA IRENE, media company executive; b. Chgo., May 2, 1947; d. Wilbur Xavier and Lorraine (Baumann) D.; children: Michael, Diane. BA, Northeastern Ill. U. With Derus Media Svc., Inc., Chgo., 1965-79, gen. mgr., 1979-84, pres., owner, 1985—. Sponsor, scholarship fund donor Friends of Pub. Relations Student Soc., 1989-90. Mem. Internat. Assn. Bus. Communicators, Japan-Am. Soc., Pub. Rels. Soc. Am. (bd. dirs. 1990, com. chair 1986-90), Nat. Assn. Hispanic Publs., Publicity Club Chgo. (com.), Internat. Pub. Rels. Soc., Women in Communications, Inc. (com. 1987-88, SARA award 1989). Office: Derus Media Svc Inc 500 N Dearborn Chicago IL 60610

DERUYTER, CAROL, mathematics educator; b. Pleasantville, N.J., Jan. 1, 1948; d. Frederick C. and Theresa A. (Heumann) deR. BS, Elizabethtown Coll., 1970; MA, Fairleigh Dickinson U., 1985. Cert. tchr., N.J. Tchr. math. Galloway Twp. (N.J.) Bd. Edn., 1970—; instr. So. N.J. Consortium for Gifted/Talented, Galloway Twp., 1984—, Ctr. for academically Talented Youth, Johns Hopkins U., Balt., 1983-85. Recipient Presdl. award for excellence in math. and sci. edn., NSF, 1985, N.J. Gov.'s Tchr. Recognition award, 1986. Mem. AAAS, Assn. Supervision and Curriculum Devel., Assn. Math. Tchrs. N.J., Nat. Coun. Tchrs. Math., AAUW, Alpha Delta Kappa (pres. 1986-88), Phi Delta Kappa (sec. 1989-90), Delta Kappa Gamma. Moravian. Office: Arthur Rann Sch 8th Ave Absecon NJ 08201

DESALVO, DEBORAH LYNN, counselor; b. New Orleans, Sept. 2, 1954; d. Nicholas Frank and Dixie Estelle (Sandlin) DeS.; m. William Byron Holmes, June 24, 1989. BS, La. State U, 1976; MEd, Ga. State U., 1984, EdS, 1987. Cert. sch. counselor, Ga. Group sales mgr. Goudchaux's Inc., Baton Rouge, 1977-79; coordinator of residence life John Brown U., Siloam Springs, Ark., 1980-82; dir. admissions and recruitment Psychol. Studies Inst., Atlanta, 1982-86; counselor Mt. Paran Counseling Ctr., Atlanta, 1984-86; asst. to dean Ga. State U., Atlanta, 1986-88, adviser for doctoral students, 1988-90; sch. counselor, 1990—; facilitator Active Parenting, Atlanta, 1983—. Mem. Am. Assn. Counseling and Devel., Kappa Delta Pi. Home: 2583 Travois Way Lilburn GA 30247

DESANTIS, CAMILLE ANN, editor; b. Bronx, N.Y., Mar. 22, 1961; d. Valdo and Lucy Joan (Andreozzi) DeSantis. BS in Med. Tech. summa cum laude, Iona Coll., 1983; generalist cert., Lenox Hill Sch. Med. Tech., N.Y.C., 1983. Cert. med. technologist. Sr. technologist Hosp. for Spl. Surgery, N.Y.C., 1983-90; jr. editor Gross Townsend Frank Hoffman, N.Y.C., 1990—. Recipient Cardinal Spellman award Iona Coll., 1983; Achievement award Am. Chem. Soc., 1980. Mem. Am. Soc. Med. Technologists, Am. Soc. Clin. Pathologists (assoc.), Delta Epsilon Sigma, Beta Beta Beta. Roman Catholic. Home: PO Box 678 Harrison NY 10528

DE SANTIS, MARY ANN THERESA, nurse; b. Phila., Mar. 23, 1938; d. Americus Anthony and Mary Theresa (McCann) De S.; (div.); 1 child, Christopher. BS, St. Joseph's Coll., 1960; RN, St. Francis Coll., 1963; MS, U. Pa., 1980, PhD, 1988. RN, N.J., Pa. Tchr. Phila. Diocese, 1955-60; RN Burdette Tomlin Hosp., Cape May Court House, N.J., 1963-68; tchr. Cape May County Vocat. Sch., Cape May Court House, 1968-70; head nurse VA Hosp., Lyons, N.J., 1970-71; instr. Union County Coll., Scotch Plains, N.J., 1971-75, Cape May County Vocat. Sch., 1975-80, 84-86; sch. nurse St. Ann's Sch., Wildwood, N.J., 1980-84; nurse mgr. Burdette Tomlin Hosp., 1986-89; dir. nurses Cape May Care Ctr., Cape May Court House, 1989—. Bd. Mem. Cape May County Mental Health, 1984-88. Mem. Am. Nurses Assn., Oncology Assn., Gerontology Assn. N.J., N.J. Nurses Assn., Moose. Republican. Roman Catholic. Home: 240 E Rio Grande Ave Wildwood NJ 08260 Office: Cape May Care Ctr Rt 9 Cape May Court House NJ 08210

DESANTO, GERARDA MARIE, psychotherapist; b. Scranton, Pa., Mar. 21, 1955; d. Edward Dominick and Iola Helen (Genevese) DeS. BA cum laude, U. Scranton, 1977; MS in Counseling, Nova U., 1981, postgrad. Writer Teen Scene Mag., North Miami, Fla., 1979-80; therapist 45th St. Mental Health Ctr., West Palm Beach, Fla., 1986-87, Nova Mental Health Clinic, Coral Springs, Fla., 1987-88, Coral Ridge Psychiat. Hosp., Ft. Lauderdale, Fla., 1980—. Author children's book: The Best of Friends, 1977. Vol. Listen to Children program, Broward County Mental Health Assn., Ft. Lauderdale, 1980-81. Mem. Am. Psychol. Assn., NOW, Good Day Sunshine Beatle Fan Club. Democrat. Roman Catholic. Home: 7014 Nandian Ln Tamarac FL 33321

DESCHAINE, BARBARA RALPH, real estate broker; b. Syracuse, N.Y., Feb. 16, 1930; d. George John and Dora Belle (Manchester) Ralph; children by previous marriage: Olav Bernt Kollevoll, Kristan George Kollevoll, Eric John Kollevoll; m. Bernard Richard Deschaine, May 23, 1981. BA, St. Lawrence U., 1952; postgrad. Pa. State U., 1969-72; grad. Pa. Realtors Inst., 1973; student Realtors Nat. Mktg. Inst., 1974-75. Salesman Brose Realty, Easton, Pa., 1967-72, assoc. broker/mgr., 1973, broker, owner, 1974-85; broker, mgr. John W. Monaghan Corp. Realtors, 1985—; mem. Pa. Real Estate Polit. Edn. Com. Bd. dirs. Easton Area C. of C., 1973-79, v.p. organizational improvement, 1975-76, v.p. econ. devel., 1976-77, pres., 1977-78; mem. Greater Easton Corp. Strategy Group, 1977-78; mem. Northampton County Revenue Appeals Bd., 1984—; trustee Easton area YWCA, 1984—. Mem. NAFE, Nat. Assn. Realtors, Pa. Assn. Realtors, Bethlehem Bd. Realtors, Eastern Northampton County Bd. Realtors (bd. dirs. 1973-87, sec. 1977, v.p. 1980-81, Realtor of Yr. 1978), Ea. Northampton County Multiple Listing Service (bd. dirs. 1987—), Realtors Nat. Mktg. Inst., Homes for Living Network (state chmn. 1980), Sales & Mktg. Execs. (bd. dirs. Easton area chpt. 1976—; Disting. Sales award 1982), Phi Beta Kappa. Republican. Presbyterian. Home: 330 Paxinosa Rd W Easton PA 18042 Office: 3063-3067 William Penn Hwy Easton PA 18042

DESCOTEAUX, CAROL J., academic administrator; b. Nashua, N.H., Apr. 5, 1948; d. Henry Louis and Therese (Arel) D. BA, Notre Dame Coll., 1970; MEd, Boston Coll., 1975; MA, U. Notre Dame, 1984, PhD, 1985. Jr. high sch. instr., dir. religious studies St. Joseph's Sch., North Grosvenordale, Conn., 1970-73; jr. high sch. tchr., dir. religious edn. Notre Dame Sch., North Adams, Mass., 1973-77; jr. high sch. instr. Sacred Heart Sch., Groton, Conn., 1977-78; chairperson religious studies discipline U. Notre Dame, Grad. Theol. Union, Notre Dame, Ind., 1982-83, 84-85; pres. Notre Dame Coll., Manchester, N.H., 1985—; trustee King's Coll., Wilkes-Barre, Pa., 1987—; pres. Fedn. of Holy Cross Colls., 1985—; mem. adv. bd. Manchester Christian Life Ctr., 1978-80; treas. N.H. Coll. and Univ. Council, Manchester, 1985—; trustee N.H. Higher Edn. Assistance Found., 1986—. Mem. Manchester United Way campaign, 1985—; bd. incorporators, mem. ethics com., instl. research com. Cath. Med. Ctr., Manchester, 1986—. Named Disting. Woman Leader of Yr., So. N.H. region YWCA, 1985. Mem. Am. Acad. Religion, Coll. Theology Soc. Am., N.H. Women's Forum, Soc. Christian Ethics, AAUW, N.H. Women in Higher Edn. Democrat. Roman Catholic. Office: Notre Dame Coll Office of the Pres 2321 Elm St Manchester NH 03104

DESHIELDS, TERESA LEIGH, psychology educator; b. Fayetteville, N.C., May 6, 1959; d. Forrest Hubert and Dorothy Rovilla (McCracken) D.; m. Raymond Caldwell Tait, Sept. 18, 1988. BA, BS, Meredith Coll., 1981; MS in Clin. Psychology, U. Ga., 1983, PhD in Clin. Psychology, 1985. Lic. psychologist, Mo. With St. Louis U. Med. Ctr., 1985—, asst. dir. behavioral treatment ctr., 1987—, asst. prof. dept. psychiatry, 1990—. Contbr. articles to profl. jours. Mem. Am. Psychol. Assn., Assn. for the Advancement of Behavior Therapy, Soc. Behavioral Medicine. Democrat. Unitarian. Office: St Louis U Med Ctr 1221 S Grand Saint Louis MO 63104

DESIMONE, RORY JEAN, small business owner; b. N.Y.C., Mar. 25, 1941; d. Joseph and Lee (Giardelli) DeS.; m. William Andrew D. Hammer Jr., Dec. 16, 1972; children: Craig Simon, Alexander Joseph. BA, Marymount Coll., 1962; postgrad., NYU, 1965-72. V.p. MacKay-Shields Fin. Corp., N.Y.C., 1962-80, cons., 1980-81; v.p. Medico Corp., Gainesville, Fla., 1981-82; pres., owner Children's Computer Conjunction div. Compu-TOTS, Gainesville, 1983—; ptnr., owner Dynamic Didactic Developware, Gainesville, 1985—; instr. behavioral scis. and career devel. Bus. Coll. Fin. and Econs., Santa Fe Community Coll.; mem. adv. bd. Fla. Instructional Computing Conf.; cons. computer various profl. orgns. Author software packages. Mem. pack com., mem. advancement bd. Boy Scouts Am., 1988-89; bd. dirs. Children's Resource Ctr.; coach local youth soccer league. Mem. Assn. Supervision and Curriculum Devel., Nat. Coun. Tchrs. of Math., Am. Ednl. Rsch. Assn., Assn. Ednl. Data Systems, Math. Assn. Am., Internat. Assn. Computing Edn., So. Assn. Children Under Six, Nat. Acad. Early Childhood Programs, Pilot Internat. (co-chairperson projects 1984-85, chairperson safety 1985—, Regional Safety award 1984-85, Nat. grant Safety 1984-85, 85-86), Fla. Assn. Computing Edn., Fla. Pub. Interest Rsch. Group, Apple Programmer's and Developer's Assn., Alachua County Computer User Group, Gainesville Apple Peelers. Republican. Roman Catholic. Clubs: APPLE Co-op (Wash.); Internat. Apple User Group (Mass.). Home: 1016 NW 112th Terr Gainesville FL 32606 Also: Childrens Computer Conjunct 1016 NW 112th Terr Gainesville FL 32606

DESISTO, ELIZABETH AGNES, medical records specialist; b. Medford, Mass., May 15, 1954; d. John Anthony and Josephine Loretta (Passero) DeS. AS cum laude, Mass. Bay Community Coll., 1974; BS magna cum laude, Northeastern U., 1979. Sr. med. record technician Children's Hosp. Med. Ctr., Boston, 1974-76; asst. dir. med. records dept. Glover Meml. Hosp., Needham, Mass., 1980-82; asst. dir. med. records dept. McLean Hosp., Belmont, Mass., 1982-83, acting dir. med. records dept., 1983-84, dir. med. records dept., 1984—. Vol. Big Sister Assn. Greater Boston, 1985-86, Greater Boston Walk for Hunger, 1983—; vol. local congl. campaigns. Mem. Am. Med. Records Assn. (reg. record adminstr., mental health record sect., bd. dirs. 1987-90, chmn. 1988-89), Mass. Med. Record Assn. (bd. dirs. 1985-91, sec. 1989-90). Democrat. Roman Catholic. Home: 723 Fellsway W Medford MA 02155 Office: McLean Hosp 115 Mill St Belmont MA 02178

DESJARLAIS, ERIKA ELSE, management analyst; b. Hamburg, Germany, Oct. 28, 1934; came to U.S., 1959; d. Friedrich Heinrich Paul Franz and Else Anna (Klussman) Fehrke; m. Leo Raymond Desjarlais, 1956 (dec. 1956); 1 child, Raymond Marcel; m. Richard Alexis Poirier, 1959 (div. 1985); 1 child, Denise Simone. AS, Monterey Peninsula Coll., 1975; BA, Antioch U., 1980; postgrad., Donsbach U., 1982. Office asst. A. Rienaecker, Goslar, Fed. Republic Germany, 1952-53, J. Wenig, Oker, Fed. Republic Germany, 1953; clk. Konsumgenossenschaft "Nordharz", Goslar, 1953-55; clk. typist 2d Can. Inf. Brigade, Soest, Fed. Republic Germany, 1956; purchasing clk. U.S. Army Quartermaster Market Ctr., Frankfurt, Fed. Republic Germany, 1957-58; sec./translator V Corps Hdqrs., Frankfurt, 1958-59; accounts maintenance clk. USAF So. Command, Panama Canal Zone, 1968-69; sec. U.S. Army Combat Devel. Experimentation Ctr., Ft. Ord, Calif., 1970-83; correctional officer Sheriff's Office, Salinas, Calif., 1974-75; mgmt. analyst Texcom Experimentation Ctr., Ft. Ord, Calif., 1983-89, 7th Infantry Div. (Light) and Fort Ord, Ft. Ord, Calif., 1989—. Mem. Fed. Women's Program Adv. Com., Ft. Ord, Calif., 1975-88; mem. Advocate Governing Bd., Rape Crisis Ctr., Monterey, 1980-82; commr. Commn. on Status of Women, Monterey County, 1986-88, Affirmative Action Commn., 1986-88; advocate Women Against Domestic Violence, 1980-81, Monterey Rape Crisis Ctr., 1980-82; active YWCA. Mem. NAFE, Am. Soc. Mil. Comptrollers, Internat. Tng. in Communication Inst., Am. Nutrition Cons. Assn. Libertarian. Evangelical-Lutheran. Club: Monterey Bay Hot Jazz Soc. (publicity chairwoman 1978, corres. sec. 1977). Home: 335 Parson Circle Marina CA 93933 Office: 7th Infantry Div (Light) and Fort Ord Attn AFZW-RM-M Fort Ord CA 93941-5222

DESMOND, KATHLEEN M(AE), international development consultant; b. L.A., May 4, 1940; d. Albert James and Muriel (Williams) D. BA magna cum laude, Immaculate Heart Coll., 1967; MA in Internat. Devel., Am. U., 1978. Edn. coord. Am. Freedom From Hunger Found., Washington, 1970-72; vol. Peace Corps., Salvador, Bahia, Brazil, 1972-75; rsch. fellow Overseas Devel. Coun., Washington, 1976; assoc. dir. Campaign for Human Devel. U.S. Cath. Conf., Washington, 1976-83; mng. sr. assoc. Devres, Inc., Washington, 1983-85; ind. cons. internat. devl. Arlington, Va., 1985—; analyst Office Tech. Assessment U.S. Congress, Washington, 1985—; Writer tng. materials for WHO Med. Edn., Mgmt. Scis. for Health, Rosslyn, Va., 1988—; writer manual on monitoring and evaluation for field staff UNICEF, 1988-90; tchr., chmn. social studies dept. Immaculate Heart High Sch., L.A., 1968-70, St. Anthony Girls High Sch., Long Beach, Calif., 1964-68. Bd. dirs. Arlington Housing Corp., 1982-88, pres., 1985-86, Colonial Village West, 1988—, pres., 1990—. Grantee Fulbright Hays, NDEA, EPDA, 1967-68. Mem. Soc. Internat. Devel., Assn. Women in Devel., Coun. on Founds. (program com. 1982-83). Democrat. Roman Catholic. Home and Office: 2701 S 16th St #627 Arlington VA 22204

DE SOLA, ISABELLA MIRIAM, lawyer, poet; b. N.Y.C., Sept. 17, 1955. JD, Columbia U., 1982. Bar: N.Y. 1984, U.S. Dist. Ct. (so. dist., ea. dist.) N.Y. 1984. Pvt. practice N.Y.C., 1984—; former fashion model. Contbr. (anthologies) Something For Everyone, Poetic Voices of America, Sunrise, Sunset, American Poetry Annual, Visions, American Poetry Anthology, Of Diamonds and Rust, Vol. 2, Another Place in Time. Sec.-treas. Beyond Shelter Coalition for Permanent Housing, N.Y.C., 1989—. Harlan Fiske Stone Scholar Columbia U., Harold P. Seligson scholarships in N.Y. Civil Practice, Bankruptcy Law, Securities Law, N.Y. Real Estate Practice, Immigration Law, Practising Law Inst., 1989. Mem. ABA (litigation, bus. law, criminal justice, natural resources, energy and environmental law, internat. law, and young lawyers sects.), Assn. Trial Lawyers Am. (mem. com.), N.Y. State Bar Assn., N.Y. State Trial Lawyers Assn., N.Y. County Lawyers' Assn. (apptd. to com. family ct. and child welfare), Columbia Law Women's Assn., Trial Practice Inst., Pub. Interest Law Students Assn., Latin Am. Law Students' Assn., Profl. Karate League, Pi Upsilon Delta Honor Soc.

DESOMOGYI, AILEEN ADA, retired librarian; b. London, Nov. 26, 1911; d. Harry Alfred and Ada Amelia (Ponten) Taylor; immigrated to Can., 1966; BA, Royal Holloway Coll., U. London, 1936, MA, 1939; MLS, U. Western Ont., 1971; m. Leslie Kuti, Nov. 22, 1958; m. 2d, Joseph DeSomogyi, July 8, 1966. Librarian in spl. and pub. libraries, Eng., 1943-66; sr. instr. Nat. Coal Bd., 1957; charge regional collection S.W. Ont., Lawson Library, U. Western Ont., 1967-71; cataloger Coop. Book Centre Can., 1971; mem. staff E. York (Ont.) Pub. Library, 1971-74; librarian Ont. Ministry Govt. Svcs. Mgmt. and Info. Svcs. Library, 1975-78, Sperry-Univac Computer Systems, Toronto (Ont.) Cen. Library, 1980-81; dep. dir. gen. Internat. Biog. Centre. Contbr. articles to profl. jours. Mem. Internat. Platform Assn., English Speaking Union, Can. Orgn. for Devel. Through Edn., Consumers Assn. Can., Can. Wildlife Fedn., Ont. Humane Soc., Internat. Fund Animal Welfare, Endangered Animal Sanctuary, U. Western Ont. Alumni Assn., Royal Holloway and Bedford New Coll. Assn., Am. Biog. Inst. Research Assn. (dep. gov., nat. bd. advisors), Internat. Biog. Assn., Internat. Biog. Centre (dep. dir. gen.), Can. Mental Health Assn., John Howard Soc., Zool. Soc. Met. Toronto, Toronto Humane Soc., World Inst. of Achievement, World Federalists of Can. Roman Catholic. Home: 9 Bonnie Brae Blvd, Toronto, ON Canada M4J 4N3

DESOR, JEANNETTE ANN, consulting psychologist; b. Balt., July 11, 1942; d. Raymond Charles and Evelyn (Geiger) D. AB magna cum laude, Cornell U., Ithaca, N.Y., 1964, PhD, 1969; postgrad., Yale U., 1964-65, U. Pa., Phila., 1970-72. Lic. psychologist, Pa., Conn. Rsch. asst. Yale U., New Haven, 1965; teaching asst. Cornell U., Ithaca, 1965-69; staff scientist Monell Chem. Senses Ctr. Monell Chem. Senses Ctr., U. Pa., Phila., 1970-75; asst. prof. Sch. Medicine, U. Pa., Phila., 1973-75; rsch. assoc. VA Hosp., Phila., 1973-75; sect. head Warner Lamber Co., Milford, Conn., 1975-78, mgr., 1978; mgr. Gen. Foods Corp., Tarrytown, N.Y., 1978-82; prin. scientist Gen. Foods Corp., Philip Morris Co., Inc., Tarrytown, 1982-88; cons. psychologist Balt., 1988—; program mgr. Gen. Foods Corp., Tarrytown, 1985-87; weight control therapist U. Pa., Phila., 1974-75; dir. Mace Fremont, Inc., Balt. Patentee, author publs. in field. Ford Found. fellow, 1963-64, Yale U. fellow, 1964-65, Cornell U. fellow, 1966-68, NIH fellow, 1970, 71, 72. Mem. AAAS, Assn. Chemoreception Scis., Human Factors Soc., Soc. Ingestive Behavior, European Chemoreception Rsch. Orgn., Eastern Psychol. Assn. Office: JA Desor Cons 10630 Breezewood Circle Woodstock MD 21163

DESOUSA, KAREN EVANS, communications professional; b. Des Moines, Dec. 6, 1975; d. William G. and Jacqueline E. (Marquette) Evans; m. Michael A. DeSousa, Dec. 6, 1975; 1 child, Matthew. BS, U. No. Iowa, Cedar Falls, 1974. Asst. to editor-in-chief Houghton Mifflin Publ., Iowa City, 1977-79; mgr. tech. support Lexisoft, Inc., Davis, Calif., 1982-87; mgr. tech. publs., software control and documentation Telwatch, Inc., El Dorado Hills, Calif., 1987-88; sr. assoc. Schmidt Assocs., Inc., Rancho Cordova, Calif., 1988-90; dir. communication svcs. Objective Systems Integrators, Folsom, Calif., 1990—; Cert. supervision practices. Author various user manuals and tech. guides. Mem. NAFE, Soc. Tech. Communications, Internat. Assn. Bus. Communicators, Am. Soc. Quality Control, Phi Epsilon Omicron. Home: 3016 Moliner Dr Cameron Park CA 95682

DESPRES, GINA HELEN, lawyer; b. Sydney, Australia, Sept. 28, 1941; came to U.S., 1964, naturalized, 1972; d. George Alfred and Winifred Florence (Bush) Eviston; B.A. with honors (Commonwealth scholar 1960-64), U. Sydney, 1964; postgrad. (NDEA fellow 1966-68), U. Calif., Berkeley, 1965-70; J.D., UCLA, 1974; m. John Despres, Sept. 23, 1964; children—Sarah, Naomi. Bar: Calif. 1974, D.C. 1976. Atty. firm Irell & Manella, Los Angeles, 1974-75; mem. firm Caplin & Drysdale, Washington, 1976-77; with Dept. Energy, 1977-79, dir. internat. energy and energy security policy, 1978-79; counsel, tax and internat. affairs U.S. Senator Bradley of N.J., 1979—. Bd. editors UCLA Law Rev. 1973-74. Mem. D.C. Bar Assn. Author articles in field. Office: 731 Hart Senate Office Bldg Washington DC 20515

DESROCHES, DIANE BLANCHE, English instructor, writer-director, editor; b. Webster, Mass., Nov. 17, 1947; d. Victor Joseph and Rose Blanche Blouin; m. Roger John DesRoches, Aug. 27, 1966 (div. Apr. 16, 1974); 1 child, Bill. AA with high honors in French, Mesa Coll., 1976; BA in English magna cum laude, San Diego State U., 1979, MA, 1981. Cert. lang. arts, lit. and ABE:ESL instr., Calif. community colls. ESL instr. Coll. of English Language, 1982—, San Diego Community Coll. Dist., 1982—. Author: (short story) Something Special, 1979, Cinderella of the 80s, 1980; (software) Basic Map Reading Skills, 1981; writer (video) The College of English Language, 1989, numerous recipes, word search puzzles, variety puzzles and ednl. puzzles., 1980—; writer, dir. (video) The Challenge Is Ours, 1989; co-writer (multimedia show) Holiday Sky Show, 1988, (screen adaptation) The Wind From the Sun, 1989; contbr. articles to mags.; contbr. (reading comprehension series) Comprehension Plus, 1982, (student assessment system) CASAS, 1982; editorial cons. (multimedia shows) Dimensions, 1987, Cycles, 1987, Star Tracks, 1988, Thundering Water, 1988, Flying Blue Marble, 1988, Night on Dream Mountain, 1988, Mars, 1988, From Here to Infinity, 1989, To Worlds Beyond, 1989, Stars Over China, 1989; translator: ABC of Ecology, 1982. Recipient Gregg award Gregg Inst., 1965; fellow State of Calif., 1979; DB Williams scholar San Diego State U., 1979. Mem. Phi Kappa Phi, Psi Chi, Pi Delta Phi. Democrat. Roman Catholic. Office: 2029-F Cerrissa Ct San Diego CA 92154

DESSASO, DEBORAH ANN, association legislative specialist, freelance writer; b. Washington, Feb. 6, 1952; d. Coleman and Virginia Beatrice (Taylor) D. AS in Bus. Adminstrn., Southeastern U., 1986, BSBA, 1988. Clk.-stenographer FTC, Washington, 1969-70; sec. NEA, Washington, 1970-

72; sec. Nat. Ret. Tchrs. Assn./Am. Assn. Ret. Persons, Washington, 1972-79, assoc. adminstrv. specialist, 1979-80, adminstrv. specialist, 1980—; founding mem., sec. Andrus Fed. Credit Union, 1980. Mem. NAFE. Mem. Worldwide Ch. of God. Home: 3052 Stanton Rd SE Washington DC 20020 Office: 1909 K St NW Washington DC 20049

DESSAUER, CARIN, journalist; b. Pottstown, Pa., Dec. 31, 1963; d. Ralph and Margot (Abrams) D.; m. Marc Richard Engel, May 29, 1988. BA cum laude, Bucknell U., 1985; postgrad., George Washington U., 1987. Reporter The Polit. Report, Washington, 1986-87; off-air reporter ABC News Polit. Unit, Washington, 1988; assoc. editor Congl. Quarterly's Politics in Am., Washington, 1989; contbg. editor Campaigns and Elections mag., Washington, 1989—; head Washington polit. unit Cable News Network, 1990—. Co-author: (monograph) Running to Win, 1988. Mem. recruiting com. for sports challenge Cystic Fibrosis of Washington, 1990—. Mem. AFTRA, Women in Communications, Inc., Phi Beta Kappa. Office: Cable News Network 111 Massachusetts Ave NW Washington DC 20001

DESSERT, LYNN MARIE, management; b. Mountainhome, Idaho, Mar. 4, 1960; d. Robert Allen and Joan Marie (Haberer) D. BA Social Work, Wright State U., Dayton, Ohio, 1981; MBA in Mgmt., Miami U., Oxford, Ohio, 1983. Asst. mgr. The Kroger Co., Toledo Findlay, 1983-86; pers. adminstr. Allied-Signal Autolite Div., Fostoria, Ohio, 1986-88; supr., emp. rels. Allied-Signal Autolite Div., Spartanburg, S.C., 1988; supr. emp. rels. Allied-Signal Automotive Sector, Southfield, Mich., 1989, Allied-Signal Garrett Automotive, Torrance, Calif., 1989—. Advisor Junior Achievement, Fostoria Ohio 1986-87. Mem. Am. Mgmt. Assn. (Sec. 1987--), Am. Soc. Personnel Adminstrs., Graduate Bus. Assn. Club Oxford Ohio (Treas. 1982-83). Republican. Roman Catholic. Office: Allied-Signal Garret Automotive Torrance CA 90503

D'ESTE, MARY ERNESTINE, health administration executive; b. Chgo., Apr. 1, 1941; d. Ernest Gregory and Mary (Turcich) D'E. Student, Mundelein Coll., 1958-61. Sec. MMM, Bedford Park, Ill., 1961-69, Michael Reese Med. Ctr., Chgo., 1969-73; adminstrv. asst. Thomas Jefferson U., Phila., 1973-85, divisional adminstr., 1985-86; adminstr. dept. cardiothoracic surgery Hahnemann U., Phila., 1986—; v.p. CTS Cardiac & Thoracic Surgeons PC, Phila., 1986—. V.p. archtl. review com. GTV Homeowners Assn., Marlton, N.J., 1979-85. Mem. Med. Group Mgmt. Assn., Am. Assn. Notaries, NAFE. Roman Catholic. Office: Hahnemann U Hosp Broad and Vine MS 111 Philadelphia PA 19102-1192

DETERT-MORIARTY, JUDITH ANNE, civic worker, graphic artist; b. Portage, Wis., July 10, 1952; d. Duane Harlan and Ann Jane (Devine) Detert; m. Patrick Edward Moriarty, July 22, 1978; children: Colin Edward, Eleanor Grace, Dylan Joseph. Student U. Wis.-Madison, 1970-73, U. Wis.-Green Bay, 1984—. Cert. in no-fault grievance mediation, Minn. Legis. sec., messenger State of Wis. Assembly, Madison, 1972, 74-76; casualty-property div. clk. Capitol Indemnity Corp., Madison, 1976-77; sec./credit clk. comml. credit div. Affiliated Bank of Madison, 1977-78; word processor consumer protection div. Wis. Dept. Agr., Madison, 1978; graphics arts composing specialist Moraine Park Tech. Inst., Fond du Lac, Wis., 1978-79; free-lance artist Picas, Pictures and Promotion (formerly Detert Graphic), 1978—; prodn. asst. West Bend News, 1980-83; devel. assoc. Riveredge Nature Ctr., Inc., Newburg, Wis., 1983-84; exec. dir. Voluntary Action Ctr. of Washington County, West Bend, 1984086; devel. cons. West Bend Hospice Program, 1985; instr. community svcs. Austin (Minn.) Community Coll., 1988; art and promotional publs. dir. Michael G. & Co., Albert Lea, Minn., 1988-89; corp. art dir. Newco, Inc., Janesville, Wis., 1989—. Vol. activities include: Austin Pub. Schs. Omnibus Program polit. cartooning instr. Dane County vol. Udall for Pres., 1976; student vol. McCarthy for Pres., U. Wis., Madison, 1968, coord. student residences McGovern for Pres., 1972; Washington County campaign coord. Nat. Unity Campaign for John Anderson for Pres., 1980; Washington County ward coord. Earl for Gov., 1982; Washington County campaign chmn. Peg Lautenschlager for Wis. state senate, Washington County ward coord. Mondale/Ferraro, 1984; vol. coord. Rock County Dukakis for Pres., 1988; campaign chair Lew Mittness for Wis. State Assembly, 1990; sec., newsletter editor Dem. Party of Manitowoc County, Wis., 1986, Rock County, 1988-90; local chair Women's Polit. Caucus, 1987-88; publicity coord. Wis. Intellectual Freedom Coalition, 1981; founding exec. bd. dirs., newsletter editor Moral Alternatives, Catholics for a Free Choice Wis. community contact; newsletter editor Voice for Choice, 1989-90; bd. dirs., v.p. Wis. Pro-Choice Conf., 1981-82; pres., founder People of Washington County United for Choice, 1981-83; bd. pres. Planned Parenthood of Washington County, 1984-85, newsletter editor, mem. coms., 1980-85; bd. mem. Montessori Children's House, West Bend, 1983-85, newsletter editor, com. chmn.; artist LWV Washington County, 1984-86; newsletter artist, artist Friends of Battered Women, West Bend, 1983-86; apptd. to Austin Human Rights Commn, 1987-88; fundraiser Victims Crisis Ctr., 1987; v.p., communication officer Rock County Dem. Party, 1988-90; cartooning instr., contbg. artist Janesville Pub. Schs., 1989—; Mower County Dem. precinct chair, affirmative action officer, county sec. Dem. Party, 1988; artist LWV Rock County. Mem. NAFE, NOW (newsletter editor Dane County 1977-78, coord. Wis. state reproductive rights task force 1982-84, coord. reproductive rights task force North Suburban Chpt., 1981-84, Minn. pub. rels. coord., 1987-88, Rock County chpt.), Women in Communications, Population Inst., Nat. Assn. Desktop Pubs. Quaker. Avocations: reading, hand spinning and knitting, world wide correspondence, antiques. Home: 23 S Atwood Ave Janesville WI 53545

DETHORNE, JACQUELYN MARIE, manufacturing company executive; b. Ft. Riley, Kans., July 30, 1957; d. Raymond John and Mary Jacqueline (Steuerle) DeT.; m. Joseph Robert Falconi, Jr., May 30, 1980 (div. Apr. 1987); 1 child, Joseph Robert III. BS in Engring. Mgmt. cum laude, U. Mo., Rolla, 1978; MBA in Fin., U. Akron, 1982. Quality, mfg. engr. Gen. Electric, Warren, Ohio, 1978-80; proposal, contracts engr. Babcock & Wilcox, Fairlawn, Ohio, 1980-82; bus. planner Babcock & Wilcox, Akron, Ohio, 1982-83; mfg. fin. analyst Babcock & Wilcox, Akron, 1983; engring. cost control supr. Gould, Inc., Cleve., 1983-85, sr. fin. analyst, 1985; dept. adminstr. Cleve. (Ohio) Clinic Found., 1985-87; mgr., govt. acctg., contracts Parker Hannifin, Cleve., 1987-90, mgr. contracts, 1990—. Mentor I Have a Dream Found., Cleve., 1988-90; cons. Jr. Achievement, Warren, 1978-79, Cleve., 1987-90. Mem. Nat. Contract Mgmt. Assn. (constitution chmn., 1988-89, edn. chmn., 1989-90, 2nd v.p. 1990—, panelist, 1990). Office: Parker Hannifin 520 Ternes St PO Box 4026 Elyria OH 44036-2026

DETMAR-PINES, GINA LOUISE, school system administrator; b. S.I., N.Y., May 3, 1949; d. Joseph and Grace Vivian (Brown) Sargente; m. Michael B. Pines, Sept. 11, 1988. BS in Edn., Wagner Coll., 1971, MA in Edn., 1972; MA in Urban Affairs and Policy Analysis, The New Sch. for Social Research, 1987; post grad. studies in Bus. Adminstrn., City U., 1987—. Cert. adminstr. and supr., sch. dist. adminstr. Tchr. pub. schs. N.Y.C., 1971-82; coord. spl. projects, pub. affairs N.Y.C. Bd. Edn., 1982, spl. asst. to exec. dir. pupil services, 1983, asst. to the chancellor, 1983-84; dir. Tchr. Summer Bus. Industry Program, Bklyn., 1984—; liaison for the Tchr. Industry Program, N.Y.C. Ptnrship., 1985—. Mem. Com. to re-elect Borough pres. Lamberti, S.I., 1985. Mayor's scholar City of N.Y., 1984—. Mem. Fgn. Lang. Instrs. Assn., U.S. Seaplane Pilot's Assn., Internat. Orgn. for Licensed Women Pilots, Chinese-Am. Soc., Am. Mgmt. Assn., Acad. Mgmt., Strategic Mgmt. Soc., Ea. Acad. Mgmt., Cambridge Flying Group Club. Episcopalian. Office: NYC Bd Edn 65 Court St Brooklyn NY 11201

DE TOLEDO, CATHERINE HOLT, medical writer; b. Columbus, Ohio, May 16, 1954; d. Golden Jr. and Petrea (Giles) Holt; m. Luiz Carlos de Toledo, Mar. 10, 1979; 1 child, Laura Holt. BS, Stanford U., 1976. Med. writer Alfred I. duPont Inst., Wilmington, Del., 1976-79; tchr. English Mich. Lang. Inst., Campinas, Brazil, 1980-81; propr. Belladerme Skin Care, Campinas, 1981-84; med. writer Louisville Hand Surgery, 1984-85; freelance med. writer Ft. Worth, 1985-89. Asst. editor: Reconstruction of the Child's Hand, 1989; contbr. articles to various publs. Mem. Am. Med. Writers Assn., NAFE, Soc. Profl. Journalists, Texpac Aux. (dist. vice-chmn. 1989), Tarrant County Med. Soc. Aux. (chmn. health fair 1988, v.p. publicity 1989), Women's Club Ft. Worth, Etta Newby Club. Home and Office: 1 Lombardy Terr Fort Worth TX 76132

DE TORNYAY, RHEBA, nurse, university dean emeritus, educator; b. Petaluma, Calif., Apr. 17, 1926; d. Bernard and Ella Fradkin; m. Rudy de Tornyay, June 4, 1954. Student, U. Calif., Berkeley, 1944-46; diploma, Mt. Zion Hosp. Sch. Nursing, 1949; A.B., San Francisco State U., 1951, M.A., 1954; Ed.D., Stanford U., 1967; Sc.D. (hon.), Ill. Wesleyan U., 1974; L.H.D. (hon.), U. Portland, 1974. Faculty San Francisco State U., 1957-67, prof. nursing, 1966-67, chmn. dept., 1959-67; asso. prof. U. Calif. Sch. Nursing, San Francisco, 1968-71; prof. U. Calif. Sch. Nursing, 1971; dean, prof. Sch. Nursing, UCLA, 1971-75; dean emeritus, prof. U. Wash., Seattle, 1975—; dir. Clin. Nurse Scholars Program, Robert Wood Johnson Found. Author: Strategies for Teaching Nursing, 1971, 3rd edit., 1987, Japanese transl., 1974, Spanish edit., 1986. Mem. Am. Nurses Assn., Am. Acad. Nursing (charter fellow, pres. 1973-75), Inst. Medicine (governing council 1979-81), Soc. Health and Human Values, Nat. League for Nursing. Office: U Wash Sch Nursing SM-24 Seattle WA 98195

DETTELBACH, IONA SCHAFFER, small business owner; b. Cleve., Jan. 5, 1935; d. Louis Lazar and Beatrice Ruth (Kargher) Schaffer; m. Richard Henry Dettelbach, Sept. 19, 1955; children: Cindy Ellen, Susan Beth, Hallie Rose. Student, Ohio State U., 1953-55, Mather Coll., 1955-56. Pres. What Knots Retail Store, Chagrin Falls, Ohio, 1972-75, And Sew On, Inc., University Heights, Ohio, 1975—; seminar leader Kappie Orginals Inc., Frederick, Md., 1988--, cons. on designs, 1989--. Past pres. United Order True Sisters #30, Cleve., 1970; exec. bd. sec. Mt. Sinai Hosp. Jr. Women's Bd., Cleve., 1963, v.p. fund raising Mis-rachi Women, Cleve., 1973, credential coord. Cleve. Nat. Air Show, 1983—. Recipient numerous ribbons from various needlework assn., 1972--. Mem. The Nat. Needlework Assn. (seminar leader), Southeastern Yarncrafters Guild, United Order of True Sisters. Jewish. Office: And Sew On Inc 2243 Warr Center Rd University Heights OH 44118

DETURK, DEBORAH SUZANNE, insurance sales; b. Garden City, N.Y., May 4, 1953; d. Frederick Walter and Carolyn Dorothy (Nubel) D. BA, U. Mich., 1975; postgrad., 1988-92. Property casualty ins. broker's lic. Dir. leasing svcs. Alanthus Corp., Westport, Conn., 1976-81; sales rep. Equico Lessors, Patterson, N.J., 1981-82; asst. v.p., sales Rhulen Agency Inc., Monticello, N.Y., 1982—; speaker, various state councils, colleges, clubs., 1982--. Contbr. articles to prof. mags. Bd. dirs. Conn. Horse Coun. Republican. Home: 11 Flora St New Fairfield CT 06812 Office: Rhulen Agy Inc PO Box 6614 Richmond VA 23230-0614

DETWEILER, MARIE LOUISE, systems analyst; b. Pinckneyville, Ill., Oct. 31, 1934; d. Harlan Isophene and Vivian Lanara (Stanley) Parkerson; m. Brian Lowell Detweiler, Sept. 2, 1956 (separated); children: Lucinda Lee Detweiler Racine, Michael Jon. BA, Anderson (Ind.) U., 1957. With Social Security Adminstrn., Balt., 1968-79, supervisory computer systems analyst, 1980-89, ret., 1990. Mem. ACLU, LWV. Democrat. Home: 2116 Gillis Falls Rd Woodbine MD 21797

DEUCHLER, SUZANNE LOUISE, state legislator; b. Chgo., July 21, 1929; m. Walter E. Deuchler Jr.; children: Mark, Maryll. BA, U. Ill. Mem. Ill. Ho. of Reps., Springfield, 1980—. Mem. Aurora reg. adv. com., Ill. Dept. Children and Family Svcs., 1976, citizens adv. bd., Aurora U., 1981; bd. dirs. Copley Meml. Hosp., 1982. Mem. AAUW, Altrusa, Bus. and Profl. Women. Republican. Office: Ill State Ho of Reps 1128A Prairie St Aurora IL 60506

DEUSS, JEAN, librarian; b. Chgo.; d. Edward Louis and Harriet (Goodwin) D. B.A., U. Wis., 1944; M.S., Sch. Library Service, Columbia U., 1959. Cataloger library N.Y.C. Council Fgn. Relations, 1959-61; head cataloger research library Fed. Res. Bank N.Y., N.Y.C., 1961-68; asst. chief librarian Fed. Bank N.Y., N.Y.C., 1969-70, chief librarian, 1970-85. Editor Banking and Fin. Collections, Spl. Collections, vol. 2, No. 3, 1983. Mem. U. Wis. Found., 1977—, bd. dirs., 1983—. Mem. Spl. Libraries Assn. (assoc. treas. 1967-70, pres. N.Y. chpt. 1971-72, bd. dirs. 1972-76). Episcopalian. Home: 260 W 12th St New York NY 10014

DEUTER, KARLA JEAN, medical technologist, microbiologist; b. Sioux City, Iowa, Oct. 9, 1960; d. Lawrence Jordon and Kathleen Claire (Dennison) Rick; m. Timothy Donald Deuter, Apr. 28, 1984. BS in Microbiology, S.D. State U., 1982. Cert. med. technologist. Staff med. technologist Monticello Med. Ctr., Longview, Wash., 1984-86, Rapid City (S.D.) Regional Hosp., 1986—. Mem. Rails to Trails, Rapid City, 1988, Literacy Coun. of the Black Hills. Recipient scholarship, S.D. State U., 1978, 83. Mem. Am. Soc. Clin. Pathologists, Black Hills Soc. Med. Technologists (treas. 1986—), Rotary (mem. internat. exch. group to India and Nepal 1989). Democrat. Roman Catholic. Home: 3920 Yucca Dr A Rapid City SC 57702

DEUTSCH, ELLEN SUE, lawyer,; b. Bklyn., Nov. 2, 1942; d. Norman and Betty (Newman) Kaplan; m. John G. Williams, Jan. 2, 1984; children—Scott, Adam. B.A., Antioch Coll., Yellow Springs, Ohio, 1975; J.D., Cath. U., 1977. Atty., Office of Telecommunication Policy, Exec. Office of the Pres., Washington, 1975-77, FCC, Washington, 1977-78; dir. policy analysis Dept. of Commerce, Washington, 1978-82; cons., assoc. Irwin & Deutsch, Washington, 1982-84; ptnr. Thelen, Marrin, Johnson & Bridges, 1987—; dir. fed. regulation Bell Communications Research, Inc., Washington, 1984—; cons. Telecommunications Cons. Group, Washington, 1982-85. Mem. ABA, Fed. Communications Bar Assn., D.C. Bar Assn.

DEUTSCH, FLORENCE ELAYNE GOODILL, nursing and health care consultant; b. San Diego, Aug. 1, 1923; d. George Ehrlich and Beatrice Marie (Urick) Goodill; m. Edward Thomas Deutsch, June 27, 1953 (dec.); 1 son, George Edward. Student, San Diego State Coll., 1942-43; B.S.N., Villa Maria Coll., 1948; diploma in nursing Evanston Hosp., Northwestern U., 1947; M.Ed., Edinboro U., 1961. Staff nurse St. Vincent Hosp., Erie, Pa., 1947; clin. instr.-supr. Hamot Med. Ctr., Erie, 1948-58, dir. edn., 1958-62, dir. Sch. Nursing, 1962-66, asst. adminstr., dir. Sch. Nursing, 1969-73; exec. dir. Florence Crittenton Home, Erie, 1966-69; asst. adminstr., dir. nursing Capitol Hill Hosp., Washington, 1974-79; assoc. adminstr. profl. services Millcreek Community Hosp., 1980-82; v.p. nursing East Liverpool City Hosp. (Ohio), 1982-87; lectr., cons. on nursing and nursing law, 1988-89; lectr. Gannon U., Erie, Pa. Past bd. dirs. Columbiana County Cancer Soc. Served with USNR, 1948-53. Named Most Outstanding Nurse Erie County, 1969, Disting. Alumna Villa Maria Coll. Gannon U., 1989. Mem. Nat. League Nursing, Am. Orgn. Nurse Execs., SCORE (vice-chmn. Erie chpt. 1988-90), Soc. Law and Medicine, Sigma Theta Tau, Delta Kappa Gamma. Republican. Presbyterian. Editor: Penn League News, 1968-70; contbr. articles to profl. jours. Address: 3207 Georgian Ct Erie PA 16506

DEUTSCH, LYNNORE SUSAN, automobile company executive; b. Detroit, June 5, 1962; d. Patrick Herbert and Carol Ann (Lehman) D. BA, Mich. State U., 1984; MS, Cen. Mich. U., 1988. Mgmt. trainee Chrysler Motors Corp., Center Line, Mich., 1984-86, packaging supr., 1986-87; office mgr. Chrysler Motors Corp., Denver, 1987-88, Itasca, Ill., 1988—.

DEUTSCH, SYLVIA, municipal official, educator; b. Bklyn., July 9, 1924; d. Nathan and Dora (Siegel) Schatz; m. Leon Deutsch, Dec. 21, 1946; children: Jack, Nathaniel Mark, Jeremy Joseph. AB cum laude, Bklyn. Coll., 1947. Exec. dir. Proportional Representation Ednl. Project, 1969-70; dir. N.Y. Met. Council, Am. Jewish Congress, 1972-78; edn. cons. ,1972-78, nat. dir. field ops. and membership, 1978-81; mem. N.Y.C. Planning Commn., 1972-81, chair, 1987-89; chair N.Y.C. Bd. Standards and Appeals, 1981-87; dir. N.Y.C. Dept. City Planning, 1987-89; adj. assoc. prof. Real Estate Inst. NYU, 1990—. Mem. Mayor's Commn. Taxi Regulatory Issues, 1981-82; v.p., chmn. legis. com. United Parents Assns., 1967-72, chmn. orgn. dept. and high schs., 1962-67; mem. Citizens Commn. City U., 1969-71; co-founder, exec. v.p. Com. for Pub. Higher Edn., 1966-74; mem. Mayor's Commn. Status of Women, 1976-79. Named Alumna of Yr., Bklyn. Coll., 1974; recipient Community Service award NCCJ, 1976, Nat. award Girls' Clubs of Am., 1988. Jewish. Office: NYC Planning Commn 22 Reade St New York NY 10007

DEUTZ, NATALIE RUBINSTEIN, actress, consultant; b. Plymouth, Mass., Sept. 26; d. Louis and Lillian Rubinstein; student Simmons Coll., 1937, Modern Sch. Applied Art, 1938-40; m. Nov. 29, 1947 (dec.). Fashion buyer Wm. Filene's Sons Co., Boston, 1940-47; asst. to corp. pres. Columbia Textiles, Inc., N.Y.C., 1956-68; dir. John Robert Powers Sch., N.Y.C., 1968-72; v.p., nat. dir. fashion merchandising, dir. advt. workshop Barbizon Internat., Inc., N.Y.C., 1972-83; cons., 1983—. Mem. Nat. Acad. TV Arts and Scis., Screen Actors Guild, AFTRA.

DEVANEY, CYNTHIA ANN, real estate broker, teacher; b. Gary, Ind., Feb. 6, 1947; d. Charles Barnard and Irene Mae (Nelson) Burner; m. Harold Verne DeVaney, Nov. 23, 1974 (dec. 1981). BS, Ball State U., 1970, MS, 1972; postgrad., Ind. U. and Purdue U., 1974-76. Cert. real estate broker, Ind. Real estate broker Century 21 McColly Realtors, Merrillville, Ind., 1979-86; real estate broker Better Homes and Gardens McColly Realtors, Merrillville, 1986—, with Pres.' Coun.; tchr. Merkley Elem. Sch., Highland, Ind., 1969—. Active Schubert Theater Guild, Chgo. Mem. Calumet Bd. Realtors (bd. dirs., Million Dollar Club), Nat. Bd. Realtors, Jr. Ind. Hist. Soc., Pres. Club, Innsbrook Country Club, Match Point Tennis Club. Democrat. Methodist. Home: 607 E 78th Pl Merrillville IN 46410 Office: McColly Better Homes & Gardens 9143 Indianapolis Blvd Highland IN 46322

DEVARIS, JEANNETTE MARY, psychologist; b. Burbank, Calif., Jan. 7, 1947; d. Nicholas Propper Klein and Elizabeth (Von Lichtenberg) Schaeffer; m. Robert Lee Blake, May 20, 1967 (div. 1979); 1 child: Brendon; m. Panayotis Eric DeVaris, Jan. 25, 1988. BA, Adelphi U., 1968; MA, Fairleigh Dickinson U., 1977; PhD, Seton Hall U., 1987. Lic. psychologist, N.J. Caseworker N.Y.C. Welfare Dept., 1968-72; alcohol and drug rehab. counselor U.S. Army, Ft. Monmouth, N.J., 1972-76; psychol. intern N.J. State Intern Program, Trenton, 1977-78; psychologist Greystone Psychiat. Hosp., Greystone Park, N.J., 1979; sr. psychologist R. Hall Community Mental Health Ctr., Bridgewater, N.J., 1979—; pvt. practice South Orange, N.J., 1988—; tng. supr. Grad. Sch. Applied and Profl. Psychology. Mem. Am. Psychol. Assn., N.J. Psychol. Assn. (children and families com., interprofl. rels. com.). Office: Psychology Svcs Inc 18 Harding Dr South Orange NJ 07079

DE VAUGHN, DEBORAH A., broadcasting executive; b. Chgo., Jan. 5, 1955; d. Ralph Alfred and Dorothy Viola (Philips) De V. BS, Ill. State U., 1976; student, Chgo. Music Coll., 1979, Elmhurst Coll., 1979; MA, Govs. State U., 1979. Producer Sta. WCFC-TV, Chkgo., 1980-87; dir. ops. WYCA Crawford Broadcasting Co., Hammond, Ind., 1988-89; producer, host LeSea Broadcasting Co., South Bend, Ind., 1989—; speaker on youth motivation, Chgo., 1979-83; dir. Global Prayer Line Action Network, Homewood, Ill., 1987—. Pianist, actress Chgo. Actors Repertory Co., 1970-72. Bd. dirs. Concerned Women for Am., Washington, 1986-88, media coord., 1986—. Mem. Soc. Broadcast Engrs., Women in Film, NAFE, Delta Kappa Delta (v.p. 1974-76). Republican. Home: 1519 E 71st Pl Chicago IL 60619 Office: LeSea Broadcasting Co 61300 Ironwood Rd South Bend IN 46614

DE VÉLEZ, EILEEN MCLELLAN, social welfare administrator; b. Boston, Apr. 26, 1955; d. Robert Francis and Mary Joan (Mc Nulty) McLellan; m. Luis Arnaldo Vélez-Cortés. Bachelor in Journalism, Suffolk U., 1977. Eligibility worker Dept. Pub. Welfare, Quincy, Mass., 1977-78; adminstrv. asst. Dept. Pub. Welfare, Quincy, 1978-80; sr. interviewer Div. Employment Security, Boston, 1980; social work tech. Dept. Social Services, Quincy, 1980-81, social worker, 1981—; hotline counselor Survival Crisis Lines, Quincy, 1978-80. Vol. AIDS Action Com., Boston. Named Social Worker of Yr., Mass. Foster Parent Assn., 1989. Mem. PFLAG (fund raising), Gamma Sigma Sigma. Democrat. Roman Catholic. Home: 1153 Hyde Park Ave Hyde Park MA 02136 Office: Dept Social Svcs 6 Fort St 2d Fl Quincy MA 02169

DEVEREUX, FRANCES, advertising agency executive. Former sr. v.p., now exec. v.p. and U.S. pers. dir. Ogilvy & Mather Advt., N.Y.C. Office: Ogilvy & Mather Advt Worldwide Pla 309 W 49th St New York NY 10019*

DEVEREUX, LANE GUSTAFSON, telecommunications executive, consultant; b. Grand Forks, N.D., Aug. 17, 1950; d. Arthur Alexander and Jeanne (Paul) Gustafson; m. Earler Jones Jr., Sept. 15, 1973 (div.); m. Michael J. Devereux, Dec. 21, 1976; children: Alexandra Gustafson, Nicholas Gustav. BA in English Lit., Webster U., 1972; MA in Tech., Washington U., St. Louis, 1975. Lead recruiter, coach Near Southside Neighborhood Assn., St. Louis, 1975-76; coord. St. Louis Agy. on Tng. and Employment, St. Louis, 1976-77; communications cons. Southwestern Bell Telephone, St. Louis, 1977-78; sales mgr. TSI, St. Louis, 1978-81; regional sales mgr. Contel Corp., St. Louis, Kansas City and San Diego, 1981-86; telecommunications cons. The Devereux Group, Escondido, Calif., 1986-88; mgr. telecommunications dept. Horizons Tech., Inc., San Diego, 1988-89; dir. tng. KBLCOM, Inc., Houston, 1989—; adj. prof. telecommunications mgmt. Nat. U., San Diego, 1985-89. Contbr. articles to profl. jours. Chair Helen Meyers Forum Com., San Diego, 1987-89. Webster U. presidential scholar, 1968-69; Washington U. scholar, 1972-74; Nat. Inst. Edn. fellow, 1974-75, Dorland Mountain Colony fellow, 1988. Mem. PEN, AAWU. Democrat. Unitarian. Office: KBLCOM Inc 800 Gessner Ste 700 Houston TX 77024

DEVIGNE, KAREN COOKE (CAR), amateur athletics executive; b. Phila., July 31, 1943; d. Paul and Matilda (Rich) Cooke; m. Jules Lloyd Devigne, June 26, 1965; children: Jules Paul, Denise Paige, Paul Michael. AA, Centenary Coll., Hackettstown, 1963; student, Northwestern U., 1963-65; BA, Ramapo Coll., Mahwah, 1976; MA, Emory U., Atlanta, 1989. Founder, owner GYMSET, Marietta, Ga., 1981--. Cons. Girls Club Am. Marietta, 1989; vol. Cobb County Gymnastic Ctr., Marietta, 1976-81, Atlanta Lawn Tennis Assn., Marietta, 1976—, Ga. Youth Soccer Assn., Atlanta, 1976—; fundraiser Scottish Rite Children's Hosp., Atlanta, 1989—. Recipient recognition awards from various youth groups, Atlanta, 1976—; named Nominee Woman of Yr. ABC News, Atlanta, 1984. Mem. U.S. Gymnastic Fedn, U.S. Assn. Ind. Gymnastic Clubs, Amateur Athletic Union, Ga. Gymnastic Coaches Assoc. Home: 3701 Clubland Dr NE Marietta GA 30068 Office: GYMSET 4957 Lower Roswell Rd NE Marietta GA 30068

DEVINE, KATHERINE, environmental consultant; b. Denver, Oct. 19, 1951. BS, Rutgers U., 1973, MS, 1980; postgrad., U. Md., 1981-82. Lab. technician, 1974-76; econ. and regulatory affairs analyst US EPA, Washington, 1979-81, 82-89; pres. DEVO Enterprises, Inc., Washington, 1990—; analyst U.S. EPA, Washington, 1984-88, program mgr., 1989; cons. Washington, 1989—; ind. cons., 1989—; exec. dir. Applied BioTreatment Assn., Washington. Author: N.J. Agricultural Experiment Station of Rutgers University. Recipient numerous fed. govt. awards. Mem. NAFE, Met. Washington Environ. Profls., Futures for Children, Alpha Zeta. Home: 704 9th St SE Washington DC 20003-2804 Office: Applied BioTreatment Assn PO Box 15307 Washington DC 20003-9997

DE VINE-KIRK, VALARIA ANN, entrepreneur, author; b. Chgo., June 14, 1951; children: Stacy, Stephen, Scott. Student, So. Ill. U., 1969, Lewis U., 1976-77. Asst. gen. mgr. Hilton-Stauffers, Chgo., 1970-73; v.p. Universal Temperature Control, Glendale Heights, Ill., 1974-77; sales rep. Matthew-Bender & Co., N.Y.C., 1977-79, D & S Pubs., Clearwater, Fla., 1979-80; assoc. pub., bus. mgr., pub. cons. Rep-Insider mag., Ft. Lauderdale, Fla., 1980-81; pres. Galaxy Distbg., Inc., Charlotte, N.C., 1982-87, Trailers by Squires, Inc., Matthews, N.C., 1988, Bus. Starters, Inc., Charlotte, 1988—; v.p. Kirk Devel. Co., Inc., Charlotte, 1985—; lectr., cons. small bus.; pres. New Homes and Condominium Ctr., Ft. Lauderdale, 1980-81. Mem. NAFE. Office: 4113 Yancey Rd Charlotte NC 28217

DEVINEY, ELIZABETH CATHERINE, psychotherapist; b. New Brunswick, N.J., Apr. 16, 1943; d. Elton Taylor and Frances Kathleen DeV. BS, Trenton State Coll., Ewing, 1964; MA, Jersey City State U., 1971; MSW, Rutgers U., 1972; postgrad., Fielding Inst. Lic. marriage counselor, N.J., social worker, N.Y. Tchr. East Brunswick (N.Y.) Pub. Schs., 1965-66; founder, dir. Rutkowski Sch. Emotionally Disturbed Children, New Brunswick, N.J., 1967-76; adminstr. Morristown (N.J.) Mem. Hosp., 1976-86, dir. child & adolescent services, 1976-86; pvt. practice psychotherapist Bernardsville, N.Y., 1982—; sheep breeder Clover Hill Farm, Flemington,

N.Y., 1976—; cons. N.J. Assn. Brain Injured Children, 1974-78, Dept. Youth and Family Svcs., Somerset and Hunterdon counties, 1982—, Women's Crisis Ctr., Hunterdon county, 1987—. Contbr. articles to profl. jours. Mem. Nat. Assn. Social Workers (diplomate), N.J. Battered Women's Assn. (pres. 1978-80), Am. Platform Assn., Victorian Soc. Office: Flemington Ctr Psychotherapy Clover Hill Farm Flemington NJ 08822

DEVIVO, ANGE, small business owner; b. Bay Shore, N.Y., Oct. 20, 1925; d. Romeo Zanetti and Karolina (Hodapp) King; m. John Michael DeVivo, Dec. 30, 1950; 1 child, Michael. Student, Washington Sch. for Secs., N.Y.C., 1945-46. Sec. Am. Airlines, N.Y.C., 1946-51; exec. sec. W.C. Holzhauer, N.Y.C., 1951-52; dist. sales mgr. Emmons Jewelers, Inc., Bound Brook, N.J., 1952-53; adminstrv. sec. Mercy Hosp., Charlotte, N.C., 1973-81; pres. Secs., Plus, Convs., Plus, Charlotte, 1983—. Active Human Svcs. Coun., Charlotte, 1984-88, Emergency Med. Svcs. Adv. Coun., Charlotte, 1981—, chmn., 1988-90, Charlotte Women's Polit. Caucus, 1972—, Mecklenburg Evening Rep. Women's Club, Charlotte, 1970—, citizen's adv. com. Conv. and Vis. Bur., 1986—; co-chair pub. Minority and Women-Owned Businesses Directory, 1988. Recipient Order Long Leaf Pine award Gov. of N.C., 1974. Mem. Women Bus. Owners (Entrepreneur of Yr. 1987), Meeting Cons. Network, Greater Charlotte C. of C. (small bus. action coun. 1983-86, 88-89, chair bus. opportunity network and mixer exhibit 1987, discount com. 1985, minority/women bus. entrepreneurs dir. chair 1988, chair Carolina Bus. Fair 1989). Roman Catholic. Office: Secs Plus/Convs Plus 2 Fairview Pla Ste 620 5950 Fairview Rd Charlotte NC 28210

DEVLIN, BARBARA JO, school district administrator; b. Milw., Oct. 6, 1947; d. Raymond Peter Seeley and Lois Elsa (Dahl) Young; m. John Edward Devlin, June 23, 1973; children: Christine Elizabeth, Kathleen Megan. BA, Gustavus Adolphus Coll., 1969; MA, U. Mass., 1971; PhD, U. Minn., 1978. Cert. tchr., sch. prin., supt., Minn.; cert. supt., Ill., Minn. Tchr. Worthington (Minn.) High Sch., 1971-75; rsch. assoc. Ednl. R & D, Mpls.-St. Paul, 1975-76, 76-77; coord. edn. svcs. Ednl. Coop. Svc., Mpls.-St. Paul, 1977-79; dir. personnel Minnetonka Pub. Schs., Excelsior, Minn., 1979-85, asst. supt., 1985-87; supt. Sch. Dist. 45, Villa Park, Ill., 1987—; editor working papers Gov.'s Coun. on Fluctuating Enrollments, St. Paul, 1976. Contbr. articles to ednl. jours. Participation chair Villa Park 75th Anniversary Com., 1988-89; chair Village Complete County Commn., Villa Park, 1990. Ednl. Policy fellow George Washington U., 1977-78; mem. fellows program Bush Found. Pub. Schs., 1984-85. Mem. Rotary Internat. (membership chair Villa Park unit 1989-91). Methodist. Home: 524 Kelly Ct Lombard IL 60148 Office: Sch Dist 45 255 W Vermont St Villa Park IL 60181

DEVLIN, JEAN THERESA, educator, professional storyteller; b. Jamaica, N.Y., Apr. 14, 1947; d. Edward Philip and Frances Margaret (Tillman) Creagh; div.; children: Michael, Bernadette, Patrick. BA, Queens Coll., 1972; MA, St. John's U., Jamaica, 1987; postgrad., So. Ill. U., 1987—. Substitute tchr. Diocese of Bklyn., 1969-75; tchr. St. Gregory's Sch., Bellerose, N.Y., 1975-82; dist. mgr. Creative Expressions, Robesonia, Pa., 1980-83; asst. to dean St. John's Coll. St. John's U., Jamaica, 1983-87; grad. asst., then doctoral fellow dept. English So. Ill. U., Carbondale, 1987—; cons. Family Literacy Project; supr. workshops Children's Lit. Assn., 1990, Stories: A Centennial Celebration, Laramie, 1990, IATE Conv., 1990; presenter poetry readings, dramatic interpretation, numerous storytelling presentations; showcased at Nat. Congress of Stroytelling. Den leader Boy Scouts Am., Bayside, N.Y., 1975-80; troop leader Girl Scouts U.S., Flushing, N.Y., 1976-78; vol. Alice Wright Day Care Ctr., Carbondale, 1989—. Mem. Nat. Coun. Tchrs. English, MLA, ALA, Nat. Assn. for Preservation and Perpetuation of Storytelling, Assn. Libr. Svc. to Children, Ill. Assn. Tchrs. English, Children's Lit. Assn., Riverbend Storytelling Guild, Northlands Storytelling Network, North Shore Storytelling Guild, Nat. Cath. Edn. Assn., Direct Mktg. Assn., Story Ent., Ladies Anchient Order Hibernians (chpt. founder, pres. 1984-85), Beatrix Potter Soc., Alpha Sigma Lambda, Sigma Tau Delta, Phi Delta Kappa. Home: Rte 5 Warren Rd Chateau 10 Carbondale IL 62901

DEVOKAITIS, JUDITH OHLSON, elementary educator; b. New Britain, Conn., Nov. 24, 1944; d. Frank A. and Ruth Eleanor (Young) Ohlson; m. Andrew B. Devokaitis, June 18, 1969. BS, Conn. State U., New Britain, 1966, MA, 1973, 6th Year adminstr./supr., 1988. Cert. in elem. edn., adminstrn./supervision. Tchr. 3d grade Hatton Sch. Southington (Conn.) Pub. Schs., 1966-68; tchr. 4th grade Griswold Sch. Berlin (Conn.) Pub. Schs., 1968—, acting prin. Griswold Sch., 1977—. Bd. dirs. Spring Lake Village Condominiums, Southington, 1986—. Named Tchr. of Yr., Town of Berlin, 1988. Mem. AAUW (membership v.p. 1988-90), NEA, Conn. Edn. Assn. (Human Relation award 1976), Berlin Edn. Assn. (pres. 1975-86), Alpha Delta Kappa (pres. chpt. 1986-88), Phi Delta Kappa. Office: Berlin Pub Sch Griswold Sch 133 Heather Ln Berlin CT 06037

DEVORE, JUDITH T., executive recruiter; b. Detroit, Sept. 13, 1959; d. Thomas E. and Lillian A. (Appenzeller) DeV. BGS, Oakland U., Rochester, Mich., 1988. Sr. human resources rep. CIS Corp., Bloomfield Hills, Mich.; personnel staff asst. Campbell-Ewald Co., Advt., Warren, Mich.; recruiting specialist Kelly Assisted Living, Troy, Mich. Mem. NAFE, Soc. Human Resource Mgmt. Home: 12342 Canterbury Warren MI 48093

DEVRIES, NANCY LYNNE, photographer; b. Pueblo, Colo., Oct. 9, 1956; d. Warren Thomas and Mary Ann E. (Butkovich) DeV. Student, Fashion Inst. Design and Merchandising, 1974, UCLA, 1975-78. Photographer L.A., 1978—; guest lect. UCLA extension and Pierce Coll., 1980-86. Exhibited in group shows at L.A. Gallerie, 1980, Art Store, 1984, Artists Soc. Internat. Gallery, 1987; represented in permanent collections John Portman & Assocs. Permanent Collection, Atlantic Richfield Corp. Art Collection. Office: PO Box 64424 Los Angeles CA 90064

DEVUONO, ANDREA JANE, advertising sales; b. Takapuna, Auckland, New Zealand, June 6, 1962; came to U.S.; d. John Frederick Hawcridge and Jillian Siobhan (Walker) McGredy; m. Patrick Michael DeVuono, Apr. 16, 1950. BA, U. Hawaii, 1985. Journalist The Garden Island Newspaper, Lihue Kauai, Hawaii, 1985-86; telemarketer Petersen Pub. Co., L.A., 1986-88, mem. advt. sales staff, 1988—. Mem. NAFE. Office: Petersen Pub Co 8490 Sunset Blvd Los Angeles CA 90069

DEW, LINDA SUE, health science facility administrator; b. Bastrop, La., Aug. 21, 1956; d. Jewel Clinton and Christien Cora (Hughes) D. Student, La. Tech. U., 1974-75; AAS, Tidewater Coll., 1977. With counter sales Taylor Rentals, Portsmouth, Va., 1977-80, party cons., 1978-80; asst. mgr. Patient Aids & Party Rentals, Norfolk, Va., 1980-81; gen. mgr. Aids for Health Care, Norfolk, 1983-87; div. mgr. Medequip Ctr. Inc., Norfolk, 1987; pres., owner Rehab Health Care, Norfolk, 1987—; cons. Hosp. Corp. Am., Nashville, 1987—; v.p. Home Care Systems Inc., Portsmouth, 1988—; v.p., owner Clare Med. Inc., Portsmouth, 1989; bd. dirs. Albemarle Home Care Systems, Elizabeth City, N.C., Independence Living Ctr., Norfolk, Va. Mem. Health Industry Digest Assn., Portwheelers Club (chmn. bd. 1990—). Democrat. Mem. Ch. of Christ. Home: 2920 Seashore Point Virginia Beach VA 23454 Office: Rehab Health Care 5873 Poplar Hall Dr Norfolk VA 23502

DEW, MARY AMANDA, psychology educator; b. Arlington, Va., Oct. 24, 1955; d. Elkin Stewart and Helen Margaret (Yerger) D.; m. James Thompson Becker, July 12, 1980; children: Ian Louis, Colin Stewart. BA in Psychology, MA in Psychology, Johns Hopkins U., 1979; MA in Social Psychology, Harvard U., 1983, PhD in Social Psychology, 1984. Teaching fellow Harvard U., Cambridge, Mass., 1980-84; sr. project coord. U. Pitts. Sch. Medicine, 1984-87, asst. prof. psychiatry, psychology and epidemiology, 1987—, dir. consultation-liaison psychiatry rsch., 1990—; cons. Am. Mgmt. Assns., N.Y.C., 1981-87; mem. rsch. and registry subcom. Vietnam Vets. Health Initiative Commn., Pa. Dept. Health, Harrisburg, 1989—. Author manual; contbr. articles to profl. jours. Chmn. rsch. rev. bd. Carriage House Children's Ctr. and Infant Toddler Ctr. Squirrel Hill, Pitts., 1987—. Fellow Harvard U., 1979-84; fellow NIMH, 1985-87, grantee, 1987—. Mem. AAAS, APA, APHA, Am. Psychol. Soc., Am. Psychopath. Assn., Internat. AIDS Soc., N.Y. Acad. Scis. Episcopalian. Office: U Pitts Dept Psychiatry 3811 O'Hara St Pittsburgh PA 15213

DEWALD, GRETTA MOLL, county official; b. Kutztown, Pa., Oct. 26, 1929; d. Lloyd A. and Olga (Wuchter) M.; m. Charles Frederick Dewald, Dec. 20, 1951; children: Michael S., Jonathon G., Henry L., Janie P., Joseph C. BA, Agnes Scott Coll., 1950. Tchr. secondary schs. Eastman City Schs., Ga., 1950-51, Bass High Sch., Atlanta, 1951-52; project exec. sec. Appalachian project Day Care and Child Devel. Coun. Am., Atlanta, 1971-73; researcher Ga. Senate, Atlanta, 1973-74; aide to commr. DeKalb Bd. Commrs., 1974-77; community rels. officer Met. Atlanta Rapid Transit Authority, 1976-77, bd. dirs., 1977; dir. women's div. Democratic Nat. Com., Washington, 1977-80; exec. asst. to chief exec. officer and bd. commrs. DeKalb County, Decatur, Ga., 1981-89; coord. DeKalb County Pretrial Svcs., 1989—. Mem. Ga. Commn. on Volunteerism, 1970-74, Ga. Women's Adv. Com., 1972-74, Nat. Adv. Com. of Women, 1977-80. Chmn., DeKalb County Dem. Com., 1972-74, 4th Congl. Dist. Ga. Com., 1974-77; campaigner, Peanut Brigade, N.H., Vt., Md., Ohio, Wi., Fla., Pa., 1976; del. Dem. Nat. Conv., 1972, 74, 76, 80; mem. adv. bd. Ga. Women's Polit. Caucus, 1983-86; So. regional coord. Dem. Task Force, Nat. Women's Polit. Caucus, 1983-85; organizer, mem. adv. bd. DeKalb Women's Network, 1983-86; bd. dirs. DeKalb Libr. System, 1983-89; bd. dirs. DeKalb Humane Soc., 1985—; bd. dirs. Our House, Inc., 1987-89; mem. Women's Resource Ctr. DeKalb, 1986-88. Mem. Nat. Assn. County Adminstrs., Ga. Coun. County Adminstrs. and Mgrs. (v.p. 1986-87, pres. 1987-88), Nat. Assn. Counties (steering com. intergovtl. rels. 1981-89, mem. women ofcls. chpt.), Women's Coun. Nat. Assn. Counties, Assn. County Commrs. Ga. (bd. dirs. 1986-88), Abigails (organizer), 1984—. Presbyterian. Home: 5428 Pheasant Run Stone Mountain GA 30087-1237 Office: Pretrial Svcs DeKalb County Office 410 Callaway Bldg 120 W Trinity Pl Decatur GA 30030 also: Pretrial Svcs DeKalb County Pub Safety Bldg 4400 Memorial Dr Complex Decatur GA 30032

DEWALL, BETH BARCLAY, museum administrator; b. Mpls., Sept. 20, 1954; d. Richard Allison and Diane Barclay (Prettyman) DeW. BA, Agnes Scott Coll., Decatur, Ga., 1976; MA, U. Cin., 1980. Mgr. photographic svcs. Cin. Art Mus., 1979-87, mgr. publs. svcs., 1982-87; merchandising mgr. Cin. Art Mus., 1988—; cons. Dayton (Ohio) Art Inst., 1987, Columbus (Ohio) Mus. Art, 1989; chmn., co-founder Mus. Shops Cin., 1985—. Contbr. articles to profl. publs. Mem. Mus. Store Assn. (various coms.), Jr. League Cin. (co-chmn. com.). Home: 3776 Ashworth Dr Cincinnati OH 45208 Office: Cin Art Mus Eden Park Cincinnati OH 45202

DEWAR, MARY REED, nursing educator; b. Orange, N.J., Oct. 27, 1922; d. Alexander Blanchard and Sara Willard (Reed) D. BA, Oberlin Coll., 1943; postgrad., Western Reserve U., Cleve., 1946; MA, N.Y. U., 1972. Reg. Nurse, Ohio, 1946. Missionary nurse United Ch. Bd. for World Ministries, NYC, 1946-70, Shansi, China, 1947-51, Dondi, Angola, 1952-58, Mt. Silinda, Zimbabwe, 1960-65, Wora Wora, Ghana, 1965-66; missionary nurse World Coun. Churches, Geneva, 1968-70; asst. prof. nursing Sch. of Nursing, Adelphi U., N.Y., 1972; examiner, faculty com. Regents Coll. degrees, Albany, 1983, rep. Internat. Council of Nurses to UNICEF, Geneva, 1983. Mem. AAUP, Am. Pub. Health Assn., N.Y. State Nurses Assn., Sigma Theta Tau. Democrat. Home: 244 16 129 Rd Rosedale NY 11422 Office: Adelphi U Sch Nursing PO Box 516 Garden City NY 11530

DEWBERRY, BETTY BAUMAN, law librarian; b. Dallas, Jan. 18, 1930; d. William Allen Bauman and Julia Ella (Owen) Hurt; m. James A. Dewberry Jr., Mar. 22, 1952 (div. Apr. 1976); children: Mary Julienne, Jennifer Camille, Robert Bruce. BA, U. Tex., 1951; MLS, Tex. Women's U., 1982. Asst. librarian Johnson & Swanson, Dallas, 1979-85; dir. libraries Johnson & Gibbs, Dallas, 1985—. Mem. Am. Assn. Law Libraries, Southwestern Assn. of Law Librarians, Dallas Assn. Law Librarians, Spl. Libraries Assn. Democrat. Presbyterian. Club: Lakeside Browning.

DEWBERRY, CLAIRE DEARMENT, engineering librarian; b. Youngstown, Ohio, Oct. 12, 1937; d. Eugene Howard and Ruth (Bright) DeA.; m. Carl R. Meinstereifel, 1956 (div. 1966); children—Paul, Dawn; m. Olin Jerry Dewberry, Jr., 1974 (div. 1979). B.S., Clarion State U., 1967; M.L.S., Ga. State U., 1977. Cert. libr. media specialist, Ga. Libr. Henry County, Stockbridge, Ga., 1967-69; head libr. Russell High Sch., East Point, Ga., 1969-84; engrng. libr. Rockwell Internat., Duluth, Ga., 1984—; rep. GIDEP, Corona, Calif., 1984-88; libr. Raytheon Co., MSD, Bristol, Tenn., 1988—. Author newsletter: Blueline. Mem. Spl. Librs. Assn., Mensa, AIAA. Democrat. Avocations: computers; flea market selling; writing. Home: PO Box 3049 Bristol TN 37625 Office: Raytheon Co 100 Vance Tank Rd Bristol TN 37620

DEWEY, ANNE ELIZABETH MARIE, lawyer; b. Balt., Mar. 16, 1951; d. George Daniel and Elizabeth Patricia (Mohan) D.; m. Peter Michael Barnett, Aug. 27, 1977; children: Brendan M., Andrew P. BA, Mich. State U., 1972; JD, U. Chgo., 1975; grad., Stonier Grad. Sch. Banking, East Brunswick, N.J., 1983. Bar: D.C. 1976. Atty. FTC, Washington, 1975-78; atty. enforcement div. Comptroller of Currency, Washington, 1978-81, sr. atty. office legis. counsel, 1981-83; sr. atty. dist. office Comptroller of Currency, Dallas, 1983-86; sr. atty. legal adv. services div. Comptroller of Currency, Washington, 1986; assoc. gen. counsel corp. and adminstrv. law Farm Credit Adminstrn., McLean, Va., 1986-87, gen. counsel, 1987—. Mem. ABA (bus. law sect., banking law com.), Fed. Bar Assn. (bd. dirs. D.C. chpt. 1988—), D.C. Bar Assn., Women in Housing and Fin. (bd. dirs. 1982-83). Roman Catholic. Home: 833 Fontaine St Alexandria VA 22302 Office: FCA 1501 Farm Credit Dr McLean VA 22102-5090

DEWEY, DOLORES GAY (DOLLY DEWEY), sheet metal company executive, nurse, consultant; b. Buffalo, Nov. 2, 1932; d. Joseph Stanley and Jeannette (Pachla) Gay; m. John William Dewey, Aug. 23, 1958 (div. 1982); children—Mari Lynn, Karen Ann. B.S. in Nursing Niagara U., 1954; postgrad. Canisius Coll., Buffalo, 1955-56. R.N. Head nurse Mt. St. Mary's Hosp., Niagara Falls, 1955-58; pres. Gay Sheet Metal Dies, Buffalo, 1964—; exec. bd. Medical Care Adv. Commn., Raleigh, N.C., 1975-77; cons. speaker Ostomy Orgn., N.C., 1977—. Chmn. N.C. Republican 4th Congl. Dist., Wake, 1977-81; chmn. County Rep. Party, 1975-77; exec. bd. Capital Health Systems Agy., Durham, N.C., 1976-81; corr. sec. AAUW, Raleigh, Named Woman of Yr., Wake County Rep. Womens Club, 1975. Mem. Nat. Fedn. Ind. Bus., N.C. Nurses Assn., Nat. Assn. Female Execs. Roman Catholic. Club: U.S. Senatorial. Avocations: painting; water skiing; ice skating; traveling. Home: PO Box 17604 Raleigh NC 27619 Office: Gay Sheet Metal Dies 301 Hinman Ave Buffalo NY 14216

DEWEY, PAT PARKER, broadcast executive, composer; b. Berkeley, Calif., Jan. 27, 1923; d. George and Mildred (Johnston) Parker; student Sullins Jr. Coll., 1940-41; Mus.B., U. Miss., 1943; m. Grayson Headley, Dec. 30, 1946 (dec. 1961); m. 2d, M. Lee Williams, Dec. 18, 1964 (div.); 1 son, Philip Lee Williams; m. Ralph B. Dewey, Dec. 26, 1976. Woman's dir. radio sta. WNNT, Warsaw, Va., commentator daily women's program, Chat with Pat, 1952-60, now owner, pres. radio station WNNT AM-FM; partner WKWI-FM, Kilmarnock, Va.; asst. soc. editor Jackson Daily News, 1943-44. Composer: concerto for piano and orch., Rhapsody of Youth, performed by Nat. Air Force Symphony, Washington, Lisner Auditorium, 1947, guest pianist with Nat. Air Force Symphony, 1964, 75; (song) Cotton Picking Blues, featured in several musicals in Miss., Washington; (song) Maid of Cotton, used as theme song Nat. Cotton Council, 1945-51; (song) Lucky X, ofcl. song Chi Omega. Chmn., Red Cross water safety program, Lancaster County, Va., 1950-56; mem. exec. com. Jr. Assembly, Washington; jr. chmn. Home Hospitality Com., Washington, 1943-46; jr. chmn. UN Club activities, Washington, 1943-48. Mem. Am. Women in Radio and Television (dir. Va. 1962-65), Nat. Soc. Arts and Letters (music chmn. Washington chpt. 1964-65), Va. Assn. Broadcasters, Internat. Platform Assn., Nat. Assn. Am. Composers and Conductors, Women's Com. for Nat. Symphony Orch., Nat. Mus. Women in Arts (founder 1986, mem. women's com.), Chi Omega, Delta Beta Sigma, Sigma Alpha Iota, Alpha Psi Omega. Episcopalian. Clubs: Friday Morning Music; Debutante of Miss., Women's (chmn. music div. Lancaster County, Va. 1956-60), Washington, Kenwood Garden, Congl. Golf, Indian Creek Yacht and Country. Home: 6211 Garnett Dr Chevy Chase MD 20815

DEWHURST, COLLEEN, actress; b. Montreal, Que., Can., June 3, 1926; m. James Vickery, 1947 (div. 1959); m. George C. Scott (div.); 2 sons. Student, Downer Coll., Milw., Am. Acad. Dramatic Art; pupil of Harold Clurman and Joseph Anthony. First profl. appearance in The Royal Family, 1946; Broadway appearances include Desire Under the Elms, 1952, Tamberlain the Great, 1956, Camille, 1956, The Eagle Has Two Heads, 1957, The Country Wife, 1957, All the Way Home, 1960 (Tony award 1961), Great Day in the Morning, 1962, Ballad of the Sad Cafe, 1963, Taming of the Shrew, Macbeth, Hello and Goodbye, Good Woman of Setzuan, Children of Darkness, Moon for the Misbegotten, 1974 (Tony award 1974, Sarah Siddons award 1974), The Big Coca-Cola Swamp in the Sky, Mourning Becomes Electra, An Almost Perfect Person, The Queen and the Rebels, The Dance of Death, You Can't Take It With You, Who's Afraid of Virginia Woolf, 1977, Rainshakes, 1984, one woman show My Gene, N.Y., 1987, Real Estate, 1986, Long Day's Journey Into Night and Ah Wilderness in Repertory, New Haven and N.Y.C., 1988, Love Letters, 1989; appearances with N.Y. Shakespeare Festival include My Gene, 1985-86; films include The Nun's Story, 1959, The Cowboys, 1972, McQ, 1974, Annie Hall, 1977, Ice Castles, 1979, When a Stranger Calls, 1977, Final Assignment, 1980, Tribute, 1980, The Dead Zone, 1983, The Boy Who Could Fly, 1986; dir. Broadway play Ned and Jack, 1981; numerous TV appearances, 1957—; appeared in TV films The Story of Jacob and Joseph, 1974, Silent Victory: The Kitty O'Neil Story, 1979, Studs Lonigan, 1979, And Baby Makes Six, 1979, Mary and Joseph: A Story of Faith, 1979, Death Penalty, 1980, Escape, 1980, Guyana Tragedy: The Story of Jim Jones, 1980, The Women's Room, 1980, A Perfect Match, 1980, Baby Comes Home, 1980, A Few Days in Weasel Creek, 1981, Johnny Bull, 1986, Sword of Gideon; appeared in TV miniseries The Blue and the Gray, 1982, A.D., 1985, Anne of Green Gables, 1986 (Gemini award 1987, ACE award), Anne of Avonlea, 1988. Recipient Obie award, 1957, 63, Lola D'Annunzio award, 1961, Sylvania award, 1960, Theatre World award; Emmy awards for Between Two Women, 1986, for Those She Left Behind (best supporting actress in a miniseries or special), 1989. Mem. Actors Equity Assn. (pres. 1985—). Office: Actors Equity Assn 165 W 46 St New York NY 10036*

DE WINDT, HERMA ILEAN, retail credit executive; b. N.Y.C.; d. Ernold G. and Benjamina (Jackson) Sewell. BS, CUNY, 1982; MA, New Sch. Social Research, 1985. Staff supr., R.H. Macy's & Co., Inc., 1967-68, jr. exec., 1968-73, alt. exec., 1971-73, asst. to dept. mgr., 1973-74, credit exec., 1974-81, divisional mgr. credit fraud, 1981—. Fellow Am. Mgmt. Assn.; mem. Am. Mktg. Assn., Am. Soc. Personnel Adminstrn., AAUW, Am. Assn. Female Execs., Sigma Iota Epsilon, Sigma Alpha Delta. Democrat. Episcopalian. Office: Credit Dept R H Macy's & Co Inc 151 W 34th St New York NY 10001

DEWIR, HARRIET, psychopharmacologist; b. Ottawa, Ont., Can., Sept. 12, 1948; came to U.S., 1981; d. REinout and Neeltje (Wibaut) deW. BA in Psychology, U. Calgary (Can.), 1970; MA in Exptl. Psychology, Concordia U., Montreal, Can., 1976, PhD in Exptl. Psychology, 1981. Lic. psychologist, Ill. Rsch. asst. dept. psychology Oxford U., Eng., 1971-73, McGill U., Montreal, 1973-74; rsch. assoc. dept. psychiatry U. Chgo., 1981-83, rsch. assoc., asst. prof. dept. psychiatry, 1984-87, asst. prof. dept. psychiatry, 1987—; associated faculty dept. psychology Com. on Biopsychology, U. Chgo., 1988—; SRC mem., site visitor drug abuse clin. and behavioral rsch. rev. com. and drug abuse biomed. rsch. rev. com. Nat. Inst. on Drug Abuse, 1987; mem. drug adv. com. FDA, 1987—; mem. adv. com. Clin. Rsch. Ctr., U. Chgo., 1989—; supr. clin. tng. in behavioral medicine and substance use dept. psychiatry U. Chgo., 1981-84, supr. outpatient drug abuse treatment, relapse prevention Lakeshore Hosp., Chgo., 1988-89; presenter in field. Contbr. articles and abstracts to profl. jours.; editorial bd. Drug and Alcohol Dependence, Psychopharmacology; reviewer Jour. Pharmacology and Exptl. Therapeutics. Grantee Nat. Inst. on Drug Abuse, 1987, 89-92, Alcoholic Beverage Med. Rsch. Found., 1988-89; Non-Med. Use of Drugs Directorate of Can. scholar, 1975; Pre-Doctoral fellow Province of Quebec (Can.), 1977-80. Mem. Am. Psychol. Assn., Can. Psychol. Assn., Rsch. Soc. on Alcoholism, Behavioral Pharmacology Soc., Internat. Study Group Investigating Drugs as Reinforcers (pres. 1989—). Home: 5550 S Dorchester Chicago IL 60637 Office: U Chgo Dept of Psychiatry 5841 S Maryland Ave Chicago IL 60637

DEWITT, KAREN KELLY (LEE), computer information consultant; b. San Francisco, Apr. 13, 1963; d. Martin Johann and Dixie Lee (Mayhak) Whitted; m. Abel M.V. Garcia, Dec. 1, 1984 (div. Aug. 1986); m. Robert Martin DeWitt, Jan. 1, 1990. Student, Mills Coll., Oakland, Calif., 1981-82. Mgr. Video Outlet, Pitts., 1983-84; asst. mgr. ECX Computers, Walnut Creek, Calif., 1984-90; accounts payable mgr. Byte & Floppy Computers, San Diego, 1990—; owner Microbyte, Concord, Calif., 1988-90, Pvt. Res. Products, National City, Calif., 1990—; cons. Svcs. Aiding Ind. Living, Concord, 1985-90, U.S. Submarine Vets. of W.W. II, Vallejo, Calif., 1985-90. Sponsor Save the children, Mali, Africa, World Wildlife Fund, 1988. Mem. NAFE.

DEWITT, MARY SCHILLER, private investigator, commercial property management and marketing consultant; b. Chgo., Aug. 25, 1948; d. Robert Baldwin and Helen (Rossman) DeW.; m. Geoffrey M. Tait, Aug. 1, 1988. AA, Coll. of DuPage, 1968; BA in Edn., U. Wis., Whitewater, 1969. With customer relations dept. John M. Smyth Furniture, Oak Brook, Ill., 1968-71, Wiggs Furniture, Bloomfield Hills, Mich., 1971; dir. pub. relations Hotel de las Hadas, Manzanillo, Mex., 1972; dir. promotion Ramco-Gershenson, Southfield, Mich., 1973-75; dir. mktg. Homart Devel. Co., Florence, Ky., 1975-76, Melvin Simon & Assocs., Inc., Hurst, Tex., 1976-79; pres. Mary DeWitt Co., Ft. Worth, 1979-85; v.p. mktg. Southmark Comml. Mgmt., Dallas, 1986-87; prin. DeWitt Group and subs. Cat's-Eye Intelligence Svc., Dallas and Ft. Worth, 1988—; cons. logistics and documentation one team Internat. Group for Hist. Aircraft Recovery, The Phoenix Group South Pacific, 1989. Founder, co-dir. Svc. to Enlist Resident Vols. in Euless, Tarrant County, Tex., 1989—. Recipient award of excellence Jones Report, 1978. Mem. Internat. Council Shopping Ctrs., Pub. Relations Soc. Am. Democrat. Episcopalian. Home: 1905 Cripple Creek Dr Euless TX 76039

DEWITZ, JEAN LAURA, freight company executive; b. Phila., Sept. 30, 1946; d. William C. and Louse Hattie (Gifford) Dewitz; m. Ronald William Alice (div. 1974); m. John Walter Hummel, Apr. 10, 1941. BA, Wayne State U., 1974; student, George Washington U., 1964-66. Exec. sec. Dairy Council of Mich., Detroit, 1970-72; asst. office mgr. Acme Ct. Reporters, Detroit, 1974-77; exec. sec. Jacobson Mfg. Co., Detroit, 1977-79, Carolina Freight Carriers, Cherryville, N.C., 1980-84; line haul supr. Carolina Freight Carriers, Carlisle, Pa., 1984—; beauty cons. Mary Kay Cosmetics, 1989—; freelance model and instr. Cinderella Modeling Sch., 1964-66. Mem. AAUW. Democrat. Roman Catholic. Office: Carolina Freight Carriers Carlisle PA 17013

DEWOLFE, MARTHA ROSE, police officer; b. Arlington, Tex., Nov. 30, 1959; d. Homer C. and Grace R. DeWolfe; married; stepchildren: Jeff, Debbie. Student, N. Tex. State U., 1978-79, Larimer County Vocat.-Tech., Ft. Collins, Colo., 1983; cert. peace officer, Tarrant County Jr. Coll., Euless, Tex., 1984; student, North Central Tex. Coun. Govts., 1984—, Southwestern Law Enforcement Sch. of Police Supervision. Police officer Grand Prairie (Tex.) Police Dept., 1984-88, sgt., 1989—; mem. Police Employee Rels. Bd., 1990—. Sec. Grand Prarie Police Assn., 1985-86. Mem. NAFE, Nat. Assn. Women Police, Tex. Assn. Women Police, Tex. Police Assn., Fraternal Order Police, Grand Prairie Police Assn. (sec. 1984-88), Mensa, SW Karate Assn. (achieved 9th degree orange belt), Leo Club (sec. 1976-78). Club: Leo (sec. 1977-78). Home: PO Box 531508 Grand Prairie TX 75053

DEWSNAP, BARBARA EVERITT, educator; b. Pelahatchie, Miss., Jan. 23, 1933; d. John C. and Irene L. (Measells) Everitt; m. Paul D. Dewsnap, May 9, 1970 (div. 1977); children: Everitt D., John Paul; 1 stepchild, Jennifer J. BS in Biology, U. So. Miss., 1953; MS in Gen. Sci., Fla. State U., 1965. Cert. tchr., Fla. Tchr. Moss Point (Miss.) Schs., 1953-55, Key West (Fla.) High Sch., 1955-59, Broward County Sch., Ft. Lauderdale, 1960-70, 77-79, 1981—. Foster parent, Broward Foster Care, Ft. Lauderdale, 1984—. Grantee NSF, 1965-67. Republican. Baptist. Office: Sunrise Middle Sch 1750 NE 14th St Fort Lauderdale FL 33304

DE WYNGAERT, LAURA PATRICIA, artist, educator; b. Boston; d. George Edward and Gertrude Marie (Connolly) Lane; m. Paul Herbert De Wyngaert Jr., Oct. 18, 1947; children: Mark Alan, Paul Herbert III, Jude

Maria, Karl. Diploma, Sch. Practical Art, Boston, 1943; BFA, Monmouth Coll., 1966, MS in Adminstrn., summa cum laude, 1969. Artist Cronin, Whinnem & Goode Advt. Agy., Boston, 1944; film animator MIT, Cambridge, 1945-46; artist, illustrator Watson Labs., Eatontown, N.J., 1947-48; artist, co-owner Precision Color Printing Co., Newark, 1949—; tchr. of gifted and talented Middletown (N.J.) Twp. Sch. System, 1985—; tchr. fine arts, various programs throughout state, N.J. Dept. Edn.; tchr. adult animation, Brookdale Community Coll., Lincroft, N.J., 1981; coord., judge art shows for bus. and community agys.. Contbr. numerous articles to profl. jours.; one-women show Middletown Town Hall, Monmouth Mus., Lincroft, N.J.; presenter in field. Mem. bicentennial com. U.S. Constn, N.J., 1986-89. Recipient numerous awards including Outstanding Educator award Middletown Jaycees, 1982, Most Outstanding Person in Arts award, 1984, others. Mem. AAUW, N.J. Art Educators, Assn. Curriculum Supervision and Devel., Monmouth County Hist. Soc., Zonta (internat. pres. 1980-82, bd. dirs. 1985-87), Bus. and Profl. Women, Lambda Sigma Tau, Alpha Delta Kappa (pres. 1980-82, 86, state historian 1984-86, Most Honoured Mem. award N.J. chpt.), Phi Delta Kappa. Home: 270 Sunrise Rd Belford NJ 07718 Office: Thorne Sch 70 Murphy Rd Port Monmouth NJ 07758

DEXHEIMER, MARION LOUISE (MARION LOUISE HINES), retired educator; b. Chgo., Dec. 31, 1920; d. Herbert Waldo and Helen (Gartside) Hines; m. Fred J. Dexheimer, Sept. 28, 1947; children: Gary Frederick, Helen Louise, William Henry. BS in Spanish, U. Ill., 1943; BS in Comml. Sci., Boston U., 1947; MS in Teaching, U. Wis., Whitewater, 1975. Sec. Fed. Civil Svc. AFB, Orlando, Fla., 1948, USDA, Madison, Wis., 1949; tchr. Spanish jr. and sr. high sch. Jefferson, Wis., 1963-65; tchr. Spanish and typing sr. high sch. Ft. Atkinson, Wis., 1965-80; ret., 1980. Treas. Women's Fellowship Congl. Ch., 1990—; mem. bd. trustees, bd. deaconesses Union Congl. Ch., Tavares, Fla.; participant hosp. aux. Waterman Med. Ctr. Lt. (j.g.) USNR, 1944-46. Mem. AAUW (past treas. Ft. Atkinson br., past membership v.p., past v.p. programs, past treas. past pres. Lake County br., spl. recognition award 1989), Lake County WAVES (publicity chmn. 1989—), Lake Frances Estate Residents Assn. (bd. dirs. activities com. 1986—). Home: 1437 Apache Circle Tavares FL 32778

DEXTER, DALLAS-LEE, insurance executive, consultant; b. Rockville Center, N.Y., Nov. 30, 1950; d. David D. and Jane (Nesbitt) D.; m. Leonard Eugene Carter, Nov. 6, 1975 (div. 1982). Student numerous dance courses; BS, Mills Coll., 1972; MA, Tchrs. Coll. Columbia U., 1974; postgrad., Nat. U. Mex., 1974, Lesley Coll., 1974, Fgn. Service Inst., 1977, Johns Hopkins Sch. Advanced Internat. Studies, 1982, Middle East Inst., 1982-83, U. N.C., 1982-86. Cert. ins., securities, teaching. Tchr. Am. Sch., Hawalli, Kuwait, 1975-76, Copenhagen Internat. Sch., Hawalli, Kuwait, 1977-79, Rygaards Internat. Sch., Hellerup, Denmark, 1980-81; mktg. contractor Nat. Right to Work Com., Hellerup, Denmark, 1986—, 21st Century Telemedial Mktg. Services, Inc., Hellerup, Denmark, 1986; sales mgr. Best Programs, Inc., Arlington, Va., Denmark, 1986, 1987—; cons. Success, Inc., Palm Beach, Fla., 1985-86, Resources Planning Systems, 1983-86, Mgmt. Engring. Affiliates, Calabasa, Calif., 1984, Aerojet Gen., Washington, 1983; ednl. cons. Mayors Program on Summer Youth Employment, Washington, 1986, Islamic Saudi Acad. of Kingdom of Saudi Arabia, Dunn Loring, Va., 1986-87; mktg. cons. Nat. Right to Work Com., Springfield, Va., 1986—; cons., adminstr. Kingdom Of Saudi Arabia: Islamic Saudi Acad., 1986-87; sales rep. First Investors Corp., Arlington, Va., 1985-86; assoc. Potomac Ins. and Fin. Planning Group, Rockville, Md., 1985—; mgr. telesales div. Best Programs, Inc., Arlington, Va., 1987—; dancer Twyla Tharp Dance Co., 1969-70, James Cunningham Co., 1970, others. Campaign worker Reagan-Bush, Washington, 1983-84; active Rock Creek Women's Republican Club, Chevy Chase Women's Rep. Club, Montgomery County Rep. Club, Nat. Fedn. Rep. Women; mem. women's com. Nat. Symphony Orch.; charter mem., sponsor Assn. of Friends of Mus. Modern Art of Latin Am. Mem. Nat. Assn. Life Underwriters, U.S. C. of C., D.C. Life Underwriters Assn., NAFE (network dir. 1985-87), Internat. Educators Inst., World Affairs Council, Soc. for Internat. Devel., Middle East Inst., Middle East Studies Assn., Nat. Acad. TV Arts and Scis., Am. Def. Preparedness Assn., AAUW, Renaissance Women Club, Columbia Univ. Club, Univ. Club, Phi Delta Kappa. Unitarian. Home: 34 Hamilton Pl Garden City NY 11530

DEXTER, DEIRDRE O'NEIL ELIZABETH, lawyer; b. Stillwater, Okla., Apr. 15, 1956; d. Robert N. and Paula E. (Robinson) Maddox; m. Terry E. Dexter, May 12, 1977; children: Daniel M. II, David Maddox. Student, Okla. State U., 1974-77; BS cum laude, Phillips U., 1981; JD with highest honors, U. Okla., 1984. Bar: Okla., U.S. Dist. Ct. (no. and ea. dists.) Okla. 1985, U.S. Dist. Ct. (we. dist.) Okla. 1987, U.S. Ct. Appeals (10th cir.) 1987; grad. Nat. Inst. Trial Advocacy Advanced Trial seminar, 1990. Jud. intern Supreme Ct. Okla., Oklahoma City, summer 1983; assoc. Conner & Winters, Tulsa, 1984-90, ptnr., 1990—. Article editor Okla. U. Law Rev., 1982-84. U. Okla. scholar, 1983. Mem. ABA, Okla. Bar Assn., Tulsa County Bar Assn., Order of Barristers, Order of Coif, Am. Inns of Court (barrister Robert D. Hudson chpt. 1990—), Delta Theta Phi. Republican. Episcopalian. Office: Conner & Winters 2400 First National Tower Tulsa OK 74103

DEXTER-ROSELL, MILDRED, piano teacher; b. Bladen County, N.C., Apr. 24, 1932; d. Robert S. and Janie Elizabeth (Edge) Dyson; m. Theodore J. Dexter, Feb. 4, 1951 (div. Apr. 1980); children: Linda Leigh Allen, John Dexter; m. Thomas G. Rosell, Dec. 31, 1983. BA cum laude, Meth. Coll., N.C., 1976. Profl. pianist, organist, 1957—; piano tchr. Fayetteville, N.C., 1963—. Mem. Fayetteville Rep. Woman's Club, 1974—, Fayetteville Symphony Orchestra, Fayetteville Lafayette Soc.. Named one of Top Community Vols., Carolina Telephone Telegraphs Co., 1989. Mem. Community Concerts (pres. 1985—), Nat. Music Tchrs. Assn. (certification), N.C. State Music Tchrs. Assn. (certification), Am. Coll. Musicians, Fayetteville Piano Tchrs. Assn., Meth. Coll. Alumni Assn., Retired Officer's Wives Club, Fayetteville Woman's Club, Chaminade Music Club. Methodist. Home and Studio: 544 Hilliard Dr Fayetteville NC 28311

DEY, CAROL RUTH, logistics management; b. N.Y., Mar. 9, 1943; d. Robert Lewis Adelson and Anne Millman; m. John Peter Dey, Feb. 9, 1968 (div. Feb. 1978). AA, San Bernardino Valley Coll., 1965; BA, Calif. State U., Sacramento, 1969; MBA, Calif. State U., San Bernardino, 1983. Sec. U.S. Dept of Interior, USAF, Retail Industry, San Bernardino, Sacramento, Calif., 1960-80; logistics mgr. USAF, San Bernardino, 1980—. Dancer Coppélia, San Bernardino, Calif., 1984; mem. St. Anne's Ch., San Bernardino, 1978—. Mem. Am. Bus. Women's Assn. (Calif. State Coll. scholar), Nat. Contract Mgmt. Assn., Smithsonian Inst., AF Assn. Republican. Roman Catholic.

DEYOUNG, KAREN JEAN, journalist; b. Chgo., Jan. 4, 1949; d. Edward Leonard and Jeanette K. (Clausen) DeY.; B.S. cum laude in Journalism and Communication, U. Fla., 1971. Features writer St. Petersburg (Fla.) Times, 1972-74; freelance reporter, Western Africa, 1974-75; Latin Am. corr. Washington Post, 1977-80, dep. fgn. editor, 1980-81, fgn. editor, 1981-85, London Bur. chief, 1985-89, nat. editor, 1989—. Recipient Disting. Svc. award fgn. reporting Sigma Delta Chi, 1979, Fgn. Corr. award Inter-Am. Press Assn., 1979; Maria Moors Cabot award Columbia U., 1981. Office: Washington Post 1150 15th St NW Washington DC 20071*

DEYOUNG, YVONNE MARIE, senior computer programmer, analyst; b. Milw., Dec. 9, 1951; d. Eugene Owen and Julia Ann (Mann) DeY. BBA in Acctg. and Data Processing, U. Wis., Eau Claire, 1975. Acct. Lab. Computing Inc., Madison, Wis., 1975-78, Tel. & Data Systems, Madison, 1978-79; programmer Wis. Dairy Herd Improvement Coop., Madison, 1979-80; programmer, analyst Profl. Ins. Mgmt. Co., Jacksonville, Fla., 1980-81; sr. programmer, analyst Rayovac Corp., Madison, 1981—; sec. bd. dirs. Rayovac Credit Union, Madison, 1985-87, chmn., 1987-89, vice chmn., 1989—; sales rep. Avon Products, Inc., Morton Grove, Ill., 1986—. Active Madison Civic Music Assn., 1975—, St. Bernard's Sr. Choir, Madison, 1975—, Edgewood Coll. Tour Choir, Madison, 1987—, 1st Brigade Band, Milw., 1989—. Mem. Data Processing Mgmt. Assn., Avon Products Pres.'s Club, Avon Products Honor Soc., Tuesday Night Live League (treas. 1986-87), Ladies of the Evening League (pres. 1989—). Roman Catholic. Home: 5216 Piccadilly Dr Madison WI 53714-2018 Office: Rayovac Corp 601 Rayovac Dr PO Box 4960 Madison WI 53711-0960

D'HARNONCOURT, ANNE, museum director; m. Joseph J. Rishel, June 19, 1971. B.A., Radcliffe Coll., 1965; M.A. with distinction, Courtauld Inst. Art, U. London, 1967. Curatorial asst. Phila. Mus. Art, 1967-69; asst. curator 20th Century art Art Inst. Chgo., 1969-71; curator 20th Century art Phila. Mus. Art, 1971-82, the George D. Widener dir., 1982—. Organizer: (with McShine) exhbn. Marcel Duchamp, 1973-74, (with others) Philadelphia: Three Centuries of American Art, 1976, Eight Artists, 1978, (with Percy) Violet Oakley, 1979, Futurism and the International Avant-Garde, 1980, (with Sims) John Cage: Scores and Prints, 1982; author: (with Walter Hopps) Etant Donnes. . .Reflections on a New Work by Marcel Duchamp, 1969, The Cubist Cockatoo: Preliminary Exploration of Joseph Cornell's Hommages to Juan Gris, 1978. Office: Phila Mus Art Benjamin Franklin Pkwy PO Box 7646 Philadelphia PA 19101

DIAGONALE, JOSEPHINE CARMELA, human resources specialist; b. N.Y.C., July 1, 1941; d. Michael and Maria Carmela (Puoti) D. BA, Coll. New Rochelle (N.Y.), 1962; MA, NYU, 1965. Tchr. Gallander U., Washington, 1968-76; sr. assoc. Mainstream Access, Inc., N.Y.C., 1978-81; ptnr. Career Perspectives, Stamford, Conn., 1981-83; pres., owner Diaconia Group, Inc., Teaneck, N.J., 1983—. Author three career guides. Mem. Am. Soc. Tng. and Devel., N.Y. Orgn. Devel. Network. Office: PO Box 3069 Teaneck NJ 07666

DIAMANT, BARBARA GREENSTEIN, physical therapist; b. N.Y.C., Dec. 3, 1932; d. Harold and Gertrude (Baliner) Greenstein; m. Chester J. Deutsch, Apr. 7, 1957 (dec. May 1977); children: Gary Deutsch, David Deutsch, Kenneth Deutsch; m. Benjamin Diamant, Apr. 8, 1979; children: Michael, David, Adena, Aaron. BS in Phys. Therapy, Columbia U., 1954; postgrad., NYU, 1954-56. Lic. phys. therapist, N.Y., Conn. Staff phys. therapist Hosp. for Spl. Surgery, N.Y.C., 1954-56; home care coord. Coney Island Hosp., Bklyn., 1956-57; outpatient phys. therapist United Hosp., Port Chester, N.Y., 1957-59; staff phys. therapist Rehab. Ctr. of South Fairfield, Stamford, Conn., 1967-70; supr. Abbott Manor, Bridgeport, Conn., 1970-72; sr. therapist Courtland Gardens, Stamford, 1972-74; pvt. practice Stamford, 1974-81; phys. therapist Jewish Home for Elderly, Fairfield, Conn., 1981-84; dir. phys. therapy Concourse Nursing Home, Bronx, N.Y., 1985-87; orthopedic phys. therapy Drs. Kwock, Scheinzeit, Fink, and Kirby, Poughkeepsie, N.Y., 1988—. Pres. PTA, Stamford, 1960-62; com. chmn. Dem. Party, Stamford. Mem. Phys. Therapy Assn. (orthopedic sect.), Geriatric Phys. Therapy, Home Care Assocs. Cons. (bd. dirs. 1985-87). Jewish. Home: 17A Miller Hill Dr La Grangeville NY 12540

DIAMOND, ADELINA, writer; b. Chgo., Oct. 9, 1927; d. Herbert C. and Jennie (Friedman) Lust; A.B., U. Chgo., 1947; M.P.A., N.Y. U., 1972, postgrad., 1981; m. Edwin Diamond, Dec. 5, 1948; children—Ellen, Franna, Louise. Sportswear buyer Mandel Bros., Chgo., 1947-49, advt. copywriter, 1949-50; fashion reporter Womens Wear Daily, Chgo., 1950-52; editor Hyde Park Herald, Chgo., 1953-56; assoc. Center for Housing Partnerships, N.Y.C., 1970-72; Eastern public affairs rep. U. Chgo., 1972-78; dir. public relations Carnegie Council on Children, 1978-81; cons. Children's Def. Fund, 1978-81; founding mem. Women U.S.A., Friends of NOW, N.Y.C.; founder, chairperson Friends of ERA. Home: 20 Waterside Pla New York NY 10010

DIAMOND, ALISA ROBIN, broadcasting/media company executive; b. N.Y.C., July 13, 1962; d. Michael Kalman and Deena Diane (Heller) D. BA, NYU, 1984. Account exec. Izod Lacoste, N.Y.C., 1981-84; adminstrv. asst. Price Communications Corp., N.Y.C., 1984-86, adminstr. corp. svcs., 1986-87, asst. sec., 1987-89, v.p. corp. affairs, 1989—; asst. sec. TLM Corp., N.Y.C., 1988—. Mem. Am. Soc. Corp. Secs., Women in Communications, Am. Soc. Profl. and Exec. Women, Internat. Radio and TV Soc. Home: 2 Fifth Ave Apt 2E New York NY 10011 Office: Price Communications Corp 45 Rockefeller Plaza Suite 3201 New York NY 10020

DIAMOND, ANN BERKMAN, financial analyst; b. New Brunswick, N.J., Feb. 8, 1951; d. Nathan and Charlotte (Goldstein) Berkman; m. Lawrence S. Diamond, Feb. 29, 1976; 1 stepchild, Lori Sharon. Student, U. Madrid, 1969-70; BA, Rutgers U., 1972. Chartered fin. cons. V.p., dir. Seiden & de Cuevas Inc., N.Y.C., 1972-87; fin. counselor Chen Planning Cons., Inc., N.Y.C., 1987-89; prin. Ann B. Diamond, Chartered Fin. Counselor, N.Y.C., 1989—; speaker fin. mgmt. seminars, N.Y.C., 1987—. Mem. adv. coun. Women in Need, N.Y.C., 1988—; bd. dirs. Lenox Group Hadassh, N.Y.C., 1988—. Mem. Internat. Assn. Fin. Planning, Am. Soc. CLU and Chartered Fin. Cons., Fin. Womens Assn. Office: 509 Madison Ave Ste 1400 New York NY 10022

DIAMOND, DOROTHY B., lawyer; b. July 22, 1918; d. Max and Sadie (Hoffman) Bernstein; m. Adrian Diamond, Sept. 6, 1942; children: A. Stephen, Peter A., Diane Diamond Capps, Ted A., Dinah Diamond Shelley, Delilah Diamond Adair. BA, U. Cin., 1940, JD, 1942. Home and Office: 3417 Section Rd Cincinnati OH 45237

DIAMOND, JANE SYDNEY, editor; b. Bronx, N.Y., May 21, 1952; d. Herbert and Sydell (Weisbar) D.; m. Tommy Eugene Peterson, Mar. 10, 1985; 1 child, Kara Robyn. BA cum laude, Clark U., Worcester, Mass., 1974; MPH, U. N.C., 1977. Scheduling officer Univ. Hosp., Boston, 1974-75; adminstr. N.C. Occupational Safety & Health Project, Durham, N.C., 1977-78; health specialist Migrant and Seasonal Farmworkers Assn., Atlanta, 1978-81; manuscript editor, Arthritis and Rheumatism Am. Coll. Rheumatology, Atlanta, 1982-83, mng. editor, 1983—. Bd. dirs. Coalition Against Unnecessary Thoroughfares in Older Neighborhoods, Atlanta, 1984-88. Mem. Coun. Biology Editors, Successful Mag. Pubs. Group, Soc. Scholarly Pub., Am. Med. Writers Assn. Home: 1149 Alta Ave NE Atlanta GA 30307 Office: Am Coll Rheumatology 17 Executive Park Dr NE Atlanta GA 30329

DIAMOND, PAMELA ANN, accountant; b. Manhasset, N.Y., June 22, 1963; d. Jack and Phyllis (Novick) D. BSBA, Boston U., 1985. CPA, N.Y. Mem. staff Ellenbogen, Freeman & Co., CPAs, N.Y.C., 1985-87; sr. acct. Ellenbogen & Dolowich, CPAs, N.Y.C., 1987-89, Ellenbogen, Rubenstein & August, CPAS, N.Y.C., 1989—. Mem. AICPAs, N.Y. State Soc. CPAs, NAFE. Office: 270 Madison Ave New York NY 10122

DIAMOND, SHARI SEIDMAN, editor, psychology educator; b. Chgo., Mar. 17, 1947; d. Leon Harry and Rita (Wolff) S.; m. Stewart Howard Diamond, Nov. 1, 1970; 1 child, Nicole. BA in Psychology, Sociology, U. Mich., 1968; MA in Psychology, Northwestern U., 1970, PhD in Social Psychology, 1972; JD with honors, U. Chgo., 1985. Bar: Ill. 1985. Rsch. assoc. Sch. Law U. Chgo., 1972-73; asst. prof. psychology and criminal justice U. Ill., Chgo., 1973-79, assoc. prof., 1979—; assoc. Sidley & Austin, Chgo., 1985-87; sr. rsch. fellow ABF, Chgo., 1987—; cons. govtl. and pub. interest groups; acad. visitor dept. law London Sch. Econs., 1981; hon. fellow Ctr. for Urban Affairs Northwestern U., Evanston, Ill., 1972-73; hon. rsch. assoc. U. London, 1970; speaker, lectr. in field. Editor Law and Soc. Rev., 1988-91; mem. editorial bd. Law and Soc. Rev., 1983-88, Law and Human Behavior, Crime and Justice Annual; past mem. editorial bd. Evaluation Rev.; reviewer NSF; contbr. articles to profl. jours. Chair Coll. Edn. Policy Com., 1979-80; dir. tng. grant NIMH Crime and Delinquency, 1979-80. Fellow Northwestern U. 1968-69, NIMH, 1969-71; grantee Spencer Found., 1972-74, Law Enforcement Assistance Adminstrn., 1974-76, Ctr. for Crime and Delinquency NIMH, 1976-81, NSF, 1980-83. Fellow Am. Psychol. Assn.; mem. Am. Psychology-Law Soc. (pres. 1987-88), Law and Soc. Assn. (trustee 1979-82). Office: ABF 750 N Lake Shore Dr Chicago IL 60611

DIAMOND, SUSAN ZEE, management consultant; b. Okla., Aug. 20, 1949; d. Louis Edward and Henrietta (Wood) D. AB (Nat. Merit scholar, GRTS scholar), U. Chgo., 1970; MBA, DePaul U., 1979; m. Allan T. Devitt, July 27, 1974. Dir. study guide prodn. Am. Sch. Co., Chgo., 1972-75; publs. supr. Allied Van Lines, Broadview, Ill., 1975-78, sr. account svcs. rep., 1978-79; pres. Diamond Assocs. Ltd., Melrose Park, Ill., 1978—; condr. seminars Am. Mgmt. Assn. Mem. Nat. Assn. Accts., Adminstrv. Mgmt. Soc., Assn. Records Mgrs. and Adminstrs., Internat. Records Mgmt. Coun., Records Mgmt. Soc. Great Britain, Nuclear Info. and Records Mgmt. Assn., Nat. Fire Protection Assn., Assn. Info. and Image Mgmt., Delta Mu Delta. Author: How to Talk More Effectively, 1972, Preparing Administrative Manuals, 1981, How to Manage Administrative Operations, 1981, How to be an Effective Secretary in the Modern Office, 1982, Records Management: A Practical Guide, 1983; co-author: Finance Without Fear, 1983; editor Mobility Trends, 1975-78; contbr. numerous articles to profl. jours. Office: 2851 N Pearl Ave Melrose Park IL 60160

DIAZ, ANA ROSA, international civil servant; b. N.Y.C., Aug. 30, 1963; d. Jose Diaz and Yolanda E. Diaz-Lopez. BA, Manhattanville Coll., Purchase, N.Y., 1985. Asst. sec. Bankers Trust Co., N.Y.C.; corp. trust adminstr. The Fuji Bank & Trust Co., N.Y.C.; internat. civil servant UNIDO, Vienna, Austria. Mem. NAFE. Home: 22-03 Whitestone Pkwy Whitestone NY 11357

DIAZ DE TORRES, MYRTHA I., nursing educator, consultant; b. Ponce, P.R., Jan. 23, 1944; d. Manuel and Monsita (Medina) Torres; Samuel Torres, July 26, 1964; children: Samuel, Ivette, Maria del Mar, Manuel, Mirsa. BS in Nursing, Cath. U. P.R., 1965; MS in Nursing, U. P.R., 1971, cert. in gerontology, 1983. Staff nurse San Jorge Hosp., Santurce, P.R., 1965-67; instr. Sch. Nursing P.R. Med. Ctr., Rio Piedras, 1967-69; instr. Sch. Nursing U. P.R., San Juan, 1971-76, asst. prof., 1976-83, assoc. prof., 1983—, instr. cardiology, 1980-84, dir. nursing program, 1985—; mem. Bd. Nurse Examiners P.R., San Juan, 1971-75; speaker 2d Inter-Am. Conf. Cardiology, 1980, 10th World Congress Cardiology, Washington, 1986. Contbr. articles to profl. jours. Mem. sci. com. P.R. chpt. Am. Heart Assn., Hato Rey, 1979-80, mem. hypertension com., 1982—, pres., 1987-88, rep. Coun. Cardiovascular Nursing, 1987—; mem. reading group Holy Ghost Parish, Levittown, P.R., 1986. Named Disting. Citizen, Jr. C. of C., Toa Baja, P.R., 1982. Mem. Coll. Profl. Nurses P.R. (bd. dirs. San Juan chpt. 1983-85, pres. 1988—), Sigma Theta Tau. Roman Catholic. Home: Paseo Alegre #E-2309 Levittown PR 00949 Office: U PR-Med Scis Campus Sch Nursing PO Box 5067 San Juan PR 00936

DIBELL, HELEN MARIE, executive assistant; b. Ellwood City, Pa., Apr. 9, 1941; d. Nicholas J. and Helen (Pintea) Savu; m. David L. Dibell, July 8, 1961 (div. 1986); children: Marta, Todd, Troy, Mark. Student, Geneva Coll., Beaver Falls, 1959-61, U. Ill., 1962. Payroll acct. Babcock & Wilcox Steel Corp., Beaver Falls, Pa., 1960-62; admininstrv. asst. U. Ill., Urbana, 1962-63, Lockheed Missiles & Space Co., Vandenberg AFB, Calif., 1963-64; acct. tng. Vanda Beauty Counselor, N.Y., 1964-78; adminstrv. asst. Okaloosa Walton Jr. Coll., Niceville, Fla., 1977-78; adminstrv. asst. Tex. Instruments, Va., 1978-79; exec. asst. Allied Signal Bendix Aerospace, Arlington, 1979-89, Orion Group Ltd., Dr. Richard DeLauer and Matra Aerospace Inc., Arlington, 1988-89; asst. to bd. dirs. Fairchild Space and Def. Corp., Germantown, Md., 1989—. Mem. Women Def., Army Assn., Am. Def. Preparedness Assn., Air Force Assn. Republican. Presbyterian. Home: 8324 Lilac Ln Alexandria VA 22308 Office: Fairchild Space & Space Corp 20301 Century Blvd Germantown MD 20874

DIBENEDITTO, BARBARA JEAN, video technician, producer; b. Waterbury, Conn., Nov. 13, 1959; d. John Ralph and Angelina (Dantino); m. Gregory A. Lewis, Oct. 25, 1986. BA, Bethany Coll., 1981. Ops. coord. Showtime Entertainment, N.Y.C., 1981-82; coordinator, graphics Magno Sound & Video, N.Y.C., 1982-83; asst. camera operator Video People Inc., N.Y.C., 1983-84; tech., editor Freelance CNN, Lifetime, HBO, Metro Area. Vol. Moundsville State Penat, 1978. Mem. AD NET. Roman Catholic. Home and Office: 348 E 51st St #4B New York NY 10022

DIBIASIO, LINDA APRIL, editor; b. Phila., Apr. 7, 1944; d. Fred Arthur and Myrtle Clara (Gardner) DuFresne; m. James DiBiasio, Oct. 14, 1966; children: Jamie, Christopher. BA, West Chester State U., 1967; postgrad., Drexel U., 1986—. Writer Sea Hawk mag., Yokosuka, Japan, 1967-68; editor, libr. Bucks County Hist. Soc., Doylestown, Pa., 1973-76, Bucks County Courts, Doylestown, 1976-78; writer, editor Doylestown Hosp. Pub. Rels., 1978-82, Profl. Press, Horsham, Pa., 1982—. Mem. Computer Press Assn., Internat. Trade Devel. Assn., Assn. Bus. Pubs. Office: Profl Press 101 Witmer Rd Horsham PA 19044

DICAMILLO, DEBRA ALLEN, international tax specialist; b. Bethesda, Md., July 12, 1957; d. David Marcelle and Mary Clarissa (Andes) Allen; m. Thomas B. Hites, (div. Dec. 1984); m. Pasqual R. DiCamillo, Mar. 1989. BS in Bus. Psychology, La. State U., Shreveport, 1983. Tax auditor IRS, Shreveport, 1983-84; internat. tax auditor IRS, Washington, 1984-86, internat. tax mgr., 1986-87; tax sr. Beers and Cutler, CPA, Wash., 1988; sr. tax specialist Marriott Corp. Internat., Bethesda, Md., 1988-90; tax cons. pvt. practice, 1987—. Mem. Am. Bus. Women's Assn., Shreveport, La., 1983-84, Alexandria, 1984-86; dive master, Profl. Assn. Dive Instrs., 1986—; campaign mem. elect G. Bush Pres., Alexandria, 1988—; vols. Washington Humane Soc., 1987—. Mem. Assn. Govt. Accts. Republican. Home: 11616 Lighthouse Dr Laurel MD 20708

DICAMILLO, LORETTA SMIMMO, utilities executive, educator; b. Bklyn., Apr. 10, 1935; d. James Joseph and Viola Catherine (Mancia) Smimmo; m. James R. DiCamillo, Nov. 5, 1955 (dec. 1972); children: Linda, Dianna, Dolores, Loretta Anne. AAS, N.Y.C. Community Coll., 1955; BA, Queens Coll., 1972; MA, NYU, 1975. Cert. tchr.; cert. home economist. Tchr. jr. high sch. home econs. N.Y.C. Bd. Edn., Bklyn., 1971-75; with Consol. Edison Co of N.Y., N.Y.C., 1975—, mgr. consumer edn. dept., 1982-89, dir. consumer edn. dept., 1989—; cons. N.Y. State Bd. Regents, Albany, 1983-87; mem. adv. bd. Mayor's Office for the Handicapped, N.Y.C., 1984—; arbitrator N.Y. Better Bus. Bur., N.Y.C., 1986—; coord. Nat. Coalition for Consumer Edn., N.Y.C., 1989—. TV radio and spokesperson utility pub. affairs and community affairs programs, 1980—. Mem. Home Econs. in Bus., Am. Home Econs. Assn. (pres. southeastern dist. 1988-89), Elec. Women's Round Table Inc. (pres. N.Y. chpt. 1987-90). Office: Consol Edison Consumer Edn 4 Irving Pl Rm 1625-S New York NY 10003

DICARLO, SUSANNE HELEN, financial analyst; b. Greensburg, Pa., Nov. 24, 1956; d. Wayne Larry and Clara Emogene (Weaver) Gower; m. John Joseph DiCarlo, June 21, 1980; children: Sarah Rose, Kristen Marie. BS in Acctg., Va. Poly. Inst. and State U., 1978. Auditor U.S. Army Audit Agy., Ft. Monroe, Va., 1978-79; acct. technician Fleet Combat Tng. Ctr., Virginia Beach, Va., 1980-82, supervisory auditor, 1982-83; fin. analyst Comml. Activity Mgmt. Team, Norfolk, Va., 1983—; fed. women's program mgr. Fleet Combat Tng. Ctr., 1980-83. Creator newsletter Fed. Women's Program Manager, 1980-83. Mem. Am. Soc. Mil. Comptrollers. Club: Seaside Mountaineers (Va. Beach) (treas. 1986-88). Home: 4013 Dillaway Ct Virginia Beach VA 23456

DICE, RHONDALEE ROHLEDER, marketing executive; b. New Castle, Pa., Apr. 23, 1958; d. J. Russell and Thelma Marie (Kash) Rohleder; m. L. Allen Dice, Apr. 16, 1988. BA, U. Pitts., 1985; MBA, U. Phoenix, 1991. Systems cons. BMG Telecommunications, Inc., Tempe, 1982-83; configuration data analyst Motorola Inc., Scottsdale, Ariz., 1985-86; sr. configuration data analyst Motorola Inc., Tempe, Ariz., 1987-88; product mktg. specialist Motorola Inc., Chandler, Ariz., 1988-89; account exec. Teledata Resources, Tempe, 1990—. Vol. Project for Literacy in U.S., 1987; pres. Search Triad Inc., 1988-89, exec. bd. 1984—. Mem. NAFE. Home: 6507 S Hardy Dr #245 Tempe AZ 85283 Office: 537 S 48th St Ste 103 Tempe AZ 85281

DICH, LOIS BOYD, insurance agent; b. Mobile, Ala., July 22, 1944; d. Malcolm Luther and Norma (Tagert) Boyd; 1 child, Marc Alan. Cert. in gen. ins., Ins. Inst. Am., Malvern, Pa., 1974. Assoc. in automation mgmt. Ins. Inst. Am., Malvern, 1989; CPCU, Am. Inst. Property & Liability Underwriters, 1985; cert. voc. tchr., Fla. Typist State Farm Ins., New Orleans, 1963-64; agent Davis Ins., Ocala, Fla., 1965-70, Chazal-Blair Ins., Ocala, 1970-76, Lykes Bros. Ins., Tampa, Fla., 1976-77, Adcock/Adock Ins., Tampa, 1981-82; asst. mgr. Bransford Ins., Tampa, 1977-81; adminstrv. asst., agent Robbins Ins. Inc., Tampa, 1982-88; commercial lines account rep. large accounts Goodwin, Loomis & Britton Inc., Hartford, Conn., 1988-89; comml. lines account rep. Blumberg Agy., Hartford, Conn., 1989—. Mem. Soc. CPCUs, Nat. Assn. Ins. Women (CPIW cert. 1973), Hartford Assn. Ins. Women, Independent Agents Conn., Profl. Ins. Agents Conn. Democrat. Baptist. Home: 63 Elm St Apt 103 Manchester CT 06040 Office: Blumberg Assocs Inc 100 Constitution Plaza 18th fl Hartford CT 06103

DICK, NANCY E., former lieutenant governor; b. Detroit, July 22, 1930; widowed; children: Margot, Timber, Justin. BA in Bus. Adminstrn., Mich. State U.; law student, U. Denver. Worked in product devel. marktg.; mem. Colo. Gen. Assembly, 1974-79; lt. gov. State of Colo., 1979-86; fin. chmn. Fedn. Rocky Mountain States; del. Nat. Democratic Party Conv., 1980; exec. bd. Gov's. Interstate Indian Council, 1981-83; chmn. regional selection White House Fellows, 1981, panelist, 1979-80; chmn. Colorado-Hunan (People's Republic China) Indsl. Conf.; del. Women's Leadership Conf. on Nat. Security. Candidate U.S. Senate, 1983; trustee Denver Symphony Assn.; hon. chmn. Friends of the Urban League; mem. rural health com. Colo. Med. Soc., 1975-76; exec. bd. U.S. Army War Coll., 1981, USAF War Coll., 1984. Recipient Disting. Alumni award Mich. State U., 1980; recipient Florence Sabin award Colo. Pub. Health Care Assn., 1980, Outstanding Alumnus award Coll. Bus., Mich. State U., 1981, Outstanding Citizen Nat. Rural Primary Care Assn., 1981, Found. scholarship Nat. Ctr. Creative Leadership, 1981, 83. Democrat.

DICKENS, DORIS LEE, psychiatrist; b. Roxboro, N.C., Oct. 12; d. Lee Edward and Delma Ernestine (Hester) Dickens; B.S. magna cum laude, Va. Union U., 1960; M.D., Howard U., 1966; m. Austin LeCount Fickling, Oct. 15, 1975. Diplomate Nat. Bd. Med. Examiners. Intern, St. Elizabeth's Hosp., Washington, 1966-67, resident, 1967-70; staff psychiatrist, dir. Mental Health Program for Deaf, St. Elizabeth's Hosp., Washington, 1970-87; clin. prof. Howard U. Coll. Medicine, 1982—. Co-founder Nat. Health Care Found. for Deaf; med. officer Region 4 Community Mental Health Ctr., Washington, Commn. on Mental Health, 1987—. Recipient Dorothea Lynde Dix award, 1980. Mem. Am. Psychiat. Assn. (achievement awards bd. 1988-89), Washington Psychiat. Soc., Alpha Kappa Mu, Beta Kappa Chi. Author: How and When Psychiatry Can Help You, 1972; You and Your Doctor; contbg. author: Hearing and Hearing Impairment, 1979; contbg. author Counseling Deaf People, Research and Practice. Home: 12308 Surrey Circle Tantallon MD 20022

DICKENS, ESTHER ANNE, industrial chemist; b. Cleve., Aug. 17, 1931; d. Hubert R. and Esther (Roush) Yerger; m. John E. Dickens, Oct. 20, 1956; children: James A., Timothy E. BA, Coll. Wooster, 1952; PhD, Northwestern U., 1956. Research chemist radiology Einstein Med. Ctr., Phila., 1958-61; chemist E.I. DuPont, Towanda, Pa., 1973-80, Parlin, N.J., 1980—. Contbr. articles to profl. jours. Guide Del. Nature Ctr., Wilmington, 1970-71; research vol. U. Research Expeditions, Kenya, Tanzania, Nepal, 1987, 1988, 1989, Earthwatch Expeditions, Zaire, Zimbabwe, Tonga, 1983, 1985, 1986. Mem. Sigma Xi. Office: E I DuPont IMG Dept Cheesequake Rd Parlin NJ 08859

DICKENS, INEZ ELIZABETH, real estate executive; b. N.Y.C., July 15, 1949; d. Lloyd Everett and Georgie Elsie (Yerby) D.; m. John Frank Russell, Sept. 25, 1982. BA, Howard U., 1972. Property mgr. Branch & Merritt, Inc., N.Y.C., 1972-75; owner, corp. pres. 1389 Constrn. Corp., N.Y.C., 1975-88, 88—; owner, corp. sec. Lloyd's Funding Corp., N.Y.C., 1975—; cons., Ennis Francis Houses, N.Y.C., 1989. Committee woman, N.Y.C. Jud. Com., 1975—, N.Y. State Dem. com., 1988—; chair bd. dirs., Langston Hughes Child Devel., N.Y.C., 1975-79. Mem. Nat. Soc. Real Estate Appraisers, Greater Harlem Real Estate Bd. N.Y., Nat. Assn. Real Estate Brokers, N.Y. State Soc. Real Estate Appraisers, Real Estate Bd. N.Y., N.Y.C. Soc. Real Estate Appraisers (committee woman 1974—), Uptown C. of C. (bd. dirs. 1988—), Nat. Assn. Negro Bus. Women (chair housing com. 1988—), 100 Black Women, Martin Luther King Club, Dem. Club. Roman Catholic. Home: 201 W 139th St New York NY 10030 Office: 2153 7th Ave New York NY 10027

DICKENS, VERA JOSIE, beauty supply company executive; b. Dixon, Mo., Nov. 27, 1933; d. Thomas Leddel and Lydia Louise (Tackett) Bacon; m. Harold Freddie Dickens, June 4, 1949; children—Harold Joseph, William Lee. Br. mgr. Midwest Beauty Supply, Jonesboro, Ark., 1964-76; mgr. Cache Beauty Supply, Jonesboro, 1976-83, corp. pres., 1983—. Mem. Beauty and Barber Supply Inst. Mem. Christian Ch. Lodge: Eastern Star. Office: Cache Beauty Supply Inc 2826 E Highland Dr Jonesboro AR 72401

DICKERSON, AMY ELIZABETH, marketing professional; b. Kalispell, Mont., June 5, 1965; d. Davis Warren and Linda Louise (Weber) D. BS in Mgmt. and Mktg. magna cum laude, U. Nebr., 1987; cert. in internat. studies, U. Växjö, Sweden, 1987. Asst. mgr. McDonald's Restaurant, York, Nebr., 1981-83; conf. hall dir. U. Nebr., Lincoln, 1986-87; retail sales rep. Black & Decker, San Francisco, 1988-89; nat. sales coord. Black & Decker, Hunt Valley, Md., 1990—. Sec. AIESEC, Lincoln, 1985; co-chair Alcohol Task Force, Lincoln, 1986. Nebr. State Regent's scholar U. Nebr., 1983-87. Mem. Am. Mgmt. Assn., Mortar Bd. (v.p. Lincoln chpt. 1986). Office: Black & Decker 10 North Park Dr Hunt Valley MD 21030

DICKERSON, CLAIRE MOORE, lawyer; b. Boston, Apr. 1, 1950; d. Roger Cleveland and Ines Idelette (Roullet) Moore; m. Thomas Pasquali Dickerson, May 22, 1976; children: Caroline Anne, Susannah Moore. AB, Wellesley Coll., 1971; JD, Columbia U., 1974; LLM in Taxation, NYU, 1981. Bar: N.Y. 1975, U.S. Dist. Ct. (ea. and so. dists.) N.Y. 1975, U.S. Ct. Appeals (2d cir.) 1975, U.S. Supreme Ct. 1980. Assoc. Coudert Brothers, N.Y., 1974-82, ptnr., 1983-86; assoc. prof. law St. John's U., Jamaica, N.Y., 1986-88, prof., 1989—. Contbr. articles to profl. jours. Trustee Rye (N.Y.) Presbyn. Nursery Sch., 1988—. Mem. ABA, Assn. of Bar of City of N.Y., Union Internat. des Avocats, Shenorock Club. Democrat. Office: St John's U Sch Law Grand Central and Utopia Pkwys Jamaica NY 11439

DICKERSON, NANCY HANSCHMAN, television producer, news correspondent; b. Milw.; d. Frederick R. and Florence (Conners) Hanschman; m. Claude Wyatt Dickerson, 1962 (div. 1983); children: Elizabeth, Ann, Jane, Michael, John; m. John C. Whitehead, Feb. 25, 1989. Student, Clarke Coll., Dubuque, Iowa, 1945-46; BS in Edn., U. Wis., 1948; HHD (hon.), Am. Internat. Coll., Springfield, Mass.; ArtsD (hon.), Pine Manor Coll., 1988. Sch. tchr. Milw.; staff asst. Senate Fgn. Relations Com., Washington; producer CBS News, 1956-60, 1st woman news corr., 1960-63; news corr. NBC, 1963-70; news analyst Inside Washington (syndicated nationally for TV stas.), 1971—; producer spl. syndicated TV programs, pres. Dickerson Co., 1971—; polit. commentator Newsweek Broadcasting Service; founder, exec. producer Television Corp. Am., 1980—; reporter Pres. Kennedy's funeral, Republican and Democratic convs., Civil Rights March on Washington, Kennedy, Johnson and Nixon inaugurations; represented Pub. Broadcasting Corp. (on all-network Conversation with Pres. Nixon), 1970; lectr.; commentator Fox TV News, 1986—. Author: Among Those Present, 1976. Trustee Am. U. Recipient Collegian award LaSalle Coll., Phila; Spirit of Achievement award Albert Einstein Coll., Yeshiva U.; Sigma Delta Chi award Boston U.; Pioneer award New Eng. Women's Press Assn.; Assoc. fellow Pierson Coll., Yale, 1972—; Peabody award for 1982 TV program on Watergate; Silver Gavel award for 1982 TV program on Watergate ABA. Mem. Radio-Television News Analysts. Club: Washington Press (past v.p.).

DICKERSON, PAMELA MAY, writer; b. Orange, Calif., June 6, 1961; d. Joseph Beattie, III and Norma May (Miller) D. BBA, BA in English summa cum laude, Chapman Coll., 1980. Free-lance writer, editor, Garden Grove, Calif., 1980-84; documentation mgr. Am. Data Industries, Irvine, Calif., 1984-89, dir. corp. communications, 1989—; pres. Pamela Dickerson and Assocs., 1989—. Contbg. editor: The HP Chronicle; contbr. articles to profl. jours. Mem. NAFE, Am. Mgmt. Assn., Soc. for Tech. Communication.

DICKESON, LUDMILA WEIR, teacher; b. Maryville, Mo., June 16, 1941; d. Benjamin Franklin and Ludmila Martha (Vavra) Weir; m. Robert Celmer Dickeson, June 22, 1963; children: Elizabeth Ann, Cynthia Marie. BSE, U. Mo., 1963, MEd, 1966. Cert. tchr., Colo., Ariz., Mo. Tchr. Columbia (Mo.) Pub. Schs., 1963-69; tchr., tutor Madison Sch. Dist., Phoenix, 1979-81; first lady U. No. Colo., 1981—; dir. Right to Read of Weld County, Inc., 1989—; com. mem. Ariz. Bd. of Edn. Statewide Textbook Adoption Com., Phoenix, 1979-80. Campaign chair United Way of Weld County, 1988; pres.-elect Greeley (Colo.) Philharmonic Orch. Assn., 1989; coun. pres. No. Colo. Coun. of Camp Fire, Inc., Windsor, Colo., 1985-87; trustee Flagstaff (Ariz.) Community Hosp., 1979. Mem. AAUW (recording sec. 1968-69), Delta Kappa Gamma, Pi Lambda Theta, Kappa Alpha Theta, Rotary, PEO Sisterhood (pres. 1974, 1984). Congregational. Home: 1862 Tenth Ave Greeley CO 80631

DICKEY, BETTE ELLYN, real estate company official; b. Ottumwa, Iowa, Jan. 25, 1936; d. Henry Albert and Mary Margaret (Donovan) Hammen; m. Valjean Joseph Dickey, June 7, 1958; children: Charles Joseph, Sarah Elizabeth. AA, Scottsdale (Ariz.) Community, 1976; BS in MMgmt. magna cum laude, Ariz. State U., 1979. Lic. real estate profl. Bookkeeper Union Bank, Ottumwa, 1956-58; fingerprint classifier FBI, Washington, 1958-59; bookkeeper, sec. Beneficial Fin., Ottumwa, 1959-62; adminstrv. asst. Kiva Elem. Sch., Scottsdale, 1966-74; real estate salesperson Russ Lyon Realty Co., Scottsdale, 1980—. Chmn. Russ Lyon dinner-auction Muscular Dystrophy Assn., Scottsdale, 1987; campaign worker Bruner for County Supr., Scottsdale, 1988; eucharist minister Women's Guild, St. Maria's Ch.. Named to top 25 residential real estate agts. in area, Bus. Jour., Phoenix, 1987. Mem. Ariz. State U. Bus. Coll. Alumni Assn. (bd. dirs., pres. 1989-90, sec., v.p. 1986-89), AAUW, LWV, Internat. Real Estate Inst., Womens Coun. Realtors, Scottsdale C. of C., Phi Theta Kappa, Phi Kappa Phi, Beta Gamma Sigma, Sigma Iota Epsilon. Republican. Roman Catholic. Office: Russ Lyon Realty Co 7150 E Lincoln Rd Scottsdale AZ 85253

DICKEY, JULIA EDWARDS, management and promotional consultant; b. Sioux Falls, S.D., Mar. 6, 1940; d. John Keith and Henrietta Barbara (Zerell) Edwards; m. Joseph E. Dickey, June 18, 1959; children: Joseph E., John Edwards. student DePauw U., 1958-59; A.B., Ind. U., 1962, M.L.S., 1967, postgrad., 1967. Asst. acquisitions librarian Ind. U. Regional Campus Libraries, 1965-67; head tech. services Bartholomew County Library, Columbus, Ind., 1967-74; dir. reference services Southeastern Ind. Area Library Service Authority, Columbus, 1974-78, exec. dir., 1978-80; pres. Jedco Enterprises, 1981—; legis. strategy chmn. Ind. Library Coop. Devel., 1975; dir. Ind. Library Trustees Assn. Governance Project, 1982. Mem. Columbus exec. bd. Mayor's Task Force on Status of Women, 1973-76; del. Ind. Sch. Nominating Assembly, 1973-75, 75-77; bd. dirs. Human Services Inc. (Bartholomew, Brown and Jackson Counties community action program), 1975, pres., 1976-78; mem. adv. council Ind./Nat. Network Study, 1977-78; adv. council Salvation Army Local, 1984-88; bd. dirs. Columbus Women's Center; precinct coordinator Vols. For Bayh, 1974; sheriff Columbus 1st precinct, 1975, clk., 1976-77, insp., 1978, judge, 1980-83; treas. Hayes for State Rep. Com., 1978, 82—. Named Outstanding Young Woman Am., 1973. Mem. ALA, Ind. Library Assn. (dist. chmn. 1972-73, chmn. library edn. div. 1980-81, ad hoc com. on legis. effectiveness, 1982, various coms.), Library Assts. and Technicians Round Table (chmn. 1968-69), Tech. Services Round Table (chmn. 1971-72, sec. library planning com. 1969-72), AAUW (pres. 1973-75), Bartholomew County Library Staff Assn. (pres. 1975-76), Exptl. Aircraft Assn. (charter pres. chpt. 729, Inc. 1981, advisor 1982, sec. 1984-85, Ind. chpt. 1988—, major achievement award Oshkosh, mem. internat. conv. antique and classic mgmt. team, 1988—), Ind. EAA Council (pres. 1982-88, advisor 1988—, internat. conv. antique/classic mgmt. team 1988—), Internat. Expt.. Aircraft Assn. (Major Achievement aware 1983, Antique Airplane Assn.,, First Tuesday, Psi Iota Xi (thrift shop steering 1985—, v.p. thrift shop chmn. 1986-87, Mem. of Yr. 1988-89). Club: Zonta. Home and Office: 511 Terrace Lake Rd Columbus IN 47201

DICKEY, LOUISE PARKE, flutist; b. Iowa City, Iowa, Feb. 17, 1942; m. David J. Pinkow, July 18, 1967. Student, Acad. de Musica de Maracaibo, Venezuela, 1960; MusB, U. Tulsa, 1964; MusM, U. Rochester, 1966. 2d flautist Orquesta Sinfonica de Maracaibo, 1958-60, Tulsa Philharm., 1961-64; prin. flautist Huntington Chamber Orch., 1971-72; faculty Lebanon Valley Coll., 1972-74, U. Ga., 1974-78; flutist, founding mem. Am. Chamber Players, 1978—; soloist various chamber orchs., U.S., Mex. and France; performer numerous recitals U.S., Europe, S.Am., Mex. Fulbright fellow, 1966-67. Mem. Nat. Flute Assn., Music Tchrs. Nat. Assn., Sigma Alpha Iota. Office: care LDP Artist Mgmt PO Box 3253 Boulder CO 80307

DICKEY, SHARON RUTHANE, pharmacist; b. Valdosta, Ga., Jan. 11, 1959; d. Charles Quay and Barbara Annette (Williams) D. BS in Biology, Phy. Sci., Miss. U. for Women, 1981; BS in Pharmacy, U. Miss., 1985. Cert. pharmacist. Hosp. pharmacy resident U. Med. Ctr., Jackson, Miss., 1985-86; staff II pharmacist U. Hosp., Jackson, 1986—. Mem. Am. Soc. Hosp. Pharmacists, Miss. Pharm. Assn. (named Disting. Young Pharmacist in Miss. 1988), Miss. Soc. Hosp. Pharmacists (newsletter editor 1987-89). Mem. Church of Christ. Office: U Med Ctr Pharmacy Dept 2500 N State St Jackson MS 39216

DICKINSON, CATHERINE SCHATZ, microbiologist; b. Cin., Jan. 6, 1927; d. Ralph Marvin and Mabel (Dare) Schatz; student U. Cin., 1944-46, postgrad. 1952; A.B., Miami U., Oxford, Ohio, 1948; m. Willard C. Dickinson, Jr., June 23, 1956; children—Kellie Dare, Bradley Clark. Supr., Bacteriology Lab., Children's Hosp., Cin., 1948-53; supr., sect. head Microbiology Lab., Ochsner Found. Hosp., New Orleans, 1953—; lectr. in field. Mem. New Orleans Area Soc. for Microbiology (pres. 1979), Am. Soc. Microbiology, Am. Soc. Clin. Pathologists (specialist in microbiology), New Orleans Soc. Microbiology, Nat. Registry for Microbiologists, Delta Zeta. Episcopalian. Club: Order Eastern Star. Home: 10001 Hyde Pl River Ridge LA 70123 Office: 1516 Jefferson Hwy New Orleans LA 70121

DICKINSON, DANA LYNNE, engineer; b. Fairborn, Ohio, Oct. 6, 1951; d. John David and Hertha Doris (Whitford) D.; m. Arthur Halliday Laurent, May 6, 1989. SB, SMChemE, MIT, 1974. Cons. engr. Arthur D. Little, Inc., Cambridge, Mass., 1975-76; prin. engr. GE Knolls Atomic Power Lab., Schenectady, N.Y., 1976-88; software engr. GE, Springfield, Va., 1988-90, TAMSCO, Arlington, Va., 1990—; freelance computer programmer, 1984-88. Avocations: bicycling, piano, volleyball, swimming. Home: 5409 Tripolis Ct Burke VA 22015 Office: TAMSCO 1225 Jefferson Davis Hwy Ste 1107 Arlington VA 22202

DICKINSON, JANE W., social services administrator; b. Kalamazoo, Sept. 27, 1919; d. Charles Herman and Rachel (Whaler) Wagner; student Hollins Coll., 1938-39; B.A., Duke U., 1941; M.Ed., Goucher Coll., 1965; m. E.F. Sherwood Dickinson, Oct. 23, 1943; children: Diane Jane Gray Clem, Carolyn Dickinson Vane. Exec. sec. Petroleum Industry Com., Balt., 1941-43; exec. sec. Sherwood Feed Mills Inc., Balt., 1943-79. Mem. exec. com. Children's Aid Md., 1960-61; mem. bd. women's aux. Balt. Symphony Orch., 1958-60; dist. chmn. Balt. Cancer Drive, 1958; dist. chmn. Balt. Mental Health Drive, 1957; co-chmn. Balt. United Appeal, 1968; bd. mgrs. Pickersgill Retirement Home. Mem. Alpha Delta Phi. Republican. Episcopalian. Clubs: Three Arts (sec. 1958-60, bd. govs. 1960-64, 67-70, pres. 1970-72) (Balt.); Women's (bd. govs. 1960-64, 86-88) (Roland Park); Cliff Dwellers Garden. Home: 1708 Killington Rd Baltimore MD 21204

DICKINSON, JOANNE WALTON, lawyer; b. Windsor, N.C., Nov. 17, 1936; d. John Odell and Lois (King) Walton; m. Charles Cameron Dickinson III; children: Richard E.P. Eaton, John W.T. Eaton, Edward V.H. Eaton. Student Wake Forest Coll., 1961-62; BA, W.Va., U., 1975, JD, 1978. Bar: W.Va. 1978. Actress, W.Va., 1968-78; contbg. editor Victorian Poetry W.Va. U., Morgantown, 1970-75; assoc. Love, Wise, Robinson & Woodroe, Charleston, W.Va., 1978-82; adj. prof. U. Charleston, 1982-85 ; prof. Hebei Tchrs. U., Shijiazhuang, Hebei Province, People's Republic China, 1983-84; lectr. Erikson Ctr./Harvard Med. Sch., 1985-88; lead articles editor W.Va. Law Rev., Morgantown, 1977-78; asst. editor Mountain State Press, Charleston, 1980-83; cons. Charles C. Dickinson III Trust. Contbr. articles to profl. jours. Bd. dirs. Women's Health Ctr., Charleston, 1980-81; bd. dirs. Legal Aid Soc., Charleston, 1980-81. Recipient 1st prize Nathan Burkan Competition ASCAP, W.Va., 1977. Fellow Royal Soc. Arts; mem. ABA, W.Va. State Bar Assn., Boston Athenaeum, Univ. Club (Wichita Falls), Harvard Club (France, Boston), Am. Club Paris, Cercle de L'Union Interalliée (Paris), Phi Beta Kappa. Home: 2100 Santa Fe #903 Wichita Falls TX 76309 Office: 1111 City National Bldg Wichita Falls TX 76301-3309

DICKINSON, WENDY ARMOUR, pension specialist; b. Meadville, Pa., July 20, 1957; d. Edwin Robert and Marilyn Alice (Kohler) Armour; m. Franklin Shivery Dickinson, Sept. 8, 1979. BS in Math., Westminster Coll., 1979. Revenue requirements analyst Gen. Telephone Ohio, Marion, 1979; teller Hill Fin., Harrisburg, Pa., 1979-80; tchr. bus. adminstrn. Thompson Inst., Harrisburg, 1980-81; employment counselor Scranton, Pa., 1981-82; office mgr. Tall trees Apts., Scranton, 1982-83, Pocal Industries, Moscow, Pa., 1983; pension technician Fin. Planning Assocs., Camp Hill, Pa., 1983-86; pension adminstr. New England Fin. Group, Harrisburg, 1986—. Mem. AAUW (Harrisburg branch dues treas. 1986-88, pres.-elect 1988-89, pres. 1989-90, bd. dirs. Pa. div., co-chair pub. policy 1990—), Delta Zeta (pres. Harrisburg alumnae 1985-89). Republican. Methodist. Home: llll Pheasant Dr N Carlisle PA 17013 Office: New Eng Fin Group 2213 Forest Hills Dr Harrisburg PA 17112

DICKINSON-MCDONALD, VICTORIA ANN, visual arts administrator; b. Phila., Oct. 3, 1951; d. Paul Oliver Jr. and Eleanor Louisa (Briscoe) D.; m. Willis C. McDonald, Apr. 22, 1989; 1 child, Geoffrey Lloyd. BA, U. Del., 1974; MA, NYU, 1988. Bus. mgmt. cons. Charles Colombo, Artist, Wilmington, Del., 1984-86, Susan Isaacs Gallery, Wilmington, 1987-88, Station Gallery, Wilmington, 1987, M. Knoedler & Co., N.Y.C., 1987, Jean Davidson, Artist, N.Y.C., 1987—, Melita Brecher, Sculptor, Bar Harbor, Maine, 1988—, Francis Hamabe, Artist, Blue Hill, Maine, 1985—, Joan Julien Grant, Sculptor, L.A., 1990; cons. Sharpe Gallery, N.Y.C., 1987. Episcopalian. Office: Dickinson-McDonald Art Mktg Ltd 1817-A Morgan Ln Redondo Beach CA 90278

DICKISON, CAROLYN HOPE CARPENTER, teacher; b. Fountain City, Tenn., May 5, 1933; d. Edward Leroy and Bessie Belle (Starr) Carpenter; m. Donald Roy Dickison, Aug. 17, 1957 (div. Feb. 1964). BA, Aurora (Ill.) U., 1955; MA, U. R.I., 1967. Cert. tchr., Ill. Tchr. E. Aurora Pub. Schs., 1955-56; tchr. S. Kingstown Pub. Schs., Wakefield, R.I., 1956%, prin., 1961-64; dir. sch. play S. Road Sch., S. Kingstown, 1964—; presentor teaching techniques U. R.I., Kingston. Mem. R.I. State Championship softball team, 1960-73; co-founder, organizer, umpire Softball Leagues, South Kingstown, 1981, player on 1st state championship team, 1964; sec. for Tuckertown Pk. Com., South Kingstown, 1984-86; nat. and state women and girls' basketball referee for high schs. and colls.; first woman umpire for men's softball; commr. South Kingstown Recreation and Pks. Commn., 1982-88, chairperson, 1986, 87; past supt. Sunday sch., chmn. bd., youth leader, past pres. R.I. and Mass. youth group, pianist Bible tchr. Rocky Brook Advent Christian Ch. Mem. NEA, S. Kingstown Tchrs. Assn. (bldg. rep., exec. bd.), Nat. Recreation and Pks. (commn. bd. dirs. 1984-88, rep. citizens bd. 1984-88), Winnapaug Country Club. Republican. Home: 37 Sweet Fern Ln Peace Dale RI 02883 Office: South Rd Elem Sch 1157 South Road Peace Dale RI 02879

DICKS, JOYCE CAROLEE, adult education administrator; b. Centerville, Iowa, Mar. 21, 1936; d. Max Arlee and Laura Jean (Oehler) Martin; m. Donald Dean Dicks, May 5, 1955; children: Stephanie Lynn Dicks Hall, Dawn Michelle. AA in Social Sci., Ohlone Coll., Fremont, Calif., 1978; BA in History, Calif. State U., Hayward, 1980, MA, 1984; Adminstrv. credential, San Jose State U., 1987. Instrnl. aide GATE program Fremont Unified Schs., 1972-77; instr. social scis. Fremont Adult Edn., 1980-88; instr. history Ohlone Coll., 1982—, DeAnza Coll., Cupertino, Calif., 1986-88; asst. dir. East Side Adult Edn. Program, San Jose, Calif., 1988—; lectr. Ottawa (Kans.) U., 1979-80; cons. Calif. Adult Schs. Assessment System Task Force, Sacramento, 1987—. Founding editor The Student Historian, Calif. State U., 1981; reviewer The Pacific Historian mag., Stockton, Calif., 1984—; author, narrator several video study programs. Active Fremont PTA, 1970-76; founding pres. Parents of Gifted Children, Fremont, 1975; charter mem. Ohlone Coll. Mus. Com., 1978—. Mem. Assn. Calif. Sch. Adminstrs., Calif. Council for Adult Edn., Orgn. Am. Historians, Inst. Hist. Study, Washington Twp. (Calif.) Hist. Soc. Home: 4641 Boone Dr Fremont CA 94538 Office: East Side Adult Edn Program 625 Educational Park Dr San Jose CA 95133

DICKSON, CAROL JEAN, clinical pharmacist; b. Oswego, N.Y., Oct. 14, 1955; d. James Gordon and Mabel Luella (Stevens) D. BA in Zoology, SUNY, Oswego, 1977; BS in Pharmacy, Albany Coll. Pharmacy, 1981; PharmD, SUNY, Buffalo, 1983. Registered pharmacist, N.Y., Mass. Resident Imogene Bassett Hosp., Cooperstown, N.Y., 1983-84; asst. prof. U. R.I. Coll. Pharmacy, Kingston, 1984-85, Albany (N.Y.) Coll. Pharmacy, 1985-87; sr. asst. clin. sci. Parke-Davis Pharms. Co., Ann Arbor, Mich., 1987-88; clin. pharmacist Baystate Med. Ctr., Springfield, Mass., 1988—; cons. Hospice of R.I., Providence, 1984-85, VA Palliative Care, Albany, N.Y., 1985-87, Long Term Care-Hospice, Springfield, Mass., 1988—. Contbr. articles to profl. jours. Profl. edn. pharmacy subcom. Am. Cancer Soc., Albany, N.Y., 1986-87. Mem. Am. Soc. Clin. Oncology, Am. Soc. Hosp. Pharmacists, Am. Coll. Clin. Pharmacy, Am. Soc. Cons. Pharmacists, Keith Clan Soc., Rho Chi. Methodist. Office: Baystate Med Ctr Pharmacy 759 Chestnut St Springfield MA 01199

DICKSON, CAROL WARD, training and development administrator; b. Radford, Va., Dec. 27, 1951; d. George Truman and Margaret Ann (Hall) Ward; m. Brian Douglas Dickson, Apr. 28, 1984; children: Christopher Ward, Joshua Ryan. BA in English, Wake Forest U., 1972; MBA, Frostburg State Coll., 1985. Rep. customer service Tektronix, Inc., Blue Bell, Pa., 1973-74, supr. support services, 1974-79; staff asst. to regional mgr. Gaithersburg, Md., 1979-80, specialist mgmt. devel. tng., 1980-84; tng. adminstr. Fairchild Space Co., Germantown, Md., 1984, supr. mgmt. devel. and tng., 1984-88, mgr. tng. and devel., 1988—. Mem. Am. Soc. Tng. and Devel., AAUW, Frederick Personnel Assn., Nat. Mgmt. Assn. (v.p. ops. 1989—), Toastmasters (pres., sec.-treas. NUS chpt., founder Fairchild chpt. 1986, pres. 1986—, Competent Toastmaster award 1986, Area Pres. of Yr. 1986-87). Republican. Baptist. Club: Toastmasters (pres., sec.-treas. NUS chpt., founder Fairchild chpt. 1986, pres. 1986—; Competent Toastmaster award 1986, named Area Pres. of Yr. 1986-87). Home: 301 W College Terr Frederick MD 21701 Office: Fairchild Space Co 20301 Century Blvd Germantown MD 20874

DICKSON, EVA MAE, credit bureau executive; b. Clarion, Iowa, Jan. 16, 1922; d. James and Ivah Blanche (Breckenridge) D. Grad. Interstate Bus. Coll., Klamath Falls, Oreg., 1943. Reporter, Mchts. Credit Service, Klamath Falls, 1941; credit dept. Montgomery Ward, Klamath Falls, 1941-42; bookkeeper Heilbronner Fuel Co., Klamath Falls, 1942; stenographer City of Klamath Falls, 1943, bookkeeper, office mgr., 1943-52; owner, operator All Star Bus. Service, Klamath Falls, 1953-58, Ace Mimeo Service, Klamath Falls, 1958-73; mgr. Mchts. Credit Service, 1973-87; customer service rep. CBI/Credit N.W., 1987—. Bd. dirs. United Way, Klamath Falls, 1980—; sec. Klamath Community Concert Assn., 1956—; treas., memls. chmn. Klamath County chpt. Am. Cancer Soc.; bd. dirs., treas. Hope in Crisis; mem. Klamath County Centennial Com., 1982, Unification for Progress Joint Planning Com., 1985; mem. nursing adv. com. Oreg. Inst. Tech., 1982—; mem. Klamath Employment Tng. Adv. Com., 1983-86; bd. dirs., sec., treas. Klamath Consumer Council; sec. Unified City for Progress Task Force, 1983-84, Snowflake Winter Festival, 1984—. Recipient Bronze Leadership award Assoc. Credit Burs., Inc., 1976. Mem. Consumer Credit Assn. Oreg. (pres. 1984-85), Credit Women Internat. (treas. dist. 10 1984-85, 2d v.p. dist. 10 1987-88, 1st v.p. 1988-89, pres. 1989-90), Assoc. Credit Bur. Pacific N.W. (pres. 1981-82), Assoc. Credit Bur. Oreg. (pres. 1978-80), Klamath Basin Credit Women-Internat. (pres. 1976-78), Soc. Cert. Consumer Credit Exec., Internat. Consumer Credit Assn., Klamath County C. of C. (pres. 1979, ambassadors com. 1980—0, Nat. Fedn. Bus. and Profl. Women's Club (chmn. nat. fin. com. 1983-84, nat. fin. com. 1982-83), Oreg. Fedn. Bus. and Profl. Women's Club (state pres. 1971-72), Klamath Falls Bus. and Profl. Women's Club (pres. 1966-67, 76-77), DAR (past regent local chpt.). Republican. Presbyterian. Club: Quota (pres. 1958-59, dist. gov. 1969-70). Avocations: painting, traveling.

DICKSON, PHYLLIS WEBSTER, retired travel agency owner; b. Elgin, Ill., Dec. 29, 1926; d. Edwin Herbert and Pauline (Kennedy) Webster; children: Pamela, Deborah, Daniel, Brian. BA, UCLA, 1947. Cert. travel counselor. Travel agt. One Stop Travel, Santa Barbara, Calif., 1981-89. Mem. Bus. and Profl. Women, Santa Barbara Women's Club (program chmn.), Assistance League (tour chmn., 2d v.p.). Republican. Home: 334 E Padre St Santa Barbara CA 93105

DICKSON-PORTER, CLAUDIA BLAIR, librarian; b. Memphis, Oct. 22, 1925; d. Walton Avery and Annie Laurie (Tate) Tucker; B.S., U. Nebr., Omaha, 1964; M.L.S., N. Tex. State U., Denton, 1971, Ph.D., 1979; m. Benjamin A. Dickson, June 5, 1945 (div.); children: Susan Dickson Morrison, Andrea Dickson Darby, Donna Dickson Stephens, Reid W., Bryan A.; m. 2d, William G. Porter, Feb. 8, 1978. Tchrs. schs. in Nebr. and Hawaii, 1964-71; librarian Nat. Assn. Retarded Citizens, Arlington, Tex., from 1971;

dir. Regional Office TAS VI, Research and Tng Center in Mental Retardation Tex. Tech. U.; dir. planning Tex. Planning Council for Devel. Disabilities, Tex. Dept. Mental Health/Mental Retardation, 1979-80; program specialist Office of Devel. Disabilities, Office of Human Devel., Fed. Region VI, Dallas, 1980-82, grants mgmt. specialist Office of Fiscal Ops., 1982-83; Head Start Community rep. Adminstrn. for Children, Youth and Families, 1983-84; program specialist So. Region Adminstrn. on Developmental Disabilities, Fed. Region VI, 1984—; tchr. community services courses El Centro Jr. Coll., Dallas. Recipient Disting. Alumnus award North Tex. State U., 1984, Regional Leadership award HHS. Mem. Spl. Libraries Assn., Southwestern, Tex. library assns., Am. Assn. Mental Deficiency, Council Exceptional Children, Soc. S.W. Archivists, Local History Soc., Phi Delta Kappa. Author, compiler in field. Home: 2413 Lakeside Dr Arlington TX 76013 Office: 1200 Main Tower Dallas TX 75202

DIDIER, MICHELLE ANN, computer programmer. BS, BA, U. Toledo, 1977; MA, Bowling Green State U., 1983. Supr. documentation and tng. The Calvert Group, Bethesda, Md., 1987-88, programmer, analyst, 1988—; instr. U. Md. Univ. Coll., College Park, 1988—, U.S. Dept. Agr. Grad. Sch., Washington, 1988—. Author numerous user guides and other documentation. Recipient Disting. Tech. Communication award Tech. Pubs. Competition, Washington, 1988. Mem. NAFE, Am. Med. Writers Assn., Soc. Tech. Communications (past chpt. pres., newsletter editor, award of merit 1986, award of excellence 1987), Assn. Women in Computing, Washington Ind. Writers.

DIDION, JOAN, author; b. Sacramento, Calif., Dec. 4, 1934; d. Frank Reese and Eduene (Jerrett) D.; m. John Gregory Dunne, Jan. 30, 1964; 1 child, Quintana Roo. B.A.., U. Calif.,, Berkeley,, 1956. Assoc. feature editor Vogue mag.,, 1956-63; former columnist Saturday Evening Post, Life, Esquire; now contbr. The N.Y. Rev. of Books, The New Yorker. Novels include: Run River, 1963, Play It As It Lays, 1970, A Book of Common Prayer, 1977, Democracy, 1984; books of essays: Slouching Towards Bethlehem, 1968, The White Album, 1979; non-fiction Salvador, 1983, Miami, 1987; co-author: (with John Gregory Dunne) screenplays for films The Panic in Needle Park, 1971, Play It As It Lays, 1972, A Star Is Born, 1976, True Confessions, 1981. Recipient 1st prize Vogue's Prix de Paris, 1956, Morton Dauwen Zabel prize AAAL, 1978. Mem. Am. Inst. Arts and Letters, Am. Acad. Arts and Scis. Office: care Simon & Schuster 1230 Ave of the Americas New York NY 10020*

DIDRICKSON, LOLETA ANDERSON, state legislator; b. Chgo., May 22, 1941; d. J. Henning and Ruth (Anderson) Anderson; m. Charles E. Didrickson, June 17, 1961; children: Abby, Charles E. Jr., John. Student U. Ill., 1958-61; BA, Governors State U., 1974. Legis. aide state senator 1979-82; gen. mgr. Titan Jack Mfg., Chicago Heights, 1981-82; mem. Ill. Ho. of Reps., 1982—; minority spokesperson labor and commerce com.; mem. elem. and secondary edn., elections and ins. coms.; mem. select com. on housing, Ill. adv. coun. Alcohol and Substance Abuse; appointee Legis. Research Unit. Mem. Jr. League Am.; pres. Homewood-Flossmoor (Ill.) High Sch. Parents Bd., 1981; Chicago Heights, 1982-83; mem. Ill. Dangerous Drugs Adv. Council, Chgo., 1985—; bd. dirs. Y-Me Breast Cancer Orgn., Homewood, Ill., 1984—, Ingall's Meml. Hosp., South Suburban Focus Coun., Operation Snowball Region II, Cook County Bd. Nat. Rep. Women; alt. del.-at-large Rep. nat. conv., 1984; mem. adv. bd. South Suburban Family Shelter, Matteson; chairperson Ill. Elected Officials for Reagan-Bush, 1984; pres. Rich Twp. Rep. Women's Club, 1987-89. Recipient Friend of Edn. award Ill. State Bd. Edn., 1985, Treasure award South Suburban Focus Council, 1986, Outstanding Citizen awrd South Suburan Assn. Commerce and Industry, 1987, Legislator of Yr., Ill. Nurses Assn., 1987, Women of Achievement award, Women in Mgmt., 1987. Mem. Taylor Inst., South Suburban Assn. Commerce, LWV. Home: 1111 Brassie Ave Flossmoor IL 60422 Office: 2023 Ridge Rd Ste 2NW Homewood IL 60430

DIE, ANN MARIE HAYES, psychologist, educator; b. Baytown, Tex., Aug. 15, 1944; d. Robert L. and Dorothy Ann (Cooke) Hayes; m. Jerome Glynn Die, June 5, 1971; 1 child, Meredith Anne. BS with highest honors, Lamar U., 1966; MEd, U. Houston, 1969; PhD, Tex. A&M U., 1977. Lic. psychologist. Asst. prof. dept. psychology Lamar U., Beaumont, Tex., 1977-82, assoc. prof., dir. Psychol. Clinic, 1982-86, dir. grad. programs in psychology, 1981-86, Regents prof. psychology, 1986, pres. faculty senate, 1985-86; pvt. practice clin. psychology Beaumont, 1979-87; prof. Tulane U., New Orleans, 1988—, dean Newcomb Coll., 1988—; adminstr. adolescent residential unit Mental Health/Mental Retardation of S.E. Tex., 1979-80; cons. in field; coordinating bd. Tex. Coll. and Univ. System Internship, 1986. Contbr. articles to profl. jours. Active community adv. com. Beaumont State Ctr. Human Devel., 1981-88, Mental Health/Mental Retardation S.E. Tex., 1981-87; participant Nat. Identification Program for Women, Am. Coun. on Edn., 1985; bd. dirs. Beaumont Civic Opera, Lamar U. Meth. Student Ctr. Fellow Coll. William and Mary, 1986-87; recipient Regents Merit award, 1979, Coll. Health and Behavioral Sci. Merit award, 1982. Fellow Am. Coun. on Edn.; mem. Am. Psychol. Assn., Southwestern Psychol. Assn., Family Svcs. Assn. (bd. dirs. 1988-89), Tex. Psychol. Assn. (dir. div. of psychologists 1986), SE Tex. Psychol. Assn. (treas. 1978-79, 79-80, pres. 1983), Tex. Coun. Family Rels., Nat. Coun. Family Rels., Mental Health Assn. Jefferson County, Nat. Register Health Svc. Providers in Psychology, Beaumont Art Mus. Methodist. Home: 43 Newcomb Pl New Orleans LA 70118 Office: Tulane U Newcomb Coll 108 Newcomb Hall New Orleans LA 70118

DIEDERICH, SISTER ANNE MARIE, college president; b. Cleve., Apr. 8, 1943. BA in English, Ursuline Coll. for Women, 1966; MA in Ednl. Adminstrn., John Carroll U., 1975; PhDin Edn. Policy and Leadership, Ohio State U., 1988. Joined Order St. Ursula, Roman Cath. Ch., 1961. Tchr. Villa Angela Acad., Cleve., 1966-70, asst. prin., 1971-76, prin., 1976-82; tchr. Beaumont Sch. for Girls, 1982-84; pres. Ursuline Coll., Pepper Pike, Ohio, 1986—. Mem. Leadership Cleve. '89. Dan H. Eikenberry scholar Ohio State U., 1985; William R. and Marie A. Flesher fellow Ohio State U., 1986. Mem. Ohio Tchr. Edn. and Adv. Commn., Phi Kappa Phi. Office: Ursuline Coll 2550 Lander Rd Cleveland OH 44124

DIEDERICHS, JANET WOOD, public relations executive; b. Libertyville, Ill.; d. J. Howard and Ruth (Hendrickson) Wood; m. John Kustings Diederichs, 1953. BA, Wellesley Coll., 1950; Sales agt. Pan Am. Airways, Chgo., 1951-52; regional mgr. pub. relations Braniff Internat., Chgo., 1953-69; pres. Janet Diederichs & Assocs., Inc., pub. relations cons., Chgo., 1970—; lectr. Harvard U.; mem. exec. com. World Trade Conf., 1983, 84. Com. mem. Nat. Trust for Historic Preservation, 1975-79, Marshall Scholars (Brit. Govt.), 1975-79; trustee Northwestern Meml. Hosp., 1985—; bd. dirs., mem. exec. com. Chgo. Conv. and Visitors Bur. 1978-87; bd. dirs. Internat. House, U. Chgo., 1978-84, Com. of 200, 1982-84, Latino Inst., 1986-89, Chgo. Network, 1987—; com. mem. Art Inst. Chgo., 1980-83; mem. exec. com. Vatican Art Council Chgo., 1981-83; pres. Jr. League Chgo., 1968-69. Mem. Nat. Acad. TV Arts and Scis., Soc. Am. Travel Writers, Chgo. Assn. Commerce and Industry (bd. dirs. 1982-89, exec. com. 1985-88), Pub. Relations Soc. Am., Pub. Relations Exch., Publicity Club Chgo., Chgo. Network, Econ. Club, Mid-Am. Club (dir. local chpt. 1977-79), Woman's Athletic Club of Chgo., Comml. Club of Chgo. Office: Janet Diederichs & Assocs 333 N Michigan Ave Chicago IL 60601

DIEHL, LESLEY ANN, psychologist; b. Oregon, Apr. 9, 1943; d. John Eldon and Lois Evelyn (Merryman) Diehl. BA, Cen Coll., 1965; MA, U. S. D., 1966; PhD, U. Ga., 1971. Lic. psychologist;. Cons. psychologist Head Start, Athens, Ga., 1968; instr. psychology Augustana Coll., Sioux Falls, S.D., 1966-67; asst. prof. psychology SUNY, Oneonta, 1970-83, assoc. prof. psychology, 1983-88, prof. pschology, 1988—; asst. dean liberal studies SUNY, 1989—; coord. women's studies program SUNY. Contbr. articles to profl. jours. Mem. Aid to Battered Women, Oneonta, 1978. Mem. Am. Psychol. Assn., Assn. Women in Psychology, Sigma Xi, Phi Kappa Phi. Home: RD 1 Box 1322 Maryland NY 12116 Office: SUNY Dept Psychology Oneonta NY 13820

DIEHL-CALLAWAY, LINDA JO, secretarial services company executive; b. Chgo., Dec. 1, 1955; d. Richard Eugene and Dolores Lillian (Domres) Diehl; m. Joseph W. Trybulec, Jr., June 1981 (div. Dec. 1983); m. Lloyd Callaway, Jr., Aug. 29, 1987. BA in Spanish and Linguistics summa cum laude, Northeastern Ill. U., 1983—. Asst. personal banker Continental Bank, Chgo., 1976-77, personal banker, 1977-80; sec. Ravenswood Hosp., Chgo., 1980-82, exec. sec., 1982-84; adminstrv. asst. United Blood Svcs., Chgo., 1984-85; owner, operator Abecedarius, Barrington, Ill., 1985—. Mem. Nat. Assn. Secretarial Svcs., Profl. Assn. Secretarial Svcs., Barrington Area C. of C. Home and Office: 106 N Lake Shore Dr Barrington IL 60010

DIENER, BETTY JANE, marketing educator, former university administrator; b. Washington, Sept. 15, 1940; d. Edward George and Minnie (Feild) D. AB, Wellesley Coll., 1962; MBA, Harvard U., 1964, DBA, 1974. Account exec. Young & Rubicam, Inc., N.Y.C., 1964-70; product mgr. Am. Cyanamid Co., Wayne, N.J., 1970-72; asst. dean, Sch. Bus. Case Western Res. U., Cleve., 1974-79; dean Sch. Bus. Adminstrn., Old Dominion U., Norfolk, Va., 1979-82; sec. commerce and resources Commonwealth of Va., Richmond, 1982-86; prof. mktg. Old Dominion U., Norfolk, Va., 1986-87; provost, vice chancellor acad. affairs U. Mass., Boston, 1987-88, prof. mktg., 1988—. Contbr. articles to profl. publs. Commr. Norfolk Indsl. Devel. Authority, 1979-82; mem. Citizens Coun. for Chesapeake Bay, 1986-87; bd. dirs. Norfolk Conv. and Visitors Bur., 1979-82, Norfolk C. of C., 1979-82, Greater Norfolk Corp., 1986-87, Va. Orch. Group, 1982-87, Va. Stage Co., 1986-87, Karamu House, 1975-79, Womenspace, 1975-79, Rapid Recovery, 1975-79, Woodruff Hosp., 1975-79, Women's City Club Cleve., 1976-79; adviser Jr. Achievement, 1963-64, Plans for Progress, 1968-70, Leadership Met. Richmond, 1980-82; adv. com. on state and local govt. programs John F. Kennedy Sch. Govt., Harvard U., 1986-88; mem. Mass. gov.'s adv. com. on sci. and tech., 1988—. Named Outstanding Working Woman, Glamour Mag., 1979, one of 10 Outstanding Career Women of Decade, Glamour Mag., 1984; recipient Honor award Soil Conservation Soc., 1984. Democrat. Home: 2001 Marina Dr #408W North Quincy MA 02171 Office: U Mass at Boston Harbor Campus Boston MA 02125

DIENST, EVELYN (RICKI DIENST), psychologist, educator; b. Bklyn., Oct. 18, 1943; d. Louis A. and Ann B. (Hein) D.; m. Robert W. Moulton, Aug. 15, 1973. Student, U. Fla., 1961; BA, Bklyn. Coll., 1965; MA, U. Calif., Berkeley, 1966; PhD, U. Calif., 1971. Asst. rsch. psychologist U. Calif., Berkeley, 1966-72; postdoctoral fellow Dept. Psychology U. Calif., 1971-73, asst. clin. prof. Sch. of Medicine, 1975—; psychology trainee VA Hosp., San Francisco, 1972-73; pres./prin. cons. Organizational Data, Alameda, Calif., 1985—; prof. Calif. Sch. Profl. Psychology, Berkeley/Alameda, 1982—; cons./dir. counseling Calif. Coll. Podiatric Medicine, San Francisco, 1984—; consulting psychologist Cancer Support Community, San Francisco, 1989—. Author: College Professors and Their Impact on Students, 1973; contbr. articles profl. jours. Recipient scholarship N.Y. Bd. Regents, 1962-65. Mem. Am. Psychol. Assn. Jewish. Home: 535 Spruce St Berkeley CA 94707 Office: Calif Sch Profl Psychology 1005 Atlantic Ave Alameda CA 94501

DIERAUF, LESLIE ANN, veterinarian, consultant; b. Boston, Feb. 7, 1948; d. Curtis John and Adeline M. (Kirk) D. BS in Microbiology, English cum laude, U. Mass., 1970; VMD, U. Pa., 1974; postdoctoral, U. Calif., Davis, 1974-77. Lic. vet. Calif., Nev., N.Y., Vt.; cert. community coll. tchr., Calif. Instr. physiology U. Calif., Davis, 1976-77; staff vet. Elk Grove (Calif.) Vet. Clinic, 1977, Midtown Animal Hosp., Sacramento, 1978-79, Marin County Vet. Emergency Clinic, San Rafael, Calif., 1979-87; independent cons., 1988—; staff vet. Calif. Marine Mammal Ctr., Ft. Cronkhite, 1979-82, dir. vet. services, 1982-84, bd. sci. advisors, 1984—; instr. animal health tech. Western Sch. Allied Health Professions, Sacramento, 1977-79; cons. Marine Mammal Cons. Services, Novato, Calif., 1985—; cons. Naval Ocean Systems Ctr., 1984—, Calif. Marine Mammal Ctr., 1984—, Pribilof Island Fur Seal Program, 1981-84, San Francisco Zoo, 1979-84, Calif. State U., Hayward, 1979-84, ; bd. sci. advisors West Quoddy Marine Research Sta., Lubec, Maine, 1979—; bd. examiners Calif. Dept. Consumer Affairs, 1978-85. Editor: Handbook of Marine Mammal Medicine: Health, Disease and Rehabilitation, 1989; mem. editorial bd. Diseases of Aquatic Organisms, 1985—; contbr. articles to profl. jours. Mem. com. to Save Squaw Valley Meadow; dir. Calif. Marine Mammal Ctr. Run for Seals; mem. Wildlife Care Assn., Sacramento, Sacramento Jr. Sci. Mus., Sacramento Community Orch., Sacramento Intramural Softball and Volleyball; vol. Belchertown State Hosp., Vet. Assistance, Nicaragua, 1988, Pakistan, 1989. Recipient Erickson Ednl. Found. award 1982-83; Thouron scholar U. Pa., 1974, U. Pa. scholar 1970-73; U. Calif., Davis grantee 1974-76; U. Calif. fellow, 1974-75, Teaching fellow U. Calif., 1975-77. Mem. AVMA (editorial asst. 1986, Congl. fellow 1990-91), Calif. Vet. Med. Assn. (editorial asst. 1988—), Internat. Assn. Aquatic Animal Medicine (pres. 1986-87, chair sci. govt. laiason com. 1989—), Soc. Marine Mammalogy, Am. Assn. Wildlife Vets., Am. Animal Hosp. Assn., Am. Assn. Avian Vets., Women's Vet. Med. Assn., Sierra Nev. Vet. Med. Assn., Wildflife Disease Assn., Calif. Vet. Med. Assn., Am. Assn. Vet. Immunology, Calif. Acad. Scis., Calif. Marine Mammal Ctr., Friends of Sea Otter. Democrat. Episcopalian. Home and Office: PO Box 2925 Olympic Valley CA 95730

DIERSEN, KAREN ANNETTE, corporate secretary; b. Chgo., Dec. 2, 1950; d/ Franklin Paul and Maria Eleanor (Ruhl) Gassner; m. David John Diersen, Apr. 1, 1978. BS in Fin., DePaul U., 1986. Stenographer FBI, Chgo., 1968-70; sec. U.S. League of Savs. Instns., Chgo., 1970-71; exec. sec. U.S. League of Savs. Instns., 1971-75, adminstrv. asst., 1975-80, corp. sec., 1980—. Mem. AAUW (sec. 1988-90, treas. 1990— Wheaton-Glen Ellyn Ill. br.), Am. Soc. Corp. Secs., Am. Mgmt. Assn., Assn. of Records Mgrs. and Adminstrs., NAFE. Republican. Roman Catholic. Home: 915 Cove Ct Wheaton IL 60187

DIESTELKAMP, DAWN LEA, laboratory data processing specialist; b. Fresno, Calif., Apr. 23, 1954; d. Don and Joy LaVaughn (Davis) Diestelkamp. B.S. in Microbiology, Calif. State U.-Fresno, 1976, M.S. in Pub. Adminstrn., 1983. Lic. clin. lab. technologist, Calif.; cert. clin. lab. dir. Clin. lab. technologist Valley Med. Ctr., Fresno, Calif., 1977-82, quality control coordinator, 1983-84; cons., instr. in field. Mem. Nat. Assn. Female Execs. Democrat. Office: 445 S Cedar Ave Fresno CA 93702

DIETER, ALICE HUNT, journalist; b. Denver, Apr. 16, 1928; d. Thomas Addison and Alice (McCullough) Hunt; BA cum laude in English Lang., U. Colo., 1949; m. Leslie Louis Dieter, Sept. 10, 1948; children: Alice Dieter Crowley-Mize, Philip Leslie, Paul Wesley. Columnist, reporter, feature writer Intermountain Observer, Boise, Idaho, 1962-72, asst. editor, 1965-72, also TV news reporter Sta. KBOI, and news librarian, 1966-73; stringer Newsweek mag., 1970-73; editorial assoc. corp. communications Boise Cascade Corp., 1973-83; ret., 1983; weekly editorial columnist Idaho Daily Statesman, 1977-85. Chair, Idaho Assn. Humanities, 1972-78; bd. dirs. Idaho Farm Workers Svcs., Inc., 1963-69, pres., 1965-69; bd. dirs. "Friends of Four" (pub. TV sta. KAIO), 1988—; mem. Boise Com. Fgn. Rels.s, 1975—; mem. Idaho Gov.'s Commn. on Excellence in Edn., 1983; mem. Idaho Selection Com. for Rhodes Scholars, 1983-84; pres. Boise LWV, 1957-59; Idaho rep. UNICEF, 1963-65; mem. Boise Valley World Affairs Assn., 1956-65; mem. Boise City Park Bd., 1964-79; co-chair Idaho Johnson for Pres., 1964, Citizens for Andrus for Gov., 1966; del. Women's Conf., Houston, 1978; active YWCA, St. Michael's Episc. Parish, Boise Philharm., Friends of Boise Library, Idaho Hist. Soc. Recipient Idaho Press awards for feature writing and news photography, 1967, for gen. interest column, 1983. Mem. Idaho Press Club (bd. dirs.), Phi Beta Kappa. Home: 1147 Santa Maria Dr Boise ID 83712

DIETRICH, MARTHA JANE (MARTHA JANE SHULTZ), genealogist; b. Brazil, Ind., Aug. 19, 1916; d. Charles Russell and Florence Delilah (McIntire) Shultz; grad. Ind. State U.; m. E(arl) Donald Dietrich, June 17, 1939; children: Florence Ann Dietrich Harris, Jean Carol Dietrich Litterst, Charles Donald. Clk., CSC, Washington, 1937-43; personnel officer Armed Forces Med. Library, Washington, 1948-54; personnel staffing specialist Navy Dept., Washington, 1954-70, ret., 1970; prof. free lance genealogist, College Park, Md., 1970—. Cert. Am. lineage specialist; authorized Bd. Cert. of Genealogists, Washington. Mem. Ky. Hist. Soc. (life), Ind. Hist. Soc., Clay County (Ind.) Geneal. Soc. (life), Somerset County (Pa.) Geneal. Soc. (life), Geneal. Soc. Pa., DAR, Nat. Officers Club (bd. dirs. Eastern region 1988-90), DAR, (state registrar 1973-76, state vice regent 1976-79), Md. DAR (state regent 1979-82, hon. state regent 1982—), Md. State DAR Officers Club, Colonial Dames XVII Century Nat. Officers Club (registrar gen. 1974-79), Daus. Am. Colonists (state chmn. 1977-79), Daus. Colonial Wars, UDC (2d v.p. gen. 1988—), Daus. of 1812, Sons and Daus. of Pilgrims (lt. gov. Md. br. 1988—), Magna Charta Dames, Order Crown of Charlemagne (registrar gen. 1983-86, hon. registrar gen. life 1986), Soc. Ind. Pioneers (life), Order Ky. Cols., Clan MacIntyre Assn. (genealogist 1978-84), Daus. Barons of Runnymede, Colonial Dames XVII Century (state pres. D.C. state soc. 1975-77, acting registrar gen. 1974-75, registrar gen. 1975-79, service awards 1977, 78), Soc. Ky. Pioneers, Colonial Daus. Seventeenth Century, Flagon and Trencher (life), Hereditary Order Descendants Twin Territories (life), Kappa Kappa, Kappa Kappa Kappa (Ind.). Episcopalian. Home and Office: 4616 Guilford Rd College Park MD 20740

DIETRICH, RENÉE LONG, educational administrator; b. Emerald, Pa., Oct. 10, 1937; d. Emmett A. and Arlene I. (Fenstermaker) Long; m. Bruce L. Dietrich, Nov. 25, 1959; children: Dodson, Katie. BS, Kutztown (Pa.) U., 1959; MLS, Rutgers U., 1966. Tchr. history Reading (Pa.) Pub. Schs., 1959-65, librarian, 1965-69; coordinator coop. edn. Reading (Pa.) Area Community Coll., 1978-81, program adminstr. title III grant, 1982—, coordinator community and legis. relations, 1983—; exec. dir. Found. for Reading (Pa.) Area Community Coll., 1986—; cons. California U. of Pa., California, Pa., 1987—, Pa. Power and Light Co., Allentown, 1981—, U.S. Office of Edn., Washington, 1990—; coordinator Berks County Women's Conf., Reading, 1980. Contbr. articles to profl. jours. Bd. dirs. Kutztown U. Found., 1981; chmn. bd. trustees Kutztown U., 1976-81; mem. LWV, host-moderator "LWV Presents..." TV talk show. Recipient Disting. Alumni award, Kutztown U., 1981. Mem. AAUW, Council for Support and Advancement of Edn., Coll.-Univ. Pub. Relations Assn. Pa., Nat. Soc. Fundraising Execs., Delta Kappa Gamma (hon. edn. soc.). Mem. United Ch. of Christ. Home: 1546 Dauphin Ave Wyomissing PA 19610 Office: Reading Area Community Coll 10 S 2d St Box 1706 Reading PA 19603

DIETRICH, SUZANNE CLAIRE, instructional designer; b. Granite City, Ill., Apr. 9, 1937; d. Charles Daniel and Evelyn Blanche (Waters) D.; B.S. in Speech, Northwestern U., 1958; M.S. in Pub. Communication, Boston U., 1967; postgrad. So. Ill. U., 1973—. Intern, prodn. staff Sta. WGBH-TV, Boston, 1958-59, asst. dir., 1962-64, asst. dir. program Invitation to Art, 1958; cons. producer dir. dept. instructional TV radio Ill. Office Supt. Pub. Instruction, Springfield, 1969-70; dir. program prodn. and distbn., 1970-72; instr. faculty call staff, speech dept. Sch. Fine Arts So. Ill. U., Edwardsville, 1972—, grad. asst. for doctoral program office of dean Sch. Edn., 1975-78; research asst. Ill. public telecommunications study for Ill. Public Broadcasting Council, 1979-80; cons. and research in communications, 1980—; exec. producer, dir. TV programs Con-Con Countdown, 1970, The Flag Speaks, 1971. Roman Catholic. Home: 1011 Minnesota Ave Edwardsville IL 62025

DIETZ, JANIS CAMILLE, manufacturing company executive; b. Washington, May 26, 1950; d. Albert and Joan Mildred (MacMullen) Weinstein; m. John William Dietz, Apr. 10, 1981. BA, U. R.I., 1971; MBA, Calif. Poly. U., Pomona, 1984. Customer service trainer People's Bank, Providence, 1974-76; salesman, food broker Bradshaw Co., Los Angeles, 1976-78; salesman Johnson & Johnson, Los Angeles, 1978-79, Gen. Electric Co., Los Angeles, 1979-82; regional sales mgr. Leviton Co., Los Angeles, 1982-85; nat. sales mgr. Jensen Gen. div. Nortek Co., Los Angeles, 1985-86; retail sales mgr. Norris div. Masco, Los Angeles, 1986-88; nat. sales mgr. Thermador Waste King div. Masco, Los Angeles, 1988—; sales trainer, Upland, Calif., 1985—; instr. Calif. Poly. U., 1988—. Dir. pub. relations Jr. Achievement, Providence, 1975-76. Recipient Sector Service award Gen. Electric Co., Fairfield, Conn., 1980, Outstanding Achievement award, 1988. Mem. Nat. Assn. Female Execs., Sales Profls. Los Angeles (v.p. 1984-86). Unitarian. Club: Toastmasters (adminstrv. v.p. 1985). Avocations: sewing, running. Office: Thermador Waste King 5116 District Blvd Los Angeles CA 90040

DIETZ, MARGARET JANE, retired public information official; b. Omaha, Apr. 15, 1924; d. Lawrence Louis and Jeanette Amalia (Meile) Neumann; m. Richard Henry Dietz, May 30, 1949 (dec. July 1971); children: Henry Louis, Frederick Richard, Susan Margaret, John Lawrence (dec.). BA, U. Nebr., 1946; MS, Columbia U., 1949. Wire editor Kearney (Nebr.) Daily Hub, 1946-47; state society editor Omaha World-Herald, 1947-48; library aide Akron (Ohio) Pub. Library, 1963-66, publicity and display dir., 1966-74, editor Owlet, 1966-74; pub. info. officer Northeastern Ohio Univs. Coll. Medicine, Rootstown, 1974-85, dir. Office of Communications, 1985-87, ret. 1987; writer Ravenna (Ohio) Record-Courier, 1988—; cons. Kent (Ohio) State U. Sch. Music, 1988—. Mem. culture and entertainment com. Goals for Greater Akron, 1976; pres. bd. Weathervane Community Playhouse, Akron, 1982-85; trustee Family Svcs. Summit County, Ohio, 1980—, Am. Heart Assn., Akron dist., 1986—, Mobile Meals Found., Akron, 1988—; v.p. Friends of Akron-Summit County Pub. Libr., 1988—; student tutor LEARN Literacy Coun., 1988—. Mem. Pub. Relations Soc. Am., Women in Communications, Assn. Am. Med. Colls. Group on Pub. Relations, LWV (edn. found. 1989—, newsletter editor Akron 1957-60). Clubs: College, Press, Akron Woman's City. Home: 887 Canyon Trail Akron OH 44303

DIETZ, SHARON LYNN, marketing communications executive; b. Bklyn., July 21, 1958; d. William Arthur and Irene Dolores (Stutzbach) D. AA in Gen. Studies, U. Md., 1980; BA in Art History, Manhattanville Coll., 1982; MA in Communications, Fordham U., 1986. Editorial asst. Pergamon Press/Maxwell Communication Corp., Elmsford, N.Y., 1982-83; acct. exec. Hill & Knowlton, N.Y.C., 1985-87; deputy editor, new bus. researcher Maxwell Communication Corp., N.Y.C., 1987-89; sr. account exec. McDonald's account Core Communications, Boston, 1990—; cons. Hill & Knowlton Pub. Rels., N.Y.C., 1985-87. Photographer (editorial) British Airways, 1988. Rep. World Affairs Coun., Conn., 1990. With U.S. Army, 1977-80; vol. Wadsworth Atheneum, 1989-90. Recipient academic scholarship Manhattanville Coll., Purchase, N.Y., 1980-82, grad. assistantship scholarship Fordham U., Bronx, 1984-86. Democrat. Roman Catholic. Home: 25 Birchwood Ave Longmeadow MA 01106

DIETZE, DAYREL ELIZABETH, systems engineer; b. Ormand Beach, Fla., Jan. 30, 1961; d. Arthur Harry and Edna (Edwards) D. BS, Rider Coll., 1984; degree in data communications, NYU, 1990. Registered profl. engr., N.Y. Communications cons. MCI, N.Y.C., 1986-88; systems engr. Rolm, N.Y.C., 1988—. Office: Rolm 237 Park Ave New York NY 10017

DIFILIPPO, FRANCINE CARMELLA, business consultant; b. Cleve., Oct. 24, 1950; d. Anthony Michael and Helen Stella (Sewalk) DiF.; m. Peter Edward Kent, Nov. 11, 1986; 1 child, Skye. BGS in Comparative Arts, Ohio U., 1973; MS in Guidance and Counseling, Cen. Conn. State U., 1975; postgrad., Nova U., 1986—. Asst. dir. student union U. Conn., Storrs, 1975-77; dean student svcs. Cen. New Eng. Coll., Worcester, Mass., 1977-79; v.p. creative svcs. Griffer Studios, Worcester, 1979-82; adminstr. Data Gen. Corp., Westboro, Mass., 1982-83; owner DiFilippo Bus. Devel., Sarasota, Fla., 1984—; pres. The Heldi Corp., Inc.; owner Downtown Bus. & Secretarial Svcs.; v.p. KDMB Corp.; bd. dirs. Osso Corp. Mem. Sarasota County Arts Coun., 1987—, sec., 1988-89, treas., 1989-90; bd. dirs. Fla. Ctr. for Bus. Devel. and Tng. Mem. Am. Mktg. Assn. (exec. profl.), Fla. Freelance Writers Assn., Fla. Women's Alliance, Sarasota C. of C., Am. Cons. League (cert.). Republican. Home: 7235 Saddlecreek Circle Sarasota FL 34241 Office: 1379 McAnsh Sq Sarasota FL 34236

DIGERONIMO, CLAIRE R., marketing professional; b. Locamo, Switzerland, Nov. 8, 1965; d. Anthony J. and Anita G. (Flaccomio) Nistico. BS in Mktg. and Advt., Syracuse U., 1987. Intern Walt Disney Prodns., London, 1986; account exec. Young & Rubicam, N.Y.C., 1985-88, SSC&B Lintas, N.Y.C., 1988-89, LeDonne & Wilner Entertainment, N.Y.C., 1989-90, Marketshare Internat., N.Y.C., 1990—. Mem. NAFE, Am. Mktg. Assn., Delta Delta Delta. Roman Catholic. Home: 244 West 4th St #1A New York NY 10014

DIGGS, LYNNE DOROTHY, physician; b. Balt., May 1, 1960; d. Robert H. and Phyllis A. Diggs. BA, U. Pa., 1981; MD, U. Md., 1985. Diplomate Am. Bd. Internal Medicine. Intern in internal medicine St. Lukes Roosevelt Hosp., N.Y.C., 1985-86; resident physician Washington Hosp. Ctr., 1987-89; emergency rm. physician EMSA, Cambridge, Md., 1988—; staff physician Group Health Assn., Washington, 1989—. Recipient Merit award U. Pa.,

1981. Mem. Montgomery County Med. Soc. (pub. health com. 1989-90), Am. Med. Women's Assn., Med.-Chi Med. Soc. Md. Democrat.

DIGGS, PHYLLIS ALLEN, mental health center administrator; b. Balt., June 19, 1926; d. George Shafter and Juanita C. (King) Allen; m. Robert H. Diggs, Nov. 2, 1957 (div. Jan. 1979); 1 child, Lynne D. BS, Howard U., 1946; MA, Cath. U., Washington, 1948; MPH, Johns Hopkins U., 1973; cert., NIMH Staff Coll., Rockville, Md., 1981. Cert. Mental Health Adminstr. Caseworker, children's svcs. coord. home finding Balt. Dept. Social Systems, 1949-57; sr. personnel technician Balt. Civil Svcs. Commn., 1957-60; sr. clin. psychologist, supr. psychol. svcs. Balt. City Pub. Schs., 1961-72, coord. social work and psychol. svcs., 1973-74; exec. dir. N. Balt. Ctr., Inc., 1974-85; asst. chief, adminstrv. officer County Execs. Office Prince Georges County Govt., Upper Marlboro, Md., 1985-87; pvt. practice cons. Balt., 1987; dir. community programs Sheppard & Enoch Pratt Hosp. Systems, Balt., 1987; pres., chief exec. officer CAMcare Community Mental Health Ctr., Camden, N.J., 1987—. Bd. dirs. Central Md. Health Systems Agy., Balt., 1979-82, Bryn Mawr Sch., Balt., 1971-79; mem. Fifth Dist. Dem. Assn., Balt., 1983-85, Md. Women's Health Coalition, Balt., 1983-86; bd. dirs. Burlington, N.J. chpt. ARC, 1990. Recipient Disting Svc. award Md. Psychol. Assn., 1983. Mem. Assn. Mental Health Adminstrs., Am. Coll. Healthcare Execs., Am. Coll. Mental Health Adminstrn., Bon-Bon's (pres. 1981-83), Viva Club (pres. 1979-81), Rotary (bd. dirs. Camden chpt. 1990). Democrat. Episcopalian. Office: CAMCare Community Mental Health Ctr 400 Market St Camden NJ 08101

DIGHE, JUDITH GINAINE, early childhood educator; b. St. Louis, Nov. 25, 1938; d. Vincent and Edna (Wold) Ginaine; m. Shrikant V. Dighe, Sept. 12, 1964; children: Ranjit, Anand. BA, Thomas More Coll., 1963; MA, U. Md., 1974. Cert. early childhood tchr., Md. Dir. girls activities Seven Hills Neighborhood Houses, Inc., Cin., 1963-65; head tchr. Rockville (md.) Gardens Parent-Child Ctr., 1971-72; tchr., co-dir. Bethesda-Chevy Chase (Md.) Nursery Sch., Md., 1972-78; tchr. Head Start Montgomery County Pub. Schs., Rockville, Md., 1978-89; tchr. specialist Head Start program Montgomery County Pub. Schs., Rockville, Md., 1986—. Book rev. editor: Parent Cooperative Nursery School International Jour., 1977-86, assoc. editor, 1980-82. Mem. Nat. Assn. for the Edn. Young Children, Md. Coun. Parent Participation Nursery Schs., Md. Assn. for the Edn. Young Children, Potomac Assn. Coop. Tchrs. (workshop leader), Md. Community Assn. for the Edn. Young Children (co-pres. 1989—), Montgomery Child Date Care Assn. (exec. bd. 1990—). Home: 9811 Wildwood Rd Bethesda MD 20814 Office: Montgomery County Schs 4910 Macon Rd Rockville MD 20852

DIGIAMARINO, MARIAN ELEANOR, zoning and code specialist; b. Camden, N.J., July 23, 1947; d. James and Concetta (Biancosino) DiG. BS in Mgmt., Rutgers U., 1978. Clk. stenographer transp. div. Dept. of Navy, Phila., 1965-70, sec., 1970-73, realty asst. Profl. Devel. Ctr.. program, 1973-75, realty specialist, 1975-81, supervisory realty specialist, head acquisition and ingrant sect., 1981-85, supervisory realty specialist, mgr. ops. br., 1985—; instr. USNR, Phila., 1983, 88. Contbr. articles to profl. jours. Mem. AAUW, Soc. Am. Mil. Engrs., Nat. Assn. Female Execs., Phi Chi Theta (pres. Del. Valley chpt. 1984-86, nat. councillor 1984, nat. fundraising com., pres. and corr. sec. (Alpha Omega chpt. 1976-78). Office: Dept of Navy No Div Naval Facilities Engring Command Real Estate Div US Naval Base Philadelphia PA 19112

DIGIOVANNI, ELEANOR ELMA, scaffold installation company executive; b. Long Island City, N.Y., May 14, 1944; d. Charles and Josephine (Laureni) DiG. Student Queensboro Coll. Collector Atlas/Re/Sun Ins. Co., N.Y.C., 1965-69; instr. Oak Manor Equitation, Weyers Cave, Va., 1970-76; dispatcher, salesperson Safway Steel Products, Long Island City, N.Y., 1977-83; ops. mgr. York Scaffold, Long Island City, 1983—. Mem. Mus. Natural History, Nat. Assn. Female Execs., Women in Constrn., Internat. Platform Assn. Democrat. Roman Catholic. Avocations: reading, horseback riding, needlepoint. Home: 14-34 30th Rd Astoria NY 11102 Office: York Scaffold Equipment Corp 37-20 12th St Long Island City NY 11101

DI GIOVANNI, PAMELA, labor relations executive; b. Cin., Nov. 16, 1946; d. Theodore Anderson and Shirley Mae (Meier) Chapman; m. Robert Anton Mayer, Aug. 7, 1971 (dec. Sept. 1971); m. Richard F. Di Giovanni; 1 stepchild, Michael David. BS in Edn., No. Ariz. U., 1968. With 20th Century Fox Film Corp., L.A., 1972—; now v.p. Fox, Inc.; trustee Motion Picture Health and Welfare Fund, 1981—, chairperson, 1982; trustee Motion Picture Industry Pension Plan, 1981—, Dirs. Guild Health and Welfare Fund, 1984—, Dirs. Guild Pension Plan, 1984—; bd. dirs. Contract Svcs. Adminstrv. Trust Fund, Dirs. Guild of Am. Contract Adminstrs. Republican. Presbyterian. Office: 20th Century Fox Film Corp 10201 W Pico Blvd Los Angeles CA 90035

DIGUGLIELMO, ANTOINETTE TERESA, teacher; b. Mt. Vernon, N.Y., Oct. 15, 1964; d. Pasquale Antonio and Teresa (Guglielmo) D. BA cum laude, Iona Coll., 1986; postgrad., Coll. of New Rochelle, 1989—. Cert. elem. sch. and spl. edn. tchr. Tchr. New Rochelle (N.Y.) Schs., 1986—. Mem. Psychology Club, Delta Epsilon Sigma, Psi Chi, Phi Delta Kappa. Republican. Roman Catholic. Home: 148 Florence St Yonkers NY 10704 Office: Daniel Webster Sch 95 Glenmore Dr New Rochelle NY 10801

DIKE, MARGARET HOPCRAFT, retired educational administrator; b. Prescott, Ariz., July 15, 1921; d. Walter Irving and Margaret Jennie (Lindsay) Hopcraft; m. Sheldon Holland Dike, Nov. 28, 1941 (div. 1971); children: Lawrence, Walter, Robert. BA, U. N.Mex., 1941, MA, 1975. Draftsman U. Calif., Los Alamos, N.Mex., 1943-45; coord. Albuquerque Pub. Schs., 1972-85; chmn. pub. adv. com. U. N.Mex., Albuquerque, 1973-74, chmn. search com. regional v.p., 1975. Co-editor: Bicentennial '76 - Albuquerque, 1977; editor booklet New Mexico Arts Resources Survey, 1957, rsch. papers in field. Trustee Albuquerque Mus., 1969-81; chmn. Albuquerque RR Centennial, 1979-80, Albuquerque Sister Cities Bd., 1988-89, Keep Albuquerque Beautiful-Schs., 1984—. Recipient Lobo award U. N.Mex., 1968, Gov.'s award for Outstanding N.Mex. Women, Commn. on Status of Women, 1986. Mem. Albuquerque Hist. Soc. (pres. 1972-78), N.Mex. Parents and Tchrs. Assn. (life, pres. 1977-79), Exec. Women Internat. (treas. 1983-85), Edn. Forum N.Mex. (sec. 1988-89), AAUW (pres. N.Mex. div. 1989—), N.Mex. Assn. for Community Edn. Devel. (pres. 1980-82), Mortar Bd. (pres. alumni chpt. 1988-90), Phi Delta Kappa, Phi Kappa Phi, Phi Alpha Theta. Methodist.

DI LELLO, DENISE-MARIE, lawyer, photographer; b. N.Y.C.; d. Robert Franklin and Joan Teresa (Draghi) Di L.; m. Russell Van Patten, May 19, 1990. BA in Journalism, Syracuse U., 1983; JD, Georgetown U., 1986. Bar: Calif. 1986. Assoc. Gibson, Dunn & Crutcher, L.A., 1986-89; counsel Twentieth Century Fox Film Corp., L.A., 1989—. Mem. Calif. Bar Assn., Beverly Hills County Bar Assn., Order of the Coif, Phi Beta Kappa. Home: 13463 Rand Rd Sherman Oaks CA 91423 Office: Twentieth Centry Fox Film 2121 Ave of the Stars 13 Fl Los Angeles CA 90067

DILEONARDI, JOAN WALL, social services administrator, researcher; b. Chgo., Oct. 20, 1935; d. Patrick Joseph Wall and Nora (Campbell) Jacoby; stepfather: Harold L. Jacoby; m. Robert J. DiLeonardi, June 14, 1958 (div. Feb. 1976); children: Robert, Mary (dec.), Jean. BA, De Paul U., 1956; PhD, U. Ill., 1982. Research dir. Omni Youth Services, Wheeling, Ill., 1975-76; research dir. Children's Home and Aid Soc., Chgo., 1979-82, v.p., 1982—; instr. Inst. for Clin. Social Work, Chgo., 1983—, U. Chgo., 1986-87; part-time tchr. various univs., Chgo. area, 1975—; local advisor Info. Tech. Resources, Chgo., 1983-87; peer reviewer Adminstrn. for Children, Youth and Families, HHS, Washington, 1982-90; cons. in field. Author: Evaluating Child Abuse Prevention Programs, 1982, What to do When the Numbers Are In, 1987; contbr. articles to profl. jours.; presenter in field. Pres. NW Suburban Day Care Ctr., Des Plaines, Ill., 1968-77; vol. Earthwatch; trustee Mensa Edn. and Research Fedn., Phila., 1984-87; bd. dirs. The Harbor, Des Plaines, 1987—. NIMH fellow, 1978-80. Mem. Nat. Assn. Social Workers (bd. dirs. 1981-83, del. 1982-83, instr. 1979-87), Child Welfare League.

DILGER, LORRAINE ANN, advertising executive; b. Chgo., Aug. 20, 1959; d. Lawrence Anthony and Catherine Ann (Brennan) Barczak; m. David Gerard Dilger, Oct. 5, 1985. BS, U. Ill., 1981. Traffic coordinator Tatham Laird & Kudner, Chgo., 1981; media dir. Paulsen & Partners, Chgo., 1981-86; acct. exec. Esrock Advt., Orland Park, Ill., 1986—. Named Best Performance by an Employee Esrock Advt., 1988. Mem. Women in Cable of Ill., Pi Beta Phi. Roman Catholic. Home: 14638 Arboretum Dr Lockport IL 60441

DILL, ANNE HOLDEN, educator; b. Poplarville, Miss., Mar. 7, 1920; d. James Houston and Florence Elizabeth (Henley) Holden; BS, U. Ala., 1954, MA, 1955, EdS, 1970; m. Elmer Dill, Jan. 25, 1941; children: Winston Elmer, Jane Anne, Caroll Elizabeth Dill Norman. High sch. tchr., Ga., 1958-65; instr. Western world lit. U. Ga. Center, Dublin, 1965-66; instr. English, Gadsden (Ala.) Jr. Coll., 1966-83. Mem. Nat. Coun. Tchrs. English, NEA, AAUW, MLA, Southeastern Conf. English in Two-Year Colls., Conf. Coll. Composition and Communication, Ala. Coll. English Tchrs. Assn., Ala. Coun. Tchrs. English, Ala. Jr. Coll. Assn., Ala. Edn. Assn., DAR (regent James Gadsden chpt. 1983-87, dir. Ala. Soc. dist. II), Children of Am. Revolution (sr. historian Ala. Soc.), Princess Noccalula Soc. (sr. organizing pres. 1986-87, sr. pres. 87-88, 88-89), Ala. Hist. Soc., Etowah Hist. Soc., N.E. Geneal. Soc., Etowah-Gadsen C. of C. (mil. affairs com.), Gadsden Woman's Club, Gadsden Music Club. Democrat. Baptist. Home: 850 Walnut St Gadsden AL 35901

DILL, ELLEN RENÉE, minister; b. Detroit, Jan. 2, 1949; d. Clarence Lorenzo and Melvin Elizabeth (Knowles) D.; m. Norval Ignatius Brown, May 24, 1980; children: Christopher Edward Brown, Crystal Elizabeth Brown. BA, Nazareth Coll. Mich., 1972; MDiv, Garrett Evang. Sem., Evanston, Ill., 1979; postgrad., Northwestern U., Evanston, Ill., 1979-82, Chgo. Theol. Sem., 1988—. Ordained to ministry Meth. Ch., 1978. Teaching asst. Head Start St. Agnes Ch., Detroit, 1966-68; tchr. Eastside Vicariate Sch., Detroit, 1972-77; pastor St. Luke United Meth. Ch., Chgo., 1980-82; assoc. pastor First United Meth. Ch., Chgo., 1982-84; pastor Clair-Christian United Meth. Ch., Chgo., 1984-88, Community United Meth. Ch., Markham, Ill., 1988-90, Woodlawn United Meth. Ch., Chgo., 1990—; condr. seminar on women in ministry Garrett Evang. Sem., 1981, instr. continuing edn. seminar for clergy in adminstrn., 1987; bd. dirs. South Dist. Bd. Ordained Ministry, Bd. Ch. Bldg. Location; chmn. No. Ill. Conf. Bd. Edn., So. Dist. Bd. Edn.; asst. chmn. bd. edn. United Meth. Ch., mem. Detroit Conf., 1978; mem. No. Ill. conf. Elders Orders, 1985. Co-author: Teachers Guide: Two Hundred Years of American Methodism, 1981; editorial advisor The Christian Ministry jour., 1987—; contbr. articles to profl. jours. Bd. dirs. Austin Christian Law Ctr., 1983-89, Child Serve Community Coun., Chgo., 1984-88, Garrett-Evang. Sem., 1978; area chairperson Mayor's Com. to Keep Detroit Beautiful. Recipient citation Mayor's Com. To Keep Detroit Beautiful, 1966, citation for excellence in journalism Mich. Press Assn., 1978; Hartman scholar, 1979; Dempster Grad. fellow, 1980, Hartman fellow, 1981. Mem. Nat. Assn. Bus. and Profl. Women, Black United Methodists for Ch. Renewal (citation for svc. 1982), So. Suburban Clergy Cluster, Ecumenical Ministerial Assn., Lay Acad. No. Ill. Conf. Home: 8600 S Cregier Chicago IL 60617 Office: Woodlawn United Meth Ch 1208 E 64th St Chicago IL 60637

DILL, EVELENA, architect; b. Brewton, Ala., Dec. 29, 1958; d. William Roger and Helen (Robinson) D. Student, Auburn U., 1977-82. Draftsman Ala. Soils and Agronomy Lab., Auburn, 1978-79; intern architect Townsley & Assocs., Huntsville, Ala., 1981, Chapman Coyle Chapman & Assocs., Atlanta, 1981-84, Gimson Kirkland Architects, Inc., Atlanta, 1984, Joseph Perry & Assocs., Atlanta, 1985; intern architect, asst. CAD mgr. Taylor-Anderson & Assocs., Atlanta, 1985-88; intern architect, CAD mgr. Archtl. Group, Alexandria, Va., 1988-90; with Noritake Assocs., Alexandria, Va., 1990; Cadd mgr. Henningson, Durham & Richardson, Alexandria, 1990—. Mem. NAFE, Va. Assn. Female Execs., Smithsonian Assocs. Mem. Ch. of Christ. Home: 6034 Richmond Hwy Apt 703 Alexandria VA 22303 Office: Henningson Durham & Richardson 103 Oronoco St Alexandria VA 22314-2096

DILL, KAROLE EDWYNA, corporate executive; b. Brklyn., July 6, 1961; d. Harold Edward and Evelyn Elaine (Eastmond) D. AB, Harvard U., 1982. Brand supr. The Procter and Gamble Co., Cin., 1982-83; asst. sec. Mfg. Hanover Corp., N.Y., 1983-86; asst. v.p. Algemeng Bank Nederland N.V., N.Y., 1986-89, Union Bank of Switzerland, N.Y.C., 1989—. Contbr. artilces to non-profl. jours. Tutor Ctr. for Reading and Writing N.Y. Pub. Library, 1988-89. Mem. Harvard Club, Alpha Kappa Alpha. Democrat. Episcopalian. Home: 45 E 135th St Apt 9H New York NY 10037

DILL, MARY ALYSON, systems analyst; b. Aug. 30, 1951; d. William Allen and Marjorie Dill. BS, Edinboro (Pa.) State U., 1973; MS in Instl. Communications, Shippensburg U., 1979; MLS, Case Western Res U., 1982. Libr. elem. and secondary schs. Bd. Coop. Ednl. Svcs., Stamford, N.Y., 1973-76; media specialist West Point (N.Y.) Elem. Sch. U.S. Mil. Acad., 1976-81; records analyst Standard Oil of Ohio, Cleve., 1981-83, info. analyst, 1983-87; tech. writer Presearch, Aiken, S.C., 1987-88; tech. writer Maxwell Online, Inc. (formerly Pergamon ORBIT Infoline), McLean, Va., 1988-89, database design analyst, 1989—. Mem. Am. Soc. for Info. Scis. Home: 2156 Evans Ct Apt 202 Falls Church VA 22043

DILLARD, ANNIE, author; b. Pitts., Apr. 30, 1945; d. Frank and Pam (Lambert) Doak; m. R.H.W. Dillard; m. Gary Clevidence, 1980; 1 child, Cody Rose; stepchildren: Carin, Shelly. B.A., Hollins Coll., 1967, M.A., 1968. Columnist The Living Wilderness, Wilderness Soc., 1973-75; contbg. editor Harper's mag., N.Y.C., 1973-85; scholar-in-residence Western Wash. U., Bellingham, 1975-78; disting. vis. prof. Wesleyan U., 1979-83, adj. prof., 1983—, writer in residence, 1987—; Phi Beta Kappa orator Harvard/Radcliffe, 1983; mem. U.S. Writers' del. UCLA U.S.-Chinese Writers' Conf., 1982; mem. U.S. Cultural Del. to China, 1982. Author: (poems) Tickets For A Prayer Wheel, 1974; Pilgrim at Tinker Creek, 1974 (Pulitzer prize for gen. non-fiction 1975), Holy the Firm, 1978, Living by Fiction, 1982, Teaching a Stone to Talk, 1982, Encounters with Chinese Writers, 1984, An American Childhood, 1987, The Writing Life, 1989. Mem. Nat. Com. on U.S.-China Relations, 1982—. Recipient N.Y. Presswomen's award for excellence, 1975, Wash. Gov.'s award for contbn. to lit., 1978; grantee Nat. Endowment for Arts, 1980-81, Guggenheim Found., 1985-86. Mem. Poetry Soc. Am., Authors Guild, Nat. Citizens for Public Libraries, Phi Beta Kappa. Address: care Blanche Gregory 2 Tudor City Pl New York NY 10017

DILLARD, JOAN HELEN, financial executive; b. Balt., June 12, 1951; d. Anthony Joseph and Frances Helen (Waclawski) Bartynski; m. Gordon Earl Dillard, Apr. 21, 1984; 1 child, Valerie Kay. A.A., Anne Arundel Community Coll., Md., 1973; B.A., U. Md., 1977; M.B.A., U. Balt., 1984. Instr. music Acad. Music, Glen Burnie, Md., 1972-77; cash mgr. Johns Hopkins Hosp., Balt., 1979-83, Md. Casualty Co., Balt., 1983-85; v.p., asst. treas. Am. Gen. Corp., Houston, 1985-89; v.p., treas. Am. Gen. Fin., Houston, 1989—. Mem. Am. Fin. Svcs. Assn., Nat. Corp. Cash Mgmt. Assn., Houston Cash Mgmt. Assn. (v.p. 1986, pres. 1987), Nat. Assn. Corp. Treas. Office: Am Gen Fin 2929 Allen Pkwy Houston TX 77019

DILLARD, MARILYN DIANNE, property manager; b. Norfolk, Va., July 7, 1940; d. Thomas Ortman and Sally Ruth (Wallerich) D.; m. James Conner Coons, Nov. 6, 1965 (div. June 1988); 1 child, Adrienne Alexandra Coons (dec.). Student, UCLA, 1958-59; BA in Bus. Adminstrn., U. Wash., 1962. Modeling-print work Harry Conover, N.Y.C., 1945; ballet instr. Ivan Novikoff Sch. Russian Ballet, 1955; model Elizabeth Leonard Agy., Seattle, 1955-68; retail worker Frederick & Nelson, Seattle, 1962, I. Magnin & Co., Seattle, 1963-64; property mgr. Seattle, 1961—; antique and interior design John J. Cunningham Antiques, Seattle, 1968-73. Author: (poem) Flutterby, 1951; asst. chmn.: Seattle Classic Cookbook, 1980-83. Charter mem., pres. Children's Med. Ctr., Maude Fox Guild, Seattle, 1965—; organizer teen groups Episcopal Ch. of the Epiphany, Seattle, 1965-67; bd. dirs. Patrons of N.W. Civic, Cultural and Charitable Orgns., Seattle, 1976—, prodn. chmn., 1977-78, 84-85, auction party chmn., 1983-84, exec. com., 1984-85; mem. U. Wash. Arboretum Found. Unit, 1966-73, pres., 1969; mem. Jr. League Seattle, provisional class pres., 1971-72, next to new shop asst. chmn., 1972-73, bd. dirs., admissions chmn., 1976-77, exec. first v.p., exec. com., bd. dirs., 1978-79; mem., bd. dirs. Coun. for the Prevention of Child Abuse and Neglect, Seattle, 1974-75, Seattle Children's Theatre, 1984-90. Mem. N.W. Asian Am. Theatre (adv. bd. 1987—), Seattle Tennis Club. Republican. Episcopalian. Home and Office: 2053 Minor Ave E Seattle WA 98102

DILLARD, NANCY ROSE, navy officer; b. Rosebud, Tex., Oct. 31, 1950; d. Hilyard Blanchard and Rose Lee (Kuhn) D. BSEd, Ga So. Coll., 1973, MEd, 1974, EdS, 1978; MS, Naval Postgrad. Sch., 1990. Sch. health svcs. coord. Savannah/Chatham County Pub. Schs., Savannah, Ga., 1974-79; field agt. N.Y. Life Ins. Co., Savannah, 1979-81; commd. lt. USN, 1982, advanced through grades to lt., 1986, active duty, 1982—. Mem. Chatham County Alcoholic Adv. Bd., S.E. Ga. region Am. Lung Assn., Savannah, 1978, maternal and infant health care com. United Way, Savannah, 1978, combined pub. health nurses com. Chatham County Health Dept., Savannah, 1978. Decorated Navy Commendation medal, Navy Achievement medal, Navy Expert Pistol medal. Mem. U.S. Naval Inst., Pilot Club, Delta Kappa Gamma. Roman Catholic. Home: 10103 King Edward Ct Upper Marlboro MD 20772

DILLEHAY, PAMELA ANN, editor, writer; b. Berkeley, Calif., Feb. 2, 1957; s. Ronald Clifford and Valerie Ruth (Sherborne) D. BA, U. Calif.-Santa Cruz, 1980. Counselor Choice Med. Clinic, Santa Cruz, Calif., 1980-82; writer KSCO Radio, Santa Cruz, 1982; mktg. programs analyst Cygnet Tech., Inc., Sunnyvale, Calif., 1983-87; pub. rels. specialist Borland Internat., Scotts Valley, Calif., 1987-88; copy editor Turbo Technix Mag., 1988; pvt. practice copy editor, Santa Cruz, 1988—; freelance writer, editor, 1989—. Counselor Planned Parenthood, Santa Cruz, 1977-80; peer advisor U. Calif.-Santa Cruz, 1980. Undergrad. rsch. grantee U. Calif.-Santa Cruz, 1979. Avocations: scuba diving, stained glass, volleyball. Democrat.

DILLENBURG, CAROLYN EVA LAUER, educator; b. Adair County, Iowa, May 13, 1934; d. Harvey Francis and Lorna Orilda (Gilbert) Lauer; m. Dale Everett Dillenburg, May 29, 1954; children: Candace Dee Brotherton, Shari Sue Eivins, Jeffrey Dale Dillenburg. AA, Creston Jr. Coll., 1954; BS, Iowa State Coll., 1956; MSEd., Drake U., 1968. Cert. secondary tchr. Engr.'s aide GM, Indpls., 1955; math. and sci. tchr. Afton (Iowa) Independent Sch., 1957-58, Runnells (Iowa) Independent Sch., 1958-59; math. and English tchr. Winterset (Iowa) Community Sch., 1959-61; math. and sci. tchr. O-M Community Sch., Orient, Iowa, 1961-63; math. and English tchr. Creston (Iowa) Community Sch., 1964-65; math. tchr. Lenox (Iowa) Community Sch., 1968—; adj. math. tchr. Southwestern Community Coll., Creston, 1977-81. Treas. Iowa Town & Country YWCA, southwest Iowa, 1981—; pres. Creston YWCA Coun., 1981—. Mem. AAUW, NEA, Iowa State Edn., Southwest Uniserv (bd. mem. 1988-92), Lenox Tchrs. Assn., Iowa Coun. Tchrs. Math., Delta Kappa Gamma, Pi Mu Epsilon, Psi Chi. Mem. United Ch. of Christ. Home: Rte 3 Box 138 Creston IA 50801 Office: Lenox Community Sch 600 S Locust Lenox IA 50851

DILLEY, BARBARA JEAN, college administrator, choreographer, educator; b. Chgo., Mar. 13, 1938; d. Robert Vernon and Jean Phyllis (Fairweather) D.; m. Lewis Lloyd, May 1961 (div.); 1 child, Benjamin Lloyd; m. Brent Bondurant, Mar. 1977 (div.); 1 child, Owen Bondurant. BA, Mt. Holyoke Coll., 1960. Dancer Merce Cunningham Dance Co., N.Y.C., 1963-68; ind. dancer, choreographer N.Y.C. and Boulder, Colo., 1966-82; dancer Yvonne Rainer Co., N.Y.C., 1967-70; dancer, choreographer The Grand Union, N.Y.C., 1970-76; dir., faculty mem. dance program Naropa Inst., Boulder, 1974-84, pres., 1984—; artist, tchr. pvt. workshops in U.S., N.Y.C., New Haven, Conn., Northampton, Mass., San Francisco, Berkeley, Calif., 1978—, pvt. workshops in Can., Toronto, Ont., Montreal, Que., Halifax, N.S., 1978—; artistic dir. Crystal Dance, Boulder, 1978-81; choreographer numerous dance groups; mem. vis. faculty NYU, Radcliffe Coll., Cornell U., U. Colo., George Washington U., others; dir. dance symposium, 1981; adjudicator SW div. Am. Coll. Dance Festival, Loretto Heights, Colo., 1986. Mem. grants selection panel Colo. Coun. of Arts and Humanities, 1981, mem. panel on policy devel. for individual grants, 1983. NEA Choreographic fellow, 1974, 76, 81; Boulder City Arts Coun. grantee, 1981. Democrat. Buddhist. Office: Naropa Inst 2130 Arapahoe St Boulder CO 80302

DILLEY, WANDA REISS, retired social worker, civic volunteer; b. Hartford, Kans., Dec. 10, 1918; d. Levi Thomas and Ruby Edith (Vail) Scott; m. Marvin L. Reiss, Apr. 29, 1943 (dec. July 1971); children: Raena Lynn Reiss-Borth, Scott, Carolyn Reiss Howes, Barbara Reiss Dunn; m. J.P. Dilley, Oct. 11, 1986. BS in Edn., Ft. Hays U., 1940, MS in Counseling, 1973. Tchr. home econs. Chase (Kans.) High Sch., 1940-43; social worker S.W. Guidance Ctr., Liberal, Kans., 1974-86; mem. Internat. Human Learning Rsch. Group, 1975-89. Vol. counselor Resonance, Tulsa, 1986—; pres. Women's Soc. of Meth. Ch., Plains, Kans., 1962-65. Mem. AAUW (v.p., sec. Liberal chpt. 1973-89, sec. Tulsa chpt. 1989—), P.E.O. Home: 8416 E 75th St Tulsa OK 74133

DILLIER, HELEN JEAN, secondary educator; b. Dayton, Ohio, May 2, 1939; d. Arthur E. and Grace (Boyd) Hortin; m. James L. Dillier, Aug. 4, 1962; children: Elizabeth Jean, Catherine Joyce. BS in Edn., Ea. Ill. U., 1961. Cert. tchr., Ill. Bus., English tchr. Marquette High Sch., Ottawa, Ill., 1976—; sponsor Jr. Class Marquette High Sch., Ottawa, 1980—. Membership com. Community Concert Assn., Ottawa, 1989-90; past pres. Home Extension, LaSalle County, Ill.; active Ch. Ladies Circle; dir. Vacation Bible Sch., Southside Christian Ch., Ottawa. Mem. DAR, Bus. and Profl. Women's Club (Career Woman of the Month 1980), Ea. Ill. U. Alumni Club, Ill. State U. Parents Club, Delta Zeta Alumni. Home: 302 Hillside Ave Ottawa IL 61350

DILLINGHAM, MARJORIE CARTER, foreign language educator; b. Bicknell, Ind., Aug. 20, 1915; m. William Pyrle Dillingham, (dec. 1981); children: William Pyrle (dec.), Robert Carter, Sharon Dillingham Martin. PhD in Spanish (Delta Kappa Gamma scholar and fellow), Fla. State U., 1970. High sch. tchr., Fla.; former instr. St. George's Sch., Havana; former mem. faculty Panama Canal Zone Coll., Fla. State U., U. Ga., Duke U.; dir. traveling Spanish conversation classes abroad. U.S. rep. (with husband) Hemispheric Conf. on Taxation, Rosario, Argentina. Named to Putnam County Hall of Fame, 1986. Mem. Am. Assn. Tchrs. Spanish and Portuguese (past pres. Fla. chpt.), Fla. Edn. Assn. (past pres. fgn. lang. div.), La Sociedad Honoraria Hispanica (past nat. pres.), Fgn. Lang. Tchrs. Leon County, Fla. (pres.), Delta Kappa Gamma (pres.), Phi Kappa Phi, Sigma Delta Pi, Beta Pi Theta, Kappa Delta Pi, Alpha Omicron Pi, Delta Kappa Gamma. Home: 2109 Trescott Dr Tallahassee FL 32312

DILLION, THERESA LEE, human resources administrator; b. Ft. Worth, June 8, 1948; d. Vernon and Dorotha (Scott) D.; m. Michael P. Kier, Aug. 16, 1979. BA, Okla. State U., 1981. Cert. profl. in human resources. Supr. benefits Reading and Bates Corp., Tulsa; human resources planning specialist Pub. Svc. Co. Okla., Tulsa. Mem. Am. Soc. Personnel Adminstrn., Tulsa Personnel Assn. (dir.). Home: 2747 E 14th Pl Tulsa OK 74104

DILLON, JUDY REEP, management executive; b. Great Falls, Mont., Dec. 24, 1944; d. Gordon and Georgie (Pilkington) Bean; m. Thomas A. Reep, Aug. 22, 1962 (div. Sept. 1975); children: Tammy, Tomi; m. Charles Ray Dillon, Sept. 22, 1975. Student, Wake Forest U., 1963-64. Bookkeeper Wachovia Bank & Trust Co., Winston-Salem, N.C., 1964-66; asst. purchasing agt. Krispy Kreme Doughnut Corp., Winston-Salem, 1966-73; co-owner, sec., treas. Action Drives, Inc., Winston-Salem, 1973—; co-owner Action Delivery Svc., Winston-Salem, 1971—. Mem. U.S. C. of C., Purchasing Agts. Assn. Republican. Moravian. Office: Action Drives Inc 1102 Ivy Ave Winston-Salem NC 27102

DILLON, MARYANN, non-profit housing development official; b. Rockville Ctr., N.Y., Nov. 19, 1951; d. James Martin and Rosemary (Peter) D. BS magna cum laude, Buffalo State Coll., 1973; MPA magna cum laude, Baruch Coll., 1985; M in Pub. and Pvt. Mgmt., Yale U., 1987. Mgr. group home for disabled adults Inst. Applied Human Dynamics, Bronx, 1978-82; asst. dir. San Francisco Food Bank, 1982-84; asst. to dir. Maricopa County Health Svcs., Phoenix, 1984-85; econ. devel. specialist Mission Housing Devel. Corp., San Francisco, 1987-88, exec. dir., 1988—. Precinct capt. Agnos for Mayor campaign, San Francisco, 1987, Dukakis for Pres. campaign, San Francisco, 1988. Recipient Letter of Commendation, Nat. Merit Soc., 1969; N.Y. State Bd. Regents scholar, 1969; Nat. Urban League fellow, 1984-85. Mem. Beta Gamma Sigma. Democrat. Roman Catholic. Office: 1656 15th St 2111 Mission St Ste 301 San Francisco CA 94103

DILUCENTE, DÉSIREÉ A., industrial engineer, consultant; b. Pitts., Nov. 7, 1964; d. Elvio Richard and Mary Deloris (Osborn) D. BSE, Marietta (Ohio) Coll., 1987. Cert. in asbestos ops. and maintenance. Indsl. engr. E.D.L. Industries Inc., Pitts., summers 1982-87; indsl. and petroleum engr. Sacramento Crushing, Chgo., 1987-88; project engr. Am. Hosp. Assn., Chgo., 1988—. Mem. Marietta Coll. Club (v.p. 1989—), Sigma Kappa (fund raiser 1986-87). Home: 607 W Wrightwood Ave Apt 503 Chicago IL 60614 Office: Am Hosp Assn 840 N Lakeshore Dr Chicago IL 60611

DIMAIO, VIRGINIA SUE, gallery owner; b. Houston, July 6, 1921; d. Jesse Lee and Gabriella Sue (Norris) Chambers; AB, U. Redlands, 1943; student U. So. Calif., 1943-45, Scripps Coll., 1943, Pomona Coll., 1945; m. James V. DiMaio, 1955 (div. 1968); children: Victoria, James V. Owner, dir. Galeria Capistrano, San Juan Capistrano and Santa Fe, N.Mex., 1979—; founder Mus. Women in Arts, Washington; cons., appraiser Southwestern and Am. Indian Handcrafts; lectr. Calif. State U., Long Beach; established ann. Helen Hardin Meml. scholarship for woman artist grad. Inst. Am. Indian Art, Santa Fe, also ann. Helen Hardin award for outstanding artist at Indian Market, S.W. Assn. on Indian Affairs, Santa Fe; bd. dirs. Mus. of Man, San Diego, 1989. Author: (forward to Mus. of Man exhibit catalogue) Paths Beyond Tradition. Recipient Bronze Plaque Recognition award Navajo Tribal Mus., 1977. Mem. Indian Arts and Crafts Assn., S.W. Assn. Indian Affairs, Heard Mus., San Juan Capistano C. of C. Republican. Roman Catholic. Office: 31681 Camino Capistrano San Juan Capistrano CA 92675 also: 409 Canyon Rd Santa Fe NM 87501

DI MARIA, VALERIE THERESA, public relations executive; b. Bronx, N.Y., Apr. 5, 1957; d. Victor Joseph and Vivian Roslyn (D'Amico) Di Maria. BA in Journalism, NYU, 1978. Asst. dir. U.S. Div. Sidonie S. Ltd., N.Y.C., 1978-79; acct. supr. The Rowland Co., N.Y.C., 1979-82, Ketchum Pub. Rels., N.Y.C., 1982-83; pub. rels. dir. Charles of the Ritz Group Ltd., N.Y.C., 1983-84; sr. v.p. Porter/Novelli Pub. Rels., N.Y.C., 1984-89; v.p. GCI Group, N.Y.C., 1989—. Mem. Pub. Rels. Soc. Am. (Silver Anvil award 1986), The Fashion Group, Am. Film Inst., Les Amis du Vin, Food Mktg. Communications, Women's Sports Found., Phi Beta Kappa. Office: GCI Group 777 Third Ave New York NY 10017

DIMATTEO, MARYANNE ROBIN, psychology educator; b. Boston, Mar. 26, 1952; d. Joseph P. and Angeline (Morreo) DiM.; m. Michael J. Esnard, Jan. 28, 1990; 1 child, Gia. BS, Tufts U., 1972; MA, Harvard U., 1974, PhD, 1976. Lic. psychologist, Calif. Asst. prof. psychology U. Calif., Riverside, 1976-81, assoc. prof., 1981-86, prof., 1986—; resident cons. RAND Corp., Santa Monica, Calif., 1988—. Author: Achieving Patient Compliance, 1982. W.K. Kellogg fellow Kellogg Found., Battle Creek, Mich., 1976. Fellow Am. Psychol. Assn., Am. Psychol. Soc.

DIMEN, MURIEL VERA, psychoanalyst; b. N.Y.C., Sept. 24, 1942; d. Alfred and Dora (Zauzmer) D.; m. Seth L. Schein, Sept. 16, 1965 (div. Aug. 25, 1980). BA, Barnard Coll., 1964; MA, Columbia U., 1966, PhD, 1970; cert., NYU, 1983. Asst. prof. Lehman Coll., Bronx, N.Y., 1970-75, assoc. prof., 1975-81; prof. Lehman Coll., Bronx, 1981-88; pvt. practice N.Y.C., 1979—; mem. faculty New Sch. for Social Rsch., N.Y.C., 1988-89, Nat. Inst. for Psychotherapies, 1989-90; co-dir. seminar in sexual difference and psychoanalysis, N.Y. Inst. for Humanities, 1986. Author: The Anthropological Imagination, 1977, Surviving Sexual Contradictions, 1986; co-editor: Regional Variation in Modern Greece, 1976; book rev. editor: Psychoanalytic Dialogues: A Jour. of Relational Perspective. Fellow Am. Anthropological Assn., N.Y. Inst. for Humanities; mem. Columbia U. Seminar on Women and Soc., Psychoanalytic Soc. Home and Office: 312 W 20th St New York NY 10011

DIMICCO, WENDY ANN, nurse educator; b. Newark, Jan. 15, 1948; d. J. Harold and Winifred (O'Connor) Preston; m. Albert Joseph DiMicco, Aug. 23, 1969; 1 child, Michael Albert. BSN summa cum laude, Barry Coll., Miami, Fla., 1969; MSN, U. Ala., Birmingham, 1970. Staff nurse Englewood (N.J) Hosp., 1969, St. Vincent's Hosp., Birmingham, Ala., 1970; instr. U. Ala. Sch. Nursing, Birmingham, 1970-72; asst. prof. nursing U. Ala. Sch. Nursing, 1972—; cons. in field; lectr. in field. Contbr. articles to profl. jours.; producer videotapes. Mem. AlaCare Home Health Svcs. Adv. Coun., 1983-90; first aid coord. Sonat/Pepsi Vulcan Marathons, Birmingham, 1985, 86; bd. dirs., legis. chmn. Rocky Ridge Elem. Sch. PTA, 1983-85. HEW grantee, 1976-78. Mem. Am. Nurses Assn., Ala. Nurses Assn., Nat. League Nursing, Ala. League Nursing, ARC, Sigma Theta Tau. Office: Univ of Ala University Station Birmingham AL 35294

DIMINO, SYLVIA THERESA, elementary and secondary educator; b. N.Y.C., June 6, 1955; d. John Anthony and Elena (Berardesca) D. BA, St. John's U., 1977; MPA, NYU, 1980, MA in Elem. and Secondary Edn., 1982, cert. advance studies in ednl. adminstrn., 1986, cert. in advanced studies in mgmt., 1990. Cert. elem. and secondary tchr., sch. adminstr., in mgmt. practices, social studies, math., N.Y. Traffic coord. Creamer Inc., N.Y.C., 1977-79; tchr. St. Patrick's Sch., N.Y.C., 1979-82; tchr. IS 131, Manhattan, N.Y.C., 1984—, adminstr., coord., 1985-90, asst.prin., 1990—. Recipinet 2000 Most Notable Women Cert. in Mgmt. Practice. Mem. NAFE, Nat. Orgn. Women in Adminstrn., Bus. Cir. N.Y., Nat. Coun. Adminstrv. Women in Edn., Nat. Orgn. Italian-Am. Women, N.Y.C. Women's City Club. Roman Catholic. Office: IS 131 Manhattan 100 Hester St New York NY 10002

DIMMICK, CAROLYN REABER, federal judge; b. Seattle, Oct. 24, 1929; d. Maurice C. and Margaret T. (Taylor) Reaber; m. Cyrus Allen Dimmick, Sept. 10, 1955; children: Taylor, Dana. BA, U. Wash., 1951, JD, 1963; LLD, Gonzaga U., 1982, CUNY, 1987. Bar: Wash. Asst. atty. gen. State of Wash., Seattle, 1953-55; pros. atty. King County, Wash., 1955-59, 60-62; sole practice Seattle, 1959-60, 62-65; judge N.E. Dist. Ct. Wash., 1965-75, King County Superior Ct., 1976-80; justice Wash. Supreme Ct., 1981-85; judge U.S. Dist. Ct. (we. dist.) Wash., Seattle, 1985—. Recipient Matrix Table award, 1981, World Plan Execs. Council award, 1981, others. Mem. Am. Judges Assn. (gov.), Nat. Assn. Women Judges, World Assn. Judges, ABA, Wash. Bar Assn., Am. Judicature Soc. Clubs: Wash. Athletic, Wingpoint Golf and Country, Harbor. Office: US Dist Ct 911 US Courthouse 1010 5th Ave Seattle WA 98104

DIMOND, MARIE THERESE, biologist, educator; b. Valdez, Alaska, Nov. 13, 1916; d. Anthony Joseph and Dorothea Frances (Miller) D. BA, Trinity Coll., Washington, 1938; MS, Catholic U. Am., 1952, PhD, 1954. Joined Sisters of Notre Dame, 1939. Instr. in German Trinity Coll., Washington, 1938-39; high sch. instr. Trinity Prep. Sch., Ilchester, Md., 1939-48; instr. of Biology Trinity Coll., Washington, 1948-53, asst. prof. Biology, 1953-57, assoc. prof. Biology, 1957-60, prof. of Biology, 1960-82, prof. emerita Biology, 1982—; coord. secondary concentration in bioethics; mem. task force, Assn. of Catholic Coll. and U., Washington 1980-81; vis. prof. Bhopal U., India, 1979, Utkal U. Bhubaneswar, 1984, 89; coord. secondary concentration in bioethics. Author: several profl. jour. articles on Biology. Recipient U.S. Pub. Health Svc. Research Grants, 1956-57, 1958-73, Nat. Sci. Found. Faculty Fellowship, 1959-61; named U.S.-India Exchange of Scientists Program, Nat. Sci. Found., 1978-79. Mem. AAAS (rep. of World Population Soc. of Sec. K 1979-84), Am. Inst. Biol. Sci., Am. Soc. Zoologists, Am. Teilhard Assn., Nat. Assn. of Biology Tchrs., Am. Physiol. Soc. (assoc.). Democrat. Roman Catholic. Home and Office: Trinity Coll 125 Michigan Ave NE Washington DC 20017-1094

DINABURG, MARY ELLEN, artist, art gallery director; b. Bklyn., Feb. 22, 1954; d. Howard and Selma (Shpritz) D. BFA, Phila. Coll. Art, 1976; MFA, Pratt Inst., 1979. Staff admissions dept. Pratt Inst., Bkyn., 1977-79; instr. Phila. Coll. Art, 1977-79; ednl. curator Okla. Mus. Art, Oklahoma City, 1980-81; tchr. The Group, Oklahoma City, 1981-86; freelance tchr. art, lectr., cons. N.Y.C., 1986-88; dir. Jack Shainman Gallery, N.Y.C., 1988—; lectr. in field, 1979—; guest artist Fabric Workshop, Phila., 1978; cons. on art curation, N.Y., Phila., Okla., Tex., 1979—. One-woman show including Greenville (N.C.) Mus. Art, 1983, Hickory (N.C.) Mus. Art, 1983, Conduit Gallery, Dallas, 1985, 86, 88; exhibited in group shows, including ArtsPlace II, Oklahoma City, 1982, Cayman Gallery, N.Y.C., 1984, Conduit Gallery, 1985, 87. Democrat. Jewish. Office: Jack Shainman Gallery 560 Broadway 2d Fl New York NY 10012

DINALE, MARGHERITA SILVI, educator, poet; b. Pisa, Italy, Oct. 20, 1928; came to U.S., 1957, naturalized, 1961; d. Luigi and Adelia (Savelli) Silvi; Dottore in Lettere, Universita Firenze, Florence, Italy, 1949; m. Franco Dinale, June 18, 1955; children—Martina, Silvia. Instr., Smith Coll., 1955-58; assoc. prof. Italian, 1968-88, prof., 1988-89, chmn. dept. Italian, 1976—, dir. Sch. In Italy, 1957, 68, 75, 82-84; research scholar Radcliffe Coll., 1958-59; lectr. Wellesley Coll., 1959, Boston U., 1960; lectr. Middlebury Summer Sch. Langs., 1956, 58, 61. Mem. Dante Soc. Am., Am. Assn. Tchrs. Italian, Dante Alighieri Soc. (Rome), AAUP, Soroptimist Internat. Author: Tutti i luoghi che ho visto, 1977, Una quieta pazienza, 1987; contbr. poetry to Paragone-Letterature, Alfabeta, Erba d'Arno, articles to Il Mondo. Recipient Lerici-Pea Poetry prize Jury of Poets, 1987. Home: 285 Old Black Rd Niantic CT 06357 Office: Smith Coll Wright Hall Northampton MA 01063

DINER, JUDITHANNE, planetary scientist; b. L.A., May 26, 1949; d. Shef and Canneal Anne (Kurey) Windress. AA in Astronomy and Photography, Santa Monica Coll., 1977; BS in Astronomy, U. So. Calif., 1980, BA in Archaeology and Anthropology, 1980. Reconciler Bank of Am., L.A., 1967-72; emergency rm. technician UCLA Med. Ctr., East L.A., 1972-75; teaching asst. Astronomy dept. Santa Monica (Calif.) Coll., 1975-77; guide, planetarium lectr. Griffith Observatory, L.A., 1976-78; engr. Jet Propulsion Lab./NASA, Pasadena, Calif., 1978-81, planetary scientist, 1981—, astronomical lectr., 1979—; cons. Union of Concerned Scientists, Cambridge, Mass., 1980—, Planetary Soc., 1980—; speakers bur. Jet Propulsion Lab., Pasadena, 1979—. Author: The Shining Gods, 1979. Contbr. Union of Concerned Scientists, Cambridge, 1980—; community organizer Calif. League of Conservation Voters, L.A., 1990—. Mem. Am. Astron. Soc., Div. of Planetary Scientists, Phi Beta Kappa. Democrat. Home: 363 1/2 Sycamore Pl Sierra Madre CA 91024 Office: Jet Propulsion Lab 4800 Oak Grove MS 183-501 Pasadena CA 91109

DINER, WILMA CANADA, radiologist, educator; b. Monaville, W.Va., Jan. 21, 1926; d. William E. and Thelma (Rollins) Canada; m. Jack Diner, Feb. 19, 1955 (dec. Aug. 1988); children: Bradley Canada, Janelle D. Russell, Jeffrey. BS, U. Ky., 1946; MD, Duke U., 1950. Diplomate Am. Bd. Radiology. Resident in radiology Mass. Gen. Hosp., Boston, 1951-54; assoc. radiologist St. Luke's Hosp., New Bedford, Mass., 1955-56; pvt. practice Little Rock, 1962-65; from instr. to asst. prof. radiology U. Ark. for Med. Scis., Little Rock, 1956-62, from assoc. prof. to prof., 1965—; mem. courtesy staff Ark. Children's Hosp., Little Rock, 1962-65; cons. radiologist Little Rock Air Force Base, Jacksonville, 1962-65; dir. radiology residency tng. program U. Ark. for Med. Scis., 1974-89, dir. diagnostic radiology sect., dept. radiology, 1974-82; mem. mammography adv. com. Ark. State Health Dept., Little Rock, 1989—; vis. prof., vis. lectr. various colls. and univs. Reviewer manuscripts Am. Jour. Roentgenology; contbr. numberous articles to med. jours. Sec. health svcs. com. Coalition on Racial Equality, Little Rock, 1989—; mem. women's adv. bd. No. Bank, Little Rock, 1990—; past pres. Temple Congregation, Little Rock. Fellow Am. Coll. Radiology; mem. Radiol. Soc. N.Am., Am. Assn. Women Radiologists (charter, treas., Marie Curie award 1988), Assn. U. Radiologists, Soc. Gastrointestinal Radiologists, LWV, Ark. Supreme Ct. Com. on Profl. Conduct, Sigma Xi. Democrat. Jewish. Office: U Ark for Med Scis 4301 W Markham St Little Rock AR 72205

DINGLE, MARGARET CONCETTA SPARGO, elementary reading director, retired; b. New Haven, Conn., Apr. 2, 1918; d. Frank Curtlin and Clara (Eck) Spargo; m. Frederick Marvin Dingle, Sr., Aug. 23, 1941; children: Patricia, Frederick Jr., Marcia, Louise. EdB, New Haven State Tchr's. Coll., 1940; MS, So. Conn. State U., 1964. Elem. tchr. Clinton (Conn.) Grammar Sch., 1940-41, Ridge Rd. Sch., North Haven, Conn., 1949-50, Prince St. Sch., New Haven, 1950-55, Alice Peck Sch., Hamden, Conn., 1956-69; reading cons. elem. schs., Hamden, 1969-73; dir. reading grades kindergarten-12 Hamden, 1973-82. Author: (curriculum guide) Individualized Reading Program, 1975-80; contbr. Instructor mag., 1971. Recipient Recognition of Svc. Plaque Internat. Reading Assn., 1972; federal grantee, 1976-79. Mem. Conn. Assn. Reading Rsch. (rsch. chairperson), Retired Tchrs. Conn. Republican. Mem. Congregational Ch. Home: 338 Still Hill Rd Mount Carmel CT 06518

DINGLE, SUSAN, library educator; b. Kankakee, Ill., Aug. 31, 1950; d. Harold Eugene and Julia Martha (Condon) Dingle; m. Gerald Howard Cliff, June 30, 1975 (div. Feb. 1984). AB, U. Ill., 1972, MS, 1975, postgrad., 1981—. Sessional reference librarian U. Alberta, Edmonton, Can., 1975-76; pub. services librarian Grant MacEwan Community Coll., Edmonton, 1976-77; librarian Alberta Alcoholism & Drug Abuse Commn., Edmonton, 1977-81; assoc. editor Grad. Sch. Library and Info Sci. U. Ill., Urbana, 1981-86, fellow, 1986-87; asst. prof. Coll. Library Sci. Clarion U., Pa., 1987—. contbr. articles to profl. jours. Mem. ALA, LWV, Am. Soc. for Info Sci. (chair local arrangements 1979), Spl. Libraries Assn., U. Ill. Alumni Assn. (life), Beta Phi Mu. Democrat. Mem. Soc. of Friends. Office: Clarion U of Pa Coll Libr Sci Clarion PA 16214

DINGMAN, AVON MARIE, insurance specialist; b. Saratoga, N.Y., Aug. 26, 1962; d. William Charles and Joyce Elaine (Barrett) Guilder. BA, Manhattanville Coll., 1984. Account rep. MONY Fin. Svcs., Purchase, N.Y., 1985-86; office mgr. Audio Design Assocs., White Plains, N.Y., 1986; employee benefits specialist Taxter Consulting Assocs. Ltd., Briarcliff Manor, N.Y., 1987—. Mem. Nat. Assn. Life Underwriters, Life Underwriters Tng. Coun. Democrat. Methodist. Home: 3 Everett Ave Ossining NY 10562 Office: Taxter Consulting Assocs Ltd 1210 Pleasantville Rd Briarcliff NY 10510

DINGMAN, LINDA SUSAN, educator; b. L.A., Mar. 23, 1942; d. Harold Hadley Story and Esther Pidgeon (Van Vleet) Schou; m. Roger Vincent Dingman, Aug. 21, 1965; children: Charles, Margaret, Zachary, Andrew. BA summa cum laude, UCLA, 1964; MA, Brandeis U., 1965. Cert. sec. tchr., Mass.; cert. sec. English tchr., severely handicapped credential, Calif., Colo. Prin. St. Clare's Family Care Ctr., Redondo Beach, Calif., 1983-86; edn. specialist Urban League Child Care Ctr., Colorado Springs, Colo., 1988-89; primary tchr. Infant-Toddler Devel. Ctr., Calif. State U., Dominguez Hills, 1986-88, head tchr., 1989—; cons. on spl. edn. Marineland, Palos Verdes, Calif., 1987; mem. coordinating coun. Los Angeles County Implementation Pub. Law 99-457, 1988. Cub Scout leader Boy Scouts Am., Lexington, Mass. and L.A., 1970-85; vol. L.A. Unified Sch. Dist., 1971-82; leader Girl Scouts U.S.A., L.A., 1975-82. Woodrow Wilson fellow, 1964. Mem. Assn. for Edn. Young Children, Coun. for Exceptional Children, Phi Beta Kappa, Kappa Delta Pi. Democrat. Roman Catholic. Home: 1532 W 238th St Harbor City CA 90710 Office: Calif State U Infant-Toddler Devel Ctr Dominguez Hills Carson CA 90747

DINGMAN, SHEILA ELAINE, financial analyst; b. Ft. Worth, Mar. 17, 1965; d. Thomas Edward and Lenora Lou (Temple) D. BA in Psychology, Tex. Tech. U., 1987; student, U. San Luis Potosi, Mexico, 1986. Office adminstr. ACSI, Inc., Dallas, 1987-89, ops. adminstr., 1987-89; analyst MBank, Dallas, 1989-90; project analyst Bank One, Dallas, 1990—; mem. Exec. Program, 1990—; advocate CASA/FOCAS, Dallas, 1989—, guardian-ad litem, 1989—. Fellow NAFE; mem. Zookeepers, Dallas Zool. Soc., Paschal Alumni Assn. (bd. mem. 1990), Delta Delta Delta Alumni Assn. Republican. Baptist. Home: 320 Westover Ct Hurst TX 76054

DININNY, JACELYN BROWN, nurse practitioner; b. Ft. Wayne, Ind., Apr. 22, 1933; d. Howard James and Helen Iva (Janney) Brown; m. Robert Edward Dininny, June 12, 1954; children: Robert James Jr., David Russell, Kathleen Ann. BA, Allegheny Coll., Meadville, Pa., 1956; BSN, Case/WRU, Cleve., 1956; MN, U. Fla., 1975. Cert. OB/GYN nurse practitioner. Asst. head nurse U. Hosp. Cleve., 1956-57, staff nurse, 1957-59; staff nurse Albion Community Hosp., Mich., 1970-71, Calhoun County Family Planning, Albion, Mich., 1970-73, Mercer Hosp., Jackson, Mich., 1971-74; asst. dir. nursing Foote Hosp., Jackson, Mich., 1976-79; nursing instr. Kellogg Community Coll., Battle Creek, Mich., 1976; nurse practitioner Drs. Parker, O'Rourke, Jones, Bake, Jackson, Mich., 1979-89, Women's Health Care, Jackson, Mich., 1989—. Named Nurse of Yr., Mich. Nursing Assn., 1982. Democrat. Methodist. Home: 412 E Erie Albion MI 49224 Office: 761 W Mich Jackson MI 49201

DINKINS, CAROL EGGERT, lawyer; b. Corpus Christi, Tex., Nov. 9, 1945; d. Edgar H., Jr. and Evelyn S. (Scheel) Eggert; m. O. Theodore Dinkins, Jr., July 2, 1966; children: Anne, Amy. BS, U. Tex., 1968; JD, U. Houston, 1971. Bar: Tex. 1971. Adj. asst. prof. law U. Houston Coll. Law, prin. assoc. Tex. Law Inst. Coastal and Marine Resources, 1971-73; assoc., ptnr. Vinson & Elkins, Houston, 1973-81, 83-84, 85—; asst. atty. gen. land and natural resources Dept. Justice, 1981-83, dep. atty. gen., 1984-85; chmn. Pres.'s Task Force on Legal Equity for Women, 1981-83; mem. Hawaiian Native Study Commn., 1981-83; dir. Nat. Consumer Coop. Banks Bd., 1981, ELI; bd. dirs., chmn. govt. and pub. affairs com. Nat. Ocean Industries Assn. Author articles in field. Chmn. Tex. Gov.'s Task Force Coast Mgmt., 1979, Tex. Gov.'s Flood Control Action Group, 1980-81; bd. dirs. U. Houston Law Ctr. Found., 1985—, Environ. and Energy Study Inst., Houston Mus. of Natural Sci., Tex. Nature Conservancy. Mem. ABA (vice chair urban, state and local govt. sect.), State Bar Tex., Houston Bar Assn., Tex. Water Conservation Assn., Houston Law Rev. Assn. (bd. dirs. 1978—), Fed. Bar Assn. (bd. dirs Houston chpt. 1986—). Republican. Lutheran. Office: Vinson & Elkins 3300 First City Tower 1001 Fannin Houston TX 77002

DINNERSTEIN, MYRA, university official; b. Phila., Apr. 19, 1934; d. Ben and Kathryn (Sharp) Rosenberg; m. Leonard Dinnerstein, Aug. 20, 1961; children: Andrew, Julie. A.B., U. Pa., 1956; M.A., Columbia U., 1963, Ph.D., 1971. Assoc. editor Ency. Yearbook, Grolier Pub. Co., N.Y.C., 1960-63; dir. women's studies U. Ariz., Tucson, 1975—, dir. S.W. Inst. for Research on Women, 1979—; mem. Ariz. Council on Humanities, Phoenix, 1975-80, 83—, rsch. prof. women's studies, 1989—; Ariz. state coordinator Am. Council on Edn., Washington, 1978-80; dir. Nat. Council for Research on Women, N.Y.C., 1982—. Editor: Changing Perspectives on Menopause, 1982; contbr. articles to profl. jours. Pres. nat. adv. bd. New Directions for Young Women, Tucson, 1981. Recipient Faculty Achievement award U. Ariz. Alumni Assn., 1980; citation award Mortar Bd. U. Ariz., 1981; Faculty Recognition award Tucson Trade Bur., 1982; named to Mortar Bd. Hall of Fame, U. Ariz., 1985. Mem. Nat. Women's Studies Assn., Am. Hist. Assn., Phi Beta Kappa. Democrat. Jewish. Office: U Ariz 102 Douglass Bldg Tucson AZ 85721*

DINNOCENZO, DEBORAH ANNE, educator; b. Lackawanna, N.Y., Nov. 19, 1964; d. James John and Alice Rose (Nalepa) D. BS, D'Youville Coll., Buffalo, 1986. Cert. tchr., N.Y. Kindergarten bilingual tchr. Buffalo Bd. Edn., 1986—. Mem. NEA, Buffalo Teachers' Fedn. (alt. del. 1989, 90). Home: 17 Edna Pl Lackawanna NY 14218 Office: PS 33 Bilingual Magnet 157 Elk St Buffalo NY 14210

DINOVO, THERESA CHRISTINE, marketing educator; b. Greenville, Ohio, Mar. 3, 1958; d. Casmir Francis and Aletha Marlene (Detling) Smogor; m. Anthony DiNovo, May 5, 1984 (div. 1986). BS in Mktg., Miami U., Oxford, Ohio, 1980, MBA in Mktg., 1981. Account exec. Ill. Bell, Chgo., 1981-82; instr. mktg. U. Colo., Boulder, 1982-83; account exec. Colo. Alliance Bus., Denver, 1983-85; instr. mktg. Miami U., Oxford, 1985—; cons. Procter & Gamble, Cin., 1988—, OKI Systems, Cin., 1988—; reviewer Irwin and McGraw-Hill, 1987-88. Named Instr. of Yr. Delta Delta Delta, Miami U., 1989. Republican. Roman Catholic.

DINSMOOR, MARA JEAN, obstetrician-gynecologist, educator; b. Indpls., June 30, 1956; d. James Arthur and Marise Kay (Sawyer) D. AB, Dartmouth Coll., 1978; MD, Ind. U., 1982. Diplomate Am. Bd. Ob-Gyn. Intern ob-gyn. U. Vt., 1982-83, resident, 1983-86; instr. U. Tex. Health Sci. Ctr., San Antonio, 1986-88, asst. prof., 1988-89; asst. prof. Med. Coll. Va., Richmond, 1989—. Contbr. articles to profl. jours., chpts. to books. Fellow Am. Coll. Ob-Gyn. (jr.); mem. Soc. Perinatal Obstetricians (assoc.), Infectious Disease Soc. for Ob-Gyn., Am. Soc. Microbiology. Office: Med Coll Va Ob-Gyn Dept Box 34 MCV Sta Richmond VA 23298

DINSMORE, ROBERTA JOAN MAIER, library director; b. Phila., Sept. 30, 1934; d. Bert Faust and Emma Baker (Keen) Maier; m. Ray W. Dinsmore Sr., Oct. 20, 1956; children: Ray Wilson Jr., Jeffrey Maier, Debra Joan, Matthew Bert. BA, Pa. State U., 1956; MLS, Clarion U. Pa., 1990. Proofreader Aluminum Co. Am., Pitts., 1957-60; office mgr. Dinsmore, Lithographer, Punxsutawney, Pa., 1969—; dir. Punxsutawney Meml. Library, 1978—; free-lance writer Greenburg (Pa.) Tribune Rev., 1980-81; adult edn. tchr. Jeff Tech., Reynoldsville, Pa., 1981-82. Head hostess Welcome Wagon Internat., Memphis, 1976-80; ch. librarian Punxsutawney Presbyn. Ch., 1985—, mem. Jefferson County Constitution Com.; tchr. adult discussion class; chairperson numerous orgns. Mem. ALA, Pa. Library Assn., Pa. Citizens for Better Libraries, Clarion Dist. Library Assn. (pres. 1984-86), AAUW (Woman of Yr. 1987), Punxsutawney Area Hist. and Geneol. Soc., Inc. (sec. bd. dirs., charter mem.), Bus. and Profl. Women, Friends of Library, Punxsutawney Area Hosp. Auxiliary, Goschenhoppen Historians. Republican. Presbyterian. Club: Garden (past pres. Punxsutawney chpt.), Irving (past pres.). Lodge: P.E.O. Home: 808 E Mahoning St Punxsutawney PA 15767 Office: Punxsutawney Meml Libr 301 E Mahoning St Punxsutawney PA 15767

DINTZIS, RENEE ZLOCHOVER, cell biology, anatomy and biophysics educator; b. N.Y.C., Aug. 31, 1927; d. William and Molly (Maisel) Zlochover; m. Howard Marvin Dintzis, June 16, 1951; childen: William S., Joanne B., Suzanne M. BA, Hunter Coll., 1948; PhD, Harvard U., 1953. USPHS postdoctoral fellow dept. physiology Yale U. Med. Sch., New Haven, 1953-54; USPHS postdoctoral fellow dept. biochemistry Cambridge (Eng.) U., 1954-56; instr. depts. biophysics and anatomy Johns Hopkins Sch. Medicine, Balt., 1973-74, asst. prof. dept. cell biology and anatomy, dept. biophysics, 1974-85, assoc. prof., 1986—; vis. rsch. assoc. Cambridge U., 1973-74; Edward Wilson vis. prof. Eliza Hall Med. Rsch. Inst., Melbourne, 1983-84. Contbr. articles to profl. jours. Mem. Md. Acad. Scis. (sci. coun. 1983—), Am. Soc. for Cell Biology, Am. Assn. Immunologists, Biophys. Soc., Clin. Immunology Soc., Phi Beta Kappa, Sigma Xi. Home: 4413 Norwood Rd Baltimore MD 21218 Office: Johns Hopkins Sch Medicine 725 N Wolfe St Baltimore MD 21205

DIONNE, DOROTHY KAY, clinical psychologist, educator; b. Orlando, Fla., July 6, 1960; d. Wilfred Andrew and Virginia May (Losey) D.; m. David Edward Reed, Sept. 16, 1989. BA, U. Cen. Fla., 1981; MS, Fla. Inst. Tech., 1983, D in Psychology, 1985. Lic. psychologist, Fla. Psychology intern Mental Health Svcs. of Osceola, Kissimmee, Fla., 1984-85; psychology resident Affiliates for Evaluation and Therapy, Miami, Fla., 1985-86; clin. psychologist Affiliates for Evaluation and Therapy, Miami, 1986-88; coord. Family Violence Program Nova U., Community Mental Health Ctr., Ft. Lauderdale, Fla., 1988-90; sr. psychologist Tri-County Mental Health Complex, Statesville, N.C., 1990—; adj. prof. Barry U., Miami, 1985-86, St. Thomas U., Miami, 1987-88; asst. prof. Nova U., Ft. Lauderdale, 1989-90. Co-author: (book chpt.) Redefining Crime Responses to Spouse Abuse, 1990. Mem. Am. Psychol. Assn., Div. 35 Am. Psychol. Assn. Women. Office: Tri-County Mental Health Complex 130 Court St Statesville NC 28677

DIPASQUA, LUCY ANN, restaurant franchise executive; b. Norwalk, Conn., Feb. 12, 1927; d. Dominick Felix and Eva Renzulli Nardi; m. Peter M. Dipasqua, Oct. 4, 1947 (div. 1986); children: Gayle, Michael, Donna, Curtis, Lynn, Peter Jr. Sec. HCA, Norwalk, 1945--; sec., treas. Lucy Dipasqua, Inc., Maitland, Fla., 1977-86; pres. Dipasqua Enterprises, Maitland, 1986--; mem. FAF Bd. Dir., Milford, Conn., 1981--, FRA Chpt. 4, Orlando, Fla., 1986--; chairperson FRA Chpt. 4, Edn. Com., Orlando, 1989; v.p. The Taste of Cen. Fla.'s Best; pres. Perkit's Devel. Co. of Cen. Fla. Mem. Franchise Advertising Fund, (bd. dirs., recipient Plaque), Fla. Restaurant Assn. (bd. dirs., sec. chpt. 4 1989, pres. elect chpt. 4 1990). Roman Catholic. Home: 411 Melanie Way Maitland FL 32751 Office: Dipasqua Enterprises Inc 100 Sybelia Ave Ste 380 Maitland FL 32751

DIPIERRO, KAREN P., systems analyst; b. Bronx, N.Y., Nov. 7, 1964; d. Aldo and Lillian (Tassan) Payer; m. Ricardo F. DiPierro Jr., Sept. 13, 1986. BBA in Mgmt. and Info. Systems, Pace U., 1986. Coord., purchasing rsch. and adminstrv. svcs. CIBA-Geigy Corp, Ardsley, N.Y., 1986-87, analyst, info. systems and adminstrv. svcs., 1987-88, sr. programmer analyst, 1988-89; systems analyst CIBA-Geigy Corp, Ardsley, 1990—; cons., tutor. Liason, campus ministry Marist Coll., Poughkeepsie, N.Y., 1983. Mem. NAFE, Human Resources Info. Systems Profls., Assn. Info. Systems Profls., Excellent Idea Com. (chairperson 1987-88). Office: CIBA Geigy Corp 444 Saw Mill River Rd Ardsley NY 10502

DIPIETRO, JANICE DIANE, accounting educator, consultant; b. Stoneham, Mass., Apr. 11, 1957; d. Anthony Vincent and Helen Delores (Landi) Camelio; m. Joseph Anthony DiPietro, Sept. 2, 1979; children: Alexandra, Joseph Anthony. BS, Bentley Coll., 1978; MBA, Boston U., 1987, DBA, 1989. CPA, R.I. Asst. contr. Smith Kline and French, Waltham, Mass., 1977-78; audit mgr. Ernst & Whinney, Boston, Providence, 1979-83; asst. prof. acctg. Bryant Coll., Smithfield, R.I., 1983-89, Northeastern U., Boston, 1989—; cons. CPA firms, R.I., Mass., 1985—; guest lectr. Am. Soc. Women Accts., Inst. of Internal Auditors, Providence, 1985—; instr. Bryant Coll. Ctr. for Mgmt. Devel. CPA Rev. Program, Smithfield, 1984—. Fin. advisor, bd. dirs. MADD, Providence, 1982—; mem. Elizabeth Boffum Chace Home for Abused Women, 1987—. Recipient R.I. Young Career Women of Yr. Bus. and Profl. Women, 1981; grantee doctoral scholarship Boston U., 1987-88. Mem. AICPA, Am. Acctg. Assn., R.I. Soc. CPA's. Office: Northeastern Univ 404 Hayden Hall Boston MA 02115

DIPLACIDO, LISA ANN, drug and alcohol treatment specialist; b. Erie, Pa., May 20, 1967; d. Audrey DiPlacido. BA, Mercyhurst Coll., Erie, 1988, MS, 1990. Counselor Hospitality House for Women, Erie, 1987-88; community edn. coordinator Rape Crisis Ctr., Erie, 1988-89; counselor Perseus House, Inc., Erie, 1989-90; drug/alcohol prevention specialist GECAC, Erie, 1989-90; drug/alcohol treatment specialist Community House for Women, Inc., Erie, 1990; individual svcs. dir. Boys & Girls Club of Erie, Inc., 1990—; cons. Dr. Gertrude A. Barber Ctr., Erie, 1988—; mem. adv. council Millcreek Sch. Dist., Erie, 1989—. Bd. dirs. Am. Heart Assn., Erie, 1989—. Mercyhurst Coll. fellow, 1988-90. Mem. AAUW, Nat. Acad. Criminal Justice Scis., Commonwealth Prevention Alliance, NOW (an organizer 1986). Democrat. Unitarian Universalist. Home: 5710 Georgetown Dr Erie PA 16509 Office: Boy & Girls Club of Erie 130 W 8th St Erie PA 16501

DI PRIMO, MARIE ANN, lawyer; b. N.Y.C., Nov. 1, 1952; d. Dominick and Rosalie (Propper) Di P.; m. Burton Rothbard, Apr. 21, 1982; children: Brigit, Justin. AA, Nassau Community Coll., 1978; BA, Hofstra U., 1980, JD, 1985. Bar: N.Y. 1986. Ptnr. Rothbard & Di Primo, Syosset, 1986—. Mem. ABA, ACLU, N.Y. State Bar Assn., Nassau County Bar Assn., Nassau County Women's Bar Assn., Phi Beta Kappa.

DIRANIAN, NANCY LUCILLE, fashion designer; b. Cambridge, Mass., Apr. 10, 1954; d. Hiram Garabed and Lucille Rose (Dakesian) D.; m. Michael Dennis Paloain, Aug. 9, 1986; 1 child, Andrea Nevart. Cert., Parsons Sch. of Design, N.Y.C., 1976. Designer Jones N.Y., N.Y.C, 1976-79; design dir. Christian Dior, N.Y.C., 1979-81, Regatta Sport, N.Y.C., 1981-83; designer Kazmel by Nancy Diranian, N.Y.C., 1983-86; design adminstr. R.H. Macy Corp., N.Y.C., 1986-89; pvt. practice design and mdse. cons. N.Y.C., 1989—; designer Ann Taylor Stores N.Y.C. 1979-81, HBA Furs N.Y.C. 1979-81; student design critic Parsons School of Design N.Y.C. 1987. Mem. Fashion Group. Republican. Home: 7 East Ct Babylon Village NY 11702 Office: 570 7th Ave New York NY 10018

DIRIG, RICHELLE MARIE, bank management trainee; b. Ft. Wayne, Ind., Sept. 15, 1965; d. Richard John and Rebecca Ann (Bracht) D. BS, Manchester Coll., 1988. Acctg. clk. Great Fidelty Life Ins. Co., Ft. Wayne, 1985; film libr. Delmar Video, Ft. Wayne, 1986; acctg. clk. Lake City Bank, Warsaw, Ind., 1987-88; mgmt. trainee Ft. Wayne Nat. Bank, 1988—. Treas., v.p. Women in the Workplace Club, N. Manchester, Ind., 1986-88; sec. Bus. Club, N. Manchester, 1986-88. Manchester scholar, 1987, Honors scholar, 1988, Hamer Scholar, 1988, Manchester Coll. Mem. NAFE, Am. Inst. Banking. Office: Fort Wayne Nat Bank 110 W Berry Fort Wayne IN 46801

DIRK, LISA, business executive; b. Washington, Oct. 5, 1956; d. Robert Anthony and Elsi Mae (Updyke) Brenkworth; m. Douglas Michael Dirk, June 12, 1976; children: Robert Anthony, Adam Michael. BA in Criminal Justice, Moorhead State U., 1981; postgrad. N.D. State U., 1981. Sec. Harmon Glass Co., Fargo, N.D., 1976-78, N.D. State U., Fargo, 1978-81; owner Handloader Heaven, Fargo, 1981-83; exec. asst. Fargo Glass & Paint Co., 1983-88, Designed Envrionment Supply, Fargo, 1988-89, gen. mgr., 1989—. Mem. Am. Soc. Profl. Estimators (chpt. sec. 1990). Methodist. Avocations: reading, needlepoint.

DIRKS, VICKIE ELLEN, accountant, consultant; b. Mpls., Jan. 21, 1953; d. Robert Waldo and Georgina Mae (Olson) D. BS, U. Minn., 1975, BSBA, 1978. CPA, Minn. Internal auditor Bemis Co. Inc., Mpls., 1978-79, cost acct., acctg. supr., 1979-80, staff acct. to controller, 1980-81; fin. mgr. commodities div. Harvest States Co., St. Paul, 1981-83; sr. acct. DataMyte Inc., Minnetonka, Onn., 1983-84; supr. acctg., mgr. credit DataMyte Inc., Minnetonka, 1984-85, mgr. fin., MIS and credit, 1985-89, contr., 1989—. Cons. Spl. Olympics College Heights, Mpls., 1985-86; chmn. campaign com. Zaccardi for Office, Columbia Heights, 1987-88; mem. Mpls. Aquatennial Flotila Float Producer, 1989—, Hasting Riverfest Flotilla Float Producer, 1989. Mem. Am. Soc. CPA's, Nat. Assn. Accts., Nat. Assn. Credit Mgrs., Am Legion Aux. (charter), VFW (charter), AWSCPA (chmn. pub. relations com. Mpls. chpt. 1986-87). Office: DataMyte Inc 14960 Industrial Rd Minnetonka MN 55345

DI SANTO, GRACE JOHANNE DEMARCO, poet; b. Derby, Conn., July 12, 1924; d. Richard and Fannie De Marco; m. Frank Michael Di Santo, Aug. 30, 1946; children: Frank Richard, Bernadette Mary, Roxanne Judith. Student in journalism, NYU, 1941-43; AB in English, Belmont Abbey Coll., 1974. Newswriter Australian Assn. Press, N.Y.C., 1942-43; staff reporter Ansonia Sentinel, Derby, 1943-45; feature writer, drama critic Bridgeport Herald, New Haven, 1945-46; editor monthly bull. Pa. State Coll. Optometry, Phila., 1947-48; free-lance writer, 1949-54; founder, pres. bd. dirs. Investors Ltd., Morganton, N.C., 1966-67; freelance writer. Author: (poetry) The Eye is Single, Portrait of the Poet as Teacher: James Dickey; contbr. The Dream Book: An Anthology of Writings by Italian-American Women. Pres., Burke County chpt. N.C. Symphony Soc., 1968-70; mem. exec. bd. Community Concerts Assn., 1962-71; trustee N.C. Symphony Soc., 1965-68, 69-70, North State Acad., Hickory, N.C., 1974—; bd. advisors Belmont Abbey Coll., 1986—. Recipient Oscar Arnold Young Meml. award, 1982. Republican. Roman Catholic. Clubs: Grandfather Golf and Country (Linville, N.C.); Mimosa Hills Golf. Address: 218 Riverside Dr Morganton NC 28655 also: Grandfather Golf and Country Club Linville NC 28646

DISHAROON, BARBARA SCHAEFFER, college official; b. Balt., Dec. 1, 1946; d. Richard Carl and Clara (Valianti) Schaeffer; m. Donald Douglas Disharoon, Jan. 4, 1969; children: Eric Douglas, Grant Douglas. BS in Early Childhood Edn., Towson (Md.) State U., 1978; MEd, Western Md. Coll., 1984. cert. tchr., Md. Tchr. Christian Pre-Sch. Program, Westminster, Md., 1976-78, William Winchester Elem. Sch., Westminster, 1979-82; supr. student tchrs., adj. instr. Western Md. Coll., Westminster, 1983—, asst. registrar, 1985-86, registrar, 1987—, asst. dean acad. affairs, 1989—. Reader adv. panel Arithmetic Tchr. Mag., 1984-85; contbr. articles to ednl. jours. dir. publicity September Song, Westminster, 1979-85; bd. dirs. Carroll County Assn. for Retarded Citizens, Westminster, 1984-86. Mem. AAUW (pres. Carroll County br. 1989-91), Am. Assn. Coll. Registrars and Admissions Officers, Middle States Assn. Coll. Registrars and Admissions Officers, Kappa Delta Pi, Phi Delta Kappa. Democrat. Roman Catholic. Office: Western Md Coll Elderdice Hall Westminster MD 21157

DISICK, RENÉE, real estate broker; b. Bklyn., Apr. 22, 1941; d. Morris and Mary (Lubin) Sherrow; m. David Martin Disick, Aug. 15, 1971. BSBA summa cum laude, Ohio State U., 1962; MAT, Stanford U., 1967. Tchr. French Mayfield (Ohio) Schs., 1962-66, Valley Stream (N.Y.) Schs., 1967-75; pvt. practice photography N.Y.C., 1975-80; real estate broker South Village Realty, Warren, Vt., 1980-88; broker-dealer Hotel Condominium Investments, Warren, 1987—; speaker Resort Seminars, Inc., Warren, 1987—. Author: Individualizing Foreign Language Instruction, 1974, (with others) Performance Objectives and Individualization, 1971; contbr. numerous articles various publs. Mem. Phi Beta Kappa. Office: Hotel Condo Investments Inc 158 S Main St Waterbury VT 05676

DISMUKES, CAROL JAEHNE, county official; b. Giddings, Tex., July 17, 1938; d. Herbert Emil and Ruby (Alexander) Jaehne; m. Harold Charles Schumann, Feb. 7, 1959 (div. May 1970); children—Timothy, Michael, Keith, Gregory; m. Milton Brown Dismukes, Mar. 19, 1971. Student Tex. Lutheran Coll., 1958. Dep. Lee County Clk., Giddings, Tex., 1970-74, chief dep., 1975-77; accounts receivable clk. Invader Inc., Giddings, 1977-79; prodn. sec. Humble Exploration, Giddings, 1979-80; county clk. Lee County, Giddings, 1980—. Mem., Dime Box Ind. Sch. Dist. Trustees, Tex., 1972-80, pres., 1977-80; v.p. St. Johns Lutheran Ch. Council, 1982-84; chmn. Dime Box Homecoming and Mini-Marathon, 1978—; chmn. scholar com. Lee Co. Jr. Livestock Show, 1982—; sec. St. John's Luth. Ch., 1986, treas., 1987-89. Mem. County and Dist. Clks Assn. Tex. Democrat. Avocations: reading; sewing. Office: Lee County Clk PO Box 419 Giddings TX 78942

DISNEY, FRANCES LOU, retired educator; b. Great Bend, Kans., Mar. 9, 1929; d. Walter Samuel and Veva Roberta (Ewalt) D. BA, Emporia State U., 1957; MS, Ft. Hays State U., 1972; cert. reading specialist, U. Kans., 1974. Cert. elem. edn. tchr. Tchr. rural sch. Otis, Kans., 1950-51; tchr. Lincoln Elem. Sch., Sterling, Kans., 1951-53; kindergarten tchr. West Elem. Grade Sch., Osawatomie, Kans., 1953-64; tchr. Eisenhower Elem. Grade Sch., Great Bend, Kans., 1964-88; tchr. summer reading program, Great Bend, 1964-69, 71-84, Lincoln Elem. Sch., 1970; cons., supr. student tchrs. summer math. program Ft. Hays U., 1970-72. Mem. cemetery bd. Great Bend Cemetery, 1980-85, Summer Civic Band Flute, Great Bend, 1965-86; periodic mem. election bds.; mem. Young Republicans, 1947-70. Recipient Master Tchr. award NEA, Great Bend, 1984. Mem. AAUW, DAR (Jeremiah Howard chpt., chaplain 1965-88, libr. 1970-88, scholar 1985-90), Delta Kappa Gamma (pres. Iowa chpt. 1984-86, edn. com. 1985-90, polit. action com. 1980-82). Republican. Methodist. Home: 3912 12th St Great Bend KS 67530

DISQUE, CAROL SUE, educator; b. Wilmington, Del., May 15, 1951; d. William Graham and Virginia (Davis) D. BA in English and Psychology, Duke U., 1973; MEd, U. Va., 1974, PhD in Edn., 1982. Dir. placement and career devel. Wake Forest U., Winston-Salem, N.C., 1976-79; dir. placement and career devel. Ohio U., Athens, 1979-82, asst. dean, 1982-86, asst. prof. higher edn., 1986-89; assoc. dean student affairs Coll. William & Mary, Williamsburg, Va., 1989-90, dean of students, 1990—. Bd. dirs. Black Diamond coun. Girl Scouts U.S., Charleston, Va., 1985-88. Mem. AAUW (corp. rep. 1985—), Ohio Coll Pers. Assn. (Project award), Ohio Assn. Women Deans, Adminstrs. and Counselors, Am. Coll. Pers. Assn., Am. Assn. Higher Edn. Office: Coll William & Mary 211 James Blair Hall Williamsburg VA 23185

DISSETTE, ALYCE MARIE, stage and television producer; b. Flint, Mich., Mar. 16, 1952; d. Leland Richard and Carol A.R. (Scott) D. Student, Genesee Coll., 1970-72, U. Mich., Flint, 1972-73, U. Wis., 1975-76. Personal asst. Gilbert V. Helmsly Jr., Madison, Wis., 1975-78; adminstrv. asst. Presentations, Met. Opera, N.Y.C., 1977-79; co. mgr. Ballet Hispanico N.Y., N.Y.C., 1980-81; gen. mgr. Dennis Wayne's Dancers, N.Y.C., 1981-83; exec. dir. Oberlin Dance Co., San Francisco, 1983-86; producer, exec. dir. David Gordon/Pick Up Co., N.Y.C., 1986-89; pres., founder Art Producers Internat. Inc., N.Y.C., 1986-89, 1989—; project dir. A Study of Choreographers, Nat. Endowment for the Arts, Washington, 1989—; producer nat. media project Festival 2000, San Francisco, 1990—; tour program cons. Performance Space 122, N.Y.C., 1989-92; mktg. cons. Pepsico Sumerture, Purchase, N.Y., 1989. Producer (dance/theater) David Gordon's U.S., 1987-89, (dance work) Invisible Cities, 1985, choreographer Brenda Way; exec producer (TV work for BBC) My Folks, 1988. Mem. Assn. Performing Arts Presenters, Am. Arts Alliance, Oberlin Dance Co. San Francisco (bd. dirs.), Dance Theatre Workshop, Dance/USA (trustee 1989). Office: Art Producers Internat Inc 440 W 34th St 5H New York NY 10001

DITHRIDGE, BETTY (MRS. ANDREW MORRISON DITHRIDGE), civic worker; b. L.A., Sept. 11, 1920; d. Thomas Edward and Louise (Miles) Mitchell; m. Andrew Morrison Dithridge, May 11, 1940; 1 child, Andrew Morrison Jr. Student, UCLA, 1937-39. Boy scout and cub scout leader L.A. Orphan's Home Soc., 1952-69, sec. extension com., 1959-61, chmn., 1966-68; vol. worker USO; mem. L.A. Jr. Philharmonic Com., 1949—; active Symphonies for Youth Concerts, 1958-59; founder, chmn. San Marino Protection Com., 1971-72; sec. L.A. County Grand Jury, 1974-75; bd. dirs. Pasadena chpt. ARC, 1961-62, Vol. Service Bur. Pasadena; bd. dirs., treas. Wilshire Community Police Coun., 1979-81; mem. citizens adv. com. L.A. Olympics Organizing Com., 1982-84; dir. Capistrano Bay Community Svcs. Dist., 1987—; guide Doheny State Beach Interpretive Assn. Recipient awards for work with local youth groups. Mem. Wilshire C. of C. (chmn. women's bur. 1957-59), L.A.C. of C. Assocs. L.A. City Coll., Orange County Marine Inst., Friends of Huntington Libr., D.A.R., Friends of San Juan Capistrano Libr., San Juan Capistrano Hist. Soc., L.A. Grand Jurors Assn., Alpha Phi, Sigma Alpha Iota. Home: 35411 Beach Rd Capistrano Beach CA 92624

DITURNO, BARBARA ROSE, charity organization administrator; b. Cleve., Nov. 19, 1963; d. Robert Eugene and Rose Marie (Otto) Sotock; m. Vincent Robert DiTurno, Sept. 19, 1987. Student, Kent State U., 1986. Spl. projects coord. Easter Seal Soc., Cleve., 1986-87, telethon coord., 1987—. Mem. Women in Communications Inc. (bd. dirs.), Radio/TV Coun. Greater Cleve. Democrat. Roman Catholic. Office: Easter Seal Soc Greater Cleve 2800 Euclid Ave 650 Cleveland OH 44115

DITZION, GRACE, artist, playwright, songwriter; b. Montreal, Que., Can.; B.A., Hunter Coll.; M.A., NYU; children—Lynn Shaw, Bruce. Tchr., N.Y.C. Bd. Edn., 1937-74; exhibited in one woman shows at Mus. of the Air (Cable TV), 1977, Nat. Arts Club, 1977, Westchester Community Coll., 1977, Salmagundi Club (award for sculpture), 1977, 1st Fed. Savs. Bank, 1979; group shows include Nat. Acad., Allied Artists of Am., Springfield Mus., Ponce Mus., P.R., Pittsfield Mus., Hudson Valley Art Assn., Chung-Cheng Cultural Center, St. John's U., Lincoln Center Cork Gallery, others; represented in permanent collections at Milford (Conn.) Fine Arts Council, Auburn (N.Y.) Community Coll., Horace Mann Collection, City U. Grad. Center, U. Hawaii; chairperson jury Washington Sq. Outdoor Art Exhibit, 1977-79, NCCJ, 1977; vice-chmn. awards jury Salmagundi Art Club, 1978, 79, 80; chmn. sculpture jury; cons. Womanart Gallery, 1976-78; TV appearances The Price Is Right, Mid-day Live Show, Richard Roffman Focus Show, 1977, 78. Recipient numerous art awards including 1st prizes, Gold medal, Purchase prize, Award of Excellence, Council Am. Artists Socs. award, Award of Merit. Mem. ASCAP, Am. Artists Profl. League, Artists Fellowship, Inc., Am. Portrait Soc., Nat. Arts Club, Internat. Beaux Arts Club of Performing Arts, Internat. Soc. Artists, Women's Press Club of N.Y.C. Important works include portrait of author on dust jacket of book, Club, 1974; (plays) A Moment of Truth, The Decision, A Dream Within a Dream, Sliding on a Rainbow, No Escape. Home and Studio: 3635 Johnson Ave New York NY 10463

DIWAN, JOYCE JOHNSON, biologist, educator, researcher; b. Bklyn., Dec. 25, 1940; d. John Henry and Lillian Freida (Russ) Johnson; m. Romesh Kumar Diwan, Oct. 25, 1970. AB, Mt. Holyoke Coll., 1962; PhD, U. Ill., Chgo., 1967. Postdoctoral fellow U. Pa. USPHS, Phila., 1966-69; asst. prof. Rensselaer Poly. Inst., Troy, N.Y., 1969-75, assoc. prof., 1975—; vis. fellow U. Warwick, Eng., 1976-77. Editor: Advances In Membrane Biochemistry and Bioenergetics, 1987; contbr. numerous articles to profl. jours. Mem. adv. com. Hudson Valley Community Coll., Troy, 1982—. Recipient rsch. grants NIH, 1974-76, 77-81, 83-87, 88—. Mem. AAAS, AAUP, Am. Soc. Biochemistry and Molecular Biology, Am. Soc. Cell Biology, Assn. Women In Sci., Biophysical Soc., N.Y. Acad. Scis. Democrat. Home: 6 Bolivar Ave Troy NY 12180 Office: Rensselaer Poly Inst Sci Ctr Biology Dept Troy NY 12180-3590

DIX, LINDA SKIDMORE, science and engineering program administrator, editor, consultant; b. Salisbury, Md., July 15, 1948; d. Owen Donaldson Skidmore Sr. and Mabel Frances Matthews Shockley; m. Charles Raymond Dix, Sep. 13, 1969; 1 child, Lara. BA, Loyola Coll., Balt., 1972; MEd, Salisbury (Md.) State Coll., 1982. Advanced profl. Md. State Dept. Edn. Tchr. secondary schs. Balt., 1972-73; tchr. James M. Bennett Sr. High Sch., Salisbury, 1973-77, coord. English dept., 1978-81; adminstrv. asst. Commn. Human Resources Nat. Rsch. Coun., Washington, 1981-82; adminstrv. assoc. Office Sci. Engring. Pers. Nat. Rsch. Coun., Washington, 1982-84, adminstrv. officer, 1984-87, program officer, 1987-90, study dir., 1990—; instr. English Salisbury State Coll., 1979; cons. leadership tng. program for women Md. State Tchrs. Assn., Balt., 1978-81, Anne Arundel County Pub. Schs., Annapolis, Md., 1982-90; prin. investigator Engring. Personnel Data Needs in the 1990's, Edn. & Employment Engrs., Minorities Sci. and Engring.; Women Sci. & Engring.; staff officer Com. on the Internat. Exch. & Movmement Engrs., Com. Engring. Labor-Market Adjustments, Com. on Scientists and Engrs. in Fed. Govt. Editor: Women: Their Underrepresentation and Career Differentials in Science and Engineering, 1987, Minorities: Their Underrepresentation and Career Differentials in Science and Engineering, 1987, On Time to the Doctorate, 1989, (with Alan K. Campbell) Recruitment, Retention and Utilization of Federal Scientists and Engineers, 1990; author: A New Generation of Women in Science and Engineering: Changing Vision to Reality, Mapping Science Education for Girls and Women: Where We've Been, Where We Are, Where We Must Go, Recruitment, Retention, and Utilization of Scientists and Engineers in the Federal Government, Women and Minorities in Science and Engineering, Activities to Promote the Interest and Role of Women in Science and Engineering; contbr. articles to profl. jours. Mem. Nat. Arbor Day Found.; Sunday sch. tchr.; original appointee Wicomico County Commn. Women, 1977-81; Severna Park, Md. United Meth. Ch., 1985-; mem. Heartfriends, 1987-, co-chmn., 1989-. Recipient cert. of Appreciation Wicomico County Bd. Edn., 1980; named Outstanding Young Woman Wicomico County Jaycees, 1977. Mem. AAAS, AAUW (chair women's issues Sevenna Park, Md. br. 1990—), NEA, Am. Ednl. Rsch. Assn. (spl. interest group on women and edn.), Nat. Coalition for Women and Girls in Edn., Am. Women in Sci., Am. Legion Aux., Nat. Trust Hist. Preservation, Nat. Geographic Soc., Nat. Mus. Women Arts (charter), Md. State Tchrs. Assn. (chair women's caucus 1977-78, human rights com. 1979-81, meritorious svc. 1978, 80), Wicomico County Edn. Assn. (pres. 1978-79) Amnesty Internat., Smithsonian. Democrat. Home: 64 Arundel Beach Rd Severna Park MD 21146 Office: Nat Rsch Coun Office Sci & Engring Pers 2101 Constitution Ave NW Washington DC 20418

DIX, PAULA MCNICHOLAS, communications educator; b. Youngstown, Ohio, May 14, 1942; d. Paul James and Mary Frances (Dignan) McNicholas; m. John Francis Dix, July 18, 1964; children: Megan Elizabeth, John Kelly. BA, Ursuline Coll., 1964; MA, Ohio State U., 1981. Pub. info. asst. Columbus (Ohio) Mus. Art, 1982-84; dir. client svcs. Clary Communications, Columbus, 1985-89; lectr. Ohio State U., Columbus, 1989—; cons., dir. Ohio task force on drug-exposed infants Ohio Dept. Health, Columbus, 1989—. Com.mem. United Way of Franklin County, Columbus, 1987—; vol. Opera Columbus, 1988-89, League Against Child Abuse, Columbus, 1986—. Recipient Bonze Quill award Internat. Assn. Bus. Communicators, 1986, 88. Mem. Pub. Rels. Soc. Am. (com. chair, Regional award Midwest 5 state area 1989, Cen. Ohio award 1988, East Cen. Dist. Regional award Midwest 5 state area 1985), Women in Communication Inc. (Great Lakes Regional award 1987). Roman Catholic. Home: 2385 Sandover Rd Upper Arlington OH 43220

DIXON, AMY LYNNE, lawyer; b. Salt Lake City, Dec. 2, 1960; d. Melvin R. and Carol Larue (Collard) D. BA, U. Utah, 1983; JD, U. Mich., 1988. Bar: Calif. 1988, U.S. Cir. Ct. Appeals (9th cir.) 1988/. Assoc. O'Melveny & Myers, L.A., 1988—. Office: O'Melveny & Myers 400 S Hope St Ste 1237 Los Angeles CA 90071

DIXON, ANNEMARIE ANDERSON, educator; b. N.Y.C., Aug. 4, 1962; d. John David and Marianne (Clavens) Anderson; m. Jerry Wayne Dixon, Aug. 25, 1984. BS in Secondary Edn., Livingston U., 1985; postgrad. in guidance/counseling, U. So. Ala. Cert. secondary sci. tchr., Ala. Tchr. sci., chmn. dept. Choctaw County High Schs., Butler, Ala., 1985-89; secondary sci. tchr., ednl. counselor Charter Acad., Mobile, Ala., 1989—; instr. Macy Bio-prep program U. Ala., Tuscaloosa, 1986-89. Mem. Keep Choctaw County Beautiful, 1988. U. Ala. grantee, 1986; Ala. Bd. Edn. scholar, 1987, Cold Spring Harbor Labs. scholar, 1988. Mem. NEA, Ala. Edn. Assn., Ala. Sci. Tchrs. Assn. Democrat. Mem. Ch. of God. Home: 820 Deer Run Dr Saraland AL 36571 Office: Charter Academy 251 Cox St Mobile AL 36604

DIXON, CAROLE, merchandise mart director; b. Gainsville, Tex., Mar. 21, 1943; d. George C. and Ann C. (Wistrand) Dixon; ed. Keuka Coll., Penn Yan, N.Y., N.Y. U. Real Estate Inst.; children—Kristin, Shaun. Real estate sales No. Westchester Land Co., Pound Ridge, N.Y., 1970-76; exec. dir. N.Y. Mdse. Mart, N.Y.C., 1979—; dir. N.Y. Tabletop Assn. Bd. dirs. 23d St. Assn. Mem. Nat. Home Fashions League, World Assn. Mart Mgrs. Contbr. articles to profl. jours. Home: 25 W 81st St New York NY 10024 Office: NY Mdse Mart Office of Exec Dir 41 Madison Ave New York NY 10010*

DIXON, CONNIE LORRAINE, executive recruiter, corporate pilot; b. Portsmouth, Va., Nov. 16, 1965; d. Robert Lawrence and June Constance (Biehle) D. BS in Aerospace Engring., Ga. Inst. Tech., 1984. FAA cert. comml., multi-engine pilot. Corp. recruiter, account exec. MSI Internat., Atlanta, 1986-87; dir. ops. USA Career Mktg., Atlanta, 1987—. Mem. Atlanta C. of C., Atlanta Lawn Tennis Assn. (capt. 1988—, city champion 1988-89), U.S. Tennis Assn. (div. champion 1987-88), Reebok Instr. Alliance, Atlanta Track Club, Profl. Career Mgmt. Assn. (sec.-treas. 1989—). Republican. Roman Catholic. Home: 9111 Chastain Dr Atlanta GA 30342-4155

DIXON, DABNEY WHITE, chemistry educator; b. Rochester, N.Y., Aug. 2, 1949; d. Donald Wynn and Helen (Hutchins) White; m. William Thomas Dixon, Aug. 27, 1982; 1 child, William Robert. AB magna cum laude, Brown U., 1971; PhD, MIT, 1976. Postdoctoral fellow U. Calif., San Diego, 1976-79; asst. prof. chemistry Washington U., St. Louis, 1979-86; asst. prof. Ga. State U., Atlanta, 1986-90, assoc. prof. chemistry, 1990—. Contbr. chpts. to books, articles to profl. jours. Recipient Career Enhancement award NSF, 1987; AAUW fellow, 1975-76; NIH fellow, 1978-79. Mem. AAAS, Am. Chem. Soc., Biophys. Soc., Protein Soc., Am. Soc. Photobiology, Phi Beta Kappa, Sigma Xi. Office: Ga State U Dept Chemistry Atlanta GA 30303

DIXON, DOROTHY BEATRICE, school administrator; b. Albert Lea, Minn., June 1, 1921; d. Peter Bernard and Elsie Leonora (Sybilrud) Hoidale; m. James George Dixon, Jr., Aug. 14, 1941; children: Richard, Paula, Paul, James III, Peter, Deborah. Student, Biola Coll., La Mirada, Calif., 1941-43. Founder, dir. Grace Brethren Christian Schs., Temple Hills, Md., 1965-86; dir. Grace Brethren Christian Schs., Clinton and Calvert, Md., 1986—, also cons., 1987—; dir. emeritus Grace Brethren Christian Schs. Author: (Bible studies series) Pleasing Him, 1951, His Own, 1961, Hidden Beauty, 1973, How Mature?, 1987. Republican. Office: Grace Brethren Christian Sch 6501 Surratts Rd Clinton MD 20735

DIXON, IRMA MUSE, state legislator, social worker; b. New Orleans, July 18, 1952; d. Joseph Sr. and Irma (White) Muse; m. Reuben Dixon, June 26, 1976. BA, So. U. of New Orleans, 1976; MSW, Tulane U., 1979; postgrad., Harvard U., 1985. Dir. dept. devel. New Orleans, 1980, bur. chief mgmt. svcs. Office of Employment and Tng., 1981-82, dir. dept. recreation, 1982-84; undersec. Dept. Culture, Recreation and Tourism Baton Rouge, 1984-86; dir. dept. property mgmt. New Orleans, 1987-88; state rep. Ho. of Reps., New Orleans, 1988—; cons. Audubon Inst. Aquarium, New Orleans, 1985, Orleans Parish sch. bd. New Orleans Pub. Schs., 1986. Recipient Legislator of Yr. Alliance for Good Govt., 1988, Outstanding Svc. award City of New Orleans-Mayor's Office, 1988, Leadership award Earhart-Tulane Corridor Assn., 1989, Legis. Women's award La. Conf. Elected Women, 1989, Presidential award Nat. Caucus State Legislators, 1989. Mem. Am. Planning Soc., Am. Soc. Pub. Adminstrs., Nat. Orgn. Black Elected Legis. Women, Nat. Black Caucus State Legislators, Nat. Conf. State Legislators, Ind. Fee Appraisers, Harvard Club La. Democrat. Baptist. Office: 650 S Pierce 2d Fl New Orleans LA 70119

DIXON, JACQUELINE, credit and collections manager; b. Birmingham, Ala., May 19, 1949; d. Isaac Monroe and Dora (Favors) D. BSBA, Ala. A&M U., 1971. With PPG Industries, Inc., Pitts., 1971-88, supr. account reconciliation, 1978-83, credit rep., 1983-88; credit and collections mgr. Giant Eagle, Inc., Pitts., 1990—. Host parent McIntyre Shelter for Children, Pitts., 1980; bd. dirs. Allegheny County Drug & Alcohol Planning Coun., Pitts., 1982, Shuman Ctr. Juvenile Detention Ctr., Pitts., 1990—, Pa. Minority Bus. and Devel. Authority, Harrisburg, Pa., 1990—. Recipient Humanitarian award Homewood Amez Ch. Missionary Circle, 1983, Community Svc. award Negro Bus. and Profl. Women's Club, 1983, Community Citation of merit County of Allegheny, 1984. Mem. Nat. Assn. Credit Mgmt., Pitts. Credit and Fin. Devel. Div., Pitts. Minority Network, Pitts. Bus. and Profl. Forum, Delta Sigma Theta (Pitts. alumnae chpt.). Home: 2125 McNary Blvd Pittsburgh PA 15221 Office: Giant Eagle Inc 101 Kappa Dr Pittsburgh PA 15238

DIXON, JEANETTE T., state legislator; b. Kansas City, Mo., Feb. 24, 1949; d. Charles Barton and Mary Emeline (Shipman) Thistle; m. Robert Eugene Dixon, Dec. 30, 1967; children: Robert Andrew, Dana Lynn, Mary Elizabeth, Laura Mae, Thomas Alexander. Student, S.E. Mo. State U. State legislator Mo. State Legislature, Springfield. Sec. Greene County Rep. Women Club, Springfield, 1985-86; co-advisor Greene County Teenage Reps., Springfield, 1984-87. Mem. NRA, Nat. Right to Life, Nat. Fedn. Blind, Am. Legis. Exchange Coun., Eagle Forum, Boy's Club (women's aux.). Baptist. Home: 3110 E Berkeley Springfield MO 65804

DIXON, KAREN SUE, psychologist; b. Bloomington, Ill., Mar. 25, 1946; d. Charles Lewis and Faye Lanore (Wantland) Henderson; m. David Thomas Biggs, Dec. 2, 1967 (div. 1972); m. Dean Eugene Dixon Jr., Jan. 13, 1973; children: Christopher, Matthew. BA, U. Calif., Berkeley, 1966; MS, San Jose (Calif.) State Coll., 1971; postgrad., Union Inst. Lic. psychol. assoc., Alaska; cert. community coll. tchr. Cons. Alaska Youth and Parent Found., Anchorage, 1989—, Parents United, Anchorage, 1989; mental health cons. Rural Alaska Community Action Program, Anchorage, 1988; cons. Charter North Hosp., Anchorage, 1985-88, Infant Impaired Hearing Program, Anchorage, 1984-85, Parent Tng. Ctr., Anchorage, 1980-82; psychiat. social worker Langdon Psychiat. Clinic, Anchorage, 1976-80; instr. in psychology U. Alaska Community Coll., Anchorage, 1974-81; parole agt. narcotic outpatient program State Dept. Corrections, Oakland, Calif., 1972-74; group counselor II, caseworker Alameda County Probation Dept., Oakland, Calif., 1971-72; cons. psychologist Alviso (Calif.) Econ. Devel. Program, 1971-72; instr. in psychology Coll. of Alameda, 1973; faculty advisor for cooperative edn. U. Alaska Community Coll., 1975-76; pvt. practice The Counseling Ctr., Anchorage, 1980—; mem. adolescent treatment team Charter North Hosp., 1985—. Sec., liaison to bd. Susitna Sch. PTA, Anchorage, 1983-84; co-chmn. optional bd. Susitna Sch., 1984-85, chmn., 1985-86, vol. coord., 1988-89. Mem. Am. Psychol. Assn. (assoc.), Alaska Psychol. Assn. (assoc.). Democrat. Office: 121 W Firewood Ln #107 Anchorage AK 99503

DIXON, LINDA DIANE, sales professional; b. Bowie, Tex., June 4, 1960; d. Pat Ray and Norma Jean (Heath) Kennedy; m. William F. Dixon Jr., Sept. 4, 1982; children: Stephanie Diane, Heather Nicole. BBA, Tarleton State U., 1982. Sales rep. Todco Communications, Austin, Tex., 1982-86; account exec. LDX Net, Inc., Austin, 1986-87; sales mgr., br. mgr., regional sales mgr. Nat. Telecommunications, Austin, 1987—. Mem. coms. Covenant United Meth. Ch., Austin, 1983—. Mem. NAFE, Bus. Execs. Assn. (sec. Austin chpt. 1987-88, treas. 1988-89, pres. 1989—). Home: 11409 Barrington Way Austin TX 78759 Office: Nat Telecommunications 1016 LaPosada #298 Austin TX 78752

DIXON, SHARON PRATT, mayor; b. Washington, Jan. 30, 1944; d. Carlisle and Mildred (Petticord) Pratt; m. Arrington Dixon (div.); children: Aimee Arrington, Drew Arrington. BA, Howard U., 1965, JD, 1968. Bar: D.C. 1970, U.S. Dist. Ct. D.C. 1970, U.S. Ct. Appeals (D.C. cir.) 1970, U.S. Tax Ct. 1970. Assoc. Pratt & Queen, P.C., Washington, 1971-76; lawyer, prof. Antioch Sch. Law, Washington, 1972-76; assoc. gen. counsel Potomac Electric and Power Co., Washington, 1976-79, dir. consumer affairs, 1979-83, v.p. consumer affairs, 1983-86, v.p. pub. policy, 1986-89; elected mayor Washington, D.C., 1990. Chmn. Ea. regional caucus Dem. Nat. Com., Washington, 1976-85, treas., 1985—; nat. committeeperson D.C. State Com., Washington, 1977—. Recipient Disting. Svc. award Fedn. Women's Clubs, 1986, Nat. Assn. Black Women Attys., 1987, 88, Presdl. award NAACP, 1983, Disting. Leadership award United Nego Coll. Fund, 1985. Mem. Women's Rsch. and Ednl. Inst. (bd. dirs. 1986-88), D.C. Unified Bar, D.C. Bar Assn., Links Club, Jack & Jill Club. Home: 8227 W Beach Terr NW Washington DC 20012 Office: Office of Mayor D C Bldg Washington DC 20004*

DIXON, SHIRLEY JUANITA, restaurant owner; b. Canton, N.C., June 29, 1935; d. Willard Luther and Bessie Eugenia (Scroggs) Clark; m. Clinton Matthew Dixon, Jan. 3, 1953; children: Elizabeth Swanger, Hugh Monroe III, Cynthia Owen, Sharon Fouts. BS, Wayne State U., 1956; postgrad., Mary Baldwin Coll., 1958, U. N.C., 1977. Acct. Standard Oil Co., Detroit, 1955-57; asst. dining room mgr. Statler Hilton, Detroit, 1958-60; bookkeeper Osborne Lumber Co., Canton, N.C., 1960-61; bus. owner, pres. Dixon's Restaurant, Canton, 1961—; judge N.C. Assn. Distributive Edn. Assn., state and dist., 1982—; owner Halbert's Family Heritage Ctr., Canton. Pres. Haywood County Assn. Retarded Citizens Bd., 1985—, v.p., chmn. bd. dirs.; bd. commrs. Haywood Vocats. Opportunities, 1985—, treas. bd. dirs.; dist. dir. 11th Congl. Dist. Dem. Women, 1982—; state Teen-Dem. advisor State Dem. party, 1985—; del. 1988 Dem. Nat. Conv., Atlanta; alderwoman Town of Canton, N.C.; vice-chair Gov.'s Adv. Council on Aging, State N.C., 1982—; 1st v.p. crime prevention Community Watch Bd., State N.C., 1985, 86; mem. Criminal Justice Bd., N.C. Assembly on Women and the Economy; chair. Western N.C. Epilipsey Assn., Haywood County N.C. Mus. History, 1987—; co-chair Haywood County Commn. on the Bi-Centennial of Constn., 1987—; pres., chairwoman bd. Haywood County Assn. Retarded Citizens, pres. N.C. coun. Alzheimer's Disease and Related Disorders Assn.; bd. dirs. Canton Recreation Dept., Western N.C. Alzheimer's Disease and Related Disorders Assn., 1987—, v.p.; mem. legis. subcom. Alzheimers-State of N.C.; bd. dirs. N.C. Conf. for Social Services, 1987—; v.p. bd. W.N.C. Alzheimers Assn.; pres. State Coun. on Alzheimers; apptd. mem. Legis. Study Com. on Alzheimers; apptd. mem. adv. bd. on Community Care and Health State N.C. Recipient Outstanding Service award Crime Prevention from Gov., 1982, Gov.'s Spl. Vol. award, 1983, Outstanding Service award N.C. Community Watch Assn., 1984, Community Service award to Handicapped, 1983-84, Outstanding Service award ARC, 1988; named Employer of Yr. for Hiring Handicapped N.C. Assn. for Retarded Citizens, 1985. Mem. NAFE, NOW, Women's Polit. Caucus, Internat. Platform Assn., Women's Forum N.C., Nat. Bd. Alzheimers Assn. (regional del.), Canton Bus. and Profl. Women's Club (pres. 1974-79; Woman of Yr. 1984), Altrusa (Women of Yr. in N.C. 1989). Democrat. Episcopalian. Home: 104 Skyland Terr Canton NC 28716 Office: Dixon's Restaurant 30 N Main St Canton NC 28716

DLOUHY, ANNETTE STEPHANIE, advertising and public relations executive, consultant; b. Cleve., Apr. 19, 1952; d. Ruth Stephanie (Dlouhy) V. AA, Dyke Coll., 1974, BS in Mktg., 1988. Sec. Dyke Coll., Cleve., 1972-74; exec. sec. Bearings Inc., Cleve., 1974-80, adminstrv. asst., 1980-82, advt. mgr., 1982-85, mgr. advt. and pub. relations, 1985, dir. advt. and pub. relations, 1985-87; prin. Designs by Dlouhy, Independence, Ohio and Naples, Fla., 1987—. Dirs. Circle, Cleve. Mus. of Art; lector/eucharistic minister St. Paul's Shrine, Cleve., 1983—; leadership devel. program Fed. Cath. Community Services, 1986, trustee; trustee Cath. Charities Corp., 1987. Named one of Outstanding Young Women in Am, 1986. Mem. Exec. Women Internat., Bus. Profl. Advertisers Assn., Citizen's League. Roman Catholic. Club: Cleve. City, Press of Cleve. Office: 1826 Kings Lake Blvd Ste 103 Naples FL 33962

DOAK, JANICE ASKEW, banker; b. Houston, Jan. 18, 1925; d. Andrew Miller and Cleo Elizabeth Askew; B.B.A., U. Tex., Austin, 1944; m. Ira Kennedy Doak, Dec. 9, 1944; children—Barbara Sue, Carolyn M. With Bank of Houston, 1949—, cashier, 1960-62, v.p., cashier, 1962-74, v.p., 1974-86, sr. v.p., 1986—. Vol. worker St. Luke's Episcopal Hosp., 1973—; docent Harris County Heritage Soc. Mem. Nat. Assn. Bank Women, Am. Inst. Banking (past dir. Houston chpt.), Credit Women Internat. (pres. Lone Star council 1986), Credit Reps. Assn. Greater Houston Banks (bd. dirs., v.p. 1989), Houston Credit Women (pres. 1977-78, 84-85), Am. Bus. Women's Assn. (pres. Houston charter chpt. 1980-81), Fedn. Houston Profl. Women (v.p. 1982-83, honoree) Alpha Chi Omega. Episcopalian. Clubs: Altrusa (pres. 1967-68) (Houston), Order Eastern Star (worthy matron). Office: Bank of Houston 5115 Main St Houston TX 77002*

DOBBIE, DOROTHY, Canadian legislator; b. Jan. 5, 1945; d. Glenn Dobbie, 1964; children: Lori, Shauna. Founder Assn. Publs. Ltd.; mem. from Winnipeg South Ho. of Commons, 1988—. Pres. Winnipeg (Man., Can.) Conv. and Visitors Bur. Named Outstanding Bus. Citizen of Yr., Man. C. of C., 1983. Mem. Winnipeg C. of C. (1st woman pres.). Mem. Progressive Conservative Party. Office: House of Commons, Parliament Bldgs, Ottawa, ON Canada K1A 0A6*

DOBBS, KAREN KEITH, head coach, educator; b. Boston, Apr. 16, 1957; d. Albert and Margaret (Stokes) K.; married; 1 child, Franklin III. BS, Fla. State U., 1978; MEd, Boston Coll., 1989. Cert. elem., phys. edn. and sci. tchr., Mass. Head track coach Newton (Mass.) South High Schs., 1980-83; tchr., team leader adminstr. Newton Brown Jr. High Sch., 1980-86; asst. track and field coach Boston Coll., 1983-87, head men's coach, 1987—. Named Coach of the Yr., Dist. I, 1987. Mem. NCAA, Beantown Rugby Union. Home: 63 Roanoke Rd Hyde Park MA 02136 Office: Boston Coll Conte Forum Chestnut Hill MA 02167

DOBELIS, INGE NACHMAN, editor; b. Würzburg, Germany, Nov. 16, 1933; came to U.S., 1938, naturalized, 1951; d. Rudolf Hugo and Resi (Hamburger) Nachman; B.A. in English, U. Ga., 1956; m. Miervaldis C. Dobelis, May 4, 1969; 1 son, Arthur N. Editorial positions Buttenheim Publs. and Crowell-Collier, 1956-64; copy editor Gen. Book div. Readers Digest, N.Y.C., 1965-72, asso. editor, 1973-79, sr. editor, 1979-85, sr. staff editor, 1985—. Exec. bd., officer Murray Hill Democratic Club, 1968-74; exec. bd. Community Bd. No. 6, N.Y.C., 1973-78, sec., 1976, chmn. health and hosps. com., 1974-78; trustee, officer Brotherhood Synagogue, 1983—; mem. N.Y. Dem. County Com., 1967-74. Mem. Phi Beta Kappa. Assoc. editor: Reader's Digest Family Encyclopedia of American History, 1975; Reader's Digest Family Health Guide and Medical Encyclopedia, 1976; Reader's Digest Illustrated Guide to Gardening, 1978; editor: Readers Digest Family Legal Guide, 1981; Quick and Thrifty Cooking, 1984; Magic and Medicine of Plants, 1986; Great Recipes for Good Health, 1988. Club: Nat. Arts (N.Y.C.). Home: 201 E 17th St New York NY 10003 Office: Reader's Digest Gen Books 260 Madison Ave New York NY 10016

DOBERSTEIN, AUDREY K., college president; b. June 12, 1932; m. Stephen C. Doberstein; children: Carole, Stephen, Anne, Curt. B.S., East Stroudsburg State Coll., 1953; M.Ed., U. Del., 1957; Ed.D., U. Pa., 1982. Exec. dir. Title I ESEA, Del. Dept. Public Instrn., 1965-69; pres. Ednl. Research and Services, Inc., 1969-79; asso. prof. Cheyney State Coll., 1969-79; pres. Wilmington Coll., New Castle, Del., 1979—. Mem. NEA, Am. Assn. Higher Edn., AAUW, Del. Assn. Bus. and Profl. Women, Phi Delta Kappa. Office: Wilmington Coll 320 Dupont Hwy New Castle DE 19720-6491

DOBIS, JOAN PAULINE, social sciences educator; b. Staten Island, N.Y., Sept. 11, 1944; d. Victor Raymond and Rosanna Elizabeth (Dandignac) Mazza; m. Robert Joseph Dobis, Dec. 21, 1968. BA in History, Notre Dame Coll., S.I., 1966; MS in Advanced Sec. Edn., Wagner Coll., 1968; Profl. Diploma in Ednl. Adminstrn. and Supervision, Fordham U., 1979. Cert. adminstr.-supr. K-12, social scis., math. K-12, N.Y. Educator Prall Intermediate Sch., Staten Island, 1966—, adminstrv. asst., 1977-82. Mem. S.I. Hist. Soc., 1968-78, Friends of Downs Syndrome Found., S.I., 1978—, Sister Helen Flynny Scholarship Com., S.I., 1981—; Friends of Seaview Hosp. and Home, Staten Island, 1984—. Recipient scholarship N.Y. State Bd. Regents, 1962, Canadian Consulate, St. Lawrence U., 1987, Internat. Brotherhood of Teamsters, U. Calif., 1988, Nat. Geographic Soc. Geography Edn. Program, SUNY, Binghamton, 1989. Mem. N.Y. State Coun. Social Studies, S.I. Coun. Social Studies, N.Y. State Hist. Assn., N.Y.C. Coun. Social Studies, Nat. Coun. Social Studies, Notre Coll. Alumnae Assn. (S.I. regent 1978-80, pres. 1982-84), St. John's U. Alumni Fedn. (sec. exec. bd. 1988-90, chmn. 1990—), Phi Delta Kappa (Fordham U. chpt., co-founder S.I. chpt., pres. 1982-84, various positions). Republican. Roman Catholic. Home: 174 Bertha Place Staten Island NY 10301 Office: Prall Intermediate Sch 11 Clove Lake Pl Staten Island NY 10310

DOBLER, NORMA (MRS. CLIFFORD DOBLER), state legislator, civic worker; b. Haines, Oreg., May 2, 1917; d. Lester and Bessie (Bircket) Woodhouse; m. Clifford Dobler, June 14, 1941; children: Sharon Louise Dobler Vega, Carol Marie Dobler Harris, Terry Lee. Student, U. Cin., 1935-37; BS in Bus., U. Idaho, 1939. Sec. to registrar U. Idaho, 1939-41; sec. to judge, Caldwell, Idaho, 1945; sec. Am. Express Co., Seattle, 1943; lab. technician U. Idaho Coll. Forestry, Moscow, 1963-69; mem. Idaho Ho. of Reps., 1973-77, Idaho Senate, 1977-87 ; mem. health and human svcs. com. Nat. Conf. State Legislators; mem. Idaho Bd. Tax Appeals, 1987—; mem. Idaho Job Tng. Coordinating Coun.; mem. Idaho Developmemtal Disabilities Adv. Coun., 1977-81; chairperson Gov.'s Task Force Independence, alternative nursing homes; mem. Commn. on Nursing and Nursing Edn.; mem. State Edn. Equity Com., 1986-89, State Adv. Coun. on Aging, 1986—.County adv. bd. trustee Moscow Sch. Dist., 1963-69, vice chmn., 1966-69; bd. dirs. Idaho Sch. Trustees Assn., 1969; leader 4-H Club, 1951-64; pres. Moscow PTA, 1958-59, life mem. Recipient Svc. award Idaho Home Economists, 1979, Conservation Legislator of Yr. award Idaho Wildlife Fedn., 1984; named Citizen of Yr. Nat. Assn. Social Workers, Idaho chpt., 1980; Outstanding Alumna award dept. home econs. U. Idaho, 1984, Conservation Legislator of Yr. award Idaho Wildlife Fedn., 1984. Mem. AAUW (hon.), LWV (bd. dirs. Moscow 1953-68, pres. Idaho, 1968-71), Delta Kappa Gamma (hon.). Methodist (pres. Woman's Soc. Christian Svc. 1972, supt. ch. sch. 1953-65, mem. ofcl. bd. 1953-67, 72). Home: 1401 Alpowa St Moscow ID 83843

DOBRIANSKY, PAULA JON, government official; b. Alexandria, Va., Sept. 14, 1955; d. Lev Eugene and Julia Kusy D. BS summa cum laude, Sch. Fgn. Service, Georgetown U., 1977; MA, Harvard U., 1980, postgrad., 1980—. Adminstrv. aide Dept. Army, Washington, 1973-76; staff asst. Am. embassy, Rome, 1976; research asst. joint econ. com. U.S. Congress, Washington, 1977-78; NATO analyst Bur. Intelligence and Research, Dept. State, Washington, 1979; staff mem. NSC, White House, Washington, 1980-83, dep. dir. European and Soviet affairs, 1983-84, dir. European and Soviet affairs, 1984-87; dep. asst. sec. of state for Human Rights and Humanitarian Affairs, 1987—; assoc. Ctr. for Internat. Affairs, Harvard U., Cambridge, Mass. Fulbright-Hays scholar, 1978: Rotary Found. fellow, 1979; Ford Found. fellow, 1980. Mem. Internat. Inst. Strategic Studies, Am. Polit. Sci. Assn., Phi Beta Kappa, Phi Alpha Theta, Pi Sigma Alpha. Club: Harvard (bd. dirs. 1982-85) (Washington). Office: Dept State Human Rights & Humanitarian Affairs 2201 C St NW Washington DC 20520

DOBRY, SYLVIA HEARN, writer, consultant historian; b. L.A., Aug. 16, 1938; d. Joseph Charles Hearn and Leona May (Crocker) DuBay; m. Ernest John McMichael, Jr., Aug. 13, 1956 (div. 1962); children: Patricia May, Pamela Frances, Debra Stacy, Ernest John III; m. George Maynard Dobry, Oct. 12, 1985. Student, U. Hawaii, 1971-73; BA, U. Calif., Santa Barbara, 1963. Singer concerts, opera, TV, commls., 1948-63; real estate developer various firms, Hawaii, South Pacific and France, 1960—; writer Hawaii Tribune Herald, Hilo, 1965-68; pres. European Castle Restorations, Lurcy-Levis, France, 1973-83; writer, producer Hawaii Actors & Musicians Soc., Kailua-Kona, 1983-85; exec. dir. West Kauai Main St., Waimea, Hawaii, 1986-89; gen. mgr. Kauai Heritage Found., Lihue, Hawaii, 1988—; state coordinator Sister Cities of Hawaii, 1989—; dir. numerous U.S. and British corps., 1969-83; sec. Valeur Pub. Ltd., London, 1975—. Editor: Living in Kona, 1985; author: (plays) Voyage of Destiny, 1988, Island Love Song, 1989, It's Hollywood In Kauai, 1990, (book) Historical Sites and Sights of Kauai, 1989; contbr. articles numerous pubs. Commr. Kauai Historical Preservation Rev. Commn., Lihue, Hawaii, 1986—; dir. Kauai Economic Devel. Bd., Lihue, 1986-89; coord., mgr. Captain Cook Celebration, Waimea, Hawaii, 1987-88; mem. Mayor's Beautification Com., Lihue, 1986-88; pub. relations Island of Kauai, 1985—; goodwill ambassador of County of Kauai to Whitby, Eng., Cooktown, Australia, 1987, 88; mem. Kauai Historical Soc., Friends of the Kauai Musuem; bd. dirs., sec. Kauai Community Players, 1989—. Mem. Inst. Outdoor Drama, Nat. Trust for Historic Preservation, Quota Club (dir. 1989—, pres. 1990—). Home and Office: 3-3400 Kuhio Hwy #A207 Lihue HI 96766

DOBSCHENSKY, CAROLYN SUE, data processing manager; b. Midland, Mich., July 1, 1943; d. Stewart Richard Carrier and Dorothy Elenora (Munger) Ribble; m. Louis Anton Dobschensky, Aug. 17, 1963; 1 child, Anton Louis. Student, Delta Coll., Saginaw, Mich., 1961, Saginaw Valley State U., 1984. Bookkeeper Fisher Sand & Gravel, Midland, Mich., 1961-63; acctg. dept. Frutchey Bean Co., Saginaw, Mich., 1963-65; acctg. supr. Berger & Co., Saginaw, Mich., 1966-87; data processing mgr. Killmer Corp., Saginaw, Mich. Mem. Rebekah's (dist. pres. 1986), United Comml. Travelers of Am. (exec. bd.), Ladies of United Comml. Travelers of Am. (state pres. 1986-87, internat. line officer 1990—). Home: 2478 Van Wormer Saginaw MI 48603

DOBSON, BRIDGET MCCOLL HURSLEY, television executive and writer; b. Milw., Sept. 1, 1938; d. Franklin McColl and Doris (Berger) Hursley; m. Jerome John Dobson, June 16, 1961; children: Mary McColl, Andrew Carmichael. BA, Stanford U., 1960, MA, 1964; CBA, Harvard U., 1961. Assoc. writer General Hospital ABC-TV, 1965-73, headwriter General Hospital, 1973-75; producer Friendly Road Sta. KIXE-TV, Redding, Calif., 1972; headwriter Guiding Light CBS-TV, 1975-80, headwriter As the World Turns, 1980-83; creator, co-owner Santa Barbara NBC-TV, 1983—, headwriter Santa Barbara, 1983-86, exec. producer Santa Barbara, 1986-87. Recipient Emmy award Nat. Acad. TV Arts and Scis., 1988. Mem. Acad. TV Arts and Scis. (mem. com. on substance abuse 1986-88, Emmy nomination 1986), Writers Guild Am., Am. Film Inst. (mem. TV com. 1986-88). Office: 2121 Ave of the Stars Ste 656 Century City CA 90067

DOBSON, MARGARET JUNE, educational administrator, health and physical fitness educator; b. Seattle, June 20, 1931; d. James Walter and Frances May (Howard) D. BS in Health and Physical Edn., U. Oreg., 1954, MS in Physical Edn., 1959; EdD, U. Wis./U. Oreg., 1965; postgrad., Brigham Young U., 1966. Instr. health and physical edn. Portland State U., 1955-65, Lincoln High Sch., Portland, 1954-55; assoc. prof. health and physical edn. Portland State U., 1965-68, prof. health and physical edn., 1968—, various adminstrv. positions, 1972-87, exec. v.p. emeritus, 1988—; instr. Portland Bur. Parks and Recreation, Eugene Bur. Parks, 1951-54; vis. prof. Mt. Hood Community Coll., Gresham, Oreg., 1969-70; instr. U.S. Mil. Spl. Services, Okinawa, Japan, 1959. Recipient numerous athletic and softball awards. Fellow Royal Soc. Promotion Health, Am. Alliance Health, Physical Edn. Recreation and Dance; mem. Am. Assn. Higher Edn., Am. Assn. State Colls. and U., AAUW, Nat. Mus. Women Arts (charter), Japan/Am. Soc. Oreg., Pacific Ballet Co., Am. coll. Sports Medicine and Sci. and numerous other memberships. Home: 4404 SW Primrose Portland OR 97219 Office: Portland State U. PO Box 751 Portland OR 97207

DOBSON, SHARON KAY, real estate agent; b. Decatur, Iowa, Aug. 20, 1936; d. Earl William and Wilma Lucille (Rhodes) Defenbaugh; children: Michael Eugene, Steve William Dobson. Grad. high sch., Van Wert, Iowa. Real estate agt. First Realty B.H.& G., Des Moines, Iowa, 1969-74, Iowa Realty Co., 1974-84; v.p. Colechester Constr., 1977-82; gen. ptnr. Rural Village Inc., Norwalk, Iowa., 1978--; pres. D&S Investments, Des Moines. Republican. Congregationalist. Office: 2423 Ingersoll Ave Des Moines IA 50312

DOBSON, SUSANN DOUGLAS, career planning specialist; b. L.A., July 19, 1949; d. George Ernest and Shari Jaciel (Butler) Krauthoff; m. Douglas Richard Dobson, Aug. 3, 1985. AA in Comml. Art, El Camino Coll., Torrance, Calif., 1970; BA in English, Sonoma State U., Rohnert Park, Calif., 1986. With J.C. Penney Co., Torrance, Calif., 1967-68; hand decorator Metlox Pottery Co., Manhattan Beach, Calif., 1968-70; ships cook pvt. yachts, 1971-72; display artist Mandels of Calif., L.A., 1973-74; mgr. trainee The Bistro Restaurant, Montecito, Calif., 1974-76; asst. mgr. Teaser's Restaurant, Santa Barbara, Calif., 1976-77; head waitress SanYsidro Ranch, Montecito, 1977-80; ad layout designer Pay n Save Corp., Fairfield, Calif., 1980-83; career ctr. dir. Napa County Regional Occupational Prog., Calistoga, Calif., 1986-90; sex equity coordinator Calistoga High Sch., 1989-90, voc. edn. coordinator, 1988-90. Editor/advisor: (high sch. yearbook) One Last Look, 1989, newspaper, The Cat Times, 1989, 90, A Whole New Look, 1990; author: (children's fiction) The Last Leaf, 1982. Contbg. mem. Calistoga Edn. Found., 1989; mem. Napa Valley Hispanic Network, 1989; coordinator Es Su Vida Workshops for Hispanic Teens, Calistoga, 1989, 90. Nat. Masonic Found. scholar, 1985; Carl T. Perkins Sex Equity grantee, 1989, 90; recipient Napa Co. Hispanic Community Svc. award Napa Valley Hispanic Network, 1990. Mem. Nat. Assn. Career Devel., Calif. Career Edn. Assn., Soc. of Children's Book Writers. Democrat. Zen Buddhist.

DOCKERY, CINDI JO, specialty toy company executive; b. Huron, S.D., May 5, 1965; d. Dwaine Harlo Wynia and Diann Marie (Leistra) Steed; m. Larry Gene Dockery, May 1, 1987; children: Regena Anne, Melanie Jan. AS, Amarillo Coll., 1986. Softlines sales rep. Target, Amarillo, Tex., 1985-86, price change supr., 1986-87; juvenile dept. mgr. Children's Palace, Amarillo, Tex., 1987-88, asst. mgr. Mem. Amnesty Internat., Nat. Mus. of Women in Arts, Cousteau Soc., Amarillo Coll. Alumni Assn. Methodist. Office: Children's Palace 101 Westgate Pkwy W Amarillo TX 79121

DOCTOR-CANHAM, RHONDA LYNN, nursing home administrator; b. Knoxville, Tenn., Dec. 19, 1964; d. Robert Frederick Doctor and Glenda Mae (Hundley) Doctor Shropshire; m. John Stewart Canham, Dec. 6, 1989. BS, Notre Dame Coll. of Ohio, 1987; postgrad., Miami U., Oxford, Ohio, 1989. Nursing asst. Mt. Alverna Home, Parma, Ohio, 1985-87; adminstr.-in-tng. Otterbein Homes, Lebanon, Ohio, 1988; needs assessment interviewer Maple Knoll Village, Springfield, Ohio, 1988; grad. asst. Miami U., Oxford, Ohio, 1987—; adminstr. Heartland of Eaton (Ohio) Nursing and Rehab Ctr., 1090—. Mem. Ohio Rsch. Council on Aging; vol. Am. Red Cross, 1983-87. Recipient Leadership award, Community Svc. award Notre Dame Coll. Ohio, 1987. Mem. Am. Coll. Health Adminstrs., Ohio Health Care Assn. Roman Catholic. Office: Heartland of Eaton 515 S Maple St Eaton OH 45320

DODD, CAROL KELLEY, health educator, allied health administrator; b. Lexington, Ky., Sept. 24, 1947; d. William Harrison Jr. and Laura Ellen (Sallee) Kelley; m. Jerry Wayne Dodd, Aug. 12, 1972; children: Kelley Ann, Jeri Ann. BS in Med. Tech., U. Tenn., 1970; MS in Higher and Adult Edn., U. Ky., 1974. Cert. med. asst.; cert. med. technician. Rsch. asst.dept. biology U. Tenn., Knoxville, 1967-69; lab. supr. U. Tenn. Hosp., Knoxville, 1970-72; lab. technician U. Ky. Hosp., Lexington, 1972-73; lab. technician, dir. lab. Cen. Ky. Blood Ctr., Lexington, 1973-74; substitute tchr. Knoxville City Schs., 1981-84; asst. prof. allied health Knoxville Coll., 1984—, program coordinator med. assisting and health adminstrn., 1984—. Instr. ARC, Knoxville, 1986—; team mem. Fish of Knox County, Knoxville, 1981—; elder New Covenant Presbyn. Ch., 1986—. Kellogg Found. fellow, 1972-74. Mem. Am. Assn. Med. Assts., Phi Beta Kappa, Phi Kappa Phi. Home: 7048 Regency Rd Knoxville TN 37931 Office: Knoxville Coll 901 College St Knoxville TN 37931

DODD, DARLENE MAE, nurse, air force officer; b. Dowagiac, Mich., Oct. 11, 1935; d. Charles B. and Lila H. D.; diploma in nursing Borgess Hosp. Sch. Nursing, Kalamazoo, 1957; grad. U.S. Air Force Flight Nurse Course, 1959, U.S. Air Force Squadron Officers Sch., 1963, Air Command and Staff Coll., 1973; BS in Psychology and Gen. Studies, So. Oreg. State Coll., 1987, postgrad., 1987; Commd. 2d lt. U.S. Air Force, 1959, advanced through grades to lt. col., 1975; staff nurse, Randolph AFB, Tex., 1959-60, Ladd AFB, Alaska, 1960-62, Selfridge AFB, Mich., 1962-63; Cam Rahn Bay Air Base, Vietnam, 1966-67, Seymour Johnson AFB, N.C., 1967-69, Air Force Acad., 1971-72; flight nurse 22d Aeromed. Evacuation, Tex., 1963-66; chief nurse Danang AFB, Vietnam, 1967; flight nurse Yokotu AFB, Japan, 1969-71; clin. coordinator ob/gyn and flight nurse, Elmendorf AFB, Alaska, 1973-76; clin. nurse coordinator obstetrics-gynecology and pediatric services USAF Med. Center, Keesler AFB, Miss., 1976-79, ret., 1979. Decorated Bronze Star, Meritorious Service medal, Air Force Commendation medal (3). Mem. Soc. of Ret. Air Force Nurses, DAV, Ret. Officers Assn., Vietnam Vets. Am., VFW, Uniformed Services Disabled Retirees, Psy Chi, Phi Kappa

Phi. Clubs: Psychology, Women of Moose. Home: 712 W 1st St Phoenix OR 97535

DODD, VIRGINIA MARILYN, veterinarian; b. Battle Creek, Mich., Oct. 14, 1950; d. George Vernon and Marilyn Ottilie (Johnson) D. BS, Mich. State U., E Lansing, 1972; DVM cum laude, Mich. State U., East Lansing, 1974. Diplomate Am. Bd. Vet. Practitioners, Companion Animal Practice, 1982. Vet. Butler Animal Hosps. Pa., Charlotte, 1975-83; medicine resident U. Tenn., Knoxville, 1983-86; asst. prof. medicine U. Saskatchewan, Canada, 1986-87; vet. Village Vet. Clinic, Farragut, Tenn., 1987-88, Vet. Referral Service, Charlotte, N.C., 1988—; relief vet. Nashboro Animal Hosp., 1988—; vet. After Hours Vet. Emergency Clinic, Greensboro, N.C., 1989—; veterinarian Vet. Consultation & Relief Svcs., 1989—; speaker U. Tenn. Knoxville, 1984-86. Author: Med. Case Report A.V.M.A. Jour. 1986, Radiology Case Report Vet. Radiology 1987. Pres. Greater Charlotte Vet. Med. Assn., 1980-82; advisor Vet. Med. Tech. Adv. Com. Cen. Carolina Tech. Coll., Sanford, N.C.; Coord. Nat. Pet Week Mecklenburg Co. nc, 1982. Mem. Am. Vet. Med. Assn., Am. Animal Hosp. Assn., Vet. Dental Soc., Am. Assn. Vet. Clinicians, Am. Heartworm Soc., Vet. Cancer Soc., Knoxville Track Club, Sierra Club, Lupus Found. of East Tenn., Triathlon Club, Phi Zeta. Home: 2513 Shaler Ln Knoxville TN 37920

DODDS, CLAUDETTE LA VONN, radio executive and consultant; b. Lenapah, Okla., Sept. 2, 1947; d. Willie Lee and Dora (Harrell) Davis; m. Donald Howard Dodds, Jan. 14, 1965 (div. June 1982); children: Clarence Adam, Donyielle Alana, Erin Michelle. AAS with honors, Kennedy-King Coll., 1984; BA, U. Ill., Chgo., 1989. Newscaster, newswriter Sta. WKKC-FM, Chgo., 1983-84, news dir., 1984-85, program and music dir., 1985, sta. mgr., 1985-87; research asst. Vernon Jarrett Chgo. Sun Times, 1988-89; exec. asst. to pres. Sta. WVON, Chgo., 1989; asst. sta. mgr. Sta. WYCA-FM, Crawford Broadcasting Co., Chgo., Hammond, Ind., 1989-90; mem. adv. com. Coll. Broadcasting, 1985-87; cons. Chgo. Nite Life, 1985-87, Hayes & Co., 1986—, Morning Show/Danny Jack Sta. KWEZ, Monroe, La., 1986—, Sta. WKKC-FM, Future Records, 1988—; music researcher Let's Dance, Chgo., 1986-88; broadcast asst. Sta. WVON, Chgo., 1989, exec. bd. Young People's Network Sta. WKKC-FM, 1988—. Producer (TV spl.) Messiah, 1985; producer, writer (radio and TV spls.) Dr. Martin Luther King, 1985-86; producer, hostess (radio spls.) Englewood Parade, 1986, Bud Billiken Parade, 1986; mag. music reporter, 1987. Mem. Dem. Student Task Force, Chgo., 1984, Student Disciplinary Bd., Chgo., 1986; coord. Concerned Students for Broadcasting Equipment, 1984. Mem. Ill. Broadcasters Assn., Broadcasters Edn. Assn., Communications Arts Guild (corr. sec. 1982-83), Phi Theta Kappa. Clubs: WKKC Social (Chgo.) (treas., founder 1983-84), Broadcasting (Chgo.) (staff adv. 1985-86). Lodges:Order of Eastern Star, Heroines of Jericho. Home and Office: 305 W 69th St Chicago IL 60621

DODERER, MINNETTE FRERICHS, state legislator; b. Holland, Iowa, May 16, 1923; d. John A. and Sophie S. Frerichs; BA, U. Iowa, 1948; m. Fred H. Doderer, Aug. 5, 1944; children: Dennis, Kay Lynn. Mem. Iowa Ho. of Reps. 1964-69, 80—, minority whip, 1967-68, chairperson ways and means com., 1983-88, chair commerce com., 1989—; mem. Iowa Senate, 1969-79, pres. pro tem, 1975-76; vis. prof. Stephens Coll., Iowa State Coll. (both 1979); vice-chairwoman Iowa Interstate Cooperation Commn., 1965-66; Vice-chairwoman Democratic Party Johnson County, 1957-60; vice chairperson com. on budget and taxation Nat. Conf. State Legislator's; mem. Dem. Nat. Com., 1968-70, Dem. Nat. Policy Council Elected Ofcls., 1973-76; chairwoman Iowa del. Internat. Women's Yr. Del. Bd. fellows Iowa Sch. Religion. Recipient Disting. Service award Iowa Edn. Assn., 1969, Wilson award Commn. on Status of Women, 1989; named to Iowa Women's Hall of Fame, 1978. Mem. LWV, Delta Kappa Gamma (hon.). Democrat. Methodist.

DODGE, NANCY NOBLE, pediatrician; b. Detroit, Dec. 30, 1957; d. Russell Robert and Marjorie (Diem) Noble; m. Michael Carlton Dodge, Aug. 2, 1980; 1 child, Katherine Noble. BA in Biology, Oberlin Coll., 1979; MD, U. Mich., 1983. Diplomate Am. Bd. Pediatrics. Pediatric resident Children's Meml. Hosp., Chgo., 1983-86; devel. fellow Children's Hosp. Phila., 1986-88; clin. asst., prof. pediatrics Riley Children Hosp., Indpls., 1988—; med. dir. Cerebral Palsy Program, Riley Childrens Hosp., Indpls., 1989—. Fellow Am. Acad. Pediatrics; mem. Am. Acad. Cerebral Palsy and Devel. Medicine. Episcopalian. Office: Riley Childrens Hosp S139 702 Barnhill Dr Indianapolis IN 46202

DODOHARA, JEAN NOTON, music educator; b. Monroe, Wis., Feb. 21, 1934; d. Albert Henry and Eunice Elizabeth (Edgerton) Noton; BA, Monmouth (Ill.) Coll., 1955; MS, U. Ill., 1975, adminstrv. cert., 1980, EdD, 1985; m. Laurence G. Landers, June 7, 1955 (div.); children: Theodore Scott, Thomas Warren, Philip John; m. Edward R. Harris, Nov. 27, 1981 (dec.); stepchildren: Adrianne, Erica; m. Takashi Dodohara, Aug. 7, 1988; 1 stepchild, Eve D. Jones. Tchr. music schs. in Ill. and Fla., 1955-76; tchr. ch. music for children, 1957-72; tchr. music Dist. 54, Schaumburg, Ill., 1976—; teaching asst. U. Ill., 1979. Named Outstanding Young Woman of Yr., Jaycee Wives, St. Charles, Mo., 1968; charter mem. Nat. Mus. Women in Arts. Mem. NEA (life), AAUW, Music Educators Nat. Conf. (life), Ill. Music Educators Assn., Soc. Gen. Music Educators, Alliance for Arts Edn., Am. Choral Dirs. Assn., U. Ill. Alumni Assn. (life), Mortar Bd., Mensa, Delta Kappa Pi. Mem. United Ch. of Christ. Home: 1068 Hampshire Ln Elgin IL 60120

DODSON, (PATRICIA) ELAINE, personal care industry specialist; b. Waxachachie, Tex., May 10, 1944; d. Gordon Oliver and Opal Christine (McCann) Dodson; m. Preston Vice, June 6, 1964 (div. 1971); children: Kevin, Chelsea Madrigal; m. Michael Roth, Aug. 12, 1988; 1 child, Jordan. BA, McMurry Coll., 1963; BS, So. Meth. U., 1974; certs. in cosmetology, Glen & Lotties, Abilene, Tex., and Ron Renees, Dallas, 1963 and 1978; cets. in makeup artistry including, Christian Chevaux, Paris and, Theresa Black, MGM Studio, Hollywood, Calif., 1979 and 1980; stduied hair design with Vidal Sasoon, Mr. Kenneth, George Carroll, Paul Mitchell, Irvine Rusk, Trevor Sorbie, John Dellaria, Toni and Guy, others. Lic. cosmetologist/aesthetician, makeup artist, communication dynamics. Hair stylist Frances Beauty Salon, Abilene, 1962-66; stylist, mgr. Zubik Beauty Salon, Dallas, 1967-76; stylist Northpark-Mantrap, Dallas, 1976-79; owner, mgr. Backstage Dallas, 1979-83; owner, producer Elaine Dodson /Snider Plaza, Dallas, 1983-85; co-owner, mgr. Terri Ives Internat., Dallas, 1985-87; owner, stylist, producer Elaine Dodson, Inc., Dallas, 1987—; tchr., cons. A Natural Way of Beauty, Dallas, 1990—; cons. Southwest Bell Telephone, Dallas, 1970—, Am. Airlines, Ft. Worth, 1986—; tchr. Redken Joico, U.S. and Europe, 1970-85, Advanced Study Programs, Southwest, 1985-90; pioneer in beauty and health makeover salon in S.W. U.S.; pub. speaker in field. Author: Elaine Dodson Seminars, 1986; producer seminars and shows Sunbelt Circle Prodns., 1980-90; developer Look Fabulous in Minutes (make up seminar). Mem. Crime Watch, Dallas, 1980—; chmn. Dallas Revitilization Programs, Dallas, 1975—, Jimmie Carter polit. campaign, Dallas; founder Food For Life, Dallas, 1979—. Production award London Aestheticians Assn., 1981, Nat. Hair Competition, N.Y.C., 1979, Hair Styling award Internat. Hair Show, London, 1978, grant Redken Labs., Redding (Calif.) Internat., 1964. Mem. Nat. Hairdressers and Cosmetology Assn., Tex. Hairdressers and Cosmetology Assn. (sec., hair compeition award 1962), Aesthicians Internat. Assn. (Dallas spokesman), Dallas C. of C. Office: Elaine Dodson Salon 5014 McKinney Ave Dallas TX 75205

DODSON, LINDA S., librarian, investor; b. Freeport, Tex., Oct. 1, 1952; d. William Erroll and Helen Rose (McDowell) Dodson. BAin Teaching, Sam Houston State U., 1975; M Library and Info. Sci., U. Tex., 1986. Librarian Goose Creek Ind. Sch. Dist., Baytown, Tex., 1977-78, Channelview (Tex.) Ind. Sch. Dist., 1978-79, Tenneco Inc., Houston, 1979-88; core librarian Arthur Andersen and Co., Houston, 1988—. Mem. Spl. Librs. Assn., Houston Online User's Group, Houston Area Law Librs. Home: 13213 Bay Place Dr Baytown TX 77520

DODSON, R. J., speech educator; b. Burkburnett, Tex., Apr. 15, 1929; d. Robert Lester and Nellie Jane (Brown) D.; m. Barbara Ann Claborn, Jan. 24, 1959; children: Randy, Paul, Amanda. AA, Kilgore Coll., 1948; BFA, U. Tex., 1951; MS, Abilene Christian U., 1964. Speech instr. Kilgore (Tex.) Coll., 1959—, dir., Ch. of Christ Bible chair, 1959-62. Author: A Guide to Speaking in Public, 1986, revised edit., 1990. Sponsor Phi Theta Kappa, Kilgore, 1965-80. 1st lt. U.S. Army, 1951-53, Korea. Decorated Bronze Star. Mem. Tex. Jr. Coll. Tchrs. Assn. Mem. Ch. of Christ. Home: 1809 Bell Longview TX 75602 Office: Kilgore Coll 1100 Broadway Kilgore TX 75662

DODSON, VANESSA MEALAINE, program analyst; b. Newport News, Va., May 30, 1958; d. Aubrey Don and Nellie (Olgesby) Herbin. BS in Bus., Va. Commonwealth U., 1980. Sales assoc. Sears, Roebuck and Co., Richmond, Va., 1979-81; asst. mgr. Lerner Shops, Richmond, 1980-81; loan processor Home Savs., Houston, 1981-82; sales assoc., joint venture coord. Sakowitz, Houston, 1981-83; coord., acct. Texaco, USA, Houston, 1982-86; program analyst armaments R & D ctr. U.S. Army, Picatinny Arsenal, N.J., 1987—. Mem. Am. Soc. Mil. Controllers, Community Recreation Br., NAFE.

DOEBBELING, MINDA KAY, social services administrator; b. Dodge City, Kans., Apr. 16, 1942; d. Clarence and Velvyn Lena (Levan) D. BA, Wichita (Kans.) State U., 1965; MS, Fla. State U., 1967. Lic. child care adminstr., Tex.; cert. social worker, alcohol and drug abuse counselor, Tex.; diplomate Am. Bd. Clin. Social Work. Jr. probation counselor Youth Ctr., Topeka, 1967-70, clin. social worker, 1971-79; clin. social worker Tex. Dept. Mental Health and Retardation, Denton State Sch., Tex., 1981-83; instr. Odessa (Tex.) Coll., 1983—; social svcs. adminstr. Tex. Youth Commn., West Tex. Children's Home, Denton, 1983—. Mem. Nat. Assn. Social Workers, Acad. Certified Social Workers. Office: PO Box 415 Pyote TX 79777

DOELLING-BAKER-ERBISCH, CAROL SUZANNE, day care director; b. Ft. Wayne, Ind.; d. James Edwin Sr. and Susie Mae (Nutter) Doelling; m. Gerald R. Baker, June, 1962 (div. 1966); 1 child, Erin Lee; m. Jeffrey E. Baker, June, 1967 (div. 1972); 1 child, Shannon Rae; m. Gilbert Erbisch, 1985. Student, Internat. Bus. Coll., Ft. Wayne, 1961. Expeditor Wayne Fabricating, Ft. Wayne, 1971; county adminstr. Champaign (Ill.) County Bd., 1974-76; sec. WICD-TV, Champaign, 1976-77; ops. chmn. 40 Plus of Colo., Inc., Denver, 1983, v.p., 1984-85, pres., 1985-86; asst. dir. St. Anne's Extended Day Program, Denver, 1986-88, ret., 1988. Editor The Village Voice newsletter, Savoy, Ill., 1974. Chmn. Winfield Village Swimming Pool com., Savoy, 1975. Mem. Am. Bus. Women's Assn.

DOENECKE, CAROL ANNE, artist; b. Chgo., July 9, 1942; d. George John and Irene Victoria (Ostrowski) Soukup; m. Justus Drew Doenecke, Mar. 21, 1970. Student, U. Chgo., 1960-63; BFA, Sch. of the Art Inst., Chgo., 1964. Artist Polk Pub. Museum All Fla. Biennial, Lakeland, 1985. Artist: Northwest Pastel Soc., Issaquah, Wash., 1989, La. Art and Artist's Guild, Baton Rouge, 1989, Hilltop Gallery, Nogales, Ariz., 1989, Pastel Soc. of the Southwest, Dallas, 1988, Ctr. for the Arts, Vero Beach, Fla., 1988, Women's Resource Ctr., Sarasota, Fla., 1987, Pastel Soc. of Can., Toronto, 1987, Lake Worth (Fla.) Art League, 1987, Glen Gallery, Sarasota Boys Club, 1987, Vantage Gallery, Ithaca, N.Y., 1986; one woman shows include Women's Resource Ctr., Sarasota, Fla., 1987, Arts Ctr. At Maas Bros., St. Petersburg, Fla., 1990. Recipient Award of Merit, Fla. Pastel Assn. Show, Arts-on-the-Park, Lakeland, Fla., 1984, Award of Merit for pastels, Arts-on-the-Park, Lakeland, 1986, Honorable Mention Human Image (all media) Art League of Manatee County, Bradenton, Fla., 1981, Honorable Mention, 46th Annual Nat. Juried Competition, Lake Worth Art League, 1987, 1st Place VIII Annual Exhbn., mems. Fla. Pastel Assn., Ft. Lauderdale, Fla., 1988. Mem. Pastel Soc. of the SW, Fla. Pastel Assn., Art League of Manatee County, Sarasota Art Assn. Episcopalian. Home and Studio: 3943 Riverview Blvd W Bradenton FL 34209

DOERFLINGER, MARLYS IRENE, landlord, small business owner; b. Cin., Apr. 2, 1943; d. Marvin Corl and Eleanor Elizabeth (Dempsey) Kummer; m. Arthur Eugene Doerflinger, Nov. 17, 1962; children: Cynthia Louise, Mark Eugene. BBA, U. Mo., Kansas City, 1975, MS in Acctg., 1979. Landlord, 1962-66, 71—; lectr. Cen. Mo. State U., Warrensburg, 1979, asst. prof., 1979-82, 89—; landlord, 1968—; co-owner Doerflinger's Christmas Trees, Kansas City, 1984—. Mem. Nat. Assn. Accts. (Kansas City chpt., v.p. continuing profl. edn. com. 1989—, bd. dirs. 1981—), Landlords Inc. of Kansas City, Mo. Christmas Tree Producers' Assn. Home and Office: Doerflinger Christmas Trees Trees 10266 Lane Kansas City MO 64134

DOERING, AMY LEWIS, associate publisher; b. Norwalk, Conn., July 16, 1960; d. Stanley Pierson and Julia (Beals) Lewis; m. Peter Eckart Doering, Aug. 16, 1986. BA, Ohio Wesleyan U., 1982. Sales exec. Am. Lawyer Newspapers, N.Y.C., 1982-87; advt. dir. Am. Lawyer Media, N.Y.C., 1987-89, assoc. pub., 1989—. Republican. Home: 12 E 97th St New York NY 10029 Office: Am Lawyer Media LP 600 Third Ave New York NY 10016

DOERING, BARBARA JEANNE, mental health and addictions counselor; b. Bklyn., May 3, 1947; d. Larry and Sylvia (Slatas) Sloan; m. J. Ward Doering II, June 24, 1989; children: Andrew, Philip Houck. BS, Purdue U., 1969; MEd, U. S.C., 1981. Cert. alcoholism counselor; nat. cert. counselor. Case mgr. S.C. Dept. Social Svcs., Conway, 1973-78; vocat. evaluator S.C. Dept. Vocat. Rehab., Conway, 1978; dir. Horry-Georgetown Youth Bur., Myrtle Beach, S.C., 1978-83; v.p. Human Resource Edn. Inst., Meriden, Conn., 1983-86; dir. vocat. svcs. APT Found., New Haven, 1986-87; dir. John Magee House Shirley Frank Found., New Haven, 1987-88; pvt. practice Cheshire, Conn., 1986—; dir. alcohol and chem. dependency svcs. Griffin Hosp., Derby, Conn., 1988—; lectr. in field; trainer on gerontology and addictions, 1983—. Newspaper columnist, 1988-89. Bd. dirs. Nat. Assn. Vols. in Criminal Justice, 1983-85; sec. Sea Haven, Myrtle Beach, S.C., 1982-83; chairperson Vols. in Probation, 1982-83; dir. 1st vocat. accredited program for addictions. Mem. Am. Assn. for Counseling and Devel., Am. Mental Health Counselors Assn., Conn. Mental Health Counselors Assn., Conn. Assn. for Counseling & Devel., Employee Assistance Profl. Assn. (membership chair Conn. chpt. 1988-90), Rotary, Psi Chi. Office: Griffin Hosp 130 Division St Derby CT 06418

DOERR, LEXIA ETHEL, educator; b. Pierre, S.D., Aug. 9, 1931; d. Leonard Edward and Ethel Elizabeth (Evans) Serbousek; m. Ray Francis Doerr, June 15, 1950 (div. 1988); children: Rae Marie Pekas, Gary, Judy, Marvin, Andrea. Student, Black Hills State Coll., 1969, BS in Edn. magna cum laude, 1971. Cert. elem. edn. tchr., S.D. Tchr. North Pearl Sch. Dist., Onida, S.D., 1949-50, Fruitdale (S.D.) Sch., 1969-70, Glenham (S.D.) Sch., 1971-72, Smee Ind. Sch. Dist., Wakpala, S.D., 1972—. Mem.,pres., chairperson Upper Mo. Assn. for Edn. of the Young Child, 1973-82. Mem. AAUW (pres. 1978-80, 85-87, treas. 1987—, chairperson county spelling contests Mobridge, S.D. chpt. 1985—), Wakpala Edn. Assn. (sec.-treas. 1975-76, 87-88, pres. 1977-78, 81-86, 88-89, chief negotiator 1985—), S.D. Edn. Assn., Kopper Kettles Craft Club (contbr. Mobridge chpt. 1974—), Jaycees, Delta Kappa Gamma (sec. 1985-86). Democrat. Roman Catholic. Home: 1112 1st Ave W Mobridge SD 57601

DOERSCHUK, JEANCLAIRE OAKES, business owner; b. Allentown, Pa., Mar. 11, 1925; d. Charles Ernest and Anna M. (Buckley) Oakes; m. Albert Peter Doerschuk, Oct. 15, 1949; children: Claire Margarete, Peter Charles, David Oakes, John Albert. Student, Mass. Wellesley Coll., 1942-45; BA, U. Pa., 1946; MA, Columbia U., 1949. Pres., chief exec. officer JCD Press dba Minuteman Press, Boston, 1978-85, Hermes Printing, Inc., San Clemente, Calif., 1988—. Home: 2727 Via Casa Loma San Clemente CA 92672 Office: Hermes Printing 111 W Ave Palizada San Clemente CA 92672

DOESBERG, ALEXANDRINA MUNRO, risk manager; b. Glasgow, Scotland, June 6, 1931; d. John Munro and Mary MacPherson (Geekie) MacLean; m. Carlo Frank Doesberg, Feb. 1, 1964; children: Lorna Ann, John Carl. Student, Skerry's Coll., Glasgow, 1945-46. Clk. Nat. Health Svc., Glasgow, 1947-58; sec. Liberty Mut. Ins., N.Y.C., 1959-67, sr. sales asst., 1980-84; risk mgr. Time Equities, Inc., N.Y.C., 1984—. Mem. NAFE, Risk and Ins. Mgmt. Soc., Inc. Presybterian. Home: 245 Passaic Ave Passaic NJ 07055 Office: Time Equities Inc 55 Fifth Ave New York NY 10003

DOGGETT, LORI ANN, grocery store official; b. Chgo., Sept. 19, 1961; d. William Edward and Jo Ann (Gurgens) D. Cert., Boulder (Colo.) Vo-Tech., 1987. Asst. store mgr. Safeway Stores, Denver, 1980—; co-owner Created Situations, Inc., Boulder, Colo., 1989—. Mem. Zonta Foothills of Boulder County (treas. 1989-90). Democrat. Home: 532 W Arrowhead St Louisville CO 80027 Office: Created Situations Inc 1750-1 30th St Ste 432 Boulder CO 80301

DOHERTY, SISTER BARBARA (ANN DOHERTY), academic administrator; b. Chgo., Dec. 2, 1931; d. Martin James and Margaret Eleanor (Noe) D. Student, Rosary Coll., 1949-51; BA in Latin, English and History, St. Mary-of-the-Woods Coll., 1953; MA in Theology, St. Mary's Coll., 1963; PhD in Theology, Fordham U., 1979; LittD (hon.), Ind. State U., 1990. Tchr. Jr. and Sr. High Schs., Ind. and Ill., 1953-63; asst. prof. religion St. Mary-of-the-Woods Coll., Ind., 1963-67, 71-75, pres., 1983—; provincial supr. Chgo. Province of Sisters of Providence, 1975-83; summer faculty NCAIS-KCRCHE, Delhi, India, 1970. Author: I Am What I Do, 1981, Make Yourself an Ark, 1984; editor: Providence: God's Face Towards the World, 1985; contbr. articles to New Cath. Encyclop. Vol. XVII, 1982. Pres. Leadership Terre Haute, Ind., 1985-86; bd. regents Ind. Acad., 1987—; bd. dirs. 8th Day Cen. for Justice, Chgo., 1978-83. Arthur J. Schmidt Found. grantee, 1967-71. Mem. Women's Coll. Coalition (nat. bd. dirs. 1984—), Assn. Colls. Ind., Ind. Colls. and Univs. of Ind. (exec. bd.), Assn. Am. Colls., Leadership Conf. of Women Religious of USA (program chairperson nat. assembly 1982-83). Democrat. Roman Catholic. Office: St Mary of the Woods Coll Office of the President Saint Mary of the Woods IN 47876

DOHERTY, EILEEN PATRICIA, economics and finance educator, college dean, educational consultant; b. Astoria, N.Y., Aug. 21, 1952; d. Joseph John and Joan Ellen (Conway) D. BA, St. John's U., 1974, MBA, 1978, JD, 1990; MA, Columbia U., 1976, EdM, 1985. Asst. to dean admissions St. John's U., Jamaica, N.Y., 1974-75, asst. to dir. instnl. research, 1975-76, asst. dean Evening & Weekend Coll., 1976-80, asst. dean Coll. Bus. Adminstrn., 1980-81, assoc. dean St. Vincent's Coll., dir. Evening and Weekend sessions, 1981-88, adj. prof. econs., 1978-88, prof. econs. and fin., 1988—; pres. Towland Ross Ednl. Cons., 1988. Assoc. editor The Forum, 1987-89, mng. editor, 1989-90. Hosp. vol. ARC, N.Y.C., 1967; rep. of city comptroller Cen. Astoria (N.Y.) Local Devel. Corp., 1982—; mem. Queens Community Planning Bd., 1980-83. Mem. ABA (law student div. rep.), N.Y. State Bar Assn., Queens County Bar Assn., Nassau County Bar Assn., Assn. Trial Lawyers Am., Am. Assn. Higher Edn., Am. Fin. Assn., Ladies Ancient Order of Hibernians, Phi Delta Kappa, Psi Chi, Kappa Delta Pi, Phi Delta Phi, Pres. Soc. Alumni Assn. (rec. sec. 1983—). Roman Catholic. Home: 150-16 17th Ave Whitestone NY 11357 Office: PO Box 342 Whitestone NY 11357

DOHERTY, ELIZABETH ROSE, computer consultant; b. Chgo., Sept. 28, 1958; d. Quentin Leo II and Mary Ann (Leisman) D. Student, Roosevelt U., Chgo. Tech. analyst CNA Ins. Co., Chgo., 1980-89; sr. cons. Tech. Solutions Corp., Chgo., 1989-90; tech. cons. Systems Software Assocs., Chgo., 1990—. Clarinetist Chgo. All City Band, 1974-76, various community orgns., 1972—. Big sister Big Bros./Big Sister Orgn., Chgo., 1987—, vol. com., 1989—; vol. Little Bros. of Elderly. Recipient Outstanding Citizen award U. Ill., Chgo., 1979. Mem. NAFE, Data Processing Mgrs. Assn., Midrange Computer Assn., People for the Ethical Treatment of Animals. Mem. Christian Ch.

DOHERTY, EVELYN MARIE, data processing consultant; b. Phila., Sept. 26, 1941; d. James Robert and Virginia (Checkley) D. Diploma, RCA Tech. Inst., Cherry Hill, N.J., 1968. Freelance data processing programmer N.J., 1978-81; data processing cons. N.J., 1981—; lectr. data processing Camden County (N.J.) Coll.; pres. PC Lotto, N.J., pub. lottery rev. Contbr. articles in field. Chairwoman Collingswood (N.J.) Dems.. founder Babe Didikson Collingswood Softball Team for Women. Mem. Data Processing Mgmt. Assn. (chmn., mem. edn. com., bd. dirs. N.J. chpt. 1980—), Internat. Platform Assn. Roman Catholic. Office: PO Box 3780 Cherry Hill NJ 08003

DOHERTY, KAREN ANN, corporate executive; b. Elizabeth, N.J., July 6, 1952; d. Eugene Nason Godfrey and Helen L. (Andersen) D.; m. Jonathan Kent Tillinghast, June 17, 1972 (div. Oct. 1978). Account exec. The John O'Donnell Co., N.Y., 1979-80; nat. conservation rep. Sierra Club, N.Y., 1980-81; mgr. membership programs Am. Mgmt. Assn., N.Y., 1981—. Mem. Women's Econ. Roundtable, Trinity Coll. Alumnae Assn. (bd. dirs. N.Y. chpt. 1981-83), Sierra Club (exec. com. N.Y.C. group 1979-82), Direct Mktg. Assn., World Direct Trade Coun., Women In Need (corp. adv. coun.). Democrat. Roman Catholic. Home: 580 84th St Apt 5H Brooklyn NY 11209 Office: Am Mgmt Assn 135 W 50th St New York NY 10020

DOHERTY, MARY MARGARET, protective services official; b. Ft. Hood, Tex., Mar. 20, 1960; d. Richard Julian and Barbara Ann (Ward) D. BA, S.D. State U., Brookings, 1983; postgrad., Fed. Law Enforcement Training, Glynco, Ga., 1984. Law Enforcement Officer. Dep. U.S. Marshals Dept. of Justice U.S. Marshal Svc., Sioux Falls, 1984—; criminal investigator Dept. of Justice U.S. Marshals Svc., Sioux Falls, 1987—; pub. rels. speaker U.S. Marshals Svc., S.D., 1984—; recruiter interviewer U.S. Marshals Svc., Washington, 1988—. Contbr. articles to profl. jours. Recipient Special Achievement award U.S. Dept. of Justice, Sioux Falls, 1985, 1988, 89; Outstanding Performance U.S. Dept. of Justice, Sioux Falls, 1986, 1987. Mem. Internat. Assn. of Women Police. Roman Catholic.

DOHERTY, MICHEL GEORGE, alcohol and drug treatment facility administrator; b. Erie, Pa., Dec. 7, 1930; d. David Lloyd and Marie (Morris) George; m. William K. Rodstein, June 10, 1952 (dec. Apr. 1969); children: William Michael, Michael William; m. Edward L. Doherty, Aug. 14, 1982. M in Human Svc. Adminstrn., Lincoln U., Oxford, Pa., 1981. Cert. addiction profl., Pa., Fla.; cert. eating disorders therapist. Addiction counselor Livingren Found., Eldington, Pa., 1974-75; clin. dir. Vitae House Inc., Glenmoore, Pa., 1975-80; clin. dir., dir. spl. programs, projects coordinator med. students Temple U. Horsham Hosp., Ambler, Pa., 1980-83; exec. dir., chief exec. officer Roxbury, Shippensburg, Pa., 1983-84; dir. substance abuse div. First Hosp. Corp., Norfolk, Va., 1982; exec. dir., chief exec. officer The Cloisters at Pine Island, Pineland, Fla., 1984—; mem. Nat. Credentialing Commn. of Alcohol Counselors, Washington, 1978-84; co-chairperson Nat. Women's Support Network, Washington, 1982-83. Contbr. articles to newspaper and mags. Bd. dirs. alcohol/drug abuse task force Springfield (Pa.) High Sch., 1983. Recipient Outstanding Accomplishment in Field award N.Am. Women's Commn. on Alcohol/Drug Abuse, 1979. Mem. Nat. Assn. Drug-Alcohol Counselors (v.p. 1978), Pa. Addiction Counselors Assn. (pres. 1978-79, Outstanding Contbn. award 1979), Assn. Labor Mgmt. and Adminstrn. Del. Valley (v.p. 1981-83), Employee Assistance Profl. Assn. (v.p. S.W. chpt. 1990—), LWV, Bus. and Profl. Women. Republican. Roman Catholic. Home: 5341 SW 11th Ave Cape Coral FL 33914 Office: The Cloisters at Pine Island Waterfront Dr Box 1616 Pineland FL 33945-1616

DOHERTY, REBECCA FEENEY, lawyer; b. Ft. Worth, June 3, 1952; d. Charles Edwin Feeney and Annabelle (Knight) Smith; divorced; 1 child, George Jason. BA, Northwestern State U., 1973, MA, 1975; JD, La. State U., 1981. Bar: La. 1981, U.S. Dist. Ct. (mid., ea. and we. dists.) La. 1981, U.S. Ct. Appeals (5th cir.) 1981, U.S. Dist. Ct. (so. dist.) Tex. 1986, U.S. Dist. Ct. (ea. dist.) Tex. 1989. Assoc. Onebane, Donohoe, Bernard, Torian, Diaz, McNamara & Abell, Lafayette, La., 1981-84, ptnr., 1985—; adj. instr. Northwestern State U., Natchitoches, La., 1975; co-dir. secondary level gifted and talented program Webster Parish, La., 1978. Contbr. articles to profl. jours.; mem. La. Law Rev., 1980, 81. Recipient Am. Jurisprudence award Lawyers Coop. Pub. Co., 1980; inducted into La. State U. Law Ctr. Hall of Fame, 1987. Mem. ABA, La. Bar Assn., La. Assn. Def. Counsel, La. Assn. Trial Lawyers, Acadian Assn. Women Attys., Order of Coif. Home: 636 Alonda Lafayette LA 70503 Office: Onebane Donohoe Bernard Torian Diaz McNamara & Abell PO Drawer 3507 Lafayette LA 70502

DOHERTY-CHAPMAN, MARGARET ANN, college administrator; b. Providence, May 1, 1952; d. James J. and Margaret Mary (McKinnion) Doherty; m. Robert Tuliszewski, July 7, 1973 (div. Aug. 1979); m. Michael P. Chapman, Sept. 23, 1981; 1 child, Kathryn Ann. Cert. dental assisting, R.I. Community Coll., 1971; BS in Communications Mgmt., U. Portland, 1985. Staff asst. N.J. Coll. of Medicine and Dentistry, Newark, 1973-76; agy. coord. Osborn & Assocs. Advt., Portland, 1985-86; coord. Mt. Hood

Community Coll., Gresham, Oreg., 1986-88, Portland Community Coll., 1987—. Pres., bd. dirs. Childpeace Montessori Sch. Daycare, Portland, 1986-87. Bob and Delores Hope scholarship U. Portland, 1984; grantee U. Portland, 1984. Mem. Women in Communications, Inc. (v.p. membership 1988-89, bd. dirs.), Am. Soc. Tng. and Devel. Roman Catholic. Office: Portland Community Coll PO Box 19000 Portland OR 97219-0990

DOI, DOROTHY MITSUE, catering executive; b. Honolulu, Feb. 21, 1934; d. Tokuju Yano and Hisayo Kashiwabara; children: Ken Kenichi, Clare Emiko, Garret Seitoku. BS in Edn., Phillips U., Enid, Okla., 1956; postgrad., UCLA, 1958, U. Hawaii, Honolulu, 1966-67, 72-74, Chaminade Coll. Honolulu, 1972-74, 77, LaVerne (Calif.) Coll., 1970-71. Cert. tchr., Hawaii. Tchr. L.A. City Schs., 1957-58, Hawaii, 1956-57, 65, 70-71; account exec. Catering, ind. contractor, Honolulu; skin care, health and beauty cons. Honolulu, travel agt., ind. contractor; pres. Triple C Svcs., Honolulu, 1983—; researcher Manoa ethnic studies program U. Hawaii; account exec., cons. Royal Banquet, 1988-89; writer, researcher, editor, mng. editor BULLOGROUN. Mng. editor Bulldogrowl. Co-chair Jester's Ball fund raising Y-Teens, 1947-52. Mem. NAFE, Cardinal Key, Hawaii Fukuoka Kenjin Kai (sec. com. chairperson editor 35th anniversary commemorative booklet), Smithsonian Instn., Kaimuki High Sch. Alumni Assn. (charter, bd. dirs. and pub. rels. chairperson 1988-90), Okla. Sooners Club, Kappa Delta Pi. Home: 2431 Yvonne Pl Honolulu HI 96816-3431 Office: PO Box 12196 Honolulu HI 96828-1196

DOI, MARY ELLEN, research chemist, laboratory administrator; b. Memphis, Mo., Jan. 15, 1933; d. Earl Edward and Beulah Mae (Leach) Tucker; m. Minoru Doi, June 16, 1962; 1 child, Paul Edward. BS, Northeast Mo. State U., 1953. Cert. med. technologist, 1957. Tchr. chemistry, biology Princeton (Mo.) High Sch., 1953-54; tchr. sci. Evans Jr. High Sch., Ottumwa, Iowa, 1954-56; lab. technician Shelby County Hosp., Shelbyville, Ill., 1957-58; med. chemist Barnes Hosp., St. Louis, 1958-60; research chemist Monsanto Chem. Co., St. Louis, 1960-63; chief chemist, dir. lab. E.S. Erwin and Assocs., Tolleson, Ariz., 1963—. Active Rep. campaign, 1976. Mem. Am. Chem. Soc., Assn. Official Analytical Chemists, Ariz. Assn. Cert. Labs. Republican. Methodist. Club: Bus. and Profl. Women (Maryvale, Glendale, Ariz.) (past sec.-treas., v.p., pres., Woman of Yr. 1974, 79). Home: 5963 W Hazelwood Phoenix AZ 85033 Office: Nutrition-Lab Svcs PO Box 237 Tolleson AZ 85353

DOKOUDOVSKY, NINA LUDMILA, dance educator; b. N.Y.C., Nov. 7, 1947; d. Vladimir Dokoudovsky and Nina Rigmor (Ström) Stroganova; m. Antoni Francis Zalewski. Student, Ballet Arts Carnegie Hall, 1954-78, Profl. Children's Sch., N.Y.C., 1959-66, Am. Acad. Dramatic Arts, 1960-62, Am. Ballet Theater Sch., 1968-70, N.Y. Conservatory of Dance, 1978-81. Faculty Ballet Arts Carnegie Hall, N.Y.C., 1964-70; tchr. dance Dokoudovsky Sch. of Classical Ballet, Englewood, N.J., 1964-70; head adminstr. Acad. Fine Arts Music and Dance, 1974-81; faculty Washington U., St. Louis, 1983-86; co-dir. Ballet Ctr. of St. Louis, 1984—; co-assoc. artistic dir. St. Louis Ballet (formerly Mo. Concert Ballet), 1981-84, co-artistic dir., 1984—; dir. Ballet Arts Lecture Demo Co., 1967-68; dancer, soloist with Ballet Arts Workshop, 1966-68, Marvin Gordon's Ballet Concepts, 1968, Empire State Ballet, 1969, Internat. Dance Competition, Varna, Bulgaria, 1970, Buffalo Ballet, 1970-72, Am. Classical Ballet, 1972, Wolf Trapp Co., 1972, L.I. Ballet Co., 1973, Festival Ballet of N.J., 1975-77, St. Louis Ballet (formerly Mo. Concert Ballet), 1982—; coach Am. dancers Internat. Dance Competition, Moscow, 1982. Choreographer: (ballets) Dance of the Hours, 1965, While the Cat's Away, 1966, Tchaikovsky Violin Concerto, 1967, In the Park, 1968, The Nyad, 1968, Adam Pas De Duex, 1969, Adam Pas de Cinq, 1974, 83, 86, 89, Weber Piano Concerto (complete), 1986-88, Nutcracker, 1980, 81-90, La Fille Mal Gardee, 1980, Une Petite Comedie, 1984, (staged ballets) Swan Lake, 1967, 69, 79, 80, Les Sylphide, 1974, 79, 82, 84, 87, Raymonda, 1972, Don Quixote, 1972, 84, 88, Sleeping Beauty, 1976, 79, 84, La Bayadere 1989, Bronislava Nijinska's Les Biches in collaboration with Irina Nijijska, 1989, 90. Office: Ballet Ctr of St Louis 10 Kimler Dr Saint Louis MO 63043-3703 also: St Louis Ballet Co 634 N Grand #10-E Saint Louis MO 63103

DOKUPIL, INEZ LOTT, real estate and investments executive; b. New Orleans, Dec. 14, 1937; d. H. Alvin and Edna M. (Joiner) Lott; m. Harold T. Dokupil, Oct. 15, 1960; children: Elizabeth, Michael. BS, Baylor U., 1958. Lab. asst. Tex. Children's Hosp., Houston, 1956; sec. H.A. Lott, Inc., Houston, 1957, Am. Nat. Bank, Houston; researcher Tenneco, Houston, 1959-63; ptnr. Lott Properties, Houston, 1979—. Research grantee Johns Hopkins U., 1958. Republican. Mem. Ch. of God. Home: 11911 Doncaster Houston TX 77024

DOLACK, DENISE ANN, marketing research company account executive; b. Hackensack, N.J., May 4, 1962; d. Arthur and Jeanet Marie (Kologe) D. BA, Rutgers U., New Brunswick, N.J., 1984; MBA, Rutgers U., Newark, 1987. Sales and mktg. coord. Dorman-Roth Foods, Inc., Moonachie, N.J., 1986-88; asst. brand mgr. Farberware, Inc., Bronx, N.Y., 1988-89; client svc. exec. A.C. Nielsen, Hackensack, 1989-90; account exec. Nielsen Mktg. Rsch., Hackensack, 1990—. Mem. Am. Mktg. Assn. Office: Nielsen Mktg Rsch 433 Hackensack Ave Hackensack NJ 07601

DOLAN, LOUISE ANN, physicist; b. Wilmington, Del., Apr. 5, 1950. BA, Wellesley Coll., 1971; PhD in Physics, MIT, 1976. Jr. fellow in physics Harvard U., 1976-79; asst. prof. physics Rockefeller U., 1979-82, assoc. prof., 1983—; vis. scientist Ecole Normale, Paris, 1977; vis. fellow Princeton U., 1978. Recipient Maria Goeppert-Mayer award Am. Phys. Soc., 1987. Office: Rockefeller U Dept Physics 1230 York Ave New York NY 10021*

DOLAN, MARY ANNE, journalist, columnist; b. Washington, May 1, 1947; d. William David and Christine (Shea) D.; B.A., Marymount Coll., Tarrytown, N.Y., 1968, H.H.D. (hon.), 1984; student Queen Mary, Royal Holloway colls. U. London, London Sch. Econs., also Kings Coll., Cambridge U., 1966-68. Reporter, editor Washington Star, 1969-77, asst. mng. editor, 1976-77; mng. editor Los Angeles Herald Examiner, 1978-81, editor, 1981—. Recipient Golden Flame award Calif. Press Women, 1980, Woman Achiever award Calif. Fed. Bus. and Profl. Women's Clubs, 1981; bd. selectors for Neiman Fellows Harvard U.; mem. Pulitzer Prize Journalism Jury, 1981, 82. Mem. Am. Soc. Newspaper Editors, NOW. Club: Los Angeles Athletic. Office: M.A.D. Inc. 1033 Gayley Ave Ste 205 Los Angeles CA 90024*

DOLAN, MARYANNE MCLORN, writer, educator, lecturer; b. N.Y.C., July 14, 1924; d. Frederick Joseph and Kathryn Cecilia (Carroll) McLorn; m. John Francis Dolan, Oct. 6, 1951; children: John Carroll, James Francis McLorn, William Brennan. B.A., San Francisco State U., 1978, M.A., 1981. Tchr. classes and seminars in antiques and collectibles U. Calif., Berkeley, Davis, Santa Cruz, Coll. of Marin, Kentfield, Calif., Mills Coll., Oakland, St. Mary's Coll., Moraga, 1969—; tchr. writing Dolan Sch., 1978—; owner antique shop, Benicia, Calif., 1970—; lectr. Nat. Assn. Jewelry Appraisers Symposium, Tucson; mem. Vintage Fashion Expo., Oakland. Author: Vintage Clothing, 1880-1960, 1983; Collecting Rhinestone Jewelry, 1984, Old Lace and Linens, 1989; weekly columnist The Collector, 1979-88; contbr. articles to profl. jours. Mem. AAUW, Antique Appraisal Assn. Am. Inc., New Eng. Appraisers Assn., Questers, Women's Nat. Book Assn. Inc., Nat. Assn. Jewelry Appraisers, Internat. Soc. Appraisers, Calif. Writers Club, Internat. Platform Assn. Republican. Roman Catholic. Home: 138 Belle Ave Pleasant Hill CA 94523 Office: 191 West J St Benicia CA 94510

DOLAND, JUDY ANN, financial rating company administrator; b. Duluth, Minn., June 29, 1940; d. Burnham Oscar and Mary Katherine (Sederholm) D. Student, Mt. San Antonio Jr. Coll., Walnut, Calif., 1960. Subs. ledger acct. Pacific Intermountain Express, LA., 1963-64; various positions Dun & Bradstreet, L.A., 1958-63, 64-80, state sales guide rep., 1980-83; payroll cashier Dun & Bradstreet, Monterey Park, Calif., 1983-85; exec. sec. Dun & Bradstreet, Long Beach, Calif., 1985—. Office: Dun & Bradstreet 555 E Ocean Blvd Ste 900 Long Beach CA 90802

DOLE, ELIZABETH HANFORD, charitable organization administrator, former secretary of labor; b. Salisbury, N.C., July 29, 1936; d. John Van and Mary Ella (Cathey) Hanford; m. Robert Joseph Dole (U.S. Senator from Kans.), Dec. 6, 1975. B.A. with honors in Polit. Sci., Duke, 1958; postgrad., Oxford (Eng.) U., summer 1959; M.A. in Edn., Harvard U., 1960, J.D., 1965. Bar: D.C. 1966. Staff asst. to asst. sec. for edn. HEW, Washington, 1966-67; practiced law Washington, 1967-68; assoc. dir. legis. affairs, then exec. dir. Pres.'s Com. for Consumer Interests, Washington, 1968-71; dep. dir. Office Consumer Affairs, The White House, Washington, 1971-73; commr. FTC, Washington, 1973-79; chmn. Voters for Reagan-Bush, 1980; dir. Human Services Group, Office of Exec. Br. Mgmt., Office of Pres.-Elect, 1980; asst. to Pres. for pub. liaison, 1981-83; sec. U.S. Dept. Transp., 1983-87; with Robert Dole Presdl. Campaign, 1987-88; participant 1988 Presdl. and Congl. campaigns; sec. U.S. Dept. Labor, 1989-90; pres. Am. Red Cross, 1991—; mem. nominating com. Am. Stock Exchange, 1972, N.C. Consumer Council, 1972. Trustee Duke U., 1974-88; mem. coun. Harvard Law Sch. Assocs.; hon. chmn. bd. overseers Duke U. Comprehensive Cancer Ctr., 1988—; mem. vis. com. John F. Kennedy Sch. Govt. Harvard U., 1988—, bd. overseers, 1989. Recipient Arthur S. Flemming award U.S. Govt., 1972, Humanitarian award Nat. Commn. Against Drunk Driving, 1988, Disting. Alumni award Duke U., 1988; named one of Am.'s 200 Young Leaders, Time mag., 1974, one of World's 10 Most Admired Women, Gallup Poll, 1988. Mem. Phi Beta Kappa, Pi Lambda Theta, Pi Sigma Alpha. Office: Am Red Cross 17th & D Sts NW Washington DC 20006

DOLE, WANDA VICTORIA, librarian; b. Melrose Park, Ill., Sept. 10, 1942; d. Malburn Sanford and Victoria Bernice (Berner) D.; m. David Richards Helmstadter, May 7, 1966 (div.). BA magna cum laude, Lawrence U., Appleton, Wis., 1964; MA in Classics, Tufts U., 1965; MS, U. Ill., 1975. Asst. editor Scott, Foresman & Co., Glenview, Ill., 1967-68; arch. librarian U. Ky., Lexington, 1976-78; humanities bibliographer U. Ill., Chgo., 1978-80; asst. dir. collection devel. U. Miami, Coral Gables, Fla., 1980-82; reg. sales mgr. Blackwell N. Am./B.H. Blackwell Ltd., Lake Oswego, Oreg., 1982-86; head librarian Pa. State U., Abington, 1986—; mem. curriculum adv. com. So. Conn. State U. Sch. Library Sci., New Haven, 1983-85; mem. Ill.-Princeton Expedition to Morgantina, Sicily, 1970. Contbr. articles to profl. jours. Mem. ALA (bd. dirs. resources and tech. svcs. div. 1982-84), Pa. Libr. Assn., Art Librs. Soc. N.Am., Women in Math. Episcopalian. Home: 109 Fern Ave Willow Grove PA 19090 Office: Pa State Univ 1600 Woodland Rd Abington PA 19090

DOLIN, LONNY H., lawyer; b. Youngstown, Ohio, Jan. 24, 1954; d. Lawrence Joseph and Sonya (Sacks) Heselov ; m. Gordon S. Black, Aug. 20, 1988; children: Nathaniel, Brooke, Aaron, Benjamin, Lindsay. AB, Georgetown U., 1976; JD, Cath. U., 1979. Bar: Vt. 1980, N.Y. State Bar 1984, U.S. Dist. Ct. (we. dist.) N.Y. 1984. Assoc. Downs, Rachlin & Martin, Burlington, Vt., 1979-81; pvt. practice Burlington, 1981-84; assoc., then ptnr. Harris, Beach, Wilcox, Rubin & Levey, Rochester, N.Y., 1984-90; ptnr. Harris, Beach & Wilcox, Rochester, N.Y., 1990—; of counsel to U.S. Congressman Fred J. Eckert, N.Y., 1985—; bd. dirs. Monroe County Legal Services Corp. Mem. Pittsford Town and County Com., N.Y., 1983—, Town of Pittsford Bd. of Zoning Appeals, N.Y., 1984—, vice chair 1990; chmn. Monroe County Comparable Worth Task Force, Rochester, 1985—, Fred J. Eckert Women's Adv. Council, Rochester, 1985—; del. The Jud. Dist. N.Y., Rochester, 1985—, chair 1990; bd. dirs. Nat. Council Jewish Women. Recipient Corpus Juris Secundum award West Pub. co., 1979. Mem. ABA, Vt. Bar Assn., N.Y. Bar Assn., Monroe County Bar Assn. (mem. practice and perf. com.), Greater Rochester Women's Bar Assn. (treas. 1986), Assn. Trial Lawyers Am., N.Y. State Trial Lawyers Assn., Genesee Valley Trial Lawyers Assn. (treas. 1990). Republican. Home: 22 Fletcher Rd Pittsford NY 14534 Office: Harris Beach & Wilcox 130 E Main St Rochester NY 14604

DOLIN, MICHELLE CYNTHIA, insurance agency executive; b. Chgo., June 8, 1952; d. Francis Clarence and Violet Louise (Hejtmanek) Pilecek; m. James Donald Wrigley, Mar. 11, 1972 (Dec. 1979); children: Juanita Lynn, Jason Alan; m. Norman Howard, May 20, 1984. Postgrad., Eastern Ill. U., Charleston, 1971; student, John Logan Coll., Carterville, 1974; BA, Western Ill. U., Macomb, 1990. Lic. Health & Life Agent. Deli person Jewell Tea Foods, Westmont, Ill., 1968-70; cook, waitress Denny's Restaurant, Carbondale, Ill., 1974-76; waitress Denny's Restaurant, Bloomington, Ill., 1976; anesthesia tech. Mennonite Hosp., Bloomington, Ill.; mgr. Maxwell's Restaurant, Bloomington, Ill., 1984; v.p. Dolin Ins. Agy., Inc., Fla., 1984-89. Hosp. Vol. Cape Coral Hosp., 1988, 1989. Mem. Am. Bus. Women's Assn., NAFE, Nat. Assn. Health Underwriters (sec. S.W. Fla. chpt.), Fla. Assn. Health Underwriters (2d v.p. 1989-90), Cape Coral Hibiscus Soc. (sec.). Office: Dolin Insurance Agy Inc 1420 A 47th St Cape Coral FL 33904

DOLINICH, CHRISTINE, artist; b. Elizabeth, N.J., Feb. 24, 1950; d. Anton J. and Irene Marie (Kutay) D. Student, Oxford U., England, 1970-71; BA in Studio Art, Rutgers U., 1973; postgrad., Westminster Choir Coll., 1984, 86. Dir. Union County Conservatory, Rahway, N.J., 1987—, Linden (N.J.) Art and Music Studio, 1983-87; critiquer Union County Teen Arts Festival, Union Coll., Cranford, N.J., 1986-88; curator visual arts Merck and Co., Inc., Rahway, 1989—. Exhibited in group shows at Los Angeles Women's Ctr., Houston U., Utah U., 1977, Newark Mus., 1982, City Without Walls Gallery, Newark, 1982, 83, 84, 85, 86, Morris Mus., Morristown, N.J., 1987; one-woman shows include Caldwell (N.J.) Coll., 1976, 82, 89, Middlesex Coll. Art Gallery, Edison, N.J., 1985, Douglass Coll. Women Artists Series, 1986-87, Rutgers U., New Brunswick, N.J., 1987, Brookdale Coll, 1988; artists books Rutgers U., U. of Delaware, Newark Library, New Brunswick, 1982-83. Fellow N.J. State Council on the Arts, 1984-85; recipient First prize Art with Mus. Subjects Cover Contest. Mem. AAUW (radio host Sta. WFMU Women in Music and Art Series 1984-85, lectr., slide and tape presentation Women in Art and Music 1985), Women's Caucus for Art, Music Tchr. Nat. Assn. (1st prize Am. Music Tchr. 1981, 83) , Piano Tchrs. Soc. Am. (Genia Robinor Pedagogy award 1989). Home: 212-0 Greenfield Gardens Evergreen Rd Edison NJ 08837 Studio: 45 E Milton Ave Rahway NJ 07065

DOLL, ELIZABETH JANE (BETH DOLL), psychologist, educator; b. Madison, Wis., July 7, 1952; d. Eugene Carter and Mary Margaret (Nash) D.; m. Bruce Douglas Nattrass, May 25, 1973; children: Scott Richard, Christine Elizabeth. BA, Mich. State U., East Lansing, 1974; MS, Ea. Mich. U., 1976; PhD, U. Ky., 1983. Instr. dept. ednl. and counseling psychology U. Ky., Lexington, 1979-80; psychologist Scott County Pub. Schs., Georgetown, Ky., 1981-84; coord. dept. ednl. psychology Psychoednl. Clinic U. Wis., Madison, 1984-89; asst. prof. psychology, dir. sch. psychology program U. Colo., Denver, 1990—; field supr. Psychol. Corp., San Antonio, 1986-88; bd. dirs. Curriculum Based Measurement Project, Belleville, Wis. Co-editor: School Psychology in Wisconsin, 1989. Pres. Wis. Fedn. Pupil Svc. Assn., Waukesha, Wis., 1989. Recipient Spl. Recognition award Dane County Project Headstart, 1989. Mem. APA, Nat. Assn. Sch. Psychologists, Am. Ednl. Rsch. Assn., Colo. Sch. Psychologist Assn. Office: U Colo Sch of Edn 1200 Larimer St Campus #106 Denver CO 80204

DOLL, LYNNE MARIE, public relations agency executive; b. Glendale, Calif., Aug. 27, 1961; d. George William and Carol Ann (Kennedy) D.; m. David Jay Lans, Oct. 11, 1986. BA in Journalism, Calif. State U., Northridge, 1983. Freelance writer Austin Pub. Rels. Systems, Glendale, 1978-82; asst. account exec. Berkhemer & Kline, L.A., 1982-83; exec. v.p., ptnr. Rogers & Assocs., L.A., 1983—; exec. dir., Suzuki Automotive Found. for Life, Brea, Calif., 1986—; mem. strategic planning com., Gateway to Indian Am. Corp. for Am. Indian Devel., San Francisco, 1988—. Pub. rels. cons., Rape Treatment Ctr., L.A., 1986—. Mem. Ad Club L.A. (bd. dirs.), Pub. Rels. Soc. Am., So. Calif. Assn. Philanthropy, Coun. on Founds., Internat. Motor Press Assn. Democrat. Office: Rogers & Assocs Ste 1010 2029 Century Park E Los Angeles CA 90067

DOLSON, VIVIAN ANTOINETTE, sales executive; b. Chgo., July 17, 1925; d. Werner Henry and Lillian Rose (Ghilardi) Steger; student DePaul U., 1943-46; m. Sept. 10, 1948 (div.); children—Bill, David. Asst. registrar DePaul U., 1952-55, exec. sec., 1955-58; asst. personnel dir. Stat. Tabulating Co., Chgo., 1958-61; owner, operator Dolson Market Research, Chgo., 1961-75; dist. sales mgr. for Ill. and Wis., Borroughs/Lear Siegler Co., Chgo., 1975-78, asst. nat. sales mgr., Kalamazoo, 1978-81; nat. sales mgr. Marvel Metal Products, Chgo., 1981-84; pres. Dolson Associates, Inc., Honolulu, 1984—; career cons. Triton Jr. Coll. Mem. Am. Market Research Assn., Nat. Office Products Assn. Am. Mgmt. Assn., Am. Soc. Interior Designers (mem. Industry Found.), Soroptomists Internat. Home and Office: Dolson Assocs 3138 Waialae Ave Apt 218 Honolulu HI 96816

DOMAN, ELVIRA, science administrator; b. N.Y.C.; d. Andrew and Lillian (McClary) Hand; m. John H. Holder (div.); children: Paula Holder Simpkins, Rodney M. BA in Chemistry, CUNY, 1955; Ma in Biochemistry, Columbia U., 1959; MS in Molecular Biology, NYU, 1960; PhD in Physiology and Biochemistry, Rutgers U., 1965. Jr. tech. U. Hosp. N.Y.U. Bellevue Med. Ctr., 1955; sr. tech. Sloan-Kettering Inst. Cancer Rsch., N.Y.C., 1956-57; rsch. asst. Coll. Physicians and Surgeons, N.Y.C., 1959-60; rsch. asst. Sloan-Kettering Inst. Cancer Rsch., N.Y.C., 1959-60, postdoctoral assoc., 1965; rsch. assoc. Rockefeller U., N.Y.C., 1965-68; lectr. Douglass Coll. Turgers U., New Brunswick, N.J., 1970-73; asst. prof. Seton Hall U., South Orange, N.J., 1973-77; assoc. program dir. NSF, Washington, 1978—; sci. fair judge pub., pvt. schs., colls., Washington, 1975; vis. scientist Rutgers U., 1989. Bd. dirs. Math. Sci., Computer Learning Ctr. of Shiloh Bapt. Ch., Washington, 1989—. Recipient Achievement award NSF, 1986; grantee, Seton Hall U., 1975. Fellow Am. Inst. Chemists; mem. AAAS, Am. Chem. Soc., Assn. Women Sci., Minority Women Sci., Toastmasters. Office: NSF 1800 G St NW Rm #321 Washington DC 20550

DOMAN, JANET JOY, association executive; b. Phila., Dec. 16, 1948; d. Glenn J. and Hazel Katie (Massingham) D. Student, U. Hull, England, 1969-70; BA, U. Pa., 1971. Cert. tchr. Clinician Inst. Achievement Human Potential, Phila., 1971-74; dir. English Early Devel. Assn., Tokyo, 1974-75; dir. Evan Thomas Inst. Early Devel., Phila., 1975-77, Inst. Achievement of Intellectual Excellence, 1977-80; vice dir. Inst. Achievement Human Potential, 1980-82, dir., 1982—; internat. lectr. treatment of brain injured children and superiority. Chair Child Brain Devel., United Steelworkers Am., 1987. Recipient Gold medal Centro de Reabilitacion Nosa Senhora da Gloria, Rio de Janeiro, 1974, Brit. Star Brit. Inst. Achievement Human Potential, 1976, Sakura Korosho medal Japanese Inst. Achievement Human Potential, 1977, statuette with pedestal Internat. Forum Human Potential, 1980. Office: Inst for Achievement Human Potential 8801 Stenton Ave Philadelphia PA 19118

DOMBROWSKI, MAUREEN MARIE, school administrator; b. Joliet, Ill., Aug. 27, 1950; d. Francis Charles and Mary Frances (Kernc) Paul; m. Harry S. Dombrowski, Jr., June 22, 1974. BA, Coll. St. Francis, Joliet, 1972; MS in Edn., No. Ill. U., 1976. Copy editor, reporter Joliet Cath. News-Register, 1968-72; tchr. English, reading, staff developer Joliet Twp. High Schs., Dist. 204, 1972—; assoc. prof. No. Ill. U., DeKalb, Ill., 1987—; adj. prof. Governors State U., University Pk., 1988—. Mem. Suburban Reading League, Will County Reading League, Internat. Reading Assn., Assn. for Supervision and Curriculum Devel., U.S. Power Sqdn., Twin Harbors Yacht Club (bd. dirs. 1985-87), New Buffalo Yacht Club, Delta Kappa Pi. Roman Catholic. Office: Joliet West High Sch 401 N Larkin Ave Joliet IL 60435

DOMER, JUDITH ELAINE, microbiologist, educator; b. Millersville, Pa., Apr. 9, 1939; d. Richard Harvey and Dorothy Alice (Peters) Kofroth; m. Floyd Ray Domer, Apr. 15, 1965. BA, Tusculum Coll., Greeneville, Tenn., 1961; PhD, Tulane U., 1966. Diplomate Am. Bd. Med. Microbiology. Asst. prof. St. Mary's Dominican Coll., New Orleans, 1967-68; rsch. assoc. Tulane Med. Sch., New Orleans, 1968-71, asst. prof., 1972-77, assoc. prof., 1977-88, prof., 1988—; rsch. fellow Kennedy Inst. Rheumatology, London, 1971-72; guest researcher NIH, Bethesda, Md., 1984-85; diagnostic mycologist Tulane Hosp., New Orleans, 1980-83; mem. Bacteriology and Mycology Study Sects., Bethesda, 1975-79, Biomed. Sci. Study Sect., 1988-90, AIDS and Related Diseases Study Sect., 1990—. Contbr. numerous articles to profl. jours. Charles Oliver Gray scholar Tusculum Coll., 1958-61; named one of Outstanding Young Women Am., 1967. Fellow Am. Acad. Microbiology, Infectious Disease Soc. Am.; mem. Am. Soc. for Microbiology (div. chmn. 1984-85, group rep. 1987, vice chmn. annual meeting program 1988—), Med. Mycological Soc. Ams. (pres. 1987-89), Am. Assn. Immunologists, Internat. Soc. for Human and Animal Mycology, British Soc. for Mycopathology (Ian Murray Meml. lectr. 1990). Democrat. Methodist. Home: 4420 Copernicus St New Orleans LA 70131 Office: Tulane Med Sch 1430 Tulane Ave New Orleans LA 70112

DOMEYER, NANCY, psychotherapist; b. Mt. Vernon, N.Y., Oct. 28, 1941; d. George and Helen (Foley) Fasenfeld; m. A. William Domeyer (div. Apr. 1988); 1 child, Todd. AB, Fla. So. U., Lakeland, 1963; MSW, Tulane U., New Orleans, 1965. Cert. clin. social worker, cert. marriage and family therapist. Social worker Touro Infirmary, New Orleans, 1965-67, St. Louis State Hosp., 1967-69, Family Counseling Ctr., Boca Raton, Fla., 1970-74; pvt. practice psychotherapy Boynton Beach, Fla., 1974—; bd. mem. Comprehensive AIDS Program, Palm Beach County, 1988-90, Inforum AIDS Program, Palm Beach County, 1986-87, AID Ctr. One, Broward County, 1985-86. Named Social Worker of Yr., Nat. Assn. Social Workers, Fla., 1985. Home and Office: 640 E Oean Ave Ste 19 Boynton Beach FL 33435

DOMINGUE, SUSAN GAY, county official; b. Port Arthur, Tex., Nov. 21, 1947; d. Stanley Juan and Laura Mae (Carrier) D. BS in Psychology magna cum laude, Lamar U., 1970; MA in Criminology, Sam Houston State U., 1977. Cert. correctional officer, probation officer, social worker, advanced clin. practitioner. Sec. Bankers Title Co., Houston, 1970-71; juvenile probation officer Jefferson County Probation Svcs., Beaumont, 1971-73, coord. community resources, 1973-82; field underwriter N.Y. Life Ins. Co., Beaumont, 1982-83; intensive supervision probation officer Jefferson County Adult Probation Dept., Beaumont, 1983, unit supr., 1983—; adj. inst. criminal justice program Lamar U., fall 1979. Charter mem. bd. dirs. Family Violence Shelter S.E. Tex., Beaumont, 1978; mem., pres. adv. coun. Salvation Army Boys Club, Beaumont, 1978-81; vol. spl. friends program Beaumont Ind. Sch. Dist., 1986-88; vol. Beaumont Clean Community Commn., 1988-89; v.p. Park Place recovery unit, Community Citizen Adv. Com., Port Arthur, Tex., 1988—. Mem. Tex. Probation Assn. (treas. 1981-82), S.E. Tex. Social Welfare Assn. (treas. 1976), Colleen Alumnae Assn. (pres. 1987-91, advisor), Phi Kappa Phi. Democrat. Roman Catholic. Office: Adult Probation Dept 1225 Pearl St Beaumont TX 77701

DOMINIQUE, LISE MARIE, broadcasting executive, radio personality; b. Lake Forest, Ill., Mar. 5, 1956; d. Nazaire Louis and Eleanor (Steffin) D. B.S. in Radio and TV, U. Ill., 1978. Morning disc jockey Sta.-KRVE, Los Gatos, Calif., 1981-83; evening air personality Sta.-KHTT, San Jose, 1983-85, news dir., 1983-85, news dir. Stas.-KSJO/KHTT, 1984-85; relief weather person Sta. KICU-TV, San Jose, 1985; traffic reporter for KCBS-San Francisco Traffic Central, Hayward, Calif., 1985-86; weekend news anchor Sta. KGO-AM, San Francisco, 1987; news dir., traffic reporter Sta. KEZR-FM, San Jose, 1986-89; news dir., morning personality Sta. KHQT-FM, San Jose, 1989, Sta. WLUP-AM-FM, Chgo.; morning traffic reporter Shadow Traffic, Chgo., 1989—. Address: PO Box 935 Lake Forest IL 60045

DOMM, ALICE, lawyer; b. Phila., May 22, 1954; d. William Donald and Alice Frances (Day) D.; m. RIchard Coles Grubb, Sept. 26, 1987; 1 child, Stephanie Elizabeth. BA, Gettysburg Coll., 1976, JD, Rutgers U., 1981. Bar: N.J. 1981, Pa. 1981. Assoc. prof. Glassboro (N.J.) Coll., New Brunswick, N.J., 1980-81; Atty., juvenile sect. chief Office of the Pub. Defender, New Brunswick, N.J., 1982—. Bd. dirs. Police Athletic League, New Brunswick, 1982-85; mem. Middlesex County Youth Services Commn., New Brunswick; steering com. treas. Middlesex County Women Lawyers Com.; mem. Gov.'s Council on Child Abuse and Neglect, Middlesex County, Gov.'s com. childrens Services Planning Juvenile Justice Subcom.; mem. Middlesex County Commn. Child Abuse and Missing Children, Criminal Justice Planning Com. Middlesex County. Mem. ABA, N.J. Bar Assn., Middlesex County Bar Assn. (trustee), Middlesex County Women's Bar Assn. (steering com., treas.), Assn. Criminal Def. Lawyers N.J. Office: Office Pub Defender 172 New St New Brunswick NJ 08903

DOMMEL, DARLENE HURST, writer; b. Charles City, Iowa, July 11, 1940; d. Roy and Elsie (Hopkes) Hurst; B.S. with high distinction, U. Minn., 1963; m. James H. Dommel, Oct. 15, 1961; children: Diann, Christine, David. MS, 1965, grad. exec. program Grad. Sch. Bus. Administrn., 1972; postgrad. So. Meth. U., 1976-77. Pub. health nurse Combined Nursing Service, Mpls., 1963-64; contbr. articles on pottery to various collectors and antiques mags., 1967—; organizer, exhibitor of art pottery display touring fin. instns. in upper midwest, 1976—; lectr. and cons. health care, antiques, journalism; health care specialist Health Services Research Center, St. Louis

Park Med. Center, 1978-79; instr. Augsburg Coll., 1979-81. Mem. Minn. Adv. Task Force on Epilepsy, 1981-83, State Council for Handicapped, 1982-84, Dept. Pub. Welfare Adv. Council on Mental Retardation and Phys. Disabilities, 1982-84; mem. profl. adv. bd. Epilepsy Found. Minn., 1984—. Mem. Mpls. Inst. Arts. USPHS trainee, 1964-65; Sigma Theta Tau scholar, 1962-63; Martha Ripley scholar, 1961-62; U. Minn. Sch. Nursing Found. scholar, 1962. Mem. U. Minn. Alumni Assn., Nat. Writers Club, Nat. League for Nursing (regional assembly constituent leagues for nursing. exec. com. 1985-87), Minn. League for Nursing (pres. 1983-85). Gethsemane Luth. Ch. Women, Am. Art Pottery Collectors Assn., Sigma Theta Tau, Delta Delta Delta. Lutheran. Home: 510 Westwood Dr N Golden Valley MN 55422

DOMONKOS, PATRICIA MAHONEY, nurse; b. Hackensack, N.J., Mar. 13, 1949; d. Harold Joseph and Mary Ann (Skrezec) Mahoney; m. John Wyne Dean, May 1, 1971 (div. 1987); children: Kimberly, Jenette; m. Lawrence L. Domonkos, June 9, 1990. AAS in Nursing, Rockland Community Coll., Suffern, N.Y., 1970; BS in Nursing, George Mason U., 1985. RN, N.Y., Va. Staff nurse Columbia Presbyn. Hosp., N.Y.C., 1970-71, No. Va. Doctors' Hosp., Arlington, 1971-73; office nurse to pvt. physicians Burke, Va., 1974-78; instr. Loudoun County Schs., Leesburg, Va., 1980-84; asst. dir. nursing Hunt Country Home Health, Reston, Va., 1985-86; pres. TLC Health Care, Inc., Leesburg, 1986-90; instr. ARC, Washington, 1990—; cons. for state guidelines for nursing assts., lic. practical nurses, 1984-89. Mem. LWV (past officer, named Entrepreneur of Yr. 1988), Nat. Nurses in Bus., Nat. Home Care, Leesburg C. of C., Preservation Soc. Roman Catholic. Home: Rte 1 Box 491 Round Hill VA 22141

DONAGHY, DEBRA ANN, controller; b. Pasco, Wash., Feb. 9, 1957; d. Martha S. (Mantel) Rice; m. Michael James Donaghy, July 12, 1986. AA, Columbia Basin Coll., 1977; BA, Whitworth Coll., 1979; MS in Taxation, Gonzaga U., 1987. CPA. Staff acct. Christie, Lyle and Co., Spokane, Wash., 1978-81, Aspaas, Simmons and Lochmiller, Spokane, 1981-83; corp. controller Jones Wholesale Florist, Spokane, 1983-88; fin. acct. Ernest and Julio Gallo Winery, Modesto, Calif., 1988-89, mgr. fin. reporting, 1989—. Mem. Am. Soc. Women Accts. (nat. sec. 1987-88, pres. 1984-85), Am. Inst. CPA's. Republican. Presbyterian. Lodge: Order of Eastern Star. Office: E & J Gallo Winery PO Box 1130 Modesto CA 95353

DONAHUE, BARBARA LYNN SEAN, television producer; b. Trenton, N.J., Feb. 14, 1956; d. Donald Paul and Elizabeth (Anderson) D.; m. Charles R. Boyce II, Aug. 20, 1983; 1 child, Terrence Donahue Boyce. BA, U. Vt., 1978. Sports coord. ABC Sports, 1984-86. Producer Badminton Horse Trials, 1988, The Hampton Classic Show Jumping, 1988, Mercedes Grand Prix of Dallas-Show Jumping, 1988, Thomas Hearns v. Iran Barkley Championship Fight, 1988, 1987 World Water Skiing Championships, 1988, U.S. Synchronized Swimming Fedn. Indsl., 1988, Seoul Olympic Profiles, 1988, World Alpine Ski Championships, 1989, Knievel Legend Continues: Can Son Avenge Evel's Crash?, 1989, Chgo. Internt. Dog Show, 1989, World Super Heavywright Weightlifting Championships, 1989, U.S. Women's Open, 1989, Olympic Sports Festival, 1987, Sunday Showcast: Jackie Robinson, 1987, The Game of the Century: Nebr. vs. Oklahoma 1971 recap, 1987, Beauty and Soul, 1986, Volvo World Cup Show Jumping, 1986, Wide World of Sports Moments, 1985, Lake Tahoe Tennis Festival, 1985, Superbikers Motocross, 1985, N.Y.C. Mini-Marathon, 1985, UCLA Invitational Track and Field Meet, 1985, United Airlines In-Flight Movies, 1985, Sarajevo Winter Olympic, 1984, Grand Prix of Monaco, 1984, U.S. vs. The World in Amateur Boxing, 1983, Battle of the Network Stars, 1983, History of the U.S. Open Golf Championship, 1982, NCAA Football, 1982. Mem. Jr. League Greenwich, 1985—. Recipient Unity award Internat. Spl. Olympics, 1983, Christopher award, 1983, Sports Emmy award Games of the XXIII Olympiad, 1984-85. Mem. Dir. Guild Am., Am. Horse Show Assn., U.C. Combined Tng. Assn., U.S. Dressage Fedn., U.S. Equestrian Team Gold Medal Club, The Field Club. Address: 35 Mead Ave Cos Cob CT 06807

DONAHUE, CHARLOTTE MARY, lawyer; b. Columbus, Ohio, Sept. 29, 1954; d. Patrick Henry and Helen Dillon (Meany) D. AB, Holy Cross Coll., 1976; JD, U. Toledo, 1983. Bar: Pa. 1984, D.C. 1985, U.S. Dist. Ct. (ea. dist.) Pa. 1985, U.S. Ct. Appeals (3d cir.) 1985, U.S. Supreme Ct. 1990. Jud. clk. to presiding justice Commonwealth Ct. Pa., Phila., 1983-84; spl. asst. U.S. atty. U.S. Dist. Ct. (ea. dist.) Pa., Phila., 1987—; atty. HUD, Phila., 1984—. Mem. Fed., Pa., Phila. D.C. Bar Assns., Order of Barristers, Internat. Platform Assn. Home: PO Box 58862 Philadelphia PA 19102 Office: HUD 105 S 7th St Philadelphia PA 19106

DONAHUE, CLAIRE GERTRUDE, insurance company executive; b. Boston, Dec. 12, 1929; d. Daniel L. and Gertrude A. (Holland) D. Student, Chamberlaine Jr. Coll., Boston, 1966-67. Gen. clk. Met. Life Ins. Co., Cambridge, Mass., 1947-65; asst. office mgr. Met. Life Ins. Co., Arlington, Mass., 1965-69; br. adminstr. Met. Life Ins. Co., Stoneham, Mass., 1969—; sec., treas. Met. Vets. Assn., Boston, 1971-86, pres., 1985, 86, sec., treas., 1987—. Home: 103 9th St Apt 213 Charlestown MA 02129 Office: Met Life Ins Co 91 Montvale Ave Stoneham MA 02180

DONAHUE, JACOLYNNE, healthcare executive; b. Green Bay, Wis., Oct. 31, 1939; d. Roy August and Emma Elizabeth (Bruckner) Jorns; m. Sept. 14, 1957; children: Terry, John, Thomas, James, David, Judith. Grad. high sch. Sec. von Stiehl Wine Inc., Milw., 1968—; mgr. Med. Dr.'s Emergency Svc., Milw., 1970; sec.-treas. Wis. Collection Corp., Milw., 1972-76; pres., owner Heirloom Collections, Internat., Milw., 1987—; gen. mgr. von Stiehl Corp., Milw., 1981—; owner Watch Designs by Jacolynne, Milw., 1989—; mgr. M.D. Wellness Clinic, St. Helena, Calif., 1989—. Republican. Roman Catholic. Home: 1603 Main St Saint Helena CA 94574 Office: MD Wellness Clinic 1314 Main St Saint Helena CA 94574

DONAHUE, JILL B., marketing executive; b. Los Alamos, N.M., June 7, 1953; d. Melvin C. and Wanda (Thomas) Foley; m. June 21, 1975 (div. 1982); children: Amber, Amanda, Ashley. BA, Redlands (Calif.) U., 1988, postgrad., 1988—. Radiology technologist San Antonio Community Hosp., Upland, Calif., 1978-82; adminstr. Diamond Bar (Calif.) Med. Ctr., 1982-86; dir. mktg. NME-Doctor's Hosp. of Montclair (Calif.), 1986-87, dir. physician relations, 1987-90; dir. devel. San Antonio Community Hosp. Found., 1990—. Bd. dirs. Montclair-Ontario YMCA, 1988—; mem. Mt. Baldy Coalition. Recipient recognition for dedicated service from Calif. state senator and mayor City of Montclair, Congl. resolution from 65th dist. assemblyman, county supr. and congressman. Mem. Am. Mktg. Assn., Healthcare Mktg. Assn., Am. Soc. Hosp. Mktg., Montclair C. of C. (pres. 1988-89, bd. dirs. 1986—), Rotary (Rancho Cucamonga club), Soroptimist, Beta Sigma Phi. Democrat. Presbyterian. Office: San Antonio Community Hosp Found 999 San Bernadino Rd Upland CA 91786

DONAHUE, JUDITH LINNEA, manufacturing company executive; b. Worcester, Mass., May 19, 1950; d. Irving James Jr. and Barbara May (Grant) D. BA, U. Mass., 1972; degree in indsl. mgmt., Worcester Poly. Inst., 1982. Tchr. Spencer (Mass.) Pub. Schs., 1972-74; asst. dir. Shewsbury (Mass.) Health Dept., 1974-76; code inspector Worcester Code Inspection Dept., 1977-78; pres. Donahue Industries, Inc., Shrewsbury, 1978—; cons. Video Images, Shrewsbury, 1979—, Dr. Denise Cantin, D.O., Shrewsbury, 1988—; bd. dirs. Donahue Industries Inc.; adv. coun., bd. dirs. publs. com. Worcester Poly. Tech., 1988—. Career devel. chairperson Jobs for Bay State Grads., Shrewsbury, 1985—, adv. coun., 1985—; adv. coun. Worcester Poly. Inst. Sch. Indsl. Mgmt., 1979-82. Mem. LWV, Women in Mfg., Am. Engring. Soc. Office: Donahue Industries Inc 5 Industrial Dr Shrewsbury MA 01545

DONAHUE, LAURA KENT, state senator; b. Quincy, Ill., Apr. 22, 1949; d. Laurence S. and Mary Lou (McFarland) Kent; m. Michael A. Donahue, July 16, 1983. B.S., Stephens Coll., 1971. Mem. Ill. State Senate, Quincy, 1981—. Mem. Lincoln Club of Adams County, Ill. Fedn. Republican Women. Mem. P.E.O. Lodge: Altrusa. Office: 634 Maine St Quincy IL 62301-3908*

DONAHUE, SUZANNE MARY, writer, film producer; b. N.Y.C., June 1, 1956; d. John Francis and Fumiko (Tanioka) D. AB in Psychology, U. So. Calif., 1977, MFA in Cinema Prodn., 1980, PhD in Communication, Cinema, 1984. Producer Learning Corp. Am., N.Y.C., 1981-82; with Columbia Pictures, Burbank, Calif., 1985; writer Univ. Microfilms Internat. Research Press, Ann Arbor, Mich., 1986; screenwriter L.A., 1986—; pres. Montage Communications Corp., L.A. Author: American Film Distribution: The Changing Marketplace, 1986. Mem. Phi Beta Kappa. Office: Montage Communications Corp 2121 Avenue of the Stars Los Angeles CA 90067

DONALDSON, DARCY MILLER, publishing executive; b. Glen Ridge, N.J., June 17, 1953; d. Paul Richardson and Susan (Alling) Miller; m. James R. Donaldson III, Feb. 6, 1988; child, Zoe Alling. Co-founder, assoc. pub. Mus. Mag., N.Y.C., 1979-83; pub. Crop Protection Chemicals Reference, N.Y.C., 1983-85; assoc. pub. Chief Exec. mag., N.Y.C., 1986-87, pub., 1987-89, sr. v.p., pub., 1989—. Mem. ASCAP, Advt. Women of N.Y. Democrat. Episcopalian. Office: Chief Exec Mag 233 Park Ave S New York NY 10003

DONALDSON, DEANNA LYN, sales executive; b. Dothan, Ala., Jan. 11, 1961; d. Huey Gerald and Mary Suellen (Ellis) D.; m. James H. Reeves, Mar. 29, 1987 (div. 1988). BS in Acctg., Auburn U., 1984. Sr. design analyst Mgmt. Sci. Am., Inc., Atlanta; sr. installation specialist Sales Technologies, Atlanta; application specialist Computer Assocs. Internat., Inc., Atlanta; regional sales support mgr. Computer Assocs. Internat., Inc., Andover, Mass.; nat. sales support mgr. Computer Assocs. Internat., Inc., Andover; cons. New England Gas/Utilities Group, New England User Group-Masterpiece Application, Boston. Active Spina Bifida charity support, Atlanta, 1987. Mem. NAFE. Mem. Ch. of Christ. Home: 102 Brown St Methuen MA 01844

DONALDSON, JANE ELLEN, real estate company executive; b. Paterson, N.J., Aug. 4, 1947; d. William John and Violet Jane (Breckenridge) Burse; m. Dennis Preston Donaldson, Aug. 23, 1969; children: Abigail, Aaron Preston, Adam Preston. BA, Bethany (W.Va.) Coll., 1969; postgrad., Greenville (S.C.) Tech. Inst., 1978. Lic. real estate broker, S.C. Realtor ERA Joy Real Estate Co., Greenville, 1978-81, broker in charge, 1981-88; dir. corp. devel. Furman Co., Greenville, 1988—. Precinct chmn. State Sen. Rep. Party, Greenville, 1987; mem. Greenville Econ. Devel. Com., 1988-90; mem. speaker's bur. Greenville County Bd. Edn., 1989—; mem. leadership Greenville, 1989. Mem. Greenville County Bd. Realtors (life mem., Million Dollar Club), S.C. Bd. Realtors, Nat. Assn. Realtors. Presbyterian. Home: 15 Enfield Way Greenville SC 29615 Office: Furman Co 33 Villa Rd Piedmont W Greenville SC 29615

DONALDSON, JEAN ANN, health care administrator; b. Boone, Iowa, Feb. 15, 1925; d. Julius Redfield and Ellen Mable (Peterson) Erickson; m. Wilbur Dwight Donaldson, July 17, 1949; children: Ann Kari, Eric Julius. BS, Iowa State U., 1946; postgrad., U. Minn., 1978, 80-83, Tulane U., 1976. Lic. nursing home adminstr., Minn. Chief dietician Raymond Blank Meml. Hosp. for Children, Des Moines, 1948-49; dept. head, chief dietician Mary Greeley Hosp., Ames, Iowa, 1949-52; instr. dept. foods and nutrition Iowa State U., 1952; mem. nursing home rev. team, periodic med. rev. team Ramsey County (Minn.), 1971-74; coord. complaint team Minn. Dept. Health, St. Paul, 1974-76, exec. dir. Office Health Facility Complaints, 1977-81; adminstr. Camilla Rose Conv. Ctnr., Coon Rapids, Minn., 1976-77, Minn. Vets. Home, Mpls., 1981-83; exec. cons. Minn. P.E.O. Home Fund, St. Paul, 1984—; cons. VA, Washington, 1983. cons. VA, Washington, 1983. Chmn.vol. svcs., bd. dirs., mem. nominating, exec. coms. ARC, St. Paul, adv. coun. Midwest Ops. Hdqrs., St. Louis; del. dist. 12, St. Paul Community Coun.; chmn. standing rules and operating com. Charter Commn. St. Paul; chmn. Ramsey County Capital Improvement Program Adsv. Com. Recipient Outstanding Leadership award St. Paul Better Neighborhoods Program, 1988. Mem. Am. Dietetic Assn. (registered), Am. Coll. Health Care Adminstrs., Minn. Dietetic Assn., Minn. Gerontol. Soc., St. Anthony Park Assn., AAUW, P.E.O. (v.p. chpt. CW, 1984-86, pres. 1986-88, chmn. Minn. Cottey Coll. scholarship com. 1989-). Methodist. Home: 1556 Branston St Saint Paul MN 55108

DONALDSON, MARY KENDRICK, nurse; b. Tifton, Ga., June 25, 1937; d. Howard Story and Trudy (Donalson) Marlin; m. Harvey Kendrick Sr., Apr. 13, 1953 (dec. 1965); children: Jerome, Micheal, Harvey Jr., Merry, Sheila, Larry; m. Isaac Hargett, Feb. 16, 1985. AA, Compton (Calif.) Coll., 1969; BS, Pepperdine U., 1972, MA, 1976; diploma in nursing, SW Coll., Los Angeles, 1984. Staff nurse St. Francis Hosp., Lynwood, Calif., 1965-67; pvt. duty nurse Profl. Nurse's Registry, Los Angeles, 1967-82; elem. tchr. Compton Sch. Dist., Calif., 1975-80; caseworker, clk. Los Angeles County Probation Dept., 1980—; pediatric, nurse companion Personal Care Health Service, Torrance, Calif., 1984—; home economist Dept. Welfare, Compton, 1970-72; asst. dir. Century Plaza Hotel, Century City, Calif., 1971-72. Chairperson Com. To Elect Garland Hardeman For Councilman, Inglewood, Calif., 1987. Exec. Housekeeping scholarship Century Plaza Hotel, Los Angeles, 1971. Mem. Fellow Am. Home Econs. Assn., Pepperdine Alumni Assn., Pepperdine's Kappa-Kappa Sorority, Am. Nurse's Assn. Democrat. Home: 802 W 228th St Torrance CA 90502 Office: Los Angeles County Probation Dept 1601 Eastlake Ave Los Angeles CA 90033

DONATH, THERESE (PHYLLIS THERESE FREEMAN), artist, writer; b. Hammond, Ind., Dec. 14, 1928; d. Arthur Max and Lillian Louise (Donath) Helfer; children from previous marriage: Mark, Alex, Kim; m. Jefferson Richardson Scoville, 1986; step-children: Suzanne, Michelle, Thomas; student Monticello Coll., 1946-47; BFA, St. Joseph's Coll., 1975; additional study Oxbow Summer Sch. Painting, Immaculate Heart Coll., Hollywood, Calif., Penland, N.C., Haystack, Maine; radio/TV personality, 1978-90. Interviewer, producer Viewpoint, Sta. WLNR-FM, Lansing, Ill., 1963-64; reporter, columnist N.W. Ind. Sentinel, 1965; freelance writer Monterey Peninsula Herald, 1981-85; contbg. author Monterey Life mag. 1981-85; asst. dir. Michael Karolyi Meml. Found., Vence, France, 1979; one-woman shows include: Ill. Inst. Tech., Chgo., 1971; group shows include: Palos Verdes (Calif.) Mus., 1974, L.A. Inst. Contemporary Art, 1978, Mus. Contemporary Art, Chgo., 1975, Calif. State U., Fullerton, 1973, No. Ill. U., DeKalb, 1971, Bellevue (Wash.) Mus. Art, 1986-87; represented in permanent collections including Kennedy Gallery, N.Y.C., also pvt. collections; creative cons. Aslan Tours and Travel, 1983-85; instr., lectr. Penland, N.C., 1970, Haystack Mountain Sch., Deer Isle, Maine, 1974, Sheffield Poly., Eng., 1978. Bd. dirs., sec. Mental Health Soc. Greater Chgo., 1963-64; exec. dir. Lansing (Ill.) Mental Health Soc., 1963-64. Recipient awards No. Ind. Art Mus., 1966, 70, 71, 73; grantee Ragdale Found., Lake Forest, Ill., 1982. Represented in The Mirror Book, 1978, American Artists An Illustrated Survey of Leading Contemporaries, 1990; author, illustrator: Before I Die, A Creative Legacy, 1989; contbr. articles to profl. jours., newspapers; illustrator: Run Computer Run, 1983.

DONATO, MYRNA MERLE, small business owner; b. Hastings, Nebr., Mar. 30, 1939; d. Ivan F. Sr. and Merle E. (Rutten) Conaway; m. Bruce Lee Nauslar, Sept. 30, 1955 (div. Dec. 1964); children: Gregory Alan, Douglas Lee; . Kenneth C. Zinck, Jan. 13, 1968 (div. Aug. 1976); m. Louis Joseph Donato; Oct. 30, 1982. Student, Citrus Jr. Coll., Azusa, Calif., 1959-61. Office mgr., dental asst. L.M. Faustina, D.D.S., Las Vegas, Nev., 1965-84; owner, bookseller Amber Unicorn, Donato's Fine Books, Las Vegas, 1981—; office mgr., dental asst. Jeffrey L. Glynn, D.D.S., Las Vegas, 1984-88; prin. Players Panorama newspaper, Forte mag., Las Vegas, 1988—. Mem. Ariz. Antiquarian Bookseller, Am. Booksellers Assn., Antigarian Bookseller Assn. Am. Republican. Office: 2202 W Charleston #2 Las Vegas NV 89102

DONATO, NOLA, software engineer; b. Chgo., July 26, 1955; d. Dominick and Eilyanne (Sheehan) D. BS, U. Ill., 1976, MSEE, 1978. Software engr. Nuvatec, Chgo., 1976; software cons. Chgo., 1977-81; game designer GDI, Chgo., 1982; prin. engr. Mattel Electronics, Hawthorne, Calif., 1982-83, Motorola ISG, Cupertino, Calif., 1983-84; sr. staff engr. Sun Microsystems, Mountain View, Calif., 1984-88; software engr. Microsoft GBU, Menlo Park, Calif., 1989—. Inventor in field. Named to U. Ill. Book of Hons., 1976; Ill. State scholar, 1972. Mem. ACM. Roman Catholic. Home: 20990 Valley Green Dr #620 Cupertino CA 95014 Office: Microsoft GBU 2460 Sand Hill Rd Menlo Park CA 94025

DONEGAN, PATRICIA LUCILLE, entrepreneur; b. San Gabriel, Calif., May 9, 1931; d. Zellen Lurton and Lucille Florence (Miller) Andrews; m. DaWayne B. Donegan, Oct. 15, 1969 (dec.). AA, Pasadena (Calif.) City Coll., 1953; BSc, UCLA, Westwood, Calif., 1956. Electronic assembler Hewlett-Packard, Palo Alto, Calif., 1959-65; social worker Shasta County, Redding, Calif., 1965; with sales Good Humor Co., 1966-67; ind. practice The Underground, Pasadena, 1976-77, The Magickal Mind, Alhambra, Calif., 1978-90; wholesale/retail and light mfg. distbr. metaphysical supplies, 1990—; with Pacific Hotel, Wallace, Idaho, 1969; postal worker, Wallace, 1970; in home supportive svc. worker, L.A. County, 1982—; counselor, tchr. on metaphysics.

DONELSON, ANGIE FIELDS CANTRELL MERRITT, real estate executive; b. Hermitage, Tenn., Dec. 2, 1914; d. Dempsey Weaver and Nora (Johnson) Cantrell; student public and pvt. schs., Hermitage, Nashville; m. Gilbert Stroud Merritt, Dec. 15, 1934 (dec.); 1 son, Gilbert Stroud; m. 2d, John Donelson, Jr., VII, Apr. 23, 1966 (dec.); step-children: John, Agnes Donelson Williams (dec.), William Stockley. Pres., So. Woodenware Co., Nashville, 1955-61, So. Properties, Co., Inc., Hermitage, 1961—. Chmn. comml. flower exhibits Tenn. State Fair, 1951; committeewoman and v.p. Davidson County Agrl. Soil and Conservation Community Com., 1959-60; bd. mem. Nashville Symphony Assn., 1961-64, regional council mem., 1977-79; chmn. bd. Nashville Presbyn. Neighborhood Settlement House; elder Presbyn. Ch., 1989—,; founding bd. mem. Davidson County Cancer Soc.; bd. mem. Nashville Vis. Nurse Service; dist. chmn., speakers bur. Am. Red Cross. Proclaimed First Lady Donelson-Hermitage Community, 1986. Mem. Vanderbilt U. Aid, Peabody Coll. Aid, Tenn. Hist. Soc., Descs. of Ft. Nashboro Pioneers (bd. dirs. 1984-87), English Speaking Union. Clubs: Ladies Hermitage Assn. (dir. 1949-89), DAR, (chpt. regent 1941), Lebanon Rd. Garden Club (pres. 1947), Horticulture Soc. Davidson County (v.p. 1949). Clubs: Ravenwood Country, Centennial, Belle Meade. Contbr. to books and mags. on history of Tenn. Home: Stone Hall Stones River Rd Hermitage TN 37076 Office: Lebanon Rd Hermitage TN 37076

DONEY, JUDITH KAREN, minister, consultant; b. Winston-Salem, N.C., Aug. 24, 1942; d. Parks Harvey and Dorothy (Hanna) Vanderlip; m. Arnold Bokhoven, May 26, 1961 (div. Mar. 1968); m. Marion Van Wyk, Mar. 16, 1968 (div. June 1975); m. Malcolm Edwards Doney, Sept. 30, 1981. Student, U. N.C., 1965-66, Vennard Coll., 1970-71, U.S.M., 1976, Phillips Coll., 1981-82. Audit clk. Consol. Credit Corp., Charlotte, N.C., 1963-64; operating rm. technician Mercy Hosp., Charlotte, 1965-66; operating and emergency rms. technician St. Dominics Hosp., Jackson, Miss., 1975-76; acute care technician U. Miss. Med. Ctr., Jackson, 1981; co-founder, sec.-treas., bd. dirs, dir. rehab. svcs. New Beginnings Ministries, Inc., Jackson, 1983—. Campaign mgr. U.S. senatorial candidate, Mahaska County, Iowa, 1968; mem. disaster team, instr. ARC, Jackson, 1980-81. Mem. Nat. Head Injury Found. Republican.

DONICHT, JOYCE MAE, college stores supervisor; b. Chgo., Feb. 11, 1949; d. George and Erna (Tetlow) Kerstein; m. Bruce E. Donicht, Sept. 20, 1975. BS, U. Wis., Menomonie, 1971; student, Wright Jr. Coll., Chgo., 1967-68. Typist U. Wis.-Stout, Menomonie, 1976-77; clk. fire and allied lines Stewart Smith Mid Am., Inc., Chgo., 1974-75; clk. policy prodn. dept. Protection Mut. Ins. Co., Park Ridge, Ill., 1972-74; stores supr. U. Wis., Menomonie, 1977—. Mem. NAFE. Home: Rte 1 Box 169 Wheeler WI 54772 Office: U Wis Stout 817 S Broadway Menomonie WI 54751

DONISTHORPE, CHRISTINE ANN, state senator; b. Christina, Mont., May 31, 1932; d. Lambert A. and Ludmilla (Hruska) Benes; m. Oscar Lloyd Donisthorpe, 1951; children—Paul, Karen, Bruce, Brian. Student U. Mont., 1951-53, San Juan Coll., N.Mex. Real Estate Sch., 1958-70. Pres. Bd. of Edn., Bloomfield, N.Mex., 1975-81; mem. N.Mex. State Senate, 1979—, mem. edn. com., 1979, fin. com., 1980, edn. study com., 1981; mem. Bd. Realtors San Juan County, 1978-81. Adv. bd. Salvation Army, 1970-75; active C. of C. Recipient U.S. Soil and Water Conservation award, 1967; Hon. State Future Farmers Adv. award, 1975. Mem. N.Mex. Hay Growers Assn. Republican. Methodist. Home: PO Box 746 Bloomfield NM 87413*

DONNALLY, PATRICIA BRODERICK, fashion editor; b. Cheverly, Md., Mar. 11, 1955; d. James Duane and Olga Frances (Duenas) Broderick; m. Robert Andrew Donnally, Dec. 30, 1977. B.S., U. Md., 1977. Fashion editor The Washington Times (D.C.), 1983-85, The San Francisco Chronicle, 1985—. Recipient Atrium award, 1984, 87, 88, 89, Lulu award, 1985, 87. Mem. San Francisco Fashion Group, Inc. Avocation: travel. Home: 1 Lansdale San Francisco CA 94127-1608 Office: Chronicle Pub Co 901 Mission St San Francisco CA 94103

DONNELLY, BARBARA SCHETTLER, medical technologist; b. Sweetwater, Tenn., Dec. 2, 1933; d. Clarence G. and Irene Elizabeth (Brown) Schettler; A.A., Tenn. Wesleyan Coll., 1952; B.S., U. Tenn., 1954; cert. med. tech., Erlanger Hosp. Sch. Med. Tech., 1954; postgrad. So. Meth. U., 1980-81; children—Linda Ann, Richard Michael. Med. technologist Erlanger Hosp., Chattanooga, 1953-57, St. Luke's Episcopal Hosp., Tex. Med. Ctr., Houston, 1957-58, 1962; engring. R &D SCI Systems Inc., Huntsville, Ala., 1974-76; cons. hematology systems Abbott Labs., Dallas, 1976-77, hematology specialist, Dallas, Irving, Tex., 1977-81, tech. specialist microbiology systems, Irving, 1981-83, coord. tech. svc. clin. chemistry systems, 1983-84, coord. customer tng. clin. chemistry systems, 1984-87, supr. clin. chemistry tech. svcs., 1987-88, supr. clin. chemistry customer support ctr., 1988—. Mem. Am. Soc. Clin. Pathologists (cert. med. technologist), Am. Soc. Microbiology, Nat. Assn. Female Execs., U. Tenn. Alumni Assn., Chi Omega. Contbr. articles on cytology to profl. jours. Republican. Methodist. Home: 204 Greenbriar Ln Bedford TX 76021 Office: 1921 Hurd St Irving TX 75061

DONNELLY, LORI ANN, benefit consultant; b. Allentown, Pa., July 1, 1963; d. John R. and Mary E (Duch) D. BA, Moravian Coll., Bethlehem, Pa., 1985. Claims examiner CIGNA Corp., Easton, Pa.; gymnastic team coach Bethlehem YWCA; chief fin. officer Donnelly Benefit, Bethlehem. Recipient Mayor's Small Bus. Citation, City of Bethlehem. Mem. Bethlehem C. of C. Office: 2475 Willow Park Rd Bethlehem PA 18017

DONNELLY, LYNNE CAROL, writer; b. Cin., Oct. 18, 1955; d. Francis Moreland and Marion Elizabeth (Yunkes) D.; m. Ronald John Donovan, Feb. 14, 1981; 1 child, Marina Rose Donnelly Donovan. BA in Linguistics summa cum laude, U. Cin., 1977. Editor Alaska Pub. Broadcasting, Anchorage, 1981-82; free-lance writer, editor Anchorage and Rollinsford, N.H., 1982—; adj. faculty mem. Alaska Pacific U., Anchorage, 1982-85; columnist Anchorage Daily News, 1985-87; columnist, corr. Portsmouth (N.H.) Press, 1987-90. Editor Learning in Prime Time TV Guide mag., 1981-82; author over 170 articles on family, health, life styles. Bd. dirs. Tudor Community Sch., Anchorage, 1984-85. Mem. Phi Beta Kappa. Home and Office: 499 Beccaris Dr Rollinsford NH 03869

DONNEM, SARAH LUND, consultant; b. St. Louis, Apr. 10, 1936; d. Joel Y. and Erle Hall (Harsh) Lund; m. Roland W. Donnem, Feb. 18, 1961; children: Elizabeth Prince, Sarah Madison. BA, Vassar Coll., 1958. Tech. aide, computer programmer Bell Labs., Whippany, N.J., 1959-60; chmn. placement vol. opportunities N.Y. Jr. League, 1972-73, asst. treas. 1974-75, chmn. urban problems relating to mental health, 1967-69, mem. project rsch. com., 1967-71, chmn., 1973-74, mem. bd. mgrs. 1973-74; chmn. community rsch. D.C. Jr. League, 1970-71, mem. bd. mgrs., 1970-71; mem. Stratford Hall (N.Y.) Com., 1970—; bd. dirs. East Side Settlement House, Bronx, N.Y., 1972—, v.p., 1975-76, chmn. Nat. Horse Show Benefit, 1976, winter antiques show adv. com., 1988—; bd. dirs. Stanley M. Isaacs Neighborhood Ctr., N.Y.C., 1973-76, v.p., 1975-76; bd. dirs. Presbyn. Home for Aged Women, N.Y.C., 1974-76, v.p., 1976; mem. exec. bd. N.Y. Aux. of Blue Ridge Sch., 1971-75, sec., 1965-67, pres., 1973-75; budget and benevolence com. Brick Presbyn. Ch., N.Y.C., 1973-76, mem. social svc. com., 1973-74, chmn. fgn. students com., 1963-64. Bd. dirs. Search and Care, N.Y.C., 1973-76, Project LEARN, Cleve., 1990—; Friends of Project LEARN, 1986—; mem. Fedn. Community Planning, Cleve., Coun. on Older Persons, 1978-82, mem. Future Planning Task Force, 1980-81, Commn. on Social Concerns, 1982-84; trustee Golden Age Ctrs. Greater Cleve., 1979—, 1st v.p., 1980-81, pres., 1981-85, chmn. devel., 1987-88, chmn. Western Res. Antiques Show, 1979, 80 , Western Res. Historical Soc. (womens adv. coun. 1977, coord. sec. 1978); mem. women's com. Cleve. Inst. Arts, 1983-86; mem. women's com. Cleve. Orch., 1979-85, Vassar Coll. Cleve. sec. 1980-82, v.p. 1983, pres. 1984-86; AAVC Club Liason Com. 1986-89, chmn. regional program com., 1987-

89, chmn. Vassar in Chgo. Conf. 1989; bd. dirs. Cleve. Ballet, 1980—, exec. com., 1981, fin. com., 1982-88, mem. ballet sch. com., 1985-88, nominating com., 1988—; co-chmn. Yale Ball, 1983; bd. advisers Ret. Sr. Vol. Program, 1982, trustee, 1983—, chmn. long range planning comm., 1986, sec. 1987-89; mem. Family Friends Adv. Coun., 1987-89; trustee Fairmount Presbyn. Ch., 1985-88 ; mem. long range planning com. United Way, Cleve., 1985-87; coord. Friends of Voinovich, 1987-89; womens advisory com. Voinovich for Governor, 1990; chmn. Johns Hopkins Parents Fund, 1986-88, Project LEARN 15th Anniversary celebration (with Barbara Bush, hon. chmn.), 1989-90. Named Vol. of Yr. N.Y. Jr. League, 1975; recipient Sustainer Svc. award Jr. League Cleve., 1990. Mem. Nat. Inst. Social Scis. (mem. memberships com. 1972—, trustee 1984—). Nat. Soc. of Colonial Dames. Republican. Clubs: Colony (N.Y.C.); Chevy Chase (Washington); Intown, Vassar, Jr. League Cleve., Kirtland (Cleve.), Tuxedo. Address: 2945 Fontenay Rd Shaker Heights OH 44120

DONOFRIO, KAREN ALENA, infosystems specialist; b. Phila., May 29, 1955; d. Lawrence Atillio and Rosemarie Cecilia (Porrini) Pieretti; m. Joseph LaSorsa Donofrio, June 9, 1979; 1 child, Gina Marie. BS in Health and Phys. Edn., East Stroudsburg U., 1977. Office mgr. Wabash Life Ins. Co., Ft. Washington, Pa., 1977-79; racquetball instr. Ct. South, Marietta, Ga., 1979; sec., receptionist, then sr. account specialist No. Telecom, Chamblee, Ga., 1979-81; office mgr. Preferred Rsch., Greensboro, N.C., 1981-84; computer ops. adminstr. Atlanta Falcons, Suwanee, Ga., 1984—. Mem. Am. Amateur Racquetball Assn., Ga. State Racquetball Assn. (publicity dir. 1985—), Nat. Physique Com. Republican. Roman Catholic. Office: Atlanta Falcons Suwanee Rd-Interstate 85 Suwanee GA 30174

DONOGHUE, MILDRED RANSDORF, educator; b. Cleve.; d. James and Caroline (Sychra) Ransdorf; m. Charles K. Donoghue (dec. 1982); children: Kathleen, James. Ed.D., UCLA, 1962; J.D., Western State U., 1979. Asst. prof. edn. Calif. State U.-Fullerton, 1962-66, assoc. prof., 1966-71, prof., 1971—. Author: Foreign Languages and the Schools, 1967, Foreign Languages and the Elementary School Child, 1968, The Child and the English Language Arts, 1971, 75, 79, 85, 90; co-author: Second Languages in Primary Education, 1979; Contbr. articles to profl. jours., Ency. of Edn. Mem. Nat. Council Tchrs. English, Am. Dialect Soc., Am. Ednl. Research Assn., AAUP, Nat. Soc. for Study of Edn., Am. Assn. Tchrs. Spanish and Portuguese, Tchrs. of English to Speakers of Other Langs., Internat. Reading Assn., Nat. Assn. Edn. Young Children, Orange County Med. Assn. Women's Aux., Authors Guild, Assn. for Childhood Edn. Internat., Phi Beta Kappa, Phi Kappa Phi, Pi Lambda Theta. Office: Calif State U Dept Elem Edn Fullerton CA 92634

DONOHUE, EDITH M., career development speicalist, consultant; b. Balt., Nov. 10, 1938; d. Edward Anthony and Beatrice (Jones) McParland; m. Salvatore R. Donohue, Aug. 23, 1960; children: Kathleen, Deborah. BA, Coll. Notre Dame, Balt., 1960; MS, Johns Hopkins U., 1981, CASE, 1985. Dir. pub. relations Coll. Notre Dame, Balt., 1970-71, asst. dir. continuing edn., 1978-81, dir. continuing edn., 1981-86; coord. program bus. and industry Catonsville Community Coll., Baltimore County, Md., 1986-88; mgr. tng. and devel. Sheppard Pratt Hosp., Balt., 1988—; adj. faculty Loyola Coll. Grad. Studies Program. Co-author: Communicate Like a Manager, 1989; co-editor, contbg. author career devel. workshop manual, 1985. Pres. Cathedral Sch. Parents Assn., 1972-74; asst. treas., treas. Md. Gen. Hosp. Aux., 1975-78; dir. Homeland Assn., 1978-81; regional rep., leader Girl Scouts Cen. Md., 1975-76; dir. sect. Exec. Women's Network, Balt., 1983-85; adv. bd. Mayor's Com. on Aging, 1981-86; dir. Md. Assn. Higher Edn., 1985—. Recipient Mayor's Citation, City of Balt. Council, 1985. Mem. Am. Assn. Tng. and Devel (bd. dirs.), Am. Assn. Counseling and Devel., AAUW (dir., v.p. 1980-83), Order Sons of Italy in Am., Chi Sigma Iota, Phi Delta Kappa. Democrat. Roman Catholic. Avocations: tennis, theatre, aerobics, handcrafts, symphony, opera. Home: 5420 Springlake Way Baltimore MD 21212 Office: Sheppard Pratt Hosp 6501 N Charles St Baltimore MD 21285

DONOHUE, ELIZABETH ANNE, psychologist; b. Ft. Campbell, Ky., Dec. 6, 1961; d. Jeremiah Francis and Wilma Grey (West) D.; m. James Joseph Cassidy, Feb. 18, 1989. BA, U. Louisville, 1982; D Psychology, Hahnemann U., Phila., 1989. Cert. sch. psychologist. Mental health specialist Timberlawn Psychiat. Hosp., Dallas, 1982-84, rsch. asst., 1984; psychol. cons. Ctr. for Early Childhood Svcs., Phila., 1986-87; counselor Harcum Jr. Coll., Bryn Mawr, Pa., 1986-87; sch. psychologist Follow Through Project, Phila., 1987-88, Phila. Pub. Sch. System, 1988-89; cons. pediatric dept. Hahnemann U., 1987-88; psychology intern Peberdy Child Clinic, Abington, Pa., 1988-89; staff psychologist Pa. Hosp., Phila., 1989—; instr. Hahnemann U., Phila., 1988; cons. Rockford Ctr., Newark, Del., 1990—. Mem. Am. Assn. Suicidology, Am. Psychol. Assn., Mortarboard, Phi Kappa Phi. Home: 1344 Farrington Rd Philadelphia PA 19151 Office: The Counseling Program Pa Hosp 8th and Spruce Sts Philadelphia PA 19107

DONOHUE, JOYCE MORRISSEY, biochemist, educator; b. Holyoke, Mass., Jan. 27, 1940; d. Richard Charles and Anna Elizabeth (Joyce) Morrissey; m. John Thomas Donohue, Jan. 27, 1973; children: Maura Joyce, John Thomas, Sean Richard, Eric Patrick. BS, Framingham (Mass.) State Coll., 1961; MS, U. Mass., 1964; PhD, U. N.H., 1972. Cert. secondary sch. tchr.; registered dietician. Tchr. West Springfield (Mass.) High Sch., 1962-66; instr. Framingham State Coll., 1966-68, asst. prof. biochemistry and nutrition, 1971-72, assoc. prof., 1972-73; adj. prof. No. Va. Community Coll., Annandale, 1974—, Va. Polytechnic Inst. and State U., Falls Church, 1979—; health scientist VJ Cicconi & Assocs., Woodbridge, Va., 1981-89; toxicology svc. mgr. Law Environ. Washington Svc. Ctr., Woodbridge, Va., 1989-90; prog. mgr. ICAIR/Life Systems Inc., Arlington, Va., 1990—; mem. adv. com. Prince William County Sch. Food Service, 1983-85. Mem. citizens adv. com. for debris landfill study and solid waste mgmt., Prince William County, 1987—; mem. Prince William County Wetlands bd., 1989—. Recipient Alumni Achievement award Framingham State Coll., 1986. Mem. AAAS, Am. Dietetic Assn., No. Va. Dietetic Assn., Sigma Xi. Home: 11979 William and Mary Circle Woodbridge VA 22192 Office: ICAIR/Life Systems Inc 1725 Jefferson Davis Hwy Arlington VA 22202

DONOHUE, PATRICIA CAROL, university administrator; b. St. Louis, Jan. 11, 1946; d. Carroll and Juanita D.; AB, Duke U., 1966; MA, U. Mo.-Kansas City, 1974, PhD, 1982; m. James H. Stevens, Jr., Aug. 27, 1966 (div. Mar. 1984); children: James H. III, Carol Janet. Tchr. math, secondary schs., Balt., St. Louis, Shawnee Mission, Kans., 1966-71; lectr. U. Mo., Kansas City, 1975-76, research asst. affirmative action, 1976-79, coord. affirmative action, 1979-82, instl. research assoc., 1982-84, acting dir. affirmative action and acad. personnel, 1984; dir. institutional research Lakeland Community Coll., 1984-86; asst. dean acad. affairs, math., engring. and tech. Harrisburg Area Community Coll., 1986-89, dean. Sch. Bus., Engring., and Tech., 1989—, Pa. Coun. on Vocat. Edn., 1989—, Pa. Occupational Dean's chair., 1988—; bd. dirs. MANTEC Indsl. Resource Ctr., 1987—, chair tech. com. Bd. dirs., v.p. Am. Cancer Soc. Jackson County, 75-84; bd. dirs. Cen. Pa. Tech. Coun.; coun. leader Hemlock Girl Scout U.S.A. bd. dirs., 1986—, PTA, 1975-77. Recipient Outstanding Service and Achievement award U. Mo. Kansas City, 1976; Jack C. Coffey grantee, 1978, grantee AAUW, 1989; named Outstanding Woman AAUW, 1989, one of Outstanding Leaders Nat. Inst. Leadership Devel., 1986, Exec. Leadership Inst., 1990.; Mem. Nat. Coun. Tchrs. Math., Mat. Assn. Am., Am. Vocat. Assn., Nat. Coun. on Occupational Edn., Am. Assn. Women in Community and Jr. Colls. (Pa. state coord. 1988, dir. region 3 1989—), Soc. Mfg. Engrs. (chmn.-elect 1988, chmn. 1989-90), Assn. Supervision and Curriculum Devel., Women's Equity Project, Nat. Assn. Student Personnel Adminstrs., Women's Network, Assn. Inst. Research, Phi Delta Kappa, (pres. 1975, Read fellow 1989), Phi Kappa Phi, Pi Lambda Theta, Delta Gamma (past v.p., del. nat. conv. 1988, pres., 1989), Cream Rose Outstanding Service award 1970). Home: 925 Pennsylvania Ave Harrisburg PA 17112 Office: Harrisburg Area Community Coll Sch of Bus Engring and Tech 3300 Cameron Street Rd Harrisburg PA 17110

DONOHUE-BABIAK, AMY L(ORRAINE), lawyer; b. Phila., Aug. 26, 1961; d. John J. and Claire L. (P.) Donohue; m. Arthur A. Donohue-Babiak, May 28, 1983; 1 child, Nathaniel Ryan. BA in Polit. Sci., U. Pa., cum laude, 1983, MA in Polit. Sci., 1983; JD, U. Pa., 1986. Bar: Pa. 1986, N.J. 1986, D.C. 1988, U.S. Ct. Appeals (3rd cir.) 1988, Fed. cir. 1988, U.S. Claims Ct. 1988, U.S. Supreme Ct. 1989. Assoc. Morgan, Lewis & Bockius, Phila., 1986—. Vol. Phila. Vols. for Indigent, Phila., 1986—, Support Ctr. for Child Advocates, Phila., 1986—. Mem. ABA, Pa. Bar Assn., Phila. Bar Assn., Christian Legal Soc. Republican. Home: 1004 S Farragut Ter Philadelphia PA 19143 Office: Morgan Lewis & Bockius 2000 One Logan Sq Philadelphia PA 19103

DONOR, MARY ELIZABETH, library director; b. Bklyn., May 21, 1938; d. Wayne Matthew and Elizabeth Marie (Brunner) Ikola; m. Albert Edward Donor, Dec. 4, 1936; children: Albert, Brian, Alyson. AA, Naussau Community Coll., 1970; BA, L.I. U., 1972; MS in Libr. Sci., Palmer Sch. Libr. & Info. Sci., 1973; postgrad., Dowling Coll. Cert. pub. librarian, N.Y. Young adult svcs. librarian Jericho Pub. Libr., Jericho, N.Y., 1973-80; sch. librarian West Hempstead Sr. High Sch., West Hempstead, N.Y., 1980-84; librarian Hempstead Pub. Libr., Hempstead, N.Y., 1985; libr. dir. Floral Park Pub. Libr., Floral Park, N.Y., 1985-87, Jericho Pub. Libr., 1988—. Mem. ALA (product and svcs. mgmt. com.), Nassau County Libr. Assn. (sec. 1978-80, bd. dirs. 1983-84, 87-88, chair legis. com.), N.Y. Libr. Assn., L.I. Coalition Against Censorship, L.I. Libr. Resourcees Coun. (legis. com. chmn.), Pub. Libr. Dirs. Assn. of N.Y. State, Nassau County Libr. Dirs. (exec. bd.). Office: Jericho Pub Library 1 Merry Ln Jericho NY 11753

DONOVAN, GERALYN MARIE, marketing executive; b. Chgo., July 14, 1960; m. Thomas C. Donovan. BS, U. Ill., 1982; MBA, Ill. Benedictine Coll., 1990. Mktg. asst. Rixson-Firemark, Franklin Park, Ill., 1982-84; mktg. mgr. ITW Norwood Mktg. Systems, Downers Grove, Ill., 1984—. Mem. Am. Mgmt. Assn., Packaging Inst. Home: 1505 Winterberry Ln Darien IL 60559 Office: ITW Norwood Mktg Systems 2538 Wisconsin Ave Downers Grove IL 60515

DONOVAN, JANE ELLEN, child care worker; b. Wagner, S.D., Jan. 29, 1957; d. John and Lois (McCabe) D. BA, Calif. State U., 1979, postgrad., 1985; postgrad., UCLA, 1981. Child care worker Cable Data, Rancho Cordova, 1986—; tchr. Rancho Cordova (Calif.) Children's Ctr., 1987, Village Montessori Schs., Fairoaks, Calif., 1987—; tchr. presch. Children's World, Citrus Heights, Calif., 1988-89. Mem. Nat. Assn. for Edn. of Young Children. Democrat. Roman Catholic. Office: Cable Data Sacramento CA 95873

DONOVAN, LOWAVA DENISE, data processing administrator; b. Galesburg, Ill., Mar. 27, 1958; d. Richard Eugene and Lowava Jeanine (Squire) Corbin; m. James Dean Rutledge, June 17, 1977 (div. May 1981); 1 child, Tiffany Michelle; m. Neal Edwin Donovan, July 9, 1983. Computer operator cert., Carl Sandburg Coll., 1977, student, 1976-86; student, IBM Edn., Chgo., 1979-87. Keypunch operator Fin. Industry Systems, Galesburg, Ill., 1977-79; computer operator Solution Assocs., Peoria, Ill., 1979-80; programmer, data processing mgr. May Co., Galesburg, 1980-81; programmer Kirkendall Gen. Offices, Galesburg, 1981-82; programmer, data processing mgr. Munson Transp., Monmouth, Ill., 1982-85, programmer/analyst, dir. data processing, 1985-87, dir. mgmt. info. systems, 1987-89; ind. contract programmer analyst Oklahoma City, Okla., 1989—. Mem. Ch. of God. Office: 5311 Willow Cliff #125 Oklahoma City OK 73122

DONOVAN, LYNLEY KAY, quality assurance professional; b. Ft. Belvoir, Va., Nov. 16, 1962; d. Lawrence K. and Judith K. (Lemna) D. BS, U. Notre Dame, South Bend, Ind., 1984. Quality assurance technician Meloy Diagnostics, Springfield, Va., 1985-86; mgr. microbiology, molecular biology, sect. head quality assurance Chiron Corp., Emeryville, Calif., 1986—. Mem. Am. Soc. Quality Control, Am. Soc. Microbiology, Am. Mgmt. Assn., Patenteral Drug Assn. Republican. Roman Catholic. Home: 2734 Oak Rd Apt 97 Walnut Creek CA 94596 Office: 4560 Horton St Emeryville CA 94608

DONOVAN, MADELINE FRANCES, educator, nurse; b. Norwich, Conn., Dec. 2, 1926; d. Thomas Joseph and Amelia Josephine (Riordan) D. Diploma in nursing, Hosp. of St. Rapahel, 1947; cert. in pub. health, Simmons Coll., 1955; BS, Ea. Conn. State U., Willimantic, 1965, MS, 1971. RN, Conn.; cert. elem. tchr., Conn. Pub. health nurse New Haven Pub. Health Assn., 1947-48, Meriden (Conn.) Pub. Health Assn., 1948-52; sch. nurse, 1952-65; tchr. elem. Ledyard (Conn.) Bd. Edn., 1965-70, Norwich Bd. Edn., 1970—. Mem. NEA, Conn. Edn. Assn., Norwich Tchrs. League, Hosp. of St. Raphael Alumni Assn., Irish-Am. Cultural Inst., Royal Soc. Health. Democrat. Roman Catholic. Home: 129 Orchard St Norwich CT 06360

DONOVAN, MARGARET, training and development consultant; b. Yankton, S.D., Jan. 1, 1950; d. Robert Bauerle and Norma Louise (Miller) D. BA in Psychology, Loretto Heights Coll., Denver, 1973; MS in Counseling and Personnel, Drake U., 1986. Cert. substance abuse counselor II, Iowa. Service worker II div. youth services State of Colo., Denver; probation officer Woodbury County Juvenile Ct., Sioux City, Iowa; mental health, substance abuse advocate Woodbury County Ct., Sioux City; dir. chem. dependency treatment ctr. Winnebago Indian Reservation; residential dir. Intersect. United Advanced Planning Ctr., Des Moines; pvt. practice tng. and devel. Donovan & Assocs., Des Moines, 1987—; part-time instr. develop. edn. Briar Cliff Coll.; hospitalization advocate Woodbury County; coord. alcohol edn. and disabled student svcs. Iowa State U., Ames; chair steering com. U. Without Walls, 1971. Asst. editor: T'Akra, 1972-73; poet, author, 1970—. Mem. edn. com. Interfaith Resources, Sioux City, 1982-83. Mem. Nat. Rehab. Counseling Assn., Nat. Rehab. Assn., Iowa Mental Health Assn., Addiction Profls. Assn. Iowa, Nat. Assn. Student Personnel Adminstrs., Nat. Assn. Alcoholism and Drug Abuse Counselors. Home and Office: PO Box 12076 Des Moines IA 50312

DONOVAN, MARIE PHILLIPS, television executive; b. Detroit; m. Tom Donovan; children: Kathleen Marie, Kevin Thomas. Student, Wayne U. Profl. actress Actors Equity Assn., N.Y.C., AFTRA, N.Y.C.; bus. mgr. Dirs. Service Inc., N.Y.C., exec. v.p., treas. Mem. Nat. Assn. Female Execs. Clubs: Cavendish, Am. Contract Bridge League (life master).

DONOVAN, SANDRA STERANKA, chemical company executive, scientist; b. Cleve., Sept. 20, 1942; d. William and Clare Marie (Foresta) Steranka; m. Paul C. Donovan, July 16, 1966; 1 child, Todd Christopher. BA magna cum laude, Case Western Res. U., 1964, MS, 1966, PhD, 1969. Research chemist Hercules, Inc., Wilmington, Del., 1969-70; sr. research assoc. Horizons, Inc., Cleve., 1971-73, research and devel. group leader, 1973-76, mgr. research and mktg., 1976-78; mgr. comml. devel. projects Standard Oil, Cleve., 1978-81, dir. planning and devel. Indsl. Chems. div., 1982-85, v.p., gen. mgr. nitrogen chems. div. Standard Oil Chem. Co., 1985-87, v.p., gen. mgr. nitrogen chems. strategic planning, 1987-88, exec. v.p., 1988—. Mem. bd. overseers Case Western Res. U., 1972-78, mem. vis. com to sch. mgmt., 1973-79; adv. bd. Berkeley Bus. Sch., 1986—. Recipient Lubrizol award, 1962; Olin Freedman Towers prize, 1967; Jr. Achievement Service award, 1979; YWCA Woman of Achievement award, 1981. Mem. Comml. Devel. Assn. (meeting chmn. 1982-83, dir. 1984-86, pres. elect 1987, past pres. 1989-90, honor award chmn. 1990-91), The Fertilizer Inst. (bd. dirs. 1985-87, planning com. 1986), Flora Stone Mather Coll. Alumnae Assn. (dir. 1973-79, outstanding alumna citation 1988), Western Res. Coll. Alumni Assn. (dir. 1975-79), Phi Beta Kappa, Sigma Xi, Iota Sigma Pi. Contbr. articles to profl. jours. Home: 246 Hawthorne Dr Chagrin Falls OH 44022 Office: BP Am 200 Public Sq Cleveland OH 44114-2375

DOODY, BARBARA PETTETT, computer specialist; b. Cin., Sept. 18, 1938; d. Philip Wayne and Virginia Bird (Handley) P.; 1 child, Daniel Frederick Reasor Jr. Attended Sinclair Coll., Tulane U., 1973-74. Owner, mgr. Honeysuckle Pet Shop, Tipp City, Ohio, 1970-76; office mgr. Doody & Doody, CPAs, New Orleans, 1976-77; computer ops. mgr. Doody & Doody, CPAs, 1979—; office mgr. San Diego Yacht Club, 1977-79. Mem. DAR, UDC, Jamestown Soc., Magna Charta, So. Dames, Colonial Dames of 17th Century, Nat. Soc. Daus. of 1812, Daus. Am. Colonists, Dames Ct. Honor, Colonial Order of the Crown, Societe Huguenot Nouvelle-Orleans, Huguenot Soc. Manakin, Soc. Knights of the Garter, Americans of Royal Descent. Republican. Lutheran. Home: 36 Cypress Rd Covington LA 70433 Office: 821 Gravier St Commerce Bldg Ste 1160 New Orleans LA 70112

DOODY, MARGARET ANNE, English educator; b. St. John, N.B., Can., Sept. 21, 1939; came to U.S., 1976; d. Hubert and Anne Ruth (Cornwall) D. B.A., Dalhousie U., Can., 1960; B.A. with 1st class hons., Lady Margaret Hall-Oxford U., Eng., 1962, M.A., 1965, D.Phil., 1968; LLD (hon.), Dalhousie U., 1985. Instr. English U. Victoria (B.C., Can.), 1962-64, asst. prof. English, 1968-69; lectr. Univ. Coll. Swansea, Wales, 1969-76; assoc. prof. English U. Calif.-Berkeley, 1976-80; prof. English dept. Princeton U., N.J., 1980-89; Andrew W. Mellon prof. humanities, prof. English Vanderbilt U., Nashville, 1989—. Author: A Natural Passion: A Study of the Novels of Samuel Richardson, 1974; (novels) Aristotle Detective, 1978, The Alchemists, 1980; (play) (with F. Stuber) Clarissa, 1984, The Daring Muse: Augustan Poetry Reconsidered, 1985; Frances Burney: The Life in the Works, 1988; (with Peter Sabor) Samuel Richardson Tercentenary Essays, 1989. Guggenheim postdoctoral fellow, 1979; recipient Rose Mary Crawshay award Brit. Acad., 1986. Episcopalian. Office: Vanderbilt U English Dept Nashville TN 37235

DOOGS, CAROL WALLACE KAKI, art therapist; b. Jacksonville, Tex., May 3, 1941; d. Bill Ford and Alice B. (Whitehead) White; m. Cletus William Doogs, 1962 (div. 1985); children; Timothy David, Jenine Marie. RN, St. Joseph Hosp., 1962; B in Gen. Studies, Tex. Christian U., 1986; M in Profl. Studies, Pratt Inst., 1989. Nurse Ft. Worth, 1962—; owner Kaki Doogs, Artist, Ft. Worth, 1967—, Do-Good Textiles, Ft. Worth, 1976-77; art therapist Ft. Worth, 1987—; bd. dirs. Com. for An Artist Ctr., Ft. Worth, 1975-80, Together Inc., Ft. Worth., 1977-79. Founder Tarrant County Arts Alliance, 1988—. Mem. Am. Art Therapy Assn., Tex. Art Therapy Assn. Home: 5300 Northcrest Rd Fort Worth TX 76107

DOOLEY, JO ANN CATHERINE, publishing company executive; b. Cin., Nov. 24, 1930; d. Joseph Frank and Margaret Mary (Flynn) D. Ed. U. Cin., 1966. Clk. Castellini Co., Cin., 1949-52; IBM operator Kroger Co., Cin., 1952; asst. acct. Gardner Publs., Inc., Cin., 1953-67, treas., sec., 1967—, dir., 1983—, v.p. fin., 1986—, also trustee employees profit sharing trust, trustee retirement trust. Mem. Am. Soc. Women Accts. (advt. mgr. Woman CPA 1979-81, nat. pres. 1982-83, treas. 1984—, exec. com., achievement award), Cin. Women's Forum. Roman Catholic. Office: 6600 Clough Pike Cincinnati OH 45244

DOOLEY, SISTER MARY AGNES, college president; b. Sommerville, Mass., Mar. 5, 1923; d. Richard and Mary A. (O'Neill) D. BA, Elms Coll., 1944; MA, Assumption Coll., 1960, LHD (hon.), 1982; Doctorat d'Université, U. Paris, 1968; LLD (hon.) Am. Internat. Coll., 1981; DMinistry, St. Louis U. Aquinas Inst., 1983; LittD (hon.), Fitchburg State Coll., 1985. Joined Congregation of the Sisters of St. Joseph, 1944; tchr. St. Joseph's High Sch., North Adams, Mass., 1946-65; chmn. lang. dept. Elms Coll., Chicopee, Mass., 1968-70, pres., 1979—; pres. Leadership Conf. Women Religious U.S., Washington, 1978-79; pres. Congregation Sisters of St. Joseph, Springfield, Mass., 1971-79. Contbr. articles to profl. jours. Recipient Disting. Alumna award Elms Coll., 1979, Human Rels. award NCCJ, 1988; decorated chevalier dans l'Ordre des Palmes Academiques (France), 1981; named Woman of Yr. Chicopee Bus. and Profl. Women's Club, Woman of Yr. Greater Springfield C. of C., 1987. Mem. Assn. Cath. Colls. and Univs. (bd. dir. 1980-85), Leadership Conf. Women Religious, Delta Epsilon Sigma. Roman Catholic.

DOOLEY, SUE ANN, information systems specialist; b. Brockton, Mass.; d. Joseph Henry and May Isabelle (Card) Jessop; 1 child, Erika. Student, Northeastern U., Boston. Programmer, analyst Arthur D. Little Systems, Burlington, Mass., 1979-80, Wang Labs., Lowell, Mass., 1980-82; sr. programmer analyst Wang Labs., 1982-83, prin. programmer, analyst, 1983-84, project mgr., 1984-87, sr. project mgr., 1987-90, info. mgmt. cons., 1990—. Mem. NAFE. Home: 24 Winsor Park Rd Lowell MA 01852 Office: Wang Labs 1 Industrial Ave Lowell MA 01851

DOOLITTLE, SHEILA ROSE, investment executive; b. Detroit, Aug. 31, 1956; d. Leonard George and Rosemary (Macaulay) Rose; m. Douglas Burklin Doolittle, May 28, 1988. BA in Mgmt. and Bus. with deptl. honors, Barat Coll., 1980. Registered commodity broker. Asst. to pres. Goldsholl Assocs., Northfield, Ill., 1980-81; mgr. Miller-Jesser Inc., Chgo., 1981-83; ptnr. Hugo Securities, N.Y.C., 1983-85; portfolio mgr. Gofen and Glossberg Inc., Chgo., 1985—; mem. Chgo. Merc. Exchange, 1983-85. Fundraiser Lawrence Hall Sch. for Boys, Chgo., 1980—; mem. Sheffield Neighborhood Assn. Mem. Nat. Futures Assn., Chgo. Bot. Gardens, Chgo. Art Inst. Home: 1035 W Webster Ave Chicago IL 60614

DOONE, MICHELE MARIE, chiropractor; b. Oak Park, Ill., Oct. 3, 1942; d. Robert Emmett and Tana Josephine (Alioto) D. Cert., Valley Coll. of Med. and Dental Careers, 1962; student, L.A. Valley Coll., 1960-63, Dallas County Community Coll., 1983-84; D in Chiropractic summa cum laude, Parker Coll. of Chiropractic, 1986. Lic. chiropractic, Calif., Tex.; cert. Nat. Bd. of Chiropractic Examiners, radiologic tech., Calif. Med. asst. William Orlando M.D., Edwin Crost, M.D., 1962-65; nursing supr., chief radiologic technologist Vanowen Med. Group, North Hollywood, Calif., 1965-76; radiologic technologist/purchasing agt. Lanier-Brown Clinic, Dallas, 1976-83; faculty mem./ chief radiologic technologist Parker Coll. of Chiropractic, Irving, Tex., 1983-85; exam and X-Ray doctor Margolies Chiropractic Ctr., Richardson, Tex., 1986; clinic staff doctor Parker Coll. of Chiropractic, Irving, Tex., 1986-87; doctor/ mgr. contractor Accident Ctrs. of Am., Garland, Tex., 1987; clinic dir. Back Pain Chiropractic, Carrollton, Tex., 1988—; advisor health related matters Inner Devel. Inst., Dallas, 1977—; sem. com. mem. Back Pain Chiropractic, Inc., Metarie, La., 1989—, clinic dir., 1988—. Mem. Tex. Chiropractic Assn. (radiology com. chmn. 1990), Am. Chiropractic Assn., Metroplex Neurospinal Diagnostic Med. and Surgical Group, Internat. Chiropractic Assn., Parker Chiropractic Rsch. Found., Parker Coll. Alumni Assn. (Dr. of Yr. award 1990), Metrocrest C. of C., Pi Tau Delta. Home: 4837 Cedar Springs #216 Dallas TX 75219 Office: Back Pain Chiropractic 2550 Trinity Mills #116 Carrollton TX 75006

DORA, JOAN TERESA, municipal clerk; b. Jersey City, Jan. 7, 1935; d. Samuel Francis and Helen Elizabeth (Curry) Kaminsky; m. Ewald Dora, Feb. 6, 1960; children: Deborah Ann, Walter John. Student County Coll. Morris-Randolph, N.J., 1970-73, Rutgers U., 1978—. Cert. mcpl. clk., N.J. Bookkeeper, office mgr. Lake Hopatcong Water Corp., High Ridge Water Co./High Ridge Sewer Co., N.J., 1970-77; acct. Lieberman & Co., Newton, N.J., 1977-78; mcpl. clk. Borough of Hopatcong, N.J., 1978—. Trustee, corp. sec. U.S. Land & Utilities, N.Y.C., 1973-77; chairperson Hopatcong Woman's Club Community Improvement Program, 1982—, Hopatcong Constnl. Bicentennial Com., 1987—. Recipient Merit award Rotary Club, 1982, Citizenship award, Rotary Club, 1985. Mem. Hopatcong C. of C. (pres. 1982-84), N.J. Fedn. Bus. and Profl. Women (asst. treas. 1982-83), Sussex County Mcpl. Clks. Assn. (pres. 1981-82), Mcpl. Clks. Assn., Internat. Inst. Mcpl. Clks., Hopatcong Econ. Devel. Commn. Clubs: Hopatcong Women's, N.W. Morris Bus. and Profl. Women's (pres. 1982-83), Deborah Hosp. Found. (1st v.p. 1982-83). Avocations: walking, golf, yogi exercise. Home: PO Box 112 Hopatcong NJ 07843 Office: Borough Hopatcong Mcpl Bldg River Styx Rd Hopatcong NJ 07843

DORAN, BARBARA LEE, sales executive; b. Phila., May 12, 1953. BA, Pa. State U., 1975; MBA, Harvard U., 1984. Asst. to women's sports info. dir. Pa. State Sports Info., State College, 1975-76; newswoman WRSC Radio, State College, 1975-76; sr. advt. copywriter Prentice-Hall, Englewood Cliffs, N.J., 1976-78; asst. to circulation dir. Working Woman Mag., N.Y.C., 1978-79; asst. list mgr. Conde Nast, N.Y.C., 1979-80; advt. sales rep. Sports Illustrated/Time Inc., N.Y.C., 1980-82; v.p. instl. equity sales First Boston Corp., N.Y.C., 1984—; asst. field hockey coach Northeastern U., 1982; asst. lacrosse coach Harvard U., 1983. Contbr. articles to mags. and newspapers. Fundraiser Harvard Bus. Sch., Class of 1984 Reunion, Boston, 1989, Dem. Party, N.Y.C., 1988; appointee Pub. Rels. Com., U.S. Olympic Com., Colorado Springs, 1984. Named to U.S. I Team, Field Hockey, U.S. Field Hockey Assn., 1978-79, U.S. I Team, Lacrosse, U.S. Lacrosse Assn., 1975-77, 85-88. Mem. U.S. Field Hockey Assn. (fin com. 1989—), Harvard Squash Club (capt. 1987—). Home: 26 E 91st St 3A New York NY 10128 Office: First Boston Corp Park Ave Pla New York NY 10055

DORAY, ANDREA WESLEY, corporate communications director, writer; b. Monte Vista, Colo., Oct. 4, 1956; d. Dant Bell and Rosemary Ann

(Kassap) D.; m. Paul Dean Doray, Nov. 25, 1978. BA, U. No. Colo., 1977. Cert. post secondary tchr. Asst. advt. mgr. San Luis Valley Publ. Co., Monte Vista, 1977-78; mktg. dir. Stuart Scott & Assocs. (formerly Philip Winn & Assocs.), Colorado Springs, Colo., 1978-80; sr. v.p. Heisley Design & Advt., Colorado Springs, Colo., 1980-85; pres., creative dir. Doray Doray, Monument, Colo., 1985—; account svcs. dir. Praco Ltd., Advt., Colorado Springs, 1987-88; dir. corp. community rels. Current, Inc., Colorado Springs, 1988—; instr. part time Pikes Peak Community Coll., Colorado Springs, 1983-86, mem. mktg. adv. coun. 1985-89; guest lectr. Colo. Mountain Coll., 1982-84, U. So. Colo., 1983, Pikes Peak Community Coll, 1983—, U. Colo., Colorado Springs, 1988—. Author: The Other Fish, 1976, Oil Painting Lessons, 1986, Coming to Terms, 1986, Roger Douglas, 1987; editor: Current Impressions; contbg. editor Colorado Springs Bus. Mag., 1984-86; creative writer World Cycling Fedn. Championships, 1986; speaker in field. Chmn. Colorado Springs Local Advt. Rev. Program, 1985; chmn., mem. exec. com. advt. and pub. rels. task force U.S. Olympic Hall of Fame, 1986; mem. State Legis. Alert and Action Coalition, 1985-87; mem. project bus. cons. Jr. Achievement, Colorado Springs, 1985-87; trustee Citizen's Goals Colorado Springs, 1988-89; speaker Nat. Coun. Community Rels., Orlando, Fla., 1988; grad. Leadership 2000, 1988. Named One of Colorado Springs Leading Women, Colorado Springs Gazette Telegraph, 1984, One of Women of 90s, 1989; Outstanding Young Alumna, U. No. Colo., 1987. Mem. Am. Advt. Fedn. (chmn. dist. 12 legis com. 1985—, pub. rels. com. 1986, Silver medal award 1986), Pikes Peak Advt. Fedn. (pres. 1984-86, Advt. Person of Yr. award), Colorado Springs C. of C. (advt. roundtable, speaker small bus. coun. 1986—, communications task force 1989—). Office: Current Inc PO Box 2559 Colorado Springs CO 80901

DORE, ANITA WILKES, English educator; b. N.Y.C., Dec. 16, 1914; d. Abraham P. and Rose (Hirsch) Wilkes; m. Robert M. Dore, June 26, 1938; children: Marjorie Dore Allen, Elizabeth. B.A., Vassar Coll., 1935; M.A. with honors, Columbia U., 1937. Cert. English tchr., N.Y. Tchr. high sch. English, Bd. Edn., N.Y.C., 1937-41, 56-59, TV broadcaster, producer, 1961-65, coordinator English jr. high sch. div., 1959-61, chairperson English dept., 1965-67, asst. dir. English, 1967-73, dir. English, N.Y.C. schs., 1973-83, cons., 1983—; cons. Young Playwrights Dramatists Guild, N.Y.C., 1983—. Author: Premier Book of Major Poets, 1970, Emerging Woman, 1974; co-author: Distrust of Authority, 1981; also articles. Pres., bd. dirs. Sch. Settlement House, Bklyn., 1951-53; mem. edn. com. NOW, N.Y.C., 1972-75; chairperson Child Study Children's Book Com. Bank St. Coll., 1983—; sec., bd. dirs. Westport-Westport Arts Ctr., Conn., 1983—; trustee Westport Library, Conn.; 1985—. Recipient Elizabeth Dana prize in English, Vassar Coll., 1934. Fellow N.Y. State English Council (v.p. 1970-75); mem. Nat. Council Tchrs. English Lit. Commn., N.Y.C. Assn. Tchrs. English (v.p. 1962-70). Democrat. Avocations: theatre, traveling, politics. Home: 36 E 36th St Apt 9B New York NY 10016

DORE, BONNY ELLEN, film and television production company executive; b. Cleve., Aug. 16, 1947; d. Reber Hutson and Ellen Elizabeth (McNamara) Barnes; m. Sanford Astor, May 22, 1987. BA, U. Mich., 1969, MA, 1975. Cert. tchr., Mich. Dir., tchr. Plymouth (Mich.) Community Schs., 1969-72; gen. mgr. Sta. WSDP-FM, Plymouth, 1970-72; prodn. supr. pub. TV N.Y. State Dept. Edn., 1972-74; producer TV series Hot Fudge Sta. WXYZ-TV, Detroit, 1974-75; mgr. children's programs ABC TV Network, Los Angeles, 1975, dir. children's programs, 1975-76, dir. prime time variety programs, 1976-77; dir. devel. Hanna-Barbera, Los Angeles, 1977; v.p. devel. and prodn. Krofft Entertainment, Los Angeles, 1977-81, Centerpoint Prodn., Los Angeles, 1981-82; pres., owner in assn. with Orion TV The Greif-Dore Co., Los Angeles, 1983-87, Bonny Dore Prodns. Inc., Los Angeles, 1988—; mem. Caucus of Writers, Producers and Dirs., 1989—, Pioneer Women in Film Video Project, co-chair, 1989—; Marsh speaker Pres. Fund for Pres. Weekend U. Mich., 1989. Producer TV series The Krofft Superstar Hour, ABC, 1978 (2 Emmy awards 1979), comedy series The 1/2 Hour Comedy Hour (starring Arsenio Hall and Victoria Jackson), ABC, 1983-84, mini-series Sins (starring Joan Collins), CBS, 1986, comedy series First Impressions, CBS, 1987-88, mini-series Glory! Glory! (starring Ellen Greene, Richard Thomas and James Whitmore; 2 Ace cable awards), HBO, 1988-89, numerous others. Mem. fundraising com. U. Mich., 1990—; assoc. mem. Nat. Trust for Hist. Preservation, 1988—. Named Outstanding Young Tchr. of Yr., Cen. States Speech Assn., 1973; Cert. of Appreciation, Gov. of Mich., 1985, City of Beverly Hills, Calif., 1985, Coun. on Social Work Edn., 1990; recipient Action for Children's TV award, 1975, Gold medal Best TV Mini-series, Best TV Screenplay Silver medal Houston Internat. Film Festival, 1990, Best TV Actress award, 1990, Best TV Supporting Actor, 1990, Best Music, 1990, Winner Best Mini Series Houston Film Festival, 1990. Mem. NATAS, Women in Film (v.p. 1978-81, pres. 1980-81), Women in Film Found. (trustee 1981—), Nat. Cable TV Assn., Beverly Hills C. of C. (cons. 1985), Exec. Roundtable L.A. (trustee 1987—), Hollywood Radio and TV Soc., Acad. TV Arts and Scis. Office: Bonny Dore Prodns Inc 11300 W Olympic Blvd Ste 870 Los Angeles CA 90064

DORFMAN, ANDREA RANDALL, journalist; b. N.Y.C., Sept. 18, 1959; d. Irvin Sherrod Dorfman and Jane Randall. BS, Yale U., 1981. Prodn. editor Acad. Press, N.Y.C., 1981-82; asst. editor, assoc. editor to sr. writer Sci. Digest mag., N.Y.C., 1982-85; reporter, researcher Time mag., N.Y.C., 1985—. Mem. Nat. Assn. Sci. Writers, Yale Alumni Assn., Yale Club. Office: Time Mag 1271 Ave of the Americas New York NY 10020

DORIA, LEONIDA TAMONDONG, accountant; b. Dagupan City, Philippines, Dec. 18, 1946; d. Jose Tenorio and Felisa (Ramirez) Tamondong; m. Manuel Tuliao Doria,. BSBA, U. East, 1967. Acctg. prof. U. Pangasinan, Dagupan, 1968-72; acct. Dagupan City Rural Bank, 1968-72, Chemetron Corp., Chgo., 1972-73, NEX Cagamer, Inc., Atsugi, Japan, 1975-77, McMillin Devel. Co., Nat. City, Calif., 1978-80, Leaf & Cole,, San Diego, 1981-84; realtor Westwind Real Estate, Chula Vista, Bonita, 1983-87, Westwind Real Estate and Chula Vista Tarbell Realtors, Nat. City, Calif., 1987--; acct. Leonel E. Guerrero & Co., San Diego, 1985--. Mem. Scottish Rite Women's Club, Officers Navy Wives, Dagupan Assn., Pangasinan Assn. Democrat. Roman Catholic. Home: 7603 Goode St San Diego CA 92139 Office: Leonel E Guerrero & Co 1450 Frague Rd Suite 602 San Diego CA 92108

DORIAN, LINDA COLVARD, association executive. Exec. dir. Nat. Fedn. Bus. & Profl. Women's Clubs, Washington, 1987—. Office: Nat Fed Bus & Profl Women's Clubs 2012 Massachusettes Ave NW Washington DC 20036*

DORIAN, NANCY CURRIER, educator; b. New Brunswick, N.J., 1936; d. Donald Clayton and Edith (McEwen) D. B.A. summa cum laude, Conn. Coll. for Women, 1958; postgrad., Yale U., 1959-60; M.A., U. Mich., 1961, Ph.D. (Rackham fellow), 1965. Lectr. Bryn Mawr Coll., Pa., 1965-66, asst. prof. linguistics in German and anthropology, 1966-72, assoc. prof., 1972-78, prof., 1978—, William R. Kenan Jr. prof., 1980-85; vis. lectr. U. Pa., 1966, 70, U. Kiel, 1967-68. Author: East Sutherland Gaelic, 1978, Language Death, 1981, Tyranny of Tide, 1985; editor: Investigating Obsolescence, 1989; asst. editor: Internat. Jour. of the Sociology of Language; assoc. editor: Language: contbr. articles to profl. jours. Fulbright scolar, W. Ger., 1958-59; NSF grantee, 1978-79. Mem. Linguistic Soc. Am., Internat. Linguistic Assn. Democrat. Unitarian. Office: Bryn Mawr Coll Dept German Bryn Mawr PA 19010

DORJAHN, RENEE VICTORIA, marketing executive; b. Eugene, Oreg., Jan. 27, 1960; d. Vernon Robert and Janet Mae (Patterson) D. BA in Math., U. Oreg., 1982; MA, U. Pa., 1984. Market planner Digital Equipment, Maynard, Mass., 1984-85; market researcher Motorola Computer Systems, Cupertino, Calif., 1985-86; cons. Market Intelligence Rsch., Mountain View, Calif., 1986-87; strategic planner Codex Corp., Canton, Mass., 1987—. Mem. Acad. Mktg. Sci., Electronic Banking Soc. (assoc.), Prodn. Devel. and Mgmt. Assn. Office: Codex Corp 7 Blue Hill River Rd Ste H-960 Canton MA 02021

DORLAND, BYRL BROWN, civic worker; b. Greenwich, Utah, Apr. 25, 1915; d. David Alma and Ethel Myrle (Peterson) Brown; grad., Snow Coll., Ephraim, Utah, 1936; teaching cert. Brigham Young U., 1937; B.S., Utah State Coll., Logan, 1940; grad. Family Inst. Vassar Coll., Poughkeepsie, N.Y., 1978; John Robert Powers Sch. Profl. Women, N.Y.C., 1980; m. Jack Albert Dorland, June 11, 1944; children: Lynn Elise Dorland Trost, Lee Allison. Sch. tchr., Utah, 1937-39, 40-42; restored Washington Irving's graveplot in Sleepy Hollow Cemetery, North Tarrytown, N.Y. (named Nat. Hist. Landmark 1972); nat. dir. Washington Irving Graveplot Restoration Program, 1968—, designer landmark plaque for grave; mem. Nat. Council State Garden Clubs, 1959—; pres. Potpourri Garden Club, Westchester, N.Y., 1966—; nat. chmn. for graveplot programs Washington Irving Bicentennial, 1983-84; dir. Dorland Family Graveyard Restoration, N.J. Hist. Landmark, 1983—. Recipient Disting. Alumni award for community svc. Snow Coll., 1989, May Duff Walters trophy Nat. Council State Garden Clubs, 1974; nat. trophy Nat. Historic Landmark Com., 1974; citation Keep Am. Beautiful, 1974. Mem. Nat. Trust for Historic Preservation (Pres.'s award 1977), Nat. Historic Soc. Am., Gen. Soc. Mayflower Desc., Internat. Washington Irving Soc. (founder, pres. 1981—), Nat. Assn. for Gravestone Studies (hon.), Herb Soc. Am., DAR. Home and Office: 10 Castle Heights Ave Tarrytown NY 10591

DORMAN, HATTIE LAWRENCE, management consultant, former government agency official; b. Cleve., July 22, 1932; d. J. Lyman and Claire A. (Lenoir) Lawrence; m. James L. Dorman, May 16, 1959; children—Lydia, Lynda, James Lawrence. Student Fenn Coll. (Cleve. State U.), part time 1950-58, D.C. Tchrs. Coll., 1960-64, Dept. Agr. Grad. Sch., 1968-69; BA, Howard U., 1987. Clk., tax specialist, mgmt. analyst, supr., staff advisor IRS, Washington, 1954-79; spl. asst. to dep. asst. sec. adminstrn. Dept. Treasury, Washington, 1978-79; dep. dir. Interagency Com. on Women's Bus. Enterprise, SBA; Task Force on EEO, Dept. Treasury 1978-79; mem. Pres.'s Task Force on Women Bus. Owners, from 1979, now ret.; assoc. prof. continuing edn. U. D.C.; trainer and speaker in field. Sec. Linton Hall Guild, 1978-80; chmn. trainer, cons., leader Girl Scout Service Unit, 1971-80; ofcl. observer Nat. Women's Conf., Houston, 1977; bd. dirs. YWCA, 1957-62; mem. planning com. Black Women's Summit, 1981; mem. Vestry Register, St. Paul's Episcopal Ch., 1981-86. Recipient spl. achievement award Commr. IRS, 1978, thanks badge Girl Scout Nation's Capital, 1977, recognition cert. for work in Christian edn. St. Paul's Episcopal Ch., 1976, Mary McLeod Bethune Centennial award Nat. Council Negro Women, 1975, other awards and certs. of appreciation. Mem. Am. Soc. Public Adminstrs., Federally Employed Women, Alumni Fed. Exec. Inst. Club: Delta Sigma Theta. Journalist Neighbor's Inc., 1969-71.

DORMAN, KAREN GAIL, consulting firm executive; b. Akron, Ohio, Mar. 2, 1952; d. Milton and Belle (Handler) D.; m. Michael Barry Schoenburg, July 3, 1988; 1 child, Joel Daniel. Student, Albert Ludwigs U., Freiburg, West Germany, 1971-72; BA, Miami U., Oxford, Ohio, 1974; MS in Journalism, Northwestern U., 1976. Prodn. copywriter WSLR Radio, Akron, 1974-75; copywriter Needham Harper & Steers, Chgo., 1977-80, Stern Walters/Earle Ludgin, Chgo., 1980-81; dir. communication rsch., mktg. mgr. Hubbard & Assocs., Chgo., 1982-85; pres., owner ServiceSeekers, Chgo., 1986—. Author: Everything You Need to Know About Shopping Surveys, 1987. Sec. Univ. Pl. Assn., Chgo., 1989-90. Mem. Bank Mktg. Assn. (program adv. coun. 1989-90), Fin. Instns. Mktg. Assn. (peer cons. 1990), Ind. Writers Chgo. (com. chmn. 1989), Miami U. Alumni, Northwestern U. Alumni. Office: ServiceSeekers 155 N Michigan Ave Ste 700 Chicago IL 60601

DORMINEY, ELIZABETH KLINE, lawyer; b. Atlanta, Sept. 16, 1956; d. Duane Walter and Margaret (McWilliams) Kline; m. A. Blair Dorminey, June 20, 1981; 1 child, Sterling Beaumont Grant. BA, U. Ga., 1973-76; postgrad., Sorbonne, Paris, 1977-78; JD, U. Ga. Law Sch., 1978-81; LLM, Columbia Law Sch., NY, 1983-84. Admitted to Bar in Ga., Conn., NY. Atty. Jacobs, Grudberg and Belt, New Haven, 1981-83; atty., advisor Import Adminstrn., US Dept. Commerce, Wash., 1985-86; spl. asst. to gen. Counsel, US Dept. Commerce, Wash., 1986-87; sr. counsel for policy and programs US Dept Commerce, Wash., 1988-89; adjunct prof., law George Mason U. Sch. Law, Arlington, 1987—; sr. atty. Office of Policy Devel., U.S. Dept. Justice, Washington, 1990—. Co-author: U. Nebr. L. Rev., Am. U. Adminstrn. Law, 1987. Mem. Daughters of the American Revolution, Wash., 1985--. Mem. Federalist Soc. Office: US Dept Justice 10th and Constitution NW Washington DC 20250

DORN, ANNITA LYNNE, farmer, rancher; b. Collinsville, Tex.; d. Guy and Laurenia (Belcher) Stephens; m. Wesley Dorn, June 20, 1969. LLB, Wayne U., Chgo., 1972. Owner grocery store Pilot Point, Tex., 1971-76; telemarketer Lego Mktg., Denton, Tex., 1989; owner farm Collinsville, Tex. Tchr. World Bible Sch. Recipient Prison Fellowship award Prison Ministry. Mem. NAFE, Am. Quarter Horse Assn., Tex. Farm Bur., Citizens for Drug Free Am. Home: Rt 1 Box 292 Collinsville TX 76233

DORN, JENNIFER LYNN, federal agency administrator; b. Grand Island, Nebr., Dec. 7, 1950; d. Harold Clarence and Ethel Agnes D.; m. Kurt Pfotenhauer. BA, Oreg. State U., 1973; MPA, U. Conn., 1977. Account exec. J.R. Tendler Assoc., Woodbridge, Conn., 1974-75; legis. asst. Senator M. Hatfield, Washington, 1977-81; com. staff Senate Appropriations, Washington, 1981-83; spl. asst. Sec. Elizabeth Dole, Washington, 1983-84; dir. Comml. Space Transp., Washington, 1984-85; assoc. dep. sec. U.S. Dept. Transp., Washington, 1985-87; asst. sec. policy U.S. Dept. Labor, Washington, 1989—; dir. strategic planning Martin Marietta Corp., Bethesda, 1988-89. Mem. Oreg. Women's Forum. Republican. Lutheran. Home: 4603 Overbrook Rd Bethesda MD 20816 Office: 200 Constitution Ave NW Washington DC 20210

DORN, WANDA FAYE, talent agent; b. Little Rock, May 23, 1945; d. Jesse Dorn and Daisy Mae (Washington) Dorn-Jones; m. Donald Hayman, Nov. 22, 1966 (div. June 1986); 1 child, Deon Horace. Grad., Crest Modeling Sch., Chgo., Patricia Vance Sch. Modeling, Chgo., 1966; AA, Chgo. Coll. Commerce, 1970; grad. tchr. tng. program, John Robert Powers Modeling Agy., Chgo., 1979. Lic. fashion cons., retailer, modeling sch. adminstr. and instr. Ct. reporter Superior Cts., San Jose, Oakland, Calif., 1973-83; instr. Marnee Jones Modeling Sch., San Jose, Calif., 1980; freelance writer San Jose-Peninsula Metro, 1982-86; fashion writer San Francisco Sun Reporter, 1982-86; owner, founder A'Dorn Studios, San Jose and Los Angeles, 1979—; lectr., instr. modeling and personal improvement; coordinator fashion prodns.; founder Black Model of Yr. Pageant, 1982; producer, host weekly talk show Society Pages, 1986—; first black stewardess for a major airline, 1966. Author: Your Most Important Accessory - Your Appearance, 1984. Recipient Outstanding Community Service award Human Relations Com. of Santa Clara, 1986, Community Service award San Jose C. of C., Ams. Top 100 Bus. and Profl. Women award Dollars and Sense mag., 1988; appointed to Fine Arts Commn., Mayor and City Council of San Jose, 1986—. Mem. Calif. Ct. Reporter's Assn., NOW, NAACP, Nat. Council Negro Women, Inc. (past v.p., chmn. fundraising com., chmn. bylaws com., chmn. internat. com.), South Bay Black Women's Network (past pres., chmn. hotline com., chmn. structure com., founding mem.), Black Concerns Assn. (past v.p., chmn. new faces program), Black Media Coalition, Black Filmmakers Hall of Fame. Office: A'Dorn Studios 1901 Ave of the Stars Ste 1774 Century City CA 90067 also: PO Box 21668 San Jose CA 95151

DORNAN, CANDACE BUTLER, marketing professional; b. Woodbury, N.J., Dec. 27, 1952; d. Walter Hildebrand and Gladys (Gardiner) Butler. BS, W.Va. Wesleyan Coll., 1975; MEd, U. N.C., Greensboro, 1980. Supr. food prodn. Stouffer's Mgmt. Food Svc., Haverford and Broomall, Pa., 1977-78; extension home economist Rutgers Coop. Extension Atlantic County, New Brunswick, N.J., 1981-86; consumer mktg. rep. South Jersey Gas Co., Folsom, N.J., 1986—; mem. adv. council home econs. dept. Glassboro (N.J.) State Coll., 1986—; mem. adv. bd. Atlantic Food Bank, Inc., Atlantic City, 1986—. Developer teaching guide Seafood, Nothing Goes to Waist, 1988. Mem. Am. Home Econs. Assn. (cert.), So. Counties Home Econs. Assn. (chmn. 1986-89), N.J. Home Econs. Assn. (trustee 1986—), So. N.J. Nutrition Council (chmn. nutrition month 1984-87), Nat. Assn. Extension Home Economists, Alpha Gamma Delta. Home: 626 First Ave Absecon NJ 08201 Office: South Jersey Gas Co #2 Heathercroft Sq Northfield NJ 08232

DORNBUSH, RHEA L., psychologist, educator; b. N.Y.C.. BA, Queens Coll., 1962, MA, 1963; PhD, CUNY, 1967; MPH, Columbia U., 1981. Lic. pychologist, N.Y. Rsch. asst., reseach assoc., teaching fellow Queens Coll., Flushing, N.Y., 1963-65; lectr., asst. prof. Douglass Coll., Rutgers U., New Brunswick, N.J., 1965-68; from asst. prof. to assoc. prof. psychiatry N.Y. Med. Coll., N.Y.C., 1968-76; sr. rsch. scientist Reproductive Biology Research Found., St. Louis, 1976-78; clin. lectr. in med. psychology Washington U. Sch. Medicine, St. Louis, 1976-78; assoc. prof. psychiatry N.Y. Med. Coll., Valhalla, N.Y., 1978-80; prof. psychiatry N.Y. Med. Coll., 1980—; adj. prof. psychology Queens Coll. CUNY, Flushing, 1983—; lectr. Assn. for the Advancement Tng. in Behavioral Scis., 1984—. Editor: Chronic Cannabis Use, 1976, Hashish: Studies of Long-Term Use, 1977; contbr. articles to profl. jours. Bd. dirs. Riverdale Sr. Svcs., Inc., Bronx, N.Y., 1984—. NIH Predoctoral fellow, 1964-65; Rsch. grantee NIMH, 1978-80, Rsch. grantee Nat. Fund for Med. Edn., 1984-88, NIH Small Grantee, 1966-68. Mem. Am. Psychol. Assn., Soc. Biol. Psychiatry, Am. Psychopathological Assn., Nat. Acad. Neuropsychologists, Internat. Neuropsychology Soc. Office: NY Med Coll Dept Psychiatry Valhalla NY 10595

DORNER-ANDELORA, SHARON AGNES HADDON, educator; b. Morristown, N.J., Nov. 3, 1943; d. William P. and Eleanor (Dygert) Haddon; BA in Bus. Edn., Montclair State Coll., 1965, MA in Bus. Edn., 1970, MA in Guidance and Counseling, 1978; EdD in Vocat.-Tech. Edn., Adminstrn. and Supervision, Rutgers U., 1982; m. Robert Andelora, Feb. 17, 1985: children: Wendy, Meridith. Tchr., Morris Knolls High Sch., 1965-70; tchr. Katherine Gibbs Sec. Sch., Montclair, N.J., 1973-74; tchr. Leonia (N.J.) High Sch., 1974-75; tchr. bus. Woodcliff Sch., Woodcliff Lake, N.J., 1976—, adminstrv. intern to supt., 1980—; tchr. adult sch. Sussex Vocat. Sch., County Coll. Morris, Randolph, N.J. Judge, Election Bd., Montclair, 1972-82. Mem. Assn. Supervision and Curriculum Devel., Am. Vocat. Assn., Am. Vocat. Research Assn., N.J. Vocat. Assn., NEA, N.J. Edn. Assn., Bergen County Edn. Assn., Woodcliff Lake Edn. Assn. (sec. 1976-84), N.J. Bus. Edn. Assn. (co-editor Observer), Nat. Bus. Edn. Assn., Eastern Bus. Edn. Assn., Consumers League (dir. 1979—), N.J. Coll. Ednl. Leaders (v.p. 1985-89, treas. 1983-84, Northeastern regional rep. 1982-83, membership com. 1989—), Northeast Coalition Ednl. Leaders, Delta Pi Epsilon (pres. Beta Phi chpt. 1979-80, v.p. 1978-79, sec. 1976-78, newsletter editor 1974-76, 89—, nat. com. 1980-84, nat. council rep. 1981-88, nat. historian 1987—, chmn. nat. com. 1982-84), Sigma Kappa (nat. alumnae province officer 1977-81, nat. alumnae dist. dir. 1981-87), Phi Delta Kappa (pres. 1980-82 treas. 1975-79, 82-84, council del. 1977-80, 84-86, research rep. 1986-88, found. rep. 1988—), Omicron Tau Theta (pres. Delta chpt. 1987-88, v.p. 1986-87, nat. parliamentarian 1986-88). Lodges: Daus. of Nile, N.J. Eastern Star. Mem. adv. bd. Today's Sec., 1981-82. Home: 28 College Ave Upper Montclair NJ 07043 Office: 134 Woodcliff Ave Woodcliff Lake NJ 07675

DORO, MARION ELIZABETH, political scientist, educator; b. Miami, Fla., Oct. 9, 1928; d. George and Alma (Carram) D. B.A., Fla. State U., 1951, M.A., 1952; Ph.D. (Bennett fellow), U. Pa., 1959. Instr. polit. sci. Wheaton Coll., Norton, Mass., 1958-60; Ford Found. Area Studies fellow U. London, Kenya, Africa, 1960-62; asst. prof. Conn. Coll., New London, 1962-65; assoc. prof. Conn. Coll., 1965-70, prof., 1970—, Lucy Marsh Haskell prof. govt., 1983—, dir. grad. studies, 1975-79, chmn. dept. govt., 1981-84, 87—. Editor: (with N. Stultz) Governing in Black Africa, 1970, 2d edit., 1986, Africa Contemporary Record, 1988—; mem. editorial bd.: African Studies Rev.; contbr. articles and book revs. to profl. jours. Fulbright fellow Makerere U., Kampala, Uganda, 1963-64; sr. research fellow Radcliffe Inst., Cambridge, Mass., 1968-69; vis. research fellow, Am. Philos. Soc. grantee East Africa Inst. Social Sci. Research, 1971-72; AAUW Am. fellow, sr. assoc. St. Anthony's Coll., Oxford U., 1977-78; vis. faculty fellow Yale U., 1984-85. Mem. Am. Polit. Sci. Assn. (publ. com. 1987—), New Eng. Polit. Sci. Assn. (chmn. status women com. 1972-75, exec. coun. 1973-75), N.E. Polit. Sci. Assn. (exec. coun. 1974-76, 82-84), African Studies Assn. (bd. dirs. program nat. meetings 1976), AAUP, AAUW, Soc. Fellows Radcliffe Inst. (exec. coun. 1979-84), Phi Beta Kappa, Phi Kapp Phi, Pi Sigma Alpha. Office: Conn Coll PO Box 5457 New London CT 06320-4196

DOROS, MARIA HECZEY, psychology educator; b. Budapest, Hungary, Oct. 25, 1937; came to U.S., 1963; d. Gabriel Doros and Ethel Tima; m. Ivan M. Heczey, Apr. 6, 1964 (div. 1979). BA, Hunter Coll., 1973, MA, 1975; PhD, CUNY, 1977. Lic. psychologist, Ohio. Pvt. practice N.Y.C., 1975-77; instr. psychology Coll. of St. Elizabeth, Convent, N.J., 1976-77, Calif. Sch. Profl. Psychology, L.A. City Coll., 1978-79; program coord. No. Wis. Ctr. for Mental Retardation-Devel. Disabilities, Chippewa Falls, 1979-80; vis. prof. Carthage Coll., Kenosha, Wis., 1980-81; asst. prof. Marietta Coll., 1981-87; pvt. practice Marietta, Ohio, 1988-89; assoc. prof. psychology Muskingum Coll., New Concord, Ohio, 1989—. Author: Woman to Woman: On the Menstrual Cycle, 1978, (cassette tapes) Deep Relaxation Exercises, 1978; contbr. numerous articles to profl. jours., chpts. to books. Mem. Am. Psychol. Assn., Ohio Psychol. Assn., Phi Beta Kappa, Psi Chi. Republican. Presbyterian. Office: Muskingum Coll Psychology Dept New Concord OH 43762

DOROUGH, TRACEY LEIGH, teacher of handicapped children; b. Pell City, Ala., Jan. 4, 1963; d. Joseph Murl and Sandra (Daffron) D. BS in Spl. Edn., Auburn U., 1985, MA in Early Childhood-Handicapped Edn., 1989. Cert. tchr., Ala. Tchr. of mentally retarded and handicapped children Alexander City (Ala.) Bd. Edn., 1985-86, Montgomery (Ala.) Bd. Edn., 1986-89, Mountain Brook Bd. Edn., Birmingham, Ala., 1989—. Mem. Nat. Coun. Exceptional Children, Profl. Educators Mountain Brook, State Coun. Exceptional Children. Republican. Methodist. Home: 3244 Burning Tree Dr Birmingham AL 35226 Office: Mountain Brook Bd Edn 3 Church St Birmingham AL 35213

DORRIS, CATHERINE ANN, risk management consultant; b. Nashville, Feb. 28, 1963; d. Ray and Mary Catherine (Hackney) D.; m. Michael D. Bennett, Sept. 9, 1989. BA, Vanderbilt U., 1985, MBA, 1986. Assoc. risk mgmt. Fin. analyst Corroon & Black, Nashville, 1986-89, cons., 1989—; session coord. Risk and Ins. Mgmt. Soc., Atlanta, 1989; tchr. econs. Jr. Achievement, Nashville, 1989. Corroon & Black coord. United Way, Nashville, 1988. Republican. Mem. Ch. of Christ. Home: 1301 Bellshire Dr Nashville TN 37207 Office: Corroon & Black 1 Commerce Pl Ste 1500 Nashville TN 37239

DORRIS, PEGGY RAE, biologist, educator; b. Holly Bluff, Miss., Feb. 27, 1933; d. Hugh Baskerville and Alta Eugenia (Stampley) D. B.S. with distinction, Miss. Coll., 1956; M.S., U. Miss., 1963, Ph.D., 1967. Tchr. biology pub. schs., Benton, Miss., 1956-57, Wilmot, Ark., 1957-60, Pontotoc, Miss., 1960-61; grad. asst. U. Miss., Oxford, 1961-66; prof. Henderson State U., Arkadelphia, Ark., 1966-72, chmn. dept. biology, 1972-90; cons. brown recluse spider and poisonous snakes pub. schs., communities, hosps., U.S. Corps. Engrs., DeGray Lake; mem. AAUW, 1967-80, Ark. Edn. Assn., 1967-78, AAUP, 1968-78, Delta Kappa Gamma, 1967-80. Contbr. articles to jour. Miss. Acad. Sci., trans. Am. Micros. Soc., Procs. Ark. Acad. Sci., other publs. Mem. Arkadelphia Water and Sewer Commn., 1978—, Soil and Water Conservation Commn., Arkadelphia, 1983—; bd. dirs. Clark County Fair Assn., 1983—, livestock chmn., 1985—. NSF grantee, 1961-63; C.E. grantee, 1978-79. Mem. AAAS, Am. Arachnology Soc., Paris Arachnology Soc., Audubon Soc., Herpetology Soc., Ark. Acad. Sci. (mem. constl. com. 1984-85), Ark. Simmental Soc. (bd. dirs. 1978—), Beta Beta Beta, Phi Kappa Phi. Avocations: reading; cycling; hunting; fishing; ranching. Home: 125 Evonshire Arkadelphia AR 71923 Office: Henderson State U H-7544 Arkadelphia AR 71923

DORSETT, PATRICIA JEAN POOLE, educator, consultant; b. New Castle, Ind., May 26, 1935; d. George Meredith and Margaret (Bryan) Poole; m. Carroll Edwin Cleek, Jan. 8, 1954 (div. 1976); children: Cynthia Anne Cleek, Patricia Jill Cleek, Deborah Susan Cleek, David Carroll Cleek; m. John Ford Dorsett, Feb. 11, 1978. BS in Edn. cum laude, Ga. State U., 1982, MS in English Edn., 1986. Cert. tchr., Ga. Pres. Direct Systems Corp., Orchard Park, N.Y., 1969-72; coordinator reservations and travel Ciba-Geigy Corp., Greensboro, N.C., 1975-78; pvt. practice travel cons. Conyers, Ga., 1979-81; cons. property mgmt. and bus. P&J Assocs., Conyers, 1980—; tchr. language arts Cousins Mid. Sch., Covington, Ga., 1983—, staff devel. chair, 1987—; sec.-treas. P&J Assocs., 1979—. Editor: (newsletter) St. Mark's Caller, 1964-69, The Voter, 1982-87, Direct Systems Corp. Mail Order Catalog, 1969-72. Pres. Coop. Nursery Sch., Orchard Park, 1961-62; leader 4-H Club, Orchard Park, 1964-74; active Rockdale (Ga.) Arts Alliance. Mem. LWV (first pres. Rockdale County chpt. 1982-83, fin. chair 1984-85, sec. 1986-87, adminstrv. v.p. 1987—, Outstanding Svc. award 1986, chair natural resources 1987—, bd. dirs. Ga. 1987-89), Ga. Assn. Educators, Ga. Internat. Reading Assn., Ga. Coun. Tchrs. of English, Nat. Fedn. Women's Clubs (chair scholarship fund 1974-75), Phi Alpha Theta. Episcopalian. Home: 1460B Pine Log Rd Conyers GA 30207 Office: P&J Assocs 954 S Main St Conyers GA 30207

DORSEY, RHODA MARY, college president; b. Boston, Sept. 9, 1927; d. Thomas Francis and Hedwig (Hoge) D. BA magna cum laude, Smith Coll., 1949, LLD, 1979; BA, Cambridge (Eng.) U., 1951, MA, 1954; PhD, U. Minn., 1956; LLD (hon.), Nazareth Coll. Rochester, 1970; DHL (hon.), Mount St. Mary's Coll., 1976, Mount Vernon Coll., 1979, Coll. St. Catherine, 1983, Johns Hopkins U., 1986, Towson State U., 1987. Mem. faculty Goucher Coll., Towson, Md., 1954—; prof. history Goucher Coll., 1965-68, dean, v.p., 1968-73, acting pres., 1973-74; pres. Goucher Coll., Balt., 1974—; lectr. history Loyola Coll., Balt., 1958-62, Johns Hopkins, 1960-61; bd. dirs. U.S. Fidelity & Guaranty Co., Balt., Chesapeake & Potomac Tel. Co. Md., First Nat. Bank Md. Bd. dirs. Am. Friends of Cambridge U., 1978—, sec., 1989—; bd. dirs. Gen. German Aged Peoples Home, Balt. 1984—, Ind. Coll. Fund Md., 1987—, Nat. Assn. Ind. Colls. and Univs., 1990—; chmn. Md.-D.C. Com. on Selection Rhodes Scholars; mem. exec. bd. Leadership-Balt. County, 1989—; mem. ednl. adv. coun. Am. Field Svc.-USA, 1989—; adv. bd. Townson Cath. High Sch., 1988—; mem. Exec. Adv. Bd. Higher Edn. of Balt. County; trustee Balt. Coun. Coun. Fgn. Affairs, 1990—. Recipient Outstanding Woman Mgr. of 1984 U. Balt. Women's Program in Mgmt. and WMAR-TV, Outstanding Achievement award U. Minn. Alumni Assn., 1984; Andrew White medal Loyola Coll., 1985; named in survey of peers as one of 100 Most Effective Coll. and Univ. Pres. in U.S., Chronicle of Higher Edn., 1986. Mem. Md. Ind. Coll. and Univ. Assn., Nat. Assn. Ind. Colls. and Univs. (bd. dirs. 1990—). Clubs: Smith, Hamilton St. (Balt.); Cosmopolitan (N.Y.C.). Office: Goucher Coll Office of Pres Towson MD 21204

DORWARD, JUDITH A., food company executive; b. Hazleton, Pa., Apr. 16, 1941; d. Eugene Joseph and Dorothy Cecelia (Shields) McNertney; m. Douglas Dean Owens, Apr. 15, 1961 (div. 1968); children: Kevin Patrick, Kelly Shawn; m. Clifford Dorward, July 4, 1969 (div. 1974). AA, Lehigh County Community Coll., 1979; BA, Muhlenberg Coll., 1984; grad. in statis. process control, Process Mgmt. Inst., Inc., Mpls., 1986. Customer svc. clk. Pa. Power & Light Co., Allentown, 1959-61; mgr. Merle Norman Cosmetic Studios, Allentown and Bethlehem, Pa., 1968-70; adminstrv. clk. Pillsbury Co., East Greenville, Pa., 1970-85; mgr. ops. prodn. Pillsbury Co., East Greenville, 1985-87, mgr. distbn. and prodn. control, chairperson labor rels. com, 1987—. Former voting machine operator Lehigh County, Slatington, Pa.; held various offices Gen. Fedn. of Women's Clubs. Mem. Phi Beta Kappa. Democrat. Roman Catholic. Home: 1249 Knossos Dr Apt 5 Whitehall PA 18052 Office: Pillsbury Co Pillsbury Rd East Greenville PA 18041

DORWART, BONNIE BRICE, internist, rheumatologist, educator; b. Petersburg, Va., Jan. 27, 1942; d. Gratien Bertrand and Myrtle Elizabeth (Houser) Brice; m. William Villee Dorwart, Jr., June 22, 1963; children: William Bertrand, Brice Burdan, Michael Walter. AB, Bryn Mawr Coll., 1964; MD, Temple U., 1968. Diplomate Am. Bd. Med. Examiners, Am. Bd. Internal Medicine, Am. Bd. Rheumatology. Intern, then resident in internal medicine Lankenau Hosp., Jefferson Med. Coll., Phila., 1968-72; instr. medicine Hosp. of U. Pa., Phila., 1972-74; fellow rheumatology U. Pa. Sch. Medicine, Phila., 1974; instr. medicine Jefferson Med. Coll., 1974-76, asst. prof., 1976-81, assoc. prof., 1981—; assoc. investigator div. rsch. Lankenau Hosp., 1978-88, chief arthritis clinic, 1982-86, chief connective tissue disorders, 1982—; assoc. dir. Greater Delaware Valley Arthritis Control Program, 1975; mem. Gov.'s adv. bd. on Systemic Lupus Erythematosus, Phila., 1981-88. Contbr. articles to med. jours., chpts. to books. Med. career advisor, active cells workshop Merion (Pa.) Elem. Sch., 1984—; fund raiser Arthritis Found., Am. Cancer Soc., Phila., 1974—; mem. resources com. Bryn Mawr Coll., 1985—. Named Physician of Yr., 32 Carat Club, Phila., 1986; Janet M. Glasgow scholar Temple U. Sch. Medicine, 1968. Fellow ACP; mem. AMA, Am. Coll. Rheumatology, Phila. Rheumatism Soc. (pres. 1981-82), Pa. Med. Soc., Philadelphia County Med. Soc. Lutheran. Home and Office: 124 Maple Ave Bala-Cynwyd PA 19004

DOSS, DIANA LYNN, executive search consultant; b. Wheeling, W.Va., Nov. 26, 1957; d. Jack Curtis and Genevieve (Groch) Birkhimer; m. Bill R. Doss, Jr., Aug. 1, 1981; 1 child, Billy Rogers Doss, III. BA, W.Va. U., 1980; student, U. Nev., Las Vegas, 1980-81, Ariz. State U., 1981. Pers. adminstr. Bank of Scottsdale, Ariz., 1982-83; asst. dir. pers. Loew's P.V. Resort, Scottsdale, 1983-85; dir. pers. Scottsdale Hilton Safari Resort, 1985-86, Sheraton Tempe (Ariz.) Mission Palms, 1986-88; pres. Human Resource Network, Scottsdale, 1988—. Mem. task force Valley of the Sun United Way, Tempe, 1987; active Am. Heart Assn., Tempe, 1987. Mem. NAFE, Valley Innkeepers Assn., Scottsdale C. of C. Republican. Office: Human Resource Network 7150 E Camelback Rd Ste 300 Scottsdale AZ 85251

DOS SANTOS, DOMITILIA M., account executive, financial planner. Student, London Sch. Econs., 1975; BA in Polit. Sci. and History, Drew U., 1975; JD, Rutgers U., 1979; courses in acctg. and security analysis, N.Y. Inst. Fin., 1982-83. Law clk. Office of Corp. Counsel, Newark, 1977-79; assoc. legal officer Office Legal Affairs UN, N.Y.C., 1879-82; litigation mgr. Saul, Ewing, Remick & Saul, N.Y.C., 1982-83; account exec. trainee Merrill Lynch, Pierce Fenner & Smith, N.Y.C., 1983-84; account exec., fin. planner Smith Barney Harris Upham Co., N.Y.C., 1984—; adj. prof. mgmt., bus. law, introduction to bus. Borough of Manhattan Community Coll., N.Y.C., 1984—; lectr. N.Y. YMCA, 1985—, New Sch. Social Rsch., 1985—; qualified as fl. trader N.Y. Futures Exch., N.Y.C. Mem. N.Y. Fgn. Lawyers Assn., Ctr. Inter-Am. Rels., The Portugal-U.S. C. of C.

DOSWELL, MARY CUMMINGS, marketing executive; b. Atlanta, June 9, 1958; d. Robert Emery Cummings and Catherine Brierly Longyear; m. John Cabell Doswell II, July 3, 1982; children: Lindsay Cummings, Catherine Carter. BA in Physics, Mt. Holyoke Coll., South Hadley, Mass., 1980; MS in Matl. Engring., MIT, 1982. Sr. staff adminstrn. sr. coord. regulation, dir. demand-side analysis Va. Power, Richmond; dir. mkt. rsch. Va. Power. Contbr. articles to profl. jours. Regional dir. admissions Mt. Holyoke Coll. Mem. Soc. Women Engrs., Elec. Utility Mkt. Rsch. Coun., Richmond C. of C. (chmn. bus. rsch. advisors), Women's Club, Tuckahoe Woman's Club, Sigma Xi. Office: Va Power PO Box 26666 Richmond VA 23229

DOTSON, LINDA SUE, entertainment agent and manager; b. Richmond, Ky., Jan. 4, 1951; d. Mason and Ida Helen (Adams) Edington; m. Sheb F. Wooley, Dec. 30, 1985; 1 child, Shauna Michelle Dotson. AS in Nursing, U. Ky., 1978; BA in Nursing, U. Tenn., 1980. RN., Ky., Tenn. Talent buyer U.S. Govt.-Germany, Babenhausen, Fed. Republic of Germany, 1968-70; head writer Stars and Stripes, U.S. Govt., Frankfurt, Fed. Republic of Germany, 1969-70; die test, extruder Parker Hanifen, Berea, Ky., 1972-75; staff, head nurse Bapt. Hosp., Nashville, 1978-83; owner Pub. Relations/Talent Agy., Nashville, 1979—; co-owner Dotson-Wooley Entertainment Group (Film), Nashville, 1982—, Channel-Cordial Music Cos. (Pubs.), Nashville, 1982—; chief executive officer, owner Lito Internat. Inc. (Export/Import), Nashville, 1988—. Composer numerous songs; author: Elbows, 1979; assoc. TV Series, To Nashville, 1982, Cable TV show, Fandango, 1984. Named Top Ten Women in Entertainment, Performance Mag., 1988, finalist CBS Records/Am. Song Festival, 1982. Mem. ASCAP, Am. Fedn. Musicians, AFTRA, Internat. Country Music Buyers Assn., Nashville Assn. Talent Dirs. Office: Cir Rider Talent & Mgmt 123 Walton Ferry Rd 2nd Fl Hendersonville TN 37075

DOTY, ANNE ELIZABETH, marketing professional; b. Denver, Nov. 19, 1959; d. Howard McGregor and Frances Ellen (Pickett) D. BA, Colo. Coll., 1982; MBA, Northwestern U., Evanston, Ill., 1988. Dir. Carleton Fund Carleton Coll., Northfield, Minn., 1983-86; product mgr. Moore Group Inc., Atlanta, 1988—. Mem. Atlanta High Mus. Young Careers Orgn., 1988, Ga. Coun. Internat. Vis., Atlanta, 1989. Named Outstanding Newcomer in Devel., Coun. for Advancement and Support of Edn., 1983; Austin scholar Northwestern U., 1986. Mem. Am. Mktg. Assn. Home: 873 E Rock Springs Rd NE Atlanta GA 30306

DOTY, DELLA CORRINE, financial consultant; b. Marshalltown, Iowa, Apr. 12, 1945; d. Edwin Francis and Della Edna (Keller) Mack; B.S.B.A. in Acctg., Drake U., 1967; m. Philip Edward Doty, Dec. 23, 1967; children: Sarah Corrine, Anne Elizabeth. Audit staff Alexander Grant & Co., C.P.A.s, Denver, 1967-71; controller Valley View Hosp. and Med. Ctr., Denver, 1971-75; rate rev. specialist Colo. Hosp. Assn., Denver, 1975-79; pvt. fin. cons., Littleton, Colo., 1979—; lectr. in field. Dir., asst. treas. YWCA of Metro Denver, 1972-74; bd. dirs. Colo. Heart Assn., 1974-82; dir. Families First, Inc., 1987-89, chmn., bd. dirs., 1988-89; trustee Colo. Children's Chorale, 1988—; mem. Jr. League of Denver, 1979—, v.p. mktg., 1985-86; sec. Littleton Pub. Schs. Bldg. Authority, 1983-86; active various charitable orgns.; v.p. fin. and housing Alpha Phi Internat., 1974-78, trustee, 1980-86; dir., treas. Alpha Phi Found., 1978-86. Recipient Founders Merit award Healthcare Fin. Mgmt. Assn., 1976, 83, Outstanding Vol. award Jr. League of Denver, 1984; CPA, Colo. Mem. Am. Inst. CPA's, Colo. Soc. CPA's, Hosp. Fin. Mgmt. Assn., Alpha Phi (Ursa Major award 1980). Republican. Baptist. Contbr. articles to profl. jours. Address: 5981 S Coventry Ln W Littleton CO 80123

DOUCETTE, MARY-ALYCE, computer company executive; b. Pitts., Feb. 12, 1924; d. Andrew George and Alice Jane (Sloan) Newland; m. Adrian Robert Doucette, Feb. 6, 1945 (dec. June 1983); children: David Robert, Regis Robert. BS, U. Pitts., 1945. Mgr. Newland Bros., Millvale, Pa., 1946-53; gen. mgr. Newland-Ludlo, Pitts., 1953-72; mgmt. cons. D3 Software, Garden City, N.Y., 1972-80, sec., corp. officer, 1980—. Fin. sec. Cerebral Palsy Assn., Garden City, Helen Keller Svcs. for the Blind, Garden City; mem. Winthrop-Univ. Hosp. Aux., Mercy League, Friends of Historic St. George Ch. of Hempstead, N.Y. Mem. AAUW, L.I. Panhellenic, Univ. Club, Nassau County Hist. Soc. (life), Garden City Histo. Soc., Alpha Delta Pi, Pi Lambda Theta. Home: 146 Washington Ave Garden City NY 11530 Office: D3 Software PO Box 8051 Garden City NY 11530

DOUGAN, DIANA LADY, federal agency executive; b. Dayton, Ohio, Jan. 13, 1943; d. Harold Wendell and Elaine (Staggers) Lady; m. J. Lynn Dougan, Nov. 30, 1968; children: Gavin Marriott, Elena Lady. BA in Indsl. Psychology and English, U. Md., 1964; postgrad., U. Utah, 1969-70; grad. advanced mgmt. program, Harvard U., 1979. Asst. chief clk. Md. State Legis., Annapolis, 1965, 66; free lance mktg. pub. relations cons. N.Y.C., Washington, 1965-66; mktg., promotions dir. Time Inc., N.Y.C., 1966-68; ptnr. Dougan and Assoc., Salt Lake City, 1970-81; dir. Corp. for Pub. Broadcasting, Washington, 1976-83; U.S. coord., dir. bur. for internat. communications and info. policy, amb. Dept. State, Washington, 1983—; nat. adv. bd. Ctr. for Study of Presidency, 1987—; chmn. numerous U.S. dels. on telecommunications and info. policy. Exec. producer pub. affairs TV series Way of Art, 1970-72, Pub. Broadcasting System TV and Nat. Pub. Radio program The MX Debate, 1981 (Peabody award 1981); producer Pub. Broadcasting System TV spl. The Nutcracker, 1975, 76, 77. Bd. dirs. U.S. Film and Video, 1978-82, World Affairs Coun., 1989—; mem. nat. adv. bd. Ballet West, 1987—; mem. gubernatorial commn. on exec. reorgn. Utah, 1980-83; mem. Utah Telecommunications Task Force, 1978; mem. Coun. Fgn. Rels. Recipient Md. Disting. Citizen award Gov. Md., 1965, Nat. Secruity Agy. medal, 1988; named Hon. Citizen of Korea, 1965, Utah Woman of Yr. AAUW, 1978, Outstanding Woman in Communications, Women in Communications, 1980. Republican. Office: Ctr for Strategic & Internat Studies 1800 K St NW Washington DC 20000

DOUGHERTY, BARBARA CAROLYNE, utility company insurance administrator; b. Elizabeth, N.J., May 9, 1937; d. Alexander Joseph and Marie Louise (Buchwald) D.; m. Peter R. Madorma (div. July 1958); m. Frank Gencsy (div. July 1972); children: Keith R., Kim L. Madorma DiPaolo, Kelli A. Chitty, Kevin A. Model Barbizon Agy., N.Y.C., 1954-58; sec. Hartig Extruders, Mountainside, N.J., 1958-61, Albert, Frank, Gunther Law Advt., N.Y.C., 1961-65; legal sec. Rinaldo and Rinaldo, Elizabeth, N.J., 1965-77, office mgr., 1973-77; legal asst. Elizabethtown Gas Co., Elizabeth, 1977-87, ins. adminstr., 1987—. Bd. dirs. Rahway (N.J.) Day Care Ctr., 1984—, sec., 1986-87, v.p., 1987—; mem. exec. com. Rahway YMCA, 1985-88, bd. dirs., 1985-89; mem. allocations com. United Way Union County, 1988-89. C. of C. Roman Catholic. Home: 6 Tisbury Ct Scotch Plains NJ 07076 Office: Elizabethtown Gas Co 1 Elizabethtown Plaza Union NJ 07083

DOUGHERTY, BETSEY OLENICK, architect; b. Guanatamo Bay, Cuba, Oct. 25, 1950; (parents Am. citizens); d. Everett and Charlotte (Kristal) Olenick; m. Brian Paul Dougherty, Aug. 24, 1974; children: Gray Brenner, Megan Victoria. AB in Architecture, U. Calif., Berkeley, 1972, MArch, 1975. Registered architect, Calif.; cert. Nat. Coun. Archtl. Registration Bds. Designer, drafter Maxwell Starkman, L.A., 1972-73, HO & K, San Francisco, 1975-76; job capt. Wm. Blurock & Ptnrs., Newport Beach, Calif., 1976-78; assoc. architect U. Calif., Irvine, 1978-79; architect Dougherty & Dougherty, Newport Beach, 1979—. Mem. Newport Beach Specific Area Plan Com., 1985, Career Edn. Adv. Com., Newport Beach, 1986. Recipient Gold Nugget grand award Pacific Coast Builders Conf., 1989. Fellow AIA (pres. Orange County chpt. 1984, Calif. chpt. 1988, nat. bd. dirs. 1989—, design awards Orange County chpt. 1981-86, 89); mem. Newport Harbor Art Mus. Office: 3 Civic Pla Ste 230 Newport Beach CA 92660

DOUGHERTY, CAROLANN JACKSON, lawyer; b. Phila., Sept. 24, 1957; d. Frank M. and Roseann (Montgomery) Jackson; m. Stephen Leo Dougherty, June 20, 1987; children: Roseann, Elizabeth. BS, Pa. State U., 1978; JD, Widener U., Wilmington, Del., 1982. Bar: Pa. 1982, N.J. 1987. Law clk. to presiding judge Commonwealth Ct. Pa., Harrisburg, 1982-83; law clk. to presiding chief judge Pa. Supreme Ct., Phila., 1983-84; asst. to legal officer Internat. Energy Agy., Paris, 1984-86; assoc. Cozen & O'Connor, Phila., 1986—. Guild mem. St. Raphaella Marry Retreat Ho., Haverford, Pa., 1989. Mem. Pa. Bar Assn. (child adv. 1989). Democrat. Roman Catholic. Home: 301 Cherry Ln Havertown PA 19083 Office: Cozen & O'Connor 1900 Market St Philadelphia PA 19103

DOUGHERTY, DANA DEAN LESLEY, television producer, educator; b. Birmingham, Ala.; d. Paul Russell and Daisy Dean (Dunham) Lesley; m. Floyd Wallace Dougherty; 1 child, Lesley Dean. BS in Secondary and Bus. Edn., Speech Therapy, Drama, Auburn U., 1968. Cert. elem. tchr., Ala. Tchr. speech, drama, computer typing, shorthand, acctg., bus. law Jefferson State Jr. Coll., Birmingham, 1968-73; office mgr. Baker, McDaniel & Hall, Birmingham, 1973-78; tchr. Mountain Brook Bd. Edn., Birmingham, 1979—; producer, dir. drama and music TV show Dean and Company, Birmingham, 1980—. Composer various songs. Recipient numerous awards Birmingham Cable TV, 1981-89, Cable TV Vulcan award, 1989-90, World Poetry Golden Poet award, 1990. Mem. Ala. State Poetry Soc. (Poetry award), Actors and Theater Guild, So. Bus. Edn. Assn., Ala. Assn. Legal Secs., Ala. Theater Organ Soc., Nat. Theater Organ Soc., Jr. Women's C. of C., Quill Club, Thalians Lit. Club, Beta Sigma Phi. Baptist. Office: Dean and Co 1277 Centerpoint Pkwy Birmingham AL 35215

DOUGHERTY, JUNE EILEEN, librarian; b. Union City, N.J., Mar. 27, 1929; d. Robert John and Jane Veronica (Smith) Beyrer; B.A. in Edn., Peterson State Coll., 1967; postgrad. Rutgers U. Sch. Library Sci., 1959-69; m. Donald E. Dougherty, Dec. 2, 1946; 1 son, Glen Allan. With A. B. Dumont, Paterson, N.J., 1950-54; sch. librarian St. Paul's Elementary Sch., Prospect Park, N.J., 1957—; dir. North Haledon (N.J.) Free Pub. Library, 1957—; sec.-treas. Dougherty & Dougherty, Inc., North Haledon, 1968—. Den mother Boy Scouts Am., 1954-57; mem. Gov. N.J.'s Tercentenary Com., 1962-64. Mem. Am., N.J., N. Haledon library assns., Cath. Library Assn., N.J. Libraries Roundtable, Bergen-Passaic Library Club, Friends N. Haledon Library. Roman Catholic. Club: St. Paul's Social. Home: 155 Westervelt Ave North Haledon NJ 07508 Office: 129 Overlook Ave North Haledon NJ 07508

DOUGHERTY, MOLLY CROCKER, nursing educator, researcher; b. Atlanta, June 30, 1944; d. Charles Raboteau and Mary Sylva (Knox) Crocker; m. Edmund Thomas Dougherty, June 12, 1965; children: Ann Margaret, Laura Lynn. BS in Nursing, U. Fla., 1965, M of Nursing, 1968, PhD in Anthropology, 1973. RN. RN U. Rochester, N.Y., 1965-66, Pardee Meml. Hosp., Hendersonville, N.C., 1966-67, Shands Teaching Hosp., U. Fla., Gainesville, 1967; prof. Coll. Nursing, U. Fla., Gainesville, 1973—, rsch. coord., 1985—; cons. nursing rsch. Nursing Div. HRSA/DHHS, Bethesda, Md., 1975-85, Nat. Ctr. Nursing Rsch., NIH, Bethesda, 1986-90, cons. rsch. tng. 1988—; cons. nurisng rsch. Yale U., UCLA, Va. Commonwealth U., 1988—. Author: Becoming a Woman in Rural Black Culture, 1978; contbr. articles to profl. jours.; editorial bd. Jour. Community Health Nursing, 1983, Applied Nursing Rsch., 1987-89. Recipient Disting. Faculty award Fla. Blue Key, 1986, Nursing Rsch. award Fla. Nurses Assn., 1987; named Disting. lectr. Sigma Theta Tau Internat., 1990; Nat. Ctr. Nursing Rsch. NIH grantee, 1984-91. Mem. Assn. Anthropology & Gerontology (nominating com. 1980-81, program com. 1981-82), Coun. Nursing & Anthropology (sec. 1979-82), Soc. Med. Anthropology (exec. com. 1982-85, publs. policy com. 1983-84), Coll. Nursing Alumni Assn. (pres. 1984-86), Sigma Theta Tau (Alpha Theta chpt. pres. 1970-71, v.p. 1975-76). Office: Univ Fla Coll Nursing Box J-197 JHMHC Gainesville FL 32610

DOUGHERTY, MOLLY IRELAND, organization executive; b. Austin, Tex., Oct. 3, 1949; d. John Chrysostom and Mary Ireland (Graves) D. Student, Stanford U., 1968-71, Grad. Theol. Union, Berkeley, 1976; BA, Antioch U., 1980. Tchr., fundraiser Oakland Community Sch., Calif., 1973-77; assoc. producer, asst. editor film Nicaragua: These Same Hands, Palo Alto, Calif., 1980; free-lance journalist, translator, Nicaragua, 1981; ednl. programs dir. Found. for Open Co., Berkeley, 1982-83; assoc. producer, film: Short Circuit: Inside the Death Squads; exec. dir. Vecinos, A Tex. Inter-Am. Initiative, Austin, Tex., 1984—; Spanish lang. tutor St. Stephen's Episcopal Sch., Austin, 1988-89. Bd. dirs. Nat. Immigration Refugee and Citizenship Forum, Washington, 1985-88; speaker, fund-raiser Salvadoran Assn. for Rural Health, 1986—; lectr. St. Stephen's Episcopal Sch., 1989. Home: 1100 Claire Ave Austin TX 78703 Office: Vecinos A Tex Inter-Am Initiative PO Box 4562 Austin TX 78765

DOUGHERTY, SHERILYNE EARNEST, computer engineering executive, marketing director; b. Washington, Sept. 9, 1950; d. Harold T. and Dorothy (Simms) Earnest. BS, Fla. State U., 1973; MS, U. Md., 1976; M.Health Adminstrn., George Washington U., 1981, EdD in Human Resources, 1988. RN, Fla., Md., D.C. Clin. coord. ICU Univ. Med. Ctr., Jacksonville, Fla., 1973-75; instr. nursing dept. Sch. of Nursing U. Md., Balt., 1976-78; assoc. prof. Sch. of Nursing Salisbury (Md.) State U., 1978-81; dir. mktg. Staff Builders Healthcare Svcs., Balt., 1981-83; clin. specialist SRT Med. Staff Internat., Springfield, Va., 1983-85; cons. Dougherty & Assocs., Alexandria, Va., 1985-87; asst. dir. mktg. Automation Rsch. Sys., Alexandria, Va., 1988-89, dir. profl. devel. and tng., 1988—; owner, mgr. Talbot St. Joint Venture, Ocean City, Md., 1981-88. Mem. Am. Assn. for Tng. and Devel., NAFE, Washington Ski Club, Sigma Theta Tau. Roman Catholic. Home: 7120 Strawn Ct Alexandria VA 22306 Office: Automation Rsch Systems Ltd 4480 King St Ste 500 Alexandria VA 22302

DOUGHERTY, URSEL THIELBEULE, communications, marketing executive; b. Rotenburg, W. Ger., July 30, 1942; naturalized U.S. citizen, 1965; d. Hugo and Margarete (Marquardt) Thielbeule; m. Erich A. Eichorn, Jan. 3, 1979. BA summa cum laude in Polit. Sci., Cleve. State U., 1971; MA in Polit. Sci., U. Wis., 1972; MBA in Fin., Case Western Res., 1982. Journalist maj. daily, women's mag., Germany, 1962-66; assoc. editor Farm Chems., 1967; publs. mgr. Trabon Systems, 1967-68; rsch. analyst Legis. Coun., State of Wis., 1972; pub. rels. adminstr. to mgr. pub. info. Eaton Corp., Cleve., 1972-84; dir. pub. affairs Freightliner/Mercedes-Benz Truck Co., Portland, Oreg., 1984-87, v.p. chmn.'s office Daimler Benz N.A. Holding Co., Inc., Washington, 1987-90; v.p. bus. devel., corp. affairs Penske Corp., Cleve.; cons. small bus. Trustee, Lake Erie coun. Girl Scouts U.S., 1975-82, Sr. Citizen Resources, 1978-81; amb. Jr. Achievement, 1979; steering com. YWCA Career Women of Achievement, 1981; adv. bd. Women's Career Networking, 1980-84; trustee, chmn. fin. com. Young Audience Greater Cleve., 1982-84. Mem. Pub. Rels. Soc. Am., Nat. Press Club, Am. Exec. Women, Pub. Affairs Coun. Home: 1510 Crest Rd Cleveland Heights OH 44121 Office: 7600 First Pl Cleveland OH 44146-6799

DOUGLAS, CLAIRE LYNETTE, human services manager; b. Texarkana, Ark., Oct. 29, 1954; d. Edwin Melvin Jones, Sr. and Margaret Marie (Harp) Thompson; m. Anthony Ray Douglas, July 23, 1977 (div. 1986); 1 child, Erika. Student, North Tex. State U.; B of U. Studies, U. N.Mex., 1977. Mgr. Claire's Boutique, Houston; unit mgr. Anderson Cancer Ctr. U. Tex., Houston. Mem. Soc. Human Resources Mgmt., Mortar Bd. Office: U Tex MDAH 1515 Holcombe Houston TX 77030

DOUGLAS, EILEEN, news broadcaster; b. Syracuse, N.Y., Sept. 17, 1946; d. Marvin and Shirley (Nadel) Bernstein; m. Jeffrey Stewart Zients, Dec. 17, 1967 (wid. Nov. 1975); 1 child, Rachel Susan; m. Stanley Israel, Aug. 24, 1985. BA with honors, Syracuse U., 1968. Reporter WNYS-TVABC, Syracuse, 1967-68, Herald Jour., Syracuse, 1969-70, WAKY Radio, Louisville, 1970; reporter, anchorman WKLO Radio, Louisville, 1970-74, news dir., 1974-76; producer, co-host show NOW WHAS-TV CBS, Louisville, 1974-75; writer, editor WINS Radio, N.Y.C., 1976-83, anchorwoman, reporter, 1983—. Author: New York Inflation Fighter's Guide, 1983; Rachel and the Upside Down Heart, 1990; creator Lets Make a Dream, 1985—. Mem. AFTRA, Writers Guild Am. Jewish. Office: WINS Radio 888 7th Ave New York NY 10106

DOUGLAS, LOUISE THERESA, banker; b. Johnstown, Pa., Aug. 5, 1955; d. Louis Joseph and Anne Joann (Kovalchick) Bienasz; m. George Edgar Douglas, June 21, 1987; 1 child, Erin Louise. Student, Edinboro U., 1973-76; diploma in gen. banking, Am. Inst. Banking, 1982; cert. in bank mgmt., Am. Bankers Assn.-Bucknell U., 1986. Teller Keystone Bank, Washington, Pa., 1977-79, Moxham Nat. Bank, Johnstown, 1979-80; comml. teller Summit Bank (formerly Salix St. Bank), Johnstown, 1980-81, mgmt. trainee, 1981-82, personal banking officer, 1982-85, asst. sec., credit adminstr., 1982—; asst. cashier, mgr. banking ctr. Beneficial Nat. Bank, Wilmington, Del., 1986-88, asst. v.p., mgr. customer svc., 1988—; com. chairperson Am. Inst. Banking, Johnstown, 1980-83, treas., 1983, 84, v.p., 1985. Treas., bd. dirs., mem. fin. com. YWCA, Johnstown, 1980; v.p. bd. dirs. Action Home Svcs., div. of Cambria County Community Action Coun., Johnstown, 1984. Mem. Nat. Assn. Bank Women. Republican. Roman Catholic.

DOUGLAS, LUCY STOVALL, graphic artist, letterpress printer; b. Lexington, Ky., Aug. 11, 1959; d. James Reed Stovall and Rosemary Ruth (McLain) Ware. BA in Social Work, Miss. State U., 1981. Editor S. Advocate News, Ashland, Miss., 1984-85; comml. etcher J.P. Stevens Engraving Co., Atlanta, 1985—, engraver, 1985—, letterpress printer, 1985—, supr., 1987—. Artist, printer Woodcuts, 1986—; propr. The Stovall Press, 1982—; woodcuts featured in Iowa Woman mag., 1984. Mem. Nat. Arbor Day Found., Nebraska City, Nebr., 1988. Mem. Nat. Amatuer Press Assn. (artist laureate 1984, 86, 87, v.p. 1988-89), Amalgamated Press Assn. Home: 115 Olympic Pl Decatur GA 30030

DOUGLAS, MARION JOAN, labor negotiator; b. Jersey City, May 29, 1940; d. Walter Stanley and Sophie Frances (Zysk) Binaski; children: Jane Dee, Alex Jay. BA, Mich. State U., 1962; MSW, Sacramento State Coll., 1971; MPA, Calif. State U.-Sacramento, 1981. Owner, mgr. Linkletter-Totten Dance Studios, Sacramento, 1962-68, Young World of Discovery, Sacramento, 1965-68; welfare worker Sacramento County, 1964-67, welfare supr., 1968-72, child welfare supr., 1972-75, sr. personnel analyst, 1976-78, personnel program mgr., 1978-81, labor relations rep., 1981—; cons. State Dept. Health, Sacramento, 1975-76; cons. in field. Author/editor: (newsletter) Thursday's Child, 1972-74. Presiding officer Community Resource Orgn., Fair Oaks, Calif., 1970-72; exec. bd. Foster Parent's Assn., Sacramento, 1972-75; organizer Foster Care Sch. Dist. liaison programs, 1973-75; active Am. Lung Assn., 1983-87; rep. Calif. Welfare Dirs. Assn., 1975-76; county staff advisor Joint Powers Authority, Sacramento, 1978-81; mem. Mgmt. Devel. Com., Sacramento, 1979-80; vol., auctioneer sta. KVIE Pub. TV, Sacramento, 1970-84, 88—; adv. bd. Job and Info. Resource Ctr., 1976-77; spl. adv. task force coordinator Sacramento Employment and Tng. Adv. Council, 1980-81; vol. leader Am. Lung Assn., Sacramento, 1983-86 Calif. Dept. Social Welfare ednl. stipend, 1967-68, County of Sacramento ednl. stipend, 1969-70. Recipient Achievement award Nat. Assn. Counties, 1981. Mem. Mgmt. Women's Forum, Indsl. Relations Assn. No. Calif., Indsl. Relations Research Assn., Nat. Assn. Female Execs., Mensa. Republican. Avocations: real estate, nutrition. Home: 7812 Palmyra Dr Fair Oaks CA 95628 Office: Sacramento County Dept Pers Mgmt 700 H St Sacramento CA 95814

DOUGLAS, MARJORIE JAMISON, television filming house company executive; b. Cleve., Sept. 11, 1926; d. Robert Huddle and Marjorie (Carr) Jamison; m. Henry Bowman Douglas II, June 16, 1951; children: Heather Leigh Douglas Carlée, Sandra Leigh Douglas-Parker, Robert Jamison. BA, Smith Coll., 1948. Draftswoman Regional Planning Commn. Cuyahoga County, Cleve., 1949-53; landscape architect freelance, Versailles, Ohio, 1956-60; pres. Douglas House, Inc., Orangeburg, N.Y., 1981—. Bd. dirs. Jr. League of Bergen County, N.J., 1964-66, Saddle River (N.J.) Planning Bd., 1976-81, Saddle River Environ. Commn., 1977-81, Vol. Bur. Bergen County, Hackensack, N.J., 1978-81. Republican. Presbyterian. Home: 275 Kings Hwy Orangeburg NY 10962 Office: Douglas House Inc 275 Kings Hwy Orangeburg NY 10962

DOUGLAS, ROXANNE GRACE, teacher; b. Orange, N.J., Dec. 17, 1951; d. Joseph Samuel and Mary (Ferro) Battista; m. Richard Joseph Douglas, June 26, 1982; 1 child, Regina Grace. BA cum laude, Montclair State Coll., 1973; student, Sorbonne U., Paris. Cert. French and elem. sch. tchr., N.J. Tchr. social studies West Orange (N.J.) Bd. Edn., 1973-74, Orange (N.J.) Bd. Edn., 1974-75; substitute tchr. various schs. N.J., 1975-76; supplemental tchr. Irvington (N.J.) Bd. Edn., 1976-80, tchr. govtl. programs, 1980—. Recipient Creative Writing awards NJSFWC-JM, Citizenship award Am. Legion. Mem. Montclair Hist. Soc., West Caldwell Hist. Soc., Victorian Soc., N.J. Edn. Assn., Montclair Mus., Newark Mus., Nat. French Honor Soc., Nat Edn. Honor Soc., Rahway Hist. Soc., Jr. Women's Club of West Essex (co-pres.), Coll. Club Orange-Short Hills. Roman Catholic. Home: 36 Beechwood Rd West Caldwell NJ 07006

DOUGLAS, SUSAN, data processing specialist, consultant; b. Chgo., Oct. 29, 1946; d. Lawrence and Phoebe Fern (Sibbald) D.; m. John D. Hauenstein, Dec. 21, 1972 (div. June 1975). BA, U. Iowa, 1972; postgrad., U. Wis., Whitewater, 1985. Project coordinator Westinghouse Learning Corp., Iowa City, Iowa, 1967-75; echocardiology technician Chgo. Osteo. Hosp., 1975-78; systems programer, analyst Household Fin. Corp., Prospect Heights, Ill., 1978-81; applications analyst Burdick Corp., Milton, Wis., 1981-84; cons. Edgerton, Wis., 1984—. Mem. Data Processing Mgmt. Assn., System 38 User's Group, Women in High Tech. Episcopalian. Home and Office: 8203 Hwy 184 Edgerton WI 53534

DOUGLAS, TERESA LYNN, sales professional; b. Columbus, Ohio, Sept. 8, 1956; d. Edward Everett and Patricia Ann (Caldwell) Vojtech; m. James Smetak, May 27, 1974 (div. 1981); children: Tonya Lynn, James Edward Louis, Angela Dawn; m. Stephen A. Douglas III, Sept. 19, 1987. AAS, Dist. One Tech. Inst., Eau Claire, Wis., 1983. Cert. med. lab. technician. Med. lab. tech. Chem-Bio Corp., Oak Creek, Wis., 1983-86; tech. sales rep. Applied Biochemists, Inc., Mequon, Wis., 1986-88, Sargeant Welch Sci., Skokie, Ill., 1988; chief officer Marlena, Ltd., Clarkston, Mich., 1989—; tech. sales rep. Analytab Products, Plainview, N.Y., 1989—; group leader Dale Carnegie Corp., Indpls., 1988-89. Charter mem. Citizens Against Govt. Waste, Washington, 1989. Mem. NAFE, Am. Soc. Clin. Pathologists (cert.). Home: 6845 Lancaster Lake #138 Clarkston MI 48016 Office: Analytab Products 200 Express St Plainview NY 11803

DOUGLASS, BEVERLY JANE, barbecue sauce manufacturing company executive; b. Pumphrey, Md., Dec. 28, 1951; d. Haywood Walter and Lee Pearl (Smith) Cooper; m. Frederick I. Douglass; children: Charles Frederick, Melani Naima. Student, Sch. of Modern Photography, Newark, 1980; BA, Antioch U., Yellow Springs, Ohio, 1982; postgrad., Catonsville Community Coll., Balt., 1984, U. Balt. Dir. visitor info. Balt. Promotion Office, 1979-83; dir. advt. Jayson Dennas Co., Balt., 1983-86; community planning and devel. specialist U.S. Govt., Balt., 1986—; with Douglass Enterprises; fashion commentator Pauline Brooks Boutiques, Balt., 1983—, Ovella's & Act III, 1984; panelist Square Off, 1985; profl. gospel singer. Vice pres. Nat. Fedn. Rep. Women, Balt., 1988; pres. Madison Avenue Neighborhood Club, Balt., 1989—, Madison Neighborhood Improvement Assn.; mem. 40th dist. Md. Cen. Com.; mem. Nat. Flag Day Com. Recipient Second Mile award Women's Rsch. and Devel., Balt., 1984, Unsung Hero award 1987. Mem. NAFE, Women of 80's. Methodist.

DOUGLASS, ENID HART, educational director; b. L.A., Oct. 23, 1926; d. Frank Roland and Enid Yandell (Lewis) Hart; m. Malcolm P. Douglass, Aug. 28, 1948; children: Malcolm Paul Jr., John Aubrey, Susan Enid. BA, Pomona Coll., 1948; MA, Claremont (Calif.) Grad. Sch., 1959. Research asst. World Book Ency., Palo Alto, Calif., 1953-54; exec. sec., asst. dir. oral history program Claremont Grad. Sch., 1963-71, dir. oral history program, 1971—, history lectr., 1977—; mem. Calif. Heritage Preservation Commn., 1977-85, chmn. 1983-85. Contbr. articles to hist. jours. Mayor pro tem City of Claremont, 1980-82, Mayor, 1982-86; mem. planning and rsch. adv. coun. State of Calif., mem. city coun., Claremont, 1978-86; founder Claremont Heritage, Inc., 1977-80, bd. dirs., 1986—; bd. dirs. Pilgrim Pla., Claremont; founder steering com., founding bd. Claremont Community Found., 1989—, pres., 1990—. Mem. Oral History Assn. (pres. 1979-80), Southwest Oral History Assn. (founding steering com. 1981, J.V. Mink award 1984), Nat. Council Pub. History, LWV (bd. dirs. 1957-59, Outstanding Svc. to Community award, 1986). Democrat. Home: 1195 Berkeley Ave Claremont CA 91711 Office: Claremont Grad Sch Oral History Program 150 E 10th St Claremont CA 91711-6160

DOUGLASS, JANE DEMPSEY, theology educator; b. Wilmington, Del., Mar. 22, 1933; d. Hazell Brownlie and Ethel Katherine (Smith) Dempsey; m. Gordon Klene Douglass, Aug. 23, 1964; children: Alan Bruce, Anne Lorine, John Gordon. AB, Syracuse U., 1954; postgrad., U. Geneva, 1954-55; AM, Radcliffe Coll., 1961; PhD, Harvard U., 1963. Assoc. dir. Presbyn. Student Ctr., Columbia, Mo., 1955-58; teaching fellow Harvard Divinity Sch., Cambridge, Mass., 1959-62; from instr. to prof. Sch. of Theology and Claremont Grad. Sch., Claremont, Ca., 1963-85; Hazel Thompson McCord prof. hist. theology Princeton (N.J.) Theol. Sem., 1985—; pres. Am. Soc. Ch. History, 1983; v.p. World Alliance of Reformed Chs., 1989-90, pres. 1990—. Author: Justification in Late Medieval Preaching: A Study of John Geiler of Keisersberg, 1966, Women, Freedom and Calvin, 1985; also articles. Presbyterian. Office: Princeton Theol Seminary CN 821 Princeton NJ 08542

DOUMAS, GENA KATHLEEN, controller; b. Winston-Salem, N.C., Nov. 27, 1963; d. Nick Harold and Susan Ellen (Ledwith) D. AAS in Bus. Computers, Davidson County Community Coll., 1984. Computer programmer Precision Part Systems, Inc., Winston-Salem, 1984-85, contr., 1986—; computer operator Stroh Container, 1985-86; ptnr., office mgr. Artisan Prodns. Ltd., Winston-Salem, 1986—. Author numerous poems. Recipient Radio Young Am. award 1973. Republican. Greek Orthodox. Home: 3155 Stratford Rd Winston-Salem NC 27103 Office: Precision Part Systems Inc 3401 Indiana Ave Winston-Salem NC 27105

DOUMLELE, RUTH HAILEY, communications company executive, broadcast accounting consultant; b. Charlotte County, Va., Nov. 6, 1925; d. Clarrie Robert Hailey and Virginia Susan (Slaughter) Ferguson; m. John Antony Doumlele, May 8, 1943; children: John Antony, Suzanne Denise Doumlele Owen. Cert. in commerce, U. Richmond, 1968; BA, Mary Baldwin Coll., 1982. Sta. acct. WLEE-Radio, Richmond, Va., 1965-67, bus. mgr., 1967-73; area bus. mgr. Nationwide Communications Inc., Richmond, 1973-75; corp. bus. mgr., Neighborhood Communications Corp., Inc., Richmond, 1978-86, asst. v.p., 1981-86; owner Broadcast Acctg. Cons., Midlothian, Va., 1986—; treas., dir. Guests of Honor, Ltd., Richmond, 1984-89; sec., Inner Light, Inc., 1984—. Contbr. articles to profl. jours.; mem. editorial rev. bd. The Woman C.P.A., 1980—. Mem. Am. Soc. Women Accts. (chpt. pres. 1974-76, contbg. editor The Coord. 1990, Chgo. chpt.), Broadcast Fin. Mgmt. Assn., Nat. League Am. Pen Women (br. pres. 1984-86), Am. Fedn. Astrologers, Va. Assn. Amateur Athletic Union (records chmn. 1959-62), Women's Club of Powhatan (select svc. system local bd. 1989). Episcopalian. Avocations: salt water fishing, Civil War history, travel, astrology. Home and Office: 2510 Chastain Ln Midlothian VA 23113

DOUTHIT, HEATHER MARIA, management consultant; b. Clinton, Iowa, June 20, 1959; d. Walter Harold Douthit and Marisol (Vidal) Dickson. BS in Music Edn., West Chester U., 1977-81. Music tchr. educator Mary D. Lang Sch., Kennett Square, Pa., 1981-82; profl. musician pvt. practice, Newark, 1982-84; U.S. Postal Service Mail Carrier, West Chester, Pa., 1984-85; sales rep. Challenge Industries, Sparta, N.J., 1986-89, corp. liaison, 1989—; musician Alter Ego, Newark, 1981-85; guitar tchr. (part-time) West Chester, 1980-82. Composer: song book, 1985. Mem. Condominium Assn. Mem. Nat. Assn. Jazz Educators, Nat. Assn. Female Execs., Kappa Delta Pi. Republican.

DOUTHITT, SHIRLEY ANN, insurance agent; b. Mexia, Tex., Feb. 21, 1947; d. Othello Young and Hazel Lorene (Corley) Thompson; m. A. Dwane Douthitt, Nov. 24, 1966; 1 child, Steven Dwane. Student, Leonard's Tng Sch., Houston, 1979; student Tex. local recording agts. licensing course, Austin, Tex., 1980; student farmers ins. group tng. program, Austin, 1980; student life underwriters trng course, Tyler, Tex., 1987. Lic. ins. agt. Sec. Lindsey & Newsom Ins. Adjusters, Palestine, Tex., 1965-73, J. Herrington Ins. Agy., Palestine, 1973-76, Ramsey Ins. Agy., Palestine, 1976-79; agt. Farmers Ins. Group, Palestine, 1979—. Recipient Bus. Woman of Yr. Palestine Profl. Bus. Women, 1983. Mem. NAFE, Women's Club. Office: Shirley Douthitt Ins Agy 3507 W Oak PO Box 7000 Palestine TX 75802

DOUTY, LUCY EVELYN, sales and marketing executive; b. Boston, Sept. 22, 1951; d. Michael H. and Irma O. (Fusco) Gionfriddo; m. George E. Douty Jr., May 20, 1972. AS in Bus. Adminstrn., Northeastern U., 1988; postgrad., Harvard U., 1989—. Mktg. mgr. Dynamics Rsch. Corp., Wilmington, Mass., 1974-85; natl. sales mgr. United States Law News, San Juan, Calif., 1986; client svcs. mgr. Price Waterhouse, Waltham, Mass., 1987—. Author: CNC Operating Manual, 1984, Sales Training Manual, 1986. Mem. Am. Mgmt. Assn., Palmer Cove Yacht Club, Boat U.S. Club. Catholic.

DOVE, KATHLEEN MEG LINDEMANN, financial aid consultant; b. Cin., Feb. 9, 1953; d. Ott Robert and Hester (Stieringer) Lindeman; m. Jeffrey Lee Kirkland, July 27, 1974 (div. 1981); m. Mark Dove, Mar. 14, 1990. BA, Ohio State U., 1976. Law enforcement dispatcher Adams County Sheriff's Dept., Decatur, Ind., 1976-79; sr. counselor Adams County-Ft. Wayne Consortium CETA, Decatur, 1979-81; receptionist/asst. bookkeeper Midas Muffler, Cin., 1981-84; fin. aid adminstr. So. Ohio Coll. Metridata, Inc., Covington, Ky., 1984-85; fin. aid coordinator Jostens, Inc., Louisville, 1985-86; fin. aid mgr. Tri-State Semi Driver Tng. Inc., Middletown, Ohio, 1986-88; fin. aid dir. So. Ohio Coll. Carrercom, Inc., Cin., 1988-90; freelance fin. aid cons. Cin., 1990—; cons. in field; conductor workshops in field. Mem. Nat. Assn. Student Fin. Aid Adminstrs., Midwest Assn. of Student Fin. Aid Adminstrs., Ohio Assn. Student Fin. Aid Adminstrs. Episcopalian. Home and Office: 7233-1 Creekview Dr Cincinnati OH 45247

DOVE, RITA FRANCES, English language educator, writer; b. Akron, Ohio, Aug. 28, 1952; d. Ray A. and Elvira E. (Hord) D.; m. Fred Viebahn, Mar. 23, 1979; 1 child, Aviva Chantal Tamu Dove-Viebahn. BA summa cum laude, Miami U., Oxford, Ohio, 1973; postgrad., Universität Tübingen, Fed. Republic Germany, 1974-75; MFA, U. Iowa, 1977; LLD (hon.), Miami U., Oxford, Ohio, 1988, Knox Coll., 1989. Asst. prof. English Ariz. State U., Tempe, 1981-84, assoc. prof., 1984-87, prof., 1987-89; prof. U. Va., Charlottesville, 1989—; writer-in-residence Tuskegee (Ala.) Inst., 1982; lit. panelist Nat. Endowment for Arts, Washington, 1984-86, chair poetry grants panel, 1985; judge Walt Whitman Award, Acad. Am. Poets, 1990. Author: (poetry) The Yellow House on the Corner, 1980, Museum, 1983, Thomas and Beulah, 1986 (Pulitzer prize 1987), Grace Notes, 1989; (short stories) Fifth Sunday, 1985 (Callaloo award 1986); mem. editorial bd. Nat. Forum, 1984—; assoc. editor Callaloo, 1986—; adv. and contbg. editor Gettysburg Rev., 1987—, TriQuarterly, 1988—. Commr. The Schomburg Ctr. Research in Black Culture, N.Y. Pub. Library, 1987—. Presdl. scholar, 1970; Fulbright/Hays fellow, 1974-75, rsch. fellow U. Iowa, 1975, teaching/writing fellow U. Iowa, 1976-77, Guggenheim Found. fellow, 1983-84, Mellon sr. fellow Nat. Humanities Ctr., 1988-89, fellow Ctr. for Advanced Studies, U. Va., 1989—; grantee Nat. Endowment for Arts, 1978, 89; recipient Lavan Younger Poet award Acad. Am. Poets, 1986, Gen. Electric Found. award, 1987, Bellagio (Italy) residency Rockefeller Found., 1988, Ohio Gov.'s award, 1988. Mem. PEN, Poetry Soc. Am., Associated Writing Programs (bd. dirs. 1985-88, pres. 1986-87), Phi Beta Kappa, Phi Kappa Phi. Office: Univ Va Dept of English Charlottesville VA 22903

DOVE-LOWTHER, SANDRA ELIZABETH, program director; b. Portsmouth, Dominica, Apr. 20, 1955; d. Clyde Wells and Jocelyn Monica (King) Dove. Student, Culinary Inst. Am., 1983; AAS, NYU, 1989. Lectr., asst. dept. chairperson N.Y. Food & Hotel Mgmt. Sch., Manhattan, 1983-87; program coord., lectr. Sch. Continuing Edn. NYU, Manhattan, 1986—; program dir., lectr. Chinese Am. Planning Coun., Queens, N.Y., 1986-88; collections mgr. Swig, Weiler & Arnow Mgmt. Co., N.Y.C.; program coordinator NYU Mgmt. Inst., Manhattan, 1986--; program dir. Chinese American Planning Council, Flushing, 1987-88. Mem. Am. Hotel & Motel Assn. Home: 1702 73rd St Apt 2 North Bergen NJ 07047

DOVRING, KARIN ELSA INGEBORG, author, playwright; b. Stenstorp, Sweden, Dec. 5, 1919; came to U.S., 1953, naturalized, 1968; m. Folke Dovring, May 30, 1943. Grad., Coll. Commerce, Gothenburg, Sweden, 1936; MA, Lund (Sweden) U., 1943, PhD, 1951; Phil. Licentiate, Gothenburg U., 1947. Journalist several Swedish daily newspapers and weekly mags., 1940-60; tchr. Swedish colls.; rsch. assoc. of Harold Lasswell Yale U., New Haven, 1953-78; fgn. corr. Swedish newspapers, Italy, Switzerland, France and Germany, 1956-60; freelance writer, journalist, 1960—; vis. prof. Internat. U., (The Vatican) Rome, 1958-60, Gottingen (W.Ger.) U., 1962; lectr. numerous univs. including Yale U., U. Wis., McGill U., U. Iowa; rsch.assoc. U. Ill., Urbana, 1968-69; invited contbr. Social Sci. Rsch. Coun., 1988; radio and TV interviews; writer Ill. Alliance to Prevent Nuclear War, radio theater. Author: Songs of Zion, 1951, Land Reform as a Propaganda Theme, 3d edit. 1965, Road of Propaganda, 1959, Optional Society, 1972, Frontiers of Communication, 1975, (short stories) No Parking This Side of Heaven, 1982, Harold D. Lasswell: His Communication with a Future, 1987, 2d edit., 1988, Forked Tongue? Body-Snatched English in Political Communications, 1989, (novel) Heart in Escrow, 1990; contbr. numerous articles to mags. Recipient Swedish Nat. award for short stories Bonniers Pub. House Stockholm, 1951; lit. awards Internat. Acad. Leonardo da Vinci, Rome, 1982-83. Mem. NOW, Société Jean Jacques Rousseau of Geneva (hon. life), Inst. Freedom of Press (life asso.), Internat. Biog. Centre (Cambridge, England) (hon., adv. coun.). Democrat. Address: 613 W Vermont Ave Urbana IL 61801

DOW, JEAN LOUISE, school system business manager; b. Mattoon, Ill., Dec. 20, 1955; d. Paul Leroy and Maria (Brandlhofer) Smith; m. Chris Alan Pfeiffer, June 1, 1974 (div. Nov. 1979); 1 child, Lisa Marie; m. John W. Dow, Aug. 1, 1986. B.S. in Bus., Ea. Ill. U., 1977, M.B.A., 1980. Office mgr. ED Buxton & Assocs., Charleston, Ill., 1974-77; personnel mgr. Unibuilt Structures, Charleston, 1977-80; bus. mgr. Eastern Ill Area Spl. Edn., Mattoon, 1980—. Ill. Assn. Sch. Bus. Ofcls. (scholarship 1984, com. mem. 1984—), Assn. Sch. Bus. Ofcls., Ill. Adminstrs. Spl. Edn. Republican, Kappa Delta Pi. Baptist. Avocations: sewing; jogging; swimming; racquetball; tennis.

DOW, LESLIE WRIGHT, communications company executive, writer, photographer; b. N.Y.C., Apr. 28, 1938; d. Charles Leslie Kerr and Margaret Scott (MacArthur) Wright; m. William Arthur Dow, Aug., 1987; 1 child, John M. Haywood. AA, Colby-Sawyer Coll., 1957; cert., Katharine Gibbs Sch., 1958. Prodn. asst. Time Inc., N.Y.C., 1958-60; exec. asst. Jefferson-Standard Broadcasting Co., Charlotte, N.C., 1960-68, G.B. Wilkins Inc., Charlotte, 1981-83; pres., pub. relations cons. Wright Communications, Inc., Charlotte, 1983—. Contbr. photography to mags. and profl. jours.; contbr. articles to mags. Bd. dirs. Charlotte Symphony Women's Assn., 1964-71, Charlotte Symphony Orch., 1965; mem. Aux. of the Mint Mus., Charlotte, 1965—. Mem. NAFE, Am. Soc. Interior Designers (dir. pub. rels. Carolinas chpt. 1984-88), Am. Bus. Women's Assn., Am. Soc. Mag. Photographers, Profl. Photographers N.C., Profl. Photographers Am. Republican. Episcopalian. Home and Office: 3721 Pelham Ln Charlotte NC 28211

DOW, LOIS WEYMAN, physician; b. Cin., Mar. 11, 1942; d. Albert Dames and Elsie Marion (Krug) Weyman; m. Alan Wayne Dow, July 23, 1966 (div. Aug. 1979); children: Elizabeth Suzanne, Alan Wayne. BA summa cum laude, Cornell U., 1964; MD cum laude, Harvard U., 1968. Diplomate Am. Bd. Internal Medicine, Am. Bd. Hematology, Am. Bd. Med. Oncology. Intern Bronx Mcpl. Hosp. Ctr., N.Y.C., 1968-69; resident in internal medicine Presbyn. Hosp., N.Y.C., 1969-70; instr., research assoc. U. Tenn., Memphis, 1972-73, asst. prof., 1973-74; research assoc. in hematology and oncology St. Jude Children's Research Hosp., Memphis, 1974-77, asst. mem., 1977-80, assoc. mem., 1980-88; assoc. prof. pediatrics U. Tenn., Memphis, 1983-88; mem. staff St. Jude Children's Research Hosp., Bapt. Mem. Hosp., 1972-88, Med. Ctr. of Del., Newark, 1988—; pvt. practice Newark, 1988—; assoc. prof., Jefferson Med. Coll., Phila., 1988—; cons., Nat. Cancer Inst. Contbr. articles to profl. jours. Fellow ACP; mem. Am. Soc. Clin. Oncology, Am. Fedn. Clin. Rsch., Am. Soc. Hematology, Am. Assn. for Cancer Rsch., Internat. Exptl. Hematology, Cornell Club. Office: Del Clin and Lab Physician Ste 129 Med Arts Pavilion 4745 Stanton-Ogletown Rd Newark DE 19713

DOW, MARY ALEXIS, financial executive; b. South Amboy, N.J., Feb. 19, 1949; d. Alexander and Elizabeth Anne (Reilly) Pawlowski; m. Russell Alfred Dow, June 19, 1971. BS with honors, U. R.I., 1971. CPA, Oreg. Staff acct. Deloitte, Haskins & Sells, Boston, 1971-74; sr. acct. Price Waterhouse, Portland, Oreg., 1974-77, mgr., 1977-81, sr. mgr., 1981-84; chief fin. officer Copeland Lumber Yards Inc., Portland, 1984-86; ind. cons. in field, 1986—; bd. dirs. Longview Fibre Co. Mem. council and fin. com. Oreg. Mus. Sci. and Industry; bd. dirs., exec. com., chair budget com. Oreg. Trails chpt. ARC, chmn. bd. N.W. Regional Blood Svcs.; mem. budget rev. com. Multnomah County. Mem. AICPA, Oreg. Soc. CPAs, Fin. Execs. Inst. Roman Catholic. Clubs: City (bd. govs.), University (Portland), Multnomah Athletic. Contbr. articles to profl. publs.

DOWALIBY, MARGARET SUSANNE, optometry educator; b. Dover, N.H., Mar. 5, 1924; d. Abraham Edward and Helen Josephine (Rizk) D. AA, L.A. City Coll., 1946; BSc, So. Calif. Coll. Optometry, 1948, OD, 1950. Lic. optometrist, Calif. Mem. faculty ophthalmic optics dept. So. Calif. Coll. Optometry, Fullerton. Author 10 books, latest being: Practical Aspects of Ophthalmic Optics, 1987, The Art of Eyewear Dispensing, 1988. Mem. Am. Acad. Optometry, Am. Optometric Assn. Democrat. Home: 8787 Shoreham Dr Apt 103 West Hollywood CA 90069 Office: So Calif Coll Optometry 2575 Yorba Linda Blvd Fullerton CA 92631

DOWBEN, CARLA LURIE, lawyer, educator; b. Chgo., Jan. 22, 1932; d. Harold H. and Gertrude (Geitner) Lurie; m. Robert Dowben, June 20, 1950; children: Peter Arnold, Jonathan Stuart, Susan Laurie. AB, U. Chgo., 1950; JD, Temple U., 1955; cert., Brandeis U., 1968. Bar: Ill. 1957, Mass. 1963, Tex. 1974, U.S. Supreme Ct., 1974. Assoc. Conrad and Verges, Chgo., 1957-62; exec. officer MIT, Cambridge, Mass., 1963-64; legal planner, Mass. Health Planning Project, Boston, 1964-69; assoc. prof. Life Scis. Inst., Brown U., Providence, 1970-72; asst. prof. health law U. Tex. Health Sci. Ctr., Dallas, 1973-78, assoc. prof., 1978—; ptnr. Choate & Lilly, Dallas, 1989—; cons. to bd. dirs. Mental Health Assn., 1958-86, Ft. Worth Assn. Retarded Citizens, 1980—, Advocacy, Inc., 1981-85. Contbr. articles to profl. jours.; active in drafting health and mental health legis., agy. regulations in several states and locat govts. Mem. ABA, Tex. Bar Assn., Dallas Bar Assn., Nat. Health Lawyers Assn., Hastings Inst. Ethics, Tex. Family Planning Assn. Quaker. Home: 7150 Eudora Dr Dallas TX 75230 Office: Choate & Lilly 750 N St Paul St Ste 1000 Dallas TX 75201

DOWD, JANICE LEE, foreign language professor; b. N.Y.C., Jan. 6, 1948; d. Edward H. and Mary A. (Vanek) D. BA, Marietta (Ohio) Coll., 1969; MA, Columbia U., 1971, MEd, 1979, EdD, 1984. Tchr. Teaneck (N.J.) Bd. Edn., 1970—; adj. asst. prof. Queens Coll., CUNY, 1984—, Columbia U., N.Y.C., spring 1988; asst. prof. M.A. TESOL program in China, Changsha, 1986, Shanghai, 1987; SAT program adminstr. Teaneck High Sch., 1978-83, yearbook sponsor, 1975-79, newspaper sponsor, 1984—. Contbr. articles to profl. jours. Mem. program com. Philanthropic Ednl. Orgn., Teaneck, 1966—. Fellow Rockefeller Found., 1988. Mem. Tchrs. English to Speakers Other Langs., Am. Assn. Applied Linguists, Am. Coun. Tchrs. Fgn. Langs., N.J. TESOL and Bilingual Edn. Assn., N.Y. State Tchrs. English to Speakers Other Langs., Second Lang. Acquisition Circle N.Y. Home: 56 Boulevard New Milford NJ 07646 Office: Teaneck High Sch 100 Elizabeth Ave Teaneck NJ 07666

DOWDELL, DOROTHY FLORENCE, novelist; b. Reno, May 5, 1910; d. Albert Berdell and Florence Edith (Lusk) Karns; m. Joseph A. Dowdell, June 21, 1931 (dec. Sept. 1983); children: Joan Eva Moore, John Lawrence. AB, U. Calif., Berkeley, 1931. Housewife, 1931-48; tchr. elem. sch. Sacramento City Sch. Dept., 1948-61. Author: How To Help Your Child in School, 1964, Tree Farms Harvest For Future, 1965, Your Career in Teaching, 1967, Sierra Nevada: THe Golden Barrier, 1968, Careers in Horticultural Science, 1969, The Japanese Helped Build America, 1970, Your Career in World of Travel, 1971, The Chinese Helped Build America, 1972, Hawk Over Hollyhedge Manor, 1973, The House in Munich, 1975, Pretty Enough To Kill, 1976, Tahoe, 1977, Hibiscus Lagoon, 1981, The Impossible Dream, 1981, Glory Land, 1981, Women's Empire, 1984, Golden Flame, 1985, Wildcatter Woman, 1986, Seafaring Woman, 1988, Highflying Woman, 1989. Recipient Jack London award, 1977. Mem. AAUW, Calif. Writers Club. Republican. Episcopalian. Home: 120 Carlton Ave #4 Los Gatos CA 95032

DOWDING DUNCAN, MARIA LAVONNE, communication company administrator; b. Lincoln, Nebr., Sept. 10, 1954; d. Donald Lee and Ramona Lavonne (Goebel) Dowding; m. Gerald Ray Bolin, Aug. 12, 1975 (div. Jan. 1982); 1 child, Jennifer LaVonne; Albert Chistopher Duncan, June 2, 1984; 1 child, Bryan Chistopher. BA in Psychology, U. Okla., 1976; A in Physics, Math., Rose State Coll., 1979; MBA, Oklahoma City U., 1983. Dist. mgr. Info. Specialists, Oklahoma City, 1976-77; with AT&T, Oklahoma City, 1977—, process coordinator, 1981-83, supr. equipment, 1983-87, supr. purchasing, 1987-89, mfg. supr., 1989—; assoc. Abide, Oklahoma City, 1984-86; advisor Duncan Enterprises Ltd. Ptnr., Oklahoma City, 1985—. Mem. St. Eugene Ch., Oklahoma City, 1987—. Mem. Nat. Assn. Realtors (assoc.), Women Execs. Cen. Okla. (treas. 1986—), PTA. Republican. Roman Catholic. Club: Weokie (Oklahoma City) (1st v.p. 1982-83). Home: PO Box 1245 Bethany OK 73008 Office: AT&T Dept 1529 7725 W Reno Oklahoma City OK 73125

DOWELL, PATTI JO, banker; b. Logansport, Ind.; m. Jeffrey T. Dowell. BA in English, Ind. State U., MA in Criminology. Rsch. assoc. Ctr. for Govtl. Rsch., Rochester, N.Y.; analyst City of Rochester, police officer; v.p., human resources Chase Lincoln First Bank of Va.; sr. v.p., mgmt. resources Monroe Savs. Bank; vice-chmn. Crime Stoppers, Rochester; treas. Monroe County Human Rels. Commn.; bd. dirs. Rochester Inst. Tech. Co-op Adv. Bd. Contbg. author rsch. studies on topics in field. Adv. bd. Women's Endowment Fund, Rochester. Mem. Am. Soc. Personnel Adminstrs. (bd. dirs. local chpt.), Rochester Women's Network, Nat. Assn. Bank Affirmative Action Dirs., Internat. Employee Benefits Assn., Am. Compensation Assn. Office: Monroe Savs Bank 300 E Main St Rochester NY 14604

DOWIS, LENORE, lawyer; b. N.Y., Nov. 7, 1934; d. Thomas and Julianna (Csitkovits) Esteves; widow; children: Daniel, Lenore, Denise, Jonathan. AAS, Suffolk County Community Coll., 1981; BA, SUNY, Stony Brook, 1983; JD, Touro Coll., 1987. Bar: N.Y. 1988, U.S. Dist. Ct. (3d dist.) N.J. 1988. Tel. operator N.Y. Tel. Co., L.I., 1951-58; real estate sales broker Gen. Devel. Corp., Hauppauge, N.Y, 1974-75; ptnr./owner Davis Trucking Co., Huntington, N.Y., 1957-67; law clk. to assoc. judge appellate div. N.Y. Supreme Ct., Bklyn., N.Y., 1986; staff atty. Nassau/Suffolk Law Svcs., Bay Shore, N.Y., 1988; pvt. practice law Smithtown, N.Y., 1988—. Mem. ABA, Suffolk County Bar Assn., N.Y. State Bar Assn., Phi Theta Kappa, Alpha Beta Gamma. Republican. Home and Office: 33 Beverly Rd Smithtown NY 11788

DOWLING, JACQUES MACCUISTON, sculptor, painter, writer; b. Texarkana, Tex., Oct. 19, 1906; d. Charles Edward and Viola John (Estes) MacCuiston. Tchrs. cert., Coll. Marshall, 1923; student of art, Loyola U., Frolich's Sch. Fine Art, L.A., NAD, Art Students League, N.Y.C.; Ph.D., Colo. State Christian Coll. One woman shows include Fedn. Dallas Artists, 1950, 52, Rush Gallery, 1958, Sartor's Gallery, 1958, Sheraton-Dallas Hotel, 1960, Dallas Meml. Auditorium, 1960; exhibited in group shows at Dallas Mus. Fine Arts, Mus. of N.Mex., Fedn. Dallas Artists, Sartor's Galleries,

Ney Art Mus., Oak Cliff Soc. of Fine Arts, Sartor's Gallery, Shuttles Gallery, Sheraton-Park Internat. Platform Assn., 1966-68, Phillips Mills Art Assn., 1967-74, Yardley Ann. Exhbn., 1968-73, Tincum Art Festival, 1968, Woodmere Art Gallery (life mem.), 1972-74, others; selected sculpture 1st S.W. ann. show Mus. N.Mex., 1958; represented in permanent collections several corps., many pvt. homes. Recipient 1st Sculpture Fedn. Dallas Artists, pinned (all awards jewels); Recipient Sweepstakes award SW Ann. Art Show, 1953, Hon. Cert. award Dallas Fed. Bus. Assn., 1964, 2 1st awards N.J. Fedn. Womens Clubs, 1972, 2 1st awards, 1974, 1st and 2d awards, 1975, Gold medal Accademia Italia, 1979, Golden Centaur award Accademia Italia, 1982, Gold medal Internat. Parliament (U.S.A.) of Safety and Peace, 1983, Centro Studi e Ricerche delle Nazioni, Parma, Italy, 1986, statue of victory, 1983; Oscar d' Italia, Accademia Italia, 1985; named Cavalier of Arts, Accademia Bedriacense, 1985, many others, including 3 awards for journalism, 1962-63; 2 Golden Flame awards World Parliament (U.S.A.), 1986. Fellow Internat. Inst. Arts and Letters (life); mem. Cousteau Soc. (founding), U.S. Chess Fedn., Am. Contract Bridge League, Internat. Acad. Lit., Arts and Sci. (hon. life mem., Tommaso Campanello with gold medal award 1972), C. of C. South Hunterdon (charter), Order Eastern Star (past grand officer, past matron). Republican. Episcopalian. Address: 2005 Halmrock Pl Sun City Center FL 33573

DOWLING-BACHAND, PATRICIA ANN, dance academy executive, writer; b. Woonsocket, R.I., Aug. 4, 1934; d. Edward Joseph and Julia Cecelia (Chester) Dowling; m. Paul Vincent Bachand, Aug. 25, 1956; children: Peter Christopher, Patrick Chester. Student, U. R.I., North Kingston, 1954. Sec. to v.p. Middlebury (Vt.) Coll., 1956-59; cons. Sergio's Restaurant, Westlake Village, Calif., 1987-88; pres. Warner Dance Ctr. West, Woodland Hills, Calif., 1988—; v.p. Chetter Prodns., L.A., 1980—. Recipient 2d place award N.Y. Hort. Soc., 1965. Mem. Woodland Hills C. of C., Boston Mineral Club Harvard U., Actors and Others for Animals. Republican. Roman Catholic. Home: 6442 Ellenview West Hills CA 91307 Office: Warner Dance Ctr West 6275 Variel Ave Woodland Hills CA 91367

DOWNEY, D'ANN BARBARA, science administrator; b. Medford, Oreg., Feb. 16, 1940; d. Myron Marcus and Marianna (Koepsell) D. BA in Econs., Calif. State U., Hayward, 1979; postgrad., UCLA, 1980-81, Golden Gate U., 1986—, Calif. State U., 1989—. Proposal analyst Stanford (Calif.) U., 1969-73, asst. research adminstr., 1973-75, contracts officer, 1975-80; sr. contracts adminstr. Jet Propulsion Lab., Pasadena, Calif., 1980-81; sr. subcontract buyer GTE-Govt. Systems Corp., Mountain View, Calif., 1981-85, procurement specialist, 1985—; cons. NCI, Bethesda, Md., 1973-79. Mem. Nat. Contract Mgmt. Assn., Soc. Research Adminstrs. Republican. Mormon.

DOWNEY, DEOBORAH ANN, systems specialist; b. Xenia, Ohio, July 22, 1958; d. Nathan Vernon and Patricia Jaunita (Ward) D. Assoc. in Applied Sci., Sinclair Community Coll., 1981, student, 1986—. Jr. programmer, project mgr. Cole-Layer-Trumble Co., Dayton, Ohio, 1981-82; sr. programmer, analyst, project leader Systems Architects Inc., Dayton, 1982-84, Systems and Applied Sci. Corp. (now Atlantic Rsch. Corp. Profl. Svcs. Group), Dayton, 1984; analyst Unisys, Dayton, 1984-87; systems programmer analyst Profl. Svcs. Group Atlantic Rsch., Fairborn, Ohio, 1987—; cons. computer software M&S Garage/Body Shop, Beavercreek, Ohio, 1986-87. Mem. Nat. Assn. for Female Execs., Am. Motorcyclist Assn., Sinclair Community Coll. Alumni Assn., Cherokee Nation Okla., Cherokee Nat. Hist. Soc. Democrat. Mem. United Ch. of Christ.

DOWNEY, JOAN CAROL, counselor; b. Waupun, Wis., Aug. 22, 1931; d. Lawrence Clarence and Johanna Gertude (VerMeer) Treffert; m. James Howard Downey, May 5, 1950 (dec. Mar. 1980); children: James, Linda, Roxe Ann, Jon. BS in Psychology cum laude, U. Wis.-Parkside, Kenosha, 1988. Cost acct. Twin Disc Corp., Racine, Wis., 1950-53; v.p. Treffert Trucking Inc., Racine, 1970-83; crisis counselor Victim Response Unit, Dist. Atty.'s Office, Racine, 1987—. Hospice vol., counselor St. Luke's Hosp., Racine, 1983-84; vol., counselor Women's Resource Ctr., Racine, 1986-87; gerontology researcher U. Wis., Kenosha, 1987-88; mem. campaign com. Rep. party, Racine, 1988; pres. PTA, Racine; mem. growth and fellowship com. First Reformed Ch. Mem. U. Wis.-Parkside Alumni Assn., Psi Chi (pres. 1986-89, outstanding mem. 1986-89). Republican. Home: 1414 Hwy V Sturtevant WI 53177 Office: Victim Response Unit 730 Wisconsin Ave Racine WI 53403

DOWNEY, JUDITH ANN, health services executive; b. Bellevue, Ohio, May 5, 1940; d. Carl Albert and Ruth Genevieve (Bowers) Krauss; m. Roland Ray Robinett, Nov. 21, 1959 (div. 1981); children: Robin, Kathy, Rachelle; m. Thomas Baker Downey, Apr. 3, 1982 (dec. 1985). Student, Bowling Green State U., 1980-81, Tiffin (Ohio) U., 1989—. Sec. Union Carbide Corp., Fremont, Ohio, 1958-59; rep. Avon, Cleve., 1966-70; cook Elmwood Ctrs., Inc., Green Springs, Ohio, 1974-88; corp. pres. Elmwood Ctrs., Inc., 1988—; missionary cook Wild Wood (Ga.) Hosp., 1988. Vol. Fairview Hosp., Fairview Park, Ohio, 1965-70, Mercy Hosp., Tiffin, 1971-82, ARC, Tiffin, 1972-76; adv. bd. Mercy Hosp., 1981-84. Republican. Office: Elmwood Centers Inc 430 N Broadway Green Springs OH 44836

DOWNEY, PATRICIA ANN, health care educator, administrator; b. Binghamton, N.Y., Dec. 14, 1953; d. Robert O'Connell and Ann Cecilia (Patrick) D.; m. William Harrold Wright, June 21, 1975 (div. 1983). AA with high honors, Broome Community Coll., 1973; BS cum laude, SUNY, Cortland, 1975; MA in Health Edn., U. Md., 1983. Substitute tchr. Binghamton City Sch. Dist., 1975; asst. mgr. Casual Corner, Johnson City, N.Y., 1975-76; adminstrv. asst. grad. studies office, Coll. Bus. and Mgmt. U. Md., College Park, 1976-77; asst. dir. health edn. U. Md., 1977-85; dir. health promotion svcs. The Arlington (Va.) Hosp., 1985-88; mgr. edn. and tng. Am. Coll. Health Assn., Rockville, Md., 1988-90; with sr. staff health svcs. div. United Info. Systems, Inc., Beltsville, Md., 1990—; lectr., presenter in health edn.; cons., CIA, Washington, 1988. Contbr. to health edn. publs.

DOWNIE, SANDRA CARROLL, health policy executive; b. St. Joseph, Mo., Feb. 10, 1939; d. William Harry Minger and Beverly (Carroll) Lee; m. R. Hayden Downie, June 1, 1963 (div. Feb. 1979); children: Whitney, Timothy, Allyson. BS, Tex. Women's U., 1960. Adjunctive therapist Menninger Meml. Hosp., Topeka, 1960-66; asst. adminstr. Hillcrest Med. Ctr., Tulsa, 1977-82; dir. Vol. Action Agy., Tulsa, 1982-83; exec. dir. Tulsa Bus. Health Group, 1983-85; v.p. Met. Tulsa C. of C., 1985—; exec. dir. Tulsa Program for Affordable Health Care, 1986—; cons. mem. Okla. Employment Security Commn., Oklahoma City, 1988—; exec. dir. Tulsa Community Found. for Indigent Health Care, 1986—. Author: editorial column Point of View, 1985—, Tulsa mag., 1985—. Count commn. appointee Tulsa Met. Area Planning Commn., 1973-81; mayor's appointee Tulsa Housing Authority, 1985-88; pres. Tulsa Met. Ministry, 1980-83; bd. dirs. ARC, Tulsa, 1971-73, 84-85. Mem. Am. C. of jC. Execs., Okla. chpt. Am. C. of C. Execs., Tulsa Tennis Club. Democrat. Roman Catholic. Office: Met Tulsa C of C 616 S Boston Tulsa OK 74119

DOWNING, CHRISTINE ROSENBLATT, theology educator; b. Leipzig, Germany, Mar. 21, 1931; came to U.S., 1935; d. Edgar Fritz and Herta (Fischer) Rosenblatt; m. George Downing, June 9, 1951, (div. Jan. 1978); children: Peter, Eric, Scott, Christopher, Sandra; m. River Malcolm, Sept. 2, 1984. BA, Swarthmore Coll., 1948; PhD, Drew U., 1966; MA, U.S. Internat. U., 1982. From instr. to assoc. prof. religion Rutgers U., New Brunswick, N.J., 1963-75; prof., chmn. dept. religious studies San Diego State U., 1974—; mem. core faculty Calif. Sch. Profl. Psychology, Pomona, 1974—. Author: The Goddess, 1981, Journey Through Menopause, 1987, Psyche's Sisters, 1988, Myths and Mysteries fo Same Sex Love Continuum, 1989; co-author: Face to Face to Face, 1975; contbr. articles to profl. jours. Fellow NEH, 1982-83. Fellow Soc. Values in Higher Edn. (bd. dirs. 1966-81); mem. AAUP, Am. Acad. Religion (pres. 1973-74). Office: San Diego State U Dept Religious Studies San Diego CA 92182

DOWNING, GWENDOLYN, mental health therapist; b. Dothan, Ala., Aug. 26, 1960; d. Morris and Janell (Griswold) D. AA, George C. Wallace Coll., Dothan, 1980; BS summa cum laude, Troy (Ala.) State U., 1981; MA in Edn., U. Ala., 1986. Cert. counselor, Ala. Counselor Ind. Living Ctr., Birmingham, Ala., 1987-88; therapist, substance abuse counselor Wiregrass Mental Health System, Dothan, 1988-90, dir. adult substance abuse svcs., 1990—; advisor Henry County (Ala.) Health Coun., Abbeville, 1989—. Mem. Arthritis Found., Dothan, 1987—. Mem. Am. Assn. for Counseling and Devel., Nat. Rehab. Assn., Am. Assn. Mental Health Counselors, Am. Rehab. Counselors Assn., Ala. Mental Health Counselors Assn. Republican. Baptist. Home: 1008 E Selma St Dothan AL 36301 Office: Wiregrass Mental Health 104 Prevatt Rd Dothan AL 36301

DOWNING, LINDA L(OU), radio sales executive; b. Smith Center, Kans., Dec. 2, 1954; d. Forrest Jack Bock and Laneta Fern (Gilbert) Bock Karsting; m. Richard Lynn Johnson, Aug. 5, 1973 (div. July 1980); 1 child, Cody Ryan; m. Michael J. Downing, July 10, 1987; stepchildren: Alyssa, Courtney. Degree in fashion merchandising Patricia Stevens Sch., Wichita, Kans., 1973. Asst. mgr. J. M. McDonald Co., Concordia, Kans. and Holdredge, Nebr., 1979-81; store mgr. Salking & Linoff Inc., Concordia and Sioux City, Iowa, 1982-83; account exec. Sentry Sta. KSEZ, Sioux City, 1983-84; sales mgr. Sta. KGLI, Cardinal Communications, Sioux City, 1984-85, gen. sales mgr. Stas. KGLI/KWSL, 1985-88; gen. mgr. Radio Stas. KKRC/KKFN-Vaughn Broadcasting, Sioux Falls, S.D., 1988—. Mem. Ad Club Sioux City, Nat. Assn. Female Execs., Sales and Mktg. Internat. Home: 1508 E 49th Sioux Falls SD 57103 Office: KKRC/KKFN 1704 S Cleveland Sioux Falls SD 57103

DOWNING, LYNDA, mortgage company executive; b. Hollywood, Calif., Jan. 10, 1949; d. Joseph Richard and Patricia Anita (Olson) Angelotti; m. John Jeffrey Downing, July 19, 1969; children: Joseph Scott, Kimberly Lynn, Lisa Michelle. AA, Moorpark Coll., 1967; cert. paralegal, Calif. Coll. Paralegal Studies, 1972; cert., Calif. Sch. Mortgage and Banking, 1979. Pvt. practice litigation paralegal Encino, Calif., 1975-79; asst. br. mgr. Transamerica Mortgage, San Diego, 1980-84; br. mgr., asst. v.p. Investors First Mortgage, San Diego, 1984-87; br. mgr. Coldwell Banker Mortgage, Encinitas, Calif., 1987-88; retail br. mgr. First Bankers Mortgage, Oceanside, Calif., 1988—. Mem. Mortgage Bankers Assn., Assn. Profl. Mortgage Women, Nat. Assn. Female Execs. Democrat. Home: 2616 Sunset Hills Escondido CA 92025 Office: First Bankers Mortgage 2424 Vista Way Oceanside CA 92054

DOWNING, MARGARET MARY, newspaper editor; b. Altoona, Pa., June 3, 1952; d. Irvine William and Iva Ann (Regan) D.; m. Gary Beaver; 1 child, Ian Downing-Beaver. B.A. magna cum laude, Tex. Christian U., 1974. Reporting intern Corpus Christi Caller Times, 1973; reporter, bur. chief Beaumont Enterprise & Jour. (Tex.), 1974-76, Dallas Times Herald, 1976-80; reporter, asst. city editor, asst. bus. and met. editor Houston Post, 1980—. Mem. Press Club of Houston (pres. 1984, bd. dirs. 1982-85), Greater Houston Hunter-Jumper Assn., Sigma Delta Chi. Episcopalian. Home: 6216 Community Dr Houston TX 77005 Office: Houston Post 4747 SW Freeway Houston TX 77001

DOWNING, MARY BRIGETTA, association executive; b. St. Louis, Jan. 28, 1938; d. William Joseph and Margaruite Mary (Callahan) Schwieder; m. George Stuart Downing, Apr. 21, 1962; 1 child, George S. Student, Corcoran Art Sch., 1954-56; BA, Catholic U., 1960. Drama specialist Army Spl. Svcs., Gelnhausen, Fed. Republic Germany, 1960-61; center dir. Am. Youth Activities, Butzbach, Fed. Republic Germany, 1961-63; cen. dir. Burrwood Indsl. Home for Blind, Cold Spring Harbor, N.Y., 1963-65; regional dir. CARE, Inc., Hicksville, N.Y., 1965-70; dir. publs. Nat. Notions Assn., N.Y.C., 1970-72; asst. dir. Lieberman, Harrison Advt., N.Y.C., 1972-74; advt. cons. M.B. Downing & Assocs., Stamford, Conn., 1974—; exec. dir. NCGR, Inc., Stamford, 1980—; pres. Mercury House Pub. Co., Stamford, 1986—. Editor, pub. NCGR jour., 1983—; pub. newsletters Geocosmic News, 1983—, Cycles Rsch., 1988; contbr. articles to profl. publs. Bd. dirs. Heart Ctr. Libr., Big Rapids, Mich., 1989—. Home: 78 Hubbard Ave Stamford CT 06905

DOWNING, ROBIN WILSON, financial analyst; b. Newton, Mass., Aug. 16, 1962; d. Robert H. and Dolores T. (Gargaro) Wilson; m. Michael F. Downing, Oct. 8, 1989. BS, Boston Coll., 1984; postgrad., Babson Coll., 1985-90. Telemktg. rep. ADP, Waltham, Mass., 1984-85; assoc. program analyst Raytheon Co., Wayland, Mass., 1985-87; program analyst Raytheon Co., Marlboro, Mass., 1987-88; program analyst Raytheon Co., Wayland, Mass., 1988-89, sr. program analyst, 1989—. Admissions vol. Boston Coll. Alumni Assn., 1985—. Mem. Sudbury/Wayland Mgmt. Club, Raytheon Mgmt. Club. Home: 3 Nobscot Rd Medway MA 02053 Office: Raytheon Co 430 Boston Post Rd Wayland MA 01778

DOWNS, CHARITY ANN, lawyer; b. Lakewood, N.J., May 7, 1943; d. William Fletcher and Hope Clyde (Robertson) D. BA summa cum laude, Georgian Ct. Coll., 1966; JD, Rutgers U., 1971. Bar: Vt. 1971, U.S. Dist. Ct. Vt. 1972, U.S. Ct. Appeals (2nd cir.) 1974. Assoc. Conley & Foote, Middlebury, Vt., 1971-80, ptnr., 1980—; mem. Profl. Conduct Bd., Vt., 1979-89. vestry mem., past jr. and sr. warden St. Paul's Ch., Wells, Vt. Mem. ABA, Vt. Bar Assn., Addison County Bar Assn. Episcopalian. Home: Box 34 Wells VT 05774 Office: Conley & Foote Drawer 391 Middlebury VT 05753

DOWNS, FLORELLA MCINTYRE, civic worker, pilot; b. Selmer, Tenn., Sept. 19, 1921; d. Edward N. and Ella Pearle (Byrd) McIntyre; m. James Harold Downs, May 27, 1946; children: Linda Downs Uellmar, William Edward, James Patrick. BA, LaVerne U., 1969. Flight instr., comml. pilot FAA, Memphis, 1945-46; pilot examiner CAA, 1946; owner, mgr. Basic Tutoring Svc., Ventura, Calif., 1982-86; civil air patrol pilot, 1956. Pres. Naval Officer;s Wives, Patuxent River, Md., 1957; active charitable orgns., Md., Italy, Ventura, 1946—; vol. Children's Home Soc., Ventura, 1962-70. Ferry pilot WASP, USAF, 1943-44, 1st lt. USAFR, 1952-56. Mem. AAUW (area rep. community issues VTA 1980-82), Women's Air Force Svc. Pilots, Toastmistress (pres. Ventura 1982-83). Democrat. Home: 751 Montgomery Pl Ventura CA 93004

DOWNS, JOETTA, city official; b. Phoenix, Nov. 7, 1944; d. William J. and Henrietta (Mason) Rose; m. Arthur C. Downs, Jr., Aug. 6, 1965; children: Andrea, Michelle. BA, U. Nev., 1980, MPA, 1983. Mgmt. asst. cable communications City of Phoenix, 1983-85, mgmt. asst. mgmt./budget dept., 1985-86, adminstrv. svcs. officer law dept., 1987—. Bd. dirs. Reno chpt. ARC. Recipient Silver Pen award, Reno. Mem. NAFE, Am. Soc. Pub. Adminstrn., Nat. Dist. Attys. Assn., Nat. Criminal Justice Assn. Office: 455 N 5th St #400 Phoenix AZ 85004

DOWNS, KATHLEEN ANNE, hospital department manager; b. Toledo, Sept. 20, 1951; d. Keith Landis and Cecelia Josephine (Wood) Babcock; m. Michael Brian Thomas, July 17, 1971 (dec. Oct. 1973); m. David Michael Downs, Aug. 8, 1981. Student, San Diego Mesa Coll., 1968-70; BS, Union Inst., 1989. Cert. med. staff coordinator. Sec. Travelodge Internat., Inc., El Cajon, Calif., 1970-73; intermediate stenographer City of El Cajon, 1973-77; adminstrv. asst. MacLellan & Assocs., El Cajon, 1977-78; sr. sec. WESTEC Services, Inc., San Diego, 1978; adminstrv. sec. El Cajon Valley Hosp., 1978-80; asst. med. staff Grossmont Dist. Hosp., La Mesa, Calif., 1980-83, coordinator med. staff, 1983-87, mgr., 1987—; tchr. The Vogel Inst., San Diego, 1986. Mem. dist. med. staff svcs. adv. com. San Diego Community Coll., 1990—. Mem. NAFE, Nat. Assn. Med. Staff Svcs. (edn. coun. 1989—, lectr.), Calif. Assn. Med. Staff Services (pres. San Diego chpt. 1986-87, treas. San Diego chpt. 1984-86, lectr.). Office: Grossmont Dist Hosp PO Box 158 La Mesa CA 92044

DOWNS, RAMONA JO, educator; b. Monett, Mo., Aug. 8, 1848; d. Earl Freeman and Elsie Joan (Cantrell) Cameron; m. John M. Thomason, June 5, 1971 (div. Feb. 1979); children: Timothy, Amanda; m. Robert Eugene Downs, Apr. 25, 1981; children: David, Daniel. BS in Home Econs., U. Mo., 1970; MA in Elem. Edn., U. Mo., Kansas City, 1974. Tchr. Early Childhood Edn. Program, Kansas City, 1970-78, spl. edn. tchr., 1978-80, ctr. dir., 1980-84; dir. U. Mo. Kansas City Enrichment Ctr., 1984—. Den leader Boy Scouts Am., Raytown, Mo., 1980-85; leader Camp Fire, Inc., 1983—. Mem. AAUW, Nat. Assn. Edn. Young Children (legis. com. 1972-82, child devel. assoc. trainer), Nat. Coalition Campus Child Care Ctrs., Assn. for Childhood Edn. Internat. Democrat. Baptist. Office: U Mo Child Enrichment Ctr 32 E 46th St Kansas City MO 64138

DOWNS, SHIRLEY GWINN, custom picture framing company executive; b. Lowell, W.Va., Sept. 17, 1936; d. Othor Dolphin and Gladys Virginia (Skaggs) Gwinn; m. Rodney Guy Downs, Dec. 27, 1958; children: Jeffrey Guy, James Preston. Grad. high sch., Radford, Va. Asst. Paint Brush Gallery, Christiansburg, Va., 1972-81; owner, mgr. Shirley's Frame Shop, Christiansburg, 1981—. Mem. Nat. Fedn. Ind. Bus., Christiansburg-Montgomery County C. of C. Presbyterian. Office: 5ll Roanoke St Christiansburg VA 24073

DOWNS, SUSAN PAULINE, travel executive; b. Providence, Mar. 1, 1950; d. Philip Elden and Dorothee Jeanne (Gauthier) D. BS, U. R.I., 1972. Owner Foster Travel Svc., Pawtucket, R.I., 1982-86; v.p. Sophisticated Traveler, Inc., Providence, 1986—; travel reporter WPRO Radio, Providence, 1987—. Telethon chmn. United Cerebral Palsy of R.I., Pawtucket 1981—; mem. corp. United Cerebral Palsy Assn. Inc., N.Y.C. 1988—, mem. campaign com., 1987—, vice chmn. N.Y.C., 1988—. Mem. United Cerebral Palsy Assn., Inc. (mem. campaign com. 1987—), United Cerebral Palsy of R.I. (exec. bd. dirs. 1978—, pres. 1988-89, Female Vol. of Yr. 1987). Office: Sophisticated Traveler Inc 285 Governor St Providence RI 02906

DOYLE, BEVERLY ANN, special education educator, psychologist; b. Hamburg, Iowa, Nov. 1, 1945; d. Robert Avery and Eunice Rose (Barsch) Scrimsher; m. Wayne Ralph Oppenheim, Mar. 7, 1960; 1 child, Alexander Wayne Oppenheim. BS, Iowa State U., 1967; MS, U. Nebr., Omaha, 1971; PhD, U. Nebr., 1977. Cert. sch. psychologist; cert. mental retardation tchr., Nebr. Tchr. Omaha Womens Job Corp., 1967, 69; dept. supr. Glenwood (Iowa) State Hosp., 1969-71; specialist learning disabilities Meyer Childrens Rehab. Inst., Omaha, 1971-77; asst. and assoc. prof. Creighton U., Omaha, 1977—; ednl. therapist Omaha Psychiat. Assn., 1985—. Contbr. articles to profl. jours. Mem. human rights rev. com. Boys Town Inst., Omaha, 1986—. Grantee Creighton U., 1979, 82, Am. Assn. Colls. for Tchr. Edn., 1984; U. Nebr.-Omaha fellow, 1971. Mem. Council for Exceptional Children, Consortium for Spl. Edn., Nebr. Assn. for Children with Learning Disabilities, Orton Soc. (pres. 1987-89). Home: 5203 Izard St Omaha NE 68132 Office: Creighton U 2500 California St Omaha NE 68178

DOYLE, CONSTANCE TALCOTT JOHNSTON, physician, educator; b. Mansfield, Ohio, July 8, 1945; d. Frederick Lyman IV and Nancy Jean Bushnell (Johnston) Talcott; m. Alan Jerome Demsky, June 13, 1976; children: Ian Frederick Demsky, Zachary Adam Demsky. BS, Ohio U., 1967; MD, Ohio State U., 1971. Diplomate Am. Bd. Emergency Medicine. Intern Riverside Hosp., Columbus, Ohio, 1971-72; resident in internal medicine Hurley Hosp. and U. Mich., Flint, 1972-74, emergency physician Oakwood Hosp., Dearborn, Mich., 1974-76, Jackson County (Mich.) Emergency Svcs., 1975—; survival flight physician U. Mich. helicopter rescue svc., 1983—; disaster cons., co-chmn. emergency med. svcs. disaster com. Region II EMS, 1978-79; course dir. advanced cardiac life support and chmn. advanced life support com. W.A. Foote Meml. Hosp., Jackson, 1979—, others; clin. instr. emergency svcs., dept. surgery U. Mich., 1981—; instr. Jackson County Emergency Med. Technician refresher courses, Jackson Community Coll. Contbr. author: Clinical Approach to Poisoning and Toxicology, 1983, 89; contbr. articles to profl. publs. Bd. dirs. Jackson County Heart Assn., 1979-83. Fellow Am. Coll. Emergency Physicians (pres. Mich. disaster com. 1987-88, bd. dir. Mich. 1979-88, chmn. Mich. disaster com. 1979-85, mem. nat. disaster med. svcs. com. 1983-85, chmn., 1987-88, cons. disaster mgmt. course Fed. Emergency Mgmt. Agy., 1982, treas. 1984-85, emergency med. svcs. com. 1985, pres. 1986-87, councillor 1986—), Nat. Am. Emergency Physicians (vice chair sect. of disaster med. svcs. 1989-90, nat. disaster subcom. 1989-90); mem. ACP, Am. Med. Women's Assn., Mich. Assn. Emergency Med. Technicians (bd. dirs. 1979-80), Mich. State Med. Soc., Jackson County Med. Soc., Sierra Club. Jewish. Home: 1665 Lansdowne Rd Ann Arbor MI 48105 Office: WA Foote Hosp Emergency Dept Jackson MI 49201

DOYLE, IRENE ELIZABETH, electronic sales executive, nurse; b. West Point, Iowa, Oct. 5, 1920; d. Joseph Deidrich and Mary Adelaide (Groene) Schulte; m. William Joseph Doyle, Feb. 3, 1956. RN, Mercy Hosp., 1941. Courier nurse Santa Fe R.R., Chgo., 1947-50; indsl. nurse Montgomery Ward, Chgo., 1950-54; rep. Hornblower & Weeks, Chgo., 1954-56; v.p. William J. Doyle Co., Chgo., 1956-80, Ormond Beach, Fla., 1980-88. Served with M.C., U.S. Army, 1942-46. Mem. Electronic Reps. Assn. Republican. Roman Catholic. Club: Oceanside Country (Ormond Beach).

DOYLE, JENNIFER LYDIA, academic administrator; b. Lubbock, Tex., Dec. 14, 1953; d. Tallie A. and Lydia (Gil) Warr; m. Jack C. Doyle, Aug. 10, 1974; children: Shannon, Ryan. BA in English, Clemson U., 1975, MEd in Couseling, 1981. Dir. career planning and placement Winthrop Coll., Rock Hill, S.C., 1987—; cons. in field. Contbr. articles to profl. jours. and newsletters. Mem. Community Task Force on Planning and Devel., Greenville, 1985. Fellow Am. Assn. Female Execs.; mem. Am. Soc. Personnel Adminstrs., Am. Mgmt. Assn., Coll. Placement Assn. (membership chmn. 1988-89). Home: 1087 Palmyra Dr Fort Mill SC 29175 Office: Winthrop Coll 638 W Oakland Ave Rock Hill SC 29730

DOYLE, JOYCE ANN, lawyer; b. Youngstown, Ohio, Aug. 13, 1937; d. Norbert Harry Doyle and Corinne (Johnson) McCoy. BA, Youngstown U., 1960; MSW, Cath. U., 1964; JD, Fordham U., 1972. Bar: N.Y. 1973, D.C. 1987. Assoc. Fogarty, McLaughlin & Semel, N.Y.C., 1973-76; asst. gen. counsel Belco Petroleum Corp., N.Y.C., 1976-85; commr. Fed. Mine Safety and Health Rev. Commn., Washington, 1985—. Mem. ABA, D.C. Bar Assn., Women's Bar Assn. D.C., Fordham Law Sch. Alumni Assn. Home: 1545 18 St NW #318 Washington DC 20036 Office: Fed Mine Safety & Health Rev Commn 1730 K St NW 6th Fl Washington DC 20006

DOYLE, JUDITH STOVALL, real estate executive; b. Dothan, Ala., Apr. 19, 1940; d. E.H. and Justine (Knowles) Stovall; m. John P. Doyle Jr., Aug. 22, 1964; children: John Patrick III, Michael D., Julie A. BS, Miss. State Coll. for Women, 1961. Tchr. math., jr. high sch., Gulfport, Miss., 1961-62; asst. dir. dept. pub. rels. SUNY-Buffalo, 1962-64; tchr. math., jr. high schs., Alexandria, Va., 1964-65, Auburn, N.Y., 1970-71; realtor, assoc. Mosher Real Estate, Auburn, 1972-80; owner, mgr. real estate property, Auburn, 1977—. Active, past pres. Mercy Aux., Auburn; chairperson Owasco Bd. Assessment Rev., N.Y., 1976—; v.p. Sacred Heart Parish Council, Auburn, 1985-89; bd. dirs. Unity House, Auburn, 1985-87. Democrat. Roman Catholic. Lodge: Ancient Order Hibernians (charter mem. Ladies Aux. 2).

DOYLE, JUDITH WARNER, marriage and family therapist, corporate executive, consultant; b. L.A., Aug. 18, 1943; d. Raymond Ross Manley and Sarah Virginia (Pletcher) Manley Flint; 1 child, Brennan Corey. BA, Calif. State U.-Long Beach, 1975, MS, 1977. Counselor Calif. State U., Long Beach, 1976-78; case mgmt. supr. Bridge/Boys Club, Wilmington, Calif., 1978-80, ElMonte Sr. Citizens Ctr., Calif., 1979-81; dir. counseling svcs. Gay/Lesbian Community Svc. Ctr., Orange County, Calif., 1985-88; owner, therapist Judith Doyle MFCC, Long Beach, 1978—; cons. AIDS Response Program, Garden Grove, Calif., 1985—; med. adv. bd. AIDS Svc. Found., Costa Mesa, Calif., 1985-88 ; exec. dir. One in Long Beach Inc., 1988-90; Golden mem. Long Beach Lambda Dem. Club, 1980—; chmn. So. Calif. Women for Understanding, L.A., 1981-85; pres., bd. dirs. Long Beach Lesbian and Gay Pride, Inc., 1983-88; co-chair, founder AIDS Walk Long Beach, 1988—; apptd. mem. Calif. State Commn. Econ. Devel. Task Force, 1984-85; trustee L. Diane Anderson Meml. Trust, 1984—. Recipient Woman of Yr. award Lambda Dem. Club, 1981, Christopher Street W., 1986, Spl. Person award Press/Telegram, 1985, Myra Riddell Svc. award So. Calif. Women for Understanding, 1985. Mem. NAFE, ACLU, Calif. Assn. Marriage and Family Therapists (bd. dirs. 1981-85, pres. 1985-86, named Disting. Clin. Mem. 1988), Greenpeace, Am. Assn. Marriage and Family Therapy, People for the Am. Way, Nat. Mus. Women in the Arts (charter), Mus. Contemporary Art (charter), Calypso Soc. Avocations: dancing, theatre, volleyball, softball.

DOYLE, KATHERINE LEE LEE, research scientist, educator; b. Sacramento, Sept. 22, 1932; d. Maurice Omar and Lorena Augusta (Merrill) D.; m. F. Vincent Brecka, Jr., May 13, 1972. B.A. magna cum laude, Dominican Coll., San Rafael, 1954; M.A., Stanford U., 1961; Ph.D., Tulane U., 1971. Research asso. Stanford Med. Sch., Calif., 1958-62; asso. research specialist U. Calif. Med. Sch., San Francisco, 1962-67; instr. Tulane Med.

Sch., New Orleans, 1967-70; asst. prof. Tulane Med. Sch., 1970-72; adj. scientist Delta Regional Primate Center, Covington, La., 1967—; prof. U. Ark. Coll. Medicine, Little Rock, 1977—; acting chmn. ob-Gyn, 1978; bd. dirs., mem. exec. bd. Ark. Family Planning Coun., 1977—, pres., 1979-80, 80-81; chmn. gov.'s task force for prevention adolescent pregnancy, 1980, 89; cons. James Bowman, Inc., 1977-78, Battelle Inst., 1977—, JWK Internat., Ark. Dept. Health, Ala. Dept. Health, Okla. Dept. Health, 1980, March of Dimes, 1980. Contbr. articles to profl. jours. Chmn. Pulaski County Task Force for Prevention Child Abuse, 1984-85, 87; pres. Planned Parenthood, 1986-88, Arkansans for Reproductive Health, 1985, Healthy Mothers Healthy Babies Coalition, 1988. Recipient Squibb award for outstanding research, 1963, leadership & service award in preventing child abuse Dept. Health & Human Services, 1985, Uppity Woman award Ark. Women's Pol. Caucus, 1985; Population Council grantee, 1963, 73; NIH grantee, 1969-72, 80-81. Mem. Am. Fertility Soc. (Rubin award 1962), Am. Assn. Planned Parenthood Physicians (program chmn. 1983), Am. Public Health Assn., Nat. Family Planning and Reproductive Health Forum, Soc. Study Reproduction, Am. Assn. Profs. Ob-Gyn., Ark. Advocates for Children and Families (bd. dirs. 1987—). Roman Catholic. Home: 211 Gorgeous View Trail Little Rock AR 72210 Office: U Ark Coll Medicine Dept Ob/Gyn Little Rock AR 72205

DOYLE, MARCIA ANN, nursing educator; b. Stockton, Calif., July 30, 1943; d. Joseph M. and Martha (Zumstein) Craig; m. Michael J. Doyle, Aug. 21, 1965; children: Michelle, Patrice, Martin. BSN, U. San Francisco, 1965; MPH, San Jose State U., 1978. Relief head nurse St. Mary's Hosp., San Francisco, 1965-66; staff nurse Kaiser Found. Hosp., Sacramento, 1967-68, Los Gatos-Saratoga Community Hosp., Los Gatos, Calif., 1970-78; dir. health edn. ctr. El Camino Hosp., Mountain View, Calif., 1978-82; clinic nursing health educator Kaiser Permanente, Santa Clara, Calif., 1983-89, charge nurse dermatology clinic, 1989—; lectr. in field. Contbr. articles to profl. jours. Mem. Sterling Community Svc. Found., Oakland, Calif., 1989. Mem. Santa Clara County Heart Assn. (chmn. pub. edn. com. 1976-78, bd. dirs. 1976-82), Calif. Nurses Assn., Sierra Club. Republican. Roman Catholic. Office: Kaiser Permanente 900 Kiely Blvd Santa Clara CA 95051

DOYLE, MARY GLADING, business owner; b. N.Y.C., Mar. 30, 1925; d. George William and Josephine Mary (Campbell) Glading; children: Douglas Alan, Claudia Ann. Student, Barnard Coll., 1945. V.p. mktg. dept. Lewtan Industries, Hartford, Conn., 1959-69; exec. v.p. Ad-Wares, Rocky Hill, Conn., 1969-72; v.p. Safety Premiums, Norwalk, Conn., 1972-86; chief exec. officer, pres. Reflectics, Norwalk, 1986—. Columnist articles Spl. Advt. Jour., 1985. Tchr. Literacy Vols., Norwalk, 1987—. Mem. Spl. Advt. Assn. Internat., Spl. Advt. Assn. N.Y., Spl. Advt. Assn. New Eng., Barnard Club (treas. N.Y. chpt. 1988—). Home: PO Box M96 Norwalk CT 06856 Office: Reflectics 71 Cedar St Norwalk CT 06854

DOYLE, P. JILL, quality assurance engineer; b. Chgo., Jan. 25, 1955; d. Russell Paul and Ruth Elaine (Dwyer) D. BS in Indsl. TEch., U. Lowell, 1983; MBA, Rivier Coll., 1988. Quality control inspector Sanders Assocs., Merrimack, N.H., 1981-82; quality assurance specialist, then quality assurance engr. Sanders Assocs., Merrimack, 1982-85; quality assurance engr. Raytheon Co., Lowell, Mass., 1985—. Mem. Product Assurance Coun., Women in Def., Raytheon Mgmt. Club. Home: 15 Hidden Valley Rd Westford MA 01886 Office: Raytheon Missile Systems Lowell MA 01852

DOYLE, PATRICIA ANNE, advertising agency executive; b. Rockville Centre, N.Y., Sept. 16, 1953; d. Thomas Edward and Anita (Maurer) D. BA in Sociology, St. Mary's Coll., 1975; MA in Sociology, Ind. U., 1977. V.p. dir. ops. Sturm Research Inc., N.Y.C., 1977-81; research supr. Ogilvy & Mather Inc., N.Y.C., 1981-83, v.p., assoc. research dir., 1983-85, sr. v.p., planning and research dir., 1985-88; sr. v.p. Lord, Geller, Federico, Einstein, Inc., N.Y.C., 1988-89, mng. dir., 1989—; chmn. mgmt. com. Lord, Geller, Federico, Einstein, Inc., N.Y.C., 1989—. Mem. Am. Mktg. Assn., Ind. U. Alumni Assn., St. Mary's Alumni Assn. Roman Catholic. Office: Lord Geller Federico Einstein 655 Madison Ave New York NY 10021

DOYLE, SHEILA MARIE, public relations executive; b. St. Louis, July 12, 1958; d. Joseph Brice and Sharon Margaret (Barber) D. Waitress Jason's Restaurant, St. Louis, 1975-77; nurse's aide Halls Ferry Meml. Home, St. Louis, 1977-78, med. records clk., 1979-80; night mgr. Sands Drug Store, St. Louis; med. records tumor registrar Normandy Osteo. Hosp. N, St. Louis, 1980-87; customer support Computerized Med. Systems, Inc., Mo., 1987--; pres. Bi-State Tumor Registrars, 1987--, sec. Mo. State Tumor Registrars, St. Louis 1987--. Author, editor: Mo. Compensation Survey, 1988. Mem. Nat. Tumor Registrars Assn., Mo. State Tumor Registrars Assn. (bd. dirs. 1988—, pres.-elect.), Am. Med. Record Assn. Home: 4110 Geraldine #4 Saint Ann MO 63074 Office: Computerized Med Systems Inc 56 Worthington Dr Maryland Heights MO 63043

DOYLE, THERESA LIPARI, real estate and marketing executive; b. Long Beach, Calif., Aug. 27, 1957; d. Joseph and Joyce Lorraine (Wagle) Lipari; m. Timothy Xavier Doyle, June 26, 1982. BA, Calif. State U., Fullerton, 1980. Fundraising asst. Am. Heart Assn., Santa Ana, Calif., 1980; account exec. Kerr & Assocs. Pub. Rels., Huntington Beach, Calif., 1980-83; dir. mktg. Covington Homes, Fullerton, Calif., 1983-86; dir. sales and mktg., Covington Homes, Orange County, Calif., 1986, v.p. sales and mktg., 1986-88; v.p. sales and mktg. Covington Homes, So. Calif., 1988—; pub. rels. cons. Am. Heart Assn., 1980-84, Family Crisis Ctr., Orange County, 1980-83. Recipient Outstanding Pub. Rels. award Publicity Club L.A., 1980, 3 Mem. Inst. Residential Mktg. awards Nat. Assn. Home Builders, 1986. Mem. Women in Communications, Inc. (Outstanding Mag. Article award 1980, Outstanding Pub. Rels. award 1980), Bldg. Industry Assn. (bd. dir. sales and mktg. coun. 1984-86, 9 Major Achievment in Merchandising Excellence awards, 1984-88), So. Calif. Women in Advertising, Calif. State U., Fullerton Alumni Assn. Republican. Roman Catholic. Office: Covington Homes 2451 E Orangethorpe Ave Fullerton CA 92631

DOYLE, ZITA MARIA, real estate corporation officer; b. Iserlohm, Germany, Sept. 20, 1961; came to U.S., 1962; d. Gary Lynn Nicholas and Grozvyda Sylvia (Serapinas) Shelhart; m. Michael V. Doyle, Nov. 12, 1980. Asst. mgr. Stottlemeyers, Pasadena, Calif., 1978-80; merchant and vault service rep., teller trainer Crocker Bank, Pasadena, 1980-86; buyer asst. staff Thrifty Corp., L.A., 1986-89; realtor Century 21 Glen Bank Realty, Glendale, Calif., 1989—. Raffle and auction coord. Jonathan Jacques Cancer Clinic, L.A., 1986-89; active March of Dimes, Glendale, 1989, Glendale Christmas Canned Food Dr. for Homeless; petition collector Calif. Ins. Initiative, L.A., 1988; mem. Daus. of Lithuania, L.A. Republican. Roman Catholic. Home: 6422 Garvanza Ave Los Angeles CA 90042

DOYLE-FARRELL, ANNE J., public relations executive, consultant, writer; b. South Bend, Ind., June 22, 1948; d. Vincent T. and Isabel (Molloy) Doyle; m. Michael J. Farrell, Sept. 21, 1985. Student U. Madrid, 1968-69; BA in Spanish, U. Mich., 1972. Intern TV news Northwestern U., summer 1972; news reporter Sta. WJIM, Lansing, Mich., 1972-73; news anchor/reporter Sta. WDEE, Detroit, 1973, Sta. WZZM-TV, Grand Rapids, Mich., 1973-77; anchor Sta. KHJ-TV, L.A., 1977-78; sports reporter, anchor Sta. WJBK-TV, Detroit, 1978-83; news editor UPI, Atlanta, 1984-85; pres. Doyle-Farrell Bus. Communications, Atlanta, 1985—; exec. producer broadcast news dept. Ford Motor Co., Detroit, 1987, mgr. broadcast news, Dearborn, 1987-89, mgr. pub. affairs Ford Parts & Svc. div., 1989; lectr. George Washington U., AAUW, others. Recipient awards UPI, AP, others. Mem. AFTRA, Sportswomen in Detroit (pres. 1980-83), Detroit Sports Broadcasters Assn., Women in Communications, Nat. Acad. TV Arts and Scis. Office: Ford Motor Co 3000 Schaeffer Rd Dearborn MI 48121

DRABANSKI, EMILY ANN, editor, publisher; b. Chgo., May 27, 1952; d. Harold John and Anna Elizabeth (Roberts) Skretny; m. John Daniel Drabanski, Nov. 25, 1972. AA in Journalism, Triton Coll., River Grove, Ill., 1972; BA in Communication, Sangamon State U., Springfield, Ill., 1975, MA in Communication, 1976. Reporter Ill. Coll. Press Assn., Springfield, 1973-74; radio announcer WSSR Radio, Springfield, 1974-75; med. TV Producer, writer So. Ill. U. Sch. Med., Springfield, 1974-76; feature writer The New Mexican, Santa Fe, N.Mex., 1977-82, spl. sects. editor, 1982-86; editor New Mexico Mag., Santa Fe, 1986-88, acting pub., 1988-89; editor in chief N.Mex. Mag., Santa Fe, 1989—. Editor: The Waning of the West, by Stan. Steiner, 1989; author: (with others) Explore New Mexico, 1989, Indians of New Mexico, 1990. Recipient project dir. grant N.Mex. Humanities Coun./ NEH, 1987. Mem. Nat. Press Women (pres. Santa Fe chpt. 1986-88, 1st place Mag. Spl. Issue 1988, 1st place 4-color Mag. Editing. 1988), Regional Pubs. Assn. Office: N Mex Mag Montoya Bldg 1100 St Francis Dr Santa Fe NM 87503

DRAG, MICHELLE MARY, accountant; b. Chgo., July 15, 1963; d. Edward John and Sally Cecilia (Wawrzaszek) Kocik; m. Alan Joseph Drag, Apr. 7, 1990. BA, Sweet Briar Coll., 1984. Acctg. clk. I MCI Telecom, Chgo., 1984-85, acctg. clk. II, 1985-86, staff asst. I, 1987-88, staff asst. II, staff adminstr., 1988; sr. acct. HealthCorp Affiliates, Naperville, Ill., 1988—. Mem. NAFE. Home: 30W055 Penny Lane Warrenville IL 60555 Office: HealthCorp Affiliates 1151 E Warrenville Rd Naperville IL 60563

DRAGE, MICHELLE S., quality assurance engineer; b. Elyria, Ohio, July 15, 1965; d. James Edwin and Mae Matilda (Reisinger) D. BS in Elec. Engring., GMI Engring and Mgmt. Inst., Flint, Mich., 1988. Quality assurance engr. Gen. Motors, Columbus, Ohio, 1988—. Author: Arm Rest Form Line Renovations, 1988. Mission Team mem. United Meth. Ch., Rio Bravo, Mexico, 1986, Nevis, West Indies, 1988, lay speaker Norwalk (Ohio) dist., 1983—. Mem. Nat. Soc. Profl. Engrs., IEEE, Am. Soc. Quality Control, NAFE. Home: 841 Cherlyn Ct Columbus OH 43228 Office: Gen Motors 200 Georgesville Rd Columbus OH 43228

DRAGE, STARLA RAE, fashion designer; b. Santaquin, Utah, Oct. 1, 1932; d. Andrew William and Vera Mae (Chatwin) Larsen; m. James Don Drage, Feb. 3, 1951; children: William Joe, Julia Ann, Callene, Darrell Edward. Seamstress Jolene Co., Provo, Utah, 1959, fore-lady, 1960-61, pattern grader, 1963-82, purchasing and prodn. coord., 1978-83, designer 1st patterns, 1984-90; v.p., designer Weinland Mktg. Corp. div. Roanna Togs, N.Y.C., 1990—; designer, pattern grader Little Gems, Provo, 1961-63. Office: Weinland Mktg Corp 1106 S State St Ste 2 Provo UT 84606

DRAIN, TRISHA MCMAHON, editor-in-chief; b. Yonkers, N.Y.; d. Edward and Anita (Reilly) McM.; m. Eugene James Drain; children: Sean McMahon, Owen McMahon. Student, Pace U., Westchester Community Coll.; AS in Bus. Adminstrn., SUNY, Purchase; BA in English, Elizabeth Seton U. Mng. editor L'Officiel/USA, N.Y.C., 1976-81; pres. McMahon Drain Assocs., Bronxville, N.Y., 1982-88; editor-in-chief Beauty mag., N.Y.C., 1988—; cons. fashion editor Hudsan Valley mag., Poughkeepsie, N.Y., 1987-88; cons. editor-in-chief Mall mags., Cherry Hill, N.J., 1982-86. Contbr. articles to various periodicals. Mem. Cosmetic Toiletry and Fragrance Assn., The Fashion Group, Am. Soc. Mag. Editors, Am.-Irish Assn., Westchester Assn. Women Bus. Owners. Home: 47 Homecrest Ave Yonkers NY 10703 Office: Beauty Mag 404 Park Ave S New York NY 10016

DRAKE, ELLEN TAN, earth science educator, historian, writer, editor; b. Beijing, Republic of China, July 23, 1927; d. Wai Hsueh and May Jane (Chin) Tan; m. Charles Whitney Drake, June 15, 1952; children: Judith Ellen, Robert Charles, Linda Ann. BA in Geology, Bryn Mawr (Pa.) Coll., 1949; MA in Interdisciplinary Studies, Oreg. State U., 1975, PhD in Oceanography in Marine Geology, 1981. Teaching asst. geology Wesleyan U., Middletown, Conn., 1949-52; asst. editor, jr. rsch. chemist Carnegie Inst. Tech., Pitts., 1952-53; asst. to the editor journalism on alcohol studies Yale U., New Haven, 1953-55, editor, head publs. div. Peabody Mus., 1961-66; resource aide social studies Corvallis (Oreg.) High Sch., 1973-75; rsch. asst. oceanography Oreg. State U., Corvallis, 1969-73, instr. English, 1975-81, editor computer ctr., 1977-79, rsch. assoc. oceanography, 1981—; chmn. history of sci. sect. Oreg. Acad. Sci., 1980-81; mem. U.S. history of geology com. NAS/NRC, 1983-86. Founding editor Discovery jour. Yale U., 1965; editor: Evolution & Environment, 1968, Geologists & Ideas, 1985, Crater Lake: An Ecosystem Study, 1990; contbr. articles to sci. jours. Founder Friends of Corvallis Child Care Ctrs., 1971-72. Mem. AAAS (coun., coord. oceanography program Pacific div. 1984—), Geol. Soc. Am. (chmn., pres. history of geology div. 1981-82, best paper award nominee 1978, 79), Sigma Xi. Office: Oreg State U Coll. Oceanography Corvallis OR 97331

DRAKE, GRACE L., state senator; b. New London, Conn., May 25, 1926; d. Daniel Harvey and Marion Gertrude (Wiech) Driscoll; m. William Lee Drake (dec.), June 9, 1946; children—Sandra DeNobile Drake. With Am. Photographic Corp., N.Y.C., 1944-72; senator State of Ohio, Columbus, 1984—. Mem. Carmelite Guild of Cleve., 1973—, Tech. Leadership Coun., Leadership Cleve., Cleve. Music Sch. Settlement. Recipient Outstanding Woman award Nat. Fedn. Rep. Women, 1984; named Legislator of Yr. Nat. Rep. Legis's. Assn, 1988, Public Official of Yr Ohio chpt. Nat. Assn. Social Workers, 1989, Outstanding Legislator of Yr. Ohio Speech and Hearing Assn., 1989. Roman Catholic. Avocations: bridge, golf. Office: Ohio Senate Statehouse Columbus OH 43266-0604

DRAKE, LINDA KAY, postal service clerk; b. Hutchinson, Kans., Mar. 13, 1957; d. Norlis Estel and Nellye Grace (Harris) D. Student, Hutchinson Community Coll., 1975-76. Sales clk. Ben Franklin Store, Hutchinson, 1977-78; printer Lowen Sign Co., Hutchinson, 1978-81; delivery person Snack Pack, Hutchinson, 1982-83; with Retail Grocery Inventory Svc., Hutchinson, 1983-84; receptionist Reno County Weed Dept., South Hutchinson, Kans., 1983, Plumbers and Pipefitters Union, Hutchinson, 1983-84; distbn. clk. U.S. Postal Svc., Hutchinson, 1984—. Mem. Am. Postal Workers Union. Republican.

DRAKE, LYNN ANNETTE, physician; b. Albuquerque, Aug. 4, 1949; d. Olen Lester and Lucille Susan (Henry) Drake; BA, Adams State Coll., 1966, MA, 1967; MD, U. Tenn., 1971. Instr. math. Adams State Coll., Alamosa, Colo., 1966-67; intern City of Memphis Hosp., 1971-72, resident in dermatology, 1972-75, chief resident, 1974-75; mem. faculty dept. medicine, div. dermatology U. Tenn. Ctr. Health Scis., also Med. Practice Group, Inc.; asst. prof. dermatology Emory U., Atlanta; chief dermatology VA Med. Ctr., Atlanta; chmn. chemosurgery tag group VA; instr. advanced cardiac life support Am. Heart Assn.; mem. emergency room com. St. Joseph Hosp. Vol., Am. Cancer Soc., 1973-75; dir. policy and planning dept. dep. chmn. dept. dermatology, Wellman Labs Photomedicine Harvard Med. Sch., Mass. Gen. Hosp., Boston, 1988—. Diplomate Am. Bd. Dermatology (chmn. com. health care quality assurance 1984—, chair.). Robert Wood Johnson Health Policy fellow, 1986-87. Bd. trustees Chapel Feur Chaplins. Fellow Am. Acad. Dermatology (bd. dirs. 1988—); mem. AMA, ACP, Soc. for Investigative Dermatology, Am. Acad. Dermatology (com. on health planning, chmn. guidelines care com.), Women's Med. Assn., Ga. Dermatology Soc., Atlanta Dermatology Soc. (program chmn.), Am. Assn. Med. Colls., Council Acad. Scis., Women's Dermatology Soc. (housestaff liaison com., nominating com., pres. 1984-87). Dermatology Found. Home: One Longfellow Pl #2418 Boston MA 02114

DRAKE, PATRICIA ANN GLASSCOCK, psychologist; b. Barbourville, Ky., July 15, 1955; d. Vernon Thomas Glasscock and Neva (Hammons) Kaplan; m. Mark Marvin Drake, Mar. 21, 1987; 1 child, Matthew Marvin. BA, Marygrove Coll., 1977; Ma, U. Detroit, 1978; PhD, Wayne State U., 1987. Lic. psychologist, sch. psychologist, Mich. Psychologist Caknipe-Kovach Assoc., Wayne, Mich., 1987-89; sch. psychologist Warren (Mich.) Consol. Schs., 1978—. Grad. scholar Wayne State U., 1981-87; named to Honorable Order Ky. Cols., 1989. Mem. Am. Psychol. Assn., Nat. Assn. Sch. Psychologists, Mich. Women Psychologists, Macomb-St. Clair Psychol. Assn. (pres. elect 1990-91). Methodist. Home: 35634 Joy Rd Livonia MI 48150 Office: Warren Consol Schs 31300 Anita Warren MI 48093

DRAKE, SARAH FRANCES ASHFORD, electronic manufacturing company executive; b. Dallas, Jan. 31, 1943; d. Roger F. and Rosa M. (Hancock) Ashford; m. Alford Willard Smallwood, Nov. 1, 1963 (div.); children: Sonja Mozelle Smallwood Ayers, Monica Grace Smallwood Harding; m. Jerry Joe Drake, Feb. 12, 1988. Student pub. schs., Odessa, Tex. Bookkeeper, First State Bank, Odessa, 1963-64; pres. Magnum Assembly, Inc., Austin, 1974—; v.p. Microsvcs. Internat., Inc., Austin, 1989—. Recipient Outstanding Achievement for Entrepreneurship award Univ. YWCA, Austin, 1990; named Mfr. of Yr. Austin C. of C., 1990. Baptist. Avocations: running, water sports, dancing. Home: 7305 Bering Cove Austin TX 78759 Office: Magnum Assembly Inc 1915 Kramer Ln Austin TX 78758

DRAKOS, IRENE SASSO, chemist; b. Bklyn., Dec. 28, 1932; d. Peter John and Lillian (Abraham) Sasso; m. James Drakos; children: Diane Eugenia Drakos Jaeger, Melissa Ann. BA, Agnes Scott Coll., Decatur, Ga., 1954; MA, Central Mich. U., 1988. Chemist Pontiac div. GM, Pontiac, Mich., 1955-59; consumer chemist Texize Chems., Greenville, S.C., 1959-64; plant chemist Cryovac div. W.R. Grace Co., Simpsonville, S.C., 1965-66; sr. project specialist automotive ops. Rockwell Internat., Troy, Mich., 1966-90, chemistry lab. supr. automotive ops., 1990—. Mem. Smithsonian Inst., 1989—. Mem. AAAS, NAFE, Am Chem. Soc., Soc. Automotive Engrs., Soc. Plastic Engrs., Founders Soc. Detroit Inst. Arts, Soc. for the Advancement of Material and Processing Engring., Toastmasters (pres. 1984-85), Rockwell Women's Club (treas. 1983-84). Greek Orthodox. Office: Rockwell Internat 2135 W Maple Rd Troy MI 48084

DRAMMIS, HILARY PATRICIA, clinical psychologist; b. Phillipsburg, N.J., Mar. 17, 1954; d. Joseph John and Helen Penelope (McConnell) Buzas; m. John Joseph Drammis, May 20, 1989. BA summa cum laude, Armstrong State Coll., 1975; MA, Augusts Coll., 1976; PhD, Ga. State U., 1983. Registered psychologist, Ill. Intern Family System Program, Chgo., 1982-83; pvt. practice Midwest Inst. for Holistic Health, Inc., Chgo., 1983-84; dir. psychol. svcs. Ctr. for Nutritional Counseling, Glenview, Ill., 1986; behaviorist Weight Mgmt. System, Chgo., 1986; pvt. practice Chgo., 1987—. Contbr. numerous articles to profl. jours. Mem. Am. Psychol. Assn. Roman Catholic. Home: 680 N Lake Shore Dr Chicago IL 60611 Office: 625 N Michigan Ste 1740 Chicago IL 60611

DRANTZ, VERONICA ELLEN, science educator and consultant; b. Chgo., Sept. 5, 1943; d. Albert William and Veronica Grace (Crowe) D. BS with high honors, U. Ill., Urbana, 1965, MS, 1969; PhD, De Paul U., Chgo., 1987. Biological Science. Forensic analytical chemist Chgo. Police Dept., Chgo., 1970-72, asst. head forensic analytical chemist, 1972-74; instr. Ravenswood Hosp. Sch. of Anesthesia, Chgo., 1975—; instr. East-West U., Chgo., 1982-84, dir. biol. and phys. sciences, 1984—; asst. profr. East-West U., 1987-88, assoc. profr., 1988—, dir. electroneurodiagnostic technology program, 1988—; adj. prof. in MS of nursing DePaul U., Chgo., 1989—; speaker Ill. Assn. Nurse Anesthetists, 1978-80, Ill. Soc. of EEG Technicians, 1986-88; sci. cons., speaker Chgo. Tchr's. Ctr., 1989; instr. Chgo. Heart Assn., 1989—. Co-author: Population Genetics A BSCS Self Instructional Prog., 1969. Recipient Research Assistantship Nat. Science Found. U. Ill. 1965-66, Research fellow Nat. Science Found. U. Ill. 1966-70, Schmidt Acad. fellow Schmidt Found. De Paul U. 1975-80. Mem. Phi Beta Kappa. Office: 4042 N Elston Ave Chicago IL 60618

DRAPER, BARBARA ANN, nursing administrator; b. Camden, N.J., July 22, 1943; d. Earl Paul and Ann Florence (Caserta) Bennett; m. Harold C. Draper, Jr., Oct. 24, 1964; children: Kathleen, Patricia. BA in Health Sci., Glassboro (N.J.) State Coll., 1975; MA in Adminstrn., Rider Coll., Lawrenceville, N.J., 1982. RN, N.J. Instr. nursing St. Francis Sch. Nursing, Trenton, N.J., 1970-79; project coord. St. Francis Med. Ctr., Trenton, 1979-82, asst. dir. staff devel., 1982-86, dir. women's health svcs., 1986—. Cofounder, pres. P.A.C.T. (Parents of Amputee Children Together), 1978-80, editor newsletter, 1976-78; trustee Mercer Coun. on Alcoholism and Drug Addiction, 1990—. Recipient Tribute to Women in Industry and Govt. award Trenton YWCA, 1986. Mem. NAFE, Nat. Assn. Dirs. Women's Health Programs, St. Francis Alumna Assn., Glassboro State Coll. Alumni Assn., Rider Coll. Alumni Assn. Office: St Francis Med Ctr 601 Hamilton Ave Trenton NJ 08629

DRAPER, MARY LYTTON, writer; b. Staunton, Va.; d. Julius Sidney and Mary Ellen (Bright) Lytton; m. David W. Draper; children: David W. Jr., Darryl L. BA, Coll. of William and Mary, Williamsburg, Va.; MALS, Georgetown U., postgrad. Freelance writer. Mem. NAFE, Washington Opera Guild, Tamarack Civic Assn., Pi Delta Epsilon, Chi Delta Phi, Psi Chi, Sierra Club. Home and Office: 1602 Northcrest Dr Silver Spring MD 20904

DRASKOVICH, ZLATANA JENNIE, educator; b. Bklyn., Dec. 20, 1948; d. Roy L. and Nancy Corinne (Thompson) Brundidge. BS, Purdue U., Hammond, Ind., 1969, MS in Edn., 1978; MA in German, Purdue U., Lafayette, Ind., 1971. Cert. tchr. German and math. grades 7-12, Ind. Shop math. educator Hammond Vocat.-Tech. High Sch., 1971-78; math. educator Hammond High Sch., 1978-86, Morton Sr. High Sch., Hammond, 1986—. Creator Miniature Egyptian Music Salon, 1984. Judge Sci. Fair Purdue U. Calumet, Hammond, 1970—; sponsor German CLub Hammond Vocat.-Tech. High Sch., 1971-78, Calculator Tournament Ind. U., Gary, 1975—; class sponsor Hammond Pub. Schs., 1972-86; dir. Math Calculator Olympiad, Hammond, 1987—, acad. coach, Hammonds, 1987—; bd. dirs. Bethany Exec. Bd., 1971—, treas., 1978-82. Recipient 10 Years Sci. Fair Judge award Purdue U. Calumet, 1979. Mem. Nat. Council Tchrs. Math., Gary Area Council Tchrs. Math., AAUW (chairperson judges Calumet chpt. 1975—, treas. 1974-76), Am. West Indian Assn., Inc., Purdue Alumni Assn. (life). Serbian Orthodox. Home: 3736 Johnson St Gary IN 46408 Office: Morton Sr High Sch 6915 Grand Ave Hammond IN 46323

DRATTELL, DEBORAH, musical composer. PhD, U. Chgo. Assoc. prof. composition and theory Tuland U.; resident composer Denver Symphony Orch., 1987—. Music dir., conductor: First Monday Contemporary Chamber Ensemble, Vivace Festival; composer: Spanish Fly, Lilith, Fire Dances; featured composer PBS-TV spl. Women in Music; commd. work for Barlow Found., Fromm Found., Concert Artists Guild, New Orleans Symphony, Pitts. New Music Ensemble, AT&T, Denver Symphony, Eastman Sch. Music; worked with Peter Maxwell Davies. Composer/Reader's Digest Commissioning Program grantee, Meet the Composer grantee, NEA grantee, Am. Music Ctr. grantee; Leonard Bernstein fellow, Vt. Composer fellow, Yaddo fellow; appointed to Assoc. Artist Position at the Atlantic Ctr. for the Arts. Office: care Denver Symphony Orch 910 15th St Ste 330 Denver CO 80202

DRAUCKER, CLAIRE BURKE, nursing educator, psychotherapist; b. Amesbury, Mass., July 19, 1955; d. Andrew Martin and Agnes Mary (Minihan) Burke; m. Carl Alexander Draucker, Oct. 8, 1980. BSN summa cum laude, St. Anselm's Coll., Manchester, N.H., 1977; MSN, Boston U., 1978; PhD, Kent State U., 1988. R.N., Ohio. Clin. nurse specialist Concord (Mass.) Area Community Mental Health Ctr., 1978-80; therapist Western Res. Human Svcs., Akron, Ohio, 1981-84; intern in psychology South Shore Community Mental Health Ctr., Quincy, Mass., 1985-86; psychology asst., nurse psychotherapist Office of D.L. Benshoff, Ph.D., Kent, Ohio, 1986—; instr., asst. prof. Kent State U. Sch. Nursing, 1988—. Mem. Am. Psychol. Assn., Midwestern Nursing Rsch. Soc., Ohio Nurses Assn. (Sigma Theta Tau (Delta Xi chpt. faculty counselor 1989—, Peg Schiltz Meml. Rsch. Fund grant 1989). Democrat. Roman Catholic.

DRAZIN, LISA, real estate investment banker, financial consultant; b. Washington, Nov. 26, 1953; d. Sidney and Bernice Ann (Jeweler) D. A.B. with honors, Wellesley Coll., 1976; M.B.A., George Washington U., 1980. Chartered Financial Analyst. Securities analyst Geico, Inc., Chevy Chase, Md., 1982; mng. prin. Jefferson Securities Ltd., Bethesda, Md., 1983; chmn., chief exec. officer Drazin & Co., Inc., Bethesda, 1985—, Drazin Properties, Inc., Bethesda, 1985-89, Drazin Securities, Inc., Bethesda, 1985-88; chmn., chief exec. officer Woodmont Asset Mgmt., Inc., 1989—; affiliate Montgomery County Bd. Realtors; real estate investment banker Restructuring Fed. Deposit Ins. Corp. Founder, Ivy Connection, Washington, 1982. Mem. Nat. Trust for Historic Preservation. Fellow Wexner Heritage Found., Assn. for Investment Mgmt. and Rsch.; mem. Nat. Assn. Realtors, Comml. Investment Real Estate Council, Realtors Nat. Mktg. Inst., Wash. Soc. Investment Analysts, Inc., Beta Gamma Sigma. Club: Wellesley (interns coordinator, recent grads. rep. 1981-84) (Washington). Office: Woodmont Asset Mgmt Inc 6403 Kirby Rd Bethesda MD 20817

DRECHSLER, DOROTHY ROBERTA, nurse; b. Balt., Nov. 9, 1949; d. William Edward and Helen Roberta (Kirkpatrick) Drechsler; m. O. Wayne Bittinger, Jan. 23, 1974 (div. 1977). BA in Am. Studies, U. Md., 1971, BSN, 1974, MS in Nursing, 1983. RN. Med. intensive care nurse U. Md. Hosp.,

Balt., 1974-77, Johns Hopkins Hosp., Balt., 1977-78; coronary care nurse clinician Frances Scott Key Med. Ctr., Balt., 1978-80; cardiac clin. specialist Greater Balt. Med. Ctr., 1980-82; instr. Union Meml. Hosp., Balt., 1982-87; cardiac clin. specialist Harbor Hosp. Ctr., Balt., 1987-90; instr. RN Sch. Nursing-Harbor Hosp. Ctr., 1989. Author: (with others) Myocardial Infarction: A Guide to Patient Education, 1988. Healthsite task force Am. Heart Assn., Balt., 1978—. Mem. Am. Assn. Cardiovascular and Pulmonary Rehab., Am. Holistic Nurses Assn., Sigma Theta Tau. Democrat. Home: 3410 University Pl Baltimore MD 21218 Office: Harbor Hosp Ctr 3001 S Hanover St Baltimore MD 21230

DREHER, NANCY C., federal judge; b. 1942. BA, JD, U. Wis. Admitted to bar, 1967. Bankruptcy judge U.S. Dist. Ct. Minn., Mpls. Office: US Dist Ct 600 Towle Bldg 330 2d Ave S Minneapolis MN 55401*

DRENNAN, DONNA JANE, lawyer; b. Champaign, Ill., Mar. 4, 1944; d. Walter E. and Marcella (Cavanaugh) Judson; children: Judson W., James B. BA, Ind. U., 1965, JD, 1969; LLM, Georgetown U., 1975. Bar: Ind. 1969, D.C. 1971, U.S. Supreme Ct. 1973. Asst. to gen. counsel Fed. Power Commn., Washington, 1972-73; gen. counsel for policy Fed. Property Council, Washington, 1973-74; spl. asst. Fed. Power Commn., Washington, 1974-76; atty. FERC, Washington, 1976-79; ptnr. McDermott, Will & Emery, Washington, 1979-82, Pillsbury, Madison & Sutro, Washington, 1982-88, Wunder, Ryan, Cannon & Thelen, Washington, 1988—. Mem. FERC Transition Team, Pres. Elect Reagan, Wsahington, 1980-81, Presidential Pvt. Sector Task Force, Washington, 1982. Mem. ABA (chmn. adminstrv. law sect., natural resources law and pub. utility law sects.), Fed. Energy Bar Assn. (exec. council 1981-84). Club: Georgetown (Washington). Home: 5801 Hillburne Way Chevy Chase MD 20815 Office: Ross & Hardies 888 16th St NW Ste 300 Washington DC 20006

DRENNON, KAY BYROM, school counselor; b. Cedartown, Ga., Dec. 16, 1949; d. William Lee and Toppy (Hardy) Byrom; m. H.W. Drennon (div. 1976); 1 child, Christine Nicole. BS in Edn., West Ga. Coll., 1971, MEd in Guidance and Counseling, 1975, EdS in Counseling, 1979, EdS in Leadership, 1988. Cert. sch. counselor, Ga. Tchr. Douglas County Schs., Douglasville, Ga., 1971-74; high sch. counselor Cobb County Schs., Marietta, Ga., 1975-78, Floyd County Schs., Rome, Ga., 1978-84; mid. sch. counselor Marietta City Schs., 1984-87, elem. counselor, 1987—; bd. dirs. Learner's Edge, Atlanta; presenter speeches and workshops to profl. orgns. Mem. AACD (chairperson nat. film festival awards com. 1980), ASCD, Ga. Sch. Counselors Assn. (7th dist. Secondary Counselor of Yr. 1980), Ga. Assn. Supervision and Curriculum Devel., Nat. Assn. Neuro Linguistic Programming, Ga. Assn. for Suicide Prevention. Home: 725 Twin Brooks Ct Marietta GA 30067 Office: Pine Forest Sch 311 Aviation Rd SE Marietta GA 30060

DRESCHER, JUDITH ALTMAN, library director; b. Greensburg, Pa., July 6, 1946; d. Joseph Grier and Sarah Margaret (Hewitt) Altman; m. Robert A. Drescher, Aug. 10, 1968 (div. 1980); m. David G. Lindstrom, Jan. 10, 1981. AB, Grove City Coll., 1968; MLS, U. Pitts., 1971. Tchr. Hempfield Sch. Dist., Greensburg, 1968-71; children's libr. Cin. Pub. LIbr., 1971-72; br. mgr. Cin. Pub. LIbrary, 1972-74; dir. Rolling Meadows (Ill.) Pub. Libr., 1974-79, Champaign (Ill.) Pub. Libr., 1979-85, Memphis/Shelby County Pub. Libr. and Info. Ctr., 1985—; cons. HBW Assocs., Dallas, 1986—. mem. Rhodes Coll. Commn. on 21st Century, Memphis, 1986-88, Leadership Memphis, 1987—; bd. dirs. Literacy Coun. Memphis, 1986—, Memphis Literacy Found., 1988—, v.p., 1989-90; bd. dirs. Memphis NCCJ, 1989—, Goals for Memphis, 1988—, chair edn. com., 1989—; mem. allocations subcom. United Way, 1989—; mem. memphis Arts Coun., 1989—; mem. allocations com. 100 for the Arts, 1989—; mem. adv. bd. Children's Mus. Memphis, 1988—; exec. adv. coun. Memphis State U., 1989—; pres. adv. coun. Lemoyne Coll. Recipient Govt. Leader award U. Ill. YWCA, 1981. Mem. ALA (chair intellectual freedom com. 1986-87), Tenn. Library Assn., Memphis Library Council, Beta Phi Mu. Mem. United Ch. of Christ (chair deacons com. 1989—). Lodge: Rotary. Home: 1505 Vance Memphis TN 38104 Office: Memphis Shelby County Pub Libr & Info Ctr 1850 Peabody Ave Memphis TN 38104-4025

DRESS, KATHERINE CHANG, government official; b. Kwenming, People's Republic China, June 22, 1941; came to U.S., 1963; d. Lee-Min and Joan J.Y. (Kao) Han; 1 child, John Peter Chang. Attended, Chung Chi Coll., Hong Kong, 1959-61; BA magna cum laude, Haile Selassie I U., Addis Ababa, Ethiopia, 1963; MA in English Lit., Bryn Mawr Coll., 1965. Lic. real estate agt., Md., D.C., Va. Lectr. English, Community Coll. Phila., 1965-66; reservation saleswoman TWA, Phila., 1967-70; sales rep. TWA, Addis Ababa, 1971-75; info. officer, spl. asst. to sr. civil coord. Inter-Agy. Task Force, Camp Pendleton, Calif., 1975; dep. dir. Nat. Rep. Heritage Groups Coun., Rep. Nat. Com., Washington, 1982; confidential asst. to dep. dir. Minority Bus. Devel. Agy., U.S. Dept. Commerce, Washington, 1983-84; county dir. Peace Corps, Cameroon, 1984-87; dep. asst. sec. for territorial and internat. affairs U.S. Dept. Interior, 1989; confidential advisor to vice chmn. Merit Systems Protection Bd., 1990—; stringer, rep. CBS News, Addis Ababa, 1971-75; producer Radio Voice of Gospel, Addis Ababa, 1971-75, columnist Ethiopian Herald, Addis Ababa, 1971-75; assoc. SAT Internat.; regional mgr. John Kealy Co. Nat. vice chmn. Chinese Ams. for Bush, Entrepreneurs for Bush, Presdl. Campaign/Transition, 1987-88. Recipient cert. of merit for superior performance U.S. Dept. Commerce, 1983, 84, cert. of appreciation for sustained superior performance Peace Corps, 1987; Marguerite N. Farley scholar Bryn Mawr Coll. Mem. NAFE, Nat. Women's Econ. Alliance, Reagan Appointees Alumni Assn., Orgn. Chinese-Am. Women (v.p.).

DRESSEL, DEANE LISETTE, dancer, choreographer; b. Las Cruces, N.Mex., Apr. 24, 1955; d. Ralph William Dressel and Elizabheth Tupper (Taylor) Hoobler; m. Arthur Stephan Bazan, Mar. 24, 1977 (div. June 1982. BFA in Dance, U. N.Mex., 1990. Journeyman's lic. N.Mex. Apprentice electrician Internat. Brotherhood Elec. Workers Local 611, Albuquerque, 1979-82, journeyman electrician, 1982-86; relay technician apprentice Electric Generation & Plains Transmition Coop., Albuquerque, 1983-85; dancer Elizabeth Waters Dance Workshop, Inc., Albuquerque, 1985-89; dancer, choreographer Albuquerque, 1983—; dancer, choreographer Mary Wang Sch. of Dance Benefit Prodns., Grants, N.Mex., 1982-90; pres. U. N.Mex. Dance Club, Albuquerque, 1988-89; dance tchr. Devel. Dance, Albuquerque, 1988-89; mem., choreographer N.Mex. Dance Coalition, Santa Fe, 1989; mem. student prodn. adv. bd. U. N.Mex. Choreographer, dancer: (dances) Wolf Eyes, 1982, Stages, 1985, A Little Plumbing Problem, 1988, Butch Babes Don't Wear Bras, 1989. Mem. Parkland Hills Neighborhood Assn., Albuquerque, 1988-90, ACLU, 1985-90, Greenpeace, 1985-89. Recipient Disting. Undergrad. scholarship U. N.Mex., 1990, Elizabeth Waters scholarship U. N.Mex., 1987-90; named N.Mex. First Woman Journeyman Electrician. Mem. NOW, NAFE, Phi Kappa Phi, Golden Key Nat. Honor Soc. Home and Office: 500 Valverde SE Albuquerque NM 87108

DRESSELHAUS, MILDRED SPIEWAK, physics and engineering educator; b. Bklyn., Nov. 11, 1930; d. Meyer and Ethel (Teichteil) Spiewak; m. Gene F. Dresselhaus, May 25, 1958; children: Marianne Dresselhaus Cooper, Carl Eric, Paul David, Eliot Michael. A.B., Hunter Coll., 1951, D.Sc. (hon.), 1982; Fulbright fellow, Cambridge (Eng.) U., 1951-52; A.M., Radcliffe Coll., 1953; Ph.D. in Physics, U. Chgo., 1958; D. Engring. (hon.), Worcester Poly. Inst., 1976; D.Sc. (hon.), Smith Coll., 1980, Hunter Coll., 1982, N.J. Inst. Tech., 1984; Doctorat Honoris Causa, U. Catholique de Louvain, 1988; DSc (hon.), Rutgers U., 1989. NSF postdoctoral fellow Cornell U., 1958-60; mem. staff Lincoln Lab., MIT, Lexington, 1960-67; prof. elec. engring. MIT, Cambridge, 1967—, assoc. dept. head elec. engring., 1972-74, prof. physics, 1983—, Inst. prof., 1985—, Abby Rockefeller Mauzé chair, 1973-85, dir. Ctr. for Materials Sci. and Engring., 1977-83; vis. prof. dept. physics U. Campinas (Brazil), summer 1971, Technion, Israel Inst. Tech., Haifa, Israel, 1972, 90, Nihon and Aoyama Gakuin Univs., Tokyo, 1973, IVIC, Caracas, Venezuela, 1977; Graffin lectr. Am. Carbon Soc., 1982; chmn. steering com. of evaluation panels Nat. Bur. Standards, 1978-83; mem. Energy Research Adv. Bd., 1984-90; bd. dirs. The Alliance Fund, Rogers Corp., Quantum Chem. Corp. Contbr. articles to profl. jours. Bd. govs. Argonne Nat. Lab., 1986-89; mem. governing bd. NRC, 1984-87, 89—. Named to Hunter Coll. Hall of Fame, 1972; recipient Alumnae medal Radcliffe Coll., 1973, Killian Faculty Achievement award, 1986-87. Fellow Am. Phys. Soc. (pres. 1984), Am. Acad. Arts and Scis., IEEE, AAAS (bd. dirs. 1985-89); mem. Nat. Acad. Engring. (council 1981-87), Soc. Women Engrs. (Achievement award 1977), Nat. Acad. Scis. (council 1987-90, chmn. engring. sect. 1987-90); corr. mem. Brazilian Acad. Sci. Office: MIT Rm 13-3005 Cambridge MA 02139

DRESSENDOFER, JO-ANNE, telecommunications company executive; b. Phila., Feb. 10, 1960; d. Joseph and Helene (Kantor) D. BA, Rutgers U., 1982. Sales dir. Graphic Media, Fairfield, N.J.; v.p. Carter Communications, Liberty Corner, N.J.; pres. IMEDIA, Inc., Morristown, N.J. Mem. NAFE, Sigma Delta Chi. Office: 93 Washington St Morristown NJ 07960

DRESSLER, BRENDA JOYCE, sex educator, consultant; b. N.Y.C., Jan. 30, 1943; d. Herbert and Betty (Kirshner) Dressler; m. Irving Kaufman, Dec. 30, 1961 (div. Dec. 1979); 1 child, Joshua Ari. BA, CCNY, 1964; MA, CUNY, 1969; PhD, NYU, 1986. Cert. health edn. specialist, sex educator. Educator sex and health N.Y.C. Bd. Edn., 1964-75, 1979—, Sex Info. and Edn. Coun. U.S., N.Y.C., 1985-86, Bd. Edn., N.Y.C., 1979—; Queens regional coord. family living, sex edn. Bd. Edn., 1990—90; cons. PTA and Curriculum Adv. Com. Steinway Jr. High Sch., N.Y.C., 1985-87, Bayside High Sch., 1987-90; coord. and cons. on family living, 1990—. Columnist: Women Mean Business; contbr. numerous articles to profl. jours. Mem. Am. Assn. Sex Educators, Counselors and Therapists (cert.), Sex Info. and Edn. Council Am., Soc. for Sci. Study of Sex, Am. Pub. Health Assn., Kappa Delta Pi. Home: 162-41 Powells Cove Blvd Whitestone NY 11357

DREUX, JOAN ALBERT, insurance company executive; b. New Rochelle, N.Y., Aug. 14, 1951; d. John Hess and Martha Jane (Morrissey) Albert; m. Mark Stewart Dreux, Sr.; 1 child, Erin; 1 stepson, Mark Stewart, Jr. BA magna cum laude, Georgetown U., 1973; MPA, NYU, 1976. Adminstrv. asst. Household Fin. Corp., Washington, 1974; legislative rep. AVCO Corp., Washington, 1976-78; exec. dir. govt. affairs Nat. Assn. of Casualty and Surety Agts., Washington, 1978-87; v.p. Fed. Legislative and Regulatory Affairs Mut. of Omaha, Washington, 1987-90. Pres. Citizens Crusade for Land Use Integrity, Herndon, Va., 1989, Sugarland Valley Fedn., Herndon/Reston, 1990—; v.p. bd. dirs. Shaker Woods Homeowners Assn., 1989—; profl. lobbyist, fundraiser, mem. steering com. numerous congressional campaigns. Mem. Women in Govt. Relations, Women in Health Ins., Jaycees, Phi Beta Kappa, Gamma Phi Epsilon. Roman Catholic. Home: 1287 Stuart Rd Herndon VA 22070 Office: Mutual of Omaha 1700 Penn Ave NW Washington DC 20006

DREW, BETTY BERG, parliamentarian, civic worker; b. Green Bay, Wis., May 27, 1929; d. Walter Richard and Viola Marion (Holz) Berg; m. Dale Robert Drew, June 3, 1950; children—Laura Jane, John Robert, Thomas Richard, James Berg. Diploma in Nursing, Wesley Meml. Hosp. Sch. Nursing, 1950. Registered profl. parliamentarian, Mich. Judge for high sch. parliamentary competitions, local, state and nat. levels, Mich., 1978—; organizer coalition of State Organ Donor Agencies, Ann Arbor, Mich., 1982-88; lectr. for parliamentary unit Oakland-Birmingham, Mich., 1983—. Officer PTO, Bloomfield Hills, Mich., 1970, 77; moderator North Ch., 1987—; mem. Bloomfield Republican Women's Club. Mem. AMA Aux. (speaker of house 1984-86), Mich. State Assn. Parliamentarians (officer 1983—), Nat. Assn. Parliamentarians, Mich. State Med. Soc. Aux. (pres. 1983-84), Women's Nat. Farm and Garden Assn. (Vernor br. pres. 1977-78), P.E.O. (pres. chpt. 1985-87). Republican. Congregationalist. Avocations: Golf; knitting; sewing; bridge; piano. Home: 4454 Barchester Dr Bloomfield Hills MI 48013

DREW, ELIZABETH, television commentator, journalist; b. Cin., Nov. 16, 1935; d. William J. and Estelle (Jacobs) Brenner; m. J. Patterson Drew, Apr. 11, 1964 (dec. 1970); m. David Webster, Sept. 26, 1981. B.A., Wellesley Coll., 1957; L.H.D., Hood Coll., 1976, Yale U., 1976, Trinity Coll., 1978, Reed Coll., 1979, Williams Coll., 1981; LL.D., Georgetown U., 1981. Writer editor Congl. Quar., 1959-64; free lance writer, 1964-67; Washington editor Atlantic Monthly, 1967-73; host TV interview program Thirty Minutes With, 1971-73; commentator TV program Agronsky and Company, 1973—; commentator syndicated TV program now called Inside Washington, 1973—; corr. New Yorker Mag., Washington, 1973—. Author: Washington Journal, 1975; American Journal, 1977; Senator, 1979; Portrait of An Election, 1981; Politics and Money, 1983; Campaign Journal, 1985, Election Journal, 1989; contbg. author various mags. and jours. Recipient award for excellence Soc. Mag. Writers, 1971, Wellesley Alumnae Achievement award, 1973, DuPont award, 1973, Mo. medal, 1979, Sidney Hillman award, 1983, Ambassador of Honor award Books Across the Sea, 1984, Literary Lion award N.Y. Pub. Library, 1985, Edward Weintal prize, 1988. Home: 3000 Woodland Dr Washington DC 20008 Office: 1717 Massachusetts Ave NW Rm LL220 Washington DC 20036

DREW, ELIZABETH HEINEMAN, publishing executive; b. Evanston, Ill., Aug. 26, 1940; d. Ben Harlow and Marion Elizabeth (Heineman) D. BA, U. Wis., 1961. With Doubleday & Co., Inc., N.Y.C., 1961-84, prodn. asst., 1961-63, personal asst. to editor in chief, 1963-66, adminstrv. asst. to editor in chief, 1963-69, editorial asst. to editor in chief, 1969-71, assoc. editor, 1971-74, editor, 1974-77, sr. editor, 1977-79, exec. editor, editorial dir., 1979-84; v.p., sr. editor William Morrow and Co., N.Y.C., 1984—; tchr. NYU Sch. Continuing Edn., 1981-82. Mem. PEN (N.Y. chpt.), Women's Media Group (treas. 1982-84, pres. 1985-86), Nat. Press Club (Washington), Assn. Am. Pubs. (internat. freedom to pub. com. 1978—, chmn. 1990—, mem. freedom to read com. 1988—). Democrat. Episcopalian. Office: William Morrow & Co Inc 105 Madison Ave New York NY 10016

DREW, JUDITH LOWERY, rehabilitation counselor; b. Providence, Dec. 23, 1950; d. Paul Wesley and Lela Marie (Richart) Lowery; m. Robert M. Jr. Drew, Aug. 25, 1973; 1 child, Jonathan. BA, R.I. Coll., Providence, 1976, MA, 1985. Cert. rehab. counselor. Tchr. spl. edn. Harmony High Sch., Chepachet, R.I., 1976-80; trainer Job Corps U.S. Dept Labor, Washington, 1980-82; dir. vocat. rehab. Mental Health Svcs., Johnston, R.I., 1984-88; counselor rehab. ConServ Co., Swansea, Mass., 1988-89, Rehab. & Re-Employment, Providence, 1989—; adj. faculty Assumption Coll., Worcester, Mass., 1985—; cons. Blackstone Valley Assn. Retarded Citizens, Pawtucket, R.I., 1987, New Bedford (Mass.) Ctr. Human Svcs., 1989-90. Vice-pres. Johnston (R.I.) C. of C., 1986-87; den leader Cub Scouts Am., Cumberland, R.I., 1989-90. Grantee State of R.I., 1986, U.S. HHS, 1987. Mem. Nat. Rehab. Assn., R.I. Rehab. Assn. (v.p. 1986-87). Baptist. Office: Reahab & Re-Employment 1 Richmond Sq Providence RI 02906

DREW, JUDY MORINE, life insurance executive; b. Chgo., June 26, 1951; d. Paul Raymond and Vurnis Gwendolyn (Dudley) Jonns; m. Douglas C. Drew, July 6, 1979; children: Michael, Kelly. Student, No. Ill. U., 1969-73. Libr. Eisenhower Jr. High Sch., Darien, Ill., 1973-74; mgr. regional mktg. office Aetna Life Casualty, Glen Ellyn, Ill., 1974-77; mgr. CNA Life and Annuity Co., Chgo., 1977-82; dir. Kemper Investors Life, Chgo., 1982-86; v.p. Xerox Life, Lisle, Ill., 1986—. Fundraiser Am. Cancer Soc., Wheaton, Ill., 1986-87. Mem. Inst. Cert. Fin. Planners, Network Industry Info. Exch. Roman Catholic. Home: 655 Riford Rd Glen Ellyn IL 60137 Office: Xerox Life 1001 Warrenville Rd Lisle IL 60532

DREW, K., human resource consultant; b. Freeport, N.Y., Feb. 6, 1939; d. Harry P. and Kathleen (Isdal) Barton; m. Peter Pantazes; children: Karen, Donna. BA, U. Ga., 1960; postgrad., U. Ill., 1961. Dir. YWCA, Corpus Christi, Tex., 1969-72, Dwoskin Nat. Wallcovering Co., Atlanta, 1974-76; dep. asst. fin. presdl. campaign, 1976-77; dir. fin. Presdl. Inaugural, Washington, 1976; dep. adv. for small bus. SBA, Washington, 1977-80, asst. to adminstr., 1980-82; v.p. Alpha Systems, Inc., Washington and Athens, Greece, 1980-85; human resource cons. MBA Mgmt., Inc., McLean, Va., 1982-84; bus. cons. Drew Cons., McLean, 1984-86; cons. assoc. Walling, June & Assocs., Old Town Alexandria, Va., 1986—. State rep. poverty program and suicide prevention bds. Corpus Christi Bus. Coun., 1969-71; bd. dirs. YWCA, Washington, 1983-385; head speaker's bur. Fairfax Symphony, 1979-85, mem. exec. devel. com., 1979-86; memm. Mental Health Exec. Bd. Dirs., Washington, 1983-88; deacon Nat. Presbyn. Ch., Washington, 1988—; asst. to exec. dir. T. Monk Found. Jazz Sch., Duke U., 1987-89; event dir. Easter Seal Soc., 1990—; mem. youth for tomorrow devel. com. Joe Gibbs Charities, Washington, 1990. Mem. Nat. League Am. Pen Women (v.p., pres. Washington Capital chpt. 1987-79, nat. bd. dirs. 1987—, nat. roster chmn. 1989—), Bus. and Profl. Women WWashington, Nat. Platform Assn., Alpha Gamma Delta. Office: 8350 Greensboro Dr Ste 1-121 McLean VA 22101

DREW, KATHERINE FISCHER, history educator; b. Houston, Sept. 24, 1923; d. Herbert Herman and Martha (Holloway) Fischer; m. Ronald Farinton Drew, July 27, 1951. B.A., Rice Inst., 1944, M.A., 1945; Ph.D., Cornell U., 1950. Instr. history Rice U., 1946-48; asst. history Cornell U., 1948-50; mem. faculty Rice U., 1950—, prof. history, 1964—, Harris Masterson, Jr. prof. history, 1983-85, Lynette S. Autrey prof. history, 1985—, chmn. dept. history, 1970-80; editor Rice U. (Rice U. Studies), 1967-81, acting dean humanities and social scis., 1973. Author: The Burgundian Code, 1949, Studies in Lombard Institutions, 1956, The Lombard Laws, 1973, Law and Society in Early Medieval Europe, 1988; editor: Perspective in Medieval History, 1963, The Barbaraian Invasions, 1970; also articles; bd. editors: Am. Hist. Rev., 1982-85, AHA Guide to Hist. Lit., 1987—; contbr.: Life and Thought in the Middle Ages, 1967. Guggenheim fellow, 1959; Fulbright scholar, 1965; NEH Sr. fellow, 1974-75. Fellow Mediaeval Acad. Am. (coun. 1974-77, 2d v.p. to pres. 1985-87, del. to Am. Coun. Learned Socs. 1977-81); mem. Am. Hist. Assn. (coun. 1983-86), Am. Soc. Legal History, So. Hist. Assn. (vice chair, chair European sect. 1986-88, exec. com. 1989-90), Phi Beta Kappa. Home: 509 Buckingham Houston TX 77024

DREWERY, IDA MAE MOORE, health science facility administrator; b. Munson, Fla., Nov. 15, 1927; d. Isaiah Moore and Gertrude (Flowers) Johnson; divorced; children: Marcalene R. Dickerson, Edward Aubrey McBride. Grad. high sch., Pensacola, Fla. Comml. cook Kings Nursing Home, Detroit, 1958-66; supr., machine operator McCarthy Plastic Co., Detroit, 1966-74; adminstr. adult foster care home Detroit Dept. Social Services, 1974—. Mem. Women of Concerned Citizens, Detroit, 1984—, Mus. of African Am. Hist., fund raiser, 1965—. Named Provider of Yr., State of Mich., 1940; recipient Resolution County of Wayne, Mich., 1947. Home: 731 E Grand Blvd Detroit MI 48207

DREXLER, CARYL RING, insurance agent; b. Macomb, Ill., Aug. 15, 1951; d. John Richard and Kathryn Jane (Luck) Ring; m. Thomas Michael Drexler, July 12, 1975 (div. 1989); children: Kathryn Marie, Anna Elizabeth. Student, Stephens Coll., 1969-71. Sales assoc. A.L. Ring & Son, Macomb, 1965-71; buyer A.L. Ring & Son, 1971-80, ptnr., 1980-88; vol. coord. Vols. for McMillan, Macomb, 1988; friends coord. CONVOCOM, Macomb, 1989; ins. agt. Profl. Mktg. Systems Inc., Macomb, 1989; bd. dirs. McDonough County Tourism Coun., Macomb, Mayor's Adv. Coun. Bd. dirs. Macomb Area Indsl. Devel. Corp., 1987; dinner dance chair McDonough County United Way, Macomb, 1986-88; lunch chair Arthritis Found., Quincy, Ill., 1989; vol. leader Two Rivers coun. Girl Scouts U.S., Macomb, 1986; precinct committeeman McDonough County Rep. Cen. Com., Macomb, 1987-89; 6th Ward alderman Macomb City Coun., 1989-93. Recipient Mayor's Key to the City, Macomb, 1980, Mayor's Award for Outstanding community Svc., Macomb, 1981, 89. Mem. NAFE, Macomb Area C. of C. (pres. 1988), McDonough County Rep. Women (ways and means chair 1986-89). Lutheran. Home: 234 W Adams Macomb IL 61455 Office: Profl Mktg Systems Inc PO Box 412 Macomb IL 61455

DREXLER, MARY SANFORD, management; b. Pontiac, Mich., Apr. 19, 1954; d. Arthur H. and Kathryn S. (Sherda) Sanford; m. Brian Day, 1975 (div. 1978); m. York Drexler, 1980. BS, Eastern Mich. U., Ypsilanti, 1976, MA, 1979; postgrad., Walsh Coll., Troy, Mich., 1983. CPA, Mich. Spl. edn. tchr. Oakland Schs., Pontiac, Mich., 1976-83; staff auditor Coopes & Lybrand, Det., 1983-84; sr. auditor Cooper & Lybrand, Det., Mich., 1984-86; asst. controller Webasto Sunroofs Inc., Rochester Hills, 1986-88; controller Infalfa Hollandia Inc., Farmington Hills, Mich., 1988--; bd. dirs. Council for Exceptional Children, Oakland County 1976--83. Bd. Dirs. Neighborhood Civic Assn., Troy Mich. 1986--. Mem. Nat. Assn. Accts. Oakland County, Mich. Assn. CPA Mich. Office: Inalfa Hollandia Inc 26700 Haggerty Rd Farmington Hills MI 48331

DREYFUSS, NANCY MATIS, speech pathologist; b. Chgo., Sept. 20, 1954; d. Jacob David and Rosalie Bette (Metzger) Matis; m. David Michael Dreyfuss, June 7, 1987. B.A., Columbia U., 1976; M.S., Tchrs. Coll., Columbia U., 1978. Staff speech pathologist diagnosis, program planning, treatment of multiply handicapped pre-sch.-age children St. Agnes Hosp., White Plains, N.Y., 1978-82; sr. speech pathologist infant/toddler devel. program North Shore Univ. Hosp., Westbury, N.Y., 1982-88; pvt. practice speech therapy, 1983—. Chmn. Young Adults Forum, Congregation Rodeph Sholom, 1983-87. Mem. N.Y. Speech and Hearing Assn., Am. Speech and Hearing Assn. (cert. clin. competence), N.Y.C. Speech/Lang./Hearing Assn. Home and Office: 25 Central Park W New York NY 10023

DREYFUSS, PATRICIA, chemist researcher; b. Reading, Pa., Apr. 28, 1932; d. Edmund T. and Anna J. (Oberc) Gajewski; m. M. Peter Dreyfuss, Jan. 30, 1954; children: David Daniel, Simeon Karl. BS Chemistry, U. Rochester, 1954; PhD, U. Akron, 1964. Postdoctoral fellow U. Liverpool (Eng.), 1963-65; rsch. chemist BF Goodrich, Brecksville, Ohio, 1965-71; rsch. assoc. Case Western Res. U., Cleve., 1971-73, sr. rsch. assoc., 1973-74; rsch. assoc. Inst. Polymers Sci., U. Akron (Ohio), 1974-84; sr. rsch. scientist, rsch. prof. Mich. Molecular Inst., Midland, Mich., 1984—; vis. rsch. fellow U. Bristol, 1972; cons. in field, 1974—; vis. prof. Polish Acad. Scis., Poland, 1974; adj. prof. Cen. Mich. U., Mich. Tech. U., Mt. Pleasant, Mich., Houghton, Mich., 1986—. Author: Poly (Tetrahydrofuran), 1982; contbr. articles to profl. jours.; co-author books; patentee in field. Flutist West Suburban Philharmonic Orch., Lakewood, Ohio, 1969-75, Explorer advisor Explorer post 2069 Boy Scouts Am., Akron, 1975-81; sec., bd. dirs. Adhesion Soc., 1976-88; treas. LWV, 1959-60; mem. ensemble Blessed Sacrament Ch., Midland, Mich., occasional flute soloist. Centennial scholar U. Rochester, 1950-54; Sohio fellow U. Akron, 1960, NSF Coop. Grad. fellow, 1961-63, NIH Spl. fellow, 1972-73. Mem. Am. Chem. Soc. (cen. region meeting chmn. 1984-90, loc. sec. chmn., vice chmn., sec. and bd. dirs. Akron chpt. 1974-84, bd. dirs. Midland chpt. 1985—, Outstanding Leadership Performance award 1981, Disting. Svc. award Akron chpt. 1985), AAUW (bd. dirs. Akron chpt., Internat. fellow 1964-65). Home: 3980 Old Pine Trail Midland MI 48640 Office: Mich Molecular Inst 1910 W St Andrews Rd Midland MI 48640

DRILLETTE, ELYSA JEAN, naval officer; b. Danvers, Mass., Feb. 9, 1960; d. Harold James and Barbara (Teel) McD.; m. Thomas Ray Drillette, Sept. 1, 1985; 1 child, Casey Haller. BSE in Indsl. Engring. cum laude, U. Mich., 1982. Designated naval aviator tactical jets A-7 Corsair. Commd. ensign USN, 1982, advanced through grades to lt., 1986, lt. tactical electronic warfare squadron, 1986-88, comdr.naval air forces, hdqrs. staff, 1988—. Recipient numerous awards. Mem. U. Mich. Alumni Assn., Tail Hook Assn., World Affairs Coun. San Diego, Assn. Women Pilots, Commercial Pilot. Roman Catholic. Office: CNAP Code 33 NASNI San Diego CA 92135-5100

DRILLMAN, PAULA, advertising agency executive. PhD in Psychology. Exec. v.p., dir. strategic planning & rsch. McCann-Erickson/NY. Office: McCann-Erickson/NY 750 3d Ave New York NY 10017*

DRISCOLL, SISTER BRIGID, college president; b. N.Y.C.; d. Daniel Driscoll and Delia Duffy. B in Math., Edn., Marymount Manhattan Coll., 1954; M in Math., Cath. U., 1957; PhD in Math., CUNY, 1967; EdD (hon.), Siena Coll. Joined Religious of Sacred Heart of Mary, Roman Cath. Ch., 1954. Prof. math., assoc. acad. dean, dir. continuing edn. Marymount Coll., Tarrytown, N.Y., founder Weekend Coll., 1975, pres., 1979—; mem. Commr. of Edn.'s Adv. Council on Post-Secondary Edn. in N.Y. State; trustee Commn. on Ind. Colls. and Univs. Bd. dirs. Girl Scouts U.S., Phelps Meml. Hosp. Ctr., North Tarrytown, N.Y., Axe-Houghton Funds; bd. dirs. Westchester/Putnam chpt. United Way, mem. nat. vol. involvement com. 2d Century Initiative; mem. Statue of Liberty/Ellis Island Commn.; trustee Marymount Sch., N.Y.C. Named Woman of Yr. Sleepy Hollow C. of C., 1982; honored for disting. service Westchester (N.Y.) chpt. NCCJ; NASA fellow, 1967. Mem. Assn. Cath. Colls. and Univs. (bd. dirs., chairwoman Neylan Commn.), Commn. on Ind. Colls. and Univs. (trustee). Office: Marymount Coll Office of Pres Tarrytown NY 10591-3796*

DRISCOLL, DAWN-MARIE, lawyer; b. Framingham, Mass., Nov. 5, 1946; d. Paul Francis and Wanda Louise (Haznar) D.; m. Norman Marcus, Apr. 8, 1978; 1 child, Christopher Marcus. BA, Regis Coll., 1968; JD, Suffolk U., 1973. Bar: Mass. 1973. Asst. counsel Mass. Senate, Boston, 1973-78; counsel William Filene's Sons Co., Boston, 1978-80, v.p., counsel, 1980—; mem. adv. council div. employment security State of Mass., 1985—; bd. dirs., mem. exec. com, v.p. Boston Mcpl. Research Bur., 1978—; lectr. Law Sch., Suffolk U., 1975, Law Sch., Boston Coll., 1976; bd. dirs. New Eng. Legal Found., Boston, 1980-85. Trustee, mem. exec. com. Regis Coll., Weston, Mass., 1983—; trustee, bd. dirs. Roxbury Community Coll. Found., 1985—; mem. Mass. Gov.'s Commn. on Mature Industries, 1983-84; bd. dirs. Downtown Crossing Assn., Boston, 1980—, chmn., 1980-83; bd. dirs. Better Bus. Bur., 1984, Social Policy Research Group, 1985—. Mass. grad. legis. fellow, Boston, 1969-70. Mem. ABA, Boston Bar Assn. (council 1981-84, subcom. chmn. corp. counsel com. 1980-82), Mass. Bar Assn., Mass. Assn. Mental Health (bd. dirs. 1985—), Boston C. of C. (co-chmn. Ctr. City task force 1980-82). Clubs: Boston, Union. Office: Palmer & Dodge 1 Beacon St Boston MA 02108

DRIVER, CHERYL ANNE, software specialist; b. Shirley, Mass., Nov. 1, 1954; d. Henry and Rita Louise (DiBenedetto) Lord; m. Thomas Piche, 1974 (div. 1975); m. Larry Dwaine Driver, Apr. 1, 1984 (div. June 1989); children: Brandon James, Alicia Marie (dec.). Student, Pikes Peak Community Coll., 1983, Regis Coll., Colorado Springs. Shipfitter Gen. Dynamics, North Kingstown, R.I., 1974-76; planner Gen. Dynamics, North Kingstown, 1976-81; electronics tech. Digital Equipment Corp., Colorado Springs, Colo., 1983-86; customer response Digital Equipment Corp., Colorado Springs, 1986-88, software specialist, tech. instr., 1988—. Office: Digital Equipment Corp 305 Rockrimmon Blvd Colorado Springs CO 80919

DRIVER, SHARON HUMPHREYS, marketing executive; b. Staten Island, N.Y., Jan. 5, 1949; d. William Edward and Gloria Patra (McCrave) Humphreys; m. William Weston Driver, Jr., June 3, 1972; children: Christopher John, Andrea Nicole. BA, Manhattanville Coll., Purchase, N.Y., 1970; MA, Coll. New Rochelle (N.Y.), 1973. Lic. tchr., N.Y. Tchr. Somers (N.Y.) Cen. Sch. Dist., 1970-76, Ossining (N.Y.) Village Recreation Dept., 1983-87; media coord./bookkeeper Equation Communications, White Plains, N.Y., 1986-89; media dir. Sims Freeman O'Brien, Elmsford, N.Y., 1989—. Trainer/facilitator Jr. League, Tarrytown, N.Y., 1987-88; sustainer, past sec. tng. liaison Jr. League Westchester-On-Hudson, 1982—; pres. Parish Coun. St. Teresa's, Briarcliff Manor, N.Y.; sec. bd. dirs. Ossining Open Door Health Clinic, 1985-89. Mem. Women in Communications. Roman Catholic. Home: 197 Macy Rd Briarcliff Manor NY 10510

DROEGKAMP, JANIS MILDRED, experiential learning educator, consultant; b. Milw., Mar. 8, 1946; d. Harold John and Geraldine Delores (Zimmerman) Droegkamp; 1 child, John Steven. BS, Carroll Coll., 1968; MEd, Marquette U., Milw., 1971; EdD, U. Mass., 1982. Cert. sch. counselor, Wis. Elem. tchr. New Berlin (Wis.) Pub. Schs., 1969-70; tchr. trainer Ch. Tchrs. Coll. Peace Corps, Mandeville, Jamaica, 1972-74; sr. edn. officer Ministry of Edn. Peace Corps, Maseru, Lesotho, 1974-77; evaluation cons. self reliance project World Bank, Maseru, 1975, 77, 80; trainer, instr. ctr. for internat. edn. U. Mass., Amherst, 1978-84, project adminstr., 1981-82; tng. project dir. Peace Corps, Kenya, Fiji, U.S.A., 1982-84; tng. cons. ctr. for tng. and assessment Peace Corps, Washington, 1982—; assoc. prof. Sangamon State U., Springfield, Ill., 1985—; tng. cons. Ministry of Edn., Bangkok, Thailand, 1979, Ill. Coalition Against Domestic Violence, Springfield, 1988, Ounce of Prevention, Chgo., Springfield, 1988—; assessment coord. Peace Corps, Nairobi, Kenya, 1983. Co-author: Women-Centered Training, 1979, Peace Corps Center for Reassessment and Training Manual, 1984. V.p. for edn. Parents Without Partners, Springfield, 1987-88; bd. dirs. Montessori Children's House, 1989—. Recipient scholarship U.S. Agy. for Internat. Devel., 1980. Mem. NOW (organizer Amherst chpt. 1982), Nat. Women's Studies Assn., Nat. Coun. Returned Peace Corps Vols., Coun. Adult and Experiential Learning (institutional), Phi Delta Kappa, Alpha Delta Kappa. Unitarian. Office: Sangamon State U Shephard Rd Springfield IL 62794-9243

DROLC, LUANN, management consultant; b. Chgo., Feb. 1, 1955; d. Louis and Anne (Miller) D.; m. Christopher G. Fortune, June 4, 1988. Student, U. Chgo., 1972-74; BA, San Francisco State U., 1977; postgrad., U. Calif., 1978-79. Tour escort Trade Wind Tours, San Francisco, 1976-77; travel agt. Bulanti Travel, Redwood City, Calif., 1977-78; automation specialist United Airlines, San Francisco, 1978-85; ops. mgr. Ambassador Travel, Santa Clara, Calif., 1985; cons. dir. Sontag Annis & Assocs., Rockville, Md., 1985-87; v.p. Citicorp Info. Mgmt. Svcs., Rockville, 1987-89, mgmt. cons., 1989—. Pres. Am. Bus. Woman's Assn., San Francisco, 1984-85; vol. Lighthouse for the Blind, San Francisco, 1978-84; advisor Jr. Achievement, San Francisco, 1979-81. Democrat. Roman Catholic. Home: 5305 Broad Branch Rd Washington DC 20015 Office: Consulting Svcs 5305 Broad Br Rd Washington DC 20015

DROSSEL, NORLEN ELTOFT, lawyer; b. San Mateo, Calif., Jan. 8, 1944; d. Norman J. and Helen (Eltoft) D.; m. Robert P. Anderson, Nov. 22, 1977; 1 child, Signe Anderssel. AB, U. Calif., Berkeley, 1965; JD, San Francisco Law Sch., 1979; LLM, Golden Gate U., 1985. Bar: Calif. 1979. Law clk. to superior ct. judge San Francisco, 1978-79; ptnr. Law Offices Anderson & Drossel, Berkeley, 1980—; judge/referee pro tem Alameda County Superior Ct., Oakland, Calif., 1988—; panel mem. Ct. Appointed Atty. Juvenile Ct., Berkeley, 1980—. Author: (jour.) Tax Exchange, 1986; editor: (newsletter) Women Lawyers, Alameda County, 1981-83. Bd. dirs. ARC, Oakland, 1985—; mem. com. Alta Bates Hosp., Berkeley, 1988—. Mem. Berkeley-Algany Bar Assn. (past bd. dirs.), Alameda County Bar Assn., Women Lawyers Alameda County (past bd. dirs.). Democrat. Home: 933 Shattuck Ave Berkeley CA 94707 Office: Law Off Anderson & Drossel 2150 Shattuck Ave 810 Berkeley CA 94704

DROUKAS, ANN HANTIS, management executive; b. Boston, Aug. 27, 1923; d. Charles George and Paula (Kanaris) Hantis; m. Peter Droukas Jr., Sept. 28, 1941; children: P. Ronald, Paulette D., Roger C. Grad. high sch., Roxbury, Mass. With Droukas Cut Sole, Inc., Brockton, Mass., 1947—, pres., treas., 1985—; with DBA Drew Leather, Brockton, 1985—; pres., treas. DBA Campello Tanning, Brockton, 1985—. Contbr. to translater textbooks from Spanish and Greek to English. Past adult participant, Boy Scouts Am., Girl Scouts U.S.; mem. Two/Ten Nat. Found., Mothers Club, Brockton Art Mus. Mem. The Two/Ten Natl. Found. New England Tanners Club, Shoe and Leather Club of Cinc., Natl. Federn. of Ind. Bus., Assoc. Ind. of Mass., USA C. of C., Order of Eastern Star. Mem. Nat. Fedn. Ind. Bus., Greek Ladies Philophotos Soc. (past treas.), Brockton Hist. Soc., Assn. Industries Mass., U.S. C. of C., Order Ea. Star. New Eng. Tanners Club, Shoe & Leather Club Cin. Office: 98 Spark St Brockton MA 02402

DROZDA, HELEN DOROTHY, psychiatric social worker; b. Omaha, Mar. 21, 1924; d. Joseph J. and Mary E. (Sabatka) D.;. BS, U. Nebr., 1955; MS, So. Ill. U., 1965; postgrad., Tex. Tech U., 1969, Midwestern U., 1968-69; PhD, Colo. State Christian Coll., 1973. Diplomate Clin. Social Workers; cert. social worker, advanced clin. practitioner, Tex., rehab. counselor. Supervising group counselor San Diego Probation Dept., 1956-57; health edn. dir. YWCA, Omaha, 1954-56; Y-teen dir. YWCA, Alton, Bloomington and Peoria, Ill., 1958-62; guidance dir. Acad. of Our Lady, Peoria, 1962-64, St. Teresa Acad., East St. Louis, Ill., 1964-67, Knox County Pub. Schs., Benjamin, Tex., 1967-69, Wilbarger County Pub. Schs., Vernon, Tex., 1969-70; exec. dir. Burk Guidance and Counseling Services, Burkburnett, Tex., 1970-86; social service supr. Western unit Wichita Falls State Hosp., Burkburnett, Tex., 1970-86. Named Social Worker of Yr., 1984. Mem. Am. Legion, Air Force Assn., Am. Guidance and Personnel Assn., Nat. Assn. Social Workers (past chmn. Red River unit, diplomate), Midwest Soc. Individual Psychology, Tex. Pub. Employees Assn., Tex. Social Psychotherapy Assn., Acad. Certified Social Workers, Nat. Rifle Assn., Am. Assn. Ret. Persons. Home: 820 Sheppard Rd Burkburnett TX 76354 Office: Burk Guidance and Counseling Burkburnett TX 76354

DRUCKER, MINDY M., editor, writer; b. Newark, Apr. 25, 1957; d. Burton and Shirley Drucker; m. Richard Gold, Apr. 30, 1989. BA, Rutgers U., 1979; diploma, NYU, 1983. Assoc. editor Time Capsule, Inc., N.Y.C., 1979-80; proofreader, editor Grolier Inc./The Scarecrow Press, Metuchen, N.J., 1980-83; copy editor spl. publs. House Beautiful mag., N.Y.C., 1983-86; mng. editor Hotel and Resort Industry mag., N.Y.C., 1986-87; copy editor Colonial Homes mag., N.Y.C., 1987-89; mng. editor Target Mktg., Phila., 1989—. Co-author: Recipes for Surfaces: A Guide to Decorative Painting Techniques, 1990; contbr. articles to various mags. Office: North American Pub Co 401 N Broad St Philadelphia PA 19108

DRUECKE, JACQUELINE PAULA, advertising executive; b. Hammond, Ind., Oct. 27, 1957; d. Jacob Paul and Antionette (Esplandiu) Schmidt; m. Charles Scott Druecke, Aug. 18, 1979. BS in Psychology, U. Wis., 1979. Asst. to controller Hoffman York & Compton, Milw., 1981-82, media planner, supr., 1982-87, assoc. media dir., 1987-88, v.p., media dir., 1988—; Mem. mktg. adv. com. MATC, 1989—. Co. rep. United Way, Milw., 1988. Recipient 2d place Addy award, 1988.

DRUFENBROCK, DIANE JOYCE, mathematics educator, computer consultant; b. Evansville, Ind., Oct. 7, 1929; d. George Lehning and Bessie Julia (Litmer) D. BA in Math. and Biology, Alverno Coll., Milw., 1953; MS in Math., Marquette U., Milw., 1959; PhD in Math., U. Ill., 1962; grad., Inst. Retraining Computer Sci., 1986; postgrad., St. Mary-of-the-Woods Coll., Ind., 1989—. Tchr. St. Matthias Sch., Milw., 1951-52, Sacred Heart Sch., Lombard, Ill., 1952-57; tchr. math. St. Joseph High Sch., Kenosha, Wis., 1957-59; prof. math. Alverno Coll., 1962-74; co-dir. Walker Point House, Milw., 1974-79; tchr. math. St. Joan Antida High Sch., Milw., 1979-80; lectr. U. Wis.-Parkside, Racine, 1980-81; prof. math. St. Mary-of-the-Woods Coll., 1981—, computer cons., 1986—. Contbr. articles to profl. jours. Nat. treas. Socialist Party, U.S.A., N.Y.C., 1977—, mem. nat. com., 1980—; candidate for U.S. vice pres., 1980; computer cons. Mountain Women's Exchange, Jellico, Tenn., 1989—; dir. parent union Higher Edn. Act, Title I, Milw., 1975-78; dir. Eugene V. Debs Found., 1981-83. NSF fellow 1960-61. Mem. Sch. Sisters St. Francis (provincial 1970-72), Math. Assn. Am. (regional gov. 1965-66), Am. Math. Soc., Franciscans for Socialism, Coll. Community Orch. Roman Catholic. Home: 1350 Elm St Terre Haute IN 47807 Office: St Mary-of-the-Woods Coll Sci Bldg Saint Mary-of-the-Woods IN 47876

DRUM, JOAN MARIE MCFARLAND, federal agency administrator; b. Waseca, Minn., Mar. 31, 1932; d. Leo Joseph and Bergetthe (Anderson) McFarland; m. William Merritt Drum, June 13, 1954; children: Melissa, Eric. BA in Journalism, U. Minn., 1962; MEd, Coll. William and Mary, 1975, postgrad., 1984-85. Govt. official fgn. claims br. Social Security Adminstrn., Balt., 1962-64; freelance writer Polyndrum Publs., Newport News, Va., 1967-73; tchr. Newport News (Va.) Pub. Schs., 1975-79; writer, cons. Drum Enterprises, Williamsburg, Va., 1980-82; developer, trainer communicative skills U.S. Army Transp. Sch., Ft. Eustis, Va., 1982-86; govt. ofcl. test assistance div. U.S. Army Tng. Ctr., Ft. Eustis, 1986—; adj. faculty English dept. St. Leo Area Coll., Ft. Eustis, 1975-78; del. Communicative Skills Conf., Ft. Leavenworth, Kans., 1983; lectr. in field. Author: Ghosts of Fort Monroe, 1972, Travel for Children in Tidewater, 1974; editor: army newsletter for families, 1968-73, Social Services Resource Reference, 1970; contbr. articles to profl. jours. Chmn. Girl Scouts U.S., Tokyo, 1964-66, Army Community Svc., Ft. Monroe, Va., 1967-68; chmn. publicity Hist. Home Tours, Ft. Monroe, 1971-73; adv. bd. James City County Social Svcs., 1989, chmn. adult svcs., 1989-90. Recipient numerous civic awards including North Shore Community Service award, Hialeah, Hawaii, 1966, Home Bur. Service award, 1975, Service award Girl Scouts U.S., Tokyo, 1965. Mem. Nat. Assn. Govt. Communicators, Nat. Soc. for Performance Instrn., Internat. Platform Speakers Assn., Va. Writers Club, Tidewater Writers' Assn., Kappa Delta Pi. Home: 9 Bray Wood Williamsburg VA 23185 Office: US Army Tng Ctr Test Assistance Div Individual Tng Evaluation Directorate Fort Eustis VA 23604

DRUMMOND, CAROL CRAMER, voice teacher, singer, artist, writer; b. Indpls., Mar. 5, 1933; adopted d. Burr Ostin Welch; d. Rosalind (Franklin) Bero; m. Roscoe Drummond, 1978 (dec. 1983). Student, Butler U., 1951-53; studied with Todd Duncan, and Rosa Ponselle. Singer Am. Light Opera Co., Washington; charter performer Concerts in Schs. Program, Washington Performing Arts Soc., 1966—; soloist 5th Ch. of Christ, Scientist, Washington, 1974—; pvt. tchr. voice and speech Mt. Desert Island, Maine, 1987—; painter, artist, 1980—; soloist numerous oratorio socs., appearances with symphony orchs., including Nat. Symphony Orch., Fairfax (Va.) Symphony Orch.; voiceover radio and TV commls., 1975—, U.S. Govt.; host The Sounding Bd., Sta. WGTS-FM, Washington, 1985—. Former columnist Animal Crackers; writer newspaper and mag. articles and stories; exhibited in art group shows. Trustee, bd. dirs. Internat. Soundex Reunion Registry, Carson City, Nev., 1978—. Mem. Nat. League Am. Pen Women, Am. Art League, Nat. Press Club (Washington), Maine State Soc. (life), Internat. Neighbors Club (Washington), Kappa Kappa Gamma. Republican. Episcopalian. Home: Dream Come True PO Box 791 Southwest Harbor ME 04679 Office: 1350 Beverly Rd Ste 115-135 McLean VA 22101

DRUMMOND, DORIS WIGGINS, psychologist; b. Ranburne, Ala., Nov. 2, 1938; d. Lee Otis and Lora Lee (Coley) Wiggins; m. J. Ferrell Drummond, Jan. 20, 1961; children: Nancy Lora, Franklin Joseph. AA, Young Harris (Ga.) Coll., 1959; BS, Jacksonville State U., 1963; MEd, West Ga. Coll., 1973; postgrad., Wesley Coll., Bristol, Eng., 1977-78, Augusta Coll., 1986, Ga. So. Coll., 1987. Tchr. of bus. Carroll County Sch. System, Mt. Zion, Ga., 1964-66; Bowdon, 1973-74; tchr. Carrollton City Schs., Mt. Zion, Bowdon, Ga., 1968-72; tchr. of bus. Jacksonville (Ala.) City Schs., 1966-67; behavioral psychologist Rome (Ga.) City Schs., 1981-82, Richmond County Schs., Augusta, Ga., 1982-86, DeKalb County Schs., Atlanta, 1986-90, Carrollton, Ga.; counsellor, Augusta, 1985-86. Ch. sch. tchr. United Meth. Chs., lay minister, Rome, Augusta, Bristol, Eng.; publicity chairperson North Ga. Conf. United Meth. Minister's Wives, Atlanta, 1988-89. Mem. Coun. for Exceptional Children. Home: 85 Azalea Trail Carrollton GA 30117

DRUMMOND, GILLIAN M., home furnishings company executive; b. Haywardsheath, Eng., Apr. 3, 1943; came to U.S., 1951; d. Bernard Gilbert and Margaret (Soot Hutcheson) D. Cert. N.Y. Sch. Interior Design, 1965; student U. Geneva, 1961-62. Asst. designer B. Altman & Co., N.Y.C., 1966-68; interior designer Tate & Hall, N.Y.C., 1968-72; Practice interior design, N.Y.C., 1972-75; mgr. customer relations Marcel Dekker Inc., N.Y.C., 1975-78; exec. dir. S.M. Hexter, N.Y.C., 1978-80; exec. dir. East Coast Winfield Design Assocs., N.Y.C., 1980-82; home furnishings cons., N.Y.C., 1982-85; pres. Gillian Drummond Inc., Wilmington N.C., 1985—. Conservative candidate N.Y. Congress, 1974; bd. dirs. Arts Council Lower Cape Fear; program chmn. St. Thomas Celebration of Arts. Mem. Decorative Fabrics Assn. (membership chmn. 1982-84), Nat. Home Fashions League, Decorative Arts Assn., Nat. Assn. Female Execs., Nat. Trust Historic Preservation, Historic Wilmington Found. Republican. Home: 117 Nun St Wilmington NC 28401 Office: 16 Wilkinson Alley Wilmington NC 28401

DRURY, CATHERINE ANNE, systems analyst; b. New Brunswick, N.J., Nov. 22, 1939; d. Eugene Ambrose and B. Anne (Morgan) D. BA in Math., Coll. of St. Elizabeth, Convent, N.J., 1963; MA in Math., Boston Coll., 1968; MS in Computer Sci., N.J. Inst. Tech., 1989. Cert. math. tchr., N.J. Tchr. St. Mary's Sch., Plainfield, N.J., 1963-68, St. Patrick's High Sch., Elizabeth, N.J., 1968-69; tchr., dept. chmn. Mother Seton Regional High Sch., Clark, N.J., 1969-81; asst. supt. Archdiocesan Schs., Newark, 1981-83; instr. math. St. Peter's Coll., Jersey City, 1983-84, Felician Coll., Lodi, N.J., 1984-86; systems analyst St. Mary's Hosp., Passaic, N.J., 1986—, asst. v.p. info. systems, 1989—; bd. dirs. Ednl. Improvement Ctr., West Orange, N.J., 1981-83. Trustee St. Elizabeth Hosp., Elizabeth, N.J., 1979-87. NSF grantee, 1970-79. Mem. Assn. for Computing Machinery (publicity chmn. 1983—), IEEE Computer Soc., Healthcare Info. and Mgmt. System Soc. of Am. Hosp. Assn., Upsilon Pi Epsilon. Roman Catholic. Home: 1136 Westfield Ave Clark NJ 07066 Office: St Mary's Hosp 211 Pennington Ave Passaic NJ 07055

DRUSE, MARGARET DOBSON, volunteer; b. Canastota, N.Y., Mar. 21, 1921; d. David Stanton and Nellie Catherine (Brundige) Dobson; m. Frederick Walter Druse, Oct. 3, 1943; children: Barbara Druse Cece, David Frederick. BA cum laude, Keuka Coll., 1943. Copy editor The Instr., Dansville, N.Y., 1943; receptionist, registrar SUNY, Alfred, 1946-48; mem. citizens adv. com. Palmer Twp., Easton, Pa., 1973-80; mem. Rep. Com., polit. worker Palmer Twp., Easton, 1986-87; mem. allocations com., fund dr. worker United Way, Easton, 1974-75; leader, trainer Great Valley council Girl Scouts U.S., 1956—, v.p., 1971-74; active Easton br. AAUW, 1954—, v.p. Easton br., 1967-69; corr. sec., v.p. Palmer Twp. Hist. Soc., 1975-84; mem. bd. Northampton County Tourism Coun., 1979-82; fin. sec. Northampton County Hist. and Geneal. Soc., 1978-85. Asst. editor: Our Hidden Heritage: Pennsylvania Women in History, 1983; compiler booklet. Recipient Service to Mankind award Sertoma Club, 1978. Mem. Pi Gamma Mu, Sigma Lambda Sigma. Home: 610 Morris St Easton PA 18042

DRUYAN, MARY ELLEN, biochemistry professor, researcher; b. Washington, July 14, 1938; d. Theodore and Anne Beverly (Sherr) Spector; m. Robert Druyan, Nov. 25, 1961 (div. 1979); children: Lara Catherine, Kira Elizabeth; m. Duane Merlin Mills, Apr. 25, 1981. BA in Polit. Sci., Wellesley Coll., 1960; MS in Biology, Tufts U., 1962; PhD in Biochemistry, U. Chgo., 1972; MPH, U. Ill., 1988. Postdoctoral appointee Argonne (Ill.) Nat. Lab., 1972-74; rsch. chemist Hines (Ill.) VA Hosp., 1974-76; asst. prof. biochemistry Loyola U. of Chgo., Maywood, Ill., 1976-82, assoc. prof. biochemistry, 1982—, dir. oral biology, 1987—; cons. Hines VA Hosp., 1976—. Mem. Com. of 100, Hinsdale, Ill., 1986—, Theatre of Western Springs. Mem. AAUW, N.Y. Acad. Sci., Am. Dietetic Assn. (cons. Chgo. chpt.), Am. Assn. Dental Schs. (sect. officer), Bd. Govs. Office: Loyola U Chgo Med Ctr 2160 S 1st Ave Maywood IL 60153

DRYDEN, MARY ELIZABETH, legal librarian, writer, actress; b. Chgo., Oct. 18, 1952; d. James Heard and Hazel Anne (Potts) Rule; m. Ian Dryden, Nov. 22, 1975. Student, U. London, 1969, Bath U., 1970; BA, Scripps Coll., 1971; postgrad. U. Edinburgh, 1971-74. Head librarian Hahn, Cazier & Leff, San Diego, 1980, Fredman, Silverberg & Lewis, San Diego, 1980-83, Riordan & McKinzie, Los Angeles, 1983—; freelance photog. model, 1973—. Theatrical appearances include Antony and Cleopatra, McOwen Theatre, London, 1984, Table Manners, Los Angeles, 1985, Harliquinade, Los Angeles, 1985, Julius Caesar, Los Angeles, 1986, Witness for the Prosecution, Los Angeles, 1987, Come and Go, Los Angeles, 1988, The Actor's Nightmare, 1989, The Dresser, 1989, (film) Private Collections, 1989, also music videos and TV Commls.; book critic Los Angeles Times; contbr. articles to newspapers. Mem. Brit. Equity, So. Calif. Soc. Law Librarians, Am. Film Inst., Theatre Palisades, Mensa, Phi Beta Kappa. Avocations: photography, wine, architecture, fine art, languages. Office: Riordan & McKinzie 29th Floor 300 S Grand Ave Los Angeles CA 90071

DRYER, DOROTHEA MERRILL (MRS. EDWIN JASON DRYER), lawyer; b. Salt Lake City; d. George Edmund and Lillian (Chapman) Merrill;m. Edwin Jason Dryer, Feb 28, 1942; children: Diana Claire Dryer Wright, Faith Ellen. AB, StanfordU., 1936; LLB, Yale U., 1940. Bar: Utah 1941, U.S. Supreme Ct., U.S. Ct. Mil. Appeals. Clk. to chief justice Utah Supreme Ct., 1941; atty. Bur. Immigration Dept. Justice, Washington, 1941-42; pvt. practice Salt Lake City, 1943-47, Washington, 1948—; dep. county atty., Salt Lake City, 1947-48. Fellow Am. Assn. Criminology; mem. ABA, Fed. Bar Assn., Utah Bar Assn., Nat. Assn. Women Lawyers, Am. Judicature Soc., Nat. Assn. for Gifted Children, Assn. for Gifted, Oral History Assn., Jr. League Washington Club, Potomac Bus. and Profl. Women's Club, Nat. Lawyer's Club. Unitarian. Home: 1210 Mottrom Dr McLean VA 22101

DRYFOOS, NANCY PROSKAUER, sculptor; b. New Rochelle, N.Y., Mar. 25; d. Richman and Edith (Harris) Proskauer; m. Donald Dryfoos. Cert. Sarah Lawrence Coll., 1939; postgrad. Columbia U. Extension Sch., 1945-46. One-person shows include: Contemporary Arts Gallery, N.Y.C., 1952, Silvermine Guild Gallery, 1954, Wellons Gallery, 1956, Bodley Gallery, 1958, Collectors Gallery, 1960, Dime Savs. Bank, Bklyn., 1969, Lincoln Savs. Bank, N.Y.C., 1975-76, 87, Donnell Libr., N.Y.C., 1987 (Pen and Brush solo show winner, 1989); group shows include: Lever Bros., Warner Communications Corcoran Gallery, Pa. Acad. Fine Arts, 1947, Syracuse Mus., 1948, Bklyn. Mus., 1952, Corcoran Gallery, 1954, Nat. Acad. Fine Arts, N.Y.C., 1952-76, Lincoln Savs. Bank, 1987, Donnell Libr. Ctr., 1987, others; v.p. Fine Arts Fedn. of N.Y. Contbr. articles to profl. publs. Mem. Sculptor's League. Fellow Nat. Sculpture Soc. (rec. sec. 1973, bd. dirs. 1988—, chmn. religious com. 1987—); mem. Allied Artists America (Medal of Honor 1978), Audubon Artists (exhbn. dir. 1983-84, asst. treas. 1987-88, prize), Am. Soc. Contemporary Artists (dir., exhbn. dir., prize), Contemporary Artists Guild (dir.), N.Y. Soc. Women Artists (dir.), Fine Arts Fedn. N.Y. (v.p.), Pen and Brush Club (Joyce and Eliot Listen award 1985, Bedy Marky Art Foundry award 1982, award of merit 1986, Emily Nichols Hatch award 1988), Nat. Trust for Hist. Preservation, Network Visual Arts Ctr. (dir.), Brandeis Creative Arts Commn. (dir.), Artists Equity Assn. (bd. dirs. 1978-80), Mcpl. Art Soc., Womens City Club N.Y. Avocations: printmaking, enameling. Home: 45 E 89th St New York NY 10128

DRYLIE, LORI L., accountant; b. Uniontown, Pa.; d. Robert and Catherine P. (Ainsley) D. BS, Calif. U., 1987. Accts. receivable clk. Brownsville (Pa.) Gen. Hosp., 1981-84; data transcriber Brownsville Gen. Hosp., 1984-88; internal auditor Allegheny Power System, Greensburg, Pa., 1988-90; acct. Allegheny Power System, Greensburg, 1990—. Home: PO Box 233 Greensburg PA 15601 Office: Allegheny Power System 800 Cabin Hill Dr Greensburg PA 15601

DRYNAN, MARGARET ISOBEL, music teacher, retired consultant; b. Toronto, Ont., Can., Dec. 10, 1915; d. William James and Ellen (Rowney) Brown; Mus.B., U. Toronto, 1943; m. George Drynan, July 3, 1940; children: Judith, John, James. Mem. nat. exec. bd. Royal Can. Coll. after 1951, nat. 1st v.p., 1980-82, nat. pres., 1982-84; charter mem., pres. Oshawa Coun. for the Arts, Ont., Can., 1972-74; founder, dir. Canterbury Singers, Oshawa, 1952-69; music supr., cons. Durham Bd. Edn., 1960-81; bd. dirs. Oshawa Symphony, 1960-80, 1st v.p., 1984-86, pres., 1986—, percussionist. Organist, choirmaster St. Matthew's Anglican Ch., Oshawa; dir. Oshawa Sr. Citizens Choir; adjudicator for piano and choral music Ontario Festivals. Recipient award Royal Conservatory Toronto, 1975, other awards. Hon. fellow Royal Can. Coll. Organists; mem. Fedn. Women Tchrs., Can. Fedn. Adjudicators, Registered Music Tchrs. (past pres.). Anglican. Clubs: Univ. Women's (past pres.); Heliconian of Toronto. Compositions include: Songs for Judith, Why do the bells?, Including Me, Missa Brevis in F, The Fate of Gilbert Gim, The Canada Goose (operetta), British Columbia, Rainy Day Song, Superjogger, Roller-skating, November, To Mary and Joseph, Prelude and Fugue in C minor for organ. Home: 589 Pinewood St, Oshawa, ON Canada L1G 2S2

DU, JULIE YI-FANG TSAI, toxicologist, biochemist; b. Republic of China, Mar. 23, 1937; came to U.S., 1961; d. Fu-Yuan and Chin-Tien (Sui) Tsai; m. Li-Jen Du, Sept. 12, 1964; 1 child, Annie. BS in Chemistry, Nat. Taiwan U., Taipei, 1959; MS in Chemistry, Tex. Tech U., 1963; PhD in Physiol. Chemistry, Ohio State U., 1970. Grad. asst. Ohio State U., Columbus, 1965-70; rsch. assoc. U. Louisville, 1970-80, Georgetown U., Washington, 1981-84; chemist U.S. EPA, Washington, 1984-87, toxicologist, 1987—. Contbr. papers to profl. jours. Mem. Soc. Toxicology. Office: US EPA 401 M St SW Washington DC 20460

DUARTE-MARSHALL, PATRICIA, real estate and insurance broker; b. Truro, Mass., Feb. 23, 1938; d. Antone Jr. and Marjorie (Beckley) Duarte. Grad. high sch., Provincetown, Mass. Lic. ins. and real estate broker; constrn. supt. Sec. various ins. agys., Amherst, Mass., 1957-60; ins. and real estate agt. Duarte Ins. & Real Estate, Truro, 1960-66, owner, prin. agt., 1966-78; ins. risk mgr. J.L. Marshall & Sons, Inc., Pawtucket, R.I., 1979—; owner, mgr. Patricia-Duarte-Marshall Real Estate, Rockport, Maine, 1988—; restorer antique homes New Eng., Mass., 1979—. Mem., sec. Truro Planning Bd., 1965-72, chmn., 1974-78; mem. exec. com. Cape Cod Planning and Econ. Devel. Com., 1971-76; mem. re-elect Brawn for Senate Com., Camden, Maine, 1988; bd. dirs., chmn. Cape Cod chpt. Am. Heart Assn., 1963-70. Mem. Penobscot Bay Bd. Realtors, Profl. Ins. Agts. New Eng. (bd. dirs. 1974-76), Gen. Fedn. Women's Clubs (2nd v.p. Camden chpt. 1989). Republican. Roman Catholic. Home and Office: 46 Pascal Ave Rockport ME 04856

DUBAN, BEVERLY ANN, immigration consultant; b. Chgo., Jan. 15, 1944; d. Bernard and Bernice (Plotkin) D.; children: Steven Breit, Carolyn Small. AA in Child Devel., L.A. City Coll., 1978, AA in Psychology, 1980; BA in Liberal Studies, U. Eng., Oxford, 1980, PhD in Social Work, 1983,

MA in Telecommunications & Elem. Edn., 1985; BA in Child Devel. and Psychology, U. Without Walls, 1981; diploma in legal investigation, Comml. Tech. Inst., Little Falls, N.J., 1985; MA in Marriage, Family, Child, and Career Counseling, U. N.Am., 1988; postgrad., City U., 1990—; numerous certs., Am. Police Acad., 1983, 87, 90. Cert. adult sch. tchr., legal asst., legal sec., med. dental asst.; cert. in process serving, bail bonding. Disc jockey Am. Radio Network, L.A., 1985-89; immigration cons. L.A., 1988—, fingerprint cons., 1988—; notary public. Mem. Nat. Notary Assn., Am. Fedn. Police, Nat. Chaplains Assn., Nat. Bailbonders Assn. Home: 529 N Detroit St Los Angeles CA 90036

DUBAY, GWEN ANN, sales and marketing professional; b. Lewiston, Maine, Mar. 25, 1951; d. Ronald N. and Alice M. (Fellows) Johnson; widowed Feb. 1985; children: Ty Brandon, Tara Lee. BA in Sociology, U. Maine, Orono, 1972. Social worker State of Maine, Bangor, 1972; office mgr. S.C. Clayton Co., Marlboro, Mass., 1972-74; sec., treas. Dubay Sales & Mktg., Zionsville, Ind., 1983-85, pres., 1985—; sales adminstr. Woods Wire Products, Inc., Carmel, Ind., 1985—; vis. artist intern Ind. Arts Commn., Indpls., 1983-84. treas. PTO, Zionsville, 1982-83; vol. tchr. for gifted Eagle Elem. Sch., Zionsville, 1983-85. Republican. Methodist. Home: 200 Governors Ln Zionsville IN 46077 Office: Woods Wire Products Inc 510 Third Ave SW Carmel IN 46032

DUBBERKE, JANE CAROL, personal care industry executive; b. Hampton, Iowa, July 27, 1947; d. Harold Martin and Julia Ann (Wasson) D. Cert. Cosmetology, Piztes-Waterloo Sch. of Beauty, Waterloo, Iowa, 1966. Cosmetologist Molly's Beauty Salon, Hubbard, Iowa, 1966-68, Quakerdale Children's Home, New Providence, Iowa, 1969-83, Jane's House of Beauty, Hubbard, 1968—. Bd. dirs., sec. Hubbard Med. Bd., 1968-87; co-chmn. Hardin County Reps., Eldora, Iowa, 1980—; chmn. for candidates Rep. congress and rep., Iowa, 1980, 82, 88, 90. Nominated to the first Physicians Asst. Examining Bd. for Iowa, Gov. Terry Branstad, Des Moines, 1989-91. Mem. Nat. Hairdressers, Dist. Nat. Hairdressers (sec., treas. 1970-72), Hardin County Hairdressers (various offices), Hubbard C. of C. (sec. 1968-69). Lutheran. Home and Office: 110 W Chestnut Hubbard IA 50122-0053

DUBBERT, PATRICIA MARIE, psychologist; b. Mexico, Mo., Mar. 7, 1947; m. Randy L. Stranghoener; 2 children. BSN cum laude, U. MO., 1972; MA in Psychiat. and Mental Health Nursing, NYU, 1972; MS in Psychology, Rutgers U., 1980, PhD in Psychology, 1982. Intern in psychology U. Miss. Med. Ctr., 1980-81, Jackson VA Med. Ctr., 1980-81; instr. in nursing L.I. Coll. of Nursing, 1972; instr. dept. nursing Herbert H. Lehman Coll. CUNY, N.Y.C., 1973-77; instr. Sch. of Medicine U. Miss., 1981-82, asst. prof. dept. psychiatry and human behavior, 1982-86, assoc. prof. dept. psychiatry and human behavior, 1986—; participating investigator VA Coop. Studies Program, 1990—. Mem. cons. editor: Behavioral Medicine Abstracts, 1982-85; mem. editorial bd. Behavior Therapy, 1984-86, 88—, Annals of Behavioral Medicine, 1987—; contbr. numerous articles to profl. jours. USPHS grantee, 1976-77; VA Merit Review grantee, 1987-90. Mem. Am. Psychol. Assn., Assn. for Advancement of Behavior Therapy, Soc. Behavioral Medicine (bd. dirs.), Southeastern Psychol. Assn., Miss. Psychol. Assn., Assn. VA Chief Psychologists, Sigma Theta Tau. Office: VA Med Ctr Dept of Vets Affairs Jackson MS 39216

DUBIN, ELLEN FENTON, management consultant; b. N.Y.C., Apr. 3, 1953; d. Edward Nathan and Joan (Sohn) Fenton; 1 child, Joanna Michelle. Student, Mt. Holyoke Coll., 1970-71; BA, U. Rochester, 1974. Personnel counselor Am. Personnel Services, Wash., 1974-75, mgr., 1975-77; dir. adminstrv. support services Children's Hosp. Nat. Med. Ctr., Wash., 1977-84; instr. George Washington U., 1985—; mgmt. cons., pres. Practice Mgmt. Cons., Inc., Potomac, Md., 1984—. Speaker Inst. on Occupational Health, Wash., Iona House Retreat, Wash., Alexandria Office on Women; bd. dirs. The Harbor Sch., Bethesda, Md., 1988—. Democrat. Jewish.

DUBIN, SHERI, promotions coordinator; b. Bronx, N.Y., Sept. 15, 1953; d. Lawrence Michael and Elaine Sylvia (Dardeck) D. Student, Queensboro Community Coll., 1971-72. Administr. asst. RCA Direct Marketing, 1975-77; trade show coord. World Cote Inc, 1979-82; office mgr., sales coord. Diamond Sales/J&H Diamond, W. Los Angeles, 1983-86; project coordinator G.T. Water Products, 1986-87; advt. and promotions coord. Sterling Software Dylakor Division, 1986—. Contbr. articles to prof. jours. Named Woman of Yr., Vly Outreach Synagogue, 1987. Mem. Moonlighters Square Dance Club (founder 1985), Vly. Outreach Synagogue, (founder 1986). Democrat. Jewish.

DUBLIN, ELVIE WILSON, clinical psychologist; b. Athens, Greece, May 18, 1937; d. Anthony I. and Rosa (Protecdicos) Nicolopoulos; m. John Wilson, Oct. 29, 1958 (div. 1967); children: David Wilson, Toni Wilson; m. James Dublin, Dec. 21, 1973 (div. 1978). BA, Ind. U., 1966, PhD, 1972. Cons. Hospitality House Nursing Home, Bedford, Ind., 1972-73; psychotherapist Choice, Inc., 1973-79, sec.-treas., 1973-79; pres. Studentworld, Inc., 1978-81; pvt. practice psychology, Bloomington, Ind., 1979—; Arabian horse breeder, founder, owner Tall Oaks Arabians, 1980-86, DUblin racig Arabians, 1986—; bd. dirs. Midwestern Psychotherapy Inst., 1977. Trainee NSF, 1965-67, USPHS, 1967-70. Mem. Am. Psychol. Assn., Ind. Psychol. Assn., Assn. Advancement Psychology, Internat. Arabian Horse Assn., Arabian Horse Registry of Am. (assoc.), Phi Beta Kappa. Clubs: Arabian Jockey, Ind. Arabian Horse. Home: 9401 E St Rd 46 Bloomington IN 47401 Office: 4151 E 3rd St Bloomington IN 47401

DUBOIS, MELODEE ANN, performing company executive; b. Vincennes, Ind., July 14, 1948; m. James E.N. Huntley, June 14, 1986; 1 child, Alexandra Mireille. AB in Philosophy, Ind. U., 1972, MA in Arts Adminstrn., 1976. Curator performing arts John Michael Kohler Arts Ctr., Sheboygan, Wis., 1974-76; adminstr. performing arts Detroit Inst. Arts, 1976-77; fundraising com. specialist Camp Fire Girls Detroit Coun., 1977-78; v.p., mng. dir. Detroit Grand Opera Assn., 1978-85, Mich. Opera Theatre, Detroit, 1985—. Bd. dirs. New Ctr. Area Coun., Detroit, 1986—, Cultural Ctr. Arts Festival, Detroit, 1987—. Mem. Nat. Soc. Fundraising, Mich. Presenters Network, Mensa. Office: Mich Opera Theatre 6519 2nd Ave Detroit MI 48202

DUBOSE, BARBARA JANE, retired educator; b. Longmont, Colo., Feb. 14, 1922; d. James Keith and Grace Ethel (Green) Webb; m. James Hassel DuBose, Apr. 14, 1946; children: Dennis Alan, Diane DuBose Arbones. BA in Art, Calif. State U., Fresno, 1944; postgrad., Amarillo (Tex.) Coll., West Tex. State U., Tex. Tech. U. Cert. tchr., Calif., Tex. Display artist Gottschalks Dept. Store, Fresno, 1944-45; tchr. art, math. Kingsburg (Calif.) High Sch., 1945; artist, writer Bible Fellowship Hour, Fresno, 1945-46; art tchr. Amarillo Pub. Schs., 1959-77; ret., 1977. Choir mem., soloist Hammer Field Airbase Choir, Fresno, 1941-46; youth leader, Sunday sch. supt., tchr. assorted Bapt. chs., Amarillo, Lancaster and Sweetwater, Tex., Fresno and Somerset, Ky., 1951-70; Sunday sch. tchr., leader sr. adults 1st Bapt. Ch., Amarillo, 1978-90, program chmn. Mission Soc., coun. mem., 1980-88. Mem. AAUW (historian 1988-90, courtesy chmn, 1990—), Amarillo Ret. Tchrs., Tex. State Ret. Tchrs. Assn., Amarillo Fine Arts Assn., Amarillo Sr. Citizen Assn., Nat. Mus. Women in Arts (charter). Home: 2510 Redwood St Amarillo TX 79107

DUBOSE, CAROL ANN, human resources consultant; b. Beaumont, Tex., Feb. 2, 1954; d. Edward Francis and Patricia (Lee) DuBose. BS, Tex. Woman's U., Denton, 1976. Cert. indsl. recreation adminstr. Supr. XEA Xerox Corp., Dallas, 1976-80; human resources recruiter Zale Corp., Irving, Tex., 1980-83; sr. recruiter Zale Corp., 1983, mgr. EEO, 1983-84, mgr. employee rels., 1984-85; sr. assoc. Drake Beam Morin, Inc., Dallas, 1985-86; v.p. Drake Beam Morin, Inc., 1986—. Vol. Dallas Arboretum and Bot. Soc., Dallas, 1985, 89. Recipient Profl. Excellence award, Drake Beam Morin, 1987. Mem. Am. Soc. Tng. and Devel. Republican. Office: Drake Beam Morin Inc 5005 LBJ Fwy #900 Dallas TX 75244

DUBOUX, PATRICIA JANE, advertising agency and human resources executive; b. Chgo., Mar. 26, 1956; d. Carl Andrew and Rita Ann (Sullivan) Hulik; stepmother, Mercedes Elizabeth (Rusch) Hulik; m. Dennis Vincent DuBoux, May 17, 1986. BA in Advt., Mich. State U., 1978; MS in Indsl. Relations, Loyola U., Chgo., 1985. Media asst. Joint Commn. on Accreditation Health Care Orgns., Chgo., 1978-79, brochure asst., 1979-80, mktg. coord., 1980-81, recruitment/compensation coord., 1982-84, recruitment/employee relations mgr., 1984-86; human resources mgr. DDB Needham Worldwide, Chgo., 1986-87, dir. personnel adminstrn., 1987-89, dir. human resources, 1989—. Mem. Human Resources Mgmt. Assn. Chgo., Am. Soc. for Personnel Adminstrn. Home: 1025 Prairie Ave Park Ridge IL 60068 Office: DDB Needham Worldwide 303 E Wacker Dr Chicago IL 60601

DUBROW, MARSHA ANN, high technology company executive, composer; b. Newark, Dec. 27, 1948; d. Leo and Rose (Haberman) Dubrow; m. Daniel Leon Chaykin, Jan. 17, 1970 (div. 1985); 1 child, Alexander; m. David Lorin Rosenberg, July 3, 1988; 1 step-child, Oliver. BA cum laude, U. Pa., 1970; MA, NYU, 1975; MFA, Princeton U., 1977, postgrad., 1977-78, 81-82; postgrad., Tufts U., 1987, Am. Women's Econ. Devel. Corp. Inst., 1987-88, Leadership Am., 1988, Leadership N.J., 1990. Prodn. coord. Children's TV Workshop, N.Y.C., 1970-73; instr. Princeton (N.J.) U., 1976-78; mgr. mktg. communications, ops., human resources AT&T/Techs., Inc., Morristown, N.J., 1978-80; dir. mktg. and ops. Acadia Communications, N.Y.C., 1980-83; dir. planning and mktg. Access Methods, Inc., N.Y.C., 1984-85; prin. Marsha Dubrow Assocs., East Rutherford, N.J., 1981—; pres., chief exec. officer Technolog, Inc., East Rutherford, N.J., 1985—. Mem. program com., life mem. bus. and profl. group Nat. Coun. Jewish Women, Essex County, N.J., 1983—; mem. The Gathering, Whole Theater, Montclair, 1987—, BMI Musical Theatre Workshop, N.Y.C, 1989—; mentor U.S. Small Bus. Adminstrn., Office of Women Bus. Ownership, Washington, 1989—. Recipient Theodore Presser award U. Pa., 1970; William C. Langley fellow NYU, 1974, Princeton U. fellow, 1976-78, Josephine de Karman fellow Aerojet-Gen. Corp., 1981, Composer's fellow in Opera-Musical Theatre N.J. State Coun. Arts, 1990. Mem. NAFE, Am. Women Entrepreneurs, Am. Mgmt. Assn., Leadership Am. Alumnae Assn., Hadassah (life mem. Essex County chpt.). Home: 34 Marion Rd Upper Montclair NJ 07043 Office: Technolog 1 Maple St East Rutherford NJ 07073

DUBUC, MARY ELLEN, teacher; b. N.Y.C. July 20, 1950; d. Patrick Joseph and Catherine (McKenna) Reynolds; BA cum laude (scholar), Marymount Manhattan Coll., 1972; MA, Columbia U., 1973; cert. advanced grad. studies R.I. Coll., 1985; m. Leo Dennis Dubuc Jr., Sept. 9, 1978; children: Brian Robert, Kimberly Ann. Spl. edn. tchr. Cardinal Cushing Sch., Hanover, Mass., 1973-76, Ferncliff Manor Sch., Yonkers, N.Y., 1976-77; program coordinator Bronx Devel. Services, 1977-78; dir. edn. R.I. Assn. Retarded, Woonsocket, 1978-84, spl. edn. cons., 1984—; qualified med. retardation profl. Seacliff, Inc., Cumberland, R.I., 1988—; tchr. BICO Collaborative Program, North Attleboro, Mass., 1989—. Fed. trainee, 1971, 72. Mem. North Smithfield PTA, 1986—. Mem. Assn. Severely Handicapped, R.I. Assn. Retarded Citizens, NAFE, R.I. Assn. Adult and Continuing Edn. (v.p. pub. relations 1986-89), Alpha Chi. Democrat. Roman Catholic. Office: No RI Chpt RIARC Inc 80 Fabien St Woonsocket RI 02895

DUCATT, JODY LYNN, advertising consultant; b. Cass City, Mich., Mar. 26, 1962; d. Harold Lee and Carolyn Mary (Lowe) Donaghy; m. Matthew Kevin Ducatt, June 18, 1988. BS in Advt./Graphic Design, The Coll. of St. Rose, 1985. Graphic artist Artography, Albany, N.Y., 1985-86; art/media dir. Sound Advice Advt., Saginaw, Mich., 1986-87; advt. cons. R.B. Decker Advt., Inc., Delhi, N.Y., 1987—. Mem. Greenpeace, World Wildlife Fund. Republican.

DUCHESNE, KAY ELLEN, systems engineer; b. Milw., Sept. 17, 1942; d. Hallie D. and Phyllis (Record) Carnes; m. Robert G. Duchesne, Aug. 25, 1967; children: Robert, Michael, Susan, Gayle, Catherine. BS, Franklin Pierce Coll., Salem, N.H., 1988. Software test engr. Signatron, Inc., Lexington, Mass., 1980-87, GE, Wilmington, Mass., 1987-88; systems engr. MITRE Corp., Bedford, Mass., 1988—. ESL tutor Commonwealth Literacy Corps, 1989—. With USAR, 1975-85. Mem. Nat. Mil. Intelligence Assn., Armed Forces Communications and Electronics Assn., Assn. Old Crows. Home: 123 Cogswell St Haverhill MA 01832 Office: Burlington Rd Bedford MA 01730

DUCKETT, JOAN, law librarian; b. Bklyn., Oct. 21, 1934; d. Stephen and Mary (Wehrum) Kearney; m. Richard Duckett, Aug. 25, 1956; children: Richard, David, Daniel, Deirdre. BA, Kean Coll., 1974; MLS, Rutgers U., 1977; JD, Suffolk U., 1983; postgrad., Oxford (Eng.) U., 1986. Bar: Mass. 1983, U.S. Ct. Appeals (fed. cir.) 1984. Media specialist Oak Knoll Sch., Summit, N.J., 1976-80; law clk. Dist. Atty. Suffolk County, Boston, 1982; vol. atty. Cambridgeport Problem Ctr., Cambridge, Mass., 1984-85; reference libr. Harvard Law Sch. Libr., Cambridge, 1982-84, coord. The New Eng. Law Libr. Consortium, 1984-87, head reference svcs., 1987—, profl. devel. com., chmn. Bryant fellowship award panel, 1987—. Protocol hostess L.A. Olympic Com., 1984. Mem. Mass. Bar Assn., Boston Bar Assn., Am. Assn. Law Librs., Law Librs. New Eng., Assn. Boston Law Librs., Alpha Sigma Lambda, Beta Phi Mu. Office: Harvard Law Sch Langdell Hall Cambridge MA 02138

DUCKETT, KAREN IRENE, interior architecture executive; b. Rochester, N.Y., June 12, 1947; d. Wardell Duckett, Dec. 28, 1973; children: Chioke, Shani, Makiri. BFA in Architecture, Ohio U., 1969; MA Urban Studies in Urban Planning, Yale U., Occidental Coll., 1974; JD, Woodrow Wilson Coll., 1981. Interior designer, project mgr. Xerox Corp., Stamford, Conn., 1969-73; dir. planning City of Flint (Mich.), 1973-75; phys. devel. adminstr. City of Atlanta, 1975-78; cons. Atlanta, 1978-85; pres. Duckett Marchant, Atlanta, 1985-89, Duckett and Assocs, Inc. (formerly Duckett Marchant), Atlanta, 1990—. Handbook chair socila and exec. com. Leadership Atlanta, 1986—, oriental chair exec. com., 1988—; sec., bd. dirs. Met. Atlanta Coalition of 100 Black Women, 1987—; mem. Leadership Ga., 1989. Nat. Urban fellow, 1974. Mem. Am. Soc. Interior Designers (cert contract interior designer), Inst. Bus. Designers, Atlanta C. of C. (com. chair 1985—). Office: Duckett and Assocs Inc 2555 Cumberland Pkwy Atlanta GA 30339

DUCKLES, SUE PIPER, pharmacology educator; b. Oakland, Calif., Mar. 1, 1946; d. Carl Frank and Joan (Brashares) Piper; m. Lawrence Taylor Duckles, Mar. 20, 1968; children: Ian Muir, Galen Vincent. BA, U. Calif., Berkeley, 1969; PhD, U. Calif., San Francisco, 1973. Postdoctoral fellow UCLA, 1973-76, asst. prof. in residence, 1976-79; asst. prof. Dept. Pharmacology U. Ariz., Tucson, 1979-83, assoc. prof., 1983-85, , U. Calif., Irvine, 1985-88, prof., 1988—. Contbr. articles to profl. jours.; assoc. editor Life Scis., 1980—; field editor Jour. Pharmacology and Exptl. Therapeutics, Bethesda, Md., 1983—. Mem. Am. Soc. Pharmacology and Exptl. Therapeutics, Am. Heart Assn., Soc. for Neurosci., Western Pharmacoloy Soc., Phi Beta Kappa. Office: U Calif Dept Pharmacology Irvine CA 92717

DUCKWORTH, CAROL KAY, university administrator, consultant; b. Wichita, Kans., Apr. 21, 1941; d. Elmer Floyd and Cynthia Ruth (Dodson) D. BA, Okla. Baptist U., 1965; MSE, Ark. State U., 1975; postgrad., U. Ark., 1984, Okla. State U., 1988—. Cert. secondary adminstr., counselor, vocat. prof., human relations trainer/coordinator. Tchr. bus. Midway High Sch., Denton, Kans., 1965-69; tchr., counselor, dir, cooperative edn. Green Forest (Ark.) High Sch., 1969-72; prof. bus. adminstrn., computer sci. Weatherford (Tex.) Coll., 1972-75; dir. cooperative edn. North Ark. Community Coll., Harrison, Ark., 1975-80; prof. computer sci. bus. adminstrn. North Ark. Community Coll., Harrison, 1976-87; asst. registrar Kans. State U., Manhattan, Kans., 1980-84; counselor Rogers (Ark.) High Sch., 1984-87; registrar U. Ozarks, Clarksville, Ark., 1987-88; asst. prof. adult edn. Okla. State U., Stillwater, 1988—; cons. grant reader U.S. Office Edn., Washington, 1980-83, cons. grant writer numerous nationwide univs., 1976—. Author: Individualized Instruction in the Business Education Classroom, 1972, Computerized Instruction in Advanced Development, 1985. Named Outstanding Bus. Student Okla. Bapt. U., 1965. Mem. Am. Assn. Bus. Women (pres. 1979, 86-87), Phi Delta Kappa (pres. 1980-81 v.p. 1986), Phi Beta Kappa (v.p. 1975). Republican. Baptist. Lodge: Order of Eastern Star (conductress 1987—). Home: 350 North Giles PO Box 434 Gentry AR 72734

DUCKWORTH, KIM PELTO, marketing executive; b. Fresno, Calif., Dec. 15, 1956; d. William Armos and Marjorie Mae (Haninger) Pelto; m. David Paul Duckworth, Aug. 16, 1986; 1 child, Heather Ann. BA in Communications, Stanford U., 1978. Asst. dir. membership club Westin Internat. Hotel, San Francisco, 1978; mktg. trainee IBM, Palo Alto, Calif., 1978-79, mktg. rep., 1979-82; account mktg. rep. IBM, San Francisco, 1982-83; with advt. staff IBM, White Plains, N.Y., 1983-85; mgr. mktg. IBM, Sunnyvale, Calif., 1985-88; regional mktg. mgr. software IBM, San Jose, Calif., 1989—. Mem. Young Reps. Los Gatos; precinct leader United Way, Palo Alto, 1985, vol. canvasser White Plains, 1984; vol. Am. Heart Assn., March of Dimes, Los Gatos, Calif., 1988—. Mem. Stanford Alumni Assn., Female Exec. Assn. Republican. Episcopalian. Clubs: Stanford (Los Gatos), Los Gatos Athletic. Office: IBM 2099 Gateway Pl San Jose CA 95101

DUCKWORTH, LYNN ALLISON, childrens apparel executive; b. Toms River, N.J., Mar. 6, 1948; d. Harry Albert Duckworth and Janet Louise (Loveman) Taber; m. John Welles Pendleton, Dec. 1, 1984; 1 child, Allison Welles. BA in Psychology, Elmira Womens Coll., 1970. Exec. trainee Bamberger's, Newark, 1971, sales mgr., 1971-75; with Health-Tex, N.Y.C., 1975-85, assoc. mdse. mgr., mdse. mgr., v.p. mdse. infant/toddlers, v.p. new product devel.; pres. Baylis Co., N.Y.C., Cin., 1985-87, Absorba, Inc., N.Y.C., 1988—; showroom mgr. Health-Tex, N.Y.C. Mem. Women's Club of Ridgewood, N.J., 1989—; deacon West Side Presbyn., Ridgewood. Mem. CMA, K.I.D.S. Republican. Home: 405 Heights Rd Ridgewood NJ 07450

DUCO, JOSEPHINE DIANE, title insurance company financial executive; b. Detroit, Apr. 28, 1947; d. Henry Leopold and Antoinette (Bono) D. B.A. in Sociology, U. Mich., 1969; M.B.A. with distinction in Acctg., L.I. U., 1981. Head teller Am. Savs. Bank, N.Y.C., 1975-77, customer service rep., 1977-78, acct., 1978-79; staff acct. Radio City Music Hall, N.Y.C., 1980; chief acct. N.E. region Am. Title Ins. Co., N.Y.C., 1980-81, asst. regional controller, 1981-83, regional controller, 1983—, v.p., 1984—, asst. sec., 1986—. Mem. NAFE, Nat. Assn. Accts. (mem. of yr. 1986-87), LWV. Office: Am Title Ins Co 675 3d Ave New York NY 10017

DUCOTE, MARJORIE ELLEN, chemist, researcher; b. Chattanooga, Oct. 28, 1938; d. David S. and Beatrice Allene (Harrell) Tate; m. Calvin L. Cucksee, Jan. 1, 1962 (div.); 1 child, Brian E.; m. Jere D. Ducote Sr. (dec. March 1986); children: Melissa L., Jesse H. AB, U. Chattanooga, 1959; student, U. Tenn., 1959-60, Southeastern Inst. Tech., 1984-86. Research and devl. chemist Eastman Chem. Products, Kingsport, Tenn., 1960-62; chemist Newport News (Va.) SS&DD Co., 1962-64; research chemist U.S. Army MICOM, Huntsville, Ala., 1964—; facilitator CPO-EEO Program, Ala.; investigator U.S. Army Grievance Investigation, Ala. Instr. karate YMCA, 1978-80, instr. self def. U. Ala., Huntsville, 1979. Recipient Mary Jane Hearn award Toastmistress, 1984, two U.S. Army MICOM Sci. and Engring. awards, 1979, 84. Mem. Federally Employed Women (pres. 1986-87), Am. Def. Preparedness Assn., VFW,Am. Legion Aux. Club: Toastmistress (pres. 1984). Lodge: Elks. Home: 2037 Bankhead Pkwy Huntsville AL 35801 Office: US Army MICOM AMSMI-RD-PR-T Redstone Arsenal AL 35898-5249

DUCOTE-COOPER, MARGARET ANN, director of news and public affairs; b. Baton Rouge, July 6, 1961; d. Magnus Michael and Elma (Rachel) D; m. Billy W. Cooper, Jr., Oct. 28, 1989. BA, Northwestern State U., 1983. News anchor, reporter KNOC/KDBH, Natchitoches, La., 1982-83; afternoon news producer WJBO, Baton Rouge, 1984-87; news dir. KIXK, El Dorado, Ark., 1987-88; bd. operator KCXY, Camden, Ark., 1987-88; news dir. WMJW, Ridgeland, Miss., 1988—. Community rels. St. Francis Catholic Ch., Madison, Miss., 1989—; adopt a sch. coord. Jackson (Miss.) Pub. Schs., 1989—; mem. MADD, Jackson, 1988-89. Mem. Sigma Kappa. Republican. Roman Catholic. Home: 4750 Chastain Dr Jackson MS 39206 Office: WMJW-MAJIC 107 715 S Pear Orchard Ste 305 Ridgeland MS 39157

DUCRET, LUCETTE, laboratory administrator, researcher; b. Evian Les Baines Haute, Savoie, France, May 18, 1948; d. Alfred Noel and Marie Louise (Buffet) D.; m. Slimane Bessioud, June 28, 1973 (div. May 1978); 1 child, Myriam Bessioud. BA, Lycee-Thonon, Lyon, France, 1966; MD, Faculte Medecine, Lyon, France, 1975, cert. in sexology, 1980, cert. in gynecology, 1981, cert. in sonography, 1982, cert. in andrology, 1985. Physician Mutelle Nationale Etudiants de France, Lyon, 1976-78; pediatric cons. Direction Dept. Action Sanitaire & Sociale, Lyon, 1977-78, gynecologist in family planning, 1979-84; gynecologist Hosp. Vienne, Lyon, 1977-84; gynecologist, sonographist Hosp. E. Herriot, Lyon, 1981-84; co-mgr. Inst. Rhone Alpin, Lyon, 1984-88; lab. dir. Augusta (Ga.) Reproductive Biology Assn., 1988—; mem. Departmental Direction Social and Sanitary Orgn., Lyon, 1977-88. Participant: book Desir d'enfant Refus d'enfant, 1980; author: (with others) Future Aspects i Human IVF, 1987; contbr. articles to profl. jours. Mem. Societe Francaise Fertilite, Am. Soc. Andrology, Am. Fertility Soc., European Soc. Human Reprodn. and Embryology, Les Amis de L'Universite. Office: Augusta Reproductive Biology Assocs 812 Chafee Ave Augusta GA 30904

DUDASH, LINDA CHRISTINE, insurance executive; b. Pitts.; d. Andrew Daniel and Lillian (Reynolds) D. BA in English, Point Park Coll., 1969. Tech. writer Am. Insts. for Rsch., Pitts., 1968-69; claim svc. rep. Reliance Ins. Co., Pitts., 1969-70, claim rep., 1970-71; claim mgr. Reliance Ins. Co., Jacksonville, Fla., 1971-73, Harrisburg, Pa., 1973-80, Chgo., 1980-86; H.O. sr. claim supr. Zurich-Am. Ins. Group, Schaumburg, Ill., 1986-88, asst. v.p., mgr. liability claims, 1988—. Office: Zurich Am Ins Group Zurich Towers 800 American Dr Schaumburg IL 60196

DUDICS-DEAN, SUSAN ELAINE, interior designer; b. Perth Amboy, N.J., Oct. 22, 1950; d. Theodore W. and Joyce M. (Ryals) D.; married Apr. 30, 1989. BS in Sociology, W.Va. U., 1972; postgrad. Rutgers U., 1975-78, U. Calif., Irvine, 1979-81, Can. Coll., 1981-89. Programmer Prudential Life, Newark, 1972-73; sr. systems analyst residential interior design Johnson & Johnson, New Brunswick, N.J., 1973-78, Sperry Univac, Irvine, Calif., 1978-80; sr. systems analyst, project leader Robert A. McNeil, San Mateo, Calif., 1981-83; design dir. TransDesigns, Woodstock, Ga., 1982—. Contbr. articles to profl. jours. High sch. mentor Directions, San Francisco, 1985—. Mem. Women Entreprenuers (membership com., treas. 1983-87), Cen. N.J. Alumni Assn. (assoc. sec., founder, pres.), San Francisco C. of C., Nat. Assn. of Profl. Saleswomen, Am. Soc. Interior Designers (allied mem. 1989—), Delta Gamma. Recipient awards TransDesigns, Woods ock, Ga., 1984, 85, 86, 87, 89. Avocations: skiing, sewing, scuba diving, ballet, hand crafts. Office: Celestial Designs/TransDesigns 19 Molimo Dr San Francisco CA 94127

DUDLEY, ELIZABETH HYMER, security manager; b. Hibbing, Minn., Mar. 12, 1937; d. Howard Golden and Esther Juliette (Wanner) Hymer; m. Richard Walter Dudley, 1962. BA Brown U., 1959; postgrad. U. Calif., Berkeley. With AT&T Bell Labs., Murray Hill, N.J., 1959-89, systems programmer, personnel info., 1965-67, systems analyst, personnel info., 1967-71, sr. systems analyst, mgmt. info. and adminstrv. systems, 1971-77, applications systems coordinator mgmt. info. and adminstrv. systems, 1977-78, group supr. affirmative action compliance and reports, 1978-81, group supr. service ops. system support group, 1982-84, mgr. security, 1984-85, mgr. govt. security, 1986-89; ret., 1989. Mem. Nat. Security Indsl. Assn., Women's Rights Assn. (treas. 1977, v.p. 1978), Am. Soc. Indsl. Security, Nat. Classification Mgmt. Soc., Brown Network. Club: Pembroke Coll. of N.J. (publicity chmn. 1965-69, v.p. 1969-70). Office: AT&T Bell Labs Whippany Rd Whippany NJ 07981

DUDLEY, GLENNA GAIL, campus relations director; b. New Tazewell, Tenn., Dec. 3, 1944; d. Thomas G. and Cassie L. (Whitaker) Tolbert. AB, Ind. U., 1967, MA, 1974; JD cum laude, Ind. U., Indpls., 1979, postgrad. bus. adminstrn., 1986—. Bar: Ind., U.S. Dist. Ct. (so. dist.) Ind. Reporter Herald-Argus, La Porte, Ind., 1966; teaching asst. Ind. U., Bloomington, 1967-68; state house reporter Sta. WLWI-TV, Indpls., 1968-71; adminstrv. asst. Ind. Bur. Motor Vehicles, Indpls., 1971-72; info. dir. drug abuse div. Ind. Dept. Mental Health, Indpls., 1972-73; asst. dep. commr. Ind. Dept. Revenue, Indpls., 1973-76, dep. commr., 1976-86; govt. affairs counsel Blue Cross & Blue Shield Ind., Indpls., 1986-89; community resl. dir. Ind. U.-Purdue U., Indpls., 1989—; adj. prof. polit. sci. Ball State U., Muncie, Ind., 1986—; mem. com. on character and fitness Ind. Bd. Law Examiners, 1988—; mem. plan design task force Ind. Gov.'s Long Term Care Project, 1988—; bd. dirs. Ind. Life & Health Ins. Guaranty Assn.; subcom. chair adv.

com. State Health Policy Commn., 1990—. Mem. protocol com. Pan Am. Games, Indpls., 1985-87; mem. spl. events com. Ind. div. Am. Cancer Soc., 1986—; mem. Greenfield Redevelopment Commn., 1990—; bd. dirs. Indpls. Better Bus. Bur., 1986—; co-chmn. Hancock County Children's Fund, Riley Hosp., 1989. Recipient Casper award Indpls. Community Svc. Coun., 1969, Sagamore of Wabash award Gov. Ind., 1979, 88. Mem. Ind. Bar Assn., Hancock County Bar Assn., Indpls. Bar Assn. (ethics com. 1979—), Indpls. Press Club (program com.), Columbia Club (membership com.), Econs. Club Indpls. Methodist. Home: 115 McClellan Rd Greenfield IN 46140 Office: Ind U-Purdue U Indpls 355 N Lansing St #109 Indianapolis IN 46202

DUDLEY, LAQUITA JOY, resource specialist; b. Amherst, Tex., May 26, 1932; d. James Henry and Mable Claire (Bostick) Dillingham; m. Harold Clay Dudley; children: Harold Scott, Janet Ellen. BA in History, Mills Coll., Oakland, Calif., 1953; MA in Spl. Edn., Chapman Coll., Monterey, Calif., 1980. Tchr. Salinas (Calif.) City Schs., 1954-64, tchr., 1972-82, resource specialist, 1982—. Mem. AAUW, Calif. Sch. Leadership Acad., Monterey County Reading Assn., Calif. Reading Assn., Calif. Tchrs. Assn., NEA, Calif. Assn. Resource Spl., Monterey Bay Resource Spl. (pres. 1986-88), Monterey Mills Club (pres. 1962-63), Delta Kappa Gamma (pres. 1988-90), Salinas Elem. Tchrs. Coun. (rep., scholarship com. 1975-90). Democrat. Presbyterian. Office: Monterey Park Sch 410 San Miguel Ave Salinas CA 93901

DUERR, DIANNE MARIE, physical education educator, professional sports medicine consultant; b. Buffalo, July 14, 1945; d. Robert John and Aileen Louise (Scherer) D. BS in health and phys. edn., SUNY, Brockport, 1967; cert., SUNY, Oswego, 1982; postgrad., Canisius Coll., 1970-71. Cert. tchr., N.Y. Tchr. North Syracuse (N.Y.) Sch. Dist., 1967—; cons. sport medicine dept. orthopedic surgery Dept. Orthopedic Surgery SUNY Health Sci. Ctr., Syracuse, 1982—; creator Inst. for Sports Medicine and Human Performance SUNY Health Sci. Ctr., Syracuse, 1988; coord. scholastic sports injury reporting system project SUNY, 1985—. Author: SSIRS Pilot Study Report, 1987, SSIRS Fall Study Report, 1988; creator Scholastic Sports Injury Reporting System, 1985, Scholastic Head and Spine Injury Reporting System, 1989. Co-chmn. Sports Medicine USA, Amateur Athletic Union, Nat. Jr. Olympic Games, Syracuse, 1987, vol. Sports Medicine Empire State Games, Syracuse, 1987, active Girl Scouts U.S.; YMCA. Mem. Am. Coll. Sports Medicine, United Univ. Professions, AAHPERSD, Am. Fedn. Tchrs., N.Y. United Tchrs., North Syracuse Tchrs. Assn. Home: 418 Buffington Rd Syracuse NY 13224 Office: SUNY Dept Orthopedic Surgery 550 Harrison Ctr Syracuse NY 13202

DUERR, MARY JANE, medical transcriptionist; b. Ft. Smith, Ark., Sept. 8, 1955; d. Joseph Henry and Mary Rita (Gorrell) D. AAS, Tulsa Jr. Coll., 1975. Med. transcriptionist Holt-Krock Clinic, Ft. Smith, 1975—. Mem. Am. Assn. Med. Transcription (cert., v.p. Western Ark. chpt. 1984-90). Republican. Roman Catholic.

DUFFEY, JEANNE CHRISTAKOS, community relations director; b. East St. Louis, Ill., Oct. 6, 1945; d. Charles and Helen (Demetrulias) Christakos; chidren: Ellen Elizabeth, Polly Susan. BJ, U. Mo., 1967. Newspaper reporter Columbia (Mo.) Tribune, 1967-68; advt. copywriter Sears Nat. Hdqrs., Chgo., 1968-69; community rels. dir. Florissant Valley Coll., St. Louis, 1969-70; advt. copywriter Sears Retail Store, Huntsville, Ala., 1970-71; asst. to editor Wood River (Ill.) Jour., 1971-72; prodn. mgr. Am. Oil Chemists Soc., Champaign, Ill., 1972-74; pub. rels. dir. Ozarks Area Community Action Corp., Springfield, Mo., 1978-79; v.p. Doulgas Kelly & Assoc., Springfield, 1979-88; community rels. dir. Springfield-Greene Cuonty Libr. Dist., 1989—. Mem. Women in Communications, Inc., Pub. Rels. Soc. Springfield (chair spl. events com.), Mo. Libr. Assn. (pub. rels. coun.), Springfield Ad Club. Home: RR2 Box 80 Rogersville MO 65742 Office: Springfield Greene County Libr PO Box 760 Springfield MO 65801

DUFFEY, MERLEE H., nurse; b. Monroe, Mich., Apr. 10, 1939; d. Walter William and Helen Merlee (Waldvogel) Grams; m. Dean R. Duffey, Aug. 31, 1958 (div. Sept. 1983); children: Tammy, Dawn. Assoc., Oakland Community Coll., 1970; BSN magna cum laude, U. Mich., 1976, MS, 1978; postgrad., Wayne State U. RN. Staff nurse, head nurse Pontiac (Mich.) State Hosp., 1970-71; staff nurse Ont. Sch. for Deaf, Milton, Can., 1972-73; dir. in-svc. edn., dir. nursing Monroe Care Ctr., 1973-74; dir. nursing edn. Met. Regional Psychiat. Hosp., Westland, Mich., 1978-79; program dir. case mgmt. Monroe County Community Mental Health Ctr., Monroe, 1979-81; dep. dir. Wayne Ctr., Detroit, 1981-85; dir. client svcs. Vis. Nurse Assn. Huron Valley, Ann Arbor, 1985-87; dept. analyst VII Mich. Dept. Mental Health, Lansing, 1987—. Mem. Ann Arbor Myasthenia Gravis Patient Support Group, 1986-87; active Big Brothers/Big Sisters Greater Lansing, 1989—; mem. devel. disabled area group Detroit Wayne County Community Mental Health Bd., 1981-85. NIMH fellow, 1976-78. Mem. Am. Nurses Assn., Mich. Nurses Assn., U. Mich. Nurses Alumni Assn., Myasthenia Gravis Assn., Sigma Theta Tau. Unitarian Universalist.

DUFFY, ELAINE MARIE, psychologist; b. N.Y.C., Dec. 22, 1954; d. Joseph and Zoila Duffy. BA, Canisius Coll., 1977; MA, Hofstra U., 1981, PhD, 1984. Cert. clin. psychologist, sch. psychologist. Dir. learning disabilities ctr. Hofstra U., Hempstead, N.Y., 1982-84; sch. psychologist Farmingdale (N.Y.) Pub. Schs., 1983-84; v.p. Brittain Assocs., N.Y.C., 1984-88; pvt. practice clin. psychologist East Hills, N.Y., Manhattan, N.Y., 1985—; rsch. scientist dept. medicine, appointee dept. psychiatry SUNY at Downstate, Bklyn., 1989—; prin. Lazar, Duffy & Lazar Assocs., Glen Cove, N.Y., 1990—; cons. TriSource Group, Inc., New Rochelle, N.Y.,1 987—, Drake, Beam, Marin Inc., N.Y.C., 1986-89, Swain & Swain, Inc., N.Y.C., 1984—, South Nassau Communities Hosp., Oceanside, N.Y., 1984—; NIH rsch. scientist SUNY at Downstate Med. Ctr., 1989—. Co-author: Industrial Behavior Modification, 1982. Bd. dirs. Ctr. for Organizational Effectiveness, N.Y.C., 1989—; bd. dirs. Parkinson Found. Long Island, 1987—. NIH Rsch. grantee social impact rsch., 1977. Mem. Am. Psychol. Assn., Nassau County Psychol. Assn. Home: 150 Joralemon St 11B Brooklyn NY 11201 Office: 211 W 56th St Ste 36A New York NY 10019

DUFFY, ESTHER RODGERS (MRS. ROGER FRANCIS DUFFY), librarian; b. Pitts., Aug. 14, 1911; d. Arthur Gregory and Charlotte Catherine (Nagle) Rodgers; B. Music and B.S. in Music Edn., Seton Hill Coll., 1932; postgrad. U. Pitts., 1933, Carnegie Inst., 1935, Simmons Coll., 1941-42; m. Roger Francis Duffy, Nov. 14, 1945; children—Katherine, Mary Anne, Roger. Instr. music Coll. Misericordia, Dallas, Pa., 1932-37; music librarian Cornell U., Ithaca, N.Y., 1937-41; asst. music librarian Columbia U., N.Y.C., 1942-43; research librarian OSS, State Dept., 1943-44, Balkans outpost rep. Office War Info., 1944-46, Balkans regional rep. USIS, 1946; asst. to pres. Juilliard Sch. Music, N.Y.C., 1947-49; asst. to mng. dir. U.S. Internat. Book Assn., N.Y.C., 1945-47; librarian fine arts Greenwich (Conn.) Library, 1961-81. Mem. adv. com. Greenwich Sr. Center. Mem. Greenwich Arts Council, AAUW, Kappa Gamma Pi. Home: 2 Peters Rd Riverside CT 06878

DUFFY, NANCY KEOGH, TV broadcast professional; b. Washington, Nov. 24, 1947; d. William Francis and Gertrude K. (Keogh) D.; divorced; children: Peter Patrick, Matthew Michael. Student, St. Mary of the Woods Coll.; AB, Marywood Coll., 1967. News reporter Sta. WHEN TV and Radio, Syracuse, N.Y., 1967-70; city press sec. City of Syracuse, 1970; news reporter Sta. WTVH, Syracuse, 1971-77; news anchorperson Sta. WIXT-TV, Syracuse, 1977—; talk show host Syracuse New Channels, 1986-87; talk show host, producer Community Connections, 1987-89; instr. Syracuse U. Producer t.v. series Duffy's People. Founder Syracuse St. Patricks Parade, 1983; organizer Cooperstown 50th Anniversary Baseball Hall of Fame Parade, 1989; organizer opening ceremonies Empire State Games, 1990; co-organizer Save our Syracuse Symphony, 1984; active Project Children, Syracuse, YMCA; telethon host Muscular Dystrophy Assn.; bd. dirs. The Media Unit, 1977—, Onondaga County Traffic Safety Bd., 1977-90; producer Talent Bank; cons. Jr. League, J. Dist. 4 Nurses. Recipient Nat. Angel award Best Spl. Religion in Media, Post Standard Woman of Achievement award, First Downtown award for Excellence 1986, Mayor's Achievement award 1985, Outstanding Communicator award Sta. WICI. Mem. Am. Women in Radio and TV (nat. award 1973), Women in Communications, Syracuse Press Club (bd. dirs. 1987—, v.p. 1990), Syracuse Rotary (pub. rels. 1989). Roman Catholic. Office: Sta WIXT-TV 5904 Bridge St Syracuse NY 13057

DUFRESNE, JERILYN CLARE, social services executive; b. Quincy, Ill., Aug. 2, 1947; d. Edward Arthur and Elaine Catherine (Kuhlman) Bozarth; m. Phillip Burns, Sept. 2, 1967 (div. Mar. 1978); m. John R. Dufresne, Aug. 23, 1980 (div. June 1983); children: Robert, Jill. Student, Quincy Coll., 1965-67; BS summa cum laude, Troy State U., 1979; M of Social Work, Washington U., St. Louis, 1984. Rehab. counselor Goodwill Industries of Chattahoochie Valley, Inc., Columbus, Ga., 1977-79; caseworker Chaddock, Quincy, Ill., 1979-81; team coord., 1981-82; asst. to v.p. Chaddock, Quincy, 1982-83, dir. tng., 1984-85, unit dir., 1985-86, dir. rsch. and program devel., 1986-87, dir. community based svcs., 1987-89, v.p. for programs, 1989—. Co-chair Pax Christi, Quincy, 1986—; mem. Diocesan Justice and Peace commn., Springfield, Ill., 1985-88, Govtl. Affairs Commn., Child Care Assn., Springfield, 1987—; chmn. Social Action Commn., Quincy, 1987-88; pres. St. Francis Parish Council, Quincy, 1988-89; mem. Diocesan Pastoral Council, 1987—, exec. com., 1988-89. Mem. Acad. of Cert. Social Workers, Nat. Assn. of Social Workers, Child Care Assn. of Ill., Ill. Council on Tng. (treas. 1986-89, vice chair 1989—). Democrat. Roman Catholic. Home: 709 Oakland Ave Quincy IL 62301 Office: Chaddock 205 S 24th St Quincy IL 62301

DUGAN, KIMIKO HATTA (MRS. WAYNE ALEXANDER DUGAN), anatomist, educator; b. Kyoto City, Japan, Oct. 21, 1924; came to U.S., 1948, naturalized, 1956; d. Shinzo and Sano (Hatta) Hatta; student U. Md., 1957-58; B.A., Okla. Coll. Women, 1961; M.S., U. Okla., 1965, Ph.D., 1970; m. Wayne Alexander Dugan, Aug. 18, 1947 (dec. Aug. 1971). Grad. fellow dept. anatomy Sch. Medicine, U. Okla., Oklahoma City, 1964-69, instr. dept. anat. sci. Coll. Medicine, 1969-71, asst. prof., 1971-78, assoc. prof., 1978—. Recipient Undergrad. Chemistry Achievement award Okla. Coll. Women, 1960; elected to U. Sci. and Arts Okla. (formerly Okla. Coll. Women) Alumni Hall of Fame, 1977. Mem. AAAS, AAUW, Am. Assn. Anatomists, Am. Inst. Chemists, Inc., Okla. Acad. Sci., Am. Chem. Soc., Am. Soc. Zoologists, Electron Microscopy Soc. Am., N.Y. Acad. Sci., Internat. Soc. Devel. Comparative Immunology, Sigma Xi. Episcopalian. Home: 1139 NW 63d St Oklahoma City OK 73116 Office: U Okla Health Scis Ctr Coll Medicine Dept Anat Scis PO Box 26901 Oklahoma City OK 73190

DUGAN, LINDA HERRINGTON, nurse, educator; b. Indpls.; d. Malcolm Truman and Anna Charlene (Halstead) Herrington; m. Robert Timothy Dugan; children: Kristen Elizabeth, Michael Gregory. BS in Nursing, Ind. U., 1976, MS in Nursing, 1978. Various positions Child Guidance Clinic, Indpls., 1975-76; student nurse Ind. U. Hosp., Indpls., 1975-77; psychiat. nurse specialist Gallahue Mental Health Ctr., Indpls., 1977-82; clin. nurse specialist, psychiatry Community Hosp., Indpls., 1982-86; acting co-chair, program dir. dept. nursing Marian Coll., Indpls., 1986—; counselor, cons. BDGW, Indpls., 1988—; chair mental health com. Community Adv. Bd. St. Vincent's Stress Ctr., Indpls., 1989—. Contbr. articles to profl. jours. Mem. Task Force Child Abuse and Neglect, Indpls., 1975-77, Ind. Youth Legis. Task Force, Indpls., 1987—, edn. comm. Mental Health Assn., Marion City, Ind., 1987—; vol. Amer. Heart Assn., Indpls., 1983, 85. Mem. Ind. Advocates Child Psychiat. Nursing (program chair 1984-86, conf. chair 1986-88, state chair 1988—), Nat. Advocates Child Psychiat. Nursing, Marian Coll. Nursing Honors Soc., Sigma Theta Tau. Office: Marian Coll 3200 Cold Springs Rd Indianapolis IN 46222

DUGGAN, CAROL COOK, researcher; b. Conway, S.C., May 25, 1946; d. Pierce Embree and Lillian Watkins (Eller) Cook; m. Kevin Duggan, Dec. 29, 1973. BA, Columbia Coll., 1968; MS, U. Ky., 1970. Reference asst. Richland County Pub. Library, Columbia, S.C., 1968-69, asst. to dir., 1970, chief adult services, 1971-82; dir. Maris Research, Columbia, 1982—; lectr. mem. Friends of Richland County Pub. Library, 1977—, Greater Columbia (S.C.) Literacy Council, 1973—; mem. worship com. Washington St. United Meth. Ch., Columbia, 1985-86, mem. staff-parish relations com., 1986—, mem. history and archives com., 1988—; mem. exec. bd. United Meth. Women 1983—, treas. unit 7, 1989—. Recipient Sternheimer award, 1968. Mem. ALA (councilor 1980-82, chmn. state membership com. 1979-83), S.C. Library Assn. (sec. 1976, exec. bd. 1976, 78-82), S.C. Pub. Library Assn. (pres. 1980-81), Beta Phi Mu. Methodist. Club: PEO (pres. 1983-85, chmn. amendments and recommendations com. 1983-85, historian 1986-87, treas. State conv., 1987-88), Columbia Coll. Afternoon of S.C. Home: 2101 Woodmere Dr Columbia SC 29204

DUGGAN, JOAN, social services administrator; b. Cleve., July 12, 1935; d. Joseph John and Norberta (McAuliffe) Colosimo; m. Patrick James Duggan, Aug. 24, 1957; children: Michael, Daniel, James, Robert, Timothy. BS in Nursing, Madonna Coll., 1973; MPA, U. Mich., Dearborn, 1987. RN, Mich. Psychiatric nurse Detroit Receiving Hosp., 1957-58; asst. research Wayne State U., Detroit, 1958; clin. instr. nursing Madonna Coll., Livonia, Mich., 1973; dir. vol. svcs. City of Livonia, 1974-76, dir. Dept. Community Resources, 1976-84, exec. asst. to mayor, 1984-87; pres., treas. Out-Wayne County Human Svcs., Inc., Northville, Mich., 1981-86, cons., 1987—; coord., cons. Mich. Tng. and Resource Ctr., Northville, 1987—; mem. project adv. coun. Mich. Dept. Social Svcs., Lansing, 1989—. Co-author tng. manuals for youth; editor: Livonia 2000, 1986. Candidate for mayor City of Livonia, 1987; bd. dirs. McNamara Charity Fund, Livonia, 1989; mem. exec. bd. Pvt. Industry C un. County of Wayne, Livonia, 1988—; conf. speaker Mich. Mcpl. League, 1976-86, mem. tng. adv. com., 1986-87. Recipient Salute to Woman award AAUW, Livonia, 1974, Nat. Vol. Activist award Nat. Ctr. for Voluntary Action, Washington, 1977, Creativity in Govt. award Mich. Conf. Mayors, Lansing, 1977. Mem. Nat. Assn. Women Cons.'s, Madonna Coll. Alumni Assn. (v.p. 1988—), Livonia Jaycee Aux. (pres. 1963-64, Woman of Yr. award 1975), Women's Econ. Club., Lawyers' Wives Club. Republican. Roman Catholic. Home: 15698 Riverside Livonia MI 48154

DUGGAN, KELLY MARIE, ; b. Newburyport, Mass., Jan. 6, 1963; d. John Wright and Raelene F. (Noyes) D. Student, No. Essex Community Coll., Haverhill, Mass., 1987—. Mgr. Swartz's Grocery Store, Newburyport, Mass., 1981-84; sec. Waverly News Co., Inc., Newburyport, Mass., 1984-86. Vol. swim instr. YWCA, Newburyport, 1979-80, vol. ann. road race, 1979-89. Scholar No. Essex Community Coll. Alumni Assn., 1989, No. Essex Community Coll. Found., 1989. Home: One Whites Ct Newburyport MA 01950

DUGGAN, M. JANE, marketing executive; b. East Orange, N.J., Nov. 5, 1949; d. Joseph P. and Mary (Winters) Militano. BA, Montclair State Coll., Upper Montclair, N.J., 1970; MBA, U. Pa., 1984. Tchr. French-Italian Summit (N.J.) Bd. Edn., 1971-79; reg. mgr. Burroughs Corp., Paramus, N.J., 1980-83; mktg. assoc. Estee Lauder Cosmetics Ltd., London, 1985-86; product mgr. Estee Lauder Internat., Inc., N.Y.C., 1986-87; dir. mktg. Estee Lauder Cosmetics Ltd., Toronto, Ont., Can., 1987; internat. area dir. Calvin Klein Cosmetics Corp., N.Y.C., 1988-89; dir. mktg. Fragrance div. Tiffany & Co., N.Y.C., 1989—. Fulbright-Hayes fellow, 1974, 79. Mem. Cosmetic and Exec. Women, Olympus Inc. (activities dir.), Summit Edn. Assn. (pres. 1976-78), Fashion Group Internat., Am. Soc. for Prevention of Cruelty to Animals, People for Ethical Treatment of Animals, Humane Soc. Democrat. Roman Catholic. Home: 3 Hanover Sq #2L New York NY 10004

DUGGINS, MARIAN BARBER, retired nurse administrator; b. Eden, N.C., Jan. 13, 1925; d. Odell Hillard and Autney (Hughes) Barber; m. William Paul Duggins, June 24, 1949; children: Eva Ruth Haywood, William Odell. Student, Bob Jones U., 1942-43; RN, N.C. Bapt. Hosp., 1946; cert. in pub. health, U. N.C., 1947. Staff nurse Forsyth County Health Dept., Winston-Salem, N.C., 1947-51, nurse adminstr., 1957-59; clinic coord. Forsyth County Mental Health Dept., Winston-Salem, 1959-74; treatment coord. Mandala Psychiat. Hosp., Winston-Salem, 1974-78; nurse supr. New Hanover County Health Dept., Wilmington, N.C., 1978-80; nurse adminstr. New Hanover County Health Dept., Wilmington, 1980-90; ret., 1990; cons. Forsyth County Half-Way House, Winston-Salem, 1960-74, Goodwill Industries, Winston-Salem, 1961-74. Co-author: Nurses Teach Mothers, 1949. Pres. Prince Ibraham PTA, Winston-Salem, 1962, Mineral Springs PTA, 1968; chair Operation Santa Claus, John U. Hosp., Butner, N.C., 1965; mem. awards selection com. YWCA, Wilmington, 1986. Recipient Margaret B. Dolan award N.C. Pub. Health Nurse, 1986. Mem. N.C. Pub. Health Assn. (Svc. award 1984, Outstanding Career Achievement award 1986, program chair ea. dist. 1984-85, program chair maternal child health sect. 1986-87), Forsyth County Mental Health Assn. (chair 1965-66). Republican. Baptist. Home: 3851 Malvern Rd Wilmington NC 28403

DUGUAY, BERNADETTE ANN, service company owner, real estate broker; b. Manchester, N.H., Mar. 16, 1963; d. Bertha Germaine (Gamache) Kennedy. BS, Keene (N.H.) State Coll., 1985. Lic. real estate broker, N.H. Supr. Svc. Master, Concord, N.H., 1985-86; mail clk. State of N.H., Concord, 1986-87; owner, prin. B&V Clean Care, Pembroke, N.H., 1987—; realtor Century 21 Raymond & Marden, Hooksett, N.H., 1988—. Mem. Nat. Assn. Realtors, Home Builders Assn. Democrat. Roman Catholic. Home: RFD 3 Leavitt Rd Box 3144 Pittsfield NH 03263 Office: Century 21 Raymond & Marden 38 Whitehall Rd Hooksett NH 03106

DUHME, CAROL MCCARTHY, civic worker; b. St. Louis, Apr. 13, 1917; d. Eugene Ross and Louise (Roblee) McCarthy; AB, Vassar Coll., 1939; m. Sheldon Ware, June 12, 1941 (dec. 1944); 1 son, David; m. 2d, H. Richard Duhme, Jr., Apr. 9, 1947; children: Benton (dec.), Ann, Warren (dec.). Tchr. elem. sch., 1939-41, 42-44; moderator St. Louis Assn. Congl. Chs., 1952; dir. Christian edn. First Congl. Ch., St. Louis, 1959-62, trustee, 1964-66, mem. ch. council, 1974-75, 88—, bd. deaconesses, 1978-81, bd. deacons, 1982-85, chmn. bd. Christian Edn., 1987-88; former bd. dirs. Community Music Schs., St. Louis, Community Sch., Ch. Women United, John Burroughs Sch., St. Louis Bicentennial Women's Com., St. Louis Jr. League; pres. St. Louis Vassar Club; pres. bd. dirs. YWCA, St. Louis, 1973-76, chmn. ann. fund, 1989-90; bd. dirs. North Side Team Ministry, 1968-84, Chautauqua (N.Y.) Instn., 1971-79, mem. adv. coun. to bd., 1987—; adv. coun. Mo. Bapt. Hosp., 1973-89; exec. com. bd. dirs. Eden Theol. Sem., 1981—, presdl. search com. 1986-87; sec. bd. dirs. UN Assn., St. Louis, 1976-84; pres. bd. dirs. Family and Children's Svc. Greater St. Louis, 1977-79; mem. chancellor's long-range planning com. Washington U., 1980-81, mem. Nat. Coun., Sch. Social Work, 1987—; chmn. Benton Roblee Duhme Scholarship Fund; pres., trustee Joseph H. and Florence A. Roblee Found., St. Louis, pres. 1984—; chmn. Chautaugua Bell Tower Scholarship Fund, 1960—. Mem. corp. assembly Blue Cross Hosp. Svc. of Mo., 1978-86. Recipient Mary Alice Messerley award for volunteerism Health and Welfare Coun. St. Louis, 1971; Vol. of Yr. award, YWCA, 1976; Woman of Achievement award St. Louis Globe Democrat, 1980. Home: 8 Edgewood Rd Saint Louis MO 63124

DUKAKIS, KATHARINE (KITTY DUKAKIS), wife of governor of Massachusetts, civic worker; d. Harry Ellis Dickson; m. John Chaffetz (div.); 1 child, John; m. Michael Dukakis, 1963; children: Andrea, Kara. Former modern dance tchr., TV reporter; dir. Pub. Space Ptnrships. Project Harvard U., Cambridge, Mass. Author: (with Jane Scovell) Now You Know, 1990. Former mem. U.S. Commn. on the Holocaust; former chmn. Mass. Gov.'s Adv. Com. on Homeless. Democrat. Jewish. *

DUKAKIS, OLYMPIA, actress; b. Lowell, Mass., June 20, 1931; d. Constantine S. and Alexandra (Christos) D.; m. Louis Zorich; children: Christina, Peter, Stefan. BS, Boston U., MFA. Co-founder, artistic dir. Whole Theatre, Montclair, N.J., 1970-90; co-founder Charles Playhouse, Boston; master tchr. NYU, 1970-85. rppeared in over 125 prodns. for regional theatres, N.Y. Shakespeare Theatre, Circle Repetory Theatre, American Place Theatre and numerous Off-Broadway theatres; appearances in film include King of America, Moonstruck, 1987 (Golden Globe, Academy Award Suppporting Actress), Steel Magnolias, 1988, Look Who's Talking, 1988, Made for Each Other, Dad, 1989, In the Spirit, 1990. Del. Dem. Nat. Convention, 1988. Recipient 2 Obie awards, Los Angeles Film Critics award, 1988. Mem. Actor's Equity Assn., Screen Actors Guild, Am. Fedn. TV and Radio Artists. Office: care Whole Theatre 544 Bloomfield Ave Upper Montclair NJ 07042

DUKE, ELLEN KAY, public relations professional, community activist; b. Indpls., June 7, 1952; d. Richard Thomas and Ruby Mae (Wright) D. Student Chapman Coll., Orange, Calif., 1972; B.S. in Pub. Affairs, Ind. U.-Bloomington, 1975; postgrad. Portland State U., 1980-81. Cert. Dale Carnegie Pub. Speaking Instr., 1987—; News reporter, Salem Statesman, Corvallis, Oreg., 1976-78; com. adminstr. Oreg. State Legislature, Salem, 1979-80; pub. involvement coordinator Met. Regional Service Dist., Portland, 1981-82; account mgr. Thunder & Visions, Portland, 1982-83; project asst. Amdahl Corp., Sunnyvale, Calif., 1983-84; spl. project coordinator Computerland Corp., Hayward, Calif., 1984-89; producer, lead facilitator Sage, Inc., Walnut Creek, Calif., 1982—; pub. rels. dir. local YMCA. Co-author: (ednl. film) Communication Skills, 1975. Chairperson Corvallis Budget Commn., Oreg., 1978; commr. Hayward Library, Calif., 1985—, Alameda County Consumer Affairs, Oakland, 1985; rep. Nat. Democratic Conv., N.Y.C., 1982. Named Able Toastmaster Toastmasters Internat., 1981. Mem. Nat. Assn. Female Execs., Am. Mktg. Assn., Sierra Club (San Francisco). Office: YMCA of East Bay 2330 Broadway Oakland CA 94612

DUKE, LOIS LOVELACE, government educator, public information officer; b. Bessemer City, N.C., Feb. 13, 1935; d. Fred R. and Pearl (Kiser) Lovelace; widowed; children: Bruce F., Mary Louanne. BA, U. S.C., 1976, MA, 1979, PhD, 1986. Prof. Am. govt. and polit. theory U. S.C., Clemson U. and Auburn U., Montgomery, Ala., 1980-89; asst. prof. U. Ala., Tuscaloosa, 1989—; pub. relations cons. Pub. Relations/Mktg. Assocs., Charlotte, N.C., 1982-85; chief pub. info. and community relations officer, Pub. Affairs Office, Fort Jackson, S.C. Organist and choir dir. United Meth. Ch.; officer PTO; leader Indian Waters Council Boy Scouts Am.; leader Congaree area Girl Scouts Am. Mem. Pub. Relations Soc. Am. (pres.), Am. Women in Radio and TV (pres. Palmetto Chpt.), Gamma Tau Alpha, Sigma Delta Chi, Pi Sigma Alpha, Beta Sigma Phi. Clubs: Columbia Media (pres.), Columbia Advt. Home: 129 Garden Springs Rd Columbia SC 29209 Office: Clemson U Dept Polit Sci 403 Strode Tower Clemson SC 29634-1509

DUKE, PATTY (ANNA MARIE DUKE), actress; b. N.Y.C., Dec. 14, 1946; d. John P. and Frances (McMahon) Duke; m. John Astin, 1973 (div. 1985); children: Sean, Mackenzie; m. Michael Pierce, March 15, 1986. Grad., Quintano's School for Young Profls. Pres. Screen Actors Guild, 1985—, lecturer Am. Film Inst., 1988. TV appearances include Armstrong Circle Theatre, 1955, The Prince and the Pauper, 1957, Wuthering Heights, 1958, U.S. Steel Hour, Meet Me in St. Louis, 1959, Swiss Family Robinson, 1958, The Power and the Glory, 1961, (series) Patty Duke Show, 1964-66, Before and After, 1979, Women in White, The Baby Sitter, The Women's Room, All's Fair, 1981-82, Something So Right, Best Kept Secrets, September Gun, (series) It Takes Two, 1983, (TV film) A Time to Triumph, George Washington: The Forging of a Nation, 1984, Fight for Life, numerous others; theatrical appearances include The Miracle Worker, 1959-61, Isle of Children, 1962; motion picture appearances in The Miracle Worker, 1962 (Acad. award as best supporting actress 1962), Valley of the Dolls, 1967, Me, Natalie, 1969 (Golden Globe award as best actress 1970), My Sweet Charlie, 1970, Captains and the Kings, 1976, The Miracle Worker, 1979, Something Special, 1987; co-author Surviving Sexual Assault, 1983, Call Me Anna, 1987. Nat. corp. council Muscular Dystrophy Assns. Am. Recipient Emmy Awards, 1964, 69, 76, 79. Mem. AFTRA. Office: care The Agy 10351 Santa Monica Blvd Suite 211 Los Angeles CA 90025*

DUKE, ROBIN CHANDLER TIPPETT, corporate professional; b. Balt., Oct. 13, 1923; d. Richard Edgar and Esther (Chandler) Tippett; m. Angier Biddle Duke, May 1962; children: Jeffrey R. Lynn, Letitia Lynn Valiunas, Angier Biddle Jr. Grad. high sch., Balt. Fashion editor N.Y. Jour. Am., N.Y.C., 1944-46; freelance writer N.Y.C., 1946-50; rep. Orvis Bros., N.Y.C., 1953-58; mem. pub. relations staff Pepsi Cola Co., Internat., N.Y.C., 1958-62; bd. dirs. Am. Home Products, N.Y.C., Rockwell Internat., Pitts., Internat. Flavors & Fragrances, N.Y.C., Dreyfus, N.Y.C., East River Savs. Bank, New Rochelle, N.Y. Vice-chmn., bd. dirs. Inst. Internat. Edn., N.Y.C., 1975—; co-chmn. Population Crisis Com., Washington, 1972; bd. dirs. Alan Guttmacher Inst., N.Y.C., 1976, Guggenheim Mus., N.Y.C., 1980. Mem. Colony Club, River Club. Democrat. Home: 435 E 52d St New York NY 10022

DUKE, VERONICA MURRAY, social worker; b. Cape May, N.J., Sept. 28, 1931; d. Thomas Patrick and Cora Beatrice (Davies) Murray; student U. Tampa, 1949-51; B.S., U. Fla., 1953; M.S.W., U. Mo., 1959; m. Alvah G. Heideman, Jr., 1955 (div. 1976); children—Alvah G. III, Sara Elizabeth; m. 2d, George Duke, Jr., 1979 (dec. 1989). Caseworker, Hillsborough County,

Tampa, Fla., 1954-56; caseworker State of Mo., Fulton, 1956-59; chief social worker Mo. State Sch., 1959-60; psychiat. social worker State of Alaska, Anchorage, 1970-72; chief social worker Alaska Psychiat. Inst., U. Alaska, Anchorage, 197287; pvt. cons., Anchorage, 1987—; field instr. U. Wash.-Yeshiva U. Republican Committeewoman, Columbia, Mo., 1969; pres. Camp Fire Girls Council, 1969-70; pres. aux. bd. Providence Hosp., 1989-90. Served as ensign USNR, 1953-54: Korea. Diplomate Nat. Assn. Social Workers; mem. Soc. Dirs. Hosp. Social Work, Acad. Cert. Social Workers, U.S. Ski Assn., Mo. Alumni Assn., Clin. Social Work Registry, Circle of Friends, U. Pacific. Republican. Episcopalian. Clubs: Soroptimists, Women's of Am. Home: 1710 Eastridge Dr Anchorage AK 99501 Office: 2900 Providence Rd Anchorage AK 99508

DUKEK, NANCY BOWMAN, travel consultant; b. Harrisburg, Pa., Jan. 8, 1916; d. Ernest Lavern and Gertrude (Horning) Bowman; m. Roger Withrow Williams, June 17, 1939 (dec. Dec. 1954); children: Cynthia Hinchman, Todd, Janet B.W., Patricia D.; m. William G. Dukek, June 30, 1956. BA with honors, Ohio Wesleyan U., 1936; MSc in Retailing, NYU, 1937. Feature publicity dir. Abraham & Straus Inc., Bklyn., 1937-39; pub. rels. dir. Hwy. Furniture Shop, North Plainfield, N.J., 1939-40, Plainfield (N.J.) Bd. Edn., 1940-42; adj. prof. Sch. Retailing NYU, N.Y.C., 1955-56; travel cons. Travelong, Inc., Elizabeth, N.J., 1960-61; owner Dukay Travel, Summit, N.J., 1961-87, cons., 1987—. Mem. Beacon Hill Club, Canoe Brook Country Club, Fortnightly Club, Coll. Club, LWV, Mortar Bd., Phi Beta Kappa. Democrat. Unitarian. Home: 11 Ridge Rd Summit NJ 07901 Office: Dukay Travel 110 Summit Ave Summit NJ 07901

DUKERT, BETTY COLE, television producer; b. Muskogee, Okla., May 9, 1927; d. Irvan Dill and Ione (Bowman) Cole; m. Joseph M. Dukert, May 19, 1968. Student, Lindenwood Coll., St. Charles, Mo., 1945-46, Drury Coll., Springfield, Mo., 1946-47; B.J., U. Mo., 1949. With Sta. KICK, Springfield, Mo., 1949-50; adminstrv. asst. Juvenile Office, Green County, Mo., 1950-52; with Sta. WRC-TV-NBC, Washington, 1952-56; assoc. producer Meet the Press, NBC, Washington, 1956-75; producer Meet the Press, NBC, 1975—; mem. Robert F. Kennedy Journalism Awards Com., 1978-82. Trustee Drury Coll., Springfield, Mo., 1984—. Recipient Disting. Alumna award Drury Coll., 1975; Disting. Alumni award U. Mo., 1978; Ted Yates award Washington chpt. Nat. Acad. TV Arts and Scis., 1979; Pub. Relations award for pub. service Am. Legion Nat. Comdrs., 1981. Mem. Am. Women in Radio and TV, Am. News Women's Club, Radio/TV Corrs. Assn., Women's Forum Washington, Soc. Profl. Journalists (dir. 1983-84), Silver Circle Broadcasting, Nat. Acad. TV Arts and Scis. Club: Nat. Press. Office: NBC News 4001 Nebraska Ave NW Washington DC 20016

DUKES, JOAN, state legislator; b. Tacoma, Wash.. Mem. Oreg. State Senate. Democrat. Home: Rte 2 Box 503 Astoria OR 97103*

DUKES, JOYCE LEAK, small business owner; b. Winston-Salem, N.C., May 3, 1954; d. Willie Thomas Sr. and Elizabeth (Lewis) Leak; m. Richard Dukes, Nov. 19, 1978; children: Richard Jr., ShaShonda Latrice, Melanie Diane. BA in Sociology, S.C. State Coll., 1976. Mgr. Quality Care Nursing Svc., West Hartford, Conn., 1980-86; pres. Joyce's Childcare Registry, Kernersville, N.C., 1986—. Mem. NAFE. Home and Office: 1385 Dora Dr Kernersville NC 27284

DUKES, REBECCA WEATHERS (BECKY DUKES), musician, singer, songwriter; b. Durham, N.C., Nov. 21, 1934; d. Elmer Dewey Weathers and Martha Rebecca (Kimbrough) Weathers-Hall; m. Charles Aubrey Dukes Jr., Dec. 20, 1955; children: Aurelia Ann, Charles Weathers, David Lloyd. BA, Duke U., 1956. Lic. elem. sch. tchr. Tchr. Durham City Schs., 1956-57; sec. USMC, Arlington, Va., 1957-58; tchr. Arlington County Schs., 1958-59; office mgr. Dukes and Kooken, Landover, Md., 1976; musical performer Washington and various locations, Va., Md., 1982—. Vocal student Todd Duncan; pianist, vocalist Back Alley Restaurant Lounge, 1982;orginal program, A Life Cycle in Song, presented throughout mid-Atlantic states and Washington; full operatic solo recital, 1983; featured performer benefit for Nat. Symphony Orch.; frequent performer pvt. functions, athletic, civic, religious and cultural events including appearances at Capitol Ctr., Cole Field House, George Washington U., Smith Ctr.; operatic solo concert with pianist Glenn Sales, 1985; benefit appearance U. Md. Concert Series, 1986, 87; holds copyrights for over 90 original songs including Between the Lovin' and the Leavin', Covers of My Mind, Gentle Thoughts (lead song Nat. Capitol Area Composers Series), Headin' Home Again, I Would Like to Be Reborn, Miss You, Tears, You Played a Part in My Life; author: (poems) Pottery. Pres. Nat. Capitol Law League, Washington, 1976-77; pres. women's group, deacon Riverdale Presby. Ch., Hyattsville, Md., 1968-70; chmn. event honoring wives of Supreme Ct. justices, 1981; mem. women's com. Nat. Symphony, 1980—. Recipient Friend of Yr. award Md. Summer Inst. for Creative & Performing Arts U. Md., 1986; named hon. trustee Prince George's (Md.) Arts Council, 1984—. Mem. Songwriter's Assn. Washington, William Preston Few Assn. of Duke U. (pres. couns., exec. bd. of ann. fund.), Internat. Platform Assn. Republican. Clubs: Founders of Duke U.; Pres.' of U. Md.; Univ. (Balt.). Home and Office: 7111 Pony Trail Hyattsville MD 20782

DUKES, TAMARA DOWNHAM, real estate executive; b. Lafayette, Ind., Sept. 22, 1962; d. Robert Henry and Sally (Ingleman) D.; stepfather: William E. Miller. BA, Wheaton (Ill.) Coll., 1984. Exec. v.p. corp. accounts Spencer Realty Co., N.Y.C., 1984—; singer, actress N.Y. area, 1986—. Mem. Nat. Assn. Female Execs. Baptist. Office: Spencer Realty 274 Madison Ave New York NY 10016

DULA, LUCILE NOELL, retired teacher; b. Hillsborough, N.C., May 18, 1914; d. Frederick Young and Mary Rebecca (Lloyd) Noell; m. Thomas Harshaw Dula; children: Thomas Hunter, Harry Sutton, Frederick Lloyd (dec.). BA, East Carolina U., 1934; MEd, Duke U., 1951. English and algebra tchr. Hillsborough High Sch., 1935-36; English and history tchr. Aberdeen (N.C.) High Sch., 1937, Hillsborough High Sch., 1937-40; English tchr. Garner (N.C.) High Sch., 1942-43; tchr. Caldwell High Sch., Rougemont, N.C., 1943-44, Elon College (N.C.) High Sch., 1944-45; English and history tchr. Aycock High Sch., Cedar Grove, N.C., 1945-48; English Tchr. Burlington (N.C.) High Sch., 1948-51; English, speech and advanced composition tchr. Walter Williams High Sch., Burlington, 1951-74; speech events coach Burlington High Sch., Williams High Sch., 1948-74; mem. com. readers N.C. English Tchrs., 1964-84. Author: Pelican Guide to Hillsborough, 1979, rev. edit., 1989, Morsels for Miscellaneous Moments, 1986; contbr. prose, fiction, poems to lit. publs. Editor newsletter St. Matthew's Episcopal Ch., Hillsborough, 1983, lay reader, 1982-85; judge local speech events; speaker to schs., civic and religious groups. Recipient citations VFW, 1959-61, Degree of Distinction, Nat. Forensic League, 1957, Honor plaques Freedom's Found. Valley Forge, 1969-72, Extraordinary Woman of N.C. award Lady Stetson div. Coty, 1987, light verse awards Idaho Writers League, 1988, N.C. Poetry Soc., 1989, Valley Forge Tchrs. award, 1974; Nat. Coun. Tchrs. of English grantee English Inst., Duke U., 1961. Mem. AAUW, AARP, Acad. Am. Poets, N.C. Poetry Soc., Nat. Coun. Tchrs. English, Hillsborough Bus. and Profl. Women (Woman of Yr. 1989),Hillsborough Hist. Soc., Kappa Delta Pi. Democrat. Home: PO Box 222 Hillsborough NC 27278

DULANY, ELIZABETH GJELSNESS, university press administrator; b. Charleston, S.C., Mar. 11, 1931; d. Rudolph Hjalmar and Ruth Elizabeth (Weaver) Gjelsness; m. Donelson Edwin Dulany, Mar. 19, 1955; 1 son, Christopher Daniel. BA, Bryn Mawr Coll., 1952. Proofreader, editor Books in Print, R.R. Bowker Co., N.Y.C., summers 1948-51, mng. editor, summer 1952; med. sec., editor dept. pediatrics U. Mich. Hosp., Ann Arbor, 1953-54; editorial asst. E.P. Dutton & Co., N.Y.C., 1954-55; editorial asst. U. Ill. Press, Champaign, 1956-59, asst. to editor, 1959-60, asst. editor, 1960-67, assoc. editor, 1967-72, mng. editor, 1972—, asst. dir., 1983—. Democrat. Episcopalian. Home: 73 Greencroft Champaign IL 61821 Office: U Ill Press 54 E Gregory St Champaign IL 61820

DULEY, SUSAN INGE, dental hygiene educator, consultant; b. Flint, Mich., Feb. 15, 1947; d. Van Howard and Eileen Rebecca (Terry) Young; m. Lee Aldon Duley, Nov. 22, 1979; children: Linda S. Duley Christian, David D., Jonathan L. BS, U. Detroit, 1978, MS, 1980, EdS, 1983; EdD, Western Mich. U., 1989. With Mott Community Coll., Flint, 1973—, div. chairperson, 1985-86, adminstr. human resource devel., 1988—; counselor 1st Presbyn. Ch., Flint, 1983; cons. Performax Corp., Minn., 1985—. Precinct del. Rep. Party, Flint, 1981. Mem. Mich. Dental Hygiene Assn. (pres. 1976), Am. Assn. Women in Community and Jr. Colls. (Leadership award 1987), Mich. Edn. Assn., Jr. League, Flint Women's Forum. Presbyterian. Office: Mott Community Coll 1401 E Court St Flint MI 48502

DULIN, PATRICIA ANN, accountant; b. Muleshoe, Tex., Mar. 24, 1952; d. Woodroe G. and Donna (Radosevich) D. BSBA, U. Nev., Las Vegas, 1975. CPA, Nev. Staff acct. Alex Logan & Co., Las Vegas, 1975; staff acct. Goussak & Raben, Ltd., Las Vegas, 1976-84, acct., owner, ptnr., 1980-84; acct., owner, ptnr. Goussak, Raben & Co., Las Vegas, 1984-88, Dulin & Raben, Ltd., Las Vegas, 1988—. Bd. dirs., officer Frontier coun. Girl Scouts U.S., 1980—; bd. dirs. Jr. League Las Vegas, 1983—, Clark County chpt. ARC, 1987-89, So. Nev. div. Desert S.W. chpt. Multiple Sclerosis Soc., 1989—. Recipient appreciation pin Frontier Coun. Girl Scouts U.S., 1986. Mem. AICPA, Nev. Soc. CPA's, Am. Soc. Women Accts. (bd. dirs. officer 1976-79). Office: 1785 E Sahara Ste Ste 245 Las Vegas NV 89104

DULLINGER, GLORIA, health science association administrator; b. St. Cloud, Minn., Aug. 27, 1962; d. George Paul and Celestine (Warzecha) Lentner; m. Wayne Allen Dullinger, Aug. 2, 1986; children: Nicole, Wesley. BS, U. Minn., 1985; MS, St. Mary's Coll., Minn., 1988; Nurse Anesthetist with honors, Abbott Northwestern Sch., Mpls., 1988. RN, Minn. Nurses aide U. Minn. Hosp., Mpls., 1981-83, student nurse, 1983-84, nurse, 1985-87; lab. processor Lufkin Med. Lab., Mpls., 1980-85; salesperson Donaldson's Dept. Store, Mpls., 1987; nurse anesthetist Riverside Med. Ctr., Mpls., 1988-89; asst. dir. VA Med. Ctr., Mpls., 1989—. Mem. Am. Assn. Nurse Anesthetists, Am. Vet. Assn. Nurse Anesthetists, Minn. Assn. Nurse Anesthetists (rules and regulation com. 1989—), Sigma Theta Tau, Alpha Tau Delta. Democrat. Roman Catholic. Home: 835 Lois Ln Lino Lakes MN 55014

DUMAS, CLAUDIA JEAN, lawyer; b. Kingston, N.Y., Aug. 2, 1959; d. Allan Mason and Virginia Nellie (Bell) D. AB, Wellesley Coll., 1981; JD cum laude, Cornell U., 1984. Bar: Mass. 1985, N.Y. 1987. Assoc. Peabody & Brown, Boston, 1984-86, Shearman & Sterling, N.Y.C., 1986-89; atty. IBM Corp., Stamford, Conn., 1989—. Durant scholar Wellesley Coll., 1981. Mem. Phi Beta Kappa. Office: IBM Credit Corp 290 Harbor Dr PO Box 10399 Stamford CT 06904

DUMAS, LINDA JEAN, telecommunications executive; b. Paris, Tenn., July 8, 1959; d. Williams Tharpe and Peggy Jean (French) D. BS, Murray State U., 1981. Tech. cons. South Cen. Bell Tel. Co., Louisville, 1981-82; tech. cons. AT&T, Louisville, 1983-85, account exec., 1986-87; mktg. mgr. AT&T, Bridgewater, N.J., 1988—. Mem. Am. Mktg. Assn. Republican. Methodist. Office: AT&T 55 Corporate Dr Bridgewater NJ 08807

DUMAS, RHETAUGH ETHELDRA GRAVES, nursing school dean; b. Natchez, Miss., Nov. 26, 1928; d. Rhetaugh Graves and Josephine (Clemmons) Graves Bell; m. A.W. Dumas, Jr., Dec. 25, 1950; 1 child, Adrienne. BS in Nursing, Dillard U., 1951; MS in Psychiat. Nursing, Yale U., 1961; PhD in Social Psychology, Union Grad. Sch., Union for Experimenting Colls. and Univs., Cinn., 1975; also various other courses; D Pub. Svc. (hon.), Simmons Coll., 1976, U. Cin., 1981; LHD (hon.), Yale U., 1989; LLD (hon.), Dillard U., 1990. Instr. Dillard U., 1957-59, 61; research asst., instr. Sch. Nursing Yale U., 1962-65, from asst. prof. nursing to assoc. prof., 1965-72, chmn. dept. psychiat. nursing, 1972; dir. nursing Conn. Mental Health Ctr., Yale-New Haven Med. Ctr., 1966-72; chief psychiat. nursing edn. br. Div. Manpower and Tng. Programs, NIMH, Rockville, Md., 1972-76; dep. dir. Div. Manpower and Tng. Programs NIMH, 1976-79, dep. dir., 1979-81; dean U. Mich. Sch. Nursing, 1981—; dir. Group Relations Confs. in Tavistock Model; cons., speaker, panelist in field; fellow Helen Hadley Hall, Yale U., 1972, Branford Coll., 1972; dir. Community Health Care Ctr. Plan, New Haven, 1969-72; mem. U.S. Assessment Team, cons. to Fed. Ministry Health, Nigeria, 1982; mem. adv. com. Health Policy Agenda for the Am. People, AMA, 1983-86; cons. NIH Task Force on Nursing Research, 1984; mem. Nat. Commn. on Unemployment and Mental Health, Nat. Mental Health Assn., 1984-85; mem. com. to plan maj. study of nat. long-term care policy Inst. Medicine, 1985; mem. adv. com. to dir. NIH, 1986-87. Author profl. monographs; contbr. articles to profl. publs.; mem. editorial bd. Community Mental Health Rev., 1977-79, Jour. Personality and Social Systems, 1978-81, Advances in Psychiat. Mental Health Nursing, 1981. Bd. dirs. Afro Am. Ctr., Yale U., 1968-72; mem. New Haven Bd. Edn., 1968-71, New Haven City Demonstrations Agy., 1968-70, Human Rels. Coun. New Haven, 1961-63, Nat. Neural Circuitry Database Com., Inst. Medicine, Nat. Acad. Scis.; mem. commn. on future structure of vets. health care U.S. Dept. Vets. Affairs, 1990. Named Disting. Alumna Dillard U., 1966; recipient various awards, including cert. Honor NAACP, 1970, Disting. Alumnae award Yale U. Sch. Nursing, 1976, award for outstanding achievement and service in field mental health D.C. chpt. Assn. Black Psychologists, 1980. Fellow A.K. Rice Inst., Am. Coll. Mental Health Adminstrs. (founding), Am. Acad. Nursing (charter, pres. 1987-89); mem. Inst. Medicine NAS, Am. Nurses Assn., Nat. Black Nurses Assn., Am. Assn. Colls. Nursing (govtl. affairs com. 1990—), Am. Pub. Health Assn., NAACP, Sigma Theta Tau Internat. (mentor award 1989), Delta Sigma Theta. Office: U Mich Sch Nursing Rm 1320 400 N Ingalls Bldg Ann Arbor MI 48109-0482

DUMDI, ELEANOR STILES, county commissioner; b. Harwich Port, Mass., May 16, 1932; d. Roger Shackelton and Marian Anita (Hillhouse) Stiles; m. Cleve E. Dumdi, Jan. 10, 1959; children: Doug, Mark. BA, Wilson Coll., 1954; MA, U. Oreg., 1970. Cert. French tchr., Oreg. Med. asst., sec. Lee M. Cole, St. Thomas, V.I., 1955-56, Clarence Adams, San Francisco, 1956-57; dir. recreation Dept. Army, Germany, 1957-59; tchr. French, vice prin. Sch. Dist. 4J, Eugene, Oreg., 1970-76; coord. coop. work experience Sch. Dist. 69, Junction City, Oreg., 1976-82; coord. vocat. edn. and leadership tng., prof. devel. Oreg. State U., Corvallis, 1982-85; coord. coop. work experience bus. dept. Lane Community Coll., Eugene, 1986; commr. Lane County, Eugene, 1987—; chair Lane County Bd. Commrs., Eugene, 1988. Active, sustaining mem. Jr. League of Eugene, 1967—; appointed com. mem. Lane County Youth Svcs. & Econ. Devel., Eugene, 1978-82; mem. Lane Regional Air Pollution Authority, 1987—, chairwoman, 1989—; mem. Bach Festival Bd., 1988—, Eugene-Springfield Partnership, 1988—, Lane County Youth Devel. Commn., 1989—. Named Sr. Woman of Yr., 1990; recipient Community Svc. award Jaycettes, 1967, Woman of Achievement award, 1988. Mem. Nat. Assn. of Counties (steering com.), Women Nat. Assn. of Counties, So. Willamette Pvt. Industry Coun., Bus. and Profl. Women , Florence Area C. of C. (pres. 1979-81, Citizen of Yr. 1988), Junction City-Harrisburg Area C. of C., AAUW (bd. dirs. Eugene chpt. 1965-66), Soroptomists (pres. Junction City chpt. 1980-81, Women Helping Women, 1990), Elks, Moose, Epsilon Sigma Alpha. Republican. Episcopalian. Office: Lane County 125 E 8th Ave Eugene OR 97401

DUMITRESCU, DOMNITA, educator, researcher; b. Bucharest, Romania; came to U.S., 1984; d. Ion and Angela (Barzotescu) D. Diploma, U. Bucharest, 1966; MA, U. So. Calif., L.A., 1987, PhD, 1990. Asst. prof. U. Bucharest, 1966-74, assoc. prof., 1974-84; asst. lectr. U. So. Calif., 1985-89; asst. prof. Calif. State U., L.A., 1987-90, assoc. prof., 1990—. Author: Gramatica Limbii Spaniole, 1976, Indreptar Pentru Traducerea Din Limba Romana in Limba Spaniola, 1980; translator from Spanish lit. to Romanian; contbr. articles to profl. jours. Mem. Am.-Romanian Acad. Arts and Scis., Am. Assn. Tchrs. Spanish, Modern Lang. Assn., Linguistic Soc. Am., Internat. Assn. Hispanics, Sigma Delta Pi. Office: Calif State U 5151 State University Dr Los Angeles CA 90032

DUMONT, SANDRA JEAN, publishing executive; b. Boston, Apr. 30, 1955; d. Donald Edward and June Marie (Carpenter) D. AA in Humanities, Dean Jr. Coll., Franklin, Mass., 1975; BA in Internat. Studies, Am. U., 1977. Asst. promotion mgr. Univ. Press Am., Washington, 1978-79; mktg. coord. Nat. Sch. Bds. Assn., Washington, 1979-80; sr. mktg. assoc. Am. Chem. Soc., Washington, 1981-83; circulation mgr. AIA, Washington, 1984; advt. account mgr. Data Base Publs., Inc., Austin, Tex., 1985-87; advt. dir. Ariel Communications, Inc., Austin, 1987-88, Acad. Computing Publ., Inc., Austin, 1990—; cons. Dumont Assocs., Austin, 1990—. Recipient 1st place award conv. promotion Assn. Trends Mag., 1979. Home: 8706 Bridgeport Dr Austin TX 78758

DUNAGAN, DORIS DEANE, administrative assistant; b. Dennison, Ohio, May 5, 1933; d. Homer Fred and Pearl Belle (Bower) Mason; m. Forest B. Dunagan, Dec. 29, 1956; children: S. Diane Todd, Linda M. Rogers. AA, Valley Jr. Coll., San Bernardino, Calif., 1963; postgrad., Trinity Coll., Atlanta, 1990—. Office mgr. State of Calif., Indsl. Accident Commn., San Bernardino, 1957-59; substitute tchr. Riverside (Calif.) pub. schs., 1966-68, Howell (N.J.) pub. schs., 1974-76; acting pers. mgr. ProdeLin, Hightstown, N.J., 1979-81; adminstrv. asst. State of Ga./DOAS, Atlanta, 1987-89; ret., 1989. Alpha Gamma Sigma scholar. Mem. Order Eastern Star. Republican. Home: 3670 Southpoint Ct NE Marietta GA 30062

DUNAVAN, ILENA ABRAMS (LENI DUNAVAN), travel agency executive; b. Bklyn., May 13, 1938; d. Sidney Charles and Lilian Lucille (Lustgarten) Abrams; m. Lawrence A. Dunavan, Dec. 16, 1974. BA, U. Fla., 1960. Classroom tchr. various schs., U.S. and abroad, 1960-67; hosp. field dir. ARC, Washington, 1967-76; travel cons. Montgomery Village Travel, Gaithersburg, Md., 1983-84, Gelco Travel Services, Rockville, Md., 1984-85; mgr. Montgomery Travel Ctr., Gaithersburg, 1985-86; ops. mgr. Travelogue Tours, Washington, 1986-88; mgr. Uniglobe Full Svc. Travel, Washington, 1988, G.M.O. Travel, Inc., Washington, 1989—, 1989—. Mem. adv. council Kaiser-Permanente Med. Ctr., Gaithersburg, 1982-85; leader Jr. Girl Scouts USA, Gaithersburg, 1982-83. Named one of Outstanding Young Women Am., 1973. Mem. Inst. Cert. Travel Agts. (cert.), Pacific Area Travel Assn., Upper Montgomery C. of C. Democrat. Jewish. Office: GMO Travel Inc 1730 Rhode Island Ave NW Ste 306 Washington DC 20036

DUNAWAY, (DOROTHY) FAYE, actress; b. Bascom, Fla., Jan. 14, 1941; d. John and Grace D.; m. Peter Wolf, Aug. 7, 1974; m. Terrence O'Neill; 1 son. Student, U. Fla., Boston U. An original mem. Lincoln Center Repertory Co.; appeared off-Broadway in Hogan's Goat; played Bonnie in motion picture Bonnie and Clyde, 1967; appeared in motion pictures: Hurry Sundown, 1967, The Happening, 1967, The Thomas Crown Affair, 1968, A Place For Lovers, 1969, Little Big Man, 1970, Doc, 1971, The Getaway, 1972, Oklahoma Crude, 1973, The Three Musketeers, 1973, Chinatown, 1974, Three Days of the Condor, 1975, Network, 1976 (Academy award for best actress), The Voyage of the Damned, 1976, The Towering Inferno, 1976, The Eyes of Laura Mars, 1978, The Champ, 1979, The First Deadly Sin, 1980, Mommie Dearest, 1981, The Wicked Lady, 1982, Supergirl, 1984, Barfly, 1987, Burning Secret, 1988, The Handmaid's Tale, 1990, others; TV movies include: After the Fall, 1974, The Disappearance of Aimee, 1976, Evita Peron, 1981, Ellis Island, 1986, 13 at Dinner, 1985, Beverly Hills Madame, 1986; appeared in play The Curse of an Aching Heart, 1982. Recipient Most Promising Newcomer Award Brit. Film Acad., 1968. Address: care Creative Artists Agy Inc 9830 Wilshire Blvd Beverly Hills CA 90212*

DUNAYEVSKAYA, ALLA, radiologist; b. Odessa, USSR, July 25, 1920; came to U.S. 1982; d. Leo and Isabella (Feldman) Shmulyan; m. Victor Dunayevsky (dec. 1965); 1 child, Valery Dunaevsky. MD, Med. Inst. Rostov-Don, Russia, 1947. Resident in radiology Inst. for Qualification fo Physicians, Leningrad, 1948; resident in roentgen diagnosis Roentgeno Radiol. Inst., Moskow, 1951, 53, 64; resident in radiol. diagnoses of cardiovascular diseases Acad. Med. Sci. of Surgery of Cardiovascular Diseases, Moscow, 1969; resident in radiol. diagnosis of bone and joint diseases Radiol. Inst. for Qualification of Physicians, Kiev, 1977; mgr. radiology Dist. Polyclinic, Murmansk, Russia, 1948-60; chief radiologist Council of Trade Union of Health Resorts of Latvien Rep., Russia, 1961-81; vol. Forbes Reg. Health Ctr., Pitts., 1982-85; researcher in med. statistics and quality assurance Forbes Health Sys., Pitts., 1985—; cons. in field. Contbr. articles to profl. jours. Mem. AAUW, Internat. Womens Club. Jewish. Office: Forbes Health Systems 2570 Haymaker Rd Monroeville PA 15146

DUNBAR, BONNIE J., engineer, astronaut; b. Sunnyside, Wash., Mar. 3, 1949; d. Robert Dunbar; m. Ronald M. Sega. BS in Ceramic Engring., U. Wash., 1971, MS in Ceramic Engring., 1975; PhD in Biomed. Engring., U. Houston, 1983. With Boeing Computer Svcs., 1971-73; sr. rsch. engr. space div. Rockwell Internat., Downey, Calif.; with NASA, 1978—, astronaut, 1981—, mission specialist flight STS 61-8, 1985, mission specialist flight STS-32, 1990; vis. scientist Harwell Labs., Oxford, Eng., 1975; adj. asst. prof. mech. engring. U. Houston. Mem. AAAS, Am. Ceramic Soc., Soc. Biomed. Engring., Materials Rsch. Soc., Tau Beta Pi. Address: NASA Johnson Space Ctr Astronaut Office Houston TX 77058*

DUNBAR, HOLLY JEAN, graphic designer; b. Plainfield, N.J., May 15, 1960; d. Robert Kenneth and Marian (DuBets) D. BA, Rutgers U., 1982. Graphic designer Chubb & Son, Inc., Warren, N.J., 1983-86; freelance writer, 1984—; graphic designer, archivist AT&T Bell Labs., Warren, 1986-88; self-employed graphic designer North Plainfield, N.J., 1986-88; direct response mktg. coord. Beneficial Mgmt. Corp., Peapack, N.J.; artist, graphic designer, editor St. Luke's Roman Catholic Ch., North Plainfield, N.J., 1987—; cons. Rutgers Coop. Extension Svc. 4-H Program, Bridgewater, N.J. photographer: (survey) Tark Farm Site Monmouth Battlefield, 1982, Ellis Island Restoration, 1988-90; artist: Official Logo of Somerset County N.J., 1985 (winning entry). Recipient Photography award, Cook Coll., New Brunswick, N.J., 1981, Photography award, Chubb & Son, Inc., Warren, N.J., 1984; cited for Distinctive Contbr. N.J. Culture & History Am. Studies Dept., Douglass Coll., New Brunswick, N.J., 1982. Mem. AAUW, DAR (dep. rep. Nat. Soc. to Vet. Affairs Vol. Svc., 1983—, state chmn. Am. Heritage-Art N.J. Soc. 1989-92, artist N.J. Soc. 1989—, nat. and N.J. state page 1983—), Douglass Coll. Alumnae Assn. Home: 725 Ayres Ave North Plainfield NJ 07063 Office: Beneficial Mgmt Corp of Am 200 Beneficial Ctr Peapack NJ 07977

DUNBAR, ISOBEL MOIRA, former environmental scientist; b. Edinburgh, Scotland, Feb. 3, 1918; d. William and Elizabeth Mary (Robertson) D. B.A., Oxford U., 1939, M.A., 1948. With div. earth sci. Can. Def. Research Bd., Ottawa, Ont., 1947-78, dir., 1975-77, sr. scientist, 1977-78; mem. Can. Environ. Adv. Council, 1972-78. Contbr. articles to profl. jours. Recipient Centennial award Can. Meteorol. Service, 1971; Massey medal Royal Can. Geog. Soc., 1972; Decorated Order of Can., 1976. Fellow Royal Soc. Can., Arctic Inst. N. Am. (gov. 1966-69), Royal Can. Geog. Soc. (dir. 1974-88); mem. Internat. Glaciological Soc. Home: RR 1, Dunrobin, ON Canada K0A 1T0

DUNBAR-WEBB, EVELYN LOUISE, computer systems business owner, consultant; b. New Haven, Apr. 6, 1954; d. Marshall Nelson and Evelyn Louise (Clinton) Dunbar; m. John Henry Webb, Aug. 9, 1986; children: Jennifer Ann, Heather Merri. Student, U. New Haven, 1972, Monegan Community Coll., Norwich, Conn., 1983-84, Conn. Coll., New London, 1984—. Travel cons. Tours, Inc., Cheshire, Conn., 1972-73; credit collector W.T. Grant Co., Wrightstown, N.J., 1973-74; data entry clk. Thomas G. Faria Corp., Uncasville, Conn., 1982-83; sec., office mgr. adminstrv. partial hospitalization program Lawrence & Meml. Hosps., New London, Conn., 1983-84; sec., office mgr. planning dept. Lawrence & Meml. Hosps., New London, 1984-85; computer systems' cons. Gremlin Systems, Old Lyme, Conn., 1985—; seminar cons. Conn. Small Bus. Devel. Ctr., New London and Groton, 1987—; pub. rels. dir. Triangle Prodns., Bridgeport, 1990; designer software Rental Realty Mgmt., Acctg. Systems Mgmt., 1986. State of Conn. scholar, 1972; Conn. Coll. scholar, 1984, 86-87. Mem. NAFE, Conn. River Valley Women's Network (bd. dirs. 1989-90), Old Saybrook C. of C. Episcopalian. Home and Office: 126 Boston Post Rd Old Lyme CT 06371

DUNCAN, ANN HUBERTY, administrator; b. Sacramento, Sept. 21, 1933; d. Martin R. and Gertrude (Turner) Huberty; m. John B. Duncan, June 30, 1957 (div. July 1971); children: Robert Martin, Kenneth Ross. BA, U. Calif.-Berkeley, 1956; MA, Calif. State U.-Hayward, 1977; EdD, Pepperdine U., 1988. Cert. tchr., personnel dir. Calif. Sch. Employees Assn., 1973-75; assoc. personnel analyst City of Oakland, Calif., 1975-76; dir. employer-employee relations City of Livermore, Calif., 1976-80; pres. mgmt. cons. firm Duncan & Assocs., Los Angeles and Castro Valley, Calif., 1980—; asst. dir. Ctr. Edn. Leadership, Pepperdine U., Los Angeles, 1984-87; prof. Grad. Sch. Pub. Adminstrn., J.F.K., Orinda, Calif., 1979-84; lectr. career devel. San

Jose State U., 1974-84, Santa Monica City Coll., 1986—, also mem. acad. senate; state dir. Calif. Community Colls., 1981-84. Chmn. Robert Cummings Student Loan Fund, 1970; commr. Hayward Bd. of Zoning Adjustments, 1970-71; trustee Chabot Coll., Hayward, 1971-84, emeritus, 1984, pres. bd., 1975, 79; factfinder Pleasanton (Calif.) Sch. Dist., 1975; candidate for Calif. State Legis., 1982; del. People's Rep. China. Recipient Pub. Service award Alameda County Sch. Bd. Assn., 1975, 79; fellow Pepperdine U., Kappa Kappa Gamma). Mem. Calif. Elected Women's Assn. for Ednl. Research (charter, state bd. dirs.), U.S.-China Peoples Friendship Assn., LWV (chpt. pres. 1968-70), Internat. Personnel Mgmt. Assn. (ethics com.), No. Calif. Personnel and Employee Relations Assn. (pres. 1979-80), Calif. Community Colls. Trustees Assn. (bd. dirs. 1982-84, speaker), Am. Assn. Community and Jr. Colls. (speaker), Am. Assn. Women in Community Colls., Calif. Assn. Community Colls., Kappa Kappa Kappa. Avocations: travel, reading, museums. Home and Office: 1250 Monaco Pacific Palisades CA 90272

DUNCAN, DOROTHY WILBER, retired educator; b. Chattanooga, Mar. 12, 1908; d. William Henry and Hattie Christian (Mitchel) Wilber; m. Alvin Campbell Shipp, 1934 (div. 1942); children: Jaqnice L., Alvin W.; m. Earl James Duncan, 1946 (div. 1956). BA, U. Chattanooga, 1930; MA, Appalachian State Tchrs. Coll., Boone, N.C., 1961. Music tchr. Hamilton County Bd. Edn., Chattanooga, 1931-34; tchr. Chattanooga Bd. of edn., 1938-44; tchr. retarded children The Matthews Sch., Balt., 1944-45; owner, tchr. kindergarten Chamblee, Ga., 1949-51; tchr. DeKalb County Bd. Edn., 1951-54; desk mgr. Main Post Libr., Ft. Bragg, N.C., 1954-56; elementary tchr. Jacksonville/DuVall County Bd. Edn., Fla., 1956-57, Brevard County Bd. Edn., 1957-77; ret. Vol. Ret. Sr. Vol. Prog., Cocoa, Fla., 1977—, Mus. History & Sci., Cocoa, 1985—; mem. vestry/sr. warden St. Mark's Episcopal Ch., Cocoa, 1962—; sec., Americanism chmn. Merritt Island Federated Rep. Women; mem. vol. exec. bd. Cen. Brevard Sharing Ctr., Cocoa, 1977—. Recipient awad for extraordinary svc. to AAUW, 1989, Evelyn Peter Kyle award fo r outstanding svc. Cen. Brevard Alumnae Club of Pi Beta Phi, 1983; named Tchr. of Yr., Mila Elementary Sch., 1972-73, others. Mem. AAUW (edn. chmn. 1977—), Community Woman's Club Cocoa, Pi Beta Phi (charter mem. alumnae club, past pres.), Beta Sigma Phi (recording sec., treas. 1984, pres. 1990-91, Valentine Queen, State Girl of the Yr. 1980, Chpt. Girl of the Yr. 1988). Republican. Episcopalian. Address: 28 Ocean St Merritt Island FL 32952

DUNCAN, ELIZABETH CHARLOTTE, marriage, family therapist, educational therapist, educator, psychologist; b. L.A., Mar. 10, 1919; d. Frederick John de St. Vrain and Nellie Mae (Goucher) Schwankovsky; m. William McConnell Duncan, Oct. 12, 1941 (div. 1949); 1 child, Susan Elizabeth Duncan St. Vrain. BA, Calif. U., Long Beach, 1953; MA, UCLA, 1962; PhD, Internat. Coll., 1984; cert. marriage and family therapist, Wash. Dir. gifted program Palos Verdes Sch. Dist., Calif., 1958-64; TV tchr., participant ednl. films L.A. County, 1961-64; dir. U. So. Calif. Presch., L.A., 1965-69, Abraham Maslow rsch. assoc., 1962-69; pvt. practice family counselor, Malibu and Ventura, Calif., Eastsound, Wash., 1979—; pub. speaker, lectr. communications; cons., counselor, 1989—; resident psychologist for film series Something Personal, 1987—; mem. Rsch. Inst. of Scripps Clinic, La Jolla, Calif.; charter mem. Inst. Behav. Med., Santa Barbara, Calif.; TV performer: (documentary) The Other Side, 1985. Creator (TV mini-series) Persephone's Child, 1988; author: Do Hearts Really Break? 1990. Active Chryalis Ctr., L.A., 1984-86, Ventura County Mental Health Adv. Bd., Calif., 1985-86, United Way, L.A., 1985-86; mem. adminstrv. bd. San Juan County, 1990; mem. Menninger Found. San Juan County, Wash., 1990; adv. bd. North Sound Regional Support Network, 1990. Recipient Emmy award for best documentary Am. TV Arts and Scis., 1976, Child Adv. of Yr. Calif. Mental Health Adv. Bd., 1987. Mem. Transpersonal Psychol. Assn., Am. Assn. for Counseling and Devel. (Disting. Svc. award 1990), Calif. State Orgn. Gifted Edn. (sec. 1962-64), Internat. Platform Assn., Am. Assn. for Marriages and Family Therapy. Democrat. Avocations: swimming, plays, concerts, boating, political issues, especially women and child abuse.

DUNCAN, FRANCES MURPHY, educator; b. Utica, N.Y., June 23, 1920; d. Edward Simon and Elizabeth Myers (Stack) Murphy; m. Lee C. Duncan, June 23, 1947 (div. June 1969); children: Lee C., Edward M., Paul H., Elizabeth B., Nancy R., Richard L. BA, Columbia U., 1942; MEd, Auburn U., 1963, EdD, 1969. Head sci. dept. Arnold Jr. High Sch., Columbus, Ga., 1960-63; tchr. physiology, Spanish, Jordan High Sch., Columbus, 1963-64; tchr. spl. edn. mentally retarded Muscogee County Sch. System, Columbus, 1964-65; instr. spl. edn. Auburn (Ala.) U., 1966-69; asso. dir. Douglas Sch. for Learning Disabilities, Columbus, 1969-70; prof. edn. and spl. edn. Columbus Coll., 1970-85; ret., 1985; dir. Columbus Devel. Ctr.; lectr. Troy State U., Phenix City, Ala. Past sec. exec. bd. Muscular Dystrophy Assn., 1968-70; 73-74; mem. Gov.'s Commn. on Disabled Georgians; past trustee Listening Eyes Sch. for Deaf; mem. adv. bd. Columbus Health Dept. Tng. Centers; chmn. Consumer Adv. Bd. Vocat. Rehab., Mayor's Com. on Handicapped; mem. team for evaluation and placement of exceptional children Columbus Public Schs. Fellow Am. Assn. Mental Retardation; mem. AAUP, AAUW (pres. 1973-75, div. rec. sec. 1975—), Council Exceptional Children (legis. chmn. 1973-74), Kappa Delta Pi, Psi Chi, Phi Delta Kappa. Roman Catholic. Home: 1811 Alta Vista Dr Columbus GA 31907

DUNCAN, JOYCE LOUISE, real estate broker; b. Canton, Ohio, Jan. 11, 1946; d. William Clayton and Virginia Ruth (Wilgus) Sommers; m. Daniel Bruce Duncan, Mar. 3, 1989 (dec. 1990); children: David Michael, Traci Lyn; m. Daniel Duncan. Student, U. Chattanooga, 1963-65. Cert. property mgr. Property mgr. Niebel Realty, North Canton, Ohio, 1981-85, Century 21 Americana Properties, St. Petersburg, Fla., 1987, Royal Estate Mgmt. Corp., Canton, 1989; broker, pres. Greystone Realty, Inc., Canton, 1989—. Mem. Women's Coun. Realtors (phone chmn. 1982, publicity chmn. 1983, treas. 1984, pres.-elect 1985, phone com. 1990), Canton/Massillon-St. Petersburg Bd. Realtors (program com. 1982-85, bldg. com. 1985, equal opportunity in housing com. 1990), Inst. Real Estate Mgmt., Greater Canton C. of C.

DUNCAN, NANNA SUE, nurse; b. Rogers, Ark., Mar. 9, 1936; d. John Parker and Esther (Kelley) Weddington; m. Doyle Clayton Duncan, Mar. 30, 1957, (dec. June 30, 1982); children: Janet Sue, David Doyle. Nursing (diploma), Springfield Baptist Hosp., 1956. Cert. RN. Industrial nurse Lily Tulip Cup Corp., Springfield, 1964-68, General Electric Co., Springfield, 1971-73; staff nurse/gynecology Conrad-Walker Mclaughlin Clinic, Springfield, 1973-75; utilization review coordinator/surgical nurse St. John's Regional Health Ctr., Springfield; sch. health nurse Richard's and Fairview Sch., West Plains, 1979-83; utilization review coordinator St. John's Regional Health Ctr., 1983-84; review coordinator Mo. Patent Care Review Found., Springfield, 1984-87; med. svc. advisor, med. dept. supr., med. and employee ins. dept. mgr. Zenith Electronics Corp., Springfield, 1987—; surgical nurse Surgical Mission Team, Haiti, 1978. Teacher, Sunday Sch.-Baptist Chs., Springfield, 1970—, leader, Camp Fire, Springfield, 1967, mission's speaker, local Chs., Springfield, 1978, advisor, David Duncan Political Campaign, Springfield, 1988. Mem. C. of C. Health Care Coalition, Ozarks Safety Council; Gideon Auxiliary, Beta Sigma Phi. Republican. Office: Zenith Electronics Corp 2500 E Kearney Springfield MO 65801

DUNCAN, PENNY R., nurse; b. Cin., Mar. 29, 1953; d. Orville R. and Doris (Noyes) D.; 1 child, Jeremiah R. BA, Carthage Coll., Kenosha, Wis., 1989; RN, Gateway Tech. Inst., Kenosha, Wis., 1980; postgrad., U. Wis., Milw. Nursing supr. Hospitality Manor Nursing Home, Kenosha, Upjohn HealthCare Svcs., Racine, Wis., Westview Nursing Home, Racine. Nurse Kenosha Summer Marching Band. Mem. NAFE, Am. Assn. for Counseling and Devel., Am. Rehab. Counseling Assn., Gamma Sigma Sigma (Outstanding Sister award), Psi Chi (Svc. award, Outstanding Officer award). Democrat. Lutheran. Home: 5120 28th St Kenosha WI 53140-3004

DUNCAN-POITIER, JOHANNA MONICA, education administrator; b. N.Y.C., Oct. 25, 1955; d. Gilbert Hoffman and Johanna Margarete (Sauer) D.; m. Philip Poitier, June 25, 1987. BA, CUNY, 1974, MPA, 1981; cert. advanced mgmt. and leadership devel., Atlanta U., 1981. Dir. career devel. Bronx Community Coll., CUNY, 1975-77, dir. spl. programs York Coll., 1977-80; dep. dir. Inst. Family and Community Life, Queens Coll., CUNY and N.Y.C. Bd. Edn., 1980-81; dir. evaluation rsch. and devel., Ctr. Labor and Urban Programs, Research and Analysis, Queens Coll., 1981-85; dir. adminstrn. Northside Ctr. for Child Devel., Inc., 1985-87; chief Bur. Audit Occupational Continuing Edn!. Program Support, N.Y. State Edn. Dept., 1987—; cons. Pres.'s Office on Devel., Employment and Tng. Research Ctr., 1980-81; seminar instr. Aviation Devel. Council and York Coll., 1977-78, Aviation Devel. Council and Queens Coll., 1980-81. Co-author: When a College Works with a Public School, 1984. Mem. Assn. Equality and Excellence in Edn. (v.p. chpt. 1979-81). Democrat.

DUNEIER, DEBRA HOPE, corporate gift service executive, gemologist; b. N.Y.C., Aug. 30, 1954; d. Jacob and Anita Arkow; student Queens Coll., 1976; grad. Gemological Inst. Am., 1980; m. Dana Brad Duneier, Sept. 2, 1971; children—Jamie Troy, Danielle Taylor. With Clyde Duneier Inc., N.Y.C., 1975-88 , v.p. loose stone div., 1980-88; pres. Debra Hope Creations Bellmore, N.Y., 1988—; lectr., seminar leader in field. Mem. Am. Gem Soc., Women's Jewelry Assn., Assn. Women Gemologists, Am. Gem Trade Assn. Retail Jewelers Am., Trends Orgn., Am. Biog. Inst. Research (bd. advisors nat. div. 1986—). Address: 1212 Ave Americas New York NY 10036

DUNFORD, KAREN LYNN, vessel documentation company official; b. Buffalo, Oct. 9, 1957; d. Robert Eugene and Joann Helen (Weigel) D.; m. David Allen Devonshuk, Mar. 6, 1982 (div. June 1985). BS in Intermediate-Upper Edn., So. Conn. State U., 1979. Elem. tchr. Sacred Heart-St. Anthony Sch., Bridgeport, Conn., 1979-80; tchr. math. St. James Sch., Stratford, Conn., 1980-83, St. Pancratius Sch., Long Beach, Calif., 1983-85; mgr. Marine Documentation Svc., Fairfield, Conn., 1985—; owner, cons. Cameo Rose, wedding invitation svc., Derby, Conn., 1985—; bridal cons. Assn. Bridal Cons., New Milford, Conn., 1990—. Mem. Conn. Marine Trades Assn. Democrat. Roman Catholic. Home: 273 Derby Ave Apt 803 Derby CT 06418 Office: Marine Documentation Svc 1055 Post Rd Fairfield CT 06430

DUNHAM, ALICE CLARKE, painter; b. Mt. Holly, N.J., Oct. 10, 1905; d. Raymond Samuel and Frances Yarnall (Caley) Clarke; m. Barrows Dunham, June 14, 1930; 1 child, Clarke. AB, Wellesley Coll., 1928; postgrad., Pa. Acad. Fine Arts, Phila., 1928-30, Boston Art Mus. Sch., 1932; MFA, Temple U., 1943. Art instr. in young people's classes, docent Phila. Mus. Art, 1944-58; team tchr. in art history and philosophy with Barrows Dunham Montgomery County Community Coll., Bluebell, Pa., 1970-85; art instr. Tyler Sch. Art Temple U., Phila., 1945-48. One-man shows, 1947, 48, 52-68; exhibited in group shows. Mem. fin. com. Women's Internat. League for Peace and Freedom, Phila., 1948—. Mem. Artists' Equity Assn. Home: 127 Bentley Ave Bala-Cynwyd PA 19004

DUNHAM, ANEVA JO, educator; b. Portsmouth, Va., Mar. 20, 1938; d. Joseph William and Rachel Lorraine (Kight) D.; B.S. in Edn. cum laude, S.E. Mo. State Coll., 1960; M.Ed. in Elem. Edn., St. Louis U., 1972; M.A. in Mgmt., Webster U., 1983. Tchr., Ritenour Consol. Sch. Dist., St. Louis, 1960—; Tri-Hi-Y coordinator YMCA, Overland, Mo., 1963-68; mem. nominating com. Ednl. Employees Credit Union, 1976-77, bldg. rep., 1975—. Bd. dirs. The Connection, 1986-89; mem. tng. program Coro Found. Women in Leadership, 1984. Mem. NEA (2nd v.p. 1986—, Women's Polit. Caucus. Kappa Delta Pi, Phi Alpha Theta. Democrat. Presbyterian. Home: 16 Coach Ct Saint Peters MO 63376 Office: 2318 Woodson Rd Saint Louis MO 63114

DUNHAM, JOANNE KROK, marketing executive; b. Chgo., Sept. 2, 1957; d. Julius James and Helen Francis (Ropski) Krok; m. David A. Dunham, Oct. 22, 1983. Student, Chgo. Coll. Commerce, 1976-78, Mundelein Coll., Chgo., 1982. Controller Dainichi Machinery, Elk Grove Village, Ill., 1984-86; adminstrn. support mgr. Galileo Co., Ltd., Rosemont, Ill., 1986—; mktg. cons. Future Trend Systems, Inc., Prospect Heights, Ill., 1988—. Officer, Arlington Heights (Ill.) Newcomers, 1989—, chmn. charity com., 1989—. Roman Catholic.

DUNHAM, MEGGIN MARIE, travel agency executive; b. Seward, Alaska, June 27, 1956; d. Willard Eugene and Beverly Dawn (Abrahamsen) D. Grad. high sch. Cert. cruise specialist, Sabre and Apollo systems specialist. Mgr., travel cons. Horizons Travel, Seward; mgr. World Express Travel, Seward. Active many community groups and functions, including Christmas fund raisers for poor children; vol. cleaning otters oiled by Exxon Valdez oil spill. Mem. NOW, Am. Soc. Travel Agts., Bus. and Profl. Women's Club, Seward C. of C., Am. Legion (v.p., sec. treasury). Episcopalian. Office: World Express Travel 300 4th Ave PO Box 2129 Seward AK 99664

DUNHAM, SELENA L., marketing executive; b. Severn, Md., Sept. 11, 1952; d. James M. and Pearl Elizabeth (Burley) Sewell; m. Kirk Dunham; children: Margo, Eric. Student, U. Md., U. Colo., Denver, Inst. Fin. Edn. Savs. tng. supr. Columbia Savs. & Loan, Denver, 1975-81, asst. savs. trainer mgr., 1981-83, asst. v.p., mgr. tng./br. adminstrn., 1983-86; pres., chief exec. officer Dunham and Assocs., Inc., Denver, 1986—; v.p., dir. mktg. and tng., 1988—; mktg. mgr. metro region Affiliated First Colo. Bank & Trust, Denver, 1988—. Mem. fin. adv. com. Arapahoe Community Coll.; bd. dirs. Denver Mental Health Ctr. Mem. Inst. Fin. Edn. (bd. dirs.), Mile High Bankers Assn. (prog. dir.), Nat. Assn. Urban Bankers, Am. Soc. Tng. and Devel., Nat. Soc. Performance and Instrn., Am. Mgmt. Assn., Rocky Mountain Bank Mktg. Assn., Nat. Bank Mktg. Assn. (program adv. coun.), Fin. Women Internat. Home: 2696 S Colorado Blvd Denver CO 80222

DUNKEL, FLORENCE VACCARELLO, entomologist; b. Kenosha, Wis., Oct. 10, 1942; d. Vincent James and Mildred (Behr-Naegeli) Vaccarello; m. Thomas Beatty Dunkel, Dec. 27, 1964 (div. 1982); children: Anne-Marie C., Alexander J., Marylynn S.; m. Robert Eller Diggs, June 20, 1987. Student, Lawrence U., 1960-62; BS in Zoology, U. Wis., 1964, MS in Zoology, 1966, PhD in Entomology, 1969; postgrad. studies, U. Minn., 1973-75. Rsch. fellow dept. entomology U. Minn., St. Paul, 1975-84; team leader USDA Office Internat. Cooperation, People's Republic China, 1982; project dir. internat Agril. programs U. Minn., 1983-87; pres., cons. Internat. Postharvest Systems, Inc., Minnetonka, Minn., 1985—; head and assoc. prof. entomology rsch. lab. Mont. State U., Bozeman, 1988—. Vis. Scholar Nat. Acad. Scis. Zhongshan U., 1981; recipient numerous grants for rsch. 1977—. Mem. AAAS, Entomol. Soc. Am., Am. Soc. Mammalogists, Am. Assn. Cereal Chemists, Sigma Xi, Gamma Sigma Delta. Club: PEO Sisterhood. Home: 23 Hitching Post Rd Bozeman MN 59715 Office: Mont State U 324 Leon Johnson Hall Bozeman MT 59717

DUNKLE, CATHLEEN BROOKE, insurance executive; b. Jacksonville, Fla., Feb. 24, 1963; d. Richard and Julia Olive (Craig) Brooke; m. Kurt Hughes Dunkle. BA, Sweet Briar (Va.) Coll., 1985; MA in Mass Communications, U. Fla., 1987. Intern William Cook Advt., Jacksonville, Fla., 1986; freelance pub. rels. writer Lakeland, Fla., 1987-88; asst. to dir. Lakeland Econ. Devel. Coun., 1988; editor, corp. writer Ind. Life Ins., Jacksonville, 1988—. Bd. dirs. Sweet Briar Coll., 1985-88, Am. Heart Assn., Jacksonville, 1989—; mem. Jr. League of Jacksonville, 1988—. Mem. Internat. Assn. Bus. Communicators. Republican. Episcopalian. Office: Ind Life Ins Co 1 Independent Dr Jacksonville FL 32276

DUNLAP, ELLEN S., museum and library administrator; b. Nashville, Oct. 12, 1951; d. Arthur Wallace and Elizabeth (Majors) Smith; m. Arthur H. Dunlap, Jr., Dec. 27, 1972 (dec. 1977); m. Frank Armstrong, May 11, 1979; 1 child, Libbie Sarah. B.A., U. Tex., Austin, 1972, M.L.S., 1974. Research assoc. Humanities Research Ctr. U. Tex., Austin, 1973-76, research librarian, 1976-83; exec. dir. Rosenbach Mus. and Library, Phila., 1983—; dir. Conservation Ctr. for Art and Hist. Artifacts, Phila., 1985—, Greater Phila. Cultural Alliance, 1985—; mem. exec. com. Phila. Area Consortium Spl. Collections Libraries, 1985—. Chmn. archives manuscripts and spl. collections program com. Rsch. Librs. Group, 1989—. Mem. ALA. Clubs: Grolier (N.Y.C.); Philobiblon (Phila.). Home: 13 Dickens Ln Mount Laurel NJ 08054 Office: Rosenbach Mus & Libr 2010 Delancey Pl Philadelphia PA 19103-6584

DUNLAP, KATHLEEN POWERS, investment banker, pension investment administrator; b. Danvers, Mass., Mar. 22, 1958; d. Richard James and Joan Marie (Kiley) Powers. AS, SUNY, Delhi, 1978; BS in Econs., U San Francisco, 1985. Stockbroker Merrill Lynch, San Francisco and, Conn., 1979-82, Bear Stearns, San Francisco, 1981-82, Kidder Peabody, San Francisco, 1982-84; regional pension cons. Aetna Life Ins., San Francisco, 1984-87; v.p., regional sales mgr. Wells Fargo Bank, Sacramento, 1987-89. Mem. Am. Soc. Pension Actuaries, Nat. Inst. Pension Adminstrs., Western Pension Conf., Employee Benefits Roundtable. Roman Catholic. Home: 4801 Manzanillo Fair Oaks CA 95628 Office: Wells Fargo Bank 500 Capitol Mall 3d Fl Sacramento CA 95814

DUNLAP, LINDA LOUISE, psychology educator; b. Kansas City, Kans., Aug. 3, 1954; d. Donald Warren and Olive Lucile (Ater) Potter; m. Gregory Lee Dunlap, Aug. 16, 1975; children: Jason Lee, Jennifer Louise. BA, Kans. State U., 1976; MA, U. Iowa, 1978, PhD, 1980. Researcher Mid-Am. Btr. for Bilingual Material, Iowa City, Iowa, 1978, Am. Coll. Testing, Iowa City, 1979; instr. U. Iowa, Iowa City, 1980, Kirkwood Community Coll., Cedar Rapids, Iowa, 1979-80; instr. psychology Ulster (N.Y.) Community Coll., 1981-82, SUNY, New Paltz, 1981-84, Dutchess Community Coll., Poughkeepsie, N.Y., 1981-85; devel. psychology cons. presch. program St. Francis Hosp., Poughkeepsie, 1987—; asst. prof. psychology Marist Coll., Poughkeepsie, 1984—; cons. N.Y. Times, News Week, 1988—, Am. Baby, Working Women, Children's Mag., Child, Working Woman, U.S.A. Today, 1990—; devel. cons. St. Francis Hosp., 1987—' guest NBC House Party TV Show, 1990. Contbr. articles to profl. jours. IBM grantee, 1989. Mem. Ea. Psychol. Assn., Am. Psychol. Assn., Soc. Rsch. in Child Devel., Dutchess County Mental Health Assn. (treas., bd. dirs. 1988-90). Home: 49 Saddle Rock Dr Poughkeepsie NY 12603 Office: Marist Coll Poughkeepsie NY 12601

DUNLAP-BAKER, JOYCE ANN, nurse, anesthetist; b. Waynesboro, Pa., July 30, 1950; d. Paul Ezra and Anna Mary (Stouffer) Dunlap; m. Francis Warren Baker, July 13, 1985. Diploma, Washington Hosp. Sch. Nursing, 1971; BSN, U. Md., 1981; diploma, Prince George's Hosp., 1983; BS, George Washington U., 1983. RN, D.C., Calif., Md. Nurse Washington Hosp. Ctr., 1971-74, Huntington Meml. Hosp., Pasadena, Calif., 1974-75, Prince George's Gen. Hosp. and Med. Ctr., Cheverly, Md., 1980-88; nurse anesthetist Md. Inst. for Emergency Med. Svcs. System, Balt., 1983—; nurse, anesthetist Howard County Hosp., Columbia, Md., 1984—; pvt. practice anesthesia Ft. Meade, Md., 1988—. Mem. Howard County Citizens Assn., 1989—. Mem. Am. Assn. Nurse Anesthetists, Md. Assn. Nurse Anesthetists, Legis. Update Com. Office: PO Box 418 Fulton MD 20759

DUNLAVEY, MARY ANN, police captain; b. Keokuk, Iowa, Mar. 14, 1929; d. Ralph Anthony and Ruth Irene (Cramer) Wilkens; m. Richard Emile Dunlavey, Aug. 12, 1948; children: Michael R., Mark A., Cheryl A., James P. AA in Adminstrn. Criminal Justice, Ill. Cen.Coll., 1971; BS in Adminstrn. of Criminal Justice, Bradley U., 1973, MA in Counseling, 1975; MA in Adminstrn. of Criminal Justice, Sangamon State U., 1978; Cert. Delinquency Control Inst. U. So. Calif., 1980; cert. Bus. Mgmt., Bradley U., 1979; cert. Sr. Mgmt. Inst. for Police, 1986. Police officer Peoria Police Dept., Ill., 1964-69, police sgt., 1969-77, police lt., 1977-82, police capt., 1982—. Contbr. articles to profl. jours. Mem. Internat. Police Mgmt. Assn. (bd. dirs., founding mem.), Internat. Assn. Chiefs of Police, Ill. Assn. Chiefs of Police, Peoria Police Benevolent and Protective Assn. (local and state). Avocations: aerobics, gardening, crafts, biking, fishing. Home: 4904 Lionel Ct Mapleton IL 61547 Office: Peoria Police Dept 542 S W Adams St Peoria IL 61602

DUNLEAVY, KRISTIE LYN, direct marketing and advertising executive; b. Washington, July 21, 1957; d. James Elliot and Betty Jean (Heflin) D. With AB&C, Alexandria, Va. Mem. Direct Mktg. Assn. Washington (bd. dirs. 1990-93, Vol. of Yr. award 1988, MMAXI gold award 1989), Nat. Bus. Forms Assn. Roman Catholic. Home: 2842 Dover Ln Apt 103 Falls Church VA 22042 Office: AB&C 2010 Eisenhower Ave Alexandria VA 22314

DUNLOP, BECKY NORTON, former government official; b. Mpls., Oct. 2, 1951; d. Carl J. and Helen L. (Betow) Norton; m. George S. Dunlop, Sept. 17, 1977. BA, Miami U., Oxford, Ohio, 1973. Polit. dir., cons. Am. Conservative Union, Washington, 1973-77; pres., founder Century Communications Inc., Washington, 1977—; assoc. dep. dir. pers. The White House, Washington, 1981-82, spl. asst. to pres., 1982-83, dep. asst. to pres., 1983-85; asst. to atty. gen. Dept. Justice, Washington, 1985-87; dep. undersec. Dept. Interior, Washington, 1987-88, asst. sec. Office of Fish and Wildlife and Pks., 1988-89; bd. dirs. Renaissance Women, Washington, Fed. Law Enforcement Tng. Ctr., Glynco, Ga.; commr. Gt. Lakes Fisheries Commn., Washington, 1988—. Bd. dirs. Here's Life, Washington, 1987-88. Recipient Outstanding Svc. award Federalist Soc., 1988. Mem. Izaak Walton League Am. Republican. Baptist. Home: 2816 S Joyce St Arlington VA 22202 Office: 470 L'Enfant Pla E Bldg #7112 Washington DC 20024

DUNMEYER, SARAH LOUISE FISHER, health care consultant; b. Ft. Wayne, Ind., Apr. 13, 1935; d. Frederick Law and Jeanette Blose (Stults) Fisher; m. Herbert W. Dunmeyer, Sept. 9, 1967; children: Jodi, Lisa. BS, U. Mich., 1957; MS, Temple U., 1966; EdD, U. San Francisco, 1983. Lic. Clin. Lab. Technologist, Calif. Instr. med. tech. U. Vt., Burlington, 1966-67; instr. med. tech. Northeastern U., Boston, 1967-68, instr. lab. asst. program, 1968-70; educator, coordinator sch. med. tech. Children's Hosp., San Francisco, 1970-73; dir. continuing edn. program Pacific Presbyn. Med. Ctr., San Francisco, 1974-82; project mgr., cons. Peabody Mktg. Decisions, San Francisco, 1983-87; sr. rsch. assoc. Inst. for Health and Aging, U. Calif., San Francisco, 1986-89; external cons. Health Care Consulting Services, San Francisco, 1986-89; seminar presenter Am. Assn. Blood Banks, San Francisco, 1976, Am. Soc. Clin. Pathologists, Miami Beach, Fla., 1977, Ann. Meeting of Am. Soc. Med. Technology, Atlanta, 1977; site surveyor Nat. Accrediting Agy. for Clin. Lab. Scis., Chgo., 1974-80. Contbr. articles to profl. jours. Vol. French-Am. Internat. Sch., San Francisco, Buck Ctr. for Rsch. on Aging. Mem. Am. Soc. on Aging, Am. Pub. Health Assn., Health Care Forum, San Francisco Med. Tech. Soc. Club: U. Mich. Alumni (San Francisco).

DUNMIRE, RUTH MARCH, instructor, consultant; b. Conneaut, Ohio, May 28, 1930; d. Carl Herman and Lucy Ann (Dennis) March; m. Raymond Veryl Dunmire, Apr. 4, 1953; children: Perry Carl, Cary Allan, Barry Ivan. BS, Thiel Coll., 1952; MS, Fla. State U., 1956. Instr. bus. Southeastern Community Coll., Whiteville, N.C., 1965-69, Nettleton Coll., Sioux Falls, S.D., 1970-73; chair bus. edn. dept. Augustana Coll., Sioux Falls, 1973-81; asst. acct. Sta. KSOO, Sioux Falls, 1981-83; instr. bus. Nat. Edn. Ctr., Birmingham, Ala., 1984-86, So. Tech. Coll., Birmingham, 1986-87, Birmingham Area Skills Ctr., 1987—, U. Ala., Birmingham, 1988—; office cons. Southeastern Community Coll., 1965-69, Augustana Coll., 1973-81, Birmingham Area Skills Ctr., 1987—. Mem. Nat. Bus. Edn. Assn., Ala. Bus. Edn. Assn., Ala. Coun. for Computer Edn., Southeastern Bus. Edn. Assn., AAUW (treas. Sioux Falls chpt. 1975-77), Order of Eastern Star, Amaranth (line officer Greenville, Pa. chpt. 1963-65). Lutheran. Office: W Cen Ala Skills Ctr PO Box 86 Montevallo AL 35115

DUNN, BONNIE BRILL, scientist; b. Bethesda, Md., Mar. 10, 1953; m.; 2 children. AA, Montgomery Coll., 1972; BS in Food Sci., U. Md., 1974, MS in Food Chemistry and Statistics, 1978, PhD in Food Chemistry, 1982. Rsch. asst. U. Md., College Park, 1976-79, teaching asst., 1977-80; researcher div. chemistry and physics U.S. FDA, Washington, 1979; statistian USDA, Beltsville, Md., 1980, researcher, 1980-82; radiochemist Positron Emission Tomography, 1984-86; head quality assurance NIH, Bethesda, 1986—. Contbr. numerous articles to profl. jours. Home: 10008 Markham St Silver Spring MD 20901 Office: NIH Dept Nuclear Medicine 9000 Rockville Pike Bethesda MD 20892

DUNN, DEBORAH DECHELLIS, trust administrator, assistant treasurer, bank operations manager; b. Plainfield, N.J., Jan. 16, 1960; d. Anthony and Joan Dora (Brown) DeChellis; m. Paul Michael Dunn, May 13, 1989; 1 child, Joseph Daniel. BS in Elem. Spl. Edn., U. Hartford, 1982. Spl. edn. tchr. Hartford (Conn.) Pub. Schs., 1982-83, East Hartford (Conn.) Pub. Schs., 1983-84; individual retirement account ops. supr. Conn. Nat. Bank, Hartford, 1984-87; individual retirement account adminstr. Glastonbury (Conn.) Bank & Trust, 1987, mgr. fin. mgmt. svc. ops., 1987—; asst. treas. Glastonbury (Conn.) Bank & Trust, 1988—; ind. edn. cons. Democrat.

Methodist. Office: Glastonbury Bank & Trust Co 2461 Main St Glastonbury CT 06033

DUNN, DEBORAH JANE, newspaper editor; b. Twin Falls, Idaho, Apr. 1, 1954; d. Jack A. and Vivian J. (Lancaster) D. BS, Western Oreg. State Coll., 1977. Family editor The Argus Observer, Ontario, Oreg., 1977-80, reporter, 1983-88; arts adminstr. Ea. Oreg. Regional Arts Coun., La Grande, 1980-82; editor The Independent Enterprise, Payette, Idaho, 1988—. Supporting mem. Project Dove-Abuse Prevention, Ontario. Recipient awards Wick Communications, 1988, 3d nat. writing award Muscular Dystrophy Assn., 1980. Mem. AAUW. Libertarian.

DUNN, DOROTHY JEAN, city official; b. Hinsdale, Ill., May 13, 1933; d. Alex Joseph and Lottie Helen (Jakubowski) Zasadzinski; m. Kenneth Henry Dunn, Oct. 27, 1960 (div. 1971); children: Lawrence Allen, Julie Susanne Dunn Bellora, Terrence Henry, Timothy Kenneth. AS, Broward Community Coll., Coconut Creek, Fla., 1982. Cert. mcpl. clk. Research librarian Sears, Roebuck & Co., Chgo., 1955-60; real estate broker various cos., Fla., 1968—; adminstrv. asst. City of Delray Beach, Fla., 1974-80; purchasing dir. City of Delray Beach, 1980-82; city clk. City of Sunrise, Fla., 1982—. Editor The Viewpoint. Instr./choir mem. 1st Presbyn. Ch., Pompano Beach, Fla., 1981-82. Mem. Broward County Mcpl. Clerk's Assn. (sec.), Bus. and Profl. Women's Club, Internat. Inst. Mcpl. Clks. (com. 1987-88), Fla. Assn. City Clks. (bd. dirs. 1988-89, chmn. manual rev. com. 1988-89), Women's Coun. Pompano Beach Real Estate Bd., Assn. Record Mgrs. and Adminstrs., Amnesty Internat., Greenpeace, Sierra Club, Toastmasters, Eagles (pres. 1955). Democrat. Presbyterian. Home: 511 SE 13th Ct Deerfield Beach FL 33441 Office: City of Sunrise 10770 W Oakland Park Blvd Sunrise FL 33351

DUNN, GRACE VERONICA, retired executive secretary; b. Bklyn.; d. Richard William and Grace Veronica (Mason) D. BA, Our Lady of the Lake U., 1940; postgrad., Columbia U., 1958. Sec. Hunt Oil Co., Dallas, 1947-48, Standard Oil Co. (N.J.), N.Y.C., 1955-59, Pan Am. Health Orgn., Washington, 1964-76. Mem. Stephanie Roper Com., Upper Marlboro, Md., 1987—; soprano soloist Holy Trinity Cath. Ch., Dallas, 1945-47, Ch. of the Incarnation Episcopal Ch., Dallas, 1945-47; soloist White House Christmas Tree, 1988. Grad. fellow Karl Schultz Found., 1940; pvt. scholar Mme. Elizabeth Schumann, N.Y.C., 1948-52. Roman Catholic.

DUNN, LINDA KAY, physician; b. Grand Rapids, Mich., Jan. 11, 1947; d. Roger John and Mary Kathryn (Bouwer) Kloote; m. Jeffrey Marc Dunn, June 3, 1972; children: David Alan, Kathryn Ann. AB in Chemistry, Hope Coll., 1968; MD, U. Mich., 1972. Diplomate Am. Bd. Ob-Gyn, Am. Bd. Maternal Fetal Medicine. Resident in Ob-Gyn. U. Mich., Ann Arbor, 1972-75; hon. research registrar St. Mary's Hosp., London, 1977-78; dir. of perinatology Temple U., Phila., 1978-79; dir. subsection on genetics Pa. Hosp., Phila., 1980—; pres. Medigen, Inc., Phila., 1987—; com. chmn. Dept. of Ob-Gyn Ethics, 1988—; med. dir. Comprehensive Maternal and Infant Svcs., Phila., 1987—. Fellow Am. Coll. of Ob-Gyn.; mem. Soc. of Perinatology Obstetricians, Am. Soc. of Human Genetics, Am. Med. Women's Assn., Pa. State Med. Soc., Phila. Obstet. Soc. Mem. Soc. of Friends. Office: Pa Hosp Dept of Ob-Gyn 8th Spruce Philadelphia PA 19107

DUNN, LORETTA LYNN, lawyer; b. Owensboro, Ky, Dec. 3, 1955; d. John Edwin and Arnetta Mae (Trunnell) D.; m. Herbert S. Lunenfeld, Oct. 18, 1985; 1 child, Jack W. BA, U. Ky., 1976, JD, 1979; LLM, Georgetown U., 1983. Bar: Ky. 1979, D.C. 1984. Staff atty. U.S. Senate Com. Commerce, Sci. and Transp., Washington, 1979-86, minority counsel, 1982-86, sr. trade counsel, 1987—. named Order of Coif. Mem. D.C. Bar Assn., Ky. Bar Assn., Washington Internat. Trade Assn., Women Internat. Trade, Phi Beta Kappa. Office: Senate Commerce Com SH-428 Washington DC 20510

DUNN, MARGARET MARY COYNE, journalist; b. Pittsfield, Mass.; d. Robert Joseph and Margaret Jane (O'Neill) Coyne; m. John Raymond Dunn, May 29, 1933 (dec.); children—Joyce Dunn Higgins, John Raymond, Joel. Student Berkshire Bus. Coll., Pittsfield, Mass.; cert. in Western lit. Radcliffe Coll., 1964. Freelance contbr. articles to numerous newspapers, including Boston Post, Boston Globe, The Pilot, Beverly Times, Providence Jour., The Tablet, Montreal Herald and Weekly Star, 1937—, to mags. including Better Homes and Garden, Yankee, Conn. Circle, Modern Baby, Family Digest, others; lectr. in field. Mem. Nat. League Am. Pen Women (pres. Boston br. 1968-70, 74-76, rec. sec. 1970-72, membership chmn. 1972-74, nat. charter chmn. 1974-76, mature women's scholarship com. 1978—, Mass. State pres. 1978-80, nat. auditor 1978-80, nat. roster chmn. 1978-80, nat. orgn. and bylaws chmn. 1982-84, nat. bylaws chmn., 1986-88; docent JFK Libr. and Mus., Boston, 1990—; co-editor Fifty Year history Boston br.; contbg. editor Pen Woman mag., assoc. editor 1980-82, 87—, pres. Conn. valley br. 1987—, nat. bylaws chmn. 1986-88), Boston Authors Club (rec. sec. 1973, 1st v.p. 1980-82, pres. 1982-86, treas. 1986—), Dickens Fellowship (coun. mem. 1972-77, treas. 1977-82), Boston Browning Soc. Club: Women's City (heritage com.). Author: (with Barbara B. Reese) Capture of the Johnson Family (hist. pageant for Charlestown, N.H.), 1954; editor Between Branches, 1974-80. Home: 19 Pilgrim Rd Wellesley MA 02181

DUNN, MARY BETH, law librarian; b. Mpls., June 21, 1949; d. Edward James and Elizabeth Antoinette (Malat) McConville; m. Paul William Dunn, Aug. 19, 1972; children: Nora Rose, Will Patrick, Hugh Michael, Eileen Elizabeth. BA, Coll. of St. Catherine, St. Paul, 1971; MLS, Syracuse U., 1977. Law libr. Supreme Ct. Libr., Syracuse, N.Y., 1978—; ptnr. Law Libr. Cons., Syracuse, 1980—. Mem. Am. Assn. Law Librs. (coun. of chpt. pres. 1983-85, chmn. legal info. to pub. com. 1987-88, interlibr. communications com. 1987-88), N.Y. State Unified Ct. Law Librs. Assn. (pres. 1986-87), Assn. Law Librs. Upstate N.Y. (bd. dirs. 1981-83, 85-86, pres. 1984-85), Cen. N.Y. Libr. Resources Coun. (bibliographic svcs. com. 1985—), NAFE, Irish Cultural Dance Soc. Cen. N.Y. Roman Catholic. Office: Supreme Ct Libr 500 Court House Syracuse NY 13202

DUNN, MARY MAPLES, college president; b. Sturgeon Bay, Wis., Apr. 6, 1931; d. Frederic Arthur and Eva (Moore) Maples; m. Richard S. Dunn, Sept. 3, 1960; children—Rebecca Cofrin, Cecilia Elizabeth. BA, Coll. William and Mary, 1954, LHD (hon.), 1989; MA, Bryn Mawr Coll., 1956, PhD, 1959; LLD (hon.), Marietta Coll., 1987, Amherst Coll., 1987; LittD (hon.), Lafayette Coll., 1988, Brown U., 1989. Mem. faculty Bryn Mawr Coll., 1958-85, prof. history, 1974-85; acting dean Undergrad. Coll. Bryn Mawr (Pa.) Coll., 1978-79, dean, 1980-85; pres. Smith Coll., Northampton, Mass., 1985—. Author: William Penn: Politics and Conscience, 1967; editor: Political Essay on the Kingdom of New Spain (Alexander von Humboldt), 1972, rev., 1988, (with Richard S. Dunn) Papers of William Penn, vols. I-IV, 1979-87. Trustee The Clarke Sch. for the Deaf, 1985, Acad. Mus., 1985, Hist. Deerfield, Inc., 1986—, Bingham Fund for Teaching Excellence at Transylvania U., 1987—; dir. Bank of New England West, 1986. Recipient Lindbeck Found. award distinguished teaching, 1969; Fellow Inst. Advanced Study Princeton U., 1974. Mem. Berkshire Conf. Women Historians (pres. 1973-75), Coordinating Com. Women Hist. Profession (pres. 1975-77), Am. Hist. Assn., Inst. Early Am. History and Culture (chmn. adv. council 1977-80), Mass. Hist. Soc., Phi Beta Kappa. Office: Smith Coll Office of Pres Northampton MA 01063

DUNN, PATRICIA ANN, academic coordinator, educator; b. Englewood, N.J., Mar. 17, 1942; d. Thomas Joseph and Rosanna Valerie (Cummings) D.; m. James Edward Egan, 1963 (div. 1974); 1 child, Deirdre Tracy. BA in English Edn., William Paterson Coll., 1963, MA in Communication Arts, 1974; postgrad., Montclair (N.J.) State Coll., 1986—. Cert. tchr., N.J., N.Y.; cert. prin., supr., N.J. Tchr. English, Intermediate Sch. Dist. 218, Bklyn., 1965-66, tchr., English and humanities, 1966-67, co-chmn. dept. humanities, 1967-68; tchr. English and humanities Midland Park (N.J.) Schs., 1969—, staff devel. coordinator, 1986—; coordinator bus. workshops Women in Bus., 1983, Stress, 1983. Editor N.J. Staff Devel. Coun. Newsletter, 1988-91; contbr. articles to profl. publs. Co-founder, coord. Ministry for Separated and Divorced Caths., Montclair, 1983-86. Mem. NEA, N.J. Edn. Assn., Nat. Staff Devel. Coun., N.J. Staff Devel. Coun. (co-founder), Bergen County Edn. Assn., Midland Park Edn. Assn. (rep. coun.), Nat. Assn. Secondary Sch. Prins., Assn. Supervision and Curriculum Devel., Internat. Platform Assn., Le Terrace Club (Nutley, N.J.). Democrat. Roman Catholic. Office: Midland Park High Sch 250 Prospect St Midland Park NJ 07432

DUNN, PATRICIA ELLEN, marketing and sales executive; b. Norwalk, Conn., Mar. 3, 1958; d. M. Joseph and Catherine (Clayton) D. BA in Govt., Wheaton Coll., 1980. New bus. underwriter MONY, N.Y. C., 1980-81, pension termination specialist, 1981-82, pension service rep., 1982-83; northeastern account exec. CNA, N.Y. C., 1983-84; cons. Johnson & Higgins, N.Y. C., 1984-86, mktg. cons., 1986; dir. bus. devel./cons. The Wyatt Co., N.Y.C., Stamford, Conn., 1986—, Little Falls, N.J., 1986—. Mem. Working in Employee Benefits (bd. dirs.), Wheaton Club (N.Y.C.), Women's Bond Club N.Y. (bd. dirs., sec.). Home: 539 E 81st St Apt 2G New York NY 10028 Office: The Wyatt Co 461 Fifth Ave New York NY 10017

DUNN, REBECCA DIANE, personnel specialist; b. Roanoke, Ala., May 8, 1948; d. Avery Moore and Iva Delle (Brewer) Cunningham; m. Robert Lewis Dunn Jr., Sept. 8, 1968 (div.); children: Elizabeth, Catherine. Student, Jacksonville (Ala.) State U., 1968. Pvt. practice piano tchr. Alexander City, Ala., 1971-85; mfg. interviewer personnel Russell Corp., Alexander City, 1985-87; lead tchr. Horizons for Learning subs. Russell Corp., Greensboro, N.C., 1983-86; supr. clerical dept. and hourly employees Russell Corp., Alexander City, 1987-89; personnel mgr. Corporate Svcs., 1989—; corp. rep. Adult Basic Edn. Adv. Bd., Alexander City, 1986—; chmn. bus. edn. craft com. Area Vocat. Tng. Ctr., Alexander City, 1987-89, pres. adv. bd. 1989-90. Mem. NAFE, Bus. and Profl. Women, Laubach Literacy Action. Baptist. Office: Russell Corp Lee St PO Box 272 Alexander City AL 35010

DUNN, SANDRA PUNCSAK, marketing communications executive; b. Melbourne, May 28, 1946; d. Frank and Thelma May (Maher) Puncsak; (div. 1978); m. Roger G. Dunn, Feb. 24, 1983. BA in Environ. Design, U. Calif., 1968; MA in Spl. Edn., San Francisco St. U., 1970; MA in Counseling and Guidance, Lewis and Clark Coll., 1974; certificate, Brookings Inst., 1983; postgrad., Columbia U. Dir. project Community Experiences for Career Edn., Tigard, Oreg., 1973-78; dir. dep. ctr. Portland (Oreg.) Job Corps Ctr., 1978; mgr. mktg. edn. div. Ea. and Western regions Singer Co., Washington, 1978-81; mgr. corp. pub. affairs Kaiser Aluminum and Chemical Corp., Oakland, Calif., 1981-84; dir. exec. edn. Pacific Telesis Group, San Francisco, 1984-85; asst. exec. dir. consumer affairs, acting dep. exec. dir. Dallas Area Rapid Transit, 1985-88; assoc. v.p., dir. univ. relations So. Meth. U., Dallas, 1988—. Past pres. Calif. State Coun. Vocat. Edn.; past chmn. Gov.'s Task Force on Youth Employment; mem. Leadership Tex., 1987, Leadership Dallas, 1990—; trustee Tex. coun. Girl Scouts U.S.; bd. dirs. Dallas chpt. Am. Diabetes Assn., USA Film Festival, Dallas; mem. Dart Citizens Adv. Coun. Recipient Twin award Nat. YWCA, 1983, Presdl. White House award, 1984, Matrix award, Grand Gold awards, 1987, 88, Clarion award; named Rising Star, Dallas-Ft. Worth Home and Garden mag., 1987. Mem. Tex. Pub. Relations Assn. (Best Texan award 1985-86), Tex. Women's Alliance, Exec. Women Dallas. Home: 7702 Marquette St Dallas TX 75225

DUNN, SUSAN, singer; b. Malvern, Ark., July 23, 1954. BA, Hendrix Coll., 1976; MM, Ind. U., 1980. Profl. debut in Aida with Peoria (Ill.) Opera Co., 1982; La Scala, Milan, debut in Aida, 1986; Carnegie Hall debut in concert performance Verdi's Requiem; other significant appearances include La Forza del Destino (Verdi), Lyric Opera, Chgo., 1988, Un Ballo in Maschera (Verdi), Vienna State Opera, 1988, Otello, Australian Opera, 1988, Il Trovatore, Washington Opera, San Diego Opera; also performances with leading symphony orchs. including N.Y. Philharm., Chgo. Symphony, Boston Symphony, Orch. de Paris, Concertgebouw Orch., Amsterdam, The Netherlands; recordings of Mass in C (Beethoven), Requiem (Verdi), Gurrelieder (Schoenberg), Wagner and Verdi Arias. Recipient Met. Opera Nat. Council award, 1981; winner Phila. Opera Co./Pavarotti Internat. Vocal Competition, 1981, WGN-Ill. Opera Competition, 1983; G.B. Dealey first prize Dallas Morning News-Dallas Opera, 1983; Richard Tucker award, 1983. Mem. Mu Phi Epsilon. Office: care Herbert H Breslin Inc 119 W 57th St New York NY 10019

DUNN, SUZAN MCVAY, computer education specialist; b. Mobile, Ala., Nov. 14, 1953; d. William Frederic and Mary Irene (Lomax) D.; m. Joseph Austin Davis, Feb. 14, 1987. BS, U. S. Ala., 1976, MEd, 1980; EdD, Auburn U., 1985. Tchr. Mobile County Schs., 1977-81; asst. curriculum coord. Brewton (Ala.) City Schs., 1983-85; computer edn. specialist Ala. State Dept. Edn., Montgomery, 1985—; sales cons. Tapestry Learning Corp., Montgomery, 1990—; instr. Auburn U., Montgomery, 1990—; cons. Apple Computer, 1986—. Co-author, editor: Computer Education Curriculum Guide, 1989. Mem. Women's Civitan Club (news editor 1990), Phi Delta Kappa. Democrat. Episcopalian. Office: State of Ala Dept Edn 50 N Ripley St Montgomery AL 36130

DUNN, THERESA ROSE, small business owner, cosmetologist; b. Seattle, Dec. 3, 1962; d. Richard Arnold Dunn and Vickie Rae (Mulka) Lutz; children: Angelina Marie Sprayberry, Marty Robbin Sprayberry, Willie Ray Sprayberry, James Roland Sprayberry, Krystalina Rose Sprayberry. AAS in Cosmetology, Spokane Community Coll., 1989. Lic. cosmetologist, Wash. Hostess Davenport Hotel, Spokane, Wash., 1977-79; rep. Avon Cosmetics, Spokane, 1977-78; cashier The Crescent, Spokane, 1978-79, Goodwill Industries, Spokane, 1979; waitress Perkins Restaurant, Spokane, 1980; rep. Mason Shoes, Spokane, 1980-87; beauty cons. Aloette Cosmetics, Spokane, 1987-90; owner, rep. Hemple Fin. Corp., Spokane, 1989—. Active Wash. Adoptees Rights Movement, Seattle, 1986, Save Our Family Ties, Spokane, 1985, Soc. Against Family Endangerment, Spokane; alternate Head Start Policy Coun., Spokane, 1985. Recipient 1st Place award Vocat. Indsl. Clubs Am., 1989, 3d Place award, 1988. Mem. NAFE, Future Stylists Am. Home and Office: E 3828 Ermina Spokane WA 99207

DUNN, VICKI LYNN, psychologist; b. Charleston, W.Va., Nov. 9, 1949; d. Robert Sherman Snodgrass and Lorene (King) Mullins; m. George R. Dunn, Jr., May 3, 1975; 1 child, Tiffani Brooke. BS in Edn., Morris Harvey Coll., Charleston, 1972; MA in Guidance and Counseling, U. South Fla., 1975, PhD in Counseling Psychology, 1983. Occupational specialist Hillsborough County Adult Edn., Tampa, Fla., 1972-73, Leto High Sch., Tampa, 1973-75; tchr. trapeze Jefferson Adult High Sch., Tampa, 1974-75; prin. Yongsan High Summer Sch., Seoul, 1976; program dir. 121st Evacuation Hosp., Seoul, 1976-77; edn. svcs. specialist USN, Norfolk, Va., 1981-82; edn. specialist MacDill AFB, Tampa, 1982-85, Dept. Army, Ft. Campbell, Ky., 1978-81; coord. family support Dept. Army, Ft. Ord, Calif., 1985-87; chief human resources Dept. Army, Honolulu, 1987-89; edn. svcs. officer U.S. Army, Atlanta, 1990—. Author: Train To Gain, 1973, Keep It Light, 1985, This Child is Driving Me Crazy, 1990. Mem. Nat. Mil. Families Assn. Home: 3110 Mt Zion Rd Apt 808 Stockbridge GA 30281

DUNNAVAN, CAROL CHAMBLIN, educator; b. Maysville, Ky, Feb. 5, 1954; d. Kenneth Harold and Anna Elizabeth (King) Chamblin; m. J. Calvin Dunnavan Jr., July 7, 1979; 1 child, Elizabeth Ann. Student Cin. Bible Coll., 1972-74; B.A., Morehead State U., 1976, M.A., 1980, Rank I in Edn., 1985. Cert. elem. tchr., Ky. Tour guide Washington Hist. Soc., Ky., 1972-75; tchr. Washington Elem. Sch., Maysville, 1976-78, Mason County Elem. Sch., Maysville, 1978-80; tchr. Straub Elem. Sch., Maysville, 1980—; supervising tchr. for student tchr. tng. Morehead State U., 1980, 83-84, 86, 88; tchr. in film Emergency Preparedness, Ky. Dept. Edn., 1983; activities demonstrator on Edn. Notebook, TV Program, 1985. Active Germantown Christian Ch., Ky., 1975—, Vacation Bible Sch., 1989, Maysville-Mason County PTA, 1976—; camp counselor Northward Christian Assembly, Falmouth, Ky., 1973. Named Outstanding Elem. Tchr. at Morehead State U. Sci. Fair, 1981, 84. Mem. Commonwealth Inst. for Tchrs. (distinguished mem.), NEA, Eastern Ky. Edn. Assn., Mason County Edn. Assn., AAUW, Kappa Delta Pi. Democrat. Club: Mason County Homemakers. Avocations: Interior decorating, floral arranging, needlework, reading. Home: 463 S Shawnee Rd Maysville KY 41056 Office: Straub Elem Sch 387 Chenault Dr Maysville KY 41056

DUNNING, ANN MARIE, architect; b. Canton, Ohio, Oct. 16, 1942; d. John Wesley and Marie E. (Wagner) D. BArch, Kent State U., 1965. Registered architect, Ohio, Mich., N.Y., Ky. Architect Little and Dalton, Cleve., 1965-67, Dalton Van Dijk Johnson, Cleve., 1967-70, Madison-Madison Internat., Cleve., 1970-71, Siebert Worley Cady Kirk, Cleve., 1971-72, Urs Dalton, Cleve., 1972-79; pvt. practice Chagrin Falls, Ohio, 1979—; dir. design and engring. Sea World of Ohio, 1986-87; cons. DuPont Co., Wilmington, Del., 1983—; mem. State of Ohio Bd. Examiners of Architects (1987-89). Mem. editorial bd. Cleve. Home & Flower Show Plan and Print Mag., 1990—; contbr. articles to profl. jours. Bd. dirs. Valley Art Ctr., Chagrin Falls, 1983, Cleve. Home and Flower Show, 1985-90. Named Career Woman of Yr., YWCA, 1986. Mem. AIA (pres. Cleve. chpt. 1986), AE Computer Task Force (organizer), Cleve. Fine Arts Adv. Panel, Chagrin Falls C. of C. Home and Office: 71 W Summit St Chagrin Falls OH 44022

DUNNING, KAREN ELLEN, electronics manufacturing company executive; b. Danville, Ill., Mar. 16, 1956; d. Thomas Wesley and Sarah Anne (Lewis) D. B.B.A. in Fin., Fla. Atlantic U., 1979, M.B.A., 1981. Researcher, Fla. Atlantic U., Boca Raton, Fla., 1979-81, cons., research assoc., 1981-85; research analyst asst. IBM, Boca Raton, 1985-86, Motorola, Inc., 19—; freelance computer programmer and cons., Boca Raton, Fla., 1983—; adj. instr. fin. Fla. Atlantic U. Mem. Beta Gamma Sigma, Phi Kappa Phi. Republican. Avocations: golf; tennis; woodworking; mechanic; running. Home: 8176 A Thames Blvd Boca Raton FL 33433 Office: 8000 W Sunrise Blvd Fort Lauderdale FL 33322

DUNPHY, MAUREEN ANN, educator; b. Springfield, Mass., Feb. 25, 1949; d. Donald J. and Mary C. (Tabb) Milbier; m. Terrence Michael Dunphy, June 30, 1979. BS in Edn., Westfield State Coll., 1971, MEd, 1975, Cert. Advanced Grad. Study, 1988. Tchr. Thornton Burgess Intermediate Sch., Hampden, Mass., 1971-75; reading specialist, dept. head West Spring (Mass.) Jr. High Sch., 1975—; acting asst. prin. W. Springfield Jr. High Sch., spring, 1989; cons. Nat. Evaluations Systems, Amherst, Mass. Mem. Long Range Bldg. Needs Com., Westfield, 1986-87. Mem. Pioneer Valley Reading Council (pres. 1977-79), Mass. Reading Assn. (dir. 1977-81), W. Springfield Edn. Assn. (negotiations sec.), Mass. Tchrs. Assn., Hampden Co. Tchrs. Assn. Home: 282 Steiger Dr Westfield MA 01085 Office: West Springfield Jr High Sch 115 Southworth St West Springfield MA 01089

DUNSMOOR, BARBARA JANET, school system administrator; b. New Haven, Oct. 2, 1944; d. Warren George and Frances Helen (Mitchell) Atnes; m. Earl Worcester Dunsmoor Jr., June 27, 1970; children: Rebecca, Sara, Katherine. BA, Albertus Magnus Coll., 1966. Tchr. English Wilbur Cross High Sch., New Haven, 1966-68, Pacific Grove (Calif.) High Sch., 1968-70; mem. Manhattan Beach (Calif.) Edn. Found., 1984-87, pres., 1986-87; mem. Manhattan Beach Bd. Edn., 1987—, pres., 1989-90. Candidate Manhattan Beach Bd. Edn., 1987. Mem. Assn. for Supervision and Curriculum Devel., Calif. Sch. Bds. Assn., Calif. Elected Women's Assn. for Edn. and Rsch., Calif. League of Middle Schs., L.A. County Sch. Trustees Assn., AAUW. Home: 1623 Ruhland Ave Manhattan Beach CA 90266 Office: Manhattan Beach City Sch 1501 Redondo Ave Manhattan Beach CA 90266

DUNWIDDIE, CHARLOTTE, sculptor; b. Strasbourg, France, June 19, 1907. Student, Acad. Fine Arts, Berlin, Mariano Benlliure, Madrid, Alberto Lagos, Buenos Aires, Argentina. Nat. Academician. Editorial bd.: Nat. Sculpture Rev; One-woman shows, Kennedy Galleries, N.Y.C., Salon de Bellas Artes, Buenos Aires, Nat. Horse Show, Madison Sq. Garden, N.Y.C., Aqueduct Racetrack, N.Y.C., Pimlico Racetrack, Balt., Nat. Arts Club, N.Y.C., group shows include, NAD, N.Y.C., Nat. Sculpture Soc. N.Y.C., Allied Artists Am., N.Y.C., Am. Artists Profl. League, N.Y.C., Hudson Valley Art Assn., Pen and Brush, N.Y.C.; represented in permanent collections including, Mus. Brookgreen Gardens, Myrtle Beach, S.C., Marine Corps Mus., Washington, Mus. Am. Art, New Britain, Conn., O'Bannon Hall, USMC, Quantico, Va., Sem. of Redemptorist Fathers, Suffield, Conn., Ch. of Good Shepherd, Lima, Peru, Nuncio Palace, Lima, also pvt. collections. Recipient numerous awards including 15 gold medals. Fellow Allied Artists, Nat. Sculpture Soc. (pres. 1982—), Royal Soc. Arts (London); mem. Am. Artists Profl. League, Pen and Brush (pres. 1964-68). Club: Cosmopolitan.

DUPEY, MICHELE MARY, communications specialist; b. Bronx, N.Y., Feb. 26, 1953; d. William B. and Sandra Nancy (Raia) D.; m. Daniel Michael Gieser, July 14, 1980 (separated Aug. 1989). BA, Montclair State Coll., 1975; cert. in Copywriting. NYU, 1981. Product analyst Internat. Playtex, Paramus, N.J., 1975-79; child care counsellor Bergen Residential Ctr., Rockleigh, N.J., 1979-80; asst. to editor Standard & Poor's Corp., N.Y.C., 1981-84; sec. DDB Needham Worldwide Inc. Advt. (formerly Doyle Dane Bernbach Advt. Co.) N.Y.C., 1985-88; asst. communications dir. Hudson County, N.J., 1988—; creator 1st and 2nd ann. women's history month program; film industry liaison; freelance copywriter, Jersey City, 1988—. In-house planning com. chair 150th anniversary celebration of Hudson County. Contbr. articles to profl. publs. Mem. NOW (pres. local chpt. 1982-83, 84-86, chmn. fin. com. N.J. orgn. 1984-85, chmn. fund raising com. 1984-85, mem. N.J. state bd. 1982-86), Women's Direct Response Group (writer newsletter 1988), N.Y. Open Ctr. (ad writer catalog promotion 1988). Democrat. Roman Catholic. Home: 206 Washington St Apt 3A Jersey City NJ 07302

DUPLESSIS, SUZANNE, Canadian legislator; b. Chicoutimi, Que., Can., June 30, 1940; d. Jean-Julien and Pearl (Tremblay) Fortin; m. Maurice Duplessis, Dec. 26, 1959; children: Jean-Maurice, Claude. BA, Laval U. Alderman Ste.-Foy, Que., 1981-84; mem. Can. Ho. of Commons, 1984—; v.p. Can. sect. Interparliamentary Union. Bd. dirs. Que. Opera Found. Mem. Ste.-Foy C. of C., Que. Provincial Assn. for Progressive Conservative Party (1st v.p. 1979—). Roman Catholic. Club: Richelieu. Address: 1070 Long Sault, Sainte-Foy, PQ Canada G1W 3Z9*

DUPRE, ANNE-MARIE, physical therapist; b. Woonsocket, Feb. 6, 1962; d. Roger Philip and Blanche J. (Lefebvre) D. BS in Phys. Therapy, Simmons Coll., 1984; postgrad., MGH Inst. Health Profls., Boston, 1987—. Sr. phys. therapist Youville Hosp. & Rehab. Ctr., Cambridge, Mass., 1985-87, clin. supr., 1987—. Mem. Neurodevel. Technique Assn. (cert.).

DUPRE, JUDITH ANN NEIL, real estate agent, interior decorator; b. Houma, La., May 7, 1945; d. Herbert Joseph and Doris Mae (LeFouef) Neil; m. Michael Anthony Dupre, Jan. 7, 1962 (div. Aug. 1987); children: Arienne Danielle, Travis Lance. BA in Psychology, Southeast Okla. State U., 1982. Fin. mgr., supr. Gen. Fin. Loan Co., La., Colo., 1960-69; exec. sec. Progressive Bank & Trust Co., Houma, La., 1973-74; health coordinator Spring Cypress Cultural & Recreation Ctr., 1974-75; bus. mgr., buyer June Morris Boutique, Ardmore, Okla., 1978-79; actress, model David Payne Agy., Dallas, 1985—; real estate agt. Vonnie Cobb Inc. Realtors, Sugar Land, Tex., 1986—; nat. mktg. asst. North American Mortgage Co. (subs. MONY Mut. N.Y.), Houston, 1987-88; mgr., care coord. Sanus N.Y. Life, Inc., 1988-89; mgr. PPO Am. Health Network, 1989—. Mem. Strake Jesuit-Mothers' Club, Houston, 1985-87, St. Agnes Acad. Women's Club, Houston, 1985-87, Ft. Bend Republican Women, Sugar Land, 1985-86; chmn. Texans War on Drugs, Sugar Land, 1985-86; bd. dirs. MUD (Dist. 6), Sugar Land, 1986—. Mem. Cath. Daus. of the Americas, Nat. Assn. Realtors, Tex. Assn. Realtors, Bal Harbour Homeowners Assn., Assn. Profl. Mortgage Women, Alpha Chi. Roman Catholic. Clubs: Sweetwater Ladies Golf Assn., Sweetwater Country (Sugar Land). Avocations: tennis, golf, fishing, boating, dancing. Address: 18038 Bal Harbour Dr Nassau TX 77058

DUPREY, JANET MARIE, county official; b. Plattsburgh, N.Y., Nov. 27, 1945; d. Peter Joseph and Edna Mae Lacy; student Empire State Coll., 1979—; m. Elmer C. Duprey, Sept. 9, 1967; children—John, Michelle. Exec. sec. Eastman Kodak Co., Rochester, N.Y., 1965-66; legal sec. John L. Bell, Plattsburgh, 1966-68; legis. asst. to Sen. Ronald B. Stafford, Plattsburgh, 1968-70; co-owner Rustic Restaurant, Peru, 1967-85; mem. Clinton County Legislature, 1976-86, chmn., 1981-82; treas. Clinton County, 1986—; mem. Champlain Valley Physicians Hosp. Med. Ctr. Corp. Mem. N.Y. State Dept. Social Services Statewide Adv. Council, 1979-81; Clinton County Social Services Adv. Council, 1976-86, Office Aging Adv. Council, Child Abuse Task Force. Mem. adv. bd. Clinton County Div. for Youth; bd. dirs. ARC, Hospice Care Services, Council Community Services, Clinton County ARC; mem. SUNY-Plattsburgh Coll. Found. Mem. LWV, SUNY Plattsburgh Coll. Found., Clinton Community Coll. Found., N.Y. State Treas. Assn., Clinton County Hotel, Restaurant and Liquor Dealers Assn. (past pres.), Champlain Valley Bus. and Profl. Women's Club (Woman of Yr. award 1985), Delta Kappa Gamma (hon.). Republican. Roman Catholic. Club: Plattsburgh AFB

Officers (hon.). Home: Telegraph St Peru NY 12972 Office: 137 Margaret St Plattsburgh NY 12901

DUPREY-GUTIERREZ, IRENE CATHY, writer, educator; b. New Bedford, Mass., Oct. 4, 1941; d. William Hector and Nora Marie (Ouimette) Duprey; m. Rafael Gutierrez-Cortez, June 10, 1965 (div. 1970); 1 child, Cathy Nora. BS in Edn., Bridgewater State Coll., 1963; MA in Edn., Calif. State U., San Fernando, 1971; EdD, U. Mass, 1988. Cert. tchr., adminstr., Calif., Mass. Tchr. L.A. Pub. Schs., 1963-65, Simi Valley (Calif.) Pub. Schs., 1967-71, New Bedford Pub. Schs., 1971-88; non-traditional outreach coord. Old Colony Vocat. Tech. High Sch., Rochester, Mass., 1989—; instr. edn. Newbury Coll., New Bedford, 1980—; freelance writer various newspapers and mags.; cons. various child abuse-parenting orgns., Mass., 1976—; ednl. rep. Challenger Space Conf., 1986, Fact-Finding Com. to Nicaragua, 1987; del. Alliance for Hispanic Edn., Washington, 1989. Author: That's Phenomenal, 1982, Stranger Than Fiction, 1985; contbr. children's stories and child abuse articles to various publs. Active various local civic orgns.; mem. pub. rels. com. New Bedford YWCA, 1988—; mem. regional adv. bd. Bay State Ctrs. for Displaced Homemakers. Named Tchr. of Yr., New Bedford Schs., 1979, Bristol County Tchrs. Assn., 1988, Outstanding Alumni, Bridgewater State Coll., 1986, Woman of Yr., Internat. Wome's Day, New Bdford, 1988. Mem. New Bedford Educators Assn. (v.p., bd. dirs., editor newsletter, mem. contract adv. bd., coms. 1974—), Mass. Tchrs. Assn., NEA, Nat. Edn. Editors Assn. (Humanitarian award), Bridgewater State Coll. Alumni Assn. (pub. rels. com. 1980-83, v.p. 1985-87, assoc. editor alumni publs. 1986-88, bd. dirs.), AAUW (pub. rels. com. Mass. div. 1986—, pub. edn. com. 1987-88, v.p. membership com. 1988—), NAFE, Ednl. Expertise (founder 1989), Speakers USA, Inc., Rosicrucian. Republican. Home and Office: 1630 Padanarum Ave New Bedford MA 02740

DUPUIS, BONNIE JEANNE, mortgage broker; b. Oceanside, Calif., Mar. 7, 1949; d. Lawrence Joseph and Dorothy Jeanne (Foye-Rost) D.; m. William James Dynes III, Apr. 13, 1968 (div. 1977); children: William James Dynes IV, Ryan Christopher Dynes. Grad. high sch., Vista, Calif. Loan processor Bankers Mortgage Co. (now Transam.), Walnut Creek, Calif., 1969-70; office mgr., sr. loan processor Guild Mortgage Co., Oakland, Calif., 1970-72; loan processor Pacific Mortgage and Loan Co., Oceanside, 1977; br.and office mgr. Keystone Fin., Inc., Vista, Calif., 1977-78; office mgr. Approved Mortgage Corp., La Mesa, Calif., 1978-79, Sunset Mortgage Corp., Vista, 1979-80, Mission Bay Mortgage Co., Escondido, Calif., 1979-80; Office mgr. Internat. Mortgage Corp., Carlsbad, Calif., 1980-81; office and br. mgr. Allstate Enterprises Mortgage Corp., Carlsbad, 1981-82; office mgr. Meritor Mortgage Corp. W. (formerly PSFS Mortgage Corp. W.), San Diego, 1982-85, United Western Funding, Inc., San Diego, 1985, 1st Calif. Funding, Inc., Escondido, 1986; v.p. underwriting, processing, closing Ocean Pacific Fin., Escondido, 1986-88; part-owner Network Mortgage, San Marcos, 1988; v.p. W.C. Fin., Escondido, 1988—; owner B.J. Dupuis Underwriting Svcs., Vista, 1988-89; owner Mortgage Svcs., Valley Ctr., Calif., 1989—, Temecula, Calif. Democrat. Lutheran. Office: Mortgage SvcsTemecula Valley Mortgage Corp Anza Valley Mortgage 41690 Enterprise Circle N #100 Temecula CA 92390

DUQUE, SARAH, painter; b. L.A., May 30, 1929; d. Victor Anthony and Sarah (Millholland) D. Student, Stanford U., Calif., Georgetown U.; BA, Dominican Coll, San Rafael, Calif., 1951; MA, Villa Schifanoia, Florence, Italy, 1961; MFA, Rosary Coll., 1971; postgrad., U. Edinburgh, Scotland, 1971-73, Johns Hopkins U., 1977. Tchr. North Ranchito Sch. Dist., 1951-53; supervising tchr. L.A. City Schs., 1953-64; prof. art North Orange County Community Coll. Dist., Fullerton, Calif., 1964-85, prof. emeritus, 1985—. One person shows include Serra Gallery, San Francisco, 1963, Loyola-Marymount U., L.A., 1963, Galleria Mazzucchelli, San Domenico, Italy, 1964, Galleria del Parione, Firenze, Italy, 1971, Fullerton (Calif.) Coll., 1974, Galleria San Marco, Firenze, 1981, Brea (Calif.) Civic Ctr., 1983, Woollahara Gallery, Sydney, Australia, 1983, Palazzo Soliano, Orvieto, Italy, 1988, Mescana, Orvieto, 1990; exhibited in group shows at Wis. State Drawing Show, Madison, 1962, Butler Inst. Am. Art, Youngstown, Ohio, 1963, Santa Paula (Calif.) Exhbn., 1964, Miracle Mile Exhbn., L.A., 1965, Nat. Art Exhbn., Cranbrook, Mich., 1977, Nat. Tapestry Exhbn., Detroit, 1979, Galleria Torra, Campania, 1982, Santuario della Verna, Tuscany, Italy, 1982, St. Thomas More Foyer, N.Y.C., 1987, The Russian Tea Rm., N.Y.C., 1987. NEA scholar, 1970; Nat. Endowment for Humanities grantee, 1977. Home and Studio: 2384 Carrotwood Dr Brea CA 92621

DUQUENOY, LINDA IRENE, health services administrator; b. Providence, R.I., Jan. 2, 1960; d. Dennis Matthew and Irene May (MacIsaac) Lynch; m. Gordon Charles Duquenoy, July 25, 1981; children: Katlyn Ann, Jonathan Dallas. BS in Health Svcs. Adminstrn., Providence Coll., 1982. Exec. intern Office of Gov. of R.I., Providence, 1980-82; adminstrv. asst. Pawtucket (R.I.) Heart Health Program, 1982-84; tng. specialist R.I. Div. of Substance Abuse, Cranston, 1984-89; coord. of prevention, edn. and tng. unit R.I. div. of Substance Abuse, Cranston, 1989-90, assoc. adminstr., 1990—; mem. Gov.'s Refugee Task Force, Gov.'s AIDS Adv. Com., Gov.'s Com. on Youth Alcohol and Sustance Abuse, Gov.'s Substance Abuse Adv. Coun. Campaign worker Dennis M. Lynch for Mayor, Pawtucket, 1972-81; campaign vol. J. Joseph Garrahy for Gov., R.I., 1978-84; campaign worker, cons. William J. Lynch for Councilman, Pawtucket, 1986; active Gov.'s Prevention Edn. and Tng. Commn., R.I., 1984—. Recipient Community Svc. award R.I. Assn. Alcholism and Drug Abuse Counselors, 1989. Mem. R.I. Joint Edn. Com. (sec., 1985—, chair 1986—), R.I. Trainers Council, R.I. Drug Cert. Bd., R.I. Chem. Dependency Profl. Cert. Bd. Democrat. Roman Catholic. Office: RI Div of Substance Abuse Substance Abuse Adminstrn Bldg Cranston RI 02920

DURAN, KARIN JEANINE, librarian; b. Burbank, Calif., Aug. 31, 1948; d. Jose Antonio and Sophia (Cortez) D.; m. Richard Mark Nupoll, Sept. 5, 1971. AA, L.A. Pierce Coll., Woodland Hills, Calif., 1968; BA, Calif. State U., 1970; MLS, U. So. Calif., 1972, PhD, 1986. Libr. Calif. State U., Northridge, 1972—; lectr. Calif. State U., Northridge, 1977-84. Mem. Comision Feminil Nacional, San Fernando Valley, Calif., 1987—. Named Woman of Year Calif. Women Higher Edn., Northridge, 1989, Bicentennial Woman, L.A. Human Rels. Com., 1976. Mem. ALA, Nat. Assn. Chicano Studies, Calif. Libr. Assn., Calif. Acad. Rsch. Librs., Women's Coun. Calif. State U., Assn. Governing Bds., REFORMA, Computer Using Educators. Office: Calif State U Northridge Libr 18111 Nordhoff St Northridge CA 91330

DURAND, CATHERINE LOUISE, probation and parole supervisor; b. Flint, Mich., May 21, 1948; d. Gerald Frederick and Joyce Leone (Sewell) D. BA in Theology, St. Louis U., 1971, MA in Bibl. Lang. and Lit., 1974. Campus minister St. Louis U., 1972-74, Marygrove Coll., Detroit, 1974; probation, parole officer Mo. Probation and Parole, St. Louis, 1975-77, asst. supr., 1977-79, dist. supr., 1979-82, sr. dist. supr., 1982—; mem. adv. bd. Higher Edn. Council on Ednl. Opportunity Ctrs., St. Louis, 1978—, Human Services Dept. St. Louis Community Coll. At Florissant, Mo., 1983—. Sister Servants of the Immaculate Heart of Mary, Monroe, Mich., 1966-74. Recipient Outstanding Service award Gov. of Mo., 1976. Mem. Am. Correctional Assn., Mo. Correctional Assn., Nat. Assn. Female Execs., Nat. Wellness Inst. Roman Catholic. Home: 8 Hickory Hill Dr O'Fallon MO 63366 Office: Mo Probation and Parole 9165 W Florissant Ferguson MO 63136

DURBIN, (MARGARET) ROSAMOND, marketing executive; b. Shelbyville, Ind., Feb. 25, 1952; d. Willard Clyde and Irma Frances (Havens) Sandefur; m. Timothy Mark Durbin, Dec. 27, 1986. BA in English, Xavier U., 1974. Office mgr. Pryde, Inc., Cin., 1975-77; media mgr. Intermedia, Inc. (merger Dektas and Eger, Inc. 1979), Cin., 1977-80; media dir. Caldwell-Van Riper, Inc., Ft. Wayne, Ind., 1980-82; media supr. Jerrico/Abbott Advt., Lexington, Ky., 1982, Marsteller, Inc., Chgo., 1982-85; mgr. Midwest mktg. Pearle Vision Ctr., Chgo., 1985-86; v.p., gen. mgr. Bonsib Inc. Mktg. Svcs., Indpls., 1986—; cons. YWCA Ft. Wayne, 1981, 82. Columnist Marketing and Media Decisions mag. Mem. Am. Mktg. Assn., Nat. Wildlife Fedn., Xavier Alumni Assn., Ind. Fedn. Advt. Agys. (bd. dirs.). Republican. Roman Catholic. Office: Bonsib Mktg Svcs Inc 8400 Woodfield Crossing Blvd #175 Indianapolis IN 46240

DURDAHL, CAROL LAVAUN, psychiatric nurse; b. Crookston, Minn., Jan. 18, 1933; d. Elmer Oliver and Ovidia (Olson) Durdahl; m. Hans A. Dahl, May 22, 1956 (div. 1983); children: Hana Sorensen, Carla Pederson. RN, St. Lukes Hosp., Duluth, Minn., 1953; BA in Human Svcs., Met. State U., St. Paul, 1982. Staff nurse various hosps., Minn., 1953-59; human svcs. tech. Willmar (Minn.) State Hosp., 1970-74, supplemental tchr., 1974-83; staff nurse Rice Meml. Hosp., Willmar, 1983-86; utilization rev. various nursing homes, Willmar, 1985-86; tchr. Willmar Area Vocat. Tech. Inst., 1986; dir. nurses Glenmore Recovery Ctr., Crookston, Minn., 1986-88; shift supr. Golden Valley (Minn.) Health Ctr., 1988—. Contbr. articles to profl. jours. Mem. AAUW, Bus. and Profl. Women, League Women Voters (pres. and state bd.), Federated Women, Does. Republican. Lutheran. Home: 6450 York Ave S #403 Edina MN 55435 Office: Golden Valley Health Ctr 4101 Golden Valley Rd Golden Valley MN 55422

DURDEN-SIMMONS, GWENDOLYN MARIE, sales executive; b. New Orleans; d. Richard Elmer and Viola (Gardiner) Durden; m. Paul Ronald Simmons, Aug. 28, 1982. AA, Delgado Coll., New Orleans, 1968; BS, Trenton State Coll., 1973, MEd, 1975. Sec. NAACP, New Orleans, 1966-67; tchr. Trenton (N.J.) Pub. Schs., 1973-75; ednl. sales rep. Houghton Mifflin Co., Hopewell, N.J., 1978, dist. sales mgr. bus. edn., 1979-84; bus. edn. sales mgr. secondary bus. Houghton Mifflin Co., Princeton, N.J., 1985—; advisor N.Y.C. Bus. Edn. Assn., 1980-87, Trenton Adminstrv. Mgmt. Com., 1988—. Named Friend of Bus., Bus. Edn. Assn. Maine, 1989. Mem. Internat. Soc. Bus. Edn., Nat. Assn. Bus. Edn., Nat. Alliance Black Educators, NAACP, NAFE, Delta Pi Epsilon. Democrat. Roman Catholic. Home: 76 Clearwater Dr Willingboro NJ 08046 Office: Houghton Mifflin Co 101 Campus Dr Princeton NJ 08540

DUREGGER, KAREN MARIE, health facility administrator; b. Des Moines, Jan. 16, 1952; d. Francis William and Luella Marie (Smith) Moore; m. Michael Steven Duregger, Feb. 26, 1972; children: Chadwick Michael, Joshua William (dec.), Francis Steven. Secretarial diploma, Am. Inst. Bus., Des Moines, 1971. Cert. health care adminstr. Des Moines Area Community Coll. Sec. Harry Rodine Co., Des Moines, 1970, Iowa State Assn. Secondary Sch. Prins., Des Moines, 1971-72; asst. adminstr. Hancock County Care Facility, Garner, 1973-74, adminstr., 1974-89; adminstr. Duncan Heights, Inc., Garner, 1989, bd. dirs., recording sec., 1989—, also bd. dirs. Sec. Mental Health/Mental Retardation/Developmentally Disabled adv. bd., Garner, 1983-90; mem. Community Edn. Bd., Garner, 1989—. Mem. County Care Facility Adminstrs. (dist. pres. 1985-87, treas. 1989—), Human Svcs. Tng. Network, 1990—, Tng. Planning Group Task Force, WaTanYe. Republican. Lutheran. Home and Office: RR2 Box 48 Garner IA 50438

DUREICH, PATRICIA S., real estate executive; b. Daybrook, W.Va., Nov. 29, 1942; d. Earnest Gyren and Leona Gail (Hamilton) Wilson; m. Alexander Dureich Sr., July 9, 1960; children: Alexander Jr., Pamela Beth, Michael Scott. Student, Inst. Children's Lit., Redding Ridge, Conn., 1981; AAS in Bus. Mgmt. magna cum laude, Alpena Community Coll., Wurtsmith, Mich.; postgrad., Saginaw Valley State U., Alpena Community Coll. Religious edn. coordinator, tchr. Sacred Heart Cath. Ch., Oscoda, Mich.; exec sec. Al's Quality Refrigeration and Air Cond. Svc., Inc., Oscoda; property owner mgr. Oscoda. Poetry pub in Anthology of Midwestern Poetry, 1988, Am. Anthology of Contemporary Poetry, 1989. Mem. com. Concert Assn.; reading tutor Oscoda Area Sch. System; contbr., supporter pub. broadcasting; past mem. Gifted Children's Parent's Group, Nat. Psoriasis Found. Recipient Cert. of Appreciation. Mem. NAFE, Bus. and Profl. Women, Air Force Assn., Nat. Geog. Soc., Am. Mus. Natural History, Iosco Hist. Soc., World Future Soc., Sacred Heart Alter Soc., Oscoda Area Choral Boosters, Smithsonian Inst., Nat. Audubon Soc., Soc. Disney Plate Collectors, Saturday Evening Post Soc. Roman Catholic. Home: 206 W Michigan Ave Oscoda MI 48750-1413

DURGIN, DIANE, lawyer; b. Albany, N.Y., May 17, 1946; d. Leslie P. and Shirley A. (Albright) D. BA, Wellesley Coll., 1970; JD magna cum laude, Boston Coll., 1974. Assoc. Shearman & Sterling, N.Y.C., 1974-83; corp. sec. Ga.-Pacific Corp., Atlanta, 1983—, v.p. law, dep. gen. counsel, 1986-89, sr. v.p. law, gen. counsel, 1989—; bd. dirs. Am. Arbitration Assn. Bd. dirs., mem. exec. and nominating coms. The Alliance Theatre Co., 1985—; mem. audit com., bd. dirs. Metro Atlanta chpt. ARC, 1988—; bd. sponsors Georgian Chamber Players, Inc., 1986—. Mem. ABA, Am. Corp. Counsel Assn., N.Y. State Bar Assn., Am. Arbitration Assn. (bd. dirs.), Am. Law Inst., Nature Conservancy (bd. dirs. Ga. chpt. 1990—), Order of Coif. Clubs: India House; Ga. Exec. Women's Network, Commerce (Atlanta). Office: Ga-Pacific Corp 133 Peachtree St NE Atlanta GA 30303

DURHAM, BARBARA, state supreme court associate justice; b. 1942. BSBA, Georgetown U.; JD, Stanford U. Bar: Wash. 1968. Former judge Wash. Superior Ct., King County; judge Wash. Ct. Appeals; assoc. justice Wash. Supreme Ct., 1985—. Office: Wash Supreme Ct Temple of Justice AV 11 Olympia WA 98504-0511

DURHAM, CHRISTINE MEADERS, state supreme court justice; b. Los Angeles, Aug. 3, 1945; d. William Anderson and Louise (Christensen) Meaders; m. George Homer Durham II, Dec. 29, 1966; children: Jennifer, Meghan, Troy, Melinda, Isaac. A.B., Wellesley Coll., 1967; J.D., Duke U., 1971. Bar: N.C. 1971, Utah 1974. Sole practice law Durham, N.C., 1971-73; instr. legal medicine Duke U., Durham, 1971-73; adj. prof. law Brigham Young U., Provo, Utah, 1973-78; ptnr. Johnson, Durham & Moxley, Salt Lake City, 1974-78; judge Utah Dist. Ct., 1978-82; justice Utah Supreme Ct., 1982—; faculty Nat. Jud. coll., Reno, 1983. Pres. Women Judges Fund for Justice, 1987-88. Fellow Am. Bar Found.; mem. ABA (edn. com. appellate judges' conf.), Nat. Assn. Women Judges (pres. 1986-87), ABA, Utah Bar Assn., Am. Law Inst., Am. Judicature Soc. (bd. dirs.). Home: 1702 Yale Ave Salt Lake City UT 84108 Office: Utah Supreme Ct 332 State Capitol Salt Lake City UT 84114*

DURHAM, ERNESTINE, government agency administrator; b. Goldsboro, N.C., Jan. 22, 1951; d. Isaiah and Frances Aretha (Bennett) D. BS, A&T U., Greensboro, N.C., 1973. Br. mgr. Social Security Adminstrn., Memphis, 1980-81; spl. asst. Social Security Adminstrn., Balt., 1981-82, policy coordination, project devel. spl., 1988-89; asst. dist. mgr. Social Security Adminstrn., Dothan, Ala., 1982-85; dist. mgr. Social Security Adminstrn., Florence, Ala., 1985-88; with midlevel mgmt. devel. program Social Security Adminstrn., Balt., 1989—. Leader Girl Scout Am., 1982-86; mem. Buddies of Nashville, Memphis Literacy Coun., 1980-81, B-Racial Study Group, 1983-85, Hawk-Houston Boys Club, House of Ruth, 1984-85, Southeast Ala. Rehab., 1985, Safeplace, 1985-88, United Way of the Shoals. Mem. Kiwanis, Jaycees (S.W. Balt. County). Home: 123 Courtland Woods Circle Pikesville MD 21208

DURHAM, PEGGY J., free-lance journalist; b. Boise City, Okla., Aug. 19, 1941; d. John M. and Mildred C. (Phillips) D.; 1 dau., Erin Christine Phillips Durham. B.A. in Journalism, U. Okla., 1963. Dir. public info. U. Tulsa, 1967-70; mgr. communications Honeywell Info. Systems, Oklahoma City, 1970-75; dir. public info. Okla. Bar Assn., Oklahoma City, 1975-77; chmn. bd., partner Metro Media Ltd. Advt. Agy., Oklahoma City, 1977-78; pres. The Word Place Advt. Agy., Oklahoma City, 1978-82; pres. Okla. Feminist Enterprises, Inc., Oklahoma City, 1977-80; freelance journalist. Editor Okla. Halfway House newsletter Alternatives, 1973; founder, editor Sister Advocate newspaper, Okla.'s only feminist newspaper, 1975-80; co-pub. Red Dirt Women's Press, 1987-88. Bd. dirs. PASEO Drug Counseling Center, Oklahoma City, 1970-73; bd. dirs., co-founder Okla. Women's Ctr., 1973-74; mem. ERA coalition NOW, 1973-75. Named one of Okla.'s 10 movers and shakers in women's movement Okla. Monthly Mag., 1976. Mem. Internat. Assn. Bus. Communicators, Oklahoma City Press Club, ACLU, Okla. Press Assn. Democrat. Home and Office: 829 NW 140th St Edmond OK 73013

DURHAM, SHARON FEENEY, architect, consultant; b. L.A., Feb. 12, 1951; d. Michael James and Theda Joyce (Stewart) Feeney. BS in Architecture, U. New South Wales, Sidney, Australia, 1972; BArch, U. Western Australia, 1976. Lic. architect, Tenn. Designer McConnel, Smith & Johnson, Sydney, 1972-73, Design Farm, Perth, West Australia, 1975-76, Yakely and Assocs., Cambridge, Eng., 1977; presentation artist and designer Barge Waggoner, Sumner and Cannon, Nashville, 1977-79; project coord. Skidmore, Owings and Merril, Washington, 1979; in-house architect Gregg Constrn. Co., Nashville, 1982-83, Ted Welch Investments, Nashville, 1983—; mktg. cons. The Whitney Group, Houston, 1989. Prin. works include bldg. Branell Coll., Berryhill Square Shopping Ctr., Edgehill Office Bldg., Carmichael Pl. Shopping Ctr. Counselor Nashville br. Boy Scouts Am., 1988—; fund raiser YWCA, 1989. Recipient Scholarship, Commonwealth of Australia, 1970-72. Mem. AIA, Am. Soc. Engring. Mgmt., Interior Bus. Designers, Order of Engrs. (hon). Republican. Methodist.

DURHAM-MCLOUD, DIANNA, state agency director; b. Memphis, Sept. 30, 1947; d. Horace Cary and Charlotte Virginia (Cain) Goode; m. William Dawson McLoud Jr., Aug. 26, 1978; children: William Dawson III, Charlotte Michelle. BA in Pub. Adminstr., Purdue U., 1969; MPA, Ind. U., 1974. Community service rep. AT&T, Indpls., 1969-71; asst. dir. Urban League NW Ind., Gary, 1972-76; mgmt. asst. specialist Nat. Urban League, Chgo., 1976-79, regional coordinator, 1979-82, asst. dir., 1982-84; dep. dir. Ill. Dept. Employment Security, Chgo., 1984—. composer inspirational songs. V.p. Hull House Assn., 1982-85, also bd. dirs.; bd. dirs. Women Employed Network, 1986—, Network Black Women, 1984—; vice-chairperson Midwest Minority Womens Caucus, 1979—; co-chair UNCF Telethon, 1986; trustee, Bible instr. Ch. Christ. Recipient Outstanding Citizen award Ill. Dept. Human Rights, 1983, Disting. Service award, U.S. Dept. Labor, 1984; named one of Outstanding Young Women, 1981, Woman of the Yr. Ind. Assn. Social Service Agys., 1978. Mem. NAACP, Internat. Assn. Personnel Employment Security, Nat. Urban Affairs Council (chair telethon 1986), Delta Sigma Theta. Home: 1324 Dewey Ave Evanston IL 60202

DURKEE, SARAH BRUCE, writer, lyricist; b. Salem, Mass., Feb. 14, 1955; d. Allen Bruce and Patricia (Cole) Durkee; m. Paul Ross Jacobs, July 2, 1988. Grad. high sch., Pingree Sch., South Hamilton, Mass. Actress, tchr. Celebration Mime Theatre, various cities, 1973-76; comedian, writer Nat. Lampoon shows, various cities, 1977-79; lyricist Andy's Summer Playhouse, Wilton, N.H., 1980—; lyricist to rock singer Meat Loaf, N.Y.C., 1983-84; scriptwriter, lyricist Henson Assocs., N.Y.C., 1985; lyricist Sesame Street and Square One TV, Children's TV Workshop, N.Y.C., 1987—; freelance writer, N.Y.C., N.H. Author, editor: Free To Be...A Family, 1987, also scriptwriter-lyricist TV spl. and record album, 1988; co-author: The Book of Sequels, 1990. Recipient Gold award for ednl. children's documentary Houston Internat. Film Festival, 1987, Emmy award for music direction and composition Sesame Street, 1989-90. Mem. ASCAP, Writer's Guild, AFTRA.

DURKIN, DOROTHY ANGELA, university dean; b. Glen Cove, N.Y., June 23, 1945; d. Frank Vincent and Rose Marie Durkin; 1 child, David Francis. BA, SUNY, Stony Brook, 1968; MA, NYU, 1974. Adminstrv. asst. SUNY, Stony Brook, 1965-67; prodn. editor Holt, Rhinehart & Winston, Inc., Stony Brook, 1967-69; editor Hill & Wang Pub., Inc., N.Y.C., 1969-70; asst. dir. pub. info. Sch. Continuing Edn. NYU, N.Y.C., 1970-72, assoc. dean pub. affairs and student svcs. Sch. Continuing Edn., 1983—; cons. N.Y.C. Ctr. for Lifelong Learning, 1974; producer TV series Continuum, Sta. WNYC, 1974; speaker, cons. coll. bd. Editor: NSF student mag., 1961. Recipient Andy Advt. award of merit, 1972; Direct Mktg. Leadership award, 1977, 80, 87; Nat. Univ. Continuing Edn. Assn. awards, bronze, silver, and gold medals, 1978, 81-88, merit award Art Dirs. Club, 1980, Merit award Soc. of Illustrators, 1980, Admissions Mktg. Report awards, 3 Gold medals, Merit award, 1986, 87, 88, 89, John Caples award 1987, 88, Catalog Age award, 1988. Mem. NUCEA (group leader learn from success), Am. Coll. Pub. Rels. Assn. (nat. award 1973), Coun. for Advancement and Support of Edn. (awards 1981, 82, 83, 84, 86, 87, 88, Grand Gold and Silver award 1989, chmn. nat. award), Women in Communications (job chmn.), N.Y. Radio Broadcasters Assn. (Big Apple award 1985), Univ. Continuing Edn. Assn. (chmn. info. svcs. div. 1980-81, chair mktg. adv. com. 1989-90), Pub. Rels. Soc., Am. Demographics (adv. bd. 1989-90), Direct Mktg. Assn. (Echo Leadership award 1987, 88), SUNY Alumni Assn. (bd. dirs., speaker, cons.), Scuba Diving Club, Community Sing Club, Parent Assn. Club. Office: NYU Sch Continuing Edn 326 Shimkin Hall New York NY 10003

DUROCHER, FRANCES ANTOINETTE, physician; b. Woonsocket, R.I., Mar. 11, 1943; d. Armand D. and Teresa (Leverone) DuRocher. BA (with honors), Trinity coll., 1964; MS, Brown U., 1966; postgrad., Woman's Med. Coll., 1970. Med. resident Phila. VA Hosp. and Med. Coll. Pa., 1971-73; assoc. in internal med. Guthrie Clinic Ltd., Sayre, Pa., 1973-79, Annandale (Va.) Group Health Assocs., 1979-87; assoc. chair internal med. Annandale Group Health Assoc., 1986-87; founding ptnr. F.A. DuRocher, M.D. and B.A. Carson M.D., P.C., Fairfax, Va., 1987--. Mem. Am. Med. Women's Assn. (exec. bd. Branch I 1985—, pres. 1987-88), AMA, Med. Soc. Va., Am. Soc. Internal Medicine, Fairfax County Med. Soc. Office: FA DuRocher MD & BA Carson 9926 Main St Fairfax VA 22031

DUSENBURY, LINDA, research psychologist, consultant; b. Florence, S.C., Aug. 5, 1959; d. Richard Green and Susan (Law) D.; m. Jeffrey Conrad Laurence, July 4, 1987. BA, U. Vt., 1980, MA, 1982, PhD, 1984. Postdoctoral rsch. assoc. Ind. U. Psychology Dept., Bloomington, 1984-85; rsch. assoc. Cornell U. Med. Coll., N.Y.C., 1985-86, asst. prof., 1986—; mem. Ind. Prevention Rsch. Ctr., Indpls., 1984-85; prevention cons. Boys Clubs Am., N.Y.C., 1986; tech. cons. Carnegie Corp., Meharry Med. Coll., Nashville, 1990; mem. Disability Prevention Work Group, Dept. Health, Albany, 1990. Co-editor: Readings in Primary Prevention, 1984, Prevention, Powerlessness, and Psychopathology, 1988; author: (with others) various books; contbr. articles to profl. jours. Recipient Vt. Conf. on Primary Prevention award U. Vt., 1980; Nat. Cancer Inst. grantee, 1985-90, Nat. Inst. Drug Abuse grantee, 1988-90. Mem. Am. Psychol. Assn. Democrat. Home: 3 Briar Close Larchmont NY 10538 Office: Cornell U Med Coll 411 E 69th St New York NY 10021

DUSEPH, FLORENCE, psychiatrist; b. Singapore, Feb. 8, 1949; came to U.S., 1976; d. V. Varghese and Emerancy (Joseph) Ramsal; m. Eayo Duseph, Aug. 19, 1974; children: Roshan, Renu, Rita. MB BS, Christian Med. Coll., Vellore, India, 1975. Diplomate, Am. Bd. Psychiatry and Neurology. Intern Christian Med. Coll. Hosp., Vellore, 1974-75; resident in psychiatry U. Kans. Sch. Medicine, Wichita, 1977-81; staff physician Sankar Hosp., Quilon, Kerala, India, 1975-76, Tiruvella (India) Med. Mission Hosp., 1976; staff psychiatrist Tarrant County Mental Health/Mental Retardation, Ft. Worth, 1981-87; pvt. practice Ft. Worth, 1987—; mem. staff Psychiat. Inst., Care Unit Hosp., St. Joseph Hosp., North Hills Med. Ctr., North Richland Hills; provisional mem. staff Harris Heb Hosp., Bedford; assoc. mem. staff Richland Hosp.; provisional mem. staff South Arlington Hosp. Mem. AMA, Tex. Med. Assn., Am. Med. Soc. on Alcoholism and Other Drug Dependencies, Tarrant County Med. Soc., Am. Psychiat. Assn., Tex. Psychiat. Soc. Home: 848 Windsong Ct Bedford TX 76021 Office: 4109 Cagle Dr Ste G North Richland Hills TX 76180

DUSHANE, PHYLLIS MILLER, nurse; b. Portland, Oreg., June 3, 1924; d. Joseph Anton and Josephine Florence (Eicholtz) Miller; m. Frank Maurice Jacobson, Mar. 13, 1945 (dec. 1975); children: Karl, Kathleen, Kraig, Kirk, Karen, Kent, Krista, Kandis, Kris, Karlyn; m. Donald McLelland DuShane, July 21, 1979 (dec. 1989); stepchildren: Diane DuShane Bishop, Donald III. BS in Biology, U. Oreg., 1948; BS in Nursing, Oreg. Health Scis. U., 1968. R.N., Oreg. Pub. health nurse Marion County Health Dept., Salem, Oreg., 1968-77; pediatric nurse practitioner Marion County Health Dept., Salem, 1977—, Allergy Assocs., Eugene, Oreg., 1979-89; mem. allied profl. staff Sacred Heart Gen. Hosp., Eugene, 1979—. Mem. P.E.O., Oreg. Pediatric Nurse Practitioners Assn. (v.p. Salem chpt. 1977-78), Am. Nurses Assn., Oreg. Nurses Assn., Nat. Assn. Pediatric Nurse Assocs. and Practitioners, Am. Acad. Nurse Practitioners, Nurse Practitioners Spl. Interest Group, Salem Med. Aux. (sec. 1968), Oreg. Republican Women, Delta Gamma Alumni (v.p. 1979). Presbyterian. Home: 965 E 23d Ave Eugene OR 97405-3074 Office: Marion County Health Dept 3180 Center St NE Salem OR 97301 also: AJ Sch Dist 200 N Monroe St Eugene OR 97402 also: Eugene Pediatric Assocs 1680 Chambers St Eugene OR 97402

DUSSAULT, MARILYN BLACK, lawyer; b. N.Y.C., May 21, 1943; d. Albert Sherwood and Dorothy Margaret (Gilligan) Black; children: Robert L., Renee Lynne. BA in History, U. Conn., 1977, JD, 1980. Bar: Conn. 1980. Assoc. Winthropo, Stimson, Putnam & Roberts, Stamford, Conn.,

1980-82, Ivey, Barnam & O'Mara, Stamford/Greenwich, Conn., 1982-84; pvt. practice law Stamford, 1984—; pres., bd. dirs. The Chesterfield Assocs., Stamford, 1987—; lectr. in field. Contbr. articles to profl. jours. Mem. ABA, Stamford/Darien Reg. Bar Assn., Phi Beta Kappa. Democrat. Roman Catholic. Office: 2777 Summer St #314 Stamford CT 06905

DUTCHER, FLORA MAE, retired school teacher; b. McCook, Nebr., Jan. 26, 1908; d. Austin Wilson and Minnie Magnolia (Tucker) D. AA, McCook (Nebr.) Jr. Coll., 1936; BA, U. Nebr., 1943, MA in Edn. and Adminstrn., 1951. Tchr. rural elem. Hitchcock and Red Willow County Schs., Nebr., 1926-35; tchr. city elem. McCook (Nebr.) Pub. Schs., 1936-39; tchr. social studies McCook (Nebr.) Jr. High Sch., 1939-50; prin. North Ward Elem. Sch., McCook, 1950-55; tchr. of edn. courses McCook (Nebr.) Jr. Coll., 1955-73; tchr. high sch. Sunday sch. class First Bapt. Ch., McCook, 1946-73; pres. dist. 5 Nebr. State Edn. Assn., 1994-50; sponsor Phi Theta Kappa, McCook, 1956-73; dean women McCook (Nebr.) Jr. Coll., 1960—. Contbr. articles to jours. Vol. High Plains Mus., McCook, 1988-90; hunger enabler Am. Bapt. Chs., McCook; ch. hist. First Bapt. Ch., McCook. Recipient scholarship Sweetbrier Shop, McCook, 1947. Mem. AAUW (pres. 1945-47), Bus. and Profl. Women (pres. 1961-62, 73-74), State Staff Ret. Tchrs. (program chmn. 1974-78), McCook Area Ret. Tchrs. Assn. (pres. 1982-86, historian 1988, 89). Democrat. Baptist. Home: 605 Third West McCook NE 69001

DUTCHER THORNTON, ALICE MARILYN, musician, educator; b. Grand Rapids, Mich., Aug. 11, 1934; d. Minor David and Mary Jeanette (Croninger) Dutcher; m. William James Thornton, Mar. 3, 1984. AA, Pine Manor Jr. Coll., 1954; MusB in Voice, U. Mich., 1956, MusM in Voice, 1958; postgrad., New Eng. Conservatory, 1960-62, Goethe Inst., Blaubeuren, Fed. Republic of Germany, 1966. Instr. voice, music lit. Kans. State Coll., Pittsburg, 1959-60; chair dept. voice Pine Manor Jr. Coll., Wellesley, Mass., 1960-63; instr. voice Detroit Inst. Musical Art, 1964-66; soloist various Chs., N.Y.C., 1967-68, 69-72; mezzo soprano Nat. Artist Co., Seattle Opera, 1968-69; mgr. Wolf Trap Farm Park Co., Vienna, Va., 1972; asst. prof. voice Grand Valley State Colls., Allendale, Mich., 1972-74; assoc. prof. voice Chgo. Musical Coll., Roosevelt U., 1974-84; owner pvt. studio San Antonio, 1984—; instr. voice San Antonio Coll., 1986-90; clinician Alexander technique Trinity U., San Antonio, 1983, San Antonio Symphony, 1985, U. Okla., Norman, 1986, Sch. Music, Okla. State U., Stillwater, 1987, Sch. Music, Sam Houston State U., Huntsville, Tex., 1987, Sch. Ch. Musci, Southwestern Bapt. U., Ft. Worth, 1987, Ouachita Bapt. U., Arkadelphia, Ark., 1990, Houston Symphony Orch., 1990, others; lectr., clinician Alexander technique Incarnate Word Coll., 1990—; adjudicator Young Tex. Music Award, Conroe, 1987; soloist, clinician Nat. Assn. Tchrs. Singing Nat. Conv., 1980, 86, 88. Am. opera auditions debut Milan teatro nuovo, L'AMICO FRITZ, 1966; debut Faust, Cin. Opera, 1968; after dinner opera tour G. Stein libretti operas, 1970, 71, Die Fledermaus, Turnau Opera, 1968; debut Cin. Zoo Opera, 1967, 68; appeared in Flying Dutchman, Grand Rapids Opera, 1989; recitals, opera and concert appearances Trinity U., 1984, 89, McNay Art Mus., 1988, 90, Incarnate Word Coll., 1990, Carnegie Hall, 1974, 77, Opera Grand Rapids, 1989, U. Mich., U. Okla., State U. Okla., and others in Can. Europe; soloist Bruckner Mass in f, Albright Song to David, Tex. Bach Choir, 1988, 89, Opera Guild San Antonio, 1989, Tues. Mus. Club, 1988, Turnau Opera, 1970-72, After Dinner Opera, Detroit Symphony Orch., 1964, 73, Nat. Symphony Orch., 1972; 9 premieres, Chgo. and San Antonio. Fundraiser San Antonio chpt. Am. Cancer Soc., 1986-87; fundraiser benefit recital Temple (Tex.) High Sch. Winner Am. Opera Auditions debut; Pro Mozart scholar, 1966. Mem. Soc. Tchrs. Alexander Technique, N.Am. Soc. Tchrs. Alexander Technique, Nat. Assn. Tchrs. Singing (bd. dirs. Chgo. chpt. 1980-83, tchr., nat. conv. Chgo. 1986, soloist 1987), Nat. Soc. Arts and Letters (tchr., clinician Alexander technique 1986). Episcopalian. Club: Tuesday Musical (San Antonio). Home: 347 Sharon Dr San Antonio TX 78216 Office: San Antonio Coll San Antonio TX 78284

DUTRAM, KAY LYNN, public health nutritionist; b. Castro Valley, Calif., Mar. 28, 1958; d. Bobby Earl and Wilma Lois (Witt) Keeling; m. Paul Warren Dutram, June 7, 1981. BS, U. Ark., 1981, MS, 1984. Nutrition coord. Kennebec Valley Commn. Action Program, Waterville, Maine, 1984-86, Maine Spl. Supplemental Food Program Women Infants Children, Augusta, Maine, 1986—. Tutor Literacy Vols. Am., Waterville, 1990—. Mem. Am. Dietetic Assn. (registered, publ. review bd. pub. health nutrition practice group, 1989, nominating com., 1989-90), Maine Dietetic Assn. (legis. coord. 1986-87, pres. 1989-90, Registered Young Dietitian of Yr. 1988), Maine Nutrition Coun. (newsletter editor 1988-89). Democrat. Baptist. Home: 12 Morrill Ave Waterville ME 04901 Office: Maternal & Child Health WIC State House Sta 11 Augusta ME 04333

DUTTON, DENISE KITASHIMA, personnel assistant; b. Cheverly, Md., Nov. 12, 1965; d. Benjamin Franklin and Betty Naoe (Harada) Kitashima. B of Gen. Studies, U. Md., 1987; postgrad., Calif. State U., Chico, 1989. Pers. classification and staffing specialist U.S. Patent and Trademark Office, Arlington, Va., 1988-89; customer svc. rep. credit card div. Chevy Chase (Md.) Savs. Bank, Frederick, 1990, sr. customer svc. rep. credit card div., 1990; pers. asst. NIH, Bethesda, Md., 1990—. Mem., vol. Nat. Kidney Found., 1986—. Mem. Internat. Pers. Mgmt. Assn., World Wildlife Fund, Greenpeace, Amnesty Internat. Republican.

DUTTON, LOIS ANN, consulting firm executive; b. Pensacola, Fla., Mar. 9, 1939; d. Cecil Ivor and Juanita (Locklear) D. B.S. in Nursing, U. N.C., 1965; M.P.H., 1966; Ph.D., U. Ala., 1984. R.N., Fla., Ala.; cert. addictions profl. Program dir. Alcoholism Services, Winter Haven, Fla., 1973-77; exec. dir. Tri-County Alcoholism Services, Inc., Winter Haven, 1975-80; asst. prof. U. Ala.-Birmingham, 1980-85; cons. Comprehensive Care Corp., Irvine, Calif., 1985-86; pres. Dutton Assocs., Inc, Tampa, Fla., 1985—; cons. Fla. Adv. Bd. for Profl. Alcoholism Edn. and Tng., Tallahassee, 1978-80; chairperson community health council U. Ala.-Birmingham, 1981-83. Mem. adv. task force Gov.'s Task Force for Devel. Alcoholism Program Standards, Tallahassee, 1977-80; adv. counsel Spouse Abuse Program, Lakeland, Fla., 1979-80; mem. edn. com. Am. Cancer Soc., Birmingham, 1981-85; instructional specialist ARC, Birmingham, 1984—; active Track Club, Tampa. Recipient Outstanding Faculty award U. Ala.-Birmingham sr. nursing students, 1983. Mem. Am. Nurses Assn., Am. Pub. Health Assn., Fla. Nurses Assn., NAFE, Sigma Theta Tau, Kappa Delta Pi. Republican. Roman Catholic. Avocations: running; painting; guitar.

DUTTON, PAULINE MAE, fine arts librarian; b. Detroit, July 15; d. Thoralf Andreas and Esther Ruth (Clyde) Tandberg; B.A. in Art, Calif. State U., Fullerton, 1967; M.S. in Library Sci., U. So. Calif., 1971; m. Richard Hawkins Dutton, June 21, 1969. Elem. tchr., Anaheim, Calif., 1967-68, Corona, Calif., 1968-69; fine arts librarian Pasadena (Calif.) Public Library, 1971-80; art cons., researcher, 1981—. Mem. Pasadena Librarians Assn. (sec. 1978, treas. 1979-80), Calif. Library Assn., Calif. Soc. Librarians, Art Librarians N.Am., Nat. Assn. Female Execs., Am. Film Inst., Am. Entrepreneurs Assn., Gilbert and Sullivan Soc., Alpha Sigma Phi. Club: Toastmistress (local pres. 1974).

DUTTON, RUTH A., automotive executive, consultant; b. Bay City, Mich., Oct. 7, 1944; d. Norman A. and Ruth O. (Tennant) McConnell; m. Dormer D. Dutton, Oct. 13, 1962; 1 child, Dwayne A. Dutton. BS magna cum laude, Oakland U., 1981; MBA, Mich. State U., 1986. With Pontiac (Mich.) div. Gen. Motors Corp., 1962-88, pers. dir., 1985-87, dir. project 21 implementation, 1987-88; mgr. personnel planning Gen. Motors Corp., Detroit, 1989-90, dir. organizational and employee devel. Internat. Export Sales, 1990—; cons. Pontiac Osteo. Hosp., 1981-82. Mem. Bus. and Profl. Women's Assn. (v.p. 1983-84). Methodist. Home: 560 Lakes Edge Dr Oxford MI 48371 Office: Gen Motors Corp 3044 W Grand Blvd Detroit MI 48202

DUVA, DONNA MARIE, financial executive; b. Paterson, N.J., June 28, 1956; d. Alfred Dominick and Frances P. (D'Andrea) D. AAS, Bergen Community Coll., 1976; BS in Acctg., Ramapo Coll., 1985. Bookkeeper Passaic County Treas. Office, Paterson, 1973-77; acctg. tutor Bergen Community Coll., Paramus, N.J., 1974-76; full charge bookkeeper Weisz Supermarket, Inc., Clifton, N.J., 1977-79; acct. Beecham, Inc., Clifton, 1980-85; chief fin. officer, controller Al Duva Enterprises, Inc., Paterson, 1976—; chief fin. officer, acctg. mgr. Power Battery Corp., Paterson, 1986—; Author newspaper editorials Paterson Evening News, 1976. Mem. N.J. Soc. Notary Pubs., Ramapo Coll. Alumni Assn., Bergen Community Coll. Alumni Assn., Nat. Assn. Female Execs. Democrat. Roman Catholic. Home: 205 Vernon Ave Paterson NJ 07503 Office: Power Battery Co Inc 543-53 E 42d St Paterson NJ 07513

DUVAL, MARY ELLEN, computer programmer; b. Poughkeepsie, N.Y., Nov. 8, 1945; d. Joseph and Barbara Isabelle (Townley) Kozlarek; m. William Richard Duval, Sept. 16, 1967 (div. June 1981); 1 child, Mary Louise. Student, SUNY, Albany, 1963-64; secretarial sci. diploma, Krissler Bus. Inst., Poughkeepsie, 1965; AS in Math, Computer Sci., Dutchess Community Coll., Poughkeepsie, 1985; BS in Computer Sci., Marist Coll., 1988. Sec. IBM, Poughkeepsie, 1965-66, 81-85, computer programmer, 1985—; clk. Naval Ammunition Depot, Hawthorne, Nev., 1967-78; asst. supr. Cen. Credit, Reno, 1980-81; co-owner, mgr. AA Locksmithing, Reno, 1979-81; office administr. Nationwide Ins., Poughkeepsie, 1981. Bd. trustees Mt. Grant Gen. Hosp., Hawthorne, Nev., 1977-78; leader Girl Scouts of Am., Hawthorne, 1977-78; organizer, founder Mt. Grant Gen. Hosp. Ladies Aux., Hawthorne, 1978, Mineral County Taxpayers Assn., Hawthorne, 1978. Mem. Alpha Chi, Alpha Sigma Lambda.

DUVALL, LORRAINE, recreation center owner; b. Hamilton, Ohio, Jan. 31, 1925; d. Saul and Martha Jane (Huff) Baker; m. Ray DuVall, June 12, 1951; children: Sharon DuVall Keese, Deborah D. Velchoff, Steve, Annette. BA, U. Cin., 1951; MA, Tex. A&I U., 1963; postgrad. Miami U., Oxford, Ohio, 1958, U. Toledo, 1959, U. Tex.-Austin, 1968. Elem. tchr. Larkmoor, Lorain, Ohio, 1956-60; tchr. math. Incarnate Word High Sch., Corpus Christi, 1964-70; owner, instr. Aerobic Fitness, Corpus Christi, 1973—; owner, coach Corpus Christi Marlin Swim Team, 1972—; mgr. Corpus Christi Country Club Pool, 1973-88; pres., mgr. Club Estates Pool Chems., Corpus Christi, 1980—, Club Estates Recreation, Corpus Christi, 1977—. Vol. psychiat. ward Meml. Hosp., Corpus Christi, 1966-70; bd. dirs. vol. YWCA, Corpus Christi, 1970-77; water safety trainer ARC, Corpus Christi, 1975-82; CPR instr. Am. Heart Assn., Corpus Christi, 1980-84; vol. children's choir dir. St. John Methodist Ch., Corpus Christi, 1966-78, Asbury United Meth. Ch., 1980—. NSF grantee U. Tex.-Austin, 1968. Mem. Am. Swim Coaches Assn., Am. Harp Soc., Symphony Guild, Sierra Club. Republican. Avocations: music; swimming; tennis; skiing; backpacking. Home: 6709 Pintail Dr Corpus Christi TX 78413 Office: 4902 Snowgoose St Corpus Christi TX 78413

DUVALL, PATRICIA ARLENE, educator; b. Pitts., June 27, 1950; d. William Richard and Willene Alberta (Goode) Addison; 1 child, Tiyonda Aikee. B.A. in Math., Carnegie-Mellon U., 1972; M.Ed., U. Pitts., 1981. Long distance telephone operator AT&T, Pitts., summers 1968-71; switchboard operator Union Nat. Bank, Pitts., summers 1972; math tchr. Allegheny Intermediate Unit, Pitts., summers, 1978-79; math skills program Chatham Coll., Pitts., 1983—; tchr. math Pitts. Bd. Pub. Edn., 1972—; math instr. Kids and Teens coll. program Community Coll. Allegheny County, summer 1986, 87; tennis coach Allegheny High Sch., Pitts., 1979-81. Mem. U.S. Tennis Assn., Am. Alliance for Health, Phys. Edn., Recreation and Dance, Women's Internat. Tennis Assn., Nat. Coun. Tchrs. Math. Jehovah's Witness. Avocations: stamp collecting, tennis, reading, collecting comic books, home computers.

DUVALL, SHELLEY, actress; b. Houston, 1949; d. Robert Duvall and Bobby Crawford. Founder Amarillo Prodns. Actress: films (debut) Brewster McCloud, 1970, McCabe and Mrs. Miller, 1971, Thieves Like Us, 1974, Nashville, 1975, Buffalo Bill and the Indians, 1976, Three Women, 1977 (Cannes Film Festival Best Actress award), Annie Hall, 1977, Popeye, 1979, The Shining, 1980, Time Bandits, 1981, Roxanne, 1987, (TV movies) Bernice Bobs Her Hair, 1977, Lily, 1986, (TV episode) Twilight Zone, 1986; exec. producer: Showtime pay TV series Faerie Tale Theatre, 1983— (Peabody award), Shelley Duvall's Tall Tales and Legends, 1985—, The Strange Case of Dr. Jekyll and Mr. Hyde, 1989. Founder, Think Entertainment prodn. co., 1988. Mem. Nat. Acad. Cable Programming (bd. govs.). Office: William Morris Agy 151 El Camino Beverly Hills CA 90069*

DUVALL-ITJEN, PHYLLIS, retail sales executive; b. Passaic, N.J., Oct. 13, 1951; d. August Richard and Joanne (Aquilina) D'Alessandro; m. Brian Alan Itjen, Apr. 1, 1979; 1 child, Shannon Alys. Office mgr. Servometer Corp., Cedar Grove, N.J., 1972-82; owner, mgr. Sweet Shoppe, Etc., Lyndhurst, N.J., 1979-82; adminstr.-pers. coord. Watson Machine Co., Paterson, N.J., 1982-88; pres. S.A.I. Personnel Svcs., West Paterson, N.J., 1988—, S.A.I. Expressions Unltd., Inc., West Paterson and Wayne, N.J., 1988—. Active children's day care field, West Paterson, N.J., 1988—. Mem. NAFE. Republican. Roman Catholic. Home: 220-A Overmount Ave West Paterson NJ 07424 Office: SAI Expressions Unltd Inc 26 West Belt Pla Wayne NJ 07470

DUVALL-KELLAR, DONNA SUSANN, sales professional; b. Bandon, Oreg., May 8, 1951; d. Wallace Woodrow and Ione Rose (Widing) Winquist; m. Robert Steven Kellar, June 9, 1989; children: Lisa Michelle, Kristin Susann. BSN, Oreg. Health Scis. U., 1974; MSN, U. Wash., Seattl, 1976. Terr. mgr. Wyeth-Ayerst, Portland, Oreg.; assoc. prof. U. Portland, 1976-78; nurse practitioner Kaiser Found., Portland, 1978-81; nurse practitioner women's health care Douglas Blatchford MD, P.C., Portland, 1981-86; pvt. practice Portland, 1986—. Mem. Nurse Practitioner Spl. Interest Group, NAFE, Nurses Assn. Coll. Ob-Gyn. Home: 12707 SE 24th St Vancouver WA 98684 Office: 10202 SE 32d Ave #701 Milwaukie OR 97222

DUVER-MICLOT, STEPHANIE ANNE, communications executive; b. Des Moines, Dec. 18, 1956; d. William Carl and Catherine Anne (Rodine) Duver; m. Jonathan Miclot; children: Carl, Susanne, Eric. BA in Journalism, Iowa State U., 1978; BA in Communications, U. West. Fla., 1982; MBA in Mktg., Nat. U., 1985; student in children's lit., Mary Wash. Coll., 1979. Tech. asst. writer The Bankers Life, Des Moines, 1978; staff editor The Havelock (N.C.) Progress Newspaper, 1980-81; staff writer, assoc. editor The Tides and Times Newspaper, Laguna Beach, Calif., 1981-84; asst. advt. coordinator Toshiba Am., Inc., Irvine, Calif., 1981-86; dir. public relations, sales & mktg. Personnel Pool of San Joaquin Valley, Inc., Fresno, Calif., 1986—; mktg. supr. The Fresno (Calif.) Bee, 1987-88; mktg. communications specialist TRW Inc., Orange, Calif., 1988—; instr. English, 4Cs Bus. Coll., Fresno, 1987-88, Nat. Coll., Fresno, 1987—, South Coast Coll. Ct. Reporting, Westminster, Calif., 1989—; cons. Words, Unltd., Fresno, 1987—; judge student journalism publs. Nat. Scholastic Press Assn./Assoc. Collegiate Press, 1987—. Mem. Women in Communications, NAFE, AAUW, Bus. and Profl. Women's Network.

DUVO, MECHELLE LOUISE, oil executive, consultant; b. E. Stroudsburg, Pa., Apr. 25, 1962; d. Nicholas and Arlene Birdie (Mack) D. AS, Lehigh County Community Coll., 1982. Intern N.C.A.C.C., Northampton, Pa., 1980-82; rehab. counselor Phoenix Project, Bakersfield, Calif., 1982-84; nat. sales mgr. Olympia Advt., L.A., 1984-85; oil exploration cons. Cimmaron Mgmt., Nashville, 1985-86; exec. sec. Pueblo Resources Corp., Bowling Green, Ky., 1986-87; nat. oil cons. El Toro, Inc., Bowling Green, 1986-87; founder, pres. Majestic Mgmt. Corp., Bowling Green, 1987—; nat. oil cons. Impact Oil, Inc., Bowling Green, 1987—; lease procurator El Toro, Inc., 1986-87, Impact Oil, Inc., 1987—. Fundraiser Am. Cancer Soc., L.A., 1984-85; vol. Humane Soc., Nashville, 1985-86, Humane Soc., Bowling Green, 1986—; counselor Salvation Army, Bakersfield, 1982-84. Mem. NAFE, Ky. Ind. Petroleum Producers Assn. Office: Majestic Mgmt Corp 551 Scott Ln Bowling Green KY 42103-4718

DVOOR, DEBORAH ANN, senior center director; b. Flemington, N.J., Aug. 20, 1959; d. Melvin and Marilyn Judith (Hayfer) D. BS in Gerontology, U. Bridgeport (Conn.), 1981; postgrad. in human svc. adminstrn., Rider Coll. Recreation dir. Stone Arch Health Care Ctr., Pittstown, N.J., 1982-83, Raritan (N.J.) Health and Extended Care Ctr., 1983-87; dir. N. Hunterdon Sr. Ctr., Inc., Califon, N.J., 1987—; mem. adv. bd. Hunterdon County Sr. Health Svcs., Flemington. Vol. Hunterdon Hospice, Inc., Flemington, 1985—. Mem. N.J. Assn. Sr. Ctr. Dirs., Nat. Coun. on Aging (Sr. Ctrs. Nat. Inst. Sr. Ctrs. affiliate). Home: 83 Broad St Flemington NJ 08822 Office: N Hunterdon Sr Ctr Inc Box 398 RD 2 Rt 513 Califon NJ 07830

DWECK, SUSAN, business consultant; b. Washington, July 26, 1943; d. Samuel Ralph and Rena (Cohen) Dweck. BA, Am. U., 1965, MS, 1988. Tchr. Montgomery County (Md.) Pub. Schs., 1966-68; rsch. asst. U. Rsch. Corp., Washington, 1969-72; rsch. specialist Exec. Office of the Pres., Washington, 1972-73, Office Asst. Sec. Planning and Evaluation, Washington, 1973-78; program analyst Nat. Inst. Edn., Washington, 1978-79; sr. program analyst Office of the Sec. Dept. Health & Human Svcs., Washington, 1978-84; pvt. practice bus. and organizational devel. cons. Washington, 1984—; bd. dirs. Assn. Part-Time Profls., Falls Church, Va., United Jewish Appeal Fedn., Washington. Co-author: Women Education and Career Development, 1974; contbr. articles to profl. jours. Mgr. Dem. Polit. Campaign, Washington, 1960-73; fundraiser WAMU Pub. Radio, Washington, 1978—, mem. vol. bd., 1980-85, Washington Tennis Found. 1980-90; vol. Women's Ctr. of No. Va., Vienna, Va., 1989—, United Jewish Appeal Fed., Rockville, Md., 1980—. Mem. Orgnl. Devel. Network, Am. Soc. Tng. and Devel., Am. Univ./Nat. Tng. Lab. Assn. (bd. dirs. 1988—, program coord. 1989), Kappa Delta Epsilon, Psi Chi. Jewish. Home and Office: Susan Dweck & Assocs. 2737 Devonshire Pl NW Washington DC 20008

DWORSKY, CLARA WEINER, merchandise brokerage executive, lawyer; b. N.Y.C., Apr. 28, 1918; d. Charles and Rebecca (Becker) Weiner; m. Bernard Ezra Dworsky, Jan. 2, 1944; 1 child, Barbara G. Goodman. BS, St. John's U., N.Y.C., 1937, LLB, 1939, JD, 1968. Bar: N.Y. 1939, U.S. Dist. Ct. (ea. dist.) N.Y. 1942. Pvt. practice, N.Y.C., 1939-51; assoc. Bessie Farberman, N.Y.C., 1942; clk., sec. U.S. Armed Forces, Camp Carson, Colo., Camp Claiborne, La., 1944-45; abstractor, dir. Realty Title, Rockville, Md., 1954-55; v.p. Kelley & Dworsky Inc., Houston, 1960—; appeals agt. Gasoline Rationing Apls. Bd., N.Y.C., 1942; bd. dir. Southlan Sales Assocs., Houston. Vol. ARC, N.Y.C.; vice chmn. War Bond pledge drive, Bklyn.; vol. Houston Legal Found., 1972-73; pres. Women's Aux. Washington Hebrew Acad., 1958-60, v.p. bd. trustees, 1959-60; co-founder, v.p. S. Tex. Hebrew Acad. (now Hebrew Acad.), Houston, 1970-75, hon. pres. women's div., 1973. Recipient Cert. award Treas. of U.S., 1943; Commendation Office of Chief Magistrate of City N.Y., 1948; Pietas medal St. Johns U., 1985. Mem. ABA (chmn. sub-com. social security and fed. disability com. sr. lawyers div. 1989—, mem. sr. lawyers div. coun.), N.Y. State Bar Assn., Nat. Assn. Women Lawyers (chmn. organizer Juvenile Delinquency Clinic N.Y. 1948-51), St. Johns U. Alumni Assn. (coord. Houston chpt. 1983-86, pres. 1986), Delphians Past Pres.'s Club, Amit Women Club, Hadassah. Jewish. Home: 9726 Cliffwood Dr Houston TX 77096

DWYER, ANN ELIZABETH, equine veterinarian; b. Syracuse, N.Y., Oct. 26, 1953; d. John Wright and Jean Knox (McAllister) D. BA cum laude, Mt. Holyoke Coll., 1975; DVM, Cornell U., 1983. Veterinarian Genesee Valley Equine Clinic, Scottsville, N.Y., 1983—; dir. N.Y. State Horse Coun., Inc., 1989—. Mem. choir Union Presbyn. Ch., Scottsville, 1987. Mem. Am. Assn. Equine Practitioners, Am. Vet. Med. Assn., Am. Soc. Vet. Ophthalmology, N.Y. State Vet. Med. Assn., Genesee Valley Vet. Med. Assn. (exec. bd.), Phi Zeta. Home: 25 Belcoda Rd Churchville NY 14428 Office: Genesee Valley Equine Clinic 1089 Bowerman Rd Scottsville NY 14546

DWYER, DIANE MARIE, lawyer; b. Amityville, N.Y., Nov. 5, 1958; d. Joseph R. and Geraldine (Burchell) D. BA, Molloy Coll., 1980; JD, St. John's U., 1983. Bar: N.Y. 1983. Assoc. Deutsch & Schneider, Bklyn., 1983-84; pvt. law practice Wantagh, N.Y., 1984—; dep. county atty. Nassau County (N.Y.), 1984—; advisor community legal instrn. program St. John's U., Jamaica, N.Y., 1984. Mem. ABA, Nassau County Bar Assn. (com. mem. 1987), Molloy Coll. Alumni Assn. (v.p. 1986-89, pres. 1989—, admissions recruiter 1988—). Home: 1539 Lakeside Dr Wantagh NY 11793

DWYER, JOHANNA TODD, medicine educator; b. Syracuse, N.Y., Oct. 20, 1938; d. M. Harold and Frances (Markey) D. BS with distinction, Cornell U., 1960; MS, U. Wis., 1962, Harvard Sch. Pub. Health, Boston, 1965; DSc, Harvard Sch. Pub. Health, Boston, 1969. Asst. prof. Harvard Sch. Pub. Health, 1969-73; home economist Proctor & Gamble, Cin., 1962-64; rsch. asst. U. Wis., Madison, 1960-62; assoc. prof. Tufts Med. Sch., 1974, prof. nutrition, 1989—; sr. scientist human nutrition rsch. USDA, Boston, 1988—; dir. Frances Stern Nutrition Ctr., New Eng. Med. Ctr., Boston; adj. prof. Harvard Sch. Pub. Health, 1988—. Author of 3 books, 1979, 83; contbr. 300 articles to profl. jours. Mem. Mass. Nutrition Bd., Boston, 1980—; cons. Exec. Office of The Pres., Washington, 1976; mem. bd. sci. counselors Nat. Cancer Inst., 1985-89. Recipient Lenna Frances Cooper award Am. Dietric Assn.; Robert Wood Johnson Health Policy fellow, 1980-83, John Stalker award Am. Sch. Food Svc. Assn., 1990. Mem. Soc. Nutrition Edn. (bd. dirs. 1975-77, pres. 1976, sec. 1990—, J. Harvey Wiley award 1983), Am. Soc. Parenteial and External Nutrition (adv. bd. 1978—), Inst. Medicine Nat. Acad. Scis. (food and nutrition bd.). Home: 31 Lakeville Rd Apt 1 Jamaica Plain MA 02130 Office: New Eng Med Ctr 750 Washington St Box 783 Boston MA 02111

DWYER, MARGARET ANN, university administrator; b. Syracuse, N.Y.; d. Edward P. and Margaret M. (O'Donnell) D. AB, Le Moyne Coll., 1954; MEd, Boston Coll., 1956. Tchr. Kingsford Park Pub. Schs., Oswego, N.Y., 1955-56; med. sch. worker St. Joseph's Hosp., Syracuse, 1956-60; registrar Le Moyne Coll., Syracuse, 1960-62, dean of women, 1962-71, asst. acad. dean, 1971-73; exec. asst. to pres. Boston Coll., 1973-75, v.p., asst. to pres., 1975—; consumer's advisers bd. Dey Bros. Dept. Store, 1966-70; bd. dirs., dir. Bay Bank Newton Waltham (now Baybank Middlesex), 1976—. sec. sdv. bd. St. Mary's Hosp., Syracuse, 1965-70; trustee Cath. Charities Archdiocese Boston, Le Moyne Coll., Syracuse, 1988—; mem. United Way (Mass.); chmn. bd. Syracuse chpt. ARC. Mem. AAUW, Nat. Assn. Women Deans and Counselors. Home: 40 Carver Rd Wellesley Hills MA 02181 Office: Boston College Chestnut Hill MA 02167

DWYER, MARY ELLEN, art educator, sculptor; b. Logansport, Ind., Mar. 22, 1946; d. Michael James and Alice Mercedes (Kavanaugh) D. BFA, St. Mary's Coll., 1969; postgrad., U. Veracruz, Xalapa, Mex., 1973, Purdue U., 1970-72; MFA in Ceramics, Ohio U., 1975. Art tchr. City of Gary (Ind.) Schs., 1970; field dir. Tribal Trails Girl Scout Coun., Logansport, Ind., 1971-72; lab asst. ceramic studio Purdue U., West Lafayette, Ind., 1971-72; grad. asst. resident life program Ohio U., Athens, 1972-73, teaching asst. ceramic dept., 1974-75; Raku specialist Camp Wah-Nee, Torrington, Conn., 1975; art tchr. Northwest Allen County Schs., Ft. Wayne, Ind., 1977; instr. art Ohio U., Zanesville, 1977-82, asst. prof., 1983—. One-woman shows include Marshall U. Art Gallery, Huntington, W.Va., 1979, Jay County Arts Coun., Portland, Ind., 1980, Otterbein Coll., Westerville, Ohio, 1986, Meth. Theol. Sem. Gallery, Delaware, Ohio, 1986; exhibited in group shows at Zanesville (Ohio) Art Ctr. May Show, 1982, 1985-87, 1989, Louis Palmer Gallery, New Concord, Ohio, 1986, Art Phase I Gallery, Chgo., 1987-88, Gallery Upstairs, Granville, Ohio, 1988, Denison U. Art Gallery, Granville, 1989, Artlink Gallery, Ft. Wayne, 1989, numerous others; contbr. articles to profl. jours. Vol. Leon Gto., Mex. with Conf. on Inter-Am. Student Projects, 1965, Logansport (Ind.) Mental Hosp., 1976, Girl Scout Day Camp, Logansport, 1977, 81, Good Samaritan Med. Ctr., Zanesville, 1981-84, Heart of Ohio Girl Scout Coun., Zanesville, 1982—. Recipient Disting. Art Educator award for eastern Ohio region Ohio Art Edn. Assn., 1984; faculty grantee Ohio U., 1978, 80, 81, 83, 84, 89. Mem. Soc. of Layerists in Multi-Media, Artlink, Ohio Women's Caucus for the Arts. Democrat. Roman Catholic. Office: Ohio U 1425 Newark Rd Zanesville OH 43701

DWYER, SANDRA SUNDERMAN, school system counselor; b. Roxboro, N.C., Sept. 10, 1946; d. Colonel Everett Chris and LottieLou (Chandler) S.; m. William Karl Dwyer, June 13, 1946; children: Jennifer Leah, Todd Everett. BS in Edn., U. North Tex., 1968, MEd, 1975; postgrad., U. Houston, 1988. Tchr. Dallas ISD, 1968-69, Nansemond County Schs., Suffolk, Va., 1972, Borger (Tex.) ISD, 1974, Deer Park (Tex.) ISD, La Porte (Tex.) ISD, 1977-82; counselor La Porte (Tex.) ISd. Sec. Bay Area Youth Symphony, 1987-88, tchr. Clear Lake Presbyterian Ch., Houston, 1989, lay pastor, 1990. Mem. Phi Delta Kappa.

DWYER-DOBBIN, MARY ALICE, communications executive; b. St. Louis, Dec. 22, 1942; d. Paul Arthur and Mary Albertina (Goessling) Dwyer; m. Leon Dobbin, July 29, 1973. BA in Speech and Drama, Webster U., 1963; MFA in Theatre, Cath. U., 1967. Chmn. speech and drama dept. St. Joseph's Acad., St. Louis, 1963-65; stage mgr. Olney (Md.) Theatre, 1967;

asst. to producer Bob Stewart Prodns., N.Y.C., 1968-70; producer Rankin/Bass Prodns., N.Y.C., 1970-73; mgr. daytime program, dir. children's program ABC, N.Y.C., 1974-77; dir. daytime and children's programs, v.p. children's program NBC, N.Y.C., 1977-81; v.p. programming Daytime cable network Hearst/ABC Video Svcs., N.Y.C., 1981-83; v.p. programming Lifetime cable network Hearst/ABC/Viacom Entertainment Svcs., N.Y.C., 1983-86; v.p. daytime programming east coast Capital Cities/ABC, Inc., N.Y.C., 1986-90; v.p. daytime programming ABC TV Network, N.Y.C., 1990—. Recipient Maggie award for TV documentaries Planned Parenthood Fedn. Am., 1982, Ace award for best mag. show, 1983, Clean Air Week award Am. Lung Assn., 1989. Mem. NATAS (bd. dirs. 1985-87), Nat. Cable TV Assn. (chmn. Ace awards com. 1983-84). Office: Capital Cities/ABC 77 W 66th St New York NY 10023

DYAR, KATHRYN WILKIN, pediatrician; b. Colquitt, Ga., Feb. 20, 1945; d. Patrick McWhorter and Virginia (Wilkin) Dyar; m. James Ansley Patten, Jan. 1, 1985. BS in Biology, Emory U., Decatur, Ga., 1966; MD, Med. Coll. Ga., Augusta, 1970. Resident in pediatrics Eugene Talmadge Meml. Hosp., Augusta, Ga., 1970-72, Georgetown U. Hosp., Washington, 1972-73; pediatrician Children's Clinic, Tifton, Ga., 1973-74, Children & Youth Project, Norfolk, Va., 1974-83; dir. Children & Youth Project, Norfolk, 1990—; pediatrician Hampton (Va.) Health Dept., 1983-90. Fellow Am. Acad. Pediatrics. Office: Children & Youth Project 606 W 29th St Norfolk VA 23508

DYBAS, SUSAN LOUISE, financial executive; b. Gowanda, N.Y., Feb. 16, 1961; d. Richard Dale and Betty Louise (Smith) Shellenbarger; m. Michael J. Dybas, Feb. 13, 1988. BS, Rochester Inst. Tech., 1983; MBA, Canisius Coll., Buffalo, 1988. Corp. trust ops. mgr., trust ops. project coordinator Mfrs. and Traders Trust Co., Buffalo, 1986-87; fin./EDP mgr. Maggs and Zack, THE Bus. Ins. Brokers, Inc., Schenectady, 1988-89; acctg. mgr. St. Francis Hosp., Buffalo, 1990—. Mem. NAFE, Nat. Assn. Bank Women, NCS Trust Users Group. Home: RD 1 Box 295 South Dayton NY 14138

DYBELL, ELIZABETH ANNE SLEDDEN, clinical psychologist; b. Buffalo, Sept. 25, 1958; d. Richard Edward and Angela Brigid (Scimone) Sledden; m. David Joseph Dybell, Nov. 30, 1985. BA in Psychology summa cum laude, U. St. Thomas, Houston, 1980; PhD in Psychology, Tex. Tech. U., 1986. Lic. clinical psychologist, Tex. Rsch. asst. health sci. ctr. Tex. Tech. U., Lubbock, 1983-84, psychol. cons. health sci. ctr. neurology dept., 1982-84; psychology intern U. New Mex., Albuquerque, 1984-85; psychotherapist Katz & Assocs. P.C., Houston, 1985-88. Author: (monograph) When Will Life Be Normal?, 1989; contbr. articles to numerous publs. choir mem. St. Thomas More Ch., Houston, 1974-87. Mem. Am. Psychol. Assn., Assn. for the Care of Childrens Health, Nat. Ctr. Clin. Infant Programs, Soc. Pediatric Psychology, Southwestern Psychol. Assn., Tex. Psychol. Assn., Houston Psychol. Assn., Am. Psychol. Soc. (charter). Roman Catholic. Office: Meyer Ctr for Developmental Pediatrics 8080 N Stadium Dr #2300 Houston TX 77054

DYCHTWALD, MADDY KENT, multimedia producer; b. Newark, Feb. 13, 1952; d. Stanley and Sally Susan (Gordet) Kent; m. Kenneth Mark Dychtwald, Nov. 24, 1983; 1 child, Casey. Student in media communications, U. Wis.-Madison, 1968-70; B.A., NYU, 1974. Actress, N.Y.C. and Los Angeles, 1974-83; dir. spl. projects Dychtwald & Assocs., Emeryville, Calif., 1983-86; dir. communications Age Wave, Inc., Emeryville, 1986, v.p. communications, 1987—. Designer, producer slide shows, videos, mktg. and communication materials; author, speaker: Third Age America: The Shape of Things to Come, 1988. Mem. Screen Actor's Guild, Am. Fedn. TV and Radio Actors, Am. Film Inst., Internat. Assn. Bus. Communicators (Award of Merit for logo design), Nat. Assn. Female Execs. Office: Age Wave Inc 1900 Powell St #700 Emeryville CA 94608

DYCKOFF, HEIDI MAE, accountant; b. N.Y.C., Sept. 2, 1961; d. Bernard and Beatrice D. Student, SUNY, Stony Brook, 1977-78, L.I. U., 1978-79, Kingsborough Coll., 1981. Asst. bookkeeper H&R Block, Bklyn., 1978-79, tax preparer, 1979-84, fgn. state tax preparer, dist. mgr., 1984-85; owner, acct. It's a Cinch, Ellenville, N.Y., 1985—. Author tax column, 1986-87. Mem. NAFE, Nat. Assn. Tax Profls., Profl. Ins. Agts., E.R. Murrow Alumni Assn. (pres. 1977—). Democrat. Jewish. Office: It's a Cinch 1 Terrace Hill Ellenville NY 12428

DYE, JUDY ANN, hospital department director; b. Tucson, July 23, 1950; d. Joseph Roy and Betty C. (Cook) Confer; m. Edward O'Neal Dye, Dec. 19, 1970; children: Kelly Ann, Justin O'Neal. BS, U. Ariz., 1973; MA, U. Phoenix, 1985. Med. technologist Univ. Med. Ctr., Tucson, 1973-81; tech. dir. Univ. Med. Ctr., 1981-87, dir. radiation oncology, 1987—; inspector Coll. Am. Pathology, Southwest U.S.A., 1982-87; judge Ariz. State Soc. Med. Tech., Tucson, 1983-85; del. Wellness Coun. Tucson, 1986-87; speaker Ariz. Cancer Ctr., Tucson, 1989. Contbr. articles to Journ. Clin. Pathology, 1978, Clin. Chemistry, 1981, Clin. Toxicology, 1983. Christian edn. tchr. Christ Presbyn. Ch., Tucson, 1980-85, St. John's on the Desert, Tucson, 1985—; crisis counselor So. Ariz. Ctr. Against Sexual Assault, Tucson, 1988—. Mem. Am. Coll. Healthcare Execs., Am. Healthcare Radiology Adminstrs., Nat. Assn. for Female Execs., Am. Assn. for Clin. Chemistry, Soc. for Radiation Oncology Adminstrs. Office: Univ Med Ctr 1501 N Campbell Ave Tucson AZ 85724

DYE, KIMBERLY ANDERSON, public relations professional; b. Louisville, Sept. 13, 1961; d. Joseph F. and Doris J. (Brunner) A.; m. Victor Edward Dye, May 19, 1990. BA in Psychology and Communications, Spalding U., 1983. Advt. media buyer Snyder's Dept. Store Inc., Louisville, 1984-87; printing mgr. Hess's Dept. Store Inc., Louisville, 1987-88, pub. rels. coord., 1988—. Active Alumni Mentor Program, Spalding U., 1990; mem. promotions com. Children's Hosp. Found., 1990, Kosair Children's Hosp., 1990. Mem. NAFE, Delta Epsilon Sigma, Psi Chi. Home: 206 Southampton Rd Louisville KY 40223

DYE, MOLLY BALL, city official; b. Hattiesburg, Miss., Dec. 20, 1951; d. David Jr. Ball and Molly (Bethea) Burke; children: Dennis David, Ernest Franklin. Student, U. Tex., 1970-71, U. So. Miss., 1971-72, U. Miss., 1975-76. Cert. pub. housing mgr. Receptionist Hattiesburg Clinic, P.A., 1972-73; med. records technician North Panola Hosp., Sardis, Miss., 1974-75; exec. dir. Sardis Housing Authority, 1975—. Founder, Cubmaster Boy Scouts Am., Sardis, 1988—; former tchr. 1st United Meth. Ch., Sardis. Mem. Miss. Assn. Housing and Redevel. Ofcls., Southeastern Regional Coun. Republican. Home: Rte 1 Box 17-C Sardis MS 38666 Office: Sardis Housing Authority 321 Greenhill Circle Sardis MS 38666

DYER, ALICE MILDRED, psychotherapist; b. San Diego, July 4, 1929; d. William Silas Cann and Louise Lair (Addenbrooke) Vaile; divorced; children: Alexis Dyer Guagnano, Bryan, Christine Dyer Murphy; m. James Vawter, Dec. 26, 1972. BA, Calif. State U., Fullerton, 1965, MA, 1967; PhD, U.S. Internat. U., 1980. Coord., counselor Brea (Calif.)-Olinda High Sch., 1968-72; sch. psychologist Cypress (Calif.) Sch. Dist., 1972-86; instr. North Orange County Community Coll., Fullerton, 1975-77; pvt. practice ednl. psychology Long Beach and Fountain Valley, Calif., 1978—; pvt. practice marriage and family therapy Fullerton and Brea, Calif., 1979—; psychologist, cons. Multiple Sclerosis Soc. Orange County, 1986—; facilitator adult mental health La Habra (Calif.) Community Hosp., 1988-89. Bd. dirs., officer Friends of Fullerton Arboretum, 1974-90; bd. dirs. Fullerton Beautiful, 1987-88, Brea Ednl. Found., 1988-89; therapist Orange County Juvenile Connection Project, 1988—. Recipient Appreciation award Gary Ctr., La Habra, 1975, Multiple Sclerosis Soc. Orange County, 1987. Mem. Am. Psychol. Assn., Calif. Psychol. Assn., Calif. Assn. Marriage and Family Therapists, Assn. for Children and Adults with Learning Disabilities (cons. 1970—, bd. dirs., facilitator), AAUW, Am. Bus. Women Assn., Soroptomists (health chmn. Brea chpt. 1987-88). Republican. Unitarian. Office: Brea Mental Health Assocs 1203 W Imperial Hwy Ste 102 Brea CA 92621

DYER, DORIS ANNE, nurse; b. Washington, Jan. 14, 1944; d. William Edward and Helen Gertrude (Smith) Swain; R.N., Sibley Nursing Sch., Washington, 1964; B.S., Am. U., 1966, M.Ed., 1969; m. Robert Francis Dyer, Jr., June 27, 1970; children—Robert Francis, William Edward, Anne-Marie Helen Sallie, Scott Robertson McGavin. Mem. staff emergency medicine dept. George Washington U. Hosp., 1960-69, emergency specialist protective services clinic, 1967-70, adminstr. asst. to dir. clinic, 1970-78; nurse cons., 1987—. Trinity Coll. scholar, 1960; Lucy Webb Hayes scholar, 1964; recipient Martha Washington award Md. Soc. SAR, 1977; Community Leaders award, 1979; Washington medal, 1984, Disting. Women of Washington award 1987; decorated Comdr. Order of St. Lazarus, 1984, medal of Merit, 1989; created dame Order of Sovereign Mil. Order, 1980. Mem. Am., D.C. nurses assns., Am. Acad. Ambulatory Nursing Adminstrs., Washington Med.-Surg. Soc. Aux. (pres.), Am. U. Grads. Assn., DAR, Washington Assembly. Clubs: Washington, Annapolis Yacht, Kenwood Golf and Country. Author: Say Ah, 1971; also articles. Address: 5608 Albia Rd Bethesda MD 20816

DYER, ELAINE DEDRICKSON, nurse educator; b. Spanish Fork, Utah, Nov. 9, 1923; d. Gilbert and Alberta (Larsen) Dedrickson; m. Gordon W. Dyer, Sept. 21, 1955. BS, RN, St. Mary's Wasatch Coll., S.L.C., 1946; MS, U. Utah, 1955, PhD, 1967. RN, Utah, registered psychologist, Utah. Operating room supr. VA, S.L.C., 1948-60, surg. svc. supr., 1961-63; chief nursing rsch. VA, S.L.C., Washington, 1967-75; dir. nursing rsch. Brigham Young U., Provo, Utah, 1975-78, dean coll. nursing, 1979-86, prof. grad. program, 1987-90; cons. Medicus Corp., Chgo., 1974-76, Joint Commn. for Accreditation Hosps., Chgo., 1975-76, New England Hosps. Nursing Rsch. Conf., L.I., 1977-79. Author: (with others) Problem Oriented Nursing, 1974, Nurse Evaluator in Education and Service, 1978; contbr. articles to profl. jours. Bd. dirs., chmn. youth orgn. Latter Day Saints Ch., S.L.C., 1958-72. NIH grantee, 1971. Fellow Am. Acad. Nursing; mem. Utah Nurses Assn. (Nurse Researcher of Yr. 1975, pres. 1969-71), Utah Psychol. Assn., ANA, Am. Psychol. Assn. Republican. Home: 763 S 850 E Orem UT 84058 Office: Brigham Young U Provo UT 84062

DYER, ELIZABETH, bank executive; b. MotherWell, Scotland, U.K., Nov. 28, 1928; Arrived in US 1955.; d. Charles and Mary Ann Carlin; m. John S. Dyer. Student, Am. Inst. Banking, N.J., 1970. Teller Midland Bank, Englewood, N.J., 1965; adminstr. asst. Midland Bank, Englewood; asst. sec. Midland Bank, Tenafy, N.J.; asst. v.p. Midland Bank, Englewood; v.p. Midland Bank, Paramus, N.J.; v.p. new bus. devel. Vol. treas. Salvation Army, Englewood. Mem. Cresskill Demarest Rotary Club, Army-Englewood Club, Zonta Internat., Nat. Assn. Bank Women. Home: 30 Woodland Rd Demarest NJ 07627

DYER, GERALDINE ANN (GERI DYER), artist; b. Bklyn., Nov. 4, 1921; d. Edward and Chattie (Holmes) Bingham; m. Ralph Dyer, Oct. 1956. Student, N.Y. Phoenix Sch. Design, N.Y.C., 1946-48, Bklyn. Mus. Art Sch., 1959, Bklyn. Coll., 1939; pvt. studies in voice with Julia Gille, 1947-50. Commd. U.S. Army, 1941, ret. USCG, 1979. One-woman shows include Henry Hicks Gallery, N.Y.C., 1978-79, 81, Womanart Gallery, N.Y.C., 1980, Keane Mason Gallery, N.Y.C., 1981, Esta Robinson Gallery, N.Y.C., 1983, Bklyn. Heights Br. Libr., Bklyn., 1986-89; exhibited at numerous group shows; represented in permanent collection Samuel Schulman Inst., Bklyn. Recipient numerous awards, award Art Horizons Internat. Art Competition, 1988. Mem. Womeninterart Ctr., Drawing Ctr., Artists Equity Assn., Poetry Soc. Am., Officers Club (N.Y.C.), Bklyn. Poetry Circle (v.p. 1990). Avocation: writing poetry.

DYER, SUSAN KRISTINE, librarian; b. Coos Bay, Oreg.; d. Stanley Keith and Betty Loray (Jameson) D.; m. Michael E. Gehringer. BA, U. Oreg., 1967, MLS, 1968; MBA, Golden Gate U., 1983. Librarian Morrison & Foerster, San Francisco, 1968-75, info. and gen. svcs. mgr., 1975-80; law librarian, records mgr. Thelen, Marrin, Johnson & Bridges, San Francisco, 1980-83; librarian World Bank Sectoral Library, Washington, 1984-89; ops. mgr. Faxon Co. Fed. Div., Herndon, Va., 1989-90, dir., 1990—. Author: Manual of Procedures for Private Law Libraries Supplement, 1984. Bd. dirs. Miriam's Kitchen, Washington, 1986-88. Mem. ALA, Am. Assn. Law Librs. (editor Recruitment Checklist 1974, newsletter editor 1976-79, pres. Western Pacific chpt. 1977-79, exec. bd. 1979-82), Spl. Librs. Assn., D.C. Libr. Assn. Office: Faxon Co Fed Div 450 Spring Pk Pl Ste 100 Herndon VA 22070

DYKEMA, DOROTHY ETHEL, retired counselor; b. Chgo., Jan. 26, 1923; d. Herbert H. and Ethel (Erikson) D. BA, Am. Conservatory of Music, 1946; MS in Rehab., So. Ill. U., 1964, MA in Music, 1985. Tchr., counselor Ill. Div. Rehab. Svcs., Chgo. and Peoria, Ill., 1946-66; mental health counselor Ill. Dept. Mental Health, Anna, 1967-80; ret. Author: They Shall Have Music, 1986. Vol. Crisis Line, Carbondale, Ill., 1980-85; bd. dirs. Jackson County Mental Health, Carbondale, 1982-88, Radio Reading Svc., Carbondale, 1985—. Mem. Morning Etude Club (pres. 1989—). Presbyterian. Home: 604 N Allyn Carbondale IL 62901

DYKEMAN, THERESE MARIE BOOS, rhetoric educator; b. Anamosa, Iowa, Apr. 11, 1936; d. Leonard Paul and Alvina Marie (Marek) Boos; m. King J. Dykeman, Feb. 7, 1959; children: John, Andria Camille, Kristen. BS in English, Creighton U., 1958; MA in English, Loyola U., Chgo., 1966; PhD in Rhetoric, Union Grad. Sch., 1980. Lectr. Chgo. City Coll., 1965-67, Housatonic Community Coll., Bridgeport, Conn., 1970-80, U. Bridgeport, 1981—, U. Conn., Stamford, 1984-85, Fairfield (Conn.) U., 1986—, U. Bridgeport Law Sch., 1986; pres. Ctr. for Ind. Study/Yale Station, New Haven, 1989—; bd. dirs. Danforth Assoc. of New England, Plymouth, N.H., 1987—. Contbr. numerous articles to Rhetoric Soc. Quarterly, Coll. Communication & Composition, Choice, Darshana International, Teaching English in the Two-Year College; contbr. poetry Weston Voice, 1987-89. Founder Pioneering Parents of Adopted Adolescents, Fairfield, 1989; bd. dirs. Fine Art Acad., Fairfield, 1985; dir. Marriage Encounter Conn., Stratford, 1975. Recipient Mini-grant for Conf. on Rhetoric in Tex. Ctr. for Ind. Study, 1988, grant for writing booklet Alcohol Coun., 1982, Mini-grant for teaching poetry Children's Mus., 1982. Mem. Rhetoric Soc. Am., Conn. Poetry Soc., AAUW (bd. dirs. 1989). Democrat. Roman Catholic. Home: 47 Woods End Rd Fairfield CT 06430 Office: Ctr for Ind Study Box 3193 Yale Station New Haven CT 06520

DYKES, VIRGINIA CHANDLER, occupational therapist; b. Evanston, Ill., Jan. 10, 1930; d. Daniel Guy and Helen (Schneider) Goodman; children: Ron Lee, Chuck Lee. B.A. in Art and Psychology, So. Methodist U., 1951; postgrad. in occupational therapy Tex. Women's U., 1953; cert. ins. rehab. specialist; cert. in work adjustment and vocat. evaluation. Occupational therapist Beverly Hills Sanitarium, Dallas, 1953-55; dir. occupational and recreational therapy Baylor U. Med. Ctr., Dallas, 1956-60, 68-89; pvt. practice, Dallas, 1989—; dir. occupational and recreational therapy Fla. Hosp., Orlando, 1962-65; staff therapist Parkland Meml. Hosp., Dallas, 1965-68; cons. Arthritis Found., 1974—. Mem. coordinating bd. allied health adv. com. Tex. Coll. and Univ. System, 1980-88; bd. dirs. Tex. Arthritis Found., chmn. patient svcs. com., 1985-89, exec. bd. sec.; bd. sponsors Kimball Art Mus.; bd. dirs. Dallas Opera and Womens Bd. of Dallas Opera. Named Tex. Occupational Therapist of Yr., 1985. Mem. Tex. Occupational Therapy Assn. (life mem. award), Am. Occupational Therapy Assn. (del. Fla. 1964, Tex. 1980-88), World Fedn. Occupational Therapists (participant 8th Internat. Congress, Hamburg, Germany, 1982, del. to 10th European Congress on Rheumatology, Moscow 1983), Chi Omega. Club: Boomerang (dir. 1971-88). Author: (manual) Lightcast II Splints, 1976; Adult Visual Perceptual Evaluation, 1981; contbr. articles to profl. jours. Home: 3203 Alderson Dallas TX 75214 Office: 3203 Alderson Dallas TX 75214

DYMOND, BARBARA LOUISE, veterinarian; b. Kingston, Pa., Feb. 8, 1956; d. Richard Dallas and Janet Ruth (Howell) D.; m. Joseph John Frederick Jr., June 29, 1985; children: Victoria Janet, Joseph John III. VMD, U. Pa., 1982. Vet. assoc. Bloomsburg (Pa.) Vet. Hosp., 1982-84; owner, veterinarian Exeter (Pa.) Animal Hosp., 1984—. Mem. DAR, Pa. Vet. Med. Assn., Am. Vet. Med. Assn., Am. Assn. of Small Rumisnant Practioners, Cornell Feline Health Research, Nature Conservancy. Republican. Methodist.

DYSTEL, JANE DEE, literary agent; b. Chgo., Aug. 8, 1945; d. Oscar and Marion (Dietler) Dystel; m. Steven G. Schwinder; 1 dau., Jessica Fanny. B.A. in Polit. Sci. cum laude, NYU, 1967. Mng. editor, then editor Grosset & Dunlap Pubs., N.Y.C., 1973-76; sr. editor A&W Pubs., Inc., N.Y.C., 1976-77; pub., v.p. World Almanac and Book of Facts, N.Y.C., 1977-85; ptnr.-lit. agt. Acton and Dystel, N.Y.C., 1986—. Cons. Multiple Sclerosis Read-a-Thon.; bd. dirs. Hamilton-Madison House. Mem. Womens Media Group, Phi Beta Kappa. Home: 1172 Park Ave New York NY 10128 Office: Acton & Dystel Inc 928 Broadway New York NY 10010

DYWASUK, COLETTE MARIE, marketing executive; b. Detroit, Feb. 6, 1941; d. Frank Anthony and Anne Rita (Wisniewski) Taube; m. Gerald Andrew Dywasuk, May 7, 1960; children: Gerald, Jeffrey, Cheryl, Mark, Janette. AA with high honors, Macomb Community Coll., 1980; BS with commendation in Mktg., Oakland U., 1982; MBA, U. Mich., Flint, 1987. Freelance writer Warren, Mich., 1969-75; spl. projects editor CECO Pub. Co., Warren, 1975-82; mktg. communications mgr. Vickers, Inc. (a Trinova Co.), Troy, Mich., 1983—. Author: (book) Adoption--Is It For You?, 1973, Adoption And After, 1974. Recipient Outstanding Cultural Achievement award City of Warren, 1976, Nat. Communications award Internat. Assn. Bus. Communicators, 1977, 79, Gold Caddy award Creative Advt. Club, Detroit, 1979. Mem. Exec. Bus. and Profl. Advt. (officer 1987—), Am. Mgmt. Assn., Women in Communications, Detroit Women Writers, Detroit Club (bd. dirs.). Roman Catholic. Office: Vickers Inc 5445 Corporate Dr Troy MI 48007-0302

DZIAK, ROSEMARY, cell physiologist, educator; b. Pittston, Pa., Apr. 11, 1946; d. Andrew and Susan (Pribula) D.; m. Juris Smiltins, Mar. 21, 1983; 1 child, George Andrew Arnold Smiltins. BS, Coll. Misericordia, Dallas, 1967; MS, U. Rochester (N.Y.), 1970, PhD, 1974. Postdoctoral fellow Northwestern U. Med. Sch., Chgo., 1974-75; instr. La. State U., New Orleans, 1975-76; asst. prof. SUNY, Buffalo, 1976-83, assoc. prof., 1983-90, prof., 1990—, dir. grad. studies, oral biology, 1980—, dir. young scholars program, 1989-90. Contbr. articles to profl. publs. NIH grantee, 1979—; recipient Rsch. Career Devel. award NIH, 1980-85. Mem. Am. Soc. Bone and Mineral Rsch. (program com. 1983), Endocrine Soc., Am. Assn. Dental Rsch. (program com. 1989-90). Democrat. Roman Catholic. Office: SUNY 320 Foster Hall Buffalo NY 14214

DZIARSKI, AGNES, dentist; b. Warsaw, Poland, Dec. 20, 1949; came to U.S., 1977; d. Henryk and Maria (Kiersnowska) Rewkiewicz; m. Roman Dziarski, Feb. 20, 1971; 1 child, Matthew. BSc, U. Warsaw, 1970, MSc, 1971; DMD, U. Pa., Phila., 1986. Rsch. asst. Dept. Physiology U. Warsaw, 1971-74, rsch. assoc. Dept. Physiology, 1974-77; rsch. specialist Dept. Neurology U. Pa. Sch. Medicine, Phila., 1978-79, rsch. specialist Dept. Allergy and Immunology, 1979-82; gen. dentist Glenwood (Ill.) Dental Assocs., 1986-88; pvt. practice Flossmoor, Ill., 1988—. Contbr. articles to profl. jours. Warner-Lambert Preventive Dentistry scholar, 1985. Mem. ADA, Acad. Gen. Dentistry, Matthew Cryer Honor Soc., Omicron Kappa Upsilon. Home and Office: 2010 Collett Ln Flossmoor IL 60422

DZIUBA, JOANNE CAROL, marketing professional; b. Batavia, N.Y., Nov. 24, 1951; d. Theodore Francis and Mary Agnes (Weldgen) D. Grad. high sch., Rochester, N.Y. From clk. to service cons. AT&T, Rochester, 1969-80; from market adminstr. to systems cons. AT&T, Dallas, 1980—. Contbr. articles to profl. pubs. Sec. Henrietta Wildlife Orgn., Mesquite, Tex., 1988, River Oaks Bd.-Community Orgn., Dallas, 1989. Mem. N. Dallas C. of C. Republican. Roman Catholic. Home: 4859 Cedar Springs #356 Dallas TX 75219

DZUBERA, PATRICIA, accounting, director; b. Passaic, N.J., Apr. 27, 1951; d. John and Marie (Drelich) D. BA, Montclair State Coll., 1973; MBA, Fairleigh Dickinson U., 1979. CPA, N.J., N.Y. Staff acct. Touche Ross & Co., Newark, 1973-75; sr. acct. Haskins & Sells, Newark, 1975-77; sr. ops. auditor Pfizer, Inc., N.Y.C., 1977-79; fin. mgr. cen. rsch. div. Pfizer, Inc., Maywood, N.J., 1979-80; divisional controller distbn. and transp. svc. div. Pfizer, Inc., N.Y.C., 1980-88; dir. acctg. Lex Electronics, Jericho, N.Y., 1988-89; fin. systems cons. JWP Inc., Purchase, N.Y., 1990—. Mem. AICPA's, N.J. State Soc. CPA's, Am. Women's Soc. CPA's. Office: Lex Electronics Jericho Turnpike Westbury NY 11590

EADS, M. ADELA, state legislator; b. Brooklyn, N.Y., Mar. 2, 1920. Ed. Sweet Briar Coll. Mem. Conn. Ho. of Reps., from 1976; now mem. Conn. Senate. Republican. Mem. Conn. Bd. Edn., 1972-76. Office: Conn State Senate State Capitol Bldg Hartford CT 06106 Home: R 1 Box 395 Kent CT 06757*

EAGAN, M. PATRICIA, productivity management consultant; b. Darby, Pa., Sept. 30, 1952; d. Joseph A. and Eileen (Nunan) E. BA, Am. U., 1974; MBA, Villanova U., 1984. Cons. Fine Art Gallery, Ardmore, Pa., 1984-87; travel coord. Bryn Mawr (Pa.) Coll., 1984-87; asst. program dir. World Affairs Coun., Phila, 1987; sr. trainer Integrated Control Systems, Litchfield, u.s. employment mgr., 1988--; U.S. cons. The Words and The Stones Exhibit., Glasgow, Scotland, 1988--. vol. canvasser, Mayoral Campaign, Phila., 1974. Republican. Roman Catholic. Home: 624 Spruce Lane Villanova PA 19085 Office: Integrated Control Systems Beach St Litchfield CT 06759

EAGAN, MARIE T. (RIA EAGAN), chiropractor; b. Rockville Ctr., N.Y., June 17, 1952; d. John F. and Mary (Ebner) E. BA, Goddard Coll., 1975; D in Chiropractic Medicine, N.Y. Chiropractic Coll., 1983. Pvt. practice chiropractic medicine N.Y.C., 1983—; bd. dirs. Chalice Found., L.A., 1986. Fellow N.Y. Chiropractic Assn., Am. Chiropractic Assn., Internat. Chiropractic Assn. Democrat. Office: 231 W 21st St #B New York NY 10011

EAGAN, SHIRLEY C., extension specialist, home economist; b. Charleston, W.Va., Mar. 29, 1942; d. Joseph Emerald Campbell and Genevieve C. (Grimm) Cottrill; m. Gerald V. Eagan, Aug. 20, 1976; 1 stepchild, Jere Michelle. BA, Marshall U., 1964; MEd, N.C. State U., Raleigh, 1969; EdD, W.Va. U., 1985. Home demonstration agt. W.Va. Extension Svc., Ripley, 1964-67; extension edn. coord. W.Va. Extension Svc., Parkersburg, 1968-69; extension specialist W.Va. Extension Svc., Morgantown, 1969—, interim div. leader, 1977-78, 90—; state advisor W.Va. Extension Homemakers Coun., 1969—; co-coord. W.Va. Family Community Leadership, 1987—. W.K. Kellogg Found. fellow N.C. State U., 1967-68. Mem. Am. Home Econs. Assn. (chair nat. com. 1989—), W.Va. Home Econs. Assn. (pres. 1987-88, Past Pres.'s plaque 1988), Nat. Assn. Extension Home Economists, W.Va. Assn. Extension Home Economists, W.Va. Adult Edn. Assn. (pres. 1969-70), Extension Assn. of W.Va. Office: 608 Knapp Hall PO Box 6031 Morgantown WV 26506-6031

EAGLE, CANDY KERR, environmental products distributor; b. Winston-Salem, N.C., Apr. 19, 1949; d. William Joseph and Mary Catherine (Hall) E. BA, Huntingdon Coll., 1971; MA, Covenant Sem., St. Louis, 1976. Prin., owner AAA Health & Safety Products, St. Louis, 1988—. Dir., Women Exploited by Abortion, St. Louis, 1984—; bd. dirs. Mo. Citizens for Life, St. Louis, 1985-88; coord. Salt & Light, St. Louis, 1986—. Republican. Office: AAA Health & Safety Product 2807 Glenrose Dr Saint Louis MO 63043

EAGLE, JOANN MARIE, food service management; b. Goodrich, Mich., June 28, 1955; d. Donald and Olga E.; children: Daniel Jay, Mark Anthony. Diploma, N.E. Oakland Vocat. Ctr., 1972-74; student, Lansing Community Coll. Dinner theater North Mich. U., Marquette, Mich., 1975-77; dietary aide, housekeeper Marquette Gen. Hosp., 1975-77; cook, caterer Huron Mountain Club, Marquette, 1975-80; stage hand Marquette Community Theater, Marquette, 1974-80; asst. mgr. Gen. Office Bldg. Cafeteria, Lansing, Mich., 1981-83, Ottawa St. Bldg. Cafeteria, Lansing, 1983-86; owner, operator The Coffee Cup Restaurant, Lansisng, 1986-87, Plaza One Coffee Shop, Lansing, 1987-88; v.p., co-founder Lansing Hospitality Corp., 1987—. Fund raiser Nat. Fedn. of the Blind, Lansing, 1984-85; clinet adv. Mich. Commn. for the Blind, Lansing, 1983—; organizer, promoter Lansing Council on Alcoholism & Substance Abuse, 1987—. Mem. Mich. Restaurant Assn.. Home: 4312 Appletree Ln Lansing MI 48917

EAGLER, JEAN-MARIE, photojournalist; b. Washington, Oct. 17, 1951; d. Anthony Charles and Lois Mae (Goode) Romano; m. John Joseph Eagler, Oct. 30, 1976; children: Hogan James, Jessalyn Marie. Student, U. Md., 1969-73. Prin. Eagler & Assocs., Raleigh, N.C., 1978-81, Chesapeake, Va., 1981—; writer, photographer Maryview Med. Ctr., Portsmouth, Va.; contbg. editor Women's Network of Hampton Rds., Norfolk, Va., 1985-86; contbg.

editor, brochure designer Va. Tech., Va. Coop. Extension Svc., 1988—; contbg. writer, photographer, brochure designer Norfolk County Hist. Soc., Chesapeake, 1988—; asst. chmn. Small Bus. Conf., Va. Coop. Extension Svc., Chesapeake, 1986—. Photographer, editor Chesapeake Historic Structures, 1988—; contbr. Hampton Rds. Mag., Va. Pilot and Ledger Star, Mil. Newspapers Va., Navy News; assoc. editor, photographer The RCRC Observer, 1988—; contbg. editor, photographer Chesapeake Monthly, 1984-85; designer brochures, letterhead, bus. cards, newsletters. Candidate Chesapeake City Coun., 1990; pres. Millwood Ave. Civic League, 1990—. Recipient letters of commendation Senator M.L. Earley and Del. J.R. Forbes for role as consumer activist. Mem. Nat. Fedn. Press Women (3d pl. award 1-3 color bus. brochure 1988), Va. Press Women (1st place award for news reporting 1987, 1st pl. award 1-3 color bus. brochure 1988), Norfolk County Hist. Soc. (oral history chmn.), Women's Network Hampton Roads. Baptist. Home and Office: Eagler & Assocs 609 Hassell Dr Chesapeake VA 23320-5411

EAGLY, ALICE HENDRICKSON, social psychologist; b. Los Angeles, Dec. 25, 1938; d. Harold Martin and Josara Alberta (Whyers) Hendrickson; m. Robert Victor Eagly, Sept. 8, 1962; children: Ingrid Victoria, Ursula Elizabeth. BA, Radcliffe Coll., 1960; MA, U. Mich., 1963, PhD, 1965. Asst. prof. Mich. State U., East Lansing, 1965-67; asst. to assoc. to full prof. U. Mass., Amherst, 1967-80; vis. asst. prof. U. Ill., Champaign, 1970-71; vis. assoc. prof. Harvard U., Cambridge, Mass., 1974-75; prof. social psychology Purdue U., West Lafayette, Ind., 1980—; MacEachern Meml. lectr. U. Alta., 1985; lectr. in field. Contbr. articles to profl. jours.; author: Sex Differences in Social Behavior: A Social Role Interpretation, 1987; cons. editor Jour. Personality and Social Psychology: Attitudes and Social Cognition, 1979—, Psychology of Women Quar., 1978-86, others; mem. editorial bd. Jour. Applied Social Psychology, 1983—, others. Recipient Disting. Pub. award, Assn. for Women in Psychology, 1978, Gordon Allport Intergroup Rels. prize, Soc. Psychol. Study Social Issues, 1976; Nat. Merit scholar, 1956-60, Fulbright fellow, 1960-61, Woodrow Wilson fellow, 1961-62, NSF fellow, 1962-65; various rsch. grants. Mem. Soc. Personality and Social Psychology (pres. 1981), Soc. for Exptl. Social Psychology (exec. com. 1973-76, 81-83), Am. Psychol. Assn., Interam. Soc. Psychology, Midwestern Psychol. Assn., Phi Beta Kappa, Sigma Xi. Office: Purdue U Dept Psychol Scis West Lafayette IN 47907

EAKLE, ARLENE H., genealogist; b. Salt Lake City, July 19, 1936; d. Thomas E. and Margaret (Mitchell) Haslam; m. Alma D. Eakle, Jr., Feb. 8, 1957; children: JoAnn, Richard, Linda, John. MA, U. Utah, PhD in English/History; AA in Nursing, Weber State U. Pres., founder The Genealogical Inst., Salt Lake City. Author: The Source: A Guidebook for American Genealogy (with John Cerny), 1984; co-author: Family History for Fun and Profit (with John Cerny), 1985. Recipient Higher award, Inst. of Heraldic and Genealogical Studies, Canterbury, Eng.; fellow of the Utah Genealogical Assn. in recognition of meritorious svc. rendered to advancement of genealogy and family history, 1987, Award of Merit, Fedn. of Genealogical Socs., 1984, The Grahame Thomas Smallwood Jr. award of Merit for personal commitment and outstanding svcs. to Assn. Profl. Genealogists. Office: PO Box 22045 Salt Lake City UT 84087

EARLE, JEAN BUIST, hospital administrator; b. Newton, N.J., Oct. 5, 1951; d. Richardson and Jean (Mackerly) Buist; m. Terry Dean Earle, Mar. 4, 1989. AB, Cornell U., 1973; MEd, Coll. William and Mary, 1974; MBA, U. Pa., 1987. Mgr. The Korman Corp., Jenkintown, Pa., 1975-77; v.p. ops. Community Assn. Mgmt. Co., Havertown, Pa., 1977-78; adminstrv. asst. Albert Einstein Med. Ctr., Phila., 1978-83; assoc. adminstr. Meml. Hosp. Burlington County, Mt. Holly, N.J., 1983-87; v.p. Overlook Hosp., Summit, N.J., 1987—. Mem. Am. Coll. Healthcare Execs., Am. Hosp. Assn., Cornell Club (no. N.J. chpt.), Wharton Alumni. Home: 20 Woodland Rd Bernardsville NJ 07924 Office: Overlook Hosp Summit NJ 07901

EARLE, SYLVIA ALICE, research biologist, oceanographer; b. Gibbstown, N.J., Aug. 30, 1935; d. Lewis Reade and Alice Freas (Richie) E. BS, Fla. State U., 1955; MA, Duke U., 1956, PhD, 1966; PhD (hon.), Monterey Inst. Internat. Studies, 1990. Resident dir. Cape Haze Marine Lab., Sarasota, Fla., 1966-67; research scholar Radcliffe Inst., 1967-69; research fellow Farlow Herbarium, Harvard U., 1967-75, researcher, 1975—; research assoc. in botany Natural History Mus. Los Angeles County, 1970-75; research biologist, curator Calif. Acad. Scis., San Francisco, from 1976; research assoc. U. Calif., Berkeley, 1969-75; fellow in botany Natural History Mus., 1989—; founder, pres., chief exec. officer, bd. dirs. Deep Ocean Tech., Inc., Oakland, Calif.; founder, pres., chief exec. officer Deep Ocean Engring., Oakland. Author: Exploring the Deep Frontier, 1980; editor: Scientific Results of the Tektite II Project, 1972-75; contbr. 70 articles to profl. jours. Trustee World Wildlife Fund U.S., 1976-82, council mem., 1984—; trustee World Wildlife Fund Internat., 1979-81, council mem., 1981—; trustee Charles A. Lindbergh Fund., Ocean Trust Found.; council mem. Internat. Union Conservation Nature, 1979-81; corp. mem. Woods Hole Oceanographic Inst.; mem. Nat. Adv. Com. Oceans and Atmosphere, 1980-84. Recipient Conservation Service award U.S. Dept. Interior, 1970, Boston Sea Rovers award, 1972, 79, Nogi award Underwater Soc. Am., 1976, Conservation service award Calif. Acad. Sci., 1979, Lowell Thomas award Explorer's Club, 1980, Order of Golden Ark Prince Netherlands, 1980, David B. Stone medal New Eng. Aquarium, 1989, Gold medalist Soc. of Women Geographers, medal Radcliffe Coll., 1990; named Woman of Yr. L.A. Times, 1970, Scientist of Yr., Calif. Mus. Sci. and Industry, 1981. Fellow AAAS, Marine Tech. Soc., Calif. Acad. Scis., Explorers Club, Calif. Acad. Sci.; mem. Internat. Phycological Soc. (sec. 1974-80), Phycological Soc. Am., Am. Soc. Ichthyologists and Herpetologists, Am. Inst. Biol. Scis., Brit. Phycological Soc., Ecol. Soc. Am., Internat. Soc. Plant Taxonomists, Explorers Club (fellow, bd. dirs. 1989—). Home: 12812 Skyline Blvd Oakland CA 94619 Office: Calif Acad Scis Golden Gate Pk San Francisco CA 94118

EARLES, DOROTHY ROBERTSON, microbiologist; b. Radford, Va., Sept. 24, 1946; d. Harry Lee and Juanita (Calfee) R.; m. Alvin Cecil Earles, Dec. 28, 1963; children: Nikki Lynn, Brian Scott. Student, Wytheville Community Coll., Va., 1975, 88, 90, New River Community Coll., Dublin, Va., 1979, 80, 83, John Tyler Community Coll., Richmond, Va., 1986. Cert. water plant operator class II. Orthodontist's asst. Dr. M.R. Hamill, Inc., Radford, 1971-82, Dr. R.L. Turner, Blacksburg, Va., 1982-84; office mgr. Dr. Graham Hoskins, Radford, 1984-85; microbiologist Radford Water Treatment Plant, 1986—. Mem. Am. Water Works Assn., Va. Cross Connection Control Assn., Christian Women's Fellowship (treas.). Mem. Christian Ch. Home: 123 Hammett Ave Radford VA 24141

EARLS, IRENE ANNE, art historian; d. William Thomas and Constance Ellen (Yanalavage) O'Connor; m. Walter Edward Earls, June 21, 1958. BA, U. Miami, Coral Gables, Fla., 1959; MA, U. Colo., 1968; PhD, U. Ga., 1975. Tchr. advanced placement history of art Orlando (Fla.) pub. schs.; rsch. assoc. U. Cen. Fla., Orlando. Author: Book Renaissance Art, 1987; contbr. articles to profl. jours. Mem. exec. com. lay adv. bd. dept. history Univ. Fla., Gainesville. Named Tchr. of the Yr., 1987-88, Nat. Honor Soc. Tchr. of the Yr., 1987-88, others. Mem. Western Soc. French History (officer of program coun.), Soc. for French Hist. Studies, Consortium On Revolutionary Europe. Office: 1625 S Beulah Rd Winter Garden FL 32787-4489

EARLY, KAREN HELENE, public relations executive; b. Elizabeth, N.J., Dec. 20, 1954; d. Erick Helmuth and Helen (Elko) Barsohn; m. Patrick Martin Early, May 22, 1976; 1 child, Frances Anne. BA, Georgetown U., 1975. Newspaper reporter Lynchburg (Va.) Daily Advance, 1976-78; communications asst. Lynchburg Gen. Hosp., 1978-79; copywriter Leggett Dept. Stores, Lynchburg, 1979; issues graphics mgr. Pa. Blue Shield, Camp Hill, Pa., 1982—. Mem. Pub. Relations Soc. Am. (bd. dirs. 1987-88, v.p. 1988-89). Office: Pennsylvania Blue Shield PO Box 890089 Camp Hill PA 17089-0089

EASBEY, MARION MORIARTY, retired telephone company official, writer; b. New Bedford, Mass., Apr. 8, 1930; d. Walter Vincent and Marion Elizabeth (Rigby) Moriarty; B.S., U. R.I., 1947-51; student Bell System Center for Tech. Edn., 1973-86. Service rep. N.E. Telephone & Northwestern Bell, Providence and St. Paul, 1952-58; office supr. Northwestern Bell, St. Paul, 1958-63, engring. staff asst., 1963-64; engring. technician, asso. engr. and engr. Northwestern Bell, St. Paul and N.E. Telephone, Providence, 1967-79, project mgr. N.E. Telephone, Framingham, Mass., 1979-86; engr. chief clk. Northwestern Bell, 1964-67. Practical politics instr. St. Paul C. of C., 1970; Lake Elmo Precinct chmn. and county conv. del., 1973; bd. dirs., co-chmn. privacy com. ACLU. Recipient cert. of Accomplishment, CAP, 1968, cert. of Merit, 1968. Mem. Common Cause (state network chmn. 1976-79), Assn. Mgmt. Women, Nat. Assn. Female Execs., Am. Mgmt. Assn., AAUW, ACLU, NOW. Democrat Unitarian. Club: Appalachian Mountain. Home: PO Box 9556 Warwick RI 02889

EASLEY, BETTY, state agency administrator; b. Victoria, Tex., Aug. 5, 1929; d. Clifford Pennington and Inez (Cary) Chapman; student U. Tex., 1947-49; B.A. in Pub. Adminstrn., Eckerd Coll., 1984; m. Kenneth E. Easley, Nov. 11, 1966; children—Cary, Barbara, Katherine, Virginia, William (dec.). Med. illustrator Walter Reed Med. Center, Washington, 1952-55; owner B&K Acctg. System, Tampa, Fla., 1962-66; newspaper columnist, Clearwater, Fla., 1969-72; mem. Fla. Ho. of Reps., 1972-86, minority leader pro tempore, 1984-86, asst. Sec. State, 1987-89; pub. svc. commr. State of Fla., 1989—. Vice chmn. Fla. Human Relations Commn., 1974-75; women's chmn. United Cerebral Palsy of Fla., 1973-75; mem. Fla. State Adv. Com. on U.S. Commn. Civil Rights, 1972-74, Pinellas County Met. Criminal Justice Planning Unit, 1972-80; bd. dirs. Morton Plant Hosp., 1984-88, Eckerd Coll., 1985-88; mem. U.S. Intergovtl. Policy Adv. Com., 1984-88, U.S. Comml. Motor Vehicle Safety Regulatory Rev. Panel, 1985—, U.S. Adv. Council on Edn. Stats., 1984-85; mem. Intergovtl. Adv. Council on Edn., 1986-88; co-chmn. Fla. Reagan-Bush, 1984; del. Republican Nat. Conv., 1976, 84; chmn. Pinellas Legis. Del., 1978-79; mem. Dist. V Mental Health Bd., 1974-78; bd. dirs. Upper Pinellas Assn. for Retarded Citizens, 1984-88, Dick Howser Ctr. for Cerebral Palsy, 1989—; mem. Women's Living and Learning Program Adv. Council, Fla. State Panel Am. Council on Edn., Fed. Edn. Data Acquisition Council. Recipient legis. award, Property Appraiser's Assn. Fla., 1981, presdl. award, 1981; legis. awards Fla. Phosphate Council, 1982, Juvenile Welfare Bd., 1976, Commn. on Human Rights, 1977, Fla. Assn. Community Colls., 1977, 80, 83, 84; TIGER award, 1977, 79, 80, 81; Fla. Sch. Bd. Assn. award, 1979, 80, 81, 82, 84; Friend of Edn. award, Pinellas Classroom Tchrs. Assn., 1980, 82; Gavel of Authority award Fla. Assn. Sch. Adminstrs., 1981, 82, 84; Allen Morris award, 1981; named rep. of year Fla. Assn. Community Colls., 1979, 81, 82, 84; nominated Most Valuable Mem. of the House, St. Petersburg Times, 1979, 80; Legislator of Yr. award Nat. Rep. Legislators Assn., 1983; Legis. award for disting. service Fla. Vocat. Assn., 1983, 84; Rep. Leadership award, 1984; Outstanding Layman award Phi Delta Kappa, 1983; service award Fla. Assn. Broadcasters, 1985; PACE award Pinellas Emergency Mental Health Services, 1985. Mem. Bus. and Profl. Women's Club, Fla. Fedn. Rep. Women's Clubs, Nat. Order Women Legislators (pres. 1982-83), Nat. Conf. State Legislators (SFA vice chmn.), Nat. Rep. Legislators Assn. (treas.), Beta Sigma Phi, Phi Theta Kappa. Episcopalian. Clubs: Zonta, Suncoast Tiger Bay. Office: Fla Pub Svc Commn 101 E Gaines St TAllahassee FL 32301

EASLEY, LOYCE ANNA, painter; b. Weatherford, Okla., June 28, 1918; d. Thomas Webster and Anna Laura (Sanders) Rogers; m. Mack Easley, Nov. 17, 1939; children: June Elizabeth, Roger. BFA, U. Okla., 1943; postgrad., Art Students League, N.Y.C., 1947-49; 1977; postgrad., Santa Fe Inst. Fine Arts, 1985. Tchr. Pub. Sch., Okmulgee, Okla., 1946-47, Hobbs, N.Mex., 1947-49; tchr. painting N.Mex. Jr. Coll., Hobbs, 1965-80; tchr. Art Workshops in N.Mex., Okla., Wyoming. Numerous one-woman and multiple painting exhibitions in mus., univs., galleries, including: Gov.'s Gallery, Santa Fe, Selected Artists, N.Y.C., Roswell, N.Mex. Mus., N.Mex. State U., Las Cruces, Tex., West Tex. Mus., Tex. Tech. Coll., Lubbock and many others; paintings in permnent collections include: USAF Acad., Colo. Springs, Colo., Roswell Mus., Carlsbad, N.Mex. Mus.. Coll. of Santa Fe and others in private and pub. collections; featured in S.W. and Art and Santa Fe Mag., 1981, '82. Named Disting. Former Student, U. Okla. Art Sch., 1963; nominated for Gov's. award in Art, N.Mex., 1988. Mem. N.Mex. Artists Equity (lifetime mem. 1963). Democrat. Presbyterian. Home: 817 E Zia Rd Santa Fe NM 87505

EASLEY, PATSY FLETCHER, interior designer; b. Amarillo, Tex., Jan. 7, 1931; d. Lowery Thurman Fletcher and Winnie Ozella (Hart) Leverett; m. Jack Wayne Easley, June 7, 1948; 1 child, James William. Student, Nicholls State U., Thibodaux, La., 1974-76; B in Interior Design, La. State U., 1990. Co-owner, treas., designer Easley's Fabrics/Interiors, Morgan City, La., 1964-72; owner, designer Pat Easley-Interior Designer, Morgan City, 1973—; mgr., dir. Leah Norman Schreier Community Ctr., Morgan City, 1986-88. Designer Am. Soc. Interior Designers Showcase "Cityscapes" at Fed. Fiber Mills Bldg., New Orleans, La., 1986. Bd. dirs. Morgan City Community Concert Assn., 1966-72; mem. St. Mary Arts and Humanities Council, 1984—, Preservation Resource Ctr., New Orleans, 1986—. Mem. Am. Soc. Interior Designers, Lic. Interior Designers La., Nat. Trust for Hist. Preservation, La. Watercolor Soc., New Orleans Mus. of Art (assoc.), Artists Guild Unltd. (treas. 1974-76, v.p. 1976-81, pres. 1984-86), Wives of U.S. Submarine Vets. World War II, Gamma Beta Phi. Baptist. Club: Ladies Petroleum (pres. 1981-82). Lodge: Eastern Star. Home and Office: 412 Saturn Morgan City LA 70380

EAST, CAPRICE DOREAN, interior designer; b. Chattanooga, Sept. 14, 1951; d. Daniel Sidney and Dora Nadean (McDaniel) E.; m. Robert Harley Blackmon, July 16, 1976. BA in Interior Design, Lambuth Coll., 1984. Div. product specification mgr. Kellwood Co., Rutherford, Tenn., 1969-75; interior designer Dabney's, Jackson, Tenn., 1975-84; owner, mgr. Capricious Interior Design, Jackson, 1984—. Crusade chmn. Madison County chpt. Am. Cancer Soc., 1987-89. Mem. Am. Soc. Interior Designers (allied), Bus. and Profl. Women (lst v.p. 1989—). Democrat. Methodist. Home: 610 Russell Rd Jackson TN 38301 Office: 610 Russell Rd Jackson TN 38301

EASTERLY, VALERIE FRANCES, small business development center director; b. Camden, N.J., May 19, 1951; d. William and Mildred (Musto) Caccese; m. Eric Easterly, June 23, 1973; children: Susannah, Shannon. BA, Vassar Coll., 1973. Lending officer Hibernia Bank, San Francisco, 1973-76; v.p. Seattle Trust, 1976-84; dir. bus., mgmt. cons. Nev. Small Bus. Devel. Ctr., Elko, 1985—. Bd. dirs., chairperson N.E. Nev. Devel. Authority, Elko, 1988—, PBS Affiliates in Elko, Friends of 14, 1988—; adv. bd. City of Elko Animal Control Bd., 1988—. Mem. AAUW, Elko C. of C., PEO, Soroptimist. Democrat. Roman Catholic. Home: 603 Pine St Elko NV 89801 Office: Nev Small Bus Devel Ctr 901 Elm St Elko NV 89801

EASTLINE, DOROTHY, advertising executive; b. Chgo., Aug. 3, 1929; d. Henry E.W. and Eleanor (Harstad) Bergst. BS in Journalism, U. Ill., Champaign. Advt. mgr. Schnadig Corp., Chgo., 1953-59, The Dearborn Co., Chgo., 1959-63, The Merchandise Mart, Chgo., 1963-72; pres., owner Eastline Communication, Chgo., 1972--. Mem. Nat. Assn. Women Bus. Owners. Home: 175 East Delaware #4907 Chicago IL 60611 Office: Eastline Communications 612 North Michigan Chicago IL 60611

EASTMAN, CAROLINE MERRIAM, computer science educator; b. Columbus, Ohio, Dec. 25, 1946; d. Robert Merriam and Kathryn Parmelee (Benedict) E.; m. Robin Michael Carter, Mar. 31, 1968. AB magna cum laude, Radcliffe Coll., 1968; MS in Computer Sci., U. N.C., 1974, PhD in Computer Sci., 1977. Asst. prof. dept. math. and computer sci. Fla. State U., Tallahassee, 1977-82; asst. prof. dept. computer sci. and engring. So. Meth. U., Dallas, 1982-84, assoc. prof., 1984-85; program dir. NSF, Washington, 1984-85; assoc. prof. dept. computer sci. U. S.C., Columbia, 1986—. Contbr. articles to profl. jours. Rsch. grantee NSF, Fla. State U., 1980-82, So. Meth. U., 1982-84, Air Force Office Sci. Rsch., Fla. State U., 1981-82. Mem. Assn. Computing Machinery (v.p. N.W. Fla. chpt. 1978-79), Assn. Women in Computing (at large bd. mem. 1979-83), AAAS (nominating com. electorate 1987-90), Am. Soc. Info. Sci. Office: Dept Computer Sci U SC Columbia SC 29208

EASTMAN, CAROLYN ANN, microbiology company executive; b. Potsdam, N.Y., Sept. 8, 1946; d. Frank Orvis and Irene (Rheaume) Eastman. BS in Biology, Nazareth Coll., 1968; AAS in Photography, Rochester Inst. Tech., 1976. Technician U. Rochester, N.Y., 1968-69; chemist Castle/Sybron, Rochester, 1969-79; owner, v.p. Sterilization Tech. Svcs., Rush, N.Y., 1979—; owner Fairfield Cosmetics, Rush, 1986—; ptnr. EFC Properties, 1983—; owner Microdispersions, Inc., 1988—, Medisperse L.P., 1988—. Contbr. articles to profl. jours.; patentee in field. Recipient various awards for photography, sculpture and painting. Mem. NOW, Assn. for Advancement of Med. Instrumentation, Sierra Club, Henrietta Art Club. Democrat. Roman Catholic. Home: 6 Genesee St Scottsville NY 14546 Office: Sterilization Tech Svcs 7500 W Henrietta Rd Rush NY 14543

EASTMAN, CAROLYN BERTHA, drug and alcohol counselor; b. Madison, Wis., Feb. 12, 1933; d. Edward William and Lillian (Rude) Rogers; m. Donald Duane Eastman, Aug. 28, 1954 (dec. 1980); children: Debra Riches, Donald, Mary, Cathy, Roger. AAS, Glendale Community Coll., 1984; BEd, Ariz. State U., 1985; postgrad., No. Ariz. U., 1986, St. Francis Coll., 1988-89. Cert. addiction counselor, Ariz. Sec. drug and alcohol unit Valley View Hosp, Youngtown, Ariz., 1982-85, drug and alcohol counselor, 1985-86; drug and alcohol counselor New Beginnings, North Las Vegas, Nev., 1987—. Mem. NAFE, Am. Bus. Women's Assn., Assn. for Death Edn. and Counseling. Roman Catholic. Home: 1750 E Karen Apt 184 Las Vegas NV 89109 Office: New Beginnings 1409 E Lake Mead Blvd North Las Vegas NV 89114

EASTMAN, LINDA SUZANNE, consulting organization executive, corporate image consultant; b. Evanston, Ill., Sept. 21, 1946; d. Robert William and Ardath Louis (Stoddard) Ellis; m. Albert Henry Eastman, Nov. 20, 1971; 1 child, Suzanne Elisabeth. Student, No. Ill. U., 1965-66, U. Louisville, 1986—. Model, Jack Winter, Chgo., 1969-71, Saks Fifth Avenue, N.Y.C., 1969; stewardess Am. Airlines, Chgo. and N.Y.C., 1969-71; owner, operator Louisville Model Agy., 1973—; pres. The Profl. Woman Network, Prospect, Ky., 1981—; corp. image cons. Author: The Professional Woman; The Teen Image Guide, 1984. Mem. Nat. Assn. Female Execs., Am. Soc. Tng. and Devel., Am. Assn. Women Bus. Owners. Republican. Episcopalian. Club: Louisville Tennis. Avocations: tennis, water skiing.. Home: 14107 Harbour Pl Prospect KY 40059 Office: The Profl Woman Network PO Box 333 Prospect KY 40059

EASTON, CAROL LEE, hospital official; b. Brockville, Ont., Can., Nov. 25, 1939; came to U.S., 1962; d. Robert Leroy and Luella Mae (Smith) Armstrong; m. J. Don Enterline, May 4, 1963 (dec. Apr. 1967); m. William Ivie Stevenson Easton, Apr. 15, 1972. Student, Brockville Bus. Sch., 1959; student med. records, Hotel Dieu Hosp., Kingstong, Ont. Registered record libr., Can. Asst. dir. med. records Kingstong Gen. Hosp., 1960-62; dir. med. records Kings View Hosp., Reedley, Calif., 1962-64, Community Hosp. Monterey Peninsula, Monterey, Calif., 1967—; mem. med. assisting adv. com. Monterey Peninsula Coll., 1987—. Mem. Am. Med. Records Assn. (assoc.), Am. Med. Transcription Assn. (assoc.), Calif. Med. Records Assn. (assoc.), Calif. Med. Transcription Assn. (assoc.). Home: PO Box A Carmel CA 93921 Office: Community Hosp Monterey PO Box HH Monterey CA 93921

EASTON, JILL JOHANNA, state official; b. Nassua County, N.Y., June 6, 1949; d. E. Paul and Thelma R. Easton. BA, U. So. Miss., 1971, MPA, 1986. Mgr. classified advt. Thibodeaux (La.) Daily Comet, 1971-73; on-air personality Sta. WNAT, Natchez, Miss., 1973-74; classified sales rep. Natchez Democrat, 1974; co-owner House of Pisces Pet Shop, Vidalia, La., 1974-75; employment interviewer Miss. Employment Svc., Gulfport, 1976-80; pub. relations rep. Miss. Dept. Health, Gulfport, 1980-83, health program rep., 1983—; pres. J & K Divers, underwater photography and archaeology co., 1990. Mem. speaker's bd. Am. Cancer Soc., Biloxi, Miss., 1986-88; bd. dirs. Miss. Coalition Mothers and Babies. 1984-88. Mem. Divers Alert Network, Gulf Coast Divers Assn. (prin. officer 1986-87), Miss. Archaeol. Rsch. Group (bd. dirs. 1987—), Miss. Polit. Sci. Assn., Sierra Club, Civitan (bd. dirs.), CEDAM Internat. (Croton-on-Hudson, N.Y.), Miss. Jaycees (outstanding devel. v.p.), Gulfport Jaycees (Jaycee of Yr.). Lutheran. Home: Q-98 Penthouse Gardens Pass Christian MS 39571 Office: Coastal Plains Pub Health D PO Box 3749 15164 Deadeux Rd Gulfport MS 39505-3749

EASTON, JOAN MARIE, educator; b. Bklyn., May 4, 1935; d. John and Honor Angela (Sheehan) Wardenier; m. Edward R. Easton, Dec. 23, 1970; 1 child, Sean. BA, Hunter Coll., 1954, MA, 1957; postgrad. doctoral studies, NYU, 1968-74. Instr. Pace U., N.Y.C., 1963-70, asst. prof., 1970-76; spl. lectr. Univ. Coll., Cork City, Ireland, 1980-82; adj. asst. prof. Coll. Santa Fe, 1982-85, adj. assoc. prof., 1985-86, asst. dir. Sch. of Open Studies, 1984-86; acting dir. Sch. of Open Studies, Coll. Santa Fe, 1985; assoc. prof., faculty advisor Capital U., Columbus, Ohio, 1986—; ptnr. Potential Plus, Columbus; founder, headmistress The Little Sch., Schull, Ireland, 1975-82; bd. dirs. Nursing Ventures; cons. in field. vol. counselor Stop Child Abuse Now, Santa Fe, 1982-83; exec. dir. Santa Fe Girls Club, 1983-84. Recipient citation City of Santa Fe, 1983. Mem. Nat. Women's Studies Assn., Nat. Council of Tchrs. of English, AAUP. Roman Catholic. Office: Capital U Adult Degree Program Columbus OH 43209

EASTON, MICHELLE, federal agency administrator; b. Phila., Aug. 12, 1950; d. Glenn H. Jr. and Jeanne (Mulhall) Easton; m. Ron Robinson, Sept. 14, 1974; children: Ronald Jr., Daniel, Thomas. AA, BA, Briarcliff Coll., 1972; JD, Am. U., Washington, 1980. Bar: Va. 1981. Asst. to exec. dir. Young Ams. for Freedom, Sterling, Va., 1973-78; asst. to dir. pub. rels. Nat. Right to Work Com., Springfield, Va., 1978; legal asst. Nat. Right to Work Legal Def. Found., 1979; transition team mem. Office of Pres.-Elect, Equal Employment Opportunity Commn., Washington, 1980-81; atty. U.S. Dept. Justice, Washington, 1981; spl. asst. to gen. counsel U.S. Dept. Edn., Washington, 1981-83; pvt. vol. orgns. liaison officer, Africa Bur. Agy. for Internat. Devel., 1984; dir. Missing Children's Program Office of Juvenile Justice and Delinquency Prevention, U.S. Dept. Justice, 1985-87; dir. intergovtl. affairs U.S. Dept. Edn., Washington, 1987-88, dep. under sec. for intergovtl. and interagy. affairs, 1988—. Republican. Episcopalian. Office: US Dept Edn 400 Maryland Ave SW Washington DC 20202-3500

EASTON, SHEENA, rock vocalist; b. Bellshill, Scotland, Apr. 27, 1959. Grad., Royal Scottish Acad. Music and Drama, 1979. Albums include Take My Time, 1981, You Could Have Been with Me, 1981, Madness, Money and Music, 1982, Best Kept Secret, 1983, A Private Heaven, 1984, The Lover in Me, 1988, Greatest Hits, 1989, (with Luis Miguel) Me Gustas Tal Como Eres (Grammy award for Mexican-Am. performance 1984). Recipient Grammy award for best new artist, 1981. Office: Harriet Wasserman Mgmt 5954 Wilkinson Ave North Hollywood CA 91607*

EASTWOOD, DELYLE, chemist; b. Upper Darby, Pa., Nov. 19, 1932; d. Earl Vivian and Thelma Bernice (Yelton) E. MS in Phys. Chemistry, U. Chgo., 1955, PhD in Phys. Chemistry, 1964; MS in Mgmt. Sci., Rensselaer Poly. Inst., 1982. Postdoctoral rsch. fellow Harvard U., Cambridge, Mass., 1964-66; rsch. assoc. U. Wash., Seattle, 1966-69, Northeastern U., Boston, 1970-71; sr. scientist Baird Atomic Corp., Bedford, Mass., 1971-72; project chemist Bendix Rsch. Ctr., Southfield, Mich., 1972-73; rsch. chemist USCG Rsch. and Devel. Ctr., Groton, Conn., 1974-81; sr. staff scientist Brookhaven Nat. Lab., Upton, N.Y., 1981-83; Nat. Superfund design ctr. chemist U.S. Army Corps Engrs., Omaha, 1983-88; sr. staff scientist Lockheed Engring. and Scis. Co., Las Vegas, Nev., 1988—; adj. prof. physics U. Nev., Las Vegas, 1990. Editor books in field; contbr. articles to profl. publs., chpts. to books. Recipient Silver medal for Meritorious Svc. U.S. Dept. Transp., 1978. Fellow Am. Inst. Chemists; mem. Soc. Applied Spectroscopy (chair Nev. chpt. 1989-90), ASTM (chair subcom., exec. bd. 1983—, chair task group 1974—), Assn. Women in Sci. (facilitator, nat. contact So. Nev. chpt. 1989-90), Am. Chem. Soc., Am. Phys. Soc. Office: Lockheed Engring and Scis 1050 E Flamingo Rd Ste 301 Las Vegas NV 89119

EATON, ANN BERRIEN, automotive company executive; b. Grosse Pointe, Mich., Aug. 15, 1960; d. Berrien Clark and Charlotte Capers (Keyser) Eaton. BJ, U. Tex., 1984. News reporter WLUC-TV, Marquette, Mich., 1984-85, WCPO-TV, Cin., 1985-87; dist. mgr. Chrysler Motors, Cin., 1987—. Mem. Sigma Gamma, Kappa Kappa Gamma. Republican. Episcopalian. Office: Chrysler Motors 11300 Cornell Park Dr Cincinnati OH 45202

EATON, ARIANA VAN DER HEYDEN, advertising executive; b. New Haven, Conn., Nov. 18, 1955; d. Frederik Selden and Mary (Bean) E. Student, Bennett Coll., 1973-74, U. New Haven, 1974-75. Printing cons. Corbett Press, Woodbridge, Conn., 1978-79; media buyer, prodn. mgr. Pace Advt., Woodbridge, Conn., 1979-82, traffic mgr., 1982-84, asst. v.p., 1984-

88, v.p. mktg. comm., 1988—. Mem. Bethany Athletic Assn., Ad Club (v.p. 1987—), Rotary (del. to U.K. group study exch. team). Protestant. Office: Pace Mktg Comm 1021 Village Walk Guilford CT 06437

EATON, DORLA DEAN See KEMPER, DORLA DEAN

EATON, EDNA DOROTHY, home health care administrator; b. Van Meter, Iowa, Mar. 21, 1938; d. Walter Clifford and Rosemarie Rose (Lienemann); m. Edward Eugene Eaton, July 1, 1962; children: David Clifford, Thomas Eugene. BS in Nursing, RN, U. Iowa, 1961. Staff nurse Shenandoah Hosp., Iowa, 1961-62, 63-65, Hamburg Community Hosp., Iowa, 1965-73; surg. supr. Grape Community Hosp., Hamburg, 1973-79, dir. nursing, 1979-87; health care administr. S.W. Iowa Home Health Services, Sidney, Iowa, 1987-88; med. surg. staff nurse Mercy Hosp., Council Bluffs, Iowa, 1988—; med. reviewer Blue Shield & Blue Cross of Nebr., 1989—. Bd. govs. Iowa Bd. Nursing, 1984—. Named Booster of Yr., Booster Club Sidney, 1985. Republican. Lutheran. Home: Box 429 Sidney IA 51652 Office: Blue Cross & Blue Shield PO Box 3248 Omaha NE 68180

EATON, JEAN BONNIE, fashion design instructor; b. Marshalltown, Iowa, Sept. 17, 1951; d. Carl Frank and Georgianna (Kubik) Uchytil; m. Thomas Sohner Eaton, Aug. 18, 1973; children: Andrew James, Jeffrey Charles. AA, Ellsworth Jr. Coll., Iowa Falls, Iowa, 1971; BA in Bus., Home Econs., U. of Northern Iowa, 1973; postgrad. studies, Mankato (Minn.) State U. Licensed instructor, Minn. Sec. Ellsworth Jr. Coll. Fashion Dept., Iowa Falls, Iowa, 1969-71, U. Northern Iowa, Cedar Falls, 1971-72; sales cons. Hazel's Fashion Fabrics, Tame, Iowa, 1968-69, Seiferts, Waterloo, Iowa, 1972-73; sales cons., cosmetic buyer Anderson's Fashions, Albert Lea, Minn., 1973-76; asst. mgr. Fusfields, Albert Lea, 1976-77; instr. Albert Lea Tech. Coll., 1977—; mem. Task Force State Dept. Edn., St. Paul, Minn., 1986—; judge County Fairs, Bus. & Profl. Women's awards, Owatonna, Albert Lea, Waseca, Minn., 1981—. Author: (Fashion Programs) Fashion Dos and Donts, Capsule Dressing, 1985-89, 1st place award, Minn. State Fair. Pub. Relations Com. United Way, Albert Lea, Minn., 1987—; fundraiser Albert Lea Family Y Youth Drive; mem. Southwest Jr. High PTO. Named Leader in Sex Equity Minn. Tech. Bd. of Edn., 1984. Mem. Minn. Mktg. Educators (Mkg. Educator of Year 1986), DECA (v.p., bd. dirs., sec., 1987—), Albert Lea Edn. Assn. (rep., 1979-81, Teacher of Year, 1987), Albert Lea TC (enrollment mgmt team 1989—) PEO (dir. programs, scholarship com. 1987-88), TTT (camp chmn. 1986-88, historian), Albert Lea C. of C. (chmn. mktg. com.); Minn. Edn. Assn. (Teacher of Excellence 1988). Home: 515 Park Albert Lea MN 56007 Office: Albert Lea Tech Coll 2200 Tech Dr Albert Lea MN 56007

EATON, KATHERINE GIRTON, retired library educator; b. St. Paul, Mar. 9, 1924; d. John Frances and Mary Ahleen (Peck) Girton; m. Burt Elliott Eaton, Oct. 18, 1947; children: John Girton, Marilee Eaton Warkentin, David Elliott. BA in Journalism, U. Mpls., 1944; MS in Journalism, U. Oreg., 1952, MLS, 1968. Reporter Bakersfield Calif., 1945-46; women's editor Rochester (Minn.) Post Bulletin, 1946-47; legal sec. Broady Law Offices, St. Paul, 1949-51; editor Oreg. State System Higher Edn., Eugene, 1952-53; cons. Oreg. State Libr., Salem, 1968-70; head pub. affairs libr. U. Oreg., Eugene, 1970-85, assoc. prof. emeritas, 1985—. Author and editor rsch. reports. Chairperson, Lane County Mental Health Bd., Eugene, 1964-88, Lane County Libr. Bd., Eugene, 1981-85, Eugene City Budget Com., 1988—, Citizens for Lane County Librs., 1980—, Human Resources Planning Project, Lane County, 1986-89. Named Outstanding Young Woman, Eugene Jaycettes, 1956, Outstanding Woman Ur., Lance coun. Orgns., 1974; recipient Gulick, Seaton, Hiitina awards Camp Fire, Inc., 1959, 66, 71. Mem. AAUW (pres. Oreg. 1975-77, nat. exec. v.p. 1981-85), ALA (coun. 1976-80), Oreg. Libr. Assn. (hon. life, pres. 1973-74), Nat. Coun. Planning Librs. (pres. 1978-79, 88-89), League Women Voters Oreg. (1st v.p. 1989—), League Women Voters Lane County (pres. 1963-65), Pacific Northwest Libr. Assn. (editor quarterly 1985—). Democrat. Presbyterian.

EATON, LYNDA LOU, aircraft manufacturing company executive; b. Nevada, Mo., Aug. 31, 1946; d. Ira and Anna Mae (Welch) E.; B.S. in Chemistry, Central Mo. State U., Warrensburg, 1967; M.B.A., Pepperdine U., 1981; m. John C. Carlisle, Dec. 1980. Blood bank supr. St. Luke's Hosp., Kansas City, Mo., 1968-71; acting blood bank supr. Hoag Meml. Hosp., Newport Beach, Calif., 1971-72; blood bank supr. City of Hope Nat. Med. Center, Duarte, Calif., 1975-77; mgr. Immuno-Science, Inc., Los Angeles, 1977-82; materials mgr. Ortho Diagnostic Systems, Inc., Irvine, Calif., 1982-85; br. mgr. Douglas Aircraft Co., Long Beach, Calif., 1985-88, mgr. components, 1988—. Mem. Am. Soc. Clin. Pathology (med. technologist, specialist in blood banking), Am. Assn. Blood Banks, Am. Prodn. and Inventory Soc. Republican. Home: 6 Palos Irvine CA 92715 Office: Douglas Aircraft Co 3855 Lakewood Blvd Long Beach CA 90846

EATON, MARGARET ANN, educator; b. Lynwood, Calif., June 5, 1953; d. Stephen William and Dolores Ann (McCarthy) DeMott; m. Jerold B. Eaton, Dec. 31, 1989. BA in Spanish, Immaculate Heart Coll., L.A., 1980; MA in TESOL (Teaching English to Speakers of Other Languages), Monterey Inst. Internat. Studies, 1983. Cert. English and ESL tchr., Calif. Tchr. English and ESL Laloma Jr. High Sch. Modesto (Calif.) City Schs., 1983-85, 86—, Gonzales (Calif.) Union High Sch. Dist., 1985-86; part-time tchr. ESL Modesto Jr. Coll., 1989—; essay corrector Ednl. Testing Svc., Berkeley, Calif., summers 1987, 88. curriculum writer ESL, Modesto City Schs., spring 1989. Vol. Stanislaus Wildlife Care Ctr., Ceres, Calif., 1987—. Mem. Calif. Assn. Tchrs. of English to Speakers of Other Langs. Office: La Loma Jr High Sch 1800 Encina Ave Modesto CA 95354

EATON, NANCY L., librarian; b. Berkeley, Calif., May 2, 1943; d. Don Thomas and Lena Ruth (McClellan) Linton; m. Edward Arthur Eaton III, June 19, 1965 (div. 1980). AB, Stanford U., 1965; MLS, U. Tex., 1968, postgrad., 1969. Cataloger U. Tex. Library, Austin, 1968-71, head MARC unit, 1971-72, asst. to librarian, 1972-74; automation librarian SUNY, Stony Brook, 1974-76; head tech. services Atlanta Pub. Library, 1976-82; dir. libraries U. Vt., Burlington, 1982-89; dean libr. svcs. Iowa State U., Ames, 1989—; del. user's coun., mem. exec. com. Online Computer Libr. Ctr., Inc., Dublin, Ohio, 1980-82, 86-88, trustee, 1987—; mgr. Nat. Agrl. Text Digitalizing Project, 1986, bd. dirs., New Eng. Libr. Network, 1987-89. Co-author: Optical Information Systems: Implementation Issues for Libraries, 1988.; co-editor: A Cataloging Sampler, 1971, Book Selection Policies in American Libraries, 1972; contbr. articles to profl. jours. U.S. Office of Edn. postmaster's fellow, 1969; Dept. Edn. Title II-C grantee, 1985, 87. Mem. ALA, Libr. and Info. Tech. Assn. (pres. 1984-85, bd. dirs. 1980-86), Iowa Libr. Assn., AAUW. Democrat. Home: 3320 Kingman Rd Ames IA 50010 Office: Iowa State Univ 302 Parks Library Ames IA 50011

EATON, PAULINE, artist; b. Neptune, N.J., Mar. 20, 1935; d. Paul A. and Florence Elizabeth (Rogers) Friedrich; m. Charles Adams Eaton, June 15, 1957; children: Gregory, Eric, Paul, Joy. BA, Dickinson Coll., 1957; MA, Northwestern U., 1958. Lic. instr., Calif. Instr., Mira Costa Coll., Oceanside, Calif., 1980-82, Idyllwild Sch. Music and Arts, Calif., 1983—; juror, demonstrator numerous art socs. Recipient award Haywood (Calif.) Area Forum for the Arts, 1986. Exhibited one-woman shows Nat. Arts Club, N.Y.C., 1977, Designs Recycled Gallery, Fullerton, Calif., 1978, 80, 84, San Diego Art Inst., 1980, Spectrum Gallery, San Diego, 1981, San Diego Jung Ctr., 1983, Marin Civic Ctr. Gallery, 1984, R. Mondavi Winery, 1987; group shows include Am. Watercolor Soc., 1975, 77, Butler Inst. Am. Art, Youngstown, Ohio, 1977, 78, 79, 81, NAD, 1978; represented in permanent collections including Butler Inst. Am. Art, St. Mary's Coll., Md., Mercy Hosp., San Diego, Sharp Hosp., San Diego, Redlands Hosp., Riverside, 1986; work featured in books: Watercolor, The Creative Experience, 1978, Creative Seascape Painting, 1980, Painting the Spirit in Nature, 1984, Exploring Painting (Gerald Brommer); author: Crawling to the Light, An Artist in Transition, 1987. Trustee San Diego Art Inst., 1977-78, San Diego Mus. Art, 1982-83. Mem. Nat. Watercolor Soc. (exhibited traveling shows 1978, 79, 83, 85), Rocky Mountain Watermedia Soc. (Golden award 1979, Mustard Seed award 1983), Nat. Soc. Painters in Acrylic and Casein (hon.), Watercolor West (Strathmore award 1979, Purchase award 1986), Marin Arts Guild (instr. 1984—), San Diego Watercolor Soc. (pres. 1976-77, workshop dir. 1977-80), Artists Equity (v.p. San Diego 1979-81), San Diego Artists Guild (pres. 1982-83), Western Fedn. Watercolor Socs. (chmn. 1983, 3d prize 1982, Grumbacher Gold medal 1983), West Coast Watercolor Soc. (exhbns. chmn. 1983-86, pres. 1989—), Eastbay Watercolor Soc. (v.p. 1988—). Democrat. Presbyterian. Home: 10 Alta Mira Ave Kentfield CA 94904

EATON, SANDRA SHAW, chemistry educator; b. Boston, Jan. 23, 1946; d. James Headon and Vera (Chapman) S.; m. Gareth Richard Eaton, Mar. 29, 1969. BA, Wellesley Coll., 1968; PhD, MIT, 1972. Asst. prof. U. Colo., Denver, 1973-80, assoc. prof. chemistry, 1980-86, prof., 1986-89; prof. chemistry U. Denver, 1990—. Contbr. articles to profl. jours. Predoctoral fellow NSF, 1969-71. Mem. Am. Chem. Soc., Phi Beta Kappa, Sigma Xi. Office: U Denver Chemistry Dept University Park Denver CO 80208

EBBEN, JOYCE MARIE, psychologist; b. Stanley, Wis., Nov. 11, 1952; d. Delton Joseph and Marie Elizabeth (Benzschawel) E. BA, U. Wis., Eau Claire, 1974, MS, 1977; MA, Calif. State U., Northridge, 1984; PhD, Claremont Coll., 1989. Sch. psychologist Sunnyside Pub. Schs., Tucson, 1977-78, Amphitheater Pub. Schs., Tucson, 1978-80; human factors specialist Hughes Aircraft Co., Canoga Park and Fullerton, Calif., 1982—; pvt. practice cons., human factors psychologist Claremont, Calif., 1986—. Mem. Human Factors Soc., Sigma Xi, Phi Kappa Phi.

EBERLE, ANNE RINEHART, artist; b. St. Louis, Mar. 21, 1932; d. Chandler Fay and Elizabeth Sarah (Milbank) Rinehart; m. Robert Todd Eberle, Apr. 12, 1958; 1 child, Sarah Conway. BA in Applied Design, Purdue U., West Lafayette, Ind., 1954; MA in Painting, Northeast La. U., Monroe, 1975; student, Kansas City Art Inst., 1954-56; postgrad., La. Tech. U., Ruston, 1978-86. Staff artist Hallmark, Inc., Kansas City, Mo., 1954-56; instr. People's Art Ctr., St. Louis, 1956-58; grad. asst. N.E. La. U., Monroe, 1973-75, instr., 1982; instr. Masur Mus. Art, Monroe, 1980—; freelance artist Monroe, 1975—. Mem. Mayor's Com. for Visual Arts, Monroe, 1979-82; pres., edn. chmn., trustee Twin City Art Found., Monroe, 1974—. Recipient 1st Pl. award painting La. Festival Art, Masur Mus., Monroe, 1987, award Mid-South Watercolorists, Little Rock, 1989. Mem. Women in Communications, Am. Watercolor Soc. (assoc.), La. Watercolor Soc., Mid-South Watercolorist, Monroe Art Assn. (sec. 1968-70), Phi Kappa Phi, Chi Omega (local pres. 1970-71). Episcopalian. Home: 2009 Lexington Ave Monroe LA 71201

EBERLE, KATHY MAE, business owner; b. Bismarck, N.D., May 26, 1966; d. Arthur F. and Vivian S. (Johnson) Forsman; m. Ron F. Eberle, June 6, 1987. Student, Dickinson (N.D.) State Coll., 1986, Minot (N.D.) State Coll., 1987. Adminstrv. asst. First Am. Bank, Minot, 1986-88; exec. sales asst. Sta. KMOT-TV, Minot, 1988-89; pvt. practice med. transcriber Bismarck and Mandan, N.D., 1989—. Mem. NAFE.

EBERLEIN, SHIRLEY ANN, educator; b. Cuba City, Wis., June 21, 1932; d. Edward H. and Bessie (Powers) Hartung; m. Fred S. Eberlein, Aug. 18, 1956; children: Nancy, John, Mark, Scott, Steven. BS in Edn., U. Wis., Platteville, 1954; MS in Edn., U. Wis., Madison, 1959; doctoral studies, 1989—; BS in Music cum laude, U. Wis., Platteville, 1977, MS magna cum laude, 1986. Cert. tchr., Wis. Tchr. Madison Pub. Schs., 1954-61; supr. student teaching U. Wis., Madison, 1954-61; instr. U. Wis., Platteville, 1968-73, supr. student teaching, 1968-73; dir. early childhood program Doudna Lab. Sch., U. Wis., Platteville, 1968-73; tchr. Platteville Pub. Schs., 1973-89; pvt. piano and organ tchr., Middleton, Platteville, Wis., 1958-86; ch. organist, Middleton, Platteville, 1961-89; vis. educator British Primary Sch., London, 1986; workshop presenter U. Wis.-Stout, Menomonie, 1987-89; cons. edn. U. Wis., Platteville, 1973-86; mem. curriculum com. U. Wis., Platteville, 1968-73. Clarinetist City Band, Platteville, 1968-70; mem. Hosp. Aux., Platteville, 1970-75; treas. U. Wis., Madison Alumni chpt., Grant County, 1970; mem. Anne Hathaway Guild, Shakespeare Festival, U. Wis., Platteville, 1985—; com. mem. Needs of Women Commn., City of Platteville, 1986-88, sec. Water and Sewer Commn., 1987-88, pres. 1988-89; mem. task force Wis. Women's Network, Madison, 1986—. Recipient Teaching Svc. award S.W. Wis. Inservice Conf., U. Wis., Platteville, 1987. Mem. NEA, Wis. Edn. Assn., Platteville Edn. Assn. (bldg. rep. 1981-89, negotiator 1981-83, adv. mem. dist. adv. com. negotiations 1983—), AAUW (bd. mem. 1979-80), Wis. Kindergarten Assn., Nat. Assn. for Edn. Young Children, Am. Guild Organists Colleague, Organ Hist. Soc., Pi Lambda Theta (pres. 1960-61), Phi Delta Kappa. Home: 500 W Mineral St Platteville WI 53818

EBERLEY, HELEN-KAY, opera singer, classical record company executive; b. Sterling, Ill., Aug. 3, 1947; d. William Elliott and P. (Conneely) E.; m. Vincent P. Skowronski, July 15, 1972. MusB, Northwestern U., 1970, MusM, 1971. Chmn., pres. Eberley-Skowronski, Inc., Evanston, Ill., 1973—; artistic coord. Eberley-Skowronski, Inc., 1973—; founder EB-SKO Prodns., 1976, tchr., coach, 1976; exec. dir., performance cons. E-S Mgmt., 1985; featured artist Honors Concert, Northwestern U., 1970; Master Class and guest lectr. various colls. and univs.; numerous TV and radio talk show appearances and interviews. Operatic debut in Peter Grimes, Lyric Opera, Chgo., 1974; starred in: Cosi Fan Tutte, Le Nozze Di Figaro, Dido and Aeneas, La Boheme, Faust, Tosca, La Traviata, Falstaff, Don Giovanni, Brigadoon, others; jazz appearances with Duke Ellington, also with Dave Brubeck; performing artist Oglebay Opera Inst., Wheeling, W.Va., 1968, WTTW TV/PBS, Chgo., 1968; solo star in: Continental Bank Concerts, 1981-89, United Airlines-Schubert, Schumann, Brahms, Mendelssohn, Fauré, Mozart, Supersta. WFMT Radio, Chgo., 1982—; featured artist with North Shore Concert Band, 1989; producer/annotator Gentleman Gypsy, 1978, Skowronski: Strauss & Szymanowski, 1979, One Sonata Each: Franck & Szymanowski, 1982; starring artist/exec. producer Separate But Equal, 1976, Opera Lady, 1978, Eberley Sings Strauss, 1980, Helen-Kay Eberley: American Girl, 1983, Helen-Kay Eberley: Opera Lady II, 1984; performed Am. and Can. Nat. Anthems for Chgo. Cubs Baseball Team, 1977-83, Chgo. Bears Football, 1977; also star in numerous concert recital and symphony appearances, Europe, Can., U.S. Mem. Mayor's founding com. Evanston Arts Council, 1974-75; judge Ice-skating Competition Wilmette (Ill.) Park Dist., 1985-88; fin. chmn. Chgo. Youth Orchestra, 1974-77, bd. dirs. 1973-77. Recipient Creative and Performing Arts award Ind. Jr. Miss. and South Bend Jr. Miss, 1965, Milton J. Cross award Met. Opera Guild, 1968; prize winner Met. Opera. Nat. Auditions, 1968; F.K. Weyerhauser scholar Met. Opera, 1967. Mem. Am. Guild Mus. Artists, Internat. Platform Assn. Clubs: St. Mary's Acad. Alumnae Assn., Delta Gamma. Office: EB-SKO Prodns 1726 Sherman Ave Evanston IL 60201

EBERSOLE, MARY ELLEN FRANCES, nurse, electrologist; b. Washington, Oct. 4, 1940; d. William Ignatius and Madelina Rose (Daidone) Hayes; m. Harold Robert Ebersole, Feb. 20, 1965; children: Eileen Marie, Kathleen. Diploma with honors, Meml. Hosp. Roxborough, 1964; cert. in electrolysis, U. Md., 1976, Eastern Inst. Practical Electrolysis, 1977. Cert. Internat. Bd. Electrologists, Nat. Commn. Electrologists. Perioperative nurse Washington Hosp. Ctr., 1964-65, operating room head nurse, 1966-68, operating room coordinator, 1969-73; perioperative nurse VA Med. Ctr., Washington, 1973-76, urodynamics clinician, perioperative endourology nurse, charge nurse urology clinic, 1976—, RN orientation instr., with med. student orientation staff, 1979—; electrologist Columbia (Md.) Electrolysis, 1978-87; electrologist, pres. Exec. Electrolysis, Laurel, Md. and Columbia, 1987—; instr. Basic Cardiac Life Support Am. Heart Assn.; chmn. bd. Mail Box Etc, Inc., College Park, Md. Mem. Help for Incontinent People, Union, S.C., 1984—. Recipient Outstanding Service award Disabled Am. Vets., 1979. Mem. Am. Urologists Assn. of Allied Health Profls. of Mid-Atlantic, Urodynamic Sub Specialist Group, Am. Assn. Operating Room Nurses (cert.), Am. Electrology Assn. (chair infection control standards com. 1987, co-chair hygiene and safety com. 1988—, Pres.'s award 1988), Md. Assn. Profl. Electrologists (recording sec. 1980, corr. sec. 1981), Am. Running and Fitness Assn., Nat. Assn. Female Execs. Democrat. Roman Catholic. Home: 11038 Montgomery Rd Beltsville MD 20705 Office: Exec Electrolysis 10794 Hickory Ridge Rd Hawthorne Office Pk Columbia MD 21044 also: Montpelier Exec Ctr 9811 Mallard Dr Laurel MD 20708

EBERSOLE, PATRICIA SUE, advertising and marketing executive, educator; b. Poughkeepsie, N.Y., Nov. 6, 1952; d. Edward and Virgnia Mae (Van Derof) E.; m. Daniel Joseph Burke, Sept. 10, 1988. AAS, Dutchess Community Coll., Poughkeepsie, 1974; student, Art Ctr. Coll. of Design, 1976-77; BS, SUNY, 1981. Graphic artist So. Dutchess News, Wappingers Falls, N.Y., 1974; asst. illustrator Jarvis Studio, Westwod, Calif., 1975-78; freelance illustrator Poughkeepsie, N.Y., 1978—; graphic dir. Ulster County Coun. for the Arts, Kingston, N.Y., 1979; art dir. Diversified Creative Svcs., Kingston, 1979; graphic designer Advertiser's Graphic Svcs., Poughkeepsie, 1981-82; pres. Ebersole Graphiks, Poughkeepsie, 1982—; adj. instr. Dutchess Community Coll., 1980-87. Recipient Recognition award IBM Corp., 1987, Cert. of Excellence, Strathmore Graphics Gallery, 1988, Desi award Graphic Design, 1984, 88, Excellence award Printing Industries of Am., 1988, Activities award Nat. Assn. for Campus Activities, 1985, Gold and Silver awards HUAMA ECLAT, 1989. Mem. Graphic Artists Guild of N.Y., Mid-Hudson Mktg. Assn., Nat. Fedn. Ind. Bus., C. of C., Aquatic Explorers, So. Dutchess Horseman's Assn., Creative Club. Office: Ebersole Graphiks 9 High Ridge Rd Hopewell Junction NY 12533

EBERT, JENNIFER ANN, writer; b. Syracuse, N.Y., Apr. 13, 1966; d. Robert John and Renee Ann (Canonico) E. BA in History, SUNY, Geneseo, 1988. Communication editor CPAC, Inc., Leicester, N.Y., 1987-89; asst. dir. devel. Cath. Diocese Syracuse, 1989—; freelance writer Bath, Inc., Syracuse. Vol. ARC, Syracuse, Spl. Olympics Livingston County, Geneseo, N.Y., 1987-88. Mem. Nat. Orgn. for Female Execs., Pub. Rels. Soc. Am. Republican. Roman Catholic. Home: 301 Orchard St Apt B3 Fayetteville NY 13066 Office: Cath Diocese Syracuse 1342 Lancaster Ave Syracuse NY 13201

EBERT, NORMA J., small business owner; b. Bowling Green, Ohio, Sept. 7, 1931; d. James C. Heckman and Mabel E. Heaton; m. George A. Walton, Nov. 5, 1950 (div. 1979); children: Rickey A., Jeffrey, A. Wesley A. Brentley A; m. Alfred V. Ebert, June 5, 1982 (dec. 1987). Student, Terra Tech. Coll., 1980. Laser disc operator Ohio No. Tel. Co., Bowling Green, Ohio, 1949-51; credit dept. So. Calif. Music Co., San Diego, 1951-52; pvt. br. exch. operator Bank of Am., Chula Vista, Calif., 1952-56; sec., clk. Moline (Ohio) Mcpl. Ct., 1956-61; pvt. Kolonial Kiddie Kare Day Care, Moline, 1961-65; dir. asst. Dr. Richard Semon, Ohio, 1975-77; social worker Dept. Human Svcs. Ottawa County, Port Clinton, Ohio, 1977-82; sec., v.p. Louis Ebert & Son Paint & Decorating Co., Cleve., 1982-86; real estate developer, prin. Ebert Walton Inc., Lakeside, Ohio, 1987—; social worker Dept. of Human Svcs. Adult Social Svcs., 1977-82; sales cons. West Harbor Landings, Marblehead, Ohio. Trustee United Meth. Ch., Lakeside, 1988—; v.p. Lake Twp. PTA, 1962-64. Mem. Team Bowling Assn. (pres. 1978-79), Lake TWP Mothers Club (pres. 1961-62), Elks Lodge. Republican. Methodist. Home: 465 Westwood Lakeside OH 43440 Office: 8850 Hartshorn Rd Lakeside OH 43440

EBITZ, ELIZABETH KELLY, lawyer; b. LaPorte, Ind., June 9, 1950; d. Joseph Monahan and Ann Mary (Barrett) Kelly; m. David MacKinnon Ebitz, Jan. 23, 1971 (div. 1981). AB with honors, Smith Coll., 1972; JD cum laude, Boston U., 1975. Bar: Maine 1979, Mass 1975, U.S. Supreme Ct 1982, U.S. Dist. Ct. Mass. 1976, U.S. Dist. Ct. Maine 1979, U.S. Ct. Appeals (1st cir.) 1976. Law clk. Boston Legal Assistance Project, 1973-75; law clk., assoc. Law Offices of John J. Thornton, Boston, 1974-76; ptnr. Ebitz & Zurn, Northampton, Mass., 1976-79; assoc. Gross, Minsky, Mogul & Singal, Bangor, Maine, 1979-80; pres. Elizabeth Kelly Ebitz, P.A., Bangor, 1980—. Pres. Greater Bangor Rape Crisis Bd., 1983-85; bd. dirs. Greater Bangor Area Shelter, 1985—, Maine Women's Lobby, 1986-89, No. Maine Bread for the World, 1987—; bd. dirs. Am. Heart Assn., Maine, 1989—; mem. various peace, feminist and hunger orgns., Bangor, 1982—. Named Young Career Woman of Hampshire County, Nat. Bus. and Profl. Women, Northampton, 1979. Mem. ABA, Assn. Trial Lawyers Am., Sigma Xi. Democrat. Roman Catholic. Home: 111 Maple St Bangor ME 04401 Office: 15 Columbia St PO Box 641 Bangor ME 04401

EBLE, SUSAN LOUISE, interior designer; b. Grand Rapids, Mich., Aug. 31, 1961; d. Robert Earl and Beatrice Elizabeth (Bauman) H.; m. William Earnest. Assoc. degree, St. Clair County Community Coll., Port Huron, 1979-81. Designer/sales Thompsosn's of St. Clair, St. Clair, Mich., 1981-85; interior design instr. St. Clair County Community Coll., Pt. Huron, 1984-85; designer/sales Co-ordinated Industries, Livonia, Mich., 1987-88, sales mgr., 1988-90; designer, sales Schwark Furniture, St. Clair, 1986-87, Bus. Resources, Southfield, Mich., 1990—. Author: Accent on Dessign, 1985, 1986. Mem. Community Devel. planning com., Livonia C. of C., Livonia, 1987—. Mem. Interior Design Soc. (Detroit chpt. pres. 1988-89 chmn. bd.), Jaycees (Rochester). Republican. Methodist.

EBRAHIMI, FERESHTEH, materials science and engineering educator; b. Tehran, Iran, Jan. 2, 1951; came to U.S., 1979; d. Soltan Ali and Rokhsare (Zia) E.; m. Salman Zia-Ebrahimi, 1971 (div. 1984); 1 child, Sara. PhD in Metallurgy, Colo. Sch. Mines, 1982; MPhil in Metallurgy, Surrey (Eng.) U., 1976; BS in Metall. Engring., Arya-Mehr U. Tech., Tehran, 1972. Instr. dept. metall. engring. Arya-Mehr U. Tech., 1972-77; cons. Internat. Tng. Cons., Tehran, 1977-78; rsch. asst. dept. metall. engring. Colo. Sch. Mines, Golden, 1979-82, postdoctoral assoc., 1982-83; rsch. scientist fracture and deformation div. Nat. Bur. Standards, Boulder, Colo., 1983-84; asst. prof. dept. materials sci. and engring. U. Fla., Gainesville, 1984-89, assoc. prof., 1989—; cons.to workshop in field, 1985. Contbr. articles to profl. jours. Grantee DARPA, 1988—, GM Corp., 1987-88, Oak Ridge Assoc. Univs., 1985-87, Nat. Bur. Standards, 1985-87, Materials Engring. Assocs., Inc., 1984-87. Mem. Am. Soc. Metals (session co-chmn. 1985), Metall. Soc. AIME (mem. com.), ASTM (publ. award 1989), Sigma Xi. Office: U Fla Materials Sci and Engring Gainesville FL 32611

ECHOLS, DOROTHY JUNG, geological consultant; b. N.Y.C., Sept. 9, 1916; d. John Frederick and Dorothy Kathy (Meyerhoff) Jung; widowed; children: Leonard, Jon, Lizette, William. BA, NYU, 1936; MA, Columbia U., 1938. Geologist Am. Republics, Houston, 1938-41, The Texas Co., N.Y.C., 1941-42, Pond Fork Oil & Gas, W.Va., 1942-45; rsch. assoc., prof. Washington U., 1951-82; cons. Curtis & Echols, Bellaire, Tex., 1979—. Home: 218 Calverton Rd Ferguson MO 63135 Office: Curtis & Echols 800 Anderson Bellaire TX 77401

ECHOLS, IVOR TATUM, educator, assistant dean; b. Oklahoma City, Dec. 28, 1919; d. Israel E. and Katie (Bingley) Tatum; AB, U. Kans., 1942; postgrad. (A.R.C. scholar) U. Nebr., 1945-46; MS in Social Work (Nat. Urban League fellow, Porter R. Lee fellow), Columbia, 1952, postgrad. (NIMH fellow), U. So. Calif., 1961-62, D.S.W., 1968; m. Kenneth Johnston, Dec. 28, 1948 (div. June 1951); 1 child, Kalu Helene; m. 2d, Sylvester J. Echols, June 13, 1954 (div. 1976); 1 child, Kim Arnett. Tchr. social studies high sch., Holdenville, Okla., 1942-43, Geary, Okla., 1943-45; caseworker A.R.C., Chgo., 1946-47; resident group worker, Dosoris House for Teen-Age Girls, Community Svcs. Soc., N.Y.C., 1950-51; supr. group work Walnut Grove Ctr. Neighborhood Clubs, Oklahoma City, 1948-51; program dir. Camp Lookout YWCA, Denver, 1951; dir. program svcs. Presbyn. Neighborhood Svcs., Detroit, summer 1960, supr. group work Merrill-Palmer Inst., Detroit, 1951-70; asst. dir. Merrill-Palmer Camp, Dryden, Mich., 1951-59; prof. Sch. Social Work, U. Conn., West Hartford, 1970-89, also asst. dean; ret., 1989; del. Inter-Univ. Consortium of Social Devel., Hong Kong, 1980; chairperson Conn. adv. com. U.S. Commn. Civil Rights. Mem. Ad Hoc Com. Citizens Concerned with Equal Ednl. Opportunity, Detroit, 1964—; cons. to N.E.A. Conf. Family Camping Washington, 1959, ednl. film Scott Paper Co., Phila., 1963, 64; summer study skills project Presbyn. Ch. Bd. Nat. Missions, Knoxville, Tenn., 1965—; sec. United Neighborhood Ctrs. Am.; pres. Protestant Community Svcs., Detroit, 1969-70; trustee Conn. Energy Found., 1987—; commr. Conn. Hist. Commn., 1986—. Recipient Educator Human Rights award UN Assn. , 1987, Sojourner Truth award Detroit chpt. Nat. Assn. Negro Bus. and Profl. Women, 1969, UN Assn. award for Edn. and Women's Rights, 1987; named Conn. Social Worker of Year, 1979. Mem. Nat. Assn. Colored Women's Clubs (participant White House Conf. on Children and Youth 1960), A.M.E. Ministers Wives, Acad. Certified Social Workers, Delta Sigma Theta. Mem. A.M.E. Ch. Home: 51 Chestnut Dr Windsor CT 06095 Office: U Conn 1800 Asylum Ave W Hartford CT 06117

ECHOLS, M. EILEEN, lawyer; b. Oklahoma City, Mar. 16, 1951; d. O.C. Steve and Eileen E. (Carter) Dodson; m. David W. Echols, Aug. 12, 1977; children: Matthew, Jonathan, Meredit. BS, Cen. State U., Edmond, Okla., 1974; MBA, Cen. State U., 1975, PhD, 1979; JD, Oklahoma City U., 1979. Bar: Okla., U.S. Dist. Ct. (we. dist.) Okla. Tchr. mentally handicapped students Oklahoma City pub. schs., tchr./coordinator; pvt. practice law Oklahoma City; judge Spl. Dist. Ct. Oklahoma City, 1989—. Contbr. articles to profl. jours. Mem. Okla. Bar Assn. (chairperson jud. com., family rels. sect.), Okla. County Bar Assn., Lions Internat. Home: 8501 S Pennsylvania Oklahoma City OK 73159 Office: Oklahoma County Courthouse 602 Oklahoma Courthouse Oklahoma City OK 73102

ECK, ANDREA LOUISE, marketing executive, human resources recruiter; b. Easton, Pa., Oct. 31, 1962; d. Charles Anthony Bottiglieri and Almeda Louise (Eck) Migliazza; m. Anthony Imperato. Student Northampton County Area Community Coll., Boston Ctr. for Edn., Weist Barron Acting, Walnut St Theatre Sch. Asst. mgr., salesperson Sigals Country Corner Shoe Dept., Easton, Pa., 1980; telemarketing rep. Sammons Communications, Easton, 1981; customer service rep. Christmas Club Corp., Easton, 1980-81, mgr., 1982-83, account exec., Framingham, Mass., 1984-86; self-employed advt. sales and mktg. exec., Phila., 1986-87; telemktg. rep. Phila. Drama Guild, 1986—; dir. admissions, talent and model recruiter John Casablancas Modeling and Career Ctr., Phila., 1988—, Millside Glen Devel. Corp., Elmsford, N.Y., 1989—. Reviewer theater sect. TV and Radio Reporter, 1986—, Steppin' Out TV mag. Sponsor Christian Children's Fund, Richmond, Va., 1984, 85, 86; fund-raiser Spl. Olympics, 1987, 89. Recipient Disting. Achievement award Christmas Club Corp., 1985—. Mem. Am. Fedn. TV and Radio Artists. Lutheran. Avocations: acting, travel, sports, aerobics. Home: 2449 Esplanade Ave Bronx NY 10469 Office: Millside Glen Devel Corp 60 Glen Rd Eastchester NY 10709

ECK, DOROTHY FRITZ, state senator; b. Sequim, Wash., Jan. 23, 1924; d. Ira Edward and Ida (Hokanson) Fritz; B.S. in Secondary Edn., Mont. State U., 1961, M.S. in Applied Sci., 1966; m. Hugo Eck, Dec. 16, 1942 (dec. Feb. 1988); children: Laurence, Diana. Mgr. property mgmt. bus., 1955—; conf. coord. Am. Agrl. Econs. Assn., 1967-68; state-local coord. Office of Gov. Mont., Helena, 1972-77; mem. Mont. State Senate, 1981—; mem. Mont. Environ. Quality Council, 1981-87. Bd. dirs. Methodist Youth Fellowship, 1960-64, Mont. Council for Effective Legislature, 1977-78, Rocky Mountain Environ. Council, 1982—; del., Western v.p. Mont. Constl. Conv., 1971-72; chmn. Gov.'s Task Force on Citizen Participation, 1976-77; mem. adv. com. No. Rockies Resource and Tng. Center (now No. Lights Inst.), 1979-81. Recipient Outstanding Alumna award Mont. State U., 1981, Centennial Equity award, 1989. Mem. LWV (state pres. 1967-70), Common Cause, Nat. Women's Polit. Caucus. Democrat.

ECKARDT, GLADYS EVANGELINE (MRS. KARL PAUL KONRAD ECKARDT), librarian; b. Hartland, N.Y., Sept. 7, 1912; d. Isaac John and Flora Caroline (Hofmeister) Beach; student U. Buffalo, 1930-32; m. Karl Paul Konrad Eckardt, Oct. 19, 1940; 1 dau., Susan (Mrs. Edward Misiewicz). Dir. Wood-Ridge (N.J.) Pub. Library, 1956-59, Rutherford (N.J.) Pub. Library, 1959-85; ref. librarian, Jane Bancroft Cook Library, U. South Fla., Sarasota, 1986—. Trustee Wood-Ridge Pub. Library, 1954-56. Mem. Am., N.J. (sec. 1964-65, chmn. N.J. insts. 1968), Bergen-Passaic (pres. 1964-66), N.Y. library assn., Pub. Relations Council, Bergen County Small Libraries (v.p. 1963), Rutgers Alumni Assn., Friends of Library. Club: Rutherford Women's College. Office: U South Fla Jane Bancroft Cook Libr 7236 Pennsylvania Ave Sarasota FL 34243

ECKERSON, NANCY FIEDLER, dietitian; b. Milw., Sept. 24, 1940; d. Lawrence Louis and Catherine Jeanne (McCarten) Fiedler; m. Raymond Grover Eckerson, July 27, 1984. BA, Rosary Coll., 1962; MS, No. Ill. U., 1979; postgrad., Gov.'s State U., 1989. Dietetic intern St. Louis U., 1963; clin. dietitian Presbyn. St. Luke's Hosp., Chgo., 1963-79; coordiantor dietetics and patient food svc. Ingalls Meml. Hosp., Harvey, Ill., 1981—; instr. Rush U., Chgo., 1980-81. Author: Quality Assurance Manual for Dietitians, 1976, A Nurse's Guide to Diabetes, 1979. Mem. Am. Dietetic Assn. (quest subcom. 1985-87, Outstanding Svc. award 1987), Ill. Dietetic Assn. (co-chair legis. 1981-83, licensure 1983-86, Outstanding Svc. award 1985), Am. Coll. Healthcare Execs., Suburban Planning Agy., South Suburban Dietetic Assn., Omicron Nu. Office: Ingalls Meml Hosp One Ingalls Dr Harvey IL 60426

ECKERT, ARLENE GAIL, child protective services specialist; b. Euclid, Ohio, July 28, 1956; d. Robert S. and Madolyn A. (King) Lough; m. Theodore Eckert III, May 14, 1983 (div. Oct. 1985). BS in Law Enforcement, U. No. Ala., 1978. Cert. social worker. Probation, parole officer Tenn. Dept. Corrections, Columbia, 1978-83; child protection svc. specialist II Tex. Dept. Human Svcs., Killeen, 1984-86; child protective svcs. specialist IV, Tex. Dept. Human Svcs., Gatesville, 1988—; coord. employees assistance project Associated Counseling Svcs., Harker Heights, Tex., 1986-88. Bd. dirs. Truancy Bd. Pulaski, Tenn., 1978-84, Truancy Bd., Lawrenceburg, Tenn., 1978-84, Multidisciplinary Child Abuse Rev. Team, Columbia, Tenn., 1979-84. Mem. Am. Correctional Assn., Tenn. State Employees Assn., NAFE. Lutheran. Office: Gatesville Dept Human Svcs 1309-A E Main St Gatesville TX 76528

ECKERT, BRENDA LYNNE, nurse; b. Harrisburg, Pa., Aug. 27, 1961; d. Ralph Eugene and Lois Ann (Starr) E. BS in Nursing, York Coll. of Pa., 1983. Cert. med./surg. nurse. Staff nurse U. Hosp., Hershey (Pa.) Med. Ctr., 1983, nurse clinician, 1983-86, primary nurse clinician, 1986-89, sr. staff nurse, 1989—. Mem. Disaster Health Svcs. Team, Harrisburg Area Chpt. Am. Red Cross; basic cardiac life support instr. Am. Heart Assn., South Cen. Pa. Dist., Lancaster, 1987—. Mem. Pa. Nurses' Assn. (bd. dirs. Dist. 15 1985-89, nominating com. 1984-85, by-laws com. 1988-89), Soc. for Peripheral Vascular Nursing, Am. Nurses' Assn. Council on Med. Surgical Nursing Practice, Am. Nurses' Assn., Sigma Theta Tau, New Horizons. Republican. Methodist. Home: 111 E Coover St Mechanicsburg PA 17055-4220

ECKERT, GERALDINE GONZALES, language professional, educator, entrepreneur; b. N.Y.C., Aug. 5, 1948; d. Albert and Mercedes (Martinez) Gonzales; m. Robert Alan Eckert, Apr. 1, 1972; children: Lauren Elaine, Alison Elizabeth. BA, Ladycliff Coll., Highland Falls, N.Y., 1970; student, U. Valencia, Spain, 1968; MA, N.Y.U., 1971; student, Instituto de Cultura Hispanica, Madrid, 1970-71. Tchr. Spanish Clarkstown High Sch. N. (N.Y.), 1971-73, Rambam Torah Inst., Beverly Hills, Calif., 1973-75; translator election materials City of Beverly Hills, 1976-83; edn. cons. Los Angeles County of Calif. Dept. Forestry, Capistrano Beach, 1982-84; lang. services and protocol Los Angeles Olympic Organizing Com., 1983-84; pension adminstr. Pension Architects, Inc., Los Angeles, 1984-87; instr. El Camino Coll., Torrance, Calif., 1987-88, Santa Monica (Calif.) Coll., 1975-89; owner, pres. Bilingual Pension Cons., L.A., 1987—; bd. dirs. Institute for Hispanic Cultural Studies, Los Angeles; spl. asst. to Internat. Olympic Com., Lausanne, Switzerland, 1983—. V.p. Notre Dame Acad. Assoc., West L. A., 1987—; mem. L.A. March of Dimes Ambassadors Group, 1987; co-founder, pres. Blind Cleaning Express, L.A., 1989—; bd. dirs. Inst. Hispanic Cultural Studies, L.A., 1984-89; spl. asst. to pres. Internat. Olympic Com. Lausanne, Switzerland, 1983—. Democrat. Roman Catholic. Clubs: Five Ring, Los Angeles, Friends of Sport, Amateur Athletic Found., Los Angeles. Office: 3728 Overland Ave Los Angeles CA 90034

ECKERT, HELEN ANN, hospital executive; b. Huntington, Ind., Aug. 20, 1940; d. Francis Anthony and Helen Elizabeth (Hartman) Fink; m. Patrick E. Eckert, Jan. 30, 1965 (div. 1978); children: Patricia, Michelle, Chris, Michael, Laura. BS in Nursing, Marquette U., 1964; MS in Nursing, Ind. U., Indpls., 1984; MPA, Ind. U., Ft. Wayne, 1988. R.N., Ind. Staff nurse Parkview Meml. Hosp., Ft. Wayne, 1964; instr. pediatric nursing Parkview HSch. Nursing, Ft. Wayne, 1964-65; staff nurse, then dir. ob. Huntington (Ind.) Meml. Hosp., 1974-79, v.p., dir. nursing, 1979-88, sr. v.p., 1988—. Bd. dirs. Pathfinder, Inc., Huntington, 1983-89, chmn. bd. dirs., 1988. Mem. Am. Orgn. Nurse Execs., Ind. Orgn. Nurse Execs. (pres. 1986), Northeast Ind. Orgn. Nurse Execs. (pres. 1988-89), Rotary, Sigma Theta Tau, Pi Alpha Sigma, Kappa Kappa Kappa (pres. 1971). Republican. Roman Catholic. Home: 1235 Terrace Dr Huntington IN 46750 Office: Huntington Meml Hosp 1215 Etna Ave Huntington IN 46750

ECKERT, JACQUELYN MARIA, editor; b. Buffalo, June 6, 1952; d. George Henry and Patricia Ann (Rott) Bilkey; m. Timothy Paul Murphy, Jan. 29, 1970 (div. May 1981); children: Paul Jeffrey, Jeremy Michael; m. Warren Lee Eckert, Dec. 5, 1987. Student, Ind. U., 1984. Adminstrv. asst. Western N.Y. Cath. Visitor, Buffalo, 1979-81; sec. religious edn. Our Sunday Visitor, Huntington, Ind., 1981-84, editorial asst. periodicals dept., 1985, staff editor periodicals and books, editor My Daily Visitor, 1985—, coord. Diocesan edits., 1986-88, assoc. editor books, 1987—. Editor, complier: Photo Directory of U.S. Catholic Hierarchy, 1987, 90. Candidate for rep. Ind. Gen. Assembly 21st Dist., 1984; mem. LaFontaine Arts Coun., Huntington County, 1985-88; mem. Huntington County Dems., 1986-88. Mem. Cath. Press Assn. Office: Our Sunday Visitor Pub 200 Noll Pla Huntington IN 46750

ECKERT, JEAN PATRICIA, educator; b. Pitts., July 22, 1935; d. Homer Michael and Berdena Leona (Kessler) Canel; m. William L. Eckert, June 13, 1959; 1 child, Suzanne Mary. BS, Indiana U. Pa., 1957; postgrad., U. Pitts., 1958-59, U. San Diego, 1981. Cert. pub. instrn., Pa. Elem. tchr. Pine-Richland Sch. Dist., Gibsonia, Pa., 1957-60; substitute tchr. Pine-Richland Sch. Dist., 1963-65; elem. tchr. Shaler Twp. Sch. Dist., Glenshaw, Pa., 1965-66, St. Scholastica Sch., Diocese of Pitts., Aspinwall, Pa., 1966—. Judge election 4th dist. Republican Party, Aspinwall, 1962-65. Mem. AAUW, Nat. Cath. Edn. Assn., Cath. Lay Edn. Assn., Vols. in Teaching Alternatives, Ind. U. Pa. Alumni Assn., Delta Zeta (sec. 1955, pres. 1956 Gamma Phi chpt.). Roman Catholic. Home: 210 12th St Aspinwall PA 15215

ECKERT, LISA LORETTA, creative director; b. Detroit, Oct. 1, 1961; d. Philip Henry and Mary Loretta (Kalinin) E. BFA in Visual Communication, No. Ill. U., 1984. Graphic designer Mark Anderson Assocs., Arlington Heights, Ill., 1984-87; creative dir. Mark Anderson Assocs., Indpls., 1988-89; art dir. Starmark Advt., Chgo., 1987; freelance art dir. Eckert Design, Chgo., 1987-88, 89—; ptnr. MacLean/Eckert Communications, Chgo., 1989—; co-founder Art for Art's Sake, Chgo., 1989—. Vol. John Holowinski for Congress, Chgo., 1988, Young Irish Fellowship, Chgo. Area Runners Assn. Mem. Soc. Typog. Arts, Art Dirs. Club Ind. Democrat. Roman Catholic. Home: 1842 W Cortland Chicago IL 60622 Office: PO Box 47761 Chicago IL 60647

ECKERT, OPAL EFFIE, education educator, retired; b. Bolckow, Mo., Mar. 19, 1905; d. Price Wallingford and Mary Jane (Pittsenbarger) Calvert; m. Thomas H. Eckert, June 19, 1929 (dec.). BS in Edn., Northwest Mo. State U., 1928, AB, 1944, MS in Edn., 1963. Instr. prin. Butler, Bolckow, Pickering, Butler Blockow, Mo., 1928-44; instr. dir. pub. Maryville (Mo.) High Sch., 1944-65; freelance writer, feature writer, columnist Maryville Daily Forum, St. Joseph Gazette, Newspress, Mo., 1955—; dir. journalism workshops Northwest Mo. State U., Maryville, 1963-74; instr. English, journalism, chmn. Northwest Mo. State Univ., Maryville, 1965-74; cons. Project Communicate, Northwest, Mo., 1964-67. Author: Grassroot Reflections, vols. I and II; contbr. articles to profl. jours. Delegate, U.S. White House Conf. Aging, Wash., 1981; sec., treas. Mo. Div. AAUW. Named Journalism Tchr. of Yr. Newspaper Fund, Inc., 1963, one of Mo. Outstanding Vols., 1981, Pioneer Educator, 1979, Disting. Mo. Woman AAUW-Mo. div., 1990. Mem. Mo. Assn. Tchrs. of English (pres., life mem.), Mo. Writers' Guild, Maryville C. of C. Democrat. Home: 610 W Halsey #5 Maryville MO 64468

ECKERT-BURTON, SUZANNE MARY, technical communications administrator; b. Pitts., May 11, 1960; d. William Lawrence and Jean Patricia (Canel) Eckert; m. William Robert Burton; 1 child, William Cody. Student, U. N.C., 1978-79, U. San Diego, 1981; BS in Indsl. Adminstrn., Carnegie-Mellon U., 1982; postgrad., U. Pa., Wharton, 1986. Sec. Liken Svcs., Pitts., 1978; mgr. various engring. positions Bell Atlantic, Arlington, Va., 1982—, mgr. systems planning, 1990—; tech. intern Bell Communications Rsch., Morristown, N.J., 1986-87. Vol. tchr. Vols. in Teaching Am., Langhorne, Pa., 1986; notary pub. Allegheny County, Pitts., 1982-84; exec. advisor Jr. Achievement, 1982-84; disbursal subcom. Bell Atlantic Polit. Action com., Phila., 1985-87. Scholar Carnegie-Mellon U. Women's Club, 1981. Mem. Carnegie-Mellon U. Alumni Soc., Mortar Bd., Lambda Sigma. Home: 15132 Athey Rd Burtonsville MD 20866

ECKHAUS, ELEANOR ANNETTE, portfolio manager; b. N.Y.C., Sept. 3, 1956; d. Abe and Faye (Flam) E. Cert. in french lit., U. Caen, Normandy, France, 1975; BA in Comparative Lit. and French, SUNY, Binghamton, 1977. Rsch. and securities analyst Prescott, Ball & Turben, N.Y.C., 1977-79; portfolio mgr. Sequa Corp., N.Y.C., 1979—; speaker at profl. confs. Mem. The Nat. Option and Futures Soc. (dir. 1988—), Tribute to Women and Industry (twin award 1989). Office: Sequa Corp 200 Park Ave New York NY 10166

ECKHOFF, ROSALEE, nurse; b. Falls City, Nebr., Apr. 24, 1930; d. George and Blanche (Montague) Rieger; R.N., Nebr. Meth. Sch. Nursing, 1951; m. Robert Dale Eckhoff, Feb. 21, 1954; children—Dixie Dee, Monte Ray. Dir. nursing Sutherland (Nebr.) Hosp., 1952-55; head nurse med. ward Hastings (Nebr.) Regional Center, 1957-61; night supr. Good Samaritan Village, Hastings, 1962; charge nurse pediatrics Mary Lanning Hosp., Hastings, 1962-65; night supr. Broken Bow (Nebr.) Hosp., 1965-66; dir. nursing Bethel Nursing Home, Ainsworth, Nebr., 1966-67, adminstr., 1967-69; part-time staff nurse Ainsworth Hosp., 1969-70; nursing home counselor Norfolk (Nebr.) Regional Center, 1970-72; night supr. Albion (Nebr.) Boone County Hosp., 1970-75; adminstrv. dir. Mideast Nebr., Albion and Columbus Mental Health Clinic, 1975-76; dir. nursing Phelps Meml. Health Center, Holdrege, Nebr., 1976—. Mem. Nebr. Soc. Nursing Service Adminstrs. (sec.-treas.), Nebr. Mental Health Assn., Luth. Ch. Women, Dist. 4 Hosp. Assn. (dir. nurses), Am. Orgn. Nurse Execs., Nebr. Orgn. Nurse Execs.(pres. elect 1989, pres. 1990). Home: 1015 West Ave Holdrege NE 68949 Office: 1220 Miller St PO Box 828 Holdrege NE 68949

ECKLAND, DIANE MARIE, employee relations specialist; b. Worcester, Mass., Nov. 11, 1958; d. Philip Donald and Christine Ann (Giovannucci) Eckland. BA, Boston Coll., 1980; MBA, U. Mass., 1982. Employee rels. asst. Celanese Corp., Narrows, Va., 1982-83, employee rels. rep., 1983-85; employee rels. rep. Celanese Corp., Charlotte, N.C., 1985-87, Mobil Corp., Woodland, Calif., 1987-88; employee rels. advisor Mobil Corp., Temple, Tex., 1988-89; career devel. advisor Mobil Corp., Rochester, N.Y., 1989—. Dir. ski race team Charlotte Skibees, 1986, 87; mem. March of Dimes Walk-Am. Named Top Achievement Advisor, Jr. Achievement, 1985, 86. Mem. Am. Soc. Personnel Adminstrs. (corp. challenge com. 1988, Honor 1989), Temple C. of C., Rotary, Charlotte Jaycees (v.p. 1986-87, Rookie of Qtr. 1985, Keyman award 1986, Dir. of the Yr. 1986, 87), N.C. Jaycees (mem. all star team 1986-87, Jaycee Speak Up award 1985). Republican. Roman Catholic. Home: 59 Lac Kine Dr Rochester NY 14618 Office: Mobil Chem 1150 Pittsford-Victor Rd Pittsford NY 14534

ECKLEY, ALICIA KATHRYN, writer, editor, public relations specialist; b. Columbus, Ohio, Mar. 31, 1959; d. Richard McCoy and Helen Louise (Martin) E. BA in Journalism, Ohio State U., 1981. Editorial asst. Diagnostic Imaging Mag., Miller Freeman Publs., San Francisco, 1982-83, asst. editor, 1983-84; pub. affairs mgr. Squibb Corp., Princeton, N.J., 1984-87; pub. relations mgr., Diasonics, Inc., South San Francisco, Ca., 1987-89; prin. Communication Essentials, San Francisco, 1989—. Mem. Pub. Relations Soc. Am., Media Alliance, Differently Employed Women.

ECKSTEIN, MARLENE R., vascular radiologist; b. Poughkeepsie, N.Y., Sept. 6, 1948; d. Marc and Lola (Charm) E.; A.B., Vassar Coll., 1970; M.D., Albert Einstein Coll. Medicine, 1973. Diplomate Nat. Bd. Med. Examiners; cert. Am. Bd. Radiology. Intern in medicine Yale-New Haven Med. Center, 1973-74, resident in diagnostic radiology, 1974-77; asst. radiologist, chief vascular radiology sect. South Nassau Communities Hosp., Oceanside, N.Y., 1977-78, asso. radiologist, chief vascular radiology sect., 1978-81, asst. dir. dept. radiology, chief vascular radiology sect., 1981-83; asst. prof. clin. radiology SUNY-Stony Brook Med. Sch., 1980-83; instr. radiology, Harvard Med. Sch., 1983-84, asst. prof., 1984—; asst. radiologist Mass. Gen. Hosp., 1983-87, assoc. radiologist, 1987—. Mem. exec. com. and hosp. chmn. United Jewish Appeal of Physicians and Dentists of Nassau County (N.Y.), 1981-83. Fellow Am. Coll. Angiology, Soc. Cardiovascular and Interventional Radiology; mem. Internat. Platform Assn., Am. Coll. Radiology, Am. Inst. Ultrasound in Medicine, Mass. Radiol. Soc., Am. Assn. Women Radiologists, Am. Med. Women's Assn., AMA, Mass. Med. Soc., New Eng. Soc. Cardiovascular and Interventional Radiology (pres. 1985-86), Radiol. Soc. N.Am., Designer and developer line of vascular catheters. Avocations: writing poetry, exercising, video and electronic equipment. Home: 141 Fulton Ave # 312 Poughkeepsie NY 12603 Office: Mass Gen Hosp Vascular Radiology Sect Boston MA 02114

ECTON, DONNA R., dietary products and services company executive; b. Kansas City, Mo., May 10, 1947; d. Allen Howard and Marguerite (Page) E.; m. Victor H. Maragni, June 16, 1986; children: Mark, Gregory. BA, Wellesley Coll., 1969; MBA, Harvard U., 1971. V.p. Chem. Bank, N.Y.C., 1972-79, Citibank, N.A., N.Y.C., 1979-81; pres. MBA Resources, Inc., N.Y.C., 1981-83; v.p. adminstrn., officer Campbell Soup Co., Camden, N.J., 1983-89; chmn. Triangle Mfg. Corp. subs. Campbell Soup Co., Raleigh, N.C., 1984-87; sr. v.p., officer Nutri/System, Inc., Willow Grove, Pa., 1989—; bd. dirs. Mellon Bank East, Phila., Barnes Group, Inc., Bristol, Conn.; commencement speaker Pa. State U., 1987. Bd. overseers Harvard U., 1984-90; vis. com. Sch. Bus. Adminstrn. Harvard U., 1986-90; mem. Coun. Fgn. Rels., N.Y.C., 1987—; trustee Inst. for Advancement of Health, 1988—; mem. bus. adv. coun. Carnegie-Mellon Grad. Sch. Indsl. Adminstrn., 1988—. Named One of 80 Women to Watch in the 80's, Ms. mag., 1980, One of All Time Top 10 of Last Decade, Glamour mag., 1984, One of 50 Women to Watch Bus. Week mag., 1987, one of 100 Women to Watch Bus. Month mag., 1989; recipient Wellesley Alumnae Achievement award, 1987; Fred Sheldon Fund fellow, 1971-72. Mem. Harvard Bus. Sch. Assn. (pres. exec. council 1983-84), N.Y.C. Harvard Bus. Sch. Club (pres. 1979-80), Wellesley Coll. Nat. Alumnae Assn. (bd. dirs., 1st v.p.). Office: Nutri/System Inc 8 Sentry Pkwy Blue Bell PA 19422-2332

EDDISON, ELIZABETH BOLE, entrepreneur, information specialist; b. Bronxville, N.Y., June 3, 1928; d. Hamilton Biggar and Elizabeth Owsley (Boyle) Bole; m. John Corbin Eddison, Feb. 10, 1951; children: Jonathan B., Elizabeth O., Martha C. AB, Vassar Coll., 1948; MS, Simmons Coll., 1973. Pres., bd. dirs. Lahore (Pakistan)-Am. Sch., 1959-61; chmn. evaluation com. Karachi (Pakistan)-Am. Sch., 1961-63; treas. bd. dirs. La Paz Coop. Sch., Bolivia, 1963-65; v.p. Assn. Am. Fgn. Svc. Women; coord. social svcs. Urban Svc. Corps, Washington Pub. Schs., 1965-69; sec. bd. dirs. Colegio Nueva Granada, Bogota, Colombia, 1969-71; chmn., treas. Warner-Eddison Assocs., Inc., Cambridge, Mass., 1973-88, pres., 1981-88; chmn., v.p. Inmagic Inc., Cambridge, 1984—; mem. steering com. State House Conf. on Small Bus., Mass., 1986-88; mem. bd. advisors Internat. Sch. Info. Mgmt., Irvine, Calif., 1984—, adv. coun. Engring. Info., Inc., N.Y., 1988—; mem. computer applications com. Cary Meml. Libr., Lexington, Mass., 1986. Compiler: Words that Mean Business, 1981; contbr. articles to profl. jours. Mem. adv. com. on internat. investment and tech. devel. U.S. Dept. State, 1980-83; mem. small bus. com. Gov.'s Bus. Adv. Coun., Commonwealth of Mass., 1985-89; co-chair Lexington Dem. Town Com., 1990—. Recipient Alumni Achievement award Simmons Coll., 1986, Disclosure Achievement award Libr. Mgmt. Bus. and Fin. div. Spl. Librs. Assn., 1987. Mem. Info. Industry Assn. (chair emeriti com. 1983-88, co-chair publs. com. 1984-87, chair small bus. forum 1986-89, mem. steering com. mgmt. and tech. coun. 1987-89, chair entrepreneur award com. 1989—, Entrepreneur award 1989), Assoc. Info. Mgrs. (chair publs. com. 1984-86, bd. dirs. 1984-86, Knox award 1988), Spl. Librs. Assn. (chmn. program com./libr. mgmt. div. 1984-85, chmn. profl. devel. com. 1987-88, chmn.-elect 1988, chair 1989-90), Am. Soc. Info. Scientists, Beta Phi Mu. Democrat. Office: Inmagic Inc 2067 Massachusetts Ave Cambridge MA 02140

EDDOWES, E(LIZABETH) ANNE, education educator; b. Sandusky, Ohio, Nov. 23, 1931; d. Carl Emerson and Helen Ruth (Sutter) Evans; m. Edward Everett, June 17, 1956; children: Andrew Wayne, Scott Edward. BS, Ohio State U., Columbus, 1953; MEd, U. Mo., St. Louis, 1969; PhD, Ariz. State U., Tempe, 1977. Tchr. Sandusky (Ohio) Pub. Schs., 1954-56, Alachua County Pub. Schs., Gainesville, Fla., 1957-59; dir. Florissant (Mo.) Coop. Nursery Sch., 1967-70; instr. Florissant Valley Community Coll., Ferguson, Mo., 1970-73; grad. and faculty assoc. Ariz. State U., Tempe, 1974-78, coord. student teaching, 1979-84; child devel. assoc. rep. Coun. for Early Childhood Profl. Recognition, Washington, 1978—; asst. prof. U. Ala., Birmingham, 1985—; validator Nat. Assn. Edn. Young Children, Washington, 1986—; cons. Southside Bapt. Child Devel. Assoc., Brookwood Forest Child Devel. Ctr., Mountain Brook, 1986—. Contbr. articles to profl. jours. Pres., v.p. Family Resource Ctr., Tempe, 1977-79, children's ctr. bd. Desert Palm United Ch. of Christ, Tempe, 1978-84. Recipient Outstanding Svc. award Ariz. State U., 1984. Mem. Orgn. Mondiale pour Edn. Prescolaire, Ala. Assn. on Young Children (pres. 1989-90), Ala. Assn. Early Childhood Tchrs., Jefferson County Assn. Young Children, Phi Delta Kappa, Alpha Phi. Office: U Ala Dept Curriculum & Instrn University Sta Birmingham AL 35294

EDDY, COLETTE ANN, aerial photography studio owner, photographer; b. Sept. 14, 1950; d. William F. and Jeanne (Valeski) Trump; m. Robert K. Eddy, Aug. 21, 1976. AA, St. Petersburg (Fla.) Jr. Coll., 1970; BA, U. South Fla., 1973; MS, Nova U., 1988. Yacht caretaker The Sundowner, St. Petersburg, 1972-73; mgr. Aunt Hattie's Restaurant, St. Petersburg, 1973-79, Johnathan Jones, Inc., St. Petersburg, 1979-80; photographer, sales rep. Smith Aerial Photos, Tampa, Fla., 1980-87; owner, aerial photographer Aerial Innovations, Inc., Tampa, 1987—. Mem. Tampa Mus. Art. Mem. Profl. Photographers Am., Fla. Profl. Photographers (award of Merit 1990), Profl. Aerial Photographers Assn., Tampa C. of C. Republican. Home: 40 Martinique Ave Tampa FL 33606 Office: Aerial Innovations Inc 1413 S Howard Ave Ste 206 Tampa FL 33606

EDDY, DARLENE MATHIS, educator, poet; b. Elkhart, Ind., Mar. 19, 1937; d. William Eugene and Fern (Paulmer) Mathis; m. Spencer Livingston Eddy, Jr., May 23, 1964 (dec. May 1971). B.A., Goshen Coll., 1959; M.A., Rutgers U., 1961, Ph.D., 1967. Instr., lectr. Douglass Coll. and Rutgers U., 1962-64, 66-67; asst. prof. English Ball State U., Muncie, Ind., 1967-70; assoc. prof. Ball State U., 1971-75, prof., 1975—, poet-in-residence, 1989—. Author: The Worlds of King Lear, 1968, Leaf Threads, Wind Rhymes, 1985, Weathering, 1990; poetry editor Forum, 1985-89; contbg. editor Snowy Egret; contbr. articles to English Lang. Notes, Am. Lit., other; contbr. poetry to various publs. Recipient numerous research, creative teaching and creative arts grants; Woodrow Wilson Nat. fellow, 1959-62; Rutgers U. grad. honors fellow, 1964-65. Mem. Nat. Council Tchrs. of English, MLA, AAUP, Shakespeare Assn., DAR (Mayflower chpt. D.C.). Home: 1409 W Cardinal St Muncie IN 47303 Office: Ball State Univ 207B English Muncie IN 47303

EDDY, ESTHER DEWITZ, pharmacist; b. Buffalo, 1926; d. Charles Frederick and Shirley Beulah (Sanderson) Dewitz; m. Russell Warren Eddy, June 8, 1948 (div. May 1977); children: Carl W., James R., Richard G. BS in Pharmacy, U. Buffalo, 1948. Community pharmacist various pharmacies, Buffalo, 1948-57; hosp. pharmacist Niagra Falls (N.Y.) Meml. Hosp., N.Y., 1964-68, Deaconess Hosp., Buffalo, 1968-69; staff pharmacist Children's Hosp. Buffalo, 1969-76, asst. dir. pharmacy, 1976-78, dir. dept. of pharmacy svcs., 1978—; adminstrv. dir. WNY poison control ctr. Western N.Y. poison control ctr., 1978—. Recipient Pharmacy Hall of Fame Pharm. Soc. of Western N.Y., 1989. Mem. N.Y. State Bd. Pharmacy (chmn. 1988-89), Am. Soc. Hosp. Pharmacists, N.Y. State Coun. Hosp. Pharmacists (bd. dir. 1974-76), Advisory Coun. Poison Prevention & Control, Western N.Y. Soc. of Hosp. Pharmacists (treas. 1968-69, pres. 1972), Pharmacy Assn. of Western N.Y., numerous others. Office: Children's Hosp of Buffalo 219 Bryant St Buffalo NY 14222

EDDY, LINDA JOAN, computer consultant; b. South Weymouth, Mass., Dec. 20, 1949; d. LaRue Ernest and Ruth (Adams) E. AA, Palm Beach Jr. Coll., 1969; BS in Edn., Fla. Atlantic U., 1971. Cert. tchr., Fla. Tchr. math. Lyman High Sch., Longwood, Fla., 1971-81; tng. dir., asst. v.p. Citizens Mortgage Corp., St. Petersburg, Fla., 1981-82, compliance officer, v.p. Loan Am. Fin. Corp., 1982-85, v.p. spl. projects to pres., 1985-86, sr. v.p. adminstrn., 1986-87; bank tng. officer CenTrust Savs. Bank, 1987-90; founder, owner R.A. Adams Assocs., Orlando, Fla., 1987—. Squadron comdr. CAP, Orlando, Fla., 1972-75, group dep. for cadets, 1976-77, group comdr., 1979-80, sector comdr., 1980-81, wing dep. dir. for cadets, 1982-87, chief of staff group 9, Dade and Broward Counties, 1987, Fla. wing dir. cadet programs, 1990—; mem. CAP. Recipient various awards, 1974, 76, 78, 81; creator Encampment Cadet Command and Staff Sch., 1981-85, 87—. Mem. NAFE, Mortgage Brokers Assn, Am. Soc. Tng. and Devel., Seminole-Orange County Bd. Realtors, Positive Thinkers Club.

EDE, JOYCE KINLAW, counselor, marketing executive; b. Lumberton, N.C., Aug. 9, 1936; d. Neil Archibald and Myrtle Carolyn (Kinlaw) Kinlaw; m. William L. Schmid, Sept. 17, 1954 (dec. Nov. 1956); 1 child, Cheryl Ann; m. Archie L. Phillips, Jr., Nov. 11, 1960 (div. July 1973); children: Archie L. III, Michael Bartley, John Wade; m. Kenneth Russell Ede, Dec. 27, 1984. Certs. Lake Sumter Community Coll., 1976, 77, 79, Volusia Community Coll., 1977, Ocala Jr. Coll., 1979, Univ. Central, Orlando, Fla., 1980, Triton Coll., 1981. Counselor, social worker Epilepsy Assn. Cen. Fla.-Lake County, 1973-76; social worker Lake Sumter Community Mental Health, Med. Social Svcs., Leesburg, Fla., 1976-79; counselor, social worker Epilepsy Assn. Cen. Fla.-Lake County, 1979-81; mktg. coord. Friendship Village, Schaumburg, Ill., 1981-84; retirement counselor Health Care Assocs., Winter Haven, Fla., 1984-85; in mktg. Cambridge Park Manor, Wheaton, Ill., 1985—; pres. Lake County Svcs. Coun., Leesburg, 1978-79; del. central Fla. Nat. Conf. on Epilepsy, Washington, 1975; mem. State Conf. on Epilepsy, Tampa, Fla., 1977-81; dir. Lake County, Epilepsy Job Tng., Tavares, Fla., 1979-81; mem., advocate Lake/Sumter County Geriatric Program, 1979; chairperson Epilepsy Bd. Fla., Tavares, 1974-75. Contbr. articles on epilepsy to profl. jours. Mem. Lake County PTA, Leesburg, 1970-76; mem. Parents Adv. Coun., Lake County, Leesburg, 1977-80; mem. Parents Coun., Dixie Youth Baseball League, Fruitland Park, Fla., 1980. Recipient Certs. Epilepsy Assn. Central Fla., Orlando, 1980, Kiwanis Clubs, Leesburg and Mt. Dora, Fla., 1974, Rotary Clubs, Leesburg, Mt. Dora, Groveland, Fla., 1974, Lions Clubs, Leesburg, Mt. Dora, Tavares, 1974-75. Mem. Am. Bus. Women's Assn. (hosp. chairperson 1979-80), Concerned Women for Am., Nat. Assn. Female Execs. Avocations: reading, sports, art, music, cooking, crafts, visiting library, playing piano. Home: 17 W 365 3rd Ave Bensenville IL 60106

EDELEN, MARY BEATY, state legislator; b. Vermillion, S.D., Dec. 9, 1944; d. Donald William and Marjorie (Heckel) Beaty; m. Joseph Ruey Edelen, Jr., June 8, 1968; children: Audra Angelica, Anthony Callaghan, Jarrod Arthur. Student Cottey Coll., Nevada, Mo., 1963-64; BA, U. S.D., 1967; MA, Trinity U., San Antonio, 1971. Asst. med. librarian U. S.D., Vermillion, 1965-67; lectr. U. S.D., Vermillion, 1969-70, Yankton (S.D.) Coll., 1973-74; mem. S.D. Ho. of Reps., 1972-80, 82—. Chmn. Clay County Reps., Vermillion, 1990; mem. exec. com. Southeastern Council of Govts.; mem. U. S.D. Community Edn. Adv. Council; mem. S.D. Safety Council's Restraint Coalition Svcs., 1987-89, S.D. Autocap Panel. Recipient Burgess Book award U. S.D., 1966; S.D. Safety Council award, 1984, Friends of Library award S.D. Library Assn., 1986, Legis. Leadership award Mountain Plains Library Assn., 1986. Mem. AAUW (life), U. S.D. Found., Vermillion C. of C., Southeastern S.D. Quota Club, Zeta Phi Eta. Mem. United Ch. of Christ. Lodges: Order Eastern Star (worthy matron), PEO. Avocations: running, camping, snowmobiling. Home: 311 Canby St Vermillion SD 57069

EDELIN, RAMONA HOAGE, association administrator. BA magna cum laude, Fisk U., 1967; MA, U. East Anglia, Norwich, Eng., 1969; PhD, Boston U. Asst. to dean of students Northeastern U., Boston, 1974-75, chmn. Afro-Am. studies program; instr. philosophy Emerson Coll., 1974-75; exec. asst. to pres. Nat. Urban Coalition, Washington, 1977-79, dir. ops., 1979-81, v.p. ops., 1981-82, v.p. programs and policy, 1982—, also pres., chief exec. officer. Mem. D.C. Humanities Coun. Mem. Phi Beta Kappa. Office: Nat Urban Coalition 8601 Georgia Ave Ste 500 Silver Spring MD 20910*

EDELMAN, JUDITH HOCHBERG, architect; b. Bklyn., Sept. 16, 1923; d. Abraham and Frances (Israel) Hochberg; m. Harold Edelman, Dec. 26, 1947; children: Marc, Joshua. Student, Conn. Coll., 1940-41, NYU, 1941-42; B.Arch., Columbia U., 1946. Designer, drafter Huson Jackson, N.Y.C., 1948-58; Schermerhorn traveling fellow, 1950, pvt. practice architecture, 1958-60; partner Edelman & Salzman, N.Y.C., 1960-79, Edelman Partnership (Architects), N.Y.C., 1979—; adj. prof. Sch. Architecture, City U. N.Y., 1972-76; vis. lectr. urban renewal New Sch., 1968; vis. lectr. Washington U., St. Louis, 1974, U. Oreg., 1974, Mass. Inst. Tech., 1975, City U. N.Y. Grad. Program Environ. Psychology, 1975, Pa. State U., City U. N.Y. Grad. Program Environ. Psychology, 1977, Rensselaer Poly Inst., 1977, Columbia U., 1979; First Claire Watson Forrest Meml. lectr. U. Oreg., U. Calif.-Berkeley, U. So. Calif., 1982. Major archtl. works include: Restoration of St. Mark's Ch. in the Bowery, N.Y.C., 1970-82, Two Bridges Urban Renewal Area Housing, 1970-86, Jennings Hall Sr. Citizens Housing, Bklyn., 1980, Goddard Riverside Elderly Housing and Community Ctr., N.Y.C., 1983, Columbus Green Apartments, N.Y.C., 1987. Recipient Bard 1st honor award City Club N.Y., 1969, Bard award of merit, 1975, 82; Residential Design award AIA, 1969, award for design excellence HUD, 1970, Honor award N.Y. State Assn. Architects-AIA, 1975, 1st prize Nat. Trust Historic Preservation, 1983, award of merit Mcpl. Art Soc. N.Y., 1983, Pub. Svc. award Settlement Housing Fund, 1983, Woman of Vision award NOW, 1989, 1st prize for design excellence C. of C., Borough of Queens, N.Y., 1989. Fellow AIA (dir. N.Y. chpt., chmn. commn. archtl. edn. 1971-73, chmn. nat. task force on women in architecture 1974-75, v.p. N.Y. chpt. 1975-77, chmn. ethics com. 1975-77, Pioneer in Architecture award N.Y. chpt. 1990); mem. Alliance of Women in Architecture (founding mem., mem. steering com. 1972-74), Architects for Social Responsibility (exec. com. 1982-85), Columbia Archtl. Alumni Assn. (dir. 1968-71). Home: 13 Bank St New York NY 10014 Office: Edelman Partnership 434 6th Ave 6th Fl New York NY 10011

EDELMAN, LONY MARIA, volunteer; b. West Hempstead, N.Y., May 13, 1930; d. John and Lina Karolina (Schlegel) Erler; m. Herbert John Edelman, Feb. 14, 1954; children: Linda Edelman Moxley, William Thomas Edelman. Student, Adelphi U., 1970. Comptometer operator Oxford Filing Co., Garden City, N.Y., 1948-53; owner Pink Canary Luncheonette, Baldwin, N.Y., 1953-69, Pink Canary Card Shop, Baldwin, 1953-69; treas., newsletter editor PTA, Baldwin, 1966-76; arts and crafts instr. Baldwin Brookside Gardens, 1971-73; housekeeper Holiday Inn, Hempstead, N.Y., 1972-76; salesperson, notary Sid Lieberman Realty, Freeport, N.Y., 1976-88; vol. South Nassau Community Hosp., Oceanside, N.Y., 1981—.

EDELMAN, MARIAN WRIGHT (MRS. PETER B. EDELMAN), lawyer; b. Bennettsville, S.C., June 6, 1939; d. Arthur J. and Maggie (Bowen) Wright; m. Peter B. Edelman, July 14, 1968; children: Joshua, Jonah, Ezra. Merrill scholar, Univs. Paris, Geneva, 1958-59; BA, Spelman Coll., 1960; LLB (J.H. Whitney fellow 1960-61), Yale U., 1963, LLD (hon.); LLD (hon.), Smith Coll., 1969, Lowell Tech. U., 1975, Williams Coll., 1978, Columbia U., U. Pa., Amherst Coll., St. Joseph's Coll., Hartford, Conn.; DHL (hon.), Lesley Coll., 1975, Trinity Coll., Washington, Russell Sage Coll., 1978, Syracuse U., Coll. New Rochelle, 1979, Swarthmore Coll., 1980, SUNY Old Westbury, Northeastern U., 1981, Bard Coll., 1982, U. Mass., 1983, Hunter Coll., U. So. Maine, SUNY, Albany, 1984, Columbia U., U. Pa., Yale U., 1985, Rutgers U., Bates Coll., Maryville Coll., Bank St., 1986, Claremont Grad Sch., Lincoln U., Georgetown U., Chgo. Theol. Coll., 1987, Wheaton Coll., Tulane U., Grinnell Coll. Brandeis U., Wheelock Coll., Dartmouth Coll., U. S.C., U. N.C., Grad. Ctr. CUNY, U. Wis. Milw., 1988, Interdenom. Theol. Ctr., Hofstra U., Tufts U., Borough Manhattan Community Coll., Wesleyan U., Calif. State U. L.A., Dillard U., U. Md., U. Miami, 1989, Howard U., Beloit Coll., Queens Coll., Am. U., New Sch. of Social Rsch., Coll. of Notre Dame, DePaul U., 1989. Bar: D.C., Miss., Mass. Staff atty. NAACP Legal Def. and Edn. Fund, Inc., N.Y.C., 1963-64; dir. NAACP Legal Def. and Edn. Fund, Inc., Jackson, Miss., 1964-68; Congl. and fed. liaison Poor People's Campaign, summer 1968; partner Washington Research Project of So. Center for Pub. Policy, 1968-73; dir. Harvard U. Center for Law and Edn., 1971-73; pres. Children's Def. Fund, 1973—. Mem. exec. com. Student Non-Violent Coordinating Com., 1961-63; mem. adv. council Martin Luther King, Jr. Meml. Library; mem. adv. bd. Hampshire Coll.; mem. Presdl. Commn. on Missing in Action, 1977, Presdl. Commn. on Internat. Yr. of Child, 1979, Presdl. Comm. on Agenda for 80's, 1980; bd. dirs. Eleanor Roosevelt Inst., NAACP Legal Def. and Ednl. Fund; trustee Spelman Coll., Atlanta, Arts, Edn. and Ams., Carnegie Council on Children, 1972-77, Martin Luther King, Jr. Meml. Center; trustee March of Dimes, Joint Ctr. for Polit. Studies; mem. Yale U. Corp., 1971-77, Aetna Found. Named one of Outstanding Young Women of Am., 1966; recipient Mademoiselle mag. award, 1965, Louise Waterman Wise award, 1970, Washington of Yr. award, 1979, Whitney M. Young award, 1979, Profl. of Yr. award Black Ent., 1979, Leadership award Nat. Women's Polit. Caucus, 1980, Black Womens Forum award, 1980, medal Columbia Tchrs. Coll., Barnard Coll., 1984, Eliot award Am. Pub. Health Assn., John W. Gardner Leadership award of Ind. Sector, Pub. Svc. Achievement award Common Cause, Compostela award Cathedral St. James, 1987, MacArthur prize fellow, 1985, Albert Schweitzer Humanitarian prize Johns Hopkins U., 1987, Philip Hauge Ahelson award AAAS, 1988, Hubert Humphrey Civil Rights award, AFL-CIO award, 1989, Radcliffe Coll. medal, 1989, Fordham Stein prize, 1989, Gandhi Peace award, 1990, many others; hon. fellow U. Pa. Law Sch. Hon. mem. Phi Beta Kappa. Address: Childrens Def Fund 122 C St NW Washington DC 20001

EDELMAN, MICHELLE ROBYN, publications executive, creative director; b. St. Louis, Sept. 12, 1964; d. Alan H. and Sybil M. (Kessler) E. BS in Biochemistry, Northwestern U., 1985, MPH, 1987, BA in Econs., 1988. Med. systems cons., tech. writer Genisys Decision Corp., Park Ridge, Ill., 1988-89; dir. tech. pubs., creative cons. Midco Internat., Inc., Chgo., 1989—. Mem. MADD, Chgo., 1988—, Horizons Program for Underpriviledged, Chgo., 1986—. Mem. AMA (ethics com. Chgo. chpt. 1987—, chmn. med. mgmt. com. 1988-89), Ill. Med. Soc. (cons. ethics com. Chgo. chpt. 1988-89), Chgo. Med. Soc., NAFE, MENSA (Chgo. chpt.), Gamma Phi Beta. Republican. Jewish. Office: Midco Internat Inc 4140 W Victoria St Chicago IL 60646

EDELSON, MARY BETH, artist, educator; b. East Chicago, Ind.; d. Albert Melvin and Mary Lou (Young) Johnson; children: Lynn Stauss, Nick. Student, Art Inst. Chgo., 1953-54; BA, DePauw U., 1955; MA, NYU, 1959. Instr. Corcoran Sch. Art, Washington, 1970-75; artist in residence U. Ill., Chgo., 1982, 88, U. Tenn., Knoxville, 1983, Ohio U., Columbus, 1984, Md. Inst. Art, Balt., 1985, Kansas City Art Inst., Mo., 1986; lectr. at various art gatherings. Group exhbns. include Internat. Feministiche Kunst, Stichting de Appel, Amsterdam, The Netherlands, 1980, Gracie Mansion, N.Y.C., 1987, Tweed Mus. Art, N.Y.C., 1987, Mendel Gallery, Mus. du Que., Phillips Gallery, Can., 1986-88, Queens (N.Y.) Mus., 1988, Corcoran Gallery Art, Washington, 1989, Mus. Modern Art, N.Y.C., 1988-89, Walker Art Ctr., Mpls., 1989, W.P.A., Washington, 1989, Dolan/Maxwell Gallery, N.Y.C., 1989, 90; represented in collections: Walker Art Ctr., Nat. Mus. Am. Art, Washington, Nat. Collection, Washington, Nat. Mus. Women in the Arts, Washington, Guggenheim Mus. Art, N.Y.C., Mus. Contemporary Art, Chgo., and others; subject of 15-yr. retrospective travelling to numerous art and ednl. instns. throughout U.S., 1988—; author: Seven Cycles: Public Rituals, 1981, To Dance: Painting with Performance in Mind, 1985, Seven Sites, 1988, Shape Shifter: Seven Mediums, 1990; contbr. articles to profl. jours. Recipient Visual Arts grant NEA, 1981, Creative Artists Pub. Svc. grant State of N.Y., 1982. Mem. Conf. Women in Visual Arts (founding mem.), Heresies Mag. Collective (founding mem.). Home: 110 Mercer St New York NY 10012

EDELSON, ZELDA SARAH TOLL, editor; b. Phila., Oct. 18, 1929; d. Louis David and Rose (Eisenstein) Toll; m. Marshall Edelson, Dec. 27, 1952; children—Jonathan Toll, Rebecca Jo, David Jan. B.A., U. Chgo., 1949, postgrad., 1949-52. Editor-writer Consol. Book Pubs., Chgo., 1953-56; social worker Balt. City Dept. Pub. Welfare, 1956-57; pub. relations writer Md. Dept. Employment Security, Balt., 1958-59; museum editor Yale Peabody Mus., New Haven, 1970-76, head publs., 1976—, editor mus.'s Discovery mag., 1983—; lectr. in sci. writing Yale U., 1983-84. Editor numerous publs. including: A Guide to the Age of Mammals, 1978. U. Chgo. scholar, 1947-51. Mem Council Biology Editors, Soc. Scholarly Publishing, Am. Assn. Museums (awards of distinction 1985, 86, award of merit 1989), New Eng. Conf. Museums. Office: PO Box 6666 Publs Office Yale Peabody Mus Natural History 170 Whitney Ave New Haven CT 06511

EDELSTEIN, ROSE MARIE, nurse educator, consultant; b. Drake, N.D., Mar. 3, 1935; d. Francis Jerome and Myrtle Josephine (Merbach) Hublou; m. Harry George Edelstein, June 22, 1957; children—Julie, Lori, Lynn, Toni Anne. B.S. in Nursing, St. Teresa's Coll., 1956; M.A. in Edn., Holy Names Coll., 1977; Ed.D., U. San Francisco, 1982, postgrad., 1987; postgrad. U. Ariz., 1985—; cert. public health nurse U. Calif., Berkeley, 1972. Dir., clin. supr. San Francisco Sch. for Health Professions, 1971-74, Rancho Arroyo Sch. of Vocat. Nursing, Sacramento, 1974-75; intensive care nurse Kaiser-Permanente Hosp., San Rafael, Calif., 1976-77; dir. inservice edn. Ross Hosp., Calif., 1977-78; assoc. dir. nursing, nursing edn. St. Francis Meml. Hosp., San Francisco, 1978—; nursing cons., med.-surg. staff RN met. hosps., San Francisco, 1985—; med.-legal cons.; instr. CPR; pvt. med.-legal cons., 1990—; invited mem. People to People Nursing Edn. and Adminstrn., candidate to East Asia, Philosophy Inst. U. Zurich, Switzerland, 1988. Mem. U.S. Senate Inner Circle, 1988. Served to lt. col. USAR Med. Res. Mem. Calif. Nurses Assn., Am. Heart Assn., Sigma Theta Tau. Roman Catholic. Author: (with Jane F. Lee) Acupuncture Atlas, 1974; The Influence of Motivator and Hygiene Factors in Job Changes by Graduate Registered Nurses, 1977; Effects of Two Educational Methods Upon Retention of Knowledge in Pharmacology, 1981. Home: PO Box 696 Ross CA 94957-0696

EDEN-FETZER, DIANNE TONI, nurse, project coordinator; b. Washington, Mar. 1, 1946; d. Lawrence Antonio Laurenzi and Eleanor Charlotte (Sparrough) Watson; m. William Earle Eden, Aug. 5, 1967 (div. 1982); 1 child, Christopher Lance; m. John Thompson Fetzer, Sept. 2, 1987. AA in Nursing, SUNY, Farmingdale, 1978; BS in Nursing, Towson (Md.) State U., 1990. RN, N.Y., Md. Charge nurse dept. neurosurgery U. Md. Hosp., Balt., 1978-79, nurse clincian I, 1979-84, dept. nursing and neurology project coord. Nat. Stroke Data Bank, 1984—, nursing edn. cons. dept. neurology and neurosurgery, 1984—. Fellow Stroke Coun. Am. Heart Assn.; mem. Am. Assn. Neurosurg. Nurses, Sigma Theta Tau. Democrat. Roman Catholic. Home: 1303 Maywood Ave Ruxton MD 21204 Office: Univ Md Hosp 22 S Greene St Baltimore MD 21201

EDERER-SCHWARTZ, JANE, pycholanalyst, social worker; b. N.Y.C., Dec. 1, 1939; d. Abel and Gertrude (Glass) Ederer. A.B., Queen's Coll., City U. N.Y., 1961; M.S.W., Columbia U., 1966, M.A., 1975. Cert. in psychoanalysis, comprehensive psychotherapy, social worker. Movement therapist Day Hosp., St. Luke's Hosp., N.Y.C., 1975-79; program dir. Shellbank Jewish Ctr., Bklyn., 1978—; movement therapist Shaaray Tefila, N.Y.C., 1978—, Creative Arts Rehab. Ctr., N.Y.C., 1979—; faculty dept. dance N.Y.U., 1980-87; field work instr. Fordham U. Sch. Social Svc., N.Y.C., 1987—, Hunter Coll. Sch. Social Work, 1988—; psychotherapist Nat. Inst. for Psychotherapies, N.Y.C., 1985—; pvt. practice, supr. dance therapy, psychoanalysis. Founding bd. dirs. Laban Inst. Movement Studies, N.Y.C., 1977—, cert. movement analyst. Grantee NIMH, 1964-66. Mem. Nat. Assn. Social Workers, Am. Dance Therapy Assn. (chmn. edn. N.Y. State 1980—, chmn. N.Y. State 1985—). Office: 251 W 51st St New York NY

EDGAR, KIMBERLY SUE, materials coordinator; b. Syracuse, N.Y., Sept. 29, 1964; d. Austin James and Donna Rae (Alexander) E. BS, Purdue U., 1986; postgrad., Northeastern U., Boston, 1986-87; MS, Hahnemann U., 1989; postgrad., Villanova (Pa.) U., 1989—. Vet. assoc. Manlius (N.Y.) Vet. Hosp., 1981-82; lifeguard Skyridge Family Club, Fayetteville, N.Y., 1982, Longley-Jones Real Estate, Syracuse, 1983; vet. assoc. Stack Hosp. for Pets, Fayetteville, 1986, Lyndon (N.Y.) Vet. Clinic, 1987, Soc. Hill Vet. Hosp., Phila., 1987-88; rsch. biologist Penrose Rsch. Labs., Phila., 1988; coord. animal sci. lab. Merck, Sharp & Dohme Rsch. Labs., West Point, Pa., 1989—. Home: Salt Springs Rd Chittenango NY 13037 Office: Merck Sharp & Dohme Rsch Labs Sumneytown Pike West Point PA 19486

EDGAR, RUTH R., educator; b. Great Falls, S.C., Jan. 7, 1930; d. Robert Hamer and Clara Elizabeth (Ellenberg) Rogers. AA, Stephens Coll., Columbia, Mo., 1949; BS, So. Meth. U., 1951; MA, Appalachian State U., Boone, N.C., 1977; postgrad., Limestone Coll., Gaffney, S.C., 1971. Lic. real estate salesman, broker. Home economist Southwestern Pub. Svc. Co., Amarillo, Tex., 1951-53, So. Union Gas Co., Austin, Tex., 1953-56, Lone Star Gas Co., Dallas, 1956-57; with Peeler Real Estate, 1970-71, Burns High Sch., Lawndale, N.C., 1971-73, Cen. Cleveland Mid. Sch., Lawndale, 1973-77, Burns Jr. High Sch., Lawndale, 1977-88; resource tchr. Elizabeth Elem. Sch., Shelby, N.C., 1988-90, Shelby, 1990—. Mem. supts. adv. coun., Cleveland County, 1971-75, Cleveland County Art Soc., 1972-73. Mem. N.C. Assn. Educators, NEA. Home: 401 Forest Hills Dr Shelby NC 28150

EDGE, IRENE ELIZABETH, computer center manager; b. Ashtabula, Ohio, Sept. 19, 1961; d. Arthur G. and Barbara A. (Burgett) Smith; m. Theodore G. Edge Jr., May 28, 1983. Assoc. Applied Bus. in Computer Tech., Kent State U., 1982, student in computer sci. Adviser computer club Kent State U., Ashtabula, 1982—. Mem. Data Processing Mgmt. Assn. (sec. Northeastern Ohio chpt. 1990, coord. student chpt. 1990). Baptist.

EDGERTON, BRENDA EVANS, soup company executive, treasurer; b. Halifax, Va., June 15, 1949; d. Elmer Keith and Bernice (Chalmers) Evans; children from previous marriage: Lauren, Eric. Student, Pa. State U., 1967-69; BA, Rutgers U., 1970; MBA, Temple U., 1976. Mgr. acctg. Scott Paper Co., Phila., 1976-78; mgr. project fin. Scott Paper Co., 1978-82, mgr. money and banking, 1982-83; dir. fin. Campbell Soup Co., Camden, N.J., 1984-85, asst. treas., 1985-88, dep. treas., 1988-89, v.p., treas., 1989—. Office: Campbell Soup Co Campbell Pl Camden NJ 08103-1799

EDGERTON, LYNNE TODD, lawyer; b. Nashville, Oct. 26, 1947; d. Kirkland Wiley and Adrienne (Hill) Todd; m. Bradford Wheatly Edgerton, Dec. 28, 1970; children: Bradford Wheatly Jr, Lauren Harrington. BA Vanderbilt U., 1969, JD, 1972; LL.M., Yale, 1979. Bar: Tenn. 1972, Va. 1975, N.Y. 1980. Law clk. U.S. Ct. Appeals (4th cir.) Va., 1973-74; dir. Pub. Interest Law Ctr., Charlottesville, Va., 1974-78; assoc. Whitman & Ransom, N.Y.C., 1979-82; sr. staff atty. Natural Resources Defense Council, Inc.,L.A., 1983—; bd. dirs. NOW, 1973-74, Adirondack Council, 1983-89, Manitoga Nature Ctr., 1986-89, Coalition to Restore Coastal La., 1988-89; bd. advisors Climate Inst., 1990—, Earth Communications Office, 1989—. Mem. Assn. of Bar of City of N.Y.

EDGERTON, STEPHENIE GROVER, educator, researcher; b. Grantsburg, Wis., May 1, 1931; d. Stephen Freeman and June Agnes (Strike) Grover; m. Alonzo Jay Edgerton (div. 1957). BA, U. Minn., 1952, BS, 1959, MA, 1959, PhD, U. Ill., 1965. Asst. prof. U. Wis., Madison, 1965-67; assoc. prof. NYU, 1967-72, prof., 1972—. Author: Fallibilism and Education, 1980. Fellow Philosophy of Edn. Soc. Democrat. Home: 100 Bleecker St New York NY 10012 Office: NYU Washington Sq New York NY 10003

EDGREN, GRETCHEN GRONDAHL, magazine editor; b. Portland, Oreg., Mar. 17, 1931; d. Jack W. and Alice Belle (Wells) Grondahl; m. James McNeese, Oct. 22, 1955 (div. Nov. 1974); children: Amy, Terence James; m. Alvin H. Edgren, Dec. 14, 1984. BJ, U. Oreg., 1952. Staff writer The Oregonian, Portland, 1952-61; editor Sunday mag. The San Juan (P.R.) Star, 1963-65; inventory and info. specialist USAF and U.S. Army Recruiting Command, San Antonio and Chgo., 1965-67; assoc. editor VIP mag. (Playboy Clubs), Chgo., 1967-69, mng. editor, 1969-70; assoc. editor Playboy mag., Chgo., 1970-74, sr. editor, 1974—. Editor: New Credit Rights for Women, 1976; contbr. articles to mags. Adv. bd. Old Oreg. Alumni mag., U. Oreg., Eugene, 1988—; pres. bd. dirs. Civic Arts Coun., Oak Park, Ill., 1976-84; bd. dirs. Village Players, Oak Park-River Forest (Ill.) Symphony Assn., Oak Park Concert Chorale, 1975—; mem. Oak Park Cable TV commn., 1984-86. Mem. Heritage Chorale, Confrerie des Vignerons de St. Vincent Mâcon (maitresse du chpt. 1988—), Webfoot Soc. U. Oreg., Phi Beta Kappa, Delta Delta Delta. Episcopalian. Office: Playboy Mag 680 N Lake Shore Dr Chicago IL 60611

EDINBERG, JOYCE FELSEN, writer; b. L.A., June 26, 1928; d. Louis and Marguerite Trafton (Ritchie) Felsen; m. Norman Joseph Edinberg, Sept. 7, 1952; children: James Ritchie, David Louis, Sara Ritchie. BA, UCLA, 1951; MA, Columbia U., 1952. Tchr. history Colegio Karl C. Parrish, Barranquilla, Colombia, 1953-55, Colegio Campo Alegre, Caracas, Venezuela, 1965-73; editor arts The Daily Jour., Caracas, 1976-78; pvt. practice writing N.Y.C., 1980—. Contbr. numerous articles on visual arts, celebrities and N.Y.C. to mags., 1976—. Pres. Venezuelan Am. Assn. Univ. Women, Caracas, 1974-76. Mem. Pi Beta Phi.

EDISON, HALI JEAN, economist; b. Santa Monica, Calif., May 28, 1953; d. Jack and Suzanne (Braveman) E.; m. James H. Berry, Sept. 25, 1988. BA, U. Calif., Santa Barbara, 1975; MS, London Sch. Econs., 1976, PhD, 1981. Economist Amex Bank, London, 1978; vis. lectr. U. Bergen, Norway, 1981-82; economist Fed. Res. Bd., Washington, 1982—; cons. Norwegian Cen. Bank, Oslo, 1987; lectr. U. Md., College Park, 1988. Contbr.: The ECU Market, 1987, Economic Modelling in OECD, 1988. Mem. Econometric Soc., Royal Econs. Soc., Am. Econ. Assn. Democrat. Office: Bd Govs Fed Res Bd Washington DC 20551

EDLIN, RITA MELAMED, family and marriage therapist; b. Cleve., Nov. 2, 1929; d. Alex and Frances (Senior) Melamed; m. Philip Edlin, Sept. 23, 1951; children: Dale, Brian, Jory, Lisa. BA, Ohio U., 1950; postgrad., Smith Coll., 1951; MSW, Ohio State U., 1967; postgrad., Gestalt Inst., 1979. Cert. social worker, Ohio. Caseworker Jewish Family Svc., Cin., 1950-51, Children's Home, Cin., 1970-71; counselor, therapist Family Svcs., Butler County, Hamilton, Ohio, 1972-82, family life educator, 1982—; instr. Miami U., 1978-80. Pub. Jonova, 1976; columnist Am. Israelite, Jewish Post and Opinion; contbr. articles to profl. jours. Docent Hebrew Union Coll., Cin 'ti, Oh Skirball Mus. Fed. Govt. Info. and Referral for Aging grantee, Butler County, Ohio, 1973, Fed. Homemaker-Home Health Aide Svc. grantee, 1973. Mem. Nat. Assn. of Social Workers, Acad. of Cert. Soc. Workers. Home: 2412 Ingleside Ave Cincinnati OH 45206

EDLOW, ESTHER, food services executive; b. Newark, July 14, 1925; d. Harry and Yetta (Leibel) Blonsky; m. Harold Edlow, Nov. 28, 1954; children: Jeremy, Helen. BS, Pratt Inst., 1947; postgrad., Rutgers U., 1950, Fairleigh Dickinson U., 1968. Chief dietitian Elizabeth (N.J.) Gen. Hosp., 1947-50; dist. mgr. Interstate United, N.Y. & N.J, 1950-60; regional v.p. Svc. Systems Corp., N.Y. & N.J, 1966-86; regional v.p. ops. Marriott Corp., N.Y.C., 1986—. Mem. Am. Dietetic Assn., Nat. Hosp. Assn., Dietitians in Bus. and Industry, Nat. Auto Mdse. Assn., Soc. Food Mgmt. Jewish. Home: 238 Lincoln Ave Elizabeth NJ 07208 Office: Marriott Corp 140 West St New York NY 07208

EDMANDS, SUSAN BANKS, research company executive; b. New Rochelle, N.Y., Oct. 7, 1944; d. George Dixon and Marian (Lepied) Banks; children: Whatleigh Winthrop, Benjamin Bruce II. BS, Boston U., 1966; cert. in libr. sci., Northeastern U., Boston, 1974. Tchr. project head start Office Econ. Opportunity, Washington, 1966; English tchr. Wattana Sch., Bangkok, 1969-71; market researcher Pauline Rendell Assocs., Somerville, Mass., 1971-72; food info. specialist Find/SVP, Inc., N.Y.C., 1977-80, mgr. tech. and indsl. group, 1980-90, rsch. dir. info. ctr., 1990—. Trustee Packer Collegiate Inst., Brooklyn Heights, N.Y., 1987—. Mem. Nat. Assn. Info. Mgrs., Soc. Plastics Industries, Soc. Chimie Industrielle (v.p. Am. sect.), Chem. Mktg. Rsch. Assn., Chemists Club (trustee). Home: 170 Pacific St Brooklyn NY 11201 Office: Find/SVP Inc 625 Ave of Americas New York NY 10011

EDMISTEN, JANE MORETZ, lawyer; b. Boone, N.C., Oct. 25, 1938; d. Ralph D. and Lola (Thompson) Moretz; 1 child, Martha. BA with honors, U.N.C., 1960, MA with honors, 1962; JD with honors, George Washington U., 1967. Research analyst Georgetown U., 1962-63, Herner & Co., Washington, 1964; mil. assistance analyst USAF, Washington, 1964-66; chief, legis. reference sect. NASA, 1966-69; admitted to N.C. bar, 1967, D.C. bar, 1967, U.S. Supreme Ct. bar, 1972; faculty N.C. Central Law Sch., Durham, 1975-76; individual practice law, 1975-76; trial atty. tax div., appellate sect. U.S. Dept. Justice, Washington, 1970-74, 76-77; asst. gen. counsel HUD, 1977-79; dep. gen. counsel Merit Systems Protection Bd., 1979-81; mem. firm Moore & Foster, Washington, 1981-82; ptnr. Prokop & Edmisten, Washington, 1983-85; pvt. practice, Washington, 1985—; adj. faculty Am. U. Sch. Law, Washington, Nat. Law Ctr., George Washington U., D.C. Sch. Law. Contbg. author BNA Portfolio. Recipient Outstanding Adj. Faculty award Am. U., 1984, 89. Mem. Am. Bar Assn., D.C. Bar Assn., Md. Bar Assn., Kappa Beta Pi, Phi Delta Delta. Office: 4400 Jenifer St NW Ste 350 Washington DC 20015

EDMISTON, MARILYN, clinical psychologist; b. Lewiston, Maine, Dec. 9, 1934; d. Lewis Walter and Anne (Nezol) Burgess; divorced; children: John Laing, Eric James. BA summa cum laude, Fla. Atlantic U., 1967, MA, 1969; PhD, U. Ga., 1973. Lic. psychologist, Calif., Fla. Clin. psychologist, childrens and adolescent unit Central Ga. Regional Hosp., Milledgeville, Ga., 1973-74, chief psychologist, 1974-75; clin. psychologist Psychol &

Guidance Ctr., San Diego, Calif., 1975; clin. psychologist, adolescent unit South Fla. State Hosp., Pembroke Pines, 1976-77; state psychol. cons. Dept. Health & Rehab. Svc., Tallahassee, 1977-83; clin. psychologist, forensic svcs. Fla State Hosp., Chattahoochee, Fla., 1983—; expert witness for testimony in Fla. courts., 1983—. Mem. Nat. Register of Health Svc. Providers in Psychology, Am. Psychol. Assn., Capital Area Psychol. Assn. Home: 2161 Shangri-La Ln Tallahassee FL 32303 office: Florida State Hospital Forensic Service Chattahoochee FL 32324

EDMISTON, NORMA, financial executive; b. Majagua, Cuba, Sept. 15, 1956; came to U.S., 1970; d. Joaquin Benjamin and Zenaida (Loveira) Prieto; m. Joseph Peter Edmiston, May 20, 1979; children: Christine, Robert. BS summa cum laude, Fairleigh Dickinson U., 1978. CPA, N.J. Sr. auditor Peat, Marwick Mitchell & Co., Short Hills, N.J., 1978-80; sr. auditor McGraw-Hill Inc., N.Y.C., 1980-81, sr. fin. analyst, 1981-84, asst. contr., 1984-85, acquisition analyst, 1985-87, contr. human resources dept., 1987-88, v.p. fin. info. and tech. dept., 1989—. Mem. AICPA, N.J. Soc. CPAs, Am. Woman's Soc. CPAs. Republican. Roman Catholic. Home: 17 MacArthur Dr Clifton NJ 07013 Office: McGraw-Hill 1221 Ave of the Americas New York NY 10020

EDMISTON, THERESA F., accountant; b. Globe, Ariz., Dec. 9, 1950; d. John H. and Melba F. (Cobb) Parker; children: Melanie, Amanda, John. Student, Shelby State Coll., Memphis, Memphis State U. Exec. sec. Lebohheur Children's Hosp., Memphis; adminstr. Svc. Corp. Internat., San Diego; bus mgr. Leite-Parrish & Assocs., Germantown, Tenn. Active Memphis Heart Assn., Shelby Youth Sports, Jr. Olympic Sports. Mem. NAFE, Memphis C. of C. Republican. Baptist.

EDMONDS, ANNE CAREY, librarian; b. Penang, Malaysia, Dec. 19, 1924; d. William John and Nell (Carey) E. Student, U. Reading, Eng., 1942-44; BA, Barnard Coll., 1948; MSLS, Columbia U., 1950; MA, Johns Hopkins U., 1959; postgrad., Western Res. U., 1960-61. With War Damage Commn., London, Eng., 1944-46; children's asst. Enoch Pratt Free Libr., Balt., 1948-49; reference libr. Sch. Bus. Adminstrn., CCNY, 1950-51; reference libr., then asst. libr. readers' services Goucher Coll., Balt., 1951-60; exchange reference libr. European svcs. libr. BBC, London, 1955; instr. Sch. L.S., Syracuse U., summer 1960; libr. Douglass Coll., Rutgers U., New Brunswick, N.J., 1961-64, instr., summer 1962, fall 1963; libr. Mt. Holyoke Coll., 1964—; vis. librarian U. North, Turfloop, South Africa, 1976-77; mem. libr. vis. com. Wheaton Coll., Norton, Mass., 1978—; mem. local systems adv. group Online Computer Libr. Ctr., Inc., 1984-87, mem. adv. com. on coll. and univ. librs., 1988-89. Author: A Memory Book: Mount Holyoke College, 1837-1987, 1988. Mem. South Hadley (Mass.) Bicentennial Com., 1975-76; mem. accreditation teams Middle States Assn. Colls. and Secondary Schs., 1963—, New Eng. Assn. Schs. and Colls., 1986—; bd. dirs. U.S. Book Exchange, 1973-76, 80-83; exec. com. New Eng. Libr. Info. Network, 1974-76, 79-85, chmn., 1982-84; mem. Adv. Commn. Historic Deerfield, 1975-81, 86—. Mem. ALA, Am. Hist. Assn., Assn. Coll. Rsch. Libraries (pres. 1970-71, chmn. constn. and bylaws com. New Eng. chpt. 1975-76, pres. New Eng. chpt. 1983-84), AAUP, AAUW. Home: 79 Cold Hill Granby MA 01033

EDMONDSON, JANE P., television company executive; b. Paterson, N.J., Feb. 17, 1946; d. Charles Anthony and Anita Rose (Van Hook) Pasolle; m. James Henry Edmondson, July 25, 1987; children: Bes Miller, Mark, Jeff, Lauren. BA in History, Mt. Holyoke Coll., 1967; M.A.T., U. Mass., 1970. Staff cons. to Congressman U.S. Ho. of Reps., Washington, 1971-73; legal asst. Arnold & Porter, Washington, 1973-79; various mgmt. positions Nat. Captionery Inst., Falls Church, Va., 1979-87; v.p. mktg. Nat. Captionery Inst., 1987—; consumer adv. bd. Greater Washington Telecommunication for the Deaf, Washington, 1983-84. Contbr. articles to profl. jours. Mem. Video Software Dealers Assn., Community Swim/Tennis Club (McLean, Va., treas. 1984-86). Democrat.

EDNEY, RUTH ANN, reading educator; b. Morgantown, W.Va., Feb. 1, 1944; d. George Foster and Margaret Luella (Fox) Peer; m. William Elton Jones II, Aug. 13, 1966, (div. Jan. 1982); 1 child, William Elton III; m. Gerry Robert Edney, Sept. 2, 1983. BA, So. Meth. U., 1966; student, Tex. Tech. U., 1966; MEd, Trinity U., San Antonio, 1980. Cert. sec., elem. tchr., reading specialist, Tex. Jr. high tchr. Lubbock (Tex.) Pub. Schs., 1966-67; tchr., third grade Westmont/Clarendon Hills Schs., Westmont, Ill., 1968-69, PORTA, Petersburg, Ill., 1969-71, Floresville (Tex.) ISD, 1979-80; jr. high tchr. Edgewood Ind. Sch. Dist., San Antonio, 1980-82; tchr., third grade Ector County Ind. Sch. Dist., Odessa, Tex., 1982-83, tchr., chpt. I Reading, 1983—. Mem. Odessa Symphony Guild, 1983—, Heritage of Odessa, 1985—, Art Inst. of the Permian Basin, Odessa, 1987—, Dallas Mus. Art, 1988-89; vol. Presdl. Mus., Odessa, 1985—, White-Pool House, Odessa, 1989—. Mem. AAUW, Permian Basin Reading Assn., Tex. State Reading Assn., Internat. Reading Assn., Assn. Tex. Profl. Educators, Odessa Profl. Edn. Assn., Odessa Panhellenic (v.p. 1988-90), Kappa Kappa Iota, Beta Epsilon Conclave (pres. 1987-88, v.p. 1988-89), Gamma Phi Beta Alumni Assn. (sec., treas. 1986-90).

EDNIE, EILEEN ROSE, nurse consultant; b. San Diego, Sept. 20, 1951; d. Joseph John and Helen (Kopka) McDonald; m. Charles Edward Ednie, July 29, 1972; 1 child, Charles Edward Jr. BS in Nursing, Otterbein U., 1986; postgrad., Wright State U., 1987—. RN critical specialist. RN Children's Hosp., Columbus, Ohio, 1975-80, Associated Pediatrics, Columbus, 1980-83; program med. mgr. Goodwill Rehab. Ctr., Columbus, 1983-85; nurse cons. Upjohn Health Care, Worthington, Ohio, 1985-88, Conservco, Columbus, 1988—; bus. adv. coun. Goodwill, Columbus, 1985—; bus. coun. Rehab. Inst., Columbus, 1987—. Mem. St. Pius Home/Sch. Assn., Reynoldsburg, Ohio, 1980—. Mem. NAFE, Rehab. Nurses Assn., Ohio Nurses Assn., Sigma Theta Tau. Democrat. Roman Catholic. Office: Conservco PO Box 16676 Columbus OH 43216

EDROZO, ROSALYN SUE, chemical engineer, environmental engineer; b. Texas City, Tex., Sept. 5, 1959; d. Harry Swan and Nelle Rosalyn (Craig) Leach; m. Lawrence Richard Edrozo, Aug. 8, 1981; children: Robert Allen, Laura Sue. BS, U. Tex., 1981. Process engr. Monsanto, Texas City, Tex., 1981-85; Process engr. Amoco Oil Company, Texas City, 1985-89, environ. engr., 1989—. Mem. Clear Lake (Tex.) Symphony, 1981-86; elder First Presbyn. Ch., Texas City, 1985-88; mem. Pasadena Mcpl. Band, 1989—; campaign treas. for Larry Edrozo Dem. candidacy for Justice of the Peace the 5th precinct. Mem. AAUW. Democrat. Office: Amoco Oil Co PO Box 401 Texas City TX 77590

EDSON, MARIAN LOUISE, communications executive; b. Sidney, Mont., Mar. 21, 1940; d. David Ira and Myrtle (Ewing) Drury; m. James Arthur Edson, Oct. 14, 1961; children: Nadine L. Mykins, Jeanine Clare Edson. Student, U. Wash., 1961-62; BS, Mont. State U., 1962; postgrad., SUNY, Binghamton, 1975-76. Cert. tchr. Mont., Wash., N.Y. Lead editor, flight data file Johnson Space Ctr., Houston, 1980-85, coordinator for payload reconfiguration data collection, 1985-86, supr. flight data file, 1986-87; lead technical editor Bell Aerospace/Textron, Buffalo, N.Y., 1987; prodn. mgr. ASYST Software Tech., Rochester, N.Y., 1987-88, publ. mgr., 1988—. Edn. com. Bay Area League Women Voters, Houston, 1984-85; assoc. Rochester Women's Network, 1987—; founding mem. Macedon (N.Y.) Reading Ctr., 1968—. Fellow Life Office Mgmt. Assn.; mem. Soc. Tech. Communicators, Nat. Mgmt. Assn., Nat. Assn. Purchasing Mgrs., AIAA. Republican. Home: 4 Boulevard Pkwy Rochester NY 14612 Office: ASYST Software Tech 100 Corporate Woods Rochester NY 14623

EDSON, VIRGINIA ELIZABETH, educator; b. Worcester, Mass., Dec. 21, 1936; d. Theodore Rogers and Beatrice (Manning) E. BS, Framingham (Mass.) State Coll., 1959; MS, Simmons Coll., Boston, 1966. Tchr. Pelham (N.Y.) Meml. High Sch., 1959-61; tchr. Wellesley (Mass.) pub. schs., 1961—, head home econ. dept., 1967-76. Bd. dirs. Cath. Social Network, Boston, 1988—. Mem. Am. Home Econs. Assn., Mass. Home Econs. Assn., Ea. Mass. Home Econs. Assn. (bd dirs.), NEA, Mass. Tchrs. Assn., Wellesley Tchrs. Assn. (treas. 1976-79), AAUW, Framingham State U. Alumni Assn., Nat. Soc. DAR, Nat. Soc. Colonial Dames of XVII Century, Nat. Soc. New Eng. Women, Cath. Alumni Club. Home: 15 Wilde Rd Wellesley MA 02181 Office: Wellesley Middle School Kingsbury St Wellesley MA 02181

EDWARDS, ALBERTA ROON, public affairs executive; b. Landeshut, Germany, Oct. 9, 1926; d. Max H. Burger and Karin Roon; m. Roger Borgeson, 1951 (div. May 1956); m. Roger Edwards; children: Jeff, Julie, Chris. BA in Econs., Oberlin (Ohio) Coll., 1946. Asst. to treas. Savs. Bank Life Ins. Fund, 1946-48; market research analyst Dun & Bradstreet, 1948-49; market analyst Charles Pfizer & Co., 1949-52, mgr., fgn. market research, 1952-56; with Schering-Plough Corp., Kenilworth, N.J., 1956-72; dir. mktg. info. and analysis Schering Corp., Kenilworth, N.J., 1972-74, dir. mktg. adminstrv., 1974-80, staff v.p. planning and adminstrn., 1980-84, staff v.p. internat. pub. affairs, mktg. services, 1984-87, staff v.p. planning, pub. affairs, market devel., 1987-88; v.p. pub. affairs Schering-Plough Internat. Corp., Kenilworth, N.J., 1988—; mem. First Am. Mktg. Del. to USSR, 1960. Contbr. articles to profl. jours. Mem. Pharm. Mfrs. Assn., Am. Mktg. Assn. (v.p. 1973-75), Internat. Mktg. Fedn. (v.p. 1972-74), Internat. Pharm. Mktg. Research Group (pres.). Office: Schering-Plough Internat Inc 2000 Galloping Hill Rd Kenilworth NJ 07033

EDWARDS, AMY WILLIAMS, administrative supervisor; b. Glenn, Ga., Dec. 21, 1930; d. William F. and Ruby (Irvin) Williams; m. Fred R. Edwards Jr., Nov. 23, 1951 (div. Nov. 1974); children: Raymond L. Edwards, Karen E. Carey, Cynthia E. Utley, Melissa E. Covey. Grad. high sch., La Grange, Ga., 1949. From file clk. to claim office supr. Allstate Ins. Co., Jacksonville, Fla., 1967-75; office ops supr. Allstate Ins. Co., Orlando, Fla., 1975-80; claim div. supr. Allstate Ins. Co., Jacksonville, Fla., 1980-87; claim adminstrv. supr. Allstate Inc. Co., Jacksonville, Fla., 1987-89, ret., 1989; part-time clerical asst. Jewish Family and Community Svc, Jacksonville, 1990—. Mem. Violet Garden Circle. Republican. Baptist.

EDWARDS, BERYL MARGARET, health science facility administrator; b. Hayes, Kent, Eng., May 3, 1932; came to U.S., 1962; d. Sidney McLuan and Florence Edith (Lister) Hunter; m. Bill Edwards, Dec. 25, 1979; 1 child, Michael David Hunter. BA in Nursing, U. London, 1953; BA in English, U. Hawaii, Honolulu, 1969; DD, U. Life Ch., Honolulu, 1978. RN, Eng. Squadron officer Women's Royal Air Force, Eng., 1953-61; med. record adminstr. Sunrise Hosp., Las Vegas, Nev., 1962-64; mgr. The Fronk Clinic, Honolulu, 1964-74; quality assurance coord. The Queen's Med. Ctr., Honolulu, 1974-87; health svc. analyst Desert Hosp., Palm Springs, 1988-89, quality improvement specialists, med. staff, 1989—; chmn. adv. com. Kapiolani Community Coll., Honolulu, 1965-74; cons. The Hunter Trust, Honolulu, 1968-87. Bibliographer: Book. A Study in Literary Romance 1968, The Life and Works of Oliver Onions 1971. Min. Weddings in Paradise, Honolulu, 1978-87. Mem. Cancer Soc. Hawaii Honolulu, Mental Health Assn. Honolulu Hawaii, Hawaii Med. Record Assn., Am. Med. Record Assn., Calif. Med. Record Assn., Hawaii Med. Record Assn. (pres. 1971-73, 85-87), Am. Record Mgmt. Assn., Hawaii Humane Soc., Hist. Hawaii Found. Democrat. Home: 62381 Belmont St Joshua Tree CA 92252

EDWARDS, BETTY, religious executive; b. Balt., Mar. 29; d. John Robert and Janie G. (Frazier) Davis; m. Robert Lee Edwards, Oct. 26, 1966; children: Belinda Edwards. Student, Catonsville Community Coll., Balt.; stenographer, Cortez Peters Bus. Sch., Balt., 1965. Clk. typist Md. Nat. Bank, Balt.; adminstrv. asst., sec.. to dist. supt. United Meth. Ch., Balt.; office mgr. to Dist. Supt. Balt. Conf., United Meth. Ch. sec. Cedar/Morris Hills Improvement Assn., 1970-84; treas. Cedar/Morris Hills Woman's Aux., 1975—, sec. Mem. NAFE, Profl. Assn. United Meth. Ch. Secs. Office: 5124 Greenwich Ave Baltimore MD 21229

EDWARDS, CAROLE A., sales executive; b. Chgo., June 25, 1954; d. Edward J. and LaVerne Marie (Carlson) E.; m. Edward F. Bywalec, Oct. 17, 1981. BA in Psychology, North Park Coll., Chgo., 1976; MBA, Loyola U., Chgo., 1990. Tchr. Chgo. pub. schs.; dir. customer svc. Ency. Britannica Edn. Corp., Chgo. Ill. State scholar. Mem. NAFE. Home: 7717 W Myrtle Chicago IL 60631 Office: Ency Brit Edn Corp 310 S Michigan Ave Chicago IL 60604

EDWARDS, CHRISTINE UTLEY, health administrator; b. Key West, Fla., Nov. 12, 1951; d. Samuel Tracy and Shirley (White) Utley; m. Lester G. Edwards, Aug. 11, 1973. B in Eng., U. Southwestern La., Lafayette, 1974; MPA, Syracuse U., 1980. Rsch. asst. So. Mut. Help Assn., Abbeville, La., 1974; dir. women's options Oneida Co. Coop. Extension, New Hartford, N.Y., 1975-76; planning specialist Oneida Co. Community Action, Utica, N.Y., 1980-81; dir. crisis services YWCA, Utica, N.Y., 1981-89; dir. edn. Planned Parenthood Mohawk Valley, Utica, N.Y., 1989; mem. com. for rape crisis ctrs. N.Y. State Dept. Health, Albany, 1984-89; cons. trainer Pvt. Devel. Orgnl. Devel., Domestic, and Sexual Violence Related Topics, Ilion, N.Y., 1986—; adj. faculty mem. Mohawk Valley Community Coll., Utica, 1989—. Founding mem. Rape Crisis Svcs., Utica, 1975; mem. Mt. Markham Family Life Edn. Adv. Com., West Winfield, N.Y., 1988—; mem. adv. com. rape crisis svcs. YWCA, Herkimer, N.Y., 1989—. Recipient Women of Merit award Mohawk Valley Women's History Project, Utica, N.Y., 1985, Kirkland Art Ctr. Color Photography award, 1989. Mem. N.Y. Coalition Against Sexual Assault (pres. 1988—), Nat. Coalition Against Sexual Assault (bd. dirs. 1985-87), Mowhawk Valley Com. Against Child Abuse (bd. dirs. 1985-88). Democrat. Home: RD 2 Box 411 Ilion NY 13357

EDWARDS, CONNIE LYNN, health care executive; b. Denison, Tex., Nov. 18, 1946; d. Charles J. and Frances Jo (Lankford) Taylor; m. Robert W. Edwards, Sept. 1, 1967; children: Charles, Robert Jr., Stephanie. AAS, Byrne Coll., Irving, Tex., 1967. Collection mgr. Zale Corp., Dallas, 1972-75; br mgr. USLIFE Credit Corp., Durant, Okla., 1975-81; asst. dir. bus. svc. Texoma Med. Ctr., Denison, Tex., 1981-86; dir. bus. svc. Med. Arts Clinic, Corsicana, Tex., 1986—. Mem. Am. Guild Patient Accts. Mgmt., NAFE. Baptist. Home: Rte 3 Box 2542 Corsicana TX 75110 Office: 301 Hospital Dr Corsicana TX 75110

EDWARDS, CYNTHIA ANN, English educator of the deaf; b. Schenectady, N.Y., Nov. 3, 1954. BS, SUNY, Geneseo, 1976; MA, Gallaudet U., 1979, EdS, 1986. Tcht. of deaf Windsor (N.Y.) High Sch., 1979-83; instr. English Gallaudet U., Washington, 1983-86, asst. prof., 1986—, program cons., 1988—. Mem. Nat. Assn. of Deaf, Assn. Supervision and Curriculum Devel., Internat. Educator, Nat. Coun. Tchrs. of English, Smithsonian Instn., Gallaudet U. Alumni Assn. Office: Gallaudet U PO #4392 1640 Kalmia Rd NW Washington DC 20012

EDWARDS, DEANNE BAHR, research associate; b. Newport Beach, Calif., Oct. 9, 1960; d. Dean Marvin and Jendon (Carstensen) Bahr; m. Peter Blair Edwards, Sept. 12, 1987. BS, Calif. Polytech. State U., San Luis Obispo, 1983; MS, U. Calif., Davis, 1989. Product devel. scientist Ortho Diagnostic Systems Inc., Carpinteria, Calif., 1983-84; lab. tech. Scripps Clinic Rsch. Found., La Jolla, Calif., 1984-86; rsch. asst. U. Calif., Davis, Calif., 1986-89; staff rsch. asst. Scripps Inst. Oceanography, La Jolla, Calif., 1989—. Mem. Am. Soc. Microbiology. Democrat. Office: Scripps Inst Oceanography 8602 La Jolla Shores Dr La Jolla CA 92093

EDWARDS, DENISE ALTHEA MICHELLE, department store official; b. London, Apr. 28, 1965; came to U.S., 1981; d. Cynthia Victoria (Donaldson) E. BBA, SW Tex. State U., 1986. Sales promotion account rep. Joseph E. Seagram & Sons, N.Y.C., 1987-88, advt. coord., 1988-89; dept. mgr. Stern's/Allied Corp., Flushing, N.Y., 1989—. Mem. NAFE, Alpha Kappa Psi. Roman Catholic. Home: 84-23 Manton St Apt 3A Briarwood NY 11435 Office: Stern's/Allied Corp 136-50 Roosevelt Ave Flushing NY 11435

EDWARDS, DONNA REED, nurse; b. Pine Bluff, Ark., Jan. 12, 1955; d. Ray and LaVerne (Doman) Reed; children: Christopher, Michael. ADN, U. Ark., Monticello, 1975; student, SUNY, Albany. RN, Ark.; CCRN; AACN; cert. in BCLS. Staff nurse med. stepdown Little Rock VA Med. Ctr., charge nurse surg. ICU; head nurse post-anesthesia care unit John L. McClellan Meml. VA Med. Ctr., Little Rock. Contbr. articles to profl. jours. Mem. AACCN, Nurses Orgn. of VA, Am. Heart Assn., Am. Soc. Post Anesthesia Nurses, Post Anesthesia Care Nurses Ark. Mem. Assembly of God Ch. Office: JL McClellan Meml VA Med Ctr PACU 4300 W 7th Little Rock AR 72202

EDWARDS, ELEANOR CECILE, comptroller; b. N.Y.C., July 23, 1940; d. Clifford Thaddeus and Lillian Louise (Taitt) Butte; m. Warren Thaddeus Edwards, Dec. 17, 1961; children: Angelique, Kelby. BBA and Acctg. summa cum laude, Mercy Coll., 1982. Supr. billing Formulette Co., Inc., Long Island City, N.Y., 1960-62; keypunch operator Temporary Agys., N.Y.C., 1963-68; tng. instr. Setab Computer Inst., N.Y.C., 1968-70; asst. office mgr. Kendrick Sytems, Inc., Elmsford, N.Y., 1970-71; office mgr. LPJ Computer Corp., Millwood, N.Y., 1972-75; full charge bookkeeper Lockwood Manor Home for Adults, New Rochelle, N.Y., 1975-77; comptroller Margaret Chapman Sch., Hawthorne, N.Y., 1977—; dir. Bradhurst Ctr. Corp., Hawthorne, 1980-88; cons. acct. Very Spl. Arts N.Y., 1983—. Vol. Spl. Olympics, Westchester, N.Y., 1980—, Very Spl. Arts N.Y., 1982—. Mem. Nat. Assn. Accts., Nat. Notary Assn., Delta Mu Delta, Alpha Chi. Democrat. Office: Margaret Chapman Sch 5 Bradhurst Ave Hawthorne NY 10532

EDWARDS, ELEANOR MATTIASICH, singer, voice educator; b. Mt. Vernon, N.Y., May 14, 1938; d. Anton Casimir and Eleanor (Gallessich) Mattiasich; m. Peter L. Edwards, Sept. 4, 1960; 1 child, Jonathan Anthony. Mus.B., Oberlin Coll., 1960; Mus.M., New Eng. Conservatory, Boston, 1963; Sommer Akademie cert. Das Mozarteum, Salzburg, Austria, 1959. Soprano soloist Temple Israel, Brookline, Mass., 1964-76, Trinity Ch., Boston, 1966-80, Boston Pops Orch., 1965, 74; presented by Concert Artists Guild in recital Town Hall, N.Y.C., 1967; voice tchr. pvt. studio, 1972—, South Shore Conservatory, Hingham, Mass., 1978-86; owner Music For Sale purchasing svc.; soprano soloist with maj. choral orgns. in Boston area; soloist numerous chs., temples; recitalist Isabella Stewart Gardner Mus., other New Eng. locations; soloist European Choral Symposium, Salzburg and Linz, Austria, 1980; chmn. voice dept. Thayer Acad., Braintree, Mass.; mem. bd. trustees, choir mem. Old South Union Ch. (Congregational), South Weymouth, Mass., 1980—. Recipient 2d place award Met. Opera Auditions, Boston, 1966. Mem. Fedn. Internat. League Officiails, Nat. Assn. Tchrs. of Singing, Pi Kappa Lambda. Democrat. Avocations: needlework, old house restoration, hockey, luge. Address: 779 Main St South Weymouth MA 02190

EDWARDS, EMMA JEAN, publishing executive; b. Trenton, N.J., Nov. 17, 1961; d. Robert James and Mary Emma (Hatchell) E. Student, Rutgers U., 1984. Asst. mgr. IGA Supermarket, Trenton, 1984-86; supr., team leader Ednl. Testing Svc., Princeton, N.J., 1986-89, program assoc., 1989—. Active NAACP, Trenton, 1985—; mem. Young People Progress, Urban League Met. Trenton. Mem. Nat. Supervisory Coun., Nat. Assn. for Exec. Women, Trenton Ednl. Soc. (asst. dir. 1984—). Democrat. Pentecostal. Home: 34 Delawareview Ave Trenton NJ 08618

EDWARDS, EVA K., field underwriter; b. Pontllanfraith, S. Wales, U.K., Sept. 18, 1942; came to U.S. 1963, naturalized 1967; d. Sydney James and Kathleen (Jones) Edwards; 1 child, Scott Jason. Basic Tng. Degree, U. Ill., 1972; A.Criminal Justice, Prairie State Coll., 1974. Field underwriter N.Y. Life Ins., Oak Brook, Ill., 1977-79, sales mgr., 1979-85, field underwriter, 1985—; sr. mktg. rep. Datavision Inc., Westmont, Ill., 1987-88; comml. sales mgr., Phoenix Pest Control, 1989—; juvenile officer Glenwood Police Dept., Ill., 1965-69; police officer Olympia Fields Police Dept., Ill., 1969-77. Contbr. articles to profl. jours. Named Boss of Year, Profl. Bus. Women's Assn., 1985; Rookie of Year, N.Y. Life Ins. Co., 1978; Counselor of Year, Rich Central High Sch., 1975. Avocations: singing.

EDWARDS, FRANCES SUE, county education administrator; b. Galena Park, Tex., Apr. 21, 1933; d. Philip Duncan and Claribel (Miller) Elkins; 1 child, Michael Douglas. MS in Bus. Edn., U. Houston, 1978; MS in Vocat. Guidance and Counseling, Sam Houston State U., 1980; cert. administrv. supervision, U. Houston. Legal asst. Bracewell & Tunks, Attys., Houston, 1955-60; pub. rels. dir. May Alvin Baggett, Galena Park, 1965-70; tchr., counselor Galena Park Ind. Sch. Dist., 1975-81; pub. info. officer Sheldon Ind. Sch. Dist., Houston, 1981-85; coord. of printing svcs. Harris County Dept. Edn., Houston, 1985—; cons., speaker on self esteem; owner KEME Emterprises. Coord. March of Dimes Campaign, Galena Park, 1960, Centennial Celebration, City of Galena Park, 1958; campaign chmn. for local, mcpl. and sch. rep. elections, Galena Park; pres. Galena Park Area Coun. PTAs, 1965, Galena Park Baseball Aux., 1967, Galena Park Riding Club. Named Lady of Yr., Galena Park C. of C., 1973, Bus. Women of Yr., Athena North Channel Area C. of C., 1984. Mem. Nat. Congress PTAs (life). Roman Catholic. Home: 1800 Leggett Dr Galena Park TX 77547 Office: Harris County Dept Edn 6300 Irvington Blvd Houston TX 77022

EDWARDS, HELEN THOM, physicist; b. Detroit, May 27, 1936; d. Edgar Robertson and Mary (Milner) Thom; m. Donald A. Edwards. BS in Physics, Cornell U., 1957, MA in Physics, 1963, PhD in Physics, 1966. Rsch. assoc. Cornell U., Ithaca, N.Y., 1966-70; assoc. head booster Fermi Nat. Accelerator Lab., Batavia, Ill., 1970-71, staff physicist, M.R., 1971-75, head switchyard extraction group, 1975-78, leader tevatron design group, 1978-79, dep. head saver div., 1980-81, dep. head accelerator div., 1981-86, head accelerator div., 1987-88; head accelerator constrn. div. SSC/URA, Dallas, 1989—. Recipient Achievement in Accelerator Physics and Tech. U.S. Summer Sch. on Particle Accelerator Prize, 1985, Ernest O. Lawrence award Dept. of Energy, 1986, Nat. Medal Tech., 1989; MacArthur Found. Chgo. fellow, 1988. Fellow Am. Phys. Soc.; mem. NAE. Office: SSC/URA 2550 Beckleymeade Ave Ste 125 Dallas TX 75237*

EDWARDS, IDA WIERSCHEM, teacher; b. St. Louis, July 15, 1938; d. George Raymond and Mildred Birtha (Eschman) Wierschem; m. David Leroy Edwards, Sept 9, 1976; 1 child, Kathryn Rae. BS in Edn., U. Mo., 1960. Cert. elementary tchr., Mo., standard life teaching certificate, Calif. Tchr. Norfolk (Va.) Pub. Schs., 1960-61, Scottsbluff (Neb.) Pub. Schs., 1961-62, Rialto (Calif.) Unified Sch. Dist., 1963-83, Shasta County Office of Edn., Redding, Calif., 1983-88, Cascade Union Elem. Schs., Anderson, Calif., 1988—; editor Rialto Tchrs. Assn. Newsletter, 1970-72, Anderson Heights Sch. Newspaper, 1989—, Small Talk Kindergarten Newsletter, 1988. Vol. Mercy Hosp. Guild., Redding, Calif. Mem. AAUW, NEA, Calif. Tchrs. Assn., Anderson Tchrs. Assn., Alpha Delta Kappa, Alpha Gamma Delta.

EDWARDS, JANE KATHERINE, hospital superintendent; b. Aberdeen, S.D., Aug. 21, 1936; d. Willis Justin and Edna Evelyn Welsh; m. James Edward Edwards, Sept. 6, 1958; children: William David, Patrick James. BS in Nursing, Mont. State U., 1958. RN, Nursing Home Adminstr., Cert. Mental Health Profl. Instr., supr. psychiatric nursing Warm Springs (Mont.) State Hosp., 1958-61, 68-71, dir. sch. of practical nursing, 1971-73, dir. nursing, 1973-78, dir. quality assurance, 1978-81; dir. treatment, residential svcs. Montana State Hosp., Warm Springs, 1981-86, supt., 1986—. Adv. com. Mont. State U. Sch. of Nursing, Bozeman, 1974-79; Mental Health adv. coun. State of Mont., 1974-79, Com. on Insts., State of Mont., 1974-78, Mental Health Admission and Discharge Rev. Team. Speaks on mental health issues at numerous, conferences, seminars, ednl. insts., conventions, etc. Named to Mont. Honor Soc. of Nursing, 1980. Mem. Am. Nurses Assn., Mont. Nurses Assn. (commn. nursing svc facilities 1980-81, task force nursing supply), Western State Hosp. Assn. (bd. dirs. 1989—), Alpha Tau Delta, Phi Kappa Phi, Elks Auxl., Hibernian Auxl., Jayceens. Home: 2005 Washoe Ave Anaconda MT 59711 Office: Mont State Hosp Warm Springs MT 59756

EDWARDS, JOELL LOUISE, handwriting expert; b. Mpls.; children: Leona Ruth, Lorell Jo, Lynda Louise, Marvin Louis. Gen. Cert., Internat. Graphoanalysis Inst., Chgo., 1970; MA, Internat. Graphoanalysis Inst., 1979. Organizer, bus. agt. East Bay Offset and Reprodn. Artisan's Local 473, Oakland, Calif.; clinic co-dir., cons., counselor Fr. Bernard Reiser, Priest-counselor, Coon Rapids, Minn.; newspaper editor, reporter, columnist, children's writer San Leandro (Calif.) pubrs., Fridley (Minn.) pubrs.; sec. Indsl. Devel. Commn., Human Resources Dir.; owner Art and Hobby Shop, Mora, Minn.; city clk. City of Coon Rapids, Minn.; profl. practice as therapist, graphokinesiologist Ojai, Calif.; cons. in field; lectr. in field. Contbr. articles to profl. jours. dir. YWCA, 1964-68, pub. rels. com.; active Family Svc. Agy, charter guild pres. 1967-68. Recipient Golden Poet award, Calif. Poets Assn., 1988. Mem. NAFE, DAR, Bus. and Profl. Women's Orgn., Graphoanalysis Soc. Mem. Worldwide Ch. of God. Home: 24000 Second St #308 Hayward CA 94541

EDWARDS, KATHRYN INEZ, instructional media consultant; b. L.A., Aug. 26, 1947; d. Lloyd and Geraldine E. (Smith) Price; m. Gregor Quentin Edwards, June 7, 1969; 1 child, Bryan. BA in English, Calif. State U., L.A.,

1969, supervision credential, 1974, adminstrn. credential, 1975; MEd in Curriculum, UCLA, 1971; PhD, Claremont Grad. Sch., 1979. Tchr., L.A. Pub. Schs., 1969-78, adv. specially funded programs, 1978-80, advisor librs. and learning-resource program, 1980-81, instructional specialist, 1981-84; cons. instructional media L.A. County Office of Edn., Downey, Calif., 1984-90; coord. ednl. media and tech. Pomona (Calif.) Unified Sch. Dist., 1990—; cons. Walt Disney Prodns., Alfred Higgins Prodns., others. Author guides and curriculum kits. Appointed by assembly speaker Willie Brown to Calif. Ednl. Tech. Com., 1990-92. Recipient Resolution award mem. Gwen Moore Calif. State Assembly, 1988, Cert. Commendation Senator Diane Watson, 1988; Mabel Wilson Richards scholar, 1968, Calif. Congress Parents and Tchrs. scholar, 1968; UCLA fellow, 1968; named Outstanding Woman of Yr. L.A. Sentinel, 1987. Mem. Nat. Assn. Minority Polit. Women, Internat. Reading Assn. (speaker nat. conv. 1988), L.A. Reading Assn. (pres.), Calif. Assn. Tchrs. of English (conf. del. 1982), Assn. Supervision and Curriculum Devel., Calif. Media and Libr. Educators Assn. (state conf. co-chair 1989), Nat. Assn. Media Women (Media Woman of Yr. 1987), Alpha Kappa Alpha. Democrat. Roman Catholic. Avocations: reading, gardening, sewing. Office: LA County Office Edn 9300 E Imperial Hwy Downey CA 90242

EDWARDS, KATHRYN LOUISE, plant physiologist; b. Washington, Pa., May 8, 1947; d. Edgar Owen and Jean Elizabeth (Lotz) E. AB, Oberlin, 1969; PhD in Botany, U. N.C., 1974. Rsch. assoc. Yale U., New Haven, 1974-76; asst. prof. Rollins Coll., Winter Park, Fla., 1976-78; asst. prof. Kenym Coll., Gambier, Ohio, 1978-84, assoc. prof., 1984—; dept. chmn., 1990—; vis. rschr. Ohio State U., Columbus, 1982-83, Jewish Hosp., St. Louis, 1986-87; vis. assoc. prof. Washington U., St. Louis, 1985-87. Author: (with others) Cell Surface In Signal Transduction, 1987; contbr. articles to profl. jours. Organizer, founder Women in Plant Physiology, 1984-85; v.p. Denison-Kenyon Sigma Xi, 1981-82. Rsch. grantee NASA, 1984, 85, 86, 87, 90. Mem. Am. Soc. Plant Physiologists, Am. Soc. Gravitational and Space Biology, Biophysical Soc., Soc. for Woman in Philosophy, Nat. Women's Studies Assn. Democrat. Office: Kenyon Coll Biology Dept Gambier OH 43022

EDWARDS, LAURIE ELLEN, home-based services company executive, educator; b. San Diego, June 3, 1951; d. Donald Morgan and Doral (Erickson) Hurd. Student Calif. Poly. State U., 1977; BA, Nat. U., San Diego, 1978; postgrad. U. Calif., San Diego, 1982-84; MS, Chapman Coll., 1986. Founder, owner La Jolla Village Secretarial Services, Calif., 1981-82; founder, owner Am. Med. Claims, La Jolla, 1981-86; pres., originator At Your Home Svcs., San Diego, 1985—; instr. bus. Palomar Coll., Mira Costa Coll., San Diego Community Colls., 1981—; lectr. in field. Columnist University City Gazette, 1982. Mem. La Jolla Town Council, 1981-84; assoc. Indsl. Recreational Council, San Diego, 1983-85. Mem. NAFE, Calif. Bus. Edn. Assn., Am. Soc. Tng. and Devel., Older Womens League, Womens Internat. Ctr., Nat. U. Alumni Assn. Avocations: photography, travel, exercising. Office: At Your Home Svcs 4350 Executive Dr Ste 200 San Diego CA 92121

EDWARDS, LYDIA JUSTICE, state official; b. Carter County, Ky., July 9, 1937; d. Chead and Velva (Kinney) Justice; m. Frank B. Edwards, 1968; children: Mark, Alexandra, Margot. Student, San Francisco State U. Began career as acct., then Idaho state rep., 1982-86; treas. State of Idaho, 1987—; legis. asst. to Gov. Hickel, Alaska, 1967; conf. planner Rep. Gov.'s Assn., 1970-73; mem. Rep. Nat. Commn., 1972, del. to nat. conv., 1980. Mem. Rep. Womens Fedn. Congregationalist. Office: State Treas's Office State Capitol Bldg Rm 102 Boise ID 83720*

EDWARDS, MARIE BABARE, psychologist; b. Tacoma; d. Nick and Mary (Mardesich) Babare; B.A., Stanford, 1948, M.A., 1949; m. Tilden Hampton Edwards (div.); 1 son, Tilden Hampton Edwards III. Counselor guidance center U. So. Calif., Los Angeles, 1950-52; project coordinator So. Calif. Soc. Mental Hygiene, 1952-54; pub. speaker Welfare Fedn. Los Angeles, 1953-57; field rep. Los Angeles County Assn. Mental Health, 1957-58; intern psychologist UCLA, 1958-60; pvt. practice, human relations tng., counselor tng. Mem. Calif., Am., Western, Los Angeles psychol. assns., AAAS, So. Calif. Soc. Clin. Hypnosis, Internat. Platform Assn. Author: (with Eleanor Hoover) The Challenge of Being Single, 1974, paperback edit., 1975. Office: 6100 Buckingham Pkwy Culver City CA 90230

EDWARDS, MARY, social worker; b. Charleston, S.C., Feb. 14, 1949; d. George and Laura (Smalls) E.; m. Morris Alexander Simmons, Feb. 14, 1988. BA, Benedict Coll., 1971; MSW, U. Pitts., 1973; postgrad., Trident Tech. Coll., 1989-90. Licensed Social Worker, Registered Securities Broker. Planner, researcher Allegheny County Children Ser., Pitts., Pa., 1973-79; couselor Family Services of Charleston, S.C., 1979-81; medical social worker Franklin C. Fetter Family Ctr., Charleston, S.C., 1981-82; field underwriter N.Y. Life Insurance Co., Charleston, S.C.; counselor Educational Opporunity Ctr., Charleston, S.C., 1987--; Instr. Insurance Companies, Charleston, 1988--. Notary Pub., Notaries of Am., 1987, Sunday Sch. Tchr., Memorial Ch., Charleston, 1980-89. Named Outstanding Woman of the Yr. Charleston, 1985. Mem. Nat. Assn. Social Workers. Republican. Protestant.

EDWARDS, MARY L., retail executive; b. Sacramento, Dec. 1, 1943; d. Louis R. Sisco and Mary M. (Bowen) Lammie; 1 child, Ted. BA in Elem. Edn., San Diego State, 1965. Gen. store and merchandise mgr. K Mart Corp., Albuquerque; retail mgmt. cons. Reston, Va.; bus. adv. counc. N.Mex. Bd. Edn. Named Cons. of Yr., Outstanding Sr. Cons. Ga. Wright Corp. Mem. Am. Bus. Assn. (past bd. dirs.).

EDWARDS, PHYLLIS MAE, accountant, graphologist; b. Wichita, Kans., June 25, 1921; d. William Noble and Nettie Mae (Riggs) Merry; m. Joseph Andrew Edwards, Sept. 19, 1945; children: Joseph Noble (dec.), James Richard, Robert Andrew, Jacqueline Merry. BA in Journalism, Wichita State U., 1944; grad. advanced graphologist, Sampson Inst. Graphology, 1967; cert. of proficiency, Tao Acupuncture, 1975; D of Graphology Sci., Rocky Mountain Graphology, 1978. Cert. profl. graphologist. Sec., bookkeeper Healy & Co., Wichita, 1939-42, Wichita State U., 1942-43; acct. Moberly & West, Pub. Accts., Wichita, 1943-45, McQuain, Edwards, & Teffs, Oakland, Calif., 1952-55; acct., graphologist Rocky Mountain Graphology Sch., Denver, 1972-81; prin. Multi-Pro Svcs., Denver, 1976—; acct. Indsl. Hard Chrome Plating Co., Denver, 1957—; expert witness for all levels of ct., Colo., Wyo., 1976—; pub. and pvt. speaker, Colo., Wyo., 1976—; sec., treas. Indsl. Hard Chrome Plating Co., Denver, 1990. Den mother Aurora (Colo.) Cub Scout Troop, 1956-59; asst. troop leader Girl Scouts U.S., Denver, 1960-64; charity fund raiser various churches, schs., and non-profit orgns., 1967—. Mem. AAUW (Denver br. treas. 1975-77, bull. editor 1980-81, sec. 1986-88, roster/circulation editor, pres. elect 1988-90, pres. 1990—), Am. Handwriting Analysts Found. (Rocky Mountain chpt.), Am. Assn. Handwriting Analysts, Coun. Graphological Socs., Rocky Mountain Graphology Assn. (treas. 1972-81), U. Denver Women's Libr. Assn., Denver Assistance League (prof. aux.). Home: 2986 S Fairfax St Denver CO 80222 Office: Indsl Hard Chrome Plating 919 Santa Fe Dr Denver CO 80204

EDWARDS, RENEE CAMILLE, acquisition logistics engineer; b. Falls Church, Va., Aug. 6, 1961; d. Walter Thomas and Elizabeth Ann (Wills) Holt. BS, George Mason U., Fairfax, 1983; MS, Central Mich. U., Merrifield, 1988; grad. program mgmt. course, Def. Systems Mgmt. Coll., 1990. Logistics analyst The BDM Corp., McLean, Va., 1983-85; deputy program mgr. COMARCO/IBS, Arlington, Va., 1985-88; logistics mgr., speaker, briefer SWL, Inc., Arlington, Va., 1988-89; mem. profl. staff Def. Systems Mgmt. Coll., Ft. Belvoir, Va., 1989—. Contbr. articles to profl. jours. Bd. dirs. Woodwalk Condominium, Burke, Va., 1987--. Named Best Speaker Toastmasters, McLean, 1985, Best Evaluator Toastmasters, McLean, 1985. Mem. Soc. of Logistics Engrs. Republican. Episcopalian. Office: Def Systems Mgmt Coll Fort Belvoir VA 22060

EDWARDS, SUSAN ARVILLÉ REYNOLDS, office assistant, nurse; b. Grand Rapids, Mich., Nov. 11, 1944; d. Grant Meredith and Lilian Bea (Geer) Reynolds; m. John Reed Edwards, Dec. 28, 1963; children: Elizabeth Ann, Scott Alan, Julie Christine. BS in Nursing, Mich. State U., 1966. RN, Ga. Staff nurse Edward W. Sparrow Hosp., Lansing, Mich., 1966; psychiatric nurse Coosa Valley Community Mental Health Ctr., Rome, Ga., 1971-78; office asst. Skinny Reed's Home Ctr., Rome, Ga., 1979--. Bd. dirs. Murphy-Harpst-Vastiti Home, United Meth. Com. Relief, Gen. Bd. Global Ministries United Meth. Ch., Women's Div. United Meth. Ch., Wesley Community Ctrs. Atlanta; active in Mental Health Assn. Floyd County, Rome Coun. for the Arts, Rome Symphony Chorus, Rome Little Theatre. Mem. AAUW, PEO. Republican. Home: 339 Mt Alto Rd SW Rome GA 30161 Office: Skinny Reeds Home Ctr 2937 Alabama Hwy Rome GA 30161

EDWARDS, SUSIE LAVERNE MATTHEWS, elementary school educator; b. Plato, Mo., Nov. 9, 1920; d. Reuben Arthur and Gladys Elsie (Crismon) Matthews; m. Don Sneed Edwards, June 1, 1941; children: Jimmie Don, Lewis Dwayne, Bobby Joe. BS in Edn. cum laude, Southwest Mo. State U., 1962; MA in Edn., Drury Coll., 1968. Elem. sch. tchr. Black Jack Sch., Plato, 1939-41, Ivey Sch., Lebanon, Mo., 1941-43, Stoutland (Mo.) Sch., 1954-55; sch. sec., bookkeeper Macks Creek (Mo.) Sch., 1955-56; elem. sch. tchr. Hurricane Deck Sch., Sunrise Beach, Mo., 1962-75, Camdenton (Mo.) Sch., 1975-80. Named Tchr. of the Yr., Camdenton Sch., 1979-80. Mem. AAUW, Mo. State Tchrs. Assn., Camdenton Tchrs. Assn. (past sec.), Royal Neighbors of Am., New Hope Womens Missionary Union (pres. 1989—). Democrat. Baptist. Home: Rt 19 Box 135 Lebanon MO 65536

EDWARDS, VIRGINIA DAVIS, concert pianist; b. Syracuse, N.Y., Jan. 8, 1927; d. Leslie Martz and Elsie (Gannon) Davis; m. William B. Edwards, Jan. 12, 1954. BA magna cum laude, Marshall U., 1948; MusB, Cin. Conservatory of Music, 1950, MusM, 1950; postgrad., U. Chgo., 1950-56, U. Calif., Berkeley, 1963. Pianist, young artists series Conservatory of Music, Cin., 1949-50; piano instr. Conservatory of Music, Evanston, Ill., 1955-56; music instr. Harvard Sch. for Boys, Chgo., 1954-55; pianist Opera Studios of Dimitri Onofrei/Bianca Saroya, Chgo., 1957-61; piano instr. Community Music Ctr., San Francisco, 1962-63; v.p. Gold Rush Gun Shop, Benet Arms Co. Imports, San Francisco, 1963-68, Afton, Va., 1968—; pvt. practice Afton, Va., 1978—; piano instr. Mary Baldwin Coll., Staunton, Va., 1988—; lecturer AAUW, Waynesboro, Va., 1979-80. Soloist Marshall U. Symphony Orchestra, 1948, Chgo. Pops Concert Orchestra, Duluth, Minn., 1961; recitalist Curtis Hall, Chgo., 1961, Legion of Honor, San Francisco, 1966, WRFK (FM), Richmond, Va., 1979; producer and performer Presbyn. Hunger Program series, 1984-87, St. John's Cath. Ch., Waynesboro, Va., 1985, Basic Meth. Ch., 1989, Augusta Hosp. Corp. Benefit, 1989; author: Conspiracy of 30--Their Misuse of Music from Aristotle to Onassis, 1990. Mem. AAUW, DAR, Va. Museum Soc. Presbyterian. Home: PO Box 87 Waynesboro VA 22980

EFRON, MERYL JOY, dentist; b. Bklyn., Oct. 14, 1957; d. Albert and Harriet (Levine) E. BS, Wagner Coll., 1979; DDS, NYU, 1983. Resident in gen. practice S.I. (N.Y.) Hosp., 1983-84; dentist Tager, Lew, DeGaetano & Efron, S.I., 1984—; attending dentist Staten Hosp. Dept. Dentistry, 1984—; clin. instr. dept. oral medicine NYU Coll. Dentistry, N.Y.C., 1984-87; instr. dental asst. tng. program CUNY and Staten Island Hosp., 1988—. Mem. Staten Island Hist. Soc., 1975—, Staten Island Inst. Arts and Scis., 1987—. Recipient Pierre Fauchard award Pierre Fauchard Acad., 1983. Fellow Acad. Gen. Dentistry; mem. Richmond County Dental Soc. (sec. 1988-89, treas. 1989-90, v.p. 1990—), Am. Acad. History of Dentistry, Am. Soc. Dentistry for Children, Alpha Omega Dental Fraternity (sec. 1981-82, v.p. 1982-83). Democrat. Jewish. Office: 3930 Richmond Ave Staten Island NY 10312

EGAN, CATHERINE DENISE, advertising and public relations executive; b. Paris, Ill., Mar. 13, 1952; d. Dennis Lee and Mary Lou (McMullen) Adams; m. Jerry R. Egan, Jan. 11, 1974; children: Lindsey Leigh, Cody Adams. BS in Edn., Eastern Ill. U., Charleston, 1973. Cert. elem. tchr. Tchr. Paris Union Dist. 95, 1974-79; salesperson Inn Fashions, Paris, 1983-89; news corr. Terre Haute (Ind.) Tribune-Star, 1986-89; tchrs. aide Paris Union Sch. Dist. 95, 1989—; with advt./pub. rels. First Fed. Bank, Paris, 1989-90; kindergarten tchr. Kansas (Ill.) Community Unit Sch. Dist. #3, 1990—. Campaign coord. Sue Suter for Ill. Comptroller, Edgar Cunty, 1990; organizer Women's Health Expo, Eastern Ill. U., Charleston, 1987, 88; mem. adv. bd. Coalition Against Domestic Violence. Mem. Paris Jr. Woman's Club (pres. 1984-86). Republican.

EGAN, DOROTHY ANN, English educator; b. Hartford, Conn., Jan. 31, 1934; d. James John and Adeline Katherine (Ebersold) E. Student, Boston Coll., 1969, 71-73; BA in German, Conn. Coll., 1957; MA in English, Trinity Coll., Hartford, Conn., 1960; postgrad., Indiana U. of Pa., 1984—. Tchr. English Colby-Sawyer Coll., New London, N.H., 1962—, dean of studies, 1976-83, chair humanities dept., 1969, 87; chair nursing search com. Colby-Sawyer Coll., New London, 1984-85, chair faculty pers. com., 1985-87, chair standing com., 1987-89, dir. acad. devel. ctr., 1987—, chair faculty grievance com. 1990—. Author: Manual for Tutors, 1987, Writing Lab Manual, 1987, Communications Skills: Reading, 1984, Directory of Career Information and Curriculum Requirements, 1979-83, Faculty Adviser's Directory, 1982. Co-founder College-Community Coun., New London, 1979; reader Talking Books Div., Concord, N.H., 1981—. Mem. AAUP, AAUW, Nat. Coun. Tchrs. English, New Eng. Assn. Tchrs. English. Office: Colby Sawyer Coll Main St New London NH 03257

EGAN, EILEEN MARY, university president; b. Boston, Jan. 11; d. Eugene O. and Mary B. (Condon) E. A.B., Spalding U., 1956; M.A., Cath. U. Am., 1963, Ph.D. (Bd. Trustees scholar), 1966; J.D., U. Louisville, 1981. Bar: Ky. 1981. Joined Sisters of Charity of Nazareth, Roman Catholic Ch., 1944; tchr. secondary schs. Wakefield, Mass., 1956-60, Memphis, 1960-62; mem. faculty English dept. Cath. U. Am., Washington, 1963-66; chmn. dept. English, Spalding U., Louisville, 1966-67, v.p., 1968-69, pres., 1969—; prof. U. Louisville Law Sch., 1982-83; adminstrv. intern Smith Coll., Northampton, Mass., 1967-68; mem. Ky. State Commn. on Higher Edn., 1969-72, 75-77; chmn. Louisville br. Fed. Res. Bank, 1981, 84. Exec. bd. Old Ky. Home council Boy Scouts Am., 1976-87; mem. bishop's pastoral council Archdiocese of Louisville, 1975-78; mem. Louisville Com. Fgn. Relations, 1978-83; chmn. open spaces adv. com. City of Louisville, 1975-81; bd. dirs. Met. United Way, 1976-80; bd. dirs. chpt. NCCJ, 1973-84; bd. dirs. Better Bus. Bur. Greater Louisville, 1974-79, v.p., 1975-79; bd. dirs. St. Joseph Infirmary, 1970-71, trustee, 1971-76, chmn. bd. trustees, 1975-76; trustee Ky. Ind. Coll. Found., 1970—; bd. dirs. Kentuckiana Metroversity, 1972—, chmn., 1982-83, exec. com., 1977—, bd. pres., 1990—; trustee JH Systems, 1984-89, bd. trustees, 1989—, Jewish Hosp., 1982-88; mem. County Judge Execs. Adv. Com. on Ethics, 1986—, Ky. Exec. Adv. Bd. for the Div. of Mental Health in Corrections, 1987—; bd. dirs. Ky. Country Day Sch., 1982-88. Recipient Equality award Louisville Urban League, 1978, award Phi Delta Kappa, 1979, Blanche B. Ottenheimer award Louisville Jewish Community Center, 1978, Brotherhood award NCCJ, 1979, Disting. Service award Louisville chpt. Am. Jewish Com., 1987, Women of Achievement award, Louisville Bus. and Profl. Women, 1989; Inst. Internat. Edn. fellow, 1963; Cultural Exchange Guest to Republic of China, 1985. Mem. Am. Assn. Higher Edn., So. Assn. Colls. and Schs., Nat. Cath. Edn. Assn. (exec. com. 1973-76), Louisville C. of C. (public edn. com. 1978-83, dir. 1981-84), English Speaking Union, AAUW, ABA, Ky. Bar Assn., Louisville Bar Assn., Am. Judicature Soc., Am. Future Soc. Democrat. Office: Spalding U 851 S 4th St Louisville KY 40203

EGAN, SHIRLEY ANNE, retired nursing educator; b. Haverill, Mass.; d. Rush B. and Beatrice (Bengle) Willard. Diploma, St. Joseph's Hosp. Sch. Nursing, Nashua, N.H., 1945; B.S. in Nursing Edn., Boston U., 1949, M.S., 1954. Instr. sci. Sturdy Meml. Hosp. Sch. Nursing, Attleboro, Mass., 1949-51; instr. sci. Peter Bent Brigham Hosp. Sch. Nursing, Boston, 1951-53, ednl. dir., 1953-55, assoc. dir. Sch. Nursing, 1955-59, med. surg. coordinator, 1971-73, assoc. dir. Sch. Nursing, 1973-79, dir., 1979-85; cons. North Country Hosp., 1985-86; infection control practitioner, 1986-87; contract instr. Natchitohes Area Tech. Inst., 1988-90, Sabine Valley Tech Inst., 1990—; nurse edn. adviser AID (formerly ICA), Karachi, Pakistan, 1959-67; prin. Coll. Nursing, Karachi, 1959-67; dir. Vis. Nurse Service, Nashua, N.H., 1967-70; cons. nursing edn. Pakistan Ministry of Health, Labour and Social Welfare, 1959-67; adviser to editor Pakistan Nursing and Health Rev., 1959-67; exec. bd. Nat. Health Edn. Com., Pakistan; WHO short-term cons. U. W.I., Jamaica, 1970-71; mem. Greater Nashua Health Planning Council. Contbr. articles to profl. pubs. Bd. dirs. Matthew Thornton health Ctr., Nashua, Nashua Child Care Ctr.; vol. ombudsman N.H. Council on Aging; mem. Nashua Service League. Served as 1st lt., Army Nurse Corps., 1945-47. Mem. Trained Nurses Assn. Pakistan, Nat. League for Nursing, Assn. for Preservation Hist. Natchitoches, St. Joseph's Sch. Nursing Alumnae Assn., Boston U. Alumnae Assn., Brit. Soc. Health Edn., Cath. Daus. Am. (vice regent ct. Bishop Malloy), Statis. Study Grads. Karachi Coll. Nursing, Sigma Theta Tau. Home: Rte 1 Box 1268A Natchitoches LA 71457

EGATZ, LAURA ANN BRUGOS, continuing education executive; b. Passaic, N.J., Dec. 17, 1942; d. Frank and Anna (Horvath) Brugos; m. Roy A. Egatz, July 17, 1965; 1 child, Ron. BA, Montclair State Coll., 1964, MA, 1979. Cert. tchr., prin., supr., N.J. Tchr. Berkeley Coll. of Bus., W. Paterson, N.J., 1978-79; founder continuing edn. div., dir. Garret Mountain campus The Berkeley Sch., 1980-83, acad. dean, 1983-84; pres. The Berkeley Sch., White Plains, N.Y., 1984-86; v.p. for continuing edn. Berkeley Coll. of Bus., W. Paterson, 1986—; founder, v.p. continuing edn. div. Bergen campus. Mem. Nat. Bus. Edn. Assn. (contbr. to yearbook 1984), Ea. Bus. Edn. Assn., Nat. Assn. Lifelong Learning, Delta Pi Epsilon. Office: Berkeley Coll Bus 44 Rifle Camp Rd West Peterson NJ 07424

EGELAND, ELIZABETH VOWELL, food products corporation executive; b. Martin, Tenn., Mar. 26, 1936; d. Vertrees and Elizabeth (Tate) Vowell; m. Elmer M.H. Nolte (div. Mar. 1976); children: Steven Martin, Stanley Vowell; m. Duane R. Egeland. AB, Memphis State U., 1956. Instr. Cobb County Mentally Retarded, Marietta, Ga., 1970-73; sales rep. Rittenbaum Bros., Atlanta, 1973-75, Nat. Labs., Montuale, N.J., 1975-77; dir. instl. sales New South Mfg. Co., Atlanta, 1977-78; nat. sales merchandiser Cornelius Co., Anoka, Minn., 1978-80; sr. nat. account mgr. Nestle Food Corp., Purchase, N.Y., 1980—. Pres. Marietta (Ga.) Council of Garden Clubs, 1968, Atlanta Kiwi Club, 1970; bd. dirs. Nat. Little League, Marietta, 1974-75. Mem. Nat. Assn. Exec. Women, Nat. Orgn. Women in Food Service Sales and Mktg. Office: Nestle Food Corp 904 Dunwoody Chace Atlanta GA 30328

EGELSTON, ROBERTA RIETHMILLER, writer; b. Pitts., Nov. 20, 1946; d. Robert E. and Doris (Bauer) Riethmiller; m. David Michael Egelston, Oct. 10, 1975; 1 child, Brian David. BA in Bus. Administrn., Thiel Coll., 1968; MLS, U. Pitts., 1974. Bus. mgr. Pitts. Pastoral Inst., 1968-70; administrv. asst. Coun. Alcoholism and Drug Abuse, Lancaster, Pa., 1970-72; dir. career planning libr. U. Pitts., 1974-78; writer, 1978--; book reviewer Coll. Placement Coun., Bethlehem, Pa., 1977-78; cons. State Affiliated Colls. and Us., 1976; group leader Johns-Norris Assocs., Pitts., 1975-76. Author: Career Planning Materials, 1981, Credits and Careers for Adult Learners, 1985. Bd. dirs. Lauri Ann West Libr., Pitts., 1983-84; active in PTA, 1985-88. Mem. AAUW (bd. dirs. Fox Chapel Area br. 1980—), Les Lauriers (sr. women's hon., Thiel Coll.), Beta Phi Mu.

EGENDORF, NORMA LUCY, advertising agency executive; b. Phila., Oct. 7, 1928; d. Louis R. and Alice J. (Petrarch) Testardi; m. Irwin A. Egendorf, Feb. 10, 1961 (div. 1980); m. Jerome Maxwell Pomerantz, Sept. 27, 1986. Student in journalism Temple U., 1950-52; Assoc., Charles Morris Price Sch. Advt. and Journalism, 1948. Advt. asst. Internat. Resistance Co., Phila., 1952-54, advt., sales promotion mgr., 1954-61; account exec. Mel Richman, Inc., Bala Cynwyd, Pa., 1961-68, v.p., acctg. supr., 1968-72; pres. The Advt. People, Inc., Bala Cynwyd, 1972—; instr. Intro. to Advt. program; lectr. in field. Contbr. numerous articles to profl. jours. Bd. dirs. Muscular Dystrophy Assn., Southeastern Pa., 1972-74, pres., 1976-88; bd. dirs. Com. of 70, Phila., 1982-88, vice chmn., 1982-84; bd. govs. Main Line YMCA, Pa., 1975-79; trustee Charles Morris Price Sch., chmn. 1982-84, com. mem. 1980—; pub. relations com. Am. Swedish Hist. Mus., 1985-86. Recipient Silver Medal award Am. Advt. Fedn., 1980, award of Merit Artist's Guild of Del. Valley, 1981, Distinguished Alunma award Charles Morris Price Sch., 1982, 3 awards of Recognition Muscular Dystrophy Assn., 1978-88. Mem. Poor Richard Club (pres. 1984-86, bd. dirs. 1980-88), Mktg. Communications Execs., Internat. (program chmn. 1982-85, bd. dirs. 1982-85), Inst. Contemporary Art (pub. relations chmn. 1980-81), Direct Mktg. Assn. (Gold Mail Box award 1968, promotion chmn. 1975-76), Phila. Club Advt. Women. Club: Germantown Cricket (Phila.) (pub. relations and promotion chmn. 1982-84). Avocations: tennis, art, sculpture, theatre. Home: 730 S American St Philadelphia PA 19147 Office: The Advt People Inc 215 N Presidential Blvd Bala-Cynwyd PA 19004

EGGERS, CECILIA DEMOVICH, educator; b. Raritan, N.J., Nov. 23, 1942; d. Frank C. and Florence S. (Bortolanzo) Demovich; m. William A. Eggers Jr., June 26, 1966; 1 child, Jennifer Christine. BA, St. Francis Coll., Loretto, Pa., 1964. Cert. sch. librarian, N.J., Ohio. Librarian Somerville (N.J.) Bd. Edn., 1964-66, Fairborn (Ohio) Bd. Edn., 1966-67; dir. youth recreational activities Bitburg AFB, Fed. Republic Germany, 1970-72; dir. adult edn. Allentown (Pa.) State Hosp., 1984—. Mem. Pa. Assn. Continuing Edn. Roman Catholic. Home: 3891 Pleasant Ave Allentown PA 18103

EGGERS, IDAMARIE RASMUSSEN, pharmaceutical manufacturing and research; b. Grand Rapids, Mich., Oct. 19, 1925; d. Nels Peter Victor and Karen Agnes (Feldt) Rasmussen; m. Raymond Frederick Eggers, Jr., May 29, 1955; children: Karen Elizabeth Eggers Baird, Raymond Frederick III. BS in Chemistry, U. Mich., 1945, MS, 1946. Chemist Merck & Co. Inc., Rahway, N.J., 1946-57, chem. biol. data coordinator, 1965-69, sect. head biol. data, 1969-77, mgr. biol. data, 1977-86; agt., broker Ray Eggers Agy., Rahway, 1958—. Patentee in field. Librarian Rahway Hist. Soc., 1969—, treas., 1972-84. Scholar Grand Rapids Woman's Club, 1942, U. Mich. Regents, 1944-46. Mem. AAAS, ACS, Metro. Women Chemists, N.Y. Acad. Sci., Rahway C. of C., Rahway Woman's Club (pres. 1988—). Episcopalian. Home and Office: 208 W Milton Ave Rahway NJ 07065

EGGERS, RENEE MARLENE, management executive; b. Ft. Worth, Feb. 8, 1956; d. Gordon M. and Ozella M. (Beebe) E. BA, Youngstown (Ohio) State U., 1978, MS in Edn., 1982, AAS, 1983, BS in Applied Sci., 1986; postgrad., Kent State U., 1988—. Tchr. Howland Christian Sch., Warren, Ohio, 1979-80; grad. asst. Youngstown (Ohio) State U., 1981-82, adj. faculty, 1982-83, adminstrv. asst. reading lab., 1983; reading instr., tutor Pa. State U., Sharon, 1983-84, lang. ctr. coord., 1984-89; co-owner CORD Techs., Hubbard, Ohio, 1989—. Contbr. articles to profl. jours. Recipient Pa. State U. Adv. Bd. grantee, 1984, 86. Mem. Assn. Ednl. Communications and Tech. Democrat. Baptist. Home: 7023 Chestnut Ridge Rd SE Hubbard OH 44425 Office: CORD Techs 7023 Chestnut Ridge Rd SE Hubbard OH 44425

EGGINTON, WYNN MEAGHER, university researcher and program facilitator; b. Portland, Oreg., Oct. 18, 1944; d. George Shaw and Florence Marion (Marriott) Meagher; m. Kendall Watson De Bevoise, Dec. 23, 1966 (div. 1984); children: Jan, Ana, Lyn; m. Everett Egginton, Sept. 27, 1986; 1 child, William Everett. BA, Stanford U., 1966; MA, U. Oreg., 1985. Intern HUD, San Francisco, 1966-68; planning officer Oakland (Calif.) Redevel. Agy., 1968; Coll. English tchr. US Peach Corps, Thailand, 1969-73; English tchr. Internat. Sch., Santiago, Chile; instr. English Lane Community Coll., Eugene, Oreg., 1980-81; document analyst U. Oreg., Eugene, 1981-82, coord. communications Coll. Edn., 1982-84; asst. to dean Sch. Edn. U. Louisville, 1984--; coord. joint com. of Jefferson County Pub. Schs. and U. Louisville, 1987—; cons., speaker sch. dist./univ. collaboration to various ednl. orgns., 1985—. Contbr. articles to profl. jours. Mem. Atherton High Sch. Bd., Louisville, 1987—; mem. choir St. Andrews Episcopal Ch., Louisville, 1986—, U. Louisville Collegium, 1987-88. Recipient Outstanding Svc. award Jefferson County Coun. for Retarded Citizens, 1986, Disting. Achievement award Wash. Edn. Press Assn., 1987. Mem. Am. Ednl. Rsch. Assn., Phi Delta Kappa. Democrat. Episcopalian.

EGLITIS, IRMA L., retired dermatology educator; b. Riga, Latvia, USSR, Oct. 13, 1907; came to U.S., 1950; d. Juris Georgs and Elizabete (Kronenberg) Liepins; m. John Arnold Eglitis, Apr. 17, 1938. MD magna cum laude, U. Latvia, 1931. Diplomate State Bd. in Dermatology and Venereal Diseases, Latvia. Asst. instr. Faculty of Medicine, U. Latvia, Riga, 1932-36, jr. instr., 1936-37, instr., 1937-44; instr. Faculty of Medicine, Erst Mortiz Arndt U., Greifswald, Fed. Republic Germany, 1944-45; instr. Coll. of Medicine, Ohio State U., Columbus, 1952-56, asst. prof., 1956-62, assoc. prof., 1962-67, prof., 1967-78, prof. emeritus, 1978—; cons. specialist for dermatology and venereal disease Brit. Control Commn. Med. Svc., Fed. Republic Germany, 1945-50; pvt. practice specializing in dermatology and venereal disease, Schleswig, Fed. Republic Germany, 1945-50. Co-author: Anatomy and Histology of the Eye and Orbit in the Domestic Animals, 1960, The Rabbit in Eye Research, 1964; contbr. articles to profl. jours.

Recipient Cert. of Merit AMA, 1982, Community Leaders and Noteworthy Am. award editorial bd. of Am. Biog. Inst., 1975. Mem. Am. Assn. Anatomists, Columbus Med. Women's Assn. (sec.-treas. 1958-59, sec. 1965-67, v.p. 1959-60, pres. 1961-63, 68), Med. Women's Internat. Assn., Coun. Inst. for Rsch. in Vision, Am. Med. Women's Assn. (nat. exec. bd., nat. sec. 1969, nat. chmn. med. edn. and practice com. 1967, nat. chmn. med. opportunities and practice com. 1968, nat. constn. and by-laws com. 1970, nat. chmn. resolutions com. 1972), Omicron Kappa Upsilon. Office: Ohio State U Coll Medicine 333 W 10th Ave Columbus OH 43210

EGNER, BETTY JANE, travel agency professional; b. Quakertown, Pa., Oct. 7, 1951; d. Charles Franklin and Frances (Webber) E. BS, Valparaiso U., 1973; MBA in Fin., Am. U., 1983. Purchasing agt. UMI Corp., Wood Dale, Ill., 1974-76; regional buyer Mobil Oil Corp., Schaumburg, Ill., 1976-78; hdqrs. buyer Mobil Oil Corp., N.Y.C., 1979-80; internat. buyer Mobil Oil Corp., Fairfax, Va., 1980-87; group cruise specialist Cruise Co. Georgetown, Washington, 1988-89; owner Cruise Travel Cons., Inc., Santa Fe, N.Mex., 1989—; mktg. cons. Am. Indian Nat. Bank, Washington, 1983. Bd. dirs. No. Va. chpt. Am. Cancer Soc., 1985—; chmn. charity cruise Children's Oncology Services, Washington, 1988; active Wolftrap Assocs., Washington Performing Arts Soc., Friends of Kennedy Ctr., Smithsonian Resident Assocs. Mem. Queen Elizabeth II World Cruise Soc., Princess Cruises Cruisemaster Club, Nat. Assn. for Cruise Only Agys., Pacific Asia Travel Assn., Rep. Senatorial Inner Circle, Tall Club of Greater Washington, Washington Ski Club, Sierra Club. Republican. Office: Cruise Travel Cons PO Box 15515 Santa Fe NM 87506

EHLEN, JUDY, geologist; b. Portland, Oreg., June 27, 1944; d. E.A. and Mina (Cowgill) E. BA in German, U. Oreg., 1966, BA, MA in Geology, 1969; MA in History, George Mason U., 1980; PhD, U. Birmingham, Eng., 1990. Geologist USA Engr. Topographic Labs., Ft. Belvoir, Va., 1972—. Contbr. articles to profl. jours. Mem. Geol. Soc. Am., British Geomorphological Rsch. Group, Geol. Soc. of Washington (councillor 1989—), Ussher Soc., Sigma Xi. Office: USA Engr Topographic Labs Fort Belvoir VA 22060-5546

EHLERS, ELEANOR MAY COLLIER (MRS. FREDERICK BURTON EHLERS), civic worker; b. Klamath Falls, Oreg., Apr. 23, 1920; d. Alfred Douglas and Ethel (Foster) Collier; BA, U. Oreg., 1941; secondary tchrs. credentials Stanford, 1942; m. Frederick Burton Ehlers, June 26, 1943; children: Frederick Douglas, Charles Collier. Tchr., Salinas Union High Sch., 1942-43; piano tchr. pvt. lessons, Klamath Falls, 1958—. Mem. Child Guidance Adv. Coun., 1956-60; mem. adv. com. Boys and Girls Aid Soc., 1965-67 ; mem. Gov.'s Adv. Com. Arts and Humanities, 1966-67; bd. mem. PBS TV Sta. KSYS, 1988—, Friends of Mus. U. Oreg., 1966-69, Arts in Oreg., 1966-68, Klamath County Colls. for Oreg.'s Future, 1968— ; co-chmn. Friends of Collier Park, Collier Park Logging Mus., 1986-88, sec. 1988—; chpt. pres. Am. Field Svc., 1962-63; mem. Gov.'s Com. Governance of Community Colls., 1967; bd. dirs. Favell Mus. Western Art and Artifacts, 1971—, Community Concert Assn., 1950— , pres., 1966-74; established Women's Guild at Merle West Med. Ctr., 1965, sec. bd. dirs, 1962-65, 76-90, bd. dirs., 1962—, mem. bldg. com. 1962-67, mem. planning com., chmn. edn. and rsch. com. hosp. bd., 1967—; pres., bd. dirs. Merle West Med. Ctr., 1990—. Named Woman of Month Klamath Herald News, 1965; named grant to Oreg. Endowed Fellowship Fund, AAUW, 1971; recipient greatest Svc. award Oreg. Tech. Inst., 1970-71, Internat. Woman of Achievement award Quota Club, 1981, U. Oreg. Pioneer award, 1981. Mem. AAUW (local pres. 1955-56), Oreg. Music Tchrs. Assn. (pres. Klamath Basin dist. 1979-81), P.E.O. (Oreg. dir. 1968-75, state pres. 1974-75, trustee internat. Continuing Edn. Fund 1977-83, chmn. 1981-83), Friends of Collier State Park Logging Mus. (sec. 1988—), Pi Beta Phi, Mu Phi Epsilon, Pi Lambda Theta. Presbyterian. Address: 1338 Pacific Terr Klamath Falls OR 97601

EHMANN, JOHANNA LOMBARDO, oncology nurse; b. Albany, N.Y., Feb. 6, 1952; d. Pasquale and Angelina (Bagnardi) Lombardo; m. David Ehmann, Dec. 1, 1979; children: Donna, John. AAS, Maria Coll., Albany, N.Y., 1972. Cert. nurse oncologist; cert. mastectomy fitter. Cons. Appearance Concepts Cons. Group, Seattle; oncology nurse Albany (N.Y.) Med. Coll.; pvt. practice oncology nursing Johanna's of Albany Ltd. Mem. Oncology Nursing Soc. Home: 161 Holmesdale Albany NY 12208 Office: 199 New Scotland Ave Albany NY 12208

EHMER, MARJY ARDUINA NICCOLL, psychologist, educator; b. N.Y.C., Feb. 3, 1927; d. George A. and Ray (Haberman) Niccoll. B.A. cum laude, Bklyn. Coll., 1947; postgrad., NYU, 1947-49; Ph.D., U. Rochester, 1959; assoc. fellow Inst. Advanced Study in Rational Psychotherapy, N.Y.C., 1976-77; m. Richard Ehmer, Jan. 23, 1948 (div. Sept. 1965); 1 child, George; m. Jess L. Dow, Sept. 1971. Lab. asst. Bklyn. Coll., 1946-48, instr., 1947-48; rsch. asst. U. Rochester, N.Y., 1948-51, Tufts Coll., Medford, Mass., 1951-54; instr. Brandeis U., Waltham, Mass., 1952; instr. U. R.I., Kingston, 1954-58, asst. prof., 1958-60, U. Bridgeport (Conn.), 1960-61, assoc. prof., 1961-62; trainee VA Hosp., West Haven, Conn., 1962-63; assoc. prof. So. Conn. State U., New Haven, 1963-69, prof., 1969-85, prof. emeritus, 1985—, dir. mental health specialization psychology dept., 1979-85; pvt. practice psychology, 1977—. Contbr. articles to profl. jours. Dist. cons. Dept. of Rehab. Svcs., 1989—. Bd. dirs., chmn. safety svcs. com. So. Cen. Conn. chpt. ARC, 1979-84, also mem. exec. com. Mem. Am. Psychol. Assn., Eastern Psychol. Assn. (election com. 1958), New Eng. Psychol. Assn. (steering com. 1982-85, 87—, pres.-elect 1985, pres. 1986, past pres. 1987, editor NEPA Newsletter 1989—), Conn. Psychol. Assn. (co-chmn. continuing edn. com. 1977-79, editor Conn. Psychologist 1979-80), Internat. Coun. Psychologists, AAAS, Race Brook Country Club, Mount Sunapee Ski Club, Sigma Xi, Psi Chi. Address: 497 Dogwood Rd Orange CT 06477

EHRENBERG, MIRIAM COLBERT, psychologist; b. N.Y., Mar. 16, 1930; m. Otto Ehrenberg, Sept. 20,1956; children: Ingrid, Erica. BA, Queens Coll.; MA, CUNY; PhD, New Sch. Social Rsch. Psychologist pvt. practice, N.Y., 1970—; dir. psychotherapy Spence Chapin, N.Y., 1980-84. Author: The Psychotherapy Maze, 1987, Optimum Brain Power, 1985, The Intimate Circle, 1988. Office: 141 E 55th St New York NY 10022

EHRENKRANZ, SHIRLEY MALAKOFF, university dean, social work educator; b. N.Y.C., Nov. 9, 1920; d. Isidore and Diana Frances (Lewis) Malakoff; m. Gilbert Ehrenkranz, Mar. 29, 1946 (dec.); children: Jean, Joel, Pamela; m. Fred Kasoff, July 11, 1982. A.B., Hunter Coll., 1939; M.A., Bryn Mawr Coll., 1943; M.S.W., U. Pa., 1945; D.S.W., Columbia U., 1967. Case worker Jewish Welfare Soc., Phila., 1943-44; case supr. S.I. Social Svc., N.Y., 1945-48, United Family and Children's Svc., Plainfield, N.J., 1949-53; field instr. Rutgers U., 1960-62; rsch. asst. Columbia U., N.Y.C., 1964-65; asst. prof. social work NYU, N.Y.C., 1966-68, assoc. prof. social work, 1968-73, prof. social work, 1973—, assoc. dean Sch. Social Work, 1969-76, acting dean, 1976-77, 1977—. Co-editor: Clinical Social Work with Maltreated Children and Their Families, 1989; contbr. book revs., articles on social work to profl. jours., chpts. to textbooks. Recipient Disting. Alumna award U. Pa., 1970, ann. award for svc. to community NYU Jewish Culture Found., 1988; NIMH grantee, 1963-64, 65. Mem. N.Y. State Assn. Deans (v.p. 1979-80, pres. 1980-81), Nat. Assn. Social Workers, Acad. Cert. Social Workers, N.Y. State Assn. Deans of Social Work Schs. (pres. 1988-89). Office: NYU Sch Social Work 3 Washington Sq N New York NY 10003

EHRINGER, SUSANN, transportation executive; b. Toronto, Aug. 22, 1960; came to U.S., 1961; d. Hans Juergen and Marion (Friedrich) E. AA, Santa Monica (Calif.) Coll., 1980; BA, UCLA, 1983. Adminstrv. asst. Flying Tiger Line, Inc., L.A., 1983-86; reservations coord. Americantours Internat., Inc., L.A., 1986-87, reservations supr., 1987-88, ops. supr., 1988-89, mgr. fit ops., 1989—. Contbr. poet: Poetic Voices of America, 1990, American Poetry Anthology, 1990. Mem. German Am. Club Santa Monica, NAFE. Office: Americantours Internat 9800 Sepulveda Blvd Los Angeles CA 90045

EHRLICH, AVA, television producer; b. St. Louis, Aug. 14, 1950; d. Norman and Lillian (Gellman) Ehrlich; m. Barry K. Freedman, Mar. 31, 1979; 1 child, Alexander Zev. BJ, Northwestern U., 1972, MJ, 1973; MA, Occidental Coll., 1976. Reporter, asst. mng. editor Lerner Newspapers, Chgo., 1974-75; reporter, news editor Sta. KMOX, St. Louis, 1976-79; producer Sta. WXYZ, Detroit, 1979-85; exec. producer Sta. KSDK-TV, St. Louis, 1985—; guest editor Mademoiselle mag., N.Y.C., 1971; free lance writer, coll. prof. Detroit, Chgo., St. Louis, 1974—. Trustee CORO Found., St. Louis, 1976-77, 86—; bd. dirs. Nat. Kidney Found., St. Louis, 1987. Named Outstanding Woman in Broadcasting Am. Women in Radio & TV, 1983, Clarion award WICI, 1989, Journalism award Am. Chiropractic Assn., 1989, Best in Midwest Feature award, 1989, AP award Ill. UPI, 1989; CORO Found. fellow in pub. affairs, 1975-76, Women in Communications Nat. award, 1988, 6 local emmy awards. Mem. Nat. Acad. TV Arts and Scis. (com. mem. 1986—, local Emmy award 1986), Women in Communications (sec. 1978-79), Soc. Profl. Journalists. Democrat. Jewish. Home: 7469 Teasdale Saint Louis MO 63130 Office: Sta KSDK-TV 1000 Market Saint Louis MO 63101

EHRLICH, ELIZABETH, journalist; b. Detroit, Oct. 12, 1954; d. Howard B. and Sarah Lillian (Stocker) E.; m. Leon A. Potok, Sept. 22, 1984; children: Amalia G., Louis A. BA, U. Mich., 1977. Com. aide Mich. State Legislature, Lansing, 1978-80; staff editor Bus. Week, N.Y.C., 1981-84, corp. fin. editor, 1984-86, social issues editor, 1986-89, assoc. editor, 1989—. Author: Nellie Bly, 1989. Office: Bus Week 1221 Ave of Americas New York NY 10020

EHRLICH, EVELYN JOAN, marketing executive; b. Pitts., June 13, 1950; d. Fritz J. and Liesel (Levi) E. BA, Barnard Coll., 1972; MS, Columbia U., 1976; PhD, NYU, 1982. Asst. prof. communications and film U. Vt., Burlington, 1980-81, NYU, N.Y.C., 1983-84, Baruch Coll./CUNY, N.Y.C., 1985-88; pres. EC Communications, N.Y.C., 1982—; cons. Lexington Sch. for Deaf, N.Y.C.; speaker at profl. meetings. Author: Cmema of Paradox, 1985; contbr. articles to various publs. Mem. Fin. Womens Assn., Am. Mktg. Assn., Bank Mktg. Assn. Office: EC Communications 7 W 14th St New York NY 10011

EHRLICH, GERALDINE ELIZABETH, food service management consultant; b. Phila., Nov. 28, 1939; d. Joseph Vincent and Agnes Barbara (Campbell) McKenna; m. S. Paul Ehrlich, Jr., June 20, 1959; children: Susan Patricia, Paula Jeanne, Jill Marie. BS, Drexel Inst. Tech., 1957—. Supervisory dietitian ARA Svc. Co., Phila. and San Francisco, 1959-65; dietary mgmt. cons. HEW, Washington, 1967-68; nutrition cons., hypertension rsch. team U. Calif. Micronesia, 1970; regional sales dir. Marriott Corp., Bethesda, Md., 1976-78; dir. sales and profl. svcs. Coll. and Health Care div. Macke Co., Cheverly, Md., 1978, gen. mgr., 1978-79; v.p. ops., div., 1979-80, pres. Health Care div., 1980-81; regional v.p. Custom Mgmt. Corp., Alexandria, Va., 1981-83, v.p. mktg., 1983-87; v.p. mktg. and healthcare sales Morrison's Custom Mgmt., Mobile, Ala., 1987-88; v.p. sales, ARA Svcs., Phila., 1988—; cons. mktg. The Green House, Tokyo, 1987-88; chmn. bd. Mktg. Matrix, Falls Church, Va., 1984-88. Mem. Health Systems Agy. No. Va., 1976-77; chmn. Health Care Adv. Bd. Fairfax County Va., 1973-77; vice chmn. Fairfax County Community Action Com., 1973-77; treas. Fairfax County Dem. Com., 1969-73; trustee Fairfax Hosp., 1973-77; bd. dirs. Tennis Patrons, Washington, 1984-88. Mem. Internat. Women's Assn., Am. Mgmt. Assn., Nat. Assn. Female Execs., Roundtable for Women in Food Service, Soc. Mktg. Profls. Club: Internat. (Washington). Avocation: reading. Home: 6512 Lakeview Dr Falls Church VA 22041 Office: ARA Svcs 1101 Market St Philadelphia PA 19107

EHRLICH, LESLIE SHARON, communications executive, lawyer; b. Bklyn., July 30, 1952; d. Abraham and Evelyn (Kuznetz) E.; m. Lee Marc Kaswiner, Aug. 11, 1979; children: Adam Jason, Jessica Sara. BA, Hofstra U., 1973; paralegal cert., Adelphi U., 1974; MA, Montclair State U., 1977; JD, Pace U., 1981. Owner Paralegal Corp., Newark, 1975-77; supr. paralegal AT&T, N.Y.C., 1977-79, law clk. with sales dept., 1979-81; mgr. state regulatory N.Y. Telephone Co., N.Y.C., 1981-82; atty. Bell Communications Research, N.Y.C., 1983-84; mgr. contracts AT&T-IS, Morristown, N.J., 1984-86; mgr. contracts, adminstrn. and policies Timeplex, Woodcliff Lakes, N.J., 1986-87; v.p., gen. counsel M&SD, Lyndhurst, N.J., 1987-88; gen. counsel Belgioive Enterprises, Inc., 1988-89; adj. prof. Am. Paralegal Inst., South Orange, N.J., 1982-83, Seton Hall, Newark, 1983-84; chairperson Nat. Coun. Jewish Women, N.J., 1981-82, Edn. and Programming, Suburban Jewish Ctr., Florham Park, N.J., 1984—; attendee Brookings Inst., Washington, 1986. Chairperson Nat. Council Jewish Women, N.J., 1981-82, Edn./Programming, Suburban Jewish Ctr., Florham Park, N.J., 1984—; attendee Brookings Inst., Washington, 1986. Mem. ABA (vice chairperson young lawyers corp. council sect. 1984-88, pub. utility com. 1986—, student liaison antitrust com. 1979-80, Silver Key award 1979, Gold Key award 1980), N.Y. Bar Assn., N.J. Bar Assn., Exec. Women of N.J. (sec. 1987—). Democrat. Jewish. Home: 8 Pheasant Way Florham Park NJ 07932 Office: M&SD Lyndhurst NJ 07071

EHRLICH, MARGARET ELIZABETH GORLEY, systems engineer, mathematics educator, consultant; b. Eatonton, Ga., Nov. 12, 1950; d. Frank Griffith and Edith Roy (Beall) Gorley; m. Jonathan Steven Ehrlich. BS in Math., U. Ga., 1972; MEd, Ga. State U., 1977, EdS, 1982, PhD, 1987; postgrad. Woodrow Wilson Coll. of Law, 1977-78. Cert. secondary tchr., Ga. Tchr. DeKalb County Bd. Edn., Decatur, Ga., 1972-83; chmn. dept. math. Columbia High Sch., Decatur, 1978-83; with product devel. Chalkboard Co., Atlanta, 1983-84; math instr. Ga. State U., Atlanta, 1983—; pres. Elise, Atlanta, 1983—; course specialist Ga. Pacific Co., Atlanta, 1984-86; systems engr. Lotus Devel. Corp., 1986-89; asst. prof. math. Ga. State U., Atlanta, 1989—; research assoc. SUNY-Stony Brook, 1976; modeling instr. Barbizon Modeling Sch., Atlanta, 1977-81; instr. Ga. State Coll. for Kids, 1984-85; test-taking cons., hon. mem. Communication Workers of Am., Atlanta, 1985—; tng. cons. Lotus Devel. Corp. Author: (software user manual) Micro Maestro, 1983, Music Math, 1984. Mem. editorial bd. CPA Computer Report, Atlanta, 1984-85. Active DeKalb LWV, 1980, Atlanta Preservation Soc., 1985, Planned Parenthood; tchr. St. Phillips Ch. Sch., Atlanta, 1981-88; vol. Joel Chandler Harris Assn., Atlanta, 1984-87. Named STAR Tchr. DeKalb County Bd. Edn., 1979, 80, 81, Most Outstanding Tchr., Barbizon Schs. of Modeling, 1980, Colo. Outward Bound, 1985, Disting. Educator, Ga. State U., 1987. Mem. LWV, Math. Assn. Am., Nat. Council Tchrs. Math., Ga. Council Tchrs. Math., Math. Assn. Am., Assn. Women in Math. (del. to China Sci. and Tech. Exch., 1989-90), Am. Soc. Tng. and Devel. Greater Atlanta, Atlanta Women's Network, DeKalb Personal Computer Instr. Assn. (pres. 1984), Aux. Med. Assn. Ga., Daus. of Confederacy, Atlanta Track Club. Democrat. Episcopalian. Avocations: piano; creative crafts; aerobics; jogging; fashion modeling. Home: 240 Cliff Overlook Atlanta GA 30350 Office: Ga State U Dept Math University Pla Atlanta GA 30303

EHRMAN, LEE, biologist; b. N.Y.C., May 25, 1935; m. Richard Ehrman, 1955; children: Esther, Judith. B.S., Queens Coll., 1956; M.S., Columbia U., 1957, Ph.D. in Genetics, 1959. Mem. faculty Barnard Coll., 1956-58; postdoctoral fellow in genetics Columbia U., N.Y.C., 1959-61; assoc. seminar on population biology Columbia U., 1981—; mem. faculty SUNY-Purchase, 1970—, prof. div. natural scis., 1972—; mem. spl. study sect. NIH, NIMH, 1979-80; vis. disting. prof. U. Miami, Coral Gables, Fla., 1981; vis. lectr. U. Puerto Rico, Rio Piedras, 1987; coordinator, panelist workshops, programs in field. Author: Behavior Genetics and Evolution, 2d edit., 1981, 2 other books; assoc. editor Evolution; assoc. editor for genetics and cytology Am. Midland Naturalist; co-editor: Behavior Genetics; assoc. editor, exec. com. Soc. Am. Naturalists, 1977-85, pres.-elect 1990; contbr. nearly 500 articles to profl. jours. Recipient Lit. Soc. Found. medal in German, 1956, chancellor's award for excellence in teaching SUNY, 1977 ; Shirley Farr postdoctoral fellow, 1961-62; USPHS postdoctoral fellow, 1959-61; faculty exchange scholar, 1974—; NSF grantee, 1979-84; Sr. Scientist award Whitehall Found., 1987—; gen. med. scis. grantee NIH, 1987—; SUNY travel grant, 1988—. Fellow AAAS, Inst. Soc. Ethics and Life Scis; mem. AAUW, Am. Soc. Naturalists (pres. 1990), Behavior Genetics Assn. (pres. 1978, Dobzhansky award for lifetime resch. 1988), Soc. for Study of Evolution (exec. council 1986—), Phi Beta Kappa, Sigma Xi. Home: 2 Jennifer Ln Rye Brook NY 10573 Office: SUNY Div Natural Scis Purchase NY 10577

EHRMAN, MADELINE ELIZABETH, government administrator; b. N.Y.C., July 4, 1942; d. Donald McKinley and Marie Madeleine (Brandeis) Ehrman. BA summa cum laude Brown U., 1964, MA, 1965; M of Philosophy, Yale U., 1967; PhD, The Union Inst., 1989. Sci. linguist U.S. Dept. State, Washington, 1969-73, regional lang. supr. U.S. Embassy, Bangkok, Thailand, 1973-75, lang. tng. supr. U.S. Dept. State, Washington, 1975-84, curriculum and tng. specialist, 1984-85, acting chmn. dept. Asian and African Langs., 1985, chmn. dept. Asian and African Langs., 1986-88, acting assoc. dean Sch. Lang. Studies, 1987-88, dir. rsch., evaluation and devel., 1989—. Author: The Meanings of the Modals in Present Day American English, 1966, Contemporary Cambodian, 1975, Indonesian Fast Course, 1982, Communicative Japanese Materials, 1984, Ants and Grasshoppers, Badgers and Butterflies: Qualitative and Quantitative Exploration of Adult Language Learning Styles and Strategies, 1989. Mem., ESOL/HILT Citizen's Adv. Council, Arlington County, Va., 1985-89; associated staff psychotherapist Meyer Treatment Ctr. Washington Sch. Psychiatry, 1989—. Woodrow Wilson Found. fellow, 1964; NSF fellow, 1964-69; recipient Meritorious Honor award U.S. Dept. State, 1983. Mem. Am. Psychol. Assn., Tchrs. of English to Speakers of Other Langs., Am. Assn. Asian Studies, Assn. for Psychol. Type, Am. Orthopsychiat. Soc., Phi Beta Kappa, Psi Chi. Avocations: reading, bicycling, gardening. Office: Fgn Svc Inst 1400 Key Blvd Arlington VA 22209

EI, SUSAN MICHELLE, English language educator; b. Detroit, Apr. 3, 1952; d. Raymond Denis Ei and Eileen Winifred (Clawson) Willson. BA, U. Mich., 1974, MA, 1985. Sales rep. Typographic Insight, Ann Arbor, Mich., 1980-86; theater mgr. Fifth Forum Theater, Ann Arbor, Mich., 1972-78; photographer's asst. Stan Ries Studios, N.Y.C., 1987—; pvt. tutor, English as a second lang. N.Y.C., 1986—; cons. in field, English as a second lang., N.Y.C., 1988—. Mem. Nat. Wildlife Fedn., Internat. Fund for Animal Welfare, Fund for Animals, Environ. Def. Fund, Foote Family Assn. of Am. (historian 1988—). Democrat. Unitarian. Home and Office: 309 W 76th St #4B New York NY 10023

EICHER, JOANNE BUBOLZ, design educator; b. Lansing, Mich., Sept. 18, 1930; d. George C. and Stella L. (Mangold) Bubolz; m. Carl K. Eicher, June 8, 1952 (div. Dec. 1974); children: Cynthia, Carolyn, Diana. BA, Mich. State U., 1952, MA, 1956, PhD, 1959. Instr., asst. prof. dept. social sci. Boston U., 1957-61; asst. prof. dept. human environment and design Coll. Human Ecology, Mich. State U., 1961-69, asso. prof., 1969-72, prof., 1972-77; prof. U. Minn., 1977—, head dept. textiles and clothing, 1977-83, head dept. design, housing and apparel, 1983-87, prof. design, housing and apparel, 1987—; dir. Goldstein Gallery, 1983-87; research assoc. Econ. Devel. Inst., U. Nigeria, 1963-66; cons. Time-Life, Inc., Howard U., Prentice Hall, Inc. Author: (with Mary Ellen Roach) Dress, Adornment and the Social Order, 1965, The Visible Self: Perspectives on Dress, 1973; African Dress: A Select and Annotated Bibliography of Subsaharan Countries, Vol. I, 1970; Nigerian Handcrafted Textiles, 1976; (with Erekosima and Thieme) Pelete Bite: Kalabari Cut-Thread Cloth, 1982; (with Pokornowski, Thieme and Harris) African Dress Bibliography, Vol. II, 1985. Contbr. articles to profl. jours. Research grantee Internat. Programs, Mich. State U., 1963-64, African Studies Center, 1965-66, 4-H Programs grantee Ethnic Heritage Program, 1974, research grantee Midwest U. Consortium for Internat. Affairs, 1968, 81; Ford Found. individual grantee, 1973; resident scholar Rockefeller Found. Study and Conf. Center, Bellagio, Italy, 1973; research grantee Buguma Internat. Affairs Soc., 1982, 84. Mem. Costume Soc. Am., Walker Art Ctr., Textile Mus., Mpls. Inst. Art, Am. Home Econs. Assn., Am. Sociol. Assn., Assn. Coll. Profs. Textiles and Clothing, Costume Soc. (London, Eng.), Nigerian Nat. Mus. Soc., African Studies Assn., Gamma Sigma Delta, Phi Kappa Phi, Alpha Kappa Delta, Tau Sigma, Alpha Gamma Delta. Democrat. Lutheran. Home: 2179 Folwell St Saint Paul MN 55108

EICHINGER, MARILYNNE H., science museum administrator; m. Martin Eichinger; children: Ryan, Kara, Julia, Jessica, Talik. AB in Anthropology and Sociology magna cum laude, Boston U., 1965; MA, Mich. State U. With emergency and outpatient staff Ingham County Mental Health Ctr., 1972; founder, pres., exec. dir. Impression 5 Sci. and Art Mus., Lansing, Mich., 1973-85; pres. Oreg. Mus. Sci. and Industry, Portland, 1985—; instr. Lansing (Mich.) Community Coll., 1978; ptnr. Eyrie Studio, 1982-85; conductor numerous workshops in interactive exhibit design, adminstrn. and fund devel. for schs., orgns., profl. socs.; bd. dirs. Assn. Sci. Tech. Ctrs., 1980-84, 88—; mem. adv. bd. Portland State U. Author: (with Jane Mack) Lexington Montessori School Survey, 1969, Manual on the Five Senses, 1974; pub. Mich. edit. Boing mag. Founder Cambridge Montessori Sch., 1964; mem. pres.'s adv. coun. Portland State U., 1986—; bd. dirs. Lexington Montessori Sch., 1969, Mid-Mich. South Health Systems Agy., 1978-81, Community Referral Ctr., 1981-85, Sat. WKAR-Radio, 1981-85; active Lansing "Riverfest" Lighted Boat Parade, 1980; mem. state health Coordinating Coun., 1980-82; mem. pres.' adv. bd. Portland State U., 1987—. Recipient Diana Cert. Leadership, YWCA, 1976-77. Mem. Am. Assn. Mus., Oreg. Mus. Assn., Assn. Sci. and Tech. Ctrs. (bd. dirs. 1980-84), City of Portland Club, Internat. Women's Club, Rotary. Club: City of Portland, Internat. Womens Club. Lodge: Zonta (founder, bd. dirs. East Lansing club 1978), Rotary (Portland). Office: Oreg Mus Sci & Industry 4015 SW Canyon Rd Portland OR 97221

EICHLER, CARLA ELISE, educational administrator; b. Wahiawa, Hawaii, May 10, 1960; d. Renald Carl and Mary Gaye (Holcomb) E. BS cum laude, U. Tenn., Chattanooga, 1978; MEd, Vanderbilt U., 1982, postgrad., 1984—. Cert. spl. edn. tchr., Tenn. Instrnl. aide Inst. of Learning Rsch., Nashville, 1974-78, tchr. spl. edn., 1982-85; typist Child Devel. Inst., Chattanooga, 1979-80; clerical asst. Hamilton County Dept. Edn., Chattanooga, 1981-82; clin. educator Cumberland Hall Acad., Nashville, 1985-87; asst. prin. Cumberland Hall Psychiat. Hosp., Nashville, 1987-89; program dir. Cumberland Hall of Meharry, Nashville, 1989—; cons. Cavert Sch., Nashville, 1987-88. Mem. Blue Key, Mortar Bd., Kappa Delta Pi. Office: Cumberland Hall of Meharry 1005 DB Todd Blvd Nashville TN 37208

EICHLING, MARY TOUROND, social services administrator, social worker; b. Washington, Oct. 3, 1947; d. Frank J. and Elizabeth (Price) Tourond; m. James B. Eichling, Aug. 1968; 1 child, Philip Beau. BS in Biology, East Carolina U., Greenville, N.C., 1970; MEd in Counseling, U. Va., 1980. Family group home parent Attention Home, Charlottesville, Va., 1976-79; probation and parole officer Va. Dept. Corrections, Madison, 1979-80; social worker Touhy Terrace Nursing Ctr., Chgo., 1980-81; child protective svcs. officer Ill. Dept. Child & Family Svcs., Chgo., 1981-85, supervising social worker, 1985-88; dir. emergency svcs., dir. ind. living Transitional Living Program, Chgo., 1988-89; clin. coord. Hemophilia Found., Chgo., 1989—; sr. adminstr. child welfare South Cen. Community Svcs.s, Chgo., 1989—; workshop leader Mayor's Conf. Child Abuse, Evanston, Ill., 1987; chmn. Foster Care Initive, Chgo., 1985-86, com. person, 1985-87. Democrat. Congregationalist. Home: 1118 Maple Evanston IL 60202 Office: South Central Community Svc 8316 S Ellis Chicago IL 60619

EICHTEN, PATRICIA JEAN, brewing company executive; b. New Ulm, Minn., Mar. 21, 1960; d. Donald Carl and Dorothy Mae (Steger) E. BSBA, Marquette U., 1982. With Miller Brewing Co., Milw., 1982—, mktg. svcs., 1983-85, coord. promotional incentives, 1985-86; price analyst, 1986, merchandising coord., 1983-84, coord. promotional incentives div., 1984-85; coord. profl. sports mktg. Miller Brewing Co., Milw., 1985-88, mgr. amateur sports mktg., 1988-89, mgr. brand promotion, 1989—. Mem. Friends of United Cerebral Palsy, Women's Sports Advocates. Home: 2024 E Webster St Milwaukee WI 53211 Office: Miller Brewing Co 3939 W Highland Ave Milwaukee WI 53208

EICKHOFF, BARBARA B., office manager; b. Denver, July 5, 1939; d. Charles Albert Sydney and Ethel Marie (Grimes) Chipperfield; m. James David Brock, June 7, 1959 (div. June 1975); children: David William, Daniel James, Douglas Albert, Diane Louise; m. David Robert Eickhoff, Jan. 16, 1988; children: Laurie Ann Eickhoff Siefke, Susan Rachelle. Student, Solano Community Coll., Suisun City, Calif., 1987—. Office mgr. Lifespring, Inc., San Francisco, 1984; adminstrv. mgr. Peabody Travel, San Mateo, Calif., 1984-86; asst. dir. ops. Lifespring, Inc., San Rafael, Calif., 1987; office mgr. Presnick Chiropractic Office, Pleasant Hill, Calif., 1987—. Mem. Order Eastern Star. Republican. Home: 1417 Humbolt Dr Suisun City CA 94585

EICKMAN, JENNIFER LYNN, art gallery director, writer, artist; b. Urbana, Ill., Nov. 7, 1946; d. Marvin A. and Emma L. (Hartrick) Smith; B.F.A., U. Ill., 1967, postgrad. in Art History, 1967-70; m. Gary Edwin Eickman, June 9, 1968. Tchr., Univ. High Sch., Urbana, 1968, Champaign (Ill.) Public Schs., 1969-70; mem. faculty U. Ill., 1968-77, Richland Coll.,

Decatur, Ill., 1975-77; asst. to dir. of extension in visual arts U. Ill., 1969-70, program dir. Allerton House Conf. Center, 1974—; dir. Allerton Art Inst., 1984—; bd. dirs. Monticello Design and Mfg.; pres. The Farms; guest lectr., tchr. art workshops. Mem. Pacific Tropical Bot. Gardens, Defenders of Wildlife, Nat. Trust Hist. Preservation, Internat. Platform Assn., Kappa Alpha Theta (delta chpt. corp. pres.). Staff writer Champaign-Urbana mag.; contbr. articles on art history, music, edn. and natural history. Home: Gate House Allerton Park Monticello IL 61856 Office: Allerton House Allerton Park Monticello IL 61856

EIDE, MARLENE, county government official, law firm executive; b. Great Falls, Mont., Mar. 4, 1932; d. Howard A. and Maud (Ray) Lund; m. Donald H. Eide, Apr. 2, 1952; children: David, Don Allen, Kjersti, Jennifer. Student, U. N.D., 1949-50. Coord., editor, writer Williams County Hist. Soc., Williston, N.D., 1974-77; legal asst. Bjella Neff Rathert Wahl & Eiken, Williston, 1977-87, bus. mgr., 1988—; mem. Ft. Buford-Ft. Union Council, Williston, 1977-87; commr. Williams County, Williston, 1981—; mem. N.D. State Banking Bd., Bismark, 1986—. Author, editor: Wonder of Williams, 1976; contbr. articles to profl. jours. Clk.-treas. Williston Twp., 1975-80; active N.W. Human Resources, 1982-88; mem. yr. of family steering com. , 1988-89. Named Outstanding Woman, Williston Jaycettes, 1976; recipient appreciation cert. for service on bd. Williston Community Libr., 1985. Mem. N.D. Press Women, Assn. Oil and Gas Producing Counties (v.p. 1981—), N.D. County Commrs. Assn. (exec. com. 1982, treas. 1982-87), Nat. Assn. Counties (steering com. on transp. 1987—), N.D. Assn. Counties (com. on future 1988—, transportation steering com., 1987—), Nat. Dem. County Ofcls. Lutheran. Lodges: Order Eastern Star (worthy matron 1962-63), Rainbow Girls (mother advisor 1961-63). Home: Rte 1 Box 56-E Williston ND 58801 Office: Williams County Courthouse PO Box 1246 201 E Broadway Williston ND 58801

EIDENSHINK, CARLA KAY, insurance company executive; b. Cherokee, Iowa, Dec. 9, 1959; d. Lloyd Henry and Janith Kay (Williams) Glawe; 1 child, Jessica Kay. AAS, Western Iowa Tech. Coll., Sioux City, Iowa, 1982. Acct. 1Vic and Van Data Processing, Inc., Ft. Dodge, Iowa; bd. sec., bus. mgr. Woodbury Cen. Schs., Moville, Iowa; automation and acctg. staff Luse-Etler-Goodwin Ins., Inc., Moville, Farmers Mut. Ins. Assn., Moville. Mem. NAFE, Am. Inst. Profl. Bookkeepers. Lutheran. Home: 511 Jackson Moville IA 51039

EIFFLER-ORTON, CAROL ANN, company executive; b. Chgo., Dec. 25, 1948; d. Peter Anthony and Anne (Coop) Chernetzki; m. George Elmer Eiffler (div. July 1972) m. Raymond Mervyn Orton, June 18, 1975. BA, Elmhurst Coll., 1982; MBA, Rosary Coll., 1985. Correspondent Beeline Fashions, Bensenville, Ill., 1966-67; sec. to asst. regional mgr. Alcan Aluminum, Melrose Park, Ill., 1967-71; sec. to exec. v.p., pres. Glogau, Inc., Melrose Park, 1971-72; legal sec. ITT Midwest Legal Office, Chgo.; sec. to chmn. bd. Warren Barr Supply Co., Chgo., 1973-74; 2d v.p. Inryco, Inc., Northlake, Ill., 1974-82; pres. Words by CEO, Northlake, Ill., 1982—. Author: Seniors Pastime, 1982. Mem. Assoc. MBA Execs., Nat. Network Women in Sales (sec. 1987, pres. chair, 1988—), Nat. Assoc. Female Execs. (network dir. 1988—), Northlake Women's Club (dir. 1983-84), Moose. Democrat. Roman Catholic. Home and Office: Words by CEO 304 E Lyndale Northlake IL 60164

EIGEN, BARBARA HELEN, artist; b. Dayton, Ohio, Jan. 15, 1945; d. Leonard and Lila (Gams) Goldman; m. Eric Franklin Eigen, Sept. 3, 1967; children: Zev, Ron. BA, Cornell U., 1967. Writer Boston U. Dept. Pub. Relations, 1969-71; prof. U. Costa Rica Sch. Fine Arts, San Jose, 1973-76; owner Eigen Arts, N.Y.C., 1977-89; Jersey City, 1989—; designer Bellini, Florence Italy 1983--, Block China N.Y. 1987--. Copyrights Ceramic Designs, Melon Tea Set and many others 1977--; Participant Designer Tables at Tiffany & Co. 1982. Mem. Crafts Council, Hadassah Club N.Y.C. Democrat. Office: Eigen Arts Inc 150 Bay St Jersey City NJ 07302

EIGHNER, RENNA BURKES, business official; b. York, Ala., Jan. 13, 1958; d. William R. and Sue S. Burkes; m. David C. Eighner (div. Sept. 1988); 1 child, Cade Austin. Student, Indian River Community Coll., Ft. Pierce, Fla., 1976-78. Loan clk. Barnett Bank Okeechobee (Fla.), 1978-80; with investments dept. Sun/Bank Okeechobee, 1980-84; exec. asst. Family Homes/Henry C. Kelly, Okeechobee, 1984—. Kick-off coord. March of Dimes, Okeechobee, 1984—; reenactment-fundraiser chmn. Battle of Okeechobee, 1987; crusade dir. Am. Cancer Soc., Okeechobee, 1987-89. Recipient svc. award March of Demss, 1984. Mem. Am. Am. Bus. Women's Assn. (v.p. Okeechobee 1987—, chmn. fashion show and Bus. Woman's Day 1988), Okeechobee C. of C. (bd. dirs. 1987—, Dir.'s svc. award 1988), Okeechobee Jaycees. Democrat. Baptist.

EIKE, BONNIE MAYE, health facility administrator; b. Whitemore, Iowa, Oct. 2, 1928; d. Lawrence Ames and Ermal Elsie (Ames) E.; m. William Thomas Allen, Jan. 2, 1957 (div. Mar. 1976); children: Tami Lynette, William Lawrence. AA, Harbor Coll., 1971; BS in Nursing magna cum laude, U. Phoenix, 1989; postgrad., U. LaVerne, 1989—. Staff, charge RN Long Beach (Calif.) Meml. Hosp., 1971-73; staff Norell Nurses Registry, Van Nuys, Calif., 1973-77; operating room supr. Grundy Meml. Hosp., Grundy Center, Iowa, 1977-80; supr., dir. staff devel. Woodview Calabasas (Calif.) Hosp., 1980—. Precinct vol. Thousand Oaks, Calif., 1973—; leader Girl Scouts U.S., Torrance, Calif., 1965-73. Mem. NAFE, Calif. Nurses Assn. Mem. Christian Ch. Home: 827 Bright Star St Thousand Oaks CA 91360

EIKENBERRY, CHING YUAN, state official; b. Seng-Yang, People's Republic China, Nov. 25, 1947; came to U.S., 1968; d. Ji and Su-Chun (Fang) Hou; m. Winston C. Yu, Sept. 4, 1971 (div. Dec. 1986); children: Jennifer, Ying-Shin; m. Karl Winfrid Eikenberry, Jan. 3, 1989. Diploma, World Coll. Journalism, Taipei, Republic of China, 1969, Internat. Trade Commn., Taipei, 1976; BA, Okla. State U., 1971. Mgr. U.S. mktg. Tong-Yong Enterprises, Taipei, 1979-82; mng. dir. Asian br. C.O. Lynch Enterprises, Mpls., 1982-83; Asian trade mgr. Minn. Dept. Agr., St. Paul, 1983-87, asst. dir. agrl. trade, 1987—. Recipient Human Rels. award Dale Carnegie Inst., Mpls., 1983, achievement award Minn. Dept. Agr., 1984, 85, 86, Pub. Svc. award Roseville Area Schs., 1985. Mem. Internat. Trade Assn. China (hon., President's award 1985), Minn. World Trade Assn., Orgn. Chinese Ams. (pres. Minn. chpt. 1989—), Chinese Am. Assn. Minn. Home: 130 Canabury Ct Little Canada MN 55117 Office: Minn Dept Agr 90 W Plato Blvd Saint Paul MN 55107

EINIGER, CAROL BLUM, investment banker; b. Phila., Nov. 30, 1949; d. Bernard Michael and Bella (Karff) Blum; m. Roger William Einiger, Dec. 21, 1969; 1 child. BA, U. Pa., 1970; MBA, Columbia U., 1973. With Conde Nast Publs., N.Y.C., 1970-71, Goldman, Sachs & Co., N.Y.C., 1971-72; with 1st Boston Corp., N.Y.C., 1973-88, with corp. fin. dept., 1973-79, with capital markets dept., 1979-88, mng. dir., 1982-88, head short-term fin. dept., 1983-88, head capital markets dept., 1985-88; vis. prof., exec.-in-residence Sch. Bus. Columbia U., N.Y.C., 1988-89; mng. dir. Wasserstein Perella & Co. Inc., N.Y.C., 1989—. Trustee Horace Mann-Barnard Sch., 1988—, U. Pa., 1989—; bd. overseers Columbia Bus. Sch., 1988—. Mem. UJA Fedn. (steering com. Wall Street div. 1989—). Office: Wasserstein Perella & Co 31 W 52nd St 27th Fl New York NY 10019

EINODER, CAMILLE ELIZABETH, educator; b. Chgo., June 15, 1937; d. Isadore and Elizabeth T. (Czerwinski) Popowski; student Fox Bus. Coll., 1954; B.Ed. in Biology, Chgo. Tchrs. Coll., 1964; M.A. in Analytical Chemistry, Gov.'s State U., 1977; MA in Adminstrn. and Supervision, Roosevelt U., 1986; postgrad. m. Joseph X. Einoder, Aug. 5, 1978; children—Carl Frank, Mark Frank, Vivian Einoder, Joe Einoder, Tim Einoder, Sheila Einoder, Jude Einoder. Secretarial positions, Chgo., 1955-64; tchr. biology Chgo. Bd. Edn., 1964—, tchr. biology and agr., 1975-81, tchr. biology, agr. and chemistry, 1981—; human rels. coord. Morgan Park High Sch., Chgo., 1980—, tchr. biology Internat. Studies Sch., 1983—, mem. adv. bd., 1989—; career devel. cons. for agr. related curriculum. Bds. dirs., founding mem., author constn. Community Coun., 1970—; bd. dirs., edn. cons. Neighborhood Coun., 1974; rep. Chgo. Tchrs. Union, 1969. Mem. Phi Delta Kappa. Home: 10637 S Claremont St Chicago IL 60643 Office: 1744 W Pryor St Chicago IL 60643

EINSTEIN, MARGERY A., food technologist; b. Mineola, N.Y., Sept. 1, 1943; d. Frederick W. and Ruth (Trebing) Andersen; m. Albert Brooks Einstein, Jr., Aug. 28, 1965; children: William Trebing, Matthew David, Christina Janet, Frederick Brooks. BS magna cum laude, Syracuse U.; MS, Cornell U. Food technologist Gen. Foods Corp., Tarrytown, N.Y., 1965-67, USDA, Beltsville, Md., 1967-69, McCormick & Co., Balt., 1969-71; rsch. scientist Rainier Brewing, Seattle, 1971-76; cons. in food tech. Mercer Island, Wash., 1976-87; pres. SensTek Inc., Mercer Island, 1987—. Contbr. articles to profl. jours. Active various charitable, civic orgns. Mem. Inst. Food Technologists, ASTM. Republican. Episcopalian. Office: SensTek Inc 6870 W Mercer Way Mercer Island WA 98040

EIS, LORYANN MALVINA, educator; b. Muscatine, Iowa, Apr. 3, 1938; d. Chester N. and Anna M. (Lenz) E. AB, Augustana Coll., 1960; MEd, U. Ill., 1963; postgrad., Montclair State Coll., 1965-67, Indiana U. of Pa., 1968, U. Iowa, 1970, Western Ill. U., 1978-80. Cir. analysis engr. Automatic Electric Co., Northlake, Ill., 1960-61; math. tchr. Orion (Ill.) Community Sch. Dist., 1961-63; math. tchr., chmn. div. math. and sci. United Twp. High Sch., East Moline, Ill., 1963—; lectr. Augustana Coll., Rock Island, Ill., 1982—. Cons. General Mathematics Textbook, 1978-79. Chmn. math. task force Edn. Svc. Ctr. #8, 1986-89; bd. sec. Citizens to Preserve Black Hawk Park Found., 1977—; v.p. coun. Salem Luth. Ch.; sec. Salem Luth. Endowmen Com.; pres. Augustana Coll. Hist. Soc. Bd. Mem. NEA, Ill. Edn. Assn., Nat. Coun. Tchrs. of Math., Ill. Coun. Tchrs. of Math., Classroom Tchrs. Assn., Assn. Supervision and Curriculum Devel., Rock Island Scott Counties Sci. and Math. Tchrs. Assn., Women in Ednl. Adminstrn., AAUW (past state pres., past regional dir. Great Lakes chpt., grantee 1975-76), Delta Kappa Gamma (state treas., chair, internat. fin. com.), Am. Philatelic Soc., TransMiss. Philatelic Soc., Quad City Stamp Club. Republican. Home: 2037 15th St Moline IL 61265 Office: 1275 42nd Ave East Moline IL 61244

EISENBERG, AMY MARCIE, financial executive; b. N.Y.C., Nov. 1, 1956; d. George and Blanche Joice (Schmell) E. BA cum laude, CCNY, 1978. Adminstrv. asst. Saxton Communications Group, Ltd., N.Y.C., 1978-79, E.T. Howard Advt., N.Y.C., 1979-80; asst. account exec. Grey Advt., N.Y.C., 1980-83, account exec., 1983-84; adminstrv. asst. Am. Express, N.Y.C., 1985-88, asst. to sr. v.p., 1988—. Mem. NAFE. Office: Am Express 200 Vesey St New York NY 10285-3700

EISENBERG, ELEANOR, lawyer; b. N.Y.C., Jan. 27, 1941; d. Philip and Minnie (Hartman) Chatzky. BA, Bard Coll., 1961; JD, Glendale U., Calif. Bar: Calif. 1976, U.S. Dist. Ct. (cen. dist.) Calif. 1976, U.S. Dist. Ct. (no. dist.) Calif. 1979. Assoc. Margolis, McTernan, et al, Los Angeles, 1976-78; exec. dir. Legal Aid Soc., Santa Cruz, Calif., 1978-88, Socorro Soc., San Francisco, 1989—. Mem. exec. com. Project Adv. Group, Wash., 1984-88. Mem. ABA, State Bar Calif. (chair legal svcs. sect.), Calif. Women Lawyers (bd. dirs.). Democrat. Home: 415 Sherwood Dr #103 Sausalito CA 94965 Office: Socorro Soc 1663 Mission St Ste 602 San Francisco CA 94103

EISENBERG, KAREN SUE BYER, nurse; b. Bklyn., Mar. 11, 1954; d. Marvin and Florence (Beck) Byer; m. Howard Eisenberg, May 11, 1974; children: Carly Beth, Mariel Bryn. Diploma nursing L.I. Coll. Hosp. Sch. Nursing, 1973; BSN, L.I. U., 1976, M in Profl. Studies, 1977. Nurse recovery room and surg. intensive care unit Downstate Med. Ctr., Bklyn., 1973-75; utilization rev. analyst Bezallel Health Related Facility, Far Rockaway, N.Y., 1975-76; utilization rev. analyst, R.N. supr. Seagirt Health Related Facility, Far Rockaway, 1976; staff nurse neurosurg. and rehab. nursing Downstate Med. Ctr., Bklyn., 1978, nurse intensive care unit, 1978-79, asst. nursing dir. pathology, clin. rsch. assoc. Rsch. Found., 1979—. Mem. Oncology Nursing Soc., Am. Nurses Assn., N.Y. State Nurses Assn., N.Y. Acad. Scis., L.I. Coll. Hosp. Alumnae Assn. Contbr. articles to profl. jours. Office: 450 Clarkson Ave Box 25 Brooklyn NY 11203

EISENBERG, MARILYN, hotel executive, demiurge; b. Chgo., Mar. 3, 1941; d. Frank and Rose (Kreisman) Spiegel; m. Jack Leo Eisenberg, Nov. 28, 1965; children: Erik, Amy Ilene. Exec. mgr. Knickerbocker Hotel, Chgo., 1966-70, Ambassador West Hotel, Chgo., 1976-85; tchr. hotel mgmt. City Coll. of Chgo., 1986-88. Co-founder, pres. Edn. Resource Ctr., Chgo., 1974-80; co-founder Express-Ways Children's Mus., Chgo., 1980, pres., 1983-86, bd. dirs. 1980—; vol. tchr. Nr. North High Sch., Chgo., 1983-90; bd. dirs. Hild Arts Ctr., Chgo., 1989—, vice chmn., 1989—; bd. dirs. Body Politic Theatre, 1977-79. Home: 3100 N Sheridan Rd Chicago IL 60657

EISENBERG, ROBIN LEDGIN, education educator; b. Passaic, N.J., Jan. 10, 1951; d. Morris and Ruth (Miller) Ledgin; m. Gary Eisenberg, Mar. 18, 1979. BS, West Chester State U., 1973; M Edn., Kutztown State U., 1977. Administrv. asst. Kenesseth Israel, Allentown, Pa., 1973-77; dir. edn. Cong. Schaarai Zedek, Tampa, Fla., 1977-79, Kehilath Israel, Pacific Palisades, Calif., 1979-80, Temple Beth El, Boca Raton, Fla., 1980--. Contbr. Learning Together, 1987. Chmn. edn. info., Planned Parenthood, Boca Raton Fla. 1989. Recipient Kamiker Camp award, Nat. Assn. Temple Educators. Mem. Nat. Assn. Temple Educators (1st v.p.), Coalition Advancement of Jewish Edn. Home: 67 SW 12th Ter Boca Raton FL 33486 Office: Temple Beth El 333 SW 4th Ave Boca Raton FL 33432

EISENBERG, SONJA MIRIAM, artist; b. Berlin, June 10, 1926; came to U.S., 1938, naturalized, 1947; d. Adolf and Meta Cecilie (Bettauer) Weinberger; student Queens Coll., 1943-46, Middlebury Coll., 1945; NYU, 1952-54; BA, NYU, 1954; postgrad. Nat. Acad. Sch. Fine Arts, 1961; m. Jack Eisenberg, Mar. 31, 1946; children: Ralph, Lynn, Lauren. One-woman shows: Bodley Gallery, N.Y.C., 1970, 73, 75, 80, Galerie Art du Monde, Paris, 1973, Buyways Gallery, Sarasota, Fla., 1973, 74, 75, 78, Galerie de Sfinx, Amsterdam, Netherlands, 1974, Huntsville (Ala.) Mus. Art, 1974, Anglo-Am. Art Mus., Baton Rouge, 1974, Comara Gallery, Los Angeles, 1974, Palm Spring (Calif.) Desert Mus., 1975, Fordham U., N.Y.C., 1976, Omega Inst., New Lebanon, N.Y., 1979, Am. Mus., Hayden Planetarium, N.Y.C., 1980, Avila Graphics, Ltd., 1981, YWCA, N.Y.C., 1981, Cathedral of St. John the Divine, N.Y.C., 1983, 85, The Millbrook (N.Y.) Gallery, 1989; group shows include: Mus. Fine Arts, St. Petersburg, Fla., 1973, Am. Watercolor Soc., 107th, 108th Exhbn., 1974, 75, Galerie Frederic Gollong, St. Paul de Vence, France, 1978, Betty Parson's Gallery, N.Y.C., 1981, Foster Harmon Galleries of Am. Art, Sarasota, Fla., 1988, Tokyo Met. Art Mus. 14th Internat. Art Friendship Exhbn., 1989; represented in permanent collections: Archives Am. Art, Smithsonian Inst., Jewish Mus., N.Y.C., Fordham U. Mus., N.Y.C., Palm Springs Desert Mus., Omega Inst., Cathedral of St. John the Divine; artist-in-residence Cathedral of St. John the Divine, N.Y.C.; designer WFUNA cachet for UN Water Power Conf., 1977, UN Internat. Yr. of Disabled Persons, 1981. Regent Cathedral of St. John the Divine, N.Y.C., 1990. Recipient gold medal for artistic merit Internat. Parliament for Safety and Peace, 1983, Palma D'Oro Europe, 1986. Mem. Accademia Italia delle Arti e del Lavoro (Gold medal 1981). Completed project Seeing the Gospel According to St. John (text and 41 paintings) for Cathedral of St. John, 1987. Home and Office: 1020 Park Ave New York NY 10028

EISENBISE, JANET K., elementary teacher; b. Pendleton, Ind., Nov. 2, 1941; d. John David and Precious Jewel (McDonald) Mercer; m. David Eisenbise, July 8, 1961 (div. Sept. 1987); children: Ruth, Jennifer, Rachel. BS, Ball State U., Muncie, Ind., 1973, MA, 1977. 3d grade tchr. Jackson Elem Sch., Anderson, Ind., 1973-75, 1st grade tchr., 1975-81; 1st grade tchr. Lapel (Ind.) Elem. Sch., 1981-85, 2d grade tchr., 1985—. Pres. Twonship Adv. Bd., 1982-86, sec. Madison County 4-H Assn., 1975-81, guardian coun. Internat. Order Jobs Daughters, 1980-82. Mem. AAUW (treas. 1989—), NEA, Order Ea. Star. Republican. Mem. Christian Ch. Home: 2642 W Mercer Dr Pendleton IN 46064

EISENBRAUN, DOREEN KAREN, insurance educator; b. St. Louis, Mo., Nov. 5, 1942; d. Julius and Esther (Mueller) N.; children: Mark S. Griffith, Michael B. Griffith; m. Darrell J. Eisenbraun, Nov. 8, 1980. BA, Bellevue Coll., Bellevue, 1978. Ins. sales Prudential Ins. Co., Omaha, 1978-79; ins. sales State Farm Ins., Omaha, 1979-80, Albuquerque, 1980-87; with staff tng. ins. DOE Enterprises Sales & Office Mgmt., Phoenix; real estate sales Tom Jackson & Assoc., Phoenix, 1988—; ins. office mgmt. State Farm Ins., Ariz., 1989—; instr. Ariz. Sch. of Ins., Scottsdale, Ariz., 1988—; staff consultation, State Farm Ins. Agts., Phoenix, Ariz. Mem., Nat'l Bd. of Realtors, Nat'l Assn. of Life Underwriters. Republican.

EISENER, LAURA DAWN, small business owner; b. Lynn, Mass., Aug. 10, 1955; d. Lawrence Watson Eisener and Bernice Irene (Cook) Sarno. BA, Conn. Coll., 1977; MLA, U. Mass., 1980. Teaching assoc. U. Mass., Amherst, 1977-80; instr. Wisteria House, Ogunquit, Maine, 1982; landscape designer Blueview Nurseries, Canton, Mass., 1982-84; instr. Wells (Maine) Continuing Edn. Program, 1985-87; pin. Laura D. Eisener Landscape Design, Waltham, Mass., 1984—; instr. Mass. Horticulture Soc., Boston, 1989, Endicott Coll. Ctr. for Continuing Edn., Beverly, Mass., 1985—, Radcliffe Seminars: Landscape Design Program, Cambridge, Mass., 1984—. Contbr. articles to profl. jours. Judge Mass. Horticulture Soc., Boston, 1989; abstract reviewer Council of Educators in Landscape Architecture, Fla., 1989; landscape coordinator-vol. Habitat for Humanity, Boston, 1989. Recipient Merit Award Single Family Residential Design Boston Soc. Landscape Architects, 1987. Mem. Am. Soc. Landscape Architects, Green Industry Council, Garden Writers Assn. Am., Perennial Plant Assn., New England Wildflower Soc., Friends of Arnold Arboretum, Friends of Conn. Arboretum, Assn. Profl. Landscape Designers. Democrat. Unitarian. Home: 469 Massachusetts Ave Lexington MA 02154 Office: Laura D Eisener Landscape 59 Maple St Ste 3 Waltham MA 02154

EISENHOWER, JEAN ANN, community relations specialist; b. Woodland, Calif., July 7, 1952; d. Arthur John and Lila (Petersen) E.; m. John Patterson, Dec. 31, 1987; children: Michael, Stephanie. BA in Media Arts, U. Ariz., 1983. Feature reporter Sta. KUAT Radio, Tucson, 1983-84; media specialist Godwin & Sarlat Pub. Rels., Tucson, 1984; dir. underwriting Sta. KXCI Community Radio, Tucson, 1984-85; dir. Jean Eisenhower Community Rels., Tucson, 1986-89; exec. dir. InterACT Community Rels., Tucson, 1990—; pres. North Am. Premaculture, 1989—. Contbg. editor internat. jour. Sustainable Living in Drylands, 1988-90. Mem. Coord. Coun. on Sexual and Domestic Violence, Tucson, 1986-88; pub. rels. chair So. Ariz. Task Force on Sexual and Domestic Violence, Tuscon, 1986-87; aactive Leadership Tucson-So. Ariz. Perspective, 1989, Leadership Alumni, 1990. Recipient First Place Radio Feature award UPI, 1983, Schoolbell award Ariz. Edn. Assn., 1983. Mem. NAFE, West Univ. Neighborhood Assn. (bd. dirs. 1986-88), Resources for Women (group leader 1987—). Home: 720 E University Tucson AZ 85719 Office: 738 N 5th Ave #212 Tucson AZ 85705

EISENMAN, TRUDY FOX, dermatologist; b. Chgo., Oct. 14, 1940; d. Nathan Henry and Bernice (Greenberg) Fox; student U. Ill. at Navy Pier, Chgo., 1958-60; M.D., U. Ill., 1964; m. Theodore S. Eisenman, Aug. 19, 1962 (div. 1985); children—Lawrence, Robert. Rotating intern Milw. County Gen. Hosp., 1964-65, med. resident, 1965-66; resident in dermatology Northwestern U. Med. Sch., Chgo., 1970-73, instr., 1973—; practice medicine specializing in dermatology, Chgo., 1973—; attending dermatologist Louis A. Weiss Meml. Hosp., Chgo., 1973—. Diplomate Am. Bd. Dermatology. Fellow Am. Acad. Dermatology; mem. Chgo. Dermatol. Soc., Am. Med. Women's Assn., AMA, Chgo. Med. Soc., Alpha Omega Alpha. Home: 2526 Thornwood Ave Wilmette IL 60091 Office: 4640 N Marine Dr Chicago IL 60640

EISENSTADT, ARLENE ELLEN, marketing professional; b. Providence, Apr. 24, 1954; d. Nathan and Blanche (Goldberg) E. BA, R.I. Coll., 1976. Cert. mktg. dir. Program coord. March of Dimes Birth Defects Found., Cranston, R.I., 1976-79; mktg. dir. North Dartmouth (Mass.) Mall, 1979-83, The Boulevard Mall, Las Vegas, 1983-88; mktg. mgr. Tracey Hall & Assocs., Newport Beach, Calif., 1988-90; regional mktg. mgr. The O'Connor Group, Laguna Hills, Calif., 1990—; sec. Greater Las Vegas Advt. Fedn., 1983-88. Mem. Saddleback Valley C. of C., Internat. Coun. of Shopping Ctrs. (Maxi award 1989), So. Calif. Mktg. Dirs. Assn. Jewish. Home: 108 Birchwood Ln Laguna Hills CA 92656 Office: The O'Connor Group 24155 Laguna Hills Mall Laguna Hills CA 92653

EISENSTADT, DEBBIE MIRIAM, Hebrew educator; b. Bayside, N.Y., Dec. 17, 1951; d. Morton and Pearl (Fox) Siegel; m. Howard Gary Eisenstadt, Aug. 9, 1983. BA in Hebrew & Religion, Queens Coll., 1973; cert., SUNY, Buffalo, N.Y., 1973-74, SUNY, Stonybrook, N.Y., 1975-76; postgrad., Fla. Internat. U., 1977-81. Cert. Hebrew educator, N.Y. Youth leader U.S. Youth, N.Y., 1973-74; educator Kadmal Sch., Buffalo, 1973-74, Hebrew Acad. Suffolk City, Suffolk County, 1975-76, Temple Yeshiva, North Miami Beach, Fla., 1977-83; art educator Haramah Sch. for Girls, Bklyn., 1984-85; educator Sol Schelter Day Sch., L.I., 1987-88; sales woman Fuller Brush Indsl., L.I., 1989—; acct. exec. American Soundcraft, L.I., 1990—. Mem. Young Israel of Plainview, L.I., 1986—, Nassau County PTA, L.I., 1986—, Emmanuel Women, L.I., 1980—.

EISENSTADT, PAULINE DOREEN BAUMAN, investment company executive, state legislator; b. N.Y.C., Dec. 31, 1938; d. Morris and Anne (Lautenberg) Bauman; BA, U. Fla., 1960; MS (NSF grantee), U. Ariz., 1965; postgrad. U. N.Mex.; m. Melvin M. Eisenstadt, Nov. 20, 1960; children: Todd Alan, Keith Mark. Tchr., Ariz., 1961-65, P.R., 1972-73; adminstrv. asst. Inst. Social Research U. N.Mex., 1973-74; founder, 1st exec. dir. Energy Consumers N.Mex., 1977-81; dir., host TV program Consumer Viewpoint, 1980-82; chmn. consumer affairs adv. com. Dept. Energy, 1979-80; v.p. tech. bd. Nat. Center Appropiate Tech., 1980—; pres. Eisenstadt Enterprises, investments, 1983—; mem. N.Mex. Ho. of Reps., 1985—, chairwoman majority caucus, chair rules com. N.Mex. House of Reps., 1987—, chair sub. com. on children and youth, 1987; mem. exec. com., vice chair pvt. coun. Nat. Conf. State Legislators, 1987; vice chmn. Sandoval County (N.Mex.) Democratic Party, 1981—; mem. N.Mex. Dem. State Central Com., 1981—; N.Mex. del. Dem. Nat. Platform Com., 1984, Dem. Nat. Conv., 1984; pres. Sandoval County Dem. Women's Assn., 1979-81; vice chmn. N. Mex. Dem. Platform Com., 1984—; mem. Sandoval County Redistricting Task Force, 1983-84; mem. Rio Rancho Ednl. Study Com., 1984—.; mem. N.Mex. First. Mem. NEA, LWV, NOW. Author: Corrales, Portrait of a Changing Village, 1980. Mem. Kiwanis (1st woman mem. local club). Home: PO Box 658 Corrales NM 87048

EISENSTAT, MAXINE EDITH, medical marketing professional; b. Bronx, N.Y., Sept. 13, 1945; d. Max and Rita Adeltha (Hibbard) E.; m. Sidney M. Bernstein, Sept. 24, 1967 (div. 1974); 1 child, Gregory M. Bernstein. Student, Vanderbilt U., 1963-65; BS, Fairleigh Dickinson U., 1967. Word processor CIBA Corning Diagnostics Corp., East Walpole, Mass., 1979-80, customer svc. correspondent, 1980-81, tech. coord., 1981-82; account rep. CIBA Corning Diagnostics Corp., N.Y., N.J., 1982-85; sr. account rep. CIBA Corning Diagnostics Corp., Phila., 1985-87; product mgr. CIBA Corning Diagnostics Corp., East Walpole, 1987—. Mem. Clin. Ligand Assay Soc. (regional bd. Wayne, Mich. 1986-87), Biomed. Mktg. Assn. Home: 133 Westfield Dr Holliston MA 01746 Office: CIBA Corning Diagnostics 333 Coney St East Walpole MA 02032

EISENSTEIN, SHERYL FAY, clinical psychologist; b. San Antonio, Aug. 30, 1961; d. Elliot Martin and Carole Anita (Isenberg) E. BA in Psychology, Rutgers U., 1983; MA in Psychology, New Sch. for Social Rsch., N.Y.C., 1985. Tchrs. aide Douglas Devel. Disabilities Ctr., New Brunswick, N.J., 1981-82; rsch. asst. Douglas Devel. Disabilities Ctr., New Brunswick, 1982-83; bank teller Midlantic Nat. Bank, Cedar Grove, N.J., 1983-85; crisis intervention counselor St. Clare's Hosp., Denville, N.J., 1985-86; clin. psychology intern Bergen Pines County Hosp., Paramus, N.J., 1986-87; staff clin. psychologist Bergen Pines County Hosp., Paramus, 1987—; asst. coord. Bipolar Disorder Psychoeducation Family Group Rsch., Bergen Pines County Hosp. with Columbia U., Paramus, 1990—. Mem. Am. Psychol. Assn. (assoc.), N.J. Psychol. Assn. Home: 59 Knight Rd Wayne NJ 07470 Office: Bergen Pines County Hosp East Ridgewood Ave Paramus NJ 07652

EISENZIMMER, BETTY WENNER, insurance agency executive; b. Twisp, Wash., July 25, 1939; d. Bren William and Julia Emogene (Salmon) Wenner; m. Erwin LeRoy Cook, June 19, 1955 (div. 1960); 1 child, Richard Jeffrey; m. Jerome Anthony Eisenzimmer, Feb. 18, 1966. Cert. in gen. ins. Ins. Inst. Am., 1981; cert. profl. ins. woman. Clk. typist MR Ins., Seattle, 1957-59; records clk. Assigned Risk Plan, Seattle, 1959-61; acct. asst. Robinson Jenner, Inc., Seattle, 1961-66; sec., acct. asst. Falkenberg & Co., Seattle, 1966-75, adminstrv. asst., 1975-77; ins. agt., corp. officer Service Ins. Inc., Seattle, 1975—; mem. adv. bd. Sch. Ins., Wash. State U. Coll. Bus., 1981-90. Asst. editor Today's Ins. Woman, 1980-81. Exec. bd. Wash. chpt. Cystic Fibrosis Found., 1978-86, pres., 1983-85, recipient Disting. Svc.

award, 1984, named Vol. of Yr. Wash. chpt., 1980; mem. Wash. State Centennial Speakers' Bur., 1987-89; mem. long range planning com. Cedar Cross United Meth. Ch., 1986-87, mem. worship com., 1988—. Mem. Seattle C. of C., Ins. Women Puget Sound (pres. 1970-72, Ins. Woman of Yr. 1978, 81, Industry award 1984 Wash. State Communicate with confidence speakoff winner, chmn. 1992 conf.), Ins. Women's Assn. Seattle (Ins. Woman of Yr. 1981), Nat. Assn. Ins. Women (nat. sec. 1976-77, regional dir. 1981-82, mem. exec. bd. 1976-77, 81-82, You Make the Difference award 1977, Regional IX Lace Speakoff winner 1983), Ind. Ins. Agts. and Brokers Wash. (edn. com. 1982-83), Ind. Ins. Agts. and Brokers King County (chmn. by-laws 1984-85), Profl. Ins. Agts. Wash. (edn. com. 1982-86, chmn. 1983-86), Wash. Ins. Council (mem. speakers bur. 1980—), Nat. Assn. Life Underwriters, Women Life Underwriters Conf. (nat. bd. dirs., region I dir. 1987-88), Acad. Producer Ins. Studies (fellow of acad.), Seattle Assn. Life Underwriters. Club: Toastmasters (pres. Wallingford chpt. 1986-87, ednl. v.p. 1987-88, dist. 2 area 5 gov. 1987-88, dist. 2 sec. 1989-90, dist. 2 admin. lt. gov., 1990—, mentor Northgate chpt. 1988—, Gov.'s Honor Roll dist. 2 1987, NC div. Lt. Gov. 1988-89, dist. 2 area Gov. of Yr, 1988, dist. 2 div. Gov. of Yr. 1989, able toastmaster silver 1988, Disting. Toastmaster 1989, Gov.'s Trophy, 1990 and other awards and positions). Home: 8932 240th St SW Edmonds WA 98020 Office: Svc Ins Inc 717 Securities Bldg 1904 Third Ave Seattle WA 98101-1179

EISERT, DEBRA CLAIRE, pediatric psychologist; b. Portland, Oreg., Nov. 28, 1952; d. Delmer Louis and Charlotte May (Johnson) E.; m. Lynn R. Kahle, Aug. 19, 1978; 1 child, Kevin Eisert Kahle. BA in Biology summa cum laude, Pacific Luth. U., 1975; MA in Devel. Psychology, U. Nebr., 1977, PhD in Devel. Psychology, 1978. Intern, postdoctoral profl. Children's Hosp. of Mich., Detroit, 1978-80; dir. of psychology Lenox Baker Children's Hosp., Durham, N.C., 1980-83; asst. prof. med. psychology Oreg. Health Scis. U., Eugene, 1989—; rsch. assoc. U. Oreg., Eugene, 1984—; instr. child devel. U. Nebr., Lincoln, 1976; rsch. supr. Accent on the Devel. Abstract Processes of Thought, 1975-78; instr. child devel. Oreg. Grad. Sch. Profl. Psychology, Portland, 1984; presenter in field. Author: (with others) Future Directions in Human Resource Management, 1986, Psychological Assessment of Special Children, 1986, Social Values and Social Change, 1983, Social Development in Youth, 1981, Piagetian Theory and its Implications for the Helping Professions, 1979; contbr. articles to profl. jours. F.E. and O.M. Johnson fellow U. Nebr., Lincoln, 1977-78. Mem. Am. Psychol. Assn. (sect. on clin. child psychology and sec. of pediatric psychology), Soc. for Rsch. in Child Devel. Office: U Oreg 901 E 18th Eugene OR 97403

EISINGER, MIKI LYNNE, systems analyst; b. N.Y.C., Dec. 5, 1948; d. Jerome and April Blossom (Kramer) Silverberg; m. Fred Gary Eisinger, May 3, 1970; 1 child, Joshua David. BA in English, CCNY, 1969. Asst. circulation dir. Marvel Comics Group, N.Y.C., 1971-73; asst. to v.p. sales Warner Communications, N.Y.C., 1973-74; programmer/analyst NL Industries, Hightstown, N.J., 1980-82; data processing cons. Princeton, N.J., 1983-87; program advisor McGraw-Hill, Hightstown, 1987—. Mem. county com. Dem. Party, Queens, N.Y., 1974-75. Regent scholar N.Y. State, 1965. Home: 889 Jamestown Rd East Windsor NJ 08520

EISLER, RIANE TENNENHAUS, lawyer; b. Vienna, Austria, July 22, 1931; came to U.S., 1946; d. David and Lisa (Greif) Tennenhaus; children: Andrea Suzanne, Loren Claire. BA, UCLA, 1952, JD, 1965. Bar: Calif. 1965, U.S. Supreme Ct. 1970. Assoc. Zagon, Schiff, Hirsch and Levine, Beverly Hills, Calif., 1966-68; sole practice L.A., 1968-78; co-dir. Inst. Futures Forecasting, Carmel, Calif., 1978—, Ctr. for Partnership Studies, Carmel, 1987—; founding dir. Los Angeles Women's Ctr. Legal Program, 1969-71; lectr. dept. anthropology UCLA, 1972, social sci. Immaculate Heart Coll., Los Angeles, 1972. Author: The Equal Rights Handbook, 1978, Dissolution, 1977, Paean to Women: A Call to Unity, 1985, The Chalice and The Blade: Our History, Our Future, 1987; contbr. articles to profl. jours. Bd. dirs. YWCA, Los Angeles, 1971, Monterey (Calif.), 1984-85, Women's Clinic, Los Angeles, 1975-78, ACLU, Monterey; mem. adv. bd. Women's Rights Reporter, 1971; NOW rep. Monterey Peninsula Women's Orgns. Network, 1981-83; mem. Nat. Women's Polit. Caucus. Mem. NOW, State Bar Calif., Gen. Evolution Research Group, Western Assn. Women Historians, Nat. Women's Conf. Com. (ERA task force 1985-86), Acad. Peace Development (research adv. bd.), Internat. Soc. Gen. Systems Research, Phi Beta Kappa, Pi Gamma Mu.

EISLER, SUSAN KRAWETZ, advertising agency executive; b. N.Y.C., Aug. 18, 1946; d. Aaron and Bertha (Platt) Krawetz; m. Howard Irwin Eisler, June 8, 1980; 1 stepchild, Robin Joy, 1 adopted son, Joseph. BA, U. Pitts., 1967; MA, New Sch. for Social Research, 1971. Analyst, Marplan, Inc., N.Y.C., 1968-69; project dir. Market Facts, Inc., N.Y.C., 1969-70; assoc. rsch. mgr. Gen. Foods, Inc., White Plains, N.Y., 1970-75, product mgr., 1975-80; rsch. dir. Elizabeth Arden, N.Y.C., 1980-81; v.p., assoc. rsch. dir. SSC&B: Lintas Worldwide, N.Y.C., 1981-87; sr. v.p., assoc. research dir., 1987—. Named Woman of Yr. YWCA Acad. Women Achievers, 1989. Mem. Am. Mktg. Assn., Advt. Women N.Y., Advt. Rsch. Found. (copy rsch. coun.). Office: SSC&B Lintas Worldwide 1 Dag Hammarskjold Pla New York NY 10017

EISMAN, ESTHER, international sales director; b. Linz, Austria, June 10, 1950; came to U.S., 1951; d. Hilel and Gusta (Rosenberg) E. BA, Butler U., 1972; MBA, Ind. U., 1979. Assoc. editor Hardware Retailing Mag., Indpls., 1972-76; dir. mktg. Blue Lustre Home Care Products, Inc., Indpls., 1976-84; dir. advt., pub. relations Howard W. Sams & Co. div. Macmillan, Inc., Indpls., 1984-85; dir. internat. sales Macmillan Computer Pub., Carmel, Ind., 1985—. Mem. Am. Mktg. Assn. (v.p. communications), Ind. U. Sch. Bus. Alumni Assn. (advisor cathedral arts coun.). Home: 5847 N Rural Indianapolis IN 46220 Office: Howard W Sams & Co 11711 N College Ave Ste 141 Carmel IN 46032

EISNER, CHRISTINE LEUTHOLD, marketing and public relations consultant; b. Greenwich, Conn., Jan. 2, 1959; d. Adolph Edwin and Annette Louise (Nebel) L.; m. Dean Harris Eisner, Sept. 7, 1986. BS in Chinese and Bus., Georgetown U., 1981; BA in Chinese and Lang. Civilization, U. Paris, 1980. Pub. rels. asst. Sotheby's Internat. Realty, N.Y.C., 1981; asst. treas. Bank of Am., N.Y.C., 1981-83; account supr. Atwood Internat., N.Y.C., 1983-85; prof. Shanghai (China) Forman Studies U., 1985; mktg. mgr. Douglas Elliman Knight Franic, N.Y.C., 1985-87; asst. dir. pub. rels. Paol Ralph Lauren Corp., N.Y.C., 1987-89; pres. Kavela Corp., Irvington, N.Y., 1989—. Mem. Women in Communications, Inc., Am. Mktg. Assn. Home: 331 Birch Ln Irvington NY 10533

EISNER, SISTER JANET MARGARET, college president; b. Boston, Oct. 10, 1940; d. Eldon and Ada (Martin) E. AB, Emmanuel Coll., 1963; MA, Boston Coll., 1969; PhD, U. Mich., 1975; LHD (hon.), Northeastern U. Joined Sisters of Notre Dame de Namur, Roman Catholic Ch.; dir. admissions Emmanuel Coll., 1967-71; dir. Emmanuel Coll. and City of Boston Pairings, 1976-78, asst. prof. English, 1976-78, chmn. dept., 1977-78, acting pres., 1978-79, pres., 1979—; lectr., teaching asst. U. Mich., 1971-73; mem. Mass. Bd. Regents, chair regents planning com., 1980-86. Trustee Trinity Coll., 1979-85, mem. adv. coun. on enrollment planning, 1981-82; adv. coun. pres. Assn. Governing Bds., 1982-88; mem. commn. on women in higher edn. Am. Coun. on Edn., 1985-87; mem. adv. bd. Ctr. for Religious Devel., Cambridge, Mass., 1983—, Synod of Archdiocese of Boston, 1988, Anti-Defamation League Dinner Com., 1988-89; chair four-yr. coll. div. United Way Campaign, 1989; mem. NAICU/NIIC joint task force Minority Participation in Ind. Higher Edn., 1989; mem. govs. award com. Carballo Scholarships, 1989. Rackham prize fellow, Ford Found. fellow, 1973-75. Mem. Assn. Ind. Colls. and Univs. in Mass. (exec. com.). Office: Emmanuel Coll Office of the Pres 400 The Fenway Boston MA 02115

EISSLER, VEDA ALICIA, teacher, musician; b. Houston, Feb. 19, 1960; d. William Eugene and Veda Mae (Greb) E. MusB, U. Houston, 1982, MusM, 1986, student, 1989—. Actress, singer and musician The Lone Star Hist. Drama, Galveston, Tex., 1977; music and fine arts instr. Fleming Fine Arts Acad., 1982-86; head orch. dir. and fgn. lang. instr. Strack Intermediate Sch., Klein, Tex., 1986—; violinist and violist Houston Instrumental Ensemble, 1976-81, Summer Arts Festival Orch., San Luis Potosi, Mex., 1982. Co-author: Headstart to Spanish, 1989, Headstart to French, 1989, Headstart to German, 1989. Bicentennial courier Am. Bicentennial Commn., Montevideo, Uruguay, 1976; dir. handbell choir Meml. Drive Presbyn. Ch., 1986-87; rep. Dem. Precinct Conv., Houston, 1978, Rep. Precinct Conv., 1980, Rep. Congl. Dist. Conv., 1980, Rep. State Conv., 1980. Mem. Music Educators' Nat. Conf., Am. String Tchr. Assn., Tex. Music Educators' Assn., Tex. Orch. Dir. Assn., Tex. State Tchr. Assn. Home: 9527 Meadowcroft Houston TX 77063 Office: Strack Intermediate Sch 18027-S Kuykendahl Klein TX 77379

EITNIER, CYNTHIA KAY, nurse; b. Lancaster, Pa., June 16, 1953; d. C. Quentin and Nancy Lee (Fisher) Martin; m. William B. Eitnier, May 24, 1986. Lic. Practical Nurse, Willow State Vocat.-Tech. Coll., 1972; Assoc. Nursing, Harrisburg Area Community Coll., 1981; B.S. in Nursing, Millersville U., 1984; postgrad. U. Ariz., 1985; M in Nursing, U. S.C., 1988. RN; cert. advanced nursing adminstrn. Practical nurse Conestoga View, Lancaster, 1973-77, Polyclinic Med. Ctr., Harrisburg, Pa., 1977-81; nurse, 1981-85, St. Joseph Hosp., Tucson, 1985-86, mem. code team, pulmonary rehab. teams, 1985-86; nursing supr. Brian Ctr., Columbia, S.C., 1986-87, asst. dir. nursing, 1987-88; dir. nursing Rheems (Pa.) Nursing Ctr., 1988, Brian Ctr., Yanceyville, N.C., 1989-90, Brian Ctr., Jeffersonville, Ga., 1990—. Mem. NAFE, Pa. Nurses Assn., NADONA. Democrat. Avocations: computers, swimming, hiking. Home: 2050 Old Clinton Rd Atp C-8 Macon GA 31211

EKSTRAND, MARGARET ELIZABETH, editor, public relations executive; b. Mpls., May 1, 1952; d. Robert Lawrence and Eleanor Mae (Anger) E.; m. Daniel Joseph Barnett, July 1, 1978. BA, U. Minn., 1973; MA, U. Colo., Denver, 1990. Sales rep. Lincoln MacCallum Desnick, Inc., Mpls., 1975-76, Investor Diversified Svcs., Inc., Denver, 1976-77, Hanes Knitwear, Inc., Denver, 1977-79; sales supr. Fortune of Denver, Inc., 1979-81; merchandising mgr. Joslins, Inc., Denver, 1982-85; coord. pub. rels. Hist. Denver, Inc., 1985-86; editor, coord. pub. rels. Colo. Hist. Soc., Denver, 1986—. Author: (monograph) Bishop Matz: The Builder Bishop, 1988; co-author: The University Club, 1891-1991; editor Colo. History News, 1985—. Mem. Colfax on Hill, Denver, 1987-; tour coord. Capitol Hill United Neighborhoods, Denver, 1988-89. Mem. Pub. Info. Officers Assn., Women in Communications, Govt. Communicators Assn., Denver Women's Press Club, Zonta (pres. Denver chpt. 1989-90), Phi Alpha Theta. Home: 1326 Emerson Denver CO 80218 Office: Colo Hist Soc 1300 Broadway Denver CO 80203

EKSTROM, KATINA BARTSOKAS, educator, artist; b. Springfield, Ill., Nov. 8, 1929; d. Tom A. and Elsie (Heinrich) Bartsokas; m. John Warren Ekstrom (div. Feb. 1978); children: John A., Kenneth M., Richard M., Timothy W., Christopher P. BFA, U. Ill., 1955, MAE, 1975. Tchr. art Urbana (Ill.) Jr. High Sch., 1974-89, Bronx (N.Y) Sch. Dist., 1990—; tchr. adult edn., 1975-80, Urbana Pk. dist., 1977-88; artist Colwell Collection catalog, Champaign, Ill., 1985; juror Chgo. Ann. Met. History Fair, 1985, Cen. Ill. Scholastics High Sch., Springfield, 1988-89, also others; Fulbright cultural exch. tchr., 1986. Exhibited in group show Champaign Arts and Humanities Assn., 1983-84, Swoope Gallery, Ind. Artist Peace Coalition Concerts, Champaign, 1985-86, U. Ill. Sinfonia, Champaign, 1986-88. 2d pl. award in painting Ill. 28th Ann. Art Exhbn. Mem. Urbana Educators Assn. (Outstanding Educator award 1986), Ind. Artists Ill., U. Ill. Alumni Assn., Kappa Delta, Phi Delta Kappa. Democrat. Methodist. Home: 30 W 96th St 2D New York NY 10025

EKSTROM, RUTH BURT, psychologist; b. Bennington, Vt., July 2, 1931; d. Ralph Amos and Bertha Paisley (Lambert) Burt; A.B., Brown U., 1953; Ed.M., Boston U., 1956; Ed.D., Rutgers U., 1967; LLD (hon.) Brown U., 1988; m. Lincoln Ekstrom, Nov. 9, 1957. Public sch. tchr., Beverly, Mass., 1953-57; sr. research asst. Ednl. Testing Service, 1957-64; vis. lectr. Rutgers U., 1958-60; dir. documentation services Ednl. Testing Service, Princeton, N.J., 1964-68, research scientist, 1968-80, sr. research scientist, 1980—. Mem. corp. (governing bd.) Brown U., 1972-88, trustee, 1972-77, fellow, 1977-88, sec. corp., 1982-88. Fellow Am. Psychol. Assn., AAAS; mem. Am. Assn. Counseling and Devel., Am. Ednl. Research Assn. (chmn. research on women and edn. 1984-85), Am. Assn. Higher Edn., Nat. Council Measurement Edn. Co-author: Education and American Youth: The Impact of the High School Experience, 1988; co-editor: Kit of Factor-Referenced Cognitive Tests, 1976; editor: Measurement, Technology and Individuality in Education, 1983; mem. editorial bd. Psychology of Women Quar., 1978-86, Jour. Counseling and Devel., 1982-85, Measurement and Evaluation in Counseling and Devel., 1989—; contbr. articles to profl. jours. Home: 78 Westerly Rd Princeton NJ 08540 Office: Ednl Testing Svc Princeton NJ 08541

ELBAUM-DAVID, JEAN, clinical team leader; b. N.Y.C., Feb. 12, 1960; d. Chaim and Sara (Bluzer) Elbaum; m. Jeffrey Owen David, Apr. 6, 1986. BA, N.Y.U., 1981, MA, 1983. Staff psychologist United Cerebral Palsy, Roosevelt, N.Y., 1985-88; clin. team leader Transitions of Long Island, Manhasset, N.Y., 1988—. Mem. Am. Psychol. Assn. (assoc.).

ELBERY, KATHLEEN MARIE, accountant; b. Boston, Nov. 30, 1959; d. Norman F. and June E. (Ramsay) E. BSBA with high honors, Northeastern U., 1983; JD cum laude, Suffolk U., 1990. CPA, Mass. Acct. Gately & Assocs., P.C., Wellesley, Mass., 1983-87, Peat Marwick, Boston, 1988—; cons. Kathleen M. Elbery, CPA, Medfield, Mass., 1988—. Merit scholar Northeastern U., 1978. Mem. AICPA, Mass. Soc. CPA's, Beta Alpha Psi, Beta Gamma Sigma, Phi Kappa Phi, Phi Delta Phi.

ELDER, CAROL See STEINHART, CAROL

ELDER, JEAN KATHERINE, education administrator; b. Virginia, Minn., May 30, 1941; d. Clarence Adrian and Katherine C. (Miltich) Samuelson. BS, U. Mich., 1963, AM, 1966, PhD, 1969; LHD (hon.), Davis and Elkins Coll., 1985; D in Pub. Service (hon.), Ferris State U., 1987. Tchr. 5th grade Ypsilanti (Mich.) Pub. Schs., 1963-64; tech. educable mentally retarded Quantico Marine Corps Dependent Sch., Va., 1964-65; dir. remedial reading program Iron Mountain (Mich.) Pub. Schs., 1965-66; research asst. U. Mich., Ann Arbor, 1966-69; asst. prof. spl. edn. Ind. U., Bloomington, 1969-71; dir. delinquency modification through edn. project Marquette (Mich.)-Alger Intermediate Sch. Dist.-Marquette County Probate Ct., 1971-72; asst. prof. edn. No. Mich. U., Marquette, 1972-76, assoc. prof., 1977-78, coordinator Title IX, 1975-76; project dir., assoc. scientist Specialist Office Three, Wis. Research and Devel. Ctr. for Cognitive Learning, U. Wis., Madison, 1976-77; assoc. prof. med. edn. Coll. Human Medicine, Mich. State U., East Lansing, 1978-82; commr. Adminstrn. of Devel. Disabilities, Washington, 1982-86; asst. sec. Office of Human Devel. Services, Washington, 1986-88; v.p. Performance Learning Systems, Inc., Farmington Hill, Mich., 1988—; cons. in field. Author: (with others) Planning Individualized Education Programs in Special Education, 1977, Pathways to Employment for Developmentally Disabled Adults, 1986; contbr. articles to profl. jours. Bd. dirs. Rehab. Internat., Am. Assn. on Mental Retardation; mem. Pres.'s Com. on Mental Retardation, 1976-79, Commn. on Presdl. Scholars, 1982-85; mem. Pres.'s Com. on Employment of People with Disabilities, 1989—. U.S. Office Edn. fellow, 1966-69. Fellow Am. Assn. Mental Retardation; mem. Assn. Retarded Citizens U.S., Council Exceptional Children, AAUW, Pi Lambda Theta, Phi Delta Kappa, Delta Kappa Gamma, Sigma Kappa. Lutheran. Home: 43050 Twelve Oaks Crescent C101 Novi MI 48377 Office: Performance Learning Systems Inc 31000 Northwestern Hwy Farmington MI 48334

ELDERS, M. JOYCELYN, public health administrator, endocrinologist; b. Schaal, Ark., Aug. 13, 1933; d. Haller Jones; m. Oliver B. Elders, Feb. 14, 1960; children: Eric D., Kevin M. BA, Philander Smith Coll., 1952; MS, U. Ark., 1967. Pediatric intern Univ. Minn. Hosp., Mpls., 1960-61; pediatric resident Univ. Ark. Med. Cen., Little Rock, 1961-63, chief pediatric resident, 1963-64, pediatric rsch. fellow, 1964-67, asst. prof. of pediatrics, 1967-71, assoc. prof. of pediatrics, 1971-76, prof. of pediatrics, 1976-87; dir. Ark. Dept. of Health, Little Rock, 1987—; Bd. dirs. Nat. Bank of Ark., North Little Rock, 1979-89. Editorial bd. Jour. Pediatrics, 1981—; contbr. articles on pediatrics to profl. jours. Bd. dirs. Northside YMCA, Little Rock, 1973—; vol. vols. in pub. schs., Little Rock, 1973—. 1st lt. U.S. Army, 1953. Recipient Worthen Bank's Ark. Profl. Woman of Distinction award, 1987; named one of 100 Women of Ark., 1980, Ark. Dem. Woman of Yr. statewide newspaper, 1988. Mem. So. Soc. Pediatrics (rsch. pres. 1979-80), Lawson Wilkins Endocrine Soc. (com. chair 1976), Ark. Sci. and Tech. Commn. (sec. 1975-89), Little Rock C. of C. (bd. dirs. 1980—), Endocrine Soc., Acad. Pediatrics, Am. Pediatric Soc. Office: Ark Dept Health 4815 W Markham Little Rock AR 72205

ELDRIDGE, MARIE DELANEY, statistician, education researcher; b. Balt., June 1, 1926; d. James Howard and Mathilda (Belz) Delaney; A.B. in Math., Coll. Notre Dame Md., 1948; Sc.M. in Biostatistics, Johns Hopkins U., 1953; m. Paul Eldridge, Apr. 3, 1961; children—Julia Delaney, Dan Pattengill. Statistician, indsl. quality control Revere Copper and Brass, Balt., 1948-49; statistician Ralph Parsons & Co., Frederick, Md., 1953-54, U.S. Govt., 1954-60; instr. U. Balt., 1958-60; supr. statistician HEW, Washington, 1960-65; with Office Statis. Programs and Standards, U.S. Postal Service, Washington, 1965-72, dep. dir., 1968-70, dir., 1970-72; dir. math. analysis div. Nat. Hwy. Traffic Safety Adminstrn., Dept. Transp., 1972-73, dir. office stats. and analysis, 1973-75; adminstr. Nat. Center Edn. Stats., Dept. Edn., Washington, 1976-84; dir. ctr. for ednl. studies Research Triangle Inst., Research Triangle Park, N.C., 1984-88; chair Durham Math. Collaborative N.C. Sch. Scis. and Math., 1987-88; cons. stats., 1988— ; mem. Edn. Commn. of States, 1976-84; mem. tech. adv. com. Calif. Assessment Program, 1978—; mem. nat. accident sample adv. com. Dept. Transp.; professorial lectr. George Washington U., 1981-84; adj. faculty Fed. Exec. Inst., 1982-84. Recipient Superior Accomplishment award U.S. Postal Service, 1970; Outstanding Performance award Dept. Transp., 1975; cert. recognition HEW, 1976, 80; Presdl. Rank award, 1981. Fellow Am. Statis. Assn. (exec. council 1975-79, co-chmn. subcom. tng. statisticians for govt. 1979-81, com. fellows 1978-80, cons. com. on govt. stats. 1985-88); mem. Am. Edn. Research Assn., Internat. Assn. Survey Statisticians, Internat. Statis. Inst., Fed. Exec. Inst. (dir. 1982-85), Washington Statis. Soc. (pres. 1976-77), Durham Math. Council (bd. dirs. 1985—, chmn. bd. 1987-88), Phi Delta Kappa. Democrat. Episcopalian. Home: 2819 Chelsea Circle Durham NC 27707

ELENT, ROZA, buyer; b. Leninabad, USSR, Sept. 26, 1944; d. Moysei and Sarra (Khasin) Levin; m. Leonid Elent, aug. 10, 1968; children: Svetlana, Elena. Cert. in acctg., Cambridge Sch., N.Y.C., 1979. Tchr. English Faculty Fgn. Lang. Pedagogical Inst. Leninabad, Odessa, USSR, 1967-78; asst. bookkeeper Atlas Optical, Bklyn., 1979-80; finished goods stock supr. Whaledent Internat., N.Y.C., 1980-82; customer svc. rep. Whaledent Internat., 1982-85, asst. to a buyer, 1985-86, purchasing agt., 1986-88, sr. buyer, 1988—. Office: Whaledent Internat 236 Fifth Ave New York NY 10001

EL-FAYOUMY, JOANNE QUINN, writer, educator; b. L.I., N.Y., Oct. 7, 1930; d. Thomas Joseph and Helen Veronica (Foster) Quinn; m. Saad G.A. El-Fayoumy, Sept. 8, 1963 (dec. 1989). BA, Barnard Coll., 1952; MA, Columbia U., 1964. Copy trainee, sec. J. Walter Thompson & Co., N.Y.C., 1952-55; sec. BBDO, N.Y.C., 1955-56; pub. relations asst., writer Helena Rubenstein Inc., N.Y.C., 1956-59; asst., writer Bob Taplinger Assocs., N.Y.C., 1959-60; adminstrv. asst. Protestant Coun. of City of N.Y., 1964-67; instr. Norfolk (Va.) State U., 1967-74, asst. prof., 1974-88; rsch. guest lectr. U. Jordan, Amman, 1986-87; numerous poetry readings. Author poetry anthology; editor: New Accounting Systems, 1984, New Budgeting Systems, 1984, Agricultural and Commercial Banking (Saad El-Fayoumy), 1984. Founding mem. Coptic Orthodox Ch. N. Am., 1964; sec. Am. Arab Anti-Discrimination Commn., Hampton Roads, Va., 1990. Recipient award, Tidewater Writers Conf.; honoree Irene Leach Meml. Contest. Mem. Arab Am. Assn. Va. (founding mem. 1973-80), AAUW (leader 1967-70), World Affairs Coun. (dir. 1970-72). Republican. Coptic Orthodox. Home: 652 Greentree Dr Virginia Beach VA 23452

ELFORD, CATHERINE WILLIAMS, management; b. Tacoma, Feb. 2, 1951; d. George Albert and Carolyn (Fogg) Williams Jr.; m. William J. Elford,. BA in Fgn. Languages, Wash. State U., 1973; MBA, Pacific Lutheran U., 1983. Supr. exec. Compensation Weyerhaeuser, Tacoma, 1980-82, mgr. position evaluation, 1982-84; dir. human resources Weyerhaeuser Co., Tacoma, 1984—. Bd. dirs. Ednl. Opportunity Program Univ. Wash., 1989. Mem. Human Resources Planning Soc., PTA, Phi Beta Kappa. Office: Weyerhaeuser Co Weyerhaeuser Tech Ctr Tacoma WA 98477

ELFREY, PRISCILLA, federal agency administrator; b. Orange, N.J., May 6, 1930; d. George Benjamin and Stella Halton (Binder) R.; m. George William Hartkejr (div. 1970); children: Stephen Paul, Kristen Ellen; m. John Vincent Elfrey. AB in Eng. & Am. Studies, Barnard Coll., 1952; postgrad. in drama, Columbia U., 1961-63; postgrad. in linguistics, NYU, 1968-70. Dir. dramatics Calhoun Sch., N.Y.C., 1961-64; asst. dir. admissions Finch Coll., N.Y.C., 1964-67; tng. supr. Mobilization for Youth, N.Y.C., 1967; pers. mgr. Am. Arbitration Assn., N.Y.C., 1967-68; tng. mgr. NYU, N.Y.C., 1968-72; mgr. employee communication and tng. Yale U., New Haven, 1972-73, assoc. dean, career counseling, 1973-79; exec. devel. officer NASA, Washington, 1979-82; strategic planning and spl. projects mgr. payloads NASA, Fla., 1982—; pres. Otec Career and Mgmt. Cons., Cocoa Beach, Fla., 1983—; mem. Space Coast Pub. Relations, Brevard County, Fla., 1981-85. Author: The Hidden Agenda, 1982; contbr. articles to profl. publs. Founder, bd. dirs. Am. Place Theater, N.Y.C., 1961-70. Yale U. fellow, 1973-79. Mem. Aerospace Women's Assn., NAFE, Fla. Women in Film. Democrat. Episcopalian. Home: 320 Barrello Ln Cocoa Beach FL 32931

ELGAVISH, ADA, biochemist; b. Cluj, Romania, Jan. 23, 1946; came to U.S. 1979; d. David and Malca (Neuman) Simchas; m. Gabriel A. Elgavish, Dec. 28, 1968; children: Rotem, Eynav. BSc, Tel-Aviv U., 1969, MSc, 1972; PhD, Weizmann Inst. Sci., Rehovot, Israel, 1978. Postdoctoral vis. fellow NIH, Balt., 1979-81; instr. U. Ala. Sch. Medicine, Birmingham, 1981-82, rsch. assoc., 1982-84, rsch. asst. prof., 1984-89, asst. prof. comparative medicine, 1989—; assoc. scientist Cystic Fibrosis Ctr., Birmingham, 1984—. Am. Lung Assn. Career Investigator awardee, 1987—; grantee, Cystic Fibrosis Found., 1986—, NIH, 1989—. Mem. AAAS, N.Y. Acad. Sci., Ala. Acad. Sci., Southeastern Pharmacology Soc., Am. Thoracic Soc., Sigma Xi. Home: 1737 Valpar Dr Birmingham AL 35226 Office: Univ of Ala Sch Medicine Dept Comparative Medicine Birmingham AL 35294

ELGIN, SARAH CARLISLE ROBERTS, biology researcher and educator; b. Washington, July 16, 1945; d. Carlisle Bishop and Lorene (West) Roberts; m. Robert Lawrence Elgin, June 9, 1967; children—Benjamin Carlisle, Thomas James. B.A. in Chemistry, Pomona Coll., 1967; Ph.D. in Biochemistry, Calif. Inst. Tech., 1971. Research fellow Calif. Inst. Tech., Pasadena, 1971-73; asst. prof. biochemistry and molecular biology Harvard U., Cambridge, Mass., 1973-77, assoc. prof., 1977-81; assoc. prof. biology Washington U., St. Louis, 1981-84, prof., 1984—. Mem. editorial bd. Jour. Cell Biology, N.Y.C., 1980-82; exec. editor Nucleic Acids Research, 1983-88; editorial bd. Jour. Biol. Chemistry, 1985-88, Molecular Cellular Biology, 1989—; contbr. papers in field. Mem. molecular biology study sect. NIH, 1986-89. Rsch. grantee NIH, 1987, 88, NSF, 1986). Fellow AAAS; mem. Am. Chem. Soc., Am. Soc. Biol. Chemists (program com. 1984), Am. Soc. Cell Biology (coun. 1983-85, publs. com. 1989—), Genetics Soc. Am. Office: Washington U Biology Dept Box 1137 Saint Louis MO 63130

ELIAS, DIANA LINDA, plastic surgeon; b. Miami, Fla., Oct. 14, 1955; d. George Frances and Dolores (Serra) E.; m. Mark David Herbst. BA, U. S. Fla., 1979; MD, Emory U., Atlanta, 1983. Intern, resident Emory U. Affiliated Hosps. Contbr. articles to profl. jours., 1984, 86, 88, 89. Mem. Planetary Soc. 1988. Mem. ACS, Assn. Women Surgeons, Southeastern Surg. Soc., Am. Soc. Plastic & Reconstructive Surgeons.

ELIAS, ELLEN VICTORIA, social science and computer educator; b. Miami Beach, Fla., May 23, 1959; d. Alvin and Lenore (Gold) E. AA, Emory U., 1978; BA, U. Fla., 1980; MS, Barry U., 1982. Cert. secondary social studies tchr., Fla. History tchr. Dade County Schs., Miami, Fla., 1981-83, dept. head, 1983-86, computer applications educator, 1986-87; adj. tchr. Dade Acad. for Teaching Arts, Miami, 1987—. Editor: Curriculum Development In the Social Studies, 1989. Publicity chairperson Miami Project to Cure Paralysis, 1982—; vol. Bob Graham for U.S. Senator, 1986. Named Tchr. of Yr. Carol City Jr. High Sch., 1983, Outstanding Young Women in Am., Master Tchr. State of Fla., 1986. Mem. Nat. Coun. for Social Studies, Fla. Assn. Computer Educators, Dade County Coun. for Social Studies, United Tchrs. of Dade.

ELIAS, SARAH DAVIS, English language educator; b. Chgo., Aug. 9, 1934; d. Calvin Paul and Julia Elizabeth (Bush) D.; m. Antoine Jack Elias, Aug. 28, 1960. BA, Roosevelt U., 1957; MA, Morgan State U., 1973; MS, Johns Hopkins U., 1983. Cert. tchr., Ill., Calif., Md. Elem. tchr. Chgo. Pub. Schs., 1958-62, Palo Alto (Calif.) Unified Sch. Dist., 1969-70; tchr. Balt. City Schs., 1961-69, 70—, chmn. reading dept., 1978-81, English tchr., 1982—; supervising tchr. Coppin State Coll., Balt., 1973-75; resource coordinator, tutor Johns Hopkins Tutorial Projects, Balt., 1968; social studies text cons. Harcourt, Brace, Jovanovich Pub., Balt., 1972. Mem. Mayor's Task Force on Edn., Balt., 1967-69, Mayor's Bicentennial Com., 1974-76. Am. Fedn. Tchrs.-Cornell U. fellow, 1967. Mem. Balt. Tchrs. Union (contract negotiator 1967-69), Internat. Reading Assn., Md. Council Tchrs. of English and Lang. Arts, Herbert M. Frisbey Hist. Soc., NAACP, Delta Sigma Theta. Democrat. Baptist. Club: Chums. Home: 20 Olmsted Green Baltimore MD 21210 Office: Balt City Schs 200 E North Ave Baltimore MD 21202

ELIAS, SHARON LOUISE, plastic surgeon; b. Nebr., Oct. 6, 1941; d. Houghton Francis and Ruth Eleanor (Bronson) E. BA, LeLand Stanford Jr U., 1965; MD, LeLand Stanford Jr. U., 1967. Dip. Am. Bd. of Plastic Surgery, 1976. Intern in surgery Univ. N.C., Chapel Hill, 1967-68, resident in surgery, 1968-69; resident in surgery U. Ariz. Hosps., Tucson, 1969-72, Med. Coll. of Wis., Milw., 1972-74; plastic surgeon Columbia Hosp., Milw., 1974—, mem. governing staff, 1987—. Mem. Am. Assn. for Hand Surgery, Midwest Assn. Plastic Surgeons, Am. Coll. Surgeons, Am. Soc. Plastic and Reconstructive Surgeons. Republican. Presbyterian. Office: 400 W Silver Spring Milwaukee WI 53217

ELIASON, NANCY CAROL, community college management; b. Washington, Feb. 24, 1929; d. Lester Frank Kirchener and Nancy Lee (Rhea) Wiebe; m. William A. Eliason, Jan. 29, 1956 (div. June, 1969) (rem. May 30, 1970); children: Charles Henry, William T., Leslie C. AB, Mary Baldwin Coll., 1950; MA, U. Md., 1953. Editor, writer Telenews, Inc., Washington, 1951-53; exec. dir. Blue Ridge Area Girl Scout Coun., Inc., Winchester, Va., 1954-55; asst. registrar Wheaton Coll., Norton, Mass., 1966-68; registrar and instr. Social Scis. Massasoit Community Coll., North Abingdon, Mass., 1968-70; assoc. prof. Social Scis. Lehigh County Community Coll., Schnecksville, Pa., 1970-76; dir. devel. and spl. projects Am. Assn. of Community and Jr. Colls., Washington, 1976-85; edn. policy analyst Nat. Govs. Assn., Washington, 1985-86; dir. devel. Close Up Found., Arlington, Va., 1986-88; cons., evaluator Fund for Improvement of Post Sec. Edn., Title III and Voc. Edn. Progs. Contbr. articles and booklets to profl. mags. and jours. on various areas of small bus. Mem. Nat. Adv. Com. on Small Bus. Devel. Ctrs., 1985—, Univ. Bus. Collaboration/Am. Assn. State Colls. and Univs., 1985-87, Nat. Ctr. for Rsch. in Vocat. Edn., 1978-80, Nat. Adv. Bd. Adult Learning, College Bd., 1979-86, Office Adult Learning Svcs., 1983-87; Nat. Evaluation Com. on Future Funds for Post-Secondary Edn., 1978-79. Nominee, Rockefeller Pub. Svc. award, 1981. Mem. AAUP, AAUW, Am. Assn. of Community and Jr. Colls. (Woman of Year 1977, Nat. Coun. community Svc. and Continuing Edn. Person of Year, 1983), Alpha Xi Delta. Home: 2112 Deborah Dr Punta Gorda FL 33950

ELIN, CAREN MINDY, chiropractor; b. Patterson, N.J., Nov. 24, 1950; d. Rudy Robak and Suzanne (Cohen) Spitzer. BS, U. Minn., 1968-72; MS, Hunter Coll., N.Y.C., 1974-77; postgrad., LA Coll. of Chiropractic, 1981-85. Tchr. NYC Bd. Edn., 1972-79, San Diego Juvenile System, 1979-81, LA Unified and LA County, 1981-85; studio tchr. Calif. State; pres. Comprehensive Muscular Skeletal Care Ctr., Los Angeles, Calif., 1985--; ptnr. with Bjoen Eek M.D. Bjorn Eek, M.D., Calif., 1987—; assoc. United Lodge Theosophists, N.Y.C., Los Angeles, 1975—; mem. Theosophical Soc., Philipines, 1987—. Co-author with Sylvia Cranston, Reincarnation a New Horizon in Sci. Religion and Soc., 1984; asst. editor: Theosophical Digest, 1988—. Mem. Am. Chiropractic Assn., Calif. Chiropractic Assn. Home: 5964 Hayes Ave Los Angeles CA 90042

ELINS, ROBERTA, public relations agency; b. New Brunswick, N.J., Apr. 20, 1955; d. Jack Jerome Elins and Florence (Brown) Schoenbrun; m. Steven Richard Dinkes, June 25, 1988. AB, Vassar Coll., Poughkeepsie, 1976. Adminstrn. asst. The Rowland Co., Inc., N.Y.C., 1976-79; acct. supr. Fishman Cairns Communications, N.Y.C., 1979-81; pres. Roberta Elins/Pub. Rels., N.Y.C., 1981-88; exec. v.p., creative dir., ptnr. Communications Specialty Group Ltd., N.Y.C.; faculty adv. and communications dept. Fashion Inst. of Tech., N.Y.C., 1986—. Co-author: Be Your Own Makeup Artist, 1983, Stress Breakers, 1985. Mem., Women's Jewelry Assn., Vassar Club (admission com., N.Y.C., chmn. publicity and exec. com. You Gotta have Park 1989—). Office: Communications Specialty 1133 Broadway New York NY 10010

ELINSON, ELAINE, public relations consultant; b. Washington, May 26, 1947; d. Jack and May Gomberg E.; m. Brian Nicholson, July 19, 1975; div. 1982; 1 child: Matthew. Student, Smith Coll., 1964-65; BA (with honors), Cornell U., 1968. Researcher Mus. Natural History, New York, N.Y., 1968; reporter, editor Pacific News Service, San Francisco, Calif., 1970-73; advance rep. Free theatre Assoc., Asia, 1971-72; internat. rep. United Farm Workers, AFL, CIO, London, Stockholm, 1974-75,1969-70; groups officer Nat'l Coun. for Civil Liberties, London, 1975-77; press officer Nat'l Assn. of Local Govn. Officers, London, 1977-79; editor ACLU News, San Francisco, 1980—; cochmn. Friends of Nicaraguar Cultural Oakland, Calif., 1983—. Co-author book Devel. Debacle, 1982; author, article in book banking on poverty, 1984. Bd. mem. Literacy. Mem. San Francisco-Oakland Newspaper Guild, Media Alliance. Home: 2437 Grant St Berkeley CA 94703 Office: ACLU-NC 1663 Mission St #460 San Francisco CA 94103

ELION, GERTRUDE BELLE, research scientist, pharmacology educator; b. N.Y.C., Jan. 23, 1918; d. Robert and Bertha (Cohen) E. AB, Hunter Coll., 1937, DSc (hon.), 1989; MS, NYU, 1941, DSc (hon.), 1989; DMS (hon.), Brown U., 1969; DSc (hon.), George Washington U., 1969, U. Mich., 1983, N.C. State U., 1989, Ohio State U., 1989, Poly. U., 1989, U. N.C., 1990, Russell Sage Coll., 1990. Lab. asst. biochemistry N.Y. Hosp. Sch. Nursing, 1937; research asst. in organic chemistry Denver Chem. Mfg. Co., N.Y.C., 1938-39; tchr. chemistry and physics N.Y.C. secondary schs., 1940-42; food analyst Quaker Maid Co., Bklyn., 1942-43; rsch. asst. in organic synthesis Johnson & Johnson, New Brunswick, N.J., 1943-44; biochemist Wellcome Rsch. Labs., Tuckahoe, N.Y., 1944-50; sr. rsch. chemist Wellcome Rsch. Labs., 1950—, asst. to assoc. rsch. dir., 1955-62, asst. to the research dir., 1963-66, head exptl. therapy, 1966-83, sci. emeritus, 1983—; adj. prof. pharmacology and exptl. medicine Duke U., 1970, rsch. prof. pharmacology, 1983—; adj. prof. pharmacology U. N.C., Chapel Hill, 1973; cons. USPHS, 1960-64; Chmn. Gordon Conf. on Coenzymes and Metabolic Pathways, 1966; mem. bd. sci. counselors Nat. Cancer Inst., 1980-84; mem. council Am. Cancer Soc., 1983-86; mem. Nat. Cancer Adv. Bd., 1984—. Contbr. articles to profl. jours.; patentee in field. Recipient Garvan medal, 1968, Pres.' medal Hunter Coll., 1970, Disting. Chemist award N.C. Inst. Chemists, 1981, Judd award Meml. Sloan-Kettering Cancer Ctr., 1983; corecipient Nobel prize in medicine, 1988, Bertner award U. Tex. M.D. Anderson Hosp., 1989; named to Hunter Coll. Hall of Fame, 1973. Fellow N.Y. Acad. Scis.; mem. Am. Chem. Soc., AAAS, Nat. Acad. Scis., Chem. Soc. (London), Am. Soc. Biol. Chemists, Am. Assn. Cancer Rsch. (bd. dirs. 1981, 83, pres. 1983-84, Cain award 1984), Am. Soc. Hematology, Transplantation Soc., Am. Soc. Pharmacology and Exptl. Therapeutics. Home: 1 Banbury Ln Chapel Hill NC 27514 Office: 3030 Cornwallis Rd Research Triangle Park NC 27709

ELIOT, JUDI, personnel consulting company executive; b. Phila., Apr. 9, 1946; d. Harry and Bernice (Page) Katz. Student Temple U., Media buyer, adminstrv. asst., copywriter Elkman Advt. Co., Bala Cynwyd, Pa., 1967-70; mgr., cons. C.W. Harvey Personnel, Phila., 1971-75; pres. Judi Eliot, Inc., Phila., 1976—, also cons.; leader seminars in field. Author articles. Bd. dirs. Am. Cancer Soc., Phila., 1980-83, mem. spl. events steering com., 1983-86, corp. sponsor Triathlon, 1985; fundraiser Sunshine Found., Phila., 1984-87; mem. Orgn. for Rehab. Through Tng., Phila., 1970—. Recipient Outstanding Service award Am. Cancer Soc., 1981, 82, Human Resource Profl. of Yr. award, 1986-87. Mem. Internat. Assn. for Personnel Women (bd. dirs. Phila. affiliate, dir. communications 1983, v.p. 1984-85, pres. 1985-86, past pres. philanthropic co-chmn 1986-87), Internat. Assn. for Personnel Women, Exec. Women Internat. Democrat. Jewish. Avocations: neuro-linguistics; communication theory; psychology; creative writing; travel.

ELIOT, LUCY CARTER, artist; b. N.Y.C., May 8, 1913; d. Ellsworth and Lucy Carter (Byrd) E. B.A., Vassar Coll., 1935; postgrad., Art Students League, 1935-40. tchr. painting and drawing Red Cross Bronx Vets. Hosp., N.Y.C., 1950, 51. Exhibited one-woman shows, Rochester Meml. Art Gallery, 1946, Cazenovia Coll., 1942, 47, 62, Syracuse Mus. Fine Arts, 1947, Wells Coll., 1953, Ft. Schuyler Club, Utica, N.Y., 1971, Nat. Shows, Pa. Acad. Fine Arts, Phila., 1946, 48, 49, 50, 52, 54, Corcoran Biennial, Washington, 1947, 51, Va. Biennial, Richmond, 1948, NAD, N.Y.C., 1971, 78, 90, Butler Inst. Am. Art, 1965, 67, 69, 70, 72, 74, 81, Cooperstown Art Assn. ann. exhbn., 1978, 80, 90; represented in permanent collections: Rochester Meml. Art Gallery, Munson-Williams-Proctor Inst., also pvt. collections. Bd. dirs. Artists Tech. Research Inst., 1975-79. Recipient First prize Rochester Meml. Art Gallery, 1946; recipient Purchase prize Munson-Williams-Proctor Inst., 1949, Painting of Industry award Silvermine Guild, 1957, 1st prize in oils Cooperstown Art Assn., 1978. Mem. N.Y. Artists Equity, N.Y. Soc. Women Artists (pres. 1973-75), Audubon Artists (dir. oil 1983-85, chmn. awards 1986-88), Am. Soc. Contemporary Artists, Pen and Brush Club N.Y.C. (Liquitex art award spring oil exhbn. 1989, 90), Cazenovia Club, Cosmopolitan Club. Episcopalian. Home: 131 E 66th St Apt 11 G New York NY 10021 also: 70 Sullivan St Cazenovia NY 13035

ELIZONDO, ANN MOCK, advertising executive; b. Pitts., Apr. 6, 1957; d. Lawrence Edward and Mary Ann (McCoy) Mock; m. Michael Lee Elizondo, Aug. 23, 1981; 1 child, Maxwell Lee. BBA, Emory U., 1979; MBA, Ga. State U., 1981. Mgmt. cons. Booz-Allen & Hamilton, Atlanta, 1979-81; brand mgr. H.P. Hood, Boston, 1981-83; mktg. mgr. Coca-Cola Co., Atlanta, 1983-86; v.p. McCann-Erickson, L.A., 1986-88, sr. v.p., 1988—. Office: McCann-Erickson 6420 Wilshire Blvd Beverly Hills CA 90048*

ELKIND, SUE NATHANSON, psychologist; b. Washington, Aug. 11, 1943; d. Milton Norman and Maria Sylvia (Philips) Nathanson; m. Peter Freudenheim Elkind, Dec. 30, 1966; children: Lauren, Perrin, Ethan. BA, Wellesley Coll., 1964; PhD, U. Calif., Berkeley, 1968. Postdoctoral fellow Mt. Zion Hosp., San Francisco, 1968-69, staff psychologist, 1969-71; pvt. practice psychologist Orinda, Calif., 1971—; supr. Psychotherapy Inst., Berkeley, 1975—; attending staff Mt. Zion Hosp., San Francisco. Author: Soul-Crisis, 1989; contbr. articles to profl. jours. Mem. Am. Psychol. Assn., Contra Psychol. Assn. Democrat. Jewish. Office: 8 Orinda Way Orinda CA 94563

ELKINS, PATRICIA A., healthcare executive, nurse; b. Medford, Mass., Feb. 5, 1941; d. Stanley Joseph and Dorothy (Harris) Crawford; m. Jay Henry VandenBasch, Oct. 26, 1962; children: Danielle, Andrea, Mark, Michelle, Joseph, John, James; m. Robert William Elkins, July 28, 1977. BS in Chemistry, U. Miami, Fla., 1971, BSN, 1981. Sec., treas. Elkins Orthopedic Coll., Danville, Va., 1982—; owner Healthcare, Inc. of Va., Danville, 1982—; owner, pres. Futuristics Trading, Milton, N.C., 1985—; owner, sec., treas. Futuristics Rehab., Danville, 1985—; owner, pres. Profl. Phys. Therapy & Rehab., Chesapeake, Va., 1986—, Progressive Phys. Therapy & Rehab., Chatham, Va., 1986—, Healthcore Inc., of N.C., Milton, 1987—, Patricia A. Elkins & Assoc., Danville, 1987—; cons. Eagle Cons., Inc., Milton, 1988—, Elkins Orthopedic Group, Danville. Bd. dirs. Nat. Youth Sport Coaches Assn., West Palm, Fla., 1982—, Coaches Adv. Round Table, N.Y., 1984—. Fellow Am. Back Soc.; mem. NAFE, ANA, Va. Nurses Assn., Phi Lambda Pi (pres. 1980). Democrat. Roman Catholic. Home: Rt 1 Box 472B Mt Hill Rd Milton NC 27305 Office: Healthcare Inc 110 Exchange St Danville VA 24541

ELLENBERGER, DIANE MARIE, nurse, consultant; b. St. Louis, Oct. 5, 1946; d. Charles Ernst and Celeste Loraine (Neudecker) E.; R.N., Barnes Hosp., St. Louis, 1970; B.S. in Nursing St. Louis U., 1976; M.S., U. Colo., 1977. Staff nurse hosps., clin. nurse, St. Louis, 1973-76; nurse clinician, Sedalia, Mo., 1977-78; nurse clinician, educator Bothwell Hosp., Sedalia, 1977-78; clin. nurse specialist, coordinator perinatal outreach edn. Cardinal Glennon Meml. Hosp. Children, St. Louis, 1978-80; instr. McKendree Coll., Lebanon, Ill., 1980; asst. prof. Maryville Coll., St. Louis, 1982-85; nurse cons. Carr, Korein, Tillary, Kunin, Montroy, Glass & Bogard, Attys. at Law, 1986—; owner, operator Diane Designs Needlepoint, St. Louis, 1981—. Served with Nurse Corps, USAF, 1970-72. Mem. Am. Nurses Assn., Nurses Assn. Am. Coll. Ob-Gyn, Nat. Perinatal Assn., Mo. Nurses Assn., Mo. Perinatal Assn. (v.p. 1980), Sigma Theta Tau. Mem. Divine Sci. Ch. Contbr. articles profl. jours. Office: 412 Missouri Ave East Saint Louis IL 62201

ELLENBERGER-THOMAS, MARGARET ANN, art educator; b. Waukesha, Wis., June 19, 1951; d. Melvin Michael and Elizabeth (Brewer) Thomas; 1 child, James Michael. BA in Art Edn., Beloit Coll., 1974; MA in Edn., U. Wis., Whitewater, 1981; postgrad., U. Wis., Madison, 1987. Cert. elem. tchr., Wis. Tchr. Beloit Pub. Schs., 1974-87, muralist, 1985-87, art specialist gifted and talented students, 1987—; tchr. Beloit Coll.; summer tchr. Janesville (Wis.) Pub. Schs., 1985; muralist Graphics Unltd., Beloit, 1986, 87; dir., founder Summer Explorers, Saturday Explorers Beloit Coll., 1986-90, dir. Rock Prairie Showcase Festival, 1986, Beloit and Vicinity Art Show, 1983-85. Co-author: Effective Schools and Effective Teachers, 1988; contbr. chpt. to book: Teaching and Counseling Gifted and Talented Learners in Regular Classrooms. Pres. bd. dirs. YWCA, Beloit, 1987-90. Mem. Wis. Coun. for the Gifted and Talented (bd. dirs. 1984-87, v.p. 1985-86, pres. 1986-87), Wis-Gate Found. (bd. dirs. 1985-87), Future Problem Solving (bd. dirs. 1986-87), Wis. Racquetball Assn. (bd. dirs. 1986-87). Home: 3211 Canterbury Ln Janesville WI 53545

ELLENBOGEN, TINA ROCHELLE, veterinarian; b. L.A., July 15, 1952; d. Albert Louis and Evelyn Renee (Stevens) E. BS, U. Calif., Davis, 1974; DVM, U. Calif., 1979. Lic. veterinarian, Wash. Assoc. veterinarian Bainbridge Island Vet. Clin., Winslow, Wash., 1979-80, S. Whidbey Animal Clin., Clinton, Wash., 1980-83, Animal Emergency Svcs., Kirkland, Wash., 1984-86; owner Mobile Veterinary Svcs., Bothell, Wash., 1987—; part-time dir. info. svcs. Delta Soc. Nat. Hdqrs., Renton, Wash., 1987—. Co-founder, vol. Doney Meml. Pet Clin., Seattle, Pet Support Network, Seattle, 1989. Mem. Am. Vet. Medicine Assn., Am. Assn. House Call Veterinarians (bd. dirs.), Wash. Vet. Medicine Assn., Seattle King County Vet. Medicine Assn., Delta Soc. (bd. dirs. Puget Sound chpt. 1986-89). Office: Mobile Vet Svcs PO Box 1744 Bothell WA 98041-1744

ELLENDER, PATTI JEAN, pharmacist; b. Lake Charles, La., Oct. 9, 1960; d. Louis Eugene Ellender and V. Ruth (Warrens) Vaughan; m. Ronald J. Schell, Apr. 4, 1987 (div. Feb. 1990). Student, McNeese State U., 1978-81; BS in Pharmacy, Northeast La. U., 1983. Registered pharmacist. Staff pharmacist Kroger Pharmacy, Lake Charles, 1984-85, Owen Healthcare, Inc., Dallas and Lake Charles, 1985-86; dir. pharmacy Doctor's Nursing Ctr., Dallas, 1986-87, asst. dir. pharmacy, 1988—; clin. staff pharmacist Parkland Meml. Hosp., Dallas, 1987-88; clin. staff pharmacist II Presbyn. Hosp., Dallas, 1988—. Mem. North Cen. Tex. Soc. Hosp. Pharmacists, Am. Soc. Hosp. Pharmacists. Republican. Roman Catholic. Office: Presbyterian Hosp of Dallas 8200 Walnut Hill Lane Dallas TX 75231

ELLER, BRENDA ANN, educator, recreational director; b. Akron, Ohio, Apr. 25, 1959; d. Paul Ray and Wanda Ann (Ammons) Miller; m. Daniel Paul Eller, Aug. 31, 1985. BA, Bob Jones U., 1981; postgrad., U. Akron, 1985. Cert. learning disabilities tchr., Ohio. Tchr. kindergarten Massillon (Ohio) Christian Sch., 1981-83, Henry Ctr. for Learning, Akron, 1984-85, Summit County Schs., Akron, 1985-86; tchr. high sch. Plain Local Schs., Canton, Ohio, 1986-90; tchr. learning disabilities resource Chicora Elem. Sch., Charleston, S.C., 1990—; instr. evening classes Jackson Community Edn., Canton, 1986-88; exec. dir. Ohio Bapt. Acres, Massillon, 1988-89. Mem. AMA (aux. 1987-89) Stark County Med. Aux., Aultman Hosp. Residents Spouses Orgn. (pres. 1987-88). Republican.

ELLER, LEONA ZIGLER, educator, civic leader; b. Harrisonburg, Va., Feb. 24, 1910; d. Samuel David and Elizabeth Susan (Wenger) Zigler; m. William Harold Row, Sept. 12, 1934 (dec. 1971); children: William Harold, Bette Joanne; m. John C. Eller, Dec. 24, 1979. BA, Bridgewater Coll., Va., 1934; MS in Edn., No. Ill. U., 1964; postgrad., U. Md., 1973. Tchr. Washington Sch., Elgin, Ill., 1954-58; prin. Grant Sch., Elgin, 1958-63, Garfield Sch., Elgin, 1963-69; tchr. 4th grade Prince George's County, Woodley Knoll Sch., Upper Marlboro, Md., 1969-75; ret. Devel. bd. Bethany Hosp., Chgo., 1979-84, Human Devel. Ctr., Chgo., 1986—; interpreter Brethren Health & Welfare, 1988-89. Mem. AAUW. Democrat. Ch. of the Brethren. Address: 245 Oak Ave #714 Sebring FL 33870

ELLERBEE, LINDA, broadcast journalist; b. Bryan, Tex., Aug. 15, 1944; m. John David Klein; children: Vanessa, Joshua. Ed., Vanderbilt U. Newscaster, disc jockey Sta. WVON, Chgo., 1964-67; program dir. Sta. KSJO, San Francisco, 1967-68; reporter Sta. KJNO and AP, Juneau, Alaska, 1969-72, Sta. KHOU-TV, Dallas, 1972-73, Sta. WCBS-TV, N.Y.C., 1973-76; Washington corr. NBC News, 1975-78; co-anchor Weekend, NBC News, NBC-TV, 1978-80; reporter NBC Nightly News, 1980-82; co-anchor NBC News Overnight, 1982-84; corr., reporter Today Show, NBC-TV; with Lucky Day Prodns., N.Y.C.; commentator Cable News Network, 1989. Author: And So It Goes, 1986. Office: Putnam Berkeley Group 200 Madison Ave New York NY 10016*

ELLERT, MARTHA SCHWANDT, physiologist, educator; b. Jersey City, Nov. 27, 1940; d. Harry Richard and Emily (Brando) Schwandt; m. William Sam Hunter, Aug. 3, 1972; children—Anthony Martin, William Fritsche. B.S., Barry Coll., 1962; Ph.D., U. Miami, Fla., 1967. Instr. physiology St. Louis U. Sch. Medicine, 1967-70, asst. prof., 1970-75, dir. summer program, 1971-75; assoc. prof. physiology Sch. Medicine, So. Ill. U., Carbondale, 1975—, assoc. prof. med. edn., 1987—, asst. dean for curriculum, 1981—. Precinct committeeman Dem. Party, Makanda, Ill., 1978—; pres. exec. bd. Carbondale New Sch., 1983-85; mem. exec. bd. Makanda Community Devel. Council, 1980-83, consumer adv. bd. Family Practice Ctr., Carbondale 1976-80; mem. steering com. Women's Coalition for So. Ill., 1990—. Mem. Am. Physiol. Soc., AAUP (nat. coun. 1976-79, chpt. pres. 1973-74, 79-80), Sigma Xi. Mem. Christian Church. Avocations: singing, politics, raising dairy goats. Office: So Ill Univ Sch Medicine Carbondale IL 62901

ELLINGSWORTH, MARILYN L., small business owner; b. Fillmore, N.Y., Mar. 24, 1947; d. Leon Wells and Alice Glena (Dildine) Hopkins; m. Dyo Chrisler Ellingsworth, July 7, 1979; children: Diane, David, Edward, Robert, Patrick, Angela Ellingsworth; Valerie, Lorraine, Donald McCaffery. Gen. secretarial diploma, Olean Bus. Inst., 1966; AAB with high honors, Lorain County Community Coll., 1979. Cert. secondary educator in acctg. and computers, Ohio. Acct. Jacobs, Visconsi, and Jacobs Co., Westlake, Ohio, 1973-85; acctg. mgr. The Timms Spring Co., Elyria, Ohio, 1985-89; owner, mgr. ME Acctg. & Tax Svc., Wellington, Ohio, 1984—. Mem. NAFE. Home and Office: 51257 Betts Rd Wellington OH 44090

ELLIOT, ELISA LOUISE, research microbiologist, educator; b. Mpls., Nov. 21, 1956; d. Arthur McAuley and Carol Ann (Brand) Elliot. Student, Tex. A&M U., 1974-76; BS in Microbiology, Tex. Tech U., 1977; PhD, U. Md., 1984. Med. technician, med. technologist Scott and White Clinic and Hosp., Temple, Tex., 1977-78; grad. teaching asst. U. Md., College Park, 1978-79, 82-84; asst. prof. seafood microbiology U. Alaska-Fishery Indsl. Tech. Ctr., Kodiak, 1984-87; microbiologist U.S. Dept. Agr. Food Safety and Inspection Svc., Beltsville, Md., 1987-89; part-time instr. Univ. Coll., U. Md., College Park, 1987—; microbiologist FDA, Washington, 1989—. Contbr. chpts. to books, articles to profl. jours. Bd. dirs. Kodiak Women's Resource and Crisis Ctr., 1986-87; worker Episcopal Ch. Loaves and Fishes Kitchen, Washington, 1989—. NSF grantee, 1973; NSF grad fellow, 1979-82. Mem. Am. Soc. for Microbiology (sec. Alaska br. 1985-87, councillor Alaska br. 1986-87), AAUW, Assn. Women in Sci., Inst. Food Technologists, Nat. Shellfisheries Assn., Nature Conservancy, Sierra, Alpha Lambda Delta, Phi Kappa Phi. Office: FDA HFF-234 Ctr for Food Safety & Applied Nutrition 200 C St SW Washington DC 20204

ELLIOT, JANET LEE, occupational physician; b. Hannibal, Mo., Aug. 6, 1955; d. Bobby Neal and Mary Elizabeth (Ford) Vandiver; m. Roger Larry Elliot, July 26, 1986. Student, U. Mo., 1979, MD, 1981. Lic. gen. practitioner, surgeon. Intern Lockport, Ill.; resident Truman Med. Ctr., Kansas City, Mo.; with occupational gen. Landmark Med. Ctr., Kansas City, Mo., 1982-84, North Indsl. Clinic, Kansas City, 1984-88; aviation med. examiner N.J., 1985; with mini residency occupational medicine Robert Wood Johnson Med. Sch., U. of Medicine and Dentistry of N.J., 1987; dir. of occupational medicine Suburban Heights Med. Ctr., Chicago Heights, Ill., 1988—. Mem. VFW, Troy, Mo., 1972—. Mem. Am. Occupational Assn., Am. Acad. of Family Practice, Am. Assn. of Railway Surgeons, Norfolk and Western Ry. Assn. Republican. Roman Catholic. Office: Suburban Heights Med Ctr 333 Dixie Hwy Chicago Heights IL 60411

ELLIOTT, CANDICE K., small business owner; b. Cedar Rapids, Iowa, Aug. 29, 1949; d. Charles H. and Eunice A. (Long) Goodrich; m. John William Jr. Elliott, Jan. 27, 1973; 1 child, Brandon Christian; 1 stepchild, John William III. BA, U. Iowa, 1971. Interior designer Dayton's, Mpls., 1971-76, Candice Interior Space Planning and Design, Guilford, Conn., 1981-87; owner, interior designer Sofa Works, King of Prussia, Pa., 1987-90; interior designer Jerrehians's Home Furnishings, West Chester, Pa., 1990—. Bd. dirs. The Old Capitol Restoration Com., Iowa City, 1970-76; curator Guilford Keeping Soc., 1983-88; cons. Zion Episcopal Ch., North Branford, Conn., 1985-88. Mem. Am. Soc. Interior Designers (bd. dirs. Conn. chpt., profl. mem.). Republican. Home: 13 Windsor Circle Wayne PA 19087

ELLIOTT, DESIREE, data processing executive; b. Phila., June 21, 1966. Bachelor's degree, LaSalle U., 1989. Statis. analyst U.S. Dept. Labor, Phila., 1986-88; office mgr. Dr. Angela Lisa, Phila., 1988-89; data coord. The Hay Group, Inc., Phila., 1990—. Fellow NAFE. Home: 1805 N Gratz St Philadelphia PA 19121

ELLIOTT, DIANA BEVERLY, management consulting executive, consultant; b. Yuma, Ariz., June 3, 1943; d. William Earney and Gladys Evelyn (Davis) Scarbrough; m. Odus Vernon Elliott Jr., Oct. 8, 1965; children: Lara Evelyn, Devin Odus. BA in Edn., U. Ariz., 1966, MEd, 1976; postgrad., Ariz. State U., Tempe, 1989—. Mem. faculty Canyon del Oro High Sch., Tucson, 1966-70; instr. in English Pima Coll., Tucson, 1976-79, Mesa (Ariz.) Coll., 1979-81; faculty Ottawa U., Phoenix, 1981-84; adminstrv. intern Maricopa Community Coll. Dist., Phoenix, 1984-85; dir. edn. Superior Tng. Svcs., Inc., Phoenix, 1985-86; v.p. EFG Assocs., Inc., Mesa, 1986-89, pres., 1989—; bd. dirs. Work-Life Options, Phoenix. Pres. Mesa Elem. Sch. PTA, 1981. Ford Found. Rsch. grantee, 1988. Mem. Ariz. Adult Edn. Assn., ASTD, Am. Mgmt. Assn. Home: 2205 S Las Flores Mesa AZ 85202 Office: EFG Assocs Inc PO Box 16200-367 Mesa AZ 85201

ELLIOTT, DIANA MARIE, investments company executive, company owner; b. St. Louis, Dec. 6, 1952; d. James E. Jr. and Aline (DollBear) Herrin; m. James W. Elliott Jr., Aug. 18, 1986; children: Peyton, Paj. Student, East Cen. Jr. Coll., Decatur, Miss., 1971; barber lic., Jett Barber Sch., Memphis, 1973; manicurist lic., Baldwin County Sch Cosmotology, Daphne, Ala., 1988. Lic. manicurist, Ala., Miss. Adminstrv. asst., asst. mgr. Avco Fin. Svcs., Memphis, Mobile, Ala., 1975-81; loan officer C&S Fin. Svcs., Mobile, 1981-85; real estate loan underwriter United Cos., Mobile, 1985-86; owner Acme Metals Co., Mobile, 1986—; v.p., sec., treas. S & E Investments, Inc., Mobile, 1986—; manicurist Ala., 1988—, Miss., 1989—; notary State of Ala., Mobile, 1985—; fin. cons. Acme Metals Co., Mobile, 1986—. Mem. Resurrection Cath. Sch. PTA, 1989—. Named nominee 2000 Notable Women. Mem. NAFE. Republican. Roman Catholic. Home and Office: SVE Investments Inc 3809 Quinn Dr Pascagoula MS 39567

ELLIOTT, DOROTHY GALE, library administrator; b. Waltham, Mass., Mar. 6, 1948; d. Robert Straight and Grace Moore (Mills) Sanborn; m. W. Mitchell Elliott, Oct. 10, 1970. BA, Wellesley Coll., 1970; MA, U. Mo., 1977. Exec. sec. Coun. for Pub. Schs., Boston, 1970-72; asst. Jerry Litton for Congress, North Kansas City, Mo., 1972; exec. sec. Stephens Coll., Columbia, Mo., 1972-74; coord. Univ. Without Walls, Stephens Coll., Columbia, Mo., 1975-76; pub. svcs. libr. St. Joseph Pub. Libr., Mo., 1977-78, dir., 1978-89, dir. River Bluffs Regional Libr., 1989—. Sec., Grand River Libr. Conf., 1982-84; bd. dirs. Mo. Librs. Film Coop., 1980-83; sec./treas. Mo. Librs. Network Bd., 1984-85; pres. N.W. Mo. Library Network Bd., 1983-85; pres. adv. coun. Sch. Libr. and Info. Sci., U. Mo., Columbia, 1985-89; mem. libr. adv. com. Mo. Coordinating Bd. for Higher Edn., 1987-89, Gov.'s Adv. Coun. on Literacy, 1987-89, Project Literacy U.S. Task Force, 1986—; mem. exec. bd. Friends of St. Joseph Pub. Libr., 1982—; active Mo.

Gov.'s Conf. Com. on Libr. and Info. Svcs., 1987—. Editor newsletter Jr. League St. Joseph, 1985-86. Bd. dirs. Mental Health Assn. St. Joseph, 1978-81; com. mem. United Way Greater St. Joseph, 1981—, com. Leadership St. Joseph; bd. dirs. Interfaith Community Services, 1982-85; mem. steering com. Lifelong Learning, St. Joseph, 1983—; mem. St. Joseph Area Women's Career Network, 1983-87, Downtown St. Joseph, Inc., 1983-87. Wellesley scholar, 1969; recipient Literacy St. Joseph award, 1988. Mem. ALA, Pub. lbr. Affiliates (network 1988—), Mo. Libr. Assn. (sec. 1983-84, chmn. legis. com. 1986-87, v.p., pres.-elect 1987-88, pres. 1988-89), Beta Phi Mu, Wellesley Club (Kansas City), Runcie Club (St. Joseph), St. Joseph Women's Press Club. Democat. Disciples of Christ. Office: River Bluffs Regional Libr 10th and Felix Sts Saint Joseph MO 64501

ELLIOTT, ELAINE SALLY, psychologist, researcher; b. St. Louis, Feb. 17, 1951; d. Walter Leonard and Helen (Krelo) E. BA in Psychology, U. Mo., 1973; MA in Psychology, San Diego State U., 1977; PhD in Psychology, U. Ill., 1980. Vis. rsch. assoc. Lab. Human Devel., Harvard U., Cambridge, Mass., 1980-81; lectr. dept. psychology Brandeis U., Waltham, Mass., 1981; fellow Ctr. for Cognitive Therapy, U. Pa., Phila., 1982-83; cons. Presbyn. U. Pa. Med. Ctr., Phila., 1984-85; pvt. practice Newton Centre, Mass., 1985—; ptnr. OSM Assocs., Newtonville, Mass., 1986—; dir. Ctr. for Cognitive Therapy Greater Boston, Newton Centre, 1988—. Author: chpt. Carmichael's Handbook of Child Psychology, 1983, Advances in Psychology, 1989. Nat. Inst. on Aging grantee Brandeis U., 1988. Mem. Am. Psychol. Assn., Assn. for Advancement Behavior Therapy, Mass. Psychol. Assn. Office: Ctr for Cognitive Therapy 10 Langley Rd Ste 200 Newton Centre MA 02159

ELLIOTT, ELIZABETH ANN, market researcher; b. Cin., Apr. 27, 1932; d. Howard E. Elliott and Kathryn E. (Forsman) Byers. BA, Denison U., 1954. Interviewer market research dept. Procter & Gamble Co., Cin., 1954-55, field supr., 1955-58, chief field supr., 1958-60, personnel dir. and scheduler, 1960-77, tech. cons., 1977—; career adv. Denison U., 1980—; market rsch. cons. Community Chest and other svc. agys., 1983—. Mem. NAFE, Delta Gamma. Republican. Presbyterian. Avocations: photography; travel; antiques; gardening; music. Home: 1326 Deliquia Dr Cincinnati OH 45230 Office: 2 Procter & Gamble Pla Cincinnati OH 45201

ELLIOTT, H. MARGARET, mathematics educator; b. Galveston, Tex., Aug. 16, 1925; d. Monroe L. and Helen (Marrs) E.; m. Karl D. Larsen, Dec. 24, 1970 (dec. Feb. 1990). BA, Rice U., 1945; MA, U. Calif., Berkeley, 1946; PhD, Radcliffe-Harvard, 1948. Instr. math. Washington U., St. Louis, 1949-51, asst. prof. math., 1951-55, assoc. prof. math., 1955-64; prof. math. Coll. of William and Mary, Williamsburg, Va., 1964-65; prof. math. U. Bridgeport (Conn.), 1968—, chmn. math., 1969-73; ONR rsch. contract Harvard U., Cambridge, Mass., 1952; tchr. ednl. and comml. TV, St. Louis, 1955-59. Vol. St. Louis Children's Hosp., St. Louis, 1949-52; sec. Internat. House Assn., St. Louis, 1952-55; bd. trustee, sec. 1st Congregationalist Ch., Stratford, Conn. 1987-88. NSF Sci. Faculty fellow MIT and Harvard U., 1957-58, Rsch. fellow Harvard U., 1948-49, 57-58, Benjamin White Whitney fellow Radcliffe, 1947-48, Ruth Lansing fellow Radcliffe, 1946-47. Mem. Am. Math. Soc., Math. Assn. Am., Nat. Coun. Tchrs. Math., AAUP, Phi Beta Kappa, Pi Delta Phi, Pi Mu Epsilon, Sigma Xi. Office: U Bridgeport Dept Math Bridgeport CT 06601

ELLIOTT, JEANNE MARIE KORELTZ, transportation executive; b. Virginia, Minn., Mar. 9, 1943; d. John Andrew and Johanna Mae (Tehovnik) Koreltz; m. David Michael Elliott, Apr. 30, 1983. Student, Ariz. State U., 1967, U. So. Calif. Cert. aviation safety inspector. Tech. asst. Ariz. State U., Tempe, 1966-68; from supr. to mgr. inflight tng./in-svc. programs Northwest Airlines Inc. (formerly Republic Airlines, Hughes Airwest, Air West Inc.), Mpls., 1968—; air carrier cabin safety specialist Flight Standards Service, FAA, Washington, 1975-76; cons. Interaction Research Corp., Olympia, Wash., 1982—. Contbg. editor Cabin Crew Safety Bull., Flight Safety Found., 1978—. Recipient Annual Air Safety award Air Line Pilots Assn., Washington, 1971, Annual Safety award Ariz. Safety Council, Phoenix, 1972; first female to hold FAA cabin safety inspector's credential, 1976. Mem. Soc. Air Safety Investigators Internat., Survival and flight equipment Assn., Assn. Flight Attendants (tech. chmn. 1968-85), Internat. Brotherhood Teamsters Airline Div., Soc. Automotive Engrs. (assoc.) (chmn. cabin safety provisions com. 1971—). Republican. Roman Catholic. Home: 16215 SE 31st St Bellevue WA 98008 Office: Northwest Airlines Inc Inflight Services Dept Minneapolis-St Paul Internat Airport Saint Paul MN 55111

ELLIOTT, LEE ANN, psychologist; b. Tulsa, Jan. 22, 1923; d. John Lewis and Evelyn (Peters) Moore; m. Craig Judson Elliott (dec. Feb. 1971). B.S., Okla. State U., 1945; postgrad., UCLA, 1947-50. Part owner Profl. Guidance Assocs., Sherman Oaks, Calif., 1961-66; owner, adminstr. health and human svcs. Woodland Self Motivation Home, Calif., 1967-78; owner Ray of Hope Hotel, Calif., 1978—; mgr., dir., spokesperson Alpha Oxi Omega, North Hollywood, Calif., 1967—; vis. nurse Vis. Nurses Assn., Hollywood, Calif., 1977-78, 1978—. Mem. Republican Presdl. Task Force, U.S. Senatorial Club, 1984—. Fellow NAFE, Smithsonian Inst.; mem. Internat. Platform Assn., Heritage Found. Home: 5251 Strohm St North Hollywood CA 91601 Office: Alpha Oxi Omega 5149 Bakman St North Hollywood CA 91601

ELLIOTT, LETHA ELAINE CRANFORD, non-profit organization administrator; b. Memphis, Oct. 21, 1936; d. Leland H. and Letha Louise (Shofner) Cranford; m. John Stanley Peterson, Feb. 9, 1959 (div. Mar. 1967); m. Clinton Carson Elliott, June 21, 1968 (div. Apr. 1981); 1 child, Leland Clinton. AA, Sullins Coll., 1956; BS, Memphis State U., 1963. Dancer, actress Memphis Civic Ballet, Front St. Theatre, 1950-66; arts editor, columnist Memphis Sunday Times, 1964-65; actress Theatre Memphis, 1987-89; fundraising asst. Memphis Arts Coun., 1965-66, administr., 1989—; researcher, writer Wildrick & Miller Advt., N.Y.C., 1966-68; asst. adminstr. Congregation Rodeph Sholom, N.Y.C., 1972-84; adminstr. Community Ch. of N.Y., N.Y.C., 1984-87; administr. G.H. Avery Co. Inc., Memphis, 1987-88; adminstr. Memphis Arts Coun., 1989—. Choreographer (ballets) Take Care, Memphis, 1962, Paganini Variations, Memphis, 1963; editor: 84th St. Greenery Fund (newsletter), N.Y.C., 1985-87; contbr. poetry to Christian Sci. Monitor, 1985-86, Wilderness Mag., 1990—, articles to profl. jours. Vol. Rodeph Sholom Shelter for Homeless, N.Y.C., 1984-87; active Nature Conservancy, Vt., Tenn., Memphis Symphony Chorus. Mem. NAFE, NOW, Nat. Assn. Ch. Bus. Adminstrs. (past sec. N.Y. chpt. 1986-87), Audubon Soc., Wilderness Soc., MENSA, Sierra Club, Network, Alpha Psi Omega. Democrat. Jewish. Office: Memphis Arts Coun 2714 Union Ave Extension Memphis TN 38112

ELLIOTT, LINNÉA CONSTANCE, publisher; b. N.Y.C., Feb. 23, 1948; d. Samuel and Edith Anna (Peterson) Whyte, Jr.; m. Peter Thomas Elliott, Aug. 31, 1969. Ground hostess Japan Airlines, N.Y.C., 1967-68; asst. to mng. editor Southmayd Corp., Yonkers, N.Y., 1968; public relations model Seagrams Corp., N.Y.C., 1968; prodn. editor, mgr. jours., editorial dept. Pergamon Press, Elmsford, N.Y., 1968-74; assoc. pub. Appleton Century-Crofts div. Prentice-Hall, East Norwalk, Conn., 1974-84; dir. mkgt. services HP Pub. Co., N.Y.C., 1986-88, assoc. publisher, 1988, gen. mgr. spl. programs div., 1989—; cons. in field. Mem. Healthcare Businesswomen's Assn., Pharm. Advt. Council, Assn. Ind. Clin. Pubs. (treas. 1981-83, pres.-elect 1984), Nat. Assn. Female Execs. Episcopalian. Mng. editor Jour. Family Practice, 1974-83, Jour. Nat. Med. Assn., 1975-79. Home: Colonial Hill RFD #1 Mount Kisco NY 10549 Office: HP Publishing Co 10 Astor Pl New York NY 10003

ELLIOTT, MELINDA JEAN, neonatologist, researcher; b. Steubenville, Ohio, Oct. 26, 1958; d. Gene Luther and Carolyn Jane (Harvey) E.; m. William Frank Cassano, May 13, 1989. BS in Biology, Bethany (W.Va.) Coll., 1980; MD, W.Va. U., 1984. Diplomate Am. Bd. Pediatrics. Intern, then resident in pediatrics U. Fla., Gainesville, 1984-87, chief resident in pediatrics, instr., 1987-88, clin. rsch. fellow div. neonatology and pediatrics, 1988—. Mem. Am. Acad. Pediatrics, Alpha Omega Alpha. Republican. Methodist. Office: U Fla Dept Pediatrics Box J 296 JHMHC Gainesville FL 32610

ELLIOTT, PEGGY GORDON, university chancellor; b. Matewan, W.Va., May 27, 1937; d. Herbert Hunt and Mary Ann (Renfro) Gordon; children from previous marriage: Scott Vandling III, Anne Gordon. B.A., Transylvania Coll., 1959; M.A., Northwestern U., 1964; Ed.D., Ind. U., 1975. Tchr. Horace Mann High Sch., Gary, Ind., 1959-64; instr. English Ind. U. N.W., Gary, 1965-69, lectr. Edn., 1973-74, asst. prof. edn., 1975-78, assoc. prof., 1978-80, supr. secondary student teaching, 1973-74, dir. student teaching, 1975-77, dir. Office Field Experiences, 1977-78, dir. profl. devel., 1978-80, spl. asst. to chancellor, 1981-83, asst. to chancellor, 1983-84, acting chancellor, 1983-84, chancellor, 1984—; instr. English Am. Inst. Banking, Gary, 1969-70; vis. prof. U. Ark., 1979-80, U. Alaska, 1982; bd. dirs. Gainer Bank and Corp. Author: (with C. Smith) Reading Activities for Middle and Secondary Schools: A Handbook for Teachers, 1979, Reading Instruction for Secondary Schools, 1986, How to Improve Your Scores on Reading Competency Tests, 1981; (with C. Smith and G. Ingersoll) Trends in Educational Materials: Traditionals and the New Technologies, 1983; also numerous articles. Bd. dirs. Meth. Hosp., N.W. Ind. Forum, N.W. Ind. Symphony, N.W. Ind. World Affairs Council, Boys Club N.W. Ind. Recipient Disting. Alumni award Northwestern U., numerous grants; Am. Council on Edn. fellow in acad. adminstrn. Ind. U., Bloomington, 1980-81. Mem. Assn. Tchr. Educators (nat. pres. 1984-85,Disting. Mem. 1990), Nat. Acad. Tchr. Edn. (dir. 1983—), Ind. Assn. Tchr. Educators (past pres.), North Cen. Assn. (commn. at large), Leadership Devel. Council ACE, Internat. Reading Assn., Phi Delta Kappa (Outstanding Young Educator award), Delta Kappa Gamma (Leadership/Mgmt. fellow 1980), Pi Lamda Theta, P.E.O., Chi Omega. Episcopalian. Home: 2037 Kenilworth Highland IN 46322 Office: Ind U NW 3400 Broadway Gary IN 46408

ELLIOTT, SUSAN LAVERNE, computer console helpdesk specialist; b. Denver, Nov. 24, 1955; d. Richard E. and Doris E. (Wimberly) Bassett; m. Brian Louis James, June 5, 1976 (div. 1987); 1 child, Richard; m. Gary Lee Elliott, Dec. 19, 1987; children: Richard, Tiffany. Student, Wheat Ridge high sch., Colo., 1974. Sales clerk K-Mart, Denver, 1974-75; dir. assistance Mountain Bell, Denver, 1975-76, acctg. clerk, 1976-77, computer equipment operator, 1978-82; sr. check processing clerk Colo. Nat. Bank, 1982; computer console operator AT&T Bell Labs, Denver, 1982--; chmn. speakers sub-com. the career day AT&T Bell Labs, Denver 1988--. Author: Manual, UNIX Operators Manual 1986. Tutor Wheat Ridge High Elem. Tutoring, Denver 1973; Career Awareness Program Speaker AT&T Affirmative Action, Denver 1988--; Elem. Sci. Fair Parr Elem., Denver 1988. Recipient Lump Sum award AT&T Bell Labs Denver 1988, Dinner For Two award AT&T Bell Labs Denver 1989. Office: 11900 North Pecas Denver CO 80234

ELLIOTT, VICKIE F., child support recovery agent; b. Harlingen, Tex., Mar. 3, 1956; d. Frederick Elliott and Frankie (Griffin) Shue. BA in English, Valdosta (Ga.) State Coll., 1979. Community svc. supr. Coastal Plain Area EOA, Inc., Valdosta, 1983-87; child support agt. Dept. Human Respurces State of Ga., Nashville, Ga., 1988—. Pres. So. Ga. Toastmasters, 1986; Valdosta Lowndes Co. Civic Round Table, 1987, sec. Habitat for Humanity, 1987. Home: 1961 Ray City Hwy Nashville GA 31639

ELLIS, ALLISON ALLEGRA, public relations executive; b. Seattle, Dec. 29, 1964; d. William H. Jr. and Beverly Bob (Woodruff) E. BA, Baylor U., 1986. Sr. account exec. Keller Crescent Co., Dallas, 1988-90; account exec. Davd Margulies Media Rels., Dallas, 1987-88. Mem. Women in Communications (bd. dirs. 1990-91, Rookie of Yr. 1989). Republican. Baptist. Home: 9831 Walnut P106 Dallas TX 75243 Office: Keller Crescent 102 Decker Ct Ste 100 Irving TX 75062

ELLIS, ANNE ELIZABETH, fundraiser; b. Orngestad, Aruba, Aug. 21, 1945; d. Thomas Albert and Anne Elizabeth (Belis) Wolfe; m. Earl Edward Ellis, Feb. 14, 1970. BS, La. State U., 1967. Fashion coord. Baton Rouge, 1962-67; textile researcher La. State U., Baton Rouge, 1965-67; buyer I.H. Rubensteins., Baton Rouge, 1967-68; fashion distbr. J.C. Penney, Inc., Arlington, Tex., 1969-70; asst. buyer J.C. Penney, Inc., Dallas, 1970-73; exec. dir. Nassau County Mus. Fine Art Assn., Roslyn, N.Y., 1985-88; speaker C.W. Post U., Greenvale, N.Y., 1988—; cons. in field. Chmn., editor: (cookbook) Specialities of the House, 1981-83. Bd. dirs., com. chmn. Congregational Ch., Manhasset, N.Y., 1975—; exec. vp., bd. dirs., com. chmn. Jr. League L.I., Roslyn, 1977—, Area I Coun. Jr. League Internat.; benefit gala chmn., com. chmn. Grenville Baker Boys & Girls Club, Locust Valley, N.Y., 1983—; pres. bd., vice-chmn. community outreach, benefit gala chmn. Tilles Performing Art Ctr. L.I. U., Greenvale, N.Y., 1985—; bd. dirs., benefit co-chmn. Nassau County Family Assn. Svcs., Hempstead, 1988—; benefit vice-chmn. Glen Cove/North Shore Community Hosp., 1989—; trustee WLIW, L.I. Pub. TV, 1990—. Recipient Vol. of Yr. award Jr. League L.I., 1984, 85, Outstanding Vol. Svs. and Commitment, County of Nassau, 1989. Mem. P.E.O. (pres. 1985-87), The Creek Inc., Meadowbrook Club Inc., Lost Tree Club, Kappa Kappa Gamma (alumna pres. 1971-72). Republican. Congregationalist.

ELLIS, BERNICE, financial planning company executive, investment advisor; b. Bklyn., July 14, 1934; d. Samuel and Clara (Schrier) H.; m. Seymour Scott Ellis, Feb. 7, 1954; children: Michele, Wayne. BA, Bklyn. Coll., 1956; MS, Queens Coll., 1970. Cert. fin. planner, N.Y. 1987, elem. educator, N.Y.C. Elementary tchr. L.I. Sch. Dists., Merrick, N.Y., 1956-60; tchr. reading N.Y.C. Bd. of Edn., Bklyn., 1972-73; coordinator Reading is Fundamental, Lawrence, N.Y., 1973-75; pres., founder N.Y. State Assn. for the Gifted and Talented, Valley Stream, N.Y., 1974-87; pres. Ellis Planning, Valley Stream, N.Y., 1984-90; cons. Nassau County Bd. Coop. Ednl. Services, Westbury, N.Y., 1973-74; adminstrv. intern region II U.S. Office Edn., 1977-78; adj. asst. prof. Nassau Community Coll., Garden City, N.Y., 1975—. Contbr. articles to profl. jours and fin. newsletters. Recipient Ednl. Professions Devel. Act fellow CUNY Inst. for Remediations Skills for Coll. Personnel, Queensborough Community Coll., 1970-73. Mem. Inst. for Cert. Fin. Planners, Inst. for Cert. Fin. Planner of L.I. (bd. dirs.), Internat. Assn. for Fin. Planners (legislative com. 1986-87 L.I. chpt.), N.Y. State Reading Assn., Adj. Faculty Assn. Nassau Community Coll., Sales Exec. Club of N.Y., L.I., N.Y. C. of C. Office: Ellis Planning Inc 628 Golf Dr Valley Stream NY 11581

ELLIS, BERNICE ALLRED, personnel executive; b. Lincoln, Ala., Mar. 15, 1932; d. Bernard Bobo and Lucille (Hogue) Allred; m. Marvin Leonard Ellis; 1 child, Jeffrey Craig. Student, Ala. A&M U., 1990, U. Ala., Huntsville, 1990. Personnel staffing specialist Bd. of U.S. Civil Svc. Examiners, Anniston, Ala., 1957-66; personnel mgmt. specialist Dept. of Army, Anniston, 1966-73; tech. svcs. officer Dept. of Army, 1973-74; personnel mgmt. specialist Dept. of Army, Redstone Arsenal, Ala., 1974-79; supervisory personnel mgmt. specialist U.S. Army Europe, Mannheim, Fed. Republic of Germany, 1979-83; tech. svcs. officer U.S. Army Europe, Darmstadt, Fed. Republic of Germany, 1983-86; supervisory personnel mgmt. specialist Dept. of Army, Fort Ritchie, Md., 1986-87; ret., 1987. Vol. Huntsville Bot. Gardens, 1989-90; mem. local group Master Gardeners, Huntsville, 1990, Huntsville Wildflower Assn., 1990—. Mem. CAP (lst lt.). Home: 82 Ty Pl Ohatchee AL 36271

ELLIS, DEEANN, real estate executive; b. Oklahoma City, Oct. 16, 1957; d. Stephen Wayne and Shirley Mae (Wasserbeck) Ellis. BS in Hotel & Restaurant Adminstrn., Oklahoma State U., 1981. Cert. real estate sales assoc. Owner's rep. First Office Mgmt., Oklahoma City, 1982-83; dir. property mgmt. Citcor Properties, Inc., Oklahoma City, 1983-86, Wiggin Properties, Inc., Oklahoma City, 1986-89; real estate mgr. Coldwell Banker Comml., Oklahoma City, 1989—. Mem. Oklahoma City Art Mus., 1986—, The Com. of Ballet Okla., Oklahoma City, 1988—; vol. Red Andrews Christmas Dinner, Oklahoma City, 1988—, Okla. Found. for the Disabled, Oklahoma City, 1986-89. Mem. Bldg. Owners and Mgrs. Assn., Soc. Real Property Adminstrs., Nat. Assn. Indsl. & Office Parks, Oklahoma City Boat Club. Republican. Methodist. Home: 17629 Iron Ln Edmond OK 73034 Office: Coldwell Banker Comml 200 N Robinson Ste 300 Oklahoma City OK 73102

ELLIS, DENISE KAY, nurse; b. Burlington, Iowa, Sept. 3, 1966; d. Darrel LaVon and June Eleanor (Zern) E. ADN, Southeastern Community Coll., West Burlington, Iowa, 1987. RN, Iowa, Ill. Nurse Fort Madison (Iowa) Community Hosp., 1987-88, Carthage (Ill.) Meml. Hosp., 1988-89, Blessing Hosp., Quincy, Ill., 1989—. Vol. Lamaze Childbirth classes, Carthage, 1988, Red Cross Bloodmobile, Dallas City, Ill., 1987-89, Lion's Club Glaucoma Unit, Dallas City, 1987. Mem. Iowa Assn. for Assoc., Degree Nurses. Democrat. Home: 1014 Locust PO Box 66 Quincy IL 62301

ELLIS, EVA LILLIAN, artist; b. Seattle, June 4, 1920; d. Carl Martin and Hilda (Persson) Johnson; m. Everett Lincoln Ellis, May 1, 1943; children: Karin, Kristy, Hildy, Erik. BA, U. Wash., 1941; MA, U. Idaho, 1950; M in Painting (h.c.), U. delle Arti, 1983. Assoc. dir. art Best & Co., Seattle, 1943; dir. Am. Art Week, Idaho, 1949-55; mem. faculty dept. art U. Idaho, 1946-48; dir., tchr. Children's Art Oreg., 1966-71; mem. faculty aux. bd. U. Wash., Seattle, 1987—, faculty chair, 1988—; freelance artist, 1943-46; lectr. in art, New Zealand, 1971-73. Author: A Comparison of the Use of Color of Old and Modern Masters, 1950. Works include: Profilo d'Artisti Contemporanei Premio Centauro D'Oro, 1982; exhbns. shows include Henry Gallery, U. Wash., 1941, Immanuel Gallery, N.Y.C., 1943-46, Rackham Gallery, U. Mich., 1956-64, Detroit Inst. Art, 1959, Kresge Gallery, 1959-64, Portland Art Mus., 1967, Corvallis Art Ctr., Oreg., 1966, U. Idaho, 1946-56, U. Canterbury, N.Z., 1979, Boise Mus., 1949-55, CSA, 1972, 79, small gallery, Sydney, Australia, 1971-73, Survey of New Zealand Art, 1979, Shoreline Mus., Seattle, 1981, N.Z. Embassy, London, 1979, Karlshamn Art Soc., Sweden, 1979, Italian Acad. Art, 1982, Palos Verdes (Calif.) Art Ctr., 1982, Swedish Embassy, 1982, Aigantighe Gallery, N.Z., 1983; represented in permanent collections U. Calif.-Berkeley, U. Wash.; guest appearances on NBC-TV, N.Y.C. Counselor Cancer Soc.; active Girl Scouts U.S., People to People Friendship Worldwide, 1943-90, Art in Embassies Abroad Program, U.S., 1980-90; elected to Acad. of Europe, 1980; mem. sister com. Christ Ch., New Zealand and Seattle, 1981-83. Recipient awards Acad. Art and Sci., 1958-66, Ann Arbor Women Painters, diploma with gold medal, Italian Acad. Art, 1980, hon. diploma fine art, 3 Nat. awards Nat. League Profl. Artists, N.Y.C.; World Culture prize, 1984; Internat. Peace award in Art, 1984; Internat. Art Promotion award, 1986, others. Fellow I.B.C. (Cambridge, Eng. chpt.); mem. Mich. Acad. Art and Sci., Nat. League Am. Pen Women, Nat. Mus. Women in Arts (charter mem.), Royal Overseas League (London), Fine Arts Soc. Idaho, Canterbury Soc. Art New Zealand, Copley Soc. Fine Arts (Boston), Inst. D'Atre Contemporanea Di Milano (Italy), Nat. Slide Registry of Artists (New Zealand and Australia), Omicron Pi. (featured in nat. mag.), Scandinavian Club (pres. 1977—), Faculty Wives Club (pres. 1979). Address: 19614 24th Ave NW Seattle WA 98177

ELLIS, GEORGIANN, health care administrator; b. South Bend, Ind., Apr. 21, 1947; d. George Frank and Ann Evelyn (Johnson) E. BS, Western Mich. U., 1969; MA, Cen. Mich. U., 1978; MBA, U. Chgo., 1984. With Borgess Med. Ctr., Kalamazoo, Mich., 1969—, dir. lab., 1981-86, v.p. profl. and ambulatory svcs., 1988—; bd. dirs. Gryphon Place, Kalamazoo, Kalamazoo Hosp. Oncology Program. Mem. Am. Soc. for Med. tech., Am. Coll. Hosp. Execs., Southwestern Mich. Soc. Med. Tech. (pres. 1970-72), NAFE, Exec. Program Club. Office: Borgess Med Ctr 1521 Gull Rd Kalamazoo MI 49001

ELLIS, GRACE CAROL, real estate executive; b. Fairview, Mo., Dec. 4, 1935; d. Leo Leslie and Grace (Allinder) Eurit; m. Leonard Eugene Ellis, Dec. 17, 1955; children—Susan Diane, Linda Jeanne, Leonard Eugene. Grad. Draughon's Bus. Sch., 1954. Real estate broker, Stillwater, Okla., 1970—; ptnr., mgr. Crestview Estates, Stillwater, 1971-85, Crestview Quick Shop and Laundry, 1971—. Republican. Baptist. Avocations: reading; gardening; traveling. Office: Crestview Quick Shop 2319 E 6th St Stillwater OK 74074

ELLIS, JEANETTE CHRISTINE, geriatric case manager; b. Sept. 3, 1962. AAS, Mercer County Community Coll., 1985; BA, Trenton State Coll., 1987, MA, 1990. Computer operator Ednl. Testing Svc., Princeton, N.J., 1985-86; project coord. Coun. Community Svcs., Princeton, 1986-87; social svc. designee Univ. Ctr. for Continuing Care, Mercerville, N.J., 1987-88; case mgr. Pub. Guardian for Elderly Adults, Trenton, N.J., 1988—. Mem. Am. Assn. Counseling & Devel., N.J. Profl. Counseling Assn., Assn. for Adult Devel. & Aging, Psi Chi, Phi Kappa Phi, Chi Sigma Iota, Sigma Phi Omega. Home: 222 Mercer St Hightstown NJ 08520 Office: Pub Guardian for Elderly Adults 216 W State St Trenton NJ 08625-0812

ELLIS, JUDITH KAY, guidance counselor, educator; b. Taylorville, Ill., Sept. 26, 1939; d. Richard Floyd and Elsie Marie (Reynolds) Murray; m. Jeffrey Thomas Ellis, May 26, 1979; children: Lisa Lachelle, Fred Forest. BS in Bus. Adminstrn., Eastern Ky. State U., 1963; license Real Estate, Realtors Bd., Montgomery, Ala., 1977; MEd in Counseling, U. Auburn, Montgomery, 1978; MEd spl. Edn., Diagnosis, Midwestern State U., Wichita Falls, Tex., 1981. Cert. elem. tchr., counselor, spl edn., Tex., Ala., Ga., Okla., Ky, Va.; lic. real estate broker Ala. Personnel staff Square D Co., Lexington, Ky., 1959, Standard Oil Co. (Ky.), Louisville, 1961-62; tchr. many sch. systems in U.S. Hon. pres. Air Force Family Support Svcs., 1984-86. Mem. NEA, TEDA, Officers Wives Club (hon. v.p. 1982-84, hon. pres. 1984-86, hon . paliamentarian 1988-90), Allied Officers Wives Club (Vicenza Italy chpt., hon. v.p.), Ederle Officers Wives Club (hon. v.p. 1990—), Military Civilian Club San Antonio (hist. 1986-87), Pan Am. Club (hon. pres. Del Rio Tex. 1984-86), Garden Club (hon. pres. 1984-86). Republican. Methodist. Home: 416 N Prairie Union Springs AL 36089

ELLIS, KERRI ANNE, management training program instructor, compensation coordinator; b. Farmersville, Tex., Jan. 29, 1964; d. Gerald Lee and Lane Harris (Smith) McDonald; 1 child, Whitney Lee Anne. East Tex. State U.; Postgrad., E. Tex. State U., 1990—. Purchasing agt. Personal Touch Interiors, Plano, Tex., 1984-86; human resources adminstr. Trailways Lines, Inc./Trailways Food Svcs., Dallas, 1986-87; coord. compensation, mgmt. tng. program instr. Greyhound Lines, Inc., Dallas, 1987—. Coord. Greyhound Lines United Way. Mem. NAFE, Dallas Personnel Assn., Soc. for Human Resources Mgmt., Alpha Lambda Delta (past pres.), Phi Eta Sigma Honor Soc. Home: 6000 Ohio Dr #1624 Plano TX 75093

ELLIS, LINDA ANN, government official; b. Washington, Apr. 26, 1944; d. James Bernard Lee and Mary Belinda (Frock) Gordon; m. Arthur J. Hill, Aug. 17, 1963 (div.); children: Suzette, Arthur, Jana-Lyn; m. Michael Ray Ellis, Dec. 10, 1982; children: Therese, Michael. BS in BA, Marywood Coll., Scranton, Pa., 1985. Staff asst. to U.S. Senator Washington, 1970-73; adminstrv. asst. to VA congl. liaison U.S. Senate, Washington, 1973-76; contact rep. Social Security, Houston, 1980-83; freelance writer Houston, 1981; intelligence research specialist U.S. Customs Svc., Houston, 1987—; coordinator for 1-800 Be-Alert Drug Smuggling Hotline, 1988—; pub. relations cons. McGraw Hill Chem. Expo, Houston, 1986. Author weekly column, Kingwood Observor, 1981-82; contbr. articles to profl. jours. Tchr. CCD, Cath. Ch., Kingwood, Tex., 1982—. Mem. Internat. Assn. Law Enforcement Intelligence Analysts, Internat. Women Writers Guild, Nat. Assn. Female Execs., Internat. Narc Enforcement Officers Assn., Tex. Law Enforcement Intelligence Units Assn. Republican. Roman Catholic. Home: PO Box 6358 Kingwood TX 77325-6358 Office: US Custome Svc 5850 San Felipe Houston TX 77057

ELLIS, MARY LOUISE, state official; b. Albert Lea, Minn., May 29, 1943; d. Stanley Orville and Neoma Lois (Guthier) Helgeson; m. Melvin Eugene Ellis, July 31, 1966; children: Christopher, Tracy. BS in Pharmacy, U. Iowa, 1966; MA in Pub. Adminstrn., Iowa State U., 1982, postgrad., 1982-83. Faculty Duquesne U., Pitts., 1977; cons. in pharmacy, Colville, Wash., 1978-79; dir. pharmacy Mt. Carmel Hosp., Colville, 1978-79; clin. pharmacist Iowa Vets. Home, Marshalltown, Iowa, 1980-81; instr. Iowa Valley Community Coll., Marshalltown, 1981-83; dir. Iowa Dept. Substance Abuse, Des Moines, 1983-86; dir. pub. health, dir. Iowa Dept. Pub. Health, Des Moines, 1986-90; spl. cons. health affairs Blue Cross/Blue Shield of Iowa, 1990—; chair Iowa Health Data Commn., Des Moines, 1986—; bd. dirs. Health Policy Corp. Iowa, 1986—; adj. asst. prof. U. Iowa, Iowa City, 1984—; comd. officer U.S. Food & Drug Adminstrn., 1989-90; mem. adv. coun. U. Iowa Coll. of Pharmacy, 1989—. Mem. Iowa State Bd. Health, 1981-83, v.p., 1982-83; mem. adv. council Iowa Valley Community Coll., 1983-85. Recipient Woman of Achievement award Des Moines YWCA, 1988. Mem. AAUW, Am. Pharm. Assn., Iowa Pharmacists Assn., Am. Pub. Health Assn., Iowa Pub. Health Assn. (bd. dirs., Henry Albert award 1990), Alpha Xi Delta, Phi Kappa Phi, Pi Sigma Alpha. Republican. Home: 2801 Woodland Ave W Des Moines IA 50265 Office: Blue Cross and Blue Shield Iowa 636 Grand Des Moines IA 50309

ELLIS, MAXINE ETHEL, social services administrator, educator; b. Kansas City, Apr. 2, 1941; d. Charles Boyd and Ethel Freda (Zeebe) Armstrong; m. Herbert Joseph Ellis, June 15, 1974; children: Carine Elizabeth, Alina Suzanne. BA in Biology, William Jewell Coll., Liberty, Mo., 1963; MS in Biology, Kans. State Coll., Emporia, Kans., 1967; AS, Moraine Parktech Coll., West Bend, Wis., 1982; postgrad., U. Mo., 1968-73. Cert. tchr. Kans., Wis. Sci. tchr. Indian Hills Jr. High, Prarie Village, Kans., 1963-69; Bio. tchr. Shawnee Mission East High Sch., Prairie Village, 1969-74; bus. mgr. Hartford (Wis.) Com. Day Care, Inc., 1978-83; workshop writer CESA Local Watershed Problems, Madison, Wis., 1979-81; substitute tchr. Hartford/West Bend (Wis.) Schs., 1974-83; econ. asst. worker Washington Co. Dept. of Soc. Svcs., West Bend, Wis., 1983—. Writer and presentor, Curriculum Guide, Local Watershed Problems Study Guide, 198l; Contbr.: book, Wis. Women: A Gifted Heritage, 1982. Curriculum Com. & Vol., Lac Lawrann Conservacy, West Bend, Wis., 1987—; mem. Riveredge Nature Club, Newburg, Wis., 1976—. Named Top 5 Finalist, Star Student Award, Moraine Park Tech. Coll., West Bend, 1982. Mem. Am. Assn. of U. Women (treas. 1989-91), Am. Fedn. of State, County & Mcpl. Workers (treas. 1985-89), Nat. Sci. Tchrs. Assn. (life mem.). United Ch. of Christ. Home: 5818 Wildlife Dr Allenton WI 53002

ELLIS, SOPHIA LUGENE, educator; b. Detroit, Jan. 30, 1927; d. Major Quincy and Ethel Lee (Jones) Holley; m. James Thomas Ellis, Feb. 17, 1968 (div. Feb. 1988); children: John Thomas, Holley Elizabeth. BA in Biology and German, U. Mich., 1949, MS in Botany, 1950, MA in German, 1964. Mid. sch. tchr. English, Oxnard (Calif.) Pub. Schs., 1968-69; elem. sch. tchr. sci. Cambridge (Mass.) Pub. Schs., 1969-71, City Sch. Detroit, 1973-75; instr. zoology Wayne County Community Coll., Detroit, 1976-77; elem. and high sch. tchr sci., biology and earth sci. Detroit Bd. Edn. Pub. Schs., 1950-68, high sch. tchr. biology and horticulture, 1978-85, tchr. sci. and lang., 1985-86, tchr. German, 1986—; book and sch. evaluator North Cen. Assn., 1984, 85, 89; cons. Ea. Mich. U. World Coll. in Germany, Ypsilanti, 1989—. Coord. United Found., Detroit, 1973-77; pres. black leadership alumni coun. U. Mich., Ann Arbor. Named Tchr. of Yr. western div. Newsweek mag., 1988; Student Aid Found. scholar, 1945-50. Mem. Am. Assn. Tchrs. German, Mich. Fgn. Lang. Assn., Met. Detroit Fgn. Lang. Assn., U. Mich. Alumni Assn. (life, family camping bd. 1977-79), Alpha Kappa Alpha. Democrat. Episcopalian. Office: Martin Luther King High Sch 3200 E Lafayette St Detroit MI 48207

ELLIS, SUSAN GOTTENBERG, psychologist; b. N.Y.C., Jan. 24, 1949; d. Sam and Sally (Hirschman) Gottenberg; B.S., Cornell U., 1970; M.A., Columbia U., 1971; M.A., Hofstra U., 1975, Ph.D., 1976; m. David Roy Ellis, July 23, 1972; children—Sharon Rachel, Dana Michelle. Instr. health edn. Nassau Community Coll., Garden City, N.Y., 1971-73; sch. psychologist public schs., Somerville, N.J., 1976-77; clin. psychologist Somerset County Community Mental Health Center, Somerville, 1976-77; sch. psychologist, Pinellas County, Fla., 1977-78; instr. St. Petersburg (Fla.) Jr. Coll., 1978; clin. psychologist, Largo, Fla., 1977—; cons. Fla. Dept. Health and Rehab. Services, Med. Center Hosp., Largo, Morton Plant Hosp., Clearwater, Fla., N.Y. State Regents scholar, 1966-71; adj. prof. Eckerd Coll. St. Petersburg, 1988. Author: Interpret Your Dreams, 1987, A Dream Primer, 1988, Make Sense of Your Dreams, 1988. Mem. Am. Psychol. Assn., Fla. Psychol. Assn., Pinellas Psychol. Assn. (treas. 1978, polit. action chmn. 1979), Kappa Delta Pi. Club: Cornell U. Suncoast (v.p. 1979-80). Home: 1904 Oakdale Ln North Clearwater FL 34624 Office: 3233 E Bay Dr Suite 100 Largo FL 34641

ELLIS, VIVIAN ELIZABETH, obstetrician-gynecologist; b. Biloxi, Miss; d. James A. and Aida (Fernande) E. BA with spl. honors, U. TEx., 1973; DO, Tex. Coll. of Osteopathic Med., 1978. Diplomate Am. Bd of Ob-Gyn. Commd. ensign USN, 1977, advanced through grades to comdr., 1987; intern Naval Regional Med. Ctr., Portsmouth, Va., 1978-79; gen. med. officer Miramar Naval Air Station, San Diego, Calif., 1979-80; resident ob-gyn Naval Regional Med. Ctr., San Diego, 1980-83, chief resident, 1983; attending staff Naval Regional Med. Ctr., Okinawa, Japan, 1983-84, Camp Pendleton, Calif., 1984-86; resigned, 1986; staff Scripps Clinic and Rsch. Found., La Jolla, Calif., 1987—. Comdr. USNR, 1986—. Recipient Teaching award, Family Practice Residents, Camp Pendleton, Calif., 1986. Fellow Am. Coll. Ob-Gyn.; mem. AMA, Calif. Med. Assn., San Diego County Med. Soc. (young physicians com., north county physicians com.), Am. Assn of Gynecologic Laparoscopists, San Diego Gynecol. Soc., Am. Inst. Of Ultrasound Medicine, N.Y. Acad. of Scis., Am. Fertility Soc., Am. Women's Med. Soc. Office: Scripps Clinic & Rsch Found 10666 N Torrey Pines Rd La Jolla CA 92037

ELLISON, CORI JEAN, music journalist; b. N.Y.C., Mar. 21, 1954; d. Daniel S. and Ethel (Olshinetsky) Ellison. BFA, Hofstra U., 1975; Diploma, Manhattan Sch. Music, N.Y.C., 1978. Singer N.Y. City Opera, 1981—, author, 1985—; singer Metro. Opera, N.Y.C., 1981—; program annotator Metro. Opera, 1984—; program annocator Lincoln Ctr., N.Y.C., 1985—; adj. asst. prof. NYU, 1986—; lectr. in field. Contbg. editor Stagebill mag., N.Y.C., 1988—; contbr. New Grove Dictionary of Opera, London, 1989—; contbr. articles to profl. jours. William Matheus Sullivan Found. grantee, 1982. Mem. Am. Guild Musical Artists, Profl. Women Singers assn., Basenji Club Am. Democratic. Home and Office: 314 W 56th St Apt 4A New York NY 10019

ELLISON, ELAINE, primary school educator, reading specialist; b. Lewis, Kans.; Aug. 23, 1926; d. Clarence Elmer and Helen Gwendolyn (Smith) Cross; m. Dale Emmerson Ellison, June 2, 1946; children: Barbara Caywood, Tina Fardella, Mary Jane Horacek, Lora Gilbert, Dean. Student, George Washington U., 1944-45; BS, Ft. Hays State U., 1966, MS, 1972, reading specialist, 1980. 6th gr. tchr. Sch. Dist. 352, Goodland, Kans., 1945-46; summer migrant sch. tchr. Sch. Dist. 352, Goodland, 1969-72, 5th gr. and jr. high sch. tchr., 1969-86, reading specialist, 1986—; 5th gr. tchr. Sch. Dist. 314, Brewster, Kans., 1966-69; mem. com. to organize 1st migrant sch. in county, Goodland, 1966-70. Mem. Friends of Libr., Goodland, 1980—; sec. to bd. dirs. City Mus., Goodland; del. Local Pride Orgn., 1989—. Mem. NEA (state and local del.), AAUW, Internat. Reading Assn., High Plains Reading Assn. (pres. 1969-70), Am. Legion Aux., Delta Kappa Gamma (sec. 1983-85). Democrat. Methodist. Home: RR 2 Box 170A Goodland KS 67735 Office: US Sch Dist 352 700 E 4th St Goodland KS 67735

ELLISON, KATHERINE ESTHER, journalist; b. Mpls., Aug. 19, 1957; d. Ellis and Bernice June (Bender) E. BA in Internat. Relations, Stanford U., 1979. Intern reporter Washington Post, 1979, Newsweek, London, 1979-80; reporter San Jose (Calif.) Mercury, 1980—; bur. chief San Jose (Calif.) Mercury, Mexico City; bd. dirs. Media Alliance, San Francisco, 1986—. Coauthor articles including Hidden Billions: The Draining of the Philippines, 1985 (Pulitzer prize 1986, George Polk Meml. award 1986, Investigative Reporters and Editors award 1986); author: Imelda: The Philippines' Steel Butterfly, 1988. Office: care San Jose Mercury News, Presidente Carranza 52, Casa 4 Colonia Coyoacan, Mexico City Mexico*

ELLISON, KATHERINE RUFFNER WHITE, psychologist, educator; b. Charleston, W.Va., Jan. 17, 1941; d. Christian Streit and Katherine Ruffner (Hughey) White. BA, Agnes Scott Coll., 1962; PhD, CUNY, 1976. Prof. Montclair State Coll., Upper Montclair, N.J., 1977—; cons. various law enforcement agys., 1973—. Author: Psychology & Criminal Justice, 1981, Stress & The Police Officer, 1983; contbr. articles to profl. jours. Ruling elder Maywood (N.J.) Presbyn. Ch., 1987—. Mem. Am. Psychol. Assn. (sec., treas. police psychology sect. 1977—), Internat. Assn. Chiefs of Police, Phi Beta Kappa. Democrat. Office: Montclair State Coll Psychology Dept Upper Montclair NJ 07043

ELLISON, PAMELA JO, construction and real estate executive; b. Wiesbaden, Fed. Republic of Germany, Dec. 14, 1956; came to U.S., 1957; d. James Roy and Ellen (Wells) Ellison; m. Thom D. Kay, Aug. 16, 1985. BS, Tex. A&M U., 1979; MBA with honors, Notre Dame, Belmont, Calif., 1987. Lic. real estate broker. Outside claims rep. Aetna Life & Casualty, Dallas and Longview, 1979-81; mng. dir. Ellison's Greenhouses, Inc., Brenham, Tex., 1981-82; sales cons. Dallas World Trade Ctr., 1982-84; adminstr. Inforite Corp., San Mateo, Calif., 1984-85; mgr. Upjohn Health Care Svcs., San Mateo and Santa Ana, Calif., 1986-88; pres., chief exec. officer Ellison-Kay, Inc., Diamond Bar, Calif., 1987—; pres., chief exec. officer, broker Ellison-Kay Real Estate, Inc., Diamond Bar, 1989—; v.p., bd. dirs. Ellison's Greenhouses, Inc., 1975—, The Flower Market, Brenham, 1976—. Youth dir. Millbrea (Calif.) Meth. Ch., 1986. Mem. NAFE, Nat. Assn. Realtors, Women Constrn. Owners and Execs., Calif. Assn. Realtors, Calif. Notre Dame MBA Assn. (pres. 1987—), Diamond Bar C. of C. Republican. Office: Ellison-Kay Inc 2040 S Brea Canyon Rd Ste 240 Diamond Bar CA 91765

ELLISON, STEPHANIE ELISE, computer infosystem scientist; b. Kans. City, Kans., July 26, 1962; d. Benoyd Myers and Lee Ann (Parks) Ellison. BA in Bus. Adminstrn., Wichita State U., 1984. Adv. mktg. support rep. IBM, Kansas City, Mo., 1985—. Mem. Alpha Kappa Alpha. Democrat. Methodist. Office: IBM 2345 Grand Ave Kansas City MO 64108

ELLMANN, SHEILA FRENKEL, investment company executive; b. Detroit, June 8, 1931; d. Joseph and Rose (Neback) Frenkel; BA in English, U. Mich., 1953; m. William M. Ellmann, Nov. 1, 1953; children: Douglas Stanley, Carol Elizabeth, Robert Lawrence. Dir. Advance Glove Mfg. Co., Detroit, 1954-78; v.p. Frome Investment Co., Detroit, 1980—. Mem. U. Mich. Alumni Assn., Nat. Trust Hist. Preservation. Home: 28000 Weymouth Ct Farmington Hills MI 48334

ELLMYER, VIRGINIA RUTH, psychiatric nurse; b. New Brunswick, N.J., Aug. 5, 1958; d. John Robert and Ruth Evelyn (McGowen) E. BS in Nursing, Seton Hall U., 1980; MS, Boston U., 1987. Cert. psychiatric nurse. Staff nurse Bergen Pines County Hosp., Paramus, N.J., 1980-82; pub. rels. asst. Allied Van Lines, Boston, 1983-89; staff nurse U. Hosp., Boston, 1983; staff nurse, patient care coordinator Highpoint Hosp., Port Chester, N.Y., 1984-85; staff nurse, cons. Charles River Hosp., Wellesley, Mass., 1983-84, 85—; clin. specialist psychiatric nursing Community Support Systems, Newton, Mass., 1987—. Co-author: (video) Cultural Aspects of Nursing, 1979, Strategic Family Therapy, 1987. Mem. Women's Ednl. and Indsl. Union, Boston, 1988—. Mem. Mass. Nurses Assn., Nurses United for Responsible Svcs., Mass. Council Psychiatric and Mental Health Nurses. Democrat. Roman Catholic. Home: 76 Elm St 404 Jamaica Plain MA 02130 Office: Community Support Systems 1310 Centre St Newton MA 02159

ELLNER, CAROLYN LIPTON, university dean, consultant; b. N.Y.C., Jan. 17, 1932; d. Robert Mitchell and Rose (Pearlman) Lipton; m. Richard Ellner, June 21, 1953; children: David Lipton, Alison Lipton. AB cum laude, Mt. Holyoke Coll., 1953; A.M., Columbia Tchrs. Coll., 1957; PhD with distinction, UCLA, 1968. Tchr., prof., adminstr., N.Y. and Md., 1957-62; prof. dir. tchr. edn., assoc. dean Claremont Grad. Sch. (Calif.) 1967-82; prof., dean sch. edn. Calif. State U., Northridge, 1982—. Co-author: Schoolmaking, 1977; Studies of College Teaching (Orange County Authors award 1984), 1983. Trustee Ctr. for Early Edn., Los Angeles, 1968-71, Oakwood Sch., Los Angeles, 1972-78, Mt. Holyoke Coll., South Hadley, Mass., 1979-84; commr. Economy and Efficiency Com., Los Angeles, 1974-82, Calif. Commn. Tchr. Credentialing; bd. dirs. Found. for Effective Govt., Los Angeles, 1982, Calif. Coalition for Pub. Edn., 1985—; commr. Calif. State Commn. Tchr. Credentialing, 1987—; founding dir. Decade of Edn., 1990. Ford Found. fellow, 1964-67, fellow Ednl. Policy Fellowship Program, 1989-90; recipient Office of Edn. award U.S. Office of Edn., 1969-72; W. M. Keck Found. grantee, 1983. Mem. Am. Edn. Rsch. Assn., Am. Assn. Colls. for Tchr. Edn., Assn. for Supervision and Curriculum Devel., Nat. Soc. for Study of Edn., Valley Industry and Commerce Assn. (bd. dirs. 1989-90). Office: Calif State U Sch of Edn 18111 Nordhoff St Northridge CA 91330

ELLSTEIN, CAROL GAIL, psychologist; b. Detroit, Nov. 29, 1951; d. Ben David and Jennie (Noble) Krugel; m. Charles Lawrence Ellstein, Mar. 26, 1972; 1 child, Melissa Beth. BA, Wayne State U., 1972, MA, 1981; PhD, Mich. State U., 1989. Ltd. lic. psychologist, Mich. Sch. psychologist Avondale Sch. Dist., Auburn Hills, Mich., 1981-83; teaching asst. Mich. State U., East Lansing, 1983-85, rsch. asst., 1985-86; psychologist Clinton-Eaton Ingham Community Mental Health and Community Svcs. Developmentally Disabled, Lansing, Mich., 1986—. Mem. Mothers Against Drunk Driving, Mich., 1987—. Mich. Dept. Mental Health grantee, 1988. Mem. Am. Psychol. Assn., Mich. Psychol. Assn., Mich. Women Psychologists, Am. Assn. Mental Retardation, Soc. for Disability Studies, Behavior Analysis Assn. Mich. Home: 521 Ardson East Lansing MI 48823 Office: Clinton-Eaton Ingham Community Mental Health Community Svcs 838 Louisa Lansing MI 48823

ELLSTROM-CALDER, ANNETTE, clinical medicine educator; b. Duluth, Minn., Dec. 19, 1952; d. Raymond Charles Ellstrom and Ruth Elaine (Bloomquist) Larson; m. Jeffrey Ellstrom-Calder, July 30, 1982; 1 child, Hannah. BA in Social Work, Psychology, Sociology, Concordia Coll., 1974; MSW, U. Wis., 1978. Group therapist N.D. State Indsl. Sch., 1973; social worker Fergus Falls (Minn.) State Hosp., 1974, Jackson County Dept. Social Services, Black River Falls, Wis., 1975-77; sr. clin. social worker U. Wis. Hosp., Madison, 1979-90, clin. instr. in medicine, 1989—; cons. Waupun (Wis.) Meml. Hosp., 1979-84; lectr. grad. sch. social work U. Wis., Madison, 1979—, lectr. U. Wis. Med. Sch., Madison, 1979-82, prin. investigator in rsch. U. Wis. Hosp., Madison, 1985—. Editor: A Guide to Patients and Families, 1984; contbr. articles to profl. jours. Del. trustee, bd. dirs. Nat. Kidney Found., N.Y.C., 1983—, chmn. bd. dirs., Milw., 1985-87, vice chmn., 1983-85, sec., 1982-83, chmn. patient svcs. com., 1981-82, bd. dirs., 1981—, chmn. nat. tng. and edn. com., N.Y., 1987—, mem. nat. patient svcs. com. N.Y., 1987—, mem. pers. com.; bd. dirs. Madison chpt., 1979—, Combined Health Appeal of Wis., 1990—; mem. nat. rsch. com. Am. Assn. Spinal Cord Injury Psychologists and Social Workers, N.Y.C., 1988-90. Recipient Health Advancement award Nat. Kidney Found. Wis., 1985, Vol. Yr. award Nat. Kidney Found. Wis., 1984, Vol. Service award Nat. Kidney Found. Wis., 1983, Nat. Nephrology Social Worker of Yr. Merit award Nat. Kidney Found. and Council of Nephrology Social Workers, 1987; hon. adoptee Winnebago Indian Tribe, 1978; named Outstanding Young Wisconsinite Wisc. Jaycees, 1988. Mem. Council Nephrology Social Workers (nat. v.p. 1984-86, nat. exec. com. 1984-86, Nat. Nephrology Social Worker Yr. award 1987), Nat. Assn. Social Workers, Pi Gamma Mu. Democrat. Office: U Wis Hosp 600 Highland Ave H4/510 Madison WI 53792

ELLSWEIG, PHYLLIS LEAH, psychotherapist, retired; b. Irvington, N.J., Apr. 19, 1927; d. Sumar and Jeanette (Geffner) Schwartz; m. Martin Richard Ellsweig, Dec. 25, 1947; children: Bruce, Steven. BS, East Stroudsburg U. (Pa.), 1947; EdM, Lehigh U., 1966, EdD, 1972. Tchr. Stroud Union High Sch., 1963-66; guidance counselor East Stroudsburg Schs., 1966-68; asst. prof. edn. East Stroudsburg U., 1968; staff psychologist, outpatient supr. Mental Health Center Carbon, Monroe and Pike Counties, Stroudsburg, 1968-80; pvt. practice in psychotherapy and clin. hypnosis Stroudsburg, 1969-87; mem. staff Pocono Hosp., 1968-88; pub. speaker in field; cons. to schs. and pvt. orgns.; tchr. adult edn. Pal Beach County, Fla. Mem. Am. Psychol. Assn., Am. Soc. Clin. Hypnosis, Internat. Soc. Hypnosis, NOW (profl. cons. 1973—). Home: 2584 NW 12th St Delray Beach FL 33445

ELLWOOD-FILKINS, LEA BEATRICE, computer executive; b. Wyandotte, Mich., May 27, 1955; d. Alvin Harold and Rhoda Martha (Krahnke) Ellwood; m. John C. Filkins, July 16, 1977; 1 ward, Kim Ruth. Student, Wayne State U., 1973-74, Wayne Community Coll., 1983-87. Office and prodn. dir. Doré Inc., Detroit, 1973-75; asst. traffic dir. Sta. WDEE, Southfield, Mich., 1975-77; word processing operator Miller Canfield Paddock and Stone, Detroit, 1977-78, word processing asst. supr., 1978-80, word processing supr., 1980-82, systems coordinator, 1982-84, tng. coordinator, 1985-88; dir. mgmt. info. systems, systems adminstrv. Clark, Klein and Beaumont, Detroit, 1988—; dir. edn., speakers bur. Greater Metro Detroit Assn. of Info. Systems Profls., 1985-87, sec. 1986-87. Set designer The Islanders, Grosse Ile, Mich., 1985-88. Dir. Christian edn. St. James Episcopal Ch., Grosse Ile, 1984-86. Mem. NAFE, Assn. Info. Systems Profls., Detroit Area Trainers' Assn., Detroit Inst. Arts Founders Soc. Club: West Shore Sail (mem. race com. 1988-90, protest com. 1989—). Office: Clark Klein and Beaumont 1001 Woodward Ave Detroit MI 48226

ELLZY, MISHA THERESE, small business owner; b. Columbus, Ohio, Aug. 16, 1962; d. Luther E. and Lorraine T. (Petersen) Colter; m. Gregory L. Ellzy, Apr. 30, 1983. Receptionist, sec. Am. Temporary Svcs., Feasterville, Pa., 1982-83; exec. sec. Trevose (Pa.) Rental & Sales, 1983-85; exec. asst. Unique Profl. Cleaners, Langhorne, Pa., 1985-90; owner Tender Loving Affairs, 1989—. Mem. NAFE, NAACP. Home and Office: 242 Thunder Circle Bensalem PA 19020

ELMAN, NAOMI GEIST, artist, producer; b. Chgo.; d. Harry and Rita (Goldstein) Geist; m. Murray Elman, May 29, 1946 (dec.Dec. 1965); 1 child, Margaret Gillespie. Student, Hamilton Inst. for Girls, NAD, Art Students League. Personal mgr. in performing arts N.Y.C. and Hawaii, 1968-80. One-woman show Churchill Gallery, 1962, Pen and Brush Club, 1986; exhibited in group shows. Vol. nurses aid pvt. and army hosps., ARC, 1939-44; v.p. N.Y. Diabetes Assn., 1955-58; mcpl. chmn. Dem. Club, Tenafly, N.J., 1958; Dem. com. woman, 1959-61; bd. dirs. Nat. Children's Cardiac Home, N.Y.C., 1940-49, Bergen County Dem. Club, 1958-60. Recipient Margareet Sussman award, 1985, Salamagundi award, 1987, Julia Lucille award, 1988. Mem. Pen and Brush Club, Artist Equity. Democrat. Address: 500 E 77th St New York NY 10021

ELMEGREEN, DEBRA ANNE MELOY, astronomy educator; b. South Bend, Ind., Nov. 23, 1952; d. Thurston George and Anne Elizabeth (Clubb) Meloy; m. Bruce Gordon Elmegreen, Aug. 21, 1976; children: Lauren Anne, Scott Gordon. AB cum laude, Princeton U., 1975; postgrad., U. Calif., Santa Cruz, 1975-76; AM, Harvard U., 1977, PhD, 1979. Carnegie postdoctoral fellow Observatories of the Carnegie Inst. Washington, Pasadena, Calif., 1979-81; vis. scientist IBM Watson Rsch. Ctr., Yorktown Heights, N.Y., 1981-88; vis. asst. prof. Vassar Coll., Poughkeepsie, N.Y., 1985-90, assoc. prof. dept. physics and astronomy, 1990—; cons. Nat. Geog. Soc., 1985-89. Author: Universe, 1988, (book supplement) Extragalactic Astronomy, 1987; contbr. articles to profl. jours. Amelia Earhart Grad. fellow Zonta Internat., 1977, 78, 79; recipient Fullam/Dudley award Dudley Observatory, 1989-90. Mem. Am. Astron. Soc. (com. on the status of women astronomers 1990-92), Internat. Astron. Union. Office: Vassar Coll Dept Physics & Astronomy Poughkeepsie NY 12601

ELMER, JEAN RADLEY, psychotherapist; b. Clifton Springs, N.Y., Aug. 6, 1946; d. Vaughn Ferris and Sara (Sutman) Radley; 1 child, William VII. BA, U. Maine, 1968; MSW, Boston U., 1971; postgrad., U. Wash., 1977-79. Caseworker Rensselaer County Dept. Social Services, Troy, N.Y., 1968-69, State of Hawaii, Honolulu, 1971-72, Seattle Children's Home, 1973-74; psychotherapist Divorce Lifeline, Olympia, Wash., 1977; outpatient therapist Mental Health N., Seattle, 1974-76, 78-82; pvt. practice psychotherapy Seattle, 1982—; pub. speaker KIRO-Radio sta., Seattle, 1984, Nat. Assn. Women in Constrn., Everett, Wash., 1986, Bothell (Wash.) C. of C., 1986, Civitan, Bellevue, Wash., 1985, Rotary Club, Seattle, 1985, Women Bus. Owners, Seattle, 1986. Contbr. articles to profl. pubs. Arbitrator Floating Homes Assn., Seattle, 1981. Mem. Am. Group Psychotherapy Assn., N.W. Group Psychotherapy Assn. (sec. 1983-85), Nat. Assn. Social Workers, Wash. State Soc. Clin. Social Workers, Assn. Women in Psychology, Women's Bus. Exchange, Women Bus. Owners. Democrat. Presbyterian. Club: Toastmasters. Home: 2349 Fairview Ave E Seattle WA 98102 Office: 1424 4th Ave Suite 903 Seattle WA 98101

ELMORE, GERALDINE CATHARINE, legal association administrator; b. Rahway, N.J., Aug. 13, 1936; d. Isaac Adrian and Mary Adele (Van Orden) Maier. BS, U. San Diego, 1955; paralegal degree, Acad. Paralegal, Matawan, N.J., 1987; BA magna cum laude, Acad. Little Flower, San Luis Rey, Calif., 1953. Reservation agt., protocal agt. Pacific S.W. Airline, San Diego, 1953-73; v.p. Soc. for Prison Reformist Alt., San Diego, 1964-79; adv. bd. mem. Project 86Plus, San Diego, 1965-78; bd. rep. San Diego Area Inst., 1983—; paralegal Bernal's Paralegal Svc., San Diego, 1985—. Adv. mem. San Diego Coalition for Human Care Service, 1986. DAR. Roman Catholic. Office: Bernals Paralegal Svc 3585-A VanDyke Ave San Diego CA 92105

ELROD, LINDA ANN, corporate data processing executive; b. Scott City, Kans., Sept. 14, 1949; d. Billy George Storey and Bette Ann (Snell) Ford; m. Charles Patrick Grommes (div.); 1 child, Danielle Louise Grommes; m. James Robert Elrod, Jan. 7, 1988. Grad. high sch., House Springs, Mo., 1967. Data entry operator Wyatt Mfg., Salina, Kans., 1975-78; computer operator Rickel Mfg. Corp., Salina, 1978-79, programmer, 1979-80, data processing mgr., 1980-81; data processing mgr. Curtis Machine Co., Dodge City, Kans., 1981-86; sr. system analyst Almet Lawnlite, Portland, Tenn., 1986-87; corp. data processing mgr. W&J Rives, High Point, N.C., 1987—; cons. J&Y Transport, Knoxville, Tenn., 1989—, Rickel Mfg., Kansas City, Kans., 1979-80. Helper, vol. Liberty House Nursing Home, Thomasville, N.C., 1990. Mem. NAFE. Methodist. Home: 319 Polk St Thomasville NC 27360

ELROD, MARGARET ANN, nurse, consultant; b. Fitzgerald, Ga., Dec. 13, 1919; d. Joseph Thomas and Della Ann (Booker) Hendricks; m. James William Elrod, Sept. 9, 1942 (div. 1967, dec.); children—Linda Sue, James Thomas (dec.), Robert Lee (dec.). Student Middle Ga. Coll., Cochran, 1936-37; R.N., Macon City Hosp., 1942. Pvt. duty nurse, Macon, Ga., 1942-49; dir. nurses Mitchell County Hosp., Camilla, Ga., 1953-57, Howard Hosp., Pelham, Ga., 1957-63, Rest Awhile Nursing Home, Moultrie, Ga., Jesup, Ga., 1963-67, Templeton Nursing Homes, Valdosta, Ga., 1967-78; dir. phys. health Parkwood Devel. Ctr., Valdosta, 1978-87, ret. 1987. Mem. Civic Round Table of Valdosta; bd. dirs. Long Term Care Ombudsman Adv. Bd., Am. Cancer Soc. (chmn. svc. and rehab. com.); vol. reader Talking Book Program, 1988; hospice vol.; bloodbank vol. Mem. Ga. State Nurses Assn. (pres. 15th dist. 1970-71, 1st v.p. 15th dist. 1988-89), Loundes County Mental Health Assn. (v.p. 1984-85, pres. 1985-86), Loundes Assn. Retarded Citizens (bd. dirs. 1983-85, service award 1983, 85-86). Democrat. Methodist. Clubs: United Spanish War Aux. (state pres. 1973-74); Pilot of Valdosta (pres. 1975-76, 77-78, 84-85); VFW Aux. Avocation: fishing. Home: Rt 12 Box 225 Lot 10 Valdosta GA 31602

EL SAFFAR, RUTH SNODGRASS, Spanish language educator; b. N.Y.C., June 12, 1941; d. John Tabb and Ruth (Wheelwright) Snodgrass; m. Zuhair M. El Saffar, Apr. 11, 1965; children: Ali, Dena, Amir. B.A., Colo. Coll., 1962; Ph.D., Johns Hopkins U., 1966; DHL (hon.), Colo. Coll., 1987. Instr. Spanish, Johns Hopkins U., Balt., 1963-65; instr. English Univ. Coll. Baghdad, 1966-67; asst. prof. Spanish U. Md.-Baltimore County, 1967-68; asst. prof. U. Ill.-Chgo., 1968-73, assoc. prof., 1973-78, prof., 1978-83, research prof. Spanish, 1983-88; prof. Northwestern U., Evanston, Ill., 1988-89; rsch. prof. U. Ill., Chgo., 1989—; dir. summer seminar on Spanish Golden Age lit. NEH, 1979, 82. Author: Novel to Romance: A Study of Cervantes's Novelas Ejemplares, 1974, Distance and Control in Don Quixote, 1975, Cervantes's Casamiento engañoso and Coloquio de los perros, 1976, Beyond Fiction, 1984; editor Critical Essays on Cervantes, 1986, Studies in Honor of Elias Rivers; adv. bd. PMLA; editorial bd. Cervantes, The Comparatist, Hispanic Issues. Woodrow Wilson fellow, 1961, NEH fellow, 1970-71, Guggenheim fellow, 1975-76, Newberry Libr. fellow, 1982, U. Ill. Inst. Humanities fellow, 1985-86, NEH fellow, 1990-91, Danforth assoc., 1973-79, Am. Coun. Learned Socs. grantee, 1978, sr. univ. scholar U. Ill., 1986—. Mem. MLA (exec. council 1974-78, commn. on future of the profession 1980-82, exec. com. div. on Spanish Golden Age poetry and prose 1977-82), Am. Assn. Tchrs. Spanish and Portuguese, Midwest MLA, Cervantes Soc. Am. (exec. com. 1979-82, 86—, v.p. 1989—). Home: 7811 Greenfield River Forest IL 60305 Office: Univ Ill Dept Spanish Chicago IL 60680

ELSDON, MARGARET BUCHANAN, educator; b. Barton, N.Y., Mar. 28, 1949; d. John George and Helen Scott (Hall) E.; m. Joseph O. Fattorusso, June 19, 1971 (div. July 1976); 1 child, Elizabeth Anne Fattorusso; m. Michael J. Jacaruso, Dec. 27, 1982. BS, Mills Coll. Edn., 1971; M.A.T., Manhattanville, 1976. Cert. elem. tchr., N.Y. Tchr. Harrison C.S.D., Harrison, N.Y., 1971—; mem. steering com. middle states Harrison C.S.D., 1987—, rep. edn. adv. coun., 1986—, chairperson staff devel. com., 1990; presenter-cons. SUNY-Purchase Partnership, Purchase, 1989; mem. negotioting team Harrison Assn. Teachers, 1990. Mem. Assn. Childhood Edn. Internat., Assn. Supervision and Curriculum Devel., Nat. Assn. for Edn. Young Children, N.Y. State United Tchrs. Home: 250 Commerce St Hawthorne NY 10532 Office: SJ Preston Sch West Harrison NY 10604

ELSE, CAROLYN JOAN, library system administrator; b. Mpls., Jan. 31, 1934; d. Elmer Oscar and Irma Carolyn (Seibert) Wahlberg; m. Floyd Warren Else, 1962 (div. 1968); children—Stephen Alexander, Catherine Elizabeth. B.S. Stanford U., 1956; M.L.S., U. Wash., 1957. Cert. profl. librarian, Wash. Librarian Queens Borough Pub. Library, N.Y.C., 1957-59, U.S. Army Special Services, France, Germany, 1959-62; info. librarian Bennett Martin Library, Lincoln, Neb., 1962-63; br. librarian Pierce County Library, Tacoma, Wash., 1963-65, dir., 1965—. Bd. dirs. Campfire, Tacoma, 1984. Mem. South Sound Women's Network (bd. dirs.), Wash. Library Assn. (v.p. 1969-71), Pacific Northwest Library Assn. (sec. 1969-71), ALA. Club: City (Tacoma). Office: Pierce County Libr Dist 2356 Tacoma Ave S Tacoma WA 98402*

ELSENHANS, VIRGINIA DELONG, association executive; b. Bronxville, N.Y., Apr. 1, 1947; d. Charles Frederick and Dorothy Potter (Hobbs) Delong; m. David Williams Elsenhans, June 7, 1973 (div. 1979); m. Jon Chadwick Haitsma, Oct. 21, 1988. BA, Elmhurst Coll., 1969; A in Applied Sci., Montgomery County Community Coll., 1976; EdM, Temple U., 1982, MBA, 1986. Cert. adult nurse practitioner, Pa. RN Temple U. Med. Ctr., Phila., 1976-80, educator community health, 1980-82, adult nurse practitioner, 1982-85; grad. asst. Sch. Bus. Adminstn. Temple U., Phila., 1985-86; adminstrv. fellw U. Mich. Hosps., Ann Arbor, 1986-88; coord. mem. edn. Group Health Assn., Washington, 1989—; cons. Meml. Hosp., Roxborough, Pa., 1982-83; rep. State Nurse Practitioner's Coalition, southeastern Pa., 1983-85; mem. adv. bd. SBI, Inc., Bala Cynwyd, Pa., 1987—. Mem. editorial bd. Jour. of Patient Edn. and Counseling; contbr. articles to profl. jours. Mem. program com. Am. Heart Assn., Phila., 1982-84, adv. bd. Domino's House, Ann Arbor, 1987-88; vice-chair dist. 1 Primary Care Clinician's and Practitioners, Phila., 1983-85; dir. Southeastern Pa. High Blood Pressure Control Program. Recipient award Am. Heart Assn., 1984. Mem. Healthcare Forum, Med. Group Mgmt. Assn., Internat. Patient Edn. Coun., Am. Pub. Health Assn. Home: 5111 Woodmere Dr Apt 203 Centreville VA 22020 Office: Group Health Assn 2000 L St NW Washington DC 20036

ELSON, SUZANNE GOODMAN, association official; b. Memphis, Oct. 17, 1937; d. Charles F. and Isabel (Ehrlich) Goodman; m. Edward Elliott Elson, Aug. 24, 1957; children—Charles Myer, Louis Goodman, Harry II. Student Randolph-Macon Women's Coll., Lynchburg, Va.; B.A., Agnes Scott Coll., 1959. Vice pres. mktg. Elson's, Atlanta, 1977-84. Ga. coordinator 51.3 Women's Com. for Carter campaign, 1975-77; sec. Nat. Council Jewish Women, N.Y.C., 1977-79; pres. Mental Health Assn. Ga., 1977-78; v.p., Nat. Mental Health Assn., 1980-82, pres., 1987; trustee Met. Atlanta Community Found., Randolph Macon Woman's Coll., Am. Craft Mus. Recipient Human Rels. award Atlanta Jewish Com., 1975; Community Svc. award Channel 11, Atlanta, 1976. Named in 100 Shapers of Future article, Atlanta Mag. Mem. Am. Craft Coun. (chmn. 1989—), High Mus. Art. (v.p. 1980-82). Home: 65 Valley Rd NW Atlanta GA 30305 Office: Elson's 65 Valley Rd NW Atlanta GA 30305

ELVIG, MERRYWAYNE, real estate manager; b. Anoka, Minn., Jan. 16, 1931; d. Wayne Leroy and Erma Lou (Greenwald) Ridge; m. Donald Keith Elvig, June 15, 1955 (div. 1972); children: Amy, David. AA, Cottey Jr. Coll., 1951; BS, U. Minn., 1953. Tchr. Anoka Hennepin Sch. Dist., Anoka, 1953-56; with med. records div. East Main Clinic, Anoka, 1972-78; real estate mgr. Skurdal Properties, Anoka, 1978-79; mgr. Belma Properties, Anoka, 1986—, Bridge Ct. Bldg. Complex, Anoka, 1987—; owner, mgr. ABC Travel, Anoka, 1979—. Commr. Housing Redevel. Authority, Anoka 1978, chmn., 1984—; bd. dirs. Walker Sr. Housing Corp., Anoka, 1986—; treas. Anoka Devel. Corp., 1986—; charter and life mem. aux. Mercy Med. Ctr., Coon Rapids, Minn., 1965—, bd. dirs., 1965-71; moderator 1st Congl. Ch., Anoka, 1984-86; mem. Greehaven Study Com., Anoka. 1986—; vol. Anoka Girl Scout Council, 1963-65; chmn. Am. Cancer Drive, 1962-65. Mem. Am. Soc. Travel Agts. (bd. dirs. 1986—), Assn. Retail Travel Agts., Minn. Exec. Women in Tourism, Internat. Fedn. Women's Orgns., Anoka Landowner's Assn., Anoka Area C. of C. (pres. 1985), Kiwanis (bd. dirs.), Philanthropic Ednl. Orgn. Sisterhood (pres. 1966-68), Philolectian Club (pres. 1965-67), Greenhaven Women's Golf Club (pres. 1987—). Republican. Home: 1933 Cressy Ave Anoka MN 55303 Office: ABC Travel 102 E Main St Anoka MN 55303

ELWART, NANCY M., nurse; b. Wausau, Wis., Dec. 10, 1939; d. Arthur and Stella Walker; m. Thomas G. Elwart, Feb. 15, 1960; children: Deborah L., James M. BS in Nursing, DePaul U., 1981, MS, 1983. Staff nurse West Surburban Hosp., Oak Park, Ill., 1961-62; charge nurse surg. unit Loretto Hosp., Chgo., 1962-64; pvt. duty nurse Chgo., 1964-67; staff nurse coronary care unit St. Mary Nazareth Hosp., Chgo., 1967-69; evening supr. St. Anne's Hosp., Chgo., 1969-80; night supr. critical care Lutheran Gen. Hosp., Park Ridge, Ill., 1980-83; clin. dir. Edgewater Hosp., Chgo., 1983-88; dir. Swedish Covenant Hosp., Chgo., 1988—. Mem. NAFE, DePaul Nurses' Alumni Assn., Chgo. Met. Assn., Am. Nurses' Assn. (cert. nursing adminstr.). Roman Catholic. Office: Swedish Covenant Hosp 5145 N California Ave Chicago IL 60625

ELWELL, ELLEN C., sales training and marketing promotions executive, instructional design and marketing promotions consultant; b. Jacksonville, Fla.; d. Merrill K. and Hermine (Chalfin) Cohen; B.A., U. Mich., 1967; M.A., N.Y.U., U. Ill., 1968; m. John Lee Elwell, Feb. 10, 1968; 1 dau., Melissa Mae. Advanced mktg. support rep. IBM, Oklahoma City, 1969-73, program planner/designer sales tng. programs, Dallas, St. Louis, 1973-79; owner, operator Elwell Assos., Inc., Dallas and St. Louis, 1979—; dir. Indsl. Catering Co., Indpls., A. Rose Prodns., Crystal Services Inc., St. Louis. Recipient Outstanding Contbn. award IBM, 1976, Notable Women of Tex. award. Mem. Am. Soc. Tng. and Devel., Am. Soc. Profl. Cons., Am. Mgmt. Assn. Author numerous corp. tng. books, 1976—. Office: 8140 Walnut Hill Ln #101 Dallas TX 75231 Office: 1231 Hanley Industrial Park Saint Louis MO 63144

ELY, MARICA MCCANN, interior designer; b. Pachuca, Mex., May 2, 1907 (parents Am. citizens); d. Warner and Mary Evans (Cook) McCann; m. Northcutt Ely, Dec. 2, 1931; children: Michael and Craig (twins), Parry Haines. B.A., U. Calif.-Berkeley, 1929; diploma Pratt Inst. of Art, N.Y.C., 1931. Free-lance interior designer, Washington and Redlands, Calif., 1931—; lectr. on flower arranging and fgn. travel, 1931—; prof. Sogetsu Ikebana Sch., Tokyo, 1972. Art editor (calendar) Nat. Capital Garden Club League, 1957-58. Pres. Kenwood Garden Club, Md.; bd. dirs. Nat. Library Blind, Washington; v.p. bd. dirs. Washington Hearing and Speech Soc., 1969; cofounder Delta Gamma Found. Pre-Sch. Blind Children, Order of Delta Gamma Rose, PWashington. Finalist Nat. Silver Bowl Competition, Jackson-Perkins Co., 1966; garden shown on nat. tour Am. Hort. Soc., 1985. Mem. Calif. Arboretum Found., Redlands Hort. and Improvement Soc. (bd. dirs. 1982—), Redlands Panhellenic Soc., Yucaipa Valley Garden Club, Town and Country African Violet Soc., Redlands Country Club, Washington Club, Chevy Chase Club (D.C.), Berkeley Tennis Club, Order of Delta Gamma Rose.

EMANUEL, DIANE MARIE, labor relations executive; b. Mpls., Apr. 17, 1947; d. Clinton David and Muriel Ruth (Jensen) Gustafson; m. Bruce A. Bakke, June 29, 1967 (div.); 1 son, Brian Allen; m. David Harris Emanuel, Jan. 28, 1978; 1 son, Frederick Paul. Cert. profl. in human resource. Student U. Minn., 1973-77, North Tex. State U., 1978-79, 85; A.A., A.S., Tarrant County Jr. Coll., 1984. Personnel mgr. ITT Thermotech, Hopkins, Minn., 1967-77; mgr. employment and equal opportunity Fingerhut Corp., Minnetonka, Minn., 1977-78; personnel mgr. Automatic Data Processing, Dallas, 1978-79; compensation adminstr. Sky Chefs, Arlington, Tex., 1979-81, employee relations specialist, 1981-83, mgr. labor relations, 1983—; cons. Assoc. Clerical Specialist, Mpls., 1976-78. Editor: Fingerprints, 1977-78, ITT Thermotech News, 1970-77, ADP News, 1978-79. Dir. concessions Coppell Pee Wee Football Assn. (Tex.), 1983-85; den leader Coppell council Boy Scouts Am., 1982, asst. den leader Webelos, 1983; campaign chmn. City Council election campaign City of Coppell, 1983. Mem. Am. Soc. Personnel Adminstrn., Twin City Personnel Assn., Dallas Personnel Assn., Mid-Cities Personnel Assn., Nat. Assn. Female Execs. Home: 541 Rolling Hills Rd Coppell TX 75019 Office: Sky Chefs Dallas-Fort Worth Airport PO Box 619777 Dallas TX 75261

EMANUELSON, KAREN SUE, marketing and desktop publishing professional; b. Detroit, May 19, 1959; d. Leo J. and Margaret Barbara (Klimek) Chromen; m. James Robert Emanuelson, Jr., Mar. 28, 1981; 1 child, Sydney Anne. BBA in Mktg., Bowling Green State U., 1981. Authorized Ventura Pub. instr. Mktg. asst. Bruce Hardwood Fls., Dallas, 1981-82; mktg. coord. Touche Ross & Co., Dallas, 1982-85; mgr., pub. rels. Systems Specialists, Inc., Dallas, 1985-87; mgr., mktg. commn. Datamatic, Inc., Richardson, Tex., 1988-89; mgr. desktop pub. svcs. Micro E's, Richardson, Tex., 1989—. Editor: (newsletters) Ex-Press, 1983-86, On Site, 1986-87, Datamatic Ink, 1987-89., The ManuScript, 1990—, The Cuda Times, 1990—, North College Park News, 1990—. Sec., treas. Young Am. Bowling Alliance, Dallas, 1986-90. Mem. Internat. Assn. Bus. Communicators, Women in Communications, Nat. Desktop Pubs. Assn. Office: Micro E's PO Box 850363 Richardson TX 75085-0363

EMBREY, CATHY GRAHAM, infosystems specialist; b. Ft. Sill, Okla., Sept. 25, 1956; d. Harold William and Lorraine Mary (Sipperly) Graham; m. Lance Glaze Embrey, Dec. 31, 1988. Student, George Mason U., 1974-75, No. Va. Community Coll., 1976-77, Am. U., 1978-79; cert., Nat. Inst. Real Estate, 1986. Asst. mgr. Boat U.S., Alexandria, Va., 1979-81, Magic Pan Creperie', Falls Church, Va., 1981; mgr. Entre' Computer Ctrs., Inc., McLean, Va., 1981-88; mgr. mktg., purchasing, distbn., info. systems Entre' Computer Ctrs., Inc. (merged with Intelligent Electronics, Inc.), Chantilly, Va., 1988—; mgr. systems planning and automation, 1989—; mgr. systems planning and automation, mgr. user support and info. cons.; cons. Speakers Bur., Washington, 1978; adj. prof. Am. U., Washington, 1986. Contbr. articles to profl. jours. Tchr. Touch for Health Found., Manassas, Va., 1987—, LDS Ch., Manassas, 1989—. Mem. Am. Mgmt. Assn. (assoc.). Republican. Office: Intelligent Electronics 4260 Entre Ct Chantilly VA 22021

EMBRY, DIANNE C., psychologist; b. Portland, Maine, Apr. 22, 1932; d. Daniel Wheeler and Dorella Marie (Viel) Nudd; m. Richard E. Pierce, Nov. 30, 1950 (div. 1958); children: Richard, Patricia Pearce Wilder (dec.), Pamela Pearce Miller, Linda M. Pearce Prestley; m. Jay Creston Embry, June 17, 1959; children: Joel Patrick, Barbara Leigh, Susan Ellen; stepchild, Stephen C. BA in Psychology, Conn. Coll., 1977; EdM, Harvard U., 1978; PhD in Psychology, U.S. Internat. U., 1983. Lic. psychologist, Wis. Postdoctorate fellow Tex. A&M U., College Station, 1984; counselor U.S. Naval Base, New London, Conn., 1973, Norwich (Conn.) State Hosp., 1974; psychotherapist, counselor Tex. A&M U., 1984; lectr. Nat. U., San Diego, 1985; clin. coordinator, postdoctoral fellow Camarillo (Calif.) State Hosp., 1987; staff psychologist Calif. Instn. for Men, Chino, 1987-89; cons. psychologist Kettle Maraine Hosp., Oconomowoc, Wis., 1990; staff psychologist St. Francis Med. Ctr., La Crosse, Wis., 1990—. Dir. dist. campaign State Rep. Conn., Groton, 1972-74; mem. Charter Revision Commn., Groton, 1974-76; mem. Groton Govtl. Study Commn., 1975; vol. therapist Conn. Valley Hosp., Middleton, 1972. Mem. Tex. Psychol. Assn., Ventura County Psychol. Assn., Am. Psychol. Assn., Phi Delta Kappa, Psi Chi. Democrat. Roman Catholic.

EMBRY, SUSAN FLEMING, electronics engineer; b. Guntersville, Ala., Feb. 5, 1954; d. Burl Russell Fleming and Hazel Lucille (Thompson) F.; 1 child, Chris. BS in Physics and Math., Athens State Coll., Ala., 1981; BSE, U. Ala., 1985; MSE in Sensor Systems, Southeastern Inst. Tech., Huntsville, Ala., 1988. Math. technician, physicist, electronics engr. Tactical Air Def. Directorate U.S. Army Missile Intelligence Agy., Redstone Arsenal, Ala., 1980-85; math. technician, physicist, electronics engr. Directed Energy Weapons Directorate U.S. Army Strategic Def. Command, Huntsville, 1985-87, gen.-electronics engr., systems integration engr., 1987-89, chmn. N-Site Network configuration control bd. system analysis and battle mgmt., 1988-89, lead engr. sensor/signal processing ground-based surveillance tracking system, 1989—. Contbr. govt. documents. Mem. Women in Electronics. Office: US Army Strategic Def 106 Wynn Dr PO Box 1500 Huntsville AL 35807

EMBRY-WARDROP, MARY RODRIGUEZ, mathematics educator; b. Monroe, La., Aug. 22, 1933; d. William Drane Haddox and Edith Dupré (Brown) Rodriguez; m. Robert Frear Wardrop, May 12, 1977. BS, Southwestern at Memphis, 1955; MA, U. Va., 1958; PhD, U. N.C., 1964. Lectr. math. Southwestern at Memphis, 1958-59, Inst. for Am. Univs., Aix-en-Provence, France, 1959-60, Lausanne Sch. for Girls, Memphis, 1960-61; asst. prof. math. U. N.C., Charlotte, 1964-68, assoc. prof., 1968-72, prof., 1972-77; prof. math. Cen. Mich. U., Mt. Pleasant, 1977-90, prof. emeritus, 1990—. Co-author: Calculus and Analytical Geometry, 1973; contbr. articles to math. jours. Recipient teaching excellence award U. N.C., Charlotte, 1968, award Cen. Mich. U. and Mich. Assn. Governing Bds., 1987. Mem. Am. Math. Soc., Math. Assn. Am. (assoc. editor Monthly 1980-86). Home: 901 Canal Rd Mount Pleasant MI 48858 Office: Cen Mich U Math Dept Mount Pleasant MI 48859

EMEK, SHARON HELENE, business consultant; b. Bklyn., Oct. 23, 1945; d. Hyman Sampson and Cynthia Gertrude (Roth) Rabinowitz; children: Aleeza Judith, Joshua Michael, Elana Yael. B.A., CCNY, 1967; M.A., Bklyn. Coll., 1970; Ed.D., Rutgers U., 1977; cert. ins. counselor. Dir. preliminary program for small coll. Bklyn. Coll., 1969-71, 73-74; dir. Am. Ctr. Reading Skills, Tel Aviv, 1972; asst. prof. Brookdale Community Coll., Lincroft, N.J., 1975-77, Rutgers U., New Brunswick, N.J., 1977-82; v.p. Radzik & Emek, Princeton, N.J., 1980—; speaker profl. meetings. Author (with Adam Radzik); Answers For Managers, 1986; Dealing Successfully with Key Management Issues, 1986. Contbr. articles to profl. jours. Recipient Promising Research award Nat. Council Tchrs. of English, 1978. Mem. Am. Mgmt. Assn., Am. Cons. Leauge. Avocations: writing; reading; jogging; tennis; travel. Office: Radzik & Emek 622 Eagle Rock Ave West Orange NJ 07052

EMERING, SANDRA ANN, actuary; b. Chgo., Sept. 12, 1949; d. Adrian Douglas and Marie (Wojnowiak) Troutman; m. Edward John Emering, July 11, 1981; 1 child, Daniel T., Edward Ina. B.S. in Math., U. Ill., 1970. Enrolled actuary. Mgr. CNA Ins. Co., Chgo., 1970-75; pension actuary Reed Ramsey, Inc., Oakbrook, Ill., 1975-77, Kemper Life Ins. Co., Long Grove, Ill., 1977-78; actuary Karel & Assocs., Northbrook, Ill., 1979-80; pres. Consulting Actuarial Group, Northfield, 1981—. Adviser Northfield Community Ch., 1982. Mem. Am. Acad. Actuaries, Am. Soc. Pension Actuaries, Women in Mgmt., Nat. Assn. for Female Execs., Inc., Chgo. Council on Foreign Relations, Nat. Assn. of Women Bus. Owners, Smithsonian Assocs. Republican. Congregationalist. Clubs: Chgo. Actuarial, East Bank (Chgo.). Office: Cons Actuarial Group 778 Frontage Rd Northfield IL 60093

EMERLING, CAROL FRANCES, consumer products company executive; b. Cleve., Sept. 13, 1930; d. Bernard and Florence A. Greenbaum; m. Norton Harvey Noll, Oct. 1, 1950 (dec. July 1951); m. Stanley Justin Emerling, May 2, 1953 (div. Aug. 1971); children—Keith S., Susan C.; m. Jerrold A. Fadem, Aug. 24, 1974 (div. Oct. 1978). Student, Vassar Coll., 1948-49, Case Western Res. U., 1949-50; LL.B. summa cum laude, Cleve. State U., 1955. Bar: Ohio 1955, U.S. Supreme Ct. 1971, Calif. 1975, N.Y. 1982. Instr. Cleve. Coll., 1956-59; from staff atty. to atty.-in-charge Legal Aid Defenders Office, Cleve., 1962-70; regional dir. FTC, Cleve., 1970-74, Los Angeles, 1974-78; sec. Am. Home Products Corp., N.Y.C., 1978—; adv. com. criminal rules Supreme Ct. Ohio, 1970-73; chmn. Cleve. Fed. Exec. Bd., 1973. Co-author: The Allergy Cookbook, 1969; Contbr. articles to legal jours. Founder Pepper Pike (Ohio) Civic League, 1959; sec. Pepper Pike Charter Commn., 1966. Recipient Claude E. Clarke award Legal Aid Soc., 1967; Disting. Service award FTC, 1972. Mem. ABA, Assn. Bar City of N.Y., State Bar of Calif. Republican. Office: Am Home Products Corp 685 3rd Ave New York NY 10017

EMERSON, ALICE FREY, college president; b. Durham, N.C., Oct. 26, 1931; d. Alexander Hamilton and Alice (Hubbard) Frey; divorced; children: Rebecca, Peter. A.B., Vassar Coll., 1953; Ph.D., Bryn Mawr Coll., 1964. Tchr., Newton (Mass.) High Sch., 1956-58; mem. faculty Bryn Mawr (Pa.) Coll., 1961-64; mem. faculty U. Pa., Phila., 1966-75, asst. prof. polit. sci., 1966-75, dean of women, 1966-69, dean of students, 1969-75; pres. Wheaton Coll., Norton, Mass., 1975—; dir. Bank of Boston Corp., First Nat. Bank of Boston; trustee Penn Mut. Life Ins. Co.; adv. bd. HERS Mid-America. Mem. adv. bd. Com. for Nat. Security, 1982—, Nat. Corp., Legal Def. and Edn.; bd. dirs. Corp. for Public/Pvt. Ventures, 1978-82, 86—, World Resources Inst., 1987—; pres. Sturdy Meml. Hosp., 1977—; mem. adv. bd. Great Woods Ednl. Forum, 1987—. Mem. AAUP, NOW (legal defense and edn. fund), Am. Polit. Sci. Assn., Am. Coun. Edn. (commn. on leadership devel. 1979-82, com. on collegiate athletics 1979—, nominating com. 1980-82), Coun. Fgn. Rels., Am. Judicature Soc. Home: 28 E Main St Norton MA 02766 Office: Wheaton Coll Office of Pres Norton MA 02766

EMERSON, ANN PARKER, dietitian; b. Twin Lakes, Fla., Dec. 3, 1925; d. Charles Dendy and Gladys Agnes (Chalker) Parker; B.S., Fla. State U., 1947; M.S., U. Fla., 1968; m. Donald McGeachy Emerson, Sept. 22, 1950; children—Mary Ann, Donald McGeachy, Charles Parker, William John. Research dietitian U. Chgo., 1948-50; adminstrv. research dietitian U. Fla. Coll. Medicine, Gainesville, 1962-68, dir. dietetic edn., 1968-74, dir. dietetic internship program, 1968-75, dir. program in clin. and community dietetics, 1974-83; mem. Commn. on Dietetic Registration, 1974-77, Commn. on Accreditation, 1980-83. Pres., Gainesville chpt. Altrusa, Internat., 1977-78. VA Allied Health Manpower grantee, 1974-81; HEW Allied Health Manpower grantee, 1975-78, 78-81. Mem. Am., Fla. Dietetic Assns. Republican. Roman Catholic. Club: Jr. League (Gainesville, Altuisa). Office: PO Box J-184 JHMHC Gainesville FL 32610

EMERSON, MADONNA SUE, motel manager; b. Paintsville, Ky., Oct. 16, 1942; d. Louis Frank Spears and Pauline (Collins) Spears Kennedy; m. Carroll Dean Emerson, Dec. 14, 1960 (div. 1981); children: James Franklin (dec.), Anthony Dean, Troy David. Grad. edult edn., Elk City, Okla. Factory employee Messenger Corp., Auburn, Ind., 1975-82; housekeeping Terrace Inn, Ardmore, Okla., 1982-84; night audit HiWay Inn, Ardmore, 1984-86; mgr. Exec. Inn, Elk City, Okla., 1986-89; asst. Super Shop Convenience Stores, Elk City, 1988-89; printer Renaissance Pub. Co., Inc., Hicksville, Ohio, 1989—; asst. Super Shop Convenience Stores, Elk City, 1989—; cons. in field. Mem. NAFE, Am. Legion Aux.

EMERSON, ROSE, career consultant; b. N.Y.C., Jan. 18, 1945; d. Aron and Leah (Zeiss) E.; m. Nov. 16, 1975; children: Michael, Peter, Noah. BS, CUNY, 1966, MS, 1972. Tchr. N.Y.C. Bd. Edn., 1966-71, dir. career programs, 1973-77; exec. v.p. Michael Simon Assocs. Inc., Mt. Kisco, N.Y., 1977-86; pres. Career Relocation Corp. Am., Purchase, N.Y., 1986—; cons. to Fortune 500 firms throughout U.S., 1981—. Contbr. articles to mags., newspapers; creator Spouse Employment Assistance Program, 1986. Mem. C. of C. (Best Small Bus. award 1988), Employee Relocation Coun., Assn. Outplacement Cons. Firms. Office: Career Relocation Corp Am 2900 Westchester Ave Purchase NY 10577

EMERSON, SARAE SUSAN, educator; b. Balt., Apr. 5, 1947; d. Manuel Nathan and Zelda (Saval) Jacobson; m. George Herman Emerson, Dec. 20, 1969 (div. 1987); children: John Dale, Peter Scott. BA, U. Fla., 1967; MEd, U. Miami, Coral Gables, Fla., 1970. Cert. tchr., Fla. Reading clinician McGlannan Lang. Arts Ctr., Miami, Fla., 1970-73; ind. learning disability cons. Miami, 1974-77; sr. assoc. prof. math Miami-Dade Community Coll., 1978—; software reviewer IBM-Miami Dade Community Coll., 1990. Developer computerized feedback for basic math. lab., 1979, for algebra lab., 1989—; contbr. articles to profl. publs.; author classroom manuals. Campaigner state polit. offices, 1987; libr. Temple Israel, 1986-88; mem. new beginnings group Temple Beth Am, 1990. Mem. Macrobiotic Found. Fla. (bd. dirs. and treas. 1989—), Nat. Coun. Staff, Program and Orgnl. Devel., Parents Without Ptnrs., Jewish Community Ctr. Democrat. Office: Miami Dade Community Coll 11011 SW 104th St Miami FL 33176

EMERSON, TYRA KIM, arts council official; b. Queens, N.Y., Aug. 14, 1957; d. Benjamin Franklin and Ada (Spells) Williams; m. Dennis L. Emerson, Apr. 22, 1978 (div. June 1984). BA, L.I. U., 1985. Office mgr. USCG Supply Ctr., Bklyn., 1976-78, St. Clair County Community Coll., Port Huron, Mich., 1978-84; fiscal clk. office compt. Pratt Inst., Bklyn., 1981-84; dir. grants Queens Coun. on the Arts, Jamaica, N.Y., 1984-90; dir. programs Queens Coun. on the Arts, 1990—. Fellow NAFE. Democrat. Baptist. Home: 134-28 155th St Springfield Gardens NY 11434 Office: Queens Coun on the Arts 161 04 Jamaica Ave Jamaica NY 11432

EMERSON-SMITH, LUANNE BENNETT, insurance company exective; b. Richmond, Ind., Dec. 12, 1936; d. Everett W. and Marjorie H. (Thornburg) Bennett. Ind. U. East, U. Dayton. Mem. mgmt. devel. staff AMI, L.A., 1985-86; regional mgr. network operations Provident Life & Accident, Chattanooga, 1986—. Bd. trustees Nat. Multiple Sclerosis Soc. Mem. Healthcare Fin. Mgmt. Assn., Order of Ea. Star. Republican. Roman Catholic.

EMERY, CHRISTINE VIENTIANE, consulting firm executive; b. Vientiane, Laos, Sept. 9, 1957; parents U.S. citizens; d. Weston Lewis and Brigitte Jaqueline (LeMaire) Emery. BA, George Washington U., 1982; student, U. Mass., 1975-76. Pres. Alianza Ibero-Americana, Washington, 1985-87, 87-89, Internat. Cultural Affairs, Washington, 1986-88, Amerisphere Group, Ltd., Washington, 1988—; adv. bd. Inter-Americas Cultural Ctr., Washington, 1986-88; v.p. PanAm Roundtable, Washington, 1989—, Coun. U.S.-Mex. Rels., Washington, 1988—; v.p. Inter-Am. Coun., Washington, 1990-91, sec. 1989-90. V.P. George Washington U. Alumni, 1988-89, PanAm Liaison Com., Washington, 1989-90; v.p. Bd. Assoc. Nat. Rehab. Hosp., Washington, 1990-91; adv. bd. Nat. Vintners Assn., Washington, 1989—, Mosaic Mag. 1990—. Mem. Rock Creek Womens Rep. Club. Office: Amerisphere Group Ltd 1776 K St NW Ste 210 Washington DC 20036

EMERY, JILL HOUGHTON, state agency administrator; b. Bangor, Maine; d. Seward L. Houghton and Marcia Poillon; m. James L. Emery; 1 child, Patrick. BS, SUNY, Genesco, 1965. Educator, 1971-83; pres. Emery Corp., Geneseo, N.Y., 1983-84; dir. Women's Bus. Ownership Office, SBA, Washington, 1985; dep. dir. Women's Bur. U.S. Dept. Labor, 1985-88, dir., 1988—. Bd. dirs. Western N.Y. State Child Care Coun.; mem. adv. com. Women Vets., Congressional Task Force on Women, Minorities and the Handicapped in Sci. and Tech.; chairperson Am. Heart Assn. (Volunteer of Yr. 1979); mem. Nat. Fedn. Rep Women. Mem. Women's Econ. Alliance, Women Execs. in Govt., Phi Delta Kappa (treas.). Office: Dept Labor Women's Bur 200 Constitution Ave NW Washington DC 20210

EMERY, LYNNDA JOYCE, occupational therapist; b. San Antonio, Sept. 26, 1953; d. Leo Lloyd and Joyce Winifred (Prins) E. BA magna cum laude, Marshall U., 1975; MEd, U. Mo., Columbia, 1980; EdD, U. Ark., Fayetteville, 1989. Occupational therapist Mo. Dept. Mental Health, Fulton, 1980-81, St. Joseph Med. Ctr., Wichita, Kans., 1982-85; pvt. practice occupational therapy Claremore, Okla., 1985-89; occupational therapy faculty U. Tenn., Memphis, 1989—. Mem. Am. Occupational Therapy Assn., Am. Mgmt. Assn., Nat. Assn. Female Execs., Kappa Delta Pi. Office: U Tenn 822 Beale Ste 345 Memphis TN 38163

EMERY, MARCIA ROSE, parapsychologist; b. Phila., Mar. 19, 1937; d. David Gelfand and Naomi (Carner) Rose; m. Gordon M. Becker, 1970 (div.); m. James D. Emery, 1982; stepchildren: Stephen, Alicia, Jamie. B.A. in Psychology, Adelphi U., Garden City, N.Y., 1958; M.S. in Clin. Psychology, CCNY, 1960; M.A. in Social Psychology, New Sch. Social Rsch., 1964, Ph.D., 1968. Rsch. asst. Office Instl. Rsch., Hunter Coll., N.Y.C., 1959-62, Community Svcs. Soc., N.Y.C., 1962-65; lectr. psychology Hunter Coll., 1965-67; assoc. prof. psychology, chmn. M.A. program in community psychology Fed. City Coll., Washington, 1968-74; pvt. practice psychology and astrological counseling Hollywood, Fla., 1981—; pres. Intuitive Mgmt. Cons. Corp.; adj. faculty Aquinas Coll., Grand Rapids; psychologist Renaissance Revitalization Ctr., Nassau, Bahamas, 1975; lectr., coord. counseling Coll. Bahamas, 1976-80; condr. workshops in parapsychology throughout U.S. Author: Dr. Marcia Emery's Intuitive Management Workout. Grantee NIMH, 1972. Mem. Am. Psychol. Assn., Assn. Humanistic Psychology, Parapsychol. Assn., Spiritual Frontiers Fellowship, Assn. for the Study of Dreams, Am. Soc. Psychical Rsch., Am. Fedn. Astrology, Assn. Past Life Rsch. and Therapy. Mem. Unity Ch. Address: 3512 McCoy SE Grand Rapids MI 49506

EMERY, MARY ALICE, bank officer; b. Petersborough, N.H., Jan. 9, 1924; d. Harold and Helen F. (Barry) Naglie; m. Stanley F. Emery, May 4,

1946; children: Susan, Karen. Asst. treas.to v.p. Peterborough (N.H.) Savs. Bank, 1967-77, v.p. to trustee, 1978-80, ret. exec. v.p., 1989. Mem. St. Peters Ch., Red Cross, March of Dimes, Am. Legion Aux. Recipient Banker of the Yr. award. Mem. N.H. Bankers Assn., Fin. Women Internat., Am. Legion Aux., U.S.-USSR Bridges for Peace. Home: 3 Oak St Peterborough NH 03458

EMERY, SUE, bulletin editor, owner bridge studio; b. Wichita County, Tex., Feb. 23, 1920; d. Billy J. and Trula V. (Mayfield) McHam; m. Horace B. Camp (div. 1958); children: Ann Camp McGrath, Connie Camp Phyllis, Billy Brit; m. John Walter Emery (dec. 1972). B.A., Harding Coll., 1939. Tchr., 1939-40; with U.S. Civil Svc., 1941-45; reporter Wichita Daily Times, Tex., 1945-46; ind. bridge club owner-operator, freelance tournament dir., daily bull. editor; editor Am. Contract Bridge League Bridge Bull., Memphis, 1972—; staff mem. Tex. Bridge Mag., 1960's. Author, researcher: No Passing Fancy, 1977; contbr. articles to mags. Active Womanpower for Eisenhower, 1950's, Democrats for Eisenhower, Tex., 1950's. Home: 1565 Hayne Rd Memphis TN 38119 Office: Contract Bridge Bull 2990 Airways Memphis TN 38116-3847

EMILITA, MARIE BERNADETTE, advertising agency executive; b. Passic, N.J., Aug. 28, 1945; d. Chester J. and Sophia H. (Zawadzki) Lewandowski; m. Charles Peter Emilita, Dec. 19, 1970; 1 dau., Amy. B.A., Skidmore Coll., 1966. With J. Walter Thompson U.S.A., Inc., N.Y.C., 1966—, creative dir., 1979—, now sr. v.p. Home: 174 Terrace Ave Hasbrouck Heights NJ 07604 Office: J Walter Thompson USA Inc 466 Lexington Ave New York NY 10017

EMLEY, SUZANNE ELAINE, nurse; b. Fort Wayne, Ind., May 24, 1949; d. Harry Edward and Dorothy Elaine (Roehm) Boze; m. Glenn Alan Emley, Oct. 13, 1984. BS in nursing, Purdue U., Fort Wayne, Ind., 1975. Charge nurse Home Hosp., Lafayette, Ind., 1973-74; asst. head nurse Luth. Hosp., Fort Wayne, Ind., 1974-77; head nurse Luth. Hosp., Fort Wayne, 1977-80; nurse, specialist Luth. Hosp., 1980-90; physician extender Cardiology Cons., P.C., 1990—. Mem. Am. Assn. Clin. Nurses (treas. 1975—), Am. Assn. Critical Care Nurses, Delta Gamma. Republican. Lutheran. Home: 4612 Scotia Dr Fort Wayne IN 46804 Office: 3000 S Wayne Ave Fort Wayne IN 46807

EMMERICH, JO ANN, broadcasting executive; b. St. Louis, Sept. 1; d. William K. and Leora M. (Wolff) E. B.A., Catholic U. Am., 1964, M.A., 1971. Drama specialist Dept. State, Europe and Middle East, 1965-66; exec. staff Olney Theatre (Md.), 1967-68; agt. TV dept. Internat. Famous Agy., N.Y.C., 1972-75; asst. producer As the World Turns, CBS, N.Y.C., 1975-76; mgr. daytime programming ABC, N.Y.C., 1976-77, dir. daytime programming, 1977-80, v.p. daytime programs East Coast, 1980-86, v.p. daytime programs, 1986-88, sr. v.p. daytime programs, 1988—. Mem. Am. Film Inst., NATAS. Office: Capital Cities/ABC Inc 77 W 66th St New York NY 10023

EMMONS, JUDITH CRANE, sales executive; b. Boston, Sept. 17, 1954; d. John Grimes and Marjorie Marie (Coughlin) E. BA, Boston Coll., 1972-76. Elem., special edn. tchr. Rogers-Pierce Children's Ctr., Arlington, Mass., 1976-81; pres. Servicemaster of North Shore Inc., Swampscott, Mass., 1981—. Bd. dirs. Rogers-Pierce Children's Ctr., 1979-81, Somerville (Mass.) Coun. Children. Mem. NAFE, North Shore Women Bus., Boston Coll. Alumni Assn. (alumni advisor 1980—). Roman Catholic. Home: 43 Timson St Lynn MA 01902 Office: Servicemaster of N Shore Inc 17 Columbia Ave Swampscott MA 01907

EMMONS, LINDA NYE, state legislator; b. Ridgewood, N.J., July 8, 1937; d. Drake and Helen N. Pinkney; A.A., Centenary Coll. Women, Hackettstown, N.J., 1957; m. Richard L. Emmons, Dec. 13, 1958; children: Mark Richard, Dwight Nye. B.A., Conn. Coll., 1972. Staff asst. AT&T Co., 1957-61; self-employed accountant, 1975—; mem. Conn. Ho. of Reps. from 101st dist., 1977—, mem. com. on revenue, bonding and fin., 1977-81, 83—, house chmn. com. on appropriation, 1981-83, ranking mem., 1981-85, asst. minority leader for fiscal affairs; mem. Conn. Bond Commn. Mem. Madison (Conn.) Charter Commn., 1967-69, Madison Republican Town Com., 1970-77; chmn. Madison Bd. Fin., 1977-79; bd. dirs. E.C. Scranton Meml. Library, 1973-89. Mem. Order Women Legislators, LWV (voters service chmn. 1968-69). Home: 111 Yankee Peddler Path Madison CT 06443

EMORY, MARTHA KELLER, history educator, counselor; b. Lexington, Ky., July 10, 1949; d. John Bernard and Florence (Doyle) Keller; m. Derald Edgar Emory, Nov. 17, 1973; children: Shannon Elizabeth, Matthew Scott. BA in History and English, U. Ky., 1971; MS in Counseling, San Francisco State U., 1989. Cert. history and English tchr., Ky.; cert. student pers. counselor, Calif. Tchr. adult edn. Army Continuing Edn., Burtonwood, Eng., 1980-81, San Francisco, 1986; career counselor San Francisco State U., 1987-88, Alumnae Resources, San Francisco, 1988-89; instr. Am. history and orientation Northwestern State U. La., Leesville, 1989—. Contbr. articles to Pelican Pipeline. Lay minister Presidio of San Francisco, 1985-89, St. Francis of Assisi Ch., Ft. Polk, La., 1989—; crisis counselor Army Community Svcs., San Francisco, 1987-88, group facilitator for leadership, career counselor, Ft. Polk, 1989—. Recipient Outstanding Community Vol. award U.S. Army, San Francisco, 1987, 88; Officers Wives Club scholar, 1987-88. Mem. Am. Assn. for Counseling and Devel., Am. Coll. Pers. Assn., Nat. Career Devel. Assn., Nat. Mil. Family Assn. (field rep. 1989—), AAUW, Chi Sigma Iota.

EMRICH, NANCY JONES, school director, fundraiser; b. Evanston, Ill., May 3, 1950; d. James W. and Vera Virginia (Allen) Jones; m. Jeffrey P. Emrich; children: Charles William Haddaway, Parker Henry van Nes. BA in Psychology, Wheaton Coll., 1972. Asst. admissions and devel. dept. Foxcroft Sch., Middleburg, Va., 1972-73, dir. admissions, 1973-81; dir. devel. North Shore Day Sch., Winnetka, Ill., 1981—. Treas. women's bd. Traveler's & Immigrants AID, Chgo., 1987-89; asst. producer Brillanteen, McGaw YMCA of Evanston, 1983—. Mem. Soc. Fundraising Execs., Coun. for Advancement and Support Edn., Jr. League Chgo. (nominating com. 1986-87, 89—).

ENDLEIN, KATHRYN ANN, corporate childcare and eldercare consultant; b. Camden, N.J., Jan. 10, 1955; d. Carl Albert and Theresa (Rockwell) E. BA in Art History and History, James Madison U., 1977; postgrad., Rutgers U., Camden, 1978-79. Acting pers. mgr. Rice & Holman Ford, Mt. Laurel, N.J., 1977-79; asst. pers. mgr. Whitehall Labs., Hammonton, N.J., 1979-83; art sales, Mt. Laurel, 1983-84; pers. officer Fidelity Bank, Phila., 1984, sr. pers. officer, 1984-85, asst. v.p. human resources, 1986-89, corp. affirmative action officer, 1984-89; cons., v.p. client rels. Metro Day Care Systems, Upland, Pa., 1990—. Cons. Bus. Vols. for Arts, Phila., 1985—; advisor Delaware County Opportunities Industrialization Ctrs., Chester, Pa., 1985-89 (Pathfinder award 1988, Vol. award 1989); vol. Cherry Hill (Pa.) Arts Adv. Bd., 1990—. State of N.J. scholar, 1973, Stratford Players Theatrical Assn., 1977. Mem. Nat. Assn. Banking (pres. 1988-89), Affirmative Action Dirs. (sec. 1986-87, v.p. 1987-88), West Jersey Field Hockey Assn. (rec. sec. 1980-84), Burlington County Footlighters (set chmn. 1987-90, dir. communications 1990—, best set award 1987, 88, 89). Office: Metro Day Care Systems 600 Upland Ave Upland PA 19015

ENDRASKE, MARILYN JOANN, financial administrator; b. St. Charles, Mo., Feb. 24, 1947; d. Joseph Matthew and Rose Lea (Martinek) Podhorsky; m. Stanley Joseph Endraske, Feb. 24, 1968; children: Stanley J., Jeffrey L., Jaclyn R., Matthew B. BS, Lindenwood Coll., 1983. Lead key punch operator data entry dept. AT&T, St. Louis, 1970-77, assignment coord. data entry dept., 1977-80, computer equip. operator data entry dept., 1980-83, fin. analyst fin. dept., 1983, acct. forecaster fin. dept., 1983-84, acct. analyst billing dept., 1984-85, collection assoc., 1985-88; credit specialist AT&T, Atlanta, 1988-89, asst. mgr. accounts receivable, 1989—. Leader Girl Scouts of U.S., St. Louis, 1969-87, Atlanta, 1987-89; cons. Jr. Achievement, St. Louis, 1986-88; chairperson Hug-A-Bear program. Mem. NAFE, Female Exec. of N. Am., Nat. Assn. Credit Mgmt., Telephone Pioneers.

ENDTHOFF, GERTRUDE ELLEN, retired educator; b. McCord, Wis., Jan. 14, 1918; d. Bernhard Johannes and Bertha Elizabeth (Fusek) Moe; m. Fredrick Fay Endthoff, May 24, 1942 (dec. June 1971). Diploma, Rusk County Normal, Ladysmith, Wis., 1945; BS in Edn., U. Wis., Milw., 1960, MS in Edn., 1971. Rural tchr. Eight Mile Corner, Town of Big Falls (Wis.), 1937-39, Oak Grove, Tony, Wis., 1939-42; tchr. Village of Tony, 1942-50, Ramsey Ave., Victory Sch., Milw., 1950-52, Rawson Sch., South Milwaukee, Wis., 1952-56; spl. reading tchr. South Milwaukee Pub. Schs., 1956-83, city reading coord., 1976-83; curator-historian South Milwaukee Hist. Soc., 1971—, lectr., 1976. Author, editor: South Milwaukee-Then to Now, 1954, 75; author: South Milwaukee, 1976, The Settlement Along Oak Creek, 1835-1985. Mem. Milw. Area Reading Assn. (pres. 1965), Internat. Reading Assn. (charter mem.), NEA, Wis. Edn. Assn., Milw. Suburban Edn. Assn. (del. 1950-70), Milw. Area Ret. Tchrs. Assn., NEA Ret., Am. Assn. Ret. Persons, Homemakers of South Milw., 1918 Club Internat., Nat. button Soc., Wis. Button Soc., Woman's Club South Milw. (pres. 1988-90), AAUW, South Milw. Hist. Soc., Alumni U. Wis. Milw., Pi Lambda Theta. Mem. Milw. Area Reading Assn. (pres. 1965), NEA, Wis. Edn. Assn., Milw. Suburban Edn. Assn. (del. 1950-70), Milw. Area Retired Tchrs., Wis. Ret. Tchrs., NEA Retired, Am. Assn. Retired Persons, Homemakers of South Milw., 1918 Club Internat., Nat. Button Soc., Wis. Button Soc., Woman's Club South Milwaukee (pres. 1988-90), AAUW, South Milw. Hist. Soc., Alumni U. Wis. Milw., Pi Lambda Theta. Republican. Lutheran. Home: 1520 Menomonee Ave South Milwaukee WI 53172

ENDYKE, DEBRA JOAN, marketing professional; b. Manchester, N.H., July 24, 1955; d. Paul Ronald and Theresa Joan (Smith) Cote; m. Michael Thomas Pidgeon, May 15, 1976 (div. Aug. 1984); m. Thomas Allen Endyke, Sept. 21, 1985. BS in Computer Sci., N.H. Coll., 1984. Mktg. specialist Bedford (N.H.) Computer Corp., 1981-84; sales and mktg. dir. electronic services program First Software Corp., Lawrence, Mass., 1984-86; account exec. Genesys Software Systems, Inc., Lawrence, 1986-87; group sales mgr. N.E. data communications div. Panasonic Co., Secaucus, N.J., 1987-88; sr. account exec. Bus. Systems Sales Group Gen. DataComm, Inc., Middlebury, Conn., 1988-89; sr. cons. Hollis (N.H.) Info. Assocs., 1989—; applications engr. Octocom Systems, Inc., Wilmington, Mass., 1989—; cons. data communications, ind., Derry, N.H., 1987—; applications engr. Octocon Systems, Inc., Wilmington, 1989—. Republican. Roman Catholic. Home: 77 Drew Rd Derry NH 03038 Office: Hollis Info Assocs 153 N Pepperell Rd Hollis MA 03049

ENG, ANNE CHIN, television executive; b. N.Y.C., Aug. 9, 1950; d. Fuen and Suit Fong (Mark) Eng; m. George Chin, June 28, 1978; 1 child, Lauren. A.A.S., Manhattan Community Coll., 1970; student Baruch Coll., 1972. Sales asst. AVCO Radio Sales, N.Y.C., 1972; asst., jr. media buyer R.D.R. Timebuying Services, N.Y.C., 1972-74; TV media buyer, planner Ogilvy & Mather Advt., N.Y.C., 1974-78; broadcast account exec. H.R. Television, N.Y.C., 1978-79, RKO TV Reps., N.Y.C., 1979-80, Petry TV, N.Y.C., 1980—. Avocations: Plate collecting; exercise; skiing. Office: Petry TV 3 E 54th St New York NY 10022

ENG, INGRID ONG LEE, structural engineer; b. Tucson, Aug. 21, 1962; d. Gin Him and Helen (Chin) Lee; m. Steven Eng, June 21, 1987. BSCE, U. Ariz., 1984; postgrad., Columbia U., 1985-86. Cert. engr.-in-tng., Ariz., N.Y. Project adminstr. Parsons, Brinckerhoff, Quade & Douglas, Inc., N.Y.C., 1984-85, deptl. adminstr., 1985, asst. engr., 1985-89, engr. I, 1989-90, engr. II, 1990—; pres., bd. dirs. GIH Constrn. Co., Tucson, 1988—. Baird scholar U. Ariz., Tucson, 1980, Gen. Residency Acad. scholar, 1980. Mem. ASCE (assoc.; v.p. 1983-84), Soc. Women Engrs. (assoc.; sec. 1983-84). Democrat. Baptist.

ENGEL, ANNE RICE, marketing professional; b. Chapel Hill, N.C., Jan. 11, 1963; d. David Hamilton and Nancy (Garfield) Rice; m. Mark Scott Engel, June 18, 1988. BA, Wheaton Coll., Norton, Mass., 1985; MBA, Northwestern U., 1989. Asst. to treas. Continental Cablevision, Inc., Boston, 1985-87; assoc. mktg. mgr. Pepsi-Cola Co., Somers, N.Y., 1989—. Office: Pepsi-Cola Co Rte 100 & Rte 35 Somers NY 10589

ENGEL, BARBARA MARCUS, pediatrician; b. N.Y.C., May 26, 1946; d. Edward and Dorothy Evelyn (MosKowitz) Marcus;m. Mark Leslie Engel, May 2, 1971; children: Jarrett, Stephen, David. BA in Biology, Wheaton Coll., 1967; MD, SUNY, Bklyn., 1971. Pvt. practice pediatrician Holmdel, N.J., 1980—; chmn. dept. pediatrics Bayshore Community Hosp., Holmdel, 1986—. Mem. Momouth Med. Soc., Am. Acad. Pediatrics, N.J. Acad. Pediatrics, Phi Beta Kappa. Office: 719 N Beers St 2B Holmdel NJ 07733

ENGEL, CHARLENE STANT, artist, art historian; b. Norfolk, Va., Nov. 5, 1946; d. Vernon Earl Sr. and Mary Elizabeth (Rawles) Stant; m. Wilson F. Engel III, May 11, 1969; children: Grace Elizabeth, Wilson F. IV. BFA, Old Dominion U., 1968; MA, U. Wis., 1974, PhD, 1976. Vis. asst. prof. U. N.M., Albuquerque, 1976-77; adjunct prof. Allentown Coll. St. Francis de Sales, Center Valley, Pa., 1977-79; curator of art collection Moravian Coll., Bethlehem, Pa., dir. gallery, asst. prof., 1979-84; adj. prof. Christopher Newport Coll., 1987; artist, art historian Newport News, Va., 1984—; Solo Exhibition, Eastern Va. Med. Sch., 1988, Crestar Bank Gallery, 1988, Thomas Nelson Coll., 1977-89, Twentieth Century Gallery, Williamsburg, 1989. Contbr. articles to profl. jours. Hermitage Foundn. Mus. fellow, 1965, Va. Museum fellow, 1964, 67, Kress fellow, 1975. Mem. Coll. Art Assn., Va. Watercolor Soc. Home: 18 Delta Circle Newport News VA 23601

ENGEL, FRANCES HOLIDAY, volunteer; b. Detroit, May 1, 1915; d. Frank E. and Besse Blanche (Begg) Holiday; m. Ruben William Engel, June 27, 1939; children: Nancy E. Barlow, Bonnie E. Hupton, William Frederick. BA, Wayne State U., Detroit, 1939; MS, Auburn (Ala.) U., 1944. Sec. Auburn U., 1939; vol. sec. Auburn Meth. Ch., 1940—, instr. in English and pub. speaking, 1946-52; sec. Blacksburg (Va.) Meth. Ch., 1952-55, Va. Poly. Inst. Found., Blacksburg, 1955-60; instr. in English and pub. speaking Va. Poly. Inst. & State U., Blacksburg, 1960-65. Author: Sightseeing in & Around Manila, 1972, Phillippine History; A Brief Digest, 1974, Pearls & Coconuts, 1980. Recipient Calesa award Phillipine Dist. Girl Scouts U.S., 1976-77, Ambassador award David O. Newsome-U.S. Ambassador to the Philippines, 1978. Mem. AAUW (treas., com. chmn. and state pres. Blacksburg chpt. 1967), Va. Poly. Inst. & State U. Faculty Women's Club (founder, 2d pres. Blacksburg chpt. 1966-68). Methodist.

ENGEL, JOAN MARCIA, psychology educator; b. Boston, June 7, 1946; d. Morris and Thelma M. (Goldman) Lezar; m. Robert Lee Engel, Feb. 2, 1969 (div. 1982). BA, U. Mass., Boston, 1970; MA, New Sch. for Social Rsch., 1977; PhD, Fordham U., 1989. Asst. rsch. scientist NYU Med. Ctr., N.Y.C., 1988; adj. asst. prof. Coll. Mt. St. Vincent, Riverdale, N.Y., 1989-90, Lehman Coll., Bronx, N.Y., 1990, John Jay Coll., N.Y.C., 1990, Coll. of New Rochelle (N.Y.), 1990; asst. prof. Marist Coll., Poughkeepsie, N.Y., 1990—. Author: Manual for Foster Parent Training, 1980. Mem. Am. Orthopsychiat. Assn., Am. Psychol. Assn., Soc. for Rsch. in Child Devel. HOme: 111 E Hartsdale Ave 5H Hartsdale NY 10530

ENGEL, MELISSA HALE, editor; b. Hartford, Conn., July 30, 1956; d. Peter Gray and Patricia (Norton) E.; m. Stephen August Zawisza, Oct. 8, 1988. BS in Mass Communication and Journalism, U. Hartford, 1978. Editor, tchr. Town of Cromwell, Conn., 1978-79; reporter, editor Shoreline Newspapers, Old Saybrook, Conn., 1979-85; mng. editor Hartford Ins. Group, 1985—; dir. recreation Markham Meadows Campground, East Hampton, Conn., 1978—. Charter mem. Old Home Day Assn., East Hampton, 1979—; founder Fun Day in East Hampton, 1985—; publicist Rep. Town Com., East Hampton, 1978—, Lanzi Invitational Tennis Tournament, 1979-89. Mem. Women in Communications (publicity asst. 1986—). Congregationalist. Office: Hartford Ins Group Hartford Pla Hartford CT 06115

ENGEL, PAMELA MARIE, education educator; b. Antigo, Wis., Apr. 22, 1956; d. Donald Otto and Dorothy Ann (Janssen) Wirth; m. Richard Alvin Engel, July 14, 1979; children: Erike Pamela, Richard Alvin, Jr. BS, U. Wis. Stevens Point, 1978; student, U. Wis. Whitewater, 1988, U. Wis. Green Bay, 1988. Cert. Tchr., Wis. Summer info. booth attendant Langlade County Economic Devel. Com., Antigo, Wis., 1974-78; tchr. St. John's Elem., Antigo, Wis., 1978-79; receptionist Mallard Coach, West Bend, Wis., 1979-80; receptionist, acct. payable Zenith Sintered Products, Menomonee Falls, Wis.; receptionist, typist Lieds Nursery, Sussex, Wis., 1980-81; social studies tchr. Howard Suamico Sch. Dist., Wis., 1981-86, Pulaski Community Schs., Wis., 1986--; jr. varsity volleyball coach Bay Port High Sch., Green Bay Wis. 1981-82; pol. club adv. Bay Port High Sch. Green Bay Wis., 1981-82; Nat. Honor Soc. Co-Advisor Pulaski Wis. 1986--. Coord. for Nursery Schedule Atonement Luth. Ch., Green Bay Wis., 1987-88, Sunday Sch. Tchr., 1985-89; mem. choir Atonement Luth. Ch., 1985. Mem. Edn. Com. Atonement Lutheran Ch. Green Bay Wis. Democratic. Lutheran. Home: 2418 Pecan St Green Bay WI 54311

ENGEL-ARIELI, SUSAN LEE, physician; b. Chgo., Oct. 7, 1954; d. Thaddeus S. Dziengiel and Marian L. (Carpenter) Kasper; m. Udi Arieli. BA, Northwestern U., 1975; MD, Chgo. Med. Sch., 1982. Med. technician G.D. Searle, Skokie, Ill., 1972, 73, assoc. dir., 1983-84; dir. U.S. Regional Clin. Support G.D. Searle, 1984-86; rsch. editorial asst. U. Chgo., 1974; rsch. assoc. Loyola U., Maywood, Ill., 1977-78; intern Rush Presbyn. St. Lukes Hosp., Chgo., 1982-83; resident U. Chgo., 1983; mgr. hosp. products div. Abbott Labs., Abbott Park, Ill., 1986—; bd. govs., dep. gov. Am. Biographical Inst. Rsch. Assn., 1988; vis. prof. Rush Presbyn.-St. Luke's Hosp., Chgo., 1985, faculty assoc., 1985; assoc. investigator, asst. prof. medicine King Drew Med. Ctr., UCLA, 1985—; practical cardiology panel experts, 1988; Med. World News Rev. panel, 1988. Contbr. articles to profl. and scholarly jours. Bd. govs. Art Inst. of Chgo., 1985—, aux. bd., 1988—, mem. multiple benefit coms., 1984—, vice chmn. Capital Campaign, 1984-85; mem. pres. com. Landmark Preservation Council, Chgo., 1984—, chmn. multiple coms. polit. candidates, 1986; bd. dirs. Marshall unit Chgo. Boys Clubs, 1984—; mem. benefit com. Hubbard St. Dance Co. 10th Gala, 1988, Victory Garden's Theatre Annual Benefit, 1988. Internat. Coll. Surgeons fellow, 1982. Mem. AMA, Am. Coll. Physicians, Am. Fedn. for Clin. Research, So. Med. Assn., Ill. State Med. Soc., Chgo. Med. Soc., Am. Acad. Med. Dirs., Nat. Acad. Arts & Scis., Dizziness and Balance Disorders Assn. Am. (bd. dirs.).

ENGELBERG, ELAINE A., educator; b. N.Y.C., Mar. 18, 1930; d. Hyman and Anna (Fried) Rosen; m. Edward Engelberg, July 27, 1950; children: Stephen Paul, Michael Joseph, Elizabeth Joyce. BA, Bklyn. Coll., 1951; postgrad., London Sch. Econs., 1975-76; MA, Boston U., 1981; postgrad., Brandeis U., 1982—. Personnel asst. USES, Eugene, Oreg., 1951-52; statis. asst. Dept. Army, Madison, Wis., 1952-55, Cavendish Lab., Cambridge, Eng., 1956-57; rsch. asst. U. Mich., Ann Arbor, 1959-60; tchr. Lexington (Mass.) High Sch., 1968—; master tchr. in charge curriculum and student tchrs., 1988-89; on sabbatical leave on gender issues Brandeis U., 1982-83. Recipient Outstanding Tchr. award U. Chgo., 1983, Tchr. of Global Issues award Clark U., 1989. Mem. Mass. Coun. Social Studies, Am. Psychol. Assn. (high sch. affiliate), Edn. for Living in Nuclear Age, Educators for Social Responsibility (organizer), NOW, MADD, Phi Beta Kappa, Pi Lambda Theta. Jewish. Home: 58 Turning Mill Rd Lexington MA 02173 Office: Lexington High Sch 251 Waltham St Lexington MA 02173

ENGELEITER, SUSAN SHANNON, federal official, former state legislator; b. Milw., Mar. 18, 1952; m. Gerald Engeleiter; children: Jennifer, Brian. B.S., U. Wis., 1974, J.D., 1981. Mem. Wis. Assembly, 1974-79; legis. asst. to Gov. Lee Dreyfus, 1979-80; mem. Wis. Senate, 1980-89, asst. minority leader, 1982-84, minority leader, 1984-89; adminstr. SBA, Washington, 1989—. Recipient award 1 of 10 best Rep. state legislators Nat. Rep. Legis. Assn., 1986, award Wis. Assn. Future Farmers Am., 1986. Mem. AAUW, ABA, Wis. Bar Assn., Camelot Forest Civic Assn. (past pres.), Nat. Woman's Bus. Coun. (chair. 1989—). Lutheran. Office: SBA 1441 L St NW Washington DC 20416 also: SBA 1441 L St NW Rm 926 Washington DC 20416*

ENGELHARD, DIANE MARY, public relations executive; b. Merrill, Wis., Apr. 23, 1964; d. Robert John and Karen Rae (Beebe) E. BS, U. Wis., Stevens Point, 1982-86. Youth coord., field rep. U.S. Sen. Robert W. Kasten, Jr., Milw., 1986; account exec. Bishea, Meili & Assocs., Inc., Milw., 1987-89; dir. pub. rels. Universal Med. Bldgs., L.P., Milw., 1989—. State chairperson Wis. Coll. Rep., Stevens Point, 1985-86; mem. Milw. Art Mus. Mem. Walker's Point Ctr. Arts. Roman Catholic.

ENGELHARDT, SISTER M(ARY) VERONICE, educational psychologist, nun; b. Syracuse, N.Y., Mar. 29, 1912; d. Herman Joseph and Ella Marguerite (Collins) E. B.S.Ed., Cath. U., 1937, M.A., 1938, Ph.D., 1962. Joined Third Franciscan Order Roman Catholic Ch., 1929; tchr. elem. and secondary schs., 1933, 38-52; instr. edn. St. Francis Normal Sch., Syracuse, 1942-56, diocesan and community sch. supr., 1952-56; dean women, head dept. edn. and psychology Chaminade Coll. Honolulu, 1957-60; clin. instr. Child Ctr. Cath. U., Washington, 1961, supr. student teaching, 1962; instr. edn., 1961-62; head dept. edn. and psychology Maria Regina Coll., Syracuse, 1962-68, founder, dir. Reading and Speech Clinics, 1962-68; founder, dir. Franciscan Learning Ctr., Franciscan Acad., Syracuse, 1968-85; asst. mother gen. Third Franciscan Order, 1965-71, chmn. personnel bd., 1972-75, chmn. communications bd., 1972-78, also editor community newsletter, 1983-89; with Tutorial Program Maria Regina Ctr., Syracuse, N.Y., 1989—; counselor, ednl. psychologist Most Holy Redeemer Sch., Tampa, Fla. Author: Looking at God's World, Creatures in God's World, Learning More About God's World; editor: Creative Arts, 1981-83. Mem. Am. Psychol. Assn., Am. Ednl. Research Assn., Internat. Reading Assn., Nat. Soc. Poets, Nat. League Am. Pen Women (1st v.p. Central N.Y. br. 1981-83). Address: Tutorial Program Maria Regina Ctr 1024 Court St Syracuse NY 13208

ENGELKING, ELLEN MELINDA, pattern company executive, real estate broker; b. Columbus, Ind., May 12, 1942; d. Lowell Eugene and Marcella (Brane) E.; children: Melissa Claire Fairbanks John David Prohaska, Ellen Margaret Prohaska. Student Sullins Coll., 1961, Franklin Coll., 1961-62, Ind. U., 1963. Vice chmn., pres., chief exec. officer Engelking Patterns, Inc., Columbus, Ind., 1980—; guest speaker bus. sch. Ind. U., Bloomington, 1985-86, Ball State U., Muncie, Ind., 1986. Campaign chmn. Am. Heart Assn., Bartholomew County, 1980-81; chmn. Mothers March of Dimes, Bartholomew County, 1967; sec. Bartholomew County Rep. Com., 1976-80; bd. dirs. Found. for Youth, 1975-78, Quinco Found., 1978-79; protocol hostess Pan Am. Games X, Indpls., 1987. Mem. Alumni Coun. Franklin Coll., U.S. C. of C., Ind. C. of C., Columbus Area C. of C. (vice chmn. bd. 1990), Ind. Mfg. Assn., Am. Foundrymens Soc., Internat. Platform Assn., Acad. of Model Aeronautics, Jr. Achievement Mfg. Assn. (bd. dirs. 1990—), Delta Delta Delta. Roman Catholic. Avocations: study and present adaptation of Shaker work ethic, remote-controlled aircrafts, literature, oil painting. Office: Engelking Patterns Inc PO Box 607 Columbus IN 47202

ENGEMAN, MRS. JACK See BEER, ALICE STEWART

ENGERRAND, DORIS DIESKOW, educator; b. Chgo., Aug. 7, 1925; d. William Jacob and Alma Willhelmina (Cords) Dieskow; BS in Bus. Adminstrn., N. Ga. Coll., 1958, B.S. in Elementary Edn., 1959; M. Bus. Edn., Ga. State U., 1966, Ph.D., 1970; m. Gabriel H. Engerrand, Oct. 26, 1946 (dec. June 1987); children: Steven, Kenneth, Jeannine. Tchr., dept. chmn. Lumpkin County High Sch., Dahlonega, Ga., 1960-63, 65-68; tchr., Gainesville, Ga., 1965; asst. prof. Troy (Ala.) State U., 1969-71; asst. prof. bus. Ga. Coll., Milledgeville, 1971-74, asso. prof., 1974-78, prof., 1978—, chmn. dept. info. systems and communications, 1978—; cons. Named Outstanding Tchr. Lumpkin County Pub. Schs., 1963, 66; Outstanding Educator bus. faculty Ga. Coll., 1975, Exec. of Yr. award, 1983. Fellow Assn. for Bus. Communication (v.p. S.E. 1978-80, 81-84, bd. dirs.), So. Mgmt. Assn., Nat., Ga. (Postsecondary Tchr. of Yr. award 10th dist. 1983, Postsecondary Tchr. of Yr. award 1984) bus. edn. assns., Am., Ga. (Educator of Yr. award 1984, Parker Liles award 1989) vocat. assns., Profl. Secs. Internat., Office Systems Rsch. Assn., Ninety-nines Internat. (chmn. N. Ga. chpt. 1975-76, named Pilot of Year N. Ga. chpt. 1973). Methodist. Contbr. articles on edn. to profl. publs. Home: 1674 Pine Valley Rd Milledgeville GA 31061 Office: Ga Coll Milledgeville GA 31061

ENGHOLM, MARY KORSTAD MUELLER, art education consultant, author; b. Seattle, May 7, 1918; d. Martin and Mary Emily (Green) Korstad; BE, UCLA, 1940; MEd, St. Lawrence U., 1949; postgrad. Syracuse U., 1950-52; m. Walter Weigel, Dec. 22, 1949 (div. 1967); 1 child, Erica K. Weigel; m.

Paul G. Mueller, Nov. 9, 1968 (dec. 1976); m. Glenn S. Engholm, Aug. 6, 1982. Tchr. art Riverside (Calif.) City Schs., 1944-46; art supr. Canton (N.Y.) Sch. Dist., 1946-48; asst. prof. art SUNY, Potsdam, 1948-58; art supr. Watertown (N.Y.) City Sch. Dist., 1962-67; cons., lectr. U. Nebr., Lincoln, 1966; art supr. Bakersfield (Calif.) City Sch. Dist., 1967-78; instr. art, continuing edn. Calif. State U., Bakersfield, 1971-74, 76, adj. instr., lectr., 1982-83; free-lance art cons., Bakersfield, 1978-84. Trustee Kern County Arts Council, 1976-83, Bakersfield Sister City Com., 1978-83, H. Weil Child Guidance Clinic, 1980-83, Kern County Mus. Alliance, 1978-84; pres. Kern County chpt. Young Audiences of Am., 1978-83; pres. bd. dirs. H. Weill Meml. Child Guidance Clinic, 1981-83; community adv. Jr. League Bakersfield, 1980-83; v.p. cen. coast Am. Scandinavians Assn., 1986-87, pres., 1987-88; bd. dirs. Lori Brock Jr. Mus., 1975-78. Recipient Bienniel Nat. Colby award Sigma Kappa, 1990. Mem. AAUW, Nat. Art Edn. Assn., Monterey History & Art Assn. (bd. dirs. 1986—), Nat. League Am. Pen Women, Inc., Greater Bakersfield C. of C. (Woman of Yr. 1983), Calif. Art Edn. Assn. (trustee 1979-82), Kern County Art Edn. Assn. (pres. 1982-83), Calif. Tchrs. Assn., Delta Kappa Gamma. Episcopalian. Author: (with Thomas and Wells) Elementary Art, 1967, Murals: Creating an Environment, 1979, One to Follow: A Tale of Two Women, 1990; contbr. articles to profl. jours.

ENGLAND, BRENDA, air transportation financial executive; b. Pine Bluff, Ark., May 24, 1940; d. W.D. and Hortense (Jones) E.; m. Joseph N. Norris, Sept. 1980; children: Billy, Sharon, Kthy, Ken, Benjy, J.J., Kellye. Student, U. Ark., 1969, Stephen Coll., 1977, La. State U., 1988. Owner The Parsons Co., Pine Bluff, 1970-74, Nat. Tax Svc., Ft. Smith, Ark., 1974-80, Palace Grocery, Alexandria, La., 1980-82; chief fin. officer La. Air Freight Corp., Alexandria, 1982—; founded, owned and operated several businesses. Recipient Youth award, 1965. Mem. Mental Health Assn., Local & State, Women's Info. and Networking Group (originator, dir.), Soroptimists (pres. 1977, nat. bd. dirs.). Home: PO Box 3988 Baton Rouge LA 70821

ENGLAND, LYNNE LIPTON, lawyer, speech pathologist, audiologist; b. Youngstown, Ohio, Apr. 11, 1949; d. Sanford Y. and Sally (Kentor) Lipton; m. Richard E. England, Mar. 5, 1977. B.A., U. Mich., 1970; M.A., Temple U., 1972; J.D., Tulane U., 1981. Bar: Fla. 1982, U.S. Dist. Ct. (mid. dist.) Fla. 1982, U.S. Ct. Appeals (11th cir.) 1982; cert. clin. competence in speech pathology and audiology. Speech pathologist Rockland Children's Hosp. (N.Y.), 1972-74, Jefferson Parish Sch., Gretna, La., 1977-81; audiologist Rehab. Inst. Chgo., 1974-76; assoc. Trenam, Simmons, Kemker, Scharf, Barkin, Frye & O'Neill, Tampa, Fla., 1981-84; asst. U.S. atty. for Middle Dist. Fla., Tampa, 1984-87, asst. U.S. trustee, 1987—. Editor Fla. Bankruptcy Casenotes, 1983. Recipient clin. assistantship Temple U., 1972-74. Mem. Am. Speech and Hearing Assn., Fla. Bar Assn., ABA, Hillsborough County Bar Assn., Assn. Trial Lawyers Am., ALTA, Am. Bankruptcy Inst., Fed. Bar Assn., Order of Coif. Jewish. Avocations: tennis, golf, playing French horn and piano. Office: US Trustees Office 4921 Memorial Hwy Ste 340 Tampa FL 33634

ENGLANDER, PAULA TYO, lawyer; b. Syracuse, N.Y., Dec. 25, 1951; d. Howard James and Pauline Harriet Henderson; m. Ronald Englander, Jan. 24, 1971; children: David, Lisa. BA, SUNY, 1978; JD, Syracuse U., 1981. Bar: Colo. 1982, U.S. Dist. Ct. Colo. 1983, U.S. Ct. Appeals (10th cir.) 1983. Law clerk Kintzele & Collins, Denver, 1982-83; pvt. practice law Denver, 1983—; cons. Orthotic and Prosthetic Assn., 1980; bd. dirs. Orthopedic Techs., Inc., Syracuse, Aurora (Colo.) Orthopedics, Inc., Gaines Brace & Limb, Inc., Lakewood, Colo., 1981. Editor The Prism, 1989—; contbr. articles to profl. jours. Asst. founding mem., asst. coordinator Export Assistance Program, 1984-87. Mem. ABA (legal econs. sect.), Alliance Profl. Women (founding mem., publs. com. 1988-89, bd. dirs. 1988—), Colo. Women's Bar Assn., Colo. Bar Assn. (gen. and small firm sect., coun. mem., sec.). Home and Office: 303 E 17th Ave Ste 700 Denver CO 80203

ENGLE, JANET PATRICIA, clinical pharmacist, educator; b. Summit, N.J., Aug. 25, 1959; d. Thomas Edward and Patricia (Walsh) E.; m. Andrew J. Donnelly, Aug. 2, 1986. BS in Pharmacy, Rutgers U., Piscataway, 1982; PharmD, U. Ill., Chgo., 1985. Lic. pharmacist, N.J., Ill. Nat. Pharm. Coun. and SAPhA intern Schering Corp., Kenilworth, N.J., 1981; staff-clin. pharmacist Overlook Hosp., Summit, 1979-83; pharmacist practitioner Eye and Ear Infirmary U. Ill. Hosp., Chgo., 1983-85; cons. pharmacist Clin. Pharmacy Cons., Inc., Morton Grove, Ill., 1986; staff pharmacist Walgreen's Pharmacy, Chgo., 1984-87; clin. pharmacy coord. West Side VA Med. Ctr. U. Ill., Chgo., 1986—; clin. asst. prof. Coll. of Pharmacy U. Ill., Chgo., 1986—; lectr. various profl. and community groups; reviewer of profl. books, manuscripts, papers. Contbr. articles to profl. jours. Chmn. Bldg. com. Vernon Pk. Townhomes Assn., Chgo., 1989. Recipient grants Roche Pharms. 1986-87, 87-89, 89—, Am. Cyanamid 1987-88; named one of Outstanding Young Women Am., 1988. Mem. Internat. Pharmacy Fedn. (hosp. pharmacists sect., acad. sect.), Am. Assn. Colls. of Pharmacy (profl. affairs com. 1988—, chmn. tchrs. pharmacy practice awards com. 1988-90, acad. mgmt. system 1988—), Am. Pharm. Assn. (chmn. elect acad. pharmacy practice and mgmt. sect. 1989—, vice chmn. publs. com. 1989, mem. various coms.), Am. Soc. Hosp. Pharmacists Assn. (pres. Greater Chgo. chpt., bd. dirs. 1988—, pres. 1989-90, mem. various coms.), Ill. Coun. Hosp. Pharmacists, Phi Lambda Sigma. Office: U Ill Coll of Pharmacy 833 S Wood St M-C 886 Chicago IL 60612

ENGLE, JEANNETTE CRANFILL, medical technologist; b. Davie County, N.C., July 7, 1941; d. Gurney Nathaniel and Versie Emmaline (Reavis) Cranfill; m. William Sherman Engle (div. 1970); children: Phillip William, Lisa Kaye. Diploma, Dell Sch. Med. Tech., 1960; BA, U. N.C., Asheville, 1976. Instr. Dell Sch. Med. Tech., Asheville, 1960-67; rotating technologist Meml. Mission Hosp., Asheville, 1967-68, asst. supr. hematology, 1968-71; supr. Damon Subs. Pvt. Clinic Lab., Asheville, 1971-73; chemistry technologist VA Med. Ctr., Durham, N.C., 1973-74, 75-76, supr., 1974-75; asst. supr. microbiology VA Med. Ctr., Salem, Va., 1976-79; supr. rsch. Med. Svc. Lab., Salem, 1979—; reviewer Jour. Club, Roanoke-Salem, Va., 1980—. Author: (poem) Reflections on a Comet, 1984; contbr. numerous articles and abstracts on med. tech. to profl. jours., 1982—. Mem. The Acting Co. Ensemble. Democrat. Episcopalian. Home: 4775 Green Valley Rd Huntington WV 25701 Office: VA Med Ctr Lab 1540 Spring Valley Dr Huntington WV 25704

ENGLE, MARY ALLEN ENGLISH, physician; b. Madill, Okla., Jan. 26, 1922; d. Russell C. and Vera (Apperson) English; m. Ralph Landis Engle, Jr., June 7, 1945; children: Ralph Landis III, Marilyn Elizabeth. A.B. cum laude, Baylor U., 1942; M.D., Johns Hopkins U., 1945; D.Sc. (hon.), Iona Coll., 1982. Diplomate: in pediatric cardiology Am. Bd. Pediatrics. Intern pediatrics Johns Hopkins Hosp., 1945-46, asst. dir. pediatrics out-patient dept., 1946-47, fellow pediatric cardiology, 1947-48; asst. resident Sydenham Hosp. Contagious Diseases, Balt., 1946; asst. resident N.Y. Hosp., 1948-49, asst. attending pediatrician, 1952-60, assoc. attending pediatrician, 1960-62, attending pediatrician, 1962—; instr. pediatrics Johns Hopkins, 1946-48; fellow pediatrics Cornell U., 1949-50, faculty pediatrics, 1950—, prof., 1969—, Stavros S. Niarchos prof. pediatric cardiology, 1979—; med. dir. Insts. in Care Premature Infant, 1952-55, dir. pediatric cardiology, 1963—; Mem. Pres.'s Adv. Panel on Heart Disease, 1972. Mem. editorial bd. Jour. Am. Coll. Cardiology, Am. Heart Jour., Heart and Lung, Yearbook of Cardiology. Recipient Spence-Chapin award for contbns. to pediatrics, 1958; award of merit Philoptochos Soc. N. and S. Am., 1978; Woman of Conscience award Nat. Council Women, 1979; citation Nat. Bd. Med. Coll. Pa., 1979; Disting. Achievement award Baylor U., 1981, Disting. Alumna award Baylor U., 1988; hon. fellow Cornell U. Med. Coll. Alumni. Mem. Am. Acad. Pediatrics (charter mem. sect. cardiology, founder's award cardiology sect. 1983), Am. Heart Assn. (Award of Merit 1975, Helen B. Taussig award 1976, dir. 1976-78), N.Y. Heart Assn. (dir. 1980-86), N.Y. Acad. Medicine, N.E. Pediatric Cardiology Soc., Harvey Soc., Soc. Pediatric Research, Assn. European Pediatric Cardiologists (corr.), Royal Soc. Med. (dir. Found. 1983—), Am. Coll. Cardiology (master tchr. 1969, 73, 76, trustee 1974-79, Theodore and Susan Cummings Humanitarian award, 1973, 76), Am. Pediatric Soc., Pediatric Cardiology Soc. Greater N.Y., N.Y. Cardiology Soc. (dir., pres. 1986-87), Explorers' Club, Internat. Garden Club, Phi Beta Kappa, Alpha Omega Alpha. Presbyterian. Home: 1 Country Club Ln Pelham Manor NY 10803 Office: NY Hosp Pediatric Cardiology 525 E 68th St New York NY 10021

ENGLE, PEGGY LORRAINE SMALLING, nursing director; b. Hutchinson, Kans., Jan. 27, 1956; d. Charles E. and Callie E. (Peterson) Smalling; m. Dale L. Engle, Oct. 14, 1978; 1 child, Christopher M. Student in pre-nursing, Mid-Am. Nazarene Coll., Olathe, Kans., 1977; AD in Nursing, Johnson County Community Coll., 1981. Co-owner Englesoft, Oketo, Kans.; staff nurse Community Meml. Hosp., Marysville, Kans.; dir. nursing Wymore (Nebr.) Good Samaritan Ctr.; dir. nursing Nebr. Health Care Assn., 1986, Good Samaritan Soc. Workshop for Dir. of Nursing, 1986, AIDS on Long Term Care, 1987; organizer Health Fair, Wymore Good Samaritan Ctr., Quality Assurance Program; revised care plan program at H. Hosp. Vol. blood mobile, blood pressure clinic ARC, Wymore; mem. adv. bd. for lic. pratical nurse program and assoc. degree nursing program S.E. Community Coll.; nurse cons., mem. Steve Boyda senatorial campaign, 1988. Mem. Nat. Gerontol. Nursing Assn., Nebr. Nurses Assn., Nebr. Health Care Assn. (vice chairperson 1988-89, chairperson 1989-90), Am. Nurses Assn. Home: Rte 1 Box 109 Oketo KS 66518 Office: Wymore Good Samaritan Ctr 105 East D St Wymore NE 68466

ENGLE, SANDRA LOUISE, state agency administrator; b. Grand Haven, Mich., Aug. 5, 1949; d. J. Edward and Ethel Caroline (Westerhouse) E. AA, Muskegon Community Coll., 1969; BA in Bus. Adminstrn., Mich. State U., E. Lansing, 1971; postgrad., Mich. State U., 1984-86. Clk. and dept. mgr. Meijers Inc., Muskegon, Grand Haven, Grand Rapids, Mich., 1971-74; ins. agt. Prudential Ins. Co., Muskegon, 1974; bookkeeper Muskegon Correctional Facility, 1974-75; bus. office mgr. Kent County Dept. of Social Svcs., Grand Rapids, Mich., 1975-76; budget and fin. dir. Mich. Dept. of Licensing and Regulation, Lansing, 1976-86; mgmt. svcs. div. dir. Mich. Dept. of State, Lansing, 1986-87; dept. svcs. area dir. Mich. Dept. of Edn., Lansing, 1987; dep. bur. dir. Mich. Dept. of Labor, Lansing, 1987-89; asst. treas. Mich. Employment Security Commn., Detroit, 1989-90; adm. svc. dir. Mich. Dept. Labor, Lansing, 1990—. Bd. dirs. R.E. Olds Transp. Mus., 1989. Mem. Humane Soc. of U.S., Mich. Region Nat. Coun. Corvette (sec., treas. Lansing chpt. 1977-82, 84), Greater Lansing Vintners Club, World Wildlife Fund, Doris Day Animal League, Habitat for Humanity. Home: 3201 Continental Ave Lansing MI 48911 Office: Mich Dept of Labor 1 W Ottawa St Lansing MI 48909

ENGLEHART, JOAN ANNE, trade association executive; b. Susquehanna, Pa., Sept. 15, 1940; d. George Louis and Muriel Elois (Washburn) Wanatt; m. Dale John Englehart, Nov. 24, 1958. AAS, Broome Community Coll., 1981; BS in Cultural Studies, Empire State Coll., 1984; postgrad., SUNY, Binghamton, 1984. Office mgr., coord. sales Bush Transformer Corp., Endicott (N.Y.), Boston, 1959-65; mgr., cons. Snelling & Snelling, Binghamton, Endicott, 1965-71; tchr., mgr. Can. Acad., Kobe, Japan, 1971-72; adminstrv. asst. GAF Corp., Binghamton, 1973-80; owner Typewriting, Endicott, 1980-85; exec. v.p. Tioga County C. of C., Owego, N.Y., 1985-87, pres., 1988—; exec. v.p. Chamber Found., 1987—. Mem. Broome Community Coll. Found., Binghamton, 1984-87; mem. scholarship com. Civic Club Binghamton, 1984-87; mem. Health Fair Adv. Bd., Broome and Tioga Counties, 1985-87; sec.-treas. Tioga County C. of C. Found., 1987—; chmn. sustaining membership com. Broome United Way, Binghamton, 1986-87; mem. planning process com. Broome-Delaware Tioga BOCES Svc. Area, 1989—; bd. dirs. N.Y.-Pa. Health Systems Agy., 1989—. Recipient award Boy Scouts Am., 1979, Evening Student Assn., 1981, award Friends Binghamton Libr., 1982, Athena award C. of C., 1986; named Woman of Achievement Broome County Status of Women Coun., 1978. Mem. AAUW (life, pres. 1986-87), Nat. Assn. Women in C. of C.'s (charter mem.), Assn. C. of C. Execs., Zonta (pres. Tioga County area club 1985-89, mem. Internat. Bd., Gov. Dist. II 1982-84, named Woman of Achievement 1985, 86, 87, 88). Republican. Baptist. Home: 4 Lancaster Dr Endicott NY 13760 Office: Tioga County C of C 188 Front St Owego NY 13827

ENGLER, MARKY ANN, financial analyst; b. Winona, Minn., Apr. 18, 1956; d. Phillip Peter and Haryette Louise (Zimdars) Newman; m. Robert Wayne Engler. BA in Acctg., Winona (Minn.) State U., 1977; postgrad., U. Wis., LaCrosse, 1989—. Supr. Hawkins, Ash, Baptie & Co., LaCrosse, Wis., 1984-87; dir. adminstrn. and fin. Catholic Charities, Inc. Diocese of LaCrosse, Wis., 1987-90; exec. dir. Catholic Charities, Inc. Diocese of LaCrosse, 1990—. Mem. Wis. Inst. CPA's, Am. Inst. CPA's, Jaycees (Treas.). Home: N6948 Sunrise Ln Holmen WI 54636

ENGLISH, CINDY MARIE, attorney; b. Jacksonville, Ark., Jan. 5, 1957; d. Richard L. and Ruby Nell (Davis) E.; m. Philip B. Gallaher, Aug. 11, 1979. BA, Ark. State U., 1974-78; JD, U. Ark. Sch. of Law, 1978-81. Asst. atty. gen. Arkansas Atty Gen., Little Rock, Ark., 1981-82; assoc. Cathy, Goodwin, Hamilton and Moore, Attys., Paragould, Ark., 1982-84; trust officer First Commercial Bank, Little Rock, Ark., 1984-85; assc. counsel Arkansas Ins. Dept., Little Rock, Ark., 1985—. Mem. Ark. Bar Assn., ABA, Pulaski County Bar Assn. Unitarian. Office: Ark Ins Dept Univ Tower Bldg Little Rock AR 72204

ENGLISH, ELIZABETH STACY, programmer/analyst, consultant; b. Milford, Pa., July 16, 1959; d. Henry Bruce and Elizabeth Deborah (Hodges) Copelman; m. Curtis R. English III, Nov. 27, 1982; 1 child, Elizabeth Deborah. BA, Pa. State U., 1982; postgrad., West Chester U., 1983-85. Programmer-analyst Info. System Consultants, Springhouse, Pa., 1983-85, C.G.A., Phila., 1985-86, Matrix Orgn., Inc., Wayne, Pa., 1986—. Mem. Chester County (Pa.) Pro Choice Coalition, 1989—, Young Dems. of Chester County, 1976, Arbor Day Found., 1990; jr. mem. Chester County Soc. Prevention Cruelty to Animals, 1975-77, Ams. for Religious Liberty, 1990—. Mem. Pa. State Alumni Assn. (life), Chester County Pa. State Alumni Assn., NOW. Republican. Methodist. Home: 218 Llandovery Dr Exton PA 19341 Office: Matrix Orgn Inc 950 W Valley Rd Suite 2602 Wayne PA 19087

ENGLISH, ELLEN DARLENE, elementary school educator; b. Mattoon, Ill., Dec. 16, 1952; d. Floyd Dale and Irma Jane (Hensley) Robinson; m. William Dean English, Feb. 13, 1971; children: Gregory David, William Scott, Joseph Dean, Brian Matthew. BS, Ind. State U., 1987. Cert. elem. educator, Ill. Reading tchr. Marshall (Ill.) Community Dist. 2, 1987—; libr. City of Marshall, 1986—; dir. summer camp Clark County Handicapped Assn., Marshall, 1988—. Mem. Home Extension Club, Kappa Delta Pi. Roman Catholic. Home: Rte 3 Box 173 Marshall IL 62441 Office: Marshall Community Unit Schs 503 Pine St Marshall IL 62441

ENGLISH, LINDA RYAN, human resources executive; b. Atlanta, Mar. 27, 1951; d. James Robert and Eva Louise (Robinson) Smith; m. Kent Alan Ryan, July 3, 1970 (div. July 1981); children: Kevin Michael, Kristen Margaret; m. Patrick Irl English. AA, DeKalb Community Coll., Clarkston, Ga., 1977; BA, Ga. State U., 1979. Mgr. pers. and benefits Neptune Internat., Atlanta, 1972-74; regional asst. Denny's, Inc., Atlanta, 1974-76; legal sec. Powell, Goldstein, Frazer & Murphy, Atlanta, 1976-80; mgr. benefits J.M. Tull Industries, Norcross, Ga., 1980-82; regional asst. Talbert, Cox & Assocs., Atlanta, 1982-84; dir. human resources U. Tampa, Fla., 1985-90; v.p. human resources U. Tampa, 1990—; cons. Prime Design Engring. Cons., Tampa, 1988. Author: A Southern Heritage, 1981. Troop leader Girl Scouts Am., Tampa, 1984-86; mem. The Tampa Connection, 1987, Bay Area Group on Health. Recipient Outstanding Service award Girl Scouts Am., 1985, Pierce Jr. High Sch., Tampa, 1986. Mem. NAFE, ASPA. Republican. Lutheran. Office: U Tampa 401 W Kennedy Blvd Tampa FL 33606

ENGLISH, RUTH ANN COWDER, personnel consultant; b. Kearney, Nebr., June 3, 1948; d. John Leonard and Ethel Lou (Brower) Cowder; m. J.D. English, Aug. 7, 1971; 1 child, Liesl Michele. BS, SW Tex. State U., 1970; MA, U. No. Colo., 1978. Tchr. Churchill High Sch., San Antonio, 1971-72; edn. dir. Houston Telephone Fed. C.U., 1972-73; property mgr. English Properties Mgmt., San Antonio, 1972—; instr. ESL U.S. Civil Service, San Antonio, 1975-79; instr. continuing edn. Alamo Community Coll. Dist., San Antonio, 1984—; pres., cons., instr. Profl. Growth Systems, San Antonio, 1986—. Vol. Keystone Sch., San Antonio, tchr., 1989—; troop leader San Antonio Area council Girl Scouts U.S., 1984—. Presbyterian. Home and Office: 3734 Litchfield St San Antonio TX 78230

ENGLISH, RUTH HILL, artist, consultant, educator; b. Andover, Mass., Feb. 7, 1904; d. Herbert Hudson and Ada Jane (Wells) Hill; grad. Abbot Acad., Andover; received pvt. instrn.; m. A. Evans Rephart, June 28, 1929; children—Susan K. (Mrs. Howard K. Simpson), Katharine K. (Mrs. Christopher R. Barnes); m. 2d, E. Schuyler English, July 4, 1959. Faculty Hampton Inst., 1924-25, Bryn Mawr Art Center (later Main Line Center of Arts), 1945-65, Wayne Art Center, 1947-49; dir. Hedgeabout Studio, Gladwyne, Pa., 1965—; lectr., art cons. throughout East, 1960-70. Past mem. womens bd. Pa. Hosp.; mem. womens bd. Babies Hosp., 1934-39. Mem. Hist. Soc. Early Am. Decoration (pres. William Penn chpt. 1950-51), Pa. Craftsmans Guild (dir. 1952-54). Republican. Episcopalian. Clubs: Acorn, Skytop (Pa.), Athenaeum. Home: 47 E Wynnewood Rd Merion PA 19066 also: Skytop PA 18357 Studio: 1124 Rose Glen Rd Gladwyne PA 19035

ENGLISH, SALLY ANN, computer executive; b. Portsmouth, N.H., May 2, 1946; d. Anthony Joseph and Sally May (Griskiewicz) Daniels; m. Robert Glenn English, Jan. 25, 1969; children: Kimberly, Melissa, Jill. BS, U. N.H., 1968, M, 1976. Med. technologist Deaconess Hosp., Boston, 1968-69; med. technologist Exeter (N.H.) Hosp., 1970-75, lab. mgr., 1975-80; asst. chief technologist data processing Emory Hosp., Atlanta, 1980-81; ednl. rep. HBO & Co., Atlanta, 1982-83, installation rep. of new tech., 1983-84, product specialist, 1984-85, mgr. clin. systems installation and support, 1985-86, nat. mgr. clin. services, 1986-87, nat. sales exec., 1987-88, div. sales exec., 1988-89; nat. sales specialist ADAC Labs., Milpitas, Calif., 1989—. Mem. NOW, Nat. Assn. Profl. Saleswomen, Nat. Assn. Female Execs. Republican. Roman Catholic.

ENGLUND, GAGE BUSH, dancer, educator; b. Birmingham, Ala., Sept. 7, 1931; d. Morris Williams and Margaret Wallace (Gagé) Bush; student Sweet Briar Coll.; student (Ford Found. scholar) Sch. Am. Ballet, 1960; m. Richard Bernard Englund, Dec. 1, 1959; children: Alixandra, Rachel Rutherford. Founder, Birmingham Civic Ballet, 1952; mem. Robert Joffrey Ballet, N.Y.C., 1957-60, soloist, 1959-60; mem. Am. Ballet Theatre, N.Y.C., 1960-63, Huntington Dance Ensemble, L.I., N.Y., 1968-69; soloist Dance Repertory Co., 1969-72; tchr. ballet, assoc. chmn. Friends of Am. Ballet Theatre, N.Y.C., 1972—; rehearsal coach Am. Ballet Theatre II, 1973-85; mem. scholarship com. Am. Ballet Theatre Sch., N.Y.C., 1974—; dir. Ala. By-products Corp., 1971-77; rehearsal coach Joffrey Ballet II, 1985—. Bd. dirs. Children's Hosp. Clinic, Birmingham, 1955-57, Spoleto Festival, U.S.A., 1980-83, Ala. State Ballet, 1967—, Birmingham Civic Ballet, 1952-67; trustee Ballet Theatre Found., 1974-87, v.p., 1980-81; trustee Episcopal Sch. of N.Y., 1979-83, Chapin Sch., 1982—, Animal Med. Center, N.Y.C., 1982—, Cancer Research Inst., 1984—. Recipient Silver Bowl award Birmingham Festival of Arts, 1955; named Queen of Birmingham Festival of Arts, 1957. Mem. Am. Guild Mus. Artists, Colonial Dames Ala., Jr. League N.Y.C. Episcopalian. Clubs: Lakewood Country, The Colony. Home: PO Box 469 Point Clear AL 36564

ENGLUND, LORI JEAN, financial products company executive; b. Omaha, Sept. 20, 1961; d. Earl Winston and Barbara Jean (Van Wie) McClellan; m. Leslie Donald Englund, Feb. 12, 1960; 1 child, Jessica Marie. BS, Ariz. State U., 1983. Mktg. rep. GNA, Austin, Tex., 1983-84, sr. mktg. rep., 1985-86; regional acct. exec. GNA, Austin and Long Beach, Calif., 1987; regional mktg. dir. GNA, Long Beach, 1988—. Mem. Nat. Assn. Female Execs., Fin. Inst. Mktg. Assn. Republican. Roman Catholic. Office: GNA 320 Golden Shore Ave Suite 120 Long Beach CA 90802

ENGRAM, BEVERLY LEIGH, state legislator; b. Feb. 2; m. Del Engram. Mem. from dist. 34, Ga. Senate. Democrat. Office: Ga State Senate Atlanta GA 30334 Other: PO Box 908 Fairburn GA 30213*

ENIS, EVA MARIE, English language educator; b. Champaign, Ill.; d. Leo Clarence Beasley and Bernice Martin; m. Vert Enis, Sept. 4, 1942;. Student, Joliet (Ill.) Jr. Coll., 1964; BA, Coll. St. Francis, Joliet, 1968; MA in English, Ea. Ill. U., 1981. Tchr. English lang. St. Francis Acad., Joliet, 1968-73; grad. asst. Ea. Ill. U., Charleston, 1979-80; owner Eva's Plamor Golf, Mattoon, Ill., 1973—; instr. Lake Land Coll., Mattoon, 1981—. Conbr. articles to profl. jours. Named: Initate Mem., Lambda Iota Iau Literary Hon. Soc., 1965. Mem. AAUW, Delta Kappa Gamma. Republican.

ENNIS-SUTHERLAND, JANINE MARIE, investigator; b. Albany, N.Y., May 15, 1958; d. Bernard Woodrow and Awanda Elizabeth (Ahrens) Herbert; m. Patrick Sean Ennis,Nov. 2, 1986 (div. Dec. 1988); m. Keith E. Sutherland, Apr. 21, 1990; children: Nicholas Bernard Ennis, Grant Edward Sutherland. BS in Adminstrn. of Justice, MacMurray Coll., 1984. Pvt. investigator Profl. Investigations, Springfield, Ill., 1984-85; ins. claims investigator Quality, Inc., Tulsa, 1985; pvt. practice paralegal investigator Springfield, Ill., 1985-90; pvt. investigator R.L. Emmons & Assocs., Dayton, Ohio, 1990—. Author: (book) Crystal Images, 1976; newspaper exposé series, 1984. Vol. chmn. Mental Health Assn., Springfield, Ill., 1969-76; mem. Com. for Children, 1988—. Recipient Golden Poets award, 1989, 90. Mem. Nat. Com. for the Prevention of Child Abuse, World Democrat. Family Club Internat.(pres. 1979—). Republican. Lutheran. Office: RL Emmons & Assocs 7865 Paragon Rd Ste 108 Dayton OH 45459

ENRIGHT, STEPHANIE VESELICH, financial company executive; b. L.A., Mar. 24, 1929; d. Stephen P. and Violet (Guthrie) Veselich; m. Robert James Enright (dec. Sept. 1982); children: Craig James, Brent Stephen, Erin Suzanne, Kyle Stephen. BA, U. So. Calif., 1952, MS, 1975. Fin. and engring. cons. Orange County, Santa Ana, Calif., 1976-79; fin. cons. The Sim-Ehrflo Group, Newport Beach, Calif., 1979-81; pres. Enright Fin. Cons., Torrance, Calif., 1981—; fin. columnist Copley Newspapers, 1987—; adj. faculty mem., UCLA, U. So. Calif.; pres. Pacific Home Builders. Contbr. articles to profl. jours. Mem. Com. Assn. of the Peninsula, Palos Verdes, Calif., 1986; found. dir. Little Co. of Mary Hosp., Torrance; bd. dirs. local chpt. YWCA. Mem. Internat. Assn. Fin. Planning (bd. dirs. and officer 9182-84, Planner of Month 1984), Inst. Cert. Fin. Planners, Nat. Assn. Women Bus. Owners, Nat. Assn. Fin. Edn., Registry of Profl. Planners, Torrance C. of C., Centurion Club, Women in Constrn., Trojan Club and League (bd. dirs. 1978-79). Republican. Roman Catholic. Office: Enright Fin Cons Union Bank Tower Ste 900 21515 Hawthorne Blvd Torrance CA 90503

ENRIQUEZ, CAROLA RUPERT, museum director; b. Washington, Jan. 2, 1954; d. Jack Burns and Shirley Ann (Orcutt) Rupert; m. John Enriquez, Jr., Dec. 30, 1989. BA in history cum laude, Bryn Mawr Coll., 1976; MA, U. Del., 1978, cert. in mus. studies, 1978. Personnel mgmt. trainee Naval Material Command, Arlington, Va., 1972-76; teaching asst. dept. history, U. Del., Newark, 1976-77; asst. curator/exhibit specialist Hist. Soc. Del., Wilmington, 1977-78; dir. Macon County Mus. Complex, Decatur, Ill., 1978-81; dir. Kern County Mus., Bakersfield, Calif., 1981—; tchr. mus. studies course U. Calif.-Santa Barbara Extension, 1982; advisor Kern County Heritage Commn., 1981-88; chmn. Historic Records Commn., 1981-88; sec.-treas. Arts Council of Kern, 1984-86, pres. 1986-88; county co-chmn. United Way, 1981, 82; chmn. steering com. Calif. State Bakersfield Co-op Program, 1982-83; mem. Community Adv. Bd. Calif. State Bakersfield, Anthro; Soc. 1986—; bd. dirs. Mgmt. Council, 1983-86, v.p., 1987, pres. 1988; bd. dirs. Calif. Council for Promotion of History, 1984-86, v.p., 1987-88. pres., 1988—; Community Adv. Bd. mem. Calif. State U.-Bakersfield Sociology Dept., 1986-88; mem. Girl Scouts Women's Adv. Com., 1989—. Hagley fellow Eleutherian Mills-Hagley Found., 1977-78; Bryn Mawr alumnae regional scholar, 1972-76. Mem. Nat. Trust for Hist. Preservation, Am. Assn. Mus., Am. Assn. for State and Local History. Unitarian Universalist. Office: Kern County Mus 3801 Chester Ave Bakersfield CA 93301

ENROTH-CUGELL, CHRISTINA ALMA ELISABETH, neurophysiologist, educator; b. Helsingfors, Finland, Aug. 27, 1919; came to U.S., 1956, naturalized, 1962; d. Emil and Maja (Syren) E.; m. David W. Cugell, Sept. 5, 1955. M.D., Karolinska Inst., 1948, Ph.D., 1952. Resident Karolinska Sjukhuset, 1949-52; intern Passavant Meml. Hosp., 1956-57; with Northwestern U., Evanston, Ill., 1959—; prof. neurobiology and physiology dept. biomed-engring. Northwestern U., 1974—; mem. vision research program com. Nat. Eye Inst., 1974-78, mem. nat. adv. eye council, 1980-84. Contbr. articles to profl. jours. Recipient Ludwig von Sallman award Internat. Assn. Research in Vision and Ophthalmology, 1982. Mem. Am. Assn. Research in Vision and Ophthalmology (co-recipient Friedenwald award 1983), Soc. Neurosci., Am. Physiol. Soc., Am. Acad. Arts and Scis., Physiol. Soc. (U.K.) (assoc.). Office: Northwestern U McCormick Sch Engring Technl Inst 2145 Sheridan Rd Evanston IL 60208

ENSOR, PATRICIA LEE, librarian; b. Birmingham, Ala., July 28, 1959; d. William Lee Ensor and Sharon Patricia (Garrick) Tavari; m. Jeffrey Coleman Binyon, Dec. 17, 1983; children: Leslie Patricia, Bryant Weigand. BA, U. Ala., Birmingham, 1979; MLS, U. Ala., Tuscaloosa, 1981. Libr. intern IBM Programming Lab., Santa Tusca, Calif., 1980; libr. asst. Health Scis. Libr. U. Ala., Tuscaloosa, 1980-81; reference libr. Calif. State U., Long Beach, 1981-83; info. svcs. libr. Ind. State U., Terre Haute, 1984—; cons. Applied Computing Devices, 1988, Rose-Hulman Inst. Tech., 1986—. Contbr. articles to profl. jours. Mem. AAUW (pres. 1990—), Ind. Online Users Group (pres. 1986-87). Democrat. Home: 621 S Center Terre Haute IN 47807 Office: Ind State U Libraries Terre Haute IN 47809

ENTINE, LYNN BERGMANN, freelance writer; b. Detroit, Apr. 28, 1947; d. Kenneth Frederick and Frances Jean (Marsh) Bergmann; m. Steven Mark Entine, June 13, 1970; children: Caryn Elizabeth Aldrich, Jeffrey Aaron Bergmann. BA in English, Mich. State U., East Lansing, 1964; MA in English, SUNY, Buffalo, 1972; MS in Agrl. Journalism, U. Wis., 1978. Program coord. Madison extension U. Wis. Ext., Madison, 1972-82; free-lance writer Madison, 1983—; editorial cons. Md. Computing Mag., N.Y.C., 1984-89; newsletter editor engring. dept. U. Wis., Madison, 1983—. Contbr. articles to profl. jours.; author (with curriculum guide) Our Great Lakes Connection, 1985; author: (with others) (booklet) Getting the Word Out, 1980. Nate Haseltine Meml. fellow Coun. for Advancement of Sci. Writing, 1977. Mem. Wis. Regional Writers, Midwest Writers Assn., Coun. for Wis. Writers (newsletter editor 1985-88, v.p. 1987-88, pres. 1988-90), Women in Communications, Inc. (newsletter editor Madison chpt. 1988-89). Home and Office: 2227 Van Hise Ave Madison WI 53705

ENTMAN, BARBARA SUE, broadcaster, writer, photographer; b. Glen Cove, N.Y., Sept. 24, 1954; d. Bernard Entman and Rose (Jacobson) Entman Pachter. BA, U. Conn., 1976. Freelance writer/photographer, 1975—; announcer, publicity dir. Sta. WHUS-FM, Storrs, Conn., 1975-76; announcer, copywriter Sta. WKAJ-AM-FM, Saratoga Springs, N.Y., 1976-77; traffic coord. Sta. WMHT-FM, Schenectady, 1977-79; ops. dir. Sta. WNIU-FM, Dekalb, Ill., 1980-82; ops. mgr. Sta. KUHF, Houston, 1982-86, announcer, 1987-88, membership dir., 1988-89; spl. projects dir. Sta. KPFT-FM, Houston, 1989—; media cons. Ill. Heart Assn., DeKalb, 1982, Sojourner Women's Bookstore, DeKalb, 1980-81; exhibited photographs in galleries and univs., 1970—; contbr. articles and poetry to mags. and newspapers; newsletter editor Congregation Aytz Chayim, Houston, 1983-84. Founder DeKalb Area Women's Network, 1981; bd. dirs. newsletter editor Art Resources Open to Women, 1977-79; mem. Chgo. Artists Coalition, 1981-82; mem. adv. bd. Houston Women's Caucus for Art, 1985-90, chairperson publicity nat. conf., 1988; del. Tex. Dem. Conv., 1984, 86, 90; mem. performing arts screening com. Houston Internat. Festival, 1989—. Mem. Houston Ctr. Photography, Houston Assn. Vol. Adminstrs. Office: Sta KPFT-FM 419 Lovett Blvd Houston TX 77006

ENTREKIN, LANG MOORE, chemical executive; b. Charleston, W.Va., Feb. 16, 1943; d. Kermit Russel and Olga Adriena (Lang) Moore; m. Wayne Gaines Entrekin, Dec. 22, 1963; children: Sonya Anne, Michael Gaines. BS in Chemistry, Newberry (S.C.) Coll., 1963; MS in Textiles and Clothing, Winthrop Coll., 1980. Chemist E.I. DuPont, New Ellington, S.C., 1963; lab technician Med. U. S.C., Charleston, 1964-67; lectr. chemistry Winthrop Coll., Rock Hill, S.C., 1980-84; pres., salesperson Lang Chem. Sales, Inc., Rock Hill, 1984—. Active Rock Hill Jr. Welfare League, 1976—, York County Med. Aux., Rock Hill. Mem. Am. Chem. Soc. (treas. 1986-87), Am. Assn. Textile Chemists and Colorists, Phi Kappa Phi, Delta Zeta. Republican. Lutheran.

EOVALDI, MARINA LUCCO, psychologist, educator; b. Highland, Ill., Oct. 3, 1940; d. Joe E. and Mary K. (Tepatti) Lucco; m. Thomas L. Eovaldi, June 9, 1962; children: Mischa, Derek. BA, U. Ill., 1962; MA, Northwestern U., 1974, PhD, 1977. Lic. psychologist, Ill. Program dir. U. Ill. YWCA, Champaign, 1962-63; tchr. Champaign High Sch., 1963-64, Bateman Sch., Chgo., 1965-66, Near North Montessori Sch., Evanston, Ill., 1967; tchr., adminstr. Chiaravalle Montessori Sch., Evanston, 1968-85; psychologist, coord. sch. and community progs. Family Inst., Chgo., 1987—; lectr., U. Wis., Ashland, Drake U., Des Moines, Beaver Coll., Jenkentown, Pa., Nat. Coll., Evanston, Northwestern U., Evanston; prof. adviser DePaul U., Chgo., 1987-89; tchr., trainer Montessori tchr. tng. courses, 1969-90; cons. to schs. and community orgns.; presenter workshops. Contbr. articles to profl. publs. Mem. Dewey Community Coun., Evanston, 1969-77, Evanston Community Child Care Coun., 1975-85; mem. task force Ill. Child Witness Project; bd. dirs. Counterpane, 1983-85, Nanny, Inc., 1983. Mem. Am. Psychol. Assn., Am. Assn. Marital and Family Therapists, Am. Montessori Soc. (bd. dirs. 1983-86), Ctr. Family Studies Alumni. Home: 2510 Sheridan Rd Evanston IL 60201 Office: Family Inst 680 N Lake Shore Dr Chicago IL 60611

EPHRON, NORA, author; b. N.Y.C., May 19, 1941; d. Henry and Phoebe (Wolkind) E.; m. Dan Greenburg (div.); m. Carl Bernstein (div.); children: Jacob, Max; m. Nicholas Pileggi. B.A., Wellesley Coll., 1962. Reporter N.Y. Post, 1963-68; free-lance writer, 1968—; contbg. editor, columnist Esquire mag., 1972-73, sr. editor, columnist, 1974-78; contbg. editor N.Y. mag., 1973-74. Author: Wallflower at the Orgy, 1970, Crazy Salad, 1975, Scribble Scribble, 1978, Heartburn, 1983; screenwriter: (with Alice Arlen) Silkwood, 1983, Heartburn, 1986, When Harry Met Sally, 1989, My Blue Heaven, 1990; co-exec. producer, co-screenwriter: Cookie, 1989. Mem. Writers Guild Am., Authors Guild, P.E.N., Acad. Motion Picture Arts and Scis. Office: care Sam Cohen ICM 40 W 57th St New York NY 10019*

EPP, MARY ELIZABETH, project manager; b. Buffalo, Aug. 7, 1941; d. John Conrad and Gertrude Marie (Murphy) Winkelman; m. Harry Francis Epp, Aug. 31, 1963. BA in Math., D'Youville Coll., 1963; MS in Math., Xavier U., 1974, MBA in Fin., 1981, MBA in Mktg., 1987. Systems analyst GE, Evendale, Ohio, 1965-71, Palm Beach Co., Cin., 1972-73; hardware systems engr. Procter & Gamble, Cin., 1973-76; systems engr. CalComp Inc., Anaheim, Calif., 1980-84; software engr. SDRC Inc., Cin., 1984-86; advanced systems project mgr. SAMI/Burke Mktg., Cin., 1986-89; ptnr. The MVI Connection, product mgr. Info. Advantage, Inc., Cin., 1989—; cons. Shelley & Sands, Zanesville, Ohio, 1983-85. Contbr. articles to profl. jours. Mem. Fairfield Charter Rev. Commn., 1981-83. Mem. AAUW (br. treas. 1975-79, state women's chair 1979-80, state treas. 1980-82), NAFE, IEEE, Assn. Computing Machinery (treas. Cin. chpt. 1987-88, pres. 1988-89, program co-chair 1989-90), Nat. Computer Graphics Assn., Nat. Fedn. Music (Ohio fedn. music parade chair 1979-81.), Mercy Hosp. Aux. Club (treas. 1978-79), Musical Arts Club. Republican. Roman Catholic. Home: 4900 Pleasant Ave Fairfield OH 45014 Office: Info Advantage Inc 655 Eden Park Dr Ste 500 Cincinnati OH 45202

EPPES, MAVIS, law records manager; b. Teague, Tex., Jan. 31, 1937; d. Rich and Ruth (Haynie) E. Student, Sam Houston State U., 1955-58. Records mgr. Vinson & Elkins, Houston, 1959—; curriculum adv. com. records mgmt. North Harris County Coll., 1983, 85, 89. Recipient Records Mgmt. award The Office, 1982. Mem. Assn. Records Mgrs. and Adminstrs. (pres. Houston chpt. 1985-86, internat. chmn. legal svcs. industry action com. 1985-87, editor newsletter, info. mgmt. achievement award Houston chpt. 1982, award of Achievement 1984, chpt. Mem. of Yr. 1986, editor Internat. Newsletter award 1988), Bus. Forms Mgmt. Assn., DAR, Colonial Dames, Daus. Founders and Patroits, Soc. Descendants of Francis Eppes I of Va., Jamestown Soc. Republican. Baptist. Home: 1310 Springrock Ln Houston TX 77055 Office: Vinson and Elkins 2968 First City Tower 1001 Fannin Houston TX 77002

EPPLEY, FRANCES FIELDEN, educator, author; b. Knoxville, Tenn., July 18, 1921; d. Chester Earl and Beulah Magnolia (Wells) Fielden; m. Gordon Talmage Cougle, July 25, 1942; children:Russell Gordon Eppley, Carolyn Eppley Horseman; m. Fred Coan Eppley, Mar. 8, 1953; 1 child, Charlene Eppley Sellers. BA in English, Carson Newman Coll., 1942; M.A., Winthrop Coll., 1963. Tchr., East Corinth (Maine) Acad., 1942-43; tchr. pub. schs., Charlotte, N.C., 1950-53, 59-83, Greenville, S.C., 1954-56, Spartanburg, S.C., 1957-58; head start tchr., summers 1964-68. Mem. hist. com. N.C. Bapt. Conv., 1985-88. Alpha Delta Kappa grantee, 1970. Mem. NEA, N.C. Social Studies Conf., Writers Assn., Alpha Delta Kappa, Pi Kappa Delta, Alpha Psi Omega. Baptist. Author: First Baptist Church of Charlotte, North Carolina: Its Heritage, 1981, History of Flint Hill, 1983, The First Astrologer, 1983, Sammy's Song, 1984, No Show Dog, 1985, Sun Signs for Christians, 1985, Astrology and Prophecy, 1987, Our Heavenly Home, 1987, Men Like-, 1987, A Hammer in the Land, 1988, Aunt Lillian's Seafoam Candy, 1988, Women's Lib in the Bible, 1988, William Penn, 1988, Columbus Was a Christian, 1988, Horoscopes of the Presidents, 1988, Messiah, 1989; (musical drama): The Place To Be, 1982, Praise in the West, 1987; (musical show): Songs of The People, 1983; (song): Katie, 1985, (cantata) How Come, Jesus?, Stubborn Stella and The Sitting Stone, 1990, Columbus: The Race Home, 1990.

EPSTEIN, BARBARA, editor; b. Boston, Aug. 30, 1929; d. H.W. and Helen (Diamond) Zimmerman; children: Jacob, Helen. B.A., Radcliffe Coll., 1949. Editor N.Y. Rev. of Books, N.Y.C., 1963—. Office: NY Rev of Books 250 W 57th St New York NY 10019

EPSTEIN, HARRIET PIKE, public relations executive; b. N.Y.C.; d. Samuel and Sonia (Kuchinok) Pike; m. Stanley H. Epstein; children: Lois N., Susan A. B.A. cum laude, NYU. Newspaper reporter Newsday, Garden City, N.Y., 1956-60; free-lance writer, 1961-69; pub. rels. exec. Townsend Communications Inc., Syosset, N.Y., 1970-75; mng. editor L.I. Bus. Rev., Plainview, N.Y., 1975-80; v.p. Howard Rubenstein Assocs., N.Y.C., 1980-81; dir. communications N.Y. State Assembly Ways and Means Com., Albany, 1981-87; v.p. GreyCom, Inc., N.Y.C., 1987-88; v.p. media rels. Fin. Svcs. Corp., N.Y.C., 1988—. Contbr. articles to various newspapers. Pres. Princeton Park Civic Assn., Jericho, N.Y., 1963-65. Mem. L.I. Women's Network (membership chmn. 1980-82), N.Y. Women in Communications, Pub. Rels. Soc. Am., N.Y. Press Club, Phi Beta Kappa. Office: Fin Svcs Corp 110 William St New York NY 10038

EPSTEIN, HELGA DREIFUSS, retired educational adminstrator; b. Cologne, Germany, Aug. 30, 1924; came to U.S., 1940; d. Leo and Margot (Steuer) Dreifuss; m. Irving A. Epstein, Feb. 15, 1948; children: Judith Ann Epstein Sciabarrasi, Jacquelyn D. Epstein Davis. Diploma, Burbank Hosp. Sch. Nursing, Fitchburg, Mass., 1947; BS, Boston U., 1967, EdM, 1970. RN, Mass.; cert. supt., prin., tchr., guidance dir., Mass. Supervisory and gen. nurse Burbank Hosp., 1947-63, instr., asst. prin. Sch. Practical Nursing, 1963-67; dir. guidance Ashby (Mass.) Sch. System, 1967-71; coord. allied health, community svc. and guidance Montachusett Regional Vocat. Tech. Sch. Dist., Fitchburg, 1971-80; dir. adult tng. and retng. Minuteman Regional Vocat. Tech. Sch., Lexington, Mass., 1981-87; instr. edn. Fitchburg State Coll., 1977-79; Former mem. Mass. community edn. adv. coun., chmn. adult edn. com., ad hoc coms., cons. Mass. Dept. Edn.; cons. Nat. Evaluations, Inc., Ednl. Tng. Svcs., Inc.; mem. adv. com. Mt. Wachusett Community Coll. Mem. Holocaust Speaker's Bur., Mass., since 1980; mem. sch. com. Mass. Regional Vocat. Tech. Sch. Dist., since 1981, past chmn., now vice chair; del. Mass. Dem. Com., 1984, 86, 88; vol. Dukakis for Pres., Mass., N.H., Ga., 1987-88; bd. dirs., leadership Series Vocat. Indsl. Clubs Am., Mass., 1987—; div. chmn. United Way North Cen. Mass., 1989; bd. dirs. Friends Children's Aid and Family Svc., Fitchburg and Leominster, 1990; guest speaker numerous profl. and community orgns. Named Mother of Yr., B'nai B'rith, Fitchburg and Leominster, 1986. Mem. Am. Vocat. Assn., Am. Assn. Sch. Adminstrs., Mass. Vocat. Assn., Mass. Assn. Vocat. Adminstrs., Mass. Sch. Com. Assn. (chmn. vocat. div. 1989—), AAUW, Phi Delta Kappa. Home: 94 Seneca St Fitchburg MA 01420

EPSTEIN, SELMA, pianist; b. Bklyn.; d. Samuel and Tillie (Schneider) Schechtman; m. Joseph Epstein, May 30, 1950. Grad. Juilliard Sch., 1949. Debut as concert pianist Carnegie Hall, N.Y.C., 1942; pianist numerous concerts, recitals; recorded numerous albums and cassettes; composer piano pieces. Most recent recitals: Luton, Eng., St. John's, London, U.S. premiere of the Percy Grainger piano concerto; numerous lecture-recitals including univs. and profl. orgns. Lectr. U.S. Info. Svc., Europe, Australia, Japan, Hong Kong, Okinawa, New Zealand, introducing music of U.S. 20th Century composers, women and black composers; editor: piano music by Lili Boulanger, Percy Grainger, Maria Hester, Parke and Dame Ethel Smyth; pianist for Epstein Duo; rec. artist: (album) Selma Epstein Plays Percy Grainger, Vol. 1, numerous cassettes of live performances. Grantee U.S Internat. Studies, 1960—. First American to teach full time at an Australian Conservatory, Newcastle Conservatory, 1972-75. Founder of Group Piano Studios and author of 8 group teaching manuals. Co-founder Md. Women's Symphony; founder, bd. dirs. Chromattica USA Chamber Music Group of Balt. Recs. of Women Composers; invited to be 1st U.S. artist in residence at RTHK in spring, 1991. Mem. Am. Grainger Soc. (pres.), Am. Thyroid Soc. (v.p. Md. chpt.), Internat. Congress Women in Music (bd. dirs. Mid-Atlantic region), West Point Parents Club of Md., Va. and D.C. (founder 1979). Avocations: painting, gardening, reading, cooking. Home and Office: 2443 Pickwick Rd Dickeyville MD 21207

EPSTEIN, WILMA GELLER, advertising agency executive; b. N.Y.C., Jan. 6, 1946; d. Jack R. and Dorothy (Brill) Geller; m. Jeffrey L. Epstein, Oct. 27, 1968; 1 child, Jill. Student, Bernard Baruch Sch. Bus., 1963-64, New Sch. for Social Rsch., 1964-65. Asst. planner Batten, Barton, Durstine & Osborne, N.Y.C., 1965-66; planner West Weir & Bartel, N.Y.C., 1966-68; planner Ogilvy & Mather, N.Y.C., 1968-76, asst. media dir., 1976-79, sr. v.p., assoc. media dir., 1979-86, mem. oper. bd., 1986—; bd. dirs., chmn. Bus. Publs. Audit, N.Y.C., 1982-88. Bd. dirs. Jewish Guild for Blind, N.Y.C., 1974-79. Named Industry Media Allstar Mktg. & Media Decisions Mag., 1987. Office: Ogilvy & Mather 309 W 49th St New York NY 10019

EPTING, CYNTHIA RENEE, tax accountant; b. Detroit, July 15, 1959; d. Comer Lee and Alma (Rhodes) De Shazo; m. Jay Edward Epting, Sept. 10, 1988. BS in Acctg., Miss. U. for Women, 1981. CPA, La. Sr. tax acct. McDermott, Inc., New Orleans, 1981-88, Arthur Young, Ft. Worth, 1988-89, Alcon Labs., Inc., Ft. Worth, 1989—. Mem. Embroidery Guild Am. Home: 5304 Ft Concho Fort Worth TX 76137

EPTING, REBECCA ANN, vocational rehabilitation counselor; b. Anderson, S.C., Aug. 30, 1940; d. Carl Lafayette and Elisabeth (Gillespie) E. BS, Clemson U., 1962. Adminstrv. asst. U.S. Dept. State, Washington, 1962; sec., adminstrv. asst. Citizens & So. Nat. Bank S.C., Columbia, 1963; casework asst. S.C. Vocat. Rehab. Dept., Columbia, 1963-67; vocat. rehab. counselor Ohio Bur. Vocat. Rehab., Columbus, 1967; vocat. rehab. counselor S.C. Vocat. Rehab. Dept. and S.C. Dept. Mental Health, Columbia, 1967-85, Anderson, 1985—. Mem. adv. bd., Clemson U. Coll. Liberal Arts, 1982—; v.p. Northlake Adv. Coun., Anderson, 1989; chmn. various ch. coms., 1989. Mem. S.C. Rehab. Counseling Assn. (treas. 1985—), Nat. Rehab. Assn., S.C. State Employees Assn., Clemson U. Class of 1962 Alumni Assn. Methodist. Home: 1912 Northlake Dr Anderson SC 29625 Office: Harris Psychiat Hosp PO Box 2907 Anderson SC 29622

ERARD, BARBARA HUGHES, lawyer; b. Indpls., Mar. 22, 1955; d. William Shannon and Marianne (Hanson) Hughes; m. Robert Edward Erard, Aug. 9, 1980; children: Matthew Shannon, Nicholas Hanson. BA magna cum laude, Amherst Coll., 1977; JD cum laude, U. Mich., 1980. Bar: Mich. 1980, U.S. Dist. Ct. (ea. dist.) Mich. 1980, U.S. Dist. Ct. (we. dist.) Mich. 1986, U.S. Ct. Appeals (6th cir.) 1987. Ptnr. Dickinson, Wright, Moon, Van Dusen & Freeman, Detroit, 1980—. Contbr. articles to legal jours. Mem. Detroit Bar Assn., Mich. Def. Trial Counsel (appellate com. 1987—), Oakland County Bar Assn., Common Cause, Amnesty Internat. Democrat. Episcopalian. Office: Dickinson Wright et al 800 1st Nat Bldg Detroit MI 46226

ERBACHER, KATHRYN ANNE, editor, art writer, marketing consultant; b. Kansas City, Mo., Dec. 11, 1947; d. Philip Joseph and Thelma Lillian (Hines) E. BS in English Edn., U. Kans., 1970; BA magna cum laude in Art, Metro State Coll., Denver, 1983. Reporter, Kansas City Star (Mo.), 1970-71; newswriter Washington U., St. Louis, 1972-76; copy editor Kansas City Star-Times (Mo.), 1976-79; editor Petro-Lewis Corp., Denver, 1979-82; assoc. Artours, Inc., Denver, 1983-84; assoc. editor arts and travel editor Denver Mag., 1984-86; freelance arts writer, editor, mktg. cons., 1986—; internat. editor Gates Rubber Co., Denver, 1987—. Creative dir. TV shorts for contemporary art collection Denver Art Mus., 1983. Mem. Metro State Coll. Alumni Bd. Dirs., 1986-87, co-chair 1987 Metro State Coll. Alumni Awards Dinner, Denver; bd. govs. Metro State Coll. Found., 1986-87; mem. program com. Colo. Bus. Com. for the Arts, 1989—; mem. pub. affairs com. Denver Ctr. for the Performing Arts., 1989—. Recipient award for arts writing Denver Partnership, 1986, award for Artbeat column in Denver mag. Colo. MAC News, 1986, also award for spl. fashion sect. Dressing the Part; co-recipient award for Gates Rubber Co. Global Communications Bus./Profl. Advt. Assn., 1988. Mem. Denver Art Mus. Avocations: visual art, theater, films, travel, Spanish language. Home: 1539 Platte St Denver CO 80202 Office: Gates Corp 900 S Broadway Denver CO 80209

ERBEZ, ELIZABETH ANNE, mutual funds executive; b. Portland, Oreg., Aug. 14, 1963; d. Richard Stephen and Cathryn Eva (Carter) Hodl; m. George Thomas Erbez, Feb. 18, 1990. BA in History, Linfield Coll., 1985. Lic. ins. agt. Asst. wholesaler John Nuveen & Co., Inc., San Francisco, 1985-86; sales assoc. Nordstrom, Walnut Creek, Calif., 1986-88; asst. wholesaler banking div. Van Kampen Merritt, Walnut Creek, 1986-87, asst. wholesaler ins. and fin. planning group, 1987-88; mutual funds specialist The Boston Co., San Francisco, 1988-89, v.p. Funds Distributor, Inc. div., 1989—. Mem. Nat. Assn. Personal Fin. Advs., Southern Calif. Planned Giving Roundtable, Clayton Women's Club, Sigma Kappa Phi (historian 1984-85, v.p. 1985, Sr. of Yr. 1985). Republican. Office: The Boston Co 400 Montgomery St San Francisco CA 94104

ERCK, RUBY JEWEL, motel owner; b. Bailey, Tex., Feb. 6, 1928; d. Grover Cleveland and Rosa Emilee (Vaughn) Shockley; m. Louis Charles Erck, June 15, 1946; children: Rose Ann, Louis Charles Jr., Phyllis, Lisa, Pennie (dec.). Grad. high sch. Office mgr. various radio stas., various locations, 1962-76; owner Reserve St. Inn, Missoula, Mont., 1981—. Sec.-treas. Missoula Hospitality Assn., 1989 , pres., 1990. Republican. Baptist. Address: Reserve Street Inn 4825 N Reserve St Missoula MT 59802

ERDEN, SYBIL ISOLDE, artist; b. N.Y.C., Nov. 30, 1950; d. Mark and Annelise (Stautner) E.; m. Philip M. Freund, July 7, 1970 (div. 1978). Student, Acad. of Art, San Francisco, 1970-71, San Francisco Art Inst., 1971-73. lectr. Calif. Coll. Arts and Crafts, 1978, Tempe (Ariz.) Fine Art Ctr., 1985, Collins Gallery, San Francisco, 1986, Collage Art Appreciation Group, Colorado Springs, Colo., 1987, South Park Sch. Dist., Fairplay, Colo., 1987, Al Collins Sch. Graphic Design, 1989-90. Shows include San Francisco Art Inst., 1973, The Bush Street Gallery, San Francisco, 1977, The Top Floor Gallery, San Francisco, 1979, I-Beam, San Francisco, 1980, Diablo Valley Coll., Walnut Creek, Calif., 1980, The Stable, San Francisco, 1982, Tempe Fine Arts Ctr., 1985, Collins Gallery, San Francisco, 1986, 89, 90—, Berkeley (Calif.) Art Ctr., 1986, The Cave, San Francisco, 1981, Alwun House, Phoenix, 1985, 87, 88, 89, 90 (award 1989), Grand Canyon Coll., Phoenix, 1988, N.Mex. Jr. Coll., 1988, 90 (award 1990), San Francisco State U., 1988, Pa. State U., 1989, Ohio State U, 1989, Mendocino Art Ctr., 1990, Jewish Community Ctr., Denver, 1990, Smithsonian Mus. Archive of Am. Art, Washington, Cerro Coso Community Coll., Kern County, Calif., 1990—; executed mural office of Dr. Peter Eckman, San Francisco, 1977, HandBall Express, San Francisco, 1981. Mem. Ariz. Visionary Alternative (founder, dir. 1984-90), Am. Surrealist Initiative, Nat. Tattoo Assn. Democrat. Jewish.

ERDMAN, BARBARA, visual artist; b. N.Y.C., Jan. 30, 1936; d. Isidore and Julia (Burstein) E. Postgrad., Chinese Inst., 1959-60; BFA, Cornell U., 1956. Visual artist Santa Fe, 1977—; guest critic Studio Arte Centro Internat., Florence, Italy, 1986; guest lectr. Austin Coll. Sherman, Tex., 1986; mem. Oracle Conf. Polaroid Corp., nationwide, 1986-88. Exhibited in numerous group shows, 1959—; one man shows include Aspen Inst., Baca, Colo., 1981, Scottsdale (Ariz.) Ctr. for the Arts, 1988; collections include N.Mex. Mus. Fine Arts, Santa Fe, IBM Corp., N.Y.C.; author: New Mexico, USA, 1985. Bd. dirs. N.Mex. Right to Choose, Santa Fe, 1981-87, Santa Fe Ctr. for Photography, 1983, pres. bd. 1985-89; mem. N.Mex. Mus. Found., Aluquerque Mus. Found. Mem. Art Student's League (life), Soc. for Photographic Edn. (guest lectr. 1987), Santa Fe Ctr. for Photography (pres., bd. dirs. 1984-89), Nat. Coun. Arts. Home and Office: 1070 Calle Largo Santa Fe NM 87501

ERDMAN, CINDY SUSAN, nurse, financial consultant; b. Allentown, Pa., Feb. 28, 1957; d. Calvin Moitis and Jean Catherine (Kratz) E. BSN, East Stroudsburg (Pa.) U., 1979. RN, Pa.; cert. in chemotherapy adminstrn., critical care, advanced concepts in pediatrics. Float nurse gen. staff St. Luke's Hosp., Bethlehem, Pa., 1979-82, CCU float nurse, 1982-83, nurse inpatient nephrology unit, 1983-87, pediatric nurse, 1987—, acting nurse mgr., 1989.

ERDRICH, KAREN LOUISE, fiction writer, poet; b. Little Falls, Minn., June 7, 1954; d. Ralph Louis and Rita Joanne (Gourneau) E.; m. Michael Anthony Dorris, Oct. 10, 1981; children: Abel, Sava, Madeline, Persia, Pallas, Aza. BA, Dartmouth Coll., 1976; MA, Johns Hopkins U., 1979. Vis. poet, tchr. N.D. State Arts Council, 1977-78; tchr. writing Johns Hopkins U., Balt., 1978-79; communications dir., editor Circle-Boston Indian Council, 1979-80; textbook writer Charles Merrill Co., 1980. Author: (textbook) Imagination, 1981, (poems) Jacklight, 1984, Baptism of Desire, 1989, (novels) Love Medicine, 1984 (fgn. edits. in over 18 langs., numerous awards including Nat. Book Critics Circle award for best work of fiction 1984), The Beet Queen, 1986, Tracks, 1988; contbr. numerous short stories, essays and poems to profl. jours. and popular mags. Johns Hopkins U. teaching fellow, 1979; Macdowell Colony fellow, 1980; Yaddo Colony fellow, 1981; vis. fellow Dartmouth Coll., 1981; Guggenheim fellow, 1985-86; recipient numerous awards for profl. excellence including Nelson Algren award, 1982, Pushcart prize, 1983, Nat. Mag. Fiction award, 1983, 87, First prize O. Henry awards, 1987. Mem. PEN (exec. bd. 1985-90), Authors Guild. Address: PO Box 70 Cornish Flat NH 03746

ERDTMANN, ELIZABETH TERRY, insurance company executive; b. Bklyn., July 27, 1961; d. Bernhard and Theresa (Muller) E. BBA, Baruch, N.Y.C., 1983; MBA, Coll. of Ins., N.Y.C., 1988. Dir. Polar Internat., N.Y.C., 1977—. photograph published žFall Stream' in Zurich, American Annual Calender, 1987. Recipient; Student Achievement award, The Wall St. Journal, 1988.

EREMIC, KATHLEEN ANN, marketing professional; b. Detroit, Feb. 23, 1952; d. Edward Harry and Helen Gabriella (Daugul) Jablonski; m. David Gregory Eremic, Jan. 8, 1983 (div. 1986). BA in Psychology and Philosophy, Oakland U., 1974; MSW, Wayne State U., 1979. Cert. profl. contracts mgr. Contract specialist Tank-Auto Command U.S. Army, Warren, Mich., 1979-83; procurement analyst Ballistic Missile Office, Norton AFB, Calif., 1983-87, Air Force Systems Command Hdqrs., Andrews AFB, Md., 1987—. Mem. Nat. Contract Mgmt. Assn. (cert., treas. San Bernardino Valley chpt. 1986-87). Roman Catholic. Home: 7902-22 Crows Nest Ct Laurel MD 20707 Office: Hdqrs Air Force Systems Command PKXB Andrews AFB MD 20334-5000

ERICHSEN-HUBBARD, ISABEL JANICE, educator; b. LaCrosse, Wis., June 18, 1935; d. Frank Peter August and Janice May (Grutzmacher) Erichsen; B.S. with honors, U. Wis., Madison, 1957, M.S., 1979, postgrad., 1980; m. Allan Paterson, Apr. 4, 1959; children—Janel Isabel, John Allan. Tchr., Kenosha (Wis.) Bd. Edn., 1957-60; tchr., supr. Madison (Wis.) Bd. Edn., 1968—; cooperating tchr. sr. program U. Wis. master tchr. seminars, 1978—; pvt. piano and vocal coach, 1950—; choir dir. St. Mary's Lutheran Ch., Kenosha, 1959-61; mem., soloist Madison Meth. Ch. Diocesan Choir, 1981-83, U. Wisc. Choral Union Choir. Program chair YWCA, 1961-65; chmn. UNICEF, 1960, Coop. Nursery Sch., 1960; info. chmn. Am. Cancer Soc., Dane County, 1960-68; bd. dirs. , sec. Friends of Meth. Hosp., 1986-87, also vol. escort, info. desk, chapel musician; R.S.V.P. Sch. Liaison, 1977-88; adjucator Wis. Assn. Music Schs., 1984; vol. Am. Players Theatre, 1987—; active Methodist Women's Soc., United Ch. Women, Madison Civic Assn., U. Wis. Cooperating Mentor Program, 1987-88, Opera Buffs, Wis. Exec. Mansion Guides, Wexford Homeowners Assn. Recipient Carol award Madison Jaycette Club, 1966, 3d grand prize Wis. State Jour. Cookbook, 1971, Golden Apple award Madison Met. Sch. Dist., 1988. Mem. NEA, Wis. Music Assn. (vocal adjucator 1985—), Wis. Edn. Assn., Madison Tchrs., Inc., Lafollette Area Lang. Arts Cadre, Madison Met. Sch. Dist. Human Relations Cadre, U. Wis. Alumni Assn. (life), Sigma Alpha Iota (Sword of Honor, past pres.), Chi Omega (alumni sec. 1970-87), Pi Kappa Delta. Clubs: Cherokee Country, Jr. Golf (dir. 1974-75). Author: Reading Techniques Using the Newspapers, Magazines, 1975; Spell It Again Sam,

1978; Hidden Curriculum, 1979; contbr. to Kenosha Kindergarten Teacher's Handbook, 1958. Home: 26 E Newhaven Circle Wexford Village Madison WI 53717-1051 Office: 2421 E Johnson St Madison WI 53704

ERICKSON, GAIL, lawyer; b. Pasadena, Calif., Feb. 9, 1934; d. Alfred Louis and Helen Hield (Baker) E. BA, Stanford U., 1955; JD, Harvard U., 1958. Bar: N.Y. 1959. Atty. W. R. Grace & Co., N.Y.C., 1958—, now sr. v.p., gen. counsel, sec. Mem. ABA. Democrat. Club: Harvard. Office: W R Grace & Co 1114 Ave of the Americas New York NY 10036

ERICKSON, LEA ELLA, dental educator; b. Pocatello, Idaho, Aug. 28, 1947; d. Jerry C. and Deloris L. (Sayler) Sims; m. Richard D. Webb; children: Nicholas Richard, Janet Marie, Amy Webb Riffe; m. John Robert Erickson, Mar. 26, 1983. AS, Idaho State U., 1969, BS, 1973; DDS, U. Md., Balt., 1978. Cert. GPR. Pvt. practice dental hygiene Pocatello, 1969-75; pvt. practice dentistry Sandy, Utah, 1979-89; clin. instr. U. Utah, Salt Lake City, 1982-89, fellow gerieatrics, 1989—; lectr. Idaho State U., 1969-75; adj. prof. Weber State Coll., Ogden, Utah, 1979-82; bd. dirs. Bethany Coll., Lindsborg, Kans.; cons. Wasatch Canyon Eating Disorders, Salt Lake City, 1985-89; speaker in field. Contbr. articles to profl. jours. Cons., Denture Access Program, Salt Lake City, 1980—; adv. com. Health Screening Ctr., Salt Lake City, 1981-86, Dental House Calls Program, Salt Lake City, 1990. Mem. ADA, Utah Dental Assn. (ho. of dels. 1988-91), Am. Soc. Geriatric Dentists, Salt Lake Dist. Dental Soc. (bd. dirs. 1988-90). Lutheran. Home: 7165 S 2780 E Salt Lake City UT 84121 Office: Univ Utah Dental Edn Bldg 518 Salt Lake City UT 84112

ERICKSON, LINDA RAE, educator; b. Huron, S.D., Aug. 17, 1948; d. Robert Emil and Esther (Schorzman) E. BS, U. Nebr., 1966; MA, U. No. Colo., Greeley, 1970; cert., U. Denver, 1990. Cert. elem. tchr., adminstr., prin. Spl. edn. resource tchr. Ignacio, Colo., 1983-85; elem. tchr. Woodland Park, Colo., 1985-86; tutor spl. edn. Am. Sch. London, 1987; elem. tchr. Borough of Brent, London, 1987, Internat. Sch. Hampstead, London, 1987-88; tchr. spl. edn. Carronhill Sch. for Handicapped, Stonehaven, Scotland, 1988-89; elem. tchr. Littleton (Colo.) Pub. Schs., 1970-83, 89—; workshop facilitator Littleton Pub. Schs., 1977-88, 90—; workshop presenter Nat. Coun. Tchrs. English, Nat. Coun. Social Studies, WNET TV Sta. Active Fawcett Soc., London, 1987-89, NEA-Colo. Edn. Assn. Women's Caucus, 1979—. Woman of Yr. nominee Littleton Jaycees, 1982; fed. grantee Use of Group Paperbacks in the Elem. Classroom, 1978—. Mem. NEA (women's leadership tng. cadre 1978-85), Colo. Edn. Assn., Littleton Edn. Assn. (bd. dirs., chair unit-bargaining team 1976-85), Internat. Reading Assn. (Pikes Peak chair 1986, workshop presenter), Colo. Assn. Sch. Execs., NOW, Alpha Delta Kappa, Phi Delta Kappa. Democrat. Lutheran. Home: 439 E Saddlewood Circle Highlands Ranch CO 80126 Office: Sandburg Elem 6900 S Elizabeth Littleton CO 80122

ERICKSON, MARILYN T., psychology educator; b. Bruckton, Mass., Apr. 30, 1936; children: Lars Carl, Nils Porter, David Lee. BA, Brown U., 1957, MA, 1959; PhD, U. Wash., 1961. Lic. psychologist. From asst. prof. to assoc. prof. U. N.C., Chapel Hill, 1961-71; assoc. prof. U. N.C., Greensboro, 1971-76; prof. psychology VA. Commonwealth U., Richmond, 1976—. Office: Va Commonwealth U Box 2018 Richmond VA 23284

ERICKSON, NANCY SALOME, lawyer, educator; b. Orange, N.J., Sept. 26, 1945; d. George Hugh and Salome Celestia (Brennesholtz) E.; 1 child, Laura. BA, Vassar Coll., 1967; JD, Bklyn. Law Sch., 1973; LLM, Yale U., 1979. Bar: N.Y. 1974, U.S. Supreme Ct. 1983. Assoc. Botein, Hays, Sklar & Herzberg, N.Y.C., 1973-75; asst. prof. to assoc. prof. N.Y. Law Sch., N.Y.C., 1975-80; asst. prof. to assoc. prof. Coll. Law Ohio State U., Columbus, 1980-88; vis. assoc. prof. Law Cornell U. Law Sch., spring 1980; disting. vis. prof. Seton Hall U. Law Sch., Newark, 1986-87; asst. corp. counsel N.Y.C. Law Dept., 1987-89; assoc. atty. legis. unit N.Y.C. Human Resources Adminstrn., 1989—. Editor-in-chief Bklyn. Law Sch. Law Rev., 1972-73; contbr. articles on sex discrimination, family law and constl. law to profl. jours. Mem. Soc. Study Women in Legal History (founder, coord. 1980), Assn. Am. Law Schs. (newsletter editor sect. women in legal edn. 1978-87), Am. Soc. Legal History, Soc. Am. Law Tchrs., Met. Women Law Tchrs. Assn. N.Y.C. (founder). Home: 619 Carroll St Brooklyn NY 11215

ERICKSON WILLIAMSON, DONNA CONSTANCE, health care products company executive; b. Schenectady, June 6, 1952; d. Albert Carl and Aurelia Alexandra Erickson; m. Scott Howard Williamson, July 24, 1976; children: Erik, Christopher. BS, Brown U., 1974; MS, MIT, 1976. Dir. domestic planning Travenol Labs., Deerfield, Ill., 1980-82, dir. strategic planning, 1982-83, v.p., 1983-85, v.p. corp. planning and bus. devel., 1985-86; pres., chief exec. officer Omnis Surg., Northbrook, Ill., 1985; corp. v.p. health cost mgmt. group, Baxter Internat., Inc., 1986—; bd. dirs. A.G. Edwards, Inc., 1988. Chief crusader Crusade of Mercy, Chgo., 1983; regional gov. MIT Sloan Club, Chgo., 1983-85, bd. govs. 1989—; trustee Brown U., 1987—; bd. dirs. ARC, Chgo., 1984—, Nat. Fund for Med. Edn., 1989—. Recipient Leadership award YWCA, Chgo., 1980. Mem. The Planning Forum (bd. dirs. 1988—). Club: Econ. (Chgo.). Avocations: cross-country skiing, sailing, bicycling, tennis. Office: Baxter Internat Inc 1 Baxter Pkwy Deerfield IL 60015

ERICSON, RUTH ANN, psychiatrist; b. Assaria, Kans., May 15; d. William Albert and Anna Mathilda (Almquist) E.; student So. Meth. U., 1945-47; BS, Bethany Coll.; MD, U. Tex., 1951. Intern, Calif. Hosp., Los Angeles, 1951-52; resident in psychiatry U. Tex. Med. Br., Galveston, 1952-55; psychiatrist Child Guidance Clinic, Dallas, 1955-63; clin. instr. Southwestern Med. Sch., Dallas, 1955-72; practice medicine specializing in psychiatry, Dallas, 1955—; cons. Dallas Intertribal Coun. Clinic, 1974-81, Dallas Ind. Sch. Dist., U.S. Army, Welfare Dept., Tribal Concerns, alcoholism, Adv. Bd. Intertribal Council. Fellow Am. Geriatrics Assn.; mem. So., Tex., Dallas med. assns., Am. (life), Tex., North Tex. psychiat. assns., Am. Med. Women's Assn., Dallas Area Women Psychiatrists, Alumni Assn. U. Tex. (Med. Br.), Navy League (life), Air Force Assn., Tex. Archaeol. Soc. (life mem.), Dallas Archaeol. Soc. (life mem., pres. 1972-73, 82-84, 89—), South Tex. Archaeol. Soc., N. Mex. Archaeol. Soc., Paleopathology Soc., Internat. Psychogeriatric Assn. (Famous Woman of the 20th Century), Alpha Omega Alpha, Delta Psi Omega, Alpha Psi Omega, Pi Gamma Mu, Lambda Sigma, Alpha Epsilon Iota, Mu Delta. Lutheran. Home: 4007 Shady Hill Dr Dallas TX 75229 Office: 2915 LBJ Freeway Ste 135 Dallas TX 75234

ERIKSON, MARY J., geologist; b. Grove City, Pa., Mar. 29, 1930; d. Emil E. and Gladys Mary (Morton) Ebner; m. Jay Arthur Erikson, Aug. 13, 1955; children: Edward, Erik, Carol. BS in Geology, U. Mich., 1952. Geologist U.S. Geol. Survey, Washington, 1952-53, Denver, 1953-56; engring. geologist Douglas Moran, Inc., Tustin, Calif., 1978-79; editor Bendix Field Engring., Grand Junction, Colo., 1979-80; program analyst Dept. Energy, Grand Junction, 1980-81; geologist U.S. Geol. Survey, Grand Junction, 1981-83; geologist Bur. Land Mgmt., Grand Junction, 1983-85, hazardous materials mgr., 1985-87; hazardous materials mgr. Bur. Land Mgmt., Santa Fe, N.Mex., 1987—. Co-editor: Uranium Resources of the U.S., 1980. Mem. Hazardous Materials Control Rsch. Inst., N.Mex. Hazardous Waste Soc. Home: 3404 Vereda Baja Santa Fe NM 87505

ERIKSON, PENNY LAUREN, advertising executive; b. San Francisco, Jan. 8, 1950; d. V. M. Jr. and Nadine (Palmerton) Hanks; m. Scott R. Erikson, Aug. 19, 1973 (div. May 1980); m. David Hooper, July 31, 1980. BA, U. Calif., Berkeley, 1971. Sales exec. CRM Inc., Del Mar, Calif., 1971-73; research mgr. W.H. Freeman Inc., San Francisco, 1973-76; research group head Ogilvy & Mather, N.Y.C., 1977-80; campaigns mgr. World Wildlife Fund Internat., Gland, Switzerland, 1979-80; v.p., assoc. research dir. Young & Rubicam, N.Y.C., 1980-85, sr. v.p., mgr. client services, 1985—. Office: Young & Rubicam NY 285 Madison Ave New York NY 10017

ERKKILA, KATHLEEN LIISA, real estate professional; b. Gloucester, Mass., Mar. 17, 1947; d. Onni R. and Barbara Louise (Howell) E. BA, U. Mass., 1970. Lic. real estate broker. Co-owner Rusty Nail Inn, Inc., Sunderland, Mass., 1972-83; mgr., buyer Hadley (Mass.) Village Barn, 1972-76; prin. Kathy Stefan Real Estate Inc., Amherst, Mass., 1976-88; mgr. broker devel., mgmt. cons., trainer Gallery of Homes, Inc., Orlando, Fla., 1989-89; pvt. practice Amherst, 1989-90; mgmt. cons. Coldwell Banker Residential Affiliates, Inc., Alexandria, Va., 1990—. Mem. Pioneer Valley Housing Assn., Hadley, 1983-88. Named Realtor of Yr., Franklin-Hampshire County Board of Realtors, 1985. Mem. Mass. Assn. Realtors (chmn. edn. 1985, dean Grad. Realtors Inst. 1985-88, state dir. 1983-84, comml. investment div. 1984-88, regional v.p. 1986-87), Realtors Nat. Mktg. Inst. (cert. residential specialist, cert. real estate brokerage mgr.), Franklin-Hampshire County Bd. Realtors (pres. 1985), Translo (dir. relocation), Zonta (bd. dirs. 1988-89). Home: 10 Quarry St Gloucester MA 01930

ERLANGER, ELLEN RENEE, investment banker; b. New Castle, Pa., Apr. 6, 1953; d. George Sidney Rubenson and Gloria Marion (Friedman) Rubenson Raffel; m. Thomas Nathan Erlanger, Aug. 24, 1985. BS in Journalism cum laude, Ohio U., 1975; postgrad., N.Y.U., 1980-85. Broker office leasing Met. Structures, Chgo., 1976-77, LaSalle Ptnrs. Inc., Chgo., 1978-80; asst. v.p. Chem. Bank-Real Estate, N.Y.C., 1980-81; assoc. real estate Eastdil Realty Inc., N.Y.C., 1982-83; assoc. real estate, investment banking Sonnenblick-Goldman Corp., N.Y.C., 1984-86; v.p. real estate capital mkts. Bankers Trust Co., N.Y.C., 1986—; prin. Erlanger Assocs., Wilton, Conn., 1989—. Claudia Bernard Meml. scholar, 1975. Mem. Young Mortgage Bankers Assn., Mortgage Bankers Assn., Young Real Estate Exec. Div. United Jewish Appeal, Women Communications Inc. (named Outstanding Member, 1975). Home: 132 Seir Hill Wilton CT 06897 Office: Bankers Trust Co 280 Park Ave 23 W New York NY 10015

ERLANSON, DEBORAH MCFARLIN, state program administrator; b. Watertown, N.Y., Oct. 17, 1943; d. Raymond Thomas and Alberta Antoinette (Schultz) McF.; m. David Norman Erlanson, Sept. 10, 1966; 1 child, Joshua David. AA in Liberal Arts, Dutchess Community Coll., 1964; BA in Psychology, Am. Internat. Coll., 1966; MS in Edn., So. Ill. U., 1972. Occupancy tng. coordinator Decatur (Ill.) Housing Authority, 1975-76, target projects program coordinator, 1976-77, spl. services coordinator, 1977-78, asst. dir. planning, 1978-82, dir. program devel., 1982—; speaker various convs., 1978—; cons. Piatt County Housing Authority, Monticello, Ill., 1985—, Woodford Homes, Inc., Decatur, 1985-86. Mem. steering com. Near West Restoration and Preservation Soc., Decatur, 1985-86, sec., 1986; bd. dirs., parent group counselor Macon County Parents Anonymous, Decatur, 1976-80; mem. health div. Decatur Council Community Services, 1978-84. Named one of Outstanding Young Women Am., 1979. Mem. Nat. Assn. Housing and Redevel. Ofcls. (mem. nat. profl. devel. com. 1983—, vice-chmn. 1987-89, nat. task force on product devel. 1987, regional exec. bd., steering com. 1983—, regional v.p. for profl. devel. 1989—, pres. Ill. chpt. 1984-87, exec. bd. Ill. chpt. 1983—, bd. govs. 1987—, chmn. nat. profl. devel. com. 1989—, task force on elderly housing issues 1989), Ill. Assn. Housing Authorities (exec. bd. 1984-87), Decatur Women's Network Assn. (founding mem. 1982, exec. bd. dirs. 1982-85). Home: 465 W Macon St Decatur IL 62522 Office: Decatur Housing Authority 1808 E Locust St Decatur IL 62521

ERLENMEYER-KIMLING, L., psychiatric and behavior genetics researcher, educator; b. Princeton, N.J.; d. Floyd M. and Dorothy F. (Dirst) Erlenmeyer; m. Carl F. E. Kimling. B.S. magna cum laude, Columbia U., 1957, Ph.D., 1961. Sr. research scientist N.Y. State Psychiat. Inst., N.Y.C., 1960-69; assoc. research scientist N.Y. State Psychiat. Inst., 1969-75, prin. research scientist, 1975-78, dir. div. devel. behavior studies, 1978—; asst. in psychiatry Columbia U., 1962-66, research assoc., 1966-70, asst. prof., 1970-74, assoc. prof., psychiatry and human genetics, 1974-78, prof., 1978—; vis. prof. psychology New Sch. Social Research, 1971—; mem. peer rev. group NIH, 1976-80; mem. work group on guidance and counseling Congl. Commn. on Huntington's Disease, 1976-77; mem. task force on intervention Pres.'s Commn. on Mental Health, 1977-78; mem. initial rev. group NIMH, 1981-85. Editor: Life-span Research in Psychopathology, 1986; issue editor: Differential Reprodn., Social Biology, 1971, Genetics and Mental Disorders, Internat. Jour. Mental Health, 1972; mem. editorial bd.: Social Biology, 1970-79, Schizophrenia Bull., 1978—, Jour. Preventive Psychiatry, 1980—. Recipient Merit award NIMH, 1989; NIMH grantee, 1966-69, 71—, Scottish Rite Com. on Schizophrenia grantee, 1970-74, 84-87, 89-91, W.T. Grant Found. grantee, 1978-86, MacArthur Found. grantee 1981. Fellow Am. Psychol. Assn., Am. Psychopath. Assn.; mem. Am. Psychol. Soc., Am. Soc. Human Genetics, AAAS, World Psychiat. Assn. (com. epidemiology and community psychiatry), Behavior Genetics Assn. (mem.-at-large 1972-74, Theodosius Dobzhansky award 1985), Soc. Study Social Biology (dir. 1969-84, sec. 1972-75, pres. 1975-78), Scientists Ctr. for Animal Welfare, Phi Beta Kappa, Sigma Xi.

ERLICHSON, MIRIAM, former fundraiser, law student; b. Bronx, N.Y., July 26, 1948; d. Jack and Bess (Hyatt) E.; m. Walter Forman, Sept. 26, 1970 (div. 1975); m. Victor Petrusewicz, July 17, 1980. BA in English, CCNY, 1969; postgrad., Hunter Coll., 1970-71, Pace Univ., 1990—; MA, CCNY, 1976. Cert. secondary tchr., N.Y. Tchr. English Edicer Rodriguez Intermediate Sch. 84, Bronx, 1972-78; sec. Union Am. Hebre Congregations, N.Y.C., 1978-79; sr. sec. to dir. ann. giving N.Y. Hosp.-Cornell Med. Ctr., N.Y.C., 1979-80, coord. ann. giving, 1980-90; sec. bd. dirs. 77th Settler Corp. Mem. NAFE, Jane Austen Soc. (Eng.), Phi Beta Kappa.

ERNEST, JUDY, food company executive; b. Cleve., Feb. 14, 1939; d. Carl John and Dorothy Amelia Harig; m. David Sears Ernest, Nov. 21, 1964 (div. 1979); children: Thomas William. BA in English, Case Western Res. U., 1961. Columnist Sun Newspapers, Cleve., 1979-84; monthly columnist New Cleve. Woman Jour, 1984-85; weekly bus. columnist Cleve. Plain Dealer, 1985-87; mgr. pub. rels. Nestle Enterprises, Inc., Solon, Ohio, 1983-89, dir. corp. affairs and communications, 1989—; lectr. to bus. groups, 1981—; creator, pub. Judy Ernests Single Parent Calendar, 1981-84; contbr. writer Living Single and Cleve. mag., 1982-84; weekly commentator Sta. WKYC-TV, NBC, Cleve., 1983-85. Editor Impressions mag., 1983—; contbr. articles to newspapers. Bd. dirs. Nat. Women's Econ. Alliance, Washington, 1987—; mem. adv. com. English dept. Notre Dame Coll., 1983-85. Recipient over 50 awards for writing and editing, 1980—, latest being lst place award Internat. Assn. Bus. Communicators, 1987, 89, Women in Communications, 1987. Mem. Soc. Profl. Journalists (bd. dirs. Cleve. chpt. 1983—), Nat. Fedn. Press Women (asst. chmn. nat. conv. 1984), Ohio Fedn. Press Women, Ohio Newspaper Women's Assn., Capital Press Women, Orphus Soc. (bd. dirs. 1983-85), Press Club Cleve. Office: Nestle Enterprises Inc 30003 Bainbridge Rd Solon OH 44139

ERNSBARGER, REBECCA FAYE, communications company administrator; b. Alvin, Tex., Sept. 9, 1949; d. Joseph Lee Mills and Bette (Stricklin) Harrell; m. Charles John Ernsbarger, Apr. 29, 1977; 1 child, Jason. Student, U. Houston, 1968-69, 86-87; Cert. in Communications, Tex. A & M, 1977, MIT, 1980. Account exec. Southwestern Bell, Houston, 1969-82; nat. account exec. AT&T, Houston, 1982-83, mgr. engring. and planning, 1983-87; dir. bus. planning and devel. System One subs. Tex. Air Corp., Houston, 1988—. Mem. Aero. Frequency Commn., Tele-Communication Assn., Nat. Assn. for Female Execs. Democrat. Roman Catholic. Office: System One Corp 1301 Fannin Ste 1800 Houston TX 77002

ERNST, JANET LEE, interior designer; b. Winston-Salem, N.C., Apr. 16, 1955; d. William Lee Ernst and Marie Keith (Shouse) Snyder. BS in Home Econs., Interior Design, U. N.C., Greensboro, 1977. Instr. arts and crafts Craft Showcase, Winston-Salem, 1977-78; display design The Ltd., Inc., N.C. and S.C., 1978-79; designer ind. retail stores Winston-Salem, 1977-81; head design dept. Butler Enterprises, Inc., Winston-Salem, 1981-86; design prin. Carolina Contract Design, Winston-Salem, 1986—; pres. Triad Design Concepts, Inc., Winston-Salem and Greensboro, 1988-90; cons. design and photography contract furniture mfr., Thomasville, N.C., 1986-89; mentor student interns U. N.C., Greensboro, 1983, 84, 87, 88, 89, 90. Vol. Humane Soc., Winston-Salem, 1977-78. Mem. Inst. Bus. Designers (affiliate, edn. com. 1987), Am. Soc. Interior Designers (allied), Nat. Trust Hist. Preservation, NAFE, Nat. Assn. for the Self Employed. Republican. Moravian. Office: Carolina Contract Design 8 W Third St Ste 235 Winston-Salem NC 27101

ERNST, MARY ANNE, mental health counselor; b. Readsboro, Vt., Aug. 25, 1944; d. Raymond Irving and Vivian (Mela) Gowdy; m. Thomas Joseph Ernst, July 30, 1966 (div. 1986); 1 child, Samantha; m. Steven Kreig, Feb. 14, 1988. BA, Keuka Coll., 1966; MA with honors, Rollins Coll., 1984. Lic. mental health counselor. Social worker Greene County Welfare Dept., Xenia, Ohio, 1967-70; instr. Brevard Community Coll., Cocoa, Fla., 1980-87; founder, counselor Stepping Stones Counseling, Merritt Island, Fla., 1981—; adj. prof. Rollins Coll., Rockledge, Fla., 1989—. Mem. chmn. Brevard Commn. on the Status of Women, Merritt Island, 1981-87; v.p., co-chmn. Thomas Jefferson Jr. High Adv. Com., Merritt Island, 1988—; mem. Cen. Fla. Presbyn. Centennial Com., Orlando, 1988—. Mem. AAUW, Internat. Transactional Analysis Assn., Am. Assn. for Counseling and Devel., Profl. Growth Assn. (treas. 1985—), Cocoa Beach C. of C. (youth leadership com. 1989, grad. leadership Brevard 1990). Republican. Presbyterian. Office: Stepping Stones Counseling 60 N Grove St Merritt Island FL 32953

ERNSTER, SISTER JACQUELYN, college president; b. Salem, S.D., Oct. 3, 1939; d. John Ernster and Eleanor (Bie) Ingalls. B.A., Mount Marty Coll., 1965; M.A., Ind. U., 1969; Ph.D., Ohio State U., 1976. Mem. faculty Mount Marty Coll., Yankton, S.D., 1970-76, v.p. acad. affairs, 1976-83, pres., 1983—; speaker S.D. Commn. on Humanities Pub. Issues Forum, 1980-82. Corp. bd. dirs. Sisters of Sacred Heart Convent, Yankton, 1976-82; trustee Madonna Profl. Care Ctr., Lincoln, Nebr., 1977-82. Mem. editorial bd. Yankton Press and Dakotan, 1984. Bush Found. fellow, 1982-83. Mem. Am. Council on Edn. (nat. identification program 1979, nat. com. on women in higher edn. 1984—), Council for Ind. Colls., S.D. Pvt. Coll. Found., Consortium for Mid-Am. (chmn. deans 1980-81), Delta Kappa Gamma (pres. 1980-82). Club: Interchange (bd. dirs. 1985) (Yankton). Office: Mt Marty Coll 1105 W 8th Yankton SD 57078

ERRICKSON, BARBARA BAUER, electronic equipment company executive; b. Pitts., Apr. 5, 1944; d. Edward Ewing Bauer and Margaret J. McConnell; m. James Jay Burcham, June 30, 1966 (div. May 1972); children: James Jay II, Linda Lee; m. William Newel Errickson, Apr. 9, 1976 (div. Feb. 1987). BA, U. Ill., 1966; MBA, So. Meth. U., 1981. Programming trainee Allstate Ins. Co., Northbrook, Ill., 1973; programmer, team leader Motorola, Inc., Chgo., 1974-78; supr. systems Tex. Instruments, Inc., Dallas, 1978-81, product line mgr. worldwide shipping systems, 1981-83, product line mgr. shipping, inventory systems, 1983-84, mgr. mktg. info. systems, 1985, mgr. benefit systems, 1986-89, mgr. S.W. case cons. and edn., 1990—; dir., billing and software developer Spring Park Home Owners, Garland-Richardson, Tex., 1984—, pres. and chmn. fin., 1985, v.p. legal, 1986. Active Dallas Women's Ctr., 1984—; mem. bus. adv. council So. Meth U. Bus. Adv. Program; mem. bus. adv. coun. El Centro Coll. Rehab. for Physically Challenged Through Data Processing, 1987—; chmn. control and adminstrn./mktg. United Way, 1986-89. Recipient Women in Leadership cert. YWCA Met. Chgo., 1977. Mem. Am. Mgmt. Assn., Am. Women in Computing (bd. dirs. 1987—, pres. 1989), Community Assns. Inst., So. Meth. U. MBA Soc., Spring Park Racquet Club, Beta Gamma Sigma. Republican. Presbyterian. Home: 6702 Lakeshore Dr Garland TX 75042 Office: Tex Instruments Inc 6500 Chase Oaks Blvd PO Box 869305 Plano TX 75086

ERSKINE, CHARLENE G., psychologist, educator; b. Stoneham, Mass., Sept. 13, 1943; d. Ervin E. and Eleanor V. (Weston) Gloor; 1 child, Frederick T. Erskine IV. BA, Atlantic Union Coll., 1966; MEd, Mass. State Coll., Fitchburg, 1971; PhD, U. Iowa, 1974. Clin. psychologist Creighton U., Omaha, 1974—, dir., adj. assoc. prof., 1978—; pvt. practice clin. psychology, Omaha, 1980—; mem. State Bd. Examiners, Nebr., 1984—. Mem. Nebr. Psychol. Assn. (sec.-treas. 1980-82), Am. Psychol. Assn., Nat. Registry Health Providers. Office: Creighton U California at 24th St Omaha NE 68178

ERSKINE, M(ARY) CARA, speech pathology and audiology educator; b. Balt., Jan. 23, 1947; d. Joseph James and Mary Bernadine (Kennedy) E. AA, Immaculata Coll., 1967; BA, Mount St. Agnes Coll., Balt., 1969; MEd, Loyola Coll., Balt., 1970. Lic. speech pathologist, Md.; lic. audiologist, Md. Asst. prof. dept. otolaryngology Johns Hopkins Med. Insts., Balt., 1970—; mem. profl. adv. com. for home care svcs., mem. utilization rev. com. for home health care program, mem. home health care quality assurance task force Johns Hopkins Hosp.; active vis. nurse assn. rev. com., Balt.; presenter various profl. and ednl. orgns. mem. prof. adv. com. for home care svcs., mem. utilization rev. com. for home health care program, mem. home health care quality assurance task force Johns Hopkins Hosp.; presenter various profl. and ednl. orgns. Head and Neck Cancer Rehab. Inst. fellow, Indpls., 1986. Mem. Am. Speech, Lang. and Hearing Assn. (certs. clin. competence in speech pathology and audiology), Am. Auditory Soc., Md. Speech and Hearing Assn. (mem. nat. congl. action contact network), Johns Hopkins Club. Democrat. Roman Catholic. Home: 20 Salthill Ct Timonium MD 21093 Office: Johns Hopkins Hosp Hearing & Speech Clinic 600 N Wolfe St Baltimore MD 21205

ERSOZ, CLARA JEAN, hospital administrator, physician; b. Pitts., Jan. 7, 1937; d. John Donald and Thelma Jean (Ward) Babb; m. Namik Ersoz; children: Nathaniel, Meryem. BS, Chatham Coll., 1958; MD, U. Pitts., 1962; M in Health Adminstrn., U. Colo., 1989. Diplomate Am. Bd. Anesthesiology, Am. Bd. Med. Mgmt. Intern Shadyside Hosp., Pitts., 1962; resident U. Toronto, 1963, Mercy Hosp., Pitts., 1964; fellow Presbyn.-Univ. Hosp., Pitts., 1965, dir. ICU, 1966-70; staff anesthesiologist St. Clair Hosp., Pitts., 1970-73, dir. ICU, house physician, 1973-76, med. dir., 1976-82, v.p. med. affairs, 1982—; mem. clin. faculty Joint Commn. on Accreditation of Healthcare Orgns., Chgo., 1985—; med. dir. Alpha Network, Pitts., 1985-87. Bd. dirs. Pitts. chpt. ARC, 1976-86. Recipient Liberty Bell award Allegheny County Bar Assn., 1976; named Woman of the Yr., Am. Trauma Soc., 1975, 77. Mem. AMA, Am. Coll. Physician Execs. Office: St Clair Hosp 1000 Bower Hill Rd Pittsburgh PA 15243

ERTEL, DENISE MARLENE, medical sales professional, nurse; b. Reading, Pa., Feb. 7, 1956; d. Dennis Joseph and Mary (Duda) E. AS in Nursing, Hahnemann U., 1981; BS in Nursing, Thomas Jefferson U., 1989. RN, Pa. Surg. ICU staff nurse, charge nurse Hahnemann U. Hosp., Phila., 1981-85; charge nurse Traveling Nurse Corp., North Broward Hosp., Pompano Beach, Fla., 1983; computer tng. specialist dept. hosp. info. systems Hahnemann U., 1985-87, systems analyst dept. hosp. info. systems, 1987-89; terr. rep. Ciba-Geigy Pharms., Summit, N.J., 1989-90, hosp. rep. Phila. area, 1990—. Writer, producer videotapes on accessing prenatal care in Phila. Mem. NAFE, Am. Assn. Critical Care Nurses, Smithsonian Assocs., Alpha Eta. Democrat. Roman Catholic. Home: 152 Woodstock Ct Cherry Hill NJ 08034 Office: Ciba Geigy Pharms Summit NJ 07091

ERTEL, GRACE ROSCOE, freelance non-fiction writer, educator; b. Santa Monica, Calif., Oct. 10, 1921; d. Thomas Benedict and Grace (Kelly) Roscoe; m. Donald Joseph Ertel, Sept. 28, 1946; children: Eileen Ariel, Adrienne Marie. BA, UCLA, 1943; teaching credential, U. Calif., Sacramento, 1970. Tchr. remedial reading Grant Sch. Dist., RioTierra-Sacramento, Calif., 1965-66; tchr. English as a second lang., other subjects Sacramento City Adult Schs., 1966-86, Grant Adult Schs., North Highlands, Calif., 1986—; freelance writer, 1975—; lectr. on writing Am. River Coll., Sacramento, 1982. Author: (booklet) Plant an Ecology Garden, 1972, 76; contbr. articles to popular mags. Mem. citizens adv. Sacramento County Solid Waste Reclamation, 1975-80. Mem. Am. Soc. Journalists and Authors, Nat. Writers Club, Am. Med. Writers, Internat. Food, Wine & Travel Writers Assn. Home and office: 6350 Dorchester Ct Carmichael CA 95608

ERVIN, ADELE QUINCY, retired educational association administrator; b. Coronado, Calif., Aug. 27, 1924; d. Robert Gilpin and Frances Quincy (Nichols) E. Lt. Can. Red Cross Motor Corps, Ottawa, Can., 1942-45, CRC Gen. Svcs., London, 1945-46; club mgr. U.S. Army Hostess Svc., Erding, Fed. Republic of Germany, 1946-47; exec. sec. alumnae assn. Westover Sch., Middlebury, Conn., 1948-63; dir. external affairs Nat. Assn. Ind. Schs., Boston, 1963-89; trustee Masters Sch., Dobbs Ferry, N.Y., 1974-77, Westover Sch., Middlebury, 1978-80, St. Mark's Sch., Southborough, Mass., 1982-89, Coun. for Religion in Ind. Schs., Washington, 1986-89. Trustee Manchester (Mass.) Pub. Library, 1970-79. Mem. LWV. Episcopalian. Home: 113 Ocean St Manchester MA 01944

ERVIN, CONNIE YVONNE, product manager; b. Buffalo, N.Y., Sept. 8, 1954; d. William C. and Jane L (Goodloe) E. BA, Barat Coll., 1975; MBA, Baldwin Wallace U., 1987. Sales rep. Moore Business Forms, Glenview, Ill., 1976-79; acct. rep. Miles Inc. Biotechnology, N.Y., 1979-83; key acct. rep. Miles Inc. Consumer Health, Cleve., Ohio, 1983-85, sales specialist, 1985-87; dist. retail mgr. Miles Inc. Consumer Health, Kansas City, Mo., 1987-88;

product mgr. Miles Incorporated, Ind., 1988--. Fellow 1490 Orgn.; mem. Assn. Black MBA's (v.p. Kansas City chpt. 1987-88), NAFE, Nat. Assn. Market Developers, Minorities in Communication (exec. bd.), Iota Phi Lambda (life). Methodist. Office: Miles Incorporated 1127 Myrtle Elkhart IN 46634

ERVIN, JANIS, communications executive; b. St. Louis, Aug. 17, 1953. BS, Washington U., St. Louis, 1977; cert. in data base adminstrn., NYU, 1988. Supr. customer service South Cen. Bell Co., New Orleans, 1978-82; mktg. support rep. N.Y. Telephone Co., N.Y.C., 1982-83, AT&T Info. Systems, N.Y.C., 1983-85; dir. telecommunications Kingsborough Community Coll., Bklyn., 1985—. Mem. IEEE, NAFE, Assn. Coll. and Univ. Telecommunications Adminstrs, Telecommunications Officer Assn. (sec. CINY 1989). Office: Kingsborough Community Coll 2001 Oriental Blvd Brooklyn NY 11235

ERVIN, SUSAN CHADWICK, lawyer; b. Aberdeen, Md., May 16, 1951; d. A.R. and Ellyn (Wiegert) E. BA, Mt. Holyoke Coll., 1973; JD, Rutgers U., 1976. Bar: N.Y. 1977, D.C. 1985. Assoc. Kronish, Lieb, Shainswit, Weiner & Hellman, N.Y.C., 1976-78, Kramer, Levin, Nessen, Kamin & Frankel, N.Y.C., 1978-83; asst. gen. counsel Commodity Futures Trading Commn., Washington, 1983-86, assoc. dir. div. of trading and markets, 1986-87, dep. dir., chief counsel div. of trading and markets, 1987—. Mem. ABA. Office: Commodity Futures Trading Commn 2033 K St NW Washington DC 20581

ERVOLINO, JOANNE MARIE, registered nurse; b. N.Y.C., Feb. 13, 1959; d. Sam Dominic and Dorothy Marie (Perry) E. BS in Nursing, Adelphi U., 1981; M, NYU, 1987. RN; cert. in Inpatient Obstetrics. From staff nurse to nurse clinician NYU Med. Ctr., 1981-85, asst. clin. coord., 1985-87; nurse cons. Bower and Gardner Med. Malpractice Law Firm, N.Y.C., 1987—; cons. med. research Bower and Gardner, N.Y.C., 1987--. mem bd dirs., v.p., sec. The Park Manor Condominium, Forest Hills, N.Y., 1989, pres. 1990. Mem. NAFE, Nat. Assn. Am. Coll. Ob-Gyn, Sigma Theta Tau. Democrat. Roman Catholic. Home: 100-25 Queens Blvd Forest Hills NY 11375 Office: Bower and Gardner 110 E 59th St New York NY 10022

ERWIN, ELIZABETH MAE, travel agency professional; b. Norfolk, Va., Oct. 31, 1951; d. Hal T. and Joan S. (Sandt) E. Assoc. degree, Taylor Bus. Sch., 1971; student, Temple U., 1983—. Asst. buyer Ideal Shoe Co., Phila., 1971-73; retail store mgr. Spencer Gifts, Atlantic City, 1973-75; teller First Pa. Bank, Phila., 1976-78; accounts payable mgr. Rosenbluth Travel, Phila., 1978-83; credit and computer mgr. Pkwy Travel, Inc., Phila., 1983—. Mem. NAFE. Roman Catholic. Office: Pkwy Travel Inc 37 S 16th St Philadelphia PA 19102

ERWIN, JANE ELIZABETH, journalist; b. St. Louis, Apr. 2, 1960; d. John Gerald Jr. and Marge Marie (Ault) Mier; m. Kenton Lane Erwin, May 15, 1982. BS, Middle Tenn. State U., 1982. Staff writer Tulsa Bus. Chronicle, 1982-84; pub. rels./practice devel. coord. Touche Ross, Tulsa, 1984-85; asst. bus. editor Tulsa World, 1985—. Contbr. articles to mags. Pub. rels. chmn. Tulsa Women's Found., Inc., 1988-89, bd. dirs., 1988—; vol. counselor Call Rape Inc., Tulsa, 1985-87; adv. bd. mem. Crosstown Day Care Ctr., Tulsa, 1989—. Mem. Women in Communications Inc. (Tulsa chpt., treas. 1989—, pres. 1985-86, progress of women chmn. 1986-87, 88-89), Sigma Delta Chi. Unitarian Universalist. Office: Tulsa World 315 S Boulder Ave Tulsa OK 74102

ERWIN, JUDITH ANN (JUDITH ANN PEACOCK), writer, photographer; b. Decatur, Ga., Jan. 4, 1939; d. Milo Eugene and Lucy Isabelle (Simpson) Peacock (dec.); m. William Wofford Erwin, Sept. 5, 1959 (div. Mar. 1982); children: William Wofford Jr., Allison Sheridan (Norton). AA, Fla. Community Coll., 1987; BA summa cum laude, Jacksonville U., 1989. Photography instr., freelance writer Jacksonville, Fla., 1986—, freelance dance photographer, 1984—; theater and dance critic Folio Weekly, Jacksonville, Fla., 1987—; pres. Ballet Guild, Jacksonville, 1973-75, Ballet Repertory Jacksonville, 1979-80; freelance costume designer, Jacksonville, 1981-86. Editorial staff Kalliope, A Jour. of Women's Art. Mem. del.'s council Art's Assembly Jacksonville, 1979-80. Mem. Nat. Soc. Arts and Letters, Fla. Freelance Writers Assn., Nat. League Am. Pen Women, Phi Kappa Phi, Phi Theta Kappa. Democrat. Episcopalian.

ERWIN-VALLEJO, TERRY ANN, alarm company executive; b. Pitts., Nov. 11, 1952; d. Earl Eugene Erwin and Rose Marie (Regina) Weckwerth; m. Abel Vallejo, Nov. 10, 1984; 1 child, A.J. Student, Fla. State Beauty Coll., Gainesville, 1970-71. From security, canine officer to mgr. cen. sta. Alarmco, Inc. Canine Patrol, Las Vegas, 1976-81, mgr. ops., 1981—. Vol. fire marshall State of Nev., 1986—. With U.S. Army, 1974-76. Mem. Sorotptimists (del. Met. Las Vegas 1982-83, chmn. growth and devel. Greater Las Vegas 1986-87). Democrat. Roman Catholic. Home: 3917 Herford Ln Las Vegas NV 89110 Office: Alarmco Inc 2007 Las Vegas Blvd S Las Vegas NV 89104

ESAU, KATHERINE, retired botanist, educator; b. Ekaterinoslav, Russia, Apr. 3, 1898; naturalized. Ph.D., U. Caif., 1931, LL.D. (hon.), 1966; D.Sc. (hon.), Mills Coll., 1962. Instr. botany, jr. botanist U. Calif.-Davis, 1931-37, asst. prof., asst. botanist, 1937-43, assoc. prof., assoc. botanist, 1943-49, prof., botanist, 1949-63; prof. botany U. Calif.-Santa Barbara, 1963-65, emeritus prof. botany, 1965—; Prather lectr. Harvard U., 1960. Recipient U.S. Nat. Medal of Sci., 1989; Guggenheim fellow, 1940. Fellow Am. Acad. Arts and Scis.; mem. NAS, AAAS, Swedish Royal Acad. Sci., Am. Philos. Soc., Bot. Soc. Am. (pres. 1951). Office: U Calif Dept Biol Sci Santa Barbara CA 93106

ESBENSHADE, KATHRYN MITCHELL, human resource manager; b. Youngstown, Ohio, Aug. 15, 1955; d. George Bennett Jr. and Mary Ann (Dongiovanni) Mitchell; m. Amos John Esbenshade Jr., Dec. 27, 1986. Student, Ohio State U., 1973-77; BS in Bus. Mgmt., Ashland (Ohio) U., 1978, MBA in Exec. Mgmt., 1983. Personnel mgr. Del-Tronics Assocs., Inc., Mansfield, Ohio, 1979-81, PMS Consol., Norwalk, Ohio, 1981-83; engring. recruiter Mgmt. Recruiters, Internat., Columbus, Ohio, 1984; personnel dir. Elyria (Ohio) United Meth. Home, 1984-85; bus. mgr. Good Shepherd, Ashland, 1985-88; human resource mgr. FSC Ednl., Inc., Mansfield, 1988—; cons. Richland Newhope Ctr., Mansfield, 1988—; bd. dirs. Cath. Social Svcs., Medina, Ohio. Author: The Effects of Flexitime on Productivity and Absenteeism, 1983. Vol. Sisters of St. Francis of Mary Immaculate, Goiania, Goias, Brazil, 1975, ARC, Ashland, 1976-85; chmn. health care panel United Appeal, Ashland, 1987-88; campaign mgr. Leininger for county commr., Ashland, 1980, 84; mem. Dem. Cen. Com., Ashland, 1978-80. Named Outstanding Sr. Woman of the Yr., Daughters of Isabella, 1973. Mem. Soc. for Human Resource Mgmt. (cons. network Alexandria, Va. chpt. 1988—), ASTD, Noon Personnel Assn., Rotary (Courage award 1973). Office: FSC Ednl Inc 905 Hickory Ln Mansfield OH 44905

ESCALERA, KAREN WEINER, public relations company executive; b. Phila., Dec. 7, 1944; d. George Joseph and Gladys (Lieberman) Weiner; m. Alfonso G. Escalera, Sept. 8, 1978; 1 child, Kent. BA cum laude, U. Pa., 1966. Assoc. editor United Bus. Publs., N.Y.C., 1967-68; account exec. Jacobson/Wallace/Westphal, N.Y.C., 1968-69; news and feature editor Hilton Internat. Hotels, N.Y.C., 1969-74, dir. pub. relations western hemisphere, N.Y.C., 1974-79; pres. Karen Weiner Escalera Assocs., N.Y.C., 1979—. Contbr. articles to profl. jours. Recipient various firm awards. Mem. Soc. Am. Travel Writers (treas. northeast chpt. 1982-84), Pub. Relations Soc. Am., Hotel Sales and Mktg. Assn., Caribbean Tourism Assn., Caribbean Hotel Assn. Avocations: cultural activities, travel. Office: 104 5th Ave New York NY 10011

ESCALÓN DELGADO, CLARA SUE, English language education specialist; b. Dayton, Ohio, Sept. 26, 1952; d. Paul and Jo Ellen (Wilson) Liesenhoff; m. Raúl Escalón, Jan. 18, 1978 (div. Sept. 1988); 1 child, Tania; m. Máximo Delgado, Feb. 23, 1990; children: Max Brian, Bridget Patricia. Degree, U. Valencia, Spain, 1972-74; BA, Murray State U., 1974; MA, Wright State U., 1984. Instr. Global Sch. of Idioms, Valencia, 1972-74; instr., interim dir. ESL program Miami U., Greenville, Ohio, 1974-77; instr. English Inst., Reynosa, Mexico, 1978; outreach worker La Raza Unida, Dayton, 1979; instr., acting dir. The English Lang. and Multicultural Inst., Dayton, 1982-86, dir., 1986—; cons. to member schs. Southwestern Ohio Coun. Higher Edn., Dayton, 1985—; cons., presenter Ohio Pub. Sch. Systems, 1985—; cons. Dayton ESL Providers, 1985—; presenter numerous cross-cultural, communication and management workshops and seminars, 1984—. Author: (book and cassette program) Speaking American English, 1985 (Program of Yr. award 1986). Founder, vol. instr. Spanish/English GED (Gen. Edn. Devel.) Program, Dayton, 1979-84; founding mem., vol. Project READ (Reading Edn. for Adults in Dayton), 1988—; founding dir. La Casa del Pueblo, Dayton, 1975-78; vol. emergency translator Vol. Bank/Dayton Cts., 1982—. Mem. NAFE, Nat. Assn. Fgn. Student Affairs, Bus. and Profl. Women, Tchrs. of English to Speakers of Other Langs., Assn. Ind. Colls. and Schs. (cons./evaluator 1989—), Dayton Coun. World Affairs, Nat. Image. Office: English Lang & Multi- Cultural Inst 2900 Acosta St Ste 140 Dayton OH 45420

ESCHETE, MARY LOUISE, internist; b. Houma, La., Feb. 8, 1949; d. Marshall John and Louise Esther (Davis) E.; m. Lorphy Joseph Bourque, July 7, 1979. BS, La. State U., 1970; MD, La. State U. Med. Ctr., Shreveport, 1974. Diplomate, Am. Bd. Internal Medicine. Resident in internal medicine La. State U. Med. Ctr., Shreveport, 1974-77; staff instr. La. State U. Med. Ctr., 1979, fellow in infectious disease, 1979; pvt. practice Houma, 1980-83; staff, dept. internal medicine South La. Med. Assocs., Houma, 1983—; chmn. infection control, Terrebonne Gen. Hosp., 1981—, South La. Med. Ctr., 1983—. Contbr. articles to med. jours. Bd. dirs., Houma Battered Women's Shelter, 1983-87, Houma YWCA, 1987-89. Mem. Infectious Disease Soc., Am. Soc. Microbiology, N.Y. Acad. Sci., AMA, So. Med. Assn. (grantee 1978), La. State Med. Soc., Terrebonne Parish Med. Soc., ACP, AAAS, Alpha Epsilon Delta, Krewe of Hyacinthians (pres. 1989-90), Houma Jr. Women's Club (reporter 1988-89, recording sec. 1990—). Democrat. Roman Catholic. Home: 3387 Little Bayou Black St Houma LA 70360 Office: South La Med Ctr 1978 Industrial Blvd Houma LA 70363

ESCO, LOIS OLIVER, retired management assistant; b. Tallassee, Ala., Oct. 14, 1916; d. George W. and Minnie (Glass) Oliver; m. Claude Harold Esco, Sept. 17, 1940 (dec. 1982); 1 child, Lois Carol. Student, Auburn U., 1939-40, Jones Law Sch., Montgomery, Ala., 1970-73. Exec. sec. VA, Montgomery, 1966-72, mgmt. asst., 1972-80; ret., 1980; sec. Reading Improvement and Managerial Devel. for Women, U. Ala., 1971. Mem. AAUW (organizer Legis. Day 1978, chmn. scholarship com. 1988—), Mus. Fine Arts Assn., English Speaking Union, Friends of Free China. Republican. Baptist. Home: 3759 MacLamar Rd Montgomery AL 36111

ESCOBAR, HILDA LOPEZ, nurse practitioner, physician assistant; b. N.Y.C., Aug. 6, 1929; d. Eladio and Josephine (Justiniano) Lopez; m. John Louis Escobar, Sept. 10, 1949; children: Linda, Michael, Jean. AAS, Nassau Community Coll., 1967; BSN, C.W. Post U., 1975; cert. in nursing mgmt. Adelphi U., 1988. Cert. hemiodialysis nurse, 1978; adult nurse practitioner, SUNY, Upstate Med. Ctr., Syracuse, 1978. Staff nurse, South Nassau Community Hosp., Oceanside, N.Y., 1967-68; staff nurse Nassau Hosp., Mineola, N.Y., 1968-78, head nurse hemodialysis unit, 1976-78; adult nurse practitioner Community Health Program, New Hyde Park, N.Y., 1978—, nurse coord. dept. medicine and urgent visit dept., 1986-89. Mem. Am. Nurses Assn. (cert. adult nurse practitioner 1988), Am. Assn. Physician Assts. (cert. 1983), Am. Assn. Nephrology Nurses & Technicians (cert. 1976), Coalition Nurse Practitioners, Phi Theta Kappa, Sigma Theta Tau (exec. bd. dirs. Alpha Omega chpt. 1978—).

ESCOBAR, MARISOL See MARISOL

ESCOTT, SHOOLAH HOPE, microbiologist; b. Stamford, Conn., May 20, 1952; d. Robert R. and Fanny (Levy) E. BS, U. Conn., 1974; MS, Northeastern U., Boston, 1985. Cert. med. technologist. Med. technologist Harvard U. Health Svcs., Cambridge, Mass., 1976-79; med. technologist, microbioly lab. New Eng. Deaconess Hosp., Boston, 1979-84; supr. microbiology Norwood (Mass.) Hosp., 1984-87, Med. Ctr. Cen. Mass., Worcester, 1987—. Named Nat. Merit Scholar, 1970; grantee, 1970. Mem. Am. Soc. Clin. Pathologists, Am. Soc. for Microbiology, N.E. Assn. for Clin. Microbiology and Infectious Disease (bd. dirs. Mass. chpt.). Office: Med Ctr Cen Mass Microbiology Lab 119 Belmont St Worcester MA 01605

ESFANDIARY, MARY SADIGH, federal agency administrator, physical scientist; b. Passaic, N.J., June 27, 1929; d. Peter J. and Veronica R. (Kida) Nieradka; m. Mohsen S. Esfandiary; children: Homayoun Austin, Dara S. BS in Chemistry, St. John's U., 1951; postgrad., Polytechnic Inst. N.Y., 1955-56. Research chemist Picatinny Arsenal, Dover, N.J., 1951-56; supr. phys. sci. Bur. Mines, Washington, 1956-61; asst. to dir. research Nat. Iranian Oil Co., Tehran, 1961-64; lectr. U. Tehran and Aryamehr Inst. Tech., Tehran, 1961-64, 69-73; dir. internat. affairs Acad. of Scis., Tehran, 1977-79; chief geog. names br. Def. Mapping Agy., Washington, 1981-86, chief prodn. mgmt. office, 1986-87, chief support div., chief inventory mgmt. div., 1987-90, chief product mgmt. dept., 1990—. Contbr. papers and articles to tech. jours., 1952-78. Pres. UN Delegations Women's Club, N.Y.C., 1967-69, v.p., program dir., 1964-67; pres. Diplomatic Corps. Com. for Red Cross, Bangkok, Thailand, 1974-76; v.p., bd. dirs. Found. for Blind of Thailand, Bangkok, 1973-77; mem. Edn. Working Group ARC, 1989-90. Recipient Badge of Honor for Social Service, Thailand, 1975, 1st Class medal Red Cross, Thailand, 1976. Mem. AAAS, Mensa. Democrat. Home: 4401 Sedgewick St NW Washington DC 20016 Office: Def Mapping Agy 6101 MacArthur Blvd Room 309 Washington DC 20315

ESH, DALIA REGINA, insurance educator, financial planner; b. Jerusalem, May 15, 1950; came to U.S., 1980, naturalized, 1989; d. Yedidya Mizrahi and Orah (Debby) Mizrahi Malka; m. David Esh; children: Odelia, Roy. Cert. proficiency in English, Cambridge U., Eng., 1969; BA, Bar Ilan U., Tel Aviv, 1972, teaching cert., 1976; postgrad., U. Mo.-St. Louis, 1981-82, Washington U., St. Louis, 1983-84; MS in Mgmt., Am. Coll., 1989. CLU; chartered fin. cons. English tchr. Lady Davis Sch., Tel Aviv, 1973-80; Hebrew tchr. Epstein Acad., St. Louis, 1981-82; sales rep. Met. Ins. Co., St. Louis, 1982-85, mktg. specialist, instr., Tulsa, 1985-86, br. mgr., Carrollton, Dallas, Tex., 1986—. Originated universal life-term sales concept, 1985. Active Jewish Community Ctrs. Assn., St. Louis, 1984-85, Tulsa, 1986, Dallas, 1987—. Human resources mgmt. grantee Washington U., 1983; recipient Career Builders award Met. Ins. Co., 1982, Leader's Conf. award, 1984, Nat. Quality award, 1984, 85, Mgmt. Conf. award, 1989; named to Million Dollar Round Table, 1985. Mem. Nat. Assn. Life Underwriters, Internat. Assn. Fin. Planning, NAFE, Am. Soc. CLU, Am. Soc. Charterd Fin. Cons., B'nai B'irth. Jewish. Avocation: folk dancing, tennis. Office: Met Ins Co 3620 N Josey Ln Carrollton TX 75007

ESHOO, BARBARA ANNE RUDOLPH, academic official; b. Worcester, Mass., Sept. 27, 1946; d. Charles Leighton and Irene Isabella (Wheeler) Rudolph; divorced; 1 child, Melissa Clinton; m. Robert Pius Eshoo, July ll, 1981. Student, Morehead State U., 1964-66, U. N.H., 1974, 75; BA, New Eng. Coll., 1976. Asst. to dir. Currier Gallery Art, Manchester, N.H., 1976-78, coord. pub. rels., 1979-82; dir. pub. rels. Daniel Webster Coll., Nashua, N.H., 1982-88, chief advancement officer, 1988—; mem. faculty Currier Art Ctr., Manchester, 1977-79; bd. advisors New Eng. Coll. Art Gallery, Henniker, N.H., 1989—; advisor on planned giving United Way, Nashua, 1989—. Com. mem. Manchester Sch. Bd., 1986—; mem. Manchester Mayor's Task Force on Youth Affairs, 1986-88; del. N.H. Sch. Bds. Assn., 1988—; trustee Manchester Hist. Assn., 1989—; mem. Mayor's Com. on Leadership, Manchester, 1988—; bd. dirs. Swiftwater Girl Scout Coun., N.H. and Vt. Mem. Nat. Soc. Fund Raising Execs., Advt. Club N.H. (bd. dirs., v.p. 1980-82). Democrat. Home: 47 Amoskeag Pl Manchester NH 03101 Office: Daniel Webster Coll 20 University Dr Nashua NH 03063

ESKESEN, RUTH ELLEN, nurse, state legislator; b. Mt. Carmel, Ohio, Mar. 7, 1939; d. Ervin E. and Elfreda Ellen (Corbin) Dameron; m. Byron Henry Eskesen, May 19, 1967. Diploma in Nursing, St. Luke's Hosp., 1964; BS in Nursing, U. Colo., 1969, MS, 1973; postgrad., U. Tex. Respiratory therapist Rose Meml. Hosp., Denver, 1960-61, clin. specialist, 1965-70; staff nurse St. Luke's Hosp., Denver, Univ. Hosp., Tucson, 1973; asst. prof. U. Ariz., Tucson, 1973-75, No. Ariz. U., Flagstaff, 1975-80; asst. instr. U. Tex., Austin, 1980; mem. Ariz. Ho. of Reps., Phoenix; treas. Ariz. Nursing Network, Phoenix, 1983-84. Editor (newsletter) Ariz. Nurses Polit. Action Com. News, 1986-87. Nurse ARC, 1964—; Rep. precinct committeewoman, Tucson, 1987—; Rep. state committeewoman, Tucson, 1989—; vice chairwoman house health com.; subcom. chairwoman house appropriations com.; mem. joint legis. budget com.; mem. joint legis. com. Ariz. Health Care Cost Containment System; mem. house counties and municipalities com., house human resources and aging com.; trustee Ariz. Nurses Polit. Action Com., Phoenix, 1984-87, chairwoman, 1987. Mem. Am. Nurses Assn., Nat. League Nursing, Nat. Order Women Legislators, Sigma Theta Tau, Phi Kappa Phi. Office: Ariz Ho of Reps 1700 W Washington Phoenix AZ 85007

ESKEW, CAROLYN ELIZABETH, human resources director; b. Campbell, Mo., Nov. 4, 1942; d. Rudolph and Helen Louise (Carrell) Preslar; m. Ambrose Ralph Eskew, Dec. 11, 1976. MusB, DePauw U., 1964; MME, Murray State U., 1969; MBA, So. Ill. U., Edwardsville, 1984. Band dir. Effingham (Ill.) Community Unit #40, Effingham, 1964-67, Calloway County Schs., Murray, Ky., 1967-69; pers. dir. Carondelet Foundry Co., St. Louis, 1970-84; pers. mgr. Monsan Mo. Electronic Materials Co., St. Peters, 1984-85; dir. human resources Absorbent Cotton Co., Valley Park, Mo., 1985—; treas., sec. v.p., pres. Human Resources Mgmt., 1982-87. Mem. Mo. C. of C. (social and labor legis. com.), Soc. for Human Resources Mgmt. (compensation and benefits com.), Personnel Assn. Greater St. Louis, Beta Gamma Sigma. Methodist. Office: Absorbent Cotton Co 401 Marshall Valley Park MO 63088

ESKOW, BONNIE MICHELE, marketing company executive; b. Bklyn., Sept. 18, 1966; d. Martin and Iris Blossom (Krell) E. BA cum laude in Econs., Bklyn. Coll., 1988. Sales mgr. Courier life Publs., Bklyn., 1983-86; pres. Competitive Edge Inc., Bklyn., 1986—. Canvasser Democratic Assemblyman, Bklyn., 1984, 86, 88; mem. N.Y. polit. interest rsch. group Bklyn. Coll., 1983-84. Recipient Recognition for Sponsoring Telemktg. Campaign, Books For Kids, N.Y.C., 1988. Mem. Ctr. for Entrepreneurial Mgmt., Am. Mktg. Assn., NAFE, Assn. Collegiate Entrepreneurs Bklyn. Coll. (alumni advisor, regional leader, pres., founder 1986—), Assn. Collegiate Entrepreneurs. Office: 9030 Fort Hamilton Pkwy Brooklyn NY 11209

ESPINO, FERN RUBY, dean; b. May 17. BA, U. Ariz., 1964, MS, 1968, PhD, 1974. Assoc. dean. instrnl. svcs. Pima Community Coll., Tucson, 1976; dean Coll. & Fin. Svcs., Coll. of Mainland, Tex. City, TX, 1976-80; assoc. dean students GMI Engring. & Mgmt. Inst., Flint, Mich., 1980-81; dean student devel. GMI Engring. & Mgmt. Inst., Flint, 1983-87. Bd. dirs. United Way Flint; bd. trustees United Way Mich.; mem. Flint Downtown Devel. Authority -Fin. Long Range Planning; v.p. communications com. Boys Scouts Am.; commr.-office of pres. Commn. Minority Bus. Devel.; mem. Nat. Hispana Leadership Initiative; supt. referent hispanic group Dept. Edn. State Mich.; bd. dirs. U.S. West Women. Named Hispanic Advocate of the Yr.. Mem. The Hundred Club of Flint, Am. Assn. Higher Edn., League of United Latin Am. Citizens. Home: 3544 Eastham Dearborn MI 48120

ESPOSITO, AMY SKLAR, lawyer; b. Bklyn., Nov. 9, 1955; d. Sidney and Rhoda (Weiner) Sklar; m. Francis Benedetto Esposito, May 4, 1985; 1 child, Melissa. BA, U. Vt., 1977; JD, Hofstra U., 1980. Bar: N.Y. 1981, Fla. 1983. Assoc. Herman & Natale, Esqs., Garden City, N.Y., 1980-81, Law Offices of Gabriel Kohn, Mineola, N.Y., 1981-84; ptnr. Ostor & Sklar, Esqs., Deer Park, N.Y., 1984—. Coach mock trials Nassau County (N.Y.) High Schs., 1984-86. Mem. N.Y. State Bar Assn., Nassau-Suffolk Women's Bar Assn. (assoc., speaker on matrimonial law). Jewish. Office: Ostor & Sklar Esqs 131 Liberty St Deer Park NY 11729

ESPOSITO, BONNIE LOU, marketing professional; b. Chgo., July 20, 1947; d. Ralph Edgar and Dorothy Mae (Groh) Myers; m. Frank Merle Esposito, Aug. 15, 1969 (div. Sept. 1985); children: Mario Henry, Elizabeth Ann. BA, George Williams Coll., 1969. Caseworker Little Bros. of the Poor, Chgo., 1969-72; organizer Community Crime Prevention, Mpls., 1978-81; dir. Little Bros.-Friends of the Elderly, Mpls., 1972-78; owner Espo Inc./Mario's Ristorante, Mpls., 1978-85; mktg. mgr. City of Mpls. Energy Office, 1981—; dir. mktg. and tng. The Energy Collaborative, 1987—; dir. mktg. Ctr. for Energy and the Urban Environment, Mpls., 1989—. Mem. NAFE (bd. dirs. Monday Night Network 1988), Midwest Direct Mktg. Assn., Minn. Multi-Housing Assn., Nat. Apartment Assn. Office: Ctr Energy Urban Environment 510 1st Ave N Ste 400 Minneapolis MN 55403

ESPOSITO, PAULETTE, human resources specialist; b. Stamford, Conn., Dec. 6, 1945; d. Peter and Juliette Marie (DeYulio) E. AS, Katharine Gibbs, N.Y.C., 1964; cert., Cornell U., 1983; BS, Marymount, 1985; cert., U. Mich., 1987. Sec. State Nat. Bank, Stamford, 1964; exec. sec. Gen. Time Corp., Stamford, 1966; office mgr. William Haight and Welch Advt., Greenwich, Conn., 1967; exec. asst. Combustion Engring., Stamford, 1968; with Champion Internat. Corp., Stamford, 1976—, supr., 1978, mgr. training devel., 1986—; lectr. Katharine Gibbs Sch., 1981; cons. tchr. Stamford Pub. Schs., 1977. Bd. dirs. Am. Red Cross, Stamford, 1983; dir. Blood Program, Stamford, 1980-85; coordinator United Way Campaign, 1983-87; v.p. Stamford Police Community Council, Stamford, 1984-86. Named Young Woman of Yr., Jaycees, 1983. Mem. Am. Soc. Training and Devel., Nat. Soc. Performance and Instrn. Democrat. Roman Catholic. Club: Midday (Stamford). Office: Champion Internat Corp 1 Champion Pla Stamford CT 06921

ESPY, MARY SUSAN, computer company executive; b. Springfield, Mo., Nov. 9, 1952; d. Reed George and Katherine Espy. BS in Computer Scis., U. Mo., Springfield, 1975. Asst. v.p. sales Fortune Systems Corp., Belmont, Calif., 1983-85, v.p. corp. devel., 1985-86; pres., chief exec. officer Tigera Corp., Redwood City, Calif., 1986-88; gen. mgr. Wang Labs., Inc., Redwood City, 1988—. Mem. Pres. Assn. Mus. Modern Art. Mem. Am. Mgmt. Assn. Republican. Presbyterian. Home: 1171 Compass Ln Foster City CA 94404 Office: Wang Labs 350 Bridge Pkwy Redwood City CA 94065

ESPY, REYNETTE COATS, personnel administrator; b. Montclair, N.J., Oct. 5, 1960; d. Andrew Bernard and Bernice (Caviness) Coats; m. Michael Bryan Espy, Sept. 8, 1984; 1 child, Lanette Clarice. BA, Upsala Coll., 1982, MA, 1985. Cert. life skills counselor. Adminstrn. asst. Montclair (N.J.) State Coll., 1982-83, U.S. Dept. Def., Nutley, N.J., 1983-84; spl. projects and pub. relations asst. Montclair Bd. Edn., 1984-86; tng. technician/counselor, cons. Univ. Medicine and Dentistry, Newark, 1986-88; employment mgr. North Jersey Devel. Ctr., Totowa, N.J., 1988-89; career cons. Essex County Community Coll., Newark, 1990—; ednl. broker, counselor Bergen Tech. Schs., Hackensack, N.J., 1990—. Mem. Internat. Assn. for Pers. Women, Nat. Assn. for Female Execs., Am. Assn. for Counseling and Devel., Nat. Employment Counselors Assn., Nat. Career Devel. Assn., Am. Mgmt. Assn. Home: 436 Lincoln Ave Orange NJ 07050

ESSA, LISA BETH, teacher; b. Modesto, Calif., Nov. 19, 1955; d. Mark Newyia and Elizabeth (Warda) Essa. B.A., U. Pacific-Stockton, 1977, M.A. in Curriculum and Instrn. Reading, 1980. Cert. tchr. elem., multiple subject and reading specialist, Calif. Tchr. primary grades Delhi (Calif.) Elem. Sch. Dist., 1978-80; reading clinic tutor San Joaquin Delta Community Coll., Stockton, Calif., 1980; tchr. primary grades Hayward (Calif.) Unified Sch. Dist., Supr., San Francisco host com. Dem. Nat. Conv., 1984. Femmes Club scholar, 1973; U. Calif. Optometry Alumni Assn. scholar, 1973; Jobs Daughters scholar, 1974. Mem. Internat. Reading Assn., Calif. Tchrs. Assn., Hayward Unified Tchrs. Assn., San Francisco Jr. C. of C., Jr. League San Francisco. Democrat. Episcopalian. Home: 1960 Clay Apt 109 San Francisco CA 94109

ESSEX, JUDY TOWNE, home economics agent; b. Jersey City, June 7, 1954; d. John Franklin and Margaret Ida (Miller) Towne; m. Paul Denison Essex, Aug. 7, 1976; children: Kyle Towne, Ryan Denison. BS, Davis and Elkins Coll., 1976; MPA, L.I. U., 1982. Cert. tchr. health and phys. edn., N.Y. Natural resource planner Town of Denning, N.Y., 1978-80; substitute tchr. Tri Valley Cen. Sch., Grahamsville, N.Y., 1980-84; night mgr. New Age Health Farm, Neversink, N.Y., 1982-84; exec. dir. Liberty Community Coalition, N.Y., 1984-86; dir. grants and rsch. Community Gen. Hosp., Harris, N.Y., 1986-89, dir. health promotion, 1987-89; home econs. agent Cornell Coop. Extension of Sullivan County, Liberty, 1989—; exec. bd. dirs. Sullivan

Diagnostic Treatment Ctr., Harris. V.p., exec. bd. dirs. Sullivan County Cares Coalition, Liberty, 1985—; mem. com. on the handicapped Town of Neversink, N.Y., 1986—; chmn. Liberty Internat. Festival and Exposition, Liberty, 1984-85; founder Parents of Challenged Children, 1987; mem. ladies aux. Neversink Fire Co.; v.p. Tri-County Maternal Infant Svcs. Network, 1989—. Mem. NAFE, Am. Soc. for Healthcare Edn. and Tng., Assn. for Care Children's Health, Sullivan County C. of C. (corr. sec., exec. bd. dirs. 1985-87). Avocations: crocheting, skiing, cooking, making candy. Home: Rte 1 Box 21 Neversink NY 12765 Office: Cornell Coop Extension of Sullivan County RR 01 P O Box 520 Liberty NY 12754

ESSLINGER, CHARLENE MARIE DOBBS, secondary educator; b. Kingsport, Tenn., Mar. 29, 1945; d. Elwood DeWitt and Elizabeth (Barron) Dobbs; divorced; children: Paul Ralph, Todd Jacob. BS, SUNY, Brockport, N.Y., 1967; MS, SUNY, Cortland, N.Y., 1971; postgrad., Roehampton U., London, 1986; cert. advanced study, SUNY, Oswego, 1989. Cert. secondary educator, N.Y. Sci. tchr. Jamesville-DeWitt (N.Y.) Cen. Sch., 1967-68, East Syracuse-Minoa Cen. Sch., East Syracuse, N.Y., 1968-77; nursery sch. tchr. Jack'n Jill, DeWitt, 1977-79; biology tchr. Syracuse (N.Y.) City Schs., DeWitt, 1981—; adj. prof. Syracuse U., 1985—. Author: Winter Science Lab Manual, 1985, N.Y. State Regents Questions in Biology, 1988-89. Medic East Area Vol. Emergency Svcs., East Syracuse, 1974-89. Named Top Sci. Educator in N.Y. State Optical Soc., 1987, Disting. Educator I.D.E.A., 1987. Mem. Nat. Sci. Tchrs. Assn., Nat. Biology Tchrs. Assn., Sci. Club (pres. 1986—), Sigma Xi. Republican. Home: 209 Washburn Dr E Syracuse NY 13057 Office: G W Fowler High Sch 227 Magnolia St Syracuse NY 13204

ESSMAN, PANSY ELLEN, retired manufacturing company executive; b. Anomoose, N.D., Dec. 11, 1918; d. Robert John and Anna (Spivack) Hurt; m. Lewis John Essman, Mar. 29, 1942 (dec. Nov. 1967); children: Caroline Lane, Katheen Kelly. Aircraft mechanic helper Civil Service, Sacramento, 1940-45; electric assembler, welder Jennings Radio, San Jose, Calif., 1945-67; electronic parts insp. Watkins & Johnson, Palo Alto, Calif., 1967-72; pres., v.p., chmn. bd. Pansy Ellen Products, San Jose, Calif., 1969-83, ret., 1983. Author: Success Secrets, 1978; Pearls of Potentiality, 1979; subject of Six Figure Women, 1983; patentee infant bath aid. Recipient Oustanding Small Bus. Woman of Yr. award Internat. Council Small Bus. Mgmt. and Devel., 1976; Nat. Ind. Nursery Furniture Retailers Assn. award, 1976.

ESTABROOK, ALISON, breast surgeon, surgical oncologist, educator; b. N.Y.C., Oct. 29, 1951; d. Edwin Burke Estabrook and Shirley (Butler) Wood; m. William Neelis Harrington, June 13, 1981. BA cum laude, Barnard Coll., 1974; MD, NYU, 1978. Diplomate Am. Bd. Surgery. Resident in surgery Columbia-Presbyn. Med. Ctr., N.Y.C., 1978-81, 82-84, fellow in surg. oncology, 1981-82, asst. prof. surgery, 1984—, Florence Irving asst. prof., 1989—, dir. Breast Clinic, 1985—, dir. surg. oncology, 1988—. Contbr. articles to med. jours. Recipient Blakemore prize for rsch. Columbia-Presbyn. Med. Ceter, 1982, 84; Florence and Herbert Irving grantee, 1989—. Fellow ACS; mem. AMA, Am. Med. Women's Assn., Am. Assn. Acad. Surgeons, Am. Fedn. Clin. Rsch., N.Y. Surg. Soc., N.Y. Met. Breast Cance Group. Office: Columbia-Presbyn Med Ctr 161 Ft Washington Ave New York NY 10032

ESTABROOK, EVELYN MARIE BASOM, musician, educator; b. nr. Farmer City, Ill., Jan. 7, 1908; d. Samuel Jay and Lura Frances (Hillman) Basom; m. Dale Russell Reeser, Oct. 20, 1929 (dec. July 1962); children: William Jay, Carolyn Jane Waugh; m. Kenneth Charlie Estabrook, Oct. 3, 1966 (dec. Jan. 1984). Diploma in Pub. Sch. Music Methods, Millikin Conservatory, 1928, degree as collegue, 1954, degree as Child Specialist, 1955. Pianist for silent movies Farmer City, 1925-26; pvt. tchr. piano, 1928—; music tchr. pub. schs. Farmer City, Mansfield, Ill., 1928-39; accompanist, asst. Grossmont High Sch., La Mesa, Calif., 1941-45; freelance dir., pianist Evelyn's Serenaders, San Diego, 1945-62; dir., accompanist various choral prodns. San Diego, La Mesa, 1945—; ballet pianist Grossmont (Calif.) Coll., 1980-85; freelance performer, choreographer various fashion shows San Diego County, 1962—; chartered accompanist Woman's Club Choral Pro Musica, La Mesa, 1947—, Community Concert and Women's Com., Grossmont, 1957—. Composer: (gospel music) America Evermore, 1960, Those Who Love and Care, 1962, (club song) Our Club, 1963, La Mesa, the Jewel of the Hills, others, occasion pieces for Air Streams All Am. Girl, 1977 , also teaching material; participant Super Bowl '88 Piano Extravaganza, San Diego; pianist, writer, dir. numerous local mus. prodns. Entertainer, accompanist various pub. and ch. activities, Ill., Calif., 1923—; pianist La Mesa C. of C., 1987—. Mem. Am. Fedn. Musicians, Soroptimist Internat. (pres. 1959-60), Ladies Philanthropic Ednl. Orgn., Music Tchrs. Assn. (cert. 1948, 55, pres. 1960-61), Delta Omicron (pres. 1927-28). Republican. Methodist. Clubs: P.E.O. (pres. 1980-81), Toastmaster (toastmistress) (La Mesa). Home and Office: 7730 Homewood Pl La Mesa CA 92041

ESTEP, JANET OLSON, sales executive; b. Bay City, Mich., July 7, 1956; d. Theodore Hendrick and Ruth Helen (Bergh) Olson; m. David Charles Estep, Dec. 18, 1955; children: Michael. BA in Econs. & Psychology, St. Olaf Coll., Northfield, Minn., 1978. Mktg. rep. IBM, Mpls., 1978-84; area mktg. rep. IBM, 1984-86; mktg. mgr. IBM, Madison, Wis., 1987—. Mem. Phi Beta Kappa. Home: 3909 Sumac Cir Middleton WI 53562

ESTEP-JOHNSTON, MEGAN ALEXANDER, hydrologist; b. Pitts., Pa., July 11, 1957; d. Bradford Colcord and Dorothy Jane (Alexander) E.; m. Carl R., Sept. 06, 1986. BS, Pa. State U., 1979; MS, Oreg. State U., Corvallis, 1983; Post Grad., U. Colo., 1985--. Grad. research asst. Oreg. State U., Corvallis, 1980-82; civil engring. tech. USDA. Forest Service, Spearfish, S.D., 1983-84; tech. project officer USDI-Office Surface Mining, Pitts., 1984-85; project leader USDI-Office Surface Mining, Denver, hydrologist, 1987-89; hydrologist U.S. Fish and Wildlife Svc. Region 6, 1989—. Author Contbr. Articles to Profl. Jours. Recipient Best Tech. Paper U. Ky. Office of Continuing Edn. 1988. Office: US Fish and Wildlife Scv Region 6 P O Box 25486 Denver Fed Ctr Denver CO 80225

ESTERLINE, SHIRLEY JEANNE, lithograph company executive; b. Paulding, Ohio, June 6, 1936; d. George Gary and Catherine Genevieve (Durbin) Sontchi; m. Meredith Esterline, Apr. 1, 1956; children: Gordon Alan, Amy Jeanne. Cert. med. technologist, Elkhart U., Ind., 1956. Lab technician, Fort Wayne, Ind., 1956-57; sec. Zollner Corp., Fort Wayne, 1957-58, Magnavox Corp., Fort Wayne, 1958-61; sales coord. Doty Lithograph Inc., Fort Wayne, 1975-77; sales mgr. Dot Line div. Dot Corp., Auburn, Ind., 1977-87, Midwest sales mgr. Falco/Sunbelt div. FL Cos., Nashville, 1987-89. Recipient Top Sales award Dot Corp., 1985. Mem. Specialty Advt. Assn. Internat. (suppliers com. 1983—, cert. advt. specialist 1985—, chmn. 100 club 1983—, seminar facilitator calendar advt. coun. 1985-89, CAS Alumni 1985—, mgmt. awards 1984, 85, 86). Methodist. Avocations: reading, gardening.

ESTERLY, JULIET KING BINDT, counselor, teacher, social worker for blind; b. L.A., May 31, 1912; d. Roy Brooks and Cora May (Hurly) King; m. Henry M. Bindt, May 30, 1937 (div. 1942); m. Everett E. Esterly, Oct. 30, 1971 (dec. 1981). BA, Scripps Coll., 1934; MA in Social Svc., U. Calif., Berkeley, 1939; cert. to teach blind, U. Wash., 1948; postgrad. in rehab., U. San Francisco. Social worker for blind Alameda County Welfare Dept., Oakland, Calif., 1939-40; home tchr. Calif. State Libr., 1940-72; counselor tchr. Calif. Dept. Rehab., 1940-72; cons. about blindness for film Magnificent Obsession, Universal Studios, 1936; sec. div. home tchrs. Am. Assn. Workers for Blind, 1944-46; charter pres. Western Conf. Home Tchrs. of Blind, 1948-52, Associated Blind of Calif., 1958-63, Braille Revival League Calif., 1987—; v.p. Nat. Braille Revival League, 1990—; bd. dirs. Calif. Coun. of Blind, 1989—, Am. Coun. of Blind, 1960-61; mem. internat. com. to create advanced Braille code, Braille Authority N.Am., Can. Nat. Inst. for Blind, Toronto, 1989—. Author: Handbook for the Blind, 1952. Legis. chair Women's Internat. League for Peace and Freedom, 1936-38; active Hollywood and Berkeley LWV, 1935-39; pres. Berkeley chpt. Nat. Fedn. Bus. and Profl. Women's Clubs, 1951, chmn. state scholarship com., 1953. Recipient Citizen of Merit award Rossmoor Retirement Community, 1985; Juliet King Esterly scholarship endowed in her honor, 1954. Mem. AAUW, Am. Assn. Ret. Persons (chpt. pres. 1983-86), Ret. Pub. Employees Assn. (chpt. pres. 1988—), Am. Coun. of Blind (Ambassador award 1978), Am. Assn. Edn. and Rehab. of Blind, Phi Beta Kappa. Democrat. Home: 2408 Ptarmigan Dr Unit 1 Walnut Creek CA 94595

ESTES, ELAINE ROSE GRAHAM, librarian; b. Springfield, Mo., Nov. 24, 1931; d. James McKinley and Zelma Mae (Smith) Graham; m. John Melvin Estes, Dec. 29, 1953. B.S. in Bus. Adminstrn., Drake U., 1953, teaching cert., 1956; M.S. in L.S. U. Ill., 1960. With Public Library, Des Moines, 1956—; coordinator extension services Public Library, 1977-78, dir., 1978—; lectr. antiques, hist. architecture, libraries; mem. conservation planning com. for disaster preparedness for libraries. Author bibliographies of books on antiques; contbr. articles to profl. jours. Mem. State of Iowa Cultural Afairs Adv. Council, 1986—, Nat. Commn. on Future Drake U., 1987-88; chmn. Des Moines Mayor's Hist. Dist. Commn.; bd. dirs. Des Moines Art Ctr., 1972-83, hon. mem., 1983—; bd. dirs. Friends of Library USA, 1986—, Henry Wallace House Found.; mem. Iowa Libr. Centennial Com., 1990-91), nominations rev. com. Iowa State Nat. Hist. Register, 1983-89. Recipient recognition for outstanding working women—leadership in econs. and civic life of Greater Des Moines YWCA, 1975, Disting. Alumni award Drake U., 1979, Woman of Achievement award YWCA, 1989. Mem. ALA, Iowa Library Assn. (pres. 1978-79), Iowa Urban Pub. Library Assn., Library Assn. Greater Des Moines Metro Area (pres.), Iowa Soc. Preservation Hist. Landmarks (bd.dirs. 1969—). Clubs: Links, Quester's, Inc. (pres. 1982, state 2d v.p. 1984-86). Lodge: Rotary. Office: Pub Libr of Des Moines 100 Locust St Des Moines IA 50308-1791

ESTES, JOAN ETHEL PELTIER, nurse, administrator; b. Two Rivers, Wis., Sept. 26, 1938; d. Milton Eli and Josephine Mary (Benzinger) Peltier; m. Jim W. Estes, Aug. 20, 1960; children: Bryan David, Laurie Ann, Steven Michael. Student, St. Mary's Hosp. Sch. Nursing, Madison, Wis., 1956-59; BS in Nursing, U. Okla., 1985, MS in Health Adminstrn., 1989. RN, Okla. Staff nurse St. marys Hosp., Madison, Wis., 1959-60, Miami (Okla.) Bapt. Hosp., 1960-62; operating room supr. Norman (Okla.) Regional Hosp., 1962-73, 82-85; dir. surg. svcs. Bapt. Med. Ctr., Oklahoma City, 1973-81; adminstrv. dir. Physicians Surg. Ctr., Norman, 1985-87; quality assurance dir., dir. nursing Moore (Okla.) Community Hosp., 1988—; facilitator, trainer AIDS resources and edn. OK Care, Okla. Dept. Health, 1989-90. Mem. Am. Nurses Assn., Okla. Nurses Assn. (bd. dirs. 1988-90), Assn. Operating Room Nurses (pres., v.p., bd. dirs. 1965—), Okla. Assn. Quality Assurance Practitioners, Okla. U. Nurses Assn. Alumni (sec.), Coll. Pub. Health Alumni. Democrat. Roman Catholic. Office: Moore Mcpl Hosp 1500 SE 4th Box 6459 Moore OK 73160

ESTES, PATRICIA LYNN, software engineer, consultant; b. Chgo., Mar. 13, 1950; d. Oliver Roy and LaVerne Marie (Kahoun) Pritchett; m. Michael Allen Estes, Mar. 18, 1972; children: Erich Allen, Scott Ward. BA, U. Fla., 1972, MEd, 1973; MS, U. Cen. Fla., 1985; MBA, Rollins Coll., 1989. Adj. instr. Rollins Coll., Winter Park, Fla., 1982-87; sr. engr. Martin Marietta Aerospace Co., Orlando, Fla., 1985-87; cons. Profl. Computer Svcs., Orlando, 1987-89; sr. analyst R.W. Beck & Assocs., Orlando, 1989—. Mem. Jr. League Orlando-Winter Park, 1982-83. Mem. IEEE, Assn. for Computing Machinery, Data Processing Mgmt. Assn., Computer Security Inst., Audubon Soc., Rotary, Phi Beta Kappa, Beta Gamma Sigma. Republican. Roman Catholic. Office: Classic Shows 308 E Par Orlando FL 32804

ESTEY, AUDREE PHIPPS, artistic director; b. Winnipeg, Man., Can., Jan. 7, 1910; d. Robert and Anna (Harrington) Phipps; student Immaculate Heart Coll., 1927-29, Ernest Belcher Ballet Sch., 1928-31, Robert Major Drama Sch., 1929-31, Koslov Ballet Sch., 1930-31; m. L. Wendell Estey, Sept. 18, 1933; children—Lawrence Mitchell, Carol.Dancer Ernest Belcher Ballet Co., Los Angeles, 1930, Fanchon and Marco Co., Los Angeles, 1930-31; actress-dancer Fox Studio, Hollywood, Calif.; 1931-32 ballet tchr. Lawrenceville and Princeton, N.J., 1938-80, Perry Mansfield Camp, Steamboat Springs Colo., summers 1949-50; head dance dept. Les Chalets Francais, Deer Isle, Maine, 1951-73; founder non-profit Princeton (N.J.) Ballet Soc., 1954, dir., cons.; founder Princeton Regional Ballet Co., 1963; founder profl. co., Princeton Ballet, 1979. Host Northeast Regional Ballet Festival-Princeton, 1968; coordinator Northeast Regional Ballet Festival-Jacob's Pillow, 1970. Apptd. by gov. N.J. State Commn. to Study Arts, 1968, trustee N.J. Sch. of the Arts, 1980; bd. dirs. Sarasota Ballet of Fla., 1989—. Recipient Rutgers U. award for contbn. to arts in N.J., 1982. Mem. N.E. Regional Ballet Assn. (pres., 1967-68, exec. v.p., 1968-71). Episcopalian. Choreographer over 20 ballets for children and young dancers including: Festival of the Gnomes, Pastels, Peter and the Wolf, Sleeping Beauty, Cinderella, Pied Piper, The Nutcracker (choreography for Act I currently used by Princeton Ballet), Chanson Innocente, Graduation Ball, Coppelia. Office: 262 Alexander St Princeton NJ 08540

ESTILL, DONNA MARIE, sales executive; b. Burlington, Wis., Aug. 18, 1935; d. Roman Nicholas and Dorothy Mary (Elverman) Terry; m. Verne Eugene Adamson, Sept. 12, 1953 (div. Mar. 1960); children: DeWayne E. Adamson, Eugena V. Adamson Houston; m. Victor Wayne Estill, Jan. 10, 1970 (div. Feb. 1985). Student, Kenosha (Wis) Sch. Real Estate, 1984; grad., Real Estate Inst., Madison, Wis., 1985. With sales Kriby Co., Kenosha, 1958-61; agt. Fidelity Life (Kemper Ins.), Kenosha, 1961-66; mgr. Fashion Two Twenty Inc., Kenosha, 1966—; ind. contractor Century 21 Colleen Realty Corp., Kenosha, 1984—; tchr. real estate law Kenosha Sch. Real Estate, 1987—. Mem. Realtor Polit. Action Com. Mem. Kenosha Bd. Realtors (bd. dirs. 1990-93, RPAC chairperson 1987-91), Kenosha Area C. of C. (ambassador 1985—), Wis. Realtors Assn., Kenosha Shrine Aux., Kenosha Women's Club. Republican. Roman Catholic. Home: 424 44th St Kenosha WI 53140

ESTIN-KLEIN, LIBBYADA, advertising executive, medical writer; b. Newark, July 13, 1937; d. Barney and Florence B. (Tenkin) Straver; m. Harvey M. Klein, Sept. 9, 1984. Student Syracuse U., 1955-57; BS, Columbia, 1960; R.N., Columbia-Presbyn. Med. Ctr., 1960; cert., N.Y. Sch. Interior Design, 1962. Med. rsch. tech. writer, N.Y.C., 1960-62; pres. Libbyada Estin Interiors, N.Y.C., 1962-65; v.p. advt. and pub. relations Behrman/Estin Inc., N.Y.C., 1965-67; account exec., dir. pub. rels. J.S. Fullerton, Inc., N.Y.C., 1967-68; med. writer L.W. Frohlich & Co., Intercon Internat. Inc., N.Y.C., 1968-69, Kallir Philips Ross Inc., N.Y.C., 1969-71; copy supr. William Douglas McAdams Inc., N.Y.C., 1971-75, Sudler & Hennessey Inc., N.Y.C., 1975-80; v.p., exec. adminstr., creative dir. Grey Med. Advt. Inc., N.Y.C., 1980-84; founder, ptnr. Estin Sandler Communications Inc., N.Y.C., 1984; v.p. Barnum Communications Inc., N.Y.C., 1984-86; sr. v.p. ICE Communications, Inc., Rochester, N.Y., 1986-87; pres. Estin-Klein Communications Inc., Rochester and Pittsford, N.Y., 1987—; bd. dirs. Grief Resource Info. Edn. Forum, Inc. Mem. Pub. Rels. Soc. Am., Advt. Women N.Y., Am. Advt. Fedn., Advt. Coun. of Rochester, Rochester Sales and Mktg. Execs. Club, Mktg. Communicators of Rochester, Am. Med. Writers Assn., Pharm. Advt. Coun., Am. Nurses Assn., Allied Bd. Trade, Columbia-Presbyn. Hosp. Alumnae Assn., Columbia U. Alumnae Assn., Syracuse U. Alumnae Assn., Sigma Theta Tau, Delta Phi Epsilon. Home and Office: 289 Garnsey Rd Pittsford NY 14534

ESTKA BERDING, JEAN THERESA, fund raiser; b. Chgo., Dec. 18, 1923; d. Joseph and Clementine (Pielaszkiewicz) Estka. Grad. high sch., Chgo. Rivetor Lockheed, Calif., 1944; field rep. Fund Raiser Meml. for Women in Mil. Svc. of Am., Washington, 1988—. Good will amb. Munich, Fed. Republic of Germany, 1965, hosp. vol. VA Hosp. Hines, Maywood, Ill., 1963-66, With U.S. Army M.C., 1944-45. Beautification award Skokie (Ill.) C. of C., 1987. Mem. VFW (bd. dirs. #3854 1963-66), Lincolnwood Lang. Bank (translator 1988—), Real Fussball Club. Roman Catholic. Home: 7431 N Kolmar Ave Skokie IL 60076

ESTRICH, SUSAN RACHEL, law educator; b. Lynn, Mass., Dec. 16, 1952; d. Irving Abraham and Helen Roslyn (Freedberg) E.; m. Martin Kaplan. BA, Wellesley Coll., 1974; JD, Harvard U., 1977. Law clk. presiding justice U.S. Dist. Ct., Washington, 1977-78, Justice John Paul Stevens, Washington, 1978-79; dep. nat. issues dir., spl. asst. Kennedy for Pres. campaign, Washington, 1979-80; sr. policy advisor Mondale-Ferraro campaign, 1984; of counsel Tuttle & Taylor, L.A., 1986-87; campaign mgr. Dukakis for Pres. campaign, Boston, 1987-88; asst. prof. law Harvard Law Sch., Cambridge, Mass., 1981-86, prof. of law, 1986—; mem. Dem. Nat. Com., Washington, 1984-88, ACLU (nat. bd.), pres. Boston chpt., 1985-86; chmn. Drafting Com./Fairness Com., 1985-86; mem. nat. governing bd. Common Cause, 1983-89. Author: Real Rape, 1987; co-author: Dangerous Offenders, 1985; contbr. articles to numerous jours. Mem. D.C. Bar, Calif. Bar, U.S. Supreme Ct. Bar. Jewish. Office: USC Law Ctr Los Angeles CA 90089-0071

ESTRIN, KARI (KAREN RUTH ESTRIN), concert producer; b. Plainfield, N.J., Nov. 5, 1954; d. Herman Albert and Pearl (Simon) E. BA with honors, Ramapo Coll. of N.J., 1976. Founder, exec. dir. Black Sheep Concerts and Publs., Inc., Cambridge, Mass., 1980-86; editor The Black Sheep Rev., 1982-85; co-producer (album) Great Acoustics, 1985; artist mgr., agt. Tony Rice/Rounder Records, 1981-85; tour mgr. Suzanne Vega/A&M Records, 1985; founder, cons. Palomine Mgmt., 1984—; asst. producer Nestle Folk Festival Prodns., Inc., N.Y.C., 1987; artist mgr. (U.S. only) 3 Mustaphas 3/Ryko Disc, 1988—; artist asst. Suzy Bogguss/Capitol Records, 1989; Assoc. producer Gr. NE Prodns., Townsend, Mass., 1986; asst. to dir. Berkshire Mountain Bluegrass Festival, Hillsdale, N.Y., 1980-81; nat. promoter Rounder Records, Cambridge Mass., 1979; bd. dirs. Sing Out! mag.; events chairperson ECO Nashville. Pub., numerous concert and festival publs. Bd. dirs. Hey, Rube Folk Music Orgn., 1983-86, Folk Arts Network, Cambridge, 1983-85, Folk Arts Ctr. of New Eng., Cambridge, 1982-84. Mem. Nat. Assn. Ind. Record Distbrs. and Mfrs. Home and Office: 1415 Sumner Ave Nashville TN 37206

ESTRIN, THELMA AUSTERN, electrical engineer; b. N.Y.C., Feb. 21, 1924; d. I. Billy and Mary (Ginsburg) Austern; m. Gerald Estrin, Dec. 21, 1941; children: Margo, Judith, Deborah. BSEE, U. Wis., Madison, 1947, MSEE, 1948, PhD, 1951; DSc. (hon.), U. Wis., 1989. Cert. clin. engr. Research engr. UCLA Brain Research Inst., 1960-70, dir. data processing, 1970-80; prof. UCLA Sch. Engring. and Applied Sci., 1980—; prof. computer sci. UCLA, 1989—; dir. div. electronics, computer and systems engring. NSF, Washington, 1982-84; dir. dept. engring., asst. dean Sch. Engring. and Applied Sci. UCLA, 1984-89; trustee Aerospace Corp., 1979-82; mem. biomed. tech. resources com. NIH, 1981-86; mem. U.S. Army Sci. Bd., 1982-83; mem. energy engring. bd. NRC, 1985-88. Contbr. articles to tech. jours. Mem. Los Angeles Women in Bus. Recipient Disting. Contbn. to Engring. Edn. award NSPE, 1985, Achievement award Soc. Women Engrs. 1981, Disting. Service citation U. Wis., 1976. Fellow IEEE (bd. dirs. 1979-80, exec. v.p. 1982, recipient Centennial medal 1984, pres. Engring. in Medicine and Biology Soc. 1977), AAAS (chair engring. sect. 1989). Jewish. Office: UCLA Sch Engring & Applied Sci Boelter Hall Rm 3732 Los Angeles CA 90024

ETCHEMENDY, JEANNE MARIE, academic administrator, lawyer; b. Leavenworth, Kans., Oct. 14, 1959; d. Leon and Ruby Adaline (Nay) E. AB in English, Stanford U., 1981; JD, U. Calif., San Francisco, 1984. Bar: Nev. 1984, Calif. 1985. Assoc. Vargas & Bartlett, Reno, Nev., 1984-85, Bidart & Assocs., Chino, Calif., 1985-86, Holtzmann, Wise & Shepard, Palo Alto, Calif., 1986-89; assoc. dir. devel. Stanford (Calif.) U., 1989—. Vol. Stanford U., 1986—. Mem. Nev. Bar Assn., Calif. Bar Assn. Democrat. Roman Catholic. Office: Stanford U Office Devel 301 Encina Hall Stanford CA 94305

ETHAN, CAROL BAEHR, psychotherapist; b. N.Y.C., May 30, 1920; d. Irving and Sadie (Goldman) Baehr; m. Sy Ethan, Mar. 18, 1955; children: Willa Capraro, Barbara Ethan. Trained Greenwich Inst. Psychoanalytic Studies, 1965-70; BA in Psychology with honors, N.Y. U., 1978; MA in Psychology, New Sch. Social Rsch., 1981. Writer, Irvington (N.J.) Herald, 1946, Walt Framer Prodns., 1949-50; tchr. Queens Coll., 1956-57; consumer psychology researcher and cons., 1950-70; staff psychotherapist Fifth Ave. Ctr. Counseling and Psychotherapy, 1965-70; pvt. practice psychotherapy, N.Y.C., 1967—; columnist Rhinebeck Gazette-Advertiser, 1981-86. Dem. committeewoman for Queens County, 1960; vol. social rehab. program Queens County Mental Health Soc., 1965-66; fellow internat. coun. sex edn. and parenthood Am. U. Recipient Founders Day award NYU, 1978. Fellow Am. Orthopsychiat. Assn.; mem. N.Y. State Assn. Practicing Psychotherapists (cert.), Am. Mental Health Counselors Assn., Divorce Mediation Coun., Am. Psychol. Assn., Internat. Acad. Behavioral Med., Counseling and Psychotherapy (clin. mem.). Address: 2 Somers Dr Rhinebeck NY 12572

ETHERTON, GLORIA ELIZABETH, retired nurse; b. Balt., Jan. 6, 1930; d. Charles Howard and Beatrice Carter (Murray) Timanus; m. Donald Francis Etherton, Apr. 23, 1955; children: Deborah, Jeffrey, Marybeth, Daniel, Michael. Student, St. Joseph's Hosp., Balt., 1950-53. RN. RN, operating room St. Joseph's Hosp., Balt., 1950-55, Kernan's Hosp., Balt., 1955-57; RN, cardiac care Easton (Md.) Meml. Hosp., 1975-85; RN, Clagget Summer Camp, Buckstown, Md., 1951-54, Camp Wright, Stevensville, Nd., 1963-80. Mem. St. Michael's Community PTA, 1963-75; vol. Remedial Reading Elem. Sch., 1965-75; chmn. St. Michael Community Ctr., 1990—; mem. xmas in St. Michaels com., 1987. Mem. Md. State Nurses Assn., Md. State Bd. of Edn., Talbot County Bd. of Edn., St. Joseph's Hosp. Alumnae, Miles River Yacht Club (v.p., treas. 1975-88), St. Michael's Women's Club. Democrat. Episcopalian. Home: PO Box S 104 A West Chestnut St Saint Michaels MD 21663 Office: Talbot County Bd Edn Talbot County Court House Easton MD 21601

ETRA, BLANCHE G., lawyer; b. N.Y.C., Mar. 8, 1915; d. Jack and Anna (Simon) Goldman; m. Harry Etra, Apr. 19, 1939; children: Aaron, Marshall, Donald, Jonathan. BA, Barnard Coll., 1937; LLB, Columbia U., 1939; DHL (hon.) Yeshiva U., 1988. Bar: N.Y. 1939, U.S. Supreme Ct. 1960. Assoc. Hautman, Sheridan & Tekulsky, N.Y.C., 1938-39; assoc. Etra & Etra, N.Y.C., 1939-77, ptnr., 1977—. Bd. dirs. Cardozo Sch. Law, N.Y.C., 1978—; bd. overseers Albert Einstein Coll. Medicine, N.Y.C. Recipient Louise Waterman Wise award Am. Jewish Congress, N.Y.C., 1975; Disting. Service award Albert Einstein Coll. Medicine, 1978. Mem. Bar of Assn. of City of N.Y., N.Y. Women's Bar Assn. Jewish. Office: Etra & Etra 655 Madison Ave New York NY 10021

ETRIS, DENISE EILEEN, anthropologist; b. Phila., Sept. 23, 1950; d. William John and Gladys Lillian (Waite) E. Diploma in nursing, Sacred Heart Hosp., Allentown, Pa., 1971; BA in Anthropology, Bloomsburg (Pa.) U., 1988; MA, Am. U., 1990. Clin. adminstr. Life Support Systems Inc., Abington, Pa., 1971-72; adminstrv. supr. Parkview Hosp., Phila., 1976-81; renal nurse specialist, transplant coordinator Geisinger Med. Ctr., Danville, Pa., 1981-85; charge nurse, substance abuse counselor White Deer/Koala Treatment Ctr., Allenwood, Pa., 1985-88; fellow Am. U., Washington, 1989—; researcher Muskegag Cree Coun., Ontario, Can., 1986-88. Publ. dir. League Women Voters, Lewisburg, Pa., 1981-82. Mem. Drug and Alcohol Nurses Assn., Phi Sigma Iota. Roman Catholic. Home: 10701-200 Hampton Mill Terr Rockville MD 20852 Office: Am U Dept Anthropology 4400 Massachusetts Ave NW Washington DC 20016

ETSITTY, SYLVIA MAE, administrator; b. Ganado, Ariz., July 23, 1957; d. Benjamin William Harding and Evelyn (Lee) McCabe; m. Bobby Leroy Etsitty, Oct. 28, 1979; 1 child, Bryant Loren. AA, Bacone Jr. Coll., Muskogee, 1978; Student, U. New Mexico, Albuquerque, 1982-83. Researcher Navajo Nation Jud. Branch, Window Rock, Ariz., 1978-78; police planner Div. Pub. Safety, Window Rock, 1979-80; mgmt. analyst Navajo Nation Div. Soc. Services, Window Rock, 1981-81; personnel analyst Navajo Nation Personnel Dept., Window Rock; prog. analyst Navajo Nation Vet. Office, Window Rock, 1984-84; project dir. Navajo Dept. Health, 1984--; dir. Ft. Defiance Hosp. Steering Community Ft. Defiance Ariz., 1984--; organizer Navajo Nation Vietnam Vet. Symposium, Window Rock, 1987-84. Author: Short Story, 1975, 89, Poetry, 1978. Vice-chmn. Local Planning Bd. Ganado, Cornfields Ariz., 1988; tech. advisor Ft. Defiance Steering Com. Window Rock, 1988; Native Am. Child Welfare Advocate. Recipient award for excellent svc. Dept. of Health, 1986, Disting. Svcs. award Ft. Defiance Hosp. Window Rock, 1987, Photography awards Navajo Nation Window Rock, 1988, 89. Mem. Red Cross Navajo Chpt. Window Rock. Democrat. Baptist. Home: PO Box 1432 Window Rock AZ 86515 Office: Navajo Nation Dept Health PO Box 1390 Window Rock AZ 86515

ETTER, CONSTANCE LYNNE, librarian, businesswomen; b. Litchfield, Ill., July 20, 1943; d. John Orla and Adeline Mae (Arkabauer) E. BA, So. Ill. U., 1965; MLS, U. Ill., 1967. Serials cataloger St. Louis U. Libr., 1967-68; libr. Alton (Ill.) Meml. Hosp. Sch. Nursing, 1968-70; from tech. svcs. dir. to ref. cons. to gen. cons. Cumberland Trail Libr. System, Flora, Ill., 1971-

76; cons. Kaskaskia Libr. System, Smithton, Ill., 1976-78; libr. Ill. State Auditor Gen.'s Office, Springfield, Ill., 1979-89; freedom info. officer Ill. State Auditor Gens. Office, Springfield, Ill., 1985-89, state auditor, 1986-89; owner, designer Horsefancy Plus, Savannah, Ga., 1990—. Vol. Kumler Neighborhood Ministries, Springfield, 1983—; mem. Women's Internat. League for Peace and Freedom, Springfield, 1984—; sec. Northwest Condominium Assn., Springfield, 1983-86, pres., 1986-87, bd. dirs. 1983-90; charter mem. Art for Peace, Springfield, 1985—. Mem. ALA, Beta Phi Mu, Lamda Iota Tau. Democrat. Presbyterian. Office: Horsefancy Plus 26 Monastery Rd Savannah GA 31411

ETTER, ZANA CLAIRE, media library director; b. Camden, N.J., June 6, 1950; d. Clair V. and Zana Irene (Clapper) Cathers; m. D.W. Early, June 29, 1974 (div. July 1981); m. Markus Ernst Etter, May 28, 1988. Student, U. Lausanne, Switzerland, 1970; BA in French, Rutgers U., 1972, MEd, 1979, MLS, 1986. Cert. French, German and ESL tchr., N.J. Cataloguer Princeton (N.J.) U., 1973-79; info. specialist Edn. Improvement Ctr., Princeton, 1979-82; supr., libr. assoc. Rutgers U. Tech. Svcs., New Brunswick, N.J., 1982-87; dir. media libr. univ. medicine and dentistry Robert Wood Johnson Med. Sch., Piscataway, N.J., 1987—; tchr. ESL West Windsor-Plainsboro (N.J.) Schs., 1978, YMCA, Princeton, 1981; tchr. French East Windsor Adult Sch., Hightstown, N.J., 1981; pvt. practice tutoring English, Plainsboro, N.J., 1981-84. Mem. Med. Libr. Assn., Health Scis. Libr. Assn. N.J. Office: Robert Wood Johnson Med Sch 675 Hoes Ln Piscataway NJ 08854

ETTL, DOROTHY ANNE, home economist, retired educator; b. Marysville, Calif., Apr. 19, 1943; d. Walter Joseph and Celia Marie (Hill) E. BS, U. Calif., Davis, 1964; MS in Home Econs., Tex. Tech. U., 1969; postgrad., U. Hawaii, summer 1970; PhD in Home Econs., U. Minn., 1976. Cert. spl. vocat. tchr., Tex., standard secondary tchr., Calif. County extension home economist Agrl. Extension Service, U. Wyo., Lusk, Wyo., 1964-67; teaching and rsch. asst. Tex. Tech. U., Lubbock, 1968-69; asst. prof. home econs. Calif. State U., Chico, 1969-73; rsch. asst. U. Minn., St. Paul, 1973-76; assoc. prof. Wash. State U., Pullman, 1976-89, mem. faculty senate, 1980-84. Contbr. numerous articles to extension publs.; author audio-visual ednl. materials; columnist Info. Kettle, 1964-67. Bd. dirs. Friends Mus. Art, Wash. State U., 1985-88. Mem. Am. Home Econs. Assn. (life; cert.), Assn. Coll. Profls. Textiles and Clothing (exec. bd. 1979-82), Nat. Assn. Extension Home Economists, Coop. Extension Assembly (v.p. 1985-88), Assn. Faculty Women Wash. State U. (treas. 1987-89), Whitman County Hist. Soc. (life), Epsilon Sigma Phi (sec. Beta chpt. 1986-88). Home: 6217 Garmire Rd Meridian CA 95957

ETTL, JOHANNA MOSELLE, county official; b. Frederick, Md., July 7, 1964; d. Dean Harrison and Patricia Minnie-Faith (Rosencrantz) E. BA, Randolph-Macon Coll., Ashland, Va., 1986; MPA, The Am. U., 1989. Intern Office of Pub. Policy State of Va., Richmond, 1986; pub. adminstrn. intern Office of Legis. Oversight, Montgomery County, Md., 1986-88; mgmt. and budget specialist Office of Mgmt. & Budget, Montgomery County, 1988—. Mem. Am. Soc. Pub. Adminstrn., Pi Sigma Alpha. Democrat. Home: 10620 Weymouth Ave Apt 4 Bethesda MD 20814 Office: Office of Mgmt & Budget 101 Monroe St Rockville MD 20805

ETZEL, BARBARA COLEMAN, psychologist, educator; b. Pitts., Sept. 19, 1926; d. Walter T. and Ruth (Coleman) E. AA, Stephens Coll., 1946; BS in Psychology, Denison U., 1948; MS, U. Miami, Fla., 1950; PhD in Exptl. Child Psychology, State U. Iowa, 1953. Staff psychologist Ohio State Bur. Juvenile Rsch., Columbus, 1953-54; asst. prof. psychology Fla. State U., Tallahassee, 1954-56; chief psychologist, child psychiatry U. Wash. Med. Sch., Seattle, 1956-61; assoc. prof. psychology Western Wash. State U., Bellingham, 1961-65, dir. grad. program in psychology, 1963-65; spl. fellow sect. early learning and devel. NIMH, Bethesda, Md., 1965-66; assoc. prof. dept. human devel. U. Kans., Lawrence, 1965-69, mem. grad. faculty, 1965—, prof. human devel., 1969—, dir. Edna A. Hill Child Devel. Lab., 1965-72, dir. Kans. Ctr. for Rsch. in Early Childhood Edn., 1968-71, assoc. dean Office of Rsch. Adminstrn. and Grad. Sch., 1972-74, dir. John T. Stewart Children's Ctr., 1975-85; vis. prof. Universidad Central de Venezuela, Caracas, 1981-82; cons. Manchester Sch. Presch. Program, U. Mex., Mexico City, 1973-75, George Peabody Tchrs. Coll., 1978, St. Luke's Hosp., Kansas City, Mo., 1981-83, Anne Sullivan Sch. for Handicapped Children, Lima, Peru, 1982-85; trustees Cambridge (Mass.) Ctr. for Behavioral Studies, 1988—; cons. Princeton Child Devel. Inst., 1987—. Author: (with J.M. LeBlanc and D.M. Baer) New Developments in Behavioral Research, 1977; contbr. articles to profl. jours.; mem. editorial bd. Behavior Analyst, 1988-91. Bd. dirs. Community Children's Ctr., Inc., 1968-71; trustee Ctr. for Rsch., Inc., U. Kans., 1975-78. Elected to U. Kans. Women's Hall of Fame, 1975; Japan Soc. Promotion for Sci. fellow, 1981. Fellow Am. Psychol. Assn. (Div. 25 Don Hake award, 1987); mem. Assn. Behavior Analysis (pres. 1987—, pres.-elect 1986-87), Soc. Rsch. in Child Devel., Midwestern Psychol. Assn., Am. Ednl. Rsch. Assn., AAAS, AAUP, Southwestern Soc. Research in Human Devel., Sigma Xi, Psi Chi, Pi Lambda Theta. Home: Woodsong at JB Ranch Rte 1 PO Box 82-E Oskaloosa KS 66066 Office: U Kans Dept Human Devel Lawrence KS 66045

ETZLER, MARILYNN EDITH, biochemist, educator; b. Detroit, Oct. 30, 1940; d. Elmer Ellsworth and Doris (Tegge) E. BS, BA, Otterbein Coll., Westerville, Ohio, 1962; PhD, Washington U., St. Louis, 1967. Asst. prof. biochemistry U. Calif., Davis, 1969-75, assoc. prof. biochemistry, 1975-79, prof. biochemistry, 1979—. Contbr. articles to sci. publs. Grantee NIH, 1970—, NSF, 1981—. Mem. Am. Soc. Biochemistry and Molecular Biology, Am. Soc. Cell Biology, Complex Carbohydrate Soc., Am. Soc. Plant Physiology, Protein Soc. Office: Dept Biochemistry/Biophysic Univ Calif Davis CA 95616

EU, MARCH KONG FONG, state official; b. Oakdale, Calif., Mar. 29, 1922; d. Yuen and Shiu (Shee) Kong; children by previous marriage—Matthew Kipling Fong, Marchesa Suyin Fong You; m. Henry Eu, July 30, 1973; stepchildren—Henry, Adeline, Yvonne, Conroy, Alaric. Student, Salinas Jr. Coll.; B.S., U. Calif.-Berkeley; M.Ed., Mills Coll., 1951; Ed.D., Stanford U., 1956; postgrad., Columbia U., Calif. State Coll.-Hayward; LL.D., Lincoln U., 1984. Chmn. div. dental hygiene U. Calif. Med. Center, San Francisco; dental hygienist Oakland (Calif.) Pub. Schs.; supr. dental health edn. Alameda County (Calif.) Schs.; lectr. health edn. Mills Coll., Oakland; mem. Calif. Legislature, 1966-74, chmn. select com. on agr., foods and nutrition, 1973-74; mem. com. natural resources and conservation, com. commerce and pub. utilities, select com. med. malpractice; sec. state State of Calif., 1975—, chief of protocol, 1975-83, sec. of state; chmn. Calif. State World Trade Commn., 1982-87; spl. cons. Bur. Intergroup Relations, Calif. Dept. Edn.; ednl., legis. cons. Sausalito (Calif.) Pub. Schs., Santa Clara County Office Edn., Jefferson Elementary Union Sch. Dist., Santa Clara High Sch. Dist., Santa Clara Elementary Sch. Dist., Live Oak Union High Sch. Dist.; mem. Alameda County Bd. Edn., 1956-66, pres., 1961-62, legis. adv., 1963. Mem. budget panel Bay Area United Fund Crusade; mem. Oakland Econ. Devel. Council; mem. tourism devel. com. Calif. Econ. Devel. Commn.; mem. citizens com. on housing Council Social Planning; mem. Calif. Interagy. Council Family Planning; edn. chmn., mem. council social planning, dir. Oakland Area Baymont Dist. Community Council; charter pres., hon. life mem. Howard Elementary Sch. PTA; charter pres. Chinese Young Ladies Soc., Oakland; mem., vice chmn. adv. com. Youth Study Centers and Ford Found. Interagy. Project, 1962-63; chmn. Alameda County Mothers' March, 1971-72; bd. councillors U. So. Calif. Sch. Dentistry, 1976; mem. exec. com. Calif. Democratic Central Com., mem. central com., 1963-70, asst. sec.; del. Dem. Nat. Conv., 1968; dir. 8th Congl. Dist. Dem. Council, 1963; v.p. Dems. of 8th Congl. Dist., 1963; dir. Key Women for Kennedy, 1963; women's vice chmn. No. Calif. Johnson for Pres., 1964; bd. dirs. Oakland YWCA, 1965. Recipient ann. award for outstanding achievement Eastbay Intercultural Fellowship, 1959; Phoebe Apperson Hearst Disting. Bay Area Woman of Yr. award; Woman of Yr. award Calif. Retail Liquor Dealers Inst., 1969; Merit citation Calif. Assn. Adult Edn. Adminstrs., 1970; Art Edn. award; Outstanding Woman award Nat. Women's Polit. Caucus, 1980; Person of Yr. award Miracle Mile Lions Club, 1980; Humanitarian award Milton Strong Hall of Fame, 1981; Outstanding Leadership award Ventura Young Dems., 1983; Woman of Achievement award Los Angeles Hadassah, 1983. Mem. Am. Dental Hygienists Assn. (pres. 1956-57), No. Calif. Dental Hygienists Assn., Oakland LWV, AAUW (area rep. in edn. Oakland br.), Calif. Tchrs. Assn., Calif. Sch. Bd. Assn., Alameda County Sch. Bd. Assn. (pres. 1965), Alameda County Mental Health Assn., So. Calif. Dental Assn. (hon.), Bus. and Profl. Women's Club, Chinese Retail Food Markets Assn. (hon.), Delta Kappa Gamma. Office: Sec of State State of Calif 1230 J St Sacramento CA 95814

EULENBERG, JULIA NEIBUHR, history and archives educator, consultant; b. San Angelo, Tex., Aug. 18, 1942; d. Ralph Waldo Niebuhr and Joy Neibuhr (Coatney) Holliday; m. George Edward Schairer, March 24, 1963 (div. 1975); children: Benjamin Baker, Sarah Niebuhr; m. Michael Eulenberg, Feb. 24, 1980. BA in Polit. Sci., U. Wash., 1965, MA in History and Archives Mgmt., 1984, Ph.C. in History, 1986. Freelance editor, 1970—; editor Battelle Seattle Research Ctr., Seattle, 1974-76; records and archives specialist Battelle Seattle Rsch. Ctr., 1981-84; mgr. info. publs. services Battelle Human Affairs Rsch. Ctrs., Seattle, 1976-81; archivist Wash. State Jewish Hist. Soc., Seattle, 1983-84; cons. archives and records mgmt., 1984—; pres. Laird Norton Archival Svcs., 1988—; owner, cons. The Corp. Archives, Seattle, 1988-89; vis. lectr. U. Wash Sch. of Library and Info. Sci., Seattle. Author: Handbook for the Recovery of Water Damaged Business Records, 1986; contbr. articles to profl. jours. Active synagogue activities. Mem. Am. Assn. for State and Local History, Assn. Records Mgrs. and Adminstrs., Immigrtion History Soc., Internat. Coun. Archivists and Records Mgrs. (corr. mem. coun. integrative com. 1981—), N.W. Archivists' Assn. (mem. publs. com., editor newsletter 1981-85), Pacific N.W. Historians' Guild (exec. bd. 1984-86), Soc. Am. Archivists, Assn. Profl. Writers and Editors (v.p. program devel. 1977-78), Seattle Area Archivits (pres. 1990—), Phi Alpha Theta. Democrat. Office: 1250 17th St E Ste 1300 Seattle WA 98112

EULER, ALINE, environmental center executive, naturalist; b. N.Y.C.; d. Henry and Alice (Revaz) E. BA, Queens Coll., 1960, MS, 1966, 77; EdD, St. John's U., 1988. Cert. permanent tchr., N.Y. Play street dir. Police Athletic League, Bklyn., 1960; elem. tchr. Bellew Pub. Sch., West Islip, N.Y., 1960-78; dir. edn. Alley Pond Environ. Ctr., Douglaston, N.Y., 1978—; instr. elem. edn. Adelphi U. Grad. Sch., Garden City, N.Y., 1981; instr. elem. sci. Queens Coll., Flushing, N.Y., 1982; instr. continuing edn. Queensborough Community Coll., Bayside, N.Y., 1988—. Contbr. articles to various publs. Sec. Orgn. Gen. Slocum Survivors, Queens Village, N.Y., 1984—; v.p. Bayside Hist. Soc., 1985-87; chmn. Oakland Lake and Ravine Conservation Commn., Bayside, 1986—. Recipient Environ. Quality award U.S. EPA, 1990, Environmental Quality award U.S. Environ. Protection Agy.-Region 2, 1970-90. Mem. Nat. Assn. for Rsch. in Sci. Teaching and Sci., N.Am. Assn. Environ. Edn., Elem. Sch. Sci. Assn. (presenter 1990), Environ. Ednl. Adv. Coun., Nat. Sci. Tchr. Assn., Queens County Bird Club (Flushing), Phi Delta Kappa. Home: 204-05 43d Ave Bayside NY 11361 Office: Alley Pond Environ Ctr 228-06 Northern Blvd Douglaston NY 11363

EUREN, MARCIA DUKE, educator; b. Indpls., Apr. 6, 1948; d. George Warren and Ethel Ruth (Trent) Duke; m. Gary Edwin Euren, June 8, 1974. BS in Edn., Ohio U., 1969. Cert. 1st grade profl. life tchr., N.D. Tchr. sci. Valley Jr. High Sch., Grand Forks (N.D.) Pub. Sch. Dist. 1, 1970—, chmn. dept., 1989—. Mem. NEA, N.D. Edn. Assn. (polit. action com. 1972—), Grand Forks Edn. Assn. (sec. 1978-81), N.D. Sci. Tchrs. Assn., Grand Forks County Hist. Soc., AAUW (chmn. ednl. founds. Grand Forks chpt. 1980—), Phi Delta Kappa, Pi Lambda Theta. Office: Valley Jr High Sch 2l00 5th Ave N Grand Forks ND 58203

EUSTER, JOANNE REED, librarian; b. Grants Pass, Oreg., Apr. 7, 1936; d. Robert Lewis and Mabel Louise (Jones) Reed; m. Stephen L. Gerhardt, May 14, 1977; children: Sharon L., Carol L., Lisa J. Student, Lewis and Clark Coll., 1953-56; B.A., Portland State Coll., 1965; M.Librarianship, U. Wash., 1968, M.B.A., 1977; Ph.D., U. Calif.-Berkeley, 1986. Asst. libr. Edmonds Community Coll., Lynnwood, Wash., 1968-73, dir. libr.-media ctr., 1973-77; univ. libr. Loyola U. of New Orleans, 1977-80; libr. dir. J. Paul Leonard Libr., San Francisco State U., 1980-86; univ. libr. Rutgers State U. N.J., New Brunswick, 1986-89, v.p. info. svcs., 1989—; cons. Union Ejidal, La Penita, Nayarit, Mexico, 1973, Univ. D.C., 1988; co-cons. Office of Mgmt. Svcs. Assn. of Rsch. Librs., 1979—; mem. adv. couns. Hong Kong U. Sci. and Tech. Librs., 1988—, Princeton U. Libr., 1988. Author: Changing Patterns of Internal Communication in Large Academic Libraries, 1981, The Academic Library Director, Management Activities and Effectiveness, 1987; contbr. articles to profl. jours. Mem. ALA, N.J. Libr. Assn., Assn. Coll. and Rsch. Librs. (pres. 1987-88) Libr. Adminstrn. and Mgmt. Assn., Soc. for Scholarly Pub. Office: Rutgers State U NJ 169 College Ave New Brunswick NJ 08903

EUSTIS, LEOLA BARNHART, nursing educator; b. Nebo, Pa., Nov. 14, 1920; d. Herbert Wilson and Ada Pearl (Murphy) Barnhart; m. George Arthur Eustis, Nov. 3, 1942 (dec. Dec. 1981); children: Carole Ann, Sarah Ruth. Diploma in nursing, Washington Hosp. Sch. Nursing, Pa., 1942; BS in Nursing Edn. magna cum laude, U. Pitts., 1957, MEd, 1964. Staff nurse Washington (Pa.) Hosp., 1942-45, supr., 1945-52, assoc. dir., nursing svc., 1965-68, dir. pers. edn., 1968-74; instr. Washington Hosp. Sch. Nursing, 1952-60, 1974-83; private duty nurse Washington Hosp., 1960-65. Mem. nat. Dem. Com., 1981—, Nat. Wildlife Fedn., 1990—, Easter Seals Soc., 1960—; bd. dirs. Am. Cancer Soc., Washington County unit, 1958-70, Washington County Mental Health Assn., 1965-70; vol. Hospice of Washington County and Washington Hosp. Mem. Washington Hosp. Nurses' Alumnae Assn. (pres. 1947-49), Am. Assn. Retired Persons, AAUW (pres. Washington county br. 1972-73, Sigma Theta Tau. Methodist.

EUSTIS, RUTHILD PANTEN, technical writer; b. Dusseldorf, Germany, Dec. 14, 1929; d. Hans and Elisabeth (Fischer) Panten; children: Renata Elisabeth, Ann Martha, Kathryn Marwick. Degree in Linguistics, Julius Maximilians U., Wurzburg, Germany, 1952; postgrad. in linguistics, Columbia U., 1955; BA, U. South Fla., 1973. Cert. educator of educably mentally retarded, elem. educator, Fla. Copy editor, proof reader Electronic Data Systems Corp., Singfield, Va.; tech. editor Electromagnetic Technology, Inc., Burke, Va.; publ. editor Sci. Applications Internat. Corp., McLean, Va.; tech. editor/writer VSE Corp., Alexandria, Va. Mem. NAFE, Washington Ind. Writers, Coun. for Exceptional Children. Home: 915 25th St NW Washington DC 20037

EUTENEUER, URSULA BRIGITTE, research cell biologist; b. Biedenkopf, Fed. Republic Germany, Aug. 26, 1949; d. Robert and Margarethe Anna Josephine (Limberger) E.; m. Manfred Paul Wilhelm Schliwa, Dec. 29, 1978. BS, U. Frankfurt, 1971, MS, 1974, PhD, 1978. Teaching asst. U. Frankfurt (Fed. Republic Germany), 1972-75, rsch. assoc., 1978-79; rsch. assoc. U. Colo., Boulder, 1979-81, U. Wis., Madison, 1981-82; staff assoc. U. Calif., Berkeley, 1982—. Co-author books; contbr. articles to profl. jours. Grad. fellow U. Frankfurt, 1975-76. Mem. Am. Soc. for Cell Biology, Electron Microscopy Soc., German Soc. for Cell Biology. Home: 309 Vassar Ave Kensington CA 94708 Office: U Calif Dept Molecular and Cell Biology Berkeley CA 94720

EVAN, CATHY EMMA, bradcaster; b. Cleve., July 4, 1958; d. Joseph and Margaret (Kanda) E. BS in Communications, Ohio U., 1980. Program dir. Sta. WIBZ-Radio, Parkersburg, W.Va., 1980-84; pub. svc. dir., on-air talent Sta. WYFE-Radio, Rockford, Ill., 1984-85; audio engr. Sta. WUAB-TV, Cleve., 1985; music dir. Sta. WBEA-Radio, Cleve., 1985-87; on-air talent Sta. WNCX-Radio, Cleve., 1987—. Winner rsch. competition Active Industry Rsch., Columbia, Ohio, 1986. Libertarian. Home: 14224 Garfield Ave Lakewood OH 44107 Office: North Coast Cable 3300 Lakeside Ave Cleveland OH 44114

EVANHOE, CLARA MAY, retired dietitian; b. Prague, Okla., Oct. 3, 1908; d. Alfred Henry and Amanda Elvira (Cansler) Burris; m. Bernard M. Evanhoe, Aug. 25, 1925 (dec. 1985); children: Patricia, Carol, Edward, Charles. BS in Lit., Okla. State U., 1927, BS in Nutrition Dietetics, 1937. Registered dietitian. Tchr. Wilson Consol., Okmuigee, Okla., 1930-31, Kendrick (Okla.) Pub. Schs., 1933-36; profl. planner W.P.A. Housekeeping Aides of Okla., Oklahoma City, 1939-41; chief mail clk. Basic Magnesium War Plant, Las Vegas, Nev., 1941-42; dietitian Okla. State U. Cafeteria, Stillwater, 1944-46; women's editor Capper's Weekly, Topeka, 1947-48; registered dietitian Topeka State Hosp., 1957-61, Stormont-Vail Hosp., Topeka, 1961-72; dietitian cons. to area nursing homes Topeka, 1972-83; ret., 1983; lectr. in field. Contbr. articles to numerous publs. Mem. AAUW, Am. Dietetic Assn., Topeka Home Econs. Assn., Kans. Author's Club. Republican.

EVANKO, MICHELLE MARIANNE, computer operator; b. Scranton, Pa., Jan. 10, 1960; d. Thomas and Evelyn Marie (Pidick) E. PA, AST, Johnson Tech. Inst., Scranton, Pa., 1980. Cert. advanced operator on VersaCAD and Computervision Cadds3. CADD operator The Babcock & Wilcox Co., Scranton, Pa., 1980-83; CADD co-mgr. operator GSGSB, Inc., Berens Bldg., Clarks Summit, Pa., 1983—. Mem. NAFE, Johnson Tech. Inst. Alumni Assn. (sec., archtl. drafting and design craft adv. com.). Democrat. Mem. Byzantine Catholic Ch. Home: 510 River St Scranton PA 18505 Office: Berens Bldg Clarks Summit PA 18411-0244

EVANOFF-MORRISON, CAROLYN YVONNE, manufacturing company executive, consultant; b. Escondido, Calif., Dec. 1, 1955; d. Chester Benson and Shirly Bernice (Pederson) E.; m. Michael Kelly Morrison, Jan. 15, 1983 (div. Nov. 1984). AA, Evergreen Valley Coll., 1986; BS in Mgmt., St. Mary's U., Moraga, Calif., 1988. Police cadet Milpitas (Calif.) Police Dept., 1972-73; cashier K-Mart, Milpitas, 1973; electronic technician Raytheon Semicondr. Co., Mountain View, Calif., 1973-75; micro electronics assembler Lockheed Missiles and Space Co., Sunnyvale, Calif., 1975-77; prodn. contr. Lockheed Missiles and Space Co., Sunnyvale, 1977-79, mfg. supr., 1979-84, product assurance supr., 1984-85, program plans specialist, 1985-90, mfg. mgr., 1986—, career counseling cons., 1979—, prodn. mgmt. cons., 1985—. Chpt. leader Young Astronauts Program, Mountain View, 1986-88. Recipient Frank G. Brewer Meml. Aerospace award CAP, Vandenberg AFB, Calif., 1987. Mem. Soc. Mfg. Engrs., Nat. Mgmt. Assn., Am. Def. Preparedness Assn., Soc. for Advancement Material and Process Engring., Challenger Soc., Am. Tropical Assn. Democrat. Pentecostal. Club: Lockheed Gun (Sunnyvale). Home: 3534 Shafer Dr Santa Clara CA 95051 Office: Lockheed Missiles and Space Co 1111 Lockheed Way Sunnyvale CA 94089-3504

EVANS, ADELINE MARIE LEMELLE, speech pathologist, educator; b. Eunice, La., June 1, 1939; d. Joseph and Elena (Laws) Lemelle; m. Virden Evans, Dec. 19, 1960; children: Anna Marie, Virden Evans III. BS, Grambling State U., 1960; MS, La. State U., 1964; Cert. in Speech Pathology, La. Tech. U., 1968; PhD, Fla. State U., 1980. Cert. clin. competency in speech pathology. Asst. prof., speech clinician Grambling (La.) State U., 1960-61, 64-73, 1975-76; asst. prof. and clin. dir. Fla. A&M U., Tallahassee, 1973-75, asst. prof. to prof. of speech, 1979—; teaching asst. Fla. State U., Tallahassee, 1978-79. Author: Speech and Language Control, 1990; co-editor: Beyond the Book, 1985, Black History calendar, 1985 (trophy); contbr. articles to profl. jours. Mem. scholarship com. Ebony Fashion Fair, Fla. A&M U., 1983-90, Coll. Level Acad. Skills Test Task Force, Tallahassee, 1982, Leon County Dem. Exec. Com., Tallahassee, 1984—; chmn. scholarship com. Tallahassee Alumnae Chpt. Delta Sigma Theta, 1986-87. Named Tchr. of Yr. Fla. A&M U., 1988, Kappa Alpha Psi Fraternity, Inc., Tallahassee, 1989, Female Faculty of Yr., Student Govt. Assn., Fla. A&M, 1988; recipient grants Fla. A&M Univ. Rsch. Com., 1985, 87, 90, fellowship John Hay Whitney, 1961. Mem. Speech Communication Assn., Fla. Communication Assn. (newsletter editor 1983-85, 2d v.p. 1987-88, editorial bd. 1988-90), Am. Speech Hearing Lang. Assn., Fla. Lang. Speech and Hearing Assn., Fla. Communication Assn., Phi Kappa Phi, Alpha Kappa Mu, Phi Delta Kappa. Democrat. Baptist. Home: 1628 Hedgefield Ct Tallahassee FL 32312 Office: Fla A&M Univ Sch of General Studies Tallahassee FL 32307

EVANS, CAROLE LYNN, programming manager; b. Lynwood, Calif., Nov. 13, 1956; d. Harold Edward and Ruby Irene (Donaldson) E. BA, Dallas Bapt. U., 1989. Programmer Dal-Tex. Optical Co., Dallas, 1977; programmer analyst Affiliated Computers Systems, Dallas, 1977-80; sr. programmer analyst Southwestern States Bankcard Assn., Addison, Tex., 1980-81; project leader Southwestern States Bankcard Assn., Addison, 1981-84, sr. programmer analyst, 1984-86, unit mgr. monetary entry systems, 1986-89, mgr. systems analyst, 1989-90; teaching asst. Brookhaven Coll., Dallas, 1982-83. Newsletter editor Dallas County Young Reps., 1987. Recipient Bronze Turbostar award Turbosuccess Personal Success Mgmt., 1989. Home: 14802 Enterprise #37B Farmers Branch TX 75234

EVANS, CHARLOTTE MORTIMER, writer, communications consultant; b. Newton, N.J., Nov. 26, 1933; d. Karl Otto and Wilhelmina (Otterbach) Pfau; student Douglass Coll., 1952-54; B.S., R.N., Columbia U. Presbyn. Hosp., 1957, postgrad., 1957-59; postgrad. N.Y.U., 1959-60; M.P.A., Coll. of Notre Dame, 1979; m. John Atterbury Mortimer, Nov. 20, 1964; children: Meredith Elizabeth, Mandy Leigh; m. G. Robert Evans, Sept. 4, 1982. Spl. assignment nurse Columbia-Presbyn. Med. Center, N.Y.C., 1957-59; med. advt. copywriter Paul Klemtner & Co., N.Y.C., 1959-61, William Douglas McAdams Agy., N.Y.C., 1961-62; account exec. Arndt, Preston, Chapin, Lamb & Keen, N.Y.C., 1962-63; Rocky Mountain corr. Med. World News, Denver, 1963-64; owner Publicite, Denver; gen. mgr. Center Mktg. Asso., Palo Alto, Calif., 1964-66; freelance writer, pub. rels. and mgmt. cons., Woodside, Calif., 1966-85; pres. Communications for Youth, 1979—. Mem. Palo Alto-Stanford Hosp. Aux., 1968-72; pub. rels. assistance Peninsula Children's Ctr., Palo Alto, 1968-73, Triton Mus. Art, San Jose, Calif., 1966-70; chmn. citizens adv. com. San Mateo County Juvenile Social Svcs.; health component Early Childhood Com., Woodside Elem. Sch. Dist.; mem. adv. com. South County Youth and Family Svcs. Program; mem. Statewide Citizens Adv. Com. on Child Abuse and Neglect Ill. Dept. Children and Family Svcs., 1987—; past chair, mem., bd. dirs. ct.-apptd. spl. advocate program CASA-Kane County , 1989—; chair adv. com. to Congressman D. Haskerton on Family and Child Legis., 1990; bd. dirs. N.J. Jr. C. of C./ UNICEF/ African Project, 1960-61; mem. San Mateo County Mental Health Adv. Bd., Friends of Woodside Libr. Bd, 1983-85; mem. Rep. Senatorial Inner Circle, 1982—; vol. Nat. Com. for Prevention Child Abuse and Neglect, 1987—. Home and Office: PO Box 710 Wayne IL 60184

EVANS, JANE, fashion retailing executive; b. Hannibal, Mo., July 26, 1944; d. L. Terrell Evans and Katherine (Rosser) Pierce; m. George Sheer, June 17, 1970; 1 child, Jonathan. BA, Vanderbilt U.; postgrad., L'Universite d'Aix Marseille. Pres. I. Miller, N.Y.C., 1970-73; v.p. internat. mktg. Genesco, N.Y.C., 1973-74; pres. Butterick Vogue Patterns, N.Y.C., 1974-77; v.p. adminstrn. and corp. devel. Fingerhut, Mpls., 1977-79; exec. v.p. fashion Gen. Mills, Inc., N.Y.C., 1979-84; pres., chief exec. officer Monet Jewelers, N.Y.C., 1984-87; gen. ptnr. Montgomery Consumer Fund, San Francisco, 1987-89; pres., chief exec. officer Inter Pacific Retail Group, San Francisco, 1989—; bd. dir. Equitable Life Assurance Soc., Philip Morris, N.Y.C., Catalyst, N.Y.C., Edison Bros. Stores, Inc. Bd. dirs. Open Hand, San Francisco. Recipient award Women's Equity Action League, 1982; Entrepreneurial Woman award Women Bus. Owners N.Y.C., 1982; named Corp. Am.'s Top Woman Exec., Savvy Mag., 1983, Fin. Woman of Yr., Fin. Women's Assn., 1986; named one of Ten Most Wanted Mgrs., Fortune Mag., 1986. Mem. Young Pres. Orgn., Com. of 200, Fashion Group N.Y., Women's Forum, Fashion Inst. Tech. (bd. dirs. 1980—). Home: 167 Saint Thomas Way Tiburon CA 94920 Office: Inter Pacific Retail Group 351 California St San Francisco CA 94104

EVANS, JANET ANN, music educator; b. Muskegon, Mich., Aug. 26, 1936; d. Burt and Mildred (Gervers) Ruffner; 1 child, Eric Alan. BMus., U. Mich., 1958, MusM, 1959. Permanent secondary teaching cert., Mich. Vocal dir. South Redford (Mich.) Schs., 1959-63, orch., band and vocal dir., 1966-79; band dir. Detroit Pub. Schs., 1979-89, local sec., mem. sch. community rels. coun., 1988-89; band dir. Stewart Sch., Detroit, 1989—; band dir. Fine Arts Honor Bands, Detroit Pub. Schs., 1980-82, 84, 86, coord. Fine Arts Festival, 1986, ret., 1989; mem. staff Nat. Music Camp, 1960-61. Author: (manual) Build Leadership NOW, 1983, Mich. NOW Policies and Guidelines, 1986; also articles. Mem. legis. liaison Older Women's League, Farmington Hills, Mich., 1981-86; del. Mich. Women's Assembly, Jackson, 1984, 86; precinct del. Mich. Dem. Party, 1984—; state chair, treas. Mich. Women's Polit. Caucus, Roseville, 1985-88. Recipient Band Scholarship award U. Mich., 1957, 58, Cert. Achievement Metro-Detroit YWCA, 1985, Cert. Spl. Recognition Detroit Pub. Schs., 1985, 88, Cert. Appreciation Mich. Dem. Party, 1986, Cert. for Outstanding Leadership Detroit Pub. Schs., 1988. Member NOW (pres., N.W. Wayne County chpt., 1980-82, developer Mich. State chpt. 1982-84, adminstrv. v.p. 1984-86, Mich. Leadership award 1981, 82, Leadership plaque N.W. Wayne County 1982), ACLU (state bd. dirs. 1985-88), Coalition of Labor Union Women (Metro Detroit chpt.), Women Internat. League for Peace and Freedom, Mich. Women's Studies Assn., Women Band Dirs. Nat. Assn. (nat. historian 1985-87, nat. recording sec. 1988—), Am. Fedn. Tchrs., Mich. Fedn. Tchrs., Detroit Fedn. Tchrs., Mich. Sch. Band and Orch. Assn., Women in the Arts, Inc. (charter), Martha Cook Bldg. Detroit Alumnae Assn. (bd. dirs. 1968-70, 86—), Bus. and Profl. Women's Club (sec. Farmington Hills chpt. 1981-82, Leadership award pin 1982), Alpha Delta Kappa (chpt. pres. 1978-80, pres. dist. II 1980-82, Pres. award pin 1980), Tau Beta Sigma (life), Sigma Alpha Iota. Democrat. Presbyterian.

EVANS, JANICE WESTON, electronic mail product manager; b. Nashua, N.H., May 18, 1946; d. William Boyd and Marjorie Ann (Kennedy) Weston; 1 child, John Derek. BA, Am. U., 1968; postgrad., U. Pa., 1968-72, Leningrad U., Leningrad, USSR, 1970. Sales IBM, Phila., 1975-78, Lexitron Corp., Phila., 1978-80; info. systems rsch. & devel. Air Products & Chemicals, Inc., Allentown, Pa., 1980—. Recipient Predoctoral Fellowship; named to Phi Kappa Phi. Mem. Exec. Women's Coun. (pres.), Allentown-Lehigh Valley C. of C., Mensa. Home: 22 Willow Run Fogelsville PA 18051 Office: Air Products & Chems Inc MIS-ET 7201 Hamilton Blvd Allentown PA 18195-1501

EVANS, JEAN ELLEN, insurance agency manager; b. Dayton, Ohio, June 23, 1950; d. Kenneth Charles and Margaret Jean (White) E. BA, Mich. State U., 1972. Materials mgr. Ashland Chem. Co., Dublin, Ohio, 1972-84; office mgr. AEI Group, Inc., Columbus, Ohio, 1984-87, Ins. Ohio Co. Agy., Columbus, 1988—. Ordained elder Presbyn. Ch., 1987—. Mem. AAUW, P.E.O. Sisterhood (pres. 1982-84), Broad St. Presbyn. Ch. Office: Ins Ohio Co Agy 40 S Third St Columbus OH 43215

EVANS, JEAN MARIE, social worker; b. Durham, N.C., May 17, 1937; d. Joseph D. and Sarah (Bynum) Stone; 1 child, Deitra L. Means. BA, N.C. Cen. U., Durham, 1954-58; MSE, U. Pa., 1960-62. Lic. driving while intoxicated assessor, N.C. Social work supervision Springfield Hosp. Ctr., Sykesville, Md., 1958-69; coordinator counseling John Hopkins Drug Program, Balt., 1969-76; social work supr. Henryton (Md.) Ctr., 1976-78; social work dir. O'Berry Ctr., Goldsboro, N.C.; from social work supr. to clin. social worker Family Svcs., Raleigh, N.C., 1983-87; field work supr. Grad. Schs. of Social Work, 1962-87, research interviewer, Research Triangle Park, 1988. Team leader Homeless Project, Durham, N.C., 1988. Mem. Continental Societies Inc. (v.p.), Acad. of Cert. Social Workers, Nat. Assn. Social Work, Bd. Marital and Family Therapist, Delta Sigma Theta Sorority. Republican. Home: 1 Poinciana Dr Durham NC 27707

EVANS, JO BURT, communications executive, rancher; b. Kimble County, Tex., Dec. 18, 1928; d. John Fred and Sadie (Oliver) Burt; BA, Mary Hardin-Baylor Coll., 1948; MA, Trinity U., 1967; m. Charles Wayne Evans II, Apr. 17, 1949; children: Charles Wayne III, John Burt, Elizabeth Wisart. Owner, mgr. Sta. KMBL, Junction, Tex., 1959-61; real estate broker, Junction, 1965-74; staff economist, adv. on 21st Congl. Dist., polit. campaign Nelson Wolff, 1974-75; asst. mgr., bookkeeper family owned ranches and rent property, Junction, 1948—; gen. mgr. TV Translator Corp., Junction, 1968—, sec.-treas., 1980—. Treas., asst. to coordinator Citizens for Tex., 1972; historian Kimble Hist. Soc.; mem. Com. of Conservation Soc. to Save the Edwards Aquifer, San Antonio, 1973; homecoming chmn. Sesquicentennial Year, Junction; treas., asst. coordinator New Constitution, San Antonio, 1974. AAUW scholarship named in honor, 1973; named an outstanding Texan, Tex. Senate, 1973. Mem. Nat. Translator Assn., AAUW, Daus. Republic Tex., Tex. Sheriffs Assn., Nat. Cattlewomens Assn., Internat. Platform Assn., Bus. and Profl. Women (pres. 1981-82). Democrat. Mem. Unity Ch. Home: PO Box 283 Junction TX 76849 Office: 618 Main St Junction TX 76849

EVANS, JODIE, health facility administrator; b. Las Vegas, Nev., Sept. 22, 1954; d. Chuck Evans and Donna (Sexsmith) Folkman; m. Jan Krajewski (div. 1985); children: Jasiu, Lala; m. Max Palevsky, Feb. 28, 1987; 1 child, Matthew Evans. BSBA, Woodbury U., 1975, postgrad., 1975-77; postgrad., Southwestern U. Sch. Law, 1977-78. Office mgr. then dir. Thriftco Ins. Co. and Devonshire Coverage Corp., 1973-84; mng. editor Tennis Illustrated, 1974-76; pub. Campaigns, 1975-79; state fin. co-chmn. Brown for Gov., 1978; dir. adminstrn. Govs. Office, 1979; treas. Brown for Pres., 1980; mgr. Brown for U.S. Senate, 1981-82; ptnr. Mayesh, Krajewski and Assocs., 1982-84; exec. dir Hereditary Disease Found., 1984-87; dir. Grief Recovery Ctr., Santa Monica (Calif.) Hosp., 1987—; bd. dirs. Calif. Econ. Devel. Coun., 1982-84, Bank of L.A., 1983-89. Bd. dirs. Women's Polit. Com., 1982—, Women's Campaign Fund, 1983—, People for Parks, 1989—, Sand County Venture Fund, 1989—, Am. Friends of Israel Mus., 1987—; bd. dirs., treas. Hereditary Disease Fund, 1985—; active Citizen Action, Earth Inst., Heal the Bay, Interfaith Task Force on Cen. Am., Nature Conservancy, No on Oil, Rape Treatment Ctr., Santa Monica Pier, Voters for Choice, Environmental Media Advocates, Nat. Women's Polit. Com., and numerous others. Office: Grief Recovery Ctr 643 E Channel Road Santa Monica CA 90402

EVANS, JOYCE GRAY, artist, educator, writer; b. Buffalo, N.Y., July 20, 1941; d. Walter W. and June (Mutton) Gray; m. James T. Evans, May 9, 1981; children by previous marriage, William Karijanian, Michael Karijanian. BS in Vocat. Edn., Buffalo State U., 1979, MS in Reading Edn., 1983. Cert. reading and vocat. edn. tchr., N.Y. Vocat. tchr. Erie Bd. Coop. Ednl. Svcs., Sanborn, N.Y., 1979-81, Niagara Orleans Bd. Coop. Ednl. Svcs., Sanborn, N.Y., 1981-83; learning skills instr. Buffalo State U., 1983-86; tutor Mercer U., Macon, Ga., 1986-87; artist Mid. Ga. Art Assn., Macon, 1986—; vol. tchr. Macon Youth Detention Ctr., 1989. Illustrator: Soil to Fly In, 1978; author: Total Harcare, 1990. Tchr., Literacy Vols. Am., 1980-86. Mem.Middle Ga. Art Assn., Bibb County Med. Aux., Bibb County Cancer Soc. Democrat. Home: 47 Capital Heights Rd Oyster Bay NY 11771

EVANS, JUDITH ANN, secondary school educator; b. Cin., Dec. 7, 1942; d. Edwin F. and Doris I. (Woltz) Eschmeyer; m. Joel Frank Evans, June 25, 1966; children: Jeffrey Frank, Jacquelyn Ann. BA in Math., Miami U., Oxford, Ohio, 1964; MEd, Miami U., 1987; postgrad., Xavier U., U. Cin. Cert. secondary, elem., computer sci. tchr., Ohio. Tchr. Forest Hills Sch. Dist., 1967-68, Little Miami Sch. Dist., Morrow, Ohio, 1978—, Cin. Sch. Dist.; mem. Warren County Computer Sci. Curriculum Com.; sec. computer sci. com. State of Ohio. Chair health com., sec., pres. Morrow Elem. PTO; v.p., sec. Little Miami Mus. Arts Assn.; sec. Little Miami Acad. Boosters. Mem. NEA, Nat. Coun. Tchrs. Math., Ohio Edn. Assn., Little Miami Tchrs. Assn. (v.p. 1988-89, pres. 1989-90, bldg. rep. 1990—), Ohio Coun. Tchrs. Math., Circle of Friends Homemakers Club (v.p., pres., chair sunshine com.). Home: 6159 Morrow-Rossburg Morrow OH 45152 Office: 605 Welch Rd Morrow OH 45152

EVANS, KATHARINE KRIEGER, veterinarian; b. Washington, Aug. 11, 1952; d. Jack Earl and Eleanor Louise (Krieger) E. BS, Va. Poly. Inst. and State U., 1974; DVM, Ohio State U., 1978. Lic. veterinarian, Ohio, Va.; accredited USDA. Pvt. practice, Winchester, Va., 1978-79, Wooster, Ohio, 1979-84, Canton, Ohio, 1984-86, Dover, Ohio, 1986—. Mem. AVMA, Ohio Vet. Med. Assn., Doberman Pinscher Club Am., Tuscarawas Valley Kennel Club, Phi Zeta, Phi Kappa Phi. Home: 5396 Overton Rd Wooster OH 44691 Office: Sifferlin Animal Hosp Rte 5 Box 443 Dover OH 44622

EVANS, LINDA, actress; b. Hartford, Nov. 18, 1942; m. John Derek (div.); m. Stan Herman, 1976 (div.). Film appearances include Twilight of Honor, 1963, The Klansman, 1974, Avalanche Express, 1979, Tom Horn, 1980; in TV series: The Big Valley, 1965-69, Dynasty, 1980-88 (Emmy nominee 1983); TV miniseries include Bare Essence, 1982, North and South Book II, 1986, The Last Frontier, 1986. Author: Linda Evans Beauty and Exercise Book, 1983. Office: care Charter Mgmt 9000 Sunset Blvd Ste 1112 Los Angeles CA 90069*

EVANS, LOIS LOGAN, investment banker, government official; b. Boston, Dec. 1, 1937; d. Harlan deBaun and Barbara (Rollins) Logan; m. Thomas W. Evans, Dec. 22, 1956; children: Heather, Logan, Paige. Student, Vassar Coll., 1954-55; BA, Barnard Coll., 1957. Alt. chief del. UN Commn. on Status Women, N.Y.C., 1972-74; bd. dirs. U.S. Commn. to UNESCO, Washington, 1974-78; pres. Acquisition Specialists, Inc., N.Y.C., 1977-81, chmn. bd. dirs.; exec. v.p. Campbell Shea Inc., N.Y.C., 1988-89; asst. chief protocol U.S. State Dept., N.Y.C., 1981-83; chmn. bd. Fed. Home Bank, N.Y.C., 1986-88, mem., 1984-88; mem. adv. bd. U.S. Export-Import Bank, 1988-90, Nat. Fin. Com.; mem. George Bush Nat. Fin. Com. Vice chair devel. council Williams Coll., N.Y., 1979-81; co-chair Reagan-Bush Campaign, N.Y., 1984; bd. dirs. Bklyn. Jr. League, 1968-72; apptd. by Pres. George Bush to South Pacific Commn., 1990—. Mem. Women's Forum, Econ. of N.Y. Club, Barnard Club, River Club. Republican. Episcopalian. Office: Acquisition Specialists Inc 745 Fifth Ave Ste 704 New York NY 10151

EVANS, LORI WAGGENER, data processing company executive; b. Colorado Springs, Colo., Jan. 8, 1959; d. Philip Alan and Elaine (Bechtold) Waggener; m. Mark Cott Evans. BA, Ohio Wesleyan U., 1981. Editor Tymshare, Inc., Cupertino, Calif., 1982-86; account exec. Miller Communications, Mountain View, Calif., 1986-87; mgr. advt. and pub. rels. McDonnell Douglas, San Jose, Calif., 1987-89; dir. mktg. Hybrid Fax, Inc., Menlo Park, Calif., 1989—. Named Area Champion, Toastmasters, 1985. Mem. Peninsula Marcom Exch. (bd. dirs. Santa Clara, Calif. chpt. 1987-88), Bus. and Profl. Advt. Assn. Democrat. Office: Hybrid Fax Inc 978 Hamilton Ct Menlo Park CA 94025

EVANS, MARGARET, publishing services company executive; b. Annapolis, Md., Oct. 6, 1938; d. Frank Joseph and Margaret Mary (Ruzicka) Wanex; m. Glen Frederick Evans, Jan. 2, 1962; 1 child, Lisa Glyn. B.A., Tulane U., 1960. Systems engr. IBM Corp., Balt., 1961-62; systems supr. U.S. Naval Acad., Annapolis, Md., 1963-67; mktg. dir. Fawcett Publs., Greenwich, Conn., 1967-77; v.p., client service dir. Neodata Services, Boulder, 1977-88; dir. mktg. and sales Palm Coast (Fla.) Data Ltd., 1988-89. Mem. Am. Mgmt. Assn. (program chmn. 1978-80), Sales Exec. Club of N.Y., Fulfillment Mgmt. Assn. (bd. dirs. 1980-84, Spl. Service award 1980), Women's Direct Response Group, Direct Mktg. Club of N.Y.C. (bd. dirs. 1981-82), Fulfillment Mgmt. Assn. (pres. 1989-90). Democrat. Avocations: reading, writing, poetry, cooking, collecting cat artifacts. Home: 122 Cedar Heights Rd Stamford CT 06905 Office: Palm Coast Data Three Park Ave New York NY 10016

EVANS, MARGARET A., civic worker; b. N.Y.C., Jan. 20, 1924; d. Bernard J. and Katherine (Walsh) Markey; B.A., Coll. Mt. St. Vincent, Mt. St. Vincent-on-Hudson, N.Y., 1944; evening student Columbia U.; m. John Cullen Evans, Jr., Nov. 24, 1951. Rep. N.Y. Telephone Co., 1944; personnel office Sak's 34th, N.Y.C., 1944-45, tng. supr., selling and non-selling depts., 1945-49, spl. assignment for store mgr. 1949-50; non-selling tng. supr. Gimbel Bros., 1950-51; rep. Gimbels and Sak's 34th at NCCJ Retail Group meeting, 1949-50. Instr. textile painting for ARC, Chelsea Navy Hosp., 1952-54, ARC vol., 1980—; bd. dirs. Marblehead Hosp. Aid Assn., 1954, pres., 1955-58; sec. Mass. Hosp. Assn. Council of Hosp. Auxiliaries, 1957-59, chmn. North Shore region, 1959-61, chmn.-elect, 1961-62, chmn., 1962-64; exofficio trustee Salem Hosp.; trustee Mary A. Alley Hosp., 1956-79, chmn. bd., 1974-79; mem. Welcome Wagon of Fairfield/Easton (Conn.), 1979-83; chmn. Fairfield/Easton Theater Group, Fifth Wheel Club of Fairfield, 1983-85 . Mem. Alumnae Assn. Coll. Mt. Saint Vincent, Arrangers of Marblehead (chmn. garden therapy 1967-79). Clubs: Marblehead Women's Newcomers (pres. 1953). Home: 108 Cedarwoods Ln Fairfield CT 06430

EVANS, MARY ELLEN, advertising executive; b. Reading, Pa., Apr. 22, 1936; d. Roland Alba and Theresa (Bartoldus) F.; m. Robert Wightman Evans, Apr. 19, 1969 (div. 1983); children: Ryan Thomas, Daniel Fulton; m. Pieter R. Wiederhold, Sept. 1, 1990. BA, U. Ariz., 1958. Fashion writer Broadway Dept. Stores, L.A., 1958-59; club dir. Spl. Svcs. Dept Army, Stuttgart, Germany, 1959-61; writer Rucker, Green & Co. Advt., San Francisco, 1961-63, Cunningham & Walsh Advt., San Francisco, 1963-67; pub. relations dir. Thomas A. Dooley Found., San Francisco, 1968-69, L.A. Model Cities Program, 1969-70; pres. Ads Etc., North Andover, Mass., 1971—. Editor: Ariz. Kitty Kat, U. Ariz., 1957-58. Bd. dirs. Internat. Inst. 1971-78, pres. 1977-78; chmn. North Andover (Mass.) Town Com., 1971-72; mem. Andover Dem. Town Com., 1975-83. Recipient Copywriter's award, San Francisco Copywriter's Club, 1965. Mem. Bus. and Profl. Advt. Assn. Roman Catholic. Home: 19 Carter Ln Andover MA 01810 Office: Ads Etc 114 Exec Park 1538 Turnpike St North Andover MA 01845

EVANS, MARY JOHNSTON, corporate director; b. Shawnee, Okla., Feb. 28, 1930; d. Paul Xenophon and Helen Elizabeth (Alford) Johnston; children by previous marriage: Marcia Lee Head, Paul Johnston Head, Eric Talbott Head; m. James H. Evans, 1984. Student, Wellesley Coll., 1947-48, U. Okla., 1949. Dir. Amtrak, 1974-80, vice chmn., 1975-79; bd. dirs. Household Internat., Inc., CertainTeed Corp., The Sun Co., Inc., Baxter Internat. Inc., Delta Air Lines, Inc., Dun and Bradstreet Corp.; adv. bd. Morgan Stanley & Co. Pres. Jr. League Oklahoma City, 1968-69; trustee Nat. Council Crime and Delinquency, 1971-75, Presbyn. Med. Center, Oklahoma City, 1969-75, Brick Presbyn. Ch., 1985-89; bd. dirs. St. Anthony Hosp., 1973-75; bd. visitors U. Pitts. Grad. Sch. Bus., 1978-85; trustee Mary Baldwin Coll., Staunton, Va., 1976-83, Carnegie Hall, 1985—. Recipient Law Day award-Liberty Bell award Oklahoma Bar Assn., 1971, Disting. Service award U. Okla., 1981; named one of Top 100 Corporate Women Bus. Week mag., 1976; named to Okla. Hall of Fame, 1978. Mem. Conf. Bd. (Sr.), Pi Beta Phi. Presbyterian (elder). Clubs: Colony, River; Maidstone (East Hampton, N.Y.). Address: 920 Fifth Ave New York NY 10021 also: Windmill Ln PO Box 488 East Hampton NY 11937

EVANS, MRS. N. LYLE See WEIR, GLORIA JANE

EVANS, ORINDA D., federal judge; b. Savannah, Ga., Apr. 23, 1943; d. Thomas and Virginia Elizabeth (Grieco) E.; m. Roberts O. Bennett, Apr. 12, 1975; children: Wells Cooper, Elizabeth Thomas. B.A., Duke U., 1965; J.D. with distinction, Emory U., 1968. Bar: Ga. 1968. Ptnr. Alston, Miller & Gaines, Atlanta, 1974-79; U.S. dist. judge No. Dist. Ga., Atlanta, 1979—; adj. prof. Emory U. Law Sch., 1974-77; counsel Atlanta Crime Commn., 1970-71. Mem. Atlanta Bar Assn. (dir. 1979). Democrat. Episcopalian. Office: US Dist Ct 1988 US Courthouse 75 Spring St SW Atlanta GA 30303

EVANS, PAMELA ROYE, marketing executive; b. Hoisington, Kans., Aug. 25, 1957; d. John Roy and Sarah Mace (Alder) E. BS in Bus., U. Kans., 1980. Sales rep. Home & Automotive Products div. Union Carbide Corp., Seattle, 1981; dist. sales mgr. Home & Automotive Products div. Union Carbide Corp., Syracuse, N.Y., 1981-82; mktg. assoc. Home & Automotive Products div. Union Carbide Corp., Danbury, Conn., 1982-84, assoc. product mgr., 1984; asst. product mgr. Grocery Products div. Ralston Purina, St. Louis, 1984-85, product mgr., 1985-86; product mgr. Eveready Battery Co. subs. Ralston Purina, St. Louis, 1986-88, group dir. mktg., 1988-90; dir. mktg. Consumer div. Esselte Pendaflex, 1990—. Home: 152 Wellington Rd Garden City NY 11530 Office: Esselte Pendaflex Corp 71 Clinton Rd Garden City NY 11530

EVANS, PAULINE, physicist, educator; b. Bklyn., Mar. 24, 1922; d. John A. and Hannah (Brandt) Davidson; B.A., Hofstra Coll., 1942; postgrad. N.Y. U., 1943, 46-47, Cornell U., 1946, Syracuse U., 1947-50; m. Melbourne Griffith Evans, Sept. 6, 1950; children—Lynn Janet Evans Hannemann, Brian Griffith. Jr. physicist Signal Corps Ground Signal Service, Eatontown, N.J., 1942-43; physicist Kellex Corp. (Manhattan Project), N.Y.C., 1944; faculty dept. physics Queens Coll., N.Y.C., 1944-47; teaching asst. Syracuse U., 1947-50; instr. Wheaton Coll., Norton, Mass., 1952; physicist Nat. Bur. Standards, Washington, 1954-55; instr. physics U. Ala., 1955, U. N.Mex., 1955, 57-58; staff mem. Sandia Corp., Albuquerque, 1956-57; physicist Naval Nuclear Ordnance Evaluation Unit, Kirtland AFB, N.Mex., 1958-60; programmer Teaching Machines, Inc., Albuquerque, 1961; mem. faculty dept. physics Coll. St. Joseph on the Rio Grande (name changed to U. Albuquerque 1966), 1961—, assoc. prof., 1965—, chmn. dept., 1961—. Mem. Am. Phys. Soc., Am. Assn. Physics Tchrs., Fedn. Am. Scientists, AAUP, Sigma Pi Sigma, Sigma Delta Epsilon. Patentee in field. Home: 730 Loma Alta Ct NW Albuquerque NM 87105 Office: U of Albuquerque Dept Physics Albuquerque NM 87140

EVANS, RENEE YVONNE, editor; b. Andrews, N.C., July 4, 1965; d. Arbie Jonathan and Doris June (Cruise) E. BA in English/Journalism, Elon (N.C.) Coll., 1987. Editor Fourth Estate, Inc., Burlington, N.C., 1987—. Author, editor features City-County Mag., 1987-90. Vol. Burlington Downtown Corp., 1989-90. Mem. Alamance County Dem. Womens Assn.

EVANS, ROSEMARY HALL, civic worker; b. Lenox, Mass., Mar. 25, 1925; d. Alfred A. and Rosamond (Morse) Hall; m. Richard Morse Colgate, Jan. 1, 1949; children: Jessie Morse, Margaret Auchincloss, Pamela Morse; m. James H. Evans, July 1, 1972 (div. 1984). Trustee Menninger Found., Topeka, Music Acad. of West, Montecito, Calif., Princeton (N.J.) Theol. Sem., U. Calif.-Santa Barbara; founding mem., life trustee Nat. Recreation and Park Assn., Washington; past trustee Nat. Audubon Soc., N.Y.C., Joffrey Ballet, N.Y.C. and L.A., Simon's Rock of Bard Coll., Gt. Barrington, Mass., Westminster Choir Coll., Princeton, N.J.; former mem. Green Acres Commn., N.J.; former mem. Equine Adv. Bd. N.J. Morgan Horse Assn.; bd. dirs., former pres. Nat. Recreation Found., N.Y.C.; former collaborator Nat. Park Svc. Mem. Colony Club (N.Y.C.), Tarratine Club (Dark Harbor, Maine), Birnam Wood Golf Club (Montecito, Calif.). Republican.

EVANS, SALLY LEES, insurance agency owner; b. Phila., Jan. 25, 1928; d. Shannon G. and Agnes (Rector) Lees. Student, Asbury Pk. Bus. Coll., 1955. Lic. ins. agt. and broker, N.J., Fla. Owner Grossinger & Heller Agy., Red Bank, N.J., 1967—. V.p. Monmouth City Fedn. Rep. Women; mem. Little Silver Rep. Club. Named First Woman appointed to Little Silver, N.J. Borough Coun., 1974. Mem. NAFE, Profl. Ins. Agts. N.J., Monmouth County Bus. Assn., N.J. Assn. Women Bus. Owners, Monmouth County SPCA, Boat Owners Assn., Humane Soc., Audubon Soc. Episcopalian. Home: 451 Point Rd Little Silver NJ 07739 Office: 18 Wikoff Pl PO Box 774 Red Bank NJ 07701

EVANS, SARAH FRANCES HINTON, nurse; b. Athens, Clark County, Ga., July 19, 1924; d. Charles Jackson and Bessie Marie (Hickman) Hinton; R.N., Macon Hosp. Sch. Nursing, 1945; B.S. in Nursing, Med. Coll. Ga., 1975; m. Omer Fountain, Oct. 9, 1948 (div. 1964); children—Anita Francine, Sarah Alice; m. John Duggan Evans, Feb. 14, 1969 (dec. Apr. 1971). Night supr. Ware County Hosp., Waycross, Ga., 1946-47; staff nurse nursery and obstetrics Mercy Hosp., Macon, Ga., 1947-48; staff nurse obstetrics Macon (Ga.) Hosp., 1952-54, 55-56, head nurse colored labor and delivery, 1956-64, obstet. staff nurse, 1964-65; head nurse newborn nursery Med. Center Central Ga., Macon, 1965-74, infection control nurse, 1974—; mem. Ga. Bd. Nursing, 1977-80. Mem. Am. Nurses Assn. (del. from Ga. 1976, 78), Assn. Practitioners in Infection Control (cert.), Ga. Heart Assn., Ga. Public Health Assn., Sixth Dist. Ga. Nurses Assn., Med. Center Central Ga. Alumnae, Med. Coll. Ga. Alumnae Assn. Baptist. Home: 6375 Houston Rd Macon GA 31206 Office: Med Ctr Cen GA Box 6000 Macon GA 31208

EVANS, SUZANNE MARIE, medicinal chemist; b. Hartford, Conn., Oct. 29, 1953; d. George Thomas and Frances Mary (Clew) E. BS magna cum laude, Fairfield U., 1975; MS, Purdue U., 1977; cert. in mgmt., Elmhurst Coll., 1982; postgrad., U. Ill., Chgo., 1985-88, Rutgers U., 1989—. Teaching and research asst. Purdue U., West Lafayette, Ind., 1975-77; chemist rsch. and devel. medicinal chemistry dept. G.D. Searle & Co., Skokie, Ill., 1978-81, rsch. chemist, 1981-82, data base coordinator, 1982-83, biomolecular structure analyst, 1983-85; sr. computational chemist Chemlab, Inc., Lake Forest, Ill., 1985-88; computational chemistry educator, cons. The BOC Group, Inc., Murray Hill/New Providenc, N.J., 1986-88; sr. scientist Tech. Ctr., New Providence, 1988—; teaching asst. U. Ill., Chgo., 1985-87; cons. computational chemist Intersoft, Inc., Lake Forest, Ill., 1985-88; speaker in field. Author: Opiates, 1986, Proceedings of First European Seminar on Computer-Aided Molecular Design, 1984; contbr. articles to profl. jours.; patentee in field. Career educator Nat. Sci. Found., 1980, Lincoln Jr. High Sch., Skokie, Ill., 1980-82, Elk Grove Village (Ill.) High Sch., 1984. Fellow U. Ill., 1987-88. Mem. Am. Chem Soc. (lectr. Milw. sect. 1985, Analytical Chemistry award 1974). Office: The BOC Group Inc Tech Ctr 100 Mountain Ave Murray Hill New Providence NJ 07974

EVANS, THELMA JEAN MATHIS, internist; b. East St. Louis, Ill., Jan. 29, 1944; d. Clemmie and Catherine (Rose) Mathis; m. Timothy Charles Evans, June 29, 1968; children: Cynthia Marie, Catherine Elizabeth (twins). BS in Zoology, U. Ill., 1967; MD, U. Ill., Chgo., 1969. Intern, then resident U. Ill. Hosp., Chgo., 1969-71, fellow in pulmonary medicine, 1971-73; med. dir., acute care unit Presbyn.-St. Luke's Hosp., Chgo., 1973-75; asst. to dir. emergency svcs. Presbyn.-St. Luke's Hosp., 1975-77; staff physician Health Specialists, S.C., Chgo., 1977-80, AT&T (Western Electric), Cicero, Ill., 1980-85, Health First, Inc., Chgo., 1985-89, Michael Reese Health Plan, Chgo., 1989—; instr., Rush Med. Coll., Chgo., 1973-84; tuberculosis control officer, infectious disease sect. Chgo. Dept. Health, 1976-77. v.p., Com. to Elect Timothy C. Evans, Chgo., 1989. Grantee, Chgo. Lung Assn., 1972-73. Mem. Am. Soc. Internal Medicine, NAACP. Democrat. African Methodist Episcopal. Office: Michael Reese Health Plan 9831 S Western Ave Chicago IL 60643

EVANS, VIRGINIA PARRISH, finance company executive; b. Waukegan, Ill., Dec. 2, 1947; d. Robert Lee and Grace Muriel (Kohl) Parrish; m. Jonathan Evans, Aug. 1, 1970; children: Jeremy Wilkins, Christine Marie. AA, Endicott Jr. Coll., 1967; MA, BE, Northeastern U., Boston, 1970; postgrad., N.H. Tech. Inst., 1983-85. V.p. Monarch Securities Inc., Springfield, Mass., 1987—; pres. VASCO, Little Rock, 1988-90; v.p. First Variable Life Ins. Co., Little Rock, 1987—, Monarch Fin. Svcs., Inc., Holyoke, Mass., 1988—. Mem. NAFE, IAFP. Home: 967 S East St Amherst MA 01002 Office: 361 Whitney Ave Holyoke MA 01040

EVARTS, HELEN COLEMAN, educator; b. N.Y.C., Apr. 7, 1928; d. Leighton Hammond and Jane (Fraser) Coleman; m. William M. Evarts, Jr., Aug. 28, 1948; children: Holly Bartow, Kate, Alice Conover. Student, Bryn Mawr Coll., 1946-48; BA, Columbia U., 1970; MA, NYU, 1973. Tchr. history Nightingale-Bamford Sch., N.Y.C., 1975—; bd. dirs. Aztec Land & Cattle Co., N.Y.C. Bd. dirs. Columbia U. Sch. Gen. Studies, The Nature Conservancy, 1984—. Mem. Assn. Tchrs. in Ind. Schs. (sec. 1980-87), Nat. Assn. Ind. Schs., Phi Beta Kappa, Cosmopolitan Club, River Club. Republican. Episcopalian. Home: 7 Gracie Sq New York NY 10028 Office: Nightingale-Bamford Sch 122 20 E 92d St New York NY 10128

EVASHWICK, CONNIE JOANN, health services administrator; b. Albuquerque, Jan. 1, 1949; d. George and Helen Elizabeth (Holding) E. BA, Stanford U., 1969, MA, 1970; MSc, Harvard U., 1971, ScD, 1974. Program specialist Mass. Dept. Pub. Health, 1974-75; asst. prof. Sch. Medicine U. N.C., Chapel Hill, 1975-77; asst. prof. Sch. Pub. Health U. Wash., Seattle, 1978-81; dir. office on aging Am. Hosp. Assn., Chgo., 1981-83; v.p. long-term care Luth. Hosp. Soc. So. Calif., L.A., 1983-85; owner, cons. CEA Consulting & Evaluation Assocs., Santa Monica, Calif., 1985—; cons., Robert Wood Johnson Found., Princeton, N.J., 1983-87; reviewer for profl. jours. Author: Managing the Continuum of Care, 1987; contbr. articles to profl. jours. Mem. Am. Coll. Healthcare Execs., Am. Pub. Health Assn. (coun. gerontol. health sect. 1985-87, governing coun. 1990-91), Am. Soc. on Aging (chmn. long-term care com. 1984-85), Gerontol. Soc. Am., Harvard Sch. Pub. Health Alumni Assn. (bd. dirs. 1987-89), Sanford U. Alumni So. Calif. (bd. dirs. 1985-87). Office: CEA 1227 E Berkeley St #5 Santa Monica CA 90404

EVENSON, ELIZABETH ANNE, corporate professional; b. Chgo., June 26, 1961; d. James Edward and Anita Barbara (Pott) E. BBA, Loyola U., Chgo., 1984. Sales rep. Carolina Freight Carriers, Cherryville, N.C., 1984-86; sales engr. Am. Design and Sales, Chgo., 1986-87; pres. Evenson & Assocs., Inc., Chgo., 1987—; sales cons. Base Assocs., Inc., Chgo., 1988—. Vol. Hooved Animal Humane Soc., Barrington, Ill., 1988. Recipient James Propst Meml. award, Carolina Freight, 1984, Heat Shrinkable Tech. diploma, Remtek Corp., Fremont, Calif., 1989. Mem. Nat. Businesswomen's Leadership Assn. Republican. Roman Catholic. Office: Evenson & Assocs Inc 7107 N Ionia Chicago IL 60646

EVENSON, S. JEANNE, small business owner; b. Wheeler County, Tex., Oct. 17, 1938; d. Glynn Edward and LaVerne (Bailey) Pugh; m. A. Berniel Evenson, May 31, 1957; children: Tara Jean Harper, Troy Berniel. BA in

Secondary Edn., Coll. Great Falls, 1972. Tchr. East Jr. High Sch., Great Falls, 1972-78; owner, operator Cattail Lawn Svc., Great Falls, 1976-80, B-J Pac-A-Part, Great Falls, 1976—. Methodist. Home: 410-25 Avenue S Great Falls MT 59405

EVERETT, DONNA RANEY, business educator; b. Corpus Christi, Tex., May 30, 1939; d. Donald Wayne and Zora Lee (Wynne) Raney; div.; 1 child, Donna Melinda. BA, Phillips U., Enid, Okla., 1961; MS, U. Houston, 1983, EdD, 1988. Adj. prof. U. Houston, 1983-88; asst. prof. bus. Tex. Tech. U., Lubbock, 1988-89, Lamar U., Beaumont, Tex., 1989-90; asst. prof. bus. edn. Tex. Tech. U., Lubbock, 1990—. Troop leader Girl Scouts U.S., Ft. Worth and Lake Jackson, Tex., 1964-80, dir. tng. Lake Jackson coun., 1980-82. Recipient Curriculum Devel. award Tex. Higher Edn. Coord. Bd., 1987-88, Disting. Paper award SWFAD, 1989. Mem. Am. Soc. Curriculum Devel., Tex. Bus. Edn. Assn. (newsletter editor 1988-91, collegiate bus. tchr. of yr. dist. 4 1989), Nat. Bus. Edn. Assn., Tex. Computer Edn. Assn., Am. Vocat. Assn. (com. mem. 1990—), Delta Pi Epsilon (pres. Alpha Gamma chpt. 1988-89).

EVERETT, JESSIE MARY, educator; b. Phila., Mar. 15, 1929; d. Bennie C. and Maggie L. (Luke) Stewart, m. James B. Everett, June 25, 1928; children: T. Keith, Mary Lisa. AA, East Central Jr., 1949; BSC, The U. Miss., 1951, MSC, 1956. Sec., mgr. Kroehler Furn. Mfg. Co., Pitts., Calif., 1951-53; faculty housing sec. The Univ. Miss., Oxford, Miss., 1954-56; bus. instr. East Central Jr. Coll., Decatur, Miss., 1956--. Editor, Newsletter, Delta Pi Epsilon, 1980, Miss. Bus. Educ. Assn., 1987. Bd. mem., Pub. Library, Decatur, 1969--, Regional Library, Kemper-Newton System, 1972--, Council, Meridale Girl Scouts, Meridian, Miss., 1987--, pres. U. Miss. Alumni. Assn., Newton County, Miss. 1988--. Mem. Miss. Bus. Educators (pres. 1981-82), So. Bus. Educators (bd. dirs. 1985-88), Nat. Bus. Educators (bd. dirs. 1985—), Women's League, Gen. Fedn. Women's Clubs, Miss. Fedn. Women's Clubs, Delta Kappa Gamma (state pres. 1985-87), Delta Pi Epsilon. Baptist. Home: Box 51 Decatur MS 39327 Office: E Central Comm Coll Box 51 Decatur MS 39327

EVERETT, LAURIE ANN, broadcast executive; b. Perth Amboy, N.J., Mar. 23, 1956; d. William and Blanche Joan (Loftus) Toth; m. Daniel Charles Everett, May 25, 1987. AA, Graham Jr. Coll., Boston, 1976; BA, Boston Coll., 1978. Prodn. sec. WGBH Ednl. Found., Boston, 1979-80, asst. unit mgr., 1980-81, unit mgr., 1981-85, coord. producer, 1985-88, dir. descriptive video svcs., 1988—. Coord. producer PBS TV spl. Hiroshima Remembered, 1985 (Emmy 1986); producer local TV spl. Ben Franklin Alive, 1987 (local Emmy 1988). Mem. Nat. Acad. TV Arts and Scis.; Rehab. and Edn. of the Visually Impaired. Home: 33 Elmore St Arlington MA 02174 Office: WGBH Ednl Found 125 Western Ave Boston MA 02134

EVERETT, MARY ELIZABETH, retirement home administrator; b. Okmulgee, Okla., June 3, 1929; d. Frederick Joseph and Harriet Lucille (Daratt) Elrick; m. Thomas Henry Everett, May 29, 1951; children: Deborah Maciolek, Thomas Stephen. BA, Salem Coll., 1951. Pres. Greater Balt. Med. Ctr. Aux., 1981-83, chmn. geriatrics, pres.; pres. Md. Assn. Hosp. Aux., Balt., 1984-86, seminar planner; pres. bd. mgrs. Wesley Home, Balt., 1986—, trustee; lectr. in field. Leader Girl Scouts U.S.A., Towson, Md.; trustee Towson Meth. Ch. Mem. Md. Assn. Hosp. Aux. (bd. dirs.). Republican. Clubs: Three Arts, Salem (Balt.) (bd. dirs.). Home: 4 Candlelight Ct Lutherville MD 21093 Office: Wesley Home 2211 W Rogers Ave Baltimore MD 21209

EVERETT, PAMELA IRENE, legal management company executive, educator; b. L.A., Dec. 31, 1947; d. Richard Weldon and Alta Irene (Tuttle) Bunnell; m. James E. Everett, Sept. 2, 1967 (div. 1973); 1 child, Richard Earl. Cert. Paralegal, Rancho Santago Coll., Santa Ana, Calif., 1977; BA, Calif. State U.-Long Beach, 1985; MA, U. Redlands, 1988. Owner, mgr. Orange County Paralegal Svc., Santa Ana, 1979-85; pres. Gem Legal Mgmt. Inc., Fullerton, Calif., 1986—; instr. Rancho Santiago Coll., 1979—, chmn. adv. bd., 1980-85, Coastline Community Coll., Costa Mesa, Calif., 1980-82, Fullerton Coll., 1989—; advisor Nat. Paralegal Assn., 1982—, Saddleback Coll., 1985—, N. Orange County Regional Occupational Program, Fullerton, 1986—; bd. dirs. Nat. Profl. Legal Assts. Inc. Author: Legal Secretary Federal Litigation, 1986, Legal Secretary Bankruptcy, 1987, Going Independent-Business Planning Guide. Mem. Orange County Paralegal Assn. (historian 1987-88), Nat. Soc. Magna Carta Dames, Plantagenet Soc. Republican. Home and Office: 406 N Adams Ave Fullerton CA 92632

EVERETT, VIVIAN DENISE, pediatrician; b. Columbia, S.C., Aug. 21, 1958; d. Percival Leonard and Dorothy Louise (Stinson) E. BS, Furman U., 1980; MD, U. S.C., 1984. Diplomate Nat. Bd. Med. Examiners, Am. Bd. Pediatrics. Intern in pediatrics Moses Cone Hosp., Greensboro, N.C., 1984-85, resident in pediatrics, 1985-87; pediatrician Cary, N.C., 1987-88, Wake County Health Dept., Raleigh, N.C., 1987—, Wake Med. Ctr., Raleigh, N.C., 1988—; dir. Child Sexual Abuse Team, Raleigh. Bd. dirs. The Women's Ctr., Raleigh, 1988—; mem. N.C. Child Abuse Coalition, Raleigh, 1990. Named to Outstanding Young Women of Am., 1985. Mem. AMA, So. Med. Assn., N.C. Pediatric Soc. (child abuse com. 1989—, state chairperson 1990), Am. Acad. Pediatrics, Am. Profl. Soc. on the Abuse of Children, Internat. Soc. Prevention of Child Abuse and Neglect, N.C. Chpt. Nat. Com. for Prevention of Child Abuse. Democrat. Methodist. Office: Wake AHEC-Pediatrics 3000 New Bern Ave Raleigh NC 27610

EVERETT-VOLGY, SANDRA SUE, psychologist, educator; b. Ft. Worth, Feb. 13, 1946; d. Barry and Maxine (Turpin) Stroup; m. Thomas J. Volgy, 1968 (div. Apr. 1985); m. Craig Ashley Everett, July 14, 1989. BA, Oakland U., 1968; MA, U. Ariz., 1972, PhD, 1975. Lic. clin. psychologist, Ariz. Chief psychologist Tucson Child Guidance Clinic, 1975-79; coord. child adv. svcs. Pima County Conciliation Ct., Tucson, 1979-84; adj. clin. faculty mem. Fla. State U., Tallahassee, 1984-86; mem. faculty S.E. Family Inst., Tallahassee, 1985-87; pvt. practice psychologist Tallahassee, 1984-87, Tucson, 1987—; mem. faculty Ariz. Inst. Family Therapy, Tucson, 1988—; cons. in child psychology HCA Sonora Desert Hosp., Tucson, 1988—; cons. Child Protective Svcs., Tallahassee, 1987-88. Co-author: Treating Borderline Family, 1988; editor: Gender Issues in Divorce, 1990; contbr. articles to profl. jours. Pres. Tucson Assn. Child Care, 1983-84. Mem. Am. Psychol. Assn., Am. Assn. for Marriage and Family Therapy (supr.). Office: 6060 N Fountain Dr Ste 150 Tucson AZ 85718

EVERIDGE, FOXENE LAMBERT, company executive, real estate broker; b. Troy, Ala., Dec. 4, 1939; d. R. Fox and Edith (Bragg) Lambert; m. Jerry F. Everidge, Dec. 23, 1957; children: J. Stanley, Steven F., Stuart L. Grad. high sch., Marianne, Fla. Owner Greater Charleston Trading Post, Goose Creek, S.C., 1971-72; sec. ERA O'Shaughnessy Realty, N. Charleston, S.C., 1973-74, adminstrv. asst. to pres., 1974-79; regional coordinator ERA of the Carolinas, Charleston, S.C., 1979-81; sales assoc. ERA O'Shaughnessy Realty, N. Charleston, 1981-84, broker, mgr., 1984—; pres. Carolina Boilers/COMAR Industries, Charleston, S.C., 1982-88; chmn. bd. COMAR Industries Inc., Charleston, S.C., 1988—. Mem. Greater Charleston Bd. Realtors, Trident C. of C. Lodge: Order Eastern Star. Home: 10 Venice Ave Hanahan SC 29418 Office: COMAR Industries Inc 2718 Azalea Dr Charleston SC 29418

EVERINGHAM, JOYCE DUBERT, library administrator; b. Hornell, N.Y., May 14, 1929; d. John Griniliffe and Genie Mae (Herda) Dubert; m. Neil Gilbert Everingham, Sept. 17, 1955; 1 child, N. Mark. B.A., SUNY-Albany; M.L.S., SUNY-Geneseo, postgrad. Librarian, East Pembroke Sch., N.Y., City Sch. Dist., Williamsport, Pa.; coordinator libraries Westhill Schs., Syracuse, N.Y.; dir. pilot project Sch. Library System Syracuse City Schs., 1979-82, supr. libraries, 1969-82; exec. dir. Western N.Y. Library Resources Council, Buffalo, 1983—; mem. N.Y. Hist. Documents Inventory State Com. Mem. ALA, N.Y. Library Assn., Western N.Y. Hosp. Library Assn., Mid-Atlantic Records & Archives, Pub. Library Sect. N.Y. Library Assn., N.Y. Documentary Heritage (steering com. 1987—), Western N.Y. Ry. Hist. Soc. Avocations: music, basketball, sports, camping, crafts. Office: Western New York Library Resources Council 180 Oak St Buffalo NY 14203

EVERINGHAM, KAREN SUE, realtor; b. Toledo, Mar. 26, 1946; d. Charles Edward and Dorthy Geneva (Clark) Raitz; m. Ronald Eugene Krueger, Nov. 21, 1964 (div. Sept. 1982); children: Ronald Eugene Jr., Robert Brian; m. Jack William Everingham, June 16, 1984. AAS in Bus. and Data Processing, U. Toledo, 1989. Salesperson LaBine Brokerage, Maumee, Ohio, 1977-79, J.H. Mason Co., Toledo, 1979-82; sales account exec. McMalon & McDonald, Toledo, 1982-88; realtor Neal South Realty, Maumee, 1988, Welles Bowen, Maumee, 1988—. Fellow Toledo Bd. Realtor; mem. Maumee Valley Exch. Club (charter, pres. elect 1989-90). Home: 626 Centee Field Maumee OH 43537 Office: Welles Bowen 1400 Dussel Dr #B9 Maumee OH 43537

EVERITT, ALICE LUBIN, labor arbitrator; b. Washington, Dec. 13, 1936; d. Isador and Alice (Berliner) Lubin; BA, Columbia U., 1968, JD, 1971. Assoc. firm Amen, Weisman & Butler, N.Y.C., 1971-78; spl. asst. to dir. Fed. Mediation and Conciliation Svc., Washington, 1978-81; editor Dept. Labor publ., 1979, pvt. practice labor arbitration, Washington, N.Y.C. and Petersburg, Va., 1981—; dean admissions Hofstra U. Sch. Law 1985-89; mem. various nat. mediation and arbitration panels including U.S. Steel and United Steelworkers. Mem. Am. Arbitration Assn., Soc. Profls. Dispute Resolution, Indsl. Rels. Rsch. Assn., Civil War Roundtable of Washington, N.Y.C. and Richmond. Office: 541 High St Petersburg VA 23803

EVERS, ANNE BIGELOW, editor; b. San Francisco, July 30, 1954; d. William Dohrmann Evers and Edwina (Benington) Leggett; m. C. Breck Hitz, Nov. 16, 1985; 1 child, Emily Anne. BA in English, U. Calif., Berkeley, 1976; MBA, St. Mary's Coll., Moraga, Calif., 1983. Asst. editor Oxford Univ. Press, N.Y.C., 1976-79; publicity dir. U. Calif. Press, Berkeley, 1979-84; editor Rsch. Svcs., San Francisco, 1984—. Participant Bus. Vols. for the Arts, San Francisco, 1987. Mem. Women in Communications, Inc., No. Calif. Book Publicists Assn. (bd. dirs. San Francisco chpt. 1980-84). Office: Rsch Mag/Golden State Mag 2201 Third St San Francisco CA 94107

EVERS, JOYCE MARY, healthcare professional; b. Milw., Sept. 22, 1954; d. Michael August and Rosemary (Langen) Grzeskowiak; m. Jeffrey Dean Evers, June 24, 1986; 1 child, Samuel. BSSW, U. Wis., 1975, MSW, 1976, MBA, 1987. Lic. social worker, Wis. Asst. dir. Children's Outing Assn., Milw., 1975-76; counselor Human Svcs. Ctr., Medford, Wis., 1977-78, Meriter Hosp., Madison, Wis., 1978-80; out-patient coord. Meriter Hosp., Madison, 1980-83, out-patient mgr., 1983—; pres. Wis. Assn. Outpatient Mental Health Facilities, 1986-88, Wis. Alcohol and Drug Treatment Providers Assn., 1990—. Bd. dirs. Middleton (Wis.) Outreach Food Pantry, 1986-88. Recipient Recognition award Big Bros./Big Sisters, 1985. Mem. Wis. Assn. Alcohol other Drug Abuse (bd. dirs. 1987-88), Nat. Assn. Social Workers, Madison Area Quality Improvement Network. Democrat. Roman Catholic. Office: Meriter Hosp NewStart Outpatient 1015 Gammon Ln Madison WI 53719

EVERS, JUDITH ANN, library/media specialist; b. Ransom, Mich., Nov. 11, 1939; d. Paul Vernon and Ival Leone (Brown) Barr; m. Orin Evers, Mar. 28, 1959; children: Brian, Kim, Shawn. BA, Western Mich. U., 1960; MA, U. Toledo, 1967. High sch. tchr. North Cen. Schs., Pioneer, Ohio, 1960-67, Hillsdale (Mich.) Community Schs., 1970-71, North Adams (Mich.) Jerome High Sch., 1971-86; media specialist tchr. Hillsdale Community Schs., 1986—; owner The Book Mark, Hillsdale, 1985-88; swim sch. dir. Evers Pvt. Pool, Osseo, Mich., 1975—. Water safety chmn. ARC, Hillsdale, 1975-89. Named Tchr. of the Yr., North Adams High Sch. Mem. AAUW (bd. dirs. 1987—), Mich. Assn. for Media in Edn. (bd. dirs. 1989—), Region 15 Mich. Assn. Media Edn. (pres. 1989-90), Delta Kappa Gamma. Methodist. Home: 5051 Monroe St Osseo MI 49266 Office: Hillsdale Community Schs 30 N West St Hillsdale MI 49242

EVERSON, CHRISTINE ARIAIL, organization communications executive; b. Spartanburg, S.C., Sept. 13, 1947; d. William Coke and Christine (Vestal) Ariail; m. Robert C. Everson III (div. 1974). BA, Va. Commonwealth U., 1972. Caseworker, protective svc. worker City of Richmond (Va.), 1972-77; editor Home Builders Assn. Va., Richmond, 1978-83; dir. communications Va. Mcpl. League, Richmond, 1983—; cons. editor Commonwealth Woman, Richmond. Com. mem. Carillon Civic Assn., Richmond, 1987—; domestic violence vol. YWCA, Richmond, 1988—; vol. foster care provider Greyhound Pets Am. Mem. Internat. Assn. Bus. Communicators (chmn. mem. svcs. Richmond 1983-89, v.p. programs 1989), Richmond Pub. Rels. Assn. Methodist. Home: 512 S Sheppard St Richmond VA 23221 Office: Va Mcpl League PO Box 12203 Richmond VA 23241

EVERSON, DIANE LOUISE, publishing executive; b. Edgerton, Wis., Mar. 27, 1953; d. Harland Everett and Helen Viola (Oliver) E. BS, Carroll Coll., 1975. Advt. mgr. Edgerton (Wis.) Reporter, 1976—; pres. Silk Screen Creations, 1981—. Pub. Directions mag., 1981—. Trustee Carroll Coll., 1987—. Democrat. Lutheran. Home: 114 Kellogg Rd Edgerton WI 53534 Office: Directions Pub 21 N Henry Edgerton WI 53534

EVERSON, JANE MCVICKER, educator; b. Arlington, Va., Oct. 13, 1958; d. George W. Everson and Mary Pat (McVicker) E. BS, U. Va., 1980, MEd, 1983; PhD, Va. Commonwealth U., 1989. Instr. spl. edn. Va. Commonwealth U., Richmond, 1983-89; dir. Helen Keller Nat. Ctr. Tech. Assistance Ctr., Sands Point, N.Y., 1990—; cons. program planning numerous states. Co-author: Transition from School to Work, 1988, Vocational Education for Multihandicapped Youth with Cerebral Palsey, 1988, numerous book chpts.; contbr. articles to profl. jours. Mem. Nat. Assn. Persons with Severe Handicaps, Phi Delta Kappa, Alpha Phi. Democrat. Office: Helen Keller Nat Ctr 111 Middle Neck Rd Sands Point NY 11050

EVERT, CHRISTINE MARIE (CHRIS EVERT), retired professional tennis player; b. Ft. Lauderdale, Fla., Dec. 21, 1954; d. James and Colette Evert; m. John Lloyd, Apr. 17, 1979 (div.); m. Andy Mill, July 30, 1988. Amateur tennis player, until Dec. 1972, profl. tennis player, 1972-89, ret., 1989; commentator NBC Sports tennis events; winner numerous tournaments including U.S. Jr. Championship, 1970, 71, U.S. Open, 1975, 76, 77, 78, 80, 82, Wimbleton Singles, 1974, 76, 81, doubles, 1976, Australian Open, 1982, 84, French Open Singles, 1974, 75, 79, 80, 83, 85, 86, Virginia Slims, 1972, 73, 75, 77, 87, European Women's Open, Geneva, 1987, Eckerd Open, 1987. Recipient Lebair Sportsmanship trophy, 1971; named Female Athlete of Yr. AP, 1974, 75, 77, 80, Athlete of Yr. Sports Illustrated, 1976, Greatest Woman Athlete of Last 25 Years Women's Sports Found., 1985. Mem. U.S. Lawn Tennis Assn. (Top Women's Singles Player award 1974), Nat. Honor Soc. Address: care Internat Mgmt Group 1 Erieview Pla Cleveland OH 44114 also: Polo Club of Boca Raton 5400 Champion Blvd Boca Raton FL 33496 also: Evert Enterprises 7100 W Camino Real Ste 203 Ste 203 Boca Raton FL 33433

EVERT, PATRICIA ANN, executive recruiter; b. Madison, Wis., Feb. 14, 1962; d. Ray Franklin and Mary Margaret (Maloney) Evert. BS/BA in Zoology and German, Duke U., 1983; MS in Exercise and Sports Sci., Pa. State U., 1985. Cert. exercise specialist Am. Coll. Sports Medicine. Educator, coach Pa. State U., Mont Alto, 1985-86; operation dir. Cardio-Sports Inc., Atlanta, 1986-89; recruiter, cons. Diversified Human Resources Group, Inc., Atlanta, 1989, mgr. internat. data search div., 1990—. Mem. Pa. State Club of Ga. (pres. 1987-88), Atlanta Jaycees (pres. 1990—). Republican. Roman Catholic. Home: 2602 Spring Creek Ln Dunwoody GA 30350 Office: Diversified Human Resources 3490 Piedmont Rd Suite 310 Atlanta GA 30305

EVERTON, MARTA VE, ophthalmologist; b. Luling, Tex., Nov. 12, 1926; d. T.W. and Nora E. (Eckols) O'Leavy; B.A., Hardin-Simmons U., 1945; M.A., Stanford U., 1947; M.D., Baylor U., 1955; postgrad. N.Y.U.-Bellevue Hosp., 1956-57; m. Robert K. Graham, Oct. 15, 1960; children—Marcia, Christie, Leslie Fox. Intern, Meth. Hosp., Houston, 1955-56; resident in ophthalmology Baylor Affiliated Hosps., Houston, 1957-59; clin. instr. ophthalmology Baylor U., 1959-60; asst. clin. prof. ophthalmology Loma Linda U., 1962-73; practice medicine specializing in ophthalmology, Houston, 1959-60, Pasadena, Calif., 1961-74, Escondido, Calif., 1974—. Mem. AMA, Am. Acad. Ophthalmology, Alpha Omega Alpha. Home: 3024 Sycamore Ln Escondido CA 92025 Office: 810 E Ohio Ave Escondido CA 92025

EVERTS, DELORES JEAN, graphic services executive; b. Madison, Wis., May 13, 1943; d. William Robert and Agnes Anna (Schwartz) Bennett; m. Gordon Clifford Conley, Nov. 30, 1963 (div. 1965); 1 child, William Earl; m. R. Alain Everts, Aug. 31, 1974. Student U. Wis.-Madison, 1961-62, Madison Area Tech. Coll., 1972-74. Pres., chmn. bd. Madison Graphic Svcs., Inc., 1980—. Editor Etchings & Odysseys mag., 1983—. With USMC, 1962. Mem. World Fantasy Conv., MadCon (v.p. 1974-85, Weirdfield award 1985), Madison Area C. of C., Madison Area Club of Printing House Craftsmen. Avocations: books, science fiction, Dr. Who. Office: Madison Graphic Svcs Inc 120 E Wilson St Madison WI 53703

EVILSIZER, MARJORIE JOAN, speech language pathologist; b. N.Y.C., Aug. 10, 1961; m. Randall Joseph Evilsizer. Cert. clin. competence, elem. sch. tchr., Okla. Speech lang. pathologist Dewey County Cooperative, Vici, Okla., 1985-87, Putman City Schs., Oklahoma City, 1987—. Recipient Headstart Svc. award Wilshire Headstart Ctr., 1982, Human Svc. award United Way. Mem. NAFE, Am. Speech Lang. Hearing Assn., Assn. for Supervision and Curriculum Devel., Cent. Okla. Speech Lang. Hearing Assn.

EVRARD, JANICE MARIE, furniture store executive, office manager; b. Washington, Ind., Apr. 16, 1959; d. Carl Bernard and Elizabeth Virginia (Wade) O'Connor; m. James Virgil Evrard, Sept. 5, 1986; children: Clint Nathaniel, Mandy Rose. AS, Vincennes U., 1979. Tchr. Center Street Day Care Ctr., Terre Haute, Ind., 1979-81; mgr. trainee Woolco Dept. Store South, Terre Haute, 1981-83; office mgr. Carl B. O'Connor D.D.S. Inc., Washington, 1984—; owner, operator Washington Furniture Mart, 1986—; participant Ind. Dental Assn., Indpls., 1983—, Palmer Assocs., Evansville, 1986, 87, Indpls., 1986. Mem. NAFE. Republican. Roman Catholic. Home: RR 1 Box 683 Montgomery IN 47558 Office: Carl B O'Connor DDS Inc 100 W VanTrees Washington IN 47501

EWART, ROBERTA MARIE, military officer; b. Akron, Ohio, Dec. 7, 1959; d. Roger Loreaux and LaVerne (Weber) E. BS in Physics, USAF Acad., 1982; BA in Physics and Philosophy, Oxford U., 1984, MA in Physics and Philosophy, 1985, MEE, 1990. Commd. 2d lt. USAF, 1982, advanced through grades to capt., 1986; shuttle flight controller NASA, Houston, 1982-83; mission controller, Global Positioning System USAF, Colorado Springs, Colo., 1985-89; Air Force ROTC asst. prof. aerospace studies Ohio State U., Columbus, 1989—. Vol. U.S. Space Found., Colorado Springs, 1985-89. Nat. Merit scholar, 1978, Marshall scholar Oxford U., 1983-85. Mem. IEEE, Laser and Electroptics Soc. Lutheran. Office: AFROTC DET 645 Columbus OH 43220

EWEN, PAMELA BINNINGS, lawyer; b. Phila., Mar. 22, 1944; d. Walter James and Barbara (Perkins) Binnings; m. Jerome Francis Ayers, Aug. 22, 1965 (div. July 1974); 1 son, Scott Dylan; m. John Alexander Ewen, Dec. 13, 1974. B.A., Tulane U., 1977; J.D. cum laude, U. Houston, 1979. Bar: Tex. 1979, U.S. Dist. Ct. (so. dist.) Tex. 1981, U.S. Ct. Appeals (5th cir.) 1981. Law clk. firm Harris, Cook, Browning & Barker, Corpus Christi, Tex., 1977-79; assoc. firm Kleberg, Dyer, Redford & Weil, Corpus Christi, 1979-80; atty. law dept. Gulf Oil Corp., Houston, 1980-84; assoc. Baker & Botts, Houston, 1984-88, ptnr., 1988—. La. Legis. scholar, New Orleans, 1976-77. Mem. ABA (forum com. on franchising 1983-85, corp., banking, bus. law sect., 1984—), Am. Petroleum Inst. (spl. subcom. to gen. com. on law, com. on product liability 1982-85), Tex. State Bar (com. on uniform communal code 1988—), Order of Barons. Office: 3000 One Shell Plaza Houston TX 77002

EWEN, PAULA ROBEY, transportation executive; b. La Plata, Md., Sept. 9, 1955; d. Kentzing Carver and Peggy Ruth (Smallwood) R.; m. Wayne Bruce Ewen, June 26, 1973. BS, U. Md., 1984; postgrad., Am. U., 1989—. Computer technician Naval Ordnance Sta., Indian Head, Md., 1974-76; computer analyst Rehab Group, Inc., Arlington, Va., 1976-77, Murry's Steaks, Inc., Forestville, Md., 1977-78; computer specialist Exec. Office of the Pres., Washington, 1978-81; computer specialist Dept. of Transp., Washington, 1981—, spl. asst., 1984-89, automation program mgr., 1989—; 1984-88, automation program mgr., 1988—. Mem. Assn. Female Execs., Charles County Bus. and Profl. Orgn. Home: Rt 1 Box 30 Port Tobacco MD 20677 Office: Dept Transp 400 Seventh St SW Washington DC 20590

EWING, CATHERINE RUTH, regional training coordinator; b. McKeesport, Pa., July 11, 1943; d. William Erskine and Elizabeth (Hughes) Duncan; married, July 14, 1990; children: Ruth Ann, Diane, Patricia, Robert, Kathleen, Heather. Regional tng. coord. Morgan's Foods Inc., Cleve., 1982—. Mem. East Suburban C. of C. Home: 1345 Cavitt Rd Monroeville PA 15146

EWING, JOAN RUTH, education educator; b. Rochester, Ind., May 8, 1932; d. Joseph Lester and Amelia Sophia (Doyle) E. AB in Spanish, Ind. U., Bloomington, 1954; postgrad., U. Notre Dame, 1960; MS in Edn., Ind. U., 1962; postgrad., U. Valencia, 1962. Spanish tchr. Ben Davis High Sch., Indpls., 1954-56; spanish tchr. Logansport High Sch., Logansport, Ind., 1956-89, 1989--. Recipient Scholarship Ind. U., Bloomington, 1950-54. Mem. Ind. Sch. Women, Ind. State Tchrs. Assn., Logansport Edn. Assn., NEA, A.A.U.W., Tourist Club, Alpha Delta Kappa, Tri Kappa Philanthropic Sorority. Republican. Baptist. Office: Logansport High Sch One Berry Ln Logansport IN 46947

EWING, MARY ARNOLD, lawyer; b. Shreveport, La., Feb. 21, 1948; d. George and Christine (Cocek) Hengy; m. Robert Craig Ewing, Aug. 30, 1981; 1 child, Kyle Ross. BA, U. Colo., 1972; JD, U. Denver, 1975. Bar: Colo. 1975, U.S. Supreme Ct. 1979. Assoc. Johnson & Mahoney, Denver, 1975-80; ptnr. Branney, Hillyard, Ewing & Barnes, Englewood, Colo., 1980-85, Bucholtz, Bull & Ewing, Denver, 1985—; asst. prof. law U. Denver, 1977-78, part time prof. 1978—; mem. faculty Nat. Inst. Trial Advocacy, 1984-89; instr. nat. session 1984, 85, 87, Nat. Bd. Trial Advocacy, regional session, 1984-89. Chmn. Denver County Task Force, 1976-77; treas. Cen. Com. 1st Congl. Dist., 1976-77; v.p. Young Rep. League Denver, 1975, pres. 1976; mem. govt. relations com. Jr. Symphony Guild, 1978—. Mem. ABA, Colo. Bar Assn. (ethics com.), Denver Bar Assn. (vice chmn. new lawyers assistance com. 1977), Colo. Women's Bar Assn., Internat. Platform Assn., Mountain States Combined Tng. Assn., Rocky Mountain Dressage Soc. (sec. High Plains chpt. 1979-80, chmn. constn. and by-laws com. 1988—), Assn. Trial Lawyers Am., Colo. Trial Lawyers Assn. (bd. govs., chmn. interprofl. com. 1980, bd. dirs. polit. action com. 1989), Douglas County Bar Assn., Am. Arbitration Assn., Nat. Bd. Trial Advocacy (cert. 1983), Am. Trakehner Assn., Rocky Mountain Trakehner Assn. (v.p. 1987),Arapahoe Hunt Club, Greenwood Athletic, Kappa Beta Pi (pres. 1977-78). Home: Nonesuch Farm 816 W Quarry Rd Littleton CO 80124 Office: Bucholtz Bull & Ewing 1666 S University Blvd Denver CO 80210

EWING-TAYLOR, JACQUELINE MARIE, business development executive; b. Elkton, Md., Feb. 7, 1953; d. Harvey Wilson and Hilda Mae (Somers) Ewing; m. Danny Lee Taylor, Dec. 27, 1983. Student, U. Miami, Coral Gables, Fla., 1971-72, Centre Coll., 1973-75, U. Nev., 1984—. Cert. compensation profl. Sales person Raleigh's, Washington, 1972-75, asst. mgr., 1975-76; mgr. pro shop Congl. County Club, Bethesda, Md., 1976-78; mgr. sales Macy's, Reno, 1978-79; trainee Nev. Nat. Bank, Reno, 1979-80, tng. specialist, 1980-81, personnel asst., 1981-84, compensation and benefits officer, 1984-86, asst. v.p., asst. personnel mgr., 1986-89, v.p. employee benefit trust, 1989; v.p. bus. devel. Security Pacific Bank, Reno, 1989—; instr. Truckee Meadows Community Coll., Reno, 1981—; lectr. U. Nev., Reno, 1982—; personnel cons. for various employers, Nev., 1985—; bd. dirs. Nev. Health Systems; tchr. Project Business, 1989. Advisor Jr. Achievement, Reno, 1980-83; bd. dirs. ACLU, Reno, 1984-87; personnel com. chmn. Planned Parenthood, Reno, 1984-86; fundraising chmn. Planned Parenthood of Nev., Reno, 1985; vice chmn., bd. dirs. Adolescent Care and Treatment, Reno. Mem. Nat. Assn. Bank Women (fundraising com. 1984-85), Am. Compensation Assn. (cert. compensation profl.), Am. Inst. Banking (speaking award 1982), No. Nev. Personnel Assn., Reno/Sparks C. of C., Toastmasters (v.p. Ad Lib 1988—, Toastmaster of Yr. 1981, 83). Republican. Home: 4640 Canyon Dr Reno NV 89509 Office: Security Pacific Bank 200 S Virginia St Reno NV 89501

EXELBERT, LOIS LOVE, nursing educator; b. Bklyn., Nov. 12, 1948; d. Samuel and Tillie (Hyman) Love; children: Eric, Janet, Ian, Brian. BS in nursing, Hunter Coll., 1970; MS, Fla. Internat. U., 1982. RN, N.Y., Fla.; cert. Childbirth Educator. Childbirth educator Bapt. Hosp. of Miami; co-developer, instr. Healthy Beginnings Prental-Postnatal Fitness Program, Miami; dir. diabetes care ctr. Bapt. Hosp. of Miami. Co-author: Diabetic's Learning Manual, 1975; contbr. articles to profl. jours. Bd. dirs. Kendale Elem. PTA. Mem. Am. Soc. for Psychoprophylaxis in Obstetrics, Am. Diabetes Assn., Am. Assn. Diabetes Educators, Fla. Orgn. Nurse Execs., Aerobics and Fitness Assn. Am., Dade County Assn. Diabetes Educators. Democrat. Jewish. Home: 9405 SW 89th St Miami FL 33176 Office: Baptist Hosp Miami 8900 N Kendall Dr Miami FL 33176

EXUM, FRANCES BELL, foreign language educator; b. Birmingham, Ala., May 11, 1940; d. Frank Kinney and Frances Henrietta (Bell) E.; BA in Spanish cum laude, Fla. State U., 1962, MA in Spanish, 1963, PhD in Spanish, 1970. Instr. Spanish, N.C. Wesleyan Coll., 1963-65, Greensboro Coll., 1965-67; asst. prof. Spanish, Winthrop Coll., 1970-73, assoc. prof., 1973-77, prof., 1977—. Mem. MLA, South Atlantic MLA (exec.com. 1986-88, Spanish I sec. 1984, chmn. 1985, nominating com. 1986-88), Assn. Internat. de Hispanistas, Am. Assn. Tchrs. Spanish and Portuguese (pres. S.C. chpt. 1979-80), Cervantes Soc. Am., Soc. Spanish and Portuguese Hist. Studies, AAUP (pres. chpt. 1976-77), Renaissance Soc. Am., Phi Beta Kappa, Phi Kappa Phi (pres. chpt. 1984-85), Pi Beta Phi. Author: The Metamorphosis of Lope de Vega's King Pedro, 1974; editor: Essays on Comedy and the Gracioso in Plays by Agustín Moreto; contbr. articles and book revs. to profl. publs. Home: 3757 Harwick Place Charlotte NC 28211 Office: Winthrop Coll Dept Modern & Classical Langs Rock Hill SC 29733*

EYMAN, LINDA MAE, nurse; b. Pitts., Jan. 8, 1945; d. Ralph Settler and Mae Aida (Wickline) E. Diploma, Allegheny Gen. Hosp. Sch., 1965; BS, St. Joseph's Coll., Windham, Maine, 1989. RN, Ohio. Nurse Cleve. Clinic Hosp., 1965-66; clin. supr. Allegheny Gen. Hosp., Pitts., 1968-75; nurse, office mgr. R. Zemel, P.C., Pitts., 1976—. Vol. tutor Greater Pitts. Literacy Coun., 1984—; sec. coun. 1st English Luth. Ch., Sharpsburg, Pa., 1988—. Mem. Soc. Gastroenterology Assts. (author jour. 1981—), Assn. Enteral and Prenatal Nutrition, Allegheny Gen. Hosp. Sch. of Nursing Alumnae Assn. (v.p. 1986-88), Soroptimist Internat. of Pitts., Inc. (v.p. 1985-88, pres. 1988—). Republican. Home: 34 B Bethany Dr Pittsburgh PA 15215 Office: R Zemel PC #527 Two Allegheny Ctr Pittsburgh PA 15212

EYRE, PAMELA CATHERINE, army officer; b. Chgo., Nov. 3, 1948; d. Francis Thomas and Jane (Burd) E.; m. Burke Owen Buntz, Jan. 10, 1986. B.A., Central State U. Okla., 1972; M.P.A., U. Okla., 1976. Commd. 2d lt. U.S. Army, 1973, advanced through grades to maj., 1986; test and evaluation officer Fort Gordon, Ga., 1982-85, research and devel. coordinator Pentagon, Washington, 1985-88, with army gen. staff Pentagon, 1988— . Fellow Armed Forces Communications Electronics Assn. Avocation: foxhunting. Home: 5011 Larno Dr Alexandria VA 22310

EZELL, ANNETTE SCHRAM, educator, university administrator; b. West Frankfort, Ill., June 19, 1940; d. Woodrow C. and Rosa (Franich) Schram; BS U. Nev., 1962, MS in Physiology, 1967, postgrad., 1969; EdD in Pub. Adminstrn., Brigham Young U., 1977; children: Michael L., Rona Maria. Mem. staff Washoe Med. Ctr., Reno, 1962; teaching asst. U. Nev., Reno, 1962-63, instr., 1963-64, 1965-67, asst. prof., 1967-71; curriculum specialist U. Nev. Med. Sch., 1971-72, project mgr. Fed. Grant Intercampus Edn. Project, 1969-71, assoc. prof., curriculum specialist rural practitioner program, 1971-73, staff assoc. Mountain States Regional Med. Program, 1974-75; cons. Nev. Dept. Edn., 1975-77; asst. dean acad. affairs U. Utah, Salt Lake City, 1977-80; acting Dean, 1981, dir., prof. doctoral program Edn. Adminstrn.; prof., dept. head Coll. Human Development, Pa. State U., 1982-85; dean Coll. Profl. Studies, prof. bus. adminstrn. U. So. Colo., Pueblo, 1985-87; sr. asst. to pres. Towson State U., Balt., 1987—; cons. higher edn., TV edn., research methology; adviser to various research, polit. and edn1. bds. Mem. Am. Ednl. Research Assn., AAAS, Am. Acad. Arts and Scis., AAUP, Am. Council on Edn., Am. Assn. Higher Edn., Soc. for Coll. & Univ. Planning, Decision Scis. Inst., Sigma Xi, Phi Kappa Phi, Delta Kappa Gamma. Home: 2515 Boston St #1006 Baltimore MD 21224 Office: Towson State U Towson MD 21204

EZELL, REVA GROSS, radio station manager, writer; b. St. Louis, Apr. 20, 1937; d. Alvin I. and Blanche R. (Marshak) Gross; m. Arnold Gross, Aug. 25, 1957 (div. June, 1977); children: Margery Gross Dellinger, Matthew David Gross; m. Henry L. Ezell, Feb. 14, 1980. AB, Ga. State U., 1960, MA, 1966; MEd, U. Ga., 1972. Cert. profl. tchr., counselor, Ga. Tchr. Gwinnet County Bd. Edn., Lawrenceville, Ga., 1960-67; tchr., counselor Upward Bound Emory U., Atlanta, 1967-70; career counselor Atlanta Bd. Edn., 1970-75; producer, writer WABE-FM, Atlanta, 1975-83, mgr., 1983—; freelance writer Atlanta Jour.-Constn., 1982—; Bd. dirs. Ga. Radio Reading Svc., 1983—. Co-author: Bus. Traveler's Guide to Atlanta, 1980; profl. radio voice, 1976—. Vol. Lupus Found., Atlanta, 1987—, Coun. Battered Women, Atlanta, 1989—. Mem. Am. Women in Radio and TV (v.p., bd. dirs. 1985-89), So. Edn. Communications Assn. (pres., bd. dirs. 1983-89), Atlanta Press Club. Office: WABE-FM 740 Bismarck Rd Atlanta GA 30324

EZELL, SHIRLEY DEE, university administrator; b. Raymondville, Tex., Apr. 14, 1938; d. William Monroe and Nina Jesse (Moon) Elliott; m. Robert Ezell, Oct. 13, 1963; children: Andrea Ezell Little, Cambrea, Christina. BS in Chemistry and Home Econs., Baylor U., 1959; MS in Textile and Costume Design, Tex. Women's U., 1961, PhD in Textile Chemistry, 1965. Chairperson costume design North Tex. State U., Denton, 1961-63; chairperson textiles and clothing Ind. State U., Terre Haute, 1967-70; chairperson dept. human devel. and consumer sci. U. Houston, 1970-79, assoc. dean acad. affairs, 1979-86, assoc. v.p. acad. programs, 1986—; active numerous coms. U. Houston, 1974—, mem. retention and admission task force, 1986-87, chairperson program planning Urban 13 Conf., 1987, liaison to So. Assn. Colls. and Schs., 1989. Author: (film series) Making It in Fashion. Recipient Tex. Higher Edn. award, 1987. Mem. ASTM (hon.), Am. Assn. Textile Chemists and Colorists, Assn. Women in Sci., Fort Bend C. of C. (chairperson edn. com. 1989—), Fashion Group (N.Y., program chmn.), Phi Kappa Phi. Republican. Baptist. Home: 1314 Plantation Dr Richmond TX 77469 Office: Univ Houston 4800 Calhoun 224 E Houston TX 77204-2162

EZZELL, LOIS RIGGINS, museum administrator; b. Nashville, Nov. 18, 1939; d. Percy Leon and Lula Belle Prather (Traughber) Von Schmittou; 1 son, Nicholas. B.S., Belmont Coll., 1968; postgrad., U. Western Ky., 1969-72, George Washington U., 1978. Cert. tchr., Ky., Tenn. Tchr. Ky. Pub. Schs., Adairville, 1962-71; tour supr. Tenn. State Capitol, Nashville, 1972-74; curator of extension services Tenn. State Mus., Nashville, 1975-77, curator edn., 1977-81, exec. dir., 1981—. Chmn. Nashville Flight of Tenn. Friendship Force, Caracas, Venezuela, 1977, Tenn. Am. Revolution Bicentennial Arts Competition, 1976; bd. dirs. Zool. Soc. Mid. Tenn., 1986-88, So. Folk Cultural Revival Project, 1986—, Tenn. Pres. Trust, 1989—, Hist. Coun., Girl Scouts U.S. Mem. Southeastern Mus. Conf. (edn. com., rep. to Am. Assn. Mus. council, publs. advt. com. 1983), Inter Mus. Council of Nashville (chmn. edn. 1980-81), Am. Assn. Mus., Am. Assn. State and Local History (edn com. 1988—). Office: Tenn State Mus 505 Deaderick St Nashville TN 37243-1120

FAATZ, JEANNE RYAN, state legislator; b. Cumberland, Md., July 30, 1941; d. Charles Keith and Myrtle Elizabeth (McIntyre) Ryan; B.S., U. Ill., 1962; postgrad. (Gates fellow) Harvard U. Program Sr. Execs. in state and local Govt., 1984; M.A., U. Colo.-Denver, 1985. children—Kristin, Susan. Instr. Speech Dept., Met. State Coll., Denver, 1985—; sec. to majority leader Colo. Senate, 1976-78; mem. Colo. Ho. Reps. from Dist. 1, 1978—, chmn. edn. com., coll. instr. Metro State Coll. Past pres. Harvey Park (Colo.) Homeowners Assn., Southwest Denver YWCA Adult Edn. Club; Southwest met. coordinator UN Children's Fund, 1969-74; mem. citizens adv. council Ft. Logan Mental Health Center; bd. mgrs. Southwest Denver YMCA. Mem. Bear Creek Republican Women's Club. Home: 2903 S Quitman St Denver CO 80236 Office: State Capitol Denver CO 80203

FABER, CAROL ANTOINETTE, petroleum company executive; b. Terre Haute, Ind., Dec. 26, 1937; d. Fred Malooley and Regina Carolyn (Collins) Breiner; m. Daniel Keith Faber, Sept. 14, 1963; children: John Craig Lund, Jeffrey Scott Lund, Lisa Anne Lund. Student, Valencia Jr. Coll., Orlando, Fla., 1979-80, Seminole Jr. Coll., 1980. Dental asst. Dr. McCormick, Indpls., 1955-57; office mgr. for various dentists Orlando, 1961-70, pvt. practice in interior design, 1978-81; gen. office worker Aero Petroleum, Inc., Orlando, 1981-82; field supr. Aero Petroleum, Inc., Bowling Green, Ky., 1982-84; pres., founder Cheyenne Petroleum, Inc., Bowling Green, 1984-89; chief exec. officer Panda Trading Co., Orlando, 1989-90, Little People Inc., Orlando, 1990—. Active Selective Service Bd., Orlando, 1983—. Mem. NAFE, Nat. Fedn. Ind. Bus., Ky. Ind. Petroleum Producers Assn. (exec. bd. 1986-87), Ky. Oil & Gas Assn., Orlando C. of C., Landmark Assn., Friends of Arts-Capital Arts Ctr., Phi Theta Kappa. Republican. Episcopalian. Office: Little People Inc 7380 Sand Lake Rd Ste 310 Orlando FL 32819

FABER, SANDRA MOORE, astronomer, educator; b. Boston, Dec. 28, 1944; d. Donald Edwin and Elizabeth Mackenzie (Borwick) Moore; m. Andrew L. Faber, June 9, 1967; children: Robin, Holly. B.A., Swarthmore Coll., 1966, D.Sc. (hon.), 1986; Ph.D., Harvard U., 1972. Asst. prof., astronomer Lick Obs., U. Calif., Santa Crux, 1972-77, assoc. prof., astronomer, 1977-79, prof., astronomer, 1979—; mem. NSF astronomy adv. panel, 1975-77; vis. prof. Princeton U., 1978, U. Hawaii, 1983, Ariz. State U., 1985; Phillips visitor Haverford Coll., 1982; Feshbach lectr. MIT, 1990; mem. Nat. Acad. Astronomy Survey Panel, 1979-81; chmn. vis. com. Space Telescope Sci. Inst., 1983-84; co-chmn. sci. steering com. Keck Observatory, 1987—. Assoc. editor: Astrophys. Jour. Letters, 1982-87; editorial bd.: Ann. Revs. Astronomy and Astrophysics, 1982-87; contbr. articles to profl. jours. Trustee Carnegie Instn., Washington, 1985—; bd. dirs. Ann. Revs., Inc., 1989—. Recipient Bart J. Bok prize Harvard U., 1978, Director's Distinguished Lectr. award Livermore Nat. Lab., 1986, Carnegie Lectr. Carnegie Inst. Washington, 1988; NSF fellow, 1966-71; Woodrow Wilson fellow, 1966-71; Alfred P. Sloan fellow, 1977-81; listed among 100 best Am. scientists under 40, Sci. Digest, 1984; Tetelman fellow, Yale U., 1987. Mem. NAS, Am. Astron. Soc. (councilor 1982-84, Dannie Heineman prize 1986), Internat. Astron. Union, Nat. Acad. Arts and Scis., Phi Beta Kappa, Sigma Xi. Office: U Calif Lick Obs Santa Cruz CA 95060

FABIAN, JEANNE, executive recruiter; b. Wilkes Barre, Pa., June 25, 1946; d. Joseph A. and Dorothy (Cannon) F.; m. Christopher Sykes, Sept. 7, 1968 (div. Mar. 1979). BBA, Baruch Coll., N.Y.C., 1969; MBA, Hofstra U., Hempstead, N.Y., 1979. CPA, N.Y. Auditor Arthur Andersen & Co., N.Y.C., 1969-73; planning analyst Avon Products, Inc., N.Y.C., 1973-75; fin. analyst Revlon, Inc., N.Y.C., 1975-77; acctg. mgr. Am. Standard, Inc., N.Y.C., 1977-78; sr. fin. analyst Texaco, Inc., Harrison, N.Y., 1979-82; asst. dir. Harper & Row Pubs., Inc., N.Y.C., 1983-86, exec. recruiter, 1986-89; owner Fabian Assocs., Inc., N.Y.C., 1989—; mgr. recoding artist. Treas., bd. dirs. Stanwix Apts. Corp., Forest Hills, N.Y., 1983—. Mem. AICPA, N.Y. State Soc. CPAs. Office: Fabian Assocs Inc 9 E 45th St Ste 305 New York NY 10017

FABIANO, DIANE FABIAN, artist; b. Calabasas, Calif., Oct. 7, 1952; d. Andrew Edward Fabiano and Mary Grace (Cataldo) Fabian. Student, Worcester Art Mus. Sch., 1972-73, Boston U., 1973-74; BFA with distinction, Calif. Coll. Arts and Crafts, Oakland, 1976; postgrad., Calif. State U., Northridge, 1981-83. One-woman shows include Antioch U. West, Venice, Calif., 1983, Prometheus Gallery, Northridge, Calif., 1986-87, Tarsh Gallery, Tarzana, Calif., 1988—; exhibited in group show at Aubes 3935 Galerie, Montreal, Que., 1986, Ashley Gallery, Sherman Oaks, Calif., 1987, Canoga Mission Gallery, Canoga Park, Calif., 1988—, Triangle Gallery, Oxnard, Calif., 1989-90, Gordon Gallery, Santa Monica, Calif., 1989-90, Barry White's Fine Art Gallery, Malibu, Calif., 1989-90, Palm Street Gallery, Ventura, Calif., 1990; represented in pvt. collections. Mem. CARE Internat. Leadership Devel. Forum, Calif., 1989, World Affairs Coun. Mem. NOW, ACLU, Womens Caucus for the Arts, Show Coalition, Artists Equity Assn., Calabasas C. of C. Home: 170 Oxbow Rd Neeham MA 02192 Studio: Contemporary Am Artist 5624 Las Virgenes Rd Studio 16 Calabasas CA 91302

FABIANO, MARION PINZOTTI, councilwoman; b. Niagara Falls, N.Y., July 23, 1937; d. Peter Joseph and Mary Beatrice (Palumbo) Pinzotti; m. Louis R. Fabiano, July 2, 1960 (div. Dec. 1988); children: Mary, Angelyn, Louis, Peter. BS in Edn., Buffalo State, 1959; MA in Edn., U. Buffalo, 1976. Tchr. Niagara Falls Bd. Edn., 1959-62; supr. student tchrs. SUNY, Buffalo, 1968-71; substitute tchr. various schs. western N.Y., 1967-70. Committeeman Grand Island (N.Y.) Dem. Com., 1989—; parish coun. mem. St. Stephens Ch., Grand Island, 1980-84; past pres. high sch./mid. sch. PTA, Grand Island; past officer various local, dist., state PTAs; formerly active pub. rels. N.Y. State PTA, honorary life mem. Home: 1011 Foxcroft Rd Grand Island NY 14072

FABINA, SUSAN LYNN, sales executive; b. Ft. Wayne, Apr. 27, 1960; d. Mathew Edward and Constance F. Student, Lutheran Hosp. Sch. of Nursing, 1983. RN. Nurse Lutheran Hosp., Ft. Wayne, 1981-86; personnel mgr. Mayhall Search Group, Fort Wayne, 1986—; med. personnel mgr., 1989—; agent Client Builder, South Bend, Ind., 1986--. mem. Nat. Assn. of Female Execs., Nat. Assn. of Life Underwriters, Delta Omega. Republican. Roman Catholic. Home: 902 W Wayne St Fort Wayne IN 46802 Office: Northwestern Mutual Life 111 E Ludwig Rd Suite 225 Fort Wayne IN 46825

FABRICANT, CATHERINE GRENCI, microbiologist; b. Davoli, Calabria, Italy, Sept. 24, 1919; came to U.S., 1920; d. Francesco Sabato and Maria Antonia (Sinopoli) Grenci; m. Julius Fabricant, Dec. 8, 1945; children: Barbara Louise, Daniel Grenci. BS, Cornell U., 1942, MS, 1948. Head med. technician infirmary Cornell U., Ithaca, N.Y., 1942-44; grad. asst. N.Y. State Coll. Vet. Medicine Cornell U., Ithaca, 1945-48, rsch. assoc., 1959-62, acting asst. prof., 1963, rsch. assoc., 1965-73, sr. rsch. assoc., 1973-85, vis. fellow, 1986—; vis. rsch. assoc. U. Aarhus (Denmark) Med. Sch., 1964-65, vis. sr. rsch. assoc., 1973. Author rsch. studies. Vol. Ithaca area Am. Heart Assn., 1980, 84, Birth Defects Soc., 1990. Grantee Morris Animal Found., 1973-74, Ralston Purina Co., 1975-82, NIH, 1976-83. Mem. Morris Animal Found.; mem. Am. Soc. Pathologists, Am. Soc. Virologists, Fedn. Am. Socs. Exptl. Biology, Sigma Xi, Sigma Delta Epsilon. Office: NY State Coll Vet Medicine Schurman Hall Cornell Univ Ithaca NY 14853

FABRIZIO, MARGARET MARY, collection agency owner; b. L.A., Apr. 6, 1954; d. Nadir Alfred and Sheila Marie (Chartrand) F. BA, U. Calif., Santa Cruz, 1976. Office mgr. Dave Richards Bail Bonds, Santa Cruz, 1977-80; family support officer Office of Dist. Atty., Santa Cruz, 1980-85; dir. info. svcs., asst. office adminstr. Grunsky, Pybrum, Ebey and Farrar, Watsonville, Calif., 1985-88; owner M. Fabrizio & Assocs., Capitola, Calif., 1988—. Co-chmn. Santa Cruz County Women's Commn., 1986—; mem. Watsonville Women's Network. Mem. NOW. Democrat. Roman Catholic. Office: M Fabrizio & Assocs PO Box 245 Capitola CA 95010

FACCIANO, PAULINE ROSE, fund raiser, public relations professional; b. Burbank, Calif., Aug. 31, 1959; d. Joseph John and Blanca Rosa (Portuguez) F. AB in English Lit., Studio Art, U. Calif., Berkeley, 1985. Devel. asst. Am. Fedn. Arts, San Francisco, 1985-86, exhbn. program asst., 1986-87; arts adminstrn. fellow Nat. Endowment for Arts, Washington, 1987; asst. to dir. Friends of Photography, San Francisco, 1987-88; asst. dir. devel. Oakland (Calif.) Mus. Assn., 1988, dir. membership campaigns, 1988-89; dir. devel. and pub. rels. Internat. Visitors Ctr., San Francisco, 1990—. Mentor, Big Sisters, San Francisco, 1990. Mem. Nat. Soc. Fund Raising Execs., Am. Assn. Museums. Democrat. Office: Internat Visitors Ctr 312 Sutter St Ste 402 San Francisco CA 94108

FADER, ELLEN STRAHS, communications company executive; b. N.Y.C., Dec. 9, 1952; d. Martin Paul and Norma (Weidenbaum) Strahs; m. Robert Steven Fader, July 30, 1976. BA, SUNY, New Paltz, 1974; postgrad. Mercy Coll., 1977, Marymount Coll., 1983. Mng. editor, prodn. mgr. Oracle newspaper, New Paltz, 1974-78; asst. editor Random House/Alfred A. Knopf, N.Y.C., 1979-81; contracts coord. Hammond Music Enterprises, N.Y.C., 1981; sr. v.p., sec. Price Communications Corp., N.Y.C., 1981-89 ; exec. v.p., sec. Rep. Broadcasting Corp., N.Y.C., 1981-89; v.p., sec. Atlas Broadcasting Corp., 1983-89, Fed. Broadcasting Corp., 1984-89, N.Y. Law Pub. Co., 1985-89, Price Outdoor Media Corp. of Am., 1985-89, Eimar Realty Corp., 1985-89, Continental Broadcasting Corp., 1987-89; sr. v.p. adminstrn. and corp. affairs Osborn Communications Corp., 1989—; bd. dirs., v.p., corp. sec. Telemation Inc., 1986-89. Recipient Haney award Met. Mus. Art, 1970, Alexander medal Bd. Edn. N.Y.C., 1969. Mem. Women in Communications, Am. Women in Radio and TV, Am. Soc. Corp. Secs., Rockefeller Ctr. Club. Avocations: traveling, reading, skiing, music. Office: Osborn Communications Corp 405 Lexington Ave 54th Fl New York NY 10174

FADER, SHIRLEY SLOAN, writer; b. Paterson, N.J., 1931; d. Samuel Louis and Miriam (Marcus) Sloan; m. Seymour J. Fader; children: Susan Deborah, Steven Micah Kimchi. B.S., M.S., U. Pa. Writer, journalist, author Paramus, N.J., 1956—; chmn., coordinator ann. writers seminar Bergen Community Coll., 1973-76. Author columns Jobmanship, People and You, Family Weekly mag., 1971-82, How to Get More From Your Job, Glamour mag., 1978-81, Start Here, Working Woman mag., 1980-88, Work Strategies, Working Mother mag., 1987-88, Women Getting Ahead, Ladies Home Jour., 1980-90, How Would You Handle It, New Idea mag., 1984—, Moving Up, Woman mag., 1989—; contbg. editor Family Weekly, 1971-82, Glamour mag., 1978-81, Working Woman mag., 1980-88, Working Mother mag., 1987-88, Ladies Home Jour., 1980-90, Woman mag., 1989—; contbr. articles to mags., U.S., Gt. Britain, Australia, Europe, 1956—; author: The Princess Who Grew Down, 1968, From Kitchen to Career, 1977, Jobmanship, 1978, Successfully Ever After, 1982, Brit. edit., 1985. Mem. Authors Guild, Am. Soc. Journalists and Authors (nat. v.p. 1976-77, mem.-at-large nat. exec. council 1976-78, 83-86), Nat. Press Club. Address: 377 McKinley Blvd Paramus NJ 07652

FAGERSTEN, BARBARA JEANNE, special education educator; b. San Francisco, Feb. 29, 1924; d. Ernest Mauritz and Louise (Hopkins) F.; m. Harold Gurish, Feb. 7, 1950 (div. 1970); children: Michael, Matthew, Jonathon. BA, San Francisco State U., 1951; MS, Dominican U., 1973, degree in spl. edn., 1975; degree in adminstrn. and supervision, 1976, degree in community coll. instruction, 1981. Personnel sec. Arabian Am. Oil Co., San Francisco, 1944-45; union sec. Jeweler's Union, San Francisco, 1946-48; med. sec. Mt. Zion Hosp., San Francisco, 1949-50; spl. edn. tchr. Marin Office Edn., San Rafael, Calif., 1967—; bd. dirs. DeWitt Learning Ctr., San Rafael, 1969. Bd. dirs. Marin Tchrs. Credit Union, San Rafael, 1978—, Marinwood Community Services, San Rafael, 1986-87; commr. Parks and Recreation Marinwood, San Rafael, 1983-86. Mem. Calif. Assn. Neurol. Handicapped Children (trustee 1973-74), Phi Delta Kappa. Democrat. Home: 272 Blackstone Dr San Rafael CA 94903 Office: Marin Office Edn 1111 Las Gallinas San Rafael CA 94903

FAGGARD, PHOEBE, marketing professional; b. Moss Point, Miss., Sept. 17, 1956; d. Norris Olen and Ruby Jane (Everett) F. BS, Miss. U. Women, 1978; MBA, Miss. Coll., 1984. Mgr. area sales McRaes, Jackson, Miss., 1981-82; mgr. pub. rels. Miller Wills Aviation, Jackson, 1982-87; field mktg. mgr. Nat. Pizza Co., Jackson, 1987-90; dir. mktg. Specialty Food Systems, Slidell, La., 1990—. Chmn., Jackson Miss. Hospitality Pageant, 1986-88, Career Women's Seminar, Jackson, 1989; vol. ARC, Jackson, 1989-90; mem. com. Strawberry Festival, Ridgeland, Miss., 1990. Recipient Vol. Svc. award Miss. chpt. Cystic Fibrosis Found., 1988, Outstanding Young Women Am., 1986. Mem. Pub. Rels. Assn. (Lantern award 1988), Jackson Sales and Mktg. Execs. (v.p., bd. dirs., Outstanding Mem. of Yr. award 1989). Baptist. Home: 312 1244 Harbor Dr Slidell LA 70458 Office: Specialty Food Systems 1320 Lakewood Dr Slidell LA 70459-4130

FAGIN, CLAIRE MINTZER, educational administrator; b. N.Y.C.; d. Harry and Mae (Slatin) Mintzer; m. Samuel Fagin, Feb. 17, 1952; children: Joshua, Charles. BS, Wagner Coll., 1948; MA, Tchrs. Coll. Columbia, 1951; PhD, N.Y. U., 1964; DSc (hon.), Lycoming Coll., 1983, Cedar Crest Coll., 1987, U. Rochester, 1987, Med. Coll. Pa., 1989. Staff nurse Sea View Hosp., S.I., N.Y., 1947, clin. instr., 1947-48; clin. instr. Bellevue Hosp., N.Y.C., 1948-50; psychiat. nurse cons. Nat. League for Nursing, N.Y.C., 1951-52; asst. chief psychiat. nursing svc. clin. ctr. NIH, 1953-54, supr., 1955; rsch. project coord. dept. psychiatry Children's Hosp., Washington, 1956; instr. psychiat.-mental health nursing NYU, N.Y.C., 1956-58, asst. prof., 1964-67, dir. grad. programs in psychiat. mental health nursing, 1965-69, assoc. prof., 1967-69; chmn. nursing dept., prof. Herbert H. Lehman Coll., CUNY, N.Y.C., 1969-77; dir. Health Professions Inst., Montefiore Hosp. and Med. Ctr., 1975-77; Margaret Bond Simon dean sch. of nursing U. Pa., Phila., 1977—; mem. task force Joint Commn. Mental Health of Children, 1966-69; gov.'s com. on children N.Y. State, 1971-75; pres. Coun. on Deans of Nursing, Sr. Colls. and Univs. N.Y. State, 1974-76; cons. to many pub. and private univs. and health care agys.; cons. Pan Am. Health Nursing, Washington, 1972-74, NIMH, HEW, 1974-76, NIMH, 1979, 83; mem. expert adv. panel on nursing WHO, 1974—; mem.-at-large Nat. Bd. Med. Examiners, 1980-83; dir. Provident Mut. Ins. Co., 1977—, audit com., 1978—, chmn., 1985—, exec. com., 1986—; mem. nat. adv. mental health coun. NIMH, 1983-88; speaker profl. convs., radio and TV; bd. dirs. Daltex Corp., 1984—, compensation com. Contbr. articles to profl. publs. Recipient Achievement award Wagner Coll., 1956, Achievement award Wagner Coll. Sch. Nursing, 1973, Achievement award Tchrs. Coll., 1975, Disting. Alumna award N.Y. U., 1979, Founders award Sigma Theta Tau, 1981, Hon. Recognition award Am. Nurses' Assn., 1988, Woman of Courage award Womens Way, 1990; NIMH fellow, 1950-51, 60-64; Am. Nurses Found. Disting. scholar, 1984. Fellow Coll. Physicians of Phila.; mem. Inst. Medicine of NAS (governing coun. 1981-83), Am. Acad. Nursing (governing coun. 1976-78), Am. Orthopsychiat. Assn. (bd. dirs. 1972-75, exec. com. of bd. 1973-75, pres. 1985-86), Nat. League for Nursing (pres. elect 1989—). Office: U Pa Nursing Edn Bldg Philadelphia PA 19104-6096

FAGNANI, MICHELE ANN, production supervisor; b. San Francisco, July 15, 1945; d. Melvin ANthony and Ann (Garetti) F.; children: Tamera Ann, Troy James. Student, San Mateo (Calif.) Bus. Coll., 1964, John Roberts Powers Coll., 1968. Draftsman Ampex, Redwood City, Calif., 1965-68; profl. model, 1967-69; draftsman Numetrics, Palo Alto, Calif., 1968-70; electronic assembler Westvalley Engring., Palo Alto, 1970-72; prodn. control planner Fairchild, San Jose, Calif., 1972-78; prodn. supr. Intel, Sunnyvale, Calif., 1978-80; prodn. mgr. Robinton Product, Inc., Sunnyvale, 1980-83, Optical Coating Labs., Santa Rosa, Calif., 1983-85, Weightronixs, Santa Rosa, 1986—; landlord rentals, San Jose and Santa Rosa, 1978; rancher, Santa Rosa, 1982-85. Democrat. Roman Catholic. Office: Weightronics 2320 Airport Blvd Santa Rosa CA 95402 :

FAHIM, AYSHE, epidemiologist, researcher; b. Ankara, Turkey, Oct. 14, 1960; came to U.S., 1966; d. Mostafa Safwatt and Zuhal (Erek) F.; m. Matthew Paul Karr, Oct. 10, 1987. BSW, U. Mo., 1982; MPH, U. Tex., Houston, 1985. Dir. family planning Serve Inc., Fulton, Mo., 1982-83; family planning counselor Planned Parenthood S.E. Tex., Houston, 1984-85; rsch. coord. Baylor Coll. Medicine, Houston, 1983-86; mktg. specialist Meth. Healthcare Network, Houston, 1986-87; dir. mktg. Beltway Community Hosp., Pasadena, Tex., 1987-88; asst. epidemiologist M.D. Anderson Cancer Inst., Houston, 1988—; pres., cons. Ginvey Health Care Internat., Houston, 1988—. Mem. Am. Pub. Health Assn., Am. Mktg. Assn., Healthcare Svcs. Mktg. Assn., Turkish-Am. Assn., H.A.R.T. Office: MD Anderson Cancer Inst 1515 Holcombe Blvd Houston TX 77030

FAHMY, RANDA, lawyer; b. Syracuse, N.Y., Feb. 4, 1964; d. Mahmoud Hussein and Irandukht (Vahidi) F. BA, Wilkes U., 1986; JD, Georgetown U., 1990. Fin. dir. Holtzman for Congress, Wilkes-Barre, Pa., 1986; lobbyist Citizens for Am., Washington, 1987; legal asst. Hamlin Blaszkow, Washington, 1987; with Koonz, McKenney & Johnson, Washington, 1988; with Willkie, Farr & Gallagher, Washington, 1989-90, assoc., 1990—. Adminstrv. editor Law and Policy in Internat. Bus., 1989-90. Mem. Rep. Nat. Lawyers Assn., Washington, 1990—. Mem. Internat. Law Soc. Georgetown U. Law Sch. (bd. dirs. Washington chpt. 1988-89).

FAHNESTOCK, JEAN HOWE, civil engineer; b. Pitts., May 22, 1930; d. James Murray and Hazel Margaret (Alberts) F. AA, Stephens, 1950; BS in Civil Engring., Carnegie-Mellon, 1955. Registered profl. engr., Ill. Sr. project mgr. De Leuw, Cather & Co., Chgo., 1955—; design mgr. De Leuw, Cather & Co., Kuwait, 1978-81, Abu Dhabi, 1981-85. Recipient Outstanding Performance award De Leuw, Cather & Co., 1981. Fellow Am.

Soc. Civil Engrs., Nat. Soc. Profl. Engrs. Republican. Presbyterian. Home: 4606 W Bryn Mawr Ave Chicago IL 60646

FAHRENBACH, JERI LYNN, librarian; b. Chgo., Sept. 24, 1948; d. Gerald Charles and Winnie (Kettles) F.; m. John Michael Cherry, Nov. 30, 1985; 1 child, Katherine Lee. BA, U. Ala., 1975, MLS, 1977. Asst. to curator U. Ala. Libr. Spl. Collections, Tuscaloosa, 1977-78; asst. dir. Fairhope (Ala.) Pub. Libr., 1978-79, Moorer & Cottage Hill Br. Libr., Mobile, Ala., 1979-82; head of reference and adult svcs. Lafayette (La.) Parish Libr., 1982-87; libr. CEL Regional Libr., Savannah, Ga., 1988-89, St. Paul's Luth. Day Sch., Savannah, 1989—. Co-editor: (newsletter) Young Adult Readers News and Services, 1979, 81. Vol., bookkeeper Habitat for Humanity, Savannah, 1987—; active Vol. Action Ctr., Savannah, 1987—. Mem. ALA, Ga. Libr. Assn., Southeastern Libr. Assn., Ala. Libr. Assn. (selections com. 1980), City Lights Theatre Guild, Savannah Area Geneal. Soc. Home: 633 Jackson Blvd Savannah GA 31405

FAHRENKAMP, BETTYE M., state legislator; b. Wilder, Tenn.; d. Earl H. and Emma (Hogue) Hargis; m. Gilbert H. Fahrenkamp, 1952 (dec.). BS, U. Tenn., 1949; MA, U. Alaska, 1962. Formerly sch. music tchr.; mem. Alaska Senate, 1978—. Chmn. dist. Democratic com., 1968-72; nat. Dem. committeewoman, 1972-78; pres. Western Legis. Conf., Coun. State Govts., 1988. With WAC, 1944-46. Mem. NAACP, Nat. Conf. State Legislators, Western Legislators Conf., Am. Assn. Ret. Tchrs., Am. Legion. Office: Alaska State Senate PO Box V Juneau AK 99811*

FAHY, NANCY LEE, food products executive; b. Schenectady, N.Y., Aug. 15, 1946; d. Christopher Mark and Frances (Lee) F.; m. Steven Neil Wohl, June 8, 1945 (div. Apr. 1978). BS cum laude, Miami (Ohio) U., 1968. Educator Palatine (Ill.) Pub. Schs., 1968-70, Glencoe (Ill.) Pub. Schs., 1970-78; sales rep. Keebler Co., Elmhurst, Ill., 1978-80, dist. mgr., 1980-82, account mgr., 1982-83, zone mgr., 1983-85, account mgr., 1985-89; regional mktg. mgr. Keebler Co., Elmhurst, 1989—. Vol. Lincoln Park Zool. Soc., Chgo., 1975-78. Mem. Food Products Club, Merchandising Execs. Club (bd. dirs. 1984-85), Grocery Mfgs. Sales Execs. Club (bd. dirs. 1984-85, asst. sec. 1987, treas. 1988, 1st v.p. 1989), Phi Beta Kappa. Office: Keebler Co 1135 Commerce Rd Morrow GA 30260

FAIKS, JAN OGOZALEK, state senator, real estate developer; b. Hempstead, N.Y., Nov. 17, 1945; d. Edmund Frank and Anna Marie (Chupella) Ogozalek. B.A., Florida State U., 1967. Tchr. Anchorage Sch. Dist., 1968-76, counselor, 1976-78; owner, mgr. Green Connection, Anchorage, 1978-81; mem. Alaska State Senate, Juneau, 1982—, pres. Author: Llama Training-Who's In Charge, 1981. Editor course devel. in career math., 1976. Bd. dirs. People Against State Income Tax, 1979—, Common Sense for Alaska, bd. dirs. Common Sense for Alaska, 1980—, research chmn., v.p., 1980-82; bd. dirs. Anchorage Symphony, 1984, Alaska Spl. Olympics; Recipient First Lady vol. award Gov. of Alaska, 1981; President's award Common Sense for Alaska, 1981; named Outstanding Secondary Tchr., Anchorage Sch. Dist., 1977. Mem. Nat. Council State Legislators, Anchorage C. of C. (bd. dirs. 1981-86, legis. chmn. 1980-82), Gen. Fedn. Women's Club (legis chmn. 1979-82), Anchorage Symphony Women's League (pres. 1980-81), Anchorage C. of C. (bd. dirs. 1987—, exec. com. 1981-82), Phi Beta Phi (pres. 1974-76). Republican. Presbyterian. Avocations: backpacking, fishing, llamas.

FAIL, MICHELLE MAXINE, advertising agency executive; b. Falmouth, Mass., Sept. 21, 1953; d. Alvin H. and Maxine Z. (Gandy) F. AA, Temple Jr. Coll., 1973; BA, S.W. Tex. State U., 1975. Account exec., media supr. McLane Mktg. Assocs., Austin, Tex., 1978-85; advt. dir. Austin Bus. Jour., 1986; cons. Innovative Mktg. Concepts, Austin, 1986-87; advt. dir. Crown Furniture, Austin, 1987-88; media dir. Fellers & Co., Austin, 1988—. Com. chmn. United Way, Austin, 1984, allocation chmn., 1986, 88, 89, 90; communication chmn. Centex Red Cross, Austin, 1987-89, sec. to bd., 1988-90, vice chair bd. 1990—. Recipient Firecracker award, Vol. of Quarter award Centex Red Cross, Austin, 1988. Mem. Austin Advt. Fedn. (bd. mem. 1979-89, silver medal award 1989), 10th Dist. Advt. Fedn. (dir. 1981-89). Office: Fellers & Co 5918 W Courtyard Dr Austin TX 78730

FAILINGER, DIANNE MARIE, personnel executive; b. Frostburg, Md., Nov. 27, 1958; d. Kermit Belvin and Thelma Josephine Failinger. B.S., Frostburg State Coll., 1980. Intern guidance counseling Braddock Jr. High, Cumberland, Md., 1980; field supr. Western Md. Consortium, Cumberland, 1980; residential services specialist Friends Aware, Cumberland, 1977-81; equal opportunity officer Allegany County Human Resources Devel. Commn., Inc., Cumberland, 1980-82, personnel officer, 1982-84; personnel adminstr. Precise Metals and Plastics, Inc., Cumberland, 1984-86; personnel specialist Meml. Hosp. and Med. Ctr., Cumberland, 1987—; v.p. Crystal Towers, Inc., Frostburg, 1987—. Bd. dirs. Community Housing Resources, Cumberland, 1982-84; program advisor Coop. Extension Service, Cumberland, 1983-86; human rights advisor Archway Sta., Cumberland, 1983—; chmn. pub. relations Gov.'s Youth Adv. Council, Balt., 1978-82; mem. Allegany County Children's Council, Cumberland, 1979-83; mem. ch. council St. Paul's Luth. Ch., Frostburg, 1984-86; sec. Frostburg Tourism Adv. Council, 1986—; mem. Cumberland Choral Soc. Recipient Letter of Appreciation/Commendation, Gov. Md., 1982; mem. community council March of Dimes, 1987—. Mem. Frostburg Bus. and Profl. Assn. (treas. local chpt. 1984-86, v.p. local chpt. 1987-88), NOW (treas. local chpt., v.p. 1987—), Delta Omicron, Psi Chi. Republican. Lutheran. Home: 109 W Main St Frostburg MD 21532 Office: Meml Hosp & Med Ctr Inc 600 Memorial Ave Cumberland MD 21502

FAILLA, PATRICIA MCCLEMENT, biomedical and environmental research administrator; b. N.Y.C., Dec. 22, 1925; s. Morgan Hall and Louise (Yandell) McClement; m. Gioacchino Failla, Jan. 22, 1949 (dec. 1961). AB in Physics cum laude, Barnard Coll., 1946; PhD in Biophysics, Columbia U., 1958; MBA, U. Chgo., 1976. Asst. physicist N.Y.C. Dept. Hosps., 1946-48; rsch. scientist Columbia U., N.Y.C., 1950-60; biophysicist Argonne Nat. Lab., Ill., 1960-71, asst. div. dir., 1971, asst. lab. dir., 1971-80, program coord., 1980-86, ret., 1986; mem. tech. electronic product radiation safety standards com., FDA-HHS, 1973-75; mem. biomed. rsch. support program subs., NIH-HHS, 1978-82; chmn. radiation com. corp. of Marine Biology Lab., 1964; mem. pres. adv. com. Med. U. S.C., Charleston, 1986—. Contbr. articles to various jours. Mem. Com. of One Hundred, Hinsdale, Ill., 1976-86. AEC predoctoral fellow Columbia U., 1948-50. Mem. AAAS, Radiation Research Soc. (councilor 1976-79), Health Physics Soc., Sigma Xi (membership com. 1970—, bd. dirs. 1975-78, 80-83). Avocations: golf, swimming. Home: 2149 Loblolly Ln Johns Island SC 29455

FAILS, DONNA GAIL, mental health services professional; b. Harlingen, Tex., Apr. 27, 1958; d. Fred R. and L. Beth (Nicholson) F. BS, Phila. Coll. Bible, Langhorne, Pa., 1982; BA in Social Work, Rutgers U., Camden, N.J., 1984, MSW, 1985. Cert. social worker. Community resource specialist March of Dimes South Jersey, Mt. Ephraim, N.J., 1982-83; case mgr., liaison Guidance Ctr. Camden County, Cherry Hill, N.J., 1983-84; outpatient coord. CamCare Mental Health Ctr., Blackwood and Cherry Hill, N.J., 1984-86; dir. partial care Comhar Mental Health Ctr., Phila., 1986-87; cons. Callahan Cons. Group, Cherry Hill, 1987-88; dir. mental health svcs., adminstr. mental health svcs. Archway Programs, Inc., Atco, N.J., 1988—; chairperson Interagy. Assessment Team of Camden County, 1989-90. Author, cons. Simon for Pres., Cherry Hill, 1988. Mem. Nat. Assn. Social Workers, Nat. Network for Social Work Mgrs., Inc., Assn. Suicidology. Mem. Free Ch. of Am. Home: 142 W Evesham Ave Magnolia NJ 08049 Office: Archway Programs Inc 197 Jackson Rd Atco NJ 08004

FAIN, KAREN KELLOGG, history and geography educator; b. Pueblo, Colo., Oct. 10, 1940; d. Howard Davis and Mary Lucille (Cole) Kellogg; m. Sept. 1, 1961; divorced; 1 child, Kristopher. Student, U. Ariz., 1958-61; BA, U. So. Colo., 1967; MA, U. No. Colo., 1977. Cert. secondary tchr., Colo. Tchr. history and geography Denver Pub. Schs., 1967—; area adminstr., tchr. coordinator Close Up program, Washington, 1982-84. Vol., chmn. young profls. Inst. Internat. Edn. and World Affairs Council, Denver, 1980—; mem. state selection com. U.S. Senate and Japan Scholarship Com., Denver, 1981—, Youth for Understanding, Denver; mem. Denver Art Mus., 1970—; vol. Denver Mus. Natural History, 1989—; bd. overseers Dept. Def. Dependents Sch., Guantanomo Bay, Cuba, 1990—. Fulbright scholar Chadron St. Coll., Pakistan, 1975; Geographic Soc. grantee U. Colo., 1986. Mem. Colo. Council Social Studies (sec. 1984-86), Nat. Council Social Studies (del. 1984), World History Assn., Nat. Geog. Soc., Rocky Mountain Regional World History Assn. (steering com. 1984-87), Colo. Geographic Alliance (steering com. 1986), Gamma Phi Beta. Democrat. Episcopalian. Home: care Dr Howard Kelogg 10140 Wolff Ct Westminster CO 80030 Office: Montbello High Sch 5000 Crown Blvd Denver CO 80239

FAIRBANKS, DEBORAH KAY MCGUIRE, instructional designer, training consultant; b. Cheatareux, France, 1954; (parents Am. citizens); d. Ed and Pat McGuire; married, 1981; children: Jessica, Justin. BA, U. Calif., San Diego, 1976; MA, Ariz. State U., 1981. Precis writer Sociol. Abstracts, San Diego, 1977; libr. Courseware, Inc., San Diego, 1977-78, instrnl. designer, 1978-82, instrnl. dir., 1982-86; instr. Ariz. State U., Tempe, 1979-81; cons. instrnl. designer Fairbanks Tng. Designs, San Diego, 1986—; trainer Self-Talk Inst., Scottsdale, Ariz., 1989—; cons. Univ. Assocs., San Diego, 1989—; instr. Palomar Coll., San Diego, 1990. Co-author: (cassette and book) Take 25: Fit Kit, 1988; mag. columnist Thoughts for Positive Living, 1990. Troop leader Girl Scouts U.S.A., San Diego, 1988-90. Mem. ASTD, AAUW (publicity chmn. 1987), Toastmasters (pres. San Diego 1989, Golden Gavel award 1989). Office: Fairbanks Tng Designs 13223 Black Mountain Rd 1-272 San Diego CA 92129

FAIRBANKS, KAREN ANN, architect; b. Mesa, Ariz., Nov. 8, 1959; d. Bruce Ronald and Margaret Mary (Osier) F. BArch, U. Mich., 1981; MArch, Columbia U., N.Y.C., 1987. Lic. architect. Designer Graham Gund Assoc., Cambridge, Mass., 1981-84; project designer Davis, Brody & Assoc., N.Y.C., 1985, Aedificare, N.Y.C., 1986; project architect Cooper, Robertson & Ptnrs., N.Y.C., 1987-89; pvt. practice arch. N.Y.C., 1989—. Dir., set designer Body Sanction: A Doric Frenzy, 1987; set designer Monkeys (dance performance) 1987, various theatre productions at Columbia U., 1986. William Kinne Fellows fellow, 1987; fellow in architecture N.Y. Found. for Arts, 1988. Mem. AIA (medal 1987), Bldg. Arts Forum, N.Y.C. Soc. Architects (Fred L. Liebman Book award 1986). Home: 212 E 29th St Apt 5 New York NY 10016

FAIRBANKS, MARY JOANNE, educational administrator; b. Massena, N.Y., Dec. 21, 1939; d. James William and Inez (Cappiello) Phillips; Assoc. in Bus. Adminstrn., Central City Bus. Inst., Syracuse, N.Y. 1959; A.S. in Accounting LaSalle Extension U., 1974; student in mgmt., Syracuse U., 1974—. Sec. elec. and computer engring. dept. Syracuse U., 1959-65, asst. to adminstrv. asst., 1965-72, publs. mgr. Assembly on U. Governance, 1970-72, coordinator computer confs., 1972-81, adminstr. short course Air Force intrasystem analysis program, 1974-78, supervisory asst. to chmn. dept. elec. and computer engring. and mgr. Air Force Post-Doctoral Program, Rome Air Devel. Center, 1972-78, adminstrv. asst. to chmn. dept. indsl. engring. and ops. research 1978-82, dir. Engring. Coop. Edn. program, 1982—; mgr. electromagnetic compatibility analysis techniques advancement program, 1978-82; coordinator workshops on computer architecture, 1977-79; ofcl. stenographer 1985 Project, USMC, 1963; mem. computer scoring team XIII Olympic Winter Games, Lake Placid, N.Y., 1980; Alpine ofcl. U.S. Ski Assn., 1980—; mem. Syracuse U. Career Planning and Placement Coun., 1988—. Pres. LWV Met. Syracuse, 1981-83, voters service dir. N.Y. State, 1983-87, publs. editor LWV of N.Y. State, 1987-89, 2d v.p. N.Y. State, 1986. Mgr., editor publs. Onondaga County Bicentennial Quilt, 1976; editor 7 elec. engring. textbooks, 1960-78; editor-in-chief A Guide to New York State Government, 1989; author: The Road to the Voting Booth, 2 vols., 1986; co-author: Career Portfolio for Volunteers, 1980, Patterns of Government in Onondaga County, 1981; contbr. articles to profl. jours. Mem. Am. Soc. Engring. Edn. (chair membership coop. edn. div. 1988-91, ann. meeting program chair cooperative edn. div.), Coop. Edn. Assn., Ohio Coop. Edn. Assn., N.Y. State Coop. and Experiential Edn. Assn., Middle Atlantic Placement Assn., Nat. Commn. for Coop. Edn. Home: 140 Edgehill Rd Syracuse NY 13224 Office: Syracuse U 367 Link Hall Syracuse NY 13244

FAIRCHILD, BEATRICE MAGDOFF, physicist; b. N.Y.C., Nov. 25, 1916; d. Samuel and Sadie (Thaler) Schwartz; m. Samuel Magdoff, 1938 (div. 1959); m. Johnson Eddy Fairchild, July, 1961. BA, Hunter Coll., 1942; MA, Bryn Mawr (Pa.) Coll., 1943, PhD, 1948. Asst. prof. physics Adelphi Coll., Garden City, N.Y., 1948-50; rsch. assoc. Bklyn. Poly. Inst., 1950-54; fellow med. rsch. coun. Cambridge (Eng.) U., 1954-55; physicist Boyce Thompson Inst., Yonkers, N.Y., 1955-61; asst. prof. Rockefeller U., N.Y.C., 1961-68; rsch. scientist coll. physicians and surgeons Columbia U., N.Y.C., 1968-85, sr. rsch. scientist, 1985—. Contbr. articles to profl. jours. NIH grantee, 1972—. Mem. Am. Crystallographic Assn., Biophys. Soc., Am. Soc. Biochemistry and Molecular Biology. Office: Columbia U Saint Lukes Hosp 114th St and Amsterdam Ave New York NY 10025

FAIREY, REBECCA LYNN OLSON, medical records professional; b. Mpls., Mar. 12, 1958; d. Richard Floyd Olson and Sharon Joann (Freed) Olson Fulk; m. Joseph Koger Fairey III, July 14, 1979; children: Katherine Rebecca, Joseph Koger IV. BS, Med. U. S.C., 1979. Dir. med. records dept. Midlands Region S.C. Dept. Mental Retardation, Columbia, 1979-81; quality assurance coord. Lexington County Hosp., West Columbia, S.C., 1981-82; project cons. Orkand Corp., Winter Springs, Md., 1982; assoc. dir. med. records dept. Orangeburg (S.C.)-Calhoun Regional Hosp., 1982-87; dir. med. records dept. Regional Med. Ctr. of Orangeburg and Calhoun Counties, Orangeburg, 1987—; med. records cons. Orangeburg Nursing Home, 1981—, Briggs Nursing Home, Silver, S.C., 1987—. Mem. S.C. Med. Record Assn. (sec. 1989-90), Am. Med. Record Assn., Orangeburg Jr. Svc. League. Methodist. Home: Hwy 601 Saint Matthews SC 29135 Office: IRMC Orangeburg 3000 Saint Matthews Rd Orangeburg SC 29135

FAIRFIELD, BETTY ELAINE SMITH, psychologist; b. Cin., Mar. 7, 1927; d. Harris E. and Bertha A. (Kilpatrick) Smith; m. John Francis Fairfield, Aug. 7, 1948; children: Gail, Gwen, Linda, Janet. BA, Oberlin Coll., 1948; MA, Fairleigh Dickensin U., 1977; Psychology D., Rutgers U., 1982. Lic. psychologist, N.J., Wash. Missionary United Ch. Bd. for World Ministries, United Ch. Christ, N.Y.C., 1948-68; Christian edn. coord. Haworth (N.J.) United Ch. of Christ, 1968-72; prin. probation officer I vol. sponsor program Bergen County Probation Dept., Hackensack, N.J., 1972-75; dir. parent workshop program Bergen County Dept. Human Svcs., Hackensack, 1976-87, clin. dir. parent workshop program, 1987-88; pvt. practice psychologist Cresskill, N.J., 1984-88, Seattle, 1988—; trustee Interpersonal Skills Inst., Englewood, N.J., 1981—. Co-author: Fairfield-Formica Parenting Program Workbook, 1983, 5th edit. revised, 1988, Leaders' Manual for Fairfield-Formica Parenting Program, 1988, (book and manual) Fairfield-Formica Sustance Abuse Prevention Workshop for Parents, 1986. Regional tng. chairperson USA Girl Scouts Far East, Tachikawa, Japan, 1965-67; ch. sch. supt. Tokyo Union Ch., 1960-64. Recipient Cert. of Commendation, Bergen County Bd. of Chosen Freeholders, Hackensack, 1977. Fellow Am. Orthopsychiat. Assn.; mem. Am. Psychol. Assn., Ill. Psychol. Assn. Mem. United Ch. of Christ. Home: 30W311 Country Lakes Dr Naperville IL 60563-9047

FAIROBENT, LYNNE ANNE, organization executive, health physicist; b. Chelsea, Mass., July 18, 1956; d. Thomas Phillip and Jeannette (Dominick) O'Reilly; m. James E. Fairobent, Apr. 10, 1982; children: Megan Elizabeth, Ryan Edward. BS in Environ. Health, Purdue U., 1978. Health physicist U.S. Nuclear Regulatory Commn., Washington, 1978-83, Sci. Applications Internat. Corp., McLean, Va., 1983-87; sr. project mgr. Nuclear Mgmt. and Resources Coun., Washington, 1987—; mem. Fed. Women's Adv. Com. NRC, 1980-81; v.p., steward Nat. Treasury Emoloyees Union, Washington, 1979-81; parliamentarian Fed. Women's Adv. Com., 1980. Recipient spl. achievement cert. U.S. Nuclear Regulatory Commn., 1981, 82. Mem. Health Physics Soc. (plenary, chmn. nat. affirmative action com. Balt.-Washington chpt. 1985-87). Democrat. Roman Catholic. Office: Nuclear Mgmt-Resources Coun 1776 I St NW Ste 300 Washington DC 20006

FAJARDO, KATHARINE LYNN, public relations executive, actress; b. Akron, Ohio, Mar. 19, 1951; d. Edwin Murray and Diane (Zabiegalski) H. BA, Johns Hopkins U., 1973; MBA, U. Calif., 1987. Dir. pub. affairs coun. Electronic Industries Assn., Washington, 1974-75; pension cons. Proskauer, Rose, Goetz & Mendelsohn, N.Y.C., 1976-77; sr. mktg. cons. The Equitable Life Assurance Soc., N.Y.C., 1977-78; dir. advt., assoc. dir. public affairs St. Joe Minerals Corp., N.Y.C., 1979-82, mgr. communications projects, 1982-83; computer cons., 1984-86; v.p. Burson-Marsteller, 1988—; actress, 1983—; leading roles include Goodbye Charlie, Picnic, Witness for the Prosecution, Barnum. Recipient Nicholson award, 1980, 81, Big Apple award, 1989; named Best Supporting Actress, Orange County, Calif., 1983. Mem. NAFE, Internat. Assn. Bus. Communicators, Am. Mgmt. Assn., Pub. Rels. Soc. Am., Internat. Platform Assn. Home: 16 Forest Hill Rd West Norwalk CT 06850

FAKES, MARY E. A., nurse; b. Sioux Falls, S.D., Sept. 4, 1962; d. Leslie L. and Kathryn A. (Nason) Lemme; m. James E. Fakes, Apr. 21, 1990. BSN, Deaconess Coll., 1987; RN, Deaconsell Coll., 1983. RN, Mo.; cert. emergency nurse. Charge nurse emergency rm. St. Louis Univ. Hosp., Alexian Bros. Hosp., St. Louis; funeral dir. Lemme Funeral Home, Festus, Mo.; occupational health nurse HealthLine, St. Louis. Named Citizen of the Month, City of St. Louis, 1988; cert. of recognition Mo. Nurse's Assn. 3d Dist., 1988, Gold medal Hosp. Assn. Met., 1988. Mem. Emergency Nurses Assn. Home: 192 Walden Ave Eureka MO 63025

FALCI, NINA LANSKY, employee benefits specialist; b. N.Y.C., Dec. 10, 1958; m. Craig M. Falci, Sept. 26, 1987. BS summa cum laude, U. Md., 1980. Cert. employee benefits specialist. Receptionist Engring. Research Assocs., Vienna, Va., 1981; personnel asst. Engring. Rsch. Assocs., 1981-82; benefits administrator Engring. Research Assocs., 1982-84, benefits specialist, 1984-86; supr. benefits and compensation Engring. Research Assocs., an E-Systems Co., 1986—. Mem. Fairfax (Va.) Choral Soc., 1984—, v.p., 1989; scholarship chmn. U. Md. Young Alumni, College Park, Md., 1983-87. Mem. Network Profls. Working in Employee Benefits, Washington Tech. Personnel Forum, Internat. Soc. Cert. Employee Benefit Specialists, Phi Kappa Phi. Office: Engring Rsch Assocs 1595 Springhill Rd Vienna VA 22182-2235

FALCO, JOANN, fundraising consultant, English educator; b. N.Y.C., Aug. 9, 1953; d. Joseph J. and Mary J. Falco. BA summa cum laude in English, Barry Coll., 1974, MA, 1976; EdD., U. Miami, 1987. Asst. dir. Fla. Pub. Interest Research Group, U. Miami, Fla., 1976-79, adminstrv. aide to asst. v.p. devel., 1980-81; ind. devel. cons., Washington and Miami, 1981—; prof. English Dade Community Coll., 1985—, pres. faculty senate, 1989—.

FALCONE, DONNA MARIE, health facility supervisor; b. Blue Island, Ill., Sept. 13, 1961; d. James Joseph and Margaret Bridget (Meegan) Reilly; m. Mark Allan. BS in Med. Tech., Marquette U., 1983; MS in Mgmt., Ill. Benedictine Coll., 1990. Med. technologist Elmhurst (Ill.) Mem. Hosp., 1983—; med. technologist quality control, cons. Bion Corp., Elmhurst, 1985-87; cons. Elmhurst Mem. Hosp., Ill. 1986—. Mem. Am. Soc. Clin. Pathologists. Republican. Roman Catholic. Home: 754 Stockley Rd Downers Grove IL 60516 Office: Elmhurst Meml Hosp 200 Berteau Elmhurst IL 60126

FALCONE, LUCILLE, lawyer; b. N.Y.C., Nov. 12, 1952; d. Joseph and Nancy (Cirillo) F.; m. Douglas Menagh, Dec. 12, 1987; 1 child, Douglas Michael. BA, Bklyn. Coll., 1972; JD, Fordham U., 1975. Bar: U.S. Ct. Appeals (2d cir.) 1976, U.S. Dist. Ct. (ea. and so. dist.) N.Y. 1978, U.S. Supreme Ct. 1984. Assoc. Corner, Finn, Dwyer & Charles, Bklyn., 1976-78; pvt. practice Bklyn., 1978-81, Manus & Weiss, N.Y.C., 1981-82; ptnr. Blutrich Falcone & Miller, N.Y.C., 1982—; bd. dirs. Savs. Bank of Rockland, N.Y. Contbr. articles to profl. jours. Counsel Friends of Mario M. Cuomo Com. Inc., N.Y., 1983-88, chairperson, 1989—. Mem. ABA, N.Y. State Bar Assn., Savs. Bank Assn. of N.Y. (assoc.). Office: Blutrich Falcone & Miller 2 Park Ave New York NY 10016

FALCONE, NOLA MADDOX, financial company executive; b. Augusta, Ga., July 8, 1939; d. Louia Vernon and Geneva Elizabeth (Fox) Maddox; m. Charles Anthony Falcone, Dec. 6, 1968; 1 child, Charles Maddox. B.A., Duke U., 1961; M.B.A., U. Pa., 1966. Security analyst, portfolio mgr. pension and personal trust dept. Chase Manhattan Bank, N.Y.C., 1961-63, 66-70; investment officer personal trust dept. Chase Manhattan Bank, 1968-70; portfolio mgr. Lieber & Co., 1974-75; br. mgr., registered rep. Lieber & Co., Arlington, Va., 1978-79; portfolio mgr. Lieber & Co., Purchase, N.Y., 1979-80; ptnr. Lieber & Co., 1981—; pres. Evergreen Total Return Fund, Inc., Lieber & Co., 1985—; bd. dirs. Evergreen Asset Mgmt. Corp., Purchase. Mem. fin. com. Jr. League, Scarsdale, N.Y., 1972-75; bd. dirs. Ea. Coll. and Ea. Sem., Pa.; trustee 1st Bapt. Ch. of White Plains, N.Y., 1973-74. Mem. Fin. Analysts Soc., CFA. Democrat.

FALCONE, PATRICIA JEANNE, administrative assistant; b. Montevideo, Minn., Oct. 12; d. Clarence I. and Eva (Corneliusen) Lalim; m. Alfonso Benjamin Falcone, Oct. 22; children: Christopher L., Steven B. BS, U. Minn., 1956; MS, U. Wis., 1958, PhD, 1962. Libr. asst. U. Minn., St. Paul, 1953-54; singer/performer Mpls., 1949-55; asst. prog. dir. U. Wis. Meml. Union, Madison, 1957-58; instr. U. Wis., Madison, 1965-66; adminstrv. asst. A.B. Falcone, M.D., Ph.D., Fresno, Calif., 1968—; pvt. investor Patricia Lalim Falcone, Ph.D., Fresno, 1968—; lectr. in field; contbr./presenter various conf., seminars. Contbr. articles to profl. jours.; author various ednl. and profl. pamphlets; artist/craftsman textile designs for U. Wis. Traveling exhibit, 1965-66. Bd. dirs. Fresno/Madera Polit. Action Com., 1985-89, 1990—; mem. Supts. Roundtable, Fresno Unified Sch. Dist., 1989; chmn. U. Calif., Fresno com. to bring UC campus to Fresno area, 1987—; chmn. Parent Adv. Com. for Gifted and Talented, 1985, mem. 1984—. U. Wis. fellow, 1958-59, scholar, 1959-62. Mem. AAUW, Med. Aux. of Fresno County Med. Soc. (exec. bd. 1989—), Assn. for Acad. Excellence (chmn. 1988—), Edison Computech Assn., Am. Scandinavian Found., Norwegian Am. Hist. Assn., Fresno Art Mus., Omicron Nu, Pi Lambda Theta, Phi Delta Gamma. Home: 1228 W Escalon Ave Fresno CA 93711 Office: 2240 E Illinois Ave Fresno CA 93701

FALENDER-ZOHN, CAROL ANN, psychologist; b. Indpls., Aug. 22, 1946; d. Allison Efroymson Falender and Dorothy Rose (Meiss) Resneck; m. Martin S. Zohn, June 8, 1980; children: David, Daniel. BA, Vassar Coll., 1968; MA, U. Wis., 1969, PhD, 1973. Lic. psychologist, Calif. Postdoctoral fellowship dept. psychology U. So. Calif. Ctr., L.A., 1978; asst. prof. Grad. Sch. Edn. UCLA, 1973-77; dir. early childhood programs GLACA-Head Start, L.A., 1977-78; head early childhood programs, asst. dir. tng. San Fernando Valley Child Guidance Clinic, Northridge, Calif., 1978—; adv. bd. CHAMP, UCLA, 1988—; chmn. profl. adv. com., Leo Baeck, L.A., 1985—. Contbr. articles to profl. jours. Mem. Am. Psychol. Assn., Soc. for Rsch. in Child Devel., Nat. Assn. for Edn. of Young Children. Office: San Fernando Child Guid Cl 9650 Zelzah Ave Northridge CA 91325

FALK, ALMA MARTHA, retired educator; b. Chgo., Apr. 18, 1910; d. Henry and Alma (Wolowski) Weihofen; m. James E. Curry, Apr. 28, 1934 (dec. Aug. 1972, 1 child, Aileen Curry-Cloonan (dec.); m. Byron A. Falk, Nov. 22, 1966 (dec. Mar. 1984). Cert. Chgo. Tchrs. Coll., 1932; BA, George Washington U., 1937, MA, 1957; postgrad., Howard U. Tchr. Hull House, Chgo., 1930-32; social worker Ill. Relief Commn., 1932-35; tchr. elem. sch., Chgo., 1937-38, 46-47; office mgr. law firms in P.R. and Washington, 1948-53; elem. tchr. Jr. Village Sch., Washington, 1953-57; reading coordinator Washington Pub. Schs., 1957-72; instr. George Washington Reading Clinic, 1957-66; pres. Greater Washington Reading Coun., 1966-67. Vol. asst. CD Milk Sta. Program, San Juan, P.R., 1942-46; instr. Urban Svc. Corps. of Vols., 1952-56; bd. dirs. Internat. Student House, Washington, 1980-88; mem. retiree coun. Mil. Dist. of Washington, 1988—, Nat. Capitol Area Retiree Coun., 1987—. Recipient citation White House Conf. on Children, 1960. Mem. AAUW (chmn. edn. com. Washington br. 1959-61, dir. 1976-80), Nat. Mil. Wives, Internat. Reading Assn., Am. Fedn. Tchrs., Women's Internat. League for Peace and Freedom, Washington Tchrs. Union (rep. reading specialists 1968-70), Am. Humanist Assn., UN Assn., Internat. Platform Assn., Phi Delta Gamma. George Washington U. Club (charter), Officers Club, Army and Navy Club (Washington), Officers' Club (Ft. Myer, Va.). Avocations: published and recorded lyricist and song writer. Home: 922 24th St NW Washington DC 20037

FALK, DONNA JOY, marketing professional; b. Bklyn., Sept. 10, 1963; d. Harold Lewis and Beverly Naomi (Lynn) Savlov; m. Jonathan Phillip Falk, Apr. 29, 1989. BS in Microbiology, Rutgers U., 1985, postgrad., 1989—. Microbiologist Interam. Juice Co., Newark, 1985-86, Akzo Chems., New Brunswick, N.J., 1986-88; sci. writer Rheometrics, Piscataway, N.J., 1988-89, tech. mktg. specialist, 1989—; freelance desktop pub., Somerset, N.J., 1989-90. Vol. Bill Grippo for Freeholder, Franklin Twp., N.J., 1989, Beacon Hill Condominium Assn., Franklin Park, N.J., 1990—. Mem. Soc. Plastics Engrs., Soc. Indsl. Microbiologists, Am. Wood Preservers Assn., Tri-Beta Biol. Honor Soc., Alpha Zeta. Democrat. Office: Rheometrics 1 Possumtown Rd Piscataway NJ 08854

FALK, ELIZABETH MOXLEY, opera and theatre producer; b. Memphis, Sept. 21, 1942; d. Warren Luke and Elizabeth Ann (Beshears) Moxley; m. Lee H. Falk, Dec. 31, 1976. Dir. mktg. Chesebrough-Pond's Internat., N.Y.C. and Beirut, 1961-65; account exec. Lintas Advt., Durban, Republic South Africa, 1965-67; mgr. mktg. Revlon Inc., N.Y.C., 1969-70; account supr. BBDO Advt. Inc., N.Y.C., 1971; dir. new product devel. Alexandra de Markoff, N.Y.C., 1972-74, Almay Cosmetics, N.Y.C., 1974-76; producer, stage mgr. Vineyard Opera Theatre, N.Y.C., 1986-89; co-mgr. New Artists Coalition, N.Y.C., 1986-88; ind. producer Elizabeth Moxley Falk Presents, N.Y.C., 1987—; founder, producer, artistic dir. PALA Opera Assn., N.Y.C., 1989—; producer Project: Music Rediscovery, 1987—; chmn. project Am. Landmark Festivals at Carnegie Hall, N.Y.C., 1988; v.p. Provincetown Acad. Living Arts, Truro, Mass. Author: The Evil Within, 1980, Mirror Images, 1981; playwright: Goldsmith's Last Rites, 1983, White Tie and Veils, 1984; producer Rossini's Il Viaggio a Reims, 1987, 88, La Gazza Ladra, 1990. Advisor Cranston for Senate, Calif., 1980, 86, Badillo for Congress, N.Y.C., 1972, 74; mem. producer's program Comml. Theatre Inst., 1990. Fellow Acad. Rossiniana; mem. NAFE, Women's Project Am. Place Theatre, Mystery Writers Am., Found. Extension-Devel. Am. Profl. Theatre, Alliance Resident Theatres, Cen. Opera Services, Am. Guild Mus. Artists (coun. for small non-union opera cos. 1988—, relief fund nat. adv. bd. 1989—), Players Club (admissions com. 1989—, entertainment com. 1990—), Nat. Opera Assn. (regional cos. com. 1990—), Conf. de la Chaine des Rotisseurs (Dame de la Chaine 1977—), Mensa. Democrat. Home and Office: 7 W 81st St #12C New York NY 10024

FALKE, BETTY LOUISE NEWMAN, accountant; b. Llano, Tex., Dec. 1, 1946; d. Travis Alger and Edith Lucile (Tate) Newman; m. Vernon George Mangold (div. July 1981); 1 child, Ian Keith; m. Joseph Renford Falke, Jan. 24, 1987; 1 child, Samantha May. Student, San Antonio Jr. Coll., 1965-66; BBA, U. Tex., San Antonio, 1985. Data claims analyst Blue Cross/Blue Shield, San Antonio, 1980-82; regional sec., acct. BioMed. Applications, San Antonio, 1982-83; with acctg. dept. Comprehensive Bus. Services, Boerne, Tex., 1983-84; acct. Cadwallader Ins. Agy., San Antonio, 1986, Data Processing Support, Inc., San Antonio, 1986-87, Archive Retrieval Systems, Inc., San Antonio, 1986-87; pvt. practice acctg. San Antonio, 1987—. Vol. Boy Scouts Am., San Antonio, 1978—, unit commr., 1989; bd. dirs. San Antonio Met. Ministries, 1987—. Scholar Women in Bus., 1983. Mem. Nat. Assn. Accts. (assoc. bd. dirs. 1988-90), Leon Springs Bus. Assn., Am. Luth. Women. Home and Office: 25403 Brewer Dr San Antonio TX 78257

FALKENBERG, MARY ANN THERESA, realtor; b. Chgo., Dec. 8, 1931; d. Joseph and Catherine (Bausch) Haselsteiner; student Barat Coll., 1953; m. Charles V. Falkenberg, Jr., Apr. 9, 1955; children—Catherine, Grace Ann, Susan Marie, Charles V., Robert, Thomas, Martin, Mary, Elizabeth, Joseph. Tchr. piano, 1946-73; organist St. Thomas of Villanova Ch., 1960—, choir dir., 1960—; sales staff Quinlan & Tyson, Realtors, Inc., Palatine, Ill., 1970-77; pres., co-owner, broker, mgr. Assos. Realty Corp., Palatine, 1978—. Named Palatine Woman of Yr., Suburban Press Found., 1962; cert. home protection cons. Mem. Women in Mgmt., Am. Mgmt. Assn., Ill. Assn. Realtors (life mem. two million dollar club, mem. three million dollar club, four million dollar club, Gold award 1988), Nat. Assn. Realtors (accredited profl. residential appraiser, cert. real property appraiser), Nat. Assn. Female Execs., N.W. Suburban Bd. Realtors (edn. com. 1977-78, non-resident com. 1982, broker-lawyer com. 1986-90, grievance com. 1988), MAP (bd. dirs. 1986-90, sec. 1988-90), Women in Sales, Barat Coll. Alumni Assn. Club: Women's. Republican. Roman Catholic. Home: 517 Warwick St Palatine IL 60067 Office: 240 E Northwest Hwy Palatine IL 60067

FALKOWSKI, PATRICIA ANN, financial analyst; b. New Brunswick, N.J., Apr. 12, 1947; d. George Francis and Letha Mae (Norman) Crawford; m. Walter Stanley Falkowski, Apr. 30, 1945; children: Karen Elizabeth, Andrew Walter. BS summa cum laude, Rider Coll., 1969; MBA in Fin., U. Chgo., 1980. Adminstrv. asst. Fed. Home Loan Bank Bd., Washington, 1970-72; analyst corp. fin. SEC, Washington, 1972-73; analyst, sr. analyst Econ. Devel. Adminstrn., Phila., 1974-76; regional analyst FDIC, Chgo., 1977-79; investment analyst Kemper Fin. Cos., Chgo., 1979-81, Harris Trust & Savs., Chgo., 1981-83, Kemper Fin. Corp., Chgo., 1983-88; pvt. practice Winnetka, Ill., 1988—. Com. chair St. Franics Hosp. Aux., Evanston, Ill., 1989. Mem. Fin. Stock Assn. Chgo. (pres. 1988-89), Chgo. Investment Analysts Soc. (com. mem. 1979-89), U. Chgo. Women's Bus. Group (com. co-chmn.). Republican. Roman Catholic. Home: 505 Sunset Rd Winnetka IL 60093

FALLENSTEIN, JUDITH FAYE, speech pathologist; b. Mankato, Minn., July 22, 1940; d. Erwin William and Frances (Miner) Bluhm; m. Thomas Gregory Fallenstein, Oct. 20, 1965; children: Nicole, Callandra. BS, Mankato State U., 1964; MSEd, U. Wis., Eau Claire, 1971. Cert. speech clinician, Minn. Speech clinician Wells (Minn.) Pub. Schs., 1964-65, Mankato (Minn.) Rehab. Ctr., 1965-66, Mankato Pub. Schs., 1966-69; instr. U. Minn., Mpls., 1971-72, rsch. fellow, 1972-73; instr. Coll. of St. Teresa, Winona, Minn., 1974-77; speech clinician Winona Pub. Schs., 1980—. Mem. NEA, Am. Speech-Hearing Assn., Winona Women's Resource Ctr., Minn. Speech-Hearing Assn., Minn. Edn. Assn., Winona Edn. Assn. (treas. 1988—), Washington-Kosciusko PTA. Democrat. Episcopalian. Home: 509 W Broadway Winona MN 55987 Office: Washington-Kosciusko Sch 365 Mankato Ave Winona MN 55987

FALLIN, BARBARA MOORE, personnel director; b. Paducah, Ky., Nov. 12, 1939; d. James Perry Moore and Margaret Arminta (Winn) Kastner; m. Jon Ball, Jan. 21, 1961 (div. July 1963); m. Ralph Daniel Fallin, May 23, 1965; children: Wade, Cathi, Cindy Pergrim, Danielle. Student, Fla. Christian Coll., 1957-58. Exec. asst. to contr. The Borden Co., Tampa, Fla., 1958-65; mktg. asst. Martin-Marietta Corp., Shalimar, Fla., 1965-71; asst. to pres. Browning-Marine, Ft. Walton Beach, Fla., 1973; pers. coord. Keltec Fla., Shalimar, 1974-78; pers. mgr. Metric Systems Corp., Ft. Walton Beach, 1979-87, pers. dir., 1987—. Mem. Job Service Employer Com., Ft. Walton Beach, 1985—; mem. adv. bd. Bay Area Vocat.-Tech. Ctr., Ft. Walton Beach, 1988—. First mistress Krewe of Bowlegs, Ft. Walton Beach, 1983-84, first lady to cap'n Billy Bowlegs XXXII, 1986-87. Mem. NAFE, Soc. Human Resource Mgmt., Emerald Coast Pers. Mgmt. Assn. (pres. 1986-88, bd. dirs. 1988—), The Nat. Mgmt. Assn., Mardi Gras Club. Republican. Methodist. Office: Metric Systems Corp 645 Anchors St Fort Walton Beach FL 32548

FALLON, KRISTINE K., architect, computer applications consultant; b. Bklyn., Jan. 28, 1949; d. William Peter and Kathleen L. (O'Connell) F. BS, Georgetown U., 1970; MArch, Va. Poly. Inst. and State U., 1977. Architect Skidmore, Owings & Merrill, Chgo., 1977-80, computer prodn. mgr., 1981-82, assoc., 1982-84, mgr. Chgo. Computer Group, 1983-84; dir. computer graphics A. Epstein and Sons Internat., Inc., Chgo., 1984, v.p., 1985-86; pres. Computer Tech. Mgmt., Inc. subs. A. Epstein and Sons Internat., Inc., Chgo., 1986—; coord. design confs. Designing for Electronic Offices, 1984, 85; lectr. in field; mem. adv. bd. Computers in Civil and Cons. Engring., 1990—. Exhibitor Chicago Women in Architecture Progress and Evolution 1974-84 Chgo. Hist. Soc., 1984; mem. editorial bd. A/E Systems Report, 1987, Design Systems Strategies, 1988—; mem. editorial contbrs. bd. Archtl. Record, 1990—. Advisor Archtl. Tech. Adv. Com. Triton Coll, River Grove, Ill., 1985—; industry sponsor Chgo. Consortium Colls. and Univs. Vocat. Instr. Practicum, 1986. Mem. AIA (Chgo. chpt. bd. dirs. 1985-89, v.p. 1985-87, del. Ill. council 1987-89), Chgo. Women in Architecture (pres. 1980-82, v.p. 1982-84), The Chgo. Network, The Cliff Dwellers. Office: Computer Tech Mgmt Inc 600 W Fulton St Chicago IL 60606

FALLON, PATRICIA ANNE, nurse; b. Boston, Nov. 26, 1951; d. Frederick Augustine and Edith Thersa (Walsh) Fallon. BS in Nursing, Northeastern U., Boston, 1974. Nurse childrens Hosp. Med. Ctr., Boston, 1972-78; nurse adult critical unit Panorama Meml. Hosp., Panorama City, Calif., 1978; Pediatric ICU nurse Valley Presbyn. Hosp., Van Nuys, Calif., 1978-89, Assoc. Health Profl., Inc., Culver City, Calif., 1985-89, Mass. Gen. Hosp., Boston, 1990—. Mem. Am. Assn. Critical Care Nurses. Home: 282 West St Reading MA 01867

FALLON, PATRICIA GAYLE, teacher's union executive; b. Phila., Feb. 1, 1945; d. William James and Sandra (Fisch) Hamilton; m. James Tobias Fallon, Jr., July 17, 1964; 1 child, James Tobias III. BA in Polit. Sci., Am. U., 1966; MEd in Ednl. Adminstrn., Sam Houston State U., 1980. Linguist, translator Nat. Security Agy., Ft. Meade, Md., 1966-68; tchr. Aldine Ind. Sch. Dist., Houston, 1969-78, North Forest Ind. Sch. Dist., Houston, 1978-80; staff rep. Houston Fedn. Tchrs., 1980-82, pres., 1982—; mem. exec. bd. Harris County AFL-CIO, Houston, 1982—. Mmem. exec. bd. KS AIDS Found., Houston, 1986-89; mem. Leadership Houston, 1986—. Fellow Am. Leadership Forum; mem. Tex. Fedn. Tchrs. (exec. bd. 1982—), Houston C. of C. Home: 2018 Cypresstree Springs TX 77373 Office: Houston Fedn Tchrs 1445 North Loop West 240 Houston TX 77008

FALLS, KATHLEENE JOYCE, photographer; b. Detroit, July 3, 1949; d. Edgar John and Acelia Olive (Young) Haley; m. Donald David Falls, June 15, 1974; children: Daniel John, David James. Student, Oakland Community Coll., 1969-73, Winona Sch. Profl. Photography, 1973-80; degree in photography, 1988, 90. Printer Guardian Photo, Novi, Mich., 1967-69; printer, supr. quality control N.Am. Photo, Livonia, Mich., 1969-76; free lance photographer Livonia, 1969-76; owner, pres. Kathy Falls, Inc., Carleton, Mich., 1976—; instr. Monroe County Community Coll. Continuing Edn., 1981-83; nat. artisan judge Congl. High Sch. Art Competition, 1985—; owner Picture Perfect, Carleton, 1987; co-owner Haleys Gift Shoppe, Dundee, Mich., 1989. Author: (booklet) Emergency Photo-Retouching for Photographers, 1988; contbr. articles to profl. jours. Represented in spl. categories in the Nat. Loan Collection, Profl. Photographers Am., 1980, 81, 83, 87; represented in permanent Collections Monroe County Hist. Mus., Archives Notre Dame. Catechist St. Patrick's Ch., Carleton, 1984-87; active Big Bros. and Big Sisters, Monroe, 1986-87; corr. sec. Monroe Women's Ctr, 1986-88. Recipient numerous awards granted by profl. photographic orgns. Mem. NAFE, Detroit Profl. Photographers Assn. (bd. dirs. 1987—, artisan chmn. 1981-82, Best of Show award 1981, 83), Profl. Photographers Mich. (artisian chairperson 1982-83, Best of Show award 1976, 81, Artist of Yr. 1980), Profl. Photographers Am. (cert. profl. photog. specialist, photographic specialist degree 1988), Am. Photographic Artisans Guild (council mem., bd. dirs. 1987—, Photographic Artisan degree 1989), Monroe County Fine Arts Council, Monroe C. of C. (chmn. council women bus. owners), Nat. Orgn. Women Bus. Owners, Profl. Photographers Am. (Photographic Craftsman degree 1990), Toastmasters, Internat. Club. Democrat. Roman Catholic. Club: Monroe Camera. Home and Office: 14554 Grafton Carleton MI 48117

FALLS, WALDTRAUT MARGRETE GOETZE, medical librarian; b. N.Y.C., June 28, 1941; d. Otto Paul and Anna Irma (Zander) Goetze; A.B., State U. N.Y. at Albany, 1963, M.A. (scholar), 1964; M.S., Columbia U., 1967; m. John Allen Falls, Jr.; children—John Francis, Michael Gregory. Asst. advt. librarian Curtis Pub. Co., N.Y.C., 1964-65; library asso. N.Y. U. Commerce Library, N.Y.C., 1965-67; librarian, instr. N.Y.C. Community Coll., Bklyn., 1967-69, 70, 73-75; med. librarian Victory Meml. Hosp., Bklyn., 1975-87, clin. librarian, U. Medicine and Dentistry N.J., Newark, 1987-88; info. mgr. otolaryngology Facial Plastic Surgery Assocs., 1988—. Mem. ALA, Med. Library Assn., Bklyn., Queens and S.I. Health Scis. Librarians, N.Y. Library Club (life). Home: 328 78th St Brooklyn NY 11209 Office: Facial Plastic Surgery Assocs 466 Bay Ridge Pkwy Brooklyn NY 11209

FALOR, MARCIA HASEK, professional volunteer; b. Cleve., Apr. 8, 1950; d. Edward Frank and Elizabeth (Sikosky) Hasek; m. Stephen Howard Falor, Dec. 29, 1973; children: Douglas Stephen, Rebecca Elizabeth. AA, Cuyahoga Comm. Coll., Parma, Ohio, 1972; BA, U. Akron, 1979, postgrad., 1979—. Cert. child development, realtor. Catering coord. Sawmill Lodge, Huron, Ohio, 1973-75; coord. Thoracic Cardiovascular Assn., Akron, Ohio, 1973-75; realtor Buy Ohio/Coldwell Banker, Westerville, 1985-87; referral realtor K&S Realty, Westerville, 1987—; v.p. Westerville (Ohio) Visitors & Conv. Bur., 1988-90, pres., 1990—; vol. Children's Hosp. Found., Columbus, Ohio,. Mem. Jr. League, Ohio, 1982-84, Westerville Ameriflora Sesquintennial Com. for 1992; trustee Inniswood Botanical Garden and Nature Preserve, Westerville, Ohio, 1983-87; Inniswood assisting bd., Westerville, 1986-88. Recipient 100 Hours Pin award, Inniswood Vol., Inc., Westerville, Ohio, 1987. Mem. Inniswood Vol. Inc. (pres. 1986-88), Ikebana Internat., Four Seasons Garden Club, Garden Club of Ohio, The Lakes Golf and Country Club, Westerville Athletic Club. Presbyterian. Home: 446 Valleyview Ct Westerville OH 43081 Office: Westerville Visitors and Co 5 W Coll. Westerville OH 43081

FALVO, DONNA R., psychology educator; b. Tuscola, Ill., Mar. 17, 1945; d. Harry Johann and Christina (Stortzum) Schmohe; m. Richard Ernst Falvo, June 4, 1977; 1 child, Michael. PhD, So. Ill. U., 1978. Lic. clin. psychologist; RN. Staff nurse Meml. Hosp., Carbondale, Ill., 1968-70; instr. VTI Nursing, So. Ill. U., Carbondale, 1970-72; instr. sch. medicine So. Ill. U., Carbondale, 1974-78, asst. prof. sch. medicine, 1978-79, dir. behavior sci. sch. medicine, dept. family practice, 1979-88, prof. rehab. inst., 1988—; cons. Milner-Fenuiex, Timonium, Md., 1986-87, Media Resources, Inc., Vancouver, Wash., 1986, VA HSR & D Grant, Marion, Fla., 1983, Soc. for Rsch. and Edn. in Primary Care-Internal Medicine. Author: Patient Education: A Guide to Increased Compliance, 1985, Principles and Practices of Vocational Rehabilitation with Hidden Disabilities, 1983; contbr. articles to profl. jours. Mary Switzer scholar Nat. Rehab. Assn., 1986. Mem. Am. Psychol. Assn. Soc. Tchrs. Family Medicine (task force mem. 1985—), Soc. for Disability Studies, Nat. Rehab. Counseling Assn., Gerontological Assn. Am. Democrat. Lutheran. Office: So Ill U Rehab Inst Carbondale IL 62901

FALVO, JANET V., advertising executive; b. S.I., N.Y.; d. John R. and Bernadette Valenza. BSBA, Bucknell U., 1981; MBA, NYU, 1989. Bus. analyst Young & Rubicam, N.Y.C., 1981-83, assoc. mgr. bus. affairs, 1983-85; bus. mgr. Wunderman Worldwide, N.Y.C., 1985-87; v.p. fin. Chapman Direct Advt., N.Y.C., 1987—. Mem. Pi Beta Phi.

FAMIGLIETTI, NANCY ZIMA, computer executive; b. Hartford, Conn., Nov. 10, 1956; d. Joseph John and Angeline (Morello) Zima; m. Arthur R. Famiglietti Jr., May 23, 1981. BA in Math., Computer Sci., Eastern Conn. State Coll., Willimantic, 1978. Sr. programmer analyst Hamilton Standard, Windsor Locks, Conn., 1978-82; system analyst Cigna Corp., Hartford, 1982-83, system designer, 1983-86, lead system designer, 1986-89; system advisor Aetna Life & Casulty Co., Hartford, 1989—. Active Conn. Trolley Mus., East Windsor, Conn. Fire Mus., East Windsor, Bushnell Carousel Soc., Hartford, Sturbridge Village, Conn. Pub. TV., Hartford, Channel 57, Springfield, Mass. Mem. Nat. Honor Soc., Kappa Mu Epsilon Math. Honor Soc. Home: 81 McGrath Rd South Windsor CT 06074

FANCHER, MARY FRANK, music educator; b. Altus, Okla., Dec. 11, 1912; d. Oscar Franklin and James Ina (Wood) Penick; m. Camillo Houston Fancher (dec. 1984); children: Suzanne Litman, Lonnie Frank, Jack Carroll, Mary Jeanne Moorman. BS in Edn., No. Tex. State U., 1967. Pianist, singer Elk City, Okla., 1928-35; tchr. various schs., Tex., 1930-39, Okla., 1945-46; piano tchr. various pvt. studios, 1946—. Organist St. Paul Episc. Ch., Altus, Okla., 1950-51; dir. piano festivals, Altus, 1940-70; actress, singer, and dancer numerous community prodns., 1982—. Docent Arts Guild, Denton, Tex., 1980—, Greater Denton Arts Coun., 1980—; active Denton Benefit League, 1973—, Denton County Dems., 1973—; vol. Friends of Symphony, Denton, 1980-87, Denton Community Theatre, 1973—, Denton Light Opera Co. Named to Hall of Fame Piano Guild USA, 1968; recipient Meritorious Service award March of Dimes, 1953-73. Mem. Altus MacDowell Club Allied Arts (pres., v.p. 1968-70), Denton Music Tchrs. Assn. (charter, archivist), Tex. Music Tchrs. Assn., Okla. Music Tchrs. Assn. (charter, v.p. Altus br., adjudicator piano contests 1953-54), Nat. Guild Piano Tchrs., Shakespeare Club (sec., v.p. fine arts dept. 1976-79, pres., v.p., sec. music dept. 1975-78), Ariel Club (del. music dept. 1989—). Baptist. Home: 1201 Austin 2 Denton TX 76201

FANK, DEBORA LYNN, transportation executive; b. Syracuse, N.Y., Mar. 4, 1952; d. Frederick Bering and Patricia Albertine (Brown) F. BA, U. Calif., Santa Barbara, 1974. Social worker Vista, Chapel Hill, N.C., 1974; bus driver City of Chapel Hill, 1975-76; engring. aide City of Corvallis, Oreg., 1978-80; transit supr. City of Albany, Oreg., 1983-85; asst. traffic engr. City of Anaheim, Calif., 1985-87, assoc. traffic engr., 1987-89, assoc. planner, 1989—; sec. Orange County (Calif.) Traffic Engring. Coun., 1989-90. Parole vol. Sheriff of Benton County, Oreg., 1982; mgr. homeless shelter County of Orange, Fullerton, Calif., 1989-90. Recipient Pub. Transit Svc. award Dept. Transp., State of Oreg., Albany, 1984, Transp. Ptnrship. award, Orange County Transp. Commn., Santa Ana, 1989. Mem. Am. Planning Assn., Inst. Transp. Engrs. (assoc.), Orange County Traffic Engring. Coun. (treas. 1989-90, chair 1990—). Democrat. Office: City of Anaheim 200 S. Anaheim Blvd Anaheim CA 92805

FANNIN, MARIANNE BENJAMIN, banker; b. Providence, Ky., May 28, 1933; d. Oliver kerney and Gwendolyn (Kemp) Benjamin; m. Thomas Newton Fannin, Aug. 28, 1953; children: Mary Todd Bills, Tamara Fannin Knappenberger. AA, Stephens Coll., 1953; student, Ariz. State U., 1973. Research analyst M.R. West Mktg. Research, Phoenix, 1973-81; prin., ptnr. Western Diversified, Phoenix, 1977—; v.p. Fannin Ins., Inc., Phoenix, 1984—; chair Republic Nat. Bank Ariz., Phoenix, 1985—. Active Rep. campaigns, Ariz., 1955—; co-chair Citizens Trans. Com., Phoenix, 1979; chair Maricopa Community Colls. Found. Bd., Phoenix, 1988; bd. dirs. Phoenix Indsl. Devel. Authority, Phoenix, 1982-89; mem. women's aux. Goodwill Industries, St. Joseph Hosp.; authority bd. Ariz. Health Facilities, 1989—. Episcopalian. Home: 77 E Missouri Phoenix AZ 85012 Office: Rep Nat Bank 2020 North Cen Phoenix AZ 85004

FANNING, BELINDA J., speech pathology professional; b. Huntsville, Ala., July 23, 1952; d. Robert A. McBride and Mary B. Beckman; m. William M. Fanning, July 24, 1970; 1 child, Mark. BS, U. Montevallo, 1983, MS, 1984; MS, U. Montevallo, 1985; AS, Calhoun Community Coll., Decatur, Ala., 1981. Lic. clin. speech pathologist, audiologist, Ga., Ala. Speech-lang. pathologist Shelby County Bd. Edn., Columbiana, Ala., 1984; audiologist Easter Seal Soc., Falls Church, Va., 1986-87; speech-lang. pathologist St. Coletta Sch., Arlington, Va., 1987-89; clin. supr., coord. Auburn U. Speech and Hearing Clinic, 1989—. Named Most Outstanding Grad. Student in Speech Pathology, 1985, Most Outstanding Grad. Student in Audiology, 1985; recipient Gormley award, 1984, Kiwanis Club scholarship, grad. honors scholarship, 1983-85, Kirby award, 1983. Mem. Am. Speech-Lang. and Hearing Assn., Speech and Hearing Assn. Ala., Am. Acad. Audiology, Health Svcs. Club of Ft. Belvior. Office: Auburn U Dept Communication Disorders 1199 Haley Ctr Auburn AL 36849

FANNING, KATHERINE WOODRUFF, editor; b. Chgo., Oct. 18, 1927; d. Frederick William and Katherine Bower (Miller) Woodruff; m. Marshall Field, Jr., May 12, 1950 (div. 1963); children: Frederick Woodruff, Katherine Woodruff, Barbara Woodruff; m. Lawrence S. Fanning, 1966 (dec. 1971); m. Amos Mathews, Jan. 6, 1984. BA, Smith Coll., 1949; LLD (hon.), Colby Coll., 1979; LittD (hon.), Pine Manor Jr. Coll., 1984; LHD (hon.), Northeastern U., 1984; hon. degree, Harvard U., 1988, Smith Coll., 1988, Babson Coll., 1988, U. Alaska, 1989, Govs. State U., Ill., 1989. With Anchorage Daily News, from 1965, editor, pub., 1972-83; editor The Christian Science Monitor, 1983-88; fall fellow Inst. of Politics Harvard U., Cambridge, Mass., 1989—; dir. AP, 1988-89; mem. nat. adv. com. The Gannett Ctr. for Media Studies; adv. bd. U. Mo. Sch. Journalism; bd. visitors Knight Fellowships for Journalists, Stanford U.; sr. adv. bd. Joan Shorenstein Barone Ctr., Harvard U.; bd. dirs. New Directions for News. Trustee Kettering Found.; bd. dirs. Ctr. for Fgn. Journalists; bd. overseers Boston Symphony Orch. Recipient Elijah Parish Lovejoy award Colby Coll., 1979, Smith Coll. medal, 1980, Mo. medal of Honor, U. Mo. Journalism award, 1980. Mem. Am. Soc. Newspaper Editors (bd. dirs. 1981—, pres. 1987-88), Soc. Profl. Journalists, Coun. Fgn. Rels., InterAm. Dialogue, St. Botolph Club (Boston), Badminton and Tennis Club (Boston). Home and Office: 330 Beacon St Boston MA 02116

FANNING, MARGARET BEVERLY, psychotherapist; b. Boston, Feb. 10, 1937; d. Alexander A. and Marion T. (Ward) Driscoll; m. George Joseph Fanning, Sept. 20, 1958; children: Jean Marie, Kathaleen, Kevin, Scott. Student, Massasoit Community Coll., 1980-82; BA in Social Work magna cum laude, Ea. Nazarene Coll., Quincy, Mass., 1984; MA in Family Counseling, Ea. Nazarene Coll., 1986. Psychotherapist Alcoholic Family Rehab., Plymouth, Mass., 1986-87; prin., owner, exec. dir. Journey Inward Counseling, Halifax, Mass., 1987—; group facilitator Plymouth County Chpt. MADD, Halifax, 1988—. Names Shawmut 1st City Bank scholar, 1981; Honor scholar Ea. Nazarene Coll., 1982-84. Mem. AACD, APA, Am. Mental Health Counselors Assn., Mass. Assn. Mental Health Counselors, Phi Delta Lambda. Office: Journey Inward Counseling 313 Plymouth St Halifax MA 02338

FANNING, MARJORIE L., newspaper editor. Mng. editor Jour. Star, Peoria, Ill. Office: Peoria Jour Star Inc 1 News Pla Peoria IL 61643*

FANNON, DIANE, advertising agency executive. V.p., then sr. v.p. Tracy-Locke, Dallas, until 1987, exec. v.p, from 1989, now dir. creative svcs.; sr. v.p. Bozell, Jacobs, Kenyon & Eckhardt, Inc., Dallas, 1987-89. Office: Tracy-Locke PO Box 50129 Dallas TX 75250*

FANTACI, MARY KATHRYN, controller; b. Rochester, N.Y., June 2, 1962; d. Arthur Raymond and Margaret Ann (Lutz) F. BA in English, Holy Cross, 1984; MBA, Suffolk U., 1985-88. Customer svc. rep. Bank New Eng., Boston, 1984-85; fin. asst. Boston Found., 1985, jr. acct., 1985-86; bus. mgr. Blackwell Sci. Publs., Boston, 1986-88; retail div. contr. Boyd Corp., Woburn, Mass., 1988-89, ops. mgr., 1989, contr. parts and svc. divs., 1989—; ops. mgr. Amana Northeast, Woburn, Mass., 1989—. Democrat. Roman Catholic. Office: Boyd Corp 15A Constitution Way Woburn MA 01801

FANTONE, CHRISTINE LYNN, paralegal; b. Summit, N.J., Aug. 25, 1951. BA, Beaver Coll., 1973; paralegal cert., N.Y. Paralegal Inst., 1974. Paralegal CBS, Inc., N.Y.C., 1974, Milberg, Weiss, Bershad & Specthrie, N.Y.C., 1974-78; paralegal supr. Reavis & McGrath, N.Y.C., 1978-85; litigation paralegal coord. Stroock & Stroock & Lavan, N.Y.C., 1985—. Mem. Legal Asst. Mgrs. Assn. Home: New York NY 10022 Office: Stroock & Stroock & Lavan 7 Hanover Sq New York NY 10004

FANUS, PAULINE RIFE, librarian; b. New Oxford, Pa., Feb. 14, 1925; d. Maurice Diehl and Bernice Edna (Gable) Rife; m. William Edward Fanus, June 20, 1944; children: Irene Weaver, Larry William, Daniel Diehl. BS, Pa. State U., 1945; MLS, Villanova U., 1961; postgrad., Temple U., 1986—. Periodical librarian Tex. Coll. Arts Industries, Kingville, 1945; tchr. nursery sch. Studio Sch., Wayne, Pa., 1953-55; librarian circulation, reference Franklin Inst., Phila., 1963-66; asst. librarian Ursinus Coll., Collegeville, Pa., 1966; catalog librarian, instr. Eastern Coll., St. Davids, Pa., 1967-71; head librarian Agnes Irwin Sch., Rosemont, Pa., 1971—. Book reviewer The Book Report. Mem. AAUP (chpt. sec. Eastern Coll. 1970-71), Pa. Library Assn. Home: Country Club Rd Phoenixville PA 19460 Office: Agnes Irwin Sch PO Box 407 Rosemont PA 19010

FAOUR, ANNA ROSE, writer, educator; b. Houston, Nov. 27, 1929; d. Jack and Alice (Emmett) Faour. B.S., U. Houston, 1952. Reporter, Houston Chronicle, 1952-53, 58-59; reporter women's dept. Houston Post, 1953-54; proof-reader McCann-Erickson, Houston, 1962-64; tchr. English, Cypress-Fairbanks Ind. Sch. Dist., Houston, 1965-79; reporter Brazosport Facts, Clute, Tex., 1981; tchr. English, Houston Ind. Sch. Dist., 1957-61, 64-65, 81-83; author, pub. TexAnna greeting cards, 1981—; freelance writer. Publicity writer Eisenhower campaign, Houston, 1956. Named Foremost Women in Communications, Foremost Am. Pub. Corp., 1970; pub. relations scholar U. Houston, 1950-52. Mem. San Jacinto Mus. History, Women in Communications. Mem. Antiochian Orthodox Christian Ch. Address: 16615 Torrington Ct Spring TX 77379

FARACE, LINDA DIANA, banker; b. Bklyn., Feb. 25, 1948; d. Leonard Paul and Sophie Cecilia (Ziemak) Karas; m. Theodore Vincent Farace, Sept. 11, 1982; step-children: Thomas, Lisa Scotti, Suzanne. BS, Pace U., 1973, student internat. fin. courses, 1968, 69. With Gen. Motors Acceptance

Corp., N.Y.C., 1966-81; sr. corp. treas. Royal Bank Can., N.Y.C., 1981-84; v.p. Nat. Bank Can., N.Y.C., 1984-87; v.p. institutional sales Credit Lyonnais, N.Y.C., 1987—. Mem. Forex Assn. Office: Credit Lyonnais 95 Wall St New York NY 10005

FARACE-EPLEY, DIANA MARIA, educator, human relations counselor; b. Bklyn., Jan. 2, 1948; d. Nicholas Vincent and Catherine (Mauro) F.; m. James Pascal Epley, Jr., July 29, 1973. AAS, Suffolk County Community Coll., 1968; BA in Psychology summa cum laude, St. Leo Coll., 1976; MA in Human Rels., Webster U., 1984. Figure cons. Barbara-Wayne Figure Salon, N.Y.C., 1970-71; evening mgr. Nu-Dimensions Figure Salon, N.Y.C., 1971-72; adminstrv. asst. to dir. sales/mktg. Hazletine Corp., Greenlawn, N.Y., 1972-73; faculty City Colls. of Chgo., Zaragoza, Spain, 1973-74, Stratford Women's Coll., Tampa, Fla., 1974; ops. mgr. Stanton & Assocs. Constrn., 1976-78; officer Richard's Auto Grooming, Inc., 1978-79; faculty Florence-Darlington TEC, Florence, S.C., 1979-81, St. Anne's Cath. Elem. Sch., 1982; tutor, tchr., counselor Darlington Acad. (S.C.), 1982; area dir. office occupations Preston Coll. Tech. and Bus. Careers, Columbia, S.C., 1983-84; owner, mental health counselor PMS Rsch. and Peripheral Treatment Clinic, 1985; ednl. resource adviser Davis-Monthan AFB Learning Ctr., Cochise Coll., Sierra Vista, Ariz., 1986—; br. safety monitor 377th CSG Housing Supply, USAF, Ramstein, Federal Republic of Germany, 1987—, civilian pers. liaison hdqrs. of electronic communications div., Kapaun, Fed. Republic of Germany, 1988—. Exhibited paintings Sumter Gallery Art, 1983; exhibited photographs various mil. points Fed. Republic of Germany, 1989. Benefactor, St. LeBre Missionary for Indians in Utah, 1983-84, Christian Appalachian Project in Ky., 1984—; mem. Florence-Darlington Tech. Coll. Ednl. Found., 1981—. Mem. Secretarial Guild Am., S.C. Ednl. Tchrs. Assn., Sumter Artists Guild, Smithsonian Assocs. Roman Catholic. Address: PO Box 6635 APO New York NY 09012

FARAGO, MARGARET ELLEN, vision service officer; b. Roselle, Ill., Feb. 9, 1954; d. Patrick Taylor and Lorayne Elizabeth (Sullivan) Hall; m. Stephen A. Farago, Nov. 16, 1975; children: Laura Christine, Tracy Ann, Elizabeth Lucille. BS, Western Ill. U., 1975; MA, U. Phoenix, 1990. Mgr. info. systems 1st Am. Health Concepts, Mesa, Ariz., 1987-89; dir. adminstrn. Outlook Vision Svcs., Inc., Phoenix, 1990—. Troop leader Girl Scouts Am., Mesa, 1984-88, neighborhood registrar, 1985-89; ct. apptd. spl. adv. Ct. Apptd. Spl. Adv., Phoenix, 1989—. Mem. Faternal Order of Police Aux. (rep. 1989—). Republican. Methodist.

FARAH, CYNTHIA WEBER, photographer, publisher; b. Long Island, N.Y., June 2, 1949; d. Andrew John and Aria Emma (Jelnikova) Weber; m. James Clifton Farah, Jan. 12, 1974; children—Elise, Alexa. B.A. in Communications, Stanford U., 1971. Prodn. staff Sta. KDBC-TV, El Paso, Tex., 1971-73; v.p. Sanders Co. Advt., El Paso, 1973-74, film critic El Paso Times, 1972-77; free lance photographer, El Paso, 1974—; pres. CM Pub., El Paso, 1981—. Photographer, co-author: Country Music: A Look at the Men Who've Made It, 1982; author: Literature and Landscape: Writers of the Southwest, 1988. Bd. dirs. N. Mex. State U. Mus. Adv. Bd., Las Cruces, 1982—; dir., vice-chmn. Shelter for Battered Women, El Paso, 1981-86; active Jr. League, 1977—, C. of C. Leadership El Paso Program, 1983-84; mem. El Paso County Hist. Comm., 1984—, vice chmn., 1986, 87, El Paso County Hist. Alliance (v. chmn. 1986-88); trustee El Paso Community Found., 1984—; adv. bd. El Paso Arts Resources dept., 1987—. Recipient J.C. Penny Golden Rule award, 1989, Vol. Svc. award El Paso Bur. United Way, 1989, Clara Barton Medallion ARC, 1979; mem. adv. coun. El Paso Bus. Com. for the Arts, 1988—; mem. adv. bd. Tex. Ctr. for the Book, 1987—. Mem. We. Writers Am., We. Lit. Assn., Juntos Art Assn., U. Tex. at El Paso Libr. Assn. (v.p. 1987-88, pres. 1989—), Tex. Profl. Photographers Assn., Stanford U. Alumni Assn. Episcopalian.

FARB, EDITH H., chemist; b. Phila., Aug. 7, 1928; d. Nathan and Rose Himelfarb; divorced; children: Irene Winicov, Diane Winicov, Joyce L. Winicov. AB, U. Pa., 1949, MS, 1951; PhD, Bryn Mawr Coll., 1958. Asst. prof. chemistry L.I. U., Bklyn., 1958-64; adj. lectr. Hunter Coll. CUNY, N.Y.C., 1964-68; adj. asst. prof. Good Counsel Coll., White Plains, N.Y., 1968-69; patent searcher Texaco Devel. Corp., N.Y.C., 1970-73; rsch. analyst N.Y.C. Dept. Health, 1973-76; environ. health scientist N.Y.C. Med. Health Rsch., 1976-82; chemist N.Y.C. Police Dept., 1983-86, N.Y.C. Dept. Environ. Protection, 1986 --; adj. lectr. York Coll. CUNY, Queens, 1982-83, Barnard Coll., Columbia U., N.Y.C., 1985-87. Recipient Bryn Mawr Coll. scholarship, 1951-56; Eastman Kodak fellow, 1957-58. Mem. ACS, N.Y. Acad. Scis., N.Y. Microscopial Soc., North Eastern Forensic Soc., N.Y. Metro Indsl. Hygiene Assn. (sec. 1981-82). Home: 63-58 78th St Middle Village NY 11379

FARBER, ROSANN ALEXANDER, geneticist, educator; b. Charlotte, N.C., Nov. 21, 1944; d. J. Wilson Jr. and June Adell (Childs) Alexander; m. Gerald Lee Farber, July 28, 1966 (div. Jan. 1969); m. Thomas Douglas Petes, July 20, 1973; children: Laura Elizabeth, Diana Christine. AB in Biology, Oberlin Coll., 1966; postgrad., U. Pitts., 1967-68, Albert Einstein Coll. Medicine, 1969; PhD in Genetics, U. Wash., 1973. Diplomate in cytogenetics Am. Bd. Med. Genetics. Postdoctoral fellow Nat. Inst. for Med. Rsch., London, 1973-75; rsch. assoc. Children's Hosp. Med. Ctr., Boston, 1975-77; from asst. prof. to assoc. prof. U. Chgo., 1977-88; assoc. prof. dept. pathology U. N.C., Chapel Hill, 1988—. Contbr. articles to profl. jours. NIH grantee, 1978—. Mem. AAAS, Am. Soc. Human Genetics. Home: 612 Morgan Creek Rd Chapel Hill NC 27514 Office: U NC CB 7525 Brinkhous-Bullitt Bldg Chapel Hill NC 27599

FARENTHOLD, FRANCES TARLTON, lawyer; b. Corpus Christi, Tex., Oct. 2, 1926; d. Benjamin Dudley and Catherine (Bluntzer) Tarlton; AB, Vassar Coll., 1946; JD, U. Tex., 1949; LLD, Hood Coll., 1973, Boston U., 1973, Regis Coll., 1976, Lake Erie Coll., 1979, Elmira Coll., 1981, Coll. of Santa Fe, 1985; children—Dudley Tarlton, George Edward, Emilie, James Dougherty, Vincent Bluntzer (dec.). Bar: Tex. 1949. Pvt. practice, 1949-65, 67-76, 80—; mem. Tex. Ho. of Reps., 1968-72; dir. legal aide Nueces County, 1965-67; asst. prof. law Tex. So. U., Houston; pres. Wells Coll., Aurora, N.Y., 1976-80. Mem. Human Relations Com., Corpus Christi, 1963-68, Corpus Christi Citizen's Com. Community Improvement, 1966-68; mem. Tex. adv. com. to U.S. Commn. on Civil Rights, 1968-76; mem. nat. adv. council ACLU; mem. Orgn. for Preservation Unblemished Shoreline, 1964—; Dem. candidate for Gov. of Tex., 1972; del. Dem. Nat. Conv., 1972, 1st woman nominated to be candidate v.p. U.S., 1972; nat. co-chmn. Citizens to Elect McGovern-Shriver, 1972; chmn. Nat. Women's Polit. Caucus, 1973-75; mem. Dem. platform com., 1988; trustee Vassar Coll., 1975-83; bd. dirs. Texans for a Bilateral Nuclear Weapons Freeze, 1983-84, Fund for Constl. Govt., Ctr. for Devel. Policy, 1983—, Mexican Am. Legal Def. and Ednl. Fund, 1980-83; chmn. Inst. for Policy Studies, 1986—. Recipient Lyndon B. Johnson Woman of Year award, 1973. Mem. State Bar Tex. Office: 1203 Central Bank Bldg 2100 Travis Houston TX 77002

FARINA, ANA BEATRIZ, electronics sales executive; b. Guayaquil, Ecuador, May 16, 1950; came to U.S., 1962; d. Luis A. and Luz Aurora (Rodriguez) Moreira; m. Manuel Jose Farina, Dec. 15, 1979; children: Kevin, Mark. AA, Latin-Am. Inst., 1971. Adminstr. asst. M&T Chem. Inc., N.Y.C., 1971-75; mgr. sales Singer Products Co., N.Y.C., 1975-78; v.p. Argil Internat. Ltd., N.Y.C., 1978-83; pres. KMA Enterprises Inc., Bklyn., 1983—. Mem. Nat. Assn. Female Execs. Roman Catholic.

FARINE, CHERYL LEE, lawyer, pharmacist; b. Brownsville, Pa., Nov. 17, 1951; d. Lionel and Lorraine (Grashion) Faux; m. Frank Joseph Farine, Nov. 30, 1974; children: Nicholas Dante, Angela Marie, Cherie Anne. BS in Pharmacy summa cum laude, W.Va. U., 1974; JD summa cum laude, Cleveland State U., 1988. Bar: Ohio 1988, U.S. Dist. Ct. (no. dist.) Ohio 1989; lic. pharmacist, Ohio. Pharmacist Mt. Carmel Hosp., Columbus, 1975, St. Luke's Hosp., Cleve., 1975-79, Marymount Hosp., Cleve., 1979-83; dir. pharmacy Brentwood Hosp., Cleve., 1983-88, dir. ancillary svc., 1987-88; assoc. Jones, Day, Reavis & Pogue, Cleve., 1988—; mem. adj. faculty U. Toledo Coll. of Pharmacy, 1981-88; clin. instr. Ohio State U. Coll. of Pharmacy, Columbus, 1985-88; mem. hosp. adv. bd. Harris Wholesale, Solon, Ohio, 1986-87. Vol. counsel Cath. Hospice Network, Cleve., 1989—; mem. legal com. ACLU, Cleve., 1989—. Mem. ABA, Cleve. Bar Assn., Ohio Bar Assn., Akron Bar Assn., Am. Soc. Hosp. Pharmacists, Cleve. Soc. Hosp. Pharmacists, Phi Alpha Delta. Democrat. Home: 9872 Pebble Beach Aurora OH 44202 Office: Jones Day Reavis & Pogue 901 Lakeside Ave Cleveland OH 44114

FARINELLI, JEAN L., public relations firm executive; b. Phila., July 26, 1946; d. Albert J. and Edith M. (Falini) F. B.A., Am. U., Washington, 1968; M.A., Ohio State U., Columbus, 1969. Asst. pub. relations dir. Dow Jones & Co., Inc., N.Y.C., 1969-71; account exec. Carl Byoir & Assocs., Inc., N.Y.C., 1972-74, v.p., 1974-80, sr. v.p., 1980-82; pres. Tracy-Locke/BBDO Pub. Relations, Dallas, 1982-87; pres. Creamer Dickson Basford, Inc., N.Y.C., 1987-88, chmn., chief exec. officer, 1988—. Recipient PR CaseBook, PR Reporter, N.H., 1984; Silver Spur, Tex. Pub. Relations Assn., Dallas, 1985. Mem. Pub. Relations Soc. Am. (Silver Anvil award 1980, 81, 85, Excalibur award Houston chpt. 1985, chmn. 1986 Silver Anvil awards, chmn. 1987 honors and awards com., chmn. 1989 Spring Conf. Counselors Acad.), Internat. Assn. Bus. Communicators (Gold Quill award 1985), Women in Communications, Women Execs. in Pub. Relations, Nat. Investor Relations Inst., Internat. Pub. Rels. Assn. (pub. rels. seminar). Clubs: Nat. Arts (N.Y.C.). Home: 333 E 56th St New York NY 10022 Office: Creamer Dickson Basford 1633 Broadway New York NY 10019

FARIS, INGRID BARTH, company executive; b. Calif., Nov. 15, 1951; d. Eugene A. Barth and Erika Beate Grande; m. W. Ray Faris, May 17, 1980. BA summa cum laude, U. Tex., 1983. V.p. Ray Faris, Inc., San Antonio. Assn. Gen. Contractors, Univ. Tex. San Antonio Alumni Assn., NAFE, Alpha Chi Soc. Republican. Episcopalian. Home: PO Box 29591 San Antonio TX 78229 Office: 15242 Tradesmen Dr San Antonio TX 78249

FARIS, LUCILE A., director nursing services; b. Phillipines, Nov. 1, 1939; d. Evaristo and Roberta Velasco; children: Cynthia, Arhur, Anthony. BSN, Cen. Philippines Coll., 1964. Charge nurse VA Hosp., N.Y.C.; supr. White Plains Nursing Home, Bronx, N.Y.; dir. nurses Health Force, N.Y.C.; dir. nursing svcs. Farand Nursing Svcs., N.Y.C. Home: 19 West 34th St Ste 1113 New York NY 10001

FARISH, TERESA IRENE, aircraft business owner; b. Evansville, Ind., June 3, 1953; d. Carman Perry and Winona Rose (Hedinger) Thomas; m. Ronald T. Farish. BS, U. Evansville, 1975. Recreational therapist Evansville Psychiatric Childrens Ctr., 1974-78; advt. assoc., mgr. Wescott Advt., Evansville, 1978; asst. dir. U. Evansville, 1978-79; free lance writer St. Louis, 1980-81; v.p., mgr., owner Ron Farish Aircraft, Tyler, Tex., 1983—; aircraft researcher Aries Aviations, Tyler, 1983. Vol.-chmn. Women's Symphony League, Tyler. Mem. NAFE, AAUW (publicity chmn. 1988), Alph Phi. Roman Catholic. Office: Ron Farish Aircraft PO Box 7 Tyler TX 75710

FARIS-STOCKEM, DEBBIE, sheet metal company executive; b. Portland, Oreg., Jan. 6, 1955; d. Ernest Duane and Elizabeth Anne (McCullough) Faris; m. Robert Allen Stockem, Oct. 18, 1975; children: Melissa Gene, Cassandra Lynn. Office mgr. Faris Sheet Metal, Inc., Portland, 1975-84, v.p., 1984-88, pres., 1988—. Mem. Nat. Assn. Women in Constrn. (bd. dirs. Portland chpt. 1987-89, pres.-elect. 1989-90), Assn. Gen. Contractors, NAFE. Office: Faris Sheet Metal Inc 102 SE 99th Ave Portland OR 97216

FARLEY, GENEVIEVE MARIE, program executive; b. Independence, Mo., Jan. 8, 1952; d. Don Everett and Nancy Elizabeth (Locke) F. B in Social Work, Graceland Coll., 1974; MSW, U. Mo., 1986. Dormitory head resident Graceland Coll., Lamons, Iowa, 1974-75; residential mgr. Greater Kans. City Found., 1975-77; clin. caseworker Kans. City Regional Ctr., 1977-87; employment program dir. Rainbow Svcs. for Youth and Families, Alpena, Mich., 1988—; group facilitator Overland Park (Kans.) Youth Diversion, 1983-85. Bd. dirs. Wellness Network Huron Shores, Alpena, Shelter Inc. Mem. Nat. Assn. Social Workers, NAFE. Democrat. Office: Rainbow Svcs 2373 Gordon Rd Alpena MI 49707

FARLEY, JENNIE TIFFANY TOWLE, industrial and labor relations educator; b. Fanwood, N.J., Nov. 2, 1932; d. Howard Albert and Dorothy Jane (Van Wagner) Towle; m. Donald Thorn Farley Jr., June 16, 1956; children—Claire Hamlin, Anne Tiffany, Peter Towle. BA, Cornell U., 1954, MS, 1969, PhD, 1970. Mem. editorial staff Mademoiselle and Seventeen mags., N.Y.C., 1954-56; freelance writer, Eng., Sweden, Peru, 1956-67; lectr., research assoc., adj. asst. prof. Cornell U., Ithaca, N.Y., 1970-72, dir. women's studies, 1972-76, asst. prof. Sch. Indsl. and Labor Relations, 1976-82, assoc. prof., 1982-89, prof., 1989—, exec. bd. dirs. women's studies program, 1970—; vis. prof. Ctr. for Women Scholars and Research on Women Uppsala U., Sweden, 1985-86; trustee Cornell U., 1988—. Author: Affirmative Action and the Woman Worker, 1979, Academic Women and Employment Discrimination, 1982; editor: Sex Discrimination in Higher Education, 1982, The Woman in Management, 1983, Women Workers in Fifteen Countries, 1985. Bd. dirs. Nat. Women's Hall of Fame, Seneca Falls, N.Y., 1986—. Recipient Corinne Galvin award Tompkins County Human Rights Commn., 1987. Mem. AAUP, Ithaca AAUW (pres. 1980-82), Grad. Women in Sci., Sociologists for Women in Soc., Tompkins County NOW. Club: Cornell Women's of Tompkins County. Home: 711 Triphammer Rd Ithaca NY 14850 Office: Cornell U Sch Indsl & Labor Rels Ithaca NY 14853

FARLEY, MARGARET MARY, physical therapist; b. San Rafael, Calif., Jan. 19, 1926; d. Angelo Joseph and Angelina (Arbini) Bertolli; m. James Vincent Farley, Jr., Aug. 25, 1951; children: Paul, Catherine, James, Loretta, Margaret, John. BA, San Francisco State U., 1948; postgrad. phys. therapy, U. Calif., med. sch., 1949. Phys. therapist U.C. Moffitt Hosp., San Francisco, 1949-50, May T. Morrison Rehab. Ctr., San Francisco, 1950-52; childbirth educator pvt. practice, San Rafael, Calif., 1953—. Recipient Recognition of Service awd. Archdiocesan Coun. Cath. Women, San Francisco, 1976, Vol. of Year awd. Marin Coun. Agcys., San Rafael, Calif., 1983,1984, 4 Those Who Care awd. KRON-TV4, San Francisco, 1984, 1985, KBAL Citizen of Day awd., KBAL Music, San Francisco, 1985. Bd. dirs. Birthright of Marin, regional cons. No. Calif. Birthright Internat., Am. Phys. Therapy Assn. (sec. San Francisco chpt., 1951-52). Republican. Roman Catholic. Home: 21 Santa Margarita Dr San Rafael CA 94901

FARLEY, MARIAN DIEDRE, librarian; b. Manhasset, N.Y., Mar. 1, 1955; d. John Joseph and Rita Sarah (Johnston) Farley. B.A., St. Bonaventure U., 1977; M.L.S., SUNY-Albany, 1978. Librarian-instr. Iona Coll., New Rochelle, N.Y., 1980-82; head circulation dept. U. Lowell (Mass.), 1982-83; library dir. Analytic Scis. Corp., Reading, Mass., 1983-90; asst. prof. Charles A. Dana Med. Libr., U. Vt., Burlington, 1990— . Mem. ALA, Spl. Libraries Assn., Route 128 Librarians, New Eng. On-Line Users Group. Democrat. Roman Catholic. Home: D6 Grandview Dr South Burlington VT 05403 Office: Charles A Dana Med Libr U Vt Burlington VT 05405-0068

FARLEY, PEGGY ANN, finance company executive; b. Phila., Mar. 12, 1947; d. Harry E. and Ruth (Lloyd) F.; m. W. Reid McIntyre, Dec. 31, 1985; 1 child, Margaret Ruth. AB, Barnard Coll., 1970; MA with high honors, Columbia U., 1972. Admissions officer Barnard Coll. N.Y.C., 1973-76; adminstr. Citibank NA, Athens, Greece, 1976-77; cons. Organization Resources Counselors, N.Y.C., 1977-78; sr. assoc. Morgan Stanley and Co., Inc., N.Y.C., 1978-84; mng. dir., chief exec. officer AMAS Securities, Inc., N.Y.C., 1984—, also bd. dirs.; bd. dirs. AMAS Group, London. Author: The Place Of The Yankee And Euro Bond Markets In A Financing Program For The People's Republic of China, 1982. Mem. Columbia U. Seminar on China-U.S. Bus., Rep. Senatorial Inner Circle, Fgn. Policy Assn. Mem. Asia Soc., China Inst. Republican. Presbyterian. Club: Metropolitan (N.Y.C.). Home: 515 E 72d St New York NY 10021 Office: AMAS Securities Inc 520 Madison Ave New York NY 10022

FARMER, CAROL ANN, retail marketing consultant; b. Columbus, Ohio, Aug. 14, 1944; d. John Edwin and Ruth Cooper F. BA, DePauw U., 1966; postgrad., Columbus Coll. Art and Design, 1969-70, Chgo. Art Inst., 1982. Sr. cons. assoc. Mgmt. Horizons, Columbus, 1971-74; owner, chief operating officer The Doody Co., Columbus, 1975-80; owner, pres. Retail Design Research, Columbus, 1980-82; exec. v.p. Lerner Stores, N.Y.C., 1982-84; v.p. market devel. Am. Can Co., Greenwich, Conn., 1984-85; pres. Carol Farmer Assocs., N.Y.C., 1985—. Chmn. Dance Cen., Columbus, 1980. Mem. Fashion Group Internat. (bd. dirs.). Office: PO Box 470 Boca Raton FL 33429

FARMER, CATHERINE SCHWALLIE, software engineer; b. Providence, Aug. 27, 1959; d. Edward Hugo and Margaret (Mullee) Schwallie; m. Douglas Jay Farmer, Aug. 16, 1986. BA, U. Mass., Boston, 1986; student, DePauw U., Greencastle, Ind., 1977-79. Installation specialist Great West Life Assurance Co., Denver, 1982-84; teaching asst. U. Mass., Boston, 1985-86; instr. Pascal Champlain Coll. Computer Camp, Burlington, Vt., summer 1986; programmer/analyst West Coast Beauty Supply Co., San Francisco, 1986-88; software engr. Jandel Sci., Corte Madera, Calif., 1988—. Vol. Dem. Calif. Primary, San Francisco, 1988. Mem. ACM, Assn. for Women in Computing. Democrat. Roman Catholic. Home: 714 Caldwell Rd Oakland CA 94611

FARMER, ELAINE F., state legislator; b. New Castle, Pa., Mar. 14, 1937; d. John R. and Pearle (McLure) Frazier; m. Sterling N. Farmer, Aug. 22, 1959; children: Heather, Drew. BBA, Case Western Reserve U., 1958, MEd, 1964. Employment supr. Stouffer Corp., Cleve., 1958-60; tchr. Lakewood Schs., Cleve., 1960-64; subs. tchr. North Allegheny Schs., Pitts., 1972-77; agt. Howard Hanna Real Estate Services, Pitts., 1977-86, mgr., 1983-86; elected mem. Ho. of Reps., Harrisburg, Pa., 1986—. Councilman Town of McCandless, Pa., 1980-86; trustee Northland Library, Pitts., 1980-85; liaison Planning Commn., McCandless, 1984-86. Mem. Nat. Order Women Legislators, Am. Legis. Exchange Council, North Hills C. of C., Airport C. of C. Republican. Presbyterian. Office: House Reps Box 178 Harrisburg PA 15237

FARMER, JANELL BETH HILTON, insurance agent; b. Indpls., Oct. 27, 1956; d. William Keith and Marilyn Beth (Bergman) Hilton; m. James Maurice Farmer, Dec. 18, 1982. BS in Agrl. Communications, Purdue U., 1978. Animal health products rep. Elanco Products Co. div. Eli Lilly, Quincy, Ill., 1979-86; life ins. agt. Mass. Mut. Life Ins. Co., Quincy, 1986—; instr. John Wood Community Coll., Quincy, 1981—. Dir. Miss Quincy Scholarship Pageant, 1989—. Mem. Quincy Sales and Mktg. Club (pres. 1989-90), Quincy Bus. Women's Network (founder, pres. 1989-90), Uptown Quincy, Inc., Nat. Assn. Life Underwriters, Purdue Alumni Assn. (life), Quincy Area C. of C. (ambassador 1987-90), Alpha Gamma Delta. Republican. Home: 2628 Midlan Quincy IL 62301 Office: Mass Mutual Life Ins Co 428 Maine Ste 360 Quincy IL 62301

FARMER, JANENE ELIZABETH, artist, educator; b. Albuquerque, Oct. 16, 1946; d. Charles John Watt and Regina M. (Brown) Kruger; m. Michael Hugh Bolton, Apr. 1965 (div.); m. Frank Urban Farmer, May, 1972 (div.). B.A. in Art, San Diego State U., 1969. Owner, operator Iron Walrus Pottery, 1972-79; designer ceramic and fabric murals, Coronado, Calif., 1979-82; executed commns. for clients in U.S.A., Can., Japan and Mex., 1972—; pvt. tchr. pottery; mem. faculty U. Calif.-San Diego; substitute tchr. Calif. community colls.; designer fabric murals and bldg. interiors, painter Coronado and La Jolla, Calif., 1982—; tchr. Blessed Sacrament Sch., San Diego, 1982-85, San Diego Unified Sch. Dist., 1985-87. Mem. Coronado Arts and Humanities Council; resident artist U. Calif.-San Diego. Recipient grant Calif. Arts Council, 1980-81; U. San Diego grad. fellow dept. edn., 1984. Mem. Am. Soc. Interior Designers (affiliate). Roman Catholic. Home: 4435 Nobel Dr #35 San Diego CA 92122

FARMER, LESLEY SUZANNE, library director; b. Spokane, Wash., June 15, 1949; d. Leslie Harlan and Emma Cecelia (Johnson) Johnson; m. Mark Lesley Farmer; 1 child, Christopher. BS in English, Whitman Coll., 1971; MLS, U. N.C., 1972; EdD, Temple U., 1981. Cert. tchr., Calif. Info. specialist Balt. County Pub. Library, Randallstown, Md., 1972-73; tech. librarian Singer Bus. Machines, San Leandro, Calif., 1974-75; instr., librarian Peace Corps, Tunis, Tunisia, 1975-77; media specialist Archdiocese Phila., 1977-81; asst. prof. Va. Commonwealth U., Richmond, 1981-82; young adult librarian Meml. Library Radnor Twp., Wayne, Pa., 1982-83; library dir. San Domenico Sch., San Anselmo, Calif., 1984—; adj. prof. Villanova (Pa.) U., 1982-83, San Jose State U., 1988—; speaker Calif. Library Assn., 1987; cons. Va. Dept. Edn., 1981-82, Marin County (Calif.) Office Edn., 1984-87. Editor: Media and the Young Adult, 1985; contbr. articles on library sci. to profl. jours. Chair Marin County Council Girl Scouts USA, 1986-88. Grantee NEH, 1986, Marin County Computer Edn. Consortium, 1984-86. Mem. ALA (chair young adult scvs. div. rsch. com. 1985-88, chair young adults svcs. div. computer applications com. 1985-88), Calif. Library Assn., Calif. Media and Library Educators Assn., Cath. Library Assn. (sect. pres. 1989—), Marin County Reference Network (chair 1987-88). Democrat. Roman Catholic. Home: 135 Golden Hind Passage Corte Madera CA 94925 Office: San Domenico Sch 1500 Butterfield Rd San Anselmo CA 94960

FARMER, MARY BAUDER, nurse practitioner; b. San Diego, Nov. 30, 1953; d. Chester Robert and Dixie (Cook) Bauder. BS, Auburn U., 1986. Exec. dir. Birmingham Woman's Med. Clinic, Ala., 1975-80; pres. Beacon Clinic, Montgomery, Ala., 1980-83; ptnr. Hill, Rose and Farmer, Atlanta, 1988—. Exec. dir. The Abortion Fund, Washington, 1978-83. Named Outstanding Young Woman of Am. Mem. Ga. Women's Agenda (founder, 1982—), LWV (mem. action com. 1982-86), Bus. Com. for the Arts, Planned Parenthood of Greater Atlanta (bd. dirs.), ODK. Democrat. Office: Hill Rose and Farmer 1810 Rockridge Pl N E Atlanta GA 30324

FARMER-DOUGAN, VALERI ANN, psychologist; b. Everett, Wash., Apr. 28, 1960; d. Richard Gary and Janice Ruth (McKay) Farmer; m. James Dudley Dougan, Dec. 28, 1985; 1 child, Erin-Kathryn. BA in Psychology, Western Wash. U., 1982; MS in Psychology, Wash. State U., 1984, PhD in Psychology, 1985. Rsch. coord. Walden Learning Ctr., U. Mass., Amherst, 1985-86; vis. asst. prof. dept. psychology Ind. U., Bloomington, 1986-90; behavioral mng. cons. Options for Better Living, Bloomington, 1986-90, Stone Belt ARC, Bloomington, 1988-90; acad. dir. The Hammitt Sch. of the Babyfold, Normal, Ill., 1990—; chair curriculum com. Bloomington Devel. Learning Ctr., 1989-90; presenter in field. Coach Spl. Programs Swimming, Bloomington, 1986, Spl. Olympics Soccer, Bloomington, 1986-88. Recipient Faculty of Week award Psi Chi, Ind. U., 1989, Student Choice Faculty award Ind. U., 1990. Mem. Am. Psychol. Assn., Assn. for Behavior Analysis, Am. Psychol. Soc., Assn. for Retarded Citizens. Roman Catholic. Office: The Hammitt School 108 E Willow St Normal IL 61761

FARNI, SUSAN HAZEL, public information officer; b. Avon Park, Fla., May 8, 1949; d. Elbert Dawson Jr. and Ann Elizabeth (Lock) Charpie; m. Michael Bruce Farni, Aug. 11, 1965; children: Natalie, Shonn, Courtland, Trent. Grad., Elcamino Coll., Torrance, Calif., 1970; student, U. S. Ala., 1985--. Controls research coordinator Hughes Aircraft, Los Angeles, 1969-70; jr. programmer Ingalls Shipbuilding, Pascagoula, MS, 1970-73; self employed contract programmer Mobile, Ala., 1973-76; programmer, analyst I Mobile (Ala.) Police Dept.; programmer, analyst II City of Mobile, 1978-81; self employed cons. Mobile, 1981-85; dir. info. systems City of Mobile, 1985--. Pres. Mothers of Twins, 1981, Exec. Women's Forum, Mobile, 1989. Mem. Nat. Assn. Female Execs., Gov. Mgmt. Info. Sciences (pres. 1987), Ala. Telecommunications Mgmt. Assn., Southeastern Telecommunications Assn., Christian Women's Club. Republican. Baptist. Home: PO Box 589 Grand Bay AL 36541 Office: City of Mobile 350 St Joseph Rm 244 Mobile AL 36602

FARNSWORTH, CHERRILL KAY, corporate executive; b. Indpls., Oct. 11, 1948; d. John Walter and Winona (Revis) Bowers; m. T. Brooke Farnsmworth, Aug. 24, 1968; children: Leslie Erin, T. Brooke Jr. BS magna cum laude, Butler U., 1970. Pres., chief exec. officer Suburban Transp. Svcs., Inc., Houston, 1974-76, Dorill Enterprises, Inc., Houston, 1976-85, Maxworth Investments, Houston, 1979-85, F&L Ventures, Inc., Houston, 1982-85; chmn. bd., pres., chief exec. officer TME, Inc., Houston, 1984—. Mem. N.W. Rep. Club, Houston, 1988—, Performing Ars League, Houston, 1984—. Named one of Women on the Move, Houston Post, 1986. Mem. Am. Assn. Ambulatory Care Profls., NAFE, Am. Mgmt. Assn., Soc. Magnetic Resonance Imaging, Tex. Exec. Women, Regents. Office: TME Inc 333 N Belt Ste 500 Houston TX 77060

FARNSWORTH, ELLEN JANE, nurse; b. Boston, May 8, 1943; d. Edward Louis and Ellen Jane (McConnell) Lynsky; m. Richard Ransom Farnsworth, Dec. 16, 1967; children: Richard Edward, Ian Scott, Ellen Jane. Diploma in nursing, New Eng. Bapt. Hosp., 1964; BS in Nursing, Boston U., 1968; MEd, Temple U., 1990. Cert. childbirth educator. Staff nurse Children's Hosp. Med. Ctr., Boston, 1965-67; staff nurse New Eng.

Bapt. Hosp., Boston, 1964-65, clin. instr., 1967-68; educator Lamaze childbirth Columbus (Ohio) Assn. Childbirth Edn., 1969-71; pvt. practice educator Lamaze childbirth Presque Isle, Maine, 1972-76, Haddonfield, N.J., 1977-82; clin. instr. Meth. Hosp., Phila., 1977-78; nurse Temple U. Health Svc., Phila., 1981-90; head nurse Temple U. Hosp., Phila., 1990—; co-founder, pres. Greater Camden Area Am. Soc. Psychoprophylaxis Obstetrics Inc., Blackwood, N.J., 1979-81; trainer Am. Soc. Psychoprophylaxis Obstetrics, Washington, 1979-81. V.p. Haddonfield Home Sch. Assn., 1979-81; dir. Peat Players, Phila., 1988-89. Recipient Mead Johnson award Nurses Ednl. Found., 1965; named Mass. Student Nurse of Yr., Mass. Student Nurses Assn., 1964. Mem. Am. Nurses Assn., AAUW (v.p. Presque Isle chpt. 1974-76), Southeastern Pa. Coll. Health Assn. (chair nominating com. 1986), Sigma Theta Tau, Eta Sigma Gamma.

FARNSWORTH, JANICE L., personal care industry executive; b. Parkersburg, W.Va., July 24, 1938; d. Robert Price Doyle and Wahneta Viola Andrews; m. Denzil F. Farnsworth, Mar. 12, 1956; children: Dana, Russell, Gregory, Steven, Sherri. Student, Parkersburg Community Coll., 1978. Lic. instr. cosmetology; advanced color cert. Mgr., instr. cosmetology Parkersburg Beauty Coll., 1983-87; master designer J.B. White's Hairstyle Ctr., Columbia, S.C., 1988-89; prin. Total Spectrum, Irmo, S.C., 1990—. Author poetry. Recipient scholarship to Clairol Internat. Mem. AARP, NAFER, Nat. Assn. Cosmetology. Democrat. Mem. Ch. of Christ. Home: PO Box 524 Lexington SC 29072

FARNSWORTH, MARJORIE ANNE WHYTE, retired genetics educator; b. Detroit, Nov. 18, 1921; d. Thomas Callan and Anna Irene (Carter) Whyte; m. Wells Eugene Farnsworth, Sept. 15, 1945; children: Samuel B., Marjorie W. BA, Mt. Holyoke Coll., 1944; MS, Cornell U., 1946; PhD, U. Mo., 1951. Lectr. zoology U. Mo., Columbia, 1946-49, AEC predoctoral fellow zoology, 1949-50, asst. prof. zoology, 1950-52; cancer cytologist Roswell Park Meml. Inst., Buffalo, 1952-53; lectr., rsch. assoc. U. Buffalo, 1953-64; assoc. prof. SUNY, Buffalo, 1964-78; adj. prof. SUNY, Buffalo, 1978-81. Author: Young Woman's Guide to Academic Career, 1974, Genetics, 1978, 2d edit., 1988; contbr. articles on devel./biochem. genetics of drosophila to profl. jours. Rsch. grantee U. Buffalo, 1954-60, NIH rsch. grantee SUNY, Buffalo, 1960-75. Home: 3 Elm Creek Dr 316 Elmhurst IL 60126

FARNSWORTH, SUSAN ELIZABETH, chemical company executive; b. Concord, Mass., Apr. 5, 1955; d. Calvin Mackintosh and Lois Mae (Nelson) F. AB, Dartmouth Coll., 1977; MBA, U. Chgo., 1981. Fin. analyst organic chems. div. W.R. Grace & Co., Lexington, Mass., 1981-83, sr. fin. analyst, 1983-84, mgr. bus. planning, 1984-86, contr., 1986, v.p. fin., 1986-90; v.p. fin. Dewey and Almy chems. div. W.R. Grace & Co., Woburn, Mass., 1990—. Nat. Merit scholar, 1973, FMC Corp. scholar, 1980. Mem. Beta Gamma Sigma. Office: WR Grace & Co Dewey and Almy Chems Div 77 Dragon Ct Woburn MA 01888

FARNSWORTH, SUSAN STEELE HIGGINS, writer; b. New Braunfels, Tex., Sept. 8, 1949; d. Walter Sayers and Marian Louise (Schumann) Higgins; B.J., U. Tex., Austin, 1971; m. Dan Collins Farnsworth, Jan. 26, 1974; 1 son, Christopher Sayers. Editor, The Greater Houston Tchrs. Jour., Media Am. Inc., 1973; tax editor/editorial supr. Peat, Marwick, Mitchell & Co., N.Y.C., 1974-77; copywriter Cannon Advt. Agy., N.Y.C., 1977; columnist The News Tribune, Woodbridge, N.J., 1977-79; writer Peat, Marwick, Mitchell & Co., N.Y.C., 1977-78, Alden & Assocs., N.Y.C., 1979-80; writer/communications cons. Peat, Marwick, Mitchell & Co., Dallas, 1979-82; dir. profl. services unit Hill and Knowlton, Inc., Dallas, 1982; owner Farnsworth & Assocs., Miami, Dallas, Phoenix, 1977—; cons. Holland & Knight, Fla. and Washington, 1983-84, Harrison & Lerch, Phoenix, 1985-86, State of Ariz., 1986-87. Named Outstanding Advt. Student, U. Tex., Austin, 1970-71. John E. McGary scholar. Mem. Nat. Assn. Female Execs. Episcopalian. Contbr. articles to profl. jours. Home: 517 Arbor Oak Dr Grapevine TX 76051 Office: Thanksgiving Tower 1601 Elm St Dallas TX 75201

FARNUM, SYLVIA ARLYCE, physical chemist; b. St. Paul, Dec. 29, 1936; d. Henry H. and Esther H. (Mettler) Ebel; m. Bruce W. Farnum, June 6, 1959; 1 child, Julie Faith. BS in Chemistry, N.D. State U., 1958, MS in Biochemistry, 1959; PhD in Phys. Chemistry, U. N.D., 1979. Instr. chemistry Washington Coll., Chestertown, Md., 1960-61; chemist interior ballistics rsch. U.S. Army, Aberdeen, Md., 1961-62; rsch. assoc. U. Del., Wilmington, 1962-64; faculty mem. chemistry Minot (N.D.) State Coll., 1964-76; rsch. supr. process chemistry Energy Rsch. Ctr., Grand Forks, N.D., 1978-86; analytical rsch. specialist 3M, St. Paul, 1986—. Contbr. to numerous books and tech. publs. Mem. Am. Chem. Soc. (past sec. fuel div. 1985-87, polymer div., polymeric material sci. and engring. div.), African Violet Soc. Am. (life), Sigma Xi. Office: 3M 3M Center 236-2B-11 Saint Paul MN 55144

FAROKHI, (HELEN) ELIZABETH DUPREE, university official; b. Augusta, Ga., Feb. 16, 1948; d. Walker Leonard and Helen (Ouzts) Dupree; m. Nasrolah Rashid Farokhi, Nov. 30, 1974; children: Amir Reza Rashid, Arman Rashid. BA, LaGrange Coll., 1970; MAT, Emory U., 1974; EdD, U. Ga., 1978. Instr. adult edn. Atlanta-Fulton County Bd. Edn., 1975-77; tchr. Cobb County Ga. Bd. Edn., Marietta, 1970-76; research asst. Inst. of Higher Edn., U. Ga., Athens, 1976-77; intern with acad. dean Clayton Jr. Coll., Morrow, Ga., 1977; high edn. cons. Clayton Jr. Coll. (now Clayton State Coll.), Morrow, 1978, Profl. Standards Commn., Atlanta, 1979-80, Govs. Com. on Postsecondary Edn., Atlanta, 1978-82; asst. coord. spl. projects Ga. Career Info. System, Ga. State U., Atlanta, 1982-83; curriculum and scheduling coord. Ga. State U., Atlanta, 1983—; conf. facilitator Assn. of Tchr. Edn. Nat. Conv., Atlanta, 1986, workshop presentation Nat. Women's Studies Assn. Ann. Conf., Atlanta, 1987, South Atlantic Regional AAUW Conf. Athens, 1988. Svc. Coun. Allocations Com. Atlanta United Way, 1988—, bd. trustees Galloway Sch., Atlanta, 1988—, pres. Galloway Sch. Parent's Assn., 1988—, numerous other positions, 1984-88. Mem. Ga. Assn. Tchr. Educators, Ga. Assn. for Supr. and Curriculm Devel., Internat. Fedn. U. Women, Am. Assn. U. Women (State div., program v.p. 1989—), U. Women (Cobb County bd. pres. 1986-88, program v.p., 1983-85, bulletin editor 1982-83), Kappa Delta Pi. Republican. Methodist. Home: 101 Hunting Creek Dr Marietta GA 30068

FARQUHAR, KAREN LEE, business forms company executive, consultant; b. Warwick, N.Y., May 27, 1958; d. Wesley Thomas and Margaret Anne (Storms) Kervatt; m. David W. Farquhar, July 17, 1982 (div. Feb. 1990); 1 child, Lauren Nichole. Assoc. Sci., Roger Williams Coll., 1978, BS cum laude, 1980. Office mgr. Price-Rite Printing Co., Dover, N.J., summer 1975-76; cons. SBA, Bristol, R.I., 1978-80; account exec. P.M. Press Inc., Dallas, 1980-90, sales trainer, 1984-85; v.p. KDF Bus. Forms Inc., Dallas, Tex., 1984-90; account exec. Jarvis Press, Dallas, 1990—; pres. Print Trends, Dallas, 1990—. Printer, Tex. Aux. Charity Auction Orgn., Dallas, 1985, Crescent Gala, Dallas, 1986, Cystic Fibrosis, Dallas, 1989—. Recipient various awards Clampitt Paper Co., Dallas, 1982, P.M. Press Inc., 1983-89, Mead Paper Co., 1985-89. Mem. Printing Industry in Am., Internat. Assn. Bus. Communicators, Nat. Bus. Forms Assn. Republican. Baptist. Avocations: piano, aerobics. Home: 429 Dillard Ln Coppell TX 75019

FARQUHAR, MARILYN GIST, pathology educator; b. Tulare, Calif., July 11, 1928; d. Brooks DeWitt and Alta (Green) Gist; m. John W. Farquhar, June 4, 1952; children: Bruce, Douglas (div. 1968); m. George Palade, June 7, 1970. AB, U. Calif., Berkeley, 1949, MA, 1952, PhD, 1955. Asst. rsch. pathologist Sch. Medicine U. Calif., San Francisco, 1956-58, assoc. rsch. pathologist, 1962-64, assoc. prof., 1964-68, prof. pathology, 1968-70; rsch. assoc. Rockefeller U., N.Y.C., 1958-62, prof. cell biology, 1970-73; prof. cell biology Sch. Medicine Yale U., New Haven, 1973-87, Sterling prof. cell biology and pathology, 1987-90; prof. pathology div. cell molecular medicine U. Calif., San Diego, 1990—. Mem. editorial bd. numerous sci. jours.; contbr. articles to profl. jours. Recipient Career Devel. award NIH, 1968-73, Disting. Sci. medal Electron Microscope Soc., 1987. Mem. NAS, Am. Soc. Cell Biology (pres. 1981-82, E.B. Wilson medal 1987), Am. Assn. Pathologists, Am. Soc. Nephrologists (Homer Smith award 1988). Home: 12894 Via Latina Del Mar CA 92014

FARR, BEVERLY AGNES, shoe manufacturing company official; b. Middleboro, Mass., Dec. 6, 1928; d. George Sampson and Bertha Josephine (Duffany) Barney; m. Stanley Thomas Farr, May 30, 1949 (dec. Mar. 1987); 1 child, Paul Thomas. A.A., Arlington Acad. Music, 1947. Prodn. clk. W.L. Douglas Shoe Co., Brockton, Mass., 1948-49; customer service rep. Commonwealth Shoe, Whitman, Mass., 1950-51; schedule and prodn. dept. Knapp Shoe Co., Brockton, 1951-53; asst. to office mgr. Givren Shoe Co., Rockland, Mass., 1953-54, Porter Shoe Co., Milford, Mass., 1954-57; purchasing mgr., leather buyer Foot-Joy, Inc., Brockton, 1957—, dir. purchasing, 1988—. Com. mem. Conservation Commn., Halifax, Mass., 1979. Mem. NAFE. Republican. Club: Boot & Shoe (com. mem., v.p., 1st woman pres. 1990). Avocations: aerobics, swimming. Home: 27 Cedar Ln PO Box 493 Halifax MA 02338 Office: Foot-Joy Inc 144 Field St Brockton MA 02403

FARR, IVANNE E., business owner, sculptor; b. Texarkana, Ark., Feb. 7, 1940; d. Franklin Lynnwood and Leone Faye (Seedig) F.; m. William D. Alsup, Aug. 27, 1960 (div. Aug. 1975); children: Joe, Mark De Witt, Lara LeAnne. Cert., Gemological Inst. Am., 1979. Founder, owner Ivanne et Cie, Inc., Corpus Christi, Tex., 1976—; v.p. Internat. Agri-Ventures, Inc., Corpus Christi, 1985—; cons. C.I.C.C., Inc., Montreal, Can., 1985, Mexican Jewellers Assn., Mexico City, 1988, Jireh Resources, Inc., Paris, 1988. Mem. Mus. Oriental Culture; bd. dirs. Chem. Dependency Unit South Tex., Coastal Bend Youth City, Palmer Drug Abuse Program,; bd. of govs., chmn. membership com. Art Mus. South Tex.; bd. of govs., co-founder Alliance for Justice Found., Inc. Mem. Gemological Inst. Am., Gulf Coast Conservation Assn., Inst. Tex. Cultures, Jewelers Assn. Am., Marine Mil. Acad. Parents Assn., Navy League (bd. dirs.), Norwegian Soc. Tex., PTA, Scandinavian Soc. South Tex. (co-founder), Tex. Jewelers Assn., Internat. Group (co-founder), Corpus Christi C. of C., Corpus Christi Area Econ. Devel. Corp. (internat. com.), Ducks Unltd., Mid-Morning Group (co-founder). Republican. Episcopalian.

FARR, JO-ANN HUNTER, psychologist; b. Brackenridge, Pa., Apr. 29, 1936; d. Francis Lytle and Dorothy (Colin) Hunter; m. William R. Hughes (div.); children: Cynthia Jo O'Hora, William Hunter, Christopher Eric, Michael Patrick, Amy Elizabeth; m. John E. Farr (div.); 1 child, John Herschel; m. James K. Medeiros, June 10, 1984. BS in Psychology and Physiology, Pa. State U., 1970, MS in Psychology, 1971, PhD in Psychology, 1974. Diplomate Am. Bd. Sexology. Dir., therapist Devel. Vision Ctr., State College, Pa., 1969-71; cons. Pk. Forest Nursery Sch., State College, Pa., 1970-71; in-take supr. psychol. clin. Pa. State U., University Park, 1972-73; cons. Centre County Youth Svc. Bur., State College, 1972-78, Juniata Tri-County Mental Health/Mental Retardation Adminstrn., Lewistown, Pa., 1974-76; asst. prof. of psychology Pa. State U., 1975-77; pvt. practice State College, 1977—; sponsored NIMH guest lectr. Kinsey Inst., Bloomington, Ind. Contbr. articles to profl. jours. Mem. Govs. Counsel for Sexual Minorities, Pa.; bd. dirs. Pa. Assoc. of Families, State Coll., Parents Without Ptnrs., State Coll. John W. White fellow Pa. State U., 1970-71, U.S. Pub. Health Svc. fellow Pa. State U., 1970-74; nominated Outstanding Pennsylvanian State Dept. of Health adm Welfare, 1986. Mem. Sex Info. and Edn. Coun. of U.S. (assoc. mem.), Am. Psychol. Assn. (full mem.), Assn. for Advancement of Behavior Therapy (full mem.), Soc. for Sci. Study of Sex (full mem.), Am. Soc. Sex Educators, Counselors, and Therapists (full mem.), Assn. Behavior Analysis (full mem.), Pa. Psychol. Assn. (full mem.), Nat. Register Health Svc. Providers, Mental Health Profs. of Cen. Pa. Office: Jo-Ann Hunter Farr & Assocs 3490 W College Ave State College PA 16801

FARR, M. PAIGE, construction company executive; b. Carlisle, Pa., Sept. 26, 1945; d. Harold Monroe and Jane Arthur Eugenia (Kean) LeBell; m. Joseph Farr, May 18, 1984. BA in Psychology summa cum laude, Mercy Coll., Dobbs Ferry, N.Y., 1983. Bookkeeping asst. Trumid Constrn. Co. Inc., Yonkers, N.Y., 1970-72, office mgr., 1972-76, corp. sec., 1976-79; v.p. JayVal Contracting Corp., Tarrytown and Peekskill, N.Y., 1979-83, Farr-Guarino Contracting Corp., White Plains, N.Y., 1983—; pres. Farr Crest Excavating Corp., East White Plains, N.Y., 1987—. Mem. Catskill Center. Mem. Contractors Assn. Westchester, Putnam and Dutchess Counties, N.Y. State Conservation Officer Assn., Catskill Forest Assn., Port Chester Obedience Tng. Club. Republican. Office: Farr-Guarino Contracting Corp 128 Fulton St White Plains NY 10606

FARR, PATRICIA HUDAK, librarian; b. Youngstown, Ohio, Mar. 10, 1945; d. Frank Francis and Anna Frances (Tylka) Hudak; m. William Howard Farr, Aug. 28, 1971; children: Jennifer Anne, William Patrick. BA, Youngstown State U., 1970; MLS, U. Md., 1980. Children's libr. Pub. Libr. Youngstown and Mahoning (Ohio), 1970-71; asst. Fla. State U. Libr. Tallahassee, 1971-73; rsch. asst. John Hopkins U. Sch. Hygiene and Pub. Health, Balt., 1974-76; asst. Mary Washington Coll. Libr., Fredericksburg, Va., 1976-79; children's libr. Cen. Rappahannock Regional Libr., Fredericksburg, 1980-84, young adult svcs. coord., 1984-89, youth svcs. libr., 1989—. Revision editor HEW pub. Thesaurus of Health Edn. Terminology, 1976; compiler Health Edn. Monographs, 1974-76. Youngstown State U. scholar, 1963-64; R.V. Lowery Meml. scholar, 1979-80. Mem. ALA, Va. Libr. Assn. Democrat. Episcopalian. Club: Rappahannock Twirlers Square Dance. Home: 618 Kings Hwy Fredericksburg VA 22405 Office: Cen Rappahannock Regional Library 1201 Caroline St Fredericksburg VA 22401

FARR, SIDNEY SAYLOR, editor, author; b. Stoney Fork, Ky., Oct. 30, 1932; d. Richard and Rachel (Saylor) S.; m. Leon Lawson, Feb. 23, 1947 (div. July 1968); children: Dennis Wayne, Bruce Alan; m. Grover V. Farr, Jan. 24, 1970. BA, Berea Coll., 1980. Assoc. editor Coun. of the So. Mountains, Berea, Ky., 1964-69; editor This Week in Asheville (N.C.) Daniels Graphics, 1970-71; editor Appalachian Heritage Berea Coll., 1985—. Author: (annotated bibliography) Appalachian Women, 1981, (narrative cookbook) More Than Moonshine, 1983. Mem. AAUW, Kiwanis (bd. mem.). Democrat. Home: 109 High St Berea KY 40403 Office: Berea Coll Berea KY 40403

FARRAR, BEVERLY JAYNE, psychologist; b. Albuquerque, N.M., Nov. 6, 1928; d. Jack Murphy and Jane Clark; m. R.L. Farrar, July 1, 1949; 1 child, Dorothy. BA, Southern Methodist U., 1949, MA, 1967; MED, East Texas U., 1972. Tchr. Allen Independent Sch. Dist., Allen, Tex., 1949; instr. Sam Houston State U., Huntsville, Tex., 1949-51; tchr. Houston Ind. Sch. Dist., Houston, Tex., 1951-52, Dallas Ind. Sch. Dist., Dallas, Tex., Houston Ind. Sch. Dist., Houston, Tex., 1953-55, Harlingen Ind. Sch. Dist., Tex., 1957-63; speech pathologist Longview Ind. Sch. Dist., Tex., 1963-69; tchr. Dallas Ind. Sch. Dist., Tex., 1969-71; assoc. Sch. psychologist Richardson Ind. Sch. Dist., Richardson, Tex., 1971–. Co-author, Early Childhood Pre-School Screening Test for Richardson Sch., 1973, Handbook For Classroom Management For Richardson Sch., 1980. Mem. AAUW, Assn. Tex. Prof. Educators, Am. Speech, Language and Hearing Assn., Pi Lambda Theta, Phi Delta Kappa, Delta Kappa Gamma (State Achievement award 1986). Republican. Methodist. Home: 10220 Mapleridge Dr Dallas TX 75238 Office: Richardson Ind Sch Dist 400 Greenville Richardson TX 75080

FARRAR, ELAINE WILLARDSON, artist; b. L.A., Feb. 27, 1929; d. Eldon and Gladys Elsie (Larsen) Willardson; BA, Ariz. State U., 1967, MA, 1969, now doctoral candidate; children: Steve, Mark, Gregory, Leslie Jean, Monty, Susan. Tchr., Camelback Desert Sch., Paradise Valley, Ariz., 1966-69; mem. faculty Yavapai Coll., Prescott, Ariz., 1970—, chmn. dept. art, 1973-78, instr. art in watercolor and oil and acrylic painting; intaglio, relief and monoprints, 1971—; one-man shows include: R.P. Moffat's, Scottsdale, Ariz., 1969, Art Center, Battle Creek, Mich., 1969, The Woodpeddler, Costa Mesa, Calif., 1979; group show Prescott (Ariz.) Fine Arts Assn., 1982, 84, 86, 89, N.Y. Nat. Am. Watercolorists, 1982; Ariz. State U. Women Images Now, 1986, 87, 89, 90; works rep. local and state exhibits; supt. fine arts dept. County Fair; com. mem., hanging chmn. Scholastic Art Awards; owner studio/gallery Willis Street Artists, Prescott. Mem. AAUW, Mountain Artists Guild (past pres.), Nat. League Am. Pen Women (Prescott br.), Ariz. Art Edn. Assn., Nat. Art Edn. Assn., Ariz. Coll. and Univ. Faculty Assn., Verde Valley Art Assn., Ariz. Women's Caucus for Art, Women's Nat. Mus. (charter Washington chpt.), Kappa Delta Pi, Phi Delta Kappa. Republican. Mormon. Home: 535 Copper Basin Rd Prescott AZ 86303 Office: Yavapai Coll Art Dept 1100 E Sheldon Rd Prescott AZ 86301

FARRAR, PAULINE ELIZABETH, accountant, real estate broker; b. Madison, Wis., July 2, 1928; d. William Charles and Mary Anna (Killalley) Selmer; m. James Walter Byers, Aug. 15, 1950 (dec. June 1972); children: Marvin Lee, Marjorie Sue; m. Robert Bascom Farrar, Apr. 14, 1974; stepchildren: Katrinka Jo Farrar Sandahl, Jon Randle Farrar. Student, U. Wis., 1946-49, U. Houston, 1956-57. Acct. Sterling Hogan, Houston, 1951-54, Lester Prokop, Houston, 1959-64, Holland Mortgage Co., Houston, 1964-68, Jetero Bldg Corp., Houston, 1968-71; real estate assoc. Mills Paulea Realtors, Houston, 1976-80, ERA, Nelson & Assocs., Missouri City, Tex., 1980-81; owner, broker Realty Execs., Ft. Bend and Sugar Land, Tex., 1981—; tax assesor, collector Sequoia Utility Dist., Houston, 1969-71. Leader Girl Scouts U.S.A., Houston, 1962-72; organizer, coordinator ladies program Stafford (Tex.) Ch. of Christ, 1978-81. Mem. Tex. Assn. Realtors (bd. dirs. 1986-87, v.p. 1986-87), Cert. Real Estate Brokers (v.p. Tex. chpt., sec.-treas. 1988-90, chpt. regional v.p.), Ft. Bend Counyy Bd. Realtors (pres. 1987—, gov. River Bend coun. 1990-91), Women's Coun. Realtors (founding chmn. Ft. Bend/S.W. Houston chpt. 1986, Tex. chpt. 1990, pres. 1988), Nat. Realtors Inst. (cert. residential specialist, cert. real estate broker, grad. realtors instr., Leadership Tng. Grad.). Office: Realty Execs 6730 Hwy 6 Sugar Land TX 77478

FARRELL, ANNE VAN NESS, foundation president; b. Peking, China, July 17, 1935; came to U.S. 1935; d. C. Peter and Virginia (Cheatham) Van Ness; m. E. Robert Farell, June 17, 1955; children: Virginia Farrell Day and Susan Farrell Johnson. BA, U. Wash., 1960. Dir. dev. Seattle Children's Home, Seattle, 1978-80; exec. v.p. The Seattle Found., Seattle, 1980-84, pres., chief. exec. officer, 1984—; dir. Council on Found. Wash., 1986—, Nat. Charities Info. Bur. N.Y.C., 1988—, Girl Scouts USA N.Y.C., 1974-83. Author: Puget Soundings, 1989. Regent Seattle U., 1986—; bd. dirs. Independent Sector, Wash., 1990—, Nature Conservancy, 1990—. Recipient Community Service Award YWCA Seattle, 1984, Girl Scout of the Year Girl Scouts, Seattle, 1986–. Mem. Pacific N.W. Grantmakers Forum (pres. 1984-85), N.W. Devel. Officers Assn. (pres. 1983-84), Wash. Women's Forum, Seattle, Jr. League, Greater Seattle C. of C. (mem. exec. com. 1987—). Republican. Episcopalian. Home: 1616 Lake Washington Blvd Seattle WA 98122 Office: The Seattle Found 425 Pike St Suite 510 Seattle WA 98101

FARRELL, JUNE ELEANOR, retired educator; b. Ft. Atkinson, Wis., Dec. 31, 1916; d. Isaac Leslie and Thora Eleanor (Huppert) Winter; m. Martin Joseph Farrell, Sept. 21, 1946; children: Leslie June Kathryn, Robert Joseph. BA, DePauw U., Green Castle, Ind., 1939. Cert. secondary tchr., Fla. Tchr. English Elmore (Ind.) Twp. High Sch., 1939-41, Beach Grove High Sch., Indpls., 1941-46, Ft. Atkinson (Wis.) Jr. High Sch., 1966-67, Venice (Fla.) Jr. High Sch., 1967-82; tchr. sci. Venice Area Mid. Sch., 1982-89, ret., 1989. Contbr. articles to profl. jours. Pres., Friends of Venice Community Ctr., 1984—. Mem. Sarasoto County Reading Coun. (pres. 1974-76), Sarasota County Tchrs. English (treas. 1975-79), Alpha Delta Kappa (pres. Omicron chpt. 1976-78, alturistic chmn. 1986-90), Delta Zeta. Republican. Methodist. Home: 640 W Venice Ave Venice FL 34285 also: 603 Van Buren St Fort Atkinson WI 53538

FARRELL, JUNE MARTINICK, public relations executive; b. New Brunswick, N.J., June 30, 1940; d. Ivan and Mary (Tomkovich) M.; B.S. in Journalism, Ohio U., 1962; M.S. in Public Relations, Am. U., Washington, 1977; m. Duncan G. Farrell, July 31, 1971. Public relations asst. Corning Glass Works, N.Y.C., 1963-65; assoc. beauty editor Good Housekeeping mag., N.Y.C., 1966; public relations specialist Gt. Am. Ins. Co., N.Y.C., 1967-68; assoc. editor Ea. Airlines, N.Y.C., 1968-82, regional public relations mgr., Washington, 1976-82; public relations dir. Nat. Captioning Inst., Falls Church, Va., 1982-83; dir. pub. rels. programs Marriott Corp., 1984—; staff cons. Office of Public Liaison, White House, 1981-82. Creator, condr. spl. career awareness program for inner city youth, Washington, 1979-80; mem. public relations com. Jr. Achievement, 1979; motivational counselor for youth Nat. Alliance of Businessmen, 1979; bd. dirs. Am. Mgmt. Svcs., 1985—; trustee Nat. Hosp. Orthopedics and Rehab., 1984—. Mem. Soc. Am. Travel Writers (mem. pub. relations com.), Am. Soc. Travel Agts., Travel Industry Assn. Am. (nat. conf. planning com., pub. relations com.), Women in Communication, Phi Mu. Republican. Clubs: Zonta, Internat. Aviation. Home: 6630 Lybrook Ct Bethesda MD 20817 Office: Marriot Hotels/Resorts One Marriott Dr Washington DC 20058

FARRELL, NAOMI, editor, correspondent, nurse researcher; b. Glasgow, Scotland, Apr. 21, 1941; came to Can., 1949, USA, 1963; d. Louis and Minnie (Przestrzeleniec) F. AAS with honors, CUNY, 1970; BSN, Hunter Coll., 1973; UN studies cert., L.I. U., 1978, MS in Social Sci. and Internat. Affairs, 1979. RN. TV performer Can., 1959-63; adminstr. Health Ins. Plan, N.Y.C., 1964-65; nurse, researcher Cornell Med. Ctr., N.Y.C., 1977-80; assoc. editor Al Hoda, New Lebanese Am. Jour., N.Y.C., 1979—; UN corr., freelance writer Globe and Mail of Can., 1980—; cons. Internat. Med. Tourism, 1985. Author numerous articles and poems for newspapers and mags. Mem. internat. adv. bd. Symphony for UN, 1986. Research paper on world hunger accepted by UN Research and Tng. Library and used in Presdl. Commn. on World Hunger, Washington, 1979. Mem. UN. Corrs. Assn. (assoc. editor 1985—), Soc. Writers of UN (v.p. 1985-86), Fgn. Press Assn., UN Assn. (citation for position paper 1978), Soc. Internat. Devel., N.Y. Acad. Scis., Am. Nurses Assn. Home: 321 E 48th St New York NY 10017

FARRELL, PAMELA BARNARD, teacher; b. Mt. Holly, N.J., Oct. 11, 1943; d. George W. and Audrey (Clerihue) Barnard; m. Joseph D. Farrell. BA, Radford Coll., Radford, 1965; MS, Radford U., Radford, 1975; MA, Northeastern U., Boston, 1988. Poetry tchr./cons. Geraldine R. Dodge Found., Morristown, N.J., 1986--; coll. tchr. Woodrow Wilson Nat'l Fellowship Found., Princeton, N.J., 1987-88; English tchr. Red Bank Regional High Sch., Little Silver, N.J.; editor The Grapevine Northeastern U. Writing Newsletter, Boston, 1986—; mem. editorial bd. The Writing Ctr. Jour., Tex., Tech. U., 1987—, Computers and Composition, Purdue U., 1987—; treas. Assembly on Computers in English. Author: Waking Dreams, 1989; editor The High Sch. Writing Ctr., 1989. Mem. Nat. Writing Ctrs. Assn. (pres.). Dem. Presbyterian.

FARRELL, SUSAN FLORENCE, air traffic control training specialist; b. Bklyn, Aug. 9, 1952; d. Louis and Florence R. (Haselton) Campbell; m. Patrick Ryan Ferrell, Mar. 2, 1947; 1 child, Amanda. BS, Bklyn. Coll., Bklyn, 1979. Asst. mgr. Macy's, Bklyn., 1970-78; museum instr. N.Y. Hall of Science, Queens, N.Y., 1974-81; tchr. N.Y.C. Bd. Edn., Queens, 1981; air traffic control specialist Fed. Aviation Administrn., Queens. Bd. mem. co-op bd. dirs. Queens, 1979-89, bd. sec., 1982-88, bd. pres., 1988-89. Recipient Cert. Appreciation Mayor's Voluntary Action Coalation, N.Y.C., 1981; Sherwood Villiage Corp., Queens, 1982; 110th Police Precinct Queens, 1983; N.Y. Neighborhood Action Coalition N.Y.C., 1984; FAA, 1986, 89. Mem. Amatuer Observers Soc. N.Y.C. Democratic. Episcopalian. Home: 590 Mead Terr North Baldwin NY 11550 Office: FAA Control Tower Bldg 155 6th Fl Jamaica NY 11430

FARRELL, SUZANNE, ballerina; b. Cin.; d. Robert Ficker and Donna (Von Holle) Holly; m. Paul Mejia, Feb. 21, 1969. Studies with Marian LaCour, Cin. Conservatory Music; LHD (hon.), Georgetown U., 1984, Fordham U., 1987, Notre Dame U., 1990; DFA (hon.), Yale U., 1988; D of Performing Arts (hon.), U. Cin., 1990. hon. lectr. dance U. Cin.; mem. faculty Sch. Am. Ballet. With N.Y. City Ballet, 1961-69, 75-89, became featured dancer, 1962, prin. dancer, 1965-69; appeared in film version Midsummer Night's Dream; Bejart Ballet of 20th Century, Brussels, 1971-75; created roles in other ballets Ah, Vous Dirais Je, Maman?; Juliet in Romeo and Juliet; The Young Girl in Rose in Nijinsky; Clown of God, 1971, Bolero, The Rite of Spring; Laura in I Trionfi; N.Y.C. Ballet in New Ravel Festival, Tzigane, In G Major, 1976; featured in TV show: Balanchine Dance in Am., Parts I-IV; author: (autobiography) Holding on to the Air, 1990. Recipient Merit award Mademoiselle mag., 1965, Dance mag. award, 1976, award of honor for arts and culture N.Y.C., 1979, Spirit Achievement award Albert Einstein Coll. Medicine, 1980, Emmy award, 1985, Golden Plate award Am. Acad. of Achievement, 1987, N.Y. State Gov.'s Arts award, 1988. Office: NYC Ballet Inc NY State Theater Lincoln Ctr Pla New York NY 10023

FARRELLY, SUZETTE L., public relations coordinator; b. New Orleans, Dec. 7, 1964; d. Durel Anthony and Rae Ann (Guerchoux) Legendre; m. Timohty P. Farrelly, Dec. 30, 1988. BA in Communications, Loyola U., New Orleans, 1986. Program coord. Women's Health Found. La., New Orleans, 1986-87; mktg., pub. rels. asst. AMI St. Jude Med. Ctr., Kenner,

La., 1987-89; pub. rels. coord. AMI St. Jude Med. Ctr., Kenner, 1989—. Mem. Knner Profl. Women's Assn., St. Jude Women's Health Found. (treas. 1987—), Women in Communication, East Jefferson Bus. Assn., New Orleans Health Care Communicators, Preferred Bus. Assn. Roman Catholic.

FARRER, CLAIRE ANNE RAFFERTY, anthropologist, educator; b. N.Y.C., Dec. 26, 1936; d. Francis Michael and Clara Anna (Guerra) Rafferty; 1 child, Suzanne Claire. BA in Anthropology, U. Calif., Berkeley, 1970; MA in Anthropology, U. Tex., 1974, PhD in Anthropology, 1977. Various positions, 1953-73; fellow Whitney M. Young Jr. Meml. Found., N.Y.C., 1974-75; arts specialist, grant adminstr. Nat. Endowment for Arts, Washington, 1976-77; Weatherhead resident fellow Sch. Am. Research, Santa Fe, 1977-78; asst. prof. anthropology U. Ill., Urbana, 1978-85; assoc. prof., coord. applied anthropology Calif. State U., Chico, 1985-89, prof., 1989—; cons. in field, 1974—; mem. film and video adv. panel Ill. Arts Coun.; mem. Ill. Humanities Coun., 1980-82; vis. prof. U. Ghent, Belgium, spring 1990. Author: Living Life's Circle: Mescalero Apache Cosmovision, 1991, Playing with Tradition, 1991; co-founder, co-editor Folklore Women's Communication, 1972; editor spl. issue Jour. Am. Folklore, 1975, 1st rev. edit., 1986; co-editor: Forms of Play of Native North Americans, 1979, Earth and Sky: Visions of the Cosmos in Native North American Folklore, 1991; contbr. numerous articles to profl. jours., mags. and newspapers, chpts. to books. Active various civic orgns. Recipient 10 awards, fellowships and grants. Fellow Am. Anthrop. Assn., Soc. for Applied Anthropology, Assn. Anthrop. Study of Play; mem. Am. Ethnol. Soc., Am. Folklore Soc., Am. Soc. Ethnohistory. Mem. Soc. of Friends. Office: Calif State U Dept Anthropology Butte 311 Chico CA 95929-0400

FARRER, ELIZABETH ANN, sales executive; b. Santa Monica, Calif., Sept. 24, 1961; d. John Allen and Eileen Anna (Auth) F. BSBA., Calif. State U., Bakersfield, 1988; BS in Interior Architecture, Calif. Poly. Inst., 1984. Mktg. rep. Sunshine Interiors, Bakersfield, 1984-85; sales rep. Am. Hosp. Supply Corp., Sunnyvale, Calif., 1985-86; sr. sales rep. Bristol-Myers U.S. Pharm., Bakersfield, 1986-89; territory mgr. Access Med. Systems, San Jose, Calif., 1989; dist. mgr. Integrated Care Systems, San Jose, 1989—. Mem. NAFE. Home: 472 9th Ave Menlo Park CA 94025

FARRIGAN, JULIA ANN, retired educational administrator, educator b. Albany, N.Y., July 19, 1943; d. Charles Gerald and Julia Tryon (Shepherd) F. BS, in Elem. Edn., SUNY Coll. at Plattsburgh, 1965; MS in Curriculum Planning and Devel., SUNY-Albany and U. Manchester (Eng.), 1973; postgrad. in adminstrv. services Calif. State U.-Fresno, 1976-78. With Monroe-Woodbury Cen. Sch. Dist., Monroe, N.Y., 1965-90; dist. coordinator gifted programs The Pine Tree Sch., 1979-90; adj. prof. Gifted Edn. Mem. AFT, NYUFT, Assn. Supervision and Curriculum Devel., N.Y. Acad. Sci., Mid-Huson Educators Gifted and Talented, Advocacy for Gifted and Talented Edn. N.Y. (state officer, editor state newsletter), DAR (William McIntosh chpt.), Monroe-Woodbury Tchr's. Assn., Delta Kappa Gamma (state asst. treas.). Democrat. Methodist. Contbr. articles in field to profl. jours.

FARRINGTON-HOPF, SUSAN KAY, plumbing and heating contractor; b. Seattle, Dec. 17, 1940; d. Donald Robert and Dorothy May (Graf) Little; m. Edwin Terry Farrington, Sept. 4, 1959 (div. Apr. 1972); children: Cathe T., Jacqueline M.; m. William Desmond Hopf, Nov. 20, 1983. BA cum laude, U.S. Internat. U., 1975, MA, 1976. Program speaker AMR Internat., N.Y.C., 1977-82; pres. Dawson Plumbing & Heating Co., Seattle, 1979—; tng. cons. Fred Sherman, Inc., San Marcos, Calif., 1982—; cons. Pacific S.W. Airlines, San Diego, 1977, Dept. Labor Job Corps, Moses Lake, Wash., 1978. Developer assertive mgmt. workshop, 1976. Mem. Seattle Execs. Assn. (bd. dirs., treas.), Am. Soc. Tng. and Devel., Nat. Assn. Plumbing Heating Cooling Contractors, Women Own Bus. Avocations: skiing, sailing, gardening. Home: 16419 261st Ave SE Issaquah WA 98027 Office: Dawson Plumbing & Heating Co 1522 12th Ave Seattle WA 98122

FARRIS, MARIE LEAZER, construction company executive; b. Gaffney, S.C.; d. S.P. and Ella Whitley Leazer; m. J.K. Farris, 1951; children: Markel, Keltner. Student, Droughes Bus. Coll., Spartanburg, S.C., Real Estate Sch., Atlanta. Cert. regional and nat. judge beauty pageants. Dir. Miss Nat. Teen Ager/Marie Farris Investments, Atlanta, Fred Astaire Dance Studio, Decatur, Ga.; pres. Farris Constrn. Co., Inc., Atlanta. Co-author: The Beauty Pageant Manual. V.p. Freedom Found. of Valley Forge. Recipient George Washington Honor medal Freedom Found. of Valley Forge, 1977. Mem. NAFE. Home: 1862 Acuba Ln Atlanta GA 30345

FARRIS, VERA KING, college president. BA in Biology magna cum laude, Tuskegee Inst., 1959; MS in Zoology, U. Mass., 1962, PhD in Zoology/Parasitology, 1965; LHD (hon.), Marymount Manhattan Coll., 1985; LLD (hon.), Monmouth Coll., West Long Branch, N.J., 1987; DSc honoris causa, Johnson and Wales Coll., 1988. Pres. Stockton State Coll., Pomona, N.J., 1983—; research assoc. U. Mich., Ann Arbor, 1965-66, instr. zoology and parasitology, 1967-68; instr. biology SUNY, Stony Brook, 1968-70, asst. prof. pathology and biology, 1970-72, assoc. prof., 1972-73, asst. to v.p. for acad. affairs, 1969-70, dean spl. programs, 1970-72; assoc. prof. biol. scis. SUNY, Brockport, 1973-77, prof., 1977-80, asst. v.p. acad. affairs, 1973, assoc. v.p. acad. affairs, 1974-77, chairperson dept. women's studies, 1975, acting dean liberal studies, 1976, acting dean social programs, 1977, acting v.p. acad. affairs, 1977-79, vice provost acad. affairs, 1979-80; prof. Kean Coll. N.J., Union, 1980-83; pres., prof. Stockton State Coll., Pomona, N.J., 1983—; speaker at schs., profl. assn., colls.; bd. dirs. Elizabethtown Gass Corp. Contbr. articles to profl. jours. Mem. adv. bd. Children's TV Workshop, N.Y.C., 1979—, Woodson Found., 1986—; apptd. to Gov.'s Commn. for Adv. Council on Holocaust Edn. in N.J., 1982—, Martin Luther King, Jr. Commemorative Commn. N.J., 1984—; mem. N.J. State Bd. Examiners, 1984—, student assistance bd. N.J. Dept. Higher Edn., 1984—; 1st vice chair N.J. Pub. Broadcasting Authority, 1984—; founding mem. Gov.'s Award Acad., 1986—; mem. commn. on minorities in higher edn. Am. Council on Edn., 1987—, bd. dirs., 1988. Recipient Meritorious Service award Brockport Students, 1980, award N.J. unit Nat. Assn. Negro Bus. and Profl. Women's Clubs, Inc., 1982, award of merit Kean Coll. Student Govt., 1982, Black History award City of Atlantic City, 1984, Kappa Alpha Psi award, 1984, award Nat. Black Women's Assn., 1984, Achievement in Edn. award NAACP, 1984, award Nat. Assn. for Equal Opportunity in Higher Edn., 1984, Presdl. citation, 1984, Service Award of Yr. Alpha Theta Lambda chpt. Alpha Phi Alpha, 1985, award Upsilon Alpha chpt. Omega Psi Phi, 1985, Humanitarian award Chapel of 4 Chaplains, 1985, Woman of Yr. award Holly Shores Girl Scouts, 1985, Disting. Community Service award Anti-Defamation League of Atlantic City B'nai B'rith, 1985, N.J. Women of Achievement award N.J. State Fedn. Women's Clubs and Douglass Coll.-Rutgers U., 1985, 86, recognition award Council of Black Faculty and Staff/Stockton State Coll., 1986, award Zulu chpt. Lambda Sigma Upsilon, 1986, cert. of appreciation B'nai B'rith, 1986, award Nat. Assn. Black Women in Higher Edn., 1986, Brotherhood/Sisterhood award South Jersey chpt. NCCJ, 1986, Educator of Yr. award Black Atlantic City Pub. Co., 1987, hon. citation Fellowship of Chs. Atlantic City, 1987, Golden Trefoil award Del. Valley council Girl Scouts U.S., 1987, People of Yr. award Galloway Twp. Edn. Found., 1988, Women's History Month award Bloomfield (N.J.) Coll. 1988; named a hon. citizen of Atlanta, 1984; named Role Model Sun Newspaper, 1988; honored as 1st Woman Coll. Pres. of N.J. by N.J. Coll. and Univ. Coalition on Women's Edn., 1983. Mem. Am. Assn. State Colls. and Univs. (com. on undergrad. edn. 1984—), Mid. States Assn. Colls. and Schs. (trustee 1982—). Home: 300 Shore Rd Linwood NJ 08221 Office: Stockton State Coll Office of Pres Pomona NJ 08240*

FARRISH, WANDA BURRUSS, small business owner, consultant; b. Page, W.Va.; d. Robert Ernest and Nancy Margaret (Settle) Burruss; m. Walter Franklin Sr., Aug. 15, 1928 (dec. Sept. 1986); 1 child, Walter Franklin Jr. Student, Beckley Coll., 1968; BS, Morris Harvey Coll., 1982. Asst. doctor's office, Oak Hill, W.Va., 1928-32; clk. variety shop, Oak Hill, 1932-41; mgr. Wanda's Variety Shoppee, Oak Hill, 1941-48, ptnr., 1948-54; owner Wanda's Bridal Shoppee, Oak Hill, 1954—; master flower show judge Nat. Coun. State Garden Club, W. Va., 1982—, master landscape critic, 1982—; bridal cons. Vol. Heart Assn., 1955-90, Fayette County Fair Assn.; past Dem. com. women Plateau Dist.; pres. Group V Oak Hill United Meth. Ch., 1975—; sch. chmn. Va. Flower Show. Recipient Woman of Yr. award Com. of Community Leaders, Oak Hill, 1954. Mem. AAUW (pres. Fayette br. 1990—), W.Va. Garden Club, Inc. (past state chmn. landscape design sch., Merit award 1987, Bee Mabely Achievement award 1989), W.Va. Flower Show Judges Coun. (v.p. 1989—), Fayette County Garden Coun. (pres. 1989—), Oak Hill Bus. and Profl. Women's Club (pres. 1990—, Woman of Yr. 1974, state membership award), Red Bud Garden Club (charter mem.), Quota Club (charter mem.). Office: Wanda's Bridal Shoppee 205 Main St Oak Hill WV 25901

FARROW, MARGARET ANN, state legislator; b. Kenosha, Wis., Nov. 28, 1934; d. William Charles and Margaret Ann (Horan) Nemitz; m. John Harvey Farrow, Dec. 29, 1956; children—John, William, Peter, Paul, Mark. Student Rosary Coll., 1952-53; B.S. in Polit. Sci., Marquette U., 1956, postgrad., 1975-77. Tchr., Archiodese of Milw., 1956-57; salesperson Bonerz Realty, Brookfield, Wis., 1971-76; trustee Elm Grove Village, Wis., 1976-81, pres., 1981-86; mem. Wis. State Assembly, 1986-89, State Senate, 1989—. Chairperson FLOW community coalition working for equitable sewer rates, New Berlin, Wis., 1982—; mem. budget com. Milw. Archdiocese, 1979—, mem. salary adminstrn. com., 1983—. Recipient community service award Elm Grove Jr. Guild, 1986. Mem. Assn. Marquette Univ. Women (bd. dirs. 1980—, 1st v.p. 1984-85), League Wis. Municipalities, League Insurance Trust (bd. dirs.), League Suburban Municipalities. Republican. Roman Catholic. Clubs: Elm Grove Woman's, Elm Grove Hist. Soc. Home: 14905 Watertown Plank Rd Elm Grove WI 53122 Office: Wis State Capitol PO Box 7882 Madison WI 53707*

FARROW, MIA VILLIERS, actress; b. Los Angeles, Feb. 9, 1945; d. John Villiers and Maureen Paula (O'Sullivan) F.; m. Andre Previn, Sept. 10, 1970 (div. Feb. 1979); children: Matthew Phineas and Sascha Villiers (twins), Lark Song, Fletcher Farrow, Summer Song, Gigi Soon Mi, Misha, Satchel. Student pub., pvt. schs. Actress appearing in TV and films. Debut in The Importance of Being Earnest, N.Y.C., 1964; starred in TV series Peyton Place; films include Hurricane, Rosemary's Baby, 1968, See No Evil, 1971, The Public Eye, 1972, The Great Gatsby, Peter Pan, A Wedding, 1978, Death on the Nile, A Midsummer Night's Sex Comedy, Zelig, The Purple Rose of Cairo, 1985, Broadway Danny Rose, Hannah and her Sisters, 1986, September, 1987, Radio Days, 1987, Another Woman, 1988, Oedipus Wrecks, 1989; appeared in stage plays Romantic Comedy, Mary Rose, The Three Sisters, The House of Bernarda Alba, Ivanov; joined Royal Shakespeare Co., London, 1974. Recipient Golden Globe award, 1967; Best Actress award French Acad., 1969; Rio de Janeiro Film Festival award, 1969; Italian Academy award, 1970. Address: ICM care Sam Cohn 40 W 57th St New York NY 10019*

FARWELL, DOROTHY ANNE, retired speech and language pathologist; b. Grand Forks, N.D., Mar. 21, 1936; d. Philip William and Tenney Constance (Johnson) West; m. Gerald Alpha Freeman, Aug. 18, 1956 (div. July 1965); 1 child, Jeffrey West; m. Robert William Farwell, June 30, 1984. BS in Edn., La. State U., 1958, MEd, 1973. Lic. in speech pathology, La.; cert. of clin. competence in speech and lang. pathology. Speech and lang. pathologist St. Helena Parish Sch. Bd., Greensburg, La., 1959-61; asst. dean women La. State U., Baton Rouge, 1961-66, supr. student tchrs., 1967-82; speech and lang. pathologist East Baton Rouge Parish Sch. Bd., Baton Rouge, 1966-82, compliance cons. pupil appraisal, 1982-84, asst. coord. pupil appraisal, 1984-86; speech and lang. pathologist St. Tammany Parish Sch. Bd., Covington, La., 1986-89; ret., 1989. Sec. Lakeside Villa Condominium Assn., Bay St. Louis, Miss., 1978-79, pres., 1980-82; v.p. Timber Creek Condominium Assn., Mandeville, La., 1986, pres., 1987, sec., 1990. Mem. Mortar Bd. (pres. alumnae Baton Rouge 1960-62), Delta Gamma (scholarship chmn. 1965-69, nominating com. 1968-70, collegiate chmn. 1970-75, awards chmn. 1975-79, rush cons. 1963-90, alumnae pres. Baton Rouge 1982, Northshore alumnae 1888-90, v.p. 1990, grad. fellowship named in her honor 1979, Cable award 1980). Republican. Presbyterian. Home: 500 Aries Dr Apt 4-B Mandeville LA 70448

FARY, DEBRA FAYE, pharmacist; b. Richmond, Va., Mar. 25, 1957; d. William Otway and Mildred Leona (Sears) F. BA in Biology, U. Va., 1979; BS in Pharmacy, Med. Coll. of Va., 1982. Registered pharmacist. Health svcs. Officer Nat. Cancer Inst., Silver Spring, Md., 1981; pharmacist Waynesboro Community Hosp., Va., 1982-85, Med. Coll. Va. Hosp., Richmond, 1985—, Peoples Drug Stores, Waynesboro, 1983-85, Kroger Pharmacy, Waynesboro, 1983-85, Standard Drug Co., Richmond, 1986—. Vol. U. Va. Hosp., Charlottesville, 1975-76. Mem. Am. Soc. Hosp. Pharmacists, Va. Pharm. Assn., AAUW (co-editor Richmond br. newsletter), Sigma Zeta, Rho Chi (scholastic recognition cert.), Kappa Epsilon (sec. 1980-81). Methodist. Avocations: travel, skiing, bicycling, reading, aerobic dancing. Office: MCV Hosp Dept Pharmacy Box 42 MCV Sta Richmond VA 23298

FASANO, JANETTE, federal agency marketing executive; b. Winthrop, Mass.; d. Guido P. and Antonia (Granese) F. BS in Bus. Administrn. and Finance summa cum laude, Boston U., 1977; MPA, Suffolk U., 1979, JD, 1987. Bar: Mass. 1987; lec. real estate broker. Presdl. mgmt. intern U.S. Small Bus. Adminstrn., 1979-81; comml. market rep. U.S. Small Bus. Adminstrn., Boston, 1981—; EEO counselor U.S. Small Bus. Adminstrn., Boston, 1982—. Chmn. Saugus Board of Selectmen, 1987—, mem. 1980—; Saugus rep. to Met. Area Planning Coun., Boston, 1982—; mem. various town coms., 1978—; former vol. Spl. Olympics, Health Alert, Mass. State Hse., Mass. Gen. Hosp. Recipient Pub. Achievement award Italian Am. Civic League, 1982. Mem. ABA, Mass. Bar Assn., Lynn Bus. and Profl. Women's Club (local and N.E. dist. Young Careerist award 1985, 86), Beta Gamma Sigma, Pi Alpha Alpha, Phi Delta Phi.

FASBENDER, CLEMENTINE MARIE SCULLY, medical center training administrator; b. N.Y.C., Apr. 2, 1936; d. William Lawrence and Clementine E. (Makray) Scully; children: William D., Edward J., Bart C. BA in English and Edn., St. John's U., Jamaica, N.Y., 1957; MS in Adult and Community Edn., CUNY, 1979. Editor, copywriter U.S. Life Ins. Co., N.Y.C., 1958-61; office mgr. Mount & Rilling, Bklyn., 1961-76; legal asst. Previte, Glasser & Farber, Jackson Heights, N.Y., 1976-77; adminstr., researcher N.Y. State Assembly, N.Y.C., 1977-79; tng. dir. Lincoln Med. and Mental Health Ctr., Bronx, N.Y., 1980—; program dir. Forest Hills (N.Y.) Adult Edn. System, 1980—; tchr. ESL, N.Y.C., 1971-80; pvt. practice cons., Jackson Heights, 1985—. Editor Capsule newsletter Lincoln Med. Ctr., 1980-88. Candidate N.Y. State Senate, 1990. Mem. AAUW, Am. Soc. for Health Edn. Trainers, Assn. Hosp. Personnel Adminstrs., Coun. Tng. Dirs. (sec. 1982-84, vice chair 1985-86), Mensa (dir. vols. Greater N.Y. area, bd. dirs., chair scholarship com.). Roman Catholic. Home: 33-11 82d St Jackson Heights NY 11372 Office: Lincoln Med and Mental Health 234 E 149th St Bronx NY 10451

FASKE, DONNA See KARAN, DONNA

FASONE, LUCILLE GERALDINE, therapist; b. Brklyn., Aug. 11, 1954; d. Joseph Angelo and Lucille Gloria (Marino) F.; divorced; 1 child, Christopher Paul. AS, Miami Dade Community Coll., 1974; BS, U. Fla., 1981. Registered respiratory therapist. Critical care therapist North Shore Hosp., Miami, Fla., 1974-78; respiratory supr. Shands Teaching Hosp., Gainesville, Fla., 1978-79; staff therapist Alachua Gen. Hosp., Gainesville, Fla., 1979-81; neonatal therapist Broward Gen. Med. Ctr., Ft. Lauderdale, Fla., 1981; ednl. coord. North Ridge Gen. Hosp., Ft. Lauderdale, Fla., 1981-82; neonatal respiratory supr. Jackson Meml. Hosp., Fla., 1982—. Mem. Am. Assn. for Respiratory Therapy, Nat. Bd. for Respiratory Therapy. Roman Catholic. Office: Jackson Meml Hosp 1611 NW 12 Ave Miami FL 33136

FASSIHI, THERESA CARMELA, journalist; b. L.A., Sept. 12, 1959; d. John Harrison Simons and Sally Elisa Graham; m. Mohammad Reza Fassihi, July 14, 1984; children: Mansoor Reza, Samad Reza Donaciano. BA in Econs. and Journalism, Stanford U., 1981. Copy editor, reporter Dallas Morning News, 1981-84; feature writer Tulsa Tribune, 1985-87; corr. Adweek mag., Dallas, 1986—; co-editor Tulsa Women, 1990—; editorial adviser S mag., Tulsa, 1985-86. pub. rels. cons. ARC, Tulsa, 1989. Mem. Women in Communications, Tulsa Exec. Exch. (v.p. 1987-88). Democrat.

FASSLER, CRYSTAL G., marketing consultant; b. Marion, Ohio, Mar. 15, 1942; d. Lloyd C. and Iola M. (Runkle) Mahaffey; student public schs., Prospect, Ohio; m. Donald D. Fassler, May 6, 1960; 1 son, Curtis A. Media buyer H. Swink Advt., Marion, 1968-73; media buyer and planner Tracey Locke Advt., Columbus, Ohio, 1973-74, Lord, Sullivan & Yoder Advt., Marion, 1974-82; pres. consultant State of Ohio Employment Services, Marion, 1982-83; nat. mktg. consultant WMRN-AM and FM, Marion, 1983-84, gen. mgr., 1985; gen. sales mgr. WRFD Radio, Columbus, 1986—. Home: 1846 Smeltzer Rd Marion OH 43302 Office: N High St E Powell Rd Columbus OH 43081

FAST, ELAINE CLAYTON, educator; b. Harper, Kans., Feb. 20, 1943; d. Harold Roy and Ruth (Bridgess) Clayton; m. Philip Eugene Fast, Feb. 14, 1969; children: Douglas, David. B in Music Edn., Wichita (Kans.) State U., 1965; M in Secondary Edn., Weber State Coll., Ogden, Utah, 1986, cert. in elem. teaching, 1975; cert. in spl. edn. teaching, Utah State U., Logan, 1980. Cert. elem. and secondary edn. tchr., Utah. Tchr. elem. Davis County Elem. Schs., 1975-79; tchr. spl. edn. Behavioral Adjustment Unit, Farmington, 1979-80, Mountain High Sch., Kaysville, Utah, 1980-88; tchr. secondary edn. Young Parents Sch., Kaysville, 1989—; cons. Davis County Job Seeker Program, 1980-84; coord. sex equity workshop com. Davis Sch. Dist., Davis County, 1987; coord. women's history workshop Utah State Bd. of Edn., Salt Lake City, 1989; facilitator Davis County Mental Health Teen Drug Sch., 1989—. Mem. single parent Econ. Ind. Demonstration Project, Davis County, 1988-89; chairperson human resources adv. bd. Davis Area Vocat. Ctr., Kaysville, 1988-89; chairperson legis. dist. 13 Davis County Dems., 1984-89. Mem. NEA, AAUW (chpt. chairperson women's worth com. 1987-89, state chairperson women's issues com. 1987-89, v.p. state div. program 1989—). Episcopalian. Home: 995 N 390 W Sunset UT 84015 Office: Young Parents Sch 264 S 500 E Kaysville UT 84037

FAUBEL, NANCY CAROLINE, business executive; b. Rochester, N.Y., July 10, 1958; d. Robert S. and Elisabeth (Torrey) F. BS, Alfred U., 1979; MBA, U. Rochester, 1983. Cert. flight instr., comml. pilot; lic. real estate agt.; notary pub. Engr. I, Babcock & Wilcox, Augusta, Ga., 1979-80, sales engr., Phila., 1980-82; v.p. Precision Equipment Services, Rochester, 1983-86; pres. Valley Aviation, Eastern W.Va. Regional Airport, 1986—; pres., owner Baron's Restaurant, Eastern W.Va. Regional Airport, 1986-89. Del., 19th Ward Community Assn., Rochester, 1986; capt. CAP, 1985—. Mem. NAFE, Rochester Pilots Assn., Rochester Real Estate Bd., Martinsburg-Berkeley C. of C. (aviation com.). Republican. Avocations: flying, carpentry, art. Home: Rt 4 Box 431-C Martinsburg WV 25401 Office: Valley Aviation W Va Regional Airport Martinsburg WV 25401

FAUDE, DIANE ELAINE, university administrative assistant; b. Medford, Wis., May 13, 1950; d. Harley Herbert and Iris Elaine (Ogle) F.; 1 child, Diana Lynn. Grad. high sch., Owen, Wis. With Manpower, Milw., 1968-69; claims adjuster ITT Life Ins. Corp. subs. ITT Corp., Thorp, Wis., 1970-75; stenographer Alaska State Bldg. Authority, Anchorage, 1975-76, sec., 1976-81, adminstrv. asst., 1981-85, adminstrv. officer, 1985-87, budget officer, 1987-88; adminstrv. asst. U. Alaska, Anchorage, 1989—. Home: 4831 Loretta Ln Anchorage AK 99507 Office: University of Alaska 3211 Providence Dr Anchorage AK 99508

FAUL, JUNE PATRICIA, education specialist; b. Detroit; d. John William and Shirley Olive (Block) Lynch; m. George Johnson Faul, Dec. 22, 1949; children: Robert Michael, Alison. Student, Coll. Sequoias, 1942-44, UCLA, 1947; BA, U. Calif., Berkeley, 1952. Cert. elem. tchr., Calif. Tchr. Tulare County (Calif.) Schs., 1945-46, Tulare City Schs., 1946-48, Visalia (Calif.) City Schs., 1948-49, Richmond (Calif.) City Schs., 1951-52, Pacific Grove (Calif.) Sch. Dist., 1965-85; designated English teaching specialist State of Calif., 1969—; with Group Four Ednl. Video Prodn.; lectr. Calif. State U., Fresno, 1969, U. Calif., Santa Cruz, 1970. Active human relations commn. City of Richmond, 1962-64; mem. adv. bd. Family Resource Ctr.; founding mem., 1st pres. Monterey (Calif.) Peninsula Child Abuse Prevention Council, 1974; hon. life mem. Calif. PTA; bd. dirs. Carmel Cultural Commn., 1964-67, Harrison Meml. Library, Carmel, Calif., 1978-84; mem., chmn. bd. Monterey Peninsula Airport Dist., 1980—. Mem. Union Concerned Scientists, Nat. Orgn. to Insure Sound Controlled Environment, Friends of Hopkins Marine Station (founder, bd. dirs.) Carmel Heritage (founder, bd. dirs.), Monterey NAACP (life), Monterey Mus. Art (life), Monterey Symphony Guild (life). Democrat. Avocation: writing. Home: PO Box 4365 Carmel CA 93921

FAULK, ELIZABETH HAMMOND, psychologist; b. Jacksonville, Fla., May 18, 1925; d. John Harrison and Cornelia Annette (Noble) F. BA, Conn. Coll., 1947; MA, U. Fla., 1950, PhD, 1955; postgrad., Columbia U. Diplomate in clin. psychology. Staff Menninger Clinic, Topeka, Kans., 1961; psychology svc. VA Hosp., Topeka, 1961-65; chief clin. psychologist Juvenile Ct. Psychiatric Clinic, Miami, Fla., 1965; sr. clin. psychologist/dir. psychol. tng. Guidance Ctr., Daytona, Fla., 1965-68; pvt. practice, pres. Psychol. & Cons. Svcs., Inc., Boca Raton, Fla., 1968—; founder Elizabeth H. Faulk Found. Vestry mem. St. Gregory's Episcopal Ch., Boca Raton, 1975-77. Fellow in clin. psychology, menninger Found., 1959-61, U. Fla., 1953-55; named Outstanding Clin. Psychologist of the Yr., Fla. Psychol. Assn., 1981. Fellow Kans. Psychol. Assn.; mem. Am. Psychol. Assn., Am. Group Psychotherapy Assn., Am. Acad. Psychotherapists, Palm Beach Psychol. Assn. (pres. 1970), Fla. POsychol. Assn., Soroptimist (pres. 1975, 83, Woman of the Yr. 1974). Episcopalian. Home: 550 NE 21st Ave #11 Deerfield Beach FL 33441 Office: Psychol & Cons Svcs 245 N Ocean Blvd Ste 205 Deerfield Beach FL 33441

FAULK, SUZANNE H., company executive; b. Portland, Oreg., Apr. 17, 1949; d. Stone Duval and Harriet Lucille (Kahlke) F.; m. Donald Lee Sullivan, Aug. 1, 1966 (div. 1969); 1 child, Anthony James; m. Bernd Hardy Paul Fritz Walter, Nov. 24, 1987. BS in Recreation and Park Mgmt., U. Oreg., 1975. Program dir. Lane County Ext. Svc., Eugene, Oreg., 1971-75; unit supr. Dept. Human Resources, Eugene, Oreg., 1975-84, employment specialist, 1975-84, adjudicator, hearing rep., 1975-84; rsch. dir. Peat, Marwick, Mitchell & Co., Dallas, 1984-86, cons., 1984-86; v.p., chief exec. officer GBR Systems Corp., Chester, Conn., 1986-89; pres., chief exec. officer Internat. Bus. Systems and Equipment Corp., Naples, Fla., 1989—; cons. Microwave Planning, Inc., Dallas, 1989—, Chris Gamboni/ind. TV and film producer, Moriches, N.Y., 1986—; bd. dirs. Berkshire Village, Inc., Naples. Author: (manuals) Bill of Rights for Volunteers, 1974, Volunteering in Community Schools, 1975; author: (curriculum) Univ. of Oreg. E.S.C.A.P.E., 1975; author: Hospitality Training Program, 1982. Vol. Naples Area Cancer Drive, 1990, Dallas Mus. of Art, 1984-86; host Dallas Rep. Welcoming Com., 1984; div. chmn. Eugene Human Rights Commn. for the Handicapped, 1978-80. Recipient Gov.'s award State of Oreg., Salem, 1975, Svc. award Sacred Heart Hosp., Eugene, 1980, Outstanding Achievement award Springfield (Oreg.) Sch. Dist., 1975. Mem. C. of C., NAFE. Episcopalian. Office: Internat Bus Systems/Equip PO Box 3041 Naples FL 33939

FAULKENBERY, MONICA ANNE, public relations administrator; b. Muskogee, Okla., Sept. 18, 1957; d. Lester Earl and Ruth Aileen (Keith) Housley; m. Allan O. Faulkenbery, Dec. 1, 1984 (dec. 1989). BA, Northeastern State U., 1979. Asst. dir. communications Bacone Coll., Muskogee, Okla., 1979-82; news coord. Tex. State Tech. Inst., Waco, 1982-84, dir. pub. info. and news, 1984—; adv. bd. Sta. KCTF-TV, Waco, 1988—. Contbr. articles to profl. jours. Chmn. media and pub. relations com. Tex. Air Expo, Waco, 1986—; vol. newsletter editor Waco Family Abuse Ctr., Waco, 1986-89. Mem. Pub. Rels. Soc. Am. (nat. and cen. tex. chpt. treas. 1990—), Nat. Sch. Pub. Rels. Assn., Tex. Pub. Rels. Assn., Advt. Club of Waco., Tex. State Inst. Women's Club, Delta Zeta Alumnae (pres. 1980-82). Mem. Christian Ch. Home: Rt 2 Box 1103 China Spring TX 76633 Office: Tex State Tech Inst 3801 Campus Dr Waco TX 76705

FAULKNER, PATRICIA ANN, addiction counselor; b. N.Y.C., Oct. 20, 1961; d. Henry Armstead and Robert (Overbey) F. BA in Psychology, Russell Sage Coll., Troy, N.Y., 1983; MA in Psychology, Jr. Coll. Albany, 1987. Bedford Stuyvesant Addiction Treatment Ctr.; Vol. rape crisis counselor Samaritan Hosp., Troy, 1981-83; relief worker ARC, Troy, 1983; alcoholism counselor, community educator Alcoholism Ctr. Rensselaer County, Troy, 1983-86; alcoholism counselor Bedford Stuyvesant ATC, Bklyn., 1983—; intern Troy Boys Club, 1985-86. Mem. N.Y. Fedn. Alcoholism Counselors, Nat. Black Alcoholism Coun., Nat. Assn. Alcoholism and Drug Abuse Counselors, Singers of Praise (pres.), Jr. Group I (v.p. 1988—). Democrat. Mem. Pentecostal Apostolic Ch. Home: 199-28 Hollis Ave

Hollis NY 11412 Office: Bedford Stuyvesant ATC 1121 Bedford Ave Brooklyn NY 11216

FAURIOL, SANDIE, agency executive; b. Tokyo, Japan, June 19, 1949; d. William Arthur and Betsy Ross (Moore) Ellis; m. Georges Alfred Fauriol, Apr. 16, 1977. Student, U. N.C., 1967-69; BA, Ohio U., 1971; postgrad., Georgetown U., Wash., 1980. Resource devel. officer, exec. dir. Planned Parenthood of Met., Washington D.C., 1976-79; v.p. for devel. Martineau Corp., Washington D.C., 1979-80; campaign dir., dir. nat. salute Vietnam Vets. Meml. Fund, Washington D.C., 1980-83; dir. devel. Youth for Understanding, Washington D.C.; co-founder, exec. dir. Project on the Vietnam Generation, Washington D.C., 1985-87; founder, pres. Ctr. for The New Leadership, 1987-90; campaign dir. Nat. Mus. Health and Medicine, 1990—; pres. Nat. Council Career Women, 1980-81, mem. adv. bd., Pub. Leadership Edn. Network, Wash., 1988-. Author: Enduring Legacies: Expressions from the Hearts and Minds of the Vietnam Generation, 1987. Mem. Nat. Soc. Fund Raising Execs. (pres. Greater Washington D.C. area chpt., 1988-90). Episcopalian.

FAUST, ALLISON LEE, marketing professional; b. Phoenix, Dec. 29, 1967; d. Charles Benjamin and Maxine Louise (Tankersley) F. Student, Abilene (Tex.) Christian U., 1986—. Staff writer The Optimist newspaper, Abilene, 1987-88; pub. rels. asst. Prodns. Plus, Sheridan, Wyo., 1983-86; program producer ACU-TV, Abilene, 1987-88; copywriter, sales asst. KORQ-FM, Abilene, 1987-89; account exec. The Optimist newspaper, Abilene, 1989; mktg. asst. Mall of Abilene, 1990—; dir. mktg. Lee Randall Consulting, Abilene and San Antonio, 1988-89. Mem. Abilene Christian U. Advt. Club (sec. 1989—), Abilene Young Reps., Alpha Epsilon Rho, Kappa Kappa Kappa, Tri Kappa Gamma. Mem. Church of Christ. Home: 1000 Justice Way Apt 1200 Abilene TX 79602

FAUST, NAOMI FLOWE, educator, poet; b. Salisbury, N.C.; d. Christopher Leroy and Ada Luella (Graham) Flowe; AB, Bennett Coll.; MA, U. Mich., 1945; PhD, N.Y. U., 1963; m. Roy Malcolm Faust, Aug. 16, 1948. Elem. tchr. Pub. Schs. Gaffney (S.C.); tchr. English, French, phys. edn. Atkins High Sch., Winston-Salem; instr. English, Bennett Coll. and So. U., Scotlandville, La., 1944-46; prof. English. Morgan State Coll., Balt., 1946-48; tchr. English, Greensboro (N.C.) Pub. Schs., 1948-51, N.Y.C. Pub. Schs., 1954-63; prof. edn. Queens Coll. of City U. N.Y., Flushing, 1964-82; lectr. in field; writer, lectr., poetry readings, 1982—. Named Tchr.-Author of 1979, Tchr.-Writer; cert. of Merit for poem Cooper Hill Writers Conf., 1970; Achievement award L.I. br. AAUW, 1985. Mem. AAUP, Nat. Coun. Tchrs. English, Nat. Women's Book Assn., Nat. Assn. Univ. Women (L.I. br.), World Poetry Soc. Intercontinental, N.Y. Poetry Forum, NAACP, United Negro Coll. Fund, Alpha Kappa Alpha, Alpha Kappa Mu, Alpha Epsilon. Author: Discipline and the Classroom Teacher, 1977; (poetry) Speaking in Verse, 1974, All Beautiful Things, 1983, And I Travel by Rhythms and Words, 1990, And I Travel by Rhythms and Words, 1990; contbr. poetry to jours. Home: 112-01 175th St Jamaica NY 11433

FAVREAU, SUSAN DEBRA, management consultant; b. Cleve., Dec. 15, 1955; d. Donald Francis and Helen Patricia (Rafferty) F. Cert., N.Y. State Police Acad., 1974; student, Cornell U., 1984, SUNY, 1986. Communications specialist N.Y. State Police, Loudonville, 1974-87; communications specialist div. hdqrs., 1987—; mgmt. cons., sec.-treas., dir. Don Favreau Assocs., Inc., Clifton Park, N.Y., 1983-86, v.p., 1986—; adj. faculty Internat. Assn. Chiefs of Police; NYSPIN coord. FBI/Nat. Crime Info. Ctr. cert. program, 1986—. Author: Teamwork in the Telecommunication Center, 1986, One More Time: How to be a Mature and Successful Telecommunications Manager, 1987; also NYSPIN cert. manuals. Recipient Dirs. commendation N.Y. State Police Acad., 1977, commendation N.Y. State Police, 1978, Supt.'s commendation, 1986. Mem. NAFE, N.Y. State Civil Svc. Assn., Emergency Communicators' Profl. Assn. (mem. adv. bd.), Colonie Police Benevolent Assn. (hon.), Am. Soc. Law Enforcement Trainers, Assoc. Pub. Safety Communications Officers (planning comm. mem. Atlantic chpt. 1986, registration chair ann. NE conf. 1986), N.Y. State Troopers Police Benevolent Assn. (hon.), Nat. Bus. Women Am., Internat. Assn. Chiefs Police, Am. Horse Shows Assn., Am. Soc. Law Enforcement Trainers, Capital Dist. Hunter/Jumper Coun. Republican. Roman Catholic. Home: 4D Hollandale Apts Clifton Park NY 12065 Office: Hdqrs NY State Police State Office Bldg Campus Bldg #22 Albany NY 12226

FAWCETT, STANCINE BRENNA, economics educator; d. Stanley A. Fawcett and Francine G. Luwe. BSBA, Ea. Mont. Coll., 1981; MS, Utah State U., 1985; postgrad., Ariz. State U. Cert. community coll. instr. Faculty acad. adviser Embry-Riddle Aeronautical U., Phoenix; faculty Golden Gate U., Phoenix; econ. forecaster, budget analyst, educator Maricopa County, Phoenix. Contbr. articles to profl. jours. Community youth leader Children's Theatre Troupe, jazz ballet ensembles LDS Ch.; tchr. primary Sunday Sch.; dir., leader summer camp for diabetic children. Named One of Outstanding Young Women Am.; recipient Presdl. fellowship, Faculty of Yr. award, 1987-88, 89-90, Lead D. Widtsoe Nat. Scholarship, 1985. Mem. NAFE, Nat. Assn. Bus. Economists, Am. Soc. Pub. Adminstrn., Am. Assn. Budget and Program Analysis, Am. Women's Econ. Devel. Assn., Women in Pub. Adminstrn., Delta Nu Alpha, Lambda Delta Sigma. Republican. Home: PO Box 973 Mesa AZ 85211

FAWELL, BEVERLY JEAN, state legislator; b. Oak Park, Ill., Sept. 17, 1930. BA, Elmhurst Coll., 1970; postgrad., No. Ill. U., 1974. Mem. Ill. Ho. of Reps., Springfield, 1981-83, Ill. Senate, Springfield, 1983—. Republican. Office: 2 S 630 Arboretum Glen Ellyn IL 60137

FAWSETT, PATRICIA C., judge; b. 1943. BA, U. Fla., 1965, MA, 1966, JD, 1973. Pvt. practice law Akerman, Senterfitt & Edison, Orlando, Fla., 1973-86; commr. 9th Cir. Jud. Nominating Commn, 1973-75, Greater Orlando Crime Prevention Assn., 1983-86; judge U.S. Dist. Ct. (mid. dist.) Fla., Orlando, 1986—. Trustee Loch Haven Art Ctr., Inc., Orlando, 1980-84; commr. Orlando Housing Authority, 1976-80, Winter Park (Fla.) Sidewalk Festival, 1973-75; bd. dirs. Greater Orlando Are C. of C., 1982-85. Mem. ABA (trial lawyers sect., real estate probate sect.), Am. Judicature Soc., Assn. Trial Lawyers Am., Fla. Bar Found. (bd. dirs. grants com.), Commn. on Access to Cts., Fla. Coun. Bar Assn. Pres.'s (pres., bd. dirs. 9th cir. grievance com.) Osceola County Bar Assn., Fla. Bar Assn. (budget com., disciplinary rev. com., integration rule and bylaws com., com. on access to legal system, bd. of cert., designation and advt., jud. adminstrn., selection and tenure com., jud. nominating procedures com., pub. rels. com., ann. meeting com., appelate rules com., spl. com. on judiciary-trial lawyer rels., chairperson midyr. conv. com., bd. dirs. trial lawyers sect.), Orange County Bar Assn. (exec. coun. 1977-73, pres. 1981-82, trustee Legal Aid Soc. 1977-81), Order of Coif, Phi Beta Kappa. Office: 611 US Dist Ct 80 N Hughey Ave Orlando FL 32801*

FAXON, ALICIA CRAIG, art educator; b. N.Y.C., July 27, 1931; d. William Donald and Clara Alicia (Harnecker) Craig; m. Richard Bremer Faxon, Feb. 21, 1953; children: Richard Paul, Thomas Hardwick. AB, Vassar Coll., 1952; MA, Radcliffe Coll., 1953, Boston U., 1971; PhD, Boston U., 1979. Lectr. New Eng. Sch. Art and Design, Boston, 1974-77; acting dir. Danforth Mus., Framingham, Mass., 1978; teaching assoc. Boston U. Sch. for Art, 1978-79; vis. lectr. Simmons Coll., Boston, 1979-80, asst. prof. art, 1980-86, assoc. prof., 1986—, chmn. dept. art and music, 1987—; lectr. Sch. for Lifelong Learning, Harvard U., Cambridge, Mass., 1978-80; program chmn. Women's Studies Adv. Bd., 1982-84. Author: Catalog Raisonné of Prints of J.-L. Forain, 1982, Pilgrims and Pioneers, 1987, Dante Gabriel Rossetti, 1989; mem. editorial bd. Woman's Art Jour., 1989—. Mem. acquisitions com. Danforth Mus., 1974-89, trustee, 1975-77. Recipient Nan award for art criticism Art New Eng., 1987; grantee Nat. Endowment for Arts, 1982, Simmons Coll., 1984, NEH, 1989. Mem. Coll. Art Assn. (chmn. preRaphaelite session 1990), Women's Caucus for Art (program co-chmn. 1986-88), Victorian Soc., 19th Century Art Historians Group, Vassar Coll. Alumnae Assn. Democrat. Episcopalian. Office: Simmons Coll 300 The Fenway Boston MA 02115

FAY, ANITRA SHARANE, psychologist; b. Ft. Smith, Ark., Sept. 23, 1954; d. Clarence Russell and Katala Ann (Green) Williams; m. Edgar Dempsey Fay, Dec. 25, 1975; 1 child, Matthew Williams. BA, U. Ark., 1976, MA, 1978, PhD, 1981. Lic. psychologist. Intern pediatric psychology U. Okla., Oklahoma City, 1980-81; psychologist Holt Krock Clinic, Ft. Smith, 1981-83, 85—, Huisman/Fay Psychol. Cons. P.A., Ft. Smith, 1982-85. Co-author: (book chapter) Handbook of Clinical Psychology, 1983. Mem. multi-disciplinary team child abuse cases Sebastian and Crawford Counties, Ark., 1990, profl. women's adv. bd. Westark Community Coll., Ft. Smith, 1988—; advisor Youth Fellowship 1st Presbyn. Ch., Ft. Smith, 1988-90. Mem. APA (div. clin. child psychology and psychotherapy), Nat. Register Health Care Providers, Soc. Pediatric Psychology, Nat. Mus. Women in Arts, Ark. Psychol. Assn., Zonta (pres. local chpt. 1986-88). Office: Holt Krock Clinic 2901 S 74th St Fort Smith AR 72903

FAY, DARCY HUNT, international training and organizational development consultant, educator; b. Cleve.; d. Horace Byron Jr. and Bette (Berne) Fay; m. Paul L. Bundick. BA in Polit. Sci., Boston Coll., 1970; M. in Internat. Adminstrn., Sch. for Internat. Tng., Brattleboro, Vt., 1979; postgrad. Fielding Inst. Cert. in intercultural tng. Tchr. Internat. Sch. Tokyo (Japan), 1971-74, Am. Sch. of Barcelona (Spain), 1974-75; dir. African/Am. Educators program AAUW Ednl. Found., Washington, 1977-81; cons. Internat. Soc. for Intercultural Edn., Tng. and Research, Washington, 1982-84; cons. Delphi Research Assocs., Washington, 1984-85, World Bank, Washington, 1984-85, Armco Steel Co., Ltd., Ohio, 1989; cons. various domestic and internat. orgns., Washington, 1986—. Contbr. articles to profl. jours. Recipient Japanese Flower Arrangement award Sogetsu Sch., Tokyo, 1974. Mem. NAFE, NOW, Asia Soc., Assn. for Women in Devel., Capital Press Women, Internat. Organizational Devel. Assn., Internat. Soc. Intercultural Edn., Tng. and Research (1984 conf. steering com., program com., chmn. conf. publs. com.), Am. Soc. Tng. and Devel., Soc. for Internat. Devel., Nat. Mus. Women in Arts (charter), OD Network. Home: 4545 Connecticut Ave NW #635 Washington DC 20008 Office: Dept State Washington DC 20521-6100

FAY, JULIE DIANE, lawyer; b. N.Y.C., Sept. 30, 1950; d. Charles I. Schwartz and Rita (Greenberg) Lauro. AB, Vassar Coll., 1972; JD, Hofstra U., 1978. Bar: N.Y. 1979, U.S. Dist. Ct. (so. dist.) N.Y. 1979, U.S. Dist. Ct. (ea. dist.) N.Y. 1984, D.C. 1985, U.S. Ct. Appeals (2d cir.) 1984. Assoc. Winthrop, Stimson, Putnam & Roberts, N.Y.C., 1978-80, 81-85, Baer, Marks & Upham, N.Y.C., 1980-81; advisor Dept. State, Washington, 1985-86; sr. counsel IBJ Schroder Bank & Trust Co., N.Y.C., 1987, asst. gen. counsel, 1988—; asst. counsel Gov.'s Jud. Nominating Com., N.Y.C., 1982. Trustee CancerCare Inc., N.Y.C., 1988—, Nat. CancerCare Found., N.Y.C., 1988—. Mem. ABA, Assn. of Bar of City of N.Y. Office: IBJ Schroder Bank & Trust Co 1 State St New York NY 10004

FAY, MARY NATALIE, civic worker; b. Hibbing, Minn., May 15, 1952; d. Bruno Anthony and Sylvia Pierrine (Banal) Perell; m. Michael James Fay, Apr. 20, 1974; children: Patrick Michael, Katherine Marie, Marie Elizabeth. BA in Math., Coll. of St. Catherine, St. Paul, 1974. Treas. ch. circle Roman Cath. Ch., Hibbing, 1980—, chmn. children's bazaar, 1981; coord. Minn. Svcs. for Handicapped Children, Hibbing, 1982—; advisor sch. computer club, Hibbing, 1988—; mem. Mesabi Regional Med. Ctr. Aux., Hibbing, 1990—; mem. Ironworld Citizen Adv. Bd., Chisholm, Minn., 1990-92; pres. PTA, Hibbing, 1982-84; city fund chmn. Am. Heart Assn., Hibbing, 1983. Mem. AAUW (bd. dirs. 1976—, treas. 1976-78, pres. 1980-82, named grant honoree 1988-89), Coll. of St. Catherine Alumni Assn. (chmn. No. Minn. 1985—, bd. dirs. St. Paul 1990—). Home: 1413 E 18th St Hibbing MN 55746

FAY, SISTER MAUREEN A., college administrator. BA in English magna cum laude, Siena Heights Coll., 1960; MA in English, U. Detroit, 1966; PhD, U. Chgo., 1976. Tchr. English, speech, moderator student newspaper, student council St. Paul High Sch., Grosse Pointe, Mich., 1960-64; chairperson English dept., dir. student dramatics, moderator student publs. Dominican High Sch., Detroit, 1964-69; co-dir. Cath. student ctr. Adrian (Mich.) Coll., 1969-71; instr. English Siena Heights Coll., Adrian, 1969-71; evaluators inst. criminal justice execs. U. Chgo., 1971-73; instr. English U. Ill., Chgo., 1971-74; dir. evaluation sch. new learning DePaul U., Chgo., 1974-75; fellow in acad. adminstrn. Saint Xavier Coll., Chgo., 1975-76, dean. grad. studies, 1979-83, dean continuing edn., 1976-83; asst. prof. No. Ill. U., Dekalb, 1980-83; pres. Mercy Coll. Detroit, 1983—; v.p. VAUT Corp, bd. dirs. four inner city high schs., Archdiocese Chgo.; mem. exec. com. Assn. Mercy Colls.; adv. com. Adult Learning Svcs., The Coll. Bd., Met. Affairs Corp. of Detroit and S.E. Mich., cons. Nat. Assn. for Religious Women, 1974-75, North Cen. Assn. Colls. and Schs., evaluator commn. on higher edn.; trustee Rosary Coll., River Forest, Ill.; emeritus mem. div. bd. Mercy Hosps. and Health Svcs. of Detroit; bd. dirs. Nat. Bank of Detroit. Asst. editor: (book rev.): Adult Education, A Journal of Research and Theory, 1971-74. Steering com. Metro Detroit GIVES; exec. com., edn. task force Detroit Strategic Planning com., 1987; trustee Mich. Opera Theatre; bd. dirs. Greater Detroit Interfaith Round Table Nat. Conf. Christians and Jews, Inc., The Detroit Symphony. Mem. Am. Assn. Higher Edn., North Cen. Assn. (cons., evaluator commn. on higher edn.), Nat. Assn. Ind. Colls. and Univs. (bd. dirs.), Assn. Ind. Colls. and Univs. of Mich. (exec. com., chairperson), Am. Assn. Cath. Colls. and Univs., AAUW, Pi Lambda Theta. Office: Mercy Coll Detroit 8200 W Outer Dr Detroit MI 48219

FAY, NANCY ELIZABETH, nurse; b. Fulton, N.Y., May 10, 1943; d. Harold and Jean (Junker) Sant; m. Ronald George Fay, July 30, 1966; step children: Rory Patrick, Ronald George Jr. R.N., Genesee Hosp., Rochester, N.Y., 1964. Cert. gerontology nurse practitioner; cert. physician's asst., cert. diabetes educator. N.Y. Head maternity nurse St. Luke's Hosp., Utica, N.Y., 1975-78, diabetes clinician, 1978-82, co-dir. diabetes out-patient clinic, 1980-82; nurse practitioner, physician's asst. Slocum Dickson Med. Group, Utica, 1982-86; gerontol. nurse practitioner Masonic Home, Utica, 1988—; diabetes educator Upstate N.Y. Spl. Profl. Pregram Eli Lilly and Co., 1988—. Chair 1st ann. Gerontol. Teaching Day Masonic Home, 1988-89, 2d, 1990, 7th ann. N.Y. State Physcians Diabetes Teaching Day, 1989. Recipient Extra Mile award St. Luke's Hosp., 1979, Outstanding Citizenship award Am. Legion, Utica, 1982; Diabetes research grantee Diabetes Project, Ctr. Disease Control Utica, 1980-82, 21st Ann. Scroll award Cen. N.Y. Acad. Medicine, . Fellow Acad. Medicine Cent. N.Y.; mem. Am. Diabetes Assn. (pres. Utica chpt. 1983—, Outstanding Vol. of Yr. 1978, bd. dirs. N.Y. State affiliate 1983—, 1st v.p. 1986-87, Program award 1985-86, profl. edn. chmn. 1983—, chair patient and pub. edn. Upstate Affiliate, 1987—, 1st v.p., 1988-89, applicant nat. com. patient and pub. and profl. edn. 1988-89, pres.-elect N.Y. State Affiliate 1987-89, pres. 1990—), Am. Acad. Physician's Assts., Am. Assn. Diabetes Educators, Womens Health and Edn. Referral Service St. Luke's Hosp. (bd. dirs. 1987—). Republican. Methodist. Avocations: doll collecting, dancing, poetry, bike riding. Home: Valley Rd PO Box J Oriskany NY 13424 Office: Slocum Dickson Med Group 430 Court St Utica NY 13502

FAY, TONI GEORGETTE, corporate professional; b. N.Y.C., Apr. 25, 1947; d. George E. and Allie C. (Smith) Fay. B.A., Duquesne U., Pitts., 1968; M.S.W. (NIMH fellow 1970-72), U. Pitts., 1972, M.Ed., 1973; cert. Yale U. Drug Dependence Inst., 1973. Caseworker, N.Y.C. Dept. Welfare, 1968-70; regional commr. Gov. Pa. Council Drugs and Alcohol, 1973-76; dir. social services Pitts. Drug Abuse Ctr., 1972-73; dir. planning and devel. Nat. Council Negro Women, 1977-79; exec. v.p. D. Parke Gibson Assocs., 1979-82; mgr. community relations Time Inc. (name now Time-Warner Inc.), N.Y.C., 1982-83, dir. corporate community relations and affirmative action, 1983—; dir. corp. community relations, 1984. Bd. dirs. N.Y.C. Pvt. Industry Council; v.p. Nat. Coalition of 100 Black Women; v.p., bd. dirs. Mary McLeod Bethune Mus. and Archives, Washington, Girls Scout U.S.A. Council of Greater N.Y., Protestant Welfare Fedn. N.Y., Coro Found., Ramapo Coll.; mem. Bus. Urban Issues Council of Conf. Bd. Named Woman of Yr., Pitts. YWCA, 1975; recipient Twin award YWCA of USA, 1987; named one 100 Top Women in Bus., Dollars and Sense Mag., 1986. Mem. Exec. Leadership Council, Alpha Kappa Alpha. Office: Time Life Bldg Rockefeller Ctr New York NY 10020

FAZIO, MARIA LENA, sales executive; b. N.Y.C., Oct. 24, 1951; d. Richard and Antoinette (Alimo) Fazio; m. Joseph Hal Fustanio (div. 1990); 1 child, Brandon Philip. AA, Elizabeth Seton Coll., Yonkers, N.Y.; BA, Fla. Atlantic U., MFA. Box office mgr. Loeb Drama Ctr. Harvard U., Cambridge, Mass., 1974-75; with prodn. dept. Tulchin Prodn. Ltd., N.Y.C., 1975; box office mgr. Burt Reynolds Dinner Theatre, Jupiter, Fla., 1978-79; freelance cons. various cities, 1980-83; sales cons. Arvida Realty Sales, Inc., Boca Raton, Fla., 1983-87, Cypress Head Realty, Inc., Parkland, Fla., 1987—. Chmn. Eminent Scholar Com., Boca Raton, 1987—. Named Best Actress Boca Raton News Critics, 1973; nominated for Carbonell award Southeast Theatre Critics, 1982. Roman Catholic. Home: 6592 Hallandaire Dr W Boca Raton FL 33433 Office: Cypress Head Realty Inc 7501 S Cypress Head Dr Parkland FL 33067

FAZZALARI, LAURA SUE, accountant; b. Hammond, Ind., May 18, 1962; d. Frank Anthony and Edith Marie (Zavatsky) F. BS in Acctg., East Carolina U., 1986. CPA, N.C. Corp. acct. Western Bank, Houston, 1984; staff auditor Deloitte & Touche, CPAs, Raleigh, N.C., 1987-89; sr. internal auditor PepsiCo, Inc., Purchase, N.Y., 1989—. Mem. choir St. Raphael Cath. Ch., Raleigh, 1987-89. Mem. NAFE, AICPA, N.C. Assn. CPAs. Republican. Home: 118 Havemeyer Pl Greenwich CT 06830 Office: PepsiCo Inc 700 Anderson Hill Rd Purchase NY 10577

FAZZINI, GEORGIA CAROL, corporate executive, business owner; b. Chicago Heights, Ill., Feb. 17, 1946; d. George and Corella A.T. (Roggeveen) Tjemmes; m. Dan Fazzini, Dec. 31, 1964; 1 child, Daniel Edward. Student, Ill. State U., Normal, 1963-64, Nat. Beauty Coll., 1979. Sec. Marshall Erdman & Assocs., Madison, Wis., 1972-73, U. Wis., Madison, 1973-74, 1974; sec. Waukegan (Ill.) Devel. Ctr., 1974-75; br. adminstr. Universal Bus. Machines, Boise, Idaho, 1982-83; owner Substitute Sec. Typing Svc., Boise, 1983-87, Revisions Resume Writing Svc., Tulsa, 1987-88; chief exec. officer Diamond Devel. Ctr., Boise, 1988—; owner Revisions Resume Writing Svc., Boise, Idaho, 1989; cons. Nat. Multiple Sclerosis Soc., Boise, 1982-86, Placed Co. Employment Agy., Boise, 1983-85; instr. resumes dept. community edn. Boise Schs., 1986—, Caldwell Schs., 1989; resume cons. Tulsa Psychiat. Ctr.'s Corp. Assistance Program, 1988; lectr. resume writing, Tulsa, 1988, Boise, 1989—. Pres. New Neighbors League, Canton, Ohio, 1978-79; vice chmn., bd. dirs., sec., con. Nat. Multiple Sclerosis Soc., Boise, Idaho, 1982-86; mem. Idaho Assn. Devel. Disability Ctrs., 1989—; guest speaker Miss Teen Pageant, Boise, 1983-84; lobbyist Boise Secretarial Svcs., 1985-86, Idaho Devel. Disability Ctrs., 1989. Recipient Rose of Month award New Neighbors League, 1979, Patient Achievement award Nat. Multiple Sclerosis Soc., 1983. Mem. NAFE, Idaho Assn. Pvt. Devel. Disability Ctrs., Nat. Fedn. Ind. Bus. Home: 3611 Gekeler Ln Apt 124 Boise ID 83706 Office: Diamond Devel Ctr 1119 Caldwell Blvd Nampa ID 83651

FEAGLER, VIRGINIA MILLER, institutional researcher; b. Princeton, Ind., Mar. 25, 1940; d. Warren Hamilton and Helen (Smith) Miller; children: Troy A., Eric C. BA in History, Ind. U., 1963, MS in Edn., 1966; MA in Librarianship, U. Denver, 1976. Library asst. Ind. U. Biology Library, Bloomington, 1963-65; serials librarian Washington U. Sch. Medicine Library, St. Louis, 1966-68; serials librarian, dir. Philsom Network Washington U. Sch. Medicine Library, 1970-73; adminstrv. asst. Colo. commn. on Higher Edn., Denver, 1974-77; asst. dir. instl. analysis Colo. State U. Office Budgets and Planning, Ft. Collins, 1977-78; assoc. dir. Colo. State U. Office Budgets and Planning, 1978-84, dir. instl. analysis, 1984-87; asst. to dean Colo. State U. Coll. Applied Human Scis., 1987-89; fin. officer Colo. Commn. on Higher Edn., Denver, 1989—; participant Acad. Mgmt. Inst., Denver, 1986-87; lectr. in field. Contbr. articles to profl. jours. Agy. liaison United Way, Ft. Collins, 1985-87. MLA scholar, 1973-74. Mem. Assn. for Instl. Rsch., Colo. Assn. PLanners and Instl. Rsch., Rocky Mt. Assn. for Instl. Rsch., Colo. Women in Higher Edn. Adminstrn. Unitarian. Home: 1213 Village Ln Fort Collins CO 80521 Office: Colo Commn Higher Edn Denver CO 80523

FEAMSTER, ELIZABETH SUSAN, lawyer; b. Frankfort, Ky., Apr. 24, 1958; d. Martin Banker and Laura Starling (Crutcher) F.; BA magna cum laude, Transylvania, Lexington, Ky., 1980; postgrad., U. Oxford, England, 1980; JD, U. Ky., 1983. Bar: Ky. 1983, U.S. Dist. Ct. (ea. dist.) Ky. 1984, U.S. Ct. Appeals (6th cir.) 1984. Assoc. Shuffett, Mooney, McCoy, Campbell, Leathers and Newcomer, Lexington, 1983-85, Fowler, Measle and Bell, Lexington, 1985—. Active in Big Bros./Big Sisters of Lexington, 1984-86; co-leader Boy Scouts Explorers Post, 1988—. Mem. Fayette County Bar Assn., Ky. Bar. Assn., Ky. Acad. of Trial Attys., Omicron Delta Kappa. Democrat. Espiscopalian. Office: Fowler Measle and Bell Bank One Pla 4th Fl Lexington KY 40507

FEARS, LOUISE MATHIS, educator; b. Washington, Ga., Dec. 31, 1935; d. Ambrose Powell Jr. and Sarah Louise (Moon) Mathis; m. Henry Beane Fears, June 22, 1958; children: Scott Powell, Douglas Edward, Leslie Louise Corinne. BA, Shorter Coll., 1958; MEd, Ga. State U., 1977. Cert. Profl. Tchr., Ga. Evaluator Ga. State Dept. Ed., Atlanta, 1958-60; asst. Pers. Dept. City of Atlanta, 1960-61; tchr. DeKalb County Ga., Bd. Edn., Decatur, 1977-90; edn. dir. Learning Solutions, Inc., 1990—. Author: A Limousine is a Magazine About Lemons, 1987. Trustee Shorter Coll., 1987—, Nat. Trust for Historic Preservation. Mem. Ga. Assn. Edn. Young Children, Southern Assn. Educators, Nat. Assn. Edn. Young Children. Democrat. Baptist.

FEASTER, SANDRA JOAN, marketing consultant; b. Darby, Pa., Mar. 25, 1954; d. William John and Magdalene M. (Linder) Crummer; m. William W. Feaster, June 27, 1981. BSN, Widener U., 1979; MS, U. Calif., San Francisco, 1984; MBA, St. Mary's Coll., Moraga, Calif., 1989. RN. Registered nurse Bryn Mawr (Pa.) Hosp., 1975-77; cardio-pulmonary specialist Children's Hosp. of Phila., 1977-81; nurse educator, staff nurse U. Calif., San Francisco, 1981-84; clin. rsch. coord. Nellcor, Inc., Hayward, Calif., 1984-85, product mgr., 1985-87, clin. edn. mgr., 1987-88; prin. Med. Industry Svcs. and Cons., Danville, Calif., 1988—. Contbr. articles to profl. jours. Chmn. fin. Blackhawk Community Charities, Danville, 1989; chmn. Ednl. Film and Video Festival, Oakland, Calif., 1989, juror, 1988. Mem. Am. Assn. Critical Care Nurses (faculty nat. teaching inst. 1988), Nat. Assn. Female Execs., Sigma Theta Tau. Office: Med Industry Svcs Cons PO Box 1738 Danville CA 94526

FEATHER, ROBERTA BROWN, psychologist, educator; b. Raleigh, N.C., Jan. 18, 1942; d. Thomas Crump Brown and Josephine (Simpson) Rhodes; m. Ben W. Feather, Sept. 13, 1969 (div. June 1976); children: Amy Kendra, Elizabeth Megan. BS, U. N.C., 1963, MS, 1965; EdD, Boston U., 1980; JD, Suffolk U., 1989. Mem. faculty Duke U., Durham, N.C., 1965-71, U. R.I., Kingston, 1973—; dir. Adult Psychiat. and Mental Health Svc., Providence, 1980—; cons. Adult Correctional Inst., Cranston, R.I., 1977-85; chairperson Div. Psychiatry, R.I. State Nurses Assn., Providence, 1975-78. Author: Moral Development of Incarcerated Females, 1980; contbr. articles to profl. jours. Chairperson Providence LWV, 1971-73; bd. dirs. Miriam Hosp., 1971-75, Butler Hosp., 1971-76, Bradley Hosp., 1971-76. Lt. col. U.S. Army, 1980—. VA scholar U. N.C., 1959-63; USPH/MH fellow, 1963-65; Bevilacqua scholar Suffolk U., 1987. Mem. R.I. Coun. Community Svcs. (bd. dirs. 1971—), Mass. Acad. Trial Lawyers, Assn. Nurse Attys., Sigma Theta Tau, Pi Lambda Theta, Pi Delta Phi. Republican. Jewish. Home: 70 Elmgrove Ave Providence RI 02906

FEATHERMAN, SANDRA, political educator; b. Phila., Apr. 14, 1934; d. Albert N. and Rebe (Burd) Green; m. Bernard Featherman, Mar. 29, 1958; children: Andrew Charles, John James. BA, U. Pa., 1955, MA, 1978, PhD, 1978. Asst. prof. dept. polit. sci. Temple U., Phila., 1978-84, assoc. prof., 1984—, asst. to pres., 1986-89, pres. faculty senate, 1985-86, dir. Ctr. for Pub. Policy, 1986—; dir. Ctr. for Pub. Policy, Temple, 1986—. Author: Jews, Black and Ethnics, 1979; contbr. articles to profl. jours. Mem. Sch. Bd. Nominating Panel, Phila., 1969-71, 79-81; bd. dirs. Citizens Com. Pub. Edn. in Phila., 1977-89, pres., 1979-81; pres. Pa. Fedn. Community Coll.; trustee Community Coll. Phila., 1970—, chmn. bd. trustees, 1984-86; life trustee Samuel Fels Found.; bd. dirs. United Way SE Pa., 1977-89, United Way Pa., 1981-84; mem. commn. jud. selection and evaluation Phila. Bar Assn., 1979-81; pres. Girls Clubs Am., Phila., 1971-73, mem. nat. bd., 1971-74; mem. Pa. Coun. on Arts, 1979-83; nat. bd. dirs. Women and Founds.-Corp. Philanthropy, 1986—; v.p. Jewish Community Rels. Coun., 1982-89, Phila., bd. dirs. 1986—; speaker Commonwealth of Pa. Humanities Coun., 1988, 90. Recipient Brooks Graves award Pa. Polit. Sci. Assn., 1982, City of Phila. Community Svc. award, 1984, Louise Waterman Wise award Am. Jewish Congress, 1988, Women's Achievement award YWCA, 1989. Mem. AAUW (bd. dir. Phila. chpt. 1975-78, 80—, pres. 1984-86, chair internat.

fellowships panel 1987—, nat. chair ednl. found. program Internat. Fellows Panel 1987—, Outstanding Woman award 1986), Am. Polit. Sci. Assn., Am. Soc. Pub. Adminstrn. Home: 2100 Spruce St Philadelphia PA 19103 Office: Temple U Broad and Montgomery Sts Philadelphia PA 19122

FECHO, CECELIA HODGES, industrial engineer; b. Washington, N.C., May 12, 1960; d. James Harold and Joyce Ann (Williamson) Hodges; m. Jeffry Allen Fecho, June 1, 1985, 1 child, Colin Andrew. BS in Indsl. Tech., E. Carolina U., 1987. Admissions clk. Beaufort County Hosp., Washington, N.C., 1980-85; work group coordinator Presbyn. Ch. U.S.A., Cap Haitian, Haiti, 1985; mfg. engr. Robert Bosch Power Tool Corp., New Bern, N.C., 1985-86; engring. tech. support intern Burroughs Wellcome Co., Greenville, N.C., 1986-87; mfg. engr. Robert Bosch Power Tool Corp., 1987-88; indsl. engr. Ametek Lamb Electric Div., Graham, N.C., 1988-89, GKN Automotive Inc., Mebane, N.C., 1990—. Burroughs Wellcome Co. fellow, 1986. Mem. Inst. Indsl. Engrs., Nat. Assn. Female Execs., Epsilon Pi Tau. Democrat. Baptist. Home: 2322 La Vista Dr #23 Burlington NC 27215 Office: GKN Automotive Inc PO Box 220 Mebane NC 27302

FEDELE, SUSAN MARIE, banker; b. Bklyn., Mar. 21, 1949; d. John Joseph and Carmela Clare (Porcelli) F. Student, Fordham U., 1975-78. Typist Mfrs. Hanover Trust, N.Y.C., 1967-71, clk., 1971-74; personnel adminstr. Phila. Internat. Bank, N.Y.C., 1974-76, supr., 1976-78, mgr., 1978-80, asst. treas., 1980-81, asst. v.p., 1982-85, v.p., 1985—, gen. mgr., 1989—, also bd. dirs.; mem. com. Council on Internat. Banking, N.Y.C. Mem. Bankers Assn. Fgn. Trade (task force on money laundering), NAFE. Democrat. Roman Catholic. Office: Phila Internat Bank 55 Broad St New York NY 10004 :

FEDELLE, ESTELLE, artist; b. Chgo.; d. John and Julia (Porebski) Szymanski. Student, Am. Acad., 1944-47, Northwestern U., 1949-51, Inst. Design, Art Inst. Chgo.; also pvt. study. Exhibited in 52 one-person shows including Wheaton (Ill.) Pub. Libr., Libertyville (Ill.) Art League; exhibited in group shows Visual Arts Ctr., Chgo., Chgo. Pub. Libr., Ill. State Fair, Grand Cen. Gallery, N.Y.C., numerous others; portraitist; pvt. art tchr., 1950—; dir. Fedelle Art Studio, Chgo.; newspaper columnist Art and You, 1974—. Author: How to Begin Painting for Fun, 1964; contbg. author: Fun Book on Painting, How to Paint from your Color Slides. Recipient 82 awards for painting including Margaret R. Dingle award, 1953; Cert. of Merit Disting. Service in Art, 1967. Mem. Oak Park Art League, Nat. League Am. Pen Women, Park Ridge, Mcpl. Art League (bd. dirs.), Regent Art League, Am. Portrait Soc., Am. Soc. Artists, Internat. Fine Arts Guild. Home: 1500 S Cumberland St Park Ridge IL 60068 Office: Fedelle Studio 6219 Northwest Hwy Chicago IL 60631

FEDERICI, MARIE VICTORIA, management executive; b. Cheverly, Md., Jan. 18, 1962; d. Vincent Federici and Carolyn Louise Smith. Student, Howard Community Coll., Columbia, Md., 1980; student in bus., Katherine Gibbs Coll., 1987. Office mgr., adminstrv. asst. Certified Surety Mgmt., Washington; gen. mgr. Bacchus Bethesda, Md.; exec. mktg. cons. Nu Skin Internat., Inc., Provo, Utah. Mem. Ch. ofChrist. Mem. NAFE. Home: 20410 Afternoon Ln Germantown MD 20874

FEDERIGHI, RENIE RIDEOUT, broadcast educator; b. Wilmington, Del., June 30, 1932; d. Owen Wilson and Irene Catherine (Ring) Rideout; m. Francis DeLage Federighi, June 25, 1955; children: Carol Ann, David Charles (dec.). BA, Oberlin Coll., 1954. Claims adjuster Liberty Mutual Ins. Cos., Boston, 1954-58; auctin mgr. Sta. WMHT-TV, Schenectady, N.Y., 1970-79; mgr. ednl. svcs. Sta. WMHT/WHMX-TV, Schenectady, N.Y., 1979—. Producer: (TV series) College Perspective, 1981, (TV programs) Holiday Choirs, 1985—. Exec. com. Consortium for Learning Techs. N.Y. State, Albany, 1981-90; CPR instr. ARC, Schenectady, 1984—. Mem. AAUW, Zonta Club Schenectady (bd. dirs. 1982-90). Home: 2109 Baker Ave Schenectady NY 12309 Office: Sta WMHT/WMHX TV PO Box 17 Schenectady NY 12301

FEDOROFF, NINA VSEVOLOD, research scientist, consultant; b. Cleve., Apr. 9, 1942; d. Vsevolod N. and Olga S. (Snegireff) Stacy; m. T. Patrick Gaganidze, June 18, 1966 (div. 1978); children: Natasha, Kyr. B.S., Syracuse U., 1966; Ph.D., Rockefeller U., 1972. Asst. mgr. transl. bur. Biol. Abstracts, Phila., 1962-63; flutist Syracuse (N.Y.) Symphony Orch., 1964-66; acting asst. prof. UCLA, 1972-74; postdoctoral fellow UCLA and Carnegie Instn. Washington, Los Angeles and Balt., 1974-78; staff scientist Carnegie Instn. Washington, Balt., 1978—; prof. dept. biology Johns Hopkins U.; mem. devel. biology panel NSF, Washington, 1979-80, sci. adv. panel Office of Tech. Assessment, Congress, Washington, 1979-80, recombinant DNA adv. com. NIH, Bethesda, Md., 1980-84, sci. adv. com. Japanese Human Frontier Sci., sci. adv. com. Competitive Rsch. Grants Office, USDA; mem. commn. on life scis., basic biology bd. NRC, NAS, Washington, 1984—; bd. dirs. Genetics Soc. Am.; mem. bd. overseers Harvard U. Contbr. articles to profl. jours., chpts. to books; editor Gene, 1981-84; editor, bd. of rev. editors Sci., 1985—. Grantee NSF and USDA, 1979-84, NIH, 1984—. Mem. AAAS, Am. Acad. Arts and Scis., Phi Beta Kappa (vis. scholar 1984-85), Sigma Xi. Office: Carnegie Inst of Washington Dept Embryology 115 W University Pkwy Baltimore MD 21210

FEDORUK, SYLVIA O., Canadian provincial official, educator; b. Canora, Sask., Can., May 5, 1927; d. Theodore and Annie (Romaniuk) F. BA, U. Sask., 1949, MA, 1951; DSc, U. Windsor, Ont., Can., 1987. Asst. physicist Saskatoon (Sask.) Cancer Clinic, 1951-57, sr. physicist, 1957; asst. prof. U. Sask., Saskatoon, 1956-89, chancellor, 1986-89, prof. emeritus, 1989—; dir. physics svcs. Sask. Cancer Found., 1966-86; lt. gov. Province of Sask., 1988—; cons. in nuclear medicine. Recipient Queen's Jubilee medal, 1977, Century Saskatoon medal, 1982. Fellow Can. Coll. Physicists in Medicine; mem. Can. Ladies Curling Assn. (past pres.), Sports Fedn. Can. (past bd. dirs.). Ukrainian Greek Orthodox. Office: Govt House, 4607 Dewdney Ave, Regina, SK Canada S4P 3V7*

FEE, CATHERINE ANN, pharmacist; b. Pitts., May 9, 1965; d. George Thomas and Frances Ann (Reed) F. BS in Pharmacy, Ohio No. U., 1990; student, U. Pitts., 1983-86. Lifeguard Crystal Pool, Fayette City, Pa., 1983-86; pharmacy intern Fee's Pharmacy, Fayette City, 1985—; pharm. lab. asst. Ohio No. U., Ada, 1987-89; pharmacy intern Blanchard Valley Hosp., Findlay, Ohio, 1989—. Named one of Outstanding Coll. Students Am., 1987. Mem. Am. Pharm. Assn., Ohio Pharm. Assn., Pa. Pharm. Assn., Lambda Kappa Sigma, Alpha Xi Delta (house mgr. 1987-88, song leader 1987-88, scholar 1988). Republican. Presbyterian. Home: 1108 William Dr Belle Vernon PA 15012

FEE, ELIZABETH, history educator; b. Belfast, Northern Ireland; came to U.S., 1968.; d. John A.T. and Deirdre F. MA, Princeton U., 1971, Cambridge (Eng.) U., 1975; PhD, Princeton U., 1978. Teaching asst. Princeton (N.J.) U., 1971-72; instr. SUNY, Binghampton, 1972-74; archivist Johns Hopkins U., Balt., 1974-78, assoc. prof. Sch. Hygiene and Pub. Health, 1974—; cons. Princeton U., 1984. Author: Disease and Discovery, 1987; editor: Women and Health, 1983, (with Daniel H. Fox) AIDS: The Burdens of History, 1988; editorial cons. Internat. Jour. Health Services; editorial bd. Jour. of the History of Medicine and Allied Scis.; contbr. articles to profl. jours. Fulbright travel grantee, 1971, Scholar Exchange program grantee, 1983, research grantee Rockefeller Archives Ctr., 1984, 85, NSF, NEH; nat. fellow W.K. Kellogg Found., 1984-87. Mem. History of Sci. Soc., Am. Assn. History of Medicine, Am. Pub. Health Assn. Office: Johns Hopkins Sch Hygiene 624 N Broadway Baltimore MD 21205

FEELEY, SISTER KATHLEEN, college president, English language educator; b. Balt., Jan. 7, 1929; d. Jerome Lawrence and Theresa (Tasker) F. B.A. in English, Coll. Notre Dame of Md.; M.A. in English, Villanova U.; Ph.D. in English, Rutgers U.; student, Claremont U. Ctr. Inst. for Study of Change. Joined Sch. Sisters of Notre Dame, Roman Cath. Ch. Am. Council on Edn. intern in acad. adminstrn., to 1971; pres. Coll. Notre Dame of Md., Balt., 1971—; asst. prof. English, then assoc. prof., then prof. Coll. Notre Dame of Md.; dir. Balt. Gas and Electric Co., Md. Econ. Devel Corp.; trustee St. Vincent Coll., Latrobe, Pa., Marian House, Notre Dame Preparatory Sch.; lectured at St. John Coll., Santa Fe, Ga. State Coll., Longwood Coll., Wheaton Coll., Fairfield U.; lectr. colls., univs., Japan, 1981. Author: Flannery O'Connor: Voice of the Peacock; contbr. articles to profl. jours. Named Woman of Yr., Jewish Nat. Fund Women's Aux., 1975, Good Will Ambassador in Israel, Am.-Israel Soc., 1976; recipient Woman of Yr. award Md. Colonial Soc., 1976, J. Jefferson Miller award Greater Balt. Com., 1979, Andrew White medal Loyola Coll., Balt., 1981, Hannah G. Solomon award Nat. Council Jewish Women, 1987, Jimmie Schwartz Found. medallion, 1987. Mem. Council on Fgn. Affairs (bd. dirs.), Assn. Catholic Colls. and Univs. (trustee). Home and Office: Coll Notre Dame of Md Caroline House 4701 N Charles St Baltimore MD 21210*

FEELEY, MARY ELIZABETH, medical records professional; b. Pottsville, Pa., May 25, 1960; d. James Joseph and Dolores Margaret (Kelly) F. BS in Health Record Adminstrn., York Coll. Pa., 1982. Transcriptionist Pottsville Hosp., 1982-84, coord., 1982-84, DRG coord., 1984-86, dir. med. records, 1986—; cons. area nursing homes, 1984—. Mem. Am. Med. Record Assn., Pa. Med. Record Assn., Cen. Pa. Med. Record Assn. (chair nominating com. 1987-88, pres. 1988-89, 2d dir. 1989-90). Office: Pottsville Hosp/ WarneClinic 420 S Jackson St Pottsville PA 17901

FEELEY, OLIVIA STADELMAN, computer professional; b. Plainfield, N.J., Feb. 1, 1939; d. Frank and Olive (Spears) Stadelman; m. J. Donald Feeley (div. May 1987); children: Donna, Dawn, Debbie. Student, Rutgers U., 1955-56. With Dictaphone Corp., 1974—, sr. data base analyst programmer, 1983-87; adminstr. data base Dictaphone Corp., Stratford, Conn., 1987—. Home: 91 Cynthia Dr Fairfield CT 06430-3001 Office: Dictaphone Corp 3191 Broadbridge Ave Stratford CT 06497

FEELEY, SHARON DENISE, marketing and management consultant; b. Chgo., Sept. 17, 1949; d. Darrell Ford and Florence Marsha (Gregorek) F. Student, SUNY, 1987—. Coll. mgr. Sara Beattie Secretarial Coll., Hong Kong, 1976-77; bus. mgr. Transplex Inc., Oak Park, Ill., 1977-79, gen. mgr., 1981-84; trade officer Far East State of Ill., Hong Kong, 1979-81; purchase agt., contract sales aide Honeywell Inc., Bensenville, Ill., 1984-86; now internat. bus. mktg. and mgmt. cons. Lake Zurich, Ill., 1986—. Editor: Tai Chi Classics, 1978. Mem. Asian Women's Mgmt. Assn. (vice chmn., founding mem. 1979-81), Mensa Club. Lodge: Rosicrucians. Home: 1183 Betty Dr Lake Zurich IL 60047

FEENEY, MARY ROSALIND, accountant; b. N.Y.C., June 13, 1951; d. John Michael and Mary Rosalind (Fitzgerald) F. BS, SUNY, 1981, MS, 1984. CPA, N.Y., V.I., Pa. Adminstrv. asst. Chase Manhattan Bank, N.Y.C., 1970-77; credit card supr. Vt. National Bank, Brattleboro, 1977-88; sr. acct. Urbach, Kahn & Werlin P.C. CPA's, Albany, N.Y., 1981-83; teaching asst. and lectr. SUNY, 1983-85; firm mgr. Brammer, Chasen & O'Connell CPA's, St. Thomas, V.I., 1985-88; asst. prof. Wilkes U., Wilkes-Barre, Pa., 1988-90; pvt. practice Albany, 1983-85, St. Thomas, 1986-88, Hunlock Creek, Pa., 1988-90. Sayles-Pierce scholar SUNY Alumni Assn., 1979-81. Mem. AICPA, Am. Woman Soc. of Cert. Pub. Acct., Am. Soc. of Women Acct. (chpt. treas. 1983-85), Pa. Inst. of Cert. Pub. Accts., NAFE, Am. Acctg. Assn., V.I. Soc. of Cert. Pub. Accts. Republican. Roman Catholic. Home: 6021 SE Landing Way #7 Stuart FL 34997

FEENEY, SANDRA BENEDICT, artist; b. Fargo, N.D., Oct. 16, 1936; m. James K. Feeney, Mar. 20, 1936; children: James, Patrick, Daniel. BA, Goddard Coll., 1980. Artist Various Exhibitions, various cities, 1984-87. Co-editor Insight: Jour. Photog. Criticism; contbr. articles to profl. jours. Recipient photography fellowship, Nat. Endowment for the Arts, 1986, R.I. State Council on the Arts, 1986. Home: 10 Cooke St Providence RI 02906

FEENKER, CHERIE DIANE, law librarian; b. Birmingham, Ala., Nov. 14, 1950; d. Marshall Ross and Joy (Martin) F. BA, U. Montevallo, 1971; MLS, U. Ala., 1979, JD with honors, 1989. Periodical librarian sci. and tech. dept. Birmingham Pub. Library, 1971-73, br. head, 1973-80, reference librarian tech. and bus. dept., 1980-84; law librarian Lange, Simpson, Robinson & Somerville, Birmingham, 1984—. Mem. vestry St. Andrew's Parish, Birmingham, 1985-87; mem. faculty CLE, 1987. Mem. ABA, Ala. Libr. Assn. (mem. faculty roundtable 1986-88, moderator 1987-88), Am. Assn. Law Librs., Beta Phi Mu. Episcopalian. Home: 2104 2d Ave N Irondale AL 35210 Office: Lange Simpson Robinson & Somerville 1700 1st Ala Bank Bldg Birmingham AL 35203

FEESE, BRENDA, marketing professional; b. Springfield, Mo., Oct. 3, 1959; d. Johnny Snow and Carol Bodenhamer; children: April, Ely. Cert., F&I Mgmt.'s Advanced Seminar, Jackie Cooper's Profl. Auto, various sales seminars. Account exec. Today's Woman Jour., Springfield; fin. and ins. mgr. Thrifty Imports, Springfield, Acura of Springfield, Douglas Toyota, Springfield; lease/office mgr. Redi-Data Systems of Am., Springfield; gen. mgr. Pay Master of St. Louis Redi-Data Systems of Am., St. Louis. Republican. Baptist. Home: 12545 Olive Blvd Ste 113 Saint Louis MO 63141 Office: Lake Level One 11885 Lackland Rd Saint Louis MO 63146

FEESER, PATRICIA, academic administrator, educator; b. Chgo., Aug. 27, 1938; d. John and Rosamaria (Klos) Reinhold; m. Larry James Feeser, Aug. 19, 1961; children: Anne Elizabeth, David John. BA, U. Color., 1962. cert. tchr., N.Y., Colo. Tchr. German and English Chartiers Valley Schs., Pitts., 1961; tchr. German Edgewood Sch. System, Pitts., 1961-62, Boulder (Colo.) Valley Schs., 1968-72; substitute tchr. Niskayuna Schs., Schenectady, N.Y., 1972-82; dir. vols. New Medico, Troy, N.Y., 1982; sr. ctr. dir. Cath. Family Svcs., Schenectady, 1982-87; staffing adminstr. Residential Opportunities, Cohoes, N.Y., 1987-88; adminstr. med. program St. Peter's Hosp., Albany, N.Y., 1988-89; intern adminstr. SUNY, Albany, 1989—. Columnist Capital Newspaper, 1988—. Dir. vols. Aids Coun. N.E. N.Y., Albany, 1989; dir. pub. rels. Hall History, Schenectady, 1990; chm. bd. Law, Order and Justice Ctr., Schenectady, 1982-86; sec. Niskayuna Rep. Com., 1989—; bd. dirs. Niskayuna Community Action Program, editor, 1988—. Recipient Community Srv. award Law, Order and Justice Ctr., 1986. Mem. AAUW (pres. Schenectady br. 1983-84), LWV (pres. local chpt. 1980-84). Home: 854 Huntingdon Dr Schenectady NY 12309 Office: SUNY 1400 Washington Ave LI85 Albany NY 12222

FEEZOR-STEWART, BARBARA YVONNE, anthropoligist, ethnohistorian, researcher; b. Salisbury, N.C., June 19, 1950; d. Walter Baxter and Winifred Sevilla (St. Pierre) Feezor; m. Johnny Leroy Stewart, Aug. 24, 1980; children: James, Autumn. Student, San Francisco State U., 1986; BA, U. Calif., Berkeley, 1987; MA, UCLA, 1989, postgrad., 1989-90. Proposal writer Qua Qui Am. Indian Ctr., Missoula, Mont., 1976-78; tchr. Intertribal Alcohol Treatment Ctr., Sheridan, Wyo., 1980-81; intern Consortium of United Indian Nations, Oakland, Calif., 1983-87; Am.-Indian recruiter UCLA Grad. Sch. Pub. Health, 1987-88; researcher, grants writer UCLA Am.-Indian Studies Ctr., 1988—; Plains Indian interpreter Custer Battlefield Nat. Monument, Crow Agy., Mont., 1985; co-founder Friends of Am.-Indian Radio, Berkeley, 1985, Qua Qui Am.-Indian Child Care, Missoula, 1978; asst. prof. Am. Indian studies Calif. State U., Long Beach; teaching asst. anthropology, UCLA, 1990—. Mem. Urban Indian Health Bd., San Francisco Bay area, 1983-88; facilitator Am.-Indian Leadership Forum, U. Calif., Berkeley, 1986—; rep. Survival Am.-Indian Assn., UN, N.Y.C., 1976; security chief 5th Ann. Am.-Indian Music Festival, Oakland, 1983; coord., arena dir. Berkeley Intertribal Pow-Wow, U. Calif., Berkeley, 1987; bd. dirs. Intertribal Tutoring Project, Berkeley, 1986-87; presenter meetings Southwestern Anthrop. Assn., 1990; workshop leader Nat. Indian Edn. Assn. Conf., San Diego., 1990; chair L.A. Am. Indian Mental Task Force, 1989—; co-organizer No. Lights Conf., Univ. Calif., Davis, 1990. Recipient Hon. Mention, 3d Ann. Martin Luther King Jr. Convocation Communion, 1985; Am.-Indian Leadership Appointment, 1987-89; Nat. Endowment For Humanities fellow, 1990, Newberry Libr. fellow, 1990—, Inst. Am. Cultures Dept. Anthropology UCLA fellow, 1990—. Mem. U. Calif. Alumnae Assn., Minn. Hist. Soc., Am. Anthropology Assn., Nat. Indian Edn. Assn., Am. Indian Grad. Student Assn., Am. Ednl. Rsch. Assn., Am. Ethnol. Soc. Republican. Home: 15180 Eagle Creek Ave Prior Lake MN 55372 Office: UCLA Dept Anthropology 314 Maines Hall Los Angeles CA 90024

FEHL, PATRICIA KATHERINE, retired educator; b. Cin., May 29, 1927; d. Norman and Gertrude (Morris) F.; A.B. cum laude, DePauw U., 1949; M.S., Ind. U., 1955, Ed.D., 1966. Tchr., Crawfordsville Schs., Ind., 1950-52; critic tchr., lab. sch., coll. methods instr. Ind. U., Bloomington, 1952-62; assoc. prof. health, phys. edn. and recreation U. Cin., 1962-73; prof., chmn. dept. gen. program Sch. Phys. Edn., W.Va. U., Morgantown, 1973-89 . Kennedy Found. grantee, 1966. Fellow Am. Sch. Health Assn.; mem. Am. Alliance for Health, Phys. Edn., Recreation and Dance (honor award 1986, v.p. recreation 1973-75, chmn. nominating com. 1985, 88, 89, 90), Midwest Dist. AAHPERD (historian, 1974-78, pres. 1978-80, Pres.'s award 1976, Honor award 1983, meritorious award 1986. parliamentarian 1973, 76, 87, 88), Ohio Assn. Health, Phys. Edn. and Recreation (v.p., chmn. div. girls and women's sports 1970-72, meritorious award 1973), W.Va. Assn. Health, Phys. Edn. and Recreation (v.p. recreation 1975; Honor award 1978, Ray O. Duncan award 1987), W.Va. Recreation and Parks Assn. (bd. dirs. 1978-81, treas. 1983, pres. 1982-84; profl. cert. 1980), Ohio Parks and Recreation Assn. (pres. 1972; Meritorious award 1974), Midwest Assn. Phys. Edn. for Coll. Women (governing bd.), Nat. Recreation and Park Assn., Phi Delta Kappa, Pi Lambda Theta, Delta Kappa Gamma. Contbr. articles to jours.; contbr. to Ohio Secondary Girls Phys. Edn. Curriculum Guide. Address: 314 Harvard Ave Terrace Park OH 45174

FEIGEL, CELESTE LOUISE, financial services administrator; b. Los Angeles, May 16, 1952; d. Emery John and Helen Louise (Bradbury) W.; m. Robert Richardson Feigel, Apr. 11, 1971 (div. 1973). BBA, Western State U., Doniphan, Mo., 1987; grad., Hypnotism Tng. Inst., Glendale, Calif., 1990. Cert. hypnotherapist. Credit mgr. accounts receivable Gensler-Lee Diamonds, Santa Barbara, Calif., 1973-74, Terry Hinge and Hardware, Van Nuys, Calif., 1975-78; credit mgr., fin. analyst Peanut Butter Fashions, Chatsworth, Calif., 1978-82; personal mgr. Charter Mgmt. Co., Beverly Hills, Calif., 1982-83; co-owner, v.p. Noreen Jenney Communicates, Beverly Hills, 1983-85; corp. credit mgr., fin. analyst Cen. Diagnostic Lab., Tarzana, Calif., 1985-89; credit mgr., fin. analyst Metwest Clin. Lab., Inc., Tarzana, Calif., 1989—; pvt. practice, 1990—; cons. Results Now, Inc., Tarzana, 1986-87. Mem. NAFE, Nat. Assn. Credit Mgmt., Credit Mgrs. Assn. So. Calif., Credit Ednl. Found., Nat. Humane Ednl. Found., Credit Mgrs. Assn. Trade Groups (bd. govs. 1988-89), Nat. Clin. Lab. Trade Group (chmn. 1988-89), Med. and Surg. Suppliers Trade Group (vice-chmn. 1988-89, chmn. 1989-90), Soc. Am. Magicians, Acad. Magical Arts, Internat. Brotherhood of Magicians, Assn. Advanced Ethical Hypnosis, Am. Coun. Hypnotist Examiners. Republican. Roman Catholic.

FEIGEN, IRENE, artist, educator; b. Bklyn., Aug. 13, 1944; d. Max and Jean (Weingarten) Marder; m. Daniel Feigen, Mar. 29, 1963; children: Erik, Nicole, Ross. BFA, Bklyn. Coll., 1964; MFA, CCNY, 1965; cert. Printmaking, NYU, 1985. Lic. tchr., N.Y.; cert. printmaker, N.Y. Tchr. fine arts N.Y.C. Bd. Edn., 1962-65; prof. fine arts Fairleigh Dickinson U., Madison, N.J., 1980-87; freelance artist, art educator Art Expo N.Y., 1980-90; artist in residence, Livingston Home and Sch. Assn., 1980—, Riker Hill Art Park, Livingston, N.J., B'nai Abraham, Livingston, 1987. Exhibitions include Robert Ward Galleries, N.Y.C., Korby Gallery, Cedar Grove, N.J., Bergen Mus., Paramus, N.J., Morris Mus., Morristown, N.J., Montclair Mus., Hebrew Home for Aged, Riverdale, N.Y., The Nese Gallery, Irvine, Calif., Newark Mus., Papermill Playhouse Gallery, Millburn, N.J., Straleys Gallery, Livingston, N.J., Whichcraft Studio, South Orange, Long Beach Island, N.J., The Key Gallery, N.Y.C., Art 3 Assocs., Livingston, Art 3 of Ft. Lee, N.J., MCI, SONY, Lewis Internat., Clifton Radiology Ctr., among others. Active Allied Bd. of Trade; bd. dirs. Arts Coun. of Livingston, 1990. Recipient numerous artistic awards. Mem. Internat. Soc. Arts, West Essex Watercolor Soc., Essex County Arts Soc. (bd. dirs. 1980-85), Livingston Arts Assn. (v.p. 1977-85, bd. dirs. 1970-85), The Printmakers Coun., Mus. Contemporary Crafts, Artists Equity. Home and Studio: 48 Blackstone Dr Livingston NJ 07039

FEIGHAN, LYNNE ROSSEN, educational administrator; b. Lakewood, Oh., Jan. 2, 1938; d. Joseph Mckinley and Marguerite (Downey) R.; m. John Thomas, June 11, 1960; children: Alison Rossen, John English. Student, Vassar Coll., Poughkeepsie, 1955-57; BA, U. Mich., 1957-59. Asst. treas. Andrews, Bartlett Assn., Cleve., 1959-60; tchr. Cleve. Pub. Schs., 1960-61; freelance editor World Pub., Cleve., 1962-64; self-employed Image Inc., Cleve.; devel. dir. Laurel Sch., Cleve., 1964—. Mem. Ohio Coun. of Fundraising Execs. (pres. 1987-88), Coun. for Advancement & Support Edn., Vassar Club (pres. 1971-73), U. Club. Office: Laurel School 1 Lyman Circle Shaker Heights OH 44122

FEIGIN, BARBARA SOMMER, advertising executive; b. Berlin, Germany, Nov. 16, 1937; came to U.S., 1940, naturalized, 1949; d. Eric Daniel and Charlotte Martha (Demmer) Sommer; m. James Feigin, Sept. 17, 1961; children: Michael, Peter, Daniel. BA in Polit. Sci., Whitman Coll., 1959; cert. of Bus. Adminstrn., Harvard-Radcliffe Program Bus. Adminstrn., 1960. Mktg. rsch. asst. Richardson-Vick Co., Wilton, Conn., 1960-61; market rsch. analyst SCM Corp., N.Y.C., 1961-62; group rsch. supr. Benton & Bowles, Inc., N.Y.C., 1963-67; assoc. rsch. dir. Marplan Rsch. Co., N.Y.C., 1968-69; exec. v.p. strategic svcs. Grey Advt. Inc., N.Y.C., 1969—, mem. agy. policy council; bd. dirs. VF Corp. Contbr. articles to profl. jours. Bd. overseers Whitman Coll. Recipient Women Achievers award YWCA, 1987. Mem. Advt. Rsch. Found. (bd. dirs. 1987). Office: Grey Advt Inc 777 3rd Ave New York NY 10017

FEIGIN, JUDITH ZOBEL, educational psychologist; b. N.Y.C., Mar. 17, 1941; d. Isador and Regina (Schwechter) Zobel; m. Ralph David Feigin, June 26, 1960; children: Susan M., Michael E., Debra F. BS, Hunter Coll., N.Y.C., 1960; MA in Edn., St. Louis U., 1977; EdD, U. Houston, 1987. Tchr. Boston pub. schs., 1960-63; spl. tchr. Briarwood Sch., Houston, 1979-81; instr. U. Houston, 1983-84, Pearland Ind. Sch. Dist., Tex., 1986-87; dir. learning support ctr. Tex. Children's Hosp., Houston, 1986—; psychometrician St. Louis Children's Hosp., 1975-76; cons. in field. Author: Development of Social Skills, 1987, Language Arts/Social Skills: A Temperament-based Curriculum, 1986; co-author: Educational Development of Child with Turner's Syndrome, 1985. Mem. Mental Health/Mental Retardation Authority of Harris County, Houston, 1981-84; v.p. Orton Dyslexia Soc., Houston, 1980-82. Mem. Am. Psychol. Assn., Tex. Assn. for Children with Learning Disabilities, Coun. for Exceptional Children, Coun. for Learning Disabilities, Phi Delta Kappa. Office: Tex Children's Hosp 8080 N Stadium Dr Houston TX 77054

FEIGON, JUDITH TOVA, physician, educator; b. Galveston, Tex., Dec. 2, 1947; d. Louis and Ethel (Goldberg) F.; m. Nathan C. Goldman; 1 child. AB, Barnard Coll., Columbia U., 1970; postgrad., Rice U. and U. Houston, 1970-71; MD, U. Tex.-San Antonio, 1976. Diplomate Am. Bd. Ophthalmology. Intern Mt. Auburn Hosp., Cambridge, Mass. Intern and clin. teaching fellow, Harvard U. Med. Sch., 1976-77; resident in ophthalmology, Baylor Coll. Medicine, Houston, 1977-80, fellowship in retina, 1980-82, clin. instr., 1982—; asst. prof. ophthalmology U. Tex. Med. Br., Galveston, 1982-85, clin. asst. prof., 1985—; pvt. practice medicine specializing in ophthalmology, vitreoretinal diseases and surgery, Houston, 1983—; physician advisor to Houston br. Tex. Soc. to Prevent Blindness, 1987-89, also bd. dirs.; mem. staff Meth., St. Lukes/Tex. Children's, John Sealy, Park Pla. Contbr. articles to profl. publs. Mem. AMA, Am. Acad. Ophthalmology, Tex. Med. Assn., Tex. Opthal. Soc., Houston Opthal. Soc., Harris County Med. Soc., U. Tex.-San Antonio Alumni Assn., Harvard Med. Sch. Alumni Assn., Vitreous Soc. Office: 6410 Fannin Ste 404 Houston TX 77030

FEILER, JO ALISON, artist; b. L.A., Apr. 16, 1951; d. Alfred Martin and Leatrice Lucille Feiler. Student, UCLA, 1969, Art Ctr. Coll. Design, L.A., 1970-72; BFA, Calif. Inst. Arts, 1973, MFA, 1975. Asst. dir. Frank Perls Gallery, Beverly Hills, Calif., 1969-70; photography editor Coast Environ. mag., L.A., 1970-72; art dir. Log/An Inc., L.A., 1975-82. One-woman shows Inst. Contemporary Art, London, 1975, Calif. Inst. Arts, Valencia, 1975, NUAGE, L.A., 1978, Susan Harder Gallery, N.Y.C., 1984; exhibited in numerous group shows, 1975—; represented in permanent collections including Nat. Portrait Gallery, London, Victoria and Albert Mus., London, Met. Mus. Art, N.Y.C., Mus. Modern Art, N.Y.C., Los Angeles County Mus. Art, Internat. Mus. Photography, Rochester, N.Y., Santa Bara Mus. Art, Oakland Mus., Mus. Fine Arts, Houston. Recipient cert. art excellence Los Angeles County Mus. Art, 1968, award Laguna Beach Mus. Art, 1976; Calif. Inst. Arts scholar, 1974. Mem. Royal Photog. Soc. Gt. Britain, Friends Photography. Democrat. Office: 251 E 51st St Ste 19G New York NY 10022

FEILER, KAREN A., sales executive; b. Ridgewood, N.J., Mar. 24, 1962; d. Edwin Knolton and Jessie (Cooper) F. AA, Bergen Community Coll., 1983; BS, Fairleigh Dickinson U., 1985, MBA, 1987. Catering svcs. mgr. Marriott Corp., Somerset, N.J., 1988; exec. meeting mgr. Marriott Corp., Somerset, 1988-89, catering mgr., 1989—. Recipient MBA Fellowship Fairleigh Dickinson U., 1985-87. Mem. Assn. for MBA Execs., Nat. Assn. for Female Execs., Hotel Sales & Mktg. Assn., Delta Mu Delta (pres. 1986-87). Republican. Home: 5406 Quail Ridge Dr Plainsboro NJ 08536 Office: Marriott Corp 110 Davidson Ave Somerset NJ 08873

FEIN, HARRIET KRONMAN, state official; b. N.Y.C., Apr. 9, 1927; d. Jacob and Anna R. (Dick) Kronman; m. Richard Saul Fein, Feb. 6, 1948; children: Ellen, Beth, Judith. PhB, U. Wis., 1948; MEd, Columbia U., 1973. Cert. rehab. counselor, alcoholism counselor, sch. psychologist, N.Y. Div. head Dutchess County Dept. Mental Hygiene, Poughkeepsie, N.Y., 1975-82; dist. mgr. Office Vocat. Rehab. N.Y. State Edn. Dept., Poughkeepsie, 1982—; bd. dirs. Dutchess County Health Planning Coun., 1976-85, treas., 1980-81, 2d v.p., 1981-82; N.E. regional rep. Nat. Rehab. Adminstrn., 1988-90, 90-92. Mem. policy guidance com., oversight com. Putnam-Dutchess Pvt. Industry Coun., 1983—, chmn. personnel, 1985-87; mem. cen. planning com. United Way Dutchess County, 1983-87, mem. admissions and grants com., 1987—. Mem. Am. Psychol. Assn. (assoc. rep. div. 1935, 1981-85), Nat. Rehab. Assn., Nat. Rehab. Counselors Assn. Office: Office Vocat/Ednl Svcs to Individuals w/Disabilities 120 Dutchess Turnpike Poughkeepsie NY 12603

FEIN, LEAH GOLD, psychologist; b. Minsk, Russia; d. Jacob Lyon and Sarah Freda (Meltzer) Gold; m. Alfred Gustave Fein, June 10, 1944; 1 child, Ira Hirsh. BS, Albertus Magnus Coll., 1939; MA, Yale U., 1942, PhD (Marion Talbot fellow), 1944. Diplomate Am. Bd. Profl. Psychology. Health educator New Haven Schs., 1930-43; asst. prof. psychology Carleton Coll., 1944-45; rsch. assoc. Conn. Interracial Commn., 1946; chief psychologist Seattle Psychiat. Clinic, 1947-48; prof. U. Bridgeport, 1946-47, 52-58; ind. clin. practice, specializing in clin., child consultation, Seattle, 1948-52, Stamford, Conn., 1952-67, N.Y.C., 1967-81, West Palm Beach, Fla., 1982-87, Stamford, Conn., 1987—; clin. cons. Conn. Commn. on Alcoholism Clinic, 1952-64; rsch. assoc. Soc. for Investigation Human Ecology; therapist Norwalk Psychiat. Clinic, 1952-64; cons. Child Edn. Found., 1953-56; dir. rsch. Sch. Nursing Norwalk Hosp., 1961-64; dir. clin svcs. cerebral palsy and mental retardation, Waterbury, Conn., 1964-65; assoc. prof. Quinnipiac Coll., Hamden, Conn., 1965-66; cons., instr., med. staff N.Y. Hosp.-Cornell Med. Ctr., White Plains, 1966-67; dir. psychology Psychiat. Treatment Ctr., N.Y., 1967-68; rsch. assoc. Roosevelt Hosp. Child Psychiatry, 1968-69; supr., cons. rsch. psychologist Bur. Child Guidance, N.Y.C. Bd. Edn., 1969-72; faculty Greenwich Inst. Psychoanalytic Studies, 1971-79; sr. rsch. scientist Postgrad. Ctr. for Mental Health, N.Y.C., 1980-82; mem. program com. Internat. Congress Social Psychiatry, 1974; rsch. cons. N.Y.C. Mayor's Vol. Action Com.,Human Resources Adminstrn., N.Y.C. Study of Delinquency and Study Abused and Neglected Children; cons., insvc. trainer Center Group Counseling, Boca Raton, Fla., 1982-84; manuscript reviewer Perceptual Motor Skills. Fellow Soc. Personality Assessment, Am. Psychol. Assn. (coun. of reps. div. 42, 1983-86), Am. Acad. Psychotherapists, Internat. Coun. Psychologists (v.p. 1961-62, 71-73, pres. 1973-75), Am. Orthopsychiat. Assn., N.Y. Acad. Sci.; mem. Nat. Assn. Gifted (v.p. 1961-62), Internat. Coun. Women Psychologists (chmn. profl. rels. among psychologists), Psychologists in Pvt. Practice (treas. 1972-78), Am. Psychol. Assn. (sec. div. psychotherapy 1966-69; coun. of reps. 1982-86), N.Y. State Psychol. Assn., Fla. Psychol Assn., Am. Assn. Group Psychotherapy and Psychodrama (council 1973-75), World Fedn. Mental Health, Nat. Council Jewish Women, Hadassah. Club: Yale (N.Y.C.). Author: The Three Dimensional Personality Test—Reliability, Validity and Clinical Implications, 1960; The Changing School Scene: Challenge to Psychology, 1974, A Rough Row to Hoe, 1990; editor Jour. Internat. Understanding, vol. 9-10, 1974; Jour. Psychology Div. Am. Friends Hebrew U.; guest editor Jour. Clin. Child Psychology, 1975; cons. editor Jour. Psychotherapy in Pvt. Practice; others; contbr. Jour. Clin. Psychology, other profl. jours. Address: Newburry Common 1450 Washington Blvd Apt N 706 Stamford CT 06902

FEIN, LINDA ANN, nurse anesthetist, consultant; b. Cin., Dec. 10, 1949; d. Joseph and Elizabeth P. (Kannady) Stofle; m. Thomas Paul Fein, Dec. 11, 1971. Nursing diploma, Miami Valley Hosp. Sch. Nursing, Dayton, Ohio, 1971, Wright State U., Dayton, 1969; postgrad. U. Cin. Med. Ctr., 1978. Nursing asst. Miami Valley Hosp., Dayton, 1969-71; staff nurse operating room Cin. Children's Hosp. and Med. Ctr., 1971, 73, Peninsula Hosp., Burlingame, Calif., 1972-73; staff nurse operating room and emergency room Doctors Hosp., San Diego, 1972; staff nurse emergency room Ohio State U. Hosps., Columbus, 1973-75, head nurse operating room, 1975-76; staff nurse anesthetist Bethesda Hosps., Cin., 1978-86; staff nurse anesthetist Mercy Hosp. of Fairfield, Cin., 1986—; childbirth educator psychoprophylactic method, 1975—; critical care nursing cons. Med. Communicators & Assocs., Salt Lake City, 1985—; co-owner Exec. Shops, Cin., 1982-85; speaker in field. Mem. search com. Cin. Gen. Hosp. Sch. of Anesthesia for Nurses, 1981-82; bd. dirs. YWCA, 1988—. Recipient Recognition of Profl. Excellence, First Nurse Anesthesia Faculty Assocs., 1982. Mem. Miami Valley Hosp. Sch. of Nursing Alumni Assn., Cin. Gen. Hosp. Sch. Anesthesia for Nurses Alumni Assn., Nurse Anesthetists of Greater Cin., Ohio Assn. Nurse Anesthetists, Am. Assn. Nurse Anesthetists, Am. Assn. Operating Room Nurses, Am. Assn. Critical Care Nurses, Nat. Registry of Cert. Nurses in Advanced Practice (cert.), Am. Soc. Critical Care Medicine, Am. Trauma Soc., NAFE, Altrusa Internat. (officer 1985—). Republican. Methodist. Lodge: Eastern Star. Avocations: antiques, gourmet cooking, African violets, roses, swimming. Home: 650 History Bridge Ln Hamilton OH 45013

FEINBERG, GLENDA JOYCE, restaurant chain executive; b. Louisville, Feb. 8, 1948; d. Harold and Winnie Esther (McIntosh) F.; divorced; 1 child, Anthony John. Student, Purdue U., 1967-68, Ind. U., 1977-79. Cert. in restaurant and personnel mgmt. Beverage mgr. Don Ce Sar Beach Hotel, St. Petersburg Beach, Fla., 1979-80; catering dir. Best Western-Skyway Inn, St. Petersburg, Fla., 1980-83; gen. mgr. Village, Inc., St. Petersburg Beach, 1983-86; banquet mgr. Tradewinds Resort Hotel, St. Petersburg Beach, 1986-87; exec. mgr. Ponderosa, Inc., Clearwater, Fla., 1987—. Mem. bd. dirs. AIDS Coalitions Pinellas. Mem. Clearwater C. of C., NOW, World Wildlife Fedn., Nat. Geographic Soc., Greenpeace, Amnesty Internat. Democrat. Office: Ponderosa Inc 1101 Cleveland St Clearwater FL 34615

FEINBERG, JILL LESLIE, communications company executive; b. N.Y.C., May 12, 1963; d. A. Herbert and Nancy Jane (Ingalsbe) F. BA, Boston U., 1985, BS, 1985. Sales asst. sta. WMRE-AM, Boston, 1986; copywriter TNT Advt., Acton, Mass., 1986-88; assoc. account rep. Sta. ABC-TV, N.Y.C., 1988-89, account rep., 1989—. Mem. Internat. Radio and TV Soc., Boston U. Alumni Soc. (Alumni Student award 1985). Home: 39 Leffler Hill Rd Flemington NJ 08822 Office: ABC TV 77 W 66th St New York NY 10023

FEINBERG, SUSAN L., school psychologist; b. Memphis, Dec. 10, 1944; d. Dave and Miriam (Phillips) Lebovitz; m. Fred B. Feinberg, Aug. 18, 1968; children: Marni, Hal. BA, U. Fla., 1966; MA, Emory U., 1971; EdS, Ga. State U., 1980. Lic. sch. psychologist Ga. Speech pathologist Atlanta Pub. Schs., 1966-70; sch. psychologist Decatur City Schs., Atlanta, 1978-80, DeKalb County Schs., Atlanta, 1978-80, Cobb County Schs., Atlanta, 1978-84, The New Sch., Atlanta, 1978-85, Floyd County, Atlanta, 1985, Buford City Schs., Atlanta, 1978-80, Trinity Sch., Atlanta, 1982—, LaGrange (Ga.) Schs., 1990—; speech pathologist Arbor Acad., Atlanta, 1970-78; mem. Fulton County Supt. Commn., Atlanta, 1988—. Recipient Leadership Atlanta, 1982.

FEINDT, MARY C., surveyor; b. Chgo., Mar. 9, 1916; d. Ernest and Lila M. (Waitt) Bastian; 1 child, Lawrence R. BS, U. Mich., 1938, MS in Civil Engring., 1944; AB, Albion (Mich.) Coll., 1937. Lic. land surveyor, Mich., Ill. Pres., owner Charlevoix Abstract & Engring. Co., Charlevoix, Mich. Contbr. articles to profl. jours. Recipient to Mary C. Feindt award. Mem. ASCE, Am. Land Title Assn. (past bd. govs.), Am. Congress on Surveying and Mapping (hon.), Mich. Land Title Assn. (past pres.), Mich. Soc. Registered Land Surveyors (past bd. dirs.), Soc. of Women Engrs. Home: PO Box 18 Charlevoix MI 49720

FEINER, ARLENE MARIE, librarian, researcher, consultant; b. Spring Green, Wis., Mar. 23, 1937; d. Herman Joseph and Cecelia Margaret (Meixelsperger) F. BA in History, Alverno Coll., 1959; MA in Libr. Sci., Rosary Coll., 1971; MA in Orgnl. Devel., Loyola U., Chgo., 1985. Gen. office worker USIA, Washington, 1959-60; adminstrv. sec. Nat. Coun. Cath. Women, Washington, 1960-62; asst. libr. Munich campus, U. Md., Fed. Republic Germany, 1962-64; preliminary cataloger, 1st editor MARC Pilot Project, Libr. of Congress, Washington, 1965-67; head libr. Acad. of the Holy Cross, Kensington, Md., 1967-70, Jesuit Sch. of Theology Libr., Chgo., 1971-79, coord. serial activities; women's studies bibliographer, Loyola U., Chgo., 1979-86; tech. svcs., collection devel. cons. DuPage Libr. System, 1986—. Editor: (bibliography) Current Serials, 1980-85; compiler: (bibliography) Guide to Women's Studies Sources, 1985; contbr. articles to profl. jours. Bd. dirs. Women's World Ctr., Chgo., 1985-88. Assn. of Theol. Schs. in U.S. and Can. grantee, 1976. Mem. ALA, NAFE, Chgo. Area Women's Studies Assn. Roman Catholic. Avocations: poetry, hiking, music. Home: 336 W Wellington Ave Apt 2102 Chicago IL 60657

FEINER, AVA SOPHIA, public affairs consultant, political economist; b. Bklyn., Feb. 13, 1950; d. Ignace and Lola (Pasternak) F.; m. Clifford Douglas Stromberg, June 25, 1972; children: Kimberly Greta, Eric George. BA summa cum laude, Yale U., 1971; MA, Harvard U., 1974, PhD in Govt., 1978. Legis. asst. to U.S. Senator Bill Bradley, Washington, 1979-82; dir. internat. trade policy U.S. C. of C., Washington, 1982-83, mgr. internat. policy dept., 1983-85; corp. program dir. IBM, Washington, 1985-87, corp. dir. pub. affairs, trade and investment, 1987; pres. Feiner Pub. Affairs Cons., Washington, 1988—; co-founder, dir. Washington Alive! Inc., 1989-90; pres. Washington (D.C.) Networks, 1990—; teaching fellow Harvard U., Cambridge, Mass., 1972-74; lectr. nat. and internat. politics and econs., 1978—; bd. dirs., World Trade Forum, Washington, 1987-89. Co-author: American Excellence in A World Economy, 1987; contbr. articles on econs., trade, fgn. policy to various publs. Del. to Atlantic Coun. Young Leadership Program, Wis. and Can., 1978, 80, Aspen Inst. Exec. Seminar, 1982, Germany-U.S. Young Leadership Conf., San Francisco, 1982. Fgn. Policy fellow Brookings Instn., 1975-76, guest scholar, 1976-77; Carnegie Endowment for Internat. Peace fellow, 1975-76. Mem. Coun. Fgn. Rels. (task force on women 1988—, term membership com. 1988—), Trade Policy Forum, Phi Beta Kappa.

FEINMAN, SUSAN MARGARET ELLMANN, health and research facility administrator, consultant; b. Atlanta, Sept. 16, 1930; d. John. I. and Mary Florence (Smith) Ellmann; m. Philip S. Birnbaum, 1953 (div. 1970); 1 child, Mary Susan; m. David M. Feinman, Jan. 22, 1972; children: Abigail Gay, Elizabeth Bonnie. BA, Wellesley Coll., 1951; MS, George Washington U., 1952, PhD, 1969. Teaching fellow microbiol. dept. George Washington U., Washington, 1966-68; supervisory microbiologist D.C. Govt., Washington, 1969-69; postdoctoral fellow Nat. Inst. Allergy and Infectious Diseases, Bethesda, Md., 1969-71; program analyst Alcohol, Drug Abuse, and Mental Health Agy., Rockville, Md., 1971-74; microbiologist FDA, Rockville, 1974-79; supervisory biologist Ctr. Food Safety and Nutrition FDA, Washington, 1987-90, U.S. Consumer Products Safety Commn., Bethesda, Md., 1979-86; health scientist adminstr. Nat. Cancer Inst. NIH, Bethesda, 1990—. Author: Environmental Impact Statement on Low Level Antibiotics in Feed, 1978, Formaldehyde Sensitivity and Toxicity, 1988; contbr. articles to profl. jours. Pres. Toastmasters, Bethesda and Parklawn, Md., 1977, 86, Fed. Employed Women, Parklawn, 1976. Mem. Am. Coll. Toxicology, Am. Soc. Microbiology, Soc. of Toxicology, Sigma Xi (pres. FDA chpt. 1978). Office: NIH/Nat Cancer Inst 5330 Westbard Ave Bethesda MD 20892

FEINSTEIN, DIANNE, former mayor; b. San Francisco, June 22, 1933; d. Leon and Betty (Rosenburg) Goldman; m. Bertram Feinstein, Nov. 11, 1962 (dec.); 1 child, Katherine Anne; m. Richard C. Blum, Jan. 20, 1980. BS, Stanford U., 1955; LLB (hon.), Golden Gate U., 1977; D Pub. Adminstrn. (hon.), U. Manila, 1981; D Pub. Service (hon.), U. Santa Clara, 1981; JD (hon.), Antioch U., 1983, Mills Coll., 1985; LHD (hon.), U. San Francisco, 1988. Fellow Coro Found., San Francisco, 1955-56; with Calif. Women's Bd. Terms and Parole, 1960-66; mem. Mayor's com. on crime, chmn. adv. com. Audit Detention, 1967-69; mem. Bd. of Suprs., San Francisco, 1970-79, pres., 1970-72, 74-76, 78; mayor of San Francisco, 1979-88; Mem. exec. com. U.S. Conf. of Mayors, 1983-88; gubernatorial candidate Calif. Dem. Party, 1990. Mem. Bay Area Conservation and Devel. Commn., 1973-78. Recipient Woman of Achievement award Bus. and Profl. Women's Clubs San Francisco, 1970, Disting. Woman award San Francisco Examiner, 1970, Coro Found. award, 1979, Coro Leadership award, 1988, Pres. medal U. Calif., San Francisco, 1988, Scopus award Am. Friends Hebrew U., 1981, Bortherhood/Sisterhood award NCCJ, 1986, Comdr.'s award U.S. Army, 1986, French Legion of Honor, 1984, Disting. Civilian award USN, 1987; named Number One Mayor All-Pro City Mgmt. Team City and State Mag., 1987. Mem. Trilateral Commn., Japan Soc. of No. Calif. (pres. 1988). Office: 909 Montgomery St Ste 400 San Francisco CA 94133

FEIRSTEIN, JANICE, real estate executive; b. Binchester, Eng., Dec. 3, 1942; came to U.S., 1967; d. Edward Mons and Mary (Watson) Walmsley; m. Laurence Feirstein, Aug. 27, 1967; 1 child, Douglas. Grad. in bus., Christison U., Spennymoor, Eng., 1961; grad. in mgmt., Inst. Fin. Edn., Ft. Lauderdale, Fla., 1980. Mgr. gift and gourmet cookware store, Lauderhill, Fla., 1977-78; exec. asst. Werbel Roth Sec., Ft. Lauderdale, Fla., 1978-79; from teller to new accounts rep. to asst. br. mgr. to br. mgr. Broward Fed. Savs. and Loan, Ft. Lauderdale, 1979-82; v.p., resort mgr. Broward Ocean View Properties, Inc., Ft. Lauderdale, 1982-88; owner Light House Cove Resort Mgmt., Inc., Ft. Lauderdale, 1988—; bd. dirs. Inst. Fin. Edn., 1981-83; mem. fin. com. Am. Resort and Recreational Devel. Assn., 1986. Vol. Gen. Hosp., Plantation, Fla., 1977-78; mem. adv. com. Broward County Sch. Bd., 1982; active Coop. Bus. Edn., Broward County, 1980-81, Nat. Adoption Ctr., 1986, Outreach Broward, 1986. Mem. NAFE, Am. Bus. Women's Assn., Light House Cove Condominium II Assn. (bd. dirs., v.p., sec. 1983-87), Light House Cove Condominium III Assn. (bd. dirs., v.p., sec. 1987-89), Light House Cove Condominium Assn. IV (bd. dirs., v.p., sec. 1985-88), Light House Cove Condominium Community Assn. (bd. dirs., v.p., sec. 1983-89), Fla. Community Assn. Mgrs. Inc., Ft. Lauderdale C. of C., Pompano Beach C. of C. Office: Light House Cove Resort Mgmt Inc 1406 N Ocean Blvd Pompano Beach FL 33062

FEIST-FITE, BERNADETTE, health and food specialist, travel consultant; b. Linton, N.D., Sept. 28, 1945; d. John K. and Cecilia (Nagel) F.; m. William H. Fite. BS in Dietetics, U. N.D., Grand Forks, 1967; MS in Edn., Troy (Ala.) State U., 1973; EdD U. So. Calif. Commd. officer USAF, 1965, advanced through grades to maj., 1983; prof. health and fitness Nat. Def. U., Ft. McNair, Washington, 1989—; pres. Feist Assocs., 1989—; speaker workshop; dir. seminar; instr. dietetic internship USAF; mgr. Coffeehouse Unitarian Ch. Mem. Alexandria Little Theatre. Decorated Air Force Commendation medal, Dept. Def. Meritorious Service medal. Mem. VFW, Soc. Internat. Edn., Tng. and Research, Am. Dietetic Assn., Internat. Food Service Execs. Assn., Assn. Mil. Surgeons U.S., Exec. Female, Air Force Assn., Soc. Nutrition Edn., Dietitians in Bus. and Industry, Sports and Cardiovascular Nutritionists, Am. Soc. Profl. and Exec. Women, Andrews Officers Club. Roman Catholic. Home: Box 7105 Alexandria VA 22307 Office: First Assocs Box 7105 Alexandria VA 22307

FEKE, DEBORAH JO, executive director; b. Cleve., Oct. 18, 1952; d. James Steve and Dolores Josephine (Nemecek) F. AB in Music Theory, Youngstown (Ohio) State U., 1975, MS in Edn., 1982. Cert. tchr., Ohio. Radio engr. Sta. WYSU-FM, Youngstown, 1973-75; tchr. Youngstown City Schs., 1978-80; caseworker Big Bros./Big Sisters, Youngstown, 1982-84, exec. dir., 1984—; TV engr. Sta. WKBN-TV, Youngstown, 1982-84; chmn. regional conf. Big Bros./Big Sisters, Ohio and Mich., 1988-89, sec., treas. profl. staff coun., exec. com., 1985-89; speaker Senate Press Conf. on Clean Air Bill, Washington, 1990. Vol. Ronald McDonald House, Youngstown, 1988—; bd. dirs. March of Dimes, Youngstown, 1983—, Am. Heart Assn., Youngstown, 1988—. Mem. Jaycees (v.p. Youngstown chpt. 1987). Democrat. Roman Catholic. Office: Big Bros/Big Sisters 325 N State St Girard OH 44420

FELBERBAUM, CAROL ANN, lighting designer; b. St. Louis, Nov. 2, 1939; d. Joseph Henry and Dorothy Helen (Ronsiek) Schilly; m. Alejo Jose Arechederra, Mar. 23, 1957 (div. 1975); children: Ann Lauren Arechederra Mercer, Scott Nicholas, Alice Tracey; m. Lew Allen Felberbaum, Jan. 23, 1987. Lighting designer William Tao & Assocs., St. Louis, 1981-84, Hellmuth, Obata & Kassabaum, St. Louis, 1984-86; pres. Lighting Design Cons., St. Charles, Mo., 1986—; adj. instr., Maryville Coll., St. Louis, 1987—. Recipient Edison award Distinction Gen. Electric, 1984, Edison Award of Merit, 1986. Mem. Illuminating Engring. Soc. (v.p. 1988-89, pres. 1989—, Edwin F. Guth award of merit 1984), St. Louis Regional Commerce and Growth Assn. Office: Lighting Design Cons 2706 Sundowner Dr Saint Charles MO 63303

FELCHLIN, MARY KATHLEEN CONROY, financial executive; b. Cleve., Feb. 16, 1951; d. Ernest J. and Margaret Jane Conroy; B.A., U. Calif., Berkeley, 1973; M.B.A., U. So. Calif., 1977. Adminstrv. asst. Mason McDuffie Investment Co., Berkeley, 1974-75; mortage mktg. staff Gibraltar Savs. & Loan, Beverly Hills, summer 1976; account officer Wells Fargo Bank, Los Angeles, 1977-79; sr. account officer Citicorp Real Estate, Inc., Los Angeles, 1979-80, asst. v.p., 1981-82, v.p., 1982—; v.p. Citicorp Real Estate Capital, 1985—; v.p. Citicorp Investment Bank, L.A., 1988-90, Citicorp Investment Mgmt., 1990—. Wittenberg fellow, 1975-76; Commerce Assos. fellow, 1976-77. Home: 8960 Wonderland Ave Los Angeles CA 90046

FELDBAUER JANSEN, MARY, producer, director; b. Rochester, N.Y., Mar. 2, 1945; d. George Francis Jr. and Irene Nicoletta (Compitello) Feldbauer; m. James A. Jansen, July 30, 1977; 1 child, Lucas. BA, Newton Coll. Sacred Heart, 1967. Staff producer Nat. Edni. TV, N.Y.C., 1969-72; script supr. NABET 15, N.Y.C., 1973-74; free-lance documentary assoc. producer N.Y.C., 1975-77, free-lance producer/dir. TV and corp. films, 1978-89; v.p. Wavelenth Prodns., Inc., N.Y.C., 1983-89. Post prodn. supr. feature Eight Men Out, 1988, telefilm Life Under Water, 1988, Little Man Tate, 1990. N.Y. State Coun. on Arts grantee, 1970. Mem. N.Y. Women in Film (pres. 1985-86). Democrat. Home: 432 23d St Santa Monica CA 90402

FELDHUSEN, HAZEL J., educator; b. Camp Douglas, Wis., Feb. 20, 1928; d. Vincent O. and Helen (Johnson) Artz; m. John F. Feldhusen, Dec. 18, 1954; children: Jeanne V., Anne M. B, U. Wis., 1965; M, Purdue U., 1968. Tchr. Suldal Sch., Mauston, Wis., 1947-50, Lake Geneva (Wis.) Schs., 1950-55, West Lafayette (Ind.) Schs., 1965—; cons. Wauwatosa (Wis.) Schs., 1981, World Conf., West Berlin, Fed. Republic of Germany 1983, Juneau (Alaska) Schs., 1986, Connersville (Ind.) Schs., 1987. Author: Individualized Teaching of the Gifted, 1990; contbr. articles to profl. jour. Vol. polit. campaign Michael Gery West Lafayette, 1983; mem.Tchr. of Yr. com., West Lafayette, 1988. Recipient Outstanding Tchr. award Elem. Tchrs. Am. 1974, Appreciation award U. Stellenbosch 1984, Appreciation award Australian Assn. for the Gifted 1987; winner Golden Apple Teaching award Greater Lafayette C. of C., 1989. Mem. NEA, Ind. State Tchrs. Assn., West Lafayette Edn. Assn. (Outstanding Achievement award 1984), Phi Delta Kappa, Delta Kappa Gamma (v.p 1983-85). Home: 2187 Tecumseh Pk Ln West Lafayette IN 47906

FELDMAN, DEBRA LYNN, nutritional research company executive; b. L.I., N.Y., Mar. 23, 1955; d. Joseph and Ruth Rebecca (Roth) Bieler; m. Gary Marc Feldman, Sept. 21, 1984. AA in Liberal Arts, Queensborough Community Coll., Queens, N.Y., 1976; BA in Communications, Queens Coll., Flushing, N.Y., 1979. Alumni dir. Queensborough Community Coll., Bayside, N.Y., 1980-86; v.p., researcher, writer Steps In Health, Ltd., Douglaston, N.Y., 1986-88, Steps in Health, Ltd., Margate, Fla., 1988—. Mem. People for the Ethical Treatment of Animals, Washington, Humane Soc. Broward County, Ft. Lauderdale, Fla.; active Listen to Children Program, Mental Health Assn. and Vol. Program of Broward County Pub. Schs., 1989. Mem. Life Extension Found., LifeNet-Biochem. Rsch. Orgn., Better Bus. Bur. S. Fla. (arbitration participant). Office: Steps In Health Ltd PO Box 63-6576 Margate FL 33063

FELDMAN, JANET DIANE, career and management development consultant; b. Mpls., Oct. 17, 1958; d. Alfred Newton and Myrna Rodel (Chasen) F. BS in Acctg., U. Minn., 1980; MS in Human Devel., St. Mary's Coll., Mpls., 1988. CPA, Minn. Sr. auditor Alexander Grant & Co., Mpls., 1981-83; registered rep. IDS/Am. Express, Mpls., 1983-84; v.p. fin. The Frankenberry Group, Mpls., 1984-85; cons. Mpls., 1985-88; cons. career mgmt. devel. Market Share, Inc., Mpls., 1989—; adj. prof. U. Minn., 1989—; edn. specialist Open U., Mpls., 1987—; cert. facilitator Parenting for Edn., Mpls., 1989—; treas. Internat. Alliance for Sustainable Ag, Mpls., 1989—. Vol. Mpls. Crisis Nursery, Mpls., 1990—, Continuum Ctr., Mpls., 1985-90, First Call for Help, Mpls., 1987; chmn. Concert/Auction Benefit Cancer Soc.,Mpls., 1982. Office: Market Share Inc 155 S 5th Ave Ste 350 Minneapolis MN 55401

FELDMAN, LAUREN, management; b. Hillsboro, Oreg., Dec. 30, 1961; d. Myron Henry and Roberta (Gerome) F. BBA, Sam Houston State U., Huntsville, Tex., 1984. Claim rep. Allstate Ins., Riverside, Calif., 1984-85, CNA Ins., Brea, Calif., 1985-86; subrogation specialist CNA INs., Brea, Calif., 1986-87; claims specialist CNA Ins., Brea, Calif., 1989—. Mem. UCI Hosp. Aux., So. Calif. Fraud Investigators Assn., Orange County Adjusters Assn. (bd. dirs.). Republican.

FELDMAN, LILLIAN MALTZ, education consultant; b. N.Y.C., Mar. 30, 1916; d. Jacob and Ida (Burko) Maltz; m. Harry A. Feldman, June 14, 1939 (dec. Jan. 1985); children: Ronald, Donna Feldman Weisman, Jeffrey, Robert. AB, George Washington U., 1937, MA, 1939; EdD in Early Childhood Edn., Syracuse U., 1987. Cert. guidance counselor, sch. adminstr., N.Y. Elem. sch. guidance counselor Syracuse (N.Y.) Sch. Dist., 1963-65, Kindergarten tchr., 1957-63, dir. early children edn., 1965-83; dir. Syracuse Head Start, summers 1968-70; cons. early childhood edn. Syracuse, 1985—; adj. instr. child, family and community studies Syracuse U., 1988-90, adj. prof., 1990—. Author invited papers in early child devel. and care, 1988, 89. Child care adv. com. Cen. N.Y. Community Found., Syracuse, 1989—; adv. com. Displaced Homemakers Regional Learning Ctr., Syracuse, 1986—, Dr. Martin Luther King Community Sch., Syracuse, 1988—, Syracuse Jewish Fedn., 1986—, JCERC; bd. dirs. Nat. Coun. Jewish Women, Syracuse, 1986—. Named Woman of Achievement Edn., Post-Standard, Syracuse, 1969; recipient Hannah Solomon award Nat. Coun. Jewish Woman, Syracuse, 1979. Mem. Syracuse Assn. Edn. Young Children (Outstanding Early Childhood Educator 1984), Consortium for Children's Svcs. (Silver Dove award 1985), Onondaga County Child Care Coun. (Community Svc. award 1983), Delta Kappa Gamma, Phi Delta Kappa. Democrat.

FELDMAN, MIRIAM ELLIN, nursing home administrator, nurse; b. N.Y.C., Dec. 12, 1924; d. Charles and Ida (Novick) Ellin; m. Herbert Feldman, Mar. 23, 1958; children: Leslie Ellin, Peter Hilton, Madeleine Elyse. RN, N.Y. State U., 1965; AAS, Queens Coll., 1965; BS, SUNY, 1974. Asst. adminstr. Five Towns Nursing Home, Woodmere, N.Y., 1963-65; cons. nursing service, N.Y., 1967-73; adminstr., developer Cerebral Palsy Domiciliary Care Program, N.Y., 1973-79; adminstr. Woodmere Health Care Ctr., N.Y., 1979—; cons. gerontology and the handicapped. Producer ednl. video tapes Patient Abuse Series, 1979-81. Recipient Outstanding Service award United Cerebral Palsy Assn., 1981. Fellow Am. Coll. Health Care Adminstrs.; mem. Am. Nursing Assn., Assn. for Help of Retarded Children. Club: Hadassah. Office: 39 Burton Ave Woodmere NY 11598

FELDMAN, SUSAN CAROL, neurobiologist, anatomy educator; b. Bklyn., Oct. 1, 1943; d. Saul Feldman and Ann Richman. BA, Hofstra U., Hempstead, N.Y., 1963; MS, Rutgers U., 1967; PhD, CUNY, 1976. Rsch. technician med. sch. Cornell U., N.Y.C., 1963-64; grad. teaching asst. CUNY, 1964-74; postdoctoral fellow Albert Einstein Coll. Medicine, Bronx, N.Y., 1975-77; postdoctoral fellow, instr. anatomy Columbia U., N.Y.C., 1977-79; asst. prof. anatomy N.J. Med. Sch., Univ. Med. Dental N.J., Newark, 1979-86, assoc. prof., 1986—. Contbr. articles to profl. jours. Mem. AAAS, Soc. Neurosci., Am. Assn. Anatomists, Am. Soc. Cell Biology, NOW. Office: Univ Med Dental NJ NJ Med Sch 185 S Orange Ave Newark NJ 07103

FELDON, JOAN SORGE, marketing researcher; b. Evanston, Ill., July 18, 1932; d. Clarence Christopher and Jane (Back) Sorge; m. Richard A. Feldon,

June 11, 1954; children—Jill Allison, Richard Alden, Reed Andrew. B.S., Northwestern U., 1954. Mktg. asst., project dir. Action Data, Inc., Cin., 1976-77, project dir. client services, 1977-80, v.p., 1980-82; pres. The Answer Group, Cin., 1982—. Vice-pres. Terrace Park Community Theatre, 1959—; mem. Cin. Music Theatre, 1960—; actor Playhouse in the Park, Cin., Edgecliff Theatre, Cin.; pres. Playhouse Prompters, Cin. Mem. Actors Equity, Am. Mktg. Assn. (sec. 1982-83, hospitality chmn. 1981-82), Mktg. Research Assn., Inc., Internat. Visitors Assn., Internat. of Frankfort (Ger.) (bd. dirs.), Women in Communications, Kenwood Country Club. Republican. Episcopalian. Avocations: tennis, golf, community theatre. Home: 3765 Chimney Hill Dr Cincinnati OH 45241 Office: The Answer Group 11161 Kenwood Rd Cincinnati OH 45242

FELDSTEIN, LISA ZOLA, art dealer, consultant; b. Santa Monica, Calif., Dec. 9, 1958; d. Donald James and Dorothy Naomi (Kahn) Zola; m. Alan H. Feldstein, Oct. 19, 1980; 1 child, Sasha Leigh. BA in History, UCLA, 1980; MBA, Pepperdine U., 1986. Theater, community svc. mgr. L.A. Trade-Tech. Coll., 1980; corp. art dir. Louis Newman Galleries, Beverly Hills, Calif., 1980-84; dir., v.p. Toluca Lake Galleries, Burbank, Calif., 1984-86; owner Zola Fine Art, L.A., 1986—; speaker, panelist Art Expo N.Y. and Art Expo Dallas, N.Y.C., 1983-90; project art cons. Litton Industries, Beverly Hills, 1984-86, Union Bank, Los Angeles, 1986—, Bateman Eichler, Hill Richards, 1988—. Contbr. articles to mag. Active Campaign for Econ. Democracy, L.A., 1986—, Hollywood Women's Polit. Com. Carnation Found. scholar, 1985, 86. Mem. Amnesty Internat., NAFE, Alpha Epsilon Phi. Democrat. Jewish. Office: 8163 Melrose Ave Los Angeles CA 90046

FELIX, JEANETTE SALZMANN, research foundation science director; b. Wausau, Wis., Feb. 13, 1944; d. Henry Lawrence and Ruth Ann (Breit) Salzmann; m. Jacob K. Felix, June 22, 1968; children: Nathan and Rebecca. BS, Edgewood Coll., Madison, 1966; PhD, U. Wis., Madison, 1971. Instr./fellow U. of Rochester Sch. of Medicine, Rochester, N.Y., 1970-76; instr./asst. profr. Johns Hopkins U. Sch. of Medicine, Baltimore, 1976-83; expert cons. Nat'l Inst. of Health, Bethesda, Md., 1983-86; dir. of science RP Found. Fighting Blindness, Balt., 1986—. Author: Research Publications (28 articles), 1968-85. Mem., Am. Assn. for Advancement of Science, Am. Soc. of Human Genetics, Assn. for Research on Vision and Ophthalmology. Home: 5706 Chilham Rd Baltimore MD 21209

FELIX, PATRICIA JEAN, steel company official; b. Baptistown, N.J., Dec. 13, 1941; d. Dmitri and Rosalia (Hryckowian) F. Student, Pratt Inst., 1960-61, Moravian Coll., Bethlehem, Pa., 1961-63. Pricing analyst Riegel Paper Corp., N.Y.C., 1966-69; placement mgr. Gardner Assocs., N.Y.C., 1969-72; buyer Bethlehem Steel Corp., 1973-78, buyer exempt, 1978-84, sr. buyer, 1984, purchasing supr., 1984—. Sec. coun. St. Nicholas Russian Orthodox Ch., Bethlehem, 1982-85, mem. coun., 1985—; sec. Bethlehem-Tondabayashi Sister City Commn., 1988—. Mem. Nat. Assn. Purchasing Mgmt. Home: 1721 Millard St Bethlehem PA 18017 Office: Bethlehem Steel Corp 701 E 3d St Bethlehem PA 18016

FELKER, ALLYN C., therapist, health facility administrator; b. Tamaqua, Pa., May 5, 1962; d. Alfred F. and Santina M. (Jacobe) B. BS, Pa. State U., State College, 1984, MEd, 1986. Cert. rehab. counselor. Intern, rehab. therapist Harrisburg (Pa.) State Hosp.; nurse's aid State Coll. (Pa.) Manor; supr., therapist, program specialist Turning Point, Pottsville, Pa. Mem. Am. Mental Health Fund. Home: 319 W Market St Apt 5 Pottsville PA 17901 Office: 210 S Centre St Pottsville PA 17901

FELKNOR, LAURIE, magagine editor; b. Cape Girardeau, Mo.; d. Francis Xavier and Ruth Cleveland (Hodges) Schumacher; m. Audley Rhea Felknor, Jr.; children: Peter Stephen, Christopher Andrew. BS in Edn., U. Mo. Tchr. English, Sikeston (Mo.) High Sch., Miss Hickey's Sch., St. Louis; asst. to editorial dir. Fleming H. Revell Pub. Co., Old Tappan, N.J., 1973-80; editor Cath. World, Paulist Press, Mahwah, N.J., 1980-86, mng. editor, 1986—. Editor: The Crisis in Religious Vocations, 1989. Mem. Cardinal's Commn. on Ecumenism, St. Louis, 1964-65. Mem. Cath. Press Assn. Office: Catholic World 997 MacArthur Blvd Mahwah NJ 07430

FELLBAUM, JEAN ANNE, training administrator; b. Teaneck, N.J., Nov. 25, 1962; d. Harold Jr. and Judith Gene (Pierce) F. Grad., Berkeley Secretarial Sch., Ridgewood, N.J., 1982; AA in Retail Mgmt., Green Mountain Coll., Poultney, Vt., 1982; BA in History, Columbia U., 1989. Adminstrv. asst. Prentice-Hall, Englewood Cliffs, N.J., 1984-85, Barnard Housing Office, N.Y.C., 1986-87; adminstrv. asst. The Computer Ctr., Inc., Montvale, N.J., 1987-88, tng. coord., 1989—, 1989—. Mem. DAR. Republican. Episcopalian. Office: The Computer Ctr Inc 112 Chestnut Ridge Rd Montvale NJ 07645

FELLENSTEIN, CORA ELLEN MULLIKIN, credit union executive; b. Edwardsville, Ill., June 2, 1930; d. Russell K. and Elberta Mable (Rheude) Mullikin; m. Charles Frederick Fellenstein, Feb. 24, 1951; children—Keith David, Kimberly Diane. Student Community Coll., 1980-83. Cert. consumer credit exec. Teller, loan officer, office mgr. Credit Union of Johnson County, Mission, Kans., 1976-84, 1st v.p., supr. lending, collections and Mastercard depts., 1984-86, exec. v.p., 1987—. Author: Moore Family History, 1987. Precinct committeewoman Johnson County Republicans, Olathe, Kans., 1976—; vol. Cerebral Palsy, 1957-66, Olathe Community Hosp., 1976—, Shawnee Mission Med. Ctr., 1986— . Mem. Internat. Credit Assn., Kans. Credit Assn., Credit Women Internat. (name now CWI: Credit Profls., dir. 1983—, Exec. of Yr. Johnson County chpt.), NAFE, DAR (treas. 1976-86), Daus. Am. Colonists (treas. 1976-86), Beta Sigma Phi. Republican. Mem. Christian Ch. Club: Friends of Historic Mahaffie Farmstead (Olathe), Soroptimist Internat. Avocations: genealogy, philately, numismatics, camping. Home: 2000 Arrowhead Dr Olathe KS 66062 Office: Credit Union Johnson County 6025 Lamar St Mission KS 66202

FELLERS, RHONDA GAY, lawyer; b. Gainesville, Tex., July 20, 1955; d. James Norman and Gaytha Ann (Sanders) F.; m. Bruce C. Hinton, Oct. 15, 1981 (div. Oct. 1985). BA, U. Tex., 1977, JD, 1980; LLM in Taxation, U. Denver, 1987. Bar: Tex. 1981, Colo. 1981, U.S. Dist. Ct. (no. dist.) Tex. 1982, U.S. Dist. Ct. Colo. 1985, U.S. Tax Ct. 1985, U.S. Ct. Appeals (5th cir.) 1986, U.S. Ct. Appeals (10th cir.) 1989. Assoc. Walters & Assocs., Lubbock, Tex., 1981-83; gen. counsel Security Nat. Bank, Lubbock, 1983; assoc. Melvin Coffee & Assocs., P.C., Denver, 1984-85, 87—; sole practice Lubbock, 1983-87. Mem. ABA, State Bar Tex., Colo. Bar Assn., Denver Bar Assn., Colo. Women's Bar Assn. Office: 2121 S Oneida Ste 336 Denver CO 80224

FELLIN, OCTAVIA ANTOINETTE, librarian; b. Santa Monica, Calif.; d. Otto P. and Librada (Montoya) F.; student U. N.Mex., 1937-39; B.A., U. Denver, 1941; B.A. in L.S., Rosary Coll., 1942. Asst. libr., instr. library sci. St. Mary-of-Woods Coll., Terre Haute, Ind., 1942-44; libr. U.S. Army, Bruns Gen. Hosp., Santa Fe, 1944-46, Gallup (N.Mex.) Pub. Libr., 1947—; post libr. Camp McQuaide, Calif., 1947; free lance writer mags., newspapers, 1950—; libr. cons.; N.Mex. del. White House Pre-Conf. on Librs. & Info. Svcs., 1978; dir. Nat. Libr. Week for N.Mex., 1959. Chmn. Red Mesa Art Ctr., 1984-88; pres. Gallup Area Arts Coun., 1988; mem. Western Health Found. Century Com., 1988, Gallup Multi-Model Cultural Com., 1988—; v.p., publicity dir. Gallup Community Concerts Assn., 1957-78, 85—; organizer Gt. Decision Discussion groups, 1963-85; mem. Gallup St. Naming Com., 1958-59, Aging Com., 1964-68; chmn. Gallup Mus. Indian Arts and Crafts, 1964-78; mem. publicity com. Gallup Inter-Tribal Indian Ceremonial Assn., 1966-68; mem. Gov's. Com. 100 on Aging, 1967-70; N.Mex. Humanities Coun., 1979; mem. U. N.Mex.-Gallup Campus Community Edn. Adv. Coun., 1981-82; N.Mex. organizing chmn. McKinley Hosp. Aux., pres., 1983; mem. N.Mex. Libr. Adv. Coun., 1971-75, vice chmn., 1974-75; chmn. adv. com. Gallup Sr. Citizens, 1971-73; mem. steering com. Gallup Diocese Bicentennial, 1975-78, chmn. hist. com., 1975; chmn. Trick or Treat for UNICEF, Gallup, 1972-77; chmn. pledge campaign Rancho del Nino San Huberto, Empalme, Mexico; bd. dirs. Gallup Opera Guild, 1970-74; bd. dirs., sec., organizer Gallup Area Arts Council, 1970-78; mem. N.Mex. Humanities Council, 1979, Gallup Centennial Com., 1980-81; mem. Cathedral Parish Council, 1980-83, v.p., 1981, century com. Western Health Found., 1988—. Recipient Dorothy Canfield Fisher $1,000 Library award, 1961; Outstanding Community Service award for mus. service Gallup C. of C., 1969, 70, Outstanding Citizen award, 1974, Benemerenti medal Pope Paul VI, 1977, Celebrate Literary award Gallup Internat. Reading Assn., 1983-84, N.Mex. Disting. Pub. Svc. award, 1987, finalist Gov's award Outstanding N.Mex. Women, 1988. Mem. ALA, N.Mex. Library Assn. (v.p., sec., chmn. hist. materials com. 1964-66, salary and tenure com., nat. coordinator N.Mex. legislative com., chmn. com. to extend library services 1969-73, Librarian of Yr. award 1975, chmn. local and regional history roundtable 1978, Community Achievement award 1983), AAUW (v.p., co-organizer Gallup br., N.Mex. nominating com. 1967—, chmn. fellowships and centennial fund Gallup br., chmn. com. on women), Plateau Scis. Soc., N.Mex. Folklore Soc. (v.p. 1964-65, pres. 1965-66), N.Mex. Hist. Soc. (dir. 1979-85), Gallup Hist. Soc., Gallup Film Soc. (co-organizer, v.p. 1950-58), LWV (v.p. 1953-56), NAACP, Gallup C. of C. (organizing chmn. women's div. 1972, v.p. 1972-73), N.Mex. Women's Polit. Caucus, N.Mex. Mcpl. League (pres. librarian's div. 1979—), Dictionary Soc. N. Am., Alpha Delta Kappa (hon.). Roman Catholic (Cathedral Guild, Confraternity Christian Doctrine Bd. 1962-64, Cursillo in Christianity Movement, mem. of U.S. Cath. Bishop's Adv. Council 1969-74; corr. sec. Latin Am. Mission Program 1972-75, sec. Diocese of Gallup Pastoral Council 1972-73, corr. sec. liturgical commn. Diocese of Gallup 1977);chmn. Artists Coop., 1985—; mem. N.Mex. Diamond Jubilee/U.S. Constitution Bicentennial Gallup Com., 1986-87. Author: Yahweh the Voice that Beautifies the Land. Home: 513 E Mesa Ave Gallup NM 87301 Office: 115 W Hill St Gallup NM 87301

FELLOWS, SUSAN MARIE, real estate property manager; b. Dec. 23, 1964; d. Richard R. and Judith (Herbst) F. BA in Real Estate and Mktg., U. Wis., Milw., 1987; grad., Wauwatosa Sch. Real Estate, 1988. Lic. in real estate, Wis. Mgr. Pizza Slices, Inc., Brookfield, Wis.; dir. mktg. and sales Art Tech, Inc., Butler, Wis.; dir. mktg. Apt. Assn. Milw.; property mgr. Nat. Realty Mgmt. Inc., Wauwatosa, Wis. Mem. Financiers and Marketers of U. Wis. Democrat. Presbyterian. Home: 3239 A S 7th St Milwaukee WI 53215 Office: 4200 W Main St Racine WI 53402

FELMLEE, VICKI PATRICIA, technical editor, consultant, writer; b. Grand Junction, Colo., Sept. 17, 1952; d. W.L. Felmlee; 1 child, William Marcus. BS, Mesa State Coll., 1978. Features editor Daily Sentinel, Grand Junction, 1977-81; owner, pres. Write Touch Syndicate, Grand Junction, 1982-86; editorial specialist UNC Geotech, Grand Junction, 1987—. Author: Cossacks--Shadow of Wolf, 1983. With Visitors and Conv. Bur., Grand Junction, 1989—. Recipient outstanding svc. award Mining and Petroleum Days, Grand Junction, 1977-79, outstanding contbn. award Grand Junction Symphony, 1980. Mem. AIME (chairwoman Colo. Plateau sect. 1985), Western Colo. Bot. Soc. (pres. 1985-88). Home: 178 Glory View Dr Grand Junction CO 81503 Office: UNC Geotech 2597 B 3/4 Rd Grand Junction CO 81503

FELSTED, CARLA MARTINDELL, librarian; b. Barksdale Field, La., June 21, 1947; d. David Aldenderfer Martindell and Dorthe (Hetland) Horton; m. Robert Earl Luna, Aug. 24, 1968, (div. 1972); m. Hugh Herbert Felsted, Nov. 2, 1974. BA in English, So. Meth. U., 1968, MA in History, 1974; MLS, Tex. Woman's U., 1978. Cert. secondary tchr., Tex.; cert. learning resources specialist, Tex. Tchr. Bishop Lynch High Sch., Dallas, 1968-72, Lake Highlands Jr. High Sch., Richardson, Tex., 1973-75; instr. Richland Coll., Richardson, Tex., 1973-76; library asst. So. Meth. U., Dallas, 1977-78; librarian Tracy-Locke Advt., Dallas, 1978-79; corp. librarian Am. Airlines, Inc., Ft. Worth, 1979-84; research librarian McKinsey & Co., Dallas, 1984-85; reference librarian St. Edward's U., Austin, Tex., 1985—; ptnr. Southwind Info. Svcs. and Southwind Bed-Breakfast, Wimberley, Tex., 1985—; bd. dirs. S.W. Fed. Credit Union, 1978-81. Editor, compiler: Youth and Alcohol Abuse, 1986. Mem. adv. bd. Sch. Libr. and Info. Scis., Tex. Women's U., Denton, 1982-84; mem. curriculum com. Wimberley Ind. Sch. Dist., 1986; bd. dirs. Hays-Caldwell Coun. on Alcohol and Drug Abuse, San Marcos, Tex., 1986-88, Inst. Cultures for Wimberley Valley, 1989—. Grantee St. Edward's U., 1986-89. Mem. ALA, Tex. Libr. Assn. (dist. program com., membership com. 1986-88), Wimberley C of C. (bd. dirs. 1987-88). Lutheran. Home: Rt 2 Box 15 Wimberley TX 78676

FELTHAM, LOUISE, Canadian legislator; b. Nfld., Can., Mar. 22, 1935; d. Herbert and Ella S. Stockwood; m. Douglas W. Feltham, June 30, 1956; children: Donna Gail, Glenn Douglas, Gary James. Councillor Municipality of Rockyview, 1974-88; mem. from Wild Horse riding, Alta. Ho. of Commons, 1988—. Progressive Conservative. Mem. United Ch. Can. Office: House of Commons, Parliament Bldgs, Ottawa, ON Canada K1A 0A6*

FELTHOUSE, PATRICIA MAE AVRIT, librarian; b. Tillamook, Oreg., Mar. 28, 1924; d. Roy Calvin and Louise (Morgan) Avrit; m. James Whitman Felthouse, May 10, 1944; children: Timothy Roy, Daphne Diane. Student, Oreg. State U., 1941-44; BA in Elem. Edn., U. Wash., 1960. Libr. Tehama County Libr., Red Bluff, Calif., 1965-85; organist United Meth. Ch., Red Bluff, 1985—. Contbr. hist. articles to profl. jours. Bd. dirs. Tehama County Mus. Found., 1980—. Mem. AAUW (pres. Red Buff-Tehama County 1974-75), Calif. Conf. Hist. Socs. (regional v.p. 1981-84). Assn. No. Calif. Records and Rsch. (bd. dirs. 1983-86), Colusi County Hist. Soc. (bd. dirs., pres. 1983-90), Bus. and Profl. Women's Club (pres. 1977-78, Woman of Yr. 1987), Tehama County Geneal. and Hist. Soc. (pres. 1986-90). Republican. Methodist. Home: 1140 Wetter Way Red Bluff CA 96080

FELTON, JUDITH R., psychoanalyst, educator; b. Phila., Aug. 21, 1942; d. Martin and Laura (Goldman) Kirshenbaum; AB in Govt., Wheaton (Mass.) Coll., 1963; MSW, Rutgers U., 1966, PhD, Rutgers U. Grad. Sch. Arts and Scis., 1983; grad. N.Y. Center for Psychoanalytic Tng., 1978; m. Stephen Felton, Feb. 8, 1966; 1 dau., Jane Jennifer. Clin. social worker VA, Newark, 1967; psychotherapist Santa Barbara (Calif.) Mental Health Services, 1967-69; supr. Santa Barbara Counselling Center, 1967-69; pvt. practice psychoanalysis, 1969—; psychoanalyst, therapist Fifth Ave. Center for Psychotherapy, N.Y.C., 1969-72; instr. Marymount Manhattan Coll., 1971; psychotherapy supr. clin. faculty, dept. psychiatry Rutgers U. Med. Sch., New Brunswick, N.J., 1972-75, teaching asst. Grad. Sch. Social Work, 1974-76; vis. lectr. Bryn Mawr Coll. Sch. Social Work and Social Research, 1980; mem. faculty N.Y. Center for Psychoanalytic Tng., 1980—, N.J. Inst. Psychoanalysis and Psychotherapy, 1982—. Bd. dirs. N.Y. Ctr. for Psychoanalytic Tng., Inst. for Psychoanalysis and Psychotherapy N.J., 1986—. NIMH fellow, 1965; diplomate Am. Bd. Psychotherapy. Recipient Disting. Faculty award Atlantic County Psychoanalytic Soc., 1987. Fellow N.J. Soc. for Clin. Social Work; mem. Nat. Assn. Soc.ial Workers, Conf. Psychoanalytic Psychotherapists, Nat. Assn. for Advancement Psychoanalysis, Groves Conf. on Family, Acad. Cert. Social Workers, Soc. for Psychoanalytic Tng. (bd. dirs. 1983—, dir. social sci. program 1983-86), AAUP, Am. Psychol. Assn. Mem. editorial bd. jour. Current Issues in Psychoanalytic Practice, 1983—; contbr. articles to profl. jours. Home and Office: 159 Valley Rd Princeton NJ 08540

FELTON, PATRICIA ANN, nurse, hospital administrator; b. Birmingham, Ala., Nov. 10, 1949; d. Perry Lee and Frankie (Walton) Brown; m. Herman Felton, Jan. 28, 1971; children: Kenneth, Karla, Felicia. Assoc. Nursing Arts, Wayne County Community Coll., 1974; B Nursing Sci., Madonna Coll., 1981; M Adminstrn., Marygrove Coll., 1987; postgrad., Mercy Coll. RN, Mich. Staff nurse oper. rm. Sinai Hosp., Detroit, 1980-82; asst. dir. Meharry Allied Health Learning Ctr., Detroit, 1982-84; dir. of nursing Universal Variable Staffing Systems, Detroit, 1982-83; clin. instr. Highland Pk. (Mich.) Community Coll., 1983-85, Mercy Coll., Detroit, 1983-85, Westland (Mich.) Med. Ctr., 1984-85; patient care educator staff devel. Grace Hosp., Detroit, 1985-87; dir. surg. svcs. Mercy Meml. Hosp., Monroe, Mich., 1988—; cons. Kitch, Saurbier, Drutchas, Wagner and Kenney, P.C., Detroit, 1986-89. Mem. NAFE, Assn. Oper. Rm. Nurses, Black Nurses Assn., Wayne County Community Coll. Nurse Alumni (sec. 1984). Democrat. Baptist. Home: 19556 McIntyre Detroit MI 48219 Office: Mercy Meml Hosp 718 N Macomb St Monroe MI 48161

FELTS, JOAN APRIL, educator; b. Tulsa, Apr. 8, 1940; d. John Hickland and Dorris Retha (Finley) Matlock; m. Wayne Keith Felts, Aug. 19, 1962; children: David Wayne, Michael Scott, Steven Doyle. BS in Edn., Northeastern State U., Tahlequah, Okla., 1962. Cert. tchr., Okla. Tchr. Ruby Ray Swift Elem. Sch., Arlington, Tex., 1962-64; co-owner Felts Family Shoe Store, Muskogee, Okla., 1966-79; tchr. Hilldale Elem. Sch., Muskogee, 1979—. Leader Neosho dist. Boy Scouts Am., 1969-78, trainer, 1978-88. Recipient Dist. award of merit Boy Scouts Am., 1982, Wood Badge tng. award Nat. coun., 1983, Silver Beaver award Tulsa coun., 1985; Tchr. of Yr. award Hilldale Ind. Schs., 1988. Mem. Hill Assn. Classroom Tchrs. (chmn. staff devel. 1985-89, newsletter editor 1988-90), Northeastern State U. Alumni Assn. (bd. dirs. 1976—, pres.-elect 1990-91), Beta Sigma Phi (Woman of Yr. award Muskogee chpt. 1987). Republican. Methodist. Home: 109 Grandview Blvd Muskogee OK 74403 Office: Hilldale Elem Sch 315 Peak Blvd Muskogee OK 74403

FELTS, MARGARET CLEMEN, environmental engrineer, consultant; b. Ft. Worth, Tex., Dec. 16, 1950; d. Arthur Taylor and Jane Jolliffe Clemen; m. Robert Louis Felts, Aug. 1, 1939; children: Shane, Jonathan, Julia. BA Orgn. Communications, Eckerd Coll., St. Petersburg, Fla., 1973; BS Petroleum Engring., La. Tech., Ruston, La., 1977; MS Energy Engring., LaSalle U., 1989. Engr. AMOCO Oil Co. Refinery, Yorktown, Pa., 1977-80; process engr. Celanese, Vernon, Tex., 1980-82; energy spl. Calif. Energy Commn., Sacramento, 1982-84; energy cons., owner Clemen Co., Sacramento, 1984-89; chief engring. div. Environ. Mgmt., McClellan AFB, Sacramento, 1985-89; owner, mgr. Clemen Environ. Svcs., 1989—; cons. Pvt. Attys. in Calif.; expert witness FERC; expert witness natural resources and utilities comns. Calif. State Assembly; cons., expert witness Calif. Pub. Utilities Commn., Calif. Energy Commn. Author: Studies and Testimonies for Calif. Pub. Utilities Com., FERC, Citizen's Energy Coun., 1984-89; article, Oil & Gas Jour., 1985; paper, Soc. of Petroleum Engring., 1986. Recipient Lee Community Leadership Award, Eckerd Coll., 1973. Assoc. mem. Soc. of Petroleum Engrs. Presbyterian. Office: SM-ALC/EME McClellan AFB CA 95624

FELTS, MARGARET DAVIS, librarian/bibliographer; b. Walla Walla, Wash., Jan. 26, 1917; d. Schuyler Ernest and Blanche Marie (Fischer) Davis; m. Wells Carter Felts, June 20, 1940 (div. 1966); children: Carol Margaret, Thomas William, Helen Elizabeth. StaBA, Stanford U., 1938; MLS, U. Calif., Berkeley, 1965. Librarian Mills Coll., Oakland, Calif., 1965-68; librarian/bibliographer U. Calif., Santa Cruz, 1968-85; ret. Author: Archives of the South Pacific Commission and Related Papers, 1971; contbr. to Catalog of the South Pacific Collection, 1978, Selection of Library Materials for Area Studies, 1990. Docent Elkhorn Slough Nat. Estuarine Rsch. Res., Moss Landing, Calif. Democrat. Home: 14 Sunset Dr Sunset Beach Watsonville CA 95076

FENDELMAN, HELAINE, art appraiser; b. Chgo., Jan. 25, 1942; d. Albert Abraham and Pearl (Loeb) Woll; m. Burton M Fendelman, July 4, 1965; chldren: Barton Douglas, Jonathon Woll. BA, Washington U., 1964; MA, C.W. Post College, Brookville, N.Y., 1967; Am. Studies Program Summer Inst., Boston U., 1978; Am. Decorative Arts Summer Inst., Winterthur (Del.) Mus., 1980. Guest curator Tramp Art Exhibition Mus. Am. Folk Art, N.Y.C., 1975; curator Tramp Art Traveling Exhibition, 1976-77, advt. dir. The Clarion, 1977-80; com. and chmn. Am. Folk Art and Country Furniture Channel 13 Ednl. TV, N.Y.C., 1978-80; curator Rye (N.Y.) Hist. Soc., 1978-81; dir. Lower Hudson Conf., 1981-82; owner Helaine Fendelman Inc., Scarsdale, N.Y., 1981—; ptnr. Fendelman & Schwartz Fine Arts, Antiques and Appraisal Firm, Scarsdale, N.Y., 1982—; adj. prof. NYU, 1990; cons. Time/Life Books, Smithsonian Instn., N.Y. State Coun. on the Arts, Westchester County (N.Y.) Hist. Soc., Scott-Fanton Mus., Danbury, Conn. Author: Tramp Art, 1976, Silent Companions: Dummy Board Figures of the 17th Through 19th Centuries, 1981, Money in Your Attic: How to Turn Your Furniture, Antiques, Silver and Collectibles into Cash, 1985, The Official Identification and Price Guide to American Folk Art, 1988; co-columnist: "What Is It...What Is It Worth?", Country Living mag. Mem. Appraisers Assn. of Am., Inc., Women in Communication, Inc., Friends of the Am. Wing Met. Mus. of Art, Westchester Assn. Women Bus. Owners, Am. Soc. Appraisers (sr.). Office: 1248 Post Rd Scarsdale NY 10583

FENNELL, DIANE MARIE, marketing executive, process engineer; b. Panama, Iowa, Dec. 11, 1944; d. Urban William and Marcella Mae (Leytham) Schechinger; m. Leonard E. Fennell, Aug. 19, 1967; children: David, Denise, Mark. BS, Creighton U., Omaha, 1966. Process engr. Tex. Instruments, Richardson, 1974-79; sr. process engr. Signetics Corp., Santa Clara, Calif., 1979-82; demo lab. mgr. Airco Temescal, Berkeley, Calif., 1982-84; field process engr. Applied Materials, Santa Clara, 1984-87; mgr. product mktg. Lam Rsch., Fremont, Calif., 1987—; founder, coord. chmn. Plasma Etch User's Group, Santa Clara, 1986-88; tchr. computer course Adult Edn., Half Moon Bay, Calif., 1982-83. Founder, bd. dirs. Birth to Three program Mental Retardation Ctr., Denison, Tex., 1974-75; fund raiser local sch. band, Half Moon Bay, 1981-89; community rep. local sch. bd., Half Moon Bay, 1982-83. Mem. Am. Vacuum Soc., Soc. Photo Instrumentation Engrs., Soc. Women Engrs., NOW. Home: 441 Alameda Ave Half Moon Bay CA 94019

FENNELL ROBBINS, SALLY, retail communications executive, editor, author; b. Greensburg, Pa., Feb. 17, 1950; d. Clifford Seanor and Charlotte Louise (Hoffman) Fennell; m. John W. Robbins, Sept. 22, 1984. BS in Journalism, cum laude, Ohio U., 1972; MA in Journalism, magna cum laude, Marshall U., 1974. Intern, reporter Tribune-Rev., Greensburg, Pa., 1972; prodn. asst. Harper's Bazaar, N.Y.C., 1972; reporter UPI, Birmingham, Ala., 1972-73; reporter, dept. editor HFD-Retailing Home Furnishings, Fairchild Pubs., N.Y.C., 1975-77; account exec. supr., client svc. mgr., v.p. Burson-Marsteller, N.Y.C., 1977-83; group mgr., v.p. pub. rels. div. Ketchum Communications, 1983-84; dir. retail communications Deloitte & Touche Retail Svcs. Group, N.Y., 1989—; grad. teaching asst. Sch. Journalism/Reporting, Marshall U., Huntington, W.Va., 1973-74. Home: 237 E 20th St New York NY 10003 Office: Deloitte & Touche 1633 Broadway New York NY 10019-6754

FENNERTY, KAREN S., banker; b. Batesville, Ind., May 26, 1962; d. Richard Dale and Mary Joyce (Crawford) Gannon; m. Brian Sean Fennerty, July 26, 1986; 1 child, Michael Sean. BS in Fin., Ind. U., 1984. Asst. v.p. First of Am. Bank, Indpls., 1984—. Office: First of Am Bank 6501 N Keystone Ave Indianapolis IN 46220

FENNESSEY, ANN MARIE, state agency administrator; b. Boston, Jan. 31, 1945; d. Thomas Jr. and Anna Ceceilia (Strausdauskais) F. Student, Mary Washington Coll., 1962-65; BA, Old Dominion U., 1967; MPA, George Mason U., 1988. Tchr. Chesapeake (Va.) Pub. Sch., 1967; corr. Blue Cross/Blue Shield, Washington, 1967-69; social svc. rep. Income Maintenance Adminstrn. D.C. Dept. Human Svcs., Washington, 1969-78, supervisory social svc. rep., 1978-88, chief food stamp sect. Income Maintenance Adminstrn., 1988—; recording sec. women's program Income Maintenance Adminstrn., 1988—. Nat. Spanish Exam. scholar, 1962. Mem. Am. Soc. for Pub. Adminstrn., Fed. Mgrs. Assn. (sec. Washington chpt. 1980-82). Home: 1220 N Pierce St #603 Arlington VA 22209 Office: DC Dept Human Svcs 645 H St NE Washington DC 20002

FENNESSY, MARSHA BEACH STEWART, sales executive, entertainment executive; b. Memphis, Jan. 17, 1952; d. Bruce Charles and Marjorie Hudson (Campbell) Stewart; m. Sean Francis Fennessy, Aug. 28, 1977. BBA in Internat. Bus., U. Tex., 1982; MFA in Arts Adminstrn./Dance Mgmt., Yale U., 1985. Mng. dir. Yale Cabaret, New Haven, 1984-85; agt. Columbia Artists Mgmt., Inc., N.Y.C., 1985-90; v.p., dir. sales Classical Artists Internat./The Entertainment Corp. USA, N.Y.C., 1990—; dancer with Louisville (Ky.) Ballet (formerly Civic), 1967-70, Actor's Theatre of Louisville, 1972, Arena Stage, Washington, 1972, Disney on Parade, NBC, S.Am., Europe, Africa, 1974, 75, 76, Geneva (Switzerland) Ballet Co., 1975, 76; dance chairwoman cultural entertainment com. U. Tex., Austin, 1981-82. Nat. Endowment for the Arts fellow 1983, 84. Mem. NAFE, Yale Alumni Assn., Yale Club (N.Y.C.), Scottish Heritage Soc., Caledonian Club. Office: Classical Artists Internat The Entertainment Corp USA 1995 Broadway Ste 1201 New York NY 10023

FENNING, LISA HILL, federal judge; b. Chgo., Feb. 22, 1952; d. Ivan Byron and Joan (Hennigar) Hill; m. Alan Mark Fenning, Apr. 3, 1977; 4 children. BA with honors, Wellesley Coll., 1971; JD, Yale U., 1974. Bar: Ill. 1975, Calif. 1979, U.S. Dist. Ct. (no. dist.) Ill., U.S. Dist. Ct. (no., ea., so., cen. dists.) Calif., U.S. Ct. Appeals (6th, 7th, 9th cir. cts.). Law clk. U.S. Ct. Appeals 7th cir., Chgo., 1974-75; assoc. Jenner and Block, Chgo., 1975-77, O'Melveny and Myers, Los Angeles, 1977-85; judge U.S. Bankruptcy Ct. Cen. Dist. Calif., Los Angeles, 1985—; bd. govs. Nat. Conf. Bankruptcy Judges, 1989—; pres. Nat. Conf. on Women's Bar Assns., Balt., 1987-88, pres.-elect, 1986-87, v.p., 1985-86, bd. dirs.; lectr., program coord. in field. Mem., bd. advisors: Lawyer Hiring & Training Report, 1985-87; contbr. articles to profl. jours. Durant scholar Wellesley Coll., 1971; named one of Am's. 100 Most Important Women Ladies Home Jour., 1988. Mem. ABA (mem. commn. on women in the profession 1987—, Women's Caucus 1987—, Individual Rights and Responsibilities sect. 1984—, Bus. and Banking Law sect. 1986—, Bankruptcy com.), Nat. Assn. Women Judges (Nat. Task Force Gender Bias in the Cts. 1986-87), Nat. Conf. Bankruptcy Judges (chair ABA liaison com.), Calif. State Bar Assn. (chair com. on women in law 1986-87), Women Lawyers' Assn. of Los Angeles (ex officio mem., bd. dirs., chmn, founder com. on status of women lawyers 1984-85, officer nominating com. 1986, founder, mem. Do-it Yourself Mentor Network 1986—), Phi Beta Kappa. Democrat. Office: US Bankruptcy Ct 312 N Spring St Rm 831 Los Angeles CA 90012

FENSTERMAKER, NANCY RUTH, business administrator, business owner; b. Columbus, Ohio, Sept. 8, 1930; d. Omar Raymond and Flora Louise (Lashley) F. Student, Ohio State U., 1947-48. Trouble shooter Pacific Fin. Corp., Chgo., 1948-56; mem. rsch. staff J. Walter Thompson Advt., Chgo., 1956-58; exec. sec. McCuskey Group, L.A., 1958-59, Nat. Steel Corp., Chgo., 1959-60, Gen. Dynamics, El Segundo, Calif., 1960-62; promoter Gospel Concerts, Redondo Beach, Calif., 1962-66; adminstr. Jake Hess Prodns., Nashville, 1966—, Danny Davis Prodns., Nashville, 1972—; prin. Dunne Enterprises, Nashville, 1986—. Producer syndicated TV program: Jake Hess & Friends, 1989. Home: 8008 Stallion Ct Nashville TN 37221 Office: Dunne Enterprises 8008 Stallion Ct Nashville TN 37221

FENSTERMAKER, SARAH, education educator; b. Indpls., Oct. 25, 1949. BA in Sociology, Goucher Coll., 1971; MA in Sociology, Northwestern U., 1973, PhD in Sociology, 1976. Rsch. assoc. Northwestern U., 1972-73; rsch. sociologist, social process rsch. inst. U. Calif., Santa Barbara, 1976—, lectr. dept. of sociology, 1976-77, asst. prof. dept. sociology, 1977-82, assoc. prof. dept. sociology, 1982-88, prof. dept. sociology, 1988—, chair, women's studies program, 1988—; lectr. Chgo. State U., 1976, The Santa Barbar Jr. League, 1977, U. Calif. Santa Barbara, 1977, Starr-King Sch. Parents Assn., 1983, UCLA, 1985, Calif. State U., 1987, Conf. for Land Grant Coll. Extension Specialist, Chgo., 1988; cons. in field. Contbr. articles to profl. jours. Grantee Spencer Found. Predoctoral Rsch. Program, 1973-74, NIMH, 1976-77, Law Enforcement Asst. Adminstrn., 1978-79, Academic Senate Opportunity Funds, 1987-88; fellow Mgmt. Inst. U. Calif., 1986, NIMH, 1975; recipient Faculty Devel. Affirmative Action award, 1980.

FENTON, MARJORIE, educational coordinator, consultant; b. Warren, Ohio, Feb. 7, 1935; d. Leland Reed and Elma Arlene (Gotthardt) Titus; m. Harold W. Fenton, June 11, 1955 (div. Sept. 1984); children: Brian, Amy. BS in Edn., Kent State U., 1985, M in Edn. Adminstrn., 1988. Treas. Champion Local Sch. Dist., Warren, 1967-80, Trumbull County Joint Vocat. Sch. Dist., Warren, 1980-89; pres., cons. Sch. Mgmt. Svcs., Inc., Southington, Ohio, 1989—; cons. Ohio Dept. Edn., Columbus, 1980-84, 89—; treas. Champion Community Sr. Housing, Inc., Warren, 1982-90; coord. Ashland (Ohio) U., 1989—. Mem. Trumbull County Bd. Edn., Warren, 1968—. Recipient Exemplary Service to Edn. award Champion Local Schs., Warren, 1980. Mem. Ohio Assn. Sch. Bus. Officials (state pres. 1979-80, state legis. chmn. 1980—, Pres.'s Disting. Service award 1984, Recognition Outstanding Service 1985), Assn. Sch. Bus. Officials Internat., Ohio Sch. Bds. Assn., Phi Delta Kappa.

FENTON, MONICA, university program officer; b. Elizabeth, N.J., Mar. 2, 1944; d. Edward B. and Veronica (Kryszczuk) Zacharczyk; m. C. Gerald Bischoff (div. 1971); m. Roger A. Fenton, July 30, 1983. Student, Union Coll., Cranford, N.J., 1962-66. Sr. rsch. tech. Bristol-Myers Co., Hillside, N.J., 1963-75; tech. adminstr., electron microscopist Albert Einstein Coll. Medicine, Bronx, N.Y., 1975-88; devel. officer, asst. to dir. Ctr. for Rsch. on Occupational and Environ. Toxicology U. Portland, 1988—. Mng. editor Third World Med. Rsch. Found., N.Y.C., 1987—, editorial cons., 1990—; copy editor (proc.) The Grass Pea: Threat and Promise, 1989, (transcripts) Toxicity of Cycads, 1988; contbr. tech. rsch. articles and abstracts to profl. jours., ghost writer 4 rsch. revs. Mem. Electron Microscopy Soc. Am., Nat. Soc. Fundraising Execs. Home: 54 W Shore Rd Mountain Lakes NJ 07046 Office: U Portland Ctr for Rsch on Occupational and Environ Toxicology 3181 SW Sam Jackson Park Rd Portland OR 97201

FENTON, PAULA BLANCHE, lawyer; b. N.Y.C., Apr. 29, 1947; d. Robert and Janet (Munk) F. BA with honors, U. Pa., 1969; JD, Columbia U., 1972. Assoc. Reavis & McGrath, N.Y.C., 1972-77; sr. clk. to presiding justice N.Y. State Supreme Ct., N.Y.C., 1977-79; ptnr. Fine, Tofel, Saxl, Berleson & Barandes, N.Y.C., 1979-83; counsel, dir. spl. events Am. Ballet Theatre, N.Y.C., 1983-87; sr. atty. Radio City Music Hall Prodns., Inc., N.Y.C., 1987—; arbitrator Am. Arbitration Assn., N.Y.C., 1979—; chmn. secondary sch. com. U. Pa., N.Y.C., 1981-84; cons. Aspen Camp for the Deaf, Colo., 1986. Bd. dirs. New Leadership Israel Bonds, 1980-82, San Diego Performances, 1987—. Recipient Award of Merit Israel Bonds, 1981. Democrat. Jewish. Office: Radio City Music Hall Prodns Inc 1260 Ave of the Americas New York NY 10020

FENWICK, LYNDA BECK, lawyer, writer; b. Great Bend, Kans., Oct. 24, 1944; d. Ralph George and Margaret Pauline (Hawk) Beck; m. Larry Dean Fenwick, Dec. 23, 1962. BS with distinction, Fort Hays State U., 1966; JD, Baylor U., 1975. Bar: U.S. Dist. Ct. (we. dist.) Tex. 1980, U.S. Dist. Ct. (no. dist.) Tex. 1986. Atty. VA, Waco, Tex., 1975-79; assoc. Pakis, Cherry, Beard & Giotes, Waco, 1979-81; sole practice Dallas, 1981-85; assoc. Taylor & Mizell P.C., Dallas, 1985-88; adj. faculty law Baylor U., Waco, 1979-81; grader exams Supreme Ct. of Tex., 1981-85. Author: Should the Children Pray? Historical, Judicial, Political Examination of Public School Prayer, 1989; assoc. editor Baylor U. Law Rev., 1974-75. Docent Dallas Mus. Art., 1982-85. Mem. ABA, Tex. Bar Assn., Ga. Bar Assn., Portrait Soc. Atlanta, Southeastern Pastel Soc., Phi Delta Phi.

FENWICK, MILLICENT HAMMOND, retired diplomat, former congresswoman; b. N.Y.C., Feb. 25, 1910; d. Ogden Haggerty and Mary Picton (Stevens) Hammond; children: Mary Fenwick Reckford, Hugh. Student, Columbia Extension Sch., New Sch. for Social Research. Assoc. editor Conde Nast Publs., N.Y.C., 1938-50; mem. N.J. Gen. Assembly, 1970-73; dir. div. consumer affairs N.J. Dept. Law and Pub. Safety, 1973-74; mem. 94th-97th Congresses from N.J. 5th Dist., 1975-83; U.S. amb. UN Food and Agr. Orgn., 1983-87. Author: Vogue's Book of Etiquette, 1948, Speaking Up, 1982. Vice chmn. N.J. advisory com. to U.S. Commn. on Civil Rights, 1958-72; mem. Bernardsville (N.J.) Bd. Edn., 1938-41; mem Bernardsville Borough Council, 1958-64. Republican. Home: Mendham Rd Bernardsville NJ 07924

FERCANA, TERRY LYNN, graphic designer; b. Youngstown, Ohio, July 23, 1962; d. Bennie A. and Ann M. (Ferl) F. BS in Advt., Kent State U., 1984. Mktg. communications asst. Akron (Ohio) Gen. Med. Ctr., 1984-85, graphic design specialist, 1985—; freelance graphic designer, Akron, 1988—. Recipient 1st place Ohio Hosp. Assn. Reach for the Stars, 1988, 2d place 1990, Gold Cert. award Strathmore Paper Co. Graphics Gallery, 1989, others. Mem. Women in Communications (merit award logo design 1989, 1st place for visual arts and layout 1990), Akron Press Club, Kent State Alumni Assn., Advt. Club Akron. Roman Catholic. Home: 38 Marshall Ave Apt 7 Akron OH 44303 Office: Akron Gen Med Ctr 400 Wabash Ave Akron OH 44307

FERENCZ, CHARLOTTE, professor epidemiology, preventive medicine; b. Budapest, Hungary, Oct. 28, 1921; came to U.S., 1954; d. Paul Ferencz and Livia deFekete. BSc, McGill U., 1944, MD, CM, 1945; MPH, Johns Hopkins U., 1970. Cert. pediatrics Royal Coll. Physicians and Surgeons, Can., pediatric cardiology Am. Bd. Pediatrics. Demonstrator McGill U., Montreal, 1952-54; asst. prof. pediatrics Johns Hopkins U., Balt., 1954-58; asst. prof. pediatrics SUNY, Buffalo, 1960-66, assoc. prof. pediatrics, 1966-73; assoc. prof. epidemiology and preventive medicine U. Md. Sch. Medicine, Balt., 1973-74, prof. epidemiology and preventive medicine, 1974—, prof. pediatrics, 1985—; Prin. investigator population based study Etiology of Congenital Heart Disease, 1981—; mem. epidemic and disease control study sect. NIH, 1984-88; pres. Delta Omega Alpha chpt. Pub. Health Soc., 1990-92. Recipient M.E.S. Abbott scholarship McGill U., 1943-45, Merit award Nat. Heart, Lung & Blood Inst., 1987, Fogarty Internat. Ctr. Health Sci. Exchange award NIH, 1988. Fellow Am. Acad. Pediatrics, Am. Coll. Cardiology; mem. Teratology Soc. Democrat. Office: U Md Sch Medicine 660 W Redwood St Baltimore MD 21201

FERENS, MARCELLA, educator, business executive; b. Pitts.; d. Ignatius and Marcella (Buzas) Slevinskas; student Greensburg Bus. Coll., 1934-35, Maison Frederic Cosmetology, 1936, Kree Inst. Electrolysis, N.Y., 1952; B.S., U. Pitts., 1957; postgrad. Mid-Western U., 1962; M.Ed., Duquesne U., 1964; m. Joseph J. Ferens, Nov. 27, 1937; children—Joseph Ferens, James. Cosmetologist and electrologist, Manor and Darragh, Pa., 1937—; research in hair regrowth, Darragh, 1954—; tchr. cosmetology Uniontown (Pa.) Vocat. High, 1954-55; tchr. algebra, reading and drama dir. Harold Jr. High Sch., Greensburg, Pa., 1958—; pres. Marcella Ferens Inc.; treas. Schumacher Labs. Inc., Darragh. Insp., Chem. Corps, Dept. Army, N.Y., 1951. Mem. Nat. Coun. Tchrs. Math., Nat. Edn. Assns., Pa. Edn. Assns. Patentee in field. Home: Box 84 Darragh PA 15625

FERGUS, PATRICIA MARGUERITA, educator emeritus, writer, editor; b. Mpls., Oct. 26, 1918; d. Golden Maughan and Mary Adella (Smith) F. B.S., U. Minn., 1939, M.A., 1941, Ph.D., 1960. Various pers. and editing positions U.S. Govt., 1943-59; mem. faculty U. Minn., Mpls., 1964-79, asst. prof. English, 1972-79, coord. writing program conf. on writing, 1975, dir. writing centre, 1975-77; prof. English and writing, dir. writing ctr., assoc. dean Coll. Mt. St. Mary's Coll., Emmitsburg, Md., 1979-81; dir. writing seminars Mack Truck, Inc., Hagerstown, Md., 1979-81; writer, 1964—; editorial asst. to pres. Met. State U., St. Paul, 1984-85; speaker in field; cons. in field; dir. 510 Groveland Assocs.; bus. mgr. Eitel Hosp. Gift Shop. Author: Spelling Improvement, 5th edit., 1990; contbr. to Minn. English Jour., Downtown Cath. Voice, Mpls., Mountaineer Briefing, ABI Digest; contbr. poems Minn. English Jour., Mpls. Muse, The Moccasin, Heartsong and Northstar Gold, The PoetryLetter, IBC Mag., others. Mem. spl. vocal octet St. Olaf Ch. Choir, St. Olaf Parish Adv. Bd. Recipient Outstanding Contbn. award U. Minn. Twin Cities Student Assembly, 1975; Horace T. Morse-Amoco Found. award, 1976; Ednl. Devel. grantee U. Minn., 1975-76; Mt. St. Mary's Coll. grantee, 1980; 3d prize vocal-choral category Nat. Music Composition Contest, Nat. League Am. Pen Women, speaker and Bronze Medalist, 13th Internat. Biographical Congress, 1986. Mem. Internat. Biog. Centre Assn., Am. Biog. Research Assn. (dep. gov. hon. research adv. bd.), Am. Biog. Rsch. Assn., AAUW, Nat. (regional judge writing awards program 1974, 76-77, state coord. 1977-79) Minn. (chmn. career and job opportunities com., mem. spl. com. on tchr. licensure, sec. legis. com.) Couns. Tchrs. English, Nat. League Am. Pen Women (pres. Minn. State Assn. br. 1990—), World Lit. Acad., Mpls. Poetry Soc. (v.p., 1st prize Haiku contest 1984, 3d prize poetry contest 1986, 1st prize poetry contest 1987, 3d prize poetry contest 1988, 2d prize poetry contest 1989), League Minn. Poets (3d prize Nature, 2d prize Humor, Autumn poetry contest 1987, 2d prize poetry contest), Midwest Fedn. Chaparral Poets (2d prize poetry contest 1987, 3d prize poetry contest 1988, 1st prize nature poetry contest 1989, 2d prize poetry contest 1989), Pi Lambda Theta. Roman Catholic. Home and Office: 1314 Marquette Ave Ste 508 Minneapolis MN 55403

FERGUSON, AMY TALLEY, social service administrator; b. Jackson, Miss., Mar. 20, 1941; d. Gilbert Arthur and Bessie Lambert (Day) T.; m. John Darrell Ferguson, Jr., Feb. 17, 1973. BA, Radcliffe Coll., 1963; MSW, Smith Coll., 1965. Cert. social worker and advanced clin. practitioner, Tex.; diplomate Am. Bd. Examiners in Clin. Social Work. Social worker U. Tex. Med. Br., Galveston, 1965-71, social work supr., 1971-83, asst. dir. dept. social work, 1983—. Mem. Nat. Assn. Social Workers, Tex. Soc. Hosp. Social Work Dirs., Soc. Hosp. Social Work Dirs. of Am. Hosp. Assn., Acad. Cert. Social Workers. Office: U Tex Med Br Dept Social Work Rte G-39 Galveston TX 77550

FERGUSON, ANNA MARIE, educator; b. Nassau, The Bahamas, Oct. 17, 1940; came to U.S., 1954; BA, Howard U., 1963; MA, U. Mich., 1978. Tchr. Cleve. Pub. Schs., 1963-64, Southeastern High Sch., Detroit, 1965-80, Cooley High Sch., Detroit, 1980—; instr. Graduate Equivalency Diploma class Cass Outreach Adult Evening Program, 1978-80; sponsor various student activities, Southeastern High Sch., 1966-80, Cooley High Sch., 1986-90; mem. adv. bd. Sta. WXYZ-TV, 1990—. Contbr. articles to community newspapers and English jours. Pres. Crary-St. Mary's Community Coun., 1981; lector St. Cypian's Episcopal Ch., 1988—; mem. NAACP, 1963-86, YWCA, 1965-86, Founders Soc. Detroit Inst. Arts, 1977—, Met. Opera Assn., 1977—, Trian's Guild of St. Cypian's Episcopal Ch., 1987—, Grand-Green Bus. Assn. Bd., 1982; chmn. Howard U., 1990. Recipient Spl. Tribute award State of Mich., 1983, 90, Cert. of Appreciation award Howard U., 1988, Fellowship award Coun. on Basic Edn., Washington, 1983; named Howardite of Yr., 1990. Fellow Coun. on Basic Edn.; mem. Nat. Coun. Tchrs. English, Mich. Coun. Tchrs. English, Detroit Fedn. Tchrs., Howard U. Alumni Club of Detroit (sec. 1977-79, 86-88, pres. 1979-81, 88—, nat. rec. sec. 1984-88, author newsletter 1979-81, 88—, souvenir booklets 1980-81, 89). Democrat. Episcopalian. Office: Cooley High Sch 15055 Hubbell Detroit MI 48227

FERGUSON, AUDRI DALE, travel executive; b. Harvey, Ill., Jan. 13, 1954; d. Dale Lloyd and Mari Lu (Parrott) Ferguson. AS, Prairie State Coll., Chicago Heights, Ill., 1974, Triton Coll., Chgo., 1976. With passenger services dept. Eastern Airlines, Chgo., 1979-85; travel cons. SATO, Inc., Chgo., 1985-89, Carlson Corp., L.A., 1989; mgr. Omega World Travel, L.A., 1989—. Treas. Rep. Womans Club, Chgo., 1986; exec. com. 42d ward Rep. Cen. Com., Chgo., 1989, precinct capt., 1989; active Tyrone Fahner campaign, Chgo., 1986, Lincoln Park Zoo, 1979-89, Anti-Cruelty Soc., 1979-89, Art Inst., 1986-88. Office: Omega World Travel 12400 Wilshire Blvd Ste 220 Los Angeles CA 90025

FERGUSON, CARMELA, social services administrator; b. Panama City, Panama, June 13, 1933; came to U.S., 1957; d. Jose Manuel and Josefa Esperanza (Caraballo) Flores; m. Raymond Alastair Ferguson, Dec. 15, 1962; 1 child, Raymond Alastair. B in Bus. Adminstrn., U. Nat. Panama, 1956; student, Bklyn. Coll., 1960-61. Sec. to br. mgr. Republic Films, Panama, 1950-55, United Artists Films, Panama, 1955-57; bilingual sec. to v.p. export sales Detector Scales, Inc., N.Y.C., 1958-65; bilingual sec. to adminstrv. asst. to corp. contr. Atlantic Richfield Co., N.Y.C., 1966-72; assoc. dir. of logistical svcs. Internat. div. Planned Parenthood Fedn., N.Y.C., 1974—. Sec. Home Sch. Assn., Queens Village, N.Y., 1972-75. Mem. NAFE. Democrat. Roman Catholic. Home: 216-28 110th Rd Queens Village NY 11429

FERGUSON, CAROLYN SUE, realtor; b. Green Sulphur Springs, W.Va., Aug. 1, 1935; d. Frank Bunyan and Effie Caroline (Johnson) Lively; m. Marion Ezekiel (Pete) Ferguson, May 28, 1955; children: Charles Ronald, Lowell Lane. Cert., Sch. of Commerce, Charelston, W.Va., 1953; grad., Realtors Inst. of W.Va., Parkersburg, 1984; cert. residential specialist, Parkersburg Community Coll., 1988; student, W.Va. State Coll., Institute, 1989—. Sec. Charleston C. of C., 1953-59; legal sec. Stanley Preiser, Esq., Charleston, 1959-61; office mgr. Union Carbide Corp., Real Estate, Charleston, 1961-70; loan closing officer Title Guaranty Co., Casper, Wyo., 1976; realtor Dobbins, Fisher and Pittman, Inc., St. Albans, W.Va., 1970-75, 77-79, Old Colony Co., Hurricane, W.Va., 1984—; chairperson equal opportunity com. Kanawha Valley Bd. Realtors, Charleston, 1987-88, chairperson-by-laws, 1989-90. Author short stories, numerous poems. Mem. Putnam County Planning Commn. Recipient Dream Maker award Multiple Listing Svc., Charleston, 1989. Mem. NAFE, Nat. Assn. Realtors, W.Va. Bd. Realtors, W.Va. Writers, Inc., Wyoming Writers, St. Albans Writers, Putnam County C. of C. (County Leadership award 1987). Democrat. Home: Whippoorwill Hollow Hurricane WV 25526 Office: Old Colony Co 4161 State Rte 34 Hurricane WV 25526

FERGUSON, DEE ANN, academic director; b. Columbus, Ohio, July 13, 1947; d. Walter Lewis and Rachel Dixon (Stone) Lucas; m. David Elton Ferguson (dec. June 1969); 1 child, Patrick Antonio. B cum laude, Ohio State U., 1966; MBA, U. Exeter, Eng., 1975. Mng. dir. Lori of London, Internat. London, 1973-80; bus. mgr., cons. Los Angeles, 1978-80; adminstr. Gussi Watches, Los Angeles, 1979-82; dir. facilities Marlborough Sch., Los Angeles, 1983—; mem. steering com. Earthquake Preparedness Marlborough Sch., 1984—. Inventor roll-r-shoe, load stabelizer, chem. formulae. Mem. Assn. Phys. Plant Admistrs. of Colls. and Univs., Am. Inst. Plant Engrs. (treas.-elect 1988, bd. dirs.). Roman Catholic. Home: 1147 N Wilcox Pl Los Angeles CA 90038 Office: Marlborough Sch 250 S Rossmore Ave Los Angeles CA 90004

FERGUSON, ELIZABETH ANN, marketing professional; b. Waterloo, Iowa, Feb. 25, 1932; d. John Richard and Eva Kathryn (Krantz) Callahan; m. Thomas R., Aug. 23, 1952; children: Mary Patrice, Thomas J., Stephen N., Dan J. Student, Iowa State Tchrs. Coll., 1950. Editorial asst. Waterloo Courier, 1967-69, feature writer, 1969-83, med. edn. reporter, 1983-85; dir. communications, publs. mktg. Allen Memorial Hosp., Waterloo, 1985—; mktg. com., Iowa Hosp. Pub. Relations., Des Moines; publ. comm., Cancer Awareness, Waterloo; sec. Cedar Valley Hospice, Waterloo, 1986-. mem. Friends of the Library, Waterloo; precinct worker, Democratic Party, Waterloo; exec. com. United Way of Black Hawk County, Waterloo, 1974-78; advisor Jr. League Waterloo Cedar Falls, 1982-87; bd. dirs. Am. Martyrs Retreat House, Cedar Falls. Roman Catholic. Home: 123 Byron Ave Waterloo IA 50702 Office: Allen Meml Hosp 1825 Logan Ave Waterloo IA 50703

FERGUSON, HELEN MOTT, exposition center official; b. Sparta, Tenn., Mar. 2, 1941; d. Lloyd Convess Mott and Eulene (Clouse) Hutchings; m. John Bainbridge Ferguson, Jr., Apr. 16, 1966; 1 child, Julie Anne. Student, Miss. State U., 1960-62. Engrng. aide TVA, Chattanooga, 1962-66; tax examiner IRS, Atlanta, 1967-69; acct. Sandpiper Enterprises, Inc., Greenville, S.C., 1979-88; adminstrv. asst. for fin. Palmetto Expn. Ctr., Greenville, 1988—. Vice pres. Merrifield Park Community Club, 1974; mem. Greenville Symphony Guild, 1974-85; vol. Meals on Wheels, 1974-89; cancer chmn., co-chmn. home life Greenville Jr. Women's Club, 1975-79; bd. dirs. Am. Cancer Soc., 1976-79, sec., 1977; bd. dirs. Carolina Ballet Theatre, 1983-86; treas. Merri-Gardeners, 1977; v.p. Pelham Trails Garden Club, 1986, pres., 1987; mem. Friends Greenville County Libr., 1977-83; treas. Stratton Place Community Club, 1985, hospitality chmn., 1986. Recipient Ballew award Greenville Jr. Women's Club, 1976, Ann Borris Meml. State Cancer award S.C. Fedn. Women's Clubs, 1978. Mem. Greenville Woman's Club. Republican. Baptist. Home: 12 Coventry Rd Greenville SC 29615 Office: Palmetto Expn Ctr Exposition Ave PO Box 5823 Greenville SC 29606

FERGUSON, JULIE ANN, corporate professional; b. Washington, Sept. 26, 1959; d. Carl Frederick Banks and Diette Agnes (Porter) Hissey; m. Joseph Pierre Ferguson, Mar. 16, 1978 (div. 1985). Student, Montgomery Coll., 1980-86; BBA with Distinction, U. Redlands, 1988. Asst. dept. mgr. Montgomery Ward Co., Gaithersburg, Md., 1978-80; sec., pubs. asst. U.S. Dept. Justice, Washington, 1979-83; project asst. Aero. and Space Engring. bd., NRC, Washington, 1983-86; adminstrv. sec. Lockheed Corp., Calabasas, Calif., 1986-88; staff asst. Lockheed Aero. Systems Co., Burbank, Calif., 1988—. Recipient Citizenship award KC, 1977. Mem. Lockheed Mgmt. Assn., NAFE, Nat. Wildlife Fedn. Democrat. Home: 507 E Cedar Ave Apt #203 Burbank CA 91501 Office: Lockheed Aero Systems Co PO Box 551 Burbank CA 91520-1020

FERGUSON, KAYE IRENE, fund raiser, marketing professional; b. Lansing, Mich., Jan. 20, 1939; d. Alfred Richard and Iris Francis (Kast) Collins; m. Stanley M. Ferguson, June 21, 1958 (div. 1983); children: Kelley Ann, Carrie Jane, Stanley M. BA, Mich. State U., 1958; postgrad., Memphis State U., 1974-75. Freelance writer Detroit, 1958-68; educator Met. Soc. for Blind, Detroit, 1968-69; media buyer, copy writer John R. Chapman Co., Royal Oak, Mich., 1969-71; talk show host Sta. KERO-TV, Bakersfield, Calif., 1971-74; creative dir. Lanigan, Inc., Memphis, 1974-75, Merritt Mosby Advt. Agy., Memphis, 1975-80; v.p., creative dir. Myers/Ferguson Assocs., Memphis, 1980-85; dir. tourism City of Memphis Conv. and Visitors Bur., Memphis, 1985-86; assoc. dir. Meth. Hosps. Found., Memphis, 1986-88; v.p. devel. Luth. Social Svcs. of Mich., 1988—; regional dir. State Tenn. Dept. Tourism, Memphis, 1986-87; profl. soprano soloist, various events, 1958—. Bd. dirs. Memphis Symphony Chorus, 1983-85, Am. Lung Assn., 1983-86; bd. dirs., past pres. Alliance for Blind and Visually Impaired, Memphis, 1985-88; mem. adminstrv. bd. Germantown United Meth. Ch., 1983-88, music dir. 1980-88, bd. dirs. 1988—; dir. music St. Paul Evang. Luth. Ch., Grosse Pointe Farms, 1989—; bd. dirs. Rackham Symphony Choir, chair devel. com. Recipient Outstanding Vol. award March of Dimes, Bakersfield, 1974, Outstanding Service award Am. Lung Assn., 1984. Mem. Memphis Advt. Fedn. (chmn. various coms. 1982-86), Nat. Assn. Female Execs., Am. Women in Radio and TV (sec. 1972-73), Nat. Assn. Hosp. Devel., Nat. Soc. Fund Raising Execs., Assn. Luth. Devel. Execs., Meth. Fellowship of Musicians (sec.-treas. 1986-87), PEO, Delta Delta Delta. Office: Luth Social Svcs of Mich 8131 E Jefferson Ave Detroit MI 48214

FERGUSON, NANCY JEAN, physician; b. Trenton, N.J., Jan. 11, 1954; d. Walter Edward Ferguson and Ruth Iseloy (Kidder) Ferguson Warga. AAS, Mercer County Community Coll., 1976; BA in Chemistry, Trenton State Coll., 1978; MD, Rutgers U., 1983. Intern/resident Hunterdon Med. Ctr., Flemington, N.J., 1983-87; med. dir. Primary Health Care Ctr. of Dade, Trenton, Ga., 1987-90, Sandmont Gala Nursing Home, Trenton, 1988-90; mem. emergency room staff Fannin Regional Hosp., Blue Ridge, Ga., 1989-90; campus physician Covenant Coll., Lookout Mountain, Ga., 1989-90; emergency rm. staff West Jersey Hosp.-No. div., Camden, N.J., 1990—; v.p. Interagy Coun., Trenton, 1989; cons. physician Family/Children's Svcs. of Dade County, 1987-90. Editor: (handbook) Physician Impairment, 1987; mem. editorial bd. Ga. Acad. Family Practice, 1989-90. Recipient Shirley Troxell award Trenton State Coll., 1978; State of Ga. drug awareness grantee, 1989. Fellow Am. Acad.Family Practice; mem. Ga. Assn. Primary Health Care, Amnesty Internat. Office: 196 George St Lambertville NJ 08530

FERGUSON, PAMELA ANASTACIA, mathematics educator, educational administrator; b. Berwyn, Ill., May 5, 1943; d. Clarence Oscar and Ruth Anne (Stroner) Anderson; m. Donald Roger Ferguson, Dec. 18, 1965; children: Keith, Amanda. BA, Wellesley Coll., 1965; MS, U. Chgo., 1966, PhD, 1969. Asst. prof. Northwestern U., Evanston, Ill., 1969-70, U. Miami, Coral Gables, Fla., 1972-77; assoc. prof. U. Miami, 1978-81, prof. math., 1981—, dir. honors program, 1985-87, assoc. provost, dean Grad. Sch., 1987—. Contbr. over 45 articles to refereed jours. Mem. Fla. Adv. Coun. for Improvement of Math. and Sci. Edn. (chair accountability com. 1989—), 1989—. NSF grantee. Mem. Am. Math. Soc., Am. Women in Math., Wellesley Club, U. Chgo. Club, Sigma Xi, Phi Beta Kappa, Omicron Delta Chi. Lutheran. Office: U Miami Grad Sch 210 Ferre Bldg Coral Gables FL 33124-2220

FERGUSON, SHARON HERMINE, nurse; b. Mansfield, Ohio, Mar. 5, 1953; d. Robert Joseph and Hermine Elizabeth (Schwartz) Frasz; m. Michael Ferguson, Mar. 23, 1974; 1 child, Marshal Joseph. Student, Ohio State U., 1972; diploma in nursing, Mid-Ohio Practical Nurse Coll., 1974. Ward sec. Mansfield Gen. Hosp., 1973-74; psychiat. nurse Bethesda Hosp., Zanesville, Ohio, 1974; pvt. duty nurse Zanesville, 1974-75; nurse Mary's Nursing Home, Zanesville, 1975; post surg. nurse Good Samaritan Med. Ctr., Zanesville, 1976—; pres. nursing class Mid-Ohio Practical Nurse Program, Mansfield, 1973-74. Vol. St. Thomas Aquinas Sch., Zanesville, 1984—; vol. support person rape survivors Survival Assistance Friendship Edn., Zanesville, 1987—. Home: 7175 Mutton Ridge Rd Zanesville OH 43701 Office: Good Samaritan Med Ctr 800 Forest Ave Zanesville OH 43701

FERGUSON, SHARON SEBASTIAN, graphic artist, government official, real estate a; b. Arlington, Va., Nov. 27, 1950; d. Richard David and Agnes Mary (Johnson) Sebastian; m. James William Ferguson, Sept. 5, 1982; 1 child, Morgan Leigh. BFA, Va. Commonwealth U., 1973; postgrad., Stanford U., 1977, Parson's Sch. Deisghn, 1979. Visual info. specialist GAO, Washington, 1973-82, art dir., 1982—; cons. and design asst. for Visual Communications Standars ma, 1984-87; freelance designer, 1981—. Mem. Art Dirs. Club Met. Washington. Home: 1615 S 23rd St Arlington VA 11101 Office: GAO 441 G St NW Room 4432 Washington DC 20548

FERGUSON, SUSAN KATHARINE STOVER, nurse, therapist; b. Warsaw, Ind., Mar. 11, 1944; d. Robert Eugene and Barbara Louise (Swaney) S.; m. Philip Charles Ferguson, May 29, 1942 (div.); children: Scott Duane, Shawn Alaine, Erin Kirsten. Diploma in nursing, Meth. Hosp.,

1966; BA in Psychology, Purdue U., 1988; postgrad., Smith Coll., 1989—. Staff nurse, health hazard appraiser Meth. Hosp. of Ind., Indpls., 1966-68; staff nurse USPHS, Bethel, Alaska, 1968-70; instr. childbirth preparation Wabash, Ind., 1975-83; nurse Family Physicians Associated, Wabash, 1976-83; rsch. asst. Purdue U., Ft. Wayne, Ind., 1986-88; staff nurse Charter Beacon Hosp., Ft. Wayne, Ind., 1988-89; intern clin. social work Clifford Beers Guidance Ctr., New Haven, Conn., 1990—; self-awareness seminar and coord. charter Beacon Hosp. Bd. dirs. Hoosiers for Safety Belts, Indpls., 1987-88, Ind. Med. Pol. Action Com., Indpls., 1986-87; coordinator, founder Safe Start Infant Safety Seat Loan Program, Wabash, 1981-87; participant in leadership devel. com. Wabash County C. of C., 1983; workshop leader Wabash County Hosp. Stop Smoking Program, 1982-83. Mem. Ind. Child Passenger Safety Assn. (pres. 1985-87), Ind. State Med. Assn. Aux. (chmn. program workbook 1982-86), Am. Psychol. Assn. (student affiliate), Sierra Club, Greenpeace, Nat. Audobon Soc., The Wilderness Soc., Nat. Wildlife Fedn., Smithsonian Assn., Kappa Kappa Kappa. Republican. Home: 2611 Neptune's Crossing Fort Wayne IN 46815

FERGUSON, THERESA LYNN, pharmacist; b. Jefferson, N.C., May 19, 1961; d. Jimmy Craig and Greta Joyce (Williams) F. BS in Pharmacy, U. N.C., Chapel Hill, 1984. Registered pharmacist, N.C. Pharmacy technician Eckard Drugs, Durham, N.C., 1982-84, Wilkes Gen. Hosp., Wilkesboro, N.C., 1983; dir. pharmacy Ashe Meml. Hosp., Jefferson, 1984—; cons. pharmacist Emerald Health Care, Jefferson, 1989—. Mem. N.C. Soc. Hosp. Pharmacists, Am. Soc. Hosp. Pharmacists, Am. Soc. Cons. Pharmacists, Blue Ridge Pharmacy Soc., Young Dems. Orgn., Jefferson Humane Soc. Methodist. Home: Rte 2 Box 848 West Jefferson NC 28694 Office: Ashe Meml Hosp PO Box 8 Jefferson NC 28640

FERGUSON MANN, SERENA DESANTOS, cable television county official; b. Washington, July 3, 1957; d. James Herman and Lena Lorraine (Santos) Ferguson; m. Charles Edward Mann, Mar. 23, 1985. BA magna cum laude, Howard U., 1979. Cinematographer Walt Disney World Co., Orlando, Fla., 1978-81; freelance editor various orgns. Washington, 1981-82; editor, producer Satellite News Channel, Washington, 1982-83; project dir. creative arts City Mission Soc., Boston, 1984; editor Sta. WGBH-TV pub. broadcasting, Boston, 1984; assoc. producer Sta. WNEV-TV 7, Boston, 1984; editor Sta. WRC-TV 4, Washington, 1985; sr. producer, dir. Mayor's Office of Communications, Balt., 1985-89; cable TV coord. Howard County Govt., Columbia, Md., 1989—; bd. dirs. Youth Communications Ctr., Balt., 1988—. Recipient Communications award Howard U., 1980, Emmy, 1985, Bronze medal N.Y. Film & TV Festival, 1985, 1st place for documentary Internat. Assn. Bus. Communicators, Balt., 1987. Mem. Internat. TV Assn., Nat. Fed. Local Cable Programmers, Nat. Assn. County Info. Officers. Office: Howard County Govt Cable 15 10650 Hickory Ridge Rd Columbia MD 21044

FERGUSON-PELL, MARGARET ALICE, health science facility press and public relations officer; b. New Haven, Aug. 14, 1951; d. Franklin Eldridge and Virginia Boardman (Porter) F.; m. Martin William Ferguson-Pell, Dec. 29, 1973; 1 child, Grace. BA in English summa cum laude, Wheaton Coll., 1973. Antiquarian book specialist John Smith & Son, Glasgow, Scotland, 1974-76; book editor Heatherbank Press, Milngavie, Scotland, 1977-78; press officer Scottish Opera Theatre Royal, Glasgow, 1978-82; pub. relations and devel. officer Helen Hayes Hosp., West Haverstraw, N.Y., 1982—. Pub. relations officer Rockland County Disaster Preparedness Team, Rockland, N.Y., 1983—; trustee Chappaqua (N.Y.) Library, 1985—; bd. dirs. Westchester Ind. Living Ctr., White Plains, N.Y., 1988—. Mem. N.Y. State Head Injury Assn. (bd. dirs. Southern region, Recognition award 1986), Nat. Union Journalists, Rockland Devel. Group, Phi Beta Kappa. Office: Helen Hayes Hosp Rt 9W West Haverstraw NY 10993

FERGUSSON, FRANCES DALY, college president, educator; b. Boston, Oct. 3, 1944; d. Francis Joseph and Alice (Storrow) Daly. BA, Wellesley Coll., 1965; MA, Harvard U., 1966, PhD, 1973. Asst. prof. Newton Coll., Mass., 1969-75; assoc. prof. U. Mass., Boston, 1974-82, asst. chancellor, 1980-82; provost, prof. Bucknell U., Lewisburg, Pa., 1982-86; pres. Vassar Coll., Poughkeepsie, N.Y., 1986—. Trustee Mayo Found., 1988—, Ford Found., 1989—. Recipient Founder's award Soc. Archtl. Historians, 1973. Office: Vassar Coll Raymond Ave Poughkeepsie NY 12601

FERLAND, DARLENE FRANCES, management consultant; b. Pawtucket, R.I., Feb. 11, 1954; d. Stephen William and Frances Grace (Masterson) Regula; m. Edward Oscar Ferland, Nov. 22, 1973; 1 child, Francesgrace. AS in Criminal Justice, Salve Regina Coll., 1975, BA in History and Polit. Sci., 1976, MA in History, 1980, postgrad. Dir. Barbizon Sch. R.I., Providence, 1979-82, Barbizon Agy. R.I., Providence, 1980-81; tchr. Bay View Acad., Riverside, R.I., 1982-84; v.p. Edward Ferland Constrn. Co., Pawtucket, R.I., 1983—; pres. Enterprising Images Inc., Pawtucket, 1985—; guest lectr. Providence Coll., 1980—. Pres. parish coun., local Roman Cath. ch., 1986—; active Am. Heart Assn. Mem. Bay View Alumnae Assn. (pres. 1981-84, Outstanding Alumna award 1983), Arrive Alive Am. (nat. bd. 1986—), Salve Regina Alumni Assn. (pres. 1986—), AAUW (Providence chpt. pres. v.p. 1983-86, legis. chair 1982-83). Democrat. Roman Catholic. Home and Office: 225 Greenslitt Ave Pawtucket RI 02861 also: Cabrita Point Saint Thomas VI 00802

FERLAZZO, ELLEN LAWSON, infosystems executive; b. Portland, Oreg., June 19, 1961; d. Robert Porter and Jene (Leggat) Lawson; m. George A. Hess Jr., Apr. 9, 1983 (div. 1985); m. Anthony Ferlazzo Jr., Aug. 1, 1986. AAS, Heald Inst. Tech., 1983; BS in Info. Systems Mgmt., U. San Francisco, 1988. Supr., tech. support and publs. Thomas Engrng. Co., Concord, Calif., 1982-86; mgr. info. svcs. ctr. Servio Logic Corp., Alameda, Calif., 1986—. Contbr. monthly column to profl. publs., 1985. Mem. Assn. for Computing Machinery, Assn. Systems Mgmt., Mt. Diablo Tech. Assn. (bd. dirs. 1989—). Home: 1392 Vailwood Ct Pleasanton CA 94566 Office: Servio Logic Corp 1420 Harbor Bay Pkwy Alameda CA 94501

FERM, LOIS ROUGHAN, religious organization administrator; b. Buffalo, Feb. 5, 1918; d. Laurence Francis and Bertha Margaret Lucy (Jopp) R.; m. Robert O. Ferm, June 28, 1941; children: Lois Esther, Rebecca Ann, Paul Robert, Stephen John. BA, Houghton Coll., 1939; MA, U. Mich., 1955; PhD, U. Minn., 1972. Cert. tchr., N.Y. Tchr. Rushford (N.Y.) Cen. Sch., 1939-41; instr. library, sociology John Brown U., Siloam Springs, Ark., 1949-51; librarian Cuba (N.Y.) Cen. Schs., 1953-55; chmn. dept. edn. Houghton (N.Y.) Coll., 1955-57; instr. edn. U. Minn., Mpls., 1959-61, mgr. Coll. Edn. Library, 1961-64; personal asst. rsch., resource coord. Billy Graham Evangel. Assn., Mpls., 1973—. Pres., Riceville Property Owners Assn., Asheville, N.C., 1982, 83, 87, 88. Mem. Soc. Am. Archivists, Oral History Assn., Christian Women's Clubs, Pi Lambda Theta, Pi Alpha Theta. Republican. Baptist. Home: 27 Patriots Dr Asheville NC 28805 Office: Billy Graham Evangel Assn 1300 Harmon Pl Minneapolis MN 55403

FERN, CAROLE L., lawyer; b. Freeport, N.Y., Sept. 2, 1958; m. Tariq Rafique. BA, Johns Hopkins U., 1979; JD, Harvard U., 1983. Bar: N.Y. 1983, Calif. 1987. Assoc. Shearman & Sterling, N.Y.C., 1987—. Dep. counsel Dukakis for Pres. Mem. ABA, N.Y.C. Bar Assn., Am. Arbitrators Assn. (panel of arbitrators), Phi Beta Kappa. Democrat. Unitarian. Office: Shearman & Sterling Citicorp Ctr 153 E 53d St New York NY 10022

FERN, TAMI LYNNE, specialty-gifted education educator; b. Bklyn., Aug. 25, 1945; d. Sidney W. and Sonia (Pinchas) F. BS, Russell Sage Coll., 1966; MS, Queens Coll., 1970; EdD, Columbia U., N.Y.C., 1989. Tchr. Franklin Square (N.Y.) Schs., 1966—; adj. prof. G.W. Post Coll., L.I.U., Columbia U., N.Y.C., 1989—. Author: Project Funny Bone, 1990. Recipient PTA awards, 1971, 79, 89. Mem. Nat. Assn. for Gifted Children, Coun. for Exceptional Children, Adv. for Gifted and Talented Edn. in N.Y. State, S.E. Adv. for Gifted and Talented Edn., L.I. Educator's Coun for the Gifted and Talented. Democrat. Jewish. Office: Franklin Square Schs Washington St Sch Franklin Square NY 11010

FERNANDES SALLING, LEHUA, lawyer, state senator; b. Lihue, Hawaii, Dec. 6, 1949; d. William Ernest Fernandes and Evelyn (Ohai) Fernandes; m. Michael Ray Salling, Aug. 14, 1971; 1 child. BS, Colo. State U., 1971; JD, Cleveland Marshall Coll., 1975. Law. Ptnr. Fernandes Salling & Salling, Kapaa Kauai, Hawaii, 1976—; mem. Hawaii Senate, 1982—. Mem. Hawaii State Bar Assn., Maile Bus. and Profl. Women's Club, Kamokila Canoe Club, Zonta. Office: 1250 Kuhio Hwy B-308 Kapaa HI 96746*

FERNANDEZ, FE, attorney; b. Havana, Cuba, Mar. 27, 1953; d. Jose Ramon and Fe F. BA with honors, Loyola U., Chgo., 1975; JD, DePaul U., 1978. Bar: Ill. 1978, U.S. Ct. Appeals (7th cir.) 1978, U.S. Dist. Ct. (no. dist.) Ill. 1978. Atty. Office of the State Appellate Defender, Chgo., 1978-81, Evanston (Ill.) Community Defender Office, 1981—; faculty Roosevelt U. Lawyer's Asst's. Program, Chgo., 1989—. Candidate for del. Dem. Nat. Conv., 1975. Office: Evanston Community Defender 828 Davis Evanston IL 60201

FERNÁNDEZ, IRIS VIRGINIA, nurse; b. N.Y.C.; d. Angel Manuel and Virginia (Rosario) F.; m. Alejandro Vásquez Jr., Mar. 4, 1972 (div. Apr. 1975); children: Alejandro III, Taina Carrero. Student, L.I. U., 1975-78; BSN, So. Conn. State U., 1985, BA in Psychology, 1985. Sr. staff nurse NYU Med. Ctr., N.Y.C., 1985-87; pvt. duty nurse N.Y.C., 1987-88; nurse analyst Empire Blue Cross/Blue Shield, N.Y.C., 1988-89, pvt. duty nurse, 1989—; asst. unit supr. Pelham Bay div. Our Lady of Mercy Med. Ctr., Bronx, 1990—; participant continuing edn. com. Cleve. Clinic Found., 1987. Mem. N.Y. State Nurses for Polit. Action. Nat. Hispanic Scholarship Fund scholar, 1981, 82, 83, 84, S.C. Women's Assn. scholar, 1981, Legion of United Latin-Am. Citizens scholar, 1983, 84, Daughters of 1853 scholar, 1983. Mem. Alpha Kappa Alpha (various coms. Eta Omega Omega chpt.). Democrat. Roman Catholic.

FERNANDEZ, ISABEL LIDIA, college administrator; b. Miami, Fla., Jan. 23, 1964; d. Rafael Juvencio and Lidia Rafaela (Morin) Fernandez. BBA, Fla. Internat. U., Miami, 1984, postgrad., 1988—. Personnel cons. Miami, 1984—; asst. dir. human resources Turnberry Isle Yacht & Country Club, Miami, 1985-87; dir. personnel Sheraton River House, Miami, 1987-88; program dir. hospitality mgmt. programs Miami-Dade Community Coll., 1988-89; dir. human resources Doubletree Hotel, Miami, 1989—. Editor newspaper The Sunblazer, 1983-84; contbr. articles to profl. jours. Named Employee of the Month, Coconut Grove Hotel, Miami, 1985. Mem. NAFE, Am. Hotel and Motel Assn. (pres. Greater Miami chpt.), Young Reps. Club (pub. rels. com.). Republican. Lutheran. Home: 9375 Fontainebleau Blvd Apt L103 Miami FL 33172

FERNANDEZ, LAURA BOVE, language educator, retired; b. Schenectady, N.Y., July 16, 1915; d. John and Josephine (Miele) Bove; m. Xavier A. Fernandez; children: Xavier J., Peter G., Anita F. Palmer. BA, SUNY, Albany, 1937; MA, Middlebury Coll., 1947; PhD, Interamerican U., Saltillo, Mexico, 1963; postgrad., San Francisco State U., 1968. Cert. tchr., N.Y. Tchr. French, Spanish, Latin various schs., N.Y., 1937-69; chmn. fgn. langs. Schalmont High Sch., Schenectady, 1957-69; cons., Bur. Fgn. Langs. N.Y. State Edn. Dept., Albany, 1953-69, supr., specialist in fgn. langs., 1969-75. Co-author: Pan y Mantequilla, 1984; co-author: Guía del español, 1970; contbr. articles profl. jours. V.p. Lee County Rep. Women, Ft. Myers, 1989; pres. Lee Rep. Women Fedn., Ft. Myers, 1990; mem. adv. bd. Edison Community Coll., Ft. Myers, 1985—; elected del. Lee County Rep. Women Conv., 1989; nominee v.p. for membership Fla. Div. AAUW, 1990-92; apptd. del. Fla. Rep. State Conv., 1990. Mem. AAUW (br. pres. 1980-84), Am. Assn. Tchrs. of French, Am. Assn. Tchrs. of Spanish (chpt. pres. 1950-52), Lee County Retired Educators Assn., N.Y. State Assn. of Fgn. Lang. Tchrs., Ft. Myers Cultural Exchange (pres. 1982-84). Republican. Roman Catholic. Home: 13401 Miniway SE Fort Myers FL 33905

FERNANDEZ, LINDA ANN, finance director; b. Ballinger, Tex., Nov. 10, 1947; d. Ivan Edward and Ann (Gottschalk) Slaughter; m. Michael Rex, June 8, 1967; 1 child, Sarah Catherine. Postgrad., U. Tex., Austin, 1976. Acct. Acct. John Hancock Life Ins., Austin, Tex., 1972-73, Home Capital Funds, Austin, Tex., 1973-75; acct., adminstrv. asst. Lyda, Boyd, Starr & Wilson, CPAs, Austin, Tex., 1975; acct. State Bar of Tex., Austin, 1975-78, controller, 1978-87; dir. of fin. State Bar of Tex., 1987--. Bd. dirs. Tex. Legal Protection Plan, Austin, Juvenile Diabetes Found., Austin, v.p., 1988-89; treas. Tex. Legal Protection Plan, Austin, 1978-80; bd. dirs. Am. Diabetes Assn., 1989—. Mem. Nat. Cash Mgmt. Assn., Austin Treasury Mgmt. Assn., Austin Soc. of Profl. Ecs. Women, Am. Soc. of Assn. Execs., Am. Diabetes Assn. (bd. dirs. 1989—). Republican. Roman Catholic.

FERNANDEZ, LINDA FLAWN, entrepreneur, social worker; b. Tampa, Fla., Sept. 14, 1943; d. Frank and Rose (D'Amico) F.; 1 child, Marci. B.S., U. South Fla., 1965; M.S., U. Nev., 1976. Social worker Hillsborough County, Tampa, Fla., 1965-67; parole officer adult div. Fla. Parole Commn., Tampa, 1967-69; dir. social services Sunrise Hosp., Las Vegas, Nev., 1969-78; ind. real estate investor, Fla. and Nev., 1965—; pres. Las Vegas Color Separations, Inc., 1978—, Las Vegas Typesetting, Inc., 1983—; LMR Enterprises, Inc., Las Vegas, 1984—; sec.-treas. Sierra Color Graphics, Inc., Las Vegas, 1983—. Founder, organizer Human Relations, pet mascots for elderly; team ofcl. girls' softball, 1985. Recipient numerous awards Ad Club Fedn. Mem. Las Vegas C. of C. (congl. com.) Women's Las Vegas C. of C., Ad Club Fedn., Citizens for Pvt. Enterprise, U.S. C. of C. Avocations: tennis; water skiing. Office: 3351 S Highland Dr Suite 210 Las Vegas NV 89109

FERNANDEZ, MAGALI, language eduator; b. Havana, Cuba, Dec. 30, 1935; came to U.S., 1960; d. Andres and Hortensia (Zamora) Hernandez; m. Raimundo Rafael Fernandez. BS in Edn., NYU, 1968, MA in Spanish Lit., 1970, PhD in Spanish Lit., 1984. Cert. tchr., N.Y. Bilingual sec. various orgns., N.Y.C., 1960-64, Spanish Mission to UN, N.Y.C., 1964-67; tchr. Newtown High Sch., Queens, N.Y., 1970-74, Ea. Dist. High Sch., Bklyn., 1974—; lectr. Spanish, Fordham U., N.Y.C., 1971, 72. Author: EL Collar, 1954, Rómulo Gallegos y Agustín Yañez: dos ensayos sobre literatura hispanoamericana, 1972, El Discurso Narrativo en la Obra de Ma. Luisa Bombal., 1988; contbr. lit. criticisms, articles to numerous publs. Mem. Am. Assn. Tchrs. of Spanish, NYU Alumni Assn.

FERNER, KATHRYN EILEEN, clinical psychologist; b. Findlay, Ohio, Feb. 23, 1944; d. Charles Craven and Lois (DeHays) Kenney; m. John William Ferner, Apr. 14, 1945; children: Matthew Charles, Christina Lynn. PsyD; BA, Coll of Wooster, 1966; MS, Millersville St. Coll., 1978; D of Psychology, Wright State U., 1985. Licensed clinical psychologist. Certified psychologist Pvt., Florence, Ky., 1979-85; therapist Clermont Counseling Ctr., Batavia, Ohio, 1985-87; clinical psychologist Pvt., Ft. Mitchell, Ky., 1985--; cons. psychologist St. Elizabeth Hosp. Family Practice Ctr., Edgewood, 1985-89. Mem. Am. Psychological Assn., Ky. Psychological Assn., Cin. Psychological Assn., Ky. Assn. for Gifted Edn. Democratic. Presbyterian. Home: 16 Woodlawn Ave Fort Mitchell KY 41017

FERRAEZ, MARTHA ELIZABETH, religious association officer; b. Tampa, Fla., May 28, 1937; d. Warren Hudson and Martha Elizabeth (Minshew) Fulton; m. Leon R. Ferraez, Apr. 19, 1961; children: Felicia Elizabeth, Leon R., Jr., Maricarmen. BA in English, Asbury Coll., 1959; MA in Bicultural Edn., U. of the Ams., 1982. Tchr. Nicholls High Sch., New Orleans, La., 1959-60, Anchorage (Alaska) High Sch., 1960-61; officer Salvation Army, Memphis, 1963, Mex., 1964-81; officer, editor territorial newsletter Salvation Army, Atlanta, 1981-83; editor program aids Salvation Army, Verona, N.J., 1984—. Contbr. articles to profl. jours. Mem. AAUW, Montclair Hist. Soc., Glen Ridge Women's Club. Republican. Home: 7 Astor Pl Glen Ridge NJ 07028 Office: Salvation Army Nat Hdqrs 799 Bloomfield Ave Verona NJ 07044

FERRANTE, OLIVIA ANN, educator; b. Revere, Mass., Nov. 9, 1948; d. Guy and Mary Carmella (Prizio) F. BA, Regis Coll., 1970; MEd, Boston Coll., 1971, postgrad., 1977-81; postgrad., Middlebury Coll., 1974, Lesley Coll., 1982, Boston Coll., 1977-81. Cert. history tchr., tchr. of blind. Chmn. Braille dept. Nat. Braille Press, Boston, 1971-74; tchr. visually impaired Revere Sch. Dept., 1974—; cons. Revere PTA, 1984—. Contbr. articles to profl. jours. Vol. Morgan Meml., Boston, 1983—; mem. Revere Com. for Handicapped Affairs, 1985—, Everett (Mass.) Chorus, 1974-76, Adult Music Ministry, 1989; soloist Revere Music Makers, 1977-79; mem. partnership com. Internat. Year Disabled, 1980-81, mem. adult choir Immaculate Conception Ch., 1966—, mem. adv. bd. Mass. Commn. of Blind, 1988—, governing bd. on ind. living, 1989; access monitor Mass. Orgn. on Disability, 1988—; mem. adv. bd. Radio Reading Svc. for Blind, 1989. Mem. NEA, Mass. Tchrs. Assn., Revere Tchrs. Assn., Nat. Space Soc., Nat. Cath. Assn. for Persons with Visual Impairment, Cath. Daus.'s of Am., Friends of Revere Pub. Libr. Democrat. Roman Catholic. Home: 115 Reservoir Ave Revere MA 02151 Office: Revere High Sch Spl Needs Dept 101 School St Revere MA 02151

FERRARA, MARY F., medical association executive administrator; b. Mt. Vernon, N.Y., Jan. 30, 1960; d. Frank Peter and Gloria Josephine (Caravetta) F. BBA in Mgmt., Iona Coll., 1982; MBA in Fin., L.I. U., DobbsFerry, 1989. Adminstrv. asst. Mt. Vernon Hosp., 1980-86; adminstr. dept. dermatology N.Y. Med. Coll., Valhalla, 1987-90, instr. Grad. Sch. Health Scis., 1989-90; adminstr. Dermatology & Med. Rsch. Assocs., 1988-90; exec. adminstr. Internal Medicine Assocs., P.C., Meriden, North Haven, Cheshire, Conn., 1990—. Mem. Adminstrs. Internal Medicine, Am. Mgmt. Assn. Home: 52 Knollwood Dr Wallingford CT 06492 Office: Internal Medicine Assocs PC 116 Cook Ave Meriden CT 06450

FERRARI, DONNA MAE, autobody and mechanical shop owner; b. Grants Pass, Oreg., Oct. 21, 1931; d. Clyde Willis and Lorene Margaret (Hart) Brewer; m. William Dominic Ferrari, June 2, 1956 (div. May 1977), m. Nov. 24, 1977 (div. June 1987); children: Julie Ann Calleja, Jennifer Lynn Brazil. Student, Humboldt State, 1949-50. Optician Dr. Ferdinand Shaw, San Francisco, 1951-57; co-owner Superb Auto Reconstrn., San Francisco, 1966-77; optician Dr. Donald Schulz, San Francisco, 1977-84; owner Superb Auto Reconstrn., San Francisco, 1987—. Mem. Calif. Autobody Assn. (asst. treas. Golden Gate chpt.), Clement St. West Merchants, Better Bus. Bur. Presbyterian. Office: Superb Auto Reconstrn Co 2535 Clement St San Francisco CA 94121

FERRARO, BETTY ANN, corporate administrator, director; b. Newport, Vt., Mar. 3, 1925; d. Clarence John and Mauretta Rowena (Potter) Morse; m. Dominic Thomas Ferraro, Oct. 8, 1964; children: Deborah, David, Susan, Barbara. Student, Mary Hitchcock Hosp. Sch. Nursing, Coll. St. Joseph, Rutland, Vt. Exec. sec. to asst. treas. Cen. Vt. Pub. Svc. Corp., Rutland, 1943-44; sec. to dean N.Y. Med. Coll., N.Y.C., 1944-46; model G. Fox Co., Hartford, Conn., 1947; corp. sec., office mgr. John Russell Corp., Rutland, 1970-80; exec. dir. Rutland Area Coordinated Child Care Com., Washington, 1977-79; adminstrv. asst. Hilinex of Vt., Rutland, 1981-83; owner Classic Connection Gift Shop, Rutland, 1983-87; adminstr. Vicon Recovery Systems, Inc., Rutland, 1987—; alderman City of Rutland, 1984-86; resource dir. Rutland City, Vt. Emergency Mgmt. Team for State of Vt., 1984—; gov.'s appointee to Community Devel. Commn., 1986; lectr. St. Peter's Parish, Rutland. Mem. Nat. Assn. Women in Constrn. (chartered, past pres.). Republican. Roman Catholic. Home and Office: 6 Tenny Brook Ct Rutland VT 05701

FERRARO, GERALDINE ANNE, lawyer, former congresswoman; b. Newburgh, N.Y., Aug. 26, 1935; d. Dominick and Antonetta L. (Corrieri) F.; m. John Zaccaro, 1960; children: Donna, John, Laura. B.A., Marymount Manhattan Coll., 1956, hon. degree, 1982; J.D., Fordham U., 1960; postgrad., N.Y. U. Law Sch., 1978, hon. degree, 1984; hon. degree, Hunter Coll., 1985, Plattsburgh Coll., 1985, Coll. Boca Raton, 1989, Va. State U., 1989, Muhlenberg Coll., 1990, Briarcliffe Coll. for Bus., 1990. Bar: N.Y. 1961, U.S. Supreme Ct. 1978. Pvt. practice, N.Y.C., 1961-74; asst. dist. atty. Queens County, N.Y., 1974-78; chief spl. victims bur., 1977-78; mem. 96th-98th Congresses from 9th N.Y. Dist.; sec. House Democratic Caucus; first woman vice presdl. nominee on Democratic ticket, 1984; fellow Harvard Inst. of Politics, Cambridge, Mass., 1988. Author: Ferraro, My Story, 1985. Chmn. Dem. Platform Com., 1984; bd. dirs. N.Y. Easter Seal Soc. Mem. Queens County Bar Assn., Queens County Women's Bar Assn. (past pres.), Nat. Dem. Inst. for Internat. Affairs (bd. dirs.), Coun. Fgn. Rels., Internat. Inst. Women's Polit. Leadership (former pres.). Roman Catholic. Office: 218 Lafayette St New York NY 10012

FERREE, ALBERTA JOYCE, home economics educator; b. Normal, Ill., May 8, 1930; d. Carl Albert and Elizabeth Ruth (Watkins) Peterson; m. Richard Bennett Ferree, June 19, 1955; children: Richard Noel, Laura Ruth, Nancy Beth. BS, Ill. State U., 1952; MEd, U. Ill., 1971. Cert. vocat. edn. tchr., Ill. Tchr. home econs. Octavia Unit Dist., Colfax, Ill., 1952-56, Univ. High Sch., Normal, 1957-58, Olympia Unit Dist., Stanford, Ill., 1965-85. Chmn. 3 M's Meth. Ch., 1989-90. Mem. AAUW (chmn. antique studies com. Marco Island, Fla. chpt. 1988-89), Women's Club (chmn. arts and crafts com. Marco Island chpt. 1990—).

FERREIRA, JACQUELINE LEE, accountant; b. Seattle, Dec. 16, 1958; d. Jack Edward and Joan Marie (Codiga) Voss; m. Dan Ferreira, Nov. 15, 1986. Student, Anchorage Community Coll., 1982, U. Alaska, 1986; Cert. Word Processing, Alaska Pacific U., 1984. Mgr. corp. cash office and acctg. br., dir. fur buying, credit mgr. Alaska Comml. Co., Anchorage, 1980-89; mgr. acctg. NutraSource, Seattle, 1989—. Chmn. Foxtree Condominiums, Anchorage, 1984-86. Recipient ACC Pres. Sterling Achievement award, 1989. Mem. Nat. Notary Assn., NAFE, Nat. Assn. Credit Mgmt. Republican. Roman Catholic. Home: 24229 26th Pl Des Moines WA 98198 Office: 4005 6th Ave S Seattle WA 98108

FERREIRA, M. JAMIE (MARY ANN FERREIRA), philosophy of religion educator; b. Alexandria, Egypt, Oct. 9, 1945; d. Joseph and Christine (Kouremetis) F. BA, Brown U., 1973; MA, Princeton U., 1975, PhD, 1977. Acting instr. religious studies Yale U., New Haven, Conn., 1976-77; asst. prof. Yale U., 1977-80, U. Va., Charlottesville, 1980-85; assoc. prof. religious studies and philosophy U. Va., 1985—; cons. in field. Author: Doubt and Religious Commitment, 1980, Scepticism and Reasonable Doubt, 1986; contbr. articles to profl. jours. Am. Coun. Learned Socs. fellow, 1983-84; faculty grantee Yale U., 1979. Mem. Soc. Philosphy of Religion (v.p. 1988-89, pres. 1989-90), Am. Philosophical Assn., Am. Acad. Religion. Office: Univ Va Cocke Hall Charlottesville VA 22903

FERRELL, GLORIA LOUISE, financial advisor, tax consultant; b. Phila., July 17, 1948; d. Robert Jr. and Lessie (Smith) McKie; m. Orey Leon Ferrell, Jr. (div. Nov. 1987); 1 child, Orey Leon III. Student, Temple U., l968-70, La Salle U., Phila., 1977-8l. Registered rep. Nat. Assn. Securities Dealers. Tax cons. H&R Block Inc., Phila., 1970-76, office mgr., tax instr., l972-76; family and youth counselor Phila. Youth Advocate Program, l98l-83; program dir. Atlantic Personnel Co., Phila., 1983-85; fin. advisor 1st Investors Corp., Ft. Washington, Pa., 1985-89; field underwriter Karr-Barth Assocs., Bala-Cynwyd, Pa., 1989—; seminar tax instr., Phila., 1974—. Fund raiser local polit. campaigns, Phila.; vol. counselor Family Counseling Orgn., Phila., 1982-86; fund raiser, fin. advisor Ivy Hill Football League, Phila., 1983—. Mem. Profl. Working Women, Black Enterprise Networking, 1st Investors Corp. Wall Street Million Dollar Club. Democrat. Baptist. Home: 2005 Sandra Rd Voorhees NJ 08043 Office: Karr-Barth Assocs 40 Monument Rd 5th Fl Bala-Cynwyd PA 19004-1712

FERRELL, KELLY LYNN, sales executive; b. Greensboro, N.C., Oct. 22, 1962; d. James Richard and Sherrell (Cogdill) F. BA in Interdisciplinary Speech, U. N.C., 1985. Sales rep. Credit Bur. Greensboro, subs. Credit Bur. Inc., 1986-88, N.C. Nat. Bank, Greensboro, 1988—. Area VII chmn. concessions Greater Greensboro Open Golf Tournament, 1989, Area IV chmn. Champions' Gala, 1990; mem. Jr. League Greensboro, 1990; chairperson Multiple Sclerosis Soc., Tour de Tanglewood Bike Race, Jamestown, N.C., 1990; aerobic instr. Sportime Racquet Club. Mem. Greensboro Jaycees, U. N.C.-Chapel Hill Young Alumni Club (co-chairperson 1989—). Republican. Methodist. Home: 3901 Hwy 220N Apt 5 Greensboro NC 27410

FERRELL, STEPHANIE RENÉ, photojournalist, writer, model; b. Radford, Va., June 4, 1963; d. Harold Orville Ferrell and Carol (Ward) Blake. AAS in Communications/Radio/TV, W.Va. State Coll., 1983, BS in Communications/Film and Theatre, 1985. Pub. rels. model HBA Fur Corp., N.Y.C., 1986, 87; underwriting adminstr. Fiduciary Ins. Co. Am., N.Y.C., 1987, 88; photojournalist 361st Pub. Affairs Detachment, Ft. Totten, N.Y., 1986, 87; broadcast photojournalist 340th Pub. Affairs Dept., Ft. Totten, N.Y., 1987—; editorial asst. Dow Jones News Svc., N.Y.C., 1989—; model, actress Belinda Dale Modeling Agy., Charleston, W.Va., 1981-86. Contbr.

articles to jours. Sgt. USAR, 1985—. Mem. NOW, Dow Jones Women's Network, Nat. Press Photographers Assn., Internat. Thespian Soc. (life). Democrat. Baptist. Office: Dow Jones News Svc 200 Liberty St 12th Fl New York NY 10281

FERRERI, JOANNE M., microelectronics engineer. BS with honors, Poly. Inst. N.Y., 1978; MBA with honors, Pace U., 1982. Project leader Western Electric Co., Newark, N.J., 1978-80; systems analyst Western Electric Co., N.Y.C., 1980-83, AT&T, N.Y.C., Berkeley Heights, N.J., 1983-87; corp. fin. and strategic analyst-mgr. on vice chmn.'s staff AT&T, Berkeley Heights, N.J., 1987-88, sr. engr. in microelectronics, 1989—. Mem. IEEE, NAFE, Soc. Women Engrs., Soc. Mfg. Engrs./Computer and Automated Systems Assn.

FERRIER, LORETTA JEAN, psychotherapist; b. Paris, Tex., Feb. 5, 1937; d. Robert Syme and Virginia (Smith) F.; m. Howard B. Franklin, Sept. 1971 (div. 1980). BA in Psychology, Antioch W. West, 1975; PhD in Psychology, Inst. Transpersonal Psychology, 1979. Ordained to ministry Ch. of Tzoddi, 1978. Adminstrv. asst. dept. sociology and anthropology San Jose (Calif.) State U., 1963-65; adminstrv. asst. dept. exobiology Stanford U., Palo Alto, Calif., 1965-67; adminstr., researcher Elmwood, Calif., 1969-70; founder, dir. Soc. Overweight Studies, San Jose, 1974-79; prin. Loretta Ferrier, A Corp., Novato, Calif., 1985—; lectr. human potential workshops, 1973—; guest speaker TV and radio; pub. relations Human Potential Movement, Calif., 1974-79; coordinator workshops, 1976—; founder Concresence-Networking, San Francisco, 1981-82; advisor to Calif. bd. dirs. Bus. Execs. for Nat. Security, 1987—; bd. dirs. Karma Triyana Dharmachakra Ctr., Woodstock, N.Y. Author: A Transpersonal Approach to the Successful Female Entrepreneur, 1980; author, editor: Dialogue, 1986, Wings, 1987; contbr. articles to Scene, Nuvo, Challenge, Sources, also other mags. Mem. forming com. Hunger Project, San Francisco, 1977-78; mem. Commn. on Juvenile Justice and Delinquency Prevention, State of Calif., 1982; advisor Ark Found., Ark Communication Inst., Lafayette, Calif., 1987—. Fellow Am. Assn. Counselors, No. Calif. Soc. Clin. Hypnosis, Profl. Women's Network; mem. Nat. Speakers Assn. Home and Office: 141 Redstone Dr Sedona AZ 86336

FERRO, DEBORAH, speech pathologist; b. Youngstown, Ohio, Oct. 12, 1956; d. Ernest Dominic and Ann R. (Pecchio) F. BA, Allegheny Coll., 1978; MA, Edinboro, 1979. Lic. Speech Pathologist. Staff speech pathologist Chantauqua County Resource Ctr., Jamestown, NY, 1979-81; dir. speech dept. Lake Erie (Pa.) Inst. Rehabilitation, 1981-86, asst. dir. speech, 1986-88; part-time instr. Allegheny Coll., Meadville, Pa., Edinboro (Pa.) U., 1987-88; pvt. cons. Pa., 1988—; dir. clin. svcs. Pegasus, 1989-90; part-time speech pathologist St. Vincents Health Ctr., Erie, 1988-89. Contbg. author: Head Injury: The Acute Care Phase, 1987. Mem. American Speech, Language Hearing Assn., PA Speech and Hearing Assn., Nat. Head Injury Found., Erie Area Head Trauma Support Group, Va. Head Injury Found. Home and Office: 1696 Treetop Dr 14B Erie PA 16509

FERRO-NYALKA, RUTH RUDYS, librarian; b. Chgo., June 2, 1930; d. Joseph F. and Anna (Serbenta) Rudys; BA, U. Chgo., 1950; MA in Library Sci., Rosary Coll., 1972; children: Keith A. Krisciunas, Kevin L. Krisciunas, Kenneth M. Krisciunas; stepchildren: Anita L. Abbate, Vincent A. Abbate; m. Frank Ferro-Nyalka; stepchildren: Eleanor, Christine, Sylvia, André, Annette Ferro-Nyalka. Tchr. elem. sch. Westmont, Ill., 1961-63; librarian Dist. 105 public schs., La Grange, Ill., 1972—, tchr. program for gifted children, 1979-81, 82-85, coordinator gifted program, 1981-82. Mem. ALA, NEA, Ill. Edn. Assn., Dist. 105 Tchrs. Assn. (pres. 1983-85), AAUW. Roman Catholic. Home: 5800 Doe Circle Westmont IL 60559 Office: 1001 Spring Ave La Grange IL 60525

FERRY, JOAN EVANS, school counselor; b. Summit, N.J., Aug. 20, 1941; d. John Stiger and Margaret Darling (Evans) F. BS, U. Pa., 1964; EdM, Temple U., 1967; postgrad., Villanova U., 1981. Cert. elem. sch. tchr., elem. sch. counselor. Indsl. photographer Bucksco Mfg. Co., Inc., Quakertown, Pa., 1958-59; math. and German tutor St. Lawrence U., Canton, N.Y., 1959-61; research asst. U. Pa., Phila., 1963; tchr. elem. sch. Pennridge Schs., Perkasie, Pa., 1964-74, 75-77, elem. sch. counselor, 1981—; pvt. practice counselor, real estate partnership Perkasie, 1981—; tutor math., German, St. Lawrence U., Canton, N.Y., 1959-61; supervisory tchr. East Stroudsburg U., Pennridge Schs., 1971-74; research asst. U. Pa., Phila., 1963; mem. acad. coms. for Pennridge Schs.; adj. faculty Bucks County Community Coll., 1983—; instr. Am. Inst. Banking, 1982—; notary pub., 1986—; mcpl. auditor, sec. bd. auditors, 1984-90, mcpl. auditor 1990—, chmn. bd. auditors 1990—; cons. in field. Author (with others) Life-Time Sports for the College Student: A Behavioral Objective Approach, 1971, 3d rev. edit. 1978, Elementary Social Studies as a Learning System, 1976. Vol. elem. sch. counselor Perkasie, 1979-81; mem. Hilltown Civic Assn., 1965-70; exec. com. chairperson Hilltown Parent Tchr. Orgn., 1965-73; mem., soloist Good Shepherd Episcop. Ch. Choir, Hilltown, 1964-77. NSF grantee, Washington, 1972-73, Philanthropic Edn. Orgn. grantee, Doylestown, Pa., 1982; recipient Judith Netzky Meml. Fellowship award B'nai B'rith, Phila., 1979, World Decoration of Excellence Medallion, 1989, Statesman's award, 1989; Durning scholar Delta Delta Delta, Arlington, Tex., 1981, Am. Mgmt. Assns. scholar, N.Y.C., 1982, Statesman's award World Inst. Achievement, 1989, Internat. Cultural Diploma of Honor, 1989, Achievement award Women's Inner Circle, 1990, Commemorative Medal of Honor, 1990, Internat. Order of Merit, 1990; named to Internat. Tennis Hall of Fame, to 2000 Notable Am. Women Hall of Fame, 1989, Community Leaders of Am. Hall of Fame, 1990, Internat. Book of Honor Hall of Fame, 1990. Fellow Internat. Biog. Assn.; mem. AAUW, NEA, NAFE, World Inst. Achievement, Pa. State Edn. Assn. (polit. action com. for edn., chair Pennridge Schs. 1986—, del. leadership conf. 1987, 89), Pennridge Edn. Assn. (faculty rep 1986-88, exec. council 1986—, negotiations resource com. 1987-89), Am. Inst. Banking (chairperson 1987), U.S. Tennis Assn. (hon. life), Pa. and Middle States Tennis Assn. (hon. life), U.S. Profl. Tennis Registry, Mid. States Profl. Tennis Registry, Women's Internat. Tennis Assn., Nat. Ski Patrol System, Pa. Elected Women's Assn., Bucks County Assn. of Twp. Ofcls., Pa. Sch. Counselors Assn., Pa. Assn. Notaries, Am. Soc. Notaries, Internat. Fedn. of Univ. Women, Internat. Platform Assn., Am. Biog. Inst. Rsch. Assn., (rsch. bd. advisors, bd. govs. 1989—), World Inst. Achievement, Shawnee-at-Highpoint Racquet Club, Pennridge Community Rep. Club (recording sec. 1986—), Mediterranean Club, Nockamixon Boat Club, Peace Valley Yacht Club, Highpoint Racquet Club, Kappa Delta Pi. Episcopalian. Clubs: Mediterranean, Nockamixon Boat, Peace Valley Yacht, Highpoint Racquet. Home: 834 Rickert Rd Perkasie PA 18944 Office: Pennridge Schs 601 N 7th St Perkasie PA 18944

FERSHTMAN, JULIE ILENE, lawyer; b. Detroit, Apr. 3, 1961; d. Sidney and Judith Joyce (Stoll) F. Student, Mich. State U., 1979-81, James Madison Coll., 1979-81; BA in Philosophy and Polit. Sci., Emory U., 1983, JD, 1986. Bar: Mich. 1986, U.S. Dist. Ct. (ea. dist.) Mich. 1986, U.S. Ct. Appeals (6th cir.) 1987. Assoc. Miller, Canfield, Paddock and Stone, Detroit, 1986-89, Miro, Miro & Weiner P.C., Bloomfield Hills, Mich., 1989—. Bd. dirs. Franklin Community Assn., 1989—; mem. Dem. Nat. Com. Mem. ABA, State Bar Mich. (exec. coun. young lawyers sect. 1989-), Common Cause, Women Lawyers Assn. Mich., Mich. Women's Hist. Ctr. and Hall of Fame, Detroit Inst. Arts Founder's Soc., Detroit Zool. Soc., Nat. Mus. Women and Arts, Soc. Coll. Journalists, Phi Alpha Delta, Omicron Delta Kappa, Phi Sigma Tau, Pi Sigma Alpha. Home: 31700 Briarcliff Franklin MI 48025 Office: Miro Miro & Weiner PC 500 N Woodward Ave Ste 200 Bloomfield Hills MI 48013

FESTERVAN, DENISE CAMPBELL, health facility administrator; b. Shreveport, La., Jan. 4, 1960; d. Sherwood Dean and Helen (Goocher) campbell; m. Rodney Cline Festervan, Jr., May 8, 1981 (div. May 1985). BS, La. State U. Med. Sch., 1983, La. State U., 1983. Staff respiratory therapist Schumpert (La.) Med. Ctr., 1981-83; head dept. respiratory care Lincoln Gen. Hosp., Rustpn, La., 1983-87; nursing home administr. Pinecrest Monor Nursing Home, Bernice, La., 1988--. Mem. La. Nursing Home Assn., Am. Health Care Assn. Democrat. Methodist. Office: Pinecrest Manor Nursing Hom 101 Reeves St Bernice LA 71222

FETSKE, RUTH BETTY, advertising agency executive; b. Rahway, N.J., Sept. 24, 1922; d. Plato Settle and Mitzie (Mihalovics) Bumgarner; student public and pvt. schs., Rahway, N.J., N.Y.C.; m. William A. Fetske, Jan. 29, 1944. Editorial asst. Woman's Home Companion mag., N.Y.C., 1941-44; photog. stylist Anton Bruehl Studios, N.Y.C., 1944-45; fashion copywriter West-Marquis Advt. Agy., Los Angeles, 1945-46; copywriter Lerner Shops, N.Y.C., 1946-47; copywriter, account exec. Dorland Internat. Advt. Agy., N.Y.C., 1947-48; advt. mgr. Marcus Breier Sons, Inc., men's outerwear, N.Y.C., 1951-53; account exec. Lester Harrison Advt. Agy., N.Y.C., 1953-60, Mervin & Jesse Levine Advt. Agy., N.Y.C., 1960-68; pres., owner Ruth B. Fetske Assocs., Inc., N.Y.C. and Conn., 1969-85. Mem. Fashion Group, Inc., Nat. Assn. Female Execs., Conn. Valley Tourism Commn. (bd. dirs. 1987-92). Contbg. writer/photographer to profl. publs. Office: PO Box 248 Cobalt CT 06414

FETTER, JEAN HOLMES, college dean; b. Swansea, Wales, Dec. 10, 1937; came to U.S., 1962; d. Frederick Henry Holmes and Nancy (Worrell) Lewis; m. Alexander Lees Fetter, Aug. 4, 1962; children: Anne Lindsay, Andrew James. BA, Oxford (Eng.) U., 1959, MA, 1962, PhD, 1962. Lectr., asst. prof. physics San Jose (Calif.) State U., 1966-74; assoc. dir. Ctr. Teaching & Learning, Stanford (Calif.) U., 1975-77; asst. to pres. Stanford U., 1977-80, assoc. dean grad. studies, 1980-84, dean undergrad. admissions, 1984—. Rose Sidgwick Meml. fellow British Fedn. U. Women, 1962. Mem. Nat. Assn. Coll. Admissions Counselors, Coll. Entrance Exam. Bd. (chmn. R & D com. 1985—). Home: 904 Mears Ct Stanford CA 94305 Office: Stanford U Undergrad Admssns Old Union Stanford CA 94305

FETTERS, DEBRA ANN, counselor; b. N.J., May 2, 1959; d. Robert Kenneth and Carole (Lewis) Rubin; m. Glenn David Fetters, Nov. 28, 1987. BSN, Edinboro (Pa.) U., 1981; MA cum laude, Rider Coll., Lawrenceville, N.J., 1989. Prog. mgr. mental health Ephrata (Pa.) Community Hosp., 1986-88; master examiner Nurse Aide Test Prog., Wayne, Pa., 1988; cons. MediQualSystems, Inc., Wayne, Pa., 1988-90. Recipient Appreciation award, Citizens of Lancaster County. Mem. Am. Psychol. Nurses Assn., Mental Health/Mental Retardation providers Assn. (bd. dirs.). Home: 1 Sycamore Ln Chester Springs PA 19425 also: 7 Kirsten St, Vandia Grove, Randburg 2194, Republic of South Africa

FETTERS, JOAN FRANCES, child care center administrator, educator; b. South Sioux City, Nebr., Apr. 4, 1939; d. Elmer David and Rose Viola (Leuenhagen) Owen; m. Harold Lee Fetters, June 9, 1958; children: Ricky Lee, Troy Dow, Mark Owen. B.A., U. No. Colo., 1960; postgrad. Mesa Coll., 1975. Tchr. pub. schs., Los Angeles, Oakland and Woodland, Calif., 1960-67, Ft. Collins, Colo., 1967-70, Crow Indian Reservation, Pryor, Mont., 1971-72; owner, mgr. Children's Workshops, Ft. Collins, 1983—, Learning Tree Children's Ctrs., Grand Junction, Colo., 1975—; chmn. bd. HLF, Inc., 1989—; sec., treas. O.T.A.H., Inc. Mem. Mesa County Dirs. Orgn. (pres. 1978-79), Larimer County Assn. for Edn. of Young Children, Nat. Assn. for Edn. of Young Children. Avocations: piano, reading, biking. Home: 3206 Norwood Ct Fort Collins CO 80525 Office: Children's Workshops 635 S Grant Fort Collins CO 80521

FETTINGER, LAURIE A., banker; b. Robert and Patricia J. (McCormack) F.; m. Andrew J. Debreceni. BS in Mgmt., Fin. magna cum laude, Rutgers U., Newark, 1986. Asst. mgr. Burger King Corp., Largo, Fla.; quotations/contract mgr. Superior Surg. Mfg. Co., Inc., Seminole, Fla.; office mgr. Deutsch and Mulvaney, Morristown, N.J.; asst. v.p., br. mgr. Citibank N.A., N.Y.C. Mem. Literacy Prog., N.Y.C. Youth; treas. Mufata Dance Co. Recipient Service Excellence award, Citibank Gold Medal, Meml. Award for Mgmt. Excellence, Citibank NYRB Svc. Soc. award. Mem. NAFE, Am. Mgmt. Assn., Phi Beta Lambda, Beta Gamma Sigma. Home: 26 Tolstoi Pl Little Falls NJ 07424

FETTWEIS, YVONNE CACHÉ, archivist; b. L.A., Nov. 28, 1935; d. Boyd Eugene and Georgette Louisa (Tilmann) Adams; m. Rolland Phillip Fettweis, July 22, 1967; children: Maurice C.B. II, Michele-Yvonne (Mrs. Paul E. Cenzer); m. Maurice Lee Caché, Jan. 8, 1955 (div. 1962). BA, Wagner Coll., 1954; postgrad, Am. U., 1973, Bentley Coll., 1981. Legal sec., asst. Judge, Davis, Stern, Orfinger & Tindall, Daytona Beach, Fla., 1961-66; head rec. sect., bd. dirs. 1st Ch. Christ Scientist, Boston, 1969-71, rsch. assoc., 1971-72, adminstrv. archivist, 1972-78, sr. assoc. archivist, 1979-84, records adminstr., 1984—. Exec. sec. Volusia County Goldwater campaign, Daytona Beach, 1964. Mem. Soc. Am. Archivist, Automated Records and Techniques Task Force, Am. Mgmt. Assn., Orgn. of Am. Historians, Ctr. for Study of Presidency, New Eng. Archivists, Ctr. for the Study of the Presidency, Assn. Records Mgrs. and Adminstrs, (bd. dirs. 1983—), Assn. Col. and Rsch. Librs., Bay State Hist. League, Order Eastern Star, Order Rainbow (bd. dirs. 1972-77). Republican. Christian Scientist. Home: 42 Edgell Dr Framingham MA 01701 Office: 1st Ch Christian Sci Christian Sci Ctr 175 Huntington Ave Boston MA 02115

FEUER, MICHELLE H., security company executive; b. Feb. 25; d. Myron and Judith (Kessler) F. BS, Stonybrook U. Ops. mgr. Wells Fargo Guard Svcs., Huntington Station, N.Y.; pers. mgr. Pinkerton's Inc., Hempstead, N.Y.; br. mgr. Profl. Security Bur., Ltd., Levittown, N.Y.; security and investigations exec. Profl. Security Bur., Ltd., Nutley, N.J., 1989—. Mem. NAFE, Am. Soc. for Indsl. Security, N.E. Assn. Women Police, ABWA.

FEUREY, BENITA, magazine editor, broadcast reporter; b. Providence, May 21, 1940; d. Benjamin Knowles and Helen Mathilde (Weinbaum) Blau; m. Theodore Vincent Feurey, May 20, 1969 (div. Apr. 1974). EdB, R.I. Coll., 1961. Tchr. Providence Sch. System, 1961-62; cons., producer documentary Sta. WJAR-TV, Providence, 1962; prodn. asst. Sta. WNET-TV, N.Y.C., 1963-65; field producer, reporter UPI TV News, N.Y.C., 1965-69; talk-show host Sta. WRVR, N.Y.C., 1971-72; field producer, consumer and gen. assignment reporter Sta. WNBC-TV, N.Y.C., 1973-80; consumer writer N.Y. Post, 1980-81; N.Y. editor Good HouseKeeping mag., N.Y.C., 1981—; consumer reporter News 12, L.I., N.Y., 1987—. Editor Success mag., 1980-82; contbg. editor House in the Hamptons, 1983—; contbr. articles to mags. Bd. dirs. Child Care Action Campaign, N.Y.C., 1984—; pres., founder Amazonian Fund, N.Y.C., 1985—; v.p. Pacific Street Block Assn., Bklyn., 1971-73; den mother Cub Scouts Am., 1972-73. Recipient 1st Ann. Stella and Charles Guttman award for spl. courage and inspiration to women Guttman Inst.; named Very Important New Yorker Child Care Action Campaign, 1985;Ford Found. grantee, 1963. Home: 185 E 85th St New York NY 10028

FEW, MELINDA MULLINIKS, stock brokerage company executive; b. Memphis, Oct. 13, 1938; d. Robert Curlee and Hallie Agnas (Marshall) Mulliniks; m. Robert Pierce Few, Jan. 13, 1962 ; 1 son, Marshall Read. Student, Memphis State U., 1956-58, v.p. Henderson, Few & Co., Atlanta, 1963-67; broker Robinson-Humphrey Co., Inc., Jacksonville, Fla., 1978-81; v.p. Blackstock & Co., Inc., Jacksonville, 1981-85; broker Interstate Johnson Lane, 1985—; sec.-treas., dir. Nat. Health Care Systems, Denticare, Inc. Active Ponte Vedra Woman's Club (bd. dirs., past pres.). Republican. Presbyterian. Home: 215 Pablo Rd Ponte Vedra Beach FL 32082 Office: Interstate/Johnson Lane & Co Inc Jacksonville FL 32202-4435

FEYLER-SWITZ, HELEN SHAFTER, artist, teacher; b. Phila., Mar. 25, 1935; d. William and Anna (Cheredarchuk) Shafter; m. Alfred E. Feyler, (dec. Mar., 1968); m. Louis J. Switz, July 31, 1971. BA, Calif. State U., Long Beach, 1964; MA, Calif. State U., 1966. Asst. to dir. The Royal Acad. of Fine Arts, The Hague, Holland, 1966; instr. Calif. State U., Fullerton, 1969, Saddleback Coll., Mission Viejo, Calif., 1969-73, Chabot Coll., Hayward, Calif., 1974-88, Ohlone Coll., Fremont, Calif., 1975-77; mem. Art Review Bd. City of Ohlone, Fremont, Calif., 1988-90. Sculptor: (Bronze) F Symbol IV 1966 (Best of Show), (Bronze) F Symbol II, 1971 (Best of So. Calif.), (Concrete) F Symbol Architectural, 1977 (purchase award); photographer: Benign, 1989 (Internat. Tour Women Photographers 1991). Judge St. Francis High Sch. Art Show, Mt. View, Calif., 1980, Bakersfield Community Coll. Art Show, 1981; commr. Chabot Coll., Hayward, 1981, Cross 1st United Meth. Ch., Fremont, 1981. Mem. Women's Caucus for Art (pres. 1985-87, achievment award 1987), Ctr. for Visual Arts, Pro Arts, Women Architects and Profls. Methodist. Home: 660 Curtner Rd Fremont CA 94539

FIAMINGO, NANCY ANNE, radiation oncology administrator; b. Elizabeth, N.J., Jan. 7, 1949; d. Eugene Gilbert and Mary Anne (Moran) Buckholtz; m. Frank Jack, Feb. 25, 1949; 1 child, Cori Anne. BS, Thomas A. Edison Coll., 1984. Staff technologist Radiology St. Elizabeth's Hosp., Elizabeth, N.J., 1971-73, Radiation Therapy United Hosp., Newark, 1973-74; staff technologist Radiation Oncology John F. Kennedy Med. Ctr., Edison, N.J., 1976-78, chief technologist, adminstrv. dir., 1984—; advisory bd. mem. St. Barnabas Med. Ctr., Radiation Therapy Sch., Livingston, N.J., 1981-83, Middlesex County Coll., Edison, 1981--. Author: Exhibit, 1980. mem. Central Jersey Health Planning Council, Middlesex County, 1984-- (sec., 1986--); bd. dir. Central Jersey Health Planning Council, N.J., 1985; bd. mgrs. Am. Cancer Soc., Middlesex County. Mem. Soc. Radiation Oncology Adminstrs. (charter), Am. Hosp. Radiology Adminstrs., Am. Soc. of Radiologic Techs., N.J. Soc. Radiologic Techs.. Democrat. Office: John F Kennedy Med Ctr Radiation Oncology James St Edison NJ 08818

FIBISH, NANCY CONNOLLY, state agency administrator; b. Balt.; d. John James and Delia (Conroy) Connolly. BA, St. Joseph Coll., Emmitsburg, Md., 1957; lic., U. Strasbourg (France), 1958; postgrad., U. Chgo., 1960-63, 66-68. Field examiner, mgmt. intern Nat. Labor Rels. Bd., Washington and Chgo., 1967-68; nat. rep. commr. Fed. Mediation & Conciliation, Washington and Chgo., 1968-81; asst. regional dir. Fed. Mediation & Conciliation, Cleve., 1981-83; fgn. svc. officer U.S. Dept. State, Washington, 1983-88; exec. dir. Maine Labor Rels. Bd., Augusta, 1988—, arbitrator. Contbr. articles to profl. publs. Vol. Chgo. Urban League, 1960-61. Fulbright scholar, 1957; Fulbright tchr., 1958; fellow U.S. Congress, 1974-75, Fed. Exec. Inst., 1980. Mem. Indsl. Rels. Rsch. Assn., Nat. Soc. Fed. Labor Rels. Profls. (program dir. 1975-76), Internat. Pers. Mgmt. Assn., Nat. Peace Inst. Found. (exec. bd. 1988—), Am. Soc. Pub. Adminstrn., Soc. Profls. in Dispute Resolution, Assn. Labor Rels. Agys., Internat. Propellor Club (v.p. London chpt. 1985-86). Office: Maine Labor Rels Bd State House Sta 90 Augusta ME 04333

FICARRA, DORI ANNE, data processing company official; b. Passaic, N.J., Sept. 22, 1965; d. Anthony Michael and Nan A. (Orlando) F. BS in Mktg., Rutgers U., 1988. Cert. payroll profl. Account exec. Automatic Data Processing, Princeton, N.J., 1988-89, dist. mgr., 1989, personal computer client trainer, 1989—. Mem. NAFE, Beta Gamma Sigma. Home: D-12 E Garden Way Dayton NJ 08810 Office: Automatic Data Processing 101 Herrod Blvd Dayton NJ 08810

FICHTER, GAY LLOYD, development coordinator; b. Lakewood, Ohio, Dec. 20, 1952; d. William Scott lloyd and Mary Josephine (Giesey) Stargle; m. Edwin Paul Fichter, Aug. 30, 1975 (div. 1986)., 1 child, Matthew. BA, La Roche Coll., 1975; MA, Duquesne U., 1980. Religious edn. coord. St. John Fisher Parish, Churchill, Pa., 1978-79; dir. religious edn. St. William's Parish, East Pittsburgh, Pa., 1979-81; substitute tchr. Bishop O'Connell High Sch., Arlington, Va., 1981-83; devel. coord. Vanguard Svcs. Unltd., Arlington, Va.; adminstrv. asst. Navy, Morale, Welfare and Recreation Fin. Br., Arlington; lit. coord., Adhoc Coalition on Drug and Alcohol Problems, National, 1988. Del., Dem. State Conv., Virginia Beach, 1988, chief election officer, Registrar Officer, Arlington, 1981-84, planning com. Family Celebration, 1988; mem. Charles Drew Health Coop. adv. com., 1989. Mem. NAFE, Va. Assn. of Drug and Alcohol Counselors. Democrat. Roman Catholic. Home: 5915 Summers Ln Fall Ch VA 22041 Office: Navy Morale Welfare & Recreation Fin Br Ste 211 Arlington VA 22202

FICKEN, KAREN VALARIE, software engineer; b. Dallas, Dec. 4, 1953; d. Roger Bedford and Alice May (Lee) Harlan; m. W. Curt Ficken, Sept. 10, 1977; children: Rob, Andrea. BBA, Stephen F. Austin State U., Nacogdoches, Tex., 1976. Sales rep. Classic BMW/Ferrari, Ricahrdson, Tex.; supr. dental/med. benefits Rockwell Internat., Ricahrdson; fin. analyst Bell No. Rsch., Ricahrdson; software reliability engr. Bell No. Rsch. Mem. bd. adjustments, City of Fairview. Mem. DAR. Home: 1130 E Arapaho Rd Richardson TX 75069

FICKEN, MILLICENT SIGLER, zoology educator; b. Washington, July 27, 1933; d. Phares Oscar and Helen Elizabeth (Richards) Sigler; m. Robert William Ficken, June 25, 1955 (div. 1989); children: John William, Carolyn Marie Ficken Powers. BS, Cornell U., 1955, PhD, 1960. Postdoctoral fellow Cornell U., Ithaca, N.Y., 1960-62; rsch. assoc. dept. zoology U. Md., College Park, 1963-67; asst. prof. zoology U. Wis., Milw., 1967-69, assoc. prof. zoology, 1969-75, prof. dept. biol. scis., 1975—, acad. program dir. field sta., 1967—. Contbr. articles on ornithology and animal behavior to sci. publs. NSF grantee, 1967-80, 87, 88. Fellow Animal Behavior Soc., Am. Ornithologists' Union; mem. AAAS, Soc. for Study of Evolution, Cooper Ornithol. Soc., Wilson Ornithol. Soc. Home: 1623 16th Ave Grafton WI 53024 Office: Dept Biol Scis Univ Wis-Milw Milwaukee WI 53201

FICKES, MARITA CLARK, financial executive; b. Chappell, Nebr., Mar. 22, 1946; d. Irven Frank and Birdie Mae (Williams) Clark; m. Allen Horton Zimmer, June 11, 1966 (div. Nov. 1973); m. Mark Blaine Fickes, Jr., June 8, 1974; children: Matthew Clark, Morriah Lynn. B.S., U. Nebr., 1969, postgrad., 1977-78. CPA, Nebr., Colo. Tchr. Neligh pub. schs., Nebr., 1969-71, Elgin pub. schs., Nebr., 1971-72; salesperson Sears Roebuck Co./Gold Key Realty, Lincoln, 1972-74; mgmt. trainee GE, Hendersonville, N.C., 1978-79; staff acct. Fred A. Lockwood & Co., CPA's, Gering, Nebr., 1979-81; prin. M.C. Fickes, CPA, Chappell, 1981-86; mgr. acctg. dept. Colo. Med. Cons.'s, Inc., Denver, 1987-88, pvt. practice cons. and acctg. svcs., Denver, 1988-89, Aurora, 1990—; pres., chief exec. officer Fin. Health, Inc., Denver, 1989-90. Sec. bd. dirs. Chappell Area Med. Svcs., 1981-86, Sidney Meml. Hosp., Nebr., 1985-86; mem. Rural Health Manpower Commn., Nebr., 1984-86, Nebr. Health Planning Com. Mem. AICPA, Nat. Bus. Assn. (rep.), Nebr. Soc. CPAs, Colo. Soc. CPAs, Denver Women CPAs, Am. Morgan Horse Assn., Phi Upsilon Omicron, Omicron Nu. Avocations: gardening, equitation, music. Home and Office: 6891 E Eagle Pl Highlands Ranch CO 80126

FIEL, MAXINE LUCILLE, writer, lecturer; b. N.Y.C.; d. William Jack and Rowena (Burton) Stempel; m. David H. Fiel; children: Meredith Susan, Lisa Beth. Student in psychology and humanities, NYU. Nat. columnist Madmoiselle Mag., N.Y.C., 1972—, Womens World, Englewood, N.J., 1979-89; contbg. editor Overseas Promotions, N.Y.C., 1979—; feature editor N.Y. Now, N.Y.C., 1980—; contbg. editor Woman's World mag., Eng., 1979-89, Bella mag., Eng., 1987-89; nat. columnist First mag. for women, 1989—; cons. legal profession jury selection, 1984—; mktg. cons. Imperial Enterprises, Tokyo and Princeton, N.J., 1983—; cons. spokesperson Rowland Co., N.Y.C., 1972-81, Allied Chem. Co., N.Y.C., 1972-75; lectr., cons. Atlanta and Fla. Bar Assns., 1986—; creator Touch Game Parker Bros., Salem, Mass., 1971-76; behavior analystand communications advisor multi-nat. bus. corps.; cons. Chesebrough-Ponds, Footwear Coun., Grand Marnier Liquor. Pioneer field polit. body lang., 1969; contbr. articles to News Am., L.A. Times, Newhouse News Svc., Newspaper Enterprises Assocs., King Features; TV appearances include A.M. N.Y., People Are Talking, The Regis Philbin Show & Eyewitness News, Cable News Network, Johnny Carson Tonight Show, Today Show, Good Morning Am., Merv Griffin Show, BBC Breakfast Show, many others. Active Sister Cities, Tokyo and N.Y.C.; charter mem. Elem. Sch. Cultural Exchange, Toyko and N.Y.C., Ctr. Environ. Edn.; bd. dirs. Periwinkle Prodns. Anti-Drug Abuse, N.Y.C. Recipient Achievement award field behavioral sci. and photojournalism, Tokyo, 1974, Outstanding Research award field psychology of gesture, Tokyo, 1976, Outstanding Achievement award Internat. Conf. Soc. Para-Psychology, 1974-75. Mem. AFTRA, Internat. Found. Behavioral Research (past v.p.), Nat. Writers Club, Authors Guild, Authors League, World Wildlife Fund, Whale Protection Fund, Cousteau Soc., Greenpeace, People for Ethical Treatment Animals, Humane Assn. U.S., Guiding Eyes for Blind, Braille Camps for Blind Children, Save the Children. Clubs: Lotos (N.Y.C.); East End Yacht (Freeport, N.Y.). Home and Office: 269-33G Grand Central Pkwy Floral Park NY 11005

FIELD, JOAN STUBER, advertising executive; b. Bronxville, N.Y., Nov. 6, 1934; d. Frederick Harold and Mildred Joyce (Vidito) Stuber; m. George Francis Field, Oct. 26, 1962; children: Alida Catherine, Frederick George. BA, Swarthmore Coll., 1956; MA, Johns Hopkins U., 1957, PhD, 1964; Fulbright student, U. Erlangen, 1958-59. Instr. in chemistry Upsala Coll., East Orange, N.J., 1972-75; prin. Zinn, Graves and Field, Inc., Livingston, N.J., 1979-82, Florham Park, N.J., 1982-89; prin. ZGF West Advt.

and Pub., Danville, Calif., 1989—. Editor: N.J. Media Guide 1989; contbr. articles to profl. jours. Candidate for mayor City of West Caldwell, N.J., 1978, candidate for coun., 1980; active Dem. County Com., West Caldwell, 1973—; bd. dirs. Citizens for Charter Change, Essex County, N.J., 1975-88, co-chmn., 1977; campaign coord. Shapiro for County Exec., West Essex, 1978; treas. Campaign to Elect Renee Lane, Essex County, 1981; bd. dirs. Friends Danville Libr., 1989—; pres. West Caldwell Residents' Assn., 1988—, newsletter editor, 1986-88, reporter, 1977—; pub. relations chmn. Hist. Soc. West Caldwell, 1988. Mem. Berkeley Macintosh Users Group, League Women Voters (pres. West Essex chpt. 1970), Greater Danville C. of C., Contra Costa Coun. (vice chairwoman waste mgmt. task force 1989—). Home and Office: ZGF West 863 El Cerro Blvd Danville CA 94526

FIELD, KAREN ANN, real estate broker; b. New Haven, Conn., Jan. 27, 1936; d. Abraham Terry and Ida (Smith) Rogovin; m. Barry S. Crown, June 29, 1954 (div. 1969); children: Laurie Jayne, Donna Lynn, Bruce Alan, Bradley David; m. 2d Michael Lehmann Field, Aug. 10, 1969 (div. 1977). Student Vassar Coll., 1953-54, Harrington Inst. Interior Design, 1973-74, Roosevelt U., 1987—. Owner Karen Field Interiors, Chgo., 1970-86, Karen Field & Assocs., Chgo., 1980-81; pres., ptnr. Field Pels & Assocs., Chgo., 1981-86; mem. top sales volume Sudler-Marling, Inc., 1989; now sales broker Rubloff, Inc., Chgo. Mem. Women's Coun. Camp Henry Horner, Chgo., 1960; bd. dirs., treas. Winnetka Pub. Sch. Nursery (Ill.), 1961-63; mem. exec. com. woman's bd. U. Chgo. Cancer Rsch. Found., 1965-66, pres. Jr. Aux., 1960-66; bd. dirs., sec. United Charities, Chgo., 1966-68, Victory Gardens Theatre, Chgo., 1979; co-founder, pres. Re-Entry Ctr., Wilmette, Ill., 1978-80; mem. br. Child Abuse Svcs., Chgo., 1981-89, Stop AIDS Real Estate Div., 1988, AIDS Walkathon Com., 1990. Recipient Servian award Jr. Aux. of U. Chgo. Cancer Rsch. Found., 1966, Margarite Wolf award Women's Bd., U. Chgo. Cancer Rsch. Found., 1967, WAIT Woman of Day. Mem. FIABCI, Chgo. Real Estate Bd., North Side Real Estate Bd. Condex, Chgo. Coun. Fgn. Rels., English Speaking Union (jr. bd. 1958-59). Office: Rubloff Inc 980 N Michigan Ave Chicago IL 60611

FIELD, MARCIA CAROLE KAPLAW, lawyer; b. N.Y.C., July 18, 1932; d. Joseph and Anne G. Kaplaw; m. Ernest R. Field, June 8, 1952; children: Joshua, Joseph, Elizabeth, Ellen. BA, Barnard Coll., 1953; JD, Hofstra U., 1976. Bar: N.Y. 1976, U.S. Dist. Ct. (ea. dist.) N.Y. 1980. Ptnr. Field & Field, P.C., Great Neck, N.Y., 1981—. Pres. Ctr. for Women's Rights, Commach, N.Y., 1985, Nassau County Coalition Against Domestic Violence, E. Meadow, N.Y., 1989—. Mem. N.Y. State Bar Assn., Nassau County Bar Assn. Office: 310 E Shore Rd Great Neck NY 11023

FIELD, SALLY, actress; b. Pasadena, Calif., Nov. 6, 1946; divorced; children: Peter, Eli; m. Alan Greisman, Dec. 1984, 1 son, Samuel. Student, Actor's Studio, 1973-75. Starred in TV series Gidget, 1965, The Flying Nun, 1967-69, The Girl With Something Extra, 1973; film appearances include The Way West, 1967, Stay Hungry, 1976, Heroes, 1977, Smokey and the Bandit, 1977, Hooper, 1978, The End, 1978, Norma Rae, 1979 (Cannes Film Festival Best Actress award 1979, Acad. award 1980), Beyond the Poseidon Adventure, 1979, Smokey and the Bandit II, 1980, Back Roads, 1981, Absence of Malice, 1981, Kiss Me Goodbye, 1982, Places in the Heart, 1984 (Acad. award for best actress 1984), Murphy's Romance (also exec. producer), 1985, Surrender, 1987, Punchline, 1987, Steel Magnolias, 1989; TV movies include Maybe I'll Come Home In the Spring, 1971, Marriage: Year One, 1971, Home for the Holidays, 1972, Bridges, 1976, Sybil, 1976 (Emmy award 1977). Office: care Creative Artists Agy 9830 Wilshire Blvd Beverly Hills CA 90212*

FIELDER, ALLYSON BETH, sales and marketing specialist, accountant; b. Tacoma, Aug. 14, 1964; d. Keith Michael and Marian Joyce (Thomas) F. BS in Managerial Econs., U. Calif., Davis, 1986. With acctg. dept. Personal Products Co., Sunnyvale, Calif., 1982-83; cons. Tech. Mktg. Programs, Santa Clara, Calif., 1987-88; bus. mgr. Advantage Imaging, San Jose, Calif., 1987-88; cons. Advantage Imaging, Mountain View, Calif., 1988-89; sales and mktg. adminstr. XMR, Inc., Santa Clara, Calif., 1988-89, coord. customer svc., 1989—. Acolyte master St. Luke's Ch., Los Gatos, Calif., 1987-89. Mem. NAFE. Republican. Episcopalian. Office: XMR Inc 5403 Betsy Ross Dr Santa Clara CA 95054

FIELDER, JUDY PARSONS, nurse; b. Columbia, S.C., Nov. 25, 1947; d. Charles Henry and Frances (Buttler) P.; m. Dennis Lee Fielder, Apr. 8, 1972 (div. June 1983); children: Keri Selden, Sara Ruth. BSN, Salve Regina Coll., 1970; M in Nursing, Emory U., 1987. RN, Ga., R.I. Staff Navy Regional Med. Ctr., San Diego, 1970-75; childbirth educator Childbirth Edn. Assn., San Diego, 1975-77, Orange Park, Fla., 1977-79; staff nurse Shallowford Community Hosp., Atlanta, 1984-87; nurse practitioner Butler & Gross Ob/Gyn P.C., Atlanta, 1987—. Pres. Four Seasons Civic Assn., Atlanta, 1980-82. Served to lt. USNR, 1970-75. Mem. Am. Nurses Assn., Nurses Assn. Am. Coll. Ob/Gyn (cert. nurse practitioner), Internat. Childbirth Edn. Assn., Am. Acad. Nurse Practitioners, Sigma Theta Tau. Home: 8110 Winged Foot Dr Atlanta GA 30350 Office: Butler & Gross Ob/Gyn PC 5675 Peachtree-Dunwoody Rd NE Atlanta GA 30342

FIELDS, BARBARA P. LINDER, marketing executive; b. Bklyn., Jan. 29, 1950; m. Steven Linder (div.); m. Nolan I. Fields, Oct. 1980; children: Brent, Adam, Stephanie, Brittany. Student, Marjorie Webster Jr. Coll., 1968-70, Am. Musical and Dramatic Acad., 1971. Showroom, nat. sales dir. Faded Glory Jeans, N.Y.C., 1974-75; owner Blazing Sadie Inc., N.Y.C., 1975-76, Personal Connections Ltd., 1976-78; internat. mktg. sales dir. Multilite USA (div. Multilite, Can.), 1979; vice pres., co-owner Nu Fields Inc. (cons. lighting and giftware industry), 1980—; owner Simply Stoned Clothing and Art Designs, 1985-89; founding pres. C.H.A.D.D. of Nassau County (Children With Attention Deficit Disorders), Bellmore, N.Y., 1989—. Office: CHADD Nassau County 3104 Susan Rd Bellmore NY 11710

FIELDS, BECKY LYNN, nurse; b. Santa Maria, Calif., Feb. 15, 1963; d. Robert Wayne and Alyce Jane (Beckman) F. BS in Nursing, Biola U., La Mirada, Calif., 1987. RN, Calif.; cert. pub. health nurse. Staff nurse neonatal ICU, Meml. Med. Ctr. Long Beach, Calif., 1987-88; staff nurse neonatal ICU, Kern Med. Ctr., Bakersfield, Calif., 1988-89, staff nurse outpatient family practice clinics, 1989—. Burt M. Lynn Meml. scholar Torrance Meml. Hosp., 1981. Republican. Office: 1830 Flower St F Ward Bakersfield CA 93312

FIELDS, BESSIE MARIE WILLIAMS, professor; b. Pasco, Wash., Sept. 14, 1940; d. Joe and Velma (Johnson) W.; m. Frederick Marshall Fields, Aug. 16, 1957 (div. Jan. 1973); children: Geretta Marie, John Duane. BS, Portland State U., 1971, MS, 1981; EdD, Nova U., 1989. Cert. counseling and devel.; cert. tchr., Ore. Counselor, instr. Portland (Ore.) State U., 1971-83; instr. Portland Community Coll., 1975-81, Marylhurst (Oreg.) Coll., 1981-82; counselor Anchorage (Alaska) Community Coll., 1983-87; prof. U. Alaska, Anchorage, 1987—; cons.Frd. Govt., 1970-73. Mem. NAACP, Urban League. Recipient Community Leaders award Ednl. Bd. Am., 1976-77, Positive Community Contributions award City of Portland, 1977, Cert. of Completion, The Seminar in Search of Excellence, 1989, Internat. Leaders in Achievement award, 1989, Cert. of Appreciation, Anchorage Sch. Dist., 1985, Appreciation with Recognition for Dedication to Edn., Supt. Anchorage Sch. Dist., 1984, Cert. of Appreciation, Anchorage Sch. Dist., 1983-84, Emerging Woman in Mgmt. cert., 1975. Mem. Am. Assn. Counseling and Devel., Alpha Kappa Alpha. Republican. Methodist. Lodges: Toastmaster Internat., AKA. Office: U Alaska 2533 Providence Ave Anchorage AK 99508

FIELDS, CHRISTINE G., nurse, poet; b. Denver, May 21, 1952; d. Dean Elwood and Charlotte Grace (Lake) Oglevie; children: Pamela Rouchelle, Gregory Peter. RN, BSN, Olivet Nazarene Coll., 1974. RN. Charge nurse Trinity Luth. Hosp., Kansas City, Mo., 1974-77; nursing audit coordinator Bethany Med. Ctr., Kansas City, Kans., 1977-79, spl. projects dir., 1978-80, adminstrv. coordinator, 1980-83, primary nurse, 1984-86; relief charge Valley Hosp. Med. Ctr., Spokane, Wash., 1986-88; patient care coordinator Hospice of N. Idaho, Coeur d'Alene, 1988—; audit cons. Olathe Community Hosp. (Kans.), 1979. Author: Patient-Centered Audit, 1984. Pres., Dist. 512 Kans. Parents Assn. for Hearing-Impaired Children, Shawnee Mission, 1983-84, 79-80; exec. Parent Adv. Council to Sch. Bd., Shawnee Mission, 1983-84. Mem. Romance Writers Am. Democrat. Home: W 6927 Prairie Post Falls ID 83854

FIELDS, DAISY BRESLEY, human resource development consultant; b. Bklyn.; student Hunter Coll., 1932-35, Am. U., 1949-53; m. Victor Fields, Aug. 2, 1936; 1 dau., Barbara Fields Ochsman. Personnel officer USAF Base, Norfolk, Va., 1942-45; asst. personnel officer Dept. Agr., Phila., 1945-47; asst. dir. personnel Smithsonian Instn., Washington, 1954-60; chief spl. programs NASA, Washington, 1960-67; spl. asst. Fed. Women's Program, VA, Washington, 1967-70; sr. program asso. Nat. Civil Service League, 1971-72; cons. Equal Employment Opportunity/Affirmative Action, 1972-75, 78—; exec. dir. Federally Employed Women, Washington, 1975-77; pres. Fields Assocs., Silver Spring, Md., 1978—; exec. dir. The Women's Inst., Am. U.; instr. Mt. Vernon Coll., 1979-80, Am. U., 1982. Chmn., Montgomery County (Md.) Personnel Bd., 1972-78; chmn. legis. com. Comm. for Women in Public Adminstrn., 1976-79; commr. Md. Commn. for Women, 1973-77; commr. Montgomery County Commn. for Women, 1979-82; editor newsletter, past pres. Clearinghouse on Women's Issues; v.p., mng. editor Women's Inst. Press; bd. dirs. Nat. Woman's Party, 1989—. Recipient award UN Assn. U.S.A., 1980. Mem. NAFE, Nat. Council Career Women, Women's Equity Action League (pres. Md. 1972-74; award 1978), Federally Employed Women (pres. 1969-71, editor newsletter 1972-77, recipient award 1974, 78), Nat. Press Club, Am. News Women's Club, Internat. Women's Writing Guild, Washington Ind. Writers;, Capital Press Women, Fedn. Orgns. Profl. Women (exec. council 1976-77, 80-82), Nat. Assn. Women Bus. Owners. Author: A Woman's Guide to Moving Up in Business and Government, 1983; contbr. articles to profl. jours. Home and Office: 13905 N Gate Dr Silver Spring MD 20906

FIELDS, FREDRICA HASTINGS, artist; b. Phila., Jan. 10, 1912; d. Theodore Mitchell and Carolyn Corlies (Baily) Hastings; student Wellesley Coll., 1930-32, Art Students League, 1933; m. Kenneth E. Fields, July 10, 1934; children: David Edward (dec.), Luellen, Stephen Francis. Designer craftsman in stained glass, 1948—; exhibited in one man show Artists Mart, Washington, 1955, First Presbyn. Ch., Stamford, Conn., 1976, Concordia Coll., Bronxville, N.Y., 1982, Greenwich (Conn.) YWCA, 1982; exhibited in group shows Nat. Soc. Arts and Letters, Washington, 1951, Smithsonian Instn., 1951, 53, 54, 57, 58, Corcoran Gallery Art, 1955, 56, Nat. Conf. on Religious Architecture, N.Y.C., 1967, Washington, 1970, Greenwich (Conn.) Art Soc. Ann. Exhbns., 1968-78, Stamford (Conn.) Art Soc., 1972, Danbury (Conn.) Public Library, 1974, Stained Glass Internat., N.Y.C., 1982, Stained Glass Assn. Am.-Corning Mus. Glass, 1987, The Gallery at Hastings-on-Hudson, N.Y., 1990; represented in permanent installations at Washington Cathedral, Marie Cole Auditorium, Greenwich Library, YWCA, Greenwich, Assn. for Research and Enlightenment Meditation/Prayer Center, Virginia Beach, Va., Conn. Hospice Inc., Branford, Concordia Coll., Bronxville, N.Y., Ch. of Holy Comforter, Kenilworth, Ill., many pvt. collections; tchr. classes in stained glass, Washington, 1950, YWCA, Greenwich, 1966, at studio, 1968-71. Recipient awards in stained glass Corcoran Gallery Art, 1955, 56, B.F. Drakenfeld award 6th Internat. Exhbn. of Ceramic Arts, Nat. Collections Fine Arts, Smithsonian Instn., 1957. Mem. Stained Glass Assn. Am. (contbr. to reference and tech. manuals vols. 1 and 2), Greenwich Art Soc. Address: 561 Lake Ave Greenwich CT 06830

FIELDS, JOAN R., chemical company executive; b. N.Y.C., Jan. 18, 1930; d. Albert and Etta (Levy) Ross; B.S., Adelphi U., 1951; cert. early childhood edn. Ann Reno Inst., 1951; children—Larry M., Paul B. Tchr., Woodward Sch., Bklyn., 1951-52, Syosset Sch. Dist., 1959-65; corp. sec. Albatross U.S.A. Inc., Long Island City, N.Y., 1966-69, pres., chmn. bd., 1969—; chmn. bd., pres. Etro Realty Corp., 1969—, Apparel Innovations Inc., 1978—; pres. J.R.F. Properties Inc., 1980—. Mem. young profl. com. United Jewish Appeal; mem. Sutton Pl. Synagogue. Mem. N.Y. Assn. Women Bus. Owners, Internat. Platform Assn., Queens C. of C. (city affairs com.), Phi Sigma Sigma. Clubs: B'nai B'rith, Excelsior. Home: 303 E 57th St New York NY 10022 Office: 36-41 36th St Long Island City NY 11106

FIELDS, KARLA JO, accountant; b. Fayette, Ala., Jan. 27, 1959; d. Bobby Frank and Dorothy (O'Dell) F. AS, Faulkner State Jr. Coll., 1979; BS, Troy (Ala.) State U., 1981, postgrad. in bus., 1983—. Staff acct. Troy State U., 1981-82; comptroller Baldwin County Commn., Bay Minette, Ala., 1982-86; sr. acct. Wood, Robertson & Assocs., Bay Minette, 1986—. Mem. vocat. adv. com. Faulkner State Jr. Coll., Bay Minette, 1983—, chair, 1986—; bd. dirs. Baldwin County Rural Transp. System, Bay Minette, 1985-86, Baldwin County Agy. on Aging, 1985-86, Robertsdale Pub. Libr.; mem. Baldwin County Transp. Bd., 1986, Laubach Literacy Action Com., South Baldwin Literacy Coun.; elected to Robertsdale City Coun.; hon. adv. rsch. bd. Am. Biol. Inst. Mem. NAFE, Am. Bus. Women's Assn. (treas.), Circle K, Phi Theta Kappa, Phi Beta Lambda. Mem. Christian Ch. Home: 23175 Pecan St Robertsdale AL 36567 Office: Woods Robertson & Assocs PO Box 699 Bay Minette AL 36507

FIELDS, KATHRYN PATRICIA, retail buyer; b. San Diego, Nov. 25, 1961; d. William Jay and Marilyn Catherine (Lamberton) F. Student in honors program, Am. U., Washington, 1981; BS in Polit. Economy, Randolph-Macon Woman's Coll., 1983. Reg. rep. N.Y. stock exchange. Constituent svcs. intern Hon. Frank Wolf U.S. Congress, Washington, 1981; adminstrn. asst. intern. div. community planning and devel. City of Lynchburg, Va., 1982; sales mgr. Va. Leisure Products, Richmond, 1983-84; sales asst., product coord. Wheat, 1st Securities Inc., Vienna, Va., 1984-86; asst. portfolio mgr. Wheat Investment Advisors Inc., Richmond, 1986-87; rsch. coord., retail stockbroker Davenport & Co. Va., Richmond, 1987-89; upholstery buyer Heilig-Meyers Co., Richmond, Va., 1989—. Mem. Soc. Fin. Analysts (assoc.), Randolph-Macon Woman's Coll. Alumni. Republican. Roman Catholic. Home: 9300-K Windy Cove Circle Richmond VA 23294

FIELDS, KATHY ANN, dermatologist; b. Waukegan, Ill., May 14, 1958; d. Maynard Bernard and Blanche (Telson) F. Student, Northwestern U., 1975-76; BS, U. Fla., 1979; MD, U. Miami, Fla., 1983. Intern in ob-gyn. Jackson Meml. Hosp., 1983-84; resident in dermatology Stanford (Calif.) U. Med. Ctr., 1984-87; laser specialist Sydney, Australia, 1987; pvt. practice San Francisco, 1988—. Fundraiser Am. Cancer Soc., San Francisco, 1988—, Child Abuse Prevention, United Jewish Appeal. Fellow Am. Acad. Dermatology; mem. AMA, Calif. Med. Assn., San Francisco Med. Soc., San Mateo Med. Soc. Office: 350 Parnassus San Francisco CA 94117

FIELDS, MYRTICE ELAINE, music educator; b. Anniston, Ala., Aug. 15, 1946; d. Willie C. and Willie Jewel (Heard) Jackson; m. William Thomas Fields (div.); 1 child, Jamal. BS, Tenn. State U., 1968, MS, 1969, postgrad., 1990—. Music specialist New London (Conn.) Bd. Edn., 1969-73; prof. music Jacksonville (Ala.) State U., 1973—; cons. Little Red Sch. House, London, 1980, USO, Europe, 1982, various univs., Romania, Bulgaria, 1983; TV host Myrtice Fields Gospel Music Showcase. Recipient awards for community svc., New London, 1973, Anniston, 1973—. Mem. Music Educators Nat. Conf., Gospel Music Workshop Am., Piano Tchrs. Forum, SCLC, NAACP, Delta Sigma Theta. Democrat. Baptist. Home: 927 Creek Trail Anniston AL 36206

FIELDS, ROBIN MAE, government official; b. Washington, Mar. 9, 1944; d. Milton and Yetta Estelle (Morgenstein) F. Student, Elon (N.C.) Coll., 1961-62, Am. U., Washington, 1969, Montgomery Coll., Rockville, Md., 1982. Budget and prog. analyst GSA, Washington, 1967-71; budget analyst Dept. of Labor, Washington, 1971-74; chief resources allocations div. Dept. of Labor, 1974-76; dep. chief mgmt. group budget Dept. of Justice, Washington, 1976-79; chief info. sys. br. Dept. Health and Human Svcs., Washington, 1979-83; chief info. and ops. br. Dept. Health and Human Svcs., 1983-86, chief sys. staffing and congl. liaison br., 1986—. Mem. citizens adv. com. Montgomery County Bd. Edn., Rockville, 1982—; bd. dirs. Jewish Community Coun. Washington, 1980—. Recipient Vol. award, Health and Human Svcs., 1980, Spl. Achievement award, 1982, 80, Sec.'s Exceptional Achievement award, 1982, Internat. Woman's Yr. award, Dept. of Labor, 1975. Mem. Am. Assn. of Budget and Prog. Analysts, Fed. Exec. Inst. Alumni Assn., B'nai B'rith, Hadassah (pres. 1973, 80-83). Jewish. Office: HHS OS ASMB BPM SSCL Humphrey Bldg Rm 503H Washington DC 20207

FIELDS, SHELIA RHONDA (SHELIA RHONDA CLINE), dietitian; b. Welch, W.Va., Aug. 27, 1953; d. Orville and Amanda (Layne) Cline; m. Dallan Fields, Sept. 22, 1974 (div. July 1981). BS Dietetics, Marshall U., 1974, MA foods and nutrition, 1984. Registered dietitian. Nutritionist Huntington (W.Va.) State Hosp., 1976-82; dir. dietary svcs., cons. Cabell County, Huntington, 1982—; cons. dietitian HCA, River Park Hosp., Huntington, 1988-89, Aivert Nursing Home, Ceredo, W.Va., 1987. Mem. Am. Dietetic Assn., Am. Soc. Hosp. Food Svc. Adminstrs., W.Va., Ohio, Ky. Dist. Dietetic Assn. (coun.-on-practice, 1989-90, nominating com. 1986-87, chmn. older Am. health fair 1981), W.Va. Pub. Employees Assn., Kappa Omicron Phi Alumni Assn. (pres. 1987—). Home: 6225 Highland Dr Huntington WV 25705

FIELDS, VIRGINIA MARY, museum curator; b. Hartford, Conn., Sept. 6, 1952; d. William Francis and Virginia Theresa (Lavelle) Monk; m. Michael Kevin Fields, June 28, 1980 (div. 1990). AB in Anthropology, San Francisco State U., 1978, MA in Anthropology, 1982; PhD in Latin Am. Studies, U. Tex., 1989. Curator native Am. collection Clarke Meml. Mus., Eureka, Calif., 1984-87; instr. dept. art Humboldt State U., Arcata, Calif., 1987; lectr. in art history U. Calif., Santa Barbara, 1988-89; asst. prof. of art history Calif. State U., Northridge, 1989; curator pre-Columbian art L.A. County Mus. Art, 1989—; cons. curator The Mex. Mus., San Francisco, 1989—; editor Pre-Columbian Art Rsch. Inst., San Francisco, 1983—; rsch. assoc. dept. anthropology Calif. Acad. Scis., San Francisco, 1984—. Contbr. numerous articles to profl. jours; editor: Fifth Palenque Round Table, 1983, Proceedings of the Sixth Palenque Round Table, Seventh Palenque Round Table, 1989. Project coord. Nat. Pub. Radio, Washington, 1990; bd. dirs. Ethnic Arts Coun., L.A., 1989—, Humboldt County Am. Diabetes Assn., Eureka, 1986-87; active Nat. Diabetes Consumer Adv. Bd. Mem. Native Am. Art Studies Assn., Soc. for Am. Archaeology. Office: LA County Mus Art 5905 Wilshire Blvd Los Angeles CA 90036

FIELO, MURIEL BRYANT, space engineer, interior designer; b. Bklyn., Dec. 11, 1921; d. Harry and Minnie (Dick) Bryant; m. Julius Fielo, June 17; 1 child, Michael Kenneth. Student, CCNY, 1938-41, Rutgers U., 1965-69; cert. N.Y. Sch. Interior Design, 1970. Gen. mgr. Fidelity Discount Corp., Irvington, N.J., adv. supr. Lincoln Loan Cos., Essex County, N.J., 1941-49; interior designer Alex Fielo Interior Decorators, Newark, 1942-49, prin., 1949-69, owner, 1969—; designer, cons. space engr. MUDGE Interior Design Studios, East Orange, N.J., 1969—. Mem. adv. panel Interior Design Mag, 1977—. Essex County freeholder clk. Bd. Freeholders, 1972-76; commr. East Orange Bus. Devel. Authority, 1977-86; mem. U.S. adv. coun. SBA-Region II, 1980-81; active LWV, 1950-55; organizer, 1st pres. South Orange chpt. Women's Am. ORT, 1952-54, mem. nat. speakers bur., 1952-65, parliamentarian No. N.J. coun., 1955-65; pres. Amity chpt. B'nai B'rith, Newark, 1946-48, v.p. No. N.J. coun., 1948-49, various nat. and state positions, 1948-80; mem. nat. com. on sect. fund raising Nat. Coun. Jewish Women, 1979-81, nat. tour. chmn., 1979-81; trustee community svcs. coun. Oranges and Maplewood, United Way of Essex and West Hudson, 1981-83; bd. dirs. East Orange Central Ave. Mall Assn., 1979-83, chmn. new voter registration drive East Orange 2d Ward, 1955—, entire city, 1969; pres. East Orange Dem. Club, 1957-58, campaign coord. for Dem. mayoral candidate, 1969, calendar coord. Essex County Dem. Party, 1970-76; mem. N.J. Bipartisan Coalition for Women's Appts., 1981—. Named Outstanding Entrepreneur of 1984 N.J. Gov., Outstanding Orgn. Pres. Kean Coll. Profl. Women's Assn., 1985, Wonder Woman of 1986, Bus. Jour. of N.J., One of 8 Women to Watch in 1987 Jersey Woman Mag., 1987; also recipient various awards for civic svc.; named Bus. Person of Yr. East Orange C. of C., 1988. Mem. Internat. Soc. Interior Designers (bd. dir. 1981-85), Nat. Home Fashions League (N.J. membership chmn. N.Y. chpt. 1981-82), Interior Design Soc., N.J. Assn. Women Bus. Owners (state bd. 1979-82), Women Entrepreneurs N.J. (pres. 1981-85, chief exec. officer 1987—), N.J. Home Furnishings Assn. (bd. dirs. 1981-84, 86—), Constrn. Specifications Inst., N.J. Soc. AIA (profl. affiliate), Guild Designer Woodworkers, Women Bus. Ownership Ednl. Coalition (N.J. State pres. 1985-87, chief exec. officer 1987—, mem. steering com. interior designers for licensing in N.Y. 1985—), East Orange C. of C. (bd. dir. 1977—, v.p. 1981-85), Bus. and Profl. Women's Club of Oranges (bd. dir. 1958-66). Jewish. Office: MUDGE Interior Design Studio 185 S Clinton St East Orange NJ 07018

FIES, MARIE JOYCE, nurse; b. Reading, Pa., Dec. 17, 1939; d. Andrea Carmine and Josephine (Scimone) Torchia; m. Robert J. Fies, Feb. 17, 1962; children: Julie, Kathleen, Robert. BSN, Lebanon Valley Coll., 1981; RN, Reading Hosp. Sch. Nursing. RN. Exec. dir. Am. Cancer Soc., Berks County Unit, Reading, Pa., 1983-75; occupational health nurse Caloric Corp., Topton, Pa., 1985-87, NGK Metals Corp., Reading, Pa., 1987-88; pres. Vis. Nurses in Industry, Inc., Reading, 1988—. Mem. ANA, Am. Assn. Occupational Health Nurses, (pres. Berks County chpt. 1989—), Pa. Nurses Assn., Berks County Nursing Alumni Assn., Reading Hosp. Sch. Nursing Alumni Assn. Mem. United Ch. of Christ. Home: RD 9184 Reading PA 19605

FIFIELD, CHERYL SCHNEIDER, human resources professional; b. Mt. Kisco, N.Y., Sept. 10, 1955; d. Walter Michael Schneider and Geraldine (O'Connor) Sadler; m. Thomas Bradley Fifield, Apr. 17, 1982. BA in Communications and English Edn., U. South Fla., 1978. Tchr. Readak Ednl. Svcs., New Orleans, 1978-80, Jeannette (La.) Sr. High Sch., 1980-82, Live Oak High Sch., Watson, La., 1982-83; broadcaster Sta. KANE, New Iberia, La., 1980-82, Sta. WFMF-FM, Baton Rouge, 1984; store exec. Mervyn's, Dallas, 1985-89; corp. recruiter Murata Bus. Systems, Dallas, 1989—; advisor Mervyn's Employee Assn., 1988-89. Mem. NAFE, Dallas Pers. Assn. Home: 2040 Oak Bluff Dr Carrollton TX 75007 Office: Murata Bus Systems 5560 Tennyson Pkwy Plano TX 75024

FIGGE, CHARLENE ELIZABETH, religious organization administrator; b. Ste. Genevieve, Mo., Apr. 16, 1948; d. William Henry and Frieda Christina (Bauman) F. B in Music Edn., Fontbonne Coll., 1970; MS, U. Dayton, 1979. Joined Sisters of Divine Providence, Roman Cath. Ch., 1965; cert. elem. vocal and instrumental tchr. Tchr. Mary Queen of Universe Sch., St. Louis, 1970-71, Mt. Providence Boys; Sch., St. Louis, 1971-75, 1978-81; tchr. St. John's Sch., Imperial, Mo., 1975-76, St. Pius X Sch., Shreveport, La., 1976-78, Ascension Sch., St. Louis, 1981-85; justice coordinator, dir. devel., asst. provincial Sisters of Divine Providence, St. Louis, 1985—. Mem. Religious Involved in Social Concerns, St. Louis, 1985—, World Peace Com., St. Louis, 1985—, Interfaith Com. on Latin Am., St. Louis, 1985-87, Midwest Coalition on Responsible Investment, St. Louis, 1985—, Nat. Cath. Devel. Conf., 1985—. Mem. Nat. Soc. Fund Raising Execs. Democrat. Office: Sisters Divine Providence 8351 Florissant Rd Saint Louis MO 63121

FIGGINS, LETHA ARLENE (LETHA ARLENE DEHN), retired teacher; b. Quenemo, Kans., July 16, 1916; d. Walter Frank and Louise May (Weis) Dehn; m. Byron Edward, Aug. 31, 1940; 1 child, Geri Sue Bauman. BA, Ottawa (Kans.) U., 1964; MS, Kans. State Tchrs. Coll., 1971. Cert. tchr., Kans. Tchr. Middleton Rural Sch., Quenemo, 1934-40, Chippewa Rural Sch., Ottawa, 1940-42, Spring Creek Rural Sch., Ottawa, 1946-66, Lincoln Elem., Ottawa, 1966-82; ret., 1982. Contbr. articles profl. jours. Mem. Pres. Reagan's Task Force, 1980-88, Pres. Bush's Task Force, 1989—; active Franklin County Rep. Women, Ottawa, 1986—, Nat. Rep. Congl. Com., Bus. Profl. Women; pres., v.p. Franklin County Tchrs. Orgns., Ottawa; v.p. Ottawa Edn. Assn., 1976, pres., 1977; vol. Phone Friend, 1988-89, 90; pres. Elm Grove Homemakers's Unit, 1985-87; mem. Friends of Ottawa Libr.; tchr. Vacation Bible Sch. Bapt. Ch., 1950-60. Named Tchr. of Yr. Finalist, State of Kans., 1980. Mem. Alpha Delta Kappa (pres. 1951—), Bus. Profl. Women (sec. 1988—), Ottawa Area Retired Tchrs. Assn. (historian 1985-89), AAUW (program leader), Assn. Childhood Edn. (past pres.), Rebekah Noble Grand (elected v.p. dist. 8, 1989, pres. dist. 8, 1990, apptd. lodge dep.), Friendship Love Truth Club. Republican. Baptist. Home: 416 E 14th St Ottawa KS 66067

FIGLAR, ANITA WISE, banker; b. Camas, Wash., Oct. 7, 1950; d. William Hulon and Mary Wise (Adkisson) Ward; m. Richard Bould Figlar, Aug. 7, 1976; children: Richard Bould II, David Wise. Student, U. Wash., 1968-70; BA in Intercultural Studies, Ramapo Coll., 1974. Mktg. coord. power and control ops. Gen. Cable Corp., Union, N.J., 1975-76, mktg. analyst power and control ops., 1976-78; various positions Potters Industries, Inc., Hasbrouck Heights, N.J., 1971-75; with highway safety programs dept. Potters

Industries, Inc., Parsippany, N.J., 1981-82, mgr. highway safety programs dept., 1982-84, mgr. bus. devel., 1985-86, industry mgr. Highway Products div., 1986-89; with customer svc. United Jersey Bank, Hackensack, N.J., 1989; fin. svc. rep. United Jersey Bank, 1989-90, asst. br. mgr., bank officer, 1990—. Contbr. articles to many profl. and govtl. pubIs. Notary pub.

FIGUEROA-CRAWFORD, DIANA JULIE, lawyer; b. Hialeah, Fla., Oct. 29, 1958; d. David Israel and Aide Irene (Cardenas) F.; m. Gary Scot Palenbaum, May 15, 1983 (div. June 1987); m. David Lock Crawford, Oct. 8, 1988. AA, Miami Dade Community Coll., 1978; BS, Fla. State U., 1980; JD, Loyola U., L.A., 1985. Cert. instr. Criminal Justice Inst. Legis. asst. Fla. Ho. of Reps., Tallahassee, 1980; legal claims rep., atty. Allstate Ins. Co., Melbourne, Fla., 1985-86; asst. state atty. Office of State Atty., Melbourne, 1986-87; ptnr. Burguet, Polan, Thompson, Figueroa & Gager, Melbourne, 1987—; asst. tchr. Criminal Justice Int., Melbourne, 1989. Asst. Gov.'s Election, Melbourne, 1987. Mem. ABA, Trial Lawyers Assn. Am., Brevard County Bar Assn., Phi Alpha Delta. Democrat. Roman Catholic. Office: Burguet Polan et al 1900 S Hickory St Melbourne FL 32901

FIKE, ELIZABETH SMITH, banker; b. Union, S.C., Dec. 17, 1960; d. James Ayers Sr. and Ruth Anne (Johnson) Smith; m. Robert Leedham Fike, June 6, 1987. BSBA in Fin., U. S.C., 1983. Claims examiner Provident Life and Accident Ins. Co., Greenville, S.C., 1983-84; staff auditor So. Bank & Trust Co., Greenville, 1985-86; staff auditor 1st Union Nat. Bank of S.C., Greenville, 1986-87, sr. auditor, 1987; sr. auditor 1st Va. Banks, Inc., Falls Church, 1987-88, supervising sr. auditor, 1988-89, asst. dept. head Cashier's Office, 1989—, asst. v.p., 1990—. Mem. Inst. Internal Auditors, Young Bankers Assn. Republican. Baptist. Home: 6017 Grayson St Springfield VA 22150 Office: lst Va Banks Inc 6402 Arlington Blvd Pla II Falls Church VA 22046

FILCHOCK, ETHEL, educator, poet. BS in Edn., Kent State U. Tchr. Cleve. Pub. Schs. Author: Voices in Poetics: Vol. 1, 1985 (Merit award); composer: Praise God, The Lord is Coming. Chmn. sch. United Way, 1985-86. Recipient Cert. of Achievement N.Y. Profl./Amateur Song Jubilee, 1986. Mem. NAFE, Am. Fedn. Tchrs. Roman Catholic. Club: Akron Manuscript.

FILER, ELIZABETH ANN, psychotherapist; b. N.Y.C., Oct. 16, 1923; d. Edwin and Edith Louise (Levy) Filer. B.S., Columbia U., 1944, M.A., 1945, M.S., 1954. Cert. bd. clin. social worker. Asst. tchr. to asst. dir. Mallay Nursery Sch., Bklyn., 1943-52; tchr., guidance staff N.Y. Sch. for Nursery Years, 1954-60; liaison social worker The Reece Sch., N.Y.C., 1954-60; cons. to schs. in N.Y.C., 1960-71; ednl. cons./therapist Ednl. Inst. for Learning and Research, N.Y.C., 1961-65; clin. social worker, psychotherapist in pvt. practice, N.Y.C., 1971—; cons. in field. Bd. dirs. Recreation Room and Settlement, N.Y.C., 1962-73. Recipient Founders Day award and Bicentennial medal Columbia U., 1954. Mem. Nat. Assn. Social Workers, N.Y. State Soc. Clin. Social Work Psychotherapists, Nat. Inst. for Clin. Social Work Advancement, Soc. for Psychoanalytic Psychotherapy, World Fedn. for Mental Health. Avocations: swimming; sports; opera; reading; needlepoint; travel. Home: 240 E 79th St New York NY 10021

FILES, EVELYN JUNE, registered nurse; b. Kauai, HI, Feb. 26, 1932; d. Louis Santos Perreira and Violet (Victorino) McCullough; m. Major Leon Files, Aug. 15, 1952; children: Eric Leon, Janet Lynn, Karen Louis. AA, Bakersfield Jr. Coll., Bakersfield, 1969; BSN, Calif. State U., 1971-73, Student. RN, PHN, CEN, TNNC. Pvt. practice custom milliner Casper, Wy., 1965-66; staff registered nurse ortho. med. surg. ICU MMCLB, Long Beach, Calif., 1969-73; supr. MMCLB, Long Beach, 1973-79; instr. Goldenwest Coll., Huntington Beach, Calif.; per dium staff St. Francis Hosp., Tulsa, 1979-83; staff registered nurse MMCLB, 1983-88; clin. eductor Meml. Med. Ctr., Long Beach, 1988—. Author: Thesis. Mem. Am. Assn. Critical Care Nurse, Emergency Nurses Assn., So. Calif. Nursing Diagnosis Assn., Sigma Theta Tau (Iota Eta chpt.). Home: 20441 Drew Cir Huntington Beach CA 92646 Office: Long Beach Meml Med Ctr Emergency Dept 2801 Atlantic Ave Long Beach CA 90801

FILIGNO, PATRICIA ANN, health science association administrator, nurse; b. Waynesburg, Ohio, Sept. 7, 1939; d. Paul Joseph and Rose Marie (Mirto) Fondriest; m. Antonio Filigno, Oct. 6, 1962. Postgrad., Mercy Sch. Nursing, Canton, Ohio, 1960; BSN, U. Akron, 1969, MEd, 1978; MS in Nursing, Kent State U., 1982. Cert. psychiatric specialist. Pediatric staff nurse Timken Mercy Med. Ctr., Canton, Ohio, 1960-63; office nurse Pvt. Family Practitioner, Canton, Ohio, 1963-66; nurse educator Mercy Sch. of Nursing, Canton, Ohio, 1966-80; dir. psychiatric program Visiting Nurse Svc., Inc., Akron, Ohio; faculty mem. Life Style Learning Ctr., North Canton, Ohio, 1989; dir., pres. Personal Growth Cons. Svcs., Ohio, 1989; coord. client care quality assurance-utilization Stark County Community Mental Health Bd., Canton, Ohio, 1989; cons., manuscript reviewer Jour. Clin. Nurse Specialists, Lakewood, Calif.; mem. Preferred Health Care, Wilton, Conn., mem. adv. com. Visicare Home Health Care, Hudson, Ohio, 1988—. Bd. dirs. Stark County Mental Health Bd., 1983-89, chair planning evaluation com. 1987-89; vol. Crisis Ctr., Canton, 1978-79. Mem. Am. Nurses Assn., Am. Nurses Psychiatric Clin. Specialists, Am. Psychiatric Nurses Assn., Stark-Carroll Dist. Nurses Assn. (1st v.p. 1968-72, 2d v.p. 1972-74, 86-88), Mercy Alumni Assn. (pres. 1966-70). Democrat. Roman Catholic. Home: 2107 Myrtle Ave NW Canton OH 44709 Office: Stark County Harrison Med Bldg Canton OH 44702-0107

FILIPI, JOAN LEAHY (JODY FILIPI), medical association executive, speech pathologist; b. Park Falls, Wis., Nov. 29, 1950; d. James Joseph and Katherine A. (Lillestrand) Leahy; m. David H. Filipi, Nov. 28, 1975; children: Kristin Brita, James Bohdan. BS in Speech Pathology Edn., U. Nebr., Omaha, 1972, MS in Speech Pathology, 1974; Cert. of Clin. Competence in Speech/Lang. Pathology, The Am. Speech and Hearing Assn. Cert. speech pathologist, Nebr. Speech lang. pathologist Ednl. Svc. Unit #4, Auburn, Nebr., 1975, Ralston (Nebr.) Pub. Schs., 1975-78; adminstrv. asst. Nebr. Acad. Family Physicians, Omaha, 1987-89, interim exec. dir., 1989, exec. dir., 1989—. Pres. Nebr. Children's Chorus, Omaha, 1985—, designer T-shirt, 1985; bd. dirs. Nebr. Alliance for Arts Edn., Fremont, 1989—; dir. vacation ch. sch. Dundee Presbyn. Ch., Omaha, 1985-87. Mem. Profl. Convention Mgmt. Assn., Am. Soc. Assn. Execs., Nebr. Soc. Assn. Execs., Nebr. Choral Arts Soc. (bd. dirs. 1987—, outstanding svc. award Nebr. Children's Chorus 1988). Office: Nebr Acad Family Physicians 401 N 117th St Ste 202 Omaha NE 68154

FILIPPELLI, ANN MARIE, computer programmer; b. Bklyn., July 27, 1961; d. Peter and Anna (Siano) F. AAS, Pace U., 1982, BBA, 1986. Programmer Cowen & Co., N.Y.C., 1979-81; programmer analyst Alexanders, N.Y.C., 1982-83; cons. Cap Genimi, N.Y.C., 1986-88; sr. programmer analyst Associated Dry Goods, N.Y.C., 1984-86, The Equitable, N.Y.C., 1988—; model, 1989. Editor newspaper, 1979. Recipient 1st pl. Future Bus. Leaders Am., N.Y.C., 1978. Mem. Murray Hill Profl. Women, Living Well Lady Club, Theater Arts Resource Club. Republican. Roman Catholic. Home: 114-06 Queens Blvd #A6 Forest Hills NY 11375

FILLA, KIMBERLY MARIE, accountant; b. St. Louis, Mar. 22, 1966; d. Donald Paul and Antoinette Marie (Woods) F. BSBA in Acctg., St. Louis U., 1988. Ops., programmer analyst Blue Cross & Blue Shield, St. Louis, 1987-88; acct. CMS Communications, Inc., St. Louis, 1988—. Home: 5653 Eichelberger Saint Louis MO 63109 Office: CMS Communications Inc 3413 Hollenberg Dr Bridgeton MO 63044

FILLER-MORRIS, HADASSA, management consulting executive; b. Haifa, Israel, July 27, 1946; came to U.S., 1968; d. Yechiel and Rosa (Midvadovskaya) Gilboa; m. Joel Nataniel Filler (div.); 1 child, Shir; m. Harvey Seth Morris, June 29, 1979. BA summa cum laude, Fordham U., 1978; PhD, CUNY, 1985; student, Alvin Ailey Sch. Dance. Lic. psychologist, N.Y., Fla. Interviewer Ctr. for Social Rsch., N.Y.C., 1979-80; dir. tng. and devel. Vector Mgmt. Systems, Osprey, Fla., 1981—; rsch. assoc. Inst. for Mid. East Peace Rsch., N.Y.C., 1980-82; supervising psychologist St. Agatha's div. N.Y. Foundling Hosp., Rockland County, 1985-87;, 1981—; cons. psychologist, N.Y.C., 1979-87; cons. GTE, Philip Morris, Sun Oil, EGI, Govt. of Australia, HP, also others, 1981—. Contbr. articles to profl. jours. With Israeli Army, 1964-67. Mem. Am. Psychol. Assn., Fla. Psychol. Assn., Am. Soc. for Tng. and Devel., Coun. for Nat. Register Health Svc. Providers in Psychology. Democrat. Jewish. Home: 3920 Casey Key Rd Nokomis FL 34275 Office: Vector Mgmt Systems 2119 S Tamiami Trail Osprey FL 34229

FILLEY, BETTE ELAINE, computer software manufacturing executive; b. Phila., June 4, 1933; d. Russell S. and Martha (Spayd) Riley; m. Laurence D. Filley, Oct. 23, 1954; children: Richard David, Barbara Nan Filley Hamilton, Patricia Lynn Filley Messenger, Kathryn Gwyn, Thomas John. Columnist, editor Johnstown (Ohio) Independent, 1957-60; illustrator, columnist Chgo. Sun-Times, 1959-60; publs. editor Sicks Rainier Brewing Co., Seattle, 1962-66; pub. Silent Majority Voice, Seattle, 1971-73; pres. The Name People, Issaquah, Wash., 1985—; freelance writer, editor Seattle, 1966—; caricature artist, various events, 1972—. Mem. Wash. Press Women, Pacific Northwest Indsl. Editors, Am. Name Soc., Can. Soc. for Study of Names, Wash. Software Assn. Republican. Home and Office: The Name People 19801 SE 123d St Issaquah WA 98027

FILLEY, DOROTHY MCCRACKEN, museum consultant, antique costume restorer; b. St. Augustine, Fla., Mar. 22, 1915; d. Fred Wellman and Rozella May (Leith) McCracken; m. Marcus Lucius Filley IV, Sept. 11, 1937; children—Leith Child Filley Colen, Linda Derrick Filley Laguerre. BS in Fine Arts, Skidmore Coll. 1936; MA in Museology, SUNY-Oneonta, 1974. Founder, dir. Rensselaer County Jr. Mus., Troy, N.Y., 1954-59; exhibits cons. to N.Y. State historian N.Y. State Edn. Dept., Albany, 1956-57; mus. cons. Hist. Soc., Saratoga Springs, N.Y.-Park Casino, 1971-74; curator, coordinator Rockefeller Empire State Mall Art Collection, Albany, 1978-80; curator exhibits and collections Albany Inst. History and Art, 1974-81, mus. cons., 1981-87; mem. N.Y. State Council on the Arts Mus. Adv. Bd., N.Y.C., 1974-75; cons. compiling history Town of Colonie, Newtonville, N.Y., 1975; mem. adv. bd. Shaker Heritage Soc., Albany, 1981-88; cons. textiles and costumes Albany Inst. History and Art, 1983-89; cons. Troy Savs. Bank Oil Painting Collection of bank presidents from 1823 to 1987 for conservation, 1988; spl. research cons. History of SUNY Univ. Plaza Bldg., 1986. Author: Recapturing Wisdom's Valley, 1975. Mem. Cooperstown Grad. Assn., Jr. League Troy (pres. 1950-51). Avocations: gardening, tennis, swimming, wildlife preservation. Home: RR 1 Box 129 Yarmouth ME 04096

FILLINGAME, SARAH ANN, psychologist; b. Las Cruces, N.Mex., Jan. 9, 1946; d. Walter Henry Fillingame and Jane Rose (Miller) O'Connell; m. Robert Macy Gelpke, Dec. 1, 1968 (div. 1982); children: Robert Macy, Jr., Jennifer Chase. BA, U. Dayton, Ohio, 1978; D. Psychology, Wright State U., Dayton, 1983. Lic. psychologist, Ohio. Dir., psychologist, psychol. asst. Children's Mental Health Program, Xenia, Ohio, 1983-85; psychologist Mental Health Resources, Xenia, 1985-86; psychologist Children's Med. Ctr., Dayton, 1986—, asst. v.p. behavioral scis., dir. psychology, 1989—; asst. clin. prof. pediatrics Wright State U. Sch. Medicine, Dayton, 1986—; presenter numerous workshops. Treas. Miami Valley Childhood Sexual Abuse Coalition, Dayton, 1988—; bd. dirs. Coalition Child Agys., Dayton, 1990—. Mem. Am. Psychol. Assn., Ohio Psychol. Assn., Dayton Area Psychol. Assn., NOW. Office: Childrens Med Ctr One Childrens Pl Dayton OH 45404

FILSKOV, SUSAN B., psychologist, educator; b. South Amboy, N.J., May 29, 1950; d. Harold T. and June (Miller) F.; widowed; children: Steven Rifkin, Laura Rifkin. BA, U. Vt., 1971, PhD, 1975. Diplomate Am. Bd. Profl. Psychology. Assoc. prof. psychology and psychiatry Coll. Medicine U. South Fla., Tampa, 1975-89; pvt. practice Tampa, 1989—; cons. VA Hosp., St. Petersburg, Fla., 1984—, Bay Pines dept. pediatrics U. South Fla., 1984—; dir. S.E. region Am. Bd. Profl. Psychology, 1990—; clin. assoc. prof. psychiatry and behavioral medicine. Editor (with T.J. Boll): Handbook of Clinical Neuropsychology, Vol. 1, 1981, Vol. 11, 1987; contbr. articles to profl. jours., chpts. to books. John Dewey fellow U. Vt., 1970. Fellow Am. Psychol. Assn.; mem. Fla. Psychol. Assn. (sec. Bay region chpt. 1984), Internat. Neuropsychol. Soc., Southeastern Psychol. Assn., Athene Soc. Home: 3301 Bayshore Blvd Ste 1604 Tampa FL 33629 Office: 3333 W Kennedy Blvd Ste 205 Tampa FL 33609

FILSON, TERESA FINCH, hospital financial executive; b. Niceville, Fla., Jan. 11, 1960; d. Leslie Ross and Betty Jean (Yon) Finch; m. Kenneth S. Filson, Dec. 19, 1981 (div. Dec. 1986); 1 child, Leslie Rochelle. AA in Bus. Adminstrn., Southwestern Jr. Coll., Waxahatchie, Tex., 1980; BA in Acctg., U. West Fla., 1982; MBA, Jacksonville U., 1988. Staff acct. Hosp. Corp. Am. Gulf Coast Hosp., Panama City, Fla., 1983; asst. controller HCA Gulf Coast Hosp., Panama City, 1983-85; controller St. Augustine (Fla.) Gen. Hosp., 1985-89, Lakeside Hosp., Metairie, La., 1989—. Treas. Big Bros./Big Sisters, St. Augustine, 1989. Mem. Healthcare Fin. Mgmt. Assn. (v.p. 1988-89). Democrat. Home: 4739 Saint Charles Apt E New Orleans LA 70115 Office: Lakeside Hosp 4700 I-10 Service Rd Metairie LA 70001

FILTER, EUNICE M., business equipment manufacturing executive; b. 1940. BA, CUNY, 1966. Former security analyst Morgan Guaranty Trust Co. N.Y.; sr. tech. analyst G.A. Saxton & Co.; sr. fin. analyst Xerox Corp., Stanford, Conn., 1973-81, dir. investor rels., 1981-84, v.p., corp. sec., 1984—. Office: Xerox Corp Long Ridge Rd Box 1600 Stamford CT 06904*

FINBERG, BARBARA DENNING, foundation executive; b. Pueblo, Colo., Feb. 26, 1929; d. Rufus Raymond and Velma Aileen (Hopper) Denning; m. Alan R. Finberg, June 21, 1953. B.A., Stanford U., 1949; M.A., Am. U. of Beirut, Lebanon, 1951. Intern U.S. Dept. State, Washington, 1949-50, fgn. affairs officer, Tech Coop. Adminstrn., 1952-53; program specialist, area chief Inst. Internat. Edn., N.Y.C., 1953-59; editorial assoc., program officer Carnegie Corp. N.Y., N.Y.C., 1959-80, v.p. program, 1980-88, exec. v.p., 1988—; program advisor A.L. Mailman Family Found. Mem. adv. council N.C. Central U. Sch. Library Sci., Durham, 1973-86; trustee Stanford U., 1976-86, v.p. bd. dirs., 1982-85; mem. accreditation com. Assn. Am. Law Schs., 1986-88; adv. coun. Beryl Buck Inst. for Edn., 1989; bd. dirs. Investor Responsibility Rsch. Ctr. Inc., 1989—; adv. com. The Henry A. Murray Rsch. Ctr. for the Study of Lives, Radcliffe Coll., 1986—; trustee N.Y. Found., 1979—, vice chmn. bd. dirs., 1983-85, chmn., 1985-89; bd. dirs. The Hole in the Wall Gang Camp Fund, Inc., 1987—. Rotary Found. fellow, 1950-51. Mem. Am. Ednl. Research Assn., Soc. for Research in Child Devel., Council on Fgn. Relations. Club: Cosmopolitan of N.Y. Home: 165 E 72nd St Apt 19L New York NY 10021 Office: Carnegie Corp NY 437 Madison Ave New York NY 10022

FINCH, CAROLYN-BOGART, speech and language pathologist, writer, speaker; b. Mineola, N.Y., June 24, 1938; d. Harold Edwin and Ruth (Waring) Bogart; m. Gordon M. Finch (div. Oct. 1982); children: David Harold, Martha Louise; m. Donald Hall Hulme; children: Wendy Harriet Hulme, Allison Elizabeth Hulme. BS, Elmira Coll., 1965; MS, Western Conn. State U., 1972; postgrad., Nova U., 1982. Cert. speech and lang. pathologist, early childhood edn., elem. edn. and communication. Speech therapist Elmira (N.Y.) City Schs., 1963-65; supervision therapist Speech and Hearing Clinic Elmira Coll., 1966-67; speech therapist Greenshire Residential Sch., Cheshire, Conn., 1968-69; speech pathologist Danbury (Conn.) City Schs., 1970-73; owner, dir. Peter Piper Sch. and Learning ctr., Brookfield Center, Conn., 1973-88, Speech Pathology Assocs., Danbury, 1974-87; mem. adj. faculty Western Conn. State U., Danbury, 1974-86, prof., 1986-87; organizer, chmn. bd. Liberty Nat. Bank, Danbury; freelance lectr., 1986-87, R. Zemper Assocs., 1987-88; pres., nat. speaker Bogart Communications, Inc, Danbury; account exec. V.R. Bus. Brokers; pres. communication Fitness Internat. div. Bogart Communications; nat. expert on body lang., speak on voice power, mind power and the multi-cultural workplace. Author: (multisensory articulation program) Portraits of Sounds, 1969, (book and posters) Survival Sign System, 1982, Universal Handtalk, 1988. Dem. nominee Danbury Town Com., 1985; mem. adv. com. Fairfield County 4-H. Recipient Mayoral Proclamation for Survival Sign System, City of Danbury, 1986. Mem. AAUP, NAFE, Conn. Speech and Hearing Assn., New Eng. Speakers Assn., Nat. Speakers Assn. Home and Office: Bogart Communications Inc 51 Cedar Dr Danbury CT 06811

FINCH, DEBRA ANN, registered nurse; b. Wyandott, Mich., Sept. 13, 1954; d. Donald William and Ellen Jane (Barr) Finch. BSN, U. Mich., 1976, postgrad., 1985—. Registered nurse, Mich. Staff nurse U. Mich. Hosp., Ann Arbor, Mich., 1976-78; sr. staff nurse South Shore Hosp., South Weymouth, Mass., 1978-80; staff nurse U. Mich. Hosp., Ann Arbor, Mich., 1980-82; asst. head nurse U. Mich Hosp., Ann Arbor, Mich.; head nurse U. Mich. Hosp., Ann Arbor, Mich., 1983--. Contbr. articles to prof mags. Mem. Soc. for Peripheral Vascular Nursing, Am. Orgn. Nurse Exec., Soc. for the Advancement of Modeling and Role Modeling, Sigma Theat Tau. Home: 830 W Huron Ann Arbor MI 48103 Office: Univ Mich Hosp 1500 E Medical Dr Rm B5224 Ann Arbor MI 48109

FINCH, DIANE SHIELDS, district merchandising manager; b. Detroit, Aug. 25, 1947; d. Earl Arthur and Carrie (Steele) Shields; m. Glenn A. Finch III, Oct. 5, 1968; 1 child, Jennifer Lynn. AA, U. Houston, 1969; student, U. St. Thomas, 1970-73, Rice U., 1980. Apt. mgr. Moonmist Manor, Houston, 1972-75; sales merchandiser Mattel Toys, Houston, 1975-77; sales merchandiser Plough Sales, Houston, 1977-79, ter. mgr., 1979-80, area mdse. mgr., 1980-84, dist. sales mgr., 1984-86; dist. mdse. mgr. Schering Plough Consumer Ops., Houston, 1986—. Area chmn. Assn. Community TV, Houston, 1985-87; mem. Friends of Ronald McDonald House; mem. Citizens Animal Protection. Mem. Nat. Assn. Female Execs., Am. Mgmt. Assn., Tex. Exec. Women (bd. dirs.), Houston Fedn. Profl. Women. Home: 10203 Huntington View Dr Houston TX 77099 Office: Schering Plough Consumer Ops PO Box 424 3030 Jackson Ave Memphis TN 38151

FINCH, LETA CECILE, risk management executive; b. Hugo, Okla., Dec. 30, 1948; d. James Phinney and Connie Williams (Gilmore); B.A., U. Hawaii, 1974; m. William N. Ryerson, Dec. 6, 1975. Tech. loss control rep. Hartford Ins. Group, Washington and Phila., 1977-79; casualty loss control cons. Alexander & Alexander, Inc., Phila., 1979-81; pres. Finch Assocs., Shelburne, Vt., 1981-87; dir. risk mgmt. U. Vt., 1982—; polit. journalist Shelburne News, 1981-83; risk mgr. U. Vt., 1983—. Bd. dirs. United Educator's Risk Mgmt. Adv. Group; Nat. Orgn. for Optional Parenthood, 1979-80; ERA coordinator LWV, Arlington, Va., 1978-79. Recipient cert. of appreciation George Washington U., 1978. Mem. Am. Soc. Safety Engrs., Univ. Risk and Ins. Mgrs. Assn. (bd. dirs. 1985—), Nat. Safety Mgmt. Soc., Nat. Assn. Coll. and Univ. Bus. Officers (task force on chem. waste 1985-86). Home: 2 Collamer Circle Shelburne VT 05482 Office: U Vt 109 S Prospect St Burlington VT 05405

FINCHER, MARGARET ANN, educator; b. Harrodsburg, Ky., June 2, 1934; d. Henry Alexander and Minnie Bee (White) Cathey; B.S. in Bus. Edn., Auburn U., 1955; M.Ed., U. New Orleans, 1978; m. Willie John Fincher, Jr., Apr. 1, 1955; children—John Richard, Joseph Michael, Judy Darlene, James Andrew. Bookkeeper, Markle's Drug Store, Auburn, Ala., 1952-54; asst. to dir. Auburn U. Library, 1955; elem. tchr., Birmingham, Ala., 1958-64; bus. edn. tchr. Abramson High Sch., New Orleans, 1964—; owner, mgr. craft shop Fanci Krafts, New Orleans, 1977-78; asst. supr. Shaklee Corp., 1979-85; libr. Abramson Sr. High Sch. Orleans Parish Sch. Bd., 1984-89. Supr. adult Bible tng. dept. Word of Faith Temple, 1982, cons. library devel., 1982, tchr., 1975-80, deaconess, 1983—; bd. dirs. Lamb Day Care Center, 1979-81; sustaining mem. Meth. Hosp. Aux., 1967—; adv./sponsor Christian Life on Campus Club. Recipient Am. Legion citation of appreciation, 1981; Future Bus. Leaders Am., award of Appreciation, 1976. Mem. ALA, Donna Villa Improvement Assn., Metro. Ednl. Media Orgn., Ch. and Synagogue Library Assn., So. Bus. Edn. Assn., Nat. Bus. Edn. Assn., La. Assn. Bus. Edn., La. Library Assn., La. Vocat. Assn., United Tchrs. New Orleans, Policemen's Assn. New Orleans (hon.), Phi Delta Kappa. Republican. Mem. Christian Ch. Office: 5552 Read Blvd New Orleans LA 70127

FINDLAY, ROBERTA, film director; b. N.Y.C., Dec. 30, 1952; d. Morris and Lillian (Isaacs) Hershkowitz. Student, CUNY. Pres. Reeltime Distbg. Corp., N.Y.C., 1979—. Dir. The Oracle, 1985, Tenement, 1986, Blood Sisters, 1986, Lurkers, 1987, Prime Evil, 1986, Banned, 1989; producer Women with Power. Mem. Ind. Feature Project, N.Y. Women in Film, Women in Communications Inc., Am. Women in Radio & TV. Office: Reeltime Distbg Corp 353 W 48th St New York NY 10036

FINDLAY, SUSAN HALTON, corporate secretary; b. Pasadena, Calif., Apr. 27, 1943; d. Edward Herbert and Sarah Felithe (Dudley) Halton; m. William Sterling Findlay; children: Kathryn, Johnathan. BA, Colo. Coll., 1966; MA, Oreg. State U., 1969. Bookkeeper, clk. Halton Tractor Co., Portland, Oreg., 1966-67; tchr. Portland Sch. Dist. #1, 1967-70; mgr. Halton Found., Portland, 1971—; corp. sec. The Halton Co., Portland, 1976—; dir. Double T. Holding Co., Portland, 1979—. Mem. Child Abuse Domestic Violence Hotline Adv. Com., State of Oreg., 1981-87; mem. Jr. League of Portland, 1966—, lobbiest, 1980-81. Named for Extraordinary Svc. Childrens Protective Svc., 1981. Mem. Assn. Oreg. Industries, Grantmakers Northwest Oreg. and Southwest Wash., The Town Club, Multnomah Athletic Club. Office: The Halton Co PO Box 3377 Portland OR 97208

FINDLER, JEAN KERCH, writer, consultant; b. Columbia City, Ind., July 4, 1951; d. Ronald Clovis and Wilma Marie (Schuman) Kerch; m. James John Miller, Apr. 21, 1984 (div. 1986); m. Richard Samuel Findler, July 25, 1989. AB in Econs., Math. with honors, Ind. U., 1973; MBA in Fin., U. Chgo., 1981. Jr. analyst, then sr. analyst Assocs. Corp. N.Am., Chgo. and South Bend, Ind., 1973-79; fin. analyst, mgr. ops. analysis Chgo. Tribune, 1979-81; sr. fin. analyst, then asst. contr. planning and analysis Union Tank Car Co., Chgo., 1981-88; freelance writer, cons. Chgo., 1988—. Mem. Alpha Lambda Delta. Home and Office: 5416 N Glenwood Chicago IL 60640

FINDLEY, MARY LOU MCBROOM, manufacturing company executive; b. Chgo., Aug. 31, 1945; d. John Kellett and Mary Jane (Kahlert) McB.; m. Leroy James Burlingame, Oct. 1, 1983; 1 child, Thomas Scott Findley; m. John William Findley, Aug. 17, 1968 (div. Dec. 1982). BA, Lawrence U., 1967; postgrad. Marquette U., 1974-76. Programmer, analyst Gen. Systems Co., Kalamazoo, 1969-71, Marine 1st Nat. Bank, Racine, Wis., 1971-72; with Twin Disc, Inc., Racine, 1972—, supr. systems and programming, 1978-79, mgr. bus. systems, 1979—. Bd. dirs. Racine Coun. Alcohol and Other Drug Abuse, 1982-88, also pres., 1984-86; cons. Jr. Achievement, 1984; bd. dirs. YMCA, Racine, 1990—. Mem. Am. Prodn. and Inventory Control Soc., Soc. Info. Mgmt. (exec. com. 1988-90). Republican. Presbyterian. Avocations: music, identifying birds and wild flowers. Home: 143 Robin Hill Dr Racine WI 53406 Office: Twin Disc Inc 1328 Racine St Racine WI 53403

FINE, JO RENÉE, audio-visual production executive; b. Norfolk, Va., June 19, 1943; d. Ruby Arthur and Tillie Fern (Goldman) F.; BA, Smith Coll., 1965; MA, NYU, 1968, PhD, 1973; m. Edward Trieber, Apr. 12, 1981; 1 child, Jessica Fine Trieber. Probation officer N.Y.C. Office Probation, 1966; res. asst. N.Y.U., N.Y.C., 1966-68, assoc. res. scientist Inst. Devel. Studies, 1968-73, res. scientist, 1973-77, adj. asst. prof. dept. ednl. psychology, 1973-76; program analyst N.Y. State Dept. Mental Hygiene, N.Y.C., 1977-78; pvt. practice psychotherapy, N.Y.C., 1978-81; pres. CVM Prodns., Inc., N.Y.C., 1978—; adj. asst. prof. ednl. communication and tech. NYU, 1989—; cons. to bds. edn., N.Y.C., also greater met. area, 1973—; adj. asst. prof. NYU, 1988—. Mem. Am. Psychol. Assn., Pharm. Advt. Council, Am. Jewish Com. (exec. bd.), Am. Soc. for Tng. and Devel. Co-author: The Synagogues of New York's Lower East Side, 1978. Home and Office: 55 W 16th St New York NY 10011

FINE, RANA ARNOLD, chemical/physical oceanographer; b. N.Y.C., Apr. 17, 1944; d. Joseph and Etta (Kreisman) Arnold; m. Shalle Stephen Fine, June 20, 1965 (div. 1979). BA, NYU, 1965; MA, U. Miami, 1973, PhD, 1975. Systems analyst Svc. Bur. Corp. subs. IBM, Miami, 1965-69; postdoctoral rsch. assoc. Rosenstiel Sch. U. Miami, 1976-77, rsch. asst. prof., 1977-80, rsch. assoc. prof., 1980-84, assoc. prof., 1984-90, prof. of marine and atmospheric chemistry, 1990—, chairperson div. marine and atmospheric chemistry, 1990—; assoc. program dir. NSF, Washington, 1981-83; mem. div. polar programs adv. com. NSF, Washington, 1987-90; mem. geophys. study com. NAS, WAshington, 1989-92; mem. adv. panel Tropical Ocean/Global Atmosphere Program, 1990-93. Contbr. articles to profl. jours. Vol. guide Vizcaya Mus., Miami, 1967-78. Grantee NSF, 1977—, NOAA, 1986—, Office of Naval Rsch., 1983-88, NASA, 1990—. Mem. AAAS, Am. Geophys. Union (sec. oceanography sect. 1986-88), Am. Meteorol. Soc., The Oceanography Soc. Office: RSMAS/MAC/U Miami 4600 Rickenbacker Cswy Miami FL 33149

FINELLI, LOUISE STEPHANIA, educator; b. Atlanta, May 26, 1919; d. Stephan and Elizabeth (Kish) Gaspar; m. Joseph Amilio Finelli, Jan. 17, 1943; children: Anton J., Joseph A. BA, Hunter Coll., 1940; MS, Herbert Lehman Coll., 1971. Tchr. St. Paul's Cath. Sch., N.Y.C., 1940-41; exec. dir. Monterey (Calif.) Peninsular Girl Scouts Coun., N.Y.C., 1943-45; field advisor N.Y.C. Girl Scout Coun., N.Y.C., 1941-43; tchr. N.Y.C. Bd. of Edn., 1955-80; pvt. practice tchr. Pleasant Valley, N.Y., 1980—; bd. dirs., sec. Trail Blazer Camps, N.Y.C., 1985—. Vol. Chippewa Dem. Club, Bronx, 1975-80. Mem. AAUW, Trail Blazer Camp Alumni Club. Democrat. Roman Catholic. Home: Rt 82 RR#3 Box 479 Millbrook NY 12545

FINELLO, TERRY LEE, communications executive; b. Trenton, N.J., Nov. 1, 1947; d. Curtis Gillikin and Joy (Urban) Rooy; m. Dennis John, June 23, 1973 (div. July 1985); 1 child, Elaine Marie. BS in Communications, Psychology, Edn., Murray State U., 1970, MS in Communications, 1971; postgrad., Cen. Conn. State U., New Britain, 1972. Tchr. Tchr., teaching asst. Murray State U., Murray, Ky., 1970-71; instr. adult edn. Wincester Bd. of Edn., Winsted, Conn., 1973-76; special lectr. Central Conn. State U., New Britain, Conn., 1975-85; lectr. communications dept. Tunxis Community Coll., Farmington, Conn., 1986—; communications lectr. U. Conn., Waterbury, 1986, Torrington, 1986—; English educator Wincester Bd. of Edn., Conn., 1971—; cons., lectr. Veteran's Hosp. Nursing Staff, Meridan, 1981, Bus. and Profl. Women, 1982; faculty cons. Conn. State Conf. Emergency Med. Techs., Hartford, 1988-90; presentor New England League of Middle Schs., Hyannis, 1988; cons. Pvt. Individuals Pub. Speaking Coach, 1976—. Home: 51 Pythian Ave Torrington CT 06790 Office: Pearson Sch 2 Wetmore Ave Winsted CT 06098

FINERTY, MARY ELLEN, nurse; b. Salisbury, Md., Mar. 30, 1947; d. Carlton Woodrow and Anna Marceda (Funds) Hurlock. BA, Asbury Coll., Wilmore, Ky., 1971; BSN, Case Western Res. U., 1973; MA, Columbia U., 1986; cert. in nursing adminstrn., Villanova U., 1989. Staff nurse Thomas Jefferson U. Hosp., Phila.; clin. nurse III Thomas Jefferson U. Hosp., nursing care coordinator; clin. coordinator Magee Rehab. Hosp., Phila. Mem. com. OUTREACH Refugee Resettlement program, Delaware County, Coalition on Caring Food Program, Delaware County. Mem. NAFE, Am. Assn. Critical Care Nurses, ARN, Nursing Edn. Alumni Assn. Home: 409 Gilpin Rd Upper Darby PA 19082

FINES FOURNIER, REBECCA EILEEN, university official; b. Alton, Ill., Oct. 10, 1960; d. Galen Wayne and Betty Jean (Phleger) Fines; m. Dennis Francis Fournier, Apr. 10, 1988. BA, So. Ill. U., Edwardsville, 1981. Dir. communications Olney (Ill.) Cen. Coll., 1981-82; asst. to pres. Muskingum Area Tech. Coll., Zanesville, Ohio, 1982-83; asst. dir. devel. Washington U., St. Louis, 1983-87; asst. dean for external affairs and devel. So. Ill. U., Carbondale, 1987—; cons. Ultimately Aloe, 1982. Active Planned Parenthood, Zanesville, 1983, Remove Intoxicated Drivers-Mo., St. Louis, 1986; bd. dirs. Univ. Christian Ministries, Carbondale, 1988. So. Ill. U. Presdl. scholar, 1978-81, Washington U. fellow, 1986. Mem. Coun. for Advancement and Support Edn., NAFE, Women in Leadership Alumnae, So. Ill. U.-Edwardsville Alumni Assn. (exec. com. 1983-89, v.p. 1987-89). Democrat. Presbyterian. Home: Rte 10 Box 100 Carbondale IL 62901 Office: So Ill U Coll Bus and Adminstrn Carbondale IL 62901

FINESTONE, SHEILA, Canadian legislator; b. Montreal, Que., Can., Jan. 28, 1927; d. Monroe and Minnie Abbey; m. Alan Finestone, June 9, 1947; children: David, Peter, Maxwell, Stephen. Ed., McGill U., Drake U. Mem. from Mount Royal riding, Que. Ho. of Commons, 1984—. Mem. Nat. Coun. Jewish Women. Mem. Orgn. Rehab. and Tng. Liberal. Office: House Commons, Parliament Bldgs, Ottawa, ON Canada K1A 0A6*

FINIZZI, MARGUERITE H(ELENE), educator; b. Allentown, Pa., Nov. 16, 1934; d. John Michael and Margaret Mary (Havrilla) Martin; BS in Secondary Edn., Kutztown State Coll., 1956; MA in English, Lehigh U., 1973; m. Joseph Anthony Finizzi, Nov. 19, 1954. Tchr. English, Harrison-Morton Jr. High Sch., Allentown, 1956-64, Louis E. Dieruff High Sch., Allentown, 1964-76, Allen High Sch., Allentown, 1976—; adviser pubs. Allen High Sch., 1978—, Quill and Scroll chpt., 1978, intramural bowling, 1990; instr. to develop. drug edn. competency for tchrs., Pa. dept. edn. Student Assistance Program and Intervention Team Tng., 1987, Lehigh U. Gifted Summer Inst., 1989—; mem. in-svc. coun. Allentown Sch. Dist., 1973-89; discussion leader for jr. classes Jewish Day Sch., 1969-71, peer coaching, 1989-90; v.p. Fearless Ladies Bowling League, 1986-89; coord. peer Leadership workshop, 1989, judge numerous acad. contests, Tchr. Expectations and Student Achievement (TESA), 1987-90, Allentown Sch. Dist. coord. for TESA Program, 1988, coord., 1989, lead tchr., 1990; lectr., speaker in field; seminar discussion leader Council of Youth, 1980; adviser Student Newspaper Adv. Program; pres. Lehigh County (Pa.) Coordinating Coun., 1967-71; mem. steering com. Allentown Sch. Dist., 1984. Recipient Meritorious award Kutztown State Coll., 1956; Newspaper Fund fellow, 1981; Commonwealth Partnerships fellow for lit. Inst. Secondary Tchrs., 1985. Mem. NEA, AAUW, Nat. Council Tchrs. English (co-chmn. conf. 1985, bd. judges 1987-90), Pa. Council Tchrs. English (bd. judges, 1990), Pa. State Edn. Assn. (editor eastern region constn.), Allentown Edn. Assn. (social chairperson 1964-79, exec. sec. 1964-69), Allentown Women Tchrs. Club (editor constn. and by-laws, welfare chmn. 1986-89, pres.-elect 1990—), Lehigh U. Alumni, Kutztown U. Alumni (pres. Lehigh County 1969-72), Columbia Sch. Press Assn. (bd. judges, 1989, 90, adviser Reflector Sci. newsletter, 1979-80), Pa. Sch. Press Assn. Home: 3025 Pearl Ave Allentown PA 18103

FINK, JOYCE ERLEEN, academic program administrator; b. Buffalo, Nov. 7, 1930; d. Frank X. and Florence (Honeck) F. AB, Rosary Hill Coll., 1952, LHD (hon.), 1973; EdM, U. Buffalo, 1959. Cons. curriculum Diocese Buffalo, 1952-54; dir. pub. rels. Rosary Hill Coll., Buffalo, 1954-57, dir. devel., 1957-59, asst. to pres., 1959-64; cons. pub. rels. Manhattan Coll., N.Y.C., 1965, N.Y. State Welfare Coun., Albany, 1964-65; from asst. dir. pub. info. to dir. publs. and spl. events SUNY, Buffalo, 1965-77, dir. pub. affairs, 1977—. Co-editor elem. sch. art course, 1954; author: Public Relations Problems in Higher Education, 1958. Trustee Kenmore (N.Y.) Mercy Hosp., 1980-82, mem. adv. bd., 1977-81; trustee Christ the King Sem., East Aurora, N.Y., 1981-84, vice chmn. bd. trustees, 1982-87, chmn. bd. trustees, 1987-88; mem. bd. govs. Buffalo Acad. of Sacred Heart, 1982-85, chmn., 1984-85; bd. dirs. Camp Fire Girls Buffalo and Erie County, 1970-72, Office of Communications Diocese of Buffalo, 1979— (St. Paul award 1988); mem. adv. bd. Buffalo Coun. World Affairs; active in United Fund Buffalo and Erie County, 1959-75. Mem. Pub. Relations Soc. Am. (pres. 1976, bd. dirs. Niagara Frontier chpt. 1977-78), 20th Century Club. Home: 346 Mill St Williamsville NY 14221 Office: SUNY 1300 Elmwood Ave Buffalo NY 14222

FINK, LINDA MARIE, hospital official; b. Loma Linda, Calif., Jan. 20, 1959; d. Ivan Leon and Elizabeth Campos (Costa) Reeve; m. David Bruce Fink, May 23, 1982; children: Aaron David, Lindsey Jennifer. Student, U. So. Calif., 1988. Office asst. Drs. Reeve & Burlison, Sierra Madre, Calif., 1974-80; microbiology asst. U. Calif., Riverside, 1978; microbiology tech. Loma Linda U., 1976-79, cardiology tech., 1978-79; cardiology tech. St. Luke's Hosp., Pasadena, Calif., 1979-80; with cardiology sect. Meth. Hosp. of So. Calif., Arcadia, 1980-81; tumor registrar, coord. pathology dept. Foothill Presbyn. Hosp., Glendora, Calif., 1981-84, 86-88; adminstrv. asst. Heart Inst. Nev., Las Vegas, 1988-89; patient billing rep. Humana Hosp. Sunrise, Las Vegas, 1989—. Democrat. Office: 3186 Maryland Pkwy Las Vegas NV

FINK, MARY ALEXANDER, health science association administrator; b. Camden, Tenn., Oct. 18, 1919; d. Mitchell Trotter and Alice (Blackwell) Alexander; m. Charles Dennis Fink, Dec. 2, 1950. BS, Okla. A&M Coll., 1939; MS, U. Mich., 1946; PhD, George Washington U., 1949; postgrad., Cambridge U., 1962. Med. technologist, chemist Fraser-Brace Engring. Co., Meadville, Pa., 1940-43; instr. dept. microbiology U. Mich., Ann Arbor, 1945-46; rsch. bacteriologist U.S. Dept. War, Frederick, Md., 1946-49; rsch. assoc. R.B. Jackson Meml. Lab., Bar Harbor, Maine, 1949-51; asst. prof. microbiology U. Colo. Med. Sch., Denver, 1951-58; rsch. microbiologist NCI/NIH, Bethesda, Md., 1959-70, program dir. immunology, 1970-74, assoc. dir. biol. rsch., 1974-77, spl. asst. to dir., 1977-84; cons. M.D. Anderson Hosp., Houston, 1964-70, Human Resource Rsch. Office, Washington, 1969. Contbr. numerous articles to profl. jours. Trustee Gordon Rsch. Confs., U. R.I. Am. Cancer Soc. grantee, 1950-58. Democrat. Home: 125 Woods Run Rd Rollinsford NH 03869

FINK, MARY VIRGINIA DANIEL, hospital administrator; b. Suffolk, Va., Feb. 28, 1951; d. Louis Mason and Nannie Wright (Williams) Daniel; m. Bryon Perry Fink,. AB in Eng., Coll. William Mary, Williamsburg, Va., 1973; MHA in HOsp. Adminstrn., Med. Coll. Va., Richmond, 1978. Adminstrn. extern. Louise Obici Meml. Hos., Suffolk, Va., 1975--76; adminstrn. resident Va. Med. Ctr., Wash., 1977--78; asst. adminstr. The Meml. Hosp., Danville, 1978-83; v.p. for adminstrn. Williamson Med. Ctr., Franklin, Tenn., 1983--. Bd. Mem, Chair. Danville Pitts. Co. YWCA, 1982-83; pres., bd. mem. Am. Heart Assn., Danville Pitts. Co. Mem. Am. Coll. Healthcare Exec., Tenn. Hosp. Assn., Am. Hosp. Assn. Methodist. Office: Williamson Med Ctr PO Box 1600 Franklin TN 37065-1600

FINK, VALERIE ANN, home economics educator; b. Chgo., Feb. 13, 1954; d. Joseph Michael and Elsie (Daghi) F. BA, Rosary Coll., 1976; MS, No. Ill. U., 1983, postgrad. Rosary Coll. Grad. Sch. Fine Arts, Florence, Italy, 1984, Iowa State U., 1986, Auburn U., 1986. Sales, gen. office Jamie Lynn Bridals, Chgo., 1976-77, Galzier Corp., Chgo., 1977-78; with Stone & Adler Advt., Chgo., 1978-79; substitute tchr. various high schs., Cook County, Ill., 1979; part-time retail salesperson I. Magnin, Oak Brook, Ill., 1985-86; tchr., dept. chmn. Westchester Dist. 92 1/2, Ill., 1980—. Author cognitive skills test: Home Economics Basic Skills Indicator, 1982. Docent Chgo. Archtl. Found., 1981-85; active Ill. Vocat. Home Econs. Curriculum Devel. Project, 1981. Mem. Westchester Edn. Assn. (treas.), Am. Home Econs. Assn., Ill. Home Econs. Assn., Nat. Trust for Hist. Preservation (vested), Omicron Nu. Roman Catholic. Avocations: travel, golf, sewing, cooking, local theater guild productions. Office: Westchester Middle Sch 1620 Norfolk Westchester IL 60154

FINKE, BLYTHE FOOTE, freelance writer; b. Pasadena, Calif., Nov. 24, 1922; d. Robert Ordway Foote and Blythe (Crawford) Mendenhall; m. John G.W. Finke, Nov. 15, 1958. B in Bus., Woodbury Coll., 1942; BA in Internat. Rels., U. Calif., Berkeley, 1946. Sec., adminstrv. clk. Union Oil Co., L.A., 1942-44; adminstrv. sec. U.S. Fgn. Svc., Vienna, Austria, 1947-49; in-house editor Shell Oil Co., Long Beach, Calif., 1950-51; asst. info. officer USIA Am. Embassy, Ankara, Turkey, 1951-53; info. officer Am. Embassy, Dusseldorf, Stuttgart, Fed. Republic Germany, 1953-58; dir. pub. rels. Bklyn. Pub. Libr., 1985-60; editor, writer, UN corr. USIA, N.Y.C., 1962-83; freelance writer, 1983—; writer in field; convenor migration com. Internat. Coun. of Women, Paris, 1989-90. Contbr. articles to profl. jours. Bd. dirs Nat. Coun. Women of U.S.A. Mem. Overseas Press Club Am., Nat. Press Club, Am. Soc. Journalists and Authors, Coun. Writers Orgns., Travel Journalists Guild, Women in Communications. Home: 45 Kyleswood Pl Inverness CA 94937-1079

FINKEL, MARCIA ROBIN, marketing professional; b. Miami, Fla., Dec. 2, 1958; d. Jack Maurice and Zelda Jean (Davidoff) F. BA in Social Work, U. Wis., 1980; MPA, Am. U., 1983. Investigator Superior Ct. of D.C., Washington, 1980-81; staff asst. Select Com. on Aging, Washington, 1981-82; rsch. asst. Louden and Co., Chgo., 1983-84; govt. affairs rep. Personnel Pool Am., Inc., Ft. Lauderdale, Fla., 1984-86, mktg. mgr., 1986—. Chpt. mem. Am. Cancer Soc., Miami, 1986—, Ft. Lauderdale Humane Soc., 1988—; bd. dirs., sec. Young Profls. Multiple Sclerosis, Miami, 1987—. Mem. Am. Coll. Health Care Mktg., Direct Mktg. Assn., Big Ten. Office: Personnel Pool Am Inc 2050 Spectrum Blvd Fort Lauderdale FL 33309

FINKEL, SHEILA BERG, marketing professional; b. Houston, Sept. 13, 1947; d. Phillip Raymond and Anna (Roth) Berg; m. Steven M. Finkel (div. June 1979). BA, Washington U., St. Louis, 1969. Lab. technician Jewish Hosp., St. Louis, 1969-70, Peoria (Ill.) Sanitary Dist., 1970-73; asst. to gen. mgr. Consol. Office Supply, Chgo., 1974, purchasing mgr., 1975-84; with Wilson Jones Co., Chgo., 1984—, mktg. info. mgr., 1988-89, promotions and telesales mgr., 1989—. Pres. Pattington Condominium Assn., Chgo., 1986, 90, sec., 1989. Mem. NAFE, Chgo. Assn. Direct Mktg. Home: 709 W Bittersweet Pl Chicago IL 60613 Office: Wilson Jones Co 3201 Old Glenview Rd Wilmette IL 60091

FINKELDAY, KAREN LYNN, manufacturing executive; b. Orange, N.J., July 21, 1944; d. Gordon Dayton and Dorothy Laura (Chesseman) Mattoon; m. John Paul Finkelday, Nov. 16, 1963; 1 child, John Paul. Student, Glassboro State Coll., 1962-63, Ocean County Coll., 1978-83. Multiple listing svc. mgr. Ocean County Bd. of Realtors, Toms River, N.J., 1976-79; acct. supr. Paco Packaging Inc., Lakewood, N.J., 1980-83; office mgr. Warne Surgical Products Inc., Eatontown, N.J., 1983-84; sales mgr. TFX Medical Inc., Eatontown, N.J., 1984-86; coord. mktg. and sales Standard-Keil Mfg. Co., Allenwood, N.J., 1986-87; exec. asst. to pres. Standard-Keil Mfg. Co., Allenwood, 1987-89; mgr. United Refrigerated Svcs., Inc., Tarboro, N.C., 1989—. Creator: (advertisement) Signatures Series, 1987, Nat. Restaurant Assn., 1987, Ptnrs. for Progress, 1988; contbr. articles to profl. jours. Mem. Greenville Mus. Art. Mem. NAFE, Am. Mgmt. Assn., N.J. Bd. Realtors, U.S. Golf Assn., Greenville Country Club. Home: 3044 Dartmouth Dr Greenville NC 27858 Office: United Refrigerated Svcs Inc PO Box 7006 Tarboro NC 27886

FINKELSTEIN, MARCIA LYN, lawyer; b. N.Y.C., Dec. 27, 1961; d. Bernard and Adele (Levine) F. BA magna cum laude, U. Pa., 1983; JD, Vanderbilt Law Sch., 1986. Admitted to N.Y. State Bar. Assoc. atty. Finley, Kumble, Wagner, Heine et al, N.Y.C., Moses & Singer, N.Y.C. Mem. World Wildlife Fund, Peta, Greenpeace. Mem. ABA, N.Y. Bar Assn., Assn. Bar City N.Y. Democrat. Jewish. Home: 77 E 12th St Apt 8G New York NY 10003 Office: Moses & Singer 1271 6th Ave New York NY 10020

FINLAY, JULIE AILEEN, magazine editor; b. Columbus, Ohio, Sept. 27, 1965; d. Paul John and Joyce Marie (Lawler) Lynch; m. Jeffrey Michael Finlay, Mar. 31, 1990. BA summa cum laude with honors, Otterbein Coll., 1987. Editor Whittle Communications, Knoxville, Tenn., 1987—. Mem. Women in Communications, Inc. (v.p. pub. rels. 1990—). Democrat. Roman Catholic. Home: 2328 Spence Pl Knoxville TN 37920 Office: Whittle Communications 505 Market St Knoxville TN 37902

FINLEY, CONSTANCE, stockbroker; b. Madera, Calif., July 16, 1952; d. Roy Clifton Finley and Freda M. (Burns) Fruin; m. Jeffrey R. Allen, May 28, 1988 (div.). BA, Lone Mountain Coll., San Francisco, 1974, MA, 1974. Psychologist Our House, Inc., Greeley, Colo., 1974-77, Southeastern Colo. Mental Health Ctr., La Junta, 1978-80; sch. psychologist Aurora (Colo.) Community Mental Health Ctr., 1977-78; tng. coord., sr. legal asst. McCutchen Doyle Brown & Enersen, San Francisco, 1980-85; stockbroker Smith Barney Harris Upham & Co. Inc., Walnut Creek, Calif., 1985—; instr. psychology Lone Mountain Coll., San Francisco, 1973, Aims Community Coll., Greeley, Colo., 1974, Naropa U., 1977-78. Mem. Civic Arts Assn., Walnut Creek, 1988—. Calif. Scholarship Fedn. scholar, 1970-74. Mem. Tech. Analysts Assn. San Francisco, Contra Costa Women's Network, AAUW (treas. Walnut Creek br. 1986-88, program chmn. Ednl. Found. 1988-89, scholarship chmn. 1989—), Dalamatian Club No. Calif. Republican. Episcopalian. Office: Smith Barney Harris Upham 1600 S Main St Ste 215 Walnut Creek CA 94596

FINLEY, KATHLEEN S., nursing educator; b. Gilroy, Calif., Nov. 19, 1949; d. Richard Herman and Juanita Dell (Black) Westergard; m. James G. Pullen, Sr., June 21, 1971 (div. June 1983); 1 child, James G. Jr.; m. Glen Finley, Sept. 9, 1989. Assoc. Sci., Pacific Union Coll., 1971; BS, Walla Walla Coll., 1973; MS, U. Portland, 1981. RN; cert. nursing adminstrn., advanced. Nursing asst. St. Helena Hosp., Deer Park, Calif., 1968-69; nursing asst. Glendale Adv. Med. Ctr., Glendale, Calif., 1969-71; charge nurse Walla Walla Gen. Hosp., Walla Walla, Wash., 1971-72; staff nurse Portland Adv. Med. Ctr., Portland, Oreg., 1972-73; dir. nurses Med. Ctr. Hosp., Portland, 1973-74; edn. instr. Glendale Adv. Med. Ctr., 1974-75; asst. dir. nursing Rogue Valley Meml. Hosp., Medford, Oreg., 1975-83; v.p. nursing Feather River Hosp., Paradise, Calif., 1983-87; v.p. patient care Littleton Hosp./Porter, Littleton, Colo., 1988-90; nursing instr. Rogue Community Coll., Grants Pass, Oreg., 1990—. Mem. Assn. Seventh-day Adventist Nurses, Nat. Assn. Female Execs., Am. Orgn. Nurse Execs. Office: Rogue Community Coll 3345 Redwood Hwy Grants Pass OR 97527

FINLEY, MARION JEAN, management and marketing executive; b. Chgo., Aug. 20, 1940; d. Ernest Augustus and Nora Crawford; m. Robert Goddard Finley, Jr., June 13, 1960; children: Robert Goddard III, Laurel Jean, Alen René, Tamar G., Marya Danielle. Student, U. Chgo., 1959-61; AAS in Math., Sci., Corning Community Coll., 1973; BS in Biochemistry, Cornell U., 1975, PhD in Genetics, 1983. Editor Naval Rsch. Project, Chgo., 1960-61; editor Woodlawn Booster, Chgo., 1961-62; mng. editor Fair Lawn News, Fair Lawn, N.J., 1962-64; editor weekly newspaper Horseheads Post, Inc., Horseheads, N.Y., 1964-66; v.p. Horseheads Post, Inc., 1966-73; lectr. human genetics Cornell U., Ithaca, N.Y., 1983-84; dir. customer svc. and mktg. Transonic Systems, Inc., Ithaca, 1986-89, Innovative Dynamics, Ithaca, 1989-90; chief executive officer In Vitro Techs. Inc., Ithaca, 1990—; pres. Warren Rd. Bus. Park Mgmt. Com., Ithaca, 1988-89. Editor Transit-Times, Ithaca, 1986-88. Clk.-trustee First Unitarian Soc, Ithaca, 1986-88; pres. UU Svc. Com., Ithaca, 1986-87; bd. dirs. Ithaca Ballet, 1977-80. Scholar Am. Agriculturist Found., 1973-75; grad. fellow Cornell U., 1976, NSF predoctoral fellow, 1977-81. Unitarian-Universalist. Home: 211 Schuyler Pl Ithaca NY 14850

FINLEY, NANCY NEWTON, risk analyst; b. Waco, Tex., Feb. 28, 1942; d. Clyde Jushce and Ruby Sue (Phillips) Newton; m. James Daniel Finley III, May 26, 1962 (div. 1982); children: Ian Brendan, Moira Lynn. BS in Chemistry, U. Tex., 1963; MS in Chemistry, San Jose (Calif.) State U., 1965. Rsch. tech. U. Calif., Donner Lab., Berkeley, 1966-68; tech. staff mem. Sandia Nat. Lab., Albuquerque, 1978—; adj. prof. U. Albuquerque, 1969-78. Contbr. articles to profl. jours. Com. chair mem. First Baptist Ch., Berkeley, Calif., 1963-68, First Congl. Ch., Albuquerque, 1980—. Democrat. Home: 6808 Hildegarde NE Albuquerque NM 87109

FINN, FRANCES M., biochemistry educator; b. Pitts., May 6, 1937; d. Stephen B. and Geraldine H. (Weber) F.; m. Klaus Hofmann, Feb. 26, 1965. BS in Chemistry, U. Pitts., 1959, MS in Biochemistry, 1961, PhD in Biochemistry, 1964. Asst. rsch. prof. biochemistry U. Pitts., 1969-73, assoc. rsch. prof., 1973-80, assoc. prof. medicine, 1980-88, prof., 1988—. Mem. Am. Chem. Soc., Endocrine Soc., Am. Soc. for Biochemistry and Molecular Biology. Home: 1467 Mohican Dr Pittsburgh PA 15228 Office: U Pitts Protein Rsch Lab 3550 Terrace St Pittsburgh PA 15261

FINN, JACQUELINE MUNLEY, science administrator; b. Balt., Sept. 28, 1945; d. Michael Francis and Jacqueline Augusta (Rouchard) Munley; m. Dennis. BA, Shepherd Coll., 1978; MAS, Johns Hopkins U., 1990. Lic. med. technologist;. Medical technologist Wyman Pk. Med. Ctr., Balt., 1982, supr. hematology, 1982-86, lab. mgr., 1986-88; lab. mgr. Johns Hopkins Hosp., Balt., 1988--. Mem. Md. Soc. Med. Tech., Am. Soc. Clin. Pathologist. Democrat. Roman Catholic. Office: Homewood Hosp Ctr 2724 N Charles St Baltimore MD 21218

FINN, JOAN LOCKWOOD, public relations executive, writer, educator; b. Plainfield, N.J., June 6, 1929; d. William Albert and Ada Louise (Dayton) F. BA in Am. History, Harvard U., 1951; MA, Columbia U., 1979, EdM, 1982, EdD, 1984. Copywriter J.C. Penney Co., Inc., 1957-58; jr. account exec. Dudley-Anderson-Yutzey, 1958-61; account exec. Theodore R. Sills & Co., 1961-63, Ted Bates & Co., 1963-67; account supr. Henderson & Roll, 1967-69; dir. press rels. Motion Picture Assn. Am., N.Y.C., 1969-73; communication specialist Coopers & Lybrand, N.Y.C., 1973-78, Urban Acad. for Mgmt., Inc., N.Y.C., 1978-82, Am. Inst. CPAs, N.Y.C., 1982-84; dir. pub. rels. KMG Main Hurdman, N.Y.C., 1984-87; account mgr. Hill, Holliday, Connors & Cosmopulos, N.Y.C., 1987-88; founder, pres. Joan L. Finn Pub. Rels., N.Y.C., 1989—; instr. communication skills Mgmt. Inst. NYU, 1987-88, Bernard Baruch Grad Schs. Bus. and Pub. Adminstrn., 1987-89. Mem. Pub. Rels. Soc. Am. (accredited). Harvard Club (N.Y.C.). Democrat. Presbyterian. Author: Heritage of Evil, 1968, Kiss More, or How to Get Across in Writing, 1977; librettist: (operetta) Chicken Little, 1973; editor Diet Ann., 1973; Diet Yearbook, 1973; contbr. articles to Motor Boating, Ideal Romances, Am. Mercury, Jack O'Dwyer's Newsletter, New Ideas for Figure and Diet, Modern Maturity, Public Rels. Jour., The Profl. Report. Home: 17 W 54th St New York NY 10019 Office: 24 W 55th St Ste 7 New York NY 10019

FINN, PATRICIA ANN, chemist, engineering systems analyst; b. Oak Park, Ill.. BS, Mundelein Coll., Chgo., 1967; PhD in Phys. Inorganic Chemistry, U. Calif., Berkeley, 1971; MBA, U. Chgo., 1986. Lab. asst. Mundelein Coll., 1963-67; teaching asst. U. Calif., Berkeley, 1967-68, rsch. asst. Lawrence Berkeley Lab., 1968-71; postdoctoral Ames Lab. Iowa State U., 1972-73; postdoctoral Ames Lab. Argonne (Ill.) Nat. Lab., 1973-75, asst. chemist, 1975-79, chemist, 1979—. Contbr. articles to sci. jours. Chmn. Adopt-a-Family Program at Christmas, St. Mary's, Downers Grove, Ill., 1989-90; co-chmn. Conf. for High Sch. Students/Argonne Sponsor, Argonne Nat. Lab., 1990. Mem. Am. Nuclear Soc. (exec. bd. Chgo. sect. 1989—), Am. Ceramic Soc., Am. Chem. Soc., Assn. Women in Sci. (pres. Chgo. area chpt. 1989—), Sigma Xi. Office: Argonne Nat Lab 9700 S Cass Bldg 205 Argonne IL 60439

FINN, PENELOPE MILLER B., clinical psychologist; b. Memphis, Mar. 3, 1951; d. Milton Andrew and Elizabeth (Collinge) Miller; m. James R. Burdett, Jr., Apr. 26, 1969 (dec. July 1972); m. Charles Carroll Finn, May 21, 1977; adopted children: April Hae Dal, Adam Yau Kam. BS, U. Tenn., 1972; MA, Loyola U., Chgo., 1979, PhD, 1980. Lic. clin. psychologist, Va. Psychology cons. on med. and surg. wards VA Med. Ctr., Salem, Va., 1979-84; group leader for women ptnrs. Vietnam vets. VA Med. Ctr., 1979-83, psychotherapist for Vietnam vets. with Post Traumatic Stress Disorder, 1982-88, leader of vocat. counseling, 1984-88, psychol. assessment coord., 1988—; trainer, profl. cons. Vietnam Vets. Am. Crisis Intervention Team, Roanoke, Va., 1985-88; author, presenter state, regional, and local workshops on stress mgmt., 1983-89, on constructive use of anger, 1979-88; author, presenter paper, state, and nat. confs. on treatment women ptnrs. Vietnam vets., 1983. Troop leader Girl Scouts U.S., Mason's Knob, Va., 1983-85. Danforth fellow Danforth Found., 1972; recipient Humanitarian Svc. award DAV, Roanoke, 1980. Mem. Am. Psychol. Assn., Va. Psychol. Assn., Vietnam Vets. Am. (hon. mem., Outstanding Community Svc. award 1985). Office: VA Med Ctr 116B Salem VA 24153

FINNERTY, EILEEN, personnel director; b. Waushara, Wis., Jan. 5, 1928; d. Clifford J. and Hazel (Baitinger) F. BA, U. Wis., 1950, sr. profl. in human resources. Personnel and tng. rep. Gimbels-Midwest, Milw., 1950-58, mgr. personnel br. store, 1958-66, asst. personnel dir., 1966-76, dir. wage and benefits, 1976-78; dir. personnel T.A. Chapman Co., Milw., 1978-80, St. Norbert Coll., De Pere, Wis., 1980—; personnel cons. pvt. practice and vol., De Pere, 1980—; speaker St. Norbert Coll., De Pere, 1980—. Mem. NE Wis. Personnel Assn. (sec., treas. 1981-83), Coll. and Univ. Personnel Assn., Am. Soc. Personnel Adminstrs., Mgmt. Women, Personnel Accreditation Inst. (cert.). Democrat. Roman Catholic. Office: St Norbert Coll De Pere WI 54115

FINNEY, JOAN MARIE MCINROY, state official; b. Topeka, Feb. 12, 1925; d. Leonard L. and Mary M. (Sands) McInroy; m. Spencer W. Finney, Jr., July 24, 1957; children: Sally, Dick, Mary. B.A., Washburn U., 1974. Mem. staff U.S. Senator Frank Carlson, Topeka and Washington, 1953-69; commr. elections Shawnee County, Kans., 1970-72; adminstrv. asst. to mayor of Topeka, 1973-74; treas. State of Kans., Topeka, 1974-91; gov. State of Kans., 1991—. Bd. dirs. Hayden High Sch. Alumni Assn., Washburn Alumni Assn., Kans. Community Service orgns., St. Francis Hosp. and Med. Ctr. Aux., Mended Hearts Inc. Mem. Nat. Assn. State Auditors (pres. 1987—), Comptrollers and Treas. , Nat. Assn. State Treas., Nat. Unclaimed Property Assn., Kans. Fedn. Women's Democratic Clubs, Reinisch Rose Garden Soc., Santa Fe Railroad Ret. Employers Club, Am. Legion Aux., Sigma Alpha Iota. Roman Catholic. Office: Office of Gov State Capitol 2nd fl Topeka KS 66612-1504*

FINNEY, PAULA MANNING, counselor, educator; b. Quitman, Tex., Mar. 18, 1959; d. Paul Webster and Dene (Nevill) Manning; m. Timothy Steven Finney, June 17, 1983; 1 child, Meredith Ann. BS in Edn., Tex. Tech

U., 1980; MS, U. Houston, 1986. Tchr. Deer Park (Tex.) Ind. Sch. Dist., 1980-88, tchr. gifted students, 1983-86, counselor, 1988—. Mem. campaign Hance for Senate, Houston, 1984, Hance for Gov., Houston, 1986. Mem. Assn. Tex. Profl. Educators (sec. Deer Park chpt. 1987-88, v.p. 1988-89, pres. 1989-90), AAUW (v.p. Pasadena chpt. 1989-90), Tex. Tech Ex-Student Assn., Alpha Pi Alumnae. Home: 4207 Woodhampton Pasadena CA 77505 Office: Deer Park Ind Sch Dist 5010 Pasadena Blvd Deer Park TX 77536

FINNIGAN, CLAIRE MARIE, media specialist, librarian; b. Putnam Valley, N.Y., Sept. 4, 1923; d. William Edward and Rose Ann (Crowell) F. BS, SUNY, Geneseo, 1945; MS, Columbia U., N.Y.C., 1952, postgrad., 1963. Sch. libr. Eden (N.Y.) Cen. Sch., 1945-47, New Paltz (N.Y.) High Sch., 1947-48; sch. libr. Peekskill (N.Y.) Elem. Schs., 1948-90, ret.; libr. U.S. Naval Air Sta., Atlantic City, N.J., summer 1948; assoc. prof. Queens Coll., Flushing, N.Y., summer 1955; cons. N.Y. State Edn.l Dept., Albany, 1953-57, Franciscan High Sch., Lake Mohengan, N.Y., 1984-86. Contbr. articles to profl. jours. bd. dirs. RIF Program, Peekskill, 1972-87; sec., bd. dirs. City Mus., Peekskill, 1982-87. Recipient Svc. award Home-Sch. Coun., 1984, Leadership award Bd. of Edn., 1987. Mem. N.Y. Sch. Libr. Media Specialists (pres., sec., treas. 1953-57, Svc. award 1987), Southeastern Sch. Libr. Media Specialists (bd. dirs., sec. 1985-87), Internat. Reading Assn. (award 1982), AAUW (sec., bd. dirs. Peekskill chpt. 1962-87, Woman Achievement award 1989), Women's Club of Peekskill (sec., treas., bd. dirs. 1962-87), Delta Kappa Gamma (v.p. No. Westchester, N.Y. chpt., pres., v.p. Alpha Omicron chpt.). Home: 1 Lakeview Dr 6L Peekskill NY 10566

FINNIGAN, SHEILA ELIZABETH, artist; b. Cleve., Nov. 27, 1942; d. John Michael and Betty (Friedberg) F.; m. James H. Feldman, July 27, 1969; children: Maureen, Abigail. BA, Ohio State U., 1963; MS, UCLA, 1968; BFA, Coll. Arts and Crafts, Berkeley, Calif., 1972. Artist, Chgo., 1973-88; represented by ARC Gallery, Chgo., 1987—. One-woman shows include ARC Gallery, Chgo., 1988, 89, Noyes Cultural Art Ctr., Evanston, Ill., 1988, Countryside Art Ctr., Arlington Heights, Ill., 1989; exhibited in group shows at Oak Park (Ill.) Art League Ann. Show, 1986, NAB Gallery, 1986, Evanston & Vicinity 7th Ann. Juried Art Exhbn., 1986, Artemesia Gallery, 1986, ARC Gallery, 1986, Skokie (Ill.) Fine Arts Commn. Ann. Show, 1986, 87, Countryside (Ill.) Art Ctr., 1987, 88, 89 (1st prize), Suburban Fine Arts Ctr., 1987 (award of excellence ann. show 1987), Esther Saks Gallery, 1987, State of Ill. Art Gallery, 1988, Limelight, Chgo., 1988, ARC at Chgo. Internat. Art Exposition, 1988, ARC at Chgo. Internat. Gallery Invitational, 1990, Muse Gallery, Phila., 1989; two-person show Ohio State U., Newark campus, 1988; work featured on Sta. WGN-TV, Chgo., 1988; work appeared in Chicago Tribune mag., 1988, Chicago Art Rev., 1989, American Artists: Survey of Leading Contemporaries, 1990; reviewed in Pioneer Press, Chgo., 1989, The New Art Examiner, 1990. Mem. Nat. Acad. Recording Arts and Scis., Chgo. Press Club, Arts Club. Studio: 999 Green Bay Rd Glencoe IL 60022

FINNIS, CHERA MILLICENT, psychologist; b. Queens, N.Y., Dec. 10, 1949; d. Joseph Francis and Millicent Kathryn (O'Brien) F. BA in Social Scis., Fordham U., 1978; MS in Sch. Psychology, Pace U., 1985, D of Psychology, 1988. Lic. psychologist, N.Y. Childcare worker Srs. of the Good Shepherd, Peekskill, N.Y., 1967-74; childcare supr. Family Reception Ctr., Bklyn., 1974-75, pvt. residence, Bklyn., 1974-75; clin. coordinator Park Slope Mini Sch., Bklyn., 1975-77; program dir. St. Germaine's Group Residence, Corona, N.Y., 1977-82; coordinator of svcs. Good Shepherd Svcs., N.Y.C., 1982-83; psychology intern Pace U. Counseling Ctr., Pleasantville, N.Y., 1984-85, Downstate Med. Ctr., Bklyn., 1985-86; psychology intern Manhattan Psychiatric Ctr., N.Y.C., 1986-87, pvt. practice, 1987—; psychologist Maria Droste Svcs., N.Y.C., 1982—. Mem. Am. Psychol. Assn., Nat. Assn. Sch. Psychology, N.Y. State Psychol. Assn., Psi Chi. Roman Catholic. Home: 400 West 23 St Apt 4-J New York NY 10011 Office: Manhattan Psychiatric Ctr 600 E 125th St Meyer 2-A New York NY 10035

FINORE, DIANE, sales and marketing executive; b. Abington, Pa., Aug. 11, 1950; d. Carmen George and Anna B. (Signore) F. AS, Tobe Coburn Sch., 1972; BA cum laude, Temple U., 1974; MA, NYU, 1984. Dir. pub. rels. and spl. events Mus. Am. Folk Art, N.Y.C., 1982-85; pub. rep. Taxi Pub. Inc., N.Y.C., 1986-87; dir. sales SALES, Inc., N.Y.C., 1987-88; pres. Finore Sales & Mktg., N.Y.C., 1989—. Roman Catholic. Office: Finore Sales & Mktg 156 W 74th St New York NY 10023

FIOCCO, M. J. K., trade association administrator; b. Cleve., Nov. 18, 1953; d. John William Littlefair and Grace Elaine (MacWilliams) F. BA in Communications, Am. U., Washington, 1975. Gen. assignment reporter Morris County Daily Record, Morristown, N.J., 1975-76, Hunterdon County Dem., Flemington, N.J., 1976; asst. sales promotion dir. Bankers Security Life Ins. Soc., Washington, 1976-77; asst. editor Traffic World, Washington, 1977-79, Daily Traffic World, Washington, 1977-79; press sec. transp. subcom. Commerce Com. U.S. Ho. Reps., Washington, 1979; dir. legis. communications Nat. Indsl. Transp. League, Washington, 1979—; Mem. Womens' Transp. Seminar, Washington, 1980—. Named to Outstanding Young Women of Am., 1980. Mem. Women in Govt. Relations (co-founder, mem. transp. task force 1986—), Nat. Press Club, Propeller Club, Road Gang. Democrat. Home: 8936 Princeton Park Dr Manassas VA 22110 Office: Nat Indsl Transp League 1700 N Moore St S-1900 Arlingtonn VA 22209-1904

FIOCK, SHARI LEE, design entrepreneur, researcher; b. Weed, Calif., Oct. 25, 1941; d. Webster Bruce and Olevia May (Pruett) F.; m. June 6, 1966 (div. 1974); children—Webster Clinton Pfingsten, Sterling Curtis. Cert. Art Instrn. Sch., Mpls., 1964; pvt. student, Lic. health, life and disability, Calif. Copywriter Darron Assocs., Eugene, Oreg., 1964-66; staff artist Oreg. Holidays, Springfield, 1966-69, part-time 1971; co-owner, designer Artre Enterprises, Eugene, 1969-74; design entrepreneur Shari & Assocs., Yreka, Calif., 1974— (retained as cons., devel. sec., chief fin. officer Cascade World Four Season Resort, Siskiyou County, Calif., 1980-86); cons., pres. Reunions, Family, Yreka, 1984—. Designer 5 ton chain saw sculpture, Oreg. Beaver, 1967; illustrator: Holiday Fun Book, 1978; creator Klamath Nat. Forest Interpretive Mus., 1979—. Author, illustrator Calling All Descendants, 1986. Residential capt. United Way, Eugene, 1972; researcher Beaver Ofcl. State Animal, Eugene, 1965-71; counselor Boy Scouts, 1983—. Mem. Nat. Assn. Interpreters, Nat. Mus. of Women in the Arts, Nat. Writers Club (founder, pres. Siskiyou chpt., past v.p. State of Jefferson chpt.). Avocations: family activities; outdoor recreation; travel; theater; music. Home and Office: 406 Walter's Ln Yreka CA 96097

FIONDELLA, JUNE LEA BELL, public utility executive; b. Meriden, Conn., May 24, 1941; d. Joseph Doran and Mildred (Hourigan) Bell; m. Louis Andrew Fiondella, Sept. 2, 1963; children: Kim Lisa, Tracy Lea. B.S. in Bus. Mgmt. cum laude, Post Coll., 1983. With Northeast Utilities, Hartford, Conn., 1959—, mgr. communications svcs., 1976-80, mgr. communications and adv. services, 1980-83, mgr. communications services and spl. projects, 1983—; chmn. Electric Council N.E. Pub. Info. Com., 1982. Recpient Pres.'s Circle of Distinction for acad. excellence, Post Coll., 1982. Mem. Women in Communications (treas. 1989, bd. dirs. 1988-89), Pub. Relations Soc. Am., Internat. Assn. Bus. Communicators, Nuclear Energy Women, Pub. Utilities Communicators Assn. (pres. 1986, regional chmn. New Eng. 1983, Maple Leaf award 1984, dir.-at-large, 1988), Advt. Club Greater Hartford, Conn. Assn. Bus. Communicators, Hartford Woman's Network, Nat. Assn. Female Execs. Democrat. Roman Catholic. Home: 1414 Meriden Ave Southington CT 06489 Office: NE Utilities Box 270 Hartford CT 06141

FIORAVANTE, JANICE C., writer/editor; b. N.Y.C., Apr. 12, 1951; d. Anthony Joseph and Josephine Rose (Scavo) F. BA in English, Bklyn. Coll., 1973. Field editor Gralla Pubs., N.Y.C., 1973-79; news features editor Fairchild Pubs., N.Y.C., 1980-84; editor-in-chief Computers In Banking, N.Y.C., 1984-86; exec. editor Fin. Sys. News, Boston, 1986-87; freelance writer/cons. Link Resources, N.Y.C., 1987-88; freelance writer/editor/cons./pres. JCF Communications, S.I., N.Y., 1988—. Mem. Women in Communications (v.p. communications 1988—, newsletter editor 1989), Women's City Club (N.Y.C.). Address: 99 Burnside Ave #2 Staten Island NY 10302

FIORE, ALICE M., director curriculum and instructional services; b. Pitts., Sept. 26, 1949; d. John E. Sr. and Mary Florentine (McCullough) Hirsch. BS in Edn., Ind. U. of Pa., 1971; MA, MEd, California U., Pa., 1973; PhD, U. Pitts., 1988; postgrad., U. Dijon, France, Harvard U. Cert. supt., exec. dir., supr. spl. edn., program specialist; cert. in French, in socially and emotionally disturbed. Tchr. French Freeport (Pa.) Area Sch. Dist.; account exec., stock broker Fin. Estate Planning, Pitts.; supr. spl. edn. programs and staff devel. Westmoreland Intermediate Unit, Greensburg, Pa.; dir. instructional svcs. Montour Area School Dist., Coraopolis, Pa. Mem. Am. Assn. Sch. Adminstrs., Pa. Assn. Sch. Adminstrs., Assn. for Supervision and Curriculum Devel., MENSA, Pa. State Edn. Assn. (exec. bd. 1988-89, spl. edn. bd. 1988-89), Assn. for Children and Adults with Learning Disabilities (adv. bd. 1984-89, chairperson spl. edn. info. com. 1984-89), Trimont Condominium Assn. (social com.). Home: 3304 Fawnway Dr Murrysville PA 15668 Office: Donohue Rd RD 12 Box 205 Greensburg PA 15601

FIORE, JOAN DE WOLFE, civic leader; b. Detroit, July 15, 1924; d. Richard Perrien and Rachel Elizabeth De Wolfe; m. Pasquale Peter Fiore, Nov. 25, 1949; children: Richard, Jill. Student, UCLA. V.p. Fitness with Finesse, Inc., Houston; historian Princeton chpt. DAR, Houston, 1974-77; chmn. Ellis Island Restoration Com., Houston, 1974-77; Seimes microfilm chmn. Washington, 1977—; state regent N.J., Nat. Soc. Magna Charta Dames.; mem. Assn. of Descs. of Knights of the Garter, Windsor Castle, Eng., Gen. Soc. Mayflower Descs., Elder William Brewster Soc.; historian First Colony of Mayflower Descs., Plantagenet Kings of Eng. Soc., Sovereign Colonial Soc. Americans of Royal Descent, Richard 3d Soc., Nat. Soc. Colonial Dames of XVII Century, Japan Soc. Vol. chmn. Med. Ctr., Princeton, N.J., 1960-77; Natural History Mus., N.Y.C., Nat. Trust Historic Preservation; mem. Whale Adoption Project, Falmouth, Mass., Kingswood Girl Sch. Alumnus Fund, Cranbrook, Med. Ctr. Princeton Aux.; mem. The Hageman Farm Restoration Fund, Middlebush, N.J. Mem. DAR (Princeton chpt. historian), Ex-Regent's Club of DAR, Colonial Order of the Crown, Emperor of The West, Present Day Club (Princeton). Mem. Soc. of Friends. Home: 18 Sturgis Rd Kendall Park NJ 08824

FIORELLA, BEVERLY JEAN, medical technologist, educator; b. Owensboro, Ky., Oct. 29, 1930; d. Gabriel and Agnes Loretta (Kurz) F. BS, Webster Coll./St. Louis U., 1952; MA, Cen. Mich. U., 1976. Chief microbiology and blood bank St. Mary's Hosp., Kansas City, Mo., 1956-67; instr., asst. prof. med. lab. scis. dept. Coll. Assoc. Health Professions, U. Ill., Chgo., 1967-74, assoc. prof., 1974-80, prof., 1980—, assoc. head dept. med. lab. scis., 1977-90, acting dept. head, 1990—, grad. program coord., 1977-81; mem. adv. panel on health ins. Subcom. Health of Com. on Ways and Means, Ho. of Reps., 1975-80; cons. lab. improvement sect. immunohematology divs. labs. Dept. Pub. Health State of Ill., 1975-85; cons. editor Clin. Lab. Scis., 1987—. Mem. bd. editors Med. Tech.-A Series, 1970-74. Named Med. Technologist of Yr., Mo. Soc. Med. Technologists, 1967. Mem. Am. Soc. Med. Tech. (pres. 1976-77), Am. Assn. Blood Banks, Ill. Med. Tech. Assn. (exec. sec. 1987—, named Ill. Med. Technologist of Yr. 1976), Chgo. Soc. Med. Technologists (treas., dir. 1969-70), Chicagoland Blood Bank Soc. (v.p. 1975-76), Internat. Assn. Med. Lab. Technologists (coun. 1988—), Acad. Clin. Lab. Physicians and Scientists, Am. Soc. Allied Health Professions, Internat. Soc. Clin. Lab. Tech., Alpha Mu Tau. Office: U Ill Chgo Dept Med Lab Scis M/C 518 PO Box 6998 Chicago IL 60680

FIPPINGER, GRACE J., telecommunications company executive; b. N.Y.C., Nov. 24, 1927; d. Fred Herman and Johanna Rose (Tesio) F. BA, St. Lawrence U., 1948; LLD (hon.), Marymount Manhattan Coll., 1980; DCS (hon.), Molloy Coll., 1982; DHL, St. Lawrence U., 1990. Dist. mgr. N.Y. Tel. Co., South Nassau, 1957-65, div. mgr., 1965-71; gen. comml. mgr. N.Y. Tel. Co., Queens, 1971—, Bklyn., 1973—; v.p., sec., treas. N.Y. Tel. Co., 1974-84; v.p., treas., sec. NYNEX Corp., N.Y.C., 1984—; mem. Manhattan East adv. bd. Mfrs. Hanover Trust Co.; bd. dirs. Conn. Mut. Life Ins., Paramount Inc., Apple Bank for Savs., Bear Stearns Co., Pfizer, Inc. Former mem. State Manpower Adv. Council; former mem. Gov.'s Econ. Devel. Adv. Council; past bd. dirs. Consumer Credit Counseling Service Greater N.Y., 1972—; hon. bd. dirs. Am. Cancer Soc., 1974—, YMCA Greater N.Y., 1975—; former dir. A.R.C., L.I., Nassau County Health and Welfare Council; trustee Citizens Budget Commn., 1974—; former dir. exec. bd. Nassau County Fedn. Republican Women. Named Woman of Yr., Bus. and Profl. Women Nassau County, 1969, Woman of Achievement, Flatbush Bus. and Profl. Women's Assn., 1974, Woman of Yr., Soroptimist Club Nassau County; hon. mem. Soroptimist Club Central Nassau, 1974; recipient John Peter Zenger award Nassau County Press Assn., 1975, Outstanding Bus. Women of 1977 award Marymount Manhattan Coll., 1978; honoree Catalyst Inc., 1977, Women's Equity Action League, 1978, Republican Women in Bus. and Industry, Cath. Med. Ctr. Bklyn./Queens, 1983, Girl Scouts, 1984, Clark Garden, L.I., 1985. Mem. Am. Mgmt. Assn. (former trustee and mem. exec. com.), Nat. Assn. Corp. Treas., Fin. Execs. Inst., Am. Soc. Corp. Secs., Am. Soc. Corp. Treas. Inc., Fin. Womens Assn. N.Y., N.Y. Chamber Commerce and Industry (chmn. mems. council 1977-79), L.I. Assn., Nat. Women's Econ. Alliance., Ladies Profl. Golf Assn. (hon.). Clubs: St. Lawrence of L.I. (N.Y.C.), Columbus, Board Room (N.Y.C.). Office: Nynex Corp 335 Madison Ave New York NY 10017

FIRE, RITA, toy manufacturing executive. BS, Ind. U., 1964. With Mattel, Inc., 1966-69, 73-79, 87—, now sr. v.p.; with Dean Witter Reynolds, 1969-70, Hunt Wesson Foods, 1970-73; owner Rita Fire Mktg., 1979-82; pres. Creata Internat., 1982-86; v.p. Arco Toys, 1986-87. Office: Mattel Inc 5150 Rosecrans Ave Hawthorne CA 90250*

FIRESTONE, DEBRA KAY, food service executive; b. Dayton, Ohio, July 6, 1958; d. Lowell Eric and Doris Ilene (Ward) Richards; m. Alfred Eugene Firestone, Oct. 25, 1987. AS in Applied Scis., Sinclair Community Coll., Dayton, 1981; BS in Tech., Bowling Green State U., 1987; sanitation-safety cert., Nat. Sanitation Found. Waitress Denny's Inc., Dayton, 1980-83, svc. coord., 1983-86, 87-88; asst. to supr. Bowling Green (Ohio) State U. Food Svc., 1985-86; banquet and catering mgr. Hara Arena Food Svc., Dayton, 1988; mgr. dining room One Lincoln Park Retirement Community, Kettering, Ohio, 1988-89; mgr. Denny's Restaurant, Springfield, Ill., 1989—. Mem. NAFE, Nat. Restaurant Assn.

FIRESTONE, ELAINE RUTH, information management and employee relations executive; b. Phila., June 5, 1959; d. Abraham I. and Frances (Reitenberg) Kimmel; m. James K. Firestone, Oct. 24, 1982; 1 child, Jason. BS, Pa. State U., 1981; postgrad., U.S. Dept. Agr. Grad Sch.; tchr.'s cert., Gratz Coll., Phila., 1979. Notary pub. Asst. to pres. Rsch. Analysis Inst., Jessup, Md., 1982-83; psychiat. coord. Columbia (Md.) Med. Plan, 1983-86; office mgr. Gen. Scis. Corp., Laurel, Md., 1986-88, corp. site coord., 1988-89, corp. info. mgr., 1989—. Mem. NAFE, Assn. Info. Mgmt. Home: 9517 Lumberjack Row Columbia MD 21046 Office: Gen Scis Corp 6100 Chevy Chase Dr Laurel MD 20707

FIRESTONE, ESTHER VIOLET, counselor; b. Xilitla, San Luis, Mex., Dec. 15, 1950; d. Ezequiel and Ruth May (Tijerina) Cepeda; m. Ronald Lee Firestone, Dec. 27, 1969; children: LeMel, Homer. AA in Social Sci., Pasadena City Coll., 1982; BA in Social Sci., Thomas Edison Jr. Coll., 1985; MA in Psychology, Nat. U., 1986. Vocat. nurse various hosps., Glendale, Calif., 1971-74; missionary nurse Ch. of God, Bolivia, 1974-78; nurse acute care unit various hosps., Riverside, Calif., 1978-79; office mgr., physiotherapist Firestone Chiropractic Clinic, Riverside and Yucca Valley, Calif., 1979—; exec. dir. Vacation Samaritans, Yucca Valley, 1984-85; psychotherapist Morongo Mental Health, Yucca Valley, 1986—; conv. speaker numerous chs. and orgns., 1974—; tchr. Bible study groups, Bolivia, U.S., 1974—. Leadership scholar Nat. U., 1986. Mem. Calif. Assn. Marriage and Family Therapists. Republican. Lodge: Soroptomist. Home: 57610 Crestview Dr Yucca Valley CA 92284

FIRESTONE, JUDITH HALL, small business owner; b. Miami, Fla., Mar. 4, 1945; d. Richard Bernard and Martha (McConnell) H.; m. Sheridan Wayne Kellogg, Feb. 22, 1968 (div. May, 1976); 1 child, Jeffry Stanley; m. Harvey Bernard Firestone, Dec. 27, 1980. BS, U. N.C., 1967; MEd, U. Del., 1975. System engr. IBM, Providence, R.I., 1967-68; tchr. Math., guidance counselor Wilmington (Del.) Friends Sch., 1968-76; dir. customer support Johnson Systems, McLean, Va., 1976-78; dir. mktg. Computer Related Svcs., Norfolk, Va., 1978-86; owner, mgr. Computer Related Svcs. North, Cleve., 1986—. Mem. Women's Bus. Owners Assn. (chmn. Trade Show, 1988, 89, bd. dirs. 1989—, 1st v.p., 1990—, vol. of year 1988-89). Democrat. Jewish. Home: 19020 Brewster Rd Aurora OH 44202 Office: Computer Related Svcs N 5910 Harper Rd Solon OH 44139

FIRESTONE, LYNN MARIE, elementary school principal; b. Ottawa, Kans., Jan. 27, 1941; d. Robert M. and Pearl E. Melton. BA, Ottawa U., 1962; MS, Emporia State U., 1967; PhD, Kans. State U., 1987. Cert. elem. tchr. K-9; cert. in social studies and English Grades 7-9. Elem. tchr. Unified Sch. Dist. 501, Topeka, 1962-82, middle sch.tchr., 1982-84; elem. prin. Unified Sch. Dist. 292, DeSoto, Kans., 1984-87, Unified Sch. Dist. 231, Gardner, Kans., 1987—. Mem. Nat. Assn. Elem. Sch. Prins., Kans. Assn. Elem. Sch. Prins., Am. Assn. Sch. Adminstrs., Assn. for Supervision and Curriculum Devel., Phi Delta Kappa. Methodist. Home: 10422 Goddard #235 Overland Park KS 66030 Office: Gardner Elem. 218 E Shawnee Gardner KS 66030

FIRTH, ANNE CATHERINE, realtor; b. Modesto, Calif., Apr. 4, 1947; d. Raymond Albert and Catherine Marie (Bone) F. Student, St. Josephs, San Francisco, 1968; student, San Francisco City Coll., 1977-79. RN, Calif. RN Georgetown U. Hosp., Washington, 1968-71; lt. USN San Diego Naval Hosp., 1971-73; RN Presbyn. Med. Ctr., San Francisco, 1973-79; sales and tech. svcs. rep. Wampole Labs. Div., Carter Wallace, N.J., 1979-81; product mgr. Wampole Labs. Div., Cranbury, N.J., 1981-82; spl. projects rep. PW Communications, N.Y.C., 1982-84; dir. spl. projects Transmedica/CBS, N.Y.C., 1984-85; realtor Cornish & Carey, Inc., Burlingame, Calif., 1985—; speaker career counseling Notre Dame High Sch., Salinas, Calif., 1974-76. Fundraiser Ctr. for Abuse Prevention, San Mateo, Calif. Named Vendor of Yr. No. Calif., VWR Scientific, 1980. Mem. Nat. Assn. Female Execs. Democrat. Roman Catholic. Home: 725 Farringdon Ln Burlingame CA 94010 Office: Cornish & Carey 360 Primrose Burlingame CA 94010

FISCELLA, MARY ANN, chiropractor; b. Bronx, N.Y., Apr. 24, 1960; d. Vincent Secondo and Carmela (Moderato) F.; m. Steven F. Vaccarella, June 2, 1990. BS in Nursing, Mt. St. Mary Coll., Newburgh, N.Y., 1982; D of Chiropractic, Life Chiropractic Coll., Marietta, Ga., 1985. Assoc. chiropractor Summit Chiropractic Ctr., East Rutherford, N.J., 1986-87; ptnr. Family Chiropractors of Ridgewood, N.J., 1987—. Mem. Internat. Chiropractic Pediatric Assn., Coun. N.J. Chiropractors, Ridgewood C. of C., Mt. St. Mary Coll. Alumni Assn., Life Chiropractic Coll. Alumni Assn. Roman Catholic. Home: 1349 Cranberry Ct Mahwah NJ 07430 Office: Family Chiropractors 20 Wilsey Sq Ridgewood NJ 07450

FISCHER, CHARLOTTE G., retail specialty chain executive; b. Hagerstown, Md., July 27, 1949; d. Charles A. Sr. and Charlotte (Green) Gibney; m. Stanley H. Fischer, Oct. 1, 1978. BS in Bus., Va. Commonwealth U., Richmond, 1971. Buyer Hochschild Kohn, Balt., 1970-76, Bloomingdale's, N.Y.C., 1976-78; mdse. mgr. Howland/Steinbach, White Plains, N.Y.C., 1978-82; v.p., gen. mdse. mgr., Picadilly Lucky Stores, Dublin, Calif.; v.p., gen. mdse. mgr., Sizes Unlimited The Limited, Secaucus, N.J., 1982-86; pres., chief operating officer, Claire's Boutiques Claire's Stores, Inc., Wood Dale, Ill., 1986--. Recipient: Guest of Honor United Jewish Appeal Fedn. of Greater N.Y.C. (Costume Jewelry Div.). Mem. Com. of 200, The Fashion Group, Nat. Retail Merchants Assn., Shopping Ctr. World Adv. Bd. Office: Claire's Boutiques Inc 1501 N Michael Dr Wood Dale IL 60191

FISCHER, DALE SUSAN, lawyer; b. East Orange, N.J., Oct. 17, 1951; d. Edward L. and Audrey (Tenner) F. BA magna cum laude, U. So. Fla., 1977; JD, Harvard U., 1980; student Dickinson Coll., 1969-70. Bar: Calif. 1980. Ptnr. law firm Kindel & Anderson, Los Angeles, 1980—; lawyer in classroom Constl. Rights Found. Mem. Legal adv. bd. Sr. Care Network. Mem. ABA, Am. Arbitration Assn. (mem. panel arbitrators), Los Angeles County Bar Assn. Home: 3695 Hampton Rd Pasadena CA 91107 Office: Kindel and Anderson 555 S Flower Los Angeles CA 90071

FISCHER, FAYNE HIRSH, audiologist; b. Macon, Ga., Feb. 3, 1965; d. Alvin Gerald and Elaine (Estroff) Hirsh; m. Daniel Bruce Fischer, Nov. 4, 1989. BA, U. Md., 1987; MA, U. Conn., 1989. Cert. clin. competence in audiology. Audiologist Leonard P. Berenholz, M.D., Phila., 1989—, Albert Einstein Med. Ctr., Phila., 1989—. Mem. Am. Speech and Hearing Assn. Home: 100 Essex Ct Lansdale PA 19446

FISCHER, IRENE KAMINKA, retired research geodesist, mathematician; b. Vienna, Austria, July 27, 1907; came to U.S., 1941; d. Armand and Clara (Loewy) Kaminka; m. Eric Fischer, Dec. 21, 1930; children: Gay A., Michael M.J. MA, U. Vienna, 1931; postgrad., Georgetown U., 1950-57; D. in Engring., U. Karlsruhe, Fed. Republic Germany, 1975. Tchr. secondary schs. Vienna, 1931-38; tchr. secondary schs. and colls. Washington, N.Y., Mass., 1941-45; researcher MIT, Cambridge, Mass., 1942-44; rsch. geodesist Army Map Svc., Def. Mapping Agy., Washington, 1952-77. Author: Geometry, 1965, Basic Geodesy, The Geoid--What's That?, 1973; contbr. hunreds of articles to profl. jours. Recipient Nat. Civil Svc. League Career award Civil Svc. League, 1976; named Fed. Retiree of Yr. Nat. Assn. Retired Fed. Employees, 1978. Fellow Am. Geophys. Union; mem. Nat. Acad. Engring., Internat. Assn. Geodsy (sec. sect. V 1963-71, chmn. study groups 1963-75). Home: 301 Philadelphia Ave Takoma Park MD 20912

FISCHER, LYNN SUZANNE, space systems engineer; b. Buffalo, Sept. 16, 1951; d. Alfred Norman and Jane Louise (Wagner) F. Student, So. Ill. U., 1970-75; BS in Physics, U. Ariz., 1977; postgrad., Calif. Inst. Tech., 1982-83, 86. Radio telescope operator Nat. Radio Astronomy Obs., Tucson, 1975-76; optical engr. Hughes Aircraft Co., Culver City, Calif., 1978-79; engr. NASA's radio astronomy program Jet Propulsion Lab., Pasadena, Calif., 1979-81, engr. meteorol. microwave, 1981, infrared data analyst IRAS, 1981-84, mem. Galileo fields and particles sci. team, 1984-85, sci. coord., software engr., 1985-87, astrometry asst., 1987; co-founder, engring. mgr. L-Com Ltd. Aircraft Intercoms, Pasadena, 1982-84; founder L-Com Tech. Design, Glendale, Calif., 1987—; astrometry asst. Univ. Calif. at L.A., 1978; pub. speaker Jet Propulsion Lab., 1982-87. Author: Galileo MAGPAC User's Guide, 1988; lead guitarist all girl rock and roll band The Honeyshoppe, 1965-68. Precinct officer L.A. County Registrar-Recorder, Altadena, 1988; pres. Caltech's Amnesty Internat. Group, Pasadena, 1981-83; tchr. Sunday sch. St. Elizabeth Ch., Altadena, 1984; sponsoring mem. Com. Concerned Scientists; coord. police dept's Local Neighborhood Watch Program, Glendale. Recipient Group Achievement award NASA, 1984, JPL Speakers Bur. awards, 1984, 86; named Outstanding Toastmaster of Yr., 1983. Mem. AAAS, Am. Inst. Physics, Am. Astron. Soc., Am. Geophys. Union, Orange County Astronomers, Planetary Soc. Home: 1113 Boynton St Glendale CA 91205

FISCHER, MARSHA LEIGH, civil engineer; b. San Antonio, May 9, 1955; d. Joe Henry and Ellen Joyce (Flake) F. BSCE, Tex. A&M U., 1977. Engring. asst. Tex. Dept. Hwys. and Transp., Dallas, 1977-79; outside plant engr. Southwestern Bell Telephone Co., Dallas, 1979-82, staff mgr. for budgets, 1982-84; engring. mgr. Southwestern Bell Telephone Co., Wichita Falls, Tex., 1984-86; mgr. facilities assignment Southwestern Bell Telephone Co., Ft. Worth, 1986-88; dist. mgr. local provisioning applications Bell Communications Rsch., Piscataway, N.J., 1988—. Mem. NSPE, Tex. Soc. Profl. Engrs., Tex. Soc. Civil Engrs., Profl. Engrs. in Industry, Tex. A&M Assn. Former Students. Republican. Home: 2 Exeter Rd Bedminster NJ 07921 Office: Bellcore 444 Hoes Ln RRC 1D353 Piscataway NJ 08854

FISCHER, MARY DEAN DUNN, secondary education educator; b. Etowah, Tenn., Mar. 3, 1928; d. Ben H. and Lois (Newman) Dunn; children: Nancy, Kenneth David, Richard, Sue Ann. BS, U. Nebr., 1981; MA, Calif. State U., San Bernardino, 1989; student, Los Andes U., Bogota, Colombia, 1970. Cert. tchr. English, social science, ESL. Tchr. Colegio Nueva Granado, Bogota; cons. ESL and basic edn. S.E. Community Coll., Lincoln, Nebr.; tchr., chmn. dept. English San Bernardino City Unified Sch. Dist.; cons. adult edn. Osceola Sch.Dist., Kissimmee, Fla. Author: Handbook for Teachers of English as a Second Language. Recipient Bilingual Svc. award San Bernardino C. of C. Mem. Internat. Reading Assn., Nat. Coun. Tchrs. English, Calif.Tchrs. Assn. Home: 3274 C Little Mountain Dr San

Bernardino CA 92405 Office: San Gorgonio High Sch 2299 E Pacific St San Bernardino CA 92404

FISCHER, THERESE MARIE, educator; b. Lead, S.D., Mar. 24, 1911; d. Ludwig Henry and Catherine (Volbach) Stadler; m. Carl Michael Fischer. BA with Distinction, San Jose State Coll., 1966; MEd, U. Oreg., 1970. Spl. edn. tchr. Los Altos (Calif.) Sch. Dist., 1966-76; edn. specialist Los Altos, 1976-85; dir. Coastside Adult Literacy, Half Moon Bay, Calif., 1985—. Mem. Bilingual Soc., Half Moon Bay, 1989. Mem. AAUW, Phi Kappa Phi. Roman Catholic. Home: 10 Sunset Terr Half Moon Bay CA 94019

FISCHLER, PAMELA FRAN, advertising agency executive; b. Bklyn., Sept. 25, 1951; s. Martin Lee and Gilda Augusta (Gerber) G.; m. Burton Fischler, July 3, 1973. Student Stephens Coll., 1969-71; BA, Hofstra U., 1973. New acct. exec. Unique Security Agy., Great Neck, N.Y., 1973-75; career counselor, acct. exec. Dartmouth Cons., N.Y.C., 1975; acct. liaison MGA, Inc., Advt., Great Neck, N.Y., 1975-76, v.p. pub. relations and media, 1977-80, exec. v.p., 1980-89; exec. v.p. Mktg. Svcs. Group, Inc., Westbury, N.Y., 1989—. Bd. dirs. Soc. of Friends of Touro synagogue, Newport, R.I. Democrat. Jewish. Home: 15 Yankee Hill Rd Ridgefield CT 06877 Office: Mktg Svcs Group Inc 28 Urban Ave Westbury NY 11590

FISCHLER, SHIRLEY BALTER, lawyer; b. Bklyn., Oct. 9, 1926; d. David and Rose (Shapiro) Balter; m. Abraham Saul Fischler, Apr. 9, 1949; children: Bruce Evan, Michael Alan, Lori Faye. BA, Bklyn. Coll., 1947, MA, 1951; JD, Nova U., Ft. Lauderdale, Fla., 1977. Bar: Fla. 1977, D.C. 1980, U.S. Ct. Appeals (D.C. cir.) 1980. Tchr., N.Y.C. Bd. Edn., 1948-50, Richmond (Calif.) Pub. Schs., 1965-66; assoc. Panza, Maurer, Maynard, Platow & Neel, Ft. Lauderdale, 1977—; pro bono atty. Broward Lawyers Care, 1982-86. Mem. South Broward Guild Philharm. Orch. Fla; bd. govs. Nova. U. Law Ctr., 1982—; mem. Commn. on Status of Women, Broward County, Fla., 1982-87, vice chair, 1983-84. Mem. Fla. Bar Assn., D.C. Bar Assn., Broward County Bar Assn. Home: 5000 Taylor St Hollywood FL 33021 Office: Panza Maurer Maynard Platow & Neel 3081 E Commercial Blvd Fort Lauderdale FL 33308

FISCHLOWITZ, BARBARA PARKER, non-profit executive; b. St. Louis, Nov. 12, 1946; d. John Louis and Gertrude Mary (Beyer) Parker; m. Merle Fischlowitz, Apr. 4, 1971; children: Benjamin Parker, Sara. BA, Elmhurst (Ill.) Coll., 1968; MA in Edn., George Washington U., 1973. Vol. Peace Corps, Trust Terriory Pacific Is, 1968-70; counselor St. Louis Sch. Nursing, 1970-71; tchr. Israeli Pub. Schs., Haifa, 1971; lectr. U. Hawaii, Honolulu, 1976-83; personnel officer Youth for Understanding, Washington, 1983-84; exec. dir. Epilepsy Found. Hawaii, Honolulu, 1984-89, Jewish Fedn. Hawaii, Honolulu, 1989—; bd. dirs. Hawaii Literacy, 1987-89; project dir. Women-U.S.A.-Hawaii, 1981, neighborhood bd. chmn., 1984-86. Producer (TV documentary) God's Ballot. Cand. Ho. of Reps., State of Hawaii, 1986; chmn. Honolulu County Com. on Status of Women, 1989—; v.p. WIN-PAC, Honolulu, 1989—; mem. Office of Disciplinary Coun., Honolulu, 1988; bd. dirs. Epilepsy Found. Hawaii, 1989—; commr. Martin LutherKing Jr. Commn., State of Hawaii, 1990—. Recipient Nat. Merit Alumni award, Elmhurst Coll., 1987, Woman of Distinction, City and County of Honolulu, 1982. Mem. AaUW (bd. dirs. 1987-89), Hawaii Women's Consortium (pres. 1987-88), Outstanding Women Leaders Assn. Democrat. Jewish.

FISCHMAN, MYRNA LEAH, accountant, educator; b. N.Y.C.; d. Isidore and Sally (Goldstein) F. BS, Coll. City N.Y., 1960, MS, 1964; PhD, NYU 1976; CPA, N.Y. Asst. to contr. Sam Goody, Inc., N.Y.C.; tchr. accounting Ctr. Comml. High Sch., N.Y.C., 1960-63, William Cullen Bryant High Sch., Queens, N.Y., 1963-66, vocat. adviser, 1963-66; instr. acctg. Borough of Manhattan Community Coll., N.Y.C., 1966-69; self employed acct., N.Y.C., 1960—; chief acct. investigator rackets, Office Queens Dist. Atty., 1969-70, community rels. coord., 1970-71; adj. prof. L.I. U., 1970-79, prof. acctg. taxation and law, 1979—, coord. grad. capstone courses, 1982-86, dir. Sch. Profl. Accountancy Bklyn. campus, 1984—; dir. Faculty Acctg. Taxation and Law Bklyn. campus, 1986—. Editor Ea. Bus. Educators Jour., 1988. Rsch. cons. pre-tech. program Bd. Edn., City N.Y.; acct.-adviser Inst. for Advancement of Criminal Justice; acct.-cons. Coalition Devel. Corp., Interracial Coun. for Bus. Opportunities; treas. Breakfree Inc., Lower East Side Prep. Sch.; mem. edn. task force Am. Jewish Com., 1972—; mem. steering com., youth div. N.Y. Dem. County Com., 1967-68, del. to Nat. Conv., Young Dems. Am., 1967, rep. assigned to women's activities com., 1967; mem. Chancellor Com. Against Discrimination in Edn., 1976—; chmn. supervisory com. Fed. Credit Union #1532, N.Y.C., 1983—; mem. legis. adv. bd. N.Y. State Assemblyman Denis Butler, 1979—; chmn. consumer coun. Astoria Med. Ctr., 1980—; mem. subcom. on bus. edn. to the econ. devel. and mktg. com. Bklyn. C. of C., 1984—. Recipient award for meritorious service Community Svc. Soc., 1969; C.P.A., N.Y. Mem. Jewish Guild for Blind, Jewish Braille Inst., Friends Am. Ballet Theatre, Friends Met. Mus. Art, Community Welfare Com., Assn. Govt. Accts. (bd. dirs. N.Y. chpt. 1984—, dir. rsch. and manuscripts 1985—, pres. elect N.Y. chpt. 1989-90), Am. Acctg. Assn., Am. Inst. CPAs, Nat., Eastern (co-chmn. ann. meeting 1967) bus. edn. assns., Nat., Eastern (chmn. ann. meeting, 1968) bus. tchrs. assns., Internat. Soc. Bus. Edn., Grad. Students Orgn. NYU (treas. 1971-73, v.p. 1973-74), Nat. Assn. Accts. (dir. N.Y. chpt. 1983—), Assn. Govt. Accts. (dir. N.Y. chpt. 1983—, pres. elect N.Y. chpt. 1989-90), NEA, AAUP, Doctorate Assn. N.Y. Educators (v.p. 1975—), Am. Assn. Jr. Colls., Young Alumni Assn.; chmn. supervisory com. Fed. Credit Union #1532, N.Y.C., 1983—; Coll. (mem. coun.), Emanu-El League Congregation Emanu-El, N.Y. (chmn. community svcs. com. 1967-68), N.Y. State Soc. CPAs (mem. com. on recruitment for CPA careers 1981—), Nat. Assn. Accts. (bd. dirs. N.Y. chpt. 1985—, dir. profl. devel. 1986-87, dir. pub. rels. 1987-88), Tax Inst. L.I. U. (dir. Bklyn. chpt. 1984—), Women's City Club (N.Y.C.), Delta Pi Epsilon (treas. 1976). Jewish. Democrat. Developed new bus. machine course and curriculum Borough Manhattan Bus. Community Coll. Office: LI U Zeckendorf Campus Brooklyn NY 11201

FISCINA, ELIZABETH GLADYS, hotel industry administrator; b. Kew Gardens, N.Y., Mar. 27, 1944; d. Elizabeth C. Gaddis; m. Peter J. Fiscina; children: Vincent P. Musac, Elizabeth D. Musac, Metz. Grad., L.I. Beauty Sch., Hempstead, N.Y., 1978. Lic. hairdresser. Cosmetologist, 1978; adminstrv. asst. I.W. Industries, Melville, N.Y., 1983-85; exec. housekeeper Woodcrest Club, Syosset, N.Y., 1986-87; head housekeeper Seawanhaka Corinthian Yacht Club, Centre Island, N.Y., 1987-88; exec. housekeeper Royal Inn Motor Lodge, Manhasset, N.Y., 1989—. Home: 7 E Main St Oyster Bay NY 11771

FISH, BARBARA, psychiatrist, educator; b. N.Y.C., July 31, 1920; d. Edward R. and Ida (Citrin) F.; m. Max Saltzman, Dec. 12, 1953; children: Mark, Ruth Saltzman Deutsch. B.A. summa cum laude, Barnard Coll., Columbia U., 1942; M.D., NYU, 1945. Diplomate Am. Bd. Psychiatry and Neurology, Am. Bd. child psychiatry. Intern Bellevue Hosp., N.Y.C., 1945-47, resident in pediatrics, 1948-49, resident in psychiatry, 1949-52; resident in pediatrics N.Y. Hosp., N.Y.C., 1947-48; practice medicine specializing in child psychiatry N.Y.C., 1952-65; instr. psychiatry Med. Coll Cornell U., N.Y.C., 1955-60; instr. pediatrics Cornell U., 1955-56, asst. prof. clin. pediatrics, 1956-60; child psychiatrist dept. pediatrics N.Y. Hosp.-Cornell Med. Center, 1955-60; mem. faculty William A. White Inst. Psychoanalysis, N.Y.C., 1957-66; assoc. prof. psychiatry sch. medicine N.Y. U., N.Y.C., 1960-70; prof. N.Y. U., 1970-72, adj. prof., 1972—, dir. child psychiatry med. ctr., 1960-72; prof. psychiatry and behavioral sci. UCLA, 1972-89, Della Martin prof. psychiatry and behavioral sci., 1989—; mem. advisory com. mental health services for children N.Y.C. Community Mental Health Bd., 1963-72; mem. profl. advisory com. on children N.Y. State Dept. Mental Hygiene, 1966-72; mem. com. cert. child psychiatry Am. Bd. Psychiatry and Neurology, 1969-77; mem. clin. program projects research rev. com. NIMH, 1976-78. Contbr. articles on the antecedents of schizophrenia and other severe mental disorders, and on the psychiat. diagnosis and treatment of children; mem. editorial bd.: Jour. Am. Acad. Child Psychiatry, 1966-71, Jour. Autism and Childhood Schizophrenia, 1971-74, Child Devel. Abstracts and Bibliography, 1974-82, Archives Gen. Psychiatry, 1975-84. Recipient Woman of Sci. award UCLA, 1978; NIMH grantee, 1961-72, 78-88, Harriett A. Ames Charitable Trust grantee, 1961-66, William T. Grant Found. grantee, 1977-83, Scottish Rite schizophrenia rsch. grantee, 1979-87. Fellow Am. Psychiat. Assn. (Agnes McGavin award 1987), Am. Acad. Child Psychiatry, Am. Coll. Neuropsychopharmacology (charter); mem. Am. Psychopath. Assn. (v.p. 1967-68), Assn. for Research in Nervous and Mental Diseases, Soc. Research in Child Devel., Psychiat. Research Soc. Home: 16428 Sloan Dr Los Angeles CA 90049-1157 Office: UCLA Neuropsychiat Inst 760 Westwood Pla Los Angeles CA 90024-1759

FISH, HELEN THERESE, educator, author; b. Mpls., Mar. 17, 1944; d. John Howard and Helen Therese (Ochs) Berg; m. Ronald Bruce Fish, Oct. 13, 1967; children: Eric James, Angela Diane, Christine Ann. BS, U. Minn., Mpls., 1966; postgrad., U. Minn., Mankato, 1969-70, U. Wis., Whitewater, 1970-72; MEd, Brenau Coll., 1986; postgrad., U. Ga., 1988—. Cert. elem. tchr., Minn., Wis., Ill., Kans., Ga. Tchr. kindergarten Lincoln Hills Sch., Mpls., 1966-68, Mapleton (Minn.) Pub. Schs., 1968-69; tchr. 1st grade Hoover Sch., Mankato, 1969-70; kindergarten tchr. Todd Sch., Beloit, Wis., 1970-73; tchr. presch., K-1 Wilson Sch., Janesville, Wis., 1973-75; tchr. gifted and reading specialist (remedial) Lakewood Sch., Park Forest, Ill., 1975-77; tchr. kindergarten, 1st and 3d grades Sibley Sch., Albert Lea, Minn., 1977-82; tchr. kindergarten Most Pure Heart Sch., Topeka, 1983-85; tchr. kindergarten Enota Sch., Gainesville, Ga., 1985-88, chronicler Danforth grant, 1988—; adj. asst. prof. Brenau Coll., Gainesville, 1988—; cons. and field test tchr. Rsch. and Devel. Ctr. U. Wis., Madison, 1970-79, Ency. Britannica Edn. Corp.; workshop leader for adminstrs. and tchrs. in Pre-Reading Skills; demonstration tchr. Internat. Reading Assn. Conv., New Orleans, 1975. Author: Starting Out Well: A Parent's Approach to Exercise and Nutrition, 1989; editor Y's Menettes newsletter, 1971-75. Sec., treas. PTA, Mpls, Mankato, Albert Lea, Beloit, Janesville, Park Forest, Topeka, Gainesville; leader Girl Scouts U.S., Blue Birds, Topeka; softball coach, Gainesville. Recipient award for contbns. to edn. and participation in Tchr. in Space Program NASA, 1986; Cert. of World Leadership, Cambridge, Eng., 1990. Mem. Ga. Edn. Assn., Assn. for Supervision and Curriculum Devel., Ga. Presch. Assn., Internat. Platform Assn., Pi Lamda Theta (Hon. Teaching Soc. award). Republican. Roman Catholic. Home: 3650 Brown Well Ct Gainesville GA 30501 Office: Enota Sch Enota Ave W Gainesville GA 30501

FISH, JEANNE SPENCER, artist, retired lawyer; b. Sedan, Ks., Jan. 15, 1921; d. Charles William and Lena (Hall) Spencer; m. Robert Irwin Fish, Jan. 6, 1947. BA, U. Kans., 1942, JD, 1945; BA in Art, Humboldt State U., 1974. Bar: Ks. 1945. Assoc. C.W. Spencer, Atty. at Law, Sedan, 1945-47; city atty. City of Sedan, 1947; asst. gen. counsel Ks. State Corp. Commn., Topeka, 1948-51; artist Eureka, Calif., 1974—. One-woman shows include oil paintings, 1977, 1986. Mem. AAUW (Edn. Found. award 1980, pres. local chpt. 1964-65), Redwood Art Assn. (pres. 1979-81, Best of Show award 1973), Humboldt Docent Coun. (pres. 1977-79), Humboldt Arts Coun. (pres. 1982-83), Phi Kappa Phi. Republican. Episcopalian.

FISH, LILIAN MANN, lawyer; b. Methuen, Mass., Sept. 6, 1901; d. Samuel Eleazer and Ella Agnes (Hobbs) Mann; m. Charles Melvin Fish, Dec. 25, 1923 (div. 1933). Student U. So. Calif., 1930's-40's; J.D. magna cum laude, Southwestern U., 1932. Bar: Calif. 1932, U.S. Dist. Ct. (so. dist.) Calif. 1932, U.S. Ct. Appeals (9th cir.) 1934, U.S. Supreme Ct. 1934. Sec. Lloyd S. Nix, Atty., San Pedro, Calif., 1926-29, Los Angeles, 1931-32; sec. Office of City Prosecutor (Lloyd S. Nix), Los Angeles, 1929-30, Victor R. Hansen, atty., Los Angeles, 1930-31; assoc. Lloyd S. Nix, Los Angeles, 1932-44, Price, Postel & Parma, Santa Barbara, Calif., 1949-71; pvt. practice, L.A., 1944-49, Santa Barbara, 1971-88; editor Ancestors West quar., 1978-88. Vice pres. Los Angeles County Young Republicans, 1939-40; bd. dirs. Santa Barbara Trust Hist. Preservation, pres., 1975, also sec.; bd. dirs., editor quarterly Santa Barbara County Geneal. Soc., 1978-88, hon. life mem.; bd. dirs. Santa Barbara Hist. Soc., 1971-76, chmn. library com., 1978-83; pres. Santa Barbara Bus. and Profl. Women, 1955-56, Nat. Bus. and Profl. Women, Los Angeles, 1945-46; registrar Mission Canyon chpt. DAR, Santa Barbara, 1965-80, 85-89 (Roll of Honor cert. 1978). Recipient Cert. of Recognition for service Calif. Senate, 1980; Cert. of Service, Bicentennial Com., City of Santa Barbara, 1975-77; named Woman of Yr., Mar Vista Bus. and Profl. Women's Assn., 1979. Mem. ABA (hon. life 1988—), Women Lawyers Club Los Angeles (pres. 1940-41), Soc. Genealogists (London), Phi Delta Delta. Republican. Mem. United Ch. of Christ. Home: 2546 Murrell Rd Santa Barbara CA 93109

FISH, RUBY MAE BERTRAM (MRS. FREDERICK GOODRICH FISH), civic worker; b. Sheridan, Wyo., July 24, 1918; d. Ryan Lawrence and Ruby (Beckwith) Bertram; R.N., St. Luke's Hosp., 1936; postgrad. Washington U., St. Louis, 1941; m. Frederick Goodrich Fish, Apr. 12, 1942; children—Bertram Frederick, Lisbeth Ann Fish Kalstein. Staff nurse Huntington Meml. Hosp., Pasadena, Calif., 1941-42; dr.'s office nurse, Denver, 1943-44; travel cons. Buckingham Travel Agy., Aurora, Colo., 1976—. Bd. dirs. Jefferson County Easter Seal Soc., 1949—, pres., 1952-53, 56-57, 66-67; pres. Colo. Easter Seal Soc., 1960-61; bd. dirs. Nat. Easter Seal Soc., 1968-69, sec. ho. of dels., 1976-77; bd. dirs. Assistance League Denver, 1968-70, 75-76, People to People for Handicapped; mem. Pres.'s Com. on Employing Handicapped, 1976—; active Rehab. Internat. of U.S.A., 1972—, Rehab. Internat., 1960—. Mem. Dau. Nile-El Mejedel. Home: 4646 Bow Mar Dr Littleton CO 80123 Office: 13741 E Mississippi Ave Aurora CO 80012

FISHER, ANITA JEANNE, English language educator; b. Atlanta, Oct. 22, 1937; d. Paul Benjamin and Cora Ozella (Wadsworth) Chappelear; m. Kirby Lynn Fisher, Aug. 6, 1983; 1 child by previous marriage, Tracy Ann. BA, Bob Jones U., 1959; postgrad., Stetson U., 1961, 87, U. Fla., 1963; MAT, Rollins Coll., 1969; PhD in Am. Lit., Fla. State U., 1975; postgrad., Writing Inst., U. Cen. Fla., 1978, NEH Inst., 1979, U. Cen. Fla., 1987, Stetson U., 1987, U. Fla., 1987, 90. Cert. English, gifted and adminstn. supr. Chmn. basic learning improvement program, secondary sch. Orange County, Orlando, Fla., 1964-65; chmn. composition Winter Park High Sch., Fla., 1978-80; chmn. English depts. Orange County Pub. Schs., Fla., 1962, 71; reading tchr. Woodland Hall Acad., Reading Rsch. Inst., Tallahassee, 1976; instr. edn., journalism, reading, Spanish, thesis writing Bapt. Bible Coll., Springfield, Mo., 1976-77; prof. English, S.W. Mo. State U., Springfield, 1980-84, instr. continuing edn., courses in music and creative writing, 1981-82, editor LAD Leaf; tchr. Volusia County Schs., Fla., 1984-88, gifted students, 1986-88; tchr. Lee County Schs., 1988—; founder Fisher=Phipps Agy. Contbr. writings to publs. in field, papers to nat. profl. confs. Vol. Greene County Action Com., 1977, Heart Fund, 1982; book reviewer Voice of Youth Advs. Writing Program fellow U. Cen. Fla., 1978. Mem. Fla. Coun. Tchrs. of English, Lee County Coun. Tchrs. of English, Nat. Coun. Tchrs. of English, Volusia County Coun. Tchrs. of English, Southern Assn. of Colls. and Schs. (steering com. 1989-90), Kappa Delta Pi. Republican. Presbyterian.

FISHER, ANNA LEE, physician, astronaut; b. St. Albans, N.Y., Aug. 24, 1949; m. William Frederick Fisher; children: Kristin Anne, Kara Lynne. B.S. in Chemistry, UCLA, 1971, M.D., 1976, M.S. in Chemistry, 1987. Physician, 1976-78; astronaut NASA Johnson Space Ctr., Houston, 1978—, mission specialist STS, 51-A, 1984. Mem. Sigma Xi. Office: NASA Johnson Space Ctr Astronaut Office Houston TX 77058*

FISHER, BONNIE LEE MICHAELSON, psychologist; b. N.Y.C., Aug. 7, 1948; d. Robert and Lillian (Pecker) Barber; m. Roger I. Michaelson, Dec. 21, 1969 (div. June 1985); m. H. Edward Fisher, Aug. 23, 1986; 1 child, Rachel Virginia. BA cum laude, NYU, 1970; MA, Temple U., 1972, PhD, 1974. Lic. psychologist, Md., Del. Dir. counseling ctr. Washington Coll., Chestertown, Md., 1973—; clin. cons. Kent County Health Dept., Chestertown, 1974-87; clin. dir. Tressler Ctr., Dover, Delaware, 1985—, Project 801 Aid-in-Dover, 1980—. Mem. Newark Symphony Orch., Del., 1976—. Mem. Am. Psychol. Assn. Home: 54 Bohemia Ln Earleville MD 21919 Office: Washington Coll Chestertown MD 21620

FISHER, ELLENA ALLMOND, librarian; b. Windsor, Va.; d. Calvin Percy and Oretha Mae (Eley) Allmond; m. Eddie Lee Fisher; children: Ellena II, Melba. BA, Va. Union U.; MS cum laude, Atlanta U. Lang. asst. Va. Union U., Richmond, tutor; libr. assoc. Atlanta U.; rsch. asst. Econ. Opportunity Atlanta; clk. typist West Employment Svc., River Forest, Ill., 1979-81; monitor testing Pasadena (Calif.) Coll. Skills Ctr.; reference librarian L.A. Pub. Libr.; young adult librarian Mark Twain Libr., L.A. Guest lect. Sheenway Sch., L.A., 1988—. Mem. Castle Heights Sch. PTA, Los Angeles, 1985-86; Doug Wilder supporter, Va. Mem. Nat. Assn. Female Execs., Our Authors Study Club, Calif. Librarians. Baptist. Home: 400 South Berendo #215 Los Angeles CA 90020 Office: Mark Twain Libr 9621 S Figueroa St Los Angeles CA 90003

FISHER, FLORENCE ANNA, association executive, author, lecturer; b. Bklyn., May 28, 1928; d. Frederick I. and Florence (Goldstein) Fisher; student pub. schs., Phila.; m. Stanley Eigenfeld, Dec. 20, 1953; 1 son, Glenn Mark Love. Founder, pres. The Alma Soc., Inc. (Adoptees' Liberty Movement Assn.), N.Y.C., 1971—; mem. Mabon Policy Advisory Council Odyssey Inst., Inc., N.Y.C., 1977-78; author: (autobiography) The Search for Anna Fisher, 1973. Office: PO Box 154 Washington Bridge Station New York NY 10033

FISHER, J. R., marketing executive; b. Greeley, Colo., Aug. 10, 1943; d. Donald L. and Mary (Nagel) Kiser; m. Larry G. Fisher, Dec. 1, 1962; children: Shannon Michelle, Michael Dean. Student, U. Nebr., Dale Carnegie Inst., Scottsbluff, Nebr. Cert. sales mgr., mktg. mgr., notary pub. Mktg. and sales mgr. Allied Chem./Prestolite, Scottsbluff; dir. mktg. and sales George Risk Industries, Kimball, Nebr.; mktg. and sales mgr. Adams, Baker, Doyle, Inc., Scottsbluff; sales mgr. western region, Wyo. state Dial-Net Systems, Scottsbluff. Mem. Profl. Bus. Women's Assn., C. of C. Address: PO Box 814 Bridgeport NE 69336 Office: Dial-Net-Systems Railway Office Pla Ste C-102 Scottsbluff NE 69361

FISHER, JEANETTE NELSON, communications executive; b. Wichita, Kans., Nov. 14, 1942; d. Russell Alan and Jean (Branch) Nelson; m. E. Gregory, M.D., June 15, 1963; children: Ted, Ann, Betsy, Matt, Kate. Student, Mt. Carmel Acad., Wichita, 1960; BA, Rosary Coll., River Forest, 1964. Chmn. 48er's Vols. Sta. WCET-TV, Cin., 1973-75; v.p. bd. dirs. Santa Maria Community Service, Cin., 1980-87; vol. coord. PRO Kids, Cin., 1986-87; chmn. Hamilton County Children's Trust Fund; reg. rep. Nat. CASA, 1988. Named Vol. of the Year Pro Kids, 1986. Mem. Hamilton County Children's, Pro Kids Bd. of Dirs., Cin. Women's Ins. Sales, Altrusa Women's Club. Democrat. Roman Catholic. Home: 1421 Herschel Ave Cincinnati OH 45208 Office: Pro Kids 222 E Central Pkwy 209A Cincinnati OH 45202

FISHER, (MARY) JEWEL TANNER, retired construction company executive; b. Port Lavaca, Tex., Oct. 31, 1918; d. Thomas M. and Minnie Frances (Dunks) Tanner; grad. Tex. Luth. Coll., 1937; m. King Fisher, Aug. 13, 1937; children—Ann Fisher Boyd, Linda Fisher LaQuay. Sec. treas. King Fisher Marine Svc., Inc., Port Lavaca, 1959-82; dir., cons. King Fisher Marine Svc.; artist. Trustee Meml. Med. Ctr., 1976-81, 90—, Golden Crescent Coun. Govts., 1980-81. Lic. pvt. pilot. Mem. DAR (regent Guadalupe Victoria chpt. 1986-88), Daus. Republic Tex., 99's, Internat. Orgn. Women Pilots. Home: Box 166 Port Lavaca TX 77979 Office: Box 108 Port Lavaca TX 77979

FISHER, JIMMIE LOU, state official; b. Delight, Ark., Dec. 31, 1941. Student, Ark. State U.; grad. John F. Kennedy Sch. Govt., Harvard U., 1985. Treas. Greene County, Ark., 1971-78; auditor State of Ark., Little Rock, 1979, treas., 1981—; sec. Ark. State Bd. Fin. Mem. Ark. Bd. Election Commrs.; trustee, ex-offico mem. Ark. Pub. Employees Retirement System, Ark. Tchr. Retirement System; trustee Ark. State Hwy. Retirement System; former vice chair Dem. State Com.; former mem. Dem. Nat. Com.; del. Dem. Nat. Conv., 1988; past pres. Ark. Dem. Women's Club. Mem. State Bd. Fin. (sec.), State Bd. Election Commrs., Nat. Assn. State Treas. (pres.). Office: Treasury Dept 220 State Capitol Bldg Little Rock AR 72201

FISHER, JOHANNA MARIE, real estate legal representative, teacher; b. Breitengussbach, Fed. Republic Germany; came to U.S., 1972; d. Manning June and Kunigunda (Fürsel) Kunigunda June; m. Herman Fisher, June 5, 1981; children: Johann, Ursula, Sabine, Herman III (stepson). B in Legal Studies cum laude, SUNY, Buffalo, 1982. Cert. legal asst. Adminstrv. asst. def. dept. Seiman's Electronics, Fed. Republic Germany, 1976-78; credit counselor Goldome Savs. Bank, Buffalo, 1983-85; with Pack, Hartman, Ball & Huckabone, Buffalo, 1985-86; tchr. Calasanctius Sch. for Gifted Children, Buffalo, 1988—; tchr. Calasanctius Prep Sch. for Gifted Children, 1988-89; cons. in field. Writer poetry, short stories. Mem. NAFE, Order Eastern Star.

FISHER, JOY DEBORAH, lawyer; b. Chgo., Mar. 15, 1952; d. J. Barry and Rochelle Barbara (Levin) F.; m. Arthur Walter Stawinski, Nov. 2, 1979; 1 child, Steven Lee Fisher-Stawinski; step children: Kathryn, Elizabeth Kline. BA, U. Ill., 1973, JD, 1976. Bar: Ill. Supreme Ct. 1976, Fed. Dist. Ct. (no. dist.) Ill. 1976. With Fisher & Sherman, Chgo., 1976-78; ptnr. J.B. Fisher & J.D. Fisher, Chgo., 1978-87; pvt. practice Chgo., Buffalo Grove, Ill., 1987—; contract atty. Ill. Sec. State, Chgo., 1981-83; mem. real estate panel Am. Arbitration Assn., Chgo., 1982—; bd. mem. Discovery Sci. Edn. Ctr. Contbr. articles to profl. jours. Vol. atty. Free Women's Legal Clin., Chgo., 1976-79; mem. steering com. Com. for ERA, Chgo., 1976-78; pro bono legal counsel for miscellanous nonprofit orgns. and abused women, Cook County, Ill., 1976—; elected mem. Bd. Edn. Wheeling (Ill.) Dist. 21, 1985—; family sponsor JCC Family to Family, Cook County, 1990. Recipient cert. appreciation Decalogue Soc. Lawyers, Chgo., 1980. Mem. AAUW (Wheeling-Buffalo Grove pub. affairs chair, 1989—), Women's Bar Assn., Greenpeace. Office: 567 Weidner Rd Buffalo Grove IL 60089

FISHER, LADDIE CARTER (ADELAIDE FISHER), free-lance writer; b. Cin., Aug. 9, 1920; d. Joshua Claude and Adelaide Louise (Wayne) Carter; m. Richard Howard Fisher, June 27, 1941; children: David Richard, Michael Robert, Ann Claudia, Catharine Louise, Mary Adelaide. BA, U. Mich., 1942; postgrad., William & Mary Coll., 1957-58, Calif. State U., Fresno, 1975, Va. Poly. Inst. & State U., 1976, 78, Hollins Coll., 1989. Tchr. English Princess Anne High Sch., Virginia Beach, Va., 1957-59; owner gift shop Virginia Beach, 1959-61; exec. dir. Mental Health Assn. Roanoke Valley, Va., 1968-74; community rels. dir. Mental Health Svcs. Roanoke Valley, 1976-81; pub. info. officer City of Roanoke, 1981-87; freelance writer Roanoke, 1987—; speaker Women's Forum, Roanoke, 1987, Regional City Clks., 1989. Author poetry; contbr. articles to profl. jours. Mem. div. adminstrn. Presbytery of Peaks, 1989—; reader play competition Mill Mountain Theater, 1989-90; bd. dirs. YWCA Roanoke Valley, 1987-90, Roanoke Valley Mental Health Assn., 1987-90. Mem. Acad. Am. Poets, Valley Writers, Blue Ridge Writers, Associated Writing Programs, Appalachian Writers Assn., Poetry Soc. Va. Presbyterian. Home: 3327G Circlebrook Dr SW Roanoke VA 24014

FISHER, MARCIA ANN, legal admininstrator; b. Geneva, Ill., Feb. 28, 1957; d. Robert L. and Beverly J. (Hopp) F. Student, Moser Bus. Sch., 1975; student, U. Ill., 1975-76; BS, U. Iowa, 1978, BS in Indsl. Relations, 1980. Paralegal Rate, Nolan, Moen & Parsons, Iowa City, 1980-82, legal adminstr., 1982—. Appointed Iowa State Foster Care Review Bd., 1987; del. Citizen Ambassador Program to People's Republic of China, 1988, to USSR, 1990. Rotary scholar, 1975. Mem. Nat. Assn. Legal Adminstrs., Iowa Assn. Legal Adminstrs., Iowa Assn. Legal Assts. (treas. 1984). Office: 22 E Court St Iowa City IA 52240

FISHER, NANCY, screenwriter, producer, director; b. N.Y.C., Oct. 21, 1941; d. Seymour and Tema F.; 1 child, Sarah Olivia. B.A., Barnard Coll., 1962. Prodn. supr. CBS, N.Y.C., 1964-66; owner, mgr. Serendipity Talent Agy., N.Y.C., 1966-68; writer, producer Grey Advt., N.Y.C., 1968-70; creative group head Benton & Bowles Advt., London, 1970-74, McCann Erickson Advt., N.Y.C., 1974-75; creative dir. Norman, Craig & Kummel Advt., N.Y.C., 1975-78; pres. Nancy Fisher Inc., Weston, Conn., N.Y.C., 1978—; pres. Creative Programming, Inc., N.Y.C., 1981-89. Creator, writer, producer TV series Womanwatch, 1982—, Celebrity Chefs, 1983—; numerous home video cassettes including Look Mom, I'm Fishing (Parents Choice award 1987), The Annapolis Book of Seamanship Video Series (Cindy award), The Christmas Carol Video, Video Dog, Video Cat, Video Baby. Recipient 5 broadcast awards Network Documentary Series, 1982-84. Mem. Dirs. Guild of Am., Wings (N.Y.C.) Office: 200 E 84th St New York NY 10028

FISHER, NAOMI YASUDA, banker; b. Kanazawa, Japan, Oct. 14, 1952; d. Naohisa and Yoshiko (Fujimaki) Yasuda; m. Arnold Stanley Fisher, June 20, 1976; 1 child, Jeffrey Akira. BA, UCLA, 1975, MA, 1980; BA,

Hiroshima (Japan) U., 1980. Loan adminstr. The Sumitomo Bank of Calif., Los Angeles, 1976-77, Security Pacific Nat. Bank, Los Angeles, 1978-79; loan officer The Fuji Bank, Ltd., Los Angeles, 1981-83, asst. v.p., 1983-84, v.p., 1985—. Scholar Japan Scholarship Soc., 1971-74, Ministry of Edn. of Japan, 1974-75. Mem. Japan-Am. Soc. of So. Calif., Japan Bus. Assn. of So. Calif., Nat. Assn Female Execs. Office: The Fuji Bank Ltd 333 S Grand Ave Los Angeles CA 90071

FISHER, NINA ANNE, environmental scientist, writer; b. Abington, Pa., Apr. 19, 1957; d. Norman J. and Doris Louise (Meyers) F. BS, Tufts U., 1979; MS, U. Va., 1982. Environ. specialist Nat. Park Svc., Bryce Canyon, Utah, 1980; rsch. asst. U. Va., Charlottesville, 1980-82; tech. cons. Time/Life Books, Alexandria, Va., 1982; cons. Coastal Rsch. Assocs., Charlottesville, 1982-83; coordinator and faculty mem. Ctr. for Northern studies, Wolcott, Va., 1981-84, 86-87; rsch. asst. and assoc. Darling Marine Ctr., U. Maine, Walpole, 1974-85; faculty mem. Nat. Wildlife Fedn., Vienna, Va., 1988; tech. writer, sr. sci. specialist Chesapeake Bay Program, Annapolis, Md., 1986—; freelance writer, graphic arts, Annapolis, 1988-89. Recycling coord., Chesapeake Bay Program, EPA, Annapolis, 1988-89. Recipient Olmstead Fellowship, Tufts U., 1979. Mem. Phi Beta Kappa, Sigma Gamma Epsilon (W.A. Tarr award 1981). Democrat. Jewish. Office: Chesapeake Bay Program 410 Severn Ave Ste 110 Annapolis MD 21403

FISHER, ROBIN LEEANN, manufacturing company executive; b. Latrobe, Pa., Oct. 12, 1955; d. Raymond William and Shirley Ann (Jones) Boring. BA in Polit. Sci., Ind. U. Pa., 1977. Insp. product assurance Westinghouse Electric Corp., Blairsville, Pa., 1978-81, product coordinator, 1983-84, 1st line supr. product assurance, 1984-89, 1st. line supr. mfg. and prodn., 1989—. Mem. NAFE, Westinghouse Foreman's Assn., Smithsonian Instn. Assocs., Ind. U. Pa. Alumni Assn., Nat. Arbor Day Found., The Nature Conservancy, Am. Mus. Natural History. Democrat. Roman Catholic. Home: RD 3 Box 437 Blairsville PA 15717 Office: Westinghouse Electric Corp Specialty Metals Plant RD 4 Box 333 Blairsville PA 15717

FISHER, ROSALIND ANITA, personnel executive; b. Jackson, Tenn., Feb. 5, 1956; d. Hartwell E. and Gwendolyn C. (Meriweather) F. BS in Psychology, Cen. Mo. State U., 1978; MS in Community Devel., So. Ill. U., 1986. Tchr. Kansas City (Mo.) Sch. Dist., 1980-82; adminstrv. asst. Urban Affairs dept. City of Kansas City, 1982, specialist Human Relations dept., 1982-85, vol. mediator, 1985—; employee relations and tng. mgr. Personnel and Risk Mgmt. dept. U. Nebr., Lincoln, 1985-87; asst. dir. personnel services dept. Kans. State U., Manhattan, 1988—; acting dir. personnel svcs. Kansas State U., Manhattan, 1988-89, dir. personnel svcs., 1989—; cons. Chancellor's Commn. on Sexual Harassment, Lincoln, 1987—; speaker women's issues. cons., trainer Stop Violence Coalition, Kansas City, 1984-85; arbitrator Cornhusker Better Bus. Bur., Lincoln, 1985-87; bd. dirs. YWCA, Lincoln, 1986-87. Recipient Appreciation award Stop Violence Coalition, 1984. Fellow Coll. and Univ. Personnel Assn., Am. Soc. for Tng. and Devel., Univ. Assn. for Adminstrv. Devel. (exec. com., chair profl. devel. 1986-87), Nat. Assn. Negro Bus. and Profl. Women (Outstanding Vol. of Yr. award 1985), Women of Color Task Force (chair 1986-87). Democrat. Baptist. Home: 724 Ridgewood Dr Manhattan KS 66502 Office: Kans State U 228 Anderson Hall Manhattan KS 66506

FISHER, SALLIE ANN, chemicals executive, consultant; b. Green Bay, Wis., Sept. 10, 1923. BS in Chemistry, U. Wis., 1945, MS, 1946, PhD, 1949. Instr. My. Holyoke Coll., South Hadley, Mass., 1949-50; asst. prof. U. Minn., Duluth, 1950-51; sr. scientist Rohm & Haas Co., Phila., 1951-60; assoc. dir. Robinette Rsch. Labs., Berwyn, Pa., 1960-72; v.p. Puricons, Inc., Berwyn, 1972-76; pres. Puricons, Inc., Malvern, Pa., 1976—. Contbg. author (5) books; patentee in field. Fellow ASTM (vice chmn. com. D-19 1972-78, Merit award 1972, Max Hecht award 1973); mem. Am. Chem. Soc., Am. Water Works Assn., Nat. Assn. Chem. Engrs., Soc. Chem. Industry of London, Engrs. Soc. West Pa. (adv. bd. Pitts. chpt. 1980—, Merit award 1984). Office: Puricons Inc 101 Quaker Ave Malvern PA 19355

FISHER, SHIRLEY MAHALEY, bank officer; b. Eastman, Ga., Feb. 25, 1943; d. Logan and Madie (Jones) Hemphill; m. David B. Fisher, Apr. 10, 1966. Grad. high sch., Eastman. From asst. cashier to asst. v.p. The Bank of Fitzgerald, Ga., 1976-90, v.p., 1990—. Baptist. Office: The Bank of Fitzgerald 302 S Main St Fitzgerald GA 31750

FISHER, SUSAN GROSSMAN, banker; b. N.Y.C., July 27, 1946; d. Bernard and Leah Irene (Gordon) Grossman; BA in Math., U. Wis., 1967; MA, Columbia U., 1968, MBA, 1976; m. Yale L. Fisher, June 17, 1968; children: Douglas Carl, Robin Leah. Asst. trust officer Mfrs. Hanover Trust Co., N.Y.C., 1971-73, asst. v.p., 1973-76, v.p. trust div., 1977-79; v.p. Wells Rich Greene, Inc., N.Y.C., 1979-80; v.p., dir. mktg. met. div. Chem. Bank, N.Y.C., 1980-82, v.p., dist. head worldwide pvt. banking div., 1982-83; sr. v.p. Marine Midland Bank, N.Y.C., 1983-85; sr. v.p. Mfrs. & Traders Trust Co., 1985-88; prin., founder The Berkshire Bank, N.Y.C., 1988—; dir. Veeco Instruments, Inc., 1983-86. Mem. leadership devel. group for execs. Brandeis U., 1976-89, Central Park Task Force, 1989; bd. dirs. Emanuel Midtown YM-YWHA, YWCA of City of N.Y., 1979-82, Dance Notation Bur., 1979-89, United Neighborhood Houses N.Y., 1982-88, Nat. Choral Coun., 1981-88, Coun. Mcpl. Performance, 1980-86, WNYC Found.; treas. Friends of the Am. Theatre Wing; women's bd. Jewish Guild for Blind; mem. Manhattan Community Bd. #5, 1981-82; nat. chmn. Rep. Nat. Com. Nat. Women's Coalition; mem. transition pers. adv. com. Bush/Quayle Campaign, 1988-89, nat. adv. coun. Benjamin N. Cardozo Sch. Law, U.S. Small Bus. Adminstrn.; gov. Space Commerce Roundtable Found., Ctr. for Study of the Presidency, Nat. Adv. Council; mem. citizens task force on pk. use and security Central Pk. Conservancy, 1989, Cen. Park Task Force, 1989. Mem. Inst. Quantitative Rsch. in Fin. (dir. 1975-79), N.Y. State Bankers Assn. (communications policy com. 1981-83), Fin. Women's Assn. N.Y. (dir. 1979-82, pres. 1980-81), Women's Forum (bd. dirs., pres. 1990—), Internat. Women's Forum (dir.), Investment Tech. Symposium (dir. 1974-78), N.Y. Chamber Commerce and Industry, Communications Industry Coun. (steering com. 1979-81), Bank Adminstrn. Inst. (trust and fin. prods. commn. 1983-86), Columbia Grad. Sch. Bus. Alumni Assn. (dir. 1981—, pres., 1985-87), Econ. Club, Beta Gamma Sigma. Office: The Berkshire Bank 600 Madison Ave New York NY 10022

FISHER, VICKI JO, medical technologist, legal intern; b. El Paso, Tex., Feb. 19, 1957; d. John Thomas and Marion Irene (Burtness) F. BS in Biology, Ea. Wash. U., 1979; postgrad., Bellevue Community Coll., 1986-88, Gonzagu U. Law Sch., 1988—. Lab. asst. Providence Med. Ctr., Seattle, 1979-80; med. technologist Providence Med. Ctr., 1980-83, 84-88, Whittaker Internat. Corp., Khamis Mushayt, Saudi Arabia, 1983-84, U. Wash., Seattle, 1987-88, Pathology Assocs., Spokane, Wash., 1988-89; legal intern U.S. Atty. Office, Spokane, 1989-90, head legal intern, 1990—. Active Group Health Hosp. Vols., Bellevue, 1987; LWV, 1987-88. Mem. ABA, Am. Assn. Clin. Pathologists, Internat. Law Soc. (pres. 1989-90), Inland Northwest World Trade Coun., Phi Delta Phi. Home: PO Box 1312 Spokane WA 99210

FISHER, WENDY ASTLEY-BELL, marketing executive; b. London, Jan. 23, 1944; came to U.S., 1947; d. Leonard Astley and Rita (Duis) Astley-Bell; m. Richard Van Mell, Mar. 21, 1970 (div. May 1980); m. Lester Emil Fisher, Jan. 23, 1981. Student, Hood Coll., 1961-63, U. Alta., Can., summer 1963; BA honors, Northwestern U., 1965; postgrad., U. Chgo., 1965-66. Lab. technician Northwestern U. Med. Sch., Chgo., 1966-67; designer Okamoto/London Studio, Chgo., 1967-71, Communications Internat., Chgo., 1971-72; freelance artist K&S Photographics, Chgo., 1972-76; dir. spl. projects Lincoln Park Zool. Soc., Chgo., 1976-81; mem. pub. rels. staff Field Enterprises, Chgo., 1981; pres., creative dir. Mailworks, Inc., Chgo., 1981—; speaker in field. Co-author: The First Hundred Years, 1975; contbr. articles to profl. jours. Bd. dirs. Jr. League Chgo., 1965-74, Vis. Nurse Assn. Chgo., 1978-82; mem. women's bd. dirs. Lincoln Park Zool. Soc., 1981-84, Crow Canyon Coun., 1989—. Recipient Gold Cert. Chgo. Savs. and Loan Assn., 1973, Award of Merit Splty. Advt. Assn., 1979; named Outstanding Women Entrepreneur Chgo. chpt. Women in Communications, 1983. Mem. Nat. Soc. Fundraising Execs. (bd. dirs. Chgo. chpt. 1982-88, Pres.'s award 1987, cert. in fundraising), Chgo. Assn. Direct Mktg. (bd. dirs. 1982-87, bd. dirs. edn. found. 1985-87), Assn. Direct Response Fundraising Counsel, Direct Mktg. Assn. (Leadership award 1978), Am. Assn. Mus., Am. Assn. Zool. Parks and Aquariums, Econ. Club Chgo. Office: Mailworks Inc 230 N Michigan Ave Chicago IL 60601

FISHMAN, DOROTHY JANET, educator; b. N.Y.C.; m. Herbert Fishman. AA, Newton Jr. Coll., 1974; BS, Boston U., 1977, MS, 1979, EdD, 1983. Registered nurse. Instr. Boston State Coll., 1979-81; spl. projects prog. dir. interactive video Am. Jour. Nursing Co., N.Y.C.; assoc. dean U. Conn. Sch. Nursing, Storrs; cons. Fishman Assocs., Farmington, Conn.; assoc. prof. nursing Sacred Heart U., Fairfield, Conn.; cons. spl. projects Am. Jour. Nursing, N.Y.C., 1985-88; assoc. prof., assoc. dean U. Conn. Sch. Nursing, 1988-89; reviewer Computers in Nursing, Phila., 1984—. Fellow Am. Acad. Nursing; mem. Nat. League Nursing, Am. Nurses Assn. (pres. Dist. I), Conn. Nurses Assn., Golf Club, Sigma Theta Tau. Home: 7 Dogwood Ln Farmington CT 06032 Office: Sacred Heart U 5151 Park Ave Fairfield CT 06432

FISHMAN, MADELINE DOTTI, management consulting executive; b. Chgo., Oct. 7, 1942; d. Martin and Anne (Sweet) Binder; m. Norton Lee Fishman, Apr. 7, 1963; children: Mark Nathan, Marla Susan. BEd, Nat. Coll. Edn., 1964, MS, 1972. Tchr., Rochester Schs. (Minn.), 1963-64, Orange County Schs., Orlando, Fla., 1967-68; reading cons. Palatine Schs. (Ill.), 1972-73; instr. Parent Effective Tng., Wilmette, Ill., 1974-76, tchr. Effectiveness Tng., 1974-76; pres. Profls. Diversified, Wilmette, Ill., 1976—; remedial and enrichment reading tchr. Waukegan (Ill.) Pub. Schs., 1986; pres. Lifeline, 1989—; mgmt. cons. World Wide Diamonds Assn., Schaumburg, Ill., 1979—, Artistic Color, Dallas, 1983-87; Pearl direct distbr. Amway Corp., Ada, Mich., 1976—. Author: Organic Gardening, 1975, The Go-Getters Planner, 1986. Leader, Camp Fire Girls, Evanston, Ill., 1963, 75. Recipient Ednl. Scholarship, Nat. Coll. Edn., 1971. Mem. Kappa Delta Pi. Jewish.

FISK, CAROL FRASER, senior manager; b. Bklyn., Mar. 2, 1946; d. John M. and Jean C. (Hardman) Fraser; m. Craig Fisk, Nov. 24, 1984. BA, Conn. Coll., 1968; Master in Urban and Regional Planning, Va. Tech., 1972; LHD, Alfred U., 1988. Mgmt. tng. program N.Y. Tel. Co., 1968-70; sr. planner No. Va. Planning Dist. Commn., Falls Church, Va., 1972-77; asst. dir. Arlington (Va.) United Way, 1977-78; coord. Youth Project Arlington (Va.) Svcs. Bd.; sr. rsch. assoc. Nat. Assn. of Countries, Washington, 1979-81; from spl. asst. to dir., regional ops. US Dept. Health and Human Svcs., Washington, 1981-84; US commissioner on aging US Dept. Health and Human Services, Washington, 1984-89; editor Aging Network News, McLean, Va., 1989; cons., 1990—; mem. US Delegation to UN World Assembly on Aging, Vienna, Austria, 1982. Mem. Am. Planning Assn., Am. Soc. for Pub. Adminstrn., Am. Soc. on Aging, Gerontological Soc. Am. Republican. Episcopalian. Office: 1014 Steeples Ct Falls Church VA 22046

FISK, PAMELA HOUSE, counselor; b. Covington, Ky., July 4, 1952; d. Leon and Virgilene (Fields) House; m. Rodney Douglas Fisk, Nov. 21, 1987; stepchildren: Casey Fisk, Elley Fisk. AS in Bus. Psychology, Thomas More Coll., 1982, postgrad., 1990—. With Procter & Gamble Co., Cin., 1971—, employment and recruiting mgr., 1985-87, recruiting and counseling mgr., 1987—; mem. Nat. Coop. Edn., Cin., 1988-90; bd. dirs. coop. Cin. Tech. Coll., Mt. St. Joseph Coll., Cin., Thomas More Coll., Crestview Hills, Ky. Mem. Ft. Wright (Ky.) Civic Club, 1989-90; vol. Cin. Youth Collaborative, 1986-90; treas. Citizens Com. on Youth, Cin., 1985-86. Mem. Ohio Coop. Edn. Assn., Cin. Human Resources Assn., Midwest Coop. Edn. Assn., NAFE. Office: Procter & Gamble Co One P&G Pla Cincinnati OH 45201

FISSELL, LILI MARLANE, community services office manager; b. Balt., Dec. 13, 1944; d. John Tony Calabrese and Hattie Martha (Painter) Sunderland; m. Kenneth Douglas Fissell, Jr., June 16, 1962; children: Darla Marlane Fissell Werner, Kenneth Douglas III. AA, Anne Arundel Community Coll., Arnold, Md., 1985. Clerk typist I Recreation & Parks, Annapolis, Md., 1975-77; Clerk typist II Fire Dept. Hdqrs., Millersville, Md., 1977-81; sec. I County Coun., Glen Burnie, Md., 1981-83; sec. III County Coun., Annapolis, 1983; adminstrv. sec. Inspections & Permits, Annapolis, 1983-85; office mgr. County Exec./community Svcs., Glen Burnie, 1985—; sec. Salary Commn., Annapolis, 1981, Maritime Commn., Annapolis, 1982-84, Sewer Allocation Commn., Annapolis, 1983-85; system operator Anne Arundel County Govt., Glen Burnie, 1986—. Leader Bluebirds/Camp Fire Girls, Millersville, 1970, Cub Scouts, Millersville, 1975; sec. Church Coun., Elvaton, Md., 1970; tchr. Christ Luth. Ch., Elvaton, 1968-80. Mem. Women of Moose. Democrat. Home: 8216 Crab Apple Ct Glen Burnie MD 21061 Office: County Exec Community Svcs 101 Crain Hwy Glen Burnie MD 21061

FISZER-SZAFARZ, BERTA (BERTA SAFARS), research scientist; b. Wilno, Poland, Feb. 1, 1928; m. David Safars; children—Martine, Michel. M.S., U. Buenos Aires, 1955, Ph.D., 1956. Lab. chief Cancer Inst. Villejuif, France, 1961-67; vis. scientist Nat. Cancer Inst., Bethesda, Md., 1967-68; lab. chief Institut Curie, Orsay, France, 1969—; vis. scientist Inst. Applied Biochemistry, Mitake, Gifu, Japan, 1986. Contbr. articles to profl. jours. Mem. European Assn. Cancer Research, Am. Assn. Cancer Research (corres. mem.), N.Y. Acad. Scis., European Cell Biology Orgn., French Soc. Cell Biology.

FITCH, IRENE L., state agency administrator; b. Corning, N.Y., Jan. 10, 1949; d. Harold E. and Vivian L. (Heaton) Manning; m. William A. Fitch Jr., Oct. 21, 1978; children: William III, Justin, Sheldon. BA, SUNY, Albany, 1972, postgrad. Claims supr. Hartford Ins. Co., Albany, 1973-78; chief labor budgeting N.Y. State Dept. Labor, Albany, 1978—. AAUW grantee. Mem. Am. Soc. Pub. Adminstrn. Home: 208 Plank Rd RD 2 Troy NY 12182

FITCH, LINDA BAUMAN, computer coordinator; b. Elmira, N.Y., Jan. 6, 1947; d. Floyd Theodore Bauman and Wilma Mildred Rennie; m. H. Taylor Fitch, Feb. 15, 1969; children: Trevor Andrew, Matthew Taylor. BS, Keuka Coll., Keuka Park, 1969. Elem. tchr. Penn Yan Cen. Sch. Dist., Penn Yan, N.Y., 1972-73; computer coord. Fitch Auto Supply, Penn Yan, 1973—. V.p. Penn Yan Cen. Sch. Bd., 1986—; mem. Fed. Rels. Network of Nat. Sch. Bd. Assocs., 1988—; chmn. BSA Troop 48 Com., Branchport, N.Y., 1986—; pub. rels. chmn. Yates Day Care Ctr. of Penn Yan, 1980-82; legis. chair 4 County Sch. Bds. Assocs., 1990—. Mem. AAUW. Republican. Presbyterian. Home: 3120 Kinneys Cors Rd Bluff Point NY 14478 Office: Fitch Auto Supply F&W Parts 211 Clinton St Penn Yan NY 14527

FITCH, MARY KILLEEN, human resources specialist; b. Carroll, Iowa, July 15, 1949; d. Michael Francis and Mildred (Pauley) Killeen; m. David Paul Fitch, July 3, 1971. BS, Iowa State U., 1971, MS, 1975; postgrad. U. Minn., 1982—. Personnel adminstr. Control Data Corp., Roseville, Minn., 1976-77; sr. compensation analyst/employee relations rep. Honeywell, Inc., Mpls., 1977-80; human resource mgr./compensation and benefits mgr. No. Telecom, Inc., Minnetonka, Minn., 1980-82; adj. instr., teaching asst. Lakewood Community Coll./U. Minn., Mpls., 1982-84; compensation cons. Gen. Mills, Wayzata, Minn., 1984-85; mgr. compensation Northwestern Nat. Life Ins., Mpls., 1985-87; prin. compensation specialist Comml. Bldgs. Group, Honeywell, Inc., Mpls., 1987; corp. dir. compensation HRIS Nat. Car Rental Systems, Inc., Mpls., 1989—; cons. exec. compensation Honeywell Inc., Mpls., 1984; cons. human resources Les Kraus & Assocs., Edina, Minn., 1984; pres. Personnel Mgmt. Services of Twin Cities, St. Paul, 1983—. Author: (with Paul Muchinsky) Organization Behavior and Human Performance, 1975; (with John Fossum) Personnel Psychology, 1985. Chmn., bd. dirs. Kathadin, United Way Agy., Mpls., 1985—; curriculum com. U. Minn., 1983-84. George Catt Iowa State U. scholar, 1970. Mem. Indsl. Rels. Rsch. Assn., AAUW, Am. Compensation Assn., Psi Chi, Phi Kappa Phi. Avocations: dressage, karate. Home: 1188 90th St E Inver Grove Heights MN 55077 Office: HR Nat Car Rental Systems Inc 7700 France Ave S Minneapolis MN 55435

FITCH, RACHEL FARR, health policy analyst; b. Deering, Mo., July 27, 1933; d. Allen Edward and Rosie Leola (Jones) Farr; R.N., St. Vincent Hosp., 1954; student Little Rock U., 1965-67; B.S., St. Louis U., 1974, M.S., 1976, Ph.D., 1983; m. Coy Dean Fitch, Mar. 31, 1956; children: Julia Anne, Jaquelyn Kay. Psychiat. staff nurse VA Ft. Root Hosp., North Little Rock, Ark., 1954-57; surg.-med. staff nurse St. Vincent Infirmary, Little Rock, 1957-65; acute care nurse Georgetown U. Hosp., Washington, 1968-69; public health nurse to adminstr. South office Vis. Nurse Assn. Greater St. Louis, 1970-73; cons. in edn. St. Louis City Health Dept., 1977-80; rsch. specialist Sen. John C. Danforth, St. Louis, 1980; owner RFF Assocs., 1983-86; project dir. study of infant mortality in city of St. Louis, 1978. Mem. community health edn. com. Am. Heart Assn., 1977—; bd. dirs. LWV of Mo., 1984—, editor newspaper, 1984-87, dir. social policy, 1987—; bd. dirs. St. Louis Met. Med. Soc. Aux., St. Louis Univ. Hosp. Aux. Mem. Am. Public Health Assn., Acad. Polit. Sci., Sigma Theta Tau.

FITCH, RITA LAVERNE PICKENS, social worker; b. Cleve., Aug. 4, 1936; d. Clarence Eugene and Lillian Beatrice (Adkins) F.; m. Kenneth Pickens, Sept. 27, 1962 (div. 1969); children: Dana Charlotte, Theodore Bryant. Student, Cuyahoga Community Coll., Cleve., 1971-73; BA, Oberlin (Ohio) Coll., 1975; MS in Social Adminstrn., Case Western Res. U., 1978. Lic. ind. social worker. Asst. land use planner Lorain County Regional Planning Dept., Elyria, Ohio, 1975-76; asst. program dir. Nord Mental Health Ctrs./O.K. Corral Program, Elyria, 1978-79; learning disabled sch. social worker Lorain (Ohio) City Schs., 1980-81; pvt. counseling practice Rita Fitch & Assocs., Lorain, Cuyahoga and Franklin Counties, Lorain, Franklin, Ohio, 1981—; geriatric social work specialist, program orgn. developer Family Svc. Assn. Lorain, 1981-86; med. social worker Cleve. Met. Gen. Hosp., 1987-88; clin. social worker VA Med. Ctr., Chillicothe, Ohio, 1988—; pvt. duty nurse, Columbus and Cleve., 1959—; pvt. practice geriatric counseling, Columbus, 1986—; ednl. fin. aid adminstr. program 1986-87; bd. dirs. Oberlin Land Use Planning Bd., 1976-78, Columbus YWCA, 1986. Author: How to Relocate to a New City, 1986, The Ultimate Secret to Finding Student Financial Aid, 1986. Mem. Oberlin Oral History Program, 1982-86, Cleve. Cen. Community Oral History Program, 1986-87; bd. dirs. Oberlin Land Use Planning Bd., 1976-78, Columbus YWCA, 1986. Grantee Ford Found., Ms. Clairol, Oberlin Coll., 1973-75, Case Western Res. U., 1976-78. Mem. Acad. Cert. Social Workers, Columbus YWCA, Nat. Assn. Social Workers, Ohio Lic. Ind. Social Workers, Oberlin Coll. Alumni Assn., Case Western Res. Sch. Applied Social Scis., Social Work Alumni Assn., Cuyahoga County Community Coll. Alunni Assn. Home: 25 S Weyant St #A Columbus OH 43213

FITE, KATHLEEN ELIZABETH, education educator. BS in Edn., S.W. Tex. State U., 1969, MEd, 1970; EdD, N. Tex. State U., 1972. Assoc. prof. S.W. Tex. State U., San Marcos, 1973—, dir. Ctr. for Study of Basic Skills, 1980, dir. Race Integration Tng. Inst., 1982-83, dir. elem. edn. dept., 1983-84, assoc. dir. sponsored projects, 1984-86, dir. sponsored projects, 1986-87; cons. and lectr. in field; active numerous departmental and campus/student orgns. at S.W. Tex. State U. Author: A Few Favorites of the Total Teacher, 1978, The Super Ideas Book, 1978, (with Sherry Mendel) Creative Art Ideas, 1979; asst. editor S.W. Tex. U. Faculty Bull., 1977-78, editor, 1978-81; contbr. numerous articles, reports and book revs. to profl. publs. Mem. sr. citizens adv. com. City Coun. San Marcos, 1978-79, 79-80, 80-81, 81-83; mem. edn. commn. First United Meth. Ch., San Marcos, 1983; facilitator, dir. numerous community workshops; many other civic activities. Named Ky. Col., 1975; grantee U.S. Dept. Edn., 1983, 84, 85, LBJ Inst., 1988, 89, others. Mem. Nat. Assn. for Edn. of Young Children, Tex. Assn. Tchr. Educators, Kindergarten Tchrs. Tex., Tex. Computer Edn. Assn. (bd. dirs. 1984-87, publs. editor, state conf. asst. 1984, 85, 86, 87, 88), San Marcos Assn. for Edn. of Young Children (treas.), Phi Delta Kappa (pres. 1981, v.p., faculty advisor, alt. del., mem. ritual team 1986-89), Kappa Delta Pi (hon.). Home: 602 La Rue San Marcos TX 78666

FITTING, MELINDA DELL, psychologist; b. L.A., Feb. 23, 1948; d. John Waldemar and Ruth Evelyn (Reynolds) F.; m. James Norman Eastham Jr., May 24, 1985; children: James III, Bradley. BA, U. Colo., 1972; MA, Stanford U., 1976; PhD, U. Denver, 1984. Lic. psychologist. Instr. Johns Hopkins U., Balt., 1984-85, asst. prof., 1985—; pvt. practice psychology Johns Hopkins U., 1986—. Contbr. articles to profl. jours. Bd. mem. Alzheimer's Assn., Balt., 1988—. Mem. Am. Psychol. Assn., Md. Psychol. Assn. (ethics com. 1990), Gerontology Soc. Am. Democrat.

FITTING-GIFFORD, MARJORIE A., mathematician, educator, consultant; b. Detroit, Nov. 29, 1933; d. Ellis John and Dorothy Jennie (Hock) Premo; m. George R. Pickering, Dec. 16, 1954 (div. 1964); children: William Russell, David Ellis, John Lawrence; m. Frederick N. Fitting, Feb. 25, 1972 (dec. 1985); m. Forrest W. Gifford, May 28, 1988. BS in Math., Mich. State U., 1954, PhD, 1968; MEd, Wayne State U., 1958; AM in Math., U. Mich., 1966. Cert. tchr., Mich., Calif. Tchr. math. secondary schs., Mich., 1954-61; instr. Lawrence Inst. Tech., Southfield, Mich., 1961-68; grad. asst. Mich. State U., East Lansing, 1966-68; prof. math. and computer sci. San Jose State U., Calif., 1968—; v.p. fin. Metra Instruments, San Jose, 1972-82; pres. Metier, San Jose, 1982—; cons. San Jose (Calif.) Unified Sch., 1969-71. Author: (software) Math Test Generation, 1983; co-author: (book series) Computer Literacy Series, 1983-85. Recipient Dean's award for teaching excellence San Jose State U., 1982; named Santa Clara County Outstanding Woman, 1979; J.C. Plant scholar Mich. State U., 1954; NSF fellow, 1965-66, Fulbright sr. lectr./rsch. grantee, Portugal, 1985-86. Mem. Math. Assn. Am., Am. Math. Soc., Nat. Coun. Tchrs. Math. (review panel 1954—), Computer Using Educators, Calif. Math. Coun. Community Colls., Calif. Math. Coun., Santa Clara Valley Math. Assn., Zeta Tau Alpha. Democrat. Roman Catholic. Avocations: gardening, rafting, kayaking. Office: San Jose State U Dept Math and Computer Sci San Jose CA 95192

FITTS, C. AUSTIN, federal agency administrator; b. Phila., Dec. 24, 1950; d. William Thomas Jr. and Barbara Kinsey (Willits) F. AA, Bennett Coll., 1970; student, Chinese U., Hong Kong, 1971; BA, U. Pa., 1974, MBA, 1978. With Dillon, Read & Co., Inc., N.Y.C., 1978-89, sr. v.p., 1984-86, mng. dir., mem. bd. dirs., 1986-89; asst. sec. for housing, urban devel. and fed. housing commr. HUD, Washington, 1989—. Mem. bd. overseers Sch. Arts & Scis., U. Pa., Phila., 1986-89; mem. N.Y. Rep. Sate Fin. Com., 1986-89, N.Y.C. Food Bank, 1987-89; bd. trustees Bank St. Coll. Edn., 1988-89; graduate adv. bd. Wharton Sch., 1986—. Recipient award Women's Bond Club N.Y., 1986. Office: US HUD 451 7th St SW Rm 9100 Washington DC 20410

FITTS, ELIZABETH ANNE, consultant, designer; b. Columbus, Ohio, May 6, 1951; d. Paul Morris, Jr. and Mary Ellen (Switzer) F.; m. Clarence Novak James, June 19, 1977 (div. May 1982). BA, U. Mich., 1972, MA, 1974. Pres., founder At Last Dancers, Inc., Ann Arbor, Mich., 1978; dir. rsch. Campaign for Mich. U. Mich., Ann Arbor, 1979-82; dir. rsch. New Sch. Social Rsch., N.Y.C., 1984-85; dir. devel. and external rels. Sch. Internat./Pub. Affairs Columbia U., N.Y.C., 1985-86, profl. schs. major gift officer Campaign for Columbia, 1986-88; exec. dir. Arts and Scis. Found., Chapel Hill, N.C., 1988-89; dir. devel. Coll. Arts and Scis., U. N.C., Chapel Hill, 1988-89, assoc. dean, 1988-89; prin., cons. Design Strategies, Ann Arbor, 1989—. Choreographer, performer Lightscape, 1979, Solo Alliance, 1979-80, Congluence, 1980, Intervisions, 1980, Compass Rose, 1981; choreographer, Space Opera One, 1981; dancer Just Moving Co., 1972. Mem. AAUW. Democrat. Office: Design Strategies 4061 Thornoaks Dr Ann Arbor MI 48104

FITZGERALD, CHICKE W., travel executive; b. Louisville, Oct. 14, 1957; d. Latham E. Jr. and Roberta Adeline (Shaw) Wright; m. Michael J. Fitzgerald. Student, Oral Roberts U., 1975; student in bus., U. Mich., 1987. V.p. CAPTURE Tech. Support; nat. sales mgr. Travelink, Denver; product mgr. product devel. Am. Airlines; mng. dir. SABRE Joint Ventures Am. Airlines, Dallas; now mng. dir. Latin Am.-SABRE Am. Airlines; presenter confs. in field. Mem. NAFE.

FITZGERALD, ELLA, singer; b. Newport News, Va., Apr. 25, 1918; m. Ray Brown (div. 1953); 1 son, Ray. Began singing with Chick Webb Orch., 1934-39; tours throughout U.S., Japan, Europe; with Jazz at the Philharmonic troupe, 1948-57; rec. artist for Decca, 1936-55, Verve, from 1956, now Pablo Records; appeared in motion picture Pete Kelly's Blues, 1955; nightclub appearances include Sahara Hotel, Caesar's Palace, both Las Vegas, Fairmont Hotel, San Francisco, Ronnie Scott's Club, London; appeared on TV in spls. with Frank Sinatra; also on All Star Swing Festival, 1972, concert with Boston Pops, 1972; later with more than 40 symphony orchs. throughout U.S.; records include At Duke's Place, 1966, Best, 1967, Clap Hands, 1961, Cote d' Azur, (with Ellington), 1967, Ella, Ella Fitzgerald; In Hamburg, 1965, Mack the Knife, Ella in Berlin, 1960, Sunshine of Your Love, Things Ain't What They Used to Be, Tribute to Porter, 1965,

Whisper Not, 1966, Watch What Happens, 1972, Take Love Easy, 1975, Ella in London, 1975, Lady Time, 1978, A Perfect Match (with Count Basie), 1979, A Tisket a Tasket, 1985, Montreux Ella, All That Jazz, 1990, numerous others. Recipient 8 Grammy awards, numerous popularity awards from Down Beat mag., Metronome mag., Musicians Poll, JAY Award Poll; named number 1 female singer 16th Internat. Jazz Critics Poll, 1968, Commander of Arts and Letters, Paris, 1990; recipient Am. Music award, 1978, Kennedy Center honor, 1979, Grammy award as best female jazz vocalist, 1981, 84; recipient Nat. Medal of the Arts, 1987. Office: care Norman Granz 451 N Canon Dr Beverly Hills CA 90210*

FITZGERALD, GLENNA GIBBS (CADY FITZGERALD), pharmacologist, toxicologist; b. Westfield, Mass., Nov. 17, 1926; d. Irving Henry and Louise Hilda (Nietzold) Cady; m. Robert DeMars Fitzgerald, July 14, 1951. BS, U. Mass., 1948, MS, 1964; PhD, Yale U., 1969. Instr. George Washington U., Washington, 1969-71; staff fellow lab. cerebral metabolism NIH, Bethesda, Md., 1971-77; pharmacologist, toxicologist FDA/HHS, Rockville, Md., 1977—. Mem. Assn. Govt. Toxicologists, Am. Soc. for Clin. Pharmacology and Therapeutics, N.Y. Acad. Scis. Office: FDA 5600 Fishers Ln Rockville MD 20857

FITZGERALD, SISTER JANET ANNE, college president; b. Woodside, N.Y., Sept. 4, 1935; d. Robert W. and Lillian H. (Shannon) F. B.A. magna cum laude, St. John's U., 1965, M.A., 1967, Ph.D., 1971, LLD (hon.), 1981. Joined Sisters of St. Dominic of Amityville, Roman Catholic Ch., 1953; NSF postdoctoral fellow Cath. U. Am., summer 1971; prof. philosophy Molloy Coll., Rockville Centre, N.Y., 1969—; pres. Molloy Coll., 1972—; chmn. L.I. Regional Adv. Council on Higher Edn., 1981-84, trustee, 1985—; trustee Commn. on Ind. Colls. and Univs., Fellowship of Cath. Scholars, 1977—, v.p., 1977-80; Roman Cath. Ch. rep. to Nat. Congress Ch.-Related Colls. and Univs., 1979; trustee Cath. Charities, Diocese of Rockville Centre, 1979-82; invited expert Internat. Meeting on Cath. Higher Edn., Rome, 1989. Author: Alfred North Whitehead's Early Philosophy of Space and Time, 1979. Mem. bd. advisors Sem. of Immaculate Conception, 1975-80; mem. adv. bd. pre-theology program Dunwoodie Sem., Archdiocese of N.Y. Recipient Disting. Leadership award L.I. Bus. News, 1988, Pathfinder award Town of Hempstead, 1990; plaque of recognition L.I. Women's Coun. for Equal Edn. Tng. and Employment, 1989. Office: Molloy Coll 1000 Hempstead Ave Rockville Centre NY 11570

FITZGERALD, JANICE S., public relations executive, academic administrator; b. Poughkeepsie, N.Y., Nov. 2, 1948; d. Lloyd Raymond and Emily Mae (Anderson) Spinner. BA magna cum laude, Cheyney U. Pa., 1972, MEd, 1973; MA, Villanova U., 1980; postgrad., Carnegie Mellon U., 1979. Prof. Cheyney U. Pa., 1972-74; dir. pub. rels. Cheyney U. Pa., Cheyney, 1974-83; dir. pub. rels. Pa. State System of Higher Edn., Harrisburg, 1983—, exec. assoc. to chancellor, dir. communications, 1985-90, exec. deputy, 1990—; reader Nat. Edn. Assn.; pres. Correct Correspondence; free lance writer. Vol. radio reader, Tri-County Assn. of Blind, Suburban Guild, Community Gen. Osteo. Hosp.; pub. rels. coun. State System of Higher Edn. Named one of Outstanding Women in Am., 1981, named Alumnus of Yr. Nat. Assn. Equal Opportunity, 1985; recipient award Chapel of Four Chaplains, 1982, Valedictory and Alumni Key award Cheyney U. Pa., 1972. Mem. Coll. and U. Pub. Relations Assn. of Pa., Pub. Relations Soc. of Am., Edn. Writers Assn. Office: Office of Chancellor Pa State System Higher Edn PO Box 809 Harrisburg PA 17108

FITZGERALD, JOYCE ISABEL, retired elementary school teacher; b. Newark, Feb. 2, 1929; d. Earl Andrew and Mary Katherine (Santo) Ellis; m. Matthew Dziekowski, Apr. 15, 1949 (div. May 1961); children: Nancy Ann, Stephen Brian; m. Edward Joseph Fitzgerald, Apr. 3, 1982. BS, Kean Coll., 1959; MEd, Rutgers U., 1961; 6th yr. level, Kean Coll., 1963. Cert. elem., early childhood edn., remediation grades K-12. Tchr. Bloomfield (N.J.) Bd. of Edn., 1958-84; tutor Project Read, 1987-90. Docent Montclair Art Mus., 1986-90. Recipient Fulbright scholarship U.S. Office of Edn., 1977-78. Mem. AAUW (treas. 1985-90).

FITZGERALD, JUDITH KLASWICK, judge; b. Spangler, Pa., May 10, 1948; d. Julius Francis and Regina Marie (Pregno) Klaswick; m. Jeffrey Lloyd Giltenboth, June 5, 1971 (div. Dec. 1982); 1 child, Kaelen Jennifer; m. Barry Robert Fitzgerald, Sept. 20, 1986; 1 child, Martha Erin. BSBA, U. Pitts., 1970, JD, 1973. Legal researcher Assocs. Fin., Pitts., 1972-73; law clk. to pres. judge Beaver County (Pa.) Ct. Common Pleas, 1973-74; law clk. to judge Pa. Superior Ct., Pitts., 1974-75; asst. U.S. atty. U.S. Dist. Ct. (we. dist.) Pa., Pitts. and Erie, 1976-87; U.S. bankruptcy judge U.S. Dist. Ct. (we. dist.) Pa., Pitts., Erie and Johnstown, 1987—. Editor: Pennsylvania Law of Juvenile Delinquency and Deprivation, 1976; contbr. articles to legal jours. Mem. Pitts. Camerata, 1978-80, Allegheny County Polit.-Legal Edn. Project, 1980, West Pa. Conservancy, 1990—, Mendelssohn Choir Pitts., 1982—; mem. coun. Program to Aid Citizen Enterprise, 1985-87. Recipient Spl. Achievement awards Dept. Justice, Spl. Recognition award Pittsburgh mag., Operation Exodus Outstanding Performance award Dept. Commerce, 1986. Mem. Fed. Bar Assn., Allegheny County Bar Assn., Women's Bar Assn. of Western Pa., Nat. Conf. Bankruptcy Judges, Am. Bankruptcy Inst., Fed. Criminal Investigators Assn. (Spl. Svc. award 1988), Nat. Assn. Women Judges, Zonta. Republican. Lutheran. Office: US Bankruptcy Ct 831 Fed Bldg 1000 Liberty Ave Pittsburgh PA 15222

FITZGERALD, MARY CATHERINE, investment advisor; b. Washington, Jan. 26, 1954; d. Joseph Everett and Jeanne Edith (Larson) F. BBA in Acctg., U. Tex., San Antonio, 1982. Athletic specialist USAF, Ramsten AB, Germany, 1972-77; acct. Gill Savs., San Antonio, 1982, Strafco, Inc., San Antonio, 1983; agt. IRS, Dallas, 1983-85; cost analyst USAF, Ft. Worth, 1985-87; lead cost analyst LTV Aerospace and Def. Co., Dallas, 1987—; ptnr. Focus Investment Advs., Arlington, Tex., 1989—. Mem. Nat. Assn. Accts., Nat. Soc. Tax Profls., Arche Scholars Honor Soc., IBM PC Users Group, Microcomputer Users Group, Beta Gamma Sigma. Republican. Roman Catholic. Home: 5715 Cedar Ridge Dr Arlington TX 76017

FITZGERALD, PATRICIA ANN, library administrator, consultant; b. Elmira, N.Y., June 14, 1949; d. Leo Joseph FitzGerald and Catherine Elizabeth (Reed) Green. BA, Syracuse (N.Y.) U., 1971, MLS, 1975; M in Pub. Mgmt., Carnegie Mellon U., 1988. Geology library supr. Syracuse U. Libraries, 1972-76, sci. reference librarian, 1976-78, acting chemistry librarian, 1978; assoc. reference librarian U. Del. Libraries, Newark, 1978-83; head sci. and tech. libraries Carnegie Mellon U. Libraries, Pitts., 1983-87, asst. dir. pub. svc., 1987-90; asst. dir. adminstrv. svc. Welch Med. Libr. Johns Hopkins U., Balt., 1990—. Trustee Pitts. Regional Libr. Ctr., 1988-90, treas., 1988-89, v.p., 1989-90. Mem. ALA, Am. Mgmt. Assn., Spl. Librs. Assn. (sec. info. tech. div. 1983-85, chmn. 1989—), Del. Online Users Group (founder, chmn. 1980-82). Office: Welch Med Libr 1900 E Monument St Baltimore MD 21205

FITZGERALD, SANDRA TUCKER, interior designer; b. Knoxville, Tenn., Jan. 19, 1955; d. Guy Virgil and Mary Frances (Smith) Tucker; m. David J. Fitzgerald, Sept. 26, 1987. BS, U. Tenn., 1977. Draftsman TVA, Knoxville, 1975-77; designer Law's Interiors, Maryville, 1977-80, McQuiddy Office Designers, Knoxville, 1980-82; facility cons. Park Nat. Bank, Knoxville, 1982-83; pres. Corp. Interiors, Inc., Knoxville, 1983—; tchr. U. Tenn., Knoxville, 1970-80. Bd. dirs. Bijou Theatre, Knoxville, 1986—, Knoxville Mus. Art, 1987; mayor apptd. mem. Private Industry Coun. Akima scholar, 1977. Mem. Inst. Bus. Designers, Am. Soc. Interior Designers, Knoxville C. of C. (diplomat), Young Profls. Knoxville Symphony Orch, U.T. Chancellor's Assocs., Exec. Women's Assn. Democrat. Episcopal. Office: Corporate Interiors Inc 318 W Depot Ave Knoxville TN 37917

FITZGERALD, SHERYL CUNNINGHAM, marketing executive; b. Chgo., Apr. 17, 1955; d. Patrick and Aileen Cunningham; m. James Carl Fitzgerald, Oct. 21, 1977; 1 child, Kathleen Cunningham Fitzgerald. BS in Psychology, Loyola U., Chgo., 1977. With sales and promotion Solar Energy Products, Skokie, Ill., 1978-82; with bookkeeping and promotion Am. Solar Chgo., Chgo., 1982-85; asst. to dir. of sales Western Golf Assn., Golf, Ill., 1985-88; dir. of sales Western Golf Assn., Golf, 1988—. Mem. NAFE, Art Inst. Chgo., Smithsonian Instn. Office: Western Golf Assn 1 Briar Rd Golf IL 60029

FITZGERALD-REDDY, KATHLEEN APRIL, environmental research administrator; b. Jamaica, N.Y., Apr. 6, 1955; d. Leo Thomas and Florence Ann (Kehoe) Fitzgerald; m. James M. Metcalfe, Jan. 17, 1981 (div. May 1982); m. John Morley Reddy, Feb. 15, 1985; 1 child, Kathleen Elizabeth. Student, U. N.H., 1973-78. Profl. model Barbizon Agy., Boston, 1974-76, Hart Agy., Boston, 1976-78; announcer Sta. WBBX Kressman Broadcasting Co., Portsmouth, N.H., 1978-80, Sta. WOKQ The Fuller-Jeffrey Group, Dover, N.H., 1980-85; environ. analyst Briggs Assocs, Inc., Rockland, Mass., 1985-86; mgr. environ. rsch. Briggs Assocs, Inc., Rockland, 1986-88; pres. KF Reddy Environ. Rsch., Inc., 1988—. Recipient Graniteer award Ad Club of N.H., 1979, Achievement Cert. in Hazardous Waste Regulations Lion Tech., 1986. Mem. Soc. for the Preservation of New Eng. Antiquities, Hampton Hist. Soc. Democrat. Roman Catholic. Home: 15 Blake Ln Hampton NH 03842 Office: KF Reddy Environ Rsch PO Box 831 Boston MA 02134

FITZGIBBON, JANE, advertising agency executive. With Yankelovich, Skelly & White; with Ogilvy & Mather, N.Y.C., 1981—, formerly head rsch., sr. v.p., group dir., 1988—. Office: Ogilvy & Mather Advt 309 W 49th St New York NY 10014*

FITZPATRICK, DARLEEN A., anthropologist; b. Greensburg, Ind., Aug. 21, 1941; d. Ferris Woodbridge Fitzpatrick and Betty Lee (Breeze) DelBuono. BA, U. Wash., Seattle, 1964, MA, 1968; PhD, U. Wash., 1986. Instr. Everett CC, 1969; cons. various Western Wash. Indian Tribes, 1986-89. Democrat. Office: Everett CC 801 Wetmore Ave Everett WA 98107

FITZPATRICK, ELIZABETH FLORIDIS, speech, language pathologist; b. Ann Arbor, Mich., Dec. 27, 1954; d. George F. and Georgia T. (Poulos) Floridis; m. John L. Fitzpatrick, Oct. 10, 1981. BS, Ind. U. of Pa., 1977; MA, Trenton State Coll., 1989. Speech and lang. specialist Lenape Regional High Sch., Medford, N.J., 1977-79; speech correctionist Edn. and Tng. Cons., Haddonfield, N.J., 1979-81, Collingswood (N.J.) Pub. Schs., 1981—. Mem. AAUW, Am. Speech-Lang. Hearing Assn. N.J. Speech-Lang.-Hearing Assn., Tri-County Speech-Lang.-Hearing Assn., Collingswood Edn. Assn. (co-chmn. grievance com. 1987-89, sec. 1989-90, 90—). Republican. Home: 719 Eldridge Ave Collingswood NJ 08107

FITZPATRICK, ELLEN, economist, consultant; b. Newark, June 22, 1957; d. Robert and Joan M. (Tampany) F. BA, Rutgers U., 1979, MA; MS, Poly. U., White Plains, N.Y. Assoc. dir., staff mgr., staff specialist N.Y. Telephone, N.Y.C.; mgr. KPMG Peat Marwick, Short Hills, N.J. Mem. Am. Econ. Assn., Nat. Assn. Bus. Economists, N.Y. Assn. Bus. Economists. Home: 180 Lafayette Ave Apt 2C Passaic NJ 07055 Office: 150 JFK Pkwy Short Hills NJ 07078

FITZPATRICK, TRACY ELIZABETH, strategic planning consultant; b. N.Y.C., Oct. 7, 1954; d. Hugh Francis Fitzpatrick and Lucy Allen (Jobson) Wierum. BA in Polit. Philosophy and Ethics, Brown U., 1976; MS in Labor Studies, U. Mass., 1983; postgrad., Harvard U./Radcliffe Coll., 1989—. Organizer Svc. Employees Internat. Union, Providence, 1977-81; adminstrv. dir. Ctr. for Popular Econs., Amherst, Mass., 1981-82; instr. labor studies U. Mass., Amherst, 1982; coord. rsch. and planning R.I. Inst. Labor Studies and Rsch., Providence, 1983-85; econ. devel. specialist State Senator John Houston, Worcester, Mass., 1985-87; asst. sec. labor Commonwealth of Mass., Boston, 1987-90; assoc. Klein & Co., Cambridge, Mass., 1990—; adj. prof. R.I. Coll., Providence, 1984-85; mem. adv. bd. Women's Inst. Labor Studies, Boston, 1987—; bd. dirs. Women's Inst. Leadership and Devel. Author: (manual) Setting Up and Running a Multi-Service Neighborhood Ctr., R.I. Dept. Community Affairs, 1976; co-author: Plant Closures & Community Recovery, 1990. Bd. dirs. Labor Rels. and Rsch. Ctr., U. Mass., 1988—. Award recipient R.I. Labor History Soc., 1989; recipient Labor Edn. award R.I. Inst. Labor Studies and Rsch., 1987, Alumni to Watch award U. Mass., 1988. Mem. Am. Soc. Tng. and Devel., Boston Labor Guild, Orgn. Devel. Network. Democrat. Office: Klein & Co 20 University Rd #410 Cambridge MA 02138

FITZPATRICK-DAVIS, JUDITH, manufacturing executive, immunochemistry researcher; b. Providence, Mar. 18, 1941; d. Walter Leo and Helen (Desmond) Fitzpatrick; m. Thomas E. Davis; children: Catherine, Laura, Diane. BA, Seton Hill Coll., 1963; MA, Syracuse U., 1968; PhD, CUNY, 1982. Cert. immunochemist. Rsch. asst. neurobiology U.S. Army, Edgewood Arsenal, Md., 1963-65; rsch. asst. Ahmadu Bello U., Nigeria, 1966-67; lectr. Cornell U., Ithaca, N.Y., 1969; v.p. Comparative Pathology Lab., Bklyn., 1970-75; sr. rsch. chemist Becton Dickinson Immunodiagnostics, Orangeburg, N.Y., 1982-84; pres. Serex Inc., Tenafly, N.J., 1984—. Contbr. rsch. articles to profl. jours., 1980-88. Pres. Bklyn Block Assn., 1972-74, Tenafly Mid. Sch., 1983; mem. Dem. Com., Bklyn. Mem. Am. Assn. Clin. Chemists (media rep. N.J. chpt. 1987—), Am. Soc. Microbiologists, Am. Assn. Sci., LWV. Home: 236 Highwood Ave Tenafly NJ 07670 Office: Serex Inc 38 Franklin St Tenafly NJ 07670

FITZSIMMONS, SOPHIE SONIA, interior designer; b. Paris, July 6, 1943; came to U.S., 1947; d. Oleg and Sophie (Ovsianico-Koulikovsky) Yadoff; m. J. Heath Fitzsimmons, Sept. 8, 1962; children: Gregory James, Raymond Heath, Douglas Paul. AAS with honors, Fashion Inst. Tech., N.Y.C., 1964. Design intern Euster Assocs., Inc., Armonk, N.Y., 1964; prin. Sophie Y. Fitzsimmons Interior Design, N.Y., Conn, 1964-77; co-owner Avon (Conn.), Interiors, Inc., 1977-89; prin. Sophie Fitzsimmons Interior Design, N.Y.C., 1989—; guest exhibitor Fashion Inst. Tech. Symposium, 1984. Chair Ann. Show of Hope Benefit, Hartford, Conn., 1975; mem. Rep. Women's Club, Simsbury, Conn., 1978-89; bd. dirs. Friends of Hartford Ballet, 1986-88. Mem. Nat. Soc. Interior Designers (adv. panel 1967), Hartford Stage Co. Stagehands, World Affairs Coun. (exec. forum), Mark Twain Meml., Wadsworth Atheneum, Bushnell Meml., Simsbury Farms Golf Assn. (bd. dirs. 1989). Office: Sophie Fitzsimmons Interior Design Ste 8A 55 Liberty St New York NY 10005

FITZSIMONS, SHARON RUSSELL, logistics and customer service executive; b. Toronto, Ont., Can., June 25, 1945; d. Leslie Alfred and Winifred Marjorie (Williston) Russell; m. John Henry Fitzsimons, Jan. 4, 1969; children: Luke Edward, Michael Russell. BA, U. So. Calif., 1968; MA, Calif. State U., 1971; MS in Bus. Adminstrn., U. Calif., Irvine, 1978. Mgr. research William Pereira Assocs., Newport Beach, Calif., 1970-71; asst. mgr. interior design Concept Environment Inc. subs. Ford Motor Co., Orange County, Calif., 1971-72; v.p. Urban Interface Group, Orange County, 1972-74; cons. in field, 1975-76; mgr. strategic planning Mission Viejo Co., Orange County, 1976-80; mgr. fin. Philip Morris Internat., N.Y.C., 1980-82, asst. treas., 1982-84, logistics exec., Melbourne, Australia, 1984-86, dir. U.S. export logistics and customer service, N.Y.C., 1987-90, dir. fin., treas., N.Y.C., 1990—. Office: care Philip Morris Internat 120 Park Ave New York NY 10017

FITZWATER-HEUMANN, KATHRYN ANNE, veterinarian; b. Lafayette, Ind., Apr. 22, 1951; d. William David Jr. and Ann (H.) Fitzwater; m. Robert Charles Heumann Jr., June 12, 1988. BS with distinction, U. N.Mex., 1980; DVM cum laude, Washington State U., 1984; DVM, Oreg. State U., 1984. Staff vet. Vet. Care Clinic, Albuquerque, 1984-85, Avenida Animal Clinic, San Clemente, Calif., 1985-86, Villa Animal Hosp., Orange, Calif., 1986—. Mem. Am. Vet. Med. Assn., Calif. Vet. Med. Assn., So. Calif. Vet. Med. Assn., World Wildlife Fund, Nat. Wildlife Fedn., Nature Conservancy, Zoolog. Soc. San Diego, Phi Beta Kappa. Home: 146 Avenida Miraman #B San Clemente CA 92672 Office: Villa Animal Hosp 4250 E Chapman Orange CA 92667

FIX-ROMLOW, JEANNE KAY, hair care products company executive; b. Madison, Wis., June 29, 1947; d. Glen H. and Violet M. (Bohnsack) Fix; m. Paul James Romlow, Nov. 7, 1985. Student, Madison Area Tech. Sch., 1966. Mgr. Fashion Fabrics, Madison, 1973-74; promotion dir. Livesey Enterprises, Madison, 1976-77; sales assoc. First Realty Group, Madison, 1977-79; territory mgr. Aerial Beauty and Barber Supply, Madison, 1979-83; regional dir. John Paul Mitchell Systems, Santa Clarita, Calif., 1983-85, v.p., 1986-87, sr. v.p., 1987—. Home: W11344 Bay Dr Lodi WI 53555 Office: John Paul Mitchell Systems 26455 Golden Valley Rd Santa Clarita CA 91350

FLACK, ROBERTA, singer; b. Black Mountain, N.C., Feb. 10, 1939; d. Laron and Irene F.; m. Stephen Novosel, 1966 (div. 1972). B.A. in Music Edn., 1958. Tchr. music and English lit. pub. schs. Farmville, N.C., Washington, 1959-67; rec. artist Atlantic Records, 1968—. Star ABC TV spl. The First Time Ever, 1973; composer: (with Jesse Jackson and Joel Dorn) Go Up, Moses; albums include: First Take, 1969, Chapter Two, 1970, Quiet Fire, 1971, Killing Me Softly, 1973, Feel Like Makin' Love, 1975, Blue Lights In The Basement, 1977, Roberta Flack, 1978, The Best of Roberta Flack, 1981, I'm The One, 1982, Born To Love, 1983, Hits and History, 1984, Roberta Flack, 1985, Oasis, 1989; writer TV theme song Valerie. Recipient Gold Record for The First Time Ever I Saw Your Face, 1972; Grammy awards for best record (The First Time Ever I Saw Your Face), 1972, (Killing Me Softly With His Song), 1973, best pop vocal duo (Where Is The Love), 1972, best female pop vocal (Killing Me Softly With His Song), 1973; winner Downbeat's reader poll as best female vocalist, 1971-73; City of Washington celebrated Roberta Flack Human Kindness Day, 1972. Mem. Sigma Delta Chi. Office: care Atlantic Records 75 Rockefeller Pla New York NY 10019*

FLAER, LORRAINE FLORENCE, executive secretary; b. Troy, N.Y., Sept. 20, 1935; d. Joseph and Yvette (Chayt) Levine; m. Ted Alan Flaer, July 3, 1955; children: Steven, Gayle, Keith. AA, Rider Coll., 1955. Typist Pub. Svc. Electric & Gas Co., Trenton, N.J., 1955-57; in sales Flaer Shoes, Inc., Burlington, N.J., 1961-75, Cinnaminson, N.J., 1966-86; receptionist CompuCom Systems, Cherry Hill, N.J., 1987-88; exec. sec. Delran Info Svcs. Ctr., Macmillan Inc., Delran, N.J., 1988—. Rec. sec. Temple Sinai Sisterhood, Cinnaminson, 1970s, bd. dirs., 1970-74; bd. dirs. Women's Am. ORT, 1962-65. Rider Coll. scholar, 1953-55. Office: Delran Info Ctr Macmillan 900 Chester Ave Delran NJ 08075

FLAHERTY, GERLINDE M. (LYNN FLAHERTY), research administrator; b. Stuttgart, Fed. Republic Germany, Feb. 19, 1942; came to U.S., 1959; d. Wilhelm and Frida (Lorenz) Klenk; m. Gerard Eugene Flaherty, June 9, 1962; children—Curt P., Wayne T. Ed., Germany. With Honeywell Corp., 1959-89, word processing coordinator, Ft. Washington, Pa., 1977-83, sr. systems rep. Bull HN Info. Systems (formerly Honeywell Inc.), Bala Cynwyd, Pa., 1983-89; exec. sec. clin. rsch. Rorer Pharm. Corp., Horsham, Pa., 1989—. Mem. Assn. Info. Systems Profls. (pres. Ft. Washington chpt. 1982-86), Am. Bus. Women's Assn. (v.p. membership 1984, pres. 1987-88, v.p. 1986, developer, organizer new chpt. 1988—, Woman of Yr. 1983), NAFE. Home: 1194 Emma Ln Warminster PA 18974 Office: Rorer Cen Rsch 800 Business Center Dr Horsham PA 19044

FLAHERTY, HEIDI ANNE-MARIE, senior financial analyst; b. Sioux City, Iowa, Feb. 9, 1962; d. Robert Thomas and Wilma Claire (Harrigfeld) F. BA, U. Calif., Santa Barbara, Calif., 1984; MBA, U. Santa Clara, 1990. Shift mgr. McDonald's Restaurant, Sunnyvale, Calif., 1978-79; busboy Velvet Turtle Restaurant, Sunnyvale, 1979-80; warehouse mgr. Recsei Labs., Inc., Goleta, Calif., 1980-84; sales rep. Executone No. Calif., Inc., San Bruno, Calif., 1984-85; engr. project analyst Westinghouse Corp., Sunnyvale, 1985-86, fin. analyst, 1986-87, dept. defense liaison, 1987-88; sr. fin. analyst Verilink Corp., San Jose, Calif., 1988-89, Pyramid Tech., Mountain View, Calif., 1989-. Mem. Mensa Soc., Churchill Club, Santa Clara Univ. MBA Assn., Alumni U. Calif. Santa Barbara Assn. Office: Pyramid Tech 1295 Charleston Rd Mountain View CA 94043

FLAHERTY, ROBERTA D., university official; b. Sharon, Pa., Aug. 7, 1947; d. Thomas and Esther Mary (Dornes) Roberts; m. Glassel D. Flaherty, Sept. 4, 1966; 1 child, Erin Leigh. BEd, Washburn U., 1970; MS in Edn., Kans. State U., 1975; postgrad. in profl. devel., Harvard U., 1985; postgrad., Kans. State U., 1985-89. With admissions office Kans. State U., Manhattan, 1970-72, transcript analyst, 1972-75, acad. advisor div. continuing edn., 1975-77, asst. dir. acad. outreach, 1977-78, dir. confs., 1978-88, assoc. dir. div. continuing edn., 1986—; mem. external rev. team consultancy U. N.D., Grand Forks, 1989. Bd. dirs. United Way Riley County, Manhattan, 1984-87, campus campaign chmn., 1986; program chmn. Future Manhattan Leadership Program, 1989. Mem. Nat. Univ. Continuing Edn. Assn. (chmn., officer region V, 1979-83, nat. chmn., officer confs. and insts. div. 1989-90, Leadership award 1988, 89), Am. Assn. Higher Edn. Home: 4427 Tuttle Cove Rd Manhattan KS 66502 Office: Kans State U Div Continuing Edn 204 College Ct Manhattan KS 66506

FLAHERTY, TINA S., corporate communications executive; b. Memphis; d. Clement Alexander and Dale (Pendergrast) Santi; m. William Edward Flaherty, Feb. 22, 1975. B.A., Memphis State U., 1961; hon. Doctorate, St. John's U., 1979. Commentator host interview program Sta. WMC-TV, Memphis, 1960-61; newscaster, commentator Sta. WHER, Memphis, 1961-62; community rels. specialist Western Electric Co., N.Y.C., 1964-66; v.p. pub. rels. div. Grey Advt., N.Y.C., 1966-72; dep. dir. corp. rels. Colgate-Palmolive Co., N.Y.C., 1972-75; dir. corp. rels. Colgate-Palmolive Co., 1975-76, corp. v.p., v.p. in charge of communications, 1976-84; v.p. pub. affairs GTE Corp., Stamford, Conn., 1984-86; pres., chief exec. officer Image Mktg. Internat., N.Y.C., 1986—. Gen. chmn. YWCA-N.Y.C., Salute to Women in Bus., 1979; former chmn. Bus. Council of UN Decade for Women; bd. dirs. Sante Fe Chamber Music Festival, York Theatre Co., Nat. Jr. Achievement, 1978—, Hugh O'Brian Youth Found.; v.p., mem. White House Pub. Affairs Advisors; nat. bd. dirs. Animal Med. Ctr.; bd. dirs. York Theatre Co. Recipient Jr. Achievement Colgate Meml. award, 1984; Named One of 8 Extraordinary Women in Bus. and Labor Women's Equity Action League, 1978; One of N.Y.C.'s Outstanding Women of Achievement NCCJ, 1978; One of 100 Top Corp. Women Bus. Week, 1976, One of 73 Women Ready to Run Corp. Am., Working Woman, 1985. Mem. Com. of 200, N.Y. Women's Forum. Home: 50 E 89th St Ste 31D New York NY 10128

FLANAGAN, ANITA MARIE, public relations professional, consultant, writer; b. South Charleston, W.Va., Sept. 25, 1940; d. Henry August and Mary Margaret (Hodge) Thormahlen; m. Shaun Michael Flanagan; children: Michael Lawrance, Sheilah Mary Catherine. AB, Northeastern U., 1963; BS, Southeastern Mass. U., 1977; MS in Environ. Health Mgmt., Harvard U., 1983. Planning cons. Town of Duxbury (Mass.), 1983; mgr. Pub. Participation Program Mass. Dept. Environ. Mgmt., Boston, 1984-86; community relations dir. Clean Harbors Inc., Braintree, Mass., 1986-88, Flanagan-Thompson Assocs., Plymouth, 1988-89; sr. pub. info. rep. Boston Edison Co., Plymouth, Mass., 1989—; hazardous waste coordinator, mem. oil spill response team Town of Duxbury, 1980-85. Mem. Am. Pub. Health Assn., Soc. for Risk Analysis, Am. Nuclear Soc., Nat. Assn. Environ. Profls.

FLANAGAN, DEBORAH MARY, lawyer; b. Hackensack, N.J., Sept. 17, 1956; d. Joseph Francis and Mary Agnes (Fitzsimmons) F.; m. Glen H. Koch, Aug. 27, 1983. BA summa cum laude, Fordham U., 1978, JD, 1981; LLM taxation, NYU, 1987. Bar: N.Y. 1982 and U.S. Dist. Ct. 1988. Sr. tax atty. McGraw-Hill Inc., N.Y.C., 1981—; sec., v.p. Internat. Archtl. Found. Inc., N.Y.C., 1982—; v.p. MHFSCO, Ltd. subs. McGraw-Hill, Inc., N.Y.C., 1984—. Mem. ABA, N.Y. State Bar Assn., Assn. of Bar of City of N.Y., N.Y. County Lawyers Assn., Fordham U. Law Alumni Assn. Home: 114 Harrison Ave Hasbrouck Heights NJ 07604 Office: McGraw-Hill Inc 1221 Ave of Americas New York NY 10020

FLANAGAN, GAIL CLAIRE, brokerage house executive; b. Rockville Centr, NY, Jan. 1, 1952; d. Eugene Edward Flanagan and Nina Lucille (Palagonia) Calabrese. BS in Bus. Adminstrn., Columbia Pacific, San Rafael, Calif., 1987--. Med. tech. Gateway Community Hosp., St. Pete, Fla., 1980-81; chemistry supr. Med. Lab. Services, Clearwater, Fla., 1981-82; account exec. Nat. Assn. Credit Mgmt., Tampa, 1982; registered rep. Prudential Ins., Largo, Fla., Olde Discount Stockbrokers, Clearwater, Fla., 1984-86; asst. regional mgr. Olde Discount Stockbrokers, Fla., 1987-89; registered rep. Dis-Com Securities, St. Pete, Fla., 1986; deferred comp spl. Holden Group, Tallahassee, Fla., 1987; registered rep. Anchor Nat. Fin. Services, Oldsmar, Fla., 1987-89; recruiter Robert Thomas Securities, Inc., St. Petersburg, 1989—. V.p. N.O.W., Pasco County, Fla., 1986-88. Mem. Nat. Assn. Female Execs., Who's Who U.S. Execs. Democrat. Roman Catholic. Office: Robert Thomas Securities 880 Carillon Pkwy Saint Petersburg FL 33716

FLANAGAN, JUDITH ANN, marketing specialist; b. Lubbock, Tex., Apr. 28, 1950; d. James Joseph II and Jean (Breckenridge) F. BS in Edn., Memphis State U., 1972. Area/parade supr. Entertainment div. Walt Disney

World, Orlando, Fla., 1972-81; parade dir. Gatlinburg (Tenn.) C. of C., 1981-85; entertainment prodn. mgr. The 1982 World's Fair, Knoxville, 1982; cons. Judy Flanagan Prodns./Spl. Events, Gatlinburg, 1982—, Miss U.S.A. Pageant, Knoxville, 1983; prodn. coord. Nashville Network, 1983; dir. sales River Terr. Resort, Gatlinburg, 1985-86; account exec. Park Vista Hotel, Gatlinburg, 1986-88; project coord. Universal Studios, Fla., 1989-90; dir. univ. rels. U. Tenn., Knoxville, 1990—; prodn. mgr. 1984 World's Fair Parades and Spl. Events, New Orleans, Neil Sedak rock video, Days of Our Lives daytime soap opera. Mem. Memphis State U. Acad. Donor Fund. Named One of Outstanding Young Women Am., 1981; recipient Gatlinburg Homecoming award, 1986. Mem. Memphis State U. Alumni Assn. Roman Catholic. Home: Rte 1 Gatlinburg TN 37738

FLANAGAN, KATHY MARIE, circuit court judge; b. Chgo., Nov. 25, 1952; d. Gerald Joseph and Rita Mary (Egan) F. BA in History, St. Xavier Coll., Chgo., 1974; JD, John Marshall Law Sch., 1979. Bar: Ill. 1979, U.S. Dist. Ct. (no. dist.) Ill. 1979. Assoc. Albert F. Hofeld, Ltd., Chgo., 1979-80, Pyrdek & Wrobel, Ltd., Oak Lawn, Ill., 1980-81; pvt. practice Oak Lawn, 1981-88; cir. ct. judge Cir. Ct. of Cook County, Ill., 1988—. Mem. Ill. Bar Assn., Chgo. Bar Assn., S.W. Bar Assn. (bd. dirs. Oak Lawn chpt. 1981-87), Coalition Suburban Bar Assn. (sec. 1985, treas. 1986, v.p. 1987). Democrat. Roman Catholic. Office: Cir Ct Cook County 50 W Washington Chicago IL 60602

FLANAGAN, LILLIAN LEE ANN, counselor, consultant; b. Boston, Feb. 15, 1933; d. Joseph E. and Nora Elizabeth (Gorman) Montague; m. M. Paul Flanagan, June 1, 1957; children: Paul, Patricia, Mark, David, Jean. AS in Mental Health, Middlesex Coll., 1979; student, U. N.H., 1975, North Shore Community Coll., Beverly, Mass., 1982, Cath. Hines Inst., Newton, Mass., 1987. Lic. mental health counselor, Mass. Spl. needs asst. Melrose (Mass.) Pub. Schs., 1976-79; counselor New Eng. Meml. Hosp., Stoneham, Mass., 1979-87, substance abuse counselor, 1982-87; esthetician St. John., V.I., 1987—; coord. social and survival skills, Melrose Pub. Schs., 1972-76; coord. ind. living skiis, EMARC, Melrose, 1977; rep. Child Search, Melrose, 1978; co-dir. Hospice Grief Work, Wakefield, Mass., 1980-82. Speaker parent groups Rotary-Lions, Melrose, 1976; coord. 766 Census, Melrose, 1973, Melrose Assn. Children Learning Disabilities, 1972-77, Our Lady of Mt. Carmel Cath. Ch. Youth Group, St. John, V.I., 1989; liaison Melrose Pub. Schs., 1974-77; implementor, Scholarship Fund for Learning Disabilities High Sch. Srs., Melrose, 1979; coord. vols. Nat. Park, St. John, 1987, 88; cons. Channel 10 TV News, St. John, 1989. Home: 10-1-1 Gluksberg Saint John VI 00830

FLANAGAN, NATALIE SMITH, state representative; b. Bradford, Mass., Aug. 6, 1913; d. Forrest Van Zandt and Blanche (Robbins) Smith; m. John Frances Flanagan. Grad. high sch., Vassalboro, Maine. Mem. N.H. Ho. of Reps., Concord, 1973—. Pres. Mass. chpt. Young Reps., 1930—; pres. bd. dirs. Haverhill (Mass.) Girls Club, 1940—; founder Rockingham (N.H.) Nutrition Program, 1979; mem. N.H. Bicentennial Commn., 1983—. Recipient Meritorious Pub. Svc. medal Sec. State, 1990. Congregationalist. Home: 132 Maple Ave Atkinson NH 03811 Office: NH State Legislature Legislative Office Bldg Rm 210 Concord NH 03301

FLANAGAN, THERESE ANN, real estate company executive; b. Chgo., Sept. 23, 1955; d. William Joseph and Margaret Eileen (McNellis) F. BA, U. Fla., 1984, MA, 1987. With First Fed. of Lake Worth, Fla., 1973-74, Fla. Nat. Bank, Palm Beach, Fla., 1974-75, 77-79; salesman Irish Realty, Inc., Lake Worth, 1979-81; asst. mgr. Sun Bay Apts., Gainesville, Fla., 1982; with Library Systems, U. Fla., Gainesville, 1982-86; pres. Flanagan & Assocs. Realty, Lake Worth, 1986—. Producer, dir. video Zora Neale Hurston, 1986. Vol. Textbook Reading for the Blind, Gainesville, 1987, The Children's Pl., West Palm Beach, Fla., 1988-89, Project Literacy, West Palm Beach, 1988-89. Mem. Modern Lang. Assn., Nat. Assn. Realtors, Fla. Assn. Realtors, Central Palm Beach County Assn. Realtors, Russian Club (treas. 1983-84), Phi Kappa Phi. Democrat. Roman Catholic. Office: Flanagan & Assocs Realty 3939 S Congress Ave Lake Worth FL 33461

FLANAGAN-HERSTEK, KATHERINE M., college administrator; b. Wilkes-Barre, Pa., Dec. 26, 1951; d. Mark Joseph and Mary Catherine (Whalen) Flanagan; m. Paul J. Herstek; children: Keith, Mark. BS in Elem. Edn., Bloomsburg U., 1973; MS in Human Svcs., Coll. Misericordia, 1988. Head tchr., chief adminstr. Children's Sch., Wilkes-Barre, 1975-77; med. social worker Wilkes-Barre Gen. Hosp., 1977-79; vol. coord. Children's Mus., Forty-Fort, Pa., 1975-81; ednl. counselor Victims Resource Ctr., Wilkes-Barre, 1981-85; coord. non credit programs Coll. Misericordia, Dallas, Pa., 1985-86, dir. experiential learning, 1986-88, asst. to acad. dean, 1988-89; dir. evening, summer and weekend programs Wilkes U., Wilkes-Barre, 1989—. Conf. organizer, presenter Luzerne County Women's Network, Wilkes-Barre, 1985-89; participant Leadership Wilkes-Barre, 1988-89; mem. adv. bd. Intercollegiate Leadership, Luzerne County, 1988-89; campus coord. United Way of Wyoming Valley, Luzerne County, 1988, vol. ednl. div., 1989, co-chair 1990 campaign. Recipient Pocono Northeast award Econ. Devel Coun. N.E. Pa., 1984. Mem. Victims Resource Ctr. Democrat. Home: 116 S Lehigh Trucksville PA 18708 Office: Wilkes U Max Roth Ctr Wilkes-Barre PA 18766

FLANDERS, DEANNE BOWMAN, advertising agency executive; b. Nashville, June 5, 1946; d. Edward Lawrence and Marie Hayley (Smith) Bowman; divorced; children: Katherine Marie, Scott Gregory. BS magna cum laude, U. Tenn., Chattanooga, 1974. Engring. asst. McMoRan Exploration, New Orleans, 1970-72; co-owner, mgr. Chattanooga's Little Shopper, 1975-82; co-owner, mgr. Dimension Advt., Chattanooga, 1979-86, owner, 1986; owner, mgr. Deanne Flanders & Assocs., Chattanooga, 1986—, Advantage Advt., Chattanooga, 1987—. Mem. steering com. March of Dimes, Chattanooga, 1985—, United Way, Chattanooga, 1988—. Mem. Chattanooga Advt. Fedn. (Chad awards 1986-89). Office: 1923 Hamill Rd Chattanooga TN 37342

FLANDERS, HELEN DRIVER, psychotherapist; b. El Paso, Tex., Dec. 1, 1947; d. Walter Williamson and Carolyn (Mayfield) Driver; m. John C. Flanders, Aug. 24, 1968 (div. 1986); children: Carolyn B., Sarah L., Laura C. BA in Communications, Stanford U., 1969; MA in Journalism, U. Colo., Boulder, 1970, MA in Edn., 1988, postgrad., 1990—. Cert. addictions counselor, Colo. Artist, gallery mgr. Longmont, Colo., 1970-87; art therapist Memonal Hosp., Boulder, 1986-88; psychotherapist incest survivors Serenity Ctr. Personal Growth, Inc., Boulder, 1988-89; psychotherapist Boulder Alcohol Edn. Ctr., 1988—; art therapist Boulder Community Hosp., 1988, 89; case mgr. inpatient psychotherapist Women's Recovery Ctr. Boulder Community Hosp., 1989—; pvt. practice Boulder, 1990—; vol. art therapist, Longmont United Hosp., 1985. Watercolor and acrylic paintings exhibited in 10 solo exhbns., numerous regional and local shows; represented in pvt. collections. Bd. dirs. Longmont LWV, 1970-75, Longmont Attention Home for Troubled Youth, 1981-82. Mem. PEO, Am. Assn. Counseling and Devel., Am. Mental Health Counselors Assn., Assn. Specialists in Group Work, Assn. Human Psychology, Soc. C.G. Jung, C.G. Jung Inst. Chgo., Nat. Disting. Svc. Registry Counseling and Devel. Assn. for Humanistic Psychology, Theta Sigma Phi, Kappa Tau Alpha, Kappa Delta Pi. Congregationalist. Office: Psychotherapist Ste 210 350 Broadway Boulder CO 80303

FLANIGAN, JEANNE MARIE, artist, animator; b. Champagne, Ill., Oct. 26, 1946; d. Harold Herbert and Mary Estelle (Walsh) Brosius; m. Jerry Hollenbeck, May 7, 1965 (div. 1972); children: Jay, Jayne, Jack; m. Michael Cletus Flanigan, Sept. 19, 1987. BFA, U. Okla., 1979, postgrad., 1979-82. Owner Hollenbeck House Costumes, Tulsa, 1967-74; animator Terry Miller Design Group, Norman, Okla., 1981-82; animator - freelance, 1980—; curator of edn. Okla. Mus. Art, Oklahoma City, 1982-84; dir. Individual Artists of Okla., Oklahoma City, 1984-85; owner Jeanne Flanigan Prodns., Norman, 1990—; tchr. animation and arts various art ctrs., schs., Okla., 1982-89. Videographer: I Had a Dream..., 1979. Bd. dirs. Norman Arts & Humanities Coun., 1988—, Progressive Independence, 1988—, Women's Studies Adv. Bd., 1980-82. Recipient 4 Addys, 1989, 3 Addys, 1990 (Oklahoma Cit6y Advt. Club), Dist. 10 Merit, Am. Advt. Fedn., 1990. lMem. NOW, Norman C. of C., Nat. Assn. Artists Orgns. (bd. dirs. 1984-86), Okla. Visual Arts Coalition, AAUW, Women's Polit. Caucus, Oklahoma City Ad Club. Home: 545 S Lahoma Norman OK 73069 Office: Jeanne Flanigan Prodns 213 W Main St Norman OK 73069

FLANIGAN, SUSAN WILSON, interior design company owner; b. Louisville, Aug. 28, 1946; d. Rollin Allen and Dorothy Ruth (Sparks) Wilson; m. Pierce John Flanigan III, Dec. 27, 1969; children: Emily Sparks, Meghan Spencer, Pierce John IV, Thomas Wilson. AB, Goucher Coll., 1968. Secondary sch. tchr. Towson (Md.) High Sch., 1968-70; vol. Balt., 1970-80; pres., owner Maison, Inc., Balt., 1980—. Fundraiser Family & Children's Svcs., Balt., 1986-90, Bryn Mawr Sch., Roland Park Country Sch., Calvert Sch., Balt., 1976-90; vice-chmn. Hunt Valley Antiques Show, Balt., 1990-91. Democrat. Presbyterian.

FLANNERY, ANNE CATHERINE, lawyer; b. N.Y.C., Nov. 2, 1951; d. John Francis and Marion Catherine (Flynn) F. BA, Marymont Manhattan Coll, 1973; JD, Bklyn. Law Sch., 1976. Bar: N.Y. 1977, U.S. Supreme Ct. 1980. Various legal positions SEC, Washington, 1976-81; assoc. regional adminstr. SEC, N.Y.C., 1981-87; of counsel Morgan, Lewis & Bockius, N.Y.C., 1987-89; ptnr. Morgan, Lewis & Bockius, 1989—. Contbr. articles to profl. jours. Recipient Meritorious Sr. Exec. award Pres. Ronald Reagan, 1987, Younger Fed. Lawyer award Fed. Bar Assn., 1986. Mem. ABA (task force SEC enforcement subcom. on fed. securities law). Office: Morgan Lewis & Bockius 101 Park Ave New York NY 10178

FLANNERY, CAROLINE OLSON, real estate broker, office manager; b. San Antonio, Apr. 28, 1942; d. Marion Alfred and Martha (Pancoast) Olson; m. John Oge Flannery, Jr., May 21, 1977. BA, U. Tex., 1963; MA, Incarnate Word Coll., San Antonio, 1975. Cert real estate broker, tchr., Tex. Biology tchr. Alamo Heights High Sch., San Antonio, 1965-72; sales and mgmt. tng. supr. Tex. Pharmacal Co., San Antonio, 1972-79; sales assoc. Guy Chipman Co., San Antonio, 1979-81, office mgr., 1981-84; pres. CF Enterprises, San Antonio, 1984-87; mktg. dir. Kuper Realty, 1987-89; office mgr. Hallmark Bradfield Properties, San Antonio, 1989—; instr. Am. Coll. Real Estate, San Antonio, 1986-89. Author: Skin Care Training Manual, 1975. Co-chmn. Bexar Couny Women's Ctr. Assn. Annual Fund Raiser, San Antonio, 1988. Recipient Jr. Goodwill Amb. award Am. Red Cross 9 European Countries, 1958. Mem. Nat. Assn. Realtors, Tex. Assn. Realtors, San Antonio Bd. Realtors, Battle of Flowers Assn., Jr. League of San Antonio, S.W. Found. Forum, Lantana Garden Club (pres. 1986-87). Republican. Episcopalian. Home: 4 Plum Ln San Antonio TX 78218 Office: Hallmark Bradfield Properties 5000 Broadway San Antonio TX 78209

FLECHNER, ROBERTA FAY, graphic designer; b. N.Y.C., June 7, 1949; d. Abraham Julius and Evelyn (Medwin) F. BA, CCNY, 1970; MA, NYU, 1972; cert. Printing Industries Met. N.Y., N.Y.C., 1974, 75, 79. Researcher, asst. editor Arno Press, N.Y.C., 1970-73; free-lance editor Random House, N.Y.C., 1973-74, graphic designer/compositor coll. dept., 1984—; graphic designer Core Communications in Health, N.Y.C., 1974-76; prodn. mgr. Heights-Inwood News, N.Y.C., 1976-77; art dir., graphic designer Jour. Advt. Research, N.Y.C., 1976-81; prin., graphic designer/compositor Roberta Flechner Graphics, N.Y.C., 1976—; graphic designer/compositor W. W. Norton & Co., Inc., 1977—, McGraw Hill, Inc., 1990—; mech. artist Fawcett, N.Y.C., 1979-80; graphic designer Avon Internat., N.Y.C., 1982; art dir., compositor, layout artist Source: Notes in the History of Art, N.Y.C., 1982—; graphic designer John Wiley & Sons, Inc., N.Y.C., 1985. Designer stationery, 1979 (Art Direction mag., Creativity-cert. distinction 1979). Art dir. enviroNews, N.Y. State Atty. Gen.'s Environ. Protection Bur., N.Y.C., 1977-78. Mem. Graphic Artists Guild, NOW, Women's Nat. Book Assn. (cons.), Nat. Assn. Female Execs., Women's Caucus for Art, Am. Inst. Graphic Arts, CCNY Alumni, NYU Alumni. Office: 106-15 Queens Blvd Forest Hills NY 11375

FLECK, JOANNE ELIZABETH TUHKANEN, medical facility administrator, program analyst; b. Duluth, Minn., Nov. 19, 1939; d. Toivo and Kathryn (Dolliver) Tukhanen; m. Marvin Charles Fleck, 1959; children: Kathryn Sarah Kockler, Toivo Paul, Tammy Ray Smith. Lic. practical nurse, Miller Dewan Sch. Nursing, St. Paul, 1959; diploma in emergency med. tng., Area Vocat. Tng. Inst., St. Cloud, Minn., 1977; AA in Mental Health/Social Work, Coll. of St. Benedict, 1981. With nursing dept. Vets. ADMX Med. Ctr., St. Cloud, 1974-79, with med. adminstrv. service, 1979-84, with occupational therapy, 1984-86, EEO cons., 1986-89, quality assurance specialist, 1984-86, patient advisor and rep., 1986—, clin. reviewer Office of Quality Assurance, 1989—. Active Girl Scouts U.S., U.S. and Italy, 1966-74; pres. Noncommd. Officers' Wives Club, Italy, 1974. Named Non-Commd. Officer Wife of Yr. Noncommd. Officers Wives Club, 1973; recipient spl. recognition award Commr. Minn. Dept. Vet. Affairs, 1988. Mem. NAFE, St. Cloud Symphony (bd. dirs.), Am. Hosp. Assn. for Patient Reps., Ambassador Club/St. Cloud C. of C. (legis. and sartell divs.), Nat. Assn. Quality Assurance Profls., Quality Assurance Profls. of Minn. (mem. editorial bd.). Home: PO Box 322 Sartell MN 56377 Office: Vets ADMX Med Ctr Saint Cloud MN 56301

FLECK, MARIANN BERNICE, health scientist; b. San Francisco, June 19, 1922; d. Erwin and Grace B. (Fisher) Kahl; m. Jennings McDaniel, June 1946; m. Jack Donald Fleck, Mar. 28, 1980; children: Gary, Eugene. B of Vocat. Edn., Calif. State U., Long Beach, 1965, BA, 1965, MA, 1968; PhD, U. Santa Barbara, 1975. Prof. life sci. div., adminstr. Fullerton (Calif.) Coll., 1960-75; profl. adminstr. Cypress (Calif.) Coll., 1975-80, prof. emeritus, 1980—; dir., owner Profl. Services Assn. Counseling, Santa Ana, Calif., 1977-80, Hypnosis Ctr., La Mirada, Calif., 1975-80; producer Dr. Mariann Health Program, Sta. KJON, Boonville, Ark., 1980-85; dir. Jack Fleck Golf and Health Acad., Magazine, Ark., 1980—; Pres. H.E.P. Internat., 1983-89; cons. and lectr. in field. U. Calif. scholar; recipient Cert. of Appreciation Ronald Reagan Commemorative medal of honor, 1988. Mem. Am. Guild Hypnotherapists (registered 1989), Am. Personnel and Guidance Assn., Calif. Personnel and Guidance Assn., Am. Running and Fitness Assn. (profl. mem.), Hypnotherapists Speakers Platform, Internat. Speakers Platform Assn. Republican. Presbyterian. Home: Route 1 Box 15A Magazine AR 72943 Office: H&P Internat Magazine AR 72943

FLEET, JHERI CHASTAIN, writer; b. Oklahoma City, May 10, 1940; d. Joe and Geraldine Frances (MacCabe) Chastain; children: John James III, Joe Chastain II, Geraldine Frances III. Student, William Woods Coll., 1958-59; BJ, U. Okla., 1961. Owner, pres. Lemon-Twist, Dallas, 1974-76, Jheri Fleet, Inc., Midland, Tex., 1977-79; dir. pub. relations Theatre Tulsa, 1979-80; freelance writer, photojournalist Tulsa and Midland, Tex., 1981-86; hist. writer Gen. Telephone Co., San Angelo, Tex., 1986-88; pub. Writer's News mag.; creator, producer (TV program) Writer's News; instr. Tulsa Jr. Coll., 1982-84, Odessa Coll., 1984-86, U. Tex., 1988. Author: Child's Guide to Dallas, 1968, to Tulsa, 1980, to Permian Basin, 1985, History of General Telephone of the Southwest, 1988; appeared in commls. and films, 1988; contbr. numerous articles to profl. jours. and popular mags. Dir. Tex. Book Fair, Dallas; dir., creator Nat. Mag. Editors Conf., Dallas. Mem. Authors League, Authors Guild, Women in Communications, Soc. Profl. Journalists, Nat. Fedn. Press Women, Austin Writers' League (exec. editor 1988-89), Okla. Writers Fedn., Internat. Women Writers Guild, Tulsa Nightwriters (v.p. 1980-84), Tex. Nightwriters (founder,pres. 1984-86), Tex. Writers Assn. (founder, exec. dir. 1989—). Republican.

FLEEZANIS, JORJA KAY, violinist, educator; b. Detroit, Mar. 19, 1952; d. Parios Nicholas and Kaliope (Karageorge) F.; m. Michael Steinberg, July 3, 1983. Student, Cleve. Inst. Music, 1969-72, Cin. Coll.-Conservatory Music, 1972-75. Violinist Chgo. Symphony Orch., 1975-76; concertmaster Cin. Chamber Orch., 1976-80; violinist Trio D'Accordo, Cin., 1976-80; asst. prin. 2d violinist San Francisco Symphony Orch., 1980-81; assoc. concertmaster San Francisco Sympony Orch., 1980-89; acting concertmaster Minn. Orch., Mpls., 1988-89, concertmaster, 1989—; violinist Ohlsson-Fleezanis-Grebanier Trio, San Francisco, 1984—; faculty mem. San Francisco Conservatory of Music, 1983-89, U. Minn., 1989—; founder Chamber Music Sundaes, San Francisco, 1980-89; bd. dirs. Bay Area Women's Philharmonic, San Francisco, 1986—. Democrat. Office: Minn Orch 1111 Nicollet Mall Minneapolis MN 55403

FLEGEAL-KIPP, SONIA RUTH, medical services executive; b. Ft. Bragg, N.C., Apr. 14, 1949; d. Foster Franklin and Helene Virginia (Eyler) F.; m. Bruce George Kipp III. BA, Schiller Coll., Heidelberg, Germany, 1971; teaching cert., Shippensburg (Pa.) U., 1973; BS, Pa. State U., 1983; MHA, Coll. of St. Francis, 1990. Translator Def. Attaches Office, US Embassy, Bad Godesberg, Fed. Republic Germany, 1971; substitute tchr. Carlisle, Pa., 1973-74; surg. and anesthesia asst. Charles L. Stoup, Jr., DDS, Carlisle, 1974-75; tri-lingual sec. Dickinson Coll., Carlisle, 1975-81; staff acct. P.R. Hoffman Co., Materials Processing, Carlisle, 1981-83; adminstr. Belvedere Med. Corp., Carlisle, 1983—. Home: 112 Horners Rd Carlisle PA 17013 Office: Belvedere Med Corp 850 Walnut Bottom Rd Carlisle PA 17013

FLEISCHER, DOROTHY ANN, electronics laboratory official; b. N.Y.C., Mar. 1, 1957; d. Lester and Rose (Schwartz) F. BS in Speech, Emerson Coll., 1979. Asst. to pub. info. dir. Community Devel. Agy. N.Y., N.Y.C., 1977; asst. to pub. rels. dir. The Real Paper, Cambridge, Mass., 1979; copy editor Design & Printing Assocs., Boston, 1980; adminstrv. asst., database mgr. CEIP Fund, Boston, 1980-85; adminstrv. asst. to dir. Rsch. Lab. Electronics, MIT, Cambridge, 1985—. Editor, writer brochure, newsletters, booklet, 1980-85; editor, staff writer Currents and Undercurrents newsletters, 1987—. Mem. Japan Karate Assn., Nat. Assn. Sci. Writers (assoc.). Office: MIT Rsch Lab Electronics 50 Vassar St 36-417 Cambridge MA 02139

FLEISCHER, MARY SUSAN, vocational nurse; b. Chgo., Feb. 2, 1956; d. Vincent Hubert and Catherine Anne (Curley) Lauer; m. Robert Fleischer, Sept. 21, 1979 (div. 1981). LVN, Pima Community Coll., Tucson, 1981; student, U. Nev., 1984-85; student in nursing, SUNY, Sacramento, 1989—. With Young's, San Francisco, 1978-79; cocktail waitress Bialey's, Tucson, 1979-80; emergency med. courier Tucson, 1980-82; nurses aide various home health agencies, Tucson, 1982-84; 21 dealer The Shy Clown Casino, Reno, Nev., 1984-85; lic. voc. nurse Truckee Meadows Hosp., Reno, 1985-87, various home health care, Reno, 1986-87, The Hawthorne Group, Inc., Reno, 1987-88; self employed lic. voc. nurse Sacramento, 1988—. Mem. Nat. Assn. Female Execs., Sacramento Poetry Soc., Quill & Scroll.

FLEISCHMAN, BARBARA GREENBERG, public relations consultant; b. Detroit, Mar. 20, 1924; d. Samuel J. and Theresa (Keil) Greenberg; BA, U. Mich., 1944; m. Lawrence A. Fleischman, Dec. 18, 1948; children: Rebecca, Arthur, Martha. Tchr., Detroit Public Schs., 1944-45, psychoanalyst's sec., Detroit, 1947-49; sec. Greenberg Ins. Agy., Detroit, 1947-49; customer/public relations cons. Kennedy Galleries, N.Y.C., 1976—. Bd. dirs. Detroit Artists Market, 1958-66; mem. women's com. Detroit Inst. Arts, 1957-66, founder, pres. vol. com., 1961-66; bd. dirs. Friends of Channel 13, 1968-80, pres., N.Y.C., 1975-79, chmn. auction, 1975, trustee, 1975-84; pres. Friends of N.Y. Pub. Library, 1979—, trustee, 1980—, v.p. bd., 1987—; trustee The Acting Co., 1986-89, pres. 1988-89; governing bd. Off the Record Luncheons, Fgn. Policy Assn., 1978-85; assoc. producer Channel 13 Auction, 1978-80; trustee Mus. Broadcasting, 1988—; vis. com. Greek and Roman Dept. Met. Mus. Mem. Cosmopolitan Club. Office: care Kennedy Galleries Inc 40 W 57th St New York NY 10019

FLEISHER, JERRILYN, financial consultant; b. Phila., May 7, 1952; d. Earl D. and Bette (Romisher) F.; m. Steven M. Bierman, May 28, 1978; 1 child, Emily Larissa. B.A., Dickinson Coll., 1973; M.B.A., Wharton Sch., U. Pa., 1975. Promotion analyst Gillette Co., Boston, 1975-77; product mgr. Chesebrough Ponds Co., Greenwich, Conn., 1977-80, Loreal Co., N.Y.C., 1980-81; account exec. Futterman Orgn., N.Y.C., 1981-83; fin. cons. Shearson Lehman Bros., Greenwich, 1983—. Mem. Internat. Platform Assn., Phi Beta Kappa. Home: 12 Martin Dale N Greenwich CT 06830 Office: Shearson Lehman Bros 2 Greenwich Pla Greenwich CT 06830

FLEISHER, MARCY BETH, television reporter, anchorwoman; b. Chgo., July 15, 1964; d. Richard Sheldon and Carol Sue (Sagett) F. BAS, U Mich., 1986. Reporter Sta. WAAM-NBC Radio, Ann Arbor, Mich., 1985-86; prodn. asst. NBC News, N.Y.C., 1986-87; anchorwoman, reporter Sta. WENY-ABC TV, Elmira, N.Y., 1987-88, Sta. WICZ-NBC TV, Binghamton, N.Y., 1988-89; reporter Sta. WTNH-ABC TV, New Haven, 1989-90, Sta. WBNS-CBS TV, Columbus, Ohio, 1990—. Bd. dirs. Pupil Assistance Learning Program, Elmira, 1987-88. Mem. Nat. Assn. Broadcast Engrs. & Technicians, Am. Fedn. TV and Radio Announcers, Sigma Delta Tau. Office: Sta WBNS-TV 770 Twin Rivers Dr Columbus OH 43216

FLEISHMAN, ELLEN MARCY, school psychologist; b. Jersey City, Nov. 29, 1952; d. Solomon and Jean (Falickman) Gerschitz; m. Edward Jay Fleishman, Nov. 27, 1977; children: Daniel, Rachel. BS magna cum laude, Bklyn. Coll., 1972; PhD, CUNY, 1978. Adj. lectr. Bklyn. Coll., 1973-77; lectr., European div. U. Md., 1978-79; psychologist Project Head Start, Piscataway, N.J., 1980; sch. psychologist N.Y.C. Bd. Edn., Bronx, 1984—; mem. profl. staff, Devel. Com., N.Y.C. Bd. Edn. Com. on Spl. Edn., 1988-89; chariperson pupil personnel com. Lorraine Hansberry Intermediate Sch., 1989—. Contbr. articles to profl. publs. Mem. Am. Psychol. Assn., Sierra Club, Phi Beta Kappa, Psi Chi. Democrat. Home: 2109 Broadway 11-41 New York NY 10023 Office: Committee Spl Edn 12 800 Home St Bronx NY 10460

FLEMING, ALICE CAREW MULCAHEY (MRS. THOMAS J. FLEMING), author; b. New Haven, Dec. 21, 1928; d. Albert Leo and Agnes (Foley) Mulcahey ; m. Thomas J. Fleming, Jan. 19, 1951; children: Alice, Thomas, David, Richard. AB, Trinity Coll., 1950; MA, Columbia U., 1951. Chmn. bd. dirs. N.Y. chpt. Medic Alert Found. Internat. Recipient Nat. Media award Family Service Assn. Am., 1973, Alumni Achievement award Trinity Coll., 1979. Mem. PEN, Authors Guild. Author: The Key to New York, 1960, Wheels, 1960, A Son of Liberty, 1961, Doctors in Petticoats, 1964, Great Women Teachers, 1965, The Senator from Maine: Margaret Chase Smith, 1969, Alice Freeman Palmer: Pioneer College President, 1970, Reporters At War, 1970, General's Lady, 1971, Highways into History, 1971, Pioneers in Print, 1971, Ida Tarbell, The First of the Muckrakers, 1971, Nine Months, 1972, Psychiatry, What's it All About?, 1972, The Moviemakers, 1973, Trials that Made Headlines, 1974, Contraception, Abortion, Pregnancy, 1974, New on the Beat, 1975, Alcohol: The Delightful Poison, 1975, Something for Nothing, 1978, The Mysteries of ESP, 1980, What to Say When You Don't Know What to Say, 1982, The King of Prussia and a Peanut Butter Sandwich, 1988; editor: Hosannah the Home Run!, 1972, America Is Not All Traffic Lights, 1976; contbr. articles to mags. Address: 315 E 72d St New York NY 10021

FLEMING, JULIA ANN, fundraising executive; b. Florence, Ala., June 26, 1947; d. Julius Davis and Margaret Montgomery (Grubb) F. MusB with distinction, Rhodes Coll., 1969; MusM, Ind. U., 1972, postgrad., 1973-75. Coordinator residence life Ind. U., Bloomington, 1972-75; asst. dir. Memphis Arts Council, 1975; dir. devel. and info. Tenn. Arts Commn., Nashville, 1975-77; assoc. dir. Affiliate Artist, Inc., N.Y., 1977-82; dir. devel. San Antonio Festival, 1982; assoc. dir. B.T.G. Mgmt., N.Y., 1983-84; dir. devel. N.J. Symphony Orch., Newark, 1984-89; dir. major gifts Carnegie Hall, N.Y.C., 1989—; evaluator major instns. La. Arts Council, Baton Rouge, 1989; chairperson fellowship panel S.C. Arts Commn., Columbia, 1984; del. People to People Internat. Women in Mgmt. Delegation, People's Republic of China, 1988. Mem. N.Y.C. Jr. League, 1985—; co-chmn. Am. Crafts Mus. Com., 1989-90; bd. advisors Solisti N.Y. Chamber Orch., N.Y., 1986—, Fonda Dance Forum, N.Y., 1984—. Mem. Nat. Soc. Fundraising Execs. (bd. dirs. N.J. chpt. 1986—), Am. Symphony Orch. League (chair regional orch. devel. dirs. 1986-87). Office: Carnegie Hall 881 Seventh Ave New York NY 10019

FLEMING, LISA L., lawyer; b. Louisville, Nov. 14, 1961; d. Joseph D. Ware. BA, Hanover (Ind.) Coll., 1982; JD, U. Louisville, 1985. Bar: Ind., U.S. Dist. Ct. (so. and no. dists.) Ind. Corp. counsel, asst. sec. Am. Comml. Barge Line Co., Jeffersonville, Ind.; career cons. Hanover Coll. Cons. Jr. Achievement; mentor Young Leaders Inst.; mem. Leadership So. Inc., 1990—. Mem. NAFE, Am. Bar Assn., Ind. State Bar Assn. (articles and bylaws com.), Clark County Bar Assn., Am. Corp. Counsel Assn., Environ. Law Inst., Jefferson County Pub. Sch System Speakers Bur., River City Bus. and Profl. Women, Ky. Women Advocated, Focus Louisville, Hanover Coll Alumni Assn. (bd. dirs. 1990—), Phi Mu. Address: 622 W St Catherine Louisville KY 40203

FLEMING, ORAMENTA DELORES, city planner, lecturer; b. Tuskegee, Ala., Mar. 21, 1955; d. Pink Fleming and Mable Fleming (Jessie) Cobb. BS in Pub. Adminstrn., Auburn (Ala.) U., 1976; MS in Pub. Adminstrn., Ga. State U., Atlanta, 1984. Proposal writer Internat. Systems, Inc., Atlanta, 1978-80, community devel. specialist, 1980, community devel. dir., 1980-83; city planner County of Cobb, Atlanta, 1983-86, rental rehab. coord., 1983-86; city planner City of Ft. Worth, 1986—; lectr. U. Tex. Sch. Social Wk., Arlington, 1989, Tex. Christian U. Bd. dirs. Fair Housing Community Resource Bd., Ft. Worth, 1987—, Tarrant County Homeless Coalition, Ft. Worth, 1989—, Habitat for Humanity, Ft. Worth, 1989—, Cath. Social Svcs., Ft. Worth, 1989—. Named Planner of the Yr., Ft. Worth Dept. Planning & Growth Mgmt., 1988; winner Tex. chpt. Am. Planning Assn. 1989 Current Planning award. Mem. Am. Planning Assn., Nat. Conf. Minority Pub. Adminstrs. (sec. 1988-89), Progressive Alliance of Cultured Women (vice chair program 1989-90), City Women's Network. Democrat. Home: 8300 Arabella Ct #515 Fort Worth TX 76120 Office: Ft Worth Dept Planning Mgmt 1000 Throckmorton Fort Worth TX 76102

FLEMING, VIRGINIA HESSE, consulting manager; b. Redondo Beach, Calif., Jan. 24, 1959; d. Frederick William Hesse and Betty (Brunson) Bathgate; m. Patrick Edward Fleming, Sept., 1987. BS in Bus. Adminstrn., Calif. State U., Northridge, 1982. Horse trainer Pacific Horse Ctr., Sacramento, 1976-79; asst. restaurant mgr. Carl's Jr. Restaurant, Agoura, Calif., 1979-80; adminstrv. acct. specialist IBM, Burbank, Calif., 1980-82; sr. cons. Arthur Andersen & Co., Costa Mesa, Calif., 1982-85; client service rep. J.D. Edwards & Co., San Francisco, 1985—. Presenter Profl. Presenters Program, San Francisco, 1986-87; v.p. Bay Area Women's Leadership Group, San Francisco, 1986-88; vol. World Peace Group, San Francisco, 1986—. Mem. Nat. Assn. Female Execs., U.S. Equestrian Team, Aircraft Owners Assn., Nat. Orgn. Women, Delta Sigma Pi. Mem. Religious Science Ch.

FLEMMER, PHYLLIS RAE, city official; b. Gettysburg, S.D., July 15, 1933; d. Josiah and Mildred Agnes (Bauer) Winters; m. Herbert Rudolph Flemmer, Dec. 26, 1951; 1 child, Donald Brian. Dental asst. A.A. Buechler, Gettysburg, S.D., 1952-63, 71-74; fin. officer Gettysburg Motor Co., 1964-71, City of Gettysburg, 1974—. Mem. S.D. Govt. Fin. Officers Assn. (adv. com. 1983, 89), S.D. Mcpl. League (Dist. 7 v.p. 1987—), Govt. Fin. Officers Assn., Gettysburg Country Club (pres. 1978). Republican. Methodist. Office: City of Gettysburg 110 E Commercial Ave Gettysburg SD 57442

FLESCHNER, MARCIA HARRIET, marketing executive, personnel consultant; b. Bklyn., Mar. 31, 1947; d. Max and Bettina (Koerner) F.; m. Arthur Mace Teicher, Nov. 23, 1974; 1 son, Craig Morgan. B.A., CUNY, 1967. Sr. vice pres. market research, placement dir. Smith's 5th Ave Agy., Inc., N.Y.C., 1965—. Mem. Am. Mktg. Assn. (2d v.p. 1987-88, dir. N.Y.C chpt. 1973-87 , cert. 1975, 82), Nat. Assn. Personnel Cons., Advt. Women N.Y., Assn. Personnel Cons. N.Y. (dir. 1979-80). Club: Castaways Yacht (New Rochelle, N.Y.). Office: Smith's 5th Ave Agy Inc 17 E 45th St New York NY 10017

FLETCHER, BETTY B., federal judge; b. Tacoma, Mar. 29, 1923. B.A., Stanford U., 1943; LL.B., U. Wash., 1956. Bar: Wash. 1956. Mem. firm Preston, Thorgrimson, Ellis, Holman & Fletcher, Seattle, 1956-1979; judge U.S. Ct. Appeals (9th cir.), Seattle., 1979—. Mem. ABA, Wash. Bar Assn., Am. Law Inst., Fed. Judges Assn. (treas.), Order of Coif, Phi Beta Kappa. Office: US Ct Appeals 9th Cir 1010 5th Ave Seattle WA 98104

FLETCHER, CATHY ANN, auditor; b. Barnesville, Ga., Aug. 23, 1949; d. John James and Dorothy Lee (Banks) Fletcher; 1 child, Lisa Faye. Student, Ohio State U., 1969-70; AS, Mass. Bay Community Coll., 1982; BS, Northeastern U., Boston, 1984. Mail clk. Fed. Reserve Bank, Boston, 1971-72; office mgr. Breckenridge Sportswear, Boston, 1973-74; asst. dir. Whittier Street Health Ctr., Boston, 1974-81; sec. to dir. Northeastern U., 1981-84; auditor Def. Contract Audit Agy., Burlington, Mass., 1984—; sec., bd. dirs. Boston Tenant Policy Coun., 1977-79; mgr. northeastern region Fed. Women's Program, 1989—; mem. adv. bd. DCAA EEO, 1989. Author: Softball Team Book, 1975. V.p., bd. dirs. Bromley Health Tenant Mgmt. Corp., Jamaica Plain, Mass., 1976—; mem. fund-raising com. Com. to Elect Jesse Jackson Pres., Boston, 1984; apptd. fed. women program coordinator State of Mass., 1988. Mem. AAUW, NAFE, Profl. Coun., Nat. Tenants Orgn., NAACP, Sigma Epsilon Rho. Club: Hawkettes Social (pres., mem. profl. coun. 1989). Lodge: Elks. Avocations: reading, swimming, cooking, walking, travel. Office: Def Contract Audit Agy Boston Br Office Thomas P O'Neill Fed Bldg Burlington MA 01803

FLETCHER, JOANNE LESLIE, nurse anesthetist, educator; b. Buffalo, Sept. 18, 1950; d. Richard Spence and Alice Jean (Harries) F. RN, Toronto (Can.) Gen. Hosp., 1972; cert. in nurse anesthesiology, Mayo Clinic Sch. Anesthesia, 1979; BSNA, U. Minn., 1981, MEd, 1986. RN, Minn. Edn. coord. Hennepin County Med. Ctr., Mpls., 1979-87; clin. coord. Mpls. Sch. Anesthesia, 1981-87; asst. dir. UHCP Sch. of Anesthesia, Pitts., 1987-89; staff anesthesist VA Med. Ctr., Pitts., 1989—. Author: (film) Pre-operative Preparation, 1988. Elder Cross Roads Presbyn. Ch., Monroeville, Pa., 1989—. Recipient Nat. Disting. Svc. award Registry in Nursing, 1988. Mem. Am. Assn. Nurse Anesthetists, Pa. Assn. Nurse Anesthetists, Anesthesia Patient Safety Found., Phi Kappa Phi. Home: 2725 Orlando Pl Pittsburgh PA 15235

FLETCHER, LAURA TRISTAN, marketing executive; b. Jonesboro, Ark., June 1, 1965; d. Donald O'Dell and Donna Lee (Stanfield) F. BBA, U. Mich., 1987; MBA, Wayne State U., Detroit, 1989. Sales rep. Avon Products, Inc., Burton, Mich., 1982-85; time office clk. CM-0Chevrolet, Flint, Mich., summer 1985; suggestion investigator GM Buick Oldsmobile Cadillac, Flint, 1985-86; mktg. coordinator Alsopure Water Co., Plymouth, Mich., 1986-88; mktg. supr. Alsopure Water Co., 1988-89; cons. U.S. Sml. Bus. Adminstrn., Detroit, 1989; mktg. analyst Atlas Technologies, Inc., Grand Blanc, Mich., 1989-90; mktg. mgr. Atlas Technologies, Inc., Fenton, Mich., 1990—. Mem. Nat. Assn. Female Execs. Address: 12095 Juniper Way #606 Grand Blanc MI 48439

FLETCHER, LOUISE, actress; b. Birmingham, Ala., 1936; d. Robert Capers F. BA, U. N.C., 1957; student acting with Jeff Corey; LHD (hon.), Gallaudet U., 1982, Western Md. Coll., 1986. Films include Thieves Like Us, 1973, Russian Roulette, 1974, One Flew Over the Cuckoo's Nest, 1975 (Acad. award as best actress), Exorcist II: The Heretic, 1976, The Cheap Detective, 1977, The Magician, 1978, Natural Enemies, 1979, The Lucky Star, 1979, The Lady in Red, 1979, Strange Behavior, 1980, Brainstorm, 1981, Strange Invaders, 1982, Once Upon a Time in America, 1982, Firestarter, 1983, Overnight Sensation, 1983, Invaders from Mars, 1985, The Boy Who Could Fly, 1985, Nobody's Fool, 1986, Flowers in the Attic, 1987, Two Moon Junction, 1987, Blue Steel, 1988, Best of the Best, 1989, Shadowzone, 1989; TV appearances include Maverick, Wagon Train, The Law-Man, Playhouse 90, The Millionaire, Alfred Hitchcock, Thou Shalt Not Commit Adultery, 1978, A Summer To Remember, 1984, Island, 1984, Second Serve, 1985, Hoover, 1986, The Karen Carpenter Story, 1988, Final Notice, 1989. Bd. dirs. Deafness Research Found.

FLETCHER, MARJORIE AMOS, librarian; b. Easton, Pa., July 10, 1923; d. Alexander Robert and Margaret Ashton (Arnold) Amos; A.B., Bryn Mawr Coll., 1946; m. Charles Mann Fletcher, May 14, 1949; children—Robert Amos, Elizabeth Ashton, Anne Kennard. Asst. to dir. research, then research asst. to pres. Pa. Mut. Life Ins. Co., 1946-49; officer A.R. Amos Co., Phila., 1949-66; part-time tchr., 1965-68; librarian Am. Coll., Bryn Mawr, Pa., 1968-77, archivist, 1973—, dir. oral history collection, 1975—, lectr. on archives, 1975—, asst. prof. edn., 1973—, dir. archives and oral history, 1977—; pres. pub. rels. MAF Enterprises, 1987—. Recipient awards Phila. Flower Show, 1965—. Mem. Spl. Libraries Assn. (pres. Phila. 1977-78), Soc. Am. Archivists (chairperson oral history sect. 1981-87, award of merit 1987), Oral History Assn., Hist. Soc. Pa., U.S. Pony Club, D.A.R., Nat. Soc. Colonial Dames in Commonwealth of Pa., Emergency Aid Pa. Found. Republican. Episcopalian. Clubs: Phila. Skating; Davis Creek Yacht; Bridlewild Pony (sponsor), Bridlewild Trails (Gladwyne). Author articles in field. Home: 1135 Norsam Rd Gladwyne PA 19035 Office: Am Coll Bryn Mawr PA 19010

FLETCHER, MARY LEE, business executive; b. Farnborough, Eng.; d. Dugald Angus and Mary Lee (Thurman) F.; B.A., Pembroke Coll., Brown U., 1951. Ops. officer C.I.A., Washington, 1951-53; exec. trainee Gimbels, N.Y.C., 1953-54; head researcher Ed Byron TV Prodns., N.Y.C., 1954; copywriter Benton & Bowles, Inc., N.Y.C., 1955-63; creative dir. Alberto-Culver Co., Melrose Park, Ill., 1964-66; v.p. advt. and publicity Christian Dior Perfumes, N.Y.C., 1967-71; v.p. Christian Dior-N.Y., N.Y.C., 1972-78, exec. v.p., dir., 1978-85; cons. Fletcher & Co., N.Y.C., 1985—. Home: 12 Beekman Pl New York NY 10022 Office: 885 3d Ave New York NY 10022-4082

FLETCHER, SHERRY LYN, educational adminstrator; b. Ashland, Kans., Dec. 29, 1947; d. James Thomas Fletcher and Maxine (Lane) Cecil; m. Baxter Barnard Brown, Nov. 1, 1982. BA in Edn., N.Mex. State U., 1968, MA in Edn., 1975, endorsement in ednl. adminstrn., endorsement in early childhood, 1984; Montessori cert., St. Nicholas Tng. Cen., London, 1976. Elem. tchr. pub. schs. pub. schs., Las Cruces, N.Mex., 1969-75; dir., founder Montessori Unltd., Las Cruces, 1976; tchr. Truth or Consequences (N.Mex.) Pub. Schs., 1983-85, elem. prin., 1983-88, coord. fed. program, 1988—; cons. McGraw Hill Pub. Support Writing Assessment Project, others 1981—; mem. steering com. State Bd. Edn., Santa Fe, 1985-86, mem. adv. com. early childhood, 1985-86, revision of state spl. edn. regulations, 1988. Mem. Elephant Butte/Caballo Leaseholders' Assn. (sec. 1985—), N.Mex. Assn. for the Edn. Young Children, Assn. Supervision and Curriculum Devel., Assn. Sch. Adminstrs. Republican. Home: Star Route N Box B Truth or Consequences NM 87901 Office: Truth or Consequences Schs Box 952 Truth or Consequences NM 87901

FLETCHER, SUZANNE WRIGHT, medical educator; b. Jacksonville, Fla., Nov. 14, 1940; d. Robert Dean and Helen Ruth (Selmer) Wright; m. Robert Hillman Fletcher, June 15, 1963; children: John Wright, Grant Selmer. BA, Swarthmore Coll., 1962; MD, Harvard U., 1966; MSc, Johns Hopkins U., 1973. Diplomate Am. Bd. Internal Medicine (bd. govs. 1981-87). Intern internal medicine Stanford U., 1966-67, resident internal medicine, 1967-68; resident internal medicine Johns Hopkins U., 1971-73; asst. prof. medicine and epidemiology McGill U. Faculty of Medicine, Montreal, Can., 1973-78; assoc. prof. medicine, clin. assoc. prof. epidemiology U. N.C. Sch. Medicine and Sch. Pub. Health, Chapel Hill, 1978-83, prof. medicine, clin. prof. epidemiology, 1983—; mem. U.S. Preventive Svcs. Task Force, 1984-88. Co-author: Clinical Epidemiology: The Essentials, 1982, founding co-editor Jour. Gen. Internal Medicine, 1984—. Fellow ACP, Am. Coll. Epidemiology; mem. Inst. Medicine, Soc. of Gen. Internal Medicine (pres. 1983-84). Office: U NC Sch Medicine 5039 Old Clinic Bldg Chapel Hill NC 27514

FLEURY, PEG MCCORMICK, college administrator; b. Madison, Wis., June 13, 1937; d. Francis Stephen and Lenore Ellen (Egan) McCormick; m. James Peter Fleury, May 12, 1962; children: Patrick McCormick, Andrew James, Anne Margaret. BS in Journalism, U. Wis., 1959, MS in Adminstrv. Leadership, 1979. Reporter UPI, Madison, Wis., 1959-60; editorial asst. Bus. Wk., Milw., 1960-62; writer pub. rels. U. Akron, Ohio, 1963-65; free-lance writer Milw., 1975-76; prog. coord. U. Wis. Ext., Milw., 1977-80; specialist off-campus instrn. U. Wis., Milw., 1980; dir. Encore/Campus P.M. Mt. Mary Coll., Milw., 1980-90, dir. enrollment, 1985-90, dir. Ewens Ctr. for Women, 1990—; conductor workshops in field. Mem. Nat. Assn. Women Deans, Counselors and Adminstrs., AAUW (v.p. programs 1990—), Milw. Coun. for Adult Learning (sec. 1988-90), Greater Milw. Assn. Phi Beta Kappa (bd. dirs. 1989—), Zool. Soc. Milw. (docent), Friends of Mus.

FLEWELLING, DIANE MAE, realtor; b. Skowhegan, Maine, Mar. 29, 1947; d. Merle Omer and Marion Elvia (McKechnie) F.;1 child Joshua Eric. Diploma, Maine Sch. Practical Nursing, 1969; AS, Manchester Community Coll., 1986; grad., Realtor's Inst., 1989. Lic. Practical Nurse. Practical nurse Redington-Fairview Gen. Hosp., Skowhegon, 1969-71, Manchester (Conn.) Meml. Hosp., 1971-87; realtor Lawrence, Martin & Park Assocs., Inc., Mansfield Center, Conn., 1987—. Designer, creator: Brochures, Newsletters, 1985-89; editor: local ch. publ., Trinity Trumpet. Mem. Evang. Covenant Ch. Mem. Nat. Assn. Realtors, Conn. Assn. Realtors, Willimantic Bd. Realtors. Republican. Office: Lawrence Martin & Park Assocs 126 Storrs Rd Mansfield Center CT 06250

FLICKER, DAWN K., paralegal; b. Santa Monica, Calif., May 16, 1960; d. Richard Daniel and Ramona Joy (Beckley) Doody; m. Kevin G. Flicker, Aug. 18, 1984; children: Michael, Johnnie. AA, West L.A. Coll., Culver City, Calif., 1980. Dept. mgr. May Co., Culver City; sr. paralegal Wolf & Wolf, Culver City. Mem. NAFE, Nat. Notary Assn., Nat. Assn. Legal Secs., Calif. Assn. Legal Secs., L.A. Westside Assn. Legal Secs. Republican. Roman Catholic. Home: 7704 Wish Ave Van Nuys CA 91406 Office: 17216 Saticoy #301 Van Nuys CA 91406

FLIEGELMAN, AVRA LEAH, editor; b. Hartford, Conn., Mar. 5; d. Irving and Rose (Bason) F.; student public schs. With publicity dept. Columbia Pictures Corp., N.Y.C., 1949; with Asso. Artists Prodns., and successor UA-TV, N.Y.C., 1955-58; with Broadcast Info. Bur. , N.Y.C., 1958—, editor-in-chief, 1969—, exec. v.p., 1979—, sr. cons., 1989—. Mem. Am. Women in Radio and TV. Democrat. Jewish. Home: 174 Dix Hills Rd Huntington Station NY 11746

FLINK, JANE DUNCAN, public relations executive, publisher; b. Atlanta, Feb. 17, 1929; d. James Archibald and Frances (Watkins) Duncan; m. Richard Albert Flink, Nov. 20, 1954; children: Jennifer, Elizabeth, Caroline, Charles Albert, James Duncan. Student Carleton Coll., U. Mo., Columbia (Mo.) Coll. Reporter, Tri-Town News, Greendale, Wis., 1958-61; reporter, photographer, feature writer, editor Cen. Mo. Rural and Farm Life mag., Centralia (Mo.) Fireside Guard, 1973-78, asst. editor, 1982-83; editor Bus. Briefs, MFA Oil Co., Columbia, Mo., 1977; editor Lifestyles, Kingdom Daily News, Fulton, Mo., 1978-82; assoc. editor Mo. Ruralist, Columbia, 1983-85; dir. external realtions Winston Churchill Meml. and Library, Westminster Coll., Fulton, Mo., 1985-89—, dir., 1989—; owner, pub. Boone County Jour., Ashland, Mo. Rep. committeewoman Ward I, Centralia, 1972, 74, 76; mem. exec. bd. Friends of Churchill Meml., Fulton; mem. Boone County Commn. on Child Abuse, 1978-81. Recipient numerous editorial awards. Mem. Nat. Fedn. Press Women (nat. achievement award 1982), Mo. Press Women (dist. v.p. 1978-79, v.p. 1985-87, chmn. honors, awards 1979-81, Woman of Achievement award 1988), Mo. Mus. Assocs., Mo. Press Assn., PEO, Sigma Delta Chi, Centralia C. of C. (bd. dirs. 1983-86—), Mo. Travel Council, English Speaking Union, Royal Oak Found., Centralia Hist. Soc. Club: Centralia Country. Home: The Clearing Rt 4 Centralia MO 65240 Office: Westminster Coll Winston Churchill Meml and Library Fulton MO 65251

FLINN, ROBERTA JEANNE, management, computer applications consultant; b. Twin Falls, Idaho, Dec. 19, 1947; d. Richard H. and Ruth (Johnson) F. Student Colo. State U., 1966-67. Ptnr., Aqua-Star Pools & Spas, Boise, Idaho, 1978—, mng. ptnr., 1981-83; ops. mgr. Polly Pools, Inc., Canby, Oreg., 1983-84, br. mgr. Polly Pools, Inc., A-One Distributing, 1984-85; comptroller, Beaverton Printing, Inc., 1986-89; mng. ptnr. Invisible Ink, Canby, Oreg., 1989—. Mem. Nat. Assn. Female Execs., Nat. Appaloosa Horse Club. Republican. Mem. Christian Ch. Home: 24687 S Central Point Rd Canby OR 97013

FLINT, CYNTHIA MARIE, air force non-commissioned officer; b. Detroit, Aug. 29, 1956; d. Clyde Everette Burgess and Frances (Flint) Algee; m. Freddie Joseph Sherman, July 15, 1985. BS in Biology, Spelman Coll., 1981; MBA, Nat. U., 1985, MA in Human Behavior, 1987. Enlisted USAF, 1982, advanced through grades to staff sgt., 1985, with, 1982—; adminstrv. specialist 307th Consol. Aircraft Maint. Squadron Strategic Air Command, Travis AFB, Calif., 1982-83, Mil. Airlift Command, Travis AFB, 1983-85, Base Comdr's Office, Travis AFB, 1985-87; pers. specialist 3415 Mission Support Squadron, Lowry AFB, Colo., 1987—; prin. New World Concepts, 1989—. Vol. ARC David Grant Med. Ctr., Travis AFB, 1983-85, Adopt-A-Sch. Program Vaughn Elem. Sch., Aurora, Colo., 1987—. Mem. Spelman Coll. Glee Club Alumnae Assn., Delta Sigma Theta. Home: 234 S Jasper Circle #17-305 Aurora CO 80017 Office: 3415 MSSQ/MSPAC Customer Svc Lowry AFB CO 80230-5065

FLINT, KATHLEEN PATRICIA, physician; b. Atlanta, July 7, 1956; d. John Austin and Ellenor Jo (Coons) F. BS, Furman U., 1978; MD, Med. Coll. Ga., 1982. Diplomate Am. Bd. Internal Medicine, Am. Bd. Rheumatology. Intern N.C. Bapt. Hosp.-Bowman Gray Sch. Medicine, Winston-Salem, 1982-83, resident, then chief resident internal medicine, 1983-86, fellow in rheumatology, 1986-88; rheumatologist Columbia (S.C.) Arthritis Ctr., 1988—; clin. instr. U. S.C. Sch. Medicine, Columbia, 1988—. Fellow Am. Coll. Rheumatology; mem. ACP, AMA, S.C. Med. Assn., Phi Beta Kappa, Alpha Omega Alpha. Office: Columbia Arthritis Ctr 1711 St Julian Pl Columbia SC 29204

FLINT, SUSAN LOUISE, public relations executive; b. Culver City, Calif., Feb. 1, 1947; d. Otto Antone and Genevieve Florence (Lindsay) Grunwald; m. Virgil Eugene Flint, Dec. 6, 1975. BA in Journalism, Pepperdine U., 1967. Pub. rels. asst. Hollywood Presbyn. Hosp., L.A., 1968; editor-in-chief So. Calif. Bus., L.A., 1968-70; pub. rels. mgr. Avco Community Developers, Inc., San Diego, 1972-75; editor-in-chief The Breeze, Carlsbad, Calif., 1975-76; pres., cons. Susan Flint Advt. & Pub. Rels., Yuma, Ariz., 1978-84; community rels. dir. San Diego Hospice Corp., 1984-85; community resources dir. Youth Devel., Inc., San Diego, 1985-86; cons. Susan Flint Advt. & Pub. Rels., Palm Springs, Calif., 1986—; pub. rels. dir. Palm Springs Desert Mus., 1987-89; pub. rels./advt. coord. City of Palm Springs (Calif.), 1989—. Bd. dirs. Easter Seal Soc. Ariz., Yuma, 1982-84; coun. mem. Desert Trail Coun. Boy Scouts, Yuma, 1983-84; vol. Home Run Hotline, San Diego, 1985—. Recipient Community Svc. award Desert Coun. Boy Scouts Am., 1984. Mem. Women in Communications (past bd. dirs.), NAFE, Nat. Fedn. Press Women, San Diego Press Club, Beta Sigma Phi. Republican. Home: 28-850 Avenida Condesa Cathedral City CA 92234 Office: Palm Springs City Hall 3200 E Tahquitz McCallum Way Palm Springs CA 92262

FLINT, SUZANNE ELIZABETH, pediatric nurse practitioner; b. Palmer, Mass., July 5, 1961; d. James Edwin and Patricia Ann (Coutu) F. BS in Nursing, Ftichburg State Coll., 1983; MS in Nursing, U. Pa., 1989. RN, Mass., Pa. Staff nurse Cooley Dickison Hosp., Northampton, Mass., 1983-88; nurse, rsch. asst. U. Pa., Phila., 1988-89; adminstr. Pediatric Care Am., Inc., Springfield, Mass., 1989—. Contbr. articles to nursing publs. Fellow Nat. Assn. Pediatric Nurse Assocs. and Practitioners (cert.); mem. Am. Heart Assn., Alumni Pa. Sch. Nursing, Alumni Fitchburg State Coll., Sigma Theta Tau. Roman Catholic. Office: Pediatric Care Am Inc 155 Maple St Ste 111 Springfield MA 01105

FLISHER, CYNTHIA DEAN, sales executive; b. Tarrytown, N.Y., June 3, 1961; d. David Anthony and Marilyn Kay (Dean) Mitchell; m. Kenneth W. Flisher Jr., Feb. 28, 1987; 1 child, Kyle William. BA, Simmons Coll., 1983. Media buyer McCann-Erickson, Inc., N.Y.C., 1983-85; sr. account exec. Sta. WVIT-TV, Hartford, Conn., 1985-89; regional sales mgr. Sta. WTWS-TV, New London, Conn., 1989—. Pres. The Theatre Group, The Hartford Stage Co., 1987—. Mem. Women in Communications, Inc. (programming com. 1987—). Home: 50 White Ave Middlebury CT 06762 Office: Sta WTWS-TV 216 Broad St New London CT 06320

FLOCKE, JENELLE LOUISE, military public affairs specialist; b. Bellville, Tex., July 3, 1949; d. Calvin Joe and Rose Army (Grubb) Mikeska; m. Robert Alfred Flocke, Oct. 5, 1968; 1 child, Catherine Rose. Student Blinn Coll., George Mason U. Bn. sec. 1st Bn., 68th Armored Div., Baumholder, Fed. Republic Germany, 1978-79; info. asst. Soldier's Mag., Alexandria, Va., 1980-81; sec., stenographer warrant officer div. U.S. Army, Alexandria, 1981-83; sec., adminstrv. asst. OASA (M&RA) Dept. Army, Pentagon, Washington, 1984-85, pub. affairs specialist, 1986—, HQDA Pentagon, 1986-88, Mil. Dist. of Washington, 1988-89, Europe Hdqrs. U.S. Army, 1989—; congl. fellow Caucus for Women's Issues, Washington, 1985-86; sec. Army Fed. Women's Program, Pentagon, 1984-87. Instr. CPR, Alexandria, 1982-86; troop leader Girl Scouts U.S.A. Troop 1685, Springfield, 1980-84, Troop 00553, Baumholder, 1977-78; chmn. bd. dirs. Timbers Community, Springfield, Va., 1986-88, Women in Def., Inc., 1986—. Recipient Outstanding Performance awards Dept. Army, 1979-85, Spl. Service award Combined Fed. Campaign, 1985, Broadcast award Soldiers Radio & TV, 1988; cert. of achievement Dept. Army, 1988, Achievement medal for civilian svc., 1989. Mem. NAFE, Federally Employed Women, Women in Def., Phi Beta Lambda (state sec. 1967-68). Lutheran. Club: Konza Klub (Brenham, Tex.). Avocations: horseback riding, reading, camping, dancing, cooking. Home: Hdqrs 21st TAACOM PAO APO New York NY 03925-3730 Office: US ARMY Hdqrs USA Europe and 7th Army APO New York NY 09403

FLOCKHART, SANDRA LAYNE, business consultant; b. Fresno, Calif., May 6, 1950; d. Fred Clark Jr. and Ebba Jean (Randall) Clark; m. Willard Dean Flockhart II, Nov. 5, 1977; children: Ian Randall, Christina Lee. BS, Fresno State Coll., 1972; cert., Exec. Etiquette Inst., Boston. Cert. wedding cons.; cert. bus. cons. Police officer U.S. Park Police, Washington; pres. Corporate Manners, Alexandria, Va. Mem. NAFE, Va. Assn. Female Execs., Alexandria C. of C. Address: 8010 Karl Rd Alexandria VA 22308

FLOCKS, MARCIA LEA HINDS, company executive; b. Snyder, Tex., May 14, 1955; d. Thomas Eugene and Peggy Ann (Jeffrey) Hinds; m. Carl J. Flocks IV; Aug. 29, 1980; 1 child, Carl J. AS, Westark Community Coll., Fort Smith, Ark., 1978; BS, BA, U. Ark., 1988. Store mgr. Hunts of Ark DBA Tom's Pants, Fort Smith, Ark., 1973-78; cashier, wire opr. A.G. Edwards and Sons, Inc., Fort Smith, Ark., 1980-84; office mgr. Big Cheif Broadcasting, KTCS AM-FM, Fort Smith, Ark., 1984-88; asst. to owner Jeffrey Sand Co., Ft. Smith, Ark., 1989—. CIP chmn. GFWC of Ark. Dist., Ft. Smith, 1988—, chmn. GFWC Jr. Civic League, 1989. Home: 6175 Grand Ave Fort Smith AR 72904

FLOM, JULIA MITTLE, civic worker; b. Bowman, S.C., Aug. 2, 1906; d. Edward Nathan and Minnie Josephine (Jackson) Mittle; m. Samuel Louis Flom (dec.); children—Joann Flom Greenberg, Edward L., Mary Sue Flom Rothenberg. Student Randolph-Macon Women's Coll., 1924-26, So. Sem., Buena Vista, Va., 1923. Bd. dirs. Univ. Community Hosp., Tampa, Fla., 1982—, Hillsborough Mental Health Assn., Tampa, 1965—, Temple Schaarai Zedek Sisterhood, Tampa, 1927—; chmn. bldg. com. Suncoast coun. Girl Scouts U.S., 1930-60; founding mem. U. South Fla., 1956—, pres's. coun., 1984-85; mem. Salvation Army, Easter Seal Guild, 1970—; Fla. Orch. & Guild, 1968—; bd. fellows U. Tampa, 1983—; mem. Jewish Welfare & Community Ctr.; mem. Coun. Jewish Women; founding mem., coun. Tampa Bay Performing Arts, 1984; mem. Tampa Mus. Patrons; mem. adv. bd. U. Tampa.; mem. bd. Community Hosp. Found., Tampa Gen. Hosp.; charter mem. St. Joseph Coun. Jewish Women. Democrat. Established scholarship U. Tampa Nursing Sch., engring. endowment scholarship U. So. Fla. Recipient Order of Elephant award Lowry Pk. Zool. Soc., Deans Soc. for Excellence award U. So. Fla. Lodge: Hadassah. Avocations: golf; painting. Address: 2403 Ardson Pl Apt 501B Tampa FL 33629

FLOOD, DIANE LUCY, marketing communications specialist; b. Plainfield, N.J., June 13, 1937; d. William Edward and Lucy (Dycker) Flood. B.A., Vassar Coll., 1959; postgrad. Fontainebleau Sch. Fine Arts (France), 1961. Advt. prodn. aide indsl. chem. div. Am. Cyanamid Co., Wayne, N.J., 1959-62, prodn. supr., 1962-64, creative coord. organic chems. div. advt., 1964-66, design art and copy mgr., 1966-70, advt. rep., 1970-72, advt. rep. paper, process chems. and resins, indsl. chem. div., 1972-77, advt. coord. water treating, mining, paper and enhanced oil recovery chems., 1977-83, mgr. mktg. communications indsl. products div., 1983—, mgr. mktg. communications Venture Chems. div., 1986-87; Chem. Products and Indsl. Products divs., 1987-89, mgr. mktg. communications Chem. Products, Indsl. Products and Internat. Chems. div., 1989-90, mgr. mktg. communications Chem. Group, 1990—. V.p., past dir. 103 Gedney St. Owners Co-op, 1985-87. Mem. Vassar Coll. Alumni Assn. Mem. Consistory of Reformed Ch. Club: Vassar of N.Y.C. Home: 103 Gedney St 3C Nyack NY 10960 Office: Am Cyanamid Co Chems Group Wayne NJ 07470

FLOOD, DOROTHY GARNETT, neuroscientist; b. Sayre, Pa., Oct. 7, 1951; d. James Murlin and Dorothy Garnett (Dietrich) F.; m. Paul David Coleman, Feb. 26, 1983. BA cum laude, Lawrence U., 1973; student, U. Ill., 1972-73; MS, PhD, U. Rochester, N.Y., 1980. Sr. instr. in anatomy U. Rochester, 1980-83, sr. instr. in neurology, 1984, asst. prof. neurology, 1984-90, assoc. prof. neurology, 1990—. Recipient Fenn award U. Rochester, 1980. Mem. AAAS, Soc. Neurosci., Am. Assn. Anatomists, European

Neurosci. Assn. Office: U Rochester Dept Neurology 601 Elmwood Ave Box 673 Rochester NY 14642

FLOOD, (HULDA) GAY, magazine editor; b. Plainfield, N.J., Aug. 14, 1935; d. William Edward and Lucy (Dycker) F.; BA, Smith Coll., 1957. Picture dept. Sports Illustrated, Time Inc., N.Y.C. 1957-58, letters dept., 1958-59, reporter, 1959-60, writer-reporter, 1960-71, asso. editor, 1971-85, sr. editor, 1985—. Life mem. Alumnae Assn. Smith Coll., Inc., Smith Students Aid Soc., Inc., Smith Coll. Club. Mem. consistory 1st Reformed Ch., Nyack, N.Y. Home: 103 Gedney St Apt 4B Nyack NY 10960 Office: Sports Illustrated Time & Life Bldg Rockefeller Ctr New York NY 10020

FLOOD, JOAN MOORE, corporate librarian; b. Hampton, Va., Oct. 10, 1941; d. Harold W. and Estalena (Fancher) M.; 1 child by former marriage, Angelique. B.Mus., North Tex. State U., 1963, postgrad., 1977; postgrad. So. Meth. U., 1967-68, Tex. Women's U., 1978-79, U. Dallas, 1985-86. Bar: Tex. 1982. Clk. Criminal Dist. Ct. Number 2, Dallas County, Tex., 1972-75; reins. libr. Scor Reins. Co., Dallas, 1975-80, Assocs. Ins. Group, 1980-83; corp./securities legal asst. Akin, Gump, Strauss, Hauer & Feld, 1983-89; asst. sec. Knoll Internat. Holdings Inc., Saddle Brook, N.J., 1989-90, 21 Internat. Holdings, Inc., N.Y.C., 1990—. Mem. ABA. Republican. Episcopalian. Home: 434 E 52d Apt 7C New York NY 10022

FLOOD, KATHLEEN ELIZABETH, systems engineer; b. Waterbury, Conn., Oct. 5, 1962; d. David Stanley and Judith Elizabeth (Delaney) F. BSEE in Computer Sci., U. Conn., 1984; MS in Computer Sci., Rensselaer Poly. Inst., 1989, postgrad. in bus. adminstrn., 1989—. Programmer analyst Pratt & Whitney Aircraft, East Hartford, Conn., 1984-86; systems support analyst Pratt & Whitney Aircraft, 1986-89, systems engr., 1989—. Tutor explorer post Boy Scouts Am., Pratt & Whitney Aircraft, East Hartford, 1984-86; carnival vol. fundraiser Spl. Olympics, Hartford, Conn., 1989; active snowball-softball com. fundraiser March of Dimes, Hartford, 1984-89, mem. gourmet gala com. fundraiser, 1987, 89; del. Girls Nation Am. Legion, summer 1979, dir. VA. Mem. NAFE, IEEE, Assn. Computing Machinery, Soc. Women Engrs. (sec. 1981-82). Democrat. Roman Catholic. Home: 13 Highcrest Dr Rocky Hill CT 06067 Office: Pratt & Whitney Aircraft 400 Main St East Hartford CT 06108

FLORA, CORNELIA BUTLER, sociologist, educator; b. Santa Monica, Calif., Aug. 5, 1943; d. Carroll Woodward and May Fleming (Darnall) Butler; m. Jan Leighton Flora, Aug. 22, 1967; children: Gabriela Catalina, Natasha Pilar. BA, U. Calif., Berkeley, 1965; MS, Cornell U., 1966, PhD, 1970. Asst. to full prof. Kans. State U., Manhattan, 1970-89, dir. population rsch. lab., 1970-78, univ. disting. prof., 1988-89; program adviser Ford Found., Bogota, Colombia, 1978-80; prof., head dept. sociology Va. Poly. Inst. and State U., Blacksburg, 1989—; cons. USAID, 1981-91. Editor: Sustainable Agriculture, 1990, RuralPolicy for the 1990s; contbr. articles to sociol. publs. Bd. dirs. Cooper House, Blacksburg, 1990—. Mem. Ruiral Sociol. Soc. (pres. 1988-89, Outstanding Rsch. award 1987), Latin Am. Studies Assn. (bd. dirs. 1982-84, pres. Midwest sect. 1989-90), Am. Sociol. Soc. Mem. Church of Brethren. Office: Dept Sociology Va Poly Inst and State U Blacksburg VA 24061-0137

FLORA, SUE ANN, real estate broker; b. Elkhart, Ind., Mar. 31, 1941; d. William Matthews and Nancy (Neu) Stubbins; m. Jack Lynn Flora (div. Oct. 1986); children: William, Jeffery. BSBA, U. Ark., 1966. Real estate broker Cressy and Everett, Elkhart, 1984—. Bd. dirs. Assn. for Disabled, Bristol; sec. Salvation Army Women's Aux., Elkhart, 1988-90. Mem. Million Dollar Club (life, Elkhart Bd. Realtors award 1989, 90), Rotary (bd. dirs. 1990—), PEO (past sec. 1987, treas. 1990—). Mem. United Ch. of Christ. Home: 701 B Kensington Ct Elkhart IN 46516

FLORCZYK-MATT, SANDRA, personnel executive; b. Syracuse, N.Y., Oct. 29, 1955; d. Alexander Stephen and Josephine (Iorio) Florczyk; m. Louis C. Matt, Jr., Nov. 1, 1980. B.A., Syracuse U., 1977; M.B.A., Nova U., 1984. Adminstr. law office Robbins, Gaynor & Bronstein, P.A., St. Petersburg, Fla., 1981—. Co-editor Community Link, 1976. Mem. Am.soc. Personnel Adminstrs., Assn. Legal Adminstrs. Republican. Roman Catholic. Avocations: art; tennis; traveling; golf. Home: PO Box 707 Mango FL 33550 Office: Robbins Gaynor & Bronstein PA 150 2d Ave N Suite 1700 Saint Petersburg FL 33701

FLOREN, GEORGIA B., real estate broker; b. Mishawaka, Ind., Aug. 25, 1931; d. Glenn W. and O. Belle (Stover) Fulp; m. John A. Floren, June 27, 1953; children: James A., Michael J. BSc., Ind. U., 1953; MSc., Butler U., Indpls., 1970. Cert. Real Estate Broker, Ind. Tchr. Arlington high sch., Indpls., 1966-72, human relations counselor, 1972-75; tchr. Bishop Chatard high sch., Indpls., 1975-77; lectr. Ind. U. Purdue U., 1977-83; edn. asst. St. Luke's United Methodist Ch., Indpls., 1983-84; sales assoc. The Bryant Co., 1986-87, Century 21 Concept, Indpls., 1987-88; real estate broker Indpls., 1989. Info. referral specialist Community Svc. Coun., Indpls., 1985; vol. The Hermitage, Indpls., 1986, Eiteljorg Mus., Indpls., 1989. Mem. Delta Kappa Gamma, Alpha Phi Frat. Republican. Methodist.

FLORENCE, LUCY MAE, investment executive; b. Shreveport, La., June 28, 1942; d. Alsie Lee and Rosie (Lee) F.; children: Tracey Matheney, Imani Matheney. BS, Kans. State U., 1969; MBA with distinction, Nat. U., San Diego, 1988; postgrad., Lone Mountain Coll., San Francisco. Lic. in security life and disability ins., variable annuity ins. Exec. dir. Watato Weusi, Inc., San Francisco; dir. children's svcs. San Francisco Coun. Chs.; investment exec. Baraban Securities Inc., Culver City, Calif. Pres. Ingleside Community Ctr., 1988-90; founding mem., co-chair mayoral task force OMI, Neighbors in Action. Mem. NAFE, Summit Orgn., Commonwealth Club of Calif. Presbyterian. Office: 363 Orizaba Ave San Francisco CA 94132

FLORENCE, VERENA MAGDALENA, small business owner; b. Interlaken, Switzerland, Nov. 4, 1946; came to U.S., 1967; d. Paul Robert and Marie (Raess) Demuth; m. Kenneth James Florence, Dec. 10, 1967. BA, U. Calif., Berkeley, 1974; MS, UCLA, 1979, PhD, 1982. Research scientist Procter & Gamble, Cin., 1983; adminstr. Swerdlow & Florence, Beverly Hills, Calif., 1984-89; pres., chief exec. officer, chmn. of bd. Böl Designs, Inc., L.A., 1989—. Contbr. articles to profl. jours. Democrat. Home and Office: 1063 Stradella Rd Los Angeles CA 90077

FLORES, KATHRYN A., healthcare administrator; b. Chgo., Apr. 27, 1954; d. Paul John and Ann Eileen (Klein) Varga; m. Jesse S. Flores, Oct. 14, 1978. BS, Purdue U., 1977; cert. in med. tech., Northwestern U., 1978; MS, Tex. Woman's U. Med. technologist N.C. Meml. Hosp., Chapel Hill, 1978-79, Cin. Gen. Hosp. U. Cin., 1979-81, Meth. Med. Ctr., Dallas, 1981-83, Parkland Meml. Hosp., Dallas, 1983-85; asst. mgr. Dallas County Hosp. Dist., Parkland Meml. Hosp., Dallas, 1985—. Block capt. Highlands Neighborhood Assn., 1987—. Mem. NAFE, Am. Coll. Healthcare Execs., Clin. Lab. Mgmt. Assn., Healthcare Fin. Mgmt. Assn., Phi Beta Kappa, Phi Kappa Phi. Roman Catholic. Office: Parkland Meml Hosp Dall County Hosp Dist 5201 Harry Hines Blvd Dallas TX 75235

FLORES, MARGARITA FRANCES, bank officer; b. Washington, Aug. 21, 1959; d. Jose Francisco and Margarita (Fernández-Mattei) F. BS in Biology, U. P.R., 1981; BBA in Corp. Mgmt., Fla. Atlantic U., 1986. Computer operator Bosch, Inc., Delray Beach, Fla., 1984; teller City Fed. Savs. Bank, Boca Raton, Fla., 1984-85, rep. new accounts, 1985-86, ops. asst., 1986-87; adminstrv. asst. C&S Nat. Bank S.C., Columbia, 1987-88, mgmt. assoc., 1988-90, asst. ops. officer, 1990—; tutor computer langs., Boca Raton, 1981-86. Mem. NAFE, Assn. MBA Execs., Am. Inst. Banking, Zool. Soc., People for the Ethical Treatment of Animals. Republican. Roman Catholic. Home: 3200 Fernandina Rd #107F Columbia SC 29210

FLORES, MARJORIE JOICE, health care facility administrator, consultant; b. N.Y.C., Dec. 19, 1937; d. Frederick and Charlotte Caroline (Koball) Repetti; divorced, 1980; 1 child, Virginia. BS in Nursing cum laude, CUNY, 1963; MPA, NYU, 1979. Cert. nursing adminstr. Nurse in charge N.Y. Hosp., N.Y.C., 1963-65; per diem nurse VA Hosp., Bronx, N.Y., 1965-66; staff nurse Ryder Meml. Hosp., Humacao, P.R., 1966; nurse in charge Clinica Pila, Ponce, P.R., 1966-67; head nurse surgery Montefiore Med. Ctr., Bronx, 1967-69, instr. inservice, 1969-71, instr. surgery, 1971-72, asst. dir. surgery, 1971-82; v.p. nursing Cooper Hosp., Camden, N.J., 1982-84; exec. dir. Hosp. HomeCare of Greater Phila., 1984-89; cons. health care mgmt. Cherry Hill, N.J., 1989—; dir. acute care svcs. Pacific Presbyn. Med. Ctr., San Francisco, 1990—; lectr. Am. Assn. Critical Care Nurses, 1980, Camden Area Health Edn. Ctr., Inc., 1983-84, Rutgers U., Camden, 1984; clin. asst. prof. Coll. Allied Health Thomas Jefferson U., Phila., 1983-89; cons. home care mgmt., 1984-89. Bd. dirs. Uxbridge Condominium Assn., 1986-88, 89—. Home and Office: 1456 47th Ave San Francisco CA 94122

FLORES, ROBIN ANN, social worker, social services administrator; b. Allentown, Pa., Oct. 6, 1949; d. Norman Henry and Ann May (Huff) Flores. B.S. in Edn., Kutztown U., 1971; M.S. in Adminstrn., U. Scranton, 1983. Caseworker gerontology Lehigh County Area Agy. for Aging, Allentown, Pa., 1973-75, info. referral outreach coordinator, 1975-78, supr. community services, 1979—; lectr. on aging process, Lehigh County, Pa., 1978—; utilization community resources, Lehigh County, 1978—. Mem. adv. bd. Community Action Com. of Lehigh Valley, 1979-82, Elder Well, 1987—; Pa. del. White House Conf. on Aging, Hershey, Pa., 1981; bd. dirs. Vis. Nurse Assn. of Lehigh County, 1982—, Women Inc., 1983-87; adv. bd. Homecare, Inc., 1982—, Geriatric Edn. Modules, Allentown Osteo. Hosp., 1979; mem. profl. adv. com. Lehigh Valley Hospice, 1984—; mem. utilization and rev. bd. Vis. Nurse Assn., 1979—; consumer rep. Pa. Power and Light Co., Nat. Assn. Female Execs., Lehigh County, Pa., 1978—; co-chmn. Human Services Tng. Coop., 1975-81. Mem. Allentown Art Mus., Old Allentown Preservation Assn., Quota Internat. Home: 237 N Lumber St Allentown PA 18102 Office: Lehigh County Area Agy on Aging 523 Hamilton St Allentown PA 18101

FLORES, SUZANNE, bookeeper, real estate company executive; b. Rosebud, Tex., May 31, 1931; d. Florentino Garza Villarreal and Maria Ynes (Cordova) Villarreal; m. Jesus Flores, May 27, 1950; children: Cynthia Anne, Denise Kaye. Cert., Cameron Bus. Coll., 1951, Real Estate Coll., 1976. Spl. interpreter adminstrn. and research Scott and White Health Clinic, Temple, Tex., 1949-60; acctg. clk. II Tex. Instruments, Dallas, 1961-68; owner, bookkeeper Flores Bookkeeping Services, Dallas, 1968—; acctg. clk. SW Med. Sch., Dallas, 1974-78; v.p., realtor Encore Real Estate, Inc., Dallas, 1984—; v.p., cons. Transplastic, Inc., Dallas, 1985-87, D. Browne Creations, Inc., Dallas, 1985-87; cons. Lancaster Investment Co. Mem. Mex. Am. Bus. and Profl. Women (founder, treas. 1972-74), Dallas Hispanic C. of C. (bd. dirs. 1981). Republican. Methodist. Home: 4124 Saranac Dr Dallas TX 75220 Office: Flores Bookkeeping Svcs 6300 N Central Expresssway Suite 105 Dallas TX 75206

FLORESTANO, PATRICIA SHERER, university administrator; b. Washington, Mar. 15, 1936; d. Wilbur L. and Virginia M. (Moriconi) F.; B.A. in Am. Civilization, U. Md., 1958, M.A. in Govt. and Politics, 1970, Ph.D. in Pub. Adminstrn. and Am. Govt., 1974; m. Thomas Florestano, Nov. 29, 1959; children—Leslie C., Thomas. Research staff State Legis. Commn. on Intergovt. Coop., 1972-75, State Gov.'s Commn. on Functions of Govt., 1973-75; staff asst. to pres. Md. Senate, 1975-78; asst. prof. Inst. Urban Studies, U. Md., College Park, 1974-79, dir. Inst. Govtl. Service, 1979-85, vice-chancellor govtl. relations, 1985—; cons. ednl. evaluation, mgmt. and survey research. Lector St. Elizabeth Ann Seton Ch., 1970—; dir. Crofton (Md.) Gymnastics Program, 1972-74; vice chmn. Anne Arundel County (Md.) Commn. on Women, 1975; mem. Anne Arundel County Schs. Adv. Forum, 1975-76, chmn. nominations com., 1976-78. Recipient Outstanding Teaching award Students Assn. of U. Md., 1979. Mem. Am. Soc. Pub. Adminstrn. (pres. 1983-84, conf. fellow), Am. Polit. Sci. Assn., So. Polit. Sci. Assn., Urban Affairs Assn. (past chmn. governing bd.), So. Consortium Univ., Pub. Service Orgns. (former editor). Democrat. Roman Catholic. Author: (with other) The States and Metropolitan Areas, 1981; Attitudes of Special Interest Groups and the Public on Chesapeake Bay Areas, 1980; also articles. Home: 1516 Farlow Ave Crofton MD 21114 Office: System Adminstrn 3300 Metzerott Rd Adelphi MD 20783

FLORIAN, MARIANNA BOLOGNESI, civic leader; b. Chgo.; d. Giulio and Rose (Garibaldi) Bolognesi; BA cum laude, Barat Coll., 1940; postgrad. Moser Bus. Sch., 1941-42; m. Paul A. Florian III, June 4, 1949; children—Paul, Marina, Peter, Mark. Asst. credit mgr. Stella Cheese Co., Chgo., 1942-45; With ARC ETO Clubmobile Unit, 1945-47; mgr. Passavant Hosp. Gift Shop, 1947-49; pres., Jr. League Chgo., Inc., 1957-59; pres. woman's bd. Passavant Hosp., 1966-68; bd. dirs. Northwestern Meml. Hosp., 1974-81, mem. exec. com., 1974-79; pres. Women's Assn., Chgo. Symphony Orch., 1974-77, founder WFMT/CSO Radiothon, 1976; chmn. Guild Chgo. Hist. Soc., 1981-84, trustee Chgo. Hist. Soc., 1981-84; life trustee Orchestral Assn., v.p. 1978-82, vice chmn. 1982-86, mem. exec. com. 1978-87; mem. women's bd. U. Chgo.; mem. vis. com. dept. music U. Chgo., 1980—; pres. bd. dirs. Antiquarian Soc., 1989—; bd. dirs. Art Inst. Chgo. (pres. 1989—), 1986—. Recipient Citizen Fellowship, Inst. Medicine Chgo., 1975. Clubs: Friday (pres. 1972-74), Contemporary; Winnetka Garden.

FLORIO, MARYANNE J., research scientist; b. Queens, N.Y., Sept. 28, 1940; d. Edgar Vincent and Helen Louise (Schultze) Spaeth; m. James J. Florio, June 25, 1960 (div. 1985); children: Christopher, Gregory, Catherine. BS summa cum laude, Trenton State Coll., 1979; MEd, Temple U., 1981, postgrad., 1982—. Cert. biofeedback therapist, tchr., N.J. Research and evaluation asst. Woodhaven Ctr., Phila., 1981-82; statis. and computer cons., program asst. Systems & Computer Tech. Corp., Phila., 1982-83; biofeedback therapist Ctr. for Creative Devel., Ardmore, Pa., 1984-85; evaluation coord. N.J. Dept. Edn., Trenton, 1987-88; computer scientist, stats. researcher N.J. Dept. Health, Trenton, 1987-88, research scientist for prenatal and neonatal care prog., 1988—; pvt. design and computing cons., 1983—; trainer computer and statis. software, N.J., Pa., 1984—, Camden County Commn. on Women, 1985—. Chmn. long-range planning, bd. dirs., 1st v.p. Camden County council Girl Scouts U.S., 1975—. Elks Club scholar, 1958, Systems and Computer Tech. Corp. scholar, 1982; Temple U. grad. fellow, 1984. Mem. Am. Edn. Research Assn., Biofeedback Soc. Am., Biofeedback and Behavioral Med. Soc. Pa. Home: 290 Evergreen Rd Barrington NJ 08007

FLORMAN, JEAN CLAIRE, mediator, writer, anthropologist; b. Washington, Aug. 14, 1952; d. Edwin Frank and Mavis Claire (Jones) F.; m. John Samuel Massa, June 24, 1980; children: Amber, Brian. BA magna cum laude, Cornell U., 1973; MA, U. Ariz., 1978, JD, 1982, postgrad. Caseworker Congressman James Howard, Washington, 1973-74; archaeologist Southside Historic Sites, Williamsburg, Va., 1974-75; legal intern U.S. Dept. Justice, Washington, 1981; editor Ariz. Law Rev., Journ. Law and Human Behavior, Tucson, 1981-83; mediator Iowa Pub. Employment Rels. Bd., Des Moines, 1988—; assoc. prof. Pima Community Coll., Tucson, 1978-79; editorial cons., 1984—. Contbr. articles, book revs. to various publs. Mem. Ariz. Task Force to Study Gender and Justice, Tucson, 1985-86, U. Ariz. Conflict Studies Com., Tucson, 1985-86; active Free Lunch Program, Iowa City, Iowa, 1987—. Mem. Women in Communications, Authors Resource Ctr. Office: 710 Giblin Dr Iowa City IA 52246

FLOTT, NANCY LEE, librarian; b. Wichita, Kans., June 8, 1932; d. Henry A. Pribbenow and Lillian I. (Torkleson) Fate; m. Richard E. Flott Sr., May 29, 1954 (div. 1966); children: Paula, Rick, Larry, Karla. BS, Emporia State U., 1954, MS, 1962; PhD, Kansas State U., 1976. Sch. librarian Lab. Sch. Emporia (Kans.) State U., 1960-63; media specialist United Sch. Dist. #345, Topeka, 1963-72; program specialist Kans. St. Dept. Edn., Topeka, 1972-82; asst. prof. Emporia (Kans.) State U., 1982-88; library dir. Cottey Coll., Nevada, Mo., 1988—; founder coord. Kans. Online Group, 1975-83, chair tech. task force Kansas Library Network Bd., 1983-85; dir. Title IV-C Classroom Improvement Grants Progran, Kans., 1981, Kans. Ednl. Dissemination/Diffusion System Resource Component, 1974-82. Contbr. articles to profl. jours. Mem. Community Theatre Bd., 1987-88, Internat. Tng. Communication, 1986—; pres. Kan-Talk of Internat. Tng. im Emporia, 1983, v.p., 1985, sec., 1986; mem.leadership tng. Vernon County, Nevada, 1988-89. Mem. ALA, Spl. Library Assn., Kansas Library Assn., AAUW (treas. 1985-88, v.p. 1989—), Bus. and Profl. Women's Club. Home: 810 S Clay Nevada MO 64772 Office: Cottey Coll 1000 W Austin Nevada MO 64772

FLOURNOY, ANDRA BROOKS, management consultant, psychologist; b. Edinburg, Tex., Oct. 22, 1956; d. James Anderson and Dorothy Grace (Long) Brooks; m. Clarence Richard Flournoy, Nov. 25, 1983. BA, Trinity U., 1976; MEd, U. Tex., 1979; PhD, Tex. A&M U., 1985. Tchr. McAllen (Tex.) Ind. Sch. Dist., 1976-79; assoc. psychologist Tex. Sch. for the Deaf, Austin, 1979-81; psychologist Career Strategies, San Antonio, 1985-89; v.p. Drake Beam Marin, Inc., San Antonio, 1989—; cons. Tex. Pub. Schs., 1981—. Fundraiser Am. Heart Assn., San Antonio, 1988—; mem. personnel com. allocations panel United Way, San Antonio, 1989-90, vice chair, 1989, chair, 1990—. Mem. APA, Tex. Psychol. Assocs., Leadership of San Antonio, Oakes Profl. Women's Assn., Greater San Antonio C. of C., Rotary. Republican. Baptist. Office: Drake Beam Morin Inc 8400 Normandale Lake Ste 470 Bloomington MN 55437

FLOURNOY, JANIE DAVIS, public relations specialist, college official; b. Shreveport, La., Mar. 15, 1950; d. Paul Robert and Dorothy Jane (Schmied) Davis; m. T. Cole Flournoy, Mar. 27, 1971 (div.); 1 dau., Frances Miller. Student, Mary Baldwin Coll., 1968-70, U. Reading, Eng., 1970-71; B.A., Centenary Coll., 1972. Writer, Shreveport Times, 1972-79; dir. pub. rels. Centenary Coll. of La., 1979—. Chmn. 4th dist. adv. bd. La. Pub. Broadcasting, 1981-84; pres. Shreveport Opera Guild, 1983-84; bd. dirs. Jr. League, 1979, 81-82. Mem. Pub. Rels. Soc. Am., Nat. Soc. of Colonial Dames Am. in State of La. (bd. dirs. Shreveport com.), Jr. League of Shreveport (bd. dirs.). Presbyterian. Home: 18 Dudley Sq Shreveport LA 71106 Office: Centenary Coll Louisiana 2911 Centenary Blvd Shreveport LA 71104

FLOURNOY, NANCY, statistics professor; b. Long Beach, Calif., May 4, 1947; d. Carr Irvine and Elizabeth (Blincoe) F.; m. Leonard B. Hearne, Aug. 28, 1978. BS, UCLA, 1969, MS, 1971; PhD, U. Wash., 1982. Statistician Regional Med. Programs, L.A., 1969-70; assoc. mem. S.W. Regional Lab. for Ednl. Rsch. and Devel., Los Alamitas, Calif., 1971-73; database mgr. U. Wash., Seattle, 1973-75; dir. clin. stats. Fred Hutchinson Cancer Rsch. Ctr., Seattle; dir. stats. NSF, Washington, 1986-88; prof. stats. The American U., Washington, 1988—; contbg. editor Inst. Mathematical Statistics, Haywood, Calif., 1989—. Contbr. articles to profl. jours. Mem. outreach com. Inst. Math. Stats., 1989—; grant reviewer AAUW, NSF, NIH. Inst. Math. Stats. fellow. Mem. AAAS, AAUW, Caucus for Women in Stats., Am. Statis. Assn. (com. of certification), Biometric Soc., Internat. Assn. for Statis. Computing, Assn. Women in Math. (joint com.), Pres. of Statis. Socs. (mem. com. scientific manpower), Inst. Math. Stats., Math. Assn. of Am., Washington Statis. Soc. Presbyterian. Office: Am U Dept Math 4400 Massachusetts Ave NW Washington DC 20016-8050

FLOWERS, AMY LEE, psychologist; b. San Antonio, July 25, 1954; d. Philip Harold Flowers and Louise Annette Lippard Wright; m. James Destrahan Warren, Dec. 3, 1983. BA, U. Tex., 1976; MEd, U. Mo., 1978, EdD in Spl Edn., 1980; PhD, U. Okla., 1985. Lic. psychologist, Ga. Caseworker, supr. Austin State Sch., 1975-76; renal counselor Ark. Reha. Svc., Little Rock, 1977-78; rehab. technician Harry Truman VA Hosp., Columbia, Mo., 1980; mental health coordinator Focal Pointe Women, Macon, Ga., 1988—; cons. in field; adj. faculty Mercer U., Macon, 1989—. Contbr. articles to profl. jours. Chmn. adult edn. com. Temple Beth Israel, Macon, 1989—; cons. Girl Scouts U.S.A., Macon, 1989—; active Soup Kitchen Macon Outreach, 1989—. Capt. U.S. Army, 1983-88. Recipient Excellence in Media award, Ga. Psychol. Assn., 1979. Mem. Am. Psychol. Assn., Ga. Psychol. Assn., Middle Ga. Psychol. Assn., Career Women's Network. Jewish. Office: Focal Pointe Women 3200 Riverside Dr Bldg C Macon GA 31210

FLOWERS, BETTY SUE, English educator; b. Waco, Tex., Feb. 2, 1947; d. Paul Davis and Betty Lou (Lewis) Marable; m. John G. Flowers III; 1 child, John Michael. BA with high honors, U. Tex., 1969, MA, 1970; PhD, U. London, 1973. With U. Tex., Austin, 1968—; dir. plan II honors program U. Tex., 1987—, assoc. dean Graduate Studies, 1979-82, 88-90. Author: Browning and The Modern Tradition, 1976, Four Shields of Power, 1987, Extending the Shade, 1990; editor: A World of Ideas, 1988, Joseph Campbell and thePower of Myth: Bill Moyers and Joseph Campbell in Conversation, 1988, (with Lynda E. Boose) Daughters and Fathers, 1988; contbr. chpts. to books, articles to profl. jours. Adv. bd. Salado Inst. for Humanities, 1980-84, bd. dirs., 1988; mem. exec. com. Tex. Com. for Humanities, 1987-90; bd. trustees Tex. Humanities Alliance, 1986-87. Recipient Amoco Teaching Excellence award 1979, Leadership Tex., 1985; Andrew W. Mellon fellow, 1976; faculty U. Rsch. Inst. grantee, 1983. Mem. MLA, Tex. Assn. Coll. Tchrs., Tex. Assn. Creative Writing Tchrs., AAUP, Nat. Poetry Therapy Assn. (bd. dirs. 1987—), NEH, Rotary, Phi Beta Kappa, Omicron Delta Kappa. Office: U Tex Dept English Austin TX 78712

FLOWERS, JUDITH ANN, communications advertising executive; b. Oxford, Miss., Feb. 21, 1944; d. Woodrow Coleman and Ola Marie (Harding) Haynes; m. Sayles L. Brown Jr., Apr. 20, 1963 (div. Apr. 1974); children: Sayles L. III, Gregory A., Matthew C., Stephen W.; m. Taylor Graydon Flowers Jr., Apr. 27, 1979. Grad. high sch., Clarksdale, Miss. Office mgr. The KBH Corp., Clarksdale, 1964-69; office mgr., estimator Willis & Ellis Constrn., Clarksdale, 1969-75; with advt. prodn. Farm Press Pub., Clarksdale, 1975-79, advt. mgr., 1979-86, dir. advt. svcs., 1986—. Counselor youth ct. County Youth Ct., Clarksdale, 1985—. Mem. NAFE, Bus. and Profl. Women (corr. sec. 1987-88, 2d v.p. 1988-89, 1st v.p. 1989-90, pres.-elect 1990—), Agri-Women Am., Nat. Agri Mktg. Assn. (v.p. mid-south chpt. 1989-90, pres. 1990—), Clarksdale C. of C. (chmn. agri bus. commn. 1989—, bd. dirs. 1989—), So. Garden History Soc., The Garden Conservancy. Republican. Baptist. Home: Box 3126 Dublin MS 38739 Office: Farm Press Pub Intersection Hwy 61 & 6 Clarksdale MS 38614

FLOWERS, SALLY A., dentist; b. Detroit, June 18, 1954; d. Willie Oscar and Mary Jane (Perry) F. Student, Ea. Mich. U., 1971-74; DDS, Howard U., 1978; MPH, Johns Hopkins U., 1980. Resident in gen. practice D.C. Gen. Hosp., Washington, 1978-79; assoc. dentist Dr. Felix, Washington, 1979, Pimlico Dental Clinic, Balt., 1979-80, Dr. Roy Baptiste, Silver Spring, Md., 1980-82, Dr. Barbara Johnson, Washington, 1981-82, Capital Hill Dental Ctr., Washington, 1981-82; pvt. practice Washington, 1982—. Sec. Kennedy St. Assn. of Mchts. and Profls., Washington, 1989-90. Mem. ADA, Acad. Gen. Dentistry, D.C. Dental Soc. (chairperson membership growth and retention com. Washington chpt. 1988), Robert T. Freeman Dental Soc., Nat. Dental Assn., Howard U. Alumni Assn., Johns Hopkins U. Alumni Assn., D.C. C. of C., Pin High Golf Club. Office: 250 Kennedy St NW Washington DC 20011

FLOWERS, VIRGINIA ANNE, state educational administrator; b. Dothan, Ala., Aug. 29, 1928; d. Kyrie Neal and Annie Laurie (Stewart) F. B.A. (State of Fla. scholar), Fla. State U., 1949; M.Ed., Auburn (Ala.) U., 1958; Ed.D. (Delta Kappa Gamma scholar, teaching asst.), Duke U., 1963. Elem. and secondary sch. tchr., adminstr. Dothan and Dalton, Ga., 1949-61; asst. prof., then prof. edn., head dept. Columbia (S.C.) Coll., 1963-68, assoc. dean, then dean, 1969-72; prof. edn. Va. Commonwealth U., 1968-69; assoc. dean, asst. provost, acting dean, vice provost Trinity Coll. Arts and Scis., Duke U., 1972-74, prof. edn., chmn. dept., asst. provost ednl. program devel., 1974-80; dean Sch. Edn., Ga. So. Coll., Statesboro, 1980-85; asst. vice chancellor Univ. System of Ga., Atlanta, 1985-88, vice chancellor, 1988—; bd. dirs., exec. com. Am. Assn. Colls. Tchr. Edn., 1979-84, pres., 1983-84; bd. dirs., exec. com. Learning Inst. N.C., 1976-80. Co-author: Law and Pupil Control, 1964, Readings in Survival in Today's Society, 2 vols, 1978; editorial bd.: Jour. Tchr. Edn, 1980-82, Ednl. Gerontology, 1979—; contbr. articles to profl. jours. Adv. trustee Queens Coll., Charlotte, N.C., 1976-78; vice chmn. continuing commn. study black colls. related to United Methodist Ch., 1973-76. Recipient Star Tchrs. award Dalton. Mem. So. Assn. Colls. and Schs. (commn. on colls.), Am. Ednl. Research Assn., Nat. Orgn. Legal Problems in Edn., Am. Assn. Higher Edn., NEA, Am. Assn. Colls. Tchr. Edn. (pres. 1983), Kappa Delta Pi, Phi Delta Kappa. Home: 619 N Superior Ave Decatur GA 30033 Office: Univ System of Ga Bd Regents 244 Washington St SW Atlanta GA 30334

FLOWERS-CHESTER, PHYLLIS DENISE, legal assistant; b. Paducah, Ky., Nov. 1, 1956; d. Stanley D. Flowers and Mary H. (Caldwell) Lanford; m. Christopher G. Chester, Sept. 28, 1985. AS, U. Toledo Community Coll., 1978; BS, U. Toledo, 1982. Legal asst. Toledo Legal Aid Soc., 1979-83; hearing officer Ohio Dept. Human Svcs., Toledo, 1983-85; legal cons. Disability Svcs., Inc., Novi, Mich., 1985-89; coord. legal program Women's Survival Ctr., Pontiac, Mich., 1989—. Chmn. awards com. People's Tribunal, Toledo, 1978; mem. paralegal tech. bd. U. Toledo, 1983-85.

Named Alumni of Yr. in Community Tech., U. Toledo, 1984. Home: 20965 Lahser Rd Apt 512 Southfield MI 48034

FLOYD, ANITA LOUISE, publishing company executive; b. Oklahoma City, Feb. 3, 1930; d. Walter Raymond and Evelyn Elizabeth (Humphrey) Kimball; m. Paul Franklin Floyd, Oct. 7, 1950; children: Paul Raymond (dec.), Eve Ann, Paula Kay, Jana Lee. BA in English, East Cen. U., Ada, Okla., 1952, MEd, 1962. Tchr. English, journalism Pasadena (Tex.) Sch. Dist., 1962-63; bookkeeper, reporter De Queen (Ark.) Bee, 1964-71, sec., comptroller, 1972-80, asst. to pub., 1980-89, v.p., 1989—, also dir. Mem. Ada Bd. Edn., 1975-80, pres., 1978; mem. Ada City Coun., 1987—; mayor City of Ada, 1990-91; founder, dir., pres. Pontotoc Animal Welfare Soc., Ada, 1981-87; elder Presbyn. Ch., Ada. Recipient Outstanding Svc. award Pontotoc Animal Welfare Soc., 1987. Mem. LWV, Ark. Press Assn., Ada C. of C. (long-range planning com.), Ninety-Nines, Rotary Internat. (bd. dirs. 1990-91), ALpha Phi (Okla. Alumna Svc. award 1988). Office: De Queen Bee Co Inc De Queen Ave De Queen AR 71832

FLOYD, DEBORAH MAE, computer hardware-software sales executive; b. Riverside, Calif., Aug. 22, 1962; d. Gary Lloyd and Caroline Mae (Fisher) Kounkel; m. Joseph Lee Floyd, Dec. 1985. BA in Biology, U. Colo., 1984. Mktg. rep. Robert Landau Assocs., Inc., N.Y.C., 1983-84; nat. rep. Chi Omega Frat., Cin., 1984-86; sales rep. Microamerica, Chantilly, Va., 1987, account rep., 1987-88, sales mgr., 1988-89, area mgr., 1989-90. Mem. nat. alumni admissions assistance programs U. Colo., Boulder, 1984—. Mem. NAFE, U. Colo. Alumni Assn., Chi Omega (scholarship adv. San Diego State U. , 1986, rush adv. George Mason U. 1987-89, mem. nat. rush team 1988-89). Republican. Lutheran. Home: 10222 Polk St Omaha NE 68127

FLOYD, LILLIAN CLAIRE, marketing director; b. Bklyn.; d. Raymond Howard and Lillian (Kane) F.; 1 child, Suzanne. BS, Kean Coll. N.J., 1977, MA, 1983. Treas. Intercontinental Plastics, Hauppauge, N.Y., 1964-67; v.p. Regency Internat. Corp., Union, N.J., 1968-82; office mgr. U.S. Congressman, Union, 1982-84; dir. mktg. Meritus Industries, Inc., Livingston, N.J., 1984—. Author poetry. Bd. dirs. Union County Commn. on Status of Women, Elizabeth, N.J., 1988—. Mem. NAFE, Kean Coll. Profl. Women's Assn., Union County Hiking Club, Friends of Lord Stirling. Democratic. Roman Catholic. Home: 845 Park Ave Elizabeth NJ 07208

FLOYD, MARGUERITE MARIE (MAITA FLOYD), publisher; b. St. Jean de Luz, France, Aug. 10, 1924; came to U.S., 1946; d. Jean Louis Branquet and Felicie Ibarrart; m. Thomas McGuire, Apr. 10, 1948 (div. 1965); m. Willard C. Floyd, May 1968 (dec. Sept. 1985). Cert., Mlle. Suertegaray, Hendaye, 1937; postgrad., Ste Bernadette, Pau, 1940, Ariz. State U., Tempe, 1967, Maricopa Tech., 1975-76, So. Mountain Community Coll., 1989. Customer svc. Trans World Airlines, N.Y., 1952-62; agt. Phoenix, 1962-82; pub. Eskualdum Pubs., Phoenix, 1982—; lectr. caregiving and bereavement. Author and illustrator: Caretakers, the Forgotten People, 1988, 89. Vol. Hospice Bereavement, Phoenix, 1987; vol. speaker Epilepsy Soc. Ariz. Mem. Toastmasters, Ahwatukee Women's Club, Ahwatukee Entertainers. Democrat. Roman Catholic. Home: 4749 E Ahwatukee Dr Phoenix AZ 85044 Office: Eskualdun Publishers PO Box 50266 Phoenix AZ 85076

FLOYD, SARA JORDON, real estate broker; b. Greensboro, N.C., Oct. 6, 1938; d. Harold Herman and Barbara (Glick) Jordon; m. John Wilson Jenrette, Dec. 20, 1960 (div. July 1975); Mary Elizabeth, Harold Hampton; Jesse Byran Floyd, June 4, 1984. BMus, Converse Coll., Spartanburg, S.C., 1960; postgrad., U. S.C., 1976. Cert. Real Estate Broker. Real estate broker Realty World , Anchor Realty, N. Myrtle Beach, S. C., 1978-; sec. Grand Strand Bd. of Realtors, N. Myrtle Beach, S.C., 1977, pub. dir., 1988. Recipient Crescent award Cleve. Hotel, Spartanburg, S.C., 1958, Am. Legion award, 1960. Mem. N. Myrtle Beach Woman's Club. Democrat. Methodist. Home: 301 11th Ave N North Myrtle Beach SC 29582 Office: Realty World Anchor Realty 211 North Kings Hwy North Myrtle Beach SC 29582

FLOYD-TENIYA, KATHLEEN, business services executive; b. Berwyn, Ill., June 23, 1953; d. David James and Phyllis L. (Lyons) Floyd; m. Robert Don Teniya, June 20, 1982; one child: James David. Cert. credit and fin. analyst, lic. realtor, Ill. Indsl. specialist Technicon Instrument Corp., Elmhurst, Ill., 1971-74, service contract adminstr., 1974-76; asst. to pres. Elmed, Inc., Addison, Ill., 1976-77; credit rep. mgr. Memorex Corp., Lombard, Ill., 1977-79; nat. sales rep. Midcontinent Adjustment Co., Glenview, Ill., 1979-83, asst. v.p. sales, 1983-86; pres., chief exec. officer, (Inteletek) Innovative Telemktg. Techniques Inc., Itasca, Ill., 1986—. Newspaper editor, publicity chmn. Dupage County chpt. Young Ams. for Freedom, 1969-70, pres.; mem. bd. edn. Trinity Luth. Sch., Lombard, Ill, 1989—; appointed mem. legal and fin., citizen advisor Village Bd., Bloomingdale, Ill., 1989—. Mem. Nat. Assn. Female Execs., Am. Soc. Profl. and Exec. Women. Lutheran. Clubs: Lombard Women's Rep., Ill. Fedn. Rep. Women. Home: 263 Evergreen Ln Bloomingdale IL 60108 Office: (Inteletek) Innovative Telemktg Techniques Inc PO Box 0163 Itasca IL 60143

FLU-ALLEN, BARBARA CARLOCK, educator; b. Muskogee, Okla., Dec. 18, 1944; d. Maurice Milton and Lois Louise (Thomas) C.; m. Harold James Flu-Allen (div. 1975); 1 child, Christopher. Cert. dental hygienist, Ohio State U., 1977, BS, 1978; MS, U. Dayton, 1989. Cert. Nat. Dental Bd.; cert. tchr., Ohio. Lab. technician II Ohio State U. Coll. Dentistry, Columbus, 1967-75, rsch. assoc., summer 1975; guidance counselor Columbus Pub. Schs., 1978-79; dental hygienist Columbus, 1977-84; pupil community asst. specialist Columbus Pub. Schs., 1979-80, tchr. on spl. assignment, 1987-88, tchr. health, 1979—; guest lectr. Bowling Green State U., 1988; co-chmn. health, physical edn. Columbus Pub. Schs. Curriculum Revision Com., 1989—. Writer AIDS Education Columbus Public Schools, 1987; writing team leader AIDS Education: Supplemental Teaching Guide Columbus and Franklin County Schs., 1988. Mem. 29th Dist. Caucus, Columbus, 1986—, The Mayor's Drug-Free Sch. Task Force, Columbus, 1989—; sec. Union Grove Bapt. Ch. Schilarship Club, 1988—; bd. dirs. Ladies Usher. Recipient Excellence in Staff Devel. award Ohio Dept. Edn., 1987; Jennings scholar, 1990. Mem. NEA, Nat. Coalition of 100 Black Women, Columbus Edn. Assn. (chairperson econ. svcs. com.), Am. Dental Hygienists Assn., Ohio Tchrs. Assn., Cen. Ohio Tchrs. Assn. (instrn. & profl. devel. com. 1983-88), Ohio State U. Alumni Assn., U. Dayton Alumni Assn. Democrat. Baptist. Home: 2846 Keystone Dr Columbus OH 43209 Office: Columbus Pub Schs 270 E State St Columbus OH 43215

FLUCK, MICHELE M(ARGUERITE), biology educator; b. Geneva, Aug. 5, 1940; came to U.S., 1972; d. Wilhelm and Henriette Alice (Delaloye) F. MS, U. Geneva, 1964, 66, PhD, 1972. Rsch. assoc. N.Y. Pub. Health Rsch. Inst., N.Y.C., 1972-73; instr. Harvard Med. Sch., Boston, 1973-78, asst. prof., 1978-79; assoc. prof. Mich. State U., East Lansing, 1979-86, prof., 1986-90, disting. prof., 1990—. Contbr. articles to profl. jours. Recipient Young Investigator's award, Nat. Cancer Inst.; grantee Nat. Cancer Inst., 1979—, Am. Cancer Soc. grantee, 1987—. Fellow Leukemia Soc. Am. (scholar 1979-85); mem. AAAS, Am. Assn. virologists. Office: Mich State U Microbiology Dept Giltner Hall East Lansing MI 48824-1101

FLUEGEL, ELIZABETH LEIGH, graphic designer; b. Rochester, Minn., Mar. 24, 1959; d. John Ormond and Eileen Margaret (O'Donnell) Fluegel. BA, Coll. St. Benedict, St. Joseph, Minn., 1982. Designer Minn. Suburban Newspapers, Edina, 1985-86; editorial designer Minn. Real Estate Jour., Edina, 1986-88; editorial design coordinator Wiliams Publs. Inc., Plymouth, Minn., 1988—. Recipient 2d place for typography and design Minn. Newspaper Assn., 1988; award of excellence Soc. Newspaper Design, 1988. Mem. LWV, NAFE, Pub. TV, Earthwatch. Democrat.

FLUELLEN, SHIRLEY ANN, optics researcher; b. Macon, Ga., Nov. 17, 1952; d. Alexander Hamilton and Mamie L. (Stanley) F. B.S., Fort Valley State Coll., Ga., 1973; postgrad. U. Mich. Dental Sch., 1973-74; O.D., Ind. U., 1979; specialist cert. Manila Central U., 1981. Cert. optometrist. Optometrist, Manila and Va., 1979—; optics research specialist Naval Space Surveillance System, Dahlgren, Va., 1982—. Chair polit. action group for Va., NAACP, 1985; organizer, pres. Fredericksburg Area Pan-Hellenic Council 1984—; mem. Nat. Council Negro Women, 1984—. Am. Fund Minority Dental Edn. scholar, 1972-74; Ga. Bd. Regents Scholar, 1969-72. Mem. Nat. Optometric Assn. (chair regional membership com.; Student Service award 1977), Beta Kappa Chi, Alpha Kappa Mu (chpt. v.p. 1972-73), Alpha Kappa Alpha, Ruby Bell Missionary Soc. Mem. Christian Methodist Episcopal Ch. Lodges: Order of Eastern Star, Daus. of Elks. Avocations: reading; travel; sewing; jogging. Home: 1292 Elmhurst Circle SE Atlanta GA 30316

FLUET, MICHELLE L., underwriter; b. Boston, June 1, 1960; d. Roland N. and Phyllis (Pizzolante) Fluet. BA, Emmanuel Coll., 1982, BFA, 1983. Cert. computer programmer;. Lead clk., night operator John Hancock Property & Casualty Ins. Co., Boston, 1985-86, underwriting asst. II, 1986-87, underwriter III, 1987-88, underwriter II, 1988-89, underwriter I, 1989—. Recipient Arts Lottary Grant; various Art Festival Prizes. Mem. Winthrop Art Assn. (bd. dirs.), Winthrop Alumni Club.

FLUGGER, PENELOPE ANN, banker; b. Chgo., June 26, 1942; d. William and Florence Bernadette (Brongiel) Grabos; B.S., U. Ill., 1964; M.B.A., Baruch Coll., 1971; m. Robert John Flugger, July 11, 1970. Sr. mgr. Price Waterhouse Co., N.Y.C., 1964-75; with Morgan Guaranty Trust Co., 1975—, auditor, 1982—, sr. v.p., 1982—. C.P.A., N.Y., Ill. Mem. Am. Inst. C.P.A.s, Nat. Assn. Accts., Fin. Execs. Inst., N.Y. State Soc. C.P.A.s, Ill. State Soc. C.P.A.s. Office: Morgan Guaranty Trust Co 60 Wall St New York NY 10260

FLUKE, LYLA SCHRAM, publisher; b. Maddock, N.D.; d. Olaf John and Anne Marie (Rodberg) Schram; m. John M. Fluke, June 5, 1937; children: Virginia Fluke Gabelein, John M. Jr., David Lynd. BS in Zoology and Physiology, U. Wash., Seattle, 1934, diploma teaching, 1935. High sch. tchr., 1935-37; tutor Seattle schs., 1974-75; pub. Portage Quar. mag., Hist. Soc. Seattle and King County, 1980—. Author articles on history. Founder N.W. chpt. Myasthenia Gravis Found., 1953, pres., 60-66; obtained N.W. artifacts for destroyer Tender Puget Sound, 1966; mem. Seattle Mayor's Com. for Seattle Beautiful, 1968-69; sponsor Seattle World's Fair, 1962; charter mem. Seattle Youth Symphony Aux., 1974; bd. dirs. Cascade Symphony, Salvation Army, 1985-87; mem. U.S. Congl. Adv. Bd.; benefactor U. Wash., 1982—, nat. chmn. ann. giving campaign, 1983-84; benefactor Sterling Circle Stanford U., 1984, Wash. State Hist. Soc., Pacific Arts Ctr.; mem. condr.'s club Seattle Symphony, 1978—. Fellow Seattle Pacific U., 1972—; mem. Wash. Trust for Hist. Preservation, Nat. Trust for Hist. Preservation, N.W. Ornamental Hort. Soc. (life, hon.), Smithsonian Assocs., Nat. Assn. Parliamentarians (charter mem., pres. N.W. unit 1961), Wash. Parliamentarians Assn. (charter), IEEE Aux. (chpt. charter mem., pres. 1970-73), Seattle C. of C. (women's div.), Seattle Symphony Women's Assn. (life, sec. 1982-84, pres. 1985-87), Hist. Soc. Seattle and King County (exec. com. 1975-78, pres. women's mus. league 1975-78, pres. Moritz Thomsen Guild of Hist. Soc., 1978-80, 84-87), Highlands Orthopedic Guild (life), Wash. State Hist. Soc, Antiquarian Soc. (v.p. 1986-88, pres. 1988—), Women's U. Club, Rainier Club, Seattle Golf Club, Seattle Tennis Club, U. Wash. Pres.'s Club. Republican. Lutheran. Address: 1206 NW Culbertson Dr Vendovi Island/Anacortes Seattle WA 98221

FLUOR, MARJORIE LETHA WADE, author; b. Christiansburg, Va., May 6, 1926; d. Hubert Dodd and Ida (Sowers) Wade; m. John Simon Fluor, Aug. 17, 1956 (dec. Sept. 1974); m. Thurman Moore, July 27, 1979. Author: (geneal. book) Birth and Death Records Floyd County, Virginia, 1980; co-author: (with Michael Evlanoff) Alfred Nobel The Loneliest Millionaire, 1969. Chmn. vols. ARC, 1960-62; mem. adv. bd. Children's Hosp., Orange County, 1965-68; bd. dirs. Orange County Symphony Assn., 1964-69, Orange County Community Chest, 1962-66, Salvation Army, 1963-68, YWCA, 1963-68, Girl Scouts U.S., 1977—, World Affairs Council Orange County, 1975—, mem. exec. bd. Holmes Research Ctr., Los Angeles, 1975—; spl. rep. Calif. Bicentennial Celebration Commn., 1967-69; trustee United Ch. Religious Sci., 1980-85. Recipient Headliner award Orange County Press County, 1966, Heart to God, Hand to Man award Salvation Army, 1968, Disneyland Community Service Program award, 1967, Practitioner Emeritus Recognition award Golden Circle Ch. of Religious Sci., 1988. Mem. DAR (past regent, state asst. chaplain), Freedoms Found. (life), Assistance League, Federated Rep. Women, Philanthropic Ednl. Orgn., Les Dames de Champagne (chmn. 1970-74), Ctr. Club, Balboa Bay Club, Santa Ana Country Club, Pro Am. Club, Order Ea. Star. Home: 1920 Heliotrope Dr Santa Ana CA 92706

FLYER, JILL S., commercial real estate professional; b. Chgo., July 25, 1942; d. Harry M. and Jeanette (Klapman) F. BA in French Lit., U. Ill., 1963, MA in French Lit., 1966. Lic. real estate broker, Ill. Promotions supr. Am. Bar Endowment, Chgo., 1968-71; adviser, organizer various grassroots polit. campaigns, Chgo., 1971-72; adminstr. Ill. Planning and Conservation League, Chgo., 1972-74; program asst. U.S. EPA, Chgo., 1974; grants adminstr. Regional Transp. Authority, Chgo., 1974-79; sales mgr. Barclay Realty, Chgo., 1979-86; owner, pres. The Urban Network, Ltd., Chgo., 1986—; sec. exec. com., bd. dirs. The River North Assn., Chgo., 1987—. Organizer Ind. Precinct Orgn., Ind. Voters of Ill., Chgo. and suburbs, 1968-75; mem. Near North Community Planning and Zoning Action Com. Mem. Comml. Real Estate Orgn., Greater N. Mich. Ave. Assn. (transp. com.). Office: Urban Network Ltd P 102 770 N Halsted St Chicago IL 60622

FLYNN, ALVA ANNE OWEN, retired family living specialist; b. Star City, Ark., Sept. 2, 1911; d. Charles Horace and Claudia Virginia (Parker) Owen; m. Aloysius James Flynn, May 6, 1941 (dec.); children: Anne Flynn-Mackin, Dennis Patrick Aloysius. Student, Monticello U. Ark., 1929-30; BS, Okla. State U., 1932; MA, Columbia U., 1939. Tchr. home-econ. Gorge-Reed, Morgan High Sch., Hamburg, Ark., 1933-34, Lauaca (Ark.) Sch. System, 1934-35; extension agt. Okla. Home-Econs. and Agr. Extension Svcs., Coalgate, Okla., 1935-38; with Inst. Euthenics Vassar Coll., Poughkeepsie, N.Y., 1939; specialist family living USDA U. Ill., Champaign, 1939-42, ret., 1942. Officer, League Women Voters, 1942—, City of Danville PTA, 1942-62; mem. Danville Music Cycle, Ill., 1942-71. Mem. AAUW (officer), Am. Family Living Assn., Omicron Nu. Republican. Home: 413 Swisher Ave Danville IL 61832

FLYNN, ANNE ELIZABETH, association executive; b. Melrose, Mass., Mar. 17, 1928; d. Wentworth and Evelyn Meredith (Crowell) Peckham; m. Walter Morse Hill, Feb. 24, 1951 (div. 1973); children: Nancy W. Kelleher, Barbara Jane Checksfield, Mary Lynn Mattern; m. J. Peter Flynn, Mar. 30, 1975. Diploma of arts, Westbrook Jr. Coll., Portland, Maine, 1947; diploma liberal arts, Dalhousie U., Halifax, Nova Scotia, Can., BA, 1950; postgrad., U. Bridgeport, U. Hartford. Cert. elem. tchr., Mass. Fgn. lang. tchr. elem. schs., South Windsor, Conn., 1962-65; elem. tchr. Tamarisk Sch., Palmdale, Calif., 1965-67; secondary tchr. Bridgeport, Conn., 1969-70; agy. mgr., v.p. Flynn-Checksfield Assn., Inc., Ipswich, Mass., 1982—; Mem. com. to study feasibility of fgn. lang. in elem. schs., South Windsor, 1961-62. 1st pres. LWV, South Windsor, 1964. Mem. Alpha Gamma Delta (Alpha Eta chpt., pres. 1948-49). Democrat. Episcopalian. Home: 500 Colonial Dr #103 Ipswich MA 01938 Office: Flynn-Checksfield Assn Inc 154 High St Ipswich MA 01938

FLYNN, ANNETTE THERESA, realtor; b. Miami, Fla., July 10, 1953; d. William Lowry and Ann Theresa (Karnafel) F. AA in Pre-Computer Systems, Miami-Dade Community Coll., 1973; BS in Computer Sci., Fla. Internat. U., 1975. Computer programer, analyst City of Miami Beach, Fla., 1975-79; project mgr. Burroughs Corp., Miami, Fla., 1979-84; sr. project mgr. Ericsson Info. Systems, Miami, 1984-87; sr. project adminstr. ISC Systems Corp., Miami, 1987-88; realtor/assoc. The Keys Co., Hollywood, Fla., 1989—. Mem. Phi Theta Kappa. Democrat. Roman Catholic. Home and Office: 7845 W Meridian St Miramar FL 33023

FLYNN, ELIZABETH ANNE, advertising and public relations company executive; b. Washington, Aug. 21, 1951; d. John William and Elizabeth Goodwin (Mahoney) F. AA, Montgomery Coll., Rockville, Md., 1972; BS in Journalism, U. Md., 1976; postgrad. San Diego State U., 1976. Writer, researcher, Sea World, Inc., San Diego, 1977-79; sr. writer Lane & Huff Advt., San Diego, 1979-80; account exec. Kaufman, Lansky, Baker Advt., San Diego, 1980-82; mng. dir. Excelsior Enterprises, Beverly Hills, Calif., 1983-84; sr. account exec. Berkhemer & Kline, Inc., L.A., 1985; pres. Flynn Advt. & Pub. Rels., L.A., 1985—; cons. Coca-Cola Bottling Co. L.A., 1982-84; U.S. corr. Aeronovum mag., 1990—. Bd. dirs. Friends of Reconstructive Surgery, Beverly Hills, 1983—. Recipient Cert. of Distinction, Art Direction Mag., 1982. Mem. NAFE., Beverly Hills C. of C., Republican. Roman Catholic. Avocations: screenwriting, short stories, painting, horseback riding. Office: Flynn Advt & Pub Rels 1440 Reeves St Ste 104 Los Angeles CA 90035

FLYNN, JANET-BETH, nurse; b. Phila., Oct. 17, 1944; d. James Fettes and Mabel (Cubbage) McCann; m. Edward Thomas Flynn, May 4, 1968; 1 child, Erin Colleen. BA, SUNY, 1973; MSN, Cath. U. Am., 1976, PhD, 1989-. Staff nurse Hosp. U. Pa., Phila., 1965-68, Lawrence & Meml. Hosp., New London, Conn., 1968; staff nurse Georgetown U. Hosp., Wash., 1974, pvt. duty nurse, 1974-78; instr. Cath. U. Am., Wash., asst. prof., 1978-81; lectr. George Mason U., Va., 1982-85; research assoc., cons. Am. Assoc. Coll. Nursing, Wash., 1986-87; author, editor, cons. Wash., 1981-. Editor, author: Nursing: From Concept to Practice, 1984, 2d edit., 1988, Technological Foundations of Nursing, 1990. Bd. dirs. No. Va. Family Svcs., Falls Church; leader Girl Scouts U.S., Gt. Falls, Va. Mem. Am. Assn. Critical Care Nurses, Sigma Theta Tau.

FLYNN, JUDITH ANNE, public relations executive; b. Hartford, Conn.; d. Jere J. and Helen P. (Kelly) F. B.A., U. Pa., 1959; M.A., Trinity Coll., Hartford, 1963. Pub. health edn. cons. Conn. Dept. Health, Hartford, 1962-64; assoc. editor Macmillan Co., N.Y.C., 1964-66; staff publicist Pub. Rels. Soc. Am., N.Y.C., 1966-68; asst. v.p. pub. rels. Bankers Trust Co., N.Y.C., 1968-75, asst. v.p., pub. rels. Marine Midland Bank, N.Y.C., 1978-80; nat. dir. pub. rels. Arthur Young & Co., N.Y.C., 1980-83; owner, dir. Flynn Communications Group, N.Y.C., 1983—; bd. dirs. Assn. for Corp. Growth, N.Y.C., Brownstone Revival Commn., N.Y.C. Mem. New Eng. Soc. (N.Y.C.), Pub. Rels. Soc. Am., English Speaking Union, Princeton Club (N.Y.C.). Office: 153 E 57th St New York NY 10022

FLYNN, JUDITH C., business executive; b. Wichita Falls, Tex., Nov. 27, 1944; d. W.H. and Teena H. Chittum; m. Harold F. Flynn, Jr.; children: Harold F. III, Peter Craig, Alison J. BA (with hons.), Grove City (Pa.) Coll., 1966; MAT (teaching fellow 1967), Brown U., 1967; MBA U. South Fla., 1987. Tchr., Franklin (N.H.) High Sch., 1967-68; internat. advt. coordinator Franklin Mint, Franklin Center, Pa., 1969-72; fin. mgr. Fire Service Agy., Annapolis, Md., 1972-74; asst. to comptroller Alcoa Marine Corp., Washington, 1974-76; v.p. fin., dir. Martel Labs., Inc., Balt., 1977-80, exec. v.p., 1982—; pres., dir. Martel Lab. Services, St. Petersburg, Fla., 1982-87; dir. Leartek Corp., 1977-80, Chgo. Aerial Survey, Inc., Des Plaines, Ill., 1982—; exec. v.p., dir. Geonex Corp., St. Petersburg, Fla., 1986—; pres., dir. ENR Group, 1987—; pres., chmn. Bd. Verde, Inc., Watsonville, Ca., 1987—; v.p., chmn. Bd. Delta Aerial Survey, Inc., Denver, 1987—; dir., chmn. ITECh, Anchorage, 1987—; bd. dirs. Unified Personnel Bd. of Pinellas County, 1985—; mem. campus adv. bd. U. South Fla., 1986—, exec. council, bus. and industry employment and devel. council of Pinellas County, 1984—; mem. state adv. com. Fla. Tng. Inst. Recipient 1988 Mid Day Bus. and Profl. Women's Women in Mgmt. award for Outstanding Profl. Achievement, Entrepreneur of Yr. award U. South Fla. Bus. Alumni Soc., 1988-89, Fla. Entrepreneur of Yr. award Arthur Young/Inc. mag., 1989. Mem. Engring. Soc. Balt., Nat. Assn. Female Execs., Internat. Oceanographic Found., Nat. Assn. Women Bus. Owners, Com. of 200 (nat. sec. 1984), Assn. Women Govt. Contractors, Beta Gamma Sigma, Phi Kappa Phi, Sigma Iota Epsilon. Republican. Episcopalian. Office: Geonex Corp 301 4th St N Saint Petersburg FL 33701

FLYNN, JUDITH E., educator; b. St. Louis, Aug. 16, 1944; d. Warren Campbell and Ruth (Tobin) F. BS, Tex. Wesleyan Coll., 1967. Cert. tchr., Tex. Tchr. Arlington (Tex.) Ind. Sch. Dist., 1967—; chairperson communications com. Arlington Schs., 1986-87, mem. policy com. sick leave bank, 1986—. Active Big Bros./Big Sisters, Inc., 1976; editor local Rep. newsletter; mem. PTA. Named to Outstanding Young Women of Am., 1977, Tchr. of Yr. Duff Elem. Sch., 1972-73, others. Mem. Assn. Tex. Profl. Educators. Baptist. Home: 3612 San Rafael Arlington TX 76013

FLYNN, MARIE COSGROVE, portfolio manager; b. Honolulu, Jan. 1, 1945; d. John Aloysius and Emeline Frances (Cael) Cosgrove; m. John Thomas Flynn, Jr., June 3, 1968; children: Jamie Marie, Jacqueline Elizabeth. BA., Trinity Coll., 1966; postgrad., U. Fribourg (Switzerland), 1964-65. Analyst U.S. Govt., Washington, 1967-70; coord. nat. reading coun. F.X. Doherty Assocs., N.Y.C., 1970-71; security analyst Corinthian Capital Co., N.Y.C., 1971-73; portfolio mgr. Clark Mgmt. Co., Inc., N.Y.C., 1973-78; v.p., sr. portfolio mgr. Lexington Mgmt. Corp., Saddle Brook, N.J., 1978—. Mem. Fin. Analysts Fedn., Inst. Chartered Fin. Analysts, Fin. Women's Assn., N.Y. Soc. Security Analysts, Bus. and Profl. Women's Club. Home: 50 Pickle Brook Rd Bernardsville NJ 07924 Office: Park 80 W Pla II PO Box 1515 Saddle Brook NJ 07662

FLYNN, MARY ANN, publishing executive; b. Plainfield, N.J., June 14, 1959; d. Raymond Joseph and Ann (Dunn) F. BA, Fairfield (Conn.) U., 1981. Legal asst. Jim Weaver, Washington, 1980-81; researcher, adminstrv. asst. to dir. sci. and tech. Smith Bucklin & Assoc., Washington, 1981-82; asst. to picture editor GEO Mag., N.Y.C., 1982-85; asst. editor Connoisseur Mag., N.Y.C., 1985-88; adminstrv. coord. to pres. Prentice Hall Trade div. Simon & Schuster, N.Y.C., 1988—; computer-mag. prodn. Film Soc. Lincoln Ctr., N.Y.C., 1987—. Contbr. articles on horses to Connoisseur Mag. Roman Catholic. Home: 513 Willow Ave Hoboken NJ 07030 Office: Prentice Hall Trade Div 15 Columbus Circle New York NY 10023

FLYNN, MARY VERONICA, town selectman, retired educator; b. Pittsfield, Mass., Dec. 15, 1919; d. Michael II and Ida Agnes (Mall) F. BSE, State Tchrs. Coll., North Adams, Mass., 1944, ME, 1945; postgrad., Yale U., 1958, Williams Coll., 1961. Cert. tchr., Mass. Tchr. New Marlboro (Mass.) Sch. System, 1941-43, Dalton (Mass.) Sch. System, 1943-61, Wahconah Regional High Sch., Central Berkshire, Mass., 1961-79; selectman Town of Stockbridge, Mass., 1978—; mus. dir. Chesterwood, Stockbridge, 1958-68, bd. dirs., 1969—; mem. Stockbridge Conservation Commn., 1967-68; sec. Stockbridge Historic Dist., 1974-76. Chmn. Dem. Town Com., Stockbridge, 1972-87, del. to state and nat. convs.; pres. Laurel Hill Assn., 1974-77. Am. Studies fellow Yale U., 1958, John Hay fellow Williams Coll., 1961; recipient Congl. Cert. merit, U.S. Ho. of Reps., 1979. Mem. Nat. Trust Historic Preservation, Berkshire County Ret. Tchrs. Assn. (pres. 1983), Norman Rockwell Mus., Berkshire County Hist. Soc., Tuesday Club (pres. 1984-86). Roman Catholic. Home: Shamrock St Stockbridge MA 01262 Office: Town of Stockbridge W Main St Stockbridge MA 01262

FOBBS, JOAN MERNA, medical technologist; b. Talladega, Ala., Mar. 3, 1943; d. Luke and Jeanette (Darden) Jenkins; 1 child, Charleston Darae. AA, Sinclair Community Coll., Dayton, Ohio, 1973; BS, Wright State U., 1975, MS, 1978; PhD, Ohio State U., 1988. Lic. profl. counselor, registered. Med. lab. technologist various corps., 1961—; counselor Sinclair Community Coll., 1977-85; adminstr. faculty U. Vermont, Burlington, 1985-89; cons. on organizational theory and policy, organizational behavior, leadership and mgmt., various schs. and colls., nationally, 1978—. Curator numerous art shows, 1978-89; editor newsletter series, 1980-87. Active on Mayor's Com. for Dr. Martin Luther King Day, Burlington, 1987-89. Recipient fellowship Ohio State U., Columbus, 1984. Mem. Black and Third World Educators (mem. exec. bd. Burlington chpt. 1985-89), Ohio Rehabilitation Assn. (pres.-elect, treas. Dayton Area chpt. 1983-85), Am. Assn. Counseling and Devel., Literary Guild (coord.), Phi Delta Kappa (pres. Vt. chpt. 1988-89). Democrat. Adventist. Home: Amber Lantern Apts B12 Essex Junction VT 05452

FOCH, NINA, actress, drama educator; b. Leyden, Netherlands, Apr. 20, 1924; came to U.S. 1927; d. Dirk and Consuelo (Flowerton) F.; m. James Lipton, June 6, 1954; m. Dennis de Brito, Nov. 27, 1959; 1 child, Dirk de Brito; m. Michael Dewell, Oct. 31, 1967. Grad., Lincoln Sch., 1939; studies with Stella Adler. Adj. prof. drama U. So. Calif., 1966-68, 78-80, adj. prof. film, 1987—; artist-in-residence U. N.C., 1966, Ohio State U., 1967, Calif. Inst. Tech., 1969-70; mem. sr. faculty Am. Film Inst., 1974-77; founder, tchr. Nina Foch Studio, Hollywood, Calif., 1973—; founder, actress Los Angeles Theatre Group, 1960-65; bd. dirs. Nat. Repertory Theatre, 1967-75; creative cons. to dirs., writers, producers of all media. Appeared in motion pictures Nine Girls, 1944, Return of the Vampire, 1944, Shadows in the Night, 1944,

Cry of the Werewolf, 1944, Escape in the Fog, 1945, A Song to Remember, 1945, My Name Is Julia Ross, 1945, I Love a Mystery, 1945, Johnny O'Clock, 1947, The Guilt of Janet Ames, 1947, The Dark Past, 1948, The Undercover Man, 1949, Johnny Allegro, 1949, An American in Paris, 1951, Scaramouche, 1952, Young Man with Ideas, 1952, Sombrero, 1953, Fast Company, 1953, Executive Suite, 1954 (Oscar award nominee), Four Guns to the Border, 1954, You're Never Too Young, 1955, Illegal, 1955, The Ten Commandments, 1956, Three Brave Men, 1957, Cash McCall, 1959, Spartacus, 1960, Such Good Friends, 1971, Salty, 1973, Mahogany, 1976, Jennifer, 1978, Rich and Famous, 1981, Skin Deep, 1988; appeared in Broadway plays including John Loves Mary, 1947, Twelfth Night, 1949, A Phoenix Too Frequent, 1950, King Lear, 1950, Second String, 1960; appeared with Am. Shakespeare Festival in Taming of the Shrew, Measure for Measure, 1956, San Francisco Ballet and Opera in The Seven Deadly Sins, 1966; also many regional theater appearances including Seattle Repertory Theatre (All Over, 1972 and The Seagull, 1973); actress on TV, 1947—, including Playhouse 90, Studio One, Pulitzer Playhouse, Playwrights 56, Producers Showcase, Lou Grant (Emmy nominee 1980), Mike Hammer; series star: Shadow Chasers, 1985, War and Remembrance, 1988; many other series, network spls. and TV films; TV panelist and guest on The Dinah Shore Show, Merv Griffin Show, The Today Show, Dick Cavett, The Tonight Show; TV moderator: Let's Take Sides, 1957-59; assoc. dir. (film) The Diary of Ann Frank, 1959; dir. (nat. tour and on-Broadway) Tonight at 8:30, 1966-67; assoc. producer re-opening of Ford's Theatre, Washington, 1968. Hon. chmn. Los Angeles chpt. Am. Cancer Soc., 1970. Recipient Film Daily award, 1949, 53. Mem. Acad. Motion Picture Arts and Scis. (co-chmn. exec. com. fgn. film award, exec. com. student film award, com. mem. spl. projects), Hollywood Acad. TV Arts and Scis. (bd. govs. 1976-77), AAUP. Office: PO Box 1884 Beverly Hills CA 90213

FODOR, JANICE HOYER, college administrator, English educator; b. Altoona, Pa., Jan. 1, 1937; d. John Jacob and Elizabeth G. (Taylor) Hoyer; m. Michael Blakney Fodor, Apr. 28, 1962; children: Joseph Edward, Nancy Elizabeth. BA in Hist., Polit. Sci., Juniata Coll., Huntingdon, Pa., 1958; MLitt, U. Pitts., 1961; EdD, No. Ill. U., 1983. Asst. dean women U. Pitts., 1959-61; supr. tng. Kaufmann's, Pitts., 1961-62; tchr. Archbishop Blenk High Sch., Gretna, La., 1969-71, Archbishop Shaw High Sch., Marrero, La., 1971-72, Hughes High Sch., Cin., 1972-74; mem. adj. faculty Coll. of DuPage, Glen Ellyn, Ill., 1974-79; dir. learning ctr. Elmhurst (Ill.) Coll., 1978—, asst. prof. English, 1981—. Bd. dirs. Summer Place Theatre, Naperville, Ill., 1984—. Mem. Am. Assn. Counseling and Devel., Nat. Assn. Women Deans, Adminstrs. and Counselors, Am. Coll. Pers. Assn. (bd. dirs. commn. on learning ctrs. 1986—), Ill. Assn. Women Deans, Adminstrs. and Counselors. Democrat. Roman Catholic. Home: 1928 Briarcliffe Blvd Wheaton IL 60187 Office: Elmhurst Coll 190 Prospect St Elmhurst IL 60126

FODREA, CAROLYN WROBEL, researcher, therapist, publisher, consultant; b. Hammond, Ind., Feb. 1, 1943; d. Stanley Jacob and Margaret Caroline (Stupeck) Wrobel; m. Howard Frederick Fodrea, June 17, 1967 (div. Jan. 1987); children: Gregory Kirk, Lynn Renee. BA in Elem. Edn., Purdue U., 1966; MA in Edn., U. Chgo., 1973; postgrad., U. Colo., Denver, 1986-87. Cert. elem. tchr., Ind. Tchr. various schs., Ind., Colo., 1966-87; founder, supr., clinician Reading Clinic, Children's Hosp., Denver, 1969-73, pvt. practice, 1973-87; creator of pilot presch.-kindergarten lang. devel. program Gary, Ind. Diocese Schs., 1987—, therapist lang. and reading disabilities, 1987—; pvt. practice Reading Clinic, Highland, Ind., 1987—, Deerfield, Ill., 1988—; founder Ctr. for Rsch. in Ednl. Ecology, Deerfield, Ill., 1989—; conducted Lang. Devel. Workshop, Gary, Ind., 1988. Author: Comprehension Program, 1985, Presch. Kindergarten Lan. Devel. Program, 1988, A Multi-Sensory Stimulation Program for the Premature Baby in its Incubator to Reduce Med. Costs and Acad. Failure, 1986, Predicting At-Risk Babies for First Grade Reading Failure Before Birth. Active Graland Country Day Sch., Denver, 1981-83, N.W. Ind. Children's Chorale, 1988—. Mem. NEA, Am. Ednl. Rsch. Assn., Internat. Reading Assn., Am. Coun. for Children with Learning Disabilities, Assn. for Childhood Edn. Internat., Colo. Assn. for Edn. of Young Children, Infant Stimulation Edn. Assn., AAUW, NAFE, Nat. Assn. for Women in Career-North Shore, Art Inst. Chgo., Smithsonian Instn., Cousteau Soc., U. Chgo. Alumni Club (Chgo. area ann. fund, Pres. fund com. 1988—, numerous positions Denver area chpt. 1974-87). Roman Catholic. Office: Ctr for Rsch Ednl Ecology 1368 Barclay Ln Deerfield IL 60015

FOEGE, ROSE ANN SCUDIERO, human resources professional; b. Bklyn., Aug. 22, 1941; d. Thomas Edward and Catherine Mary (Demarsico) Scudiero; m. William Henry Foege, Apr. 19, 1975. BA, Queens Coll., 1973; MS cum laude, Iona Coll., 1981. Cert. Am. Registry Radiologic Technologists. X-ray technician St. Clare's Hosp., N.Y.C., 1956-61; supr. x-ray N.Y. Internat. Longshoremen's Assn. Med. Ctr., N.Y.C., 1960-67, Life Extension Inst., N.Y.C., 1967-73; radiologic technologist Exxon Corp., N.Y.C., 1973-81, coordinator systems and records, 1981-86; sr. human resources specialist Exxon Cen. Services div. Exxon Corp., Florham Park, N.J., 1986—. Vol. Wykagyl Neighborhood Assn., New Rochelle, N.Y. Mem. Am. Soc. Personnel Adminstrs., Am. Mgmt. Assn., Am. Acad. Med. Adminstrs., Am. Soc. Radiologic Technologists, Nat. Assn. Female Execs., Mensa, Iona Coll. Alumni Assn. Home: 149 Wykagyl Terr New Rochelle NY 10804 Office: Exxon 180 Park Ave Florham Park NJ 07932

FOEHRKOLB, SUSAN MARY, special education educator; b. Moline, Ill., Apr. 14, 1948; d. Frank Joseph and Lenore Ethel (Huggins) Balkan; m. Lawrence Cletus Foehrkolb, Aug. 8, 1970; children: Jamie Elizabeth, Matthew Frank. BA, Clarke Coll., 1970. Tchr. lang. arts, reading and gifted East Moline (Ill.) Grade Sch. Dist. 37, 1970, chair dept. lang. arts and reading, 1985—, chair reassessment of learning objectives com., 1990; coord. dist. spelling contest East Moline Grade Sch. Dist. 37, 1985-86, mem. young citizen selection com., 1985—, rep. reading articulation com., 1986, co-chair writing curr., 1986, co-chmn. learning objectives com., 1986; mem. dist. curr. study com. on handwriting, 1986, dist. reading com., 1988—, dist. comprehensive program planning com. for Gifted, 1988-89; sch. rep. PTA pres. and tchrs. com., 1987-89, coord., faculty rep. Glenview (Ill.) Jr. High Acad. Achievement Night, 1973—. Homeroom mother Hillcrest Elem. Sch., East Moline; tiger cub mother Boy Scouts Am., East Moline, 1987-88, den leader asst., 1988—. Mem. NEA, Ill. Edn. Assn., East Moline Edn. Assn., Ill. Council for Gifted Edn. Democrat. Roman Catholic. Home: 2623 First St East Moline IL 61244 Office: E Moline Pub Sch Dist 37 836 17th Ave East Moline IL 61244

FOFFÉ, MARIA CATHERINE, business owner, consultant; b. Bklyn., Jan. 24, 1948; d. John Salvator and Viola Madeline (De Fina) F.'; m. Kenneth Richard Jameson, Sept. 25, 1988. BA cum laude, Boston U., 1969; MA, Columbia U., 1972; MBA, Fordham U., 1977. Personnel interviewer, recruiter Macy's, N.Y.C., 1969; recruiter then pers. adminstr. McGraw-Hill, N.Y.C., 1970-80; human resource cons. then v.p., group mgr. Merrill Lynch & Co., N.Y.C., 1980-89; pres., owner Global Resources Cons., N.Y.C., 1989—. Author: (manuals) International Personnel Policies, 1980, Relocation Policies, 1984, Net Pay6 Programs, 1986. Vol. various elderly orgns., N.Y.C.; mem. faculty NYU, 1990. NYU scholar, 1965. Mem. Am. Soc. Personnel Adminstrs., Global Bus. Assn., Am. Coun. on Internat. Personnel (bd. dirs. 1983-89), N.Y. Personnel Mgmt. Assn. (chairperson new mems. com. N.Y.C. chpt. 1975-78), Fordham Alumnae Assn., Downtown Athletic Club. Home: 155 Montague St Heights NY 11201 Office: Global Resources Cons Inc 200 Park Ave Ste 303 East New York NY 10166

FOGAL, RUTH ANN MALLON, nurse; b. Central Falls, R.I., Sept. 4, 1952; d. Charles Leonard Jr. and Theresa Annette (Bussey) Mallon; m. Raymond Alan LaFazia, Aug. 1972 (div. 1973); m. Ronald William Fogal, June 21, 1975 (div. 1981). AS in Nursing, Bristol Community Coll., 1975; B Profl. Studies, Barry U., 1988; postgrad., St. Thomas Sch. Law, Miami, Fla., 1989—. R.N., Maine, Ohio, Fla., Mass.; cert. in psychiat./mental health. Psychiat. nurse St. Mary's Hosp., Lewiston, Maine, 1975-76, St. Charles Hosp., Oregon, Ohio, 1976-78; psychiat. nurse U. Miami (Fla.)/Jackson Meml. Hosp., 1978-79, psychiat. nursing supr., 1979-82, psychiat. nurse specialist, 1982—. Mem. Am. Nurses Assn., Fla. Nurses Assn. (del. conv. 1988), Nurse Profl. Orgn. (nurse advocate, mem. profl. practice com. 1987-88), Dade County Mental Health Assn., Fla. Assn. Women Layers (student chpt.), Am. Heart Assn., Coral Gables C. of C., Dade Heritage Trust, Dade Hist. Soc. Home: 15820 Palmetto Club Dr Miami FL 33157 Office: U Miami Jackson Meml Hosp 1611 NW 12th Ave Miami FL 33136

FOGARTY, ELIZABETH RUMMANS, retired librarian, researcher; b. Portsmouth, Ohio, Nov. 1, 1916; d. George Rummans and Mattie Belle (Shaver) Jordan; m. Joseph Christopher Fogarty, Oct. 6, 1945 (dec. Jan. 1977); children: Patricia C., Michelle., Josephine S. BA magna cum laude, Ohio Wesleyan U., 1938; MLS, U. Ill., 1939. Post libr. U.S. Army, Camp Atterbury, Ind., 1942-45; organizer of libr. Legis. Auditor's Calif. Capitol Office, Sacramento. 1952-53; med. rsch. libr. U.S. Army Med. Ctr., Ryukyu Islands, Japan, 1967-70, U.S. Army Hosp., Ft. Polk, La., 1970-72; libr. pub. svcs. McAllen Pub. Libr., Tex., 1974-76. Researcher for Calif. state legislators and physicians. Chmn. coun. on ministries, mem. adminstrv. bd. St. Mark United Meth. Ch., McAllen, 1975—; Germany country commr. North Atlantic Girl Scout Bd. Europe, 1961-63. Mem. AAUW (pres. McAllen br. 1977-81, bd. dir. internat. rels. Tex. state div. bd. 1981-84, cond. internat. rels. workshops at Tex. state and nat. convs. 1981—, Outstanding Woman of yr. award 1980), DAR (regent Sam Maverick chpt. 1983-85), Colonial Dames 17th Century (pres. Capt. Thomas Jefferson chpt. 1985—, Tex. state bd. 1985—, v.p. 1987—, Uni985—, v.p. 1987—), United Daus. Confederacy (treas. Palo Alto chpt. 1982-84, registarar 1987—), ALA, LWV, Mortar Board, U.S. Daus. 1812, The Jamestowne Soc., Nat. Soc. Daus. Am. Colonists, Nat. Soc. Colonial Dames (state pres. Tex. 1989—), Nat. Soc. Magna Charta Dames (pres. UDC Palo Alto chpt. 1990—), Soc. of Ky. Pioneers, Phi Beta Kappa, Delta Delta Delta, Delta Sigma Rho, Phi Sigma Alpha. Methodist. Home: 405 Vermont St McAllen TX 78503

FOGEL, ADELAIDE FORST, lawyer; b. N.Y.C., July 26, 1915; d. Leon and Antoinette (Hahn) Forst; B.A., Washington Sq. Coll., 1936; LL.B., N.Y. U., 1939; m. David Fogel, June 2, 1940; children—Ann Fogel Vivell, Susan Lee Fogel Lloyd. Admitted to N.Y. State bar; individual practice law, N.Y.C., 1940—. Patron N.Y. Philharmonic; trustee Temple Israel, N.Y.C., past pres. Sisterhood. Mem. Met. Mus. Art, Mus. Natural History, N.Y. U. Law Alumni Assn.

FOGERTY, PATRICIA MARIE, marketing research company executive; b. San Diego, Apr. 20, 1943; d. Charles August and Orpha Elizabeth (Fogerty) Bremer; m. Steven Floyd James, Apr. 19, 1980. BS, Stanford U., 1966. Regional data mgr. U.S. Census Bur., Washington, 1967-69; pres., chief exec. officer Fogerty Group, Inc., San Diego, 1970—; cons. Western States Rsch., San Diego, 1987—, Accurate Data Analysis, San Diego, 1988—. Editor: Marketing Case Histories, 1985; contbr. articles to mags. Mem. Am. Mktg. Assn. (v.p. 1987-88, Membership award 1988), Market Rsch. Assn. Republican. Episcopalian. Office: 4915 Mercury St San Diego CA 92111

FOGG, CYNTHIA ANN, accountant; b. Rumford, Maine, Sept. 20, 1956; d. Raymond Joseph and Constance Jean (Roderick) Roy; m. Jeffrey Lynn Fogg, July 23, 1977; children: Desiree Lynn, Dustin James. Student, Husson Coll., Bangor, Maine, 1981-85. Bookkeeper, purchaser Thompson Trucking, Inc., Lincoln, Maine, 1978-83; pvt. practice acctg. Lincoln, Maine, 1983-86; owner, mgr. Lasting Impressions, Lincoln, 1984-88; bookkeeper H.C. Haynes, Inc., Winn, Maine, 1988-89; mgr. Whitney Energy Inc., Lincoln, 1989—. Mem. budget com. Town of Lincoln, 1986-89, councilor, 1989—; mem. Econ. Devel. Adv. Com., Lincoln, 1986—; mem. Lincoln Planning Bd., 1988-89. Mem. NAFE, Lincoln C. of C. (sec. 1984-86). Democrat. Roman Catholic. Home: RR 2 Box 955 Lincoln ME 04457 Office: Whitney Energy Inc 131 Main St Lincoln NE 04457

FOGLE, JOE ANN, film editor; b. Norfolk, Va., July 2, 1945; d. Silbert and Marie (Miller) Freshman; m. Daniel Richard Fogle, Dec. 24, 1968 (div. Jan. 1976); children: Dena Rachel, Dara Rani. Student, U. Utah. Comml. asst. Filmex West, Los Angeles, 1965-68; post-prodn. coordinator M.T.M. Enterprises, Los Angeles, 1976, film editor, 1976-84; film editor Twentieth Century-Fox Film Corp., Los Angeles, 1985, Amblin Entertainment, Los Angeles, 1985-87; free-lance editor, 1987-89; supervising editor, co-producer new series Steven Bochco Prodns., 1989—. Editor Three O'Clock High, 1987. Nominee for Emmy award Outstanding Editing for a Series, Single Camera Prodn., 1986, 87, Emmy nominee 2 hour spl. Mem. Acad. TV Arts & Scis., Am. Cinema Editors Soc.

FOIL, JACQUELINE B., educator; b. Bklyn., July 20, 1929; d. Samuel Jack and Idalie (Haak) F.; divorced, 1978; children: Kenneth, B., Gary M. Marcus. BA, Bklyn. Coll., 1960, MS, 1965; postgrad., Syracuse U., 1985—. Tchr. N.Y.C. Bd. Edn., Bklyn., 1960—; adj. prof. Southampton (N.Y.) Coll., 1979—, Coll. Staten Island (N.Y.), CW Post, Long Island U., Bklyn., 1984—; instr. Effective Teaching Program, N.Y. State United Tchrs., 1979—; mentor facilitator N.Y.C. Bd. Edn., 1988—. Co-author: Farm Workers Battle for Justice, 1969; Images of Bklyn., 1987. Mem. United Fedn. Tchrs., N.Y. United Tchrs., Am. Fedn. Tchrs., Am. Ednl. Rsch. Assn., N.Y. State Assn. for Supervision and Curriculum Devel. Home and Office: 995 E 21st St Brooklyn NY 11210

FOIL, MARY BETH, general surgeon; b. Winston-Salem, Jan. 4, 1954; d. William Charlton and Patricia (Petree) F. BA, U. N.C., 1976; MD, East Carolina U., 1981. Diplomate Am. Bd. Surgery. Resident gen. surgery E. Carolina U., Greenville, 1981-85; chief resident gen. surgery E. Carolina U., 1985-86, clin. instr., 1986-87; clin. instr., trauma fellow U. Calif. San Diego Med. Ctr., 1987-88; dir. surg. critical care Pitt County Meml. Hosp., Greenville, 1988—; assoc. dir. trauma svc. E. Caroluna U., 1988—, asst. prof. surgery, 1988—; co-dir. Adv. Trauma Life Support courses, E. Carolina U. Sch. Medicine, 1989, 90. Contbr. articles to profl. jours. Gov.'s Hwy. Safety Prog. grantee, 1989. Mem. Am. Trauma Soc. (bd. dirs.), E. Carolina U. Med. Alumni Assn. (treas.), Assn. Women Surgeons, Ea. Assn. for Surgery of Trauma, Assn. Acad. Surgeons, Soc. Critical Care, Am. Trauma Soc., Southeastern Surg. Congress, So. Med. Soc., Pitt County Med. Soc., AMA, N.C. Med. Soc., Am. Assn. Family Physicians, ACS, Am. Med. Women's Assn. (v.p. 1989), Sigma Xi, Alpha Chi Sigma. Office: PO Box 6028 Greenville NC 27835-6028

FOK, AGNES KWAN, cell biologist, educator; b. Hong Kong, British Crown Colony, Dec. 11, 1940; came to U.S., 1962; d. Sun and Yau (Ng) Kwan; m. Fok, June 8, 1965; children: Licie Chiu-Jane, Edna Chiu-Joan. BA in Chemistry, Coll. Great Falls, 1965; MS in Plant Nutrition and Biochemistry, Utah State U., 1966; PhD in Biochemistry, U. Tex., Austin, 1971. Asst. rsch. prof. pathology dept. U. Hawaii, Honolulu, 1973-74, Ford Found. postdoctoral fellow, anatomy dept., 1975, asst. rsch. prof. Pacific Biomed. Rsch. Ctr., 1975-82, assoc. rsch. prof., 1982-88, assoc. rsch. prof. biology program, 1985, rsch. prof., 1988—, grad. faculty, dept. microbiology, 1977—. Contbr. articles to profl. jours. Mem. Am. Soc. for Cell Biology, Soc. for Protozoologists, Sigma Xi (treas. Hawaii chpt. 1979—). Office: U Hawaii Dept Microbiology Honolulu HI 96822

FOL, MONIQUE ELIANE, educator; b. Courbevoie, France, June 20, 1933; came to U.S., 1957; d. Cornelius Maxime and Lucette (Adam-Mulhberg) F. Baccalaureat in Philosophy, Universite de Paris, 1952, Licence en Droit, 1955; MA, U. Calif., Berkeley, 1960; Doctorat, Universite de Nice, 1977. Councellor-at-law Paris, 1955-57; teaching asst. U. Calif., Berkeley, 1959-61, research asst., 1962-63; instr. Wellesley (Mass.) Coll., 1964-67; prof. Boston Coll., Chestnut Hill, Mass., 1967—; moderator of the french acad., Boston Coll., Chestnut Hill, 1967-69, mem. grad. EPC, 1977-80, dir. of the scholar of the Coll., 1977-78, 83-84, coord. of the honors program, 1984—, coord. of advanced composition and literary analysis, 1988—. Author: Jean de Boschere ou le chemin du retour, 1987, le Temps de la Confidence 1990; co-author: The Certain Style, 1969, Un style certain: Les Mots Pour l'Écrire, 1988, Le Cheval dans les Rougon-Macguart, 1990, Occident/Orient, rencontres; contbr. articles to profl. pubs. Founder, pres. A Will/A Way, Littleton, Mass., 1981, Handicapped organized Women, 1985 (Boston br.). Bourses Ministere de l'Education Nationale Paris, 1952-55; Harbism & Burgess research grant Princeton U., 1958, Newhouse grant U. Calif., 1958, research grants, 1961-62; Mellon Found. grant 1985-86; Ford Found. grant, 1985; faculty teaching grant, Boston Coll., 1985, research grant, 1984-85, faculty fellowship 1987. Mem. Modern Lang. Assn., Assn. of Tchrs. of French, Boston Inst. of Psychology. Democrat. Home: 97 Wellesley Ave Wellesley MA 02181 also: 108 Mabry Way San Rafael CA 94903 Office: Boston College Chestnut Hill MA 02167

FOLEY, BEVERLEY B.L., nurse; b. Norfolk, Va., Jan. 30, 1945; d. Dennis Langley and Barbara Helen (Ballantyne) F. Diploma in nursing, Mass. Gen. Hosp., Boston, 1966. Staff nurse Mass. Gen. Hosp., Boston, 1966-68; staff nurse New England Med. Ctr., Boston, 1969-71, head nurse, 1971-73; nursing supr. North Shore Childrens' Hosp., Salem, Mass.; staff nurse New England Deaconess Hosp., Boston, 1976—; expert nurse Mass. Nurses Assn. Boston, 1985—; surgical nurse liason New Eng. Deaconess Hosp., 1986. Compiler: Guide to Beneficial Care Answers for Active Critical Care Nurses, 1988. Mem. Am. Assn. Critical Care Nurses, Greater Boston Chpt. Am. Assn. Critical Care Nurses (bd. dirs. 1988, mktg. and rsch. com. 1984). Home: 177 E Lothrop St Beverly MA 01915

FOLEY, EILEEN MARY, educator; b. Greenwich, Conn., June 7, 1954; d. Joseph William and Mary Carol (Modugno) Gagon; m. William Charles Foley, July 11, 1980; 1 child, Gareth Charles. BA, U. Conn., 1976; MA, West Conn. u., 1983. Cert. tchr., Conn. Tchr. Joel Barlow High Sch., Redding, Ct., 1978-82; tchr. history Ridgefield (Conn.) High Sch., 1982-89, Wilton (Conn.) High Sch., 1989—. Developer social studies writing program. Active Danbury Preservation Trust, Conn., 1982—. Mem. NEA, Conn. Edn. Assn., Wilton Edn. Assn., Nat. Coun. Social Studies. Democrat. Roman Catholic. Home: 16 Park Ave Danbury CT 06810 Office: Wilton High Sch Wilton CT 06897

FOLEY, HELEN CLAIBORNE, university administrator; b. Columbia, S.C., June 8, 1945; d. David Bartholemew and Helen Irving (DuBose) F. BS, U. S.C., 1984; MEd, Vanderbilt U., 1986. Staff asst. U. S.C., Columbia, 1971-77; assoc. dir. U. S.C. Alumni Assn., Columbia, 1977-80; dir. devel. coll. pharmacy U. S.C., Columbia, 1980-85; dir. devel. Va. Poly. Inst., Blacksburg, 1987—. Vol. Richland Meml. Hosp., Columbia, 1970-75, Spl. Olympics, Columbia, 1976-78; tchr. Literacy Coun., Columbia, 1987. Named one of Disting. Alumni U. S.C., 1988. Mem. Rotary (chmn. mentor com. Blacksburg-Christiansburg chpt. 1989—), Blacksburg C. of C. (chmn. legis. com. 1989). Episcopalian. Home: 1202 Palmer Dr Blacksburg VA 24060 Office: Va Poly Inst Devel Office Blacksburg VA 24061

FOLEY, MRS. JOHN PORTER, JR. See ANASTASI, ANNE

FOLEY, MARY JOSEPHINE, nurse eduator; b. Woburn, Mass., Feb. 22, 1936; d. Patrick Joseph and Catherine Agnes (Burke) F. BS magna cum laude, Boston Coll., 1957, MS, 1963; postgrad., NYU, 1969-71. RN, Mass. Nurse Visiting Nurse Assn. Boston, 1957-61; instr. Simmons Coll., Boston, 1962-67, Holy Name Hosp. Sch. Nursing, Teaneck, N.J., 1979-81; asst. prof. SUNY, Buffalo, 1967-69; lectr. nursing Harlem Hosp. Sch. Nursing, N.Y.C., 1969-70; cons. test devel. Nat. League for Nursing, N.Y.C., 1971-78; asst. prof. Bunker Hill Community Coll., Boston, 1981-82, chmn. nurse edn. dept., 1982-88; dir. nursing edn. Youville Hosp. and Rehab. Ctr., Cambridge, Mass., 1988—; workshop cons. multiple choice testing, various cities, 1971-89. Mem. Am. Nurses Assn., Nat. League for Nursing (accreditation visitor 1987-88), Mass.-R.I. League for Nursing (v.p. 1989), Orgn. for Advancement Assoc. Degree Nursing, St. Charles Alumnae (pres. 1963-64), Mother Cabrini Guild (v.p. 1960-61), Sigma Theta Tau. Democrat. Roman Catholic. Home: 13 Franklin St Woburn MA 01801 Office: Youville Hosp & Rehab Ctr 1575 Cambridge St Cambridge MA 02138-4398

FOLEY, MAUREEN FRANCES, chemistry educator; b. Mass., Aug. 9, 1946; d. Albert F. and Julia (Doyle) Foley; m. C. John Blankley, Aug. 31, 1976. BS in Chemistry, Wayne State U., 1969; MS, Eastern Mich. U., 1979. Rsch. asst. Parke-Davis, Ann Arbor, Mich., 1969-73, 74-78; part-time lectr. Harper Hosp., Detroit, 1978-79, Washtenaw Community Coll., Ann Arbor, 1978-81; assoc. prof. chemistry Schoolcraft Coll., Livonia, Mich., 1984—. Mem. Am. Chem. Soc., Nat. Sci. Tchrs. Assn., Mich. Edn. Assn.

FOLEY, PATRICIA JEAN, accountant; b. Bridgeport, Conn., Jan. 12, 1956; d. John Edward and Louise (Caselli) F. AA, Housantonic Community Coll., 1978; BS, Cen. Conn. State Coll., 1980; MBA, U. Hartford, 1990. CPA, Conn. Staff acct. Spitz, Sullivan, Wachtel & Falcetta, Hartford, Conn., 1981-82, client acct., 1982-85, sr. acct., 1985-87, supr., mgr., 1987—. Pres. Woodsedge Condominium Assn., Newington, Conn., 1989-90, treas., 1985-90. Mem. AICPA (mgmt. adv. svcs. 1987-90), Conn. Soc. CPA's, Am. Womens Soc. of CPA's. Home: 35-1B Woodsedge Dr Newington CT 06111

FOLINO, BARBARA ADELE SCHALK, academic administrator, counselor; b. Chgo., Jan. 16, 1939; d. Stanley Steven and Adele Mary (Maniak) Schalk; m. July 27, 1968 (div. May 1979). BS, Coll. of St. Catherine, St. Paul, 1960; MEd, U. Pitts., 1968. Cert. tchr.; lic. counselor. Camp dir. Mpls. Girl Scout Coun., summers 1960-67; tchr. St. Margaret's Acad., Mpls., 1960-63, Community Sch. Dist., Blue Island, Ill., 1963-67; sch. counselor Shaler Area Sch. Dist., Glenshaw, Pa., 1968-69, guidance counselor, 1970—, chair guidance dept., 1989—. Mem. NEA, Pa. State Edn. Assn., Am. Assn. Counseling and Devel., Am. Sch. Counselors Assn., Allegheny County Counselors Assn. (sec. 1979—, Counselor of Distinction 1988), Pa. Sch. Counselors Assn. (conf. registrar 1983—, bd. govs. 1988—). Office: Shaler Area Sr High Sch 381 Wible Run Rd Pittsburgh PA 15209

FOLK, APRIL LYNN, software engineer; b. Cleve., Nov. 26, 1960; d. George Earl and Roberta Ann (Campbell) F. AS, Ohio Valley Coll., 1981; BS, David Lipscomb Coll., 1983; postgrad., W.Va. U., 1983-85. Computer programmer One Valley Bank, Charleston, W.Va., 1983-85; systems programmer Peoples Banking and Trust Co., Marietta, Ohio, 1985-87; sr. software specialist Digital Equipment Corp., Dunbar, W.Va., 1987—. Preparer ch. bull. South Charleston (W.Va.) Ch. of Christ, 1983-84, bible class tchr., 1983-85, Camden Ave. Ch. of Christ, Parkersburg, W.Va., 1985-88. Mem. Digital Equipment Computer Users Soc. Office: Digital Equipment Corp One Players Club Dr Charleston WV 25311-1689

FOLK, BARBARA THERESA, accountant, company financial executive; b. Stoneham, Mass., Oct. 24, 1947; d. George John and Theresa Sarah (Moylan) F. AS in Acctg., Mass. Bay Community Coll., 1967. CPA, Mass., Fla. Internat. accounts receivable and translator Addison-Wesley Pub. Co., Reading, Mass., 1967-68; payroll supr., accounts payable mgr. Nat. Uniform Sales, Woburn, Mass., 1968-70; with constrn. and accounts payable depts. Walt Disney World, Orlando, Fla., 1970-72; controller, cost acct. United Assocs., Inc., Orlando, 1972—, sec., treas., chief financial officer, 1986—, also bd. dirs.; acctg. cons. A.I.R.C.O.A., Denver, 1975-85, Cypress Hotel Mgmt. Co., Orlando, 1986—; acctg. cons., advisor to bd. dirs. Electrogame, Inc. Fundraiser Am. Heart Assn., Orlando, 1983; fundraiser, event participant Leukemia Soc. Am., Orlando, 1984, 85, 86. Mem. Legion of Mary. Democrat. Roman Catholic. Office: United Assocs Inc 1215 E Amelia St Orlando FL 32803

FOLLANSBEE, DOROTHY LELAND, publisher; b. St. Louis, Mar. 24, 1911; d. Robert Leathan and Minnie Cowden (Yowell) Lund; grad. Sarah Lawrence Coll., 1931; m. Austin Porter Leland, Apr. 24, 1935 (dec. 1975); children—Mary Talbot Leland MacCarthy, Austin Porter Jr. (dec.), Irene Austin Leland Barzantny; m. 2d, Robert Kerr Follansbee, Oct. 20, 1979. Pres., Station List Publ. Co., St. Louis, 1975—; dir. Downtown St. Louis Inc. Hon. chmn. Old Post Office Landmark Com., 1975—; bd. dirs. Services Bur. St. Louis, 1943, pres., 1951; bd. dirs. Robert E. Lee Meml. Assn.; mem. St. Louis County Parks and Recreation Dept., 1969; bd. dirs. Stratford Hall, Va., 1953—, pres., 1967-70, treas., 1970—; bd. dirs. Historic Bldgs. Commn. St. Louis County, 1959-85, Mo. Hist. Soc., 1960-77, Mo. Mansion Preservation Com., 1975-80, Chatillon DeMenil House, 1977-79. Recipient Landmarks award Landmarks Assn. St. Louis, 1974; Pub. Service award GSA, 1978; Crownenshield award Nat. Trust for Hist Preservation, 1979. Mem. Colonial Dames Am., Daus. of Cin. Episcopalian. Clubs: St. Louis Country, Fox Chapel Golf, Princeton of N.Y., St. Louis Jr. League. Home: 35 Pointer Ln Saint Louis MO 63124 also: 1001 River Oaks Dr Pittsburgh PA 15215 Office: 906 Olive St Saint Louis MO 63101

FOLLETT, MARY VIERLING, artist, art conservator, appraiser; b. Chgo., Feb. 9, 1917; d. Arthur Garfield and Grace May (Cummings) Vierling; student U. Southern Calif., 1932-34, grad. Acad. Profl. Art Conservators, 1975, Masters, 1978; m. Garth Benepe Follett, Feb. 16, 1945; 1 dau., Dawn Goshorn; 3 stepchildren. Exhibited in group shows Palette and Chisel Acad. Fine Arts, 1975, 76, 77, 78, Municipal Art League, 1972-78, others;

represented in permanent collection Fla., Calif., Italy, others; owner, operator Paintin' Place, gallery, Oak Park, Ill., 1973-90; dir. Palette and Chisel Acad. Fine Arts, Chgo., 1975-76. Vice pres. Oak Park LWV, 1952-54, welfare chmn., 1956-58; treas. Oak Park Council Internat. Affairs, 1962-74. Recipient Gold medal Palette and Chisel Acad. Fine Arts, 1976-77, 1st award Civics and Art Found. Union League Chgo., 1977. Mem. Oak Park River Forest Art League (v.p., dir. 1981-82), Pen Women Am., Municipal Art League Chgo., Art Inst. Assos. Oak Park and River Forest (women's bd. 1967—), Oak Park River Forest Hist. Soc. Club: 19th Century Women's. Home and Studio: 1440 Park Ave River Forest IL 60305

FOLLINGSTAD, CAROL ANN, nurse; b. Oak Park, Ill., June 1, 1945; d. Raymond Donald and Iris Eleane (Hofmann) F. RN with honors, Swedish Hosp. Sch. Nursing, Mpls., 1968; student, U. Minn., 1968-70, L.A. City Coll., 1971-73, 77-79; BS in Health Sci. with di, U. Redlands, 1983. Cert. lactation cons. Sr. staff nurse UCLA Ctr. for the Health Scis., Westwood Village, L.A., 1970-71; labor and delivery staff nurse Queen of Angels Hosp., L.A., 1971-74; mem. operating rm. staff; nursing cons. Trainex Corp., Garden Grove, Calif., 1973; operating room team leader St. Vincent Med. Ctr., L.A., 1975-78; night supr. Beverly Manor Convalescent Hosp., Burbank, Calif., 1978; obstetrics state nurse, perinatal nurse educator Meml. Hosp. Glendale, Calif., 1978-90; head nurse, 1979-81; physician's rep. Medela, Inc., Crystal Lake, Ill., 1987-89; infant devel. specialist Calif. State U., L.A., 1984-89; prenatal breastfeeding instr. St. Joseph Med. Ctr., Burbank, Calif., 1985—; mem. internat. immunization team to Uganda (African Enterprise), 1988-90; lactation cons. pvt. practice. Outreach coord. Emmanuel Evang. Free Ch., Burbank, 1987—. Mem. Calif. Perinatal Assn., Internat. Lactation Cons. Assn., La Leche League Internat., Nurses Assn. Am. Coll. Ob-Gyn, UCLA Lactation Alumni Assn. (treas.). Republican. Home and Office: 2021 Grismer #38 Burbank CA 91504

FOLLMAN, DOROTHY MAJOR, therapist; b. Colden, N.Y., Nov. 7, 1932; d. Francis Emri and V. Blanche (Feedham) Major; m. Roy John Follman, Nov. 26, 1954; children: John J., Mark J., Curtis J., Thomas J. BS in Recreation Edn. magna cum laude, SUNY, Cortland, 1954; MEd, SUNY, Buffalo, 1979. Cert. therapeutic recreation specialist. Asst. dir. health edn. YWCA, Niagara Falls, N.Y., 1954-55; instn. tchr. N.Y. State Dept. Corrections, Albion, 1968-70, N.Y. State Narcotic Addiction Control Commn., Albion, 1970-71, Medina, 1971-73; sr. recreation therapist N.Y. State Drug Abuse Control Commn., Medina, 1973-76, N.Y. State Office of Mental Health, Rochester, 1976-77; head recreation therapist Buffalo, 1977—; instr. Medaille Coll., Buffalo, 1983-84, mem. adv. bd. 1982-87; bd. dirs. Metcalf Endowment Fund, Cortland, 1981-87. Mem. adv. bd. SUNY, Brockport, 1986-87; choir dir. United Meth. Ch., Kenyonville, N.Y., 1965-75, United Meth. Ch., 1980—; honoree 36th Ann. Cortland Coll. Recreation Conf., 1986. Named Woman of Yr. Friends of Buffalo Psychiatric Ctr., 1986. Mem. Nat. Therapeutic Recreation Soc., N.Y. State Recreation and Parks Soc., Inc. (exec. bd. 1985—, disting. service 1985, profl. service 1987, 89), Niagara Frontier Recreation and Parks Soc. (exec. bd. 1983-86, awards chmn. 1983-86, award for excellence 1987), SUNY-Cortland Alumni Adv. Bd.

FOLLWEILER, JOANNE SCHAAF, chemistry educator; b. Phila., Aug. 8, 1942; d. Frederick carl and Olive Jean (Ireland) Schaaf; m. Douglas MacArthur Follweiler, Aug. 22, 1964; children: Dejah, Jaelieth. BS, Muhlenberg Coll., 1964; MS, U. Pa., Phila., 1968, PhD, 1977. Chemist E.I. DuPont, Wilmington, Del., 1964-66, FMC Corp., Princeton, N.J., 1968; instr. chemistry Mercer County Community Coll., Trenton, N.J., 1969; prof. chemistry Lafayette Coll., Easton, Pa., 1970—; specialist chemistry info., Easton, 1969—. editor: Handbook of Chromatography Pesticides, 1984. Mem. Sigma Xi (sec. 1988—). Office: Lafayette Coll Olin Hall Easton PA 18042

FOLSOM, WYNELLE STOUGH, retired wood products manufacturing executive; b. Bankston, Ala., July 19, 1924; d. Richard Carey and Ora Beatrice (Fowler) Stough; m. Eugene Bragg Folsom, Sept. 3, 1944; children: Don Wayne, Dana L. Student U. Ala., Livingston U., 1962-63, Draughan Bus. Coll., Montgomery, Ala., 1941-42, Alexander State Coll., Alexander City, Ala., 1967-68, Chilton Vocat. & Tech. Sch., Clanton, Ala., 1969-70. Sec., Ala. Power Co., Birmingham, 1942-44; med. librarian Santa Rosa Hosp., San Antonio, 1944-46; payroll clk. Dow Chem. Co., Freeport, Tex., 1946-48; with audit dept. Sears, Roebuck & Co., Selma, Ala., 1956-66; sec.-treas. Oakline Chair Co., Inc., Selma, 1967-83, pres., 1983-86. Chmn. publicity Cahaba Regional Libr. (Friends of the Libr.), Clanton, Ala., 1979; mem. Selma-Dallas County Historic Preservation Soc., 1982-87. Mem. Selma C. of C., Hemorcallis Garden Club (pres. 1979), Woman's Study Club (chmn. publicity 1967-69). Republican. Mem. Ch. of Christ. Avocations: needlework, fishing, reading, painting, gardening. Home: 200 Chris Circle Selma AL 36701 Office: Oakline Chair Co Inc Hwy 31 N PO Box 1698 Clanton AL 35045

FOLSTER, BONNIE, advertising executive. Former v.p., then sr. v.p. Doyle Dane Bernbach, Inc. (later DDB Needham Detroit), Troy, Mich., until 1989; exec. v.p. Brogan Kabot Advt. Consultancy, Inc., Southfield, Mich., from 1989, now ptnr. creative svcs. dept. Office: Brogan & Ptnrs Advt Consultancy Inc 3000 Town Ctr Ste 475 Southfield MI 48075*

FONDA, JANE, actress; b. N.Y.C., Dec. 21, 1937; d. Henry and Frances (Seymour) F.; m. Roger Vadim (div.); 1 child, Vanessa; m. Tom Hayden, Jan. 20, 1973 (div.); 1 child, Troy. Student, Vassar Coll. Appeared on Broadway stage in There Was A Little Girl, 1960, The Fun Couple, 1962; appeared in Actor's Studio prodn. Strange Interlude, 1963; appeared in films Tall Story, 1960, A Walk on the Wild Side, 1962, Period of Adjustment, 1962, Sunday in New York, 1963, In the Cool of the Day, 1963, The Love Cage, 1963, La Ronde, 1964, Cat Ballou, 1965, The Chase, 1966, Any Wednesday, 1966, The Game Is Over, 1967, Hurry Sundown, 1967, Barefoot in the Park, 1967, Barbarella, 1968, Spirits of the Dead, 1969, They Shoot Horses, Don't They?, 1969, Klute, 1970 (Acad. award for best actress), Steelyard Blues, 1973, A Doll's House, 1973, The Blue Bird, 1976, Fun With Dick and Jane, 1976, Julia, 1977, also producer Coming Home, 1978 (Acad. award best actress), California Suite, 1978, Comes a Horseman, 1978, also producer The China Syndrome, 1979, Electric Horseman, 1979, Nine to Five, 1980, On Golden Pond, 1981, Rollover, 1981, The Dollmaker (Emmy award best actress ABC-TV), 1984, Agnes of God, 1985, The Morning After, 1986 (Acad. award nomination best actress), Old Gringo, 1988, Stanley and Iris, 1990; author: Jane Fonda's Workout Book, 1981, Women Coming of Age, 1984, Jane Fonda's New Workout & Weight-Loss Program, 1986, Jane Fonda's New Pregnancy Workout & Total Birth Program, 1989, Jane Fonda Workout Video, 8 additional videos. Recipient Golden Apple prize for female star of yr. Hollywood Women's Press Club, 1977, Golden Globe award, 1978; rated number 1 heroine of young Ams., U.S. News Roper Poll., 1985, 4th most admired woman in Am., Ladies Home Jour. Roper Poll, 1985. Office: care Fonda Films PO Box 1198 Santa Monica CA 90406

FONS, GAIL BASSETT, publisher; b. Hartford, Conn., Dec. 30, 1961; d. Stanley Davis and Lois Estelle (Bassett) F. BA in English, Bates Coll., 1983; MS in Journalism, Boston U., 1984. News corr. Nashua (N.H.) Telegraph, 1979; staff reporter Billerica (Mass.) Minuteman, 1984, The Monadnock Ledger, Peterborough, N.H., 1985; editorial asst. The Robb Report mag., Acton, Mass., 1985-87; freelance writer Lexington, Mass., 1987-88; pres., pub. Imagic Prodns., Lexington, 1988—; publicist, cons., Auto Internat. TV show, Boston, 1988—; cons., Purity Supreme, Billerica, 1989. Contbr. articles on automotive and other topics to various publs. Mem. Internat. Motor Press Assn., Nat. Assn. Desktop Publishers, BMWCCA. Home: 214 Massachusetts Ave Lexington MA 02173 Office: Imagic Prodns Ste 207 922 Waltham St Lexington MA 02173

FONTAINE, CARLA JOAN, data processing administrator; b. Falls City, Nebr., Feb. 16, 1952; d. Marvin Dale and Clara Jean (Norton) Kermoade; m. William Francis Blazak, Aug. 15, 1976 (div. Dec. 1985); m. Normand Lionel Fontaine, Nov. 25, 1988. BS, U. Nebr., 1974; postgrad., Ohio State U., 1976-79. Tchr. aide Lincoln (Nebr.) Sch. Dist., 1974-75; typist II U. Nebr., Lincoln, 1975-76; adminstrv. asst. Ohio State U., Columbus, 1977-79, U. Calif., Davis, 1979-81; mgr. customer support Pertaine Systems, Mountain View, Calif., 1981-85; dir. client svcs. Pertaine Systems, Redwood City, Calif., 1985-89; computer trainer, consultant Salt Lake City, 1989—. Mem. NOW, 1979-81. Lutheran. Home: 3390 E Marinda Way Salt Lake City UT 84121

FONTENOT, MARY ELLEN, psychotherapist; b. Lacassine, La., Sept. 11, 1950; d. Claude Adam and Betty Jean (Foreman) F.; 1 child, Monte Fontenot McCune. BA, Met. State Coll., 1981; MA, U. No. Colo., 1983, ABD, 1986. Pvt. practice psychotherapist Aurora, Colo., 1983—; dir. counseling ctr. Lorreto Heights Coll., Denver, 1985-86, instr. psychology, 1987-88; mgr. support and recovery svcs. Adams Community Mental Health, Commerce City, Colo., 1988—. Mem. Am. Psychol. Assn., Am. Counseling Devel. Assn., Colo. Assn. Sex Therapists, Psi Chi. Democrat. Office: 8000 E Prentice D1 Englewood CO 80111

FONTES, PATRICIA J., educational psychologist; b. Providence, Dec. 10, 1936; d. Manuel William and Conceicao Elizabeth (Sousa) F. BS in Edn., Boston U., 1957; MEd, Boston Coll., 1965, PhD, 1968. Lic. psychologist. Tchr. Warwick (R.I.) pub. schs., 1957-59; religious sister/superior Sisters of Our Lady of Providence, 1959-65; asst. prof. U. R.I., Kingston, 1968-69; asst./assoc. prof. Salve Regina Coll., Newport, R.I., 1969-72; cons. psychologist Girl Scouts of R.I., Inc., Providence, 1972-73; research fellow Ednl. Research Ctr., St. Patrick's Coll., Dublin, Ireland, 1973-88; cons. psychologist Girl Scouts R.I., Providence, 1989—; lectr. in field. Author: Equality in Primary Teaching 1985; contbr. articles to profl. jours. Boston U. scholar, 1953-57; Boston Coll. fellow, 1965-68; Inst. for Portuguese Lang. and Culture grantee, 1982. Mem. Am. Psychol. Assn., Am. Ednl. Rsch. Assn., Nat. Coun. on Measurement in Edn., Am. Evaluation Assn., Internat. Coun. Psychologists, Internat. Assn. Applied Psychology. Roman Catholic. Office: Girl Scouts RI Inc 125 Charles St Providence RI 02906

FONVILLE, LINDA JEAN, educator; b. Exeter, Calif., Oct. 23, 1949; d. Amon and Barbara Jean (Dungan) F. BS, Calif. State Poly. U., 1971, credential in home econs., art and history, 1972. Charter cert. home economist, Calif. Tchr. home econs. El Sausal Mid. Sch., Salinas, Calif., 1972—, chmn. dept. fine arts, 1985—; curriculum cons.; mem. Salinas Vocat. Edn. Bd., 1972—. Mem. Cursillo Community, Salinas, 1981—. Named Outstanding Educator Monterey County, 1980. Mem. Am. Home Econs. Assn., Calif. Home Econs. Assn., Calif. Tchrs. Assn. (bldg. pres. Salinas 1979-80), DAR (state page 1984), Calif. State Poly. U. Alumni Assn., Monterey County Geneal. Soc. (treas. 1989-91), Delta Kappa Gamma (2d and 1st v.p., pres. 1989-91, treas. Theta Pi chpt.). Republican. Presbyterian. Home: 6 Pajaro Way Salinas CA 93901-2909 Office: El Sausal Mid Sch 1155 E Alisal St Salinas CA 93905

FOODY, JAN PETKUS, real estate company executive; b. Chgo., July 24, 1935; d. Charles Mathew Petkus and Grace Margaret (Watson) Newton; m. Ralph Wesley Foody, Apr. 22, 1968. Student, Wilson Jr. Coll., 1953-55, Chgo. Tchr's. Coll., 1955-57, Loyola U., Chgo. Lic. real estate broker. Tchr. Plato Sch., Chgo., 1960-61; owner Pooch & Poodle, Chgo., 1963-67; sales staff Pram Labs., Chgo., 1967-68; sales assoc. Old Colonial Real Estate, Skokie, Ill., 1969-73, Fairbanks & Taylor Real Estate, Chgo., 1973-74; sales mgr. LaThomus & Co. Real Estate, Chgo., 1974-83; v.p., mgr. 3 residential sales offices Draper and Kramer, Inc., Chgo., 1984—. Pres. Young Voters League of South Shore, Chgo. 1962; precinct capt. Republican Party, Chgo. 1963-66. Mem. Chgo. Real Estate Bd., Chgo. North Side Real Estate Bd., Condex Residential Listing Svc. (pres. 1984-85, bd. dirs. 1980—), Old Town C. of C., Lincoln Park C. of C. Republican. Presbyterian. Home: 5000 Marine Dr N Chicago IL 60640 Office: Draper and Kramer Inc 1660 N La Salle St Chicago IL 60614 also: 899 S Plymouth Ct Chicago IL also: 200 E Walton St Chicago IL 60611

FOOTE, BARBARA AUSTIN, civic foundation executive; b. Seattle, Mar. 26, 1918; d. Edwin Charles and Marion (Roberts) A.; m. Robert Lake Foote, June 14, 1941; children: Markell Foote Kaiser, Marion Roberts, Helen Foote Schloerb. AB, Vassar Coll., 1940. Tchr. Shady Hill Sch., Cambridge, Mass., 1942-43, Madeira Sch., Greenway, Va., North Shore Country Day Sch., Winnetka, Ill., 1960-71; mem. exec. com. Chgo. Community Trust, 1970-85, chmn. exec. com., 1978-85; bd. dirs. Harris Bank, Glencoe and Northbrook, Ill., The New Eng. (name formerly New Eng. Mut. Life Ins. Co.), Boston. Author book of verse, 1948. Pres. Jr. League Chgo., 1947-49, Assn. Jr. Leagues Am., 1954-56, Glencoe Bd. Edn., 1957-63; trustee Vassar Coll., 1966-74. Mem. Vassar Alumni Assn. (nat. pres. 1975-78), Phi Beta Kappa. Congregationalist. Clubs: Fortnightly of Chgo.; Cosmopolitan (N.Y.C.). Home: 587 Longwood Ave Glencoe IL 60022

FOOTE, DOROTHY GARGIS, publishing company executive; b. Sheffield, Ala., Jan. 27, 1942; d. Tracy E. and Mary Helen (Cox) Gargis; m. A. Edward Foote, Mar. 15, 1960; children: Anthony E., Kevin A., Michele. Student, U. So. Miss., 1966-67; AS in Nursing, NW Coll., 1985; BS in Nursing, U. N. Ala., Florence, 1987; MS in Nursing, U. Ala., Huntsville, 1989; postgrad., U. North Ala., England and Scotland, 1990. RN, Ala.; cert. family nurse practitioner. Real estate assoc. McWaters Realty & Appraisal Co., Athens, Ga., 1977-79; acctg. clk. U. Ga., Athens, 1979-81; nurse practitioner Mitchell Hollingworth annex Eliza Coffee Meml. Hosp., Florence, 1985—; v.p. Thornwood Books, Florence, 1980—. Editor newsletter Dames Digest, 1970. Pres. Band Boosters, Athens, 1976. Mem. Am. Nursing Assn., Ala. State Nurses Assn. (pres. dist. 1 1989—, bd. dirs. 1989—), Phi Theta Kappa, Beta Sigma Phi (pres. 1976-77, sec. 1987-88). Home: 222 Shirley Dr Florence AL 35630

FOOTE, EVELYN PATRICIA, military officer, consultant; b. Durham, N.C., May 19, 1930; d. Henry Alexander and Evelyn Sevena (Womack) F. BA summa cum laude, Wake Forest U., 1953; student, U.S. Army Command & Gen. Staff Coll., Leavenworth, Kans., 1971-72, U.S. Army War Coll., Carlisle, Pa., 1976-77; MS in Govt. and Pub. Affairs, Shippensburg State U., 1977; student, U. Va. Sch. Bus. Adminstrn., 1980; LLD (hon.), Wake Forest U., 1989. Commd. 1st lt. U.S. Army, 1960, advanced through grades to brig. gen., 1986; platoon officer WAC U.S. Army, Ft. McClellan, Ala., 1960-61; officer selection officer 6th recruiting dist. U.S. Army, Portland, Oreg., 1961-64; comdr. WAC Co. WAC Co., U.S. Army Engr. Brigade, Ft. Belvoir, Va., 1964-66; student Adj. Gen. Officer Advanced Course, Ft. Benjamin Harrison, Ind., 1966; exec. officer, chief adminstrv. div., info. office U.S. Army, Vietnam, 1967; exec. officer, office personnel ops. WAC, Washington, 1968-71, plans and programs officer OFC, dir., 1972-74; personnel mgmt. officer U.S. Army Forces Command, Ft. McPherson, Ga., 1974-76; comdr. 2d basic tng. bn. U.S. Army Tng. Brigade and Military Police Sch., Ft. McCllellan, Ala., 1977-79; faculty mem. U.S. Army War Coll., 1979-82; student Fgn. Service Inst., Dept. of State, Washington, 1982-83; comdr. 42d Mil. Police Group, Mannheim, Fed. Republic of Germany, 1983-85; spl. asst. to comdg. gen. 32d Army Air Def. Command Hdqrs., Darmstadt, Fed. Republic of Germany, 1985-86; dep., insp. gen. for inspections Hdqrs. Dept. of the Army, Washington, 1986-88; dep. comdg. gen. Mil. Dist. Washington, comdr. Ft. Belvoir, Va., 1988-89; ret. U.S. Army, 1989; free-lance lectr., cons. in def. pers. and leadership, mem. or advisor numerous bds.; mem. VA Bd. for Vets.' Affairs; lectr. various U.S. Army groups. Contbr. articles to military jours. Bd. visitors Wake Forest U.; me. Va. Gov.'s Mil. Advisors Coun. Decorated D.S.M., Legion of Merit with oak leaf cluster, Bronze Star, Meritorious Svc. medal with two oak leaf clusters; German Cross of Svc. 1st class; recipient Disting. Svc. award Wake Forest U., 1987. Mem. Assn. U.S. Army, Bus. and Profl. Women U.S.A., Exec. Women in Govt., Federally Employed Women, WAC Vets. Assn., Zonta Internat. Democrat. Lutheran.

FOOTE, FRANCES CATHERINE, association executive, sales consultant; b. Chgo., Apr. 3, 1935; d. Peter and Ellen Gertrude (Quinn) F. BS in Edn., Cardinal Stritch Coll., 1957; MS in Edn., Ill. State U., 1966. Cert. tchr., Ill. Tchr. Sch. Dist. 123, Oak Lawn, Ill., 1959-84; asst. prin. Sch. Dist. 123, Oak Lawn, 1971-80; pres. Am. Now, St. Petersburg, Fla., 1985—; instr. Geography workshops for tchrs., 1967-70, Use of Newspaper in Classroom Workshops, 1973-75; co-chairperson Social Studies Curriculum Revision; sales cons., sales rep. World Book-Childcraft, Inc., Chgo., 1990—. Officer PTA, Oak Lawn, 1973-76; mem. Rep. Nat. Com., Washington. Mem. Am. Fedn. Tchrs. Roman Catholic. Home and Office: 280 126th Ave Apt #203 Treasure Island FL 33706

FOOTE, LINDA GASS, progerty management executive; b. Livingston County, Ky., Sept. 12, 1939; d. Norman W. and Ruby (Sunderland) Gass.; m. Phillip L. Foote, Nov. 13, 1959 (div. Aug. 1976); children: Phillip L. Jr., Gerard Stuart. BA cum laude, Western Ky. U., 1960, postgrad., 1970—. Tchr. English lang., Latin, history, speech Marshall County High Sch., Benton, Ky., 1961-62, Murray (Ky.) High Sch., 1962-66, Paducah (Ky.) Tilghman High Sch., 1966-68, Hardinsburg (Ky.) High Sch., 1970-71, Glasgow (Ky.) High Sch., 1971-72, Ea. High Sch., Louisville, 1972-78; real estate broker Louisville, 1972—, gen. contractor, 1976-86; property mgr. Thompson Properties Inc., Louisville, 1981-85, I.R.E. Fin. Svcs., Louisville, 1985—; owner, mgr. Foote Property Mgmt., Louisville, 1985—; real estate broker, Ohio, 1986—; instr., conductor seminars Continuing Edn. Ctr. U. Louisville, 1988—. Vol. fundraiser Sta. KET-TV, 1988. Mem. NAFE, AARP, Bldg. Owners and Mgrs. Assn. (cert.), Inst. Real Estate Mgrs., Sales and Mktg. Execs., Kentuckiana Women's Network, Bus. and Profl. Women's Club. Democrat. Office: Profl Towers 4010 Dupont Circle Louisville KY 40207

FOOTE, SHERRILL LYNNE, manufacturing company technician; b. Marshalltown, Iowa, Apr. 19, 1940; d. Howard Raymond Ellis and Lois Ellen (Cooper) F.; m. Terry D. Downey, July 27, 1958 (div. 1978); children: Patrick L., Holly L. Harrelson; m. Frank H. Foote, Nov. 17, 1979 (div. 1989); stepchildren: Lauri K., Christopher R. Student, Marshalltown Community Coll., 1981—. Receptionist Drs. Long & Clawson, Marshalltown, 1958-59; clk. Fisher Controls, Marshalltown, 1963-73, cost estimating analyst, 1974-82, sr. cost estimator, 1982—. Contbr. limericks Des Moines Register (Contest Winner), 1976, Marshalltown Times Rep., 1986. Mem. Am. Creativity Assn., Mensa (contbr. Bulletin Wordplay 1981—, limerick editor M-Pressions Cen. Iowa newsletter 1989—). Democrat. Methodist. Home: 702 Ratcliffe Dr Marshalltown IA 50158

FOOTER, SHEILA, lawyer; b. Washington, May 30, 1938; d. Irvin J. and Frances (Jewler) Footer. BA, George Washington U., 1964; JD, Georgetown U., 1982. Bar: Md. 1982, D.C. 1983, U.S. Supreme Ct. 1987, U.S. Ct. Appeals (D.C. cir., 4th cir.) 1989, U.S. Dist. Ct. (Md. dist., D.C. dist.) 1989. Asst. state's atty. Montgomery County State's Atty.'s Office, Rockville, Md., 1983-89; atty. firm Silver, Freedman & Taff, Washington, 1989—. Contbr. articles to legal jours. Mem. Montgomery County Commn. for Women, 1989—. Mem. Md. Bar Assn., Montgomery County Bar Assn. (exec. com. 1986=87), Women's Bar Assn. Med. (Montgomery County exec. com. 1986-88), Assn. Trial Lawyers Am., Alpha Lambda Delta.

FORBES, CYNTHIA ANN, small business owner, marketing educator; b. Richmond, Calif., Dec. 27, 1951; d. James Martin and Mary Jane (Clafferty) Forbes; m. Larry Charles Osofsky, Mar. 20, 1970 (div. 1980); 1 child, Anna; m. William Charles Ham, Aug. 30, 1986. BA, U. Calif., 1977; MS, Golden Gate U., 1981. Research asst. U. Calif., Berkeley, 1975-77, Chevron Research, Richmond, 1977-79; specialist dealer affairs Chevron USA, San Francisco, 1979-80, sales rep., San Fafael, Calif., 1981-84, adminstrv. supr., San Ramon, Calif.; 1984-85, advt. mgr. Chevron Chem. Co., San Francisco, 1986—; assoc. prof. Golden Gate U., San Francisco, 1981—. Vol., lectr. child abuse prevention. Mem. Contra Costra Women's Network, Nat. Agrimarketers Assn. Democrat. Jewish. Avocations: mountaineering, bicycling. Home: 83 Acacia Dr Orinda CA 94563 Office: Golden Gate Univ 1536 Mission St San Francisco CA 94105

FORBES, EVE-LYN, management consultant, hypnotherapist; b. Salisbury, Rhodesia, Nov. 4, 1949; came to U.S., 1981; d. Fredrick Robert Belstead and Edna May Patricia (Griffiths) Downey; m. Paul Adrian Forbes, Feb. 13, 1977; children: Steve Dwain, AJ, Renford Tate. Cert. hypnotherapist Psychoneurology Found. Stable dir., mgr., horse trainer Centro Hipico De Chimoio, Mozambique, 1975-77; realtor Tarbell By the Sea, Calif., 1979-82; hypnotherapist Mind Mgmt. Tng., 1984—; workshop trainer Mind Mgmt. Tng., Ga., 1984—; pres., owner Mind Mgmt. Tng., Augusta, Ga., 1988—. Author: The Black Pot African Cook Book, 1980. Vol. drug and alcohol counsellor Georgia Regional Hosp., 1989, self esteem tchr. Orange County Juvenile Hall, 1985; editor newsletter Network Augusta, 1989. Named Top Show Horse Jumper, Mozambique, 1975. Mem. ASTD, U.S. Taekwondo Alliance (nat. 1st pl. winner 1990), Nat. Speakers Assn., Carolina Speakers Assn., Internat. Platform Assn., Am. Hypnotherapy Assn., Toastmasters Internat. (sec., treas. 1984, area gov. 1988, pres. 1990, toastmaster yr. award 1988). Home: 3622 Nassau Dr Augusta GA 30909

FORBES, JUDIE, aeronautical engineer; b. Fullerton, Calif., Sept. 27, 1942; d. James Franklin and Lois Virginia (Couse) F.; children: Laurel Alice Schader, James Joseph Resha, Edward John Resha III. BA in Physics, Calif. State U., Fullerton, 1974; MS in Engring., Calif. State U., 1979; MBA, U. So. Calif., 1983; postgrad., Claremont Grad. Sch. Engr. electromech. div. Northrop, Anaheim, Calif., 1975-80; project engr., mgr. electronic div. Northrop, Hawthorne, Calif., 1981-87; tech. staff TRW, San Bernadino, Calif., 1981; project mgr. Gen. Rsch. Corp., El Segundo, Calif., 1987-89; v.p. D.C. Caldwell & Co., Inc., Buena Park, Calif., 1987—; program mgr. TRW Technar, Irwindale, Calif., 1989—. Active Town Hall Calif., Los Angeles, 1983—. Calif. State U. Found. grantee, 1974; named Disting. Alumni Calif. State U., 1986; recipient Engring. Merit award Orange County Engring. Council, 1985. Fellow Inst. for Advancement Engring., AIAA (assoc., pres. Orange County 1986-87), Soc. Women Engrs. (pres. Los Angeles chpt. 1981-82, nat. v.p. 1983-84). Democrat. Home: 23557 Casa Loma Dr Diamond Bar CA 91765 Office: TRW Technar 5462 Irwindale Ave Irwindale CA 91007

FORBES, LAURIE JANE, health facility administrator, psychotherapist; b. Newark, Dec. 6, 1950; d. Robert Seymour and Elise May (Berger) F. BA, U. Miami, Coral Gables, Fla., 1973; MSW, Barry U., 1976. Lic. clin. social worker, Fla. Coord. aftercare svcs. Mobile Aftercare Project, 1976-79; pvt. practice cons. to nursing homes Miami, Fla., 1977-84; pvt. practice psychotherapist Miami, 1978—; coord. aftercare svcs. Douglas Gardens Community Mental Health Ctr., Miami Beach, Fla., 1979-80, North Miami Community Mental Health Ctr., Miami, 1980-81; social worker Jackson Meml. Hosp., Miami, 1981-85, supr., 1985-88, program adminstr. Rape Treatment Ctr., 1988—; adj. asst. prof. dept. psychiatry U. Miami Sch. Medicine, 1984. Mem. Nat. Assn. Social Workers, Acad. Cert. Social Workers (diplomate). Office: Jackson Meml Hosp 555 NE 34th St Ste 1609 Miami FL 33136

FORBES, MARY GLADYS, educator; b. Bend, Oreg., June 19, 1929; d. Percy Lloyd and Bertha May (Gettman) F. BA in Edn. magna cum laude, Cascade Coll., 1951; BS in Edn., Western Oreg. State Coll., Monmouth, 1954, MS in Edn., 1968. Cert. tchr., Oreg. Tchr. Christian & Missionary Alliance, Mamou, Guinea, West Africa, 1952-54, Bend (Oreg.)-Redmond Christian Day Sch., 1954-56, Dalat Sch., Asia, 1956-76; tchr. Bend-LaPine Sch. Dist. 1, Bend, 1976—, adminstr., tchr., 1981-87, tchr. kindergarten, 1989—; cons. Chpt. I Program in Spl. Edn., 1986-87; supt. Sunday sch. Christian & Missionary Alliance, 1976-80, Faith Fellowship Four Sq., Madras, Oreg., 1981-88. Mem. Citizens for the Republic, Washington, 1989; mem. Rep. Nat. Com., 1990—. Recipient Cert. of Appreciation Hale Found., 1986, 87, Skyhook II Project, 1987, Concerned Women of Am., 1987. Mem. Am. Def. Inst., Nat. Right to Life Com., Inc., Coun. for Inter-Am. Security, Nat. Assn. for Uniformed Svcs., Concerned Women for Am., Capitol Hill Women's Club. Home: 220 N 9th St Madras OR 97741 Office: Bend LaPine Sch Dist 1 520 NW Wall St Bend OR 97701

FORBES, SARAH ELIZABETH, gynecologist, real estate corporation officer; b. Currituck, N.C., May 4, 1928; d. Dexter and Mary (Brock) Forbes. BA, U. Rochester, 1949; MD, Med. Coll. of Va., 1954. Diplomate Am. Bd. Ob-Gyn. Intern Norfolk (Va.) Gen. Hosp., 1954-55; resident ob-gyn Johnston-Willis Hosp., 1955-56; resident ob-gyn Norfolk Gen. Hosp., 1956-57, chief resident, 1957-58; pres., gynecologist Sarah E. Forbes, Md., Inc., Newport News, Va., 1958—; pres., real estate investor Mary B. Forbes Land Corp., Newport News, 1972—; pres. Sebrof Corp., Newport News, 1978—, Haras, Inc., Newport News, 1984—, S.S. U.S., Inc., Newport News, 1984—; chmn. Utilization Com. Riverside Hosp., 1974; bd. dirs. Family Planning Council;teaching staff Riverside Hosp. Ob-Gyn Dept. Pres. Peninsula Soc. Prevention Cruelty to Animals, 1966—; bd. adv. Parents Without Partners, Peninsula Chpt.; bd. dirs. Newport News chpt. Am. Cancer Soc., pres. 1973-74, 1st v.p. 1972-73, 2nd v.p. 1971-72, chmn. rsch. 1961-69; candidate Newport News City Council, 1986. Recipient AMA Physician's

Recognition award for Continuing Edn., 1973-76, Twin award, Va. Peninsula Young Women's Christian Assn., 1987; named Woman of Yr. for Peninsula area, 1975. Mem. Va. Peninsula Acad. Medicine (pres. 1973-74, v.p. 1972-73, sec., treas. 1971-72); fellow AMA, Va. Med. Soc., Newport News Med. Soc. Am. Coll. Ob-Gyn, Tidewater Ob-Gyn Soc. Office: 12420 Warwick Blvd Newport News VA 23606 Home: 5 Merry Point Terr Newport News VA 23606

FORBES-RICHARDSON, HELEN HILDA, state agency administrator; b. Detroit, July 26, 1950; d. Henry and L. Trunetta (Adams) Forbes; m. Leon Richardson (div.); 1 child, Leon Ronald Jr. BA in Edn. and Human Svcs., U. Detroit, 1972; MPA, Harvard U., 1989. Cert. tchr. Mich. Substitute tchr. Detroit Bd. Edn., 1972-75; assistance payment worker State Dept. Social Svcs., Detroit, 1976-79, supr. assistance payment, 1979-85, section mgr., 1985—; adminstrv. asst. to chief dep. dir. Wayne County Dept. Social Svcs., Detroit, 1989-90; Mem. case rev. com. Mich. Dept. Social Svcs. Gen. Assistance, 1985, 87, labor relations subcom., quality initiative task force tng. com., 1985; mem. tng. com. quality initiative task force Wayne County Dept. Social Svcs., 1984, co-chairperson task force conf. planning com., 1987, client svc. subcom., 1989—, coord. employee recognition program, 1989-90, chmn. procedure com., Grand River Warren local office, 1990—, coord. state employee recognition program, Wayne County, 1989-90; chair security plan com. client info. system County of Wayne, 1989, mem. UAW Secondary Contract Negotiations Team, 1988; mem. conf. planning com. Mich. County Social Svcs. Assn., 1988; chairperson Grand River/Warren Procedures Com., 1990, employee recognition awards program level 1 Grand River/Warren Dept. Social Svcs., 1990; pres. Forbes-Richardson Ltd., 1990—; mgmt. cons. Forbes-Richardson Ltd., 1990. Coordinator Social Svc. United Found. Dr., Lafayette local office 1985, Social Svc. Black United Fund Dr. 1987, speaker Nat. Polit. Congress Black Women, 1986; student project coord. Wayne County Community Coll., Wayne County Dept. Social Svcs., 1989; coord. scholarship project Mary Holmes Coll. Spirit of Detroit Leadership award, 1985. Mem. Am. Pub. Welfare Assn. (planning com. 1986), Nat. Assn. Female Execs. Baptist. Office: Mich Dept Social Svcs Grand River/Warren Local Office Detroit MI 48208 also: Forbes-Richardson Ltd 65 Cadillac Sq Ste 3200 Detroit MI 48226 also: 5131 Grand River Warren Dist Office Detroit MI 48208

FORCE, MARIA THERESA, industrial psychologist; b. France, Feb. 20, 1958; came to U.S., 1959; d. Miklos J. and Maria (Majer) Laszlo; m. Kevin C. Force, Apr. 15, 1984; children: Rebecca, Kimberly. BA, Drew U., 1980; MS, Stevens Inst. Tech., 1982. Pvt. practice family mediation Verona, N.J.; exec. mgr. Am. Investors Group, Inc., East Hanover, N.J.; v.p., owner Guarantee Bagel Inc., West Orange, N.J. Mem. NAFE, Acad. Family Mediators, Assn. Family Conciliation Cts. Republican. Home: 87 Personette Ave Verona NJ 07044

FORD, ANN SUTER, health care consultant, planner, educator, nurse; b. Mineola, N.Y., Oct. 31, 1943; d. Robert M. and Jennette (Van Derzee) Suter; m. W. Scott Ford, 1964; children: Tracey, Karin, Stuart. RN, White Plains Hosp. Sch. Nursing (N.Y.), 1964; BS in Nursing with high distinction, U. Ky., 1967; MS in Health Planning, Fla. State U., 1971, PhD, 1975. Nurse, U. Ky. Med. Ctr., 1964-65, Tallahassee Meml. Hosp., 1968-69; guest lectr. health planning dept. urban and regional planning Fla. State U., Tallahassee, 1973-76, health planner and research assoc., 1974-76, vis. asst. prof., 1976-77, asst. prof. and dir. health planning splty., 1977-83, assoc. prof., 1982-83; health care analyst and policy cons., 1983-86; med., health program analyst Aging and Adult Services for State of Fla., 1986—; coordinator Fla. Alzheimer's Disease Initiative, 1986—; bd. dirs. Fla. Lung Assn.; mem. exec. com. human services and social planning tech. dept. Am. Inst. Planners, 1977-78. Author: The Physician's Assistant: A National and Local Analysis, 1975; contbr. numerous articles on health edn. and health planning to profl. jours.; contbr. chpts. to books; author research reports. USPHS grantee, 1965-67; HEW grantee, 1978; Univ. fellow Fla. State U., 1971-72; recipient Am. Inst. Planners' Student award, 1975. Mem. Am. Planning Assn. (charter mem. human services and social planning tech. dept. 1976—, chmn. health planning session Oct. 1978, 79, health policy liaison 1979-83, author assn. health policy statement), Am. Health Planning Assn., Phi Kappa Phi. Address: 2602 Cline St Tallahassee FL 32312

FORD, BARBARA A., marketing specialist; b. Washington, Mar. 18, 1952; d. Charles A. and Elsie C. (Duckett) Brandford; m. Gregory Ford, Aug. 5, 1972; children: Gregory, Jabbar. Student, Prince Georges Community Coll., Upper Marlboro, Md., 1989. Window clk. U.S. Postal Svc., Hyattsville, Md., supr. mails and delivery; retail mktg. specialist U.S. Postal Svc., Capitol Hts., Md. Bd. dirs. Landover Hills Boys and Girls Club; pres. Landover Knolls Assn. Mem. NAACP (chairperson Freedom Fund program, exec. bd. mem., corr. sec. 1987—), Combined Communities in Action (exec. bd. mem. 1986—), Nat. Coun. Negro Women Inc. Baptist. Address: 6509 Osborn Rd Landover Hills MD 20784

FORD, BARBARA HANNON, physical education educator; b. Whittier, Calif., Jan. 1, 1941; d. Walker and Gay (Dunsmoor) Hannon; m. Richard Donald Ford, May 21, 1960; children: Laura Ford Leathers, Richard Walker. BS, Calif. Poly. U., Pomona, 1963; MA, Calif. Poly. U., San Luis Obispo, 1965; EdD, Brigham Young U., 1983. Tchr. phys. edn., coach Montclair (Calif.) High Sch., 1964-67, Alta Loma (Calif.) High Sch., 1967-68; tchr. phys. edn., coach Calif. State Poly. U., Pomona, 1968-71, tchr. recreation, 1971—; cons. City of Corona Parks and Recreation Dept., 1985-87, State of Calif. Accreditaiton Com., Sacramento, 1989—. Co-author: Master Plan for City of Corona, 1987. Bd. dirs. Camp Fire Inc., Claremont, 1983-87. Recipient awards Calif. State Poly. U., Pomona, 1987, 88. Mem. AAHPERD (recreation chmn. S.W. dist. 1969-70), Nat. Parks and Recreation Assn., Calif. Parks and Recreation Soc. (program chmn. 1987-88), Calif. Assn., Health, Phys. Edn., Recreation and Dance (coord., recreation major 1986-89), Calif. Poly. Women's Club (pres. 1988-89), Chi Kappa Rho (svc. award 1983, 85). Home: 580 W 21st St Upland CA 91786 Office: Calif State Poly U 3801 W Temple Ave Pomona CA 91768

FORD, BARBARA JEAN, librarian; b. Dixon, Ill., Dec. 5, 1946; d. Robert Harold and Lois Hazel (Hann) F. BA, Ill. Wesleyan U., 1968; MA, Tufts U., 1969; MS, U. Ill., 1973. Dir. soybean insect rsch. info. ctr. Ill. Natural History Survey, Urbana, 1973-75; asst. documents libr. U. Ill., Chgo., 1975-79, documents libr., 1979-84; asst. dir. for pub. svcs. Trinity U. Maddux Libr., San Antonio, 1984-86, assoc. dir., 1986—. contbr. articles to libr. jours. Bd. dirs. Nat. Coun. Returned Peace Corps Vols. Mem. ALA (coun. 1980-89), Assn. Coll. & Rsch. Librs. (pres.-elect 1989-90, pres. 1990-91). Office: Trinity U Libr 715 Stadium Dr San Antonio TX 78212

FORD, BETTY BLOOMER (ELIZABETH FORD), wife of former President of U.S.; b. Chgo., Apr. 8, 1918; d. William Stephenson and Hortence (Neahr) Bloomer; m. Gerald R. Ford (38th Pres. U.S.), Oct. 15, 1948; children: Michael Gerald, John Gardner, Steven Meigs, Susan Elizabeth. Student, Sch. Dance Bennington Coll., 1936, 37; LL.D. hon., U. Mich., 1976. Dancer Martha Graham Concert Group, N.Y.C., 1939-41; model John Powers Agy., N.Y.C., 1939-41; fashion dir. Herpolscheimer's Dept. Store, Grand Rapids, Mich., 1943-48; dance instr. Grand Rapids, 1932-48; pres., bd. dirs. The Betty Ford Ctr., Rancho Mirage, Calif. Author: autobiography The Times of My Life, 1979, Betty: A Glad Awakening, 1987. Bd. dirs. Nat. Arthritis Found. (hon.); trustee Martha Graham Dance Ctr.; mem. theatre mgmt. com. Bob Hope Cultural Ctr.; trustee Eisenhower Med. Ctr., Rancho Mirage; hon. chmn. Palm Springs Desert Mus.; nat. trustee Nat. Symphony Orch.; trustee Nursing Home Adv. and Research Council Inc.; mem. Golden Circle Patrons Ctr. Theatre Performing Arts; bd. dirs. The Lambs, Libertyville, Ill. Episcopalian (tchr. Sunday sch. 1961-64). Home: PO Box 927 Rancho Mirage CA 92270*

FORD, CATHY ZOE, dentist; b. Knoxville, Tenn., June 2, 1953; d. Lester Smith and Velma (Dyer) Ford; m. James Tate McClung, Jr., June 17, 1978; children: Lindsay Hunter, Megan Ford McClung. BA, U. Tenn., 1974; DDS, La. State U., 1979. Med. rep. Arnar-Stone Labs., New Orleans, 1974-75; gen. practice dentistry, Rocky Mount, Va., 1980—; cons. Eldercare, Rocky Mount, 1982-84. Vol. Jr. League of Roanoke Valley, Va., 1982—. Recipient Achievement in Oral Surgery award La. Soc. Oral and Maxillofacial Surgeons, 1977-79, Am. Assn. Oral and Maxillofacial Surgeons award in oral surgery, 1979. Mem. Alpha Lambda Delta. Republican. Presbyterian. Avocations: golf, tennis. Home: 5119 Elk Hill Dr Roanoke VA 24014 Office: 277 S Main St Ste 201 Rocky Mount VA 24151

FORD, CYNTHIA ANN, advertising executive; b. Longview, Tex., Dec. 15, 1957; d. Doyle and Sandra Anne (Cole) F. Dist. mgr. Florafax Internat., Tulsa, 1981-82; art dir. Anderson, Baker, Beam Advt., Tulsa, 1983-85; owner The Ford Agency, Tulsa, 1985—. Recipient AddY award Oklahoma City Advt. Club, 1983, 84, Tulsa Addy, 1988, Achievement award Appleton Papers, 1984, Silver award Graphex, Cert. of Excellence Bus./Profl. Advt. Assn., 1985, 1st Place award Kimberly Clark Corp., Cert. of Merit Printing Industries Am., Corp. Design award Graphics Standard Manual, 1987, Silver Link award Pub. Rels. Soc. Am., 1988, Cert. of Merit Printing Industries Am., 1988. Mem. Art Dirs. Club of Tulsa (v.p. 1987-88, sec. 1988-89, Tulsa Addy ann. report 1989). Office: The Ford Agy 2508 E 21st St Tulsa OK 74114

FORD, EILEEN OTTE (MRS. GERARD W. FORD), modeling agency executive; b. N.Y.C., Mar. 25, 1922; d. Nathaniel and Loretta Marie (Laine) Otte; m. Gerard William Ford, Nov. 20, 1944; children: Margaret (Mrs. Robert Craft), Gerard William, M. Katie, A. Lacey. B.S., Barnard Coll., 1943. Stylist Elliot Clarke Studio, N.Y.C., 1943-44, William Becker Studio, 1945; copywriter Arnold Constable, N.Y.C., 1945-46; reporter Tobe Coburn, 1946; co-founder, v.p. Ford Model Agy., N.Y.C., 1946—. Author: Eileen Ford's Model Beauty, Secrets of the Model's World, A More Beautiful You in 21 Days; Author: Beauty Now and Forever, 1977. Bd. dirs. London Philharmonic, 1948—. Recipient Harpers Bazaar award for promotion internat. understanding., Woman of Yr. in Advt. award, 1983. Office: 344 E 59th St New York NY 10022

FORD, ELLEN HODSON, composer; b. Lincoln, Ill., Feb. 1, 1913; d. Albert and Mary (Fairclough) Hodson; m. John Joseph Janov, May 10, 1933 (dec. Sept. 1948); children: Alberta, Patricia, Jacqueline, David; m. James Gregory Ford, June 13, 1964. Studies with, Avelyn Kerr, Paul Sasstavitch, Chgo., 1940-48. Pvt. practice organ teaching Chgo., 1948-63; pub. Gabbriel Music Co., Taylorville, Ill., 1984. Composer, pub. 150 compositions, 1976-87. Recipient Cert. Recognition Josephine Oblinger, 1984, Mayor Peter Andrews Lincoln, Ill., 1989, Mayor Jim Noren Taylorville, Ill.; recognized by Queen Elizabeth II, also the Queen Mother of Eng. for compositions submitted. Mem. ASCAP, Am. Women's Composers Orgn., Music Arts Club, Women's Club, Order Ea. Star. Republican. Episcopalian. Home and Office: 421 W Franklin St Taylorville IL 62568

FORD, JANET MARIE, social worker; b. Long Beach, Calif., Mar. 19, 1941; d. Woodrow Wade and Genevieve (Williams) Partin; m. Errol Ford, Dec. 21, 1963; 1 child, Michael Edward. BA, Pepperdine U., Los Angeles, 1963; MSW, Calif. State U., 1988. Asst. teenage program dir. L.A. Harbor Y.W.C.A., San Pedro, Calif., 1963-66; sr. social worker Dept. Social Services, San Francisco, Calif., 1966-68; dir. of social services Ctr. Med. Hosp., Kentfield, Calif., 1968; sr. social worker Dept. of Social Services, San Francisco, Calif., 1968-69; social service worker Richfield Care Ctr., Richfield, UT, 1977-81; protective service worker NE Dept. of Social Services, Gering, Neb., 1982-84; case mgr. Child Protective Svcs. Napa County (Calif.) Human Svcs. Delivery System, 1984-89; co-therapist Napa County Adolescent Girls Sexual Abuse Therapy Group, 1985-89. Author: Foster Home Care of Sexually Abused Children, 1988. Mem. Nat. Assn. Social Workers. Democrat. Presbyterian.

FORD, KATHLEEN, artist, designer, writer; b. San Francisco, Mar. 3, 1932; d. Edward Francis and Mary Catherine (Donnelly) Dowd; student San Francisco Coll. for Women. 1950-53; B.A. in Design, Salinger Sch. Design, San Francisco, 1954. Head designer swimwear Gantner of Calif., San Francisco, 1954-55; asst. designer Jantzen, Inc., Seattle, 1955-56; owner, mgr. Kathleen Dowd Boutique, Sausalito, Calif., 1956-62; designer Constructions For Sound and Video, objects for manufacture, 1976—; author: The Three-Cornered House, 1968; The End (film); Last And 1/2 (film); author, designer American Point 50 (film); author screenplays The Rocker and Sweetheart, Key Grip, Kicked Out!, Bel Air Bump!; authored kits for making miniature prodns.; dir. The Loyola Internat. Art Consortium. Mem. Contemporary Authors, Writers Guild of Am. Home: 425 Castenada Ave San Francisco CA 94116

FORD, KAY LOUISE, industrial relations specialist; b. Pontiac, Mich., Aug. 2, 1944; d. Norman Avery and Elsa Katherine (Wahlsten) F.; m. Billy Wayne Reed, Aug. 20, 1965 (div. Jan. 1979); children: Matthew Wayne Reed, Bradley Ford Reed. AB, U. Mich., 1965; MA, SUNY, Brockport, 1983. Speech therapist Community Treatment Ctr., Bath, Maine, 1966-68; continuing edn. coord. SUNY, Brockport, 1974-78, grad. asst., 1978-79; contract tng. dir. Monroe Community Coll., Rochester, N.Y., 1979-86; exec. dir. Livingston Washtenaw Pvt. Industry Coun., Ann Arbor, Mich., 1986—; contract trainer Cornell U., Rochester, N.Y., 1983-86, Learning Internat., Buffalo, 1984-87; field instr. U. Mich., 1988—. Co-chmn. Internat. Spl. Olympics Ceremonies Com., Brockport, 1979-80, Washtenaw United Way Communications, Ann Arbor, 1987--, Mich. Theatre Fund Raising, Ann Arbor, 1987--; bd. dirs. Jazz for Life--On Stage for Kids, Ann Arbor, 1987--. Mem. Ann Arbor Personnel Assn., Am. Soc. Tng. and Devel., Acad. Polit. Sci., Greater Brighton Area C. of C., Mich. Rehab. Svcs., Supported Employment, Washtenaw Community Coll. (mem. bus. and labor leaders adv. com.), Eastern State Communication Assn. Office: Livingston Washtenaw Pvt Industry Coun 211 E Huron St Ann Arbor MI 48104

FORD, LEE ELLEN, scientist, educator, lawyer; b. Auburn, Ind., June 16, 1917; d. Arthur W. and Geneva (Muhn) Ford; BA, Wittenberg Coll., 1947; MS, U. Minn., 1949; PhD, Iowa State Coll., 1952; JD, U. Notre Dame, 1972. Bar : Ind. 1972. CPA auditing, 1934-44; assoc. prof. biology Gustavus Adolphus Coll., 1950-51, Anderson (Ind.) Coll., 1952-55; vis. prof. biology U. Alta. (Can.), Calgary, 1955-56; assoc. prof. biology Pacific Luth. U., Parkland, Wash., 1956-62; prof. biology and cytogenetics Miss. State Coll. for Women, 1962-64; chief cytogeneticist Pacific N.W. Rsch. Found., Seattle, 1964-65; founder, dir. Canine Genetics Cons. Svc., Parkland, 1963-69; pvt. practice, Ind., 1972—. Founder, sponsor Companion Collies for the Adult, Jr. Blind, 1955-65; dir. Genetics Rsch. Lab., Butler, Ind., 1955-75, cons. cytogenetics, 1969-75; legis. cons., 1970-79; dir. chromosome lab. Inst. Basic Rsch. in Mental Retardation, S.I., 1968-69; founder, dir. Legis. Bur. U. Notre Dame Law Sch., founder, editor New Dimensions in Legis., 1969-72; editor Butler Record Herald, 1972-76; founder, dir. Ind. Interreligious Com. on Human Equality, 1976-80; exec. asst. to Gov. Otis R. Bowen, Ind., 1973-75; founder, bd. dir. Ind. Commn. on Status Women, 1973-74; bd. dirs. Ind. Council Chs.; editor Ford Assocs. pubs., 1972-86; mem. Pres.'s Adv. Council on Drug Abuse, 1976-77. Admitted to Ind. bar, 1972. Adult counselor Girl Scouts U.S.A., 1934-40; bd. dirs. Ind. Task Force Women's Health, 1976-80; mem. exec. bd., bd. dirs. Ind.-Ky. Synod Lutheran Ch., 1972-78; bd. dirs., mem. council St. Marks Luth. Ch., Butler, 1970-76; mem. social services personnel bd.; mem. DeKalb County (Ind.) Sheriff's Merit Bd., 1983-87; founder, dir., pres. Ind. Caucus for Animal Legis. and Leadership, 1984-87. Mem. or ex-mem. AAUW, AAAS, Genetics Soc. Am., Am. Human Genetics Soc., Am. Genetic Assn., Am. Inst. Biol. Scis., Am. Soc. Zoologists, La. Acad. Sci., Miss. Acad. Sci., Ind. Acad. Sci., Iowa Acad. Sci., Bot. Soc. Am., Ecol. Soc. Am., ABA (bd. dir.), Ind. Bar Assn. (bd. dir.), DeKalb County Bar Assn. (bd. dir.) Bar Assn., Humane Soc. U.S. (bd. dir. 1970-88), DeKalb County Humane Soc. (founder, bd. dir. 1970-86), Ind. Fedn. Humane Socs. (bd. dir. 1970-84), Nat. Assn. Women Lawyers (bd. dir.), Bus. and Profl. Women's Club, Nat. Assn. Rep. Women (bd. dir.), Women's Equity Action League (bd. dir.), Assn. So. Biologists, Phi Kappa Phi. Club: Altrusa. Founder, editor: Breeder's Jour., 1958-63; numerous vols. on dog genetics and breeding, guide dogs for the blind. Contbr. over 2000 sci. and popular publs. on cytogenetics, dog breeding and legal topics; contbr. articles to Am. Kennel Club Gazette, 1970-81, also others; researcher in field. Home and Office: 336 Hickory St Butler IN 46721

FORD, LISA ANN, training consultant; b. Knoxville, Tenn., Nov. 12, 1956; d. Lester Smith and Velma (Dyer) F. BA, U. Tenn., 1977; student Alliance Française (Paris), 1976. Energy edn. specialist Oak Ridge Assoc. U., Tenn., 1977-78; tng. cons. Vernine & Assocs., Knoxville, 1978-83; tng. cons., owner Ford & Assocs., Atlanta, 1983—. Vol. High Mus. Art/Young Careers, Atlanta. Named Outstanding Alumni U. Tenn. Mem. Am. Soc. Tng. and Devel. (treas. 1978-79, bd. dirs. 1979-84), Nat. Speaker's Assn., Atlanta Womens Network. Republican. Presbyterian. Avocations: tennis, sailing, travel, antiques. Home and Office: Ford Assocs 140 Seville Chase Atlanta GA 30328

FORD, LORETTA C., nurse, educator and university dean emeritus; b. N.Y.C., Dec. 28, 1920; d. Joseph F. and Nellie A. (Williams) Pfingstel; R.N., Middlesex Gen. Hosp., New Brunswick, N.J., 1941; BS in Nursing, U. Colo., 1949, MS, 1951, EdD, 1961; DSc (hon.) Ohio State Med Coll.; LLD (hon.) U. Md., 1990; m. William J. Ford, May 2, 1947; 1 dau., Valerie. Staff nurse New Brunswick Vis. Nurse Service, 1941-42; supr., dir. Boulder County (Colo.) Health Dept., 1947-58; asst. prof., then prof. U. Colo. Sch. Nursing, 1960-72; dean Sch. Nursing, dir. nursing, prof. U. Rochester (N.Y.), 1972-86, acting dean Grad. Sch. Edn. & Human Devel., 1988-89; vis. prof. U. Fla., summer 1968, U. Wash., Seattle, 1974; mem. educators adv. panel GAO; dir. Security Trust Co., Rochester, Rochester Telephone Co.; internat. cons. in field. Bd. dirs. Threshold Alte. Youth Services, Easter Seal Soc., ARC, Monroe Community Hosp. Served with Nurse Corps, USAAF, 1942-46. Named Colo. Nurse of Year; recipient N.Y. State Gov.'s award for women in sci., medicine and nursing. Fellow Am. Acad. Nursing; mem. Nat. League Nursing (fellowship, Linda Richards award), Am. Coll. Health Assn. (Boynton award), Am. Nurses Assn., Am. Public Health Assn., Inst. Medicine. Author articles in field, chpts. in books. Office: Univ Rochester Med Ctr 601 Elmwood Ave Box HWH Rochester NY 14642

FORD, MAUREEN MORRISSEY, civic worker; b. St. Joseph, Mo., July 1, 1936; d. Albert Joseph and Rosemary Kathryne (FitzSimons) Morrissey; student U. N.Mex., 1953-54, U. Bridgeport (Conn.), 1966-68; BS, Fairfield U., 1986, postgrad. in Applied Ethics, 1986—; m. James Henry Lee Ford, Jr., Feb. 12, 1954; children: Kathryne Elizabeth, Maryellen, James Henry Lee III, William Charles, Maureen Lee. Charity and sch. vol., 1959—; fundraiser for community causes, mus., agys., 1964—; active presdl. campaign Barry Goldwater, 1963-64, congressional campaign Senator Lowell Weiker, 1968; pre-sch. tchr. Nature Ctr. Environ. Activities, 1966-68, trustee, v.p. bd. dirs., 1968-75; assoc. program in applied ethics, Fairfield U., 1986—. Author: (with Lisa H. Newton) Taking Sides: Controversial Issues in Business Ethics. V.p. Women's League, 1966-70; mem. exec. com. Republican Women's Club, Westport, 1967-68; leader, trainer Troops on Fgn. Soil br. Girl Scouts US, Caracas, Venezuela, 1971-72; founding trustee, treas. Kara Mus., Norwalk, Conn.; mem. adv. council Fairfield County (Conn.) for spl. edn. Staples High Sch.; bd. dirs. CLASP; mem. exec. com. Group Home Search; cons., facilitator life planning workshops Merideth Assocs., Westport; mem. 1st selectmen's com. on recycling, 1974-75; bd. dirs. PTA, 1976-79; mem. YWCA of Bridgeport Com. of 100 and Task Force; v.p. bd. dirs. YWCA, 1980-87, pres., 1984-85; v.p. Conf. Women's Orgns., Bridgeport; founding mem. Concerned Women Colleagues of Bridgeport; pres. Jr. League Eastern Fairfield County, Inc., 1977-78; v.p., sec. J.H.L.F. Inc., Westport. Mem. Assn. Jr. League Am., Westport Tennis Assn. Roman Catholic. Home: 299 Sturges Hwy Westport CT 06880

FORD, SARAH ANN, academic administrator; b. Gary, Ind., Aug. 29, 2951; d. Sherman Joe Rusell and Alice Selena (Johnson) F. BS, Ball State U., 1973, MA, 1974; MBA, Keller Grad Sch., 1987. Dir. Multi. cultural cnt Marquette Univ., Milw., 1974-78; arts adminstr. UW - Extension, Milw., 1978-84; small bus. program coordinator UW - Milw., 1984-88; dir. econ. devel. div. Waukesha County Tech. Coll., Pewaukee, Wis.; security agent Nat. Devel. & Investment, Brookfield, Wis., 1980-82; sec. Wis. Council on Small & Minority Bus., Madison, Wis., 1987--. Publisher: Colorlines Magazine, 1980--. pres., founder Colorlines Foundn. for Arts & Culture, Inc., Milw., 1986--; pres. Heritage Chorale, Milw., 1986--; mem. Milw. Forum, Milw., 1987--. Lt. U.S. National Guard, 1978--. Named: Outstanding Young Women, Outstanding Young Women in Am., Milw., 1985. mem. Wis. Econ. Devel. Assn., Profl. Dimensions, Delta Sigma Theta Sorority. Democrat. Baptist. Office: Waukesha County Tech Coll 800 Main St Pewaukee WI 53072

FORD, SHARON ANN, manufacturing company executive; b. Appleton, Wis.. AA with hons., Dekalb Coll., 1986; BBA, Ga. State U., 1990. Trust ops. officer Valley Trust Co., Appleton, Wis., 1968-78; group leader-adminstrn. Kimberly-Clark Corp., Roswell, Ga., 1978-90; mgr. customer svc. and adminstrn. beauty barber bus. Kimberly-Clark Corp., Balfour, N.C., 1990—. Mem. NAFE, Nat. Assn. Bus. and Profl. Women's Club, Golden Key. Home: PO Box 191 Balfour NC 28706-0191

FORD, TSY, communications design consultant; b. Denville, N.J., Nov. 15, 1957; d. John James and Anna Louise (Ammerman) F. Student, Sch. Fashion Design, Boston, 1975-76, County Coll. of Morris, Randolph, N.J., 1977-78, Parsons, N.Y.C., 1979, 81-84. Communications designer, cons. Tsy Ford Communications Design, Caldwell, N.J., 1978—; cons. Suburban Propane Gas Corp., Morristown, N.J., 1980-85, Seton Hall U., Orange, N.J., Philips Lighting Co., Somerset, N.J., 1985—; freelance, cons. The Foote System, N.J., 1984—; guest speaker for advanced pub. rels. course, Seton Hall U., So. Orange, 1987, 88. Designer creative dir., Seton U., Annual Appeal Fundraising program, 1987. Mem. Internat. Assn. Bus. Communications (exec. bd. sec. N.J. chpt. 1988, 89), IABC (N.J. Iris Awards Program, chmn. 1988, 89), Graphic Artists Guild, Advt. Club N.J. Office: Tsy Ford Communication Design PO Box 109 Caldwell NJ 07006

FORDHAM, SHARON ANN, food company executive; b. Somerset, N.J., Jan. 30, 1952; d. Thomas Anthony and Gladys Maryann (Hagaman) F. BA in History with honors, Rutgers U., 1975; MBA in Mktg., U. Pa., 1977. Asst. product mgr. Bristol-Myers (Drackett Co.), Cin., 1977-78, product mgr., 1979; product mgr. Borden, Inc., Columbus, Ohio, 1979-81; product mgr. Nabisco Brands, Inc., East Hanover, N.J., 1981-82, group product mgr., 1982-84, dir. mktg., 1984-86, sr. dir. new bus., 1986—. Originator, dir. Almost Home (Cookie Wars), 1983, Low Salt Ritz and Premium, 1985-86, Ritz Bits, Quackers, Am. Classic, 1987, Teddy Grahams, 1988. Mem. Woodbridge (N.J.) Wind Ensemble, 1982-83, Hillsborough Wind Ensemble, Somerset, N.J., 1984-87. Recipient award Point of Purchase Advt. Inst. (POPAI), 1983, 89, Gold Effie award Assn. Nat. Advertisers, 1986, New Product of Yr. award Bus. Week, 1988, Food and Beverage Mktg., 1988; New Snack Product of Yr. award Consumer Network, 1988, Gorman Pub., 1988. Mem. Am. Mktg. Assn. (New Product Marketer of Yr. award 1988, New Product of Yr. award 1988), Mensa, Wharton Club N.Y., Hillsborough Golf Club (N.J.). Republican. Roman Catholic. Office: Nabisco Biscuit Co 100 DeForest Ave PO Box 527 East Hanover NJ 07936

FORDYCE, BARBARA ANN, linen services executive; b. Moose Lake, Minn., July 2, 1955; d. Vernon Ernest and Helen Elizabeth (Viita) Beck; m. Kevin Wayne Fordyce, Apr. 17, 1989. AA, St. Mary's Jr. Coll., Mpls., 1975; BA in Applied Sci., U. Minn., 1980; cert. registered cen. svc. tech., Purdue U., 1988. Instr. McDonnell Ctr., Mpls., 1975-78, Portland Resident, Mpls., 1978-80; supr. dir. Community Hosp. Linen Svcs., Mpls., 1980—; project engr. Foussard Mgmt. Services, St. Paul, 1983-86. Mem. Assn. Operating Room Nurses, Nat. Assn. Instl. Laundry Mgrs. Democrat. Lutheran. Home: 4411 155th Ave NE Ham Lake MN 55304 Office: Community Linen Svcs 201 Royalston Ave Minneapolis MN 55405

FOREHAND, JENNIE MEADOR, state legislator; b. Nashville, Dec. 17, 1935; d. James T. and Estelle (Woodall) Meador; student Woman's Coll. of U. N.C., Greensboro, 1954-56; B.S. in Indsl. Relations, U. N.C., Chapel Hill, 1958; m. William E. Forehand, Jr., July 19, 1958; children: Virginia, John Bentley. Reporter, Charlotte (N.C.) News, 1954-56; probation counselor Juvenile Ct., Charlotte, 1958; tchr. Anne Arundel County (Md.), 1958-60; statis. analyst NIH, Bethesda, Md., 1961-62; edn. research project evaluator Montgomery County (Md.) Bd. Edn., 1973-74; interior designer, owner Antiques and Interiors, Rockville, Md., 1971—; rep. Md. Gen. Assembly, 1978—; mem. appropriations com., joint capital budget com., health and environ. subcom., Md. com. on Physical Fitness, Bd. Md. State Games; co-chair Gov's. Task Force on Sr. Citizen Ctrs., NIH Bio-Safety Com.; adv. bd. First Women's Bank of Md. Planning bd. Montgomery County Health Systems Agy., chmn. edn. and community involvement; past chmn. Rockville Civic Improvement Adv. Commn.; consumer rep. Rockville Econ. Devel. Council; mem. Montgomery County Bd. of Edn. Med. Adv. Com.; mem. Md. Community Mental Health Adv. Bd.; pres. local civic assn.; bd. dirs. Mid-Md. Lung Assn., Montgomery County Hist. Soc.; bd. dirs. local sch. PTA; adv. bd. Mont. Hospice Soc., mem. Peerless Rockville Hist.

Preservation, Ltd., Questers; bd. dirs. Md. Coll. Art and Design, Rockville Arts Place. Mem. Women's Caucus of Md. Gen. Assembly, AAUW, Md. Assn. Elected Women, Women's Polit. Caucus. Democrat. Methodist. Office: State Ho Reps 223C House Office Bldg Annapolis MD 21401

FOREMAN, ANNE N., lawyer; b. Hollywood, Calif., Oct. 16, 1947; d. Dorothy Newman Rogers; m. Dennis Irwin Foreman, Sept. 7, 1974; children: Victoria Anne, Thomas Graham, Kathleen Elizabeth. BA, U. So. Calif., 1969, MA, 1975; JD, Am. U., 1980. Bar: D.C. 1981, U.S. Dist. Ct. (D.C. dist.) 1981, U.S. Ct. Mil. Appeals 1988. Law clk. Bracewell & Patterson, Washington, 1979-81, atty., 1980-85; fgn. service officer U.S. Dept. State, Washington, 1973-77; assoc. dir. presdl. personnel National Security The White House, Washington, 1985-87; air force gen. counsel Dept. of the Air Force, Washington, 1987-89, undersec., 1989—. Mem. Phi Beta Kappa. Republican. Office: Dept Def The Pentagon Rm 4E886 Washington DC 20330-1000

FOREMAN, CAROL LEE TUCKER, business executive; b. Little Rock, May 3, 1938; d. James Guy and Willie Maude (White) Tucker; A.A., William Woods Coll., Fulton, Mo., 1958; A.B., Washington U., St. Louis, 1960; postgrad. Am. U.; LL.D. (hon.), William Woods Coll., Fulton, Mo., 1976; m. Jay Howell Foreman, June 13, 1964; children: Guy Tucker, Rachel Marian. Rsch. asst. Com. on Govt. Ops., U.S. Senate, 1961; assoc. Fed. Counsel Assocs., 1961-63; instr. Am. govt. William Woods Coll., Fulton, 1963-64; exec. asst. to Rep. James Roosevelt, 1964; dir. rsch. and publs. Dem. Nat. Com., 1965-66; Congressional liaison aide HUD, 1967-69; chief info. liaison Ctr.for Family Planning Program Devel., Planned Parenthood-World Population, 1969-71; dir. policy coordination Commn. on Population and Am. Future, 1971-72; exec. dir. Citizens Com. on Population and Am. Future, 1972-73, Paul Douglas Consumer Rsch. Ctr., 1973-77, Consumer Fedn. Am., 1973-77; asst. sec. food and consumer svcs. Dept. Agr., Washington, 1977-81; pres. Foreman & Co., 1981-86, ptnr. Foreman & Heidepriem, 1986—; bd. dirs. Adams Nat. Bank, Christianity and Crisis. Exec. dir. Ctr. for Women Policy Studies, 1983-84; mem. Interdeptl. Task Force on Women; mem. D.C. Commn. on Status Women, 1973-74; dir. Consumer's Union, 1982-83, Food Rsch. and Action Ctr., 1983—; dir. Commodity Credit Corp., 1977-81, Nat. Consumer Coop. Bank, 1979-81; vice-chmn. Ctr. Nat. Policy, 1982-84, dir., 1981—; trustee Washington U., St. Louis, 1987—. Recipient Disting. Alumni award Washington U., 1979. Mem. Women's Equity Action League (past pres. local chpt.), Nat. Planning Assn. (dir. 1985—), Woman's Nat. Dem. Club, Pi Beta Phi. Presbyterian. Home: 5408 Trent St Chevy Chase MD 20015 Office: Foreman & Heidepriem 1112 16th NW Ste 750 Washington DC 20036

FOREMAN, NANCY JEAN, interior designer; b. Balt., Feb. 21, 1949; d. Ernst and Julia (Rosenthal) Guggenheim; m. Jeff Foreman, Apr. 1, 1978. BS, U. Md., 1970. Interior designer Lucas Design Group, Balt., 1972-76; space planner Md. Casualty Co., Balt., 1976-77; interior designer Michael Asner & Assocs., Balt., 1977-78; pres. Nancy Foreman Design, Timonium, Md., 1978—. Fundraiser Kennedy Inst. for Handicapped Children, Balt., 1986; mem. Greater Balt. Com., 1985—; bd. dirs. Grant-A-Wish Found., 1988—. Mem. Am. Soc. Interior Designers (bd. dirs. 1987—), Comml. Real Estate Women, Bldg. Office Mgrs. Assn., Nat. Assn. Indsl. Office Parks, Balt. County C. of C. Office: 16 Greenmeadow Dr Timonium MD 21093

FOREMAN, NANCY NORTH, chamber of commerce executive; b. Akron, Ohio, Feb. 12, 1938; d. Willson Harvey Lawrence and Wilma Gayle (Gilhousen) Hunter; m. William Blaine Foreman, Apr. ll, 1959; children: Laurie Ann, Kathleen Guy Foreman Eliason, William Scott, James Blaine. Student, Ohio U., 1956-58. Color cons. Glidden Paint Co., Cleve, 1958-59; exec. mgr. Euclid (Ohio) C. of C., 1975—; exec. dir. Euclid Gateway Found., 1985—. Mem. Euclid Devel. Corp., 1977—, Euclid Hosp. Assn., 1981—; prs. Euclid Little Theatre, 1973, 85; co-dir. Euclid Women's Ensemble. Named Woman of Yr., Euclid Women's Caucus, 1987. Mem. U.S. C. of C., Ohio C. of C., C. of C. Execs. Ohio (sec., treas., v.p., pres. 1987-90), Ohio Devel. Assn. Republican. Presbyterian. Home: 650 Hemlock Dr Euclid OH 44132 Office: Euclid C of C 291 E 222d St Euclid OH 44123

FORER, MARGERY PATRICIA, greeting card company executive; b. N.Y.C., Mar. 17, 1922; d. David and Hattie Bregman; m. David Forer, Dec. 17, 1948; children: David Brett, Katherine Ellen. BS, Skidmore Coll., 1943. Asst. testing dept. Manhattan Project Columbia U., 1943-44; fashion reporter Women's Wear Daily, 1944-47; 1st fashion editor Footwear News, 1947-49; co-founder, sec.-treas. div. Butterick Co., Inc. Brett-Forer Greetings, N.Y.C., 1949, fashion coord., stylist-designer; mem. adv. bd. greeting card com. UNICEF; speaker, cons. in field. Mem. Greeting Card Assn. (pres. 1982). Office: 161 6th Ave NW New York NY 10013

FOREST, CHARLENE LYNN, cell biologist, educator; b. N.Y.C., Feb. 27, 1947; d. Harold Matthew and Sadie (Biller) Friedman; m. Richard Mark Forest, June 29, 1969. BS, Cornell U., 1968; MS, Adelphi U., 1972; PhD, Ind. U., 1976. Postdoctoral fellow Harvard U., Cambridge, Mass., 1976-79; asst. prof. Bklyn. Coll. CUNY, 1979-83, 84-86, assoc. prof., 1986—; prin. investigator, grant assoc. Rsch. Found. CUNY, Bklyn., 1983-84. Contbr. articles to profl. publs. Grantee NIH, 1980-83, NSF, 1983-85, 85-88; recipient Career Advancement award NSF, 1989-90. Mem. Am. Soc. Cell Biology, Genetics Soc. Am., Soc. Protozoologists, Assn. Women in Sci., N.Y. Acad. Scis., N.Y. Soc. Electron Microscopists, AAAS, Sigma Xi. Office: Bklyn Coll Dept Biology Bedford Ave and Ave H Brooklyn NY 11210

FORESTER, BETH N., real estate broker, educator; b. Salisbury, Md., Jan. 17, 1933; d. Samuel Francis and Bessiemae (Byrd) Nava; m. Richard Willard Brown; children: Lynne, Lisa, Paul. BA, U. Mass., 1954. Tutor Paxton (Mass.) Sch. System, 1958-64; tchr. head start program Mass. Sch. System, Worcester, 1964-71, prin. head start program, 1971-77; real estate salesperson TownCrier, Fairport, N.Y., 1978-87, John T. Nothnagle, Inc., Fairport, N.Y., 1984—; tchr., panel mem. Nothnagle Tng. Ctr., Rochester, 1986—. Recipient Top 5 Nat. Gallery of Homes Sales award, 1985, 86, 87, 88, 89. Mem. N.Y. State Assn. Realtors, N.Y. Women's Coun. Realtors, Fairport Woman's Assn., AAUW, U. Mass. Alumnae Club (v.p. 1960-64), Fairport Newcomers Club (treas. 1978, v.p. 1979), Kappa Alpha Theta (pres. 1960). Repbulican. Episcopalian. Home: 17 Valewood Run Penfield NY 14526 Office: John T Nothnagle Inc 65 S Main Fairport NY 14450

FORESTER, JEAN MARTHA BROUILLETTE, librarian, educator; b. Port Barre, La., Sept. 7, 1934; d. Joseph Walter and Thelma (Brown) Brouillette; m. James Lawrence Forester, June 2, 1957; children: Jean Martha, James Lawrence. BS, La. State U., 1955; MA (Carnegie fellow 1955-56), George Peabody Coll. Tchrs., 1956. Libr. Howell Elem. Sch., Springhill, La., 1956-58; asst. post libr. Fort Chaffee, Ark., 1958; command libr. Orleans Area Command, U.S. Army, Orleans, France, 1958-59; acquisitions libr. Northwestern State U., Natchitoches, La., 1960; serials libr. La. State U., New Orleans, 1960-66; mem. faculty La. State U., Eunice, 1966-85, asst. libr., 1972-85, assoc. libr., 1985-87, acting libr., 1987-88, dir. libr., 1988-89, libr. emeritus, 1989—; asst. prof., 1972-85, faculty senator, 1978-80, 85-86, 87-89; innkeeper Crown'n'Anchor Inn, Newcastle, Maine, 1989—. Coauthor: Robertson's Bill of Fare; contbr. articles to profl. jour. Active Eunice Assn. Retarded Children. Mem. La. Libr. Assn. (sect. sec. 1971-72, coord. serials interest group 1984-85), UDC, Delta Kappa Gamma (chpt. parliamentarian 1972-74, rec. sec. 1984-86), Alpha Beta Alpha, Phi Gamma Mu, Phi Mu, Order Eastern Star. Democrat. Baptist.

FORGOTSON, FLORENCE FRANCES, lawyer; b. Spotswood, N.J., Apr. 19, 1908; d. Harry and Betsy (Schiller) F.; m. John E. Adams (dec.). BS, NYU, 1929, LLB, 1929, D of Juridicial Sci., 1947. Bar: N.J. 1930, U.S. Dist. Ct. 1930, U.S. Bd. Immigration Appeals 1948, Ct. Internat. Trade 1955, U.S. Immigration Ct. 1955, U.S. Supreme Ct. 1955. Pvt. practice Red Bank, N.J., 1929—; tchr. law courses Monmouth Coll., 1948-81; Am. del. to conf. on Mid. East in Switzerland, 1948; specialist in family law. Contbr. articles to profl. jours. Pres. League of Women Voters, Hadassah, Explorer Scouts. Recipient 50th Anniversary Legal Practice award, State of N.J., 1979, Women of Achievement award, Commn. on the Status of Women, 1989. Mem. ABA (internat. law, corp. law and family law sects.), N.J. Bar Assn. (internat. law, corp. law and family law sects.), Monmouth County Bar Assn. (family law sect.), AAUW, Nat. Assn. Women Lawyers, Internat. Assn. Women Lawyers, Am. Judicature Soc., Soroptimist Club, Federated Women's Club. Home: Lone Oak Shrewsbury NJ 07702 Office: 182 Broad St Red Bank NJ 07701

FORKAN, PATRICIA ANN, association executive; b. N.Y.C., June 13, 1944; d. Robert James and Elaine May (Van Horn) F.; BA in Polit. Sci., Pa. State U., 1966; postgrad. Am. U., 1968-69. Manpower analyst Dept. Labor, Washington, 1967-69; nat. coordinator Fund for Animals, N.Y.C., 1970-76; v.p. program and communications Humane Soc. of U.S., Washington, 1976-86, sr. v.p. 1987—; mem. U.S. del. Internat. Whaling Commn., 1978, Renegotiation of Conv. for Regulation of Whaling, 1978, U.S. del. North Pacific Fur Seal Commn., 1985; mem. U.S. Public Adv. Com. to Law of the Sea, 1978-83; bd. dirs. Coun. for Ocean Law; advisor, contbr. weekly TV show Living with Animals; advisor Animal Polit. Action Com. Contbr. articles to environ. and animal welfare publs. Co-host weekly radio show, 1986-87. Office: Humane Soc of US 2100 L St Washington DC 20037

FORMAN, BETH ROSALYNE, entertainment industry professional; b. N.Y.C., Oct. 15, 1949; d. Philip and Dorothy Lea (Vilensky) F. BA in English with honors, NYU, 1971; MA with honors, Columbia U., 1972; MBA in Fin., Rutgers U., 1980. Asst. to contr. Colin Hochstin Co., N.Y.C., 1971-78; instr. Columbia U., N.Y.C., 1974-76; adj. faculty Bergen Community Coll., Paramus, N.J., 1985-87; communications cons. B.R. Forman & Co., Paramus, 1981-87; proposal mgr. Ogden Allied Svcs.Corp., N.Y.C., 1988-89; dir. tech. svcs. Ogden Allied Entertainment Svcs., Rosemont, Ill., 1990—. Bd. dirs. new leadership div. United Jewish Community Bergen County, River Edge, N.J., 1981-87, chmn. fundraiser, 1983, chmn. edn. com., 1983-86, treas., 1984-86. Pres.'s fellow Columbia U., 1973. Mem. Women in Communications, Columbia U. Club of Chgo., Mensa. Democrat. Home: 421 Yuhas Dr Paramus NJ 07652 Office: Ogden Allied Entertainment 9501 W Devon Ave Rosemont IL 60018

FORMAN, JEANNE LEACH, piano and voice educator; b. Los Angeles, Mar. 3, 1916; d. Rowland E. and Charlotte F. (Van Wickle) Leach; student U. Redlands, 1934-36, UCLA, 1937; m. Edward S. Forman, July 28, 1945; children—Bonnie Jeanne (Mrs. James Field Ottinger), Karen Lynn (Mrs. Patrick Maginnis), Wendy K. Forman (Mrs. Michael Bolduc). Pvt. tchr. piano, Pasadena, Calif., 1945-52, Tucson, 1952-58, Sunnyvale, Calif., 1958-75, Santa Barbara, Calif., 1976—; owner, dir. Jeanne Forman Studios, Sunnyvale; owner/dir. Jeanne Forman Enterprises (Music to Write By), 1982—; owner J. Forman Advt. Agy.; propr. Jeanne Forman Advt. and Enterprises; writer Los Angeles Times, 1978-80; columnist The Galeria Santa Barbara News Press, 1978—; publicity writer Music Tchrs. Assn.; tchr. of blind Santa Clara County Assistance League; lectr. on blind techniques, vocal techniques, rapport in communications; freelance writer; gen. edn. staff Brooks Inst. Photography; Santa Barbara guest appearances There is a Way, Sta. KHJ-TV, Los Angeles. Author: Security, 1984, Secret of the Pig, 1984; composer: I Love to Hear the Bells, 1986, Christmas Is Here; compositions performed by U. Calif., Santa Barbara, 1971. Mem. Calif. Assn. Profl. Music Tchrs., Music Tchrs. Nat. Assn. Home: 1119 Alameda Padre Serra Santa Barbara CA 93105

FORMAN, PAULA, advertising agency executive. Market rsch. trainee BBDO; sr. v.p., mgmt. supr. Wells, Rich, Greene; now exec. v.p., exec. mgmt. dir. Saatchi & Saatchi Advt. Worldwide, N.Y.C. Office: Saatchi & Saatchi Advt Worldwide 375 Hudson St New York NY 10014

FORMAN, TAMARA, sales executive; b. Providence, Nov. 24, 1947; d. Hyman and Sylvia (Gordon) F. Student, U. R.I., 1978, UCLA, Northwestern U., Mass. Bay Community Coll. Pers. generalist, sec. Citizens Bank, 1973-77; nat. ops. coord., br. mgr., sales rep. Adia Temp. Svcs. Inc., Menlo Park, Calif., 1977-82; asst. to mgr., constrn. and plant svcs. Am. Broadcasting Co., 1982-83; mgr. franchise devel. Drake Franchise Systems Inc., L.A., 1983—. Mem. NAFE, Am. Soc. Profl. and Exec. Women, Pers. and Indsl. Rels. Assn., Pasadena C. of C., The Firm. Address: 6071 Magnolia Ln Woodland Hills CA 91367

FORNELL, MARTHA STEINMETZ, educator, artist; b. Galveston, Tex., Dec. 19, 1920; d. Joseph Duncan and Martha Lillian (McRee) Steinmetz; m. Earl Wesley Fornell, Sept. 20, 1947 (dec. Mar. 1969). B.Mus. cum laude, U. Tex., 1943; postgrad. U. Houston, 1953-56, Lamar U., 1957-60. Music cons., fgn. program editor Voice of America, USIA, N.Y.C., 1944-46; advt. cons. fed. agys., San Antonio, 1946-47; tchr. music secondary schs., Houston, 1953-56; tchr. art Beaumont (Tex.) Ind. Sch. Dist., 1956-79; collages exhibited Galerie Paula Insel, N.Y.C., 1974-84, Ponce, P.R., 1976-79, 82, 84, 87; group show participant Ann. Am. Nat. Miniature Show, Laramie, Wyo. Recipient Circuit awards Tex. Fine Arts Assn., 1962-64, Invitational awards, 1964-65. Mem. Tex. Fine Arts Assn., Mu Phi Epsilon. Contbr. articles to Am.-German Rev. Address: 2303 Evalon Ave Beaumont TX 77702

FORNEY, VIRGINIA SUE, educational counselor; b. Little Rock, Sept. 15, 1925; d. Robert Millard and Susan Amanda (Ward) Tate; m. J.D. Mullen, Jr., Oct. 13, 1945 (div. 1966); children—Michael Dunn, Patricia Sue; m. Bill E. Forney, Apr. 29, 1967. Student Tex. State Coll. for Women, 1943-46; B.F.A., U. Okla., 1948; postgrad. Benedictine Heights Coll., Tulsa, 1957-58; M.Teaching Arts, Tulsa U., 1969; postgrad. Okla. State U., intermittently, 1969—. Cert. secondary tchr., sch. counselor, vis. sch. counselor, Okla. With Sta. WNAD, U. Okla., 1947-49; tchr. lang. arts Tulsa Bd. Edn., 1959-73; women's counselor Tulsa YWCA, 1980; vis. sch. counselor Tulsa County Supt. of Schs. Office, 1980—. Mem. budget com. United Way Greater Tulsa, 1980-86, edn. com. Planned Parenthood Greater Tulsa, 1980-86; mem. Tulsa County adv. council Okla. State U., 1983—; chairperson Tulsa Coalition for Parenting Edn., 1983-84; chairperson problems of youth study Tulsa Met. C. of C., 1984-85; mem. gen. bd. March of Dimes Greater Tulsa, 1985. Mem. Am. Assn. for Counseling and Devel., Internat. Assn. Pupil Personnel Workers (state bd. dirs. 1982-86), Okla. Assn. Family Resource Programs (regional v.p. 1982-86, state pres. 1986-87), Program Internat. Ednl. Exchange (community coordinator for Tulsa 1986—), LWV Okla. (chairperson juvenile justice study 1976-77). Democrat. Unitarian. Avocation: piano.

FORONDA, ELENA ISABEL, educator; b. N.Y.C., Jan. 15, 1947; d. Severino Deliso and LaVerne (Ibanez) F. BS in Music, Hunter Coll., CUNY, 1969, MA in Music Edn., 1971. Tchr. vocal music N.Y.C. Pub. Sch. System, 1970—; asst. dir. tchr. placement Hunter Coll., City U. N.Y., summers 1971-72; examination asst. N.Y.C. Pub. Sch. System Bd. Examiners, 1987—. Sponsor children in Philippines and El Salvador, World Vision Internat.; del. Asian Am. Women's Caucus, 1977; mem. Hunter Coll. choirs, 1968-69, 71; pianist, minister of music Ch. of The Holy Spirit, Bklyn., 1988—. Dist. winner Nat. Piano Playing Auditions, 1965; recipient N.Y. State permanent cert. Dept. Edn., 1971. Mem. Music Educators Nat. Conf., N.Y. State Sch. Music Assn., Amateur Chamber Players (Vienna, Va.), Internat. Platform Assn. Democrat. Episcopalian.

FORREST, ARLENA CORNELL, writer; b. St. Louis, Jan. 10, 1940; d. Robert and Jessie (Miller) Holmes; m. Lindbergh Cornell (div. 1976); children: Latonia, Lynn, Kimberly, Shedrick, Ingrid, Brett; m. Lamarr Forrest; 1 child, Ronald. BS in Pub. Adminstrn., U. So. Calif., 1989. With accounts receivable dept. Homer G. Phillips Hosp., St. Louis, 1970-72; psychologist asst. Family Children Services, St. Louis, 1972-74; bus driver So. Calif. Rapid Transit, 1978-85; freelance writer L.A.; freelance writer, L.A.; legal sec. St. Louis U.. Law Sch., 1972-76; with promotion and circulation dept. Media and Values mag., L.A., 1988-89. Author: The Grim Reaper, Something Old Something New. Active Jesse Jackson for President Campaign, L.A., 1984. Mem. Paralegal Assn., NAFE. Democrat. Roman Catholic. Home: 2020 Corning St #3 Los Angeles CA 90034

FORREST, BETH, insurance agency executive; b. Quincy, Mass., Aug. 13, 1960; d. Richard David and Elizabeth Anne (Veno) F. Student, Quincy Jr. Coll., 1978-79; BS, North Adams State Coll., Mass., 1982. Notary pub., Mass. Chem. svc. rep. Mahoney & Wright Ins. Agy., Weymouth, Mass., 1975-79; comml. svc. rep. Mahoney & Wright Ins. Agy., Dedham, Mass., 1983-85; mgr., v.p. Mahoney & Wright Ins. Agy., Wrentham, Mass., 1985—, mgrs. coun., 1989—. Mem. Young Agts. Mass. Democrat. Roman Catholic. Office: Mahoney & Wright Ins Agy 46 South St PO Box 929 Wrentham MA 02083

FORREST, MARION PATRICIA, marketing entrepreneur; b. Flushing, N.Y., Oct. 15, 1935; d. William and Beatrice (Giordano) Jones; m. John Fletcher, Jan. 19, 1952 (div. Jan. 1958); 1 child, John; m. Theodore Forrest, April 23, 1966 (div. 1970); children: Diane. Student, Pierce Jr. Coll., 1967-69. Model various TV and photo print, San Diego, 1961-62; mktg. Beverly Hills, Calif., 1972-74; real estate sales Jack Heller Realty, Beverly Hills, Calif., 1977-81; owner, pres. The Beverly Hills Estate, 1982-84; owner Forrest Prodns., Beverly Hills, 1982-84. Producer: film The Butterfly Garden, 1972, Culturally Speaking, 1986; originator, pub. audio tapes Culturally Speaking. Vol. social worker for Los Angeles homeless. Mem. Publisher's Mktg. Assn.

FORREST, SUZANNE SIMS, research historian; b. Pitts., Nov. 15, 1926; d. Clarence E. and Corinne Tousley (Landgraf) Sims; m. Stephen F. de Borhegyl, July 5, 1949 (dec. 1969); children: Ilona Maria, Stephen Ernest, Carl Robert, Christopher Francis; m. James T. Forrest, Sept. 16, 1978. BA, Ohio State U., 1948; postgrad., U. Okla., 1967; MS, U. Wis., Milw., 1973; PhD, U. Wy., 1987. Asst. to dir. Carnegie Institution Wash., Guatemala City, 1949-50, Inst. Nutrition for Cen. Am., Panama, Guatemala City, 1950-51; tchr. Milw. U. Sch., 1966-1973; coordinator, cont. edn. Alverno Coll., Milw.; dir. Albuquerque (N.M.) Museum, 1974-79; exec. dir. Wy. Council for the Humanities, Wy., 1979-81; curator Bradford Brinton Meml. Mus., Big Horn, Wy., 1988-90. Author: Ships, Shoals and Amphoras, 1961, Museums, 1962, Secret of the Sacred Lake, 1967, The Preservation of the Village: New Mexico's Hispanics and the New Deal, 1989. Home: PO Box 638 Placitas NM 87043

FORREST, VICTORIA KAUFMAN, journalist; b. N.Y.C., Mar. 23, 1944; d. Michael David and Elizabeth Sarah (Levy) Kaufman; m. David Mortimer Forrest, Apr. 30, 1936; 1 child, Heather Elizabeth. BS, 1964. Writer, profl. journalist, profl. model Atlanta, 1964-68; talent and mgmt. cons. Forrest and Co., Dunwoody, Ga., 1968—. Columnist, photojournalist Forsyth Daily News, Dean Image, Peachtree News, Lanier Life mag., 1987—; journalist Comments on Country, International Country, The Forum, The Crier; producer/host, entertainment writer, reviewer Georgia Speaks. Bd. dirs. scholarship fund com. Shallowford Hosp., Dunwoody, 1982-85. Mem. Internat. Photographer, Internat. Platform Assn., Am. Image News Svc., Am. Film Inst. Republican. Jewish. Home: 2396 Ledgewood Dr Dunwoody GA 30338

FORRESTER, ANN, nurse. AA in Nursing, Craven Community Coll., New Bern, N.C., 1977; LPN, Durham Tech. Inst., 1972. RN, N.C. Staff nurse ob-gyn., labor and delivery and nursery Carteret Gen. Hosp., Morehead City, N.C., 1977-78, head nurse, 1978-80; asst. dir. nursing, then dir. nursing Harborview Nursing Home, Morehead City, 1980-81; nursing supr. Calhoun County Med. Care Facility, Battle Creek, Mich., 1982-83; staff nurse, relief charge nurse med.-surg. unit Craven Regional Med. Ctr., New Bern, N.C., 1983-85, 87-88, relief nursing supr., 1984-85, asst. dir. nursing, 1985-87; asst. nurse mgr. orthopedics Britthaven Nursing Home, New Bern, N.C., 1988—; nursing supr. Britthaven Nursing Home, New Bern, 1987. Mem. Am. Nurses Assn., N.C. Nurses Assn. (cert.). Address: PO Box 2975 New Bern NC 28561

FORSHA, ANITA LOUISE, human service agency administrator; b. Williamsport, Pa., Aug. 26, 1950; d. Howard Monroe and June Eleanor (Turley) Fry; m. Frank Leroy Forsha, Nov. 15, 1974 (div. 1986). Cert., Mayer Sch. Fashion, N.Y.C., 1969; AA, Williamsport Community Coll., 1974; BA, Lycoming Coll., Williamsport, 1976; MBA, Bloomsburg (Pa.) U., 1985. Lic. nursing home adminstr., Pa. Asst. residence mgr., then residence mgr. Hope Enterprises, Inc. and Affiliates, Williamsport, 1973-76, caseworker, coord., 1977-78, dir. residential svcs., 1979-82, v.p. residential svcs., 1982-85, 86—, acting pres., 1988-89. Named Alumna of Yr. Williamsport Area Community Coll., 1989. Mem. Lycoming Assn. Retarded Citizens, Am. Mgmt. Assn., Leadership Lycoming, Pa. Assn. Rehab. Facilities, Williamsport Kiwanis Club, Williamsport Area Women's Network. Home: 1025 Rural Ave Williamsport PA 17701 Office: Hope Enterprises Inc 136 Catawissa Ave PO Box 1837 Williamsport PA 17703-1837

FORSTER, TERESA ANN, human factors engineer, consultant; b. Glen Falls, N.Y., June 3, 1961; d. Richard Lee and Leona (Sheehan) F. BA, Colby Coll., 1983; MS, Rensselaer Polytech. Inst., 1988. Adj. rsch. faculty Albany (N.Y.) Med. Coll., 1983-84; researcher Rensselaer Polytech. Inst., Troy, N.Y., 1983-84; human factors engring. intern IBM Corp., Kingston, N.Y., 1984-86; human factors engr. Data Gen. Corp., Westboro, Mass., 1986-89; human factors engring. cons. Herbst Lazar Bell, Inc., Wellesley, Mass., 1989—; mem. tech. staff TASC, Reading, Mass, 1989-90. Workshop instr. youth leadership program Toastmasters/Boy Scouts Am., Westboro, 1988. Recipient E. Parker Johnson award Colby Coll., 1983; Rensselaer Polytech. Inst. fellow, 1984-86. Mem. Human Factors Soc., Boston Computer Soc., Assn. for Computing Machinery, Data Gen. Ski Club (sec. Westboro chpt. 1987-88, pres. 1988-89), Toastmasters (v.p. mktg. com. Westboro chpt. 1988). Republican. Roman Catholic. Home: 800 Bulfinch Dr #510 Andover MA 01810

FORSTER, VIRGINIA L., facilities management and leasing consultant; b. Beverly, Mass., Feb. 20, 1953; d. Walter H. and Lucie Jacques F. AS in Bus. Mgmt., AA in Liberal Arts, Bunker Hill Community Coll., Boston, 1985. Gen. mgr. Hdqrs. Cos., Boston, 1984-87; corp. real estate, leasing and facilities mgr. Internat. Data Group, Framingham, Mass., 1987-90; facilities mgr. Nixdorf Computer Engring. Co., Cambridge, Mass., 1990—. Vol. Beverly Hosp., 1969-72, Big Sisters Am., 1983; pres. Fenway Rider's Com., 1978. Mem. Am. Mgmt. Assn., Internat. Facilities Mgmt. Assn., Am. Airlines Kiwi Club. Home: 115 W Squantum St #407 North Quincy MA 02171

FORSYTHE, ELIZABETH M., corp product development vice president; b. Pittsburg, Pa., Feb. 18, 1951; d. Norman F. and Mary Edith (Husted) Moody; m. David A. Forsythe, Sept. 16, 1978 (div. 1988); m. Brian F. Schnaly, Dec. 16, 1989. Studentt, Rumson Fair Haven, 1969; student, Vermont Coll., 1971, U. Arizona, 1973. Mgr. AGI Inc., N.Y., 1974-75; mktg. mgr. Germaine Monteil Cosmetics Inc., N.Y., 1976-79; product mgr. Estee Lauder Clinique Inc., N.Y., 1980-86; v.p. Revlon Inc., N.Y.; v.p. corp. product Estee Laude, N.Y., 1986--. Mem. Cosmitsi Exec. Women, Fashion Group. Home: 349 E 49th St New York NY 10007

FORSYTHE, MARY MACCORNACK, state legislator; b. Whitehall, Wis., May 23, 1920; d. Robert Lee and Gladys Fry MacCornack; m. Robert A. Forsythe, July 18, 1942; children: Robert A., Polly Forsythe Johnson, Jean Forsythe Peterson, Ann Forsythe Smith, Joan. MusB, St. Olaf Coll., 1942. Tchr., Viroqua, Wis., 1942-43, Whitehall, Wis., 1944-46; mem. Minn. Ho. of Reps., St. Paul, 1972-90, chmn. appropriations com., 1985-86. Mem. Guthrie Theater Found., 1973-80; mem. Minn. Commn. on Econ. Status of Women, 1976-79, Minn. News Council, 1979-86; trustee Fairview Riverside Hosp., 1980-86, Fairview-Southdale Hosp., 1986—; mem. exec. com. Seat Belt Coalition, Fairview Corp. Bd. Recipient Disting. Alumna award St. Olaf Coll., 1974; Dr. I. Michael Kuhn award Nat. Hemophilia Found., 1978; Outstanding Woman of Edina Bicentennial award, 1978; Community Service award Edina Optimists, 1982. Mem. Nat. Conf. State Legislators (vice chmn. human resources com. 1977-78), Rotary. Republican. Lutheran. Home: 5308 Brookview Ave Edina MN 55424 Office: State Office Bldg Saint Paul MN 55155

FORSYTHE, PATRICIA HAYS, foundation executive; b. Curtis, Ark.; d. John Chambers and Flora Jane (Eby) Hays; m. Kurt G. Pahl, Dec. 15, 1962 (div. Dec. 1980); children: Thomas Walter, Susan Clara; m. Robert E. Forsythe, June 20, 1981; 1 child, Nathaniel Ryan. BA, Calif. State U., Los Angeles, 1974; MSLS, U. So. Calif., 1976. Asst. to dir. devel. office The Assocs., Calif. Inst. Tech., Pasadena, 1978-81; exec. dir. Iowa City Pub. Library Found., 1982-89; dir. devel. Hoover Presdl. Libr. Assn., West Branch, Iowa, 1989—. Bd. dirs. Nat. Soc. Fund Raising Exec., Alexandria, Va., 1987-89, pres. ea. Iowa chpt., 1988-89. Recipient Outstanding Fund Raising Exec. award Ea. Iowa, 1990. Mem. LWV (editor 1985-87), ALA, Iowa City C. of C., Iowa Life Shares Assn. (bd. dirs.), Libr. Adminstrn. and Mgmt. Assn., I.C. & M. Club, Hancher Guild (audience devel. 1981-85, pres. 1985-86), Univ. Athletic Club, Rotary. Congregationalist. Home: 1806 E

Court St Iowa City IA 52245 Office: Hoover Presdl Libr Assn PO Box 696 West Branch IA 52358

FORT, CATHERINE FOARD, organizational development consultant; b. Orange, N.J., July 29, 1927; d. Henry Gilbert Foard and Catherine (Williams) Blackwell;m. James Frazier Fort, Sept. 30, 1950; children: James Frazier Jr., Keith Douglas, Catherine Williams Johnston. Student, St. Mary's Jr. Coll., 1944-45, U. Ga., 1945-47; BGS, George Washington U., 1978; MA in Applied Behavioral Sci., Whitworth Coll., 1983. Workshop instr. George Washington U., Washington, 1974-80; ind. cons. nationwide, 1970—; liason staff Intermet Sem., Washington, 1973-77; organizational cons. Congressional Clearinghouse on the Future, Washington, 1978-81; dir. Parish Intern Program Episcopal Diocese of Washington, 1978-82; coordinator Profl. Devel. Program Mid-Atlantic Assn. for Tng. and Consulting, Washington, 1976—, network cons., 1970—, vice chmn., bd. dirs., 1987—; network cons. The Alban Inst., Inc., Washington, 1977—. Contbr. articles to various newsletters and periodicals, 1978—. Pres. LWV, Alexandria, Va., 1955-56; del., Dem. State Conv. Lee Dist., Fairfax County, Va., 1981, 88, 89; sr. warden Immanuel-Episc.-Ch.-on-the-Hill, Alexandria, Va., 1984-85; mem. steering com. Assn. for Creative Change within Religious and Social Systems 1977-80, profl. devel. recognition com., 1980-84, recipient profl. recognition, 1978. Mem. Cert. Cons. Internat. (cert. 1985, profl. reviewer), Soc. Mayflower Descendants (N.C.), Nat. Tng. Labs. Inst. Home and Office: 5950 Wilton Road Alexandria VA 22310

FORT, DENISE CONLIN, clinical psychologist; b. N.Y.C., Dec. 21, 1943; d. John J. and Mary Agnes (Foley) Conlin; m. Matthew Ryan Kenney, Aug. 14, 1965 (div. 1974); children: Megan Ryan, Brendon Conlin; m. John Porter Fort, July 25, 1975. BSN, Georgetown U., 1964; MSN, Cath. U., 1967, MA, 1977, PhD in Clin. Psychology, 1984. Dir. nursing edn. Chestnut Lodge Hosp., Rockville, Md., 1967-68; instr. in psychsocial nursing U. Wash., Seattle, 1971-73; clin. intern Area A Community Mental Health Ctr., Washington, 1976-77; clin. psychology rsch. intern St. Elizabeth's Hosp., Washington, 1977-78; post doctoral fellow Sheppard Pratt Hosp., Towson, Md., 1982-83; staff psychologist Sheppard Pratt Hosp., Towson, 1983-85, Chestnut Lodge Hosp., Rockville, 1985—; candidate Washington (D.C.) Psychoanalytic Inst., 1988—; faculty Washington (D.C.) Sch. Psychiatry, 1986—. Contbr. chpts. to books. Mem. Am. Psychol. Assn., Am. Psychoanalytic Assn., Md. Psychol. Assn., D.C. Psychol. Assn., Nat. Register Health Svc. Providers in Psychology, Washington Psychologists for Study Psychoanalysis (v.p. 1989-90, pres. elect 1990—), Sigma Theta Tau. Democrat. Roman Catholic. Home: 4704 Linnean Ave NW Washington DC 20008 Office: Chestnut Lodge Hosp 500 W Montgomery Ave Rockville MD 20850

FORTENBERRY, BETTY DILLARD, educator; b. Russellville, Ala., Feb. 16, 1939; d. Charles Rainey and Lyda Thelma (Webb) Dillard; m. William Haynes Fortenberry, Aug. 15, 1975. BS, David Lipscomb Coll., Nashville, 1961; MS, Ala. A & M U., Normal, 1973. Tchr. bus. Mars Hill Bible Sch., Florence, Ala., 1961-67, Phillips High Sch., Bear Creek, Ala., 1967-71, Limestone Area Voc-Tech. Ctr., Athens, Ala., 1971-74, Huntsville (Ala.) City Schs., 1974—; part-time instr. Calhoun Community Coll., Huntsville, 1986—. Mem. Ala. Edn. Assn., Nat. Bus. Edn. Assn., So. Bus. Edn. Assn., AAUW. Mem. Ch. of Christ. Home: 7711 Oakridge Dr SE Huntsville AL 35802

FORTESCUE, MARGARET L., chemical company executive; b. Knoxville, Tenn., May 29, 1940; d. John Elliott and Frances Louise (Floyd) F.; m. Louis A. Zircher, Mar. 3, 1984; children: Louis A., Jennifer M. BS in Psychology, U. Tenn., 1963; MAT in Biology, Ga. State U., 1972; student, Pace U. Cert. secondary sci. tchr. Internat. sales mgr., bus. analyst, supr. sales edn. Union Carbide Corp., Danbury, Conn., div. mgr. customer svc.; market mgr. Union Carbides Biocide Bus., Sewickley, Pa. Pres. Queen Selwyn Condominium Assn., 1977. Mem. Inernat. Customer Svc. Assn., Women in Mgmt., Coun. Logistics Mgmt. Address: 6 Demar Dr Sewickley PA 15143 Office: PO Box 670 1 River Rd Bound Brook NJ 08805

FORTI, CORINNE ANN, corporate communications executive; b. N.Y.C., July 26, 1941; d. Wilbur Walter and Sylvia Joan (Charap) Bastian; B.A., CUNY, 1963; m. Joseph Donald Forti, Aug. 18, 1962 (dec.); 1 child, Raina. Adminstrv. asst. Ednl. Broadcasting Corp., 1963-65; adminstrv. asst. W.R. Grace & Co., N.Y.C., 1965-67, pub. relations rep., 1967-70, mgr. info. services, 1970-79, dir. info. services, 1980-86, dir. info. and advt., 1986-87; pres. Bastian-Forti Communications, 1988-89, Forti Communications Inc., 1989—; lectr. photography and graphics Am. Mgmt. Assn. Bd. dirs. YM/YWCA Day Care, Inc. Named to Acad. Women Achievers, YWCA, 1979; recipient citation award in communications Nat. Council of Women, 1979. Mem. Am. Women in Radio and TV, Chem. Mfrs. Assn., Am. Mgmt. Assn., Women Execs. in Pub. Relations. Republican. Roman Catholic. Home: 1246 Calle Yucca Thousand Oaks CA 91360

FORTNA, LIXI, member house of representatives; b. Austerlitz, Moravia, Czechoslovakia, July 1, 1913; came to U.S., 1939; d. Felix Redlich von Wezek and Marianne Loew; m. Peter Wenzel, May 26, 1936 (div. 1944); children: Victor, Rosi; m. Floyd W. Fortna, Nov. 13, 1947. LLD, U. Prague, Czechoslovakia, 1936. Office mgr. Sugarbush Ski Area, Warren, Vt., 1958-82; supr. U.S. War Damage Commn., Manila, 1947-50; mem. Ho. of Reps. State of Vt., Montpelier, 1982—; bd. dirs. Cen. Vt. Solid Waste Mgmt. Plan, Barr, Valley Med. Ctr., Waitsfield, Vt. Selectman Town Govt., Warren, pres. "Smart" Ski Municipalities Assn., Montpelier; chairperson Rep. Caucus. With USAF, 1950-54. Mem. Rotary. Roman Catholic. Home and Office: Box 31-1 Warren VT 05674

FORTNEY, DIANE ELINE OSBORN, accountant, financial analyst; b. Rockford, Ill., May 1, 1958; d. Lloyd William and Lila Jean Belle (Lidke) Osborn; m. Gary Michael Fortney, May 17, 1980. BS in Acctg., Mankato (Minn.) State U., 1980. CPA, Minn. 1984. Intern gen. acctg. PEP Svcs., Bloomington, Minn., 1979; asst. tax preparer J. Meyer Acctg., Roseville, Minn., 1979-80; staff acct. Samual Held & Assocs., St. Louis Park, Minn., 1980-82; head acct. Republic Telcom, Bloomington, 1982-84; consolidation acct. CTS Fabric-Tek, Inc., Eden Prairie, Minn., 1984-86; fin. analyst Micro Component Tech., Inc., Shoreview, Minn., 1986-90; pvt. practice acctg., Inver Grove Heights, Minn., 1983—. Tutor Mankato State U., 1978-79; treas. Salem Community Child Care Ctr., Inver Grove Heights, 1986—. Mem. AICPA, Minn. Soc. CPA's, Am. Bus. Women's Assn. (pres. Key Wakota charter chpt. 1988-89, Woman of Yr. 1987), Micro Component Tech., Inc., Employees Club (pres. 1987-90), IGH/SSP C. of C., Nat. Soc. Tax Profls. Methodist.

FORTNEY, JUDITH A., epidemiologist, researcher; b. Bebington, Cheshire, Eng., Jan. 28, 1938; came to U.S., 1959; d. Cyril and Jacqueline (Faulkner) Cooper; m. Lloyd R. Fortney, Apr. 15, 1961 (div. 1986); children: John, Emma. BS, London U., 1959; MS, U. Wis., 1963; PhD, Duke U., 1971. Various positions Family Health Internat., Research Triangle Park, N.C., 1974-87, dir. div. reproductive epidemiology, 1987—; cons. NIH, Bethesda, Md., 1985—, WHO, Geneva, 1985—; adj. assoc. prof. dept. epidemiology U. N.C. Sch. Pub. Health, Chapel Hill, S.C., 1986. Contbr. numerous articles to profl. jours. Fellow Am. Coll. Epidemiology; mem. Am. Pub. Health Assn., Soc. for Epidemiologic Rsch., Internat. Epidemiologic Assn. Democrat. Office: Family Health Internat Box 13950 Research Triangle Park NC 27709

FORTUNATO, ROBERTA ANN, educator; b. Bridgeport, Conn., Aug. 14, 1936; d. Daniel O'Connell and Alberta (Ross) Sulig; m. Frank, Apr. 6, 1958. BS in Math., Physics, Ohio Wesleyan U., 1958; MS in Energy Mgmt., N.Y. Inst. Tech., 1988. Research asst. Gruman Aerospace, Bethpage, N.Y., 1958--59; sub. tchr. Islip (N.Y.) Pub. Schs., 1969-70, Bay Shore (N.Y.) Pub. Sch., 1970--. Trustee, dp. mayor Village Brightwaters, N.Y., 1980—; sec. bd. Victims Info. Bur. Suffolk, Inc. Named Woman of Yr. Govt. Town of Islip, 1987. Mem. AAUW (pres. 1980-82, Renew Grant award 1985), Women on the Job. Episcopalian. Home: 551 Potter Blvd Brightwaters NY 11718

FORTUNE, LAUREN SUSAN PITZ, writer, editor, publications consultant; b. Cedar Rapids, Iowa, Oct. 5, 1948; d. Raymond Carl and Erna Sophia (Reihman) Pitz. Graphic Arts, Kirkwood Community Coll., Cedar Rapids, 1974; BA, Western Wash. State U., 1980; MA, Antioch U., 1986. Owner Plainswoman Bookstore, Iowa City, 1976-78, Iowa City Press, 1972-78; bus. mgr. Star Printing Co., Winchester, Mass., 1980-81; asst. to dean Kennedy Sch. Harvard U., Cambridge, Mass., 1981; conf. and procs. coord. Internat. Soc. for Optical Engrs., Bellingham, Wash., 1982-83; publs. coordinator U. Wash., Seattle, 1986-88; editor Microsoft Corp., Redmond, Wash., 1988-89; mng. editor Backbone: A Jour. of Women's Lit., Seattle, 1985-89; publs. cons. Antioch U. and U. Wash., Seattle, 1990—; mktg. cons. Antioch U., 1989-90; mng. editor President's Report, U. Wash., 1990; orgn. cons. Women's Funding Alliance, Seattle, 1985-86; co-founder Ain't I A Woman? newspaper, Iowa City, 1968-71, Iowa City Women's Press, 1971-78, The Plainswoman Bookstore, 1976-78. Vol., Nature Conservancy projects, Seattle, 1987—; vol. media corps Goodwill Games, Seattle, 1990; enumerator Census, U.S. Dept. Commerce, Seattle, 1990. Recipient award A Jour. Women's Lit., 1987, Best Lit. Mag. award, Backbone, 1987. Mem. Women in Communications, Inc., Soc. for Tech. Communications (2 awards 1989), Internat. Assn. Bus. Communicators, NOW. Democrat. Mem. Amana Church. Home: 4721 47th Ave NE Seattle WA 98105

FORTUNE, SUSAN ELIZABETH, sales executive; b. Augusta, Maine, July 20, 1964; d. Thomas T. and Ruth Ann (Pinkham) F. Student, Whitleands Coll., London, 1985-86; BS in Communication, U. So. Maine, 1986. Sales rep. Portland (Maine) Monthly mag., 1986-87; office mgr. Debt Mgmt. Svcs., Portland, 1987; sales exec. Seafood Internat. mag., London, 1987-88; U.S. sales rep. Seafood Internat. mag., Portland, 1988-90; sales mgr. N.Am. div. Seafood Internat. mag., Vancouver, B.C., Can., 1990—. Home and Office: Seafood Internat, 580 Hornnby St Ste 440, Vancouver, BC Canada V6C 3B6

FORWARD, DOROTHY ELIZABETH, legal assistant; b. Medford, Mass., Oct. 12, 1919; d. Roy Clifford and Julia (Lane) Hurd; student UCLA, 1964; m. Winston W. Forward, Sept. 29, 1942. Sec. nat. dir. fund raising ARC, Washington, 1943-46; legal sec. William W. Waters, Esq., Los Angeles, 1953-56; office mgr. Winston W. Forward, Ins. Adjuster, Arcadia, Calif., 1956-64; legal asst. John M. Podlech, Esq., Pasadena, 1964-79; dir. Calif. Probate Insts., Arcadia, 1970—; ind. probate legal asst., 1979—; condr. workshops in probate procedures, 1969—. Recipient ARC Meritorious Service award, 1945; named Legal Sec. of Yr., Pasadena Legal Secs. Assn., 1974, 75, 77; Freedom Through Edn. award, Pasadena Legal Secs. Assn., 1975. Mem. Nat. Assn. Legal Secs., Legal Secs. Inc., Calif. Assn. Legal Secs. (parliamentarian 1982-84), Pasadena Legal Secs. Assn. (pres. 1976-78), Los Angeles County Forum of Legal Secs. (chmn. 1978-80), Nat. Assn. Legal Assts. (charter). Contbg. author: Calif. Legal Secretary's Handbook, 1984, 85. Office: PO Box 311 Arcadia CA 91066-0311

FOSGATE HEGGLI, JULIE DENISE, marketing executive; b. El Paso, Tex., Feb. 17, 1954; d. Orville Edward and Patricia (Ward) Fosgate; m. Bjarne Heggli, June 20, 1980; children: Elise Mai, Kristin April. BA in Broadcasting, U. So. Calif., 1976, MA in Journalism, 1978. On-board editor Royal Viking Line, San Francisco, 1978-80; editor Stentor, Trondheim, Norway, 1981; staff Grunion Gazette, Long Beach, Calif., 1981; news editor Nine Network Australia, Los Angeles, 1981-82; editor South Coast Metro News, Costa Mesa, Calif., 1981-82; v.p. The Newport Group, Newport Beach, Calif., 1982-85; exec. editor Orange County This Month, Newport Beach, 1985; exec. dir. mktg. Gen. Group Cos., Harbor City, Calif., 1985-87; sr. v.p. mktg. Automax Corp., L.A., 1987-88, Gen. Group Internat., Harbor City, Calif., 1988—. Mem. NAFE, Phi Beta Kappa. Home: 225 Glendora Ave Long Beach CA 90803 Office: GGI 24428 S Vermont Ave Harbor City CA 90710

FOSLER, GAIL D., economist, government official; b. Los Angeles Dec. 7, 1947; d. Richard E. and Helen Elizabeth (O'Gorman) Deschner. A.B. in Econs. U. So. Calif., 1969; M.B.A. in Fin., NYU, 1972. Research analyst Chgo. Dept. Human Resources, 1970-72; research assoc. I.C.F., Inc., 1972-74; asst. v.p., economist Manufacturers Hanover, 1974-78; chief economist Senate Budget Com., Washington, from 1981, dir. and chief economist, from 1986; now chief economist The Conf. Bd., Inc., N.Y.C. Office: The Conference Bd Inc 845 3rd Ave New York NY 10022

FOSNAUGHT, PATRICIA S., art educator; b. Jersey City, Mar. 20, 1943; m. Robert A. Fosnaught, Nov. 26, 1964; 1 child, Nancy Fosnaught Mazeres. BFA, U. Dayton, 1969; M. Art Edn., Wright State U., 1973. Cert. art tchr. Art tchr. Dayton (Ohio) Pub. Schs., 1972-73; art tchr. Trotwood-Madison Schs., Trotwood, Ohio, 1973-78; instr. art Tenn. Tech. U., Cookeville, 1979—; artist in residence Tenn. Tech. U./Tenn. Arts Commn., 1989—; cons. art edn. several regional sch. systems. Photographs included in Soft Jewelry, 1977, (Nancy Howell-Koehler, author) Photo Art Processes, 1980; exhibited in many shows; contbr. articles on art and women's issues to local newspaper. Pres. AAUW, Cookeville, 1985-87; corresponding sec. Bus. & Profl. Women's Club, Cookeville, 1988-89, first v.p. 1990-91; bd. mem.-at-large Inner Wheel Club/Cookeville, 1989-90. Recipient Purchase award Tenn. Arts Com., Cookeville, 1981, Gov.'s award/arts State of Tenn., 1982. Mem. Cookeville Arts Coun. (grants com. chair 1990), Cumberland Art League, Upper Cumberland Regional Arts Coun. (charter bd. dirs. 1989-90). Home: RR 15 Box 82 Cookeville TN 38501

FOSS, MICHELLE MARIE, asbestos and insulation contractor; b. Bozeman, Mont., Apr. 4, 1964; d. Elmer Eugene and Katherine Jean (O'Connell) F. Grad. high sch., Culbertson, Mont.; student, Montana State U., 1982-83, 84. Rancher Gene Foss Ranch, Culbertson, Mont., 1975-85; cabinet maker helper Jensen's Custom Cabinets, Billings, Mont., 1986; hubworker United Parcel Svc., Billings, 1986; painter Kober Homes and Constrn., Billings, 1987; asbestos worker Envir-o-Tech dba Envir-o-Comply, Redmond, Wash., 1988—. Mem. Ctr. for Holistic Resource Mgmt. Office: Envirotech Envirocomply 2799 152nd Ave NE Redmond WA 98052

FOSS, PATRICIA HOWLAND, state legislator, insurance agency manager; b. Brattleboro, Vt., Nov. 29, 1925; d. Walter Marshall and Ruth E. (Kipp) Howland; m. James L. Foss, Sept 14, 1947. Student, U. N.H., 1943-44. Various positions to office mgr. Gen. Ins. Agy., Rochester, N.H., 1952-89; state legislator N.H. Gen. Ct., Concord, 1985-90. Bd. trustees Frisbie Meml. Hosp., Rochester; past pres. Frisbie Meml. Hosp. Aux., 1985, 86, 1st v.p., asst. treas, 1983, 84, mem. exec. bd., 1987-89. Mem. N.H. Order Women Legislators, Nat. Order Women Legislators. Republican. Home: HC 71 Box 12 Center Strafford NH 03815 Office: NH General Court Concord NH 03101

FOSSLAND, JOEANN JONES, advertising executive; b. Balt., Mar. 21, 1948; d. Milton Francis and Clementine (Bowen) Jones; m. Richard E. Yellott III, 1966 (div. 1970); children: Richard E. IV, Dawn Joeann; m. Robert Gerard Fossland Jr., Nov. 25, 1982. Student, Johns Hopkins U., 1966-67; cert. in real estate, Hogan's Sch. Real Estate, 1982. Owner Kobble Shop, Indiatlantic, Fla., 1968-70, Downstairs, Atlanta, 1971; seamstress Aspen (Colo.) Leather, 1972-75; owner Backporch Feather & Leather, Aspen and Tucson, 1975-81; regional mgr. Welcome Wagon, Tucson, 1982; realtor assoc. Tucson Realty & Trust, 1983-85; sales mgr. Home Illustrated mag., Tucson, 1985-87, gen. mgr., 1988-89; asst. pub. Phoenix/Scottsdale, Tricities, Tucson Homes Illustrated, Tucson, 1990—; pub. Tucson Deliver Ease, 1990—; speaker continuing edn. Lindquist Seminars, Tucson, 1987—; cons. Albuquerque Homes Illustrated, 1987—. Designer leather goods (Tucson Mus. Art award 1978, Crested Butte Art Fair Best of Show award 1980); pub. Tucson Deliverease, 1990—. Mem. Tucson Met. Conv. and Visitors Bur.; notary pub. State of Ariz., 1984-88; voter registrar Recorder's Office City of Tucson, 1985—; bd. dirs. Hearth Found., Tucson, 1987—, Ariz. Integrated Residential & Ednl. Svcs., Inc., 1989—; mem. The Hunger Project, The Holiday Project. Mem. NAFE, Women's Coun. Realtors (treas. Tucson chpt. 1987, sec. 1988, Affiliate of Quarter 1986, Leadership Tng. Grad. designation 1989), Tucson Bd. Realtors (Affiliate of Yr. 1986), Tucson C. of C., Rotary. Democrat. Presbyterian. Office: Homes Illustrated 426 E 7th St Tucson AZ 85705

FOSSUM, DONNA L., lawyer; b. Cedar Rapids, Iowa, Feb. 5, 1949; d. Donald E. and Esther O. (Sondreal) F. BA, U. N.Mex., 1971; MA, SUNY, Buffalo, 1974, JD, 1975, PhD, 1981. Bar: N.Y. 1976, Ill. 1978., D.C. 1978. Research atty. Am. Bar Found., Chgo., 1975-80; counsel Com. on Govt. Ops., U.S. Ho. of Reps., Washington, 1981-88; dep. assoc. adminstr. Office Fed. Procurement Policy Office of the President, Washington, 1988-89; atty. Dilworth, Paxson, Kalish & Kauffman, Washington, 1989—; adv. com. legal advocacy fund AAUW, Washington, 1981—. Contbr. articles to profl. jours., numerous speeches. Mem. planning commn. City of Alexandria, Va., 1990—. Mem. ABA (vice chair legis. coordinating com. pub. contract law sect. 1990—), U. N.Mex. Alumni Assn. (pres. Washington chpt. 1984-90), Phi Beta Kappa, Phi Kappa Phi.

FOSSUM, THERESA WELCH, veterinary medicine educator, surgery consultant; b. Douglas, Wyo., July 21, 1957; d. David Earl Welch and Marian C. (Sump) Smith. BS in Agr. with honors, U. Idaho, 1978; DVM cum laude, Wash. State U., 1982; MS in Vet. Anatomy, Ohio State U., 1986; postgrad. in vet. microbi, Tex. A&M U., 1987—. Diplomate Am. Coll. Vet. Surgeons. Medicine and surgery intern Santa Cruz (Calif.) Vet. Hosp., 1982-83; resident Coll. Vet. Medicine, Ohio State U., Columbus, 1983-86, asst. prof., 1986-87; asst. prof. small animal medicine and sugery Tex. A&M U., College Station, 1987—; presenter in field. Contbr. articles to vet. jours., chpts. to books. Potlatch Forest Inc. scholarship, 1975, 76, Delta Delta Delta, Jacob Monson and bookstore scholar, U. Idaho, 1976. Mem. Am. Coll. Vet. Surgeons, AVMA, Am. Animal Hosp. Assn., Vet. Cancer Soc., Wash. State Vet. Med. Assn., Calif. Vet. Med. Assn., Am. Vet. Laser Soc., Phi Zeta, Alpha Zeta. Home: 9101 Riverstone Ct College Station TX 77845 Office: Tex A&M U University Dr College Station TX 77843

FOSTER, BOBBIE DORE, newspaper editor; b. Abbeville, La., Nov. 28, 1938; d. Morris Allen and Mary Ann (Fontenot) Doré; m. Bernard Vance, July 28, 1979. Student, U. Washington, 1971-72, Western Washington State U., 1975-76, Portland State U., 1977-78; BA, U. Portland, 1989. Sec., receptionist Office of Publs. U. Washington, Seattle, 1971-72; exec. sec. Seattle Pub. Schs., 1972-77; office mgr. The Skanner Newspaper, Portland, Oreg., 1977-78, copy editor, 1978-79, mng. editor, 1979-84, editor, 1984—; coord. Sch. Partnership Program: Journalism, Portland, 1990—. Bd. dirs. ARC Oregon Trail chpt., Portland, 1985-88, State Scholarship Commn., Eugene, Oreg., 1988-91, Community Action Agy., Portland, 1985-86; mem. Oreg. Peace Inst., 1988-89, Urban League Adv. Com., Portland, 1982-83. Recipient Edn. and Leadership in Politics, Edn. and Community Svc. award Oreg. Women's Polit. Caucus, Women of Color Task Force, Salem, Oreg., 1979, Support of Coop. Edn. Program award Portland Community Coll., 1985, Community Svc. award Black Women's Gathering, Portland, 1987, Svc. award ARC, Portland, 1988, 2nd pl. best editorial West Coast Black Pubs. Assn., Bakersfield, Calif., 1989. Mem. Women in Communications (v.p. membership 1984-85, v.p. profl. devel. 1988-89, Outstanding Community Svc. award 1988), Black Cath. Lay Caucus (del. nat. black Cath. congress 1988), Soc. Profl. Journalists (co-chair minority mentor program 1989—), Rotary, Albina Club. Roman Catholic. Office: The Skanner Group 2337 N Williams Ave PO Box 5455 Portland OR 97228

FOSTER, CATHERINE RIERSON, manufacturing company executive; b. Balt., Mar. 14, 1935; d. William Harman and Ella Fredericka (Magsamen) Rierson; m. Morgan Lawrence Foster, Nov. 17, 1957 (dec. Jan. 1990); children: Diana Kay, Susan Ann, Morgan Lawrence, Heather Lynne. Student, Balt. City Coll., 1955, Johns Hopkins U., 1956-57, Glendale Coll., 1962-63. Sec. Martin Co., Balt., 1956-57, adminstrv. sec., 1957-58; v.p., corp. sec. Fostermation, Inc., Meadville, Pa., 1971-90, pres., chmn. bd., 1990—, also bd. dirs.; mem. adv. com. Vocat./Tech. Sch., Meadville, 1982-86. Pres. La Crescents, La Crescenta, Calif., 1962; active City Hosp. Aux., Meadville, 1969-86, Rep. Women's Workshop, Glendale, Calif., 1966-68, Com. to Elect Ronald Reagan, Glendale, 1967; bd. dirs. YWCA, Meadville, 1988-89, also chmn. fin. com., 1988-89. Mem. DAR (chpt. regent 1989—), NAFE, Order Eastern Star. Lutheran. Home: 1121 Lakemont Dr Meadville PA 16335 Office: Fostermation Inc 200 Valleyview Dr Meadville PA 16335

FOSTER, ELAINE ELIZABETH, art educator; b. Lawrence, Mass., Jan. 13, 1934; d. Ernest Webster and Elizabeth Josephine (Dubuc) F. Cert., Sch. of the Worcester Art Mus., 1955; BA, Clark U., 1957, MA, 1961; profl. diploma, Columbia U., 1965, EdD, 1970. Supr. art Auburn (Mass.) Elem. Schs., 1957-59; tchr. art Auburn Pub. Jr. High Sch., 1959-61, Auburn Pub. High Sch., 1961-65; from asst. prof. to prof. art Jersey City State Coll., 1966—. Author: Collage Film Guide, Crayon Film Guide, 1966, A Great School of Fine Arts in N.Y.C.: A Study of the Development of Art at Columbia University (1860-1914), 1970; lectr. The Brain and Art, 1975—; group shows include 25 exhbns. in N.E.; patentee for tie brooch design, 1988, 89. Mem. Nat. Art Edn. Assn., Univ. Council for Art Edn. (pres. 1980-82), Am. Assn. Univ. Profs. (pres. local chpt. 1978-80), Soc. N.Am. Goldsmiths, Am. Craft Council, Dromenon/The Possible Soc. in N.Y. Avc.

FOSTER, GOLDA MARIE, publishing and marketing consultant; b. San Angelo, Tex., Apr. 22, 1948; d. Horace Martin and Golda Marie (Triplett) F. Student, Angelo State U., 1969. News reporter San Angelo Standard-Times, 1966-67; fashion illustrator Hemphill-Wells, San Angelo, 1968-71; recreational vehicle sales mgr. Jim Bass Ford, San Angelo, 1972-74; mag. editor Anchor Pub. Co., San Angelo, 1974-75; city mgr. Nat. Car Rental, San Angelo and Abilene, Tex., 1975-82; adminstr. KNA Oilfield Svcs., Inc., Kenai, Alaska, 1983-84; prodn. mgr. Womack-Kleypas-Gette Advt., San Angelo, 1985-86; owner Hist. Mktg. & Resources, San Angelo, 1986—; owner Foster Publs. Group, San Angelo, 1987—; bd. dirs. Tricom Assn. Advt. Fedn., San Angelo. Editor: Tom Green County History, 1987-88, Founders & Settlers of Heart of Texas, 1987-88. Rep. precinct chmn. Taylor County, Abilene, 1982; pres. Confederate Air Force Cols. Ladies, Abilene, 1981-82; friend Ft. Concho Mus., San Angelo Mus. Fine Arts; mem. Abilene Centennial Com., 1981; sec., chmn. pubs. Tom Green County Hist. Commn., 1989-91, San Angelo, 1986—; co-chmn. San Angelo Incorporation Centennial, 1989; bd. dirs. Downtown San Angelo Assn., 1987—, Tom Green County Hist. Preservation League, 1987—. Recipient Addy award. Mem. Tex. State Hist. Assn., Tex. Hist. Found., Hist. San Angelo, Hist. Orient-Santa Fe Depot, Inc. (bd. dir. 1989—), Nat. Trust for Hist. Preservation, Bus. and Profl. Women's Club, West Tex. Hist. Assn., Tom Green County Hist. Soc., United Daus. of Confederacy, Colonial Dames 17th Century (sec. 1984—, registrar 1987—), Kiwanis. Episcopalian. Home: 1115 N Van Buren San Angelo TX 76901 Office: Hist Mktg & Resources PO Box 3243 San Angelo TX 76902

FOSTER, IRENE PARKS, librarian; b. Chgo., Sept. 30, 1927; d. Ira Dean and Mary Crenshaw (Bowles) Parks; 1 child, Robbe Lynn Henderson. PhD, Harold Washington Coll., 1988. Prodn. editor Ency. Brittannica, Chgo., 1963-72, graphics project dir., 1972-74, prodn. specialist, 1975-76, coord. editor, 1976-77; prodn. dir. MacMillan Pub. Co., N.Y.C., 1975; asst. prodn. mgr. AMA, Chgo., 1977-85, mktg. officer, 1985-86, fulfillment officer, 1986-88, fulfillment and videotape libr., 1988—; lectr. univs., Ill., Mich. and Wis., 1976; interaction mgmt. program, Chgo., 1982-83; small bus. workshops, Chgo., 1985. Contbr. poems, articles to jours. Bd. dirs. Weisman scholarship, Chgo. Communications, 1989—; active Dem. party, Chgo., 1945-75, ofcl. hostess Dem. Presdl. Campaign, Chgo., 1952. Named 1990 Golden Poet, World of Poetry. Mem. Advt. Print Prodn. Club (bd. dirs. 1988-90). Roman Catholic. Office: Am Med Assn 515 N State St Chicago IL 60610

FOSTER, JODIE (ALICIA CHRISTIAN FOSTER), actress; b. Los Angeles, Nov. 19, 1962; d. Lucius and Evelyn (Almond) F. BA in Lit. magna cum laude, Yale U., 1985. Acting debut in TV show Mayberry, R.F.D, 1969; numerous other TV appearances including My Three Sons, The Courtship of Eddie's Father, Gunsmoke, Bonanza, Paper Moon, 1974-75; TV spl. The Secret Life of T.K. Dearing, 1975; TV movies Rookie of the Year, Smile, Jenny, You're Dead; motion picture appearances Napoleon and Samantha, 1972, Menace of the Mountain, One Little Indian, 1973, Tom Sawyer, 1973, Kansas City Bomber, 1972, Alice Doesn't Live Here Any More, 1975, Taxi Driver, 1976 (Acad. award nominee Best Supporting Actress), Echoes of a Summer, 1976, Bugsy Malone, 1976, Freaky Friday, 1976, The Little Girl Who Lives Down the Lane, 1977, Candleshoe, 1977, Foxes, 1980, Carny, 1980, Hotel New Hampshire, 1984, The Blood of Others, 1984, Siesta, 1986, Five Corners, 1986, Reckless Endangerment, Stealing Home, 1988, The Accused, 1988 (Academy award Best Actress, 1989), The Silence of the Lambs, 1990. Recipient Golden Globe award, 1989. Office: care ICM 8899 Beverly Blvd Los Angeles CA 90048*

FOSTER, JOYCE GERALDINE, research biochemist; b. Farmville, Va., Oct. 10, 1951; d. James Monroe and Fannie Louise (Torrence) F. BS, Longwood Coll., 1974; MS, Va. Poly. Inst. and State U., 1976; PhD, 1979.

Grad. teaching/rsch. asst. dept. biochemistry and nutrition Va. Poly. Inst. and State U., Blacksburg, 1974-79, rsch. assoc. dept. biochemistry and nutrition, 1979; rsch. assoc. dept. horticulture U. Wis., Madison, 1979-80; rsch. assoc. dept. botany Wash. State U., Pullman, 1981; agrl. scientist div. plant and soil sci. W.Va. U., Morgantown, 1982; rsch. biochemist U.S. Dept. Agr. Appalachian Soil and Water Conservation Rsch. Lab., Beckley, W.Va., 1982—, acting lab. dir., 1986—; adj. asst. prof. dept. plant pathology physiology and weed sci. Va. Poly. Inst. and State U., 1983—. Contbr. articles to profl. jours. Mem. alumni bd. dirs. Longwood Coll., 1983-85; mem. rev. com. W.Va. Edn. Fund Grant Applications; ptnr. W.Va. Partnership in Edn. Program; mem. futures com. Beckley Coll. Mem. editorial bd. Plant Physiology, Jour. Agrl. and Food Chemistry. Recipient Outstanding Alumni Achievement award Va. Poly. Inst. and State U., 1986, W.Va. Outstanding Achievement in Sci. award, 1986, cert. of merit USDA-Agrl. Rsch. Svc., 1986, 87, Rsch. Leadership award, 1987, 88, Rsch. Accomplishments award, 1989, Community Svc. and Profl. Achievement award NOW, 1989, Alumni Achievement award Longwood Coll., 1989; Longwood Coll. Acad. Achievement scholar, 1974, Mary White Cox Coll. scholar, 1970; USDA Apprenticeship grantee, 1985-88, Rsch. Assoc. grantee, 1986-88, 88-90. Mem. Am. Chem. Soc. (James Lewis Howe Sr. chemistry award Blueridge sect.), Am. Soc. Plant Physiologists (sec.-treas. so. sect. 1989-90, v.p. 1990-91), Japanese Soc. Plant Physiologists, Am. Inst. Biol. Scis., Am. Soc. Agronomy, Crop Sci. Soc. Am., Plant Growth Regulator Soc. Am., AAAS, Am. Soc. for Biochemistry and Molecular Biology, Scandinavian Soc. Plant Physiology, Japan Soc. for Bioscience, Biotechnology and Agrochemistry, Phytochem. Soc. N. Am., Va. Acad. Sci. (J. Shelton Horsely rsch. award 1982), AAUW (pres. Beckley br. 1989-91, Sci. Achievement award 1987), Sigma Xi, Phi Lambda Upsilon, Phi Sigma, Phi Tau Sigma, Gamma Sigma Delta, Phi Kappa Phi (v.p. Longwood Coll. chpt. 1973-74), Omicron Delta Kappa, Kappa Delta Pi, Alpha Lambda Delta (Sr. acad. award 1974). Home: 109 Walnutview Dr Beaver WV 25813-9753 Office: PO Box 867 Airport Rd Beckley WV 25802-0867

FOSTER, KATHLEEN HURLEY, nursing administrator; b. Cambridge, Md., July 6, 1949; d. Donald Lake and Betty Lindburg (Bradshaw) Hurley; m. Joseph Taylor Foster III, Aug. 22, 1970; children: Amy, Julie. BSN, U. Md., Balt., 1978; MS in Nursing, U. Md., 1981; diploma, MacQueen Gibbs Willis Sch., 1970. RN, Md. Staff nurse Ea. Shore Hosp. Ctr., Cambridge, 1970-71, asst. head nurse, 1971-73, instr. nursing, 1973-80; adminstr. dir. Talbot County Mental Health Clinic, Easton, Md., 1980-81, acting dep. health officer, 1987-89, dir. community health nursing, 1981-87, 89—; sec. Talbot Hospice Found., 1981—. Pres. Talbot County Health Planning, 1976-78; chmn. Talbot County AIDS Task Force, 1987—. Mem. ANA, APHA, Md. Coun. Community Health Nursing Dirs. (chmn. 1989), Sigma Theta Tau. Democrat. Roman Catholic. Home: RR 5 Box 743 Easton MD 21601 Office: Talbot County Health Dept PO Box 480 100 S Hanson Easton MD 21601

FOSTER, KATHRYN CAREY, gemologist; b. Circleville, Ohio, July 24, 1955; d. Seymour Robinson and Barbara (Carey) F. AS, Bennett Coll., Millbrook, N.Y., 1975; BS in Geology, U. Miami, 1978; grad., Gemological Inst. Am., Santa Monica, Calif., 1985. Saleswoman, appraiser Minecraft, Boca Raton, Fla., 1981-83, J.B. Robinson Jewelers, Boynton Beach, Fla., 1986, Regent, Boca Raton, 1987, Moore's Jewelry, Wilton Manors, Fla., 1987; saleswoman, appraiser Carroll's Jewelers, Coral Gables, Fla., 1980, Ft. Lauderdale, Fla., 1983-85, 87—. Mem. Am. Gem Soc. (cert.), Am. Gem Soc. Alumni Assn., Miami Mineral and Lapidary Guild (faceting tchr.), Micromounters Nat. Capital Area (sec.), Micromount Group of Miami Mus. Sci. (speaker), No. Va. Mineral Club, Mineral Soc. D.C., Gemological Inst. Am. Alumni Assn. Republican. Presbyterian. Home: 114 Mayfair Ln Boynton Beach FL 33462 Office: PO Box 562 Boynton Beach FL 33425-0562

FOSTER, LAVERNE ARNETT, real estate broker; b. Snyder, Tex., June 24, 1930; d. Walter Franklin and Pearl Frances (Whatley) Arnett; m. Ralph Foster, 1949 (div. 1977). Sec. Arnett-Foster Oil Co., Snyder, 1950-52, Foster Testers Inc., Snyder, 1952-56; realtor, salesman Nova Roberts Realtors, Midland, Tex., 1971, Bunnie Kent Gallery of Homes, Midland, 1971-75; v.p., sec. Foster Testers Inc., Midland, 1975-77; realtor, broker LaVerne Foster, Realtors, Midland, 1975—. Chmn. Midland Community Concerts, 1979-83; sec. Midland County Rep., 1984, 1st v.p., 1985, pres., 1986; dir. 25th Senatorial dist. Tex. Fedn. Rep. Women, 1988-89, treas., 1990—. Mem. Midland Bd. Realtors, Tex. Assn. Realtors, Nat. Assn. Realtors, Fine Arts (sec. 1979, v.p. 1980, pres. 1981, Midland Arts Assn. (treas. 1987), Midland C. of C. (M Squad). Mem. Ch. of Christ. Mailing Address: PO Box 8336 Midland TX 79708 Home: 4915 Tattenham Corner Midland TX 79707

FOSTER, MARTHA TYAHLA, educational administrator; b. Coaldale, Pa., Apr. 22, 1955; d. Stephen and Frances (Solomon) Tyahla; m. David Marion Foster, Jan. 3, 1981. B.A., U. Va., 1977, M.Ed., 1981, Ed.S., 1981. Legis. asst. U.S. Ho. of Reps., Washington, 1977-79; asst. dean summer session U. Va., Charlottesville, 1981; program cons. campus activities U. Houston, 1981; coordinator student affairs Capitol Inst. Tech., Kensington, Md., 1982-83, asst. dean students, Laurel, Md., 1983-84, assoc. dean students, 1984-86, dean students, 1986-87; bd. dirs. Curry Sch. Edn. Found. U. Va. Mem. Arlington County Commn. on Status of Women, 1985-88. Named Woman of Yr. Bus. and Profl. Women's Club, Vienna, Va., 1986 . Mem. Va. Counselors Assn. Methodist. Lodge: Order of Eastern Star (worthy matron 1988-89).

FOSTER, MELISSA See **MCCONNELL, MELISSA**

FOSTER, MICHELE CONSIGLI, business executive; b. N.Y.C., Jan. 26, 1956; d. Joseph A. and Rita Ann (Balcar) Consigli; m. Ernie Gudmund Foster, Dec. 18, 1982. BS, U. No. Colo., 1978. Sr. terr. mgr. Johnson and Johnson, New Brunswick, N.J.; div. mgr. Whitehall Labs., N.Y.C.; regional mgr. Colgate Palmolive, Chaska, Minn.; bus. devel. mgr. Carter-Wallace Inc., N.Y.C. Bd. dirs. Columbia River coun. Girl Scouts U.S. Address: 15703 NE 26th St Vancouver WA 98684

FOSTER, NANCY HASTON, columnist, author; b. Austin, Tex., June 7; d. Arch B. and Verlea (Jones) H.; m. Joe D. Foster Jr. (div.). BJ, U. Tex., BA in Sociology. Writer, pub. rels. dept. Trinity U., San Antonio, Tex.; social worker pub. welfare dept. State of La., Lafayette; instr. sociology U. Tex., Austin; columnist San Antonio Light, 1982-83, San Antonio Express-News, 1989—; freelance writer, 1977—. Co-author: San Antonio, a Texas Monthly Guidebook, 1983, rev. edit., 1989; author: The Alamo and Other Texas Missions to Remember, 1984; contbg. editor, writer: Texas, Fodor's Travel Guides, 1985, rev. edit., 1990, Fodor's American Cities, 1986, rev. edit., 1988, Texas, a Texas Monthly Guidebook, 1989; contbr. articles to popular mags. Mem. Women in Communications, Phi Beta Kappa. Home and Office: 412 Cloverleaf #3 San Antonio TX 78209

FOSTER, PAULINE ADELE, research analyst; b. Sunderland, England, Feb. 25, 1950; d. Ambrose Lindsley and FLorence (Slack) Phillipson; m. Keith Foster, July 10, 1971 (div. 1974). BA (with honors), U. Warwick, Coventry, England, 1983; PhD, U. Warwick, 1990. Lectr. Monkwearmouth Coll., Sunderland, Eng., 1974-80; rsch. officer Sheffield (Eng.) City Poly., 1983-84; lectr. Lincoln (Eng.) Coll. Technology, 1984-85; rsch. analyst U. Wis.-Milw., 1990—. Mem. Brit. Sociol. Assn., Am. Sociol. Assn., Indsl. Relations Rsch. Assn. Home: 508 S Towne Dr #Y209 S South Milwaukee WI 53172

FOSTER, PEARL DELPHINE, physician, educator; b. N.Y.C., Oct. 23, 1922; d. Isabel A. Courtney; m. Charles C. Hunt, June 25, 1950; children—Joanne Y., Patrice M. B.S., Queens Coll., 1943; M.D., Howard U., 1948; M.P.A., C.W. Post Coll., 1980. Intern, Harlem Hosp., N.Y.C., 1948-49, resident, 1950-53; resident Freedmen's Hosp., Washington, 1949-50; tchr. internal medicine Harlem Hosp. Sch. Nursing, 1955-65; practice medicine specializing in internal medicine, St. Albans, N.Y., 1953—; assoc. in clin. medicine Columbia U., 1970; chmn. utilization and quality rev. com., mem. med. bd. Harlem Hosp.; mem. exec. com. Hillcrest Gen. Hosp., Flushing, N.Y.; mem. med. bd. St. Joseph Hosp. Recipient citation Harlem Hosp., 1958; Community Service award Nat. Urban Coalition, 1970-73. Mem. Am. Coll. Quality Assurance and Utilization Rev. Physicians, AMA (recipient Physicians Recognition award), N.Y. Heart Assn., Am. Geriatric Soc., Am. Pub. Health Assn., N.Y. State Pub. Health Assn., N.Y. Acad. Sci., N.Y. State Soc. Internal Medicine, Am. Bd. Quality Assurance and Utilization Rev. (v.p. 1980-85), Kappa Pi, Pi Alpha Alpha. Roman Catholic. Clubs: Carats, Coalition of 100 Black Women. Office: 200 15 Linden Blvd Saint Albans NY 11412

FOSTER, ROYCE PORTER, general contracting company executive; b. Wilkes County, Dec. 12, 1928; d. Lee Roy and Vassie Beatrice (Byrd) Porter; m. Roy George Foster, June 20, 1953; children—Karen Elizabeth, Melanie Ann, John Andrew. Student Draughon's Bus. Coll., 1945-46. Cert. ceramics tchr. Clk.-typist Coble Dairies, Wilkesboro, N.C., 1946-47; bookkeeper Lineberry Foundry, North Wilkesboro, N.C., 1947-53; bookkeeper Nat. Meml. Park, Falls Church, Va., 1953; bookkeeper T.A. Talley & Son, Richmond, Va., 1955-56; bookkeeper Q.M. Tomlinson, Inc., Roanoke, Va., 1965-82, exec. v.p., 1982—. Mem. adv. bd. Va. Western Community Coll., Roanoke, 1980-81, Youth Svcs., Total Action Against Poverty. Mem. Nat. Assn. Women in Constrn. (pres. 1979-81), Am. Bus. Women's Assn., Am. Mgmt. Assn., Nat. Assn. Female Execs. Democrat. Presbyterian. Office: QM Tomlinson Inc 2001 Centre Ave NW Roanoke VA 24022

FOSTER, RUTH MARY, business administrator; b. Little Rock, Jan. 11, 1927; d. William Crosby and Frances Louise (Doering) Shaw; m. Luther A. Foster, Sept. 8, 1946 (dec. Dec. 1980); children: William Lee, Robert Lynn. Grad. high sch., Long Beach, Calif. Sr. hostess Mon's Food Host of Coast, Long Beach, 1945-46; dental asst., office mgr. Dr. Wilfred H. Allen, Opportunity, Wash., 1946-47; dental asst., bus. asst. Dr. H. Erdahl, Long Beach, 1948-50; office mgr. Dr. B.B. Blough, Spokane, Wash., 1950-52; bus. mgr. Henry G. Kolsrud, D.D.S., P.S., Spokane, 1958—, Garland Dental Bldg., Spokane, 1958—. Sustaining mem. Spokane Symphony Orch. Mem. Nat. Assn. Dental Assts., Disabled Am. Vets. Aux., Spokane's Lilac City Bus. and Profl. Women (treas.), Nat. Alliance Mentally Ill., Wash. Alliance Mentally Ill, Spokand Alliance Mentally Ill, Internat. Platform Assn., Spokane Club, Credit Women's Breakfast Club. Democrat. Mem. First Christian Ch. Office: Henry G Kolsrud DDS PS 3718 N Monroe St Spokane WA 99205

FOSTER, SHARON LEE, psychology educator; b. Scranton, Pa., Mar. 3, 1949; d. Ralph Keeler and Virginia Ann (Bundy) F.; m. Thomas Donald Barton, July 26, 1980. BA, Stanford U., 1971; PhD, SUNY, Stony Brook, 1978. Lic. psychologist, W.Va. Asst. prof. psychology W.Va. U., Morgantown, 1978-83, assoc. prof. psychology, 1983-88, prof. psychology, 1988-89; prof. U.S. Internat. U., San Diego, 1989-90, Calif. Sch. of Profl. Psychology, 1990—; vis. asst. prof. W.Va. U., 1977-78; mem. bd. examiners of psychologists State of W.Va., 1983-89. Author: (with others) Negotiating Parent-Adolescent Conflict, 1989; assoc. editor Behavioral Assessment; mem. editorial bd. Psychol. Assessment, Jour. of Cons. and Clin. Psychology, Behavior Therapy Behavior Modification; contbr. articles to profl. jours. Recipient Outstanding Researcher award Coll. of Arts and Scis., W.Va. U., 1987. Mem. Assn. for Advancement of Behavior Therapy, Am. Psychol. Assn., Assn. for Behavior Analysis, Brit. Assn. for Behavioral Psychotherapy. Office: Calif Sch of Profl Psychology 6212 Farris Sq San Diego CA 92116

FOSTER, SUSAN CHANDLER, management consultant; b. Montgomery, Ala., Sept. 21, 1949; d. Horace Leonard and Mary Charles (Howell) Chandler; m. George E. Shirley, Dec. 1, 1967 (div. 1978); 1 child, Scott. BS, Troy State U., 1978; MS, U. So. Calif., Los Angeles, 1983. Chief force devel. Hdqrs. 60th Ordnance Group, Zweibrucken, Fed. Republic Germany, 1981-84; staff asst. Sec. of Army, Arlington, Va., 1984-85; program analyst Dep. Chief of Staff Logistics, Arlington, 1985-86; dept. mgr. CACI, Inc., Arlington, 1986—. U.S. Army Legis fellow, 1987.

FOSTER, SUSAN WELTHA, crochet magazine editor; b. Concord, N.H., Dec. 27, 1946; d. Albert Lewis and Gertrude Weltha (Astles) Hankins; m. Francis J. Andrews III, May 14, 1966 (div. 1977); children: Leah Michelle, James Todd; m. Ronald Arthur Foster, July 21, 1990. Diploma, Concord Hosp. Sch. Nursing, 1969; BA summa cum laude, New Eng. Coll., 1980. Staff nurse New Eng. Coll., Henniker, N.H., 1972-85; freelance writer, 1975-80; reporter Concord Monitor, 1978-79; editor House of White Birches, Berne, Ind., 1979—. Contbr. articvles to Am. Jour. Nursing, Yankee mag., N.H. Profiles mag.; contbr. fiction to Lit. Jour. Vol. blood drives ARC, Henniker, blood pressure screenings, Henniker; activist Citizens Against Nuclear Dump, 1988. Mem. Am. Creative Craft Industries, Soc. Craft Designers, U.S. Golf Assn., N.H. Women's Golf Assn., Cousteau Soc., Duston Country Club Assn. (sec. 1990, ladies club champion 1989). Home and Office: House of White Birches 6 Pearl St PO Box 776 Henniker NH 03242

FOSTER, VIRGINIA, retired botany educator; b. Joseph, Oreg., Feb. 4, 1914; d. Perry Alexander and Genevieve (Shain) F. BS, U. Wash., 1949, MS, 1950; PhD, Ohio State U., 1954. Prof. Judson Coll., Marion, Ala., 1956-58; prof. Miss. State Coll. for Women, Columbus, 1958-59, LaVerne (Calif.) Coll., 1959-60, Calif. Western U., San Diego, 1960-61, Pensacola (Fla.) Jr. Coll., 1962-84. Author: (lab. manual) The Botany Laboratory, 1976, rev. edit., 1985. Home: 9270 Scenic Hwy Pensacola FL 32514

FOSTER, VIRGINIA HIGHLEYMAN, nonprofit association executive; b. Kansas City, Mo., Apr. 15, 1935; d. Wilbur Beck and Virginia Josephine (Ledterman) Highleyman; m. Daniel Lee Foster (div. 1984); children: Kenneth Lee, Steven Harp. BA, Okla. State U., 1957; MA, Lindenwood Coll., St. Charles, Mo., 1978. Dist. dir. Girls Scouts U.S.A., Chgo., 1957-62; dir. devel. ARC, Fairfax, Va., 1975-77; exec. dir. YWCA, Fairfax, 1977-79; nat. asst. exec. dir WICS Inc., Washington, 1979-84; dir. fin. Nat. Dem. Inst. for Internat. Affairs, Washington, 1984-87; pres., exec. dir. Va. Spl. Olympics Inc., Richmond, Va., 1987—; cons. V.H. Foster Assocs., Washington, 1974—; adj. trainer Nat. Ctr. for Vol. Action, Washington, 1976-79. Chmn. bd. Hannah Harrison Career Sch., Washinton, 1984-86; pres. YWCA, Fairfax, 1972-74, Mansfield, Ohio, 1961-62, bd. trustees, 1961-62, bd. dirs., Washington, 1974-75; bd. dirs. ARC, Fairfax, 1972-75; chmn. U.S. Adv. Coun., 1988-90; mem. internat. adv. coun. Spl. Olympics Internat., 1990—. Recipient Orenda award YMCA-YWCA, 1968. Mem. Am. Soc. Assn. Execs., Nat. Assn. Spl. Olympics Profls., Am. Mgmt. Assn. Democrat. Episcopalian. Home: 4962 Sabra Ln Annandale VA 22003 Office: Va Spl Olympics Inc 100 W Franklin St Ste 400 Richmond VA 23220

FOSTER, VIRGINIA LEE See **REEDER, VIRGINIA LEE**

FOTI, LAUREL COHEN, financial services associate; b. Chgo., Dec. 1, 1943; d. Carl Eugene and Joan Adele (Arenz) P.; m. Sidney Henry Cohen, June 29, 1968 (div. Nov. 1981); children: Elizabeth Ann, David Arthur, Douglas Edward, Deborah Sue; m. Frederick Joseph Foti, Jan. 19, 1985. Diploma in RN, Swedish Covenant, 1967; BS, Moody Bible Inst., 1976. Staff nurse Overlook Hosp., Summit, N.J., 1980-82; pub. health nurse Patient Care Svc., West Orange, N.J., 1982-83; hospice nurse The Hospice, Inc., Montclair, N.J., 1984-87; fin. svc. rep. A.L. Williams & Assoc., Inc., Duluth, Ga., 1985-89, regional v.p., 1989—. State coord. La Leche League, N.J., 1976-78; hospice vol. The Hospice, Inc., 1987—; mem. MADD, Rep. Presdl. Task Force, 1989. Lt. (j.g.) USNR, 1967-69. Mem. Adoptees Liberty Movement Assn. (spokesman 1977-83). Republican. Presbyterian. Home: 18 Ruthven Pl Summit NJ 07901 Office: A L Williams 205 Rte 46 W Ste 1 Totowa NJ 07512

FOTINOS, KATHERINE, educator; b. San Francisco, Apr. 12, 1926; d. Christ Anastasios and Ageliki George (Pilarinos) F. BA, San Francisco State Coll., 1948; MA, Stanford U., 1955. Life diploma tchr. Calif. Tchr. Excelsior Sch., San Francisco, 1948-53, Ridgepoint III, San Francisco, 1953-54, Jedediah Smith Sch., San Francisco, 1954-55; head tchr. Washington Irving Sch., San Francisco, 1955-60, Jean Parker Sch., San Francisco, 1960—; curriculum designer 1951—; cons. Calif. Geog. Alliance. Co-author: Curriculum Guide for Language Arts, Curriculum Guide for Music, Curriculum Guide for Social Studies and Science (all for grades K-6 in San Francisco Unified Sch. Dist.). Designer Deaf Scrabball, 1981; ednl. advisor Sts. Constantine and Helen Greek Orthodox Ch., Vallejo, Calif., 1989—. Vol. Assn. for Deaf and Blind, 1980—; chmn., auditor Sonoma County Legislator; docent Calif. Hist. Soc., Sonoma; festival decoration chmn. Greek Orthodox Ch., Solono County 1982; vol. Sonoma Rep. Com., 1982; U.S. senatorial candidate campaign chmn. Sonoma County, 1986; scholarship chmn. Northern Div. Calif. Fedn. Rep. Women, 1987—. Mem. AAUW, Calif. PTA (hon. life), Calif. Tchrs. Assn., Stanford Edn. Club (sec. 1972-74), Sonoma Valley Chorale, Sonoma County Ballet Guild (bd. dirs.), Am. Chorale Dirs. Assn. (bd. dirs.), European Touring Concert Group, Sonoma Valley Rep. Women (charter mem.), Nat. Fedn. Rep. Women (fed. regent), Calif. Retired Tchrs. Assn. (bd. dirs.), Alpha Delta Kappa (life; pres. 1962-64). Clubs: Jack Anderson, Etude Music (scholarship chmn.). Lodge: Daus. Penelope (v.p. 1974-76). Avocations: travel, archaeology, dance, art, gardening. Home: 150 El Portola Dr Sonoma CA 95476

FOUCHÉ, HELEN STROTHER, editorial design executive; b. Washington, Apr. 19, 1939; d. James Herschel and Elizabeth Ellen (Wright) Strother; m. Robert Michael Fouché, Oct. 20, 1962; children: James Michael, David Carroll, Stephen Charles, (nephew) James Franklin Ray. BA cum laude, Auburn U., 1960; student, Belles Artes, Managua, Nicaragua, 1964-65; student Intensive Lang. Tng., Fgn. Svc. Inst., 1961, 73; grad., Am. Transp. Inst., 1983. Asst. producer-dir. Internat. TV Svcs., U.S. Info. Agy., Washington, 1960-62; diplomatic svcs. with fgn. svc. husband U.S. Dept. of State, Europe, Africa, Cen./So. Am., 1963-81; art instr. for internat. children's classes La Paz, Bolivia, 1979; community liaison officer U.S. Embassy, La Paz, 1979-81; internat. group coord. Group Travel Unlimited, Alexandria, Va., 1983-84; mng. editor Am. Leisure Industries, Lanham, Md., 1986-87; editor, cons. Washington Editorial Svcs., DC and Met. area, 1987-88; pres. Washington Editorial Svcs. Inc., Washington, Arlington, Va., 1988—; bd. dirs. Fgn. Svc. Youth Found., Washington, 1989—; cons. Overseas Briefing Ctr., Fgn. Svc. Inst., U.S. Dept. of State, Arlington, 1981—, B.C.I.U. Inst., Am. U., Washington, 1988—; media cons. designed slide shows, wrote scripts for non-profit causes. Contbg. editor, columist: Diplomatic Digest, and others; mem. editorial bd. Foreign Svc. Jour., 1989—; creative works include mural, Crippled Children's Ward, Managua Gen. Hosp., Nicaragua, 1964, Montessori Sch., La Paz, 1980; contbr. articles to profl. publs. Pres. Episcopal Ch. Women of St. Michael's, 1989-90, mem. vestry, 1990—; mem. Altar Guild 1982—, lector 1984—; mem. Yorktown High Sch. Choral Boosters. Recipient Vol. of Yr. award, Tampa, Fla., 1970; named for Exceptional Cross-Cultural Effectiveness, Fgn. Svc. Inst., Dept. of State, 1988, one of Outstanding Young Women of Am., 1973. Mem. AAUW, DAR, Assn. of Am. Fgn. Svc. Women (bd. mem., editorial com., newsletter editor), Leadership Greater Washington, Nat. Press Club, Jamestown Soc., Order of Charlemagne, Alpha Gamma Delta Alumae Assn. Democrat. Episcopalian. Home and office: Washington Editorial Svcs 1509 N Kentucky St Arlington VA 22205

FOUCHEK, PAULA TROTT, marketing professional; b. Ennis, Tex., June 19, 1951; d. Jack Starnes and Bennie Jo (Bozeman) Trott; m. Kip Richard; 1 child, Shea Daniel. BS in English and Speech, East Tex. State U., 1973. Sec. Pearcy/Christon Realtors, Dallas, 1973-74; tchr. Irving (Tex.) High Sch., 1974-77; rep. mktg. Metroplex Paper and Supply div. Motford, Inc., Dallas, 1977-79; cons. sales tng. Xerox Learning Systems, Dallas, 1978; coord. pub. rels. TexaSweet Citrus Advt., McAllen, Tex., 1980-84; exec. dir. Tex. Fresh Promotional Bd., Harlingen, 1984—. Mem. United Fresh Fruit and Vegetable Assn. (mem. fresh approach com. 1984—), Produce Mktg. Assn. (mem. nutrition task force 1984-87, consumer edn. com. 1988—, bd. drs. retail div.), Can. Fruit Wholesalers Assn., Fresh Produce Coun. Republican. Methodist. Office: Tex Fresh Promotional Bd 6912 W Expressway 83 Harlingen TX 78552-3701

FOULKE, SARAH B., lawyer; b. Westchester, N.Y., Dec. 10, 1955; d. Roy Anderson Jr. and Katherine Maureen (Hanway) F.; m. Donald Earl Bemus Jr., July 9, 1988 (dec. Apr. 1989). BA, Skidmore Coll., 1977; JD, Vt. Law Sch., 1982. Bar: N.Y. Sr. atty., owner Law Offices of Sarah B. Foulke, Saratoga Springs, N.Y., 1984—. Mem. Saratoga Springs Planning Bd., 1990—; hearing examiner N.Y. Bd. Equalization and Assessment, 1989—. Mem. DAR, ABA, N.Y. Bar Assn., Soroptimist (Saratoga County club), Saratoga Horseworks (adv. coun. 1989), Saratoga Springs Preservation Found. (award 1989), Ea. N.Y. Dressage and Combined Tng. Assn. (chairperson competitions benefiting retarded citizens 1990—). Office: 368 Broadway Ste 12 Saratoga Springs NY 12866

FOULKROD, SARAH SUTHERLAND, librarian; b. Clintwood, Va., Aug. 26, 1949; d. Benjamin Fulton and Sarah Neal (Cothron) Sutherland; m. Charles Bruce Foulkrod, Aug. 4, 1973; 1 child, Charles Matthew. BA, U. Ky., 1971; MLS, U. Pitts., 1972. Reference libr. Wilmington (Del.) Inst. Libr., 1972-77, coordinator, acquisitions, 1974-77. Trustee Free Libr. of Northampton Twp., Richboro, Pa., 1981-87; mem. Dist. Adv. Com. for Bucks County Librs., Doylestown, Pa., 1987-; sec. Friends of the Libr., Richboro, 1989-. Mem. AAUW, Pa. Libr. Assn., Embroiderers Guild of Am. Republican. Methodist.

FOUNTAIN, CAMILLE CHRISTINE, social worker; b. Washington, July 26, 1961; d. Lewis Edward and Marian (Rice) F. BS, Towson State U., 1984; MSW, Howard U., 1989. Asst. to dir. fin. and adminstrn. Children's Defense Fund, Washington, 1986-89; graduate intern WUL Pins Ctr., Washington, 1987-88; child welfare intern Children's Defense Fund, Washington, 1988-89. Pres. Assn. of Black Social Workers, Howard U., 1988-89, recording sec., Met. Washington chpt., 1990—. Mem. Nat. Assn. Social Workers, Pi Sigma Delta Social Work Honor Soc. Democrat. Catholic. Office: Children's Defense Fund 122 C St NW Washington DC 20011

FOUNTAIN, LINDA KATHLEEN, health science association executive; b. Fowler, Kans., Apr. 30, 1954; d. Ralph Edward and Ruth Evelyn (Cornelson) Young; m. Andrew Fountain. BS in Nursing, Cen. State U., Edmond, Okla., 1976. RN, Okla. Staff nurse med./surg. and coronary care unit Presbyn. Hosp., Oklahoma City, 1976-79; mgr. nursing Hillcrest Osteo. Hosp., Oklahoma City, 1979-80; staff nurse, mgr. Oklahoma U. Teaching Hosp., Oklahoma City, 1981-82; pres. New Life Programs, Oklahoma City, 1981-88, Nursing Entrepreneurs, Ltd., Oklahoma City, 1988—; mgr. Internat. Health Supply, Oklahoma City, 1988—; coord. lactation cons. program, State of Okla., 1981—, new life car seat rental program at various hosps., 1983—; cons., speaker Success Co., Oklahoma City, 1984—; owner Rainbows Overhead Graphic Media, Oklahoma City, 1984. Founder Praxis Coll., Oklahoma City, 1988. Named Mentor of Yr., Okla. Metroplex Childbirth Network, Oklahoma City, 1984. Mem. Am. Nurses Assn., Internat. Lactation Cons. Assn., Internat. Platform Assn., Bodyworkers and Wellness Therapies Assn. Office: Nursing Entrepreneurs Ltd PO Box 75393 Oklahoma City OK 75507

FOURCARD, INEZ GAREY, foundation executive, artist; b. Bklyn.; d. George W. and Frances E. (MacDonald) Garey; student Pratt Inst., 1946-48; BFA, McNeese State U., 1963; diploma Maestro di Pitturia Arti Modernea e Contemporaneo, Salsomaggiore, Italy, 1982. Waldren Arthur Fourcard, Aug. 7, 1948; children—Chrystal Frances, Sharon Lynn, Waldren Arthur, Andrea Renee, David Marquard, Anita Lynn. Exhibited in numerous one man shows throughout U.S., also in Eng., France and Spain; 3 paintings on loan to Gov. La., 1974-77; mem. gifted and talented sect. of Spl. Edn. State of La., 1971-73; mem. adv. council Child Centered/Parent Tutored Kindergarden Program, 1974—; mem. La. Task Force for Community Edn., 1974-75; v.p. La. Assn. for Sickle Cell Anemia, 1974—; named best statewide vol.; mem. Calcasieu Parish Bicentennial Com., 1974—; exec. dir. Southwestern Sickle Cell Anemia Found., Lake Charles, La., 1973—, producer, dir. 7 Sickle Cell Telethons, Sta. KPLC-TV, 1980-87, exec. dir. World Sickle Cell Orgn., Houston, 1990—; bd. dirs. World Sickle Cell Anemia Found.; del. to Dem. Nat. Convs., 1980, 84. Named Hon. Citizen of Fort Worth, 1977; recipient Award of Merit, Human Relations Council of Lake Charles Deanery, award for services to sickle cell disease Sigma Gamma Rho, award for community service Phi Beta Sigma, Gold medal first prize Accademia Italia della Arti e del Sarvo, Italy, 1980, Statua della Vittoria Centro Studie Richerche Delle Nazioni, Italy, 1985. Democrat. Roman Catholic. Important works include The Widow in pvt. collection Bertrand Russell Peace Found., London. Home: 1414 St John St Lake Charles LA 70601 Office: 1408 Jackson St Rm #21 Lake Charles LA 70601

FOURNET, MARILYN MICHELE, lawyer; b. Hammond, La., June 7, 1949; d. Francis Gary Jr. and Marilyn Rita (Delcourt) F. BA, Southeastern La. U., 1971; JD, La. State U., 1978. Bar: La. 1978, U.S. Dist. Ct. (mid.

dist.) La. 1980, U.S. Ct. Appeals (5th cir.) 1983, U.S. Dist. Ct. (we. dist.) La. 1984, U.S. Supreme Ct. 1984, U.S. Dist. Ct. (ea. dist.) La. 1986. Law clk. to presiding justice Baton Rouge, 1978-79; trial atty., chief of appellate sect. Office of Pub. Defender, Baton Rouge, 1978-83, chief of appellate sect., 1985-86; assoc. Small, Williamson, Brocato & Fournet, Alexandria, La., 1983-85; pvt. practice Law Offices M. Michele Fournet, Baton Rouge, 1986—; mem. indigent defender bd. 19th Jud. Dist. Ct. Mem. La. Task Force Women in Ct., New Orleans, 1989; bd. dirs. La. Capital Def. Project, New Orleans, 1986-88. Mem. Nat. Assn. Criminal Def. Lawyers, La. Assn. Criminal Def. Lawyers (bd. dirs. 1988—, president's commendation 1988), La. Bar Assn. (bd. dirs. criminal sec. 1989), Baton Rouge Bar of Criminal Justice (pres. 1987-88). Democrat. Roman Catholic. Home: 1959 Tulip St Baton Rouge LA 70806 Office: M Michele Fournet Atty 251 Florida St Ste 407 Baton Rouge LA 70801

FOURNEY, CATHERINE JO, educator, counselor; b. Beckley, W.Va., Sept. 21, 1965; d. Joseph Charles and Catherine Anne (Hess) Fourney. BS in Elem. Edn., W.Va. U., 1988. Pre-school tchr. Family Ctr., Beckley, 1987, Blue-Ashe Ednl. Bldg., Cin., 1988; substitute tchr. Raleigh County Bd. Edn., Beckley, 1988—, also tutor of homebound, 1989—. Bd. dirs. Family Ctr., Beckley, 1989—. Mem. Am. Fedn. Tchrs., W.Va. Edn. Assn., Delta Gamma. Republican. Roman Catholic. Home: 114 Parkway Dr Beckley WV 25801

FOURNIER, CAROL SHERMAN, technical services consultant; b. Phila., July 10, 1960; d. Edwin H. and Alberta H. (Prokop) Sherman; m. Alvaro E. Fournier Jr., May 19, 1990. Ed., Temple U. Dir. pers. Tech. Adv. Svc., Inc., Blue Bell, Pa., v.p. Mem. NAFE, Soc. for Human Resource Mgmt., Adminstrv. Mgmt. Soc. Address: 1166 DeKalb Pike Blue Bell PA 19422

FOUST, GRACE NAOMI, nutritional services administrator, dietitian; b. Palmyra, Pa., June 9, 1938; d. John Roy and Mary Ethel (Parker) Ewing; m. Larry Thomas Foust, July 16, 1961; children: Susan Lynn, Thomas Dwight, Sandra Jean. BS, Pa. State U., 1960. Home econs. tchr. Conemaugh Twp. High Sch., Davidsville, Pa., 1961-62; substitute tchr. Warren (Pa.) Area High Sch., 1971-76; nutritionist Warren-Forest County Head Start, Warren, 1978-82; dietitian Stouffer Corp., Cleve., 1960-61, Warren Gen. Hosp., 1977-85; dir. nutritional svc. Shriners Hosps. Crippled Children, Erie, Pa., 1986—; cons. dietitian, Warren Nursing Home, 1977-84, Quiet Acres Nursing Home, Spring Creek, Pa., 1978-80. Organizer, dir. self help group for diabetics, Warren, 1978-85; leader Warren Brownie Troup , 1978-80; v.p. Warren PTA, 1981; pres. Warren Music Boosters, 1984; bd. dirs. Warren Band Boosters, 1985. Mem. AAUW. Republican. Presbyterian. Home: 1560 Taylor Ridge Ct Erie PA 16505

FOUST, SHARON JEANETTE, educator; b. Ft. Worth, Oct. 30, 1953; d. Irvin Dale and Norma Jean (Wiley) Rogers; m. David Howard Foust, Apr. 3, 1982. BS, U. Tex., 1976; MEd, Sam Houston State U., 1982. Cert. profl. diagnostician. Tchr. Aldine Ind. Sch. Dist., Houston, 1977-81, spl. edn. tchr., 1981-83; ednl. diagnostician Cypress-Fairbanks Ind. Sch. Dist., Houston, 1983-84, tchr., 1984-85, reading specialist, 1985-86; tchr. Hurst-Euless-Bedford (Tex.) Ind. Sch. Dist., 1986-88, transitional first grade tchr., 1988—. Mem. PTA (publ. com. 1979-80, program com. 1981, exec. bd. 1979-81). Mem. Tex. Classroom Tchrs. Assn. (faculty rep.). Democrat. Home: 3 Country Pl Fort Worth TX 76180 Office: Hurst Euless Bedford Ind Sch Dist 1849 Central Dr Bedford TX 76022

FOUTS, DONNA DESTI, health agency director; b. N.Y.C., Feb. 4, 1949; d. Donald N. and Genenieve (Whiteley) McClure; married, Dec. 19, 1975 (dec. 1986); 1 child, Joshua. BS in Recreation, U. Wis., La Crosse, 1971; MEd, Boston U., 1977; MA in Pub. Adminstrn., Central Mich. U., 1982. Dir. camp and recreation YWCA, Honolulu, 1978-81; dir. mktg. and sales Lifestyle Mgmt. Ctr., Honolulu, 1981-82; dist. dir. Muscular Dystrophy Assn., Honolulu, 1982-86; exec. dir. United Cerebral Palsy Assn., Honolulu, 1986—; bd. dirs. Sunshine Pre Sch., Kailua, Hawaii. Bd dirs. Windward Children's Race, 1990. With AUS, 1975-77. Named Pahhellenic Woman of Yr., Hawaii, 1980. Mem. NAFE, Windward Marathon Assn. (publicity chair 1989—), Womens Island Soccer Assn., Alpha Phi. (v.p. 1988-90). Office: United Cerebral Palsy Assn 245 N Kukui St Ste A Honolulu HI 96817

FOUTS, ELIZABETH BROWNE, psychologist, metals company executive; b. New Orleans, July 5, 1927; d. Donovan Clarence and Mathilde Elizabeth (Hanna) B.; m. James Fremont Fouts, June 19, 1948; children: Elizabeth, Donovan, Alan, James. BA, Tulane U., 1948; MS, N.E. La. U., 1973, postgrad., 1984. Cert. sch. psychologist, La.; cert. reality therapist, La. Instr. spl. ed., psychol. cons. N.E. La. U., Monroe, 1971-73; sch. psychologist Ouachita Parish Schs., Monroe, 1973-87; sec.-treas Fremont Corp., Monroe, 1967—, Auric Metals Corp., Salt Lake City, 1975—; pres. Sunbelt Reality Therapist, 1989-90. Mem. exec. bd. Episc. Diocese Western La., 1986-87, commn. ministry, 1987—; bd. dirs. Assn. for Retarded Citizens, Monroe, 1982-88, treas., 1984, pres., 1987. Named Outstanding Sch. Psychologist State of La., 1987. Mem. Nat. Assn. Sch. Psychologists, Coun. for Exceptional Children, La. Sch. Psychologists Assn. (pres. 1978-79, Outstanding Woman Sch. Psychologist 1984, newsletter editor 1988—). Avocations: biking, skiing, swimming. Home: PO Box 7070 Monroe LA 71211 Office: 4002 Bon Aire Dr Monroe LA 71203

FOWKE, EDITH MARGARET FULTON, author, emeritus English language educator; b. Lumsden, Sask., Can., Apr. 30, 1913; d. William Marshall and Margaret (Fyffe) Fulton; m. Franklin George Fowke, Oct. 1, 1938. Student, Regina Coll., 1929-31; B.A. with high honors in English and History, U. Sask., 1933, M.A. in English, 1938; LL.D. (hon.), Brock U., 1974, U. Regina, 1985; D.Litt., Trent U., 1975, York U., 1982. Editor Western Tchr., Saskatoon, Sask., 1937-45; assoc. editor Mag. Digest, Toronto, Ont., 1945-50; freelance writer CBC Radio, 1950-71; assoc. prof. English, York U., Downsview, Ont., 1971-77; prof. York U., 1977-83, prof. emeritus, 1983—. Author: Folk Songs of Canada, 1954, Folk Songs of Quebec, 1957, Songs of Work and Freedom, 1960, Canada's Story in Song, 1960, Traditional Singers and Songs from Ontario, 1965, More Folk Songs of Canada, 1967, Lumbering Songs from the Northern Woods, 1970, Sally Go Round the Sun, 1969, Penguin Book of Canadian Folk Songs, 1974, Folklore of Canada, 1976, Ring Around the Moon, 1977, Folktales of French Canada, 1979, Sea Songs and Ballads from Nineteenth Century Nova Scotia, 1981, Singing Our History, 1985, Tales Told in Canada, 1986, Red Rover, Red Rover: Children's Games Played in Canada, 1988, Canadian Folklore, 1988; editor: Songs and Sayings of an Ulster Childhood by Alice Kane, 1983, Can. Folk Music Jour., 1973—; co-editor: Bibliography of Canadian Folklore in English, 1982, Explorations in Canadian Folklore, 1985. Decorated Order Can. Fellow Am. Folklore Soc., Royal Soc. Can.; mem. Writer's Union Can., English Folk Dance & Song Soc., Assn. Can. Univ. Tchrs. English, Can. Assn. Univ. Tchrs., Can. Folk Music Soc. (exec. com.), Folklore Studies Assn. Can., Mensa. Home: 5 Notley Pl, Toronto, ON Canada M4B 2M7 Office: Winters Coll, 4700 Keele St, North York, ON Canada M3J 1P3

FOWLER, ANNE VICTORIA, personnel company exeutive; b. Denver, Feb. 12, 1945; d. Nicholas John and Estelle (Sullivan) F. MS in Human Resource Mgmt., Am. U., 1988. V.p. Midland Ins. Co., N.Y.C., 1971-85; asst. v.p. E.W. Blanch Co., N.Y.C., 1985-86; owner, mgr. Norrell Svcs., Inc., Shrewsbury, N.J., 1987—. Mem. Internat. Assn. Pers. Women (treas. Monmouth County 1989—), Greater Red Bank C. of C. (bd. dirs. 1989—). Home: 150 Manor Dr Red Bank NJ 07701 Office: Norrell Svcs Inc One N Revmont Dr Shrewsbury NJ 07702

FOWLER, ARDEN STEPHANIE, music educator; b. N.Y.C., May 24, 1930; d. Arthur Simon and Lenore Irene (Strouse) Bender; m. Milton Fowler, Aug. 6, 1951; children: Stacey Alison, Crispin Laird. Student, Traphagen Sch., 1947-49; BA, Marymount Coll., Tarrytown, N.Y., 1976; MusM, U. So. Fla., 1978. Designer Rubeson's Sportswear, N.Y.C., 1949-51; free-lance designer Dobb's Ferry, N.Y., 1952-72; organist/choir dir. Children's Village, Dobb's Ferry, N.Y., 1972-74; music specialist Highland Nursery Sch., Chappaqua, N.Y., 1972-76; pvt. voice tchr., vocal coach, 1972—; music therapist Cedar Manor Nursing Home, Ossining, N.Y., 1974-76; founder, pres. Gloria Musicae Chamber Chorus, Sarasota, Fla., 1979-85, mng. dir., 1985-89; soloist various chs., choruses, N.Y. and Fla., 1953—; faculty vocal music St. Boniface Conservatory, Sarasota, 1979-81; music critic Sarasota Herald Tribune, 1986—; freelance travel writer. Mem. Nat. Assn. Tchrs. Singing, Chorus Am., Assn. Profl. Vocal Ensembles, Sarasota County Arts Council, Friends of the Arts (hon.), Sigma Alpha Iota, Phi Kappa Phi. Democrat. Episcopal. Home: 4244 Marina Ct Cortez FL 34215 Office: Gloria Musicae Inc Box 3863 Sarasota FL 34230

FOWLER, AUDRIAN HUFF, principal; b. Grangeville, Idaho, Oct. 28, 1940; d. Eral W. and Eleanor Genevieve (Gunter) Huff; m. Dwight L. Fowler (div. Dec., 1987); children: Mitchell Lynn, Heather Audrian. BS, U. Idaho, Moscow, 1962; MEd, U. Wash., Seattle, 1970; PhD, Wash. State U., 1983. Cert. Prin. Tchr. Kiona Benton City (Wash.) Sch. Dist., 1962-63, Prosser (Wash.) Sch. Dist., 1963-65; tchr., counselor Highline Sch. Dist., Seattle, Wash., 1966-74; from tchr., counselor to prin. Endicott (Wash.) Sch. Dist., 1974-85; prin. Othello (Wash.) Sch. Dist., 1985-88, Kent (Wash.) Sch. Dist., 1988—. co-founder Othello Literacy Program, 1988; mother adv. bd., bd. dirs. Rainbow for Girls, St. John, Benton City, Othello. Mem. Assn. Wash. Schs. Prins. (co-chair legis. com. 1986-88), Elem. Sch. Prin.'s Assn. of Wash. (treas.), Wash. Interscholastic Activities Assn., Altrusa, Rotary, Alpha Chi Omega. Home: 31600-126th Ave SE #132 Auburn WA 98002 Office: Fairwood Elem Sch 1660-148th Ave SE Renton WA 98058

FOWLER, BETTY JANMAE, dance company director, editor; b. Chgo., May 23, 1925; d. Harry and Mary (Jacques) Markin; student Art Inst., Chgo., 1937-39, Stratton Bus. Coll., Chgo., 1942-43, Columbia U., 1945-47; B.A., Eastern Wash. U., 1984; 1 dau., Sherry Mareth Connors. Mem. public relations dept. Girl Scouts U.S.A., N.Y.C., 1961-63; adminstrv. asst. to editor-in-chief Scholastic Mags., N.Y.C., 1963-68; adminstrv. dir. Leonard Fowler Dancers, Fowler Sch. Classical Ballet, Inc., N.Y.C., 1959-78, tchr. ballet, 1959-61; editor Bulletin, Kiwanis weekly publ., Spokane, Wash., 1978-82, adminstrv. sec. Kiwanis Club; instr. Spokane Falls Community Coll., 1978. Founder Safe Water Coalition Wash. State, 1988. Cert. metabolic technician Internat. Health Inst. Address: W 5615 Lyons Ct Spokane WA 99208

FOWLER, BETTY JO, investment company executive; b. Medesto, Calif., July 1, 1938; d. Gilbert Fredrick and Vera Margareatha (Sherman) Hildebrand; m. Robert N. Fowler, Feb. 10, 1962 (div. 1971); 1 child, Kimberlun Duane. Student, Western Schs., San Diego, 1985-87, NYU, 1987. Owner, developer B.J. Fowler & Co., 1970—; investment specialist J. Lance and Co., Bend, Oreg., 1971-74; gen. owner B.J. Fowler Constrn., Bend, 1975-79, San Deigo, 1986—; owner Redmond (Oreg.) Hotel, 1979-81; owner, mgr. B.J. Fowler Realty, Property Mgmt. & Constrn. Co., Redmond, 1981-83; investment specialist for women Portfolio Investments, La Jolla, Calif., 1984—; owner, developer art, craft and antique mini mall The OLD Creamery, Redmond, Oreg., 1989—; real estate counselor, San Diego, 1985—; speaker in field. Named to Most Outstanding Bus. People, Bend C. of C., 1975, 76. Mem. San Diego Bd. Realtors, Deschutes County Bd. Realtors, Redmond C. of C., Women Constrn. Owners and Execs., Caltrans. Office: The OLD Creamery 526 SW 6th St Redmond OR 97756

FOWLER, CECILE ANN, nurse, professional soloist; b. Paterson, N.J., Feb. 14, 1920; m. Chester A. Fowler, Mar. 9, 1942. Grad., Passaic (N.J.) Gen. Hosp. Nursing Program, 1941. Nurse Beth Israel Hosp., Newark, 1941-42, Orange (N.J.) Meml. Hosp., 1942-50; asst. receptionist Dr. Stokes, Urologist, East Orange, N.J., 1943-44; nurse Mountainside Hosp., Montclair, N.J., 1960-69, head nurse, premature and newborns, 1966-67; profl. soloist, 1952-69; part-time nurse Upper Three Hosps., 1950-60; co-founder The Oratorio Soc. of N.J., Montclair, 1952; mem. quartet First Baptist Ch., Montclair. Active various coms. PTA, 1951-62; co-founder Civilian Def., Little Falls, N.J., 1967; sponsor Met. Opera Guild of N.Y., 1977—; child sponsor World Vision, 1983—; mem. Rep. Presdl. Task Force, 1987—. Recipient Vocal Accomplishment award Griffith Music Found., 1944, 45, medal of Merit Pres. Reagan, 1988, Pres. Bush, 1990. Mem. Lincoln Ctr. for the Performing Arts, Friends of Carnegie Hall, Am. Biog. Inst. Am. (rsch. bd. advs. 1989-, dep. gov., life mem.), Heritage Found. (U.S. English mem. 1986-), U.S. Senatorial Club (preferred mem. 1988-), The Little Falls Woman's (edn. chmn.), The Montclair (gov. 1979-81), The Montclair Operetta (various chmnships 1943—, elect gov. 1990-92). Republican. Roman Catholic. Home: 9 Lotz Hill Rd Clifton NJ 07013

FOWLER, ELIZABETH MILTON, real estate executive; b. Watertown, Fla., Jan. 11, 1919; d. Arthur Wellington and Mattie Jean (Hodges) Milton; m. Albert L. Fowler, Jr., Aug. 6, 1948; children: Patricia Dawn Cecilia, Richard Gordon Sean. Student Bowling Green Bus. U., 1938-39; Cultural HHD (hon.), World U. Roundtable, 1988. Sec. to dir. Workmen's Compensation Div., Fla. Indsl. Commn., Tallahassee, 1940-41; sec. to supt. div. Gibbs Ship Yard Repair, 1942-44; sec. to elec. engrs. Reynolds, Smith & Hills, Architects and Engrs., 1946-49; sec. to pres. Aichel Steel Corp., Jacksonville, Fla., 1949-50; adminstr. office mgr. for prin., vice-prin. Am. Dependent Sch., Moron Air Base, Spain, 1961-63; owner, mgr. Elizabeth Properties, Jacksonville, 1956—. Chmn. ways and means com. Chattanooga High Sch. PTA, 1956-57; asst. den mother Cub Scout Troop, 1970; block worker Gov. Reagan's Presdl. Campaign. Recipient Spl. Appreciation award Eglin AFB, Fla., 1969. Mem. Nat. Assn. Female Execs., Am. Security Council (nat. adv. bd.), Dade County Crimewatch Orgn. Republican. Avocations: art and interior design, horseback riding, collecting fine porcelain, reading, politics and world affairs. Home and Office: 20101 SW 92d Ave Miami FL 33189

FOWLER, JOANNA S., chemist; b. Aug. 9, 1942. BA, U. South Fla., 1964; PhD in Chemistry, U. Colo., 1968. Rsch. assoc. U. East Anglia, Eng., 1968-69; rsch. assoc. in organic chemistry Brookhaven Nat. Lab., Upton, N.Y., 1969-71, chemist, 1971—. Mem. Soc. Nuclear Medicine, Am. Chem. Soc. (co-recipient Gustavus John Esselen Award for Chemistry in the Pub. Interest, northeastern sect., 1988). Office: Brookhaven Nat Lab Dept Chemistry Bldg 555A Upton NY 11973*

FOWLER, JULIANNE, professional development manager; b. Pitts., Apr. 11, 1949; d. Charles G. and Elizabeth (Harrington) Brooks; m. Paul E. Fowler, Nov. 7, 1979; children: Ryan, Scott. BS, Salem (W.Va.) Coll., 1971; MA, U. Leicester, Eng., 1974. Cert. community coll. instr., Calif.; cert. in mgmt. studies, mgmt. instrn. Cons. in pvt. practice L.A.; ednl. programs adminstr. Rockwell Internat., Canoga Park, Calif.; lectr. UCLA, U. So. Calif., L.A. Mem. Rockwell Speakers Bur. Recipient YWCA Leadership Achievement award; Rotary Internat. grad. fellow. Mem. Nat. Mgmt. Assn., Assn. for Bus. Communication, Rockwell Orgn. for Women (pres.). Address: 490 Lake Breeze Pl Wood Ranch CA 93065

FOWLER, LINDA MCKEEVER, hospital administrator, management educator; b. Greensburg, Pa., Aug. 7, 1948; d. Clay and Florence Elizabeth (Smith) McK.; m. Timothy L. Fowler, Sept. 13, 1969 (div. July 1985). Nursing diploma, Presbyn. U. Hosp., Pitts., 1969; BS in Nursing, U. Pitts., 1976, M in Nursing Adminstrn., 1980; DPub Adminstrn., Nova U., 1985. Supr., head nurse Presbyn. Univ. Hosp., Pitts., 1969-76; mem. faculty Western Pa. Hosp. Sch. Nursing, Pitts., 1976-79; acute care coord. Mercy Hosp., Miami, 1980-81; asst. adminstr. nursing North Shore Med. Ctr., Miami, 1981-84, v.p. patient care, 1984-88, Golden Glades Regional Med. Ctr., Miami, 1988-89, Humana Hosp.-South Broward, Hollywood, Fla., 1989—, assoc. exec. dir. nursing; mem. adj. faculty Barry U., Miami, 1984—, Broward Community Coll., Ft. Lauderdale, 1984—, Nova U., 1986—; cons. Strategic Health Devel. Inc., Miami Shores, Fla., 1986—. Dept. HEW trainee, 1976, 79-80. Mem. Am. Orgn. Nurse Execs. (legis. com. 1988-90), Fla. Orgn. Nurse Execs. (bd. dirs. 1986-88), South Fla. Nurse Adminstrs. Assn. (sec. 1983-84, bd. dirs. 1984-86), U. Pitts. Alumni Assn., Presbyn. U. Alumni Assn., Portuguese Water Dog Club Am. (bd. dirs. 1988-89), Ft. Lauderdale Dog Club (bd. dirs. 1981-82, 83-85, v.p. 1982-83), Sigma Theta Tau. Lutheran. Home: 1040 SW 110th Terr Davie FL 33324 Office: Humana Hosp South Broward 5100 W Hallandale Beach Blvd Hollywood FL 33023

FOWLER, NANCY CROWLEY, government economist; b. Newton, Mass., Aug. 8, 1922; d. Ralph Elmer and Margaret Bright (Tinkham) Crowley; m. Gordon Robert Fowler, Sept. 11, 1949; children: Gordon R., Nancy Pualani, Betty Kainani, Diane Kuulei. AB cum laude, Radcliffe Coll., 1943; grad. mgmt. tng. program, Harvard U.-Radcliffe Coll., 1946; postgrad., U. Hawaii, 1971-76. Econ. rsch. analyst Dept. Planning & Econ. Devel., Honolulu, 1963-69; assoc. chief rsch. Regional Med. Program, Honolulu, 1969-70; economist V and VI Dept. Planning and Econ. Devel., Honolulu, 1970-78, chief policy analysis br., 1978-85, tech. info. services officer, 1985-87, energy cons., 1988—; staff rep. State Energy Functional Plan Adv. Com., Honolulu, 1983—, Hawaii Integrated Energy Assessment, 1978-81, Energy Resources Coord.'s Report, 1988, 89. Contbr. articles to profl. jours. Recipient Employee of Yr. award Dept. Planning and Econ. Devel., Honolulu, 1977, others. Mem. Hawaii Econs. Assn. (various offices), Radcliffe Club of Hawaii, Propeller Club, Port of Honolulu Club, Navy League Club. Democrat.

FOWLER, SUSAN MICHELE, real estate broker; b. East Liverpool, Ohio, Jan. 6, 1952; d. George Robert and Mary Helen (Gilliland) F.; m. Paul Joseph Cusumano, Nov. 5, 1988. BA, West Liberty Coll., 1973. Lic. real estate broker, Ohio. Sales rep. Tropic-Cal, L.A., 1974-76; project mgr. R&B Enterprises, L.A., 1977-80; regional leasing mgr. First Union Mgmt., Inc., Cleve., 1981-82; comml. real estate broker Adler, Gavin, Rogers, Inc., Cleve., 1983-86, Coldwell Banker Comml. Real Estate, Cleve., 1986—; pres., Christopher Real Estate Investment, Cleve., 1989—, Christopher Mgmt. Co., Cleve., 1989—. Trustee, pres., West Side Community Mental Health Ctr., Cleve., 1985—; trustee, v.p. Child Conservation Coun., Cleve., 1988—; trustee, Big Bros./Big Sisters Greater Cleve., 1989. Mem. Comml. Real Estate Women, Cleve. Area Bd. Realtors (speakers bur.), Nat. Assn. Realtors, Ohio Assn. Realtors, Cleve. Mus. Art, Pine Lake Trout Club. Democrat. Roman Catholic. Home and Office: 6 Circle Dr Chagrin Falls OH 44022

FOWLER, TERRI (MARIE THERESE FOWLER), artist; b. Decatur, Ga., Sept. 26, 1949; d. John Francis and Marjorie (Benson) Herndon; m. John Charles Fowler, July 29, 1972; children: Courtney Marie, Douglas Edwin. Studied with Carolyn Wyeth, Wyeth Sch. Art, 1972. speaker to arts groups, schools. One-woman shows include Hampden Sydney Coll., 1973, Longwood Coll., 1976, C&S Bank, Camden, S.C., 1979, Benfield Gallery, 1985-89; exhibited in cen. chpt. Va. Mus., 1973 (recipient award 1973), Colonial Williamsburg, 1974-77, Md. St. House, Md. St. Senate, 1983-85; works selected by Am. Heart Assn. for Holiday Card Series, 1986-87, commnd. Prince Edward County Bicentennial Com., 1976; represented in many nat. and internat. pvt. collections. Active Girl Scouts Am. cen. Md.; sec. citizens adv. com. Annapolis Mid. Sch. Mem. Balt. Watercolor Soc., Md. Fedn. Art. Anapolis Watercolor Club., San Diego Watercolor Soc., U.S. Naval Acad. Womens Club and Garden Club. Home: 123 Groh Ln Annapolis MD 21403

FOWLER, VIVIAN DELORES, insurance company executive; b. Knoxville, Tenn., Sept. 26, 1946; d. Rance James Pierce and Margaret Wildene (Crowe) Compton; m. James Hubert Fowler, May 12, 1979. Student, U. Tenn., Knoxville. Clk. Travelers Ins. Co., Knoxville, 1967-84, adminstv. staff, 1984, comml. mktg. asst., 1984-86; comml. acctg. analyst Travelers Ins. Co., Nashville, 1986-89, sr. account analyst, 1989-90, account mgr., 1990—. Lay witness speaker, United Meth. Ch., Knoxville 1979-82; charter mem. St. Thomas Hosp. Found. Soc., 1990. Mem. Soc. Cert. Ins. Counselors (cert. 1987), Nat. Assn. Female Execs., Nat. Assn. of Ins. Women (cert. Profl. Ins. Woman 1975). Republican. United Methodist. Home: 194 Burning Tree Dr Hermitage TN 37076 Office: The Travelers Ins Co 44 Vantage Way Nashville TN 37228

FOWLKES, YVONNE LAMPKIN, small business owner; b. Fort Deposit, Ala., Nov. 4, 1947; d. Joe Albert and Lola D. (McHenry) Lampkin; m. H. Earl Fowlkes, Dec. 6, 1969; children: Tia Dawniel, Kiva Jael. BS, Auburn U., 1969; MEd, Ga. State U., 1973. Cert. high sch. tchr. Tchr. math. Bd. Edn. Sylvan High, Atlanta, 1969-74, career edn. tchr., 1974-76; engr. So. Bell Telephone Co., Atlanta, 1976-79, tng. mgr., 1979-81, cost analyst, 1981-84; asst. staff mgr. AT&T Communications, Atlanta, 1984-86, staff supr. mktg., 1986-88; pres. Mini Maid Svcs. Southside, Decatur, Ga., 1986—; instr. communications Clayton State Coll.; ptnr. Mini Maid Coop, Atlanta, 1986—. Program chmn. Bob Mathis PTA Exec. Bd., 1988-89; mem. adv. bd. U. Ga. Extension Svc. Program Adv. Com., Dekalb County Children's Emergency Shelter. Recipient Devoted Svc. award Bob Mathis PTA, Decatur, 1989. Mem. Am. Bus. Women's Assn. (pres. 1984-85, presidential award 1985, outstanding svc. award 1987), NAACP (new bus. award DeKalb County 1987), DeKalb Network for Women, nat. Coalition of 100 Black Women, DeKalb C. of C., Auburn U. Alumni Assn., Ga. State U. Alumni Assn. Democrat. Methodist. Home: 3211 Baxberry Ct Decatur GA 30034

FOX, ANNETTE JOY, marketing specialist; b. Pacific Grove, Calif., Mar. 8, 1951; d. Kenneth Fredrick and Emma Margaret (Courtney) Brosi; children: Amber Leigh, Heather Leigh; m. Frederick William Fox, Dec. 15, 1985. BA, Ind. U., 1977; MBA, Amber U., 1987. Tax investigator Ind. Dept. Revenue, Indpls., 1971-73; service rep. Ind. Bell, Indpls., 1973-81, Southwestern Bell, Dallas, 1981-83; account specialist AT&T Info. Systems, Dallas, 1983-84; account exec. Executone, Dallas, 1984-85; coordinator mktg. Contel, Dallas, 1985-88; product mgr. Contel, Merrifield, Va., 1988—. Troop leader Girl Scouts Am., Richardson, Tex., 1985—; coach Richardson Soccer Assn., 1984-85. Mem. Am. Mktg. Assn., U.S. Telephone Assn., Nat. Assn. Female Execs. Club: Toastmasters. Home: 15801 Palmer Ln Haymarket VA 22069 Office: Contel PO Box 401 Merrifield VA 22116

FOX, CAROLYN ELAINE, nurse; b. Swannanoa, N.C., Aug. 28, 1933; d. William Marion and Sereptha (West) F. Diploma in Nursing, Rutherford Hosp., 1955; B.S. in Nursing, Western Carolina U., 1978, M.A. in Edn., 1981. RN. Staff nurse Highland Hosp., Asheville, N.C., 1955-64, head nurse, 1964-71, supr., 1972-73, acting dir. of nursing service, 1974-75, 84-85, asst. dir. of nursing service, 1975-79, clin. coordinator, 1979-84, assoc. dir. nursing service, 1985—. Contbr. articles to profl. publs. Mem. Am. Nurses Assn., N.C. Nurses Assn., Dist. #1 Nurses Assn. (bd. dirs., v.p.), Council of Psychiatric/Mental Health Nursing, Sigma Theta Tau. Baptist. Avocations: crafts; spectator sports; bowling; music; art. Home: 219 Richmond Ave Swannanoa NC 28778 Office: Highland Hosp Box 1101 Asheville NC 28802

FOX, ELIZABETH REGINA, educator; b. Neptune City, N.J.; d. John R. and Janet M. (Baldwin) O'R. BA, William Paterson Coll., 1980; MEd, U. Houston, 1984. Cert. early childhood edn., elem. and reading tchr., Tex. Tchr. Houston Ind. Sch. Dist., 1980-87, instructional supr., 1987-89; prin. Will Rogers Elem. Sch., Houston, 1989—; instr. Houston Community Coll., 1984-86; cons. Calvary Episc. Sch., Richmond, Tex., 1985; trainer IMPACT Ctr. for Thinking, San Diego, 1988—. Team leader United Way, Houston, 1982-86; vol. Christmas in Montrose, Houston, 1986—, Spl. Olympics, Houston, 1986—, Friends of the Houston Library, 1988—; mem. Children's Mus., Houston, 1987—. Named Outstanding Young Educator, Jaycees, 1986. Mem. Houston Coun. Edn., Nat. Assn. for Edn. Young Children, Houston Assn. Sch. Adminstrs., Assn. for Supervision and Curriculum Devel., Houston Assn. for Supervision and Curriculum Devel. (pres., dir.), Tex. Assn. for the Improvement of Reading (state bd. mem.), Harris County Dept. Edn. (mem. early childhood edn. leadershp group), Houston Edn. Exch. (founder), Greater Houston Area Reading Coun. Democrat. Roman Catholic. Home: 626 Omar Ave Houston TX 77009 Office: Will Rogers Elem Sch 3101 Weslayan Houston TX 77027

FOX, GAIL STRONG, physical fitness consultant; b. Schenectady, N.Y., Sept. 23, 1943; d. Donald N. and Hanna L. (Van Antwerp) Strong; m. John F. Fox, Aug. 14, 1966; children: Jennifer E., Joshua A. BA, SUNY, Oreonta, 1965; postgrad., SUNY, Albany, 1965-66. Tchr. Averill Park (N.Y.) Sch., 1965-70; vol. Girl Scouts U.S., Los Alamos, N.M., 1975-81, L.A. Schs. Credit Union, Los Alamos, 1982—; aerobics instr. Los Alamos Nat. Lab., 1982—; acting aerobics coord. Los Alamos Nat. Lab. Wellness Ctr., 1987-89, cons., 1989—. Mem. Los Alamos Credit Union Bd., 1982—, Republican Campaign Com., Los Alamos, 1986, 88; exec. bd. Golf Course Pool Assn., Los Alamos, 1982-85. Mem. Interna.t Dance Exercise Assn. Democrat. Roman Catholic. Home and Office: 540 Grand Canyon Los Alamos NM 87544

FOX, GRETCHEN HOVEMEYER, freelance editor, genealogical consultant; b. Erie, Pa., Jan. 2, 1940; d. Ernst Henry and Marjory Etta (Hollister) Hovemeyer; m. Kenneth Roland Fox, Apr. 23, 1989. AB, Radcliffe Coll., 1961. Manuscript sec. Internat. Tax Program, Harvard U. Law Sch.,

Cambridge, Mass., 1961-63; copy editor Internat. Tax Program, Harvard U. Law Sch., Cambridge, 1963-65, editorial asst., 1965-66, publs. asst., 1966-76, editorial and pub. dir., 1976-89; freelance editor, cons. pub. and genealogy Cambridge, 1989—. Co-compiler: Bibliography on Taxation of Foreign Operations and Foreigners: 1968-75, 1976, Bibliography on Taxation of Foreign Operations and Foreigners: 1976-82, 1983; contbr. articles on geneal. to prof. jours.; designer computer software. Mem. New Eng. Hist. Geneal. Soc., Orange County Geneal. Soc. (pub. cons. 1983—), Sullivan County (N.Y.) Hist. Soc., DAR (chpt. registrar, chpt. historian 1978-83). Home and Office: 10 Agassiz St Apt 21 Cambridge MA 02140

FOX, JEANNE MARIE, lawyer; b. Phila., May 30, 1952; d. Samuel Cooper and Palmira Caroline (Ungerbuehler) F.; m. Stephan DeMicco, Sept. 29, 1979. BA, Douglass Coll., Rutgers U., New Brunswick, 1975; JD, Rutgers Sch. of Law, Camden, 1979; completed Program for State and Local Govt. Execs., Harvard U., 1989. Lawyer. Letter carrier U.S. Post Office, Delran, 1971, 73, 76; intern U.S. Dept. of Environ. Protection, Edison, Phila., 1974, 77; law clerk Bd. of Pub. Utilities, Newark, N.J., 1978, N.J. Supr. Court, Camden, N.J., 1978, 79; policy dir. N.J. Democrat. State Com., Trenton, N.J., 1979-80; atty. N.J. Office of the Sec. of State, 1980-82; regulatory officer Bd. of Pub. Utilities, Newark, 1982-85, deputy dir., 1985-87; dir. N.J. Bd. of Pub. Utilities, 1987-89, sr. advisor for policy and mgmt., 1989—. Contbr. articles to profl. jours. chairperson, com. on the Status of Women, Middlesex, 1985-89; pres. Middlesex County Women's Polit. Caucus, 1984-86, Women's Polit. Caucus of N.J., 1988—; mem. steering com. and adminstrn. com. Nat. Women's Polit. Caucus, 1989—; bd. dirs. Douglass Coll. Assoc. Alumnae, 1985—; trustee Rutgers U., 1989—; mem. N.J. Commn. on Sex in the Statutes, 1989—. Named Outstanding Young Woman of N.J. Outstanding Young Women of Am., 1985, N.J. Women of Achievement N.J. Women's Clubs & Douglass Coll., 1986, Jerseyan of the Week Star Ledger, 1986. Mem. N.J. State Bar Assn., Rutgers Sch. of Law Alumni Assn., Rutgers Club. Democrat. Home: 227 New York Ave New Brunswick NJ 08901 Office: Bd of Pub Utilities Gateway II Newark NJ 07102

FOX, JOAN MICHELLE, advertising executive; b. N.Y.C., Jan. 31, 1947; d. Walter Bernard and Doris (Rachelson) Strauss; m. Martin Leonard Fox, Jan. 8, 1978; children: Wendy Robyn, Jessica Randi. Assoc. in Bus. and Fin., CCNY, 1964, BA in Spl. Edn./Econs., 1966. Tchr. spl. edn. N.Y.C. Sch. System, 1967-69; controller Beaumont-Bennett Advt., N.Y.C., 1969-72; bus. mgr. Radio Sales div. Metromedia, N.Y.C., 1972-74; asst. treas. Einstein Assocs. Inc., N.Y.C., 1974-77; from controller to sr. v.p. fin. planning and adminstrn. Ogilvy & Mather U.S., N.Y.C., 1977-89; sr. v.p. adminstrn. Ogilvy & Mather, Chgo., 1989—. Mem. ASCAP, Assn. Advt. Fin. Mgrs., Corp. East Mgrs., Assn. N.Y. Treas. and Fin. Mgrs. Assn., Advt. Women of N.Y., Women's Econs. Round Table, Am. Mgmt. Assn. Office: Ogilvy & Mather 676 St Clair Chicago IL 60611*

FOX, KAREN, architect; b. Phila., Mar. 19, 1949; d. Joseph Robert and Jane (Jarrett) F. AA, Pine Manor Coll., 1969; BA, Boston U., 1971; BArch, RISD, 1974; MBA, Simmons Coll., 1989. Registered architect, D.C. Staff architect Cannon, Washington, 1975-77, Mariani, Washington, 1977-78, Arthur Cotton Moore, Washington, 1978, Wilkes & Faulkner, Washington, 1979-81, Notter Finegold, Washington, 1981-82; assoc. Stubbins Assn., Cambridge, Mass., 1982—; chair program com. Washington Women in Architecture, 1975-82. Chair cons. com. Jr. League of Boston, 1987—. Mem. Am. Inst. Architecture, Boston Soc. Architects. Republican. Quaker. Home: 41 Bowdoin St Cambridge MA 02138

FOX, KELLY DIANE, assistant buyer; b. Brockton, Mass., Sept. 9, 1959; d. James H. and Betty Jane (Calloway) F.; m. Alan David Goldberg, July 6, 1985; 1 child, Andrew Jason. B.A., Allegheny Coll., 1980; postgrad. in Bus. Adminstrn., Suffolk U., 1983-84; student Temple U., London, 1978, Syracuse U., London, 1979. Asst. mgr. Casual Male, Braintree, Mass., 1980, Hit or Miss, Braintree, 1981-82; merchandiser Foxmoor, West Bridgewater, Mass., 1982; distbr. Hill's Dept. Stores, Canton, Mass., 1982-85; asst. buyer BJ's Wholesale Club, Natick, Mass., 1985—; cheerleading coach Avon High Sch., Mass., 1982-83. Mem. Nat. Assn. Female Execs. Methodist. Avocations: dance, exercise, cooking, art galleries.

FOX, KYMBERLY COVERT, manufacturing company executive; b. Mt. Gilead, Ohio, Feb. 3, 1960; d. Donald Lacey and Martha (Rodella) Covert; m. William G. Fox, Aug. 31, 1982; 1 child, Dustin James. BA, Baldwin-Wallace Coll., 1982. Personnel dir. Covert Mfg., Inc., Galion, Ohio, 1982-84; contract adminstr., mil. div. Covert Mfg., Inc., 1985-87, gen. mgr. pump div., 1987—, also bd. dirs. Mem. Sump and Sewage Pump Mfg. Assn., Galion C. of C. (bd. dirs. 1987—), Crawford County Pvt. Industry Coun. (bd. dirs. 1987-88). Republican. Methodist. Home: 6040 Crawford Morrow LineRd Galion OH 44833 Office: Covert Mfg Inc 328 S East St Galion OH 44833

FOX, MARYE ANNE, chemistry educator; b. Canton, Ohio, Dec. 9, 1947. BS, Notre Dame Coll. of Ohio, 1969; MS, Cleve. State U., 1970; PhD, Dartmouth Coll., 1974; postgrad., U. Md., 1974076. Prof. chemistry U. Tex., Austin, 1976—, now Rowland Pettit Centennial prof.; mem. adv. bd. NRC, Commn. on Phys. Scis., Math. and Applications, 1987—, workshop on Chemistry Dept. of the Future, 1987; mem. adv. com. for chemistry NSF, 1989—, selection coms. grad. fellowships, 1985, Presdl. Young Investigators, 1986, Sci. and Tech. Ctrs., 1988, Sci. and Tech. Ctr. on Photoinduced Electron Transfer, U. Rochester, Kodak, Xerox, 1989—; mem. Med. Chemistry A Study Sect. NIH, 1987—, Com. on Recommendations, U.S. Army Rsch. Office, 1984-87; external reviewer Notre Dame Radiation Rsch. Lab., 1983, Brookhaven Nat. Lab., 1986, Lab. for Chem. Biodynamics, Berkeley, 1988. Assoc. editor: Jour. Am. Chem. Soc., 1986—; mem. adv. bd. Journ. Organic Chemistry, 1985-89; contbr. numerous articles to profl. jours. Recipient Agnes Faye Morgan Rsch. award, Iota Sigma Pi, 1984, Arthur C. Cope scholar award Am. Chem. Soc., 1988; named to Hall of Excellence, Ohio Found. Ind. Colls., 1987, The Best of the New Generation, Esquire Mag., 1984; Alfred P. Sloan Rsch. fellow, 1980-82, Camille and Henry Dreyfus tchr. scholar, 1981-85. Home: 5203 Valburn Circle Austin TX 78731 Office: Univ of Texas Dept of Chemistry Austin TX 78712

FOX, MURIEL, public relations executive; b. Newark, Feb. 3, 1928; d. M. Morris and Anne L. (Rubenstein) F.; m. Shepard G. Aronson, July 1, 1955; children: Eric R., Lisa S. Student, Rollins Coll., 1944-46; B.A. summa cum laude, Barnard Coll., 1948. Art critic, bridal editor Miami (Fla.) News, 1946; reporter U.P.I., 1946-48; polit. speechwriter, publicist, 1949-50; with Carl Byoir & Assos., N.Y.C., 1950-86; TV-radio writer Carl Byoir & Assos., 1950-52, dir. TV-radio dept., 1952-57, v.p., 1956-74, group v.p., 1974-76, exec. v.p., 1977-85; pres. subs. MediaCom Communications Tng., 1975-85, By/Media Inc., 1981-85; sr. cons. Hill & Knowlton, Inc., 1986—; dir. Harleysville Ins. Co., Rorer Group Inc.; Co-chmn. Vice Presdl. Task Force on Women, 1968; mem. steering com. Women's Forum, 1974-79, pres., 1976-78; mem. Women's Econ. Adv. Com., N.Y.C., 1974-78; mem. nat. adv. com. Nat. Women's Polit. Caucus; mem. nat. adv. bd. Women Today, Ethnic Woman. Bd. dirs. N.Y. Diabetes Assn., 1956-66; bd. dirs. Holy Land Conservation Fund, United Way of Tri-State, Internat. Rescue Com., 1977-84; v.p. Rockland Ctr. for the Arts, 1985—. Named one of 100 Top Corp. Women Bus. Week mag., 1976; recipient Matrix award Women in Communications, 1977, Bus. Leader of Year award ADA, 1979; Disting. Alumna award Barnard Coll., 1985; Eleanor Roosevelt Leadership award, 1985. Mem. Am. Women in Radio and TV (dir. 1959-61, chmn. nat. publicity com. 1955-57, chmn. nat. pub. relations com. 1957-59, Achievement award 1983), NOW (founder, v.p. 1967-70, chmn. bd. 1971-73, chmn. nat. adv. com. 1973-74, bd. dirs. Legal Def. and Edn. Fund 1974—, v.p. Fund 1977-78, pres. 1978-81, chmn. bd. 1981—), Am. Arbitration Assn. (bd. dirs. 1983-87). Home and Office: 66 Hickory Hill Rd Tappan NY 10983

FOX, PHYLLIS ANN, computer software consultant; b. Denver, Mar. 13, 1923; d. Rudolph Herzer and Karen Irene (Denton) F.; m. George Sternlieb, Apr. 25, 1958; children: David, Benjamin. BA in Math., Wellesley Coll., 1944; BSEE, U. Colo., 1948; MEE, MIT, 1949, D in Math., 1954. Programmer, differential analyzer Gen. Electric Co., Schenectady, N.Y., 1944-46; rsch. assoc. Atomic Energy Computing Ctr. Courant Inst./NYU, 1954-58; rsch. assoc. Sch. Indsl. Mgmt. MIT, Cambridge, 1958-60, rsch. assoc. Computation Ctr., 1960-62; prof. computer sci. N.J. Inst. Tech., Newark, 1963-73; mem. tech. staff Bell Labs., Murray Hill, N.J., 1973-84. Author: LISP Programmer's Manual, 1961, (monograph) Safety in Car Following, 1967; author, editor (three-vol. manual and software) PORT Math. Subroutine Libr., 1974, 84. Fellow AAAS; mem. Assn. for Computing Machinery, Soc. for Indsl. and Applied Math., Assn. for Women in Math. Home: 66 Old Short Hills Rd Short Hills NJ 07078

FOX, RENÉE CLAIRE, sociology educator; b. N.Y.C., Feb. 15, 1928; d. Paul Fred and Henrietta (Gold) F. A.B. summa cum laude, Smith Coll., 1949, L.H.D., 1975; Ph.D., Harvard U., 1954; M.A. (hon.), U. Pa., 1971; Sc.D. (hon.), Med. Coll. Pa., 1974, St. Joseph's Coll., Phila., 1978; D. honoris causa, Katholieke U., Belgium, 1978; LHD (hon.), La Salle U., Phila., 1988. Research asst. Bur. Applied Social Research, Columbia U., 1953-55, research asso., 1955-58; lectr. dept. sociology Barnard Coll., 1955-58, asst. prof., 1958-64, assoc. prof., 1964-66; lectr. sociology Harvard U., 1967-69; research fellow Center Internat. Affairs, 1967-68, research assoc. program tech. and soc., 1968-71; prof. sociology, psychiatry and medicine U. Pa., Phila., 1969—, Annenberg prof. social scis., 1978—, chmn. dept. sociology, 1972-78; Sci. adviser Centre de Recherches Sociologiques, Kinshasa, Congo, 1963-67; vis. prof. sociology U. Officielle du Congo, Lubumbashi, 1965; vis. prof. Sir George Williams U., Montreal, Que., Can., summer 1968; Phi Beta Kappa vis. scholar, 1973-75; dir. humanities seminar med. practitioners Nat. Endowment Humanities, 1975-76; maitre de cours U. Liége, Belgium, 1976-77; vis. prof. Katholieke U., Leuven, Belgium, 1976-77; Wm. Allen Neilson prof. Smith Coll., Mass., 1980; dir. d' Etudes Associé, Ecole des Hautes Etudes en Sciences Sociales, Paris, summer 1989; mem. bd. clin. scholars program Robert Wood Johnson Found., 1974-80; mem. Pres.'s Commn. on Study of Ethical Problems in Medicine, Biomed. and Behavioral Research, 1979-81; dir. human qualities of medicine program James Picker Found., 1980-83; Fal Golden Kass lectr. Harvard U. Sch. Medicine and Radcliffe Coll., 1983, Kate Hard Mead lectr. Med. Coll. Pa./Coll. Physicians Phila., 1990. Author: Experiment Perilous, 1959, (with Willy DeCraemer) The Emerging Physician, 1968, (with Judith P. Swazey) The Courage to Fail: Essays in Medical Sociology, 1979, 2d edit., 1988, L'Incertitude Medicale, 1988, The Sociology of Medicine: A Participant Observer's View, 1989; assoc. editor: Am. Sociol. Rev, 1963-66, Social Sci. and Medicine; mem. editorial com.: Ann. Rev. Sociology, 1975-79; assoc. editor Jour. Health and Social Behavior, 1985-87; mem. editorial adv. bd.: Tech. in Soc, Science, 1982-83; editorial bd.: Bibliography of Bioethics, 1979—, Culture, Medicine and Psychiatry, 1980-86, Jour. of AMA, 1981—; contbr. articles to profl. jours. Bd. dirs. Medicine in Public Interest, 1979—; mem. tech. bd. Milbank Meml. Fund, 1979-85; mem. overseers com. to visit univ. health services Harvard Coll., 1979-86; trustee Russell Sage Found., 1981-87; vice chmn. bd. dirs. Acadia Inst., 1990—. Recipient E. Harris Harbison Gifted Teaching award Danforth Found., 1970, Radcliffe Grad. Soc. medal, 1977, Lindback Found. award for teaching, U. Pa., 1989; Wilson Ctr., Smithsonian Instn. fellow, 1987-88, Guggenheim fellow, 1962. Fellow African Studies Assn., AAAS (dir. 1977-80, chmn. sect. K 1986-87), Am. Sociol. Assn. (council 1970-73, 79-81, v.p. 1980-81), Am. Acad. Arts and Scis., Inst. Medicine (Nat. Acad. Scis., council 1979-82), Inst. Soc., Ethics and Life Scis. (founder, gov.); mem. AAUP, AAUW, Assn. Am. Med. Colls., Social Sci. Research Council (v.p., dir.), Eastern Sociol. Soc. (pres. 1976-77), N.Y. Acad. Scis., Soc. Sci. Study Religion, Inst. Intercultural Studies (asst. sec. 1969-78, sec. 1978-81, 89—, v.p. 1987-89), Am. Bd. Med. Specialists, Phi Beta Kappa (senate 1982-87). Home: 135 S 19th St Philadelphia PA 19103

FOX, SIMONE MARTHA, photographer, business owner; b. Lubeck, West Germany, Apr. 13, 1961; came to U.S., 1962; d. Heinz Gunther and Elaine (Cencel) Kilian; m. James P. Fox, Nov. 11, 1989. Student, U. Ark., 1977-80, UCLA, 1986, Mass. Coll. of Art, 1987; BFA, NYU, 1988. Photographer Simone Kilian Photography, 1982-89, Fox Photography, N.Y.C., 1989—; press photographer East Village Eye, N.Y.C., 1982-83, New Mus. Express, London, 1983-84; mgr. Eyetype, N.Y.C., 1987-89; press photographer Details mag., N.Y.C., 1988. Photographer: book James, 1988. Mem. Internat. Freelance Photographer's Orgn. Episcopalian. Home and Office: 409 E 116 #4 New York NY 10029

FOX, VIRGINIA GAINES, public broadcasting executive; b. Campbellsville, Ky., Apr. 30, 1939; d. Harold Durrett and Kathryn (Arnold) Gaines; m. Victor Fox, Dec. 27, 1963. BA in Edn., Morehead State U., 1961; MSLS, U. Ky., 1969. Cert. tchr., librarian, Ky. Tchr. Franklin County Schs., Frankfort, Ky., 1961-62, Mason County Schs., Maysville, Ky., 1962-63, Whiteland Elem. Sch., Ind., 1963-64; tchr., librarian Fayette County Schs., Lexington, Ky., 1964-68; utilization specialist Ky. Ednl. TV, Lexington, 1968-69, asst. dir. edn. for evaluation, 1969-70, exec. asst. to exec. dir., 1970-71, dir. edn., 1971-74, dir. edn. and programming, 1974-75, dep. exec. dir., 1974-80; pres., chief exec. officer So. Ednl. Communications Assn., Columbia, S.C., 1980-88; exec. v.p. KET Found., Lexington, Ky., 1988—; pres. KET Endowment, Lexington, 1988—; mem. nat. adv. com. Children's TV Workshop, N.Y.C., 1979—, Teleconnect Database Mktg. Co., Cedar Rapids, Iowa, informal sci. edn. panel NSF, Washington, 1986—; dir. Editorial Integrity Project, Columbia, 1984—; cons. programming int the arts/TV adv. panel Nat. Endowment for the Arts, 1988—, Challenge III media panel, 1989. Exec. producer TV programs: Just One Day, 1979 (Eudora Welty award 1980), Vectoria, 1978 (Corp. for Pub. Broadcasting award 1979), GED. Named Woman of Yr. in Edn., Lexington Bus. and Profl. Women's Club, 1971-72. Mem. Am. Soc. Assn. Execs., Nat. Assn. Ednl. Broadcasters, ALA, Assn. for Ednl. Communications and Tech. (Edgar Dale award region V 1975), Wildlife Action. Episcopalian. Avocations: reading, golf, piano, running. Home: 135 Locust Hill Frankfort KY 40601 Office: KET Found 600 Cooper Dr Lexington KY 40502

FOX, WENDELLA PENISTER, lawyer; b. Balt., Sept. 21, 1951; d. Charles Washington Jr. and Lucille Eleanor (Penister) F. BA, U. Pa., 1973, JD, 1976. Bar: Pa. 1977, U.S. Dist. Ct. (ea. dist.) Pa. 1980, U.S. Ct. Appeals (3d cir.) 1981. Staff atty. NLRB, Phila., 1976-81; assoc. Freed and Larry, Phila., 1981-82; pvt. practice Phila., 1982; ptnr. Jackson, Fox & Evans, Phila., 1983-87; dep. chief counsel State of Pa. Dept. of Labor, Harrisburg, 1987-88; ptnr. Mylotte, David & Fitzpatrick, Phila., 1988—. Chair Phila. Zoning Bd., 1984-89; counsel to state senator Chaka Fattah and state rep. Vincent Hughes, 1988. Mem. Barristers, Phila. Bar Assn., Urban League. Democrat. Episcopalian. Office: Mylotte David & Fitzpatrick 1800 JFK Blvd 7th Fl Philadelphia PA 19103

FOX-BISWELL, EILEEN MARIE, pediatrician; b. Ft. Worth, Aug. 5, 1954; d. Richard Howell and Evelyn Marie (Mayhew) Fox; m. Donald Arthur Buswell Jr., May 25, 1985; children: Bradley Allen, Brian Andrew. BS, Tex. Christian U., 1976; MD, UTMB at Galveston, 1979. Pediatric practice Drs. Fox & Fields, Norman, Okla., 1982--; chief of staff J.D. McCarty Ctr. for Handicapped Children, Norman, 1984--; chief of pediatrics Norman Regional Hosp., 1986; sec. Med. Staff Norman Regional Hosp.; chief of staff Med. Staff J.D. McCarthy, Norman, 1984--. Bd. dirs. Juvenile Services, Norman, 1983--; big sister Big Brothers, Big Sisters, Norman, 1984-87; bd. dirs. Communicty Med. Lab., Norman, 1987--. Fellow: Am. Acad. of Pediatrics, Am. Acad. of Cerebral Palsy; mem. Pediatric Con. (chief of pediatric, 1986). Democrat. Methodist. Office: Drs Fox & Fields 500 E Robinson #2600 Norman OK 73071

FOXEN, LYNNE ANNE, insurance company executive; b. Teaneck, N.J., Mar. 8, 1950; d. Joseph Patrick and Yolanda A. (Franchini) F. BS, St. Peter's Coll., 1980. Asst. treas. arms div. Ashford Holding Corp., N.Y.C., 1975-77, fin. planning mgr. MIC div., 1977-82, asst. v.p., 1982-84; dir. Empire Blue Cross Blue Shield, N.Y.C., 1984-88; sr. bus. analyst Am. Mgmt. Systems, Roseland, N.J., 1988—. Mem. Assn. Women in Prodn., NAFE. Home: 147 Magnolia Ave Tenafly NJ 07670

FOX-FENELON, LAURA MICHELE, graphic design business owner; b. Glen Ridge, N.J., June 13, 1962; d. Dennis Michael and Julia Eileen (Francis) F. Student, C.W. Post Coll., Greenvale, N.Y., 1980-82, Parsons Sch. of Design, N.Y., 1982-83; BFA Cum Laude, Montclair State Coll., 1986. Typesetter, artist type and design shop C.W. Post Coll., Greenvale, N.Y., 1981-82; typesetter, artist Pub-Set Inc., Union, N.J., 1982-84; framer Frames and Framers, Short Hills, N.J., 1985-86; studio artist Salthouse, Torre and Ferrante, Rutherford, N.J., 1986-87; asst. to group product design dir. C&G Advt. Agy., Inc., Ciba-Geigy Pharms., Summit, N.J., 1988—, LMF Graphics, Maplewood, N.J., 1988—; mem. Hunterton Art Ctr., Clinton, 1988—, N.J. Ctr for Visual Arts, Summit, 1988-89. Leader Girl Scouts U.S.A. for Handicapped, Matheny Sch., Peapack, N.J., 1987-89. Recipient Acad. Scholarship Advt. Club of North Jersey, 1985. Home and Office: 15 Maple Terr Maplewood NJ 07040

FOX-FREUND, BARBARA SUSAN, real estate executive; b. Rocky Mount, N.C., Jan. 17, 1949; d. Albert Richard and Anita (Levinson) Fox; m. James Coleman Freund, Jan. 12, 1985. Student, Centenary Coll., 1968, Boston U., 1970. Real estate broker Whitbread-Nolan, Inc., N.Y.C., 1972-80; v.p. Stribling and Assocs., Ltd., N.Y.C., 1980-82; exec. v.p. Cross and Brown Residentials, Inc., N.Y.C., 1982-88; pres. Fox Residential Group, Inc., N.Y.C., 1988—. Bd. dirs. Riverside Symphony, N.Y.C., 1989; bd. dirs., pres. 55 W. 73d St. Corp., N.Y.C., 1986—. Mem. Real Estate Bd. N.Y. (chmn. residential com. 1986-89, ethics com. 1989—, bd. dirs. brokerage com. 1988—, tchr., 1986—). Republican. Jewish. Home: 55 W 73d St New York NY 10023 Office: Fox Residential Group Inc 43 E 78th St New York NY 10021

FOX-ROSELLINI, SUSAN EVA, marketing executive; b. N.Y.C., Apr. 8, 1956; d. William and Barbara (Weil) Fox; married, 1989. BBA, George Washington U., 1978. Teaching asst. George Washington U., 1977-78; human resource assoc. Am. Can Co., Greenwich, Conn., 1978-79; project coordinator bus. resources Am. Can Internat., Greenwich, 1979-82; dir. mktg. ops. U.S. San. de Mex. subs. Am. Can Co., Mexico City, 1982-83; sr. account mgr. Mass Mktg. Systems Internat. subs. Am. Can, N.Y.C., 1983-84; asst. v.p. Bankcard Mktg., Citicorp Credit Services Inc., N.Y.C., 1984-88; v.p. ins. Citibank, N.A., N.Y.C., 1988-89; v.p. bank products Access Am. (subs. Blue Cross/Blue Shield), 1989—. Vol. Ford Presdl. Com., Washington, 1978, Nixon Presdl. Com., N.Y.C., 1974; bd. dirs. CAD div. Am. Jewish Com., 1983—. Recipient Excellence in internat. bus. award George Washington U., 1978. Mem. Direct Mail Assn., Nat. Assn. Female Execs., N.Y. Jr. League, Excelsior Club. Office: Access Am 600 Third Ave 4th Fl New York NY 10016

FOY, DEBORAH SANFORD, social worker; b. Monroe, La., Feb. 17, 1954; d. Fred Darden Sanford and Gladys (Schoen) Thompson; m. Gary Dee Foy, May 9, 1981. BA in Sociology and Social Work, S.W. Tex. State U., 1975. Cert. social worker, Tex. Social worker Dept. Human Svcs. State of Tex., Austin, 1976-81; program coord. Day Care Assn. of Ft. Worth and Tarrant County, 1982-84; disability examiner Disability Determination div. Tex. Rehab. Commn., Austin, 1984—; cons. Social Studies, Austin and Travis County, Tex. 1984—. Vol. Hotline to Help, San Marcos, Tex., 1975-78, Big Bro.-Big Sister program, Austin, 1978-80; treas. Sandybrook Neighborhood Assn., Ft. Worth, 1981-83; chairperson Community Resources, Lockhart, Tex., 1977-79; social activities chairperson Milwood Neighborhood Assn., 1988-90. Mem. Nat. Assn. Social Workers, Nat. Assn. Disability Examiners, Tex. Assn. Disability Examiners, Milwood Neighborhood Assn. Home: 4522 Sidereal Dr Austin TX 78727-5105

FOY, HJORDIS ELSA MANNBECK, epidemiology educator; b. Stockholm, June 28, 1926; came to U.S., 1956; d. Lewi Axel Emanuel and Elsa Amalia (Lindbom) Mannbeck; m. Robert Eugene Foy, Nov. 23, 1956; children: Katherine Elisabeth, Rebecca Elsa, Clarissa Barbara. MD, Karolinska Inst., Stockholm, 1953; MS, U. Wash., 1967, PhD, 1968. Diplomate Am. Bd. Preventive Medicine. Staff neursurgery and psychiatry Southern Hosp., Stockholm, 1953; staff medicine Hosp. Infectious Diseases, Stockholm, 1953-56, Swedish Red Cross Hosp., Pusan, Republic of Korea, 1954-55; intern, fellow Johns Hopkins Hosp., Balt., 1956-58; staff Station Hosp., Ft. G. Meade, Md., 1960-61; admitting physician VA Hosp., Denver, 1963; resident, st. fellow dept. preventive medicine U. Wash., Seattle, 1963-66, asst. prof. dept. preventive medicine, 1968-70, assoc. prof. dept. epidemiology, 1970-72, prof. dept. epidemiology, 1976—; acting chmn. dept epidemiology U. Wash., Seattle, 1980, dir. preventive medicine tng., 1983-89; cons. Ministry Pub. Health, Bangkok, Thailand, 1987-88. Co-author books primarily on acute respiratory infections and pneumonia; contbr.articles to profl. jours. Capt. med. svc. Swedish mil., 1954-55. Rsch. grantee NIH Epidemiology of M. Pneumoniae Infections, 1972, Non-bacterial Infections in Obstetrics, 1974, Immunity to Mycoplasma Pneumoniae Infections, 1975, Influenza Epidemiology and Immunity, 1976, Seroepidemiological Study of Legionella Infections, 1980, Preventive Medicine Residency Tng., 1983, Long Term Studies of Infections in Families, 1984, tng. grantee Dept. Social Svcs., Bethesda, 1980, 83, 84. Fellow Infectious Diseases Soc. Am., Am. Coll. Preventive Medicine; mem. Am. Epidemiol. Soc., Internat. Epidemiol. Soc., Soc. for Epidemiol. Rsch., Am. Soc. for Virology, Internat. Soc. Mycoplasmologists. Office: Dept Epidemiology SC 36 Pacific Ave Seattle WA 98195

FOY, MARGUERITE ELISABETH, adult home administrator; b. Crillon, Oise, France, Dec. 28, 1952; d. Francis Glen and Marguerite (Thibault) F. BA, Dowling Coll., Oakdale, N.Y., 1978. Cert. adult home administr., N.Y. Libr. technician Dowling Coll., 1971-77; realtor, 1973-79; adminstr., owner Golden Villa Rest Home, Lake Ronkonkoma, N.Y., 1979—. Instr. first aid ARC, Coram, N.Y., 1989—. Mem. Empire State Assn. Adult Homes (charter), Greater Ronkonkomas C. of C. Office: Golden Villa Rest Home 58 Portion Rd Lake Ronkonkoma NY 11779

FOYE, JENNIFER WILDER, healthcare professional; b. Detroit, Aug. 17, 1959; d. William Thornton and Sara Geneva (Stewart) Wilder; m. Scott Anthony Foye, Aug. 15, 1981. BS in Speech Pathology and Audiology, Kent State U., 1981. Audiometric technician, med. asst. Luth. Med. Ctr., Cleve., 1982-85, mktg. rep., 1985-89, coord., occupational health svcs., 1989—; adv. coun. Playhouse Sq. Counseling, Cleve., 1987—; adv. bd. Vocat. Guidance Svcs., Cleve., 1988—. Exec. com. mem. Cuyahoga County Rep. Party, Cleve., 1989. Mem. Kiwanis Internat. (bd. dirs. West Park Club 1988, Cleve. Club membership, youth svcs.), Delta Gamma. Roman Catholic. Office: Luth Med Ctr 2609 Franklin Blvd Cleveland OH 44113

FRACALOSSI, SHELLEY ANN, business consultant, business owner, accountant; b. Plattsburgh, N.Y., June 14, 1954; d. William and Bertha May (Beckwith) Grube; m. Daniel H. Fracalossi, Jan. 10, 1976; 1 child, Elisabeth Mary. Student, Oxford U., 1973; BA in English, SUNY, Plattsburgh, 1976. Tax preparer H&R Block, Plattsburgh, 1976-88; owner Trinity Pk. Antiques, Plattsburgh, 1980—, Complete Bookkeeping Svc., Plattsburgh, 1986—; gen. mgr. Gowett's Trucking, Plattsburgh, 1987—. Author poetry. Crary Fund scholar, SUNY, 1972. Mem. Clinton County C. of C. Office: Complete Bookkeeping Svc 36 Miller St Plattsburgh NY 12901

FRACKMAN, NOEL, art critic; b. N.Y.C., May 27, 1930; d. Walter David and Celeste (Barman) Stern; m. Richard Benoit Frackman, July 2, 1950; 1 dau., Noel Dru. Student Mt. Holyoke Coll., 1948-50; BA, Sarah Lawrence Coll., 1952, MS, 1953; postgrad. Columbia U., 1964-67; MA, Inst. Fine Arts, NYU, 1976, PhD, 1987. Art critic Scarsdale Inquirer (N.Y.), 1962-67, Patent Trader, Mt. Kisco, N.Y., 1962-71; assoc. Arts Mag., N.Y.C., 1968—; lectr. Aldrich Mus. Contemporary Art, Ridgefield, Conn., 1967-75, Gallery Passport Ltd., N.Y.C., 1968—; curator of edn. Storm King Art Ctr., Mountainville, N.Y., 1973-75. Author (catalogue) John Storrs, Whitney Mus. of Am. Art, 1986; contbr. articles and/or revs. to various mags. including: Arts Mag., Harper's Bazaar, Feminist Art Jour., Art Voices. Sarah Williston scholar, 1948-50; recipient 1st prize, coll. publs. contest Mademoiselle mag., 1961. Mem. Internat. Assn. Art Critics, Art Table Inc., Coll. Art Assn. Home: 3 Hadden Rd Scarsdale NY 10583

FRADKIN, MINDY SUE, fashion stylist, costume and hat designer; b. Balt., June 3, 1955; d. Robert Bernard Fradkin and Dorothy (Wolfe) Hight. Student, Art Ctr., Los Angeles, 1979-81; AA with honors, Art Ctr. Coll. of Design, Los Angeles, 1983. Freelance asst. stylist, Los Angeles, 1982-83, N.Y.C., 1983-84; stylist, prodn. coord. Cailor Resnick Studio, N.Y.C., 1984; free-lance fashion stylist and costume designer for print and film, N.Y.C., 1985—. Appeared on TV in World of Photography; created costumes (film) Simple Justice, 1989, Hats by Mindy, 1989. Active Big Sisters. Mem. Nat. Assn. Broadcast Employees and Technicians, Assn. Stylists and Coordinators (sec. 1984-85), Stylists and Allied Svcs. (bd. dirs. 1985-86), The Fashion Group (publs. com., photographer), N.Y. Women in Film, 1989. Democrat. Avocations: writing, opera, classical and jazz music, reading, films. Office: 313 W 75th St 4B New York NY 10023

FRAGA, TINA ANTOINETTE, sales executive; b. Arlington, Va., Mar. 4, 1965; d. Donald Phillip and Sandra Ann (Urani) Ceccarelli; m. Michael Richard Fraga, Jan. 9, 1988. BS in Indsl. Psychology, George Mason U., 1987. Account exec. Coffee Butler Svc. Inc., Alexandria, Va., 1988, sales trainer, 1989, sales supr., 1989—. Mem. NAFE, Prince William County C. of C., Toastmasters. Roman Catholic. Office: Coffee Butler Svc Inc 3660 Wheeler Ave Alexandria VA 22304

FRAHM, GRECHEN KAI, dietitian; b. Ashland, Ky., May 5, 1959; d. Richard Paul Buyalos and Jeanette Paige (Abernathy) Nanninga; m. Perry Hayden Frahm, Sept. 5, 1987; 1 child, Jacob Hayden. BA in Foods and Nutrition, San Diego State U., 1981. With Mission Bay Meml. Hosp., San Diego, 1982-84, diet technician, 1983-84; dietetic intern Ind. U. Sch. Medicine, Indpls., 1984; clinical dietitian San Antonio Community Hosp., Upland, Calif., 1984-86; adminstrv. dietitian High Desert Hosp., Lancaster, Calif., 1986-87; clin. dietitian Palmdale (Calif.) Hosp. Med. Ctr., 1987-88, dietary dir., 1988—; adj. instr. Antelope Valley Community Coll., Lancaster, 1988—. Mem. Am. Dietetic Assn., Calif. Dietetic Assn., Phi Upsilon Omicron, Beta Sigma Phi. Republican. Home: Po Box 2037 Wrightwood CA 92397 Office: Palmdale Hosp Med Ctr 1212 East Ave S Palmdale CA 93550

FRAHM, SHEILA, state legislator; b. Colby, Kans., Mar. 22, 1945; m. Kenneth Frahm; children: Amy, Pam, Chrissie. BS, Ft. Hays State U., 1967. Mem. bd. edn. State of Kans., 1985-88, state senator from dist. 40, 1988—. Mem. AAUW (Outstanding Br. Mem. 1985), Thomas County Day Care Assn., Shakespeare Fedn. Women's Clubs, Farm Bur., Kans. Corn Growers, Kans. Livestock Assn., Rotary (Paul Harris fellow 1988). Republican. Address: 985 S Range Colby KS 67701*

FRAHM, SUE ADELE, university administrator; b. Beatrice, Nebr., Jan. 16, 1941; d. Berwin Richard and Kathryn Mary (Burroughs) Shaffer; m. Larry Dean Frahm, Aug. 17, 1963; children—Jeffrey Michael, Kristi Anne. B.A., Nebr. Wesleyan U., 1962; M.S., U. Nebr.-Lincoln, 1978. Instr., Southeast Community Coll., Lincoln, 1972-77, project asst. Ctr. on Aging, 1977-78, aging coordinator, 1978-79, asst. coord. adult edn., 1979-80; alumni dir. Wesleyan U., Nebr., 1982-89; campaign dir. United Way of Lincoln and Lancaster County; trainer Minn. Couples Communication Program, Mpls., 1977-82. Pres., 1st v.p. YWCA, Lincoln, 1978-85; bd. dirs. Lincoln council Camp Fire, 1975-78, Lincoln Ctr. for Srs., 1970-76; co-pres. Community Adv. Council, Lincoln, 1985-86. Mem. Adult Continuing Edn. of Nebr., Omicron Nu. Avocations: reading, backpacking. Home: 8033 Sanborn Dr Lincoln NE 68505 Office: United Way 215 Centennial Mall South Ste 112 Lincoln NE 68508

FRAHM, TONI ROBINSON, caterer, party consultant; b. Buffalo, July 31, 1947; d. John Stanley and Jaye (Valery) Robinson; m. Barry Hirsch Frahm, Aug. 20, 1978; 1 child, Jason Ashley. Model John Robert Powers Agy., Boston, 1966-68; stewardess United Airlines, Newark, 1968-70; dir. tour svcs. Am. Internat. Travel Svc., Newton, Mass., 1970-77; owner, caterer Talk of the Town, Inc., Greensboro, N.C., 1982—; owner, mgr. Talk of The Town Limousine Svc., Greensboro, 1984—, Incredible Edibles, Greensboro, 1988—. Contbr. to cookbooks, topical mags. Bd. dirs., Ctr. Creative Arts, Greensboro, 1982-84; fundraiser, Muscular Dystrophy, Leukemia Found., Am. Cancer Soc., all Greensboro. Mem. Greensboro C. of C., Kiwanis. Office: Talk of the Town Inc 3728 Lawndale Dr Greensboro NC 27408

FRAKE, BARBARA HOLLISS, research company executive; b. Chgo., Feb. 1, 1945; d. Harold and Josephine (Orlowski) Colby; m. Gerald Frake, Sept. 9, 1967; children: Ray, Alicia, Brian, Steve. BA, Northeastern Ill. U., Chgo., 1989. Sales assoc. Marshall Field & Co., Chgo.; product coord. Kolod Rsch., Northbrook, Ill. Den mother Cub Scouts, Boy Scouts Am., award chmn. local unit; pres. Morningstar Guild, chmn. rummage sale; treas. Athletic Boosters; vol. Art Inst., Chgo., Bot. Graden, Chgo., mem. alumni bd. Notre Dame High Sch., Chgo., other coms.; active local high sch. activities. Mem. Newcomer's Club (chmn. old peoples' home birthday, other coms.), Cath. Women's Club (various coms.), Sigma Tau Delta (pres., chmn. antique show).

FRAME, ANNE PARSONS, civic worker; b. Berkeley, Calif., Jan. 3, 1904; d. Reginald Hascall and Maude (Bemis) Parsons; A.B., Mills Coll., 1924; postgrad. Columbia, 1924-25; m. Frederic D. Tootell, Apr. 3, 1926 (div. July 1935); children: Geoffrey H., Natalie (Mrs. Oliver); m. Jasper Ewing Brady, July 31, 1935; (dec. Dec. 1944); 1 son, Hugh Parsons; m. Howard Andres Frame, Mar. 29, 1948 (dec. Dec. 1986). Dir. Parsons, Hart & Co., Seattle, Hillcrest Orchard Co., Seattle. Mem. bd. mgmt. Palo Alto br. A.R.C., 1955-61; trustee Children's Hosp. & Med. Ctr., Seattle, 1942-48; bd. dirs. Children's Health Coun., Palo Alto, Calif., 1953-63, 64-76, pres., 1954-58, assoc. mem., Seattle, 1986—; sponsor Nat. Recreation Assn., 1942-66, trustee, 1948-66; sponsor Nat. Recreation and Park Assn., 1966—, trustee, 1966-73; trustee Nat. Recreation Found., 1964—; 1st v.p. Children's Hosp. at Stanford Sr. Aux., 1965-67, bd. dirs. Hosp., 1967-85; former mem. adv. com. Holbrook-Palmer Park; trustee Mills Coll., 1952-62; bd. dirs. Holbrook-Palmer Recreation Park Found., 1968-86; bd. govs. San Francisco Symphony Assn., 1949-79; mem. Atherton (Calif.) Park and Recreation Commn., 1968-81. Mem. LWV, Bowne House Hist. Soc., San Mateo County, Seattle, Chgo., Calif. hist. socs., Calif. Heritage Council, San Francisco Mus. Art, Seattle Art Mus., Museum Soc., Nat. Trust for Historic Preservation, Nat. Soc. Colonial Dames Am. Episcopalian. Clubs: Sunset, Tennis (Seattle), Woodside-Atherton Garden (bd. dirs. 1966-68), Francisca (San Francisco), Menlo Country (Calif.), Seattle Garden Club.

FRAME, DOROTHY ELIZABETH, public relations executive; b. Bklyn.; d. Edward Francis and Edna Sophie (Groef) Feltmann; m. Manson Frame, Mar. 24, 1956 (div. 1978); 1 child, Manson Andrew. Student, Hofstra U., 1952-58, SUNY, Plattsburg, 1983, Hofstra U., 1984. Assoc. editor Sperry Rand, Great Neck, N.Y., 1955-58, editor, 1958-61; mng. editor Salvo Mag., Inc., L.I., 1964-67; dir. pub. info. North Shore Schs., Sea Cliff, N.Y., 1967-78; dir. communications Ednl. Mgmt. Inst., Glen Cove, N.Y., 1978-81; pres. Dorothy E. Frame Assocs., Inc., Glen Head, N.Y., 1981—; Bd. dirs. Ed. Com., Inc., Farmingdale, N.Y.; cons. spl. events N.Y. div. Gimbels, N.Y.C., 1975-85. Contbr. articles to profl. jours. Bd. dirs. Robert Constant Scholarship Fund, Glen Head, N.Y., 1984—. Mem. Nat. Sch. Pub. Relations Assn. (publs. awards of excellence, 1978, 82, 83), N.Y. State Sch. Pub. Relations Assn. (award of excellence 185, spl. purpose publs. 1986, 87, 88, 89), Nat. Bus. and Profl. Women's Club, Research and Investment Club of L.I. (pres. 1987—). Home and Office: 5 Cross Ln Glen Head NY 11545

FRANCA, CELIA, director, choreographer, dancer, narrator; b. London, Eng., June 25, 1921; m. James Morton, Dec. 7, 1960. Student, Guildhall Sch. Music, Royal Acad. Dancing; LLD (hon.), Assumption U. of Windsor, 1959, Mt. Allison U., 1966, U. Toronto, 1974, Dalhousie U., 1976, York U., 1976, Trent U., Peterborough, Ont., Can., 1977, McGill U., 1986; DCL (hon.), Bishop's U., 1967; DLitt (hon.), Guelph U., 1976. Mem. jury 5th Internat. Ballet Competition, Varna, Bulgaria, 1970, 2d Internat. Ballet Competition, Moscow, 1973. Debut: corps de ballet Mars, The Planets (Tudor), Mercury Theatre, London, 1936; soloist, Ballet Rambert, London, 1936-38, leading dramatic dancer, Ballet Rambert, 1938-39, guest artist, Ballet Rambert, 1950, dancer, Ballet des Trois Arts, London, 1939, Arts Theatre Ballet, London, 1940, Internat. Ballet, London, 1941, leading dramatic dancer, Sadler's Wells Ballet, 1941-46, guest artist, choreographer, Sadler's Wells Theatre Ballet, London, 1946-47, dancer, tchr., Ballets Jooss, Eng., 1947, ballet mistress, leading dancer, Met. Ballet, London, 1947-49, dancer, Ballet Workshop, London, 1949-51, founder, artistic dir., Nat. Ballet Can., Toronto, 1951-74, a prin. dancer, Nat. Ballet Can., 1951-59, co-founder, Nat. Ballet Sch., Toronto, 1959—; prin. roles include Black Queen in Swan Lake; title roles in Lady from the Sea; choreographer: ballets, including Midas, London, 1939, Cancion, London, 1942, Khadra, London, 1946, Dance of Salome, BBC-TV, 1949, The Eve of St. Agnes, BBC-TV, 1950, Afternoon of a Faun, Toronto, 1952, Le Pommier, Toronto, 1952, Casse-Noisette, 1955, Princess Aurora, 1960, The Nutcracker, 1964, Cinderella, 1968, numerous others for CBC, Can. Opera Co.; author: The National Ballet of Canada: A Celebration, 1978. Hon. patron Osteoporosis Soc. Can. Decorated Order of Can.; recipient Key to City of Washington, 1955; Woman of Year award B'nai B'rith, 1958; award for outstanding contbn. to arts Toronto Telegram, 1965; Centennial medal, 1967; Hadassah award of merit, 1967; Molson award, 1974; award Internat. Soc. Performing Arts Adminstrs., 1979; twice visited China at invitation of Chinese govt. to teach; in Beijing mounted full-length Coppelia, 1980; honored as one of founders of Can.'s major ballet cos. at Alta. Ballet Co.'s 15th anniversary, 1981; recipient Can. Dance award, 1984; Gold Card IATSE local 58, 1984; diplôme d'honneur Can. Conf. Arts, 1986, Woman Yr. award St. George's Soc. Toronto, 1987, Order of Ont., 1987. Office: 250 Clemow Ave, Ottawa, ON Canada K1S 2B6

FRANCE, HELEN WAY, corporate banker; b. Cleve., Dec. 3, 1953; d. Edward Agnew and Elizabeth Ann (Way) France; m. Peter H. Calfee, Dec. 5, 1981 (div. Feb. 1989). BA in Comparative Lit., Smith Coll., 1975. With Society Nat. Bank, Cleve., 1979—, comml. banking officer, 1980-82, asst. v.p., 1982-83, v.p., sr. relationship mgr., 1983-86, 88—, sr. relationship mgr., 1986-88. Cons. Jr. Achievement, Cleve., 1990. Recipient Cert. of Merit, YWCA, Cleve., 1983, named Woman of Achievement, 1984. Mem. Nat. Corp. Cash Mgrs. Assn. (cert.), Cleve. Treas. Club (trustee, officer 1983—), Smith Coll. Club Cleve. (treas. 1990-91), Smith Coll. Club N.Y., Cleve. Skating Club. Republican. Presbyterian. Home: 2825 S Moreland Apt 7 Cleveland OH 44120 Office: Society Nat Bank 800 Superior Ave Cleveland OH 44114

FRANCHIK, CAROL ANN, law firm administrative manager; b. Chgo., Jan. 5, 1939; d. Florian J. and Mildred E. (Backofen) Ostrowski; student Morton Coll., 1964; 1 son, Mark William. Legal sec. Hajek & Hucek, Cicero, Ill., 1956-58, Kirkland & Ellis, Chgo., 1958-59, 63-67; exec. sec. DeSoto Chem. Coatings, Chgo., 1961-63; adminstrv. mgr. Wildman, Harrold, Allen & Dixon, Chgo., 1967-79; v.p., controller Duff & Phelps, Inc., Chgo., 1979-83; adminstrv. mgr. Siegan, Barbakoff, Gomberg, Gordon & Elden, Ltd., Chgo., 1984; dir. fin. and adminstrn. Holleb & Coff, Chgo., 1984—; pres. Law Offices Mgrs. Assn., Chgo., 1976. Mem. adv. bd. Prairie State Coll., 1978-79; exec. bd. Fullersburg Homeowners Assn., 1980-81. Mem. ABA, Ill. State Bar Assn., Assn. Legal Adminstrs. Nat. Fedn. Bus. and Profl. Women's Clubs, Inc. Office: 55 E Monroe Chicago IL 60603

FRANCHINI, ROXANNE, banker; b. N.Y.C., Mar. 20, 1951; d. Tullio and Jean (Brady) F. Ed. Emerson Coll., Ricker Coll., New Sch. Social Research. With Princess Marcella Borghese div. Revlon, N.Y.C., 1972-73; stewardess TWA Airlines, 1973-74; asst. to pres. N.Y. Shipping Assn., N.Y.C., 1974-79; benefits mgr. Kidde, Inc., 1979-83; 2d v.p. pension trust fin. services Chase Manhattan Bank, N.A., N.Y.C., 1983-85, v.p. mgr. global securities, 1985-89; v.p., sr. sales mgr. global custody worldwide securities svcs. Citibank, N.Y.C., 1989—. Coord. community fund raising campaigns. Mem. NAFE, AAUW, Am. Mgmt. Assn., Fin. Women's Assn. of N.Y., Internat. Founds. Employee Benefits, Internat. Ops. Assn., S.W. Pension Conf., Nat. Investment Co. Service Assn.

FRANCIS, ALEXANDRIA STEPHANIE, psychologist; b. N.Y.C., June 5, 1952; d. Charles William and RoseMary Barbara (Beller) F.; m. Fred David Haruda, May 28, 1983. BA, Sweet Briar Coll., 1974; MA, NYU, 1977, PhD, 1982. Research assoc. NYU Med. Ctr., N.Y.C., 1977-78; program dir. Profl. Exam Service, N.Y.C., 1978-81; project dir. CTB/McGraw-Hill, Monterey, Calif., 1982-86; pvt. cons. Cen. Coast Neurol. Assocs., Salinas, Calif., 1986—; research cons. Population Inst., N.Y.C., 1976-77; program specialist CTB/McGraw-Hill, 1981. Contbr. articles to profl. jours. Vol. Aux. of Community Hosp. of Monterey Peninsula, 1982—. Recipient Helen K. Mull scholar Sweet Briar Coll., 1974. Mem. Am. Ednl. Research Assn., Am. Psychol. Assn., Nat. Council of Measurement in Edn. (reviewer of research programs 1983), Kappa Delta Pi. Home: 13485 Paseo Terrano Salinas CA 93908

FRANCIS, CAROLYN RAE, educator, musician, author, publisher; b. Seattle, July 25, 1940; d. James Douglas and Bessie Caroline (Smith) F; m. Barclay Underwood Stuart, July 5, 1971. BA in Edn., U. Wash., 1962. Cert. tchr., Wash. Tchr. Highline Pub. Schs., Seattle, 1962-64; musician Olympic Hotel, Seattle, 1962-72; 1st violin Cascade Symphony Orch., 1965-78; tchr. Bellevue (Wash.) Pub. Schs., 1965—; pres. Innovative Learning Designs, Mercer Island, Wash., 1984—; instr. string instruments; speaker insvc. workshops convs. music educators, London, Vancouver, B.C., Can., Indpls., Seattle, N.Y.C., L.A., Sacramento, Chgo., Balt., Washington, San Antonio, Fresno, Calif., Lexington, Ky., Boston, Phoenix, San Diego, Tampa, Fla., Washington, Ashland; adjudicator music festivals, Am. Band Coll. Author-pub. Music Reading and Theory Skills, Levels 1, 2, 1986, Level 3, 1984; contbr. articles to profl. jours., 1984—. Mem. Snohomish Indian Tribe. Bellevue Schs. Found. grantee, 1985-86, 86-87, 89-90. Mem. NEA, Am. String Tchrs. Assn., Music Educators Nat. Conf., Nat. Assn. Music Tchrs., Nat. Sch. Orch. Assn. Office: Innovative Learning Designs 7811 SE 27th Ste 104 Mercer Island WA 98040

FRANCIS, CLAUDE, writer; b. London. PhD, UCLA, 1965. Vis. rsch. assoc. Radcliffe U., Cambridge, Mass., 1979-81. Co-author: M. Proutst: Poèmes, 1980, Les Ecrits de S. De Beauvoir, 1989, M. Proust et les Siens, 1983, S. de Beauvoir, a Life, a Love Story (published in 12 Langs.), 1986, Prix de Elle, 1986.

FRANCIS, EULALIE MARIE, psychologist; b. Holmdel, N.J.; d. Richard Erickson and Cora Mina (Patterson) F. BS, Newark State, N.J., 1945; EDM, Rutgers U., New Brunswick, 1957, MA, 1961; PhD, Rutgers U, Harvard U., N.J., Mass., 1971, 1973. Cert. Edn. Psychology. Tchr. Elem. Edn. Pub. Schs., Middletown, N.J., 1945-51; Elem. supr. Pub. Schs., Red Bank, N.J., 1951-63; dir. learning disability and psychologist Pub. Schs., East Brunswick, N.J., 1984; Cons. Nat. Assn. Mental Health N.Y.C., Family and childrens Sorriccs Natigna, N.Y.C., Lincoln Sch. Tchrs. Coll., Columbia U. 1981-89; Dir. Rsch. Div. NEA Assn. Trenton N.J. 1988-89. Author, Editor: Book: "Kinesthetic Method of Reading", "Theory and Techniques of Auditory Perception in Reading" 1964-68. Adv. State Hist. Site Coun. Trenton N.J. 1986, Cultural and Heritage Com. Holmdel N.J. 1987-89. Mem. Arts Counc. of Princeton, Monmouth Mus. Lincroft, N.J., AAUW, Adv. Com. on Status of Women, Dir. Youth and Family Svcs., Princeton Child Devel. Inst., Rumson Country Club, Springlake Golf. Republican. Presbyterian. Home: Box 43 Holmdel NJ 07733

FRANCIS, MRS. LEE See LYBARGER, ADRIENNE REYNOLDS

FRANCIS, PEGGY ANN, marketing professional; b. St. Louis, Aug. 29, 1952; d. Wilbur Morris and Rita (Sve) Francis. BA with high honors, Northeastern Ill. U., Chgo., 1974; MS, Ind. U., 1975. Exec. dir. Julia Jameson Health Camp & Program Inc., Indpls., 1977-79; mktg. asst. Am. Salesmasters, Indpls., 1979-81; mgr. mkt. support Resort Condominiums Internat. Inc., Indpls., 1981-84; mktg. telemarketing cons. Money's Worth, Chgo., 1984-87; dir. sales and mktg. Burgess, Anderson & Tate Inc., Zion, Ill., 1987—; operator Money's Worth, Chgo., 1984—. Author: Contbr. article to Mag. 1988-. Bd. dirs. Am. Camping Assn., Martinsville, Ind., 1973. Mem. Kappa Delta. Office: Burgess Anderson & Tate Inc 2501 Deborah Ave Zion IL 60099

FRANCIS, ROBERTA WILLIAMS, community affairs director; b. Lancaster, Pa., Feb. 15, 1943; d. Robert Franklin and Emma Louise (Gibble) Williams; m. Samuel Hopkins, June 5, 1965; children: Erika Lynne, Christopher Samuel. AB summa cum, Dickinson Coll., 1964; MA in English Lit., Boston U., 1965. Editor Little Brown & Co, Boston, 1966-68; reporter Chatham (N.J.) Courier, 1981-82; women's issues dir. LWV, Trenton, N.J., 1981-85; author, researcher LWV, Washington, 1987-88; workshop coord. Ctr. for Am. Woman and Politics Rutgers U., New Brunswick, N.J., 1985, 87; project coord. Women's Rights Litigation Clinic Rutgers U., Newark, 1988-89; project specialist Inst. for Rsch. on Women Rutgers U., New Brunswick, 1989-90; dir. div. on women Dept. Community Affairs, Trenton, N.J., 1990—. Author: Changed Forever: The League of Women Voters and the ERA, 1988. Mem. N.J. Task Force on Equitable Compensation, 1984-87, Bd. Edn., Chatham, N.J., 1984-88, N.J. Adv. Com. on the Status of Women, 1987-90, Women's Agenda of N.J., Bipartisan Coalition for Women's Appointments. Mem. LWV. Democrat. Home: 68 Dale Dr Chatham NJ 07928 Office: Dept Community Affairs Div on Women 101 S Broad St CN 801 Trenton NJ 08625

FRANCIS, SUSAN GAIL, healthcare executive, nurse; b. Haverhill, Mass., Mar. 12, 1957; d. Henry Sterling and Shirley Elizabeth (Theberge) F. Diploma, Malden (Mass.) Hosp., 1978; BSN, Salem (Mass.) State Coll., 1984. Staff nurse Whittier Rehab. Hosp., Haverhill, 1978-83, unit mgr., 1983-85, dir. utilization rev. bd., 1986-87, dir. admissions, liaison with utilization rev. bd., 1987-88, v.p. patient svcs., 1988—; nurse cons. Oxford Manor Nursing Home, Haverhill, 1980-83. Mem. Mass. Quality Assurance Profls. Office: Whittier Rehab Hosp 76 Summer St Haverhill MA 01830

FRANCIS, SYBIL ELDRIDGE, academic administrator; b. L.A., Aug. 14, 1947; d. Thomas William Eldridge Sr. and Frances Pauline (Graves) Raynar; m. Paul R. Francis, Dec. 23, 1970 (dec. Mar. 1980); 1 child, Elizabeth Anne Francis; m. John Greene Herring III, June 4, 1987. AA, Quinsigamond Community Coll., Worcester, Mass., 1972; BA, N. Cen. Coll., 1974; MA, Northwestern U., 1977, PhD, 1979. Researcher, lectr. Northwestern U., Evanston, Ill., 1977-78; dir. agy. svcs. Ill. State Scholarship Commn., Deerfield, Ill., 1979-81; pvt. practice psychologist Houston, 1981-82; dir. continuing edn. program Lee Coll., Baytown, Tex., 1982-87; dir. continuing edn. and community svcs. Brunswick (Ga.) Coll., 1987—. Contbr. numerous articles to profl. jours. Edn. advisor Glynn County Leadership 90's, Brunswick, 1988-89; bd. dirs. E. Harris County Women's Ctr. & Shelter, Baytown, 1985-87, v.p., 1986-87; bd. dirs. Brunswick YWCA, 1989—. Mem. Ga. Mil. Edn. Coun. (bd. dirs.), Am. Assn. Coll. Registrars and Admissions Officers, Assn. for Instnl. Rsch., Golden Isles C. of C. (bd. dirs. Brunswick chpt. 1990—), Kiwanis. Home: 4211 7th St East Beach Saint Simons Island GA 31522 Office: Brunswick Coll Altama at 4th Brunswick GA 31523

FRANCISCO, MARCIA MADORA, data processing professional; b. Washington, Aug. 14, 1958; d. Terry Lee and Alice (Hughes) F. BS in Bus., U. Md., 1980; MBA, Pa. State U., 1986. Systems analyst Sperry Co., Harrisburg, Pa., 1980-86; cons. Touche Ross, Pitts., 1986-88; regional mgr. data processing Unisys, Arlington, Va., 1988-89; mgr. quality assurance MCI Communications Corp., Arlington, 1989—. Troop leader Girl Scouts U.S., Harrisburg, 1982-86, mgr. svc. unit, Rockville, Md., 1988—. Mem. Data Processing Mgmt. Assn., Nat. MBA Assn., Delta Sigma Theta, Phi Chi Theta. Home: 14616 Wexhall Terr Burtonsville MD 20866 Office: MCI 701 S 12th St Arlington VA 22202

FRANCK, CAROL EICHERT, health care association administrator; b. Lebanon, Pa., Dec. 12, 1937; d. Ralph F. and Mary Ellen (Beigh) Eichert; m. Michael, May 29, 1965; children: Michele, Lauren, Rebecca, Jennifer. BS, Cornell N.Y.Hosp. Sch. Nursing, 1960; MS, U. Calif., 1962; student, Tchrs. Coll., 1970; postgrad., Mich. State U., 1978. Staff nurse Cornell N.Y. Hosp., N.Y.C., 1960-61, instr., asst. prof., 1962-68; asst. prof., leadership and mgmt. Coll. Nursing, Mich. State U., 1971-75, dir., undergrad. nursing program, 1978-82; dir. govt. affairs Mich. Nurses Assn., East Lansing, 1984-86, exec. dir., 1986—; invited participant, Inst. on Care of The Dying-Yale, New Haven, Conn., 1963; advisory comm. Drop In Day Ctr.-Handicapped, Mich., 1980-81; accreditation site visitor, Animal Tech. Program, Mich., 1984. Adv. commn. Mich. Hosp. Orgn., Lansing, 1979-80; moderator Edgewood United Ch., East Lansing, 1983-84; adv. commn. Gov. Health Care Cost Mgmt. Team, Mich., 1989. Mem. Mich. Nurses Assn., Nat. League for Nursing, Sigma Theta Tau, Phi Delta Kappa, Phi Kappa Phi. Home: 1211 N College Rd Mason MI 48854 Office: Mich Nurses Assn 120 Spartan Ave East Lansing MI 48823

FRANCKE, GLORIA NIEMEYER, pharmacist, editor, publisher; b. Dillsboro, Ind., Apr. 28, 1922; d. Albert B. and Fannie K. (Libbert) Niemeyer; m. Donald Eugene Francke, Apr. 15, 1956. BS in Pharmacy, Purdue U., 1942; PharmD, U. Cin., 1971; postgrad. U. Mich., 1945; PharmD (hon.) Purdue U., 1988—. Pharmacist, Dillsboro Drug Store, 1943-44; instr. Sch. Pharmacy, Purdue U., Lafayette, Ind., 1943; asst. to chief pharmacist U. Mich. Hosp., Ann Arbor, 1944-46; assoc. editor Am. Jour. Hosp. Pharmacy, Washington, 1944-64; asst. dir. Div. Hosp. Pharmacy of Am. Pharm. Assn., Washington, 1946-56; exec. sec. Am. Soc. Hosp. Pharmacists, Ann Arbor, 1949-60; acting dir. dept. communications, Washington, 1963-64; drug lit. specialist Nat. Library Medicine, Bethesda, Md., 1965-67; clin. pharmacy teaching coordinator VA Hosp., Cin., 1967-71; asst. clin. prof. clin. pharmacy Coll. Pharmacy, U. Cin., 1967-71; chief program evaluation br. Alcohol and Drug Dependence Service, VA, Central Office, Washington, 1971-75; dir. Pharmacy Intelligence Ctr., Am. Pharm. Assn., Washington, 1975-85; mem. Roche Hosp. Pharmacy Adv. Bd., 1971-74; judge for ann. Lunsford Richardson Pharmacy awards, 1963, 64; mem. com. standards for drug abuse treatment and rehab. programs Joint Commn. Accreditation of Hosps., 1974-75. Author: (with D. E. Francke, C. J. Latiolais and N.F. H. Ho) Mirror to Hospital Pharmacy, 1964. Contbr. articles on hosp. pharmacy and clin. pharmacy to profl. jours. Recipient H.A.K. Whitney award Mich. Soc. Hosp. Pharmacists, 1953, Disting. Alumnus award Purdue U. Sch. of Pharmacy, 1985, Remington Honor medal, 1987; also various commendations. Mem. Am. Pub. Health Assn., Internat. Pharm. Fedn., Am. Inst. History of Pharmacy (exec. sec. 1968-78), Tex. Soc. Hosp. Pharmacists (hon.), Am. Pharm. Assn. (hon. chmn. 1986), Am. Soc. Hosp. Pharmacists, Drug Info. Assn., Kappa Epsilon, Rho Chi. Presbyterian. Home and Office: 3900 Cathedral Ave NW #403-A Washington DC 20016

FRANCO, ANNEMARIE WOLETZ, editor; b. Somerville, N.J., Sept. 18, 1933; d. Frederick Franz and Bertha (Laugginger) Woletz; m. Frederick Nicholas Franco, June 11, 1977. Student, Wood Coll. of Bus. Editorial asst. Internat. Musician, then assoc. editor, 1965-88, ret., 1988. Republican. Presbyterian. Home: 166 Wellstone Dr Palm Coast FL 32137

FRANCO, BETTIE WESTERVELT, guidance counselor; b. Paterson, N.J., May 30, 1932; d. Warren Herbert and Nina Elizabeth (Pennington) Westervelt; m. July 28, 1950 (div. 1972); children: Shelley Franco Bowman, Peter Franco III. BA, Paterson State Coll., 1964; MS, Montclair State Coll., 1969. Cert. elem. tchr., student personnel svcs., adminstrn. and supervision. Guidance counselor, tchr. Wayne (N.J.) Bd. Edn., 1964—. Pres. Valley Terrace Condominium Assn., Wayne, 1987-89; bd. dirs. Clifton (N.J.) Adult Opportunity Ctr., 1980-85; county committeewoman Wayne Rep. Orgn., 1988-90; mem. Pub. Svc. Electric and Gas Energy Edn. Adv. Com. Mem. NEA, N.J. Edn. Assn., Passaic County Edn. Assn., Wayne Edn. Assn. (sec. 1987-87), Passaic County Personnel and Guidance Assn., Supts. Key Communicators, DAR. Home: 15 Knox Terr Apt 2B Wayne NJ 07470

FRANK, AGNES THERESA, librarian; b. Budapest, Hungary; came to U.S., 1958; d. Julius Furedi and Maria Szlovak; m. Neil Frank (div. 1971). MLS, Columbia U., 1964. Dir. med. library French & Polyclinic Med. Sch. and Health Ctr., N.Y.C., 1970-74, St. Vincent's Hosp. and Med. Ctr., N.Y.C., 1974—. Mem. Med. Libr. Assn. (cert.). Home: 372 Central Pk W Apt 16A New York NY 10025 Office: St Vincents Hosp Med Ctr 153 W 11th St New York NY 10011

FRANK, BARBARA ANN, advertising executive, educator, artist; b. Mayfield, Ky., May 5, 1939; d. Jesse Aton and Maggie Lulillier (Scarbrough) Janes; m. James Lawrence Barker, (dec. 1962); children: Cynthia Lou, Laura LeAnn; m. William Harry Frank. BS, Murray State U., 1971, MA, 1971; postgrad., U. Ky., 1976-85. Cert. elem. educator, Ky. Art dir., tchr. St. Joseph Elem. Sch., Mayfield, Ky., 1974-76; gallery dir. The Gallery, Mayfield, 1985; dir., tchr. Treasure House Day Care, Mayfield, 1984-86; instr. Draughons's Jr. Coll. Bus., Paducah, Ky., 1983-86, Paducah Community Coll., 1983-86; photographer The Gallery, Mayfield, 1979—; hostess, sales Welcome Wagon Internat., Memphis, 1986-87, field mgr., 1987—; lectr. and instr. personnel mgmt., implementing goal, policies and hiring. Patentee in field. Prin. work includes Sculpture Prism Playhouse, 1986. Author: Beauty 'n the Beast, 1975. Publicity dir. Graves County Extension Homemakers, 1972-86; pres. Graves County Active Artists Assn., Mayfield, 1985-87. Recipient Best of Show Photo Ky. Extension Homemakers Assn., 1986, Nat. Award of Excellence Welcome Wagon Internat., 1989. Mem. AAUW, Profl. Photographers Am., Ky. Bus. & Profl. Womens Club, Purchase Area Arts Council, Council of Club Women, Burnett's Chapel Homemakers Club. Republican. Baptist. Home and Office: 1018 W Broadway Mayfield KY 42066 Office: Welcome Wagon Internat 145 Court Ave Memphis TN 42066

FRANK, CARLA, art director; b. Pitts., Jan. 17, 1960; d. Philip Lawrence and Gloria (Cervi) F. BA, Penn State U., 1982. Prodn. designer Washingtonian Mag., Washington, 1983-84, asst. art dir., 1984-85; art dir. Dossier Mag., Washington, 1985-86, Saturday Rev. Mag., Washington, 1986, Carla Frank Design, Washington and Balt., 1986—. Mem. Met. Washington Art Dirs. Club; bd. dirs. Md. Action to Prevent Child Abuse. Recipient regional ann. award Print mag., 1987, ann. award Communication Arts, 1983, ann. book award Graphis Assn., 1983, award Soc. Illustrators, 1987, award of excellence Monadnock Paper Mills, 1989. Mem. Art Dirs. Club Met. Washington (recipient annual awards 1987, 88). Office: 2330 N Charles St Baltimore MD 21218

FRANK, CAROLINE KACHURA, tax manager, consultant, finance executive; b. Queens, N.Y., June 24, 1943; d. John and Anne (Predko) Kachura; m. Richard F. Frank, Feb. 20, 1965; children: Richard, John. BS in Biology, Adelphi U., 1965, MA in Edn., 1972; postgrad., N.Y. Inst. Tech., 1985-86, L.I. U., 1986—. Tchr. chemistry St. Anthony's High Sch., Kings Park, N.Y., 1979; tax preparer H&R Block Inc., Commack, N.Y., 1981-84; mgr. bus. services H&R Block Inc., East Northport, N.Y., 1986-87; gen. mgr. Home World, Huntington, N.Y., 1984-85; tax acct. David Vermut CPA, PC, Jericho, N.Y., 1986-87, tax mgr., 1987-88; pres., chmn. bd. dirs. K.C. Frank and Assoc. Inc., Huntington, 1988-89; v.p. fin. Aviation Edn. Systems, Inc., Melville, N.Y., 1989, Sandy River Hardware, Inc., Farmingdale, N.Y., 1990; dir. pub. rels., radio and TV seminars H&R Block, 1984-85 (pub. relations award 1984, 85); bd. dirs. RSF Visual Fantasies Corp.; advisor Christian Nursing Registry Inc., Commack, N.Y., 1989—. Mem. AICPA (jr. mem.), Nat. Notary Assn., Nat. Assn. Tax Practitioners. Republican. Roman Catholic. Home: 203 Little Plains Rd Huntington NY 11743

FRANK, ELIZABETH, English literature educator, author; b. Los Angeles, 1945. Student Bennington Coll.; BA, MA, PhD, U. Calif.-Berkeley. Assoc. prof. English lit. Bard Coll., Annandale-on-Hudson, N.Y., 1982—. Author: Jackson Pollock, 1983, Louise Bogan: A Portrait (Pulitzer prize for biography 1986). Office: Bard Coll Dept Lang & Lit Annandale-on-Hudson NY 12505

FRANK, HILDA RHEA KAPLAN, dancer; b. Houston, Dec. 30, 1939; d. Sam and Bertha (Grevsky) Kaplan; m. Robert Stuart Frank, Feb. 28, 1960; children—Karen Denise Frank Hurwitz, Daniel Steven, Nancy Alyson. Student Newcomb, Coll., New Orleans, 1957-59, U. Houston, 1959-60, Butler U., 1960. Dance tchr. Joy Alexander Sch. Dance, Houston, 1955-57, Jane Browning Sch. Dance, Houston, 1965-69, Rudy Jenkins, Sch. Ballet, Houston, 1968-69, Xperience Gymnastic Team, Houston, 1972-75; dance tchr. Jewish Community Ctr., Houston, 1975-80, dance com. chmn., 1978—, bd. dirs., 1987—; dance panelist Cultural Arts Council Houston, 1980-85, 1988—; sec.-treas. Discovery Dance Group, Houston, 1981-84, pres., 1984-85; trustee Houston Dance Coalition, 1985-87. Choreographer: To Live Arother Summer, 1980; Jewish Fairy Tale, 1974; My Son, The President, 1981; dir., choreographer Emanu El Israeli Dancers, Houston, 1973—; co-chair The Jewish Festival, 1989. Recipient scholarship Jacob's Pillow Dance Festival, Lee, Mass., 1959; named Vol. of Yr., Jewish Community Ctr., Houston, 1985. Mem. Houston Dance Coalition (trustee 1985-86), Cultural Arts Council Houston. Jewish. Clubs: Hadassah, Sisterhood of Emanu El (Houston) (Israeli dance dir. 1973—). Home: 1 Woods Edge Ln Houston TX 77024

FRANK, JACQUELYN A., spouse relocation consultant; b. Sherburn, Minn., July 20, 1941; d. Glen H. Montague and Marvel (Robinson) Jones; m. John L. Frank. AA, Kirkwood Community Coll., Cedar Rapids, Iowa, 1971; BA, U. Iowa, 1973; MS, Loyola U., Chgo., 1988. Social worker Phoenix Indian Ctr., 1973-74; civil rights specialist Ariz. Atty. Gen.'s Office, Phoenix, 1974-78; dir. affirmative action Hawkeye Tech. Inst., Waterloo, Iowa, 1978-80; community organizer Hinsdale, Ill., 1980-84; staff devel. supr. Ill. Dept. Civil Rights, Chgo., 1984-85; pres. Jacquelyn Frank and Assocs., Lexington, Ky., 1987—; cons. Western Mich. U., Kalamazoo, 1987-88; numerous TV apparances on spouse relocation assistance issues; trainer family relocation and spouse relocation/employment. Mem. Blue Grass Trust for Hist. Preservation, Opera Cent. Ky. Mem. Employee Relocation Coun., Am. Soc. Personnel Adminstrs. (nat., internat.), Jpan-Am. Soc., Internat. Assn. Personnel Women, Indsl. Rels. Rsch. Assn. Home: 1095 Merrick Dr Lexington KY 40502

FRANK, MARTHA STEPS, advertising executive; b. Topeka, Dec. 22, 1939; d. William Emil and Helen Marie (Niemeier) Steps; m. Manual Frank Jr., July 8, 1967; children: Trevor Alan, Corey Lane. BA, Kans. State U., 1961; MA, San Diego State U., 1970. Editor Kans. Agrl. Situation Kans. State U., Manhattan, 1960-62; copywriter Emerson Franzke Advt. Agy., Topeka, 1962-63; program sec. KOGO Radio, San Diego, 1963-65; sr. v.p. Wilson, Frank & Assocs., San Diego, 1965—. Sec. San Diego Imperial chpt. Cystic Fibrosis Found., 1987—, bd. dirs. Mem. San Diego Assn. Advt. Agys. (pres. 1988), Gamma Phi Beta (pres., bd. dirs., 1984—, Beta Lambda scholarship found.). Republican. Methodist. Home: 6428 Coral Lake Ave San Diego CA 92119 Office: Wilson Frank & Assocs 3225 4th Ave San Diego CA 92103

FRANK, MARY LOU, educator; b. Cleve., May 15, 1915; d. William Henry and Martha Ann (Brown) Parsons; m. Russell Edward Frank, May 18, 1935; children: Richard Edward, James Russell. BS in Edn., Cleve. State U., 1960; MS in Edn., U. Akron, Ohio, 1967, Miami U., Oxford, Ohio, 1934-35; student, Baldwin-Wallace Coll., 1933-34. Cert. tchr., Ohio. Substitute tchr. Cleve. Pub. Schs., 1963; tchr. elem. Brecksville (Ohio) City Sch. Dist., 1953-71; tchr. elem. Lee County Bd. of Edn., Ft. Myers, Fla., 1971-74, ret., 1974; mem. ambassadors to China from Fla., Children's Palaces Homes Hosps., 1980. Martha Holden Jennings Found. scholar, 1963-64, grantee, 1965. Mem. U.S. Power Squadron Aux. (pilot), Collier Reading Coun., Delta Kappa Gamma. Home: 61 Impala Ct Rt 23 Fort Myers FL 33912

FRANK, NANCY GILLEN, state legislator; b. N.Y., June 15, 1943; d. Martin and Ann (McGrown) Gillen; children: Christopher, Kathleen. Founder, Sch. of Religion for Children with Special Disability; mem. State Dem. Com., Hillsbough County Com., Merrimack Town Com. Mem. N.H. Order Women Legislators, Nat. Order Women Legislators, Sheepfold Club. Home: 15 Indian Rock Rd Merrimack NH 03054

FRANK, NATALIE SUSAN, real estate broker; b. Chgo., Nov. 13, 1963; d. Mark and Irene (Kelly) Frank. BA, St. Mary's Coll., 1985; MBA, U. Notre Dame, 1987. Grad. Real Estate Inst. Real estate broker Charles T. Houha Co., Realtors, Oak Park, Ill., 1987—. Mem. Nat. Assn. Realtors, Ill. Assn. Realtors, Oak Park Bd. Realtors (chmn. assocs. com. 1989-90), Real Estate Brokerage Council, Phi Alpha Theta. Roman Catholic. Office: Charles T Houha Co 915 S Oak Park Ave Oak Park IL 60304

FRANK, PAULA FELDMAN, business executive; b. Tulsa; d. Maurice M. and Sarah (Bergman) Feldman; m. Gordon D. Frank, Dec. 15, 1955; children: Cynthia Jan, Margaret Jill. B.S., Northwestern U., 1954. Directed, wrote and appeared in TV films for Nat. Safety Coun., Chgo., 1954-55; appeared in TV commls., 1955-56; asst. prodn. mgr. Kling Films, Chgo., 1956; now pres. Gaston Ave. Optical Inc., Dallas. Social chmn. Baylor Hosp. Vol. Corp., Dallas, 1962—; asst. dir. Des Plaines (Ill.) Theater Guild, 1956-57, Pearl Chappell Playhouse, Dallas, 1962-63, Dallas Theater Center, 1964. Mem. Hockaday Alumni Assn., Tau Gamma Epsilon, Phi Beta, Sigma Delta Tau. Home: 7123 Currin Dr Dallas TX 75230

FRANK, RUBY MERINDA, employment agency executive; b. McClusky, N.D., June 28, 1920; d. John J. and Olise (Stromme) Hanson; m. Robert G. Frank, Jan. 14, 1944 (dec. 1973); children: Gary Frank, Craig. student Coll. Mankato, Minn., Aurora (Ill.) U. Exec. sec., office mgr. Nat. Container Corp., Chgo., 1943-50; owner, pres. Frank's Employment, Inc., St. Charles, Ill., 1957—; corp. sec. Sta. WFXW-FM, Geneva, 1988—; chmn. Baker Hotel, 1989—; sec. bd. trustees Delnor Hosp., St. Charles, 1959-78, chmn. bd., 1985-87; vocat. adviser Waubonsee Coll.; bd. dirs. Aurora U. Contbr. weekly broadcast Sta. WGSB, 1970-80, weekly interview program Sta. WFXW. Active mem. Women's aux.; vice chmn. Kane County (Ill.) Rep. Com., 1968-77; pres. Women's Rep. Club, 1969-77; local bd. Am. Cancer Soc.; adv. council Dellora A. Norris Cultural Arts Ctr.; bd. govs. Luth. Social Svc. Baker Hotel (sec. 1987, vice chmn. 1988); bd. dirs. St. Charles Hist. Soc., 1989; co-vice chmn. Delnor Community Health System; mem. exec. bd. Aurora Found., 1989—. Recipient Exec. of Yr. award Fox Valley PSI; Charlemagne award for community service, 1982; bd. dirs. Aurora Found. Mem. St. Charles C. of C. (pres., bd. dirs. 1976-82, amb.), Kane-DuPage Pers. Assn. (v.p. 1971—), Nat., Ill. employment assns., Ill. Assn. Pers. Cons. (dir.), Women in Mgmt. Lutheran. Clubs: St. Charles Country; Execs. of Chgo., St. Charles Ambs. Club (pres.). Home: 534 Longmeadow Circle Saint Charles IL 60174 Office: Arcada Theater Bldg 12 S 1st Ave Saint Charles IL 60174

FRANK, SANDRA KAYE, mathematics educator; b. Springfield Twp., Mich., June 11, 1941; d. Virgil Euleas and Dorothy Arliene (Wells) Noble; m. Joseph Frederic Frank, Aug. 1, 1970; 1 child, Joseph Lindbergh. B.A., Central Mich. U., 1963; M.A., U. Mont., 1967. Tchr. math. Dearborn Pub. Sch., Mich., 1963—, Edsel Ford High Sch., 1978—. Mem. Mich. Council Tchrs. Math., Mich. Assn. Computer Users and Learners, Nat. Coun. Tchrs. Math., Math. Assn. Am. Clubs: Mich. Flyers, Ninety-Nines. Home: 21222 Audette St Dearborn MI 48124

FRANK, SARAH MYERS, lawyer; b. Indpls., Jan. 19, 1937; s. Dewey Everett and Minnie Estelle (Mitchell) M.; m. Ronald Marsh, Aug. 25, 1956; children: James, John, Janet. Student Principia Coll., Elsah, Ill., 1954-56; BS, Purdue U., 1958; JD, Ind. U., 1977. Bar: Ind. 1977, U.S. Dist. Ct. (so. dist.) Ind. 1977, U.S. Ct. Appeals (7th cir.) 1984. Tchr. Colfax High Sch. (Ind.), 1958-59, Washington Twp. Schs., Indpls., 1973-74; sr. law clk. Ind. Supreme Ct., Indpls., 1977-85; staff atty. Hyatt Legal Svcs., Indpls., 1985-86, UAW Legal Svcs. Plan, Indpls., 1986—. V.p. bd. dirs. Camp Fire, Inc., Indpls., 1983-85; bd. dirs. Dela. Trails Sch., Indpls., 1967-69. Mem. Ind. Bar Assn., Indpls. Bar Assn. (co-chmn. spl. projects women's div., family law sect., probate law sect.), AAUW (bd. dirs. 1981-82). Republican. Club: Pincipia (pres. 1983-84). Office: UAW-Ford Legal Svcs Plan 5435 N Emerson Way Ste 400 Bank 1 Bldg Indianapolis IN 46226

FRANK, YAKIRA HAGALILI, English educator; b. N.Y.C., Nov. 15, 1923; d. Abraham and Sonia (Flax) Hagalili; m. Simon Frank, Oct. 28, 1945; children: Tamar, Daniel. BA, Hunter Coll., 1943; MA, U. Pa., 1945; PhD, U. Mich., 1949. Lectr. U. Pa., Phila., 1943-45, Hunter Coll., N.Y.C., 1950-55; asst. prof. U. Conn., Stamford, 1963-67, assoc. prof., 1967-74, dir. adminstrn., 1974-88, prof. English, 1974—; cons. Bi-Cultural Day Sch., Stamford, 1964—, Bridgeport (Conn.) Engring. Inst., 1981. Contbr. articles to profl. jours., 1966-79. Bd. dirs. Conn. Pub. Broadcasting, Hartford, 1984—; trustee Stamford Found., 1979—; sec., treas. Conn. Humanities Coun., Middletown, 1977-83 (Wilbur Cross award 1987); chmn. Taskforce for Women in Bus., Fairfield County, Conn., 1977-79. Recipient Visiting Scholar award Yale U., New Haven, 1988-89. Mem. AAUW (Educator of Yr. award 1981), Linguistic Soc. Am., Modern Language Assn., Nat. Coun. Tchrs. of English, Speech Communication Assn., Midday Club (Woman of Yr. award 1979, 86), Phi Beta Kappa (pres. Epsilon chpt. U. Conn. 1989-90). Home: 34 Hazelwood Ln Stamford CT 06905 Office: U Conn Scofieldtown Rd Stamford CT 06903

FRANK BAYER, ELLEN, lawyer, educator; b. Bklyn., Nov. 24, 1957; d. Leon and Gladys (Reznik) Frank. BS, Bklyn. Coll., 1979; JD, Boston Coll., 1982. Bar: N.Y. 1983, Mass. 1983. Fiscal analyst HUD, N.Y.C., summer, 1979; assoc. F. Strafaci, Bklyn., 1982-83; assoc. firm F. Lee Bailey and Aaron J. Broder, N.Y.C., 1984; pvt. practice law, N.Y.C., 1984—; tchr., coach mock trial team High Sch. Graphic Communication Arts, N.Y.C., 1985-87. Moderator Conf. on Legal Rights of Battered Women, N.Y.C., 1983; sec. 61st Civilian Patrol, Bklyn., 1979; mem. King's Hwy. Devel. Corp., Bklyn., 1982—. Recipient House Sense award Housing, Preservation and Devel., 1986, 87; U.S.-German Tchr. fellow German Marshall Fund, 1988; Impact II grantee, 1988. Mem. ABA, N.Y. Women's Bar Assn. (matrimonial law, internat. law coms.), N.Y. State Trial Lawyers Assn., New York County Lawyers Assn. (law, youth and citizenship com.), Phi Alpha Delta (publicity dir. Boston 1981-82). Democrat.

FRANKE, MARIPAT KEMPS, process engineer; b. Appleton, Wis., Nov. 12, 1960; d. Ralph Edward and Mary Lee (Marciniak) Kemps; m. Mark Steven Franke. BA in Math. and Physics, Coe Coll., Cedar Rapids, Iowa, 1983; MS in Chem. Engring., Inst. Paper Chemistry, 1987. Rsch. technician Kimberly Clark Corp., Neenah, Wis., 1984-85; process engr. Kimberly Clark Corp., Memphis, 1987-88, area process engr., 1988—. Mem. Paper Industry Mgmt. Assn., Tech. Assn. Pulp and Paper Industry, Neighborhood assn., Toastmaster Internat., Sigma Phi Sigma, Delta Delta Delta. Presbyterian. Home: 7835 Deerfield Trace Memphis TN 38133 Office: Kimberly Clark Corp 400 Mahannah Ave Memphis TN 38107

FRANKEL, BETTY SOPHIA, landscape designer, writer, photographer; b. N.Y.C., Mar. 26, 1923; d. Harry B. and Estelle Ruth (Weil) Schwartz; m. Richard William Frankel, Feb. 7, 1943; children: Martha F., Barbara A., Edward H. BS in Botany, U. Mich., 1944, M in Land Architecture, 1973. Tchr. sci. and math. Elmira (N.Y.) Schs., 1945-46; tchr. English and art Farmington (Mich.) Schs., 1962; asst. botanist Cranbrook Inst. of Sci., Bloomfield Hills, Mich., 1964-65; garden writer Detroit Free Press, 1969—; freelance garden and landscape designer Farmington, 1973—; instr. gardening Schoolcraft Community Coll., Livonia, Mich., 1987—. Author: Adventures in Landscape, 1973, chpt. Natural History of Farmington, 1976. Founding mem. Farmington Hills Beautification Commn., 1966-70, 86—, Farmington Hills Pk. Commn., 1971-80. Recipient Frieda Bottom award Met. Detroit Landscape Assn., 1976. Mem. Garden Writers Assn. of Am., Federated Garden Clubs of Mich., Landscape Critics Coun., AAUW, Mich. Botanical Club, Mich. Nature Assn. Democrat. Jewish. Home and Office: 30300 Rockshire Farmington Hills MI 48334

FRANKEL, JUDITH JENNIFER MARIASHA, clinical psychologist; b. Bklyn., May 25, 1947; m. Anthony R. D'Augelli, Sept. 1, 1968 (div. 1985); children: Jennifer Hannah, Rebecca Lindsey. BA, New Coll. at Hofstra U., 1968; MA, U. Conn., 1971, PhD, 1972. Lic. psychologist, Pa. Rsch. psychologist Family Consultation Ctr., Roslyn, N.Y., 1968, Conn. State Dept. Mental Health, Hartford, 1969-71; staff intern VA Hosp., West Haven, Conn., 1971-72; asst. prof., dir. program devel. and evaluation Addiction Prevention Lab. Pa. State U., State College, 1972-80; pvt. practice psychology State College, 1976—; psychol. cons. PYRAMID Orgn., Walnut Creek, Calif., 1975-78, N.Y. Dept. Mental Health, 1976, Nat. Inst. Alcohol Abuse Prevention, Nat. Inst. Drug Abuse Prevention, Nat. Youth Alternatives Program, 1975-79; v.p. Mental Health Profls., State College, 1978-80, pres., 1980-82; exec. bd. Cen. Pa. Psychol. Assn., 1989-90. Author: Decisions Are Possible, 1975, Communication and Parenting Skills, 1976, Helping Others, 1980; contbr. articles to profl. jours. Campaigner Stein for Rep., 1982, Wachob for Congress, 1984, Radis for Rep., 1990; community action chair Congregation Brit Shalom, State College, 1985-87, edml. liaison coord., 1985-87; v.p. women's group Jewish Community Ctr., 1988-90, pres. women's group, 1990—, trustee, 1990—. USPHS fellow, U. Conn., 1969-71. Mem. Am. Psychol. Assn., Eastern Psychol. Assn., Cen. Pa. Psychol. Assn. (exec. bd. 1989-90), Jewish Community Coun. Women (bd. dirs. 1990—), Phi Beta Kappa, Phi Kappa Phi. Democrat. Jewish.

FRANKEL, MARILYN ELLMAN, public relations consultant, writer; b. Bklyn., Sept. 19, 1942; d. Isaac and Estelle (Shapiro) Ellman; m. Haskel Frankel, May 21, 1972 (div. July, 1987); 1 child, Elizabeth Emily. BA in English, Conn. Coll., 1964. Pub. rels. asst. Yeshiva U., N.Y.C., 1964-65; with pub. rels., editor co. paper BBDO, N.Y.C., 1965-69; dir. pub. rels. Firestone Assocs. Advt., N.Y.C., 1967-69; pub. rels. profl., women's affairs and travel writer Eastern Airlines, N.Y.C., 1969-72; freelance publicist N.Y.C., 1972-75; internat. pub. rels. mgr. Estee Lauder Inc., N.Y.C., 1976-77; pub. rels. cons. Marilyn E. Frankel Pub. Rels., Westbrook, Conn., 1975—. Co-author: All My Patients are Under the Bed, 1980. Bd. dirs. Chestnut Hill Concerts, Guilford, Conn., 1985—, pres., 1989—; bd. dirs. Literacy Vols.-Valley Shore, Westbrook, 1983-86; vol. Reach for Recovery, Am. Cancer Soc., Middletown, Conn., 1985—. Jewish.

FRANKENTHALER, HELEN, painter; b. N.Y.C., Dec. 12, 1928; d. Alfred and Martha (Lowenstein) F.; m. Robert Motherwell, Apr. 6, 1958 (div.). BA, Bennington Coll., 1949; LHD (hon.), Skidmore Coll., 1969; DFA (hon.), Smith Coll., 1973, Moore Coll. Art, 1974, Bard Coll., 1976, NYU, 1979, Marymount Manhattan Coll., 1989, Adelphi U., 1989, Washington U., St. Louis, 1989; D.Art, Radcliffe Coll., 1978, Amherst Coll., 1979. tchr., lectr. Yale U., 1966, 67, 70, Hunter Coll., 1970, Princeton U., 1971, Cooper Union, N.Y.C., 1972, Washington U. Sch. Fine Arts, 1972, Skidmore Coll., 1973, Swathmore Coll., 1974, Drew U., 1975, Harvard, 1976, Radcliffe Coll., 1976, Bard Coll., 1977, Detroit Inst. Arts, 1977, also N.Y. U., U. Pa., Sch. Visual Arts, Goucher Coll., Wash. U., Yale Grad. Sch., U. Ariz., 1978, Graphic Arts Council N.Y., 1979, Harvard U., 1980, Phila. Coll., 1980, Williams Coll., 1980, Yale U., 1981, Brandeis U., 1982, U. of Hartford, 1983, Syracuse U., 1985; U.S. rep. Venice Biennale, 1966. One-woman shows include, Tibor de Nagy Gallery, N.Y.C., 1951-58, Andre Emmerich Gallery, N.Y.C., 1959-73, 75, 77, 78, 79, 81, 82, 83, 84, 86, 87, 89, Jewish Mus., N.Y., 1960, Everett Ellin Gallery, Los Angeles, 1961, Galerie Lawrence, Paris, 1961, 63, Bennington Coll., 1962, 78, Galleria dell'Ariete, Milan, 1962, Kasmin Gallery, London, 1964, David Mirvish Gallery, Toronto, 1965, 71, 73, 75, Gertrude Kasle Gallery, Detroit, 1967, Nicholas Wilder Gallery, Los Angeles, 1967, Andre Emmerich Gallery, Zurich, 1974, 80, Swathmore (Pa.) Coll., 1974, Solomon R. Guggenheim Mus., N.Y.C., 1975, Corcoran Gallery Art, Washington, 1975, Seattle Art Mus., 1975, Mus. Fine Arts, Houston, 1975, 85, 86, Ace Gallery, Vancouver, B.C., Can., 1975, Rosa Esman Gallery, N.Y.C., 1975, 83, 89, 3d Internat. Contemporary Art Fair, Paris, 1976, 81, retrospective Whitney Mus. Am. Art, 1969, Whitechapel Gallery, London, Eng., 1969, Kongress-Halle, Berlin, Kunstverein, Hannover, 1969, Heath Gallery, Atlanta, 1971, Galerie Godard Lefort, Montreal, 1971, Fendrick Gallery, Washington, 1972, 79, John Berggruen Gallery, San Francisco, 1972, 79, 82, Portland (Oreg.) Art Mus., 1972, Waddington Galleries II, London, 1973, 74, Janie C. Lee Gallery, Dallas, 1973, Houston, 1975, 76, 78, 80, 82, Met. Mus. Art, N.Y.C., 1973, Gallery Diane Gilson, Seattle, 1976, Greenberg Gallery, St. Louis, 1977, Galerie Wentzel, Hamburg, Germany, 1977, Jacksonville (Fla.) Art Mus., 1977-78, Knoedler Gallery, London, 1978, 81, 83, USIA exhbn., 1978-79, Atkins Mus. Fine Art, William Rockhill Nelson Gallery Art, Kansas City, Mo., 1978, 80, Saginaw Art Mus., Mich., 1980, Gimpel and Hanover and Andre Emerich Galleries, Zurich, 1980, Gallery Ulysses, Vienna, 1980, Knoedler Gallery, London, 1981, 83, Buschlen/Mowalt Fine Arts, Vancouver, 1989; numerous others; exhibited in group shows including, Whitney Mus., 1958, 71, 75-79, 82, Carnegie Internat., Pitts., 1955, 58, 61, 64, Columbus Gallery Fine Arts, 1960, Guggenheim Mus., 1961, 76, 80, 82, Seattle World's Fair, 1962, Art Inst. Chgo., 1963, 69, 72, 76, 77, 82, 83, San Francisco Mus. Art, 1963, 68, Krannert Mus., U. Ill., 1959, 63, 65, 67, 80, Washington Gallery Modern Art, 1963, Pa. Acad. Fine Arts, 1963, 68, 76, N.Y. World's Fair, 1964, Am. Fedn. Arts Circulating Exhbn., 1964, U. Austin Art Mus., 1964, Rose Art Mus. Circulating Exhbn., 1964, Detroit Inst. Arts, 1965, 67, 73, 77, U. Mich. Mus. Art, 1965, Md. Inst., 1966, Norfolk Mus. Arts and Scis., 1966, Venice Biennale, 1966, Smithsonian Instn., 1966, Expo '67, Montreal, 1967, Washington Gallery Modern Art, 1967, Ga. Mus. Art, Athens, 1967, U. Okla. Mus. Art, Norman, 1968, Philbrook Art Center, Tulsa, 1968, Cin. Mus., 1968, U. Calif. at San Diego, 1968, Mus. Modern Art, N.Y.C., 1969, 75, 76, 80, 82, Met. Mus., N.Y.C., 1969-70, 76, 79, 81, Va. Mus., Richmond, 1970, 74, 87, Balt. Mus. Art, 1970, 76, Boston U., 1970, Boston Mus. Fine Arts, 1972, 82, Des Moines Art Center, 1973, Mus. Fine Arts, Houston, 1974, 82, Smith Coll. Mus. Art, Northampton, Mass., 1974, El Instituto de Cultura Puertorriquena, San Juan, 1974, Basil (Switzerland) Art Fair, 1974, 76, Finch Coll. Mus. Art, N.Y.C., 1974, S.I. Mus., 1975, Denver Art Mus., 1975, Visual Arts Mus., N.Y.C., 1975, 76, Mus. Modern Art, Belgrade Yugoslavia, 1976, Galleria d'Arts Moderna, Rome, 1976, Grey Art Gallery, N.Y.C., 1976-78, 81, Bklyn Mus., 1976-77, 82, Edmonton Art Gallery, Alta., Can., 1977, 78, Albright-Knox Mus., Buffalo, 1978, Fogg Art Mus., Harvard U., 1978, 83, Nat. Gallery Art, Washington, 1981, St. Louis Art Mus., 1982, Phoenix Art Mus., 1980; represented in permanent collections, Met. Mus. Art; exhibited in group shows including, Chrysler Mus., Norfolk, Va., 1976; represented in permanent collections, Bklyn. Mus.; exhibited in group shows including, Everson Mus., Syracuse, N.Y., 1976, 79; represented in permanent collections, Solomon R. Guggenheim Mus.; exhibited in group shows including, Art Gallery of Ont., Toronto, 1979; exhibited in group shows including, Hirshorn Mus. and Sculpture Garden, Washington, 1980; Tate Gallery, London, 1981, Walker Art Ctr., Mpls., 1981, Milw. Art Mus., 1982, Mus. Fine Arts, Boston, 1982, Whitney Mus. Am. Arts, N.Y., 1982, numerous others; represented in permanent collections: NYU, Mus. Modern Art, Albright-Knox Art Gallery, Buffalo, Whitney Mus., N.Y.C., U. Mich., High Mus., Atlanta, Milw. Art Inst., Wadsworth Atheneum, Hartford, Newark Mus., Yale U. Art Gallery, U. Nebr. Art Gallery, Carnegie Inst., Pitts., Detroit Inst. Art, Balt. Mus. Art, Univ. Mus., Berkeley, Calif., Bennington (Vt.) Coll., Art Inst. Chgo., Cin. Art Mus., Cleve. Mus. Art, Columbus Gallery Fine Arts, Honolulu Acad. Arts, Contemporary Arts Assn., Houston, Pasadena Art Mus., William Rockhill Nelson Gallery Art, Mus. Fine Arts, Kansas City, Mo., City Art Mus., St. Louis, Mus. Art, R.I. Sch. Design, Providence, San Francisco Mus. Art, Everson Mus., Syracuse, N.Y., Smithsonian Instn., Walker Art Inst., Mpls., Washington Gallery Modern Art, Wichita Art Mus., Brown Gallery Art, Nat. Gallery Victoria, Melbourne, Australia, Australian Nat. Gallery, Canberra, Victoria and Albert Mus., London, Eng., Tokyo Mus., Ulster Mus., Belfast, No. Ireland, Elvehjem Art Center, U. Wis., Israel Mus.-Instituto Nacional de Bellas Artes, Phila. Mus. Art, Phoenix Art Mus., Corcoran Gallery Art, Boston Mus. Fine Arts, Springfield (Mass.) Mus. Fine Arts, Witte Mus., San Antonio, Abbott Hall Art Gallery, Kendal, Eng., Mus. Contemporary Art, Nagaoka, Japan, Guggenheim Mus., N.Y.C., 1984, others; was subject of film Frankenthaler: Toward a New Climate, 1978. Trustee Bennington Coll., 1967—. Fellow Calhoun Coll., Yale U., 1968—; recipient 1st prize for painting Paris Biennale, 1959; Gold medal Pa. Acad. Fine Arts, 1968; Great Ladies award Fordham U., Thomas Moore Coll., 1969; Spirit of Achievement award Albert Einstein Coll. Medicine, 1970; Gold medal Commune of Catania, III Biennale della Grafica d'Arte, Florence, Italy, 1972; Garrett award 70th Am. Exhbn., Art Inst. Chgo., 1972; Creative Arts award Nat. Women's div. Am. Jewish Congress, 1974; Art and Humanities award Yale Women's Forum, 1976; Extraordinary Woman of Achievement award NCCJ, 1978; Alumni award Bennington Coll., 1979, N.Y.C. Mayor's award , 1986. Mem. Nat. Inst. Arts and Letters, Am. Acad. and Inst. Arts and Letters. Office: care Andre Emmerich 41 E 57th St New York NY 10022*

FRANKHOUSER, NANCY DOBBS, food products executive; b. Reading, Pa., Aug. 20, 1935; d. William Isaac and Nora (Bott) Dobbs; m. Robert M. Frankhouser, Apr. 24, 1954; children: Robert M. Jr., Richard M. Student, Albright Coll., 1954. With Penn Dairies Inc., Lancaster, Pa., 1967—, v.p. human resources and communications, asst. sec., 1985-86, v.p. adminstrn., sec., 1986—. Bd. dirs. Drug and Alcohol Rehab. Svcs., Inc., Lancaster, 1976-86, Lancaster Community Gallery, 1986-88, Lancaster City Human Rels. Commn., 1976—, Lancaster County Human Rels. Commn., 1976—; mem. Lancaster City Zoning Appeals Bd., 1976-84, chairperson, 1983-84. Recipient Good Govt. award Lancaster Jaycees, 1984, Mktg. award Internat. Assn. Ice Cream Mfg., 1984-89, Community Svc. award Lancaster City Coun., 1986, Chmn.'s award Lancaster C. of C. and Industry, 1986; named Career Woman of the Yr., Sales and Mktg. Execs., 1985, Humanitarian award Lancaster City-County Human Rels., 1989. Mem. Internat. Assn. Bus. Communicators, Lancaster C. of C. and Industry (bd. dirs. 1987—, vice chairperson, 1989—). Republican. Methodist. Home: 333 E Orange St Lancaster PA 17602 Office: Penn Dairies Inc 1801 Hempstead Rd Lancaster PA 17604

FRANKIEWICZ, MARCIA JEAN, telemarketing executive; b. East Chicago, Ind., July 9, 1947; d. Edward Stanley and Bernice Jean (Pikula) F.; m. Richard Joseph Palchak, Apr. 22, 1989; 1 child, Sarah Frankiewicz-Palchak. BS in Edn., Western Mich. U., 1969; MS in Spl. Edn., U. Wis., Whitewater, 1981. Tchr., unit leader Wilson Elem. Sch., Janesville, Wis., 1969-79; spl. edn. tchr. Brown Deer (Wis.) High Sch., 1979-84, trainer, 1983-84; spl. svcs. mgr. Braeger Chevrolet, Inc., Milw., 1984-85; telemktg. mgr. Gander Mountain, Inc., Wilmot, Wis., 1985-86; pres., owner MJ Dimensions, Brookfield, Wis., 1986—; guest WISN Radio, Milw., 1988; speaker and seminar leader in field. Advisor mktg. edn. adv. com. Milw. Pub. Schs., 1987—. Mem. Wis. Telemktg. Mgrs. Assn. (pres. 1987-89), Sales and Mktg. Execs. Milw. (v.p. programs 1989-90), Internat. Assn. Pers. Women (bd. dirs. 1984-87), Pers. Indsl. Rels. Assn. Milw. (various coms.), Wis. Women Entrepreneurs, Alpha Omicron Pi, Kappa Delta Pi. Roman Catholic. Office: MJ Dimensions 1025 S Moorland Rd Ste 403 Brookfield WI 53005

FRANKLIN, ARETHA, singer; b. Memphis, 1942; d. Clarence L. and Barbara (Siggers) F.; m. Ted White (div.); m. Glynn Turman, Apr. 11, 1978. First record at age 12; rec. artist with Columbia Records, N.Y.C., 1961, then with Atlantic records, now with Arista Records; albums include Aretha, 1961, Electrifying, 1962, Tender Moving and Swinging, 1962, Laughing on the Outside, 1963, Unforgettable, 1964, Songs of Faith, 1964, Running Out of Fools, 1964, Yeah, 1965, Soul Sister, 1966, Queen of Soul, Take it Like You Give It, 1967, Lee Cross, Greatest Hits, 1967, I Never Loved a Man, 1967, Once in a Lifetime, Aretha Arrives, 1967, Lady Soul, 1968, Greatest Hits, Vol. 2, 1968, Best of Aretha Franklin, Live at Paris Olympia, 1968, Aretha Now, 1968, Soul 69, 1969, Today I Sing the Blues, 1969, Soft and Beautiful, Aretha Gold, 1969, Satisfaction, I Say a Little Prayer, 1969, This Girl's in Love With You, 1970, Spirit in the Dark, 1970, Don't Play that Song, 1970, Live at the Fillmore West, 1971, Young Gifted and Black, 1971, Aretha's Greatest Hits, 1971, Amazing Grace, 1972, Hey Hey Now, 1973, Star Collection, 1978, First 12 Sides, 1973, Let Me Into Your Life, 1974, With Every Thing I Feel in Me, 1975, You, 1975, Sparkle, 1976, Ten Years of Gold, 1976, Sweet Passion, 1977, Almighty Fire, 1978, La Diva, 1979, Aretha, 1980, Who's Zoomin' Who, 1985, One Lord, One Faith, One Baptism, 1987, Aretha Sings the Blues, 1965, 85, Lady Soul, 1988, Through the Storm, 1989; appeared in film: Blues Brothers, 1980; performer: (Showtime prodn.) Aretha, 1986; concert tours in U.S. and Europe. Named Top Female Vocalist, 1967; named Number One Female Singer 16th Internat. Jazz Critics Poll, 1968; recipient Grammy award for best female rhythm and blues vocal, 1967-74, 81, 85, 87, for best rhythm and blues rec., 1967, for best soul gospel performance, 1972, for best rhythm and blues duo vocal (with George Michael, 1987); Am. Music award, 1984. Address: 8450 Linwood St Detroit MI 48206*

FRANKLIN, BARBARA ANN, director of programs, educator; b. Houston, June 4, 1950; d. Thomas Watson and Dorothy Elizabeth (Barclay) Brooks; m. Robert Howard Franklin, Mar. 9, 1984; children: Raymond, Brooke, Jim, Daphne, John, Debbie. BS in Edn., Lamar U., 1972. Cert. spl. edn. tchr., Tex. Tchr., tutor South Pk. Juvenile Delinquent Alternative Sch., Beaumont, Tex., 1970-72; tchr. elem. Brazosport Ind. Sch. Dist., Freeport, Tex., 1972-76; tchr. The Children's Pl. Presch., Freeport, 1982-84, tchr. learning disabled children, 1984-88; program dir. Brazosport Meml. Hosp., Lake Jackson, 1989—; edn. chmn. Brazosport Safety Edn. Found., Lake Jackson, 1989—. Author poetry. Active box office Brazosport Music Theatre, Lake Jackson, 1988—; mem. patron com. Jr. Svc. League, Lake Jackson, 1989—; mem. fin. com. South Tex. Girl Scouts U.S. coun., Lake Jackson, 1988; co-chmn. Am. Heart Assn. Ball, Lake Jackson, 1989; sponsor Brazosport Music Theatre, 1987—; mem. Freeport PTA, 1978—, parliamentarian, 1985; mem. Brazosport Little Theatre, 1988—; chmn. Brazosport Safetytown Project, 1988—. Recipient Program award Christian Women's Club, 1979, Appreciation award Bay Area Coun. Boy Scouts Am., 1987, Civic Recognition and Appreciation award Brazosport Safety Found., 1989. Mem. AAUW (art auction chmn.), Rotary (hospitality chmn. Brazosport chpt. 1989). Democrat. Methodist. Home: 105 Sleepy Hollow Dr Lake Jackson TX 77566 Office: Brazosport Meml Hosp 100 Medical Dr Lake Jackson TX 77566

FRANKLIN, BARBARA HACKMAN, management consultant, director, educator; b. Lancaster, Pa., Mar. 19, 1940; d. Arthur A. and Mayme M. (Haller) Hackman; m. Wallace Barnes, Nov. 29, 1986. BA with distinction, Pa. State U., 1962; MBA, Harvard U., 1964; D of Bus. Adminstrn. (hon.), Bryant Coll., 1973; D of Commerce (hon.), Drexel U., 1990. Mgr. environ. analysis Singer Co., N.Y.C., 1964-68; asst. v.p. Citibank, N.Y.C., 1969-71; mem. White House staff, Washington, 1971-73; commr., vice chmn. U.S. Consumer Product Safety Commn., Washington, 1973-79; sr. fellow, dir. govt. and bus. programs Wharton Sch., U. Pa., Phila. and Washington, 1979-89; pres., chief exec. officer Franklin Assocs., Washington, 1984—; adviser to comptroller gen. U.S., 1984—; bd. dirs. Aetna Life and Casualty Co., Dow Chem. Co., Westinghouse Electric Corp., Black & Decker Corp., Automatic Data Processing, Inc., Nordstrom, Inc., Armstrong World Industries; trustee, Pa. State U.; pub. mem. Auditing Standards Bd. Planning Com., 1989. Contbr. numerous articles to profl. jours. Apptd. by Pres. Reagan then Bush to Pres.'s Adv. Com. Trade Negotiations, 1982-86, 89—, chmn. task force on tax reform, 1985-86; co-chmn. Nat. Fin. Com. George Bush for Pres., 1985-88; bd. visitors Def. Systems Mgmt. Coll., Dept. Def., 1986-89; svcs. policy adv. Com. of U.S. Trade Representatives; apptd. by Pres. Bush and confirmed by senate as alt. rep. and pub. del. 44th Session of UN Gen. Assembly, 1989; apptd. by Gov. Thornburgh to State Bd. Edn., Commonwealth Pa., 1980-81; bd. regents U. Hartford, 1986-88. Recipient Disting. Alumni award Pa. State U., 1972, Disting. Woman award Northwood Inst., 1972, Catalyst Award for Corp. Leadership, 1981, Excellence in Mgmt. award Simmons Coll., 1981, ann. award Am. Assn. Poison Control Ctrs., 1979, cert. appreciation, Am. Acad. Pediatrics, 1978, 79, Dirs. Choice award Nat. Women's Econ. Alliance, 1987, Award for Corp. Social Responsibility, CUNY, 1988; Kappa Alpha Theta Graduate fellow, 1962, Edith Gratia Stedman, Harvard U., fellow, 1962. Fellow Nat. Assn. Corp. Dirs.; mem. AICPA (bd. dirs.), Nat. Assoc. of Women Bus. Owners, Women's Forum Washington, Nat. Women's Econ. Alliance Found. (bd. govs., Dir.'s Choice award 1987), Internat. Women's Forum (founding mem.), Nat. Women's Party, Am. Newswomen's Club, Exec. Women in Govt. (founding mem., vice chmn. 1973—), Bretton Woods Com., Women's Econ. Round Table, Washington Forum, Women's Rep. Club of Lancaster County, Alumni Coun. Pa. State U., Penn State Club of Greater Washington, Harvard Bus. Sch. Club (Washington), 1925 F Street Club, Washington, Women's Nat. Rep. Club (bd. govs. 1969-71), Econ. Club N.Y. Congregational. Avocations: exercise, skiing, sailing, reading. Office: Franklin Assocs 2600 Virginia Ave NW Ste 506 Washington DC 20036

FRANKLIN, BARBARA KIPP, bank trust executive; b. Jackson, Mich., Jan. 7, 1943; d. Robert Charles and Barbara Jean (Boardman) F.; m. John Gordon Farrell, May l, 1965 (div. 1968); m. Reuel L. Howe, Jr., June 28, 1980 (div. 1983). BBA, U. Mich., Ann Arbor, 1967. Chartered fin. analyst; cert. fin. planner. Freelance journalist Various Mich. and Ohio Newspapers, 1968-71; pub. relations rep. Bayerische Motoren Werke, Munich, Germany, 1969-71; adminstrv. asst. U. Calif., Santa Cruz, Calif., 1972-75; acct. exec. Dean Witter Reynolds, Los Angeles, 1975-77; trust rep. First Interstate Bank, 1978-79; trust adminstr. Union Bank, Los Angeles, 1980-81; trust portfolio mgr. Fidelity Bank, Phila., 1981-84; trust portfolio mgr., regional trust mgr. Provident Bank, Phila., 1984—. Bd. dirs. Children's Country Week Assn., Chester County, 1988-. Mem. Phila. Securities Assn., Assn. Investment Mgmt. and Rsch., Inst. Chartered Fin. Analysts, Inst. Cert. Fin. Planners, Estate Planning Coun., U. Mich. Assn. Greater Phila., Hist. Soc. Chester County, DAR. Office: Provident Bank 137 N High St West Chester PA 19380

FRANKLIN, CAROL BERTHA, minister; b. Paris, Tex., Apr. 5, 1947; d. Forrest Treadwell and Bertha Florence (Breazeale) F. BA, U. Wash., 1969; MDiv, Southern Baptist Theo. Sem., Louisville, 1976. Tchr. Hawaii Baptist Acad., Honolulu, 1969-71, adminstrv. asst., 1972-73; reporter Baptist Joint Com. on Pub. Affairs, Wash., 1976-79; minister First Baptist Ch., Wash.; lobbyist American Baptist Churches USA, Wash., 1983-. Contbr. articles to profl. jours. Democrat. Home: 142 S Virginia Ave Falls Church VA 22046

FRANKLIN, DALE HELAINE, executive director of marketing; b. St. Louis, Mar. 12, 1940; d. Max S. and Gertrude G. (Cohen) F.; m. Ronald D. Cornelius, May 18, 1978 (div. 1986). Student, U. Miami, Fla., 1958-60. Asst. mgr. Fillmore East Theatre, N.Y.C., 1968-70; manegerial asst. The Grateful Dead, San Rafael, Calif., 1970-72; road mgr., then mgr. New Riders of the Purple Sage, San Rafael, 1972-77; exec. dir. Nashville Music Assn., 1981-85; coord. edn. and spl. projects Tenn. Performing Arts Ctr., Nashville, 1986; dir. regional alumni and devel. Vanderbilt U., Nashville, 1987-90; dir. transp. and lodging, Woodstock Festival, Bethel, N.Y., 1969; curator, archivist Gov.'s Staff Tenn. Homecoming, Nashville, 1986, exec. dir. Leadership Music, Nashville, 1989—. Bd. dirs., Nashville Inst. of Arts, 1983-87, Nashville chpt. Am. Cancer Soc., 1986—; pres., bd. dirs., Community Access Television, Nashville, 1983-86; bd. dirs., coun. mem. W.O Smith Nashville Community Music Sch., 1984—. Featured in music industry publs. Mem. Broadcast Music (writer affiliate), Country Music Assn., Leadership Nashville (prog. com. 1984-89), Leadership Music (bd. dirs. 1989—), Copyright Soc. of the South (exec. 1988—). Home: 7899 River Rd Nashville TN 37209 Office: Scene Three Inc 1813 Eighth Ave S Nashville TN 37203 also: Leadership Music PO Box 158010 Nashville TN 37215

FRANKLIN, HARRIET LEWIS, communications consultant; b. Pitts., Feb. 2, 1938; d. Edward Arthur and Freda (Jubelirer) Lewis; m. Kenneth Ronald Franklin, Dec. 27, 1960; children: Gregg Edward, Erica Gene. BA with high honors, Chatham Coll., 1959; MA, U. Pitts., 1968; PhD, Carnegie-Mellon U., 1974. adj. prof. U. Pitts., 1980—. Tchr. English, Taylor Allderdice High Sch., Pitts., 1959-64; instr. English, Community Coll. Allegheny County, Pitts., 1964-68; prof. English, U. Pitts., 1974-80; pres. Franklin Communications, Pitts., 1980—; adj. prof. U. Pittsburg, 1980—. Author: Elvis: Prophet of Power, 1984, also tng. manuals. Bd. dirs. Community Day Sch., Pitts., 1980-84, Family Resources, Pitts., 1985-88; vol. Pitts. Symphony Soc., 1982-84; vol. writer United Way, Pitts., 1980, 87. Scholar Ford Found., 1969; fellow Carnegie-Mellon U., 1969-74; named to U.S. Register of Am. Writers, 1986. Mem. Am. Soc. Tng. and Devel., Assn. Mgmt. Cons., Internat. Franchise Assn. (edn. com. 1985—), Pitts. Athletic Assn., Concordia Club. Democrat. Jewish. Home: 5840 Aylesboro Ave Pittsburgh PA 15217 Office: 4730 Centre Ave Pittsburgh PA 15213

FRANKLIN, MRS. HUGH See L'ENGLE, MADELEINE

FRANKLIN, KATHLEEN ANNA, chemical engineer; b. Columbus, Ohio, Jan. 20, 1957; d. George Joseph and Ellen Jane (Hagood) F. BSChemE, La. State U., 1982. Lab. supr. La. Cellulose Specialties, Greensburg, 1983-84; chem. engr. U.S. EPA, Washington, 1985—. Mem. Am. Inst. Chem. Engrs. Democrat. Roman Catholic. Home: 1611 S 28th St Apt #5 Arlington VA 22206 Office: US EPA TS 779 401 M St SW Washington DC 20460

FRANKLIN, MARGARET LAVONA BARNUM (MRS. C. BENJAMIN FRANKLIN), civic leader; b. Caldwell, Kans., June 19, 1905; d. LeGrand Husted and Elva (Biddinger) Barnum; m. C. Benjamin Franklin, Jan. 20, 1940 (dec. 1983); children: Margaret Lee (Mrs. Michael J. Felso), Benjamin Barnum. B.A., Washburn U., 1952; student, Iowa State Tchrs. Coll., 1923-25, U. Iowa, 1937-38. Tchr. pub. schs. Union, Iowa, 1925-27, pub. schs., Kearney, Nebr., 1927-28, Marshalltown, Iowa, 1928-40; advance rep. Redpath-Vawter-Chautauquas, 1926, Associated Chautauquas, 1927-30. Mem. Citizens Adv. Com., 1965-69; mem. Stormont-Vail Regional Ctr. Hosp. Aux.; bd. dirs. Marshalltown Civic Theatre, 1938-40, Topeka Pub. Libr. Found., 1984—. Recipient Waldo B. Heywood award Topeka Civic Theatre, 1967, award Topeka Pub. Libr., 1977; named Outstanding Mem., Mother of Kans. chpt. Alpha Delta Pi, 1971. Mem. DAR (state chmn. Museum 1968-71), AAUW, Gemini Group of Topeka, Topeka Geneal. Soc., Topeka Civic Symphony Soc. (dir. 1952-57, Svc. Honor citation 1960), Doll Collectors Am., Marshalltown Community Theatre (pres. 1938-40), Topeka Pub. Libr. Bd. (trustee 1961-70, treas., 1962-65, chmn. 1965-67), Shawnee County Hist. Soc. (dir. 1963-75, sec. 1964-66), Nat. Multiple Sclerosis Soc. (dir. Kans. chpt. 1963-66), Stevengraph Collectors Assn., Friends of Topeka Public Libr. (dir. 1970-79, Disting. Svc. award 1980), Philanthropic and Ednl. Orgn. (pres. chpt. 1956-57, coop. bd. pres. 1964-65, chpt. honoree 1969), Native Sons and Daus. Kans. (life), Nonoso, Topeka Stamp Club, Western Sorosis Club (pres. 1960-61), Minerva Club (2d v.p. 1984-85), Woman's Club (1st v.p. 1952-54), Knife and Fork Club, Alpha Beta Gamma. Republican.

FRANKLIN, PAULA ANNE, psychologist, educator, writer; b. Wheaton, Ill., Feb. 2, 1928; d. Paul Spangler and Ella Creighton (Daniels) Fowler; m. Richard Clarence Franklin, Aug. 13, 1950; children: Jan Franklin BenDor, Timothy Vickery, Edward Lee. Student, Manchester U., England, 1946-47; BSc in History, Northwestern U., 1944-45, 47-49, postdoctoral, 1975; post-grad., So. Ill. U., 1959-61; MA, W.Va. U., 1970; PhD, Union Inst., 1980. Lic. psychologist, Md. Dir. Franklinc Cons. in Applied Behavioral Sci., Balt., 1969—; mem. applied behavioral sci. faculty Johns Hopkins U., Balt., 1972—; rsch. project dir. Social Security Adminstrn., Balt., 1973—; mem. psychology faculty U. Balt., 1989—. Author: (with R. Franklin) Tomorrow's Track, 1976, (with others) Disability in the U.S., 1990; contbr. articles to profl. jours. Mem. various coms. LWV, 1950-75; various positions Girl Scouts U.S., Boy Scouts Am., 1950-70. Mem. Am. Psychol. Assn., Am. Evaluation Assn., Assn. Am. Women in Sci. (v.p. Balt. chpt. 1987-89), Md. Psychol. Assn. (mem. various coms., Cert. of Recognition 1981). Unitarian. Home: 3946 Cloverhill Rd Baltimore MD 21218 Office: DDPIS OD Soc Security Admns Annex 2223 6401 Social Security Blvd Baltimore MD 21235

FRANKLIN, SHERYL J., information services executive; b. Buffalo, June 25, 1954; d. W. Eugene and Shirley M. (Shults) F. Student, Bapt. Bible Coll., 1971-72, U. Scranton, 1974-76, Camden County Coll., Blackwood, N.J., 1979-80. Pers. clk. Met. Life Ins. Co., Clarks Summit, Pa., 1973-75; programmer Met. Life Ins. Co., Clarks Summit, 1976-77; sr. programmer/analyst First Pa. Bank, Phila., 1977-81; cons. AGS Info. Svcs. subsidiary NYNEX Corp., Phila., 1981; account supr. AGS Info. Svcs. (formerly SDA), Phila., 1981-82, tech. mgr., 1983-84, account exec., 1984, br. mgr., 1984-87, v.p., 1987—. Active ASPCA. Mem. Data Processing Mgmt. Assn., Network of Women in Computer Tech., Planetary Soc., Defenders of Wildlife, Humane Soc. U.S. Republican. Mem. Dutch Reformed Ch. Office: AGS Info Svcs Inc The Bourse Bldg Ste 560 Philadelphia PA 19106

FRANKLIN, SHIRLEY CLARKE, municipal official; b. Phila., May 10, 1945; d. Eugene Haywood Clarke and Ruth (Lyons) White; m. David McCoy Franklin, Feb. 5, 1972 (div. 1986); children: Kai Ayanna, Cabral Holsey, Kali Jamilla. BA, Howard U., 1968; MA, U. Pa., 1969. Contract compliance officer U.S. Dept. Labor, Washington, 1966-68; instr. social scis. Talledega (Ala.) Coll., 1969-71; from dir. to commr. Dept. Cultural Affairs, Atlanta, 1978-82; chief adminstrv. officer City of Atlanta, 1982-90, exec. officer for ops., 1990—. Trustee Atlanta Symphony Orch., 1977-81, Atlanta Found., 1980—; mem. Ga. Council for the Arts, Atlanta, 1979-82, adv. bd. Ga. Women's Polit. Caucus, Atlanta, 1982-84; chmn. expansion arts panel Nat. Endowment for the Arts, Washington, 1980-82; bd. dirs. Nat. Urban Coalition, Washington, 1980-83; dep. campaign mgr. Young for Atlanta, 1981-82. Recipient Disting. Alumni award Nat. Assn. for Equal Opportunity Higher Edn., 1983, Leadership award Atlanta chpt. NAACP, 1987; named to Acad. Women Achievers YWCA Greater Atlanta, 1986. Mem. Nat. Forum Black Pub. Adminstrs. Democrat. Club: Chautauqua Circle. Office: City Hall 55 Trinity Ave SW Atlanta GA 30335

FRANKOVICH, MARY JO, clinical audiologist; b. Milw., Mar. 25, 1954; d. Joseph Dale and Darlene Sue (Nix) Wolfe; m. George Robert Frankovich. AA in Liberal Arts, Northwestern Mich. Coll., 1974; BS in Communication Disorders, No. Mich. U., 1976; MA in Audiology, Wayne State U., 1978. Student, audiology fellowship Wayne State U., 1976-78; audiologist Met. Hosp., Wayne, Mich., 1978-79, Ent Assocs. - Bloomfield, Bloomfield Hills, Mich., 1979-87; sr. audiologist Pontiac Osteopathic Hosp., Mich., 1980-87; sr. audiologist, cons. With Gregory C. Roche, D.O., Pontiac, Mich., 1987—; audiology com. Mich. Speech Hearing Assn., Lansing, Mich., 1988—, planning com. mem., 1988—. Mem. Am. Speech Lang. Hearing Assn., Mich. Speech Hearing Assn., Am. Auditory Soc. Roman Catholic. Home: 3430 Ridgeview Rochester Hills MI 48309 Office: 909 Woodward Ave Ste 115 Pontiac MI 48053

FRANKSON-KENDRICK, SARAH JANE, publisher; b. Bradford, Pa., Sept. 24, 1949; d. Sophronus Ahimus and Elizabeth Jane (Sears) McCutcheon; m. James Michael Kendrick, Jr., May 22, 1982. Customer service rep. Laros Printing/Osceola Graphics, Bethlehem, Pa., 1972-73; assoc. editor Babcox Publs., Akron, Ohio, 1973-74; assoc. editor Bill Communications, Akron, 1974-75, sr. editor, 1975-77, editor-in chief, 1977-81; assoc. pub. Chilton Co./ABC Pub., Chgo., 1981-83, pub., 1983-89, group pub., Radnor, Pa., 1989—. Recipient Automotive Replacement Edn. award Northwood Inst., 1983, award for young leadership and excellence Automotive Hall of Fame, 1984. Mem. Automotive Parts and Accessories Assn. (bd. dirs., strategic planning com., show planning task force), Internat. Assn. Bus. Communicators, Am. Mgmt. Assn., Women in Communications, 500 Automotive Execs. Club (bd. dirs., pres.). Republican. Club: Knollwood Country (Lake Forest, Ill.). Office: Chilton Co/ABC Pub 201 Clinton Way Radnor PA 19089

FRANKUM, CAROLYN IRENE, dietitian; b. Memphis, Feb. 19, 1937; d. Robert Oscar and Irene Schneider (Perry) F. BS in Home Econs., David Lipscomb Coll., Nashville, 1960; MS in Nutrition, Case Western Res. U., 1963. Staff dietitian Lakewood (Ohio) Hosp., 1960-63; asst. prof. Med. Coll. Ga. Sch. Nursing, Augusta, 1963-66; instr. David Lipscomb Coll., 1966-68; dietitian Vanderbilt U. Med. Ctr., 1968—. Co-author: Change of Seasons (A Guide to Low-Salt/Sodium Living), 1986. Vol. Hospitality House, Nashville. mem. Am. Dietetic Assn. Office: Vanderbilt U Med Ctr Nutrition Svcs 21st Ave N Nashville TN 37232

FRANN, MARY, actress; b. St. Louis, Dec. 27. Student, Northwestern U. Formerly staff mem. KSDK-TV, St. Louis, later with ABC, Chgo.; various appearances Chgo. theaters; in Story Theatre, Los Angeles, N.Y.C., other theatre appearances Los Angeles; TV series: Newhart, 1982-89 , My Friend Tony, 1969, Days of Our Lives, Return to Peyton Place, King's Crossing, 1982, Mike Hammer, 1987; motion pictures for TV: Portrait of an Escort, Gidget's Summer Reunion, Eight is Enough, A Family Reunion; hostess Miss USA pageant, 1986, 87, Miss Universe pageant, 1986, 87; commentator Tournament of Roses Parade, 1985-87. Office: care William Morris Agency 151 El Camino Beverly Hills CA 90212

FRANSEN, CHRISTINE IRENE, mathematics teacher; b. Chgo., Sept. 3, 1947; d. Henry and Irene Antoinette (Ross) F. BS in Maths. Edn., U. Ill., 1969; MS in Maths., Northeastern Ill. U., 1971. Cert. maths. tchr., Ill. Tchr. Senn Met. Acad., Chgo., 1969—. Stage mgr., dancer Ensemble Espanol Dance Co., Chgo., 1977—. Recipient Outstanding Tchr. award U. Chgo., 1979, 82, 83, Honors Tchr. award NASA, 1985, Dedicated Tchr. award Kate Maremont Found., 1982, Ednl. Svc. award Blum-Kovler Found., 1989. Mem. Nat. Coun. Tchrs. Math., Ill. Coun. Tchrs. Math., Met. Math. Club Chgo.

FRANTZ, NANETTE MICHELLE, account executive; b. Columbia City, Ind., June 13, 1955; d. Fred and Vivian (Babcock) Vetor; m. James Richard Frantz, June 25, 1977; 1 child, Olivia Michelle. BA, St. Mary of the Woods, 1977; MBA, Ind. Wesleyan, 1990. Pub. rels. mgr. United Telephone of Ind., Warsaw, 1977-88; asst. comml. mgr. United Telephone of Ind., Plymouth, 1988-89; account exec. Ind. Bus. Mag., Indpls., 1989—; instr. mktg. Ind. Vocat. and Tech. Inst., Warsaw, 1989. Pres. Warsaw Found. for Pub. Edn., 1987; canvasser March of Dimes, Warsaw, 1987—. Mem. Kosciusko Assn. Female Execs., AAUW. Republican. Episcopalian. Home and office: Ind Bus Mag 176 E Dellview Dr Warsaw IN 46580

FRANTZVE, JERRI LYN, industrial psychologist, consultant, educator; b. Huntington Beach, Calif., Sept. 9, 1942; d. Rolland and Marjorie Cleone (Ferrin) Weiland. Student, Purdue U., 1964-68; BA in Psychology and History, Marian Coll., 1969; MS in Organizational Psychology, George Williams Coll., 1976; PhD in Indsl. and Organizational Psychology, U. Ga., 1979. Case worker Marion County Welfare Dept., Indpls., 1970-71; mkgt. rsch. analyst Quaker Oats Co., Barrington, Ill., 1971-75; mgmt. cons. J.L. Frantzve & Assocs., Christiansburg, Va., 1978—; asst. prof. sch. of mgmt. SUNY, Binghamton, N.Y., 1979-83; pers. rsch. advisor Conoco/DuPont, Ponca City, Okla., 1983-84; pers. rsch. coord. Conoco/DuPont, Ponca City, 1984, pers. rsch., acad. affairs coord., 1984-86; dir. welfare benefits Conoco/Dupont, Ponca City, 1986-88; cons. psychologist Allen Assocs., Northboro, Mass., 1988-89; assoc. prof. psychology Radford (Va.) U., 1989—; instrn. cons. USAF, Rome, N.Y., 1979-83; dir. Israel Overseas Rsch. Prog., Ginozar, Israel, 1982, Japanese Overseas Rsch. Prog., Tokyo, 1983; coordinator rsch. Ctr. for Gender Studies, Radford U., 1989—. Author: Behaving in Organizations: Tales from the Trenches, 1983, Guide to Behavior in Organizations, 1983; contbr. articles to profl. jours. Bd. dirs. Broome County Alcoholism Clinic, Binghamton, N.Y., 1980-83, bd. dirs. Broome County Mental Health Clinic, Binghamton, 1981-83; del. Dem. Caucus, Okla., 1985. Mem. Am. Psychol. Assn. (com. on women in psychology 1986-88), Acad. of Mgmt. (Eastern chpt. placement dir. 1982), Am. Soc. Pers. Adminstrn., Soc. for Personality and Social Psychology, Assn. for Women in Psychology, AAUW, Delta Sigma Pi. Home: 1300 Chestnut Dr Christiansburg VA 24073 Office: Radford U Dept Psychology Radford VA 24142

FRANZ, LYDIA MILLICENT TRUC, real estate executive; b. Chgo., Jan. 11, 1924; d. Walter and Lydia (Kralovec) Truc; Mus.B., Ill. Wesleyan U., 1944; Mus.M., Northwestern U., 1949; m. Robert Franz, Aug. 27, 1952 (dec. Aug. 1983). Tchr. music pub. schs., Muskegon, Mich., 1947-48; mktg. research analyst Grant Advt. Agy., Chgo., 1949; mktg. research asst. Buchen Co., Chgo., 1949-52; asst. to dir. mktg. research Sherman Marquette Advt. Co., Chgo., 1952; asst. to pres., dir. media and research Andover Advt. Agy., 1952-55; salesman Boehmer & Hedlund, realty, Barrington, Ill., 1960-63; pres. Century-21-Country Squire, Inc., Barrington, 1963-87, sr. v.p. Koenig & Strey, Realtors, Barrington, 1987—; dir. Clyde Fed. Savs. & Loan Assn., 1984—. Recipient Disting. Alumni award Ill. Wesleyan U., 1988. Mem. adv. com. Office of Real Estate Research, U. Ill., Champaign. Served with WAC, 1944-46. Mem. Women in Real Estate (pres. 1966-67), Barrington Bd. Realtors (pres. 1968-69), Ill. Assn. Realtors (dir. 1972-75, 81—, gov. Realtor's Inst. of Ill. 1972-78, exec. com. 1977—, pres. 1984, Realtor of Yr. 1988), Nat. Assn. Realtors (dir. 1982—), Realtors Nat. Mktg. Inst. (bd. govs. 1979, regional gov. 1980), Barrington C. of C. (pres. 1974, dir. 1972-75, 84—, Merit award 1985), Barrington Bus. and Profl. Women's Club, Mensa, Sigma Alpha Iota. Republican. Home: 408 E Hillside Ave Barrington IL 60010 Office: 209 Park Ave Barrington IL 60010

FRANZHEIM, BARBARA, restoration company executive, fine arts consultant; b. Newark, Feb. 7, 1939; m. Kenneth Franzheim, II, Apr. 15, 1966 (div. 1973); children—Pamela Franzheim Tower, Sabrina, Melita; m. 2d, Daniel Dror, Sept. 27, 1974 (div. 1985); 1 son, Daniel. B.A., Montclair Coll., 1962; postgrad., NYU, 1962, Fordham U., 1965-66; M.E., Seton Hall U., 1964. Tchr. English, N.J., 1962-64; with editorial dept. McGraw-Hill, N.Y.C., 1965; with Batten Barton Durstine & Osborn, N.Y.C., 1965; various positions fashion industry, N.Y.C., 1965-66; with U.S. Fgn. Service, South Pacific, N.Z., Tonga, Fiji, Samoa, 1969-72; owner Hist. Restoration Co., Tex. and N.Y.C., 1976—; chief exec. officer Three Sources Corp., Houston, 1976—. Restorations include: Cabin, Xalapa Farm, Paris, Ky., 1969, U.S. Embassy Resisdnece, Lowerhutt, New Zealand, 1981, 1412 North Blvd., Houston, 1975, Cynthiana Hall, Lexington, Ky., 1975, Gardenside, Southhampton, 1979, Bellefleur Farm, Versailles, Ky., 1983, La Favorita, Palm Beach, Fla., 1984, 635 Park Ave., N.Y.C., 1985, La Fleur Artist's Village, Southampton, N.Y., 1986; columnist, contbg. editor 713 mag., 1988—; contbg. author Bluegrass mag. Advisor Town of Versailles Main St. Assn.; bd. dirs. Tex. Children's Hosp., Houston, 1967-68, Tex. Mental Health Assn., Houston, 1968-69, Contemporary Arts Mus., Houston, 1976-80, Houston Symphony, 1981-82, Houston Grand Opera, 1975-85. Mem. U.S. Simmental Cattle Assn. (breeder), Pyramid Society Arabian Breeders, Houston Club, Houstonian Club, University (Houston) Club, Lafayette Club, Idle Hour Club, Thoroughbred Club of Am. Republican. Roman Catholic. Home: 1400 Hermann Dr Penthouse B Houston TX 77004 Address: Bellefleur Farm Clifton Pike Versailles KY 40383 Office: Historic Restoration Co 5 Chamberlain Ave Warren NJ 07060

FRANZONI, LAURYN L., editor; b. Takoma Park, Md., July 14, 1957; d. John Carlos and Kathryn Helen (Kline) F.; m. Stanley M. Pederson, Dec. 29, 1984; 1 child, Meredyth Franzoni Pederson. BA in Am. Studies, Dickinson Coll., 1978; MA in Journalism, The Am. U., 1979; postgrad. in bus. studies, Drury Coll., 1987-89. Reporter Bus. Rev. of Washington, 1979-80; editor, pub. The Franzoni Report, Washington, 1980-81; sr. staff writer Washington Bus. Jour., 1981-82; mng. editor Phillips Pub., Potomac, Md., 1982-84; v.p. pub. TeleStrategies, Inc., McLean, Va., 1984-85; editor Springfield (Mo.) Bus. Jour., 1985-86; v.p., mktg. Hedges Communications, Springfield, 1986-87; editor Retail Banking Strategist, N.Y.C., 1987—; columnist The Am. Banker, N.Y.C., 1990—. Mem. Yr. 2000 Commn., Springfield, 1988-89. Named to Outstanding Young Women of Am., 1985, 87. Mem. Bank Mktg. Assn. - Heart of Am. Chpt., Women in Communications, Springfield Ad Club (bd. dirs. 1986-89), Washington Ad Club (bd. dirs. 1980-83), Newsletter Assn. Roman Catholic. Office: PO Box 4732 Springfield MO 65808

FRASER, MARJORIE ALICE, business educator, retired, rancher; b. Ventura, Calif., Mar. 8, 1914; d. Silas Orton and Joycie Elizabeth (Totten) F. AA, Ventura Jr. Coll., 1934; BE, UCLA, 1938; MEd, U. So. Calif., 1942. Typing and history tchr. Ventura Jr. High Sch., 1938-41; evening tchr. Ventura Coll., 1938-41, 57-64; shorthand and typing tchr. Inglewood High Sch., 1941-42; with Army Air Force Depot, San Bernardino, Calif., 1942; typist U.S. Engrs., Skagway, Alaska, 1943; tchr. Nordhof High Sch., Ojai, Calif., 1949-61; clerk-typist U.S. Dept. State, Pretoria, South Africa. Author:

Investigation, Speed, and Accuracy in Typewriting, 1942; editor: Legend-Gosnell Bend to Casitas (1859-1916), 1965. Deaconess Community Presbyn. Ch., Ventura, 1950s; past bd. mem. YMCA, YWCA, 1950s; docent Ventura County Hist. Mus., 1979-88. Mem. NEA (life), AAUW, Calif. Bus. Edn. Assn. (pres. so. sect. Calif. 1950s), Ojai Valley Tchrs. Assn. (v.p. 1950s), Ojai Bus. and Profl. Womens Club (pres.), UCLA Alumni Assn. (life), Ventura C. of C. (womens div.), Buena Ventura Womens Club, Clan Fraser Assn. for Calif., Masons. Republican.

FRASER, PATRICIA LEE, secretary; b. Chgo., Jan. 7, 1944; d. Jack and Patricia Harriet (Lee) F. From sec. to sr. exec. asst. to pre. media rsch. A.C. Nielsen, Ill., 1987-90; adminstrv. sec. Sta. WTTW-TV, Chgo., 1990—. Bd. dirs. Hollywood-North Park Improvement Assn., Chgo., 1986-88. Mem. Chgo. Women's Bowling Assn. (bd. dirs. 1988—), Sportswomen's Golf. Democrat. Roman Catholic. Office: Sta WTTW Channel 11 5400 N St Louis Chicago IL 60625

FRASER, RENEE WHITE, advertising executive; b. Columbus, Ohio, June 15, 1952; d. William Burval and Ruth Ann (Stuber) White; m. William Jackson, Aug. 25, 1973 (div. 1976); m. Scott Cameron Fraser, Dec. 10, 1977; children: Nicole, Caneel, Skye. BA, U. So. Calif., 1973, MA, 1975, PhD, 1981. Prin. PLOG Rsch., Reseda, Calif., 1977-80; v.p. Leichenne Rsch., Century City, Calif., 1980-81; v.p., dir. research Young & Rubicam, L.A., 1981-84; sr. v.p., dir. strategic planning and research Bozell, Jacobs, Kenyon & Eckhardt, L.A., 1984-88; exec. v.p., gen. mgr. Bozell, Inc., L.A., 1988—; bd. dirs. Sharon Clark & Assocs., L.A.; pres., bd. govs. Vols. of Am., L.A. Author: Behavioral and Psycho-cultural Factors in Planning Health Care Systems, 1978, Environmental Health Issues in Developing Health Care Systems in Third World Countries, 1978, Psycho-social and Sociological Considerations in Developing Health Care Systems in Developing Nations, 1980, Public Health Techniques for Health Care Systems in Developing Countries, 1980. Recipient Disting. speaker award Direct Mktg. Assn., 1985. Mem. Am. Mktg. Assn., Am. Psychol. Assn., Advt. Rsch. Found., Calif. Yacht Club, Psi Chi, Sigma Chi. Democrat. Methodist. Home: 10758 National Blvd Los Angeles CA 90064 Office: Bozell Inc 12121 Wilshire Blvd Los Angeles CA 90025

FRASER-SMITH, ELIZABETH BIRDSEY, microbiologist; b. Pasadena, Calif., Apr. 19, 1938; d. William Canvin and Elizabeth Armstrong (Creswell) Birdsey; m. Antony Charles Fraser-Smith, Apr. 6, 1968; children: Julie Gaye, William Antony. BA, Stanford U., 1960, MA, 1962. From assoc. scientist to sr. scientist Lockheed Missiles and Space Co., Palo Alto, Calif., 1960-69; biologist Enviros, Los Altos, Calif., 1973-77; from biologist II to staff researcher II Syntex Rsch. Corp., Palo Alto, 1977—; tchr. exploratory experience program Palo Alto Unified Sch. Dist., 1966-68; tchr. Lyceum for Gifted Students, Palo Alto, 1978-80. Author: Child Ecology: A Resource for the Elementary School Teacher, 1974; contbr. articles to profl. jours.; patentee in field. Mem. AAAS, Am. Soc. Microbiology, Internat. Soc. Virology, Nat. Wildlife Fedn., Zero Population Growth, Sempervirens Fund, Am. Farmland Trust, Sierra Club. Home: 71 Alma Ct Los Altos CA 94022

FRAUNFELTER, BRENDA LYNN, nurse; b. Lancaster, Pa., Aug. 31, 1953; d. Floyd Samuel and Betty Jane (Lear) F. LPN, Willow St. Area Vo-Tech Sch., Pa., 1972; RN, Bucks County Grand View Sch., 1975. Cert. cardiographic technician. LPN pediatric dept. Lancaster (Pa.) Osteopathic Hosp., 1972-74, RN, 1975-77, asst. head nurse, 1977-81, staff nurse, 1981-82; nurse tech. cardiology dept. Community Hosp. of Lancaster, 1982—. Mem. We Love Lucy Fan Club. Republican. Roman Catholic. Home: 423 Hamilton St Lancaster PA 17602 Office: Community Hosp Lancaster 1100 E Orange St Lancaster PA 17604

FRAUSTO, MARIA CHRISTINA, educator; b. San Jose, Calif., Dec. 25, 1952; d. Carlos and Hortencia (Pasillas) F. BA, U. of the Pacific, 1975; postgrad., Calif. State U., San Jose, 1975—. Cert. elem. and secondary tchr., Calif. Tchr. kindergarten, 1st grade bilingual edn. San Jose Unified Sch. Dist., 1975-81; bilingual resource tchr. Santee Sch., Franklin-McKinley Sch. Dist., San Jose, 1981-85; tchr. 1st grade bilingual edn. McKinley Sch., San Jose, 1985-88; tchr. Spanish and English as a second lang. Sylvandale Middle Sch., 1988—; master tcrh. for student tchrs. San Jose State U., 1985—; presenter workshops on bilingual edn. and teaching English as a second lang.; tchr. adult edn. and English as a second lang., San Jose, 1988—. Grantee East Valley Ednl. Found., San Jose, 1987. Mem. Calif. Assn. Bilingual Edn. (chair fundraising 1982-84). Democrat. Roman Catholic. Clubs: McKinley Track (San Jose), NorCal Cheetah Track Club. Home: 2339 Ravine Dr San Jose CA 95133 Office: Franklin McKinley Sch Dist 2072 Lucretia Ave San Jose CA 95122

FRAWLEY, SISTER CLAIRE, educator; b. Elmira, N.Y., Nov. 7, 1929; d. James Edward and Alice (Keating) Frawley. BS, Nazareth Coll., 1957, BA, 1966; postgrad., Siena Coll., 1967, U. Dayton, 1967-68, Cath. U., 1969-73; MRE, Divine Word, 1972. Sch. administr., tchr. Parish Schs., Rochester, Ithaca, Elmira, N.Y., 1950-80; founder, exec. dir. St. Claires Homes, Escondido Calif., homes for homeless women and children, youth minister, Escondido, established and administered program for youth and young adults. Recipient Women Helping Women award Soroptimists, Womens Internat. Living Legacy award; scholar Nat. U. Mem. NAFE, Assn. of Christian Therapists, Calif. Mental Health Assn., Womens Internat., Coalition of Human Svc. Agencies, Child Abuse Coalition, Inland Dirs. Coalition. Home: 784 E Mission Apt E Escondido CA 92025

FRAYER, DOROTHY ANN, university administrator; b. Detroit, Nov. 1, 1938; d. Rudolph Frayer and Anna Jane Funk. BA, Mich. State U., 1960, MA, 1962; PhD, U. Wis., 1969. Asst. scientist Wis. R&D Ctr. for Cognitive Learning, Madison, Wis., 1969-72; assoc. profr. Hofstra U., Hempstead, N.Y., 1972-81; assoc. dean, sch. edn. Hofstra U., Hempstead, 1973-75, exec. dir. grants, contracts, rsch., 1976-80; dean, sch. edn. Duquesne U., Pittsburgh, 1981-88; assoc. acad. v.p Duquesne U., 1989—. Author: Conceptual Learning Development, 1974. Recipient Disting. Alumni award Mich. State U., E. Lansing, 1970. Mem. Am. Psychol. Assn., Am. Ednl. Rsch. Assn., Am. Assn. Higher Edn., Am. Assn. Univ. Administrs., Phi Delta Kappa. Democrat. Episcopalian. Home: 413 Allenberry Dr Pittsburgh PA 15237 Office: Duquesne Univ Pittsburgh PA 15282

FRAZER, ELIZABETH BURGESS, realtor; b. Hickory, N.C., July 23, 1937; d. Arthur Harry and Sara Elizabeth (Doll) Burgess; m. John Sidney Frazer, Oct. 15, 1960; children: John Martyn, Harry Lee. BA, Queens Coll., 1959. Dir. Christian edn. First Presbyn. Ch., Lincolnton, N.C., 1959-60; interim First Presbyn. Ch., Asheville, N.C., 1969-70; realtor McArthur-Sanders, Brentwood, Tenn., 1986—. Active Ira B. Jones PTA, 1968-76, sec. 1970-71; assoc. supt. Sun. sch. First Presbyn. Ch., Asheville, 1970-74, pres. Women of the Ch., 1974-76. ors, 1989. Mem. Williamson County Bd. Realtors, Women's Council Realtors, Nashville Bd. Realtors, AAUW (pres. 1970-72), Tenn. GRI (charter mem.). Home: 110 Long Valley Rd Brentwood TN 37027 Office: McArthur-Sanders Realtors 1749 Mallory Ln Brentwood TN 37027

FRAZER, PHYLLIS SEELY, hair salon and skin care company executive; b. Montclair, N.J., Oct. 25, 1953; d. Frederick Gilbert and Judith Dorothy (Moxley) F. Grad. high sch., Montclair. Hairdresser The New You, Upper Montclair, N.J., 1977-79; makeup artist Martini Skin Care Salon, N.Y.C., 1979-82; account coord. Christian Dior, N.Y.C., 1982-87; bus. mgr. Chameleon Ltd., N.Y.C., 1987—; chief exec. officer Hands on at the Cutting Corner, Pequannock, N.J., 1989—. Office: Chameleon Ltd 207 8th Ave New York NY 10011 also: Hands on at Cutting Corner 165 Newark-Pompton Turnpike Pequannock NJ 07440

FRAZER, WENDY, nurse, physician assistant; b. Steubenville, Ohio, June 3, 1943; d. Richard William and Mary Elizabeth (Sliday) F. RN, Beaver Valley Gen. Hosp., New Brighton, Pa., 1964; AAS, Cuyahoga Community Coll., 1983. RN, Ohio, Pa. Pediatrics nurse Cleve. Clinic Found., 1962-65; asst. head nurse Cardiovascular Lab., 1965-73; surg. nurse clinician cardiothoracic surgery Cleve. Clinic Found., 1978-86, 88—, genthoracic surgery nurse clinician, 1986-88; admissions officer Lakewood Hosp., 1984-85; instr. cardiovascular tech. program Cuyahoga Community Coll., Cleve., 1987—, clin. preceptor surg. asst. program, 1984-87; mem. steering com. Master's Group of Phoenix Ctr., 1986-88; physician asst. membership com. Alumnus Assn., 1986. Assoc. founder, counselor Inst. Creative Living, 1976-80. Mem. Nat. Acad. Physician Assts., Nat. Assn. Cardiovascular Physician Assts., Cleve. Zool. Soc., Nat. Geog. Soc., Sci. Club. Republican. Baptist. Office: Cleve Clinic Found 9500 Euclid Ave Cleveland OH 44106

FRAZIER, ELLEN ELIZABETH, accountant, consultant; b. Cambridge, Mass., Jan. 28, 1950; d. Helen Rhoda (Brooks) Frazier. Student So. Meth. U., 1967-69; BBA, U. Houston, 1972; MBA, Houston Bapt. U., 1984. Acctg. mgr. Baker Internat. Co., Houston, 1979-81; acct., cons. NL Industries, Houston, 1981-87; tech. cons. Baylor Coll. Medicine, 1987—; adj. prof. data processing North Harris County Coll., 1989—. Vol. Gary Hart's Presdl. Campaign, Houston, 1983—; mem. speakers' bur. United Way Campaign, 1984, Family Service Bur., 1987-88. Mem. So. Meth. U. Alumni Assn., Houston Bapt. U. Alumni Assn., Assn. for Women in Computing (pres. Houston chpt. 1987-88, nat. v.p. 1988), Fedn. Houston Profl. Women (Outstanding Houston Profl. Woman 1988). Democrat. Methodist. Club: Native Houstonian (charter mem.). Home: 1511 Burning Tree Rd Kingwood TX 77339 Office: Applied Micros Inc/SYMON 12946 Dairy Ashford Sugar Land TX 77478

FRAZIER, KIMBERLEE GONTERMAN, veterinarian; b. St. Louis, Mar. 5, 1953; d. Joseph Wilbur Jr. and Melody (Engleman) Gonterman; m. Burk Ralph Frazier, Oct. 11, 1985; 1 child, Weston James. DVM magna cum laude, U. Mo., 1979. Vet. intern U. Mo. Coll. Vet. Medicine, Columbia, 1979-80; relief veterinarian, St. Louis and Kansas City, Mo., 1980-84; account exec. Merrill Lynch, Clayton, Mo., 1984-85; owner, founder, small animal practitioner VET STOP Animal Clinics, St. Charles, St. Peters, Florissant, Rock Hill, Mo., St. Louis, Mo., 1985—; advisor Math. Sci. Network, St. Louis, 1987. Frank Wells scholar U. Mo., 1978; First Pl. in Exhibn. Sport for synchronized swimming, Munich Olympics, 1972. Mem. AVMA, Mo. Vet. Med. Assn., St. Louis Vet. Med. Assn., Mo. Bot. Garden, Friends of Zoo, Gamma Sigma Delta, Phi Zeta. Republican. Home: 4601 Maryland Ave Saint Louis MO 63108 Office: VET STOP Animal Clinics 7527 S Lindbergh Blvd Saint Louis MO 63125

FRAZIER, RUTH MAE, insurance company executive; b. East Orange, N.J., Oct. 12, 1944; d. Clarence and Ruth May (Cowan) F. BA, Kean Coll. N.J., 1982; MA, Montclair State Coll., 1990. Various positions Prudential Ins. Co., Roseland, N.J., 1962-84, rsch. analyst, 1984-86, systems analyst, 1986-88, assoc. systems mgr., 1988—. Mem. Phi Kappa Phi, Alpha Sigma Lambda, Lambda Alpha Sigma. Office: Prudential Ins Co 55 N Livingston Ave Roseland NJ 07068

FRAZIER-TSAI, KAREN LYNNE, English as second language specialist; b. Kansas City, Mo., June 2, 1952; d. Harold Allistone and Audrey Rose (Kana) Frazier; m. Chen-Lung (James) Tsai, Sept. 27, 1986; 1 child, Amy Pei-Je. BA with honors in Speech, Coll. of Wooster, 1974; MA in Linguistics, Ohio U., 1983. Mem. pub. rels. dept. Falls Savs. & Loan Assn., Cuyahoga Falls, Ohio, 1974-79, br. mgr., 1976-79; credit mgr. Burton Rubber Processing, Akron, Ohio, 1979-81; Saudi program dir. English Lang. and Multicultural Inst., Dayton, Ohio, 1983-84; dir., fgn. student advisor ESL, Coll. of Mt. St. Joseph, Cin., 1984-86; tchr. Chmn. Sch. and Hundred Dynasty Co., Taipei, Rep. of China, 1986-87; tchr., supr. Emerson Lang. Sch., Taipei, 1987; prof. Fuhsing Kang Coll., Taipei, 1987-88; dir. Chmn. Mgmt. and Cultural Svcs., Taipei, 1987-89; writer Oxford U. Press, N.Y.C., 1989—; dist. rep. Ohio Tchrs. of English to Speakers of Other Langs., 1985-86. Treas. Falls Civic Music Assn., Cuyahoga Falls, 1978-79; mem. Akron Symphony Chorus, 1977-81, Blossom Festival Chorus, Cuyahoga Falls, 1980-81, Dayton Bach Soc., 1983-84; vol. tchr. Internat. Inst., Akron, 1980-81; internat. admissions rep. Coll. Mt. St. Joseph, Taipei, 1986-89. Mem. Tchrs. English to Speakers Other Langs., Nat. Assn. for Fgn. Student Affairs. Republican. Methodist. Home and Office: 1864 Oriole Dr Elk Grove IL 60007

FREAM, ANITA SUE, psychologist, educator; b. Muskogee, Okla., Jan. 6, 1948; d. Howard H. and Irene M. (Couri) F. BA, Okla. Bapt. U., 1969; MA, Okla. U., 1976. Psychologist Cleveland County Youth and Family Ctr., Norman, Okla., 1975-79; asst. prof. U. Okla., Norman, 1979-82, program devel. specialist Nat. Resource Ctr. for Youth Svcs., 1982-87, assoc. dir. S.W. Regional Ctr. for Drug-Free Schs., 1988—; adj. asst. prof. human rels. U. Okla., 1982—. Author: Understanding Child Development, 1986; contbg. author: Using Behavior Modification, 1986; asst. editor Centerboard Jour., 1985; contbr. articles to profl. jours. Mem. Okla. Coun. on Juvenile Justice, Oklahoma City, 1989—, chair mental health com., 1984-86; mem., chair citizens adv. bd. Cleveland County Youth and Family Ctr., 1979-83. Mem. Am. Assn. for Adult and Continuing Edn., Okla. Partial Hospitalization Assn. Democrat. Office: U Okla 555 Constitution Ste 138 Norman OK 73037

FREANEY, DIANE M., financial executive; b. Boston, Sept. 15, 1943; d. James A. and Dorothy (Biddle) F.; m. R. Michael Harter, Sept. 12, 1970 (div. 1978); 1 child, Allison E. Harter. BS in Acctg., Syracuse U., 1965. CPA, N.Y., Pa. Auditor Ernst & Young, N.Y.C., 1967-76; asst. corp. controller Kenton Corp., N.Y.C., 1970-72; planning officer Citibank, N.Y.C., 1972-74; mgr. fin. control ITT Corp., N.Y.C., 1974-77; dir. bus. analysis Cigna corp., Phila., 1977-79; corp. contr. Safeguard Bus. Systems, Inc., Fort Washington, 1979-82, treas., 1982-87; v.p., chief fin. officer Windon Capital Mgmt., Bala Cynwyd, Pa., 1987-89; ptnr. Triage Inc., Lafayette Hill, Pa., 1989—. Founder Phila. Women's Network, 1978; bd. dirs. Miquon Sch., Pa., 1980-87, Ambler YMCA, 1984—, Better Bus. Bur. S.E. Pa., 1984—. Mem. AICPA, N.Y. State Soc. CPAs, Pa. Inst. CPAs, Phila. Fin. Assn., Fin. Women's Assn. N.Y., Whissahickon Valley C. of C. (bd. dirs.), Forum of Exec. Women. Office: Triage Inc 4114 Kottler Dr Lafayette Hills PA 19444

FRECHETTE, ALICE MARIE, medical records professional; b. Atlantic, Iowa, July 24, 1947; d. Gail and Glendale (Grennell) Armstrong; m. Steven C. Frechette, Dec. 30, 1972; children: Christopher, Andrew, David, Sarah. BS in Med. Record Sci., Coll. St. Mary, Omaha, 1969. Asst. dir. med. record dept. St. Luke's Hosp., Duluth, Minn., 1969-70, dir. med. record dept., 1970-78; technician med. record dept. St. Cloud (Minn.) Hosp., 1979-80, dir. med. record svcs., then mgr. med. records, 1980—; med. record cons. Lakeshore Luth. Home, Duluth, 1972-78, Cambridge (Minn.) Health Care Ctr., 1979—, Hillcrest Health Care Ctr., Rush City, Minn., 1984—, St. Benedict's Ctr., St. Cloud, 1986—, Bethesda Homes, Willmar, Minn., 1986—, GlenOaks Nursing and Retiement Ctr., New London, Minn., 1986—, Foley (Minn.) Nursing Ctr., 1987—; instr. Coll. St. Scholastica, Duluth, 1978; presenter workshops in field. Lay instr. baptismal class St. Anthony's Ch., St. Cloud; vol. Am. Cancer Soc., March of Dimes, Leukemia Soc. Mem. Minn. Med. Record Assn. (pres. Region D 1986-87, state pres. 1989-90), Northeastern Minn. Med. Record Assn. (program chair 1975-76). Home: 52 22d Ave N Saint Cloud MN 56303 Office: Saint Cloud Hosp 1406 6th Ave N Saint Cloud MN 56303

FREDERICH, KATHY W., social worker; b. Ashland, Ky., Apr. 19, 1953; d. James Greeley and Jo Ann (Sparks) Walker; divorced; m. Harry Donald Frederich, Sept. 5, 1987; stepchild, David Scott. BA with distinction, U. Ky., 1978; postgrad. in criminal justice, Ea. Ky. U., 1989—. Tng. supr. Blue Grass Assn. for Retarded Citizens, Lexington, Ky., 1971-75, Bur. Vocational Rehab., Lexington, 1976-77; social worker Ky. Dept. for Social Svcs., Lexington, 1978-79, field office supr., 1979-85; social work/domestic violence prog. specialist, conf. coord. Ky. Dept. for Social Svcs., Frankfort, Ky., 1985—, instr., 1987—; instr. Ky. Sheriff's Acad., 1986—, Lexington Fayette div. of Police, 1981-87; cons., trainer for field staff and related profls. statewide, Ky., 1983—; mem. adv. bd. Assn. for Older Kentuckians, 1989—; mem. Ky. Law Enforcement Tng. Project, 1989—. Recipient Outstanding Svc. award Lexington Fayette div. of Police, 1984, Ky. Sheriff's Acad. Hon. Grad., 1989, tributes, 1986, 87, 88, Outstanding Kentuckian award Gov. Martha Layne Collins, 1987, Outstanding Young Am. Women award, 1987, Outstanding Victim Adv. award Lexington Urban County Govt., 1990; named Ky. Col., 1985. Democrat.

FREDERICK, CHARLENE J., advertising executive, graphic designer; b. Des Moines, July 23, 1951; d. George Emory and Charlene (Lauer) Jefchak; m. Michael Lewis Frederick, May 25, 1974. BFA in Design, U. Kans., 1974, MS in Journalism, 1987. Graphic designer Meseraull Printing, Lawrence, Kans., 1974-75; illustrator Hill Advt. Agy., Lawrence, 1975-76; graphic designer U. Kans., Lawrence, 1976-83, Art For Living, Wichita, Kans., 1983; graphic designer media resources ctr. Wichita State U., 1983-88, mgr. creative svcs., 1988-89, assoc. dir. creative svcs., 1989—; adj. prof. Wichita State U., 1985; judge Kans. Scholastic Press Assn., 1983, 85, 86, 87, Health Sci. Communications Assn., 1989, others. Vol. Am. Heart Assn., Wichita, 1987-88, Wichita Radio Reading Svc., 1990—. Recipient award of merit Council for Advancement and Support of Edn., 1988-89, Silver Medal award, 1988; honor award Neenah Paper/Kimberly Clark Corp., 1987; Outstanding Achievement award Library Pub. Relations Council, 1989. Mem. Women in Communications Inc. (sec. 1986-88, pres. 1989-90), Univ. and Coll.Designers Assn., River City Women's Club (founding mem., pres. 1982-83), Phi Kappa Phi, Kappa Tau Alpha. Methodist. Office: Media Resources Ctr Wichita State U 1845 Fairmount Wichita KS 67208

FREDERICK, ELIZABETH ANN, social worker; b. Ossining, N.Y., Dec. 29, 1954; d. Anthony and Helen Jane (Garrison) F. AA, Dutchess County Community Coll., Poughkeepsie, N.Y., 1975; BA in Psychology, Marist Coll., Poughkeepsie, 1978, cert. legal asst., 1979; postgrad., SUNY, New Paltz, 1981-83; MSW, SUNY, Albany, 1985. Psychology intern Hudson River Psychiat. Ctr., Poughkeepsie, 1978; legal intern Dutchess County Pub. Defenders Office, 1978; intake counselor Women's Ctr. SUNY, New Paltz, 1980-81; intern social work Rehab. Support Services, Albany, 1983-84; aging service specialist Sr. Service Ctrs. of Albany Area, Inc., 1985—. V.p. fin. NOW, N.Y., 1980, pres. Dutchess County chpt., 1980, pres. Albany chpt., 1983; mem. Mid-Hudson Coalition for Free Choice, Poughkeepsie, 1976; del. NOW N.Y. State. Mem. Nat. Assn. Social Workers, Capital Dist. Assn. Providers of Aging Svcs., Nat. Coun. Sr. Citizens, Older Women's League, Albany Women's Bldg. Club (mem. coordinating coun., mem. maintenance com.). Democrat. Office: Sr Svc Ctrs of Albany Area Inc 25 Delaware Ave Albany NY 12210

FREDERICK, MARIJANE, human resources professional; b. Bklyn., Dec. 10, 1953; d. William Paul and Helen (Stepien) F.; m. Sewell Fletcher Hipps Jr., Sept. 8, 1979; 1 child, Matthew Frederick Hipps. BA in Secondary English Edn. summa cum laude, SUNY, Albany, 1975. Field supr. Nat. Opinion Research Ctr. Rand Corp., Fitchburg, Mass., 1975-76, field rep. Glen Slaughter and Assocs., 1976-77; systems and procedures specialist Nat. Rural Electric Coop. Assn., Washington, 1977-79, personnel specialist, 1979-81; personnel dir. Palmetto Electric Coop. Inc., Hilton Head Island, S.C., 1981—. Mem. Rotary Internat., Sigma Tau Beta. Office: Palmetto Electric Coop Inc PO Box 21239 111 Mathews Dr Hilton Head Island SC 29925

FREDERICK, VIRGINIA FIESTER, state legislator; b. Rock Island, Ill., Dec. 24, 1916; d. John Henry and Myrtle (Montgomery) Heise; B.A., U. Iowa, 1938; postgrad. Lake Forest Coll., 1942-43; m. C. Donnan Fiester (dec. 1975); children—Sheryl Fiester Ross, Alan R., James D.; m. 2d Kenneth Jacob Frederick, 1978. Free-lance fashion designer, Lake Forest, Ill., 1952-78; pres. Mid Am. China Exchange, Kenilworth, Ill., 1978-81; mem. Ill. Ho. of Reps., Springfield, 1979—, asst minority leader, 1990—. Alderman, first ward Lake Forest, 1974-78; del. World Food Conf., Rome, 1974. mem. Ill. Commn. on Status of Women subcom. pensions and employment, 1976-79; co-chmn. Conf. Women Legislators, 1982-85. Named Chgo. Area Woman of Achievement, Internat. Orgn. Women Execs., 1978. Recipient Lottie Holman O'Neal award, 1980, Jane Addams award, 1982, Outstanding Legislator award Ill. Hosp. Assn., 1986, VFW Svc. award, 1988, Joyce Fitzgerald Meml. award, 1988, Susan B. Anthony Legislator of the Yr. award, 1989. Mem. LWV (local pres. 1958-60, state dir. 1969-75, mem. nat. com. 1975-76), AAUW (local pres. 1968-70, state pres. 1975-77, state dir. 1963-69, mem. nat. commns. 1967-69), UN Assn. (dir.), Chgo. Assn. Commerce and Industry (dir.). Methodist. Home: 1540 Greenleaf Ave Lake Forest IL 60045

FREDERICK-MAIRS, T(HYRA) JULIE, alcohol agency official; b. Islip, N.Y., Jan. 4, 1941; d. Manuel and Thyra C. (Thorsen) Cajiao; BA, Adelphi U., 1961; MSW, U. So. Calif., 1972. Social worker Los Angeles County Dept. Social Svcs., 1966-67, social work supr., 1967-70; planning cons. Los Angeles County Dept. Social Svcs. and Los Angeles County Chief Adminstr.'s Office, 1972-76; dep. to supr. 4th Dist., Los Angeles County, 1976-80; asst. dir. Los Angeles County Office Alcohol Programs, 1980—. Mem. or past mem. Los Angeles Child Sexual Abuse Project, Commn. for Sex Equity, Los Angeles Unified Sch. Dist., Harbor Police Community Adv. Coun., Los Angeles; mem. Perinaial Substance Abuse Coun. L.A., San Pedro and Peninsula Family Stress Task Force, Los Angeles; mem. ops. com. Interagy. Coun. on Child Abuse and Neglect; bd. dirs. Marshall High Sch. PTA, Los Angeles; adv. com. UCLA Alcohol Research Center; mem. Westside Child Trauma Coun. U. So. Calif. fellow, 1988. Mem. Los Amigos de la Humanidad, Women in Health Adminstrn., Alpha Epsilon Delta, Beta Beta Beta. Clubs: Bus. and Profl. Women's, Soroptimists (pres. Los Angeles County 1986-88, dir. Found. of Los Angeles, 1986-88), Cath. Maritime (dir.). Author: (with others) Youth Program Planning, 1975.

FREDERICKS, JOAN DELANOY, retired health science administrator; b. Dobbs Ferry, N.Y., Feb. 27, 1928; d. Robert Bert and Amelia (DeLanoy) F. BA, Skidmore Coll., Saratoga Springs, N.Y., 1949; MA, Syracuse U., 1954. Rsch. asst. C.F. Kettering Found., Yellow Springs, Ohio, 1949-50; rsch. tech. Syracuse (N.Y.) U. Med. Sch., 1950-54, Duke U. Med. Sch., Durham, N.C., 1954-58, NIH, Bethesda, Md., 1958-88; ret., 1988; chemist Nat. Inst. Arthritis and Metabolic Diseases, NIH, Bethesda, 1958-63, scientific grant asst. Nat. Inst. Heart, Lung and Blood Diseases, Bethesda, 1963-70, asst., program dir. Nat. Inst. Arthritis Metabolism and Digestive Diseases, 1970-81, exec. sec. div. Rsch. Grants, 1981-88; cons. in field. Mem. Sumner Sq. Condominium Assn. (sec., v.p. 1988-90).

FREDERICKSEN, GAIL BERGANTINO, marketing professional; b. Waterbury, Conn., Oct. 31, 1955; d. Anthony J. Sr. and Mary Cecelia (Mrozinski) Bergantino; m. Raymond P. Fredericksen, Oct. 31, 1981 (div.). AS, Mattatuch Community Coll., 1975; BS, U. Hartford, 1985. Sales promotions mgr. Kero Sun, Inc., Kent, Conn., 1975-83; pres. Fredericksen Downes Advt., South Windsor, Conn., 1983-85; advt. mgr. Cauzin Systems, Inc., Waterbury, 1985-86; dir. mktg. TUP Info. Systems, Windsor, Conn., 19867—. Pres. bd. dirs. ACSS Ctr. Spiritual Studies, Southbury, Conn., 1988. Mem. NAFE. Republican.

FREDERIKSEN, MARILYNN ELIZABETH CONNERS, physician; b. Chgo., Sept. 12, 1949; d. Paul H. and Susanne (Ostergren) Conners; m. James W. Frederiksen, July 11, 1971; children: John Karl, Paul S., Britt L. BA, Cornell Coll., 1970; MD, Boston U., 1974. Diplomate Am. Bd. Ob-Gyn, Am. Bd. Maternal-Fetal Medicine. Instr. ob-gyn. Northwestern U., Chgo., 1981-83, asst. prof. ob-gyn., assoc. clin. pharmacology, 1983—; mem. ob-gyn. adv. panel, 1985-90 , USP Com. of Revision, Rockville, Md., 1986—; del. to 1990 USP conv. Northwestern U. Med. Sch.; mem. gen. clinic rsch. ctr. com. NIH, 1989—. Contbr. numerous articles to profl. jours. Bd. dirs. Cornell Coll. Alumni Assn., Mt. Vernon, Iowa, 1986-90. Recipient Pharm. Mfrs. Assn. Found. Faculty Devel. award, 1984-86; grantee NIH. Fellow Am. Coll. Ob-Gyn.; mem. Soc. Perinatal Obstetricians, Cen. Assn. Obstetricians and Gynecologists, Am. Med. Womens Assn., Am. Soc. Clin. Pharmacology and Therapeutics, Chgo. Gynecologic Soc., Phi Beta Kappa. Republican. Episcopalian. Home: 2002 Devon Park Ridge IL 60068 Office: Northwestern U 680 N Lake Shore Dr Ste 810 Chicago IL 60611

FREDERIKSEN, PATIENCE ANN, librarian; b. Warwick, R.I., Aug. 21, 1957; d. Robert Christian and Winifred Holmes (Valentine) F.; 1 child, Christian Lawrence Klint. BA in Creative Writing/History, Carnegie Mellon U., 1979; MLS, Syracuse U., 1986. Reference libr. Anchorage Mun. Librs., 1986-88; reference coord. Juneau (Alaska) Pub. Librs., 1988-89; documents libr. Alaska State Libr., Juneau, 1989, collection devel. libr., 1989—. Recipient Nat. Merit Scholarship, Carnegie-Mellon U., Pitts., 1975-79. Mem. Alaska Libr. Assn. Democrat. Home: 1310 4th St #6 Douglas AK 99824 Office: Alaska State Libr PO Box G Juneau AK 99811-0571

FREDETTE, BARBARA WAGNER, art educator; b. Lima, Peru, Dec. 5, 1933; came to U.S., 1934; d. Lawrence A. and Anne A. (Sherwood) Wagner; m. John W. Fredette Jr., Dec. 28, 1953 (dec.); children: John W. III, Lawrence F. BA, Chatham Coll., 1955; MEd, U. Pitts., 1963, EdD, 1969. Supr. elem. art Hampton Sch., Allison Park, Pa., 1960-64; tchr. art edn.

Carnegie Mellon U., Pitts., 1964; assoc. prof. U. Pitts., 1964—. Roundtable mem. Pitts. Fund for Arts Edn., 1988—. Mem. Nat. Art Edn. Assn., Pa. Art Edn. Assn. (Outstanding Art Educator award 1984), Am. Edn., Am. Edn. Rsch. Assn., Internat. Visual Litrarcy Assn., Phi Delta Kappa. Republican. Roman Catholic. Home: 939 Savannah Ave Pittsburgh PA 15221 Office: U Pitts 4C31 Forbes Quad Pittsburgh PA 15260

FREDMAN, SUSAN MIRIAM, interior designer; b. Chgo., Nov. 14, 1950; d. David Wolfe Fredman and Selma (Lobelson) Florio; m. Martin Donald Zitlin, Jan. 28, 1984 (div. 1988); 1 child, Amanda Beth. BS, Ill. State U., 1973. Owner, pres. Interior Accents, Ltd., Highland Park, Ill., 1975—; tchr. interior design class Deerfield/Highland Park High Sch., 1986—; commr. Appearance Rev. Commn., Highland Park, 1989—; mem. Color Mktg. Group, 1990—. Contbr. to numerous local publs. V.p. ways and means Ravinia Nursery Sch., Highland Park, 1988—. Mem. Internat. Soc. Interior Designers (bd. dirs. Ill. chpt. 1984-86), Color Mktg. Group. Office: Interior Accents Ltd 457 Central St Highland Park IL 60035

FREDRICK, SUSAN WALKER, tax company manager; b. Painesville, Ohio, Nov. 17, 1948; d. Floyd Clayton and Margaret (Merkel) Walker; m. Stephan Douglas Fredrick, Oct. 20, 1973. BS, Mt. Union Coll., Alliance, Ohio, 1970; MS, U. Conn., 1973. Research asst. Boyce Thompson Inst., Yonkers, N.Y., 1971-74; dir. quality control Lawley, Matusky, Skelly, Tappan, N.Y., 1974-75; field supr. Ecological Analysts, Middletown, N.Y., 1975-76; scientist Pandullo Quirk Assocs., Wayne, N.J., 1976-78; editor Bi-oscis. Info. Service, Phila., 1978-80; tax preparer H&R Block, Inc., King of Prussia, Pa., 1978-80, dist. mgr., 1980—; guest lectr. Temple U., 1981-86. Mem. NAFE, Nat. Assn. Enrolled Agts., Pa. Soc. Enrolled Agts., Soroptimist Internat. of Mainlin. Club: Keystone Divers (West Chester, Pa.). Lodge: Soroptimists. Office: H&R Block Inc King of Prussia Plaza Q2A King of Prussia PA 19406

FREDRICK, VICTORIA M., accountant; b. Denver, Feb. 3, 1950; d. Floyd W. and Bethel I. Fredrick; m. Mitchell J. Carleton. BA in Bus. Adminstrn., Ft. Lewis Coll., Durango, Colo., 1972; BS in Acctg., Met. State U., Denver, 1980; MBA, Boise (Idaho) State U., 1989. Cert. mgmt. acct. Sr. acct. Boise Cascade Corp., 1981-85, fin. analyst, 1985-86, acctg. specialist, 1986-89; mgr. acctg. and fin. Malacha Power Project, Inc., Boise, 1989—; cons. acctg., Denver, 1977-81; speaker beginning bus. workshops SBA, Boise, 1982-86, high schs. and univs., Boise, 1984—; mem. audit com. Boise Cascade Credit Union, 1985-87. Chairperson Boise Cascade/Boise Art Mus. Vol. Coords., 1985-88; mem. devel. com. Idaho Zool. Soc., Boise, 1990. Mem. Nat. Assn. Accts. (pres. 1986-87, bd. mem. 1982-88, most valuable mem. 1987-88). Office: Malacha Hydro Ltd Ptnrship 1555 Shoreline Dr Boise ID 83707

FREE, ANN COTTRELL, writer; b. Richmond, Va.; d. Emmett Drewry and Emily (Blake) Cottrell; grad. Collegiate Sch. for Girls, Richmond, 1934; student Richmond div. Coll. William and Mary, 1934-36; m. James Stillman Free, Feb. 24, 1950; 1 child, Elissa. AB, Barnard Coll., Columbia, 1938. Reporter Richmond Times Dispatch, 1938-40; Washington corr., Newsweek, 1940-41, Chgo. Sun, 1941-43, N.Y. Herald Tribune, 1943-46; pub. information dir. UNRRA China Mission, Shanghai, 1946-47; corr. Middle and Nr. East and Europe, 1947-48; writer-photographer Marshall Plan, Washington and Western Europe, 1949-50; Washington corr. N.Am. Newspaper Alliance, 1955-80; contbg. editor Between the Species; contbr. newspapers and mags., including Washington Star and Washington Post; Washington editor EnviroSouth Quar., 1977-82; pres. Flying Fox Press. Mem. Friends of the Rachel Carson Nat. Wildlife Refuge (hon. founding mem.); chmn. Mrs. Roosevelt's Press Conf. Assn., 1943; cons. expert Rachel Carson Coun.; v.p. Viegues (P.R.) Humane Soc.; coord. Albert Schweitzer Summer Fellows Program; bd. dirs. Albert Schweirzer Fellowship; pres. Albert Schweitzer Coun. on Animals and Environment. Recipient Dodd Mead-Boys' Life Writing award, 1963, Albert Schweitzer medal, Animal Welfare Inst., 1963, Jr. Book award certificate Boys Clubs of Am., 1964; Humanitarian of Yr. awards Washington Animal Rescue League, 1971, Montgomery County Humane Soc., 1971, Washington Humane Soc., 1983, News Writing award Dog Writers Assn. Am., 1975, 78, Rachel Carson Legacy award, 1987; recognition Dept. Interior, 1970. Mem. Soc. Woman Geographers, Nat. Press Club, Am. News Women's Club. Author: Forever the Wild Mare, 1963, Animals, Nature and Albert Schweitzer, 1982, No Room, Save in the Heart, 1987. Home: 4700 Jamestown Rd Bethesda MD 20816 also: Lantz Mill Edinburg VA 22824

FREE, BETTY IRENE, editor; b. Geneva, Ill., Aug. 17, 1940; d. Einar Eric and Helen Florence (Ross) F. BA, Wheaton Coll., 1962; Student, Nat. Coll. Edn., Evanston, 1984. Substitute tchr. Elgin Pub. Sch., Elgin, Ill., 1962-64; sec. Ch. of the Brethren Gen. Offices, Elgin, 1964-70; proofreader David C. Cook Publ. Co., Elgin, 1970, assoc. editor/contbg. editor, 1970-77; contbg. editor N000, 1971-77; editor David C. Cook Publ. Co., Elgin, 1977-84, sr. editor, 1984—; workshop seminar leader David C. Cook Publ. Co., 1977—, DuPage County Assn. for the Edn. of Young Children, Glen Ellyn, Ill., 1988. Author: Evangelizing Today's Child, 1987-88. Mem. Chgo. Assn. for the Edn. Young Children (workshop seminar leader), Nat. Assn. for the Edn. Young Children. Mem. Evangelical Covenant Ch. Office: David C Cook Pub Co 850 N Grove Ave Elgin IL 60120

FREE, WENDY ANNE, insurance underwriter; b. Colo. Springs, Colo., Apr. 24, 1956; d. Samuel Alexander and Corinne Barbara (Carlson) Barclay; m. David Michael Free, Sept. 1, 1979; Lauren Anne. BA in Bus. Mgmt., Calif. State U., Fullerton, 1979. From underwriter comml. to sr. underwriter State Farm Ins., Costa Mesa, Calif., 1979-81; field underwriter State Farm Ins., Orange, Calif., 1981-82; from service supr. II to comml. account underwriter State Farm Ins., Costa Mesa, calif., 1982-85; comml. underwriting supr. State Farm Ins., Costa Mesa, Calif.; underwriting staff asst. State Farm Ins., Bloomington, Ill., 1989—; dir. scholarship and telecommunications chartered property casulty underwriter, 1988—; chair telecommunications chartered property casulty underwriter, Orange Empire chpt., Costa Mesa, 1987-88. Team capt. Proposition 104 Tele. Bank Ins. Collation, Costa Mesa 1988, campaign dir. City Council Candidate, 1987, 1988 Tustin, Calif. Mem. Nat. Assn. of Female Execs., Irvine Bus. and Profl. Women CLub (1st v.p. 1984-85, fin. chair 1983-84, found. chair 1982-83). Republican. Office: State Farm Ins 112 E Wash Bloomington IL 61701

FREEBERG, SARAH FRANCES, executive chef; b. Altoona, Pa., Sept. 21, 1958; d. Robert Donald and Margaret (McNitt) F. BS in Bus., Juniata Coll., 1980; A.O.S., Culinary Inst., Hyde Park, N.Y., 1985. Owner, mgr. Phoenix Specialty Dist., Hollidaysburg, Pa., 1980-83; banquet chef Mariner's Inn, A Clarion Hotel, Hilton Head Island, S.C., 1985-86; instr. Johnson & Wales Coll., Charleston, S.C., 1987; chef Jilich's on East Bay, Charleston, 1986-88; exec. chef Caper's Am. Food & Spirits, Annapolis, Md., 1988—; chairperson Am. Seafood Challenge, Charleston, 1987-88; asst. The Society on Am. Cruisine, Charleston, 1987. Mem. Am. Chef's Fedn. Home: 14927 London Ln Bowie MD 20715 Office: Capers Am Food & Spirits 210 Revell Hwy Annapolis MD 29401

FREEDMAN, ANNE BELLER, public speaking and marketing consultant; b. Gardner, Mass., June 22, 1949; d. Gabriel Philip Freedman and Natalie Engler (Beller) Lyons; m. Edward A. Fischer, May 20, 1979; 1 child, Lynne Heather. BSJ U. Fla., 1971. Staff writer Coral Gables Times, Miami, 1972-73; reporter Miami News, 1973-74; assoc. editor Miami Phoenix, 1974-75; freelance writer, Miami, 1975-80; corr. Advt. Age, Miami, 1977-81; pres. Exec. S.O.S., Inc., Miami, 1980-90; pres. Speak Out, Inc., Coral Gables, 1990—; instr. Fla. Internat. U. Author: Unforgettable Speeches and Presentations in 8 Easy Steps; contbr. articles to profl. jours. Bd. dirs. Miami/Bogota-Calé Sister Cities Program, 1983-85. Mem. South Miami/Kendall C. of C. (editor monthly newsletter 1980-83, dir., 1982-85, chmn. bus. com. 1985—, editor ann. directory and buyer's guide 1986-87, 89—, Presdl. award 1983, 89), Nat. Assn. Women Bus. Owners (chair public relations 1981, dir. tng. and devel. 1987—, dir. corp. ptnrs. 1988—, v.p. 1989—), Coral Gables C. of C., Greater Miami C. of C. Clubs: Toastmasters (pres. 1984). Home: 6721 SW 113th Pl Miami FL 33173 Office: 11410 N Kendall Dr Suite 207 Miami FL 33176

FREEDMAN, BETTY, advertising agency executive. Formerly with Kenyon & Eckhardt, Foote, Cone & Belding; creative dir., v.p., now sr. v.p. Grey Advt., Inc., N.Y.C., 1970—. Recipient Clio award, others. Office: Grey Advt Inc 777 3rd Ave New York NY 10017*

FREEDMAN, JOAN M., guidance counselor, city councilwoman; b. Fitchburg, Mass., Dec. 9, 1949; d. John Patrick and Rose Ellen (Lunetta) Walsh; m. Richard Allen Freedman, June 26, 1971; children: Melissa Joan, Andrea Rose. BS in Edn., Fitchburg State Coll., 1971, MEd, 1976. Cert. tchr., counslor, sch. psychologist, Mass. Elem. guidance counselor Leominster (Mass.) Pub. Sch. System, 1983—; mem. Fitchburg City Coun., 1990—. Sec. Ward 5 Dem. Com., Fitchburg, 1986—; mem. Fitchburg Birthday Com., 1989; del. Mass. Dem. Conv., 1990. Horace Mann grantee Mass. Dept. Edn., 1989. Mem. Mass. Tchrs. Assn., AAUW (pres. 1985—). Roman Catholic.

FREEDMAN, JUDITH GREENBERG, Connecticut state senator, importer; b. Bridgeport, Conn., Mar. 11, 1939; d. Samuel Howard and Dorothy (Hoffman) G.; m. Samuel Sumner, Dec. 24, 1964; 1 child, Martha Ann. Student, Boston U., 1957-58, U. Mich., 1958-59; BS, So. Conn. State U., 1961, MS, 1972. Tchr. Hollywood (Fla.) Pub. Schs., 1961-62, White Plains (N.Y.) Pub. Schs., 1962-64, Wilton (Conn.) Pub. Schs., 1964-66; tchr. Weston (Conn.) Pub. Schs., 1966-72, tutor, 1977-80, tchr., 1982-84; owner Judith's Fancy, Wesport, Conn., 1984—; state senator from Conn., 1987—; ranking mem. human svcs. com., 1987-88, ins. com., 1987-88, appropriations com., 1989—. Pres., v.p. Rep. Women's Assn., 1976-80; pres. Rep. Women of Westport, 1976-79; mem. Bd. Edn., Westport, 1983-87, 89—, ranking mem. appropriations com. to date. Jewish. Home: 17 Crawford Rd Westport CT 06880

FREEDMAN, MARION GLICKMAN, career counselor; b. N.Y.C., Feb. 3, 1922; d. Edward and Minnie (Tokarsky) Glickman; m. Bernard M. Freedman, Nov. 29, 1941; children: Rochelle Freedman Hassen, Diane Freedman Slatz. BS, NYU, 1942, MA in Secondary Edn., 1964, MA in Guidance, 1967, postgrad., 1975-77. Cert. counselor, N.Y. BS NYU, 1942, MA in Secondary Edn., 1967; tchr. high sch., guidance counselor Bushwick High Sch., Bklyn., 1965-74; guidance counselor James Monroe High Sch., Bronx, N.Y., 1974-76, 77—; career counselor Walton High Sch., Bronx, 1976-77. Mem. Am. Personnel Assn. and Guidance Assn., N.Y. State Personnel and Guidance Assn., N.Y.C. Personnel and Guidance Assn., Nat. Bd. Cert. Counselors, NYU Alumni Assn., Delta Pi Epsilon. Jewish. Home: 6556 174th St Flushing NY 11365 Office: 1300 Boynton Ave Bronx NY 10472

FREEDMAN, PENNY MILLICENT, psychotherapist; b. Newark, Aug. 13, 1941; d. Naom Norman and Frances (Rothman) F. BA, Rutgers U., 1963; MSW, Smith Coll., 1966; PhD, Barry U., Miami Shores, Fla., 1988. Clin. social worker Mass. Mental Health Ctr. of Harvard U., Boston, 1966-68; dir. social work Cambridge City Hosp., 1968-70; dir. family svc. unit Jewish Family and Children's Svcs., Miami, Fla., 1975-76; therapist, supr., instr. Douglas A. Thom Clinic for Children, Boston U. Sch. Medicine, 1970-75; dir. family svc. unit, therapist, supr, instr. Jewish Family and Children's Svcs. Greater Miami, 1975-76; therapist, supr., instr. Jewish Family & Children's Svcs. of Greater Miami (Fla.), 1976—; pvt. practice psychotherapy Miami, 1977—; lectr. in field. Contbr. articles to profl. jours. Vol. WLRN Radio/TV, Miami, 1988—, vol. nurse Women's Emergency Network; mem. Mental Health Assn. South Fla., 1985—. Mem. LWV, Clin. Social Work Assn. South Fla. (charter, pres. 1989), Behavioral Sci. Inst. (sec. 1985-89), Fla. Psychoanalytic Soc. (assoc.), Soc. for Psychoanalytic Study of Film, NOW, Amnesty Internat., Women's Emergency Network. Democrat. Jewish. Address: 8220 SW 151st St Miami FL 33158

FREEDMAN, SANDRA WARSHAW, mayor; b. Newark, Sept. 21, 1944; m. Michael J. Freedman; 3 children. BA in Govt., U. Miami, 1965. Mem. Tampa (Fla.) City Coun., 1974—, chmn., 1983-86; mayor City of Tampa, 1987—. Bd. dirs. Jewish Community Ctr., 1974-75, Boys and Girls Clubs Greater Tampa, Hillsborough Coalition for Health, Tampa Community Concert Assn.; mem. sports adv. bd. Hillsborough Community Coll., 1975-76; sec. Downtown Devel. Authority, 1977-78; bd. dirs., v.p. Fla. Gulf Coast Symphony, 1979-80; vice chmn. Met. Planning Orgn., 1981-82; corp. mem. Neighborhood Housing Service; bd. fellows U. Tampa; mem. steering com. Hillsborough County Council of Govt.'s Constituency for Children; mem. exec. bd. Tampa/Hillsborough Young Adult Forum; chmn. bd. trustees Berkeley Prep. Sch.; trustee Tampa Bay Performing Arts Ctr., Inc., Tampa Mus.; mem. ethics com. Meml. Hosp.; mem. Tampa Preservation, Inc., Tampa/Hillsborough County Youth Council, Davis Islands Civic Assn., Tampa Hist. Soc., Met. Ministries Adv. Bd., Rodeph Sholom Synagogue, Sword of Hope Guild of Am. Cancer Soc., Friends of the Arts. Recipient Spessard L. Holland Meml. award Tampa Bay Com. for Good Govt., 1975-76, Human Rights award City of Tampa, 1980, award Soroptimist Internat. Tampa, 1981, Status of Women award Zonta of Tampa II, 1986, Woman of Achievement award Bus. & Profl. Women; named to Who's Who and Why of Successful Fla. Women, 1984. Mem. Hillsborough County Bar Aux., Greater Tampa C. of C., C. of C. Com. of 100 (exec. com.), Fla. League of Cities (bd. dirs.), Tampa Urban League, Nat. Council Jewish Women, U. Miami Alumni Assn., Athena Soc., Hadassah. Office: 306 E Jackson St Tampa FL 33602

FREEDMAN, WENDE LEE POGUST, engineer, consultant; b. Oyster Bay, N.Y., Apr. 11, 1957; d. Frederick Bernard and Beatrice (Baris) Pogust; m. Lawrence Jay Freedman, Oct. 14, 1984; 1 child, Hannah Elyse. BS in Civil Engring., Bucknell U., 1979. Registered profl. engr., N.Y. Structural designer Howard Needles Tammen Borgdorf, N.Y.C., 1979-80, URS Co., N.Y.C., 1980-82; engring. cons. McDonnell Douglas Automation, N.Y.C., 1982-83; application engr. Summagraphics, Fairfield, Conn., 1983; mktg. support analyst Prime Computer, N.Y.C., 1983-87, mktg. tech. support mgr., 1987-89; mgr. tech. svcs. Drover Technologies, Inc., Tarrytown, N.Y., 1989—. Mem. ASCE, Nat. Soc. Profl. Engrs.

FREELAND, COLLEEN LOUISE, insurance company executive; b. Erie, Pa., Dec. 23, 1957; d. Arthur Merrit and Helen Louise (Royall) F. BA, U. Edinboro, 1979; AA, Rancho Santiago Coll., Santa Ana, 1986. Loss prevention coordinator Hills Dept. Store, Kokomo, Ind., 1979-80; ins. adjustor State Farm Ins., Anaheim, Calif., 1980-88, Erie Ins. Exchange, Erie, Pa., 1989. Mem. Erie Claims Assn., Ins. Inst. of Am., Nat. Assn. Ins. Women. Methodist. Home: 406 Sparkhill Ave Erie PA 16511 Office: Erie Ins Exchange 406 Sparkhill Ave Erie PA 16511

FREELAND, SANDRA TUCKER, federal agency administrator; b. Starkville, Miss., July 22, 1948; d. John Earl and Hazel Ruth (Ballinger) Tucker. BA cum laude, Millsaps Coll., Jackson, Miss., 1969. Agt. IRS, Atlanta, 1969-82, appeals officer, 1982-85, staff asst. to RDA, 1985-86, asst. RDA, 1986-89; chief New Orleans Appeals Office, 1989-. Pres. Tucker, Ga. Edinburgh Estates Civic Club, 1983. Recipient Nat. Meth. scholarship, Millsaps Coll., 1966-69, Acad. Leadership scholarship, Millsaps Coll., 1966-69, Wall St. Jour. award, 1969. Mem. Garden Dist. Assn., Fed. Bus. Assn., Am. Soc. Women Accts. Democrat. Protestant. Club: Univ. Yacht. Office: New Orleans Appeals Office 501 Magazine St Ste 940 New Orleans LA 70130

FREEMAN, ANNE HOBSON, writer, English language educator; b. Richmond, Va., Mar. 19, 1934; d. Joseph Reid Anderson and Mary Douthat (Marshall) Hobson; m. George Clemon Freeman, Jr., Dec. 6, 1958; children: Anne Colston McEvoy, George Clemon, Joseph Reid Anderson. AB, Bryn Mawr Coll., 1956; postgrad. London U., 1956-57; MA, U. Va., 1973. Fiction writer, 1956—; reporter Internat. News Svc., Eastern Europe, 1957; editor Va. Mus. Fine Arts, Richmond, 1959-63; lectr. English, U. Va., Charlottesville, 1973-88; chmn. adv. com. Bryn Mawr Bull., Pa., 1978-81; firm historian Hunton & Williams, Richmond, 1984-88. Contbr. stories to various mags., anthologies, lit. jours. Mem. Richmond Area Dem. Woman's Club, 1968—; bd. dirs. Va. Hist. Soc., Va. Commn. for Humanities and Pub. Policy, 1985-89, Nat. Coun. Friends of Kennedy Ctr., Washington, 1983-85, Mus. of Confederacy, Richmond. Fulbright scholar, 1956-57; Va. Ctr. for Creative Arts fellow, 1981-83, 85, 89. Mem. Va. Writers Club, Country of Va. Club, Woman's (Richmond) Club. Episcopalian. Home: 10 Paxton Rd Richmond VA 23226 Office: U Va Dept English Wilson Hall Charlottesville VA 22903

FREEMAN, CAROL ANNE, public relations and marketing executive; b. Asheville, N.C., Feb. 12, 1940; d. William Allen and Anna Lou (Rhinehardt) Wheatley; m. Michael McKinnley Freeman, July 25, 1964; children: Michael and Allen (twins). BFA, U. N.C., 1963. Art educator Charlotte-Mecklenburg Schs., Charlotte, N.C., 1963-64; art educator Anderson County Schs., Anderson, S.C., 1964-67, Asheville Art Mus., Asheville, N.C., 1970-71, Asheville City Schs., 1969-75; pub. relations/mktg. dir. Highland Hosp., Asheville, 1978—; art cons. N.C. Advancement Sch., Winston-Salem, 1973, western region Environ. Edn. Ctr., Asheville, 1975-76. Editor Highland Highlights, 1983-89. Pres. Jr. League Asheville,Inc., 1979-80; bd. dirs. Camp Loquastee, Asheville, 1975-78; adv. bd. Health Adventure, Asheville, 1988—. Mem. Nat. Assn. Pvt. Psychiat. Hosps. (mktg. dirs. group), Carolinas Hosp. Pub. Relations Soc., Pub. Relations Soc. Western N.C. Democrat. Methodist. Office: Highland Hosp 49 Zillicoa St Asheville NC 28801

FREEMAN, CAROL HART, educator; b. Childress, Tex., June 17, 1955; d. Bobby Byron and Donna (Broughton) Hart; m. James Gray Freeman, Apr. 10, 1977; children: Lauren, Paige. BS, Tex. Tech U., 1977. Educator Childress Ind. Sch. Dist., 1977-78; pvt. Tiny Texan Preschool, Childress, 1984—. Sec. Am. Heart Assn., Childress, 1989, fund drive participant, ARC, 1985, Am. Cancer Soc., 1985, pageant dir. Greenbelt Bowl, bd. dirs., 1983-86; pres. PTO; chmn. coun. ministries First United Meth. Ch., 1990. Mem. AAUW, Childress Outreach Bd. of Dirs. (Woman of Yr. 1990), Creative Ext. Club, Angel Flight Club, Delta Delta Delta, Phi Kappa Phi, Alpha Lambda Delta, Kappa Delta Pi, Rho Lambda, Beta Sigma Phi (Woman of Yr. Alpha Delta Omega chpt. 1990), Alpha Delta Omega. Methodist. Home: 3 Hillcrest Addition Childress TX 79201

FREEMAN, DIANNE MENDOZA, association executive; b. Laredo, Tex., Aug. 12, 1947; d. Luis Felipe Sr. and Alicia Juanita (Puentes) Mendoza; 1 child, Dina Rochelle Uribe. BA, Our Lady of Lake U., San Antonio, 1968, MEd, 1975; MA, Incarnate Word Coll., 1973; PhD, U. Tex., Austin, 1982. Tchr. Laredo Ind. Sch. Dist., 1968-73; test instrument specialist Edgewood Ind. Sch. Dist., San Antonio, 1973-76; rsch. assoc., proj. coord. SW Edn. Devel. Lab., Austin, 1976-77; assoc. coord. office student affairs Austin Ind. Sch. Dist., 1977-79; vis. instr. Laredo State U., 1979-82; title VII migrant supr. Laredo Ind. Sch. Dist., 1982-83; dir. devel., pub. rels. Mercy Regional Med. Ctr., Laredo, 1983-86; exec. v.p. Laredo C. of C., 1986—. Mem. United Way of Laredo, 1982—, past pres.; mem. Princess Pocahontas Coun., Laredo, 1982—, George Washington's Birthday Celebration Assn., Laredo, 1982—, Aux. to Mercy Regional Med. Ctr., Laredo, 1982—, Leadership Tex., Austin, 1984—; bd. dirs. Leadership Laredo, 1986—; bd. dirs., exec. com. United Way of Tex., 1986—; alumnae bd. Leadership Am., 1988-90; 2d v.p., exec. com., bd. dirs. Hispanic Women's Network of Tex. Named one of Outstanding Young Women of Am., 1977. Mem. Women's City Club. Democrat. Roman Catholic. Home: 511 Surrey Laredo TX 78041 Office: Laredo C of C PO Box 790 Laredo TX 78042-0790

FREEMAN, ELAINE LAVALLE, sculptor; b. Boston, May 22, 1929; d. John and Ellen (Tufts) Lavalle; m. Felix Joachim Freeman, Jr., June 16, 1951 (div. 1974); children: John Lavalle, William Baker, Ellen Candler. Student, NAD, 1973, Art Students League, N.Y.C., 1947-49, 70-73; BA, Fordham U., 1986. Profl. sculptor N.Y.C. and Southampton, N.Y., 1973—; instr. sculpture Sculpture Ctr. Sch., N.Y.C., 1977-81; vol. gallery asst. Sculpture Ctr., N.Y.C., 1979—; exec. com., sec., bd. trustees Sculpture Ctr., N.Y.C., 1985—. One woman shows include Wheeler Gallery, Providence, 1979, Sculpture Ctr., N.Y.C., 1977, Southampton Gallery, N.Y.C., 1975; exhibited in group shows including Nat. Acad., Audubon Artists, Allied Artists, Parrish Mus., Nat. Arts Club, Am. Standard Corp. Gallery, Sculpture Ctr. Gallery, Huntington Twp. Art League, east End Arts Coun., 1973—. Bd. dirs. Southampton Fresh Air Home for Crippled Children, 1980-86, sec., 1981-83, treas. 1980. Recipient Judges award, Parrish Art Mus., Southampton, 1974, Am. Carving Sch. award, Allied Artists, N.Y.C., 1977, Anna Huntington Hyatt award, Catherine Lorillard Wolfe Art Club, N.Y.C., 1983. Mem. Colony Club, Meadow Club. Democrat. Episcopalian. Home: 119 W 77 St New York NY 10024

FREEMAN, FLORENCE ELEANOR, lawyer; b. Cambridge, Mass., Feb. 25, 1921; s. Elbern and Olive Blanche (Rice) F.; AB, Wellesley Coll., 1942; JD, U. Pa., 1945. Bar: Del. 1947, U.S. Dist. Ct. Del. 1948, U.S. Ct. Appeals (3d cir.) 1950, Mass. 1954, U.S. Dist. Ct. Mass. 1960. Assoc., Lynch & Hermann, Wilmington, Del., 1946-53; sole practice, Weston, Mass., 1954-69; ptnr. Freeman & Conceison, Weston, 1970-83, Freeman & White, Weston, 1984—; town counsel Town of Weston, 1968-86, spl. counsel, 1986-89. Author: (play) Portrait of a Prince, 1965. Pres. Weston LWV, 1960-62, Weston Drama Workshop, 1963-71; mem. bd. selectmen Town of Weston, 1964-68; sec., trustee So. New Eng. Conf. United Meth. Ch., Boston, 1971-74, chancellor, 1976-86 ; bd. visitors Boston U. Sch. Theology, 1978—; chmn. bd. advisors Anna Howard Shaw Ctr., 1988—; mem. council fin. and adminstrn. United Meth. Ch., Chgo., 1980-88, alt. jud. council, 1980-88, chmn. legal responsibilities com. 1980-88. Mem. ABA, Bar Assn. Club: Footlight (Boston) (pres. 1962-64); Wellesley Coll., Eastern Point Yacht. Office: Freeman & White 483 Boston Post Rd Weston MA 02193

FREEMAN, JANE ROSALIE, health facility administrator, director; b. Newton, Mass., Mar. 8, 1955; d. Isadore and Irene (Demers) Ludwin; m. Joseph William Freeman, Sept. 7, 1980. BA, Goddard Coll., 1978; MPA, Suffolk U., 1985. Various adminstrv. positions Boston, 1975-83; sr. program analyst Mass. Dept. Pub. Health, Boston, 1984-86; mgmt. cons. The Burlington (Mass.) Group, 1987-88; dir. strategic planning Jordan Hosp., Plymouth, Mass., 1988—. Vol. adult literacy program, Plymouth, 1990—; bd. dirs. Nat. Soc. for Autistic Children, Boston, 1981-82. Polaroid Found. grantee, 1982. Mem. Healthcare Mgmt. Assn., Am. Pub. Health Assn., Soc. for Hosp. Planning and Mktg., Women in Healthcare Mgmt., Am. Coll. Healthcare Execs. Office: Jordan Hosp 275 Sandwich St Plymouth MA 02360

FREEMAN, MYRNA FAYE, management; b. Danville, Ill., Oct. 30, 1939; d. Thomas Gene and Dorothy Olive (Chodera) F.; m. Lonnie Lee Choate, Aug. 16, 1959 (div. 1987); children: Leslie Rene, Gregory Lonn. BA in Pub. Adminstrn., San Diego State U., 1977, MA in Edn. Adminstrn., 1987. Employee benefits mgr. City of San Diego, 1974-84; asst. risk mgr. San Diego County Office of Edn., San Diego, 1984—; instr. sch. bus. mgrs. acad. Assn. Calif. Sch. Adminstrs., 1985--. Author: Book, Adm. Impact of Implement Leg. 1987; Author: Article Risk Mgmt.- Emp. Benefits 1985, Risk Mgmt. - Workers' Comp. 1986, Risk Mgmt. - Loss Control 1986. Mem. Kaiser Consumer Coun., 1977-87, pres., 1979-80.; bd. dirs. S.D. County Affirmative Action Bd., 1985. Recipient Award of Appreciation COMBO-Cultural Arts of San Diego 1977. Mem. Risk Ins. Mgmt. Soc. (pres. 1988), Calif. Assn. Sch. Bus. Ofcls. (chmn. risk mgmt. R&D comm. 1987-88), S.D. Employers Health Cost Coalition (vice chmn. 1987-), S.D. Group Ins. Claims Coun. (pres. 1987), Calif. Women in Govt. (bd dirs. 1983-84),Sigma Kappa, Phi Kappa Phi. Republican. Home: 4345 Cartulina Rd San Diego CA 92124-2102 Office: San Diego County Office of Edn 6401 Linda Vista Rd San Diego CA 92111-7399

FREEMAN, PATRICIA ELIZABETH, library and education specialist; b. El Dorado, Ark., Nov. 30, 1924; d. Herbert A. and M. Elizabeth (Pryor) Harper; m. Jack Freeman, June 15, 1949; 3 children. BA, Centenary Coll., 1943; postgrad., Fine Arts Ctr., 1942-46, Art Students League, 1944-45; BSLS, La. State U., 1946; postgrad., Calif. State U., 1959-61, U. N.Mex., 1964-74; EdS, Peabody Coll., Vanderbilt U., 1975. Libr. U. Calif., Berkeley, 1946-47; libr. Albuquerque Pub. Schs., 1964-67, ind. sch. libr. media ctr. cons., 1967—. Painter lithographer; one-person show La. State Exhibit Bldg., 1948; author: Pathfinder: An Operational Guide for the School Librarian, 1975; compiler, editor: Elizabeth Pryor Harper's Twenty-One Southern Families, 1985. Mem. task force Goals for Dallas-Environ., 1977-82; pres. Friends of Sch. Librs., Dallas, 1979-83. With USAF, 1948-49. Honoree AAUW Ednl. Found., 1979; vol. award for outstanding service Dallas Ind. Sch. Dist., 1978; AAUW Pub. Service grantee 1980. Mem. ALA, AAUW (dir. Dallas 1976-82, Albuquerque 1983-85), LWV (sec. Dallas 1982-83, editor Albuquerque 1984-88), Nat. Trust Historic Preservation, Friends of Albuquerque Pub. Libr., N.Mex. Symphony Guild, Alpha Xi Delta. Home: 3016 Santa Clara SE Albuquerque NM 87106

FREEMAN, PHYLLIS THERESE See DONATH, THERESE

FREEMAN, SUSAN SWARTZMAN, business executive; b. Kansas City, Mo., Nov. 25, 1957; d. Howard L. and Leatrice (Endlich) Swartzman; m. Thomas B. Freeman, Aug. 12, 1979; 1 child, Daniel Harry. BA, Wellesley Coll., 1979; MBA, Columbia U., 1983. Researcher Mitsubishi Internat. Corp., Wash., 1980-81; asst. prodn. mgr. Pfizer, Inc., N.Y.C., 1982; jr. acct. mgr. Benton & Bowles, London, 1983-84; acct. exec. D'Arcy Masius Benton & Bowles, N.Y.C., 1984-86; account supr. Young & Rubicam, N.Y.C., 1986-88; exec. dir. Tampa (Fla.) Bus. Com. Arts, 1989—. Bd. dirs. Solisti N.Y. Chamber Orch., 1987-88. Mem. Wellesley Club (alumna interviewer).

FREEMAN-BARAKA, RHONDA NICHELLE, business executive; b. Tuskegee, Ala., Mar. 9, 1962; d. Riley and Annie Mae (Lampkin) Freeman; m. Tony Colvin-Baraka, Dec. 24, 1985. BA in English, Talladega (Ala.) Coll., 1983. Reporter The Daily Home Newspaper, Talladega, 1982-83; intern reporter The Nat. Leader Newspaper, Phila., 1983; reporter The Tuskegee News, 1984, assoc. editor, 1985-86; editor, assoc. pub. The Tuskegee (Ala.) News, 1986-89; v.p., creative dir. Kuumba & Assocs. (name changed to T&R Communications, pub. rels. and consulting co.), Auburn, Ala., 1989—. Mem. Ala. Press. Assn., Ala. Press Assn. Journalism Found. (bd. dirs.). Office: T&R Communications PO Box 1110 Auburn AL 36830

FREERKSEN, DEBORAH LYNNE, biochemist; b. Calgary, Alta., Can., May 16, 1956; came to U.S., 1970; d. Hugh Alexander and Roxana Marguerite (Wheaton) Chalmers; m. Robert Wayne Freerksen, July 7, 1979; children: Michelle Anne, David Brent. BA in Chemistry and Molecular Biology, U. Colo., 1978; PhD in Biochemistry, U. Del., 1984. Rsch. biochemist med. products dept. E.I. DuPont DeNemours & Co., Inc., Wilmington, Del., 1987-88, rsch. biochemist cen. rsch. dept., 1988-89, registration specialist agrl. products dept., 1990—. Contbr. articles to profl. jours. Am. Heart Assn. fellow, 1984-86. Mem. AAAS, Am. Chem. Soc. (biochemistry chair 1989). Office: Du Pont Co PO Box 80038 Wilmington DE 19880-0038

FREES, KAREN ANN, educator; b. Manning, Iowa, Feb. 3, 1962; d. John and Margaret Ann (Lutwitze) F. BA, Iowa State U., 1984; postgrad., U. Wis., 1990—. Dir. community rels. Manning Substance Abuse Treatment Unit, 1984-85; community svcs. cons. Iowa chpt. Nat. Com. for Prevention Child Abuse, Des Moines, 1985-86; exec. dir. Ames-Iowa State U. YWCA, 1986-88; regional AIDS specialist Minn. Dept. Edn., Thief River Falls, 1988-90; on-call advocate Violence Intervention Project, Thief River Falls, 1988—; instr. personal safety course, Iowa, 1985-87; instr. HIV/AIDS ARC, 1990—. Chair, founder AIDS Coalition Story County, Iowa, 1987-88; chair, advocate Assault Care Ctr., Ames, 1983-84, 87-88; bd. dirs. Iowa Orgn. for Victim Assistance, Des Moines, 1985-88; co-pres., treas. Iowa Coalition Against Sexual Assault, Des Moines, 1985-88; co-facilitator, advocate Polk County Victim Svcs., Des Moines, 1985-88. Dan Murphy scholar Iowa State U., 1984; recipient Univ. Human Rels. Svc. award Iowa State U., 1987. Mem. NAFE, NOW, Nat. Women's Studies Assn., Altrusa Internat., Iowa Network for Women (charter), Sigma Delta Chi, Alpha Epsilon Rho. Democrat. Home: 2925 Fish Hatchery Rd Apt 206 Madison WI 53713

FREESE, MELANIE LOUISE, librarian, professor; b. Mineola, N.Y., May 12, 1945; d. Walter Christian and Agnes Elizabeth (Jensen) F. BS in Elem. Edn., Hofstra U., 1967, MA in Elem. Edn., 1969; MLS, L.I. U., 9177. Cert. tchr., N.Y. Bibliographic searcher acquisitions dept. Adelphi U. Swirbul Libr., Garden City, N.Y., 1973-79, res. desk libr., 1979-83; catalog libr., assoc. prof. Hofstra U. Axinn Libr., Hempstead, N.Y., 1984—; ch. librarian St. Peters Evang. Luth. Ch., Baldwin, N.Y., 1977—. Mem. ALA, Nassau County Libr. Assn. (corr. sec. acad. and spl. librs. div. 1986-88, v.p., pres.-elect. 1989-90), Bus. and Profl. Women's Club Nassau County (pres. 1990—). Republican. Office: Hofstra U Axinn Library 1000 Fulton Ave Hempstead NY 11550

FREI, JOHN KAREN (SISTER), university administrator; b. Jersey City, Sept. 30, 1936; d. John A. and Mae F. (Reilly) F. BA, Douglass Coll., New Brunswick, N.J., 1959; MS, Rutgers U., 1961; PhD, U. Miami, 1972; MBA, Barry U., Miami, 1982. Teaching asst. Rutgers U., New Brunswick, 1959-61; assoc. in rsch. Yale U., New Haven, Conn., 1961-64; instr. Barry U., 1964-65, 67-70, from asst. prof. to prof. biology and chmn., 1970-81, also dir., 1983, also dean, 1984, assoc. v.p., 1985—; instr. Siena Heights Coll., Adrian, Mich., 1965-66; religious formation Adrian Dominican Motherhouse, 1965-67; mem. STATUS, Miami. Contbr. articles to profl. jours. NIH grantee, 1983, 86. Mem. AAUW, Torrey Botanical Club, Am. Orchid Soc., Beta Beta Beta, Sigma Xi. Office: Barry U 11300 NW 2d Ave Miami Shores FL 33161

FREIBERG, BRENDA RANDALL, strategic planning and marketing consultant; b. Denver, May 31, 1938; d. Morton H. and Villis (Gumbiner) Randall; m. Robert D. Heller, Nov. 2, 1958 (div. 1963); 1 child, Brett Randall; m. Thomas A. Freiberg Jr., Jan.8, 1964; children: Michael T., Katherine. Student, Wellesley Coll., 1956-58; BA, U. Calif., 1964. Program dir. Constl. Rights Found., Los Angeles, 1975-77; exec. dir. Council for Peace & Equality in Edn., Los Angeles, 1977-79; v.p. Hughes Communications, Inc., El Segundo, Calif., 1979-84, Internat. Satellite Strategies, Los Angeles; dir., credit card program Am. Med. Internat., Beverly Hills, Calif., 1985; v.p. Reliant Fin., 1986, Medialink Internat., Los Angeles, 1986; mktg. cons. Los Angeles, 1988--. Bd. dirs. Los Angeles Urban League, 1981-84, Constl. Rights Fedn., Los Angeles, 1981-83, Adv. Bd. KCET, Los Angeles, 1979-81; mem. steering com. Western Branch of Watch Coms., Los Angeles, 1989--. Mem. Jr. League (chair juvenile justice com., 1973-74). Democrat. Home: 11245 Montana Ave Los Angeles CA 90049

FREIBERG, KAREN LOUISE, psychology educator, writer; b. Oneonta, N. Y., Apr. 17, 1944; d. Peter and Helen Margarethe (Nordberg) H.; m. Joseph Michael, May 9, 1969; children: Kenneth, Signelise. BS, SUNY, Plattsburgh, 1966; MS, Cornell U., Ithaca, 1968; Ph.D., Syracuse U., N.Y., 1974. Teaching asst. Cornell U., Ithaca, N.Y., 1966-67; rsch. asst. Cornell U., Ithaca, 1967-68; charge nurse Reconstruction Home, Ithaca, 1967-68; field health nurse Navajo Indian Reservation, Gallup, N.Mex.; assoc. project dir. U. of Tex. Med. Br., Galveston, Tex., 1969-70; lectr. Syracuse U., 1970-75; rsch. specialist Cornell U., Ithaca, 1976-78; asst. prof. Le Moyne Coll., Syracuse, 1978-79; assoc. prof. U. Md. Baltimore County, Catonsville, Md., 1979--. Author: Human Development, 1979, 2nd ed., 1983, 3rd ed., 1987, Educating Exceptional Children, 1987. Mem. Internat. Confron Infant Studies, Soc. for Rsch. in Child Devel., Am. Psychological Assn. Methodist. Home: 505 N Chapelgate Ln Baltimore MD 21229 Office: UMBC Psychology Dept 5401 Wilkens Ave Baltimore MD 21228

FREIDENBERGS, INGRID, psychologist; b. Latvia, Aug. 6, 1944; came to U.S, 1951; d. Olgerts and Marta (Purvins) F.; m. Jack Feder, June 21, 1980; 1 child, Paul. BA, CCNY, 1966, MS, 1970; MA, L.I. U., 1973, PhD, 1983; cert. in psychoanalysis, NYU, 1983. Lic. psychologist, N.Y. Sch. psychologist Bur. of Guidance N.Y.C. Bd. Edn., 1971-73; intern in clin. psychology Bellevue Psychiat. Hosp., N.Y.C., 1973-74; with Inst. Rehab. Medicine NYU, N.Y.C., 1974—, dir. psychology intern program Inst. Rehab. Medicine, 1983-85, dir. psychol. svcs. Cancer Rehab. Svc., 1979—; adj. asst. prof. dept. counselor edn. NYU, 1978-82, clin. instr. dept. psychiatry NYU Med. Ctr., 1981—; presenter in field. Contbr. numerous articles to profl. jours. Mem. med. adv. bd. Skin Cancer Found. NSF fellow Yeshiva U., 1966, L.I. U. fellow, 1971-72. Mem. Am. Psychol. Assn., N.Y. State Psychol. Assn., Psychoanalytic Soc. of NYU, Assn. for the Advancement of Psychology. Office: 29 W 9th St New York NY 10011

FREILICH, JOAN SHERMAN, utilities executive; b. Albany, N.Y., Nov. 3, 1941; d. Julius and Bess (Bergner) Sherman; m. Sanford J. Freilich, Jan. 24, 1965. AB in French, Barnard Coll., 1963; MA in French, Columbia U., 1964, PhD in French, 1971, MBA in Fin., 1980. Instr. CCNY, Columbia U., N.Y.C., 1965-75; tchr. Walden Sch., N.Y.C., 1970-74; asst. to the dean Coll. New Rochelle, New Rochelle, N.Y., 1974-75; dir. admissions Coll. New Rochelle, 1975-78; sr. acct. Consolidated Edison Co. N.Y., N.Y.C., 1978-81; mgr. acctg. rsch. Consolidated Edison Co. N.Y., 1981-82, controller power generation, 1982-86, gen. mgr. power generation, 1986-89, exec. asst. to pres., 1989, asst. v.p. corp. planning, 1989—. Author: Paul Claudel's "Le Soulier de satin": A Stylistic, Structuralist and Psychoanalytic Interpretation, 1973; assoc. editor Claudel Studies, 1973-78; contbr. articles to profl. jours. Publ. grantee Humanities Rsch. Coun. Can., 1972; Pres.'s fellow Columbia U., 1964, Henry Todd fellow, 1967; recipient scholarship N.Y. State Bd. Regents, 1959, Nat. Merit Found., 1959, Columbia U., 1965. Mem. Nat. Assn. Accts., Beta Gamma Sigma, Phi Beta Kappa. Office: Consolidated Edison Co NY 4 Irving Pl New York NY 10003

FREIMAN, LELA KAY, educator; b. Canton, Miss., Oct. 2, 1939; d. Lyle K. and Mae Susan (Billman) Linch; m. James F. Freiman, Sept. 5, 1965 (div. Feb. 1975); 1 child, Jennifer Leigh. Student, Northwestern State Coll., Natchitoches, La., 1957-59; BA, U. Iowa, 1962; MEd, U. Ariz., 1977. Tchr. speech, English and drama Sturgeon Bay (Wis.) High Sch., 1962-65; spl. edn. tchr. Naylor Jr. High Sch., Tucson, 1975-83; tchr. drama Sahuaro High Sch., Tucson, 1983—; summer camp dir. Sahuaro coun. Girl Scouts U.S.A., Tucson, 1977-87; mem. adv. coun. drama dept. U. Ariz., Tucson; participant Nat. faculty for Humanities, Santa Fe, Tucson, 1988-89. Former leader, trainer, camp dir. Girl Scouts U.S.A., Sturgeon Bay, Wisconsin Rapids, Waukesha, Wis., Ariz. rep. Nat. Leadership Conf., Washington, 1983; first aid com., instr. AFA, CPR and ARC, Tucson; instr. CPR, Am. Heart Assn., Tucson; Sunday sch. tchr., supt., mem. coun. Luth Chs., Wisconsin Rapids, Waukesha, now Tucson; v.p. bd. dirs. S.W. Actors Studio, Tucson, 1987—. Recipient Thanks Badge, Sahuaro coun. Girl Scouts U.S.A., 1976, 88, Cross and Crown award Luth. Scouters So. Ariz., 1983, Mainstream Tchr. of Yr. award Assn. for Retarded Citizens So. Ariz., 1989. Mem. Theatre Edn. Assn., Ariz. Theatre Educators Assn. (state sec., com. to draft curriculum guidelines for Ariz. Ho. of Reps.), NEA, Ariz. Edn. Assn., Tucson Edn. Assn. Home: 7517 E Beach Dr Tucson AZ 85715 Office: Sahuaro High Sch 545 N Camino Seco Tucson AZ 85710

FREIRE, GLORIA MEDONIS, social worker; b. Pitts., Apr. 19, 1929; d. Vincent X. and Anastasia T. (Puida) Medonis; m. Luis Francis Freire, Aug. 30, 1958; children: Michael, Charles. BA in Polit. Sci. and Econs., Carlow Coll., 1950; MSSA, Case-Western Res. U., 1955; MPA, Cleve. State U., 1986; postgrad., Union Inst., 1990—. Teen-age dir. Merrick House, Cleve., 1955-62; group psychotherapist Cleve. Psychiat. Inst., 1966-73; lectr. Sch. Applied Social Scis., Case-Western Res. U., Cleve., 1973-75; cluster dir. Golden Age Ctrs., Cleve., 1975-76; specialist Community Guidance and Human Svcs., Cleve., 1976, staff tng. and devel. coord., 1977, dir. consultation and edn., 1978-84; coord. psychiat. emergency svcs. systems Lake County Mental Health Bd. Ohio, 1984-86; adminstr. hispanic office Cath. Counseling Ctr., Cleve., 1986—. Editor: SASS mag., Case Western Res. U. Alumni, 1973-79. Chmn. steering com. East Community Task Force on Desegregation; chmn. subcoun. of Ohio Community Mental Health Ctrs. Consultation and Edn.; chmn. Consultation and Edn. Coun. Cleve.; coord. Christian Formation Community of St. Malachi, 1975-77, coord. liturgy commn., 1978-80, coord. social concerns com., 1982-84; mem. Diocesan Commn. on Cath. Community Action, 1982-88, vice chmn., 1986-87; mem. Urban League Edn. Adv. and Task Force on Minimum Competency, 1978-80. Recipient Disting. Leadership award Alumnae Assn. Carlow Coll., 1982. Mem. Nat. Assn. Social Workers (task force on desegregation 1974-83, co-chmn. 1981-83, coord. polit. action com. 1977, dir. Cleve. chpt. 1975-77, sec.-treas. Ohio coun. of chpts. 1975-76, steering com. Cleve. chpt. 1987-89), Acad. Cert. Social Workers, Am. Soc. Pub. Adminstrn. (trustee Cleve. chpt. 1987—), Am. Soc. Profl. and Exec. Women, Nat. and Cuyahoga County Women's Polit. Caucus (exec. bd.), Am. Group Psychotherapy Assn., Tri-State Group Psychotherapy Soc. Democrat. Roman Catholic. Home: 5001 Tuxedo Ave Cleveland OH 44134 Office: Hispanic Office Cath Counseling Ctr 2012 W 25th St Cleveland OH 44113

FREITAG, BARBARA JO, catalog merchandising director; b. Chgo., July 24, 1948; d. Harold Edward and Gertrude Louise (Rohde) F.; m. Ronald D. Pace, Nov. 24, 1989. BBA cum laude in Mktg., U. Miami, Fla., 1970. Exec. trainee J.G. Nef and Co., Herisau, Switzerland, 1970-71; dept. mgr. Sears Roebuck & Co., Pompano Beach, Fla., 1971-72; market comparison researcher Sears Roebuck & Co., N.Y.C., 1973; asst. nat. sales mgr. Sears Roebuck & Co., 1974-75, asst. buyer sportswear, 1976-77, asst. nat. fashion dir., 1978; buyer swimwear Sears Roebuck & Co., Chgo., 1979-81; buyer sportswear Sears Roebuck & Co., 1982-83; dir. merchandising Avon Fashions div. New Hampton Inc., N.Y.C., 1983—. Vice pres. U. Miami chpt. A.I.E.S.E.C., Fla., 1969-70. Recipient Am. Legion award Am. Legion, Miami, 1966. Mem. Fashion Group, Phi Kappa Phi. Roman Catholic.

FREITAS, CATHRYN RADIN, municipal administration; b. Larkspur, Calif., Dec. 17, 1954; d. John Paul and Clara Hester (Stackhouse) R.; m. Donald Patrick Freitas, Oct. 5, 1985. BA, U. Calif., 1977; Masters Pub. Adminstrn., George Wash. U., 1979. Asst. to city mgr. City Antioch, 1979-84; personnel officer Cen. Contra Costa Sanitary Dist., Martinez, Calif., 1984--. City planning commr., 1984-86, council mem. City Antioch, 1986--, fire commr., Riverview Fire Protection Dist., 1986-87, county transp. commr., Contra Costa County, 1987--. Mem. AAUW (pres. 1983-84), Internat. Personnel Mgmt. Assn. Democrat. Roman Catholic. Office: Cen Contra Costa Sanitary 5019 Imhoff Pl Martinez CA 94553

FRELIGH, HELEN HOLCOMB, author; b. Granby, Conn., Mar. 9, 1907; d. John Mills Jewett and Bessy Emma Holcomb; m. Fletcher James Freligh; children: Dorothy Ruth, Marcia Gertrude, Edward Fred. BA in English, U. Conn., 1969. Author: Alex, 1986; contbr. articles, poetry to profl. jours. Rep. Newington VA Hosp. for DAR, 1970-86; active in past various charitable orgns. Mem. DAR (regent 1979-81). Republican. Congregationalist. Address: 129 Knob Hill Rd Glastonbury CT 06033

FRENCH, CAROL ANN, reference librarian; b. Marion, Ohio, Feb. 13, 1944; d. Louis and Ruth Adeline (Dewiel) F.; m. Thomas Ray Franklin (dec. May 1976); m. Joseph Michael Retcho, May 6, 1990; children: Rick Furniss, Ron Furniss, Tammy Radabaugh, Toni Sewaringen De Osegueda. Assoc. in Liberal Arts, Broward Community Coll., Pembroke Pines, Fla., 1984; BFA, Fla. Atlantic U., 1989; postgrad., U. So. Fla. Reference libr. Broward County, 1984—. Artist: (pastel drawings) Inside Out, 1989 (hon. mention award 1989); reference libr. work, Pathfinder, Sculpture in the 1960s, 1990. Mem. Am. Libr. Assn., Broward County Libr. Assn. Office: Broward County Library 7300 Pines Blvd Pembroke Pines FL 33024

FRENCH, LEXIE ANNE, educator, writer; b. Idaho Falls, Idaho, Dec. 29, 1949; d. William P. and Erma (Maxfield) Fowler; m. Alan E. French, Aug. 26, 1972; children: Travis William, Mikela Alexander. BA, Idaho State U., Pocatello, 1972. Cert. secondary English and social studies tchr., Idaho. Thcr. Skyline High Sch. Dist. 91, Idaho Falls, 1977—. Author: (with others) Second Stories, 1987. Co-founder Idaho Falls Coalition for Excellence in Edn., Idaho Falls, 1989-90; pres., bd. dirs. Jr. Achievement, Idaho Falls, 1990—. Named Outstanding Tchr., Idaho Coun. of Employing the Handicapped, 1984, U. Chgo., 1987; NEH fellow Wayne State U., 1987. Mem. NEA, AAUW, Found. for Edn. Excellence (bd. dirs. 1990—), Idaho Falls Edn. Assn. (pres. 1986-87), Idaho Coun. Tchrs. of English (pres. Idaho chpt. 1984-85), East Idaho Reading Coun., Idaho Falls C. of C. (com. chair 1987—, chmn. Winter Snowfest Celebration 1989, chmn. edn. com. 1990—, bd. dirs. 1990—), Idaho Humanities Coun. (bd. dirs. 1985-89). Home: 349 Gustafson Dr Idaho Falls ID 83402 Office: Skyline High Sch 1767 Blue Sky Dr Idaho Falls ID 83402

FRENCH, STEPHANIE TAYLOR, arts administrator; b. Newark; d. William Taylor and Connie V. French; B.A., Wellesley Coll., 1972; M.B.A., Harvard U., 1978; m. Amory Houghton, III, Sept. 8, 1979; 1 dau., Christina French Houghton. Traffic mgr. Radio Sta. KFRC, 1973-74; free-lance on-air performer, producer San Francisco and Oakland cable TV stas., 1973-76; dir. European Gallery, San Francisco, 1974-75; acct. exec. Young & Rubican, N.Y.C., 1978-79; acct. supr. Rives Smith Baldwin & Carlberg, Houston, 1980-81; mgr. cultural affairs and spl. programs Philip Morris Cos. Inc., N.Y.C., 1981-86, dir., cultural and contributions programs, 1986—. Bd. dirs. The Joffrey Ballet, Twyla Tharp Dance Co., Lar Lubovitch Dance, Art Table, Am. Fedn. of Arts, Am. Council on Arts; co-chmn. producers council Bklyn. Acad. Music, Dance Theatre Workshop; co-chmn. Assocs. of Babies Hosp., Columbia Presbyn. Med. Ctr. Clubs: Harvard Bus. Sch., Wellesley. Home: 161 E 90th St Apt 2C New York NY 10128 Office: Philip Morris Cos Inc 120 Park Ave New York NY 10017

FRENCH, VIRGINIA LEE, food management company executive, dietitian; b. Superior, Mont., Aug. 4, 1939; d. William Wallace and Virginia Lee (Estes) Schneider; m. Richard George French, Aug. 16, 1958; children: Richard Mark, Leanne Rene. BS, Mont. State U., 196l; MEd, U. Mont., 197l. Registered dietitian. Staff dietitian St. John's Hosp., Oxnard, Calif., 1962, dir. food svc., 1962-63; instr. English, Chiengmai (Thailand) U., 1965; instr. food svc. Marin County, Corte Madera, Calif., 1972-73; food svc. cons. H. Troy Hosp. Svcs., Southampton, Pa., 1973-74; chief dietitian Montgomery County Geriatric and Rehab. Ctr., Royersford, Pa., 1975-77; adminstrv. dietitian Wood Co., Allentown, Pa., 1977-78, exec. group mgr., 1978-85, v.p., 1985—. Bd. dirs. Meals on Wheels United Way, Lehigh County, 1987—. Mem. Am. Dietetic Assn., Nat. Restaurant Assn. Republican. Presbyterian. Home: 420 W Philadelphia Ave Boyertown PA 19512 Office: Wood Co 608l Hamilton Blvd Allentown PA 18106

FRENGUT, RENEE HIRSCH, consumer psychologist, marketing research consultant; b. N.Y.C., May 14, 1945; d. Erich F. and Eleanore F. (Kaplan) Hirsch. BA, CCNY, 1966; MA, Yeshiva U., 1968, PhD (NIMH fellow), 1977. Cert. psychologist. Instr. dept. psychology N.Y. Inst. Tech., N.Y.C., 1968-69; clin. intern N.Y. State Psychiat. Inst., Columbia U. Coll. Physicians and Surgeons, 1969-70; staff psychologist Westchester County Community Mental Health Bd., 1970-71; staff psychologist Abbott House for Children, Irvington, N.Y., 1971-72, supr. exptl. therapeutic group homes, 1971-72; mem. faculty dept. psychology Montgomery Coll., Rockville, Md., 1972-74; staff psychologist Potomac Found. for Mental Health, Rockville, Md., 1973-75; pvt. practice clin. psychology, 1974-77; rsch. cons. social rsch. div. NBC, N.Y.C., 1976; qualitative media rsch. cons. R.H. Bruskin Assocs., New Brunswick, N.J., 1976; part-time lectr. psychology Mercy Coll., Dobbs Ferry, N.Y., 1976-78; rsch. group head The Nowland Orgn., Greenwich, Conn., 1977-78; pres. Qualitative Decisions Ctr., Inc., N.Y.C., 1978-84, Market Insights, Inc., Bronxville, N.Y., 1984—. Mem. Am. Psychol. Assn., Am. Mktg. Assn. Office: 270 Bronxville Rd Bronxville NY 10708

FRESCH, MARIE BETH, court reporting company executive; b. Norwalk, Ohio, Jan. 16, 1957; d. Ralph Roy and Vonda Mae (Brunkhorst) Spiegel; m. James R. Fresch, Aug. 5, 1978; 1 child, Alexandra Jane. AS in Bus., Tiffin U., 1977; cert. in ct. reporting, Acad. Ct. Reporting, 1979. Registered profl. reporter, Ohio. Ofcl. reporter Seneca County Common Pleas Ct., Tiffin, Ohio, 1979-80; owner, operator Marie B. Fresch & Assocs., Norwalk, 1980—. Mem. Nat. Shorthand Reporters Assn., Ohio Shorthand Reporters Assn. (student promotions and pub. relations coms. 1986—), Baron Users Group (ct. reporter computer support group), NOW (sec. Port Clinton chpt. 1984-86, treas. 1986-87), Am. Legion Aux., Kappa Delta Kappa. Democrat. Methodist. Lodge: Order of Eastern Star (esther 1979-81). Home and Office: 47 Warren Dr Norwalk OH 44857

FRESCOLN, KATHARINE PITMAN, emeritus history educator; b. Swarthmore, Pa., May 9, 1917; d. John Himes and Katharine Elsie (Anders) Pitman; m. Joseph Wright Frescoln, Jan. 6, 1942. AB, Wittenberg U., 1965; MA, W.Va. U., 1966, PhD, 1971. Social studies tchr. sch. Parsons, W.Va., 1963-65; instr., asst. prof., assoc. prof. history Shepherd Coll., Shepherdstown, W.Va., 1967-75, prof., 1975-85, prof. emeritus, 1985—. Contbr. articles to profl. jours. Samuel Sprecker scholar, 1959. Mem. DAR, Am. Hist. Assn., Am. Assn. for Advancement Slavic Studies, N.Am. Conf. on Brit. Studies, Soc. for Descendants of Schwenkfelder Exiles, Phi Alpha Theta (internat. councillor 1980-82). Home: Heatherfield PO Box 683 Shepherdstown WV 25443

FRETER, LISA, communications specialist; b. Washington, Aug. 25, 1951; d. Theodore Henry and Elizabeth Crawford (Stout) Freter; m. David O'Shea Dawkins, Dec. 20, 1975 (div. Nov. 1989); 1 child, Meghan Elizabeth. Student, Towson State Coll., 1969-70, Inst. Allende, San Miguel de Allende, Guanajuato, Mex., 1970-72, U. de las Americas, Cholula, Puebla, Mex., 1972-73; BSBA, U. Phoenix, 1991. Mgr. La Bonita Supper Club, Denver, 1974-75; adminstrv. asst. Magic Pan Inc., Denver, 1975-79; owner B&B Liquors, Denver, 1979-81; adminstrv. asst. Gt. Amusement Emporium, Englewood, Colo., 1981-83; sec. corp. Ponderosa Homes Colo. Inc., Englewood, 1983-85; dir. pubs. Gt. Western Assn. Mgmt., Denver, 1985-88; adminstrv. asst. Employment and Tng. div. Arapahoe County, Aurora, Colo., 1988—. Author: (poems) The San Miguel Writer, 1970, Xalli, 1971; exec. producer Law Enforcement Torch Run for Spl. Olympics Video, 1986, videotaped pub. svc. announcements, 1987; producer, dir. (video) Private Industry Council, 1989. Exec. dir. Colleagues Police for Edn., Support, Denver, 1983-85; liaison Colo. Assn. Chiefs Police, 1983-85, Spl. Olympics, 1986-88. Mem. Freedoms Found. Valley Forge (v.p. pub. relations Denver area chpt. 1988—, 1989-90), Colo. Gang Investigators Assn. (exec. dir. 1989-90). Home: 7275 B S Xenia Circle Englewood CO 80112-1958

FREUDENTHAL, NANCY ELLEN, medical services coordinator; b. Pacific Junction, Iowa, May 23, 1940; d. John Charles and Louise Katherine (Kirker) Long; m. Kenneth Duane Freudenthal, July 23, 19861 (div. 1973); children: Kristi Lynn, John Jorge. BS, Jennie Edmundson Sch. Nursing, 1961. Nurse Douglas County Hosp., Omaha, 1961-63, from RN intensive care to head nurse, 1968-73; RN intensive care Nebr. U., Omaha, 1964-68; RN Med. Svcs. Dept. of Corrections, Omaha, 1973—; cons. Correctional Medicine to other Cities and States, 1975-80, com. mem. AMA Adtloc Task Force, Chgo., lectr. Creighton U. and Nebr. U. sch. of Nursing, 1976-86. Author: Supervisor Nurse, 1973, AMA Correctional Medicine, 1977, 1981. Campaign area chmn. Rep. for Congress, Omaha, 1980, participant Health Fair of Midlands, Aid Vol. Group. Mem. Sweet Adelines. Home: 5072 S 105 St Omaha NE 68127 Office: Douglas County Dept Corrections 710 S 17th St Omaha NE 68102

FREUND, EMMA FRANCES, medical technologist; b. Washington; d. Walter R. and Mabel W. (Loveland) Ervin; BS, Wilson Tchrs. Coll., Washington, 1944; MS in Biology, Catholic U., Washington, 1953; MEd in Adult Edn., Va. Commonwealth U., 1988; cert. in mgmt. devel. Va. Commonwealth U., 1975, MEd, 1988; student SUNY, New Paltz, 1977, J. Sargeant Reynolds Community Coll., 1978; m. Frederic Reinert Freund, Mar. 4, 1953; children: Frances, Daphne, Fern, Frederic. Tchr. math. and sci. D.C. Sch. System, 1944-45; technician in parasitology lab., zool. div., U.S. Dept. Agr., Beltsville, Md., 1945-48; histologic technician dept. pathology Georgetown U. Med. Sch., Washington, 1948-49; clin. lab. technician Kent and Queen Anne's County Gen. Hosp., Chestertown, Md., 1949-51; histotechnologist surg. pathology dept. Med. Coll. Va. Hosp., Richmond, 1951—, supr. histology lab., 1970—; mem. exam. council Nat. Cert. Agy. Med. Lab. Personnel. Asst. cub scout den leader Robert E. Lee council Boy Scouts Am., 1967-68, den leader, 1968-70. Co-author (mini-course): Instrumentation in Cytology and Histology, 1985. Cert. Nat. Cert. Agy. for Clin. Lab. Personnel. Mem. Am. Soc. Med. Technology (rep. to sci. assembly histology sect. 1977-78, chmn. histology sect. 1983-85, 89—), Va. Soc. Med. Technology, Richmond Soc. Med. Technologists (corr. sec. 1977-78, dir. 1981-82, pres. 1984-85), Va. Soc. Histology Technicians (dir. 1979—, pres. 1982-88), Nat. Certification Agy. (clin. lab. specialist in histotech., clin. lab. supr., clin. lab. dir.), N.Y. Acad. Scis., Am. Assn. Clin. Chemistry (assoc.), Am. Soc. Clin. Pathologists (cert. histology technician), Nat. Geog. Soc., Va. Govtl. Employees Assn., AAAS, Nat. Soc. Histotech. (by-laws com. 1981—; C.E.U. com. 1981—, program com. regional meeting 1984, 85, chmn. regional meeting 1987), Am. Mus. Natural History, Smithsonian Instn., Am. Mgmt. Assn., Clin. Lab. Mgmt. Assn., Nat. Soc. Historic Preservation, Am. Biog. Inst. Research Assn. (life; recipient Commemorative medal of Honor 1986), Sigma Xi, Phi Beta Rho, Kappa Delta Pi, Phi Lambda Theta. Home: 1315 Asbury Rd Richmond VA 23229 Office: Surgical Pathology Dept Med Coll VA Hosp PO Box 240 Richmond VA 23298-0240

FREY, E(MMA) MARGARET MOORE, school psychologist; b. Hinston, W.Va., May 27, 1923; d. John Thompson and Josie May (Meadows) Moore; m. John Melvin Frey, Mar. 25, 1956; children: John William, Eleanor Josie, Andrew Patrick, Emily Jane. BS, Clarion (Pa.) State Coll., 1944; MS, Pa. State U., 1949; postgrad., Duke U., 1946, Shippinsburg (Pa.) State U., 1970-71. Lic. sch. psychologist, Pa. Elementary tchr. Clarion Limestone Sch. Dist., Strattonville, Pa., 1944-47, Bulter (Pa.) Sch. Dist., 1947-48; supr. spl. edn. Bedford and Fulton Counties, Pa., 1950-52; elementary supr., sch. psychologist Chambersburg (Pa.) Sch. Dist., 1952-56; sch. psychologist

Cumberland County, Carlisle, Pa., 1956-57, Franklin County/Lincoln Intermediate Unit #12, New Oxford, Pa., 1970-86; sch. psychologist part-time Chambersburg area schs., 1986-87, Lincoln Intermediate Unit #12, 1988-89. Bd. dirs. Chambersburg Area Community Concert Assn., 1970—, Chambersburg Area Hosp. Aux., 1988—; area sub-chmn. Chambersbur Area United Fund, 1970—; adv. bd. Christian Women's Club, 1989—; Sun. sch. supt. Cen. Presbyn. Ch., 1987—, vol. ch. choir, 1985—; vol. Released Bible Time, Children's Bible Mission, Greencastle, Pa., 1988—. Mem. Franklin County Sch. Retiree's Assn. (life), The Huguenot Soc. Pa. (life), Pa. Psychol. Assn. Republican. Home: 420 Woodland Way Chambersburg PA 17201

FREY, LINDA SUSAN, editor, advertising and public relations consultant; b. Indpls., May 22, 1951; d. Wayne R. and Mildred Louise (Kendall) Chambers; m. R. Michael Frey (div. 1975); 1 child, Ryan Kendall. BS, Ball State U., 1973. Secretarial position Am. States Ins., Indpls., 1973-74, asst. editor, 1974-76, editor employee communications, 1976—; cons. Greater Indpls. Literacy League, 1984—; cons., editor Greater Indpls. Council on Alcoholism; cons. Ind. Counselors Assn. on Alcohol and Drug Abuse. Photographer for book cover; design artist of original logo for Greater Indpls. Literacy League. Mem. Ind. Gov.'s Adult Literacy Coalition, 1986, 87; literacy tutor to adult non-readers, 1985-87; cons., speaker United Way Cen. Ind., 1974—; mem. adv. bd. North Am. Wildlife Park Found., Battleground, Ind. Recipient Excellent Performance in communications award Ind. Bus. Communicators, 1980. Mem. Women in Communications, Internat. Assn. Bus. Communicators. Office: Am States Ins 500 N Meridian Indianapolis IN 46204

FREY, RICHELLE M., legal secretary; b. Jennings, La., Dec. 29, 1961; d. Carlton Ray and Dolores (Doucet) McFarlin; m. Kenneth Paul Frey, May 2, 1987. BSBA, U. So. La., 1984, paralegal cert., 1989. Dep. clk. City Ct. of Lafayette, Crowley, La., 1984-85; legal sec., paralegal Edwards, Stefanski & Barousse, Crowley, 1985—. Treas. Am. Cancer Soc., Acadia Parish, La., 1989-90. Mem. AAUW, Crowley Bus. and Profl. Women's Club (v.p. 1987-89, Woman of the Yr. 1988). Democrat. Roman Catholic. Home: 941 W Walnut Eunice LA 70535

FREYD, JENNIFER JOY, psychology professor; b. Providence, Oct. 16, 1957; d. Peter John and Pamela (Parker) F.; m. John Q. Johnson, June 9, 1984; children: Theodore, Philip. BA in Anthropology magna cum laude, U. Pa., 1979; PhD in Psychology, Stanford U., 1983. Asst. prof. psychology Cornell U., 1983-87; assoc. prof. psychology U. Oreg., Eugene, 1987—; fellow Ctr. for Advanced Study in the Behavioral Scis., 1989-90; elected mem. Faculty Coun. of Reps., Cornell U., 1986-87; apptd. mem. Child Care Study Com., U. Oreg., 1987-89. Editorial bd. Jour. Experimental Psychology: Learning, Memory and Cognition, Gestalt Theory; guest reviewer Am. Jour. Psychology, Am. Psychologist, others; contbr. articles to profl. jours. Recipient Graduate fellowship NSF, 1979-82, Univ. fellowship Stanford U., 1982-83, Presdl. Young Investigator award NSF, 1985-90, IBM Faculty Devel. award, 1985-87, fellowship Ctr. for Advanced Study in the Behavioral Scis., 1989-90, John Simon Meml. fellowship Guggenheim Found., 1989-90, Rsch. Scientist Devel. award NIMH, 1989-94; other rsch. funding. Mem. AAAS, Am. Psychol. Assn., Am. Psychol. Soc., Psychonomic Soc., Sigma Xi. Office: Univ Oregon Dept Psychology Eugene OR 97403

FREYER, VICTORIA C., fashion consultant, interior designer; b. Asbury Park, N.J.; d. Spiros Steven and Hope (Pappas) Pappaylion; m. Cyril Steven Arvanitis, Dec. 26, 1950 (div. 1975); children: Samuel James, Hope Alexandra. BA, Georgian Court Coll., 1950; student, N.Y. Sch. Interior Design, 1971-72. Mgr. Homestead Restaurant, Ocean Grove, N.J., 1946-58; art supr. Lakewood (N.J.) Pub. Schs., 1950-51; interior designer London, 1975-76, F. Korasic Assocs., Oakhurst, N.J., 1977-78; owner, operator Virginia Interiors, McLean, Va., 1974-90; interior designer Anita Perlut Interiors, McLean, 1986; owner, operator Victoria Freyer Interiors, McLean, 1986—; fashion cons. Nordstrom Splty. Store, McLean, 1988—. Pres. Monmouth County Med. Aux., 1964; originator 1st lecture series Monmouth Coll., Long Branch, N.J., 1965; guest moderator Alexandria (Va.) Hosp. Series, 1988; mem. Women's Symphony Com., Washington, 1988—; guest speaker Girl Scouts U.S. Coun. Nation's Capitol, 1988-90, Nuclear Energy Coun., 1989, pers. dept. CIA, 1989-90, Internat. Women's Group Washington, 1989-90. Mem. AAUW (program chmn. 1968). Greek Orthodox. Office: 7630 Provincial Dr McLean VA 22102 Office: Nordstrom 1961 Chain Bridge Rd McLean VA 22102

FREYTAG, SHARON NELSON, lawyer; b. Larned, Kans., May 11, 1943; d. John Seldon and Ruth Marie (Herbel) Nelson; m. Thomas Lee Freytag, June 18, 1966; children: Kurt David, Hillary Lee. BS with highest distinction, U. Kans., Lawrence, 1965; MA, U. Mich., 1966; JD cum laude, So. Meth. U., 1981. Bar: Tex. 1981, U.S. Dist. Ct. (no. dist.) Tex. 1981, U.S. Ct. Appeals (5th cir.) 1982. Tchr. English, Gaithersburg (Md.) High Sch., 1966-70; instr. English, Eastfield Coll., 1974-78; law clk. U.S. Dist. Ct. for No. Dist. Tex., 1981-82, U.S. Ct. Appeals for 5th Circuit, 1982; ptnr. litigation and appellate sect. Haynes and Boone, Dallas, 1983—, vis. prof. law Southern Meth. U., 1985-86. Editor-in-chief Southwestern Law Jour., 1980-81; contbr. articles to law jours. Mem. ABA, Tex. Bar Assn., Dallas Bar Assn., Dallas Mus. Art, Dallas Shakespeare Soc., Dallas Inn of Ct., Barristers, Order of Coif, Phi Delta Phi, Phi Beta Kappa. Lutheran. Office: Haynes & Boone 3100 NCNB Pla Dallas TX 75202

FRIAUF, KATHERINE ELIZABETH, metal company executive; b. Balt., Oct. 13, 1956; d. John Beecher Friauf and Elizabeth Withers (Wilson) Struever. Student, Columbia Coll., Chgo., 1979-81. Cert. sound engr. Owner, operator Midwest Emery Freight System, Chgo., 1978-80; driver BCB Dispatch, Inc., Rochester, N.Y., 1980-88; dispatcher, systems analyst BCB Dispatch, Inc., LeRoy, N.Y., 1988-89; corp. controller Rochester Plating Works, Inc., 1988—; dir. Rochester Plating Works, Inc., 1988—. Mem. NAFE, Rochester Women's Network. Presbyterian. Office: Rochester Plating Works Inc Two Cairn St Rochester NY 14611-2476

FRICK, NANCY MALINOSKY, consultant, counselor, author, researcher; b. Lakewood, Ohio, July 21, 1943; d. Raymond Oliver and Bettie Marie (Leonard) Malinosky; m. Richard Louis Bruno, May 28, 1983. BA summa cum laude, Baldwin-Wallace Coll., 1965; MDiv magna cum laude, Drew U., 1968. Libr. adminstr., tchr. Gill Upper Sch., Bernardsville, N.J., 1968-72; dir. dept. social svcs. Door of Hope Home and Sch. for Emotionally Disturbed Girls, Jersey City, 1972-74; counselor sr. citizen's unit CETA Jobs Program, Jersey City, 1974-79; sr. program specialist regional tech. assistance unit Office for Civil Rights, U.S. Dept. Edn., N.Y.C., 1979-84; accessibility planner Office Spl. Svcs. N.J. Transit, Newark, 1984-85; assoc. dir., program coord., access specialist D.I.A.L. for Ind. Living, Clifton, N.J., 1985-86; adj. instr. dept. psychology Felician Coll., Lodi, N.J., 1986-87; exec. dir. Harvest Ctr., Inc., Hackensack, N.J., 1987—; mem. Tri-State Adv. Bd. on Para-Transit and Half-Fare Program for N.Y.C., 1980-81, N.J. Commn. on Recreation for Handicapped, 1985-86, N.J. Barrier-Free Sub-Code Com., 1985—; mem. staff N.J. Follow-Up Confs. to White House Conf. on Handicapped, 1981; program coord. Internat. Post-Polio Rsch. Task Force, 1984—; mem. adv. bd. Community Health Law Project, East Orange, N.J., 1985-86. Contbr. articles to profl. jours. Treas. adv. bd. Jersey City Meals-on-Wheels, 1976-78; mem. adv. bd. Hudson Health Systems Agy., 1978-80; co-founder Will Power, Inc., Hudson County, N.Y., 1979; mem. Tri-State Com. on Transp. Needs Elderly and Handicapped, 1979-82; mem. facilities needs adv. bd. N.J. Dept. Health, 1980-81; mem. adv. bd. for spl. edn. svcs. N.J. Dept. Edn., 1984-85. Named Young Career Woman, N.J. Bus. and Profl. Women's Assn., 1967; recipient cert. of merit N.J. Adv. Coun. Internat. Yr. Disabled Persons, 1981, Handicapped Profl. Woman of Yr. award N.E.-Potomac div. Pilot Club Internat., 1986, ann. award civil rights activist com. for disabled CUNY, 1986, Merit award Baldwin-Wallace Coll. Alumni Assn., 1990. Office: Harvest Ctr Inc 151 Prospect Ave Hackensack NJ 07601

FRICKE, JANIE (JANE MARIE FRICKE), singer; b. Ft. Wayne, Ind., Dec. 19, 1947; d. Waldemar and Phyllis (Kyler) Fricke; m. Randy Jackson, Sept. 16, 1982. B.E., Ind. U. Cert. elem. tchr. Albums include: Sleeping With Your Memory, Love Notes, The First Word in Memory, Black & White, 1986, Saddle the Wind, 1988, Labor of Love, 1989. Named Female Vocalist of Yr., Music City News Cover awards, 1983, 84, Female Vocalist of Yr. Acad. Country Music, 1984, Female Vocalist of Yr. Country Music Assn., 1982, 83, Top Country Female Vocalist, Billboard Mag., 1983, Cash Box Mag., 1983, Most Promising Female Vocalist, Music City News Cover awards, 1979; nominee Grammy awards, 1979, 81, 84. Office: care CBS Records 51 W 52d St New York NY 10019*

FRICKLAS, ANITA ALPER, religious organization administrator; b. Perth Amboy, N.J., Nov. 2, 1937; d. William and Dotty (Finkel) Alper; m. Richard Leon Fricklas, Dec. 22, 1957; children: Michael, Kenneth, Susan. AD in Comml. Sci., Boston U., 1957; BBA, Upsala Coll., 1959; MA in Religion, Iliff Sch. of Theology, Denver, 1985. Reform Jewish Educator. Instr. Somerset County Coll., Somerville, N.J., 1970-72; dir. edn/programming Temple Sinai, Denver, 1973-90; prof. Iliff Sch. Theology, 1986—; cons. Nat. Assn. Temple Educators, 1982—. Author: chpt. Jewish Principal's Handbook, 1984. Exec. dir. Am. Jewish Com., 1990—; sec. Hunter Hill Homeowners Assn., Englewood, Colo., 1973-74. Recipient Disting. Leadership award, 1989-90. Mem. LWV (pres. Somerset County chpt. 1967, Bridgewater Twnship. chpt. 1968-70), Nat. Assn. Temple Educators (bd. dirs. 1987—), Jewish Educators Coun. of Denver (pres. 1984-88), Nat. Coun. Jewish Women, Hadassah, Assn. for Supervision and Curriculum Devel.

FRIDLEY, SAUNDRA LYNN, internal audit executive; b. Columbus, Ohio, June 14, 1948; d. Jerry Dean and Esther Eliza (Bluhm) F. BS, Franklin U., 1976; MBA, Golden Gate U., 1980. Accounts receivable supr. Internat. Harvester, Columbus, Ohio, San Leandro, Calif., 1972-80; sr. internal auditor Western Union, San Francisco, 1980; internal auditor II, County of Santa Clara, San Jose, Calif., 1980-82; sr. internal auditor Tymshare, Inc., Cupertino, Calif., 1982-84, div. contr., 1984; internal audit mgr. VWR Scientific, Brisbane, Calif., 1984-88, audit dir., 1988-89; internal audit mgr. Pacific IBM Employees Fed. Credit Union, San Jose, 1989-90, Western Temporary Svcs., Inc., Walnut Creek, Calif., 1990—; pres., founder Bay Area chpt. Cert. Fraud Examiners, 1990. Mem. NAFE, Friends of the Vineyards. Mem. Internal Auditors Speakers Bur., Cert. Fraud Examiners (founder, pres. Bay area chpt.), Inst. Internal Auditors (pres., founder Tri-Valley chpt.), Internal Auditor's Internat. Seminar Com. Avocations: woodworking, gardening, golfing. Home: 862 Bellflower St Livermore CA 94550 Office: Pacific IBM Employees Fed Credit Union 5615 Chesbro Ave San Jose CA 95123

FRIED, BRENDA LYNNE, product management executive; b. Balt., Nov. 6, 1956; d. Jerome and Rose (Miller) F. BA, U. Md., Balt., 1979. Instr. mktg., terr. mgr. Amoco Oil Co., Balt.; sales rep. institutional products Mobile Chem. Co., S.C.; market devel. mgr. Mobil Chem. Co., Frankfort, Ill., product mgr. Mem. NAFE. Office: 437 Center Rd Frankfort IL 60423

FRIED, JOANNE BETTE, nurse; b. Cleve., Aug. 26, 1955; d. Stanley Hillman and Winifred (Fox) F. Student, Vanderbilt U., 1973-75; BS in Nursing, U. So. Miss., 1978. RN, La. Nurse Ochsner Med. Found., New Orleans, 1978—. Bd. dirs. Congregation Gates of Prayer, Metairie, La., 1986—, exec. com., rec. sec., 1989-91; bd. dirs., sec. bd. dirs. Sisterhood, 1986-88, rec. sec., 1987-89, 2nd v.p., 1989—. Mem. NOW, Am. Nurses Assn., Assn. Operating Room Nurses (cert.), Nat. Assn. Orthopedic Nurses, Am. Assn. Critical Care Nurses, Soc. Peripheral Vascular Nursing, La. Nurses Assn., New Orleans Dist. Nurses Assn., Alumni Assn. U. So. Miss., Nat. Orgn. Women, Nat. Coun. Jewish Women, Southeastern Surg. Nurses Assn., Friends of Zoo, Friends of the Aquarium, Assn. Reformed Zionists of Am., New Orleans Mus. Art, B'nai B'rith Women. Democrat. Home: 4116 Fairfield St Metairie LA 70002 Office: Ochsner Med Found 1516 Jefferson Hwy New Orleans LA 70121

FRIED, KAREN JOAN, real estate broker; b. N.Y.C., Dec. 7, 1962; d. Raymond Ralph and Dorothy (Stricks) F. AB in Econs., Lafayette Coll., 1984. Intern Office of Bus. Liaison Dept. Commerce, Washington, 1983; intern Office Pub. Liaison The White House, Washington, 1983; v.p. Cross & Brown Co., N.Y.C., 1984-88, Peter R. Friedman, Ltd., N.Y.C., 1989—; broker Real Estate Bd. of N.Y. Sec. jr. com. Pub. Health Rsch. Inst., N.Y.C., 1989—; contbr. United Jewish Appeal, N.Y.C., 1987, 88, 89. Fellow Mus. Modern Art; mem. Mcpl. Arts Soc., N.Y. Road Runners Club, Triathalon Fedn. Republican. Office: Peter R Friedman Ltd 767 Fifth Ave New York NY 10153

FRIED, RONNEE, marketing research company executive; b. N.Y.C., Dec. 16, 1947; d. Phillip Frank Fried and Gloria Edith (Pfeffer) Sandow. B.A., George Washington U., 1969. Field dir. AHF Mktg. Research, N.Y.C., 1969-73; project dir. Decisions Ctr. Inc., N.Y.C., 1973-76, Ogilvy & Mather Advt., N.Y.C., 1977; assoc. group mgr. Data Devel. Corp., N.Y.C., 1977-81; ptnr., exec. v.p. Brown Koff & Fried Inc., N.Y.C., 1981—; dir. Wats Interviewing Network Inc., Rutherford, N.J. Mem. speakers bur. Greater N.Y. Conf. Soviet Jewry, 1979—. Mem. Am. Mktg. Assn. (Effie Awards Judging co-chmn. 1982, membership com. 1981, Recognition award 1982), Advt. Women N.Y. Jewish. Club: Tarrytown Group. Avocations: 1948 Chrysler New Yorker. Home: One Fifth Ave New York NY 10003 Office: Brown Koff & Fried Inc 14 W 23rd St New York NY 10010

FRIEDAN, BETTY, author, feminist leader; b. Peoria, Ill., Feb. 4, 1921; d. Harry and Miriam (Horwitz) Goldstein; m. Carl Friedan, June 1947 (div. May 1969); children—Daniel, Jonathan, Emily. AB summa cum laude, Smith Coll., 1942, LHD (hon.), 1975; LHD (hon.), SUNY, Stony Brook, 1985, Cooper Union, 1987. Research fellow U. Calif. at Berkeley, 1943; lectr. feminism univs., women's groups, bus. and profl. groups in U.S. and Europe; founder NOW, 1st pres., 1966-70, chairwoman adv. com., 1970-72, mem. bd. dirs. legal def. and edn. fund; organizer Nat. Women's Polit. Caucas, 1971, Internat. Feminist Congress, 1973, First Women's Bank, 1973, Econ. Think Tank for Women, 1974; v.p. Nat. Assn. Repeal Abortion Laws, 1970-73; Disting. vis. prof. sch. journalism and studies of women and men in soc., U. So. Calif., 1987; vis. prof. sociology Temple U., 1972, Queens Coll., 1975; vis. lectr. Calhoun Coll., fellow Yale U., 1974; lectr. New Sch. Social Research, N.Y.C., 1971; sr. research assoc. Ctr. Social Scis., Columbia U., N.Y.C., 1979-81; bd. dirs. NOW Legal Defense and Education fund; co-chmn. Nat. Comms. Women's Equality; del. White Ho. Conf. on Family, 1980; del. UN Decade for Women Confs. in Mexico City, Copenhagen, Nairobi; mem. LORAN Commn. Harvard Community Health Plan; vis. scholar U. S. Fla., Sarasota, 1985; Disting. vis. prof. Sch. Journalism and Social Work Sch. U. So. Calif. Author: The Feminine Mystique, 1963, It Changed My Life: Writings on the Women's Movement, 1976, The Second Stage, 1982, new edit., 1986; mem. editorial bd. Present Tense mag.; contbg. editor McCall's mag, 1971-74; contbr. Atlantic Monthly; contbr. articles to New York Times, Cosmopolitan, Saturday Rev., Family Circle, Good Housekeeping, and others; papers being collected by Schlesinger Libr. Harvard U. Mem. exec. com. Am. Jewish Congress, co-chair nat. commn. women's equality, 1984-85; mem. nat. bd. Girl Scouts USA, 1976-82; mem. N.Y. County Democratic Com. Recipient Humanist of Yr. award, 1975; Inst. Politics fellow Kennedy Sch. Govt., Harvard U., 1982, Mort Weisinger award for outstanding mag. journalism Am. Soc. Journalists and Authors, 1979; named Author of Yr. Am. Soc. Journalists and Authors, 1982; Research fellow Ctr. Population Studies, Harvard U., 1982-83, Chubb fellow Yale U., 1985, Andrus Ctr. Gerontology fellow U. So. Calif., 1986. Mem. AFTRA, Author's Guild, PEN, Women's Ink, Women's Forum, Mag. Writers, Am. Soc. Journalists and Authors (Mort Weisinger award 1979, Author of Yr. 1982), Assn. Humanistic Psychology, Am. Sociology Assn., Gerontol. Soc. Am., Coffee House, Phi Beta Kappa. Address: 1 Lincoln Pl #40K New York NY 10023

FRIEDENBERG, KAREN ROSEN, real estate executive; b. Savannah, Ga., May 3, 1949; d. Emanuel F. and Thelma Z. (Reed) Rosen; 1 child, Jodi. BS in Mass Communications, Emerson Coll., 1971; student U. N.C., summer 1968, Harvard U., summer 1967, U. Ga., 1967-69. Exec. trainee Jordan Marsh, Boston, 1974-76; broadcast dir. Rich's, Atlanta, 1976-78; mktg. dir. Northlake Mall, Atlanta, 1978-80, Lenox Square, Atlanta, 1980-82; retail leasing assoc. Trammell Crow Co., Atlanta, 1982-85, Kern & Co., Atlanta, 1985-86, Retail Properties Group, 1986-89; mng. dir. Retail Realty Advisors, 1989—. Bd. dirs. Atlanta chpt. Nat. Coun. Jewish Women; patron High Mus. Art; mem. Temple Sinai. Mem. Internat. Coun. Shopping Ctrs., Atlanta Bd. Realtors, Comml. Real Estate Women, Midtown Bus. Assn., Buckhead Bus. Assn., Hadassah. Republican. Jewish. Avocations: aerobics, bicycling, hiking, rafting. Home: Four Pendleton Pl Atlanta GA 30342

FRIEDLAND, BILLIE LOUISE, human services administrator; b. Los Alamos, New Mex., Jan. 6, 1944; d. William Jerald and Harriet Virginia (Short) Van Buskirk; m. David Friedland. BS in Edn., Calif. U. of Pa., 1972, MS in Psychology, 1986. Sales mgr., buyer Friedland's Ladies Ready-To-Wear, Monessen, Pa., 1969-72; tchr. Belle Vernon (Pa.) Area Schs., 1973-74; head social scis. dept. Yeshiva Achei Tmimim, Pitts., 1974-75; caseworker Fayette County Mental Health and Mental Retardation Clinic, Uniontown, Pa., 1975; ctr. supr. Fayette County Mental Health and Mental Retardation Clinic, Uniontown, 1976; case mgr., family support svcs. coord. Diverified Human Services Inc., Monessen, 1978-89; founded first Infant/Toddler Day Care Project, Fayette County, 1976-78. Mem. NAACP, Nat. Assn. Dual Diagnoses, Pa. Conf. on Black Basic Edn. Office: Diversified Human Svcs Eastgate #8 Monessen PA 15062

FRIEDLANDER, MYRNA LOIS, psychologist; b. Washington, Dec. 10, 1947; d. Leon Herbert and Ada (Slater) F.; 1 child, Lee Kara. BA cum laude, Case Western Res. U., 1969; MA, George Washington U., 1978; PhD, Ohio State U., 1980. Lic. psychologist, N.Y. Assoc. prof. SUNY, Albany, 1981—; clin. adj. asst. prof. Albany Med. Coll., 1984—. Contbr. articles to profl. jours. Fellow Am. Psychol. Soc., Am. Psychol. Assn. Democrat. Jewish. Office: SUNY 1400 Washington Ave Albany NY 12222

FRIEDLANDER, PATRICIA ANN, marketing executive; b. Chgo., May 9, 1944; d. James Farrell and Therese Mary (Pfeiler) Crotty; m. Daniel B. Friedlander, July 3, 1971 (div. Apr. 1978); children: Michael Derek, David Colin. BA, Cardinal Stritch Coll., 1966; MA, U. Wis., Milw., 1968; postgrad., U. Chgo., 1968-69, U. London, 1968—. Instr. U. Wis., Milw., 1966-68, Chgo. State U., 1968-71, Argo Community High Sch., Summit, Ill., 1971-73, Park Dist., Park Forest South, Ill., 1973-77; counselor Will County Mental Health Clinic, Park Forest South, 1977-78; sales rep. Prentice-Hall, Inc., Englewood Cliffs, N.J., 1978-84; nat. sales mgr. Dow Jones-Irwin, Homewood, Ill., 1984-87; dir. mktg. Nat. Textbook Co., Lincolnwood, Ill., 1987-88; mgr. mktg. Scott Foresman & Co., Glenview, Ill., 1988-90; corp. advt. dir. Giltspur, Inc., Itasca, Ill., 1990—; dir. Printer's Row Bookfair, Chgo., 1985; pub. cons.; speaker in field. V.p. Townhome Assn., Park Forest South, 1978; den mother Cub Scouts Am., Park Forest South, 1981-84. Mem. Am. Book Travelers, Midwest Book Travelers (pres. 1983-87), Chgo. Book Clinic, Lincoln Park Zool. Assn. (life). Home: 2320 W Farwell Chicago IL 60645 Office: Giltspur Inc 500 Park Blvd Itasca IL 60143

FRIEDMAN, BARBARA GLATT, clinical mental health counselor; b. Newark, May 13, 1937; d. Ben Harry and Sadie (Gudis) Glatt; m. Bernard Friedman, June 11, 1955 (dec.); children: Barry Jay, Ronnie Mark, Mitchell Ira. BA, Edison State Coll., 1979; postgrad., Trenton State Coll., 1979-80; MS, U. Pa., 1982; PhD SW U., 1988. Cert. profl. counselor, Md. clin. hypnotherapist, mental health counselor, N.J., Md. Counselor Am. Youth Crisis Ctr., Oberursel, Fed. Republic of Germany, 1972-74; career counselor Vol. Employment Svc. Team, Camden County, N.J., 1977-79; counselor Glassboro (N.J.) State Coll. Counseling Ctr., also cons.; pvt. practice psychology, Cherry Hill, N.J., 1980—; tchr. adult edn., 1982—; assoc. Ednl. Info. Resource Ctr., Sewell, N.J., 1987—; cons., psychol. counselor Together, Inc., Glassboro, 1983—; bd. dir.-founder Alts. in Direction, 1983; workshop facilitator; guest lectr. in field. Mem. Parents' Campaign for Handicapped Children and Youth; bd. dirs. Frankfurt (Fed. Republic of Germany) Am. Jewish Community Chapel, 1969-72. Recipient cert. of recognition, Oberursel, 1973, presdl. cert. of honor Camden County Coll., 1978. Mem. Nat. Bd. Cert. Counselors, Am. Assn. Counseling and Devel., Am. Mental Health Counselors Assn. (holistic counseling spl. interest network), N.J. Mental Health Counselors Assn., Nat. Acad. Cert. Clin. Mental Health Counselors (cert.), Am. Guild Hypnotherapists (registered), N.J. Mental Health Counselors Assn., N.J. Profl. Counselors Assn., N.J. Career Devel. Assn., Arthritis Found., Cherry Hill C. of C. (chmn. edn. com. 1984-88, mem. speakers bur. 1985—, cert. of recognition 1985), N.J. Career Devel. Assn., Small Bus. Coun., N.J. Assn. Women Bus. Owners. Home: 16 Dartmouth Rd Cherry Hill NJ 08034 Office: 883 Cooper Landing Rd Ste 131 Cherry Hill NJ 08002

FRIEDMAN, DARLENE, communications executive, educator; b. Pitts., Sept. 2, 1955; d. Howard J. and Beverly Jean (Scharf) F. BA in Edn., U. Pitts., 1978; MA in Journalism, Temple U., 1983; postgrad., Temple U. Law Sch., 1989—. Cert. secondary edn. tchr., Pa. Tchr. English Northley Jr. High Sch., Aston, Pa., 1979, Unionville (Pa.) Middle Sch., 1979-80, O'Hara Jr. High Sch., Fox Chapel, Pa., 1980; editor Commonwealth Land Title Ins. Co., Phila., 1984-86; dir. communications Soroptimist Internat., Phila., 1986—. Mem. World Affairs Coun., Amnesty Internat., Greenpeace. Democrat. Jewish. Home: 7227 Brent Rd Upper Darby PA 19082 Office: Soroptimist Internat 1616 Walnut St Philadelphia PA 19013

FRIEDMAN, ELLEN G., English educator; b. Frunze, USSR, July 20, 1944; came to U.S., 1950; d. Jack and Lola (Freedman) Glazer; m. Max Friedman, Jan. 23, 1965;. BA, L.I. U., Bklyn., 1966; MA, CUNY, 1972; PhD, NYU, 1978. Prof. English Trenton (N.J.) State Coll., 1978—; dir. writing, women's studies Trenton State Coll., 1980—. Author: Joyce Carol Oates 1980; editor, contbr. Joan Didion 1984, Breaking The Sequence 1989; contbr. articles to profl. jours. Mem. AAUW, Modern Lang. Assn., NE Modern Lang. Assn. Office: Trenton State Coll English Dept Hillwood Lakes CN4700 Trenton NJ 08650

FRIEDMAN, FRANCES, public relations firm executive; b. N.Y.C., Apr. 8, 1928; d. Aaron and Bertha (Itzkowitz) Fallick; m. Clifford Jerome Friedman, June 17, 1950; children—Kenneth Lee, Jeffrey Bennett. B.B.A., CCNY, 1948. Dir. pub. relations Melia Internat., Madrid, N.Y.C., 1971-73; sr. v.p. Lobsenz-Stevens, N.Y.C., 1973-75; exec. v.p. Howard Rubenstein Assocs., N.Y.C., 1975-83; pres., prin. Frances Friedman Assocs., N.Y.C., 1983-84; pres., chmn. bd. dirs. GCI Group Inc., N.Y.C., 1984—. Bd. dirs. ACRMD-Retarded Children, N.Y.C., 1983-85, City Coll. Fund, N.Y.C., 1970-79; mem. adv. bd. League for Parent Edn., N.Y.C., 1961-65; editor South Shore Democratic Newsletter, North Bellmore, N.Y., 1958-61, press sec. N.Y. State Assembly candidate, 1965, N.Y. State Congl. candidate, 1968; officer Manhasset Dem. Club, N.Y., 1965-69; mem. adv. com. N.Y.C. Council candidate, 1985. Mem. Pub. Relations Soc. Am., Women in Communications (Matrix award for pub. relations 1989), The Counselors Acad., Pride and Alarm, City Club N.Y. Democrat. Jewish. Home: 860 Fifth Ave New York NY 10021 Office: GCI Group Inc 777 Third Ave New York NY 10017

FRIEDMAN, FREDRICA SCHWAB, editor, publisher; b. N.Y.C., Aug. 29, 1939; d. Joseph H. and Ruth (Landis) Schwab; m. Stephen J. Friedman, June 25, 1961; children: Vanessa V., Alexander S. BA, Vassar Coll., 1961; MA, Columbia U., 1963. Assoc. articles editor Holiday Mag., N.Y.C., 1966-68; contributing editor Travel & Leisure Mag., N.Y.C., 1969-70; editorial cons. Saturday Rev. Mag., N.Y.C., 1971-74; sr. editor Reader's Digest Press, N.Y.C., 1974-77; sr. staff editor Reader's Digest Condensed Books, N.Y.C., 1977-84; sr. editor Little, Brown & Co., N.Y.C., 1985-88, exec. editor, assoc. pub., v.p., 1988—. Mem. Women's Forum, Women's Media Group, The Peer Group. Home: 1185 Park Ave New York NY 10128 Office: Little Brown & Co 205 Lexington Ave New York NY 10016

FRIEDMAN, JUDITH BRYNA, corporate communications executive; b. Yonkers, N.Y., July 11, 1950; d. Gerald A. and Mildred A. Friedman. BA, Pa. State U., 1971; cert. in spl. studies, Harvard U., 1991. Assoc. TV producer WCVB-TV, Needham, Mass.; TV producer WBZ-TV, Boston; advt. mgr. Dayton's, N.Y.C.; tng. cons. The Travelers, Hartford, Conn.; sales promotion officer, ltd. prin. Conn. Mut. Fin. Svcs., Hartford; dir. corp. communicatons Richard Roberts Group, Avon, Conn.; dir. corp. communication MetLife-State St. Investment Svcs., Boston; v.p., mgr. editorial and creative svcs. The Putnam Cos., Boston. Active Jewish Big Bros. and Big Sisters, Jewish Family Svcs.; bd. dirs. ROFEH Internat. Address: 33 Sleeper St Unit 407 Boston MA 02210

FRIEDMAN, L. JEANNE, computer company executive; b. N.Y., Mar. 4, 1951; d. Samuel and Sylvia Friedman. BA, Brandeis U., Waltham, Mass., 1973; MBA, Harvard U., 1983. Programmer Nixdorf Computer, Irvington, N.J., 1973-74; systems analyst Consolidated Edison, N.Y., 1974-77; sr. cons. Amdahl Corp., Sunnyvale, Calif., 1978-81; dir. Wang Lab., Lowell, Mass., 1985—. Author: Design Review for a Database Enviroment, 1981. Mem.

South End Hist. Soc., Brandeis Alumni Assn., Harvard Bus. Sch. Assn. Office: Wang Lab Inc 1 Indsl Ave Lowell MA 01851

FRIEDMAN, LESLEY, temporary personnel agency executive, entrepreneur; b. Dayton, Ohio, Dec. 1, 1953; d. Howard I. and Wilma (Mann) F. BA magna cum laude, Mt. Holyoke Coll., 1975; JD, NYU, 1985. Bar: N.Y. Atty. Reavis and McGrath, N.Y.C., 1985-87; pres., chief exec. officer Spl. Counsel, Inc., N.Y.C., 1987—. Mem. Am. Bar Assn., N.Y. Women's Bar Assn., Assn. Bar City N.Y., Am. Jewish Com., U. Club (N.Y.). Office: Spl Coun Inc 19 W 34th St Ste 1018 New York NY 10001

FRIEDMAN, MARIA ANDRE, public relations executive; b. Jackson, Mich., June 12, 1950; d. Robert Andre and Mary MacLean (Thompson) Hoving; m. Stanley N. Friedman, July 22, 1973; children: Alexandra, Adam. B.A. cum laude, U. Md., 1972, M.A., 1979; postgrad., Nova U., 1987—. Writer, U.S. Bur. Mines, Washington, 1973-78; head writer Nat. Ctr. for Health Svc. Rsch. and Health Care Tech. Assessment, DHHS, Rockville, Md., 1978-85, chief publs. and info. br. Agy for Health Care Policy and Rsch., 1986-89; dir. Office Pub. Affairs Health Care Fin. Adminstrn., Washington, 1990—; pres. Medi-Systems, Inc., Silver Spring, Md., 1980—; v.p. Metro Med. Assocs., Silver Spring, 1982—, MediSystems Fin. Services, 1984—. Mem. Nat. Assn. Govt. Communicators, Acad. of Mgmt. Home: 12535 Heurich Rd Silver Spring MD 20902 Office: Health Care Fin Adminstrn 200 Independence Ave SW H Hubert Humphrey Bldg Rm 435 Washington DC 20201

FRIEDMAN, MARNA WENDY, marketing consultant; b. Pequannock, N.J., Jan. 13, 1959; d. Harold and Marcia Ruth (Nyman) F. Student, Fairleigh Dickinson U., 1977-78; BS, C.W. Post Coll., Greenvale, N.Y., 1981; MA, New Sch. Social Research, N.Y.C., 1986. Mgr. sales Macy's Dept. Store, N.Y.C., 1981-82; traffic coordinator Direct Mktg. Agy., Stamford, Conn., 1982-83; prodn. coordinator The N.Y. Community Trust, N.Y.C., 1983-86; mktg. cons. MWF, Ewing, N.J., 1986—; asst. prof. Mercer County Community Coll., West Windsor, N.J.; pres., bd. dirs. Baby Basket Co., Ltd., Ewing, 1986-89; cons. Friedman Enterprises, Ewing, 1978—, Feraioli, Wesdyk & Freifeld, Prompton Lakes, N.J., 1984-85, Helene Fuld Med. Ctr., Trenton, N.J., 1988-89. Pub. info. officer Fedn. Protestant Welfare Agys., Inc., N.Y.C., 1987—, Jr. Assocs. Com.; mem. com. Morris County Dem., Montville, 1983-84; mem. Nat. Dem. Com., Washington, 1983—. Mem. Women in Communications (edn. com.), Community Agys. Pub. Relations Assn., Internat. Communications Assn., Community Agys., Pub. Relations Assn., Am. Mktg. Assn., Am. Women Entrepreneurs. Jewish. Avocations: music, travel, gourmet cooking, calligraphy. Home: 1 Cromwell Ct Ewing NJ 08628 Office: 3 Ronit Dr Ewing NJ 08628

FRIEDMAN, PENNY, real estate portfolio manager, lawyer; b. Cleve., Dec. 24, 1951; d. Harold Emanuel and Ruth (Resnick) F.; m. Daniel Joseph Hoffheimer, June 7, 1981; children: Rachel, Leah. AB in Econs. with high honors, U. Mich., 1973, JD cum laude, 1977. Bar: Ohio 1977. Atty. Taft, Stettinius & Hollister, Cin., 1977-80; v.p. property devel. Gt. Am. Broadcasting Co. (formerly Taft Broadcasting Co.), Cin., 1980-88; real estate portfolio mgr. Bartlett & Co., Cin., 1988—. V.p. Leadership Cin. Alumni Assn., 1987-89; pres. Family Svc. Cin. Area, 1988—, v.p., 1985-88, trustee, 1979—; vice chmn. Cin. Devel. Fund, 1988—; bd. dirs. Cin. Ctr. for Devel. Disorder, 1979-85, Seven Hills Neighborhood Houses, 1981-86; trustee Devel. Corp. for Cin., 1989—. Named one of Outstanding Young Women in Am., 1988. Mem. Ohio State Bar Assn., Cin. Bar Assn., Urban Land Inst., Phi Beta Kappa. Office: Bartlett & Co 36 E 4th St Cincinnati OH 45202

FRIEDMAN, SUE TYLER, technical publications executive; b. Nürnberg, Germany, Feb. 28, 1925; came to U.S., 1938; d. William and Ann (Federlein) Tyler (Theilheimer); m. Gerald Manfred Friedman, June 27, 1948; children: Judith Fay Friedman Rosen, Sharon Mira Friedman Azaria, Devora Paula Friedman Zweibach, Eva Jane Friedman Scholle, Wendy Tamar Friedman Spanier. Student, Beth Israel Sch. Nursing, 1941-43. Exec. dir. Ventures and Publs. of Gerald M. Friedman, 1964—; owner Tyler Publs., Watervliet and Troy, N.Y., 1978-86; treas., dir. Northeastern Sci. Found., Inc., Troy, 1979—; treas. Gerry Exploration, Inc., Troy, 1982—; office mgr. Rensselaer Ctr. Applied Geology, Troy, 1983—. Pres. Pioneer Women/Na'amat, Tulsa, 1961-64, treas., Jerusalem, Israel, 1964, pres., Albany, N.Y., 1968-70; bd. dirs. Temple Beth-El, 1965—, dir. Hebrew Sch., 1965-80. Named hon. alumna Dept. Geology, Bklyn. Coll. at CUNY, 1989; Sue Tyler Friedman medal for distinction in history of geology created in her honor, Geol. Soc. London, 1988. Mem. Geology Alumni Assn. (hon.). Jewish. Home: 32 24th St Troy NY 12180 Office: Rensselaer Ctr Applied Geology 15 3d St Box 746 Troy NY 12181

FRIEDMAN, SUSAN LYNN BELL, public relations specialist; b. Lafayette, Ind., May 23, 1953; d. Virgil Atwood and Jean Loree (Wiggins) B.; m. Frank H. Friedman, July 31, 1976; 1 child, Alex Charles. B.A., Purdue U., 1975; M.S., Ind. State U., 1981. Asst. dir. pub. relations Vincennes U. Jr. Coll., Ind., 1977-83; dir. Knox County C. of C., Vincennes, 1983-84; writer/editor VSE Corp., Alexandria, Va., 1984-85; asst. to pres. Am. Assn. Community and Jr. Colls., Washington, 1985-87; owner/pres. SBF Promotions, 1987—; mgr., program developer Family Resources, Inc., 1988—; partnership coord. Beaufort (S.C.) County Sch. Dist., 1989—; cons., 1982-84; mem. Tech. Coll. of the Lowcountry (S.C.) Found. Bd. dirs., 1987—; Knox County chpt. Am. Heart Assn., 1982-84; mem. exec. bd. Leadership Vincennes, 1982-84; Hoosier scholar, 1971, 72; pres. Annandale BPW, 1987-88, bd. dirs. Beaufort-Jasper Comprehensive Health Services, Inc. Mem. Am. Assn. Women in Community and Jr. Colls. (nat. liaison 1985-87), LWV (chpt. v.p. 1982-84), Leadership Beaufort, Bus. and Profl. Women, Zonta Beaufort, Am. Civil Liberties Union. Democrat. Home: 41 Wade Hampton Dr Beaufort SC 29902

FRIEDMANN, EMILY MACCARO, accountant, company executive; b. N.Y.C., Nov. 9, 1949; d. William Anthony and Katherine Gladys (Butzgy) Maccaro; m. James Bernard Friedmann, Nov. 11, 1978; children—Katherine, Margaret. B.S., Syracuse U., 1971. Cost acct. Automatic Connectors, Commack, N.Y., 1971-76; sr. cost analyst Standard Brands, N.Y.C., 1976-77; asst. controller So. Calif. Carton, Gardena, 1977-79; mgr. fin. planning Dynachem Corp., Tustin, Calif., 1979-84; mgr. cost acctg. Targeted Coverage Inc., Glendora, Calif. Republican. Roman Catholic. Home: 716 Big Falls Dr Diamond Bar CA 91765 Office: 533 W Foothill Blvd Glendora CA 91740

FRIEDMANN, ROSELI OCAMPO, microbiologist, educator; b. Manila, Nov. 23, 1937; came to U.S., 1968; d. Eliseo Amio and Generosa (Campana) Ocampo; m. Emerich Imre Friedmann ; children: Maria Roseli, Rodolfo. BSc in Botany, U. Philippines, 1958; MSc in Biology, Hebrew U. of Jerusalem, 1966; PhD in Biology, Fla. State U., 1973. Rsch. assoc. Inst. Sci. and Tech., Manila, 1958-67; rsch. asst. Queen's U., Kingston, Ont., Can., 1967-68; teaching asst. Fla. State U., Tallahassee, 1968-73, rsch. assoc., 1973—; asst. prof. dept. biology Fla. A&M U., Tallahassee, 1975-84, assoc. prof., 1984-87, prof., 1987—. Contbr. articles to sci. jours. Recipient Resolution of Commendation, State of Fla., Tallahassee, 1978, Antarctic Svc. medal U.S. Congress, Tallahassee, 1981. Mem. Soc. Phycologique France, Phycological Soc. Am., Planetary Soc., AAAS, U.S. Fedn. Culture Collections, Am. Soc. Microbiology, Assn. Women in Sci., Sigma Xi. Office: Fla A&M U Martin Luther King Blvd Tallahassee FL 32307

FRIEDRICH, GLORIA JOY, school psychologist; b. Chgo., Feb. 20, 1936; d. George Anthony and Veronica Barbara K.; m. Robert, June 5, 1954; children: Christopher Lee, Jonathan Drew, James Todd. AA, Coll. of DuPage, Glen Ellyn, Ill., 1971; BA, Nat. Coll. of Edn., Evanston, Ill., 1982, MS in Edn., 1987; EdS, Nat. Coll. of Edn., 1990. Sch. Psychologist and Early Childhood Spl. Edn. Tchr. Tchr. St. John Luth., Darien, Ill., 1971-85, dir. Pre-Sch., 1972-85; sch. psychologist Community Unit Sch. Dist. 303, St. Charles, Ill., 1987—. Pres. LWV, Oak Lawn, Ill., 1961-62, DuPage County election judge, 1968-89; fellow Nat. Coll. Edn.; active Early Childhood Adv. Bd. Elmhurst (Ill.) Coll. Mem. Nat. Assn. of Sch. Psychologists, Ill. Sch. Psychologist Assn., West Suburban Sch. Psychologist Assn. (pres. 1990-91), DuPage Regional Unit of Chgo. Assn., Phi Delta Kappa. Lutheran. Office: Community Unit Sch Dist 303 201 S 7th St Saint Charles IL 60174

FRIEDRICH, MARGRET COHEN, guidance and student assistance counselor; b. Balt., June 4, 1947; d. Joseph Cohen and Judith (Kline) Cohen Roisman; m. Jay Joseph Friedrich, May 16, 1971; children: David Benjamin, Marc Adam, Samantha Lauren. B.Ed., U. Miami-Fla., 1969, M.Ed., 1970. Cert. alcoholism and addiction counselor. Grad. asst. U. Miami, Coral Gables, Fla., 1969-70; tchr. Balt. Bd. Edn., 1970; guidance counselor Ridgewood Bd. Edn., N.J., 1970—; student assistance counselor, 1986—, chmn. student assistance com., 1986—; alcoholism counselor Bergen County Dept. Health, Paramus, N.J., 1981-82; in-service tchr. Ridgewood Bd. Edn., 1983, supr., coordinator peer counseling program high sch., 1979—; with Assn. Mental Health and Counseling of No. N.J., 1985—; cons. N.J. Student Assistance Program, student asst. cons. N.J. Dept. Edn., chmn. student asst. com. Author tech. papers. Exec. bd. Hadassah, Ridgewood-Glen Rock, N.J., 1971—; youth leadership com. United Jewish Appeal, Bergen County, 1974-75; sec. Bergen County Youth Com. Substance Abuse, Paramus, 1980—, conf. coord. com., 1983; treas. Ridgewood Coalition Substance Use and Abuse, 1983-84, Ridgewood Substance Abuse Prevention Commn., 1989—; participant Pres.'s Drug-Free Am.; faciliatator Gov.'s N.J. Drug-Free TeleConf.; co-chmn. fundraiser, treas. United Parents/Safe Homes, Ridgewood, 1984; lectr./educator Passaic County Juvenile Conf. Com., Paterson, N.J., 1984. Reisman scholar, 1969; U. Miami teaching asst., 1970, recipient Recognition award, 1968. Mem. N.J. Assn. Alcoholism Counselors, Nat. Assn. Suicidology, N.J. Edn. Assn., Ridgewood Edn. Assn., Bergen County Edn. Assn., N.J. Task Force on Women and Alcohol, N.J. Personnel and Guidance Assn., Sigma Delta Tau. (exec. bd. 1965-69). Democrat. Jewish. Office: Ridgewood High Sch Ridgewood NJ 07451

FRIEDRICH, ROSE MARIE, travel agency executive; b. Chgo., May 17, 1941; d. Theodore A. and Ann Bernadine (Coppoth) Dlugosz; m. Gerhard K. Friedrich, Apr. 18, 1964; 1 child, Alan C. Student, Roosevelt U., 1986—. Cert. travel agt. Travel cons. Chgo. Motor Club, 1959, Drake Travel, Chgo., 1960-65; mgr. 1st Nat. Travel, Arlington Heights, Ill., 1969-71, Total Travel, Palatine, Ill., 1971-76; owner, pres. Travel Bug Ltd., Lake Zurich, Ill., 1977-89; owner Travel Edn. Concepts, Inc., Palatine, Ill., 1987—, Am. Inst. Travel, Inc., Lake Zurich, Ill., 1987—, Group Travel Specialists, Inc., Lake Zurich, 1988—; prin. Group Travel Specialists, Inc., 1988—; advisor Coll. Lake County, Grayslake, Ill., 1985—. Author: (books) Travel Career Textbook, 1980, Guide to Tour Organizing, 1984, Build Profits Through Group Travel, 1984, Independent Travel Agent, 1986. Mem. Inst. Cert. Travel Cons. (chmn. edn. forum 1981-84, appreciation award 1984), Soc. Travel and Tourism Educators, State of Ill. Council Vocat. Edn. (mem. Career Guidance Consortium, Appreciation award 1986), Lake Zurich C. of C. (pres. 1984-85). Republican. Roman Catholic. Home: 407 E Knob Hill Dr Arlington Heights IL 60004 Office: Group Travel Specialists Inc 2070 N Rand Rd Palatine IL 60074

FRIEDRICH-PATTERSON, EVELYN BETH, banker; b. Phila., Nov. 14, 1953; d. Robert E. and Judith Evelyn (Redowitz) Friedrich; m. C. William Patterson II, June 17, 1978; children: William Friedrich, Laura Sophia. Student, U. Southampton (Eng.), 1973-74; BA, Beaver Coll., 1975. Legal asst. Finley Kumble Wagner et al, N.Y.C., 1975-78; trust officer 1st Fidelity Bank-N.J., Newark, 1978-79; sr. v.p. U.S. Trust Co. N.Y., N.Y.C., 1979-90; pres. personal asset mgmt. Evans and Moxon Capital Mgmt., Inc., Yardley, Pa., 1990—; cons. C.W. Patterson Sales & Cons. Co., Yardley, Pa., 1980—. Republican. Office: Evans & Moxon Capital Mgmt Inc 33 S Delaware Ave Yardley PA 19067

FRIEL, PATRICIA ELIZABETH, speech educator, drama educator; b. Zanesville, Ohio, Sept. 25, 1956; d. Roy Henry and Martha Jane (MacMichael) F. BA in Speech Communication & French, U. Cin., 1978, MA in Speech Communication Arts, 1979; teaching cert., Xavier U., 1984-85; 2 yr. acting program, Neighborhood Playhouse, N.Y.C., 1980-82. Secondary teaching cert. in speech. French tutor U. Cin., 1975-78; rsch. asst. Renatus Hartogs, M.D., N.Y.C., 1980-81; word processor, adminstrv. asst. Merrill Lynch, Pierce, Fenner & Smith, Inc., N.Y.C., 1981-83; lectr. in speech U. Cin., 1983-86; instr. in speech and drama U. Cin., Clermont Coll., Batavia, Coll., 1986—; theatre dir. U. Cin., Clermont Coll., Batavia, 1987—, auditorium improvement project dir., 1987—, speech/drama club advisor, 1987—, speech/drama area coord., 1987—, arts series coord., 1986-87; cons. Plaza Dermatology Assocs., N.Y.C., 1982; communication cons. Randell-Heiken, Inc., N.Y.C., 1983; market rsch. cons. The Data Group, Inc., Cin., 1983; security cons. Honeywell, Inc., Cin., 1984; speaker Univ. Cin. and Women in Communications, Inc. Speakers Bureau, Cin., 1987—; asst. coord. radio scriptwriting workshop, Introductory Radio Writing and Performance Workshop, 1990; chair of com. course devel., Interdisciplinary Interpersonal Communication, 1990. Co-author: (musical play) The Circus of Life, 1979; author: (diagnostic instrument) Developing a Diagnostic Instrument for Communication Anxieties, 1990. Judge Greater Cin. Assn. Community Theatres, Cin., 1987—; bd. mem. So. Ohio Arts Region, Bethel, Ohio, 1988-89, sec. 1989. Grantee Univ. Cin. Ednl. Rsch. Coun., Cin., 1989, Ohio Arts Coun., Columbus, Ohio, 1987-88; recipient prominent alumni award Univ. Cin. Communication Arts Dept., Cin., 1989. Mem. Women in Communications Inc. (cons. 1989-90, bd. mem. 1990-91), Speech Communication Assn., Southeastern Theatre Conf., Ohio Theatre Alliance, Am. Forensic Assn., Clermont Coll. Arts Adv. Coun. (chair 1986-88), Am. Soc. for Tng. and Devel., Phi Beta Kappa, Delta Sigma Rho, Tau Kappa Alpha. Republican. Methodist. Office: Univ Cin Clermont Coll 725 College Dr Batavia OH 45103

FRIELAND, ALYCE, financial executive; b. Bklyn., May 2, 1943; d. Aaron and Sarah Estelle (Rothman) Finkelstein; m. Harry Frieland, Mar. 6, 1942; children: Jamie, Cortnie. Student, NYU, 1961-63. Sales mgr. Malom Lingerie, N.Y.C., 1962-66; sales coord. Sherman Underwear, N.Y.C., 1966-71; pub. rels. cons. Espon, Fla., 1977; organizer press confs. Fla., 1977—; pres., fin. planner Greenbelt Equities, Inc., N.Y.C., 1982-84; archtl. planner, developer, pres. Kasday Design, N.Y.C., 1977-87; pres., syndicator, developer, mgr. M & M Mgmt. Corp., Coconut Grove, Fla., 1985—; asst. chef to Isabelle Marique, N.Y.C., Albert Jorant, Paris; founder Psychic Life Counselling, Fla., 1990—. Office: M & M Mgmt Corp 2 Grove Isle Dr #1807 Coconut Grove FL 33133 also: 500 E 77th St Ste 519 New York NY 10021

FRIEMAN, HILDEGARDE, special education teacher, consultant, diagnostician; b. Balt., Jan. 11, 1948; d. Maurice and Ethel (Belson) F. BS, U. Md., 1970; MS, Johns Hopkins U., 1975, cert. advanced standing in edn., 1976; cert. minimum brain dysfunction, Temple U., 1976. Cert. spl. educator. Spl. educator Balt. City Schs., 1970—; mem. Council Exception Edn., Balt., 1970—; cons. Spl. Olympics, Balt., 1983—, also city and state legislatures and dels., 1980—. Guest lectr. Sta. WEAA-Radio, Morgan State U., 1980. Recipient resolution for outstanding work Balt. City Council, 1982, cert. of merit Parents Tchrs. Adv. Council Balt. City Schs., 1974-75. Mem. NEA, Balt. Tchr. Union, Phi Lambda Theta. Democrat. Avocations: music, theater, exercise. Home: 117 B Cross Keys Rd Baltimore MD 21210

FRIEND, MIRIAM RUTH, personnel company executive; b. Scranton, Pa., May 19, 1925; d. Benjamin and Etta (Weiss) Loewy; m. Sidney Friend, Aug. 27, 1950. BA, Syracuse U., 1947; cert., Inst. Pub. Welfare Tng. Cornell U., 1950. Social worker Child Placement div. N.Y. State Dept. Welfare, Binghamton and Ithaca, 1948-52; v.p. Office Help Temps., Yonkers, N.Y., 1954-83; pres. Friend & Friend Personnel Agy., Yonkers, N.Y., 1985—. Mem. Eliz Seton Coll. Adv. Council; pres. Pvt. Industry Council, Yonkers, 1981-82, Yonkers Gen. Hosp. Aux., 1983-84, Big Bros./Big Sisters, Yonkers, 1978-80; bd. dirs. Salvation Army, Yonkers, 1977—; publicity chmn. Sen. John E. Flynn Salute, 1986; chmn. breakfast com. Yonkers C. of C., 1978; chmn. Work Opportunities Referral for Kids; chmn.; bd. mem. Community Planning Council; trustee Yonkers Gen. Hosp., 1978—. Recipient Disting. Service award United Way, 1983, Community Service award Yonkers Council of Chs., 1984, Woman in Bus. award YWCA, 1986; named Pioneer of Industry Ind. Office Services, Hilton Head, S.C., 1984. Mem. Assn. Bus. Profl. Women, Psi Chi. Clubs: Racquet, Amackassin (Yonkers). Lodge: Soroptimists (pres. 1970-72), Rotary. Home: 11 Abbey Pl Yonkers NY 10701 Office: Friend & Friend Personnel Agy 480 N Broadway Yonkers NY 10701

FRIER, SHARON BOATWRIGHT, music educator, pianist; b. Valdosta, Ga., Feb. 24, 1942; d. Clifford Eugene and Margaret Louise (Shaw) B.; divorced; children: Laurie Lancaster Swift, John Kevin Lancaster; m. Archie A. Frier. AB in Music, Valdosta State Coll., 1963; MA in Edn., Ea. Ky. U., 1973; cert. Yamaha Music Schs. Am., 1976. Instr. Cumberland Coll., Williamsburg, Ky., 1971-75; dir. music 1st Bapt. Ch., Williamsburg, 1973-75; owner, dir. Music Lab., Valdosta, Ga., 1976-85; instr. music Valdosta State Coll., 1977-85, Troy State U., Moody AFB, 1984-87; pianist Lee St. Bapt. Ch., Valdosta, 1984-87; music specialist Park Ave. Bapt. Sch., Titusville, Fla., 1987-88; owner Frier Enterprises, 1987-88; instl. counselor Dept. Corrections, 1988—; pianist First Bapt. Ch. Titusville, 1988-89; lit. meet adjudicator Southeastern Assn. Ind. Schs., 1982, 84. Precinct committee woman Rep. Named to Outstanding Young Women Am., U.S. Jaycees, 1974. Mem. Music Tchrs. Nat. Assn., Fla. Music Tchrs. Assn. (cert., v.p. publicity and editor newsletter 1981-82), South Ga. Music Tchrs. Assn. (pres. 1978-79), Sigma Alpha Chi, Alpha Chi. Avocations: reading, gardening. Home: PO Box 6061 Titusville GA 32782

FRIERY, DONNA ELIZABETH, electrical engineer, marketing professional; b. Framingham, Mass., Mar. 25, 1957; d. James Russell and Josephine Elizabeth (Niewiera) F.; m. Steven Offenbacher (div. Aug. 1984). BS in Biology, Suffolk U., 1979; Med. Tech. Degree, Newton (Mass.) Wellesly Hosp., 1979; MSEE, Ga. Inst. Tech., 1985. Med. technologist Forsyth Dental Ctr., Boston, 1980-81, Smith, Kline & French, Tucker, Ga., 1981-82; field application engr. Fairchild Semiconductor Corp., Atlanta, 1985-87, Boca Raton, Fla., 1987; field sales engr. Nat. Semiconductor Corp., Raleigh, N.C., 1987—. Mem. IEEE (biomed. soc. Atlanta chpt. 1983-85, sec. 1983-85), NAFE, Raleigh Ski and Outing. Home: 2101 St Mary's St Raleigh NC 27608

FRIES, HELEN SERGEANT HAYNES, civic leader; b. Atlanta; d. Harwood Syme and Alice (Hobson) Haynes; student Coll. William and Mary, 1935-38; m. Stuart G. Fries, May 5, 1938. Bd. mem. Community Ballet Assn., Huntsville, Ala., 1968—; mem. nat. nurses aid com. ARC, 1958-59; dir. ARC Aero Club, Eng., 1943-44; supr. ARC Clubmobile, Europe, 1944-46; mem. women's com. Nat. Symphony Orch., Washington, 1959—, chmn. residential fund drive for apts., 1959; bd. dirs. Madison County Republican Club, 1969-70; mem. nat. council Women's Nat. Rep. Club N.Y., 1963—, chmn. hospitality com., 1963-65; bd. dirs. League Rep. Women, 1952-61; patron mem., vol. docent Huntsville Mus. Art, Huntsville Lit. Assn.; vol. docent Weeden House, Twickenham Hist. Preservation Dist. Assn., Inc., Huntsville; mem. The Garden Guild, Huntsville. Recipient cert. of merit 84th Div., U.S. Army, 1945. Mem. Nat. Soc. Colonial Dames Am., Daus. Am. Colonists, DAR, Nat. Trust Hist. Preservation, Va., Nat., Valley Forge (Pa.), Eastern Shore Va., Huntsville-Madison County hist. socs., Assn. Preservation Va. Antiquities, Greensboro Soc. Preservation, Tenn. Valley Geneal. Soc., Friends of Ala. Archives, Nat. Soc. Lit. and Arts, Va. Hist. Soc., English Speaking Union, Turkish-Am. Assn., Army-Navy Club, Washington Club, Capitol Hill Club, Army-Navy Country Club, Garden Club, Redstone Yacht Club, Huntsville Country Club, Heritage Club, Botanical Garden Club. Home: 409 Zandale Dr Huntsville AL 35801

FRIESEN, NANCY MILLER, financial systems specialist; b. Cleve., June 21, 1947; d. Storm Basberg and Eileen Mathilde (Andersen) Miller; m. George M. Lesko, Sept. 21,1968 (div. Sept. 1979); m. Frank George Friesen, Jan. 6, 1982. BS in Elem. Edn., Bowling Green State U., 1968; MBA, U. Tex., Arlington, 1983. Tchr. Palm Beach County Schs., Palm Beach Gardens, Fla., 1968-74, Tulsa Pub. Schs., 1974-78; fin. analyst Gen. Dynamics, Ft. Worth, 1978-82; fin. systems specialist LTV Aerospace and Def., Dallas, 1984—. Mem. NAFE, Personal Ancestral File Internat., Nat. Osteoporosis Found., Toastmasters Internat. Home: 6705 Glen Dale Dr Arlington TX 76017 Office: LTV Aerospace and Def W Jefferson St Dallas TX 75265

FRIESZ, LYNDA M., public relations executive; b. Idaho Falls, Idaho, Sept. 22, 1960; d. Jack and Elva (Ferritt) F. BA, Boise State U., 1982. Model, instr. John Robert Powers, Boise, Idaho; intern KBCI-TV, Boise; info. specialist Boise State U.; pvt. practice and event mktg. Lynda Friesz Pub. Rels., Boise; guest lectr. Boise State U. Address: 4212 Collister Dr Boise ID 83703

FRIMML, JAYMEE JO, chiropractor, nurse; b. Watertown, S.D., Oct. 18, 1949; d. Rodney Elsworth and Marie Ruth (Musta) Dale; m. Steven James Frimml, July 1, 1984; 1 child, Richard Mark. AS in Nursing, So. Coll., Collegedale, Tenn., 1970; student U. Ariz., 1979-81; D. Chiropractic, Palmer Coll. Chiropractic, Davenport, Iowa, 1985. Registered nurse, Tenn., Tex., Okla., Mich., Ariz., Iowa, Idaho. Emergency room nurse Madison Hosp., Tenn., 1970-71; nursing supr. Wilson N. Jones Hosp., Sherman, Tex., 1972-74; neonatal nurse specialist Lansing Gen. Hosp., Mich., 1974-78; clin. nurse leader, pediatrics Tucson Med. Ctr., 1978-81, pulmonary nurse specialist, 1981-82; chiropractor Cramer Chiropractice Clinic, Boise, Idaho, 1986; owner, chief exec. officer Northwest Health Inst., 1986—. Contbr. biweekly articles Idaho Press Tribune. Bd. dirs. Seventh-day Adventist Better Living Com., Caldwell, Idaho, 1986, 88, 89, 90; Idaho Conf. Exec. Com., Family Life Com. Mem. Am. Chiropractice Assn., Internat. Chiropractic Assn., Council on Roentgenology, Idaho Assn. Chiropractice Physicians (mem. polit. action com.), Nampa C. of C., Sigma Phi Chi (legis. com.). Seventh-day Adventist. Lodge: Soroptimists. Home: 3613 Juanita Way Nampa ID 83651 Office: Northwest Health Inst. 1203 10th St S Nampa ID 83651

FRIOU, ANN WHEELOCK, public relations executive, writer; b. Austin, Tex., Nov. 7, 1953; d. Kinch Carter and Ernestine Scott (Gibson) Wheelock; m. Thomas Claborne Friou, Sept. 14, 1985. BJ, U. Tex., 1976. Asst. editor ex-students assn. U. Tex., Austin, 1976-77; copy editor, reporter Austin Citizen Newspaper, 1977-78; asst. news bur. mgr. U. Idaho, Moscow, 1978-80, news bur. mgr., 1980-84; dir. communications Southwestern U., Georgetown, Tex., 1985-90; media rels. dir. Tex. Dept. of Commerce, Austin, 1990—; cons. Puget Sound Blood Ctr., Seattle, 1988—, Bonner Inc., Austin, 1990—. Bd. dirs. Washington-Idaho Symphony, 1982-84. Mem. Coun. for Advancement and Support of Edn. (4 Nat. awards 1978-89), Internat. Assn. Bus. Communicators, Women in Communications, Inc. (v.p. 1987-90), Tex. Nature Conservancy, Sierra.

FRISCH, ROSE EPSTEIN, population sciences researcher; b. N.Y.C., July 7, 1918; m. David H. Frisch; children: Henry J., Ruth Frisch Dealy. BA, Smith Coll., 1939, MA, Columbia U., 1940; PhD, U. Wis., 1943. Assoc. prof. population studies Harvard U., Cambridge, Mass., 1984—. Contbr. articles to profl. jours. John Simon Guggenheim Meml. fellow, 1975-76. Mem. AAAS, Endocine Soc. Am., Population Soc. Am., Sigma Xi (nat. lectr. 1989-90). Office: Harvard U Ctr Population Studies 9 Bow St Cambridge MA 02138

FRISCH, WENDI J., technical editor; b. Torrance, Calif., Sept. 3, 1960; d. John Henry and Karen Margaret (Blitz) Frisch. BA cum laude, San Francisco State U., 1984. Editorial asst. Intervisual Communications, L.A., 1985-87; tech. writer City Nat. Bank, Beverly Hills, Calif., 1987-88, tech. editor, 1988—. Mem. Soc. Tech. Communication. Home: 8633 W Knoll Dr Apt 207 West Hollywood CA 90069 Office: City Nat Bank 120 S Spalding Dr Ste 215 Beverly Hills CA 90212

FRISCHKNECHT, JACQUELINE, college program director, educator; b. Norfolk, Va., Apr. 15, 1932; d. John L. and Elizabeth (Holloway) Buck; m. George Allen (div. 1956); children: Ella Marie, Deborah; m. Frank Conrad Frischknecht, June 10, 1970 (dec. Aug. 1987); 1 child, Amalie Lucile. BS in Edn., U. Colo., 1962; MA in Libr. Sci., U. Denver, 1969, PhD in Speech Communications, 1977. Elem. sch. tchr., libr. Boulder (Colo.) Valley Pub. Sch., 1962-68; various cons. jobs, 1968-77; part-time lectr. Aprapahoe Community Coll., Littleton, Colo., 1976-83; dir. acad. affairs, applied communications U. Coll., Denver, 1985—; adj. prof. U. Coll., Denver, 1983—; pres. Communication Skills Tng., Denver, 1978—. Author: Applied Communication Curriculum of University College, 1984, Interpersonal Communication Game for the Elderly. Mem. Internat. Communication Assn., Nat. U. Continuing Edn. Assn., Am. Assn. Continuing & Adult Edn., Western Communication Assn., Colo. Communication Assn., Speech Communication Assn. Home: 169 Canyon Vista Dr Morrison CO 80465 Office: Univ Coll 2327 E Evans Denver CO 80208

FRISINA, RUTH M., counselor, writer; b. Helena, Mont., May 18, 1950; d. Frederick Robert and Luella C. (Abenroth) Miller; m. Michael Redvers Frisina, Aug. 17, 1974. BS, Mont. State U., Bozeman, 1972; postgrad., Coll. of Great Falls, Mont., 1988—. Tech. writer Mont. Energy R & D Inst., Inc., Butte, Mont., 1979-80, rsch. analyst, 1980-81; freelance documentation cons. Butte, 1981-86; career counselor Mont. Dept. Labor and Industry, Butte, 1986—; adj. lectr. Mont. Coll. Mineral Sci. and Tech., Butte, 1982-83. Chair, co-founder Butte Network Employment and Tng. Svcs., 1988—. Mont. Dept. Natural Resources and Conservation Rsch. grantee, 1973. Mem. Mont. Acad. Scis., Internat. Assn. Personnel in Employment Security, Am. Soc. for Human Resource Mgmt., Mont. Assn. Counseling and Devel., AAUW.

FRISK, SUSAN JANE, educator; b. Bennington, Vt., Nov. 14, 1936; d. Daniel Hans and Eunice Jane (Hood) Gutermann; m. Charles Everett Frisk, Nov. 25, 1960; 1 child, Tamara Jane. BS in Edn., U. So. Calif., 1959. Cert. kindergarten, primary, gen. edn. tchr. Elem. tchr. Alamitos Sch. Dist., Garden Grove, Calif., 1955-60; elem. tchr. Orange Unified Dist., Orange, Calif., 1960-70, Central Point Sch. Dist., Central Point, Oreg., 1971—. Named Woman of Yr. Beta Sigma Phi-Xi Gamma Gamma, 1979. Mem. NEA, Oreg. Edn. Assn., Central Point Edn. Assn., AAUW (hospitality Medford chpt. 1988—, sec. Oreg. State Extention chpt. 1982-89), Alpha Omicrom Pi. Republican. Home: 21440 E Evans Creek Rd White City OR 97503 Office: Central Point Sch Dist 250 N 2nd St Central Point OR 97502

FRIST, JANE ELIZABETH, real estate broker; b. Richmond, Va., Jan. 26, 1935; d. John Chester and Lois Elizabeth Frist; m. Arnold Cornelius Harms (div. 1978); children: Jane Alden, John David, Robert Dale. BA, Agnes Scott Coll., 1956; postgrad., Princeton Theol. Sem., 1956-59; Cert. in Elem. Edn., U. Denver, 1968; grad., Realtors Inst. Cert. residential specialist. Tchr. Madison Nursery Sch., 1964-67, Univ. Park Elem., Denver, 1967-73; sub. tchr. Denver Pub. Schs., 1973-78; real estate agt. Russ Wehner Realty, Denver, 1977-78, Moore and Co., Denver, 1978-80, ReMax Real Estate, Denver, 1980-82, Merrill Lynch Realty, Orlando, Fla., 1982-89, Prudential Fla. Realty, Orlando, 1989—; judge Parade of Homes, Orlando, 1985—. Illustrator: (book) No Wings in the Manse, 1955; illustrator, writer of stories, poetry mag. Aurora, 1952-56. Elder Montview Presbyn. Ch., Denver, 1976-79, 1st Presbyn. Ch., Orlando, 1986-89. Mem. Orlando-Winter Park Bd. of Realtors, Merrill Lynch 3 Million Leading Edge Soc., Orlando Country Club. Home: 1502 Oakley St Orlando FL 32806 Office: Prudential Fla Realty 211 E Colonial Dr Orlando FL 32801

FRITSCH, CHERYLE JEAN, account representative; b. Oceanside, Calif., May 25, 1962; d. Max William and Ava Lee (Siglier) F. AA in Bus., Orange Coast Coll., Costa Mesa, Calif., 1987; student, Calif. State U., Fullerton, 1987-89. Phlebotomist St. Joseph Hosp., Orange, Calif., 1981-84; sr. phlebotomist Hoag Meml. Hosp., Newport Beach, Calif., 1984-87; client svc. rep. Cen. Diagnostic Lab., Tarzanna, Calif., 1987-88; sales rep. W.W. Grainger, Riverside, Calif., 1988-90, Allied Clin. Lab., San Diego, 1990—.

FRITSMA, DARLENE KAYE, nurse; b. Grand Haven, Mich., Dec. 9, 1941; d. Douglas and Connie (Brink) Vander Zwaag; m. Donald Fritsma, Dec. 9, 1961 (div. 1982); children: Debra Lyn Fritsma DeRoy, Donald J. Jr. AA, AS, Brevard Community Coll., 1974; BS, Rollins Coll., Winter Park, Fla., 1981; MS in Nursing, U. Fla., 1985. RN, Fla. CCU staff nurse Brevard Hosp., Melbourne, Fla., 1974-79; asst. head nurse emergency room Holmes Regional Med. Ctr., Melbourne, 1979-80, nursing staff devel. coord., 1980-85; nursing supr. Fla. Hosp. Med. Ctr., Orlando, 1985—; adj. faculty U. Cen. Fla., Orlando, 1987-89; cons. in field. Contbr. articles to nursing publs.; producer TV program on nursing. Pres. Brevard CPR, Inc., 1984-85; mem. Fla. Dem. exec. com., Tallahassee, Orlando, 1989-90; treas., bd. dirs. Hyde Park Property Owners Assn., Winter Park, Fla., 1989-90; voter registrar Orange County, Orlando, 1988—; mem. health sub-com. Goals 2000-Greater Orlando C. of C., 1988—. Mem. Am. Nurses Assn. (nominating com. 1989—), Fla. Nurses Assn. (bd. dirs., dir. practice 1988—), Am. Heart Assn. (Fla. affiliate faculty), Am. Assn. Critical Care Nurses (pres. Space Coast unit 1983-84, strategic planning com. 1983-84), Fla. Hosp. Found., Commn. on Future of Nursing in Fla., Am. Cancer Soc., Phi Theta Kappa, Sigma Theta Tau. Presbyterian. Home: 1405 Hyde Park Dr Winter Park FL 32792

FRITTS, LILLIAN ELIZABETH, nurse; b. N.Y.C., July 19, 1923; d. William Franklin and Elzora Jane (Hodge) Bowen; A.D.N., R.N., Central Peidmont Community Coll., 1969; m. Thurman Luther Fritts, Aug. 5, 1944; children—William Luther, Franklin Lee, George Allen. Emergency room nurse Lexington (N.C.) Meml. Hosp., 1953-58; office nurse James T. Welborn, M.D., Lexington, 1958-60; staff nurse Haven Nursing Ctr., Lexington, 1960-61; pvt. duty nurse, 1961-63; owner, ptnr. Buena Vista Nursing Ctr., Lexington, 1964—; adult extension tchr. Davidson County Community Coll., 1978, adv. bd. nursing program, 1969-79; pres. Piedmont dist. Long Term Nursing Dirs., 1986-88, Long Term Care Piedmont Nurses Assn., 1987-89. Mem. Am. Nurses Assn., N.C. Nurses Assn., Lic. Practical Nurse Orgn. (state sec. 1958-60), N.C. Lic. Practical Nurse Assn., Dist. 9 Nurse Assn. N.C., N.C. Health Care Facilities Services Assn., Gideons Internat. Baptist. Home: Everhart Rd PO Box 419 Lexington NC 27292

FRITZ, ETHEL MAE HENDRICKSON, writer; b. Gibbon, Nebr., Feb. 4, 1925; d. Walter Earl and Alice Hazel (Mickish) Hendrickson; BS, Iowa State U., 1949; m. C. Wayne Fritz, Feb. 25, 1950; children: Linda Sue, Krista Jane. Dist. home economist Internat. Harvester Co., Des Moines, 1949-50; writer Wallace's Farmer mag., Des Moines, 1960-64; free-lance writer, 1960—. Chmn. Ariz. Council Flower Show Judges, 1983-85; media rels. Presdl. Inaugural Com., 1988. Accredited master flower show judge. Mem. Women in Communications (pres. Phoenix profl. chpt.; nat. task force com. 1980—), Am. Soc. Profl. and Exec. Women, Am. Home Econs. Assn., SW Writers' Conf., Ariz. Authors Assn., Phi Upsilon Omicron, Kappa Delta. Republican. Methodist. Club: PEO. Author: The Story of an Amana Winemaker, 1984, Prairie Kitchen Sampler, 1988, The Family of Hy-Vee, 1989.

FRITZ, JEAN GUTTERY, writer; b. Hankow, People's Republic China, Nov. 16, 1915; d. Arthur Minton and Myrtle (Chaney) Guttery; m. Michael Fritz, Nov. 1, 1941; children: David, Andrea. BA, Wheaton Coll., Norton, Mass., 1937, LittD (hon.), 1987; LittD (hon.), Washington and Jefferson Coll., 1982. Author: Fish Head, 1954, The Late Spring, 1957, The Animals of Doctor Schweitzer, 1958, The Cabin Faced West, 1958, How to Read a Rabbit, 1958, Brady, 1960, I, Adam, 1963, Magic to Burn, 1964, Early Thunder, 1967, George Washington's Breakfast, 1969, Cast for a Revolution, 1972, And Then What Happened, Paul Revere?, 1973, Why Don't You Get a Horse, Sam Adams?, 1974, Where Was Patrick Henry on the 29th of May?, 1975, Who's that Stepping on Plymouth Rock?, 1975, Will You Sign Here, John Hancock?, 1976, The Secret Diary of Jeb and Abigail, 1976, What's the Big Idea, Ben Franklin?, 1976, Can't You Make Them Behave, King George?, 1977, Brendon the Navigator, 1979, Stonewall, 1979, Where Do You Think You're Going, Christopher Columbus?, 1980, The Man Who Loved Books, 1981, Traitor: The Case of Benedict Arnold, 1981, The Good Giants and the Bad Pukwudgies, 1981, Homesick: My Own Story, 1982 (Am. Book award 1983, Child Study Book award 1983, Honor Book, Newberry Medal Book 1983), China Homecoming, 1985, The Double Life of Pocahontas, 1983 (Boston Globe/Horn Book award 1984), Make Way for Sam Houston, 1986 (Western Writers award 1987), Shh! We're Writing the Constitution, 1987, China's Long March, 1988, The Great Little Madison, 1989. Recipient Christopher award Cath. Library Assn., 1982, Regina Medal Cath. Library Assn., 1985, Laura Ingalls Wilder award ALA, 1986. Home: 50 Bellewood Ave Dobbs Ferry NY 10522

FRITZ, JOANNE LEE (JONI FRITZ), association executive; b. Bklyn., May 5, 1936; d. Theodore Roosevelt and Josephine (Chandler) L.; m. John D. Allen Jr., June 16, 1956 (div. Jan. 1970); children: John D. III, Cynthia Allen de Ramos, Victoria Lee Burnett; m. Nicholas Fritz Jr., July 4, 1970. Student, Cornell U., 1954-56; BA in Sociology with distinction, George Washington U., 1971. Tchr. Enon Elem. Sch., Chester, Va., 1958-59; med. records analyst Fairax (Va.) Hosp., 1962-66; med. asst. Drs. Apter and Morrissey Ltd., 1966-72; assoc. dir. Nat. Assn. Pvt. Residential Resources, Falls Church, Va., 1972-76, exec. dir., 1976—; panelist Office Human Devel. HHS, 1980-83; speaker pvt. residential svcs. nat. and state confs.; sec. Consortium for Citizens with Devel. Disabilities, 1974-82, chmn. housing task force, 1983-85, chmn. staff wage and hour task force, 1986-88; mem. steering com. Forum on Long Term Care, Washington, 1979-84; bd. dirs. Accreditation Coun. for Svcs. to Mentally Retarded and other Developmentally Disabled Persons, 1979-80; mem. adv. panels various orgns. Author, editor, Links, 1976—. Trustee Commn. on Accreditation Rehab. Facilities, 1984-89, chmn. standards com., 1985-87. Mem. Am. Assn. Mental Retardation, Assn. Retarded Citizens, Nat. Head Injury Found., Nat. Assn. Women Execs., Nat. Fire Protection Assn. (subcom. bd. & care). Office: Nat Assn Pvt Residential 4200 Evergreen Ln Ste 315 Annandale VA 22003

FRITZ, MARILYN JOHNSTON, educator; b. East Strodsburg, Pa., Oct. 27, 1937; d. Arnold and Ruth Eliza (Feltman) Parker; m. Alan Robert Johnston, Aug. 29, 1959 (div. Sept. 1982); children: Scott Alan, Kelly Lee; m. Joseph Gary Fritz, Dec. 26, 1983. BS, Trenton State Coll., 1959, postgrad., 1972; postgrad., San Francisco State U., 1986, Beijing Inst. Phys. Edn., People's Republic of China, 1986. Cert. health and phys. edn. tchr., N.J. Tchr. phys. edn. Neptune (N.J.) High Sch., 1959-60; elem. tchr. HEW, Ramey AFB, P.R., 1962-64; coord. spl. projects Ocean Twp. High Sch., Oakhurst, N.J., 1965-67, tchr. phys. edn., 1967—, coach field hockey, swimming, track and field, 1975—; councilor, tchr. swimming Seashore Day Camp, West End, N.J., 1960-70; tchr. Monmouth County Adult Schs., Oakhurst, 1967-72; asst. mgr. Ocean Community Pool, Ocean Twp., 1982—; dir. day camp Ocean Twp. Recreation Dept., 1982-84, also com. mem., 1970-84; chaparone student tours USSRĄ 1981, West Germany, Switzerland, Austria, 1987. Recipient select coaching award Scholastic Coach mag., 1989. Mem. NEA, N.J. Edn. Assn., Monmouth County Edn. Assn., N.J. Assn. Health, Phys. Edn. and Recreation, Collegiate Placement Svc. for Student Athletes, Elks Aux. Methodist. Office: Ocean Twp Internat Sch W Park Ave Ocean NJ 07712

FRITZ, MARY G., state legislator; b. Cambridge, Mass., May 8, 1938; d. Patrick John and Kathleen Sherry; m. William W. Fritz, Aug. 24, 1963; children: William Jr., Kathleen, Michael, Heather, Matthew, David. BA, Emmanuel Coll., Boston, 1959. Cert. tchr., Conn. Tchr. Wallingford (Conn.) Bd. Edn., 1959-64; dir., owner nursery sch., Yalesville, Conn., 1969-78; mgr. furniture store, Yalesville, 1977-81; legislator 90th dist. State of Conn., 1983-84, 87-88, 89—. Bd. dirs. Wallingford Day Care, 1985—; adv. bd. Substance Abuse Coalition, Cheshire, Conn., 1985—; adv. coun. August Early Intervention Ctr., Cheshire, 1985—. Mem. Grange Club, Kiwanis. Democrat. Roman Catholic. Home: 43 Grove St Yalesville CT 06492

FRITZKE, AUDREY ELMERE, artist; b. Utica, N.Y., Aug. 12, 1933; d. Harry Herman and Eutha Elmere (Wilcott) Laflin; m. B. William DeLia, Jan. 3, 1952 (div. 1968); children: Steven, Richard, Donna; m. Bernhardt C. Fritzke, Dec. 15, 1971. Student, SUNY, 1970-71, U. Cin., 1975, UCLA, Santa Monica, 1981-83. Painter portraits including Nancy Reagan, 1987; represented in numerous pvt. and pub. collections. Named Best Portrait, Best in Show, Ebell of L.A., 1989. Mem. Mayflower Soc., William Bradford Soc., Am. Portrait Soc., Pacific Palisades Art Assn. (bd. dirs. 1983-85, Best Oil 1983-85, Best Portrait 1984), Rodeo de Las Aguas NSDAR (regent, vice-regent 1983-90, Costume Coun. L.A. County Mus. Art, Nat. Woman in the Arts, Bay Area Artists. Republican. Home and Office: 24420 Zermatt Ln Valencia CA 91355

FRIZZELL, LUCILLE BRIDGERS, librarian; b. Yazoo City, Miss., Dec. 17, 1925; d. Thomas Alfred Bridgers and Maie Hollingsworth; m. Byron Waters Frizzell, July 24, 1952; children: Peter Graham, David Edward, Mark Dillard. BS, East Tenn. State U., 1977, MS, 1980. Cert. secondary tchr., Tenn. Sec. U.S. Steel Corp., 1946-53; libr. Steed Coll., Johnson City, Tenn., 1980-82, Bristol Coll., Johnson City, 1982-84, Draughons Jr. Coll., Johnson City, 1984—. Mem. DAR (treas. Johnson City chpt. 1959-60), Tenn. Libr. Assn., Boone Tree Libr. Assn. (v.p. 1986-87), Tri-Cities Areas Health Scis. Libr. Consortium, Nat. Soc. So. Dames (v.p. East Tenn. chpt. 1986-88, v.p. Tenn. state chpt. 1990—), Watauga Assn. Genealogists (charter), Washington County Hist. Soc. (charter), Monday Club, Delta Kappa Gamma. Republican. Baptist. Home: 1111 Southwest Ave Johnson City TN 37604 Office: Draughons Jr Coll PO Box 4103CRS Johnson City TN 37602

FRIZZELL-DONNER, JUDITH, editor, writer, marketing professional; b. Woburn, Mass., Oct. 22, 1958; d. Norman Richard and Thelma Virginia (Josephson) Frizzell; m. Phillip Louis Donner, Aug. 12, 1984 (div. Aug. 1989). Grad. high sch., 1976. Editor, mktg. dir. Arnett Press, Downey, Calif.; asst. dir. creative svcs. The Nat. Assn. of TV Program Execs., L.A.; mng. editor audio/video interiors mag. CurtCo Pub., Woodland Hills, Calif.; mng. editor Mobile Office mag. CurtCo., Inc., Woodland Hills, Calif. Producer, editor Wild Wild West TV series, 1960. Mem. Nat. League of Am. Pen Women, Publ. Prodn. Club So. Calif. Democrat. Office: CurtCo Inc 21600 Oxnard St Ste 480 21700 Oxnard St Ste 1600 Woodland Hills CA 91367

FROEHLICH, ANNA INGRID, accountant; b. Passaic, N.J., Dec. 28, 1956; d. Matthias and Anna (Knebl) F. B degree, Montclair State Coll., 1978; MBA, Fairleigh Dickinson U., 1981. Staff acct. Bache, Halsey, Stuart, Shields, Inc., N.Y.C., 1978-80; mgr. acctg. Morgan Stanley & Co., Inc., N.Y.C., 1980-85; v.p. E.F. Hutton & Co., Inc., N.Y.C., 1985-87, Drexel, Burnham, Lambert, Inc., N.Y.C., 1987-90; systems analyst Salomon Bros., Inc., N.Y.C., 1990—. Roman Catholic. Home: 201 Applegate Ln East Brunswick NJ 08816

FROEHLICH, KRISTI LYNN, association communications coordinator; b. Houston, Jan. 10, 1964; d. Robert Paul and Donna Joy (Stengler) F. BA in Journalism, Tex. Tech. U., 1986. Field rep. Am. Cancer Soc., Amarillo, Tex., 1987-88; communications coord. Dallas Police Assn., 1988—. Active Mary Immaculate Ch., Farmer's Branch, Tex.; vol. Bryan's House Children's AIDS Facility, Dallas, 1990. Mem. Women in Communications. Democrat. Roman Catholic. Office: Dallas Police Assn 2108 Jackson St Dallas TX 75201

FROEHLICH, LINDA ANN, manufacturing company executive; b. Pitts., July 20, 1947; d. Joseph A. and Mary H. (Skrip) Vodvarka; m. Richard David Froehlich, Mar. 25, 1966; children: Richard Bernard, Deanna Lyn. BA, Pa. State U., 1973. Owner Ace Wire Spring and Form Co., Inc., McKees Rocks, Pa., 1976—. Inventor giant paper clip. Mem. NAWBO, SMI, Smaller Mfg. Coun., Pitts.-Ohio Spring Mfg. (pres. 1986-87). Roman Catholic.

FROMAN, ANN, sculptor. Student, New Sch. for Social Rsch., N.Y.C., 1967, Fashion Inst. Tech., N.Y.C., 1961, Art Students League, N.Y.C., 1970, Nat. Acad. Sch. Fine Arts, N.Y.C., 1967, Palace Fontainebleau Sch. Fine Arts, France, 1961. Fashion, shoe designer, sculptor. Represented in numerous permanent collections including Survival, Bklyn. Coll., Butterfly, Shulamith Sch. for Girls, Bklyn., Lost Generation, Temple B'nai B'rith, Queen Esther, Iowa Jewish Home for the Aged, Des Moine, Sarah, Mus. Fine Art, Springfield, Mass., Three Dancers, Butler Mus. Art, Youngstown, Ohio, Jacob and the Angel, Slater Mus., Norwich, Conn., Ruth and Naomi, Richmond Library, Wichita, Kans., Temple Israel, Wiles Barre, Pa., Out of the Ashes, Congregation Emanu-El, N.Y.C., Temple DeHirsch Sinai, Seattle, Culinary Inst. Am., Hyde Park, N.Y., Holy Family, St. Raphaels Ch., Livingston, N.J.; numerous one woman shows including St. Raphaels Ch., Internat. Art Expo, N.Y., Dyansen Gallery, Beverly Hills, Calif., 1988, Artistic Investments, Atlanta, 1988, Jewish Community Ctr., Wilkes Barre, Pa., 1988, Great Artist Series, Miami, Fla., 1986, Bennington (Vt.) Mus., 1981, Judaica Mus., Phoenix, Ariz., 1979, Bodley Gallery, N.Y.C., 1978, Hebrew Coll., Boston, 1977, 82, Berkshire Mus., Pittsfield, mass., 1977, Nat. Arts & Antiques Festival, N.Y.C., 1969, 73, Bacardi Gallery, Miami, 1971, Black Starr & Frost Lt. Gallery, N.Y.C., 1970; numerous group shows including Internat. Arts Club, Nat. Arts Club, N.Y.C., Bklyn. Mus., Allied Artists Show, Vet. Artists Am., N.Y.C., Aleph Gallery, Mex. City, Ella Lerner Gallery, Lenox, Mass., Union Carbide, N.Y.C., Lever House, N.Y.C., Nelson Rockefeller Collection, N.Y.C., U.S. Customs Mus., N.Y.C., ReVann Galleries, Ft. Lauderdale, Fla., Bass Mus., Miami, Fla., Images Internat., Bethesda, Md. Recipient First Prize for Sculpture Salmagundi club, 1980, Cornavin Ltd. award Nat. Arts club, 1978, Watson Guptill award Nat. Arts Club, 1976, Ivan R. Lashin award Am. Soc. Contemporary Artists, 1975, Mortimer C. Ritter award Fashion Inst. Tech., 1971, Bklyn. Mus. Sculpture award, 1970, Shoe Design award, 1968, Packaging Design award Shoe Industry, 1965, Fashion Design award, 1959, Scholastic Mag. award, 1959. Studio: South Anson Rd Stanfordville NY 12581

FROMMELT, GAYLE MARIE, psychologist; b. Clinton, Iowa, Feb. 17, 1960; d. Robert J. and Barbara A. (Cassidy) F.; m. Robert J. Minkewicz, Oct. 11, 1986. BS, U. Colo., 1982; MA in Psychology, Northwestern U., Evanston, Ill., 1986, PhD, 1988. Lic. psychologists, N.H., Vt. Staff psychologist Nashua (N.H.) Brookside Hosp., 1988-89; psychologist Assn. Psychology, Burlington, Vt., 1989—; behaviorist Fanny Allen Hosp., Winooski, Vt., 1989—; supr. Dartmouth Med. Sch., Hanover, N.H., 1990—; lectr. dept. psychology U. Vt., Burlington, 1990—. NIH grantee, 1984-85; NIMH fellow, 1985-87, Benton J. Underwood fellow Northwestern U., 1985. Mem. Am. Psychol. Assn., Soc. for Psychotherapy Rsch., Vt. Psychol. Assn., Nat. Register of Health Care Providers. Office: Assocs in Psychology 92 Adams St Burlington VT 05401

FROMMEYER, DENISE LI, computer company executive; b. Leavenworth, Kans., Aug. 27, 1953; d. Robert William and Margaret Ann (Snowden) Barnhart; m. William Palmer Frommeyer Jr., Sept. 26, 1980; children: Rachel Jessica, Aaron Karl Robert. Student, Memphis State U., William Carey Coll., Biloxi, Miss. Lic. pvt. pilot. Computer systems designer, engrng. adminstr., draftsman Martin Marietta Manned Space Systems, New Orleans, 1977-89; account rep. Heath-Zenith Computers and Electronics, Kenner, La., 1989—. Exec. advisor to Jr. Achievement. Mem. NAFE, Nat. Mgmt. Assn. (past publicity/pub. rels. chmn. Michoud chpt.). Address: 47 Avant Garde Cir Kenner LA 70065 Office: 1900 Vets Meml Hwy Kenner LA 70062

FROMSON, ANTOINETTE DUVAL, civic worker; b. Chgo., May 22, 1925; d. Ralph A. and Yvonne (Duval) Brown; Barnard Coll., 1947; m. Howard A. Fromson, Oct. 12, 1946; children—Michele Yvonne, Michael Erik, Timothy Arthur, Brett Duval. Plaintiff, Women vs. Conn., legal action about the right of women to control their bodies, 1969; convenor, 1st chmn. Conn. Women's Polit. Caucus, 1970; organizer Westport-Weston (Conn.) chpt. NOW, 1972, organizer, convenor, pres. Southwestern conn. chpt., 1974-78; del. Conn. Democratic Conv., 1974; mem. Weston Town Dem. Com., 1972-74; bd. dirs. Westport YMCA, bd. trustees; bd. dirs. Conn. Planned Parenthood, Five Town Found. Mem. Unitarian-Universalists Women's Fedn., Barnard Alumni Assn., Cedar Point Yacht Club, Aspetuck Valley Country Club, Fairfield Organic Gardening Club. Democrat. Unitarian. Home: PO Box 1151 Weston CT 06883

FRONEK, KITTY, physiologist; b. Grenoble, France, Mar. 23, 1925; came to U.S., 1965; d. Josef and Milada (Eisen) Weiner; m. Arnost Fronek, 1950; children: Jan, Zdenka. MD, Charles U., Prague, Czechoslovakia, 1950; PhD, Czechoslovak Acad. Scis., 1960. Rsch. asst. dept. pharmacology Charles U., 1948-50, asst. prof., 1950-51; sr. investigator Inst. for Cardiovascular Diseases, Prague, 1951-60; sr. investigator, head physiol. div. Inst. for Nuclear Diagnosis, Prague, 1960-64; rsch. assoc. surg. rsch. Temple U., Phila., 1965-68; assoc. rsch. bioengring. U. Calif., San Diego, 1968-75, rsch. physiologist, 1975—; rsch. and devel. cons. NIH, Washington, 1973-74, with cardio-vascular study sect., 1975-79, site visit mem., 1977, 82. Contbr. numerous articles to profl. jours. Mem. Am. Physiol. Soc., Microcirculation Soc., Biomed. Engring. Soc. Office: U Calif San Diego M-043 La Jolla CA 92093

FRONTIERE, GEORGIA, professional football team executive; m. Carroll Rosenblum, July 7, 1966 (dec.); children: Dale Carroll, Lucia; m. Dominic Frontiere. Pres., owner L.A. Rams, NFL, 1979—. Bd. dirs. L.A. Boys and Girls Club, L.A. Orphanage Guild, L.A. Blind Youth Found. Named Headliner of Yr., L.A. Press Club, 1981. Office: Los Angeles Rams 2327 W Lincoln Ave Anaheim CA 92801*

FROOKS, DOROTHY, lawyer, author; b. Saugerties, N.Y.; d. Reginald and Rosita (Siberez) F.; LL.B., Hamilton Coll., 1918, LL.M., 1919; spl. courses Harvard U., N.Y. U., St. Lawrence U., U. N.C. Law Sch., Tulane U., Duquesne U.; Ps.D., Nat. Inst. Psychology, 1946; student Indsl. Coll. Armed Forces, 1953; m. Jay Philippe Vanderbilt. Bar: N.Y. 1920, U.S. Customs Ct., 1932, U.S. Supreme Ct., 1934, U.S. Dist. Ct. P.R., 1925, Calif. 1926, La. 1929, Alaska 1935, U.S. Ct. Claims, 1950, U.S. Ct. Mil. Appeals, 1954, Hawaii 1958. atty. Salvation Army, N.Y.C., 1921-24; organizer Poor Man's Ct., 1921; atty. for com. U.S. Coast Guard, 1939-40; counsel N.Y. State Bd. Edn., 1940-41; owner, editor Public Service Record, N.Y.C., 1920-21; pub. Murray Hill News, Oyster Bay News, 1916-19; columnist N.Y. Evening World, 1929-32; del. 1st Inter-Am. Bar Conf., Havana, 1921, Internat. Law Conf., Oxford, Eng., 1932, Atty. Gen.'s Crime Congress, Washington, 1934, Gov.'s Crime Conf., Albany, 1935; candidate for Congress-at-large State N.Y., 1934; nat. judge adv. Vets. of World War I, Inc., 1969; arbitrator Small Claims Ct., 1970—. Served as chief yeoman U.S. Navy in charge woman enrollments and recruiting, World War I; served in Judge Adv. Office, U.S. Army, World War II. Recipient medal for patriotic service by Woodrow Wilson, 1918. Mem. ABA, Nat. Assn. Woman Lawyers (organizer, pres. 1921-22, chmn. mil. and naval law com. 1946), Nat. Aero. Assn., Am. Judicature Assn., Wis. Archaeol. Soc., N.Y. State Bar Assn., Westchester County Bar Assn., Inter-Am. Bar, Women of Greater N.Y. (pres.), Murray Hill Assn. (pres.), Iota Tau Tau, Epsilon Eta Phi. Presbyterian. Clubs: Westchester Jr. League, Eastern Star, Peekskill Country (dir.). Author: The American Heart, 1919; Civilization, 1922; Criminal Obscenity, 1923; Chronology of the Catholic Church; Loves Law, 1927; Wills and Estates, 1929; All in Love, 1932; Over the Heads of Congress, 1935; Portia on Horseback, 1943; The Olympic Torch, 1946; Girls Get Their Men, 1947; How to Use the Small Claims Court, 1979; Wills, 1981; Lady Lawyer, 1975; Labor Courts-Outlaw Strikes, 1984; Poisoned with Power, 1986. Office: Route 6 Lake Mohegan Peekskill NY 10547 Law Office: 237 Madison Ave New York NY 10016

FROOME, MARIE OLIVE, educator; b. San Francisco, Sept. 29, 1933; d. Oliver and Marie (Quinones) Pruden; m. George M. Froome, Jan. 29, 1955 (div. 1975); children: Joseph D., David W. BA, Calif. State U., Chico, 1955, MA, 1979. Cert. tchr. Tchr. Red Bluff (Calif.) City Schs., 1955-60; tchr. Antelope Schs., Red Bluff, 1960-62, Title I tchr., 1968-75, tchr., 1975-77; resource tchr., bilingual (Spanish) educator Tehama County Schs., Red Bluff, 1977—; community adv. bd. No. Calif. Edl. TV Assn., Inc., 1987. Co-author: 50 Years of Rodeo, 1972; author children's stories; contbr. articles to profl. jours. Campaign worker Republican Party, Red Bluff, 1962, local election, Tehama County, 1990; mem. community adv. bd. N. Calif. Edl. TV Assn. Inc., 1980-87. Recipient trophy, Lion's Club, Tehama County, 1951, Shasta Zone, 1951. Mem. Tehama County Educators (pres. 1986-89), AAUW (former officer). Roman Catholic. Home: 12609 Wilder Rd Red Bluff CA 96080 Office: Tehama County Dept Edn Lincoln St Red Bluff CA 96080

FROST, ALLISON K., healthcare administrator; b. Alameda, Calif., Nov. 6, 1956; d. Elliott and Rhoda E. (Greendorfer) Kapchan; m. Norbert U. Frost, Aug. 13, 1978; 1 child, Lindsay R. BS, U. Calif., Davis, 1978; MS in Pub. Health, UCLA, 1980. Dir. med. staff rels. St. Marys Hosp. and Med. Ctr., San Francisco; asst. adminstr. Kaiser Permanente, Santa Clara, Calif.; asst. to v.p., regional med. ctr., adminstr. Kaiser Permanente, Oakland, Calif.; now dir. emergency preparedness Kaiser Permanente, northern Calif. Mem. Am. Coll. Healthcare Execs., Healthcare Execs. No. Calif., Women's Healthcare Execs. No. Calif. Office: 1950 Franklin St 12th Fl Oakland CA 94612

FROST, FELICIA DODEE, brokerage firm executive; b. Oklahoma City, Oct. 19, 1956; d. Carl S. Frost and Mikki (Matheny) Marcus. Student So. Meth. U., 1974-76. Gen. mgr. Keystone Readers Service, Dallas, 1976-80; adminstrv. mgr then asst. v.p. Merrill Lynch Pierce Fenner and Smith, Dallas, 1980—. Pub. Frost Reading and Math Program, 1979. Bd. dirs. North Dallas Shared Ministries, 1988—. Mem. Dallas Securities Dealers Assn., Nat. Assn. Securities Dealers (gen. securities prin., mcpl. securities rulemaking bd. prin., registered options prin., bd. arbitrators), NYSE (com. mem.). Republican. Mem. Unity Ch. of Christianity. Home: 5590 Spring Valley St Unit C 207 Dallas TX 75240 Office: Merrill Lynch Pierce Fenner and Smith 2000 Premier Place 5910 N Central Expy Dallas TX 75206

FROST, JANET I., business executive; b. Danbury, Iowa, Jan. 31, 1935; d. Clarence F. and Bertha C. (Peter) Collins; children: Scott A., Derek E. Student, Lassen Jr. Coll., Susanville, Calif., Western Nev. Community Coll. Adminstrv. sec. Nev. State Employment Security Dept., Carson City, 1967-74; adminstrv. asst. Sunnyvale (Calif.) Sch. Dist., 1975-80; exec. asst. to pres., asst. corp. sec. Dalgety, Inc., San Mateo, Calif., 1982—. Mem. NAFE, Exec. Women Internat. (pres. San Francisco chpt. 1990). Home: 3941 Pacific Heights Blvd San Bruno CA 94066 Office: 901 Mariners Island Blvd Ste 700 San Mateo CA 94066

FROST, JUANITA CORBITT, hospital foundation coordinator; b. Rockford, Ill., Aug. 4, 1926; d. Mervin Charles and Eva Marie (Moberg) Corbitt; m. Thomas Tapenden Frost, Jan. 3, 1954; children: Annamarie, Thomas Tapenden. Student, Little Rock U., Ark., 1959-61. Med. sec. asst. clinical pathology lab. VA, Whipple, Ariz., 1951-54; exec. dir. Camp Fire Girls, Temple, Tex., 1967-73; exec. sec. Scott & White Meml. Hosp. Found., Temple, Tex., 1973-82; hosp. found. coordinator, exec. asst. to bd. Scott & White Meml. Hosp., Scott Sherwood and Brindley Found, Temple, Tex., 1982—. Mem. vestry Episcopal Ch., Temple Tex. 1985-87, 88—; sr. warden Episcopal Ch., Temple Tex. 1987; mem. Com. on Bishop's Address NW Region Diocese Episcopal Ch., Houston 1988; mem. Bell County Choral Group Belton Tex. 1988—; mem. Tchr. Literacy Coun., Temple Tex. 1988—. Home: 3001 Las Moras Dr Temple TX 76502 Office: Scott & White Meml Hosp Found 2401 S 31st St Temple TX 76508

FROST, MARGARET ANNE, real estate agent; b. Cleve., Sept. 26, 1935; d. Louis Howard and Dorothy Belle (Stiles) Manchester; m. Richard E. Brown, July 1960, (div. Sept., 1963); 1 child, Sean Glenn; m. James Andrew, Nov. 9, 1963; children: Elizabeth Anne, Amy Howland. Student, Kent State U., 1955, Baldwin Wallace Coll., 1959, Case Western Res. U., 1963; Assoc., Cuy Community Coll., Cleve., 1973. RN, Ohio. Exec. sec., Chesapeake & Ohio Ry. Co., Cleve., 1955-61; corp. sec., treas. R.C. Kyle & Assocs., Fairview Park, Ohio, 1963-69; nurse various hosps., Greater Cleve., 1973-78; freelance writer Rocky River, Ohio, 1978-86; mgr. Clan Gregor Ctr., Balguhidder, Scotland, 1986; v.p., gen. mgr. Fermentia Enterprises, Ohio, 1985-86; asst. dir. Nannies of Cleve., Lakewood, Ohio, 1987; v.p. Clan Gregor Found., 1987—, also bd. dirs.; operating room nurse part-time Cleve. Met. Gen. Hosp. Author: Granny MacGregor's Favorite Recipes, 1988, Poems of Life, 1987, Caleb's Journals, 1982; contbr. articles to profl. jours. Vol. Cleve. Internat. Program, 1965-88; lobbyist, mem. Nat. Abortion Rights Action League, Cleve., 1975—; chmn. Clan Gregor Con. U.S., 1989. Recipient First Prize Poetry Kiwanis Internat., 1953, Highest Honors Grand Cross of Colors Masonic, 1953, Honored Founder Great Lakes Chpt. Clan Gregory Soc., Ohio, 1988. Mem. Nat. Assn. Realtors, Cleve. Area Bd. Realtors, West Side Realtors Roundtable, Chesapeake & Ohio Hist. Soc., Kent State U. Alumni Assn., Cuyahoga Community Coll. Alumni Assn., LWV, Audubon Soc., Gregor Soc. Scotland (founder Gt. Lakes chpt.), Cuyahoga Community Coll. Faculty Wives Assn. (pres. 1967-68), Sierra Club, Rainbow Girls, Order Eastern Star, Beta Sigma Phi. Republican. Unitarian. Office: Dolores C Knowlton Realtors 28687 Center Ridge Rd Westlake OH 44145

FROST, MONICA MCASEY, economic development company executive, accountant; b. Joliet, Ill., Jan. 12, 1959; d. Joseph Michael McAsey and Mary Joan (Whalen) Rommel; m. Marc Lawrence Frost, May 14, 1983. Student, Clarke Coll., Dubuque, Iowa, 1977-79; BBA in Fin. and Acctg., U. Iowa, 1981, postgrad., 1983-84. CPA, Iowa, Ind. Asst. bank examiner FDIC, Chgo., 1980-81; sr. asst. acct. Deloitte Haskins & Sells, Indpls., 1984-86; dir. fin. svcs. Indpls. Econ. Devel. Corp., 1986-88, v.p., asst. treas., 1988—; mem. adv. bd. Ind. Emerging Bus. Forum, Indpls., 1986—; asst. sec. Mid City Pioneer Corp., Indpls., 1986—. Vol. for run-walk Riley Hosp., Indpls., 1987, 88. Mem. AICPA, Nat. Assn. Accts., Ind. Soc. CPA's, Ind. Area Devel. Coun., Entrepreneur's Alliance Ind. (bd. dirs. 1986—), Women's Bus. Initiative (bd. dirs. 1986-87), Venture Club Ind. Republican. Roman Catholic. Office: Indpls Econ Devel Corp 320 N Meridian St Ste 906 Indianapolis IN 46204

FROST, ROSE KOBEL, library executive; b. Saginaw, Mich., Jan. 20, 1950; d. Philip Raymond and Angeline Alice (Brink) Grybowski; m. Lawrence J. Frost, Jan. 23, 1988. AA, Delta Coll., 1969; BA, Mich. State U., 1971; MA, U. S. Fla., 1977. Cert. permanent profl. librarian, Mich. Library aide, librarian Orlando Pub. Library, Fla., 1973-78; sales rep. Baker & Taylor, Momence, Ill., 1978-81; pub. relations officer Saginaw Pub. Library, 1981-83; librarian Delta Coll., University Center, Mich., 1983-85; supr. user services Grace Dow Library, Midland, Mich., 1985-88; exec. dir. Presque Isle County Library, Rogers City, Mich., 1988—; chmn. Video Cassettes in Pub. Libraries Conf., 1986; chmn. adv. coun. Northland Library Coop., 1989—. Chmn. networking YWCA, Bay City, Mich., 1985; trustee Carrollton (Mich.) Pub. Schs., 1985-88. Mem. ALA, Mich. Library Assn. (pub. relations com. 1981-84, chmn. intellectual freedom com. 1985-87, presenter Best of Show awards 1984, panel mem. conf. 1984), AAUW (newsletter editor 1983-84). Clubs: Welcome Aboard; Bay City Networking (chmn. 1985). Avocations: classical music, theater, travel, swimming, reading.

FROST, SUSAN ANN, laboratory administrative executive; b. Omaha, Mar. 14, 1945; d. Orville John and Ruth Theresa (O'Keefe) Willms; m. Michael Forbes Labora, Sept. 3, 1966 (div. Oct. 74); 1 child, John Michael; m. Marc George Frost, Aug. 2, 1980. Student, Xavier U., 1965; BS, Coll. St. Mary, Omaha, 1969. Registered med. technologist. Asst. supr. of blood bank Creighton Meml. St. Joseph Hosp., Omaha, 1969; administrv. dir. of lab. CGH Med. Ctr., Sterling, Ill., 1969—; instr. Sauk Valley Community Coll., Dixon, Ill., 1969--. Del. People to People to People's Republic China, 1989. Mem. Am. Soc. for Med. Tech., Women's Guild, Lambda Tau Lambda, Kappa Gamma Pi. Republican. Roman Catholic. Office: CGH Med Ctr 100 E LeFevre Rd Sterling IL 61081

FRUCHTMAN, SHIRLEY MILLSTEIN, accountant; b. Newark, Sept. 8, 1922; d. Harry M. and Regina (Kalmuk) Millstein; m. Harvey L. Fruchtman; children: Lois D. Pierce, Debra J. Fruchtman Rigberg, Amy M. AA in Acctg., Essex County Coll., Newark, 1976; BS in Acctg., Stockton State Coll., Pomona, N.J., 1979. Substitute tchr. So. Regional High, Manahawkin, N.J., 1977-89; vol. tax counselor for elderly Solono County, Calif., 1986, 87, 89, Ocean County, N.J., 1990. Vol. fundraising South Ocean County Hosp., 1986. Mem. AAUW (treas. 1986-89). Home: 1249 Redwood Ct Dixon CA 95620

FRUEHAN, ANNETTE SHIRLEY, marriage, family and child therapist, educator; b. Wetaskiwin, Alta., Can., July 4, 1944; came to U.S., 1953; d. Edmond and Othilia (Pohl) Yetz; m. Joel Alan Fruehan, Sept. 16, 1967; children: Anjolette, Brett. BA, Calif. State U., Long Beach, 1966; MS, Calif. State U., L.A., 1973. Rehab. counselor Calif. Dept. Rehab., 1966-71; counselor Orange Coast Coll., Costa Mesa, Calif., 1972-85, prof. psychology, ESL, 1985—; marriage, family and child therapist, Whittier, Calif., 1985—. Author: Creating Your Own Future, 1983. Speaker MADD, Orange County. Mem. Am. Fedn. Tchrs. Mem. Assemblies of God Ch. Office: Orange Coast Coll 2701 Fairview Rd Costa Mesa CA 92628

FRUEHLING, ROSEMARY T., editor; b. Gilbert, Minn., Jan. 23, 1933; d. Tony and Mary (Scalise) Leoni; children: Shirley Rae, Anya, John Daniel. BS, U. Minn., 1954, MA, 1968, PhD, 1980. Cert. vocat. tech. inst. dir.; cert. in bus. edn. Mgr. instructional svcs. State Bd. Voc-Tech. Edn., St. Paul; mgr. Minn. Software Office, State of Minn., St. Paul; mgr. office tech. Gregg, McGraw Hill, Mpls.; nat. cons. editor SRA, St. Paul, Software Solutions, Inc.; pres. Paradigm Pub. Intenat., Eden Prairie, Minn. Author: Communicating for Results, Electronic Office Procedures, Business Communications, Business Correspondence: Essentials of Communication, Psychology of Human Relations, Working at Human Relations, Your Attitude Counts, Write to the Point. Mem. Am. Vocat. Assn., Minn. Vocat. Assn., Nat. Bus. Edn. Assn., Delta Pi Epsilon. Home: 4335 Chimo E Wayzata MN 55391 Office: 6436 City W Pkwy Ste 200 Eden Prairie MN 55344

FRUHMANN, KAREN ANNE, laboratory administrator; b. Orange, N.J.; d. Robert Whitin and Anna (Harvey) Mullin; B.A. magna cum laude in Psychology and Biology, William Paterson Coll., 1974; cert. med. tech. St. Mary's Hosp., 1975; M.S. summa cum laude in Med. Tech., Fairleigh Dickinson U., 1977; postgrad. Southeastern U., 1982-85. Cert. bioanalyst, clin. lab. dir. Am. Bd. Bioanalysis. Biochemistry technologist Raritan Valley Hosp., Greenbrook N.J., 1975-76; asst. supr. enzymology, tech. writer quality assurance, diagnostic researcher, chemistry adminstr. Warner Lambert Gen. Diagnostics, Morris Plains, N.J., 1976-78; dir. lab. services Kessler Inst. for Rehab. W. Orange, N.J., 1979—. Mem. Am. Soc. Clin. Pathologists (affiliate mem.), N.Y. Acad. Scis., Am. Soc. Med. Tech., N.J. Soc. Med. Tech., Assn. for Women in Sci., Nat. Certification Agy. (clin. lab. scientist), Alpha Mu Tau. Presbyterian. Contbr. articles on hematology to profl. jours. Office: Kessler Inst 1199 Pleasant Valley Way West Orange NJ 07052

FRUTH, BERYL ROSE, physician; b. Carey, Ohio, Mar. 27, 1952; d. Oscar W. and Alice (Arnett) Fruth. BA in Chemistry magna cum laude, Asbury Coll., 1973; MD, Ohio State U., 1977. Diplomate Am. Acad. Family Practice. Intern Grant Hosp., Columbus, Ohio, 1977-78, resident, 1978-79, chief resident, 1979-80; practice medicine specializing in family practice, Columbus, 1980—; asst. dir. family practice residency Grant Hosp., 1980-81; med. dir. Columbus Dispatch, 1983—, St. Anthony Breast Evaluation Ctr., 1986—; lectr. Columbus Cancer Clinic, 1984. Contbr. Ohio State U. Med. Sch. Learning Module in Alcoholism, 1983-84. Named Alumna of Yr., Vanlue Sch., Ohio. Fellow Am. Acad. Family Physicians; mem. AMA, Am. Med. Women's Assn. Office: 20 Governors Pl Columbus OH 43203

FRY, ANNE EVANS, zoology educator; b. Phila., Sept. 11, 1939; d. Kenneth Evans and Nora Irene (Smith) F. AB, Mount Holyoke Coll., 1961; MS, U. Iowa, 1963; PhD, U. Mass., 1969. Instr. Carleton Coll., Northfield, Minn., 1963-65; asst. prof. Ohio Wesleyan U., Delaware, 1969-74, assoc. prof., 1974-80, prof., 1980—. Contbr. articles to profl. jours. Recipient Welch Teaching award Ohio Wesleyan U., 1976. Mem. AAAS, Am. Inst. Biol. Scis., Am. Soc. Zoologists, Ohio Acad. Sci., Soc. Devel. Biology, Sigma Xi. Office: Ohio Wesleyan U Delaware OH 43015

FRY, DONNA MARIE, military officer, educator; b. Altadena, Calif., Oct. 16, 1947; d. Hampton Scott and M. Genevieve (Wolff) F.; m. William Raymond Burrell, June 16, 1952; 1 child, Alicia Fay. BA, Rutgers U., 1981; MS, Air Force Inst. Tech., 1986. Enlsited USAF, 1968, advanced through grades to master sgt., advanced through grades to capt., 1981; staff cost analyst Cost Rsch. Office USAF, Bergstrom AFB, Tex., 1986-88; instr. Air Force Inst. Tech. USAF, Wright-Patterson AFB, Ohio, 1989—; cons. in field. Contbr. articles to profl. jours. Mem. Am. Soc. Mil. Comptrollers (v.p., project officer 1988—), Inst. Cost Analysis, Air Force Assn., SALSAW (pres. Dayton, Ohio chpt. 1990—). Republican. Roman Catholic. Home: 2169 Northern Dr Beavercreek OH 45431-3124 Office: USAF AFIT/LSQ Wright-Patterson AFB OH 45433-6083

FRY, LINDA SUE, cheesecake company executive; b. Detroit, May 7, 1961; d. Walter Stephen and Christine Ann (Malinowski) Stevens; m. Daniel Kennth Fry, May 28, 1983; children: Amanda Sue, Travis Michael. BS in Biology, Morningside Coll., 1983. Asst. mgr. Golden Coral Steakhouse, Shawnee, Kans., 1983-84; sales rep. Met. Life Ins. Co., Overland Park, Kans., 1984-85; sales and catering rep. Holiday Inn Downtown, Kansas City, Kans., 1985-87, dir. sales, 1987-88; ops. and adminstrv. mgr. Crissy's Old Fashioned Cheesecake, Inc., Ontario, Calif., 1988—. Mem. steering com. City of Festival Assn., Kansas City, 1985-86, pres., 1986-88; ex-officio mem. Kansas City Conv. and Visitors Bur., 1986-88; mem. orgn. com. Statue of Liberty Move to Freedom Tour, Kansas City, 1986; mem. steering com. March of Dimes, Wyandotte County, Kans., 1987, 88, United Way, Wyandotte County, 1987, 88; mem. planning com. Polish Festival Assn., Kansas City, 1986-88; state bd. dirs. Kansas City Jaycees, 1987-88; amb. Kansas City C. of C., 1986-88. Mem. Nat. Assn. Profl. Saleswoman (chpt. treas. 1985-86), Soc. Govt. Meeting Planners (charter, membership com. 1988-89), Women in Travel (membership chmn. 1987-89), NAFE, Women in Networking, Bus. Women's Network, Hotel Sales and Mktg. Assn., Nat. Assn. Life Underwriters, Women's Assn. Life Underwriters, Ontario Jaycees (state dir. 1989-90, pres. 1990—, centennial com. 1990—, christmas on Euclid com. 1990). Roman Catholic. Home: 1352 W 5th St Apt K-10 Ontario CA 91762 Office: Crissy's Cheesecake PO Box 1340 Alta Loma CA 91701

FRY, MARION GOLDA, university administrator; b. Halifax, N.S., Can., Apr. 16, 1932; d. George W. and Marion I. (Publicover) F. Grad., U. King's Coll., 1953, DCL, 1985; MA, Dalhousie U., 1955; B of Lit., Oxford U., 1958; DLitt, Trent U., 1989. Asst. prof. philosophy, asst. dean of women Bishop's U., 1958-64; prin. Catharine Parr Traill Coll., Trent U., 1964-69, assoc. prof. philosophy, 1964-86, v.p., 1975-79; pres. U. of King's Coll., Halifax, 1987—. Office: U of King's Coll, Office of Pres, Halifax, NS Canada B3H 2A1*

FRY, MILDRED HELEN, library director; b. Canton, Ohio, Mar. 31, 1940; d. Homer D. and Freda A. (Heldman) Covey; m. James W. Fry, July 26, 1957 (div. 1985); 1 child, Christine Lee Fry Clarke. BA, Capital U., Columbus, Ohio, 1982; MLS, Kent (Ohio) State U., 1986. Libr. asst. Stark County Dist. Libr., Canton, 1958-61; asst. dir. Mayne Williams Pub. Libr., Johnson City, Tenn., 1965-66; circulation desk supr. Ohio State U. Libr., Edn. and Psychology, 1966-82; training coord. Online Computer Libr. Ct., Columbus, 1982-84; asst. to dir. Cleve. Area Met. Libr. System, 1986—, acting exec. dir., 1989—. Mem. ALA Continuing Libr. Edn. Network and Exchange Round Table (exec. bd. 1990—), ALA Libr. Adminstrn. and Mgmt. Assn., Ohio Libr. Assn. (bd. dirs. 1990-93), Am. Soc. for Tng. and Devel., Ohio Women Librs., Ohio Cou. of Fundraising Exec., First Families of Ohio, Sierra Club (19th congrl. dist. coord. 1987-88). Democrat. Home: 6503 Marsol Rd Apt 541 Mayfield Heights OH 44124 Office: Cleve Area Metro Libr 3645 Warrensville Ct Rd Ste 116 Cleveland OH 44122

FRY, NENAH ELINOR, college president; b. Chgo., Nov. 5, 1933; d. August Jefter and Gladys Alberta (Bobcock) F. B.A., Lawrence U., 1955, LL.D., 1984; M.A., Yale U., 1957, Ph.D., 1964; D.Litt., Wilson Coll., 1980. Instr. Lawrence Coll., Appleton, Wis., 1959-61; asst. prof., then assoc. prof. history Wilson Coll., Chambersburg, Pa., 1963-75; dean of coll. Wells Coll., Aurora, N.Y., 1975-83; pres. Sweet Briar Coll., Va., 1983-90; evaluator Middle States Assn., Phila., 1970—; trustee Lawrence U. Bd. dirs. Lynchburg Fine Arts Ctr., Pres.'s Com., NCAA. Woodrow Wilson fellow, 1955. Mem. Am. Hist. Assn., Soc. for French History, Berkshire Conf. Women Historians, Phi Beta Kappa (assoc.). Address: PO Box 61 Sweet Briar VA 24595*

FRYBERGER, AMY JO, sales professional; b. Lancaster, Pa., Sept. 5, 1966; d. John William and Janet Irene (Wolfel) Newell; m. Brian Lorenza Fryberger, June 6, 1987. AS, Lancaster Bus. Sch., 1987; student, Lock Haven (Pa.) U., 1984; cert., Ford Life Ins. Co., Dearborn, Mich., 1989, Keith Wood Agy., 1990. Dir. pub. rels. PennAg Ind. Assn., Ephrata, Pa., 1985-87; profl. salesperson Keller Bros. Auto Co., Lititz, Pa., 1987-88; bus. mgr. Freedom Ford of Ephrata, 1988-89; profl. sales agt., divisional mgr. Keith Wood Agy., Ft. Worth, 1990—; founder employee involvement and quality commitment coms. Freedom Ford, Ephrata, 1988-89. Contbr. articles to profl. jours. Mem. NAFE, Soroptimists Internat. (del. 1989—). Democrat. Roman Catholic. Home: 124 Colonial Dr Akron PA 17501

FRYE, BOBBIE SUE, nurse; b. Hamilton, Ala., Aug. 17, 1937; d. James Thomas and Sybil Pauline (Webb) Frye. BSN, Washington U., 1968; RN, Bapt. Hosp., 1958; MS, U. N.C., 1971. Staff nurse Gen. Hosp., Greenville, Miss., 1958-59, Belleville, Ill., 1967, 68; instr. Mo. Bapt. Sch. Nursing, St. Louis, 1968-69; staff nurse N.C. Meml. Hosp., Chapel Hill, 1969-71; instr. U. N.C. Sch. Nursing, Chapel Hill, 1971-73, asst. prof., 1973-74; clin. nurse specialist U. N.C. Hosps., Chapel Hill, 1974—; adj. asst. prof. U. N.C. Sch. Nursing, 1974-76; assoc. Carolina Population Ctr., 1971—; chief nurse, USAFR, 1971-74; continuing edn. faculty NAACOG, Washington, 1974-87. Vol./capt. United Fund campaign, Chapel Hill, 1985-89; vol. 1987 Olympic Festival. Capt. USAF, 1959-67. Named Nurse of the Yr., N.C. NAACOG, 1978; Faculty award, U. N.C. Sch. Nursing Srs., 1974, others. Mem. Oncology Nursing Soc., NAACOG: The Orgn. for Obstetric, Gynecologic and Neonatal Nurses (nat. pres. 1989), Sigma Theta Tau. Baptist. Office: U NC Hosps 101 Manning Dr Chapel Hill NC 27514

FRYE, HELEN JACKSON, federal judge; b. Klamath Falls, Oreg., Dec. 10, 1930; d. Earl and Elizabeth (Kirkpatrick) Jackson; m. William Frye, Sept. 7, 1952; children: Eric, Karen, Heidi; 1 adopted child, Hedy; m. Perry Holloman, July 10, 1980. BA in English with honors, U. Oreg., 1953, MA, 1960, JD, 1966. Bar: Oreg. 1966. Public sch. tchr. Oreg., 1956-63; pvt. practice Eugene, 1966-71; circuit ct. judge State of Oreg., 1971-80; U.S. dist judge Dist. Oreg. Portland, 1980—. Office: US Dist Ct 119 US Courthouse 620 SW Main St Portland OR 97205

FRYE, JUDITH ELEEN MINOR, editor; b. Seattle; d. George Edward and Eleen G. (Hartelius) Minor; student UCLA, 1947-48, U. So. Calif., 1948-53; m. Vernon Lester Frye, Apr. 1, 1954. Acct., office mgr. Colony Wholesale Liquor, Culver City, Calif., 1947-48; credit mgr. Western Distbg. Co., Culver City, 1948-53; ptnr. in restaurants, Palm Springs, L.A., 1948, ptnr. in date ranch, La Quinta, Calif., 1949-53; ptnr., owner Imperial Printing, Huntington Beach, Calif., 1955—; editor, pub. New Era Laundry and Cleaning Lines, Huntington Beach, 1962—; registered lobbyist, Calif., 1975-84. Mem. Textile Care Allied Trade Assn., Laundry & Dry Cleaning Suppliers Assn., Calif. Coin-op Assn. (exec. dir. 1975-84, Cooperation award 1971, Dedicated Svc.award 1976), Nat. Automatic Laundry & Cleaning Coun. (Leadership award 1972), Women Laundry & Drycleaning (past pres., Outstanding Svc. award 1977), Printing Industries Assn., Master Printers Am., Nat. Assn. Printers & Lithographers, Huntington Beach C. of C. Office: 22031 Bushard St Huntington Beach CA 92646

FRYER, JOAN COOK, education counselor; b. Dothan, Ala., Nov. 3, 1952; d. Tobe J. and Berlie (West) Cook; m. William Paul Fryer, July 21, 1983;. Student, Wallace Community Coll., Dothan, Ala., 1972; BA, U. Ala., 1974; MEd, Auburn U., 1980; postgrad., Fla. State U., 1988, Troy State U., 1989. Lic. profl. counselor, Ga. Counselor, dir. career ctr. Bainbridge (Ga.) Coll., 1980—. Mem. United Meth. Women, Sunday Sch. Tchr., Wesley Fellowship Sunday Sch. Class, Epworth Sunday Sch. Class, 1982-84, Social Concern Chairperson; mem. Bainbridge Little Theatre. Recipient gold and silver medallion for outstanding accomplishment. Mem. Am. Heart Assn., Am. Assn. Univ. Women, Am. Arthritis Assn., Auburn, Bainbridge Svc. Club, Delta Kappa Gamma, Alpha Delta Kappa. Democrat. Home: 1608 Pineland Dr Bainbridge GA 31717 Office: Bainbridge Coll Hwy 84 E Bainbridge GA 31717

FRYER-MCCULLOCH, BRONWYN, marketing communications executive; b. Glendale, Calif., Sept. 29, 1954; d. Wallace Lovatt and June Carolyn (Cummings) Fryer; m. C. McCulloch, May 13, 1989. BA, U. Calif., Santa Cruz, 1978; MA, U. Calif., Berkeley, 1980. Instr. U. Calif., Berkeley; writing dir. Ralph Silver Assocs. Pub. Rels., San Francisco; editor, writer San Francisco; mgr. editorial svcs. Ingres Corp., Alameda, Calif.; mgr. mktg. communications Legato Systems Inc., Palo Alto, Calif. Contbr. articles to nat. and regional mags. Mem. Internat. Assn. Bus. Communicators (award for best press release), , Pub. Rels. Soc. Am., Peninsula Mktg. Communications Assn., Inst. for Hist. Study, Media Alliance. Home: 115 Sky Londa Dr Woodside CA 94062

FRYXELL, GRETA ALBRECHT, oceanographer, educator; b. Princeton, Ill., Nov. 21, 1926; d. Arthur Joseph and Esther (Andreen) Albrecht; m. Paul A. Fryxell, Aug. 23, 1947; children: Karl Joseph, Joan Esther, Glen Edward. BA, Augustana Coll., 1948; MEd, Tex. A&M U., 1969, PhD, 1975. Tchr. math and sci. jr. high schs. Iowa, 1949-52; research asst. Tex. A&M U., College Station, 1968-71, research scientist, 1971-80, asst. prof., 1980-83, assoc. prof., 1983-86, prof. oceanography, 1986—; vis. scientist U. Oslo, 1971; chairperson adv. commn. Provasoli-Guillard Ctr. for Culture of Marine Phytoplankton Bigelow Lab, Maine, 1985-87. Editor: Survival Strategies of the Algae, 1983; contbr. articles to profl. jours. Recipient Outstanding Woman award Brazos County, College Station, 1979, Outstanding Achievement award Augustana Coll., Rock Island, Ill., 1980; NSF grantee. Mem. AAAS, AAUW, ACLU, Phycol. Soc. Am. (editorial bd. 1976-79, 82-85, chairperson Prescott award com.), Brit. Phycol. Soc., Internat. Phycol. Soc., Am. Soc. Limnology and Oceanography, Am. Soc. Plant Taxonomists, Internat. Diatom Soc. (bd. govs. 1986—), Tex. Assn. Coll. Tchrs. Democrat. Unitarian-Universalist. Home: 210 Redmond Dr College Station TX 77840-3129 Office: Tex A&M U Dept Oceanography College Station TX 77843-3146

FUCCI, LINDA DEAN, banker; b. Roanoke, Ala., July 2, 1947; d. Alton Hershall and Irma Nell (Trimble) Dean; m. Bob Fucci, Aug. 1981; children: Allen, Debbie, Nicky, Mark. AS, So. Union State Jr. Coll., Opelika, Ala., 1974; spl. courses Am. Inst. Banking, Am. Inst. Real Estate, Auburn U., Air U., Lanett, Ala.; grad. sch. banking, La. State U., 1986. Cert. flight instr. With Bank of East Ala., Opelika, 1968-72; adminstrv. asst. Auburn (Ala.) Nat. Bank, 1972-80, asst. v.p., 1980-82, v.p., 1982-84, v.p., cashier, chief fin. officer, 1984-88, sr. v.p., chief fin. officer, 1988—; sec.-treas. Auburn Nat. Bancorporation, 1985—; sec., bd. dirs. ANB System, Inc.; recruiter, pilot Air Trans, Auburn, 1979-81; instr. Ala. Banking Sch. U. S. Ala., 1989. Treas. Lee County Heart Assn., 1979-81; crusade chmn. Lee County Cancer Soc., 1980, pres., 1980; mem. Auburn Heritage Soc. Mem. Nat. Assn. Bank Women, Am. Heart Assn., Am. Inst. Banking (pres. East Ala. chpt. 1981, state com. 1982-84, instr. 1983—), Aircraft Owners and Pilots Assn., Ala. Bankers Assn. (funds mgmt. com. 1984—, chmn. 1989). Pilots Lobby. Roman Catholic. Home: PO Box 592 Auburn AL 36830 Office: PO Box 711 Auburn AL 36830

FUCHS, ELAINE V., molecular biologist, educator; b. Hinsdale, Ill., May 5, 1950; d. Louis H. and Viola L. (Lueck) F.; m. David T. Hansen, Sept. 10, 1988. BS in Chemistry with honors, U. Ill., Urbana, 1972; PhD in Biochemistry, Princeton U., 1977. Postdoctoral fellow dept. biology MIT, 1977-80; asst. prof. U. Chgo., 1980-85, assoc. prof., 1985-88, prof. dept. molecular genetics and cell biology, 1989—, investigator, Howard Hughes Inst., 1988—. Editorial bd. Jour. Cell Biology, 1988—; contbr. articles to profl. jours. Recipient R.R. Benseley award, Am. Assn. Anatomists, 1988, Searle Scholar award, Chgo. Community Trust, 1981-84, Presidential Young Investigator award, NSF, Washington, 1984-89. Mem. Am. Assn. Cell Biology, Am. Assn. Biol. Chemists, Phi Beta Kappa. Office: U Chgo Howard Hughes Med Inst Dept Molecular Genetics 5841 S Maryland Ave Chicago IL 60637

FUCHS, MARY ALLISON, hotel company executive; b. Detroit, Feb. 10, 1926; d. Lloyd H. and Mary (Peek) Allison; m. Arthur B. Fuchs, Oct. 31, 1948; 1 child, Gregory A. Student U. So. Calif.-Los Angeles. Asst. controller Anderson-Dunham, Los Angeles, 1947-56; paymaster Frontier Hotel, Las Vegas, 1956-57; asst. controller Tropicana Hotel, Las Vegas, 1957-73; paymaster MGM Grand Hotel, Las Vegas, 1973—, v.p., dir. Employees Credit Union, 1983—. Named Boss of Yr., Am. Bus. Women's Assn., 1985. Mem. Internat. Assn. Hospitality Accts. (Las Vegas chpt.; sec. 1981, treas. 1982, v.p. 1983, pres. 1984, chmn. bd. dirs. 1985, awards 1981, 84). Avocations: travel; reading. Office: Bally's Grand Inc 3645 Las Vega Blvd S Las Vegas NV 89109

FUCHS, PAMELA MARIE, marketing executive; b. Bartlesville, Okla., Apr. 10, 1964; d. Richard Charles and Joyce Marie (Jeffrey) F. BS in Mktg. and Mgmt., Okla. State U., 1986. Mktg. analyst Hillcrest Med. Ctr., Tulsa, 1989—. Office: Hillcrest Med Ctr 1120 S Utica Tulsa OK 74105

FUCHS, SAM LIEN, business administrator; b. Rapid City, S.D., Jan. 9, 1963; d. Charles H. and Barbara J. (Vidal) Lien; m. Robert E. Fuchs, May 31, 1986. BS, U. Wyo., 1985, MBA, 1986. Indsl. engr. Boeing Comml. Airplane Co., Everett, Wash.; mgr. Nine Liens Partnership, Rapid City; pres. Ingenious Software Inc., Rapid City; indsl. engr. Pete Lien & Sons, Rapid City. Treas. Trinity Luth. Ch.; pres. Black Hills Family Bus. Coun.; mem. grad. bus. chmn. Pennington County Air Quality Rev. Bd.; commr. SD Cement Plant. Address: PO Box 440 Rapid City SD 57709

FUDGE, DAWN NATALIE, restaurant owner, chef; b. Houston, Dec. 19, 1954; d. Frank James and Retha Mae (Bass) F. BS, U. Houston, 1978. Sec. to asst. compliance officer Am. Capital Asset Mgmt., Houston, 1973-78, portfolio asst., 1978-80, asst. compliance officer, 1980-85, compliance officer, 1985-87; owner, chef Last Concert Cafe, Houston, 1986—; instr. Leisure Learning Unltd., Houston, 1986—, Klein (Tex.) High Sch. Home Econs., summer 1990. Author: Tex-Mex with a Flair, 1987. mem. Rep. Senatorial Inner Circle, 1990. Mem. Tex. Restaurant Assn., Greater Houston Conv.

and Visitors Bur., Houston Restaurant Assn., Rosecrucian. Baptist. Home: 803 William St Houston TX 77002 Office: Last Concert Cafe 1403 Nance St Houston TX 77002

FUDGE, DEBORAH ANN, chiropractor; b. Medford, Mass., Mar. 2, 1961; d. Ronald S. and Marilyn P. (Robar) F.; m. Brian E. Varga, Dec. 7, 1986. Student, U. Southern Maine, 1981. Exam. dr. Dr. John E. Scola, Port Charlotte, Fla, 1986; chiropractor Varga Chropractic, Methuen, Mass., 1986—. Mem. MerriMack Valley Chiropractic Assn., Mass. Chiropractic Soc. Republican. Office: Dr Brian E Varga 230 B Pleasant St Methron MA 01844

FUDULI, ROBIN ANN, insurance sales executive; b. Seattle, Apr. 14, 1947; d. Anthony R. and Dorothy (Tatarka) Chapetta; m. Alfredo Fuduli, Dec. 7, 1980; children: Francesca La Pelusa, Allessandra La Pelusa, Gianluca. Lic. ins. agt., Calif. Account adminstr. Frank B. Hall, L.A., 1978-80; underwriter Mission Ins. Co., L.A., 1980-82; mktg. rep. Ins. Co. of West, Encino, Calif., 1982-85; from account mgr. to account exec. Sullivan Kelly and Assocs., L.A., 1985—. Active L.A. County Mus. Mem. Am. Mgmt. Assn., Am. Soc. Profl. and Exec. Women, Calif. Assn. Risk Mgrs., So. Calif. Risk Mgrs., L.A. Athletic Club, Toastmasters (pres. local chpt.). Democrat. Roman Catholic. Office: Sullivan Kelly and Assocs 800 W Sixth St Los Angeles CA 90017

FUENNING, ESTHER RENATE, educator; b. Florence, Mo.; d. Albert Theodore and Elizabeth (Muenzinger) F. BS, U. Nebr.; MA, Columbia U., 1952; doctoral program in recreation, U. Ill., Champaign. Dean of women Carthage (Ill.) Coll., 1949-50; asst. social dir. Ill. Union U., 1955-61; dean of women So. State Tchrs. Coll., Springfield, S.D., 1961-63; asst. dir. student activities Ill. Tchrs. Coll., South Chicago, 1963-64; prof. Wilbur Wright Coll., Chgo., 1964-77; sub. tchr. Chgo. Pub. Schs., 1977-82; tchr. dept. aging and disability Sr. Citizens Ctrs., Chgo., 1980—; dir. pub. relations Wright City Coll., 1964-77; del. Internat. Leisure and Recreation Congress, Krefeld, Germany, World Leisure and Recreation Assn, USSR. Author: pamphlets in field. Tour guide adults abroad Wright City coll., 1986—; del. for sr. citizens conf. Wilbur Wright Coll., 1984, organized art fair, 1968—. Served with Civilian Br., 1943-49, CBI. Recipient Gov. Thompson Sr. Leadership award, Outstanding Service award Wright Coll. Alumni., Dedicated and Outstanding Leadership award Wright Coll., 1975; inducted Chgo. Sr. Citizen Hall Fame. Republican.

FUENTES, SONIA PRESSMAN, lawyer; b. Berlin, May 30, 1928; came to U.S., 1934; d. Zysia and Hinda (Dombek) Pressman; m. Roberto Fuentes, Oct. 24, 1970 (div. Mar. 1980); 1 child, Zia Monina. BA, Cornell U., 1950; LLB sum cum laude, U. Miami, 1957. Bar: Fla. 1957, D.C. 1959, U.S. Supreme Ct. 1961. Claims atty. Office Alien Property U.S. Dept. Justice, Washington, 1957-59; legal asst. to chmn. NLRB, Washington, 1959-65; chief legis. counsel div. EEOC, Washington, 1965-73; sr. atty. GTE Svc. Corp., Stamford, Conn., 1973-81; dir. compliance mgmt. TRW, Inc., Cleve., 1981-84; atty. HUD, Washington, 1985—; cons. U.S. Dept. labor, Women's Bur., On., Can.; witness select com. Ho. of Lords, Eng.; Am. specialist USIA, Europe, S.E. Asia, Japan; legis. fellow HUD, 1988; legis. subcom. on labor U.S. Senate, spl. asst. to Congresswoman Nancy Pelosi. Contbr. articles on employment discrimination to profl. jours. Mem. NOW (founder), Women's Equity Action League (founder), Federally Employed Women (founder), Women in Mgmt. (founder), Phi Beta Kappa. Democrat. Jewish. Office: HUD 451 7th St SW Washington DC 20410

FUGATE, VIRGINIA KIMBROUGH, sales professional; b. Birmingham, Ala., July 31, 1940; d. George Willis and Sarah Margaret (Postelle) F.; m. Neil Peter Clarke, May 21, 1970 (div. May 1973). B in Music Edn., Fla. State U., 1962. Trainee draftsman Broward County Tax Assessor's Office, Fla., 1963; from systems engr. to adv. mktg. rep. IBM, 1963-70, 78-82; programmer, analyst 1st Nat. Bank Atlanta, 1970-71; program adminstr. Ins. Systems Am., Inc., 1971-72; sr. systems analyst Trusco Data Systems/Trust Co. Bank Ga., 1972-73; from systems engr. to mktg. rep. Data 100 Corp., 1973-78; sr. sales rep. Datapoint Corp., N.Y.C., 1983-84, 85-89; account exec. Wang Labs., 1984-85; with Systems Automation Inc., Ft. Lauderdale, 1989-90; agt. ADCAHB Fin. Planners, Inc., Coral Springs, Fla., 1990—. Backstage tour guide Met. Opera Guild, N.Y.C., 1982-88, dir. vols., 1985-88. Mem. DAR, Sigma Kappa (sec. 1960-61). Republican. Presbyterian. Home: 2881 NE 32 St Fort Lauderdale FL 33308

FUGELBERG, NANCY JEAN, educator; b. Tarentum, Pa., Mar. 6, 1947; d. Stanley and Mary (Struhar) Homer; m. Darrell Marvin Fugelberg, Aug. 27, 1977. Cert. master piano classes and music lit. Mozarteum, Salzburg, Austria, 1968; B.Music Edn., Mount Union Coll., 1969; postgrad. Kent State U., 1976; EdM in Curriculum and Instrn., Ashland U., 1989. Music tchr. Alliance Sch. Dist., Ohio, 1969-70, Minerva Sch. Dist., Ohio, 1970—; ch. organist First Imamnuel United Ch. of Christ, Alliance, Ohio, 1969-85. Pianist for musicals Carnation Players, Alliance, 1969-72. Recipient award for working with handicapped children Minerva Sch. Dist., 1981; Alumni Service award Mu Phi Epsilon, 1983, 84; named One of Outstanding Young Women Am., 1981. Mem. Music Educators Nat. Conf., Minerva Tchrs. Assn., NEA, Mu Phi Epsilon (chpt. v.p. 1980-82, pres. 1982-84). Democrat. United Ch. of Christ. Avocations: plants, traveling. Address: 345 S Rockhill Ave Alliance OH 44601

FUHR, THERESA MARIE, gerontologist; b. Flushing, N.Y., Aug. 27, 1964; d. Joseph Ernest and Erika Joan (Benz) F. BA in Psychology, U. Dayton, 1986; MS in Gerontology, Med. Coll. Va., 1988. Rsch. asst. Med. Coll. Va./Va. Commonwealth U. and Beth Sholom Woods, Richmond, 1987; rsch. asst. gerontology and psychology depts. Med. Coll. Va., 1986-87; asst. dir. activities Beaufont Towers, Richmond, 1986-88; recreation, social dir. Ginter Hall West, Richmond, 1988; project dir. Va. Housing Devel. Authority, Richmond, 1988—; presenter to confs. in field. Author various publs. in field; appeared on talk show WKIE-AM radio, 1990. Recipient Notable Accomplishment award Crawford Convalescent Home, 1986; Robert Wood Johnson Found. grantee, 1989—; Commonwealth of Va. fellow, 1986-87. Mem. Am. Soc. on Aging, NAFE, Va. Assn. on Aging, Phi Kappa Phi. Republican. Roman Catholic. Office: Va Housing Devel Authority 601 S Belvidere St Richmond VA 23220

FUHRMAN, ESTHER, sculptor, business owner, jewelry designer; b. Pitts., Pa., Feb. 25, 1939; d. Harry and Lena (Bernstein) Segal; m. Robert J. Fuhrman, Oct. 29, 1961; children: Debbi Lynn, Mimi Suzanne, Karen Leigh. Student, Pa. State U., 1956-57; BFA, U. Pitts., 1960. Sculptor Fuhrman Assocs., Jenkintown, 1968—; pres. Demika, Inc., Huntington, N.Y., 1970-75; jewelry designer Esther Fuhrman Designs, Jenkintown, 1986—, Avante Products Corp., Rivers Edge, N.J., 1988—; name lic. by Calderon Bag and Belt Co., The Tana Collections; Joslyn Collection. Vice pres. bd. assocs. Fox Chase Cancer Ctr., Pa., 1985. Mem. Sculptors League N.Y. (v.p.), Nat. Assn. Women Artists (Sculpture 1980), Art Alliance Phila., Artists Equity. Home: 428 Newbold Rd Jenkintown PA 19046 Office: Avante Products Corp 7700 River Rd North Bergen NJ 07047

FUJIKAWA, EVA, automotive executive; b. Santa Monica, Calif., May 27, 1958; d. Osamu Sam and Teruko (Nakamizo) F. BA, U. of the Pacific, 1979; MBA, Loyola Marymount U., Westchester, Calif., 1985. Bus. mgr. Hughes Aircraft Co. (subs. GM), El Segundo, Calif., 1979—, Culver City, Calif., 1979—. Mem. Am. Mgmt. Assn., Nat. Contracts Mgmt. Assn., L.A. World Affairs Coun., El Segundo C. of C. (indusl. activities com. 1989—), Japanese-Am. Nat. Mus., Econ. Ventures Com. Methodist. Home: 1633 E Palm Ave Apt 4 El Segundo CA 90245

FUJIWARA, ELIZABETH JUBIN, lawyer; b. New Orleans, Dec. 20, 1945; d. Otha Ernest and Yvette Marie (Jubin) Barron; m. Ronald Toshio Fujiwara, Jan. 7, 1978; children: Jean Paul Jubin Toshiro, Maria Sachiko, Cathleen Sumiko Yonahara. Student, U. Tex., Irving, 1963-64; BA in Sociology, Loyola U., New Orleans, 1967; MSW, U. Hawaii, 1971, JD, 1983. Exec. dir. ACLU of Hawaii, Honolulu, 1975-77; specialist in equal edn. opportunity Dept. Edn., Honolulu, 1978; asst. dir. Inst. Productive Behavior, Honolulu, 1978-80; faculty rsch. asst. William S. Richardson Sch. Law, U. Hawaii, Honolulu, 1981; law clk. to presiding justice Intermediate Ct. Appeals Hawaii, Honolulu, 1984-86; pvt. practice law Honolulu, 1986-87; ptnr. Fujiwara & Fujiwara, Attys. At Law, Honolulu, 1988—. Editor: Handbook Women's Legal Rights in Hawaii, 1990. Active Hawaii Women's Polit. Action League, 1983-85, 89—, Ad Hoc Com. Abortion Rights, 1977-79; organizer Coalition Against Capital Punishment, 1976-78; Peace Corps trainee in P.R. and Guatemala, 1968. Named one of Outstanding Young Women of Yr. State Commn. on Status of Women, 1976, Outstanding Hawaii Woman Lawyer of Yr., 1988. Mem. ABA, Hawaii Bar Assn., Assn. Trial Lawyers Am., Hawaii Women Lawyers (co-chair pay equity com. 1985-87, spouse abuse and women prisoners legal penal project 1985-88, mem. legis. com. 1985-87, bd. dirs.), Clark Hatch Health Club, Women's Support Group, Kappa Beta Gamma. Democrat. Buddhist. Office: Cen Pacific Pla 220 S King St Ste 1501 Honolulu HI 96813

FUKUSHIMA, BARBARA NAOMI, accountant; b. Honolulu, Apr. 5, 1948; d. Harry Kazuo and Misayo (Kawasaki) Murakoshi; B.A. with high honors, U. Hawaii, 1970; postgrad. Oreg. State U., 1971, 73, U. Oreg., 1972; m. Dennis Hiroshi Fukushima, Mar. 23, 1974; 1 son, Dennis Hiroshi Jr. Intern, Coopers & Lybrand, Honolulu, 1974; auditor Haskins & Sells, Kahului, Hawaii, 1974-77; pres. Book Doors, Inc., Pukalani, 1977—; pres. Barbara N. Fukushima C.P.A., Inc., Wailuku. 1979—; sec. treas. Target Pest Control, Inc., Wailuku, 1979—; internal auditor, acct. Maui Land & Pineapple Co., Inc., Kahului, 1977-80; auditor Hyatt Regency Maui, Kaanapali, 1980-81; ptnr. D & B Internat., Pukalani, 1980—; instr. Maui Community Coll., Kahului, 1982-85; fin. cons. Merrill Lynch, Pierce, Fenner & Smith, Inc., 1986—. Recipient Phi Beta Kappa Book award, 1969. Mem. Am. Inst. C.P.A.s, Hawaii Soc. C.P.A.s, Nat. Assn. Accts., Hawaii Assn. Public Accts., Bus. and Profl. Women's Club. Tenrikyo. Home: 200 Aliiolani St Pukalani HI 96768 Office: 1001 Bishop St Penthouse Honolulu HI 96813

FULE, VILMA GARCIA, plastic and reconstructive surgeon; b. San Pablo City, The Philippines, May 14, 1950; came to U.S., 1976; d. Franco Ariston and Virginia (Alcaide Garcia) F.; m. Jose L. Castro, May 3, 1980; 1 child, Virginia del Carmen. BS, U. Santo Tomas, Manila, 1970, MD cum laude, 1974. Intern Phila. Gen. Hosp., 1975, Elizabeth (N.J.) Gen. Hosp., 1976-77; resident in surgery Hosp. for Joint Disease, 1977-81; fellow in plastic surgery Lehigh Valley Hosp. Ctr., 1982-84; fellow Milton S. Hershey Med. Ctr., 1984; pvt. practice Jersey City, 1984-85; cons. Christ Hosp., N.J., 1985—, St. Francis Hosp., N.J., 1985—, Palisades Gen. Hosp., North Bergen, N.J., 1985—, Jersey City Med. Ctr., 1985—. Mem. Am. Assn. Plastic and Reconstructive Surgery, Oculoplastic Fellowship Soc., N.Y. Acad. Scis., Hudson Med. Soc. Roman Catholic. Home: 1077 River Rd Apt N-904 Edgewater NJ 07020 Office: 2730 Kennedy Blvd Jersey City NJ 07304

FULGHAM, BETTY REEVES, nursing educator; b. McComb, Miss., Apr. 10, 1951; d. Richard and Ida Mae (Roberts) Reeves; m. William W. Fulgham, July 11, 1969; (div. 1985); 1 child, Richard. BS, U. So. Miss., 1977; MS in Nursing, U. Miss., 1981. Staff charge nurse S.W. Miss. Reg. Med. Ctr., McComb, 1977-86, house supr., 1986—; instr. S.W. Miss. Community Coll., Summit, 1977—; seminar presenter, 1987-88. Mem. NAFE, Miss. Profl. Educators, Orgn. for Advancement of Assoc. Deg. in Nursing, Sigma Theta Tau. Home: MR Box 18B Summit MS 39666 Office: SW Mississippi Comm Coll Summit MS 39666

FULKS, SARAH JANE See WYMAN, JANE

FULLER, BER KAREN LACKRITZ, trading company executive; b. Summit, N.J., Oct. 6, 1960; d. Robert Works and Ann (Lackritz) F. Grad. Inst. Internat. Studies, U. Calif., Berkeley, 1985; MA, Columbia U., 1985; doctoral student, London Sch. Econs., 1985-86; Diplôma, U. Geneva. Tchr. Beijing Second Fgn. Lang. Inst., 1986-87; prodn. asst. NBC News, Beijing, 1987, ABC News, Beijing, 1987-88; dir. Chinese affairs Son of Heaven-Chinese Art Exhbn., Seattle, 1988-89; adminstrv. dir., asst. to pres. China House Trading Co., Seattle, 1989; adminstrv. cons. Ocean Rsch. and Conservation Assn., Seattle, 1989—. Fellow Columbia U., 1983, research fellow London Sch. Econs., 1986. Mem. Phi Beta Kappa. Home: 6610 Fremont Ave N Seattle WA 98103

FULLER, CAROLINE CASE, lawyer; b. Great Bend, Kans., Oct. 14, 1956; d. Lowell C. and Rosemary (Callahan) Case; m. Henry S. Fuller III (dec. May 1989); 1 child, Chase. BA, So. Meth. U., 1977; JD, U. Tex., 1980. Bar: Tex. 1980, Ark. 1982, Colo. 1984, U.S. Dist. Ct. Colo. 1986. Assoc. Hancock & Piedfort, Austin, Tex., 1980-82, The Wood Law Firm, North Little Rock, Ark., 1983-84; law clk. to presiding justice U.S. Bankruptcy Ct. Colo. Dist., Denver, 1985-86; assoc. Fairfield & Woods, P.C., Denver, 1986—. Mem. ABA, Colo. Bar Assn., Tex. Bar Assn. Office: Fairfield & Woods PC 1700 Lincoln St #2400 Denver CO 80203

FULLER, CASSANDRA MILLER, retailer executive; b. Norwalk, Conn., Dec. 10, 1965; d. George Louis and Bernice (Simmons) Miller; m. David Norman Fuller, Dec. 24, 1988. BS, S.C. State Coll., 1987. Interior decorator's apprentice Marty Rae Interiors, Orangeburg, S.C., 1984-85; asst. mgr. Dairy Queen, Orangeburg, S.C., 1986-87; day mgr. The Bedford, Stamford, Conn., 1987-88; dept. mgr. Burlington Coat Factory Warehouse, Danbury, Conn.; cons. Orangeburg Metro Transit 1987. Recipient Cleanliness and Purity award Dairy Queen Orangeburg, S.C. 1986. Mem: Nat. Assn. of Female Execs., Kappa Omicron Phi. Democrat. Baptist.

FULLER, CONSTANCE CRAIN, human resources consultant; b. Union, Mo., June 3, 1947; d. Gilbert L. and Doris (Toelke) Crain; children: Peter Jonathan Briddell, Jeremy Michael Briddell. BA, Nat. Coll., Chgo., 1985; MBA, Fontbonne Coll., St. Louis, 1987. Cert. Profl. Sec. From sec. to staff cons. comml. Bethlehem Steel Corp., St. Louis, 1867-88; sr. HR cons. comml. Bethlehem (Pa.) Steel Corp., 1988-90; cons. Denver, 1990—; adjunct prof. Organizational Devel. Masters in HRD program, Webster U., St. Louis, 1988, adjunct lectr. Organizational Behavior MBA program, Lehigh U., Bethlehem, Pa., 1989. Author: "The Koetting Touch", 1984. Mem. American Soc. for Tng. and Devel. Lutheran. Home: 16525 E Alamo Pl Denver CO 80015

FULLER, DIANA LYNN, lawyer; b. Morgantown, W.Va., Nov. 16, 1952; d. William Fleming and Amelia Marie (Lattanzi) F.; m. Robert Deeb Batey, July 21, 1979. B.S., W.Va. U., 1972, J.D., 1977. Bar: W.Va. 1977, U.S. Dist. Ct. (so. dist.) W.Va. 1977, Fla. 1978, U.S. Dist. Ct. (no., mid. and so. dists.) Fla., U.S. Ct. Appeals (5th and 11th cirs.). Law clk., ct. crier to chief judge U.S. Dist. Ct. (mid. dist.) Fla., Tampa, 1977-79, arbitrator arbitration program; ptnr. Fowler, White, Gillen, Boggs, Villareal & Banker, P.A., Tampa, 1979-85; ptnr. Smith & Fuller, P.A., Tampa, 1985—; lectr. in area of constrn. law. Contbr. articles to profl. jours. Mem. ABA (del. gen. assembly 1984, litigation sect., construction litigation com.), Forum on the Construction Industry, Am. Judicature Soc., Fed. Bar Assn., Hillsborough County Bar Assn., W.Va. Trial Lawyers Assn., Greater Tampa C. of C., Nat. Coun. of W.Va. U. Coll. of Law, Phi Alpha Delta. Home: 2418 W Palm Dr Tampa FL 33629 Office: 101 E Kennedy Blvd Suite 1800 Tampa FL 33602

FULLER, DICKIE M., nutritional consultant; b. Leadville, Colo., Sept. 14, 1942; d. Richard James and Mae Maxine (Malin) Doyle; m. Norman Keith Fuller, Nov. 8, 1987; children: Paul Holcomb, Coleen Holcomb. Student, U. Ariz., U. Tex., El Paso, U. N.Mex., Inst. Nutritional Edn. Cert. nutritional counselor, colon therapist, enzyme therapist, NLP practioner. Tech. specialist, educator 21st Century Nutrition, Forsyth, Mo. Contbr. articles to profl. jours. Mem. Soc. Neuro Linguistic Programming, Psycho Neurology Found., Am. Assn. Nutritional Consultants, Occidental Inst. Rsch. Found. Home: 8870 Fiesta Terr Littleton CO 80124

FULLER, GAIL MARIE, health services executive, consultant; d. Ralph Thomas and Elizabeth Cora (Chapman) Frisk; m. Keith Edward Fuller, Nov. 9, 1968; children: Daniel Jason, Joanna Marie. BA in Secondary Edn., Elmira (N.Y.) Coll., 1971; MS in Edn., SUNY, 1979. Lectr. SUNY, Binghamton, 1979, 90; tng. coord. Savin Corp., Binghamton, 1979-83; edn. specialist IBM, Owego, N.Y., 1983; program dir. SUNY, Binghamton, 1984; mgr. tng. and devel. United Health Svcs., Johnson City, N.Y., 1985—; lectr. Broome Community Coll., Binghamton, 1986. Mem. Am. Soc. Tng. and Devel. (bd. dirs. So. Tier 1987-90), So. Tier Personnel Assn. Home: Box 303D Matthews Dr Binghamton NY 13901 Office: United Health Svcs Mitchell Ave Binghamton NY 13903

FULLER, JEWEL LADENE ADAMS, hospital administrator; b. Geneva, Ala., June 22, 1933; d. James M. and Aggie (Somerset) Adams; widowed; children: James David, Anne Fuller Warlick, Philip Ernest. BS, U. Tenn., 1978; MS, Memphis State U., 1983. Cert. med. technologist Am. Soc. Clin. Pathologists. Staff med. technician St. Francis Hosp., Columbus, Ga., 1961-66; staff med. technician Martin Army Hosp., Ft. Benning, Ga., 1966-67, VA Hosp., Atlanta, 1967-68; staff med. technologist VA Hosp., Memphis, 1968-77; mgr. Med Express Labs. Inc. Methodist Hosp., Memphis, 1977-87; adminstrv. resident St. Francis Hosp., Columbus, 1987-88; adminstrv. asst. St. Francis Hosp., 1988-89, asst. adminstr., 1989—; bd. dirs. Am. Red. Cross, Columbus, Am. Heart Assn.; group leader AIDS Task Force, Columbus, 1988-89; dept. chairperson United Way Campaign, Memphis, 1985. Vol. Counseling/Rape Crises Ctr., Memphis, 1983-84; mediator Citizens Dispute Program Shelby County Ct., Memphis, 1982-83. Mem. Am. Pub. Health Assn., Am. Soc. for Med. Tech. (treas. 1985-86). Democrat. Office: St Francis Hosp PO Box 7000 Columbus GA 31995

FULLER, JUANITA FAISON, writer; b. Greenville, Ala., Jan. 3, 1927; d. William Moody and Johnie Alma (Pryor) Faison; m. Edward Fuller, Aug. 23, 1954; 1 child, Sharon Anne Hurst. Student, Ala. Polytechnic Inst., 1946. Bookkeeper Tom Fitzpatrick CPA, Montgomery, Ala., 1947-49, Teague Hdwe Co., Montgomery, 1949-51, Regial Glove Co., Greenville, Ala., 1951-53, Thagard Finance Co., Greenville, Ala.; lab. tech. Monsanto Co., Pensacola, Fla., 1954-79; writer Ala., 1973-89. Contbr. poems to prof. jours. Asst. leader, Girl Scouts of Am., Pensacola, Fla., 1962-72, mem. Hist. Soc., Greenville, 1984-86, vol. fire dept., 1982-89, asst. leader, Boy Scouts of Am., 1987-89. Mem. Ala. State Poetry Soc. Democratic. Methodist. Home: Route 5 Box 50A Greenville AL 36037

FULLER, JULIA PAZDRAL, assistant treasurer, cash manager; b. Brenham, Tex., Apr. 20, 1945; d. George Vashie and Lucille (Brown) Pazdral; m. Jerry B. Fuller; 1 child, Suzanne. BS in Edn., Tex. Christian U., 1967. Cert. cash mgr. Tchr. Corpus Christi (Tex.) Ind. Sch. Dist., 1967-68; office mgr. Lincoln Orthodontic Clinic, Corpus Christi, 1968-69; adminstrv. asst. Tex. Industries Inc., Dallas, 1969-72, cash mgr., 1972-83, asst. treas., 1983—. Officer PTA CFBISD, 1985—; key communicator Carrollton/Farmers Br. Ind. Sch. Dist., Carrollton, 1987—; tchr. Jr. Achievement Project Bus., Irving, Tex., 1979. Mem. Dallas Cash Mgmt. Assn. (membership chairperson 1981, sec. 1982, treas. 1983), Nat. Corp. Cash Mgmt. Assn. (bd. dirs. 1989—). Republican. Methodist. Office: Tex Industries Inc 7610 Stemmons Frwy Dallas TX 75247

FULLER, JULIA RUTH, computer analyst; b. Detroit, Oct. 25, 1958; d. William James and Julia Henrietta (Thomas) Coleman; m. Darnell Fuller, Nov. 10, 1984 (div. Dec. 1988). BA in Computer Sci., Wayne State U., 1980. Programmer analyst Mich. Bell Telephone Co., Detroit, 1980-82; tech. support analyst Unisys Corp. (formally Burroughs), Detroit, 1982—. Musician Met. Community Tabernacle, Detroit, 1975-84, 88—, Greater Faith New Covenant Assembly, Detroit, 1985-87. Democrat. Office: Unisys Corp 1 Unisys Pl Detroit MI 48232

FULLER, KAREN ANN, health service administrator; b. Buffalo, Feb. 7, 1947; d. F. Robert and Phyllis (Townsend) Kirsch; divorced; children: Ray D. Fuller, Dean Alan Fuller. AAS in Nursing, Niagara County Community Coll., 1973; BS in Nursing, D'Youville Coll., 1975; MS, Southwest U., 1985, PhD, 1986. RN, N.Y., Fla.; lic. practical nurse, N.Y.; cert. adult home adminstr., N.Y. Nurse's aide Mt. View Hosp., Lockport, N.Y., 1969-73; staff nurse in-charge Lockport Meml. Hosp., 1973-75; dir. nursing Newfane (N.Y.) Health Facility, 1976-78, Erie County Home & Infirmary, Alden, N.Y., 1978-79; dir. healthcare Manpower, Inc., Buffalo, 1979-82; dir. nursing Beechwood Residence & Nursing Home, Getzville, N.Y., 1982-84, St. Francis Hosp., Buffalo, 1984-86; adminstr. Bassett Manor, West Side Manor Wegman Cos., Williamsville and Liverpool, N.Y., 1987; v.p. RKS Mgmt. Svcs., Inc., Buffalo, 1988; pres. Fuller Assocs., Inc., Lockport, N.Y., 1989—; cons. in field. Author: The Ambulatory Surgery Experience, 1986. Mem. Occupational Adv. Council, Liverpool, 1987—. Fed. grantee D'Youville Coll., 1975; Lilla Hooper Meml. scholar, 1974-75. Mem. NAFE. Republican. Presbyterian. Home: 26 Bob-O-Link Ln Lockport NY 14094

FULLER, MARGARET VIRGINIA, nurse; b. Wynne, Ark., Dec. 28, 1948; d. Earnest B. and Irene (Robinson) Fowlkes; m. John Luther Fuller, Dec. 12, 1969; children: Johnny, Mary Virginia. Diploma, Meth. Hosp. Sch. of Nursing, Memphis, 1969. RN. Head nurse of diagnostic neurology Meth. Hosp., Memphis, 1975-77, head of patient mgmt. system, instr., 1977-81, coordinator of nursing info. system, 1981-85; mgr. patient care system Healthcare Internat., Austin, Tex., 1985-89; office nurse Austin Urology Assocs., 1989—; speaker in field. Mem. Am. Nurses Assn., Tex. Nurses Assn., Tenn. Nurses Assn. Republican. Baptist. Home: 11521 Chancellroy Austin TX 78759 Office: Austin Urology Assocs 11111 Research Ste 220 Austin TX 78759

FULLER, MOZELLE JAMES, clergywoman, retired nurse; b. Greer, S.C., Aug. 10, 1909; d. William and Julie (Lipscomb) James; m. James Henry Fuller, Mar. 12, 1928; 1 child, Shirley Lindsey Berkley. Diploma, Nat. Inst. Nursing; student, Howard U.; DD (hon.), Universal Life Ch., Christ Mission, 1980. Ordained to ministry Penecostal Bapt. Ch., 1967. Personality Sta. WOL and Sta. WMMJ-FM, Washington; bd. dirs. Internat. Found. for the Performing Arts. Mem. D.C. Commn. on Aging; co-founder Ch. of What's Happening Now; missionary Peace Bapt. Ch., 1949—; founder Sr. Citizens United To Serve Humanity. Recieved Nat. Black Monitor Hall of Fame Community Bldg. award. Mem. Women Ministers Greater Washington, Ministers in Partnership, Am. Legion Aux. Democrat. Baptist. Home: 624 17th St NE Washington DC 20002

FULLER, PAULA G., travel industry executive; b. Atlanta, Dec. 18, 1949; d. Paul D. and Edith Louise (Brice) Gentle; children: Laura, George, Jennifer. AAS in Mktg., Clayton State Coll., Morrow, Ga. Cewrt. in Lotus, word processing, travel agy. ops., ct. reporting. From. rental rep. to comml. accounts Hertz Corp., Atlanta, account svc. rep. Recipient ednl. grants. Mem. NAFE, Ga. Coun. Notaries, Travel Industry Assn. Ga. Republican. Baptist. Office: 4751 Best Rd Ste 400 Atlanta GA 30337

FULLER, SHARON S., insurance agent; b. Hagerstown, Md., Sept. 6, 1946; d. Gerald Browning and Lillian Dorathy (Lane) Smith. Student schs. Hagerstown. Cert. ins. agt., Fla.; lic. ins. rep., mgr. With Washington Adventist Hosp., Takoma Park, Md., 1968-79; word processing coordinator Fla. Hosp., Orlando, 1979-84; info. systems adminstr. Broad & Cassel, Miami, Fla., 1984-85; ins. agt., Orlando, 1985—; owner, gen. mgr. Fuller Agy., 1987—. Contbr. articles to profl. publ. Active Competency Evaluation Com. Orange County Pub. Schs., Orlando, 1984-85. Mem. Assn. Info. Systems Profls. (v.p. 1985). Seventh-day Adventist. Avocations: reading; travel. Home: 8712 Gopher Ln Orlando FL 32829 Office: Fuller Agy PO Box 720356 Orlando FL 32822

FULLER, SUE, artist; b. Pitts.; d. Samuel Leslie and Carrie (Cassedy) F. B.A., Carnegie Inst. Tech., 1936; M.A., Columbia U., 1939. Producer: movies String Composition, 1970, 74; one-woman shows include Bertha Schaefer Gallery, McNay Art Inst., San Antonio, Norfolk Mus. Currier Gallery, Corcoran Gallery, Smithsonian Instn., others; exhibited in group shows including Aldrich Mus., Corcoran Gallery, Phila. Mus., Mus. Modern Art, Whitney Mus., Bklyn. Mus., Brit. Mus., London, others; represented in permanent collections Addison Gallery Am. Art, Larry Aldrich Mus., Chgo. Art Inst., Des Moines Art Ctr., Ford Found., Met. Mus., Guggenheim Mus., Whitney Mus. Am. Art, Tate Gallery London, Brit. Mus. London, Library of Congress, others; commd. works include Unitarian Ch. All Souls, N.Y.C., 1980, Tobin Library, McNay Art Mus., San Antonio, 1984. Recipient Alumni Merit award Carnegie Mellon U., 1974, CAA/WCA Nat. Honor award, 1986; Louis Comfort Tiffany fellow, 1948; Guggenheim fellow, 1949; Nat. Inst. Arts and Letters grantee, 1950; Eliot Pratt Found. fellow, 1966-68; Mark Rothko Found. grantee, 1973; U. Cin. Nat. Sculpture Conf.: Works by Women honoree, 1987. Home: PO Box 1580 Southampton NY 11969

FULLER, TRACY ANNETTE, laboratory executive; b. Oklahoma City, Apr. 11, 1962; d. Billy Newton and Barbara Sue (Barnes) F. AA in Home Econs., Abraham Baldwin Coll., 1982; BS in Home Econs. & Journ, U. Ga.,

1984. County agrl. agt., home economist Ga. Coop. Extension Svc., Douglas, 1984-87; territory mgr. sales Ross Labs. div. Abbott Labs., Marietta, Ga., 1987—. Contbr. articles to local newspaper; guest TV program, 1986 (Communication award). Recipient Young Profl. of Yr. award Ga. Home Econs. Assn., 1986. Mem. Cobb Area Pediatric Soc. (exec. sec. 1988—). Republican. Lutheran. Home: 2080 Bishop Creek Dr Marietta GA 30062 Office: Ross Labs 2080 Bishop Creek Dr Marietta GA 30062

FULLER, WANDA LOU, state representative; b. Browning, Mo., Sept. 12, 1938; d. Harry L. and Alta Eulavea (Browning) Longwell; divorced; children: Carla E., John C. and Lori K. Student, Kansas City Jr. Coll., 2956, Wichita State U., 1974. Dept. sec. Hallmark Cards Inc., Kansas City, Mo., 1955-57, U. Mo., Rolla, 1957-59; assoc. tchr. Wichita Preschool for Blind, Kans., 1975; program coord. State Republican Party of Kansas, Wichita, 1978; office adminstr. Downtown Lions Club, Wichita, Kans., 1980-82; state representative Kansas, 1981—; cons. State Republican Party, Wichita, Kans., 1982—. Recipient Woman of Yr. award Wichita Zonta Club, 1985, Thanks badge, Wichita Area Girl Scout Coun., 1974, Citizenship award Princeton (Mo.) C. of C. Mem. Citizen Participation Orgn., Wichita, Normandy Republican Women, Nat. Fedn. Republican Women, Nat. Order Women Legislators, Nat. Conf. State Legislators, Wichita Childrens Home Bd., Booth Family Svcs. Adv. Coun., Sedgwick County Mental Health Adv. Bd., Kansas Ombudsman for Corrections, Wichita-Sedgwick County (Bus. Edn. Success Team Bd.), League of Women Voters (bd. dirs. 1974-78), Womans Soc. Christian Svc. (pres. 1964-66), Girl Scout Alumni and Friends Inc. (pres. 1987—). Mem. Christian Ch. Home: 2808 Sennett Wichita KS 67211 Office: Ho of Reps Statehouse Topeka KS 66612-1591

FULLER LEVINE, JANICE CAROL, nurse; b. Detroit, Jan. 22, 1942; d. James Edward and Marjorie Ann (Brumitt) Smith; div.; children: Colleen, Lana, James, John; m. Hervert Levine. Degree in Practical Nursing, E.C. Goodwin Tech. Coll.-New Britain Gen. Hosp., 1969; diploma in Nursing, Tunxis Community Coll., 1981; student in familty therapy porgram, U. Conn., 1983-84; student, Mid State Sch. Family Therapy, 1984-85. RN Conn.; cert. psychiat. and mental health nursing A.N.A. Lic. practical nurse Geri-Care, Farmington, Conn., 1969-71; staff nurse for pvt. physician, New Britain, Conn., 1971-75, NCCB, Bristol, Conn., 1975-81; supr. nursing Nursing Care Ctr. Bristol, Bristol, 1981-84, Elmcrest Psychiat. Inst., Portland, Conn., 1984-86; exec. dir. families domestic violence Coping Ctr., Middletown, Conn., 1986—; lectr. on drugs and family violence various pub. schs. Mem. exec. bd. New Haven chpt. Am. Heart Assn., 1986; bd. dirs. sexual assault crisis service Middlesex County, 1987-88, Nat. Orgn. Victim Assistance, 1988, Am. Heart Assn. Middlesex County, 1986-88. Mem. Am. Nurses Assn., Nat. Assn. Female Execs. Office: Coping Ctr 770 Saybrook Rd Middletown CT 06457

FULLERTON, GAIL JACKSON, university president; b. Lincoln, Nebr., Apr. 29, 1927; d. Earl Warren and Gladys Bernice (Marshall) Jackson; m. Stanley James Fullerton, Mar. 27, 1967; children by previous marriage—Gregory Snell Putney, Cynde Putney Mitchell. B.A., U. Nebr., 1949, M.A., 1950; Ph.D., U. Oreg., 1954. Lectr. sociology Drake U., Des Moines, 1955-57; asst. prof. sociology Fla. State U., Tallahassee, 1957-60; asst. prof. sociology San Jose (Calif.) State U., 1963-67, asso. prof., 1968-71, prof., 1972—, dean grad. studies and research, 1972-76, exec. v.p. univ., 1976-78, pres., 1978—; bd. dirs. Assoc. Western Univs., Inc., 1980—; mem. sr. accrediting commn. Western Assn. Schs. and Colls., 1982-88, chmn., 1985-86; mem. Pres.'s Commn. Nat. Collegiate Athletic Assn., 1988—. Author: Survival in Marriage, 2d edit, 1977, (with Snell Putney) Normal Neurosis: The Adjusted American, 2d edit, 1966. Carnegie fellow, 1950-51, 52-53; Doherty Found. fellow, 1951-52. Mem. Am. Sociol. Assn., Western Coll. Assn. (exec. com., past pres.), Nat. Collegiate Athletic Assn. (pres.'s commn.), San Jose C. of C. (bd. dirs.), Phi Beta Kappa. Home: 97 E St James St #58 San Jose CA 95112 Office: San Jose State U Washington Sq San Jose CA 95192-0001

FULLERTON, MOLLIE HAYS, psychotherapist; b. Homer City, Pa.; d. Ray Atkins and Elizabeth (Nicely) Pulliam; m. James Daniel, Feb. 23, 1963 (div. 1978); children: Jeffery, Ashley, Amanda, Jonathan. MEd, Cambridge Coll., 1988. Moderator Armed Forces Radio & TV, Roykjauik, Iceland, 1970; counselor Planned Parenthood, Colorado Springs, 1978; dir. mktg., sales Sea Watch Assoc., Bourne, Mass., 1980-84; pres. Hays Holmes, Sandwich, Mass., 1984-87; intern Independence House, Hyannis, Mass., 1987—. Republican. Episcopalian. Home: 15 Pond View Rd Sandwich MA 02537

FULLERTON, SALLY ANN, human services educator; b. Portland, Oreg., Dec. 31, 1934; d. Roland and Ida (Berger) Hornecker; m. Earl R. Fullerton, June 13, 1964. BS, Oreg. State U., 1956; MA, Cornell U., 1960; PhD, U. Oreg., 1970. County 4-H Club agt. Oreg. State U. Extension, Oregon City, 1956-59; instr., asst. dean of women So. Oreg. Coll., Ashland, 1960-62, Pacific U., Forest Grove, Oreg., 1963-64; vocat. counselor Lane County Youth Project, Eugene, Oreg., 1964-66; evaluation officer regional tng. program VISTA, Eugene, 1966-68; social worker Springfield (Oreg.) Sch. Dist., 1968-70; from asst. prof. to full prof. U. Oreg., Eugene, 1970—, dept. head, 1972-77, 82—. Editor: History of Human Service Movement, 1990; contbr. articles to profl. jours. Mem. Nat. Orgn. Human Svc. Edn. (newsletter editor 1985-88, bd. dirs. 1985-90, chair profl. devel. com. 1988-90, Mirian Clubok award 1988), Am. Psychol. Assn., Mortar Bd., Phi Kappa Phi. Office: U Oreg Dept Human Svcs Eugene OR 97403

FULLERTON, SUSAN KATHRYN, chemical and environmental engineer; b. Roseville, Mich., Sept. 30, 1957; d. Albert and Florence (Martell) Minicucci; m. Charles Eugene Fullerton III, Dec. 28, 1985; children: Charles Jacob, Taylor Andrew. BSE, Mich. State U., 1980; MSE, U. Mich., 1984. Registered profl. engr., Va. Jr. engr. NIOSH, Rockville, Md., 1978, E.I. DuPont Co., Troy, Mich., 1979; sr. engr. Office Radiol. Health, Rockville, 1980-84; sr. project mgr., cons. Engring.-Sci., Inc., Virginia Beach, Va., 1984—. Lt. USPHS, 1979-84. Mem. Soc. Women Engrs. (pres. 1987-88), ASCE. Roman Catholic.

FULLING, KATHARINE PAINTER, educator, writer; b. Dodge City, Kans.; d. William George and Carrie (Lopp) Painter; m. Virgil H. Fulling, Sept. 24, 1948. BA, Northwestern U., 1940; MA, Columbia U., 1947; postgrad., Vassar Coll., 1948, San Marcos U., Lima, Peru, 1948-49, Inst. Internat. Edn., U. Madrid, Spain, 1952-53. Asst. dir. Casa Panamericana, Mills Coll., 1944; asst. to dir. Fine Arts Dept. Columbia U., N.Y.C., 1945-47; tchr. pub. schs. Port Washington, L.I., N.Y., 1953-55; lectr. Global Edn., UN, N.Y.C., 1953-56; pub. rels. dir. Nat. League Am. Pen Women, Washington, 1958-60; Non-Govtl. Orgns. rep. United Women of the Ams., UN, N.Y.C., 1959-62; lectr. Asia and Africa Halls Smithsonian Inst., Washington, 1965-69; lectr. Folger Shakespeare Libr., Washington, 1969-73; art reviewer Wyo., Denver Art Mus., 1974—. Author: The Cradle of American Art, 1948, Mantillas and Silver Spurs, 1952; columnist, contbr. articles to profl. jours. and mags., also columnist. Mem. nat. adv. bd. for Bob Dole's Presdl. campaign, 1988—, Nat. Trust for Historic Preservation, Washington, 1987—; charter mem. Nat. Mus. Women in Arts, 1987—; rep. for Colo. Pres. Bush's Nat. Senatorial Com., Washington; Wyo. Coun. for Humanities, 1979-80; bd. dirs. Am. Security Coun., Washington; vol. Denver Oasis Club for Sr. Citizens. Fellow U. Madrid, 1952-53. Mem. Internat. Ednsia Soc., Inter-Am. Ctr., AAUW, Nat. League Am. Pen Women (Woman of Achievement award 1973), LWV (pres. 1967-69), Nat. Mus. Women in the Arts (charter), Buffalo Bill Hist. Mus., Mark Twain Soc. (hon. mem.), Sigma Alpha Iota, Kappa Delta, Nat. Press Club (Washington). Address: 1295 Race St Apt 312 Denver CO 80206-2854

FULLMAN, LYNN GRISARD, editor; b. Chattanooga, Tenn., May 20, 1949; d. James Lindsay and Margaret (Conner) Grisard; m. Milton E. Fullman Jr., May 30, 1970; children: Christine, Cameron. BA in Journalism, Samford U., 1971. Writer, editor Freelance, 1973. Mem. Soc. Profl. Journalists, Am. Soc. Journalists and Authors, Internat. Food, Wine and Travel Writers Assn. Baptist. Home and Office: 2446 Monte Vista Dr Birmingham AL 35216

FULRATH, IRENE, corporate marketing executive; b. N.Y.C., Nov. 15, 1945; d. Logan and Grace (Sheehy) F. B.A., Wheaton Coll., Ill., 1967. Media exec. Doyle Dane Bernbach, N.Y.C., 1967-72; account exec., retail sales mgr. Sta. WABC, N.Y.C., 1972-84; account exec. Sta. WABC-TV, N.Y.C., 1984-86; corp. sales mgr., Am. Express Co., 1987—. Mem. Fin. Advt. and Mktg. Assn. (bd. dirs. 1981-84, sec. 1984-85, v.p. 1985-86, pres 1986-87). Republican. Presbyterian. Avocation: travel. Home: 150 E 56th St New York NY 10022 Office: Am Express Co 100 Church St New York NY 10007

FULWEILER, PATRICIA PLATT, civic worker; b. N.Y.C., Mar. 19, 1923; d. Haviland Hull and Marie-Louise (Fearey) Platt; m. Spencer Biddle Fulweiler, Oct. 5, 1946; children: Marie-Louise Fulweiler Allen, Pamela Spencer, Hull Platt, Spencer Biddle. AB cum laude, Bryn Mawr Coll., 1945; MBA, Columbia U., 1950. Jr. copywriter, asst. account exec. Dorland Internat. Pettingell & Fenton, N.Y.C., 1945-46; statistician, fin. staff treas.'s office GM, N.Y.C., 1950-52; asst. account mgr. investment dept. Fiduciary Trust Co., N.Y.C., 1953-61; bd. dirs. Chapin Brearley Exchange, Inc., 1964-74, treas., 1966-71, pres., 1971-73. Bd. dirs. Knickerbocker Greys, 1965—, treas., 1970-75; bd. dirs., treas. City Gardens Club, N.Y.C., 1974-79, chmn. ways and means com., 1974-81; bd. dirs. Nat. Soc. Colonial Dames State N.Y., 1973-82, asst. treas., 1973-82; mem. fin. com. Alumnae Assn. Bryn Mawr Coll., 1970-76; bd. dirs. Daus. of Cin., 1974-81, scholarship adminstr., 1976-81; pres. Ladies Christian Union, 1982-87, chmn. fin. com., 1987—; rec. sec. Women's Assn. St. James Ch., N.Y.C., 1972-75, co-chmn. Spring Festival, 1974-75, chmn., 1975-76, treas., 1976-81, mem. Altar Guild, 1975—; treas. Churchwomen's League for Patriotic Svc., 1982-86; mem. scholarship com. Youth Found., 1981—, pres., 1990—; membership chmn. Huguenot Soc. Am., registrar, 1986—. Mem. Soc. Sponsers of USN, Alumnae Coun. Spence Sch., Colonial Dames Am. (bd. dirs. 1987—), Nat. Soc. Colonial Dames, Colony Club, Thursday Evening Club, Wilson Point Beach Assn. Club. Republican. Home: 158 E 83d St New York NY 10028

FUNESTI, JULIE COLETTE, nurse, researcher; b. Teaneck, N.J., Jan. 3, 1962; d. John Kenneth and Margaret Ann (Kennedy) F. BS in Nursing, Cath. U. Am., 1984. RN, N.Y. Staff nurse med. fl. NYU Med. Ctr., N.Y.C., 1984-86, staff nurse ICU, 1986-87, AIDS rsch. nurse clinician, 1987—; cons. nurse Gay Men's Health Crisis, N.Y.C., 1986—. Vol. Bill Greer for Congress campaign, N.Y.C., 1986-87. Mem. Nat. League for Nursing, N.Y. State Nurses Assn., Sigma Theta Tau. Republican. Roman Catholic. Home: 340 E 34th St #6F New York NY 10016 Office: NYU Med Ctr C&D Bldg Bellevue E 27th 1st Ave 550 1st Ave New York NY 10016

FUNK, ELLA FRANCES, genealogist, author; b. Domino, Ky., Apr. 7, 1921; d. Roy William and Edna Rene (Cummins) Roach; B.Liberal Studies, Mary Washington Coll., Fredericksburg, Va., 1982; m. Eugene Boyd Funk, June 20, 1942; children: Susan Teresa, Eugene Boyd. Exec. sec. Lang. Labs., Inc., Bethesda, Md., 1969-70; office mgr. legal firm Donovan Leisure Newton & Irvine, Washington, 1970-76; genealogist, hist. researcher, writer, 1976—; vol. Assn. Preservation Va. Antiquities; mem. Lake of the Woods Ch. Named Exec. of Week, Sta. WGMS, Washington, June 1975; recipient Ribbon winner for poem Va. Fedn. Women's Clubs. Life mem. Nat. Geneal. Soc.; mem. Hist. Fredericksburg Found., DAR, Alpha Phi Sigma, Sigma Phi Gamma. Club: Woman's (Fredericksburg, Va.). Lodge: Order Eastern Star. Author: Cummins Ancient, Cummins New, vol. 1, 1978, vol. 2, 1980, Joseph Funk, a biography, 1984, Benjamin's Way, 1988, (short story) Christmas In The Abbey, 1988 (Ribbon winner 1989), (poem) The Good Ship (Ribbon winner 1990). Address: Box 557 Lake of the Woods Locust Grove VA 22508

FUNK, SUSAN ELLEN, manufacturing executive, accountant; b. Highland, Mich., May 16, 1951; d. Ralph Neil and Ellen Jean (Noble) F. BBA in Acctg., Wayne State U., 1979. Chief fin. officer, pres. Detroit Bandag, 1972—; chief fin. officer, v.p. Trico Bandag, Redford, Mich., 1977—; chief fin. officer N.F.L. Tire Svc., Warren, Mich., 1985—, Comml. Tire Svcs., Grand Rapids, Mich., 1987—. Recipient Spirit award, 1985, 86. Mem. Am. Retreaders Assn., Nat. Tire Dealers Assn., Mich. Trucking Assn. (equipment and maintenance div.), Nat. Assn. Women Bus. Owners. Republican. Methodist. Office: Detroit Bandag 750 S Dix Detroit MI 48217

FUNKHOUSER, DEIDRA ELLEN, rehabilitation counselor, supervisor; b. Alta, Iowa, Dec. 13, 1950; d. Melvin Joseph and Frances Donna Bell (Erickson) Williams; m. Steven Max Funkhouser, July 3, 1951; children: Joshua, Benjamin. BA, U. N. Colo., 1972, MA, 1977. Tchr. Milliken (Colo.) Middle Sch., 1975; rehab. counselor Profl. Counselors, Denver, 1977, Colo. Div. Rehab., Colorado Springs, 1977-83; owner, career counselor Career Potentials, Colorado Springs, 1983-89; rehab. counselor, supr. Olson Vocat. Svcs., Colorado Springs, 1989—; pres. Pikes Peak Mental Health Vocat. Bd., Colorado Springs, 1984-86; bd. dirs. Work Experience and Study Adv. Bd., Colorado Springs, 1988-89. Chmn. bd. dirs. Pikes Peak Alliance for Mentally Ill, Colorado Springs, 1986-88. Named to Outstanding Young Women Am., 1978. Mem. Nat. Assn. Counseling and Devel., Colo. Assn. for Counseling and Devel., Nat. Assn. for Career Devel., ALMACA, Kappa Delta Phi. Home: 8360 Avens Circle Colorado Springs CO 80920 Office: Olson Vocat Svcs 701 S Cascade Ave Colorado Springs CO 80903

FURAY, CATHERINE J., lawyer; b. Eau Claire, Wis., May 26, 1952; d. John B. and Elizabeth (Selbach) F.; m. James D. Sweet, Aug. 16, 1975. BA, U. Wis., Eau Claire, 1974; MS, U. Wis., Menominee, 1975; JD, U. Wis., 1980. Bar: Wis. 1981, U.S. Dist. Ct. (we. and ea. dists.) Wis. 1981, U.S. Ct. Appeals (7th cir.) 1986. Assoc. Kassner and Sweet, Madison, 1980-82; prin. James D. Sweet Law Offices, Madison, 1982-83; investigator Wis. Personnel Commn., Madison, 1983-84; pvt. practice Madison, 1983-84; assoc. Axley Brynelson, Madison, 1984—; speaker Wis. Jud. Conf., Madison, 1986; instr. gen. practice U. Wis. Law Sch., Madison, 1989—; chair State Bar Bridge-the-Gap Commn., Madison, 1987—. Producer videotape Farm Credit: Debt or Alive, 1988. Mem. fin. com. Wis. Spl. Olympics, 1987—. Mem. ABA (del. young lawyers assembly 1986-88, pub. svc. awards 1988), Wis. Bar Assn. (pres. young lawyers div. 1987-88, bd. govs. exec. com. 1988—, Comprehensive Achievement award 1988), Overtime Club. Home: 7743 Hillcrest Ave Middleton WI 53562 Office: Axley Brynelson 2 E Mifflin St Ste 200 Madison WI 53701-1767

FUREY, AGNES, social services administrator; b. Jersey City, Feb. 11, 1937; d. Eugene and Agnes (Murphy) Wedlake; children: Frank, Patricia Reed. Student, Cornell U., 1978, U. South Fla., 1985; cert. in nursing, Jersey City Bd. Edn., 1980. Cert. addictions profl. Staff nurse Christ Hosp., Jersey City, 1979-82; case mgmt. supr., charge nurse Manatee Glens Corp., Bradenton, Fla., 1982-89; dir. support svcs. Sarasota (Fla.) AIDS Support, 1989-90; project officer, primary care and substance abuse treatment integration project, alcohol and drug abuse program AIDS unit, Fla. Dept. Health and Rehab. Svcs., Tallahassee, 1990—; pub. speaker on AIDS and addiction. Pres. Bay Area Community AIDS Response; vice chmn. AIDS Resources of Manatee; mem. Women's AIDS Network, Bradenton Women's Network, Manatee Community Coun. for Children, Manatee Area Vol. Assn., Healthy Mothers, Healthy Babies, Manatee County, Community Consortium for Children and Youth, Sarasota County, Vol. Ctrs. Sarasota and Venice, others. Recipient Outstanding Profl. of Yr. award Smithers Found., 1987, Community Svc. award for AIDS edn. and svc., Ch. of the Trinity M.C.C., 1989. Mem. NAFE, Fla. Alcohol and Drug Abuse Assn., Fla. Studio Theatre., Sarasota AIDS Support Inc. (advisory bd.), Am. Bus. Women's Assn., Nat. Lesbian and Gay Health Found., Nat. Assn. Lesbian and Gay Alcoholism Profls., Nat. AIDS Minority Counc., Exec. Networks of Manatee and Sarasota. Home: 1112 S Magnolia Dr Apt A107 Tallahassee FL 32301 Office: 1317 Winewood Blvd Bldg 6 Rm 182 Tallahassee FL 32399-0700

FURGIUELE, MARGERY WOOD, educator; b. Munden, Va., Sept. 28, 1919; d. Thomas Jarvis and Helen Godfrey (Ward) Wood; B.S., Mary Washington Coll., 1941; postgrad. U. Ala., 1967-68, Catholic U. Am., 1974-76, 80; m. Albert William Furgiuele, June 19, 1943; children—Martha Jane Furgiuele MacDonald, Harriet Randolph. Advt. and reservations sec. Hilton's Vacation Hide-A Way, Moodus, Conn., 1940; sec. TVA, Knoxville, 1941-43; adminstrv. asst., ct. reporter Moody AFB, Valdosta, Ga., 1943-44; tchr. bus. Edenton (N.C.) High Sch., 1944-45; tchr. bus., coordinator Culpeper (Va.) County High Sch., 1958-82; ret., 1982; tchr. Piedment Tech. Edn. Center, 1970—. Co-leader Future Bus. Leaders Am., Culpeper, mem. state bd., 1979-82; state advisor 1978-79, Va. Bus. Edn. Assn. Com. chmn., 1978-79. Certified geneal. record Searcher; contbr. articles to profl. jours. Mem. Nat., Va. Bus. Edn. Assns., Am., Va. Vocat. Assns., Smithsonian Assos. Club: Country (Culpeper). Home: 1630 Stonybrook Ln Culpeper VA 22701

FURLONG, SUZANNE, educator; b. Phoenix, Mar. 23, 1956; d. Lovell Brown and Patricia Ann (Snuffer) Lieurance; m. Daniel Francis Furlong, Dec. 30, 1978; children: Bryce Allen, Douglas Scott, Karen Lynn. Student, Scottsdale (Ariz.) Community, 1974-76; BA in Psychology, Ariz. State U., 1978, Spl. Edn. Cert., 1980; Spl. Edn. Cert., U. Phoenix, 1979. Prog. devel. tchr. Mesa (Ariz.) pub. schs., 1980, tchr., 1980-81; Home Bound tchr. Prescott (Ariz.) Unified Schs., 1981-82; prog. devel. staff/tchr. Prescott Child Devel. Ctr., 1982-83, 90—; prog. developer Chino Valley (Ariz.) schs., 1989. Vol. Prescott Unified Schs., 1989—; v.p. bd. Prescott Child Devel. Ctr., 1990—. Named Prescott Jr. of the Mo., Prescott Jr. Woman's Club, 1983, 89, Cert. of Appreciation, Prescott Unified Schs., 1990. Mem. AAUW (pres. 1986-88). Home: 3105 Angus Dr Prescott AZ 86301 Office: Prescott Child Devel Ctr 710 Whipple Prescott AZ 86301

FURMAGE, ANN MASON, controller; b. Milw., Wis., Dec. 30, 1937; d. Lynn Erland and Marion Bernice (Lowe) Baker; m. William Joseph Furmage III, Apr. 30, 1964 (div. 1987); children: Nacre Web Fury, Kathryn Ann Furmage. B in Bus., Western Australia Inst. Tech., Bentley, 1980. Acct., adminstr. Horwath and Horwath Chartered Accts., South Perth, Western Australia, 1980-82, Wesley Cen. Mission and Wesley Property Com., Perth, Western Australia, 1982-85; contr. The Temple Found., Fairfax, Va., 1985-87, Trustbank Realty Svcs., Falls Ch., Va., 1988-90, Select Appointments Internat. U.S.A., Washington, 1990—. Vol. mem. production crew for Pub. Access TV. Mem. Australian Soc. of Accts. (cert. practicing acct.), Zonta (recording sec. Fairfax County, 1986-89). Episcopalian. Office: Select Appointments Internat USA 2050 17th St NW Washington DC 20036

FURNEY, LINDA JEANNE, state legislator; b. Toledo, Sept. 11, 1947; d. Robert Ross and Jeanne Scott (Hogan) F. BS in Edn., Bowling Green State U., 1969. Tchr. Washington Local Schs., Toledo, 1969-72, Escola Americano do Rio de Janiero, 1972-74; asst. mgr. banquets Holiday Inn, Perrysburg, Ohio, 1976-77; tchr. Springfield Schs., Holland, Ohio, 1977-83; council mem. City of Toledo, 1983-86; mem. Ohio State Senate, Columbus, 1987—; ranking minority mem. Econ. Devel. Com. Pres. Ohio NOW, 1979-81; Dem. precinct committeewoman Toledo, 1980—; mem. Toledo Bd. Edn., 1982-83. Congregationalist. Home: 1953 Brussels Toledo OH 43613 Office: Ohio State Senate Columbus OH 43215

FURR, CHRISTINE MARIE, employee leasing company executive; b. Batavia, N.Y., Nov. 12, 1960; d. Robert Earl Furr and Catherine Gladys (Peck) Miller. BS, Niagara U., 1982. Credit analyst Interpace Corp., LeRoy, N.Y., 1982; personnel asst. ROW Employee Leasing Svcs., Rochester, N.Y., 1983-84, dir. personnel, 1984-86, dir. ops., 1986-88, v.p. ops., 1988—. Mem. N.Y. State Leasing Assn. (membership chmn. bd. dirs. 1989-90), Nat. Staff Leasing Assn., Rochester Area Recreation and Employee Svc. Assn., Soc. for Human Resource Mgrs., NAFE. Republican. Roman Catholic. Office: ROW Employee Leasing Svcs 1004 Buffalo Rd Rochester NY 14624

FURREY, ANNE-MARIE, communications executive; b. Tulsa, Okla., Dec. 9, 1948; d. James Oscar and Gertrude Ella (Rutkowski) Mason; m. Richard L. Furrey, Oct. 4, 1968; 1 child, Jaclyn Marie. Student, Phoenix Coll., 1967-68, 77-78, Bellcore Tech. Edn. Ctr., 1981-83, 87-89, Rio Salado Coll., 1987. Compilation clk. Mountain Bell, Phoenix, 1968-69, analytical clk., 1969-79, engrng. records clk., 1979-80, engrng. specialist, 1980-83, mgr. corp. real estate, 1983-87; mgr. project coordination U S WEST Communications, Inc., Phoenix, 1987-89, communications mgr., 1989—. Author numerous poems (Best New Poets of 1988, 89). Chmn. U S WEST Women, sec., 1989, 90; chmn. Walk Am. March of Dimes, Phoenix, 1989, Ariz. State Poetry Soc., 1990, Ariz. State Fair Project. Mem. Business and Profl. Woman's Assn., Poetry Soc. of Am., Ariz. Authors Assn., Phoenix Poetry Soc., Soroptimists (del. Ariz. women's town hall 1990). Home: 4416 E Willow Ave Phoenix AZ 85032

FURSTENBERG, BARBARA SPAR, psychologist; b. Cambridge, Mass., Oct. 3, 1944; d. Leonard Lawrence and Ruth Eunice (Rogoff) Matthews; m. Herbert Martin Spar, Dec. 28, 1968 (dec. 1975); 1 child, Joshua David; m. Michael P. Furstenberg, May 20, 1984; 1 child, Sasha Claire. BA, Bennington (Vt.) Coll., 1966; PsyD, Mass. Sch. Profl. Psychology, Dedham, 1983. Lic. psychologist, Mass. Staff psychologist Charles River Counseling Ctr., West Newton, Mass., 1983-87; pvt. practice psychology Newton, 1985—. Mem. Am. Psychol. Assn., Mass. Psychol. Assn., Div. 39 of Mass. Psychol. Assn. Democrat. Jewish. Home and Office: 47 Lombard St Newton MA 02158

FURSTMAN, SHIRLEY ELSIE DADDOW, advertising executive; b. Butler, N.J., Jan. 26, 1930; d. Richard and Eva M. (Kitchell) Daddow; grad. high sch.; m. Russell A. Bailey, Oct. 1, 1950 (div. Oct. 1967); m. 2d, William B. Furstman, Dec. 24, 1977. Asst. corporate sec. Hydrospace Tech., West Caldwell, N.J., 1960-62; sec. to pres. R.J. Dick Co., Totowa, N.J., 1962-63, Microlab, Livingston, N.J., 1963; asst. corporate sec. Astrosystems Internat., West Caldwell, N.J., 1963-65; corporate sec. Internat. Controls Corp., Fairfield, N.J., 1965-73; sec. to pres. Global Financial Co., Nassau, Bahamas, 1974-75; office mgr. Internat. Barter, Nassau, 1975-76; sec. to pres., corp. sec. Haas Chem. Co., Taylor, Pa., 1976-77; asst. to pres., pub. Am. Home mag., N.Y.C., 1977-78; office mgr. Gilbert, Whitney & Johns, Inc., Whippany, N.J., 1979—. Home: 11A Foxwood Morris Plains NJ 07950

FURTAK, HIROKO, purchasing agent; b. June 21, 1953. Student, North Tech. Ctr., West Palm Beach, Fla., Inst. Fin. Edn., Palm Beach Gardens, Fla. Purchasing asst. St. Mary's Hosp., West Palm Beach, Klock Co. div. Gulf & Western, Palm Beach Garden; purchasing agt. Community Savs., Riviera Beach, Fla. Address: 214 2d Way West Palm Beach FL 33407

FUSCO, JACQUELINE TECCE, systems consultant; b. N.Y.C., Apr. 23, 1956; d. Sam L. and Lee M. (Malandri) Tecce; m. William Fusco, Apr. 7, 1984; children: Samantha Nicole, Nicholas Alexander. BA in Pychology St. Francis Coll., Bklyn., 1978, AAS in Bus Adminstrn., 1978. Teller Chem. Bank, N.Y.C., 1975-78; asst. dir. lease adminstrn. Brooks Fashion Stores, N.Y.C., 1979-81; coordinator info. services Richard Kove Assocs., N.Y.C., 1981-86; v.p. Bilco Mech. Corp., Port Washington, N.Y., 1985—; pres., systems cons. J.T.F. Word Processing, 1988—; . Mem. Anti-Vivisection Soc., 1978—, Save Our Strays, Bklyn., 1978—; vol. Rusk Inst., N.Y.C., 1982; mem. Citizens to Replace LILCO, 1985—. Mem. Nat. Assn. Female Execs., Ill. Mgmt. and Exec. Search Cons., Paret Resource Ctr., Psi Chi, Chi Beta Phi. Republican. Roman Catholic. Home: 1 Davis Rd Port Washington NY 11050 Office: Bilco Mech Corp & JTF Word Pros Port Washington NY 11050

FUSSELL, CATHARINE PUGH, biological researcher; b. Phila., July 13, 1919; d. Milton H. and Isabel R. (Pugh) F. AB, Colby Coll., 1941; MS, Cornell U, 1958; PhD, Columbia U., 1966. Administrv. asst. Am. Friends Svc. Commn., Phila., 1947-55; rsch. asst. Brookhaven Nat. Lab., Upton, N.Y., 1957-60; rsch. assoc. Inst. Cancer Rsch. Fox Chase, Phila., 1966-67; post doctoral fellow Fels Rsch. Inst., Phila., 1967-68; from asst. prof. to assoc. prof. Pa. State U., McKeesport, Abington, Pa., 1968-88; rsch. scientist Pa. State U., Abington, Pa., 1988-89; vis. scholar U. Pa., Med. Sch., Phila., 1990—. Contbr. articles to profl. jours. Mem. AAAS, AAUW (pres. 1985-87, Montgomery County branch), Am. Soc. Cell Biology, Botanical Soc. Am., Genetics Soc. Am. Home: 7807 Spring Ave Elkins Park PA 19117

FUTAS, ELIZABETH (DOROTHY FUTAS), library and information studies educator, program director; b. N.Y.C., May 8, 1944; d. Bart and Eleanore Rhoda (Tabak) F. BA, CUNY, 1965; MA, U. Minn., 1966; postgrad., Queens Coll., 1968-71; PhD, Rutgers U., 1980. Grad. asst. U. Minn., Mpls., 1965-66; cataloguer Ford Found., N.Y.C., 1967-68; reference bibliographer Queens Coll., N.Y., 1968-74, 76-77; adj. faculty Rutgers U., New Brunswick, N.J., 1975-76; asst. prof. Emory U., Atlanta, 1977-83, assoc. prof., 1983-85; adj. prof. U. Wash., Seattle, 1985; dir., prof. grad. sch. libr. and info. studies U. R.I., Kingston, 1986—, acting dean Coll. Arts and Scis., 1990, mem. index com. Reference and Adult Svcs., 1983-87; cons. Holt,

Rinehart, Winston, N.Y.C., 1978; chmn. mgmt. com. Dept. State Libr. Svc., Providence, 1986-88; mem. Wilson index com. Reference and Adult Svcs., 1983-87. Author: 3 books on libr. sci.; editor RQ jour., 1987—; mem. editorial bd. Collection Bldg., 1978—; contbr. articles to profl. jours. Regents scholar Brooklyn Coll., 1961-65. Mem. ALA (councilor 1978-88, exec. bd. 1984-88), Coun. Deans and Dirs. (chair 1989—), R.I. Libr. Assn., N.H. Libr. Assn. Home: 11 Misty River Terr Saunderstown RI 02874 Office: Univ RI Grad Sch Libr/Info Studies Rodman Hall Kingston RI 02881

FUTRELL, MARY ALICE HATWOOD, association executive; b. Alta Vista, Va., May 24, 1940; d. Josephine Austin; m. Donald Lee Futrell. BA, Va. State U., 1962; MA, George Washington U., 1968; postgrad., U. Md., U. Va., Va. Poly Inst. and State U.; DHL (hon.), Va. State U., George Washington U., 1984, Spellman Coll., 1986, Cen. State U., 1987; DEd, Eastern Mich. U., 1987; hon. doctorates, U. Lowell, Adrian Coll. Bus. edn. tchr. Parker-Gray High Sch., Alexandria, Va., 1963-65; bus. edn. tchr., dept. chmn. George Washington High Sch., 1965-80; pres. NEA, Washington, 1983-89; sr. fellow, assoc. dir. George Washington U. Ctr. for the Study of Edn. and Nat. Devel., 1989—; mem. adv. com. on tchr. cert. State of Va., 1977-82, adv. com. to U.S. Commn. on Civil Rights, 1978; mem. Gov.'s Com. on Edn. of Handicapped, 1977; state rep. to Edn. Commn. of States, 1982; mem. Carnegie Found.'s Nat. Panel on Study of Am. High Sch., Carnegie Forum on Edn. and Economy, task force on teaching as profession; mem. edn. adv. council Met. Life Ins. Co.; trustee Joint Council on Econ. Edn.; mem. study commn. on Global Perspectives in Edn.; mem. Va.-Israel Commn., Nat. Select Com. on Edn. Black Youth; mem. Nat. Bd. for Profl. Teaching Standards; chairperson edn. com. Nat. Council for Accreditation Tchr. Edn.; mem. task force on educationally disadvantaged Com. for Econ. Devel. Mem. editorial bd. ProEdn. mag.; bd. advisers Esquire Register, 1985. Mem. women's council Democratic Nat. Com., Dem. Labor Council; former pres. ERAmerica, nat. chairperson; mem. U.S. Nat. Commn. to UNESCO; mem. adv. council Internat. Labor Rights Edn. and Research Fund; mem. Nat. Dem. Inst. for Internat. Affairs, Nat. Labor Com. for Democracy and Human Rights; bd. advisers Project VOTE; mem. Martin Luther King Jr. Fed. Holiday Commn.; trustee Nat. History Day; bd. dirs. U.S. Com. for UNICEF, Nat. Found. for Improvement Edn., Citizen-Labor Energy Coalition. Recipient Human Rights award NCCJ, 1976, cert. of appreciation UN Assn., 1980, Disting. Service medal, Columbia Univ., 1987, Schull award Ams. for Dem. Action, Pres.'s award NAACP, numerous others; named Outstanding Black Bus. and Profl. Person, Ebony mag., 1984, One of 100 Top Women in Am., Ladies Home Jour. mag., 1984, One of 12 Women of Yr., Ms. mag., 1985, One of Top 100 Blacks in Am., Ebony mag., 1985-89; Ford Found. and Nat. Com. on U.S.-China Relations grantee, 1981. Mem. NEA (bd. dirs. 1978-80, task force on sch. vols. 1977-78, head human relations com. to 1980, sec.-treas. 1980-83) (Creative Leadership in Women's Rights award 1982), Edn. Assn. Alexandria (pres. 1973-75), Va. Edn. Assn. (pres. 1976-78) (Fitz Turner Human Rights award 1976), World Confedn. Orgns. of Teaching Profession (pres. 1990—, exec. com., v.p. 1988—, chmn. women's caucus, 1984—, women's concerns com., chmn. fin. commn., 1986-89, pres. 1990), Am. Assn. Colls. Tchr. Edn., Am. Assn. State Colls. and Univs. Office: George Washington U Sch of Edn and Human Devel 506 C Funger Hall/2201 G St NW Washington DC 20052

FUTTER, ELLEN VICTORIA, college president; b. N.Y.C., Sept. 21, 1949; d. Victor and Joan Babette (Feinberg) F.; m. John A. Shutkin, Aug. 25, 1974; children—Anne Victoria, Elizabeth Jane. Student, U. Wis., 1967-69; AB magna cum laude, Barnard Coll., 1971; JD, Columbia U., 1974, LLD (hon.); LLD (hon.), Hamilton Coll., N.Y. Law Sch.; DHL (hon.), N.Y. Law Sch. Bar: N.Y. 1975. Assoc. Milbank, Tweed, Hadley & McCloy, N.Y.C., 1974-80; acting pres. Barnard Coll., N.Y.C., 1980-81, pres., 1981—, also trustee; bd. dirs. Fed. Res. Bank of N.Y., dep. chmn.; bd. dirs. Mut. Benefit Life, com. on econ. devel. Mem. Helsinki Watch; friend N.Y.C. Commn. on Status of Women Ptnrs., N.Y.C. Partnership; bd. dirs. Consortium on Financing Higher Edn., The Am. Assembly. Recipient Spirit of Achievement award Albert Einstein Coll. Medicine Yeshiva U., Abram L. Sachar award Brandeis U., Elizabeth Cutter Morrow award YWCA. Mem. ABA, N.Y. State Bar Assn., Assn. Bar City of N.Y., Nat. Inst. Social Scis., Coun. Fgn. Rels., Cosmopolitan Club, Century Club, Phi Beta Kappa. Office: Barnard Coll Office of Pres 3009 Broadway New York NY 10027

FUZEK, BETTYE LYNN, educator; b. Knoxville, Tenn., Oct. 24, 1924; d. Wallace Paul and Bess (Wallace) Bean; m. John F. Fuzek, May 31, 1943; children: Mary Ann, Mark Lynn, Martha Elizabeth. Student, U. Tenn., 1944-45, East Tenn. State U., 1959-64; BS, Milligan Coll., 1966; postgrad. summers, various schs., 1966—. Cert. tchr., Tenn. Sci. tchr. Dobyns-Bennett High Sch., Kingsport, Tenn., 1969-72; subs. tchr. Sullivan County High Schs., Kingsport, 1973-86; violin tchr. Symphony Assn. of Kingsport Talent Edn. Prog., 1973-80, Kingsport Suzuki Assn., 1980—; violinist Kingsport Symphony Orch., 1980-85. Mem. AAUW, DAR, Suzuki Assn. Ams. Presbyterian. Home: 4603 Mitchell Rd Kingsport TN 37664

GAAR, MARILYN A. WIEGRAFFE, political science educator; b. St. Louis, Sept. 22, 1946; d. Arthur and Marjorie Estelle (Miller) W.; m. Norman E. Gaar, Apr. 12, 1986. AB, Ind. U., 1968, MA, 1970, MS, 1973. Mem. faculty Stephens Coll., Columbia, Mo., 1971-73, Johnson County Community Coll., Overland Park, Kans., 1973—; interviewer Fulbright Hayes fellowship candidates, Kansas City, Mo., 1982-88; state selection com. Congress Bundestag Youth Exch. Program, Kans., 1985; pres. faculty del. Kans. Assn. Community Colls., 1984-85. Author: Profile of Kansas in State and Local Supplement to The Amercian Democracy by Thomas E. Patterson, 1990. Pres. LWV Johnson County, Kans., 1987-89; chmn. governing bd. Johnson County Mental Health Ctr. governing bd., Overland Park, Olathe, Kans., 1985-86; vol., translator Russian Refugee Resettlement Program Jewish Family and Children Svcs., Kansas City, 1979-81; alt. mem. Rep. Party State Com., Kans., 1984-86; Rep. city chmn., Shawnee, Kans., 1982-86; bd. dirs. Substance Abuse Ctr., Johnson County, 1983-85; treas. Heart of Am., Japan Am. Soc., 1979; program chmn. Kans. Fedn. Rep. Women, 1984-87; mem. Norton Simon Mus., Pasadena, Calif., Friends of Huntington Libr., San Marino, Calif. Grantee Europaische Akademie, West Berlin, 1984, Fulbright Hayes, Netherlands, 1982, Japan, 1975; Univ. fellow NEH, 1980. Mem. Community Coll. Humanities Assn., Kans. Polit. Sci. Assn., Soc. of Fellows, Nelson-Atkins Mus. Art, Mus. Contemporary Art L.A., Dobro Slovo Nat. Slavic Hons. Soc., Phi Beta Kappa, Pi Sigma Alpha. Episcopalian. Office: Johnson Co Community Coll 12345 College Blvd Overland Park KS 66210

GAARDER, MARIE, speech pathologist; b. New Britain, Conn., July 19, 1935; d. Nicholas and Clara (Sangeloty) Sarris; B.S., U. Ill., 1957; postgrad. U. Md., 1962-63, Our Lady of Lake U. Grad. Sch. Social Work, San Antonio, 1976-77; m. Kenneth R. Gaarder, Dec. 8, 1962; children—Jason, Galen. Founder speech therapy program Flossmoor (Ill.) Sch. Dist. 161, 1957-59; speech pathologist Prince George's County (Md.) Bd. Edn., 1959-65, Sidwell Friend's Sch., Washington, 1966-67, St. Maurice Sch. for Learning Disabilities, Potomac, Md., 1968-69; pvt. practice speech therapy, Chevy Chase, Md., 1967—; adminstrv. officer Gaarder Med. Corp., Chevy Chase, 1977—. Pres., Prince George's chpt. Council for Exceptional Children, 1963-64; mem. Florence Crittenton Circle, 1966-69, Hospitality and Info. Service for Diplomats, 1967—; chmn. activities com. Jr. Teens, 1979-80; chmn. publicity YWCA Internat. Fair, 1977-79, chmn. entertainment, 1983, chmn. 1987-88; mem. internat. com. Woman's Nat. Democratic Club; co-chmn. Adv. Com. for Quality Integrated Edn. in Montgomery County, 1977-78; bd. dirs. D.C. br. YWCA, 1981-82, Washington Ctr. Music Therapy Clinic, Cath. U. Am., 1983—, The Samaritans of Washington, 1984—; chmn. Career Day, Nat. Symphony Ednl. Activities, 1981—; chmn. oral history 65th Birthday Town of Chevy Chase; chmn. Mid-Atlantic regional adv. bd. Am. Found. for the Blind, 1984-85. Recipient cert. of appreciation Opera Guild San Antonio, 1977, Outstanding and Dedicated Svc. to 1987 Internat. Fair Plaque YWCA of the Nat. Capital Area. Mem. Am. Speech, Lang. and Hearing Assn. (advanced cert.), Md. Speech, Lang. and Hearing Assn., Internat. Assn. Logopedics and Phoniatrics, World Affairs Coun. of Washington, Soc. for Internat. Devel., Asia Soc., Soc. for Preservation of Greek Heritage, Zeta Phi Eta. Greek Orthodox. Club: Capitol Speakers (sec. chpt. III 1983-84) (Washington). Contbg. author: San Antonio Cookbook II, 1976. Home and Office: 4221 Oakridge Ln Chevy Chase MD 20815

GABEL, KATHERINE, academic administrator; b. Rochester, N.Y., Apr. 9, 1938; d. M. Wren and Esther (Conger) G.; m. Seth Devore Strickland, June 24, 1961 (div. 1965). AB, Smith Coll., Northampton, Mass., 1959; MSW, Simmons Coll., 1961; PhD, Syracuse U., 1967; JD, Union U., 1970; bus. program, Stanford U., 1984. Psychol. social worker Cen. Island Mental Health Ctr., Uniondale, N.Y., 1961-62; psychol. social worker, supt. Ga. State Tng. Sch. for Girls, Atlanta, 1962-64; cons. N.Y. State Crime Control Coun., Albany, 1968-70; faculty Ariz. State U., Tempe, 1972-76; supt. Ariz. Dept. of Corrections, Phoenix, 1970-76; dean, prof. Smith Coll., 1976-85; pres. Pacific Oaks Coll. and Children's Sch., Pasadena, Calif., 1985—; advisor, del. UN, Geneva, 1977; mem. So. Calif. Youth Authority, 1986—. Editor: Master Teacher and Supervisor in Clinical Social Work, 1982; author report Legal Issues of Female Inmates, 1981, model for rsch. Diversion program Female Inmates, 1984. Vice chair United Way, Northampton, 1982-83; chair Mayor's Task Force, Northampton, 1981. Mem. Nat. Assn. Social Work, Acad. Cert. Social Workers, Nat. Assn. Edn. Young Children, Western Assn. Schs. and Colls., Pasadena C. of C., Athenaeum, Pasadena Rotary Club. Democrat. Presbyterian. Office: Pacific Oaks Coll 5 Westmoreland Pl Pasadena CA 91103

GABEL, KRYSTAL LEIGH, accountant; b. Shelby, Nebr., Aug. 6, 1964; d. Eugene Alfred and Jeanette Leigh (Daum) G. BS with distinction, U. Nebr., 1986. CPA, Nebr. With Cen. Telephone Co., Lincoln, Nebr., 1986-87, sr. acct., 1987—. Vol. coach YMCA, Lincoln, 1988—. Mem. NAFE, AICPA, Nebr. Soc. CPAs, Lincoln-Greater Nebr. Alumni Assn. (bd. dirs., sec. 1987-90—, dist. bd. dirs. 1990—), Delta Sigma Pi. Republican. Roman Catholic. Home: 1208 SW 24th St Lincoln NE 68522

GABLE, CAROL BRIGNOLI, pharmacoepidemiology research dirctor; b. N.Y.C., Dec. 28, 1945; d. Peter Joseph and Frances Veronica (Guma) Abatemarco; m. Frank Giovanni Brignoli, May 19, 1968 (div. Nov. 1981); children: Barbara, James; m. Raymond Lewis Gable, Jan. 8, 1983; 1 child, Matthew. BS, CUNY, 1968; PhD in Chemistry, U. Md., 1973, MA in Statistics, 1986. Chemist N.Y. Research Inst., N.Y.C., 1967-68; grad. asst. U. Md., College Park, 1968-73; lectr. Montgomery Coll., Takoma Park, Md., 1972-75; research assoc. USDA/CFEI, Hyattsville, Md., 1974-76; chemist FDA, Washington, 1977-89; rsch. dir. pharmacoepidemiology Systemetrics/McGraw Hill, Washington, 1989—. Contbr. articles to Biophysical Chemistry, 1978, Nutrition, 1976-77, Risk Assessment, 1989. N.Y. State Regents scholar, 1963-67; recipient NSF traineeship. Mem. Am. Chem. Soc., AAAS, Soc. for Risk Analysis. Democrat. Mem. United Ch. of Christ. Home: 7715 Glenmore Spring Way Bethesda MD 20817 Office: Systemetrics McGraw Hill 4401 Connecticut Ave NW Washington DC 20008

GABLE, MARTHA ANNE, educator; b. Phila.; d. James F. and Stella (Gingrich) G. BE, Ind. U., 1942; MEd, Temple U., 1935. Tchr., Phila. Pub. Schs., 1926-41, asst. dir. phys. and health edn., Phila., 1942-48, asst. dir. sch. and community relations, 1948-55, dir. radio-TV edn., 1955-68; editor Am. Assn. Sch. Adminstrs., Washington, 1968-73, cons. Editechnology, 1973—; mem. Pa. Gov.'s Adv. Commn. on Edn., 1956-58, White House Conf. on Edn., 1955; cons. Joint Council Ednl. TV, Washington; chmn. adv. com. Pa. Ednl. TV, 1960-68; del. Internat. Conf. Ednl. TV, London, 1954. Judge, Olympic Games, London, 1948, Helsinki, 1952, Melbourne, 1956, Rome, 1960, Tokyo, 1964; bd. dirs. Phila. Home and Sch. Council, 1950-68; v.p. Women for Greater Phila. Named Disting. Dau. of Pa.; recipient Pres.'s award Phila. C. of C., Silver Medal award Phila. Club Advt. Women, Trustee Service award Pop Warner Little League, Service award Mus. Council Phil. and Del. Valley; named to Pa. Sports Hall of Fame. Mem. AAUW, NEA, Phila. Pub. Relations Assn. (Hall of Fame), Am. Women in Radio and TV, Pub. Rels. Soc. Am., Phila. Ad Club, Am. Assn. Sch. Adminstrs., Phila. Mus. Art, Women in Communications, Am. Newswomen's Club. Presbyterian. Club: Cosmopolitan, Nat. Press. Home: 2601 Parkway Philadelphia PA 19130

GABRIA, JOANNE BAKAITIS, information processing systems equipment company executive; b. Washington, Pa., Jan. 16, 1945; d. Vincent William and Mary Jo (Cario) Bakaitis. BA in English, U. Dayton, 1965, MA in Mktg. Communications, 1973, MBA, 1979. Advt. writer Dancer-Fitzgerald-Sample, Dayton, Ohio, 1969-72; advt. coordinator Monarch Marking Systems, Dayton, 1972-73; product tech. editor Frigidaire div. GM, Dayton, 1973-77; dir. tech. communications Mead Tech. Lab., Dayton, 1977-79; publs. mgr. NCR Corp., Dayton, 1979-81, internat. product mgr., 1981-86, mgr. internat. market analysis, 1986-87, mgr. Internat. Market Rsch., 1987—. bd. dirs. Contact-Dayton, 1984-85. Author: Microwave Cooking in 3 Speeds, 1976, Communications Standards, 1978, Retail Operations, 1982; editor: Ivy Jour., 1980-82. Chair numerous coms. St. Leonard Community, Centerville, Ohio, 1978-88; telephone vol. Contact-Dayton Crisis Intervention, 1982-86; big sister Big Bros./Big Sisters, Dayton, 1985-86; bd. dirs. Miami Valley chtp. Nat. Kidney Found. of Ohio, 1987—; mem. Ohio Patient adv. com. Tri-State Renal Network, Inc., 1989—. Recipient Disting. Achievement award Contact-Dayton, 1985, Outstanding Service award Miami Valley chpt. Nat. Kidney Found. of Ohio, 1988, Edn. award, 1990. Mem. Dayton Soc. Natural History, Marianist Affiliates (co-chmn. 1981-86). Democrat. Roman Catholic. Avocations: gardening, nature, classical music. Home: 7807 Graceland St Dayton OH 45459 Office: NCR Corp World Hdqrs-2 1700 S Patterson Blvd Dayton OH 45479

GABRIEL, BARBARA JAMIESON, educator; b. Pasadena, Calif., Jan. 21, 1929; d. Hamer Hershal and Hazel (Kendall) Jamieson; m. Albert Lawrence Gabriel, June 28, 1947; children—Sam Winston, Bryn Patricia Petersen. B.A. magna cum laude, Calif. State U.-Long Beach, 1971, M.A. in Ednl. Adminstrn., 1982. Cert. tchr., sch. adminstr., Calif. Bilingual tchr. Parkview Sch., 1973-78, minimum essential tchr., 1978-80; instructional materials specialist Mountain View Sch. Dist., El Monte, Calif., 1980—, bilingual program cons., 1985—; dir. Title VII project, 1988-89. Mem. State Book Rev. Com., 1979, Four Dist. Task Force, 1979; sec. El Monte/So. El Monte Coordinating Council; mem. 1989 Cabe Conf. Planning Com.; supporting mem. Aero-Space Mus., Globe Theatre. Mem. Internat. Reading Assn., Assn. Supervision and Curriculum Devel., Nat. Council Tchrs. English, San Diego Zool. Soc., Long Beach Art Mus., Audubon Soc., Phi Kappa Phi, Kappa Delta Pi, Phi Delta Kappa. Clubs: Alamitos Bay Yacht, (Long Beach, Calif.). Office: 2850 N Mountain View Rd El Monte CA 91732

GABRIEL-REYES, ASTERIA MASANGKAY, pediatrician; b. Manila, Philippines, May 20, 1933; came to the U.S., 1963; d. Juan and Timotea (Masangkay) Gabriel; m. Oscar F. Reyes, Sept. 7, 1977. AA, U. Santo Tomas, Manila, 1951; student, U. Santo Tomas, 1956. Statt physician Pineland Hosp. & Training Ctr., Pownal, Me., 1963-65; prin. physician Paul A. Dever State Sch., Taunton, Mass., 1965-68; med. specialist 11 Long Island Devel. Ctr., Melville, N.Y., 1968-70; chief pediatrics Long Island Devel. Ctr., Melville, 1970-75, deputy dir. health services, 1979-88, dir. med. quality assurance, 1988--. Mem. Am. Acad. Pediatrics, Royal Soc. Health, Am. Pub. Health Assn., Am. Roman Catholic. Office: LI Devel Ctr 133 Carman Rd Melville NY 11747

GADDIS, DENISE RENEA, educator, consultant; b. Oklahoma City, Sept. 26, 1951; d. Lais Joseph and Vera Mae (Darrington) Bowen; m. John Lee Gaddis III, June 19, 1975 (div. Sept. 1982); 1 child, Tandalah Renea. BS in Elem. Edn., Southeastern State U., 1973; postgrad., Oklahoma City U., 1974-75, Rose State Coll., Midwest City, Okla., 1981-84; MEd, Cen. State U., 1984. Cert. bus. edn. tchr., Okla. Evaluation planning asst. Dept. Econ. Community Affairs, 1973-75; bus. educator Opportunities Industrialization Ctr., Oklahoma City, 1975-76; tchr. elem. Oklahoma City Pub. Schs., 1977-78, 87—; mem. mgmt. Extension I, Tulsa, 1978-81; adminstrv. asst., v.p. Pk. State Bank, Nicoma Park, Okla., 1981-82; bus. educator Metro-Tech, Oklahoma City, 1982-85, Okla. Jr. Coll., Oklahoma City, 1988; cons. Star Elem. Sch., Oklahoma City, 1985. Vol. Rainbow Coalition, Atlanta, 1985, Community Action, Spencer, Okla., 1986, Say No to Drugs, Spencer, 1988; mem. United Way, Oklahoma City. Recipient Cert. of Appreciation, Oklahoma City Pub. Schs., 1983. Mem. NAFE, Smithsonian Inst., AAAS, Okla. Women in Edn. Assn. Republican. Baptist. Home: 3501 Fox Ave Spencer OK 73084

GADE, SANDRA ANN, physics educator; b. Waterbury, Conn., Oct. 27, 1937; d. Leroy Carl Gustav and Elsie (Wall) Kleinschmidt; m. Edward Herman Henry III, June 10, 1960; children: Susan Jean Gade Hill, Barbara Jean Gade Leo. BS, Valparaiso U., 1959; PhD, U. Pitts., 1966. Asst. prof. physics, dept. astronomy U. Wis., Oshkosh, 1966-70, assoc. prof., 1970-80, prof., 1980—, chmn. dept., 1987—. Contbr. articles to physics jours. Recipient numerous rsch. grants Faculty Devel. Bd., U. Wis., Oshkosh, 1978—. Mem. Am. Phys. Soc. Republican. Lutheran. Home: 1015 Maricopa Dr Oshkosh WI 54904 Office: U Wis-Oshkosh 800 Algoma Blvd Oshkosh WI 54901

GADINSKY, APRIL DEANNE, utility company executive; b. N.Y.C., Apr. 12, 1963; d. Martin and Dorothy (Vitucci) G. BS in Systems Analysis, U. Miami, 1984, MBA, 1985, MS, 1989. Mgmt. cons. Deloitte Haskins & Sells, Miami, Fla., 1985-86; rate analyst Fla. Power & Light Co., Miami, 1987—; info. systems researcher U. Miami, Coral Cables, Fla., 1982-84, mgmt. sci. grad. asst., 1985; cons. Eastern Airlines, Miami, 1985, Fontainebleau Hilton Hotel, Miami Beach, Fla., 1987. Mem. Am. Cancer Soc., Miami, 1986. Mem. IEEE, Data Processing Mgmt. Assn. (v.p. student br. 1982-84), Assn. Systems Mgmt., NAFE, Inst. Mgmt. Scis., Ops. Research Soc. Am., Am. Bus. Women's Assn., Am. Heart Assn., Cystic Fibrosis Assn. Home: 10220 SW 87 St Miami FL 33173

GADOMSKI, EVELYN, sales professional; b. Oranienburg, Germany, Feb. 26, 1934; came to U.S., 1956; d. Rudi and Irmgard (Friszewsky) Hempler; m. John Anthony Gadomski, Dec. 6, 1954 (dec. Dec. 1976); children: Karin Ann, Susan Rose (dec.), Mark Steven. Student, Cedar Crest Coll., 1977-78, Muhlenberg Coll., 1982-83. Sec. Gaismeier, Ulm, Fed. Republic Germany, 1952-53; waitress U.S. Army, Ulm, 1953-54; sec. Harvey Hubbell Inc., Bridgeport, Conn., 1973-74, sales trainee, 1974-75, field salesperson, 1975-79, sr. salesperson, 1979—. Chairperson inner city ministry, St. Paul's Luth. Ch., Allentown, Pa., 1985—. Lodge: Soroptimists. Home: 26 S Jefferson St Allentown PA 18102 Office: Hubbell Inc State St and Bostwick Ave Bridgeport CT 06605

GAERTNER, CATHERINE LOUISE, broadcast journalist; b. Albany, N.Y., Apr. 6, 1968; d. Richard F. and Nancy L. (Keary) G. BA, U. Ill., 1990. Pub. affairs rep. USAF, Heath, Ohio, 1985; reporter, photographer Licking Countian Newspaper, Newark, Ohio, 1985-86; intern producer News dept. Sta. WCMH-TV, Columbus, Ohio, 1988; intern host Cablevision TV, Urbana, Ill., 1988-89; intern reporter News dept. Sta. WDWS-TV, Champaign, Ill., 1989-90; video producer U.S. Army Corps of Engrs., Champaign, 1989-90; video prodn. specialist Agr. Communications U. Ill., 1990—, lectr. journalism dept., 1990—. Author, editor Compendium Mag., 1985. Recipient First pl. Ohio Women's Press Assn., 1985, First pl. Nat. News Mag. Design Journalism Edn. Assn., 1986; communications scholarship U. Ill., 1989-90. Mem. Radio-TV News Dirs. Assn., Ill. News Broadcasters Club, Womens in Communications, Inc., Golden Key, Alpha Lambda Delta (pres. 1987-88), Kappa Tau Alpha, Phi Eta Sigma. Home: 4819 Utah Dr Ames IA 50010

GAETANO, JOYCE ANN, chemical engineer; b. Pitts., Apr. 4, 1956; d. Samuel S. and Elizabeth A. (Brandy) G. BS in Chem. Engring., U. Pitts., 1978. Engr. rsch. div. Westinghouse Corp., Pitts., 1978; tech. product rep. Mobay Corp., Pitts., 1979-81, product mgr., 1981-83, tech. mktg. specialist, 1983-85, project mgr., 1985—. Contbr. articles to profl. jours. Mem. Western Pa. Soc. Engrs., Soc. Automotive Engrs., Soc. Plastics Industry (chmn. polyurethane com. 1979—). Home: 1439 Hidden Timber Manor Pittsburgh PA 15220 Office: Mobay Corp Mobay Rd Pittsburgh PA 15205

GAFFGA, (LOIS) DIANE, parenting organization administrator, therapist; b. Abington, Pa., Oct. 18, 1947; d. Carl William and Vera Catherine (Holland) Wagenhals; m. George Taylor Gaffga, Aug. 22, 1970 (div. 1988); children: Jean Michelle, Sandra Lynn. BS, West Chester (Pa.) State U., 1969; MEd, Temple U., Phila., 1985. Tchr. Ft. Belvoir (Va.) Elem. Sch., 1970-71, Rose Tree Media (Pa.) Elem. Sch., 1971-72; childbirth instr. Childbirth Edn. Assn., Conshohocken, Pa., 1979-84, counselor for nursing mothers, 1973-80; family therapist Robt. Benjamin, M.D., P.C., Dresher, Pa., 1985—; founder, curriculum and program developer Parents' Network, Inc., Ambler, Pa., 1980—, exec. dir., coord. tng. ctr., 1989—. Contbr. articles to profl. jours. Mem. Childbirth Edn. Assn. (life), Family Resource Coalition, Am. Psychol. Assn., Wissahichon Valley Interagy. Forum. Presbyterian. Home: 1651 Edison Dr Maple Glen PA 19002 Office: Parents Network Inc 411 Susquehanna Rd Ambler PA 19002

GAFFNEY, DOROTHEA FINNEN, retired federal employee, book company executive; b. Paterson, N.J., Aug. 19, 1918; d. Charles Christopher and Mary (Mitchell) Finnen; m. Harold R. Gaffney, Aug. 25, 1951; 1 child, Hale R. Student, Am. U., 1949-51. Asst. chief supply br. spl. services, U.S. Army, 1945-51; procurement officer Quartermaster Corp., U.S. Army, 1951-55; purchasing and contracting officer U.S. Air Force, 1956-59, U.S. Coast Guard, 1959-69; chief procurement br. 3d dist. U.S. Coast Guard, 1969-75; v.p. Am. Overseas Book Co., Norwood, N.J. 1975—. Recipient Silver medal for meritorious achievement U.S. Sec. Transp., 1974. Roman Catholic. Club: Garden Club (pres. 1980-84). Home: 22 Lambeth Ln Lakehurst NJ 08733

GAFFORD, MARY MAY, educator; b. Paris, Tex., Jan. 4, 1936; d. Benjamin Earl and Mary Elizabeth (Perfect) Grimes; m. Frank Hall Gafford, Dec. 31, 1958; children: Michelle Marguerite, Georgette Marie. BA in English and Social Studies, North Tex. State U., Denton, 1957, MA in English, Spanish and History, 1958; postgrad., U. Nev., summer 1970. Tchr. English Alpine (Tex.) Pub. Schs., 1959-61; tchr. English and history Houston Sch. Dist., 1957-58; tchr. English and Spanish Grapevine (Tex.) Sch. Dist., 1958-59, Amarillo (Tex.) Sch. Dist., 1962-65; tchr. English, Spanish and Journalism Fabens (Tex.) Schs., 1965-67; tchr. English and Spanish Flagstaff (Ariz.) Schs., 1967-68, Mesa County Schs., Grand Junction, Colo., 1968-71; tchr. English Clark County Schs., Las Vegas, Nev., 1976—. Editor: War Bonnet Grand Junction mag., 1967-71. Vol. Am. Cancer Soc., Las Vegas, 1974—, So. Nev. Dem. Party, Las Vegas, 1980; vol. youth health fair Nev. Bus. Svcs., Las Vegas, 1989. Mem. Clark County Classroom Tchrs., So. Nev. Tchrs. of English, State Pks. Cultural Arts Bd., DAR (regent, vice-regent 1983-90), AAUW (life, chmn. teen-age pregnancy study group Las Vegas chpt. 1986-90, pres. 1976-77). Methodist. Home: 5713 W Balzar Ave Las Vegas NV 89108 Office: Roy Martin Jr High 2800 E Stewart Ave Las Vegas NV 89101

GAFKA, SHEILA KURLANDER, real estate professional; b. Bronx, Sept. 24, 1939; d. George and Susie (Cohen) Kurlander; m. Gerry Gafka, June 19, 1960; children: Jan Michael, George Keith. BA, Bklyn. Coll., 1960, MS, 1963; AAS, Ulster County Community Coll., 1981; GRI, Realtors Inst., 1987. Tchr. Pub. Sch. Dist. 138, Bklyn., 1960-63, Niskayuna Elem., Schenectady, N.Y., 1963-64, Wappinger Falls, Poughkeepsie, N.Y., 1964-66; realtor O'Connor-Kershaw, Kingston, N.Y., 1977-79, Chet Krom Realty, Kingston, 1980-82, Falls Realty, Raleigh, N.C., 1983-84, Ammons Pittman, Raleigh, 1984—. Mem. Raleigh Bd. Realtors. Home: 1057 Vestavia Woods Dr Raleigh NC 27615

GAGE, NANCY ELIZABETH, accountant, college administrator, educator; b. Chgo., Aug. 22, 1947; d. Winfred Paul and Anne Ellen (Osbon) Rankhorn; m. Walter Howard Crane, June 14, 1969 (div. June 1977); 1 child, Patrick; m. James Lewis Gage, June 10, 1977 (div. Oct. 15, 1981); 1 child, Laura Anne. BS, Ill. Inst. Tech., 1969; postgrad. Winona State U., 1978-80, U. Minn., 1981-82. Cert. tchr. math., Wash., Mich., Ill. Tchr. math. St. Bede Acad., Eau Claire, Wis., 1977; accounts specialist U. Minn., Mpls., 1981, asst. adminstr., 1981-82, assoc. adminstr., 1982-83; grants acct. Coll. of DuPage, Glen Ellyn, Ill., 1984, cash disbursements mgr., 1984-87, chief acct., 1987—; mem. bd./staff rels. com. Coll. DePage Bd., 1990—; chmn. supervisory com. Fed. Credit Union, 1985-86, mem. project team payroll/personnel systems implementation, 1985-87; mem. project team gen. ledger system implementation,, 1987-89. Contbg. author math. curriculum, 1972. Media contact coord. Common Cause, Manistique, Mich., 1975-76; bd. dirs. pres. Manistique Coop. Nursery Sch., 1974-75; mem. Bicentennial program com. Manistique Jr. Women's Group, Manistique, 1975-76, Chgo. Tchrs. Against the Vietnam War, 1969. Recipient Coll. of DuPage Outstanding Service award, 1987-88; State of Ill. fellow, 1970; Ill. Inst. Tech. scholar, 1964. Mem. NAFE, Coll. of DuPage Classified Pers. Assn. (bd. dirs., staff rels. com. 1990—), Am. Soc. Profl. and Exec. Women, 1967-68), Cen. Assn. Coll. and Univ. Bus. Officers (2 yr. coll. com. 1990). Nat. Assn. Univ. and Bus. Officers, Kappa Phi Delta (treas. 1967-68). Democrat. Unitarian. Club:

Manistique Extension Homemakers (treas. 1974-76). Avocations: tapestries, embroidery, singing, gardening, camping, reading. Home: 1571 Fairway Dr Apt 101 Naperville IL 60563 Office: Coll of DuPage Fin Office 22d St at Lambert Rd Glen Ellyn IL 60137

GAGLIONE, RAE ANN, lawyer; b. Brklyn., Aug. 19, 1962; d. John and Anita (Pfeiffer) G. BA, Marymount Coll., Tarrytown, N.Y., 1984; JD, Fordham U., N.Y., 1987. Staff atty. Dept. of Ports and Trade, N.Y.C., 1988—. Roman Catholic. Office: NYC Dept Ports and Trade Battery Maritime Bldg New York NY 10004

GAGNE, DEBORAH, advertising agency executive. V.p. fin., then sr. v.p., now exec. v.p. adminstrn. and fin. Mendoza, Dillon & Asociados, Inc., Newport Beach, Calif. Office: Mendoza Dillon & Asociados 4100 Newport Pla Ste 600 Newport Beach CA 92660*

GAGNÉ, GEORGETTE MARIE, computer company executive; b. New London, Conn., Apr. 1, 1950; d. Armand Joseph and Yvette Alice (Capistran) G.; m. Stephen John Cordeiro, May 22, 1982. BA, U. Mass., Boston, 1972. Phototypographer South Middlesex News, Framingham, Mass., 1973-74, advt. rep., 1974-76; proofreader Digital Equipment Corp., Maynard, Mass., 1976-78, assoc. tech. editor, 1978-81; tech. editor Digital Equipment Corp., Shrewsbury, Mass., 1981-83, sr. tech. editor, 1983-86; publishing unit mgr. Digital Equipment Corp., Marlborough, Mass., 1986—. Recipient 12 editing awards Soc. Tech. Communications. Mem. NAFE, Humane Soc., Middlesex Striders Club. Home: 65 Pearl St Holliston MA 01746 Office: Digital Equipment Corp MR02-2/D14 2 Results Way Marlborough MA 01752

GAGNE, PAMELA BASHORE, lawyer; b. Harrisburg, Pa., Oct. 19, 1955; d. Charles Eicker and Helen Louise (Adams) Bashore; m. William Roderick Gagne, Aug. 26, 1978; children: Roderick Bashore, Evan Rhodes. B.A. cum laude, Vanderbilt U., 1977; student Inst. Internat. and Comparative Law, Sorbonne, Paris, 1978; J.D., Dickinson Sch. Law, 1980. Bar: Pa. 1980, Fla. 1982. Law clk. Pa. Dept. Environ. Resources, Harrisburg, 1978-79; jud. clk. to judge Gwilyn A. Price, Pitts., 1980-82; assoc. Marshall, Dennehey, Warner, Coleman & Goggin, Phila., 1982-86, pvt. practice, Phila, 1986-87, 90—; assoc., Rotko and Creskoff, Phila., 1988-89; bd. dirs. Edwin L. Heim Co., Inc., Harrisburg; dist. coord. Pa. Mock Trial Competition, 1986-87. Mem. Lawyers for the Arts, Phila., 1983-86; fundraiser, community organizer St. Christopher's Children's Hosp., Phila., 1983—, exec. coun., 1986-87; mem. Washington Mews Condominium Coun., Phila., 1982-85, Young Lawyers Child Abuse Com., Phila., 1983—; mem. Dem. com. Springfield Twp. Montgomery County, 1990—. Recipient Am. Jurisprudence award, 1980; Merit award for Achievement in Advocacy, Dickinson Sch. Law, 1980. Mem. ABA, LWV, Pa. Bar Assn. (com. on statutory law 1985—, young lawyers youth edn. com. 1985—, chmn. zone 1 1986-89, del. exec. coun. young lawyers div. 1986-89), Fla. Bar Assn., Phila. Cricket Club, Acorn Club, Phi Alpha Delta. Presbyterian. Home and Office: 515 Cresheim Valley Rd Wyndmoor PA 19118

GAGNON, EDITH MORRISON, ballerina, singer, actress; b. Chgo., Apr. 8; grad. Chalif Sch. Dancing, N.Y.C.; student Northwestern U.; voice student Forest Lamont of Chgo. Opera Co.; grad. Chalif Sch. of N.Y.; trained with Ivan Tarasoff; m. Alfred Gagnon, Feb. 3, 1977; children by previous marriage—Joyce, Morton. Premiere ballerina Pavley and Oukrainsky Russian Ballet of Chgo., performer with Chgo., Met., Ravinia Opera Cos.; appeared Birthday of Infanta, Greenwich Follies, The Five O'Clock Girl; founder, dir., instr. Sch. of Dance, St. Louis; singer in concert, Carnegie Hall; commentator radio programs Women on the Home Front, Sta. KSD, St. Louis, and CD program Sta. WEW, St. Louis U.; voice coach, producer, performer benefit performances, St. Louis, San Francisco area. Pres. Pets Unlimited, San Francisco; bd. dirs. Artists Embassy. Mem. Pacific Musical Soc. (v.p. San Francisco), Equity Guild. Clubs: Burlingame Country; International Embassy, Francisca

GAGNON, JANICE M., communications account representative; b. Hartford, Conn., Aug. 5, 1955; d. Russell Matthew and Arlene Marie (Trainor) G. BA, U. Calif., Irvine, 1978; postgrad., U. Phoenix, Stanford U. Editor/acad. affairs U. Calif., Irvine; unit mgr. Colgate-Palmolive, Anaheim, Calif.; sales mgr. Southwestern Bell, St. Louis; communications analyst Pacific Telesis Bus. Systems, Colton, Calif.; maj. account representative US Sprint, Gardena, Calif. Mem. AAUW, Long Beach C. of C. (women's coun.). Democrat.

GAGNON, LYNNE MARIE, nurse; b. Presque Isle, Maine, Aug. 1, 1951; d. Guilford Monroe and Caroline (Folger) Smith; m. Daniel Gale Gagnon, Dec. 29, 1971; children: Amber, Dawn, Beth. Nursing diploma Mercy Hosp. Sch. of Nursing, Portland, Maine, 1972; student St. Joseph's Coll., North Windham, Maine, 1969-72, U. Maine-Orono, 1980-84; BSN SUNY-Albany, 1987. Registered nurse, Maine; cert. emergency nurse. Staff nurse St. Agnes Hosp., Balt., 1972-73, Hartford Hosp., Conn., 1973-74; staff nurse, charge nurse A.R. Gould Meml. Hosp., Presque Isle, Maine, 1974-77; staff nurse I, emergency dept. Eastern Maine Med. Ctr., Bangor, Maine, 1979-82, staff developer, 1982-88, head nurse emergency svcs. dept., 1989—, mgr.; mem. Gov.'s Adv. Bd. to Emergency Med. Services, 1983-89, chmn., 1985-86, 86-88; chmn. 11th and 14th Ann. New Eng. Symposium on Emergency Nursing, 1985. Bd. dirs. Orono Vol. Rescue Service, 1985—, v.p. 1987, pres. 1988; mem. Maine Seat Belt Coalition, 1986. Mem. Am. Nurses Assn., Maine State Nurses Assn., Emergency Dept. Nurses Assn. (chpt. pres. 1979-81), Nat. Emergency Nurses Assn. (bd. dirs. 1988—, pres.-elect 1990), Maine Emergency Nurses Assn. (pres. 1984, 85-86), Nat. Bd. Cert. for Emergency Nurses. Democrat. Roman Catholic. Avocations: cross-country skiing; sewing; reading. Home: RFD 5 Box 260 Bangor ME 04401 Office: Ea Maine Med Ctr Edn and Tng Ctr 489 State St Bangor ME 04401

GAGNON, YVONNE, public relations specialist; b. Old Town, Maine, Feb. 3, 1946; d. Louis and Florence (Sirois) Gagnon. BA, Albertus Magnus Coll., 1968; postgrad., Fgn. Svc. Inst., 1975, NYU. Tchr. Peace Corps, Fiji Islands, 1969-71, Colchester/W. Hartford, Conn. and Woburn, Mass., 1968, 72-74; manpower tng. and planning advisor Pacific Arch. & Engrs., Jakarta, Indonesia, 1975-77; owner, dir. Transcultural Rsch. Internat., W. Newton, Mass., 1977-80; pub. affairs mgr. Freeport Indonesia, N.Y.C., 1980-85; pub. rels. mgr. Nynex Internat., White Plains, N.Y., 1986-89; ptnr. YG/Film Forms, N.Y.C. and San Francisco, 1989—. Producer (film documentary) Mining Challenge, 1981. Mem. Nat. Returned Peace Corps Vols. Mem. Pub. Rels. Soc. Am., Women in Communications, Advt. Women N.Y., Fgn. Press Assn. Office: YG/Film Forms 280 Bronxville Rd #6A Bronxville NY 10708

GAI, PAULA MARCHIO, tax consultant; b. Hartford, Conn., Dec. 8, 1943; d. Anthony Paul and Anina (Lattanzio) Marchio; m. Henry J. Gai, Jr., July 22, 1967; children: Alisa Nina, Krista Mari. BS, Cen. Conn. U., 1965; postgrad., Trinity Coll., Hartford, Conn., 1966, Boston U., 1972-74. Tchr. Avon (Conn.) Pub. Schs., 1965-69; substitute tchr. Holliston (Mass.) Pub. Schs., 1977-81; tax preparer H & R Block, Inc., Marlboro, Mass., 1981-90, mgr., 1982-87; pub. rels. rep. H & R Block, Inc., Kansas City, Mo., 1982-90; tax cons. Internat. Cons. Svcs., Holliston, Mass., 1985—; tax expert ABC Network, Boston, 1990; lectr. Tax Seminars, 1982-90; speaker various groups and medias, 1983—. Contbr. articles to profl. jours., newspapers. Mem. LMW, Holliston, Mass., 1972-84, Marion Prep. Sch. adv. bd., Farmingham, Mass., 1985-89. Democrat. Roman Catholic. Home: 122 Jennings Rd Holliston MA 01746

GAILEY, MARGUERITE HENRIETTA, healthcare professional, nurse; b. San Angelo, Tex., Oct. 2, 1917; d. Oscar Augustus and Virginia Catherine (Warren) Savage; m. Luther Lewis Gailey, Nov. 4, 1937; children: Catherine Elesynna Betsill, Laura Estalee. AA, San Angelo Coll., 1937; cert., San Angelo Bus. Coll., 1942; student, Baylor U. Med. Ctr., 1965-66; cert., Howard Coll., 1972. Asst. instr. phys. edn. San Angelo Ind. Sch. Dist., 1936-37; librarian Tom Green County Library, San Angelo, 1937-38; elem. and substitute tchr. Tom Green County Rural Schs., San Angelo, 1938-41; mgr., owner restaurant San Angelo and Tularosa, N.Mex., 1946-48; floral designer Leon's Flowers, San Angelo, 1948-50; nurse, med. sec. Emergency Hosp., San Angelo, 1950-53; cost acct., payroll clk. Warner Constrn. Co., San Angelo, 1954-58; night supr. Bronte (Tex.) Hosp., 1958-62; asst. adminstr. Bapt. Meml. Ctr., San Angelo, 1985—; cons. Home Fund, Inc., San Antonio, 1964-68, NAPNES, Silver Springs, Md., 1987—. Mem. aux. Bapt. Meml. Hosp., San Angelo; com. chair, bd. dirs. El Camino Girl Scouts coun., San Angelo, 1988—. Named Woman of Yr., Bus. and Profl. Women's Club, 1972, Lady of Yr., Internat. Assn. Ladies Aux., 1987. Mem. San Angelo Coll. Alumni Assn., Tex. Soc. Human Resources Adminstrs. Democrat. Home: 902 N Main D13-N San Angelo TX 76903 Office: Bapt Meml Geriatrics Ctr PO Box 5661 San Angelo TX 76902

GAINEN, SUSAN ROSE, lawyer, consultant; b. Washington, Jan. 7, 1950; d. Herman and Letty (Cohen) G. BA in History, U. Md., 1980; JD, U. Balt., 1984. Bar: Md. 1984. Referral specialist Md. Vol. Lawyers, Balt., 1983-84; assoc. Ronald A. Silkworth, P.A., Glen Burnie, Md., 1985-86; v.p., legal recruiter Conaway Legal Search, Balt., 1986-89; prin. Susan Gainen Legal Search, Balt., 1989-90; sr. cons. The Barrister Group, Washington, 1989—. Contbr. articles to profl. jours. Chmn. bd. dirs. Md. Media, Inc., College Park, 1984—. Mem. ABA, Balt. City Bar Assn., Md. Bar Assn., U. Balt. Alumni Assn. (bd. govs. 1989—, chair law liason com.). Office: The Barrister Group 1850 M St NW STe 820 Washington DC 20036

GAINER, LEILA JOSEPHINE, public relations executive; b. Balt., Dec. 4, 1948; d. Theodore and Lela Lee (Harrison) Dworkowski; m. Robert M. Gainer, Aug. 21, 1971. BA, Frostburg (Md.) State Coll., 1970. Reporter, editor Labor Law Guide, Coll. and Univ. Report Commerce Clearing House, Inc., Washington; dir. Ctr. for Regional Action Nat. Assn. Regional Coun. Local Govts., Washington; dir. nat. affairs Am. Soc. for Tng. and Devel., Alexandria, Va.; dir. pub. rels. Lesuik, Himmelsbach, Wilson, Hearl & Dietz, Myrtle Beach, S.C.; mem. Nat. Project on Apprenticeship; mem. adv. bd. Center for Bus. and Industry. Co-author: Training in America: The Organization and Strategic Role of Training, Workplace Basics: The Essential Skills Employers Want, Workplace Basics: Training Manual, Training the Technical Workforce; author monographs. Hnored by Pres. Carter for Leadership on 1980 Rural Devel. Act. Mem. Nat. Tech. Edn. Coalition, Am. Soc. Assn. Execs., Am. League Lobbyists. Address: 327 Red Fox Circle Myrtle Beach SC 29577

GAINES, ALIDA MOIRA, advertising executive; b. Nov. 21, 1957; d. Jerry and Harriet (Fischman) G. BS, SUNY, Oswego, 1979. Network asst. N.W. Ayer, N.Y.C., 1980; network supr. J. Walter Thompson, N.Y.C., 1980-86; v.p. network dept. SSC&B/Lintas, N.Y.C., 1986-88; mgr. broadcast RJR Nabisco, N.Y.C., Atlanta, 1988—. Office: RJR Nabisco Broadcast 7 Campus Dr Parsippany NJ 07054

GAINES, ANNE PRESTON, publisher's assistant; b. Charleston, W.Va., July 25, 1950; d. William Thomas Griffiths and Elizabeth Preston Tupper; m. William Maxwell Gaines, Feb. 21, 1987. BFA, U. Colo., 1972. Sec. N.Y. Bailliage Confrerie de la Chaine des Rotisseurs, N.Y.C, 1976-81; asst. to pub. MAD Mag., N.Y.C, 1980—. Mem. Wine and Food Soc. N.Y., John More Assn. (bd. dirs. 1980-86), Ison Soc. (charter mem.). Office: MAD mag 485 Madison Ave New York NY 10022

GAINES, ELIZABETH WOLCOTT, insurance-management analyst; b. Schenectady, N.Y., Jan. 8, 1963; d. George Loweree and Margaret Earl (Greene) G.; m. J. Martin Brayboy, Oct. 14, 1989. BA, Yale Coll., 1984; MBA, Columbia U., 1988. Assoc. Jackson Ventures Internat., Balt., 1984-85; ops. coord. Md. Nat. Bank, Balt., 1985-86; sr. mgmt. analyst CIGNA Corp., Hartford, Conn., 1988—. Vol. Career Beginnings, Hartford, 1988-89, Friendly Visitors, Hartford, 1988-89. Mem. Beta Gamma Sigma.

GAINES, JEANIE, personnel specialist; b. Borger, Tex., May 13, 1953; d. Edward Orlando and Betty Lee (Kinsey) Houston; m. Mathew Edward Gaines; 1 child, Jeremy Daniel. AS, Ctr. for Degree Studies, Pa., 1985; BBM, Kenedy Western Univ., Calif., 1987. Supr. Word Processing Ctr.; asst. to dir., asst. dir. Genetics Screening and Counseling Svc., Denton, Tex.; pers. officer, adminstrv. asst. Parkside Lodge Westgate, Denton. Mem. NAFE, NOW, Am. Mgmt. Assn. Address: 2320 W Prairie Apt 106 Denton TX 76201

GAINES, KENDRA HOLLY, English educator, editorial and writing consultant; b. Chgo., Dec. 6, 1946; d. Reuben B. and Frances P. Gaines; m. Kenneth C. Wolfgang, Feb. 18, 1989. BA with distinction, Mt. Holyoke Coll., 1968; MA with honor, Claremont Grad. Sch., 1971; MA, Northwestern U., 1974, PhD, 1982. Cert. life secondary and community coll. tchr., Calif. Tchr. English, Claremont (Calif.) Collegiate Sch., 1969-72; teaching asst. Northwestern U., Evanston, Ill., 1975-78; instr. English, U. Mich., Ann Arbor, 1978-79; assoc. editor Scott, Foresman Co., Glenview, 1983-85; instr. English, career tutor U. Ariz., Tucson, 1985—; editorial cons., freelance writer, 1969—. Contbr. articles to various publs.; writer radio scripts Holiday World of Travel, 1969—. Grantee State of Calif., 1970; Mills fellow, 1971; fellow Northwestern U., 1973-76. Mem. MLA, Nat. Coun. Tchrs. English, AAUW. Home: 925 N Jerrie Ave Tucson AZ 85711 Office: U Ariz Humanities Adminstrn Tucson AZ 85721

GAINES, LA DONNA ADRIAN See SUMMER, DONNA

GAISFORD, JANA SUE, postal administrator; b. Sentinel, Okla., Jan. 17, 1952; d. Leonard Erie and Sam Geneva (Martin) Lumpkin; 1 child, Jason Charles. BS in Bus. Adminstrn., Northwestern Okla. State U., 1974; student, Autry Votech, Enid, Okla., 1987. Clk., carrier U.S. Postal Svc., Alva, Okla., 1979-84; sec. U.S. Postal Svc., Enid, Okla., 1984-87; officer in charge of detail U.S. Postal Svc., Cherokee, Okla., 1988; supr. delivery and collection U.S. Postal Svc., Enid, 1987-89; acting A.O. coord. U.S. Postal Svc., Oklahoma City, 1989; supr. postal operation U.S. Postal Svc., Ada, Okla., 1989—; dir.-at-large women's adv. coun. U.S. Postal Svc., Oklahoma City, 1985-86, vice-chair, 1986-87, chair, 1987-89. Mem. Nat. Assn. Postal Suprs., Nat. Assn. Postmasters. Mailing: PO Box 201 Ada OK 74821-0201 Home: RR 2 Box 8A Ada OK 74821 Office: 131 E 12th Ada OK 74820

GAJDA, PATRICIA ANN, history educator; b. E. Cleve., Ohio, Jan. 24, 1941; d. Thaddeus J. and Rose M. (Rusnaczyk) Gajda. BS, St. John Coll., 1962; MA, Case Western Reserve U., 1966, PhD, 1972; BA, U. Tex., Tyler, 1988. Tchr. Cleve. Catholic Sch., 1962-65; tchr., alt. prin. U.S. Dept. Def. Overseas Dependents Sch., Gelnhausen, Germany, 1965-67; lect. John Carroll U. and Cuyahoga Community Coll., Cleve., 1972-74; asst. prof. history Univ. Tex., Tyler, 1974-77, assoc. prof., assoc. v.p., 1976-83, dir. internat. program, 1977-86; prof. history Univ. Tex, Tyler, 1983--; cons. Jr. Coll. , 1977--. Author: Faces of Tyler, 1979, Postscript to Victory, 1982. Precinct chair, Democratic Party, Tyler, 1980; mem. Sister Cities. Mem. Tex. Cath. Hist. Soc. (pres.), Tex. State Hist. Assn., East Tex. Hist. Assn., Polish-Am. Hist. Assn. Roman Catholic. Office: U Tex 3900 University Blvd Tyler TX 75701-6699

GAJEWSKI, CHRISTINE, city official; b. New Britain, Con., Jan. 21, 1946; d. Stanley Constantine and Tessie (Dabrowska) Panus; m. Eugene Gajewski; children: Rose Marie, Marcel Daniel. BS, Cen. Conn. State U., 1968, MBA. Bookkeeper, office clk. A.Y.O. Packing Co., New Britain; acctg. clk. J. Edward Loughery, New Britain; bookkeeper City of New Britain, asst. dir. fin. Address: 158 Misty Mt Rd Kensington CT 06037 Office: City of New Britain Fin Dept 185 Main St New Britain CT 06051

GALANE, IRMA ADELE BERESTON, electronic engineer; b. Balt., Aug. 23, 1921; d. Dr. Arthur and Sarah (Hillman) Bereston; B.A., Goucher Coll., 1940; postgrad. Johns Hopkins, 1940-42, Mass. Inst. Tech., 1943, George Washington U., 1945, 65, 73, 77, 79, U. Md., 1958, Army Mgmt. Sch., 1964; 1 dau., Suzanne Felice Galane Duvall. Physicist, Naval Ordnance Lab., 1942-43; electronic engr. Navy Bur. Ships, 1943-49, Army Office Chief Signal Officer, 1949-51, Navy Bur. Aeros., 1951-56, Air Research and Devel. Command, USAF, 1956-57, FCC, 1957-60, NASA, 1960-62; supervisory electronic engr. USCG Hdqrs., 1962-64; sci. specialist engring. scis. Library of Congress, 1964-65; project engr. Advanced Aerial Fire Support System, Army Materiel Command, 1965-66; engr. Naval Air Systems Command, 1966-71; electronic engr. Spectrum Mgmt. Task Force, FCC, 1971-76, sr. research engr. FCC, 1976—; Judge nat. capitol awards for engrs. and architects, 1975. Registered profl. engr., D.C. Mem. IEEE (sr.), Am. Inst. Aeros. and Astronautics, Nat. Soc. Profl. Engrs. (chmn. publs. com. 1959-60, co-chmn. civil def. com. 1965, spl. asst. to pres. 1965), Soc. Women Engrs. (sr. mem.; nat. membership chmn. 1952, nat. dir. 1953, mem. nat. scholarship com. 1958), Armed Forces Communications and Electronics Assn., Fedn. Profl. Assn., Am. Ordnance Assn., Johns Hopkins Alumni Assn., AAAS, U.S. Naval Inst., Marine Tech. Soc., Internat. Platform Assn., Smithsonian Inst. (assoc.), Mensa. Editor: The Met. Washington Profl. Engr., 1958-60. Home: 4201 Cathedral Ave NW Washington DC 20016

GALANTUOMINI, CAROL BRIGIDA, probation officer; b. Reno, Nov. 22, 1959; d. Martin Joseph and Margaret Marie (Casazza) G. BS in Social Work, U. Nev., 1981, postgrad., 1988—. Lic. social worker. Runaway counselor Community Runaway and Youth Svcs., Reno, 1982-84; juvenile probation officer Washoe County Juvenile Probation Dept., Reno, 1984-89, juvenile probation unit supr., 1989—; truancy worker, liasion Washoe County Juvenile Probabation, 1988-89; group facilitator Parent's United, Reno, 1984-87. Mem. Child Abuse and Neglect Task Force of No. Nev., 1990—; religious edn. instr. Our Lady of the Snows Cath. Ch., Reno, 1982-87.

GALATTE-HOWARD, GAIL ANN, insurance training professional; b. Chgo., Oct. 3, 1959; d. Nicholas Joseph and Jeanette Marie (Notorleva) G.; m. James Clarke Howard, Mar. 7, 1981; children: Elizabeth Ashley, Kristina Lynne, Melissa Anne. BS, Ill. State U., 1980, MS, 1982. Rsch. asst. Cragan Rsch. Inc., Bloomington, Ill., 1980-84; instr. Ill. State U., Normal, 1982-83; client svc. rep. Midwest TV, Inc., Peoria, Ill., 1983-84; coord. employee communications and media rels. Country Cos., Bloomington, 1984-86, mgr. agy. and consumer communications, 1986-89, agt. tng., design specialist, 1989—; design specialist, 1989—; trainer Country Cos., 1989—. Asst. instr. St. Patricks of Merna, Bloomington, 1989; co-leader Girl Scout U.S.A., Troop 222, Bloomington, 1989. Fellow NAFE, NASD, Women in Communication, Am. Soc. CLUs; mem. Pi Beta Phi (pres. Ill. State U. chpt., house corp. 1988-90). Republican. Roman Catholic. Home: 211 W 17th Pl Lombard IL 60148 Office: Country Cos 1701 Towanda Ave Bloomington IL 61701

GALBREATH, JOYCE DALE CONDRAY, interior decorator; b. B'Ham, Ala., Mar. 11, 1930; d. Marvin Walto and Leota Francis (Cochran) Condray; m. James M. Galbreath (div. 1976); 1 child, James Marvin Jr. BA, U. Ala., 1953; postgrad., Sorbonne U., Paris, France, 1961, U. Ala., 1965. Interior decorator Galbreath Interiors, Huntsville, Ala., 1965-75, Castner Knotts, Nashville, Tenn., 1976-80, Advanced Construction Co., Nashville, N.Y., 1981-85, Mencon Ind., Melbourne Bch.; dir. Mencon Gallery, Vero Bch., Fla., 1987-88. Republican. Baptist. Home: 8040 S A1A Hwy Melbourne FL 32951

GALCHICK, JANET MAE, advertising executive; b. Salem, Ohio, June 23, 1951; d. Paul Lawrence and Lena Marie (DePietro) G.; m. Warren Phillip Yarnell, Apr. 15, 1978; children: Eric Charles, Elyse Meredith. BA, Ohio State U., 1973, MA, 1976, PhD, 1977. Rsch. assoc. Ohio State U., Columbus, 1975-77; rsch. asst., polit. scientist The Brookings Inst., Washington, 1977-79; rsch. assoc., polit. scientist Woodrow Wilson Sch. Pub. and Internat. Affairs, Princeton U., 1979-81; from rsch. account exec. to assoc. dir. rsch. Young and Rubicam, Inc., N.Y.C., 1981-87, consumer insight dir., 1987-90; rsch. dir. Arbeit & Co., N.Y.C., 1990—. Co-author: Public Service Employment: A Field Evaluation, 1981. Mem. steering com. East coast regional campaign office Ohio State U., N.Y., 1988—. Roman Catholic.

GALE, PAULA JANE, chemist; b. Joplin, Mo., July 26, 1946; d. Richard O. and Paula (Thogmartin) G.; m. Ernest David Moldrz, Mar. 23, 1968 (div. Aug. 1972); m. Bryan L. Bartz, July 6, 1985; 1 child, Elizabeth. AB, Randolph-Macon Woman's Coll., 1968; PhD, Brandeis U., 1976. Tchr. Lewis-Wadhams Sch., Westport, N.Y., 1968; analytical chemist Charles River Pollution Control Project, Cambridge, Mass., 1969; tchr. asst. Brandeis U., Waltham, Mass., 1970-74; rsch. assoc. Yale U., New Haven, Conn., 1975-77; from instr. to rsch. assoc. U. Va., Charlottesville, Va., 1977-79; sr. assoc. engr. IBM Corp., Poughkeepsie, N.Y., 1979-80; tech. staff mem. David Sarnoff Rsch. Ctr., Princeton, N.J., 1980—; rsch. asst. Mass. Gen. Hosp., Boston, 1968; rsch. physicist Wentworth Inst., 1975; vis. scientist NIH, Bethesda, Md., 1978; speaker in field for numerous orgns. Contbr. articles to profl. jours. Mem. Nat. Trust for Hist. Preservation. Mem. AAAS, Am. Soc. Mass Spectrometry (treas. 1990-92, chmn. nominating com. 1988, chmn. N.J. discussion group, 1981-83), Am. Chem. Soc. Office: David Sarnoff Rsch Ctr CN 5300 Princeton NJ 08543-5300

GALKIN, FLORENCE, social worker, writer; b. N.Y.C., Dec. 27, 1925; d. Victor and Sadie (Sobel) Greenwald; BA, Hunter Coll., 1946; MSW, U. Pa., 1951; advanced cert. Columbia U., 1961, postgrad., NIMH fellow, 1962-64; m. Bernard Galkin, Dec. 18, 1948; children: Judith, William Seth. Caseworker, Jewish Child Care Assn., N.Y.C., 1951-57; field instr. community orgn. Birds Coler Hosp., 1968; ombudsman program Community Council Greater N.Y., 1978—; research assoc. Center Policy Research, 1980—; exec. dir. Community Action and Resources for the Elderly, 1976—; nat. v.p.Am. Jewish Congress, 1986—. Bd. dirs. Nat. Coalition for Nursing Home Reform, 1978-79. Mem. Nat. Assn. Social Workers. Jewish. Author: People and Nursing Homes, 1977; (with others) Neighborhood Information Center: A Study and Some Proposals, 1966; (with Hochbaum) The New York State Patient Advocacy Program, Patients and Their Complaints, 1978, Discharge Planning: No Deposit, No Return, 1982, Medicaid Patients Need Not Apply, 1987. Home: 400 E 56th St New York NY 10022 Office: Am Jewish Congress 15 E 84th St New York NY 10028

GALL, ADRIENNE LYNN, publications manager; b. Long Branch, N.J., Jan. 25, 1960; d. Robert Conrad and Anna May (Critchfield) Gall. B.A., Hood Coll., Md., 1982. Editorial asst. Polo Mag., Fleet St. Corp., Gaithersburg, Md., 1982-83; assoc. editor Nat. Solid Wastes Mgmt. Assn., Washington, 1983-86; mng. editor Am. Soc. Tng. & Devel., Alexandria, Va., 1986-88; publ. mgr. Stratton/Petersen Publ. & Pub. Rels., Arlington, Va., 1988—. Mem. Smithsonian Assocs. Democrat. Avocations: equestrienne; historic preservation; environmental conservation. Office: Stratton/Petersen 2800 Shirlington Rd Ste 706 Arlington VA 22206

GALL, ELIZABETH BENSON, dating service executive; b. Williamson, W.Va., June 11, 1944; d. Thomas Jefferson Bluebaum and Ollie Mae (Moore) Bluebaum Walker; Charles B. Walker (stepfather); 1 child, Thomas Ethan. Ptnr., dir. Chicagoland Register, dating service, Chgo., 1974-84; cooking instr. Elizabeth Benson Internat. Cooking Lessons, 1978-84; owner Ethnic Party People Catering, 1981—, Phone-A-Friend Dating Service, Chgo., 1984—. Home and Office: 6314 N Troy St Chicago IL 60659

GALL, ROXANNE BERNADETTE, registered nurse; b. Covington, Ky., Nov. 9, 1954; d. Andrew James and Shirley Catherine (Gubser) G.; m. W. Russell Morgan, Aug. 1, 1977 (div. Dec. 1984); 1 child, W. Robert. ADN, Lexington Tech. Inst., 1978; BSN, U. Ky., 1983, postgrad., 1988—. RN, Ky. Nurse, clin. supr. paramedic program Ea. Ky. U., Richmond, 1984-85; critical care nurse St. Joseph Hosp., Lexington, Ky., 1978—, evening charge nurse recovery room, 1979-80, asst. charge nurse ICU, 1980-84, critical care quality assurance coord., 1986-88. Chmn. Foster Care Rev. Bd., Lexington, 1987-88, mem., 1989. Democrat. Roman Catholic. Home: 122 Forest Ave Lexington KY 40504

GALL, SUZANNE LEIGH, librarian; b. Columbus, Ohio, Apr. 22, 1959; d. Elmer Raymond and Dorothy Marie (Ryan) G. BA, Ohio State U., 1982; MLS, Kent (Ohio) State U., 1988. Librarian Kohrman Jackson & Krantz, Cleve., 1986—. Mem. Am. Assn. Law LIbraries, Ohio Regional Assn. Law Libraries. Office: Kohrman Jackson & Krantz 1 Cleveland Ctr 20th Fl Cleveland OH 44114

GALLAGHER, ANNE PORTER, business executive; b. Coral Gables, Fla., Mar. 16, 1950; d. William Moring and Anne (Jewett) Porter; m. Matthew Philip Gallagher, Jr., July 31, 1976; children: Jacqueline Anne, Kevin Sharkey. BA in Edn., Stetson U., 1972. Tchr. elem. schs., Atlanta, 1972-74; sales rep. Xerox Corp., Atlanta, 1974-76, Fed. Systems, Rosslyn, Va., 1976-81; sales rep. No. Telecom Inc. Fed. Systems, Vienna, Va., 1981-84, account exec., 1984-85, sales dir., 1985-87, mktg. dir., 1987—. Mem. NAFE, Armed

Forces Communications and Electronics Assn., Pi Beta Phi. Episcopalian. Avocations: skiing, aerobics, needlepoint. Home: 4052 Seminary Rd Alexandria VA 22304 Office: No Telecom Fed Systems Inc 8614 Westwood Center Dr Vienna VA 22182

GALLAGHER, CATHY LOUISE, negotiations consultant; b. Detroit, Jan. 21, 1948; d. Norman James and Vera Pearl (Prott) G. BA, Adrian (Mich.) Coll., 1970; MA, Mich. State U., 1980. Home service advisor Consumer Power Co., Muskegon, Mich., 1970-72; home economist, info. specialist, media cons. coop. extension service Mich. State U., East Lansing, 1972-81; sales rep. John Hancock Mut. Ins. Co., Southfield, Mich., 1981-82, Surgikos subs. Johnson & Johnson Co., Toledo, 1982-84, NDM Corp., Milw., 1984-85; profl. services cons. HPI Health Care Services, Inc., Milw., 1985-86; sr. cons. HPI Health Care Services, Inc., Milw. and Atlanta, 1986-88; pvt. practice cons. Milw., 1988—; speaker in field. Mem. Nat. Speakers Assn., Wis. Profl. Speakers Assn. Home and Office: 9102 N 75th St Apt 3-B Milwaukee WI 53223-2056

GALLAGHER, IDELLA JANE SMITH (MRS. DONALD A. GALLAGHER), foundation executive, writer; b. Union City, N.J., Jan. 1, 1917; d. Fred J. and Louise (Stewart) S.; Ph.B., Marquette U., 1941, M.A., 1943, Ph.D., 1963; postgrad. U. Louvain, Belgium, U. Paris; m. Donald A. Gallagher, June 29, 1938; children—Paul B., Maria Noel. Lectr. philosophy Marquette U., 1943-52, 54-56; instr. philosophy Alverno Coll., Milw., 1956-58; asst. prof. philosophy Villanova U., 1958-62; asst. prof. philosophy Boston Coll., 1962-68, asso. prof., 1968-69; assoc. prof. philosophy U. Ottawa, 1969-71, prof., 1971-73; projects adminstr. DeRance Found., Milw., 1973-80, v.p., 1981—; vis. prof. philosophy Niagara U., 1976-81. Mem. Sudbury (Mass.) Com. for Human Rights, 1963-69; trustee Mt. Senario Coll., Ladysmith, Wis., 1976-86. Recipient Sword and Shield award St. Louis U., Baguio City, Philippines, 1975. Mem. Metaphys. Soc. Am., Am. Cath. Philos. Assn. (exec. council 1967-69), Am. Soc. Aesthetics, Assn. Realistic Philosophy, AAUP, Brit. Soc. Aesthetics, Canadian Philos. Assn., Canadian Assn. U. Tchrs., Phi Alpha Theta, Phi Delta Gamma. Author: (with D. A. Gallagher) The Achievement of Jacques and Raissa Maritain, 1962; The Education of Man, 1962; (with D. A. Gallagher) A Maritain Reader, 1966; (with D.A. Gallagher) St. Augustine—The Catholic and Manichaean Ways of Life, 1966. Morality in Evolution: The Moral Philosophy of Henri Bergson, 1970. Gen. editor: Christian Culture and Philosophy Series, Bruce Pub. Co., 1965-68. Contbr. to New Cath. Ency., also articles to profl. jours. Home: 7714 W Wisconsin Ave Wauwatosa WI 53213 Office: DeRance Found 7700 W Bluemound Rd Milwaukee WI 53213

GALLAGHER, KATHY ANN, foundation administrator; b. Williamsport, Pa., Sept. 21, 1954; d. Dan LeRoy and Shirley Joann (Klein) Hoover; m. James Michael Nelson, Oct. 23, 1976 (div. 1983). BS in German Edn., Ind. U. of Pa., 1976; postgrad., Pa. State U., 1978-83. Tchr. German Hollidaysburg (Pa.) Area Sch. Dist., 1977-85; adminstr. Carlisle (Pa.) Project, 1985; dir. fin. devel. and pub. relations Am. Lung Assn., York, Pa., 1986; chief profl. officer Adams County United Way, Gettysburg, Pa., 1987—; bd. dirs. Adams Area Postal Customer Counc., Gettysburg. Press sec. Nancy Kulp's campaign for 9th Congl. Dist., Pa., 1984; mem. Downtown Gettysburg, 1987—, 125th Battle of Gettysburg Anniversary Commn., 1988; treas. Adams County Christmas Dinner, 1987—; bd. dirs. Adams County Coun. Community Svcs., 1987—, Pa. State Club of Adams County, 1989—; mem. adv. bd. Adams County Job Ctr., 1989—, Minority Youth Ednl. Inst., 1988—, Intercultural Resource Ctr. Gettsburg Coll., 1989—;mem. Adams area Postal Customer Coun., 1988-89; dir. Adams Community TV, 1987-89. Fulbright/Goethe Haus scholar, Stuttgart, Fed. Republic of Germany, 1982. Mem. NAFE, Bus. and Profl. Women, Cen. Pa. Assn. Women Execs. (charter), Kiwanis, Pa. State Alumni Assn. (life), Alpha Omicron Pi. Democrat. Lutheran. Home: 2566 Old Route 30 Orrtanna PA 17353 Office: Adams County United Way PO Box 3545 Gettysburg PA 17325-3545

GALLAGHER, LINDY ALLYN, banker; b. Kalamazoo, Mich., Sept. 27, 1954; d. Karl P. Joslow and Audrey S. Phillips; m. Thomas J. Gallagher, Nov. 29, 1975; children: James Allyn Buckley, Phillip Graham. BS, U. Pa., 1975; MBA, Columbia U., 1982. Faculty, researcher U. Pa., Phila., 1976-80; corp. banking officer Bank of Montreal, N.Y.C., 1982-84; v.p. Citibank NA, N.Y.C., 1984-89, Chase Manhattan Bank, N.Y.C., 1989-90; prin. private fin. consulting firm, 1990—; treas., dir. 957 Lexington Corp., 1981-87. Editor Columbia Jour. World Bus., 1980-82. Active Women's Nat. Rep. Club, 1986—. Mem. Doubles Club (N.Y.C.), Columbia Club, Country Club of Darien. Republican. Episcopalian.

GALLAGHER, LORIE MILLER, advertising agency official; b. Hartford, Conn., June 23, 1962; d. Lee Byron and Lois Anne (Concannon) Miller; m. Keith Ian Gallagher, Apr. 20, 1985. BA in Psychology, Trinity Coll., Hartford, 1984. Office asst. FPM, Inc., Sacramento, 1984-85; copywriter Beall-Ladymon, Shreveport, La., 1985-86; account rep. Campbell and Co., Shreveport, 1986—. Vol. United Way, Shreveport, 1989. Recipient silver award 10th dist. Am. Advt. Fedn., 1990. Mem. Shreveport-Bossier Advt. Fedn. (bd. dirs., editor newsletter ADVERB 1989-90, gold award 1990, Best of Show award 1990, Pres.'s award 1990). Home: 8801 Hollow Bluff Dr Haughton LA 71037 Office: Campbell and Co 625 Texas St Ste 202 Shreveport LA 71101

GALLAGHER, MARY BETH, sales executive; b. N.J., Aug. 17, 1963; d. James J. and Anne E. (Weierich) G. BSBA, Elmira Coll., 1985. Sales rep. Pitney Bowes, East Windsor, Conn., 1985-88; dist. mgr. Comvestrix, Lynhurst, N.J., 1988-89; cons. Mary Kay Cosmetics, Morris Plainns, N.J., 1989—. Mem. Jr. C. of C., NAFE. Home and Office: Mountain Club Bldg 38 6B Morris Plains NJ 07950

GALLAGHER, NANCY ANNE, college official; b. Henniker, N.H., July 15, 1952; d. Bernard Leon and Theresa Marie (Damour) Young; m. Joseph John Gallagher, Oct. 2, 1971; children: Jennifer Joan, James Joseph. Student, St. Anselm Coll., 1986—. Clk. bus. office New Eng. Telephone, Manchester, N.H., 1970-74; operator switchbd. St. Anselm Coll., Manchester, 1978-87, dir. telecommunications, 1987—. Tchr. St. Raphael Ch., Manchester, 1986—; vol. libr. St. Raphael Sch., Manchester, 1974-76. Mem. NAFE, Assn. Coll. and Univ. Telecommunication Adminstrs. (N.H. state coord. 1990—), N.H. Telecommunication Assn. Roman Catholic. Office: St Anselm Coll 87 St Anselms Dr Manchester NH 03102

GALLAGHER, OLIVE, communications specialist, speaker; b. Phila., Jan. 10, 1943; d. Sidney L. and Lydia May (Koff) Krawitz; m. Walter L. Schaffer, Aug. 10, 1963 (div. July 1981); children: Deborah L., Jessica Lynn. BA in Humanities, Case Western Reserve U., 1965. Pres. King's Crown Music, Cleve., 1971-73, Morning Glory Prodns., L.A., 1973-80, Lorry Music Co., Cleve. and L.A., 1973—; founder, pres. Personal Best, Inc., L.A., 1985-89, chief exec. officer, 1989—; founder, bd. dirs. Agnon Sch., Cleve. Composer, lyricist over 600 published songs; author (poetry) The Singing Heart Volume I, 1983, The Cage of the Soul vol. II, 1984, (book) Playing With a Full Deack, 1988; producer, writer (video) Those Murphy's Law Days, 1988. Entertainment chmn. Nat. Council Jewish Women, Cleve., 1963; first pres. young people's div. Israel Bonds, Cleve., 1968. Mem. Nat. Speakers Assn., Nat. Assn. Female Execs., Women's Referral Service, Women in Communications, Manhattan Beach C. of C., Women in Health, Alpha Epsilon Phi. Democrat. Jewish. Club: Leads (Manhattan Beach). Office: Personal Best Inc 1142 Manhattan Ave Manhattan Beach CA 91266

GALLAGHER, PAULA MARIE, chemical engineer; b. Lowell, Mass., May 14, 1964; d. Frederic Paul and Florence Mae (Blades) G. BSmagna cum laude, U. Lowell (Mass.), 1986, postgrad. in chem. engring. Rsch. and process devel. engr. Phasex Corp., Lawrence, Mass., 1986—. Contbr. articles to profl. jours. Mem. NAFE, Am. Inst. Chem. Engr., Soc. Women Engrs., Tau Beta Pi. Office: Phasex Corp 360 Merrimack St Bldg 9B Lawrence MA 01843

GALLANT, MAVIS, author; b. Montreal, Que., Can., Aug. 11, 1922. Hon. doctoral degree, U. St. Anne, N.S., Can., 1984, York U., Toronto, 1984, U. Western Ont., 1990. Writer-in-residence U. Toronto, 1983-84. Author: Green Water, Green Sky, 1959, 60, A Fairly Good Time, 1970; short stories The Other Paris, My Heart Is Broken: 8 Stories and a Short Novel (Brit. title An Unmarried Man's Summer), 1964, The Affair of Gabrielle Russier; introductory essay, 1971; The Pegnitz Junction, a Novella and Five Short Stories, 1973, The End of the World and Other Stories, 1974; short stories From the Fifteenth District, 1979, Home Truths, 1981, Overhead in a Balloon, 1985; play What Is To Be Done? (produced Toronto 1982), 1984, Paris Notebooks: Essays and Reviews, 1986, (short stories) In Transit, 1989; contbr. to New Yorker, 1951—. Decorated Order of Can.; recipient Gov.-Gen.'s Lit. award, 1982. Fellow Royal Soc. Lit.; fgn. hon. mem. Am. Acad. and Inst. Arts and Letters. Home: 14 rue Jean Ferrandi, Paris France VI

GALLANTY, JULIE ANN, social services administrator; b. N.Y.C.; d. Robert J. and Nancy (Dudar) G.; m. David S. Rogers, Feb. 16, 1986; 1 child, Jordana E. Rogers. BA in Psychology, SUNY, Binghamton, 1982; MA in Early Childhood and Elementary Edn., Adelphi U., 1988. Lic. tchr. nursery through grade 6, N.Y. Presch. tchr., asst. coord. family ctr. West Side YMCA Greater N.Y., N.Y.C., 1982-84, asst. youth dir., 1984-86; dir. youth and family svcs. Vanderbilt YMCA Greater N.Y., N.Y.C., 1986—; cons. child care div. Pitts. YMCA, 1988-90; cons. day camp dirs. conf. Mgmt. Resource Ctr.-YMCA, Pawling, N.Y., 1990; day camp cons. corp. office YMCA of Greater N.Y., 1990; participant, presenter various profl. seminars and confs., 1985—. Active youth com. Community Bd. 6; adult CPR instr., standard first aid instr. ARC. Mem. NAFE, Assn. Profl. Dirs. (mem. com., excellence award 1986, 88), Am. Camping Assn. (assoc. vis. 1987—). Office: Vanderbilt YMCA Greater NY 224 E 47th St New York NY 10017

GALLAUGHER, BARBARA ALICE, educator; b. Galesburg, Ill., Feb. 5, 1950; d. Arthur Doan and Mary Frances (Russell) Potter; m. Larry Alan Gallaugher, June 16, 1973 (div. 1981). BS, We. Ill. U., 1972; MEd, Ariz. State U., 1987. Cert. elem. tchr., Ariz. Tchr. Ctr. Cass Sch. Dist. 66, Downers Grove, Ill., 1972-73, Woodland Sch. Dist. 50, Gages Lake, Ill., 1973-75, Chandler (Ariz.) Unified Sch. Dist. 80, 1977—; v.p., co-owner Pavillion Prodns., Inc. Musician fund raiser Chandler Food Bank, 1985, 86; runner Food for Hungry, Scottsdale, Ariz. Named Outstanding Woman, City of Chandler, 1986. Mem. Chandler Edn. Assn., Ariz. Edn. Assn. NEA, Ariz. Small Bus. Assn., Nat. Assn. Women Bus. Owners. Decmocrat. Roman Catholic.

GALLEN, SUE S., gallery owner; b. N.Y.C., June 12, 1931; d. Solomon Samuel and Diana (Flasterstein) Goldstein; m. Gerald Gallen, June 31, 1956; 1 child, Jeffrey. BA, Bklyn. Coll., 1952; MA, Columbia U., 1955; MS, L.I. U., 1977. Cert. Spanish tchr., N.Y. Translator Lionel Essex-Internat. Internam., N.Y.C., 1952; Spanish tchr. S.J. Tilden High Sch., Bklyn., 1952-53, James Monroe High Sch., N.Y.C., 1953, Jordan Mott Jr. High Sch., N.Y.C., 1953-56, Bayside High Sch., Queens, N.Y., 1956-57, Francis Lewis High Sch., Queens, 1960-74, Jamaica High Sch., Queens, 1974-90; owner Artisans Internat. Gallery, Westhampton Beach, N.Y., 1990—. Mem. Am. Assn. Tchrs. Spanish, Phi Beta Kappa, Sigma Delta Pi. Home: 9 Wisteria Pl Syosset NY 11791

GALLI, EVELYN DIANE, advertising executive; b. N.Y.C., Oct. 28, 1954; d. Heinz Werner and Helen Adele (Stelling) Wischnewski; m. Bruce James Galli, Oct. 10, 1980. BA, Queens Coll., 1977. Media mgr. Trout & Ries Advt., N.Y.C., 1977-83; media specialist MPMS, N.Y.C., 1983-84; media dir. RMR Advt., N.Y.C., 1984-85; v.p., media dir. Herman Assocs., N.Y.C., 1985—. Mem. Lamstedter Damen Circle (v.p. Franklin Square, N.Y. chpt. 1987—). Lutheran. Office: Herman Assocs 488 Madison Ave New York NY 10022

GALLIAN, VIRGINIA ANNE, educator; b. St. Louis, Dec. 29, 1933; d. Martin Charles and Flora Olinda (Rocklage) Schake; children: John Charles, Paige Renee. BS, U. Mo., 1955, MS, 1966; student, U. San Jose, Calif., 1961, U. North Tex., Denton, 1971. Tchr. Hazelwood (Mo.) Pub. Schs., 1955, Ft. Dix Post Sch., Trenton, N.J., 1956, Ft. Bragg Post Sch., Fayetteville, N.C., 1956-58, Fergusen-Florrisant (Mo.) Pub. Schs., 1958-59; music supr. Jefferson City (Mo.) Pub. Schs., 1959-60; tchr. Union Sch. Dist., San Jose, 1960-63, 67, 68, Bridgeport (Calif.) Pub. Schs., 1963-65, Columbia (Mo.) Pub. Schs., 1965-67; music tchr. Denton Ind. Sch. Dist., 1970—. Traffic bd. City of Denton, 1983—. Mem. Tex. State Tchrs. Assn. (lobbyist 1985—, bd. dirs. 1988—), Denton Edn. Assn. (chmn. 1985—), Sigma Alpha Iota (chaplin 1972-74), Phi Delta Kappa. Republican. Methodist.

GALLIHER, MILDRED JOANNA, biology educator; b. Wichita, Kans., Aug. 2, 1944; d. Michael John Harvey and Mildred Joanna (Miezis) Galliher. BS, U. Ariz., 1965, MS, 1970. Life biol. scis. tchr.'s cert., provisional math. tchr.'s cert., Ariz. Grad. teaching asst. biology dept. U. Ariz., Tucson, 1966-69, lab. technician agrl. chemistry and soils dept., 1969-70; instr. biology Cochise Coll., Douglas, Ariz., 1970—, acting head sci. dept., 1987-88, interim div. chair sci., math. and social sci., 1989-90; text book reviewer William C. Brown Co., 1988—; participant Women's Leadership Devel. Conf., Phoenix, 1987. Author: (video tape) How To Study, 1987. Mem. Mule Mountain Citizen's Band Club, Bisbee, Ariz., 1975-80; mem. Ariz. Dem. Com., 1988—. Mem. AAAS, Nat. Assn. Biology Tchrs., Soc. Coll. Sci. Tchrs., Am. Inst. Biol. Scis., Nat. Sci. Tchrs. Assn., Human Anatomy and Physiology Soc. (charter, membership com. 1989-90), Ariz. Biology Conf., Mountain View Computer Users Group, Beta Beta Beta. Roman Catholic. Office: Cochise Coll SMASS Rte 1 Box 100 Douglas AZ 85607

GALLINGER, LOIS MAE, medical technologist; b. Hibbing, Minn., Sept. 5, 1922; d. Clarence Adolph and Dorothy Mae (Stoller) Belanger; m. Ben Elton Gallinger, Sept. 1, 1956; children: Carol Elda, Gregory John. BS, U. Minn., 1946; Med. Tech. Intern, Coll. St. Scholastica, 1948-49. Cert. med. technologist. X-ray technologist Leigh Clinic, Grand Forks, N.D., 1946-47, Nicollet Clinic, Mpls., 1947-48; med. technologist Little Traverse Hosp., Petoskey, Mich., 1949-52; med. and x-ray technologist Lakeside Med. Ctr., Duluth, Minn., 1952-60; med. technologist St. Mary's Med. Ctr., Duluth, 1961-87; retired, 1987. Treas. Benedictine Health Ctr. Aux., Duluth, 1984—, Women's Assocs. Duluth Symphony, 1986—; cookie chmn. No. Pine Girl Scouts, Duluth, 1969; bd. dirs. St. Paul's Episcopalian Women's Club, Duluth, 1970s, greeter's chmn., 1970s. Mem. Am. Soc. Med. Tech., Minn. Soc. Med. Tech. (regional historian 1969), AAUW, Duluth Women's Club. Home: 364 Leicester Ave Duluth MN 55803

GALLINOT, RUTH MAXINE, educational consultant, educator; b. Carlinville, Ill., Feb. 16, 1925; d. Martin Mike and Augusta (Kumpus) G. BS, Roosevelt U., Chgo., 1971, MA with honors, 1974; PhD, The Union Inst. (formerly Union for Experimenting Colls. and Univs.), Cin., 1978. Adminstrv. asst., exec. sec. Karoll's Inc., Chgo., 1952-66; asst. dean Cen. YMCA Community Coll., Chgo., 1966-81, dir. life planning inst., 1979-80; pres. Gallinot & Assocs., Chgo., St. Louis and Bethalto, Ill., 1980—; mem. task force Office Sr. Citizens and Handicapped, City of Chgo., 1971-79; mem. criteria and guidelines com. Internat. Assn. for Continuing Edn. and Tng., 1983-86, survey and research com., 1984-88; mem. nat. adv. council bus. edn. div. Am. Vocat. Assn., 1980-84, sec., 1982-84. Developer leisure time adult edn. time series for elderly Uptown model cities area dept. human resources City of Chgo., 1970; host show Sta. WGCI-FM, Chgo., 1975-81; editor: Certified Professional Secretaries Review, 1983; contbr. articles to profl. jours. Chmn. Commn. Status of Women in State of Ill., 1963-68; del. White House Conf. on Equal Pay, 1963, White House Conf. on Civil Rights, 1965, City of Chgo. White House Conf. on Info. and Library, 1976, State of Ill. White House Conf. Info. Services and Library Services, 1977; life mem. Mus. Lithuanian Culture, Chgo., 1973—; pub. mem. Fgn. Service Selection Bd. U.S. Dept. State, 1984; bd. dirs. Luths. for Chgo., 1978-83, also founding member; member adv. edn. com. Chgo. Commn. Human Relations, 1968-75, Task Force Office Sr. Citizens and Handicapped City of Chgo., 1975-79. Recipient Leadership in Civic, Cultural and Econ. Life of the City award YWCA, Chgo., 1972, Achievement in Field Edn. award Operation P.U.S.H., Chgo., 1975. Mem. Profl. Secs. Internat. (past pres., ednl. cons. 1980-84), Edn. Network Older Adults (v.p., sec. 1979-86), Nat. Assn. Parliamentarians (Ill. and Chgo. chpts.), Literacy Coun. Chgo. (bd. dirs. 1979-86), Zonta of Alton (treas. Chgo. club 1965-66). Lutheran. Home and Office: Gallinot & Assocs 210 James St Bethalto IL 62010-1318

GALLO, GLORIA JEAN, child psychologist; b. Kenosha, Wis., Apr. 24, 1959; d. Felix and Florence Helen (Barth) G.; m. Reed Alan Watson, July 3, 1983; 1 child, Joseph Tyler. BA in Psychology with honors, Northwestern U., 1981; MA, DePaul U., 1984, PhD, 1987. Lic. psychologist, Ill. Staff therapist DePaul U., Chgo., 1985-86; staff psychologist Orchard Mental Health Ctr., Chgo., 1988—; pvt. practice Northfield, Ill., 1990—; cons. Ptnrs. in Transition, Northfield, 1990—. Mem. Am. Psychol. Assn., Assn. Play Therapy. Office: 778 Frontage Rd Ste 123 Northfield IL 60093

GALLO, JOYCE ANNE, social services administrator; b. Buffalo, Aug. 28, 1928; d. Wesley Floyd and Florence Mae (Plugh) Bigelow; m. John Kreitner, Dec. 31, 1946 (div. 1966); children: David, James, Pamela, Deborah; m. Francis Jerome Gallo, Feb. 15, 1985. Student, SUNY, Buffalo, 1946, 64, 67, Edison Community Coll., 1974-77, Parsons Sch. Design, 1985. Teller dept. loans Marine Midland Bank, Buffalo, 1964-73; supr. dept. loans 1st Nat. Bank, Naples, Fla., 1973-74; supr. loans, credit, new accounts Barnett Bank, Naples, 1974-79; with McFadden-Sprowls Inc., Naples, 1979-81; bookkeeper, receptionist C.A. Murphy Law Offices, Naples, 1981-83; adminstrv. asst. 1st Regency Internat. Devel., Naples, 1983-85; dir. sales Vanderbilt Inn on the Gulf, Naples, 1985-86; coordinator vols. LUVS for Youth Haven, Naples, 1986—, also bd. dirs. Co-chmn. United Fund Dr., Naples, 1980; sec., rep. Erie County Bd. LWV, Buffalo, 1964; del. Fla. Women's Conf., Orlando, 1977. Mem. Am. Bus. Women's Assn. (past pres. Naples br., del. nat. conv., named Woman Yr. 1979), Nat. Assn. Female Execs. Republican. Roman Catholic. Club: Pilot. Home: 2201 Lakeway Blvd #16 Austin TX 78734

GALLO, LOUISE ANN, retail company executive; b. White Plains, N.Y., Feb. 6, 1934; d. James J. and Theresa R. (Volpe) Grippo; m. Angelo R. Gallo, Oct. 18, 1953; 1 child, Julie. Gen. mgr. A.M. Burns, Inc., Scarsdale, N.Y., 1964-84, pres., 1984—. Mem. Eastchester C. of C. (pres. 1987-89). Republican. Roman Catholic. Office: AM Burns Inc 747 White Plains Rd Scarsdale NY 10583

GALLO, MARY ELLEN, wholesale beverage distribution company executive; b. Allentown, Pa., May 2, 1957; d. Frank and Elizabeth Eugenia (Clark) Banko; m. Vincent James Gallo, Jr., Aug. 28, 1982; children: Anthony James, Megan Elizabeth Lee. BS, Purdue U., 1979, BA, 1980. Sec. Banko Beverage Co., Allentown, 1980-82, pres., 1982—. Bd. dirs. Bethlehem Musikfest Assn., Pa., 1983—, mktg. co-chmn., 1985-88, chmn. food vendor com., 1986-88; bd. dirs. Cities in Schs., Lehigh Valley, 1985—, treas., 1987-88. Named Outstanding Young Citizen, Bethlehem Jaycees, 1987. Mem. Bethlehem Area C. of C. (bd. dirs. 1985-89), Nat. Beer Wholesalers Assn., Malt Beverage Distbrs. Assn., Pa. Beer Wholesalers Assn. Democrat. Roman Catholic. Avocations: eucharistic ministry, music, dancing, needlework, walking. Home: 2201 Meadow Ln Dr Easton PA 18042 Office: Banko Beverage Co 2124 Hanover Ave Allentown PA 18103

GALLO, TERESA L., advertising agency executive. Former sr. v.p. and creative dir. DFS Dorland N.Y. (now Saatchi & Saatchi Advt.), N.Y.C., now exec. v.p. Office: Saatchi & Saatchi Advt 375 Hudson St New York NY 10014-3620*

GALLOWAY, ALENE MARSHA, marketing professional, data processing programmer; b. Bronx, Mar. 6, 1949; d. Steven Saul and Nettie (Jaffe) Crayne; m. Duane M. Galloway, Sept. 2, 1990. Student, SUNY, Plattsburgh, 1967. Keypunch operator Kobe Mfg., Huntington Park, Calif., 1968-72, Zales HQ., Dallas, 1973; coding supr. M.A.R.C., Dallas, 1973-74; programmer trainee Moore Computing, N.Y.C., 1974; programmer M.G. Data, Inc., N.Y.C., 1974-75, Data Probe, Inc., N.Y.C., 1976-78; data processing mgr. Teaman/Lehman Assoc., Inc., Norwalk, Conn., 1978-82; pres. Bolding Tab Svc., Inc., Norwalk, 1982—. Republican.

GALLOWAY, LILLIAN CARROLL, modeling agency executive, consultant; b. Hazard, Ky., Sept. 23, 1934; d. William Zion and Clemma (Lewis) Carroll; m. Thomas Roddy Galloway, Dec. 21, 1957; children: David Junkin, Scott Thomas, Donald Lewis. Student, Cumberland Coll., 1955, Ea. U., Richmond, Ky., 1956, U. Cin., 1958, John Robert Powers Sch., Cin., 1958. Tchr. Vandalia (Ohio) Elem. Sch., 1954-56, Kenwood Elem. Sch., Louisville, 1956-57, Cin. Pub. Schs., 1957-64; founder, pres. Fairfax Model Agy., Washington, 1964-67, Cin. Model Agy. Internat., 1967—, Lillian Galloway Modeling Acad., Cin., 1971—, Children Model Agy. Internat., Cin., 1985—; cons., co-owner John Robert Powers Modeling Sch., Cin., 1957-64; pres. Student Model Bds., Cin., 1984—; dir. Career Day, Cin., 1967—. Mem. Cin. Better Bus. Bur., 1967—; trustee Knox Presbyn. Ch., Cin. Named Cin.'s Outstanding Bus. Woman, Sta. WCPO-TV, 1985, Outstanding Alumni, Cumberland Coll., 1988. Mem. Modeling Assn. Am. (chmn. convs. 1975-77), Am. Modeling Assn. Internat. (pres. 1976-77), Cin. Advertisers Club (membership and program coms., Outstanding Bus. Women award 1985), Exec. Women Internat. (program com., chmn. bd. dirs. 1986, Woman of Achievement award 1986), Cin. C. of C., Cumberland Coll. Alumni Assn. (pres. 1982), English Speaking Union, Order Ky. Cols., DAR, Cin. Woman's Club, Town Club (bd. dirs. 1988—), Order Eastern Star (organist 1953—). Republican. Home: 6027 Stirrup Rd Cincinnati OH 45244 Office: 6047 Montgomery Rd Cincinnati OH 45213

GALLOWAY, LOIS, education and personal development counselor; b. Orangeburg, S.C., Feb. 28, 1941; d. Fairy Dykes and Bernice (Glover) Brown; children: Donna Patton, Darryl W., Gary W. Stephens; m. Carl Wesley I Galloway, Apr. 10, 1982; 1 child, Carl Wesley II. AA, Mira Costa Coll., 1973; BA in Psychology, U. San Diego, 1975, MA in Counseling, 1976. Counselor Mira Costa Coll., Oceanside, Calif., 1975-80; owner, figure cons. Venus De Milo, Livermore and San Pablo, Calif., 1980-83; pvt. counselor employment, cons. sales San Francisco, 1983; coordinator, counselor Palomar Coll., San Marcos, Calif., 1983—, lectr. single parenting program, 1983; lectr. single parenting Oceanside, 1975-78. Mem. NAACP, Negro Bus. and Profl. Women, Am. Women in Jr. Community Coll. Democrat. Baptist. Lodge: Order Eastern Star (Marshall of West).

GALLOWAY, MARLA LYNN, commercial airline pilot; b. Lakeland, Fla., July 18, 1961; d. Harold Clayton and Jewel (Boyer) G. B in Aero. Sci. (magna cum laude), Embry-Riddle Aero. U., 1983, M in Aerospace Sci. summa cum laude, 1990. Licensed airline transport pilot, flight instr. Flight instr. Embry-Ridle Aero. U., Daytona Beach, Fla., 1983-84; flight instr., charter pilot Butler Aviation, Savannah, Ga., 1984; pilot Atlantic S.E. Airlines, Inc., Atlanta, 1984-85; chief pilot Jet Ctr., Inc., Cin., 1985-89; pilot Airborne Express, Inc., Wilmington, Ohio, 1989—; adj. faculty mem. Embry-Riddle Aero. U. 1990—. Nominated participant in regulatory rev. FAA, Washington, 1989. Mem. Aero Sci. Indsl. Adv. Coun. (Embry-Riddle Aero U.), Internat. Soc. Women Airlines Pilots, Aircraft Owners & Pilots Assn. Republican. Baptist. Home: 24 Eagle View Ln Fort Thomas KY 41075

GALLUP, JANET LOUISE, business official; b. Rochester, N.Y., Aug. 11, 1951; d. John Joseph and Mildred Monica (O'Keefe) VerHulst; m. Robert Hicks Gallup, June 26, 1982 (div. Nov. 1985); 1 son, Jason Hicks. B.A., Hofstra U., 1973; M.A. (grad. asst.), Calif. State U.-Long Beach., 1979. Asst. trader E.F. Hutton, N.Y.C., 1973-75, Los Angeles, 1975, instr. Calif. State U.-Long Beach, 1978-79; fin. analyst Rockwell Internat., Seal Beach, Calif., 1979-85, coordinator mgmt. and exec. devel. and succession planning, 1985—. Vol. Cedar House Ctr.-Child Abuse, Long Beach, 1976. Democrat. Roman Catholic. Office: Rockwell Internat 2600 Westminster Blvd Seal Beach CA 90740

GALLUPS, VIVIAN LYLAY BESS, federal agency administrator; b. Vicksburg, Miss., Jan. 14, 1954; d. Vann Foster and Lylay Vivian (Stanley) Bess; m. Ordice Alton Gallups, Jr., July 12, 1975. BA, Birmingham So. Coll., 1975, MA in Mgmt., 1985; MA in Edn., U. Ala., Birmingham, 1975. Counselor Columbia (S.C.) Coll., 1975-76; case mgr. S.C. Dept. Social Services, Lexington, 1976; benefit authorizer, payment determination specialist then recovery reviewer Social Security Adminstrn., Birmingham, 1977-85; contract adminstr. U.S. Dept. Def., Birmingham, 1985—. Hospice vol. Bapt. Med. Ctr.-Montclair, Birmingham, 1982; trustee, treas. Resurrection House, Birmingham, 1984-85; vol. counselor Cathedral Ch. of Advent, Birmingham, 1987. Mem. Nat. Contract Mgmt. Assn. (chpt. sec. 1987, chpt. pres. 1990—). Episcopalian. Home: 566 12th Ct PO Box 126 Pleasant Grove AL 35127-0126 Office: US Dept Def Def Logistics Agy 2121 8th Ave N Suite 104 Birmingham AL 35203

GALOTTI, DONNA, publishing executive; b. Mountainside, N.J., Feb. 8, 1955; d. Jack and Analid Kalajian; m. Ron Galotti, Oct. 14, 1981. BS, Penn State U., 1975. Internat. credit analyst Irving Trust Co., N.Y.C., 1976-77; ad sales rep. BMT Pub., N.Y.C., 1977-79; ad sales rep. Woman's Day Mag., N.Y.C., 1979-81, cosmetics mgr., 1981-83, ea. mgr., 1984-87; v.p., ad dir. Ladies' Home Jour., N.Y.C., 1987-89, v.p., pub., 1989—. Home: 100 Park Ave New York NY 10017 Office: Ladies' Home Journal 100 Park Ave New York NY 10017

GALSTON, NANCY LEE, management; b. Salida, Colo., May 4, 1954; d. Leo Lyman and Mary Ann (Parrott) Locke; 1 child, Mamie Camile. AS, Colo. Mtn. Coll., Timberline Campus, Buena Vista, 1986; student, Nat. Inst. Nutritional Edn., Greenwood Village, Colo., 1988. Cert. Nutritionist, Colo. Booth chairperson High County Folklife Festival, Buena Vista, Colo., 1988-89, pres., 1989—. Bd. dirs. High County Folklife Festival, Buena Vista, 1988-90. Named Student of Yr., Nat. Inst. Nutritional Edn. 1986. Mem. Buena Vista C. of C. (bd. dirs., Citizen of Yr. 1987). Office: The Pantry PO Box 863 Buena Vista CO 81211

GAMBALE, AMY ROSE, marketing consultant, educator; b. Bklyn., Sept. 3, 1942; d. Salvatore Domenick and Rose (Juliano) G. BS in Mktg., Fashion Inst. Tech., N.Y.C., 1979. Media asst. Benton & Bowles, N.Y.C., 1967-69; rsch. analyst Ted Bates Co., N.Y.C., 1970-72; broadcast coord. Norman, Craig & Kummel, N.Y.C., 1972-74; asst. prodn. mgr. Hoechst Fibers, N.Y.C., 1974-77; v.p., mgmt. supr. Dentsu Corp. Am., N.Y.C., 1977-89; pres. Image Dynamics, N.Y.C., 1990—; adj. prof. Fashion Inst. Tech., 1989—. Recipient Disting. Alumni award Fashion Inst. Tech., 1989. Mem. The Fashion Group, Am. Found. Image Cons., Japan Soc., Underfashions Club, Am. Women Entrepreneurs. Office: Image Dynamics 310 E 44th St Ste 1224 New York NY 10017

GAMBARDELLA, ROSEMARY, federal judge. BA, JD, Rutgers U. Admitted to bar, 1980. Judge U.S. Bankruptcy Ct., Dist. N.J. Office: US Dist Ct 15 N 7th St Camden NJ 08101*

GAMBEE, ELEANOR BROWN, writer, lecturer, civic worker; b. N.Y.C., Apr. 10, 1904; d. Robert Rankins and Elizabeth (Turner) Brown; m. A. Sumner Gambee, June 1, 1928; children: Sumner Brown, Craig, Eleanor Fay, Robert Rankin. AB, Vassar Coll., 1925; postgrad., Columbia U., 1926. Free-lance writer, lectr. on herbs, horticulture, plants in industry various orgns., 1961—; cons. sect. herbs Nat. Geographic mag., 1983, Reader's Digest Guide to Gardening, 1978; researcher, chmn. Chemurgic Garden. Contbr. numerous articles to hort. publs.; editorial bd. Vassar Alumnae Mag., 1954-56. Trustee Dwight Sch., Englewood, N.J., 1957-63; publicity chair Maternal Health Ctr. Bergen County, Englewood, 1934-38; v.p., mem. bd. Planned Parenthood Assn. Bergen County, 1938-46; publicity chair No. Valley chpt. ARC, 1939-43; 1st v.p. Social Svc. Fedn., Englewood, 1948-52; Englewood Hosp. Devel. Com., 1965-75; publs. com. Hort. Soc. N.Y., 1972-75. Recipient Garden Club Am. Hort. award, 1962, Merit award, 1979; Disting. Svc. award N.Y. Bot. Garden, 1980. Mem. Herb Soc. Am. (past pres.), Corp. N.Y. Bot. Garden, Garden Club Englewood (hon.). Home: 133 H East Palisade Ave Englewood NJ 07631

GAMBILL, BETHANY LUELLA, computer programmer; b. Painesville, Ohio, Oct. 12, 1953; d. Garfield and Shirley Mae (Jones) Johns; m. Stephen Carl Gambill, Feb. 21, 1977; 1 child, Sarah Elizabeth. A.S. in Computer Programming, Inst. Computer Mgmt., Cleve., 1973; student Cuyahoga Community Coll., 1974, U. Akron, 1980, Kent State U., 1985—, Inst. of Children's Lit., 1989. Bookkeeper, asst. to art dir. Revere Chem. Corp./ Monroe Co., Solon, Ohio, 1973-74; bookkeeper Revere Chem., Solon, 1974-75; with Alltel Corp., Twinsburg, Ohio, 1975—, transmission coord., 1977-78, toll control supr., 1978-80, toll coord., 1980-85, computer programmer, 1985—. Author: (poems) The Quiet House, 1989; 1990 Dependent Care Directory, 1990. Vol. ARC. Mem. Nat. Assn. Female Execs., Nat. Fedn. Bus. and Profl. Women (2d v.p. Ohio chpt. 1982-84, dist. legis. rep. 1984, 1st v.p. 1984-86, pres. 1990—, Young Careerist award 1983), Nat. Assn. Computer Profls. Lutheran. Avocations: travel, camping, reading. Home: 95 N River Rd Munroe Falls OH 44262 Office: Alltel Corp 2000 Highland Rd Twinsburg OH 44087

GAMBINO, LORRY, systems administrator; b. Trenton, N.J., May 22, 1942; d. Jacob L. and Agatha A. (Menrath) Krebs; m. Thomas D. Gambino, Aug. 24, 1963; children: Marc David, Michael Thomas, Kimberly Sue. BA, Fordham U., 1985. Personal sec. Morton Lane Esquire, N.Y.C., 1968-69; data entry supr. Hospac Corp., N.Y.C., 1972-74; v.p. Sunrise Artistries Inc., N.Y.C., 1972—; data processing mgr. DI-COM Corp., N.Y.C., 1974-76; v.p. Umano Found., Inc., N.Y.C., 1976—; systems adminstr. Coach Leatherware Co. div. Sara Lee Corp., N.Y.C., 1977—; art dir. Sunrise Artistries Inc., N.Y.C., 1972—. Mem. Planetary Soc., Freedom House, Nat. Peace Inst. Found. Democrat. Home: 345 W 30th St 6A New York NY 10001 Office: Coach Leatherware Co 516 W 34th St New York NY 10001

GAMBLE, KAMY RAYBURN, transportation executive;b. Athens, Tenn., Dec. 31, 1960; d. Charles Edward and Nadine (Clendenen) Rayburn; m. Timothy Blair Gamble, Sept. 10, 1988. AAS, Cleve. State Community Coll., 1982; BS, Tenn. Wesleyan Coll., 1984. Y.c.c. U.S. Forest Service, Etowah, Tenn., 1978; distbn. clk. Mayfield Dairy Farms, Inc., Athens, Tenn., 1982-88; fleet and transp. Mayfield Diary Farms, Inc., Athens, Tenn., 1988--. Mem. Nat. Trust for Hist. Preservation, Washington, 1989, Scottish Tartans Soc., Comrie, Perthshire, Scotland, 1987, Etowah Festival Chorus. Mem. Office Edn. Assn., Presbyterian Women, Tenn. Scenic River Assn., Chota Canoe Club. Republican. Home: 1304 Pennsylvania Ave Etowah TN 37331 Office: Mayfield Dairy Farms Inc 806 E Madison Ave Athens TN 37303

GAMBOA, J. C., air conditioning company executive; b. Bklyn., June 7, 1951; d. Joseph Manuel and Gladys (Taylor) G.; m. Gary M. Montgomery, Aug. 19, 1972; children: Jamil I., Jalena I., Malachi J. BS, Syracuse U., Utica, N.Y., 1972. Rsch. asst. U. Pitts., 1972-73; market analyst Phila. Urban Coalition, 1975-78, mktg. mgr., 1978-80; dir. sales JWM Corp., Phila., 1980-82; sales rep. Gamboa Industries, Camden, N.J., 1982-84; v.p., gen. mgr. Penn Bus., York, Pa., 1984-87, pres., 1987-89; v.p. svc. for air conditioning systems Celsius Transit Communications, York, Pa., 1989—. Author emergency health care survey, 1976. Edn. chair Black Women's Network of YWCA, York, 1987-89; team capt. York Hosp., 1988; mem. long-range com. York City Sch. Dist., 1988, allocations com. United Way of York County, 1987. Recipient Minority Achievement award SBA, Phila., 1977; named Outstanding Young Woman NAACP, York, 1980, 81, recipient Freedom award, 1988. Mem. Minority Bus. Assn. (treas. 1988—), York Area C. of C. (bd. dirs. 1987, pres. small bus. sect. 1987), Mfrs. Assn. South Cen. Pa., Crispus Attucks Assn. (Minority Achievement award 1988), Am. Mgmt. Assn., Cen. Pa. Internat. Bus. Assn. Republican. African Methodist Episcopal. Home: 710 Maryland Ave York PA 17404

GAMBRELL, LUCK FLANDERS, corporate executive; b. Augusta, Ga., Jan. 17, 1930; d. William Henry and Mattie Moring (Mitchell) Flanders; m. David Henry Gambrell, Oct. 16, 1953; children: Luck G. Davidson, David Henry, Alice Kathleen, Mary G. Rolinson. BA, Duke U., 1950; diplome d'etudes françaises, L'Institut de Touraine, Tours, France, 1951. Chmn. bd. LFG Co., 1960—. Mem. State Bd. Pub. Safety, 1981—; bd. dirs. Atlanta Symphony Orch., 1982-85; mem. Chpt. Nat. Cathedral, Washington, 1981-85; mem. World Service Council YWCA, 1965—, council Presbytery Greater Atlanta, 1988; elder Presbyterian Ch.; trustee Student Aid Found., Atlanta, 1975—; mem. Bd. Councilors The Carter Ctr., Emory U. Mem. Atlanta Jr. League, Alpha Delta Pi.

GAMBRELL, SARAH BELK, retail executive; b. Charlotte, N.C., Apr. 12, 1918; d. William Henry and Mary (Irwin) Belk; B.A., Sweet Briar Coll., 1939; D. Humanities, Erskine Coll., 1970, U. N.C.-Asheville, 1986; m. Charles Glenn Gambrell (dec.); 1 child, Sarah Belk. Pres., v.p., dir. Belk Stores, various locations, 1947—. Trustee Princeton (N.J.) Theol. Sem., Johnson C. Smith U., Charlotte, N.C., Warren Wilson Coll., Swannanoa, N.C.; trustee nat. bd. YWCA; bd. dirs. Parkinson's Disease Found.; bd. dirs. Opera Carolina, Charlotte, Planned Parenthood, Charlotte, YWCA, Charlotte; hon. trustee Cancer Research Inst., N.Y.C.; hon. bd. dirs. YWCA, N.Y.C. Mem. Fashion Group, Inc., Jr. League N.Y.C., Nat. Soc. Colonial Dames, DAR. Home: 300 Cherokee Rd Charlotte NC 28207 Office: 6100 Fairview Rd Ste 640 Charlotte NC 28210

GAMMELL, GLORIA RUFFNER, sales executive; b. St. Louis, June 19, 1948; d. Robert Nelson and Antonia Ruffner; m. Doyle M. Gammell, Dec. 11, 1973. AA in Art, Harbor Coll., Harbor City, Calif., 1969; BA in Sociology, Calif. State U., Long Beach, 1971. Cert. fin. planner. Bus. analyst Dun & Bradstreet Inc., Los Angeles, 1971-81; rep. sales Van Nuys, Calif., 1981-89; v.p., sec. bd. dirs. Gammell Industries, Paramount, Calif., 1986—. Mem. Anne Banning Assistance League, Hollywood, Calif., 1981-82; counselor YWCA, San Pedro, Calif., 1983-84; fundraiser YMCA, San Pedro, 1984-85; mem. womens adv. com. Calif. State Assembly, 1984-89. Recipient Best in the West Presdl. Citation, 1981-86, 89. Home: 991 Channel St San Pedro CA 90731

GAMMON, GLENNA JEAN, banker; b. Upper Darby, Pa., May 29, 1951; d. Howard Jean and Glenna Jean (Hoppes) Smith; m. Garland Wayne Gammon, June 3, 1973 (div. 1977). BS, Va. Commonwealth U., 1973; student, Rockhurst Coll., 1982-83. Buyer Thalhimer's Dept. Store, Richmond, Va., 1973-76; sales rep. Hallmark Card, Tyler and Dallas, Tex., 1976-79; mktg. mgr. Hallmark Card, Kansas City, Mo., 1979-84; sales trainer Hallmark Card, Columbus, Ohio, 1984-85; officer Crestar Bank, Richmond, 1985-90, v.p. product mgmt., 1986—. Choir leader Grove Ave Bapt. Ch., Richmond, 1986—, divorce ministry group leader, 1989, 90. Office: Crestar Bank 919 E Main St Richmond VA 23219

GAMSON, ZELDA FINKELSTEIN, sociologist, researcher; b. Phila., Mar. 12, 1936; d. Samuel and Reba (Ladin) Finkelstein; m. William Anthony Gamson, July 1, 1956; children: Jennifer, Joshua. BA, U. Mich., 1958, MA, 1959; PhD, Harvard U., 1965. Study dir. Survey Rsch. Ctr. U. Mich., Ann Arbor, 1965-72, asst. prof., 1970-74, assoc. prof., 1974-78, prof., 1978-84; dir. New England Resource Ctr. U. Mass., Boston, 1988—; mem. vis. com. Harvard U., Cambridge, Mass., 1965-70; mem. study group U.S. Dept. Edn., Washington, 1984-85; cons. in field. Author: Liberating Education, 1984, Higher Education & the Real World, 1989, (with others) Academic Values & Mass Education, 1970, 75; author: (book chpts.) Black Students on White Campuses, 1978. Vice chair bd. Antioch U., Yellow Springs, Ohio, 1990—; bd. dirs. Nathan Mayhew Seminars, Martha's Vineyard, Mass., 1990—. NSF grantee, 1966, Lilly Endowment grantee, 1976, NIMH grantee, 1975, Fund for Improvement Postsecondary Edn. grantee, 1979, Pew Charitable Trusts grantee, 1989, Mellon Found. grantee, 1989. Mem. Am. Sociol. Assn. (chmn. edn. sect.), Am. Assn. for Higher Edn., Assn. for the Study of Higher Edn., Sociologists for Women in Soc., Nat. Ctr. for Employee Ownership, Collaborative Undergrad. Edn. Network. Democrat. Jewish. Office: U Mass Boston Grad Coll Edn Boston MA 02125

GANDEK, JEAN DAVIS, educator; b. Nashua, N.H., June 21, 1931; d. Townsend King and Helen Georgette (Butler) Davis; m. Andrew Gandek, Nov. 20, 1954 (dec. Aug. 1988); children: Barbara Lynne, Kathryn Lynne. BA, Mt. Holyoke Coll., 1952; MA, Columbia U., 1954. Rsch. technician Rockefeller Inst. for Med. Rsch., N.Y.C., 1952-53, 54-56, Alfred I. du Pont Inst., Wilmington, Del., 1956-57; substitute tchr. Seaford (Del.) Sch. Dist., 1977—. Leader, cons., organizer Girl Scouts U.S.A., Seaford, 1970-8l; v.p. Friends Seaford Dist. Libr., 1985-87; mem. bd. commrs. Seaford Dist. Libr., 1987—, v.p., 1988-89. Recipient Friend of Seaford Edn., Seaford Bd. Edn., 1987. Mem. AAUW (edn. rep. Del. div. 1984-86, Ednl. Found. gift in her honor Del. div. 1986, Seaford 1989), Phi Beta Kappa. Unitarian. Home: 745 Woodlawn Ave Seaford DE 19973

GANDY, JOYCE ANN, business administrator, former dance educator; b. Picher, Okla., Feb. 5, 1937; d. Sheppard Levi and Naydeen Maxine (Phillips) G.; m. Bernard Diamond, Aug. 2, 1985. A.A., Parsons Jr. Coll., 1957; dance student of Thalia Mara, Gertrude Edwards Jory, Yurik Lazowsky, Robert Joffrey, Luigi, Frank Wagner. Cert. Cecchetti Council Am. Owner, tchr. Joyce's Dance Studio, Parsons, Kans., 1953-66; gen. sec. Nat. Acad. Ballet and Theatre Arts, N.Y.C., 1966-72; sec., adminstrv. asst., conv. mgr. Am. Inst. Steel Constrn., N.Y.C., 1973-79, office mgr., Chgo., 1979-80, personnel adminstr., Chgo., 1980-81; bus. adminstr. Bernard Diamond, D.D.S., P.A., Edison, N.J., 1983—. Recipient various dance grants, 1949-66. Mem. NAFE, Internat. Platform Assn. Mem. Ch. of Christ. Avocations: drawing, music, dance, gardening. Office: Bernard Diamond DDS PA 42 Parsonage Rd Edison NJ 08837

GANDY, SUE ANN, costume designer; b. Kansas City, Mo., Apr. 26, 1951; d. Jack Silvetis and Jane Frances (DeVault) G. Student, U. Mo., Kansas City, 1972-75. Asst. costume designer (Broadway) Singin in the Rain, 1984, Design for Living, 1985, The Search for Signs of the Universe, 1987, Anything Goes, N.Y., London, 1987-89, (motion pictures) The Mosquito Coast, 1985, Biloxi Blues, 1987, January Man, 1988, Dirty Rotten Scoundrels, 1988, Q&A, 1989. Mem. United Scenic Artist.

GANESAN, ANN KATHARINE, molecular biologist; b. Denver, July 25, 1933; d. Philip Lewis and Katharine (Montgomery) Cook; m. A.T. Ganesan, Aug. 3, 1963. BA, Wilson Coll., 1954; MS, U. Wis., 1959; PhD, Stanford U., 1961. Rsch. assoc. Stanford (Calif.) U., 1972-75, sr. rsch. assoc., 1975—; mem. radiation study sect. NIH, Bethesda, Md., 1986-90. Contbr. articles to profl. jours. Am. Med. Soc., NIH grantee, 1980-83. Mem. Genetics Soc. Am., Am. Soc. Microbiology. Office: Stanford U Biology Dept Stanford CA 94305-5020

GANESH, CHERIE MARGARET, real estate project manager; b. Memphis, Jan. 17, 1950; d. Terrence Billy and Mary Margaret (Hanna) Miller; m. Robert W. Proctor, Aug. 5, 1971 (div. May 1981); m. Nagraj Ganesh, June 25, 1983. Student, Memphis State U., 1967-71; MusB, U. Ariz., 1972; grad., Inst. Fin. Edn., Chgo., 1980; postgrad., U. San Diego, 1987, Rollins Coll., 1990—. Constrn. disbursement processor Keystone Savs., Westminster, Calif., 1977-79, Home Fed. Savs., Santa Ana, Calif., 1979-80; project coordinator Home Capital Devel. Group, San Diego, 1980-86; broker, v.p. Sumukham Corp. (owned by Nagraj & Cherie), San Diego, 1984—; mgr. asset Homevest Real Estate Securities, San Diego, 1986-87; project mgr. Home Capital Devel. Group, San Diego, 1987—; bd. dirs. Community Assns. Inst., San Diego, 1983-88, pres. 1987; edn. com. Homebuilders Council BIA, San Diego, 1986. Mem. NAFE, Home Builders Assn. of Mid-Fla. Republican. Office: Home Capital Devel Group 1060 Maitland Ctr Commons #301 Maitland FL 32751

GANG, CAROLYN SUE, academic counselor; b. Enid, Okla., Nov. 15, 1952; d. Pern Lorn and Faye (Rouse) G.; m. Ed Noltensmeyer, June 23, 1990. BS, Okla. State U., 1974, MS, 1975. Membership coord. Nat. Univ. Teleconf. Network, Stillwater, Okla., 1984-85; personnel asst. Okla. State U., Stillwater, 1976-77, acad. counselor arts and scis. student svcs., 1977-79, sr. acad. counselor psychology dept., 1985-90. Recipient Outstanding Advisor award Okla. State U. Coll. Arts and Scis., 1987, 89. Mem. LWV, AAUW (pres. Stillwater 1989—), Am. Assn. for Counseling and Devel., Am. Coll. Personnel Assn., Okla. Assn. for Counseling and Devel., Okla. Coll. Personnel Assn. (newsletter editor 1978-79), Am. Bus. Women's Assn. (Woman of Yr. award Stillwater 1987), Bus. and Profl. Women (membership chmn. Okla. Fedn. 1989—, nat. young career women chmn. 1989—, Woman of Yr. award Stillwater 1986, Okla. Young Careerist 1978), Order Eastern Star, Phi Delta Kappa, Kappa Delta Pi, Beta Sigma Pi, Delta Zeta (Disting. Alumnae 1989). Democrat. Methodist. Home: 3704 W 15th Stillwater OK 74074

GANN, JEAN POPE, insurance agency executive, fine arts appraiser; b. Winfield, Ala., Dec. 5, 1917; d. Garvin and Clara (Couch) Pope; m. John Henry Gann, Apr. 6, 1935; children: John Garvin, W. Gerald, Jean Gann Nelson. Student, U. Howard Coll., 1949-52, U.Ala., 1964-68, Montevallo, Ala., 1983-84, Samford U., 1983-85. Lic. ins. agt.; cert. appraiser fine arts and antiques. Owner, mgr. Sylacauga (Ala.) Ins. Agy., 1952—; instr., trainer Sylacauga High Sch., 1960—; co-chmn. Citywide Sales Clinic, Sylacauga C. of C., 1972. Contbr. articles to profl. jours. Mem. Birmingham (Ala.) Mus. Art, 1979—; exec. bd. dirs. United Givers Fund, Sylacauga, 1978-81; charter mem. Sylacauga Mus. and Arts Ctr., 1982—; v.p. Sylacauga High Sch. PTA, 1961-62; chmn. edn. Am. Cancer Soc., South Talladega County, Ala., 1953-61; bd. dirs. Sylacauga Boys Club, 1989—; mem. Ala. Women's Polit. Caucus, 1978—, Nat. Dem. Com., Ala. Dem. Com., Ala. Citizens for ERA; tchr. adult Bible class 1st Bapt. Ch., 1945—, mem. long range planning com., 1950-58, 89—; chmn. com. that established Ave. of Flags in Sylacauga, 1972; pres. Bapt. Women's Orgn., 1964-65, 76-80; chmn. prayer breakfast Nat. Bus. Women's Week, 1979-85. Named Woman of Achievement, Sylacauga Bus. and Profl. Women's Club, 1976, Sylacauga Woman of Yr., Sylacauga Exchange Club, 1961; recipient cert. in Christian tng. Howard Coll., Samford U., 1983; cert. of recognition 1st Bapt. Ch., 1985. Mem. Soc. Fine Arts U. Ala., Ala. Ind. Ins. Agts. (legis. com. 1978-79, 84-85), Nat. Assn. Ind. Ins. Agts., Ala. Fedn. Bus. and Profl. Women's (dist. chmn. for young careerists 1972-73, legis. chmn. Sylacauga chpt. 1983—, pres. 1962, 62, 73), Sylacauga Bus. & Profl. Women's Club (legis. chmn. 1980-87, chmn. internat. com. 1987—), U.S.A. Young Careers (chmn. 1987-88, internat. chmn. 1988), Nat. Trust for Hist. Preservation, Sylacauga C. of C. (mem. com. 1952—), Sylacauga Antique Group, LWV, Nat. Mus. Women in the Arts (charter 1987—), Bus. and Profl. Women's Found., Alpha Lambda Delta. Club: Coosa Valley Country (charter mem.). Avocations: antique buff-collector, historical sites and buildings. Home: 300 W Bay St Sylacauga AL 35150 Office: Sylacauga Ins Agy PO Box 598 Sylacauga AL 35150

GANN, JO RITA, social services administrator; b. Talihina, Okla., June 2, 1940; d. Herbert and Juanita Rita (Fields) G. BS, Okla. Bapt. U., 1962; M Theatre Arts, Portland State U., 1970. Tchr. Oklahoma City Pub. Schs., 1962-64; teen dir., dir. health edn. YWCA, Oklahoma City, 1964-67; camp dir., teen dir. YWCA, Portland, Oreg., 1967-72; asst. dir., program coordinator YWCA, Flint, Mich., 1972-75; exec. dir. YWCA, Salem, Oreg., 1975—; chair N.W. regional staff YWCA, Portland, 1983; chief exec. officer bus. panel Oregonian's Pub. Co. Co-author: A New Look at Supervision, 1980. Del. UN Conf. for Non-Govtl. Orgns.; internat. study del. on world econ. interdependence to Ghana, Africa; speaker Global Concerns, Salem and Portland, 1981—; mem. pres.'s council Salem Summerfest, 1985, 86. Mem. Exec. Dirs. YWCA of U.S., Nat. Orgn. Female Execs. Democrat. Christian Scientist. Office: YWCA 768 State St Salem OR 97301

GANN, THERESA VERLYN, business educator; b. Pampa, Tex., June 16, 1943; d. Loyd and Cynthia Lorene (Hunter) Riggins; m. James Allen, Aug. 11, 1961; 1 child, Stephen Anthony. BS, U. Houston, 1979, MBA, 1980. Bookkeeper First Nat. Bank, Panhandle, Tex., 1963-64; bookkeeper Citizens State Bank, Pampa, 1967-69; loan sec. Bay Area Bank and Trust, Webster, Tex., 1971-73; confidential sec. Dart Industries, Pasadena, Tex., 1973-76; dept. chmn. San Jacinto Coll., Pasadena, 1980—; speaker San Jacinto Dist. Workshop, Pasadena, 1984, 85, Clear Creek Independent Sch. Dist. Workshop, League City, Tex., 1987. Author: Step-by-Step Approach to DisplayWrite 3, 1988, Step-by-Step Approach to DisplayWrite 4, 1988; contbr. articles to profl. jours. Mem. audit com. Clear Lake (Tex.) Bapt. Ch., 1985-89, fin. com., 1988-90; mem. Clear Lake PTA, 1976-88. Named Bus. Tchr. of Yr. Dist. IV, Tex. Bus. Educators, 1989. Office: San Jacinto Coll 8060 Spencer Hwy Pasadena TX 77505

GANNAWAY, JOANN PICKERING, social worker, family counselor, education specialist; b. Princeton, Ky., Apr. 10, 1930; d. William Goebel and Ethel Clifton (Gresham) Pickering; m. Richard Moore Gannaway, June 15, 1952; children: Dianne, Mary Lisa, Richard Moore Jr., Deborah Marel. BA, Vanderbilt U., 1952; MEd, Winthrop Coll., 1985; EdS, U. S.C., 1987. Tchr. Davidson County Schs., Nashville, 1952-53, Spartanburg County Schs., Spartanburg, S.C., 1970-72, Lancaster (S.C.) City Schs., 1974-83; social worker, family counselor, ednl. specialist Reound, Inc., rehab. ctr. for head injured, Lancaster, 1987—. Mem. Lancaster Mental Health Assn., 1980—, Lancaster Community Theater, 1983-85, Lancaster County Coun. Arts, 1985—; mem. found. bd. Will Lou Gray Opportunity Sch., Columbia, S.C., 1987—. Mem. Am. Assn. Marriage and Family Therapists (assoc.), Lancaster Garden Club. Democrat. Presbyterian. Home: ll37 Canterbury Dr Lancaster SC 29720 Office: Rebound Inc 822 Meeting St Lancaster SC 29720

GANNON, SISTER ANN IDA, philosophy educator emeritus, former college president; b. Chgo., 1915; d. George and Hanna (Murphy) G. A.B., Clarke Coll., 1941; A.M., Loyola U., Chgo., 1948, LL.D., 1970; Ph.D., St. Louis U., 1952; Litt.D., DePaul U., 1972; L.H.D., Lincoln Coll., 1965, Columbia Coll., 1969, Luther Coll., 1969, Marycrest Coll., 1972, Ursuline Coll., 1972, Spertus Coll. Judaica, 1974, Holy Cross Coll., 1974, Rosary Coll., 1975, St. Ambrose Coll., 1975, St. Leo Coll., 1976, Mt. St. Joseph Coll., 1976, Stritch Coll., 1976, Stonehill Coll., 1976, Elmhurst Coll., 1977, Manchester Coll., 1977, Marymount Coll., 1977, Governor's State U., 1979, Seattle U., 1981, St. Michael's Coll., 1984, Nazareth Coll., 1985, Holy Family Coll., 1986, Keller Grad. Sch. Mgmt., Our Lady of Holy Cross Coll., New Orleans, 1988. Mem. Sisters of Charity, B.V.M.; tchr. English St. Mary's High Sch., Chgo., 1941-47; residence, study abroad, 1951; chmn. philosophy dept. Mundelein Coll., 1951-57, pres., 1957-75, prof. philosophy, 1975-85, emeritus faculty, 1987—, archivist, 1986—. Contbr. articles philos. jours. Mem. adv. bd. Sec. Navy, 1975-80, Chgo. Police Bd., 1979—; bd. dirs. Am. Coun. on Edn., 1971-75, chmn., 1973-74; nat. bd. dirs. Girl Scouts U.S.A., 1966-74, nat. adv. bd., 1976-85; trustee St. Louis U., 1974-87, Ursuline Coll., 1978—, Cath. Theol. Union, 1983-89, DeVry Inc., 1987—, Duquesne U., 1989—; bd. dirs. Newberry Libr., 1976—, WTTW Pub. TV, 1976—, Parkside Human Svcs. Corp., 1983-89. Recipient Laetare medal, 1975, LaSallian award, 1975, Aquinas award, 1976, Chgo. Assn. Commerce and Industry award, 1976, Hesburgh award, 1982, Woman of Distinction award Nat. Conf. Women Student Leaders, 1985, Outstanding Svc. award Coun. Ind. Colls., 1989, Woman of History award for edn. AAUW, 1989. Mem. Am. Cath. Philos. Assn. (exec. coun. 1953-56), Assn. Am. Colls. (dir. 1965—, chmn. 1969-70), Religious Edn. Assn. Am. (pres. 1973, chmn. bd. 1975-78), N. Cen. Assn. (commn. on colls. and univs. 1971-78, chmn. exec. bd. 1975-77, dir.), Assn. Governing Bds. Colls. and Univs. (dir. 1979-88, hon. dir. 1989—). Address: 6363 Sheridan Rd Chicago IL 60660

GANNON, ANNE DURNEY, banker; b. Bethlehem, Pa., May 15, 1952; d. Joseph J. and Barbara J. (Graveline) Durney; 1 child, Christopher P. Gannon. BA in Polit. Sci. and History, Rosemont Coll., 1974; postgrad. in bus. adminstrn. Temple U., 1974-77, Stonier Grad. Sch. Banking, Rutgers U., 1977-80; m. Joseph H. Gannon, Oct. 11, 1980. Mut. fund adminstr. Provident Nat. Bank, Phila., 1974-76, mgr. fed. funds dept., 1976-89, head Eurodollar trader Nassau br., 1980-86, div. head, facilities mgmt., 1986-88, group mgr. electronic banking ops., 1989—. Mem. Rosemont Coll. Alumnae Assn. (dir. and treas. 1978-80), Overbrook Golf Club (Bryn Mawr, Pa., Cynwyd (Pa.) Club. Republican. Roman Catholic. Home: 4 Meredith Rd Green Hill Farms PA 19151 Office: Provident Nat Bank 120 S 17th St Philadelphia PA 19101

GANNON, CAROLYN, computer engineer; b. Long Beach, Calif., Mar. 10, 1945; d. Ray Adelbert and Mary (Shuler) Heimburger; m. Terry Lee Gannon, June 15, 1968. BA, U. Calif., Santa Barbara, 1968, MSEE, 1974; jr. coll. teaching credential, Chapman Coll., Calif., 1971. Programmer Gen. Electric TEMPO, Santa Barbara, 1967-69, 73-74, Computer & Software, Inc., Edwards AFB, Calif., 1969-73, Mission Rsch. Corp., Santa Barbara, 1973; dir. software tech. ops. Gen. Rsch. Corp., Santa Barbara, 1974-84; cons. Gannon Cons., Woodside, Calif., 1984—; tech. staff Sun Microsystems Fed., Milpitas, Calif., 1990—; instr. Antelope Valley Coll., Lancaster, Calif., 1971-73; conf. chmn. Mil. Computing Conf., Washington, 1989. Contbr. numerous papers to profl. jours. Mem. Assn. for Computing Machinery (chmn. chpt. 1980-82), IEEE, Ada-Joint Users Group (bd. dirs. 1990—, co-chmn. cost estimation working group 1989—). Office: Gannon Cons 3530 Partition Rd Woodside CA 94062 Office: Sun Microsystems Fed 1100 Cadillac Ct Milpitas CA 95033

GANNON, LOLA FERN, government official; b. Collinsville, Okla., Jan. 13, 1932; d. David Delbert and Lela Isabell (Phillips) Fisher; m. John Edward Gannon, Apr. 30, 1955; children: Rick, Marcia, Linda, Nancy. AA, Reedley (Calif.) Coll., 1951. Sec. Bank of Am., San Francisco, 1951-52; statis. clk. DOD, Presidio, Calif., 1952-55; fiscal acctg. clk. Dept. Interior, Bur. Indian Affairs, Portland, Oreg., 1955-58; head procurement support group Dept. Interior, Bonneville Power Adminstrn., Portland, 1967-76; procurement asst. Dept. Energy, Bonneville Power Adminstrn., Portland, 1976-77; procurement agt. Dept. Energy, Bonneville Power Adminstrn., 1977-78; warrented contracting officer Dept. Interior, Fish & Wildlife Svc., 1978—. U.S. del. People to People Internat., 1988, People's Republic of China. Recipient Spl. Achievement Awards, U.S. Fish & Wildlife Svc.,

Portland, 1984-88, Admistrv. Employee of the Yr., 1986. Fellow Nat. Contract Mgmt. Assn. (chpt. pres. 1982-83, chpt. dir. 1983-84); mem. NAFE, Windy Whirlers Sq. Dance (pres. 1981—). Democrat. Home: 6703 Park Way Gladstone OR 97027 Office: US Fish & Wildlife Svc 911 NE 11th Ave Portland OR 97232

GANNON, MARY CAROL, nutritional biochemist; b. Mpls., Oct. 25, 1944; d. Gerald Francis and Betty (Baumgardner) Thill; m. John Michael Gannon, Feb. 8, 1964 (div. 1968). BS, U. Minn., 1972, PhD, 1983. Technician Chemistry Lab, VA, Mpls., 1967-70, 70-73, Dept. Biochemistry, U. Minn., Mpls., 1968-70; chemist Endocrine Rsch., VA, Mpls., 1973-83; nutritional biochemist Metabolic rsch. VA, 1983—, dir. metabolic rsch. lab., 1989—; rsch. assoc. dept. medicine U. Minn., 1985-88; instr. dept. medicine —, 1988—, asst. prof. dept. food sci. and nutrition, 1988—; grad. faculty U. Minn., St. Paul, 1986—; sec.-treas. Metabolic Rsch., Inc., St. Paul, 1975—. Contbr. articles to profl. jours. Recipient Spl. Acievement award, 1977, Superior Performance award, 1983, others. Fellow Am. Coll. Nutrition; mem. Am. Diabetes Assn., Inst. Food Technologists, Am. Inst. Nutrition, European Assn. for Study of Diabetes, Am. Soc. Biol. Chemists, Iota Sigma Pi. Office: Metabolic Rsch Med Ctr Dept Vet Affairs 1 Veterans Dr Minneapolis MN 55417

GANS, ERNA IRENE, printing company executive; b. Bielsko, Poland; d. Adolf and Rosa (Pelzman) Reicher; came to U.S., 1948, naturalized, 1953; BA, Roosevelt U., 1971; MA, Loyola U., Chgo., 1974; m. Henry Gans, Apr. 16, 1947 (dec. Oct. 1987); children: Alan, Howard. Asst. prof. dept. sociology Loyola U., Chgo., 1976; pres. Internat. Label & Printing Co., Bensenville, Ill., 1972—. Chmn., Skokie (Ill.) Youth Commn., 1968-68; bd. govs. Israel Bond Orgn.; founder, chmn. Holocaust Meml. Found. Ill.; mem. U.S. Holocaust Meml. Council. Recipient Edward S. Sparling award Roosevelt U., 1987, 3d Ann. Humanitarian award Holocaust Meml. Found. Ill., 1988. Mem. Am. Sociol. Assn., Nat. Fedn. Ind. Bus., Am. Acad. Polit. and Social Sci. Republican. Jewish. Clubs: B'nai B'rith (pres. 1976—). Home: 2812 Woodland Dr Northbrook IL 60062 Office: 537 Edgewood Dr Wood Dale IL 60191

GANS, MARION LOIS, public relations executive; b. Paterson, NJ; d. Joseph George and Hattie (Alexander) Edelman; m. Irwin Gans; children: Edward M., Julie E., Robert F. BS cum laude, Syracuse U.; MA, Fairfield U., 1973. Tchr. Stamford (Conn.) High Sch.; dir. pub. relations BiCultural Day Sch., Stamford, 1972-78; owner Marion Gans Communications, Stamford, 1978-82; pres. Gans Pub. Relations, Inc., Stamford, 1982—; cons. Cahill Assocs., Westport, Conn., 1984—; mem. faculty U. Conn., 1984—. Contbr. articles to mags., newspapers. Press sec. Dem. mayoral candidate, Stamford, 1977; com. mem. Voluntary Action Council, Stamford, 1984; bd. dirs. Stamford Land Conservation Trust; v.p. Jr. Achievement Southwestern Conn., Stamford. Recipient 13 awards for pub. relations and writing. Mem. Southwestern Area Commerce and Industry Assn., Women in Mgmt. (bd. dirs. 1984—), Stamford Symphony Soc. Democrat. Jewish. Office: Gans Pub Rels 126 Woodside Green Ste 2C Stamford CT 06905

GANSE, JEAN MARIE, sales and marketing professional; b. Lancaster, Pa., Oct. 26, 1949; d. John Henry and Mary Jane (Rose) G. BA, Coll. of Mt. St. Joseph, 1971; postgrad., Loyola U., Md., 1989—. With hotel sales and mgmt. supervision, 1971-77; mgr. advt. and merchandising, mktg. svcs. supr., asst. Yorktowne A. Wickes Co., 1977-82; mktg. coord., product mgr. Dustbuster Vacuum, mktg. mgr., nat. accounts mgr., bus. devel. mgr. tool, household, svc. opers. Black & Decker, Lancaster, Pa., Hampstead, Md., Shelton, Conn., 1982—. Mem. coms. Cystic Fibrosis Found., Balt., 1989—. Mem. Assn. of Nat. Advertisers, Nat. Yellow Pages Com. Republican. Roman Catholic. Office: Black & Decker US Inc PO Box 564 Hampstead MD 21074

GANT, CYNTHIA ELEANOR, analytical chemist; b. Detroit, Oct. 23, 1948; d. Harold William and Mildred (Phillips) G. BS, Tex. Woman's U., 1970, MS, 1978. Cert. med. technologists, quality engr., computer technician. Med. technologist All Saints Hosp., Ft. Worth, 1971-74, Baylor Med. Ctr., Dallas, 1974-75; teaching asst. Tex. Woman's U., Denton, 1975-78; med. technologists Med. Plaza Hosp., Ft. Worth, 1976; asst. microbiologist Diagnostic div. Abbott Labs., Dallas, 1976-78; quality control technician Container div. Miller Brewing Co., Ft. Worth, 1978-89; analytical chemist Corp. Master Brewers div. Miller Brewing Co., Milw., 1989—. Recipient Outstanding Achievement in the Community award Sickle Cell Anemia Assn., 1980. Mem. Am. Soc. of Clin. Pathology, Am. Soc. for Quality Control, Am. Soc. of Microbiology, Soc. for Indsl. Microbiology, Order of Eastern Star. Presbyterian. Office: Miller Brewing Co 3939 W Highland Blvd Milwaukee WI 53208

GANTER, GLADYS, retired Latin teacher. Latin tchr. Hamilton, Ohio. Home: 598 Harrison Ave Hamilton OH 45013

GANTZ, SUZI GRAHN, special education educator; b. Chgo., May 17, 1954; d. Robert Donald and Barbara Edna (Ascher) Grahn; m. Louis Estes Gantz, July 11, 1976; children: Christopher, Joshua. BS in Edn., U. Ill., 1976. Tchr. hearing impaired A.G. Bell Sch., Chgo., 1976-80, 88—; sales asst. Bob Grahn & Assocs., Chgo., 1982-84; with sales dept. Isis/My Sisters Circus, Chgo., 1984-86; interpreter Glenbrook North High Sch., Northbrook, Ill., 1986-87; interpreter, aide Lake Forest (Ill.) Dist. 67, 1987-88. Mem. Northbrook Citizens for Drug and Alcohol Alliance, 1988—; cubmaster Boy Scouts Am., Northbrook, 1990—. Mem. Ill. Tchrs. of the Hearing Impaired, A.G. Bell Soc., Coun. on Exceptional Children. Home: 485 Laburnum Northbrook IL 60062 Office: AG Bell Sch 3730 N Oakley Chicago IL 60618

GANTZER, MARY LOU, research chemist; b. Mpls., Oct. 3, 1950; d. Richard John and Mary Jane (Capistrant) G. B Chemistry, U. Minn., 1972, MS, 1976; PhD in Chemistry, U. Va., 1980. Instr., postdoctoral fellow dept. chemistry U. Va., Charlottesville, 1980-81; rsch. scientist diagnostics div. Miles, Inc., Elkhart, Ind., 1981-84, sr. rsch. scientist, 1984-86, staff scientist, 1986-87, supr. R & D, 1987—; mem. Women in Mgmt. del. to People's Republic China, 1988. Contbr. articles to chemistry jours.; patentee in field. Fellow Am. Inst. Chemists; mem. Am. Chem. Soc., Am. Assn. Clin. Chemistry (chmn. Chgo. sect. 1988, Chmn.'s award 1988), N.Y. Acad. Scis., Vis. Nurses Assn. Michiana (bd. dirs. 1990—), Iota Sigma Pi. Roman Catholic. Home: 25723 Kiser Ct Elkhart IN 46514 Office: Miles Inc Diagonstics Div PO Box 70 (B1802) Elkhart IN 46515

GAPEN, DELORES KAYE, librarian, educator; b. Mitchell, S.D., July 1, 1943; d. Lester S. and Lena F. G. B.A., U. Wash., 1970, M.L.S., 1971. Gen. cataloger Coll. William and Mary, Williamsburg, Va., 1971-72; instr., asst. head Quick Editing Ohio State U., Columbus, 1972-74; head Ohio State U., 1974-77; asst. dir. tech. services Iowa State U., Ames, 1977-81; dean, prof. univ. libraries U. Ala., University, 1981-84; dean gen. library system U. Wis., Madison, 1984—; exec. com. Council U. Wis. Libraries, 1985-87; cons. Northeast Mo. State U., 1980, Assn. Research Libraries task force on biblog. control, 1981, Pa. State U., 1982, Conn. Coll., 1982; chmn. Coun. U. Wis. Librs., Madison, 1989-90; vice chmn. exec. com. of bd. trustees U. Wis. Online Computer Library Ctr., Madison, 1984-86, also mem. research libraries adv. com. (chair task force on Future of Research Library Coop. in Changing Techs. Environment, 1986-89, chmn. com. short cataloging records, 1983-84), 1989; cons. Bryn Mawr Coll. Online System Planning, 1983, Council Library Resources Edn. Task Force on Future of Library Sch. Edn., 1983, Tex. A&I U. reaffirmation team cons. for So. Assn. Colls. and Schs., 1984, Dickinson Coll. Library Autocat System, 1987; chair Assn. of Research Libraries Task Force for Govt. Info. in Electronic Form, 1986-87; mem. Assn. of Research Libraries Task Force on Scholarly Communication, 1983-87; nat. cons. scholar librarian, IBM, 1989-90. Contbr. articles to profl. pubs. Mem. AAUP, ALA, Southeastern Libr. Assn., Ala. Libr. Assn., Assn. Rsch. Librs. (chmn. task force govt. info. in electronic form 1986-87, bd. dirs. 1987-90), Bus. and Profl. Women's Assn., Beta Phi Mu, Alpha Lamba Delta. Democrat. Roman Catholic. Home: 702 Seneca Pl Madison WI 53711 Office: U Wis-Madison Meml Libr 728 State St Madison WI 53706

GARABEDIAN, SUSAN MARY, communications executive; b. Fresno, Calif., Oct. 31, 1957; d. Charles Edward and Eleanor (Mirigian) G.; m. Richard Lewis Ruffalo, Oct. 9, 1949; children: Jonathan Joseph, Jeffrey Charles Ruffalo. Postgrad., U. Southern Calif., 1978-82, U. Southern Calif., Veterans Adminstrn. Med. Ctr., Long Beach, Calif., 1982-83; MBA, George Wash. U., 1985. Assoc. dir. Ruffalo and Assocs., Clin. Pharmacology and Therapeutics, 1980-82; post-doctoral resident in ambulatory Care and Clin. Pharmacy Veterans Adminstrn. Med. Ctr., Long Beach, Calif., 1982-83; asst. dir., Clin. Pharmacy Services, George Wash. U. Med. Ctr., 1983-88; asst. prof. Howard U. Coll. Pharmacy and Pharmacal Sciences; adv. panel infectious disease, US Pharmacopeia, Bethesda, Md., 1985, adjunct asst. prof. Georgetown Med. Sch., Wash., 1987, data mgr., evaluator N.C.H.S.R., N.I.H., evaluation of appropriateness of drug therapy as prescribed by physicians and clin. pharmacist prescribers.

GARAM, MARTHA JANE, editor; b. Cleve., Aug. 8, 1947; d. William Bertram and Yetta Lillian (Shaftel) Webber; children: Jennifer Barbara, Michelle Debra. BA in Edn., U. Mich., 1969; MA in English, NYU, 1970. Cert. secondary sch. tchr., N.Y. Tchr. English George W. Hewlett High Sch., N.Y., 1971-74; project asst. Am. Council on Teaching Fgn. Langs., Hastings-on-Hudson, N.Y., 1982-83; freelance reporter The Enterprise, Hastings-on-Hudson, 1982-83, copy editor, 1983-84, editor-in-chief, 1984-88; sr. editor Housewares Executive, N.Y.C., 1988-89; mng. editor Computer Publishing, Advt. Report and Telecom Advt. Report, Larchmont, N.Y., 1989—; editor newsletter Parent-Tchr.-Student Assn., Hastings Pub. Schs., 1981-82. Mem. Hastings Creative Arts Council, 1981—. Recipient cert. of merit N.Y. State Sch. Bds. Assn., 1986, proclamation for outstanding community svc., County Bd. of Legislators, 1988. Mem. Nat. Assn. Female Execs. Office: Computer Publishing 2 East Ave Larchmont NY 10538

GARAY, ERICA BLYTHE, lawyer; b. N.Y.C., Mar. 8, 1953; d. Harold and Gladys M. (Messing) G.; m. Gary S. Schachter, Dec. 22, 1973 (dec. Aug. 1980); m. Michael B. Siehs, June 10, 1984; children: Rachel Claire, Kaitlin Anne. BA, SUNY, Binghamton, 1973; JD, St. John's U., Jamaica, N.Y., 1978. Bar: N.Y. 1979, U.S. Dist. Ct. (so. and ea. dists.) N.Y. 1979, U.S. Dist. Ct. (no. dist.) Calif. 1986, Calif. 1987, U.S. Dist. Ct. (cen. dist.) Calif. 1987, U.S. Ct. Appeals (fed. cir.) 1987. Asst. corp. counsel N.Y.C. Law Dept., 1978-82; assoc. Willkie Farr & Gallagher, N.Y.C., 1982-83, Rivkin Radler Dunne & Bayh, Uniondale, N.Y., 1983-85; ptnr. Rivkin Radler Bayh Hart & Kremer, Uniondale, 1986—. St. Thomas More scholar St. John's U., 1976-78; recipient St. Thomas More award St. John's U., 1978. Democrat. Office: Rivkin Radler Bayh Hart & Kremer EAB Pla Uniondale NY 11556-0111

GARAZI, IDA SHWARTZ, artist, interior designer; b. Havana, Cuba, Aug. 21, 1936; came to U.S., 1959; d. Moris and Pola (Levin) Shwartz; children: Susana, Diana; m. Phillip Albert Winter, Sept. 4, 1985. Cert. in Interior Design, Am. U., Havana, 1959; AA, Miami Dade Jr. Coll., 1976; student, Fla. Internat. U. Textile color coordinator David and Dash Interior Design, Miami, Fla., 1962-64; cons. in interior design Saul Siegal Fabrics, Miami, 1964-66; dist. sales Jordan Marsh Art Gallery, Miami, 1971-76; interior designer Red Tag Furniture, Miami, 1977-87; mem. coop. gallery South Fla. Art Gallery, Miami Beach, Fla., 1985—. One-woman shows include Menorah Temple, Miami, 1979, Bacardi Art Gallery, Miami, 1980, South Fla. Art Gallery, Miami, 1986, Louis Flower and Art Gallery, Bay Harbor, Fla., 1987; group exhbns. include Fla. Internat. U., Miami, 1984, 85, Barbara Gillman Gallery, Miami, 1985, North Miami Met. Mus., 1985; featured work pub. South Fla. Home and Garden Mag., 1987. Art dir. Interam. chpt. Hadassah, Miami, 1981. Mem. Women's Caucus for Art, Miami Watercolor Soc., Allied Arts, Phi Pheta Kappa. Jewish. Home: 1261 99th St Bay Harbor Islands FL 33154

GARBÁTY, MARIE LOUISE, art collector and patron; b. Berlin, Ger., Mar. 9, 1910; widowed. Patron, Met. Opera, N.Y.C. Opera; patron, hon. mem. Allentown (Pa.) Art Mus.; mem. N.Y.C. Opera Guild; fellow in perpetuity Met. Mus. Art; life fellow Mus. Fine Arts, Boston; internat. centennial patron Mus. Fine Arts, Boston; benefactor, life mem. Chrysler Mus., Norfolk, Va.; assoc. mem. Solomon Guggenheim Mus., N.Y.C., cofounder Am. Shakespeare Festival Theater, Stratford, Conn.; friend N.Y.C. Library; mem. Am. Fedn. Art, China Inst. Am. Inc., N.Y.C., Asia Soc., N.Y.C., Art Mus., Palm Beach, Fla.; donations numerous museums, libraries, profl. socs., including Met. Mus. Art, N.Y.C., U. Wash., Cooper Union Mus., Boston U. Library, Calif. State Coll. Library, Fullerton, Yale U. Library, Hoover Library, Stanford U., Library of Congress, Art Inst., Chgo., Carnegie Inst. Art, others.

GARBER, JUDITH ANN, health care services executive; b. Ville Platte, La., Dec. 6, 1949; d. Gordon Lee and Hazel (Pitre) Dardeau; children: Raegan Dyane, Dustin Paul. B.S. in Nursing, U. Southwestern La., 1972. Head nurse Rehab. Ctr., Ithaca, N.Y., 1973-74; charge nurse County Hosp., Ames, Iowa, 1975-76; nurse cons. pvt. industry, Tacoma, 1980-83; unit mgr. med. rev. Health Care Cost Containment, Orlando, Fla., 1983-86; pres. Cost Containment Cons., Casselberry, Fla., 1986—; bd. dirs. Am. Bd. Quality Assurance and Utilization Review. Speaker nat. edn. conf. Self-Insurance Inst. Am., San Francisco, 1985. Mem. NAFE, Fla. Utilization Rev. Assn., Fla. Occupational Health Nurses Assn., Self-Insurance Inst. Am., Central Fla. Claims Assn. (bd. dirs., pres.). Republican. Roman Catholic. Club: Seminole Soccer (Longwood, Fla.). Office: PO Box 915155 Longwood FL 32791-5155

GARCIA, DIANE LUTZ, social worker, psychotherapist; b. Newark, Dec. 3, 1947; d. Kenneth John and Mary Jane (Mullock) Lutz. BA, Rutgers U., 1971, MSW, 1974, PhD, 1981. Cert. social worker, qualified clin. social worker. Psychiat. social worker, asst. chief crisis intervention Univ. Medicine and Dentistry, Newark, 1974-76; program officer, data coord. Ctr. for Human Resources Planning and Devel. Inc., East Orange, N.J., 1976; rsch. asst. Rutgers U. Grad. Sch. Social Work, New Brunswick, N.J., 1976-78; cons. dir. program evaluation Youth Consultation Svc., Newark, 1978-79; psychiat. social worker Essex County Hosp. Ctr., Cedar Grove, N.J., 1979-81, 82-84; dir. social svc. and admissions Essex County Geriatrics Ctr., Belleville, N.J., 1981-82; social work specialist Ocean County Bd. Social Svcs., Toms River, N.J., 1984—; psychotherapist Shore Mental Health Ctr., Lakewood, N.J., 1986—; pvt. practice psychotherapy and care mgmt. Bricktown, N.J., 1989—. NIMH fellow, 1977-78. Mem. Nat. Assn. Social Workers, Nat. Assn. Pvt. Geriatric Care Mgrs. Office: 478 Manchester Ave Bricktown NJ 08723

GARCIA, EDNA I., secondary school educator; b. Humacao, P.R., Feb. 16, 1951; d. Agustin and Benigna Garcia; children: Clemente, Myrna. BA, Internat. Inst. of Ams., Hato Rey, P.R., 1983; postgrad., U. Bridgeport, 1985, Housatonic Coll., Bridgeport, Conn., 1989, Fairfield U., 1990—; student paralegal studies, Profl. Career Devel. Inst., Atlanta, 1990—. Notary pub.; cert. Spanish tchr. Coord. social sci. Spanish Am. Devel. Agy., Bridgeport, outreach worker; tchr. English Dept. Pub. Edn., Carolina, P.R.; ESL tchr. Bassic HIgh Sch., Bridgeport. Mem. citizen's adv. com. on contract compliance Mayors Office. Mem. NAFE, NOW, ASPIRA (founding mem.), CAUSA (official elections moderator). Address: 1575 Boston Ave Apt B-12 Bridgeport CT 06610

GARCIA, ELIZABETH, deputy clerk; b. Fajardo, P.R., Aug. 7, 1961; came to U.S., 1976; d. Lorenzo and Juana (Carrasquillo) G.; 1 child, Maria I. Pesce. Diploma in word processing, Stone Sch., New Haven, Conn., 1985. Supr. Blue Mountain Mushroom Co., Reading, Pa., 1981-82; interpreter free lance, various cities, 1980—; notary pub. State of Conn., New Haven, 1988—; dep. clk. U.S. Dist. Ct., New Haven, 1985—; notary pub., New Haven, 1988—. Democrat. Roman Catholic. Home: 36 Hotchkiss New Haven CT 06511 Office: US Dist Ct 141 Church St New Haven CT 06510

GARCIA, JOSEFINA MARGARITA, dancer, nurse, educator; b. Mascota, Jalisco, Mex., May 2, 1906; came to U.S., 1923, naturalized, 1944; d. Manuel Garcia Perez and Margarita (Garcia) Flores. Diploma Nat. Coll., Kansas City, Mo., 1933; tchrs. cert. State Tchrs. Coll., Queretaro, Mex., 1935; RN, Bethany Hosp. Sch. Nursing, 1939; diploma in psychiat. nursing Inst. of Living, Hartford, Conn., 1941; BS, Tchrs. Coll., Columbia U., 1943, MA in Health and Phys. Edn., 1945; PhD in Dance and Related Arts, Tex. Woman's U., 1958. Elem. tchr. Meth. Normal Sch., Puebla, Mex., 1934-36; dir. religious edn., nurse, coordinator phys. edn. George O. Robinson Sch., San Juan, P.R., 1939-40; psychiat. nurse psychiat. div. N.Y. Okla. White Plains, 1941-43; tchr. health Poly. Inst., San German, P.R., 1943-44; charge corrective gymnastics Hosp. for Spl. Surgery, N.Y.C., 1944-45; nurse Bellevue Hosp., N.Y.C., 1945-50; tchr., performer La Meri's Ethnologic Center, N.Y.C., 1945-47; lectr., dancer Pearl Buck's East and West Assn., 1947-49; artist, tchr., nurse Jacob's Pillow U. of Dance, Lee, Mass., summers 1949-55; pvt. duty nurse Harkness Pavillion, N.Y.C., 1952-55; supr. psychiat. div. Parkland Meml. Hosp., Dallas, 1956-58; grad. asst. in dance Tex. Woman's U., Denton, 1956-58; chmn. health, phys. edn. and recreation dept. Okla. Coll. for Women, Chickasha, 1958-63 (on leave), instr., 1934-36, 39-40, prof., 1963-64; vis. prof. edn. Miami U., Coral Gables, Fla., 1963-64; dir. dance in dept. health and phys. edn., prof. phys. edn. Madison Coll., Harrisonburg, Va., 1964-67; tchr. English as secondary lang., bilingual edn. N.Y.C. Bd. Edn.; part-time staff Grady Meml. Hosp., Chickasha, 1962-63; numerous dance recitals and workshops, 1940—; tchr. Mexican and Latin Am. dance Tina Ramirez Dance Studio, N.Y.C.; cons. Sacred Dance Guild; choreographer on Mexican themes Alliance Latin Am. Arts, summers 1973-74; artist-in-residence Spelman Coll., Atlanta, 1978-79; relief night nurse, prof. geriatric health and exercises Williams Residence, N.Y.C. Vol., Channel 13 Public TV; founder Center for Internat. Security Studies; mem. Am. Security Council; bd. govs. N.Y. chpt. Arthritis Found.; vol. Carnegie Hall. Fellow AAHPER; mem. Am., Okla., N.Y. State (dir.) nurses assns., Nat., So., Va. assns. phys. edn. coll. women, ANTA, Okla, Okla. Assn., Va. Assn. Health, Phys. Edn. and Recreation (chmn. 1962-63), AAUW, Chickasha Bus. and Profl. Women's Club (past chmn. internat. relations com.), Nat. Dance Tchrs. Guild, Nat. Council Arts in Edn., Mus. Natural History, Dance Notation Bur., Internat. Platform Assn., Pan Am. Women's Assn. (dir. 1967-78, v.p.), Dance Film Library Assn. (dir. 1967-70), Film Soc. (dir.), Profl. Dance Tchrs. Assn., Nat. Council Sr. Citizens, Met. Opera Guild, Cooper-Hewitt Mus., Nat. Geog. Soc., N.Y. YWCA, Kappa Delta Pi, Phi Sigma Iota. Contbr. articles on dance to profl. publs., Groliers Ency., Richards Ency. Home: 720 West End Ave Suite 821 New York NY 10025

GARCIA, KATHERINE LEE, comptroller, accountant; b. Portland, Oreg., Nov. 4, 1950; d. Gerald Eugene and Delores Lois (Erickson) Moe; m. Buddy Jesus Garcia; Nov. 19, 1977; children: Kevin, Brett, Rodd. BS cum laude, U. Nevada, 1976. CPA, Idaho, Nev. Retail clk. Raleys, Food King, Reno, 1968-76; sr. acct. Pieretti, Wilson and McNulty, Reno, 1976-78, Deloitte Haskins and Sells, Boise, Idaho, 1979-81; sr. acct. Washoe County, Reno, 1981-83, chief deputy compt., 1983—. Treas., bd. dirs. Friends of 4 (pub. TV), Boise, 1979-81. Recipient Cert. of Excellence in Fin. Reporting, Govt. Fin. Officer's Assn., 1982—. Mem. AICPA, Nev. Soc. CPAs (state and local govt. com. 1989—), Govt. Fin. Officers Assn. (spl. rev. com. 1989—), Nev. Govt. Fin. Officers Assn. (treas. 1989—). Republican. Home: 655 W Joy Lake Rd Reno NV 89511 Office: Washoe County PO Box 11130 Reno NV 89520

GARCIA, MARY JANE MADRID, state legislator; b. Dona Ana, N.Mex., Dec. 24, 1936; d. Isaac C. and Victoria M. Garcia. A.A., San Francisco City Coll., 1956; B.S., N.Mex. State U., 1982, B.A. in Anthropology, 1983, M.A. in Anthropology, 1985. Interpretor, translator to USAF Capt., Hotel Balboa, Madrid, Spain, 1962-63; exec. sec. to city mgr. City of Las Cruces, N.Mex., 1964-65; adminstrv. asst. RMK-BRJ, Saigon, Socialist Republic Vietnam, 1966-72; owner Billy the Kid Gift Shop, Mesilla, N.Mex., 1972-81; pres., owner Victoria's Night Club, Las Cruces, 1981—; state senator Dist. 38, N.Mex.; with archaeol. excavations N.Mex. State U. Anthropology Dept., summer 1982, spring 1983. Bd. dirs., sec-treas. Dona Anna Mutual Domestic Water Assn.; mem. Subarea Council Health Systems Agy., 1979; bd. dirs. Sun Country Savings Bank, Las Cruses, 1985; treas. Toney Anaya for U.S. Senate, 1978; active Toney Anaya for N.Mex. Gov., 1979-82. Mem. N.Mex. Retail Liquor Assn. Democrat. Roman Catholic. Home: Isaac Garcia St PO Box 22 Dona Ana NM 88032 Office: Senate of N Mex State Capitol Santa Fe NM 87503*

GARCIA, NANCY YEATTS, school system administrator; b. Altoona, Pa., June 9, 1947; d. Charles E. and Dorothy B. (Shull) Yeatts; m. José C. Garcia. AAS, Harrisburg (Pa.) Area Community Coll., 1967; B Elem. Edn., Pa. State U., 1969, M Elem. Edn., 1971; EdD, Temple U., 1985. Cert. tchr., Pa. Tchr. Camp Hill (Pa.) Elem. Sch. and Cumberland County, 1969-74; instructional advisor Capital/Area Intermediate Unit Sch. Dist. #15, Dauphin, Cumberland and Perry Counties, Pa., 1974-79; dir. Capital/Area Intermediate Unit Sch. Dist. #15, Lemoyne, Pa., 1979—; mem. Council of Exceptional Children, 1970s-80s, Children's Lit. Council Cen. Pa., 1985—. Mem. Camp Hill Jr. Civic Club, 1970s—; life mem. Humane Soc. Harrisburg, 1985—. Millersville (Pa.) Coll. grantee, 1970. Mem. Pa. State U. Alumni (life), Temple U. Alumni (life), Harrisburg Area Community (life, former bd. dirs.), Harrisburtg Bd. Realtors, Phi Delta Kappa (life mem. Harrisburg chpt.). Office: Capital Area Intermediate Unit #15 55 Miller St PO Box 489 Summerdale PA 17093-0489

GARCIA, PATRICIA ANN, banker; b. Ft. Lauderdale, Dec. 16, 1959; d. Paul Jorge and Irene Cecilia (Kenny) G. BA in Geography, Clark U., 1982. Fin. assoc. Security Pacific Merchant Bank, N.Y.C., 1982-89; cons. Bessemer Trust Co., N.Y.C., 1989-90; asst. v.p. U.S. Trust Co., N.Y.C., 1990—. Democrat. Methodist.

GARCIA, PHYLLIS JOSEPHINE, teacher, consultant; b. Chgo., Aug. 21, 1934; d. Peter Thomas and Louise Phyllis (Smietanski) Witkowski; m. Jesse Garcia, Apr. 14, 1951; children: Kenneth, Thomas, Nancy, Janet, Susan. AA, Daley Coll., Chgo., 1982, AAS, 1983; BA in Edn., Roosevelt U., 1985; MS in Edn., Chog. State U., 1987. Early childhood tchr., community worker McDowell Settlement, Chgo., 1950-55, youth leader, 1963-67; adminstrv. asst. May D&F, Denver, 1972-77; tchr. U. Chgo. Lab. Sch., 1985-86; tchr. early childhood intervention program Denver Pub. Schs., Chgo., 1988—; child devel. assoc. Rep. Coun. for Early Childhood Profl. Recognition, Washington, 1986—. Leader Girl Scouts Am., Chgo., 1963-68. Mem. Assn. for Childhood Edn. Internat., Nat. Assn. for Edn. Young Children, Assn. for Supervision and Curriculum Instrn., Assn. for Child Care Cons. Internat. Democrat. Roman Catholic. Home: 709 S Leyden Denver CO 80224

GARCIA, SANDRA JOANNE ANDERSON, psychology educator; b. Buffalo, Aug. 10, 1939; d. James Edwards and Thelma Harriet (Crawford) Anderson; m. Gerard L. Garcia, Jr., June 11, 1960 (div. 1968); 1 child, Robert Vincent. BA, Tex. Western Coll., 1966; MA, U. Tex., El Paso, 1968; PhD, Stetson U. Coll. Law, 1971; JD, Stetson U., 1985. Rsch. assoc. Human Rsch. Office, George Washington U., El Paso, 1967-68; rsch. assoc. SW Regional Lab. for Ednl. Rsch. and Devel., Inglewood, Calif., 1968-69; asst. prof. English dept. UCLA, 1970-74; asst. prof. psychology U. South Fla., Tampa, 1974-80, assoc. prof., 1989-90, prof., 1990—. Editor: Bionic Babies in High-Tech Families: New Issues in Child Psychology, 1988; coeditor: Current Perspectives in Legal, Psychological, and Ethical Issues, 1990. Recipient Equal Opportunity award U. South Fla., 1976; rsch. fellow Ford Found., Jerusalem, 1973-74, Am. Bar Found., 1989, 90, McKnight Found., 1989-90, Nat. Ctr. for State Cts., 1990—. Democrat. Home: 300 F Patriot Lane Williamsburg VA 23185

GARCIA, VALERIE LONGVAL, travel consultant; b. Tampa, Fla., June 30, 1960; d. Robert and Rose (Fernandez) Longval; m. David Anthony Garcia, June 5, 1982. Student, Hillsborough Community Coll., 1983—. Agt. TWA, Tampa, 1979-82, Continental Airlines, Tampa, 1982-85; cons. Travel Resources, Tampa, 1985-88, Ask Mr. Foster/Palm Travel, Tampa, 1989—. Mem. Tampa Bay Kennel Club (asst. show chmn. 1988—). Democrat. Roman Catholic. Home: 2009 Quail Hollow Blvd Wesley Chapel FL 33544 Office: Palm Travel Inc Carlson Travel Network Assoc 3109 W Buffalo Ste 101 Tampa FL 33607

GARCIA-PARIS, CAROLINA, computer engineer, software developer; b. Caracas, Venezuela, Dec. 19, 1962; came to U.S., 1987; d. German de la Cruz Garcia Medero and Virginia Lucia (Paris) Mesa. BS in Computer Engrng., U. P.R., 1987; MS in Computer Sci., U. Miami, 1988. Lab. asst. U. P.R., Mayaguez, 1984-85; sr. staff technologist Bell Communications Rsch., Piscataway, N.J., 1986, mem. tech. staff, 1988—. Mem. Bellcore Assn. Hispanics in Telecommunications (locational dir. 1990). Roman

Catholic. Home: 120 Royal Dr Apt 390 Piscataway NJ 08854 Office: Bell Communications Rsch 33 Knightsbridge Rd 4H-208 Piscataway NJ 08854

GARDE, SUSAN REUTERSHAN, defense contractor administrator; b. Southampton, N.Y., Sept. 5, 1953; d. Robert Gordon and Ann Patricia (Cronin) Reutershan; m. John Franklin Garde III, May 20, 1989. BS, Skidmore Coll., 1975; MBA, Fla. Inst. Tech., 1983. Budget analyst Grumman Aerospace Corp., Bethpage, N.Y., 1975-76, program planner, 1976-79; sr. budget planner Grumman Aerospace Corp., Stuart, Fla., 1979-81, program planner, 1981-82; adminstr. rsch. ctr. United Technologies, West Palm Beach, Fla., 1982-86; sr. adminstr. United Technologies Inc., West Palm Beach, 1986-87, United Technologies Optical Systems Inc., West Palm Beach, 1988—. Mem. NAFE, Am. Bus. Women's Assn. (pres. Orchid chpt. 1986-87, Sailfish chpt. 1985), Nat. Wildlife Fedn., Skidmore Alumni Assn., Skidmore Club S.E. Fla. Republican. Roman Catholic. Home: 7 Brighton Ct Palm Beach Gardens FL 33418 Office: United Technologies Optical Systems Inc PO Box 109660 West Palm Beach FL 33410

GARDIS, GILDA J., quality analyst; b. Jersey City, Jan. 16, 1944; d. William Patrick and Gilda Esther (Weber) Cornett; m. David Richard Gardis, Oct. 8, 1966 (div. 1981). Student, Oceanside-Carlsbad Jr. Coll., Santa Monica City Coll. Prin. typist clk. UCLA, 1966-69, adminstrv. asst., 1969-73, acctg. asst., 1973-75, mgmt. services officer, UCLA, 1975-79; mgmt. services officer U. Calif., San Diego, La Jolla, 1979-85; quality analyst Teledyne Kinetics, Solana Beach, Calif., 1986—; part-time sales rep. Mervyn's, Oceanside, Calif., 1986—. Active Oceanside High Sch. Booster Club, 1980-83. Recipient Tiffany award Manpower, Inc., Carlsbad, Calif., 1985. Mem. Am. Mgmt. Assn. (assoc.), Nat. Assn. Female Execs., Network Exec. Women, Am. Soc. Profl. and Exec. Women, Nat. Assn. Profl. and Exec. Women, Teledyne Kinetics Recreation Assn. (sec. 1987, chairperson 1988), Mervyn's Employee Assn. (pres. 1990). Roman Catholic. Avocations: tennis, bicycling, art, bowling. Home: 3559 Guava Way Oceanside CA 92054 Office: Teledyne Kinetics 410 S Cedros Solana Beach CA 92075 also: PO Box 1401 Oceanside CA 92054

GARDNER, BETTIANN, hair care products executive; b. 1930. With Soft Sheen Products Inc., Chgo., 1964—; now co-chmn. Soft Sheen Products Inc. Office: Soft Sheen Products Inc 1000 E 87th St Chicago IL 60619*

GARDNER, CAROL ROBIN, immunology educator; b. Bklyn., Mar. 28, 1956; d. Robert D. and Sandra (Zwickel) G. BA, SUNY, Potsdam, 1978; MS, So. Ill. U., Edwardsville, 1980; PhD, Tex. Woman's U., 1985. Teaching and rsch. asst. So. Ill. U., 1978-80, Tex. Woman's U., Denton, 1980-85; postdoctoral fellow Rutgers U., Piscataway, N.J., 1985-88, asst. rsch. prof. dept. pharmacology and toxicology, 1988—. Contbr. articles and abstracts to profl. jours., chpts. to books. Mem. AAAS, Electron Microscopy Soc. Am., Soc. for Leukocyte Biology, N.Y. Acad. Scis., Sigma Xi, Iota Sigma Pi. Jewish. Home: 85 Tices Ln Apt 8 East Brunswick NJ 08816 Office: Rutgers U Coll Pharmacy Dept Pharm and Toxicology Piscataway NJ 08855-0789

GARDNER, COLETTE YVONNE, human resources executive; b. Marianna, Fla., Jan. 27, 1958; d. Harvey Strevell and Angela Lilyan (Colette) G. BBA, U. Cen. Ark., 1980. Pers. specialist Coopers & Lybrand, Dallas, 1981-84; pers. mgr. Arthur Andersen & Co., N.Y.C., 1984-89; v.p. Bankers Trust Co., N.Y.C., 1989—; program chmn., mem. N.Y. State Soc. CPAs, N.Y.C., 1986-89. Vol. Out of Sight Blind Recreation, Long Island, N.Y., 1985-87; supporter MS Soc., N.Y.C., 1985—. Republican. Roman Catholic. Home: 410 W 53rd 204 New York NY 10019

GARDNER, GRACE DANIEL, company executive; b. Nashville, Oct. 15, 1911; d. John and Grace Olive (Knight) Daniel; m. Edwin Sumner Gardner, July 10, 1935; children: Gretchen, Patricia, Edwin Sumner. BA, Vanderbilt U., 1932. Tchr. Nashville pub. sch., 1932-33; dept. mgr. Tenn. Electric Power Co., Nashville, 1933-35; devel. officer Tenn. Performing Arts Found., Nashville, 1975-78; exec. dir. Tenn. Performing Arts Found., 1978—. Chmn. fund raising ARC, Nashville, 1947, active various other charitable orgns. Fellow: Nat. Soc. Fund Raising Execs., Centennial (dir. music com. chmn.). Episcopalian.

GARDNER, JILL CHRISTOPHER, neuroscientist; b. Winchester, Mass., Dec. 23, 1948; d. Wallace Joseph Gardner and Lyna (Christopher) Mueller. BSc with lst class honors, Dalhousie U., Halifax, N.S., Can., 1975, MS, 1977, PhD, 198l. Rsch. assoc. Dalhousie U., 1981-82; postdoctoral fellow MIT, Cambridge, 1982-85, NIH fellow in biophysics, 1987—; postdoctoral assoc. Children's Hosp., Boston, 1986-87; rsch. fellow in otolaryngology Mass. Eye and Ear Infirmary, Boston, 1987—; specialist in neurophysiology Mass. Gen. Hosp., Boston, 1987—. Contbr. articles to sci. jours., chpts. to books. Co-dir. Summer Village Camp, Marlboro, Mass., 1972; researcher Rockefeller for Pres. Com., N.Y.C., 1968; advance person Romney for Pres., N.H., 1968. Dalhousie U. Rsch. and Devel. Fund grantee, 1981, 82, Natural Scis. and Engring. Coun. grantee, 1983, 84. Mem. Soc. for Neurosci., Assn. for Rsch. in Vision and Ophthalmology, Internat. Brain Rsch. Orgn., World Fedn. Neuroscientists, Brit. Brain and Behavior Soc., Phi Theta Kappa. Office: Mass Eye and Ear Infirmary Eaton Peabody Lab 243 Charles St Boston MA 02140

GARDNER, LYNN SULLIVAN, public relations executive; b. N.Y.C., Sept. 30, 1957; d. John Joseph and Christina Mary (Broderick) Sullivan; m. Randy Alan Gardner, Oct. 9, 1982. B.A., Boston Coll., 1978; postgrad. New Sch. Social Rsch., N.Y.C., 1985. Assoc. producer Miss Universe, Inc., N.Y.C., 1979-81, Time-Life Video, N.Y.C., 1981; script supr. RG Prodns./NBC., N.Y.C. and L.A., 1981-83; agt. Elite Model Mgmt., N.Y.C., 1983-84; v.p. pub. rels. The Solomon Orgn., N.Y.C., 1984—. Admission counselor Boston Coll., N.Y.C., 1979—; activist North Shore Animal League, N.J., 1982—; foster parent Christian Children's Fund, Zambia, Africa, 1983—, Covenant House of Internat. Platform Soc.; vol. The Starlight Found. Mem. Assn. Real Estate Women, NAFE, Media Network, Am. Women in Radio and Tel., Am. Film Inst., Internat. Platform Soc., Nat. Mus. Women in Arts, ASPCA (activist 1982—, N.J. chpt.), Boston Coll. Alumni Club. Democrat. Roman Catholic. Avocations: collecting crystal cats, acting, children's theatre, reading, traveling. Home: 35 Clark St #4-D Brooklyn Heights NY 11201 Office: The Solomon Orgn 18 E 48th St New York NY 10017

GARDNER, MARGARET FENTON, publisher; b. Los Angeles, Aug. 26, 1932; d. Howard Mansfield and Leota Gustine (Courson) Fenton; m. James Stanley Gardner, June 24, 1950; children: James Stanley, Michael Alan, Steven Edward. Postgrad., Mt. San Antonio Coll., Walnut, Calif., 1970. Admitting clk. Inter Community Med. Ctr., Covina, Calif., 1961-70, 1982-86; with med. transcription dept. Wasatch County Hosp., Heber City, Utah, 1987—; pub. Abbott, Aldrich, Bailey, Courson, Crawford, Gardner, Keeler, Midway, Utah, 1980—. Mem. Police Wives Assn., Alpha Theta Rho. Republican. LDS.

GARDNER, MARJORIE HYER, science association administrator; b. Logan, Utah, Apr. 25, 1923; d. Saul Edward and Gladys Ledingham (Christiansen) Hyer; B.S., Utah State U., 1946, Ph.D. (hon.), 1975; M.A., Ohio State U., 1958, Ph.D., 1960; cert. Ednl. Mgmt. Inst., Harvard U., 1975; m. Paul Leon Gardner, June 6, 1947; children: Pamela Jean, Mary Elizabeth. Tchr. sci., journalism and English high schs., Utah, Nev., Ohio, 1947-56; instr. Ohio State U., Columbus, 1957-60; asst. exec. dir. Nat. Sci. Tchrs. Assn., 1961-64; vis. prof. Australia, India, Yugoslavia, Nigeria, Thailand, Peoples Republic of China, 1965-82; assoc. dean, dir. Bur. Ednl. Rsch. and Field Svc., College Park, Md., 1975-76; dir. Sci. Teaching Ctr., U. Md., College Park, 1976-77, prof. chemistry, 1964-84; dir. Lawrence Hall Sci., U. Calif.-Berkeley, 1984-90; div. dir. NSF, 1979-81; cons. UNESCO, 1970—; NSF grantee, 1964—; recipient Catalyst medal Chem. Mfrs. Assn., 1980, Nyholm medal Royal Soc. Can., 1987, U.S.U. Centennial award, 1987, ACS Chemical Edn. award, 1988. Fellow AAAS (coun.), Am. Inst. Chemistry; mem. Am. Chem. Soc., Chemistry Assn. Md. (pres.), Internat. Union of Pure and Applied Chemistry (exec. com.), Internat. Orgn. Chemistry in Devel. (edn. panel), Assn. Edn. of Tchrs. of Sci., Nat. Assn. Rsch. in Sci. Teaching, Nat. Sci. Tchrs. Assn., Am. Assn. Higher Edn., Soc. Coll. Sci. Tchrs. (pres.), Fulbright Alumni Assn. (pres., dir.), Phi Delta Kappa, Phi Kappa Phi. Author: Chemistry in the Space Age, 1965; editor: Theory in Action, 1964, Vistas of Sci. Series, 1961-63; Investigating the Earth, 1968, Interdisciplinary Approaches to Chemistry, 1973, 1978-79; Under Roof, Dome and Sky, 1974, Toward Continuous Professional Development: Designs and Directions, 1976; contbr. articles in on chemistry and sci. edn. to profl. jours. Home: 517 Vista Height Rd Richmond CA 94805 Office: U Calif Lawrence Hall Sci Centennial Dr Berkeley CA 94720

GARDNER, MARY BERTHA HOEFT CHADWICK, retired postmaster, small business owner; b. Vernal, Utah, June 13, 1914; d. Edward and Hazel (Burgess) Hoeft; B.S. in Elem. Edn., Utah State U., 1950; m. Rulon Chadwick, Sept. 3, 1935 (div. July 1949); children—Mary Jo Chadwick Wight, Adriana Chadwick Forsgren; m. Leon D. Gardner, July 14, 1951 (dec. May 1974). Bookkeeper, Model Dairy, 1935-49; Weber Central Dairy, 1949-51, Bishops Storehouse, 1950-51; sch. tchr., Ogden, Utah, 1950-51; clk. Post Office, Honeyville, Utah, 1956-72, postmaster, 1972-81; owner Country Store/RV Campground, Mantua, Utah. Pres., Relief Soc. Ch. Jesus Ch. of Latter-day Saints, mem. stake bd. relief soc., mem. stake bd. Sunday sch., mem. stake bd. mut. improvement assn. orgn., stake spl. interest leader 1982-86; mem. Utah State Women's Legis. Council, 1983-85. Mem. Nat. League Postmasters (exec. v.p. state br., editor newsletter), Nat. Assn. Postmasters, AAUW (treas.), Daus. Utah Pioneers, Bus. and Profl. Women's Club (treas. Brigham City, treas. treas. No. Dist. 1984-85, Logan 1985-86). Home: 8440 N Hwy 69 Honeyville UT 84314

GARDNER, NANCY HAZARD, small business owner, systems analyst; b. Washington, Feb. 17, 1949; d. Everett Browning and Vera Catherine (Rushworth) G. BS, U. Md., 1972. Trainer Equitable Trust Bank, Balt., 1970-74; program analyst U. Md., College Park, 1974-77; adminstr. Nat. Acad. Scis., Washington, 1977-80; office mgr. Ctr. for Population Options, Washington, 1980-81; compt. Carltech Assocs., Inc., Columbia, Md., 1981-83; fin. dir. Helschien Health Ctr., Columbia, 1983-84; pres. Sensitive Systems, Inc., Balt., 1982—, chmn. bd. dirs. Mem. NAFE. Office: Sensitive Systems Inc 2910 O'Donnell St Baltimore MD 21224

GARDNER, NATALIE NELLIE JAGLOM, advertising agency executive; b. Cernauti, Rumania; came to U.S., 1939, naturalized, 1946; b. Abraham and Nadia (Shoenberg) Jaglom; student Ohio State U., 1943, N.Y. U., 1944, U. Calif., Berkeley, 1945; m. Ralph David Gardner, Apr. 9, 1952; children—Ralph David, John Jaglom (dec.), Peter Jaglom, James Jaglom. Dir. Ralph D. Gardner Advt., N.Y.C., 1955—; pres. Gardner Internat., Inc., 1981—; dir. N.Y. Commodities Corp., Overseas Barters, Inc. Vol., ARC, 1944; hosp. vol. Am. Women's Vol. Services, 1944-45; active UN Host Family Program. Home: 135 Central Park W New York NY 10023 Office: 888 7th Ave 34th Fl New York NY 10106

GARDNER, SANDRA LEE, registered nurse, outreach consultant; b. Louisville, Dec. 1, 1946; d. Jane Marie (Schwab) Gardner. Nursing diploma, Sts. Mary and Elizabeth Hosp., Louisville, 1967; BSN magna cum laude, Spalding Coll., 1973; MS, U. Colo., 1975, Pediatric Nurse Practitioner, 1978. Premature coordinator Meth. Evang. Hosp., Louisville, 1967-71; charge nurse Children's Hosp., Louisville, 1971-73; staff/charge nurse Children's Hosp., Denver, 1973-74, perinatal oujtreach coord., 1974-76; asst. prof. U. Colo. Sch. Nursing, 1976-79; co-founder, vice chmn. bd. dirs. Denver Birth Ctr., 1977-79; dir., cons. Profl. Outreach Consultation, Aurora, Colo., 1980—; founding mem. Colo. Perinatal Car Council, Denver, 1975—; founding dir. Neonatal Nursing Edn. Found., Aurora, 1982—. Co-editor: Handbook of Neonatal Intensive Care, 1985, 89; contbr. articles to profl. jours. Foster parent educator Dept. Social Svcs., 1976-78; in pub. edn. KVOD Radio/Channel 2, Denver, 1978; nursing supr. 9 Health Fair, Denver, 1980. Recipient Gerald L. Hencemann award March of Dimes, Denver, 1978. Mem. Am. Nurses Assn. (Book of Yr. 1986, 90), Nat. Neonatal Nurses Assn. Democrat. Home: 12095 E Kentucky Ave Aurora CO 80012

GAREY, PATRICIA MARTIN, artist; b. State College, Miss., Nov. 11, 1932; d. Verey G. Martin and Eva Myrtle Jones; m. Donald L. Garey, Aug. 1, 1953; children: Deborah Anne Garey Furst, Elizabeth Laird Garey Spurlock. BS in Costume Design, Tex. Women's U., 1953; MFA, Tex. Tech. U., 1973; postgrad. in art history, Two-Dimensional Studio Art, 1970-73. Prodn. mgr. Cox Advt. Agy., Roswell, N.M., 1958-63; art instr. Coll. of Southwest, Hobbs, N.M., 1967-69, 72-73; artist-in-residence N. Mex. Arts Commn., Santa Fe and Hobbs, 1974-76; studio artist Hobbs, 1976—; instr. Cloudcroft (N.Mex.) Artists Sch., 1989-90. One-woman shows include N. Mex. Jr. Coll., Hobbs, 1969, Coll. of SW, 1974, 79, Sangre de Cristo Arts Ctr., Pueblo, 1979, U. Tex. of Permian Basin, Odessa, 1980, N.Mex. Jr. Coll.; represented at Beverly Gordon Gallery, Dallas, Sylvia Ullman Am. Crafts, Cleve., Design Today, Lubbock Tex., El-Dor Galleries Old-Town, Albuquerque, Galeria de la Paloma, Santa Fe; work exhibited at Roswell Mus. Art, Southeastern N.Mex. Small Painting Exhibit (2d pl., 1966), Llano Estacado Art Exhbn. 1967 (Hon. Mention Oil Painting), 68 (2d pl. Graphics), 69 (Hon. Mention Graphics, 2d pl. Sculpture, 2d pl. Acrylics), 75 (1st pl. Ceramics), 76 (1st pl. Drawing, 2d pl. Painting), Americas Gallery, Taos, 1974, Blair Gallery, Santa Fe, 1974, Mus. Fine Arts, Santa Fe, 1976, Tex. Tech. U., 1977, Little Rock Art Ctr., Ark., 1978, Hills Gallery, Santa Fe, 1979, Dallas Mus. Fine Art, 1986, 87, 88, 90, Beaux Arts Ball Art Auction, 1990, Okla. City Mus. Art, Little Rock Art Ctr., El Paso (Tex.) Sun Carnival; represented in collections Beverly Gordon Gallery, Dallas, Tex. Tech. U.; dossant Meadows Mus. of Art SMU, Dallas, 1990. Bd. dirs. S.W. Symphony, Hobbs, 1987-88. Mem. Delta Phi Delta, Chi Omega. Democrat. Methodist. Studio: 315 E Alto Hobbs NM 88240 also: Piney Woods Cloudcroft NM 88350

GARFIELD, EVELYN PICON, Spanish educator; b. Newark, Aug. 23, 1940; d. Sol G. and Edith (Haskell) Picon; m. Louis Norman Garfield, Nov. 3, 1961 (div.); children: Gene Douglas, Audrey Suzanne; m. Ivan A. Schulman, Nov. 17, 1979. AB, U. Mich., 1963; MA, Washington U., St. Louis, 1967; PhD, Rutgers U., 1972. Instr., asst. prof. Spanish and Italian dept. Montclair State Coll., Upper Montclair, N.J., 1970-74; co-dir. affirmative action U. Mass., Boston, 1974-76; asst. prof. Spanish, Brown U., Providence, 1976-80; asst. prof. Spanish, Wayne State U., Detroit, 1980-81, assoc. prof., 1981-84, prof., 1984-85; prof. Spanish, U. Ill., Urbana, 1985-86, prof. Spanish and comparative lit., 1986—, assoc. dean Coll. Liberal Arts and Scis., 1987-89; conf. presenter, guest lectr. in field; cons. to pubs., 1980—; project coord. lst exchange program colloquia on Latin Am. lit. between U.S. and USSR, 1983—, Am. Coun. Learned Socs.-Soviet Acad. Scis. Commn. on Humanities and Social Scis.; coord. 2d Symposium on Latin Am. lit. between U.S. and USSR, 1987. Author: Es Julio Cortazar un Surrealista?, 1975, Julio Cortazar, 1975, Cortazar por Cortazar, 1978, 2d edit., 1981, (with Schulman) Las entranas del vacio, 1984,Poesia modernista hispanoamericana y espanola, 1986, Las literaturas hispanicas, 1990; Women's Voices from Latin Am., 1985, Women's Fiction from Latin America, 1988, Julio Cortazar: Cartas a una pelirroja, 1990; co-editor 2 books; contbr. articles and book revs. to profl. jours., also chpts. to books. N.J. Com. for Humanities grantee, 1973, Am. Philos. Soc. grantee, 1973, NEH grantee, 1982, 83, Fulbright grantee, 1986, also others. Mem. MLA, Am. Assn. Tchrs. Spanish and Portuguese, Latin Am. Studies Assn., Instituto Literatura Iberoamericana, AAUW (chmn. com. W on status of wommen N.J. chpt. 1971-72). Office: U Ill 4080 Fgn Langs Bldg 707 S Mathews St Urbana IL 61801

GARFIELD, JOAN BARBARA, mathematics and statistics educator; b. Milw., May 4, 1950; d. Sol. L. and Amy L. (Nusbaum) G.; m. Michael G. Luxenberg, Aug. 17, 1980; children: Harlan Ross and Rebecca Ellen (twins). Student, U. Chgo., 1968; BS, U. Wis., 1972; MA, U. Minn., 1978, PhD, 1981. Assoc. prof. math./stats. The Gen. Coll., U. Minn., Mpls., 1981—, coord. rsch. and evaluation, 1984-87. Mem. Am. Statis. Assn., Am. Assn. Higher Edn., Am. Ednl. Rsch. Assn., Internat. Assn. for Statis. Computing, Internat. Study Group on Learning Probability and Stats. (sec. 1987—). Jewish. Avocations: violin, viola. Office: U Minn Gen Coll Div Sci Bus Math 216 Pillsbury Ave SE 340 Appleby Hall Minneapolis MN 55455

GARFINKEL, RENÉE EFRA, clinical services administrator; b. N.Y.C., May 26, 1950; d. Jacob Joseph and Miriam (Herc) Morgenstern; m. Jay Garfinkel, June 22, 1969; children: Elon J., Erica B. BA, Am. U., 1971; PhD, Lund U., 1975. Lic. psychologist, Pa., Md., D.C. Sr. clin. psychologist Phila. Geriatric Ctr., 1977-80; chief psychology dept. Grad. Hosp., Phila., 1980-85; dir. women's programs Am. Psychol. Assn., Washington, 1985-86; dir. Gerontology Svcs., Silver Spring, Md., 1986—; bd. dirs. Hebrew Home of Greater Washington, Rockville, Md., Hebrew Acad. of Greater Washington. Contbr. articles to profl. jours. Sec. Eldergames, Washington, 1986; bd. dirs. Sr. Citizen Judicare Project, Phila., 1983-85. Kellogg Found. scholar, 1983. Mem. Am. Psychol. Assn., Gerontol. Soc., N.Y. Acad. Scis., Nat. Coalition for Women's Mental Health, Women's Health Alliance Pa. (charter). Office: Gerontology Svcs 12017 Brookhaven Dr Silver Spring MD 20902

GARFINKLE, CARYN, tax specialist; b. N.Y.C., Dec. 17, 1951; d. Elias and Sylvia (Goldberg) Globe; m. Martin Garfinkle, Dec. 17, 1972; children: Steven, Eric. BS, Bklyn. Coll., 1973; MBA, St. John's U. CPA. Tax sr. Arthur Andersen and Co., N.Y.C.; asst. prof. acctg. Bklyn. Coll.; internat. tax mgr. Laventhol and Horwath, N.Y.C.; tax ptnr. Brand Sonnenschine and Zakheim, N.Y.C. Contbr. articles to profl. jours. Mem. AICPA, N.Y. State Soc. CPAs, Beta Gamma Sigma. Address: 377 Broadway New York NY 10013

GARGALLI, CLAIRE W., banker; b. Phila., Dec. 3, 1942; d. Robert and Kathryn Emma (LaPish) Waterhouse. B.A., Middlebury Coll., 1964. Credit analyst Fidelity Bank, Phila., 1964-68, asst. treas., 1968-70, asst. v.p., 1970-73, v.p., 1973-74, exec. v.p., 1975-84; gen. mgr. Fidelity Internat. Bank, N.Y.C., 1974-75, pres., 1977-79; sr. exec. v.p. Equibank, Pitts., 1984, pres., 1984-87, chmn., chief exec. officer, from 1987; bd dirs Gen. Coal Co., Phila. Bd. dirs. Internat. House, Phila., 1980—; bd. dirs. World Affairs Council, 1983—; mem. adv. bd. U. Pa. Com. Women's Concerns, 1978—. Republican.

GARGES, SUSAN, microbiologist; b. Chelsea, Mass., Jan. 9, 1953; d. Thomas Smith and Mary Helen (Hunt) G.; m. Arthur Lawrence Zachary, Mar. 19, 1982; children: John, Samuel. BA, U. Dayton, 1974, MS, 1978; PhD, U. Md., 1983. Teaching asst. U. Dayton, Ohio, 1974-76; faculty rsch. asst. U. Md., Coll. Pk., Md., 1976-79; microbiologist Nat. Cancer Inst. NIH, Bethesda, Md., 1979—; mem. com. on standards for virus ASTM, 1986—. Mem. Am. Soc. for Microbiology. Office: NCI NIH Bldg 37 Rm 4B10 Bethesda MD 20892

GARGIULO-KULIKOWSKI, JOAN, payroll executive; b. Teaneck, N.J., Jan. 13, 1953; d. Joseph John and Catherina (D'Angelo) Gargiulo; 1 child, Pamala Renee Kulikowski. AA cum laude, Bergen Community Coll., Paramus, N.J., 1983. Pres. Audio Rack Svc. Ctr. Inc., Westwood, N.J., 1983-88; payroll dir. Lockheed Info. Mgmt. Svcs. Co., Teaneck, N.J., 1988-90; asst. adminstr. savs. plans Lockheed Corp., Calabasas, Calif., 1990—; cons. savs. plans ADP, Clifton, N.J., 1989. Co-chmn. Union St. Sch. PTO, Hackensack, N.J., 1989-90; treas. Westwood Parents of Exceptional Children, 1989-90. Mem. NAFE, Am. Payroll Assn. Office: Lockheed Corp 4714 Park Granada Blvd #204 Calabasas CA 91302

GARIBALDI, MARIE LOUISE, state supreme court justice; b. Jersey City, Nov. 26, 1934; d. Louis J. and Marie (Serventi) G. BA, Conn. Coll., 1956; LLB, Columbia U., 1959; LLM in Tax. Law, NYU, 1963. Atty. Office of Regional Counsel, IRS, N.Y.C., 1960-66; assoc. McCarter & English, Newark, 1966-69; ptnr. Riker, Danzig, Scherer & Hyland, Newark, 1969-82; assoc. justice N.J. Supreme Court, Newark, 1982—. Contbr. articles to profl. jours. Trustee St. Peter's Coll.; co-chmn. Thomas Kean's campaign for Gov. of N.J., 1981, mem. transition team, 1981; mem. Gov. Byrne's Commn. on Dept. of Commerce, 1981. Recipient Disting. Alumni award NYU Law Alumni of N.J., 1982; recipient Disting. Alumni award Columbia U., 1982. Fellow Am. Bar Found.; mem. N.J. Bar Assn. (pres. 1982), Columbia U. Sch. Law Alumni Assn. (bd. dirs.). Home: 34 Kingswood Rd Weehawken NJ 07087 also: 583 Newark Ave Jersey City NJ 07306

GARING, IONE DAVIS, civic worker, club woman; b. Huntsville, Ala., Jan. 8, 1930; d. Drury McNary and Ione (Thompson) Davis; m. John Seymour Garing, Apr. 26, 1952; children: John Davis, Susan Carolyn. BSc in Edn. cum laude, Ohio State U., 1951. Tchr. Columbus (Ohio) Pub. Schs., 1952-54, Upper Arlington Pub. Sch., Columbus, 1957-58; libr. Newton (Mass.) Libr., 1955; interviewer audits and surveys Elmo Roper, Boston, 1956; mem. adv. com. Sch. Com. on Spl. Edn., Lexington, Mass., 1979-80; mem. adv. bd. Cary Meml. Libr., Lexington, 1989—. Active numerous civic orgns., including mem. Town Meeting, Lexington, 1980—; mem. exec. bd. Lexington Dem. Com., 1987—; del. Mass. Dem. Convs., 1986, 88, 90; mem. exec. bd. Friends Coun. on Aging, 1986, PTA's, 1965-79; vol. Meals on Wheels, 1985—; pres. United Meth. Women, Lexington, 1973-75; bd. dirs. Meth. Weekday Sch., 1971-80; co-organizer 1st town-wide hazardous waste collection in U.S., Lexington, 1983; vol. Lexington Hist. Soc., 1978—; co-chmn. Friends of Cary Libr. Orgn., 1990—. Mem. LWV (pres. Lexington 1983-85), NOW, AAUW (Mass. long range planning com.), DAR (vice regent 1977-80, Mass. chmn. scholarships and loan com. 1980-83), Florence Crittenton League, Outlook Club (pres. 1985-87, chmn. scholarships com. 1990—), North Shore Rock and Mineral Club (Lynnfield, Mass.), Alpha Chi Omega. Home: 157 Cedar St Lexington MA 02173

GARIPPA, JOAN, management consultant; b. N.Y.C., Jan. 21, 1945; d. John and Victoria (Rotteveel) Welch; m. Thomas Garippa, May 17, 1969. BBA, Bernard M. Baruch Coll., 1983. Tchr. bus. edn. N.Y.C. Bd. Edn., 1984-85; mgmt. analyst N.Y.C., 1985-90; pres. JWG Enterprises, Little Neck, N.Y., 1989—. Founding mem. Queens Women's Ctr., 1988; v.p. Little Neck Pines Assn., 1988—; pres., exec. dir. youth porgrams Little Neck-Douglaston Community Coun., 1978-82; bd. dirs. Little Neck Community Assn., 1974-83; Borough Pres.'s Transit Adv. Bd., 1983—; dep. marshal Little Neck-Douglaston Meml. Day Parade, 1982; candidate 16th dist. N.Y.C. Coun., 1981, Community Sch. bd. 26, 1989; mem., co-chmn. transp. com. Queens Community Planning Bd. No. 11, Bayside, N.Y., 1980—; mem. Concerned Citizens for Preservation of Little Neck-Douglaston Community, 1973-78. Recipient Citizenship award, cert. of recognition, 1981, Borough Pres.'s Citation for 10 yrs. svc. on Community Planning Bd., 1989. Mem. NAFE, Am. Soc. Profl. and Exec. Women, Networking Exec. Women of Queens and Western Nassau, Nat. Assn. Women Cons. Inc., Internat. Platform Assn. Republican. Roman Catholic. Home and Office: 41-31 248 St Little Neck NY 11363

GARISON, LYNN LASSITER, real estate investor; b. El Dorado, Ark., Dec. 19, 1954; d. Robert Weaver and Iris Amy (Horton) Lassiter; m. James Wallace Garison, Jr., Dec. 11, 1982. Student, Randolph-Macon Woman's Coll., 1973-76; BS, Tex. A&M U., 1978. Lic. real estate broker, Ark., Okla., Tex. From broker assoc. to regional mgr. J. B. Goodwin, Realtors, Residential, Inc., Austin, Tex., 1979-82; comml. broker assoc. Christon Co., Realtors, Inc., Dallas, 1983-87; v.p. Dallas Mkt. Ctr., Dallas, 1987-89; regional v.p. Tenenbaum-Hill and Assocs., Inc., Dallas, 1989—; bd. dirs. North Tex. Cert. Comml. Investment Bd. Bd. dirs. Dallas Coun. World Affairs; mem. Mayor's Task Force on Child Abuse, Opportunity Dallas, Highland Pk. Presbyn. Ch. Mem. LWV, DAR, Internat. Coun. Shopping Ctrs., Nat. Assn. Corp. Real Estate, Am. Soc. Assn. Execs., Cert. Comml. Investment Mem., Urban Land Inst., Comml. Real Estate Women. Home: 4317 Greenbrier Dr Dallas TX 75225

GARITY, JOAN PATRICIA, nurse, educator; b. Quincy, Mass., Apr. 29, 1944; d. Philip Francis and Virginia (Corcoran) Garity. B.S., Boston Coll., 1966; M.Ed., Northeastern U., 1971; Ed.D., Boston U., 1985. R.N., Mass. Vol. nursing clinic Mt. St. Joseph Acad., Mandeville, Jamaica, W.I., 1966-67; staff nurse Boston City Hosp., 1967-68; staff nurse Quincy City Hosp., Mass., 1968; dir. inservice edn. Quincy City Hosp., 1968-70, staff nurse recovery room, 1970-71; staff devel. specialist, dept. nursing , Mass. Gen. Hosp., Boston, 1971—, coordinator mgmt. edn., 1980-85, coordinator of student clin. placement, staff devel. services,1985— ; cons., lectr. in field; mem. adv. bd. Regis Coll. Sch. of Nursing, Weston, 1986—. Contbr. articles to profl. jours. Co-chmn. Gov.'s Adv. Council on Continuing Edn. for Nurses, Boston, 1986-87; del. to Europe People to People, 1988. Am. Orgn. Nurse Execs. scholar Am. Nurses Found., 1984. Mem. Am. Nurses Assn., Mass. Nurses Assn. (mem. Council on Continuing Edn. 1980-81, co-chair Commn. on Continuing Edn. 1982-83, Cabinet on Continuing Edn. 1984, Nursing Practice award 1985), Boston Coll. Alumni Assn. (Excellence in Sci. award 1988), Sigma Theta Tau (pres. Alphi Chi chpt. 1988—), Pi Lambda Theta, Alpha Gamma. Democrat. Roman Catholic. Avocations: novels, museums, art, concerts, traveling. Home: 9 Tingley Rd East Braintree MA 02184 Office: Mass Gen Hosp Fruit St Boston MA 02114

GARITY, MARY MARGARET, editor, writer; b. Milw., Feb. 6, 1950; d. Robert Francis and Alice Jeanette (Rynders) G. BA, U. Wis., Milw., 1971. Assoc. editor Nat. Christmas Tree Assn., Milw., 1976-79; publs. dir. Milw. Pub. Mus., 1979-89; freelance writer, editor Milw., 1989—; cons. Carnegie Mus. Natural History, Pitts., 1984, PGI, New Berlin, Wis., 1989. Vol. coord. Friends of Channels 10/36, pub. TV, Milw., 1982—; area chmn. Channel 10/36 Auction, 1990. Recipient award of distinction Am. Assn. Mus., 1983, 87, 88, award of merit, 1984, 85. Mem. Soc. for Scholarly Pub., Mid-Am. Pubs. Assn. (membership com. 1989—). Home and Office: 8049 N Santa Monica Blvd Milwaukee WI 53217

GARLAND, LARETTA MATTHEWS, educational psychologist, nurse-educator; b. Jacksonville, Fla.; d. Wilburn L. and Clyde-Marian (Chamberlin) Matthews; diploma Fla. State Sch. Nursing, 1942; BSN, Emory U., 1950, MEd, 1953; BA in Edn., U. Fla., 1951; cert. cardiologist nurse specialty Tex. Med. Center, 1965; EdD, U. Ga., 1975; postgrad. in counseling and guidance Ga. State U., 1969, grad. cert. in gerontology, 1981; Cert. nat. counselor, 1986; m. John B. Garland, Mar. 2, 1946; children: John Barnard, Brien Freeling, Amy-Gwin. Office and staff nurse, Lakeland, Fla., 1942, 45; nurse ARC, Buffalo, 1956; asst. prof. nursing Med. Coll. Ga., 1965-67; instr. Emory U., 1952-54, assoc. prof., 1967-71, prof., 1972-86; prof. emeritus, 1987—; ednl. psychologist, dir. gerontol. nurse practitioner program, 1978-80, asst. to dean, 1983-86. Served with Nurse Corps, U.S. Army, 1942-45. Decorated Bronze Star; recipient Outstanding Teaching award Emory U. Sch. Nursing Grad. Srs., 1977, appreciation award So. Region Constituent Leagues, Nat. League for Nursing award, 1987, Mabel Korsell award of appreciation Ga. League for Nursing, 1987, Spl. Recognition award Ga. Nurses Assn., 1988, appreciation Ga. Assn. Nursing Students, 1990; HEW fellow, 1967-68. Mem. Am. Psychol. Assn., Am. Assn. Counseling and Devel., Am. Nurses Assn., Nat. League Nursing, Bus. and Profl. Women, China Burma India VA Assn., Alpha Chi Omega, Sigma Theta Tau, Kappa Delta Pi, Alpha Kappa Delta, Omicron Delta Kappa. Methodist. Author: (with Carol Bush) Coping Behavior and Nursing, 1982; editor: Gerontological Nursing Handbook, 1990; contbr. articles to profl. jours. Office: Emory U Nell Hodgson Woodruff Sch Nursing Atlanta GA 30322

GARLAND, MARGIE Y., health facility administrator; b. Louisville, May 16, 1937; d. Frank L. and Ann (Epperson) Jones; children: Stephen, Renee, Michael, Timothy. BA in Psychology, U. N. Fla., Jacksonville, 1973. Mental health assoc. U. Hosp., Jacksonville, Fla., 1974-75, biofeedback therapist, 1975-77; clinic mgr. Advanced Health Systems, S.L.C., 1977-79; dir. physician, services Health Data Network, Louisville, 1977-79; mgmt. cons. NKC Hosp., Inc., Louisville, 1988-89; exec. adminstr. N. Broward Radiologists, PA, Pompano Beach, Fla., 1990—. Author: Article Computers in Healthcare 1987. Recipient Blue Key Leadership award U. Fla., 1972. Republican. Baptist. Office: N Broward Radiologists PA Pompano Beach FL 33060

GARLIN, LINDA CLAYTON, real estate broker; b. Paragould, Ark., Aug. 15, 1937; d. Swepton Taylor and Susie (Spence) Clayton; m. James C. Bullard, Feb. 3, 1957, (div.); children: Andrew Clayton, Melinda K. Bullard Holt, James Clifton Jr.; m. Cecil R. Garlin, Dec. 28, 1973 (div. Apr. 1978). Student, U. Miss., 1955-56, 57-58, U. Mo., 1956-57. Distbg. and scheduling asst. mgr. Uniroyal Inc., Kennett, Mo., 1973-75; mgr. Bradley & Noble Abstract & Title Co., Kennett, 1975-79; realtor Dan Stewart Co., Memphis, 1979-85; realtor, broker River Oaks Realtors, Memphis, 1985—. Bd. dirs. Nat. Kidney Found. West Tenn., Memphis, 1981—, v.p. 1990; pres. Chatham Village Homeowner Assn., 1986—; mem. Evergreen Hist. Dist. Assn., 1989—; Ennead Crewe Memphis Cotton Carnival Soc., 1990. Mem. Memphis Bd. Realtors (life mem. Million Dollar Club, ednl. com.). Home: 328 N Mclean Memphis TN 38112 Office: River Oaks Realtors 1926 Exeter Memphis TN 38138

GARMAN, KAREN ANN, educational media specialist; b. Phila., June 10, 1960; d. Ralph J. and Caroline (Beltley) G. BS, LaSalle U., 1982; MEd, Temple U., 1985; postgrad., U. So. Calif., 1990—. Asst. dir. audiovisual dept. LaSalle U., Phila., 1981-82; assoc. dir. TV ctr. Hahnemann U., Phila., 1982-85; dir. edn. resources U. Medicine and Dentistry of N.J., Stratford, 1985-90; exec. dir. Tng. and Edn. Cons., Phila., 1986-90; lectr. ednl. media LaSalle U., 1986-90; film producer Tucker Sports Films, Phila., 1979-83; rsch. asst. U. So. Calif. Sch. Medicine, 1990—. Active Alice Paul Found., Inc., Mt. Laurel, N.J., 1990—. HHS grantee, 1986-89. Mem. Women in Communication (v.p. 1986-89), Communication Alumni LaSalle (chmn. external affairs 1988-90), Assn. for Ednl. Communications and Tech., AAUP, Northeast High Sch. Alumni Assn. (pres. 1989-90). Home: 981 Lehigh Dr Yardley PA 19067

GARMAN, KATHLEEN ANN, human resources manager; b. Reading, Pa., Nov. 22, 1956; d. Elmer C. and Catherine E. (Rapak) G. BS, Penn State U., 1978; MBA, Lehigh U., 1985; Cert. in Bible Studies, Lancaster Bible Coll., 1990. Personnel adminstr. Easco, Reading, Pa., 1979-83; personnel mgr. Swift & Co., Birdsboro, Pa., 1983, Camsco, Maidencreek, Pa., 1983-85; human resource mgr. Timeter Internat., Lancaster, Pa., 1986-87; employment coord. R.R. Donnelley & Sons Co., Lancaster, 1987-88; human resource mgr. Kalas Mfg., Inc., Denver, Pa., 1988—; chmn. Employers Adv. Coun., Reading, 1982-86, Lancaster, 1986-88. Emergency shelter mgr. ARC, Berks County, Pa., 1984-85, CPR instr., 1983-86, 87-88; CPR instr. Am. Heart Assn., Berks County, 1983-86; vol. CONTACT, Lancaster, 1990. Named Outstanding Co-Chairperson United Way Berks County, 1983, 84; recipient Kunkle Scholarship, 1974. Mem. Soc. for Human Resources Mgmt., Lancaster Human Resources Mgmt. Assn. (bd. dirs. 1990), Am. Soc. Tng. & Devel., Bus. & Profl. Women of Berks County (v.p. 1983-85, Young Careerist 1983), Berks County Bus. Women's Network, Pa. State Employers Adv. Coun., Lancaster C. of C. (employee rels. com. 1988—). Office: Kalas Mfg Inc 25 Main St Denver PA 17517

GARMAN, TERESA AGNES, state legislator; b. Ft. Dodge, Iowa, Aug. 29, 1937; d. John Clement and Barbara Marie (Korsa) Lennon; m. Merle A. Garman, Aug. 5, 1961; children: Laura Ann Garman Hansen, Rachel Irene, Robert Sylvester, Sarah Teresa Powers. Grad. high sch., Ft. Dodge. With employee relations dept. 3M Co., Ames, Iowa, 1974-86; mem. Iowa Ho. of Reps., Des Moines, 1986—. Del. Rep. Nat. Conv., 1988; mem. Rep. Nat. Platform Com., 1988. Mem. Am. Bus. Women's Assn., Rep. Farm Policy Council, Story County Rep. Women, Friends of Mamie Eisenhower. Roman Catholic. Clubs: Boone Women's, Story County Porkettes, Farm Bur. Home: RR 2 Ames IA 50010 Office: State Capitol Des Moines IA 50319

GARMIZE, SHARON MARIE, artist, small business owner; b. Plymouth, Pa., Feb. 12, 1950; d. Michael and Josephine (Kovalick) Berish; m. Richard M. Garmize, Apr. 4, 1970 (div. Aug. 1982). Student, Pa. State U., 1967-69. Buyer Allied Stores div. Pomeroys Inc., Wilkes Barre, Pa., 1970-75, div. sales mgr., 1975-77; pres., owner SMG Sales Corp., Wilkes Barre, 1975-82; designer, owner Sharon Garmize Needlepoint Designs, Moutaintop, Pa., 1977—; owner Designs by Sharon Garmize, 1989—. Specialist in needlework miniatures with more than 50 pub. designs, 1981—; miniatrue needlework featured in Star Mag., 1988; works displayed in group shows Monaco and London chpts. of Am. Needlepoint Guild (best of show), 1982. Selected as one of subjects in book Masters in Miniature, 12 Artists at Work, by Anne Day Smith. Fellow Internat. Guild Miniature Artisans (trustee 1981-83); mem. The Nat. Needlework Assn., Nat. Assn. Miniature Enthusiasts (Acad. of Honor 1988), Am. Crafts Council. Democrat. Roman Catholic. Home and Office: 27 Yorktown Rd Mountaintop PA 18707

GARNER, CARLENE ANN, orchestra administrator; b. Dec. 17, 1945; d. Carl A. and Ruth E. (Mathison) Timblin; m. Adelbert L. Garner, Feb. 17, 1964; children: Bruce A., Brent A. BA, U. Puget Sound, 1983. Adminstrv. dir. Balletacoma, 1984-87; exec. dir. Tacoma Symphony, 1987—; cons. Wash. PAVE, Tacoma, 1983-84. Pres. Wilson High Sch. PTA, Tacoma, 1983-85; chmn. Tacoma Sch. Vol. Adv. Bd., 1985-87; pres. Emmanuel Luth. Ch., Tacoma, 1984-86; sec.-treas. Tacoma-Narrows Conf., 1987-89. Mem. Northwest Devel. Officers Assn., Am. Symphony Orch. League, Jr. Women's Club Tacoma (pres. 1975-76), Wash. State Fedn. Women's Clubs (pres. Peninsula Dist. 1984-86, treas. 1988—, Clubwoman of Yr. 1977, Outstanding FREE chmn. Gen. Fedn.). Lutheran. Home: 1115 N Cheyenne Tacoma WA 98406 Office: Tacoma Symphony PO Box 19 Tacoma WA 98401

GARNER, DOROTHY ANN, paper industry executive; b. Sparta, Wis., Feb. 12, 1959; d. Arden A. and Dorothy W. (Shepard) G. BS in Paper Sci., U. Wis., Stevens Point, 1981. From process engr. to supr. prodn. systems Internat. Paper Co., Mobile, Ala., 1981-89, supr. planning and customer svc., 1989—. Mem. NAFE, Tech. Assn. of Pulp and Paper Industry, Beta Sigma Phi (pres. Omicron chpt. 1988, Woman of Yr. 1987). Home: 7105 Deer Run E Pine Bluff AR 71603

GARNER, JO ANN STARKEY, educator; b. Ft. Hamilton, N.Y., Dec. 25, 1934; d. Joseph Wheeler and Irene Dorothy (Vogt) Starkey; m. James Gayle Garner, Mar. 2, 1957; children: Mary Vivian Pine, Margaret Susan Gillis, Kathryn Lynn. BA in History, Govt., Law, U. Tex., Austin, 1956; postgrad., Trinity U., 1973. Cert. deaf edn. and elem. tchr., Tex. Kindergarten tchr. Platenstrasse Internat. Sch., Frankfurt, Fed. Republic Germany, 1964-66; tchr. of deaf Sunshine Cottage Sch. for Deaf, San Antonio, 1966—; speech cons. Trinity U., 1978, cooperating tchr., 1978-87. Mem. Tex. Alexander Graham Bell Assn. (charter), San Antonio Geneal. and Hist. Soc., The Bright Shawl, Rep. Nat. Com., Sunshine Sch. for Deaf (supporting mem.), German-Texan Heritage Soc., Alpha Delta Pi, Pioneers of Ill., Ill. Geneal. Soc., Tex. State Geneal. and Hist. Soc. Republican. Roman Catholic. Home: 2027 Edgehill Dr San Antonio TX 78209 Office: Sunshine Cottage Sch for Deaf 103 Tuleta San Antonio TX 78209

GARNER, MARY JANE, cosmetics company executive; b. Terre Haute, Ind., Oct. 6, 1916; d. Thomas Law and Myra (Short) Kemp; m. William Stanley Garner, Jan. 11, 1941 (div. Nov. 1965); 1 child, William Stanley. Student Lindenwood Coll. for Women, 1935, John Heron Art Sch., 1936-38; grad. Parsons Sch. Design, 1940, Planning for Preservation Inst. of Govt., U. N.C., 1972; student writers workshop Ind. U., 1967. Model made-to-order dept. Bergdorff Goodman, N.Y.C., 1940-41; asst. buyer Crystal Room, Indpls., 1965-66; proof cons. fact Inc., St. Louis, 1968-69; pres., founder Mary Jane Garner Cosmetics, Chapel Hill, N.C., 1985—. Sec. Chapel Hill Hist. Soc., 1973-74, bd. dirs., 1973-75; mem. N.C. Bicentennial Com., 1974-78, also mem. grants com.; mem. Chapel Hill Bicentenial Commn., 1974-76; Republican precinct chmn., Chapel Hill, 1972; co-chmn. Holshouser for Gov., Orange County, N.C., 1972; Rep. precinct registrar, Chapel Hill, 1973-75; pres. Rep. Women's Club, Chapel Hill, 1973-74; chmn. state conv. N.C. Fedn. Rep. Women, 1974, Bicentennial chmn., 1974-76, legis. chmn., 1976-77, area v.p., 1978-80, pub. relations chmn., 1981-83, mem. credentials com. for nat. conv., 1980; mem. U.S. Senate Minority Leader's Citizens Adv. Com., 1974-76; mem. nat. adv. bd. Am. Security Council, 1978-79; mem. bldg. com. N.C. Rep. Hdqrs., 1978; mem. Nat. Presdl. Adv. Commn., 1989—. Recipient cert. appreciation Am. Revolution Bicentenial, 1976, Spl. Recognition award Am. Security Council, 1979, Presdl. Achievement award Pres. Reagan, 1982; named most improved golfer Golf Digest Mag., 1978. Club: Chapel Hill Country (bd. govs. 1975-76). Office: Mary Jane Garner Cosmetics 100 Howell Ln Chapel Hill NC 27514

GARNER, OLLIE BELLE, contracting company executive; b. Waynesburg, Ky., Feb. 6, 1928; d. Rufus D. and Nettie B. (Hubble) Stonecypher; Rogers Bus. Coll., Somerset, Ky., 1947; m. Leo M. Garner, May 26, 1947. Sec., Pulaski County (Ky.) Extension Office, Somerset, 1948-50; bookkeeper W.C. Brass & Assos., Indpls., 1951-62; sec., bookkeeper Acme Constrn. Co., Indpls., 1963-65; sec., v.p., dir., co-owner J & O Contractors, Inc., Indpls., 1965—. Mem. Early Am. Soc., Marion County Art League, Nat. Assn. Women Bus. Owners, Network of Women in Bus., Nat. Assn. Women in Constrn., Internat. Platform Assn., Indpls. Mus. Art, YWCA. Club: Economic. Home: 7515 W Mooresville Rd Camby IN 46113 Office: 3906 W Washington St Indianapolis IN 46241

GARNETT, CARLA RENÉE, staff writer; b. Washington; d. Marvin Frederick and Carolyn Virginia (Clarke) G. AAS, Fashion Inst. Tech., 1985, BS, 1987; postgrad., Am. U. Pub. affairs specialist clin. ctr. communications NIH, Bethesda, Md., 1987-88, staff writer Record, 1988—. Contbr. Kiskeya mag., NIHAA Update. Writer Mt. Carmel Newsletter, Washington; mem. Young Disciples for Christ Fellowship, Washington; v.p. intermediate usher bd. Mt. Carmel Bapt. Ch., Washington, 1989-90. U.S. Govt. fellow, 1983-87; Versie Epps scholar, 1984. Mem. NAFE. Office: NIH Record 9000 Rockville Pike Bethesda MD 20892

GAROFALO, DENISE ANNE, librarian, automation consultant; b. Norwich, N.Y., July 26, 1959; d. John Andrew and Irene Anne (Boucher) Listovitch; m. James Anthony Garofalo, Aug. 29, 1987. BA, SUNY, Albany, 1980, MLS, 1982. Libr. Pawtucket (R.I.) Pub. Libr., 1982-85; head tech. svcs. and automated systems Warwick (R.I.) Pub. Libr., 1985-87; automation cons. N.H. State Libr., Concord, 1987-89; automated systems mgr. Mid-Hudson Libr. System, Poughkeepsie, N.Y., 1989—. Reviewer Library Jour., 1983—, Library Resources and Technical Services mag., 1989—. Mem. com. Milford Town Hall renovation, 1988-89, auditorium renovation, 1988-89. Mem. ALA, NAFE, AAUW, Nat. Trust for Hist. Preservation, N.Y. Libr. Assn., Nat. Audobon Soc. Democrat. Roman Catholic. Office: Mid-Hudson Libr System 103 Market St Poughkeepsie NY 12601

GAROFALO, RENEE J., optometrist; b. Chgo., Feb. 18, 1957; d. Gasper G. and Josephine (Miserendino) G. Student, Ill. State U., 1975-78; BS in Biology, Loyola U., Chgo., 1981; BS in Visual Sci., Ill. Coll. Optometry, 1983, OD, 1985. Contact lens fellow U. Houston Coll. Optometry, 1985-86; rsch. optometrist Wesley-Jessen Corp., Chgo., 1989—, clin. optometrist, 1988-89; pvt. practice Countryside, Ill., 1986-88; vol. Vol. Optometric Svc. to Humanity, Colombia, Chile, Paraguay, 1985—. Roman Catholic. Office: Wesley Jessen Corp 400 W Superior St Chicago IL 60610

GARONZIK, SARA E., stage director; b. Phila., Jan. 12, 1951; d. Milton and Bernice (Kohn) G. BA in Spanish cum laude, Temple U., 1972. Artistic dir. The Phila. Theatre Co., 1980—. Bd. dirs. Greater Phila. Cultural Alliance. Recipient prize Sigma Delta Pi, 1972. Office: Phila Theatre Co 21 S 5th St Bourse Bldg Ste 735 Philadelphia PA 19106

GAROUFALIS, MARIA ELAINE, auditor; b. Chgo., Jan. 9, 1957; d. Byron L. and Irene (Mathews) G. BS, Manchester Coll., 1979. CPA, Ill. Sr. audit mgr. Ernst & Young, Chgo., 1979—. V.p. St. Nectarios Greek Orthodox Ch. Ladies' Soc., Palatine, Ill., 1987-88, pres., 1989—. Mem. Ill. CPA Soc., Chgo. Soc. Women CPA's, Nat. Assn. Female Execs., Manchester Coll. Acctg. Alumni Assn., Greek Women's Univ. Club Chgo. Office: Ernst & Young 1 IBM Pla 330 N Wabash Av Chicago IL 60611

GARR, TERI, actress; b. Lakewood, Ohio, 1952. Appeared in films including: The Conversation, 1974, Young Frankenstein, 1974, Won Ton Ton, The Dog Who Saved Hollywood, 1976, Oh God!, 1977, Close Encounters of the Third Kind, 1977, Mr. Mike's Mondo Video, 1979, The Black Stallion, 1979, Tootsie, 1982, One From the Heart, 1982, The Sting II, 1983, The Black Stallion Returns, 1983, Mr. Mom, 1983, Firstborn, 1984, After Hours, 1985, Miracles, 1986, Out Cold, 1989, Let It Ride, 1989, Short Time, 1990, Waiting for the Light, 1990; TV movies include Doctor Franken, 1980, Prime Suspect, 1982, The Winter of Our Discontent, 1983, To Catch a King, 1984, Intimate Strangers, 1986, Pack of Lies, 1987, Teri Garr in FlapJack Floozie, 1988; regular on TV series The Sonny and Cher Comedy Review, 1974; other TV appearances include Law and Order, 1976, Fresno. Office: care Bill Treusch Assocs 853 7th Ave Apt 9A New York NY 10019*

GARRELS, HELEN ANN, horse breeder; b. El Paso, Tex., Apr. 4, 1940; d. John James and Georgia Allen (Green) Holman; m. James John Morrissey, June 29, 1958 (div. 1982); children: James John III, David Wayne, Steve Ray, Scot Allen; 1 foster child, Gordon Anderson; m. Wilbur Dean Garrels, Apr. 17, 1982; stepchildren: Lauri Smith, Jo Ann Williams, Barbara Helenschmidt. Student, U. Tex., El Paso, 1965; student, Midwestern U., 1975-76. Clk. El Paso Police Dept., 1959-60; long distance operator Mountain States Telephone, El Paso, 1960-64; all lines liability rater Echling Irving & Crowe Ins., El Paso, 1964-70; owner Helen House of Dog Grooming, El Paso, Graham, Tex., 1960—; pvt. health care Mimi Bohner Bohner Oil Co., Burkbirnett, Tex., 1975-76; bank guard Wichita Nat. Bank, Wichita Falls, Tex., 1976-81; owner show Arabians Unicorn Valley Ranch, Graham, 1981—; owner Helen's House of Dog Grooming, Graham, Indian Trail, N.C., 1990; counselor battered women and children, rape victims, durg and alcohol abuse First Step, Wichita Falls, Graham, 1975-88. Pro-life marcher, Concord, N.C., 1990; mem. CWA Union-Griever, El Paso, 1960-64; active various charitable orgns.; donator horses for Halloween and Christmas parades, Graham, Tex., 1988, 89 and to Hemby Bridge Sch., Indian Trail, N.C. to raise money for libr. books, 1989; cand. U.S. rep. 8th Congl. Dist. N.C., 1990—. Democrat. Presbyterian. Office: Helen Garrels Campaign Com PO Box 2256 Matthews NC 76105

GARRET, PAULA LYN, publishing company executive; b. N.Y.C., Oct. 17, 1951; d. Norman and Sandra (Gilden); m. James T. Ferrise, Sept. 13, 1987. BS in Communications summa cum laude, Boston U., 1973; MBA, Case Western Reserve U., 1982. Dir. print media Stern/Frank Advt., Boston, 1973-76; dir. advt. Am. Soc. Assn. Execs., Washington, 1976-80; mktg. cons. PG & Assocs., Cleve., 1980-82; assoc. dir. advt. Calif. State Bar Assn., San Francisco, 1982-83; dir. mktg. and advt. Cars & Parts mag. div. Amos Press, Sidney, Ohio, 1983-84, dir. mktg. sales, 1984-87; v.p., pub. Amos Press, Inc., Sidney, 1987—. Co-author: (monograph) Effective Business to Business Advertising, 1982. Mem. Am. Mktg. Assn., Direct Mail Mktg. Assn., Am. Mgmt. Assn. Office: Amos Press 911 Vandemark Rd Sidney OH 45365

GARRETT, GLENDA DARLENE, distribution company executive; b. Mpls., Mar. 1, 1963; d. Floyd Ralph and Gretchen Marie (Rosch) G. BS, Corpus Christi State U., 1987. Cert. tchr., Tex. Vet. asst. Flour Buff Animal Hosp., Corpus Christi, Tex., 1979-82; sales rep. Corpus Christi Athletic Club, 1985-88, We Care Distbn. Inc., Corpus Christi, 1987—; sci. tchr. Rockport High Sch., 1988—; choreography cons. Pat Magee Models, Corpus Christi, 1987—. Asst. Gulf Coast Humane Soc., Corpus Christi, 1980-83. Named Miss Flour Bluff, Flour Bluff Assn., 1981, Miss Port Aransas, Port Aransas/Deep Sea Roundup, 1982, Miss Nueces County, 1982, Miss Dallas/Corpus Christi, 1986. Mem. NAFE, Am. Fedn. Tchrs., Pre-Profl. Soc. (Corpus Christi). Republican. Methodist. Home: 6230 Whitaker Corpus Christi TX 78412

GARRETT, GLORIA SUSAN, social services professional; b. Tampa, Fla., Nov. 30, 1951; d. Howard Leon and Marie Leonora (Garcia) G.; m. Michael Thomas McClain, May 16, 1973; children: Molly Kathleen Garrett McClain, Andrew Michael Garrett McClain. Student, Agnes Scott Coll., 1969-71, U. South Fla., 1971-72; BA, Ga. State U., 1977, MEd, 1979. Sr. caseworker DeKalb County Dept. Family and Children Services, Decatur, Ga., 1979-80, 82-84, prin. caseworker, 1980-82, 84-85, casework supr., 1985-86; sr. casework supr. Decatur, Ga., 1986—. Mem. Am. Pub. Welfare Assn., Ga. County Welfare Assn. Office: DeKalb County Dept Family and Children Svcs 178 Sams St Decatur GA 30030

GARRETT, HELEN MARIE, state senator; b. Paducah, Ky.; d. John Frank and Helen Eunice (Bean) Rickman; m. John Thomas Garrett, 1952 (dec.); children—Tom, Carol. Mem. Ky. Senate, majority whip. Democrat. Office: Ky Senate State Frankfort KY 40601

GARRETT, LAUREL A., management consultant; b. Waukegan, Ill., May 12, 1960; d. Richard W. and Eleanor A. (Schley) Augustine. Student, DeVry Inst., Chgo., Oakton Community Coll., Park Ridge, Ill. Sr. claim examiner Bankers Life Ins. Co., Lombard, Ill., 1978-81; mgr. MICA, Inc., Chgo., 1984-89; project. mgr., cons. R.N. Swanson and Assocs., Inc., Deerfield, Ill.; sole propr. Laurel Garrett Enterprises, Chgo., 1989—. Mem. NAFE, Nat. Assn. for Self Employed, Am. Mgmt. Assn. Office: 117 W Harrison Bldg Ste L-244 Chicago IL 60605

GARRETT, MELISSA JO, educator; b. Sewickley, Pa., Mar. 2, 1956; m. Allen McCain Garrett, Jr., June 23, 1977; children: Allayna McCain Garrett, Mitchell Joseph Garrett. BS in Therapeutic Recreation, Temple U., 1976; Elem. Cert., U. Pitts., 1986; MEd, Slippery Rock (Pa.) U., 1988. Cert. elem. edn., reading specialist. Ins. broker, recreation instr., tutor Phila., 1976-79; kindergarten tchr. Pitts., 1985-86; remedial reading and math. coord. Monaca (Pa.) Sch. Dist., 1986-88; tutor, instr. Youngstown (Ohio) State U., 1988-89; instr. in reading and study skills Slippery Rock U., 1989—; cons. Adult Literacy Action, Beaver County, Pa., 1988—. Councilman Patterson Heights (Pa.) Borough, 1987—, chmn. recreation, chmn. shade trees com.; commr. Blackhawk Little Cougars Football, Beaver Falls, Pa., 1989—; bd. dirs. Patterson Recreation and Blackhawk Recreation, Beaver Falls. Mem. AAUW (chmn. 1988-89), Keystone State Reading Assn., Leotta Hawthorne Reading Assn. (com. chmn. 1987-89), Internat. Reading Assn. Republican. Baptist. Home: 504 Fourth Ave Patterson Heights Beaver Falls PA 15010-3212

GARRETT, NANCY ROBERTS, editor; b. Terre Haute, Ind., Dec. 5, 1954; d. Jack Richford and Anne Marie (Dennison) Roberts; m. William H. Garrett Jr., Jan. 2, 1978 (div. Sept. 1986). BS in Journalism cum laude, Ind. State U., 1977. Sports reporter Terre Haute Tribune-Star, 1975-76; sports reporter Paris (Ill.) Daily Beacon-News, 1977-80, reporter, photographer, 1981-85, mng. editor, 1985—; editor Marshall (Ill.) Independent, 1980-81; corr. Sta. WTWO-TV, Terre Haute, 1978—; media adviser State Sen. Harry Woodyard, Chrisman, Ill., 1983-89; advt. cons. Rep. William Black, Danville, Ill., 1986-88. Author, editor Series Clark County Park Dist., 1980-81 (2d pl. award Ill. Press Assn.). Deacon Paris Presbyn. Ch., 1982, elder, 1985—; commr. to gen. assy. United Presbyn. Ch., 1990—; mgr. Paris Youth Ctr., 1981-86; pres. Edgar County Young Rep., Paris, 1987—; dir. Community Concert Assn.; cheer coordinator Mayo Middle Sch., 1987-88; drama dir. Paris High Sch., 1987—, cheerleading coordiantor, 1989—. Mem. Assn. Soc. Profl. Journalists, Sigma Delta Chi. Presbyterian. Home: 416 N Jefferson Paris IL 61944 Office: Paris Daily Beacon-News North Main St Paris IL 61944

GARRETT, RUBY GRANT, graphic designer, nurse; b. Covington, Ga., May 13, 1941; d. Robert Lee and Lola (Price) Grant; m. William Harold Garrett, Aug. 18, 1961. Cert. Nursing, Carver Vocat. Edn. Inst., 1960; BFA, Atlanta Coll. Art, 1971; postgrad., Ga. State U., 1971-72. Designer Eric Hill & Assocs., Inc., Atlanta, 1971-72; pres., owner G. Designs, Inc., Atlanta, 1972-79, Garrett Communications, Atlanta, 1979—. Mem. Nat. Assn. Market Developers (com. chair programs 1987-88, pres. Atlanta chpt. 1982-83), Atlanta Bus. League (bd. dirs. 1983-87), Black Women Entrepreneurs (com. chairperson 1982-88), Black Women's Internat. Coun., Nat. Assn. Media Women. Office: Garrett Communications PO Box 53 Atlanta GA 30301

GARRETT, RUBY JOYCE BURRISS, lawyer, educator; b. Greenville, N.C., Apr. 1, 1946. BS in Zoology with honors, U. Tenn., 19685; PhD in Physiology and Biophysics, U. Ky., 1971; JD with honors, U. N.C., 1981. Instr. dept. materia medica Coll. Pharmacy U. Ky., Lexington, 1971-72, asst. prof. div. pharmacodynamics and toxicology, 1973-77, assoc. prof. div. pharmacodynamics and toxicology, 1977-79; cons., clk. OSHA rev. bd. N.C. Dept. Labor, Raleigh, 1981-83; assoc. Vernon, Vernon, Wooten, Brown and Andrews, P.A., Lexington and Burlington, N.C., 1982-86, ptnr., 1987—; adminstrv. law judge occupational safety and health Vernon, Vernon, Wooten, Brown and Andrews, P.A., Lexington and Burlington, 1984—; vis. investigator membranes lab. N.Y. Blood Ctr., N.Y.C., 1973, 74. Note and comment editor: U. N.C. Law Rev., 1981-82; contbr. numerous articles to profl. jours. Mem. ABA, N.C. Bar Assn., Alamance County Bar Assn., S.C. Dental Assn. (hon.), Am. Soc. for Pharmacology and Exptl. Therapeutics, Rho Chi Nat. Pharmacy (hon.), Order of Coif. Home: 407 James St Carrboro NC 27510 Office: Vernon Vernon Wooten Brown & Andrews 522 S Lexington Ave PO Box 2348 Burlington NC 27216-2348

GARRETT, SHIRLEY GENE, nuclear medicine technologist; b. Evanston, Ill., Apr. 19, 1944; d. Nathan and Emma Louise (Uecker) G. AA, Oakton Community Coll., 1977; AS in Nuclear Medicine, Triton Coll., 1980; BA, Northeastern Ill. U., 1983; MA, Gov.'s State U., University Park, Ill., 1985. Cert. nuclear medicine technologist. Technologist nuclear medicine Chgo. Osteopathic Hosp., 1980-88, Little County of Mary Hosp., Evergreen Park, Ill., 1989, Luthern Gen. Hosp., Lincoln Park, Ill., 1989, Mt. Siani Hosp.,

Chgo., 1990—. Contbr. articles to profl. jours. Vol. Ravenswood Hosp., Chgo., 1986—, Mt. Sinai Hosp., 1990—. Mem. Soc. Nuclear Medicine (technologist sect., cen. chpt. bylaws com. 1982-83, 85-86, continuing edn. com. 1986-87, chmn. nominating com. 1987-88, chmn. edn. com. 1988-89, pres.-elect 1989-90), Assoc. and Tech. Affiliates Chgo. Area (edn. coord. 1981-84, adv. bd. 1983-84, 87-88, pres. 1985-87, chmn. nominating com. 1987-89). Lutheran. Office: Mt Sinai Hosp 1500 S California Chicago IL 60608

GARRICK, LAURA MORRIS, biochemistry educator; b. Chgo., Sept. 8, 1945; d. Owen John and Lillian Helena (Shannon) Morris; m. Michael David Garrick, May 26, 1970; 1 child, Amy Robyn. BS, Marquette U., 1967; PhD, U. Va., 1972. Rsch. asst. instr. dept. medicine SUNY, Buffalo, 1972-76, rsch. instr., 1976-79, rsch. asst. prof., 1979—, rsch. assoc. dept. biochemistry, 1978-86, clin. asst. prof., 1986—; rsch. fellow Harvard U. Med. Sch., Boston, 1977-78. Contbr. articles to sci. jours.; patentee method for reticulocyte evaluation by RNA detection. Grantee NIH, 1983—, Cooley's Anemia Found., 1985-86, 87-88, NSF, 1987—. Mem. AAAS, Am. Chem. Soc., Am. Soc. for Hematology, Genetics Soc. Am., Sigma Xi. Office: SUNY Dept Biochemistry Cary 25 Buffalo NY 14214

GARRIGA, ERISBELIA, business education educator, administrator; b. Aguadilla, P.R., Apr. 28, 1947; came to U.S., 1973; d. Jose Manuel and Eufemia (Illas) G.; m. Manuel A. Ramos, Dec. 18, 1976. BA, U. P.R., 1969; MA, NYU, 1971, PhD, 1988; advanced profl. diploma, Bklyn. Coll., 1989. Lic. bus. edn. and Spanish tchr., N.Y. Bus. edn. tchr. E.M. de Hostos High Sch., Mayaguez, P.R., 1969-73; secretarial scis. instr. U. P.R., Mayaguez, 1970-73, Aguadilla, 1976-77; rsch. asst. Hostos Community Coll. CUNY, Bronx, 1974-80; instr. LaGuardia Community Coll. CUNY, Long Island City, 1980-82; dir. tng. Woodhull Med. & Mental Health Ctr., Bklyn., 1982—. Mem. Nat. Bus. Edn. Assn., Assn. Supervision and Curriculum Devel., Comisión Acreditadora de Instituciones Educativas, Alpha chpt. Delta Pi Epsilon. Home: 70 Midwood St Brooklyn NY 11225 Office: Woodhull Med & Mental Health Ctr 760 Broadway Brooklyn NY 11206

GARRIS, EMILIE ROSS, psychologist, consultant; b. Rocky Mount, N.C., June 20, 1947; d. John Marshall and Wilma Little (Ross) G.; children: Robert Bruce Sharer, Jr., Marshall Lee Sharer. Student, U. N.C., Greensboro, 1965-67; BA in Edn., N.C. Wesleyan Coll., 1969; PhD in Psychology, U. N.C., 1982. Lic. psychologist. Rsch. assoc. U. N.C. Sch. Medicine, Chapel Hill, 1978-80; rsch. asst. NIMH, Rockville, Md., 1980; doctoral intern Towson (Md.) State U. Counseling Ctr., 1980-81; instr. U. Balt., 1982; coord. GUIDE-D.C. Drug Abuse Program, Washington, 1982-83; rsch. psychologist intelligence div. U.S. Secret Svc., Washington, 1983-85; psychologist Halen Group, Greensbeth, Md., 1985—, Comprehensive Counseling Ctrs., Columbia, Md., 1985—. Contbr. articles to profl. jours. Mem. Human Rels. Commn., Rocky Mount, 1974-76. Named Women of Yr. Washington Woman Mag., 1985. Mem. Am. Psychol. Assn., Nat. Register of Health Svc. Providers in Psychology, Law Enforcement Behavioral Scis. Assn., Md. Psychol. Assn., Balt. Psychol. Assn., Fedn. Practicing Jujitsuans, Phi Delta Kappa. Office: Comprehensive Cnslng Ctrs 10705 Charter Dr Ste 340 Columbia MD 21044

GARRISON, ALTHEA, health center executive, civic worker, former goverment official; b. Hahira, Ga., Oct. 7, 1940; d. Charles and Lenora Mae (Davis) G. AS, Newbury Jr. Coll., 1978; BS, Suffolk U., 1982; cert. in social studies, Harvard U., 1986; MS, Lesley Coll., 1984. Counselor, supr. Charlotte House Dorchester (Mass.), 1977-77; with EDP dept., sr. assessor Mass. Dept. Revenue, Boston, 1979-81; sr. examiner Office State Compt., Boston, 1982-90; bd. dirs. Uphams Corner Health Ctr., Dorchester, 1983—, v.p., 1987—. Charter mem. adv. bd. Cristian Record Braille, Lincoln, Neb., 1983; mem. alumna coun. Lesley Coll. Grad. Sch., Cambridge, Mass., 1986-88; mem. Nat. Rep. Congl. Com., 1988—; life mem. Rep. Presdl. Task Force, 1989—; charter founder Ronald Reagan Rep. Ctr., Washington, 1989; nominee city coun. Dorchester, 1989. Recipient Senator's citation Commonwealth of Mass., 1982, medal of merit Rep. Task Force, 1989; hon. fellow John F. Kennedy Libr., 1987-90. Mem. Am. Mgmt. Assn., Nat. Assn. Govt. Employees (negotiator, organizer 1979-81), Suffolk U. Gen. Alumni Assn. (bd. dirs. 1986-89), Heritage Found., Nat. Found. Cancer Rsch. (hon.), DAV Comdrs. Roman Catholic. Home: 18 Jerome St Apt 2 Dorchester MA 02125 Office: Uphams Corner Health Ctr 500 Columbia Rd Dorchester MA 02125

GARRISON, ANN JARDINE, economist, assistant professor; b. Colorado Spring, Colo., June 15, 1938; d. Douglas Connell and Lillian (Marshall) Jardine; m. A.D. Garrison, Sept. 8, 1956. BA, U. No. Colo., 1965, MA, 1967. Asst. prof. econs. U. No. Colo., Greeley, Colo., 1967—; cons. in field. Bd. dirs. Weld County United Way, Greeley, 1985—; mem. Weld County Planning Commn., 1985—. Grantee Greeley/Weld Econ. Action Ptnrship., 1989, grantee U. No. Colo. Rsch. Corp., 1989, grantee U. No. Colo. Found., 1989. Mem. Colo. Women's Studies Assn. (treas. 1985—), Western Econ. Assn., Am. Planning Assn. (Colo. chpt.). Democrat. Home: 23736 Weld County Rd 58 Greeley CO 80631

GARRISON, BETTY BERNHARDT, mathematics educator; b. Danbury, Ohio, July 1, 1932; d. Philip Arthur and Reva Esther (Meter) Bernhardt; m. Robert Edward Kvarda, Sept. 28, 1957 (div. 1964); m. John Dresser Garrison, Jan. 17, 1968; 1 child, John Christopher. BA, BS, Bowling Green State U., 1954; MA, Ohio State U., 1956; PhD, Oreg. State U., 1962. Teaching asst. Ohio State U., Columbus, 1954-56; instr. Ohio U., Athens, 1956-57, San Diego State Coll., 1957-59; teaching asst. Oreg. State U., Corvallis, 1959-62; asst. prof. San Diego State U., 1962-66, assoc. prof., 1966-69, prof., 1969—. Reviewer of articles and books, 1966—. NSF fellow, 1960-61, 61-62. Mem. Am. Math. Soc., Math. Assn. Am. Home: 5607 Yerba Anita Dr San Diego CA 92115 Office: San Diego State U Math Dept San Diego CA 92182

GARRISON, BRENDA JOYCE, travel agency owner; b. New Britain, Conn., Feb. 4, 1943; d. James and Justina (Fernandez) Tella; m. Wayne Garrison, Nov. 1, 1975. Student, Hartford Airline Personnel Sch., 1961-62, U. Conn., 1966, Tunxis community Coll., 1975. Supr. Allstate Ins., West Hartford, Conn., 1962-63; ins. cons. W.L. Hatch Co., New Britain, 1963-64; sales rep. Am. Mut. Ins. co., Wethersfield, Conn., 1964-69; asst. sec. Hartford (Conn.) Ins. Group, 1969-85; exec. v.p. Uniglobe Passport Travel Inc., Windsor, Conn., 1985—, also bd. dirs. Mem. Assn. Entrepreneurial Women, Windsor C. of C., Conn. Animal Welfare League. Roman Catholic. Office: Uniglobe Passport Travel 200 High St Windsor CT 06095

GARRISON, CAROLE GOZANSKY, academic administrator; b. Chgo., Oct. 18, 1942; d. William and Gertrude (Epstien) Gozansky; children: Debralin Garrison Hughes, Samantha. BA, U. Miami, Coral Gables, Fla., 1963; MPA, Ga. State U., 1977; PhD, Ohio State U., 1979. Cert. police officer. Instr. Miami (Fla.) Dade Jr. Coll., 1969-72, Miami (Fla.) Dade Detention Ctr., 1973; police officer Atlanta Bur. of Police Svcs., 1973-77; asst. prof. Kean Coll., Union, N.J.; assoc. prof. U. Akron, Ohio, 1981—; exec. bd. Ohio Council of C J Edn., 1985--, exec. counselor Div. of Women and Crime, 1987--, dir. Women's Studies, Akron, 1986--, assoc. dir. Project for the Study of Gender and Edn., Kent, Ohio, 1988--. Contbr. articles to prof. jours. Pres. Women's History Project Inc., Summit County, 1983; pres. Rape Crisis Ctr. Adv. Bd., Akron, 1985-87; bd. mem. We. Reserve Girl Scouts, Summit County, 1986-88, YMCA, Akron, 1989. Mem. North Cen. Women's Studies Assn. (coord.), Nat. Women's Studies Assn., Am. Soc. Criminologist. Democrat. Jewish. Office: U Akron Spicer Hall 120 Akron OH 44325

GARRISON, JANE GAYLE, astrologer; b. Texarkana, Ark., Dec. 8, 1951; d. Joseph Fletcher and Betty Jane (George) G. Student, Southwestern U. at Memphis, 1970-72; BA, U. Ark., Little Rock, 1984. Instr. yoga Chapel Hill (N.C.) Dept. Recreation, 1975-76, Chapel Hill YMCA, 1976-77, U. Ark., 1983-84; pvt. instr. yoga, Chapel Hill, Little Rock, 1976-86; astrological counselor, Little Rock and Raleigh, N.C., 1979—; lectr. astrological groups. Contbr. articles to astrological publs. Mem. Nat. Coun. for Geocosmic Rsch., Am. Fedn. Astrologers, NAFE, Mensa (editor, pub. Cosmic Cycles newsletter quar. 1987—), Phi Kappa Phi. Mem. Unity Ch. of Practical Christianity. Home and Office: 159 Winners' Circle Cary NC 27511

GARRISON, WANDA BROWN, paper manufacturing company employee; b. Madison County, N.C., Sept. 16, 1936; d. Roy Lee Brown and Zella Arizona (Miller) Brown Hannah; m. Charles Mitchell Garrison, July 9, 1955; children—Roy Lee, Marsha Joan; 1 step-son, Charles Mitchell, Jr. Student air-line hostess Weaver Airlines, St. Louis, 1954-55; student Haywood Tech. Coll., Clyde, N.C., 1967-68; student IBM, Asheville, N.C., 1977; student in data processing Agy. Record Control, Atlanta, 1978. Operator Day Co., Waynesville, N.C., 1954-57; driver Haywood County Schs., Waynesville, 1970-71; operator Am. Enka, N.C., 1972-75; bookkeeper L. N. Davis Ins. Co., Waynesville, 1975-80; stock preparation Champion Internat., Canton, N.C., 1980—; cons. Garrison and Assocs. Environ. Solutions, Robertsdale, Ala. Sec./treas. James Chapel Baptist Ch., Haywood County, N.C., 1965-77; pres. Fire Dept. Aux., Crabtree, N.C., 1973—; pres. Women Mission Union, Crabtree Bapt. Ch., Haywood County, 1977-80; v.p. Gideon Aux., Haywood County, 1982-84, pres., 1984-87; state aux. follow-up rep., 1984-87, state zone leader, 1987-88. Recipient Life Saving plaque Lion's Club, Waynesville, 1972. Mem. AFL-CIO. Democrat. Home: Hwy 209 Rt 1 Box 230A Clyde NC 28721

GARROTT, IDAMAE T., state legislator; b. Washington, Dec. 24, 1916; married; 2 children. AB, Western Md. Coll., 1936, LLD (hon.). Mem. Md. Ho. of Dels., 1979-87, mem. ways and means com., joint com. on energy; mem. Md. State Senate, 1987—, econ. and environ. affairs com., joint com. on fed. rels. Author: Paying Our Way, Maryland State Taxes and You, 1958. Mem. Montgomery County Coun., 1966-74, chmn. planning com., 1970-74, pres., 1971; bd. dirs. Washington Met. Area Transit Authority, 1972-74; bd. dirs. Washington Suburban Transit Commn., 1971-74, chmn., 1972; bd. dirs. Met. Washington Coun. Govts., pres., 1974, chmn. land use com., 1969-74; bd. dirs. Solid Waste Mgmt. Agy. Met. Washington, 1969-74; pres. Montgomery County Humane Soc., 1976-77; bd. dirs. Wheaton Rescue Squad, 1982-84. Recipient John Dewey award, 1982, Humanitarian award Montgomery County Humane Soc., 1983, Cert. of Appreciation Montgomery County Edn. Assn., 1984, Horn Book award, 1985, Thomas B. Cook award, 1987, Md. Assn. of Deaf award, 1987. Office: Md State Senate Annapolis MD 21401

GARSIDE, MARLENE ELIZABETH, advertising executive; b. Newark, Dec. 1, 1933; d. Abraham and Shirley (Janow) Carnow; B.S. in Commerce and Fin., Bucknell U., 1955; m. Stanley Kramer, Aug. 7, 1955 (dec. 1967); children: Deborah Frances, Elizabeth Anne; m. Martin Lutman, Aug. 27, 1969 (dec. 1981); m. Michael J. Weinstein, Apr. 9, 1983 (dec. 1984); m. Normand Garside, Apr. 5, 1986. Asst. rsch. dir. Modern Materials Handling Co., Boston, 1955-57; econ. analyst, project adminstr. United Rsch. Co., Cambridge, Mass., 1957-58; free lance tech. writer, econ. analyst, 1958-66; asst. mgr. survey planning and market rsch. IBM, White Plains, N.Y., 1967-69; mgr. rsch. svcs. McKinsey & Co., Cleve., 1969-72; former v.p., dir. Am. Custom Homes, former dir. Liberty Builders, Inc., Cleve.; owner, v.p., dir. Am. Custom Builders Inc., Cape Coral, Fla., 1978—; ptnr., dir. Star Realty Inc., Cape Coral, 1980—; account exec. Media Graphics, Inc., Naples, Fla., 1984; advt. mgr. Fox Electronics, Ft. Myers, Fla., 1984-86; v.p. Langdon Advt., Ft. Myers, 1987-88; asst. mgr. facility State of Fla. Dept. Health and Rehabilitative Svcs., Ft. Myers, 1988—; mgr. facilities svcs. Dist. 8 State Fla. Mem. Econ. and Indsl. Devel. Task Force, City of Cape Coral, 1979. Mem. Nat. Assn. Homebuilders, Bldg. Industry Assn., Constrn. Industry Assn., Nat. Bd. Realtors. Home: 1482 Sautern Dr Fort Myers FL 33919 Office: State of Fla Dept Health Rehab Svcs 6719 Winkler Ave Fort Myers FL 33919

GARSKE, KATHLEEN AGNES GAUTHIER, foundation administrator; b. Milw., July 14, 1946; d. Romeo Albert and Genevieve (Grybush) Gauthier; children: Angela Marie, Michelle Marie. BA, U. Wis., 1968; postgrad., Old Dominion U., 1987—. Family caseworker Silver Springs Neighborhood Ctr., Milw., 1968-69; adoption counselor Internat. Social Assistance, Okinawa, Japan, 1979-80; substitute tchr. Dept. of Def. Overseas Schs., 1970-86; adoption caseworker Internat. Social Svc., Frankfurt, West Germany, 1981-86; regional dir. Office Refugee Resettlement, Norfolk, Va., 1986—. Bd. dirs. European coun. Girl Scouts U.S., Fed. Republic of Germany, 1985-86, trainer, cons., Wuerzburg, Fed. Republic of Germany, 1985-86, leader, 1971-86. Recipient Community Vol. Appreciation Cert., Community of Wuerzburg, 1981-86, Svc. award Girl Scouts U.S., 1984, 85, 86. Mem. NAFE, ASPA (sec. 1990—), Peninsula Women's Network (sec. 1990—). Home: 12660 E Nettles Dr Newport News VA 23606 Office: Office Refugee Resettlement 1802 Ashland Ave Norfolk VA 23509

GARSON, KARIN BEST, nursing director; b. Bklyn., Nov. 11, 1945; d. Richard Joseph and Irene Elizabeth (Hannula) Best; m. Jan. 30, 1970 (div. Feb. 1990); children: Matthew, Aaron. Diploma in nursing, Albany (N.Y.) Med. Ctr., 1967; BA in Psychology, U. Hartford, Conn., 1974; MPA, Marist Coll., 1988. RN. Staff nurse N.Y. Hosp., N.Y.C., 1967-68, Albany Med. Ctr., 1968-69; instr. in ob.-gyn. Albany Sch. Practical Nursing, 1969-70; in-svc. coord. MediCenter of Denver, 1971-72; instr. in nursing Hartford Hosp. Sch. Nursing, 1972-74; childbirth educator YWCA/YMCA, South Salem, N.Y., 1976-82; dir. Hospice of Dutchess County, Poughkeepsie, N.Y., 1983-86; dir. of nursing Healthsavers, Inc., Poughkeepsie, 1989, Hudson Valley Home Care, Poughkeepsie, 1989—. Mem. Jr. League of Poughkeepsie, 1982-84; mem. nursing edn. com. Am. Cancer Soc., Poughkeepsie, 1990—; bd. dirs. Jr. League of No. Westchester, Mt. Kisco, N.Y., 1980-82, Vassar Temple Sisterhood, Poughkeepsie, 1985-86. Mem. N.Y. State Nurses Assn., N.Y. State Hospice Assn., Am. Assn. Pub. Adminstrs. Democrat. Jewish. Home: 8 Fox Hill Unit C2 Poughkeepsie NY 12603 Office: Hudson Valley Home Care 80 Washington St Ste 310 Poughkeepsie NY 12601

GARTLEY, CHERYLE BLUMBERG, foundation administrator; b. Ottawa, Ill., Mar. 18, 1947; d. Herman S. and Lucille (Flood) Blumberg. BS, No. Ill. U., 1969; postgrad., U. Chgo., 1976-80. Advt. mgr. State Nat. Bank, Evanston, Ill., 1973-78; pres. Simon Found., Wilmette, Ill., 1983—. Author, editor: (book) Managing Incontinence, 1983; scriptwriter: (film) The Solution Starts With You, 1985. Founder Evanston Vet's. Day, 1974, Simon Found. U.S.A., 1983, Can., 1987; co-chmn com. Bicentennial Festival, Evanston, 1976; bd. dirs. North Shore Am. Cancer Soc., bd. dirs. Srs. Action Services, Evanston, 1976-77. Mem. Internat. Continence Soc., Assn. Continence Advisors. Office: Simon Found Box 815 Wilmette IL 60091

GARTNER, LILLIAN MARY, real estate appraiser; b. Somerville, N.J., Dec. 19, 1944; d. Michael and Blanche (Sledzewski) Zamorski; divorced 1985; children: Joseph Daniel, David Michael. AAS, Reading Area Community Coll., 1983. Prodn. and inventory analyst Cabot Berylco, Inc., Reading, Pa., 1980-85; buyer AT&T Technologies, Inc., Allentown, Pa., 1985-87; real estate appraiser Blue Mountain Realty, Bernville, Pa., 1987—. Me. Nat. Assn. Realtors, Pa. Assn. Realtors (grad. realtors inst. 1988), Greater Reading Bd. Realtors, Soc. Real Estate Appraisers (candidate). Republican. Roman Catholic. Office: Blue Mountain Realty 1001 S 4th St Hamburg PA 19526

GARTZ, LINDA LOUISE, television producer, director, writer; b. Chgo., Mar. 23, 1949; d. Fred Samuel and Lillian Louise G. BA, Northwestern U., Evanston, Ill., 1970, MA in Teaching, 1972. Tchr. Chgo. Pub. Schs., 1971-72; tchr. and TV instr. Winnetka (Ill.) Pub. Schs., 1972-80; TV producer and writer Cath. TV Network, Chgo., 1980-81; free-lance producer for documentary WLS-TV (ABC), Chgo., 1981-82, TV news researcher, asst. producer, 1982-83; assoc. producer, writer for documentaries WBBM-TV (CBS), Chgo., 1983-85; pres. Linda Gartz Prodns., Chgo., 1983—. Writer, assoc. producer (TV documentary) Children and Divorce, 1984 (Emmy award 1985), The Class of '84 (silver award N.Y. Film Festival 1985); (children's spl.) The Red Jacket 1985 (Emmy award 1986), No Place Like Home, 1985 (award Ill. Broadcasters Assn. 1985, San Francisco Internat. Film Festival 1985); producer, dir., writer (TV documentary) Changing Habits, 1986 (Emmy award 1986), Hispanic Mosaic, 1987 (Emmy award 1988). Recipient cert. of Merit Chgo. Internat. Film Fest, 1981, 88, 1st place Sports award AP, 1983, 1st place documentary Columbus Internat. Film Fest, 1988, Broadcast Media award San Francisco State U., 1988. Mem. NATAS. Office: 2811 Hartzell St Evanston IL 60201

GARVEY, JANE ROBERTS, lawyer; b. N.Y.C., Oct. 21, 1919; d. George Alexander and Helen Hickson (Hernon) Roberts; m. Francis Bernard Garvey, June 1, 1946; children: Ellen, Jane, Francis B. Jr. BA, Coll. New Rochelle (N.Y.), 1938; LLB, Columbia U., 1941. Bar: N.Y. 1942, U.S. Bd. Immigration Appeals 1957, U.S. Immigration and Naturalization Svc. 1957, U.S. Supreme Ct. 1958. Jr. assoc. Wikes, Riddel, Bloomer, Jacobi & Maguire, N.Y.C., 1942-44; assoc. Jackson, Nash, Brophy, Barringer & Brooks, N.Y.C., 1944-46; ptnr. Francis B. Garvey Esq., Babylon, N.Y., 1946—. Gov., internat. dir. Zonta Internat., Chgo., 1982-86; dir. planned giving Am. Heart Assn., 1984-87. Recipient spl. commendation USN, 1946, hon. commendaion Suffolk County (N.Y.) Legislature, 1983; named Hon. Big Sister of Yr., Big Sister/Big Bros., Washington, 1977; named to Lady Comdr. Equestrian Order of the Holy Sepulchre granted by Pope John XXIII. Mem. ABA, N.Y. Bar Asssn., Babylon Yacht Club, Southward Ho Golf Club (hon.). Republican. Roman Catholic. Home: 64 W Islip Rd West Islip NY 11795 Office: Francis B Garvey PO Box 158 Babylon NY 11702

GARY, DEBORAH, air force officer; b. Phila., May 14, 1955; d. Sam and Pauline (McCoy) Hill; m. Ronald H. Gary, July 30, 1976. BA, Hampton (Va.) U., 1976; MA, George Washington U., 1987. Commd. 2d lt. U.S. Air Force, 1978, advanced through grades to maj.; info. systems concepts devel. Hdqrs. Tactical Air Command, Hampton, 1982-86; chief info. mgmt. div. 7th Communications Group USAF, Pentagon, Washington, 1986-90. asst. chmn. USAF Fin. Mgmt. Briefing Team, briefing ROTC cadets at univs. Vol. income tax preparer VITA; vol. math. tutor; air force cadet/officer mentor action program WIBC. Mem. NAFE, Ret. Officers Assn., Nat. Coun. Negro Women, Alpha Kappa Alpha. Address: 4307 Cedar Lake Ct Alexandria VA 22309

GARY, GAYLE HARRIET MARGARET, communications executive; b. N.Y.C., Dec. 23, 1920; d. Michael H. and Lilian E. (Robbins) Summers; m. Arthur John Gary, Oct. 28, 1943; 1 child, Sandra G. Student, U. Miami, 1939, NYU, 1940-43, Columbia U., 1944-45. Pres., owner Gayle Gary Assocs. Radio-TV Cons., N.Y.C., 1954—. Interviewer, producer radio program and news bur. Views and People in the News. Pres. Guild of St. Bartholomew Protestant Episcopal Ch., N.Y.C., 1954-56; mem. prize com. debutante ball N.Y. Infirmary, N.Y.C.; mem. Friends of Philharm. Com., N.Y.C., 1950—; mem. fund-raising com. Women United Hosp. Fund, N.Y.C., 1950; mem. nat. adv. com. Narconon, 1950—; mem. spl. events com. Eleanor Roosevelt Meml. Found., N.Y.C., 1958—; bd. dirs. spl. social svcs. NYU-Bellevue Med. Ctr.; mem. exec. com. Hope Cotillion, N.Y.C., 1958—; bd. dirs. Nat. Radio-TV Com. for Am. Observance Human Rights Week, 1955—; co-leader N.Y.C. Assembly Dist., 1960-70; bd. dirs., rec. sec. Churchwomen's League for Patriotic Svc. Mem. Pub. Rels. Soc. Am. (accredited), Internat. Radio and TV Execs. Soc., Nat. Inst. Social Scis., Religious Pub. Rels. Soc. Am., Am. Women in Radio and TV, Hort. Soc. N.Y., Hubbard Assn. Scientologists Internat., Sea Orgn., Navy League, English-Speaking Union, Women's Nat. Rep. Club (nat. chmn. pub. rels. coun.), Women's Chess Club N.Y. (exec. v.p. 1968—). Home and Office: 1212 5th Ave #13B New York NY 10029

GARY, JULIA THOMAS, minister; b. Henderson, N.C., May 31, 1929; d. Richard Collins and Julia Branch (Thomas) G. BA, Randolph-Macon Woman's Coll., 1951; MA, Mt. Holyoke Coll., 1953; PhD in Chemistry, Emory U., 1958, MDiv cum laude, 1986. Ordained to Meth. Ch. as deacon, 1986, as elder 1989. Instr. Mt. Holyoke Coll., South Hadley, Mass., 1953-54, Randolph-Macon Woman's Coll., Lynchburg, Va., 1954-55; from asst. prof. to prof. chemistry Agnes Scott Coll., Decatur, Ga., 1957-84, dean, 1969-84; pastor-in-charge St. Matthew United Meth. Ch., East Point, Ga., 1987—; bd. dirs. INSA, Atlanta. Contbr. articles to profl. jours. Recipient Alumnae Achievement award Randolph-Macon Woman's Coll., 1990. Mem. Zonta of Atlanta (pres. 1979-81, Zonta of the Yr. 1988), Phi Beta Kappa, Sigma Xi. Home: 117 Bruton St Decatur GA 30030

GARY, NANCY ELIZABETH, nephrologist, academic administrator; b. N.Y.C., Mar. 4, 1937; d. Walter Joseph and Charlotte Elizabeth (Sayer) G. BS, Springfield (Mass.) Coll., 1958; MD, Med. Coll. Pa., 1962. Diplomate Am. Bd. Internal Medicine, Am. Bd. Nephrology. Resident Nassau County Med. Ctr., East Meadow, N.Y., 1962-64; resident St. Vincent's Hosp. and Med. Ctr., N.Y.C., 1964-65, chief renal sect., 1967-74; fellow in nephrology Georgetown U. Med. Ctr., Washington, 1965-67; instr. medicine NYU Sch. Medicine, N.Y.C., 1968-74; asst. prof. U. Medicine and Dentistry of N.J.-Rutgers Med. Sch., Piscataway, 1974-76, assoc. prof., 1976-81, prof., 1981-88, assoc. dean, 1981-87, exec. assoc. dean, 1987-88; dean Albany (N.Y.) Med. Coll., 1988-90; sr. med. adv. to adminstr. health care financing HHS, Washington, 1990—. Contbr. chpts. to books, articles to profl. jours. Robert Wood Johnson Health Policy fellow Nat. Acad. Sci. Inst. Medicine, 1987-88. Fellow ACP; mem. Assn. Am. Med. Colls. (coun. deans), AMA, Am. Soc. Nephrology. Office: DHHS Health Care Fin Adminstrn/Adminstrs Office 200 Independence Ave SW Washington DC 20201

GARY, SHARON DELIGHT, psychological examiner; b. Decatur, Tex., June 14, 1951; d. Dorthea (Somerville) Gary; B.S. with honors in Psychology, State Coll. Ark. (name changed to U. Central Ark.), 1973; M.S. in Clin. Psychology, Memphis State U., 1975, postgrad. in clin. psychology, 1975-76. Liaison worker Foster Home and Group Home programs N.E. Community Mental Health Center, Memphis, 1975-76; psychol. examiner, asst. dir. Hutt Psychol. Group, Memphis, 1976-79; cons. psychol. examiner Sequoyah Center, Tenn. Psychiat. Hosp. and Inst., Memphis, 1976-77; coordinator, instr. foster care program Center for Govt. Tng., U. Tenn., Memphis, 1978—; owner, psychol. examiner Psychol. Services of Memphis, 1979—; cons. St. Peter Home for Children, 1982-84, Holston's Meth. Children's Home, 1983—; active workshops, seminars on learning disabilities child devel.; mem. Women's Resource Center, 1977-82, Multidisciplinary Child Abuse Rev. Team, Region IX Dept. Human Svcs. 1979—, active NOW march for ERA; mem. Tenn. Juvenile Justice Commn., 1985-88, mem. grant rev. com. Juvenile Justice Commn., 1986-88, acting chmn. grant rev. com., 1987; participant in lobbying for Ark. Assn. Children with Learning Disabilities; head panel on psychol. effects of being in foster care Juvenile Ct. Judges Ann. Conf., Tenn., 1980; resource person for adoptive families. Recipient Ark. Traveler cert., 1978, cert. of appreciation Tenn. Foster Care Assn., 1979, cert. of appreciation Boys Town, 1984. Mem. Am. Psychol. Assn., Tenn. Area Psychol. Assn., Memphis Psychol. Assn., Nat. Rehab. Assn., Assn. for Children with Learning Disabilities, Council on Adoptable Children, Psi Chi. Bd. dirs., sec. Unity Christ Ch., 1987-88. Clubs: Exec. Women Memphis (charter mem., sec. 1978-81), Zonta (pres. 1985-86) (Memphis). Author: Parenting Happy Children: Coping with Destructive Behavior, 1985. Contbr. chpt. to Juvenile Court Review Board Manual. Home: 3163 Highmeadow Dr Memphis TN 38128 Office: Psychol Svcs Memphis 2714 Union Ave Extd Ste 224 Memphis TN 38112

GARZA, JANET LOIS, social studies educator; b. Mankato, Minn., Apr. 23, 1939; d. Leo Alvan and Evelyn Lois (Mediger) Stowell; m. Antonio Garza Jr., Mar. 21, 1959; children: Ricardo, Raquel, Antonio III. BS, Eastern N.Mex. U., 1975, MA, 1976, cert. in edn., 1983. Cert. social studies tchr., N.Y., N.Mex., Mich., Pa. Tchr. social studies Clovis (N.Mex.) Mcpl. Schs., 1975-87; part-time history and geography instr. Ea. N.Mex. U., Clovis, 1980-87; tchr. social studies Mt. Markham High Sch., West Winfield, N.Y., 1987—. Author: (with others) U.S. History Books, 1 and 2, Grade 8, 1986. With USAF, 1958-59. Mem. N.Y. State Coun. for Social Studies, Nat. Coun. for Social Studies, Assn. for Supervision and Curriculum Devel., AAUW (pres. Clovis chpt. 1982-87). Republican. Lutheran. Office: Mt Markham High Sch Fairground Rd West Winfield NY 13491

GARZARELLI, ELAINE MARIE, economist; b. Phila., Oct. 13, 1951; d. Ralph J. and Ida M. (Pierantozzi) G.; BS, Drexel U., 1973, MBA, 1977; doctoral candidate NYU, 1980. With A.G. Becker, N.Y.C., 1973-84, v.p., economist, 1975-84, mng. dir., 1984; exec. v.p. Shearson Lehman Bros., 1984—; lectr. in field. Named Businesswoman of Yr. Fortune Mag., 1987. Mem. Nat. Assn. Bus. Economists, Women's Fin. Assn., Am. Statis. Assn., Women's Bond Assn. Developer Sector Analysis, econometric model for predicting industry profits and stock price movements, also predicted stock market crash of 1987. Home: 280 Butler Rd Springfield PA 19064 Office: Shearson Lehman Hutton Inc World Fin Ctr Tower C New York NY 10285

GASAWAY, LAURA NELL, law librarian, legal educator; b. Searcy, Ark., Feb. 24, 1945; d. Merel Roger and Carnell (Miller) G. BA, Tex. Woman's U., 1967, MLS, 1968; JD, U. Houston, 1973. Bar: Tex. 1974. Catalog libr. U.

Houston, 1968-70, catalog-circulation libr., 1970-72, asst. law libr., 1972-73, law libr., asst. prof. law, 1973-75; dir. law libr., prof. law U. Okla., Norman, 1975-85; dir. law libr., prof. law U. N.C., 1985—; copyright cons. Recipient Calvert prize U. Okla., 1978, 81, Compton award Ark. Librs. Assn., 1986. Fellow Spl. Librs. Assn. (H.W. Wilson award 1983); mem. ABA, State Bar Tex., N.C. Bar Assn., Am. Assn. Law Librs. (pres. 1986-87). Democrat. Author: (with Maureen Murphy) Legal Protection for Computer Programs, 1980; (with James Hoover and Dorothy Warden) American Indian Legal Materials, A Union List, 1981. Democrat. Office: U NC Law Libr CB #3385 Chapel Hill NC 27599-3385

GASKA, CHRISTINE, accountant; b. Queens, N.Y., June 25, 1965; d. Basil Charles and Helen (Bulgarides) P. AS cum laude, Nassau Community Coll., 1985; BBA, Hofstra U., 1987. Staff acct. H.G. Toys, Inc., Long Beach, N.Y., 1987-88; project acct. Johansen Orgn., Hempstead, N.Y., 1988—. Treas., sec. Sonia Lee and Dad Against Drunk Driving and Drugs, East Meadow, N.Y., 1987-88. Home: 1938 Charles St Bellmore NY 11710 Office: Johansen Orgn 91 N Franklin St Hempstead NY 11550

GASPAR, ANNA LOUISE, retired educator; b. Chgo., May 12, 1935; d. Miklos and Klotild (Weiss) G. BS in Edn., Northwestern U., 1957. Cert. elem. tchr., Calif. Tchr. 6th grade Pacific Palisades (Calif.) Pub. Schs., 1957-58; tchr. 1st grade Eastman St. Elem. Sch., L.A., 1959, Glassell Pk. Elem. Sch., L.A., 1959-62; tchr. 1st and 4th grades Stoner Ave. Elem. Sch., L.A., 1962-67; tchr. Brentwood Elem. Sch., L.A., 1967-78; tchr. 4th and 5th grades Brockton Ave. Elem. Sch., L.A., 1978-90. Mem. Nat. Ret. Tchrs. Assn., Calif. Ret. Tchrs. Assn. (Santa Monica Bay div.), Hadassah, Northwestern Univ. Alumni Assn., Travelers Century Club, Lindblad Intrepid Club. Democrat. Jewish. Home: 1430 Idaho Ave Apt F Santa Monica CA 90403

GASPARRO, MADELINE, banker; b. Jersey City, Oct. 5, 1928; d. Donato and Anna (D'Urso) D'Achille; m. Dominick J. Gasparro, Apr. 30, 1949; children: Dorothy, Joseph, Donato, Frank. Grad. high sch., Jersey City. Salesperson credit dept. and employee sales J.C. Penney, Parlin, N.J.; head teller Amboy Madison Nat. Bank, Old Bridge, N.J., bank mgr. Chpt. chmn. South Amboy Hosp., mem. fin. com.; eucharist minister St. Bernadette Ch. of Parlin. Mem. NAFE, Nat. Assn. Bank Women (past hostess), Fin. Women Internat. (chair membership 1990—), Altar Rosary Soc. (past. pres.). Address: 17 Parkway Pl Parlin NJ 08859

GASPERINI, ELIZABETH CARMELA (LISA GASPERINI), advertising professional, graphic designer; b. Newark, Sept. 26, 1961; d. Enrico Caesar and Wanda Claudia (Stanziale) G. BFA, Caldwell (N.J.) Coll., 1983. Advt. specialist J.C. Penney Corp., Wayne, N.J., 1982-83; asst. prodn. mgr. Internat. Postal Mktg. Corp., Montville, N.J., 1983-84; art dir. Healy, Dixcy & Forbes, W. Caldwell, N.J., 1984-86; sr. mktg. specialist Am. Varityper Corp., E. Hanover, N.J., 1986-88; product promotion mgr. Brother Internat. Corp., Somerset, N.J., 1988-90; with Ishida USA Inc., Parsippany, N.J., 1990—; art cons. Italico Pubs., Livingston, N.J., 1982—; owner, cons. Gasperini Graphics, Towaco, N.J., 1984—; telemarketing specialist Sears, Roebuck & Co., Fairfield, N.J., 1984—. Mem. N.J. Art Assn., N.J. Italian-Am. Assn. (cons. 1982—). Democrat. Roman Catholic. Home: 10 Willard Ln Towaco NJ 07082

GASPERONI, ELLEN JEAN LIAS (MRS. EMIL GASPERONI), interior designer; b. Rural Valley, Pa.; d. Dale S. and Ruth (Harris) Lias; student Youngstown U., 1952-54, John Carrol U., 1953-54, Westminster Coll., 1951-52; grad. Am. Inst. Banking; m. Emil Gasperoni, May 28, 1955; children: Sam, Emil, Jean Ellen. Mem. Coeurde Coeur Heart Assn., Orlando Opera Guild, Orlando Symphony Guild. Mem. Jr. Bus. Women's Club (dir. 1962-64). Presbyterian. Clubs: Sweetwater Country (owner, gen. mgr.) (Longwood, Fla.); Lake Toxaway Golf and Country (N.C.). Home: 1126 Brownshine Ct Longwood FL 32779

GASS, GERTRUDE ZEMON, psychologist, researcher; b. Detroit; d. David Solomon and Mary (Goldman) Zemon; m. H. Harvey Gass, June 19, 1938; children: Susan, Roger. BA, U. Mich., 1937, MSW, 1943, PhD, 1957. Lic. clin. psychologist, Mich. Mem. faculty Merrill-Palmer Inst., Detroit, 1958-69, lectr., 1967; mem. faculty Advanced Behavioral Sci. Ctr., Grosse Pointe, Mich., 1969-72; pvt. practice clin. psychology Birmingham, Mich., 1972—; adj. prof. psychology U. Detroit, 1969-75; cons. Continuum Ctr. Oakland U., Rochester, Mich., 1961-77, Traveler's Aid, Detroit, 1959-75; pres. Shapero Sch. Nursing, Detroit, 1967-72, cons. 1958-78; psychol. cons. Physician's Ins. Co. of Mich., 1988—, mgt. Mich. Bell Telephone, 1979-82. Mem. Adv. Com Sch. Needs, 1954-56; trustee Sinai Hosp. Detroit, 1972—; bd. dirs. Tribute Fund United Community Services, 1955-67. Fellow Am. Assn. Marriage-Family, Am. Orthopsychiatric Assn. (v.p. 1975-76); mem. Psychologists Task Force (v.p. 1977-84), Mich. Inter-Profl. Assn. (pres. 1976-78), Mich. Assn. Marriage Counselors (1979-80), Mental Health Adv. Service, Blue Cross and Blue Shield of Mich., Phi Kappa Phi, Pi Lambda Theta. Office: 30200 Telegraph Rd Birmingham MI 48010

GASS, MARGERY STOOPS, obstetrician gynecologist; b. Cin., Oct. 7, 1944; d. Jean Todd and Margaret Elizabeth (Mobberley) Stoops; m. Frederick Stuart Gass, June 19, 1966; children: Molly Margaret, David Frederick. BA, DePauw U., 1966; MA, Miami U., Oxford, Ohio, 1969; MD, U. Cin., 1980. Diplomate Am. Coll. Ob-Gyn. Lectr. Miami U., Oxford, 1972; asst. prof. clin. Ob-Gyn U. Cin. Coll. Medicine, 1984—; part-time faculty Talladega (Ala.) Coll., 1969-70. Vol. United Appeal, Am. Cancer Soc., Planned Parenthood, YWCA, Oxford, 1972-75. Fellow Am. Coll. Ob-Gyn; mem. AMA, Mortar Bd., Alpha Lambda Delta, Alpha Omega Alpha, Phi Beta Kapp. Office: Univ Cin/Dept Ob-Gyn 231 Bethesda Ave Cincinnati OH 45267-0526

GASTEYER, CARLIN EVANS, broadcast executive, museum studies educator; b. Jackson, Mich., Mar. 30, 1917; d. Frank Howard and Marian (Spencer) Evans; student Barnard Coll., 1934-35; B.A., CUNY, 1983; m. Harry A. Gasteyer, Jan. 8, 1944; 1 dau., Nancy Catherine. Clk., First Nat. City Bank, 1939-42; statistician Bell Telephone Labs., 1942-45; dir. asst. S.I. Mus., 1956-61; bus. mgr. Mus. of the City of N.Y., 1961-63; mus. adminstr., 1963-66; asst. dir. Monmouth (N.J.) Mus., 1966-67, Mus. of City of N.Y., 1967-70; vice dir. adminstrn. Bklyn. Mus., 1970-74; dir. planning Snug Harbor Cultural Center, S.I., N.Y., 1975-79; cable TV Cons., 1980—; adj. lectr. mus. studies Coll. S.I. CUNY, 1985—. Active Girl Scouts. Co-founder, pres. Jr. Mus. Guild, S.I. Mus., 1956-58. Mem. N.Y.C. Local Sch. Bd. 54, 1960-61. Mem. Am. Assn. Mus., Mus. Council of N.Y.C. Club: Cosmopolitan. Home: 50 Fort Pl Staten Island NY 10301

GASTON, JUDITH ANN, media specialist; b. Escanaba, Mich., Mar. 31, 1950; d. Elroy Willard and Wilma Mae (LeBrasseur) Zimmermann; m. Paul Lewis Gaston, Apr. 14, 1975. AA, Bay de Noc Community Coll., 1970; BA, Cen. Mich. U., 1971; MS, U. Wis., 1980; MA, U. Minn., 1990. Libr. Cass City (Mich.) Pub. Schs., 1972; from head tech. processing to acting dir. audio visual libr. svc. U. Minn., Mpls., 1972-73, dir. film and video svc., 1973—. Mem. Am. Film and Video Assn. (pres. 1987-88), Consortium Coll. and Univ. Media Ctrs. (pres. 1989-90), Minn. Assn. for Continuing Adult Edn. (pres. 1988-89), Am. Soc. for Tng. and Devel. Office: U Minn Film and Video Svc 1313 5th St SE Ste 108 Minneapolis MN 55414

GASTON, REBECCA LEE, medical sales specialist; b. Johnstown, Pa., June 5, 1952; d. Willard Calvin and Wanda Caroline (Varner) G.; m. James Allen Conner, July 23, 1976 (div. 1977). Student, Miami Valley Hosp. Sch. Radiol. Tech., Dayton, Ohio, 1970-72; A in Applied Sci. cum laude, Sinclair Coll., 1979. Instr. Miami Valley Hosp. Sch. Radiology, Dayton, 1972-79; supr. cardiovascular lab. Grandview Hosp., Dayton, 1979-84; physicians asst. Dr. James Laws, Dayton, 1982-84; med. sales specialist Honeywell Med. Corp., Balt., 1984-86, Med. Graphics Corp., Balt., 1986-88, Angiotec, Scotts Valley, Calif., 1988-89; pres. RLG ProImage, Inc., Reno, 1989—; cons. Cardiopulmonary Rehab., Balt., 1984. Mem. Am. Soc. Radiol. Tech., Nat. Soc. Cardiopulmonary Tech., Dayton Soc. Cardiopulmonary Tech. (chairperson program com. 1978), Greater Dayton Med. Imaging Soc. (pres. 1983), Washington Soc. Cardiopulmonary Technologists, Nat. Aquarium Assn., NOW. Office: PO Box 11675 Reno NV 89510

GASWICK, CAROLYN JEAN, librarian; b. York, Nebr., Dec. 14, 1042; d. Paul H. and Helen Alberta (Teale) Myers; m. Dennis Charles Gaswick, June 14, 1964; children: Christina, Wyatt. BS in Edn. and English, Nebr. Wesleyan U., 1964; MLS, Western Mich. U., 1972. Tchr. Oak Creek Sch., Albany, Oreg., 1965-67, Three Village Sch. Dist., Stony Brook, N.Y., 1968-69; libr. Litchfield (Mich.) Schs., 1972-73; reference libr. Kellogg Community Coll., Battle Creek, Mich., 1980-81; serials and documents libr. Albion (Mich.) Coll., 1981—. Mem. Mich. Libr. Assn., N.Am. Serials Interest Group, Govt. Documents Roundtable Mich. (sec. 1988-89, v.p., program chmn. 1989-90, pres. 1990-91), AAUW, P.E.O. (pres. 1978-80), Phi Kappa Phi, Kappa Delta Pi, Beta Phi Mu. Home: 123 Bushong Dr Albion MI 49224 Office: Albion Coll Libr 602 E Cass St Albion MI 49224

GATES, BARBARA ANN, nurse employment manager; b. Macon, Tenn., Sept. 7, 1941; d. James and Susie Mae (Thomas) O'Banner; m. Robert Washington, June 23, 1961 (div. 1976); children: Robert Washington Jr., Rosalyn Marie; m. Ernest Louis Gates, Aug. 31, 1976. AD in Nursing, Henry Ford Comm., 1973; BA, Madonna Coll., 1980, BS Nursing, 1982; MS, U. Mich., 1988. Mich. Bd. of Nursing, 101783. Asst. bank mgr. Security Bank and Trust Co., Southgate, Mich., 1960-73; staff nurse to supr. Veterans Adminstr., Allen Park, Mich., 1973-79; sch. nurse. Ecorse Pub. Sch., Ecorse, Mich., 1979-86; medicare adminstr. Upjohn Healthcare Services, St. Clair Shores, Mich.; clinical coord. Veterans Adminstr., Allen Park, Mich., 1986--. Sch. Bd. Candidate, River Rouge Bd. of Educ., 1974, corp. bd. mem., Southeastern Mich. Family Planning Project, Westland, 1980—. Lt. (j.g.) USNR Nurse Corps, 1990. Mem. Nurses Orgn. of Vet. Affairs. (fin. chairperson 1988—), Am. Bus. Women's Assn., Mich. Assn. of Nurse Recruiters, VA Nurse Recruiters Assn., Delta Sigma Theta Sorority, Inc. Democratic. Protestant. Home: 8575 Steel Detroit MI 48228 Office: Veterans Administration Southfield Outer Dr Allen Park MI 48101

GATES, BARBARA LYNN, school administrator, educator; b. Billings, Mont., May 13, 1954; d. Joseph Isacc and Ima Evelyn (Daugherty) G. B.S. in Elementary Edn., Eastern Mont. Coll., 1976. Cert. tchr., Mont. Tchr., Union Sch., Lindsay, Mont., 1976-79, Greycliff Sch., Mont., 1979-80; supr. Alliance Christian Sch., Lewistown, Mont., 1981-83, prin., supr., 1983-86; prin., supr. Paradise Christian Acad., Lewistown, Mont., 1986—.

GATES, BRENDA LEE, company executive; b. Boston, May 31, 1958; d. Robert Daniel and Nancy Elaine (Bucher) G. BS in Health Planning, Pa. State U., 1980; MA Health Svc. Adminstrn., George Washington U., 1987. Sr. acctg. clk. George Washington U. Med. Ctr., Washington, 1981-82, jr. acct., 1982-84; project mgr. Health Care Systems, Inc., Washington, 1984-86, v.p. data processing and ops., 1987; founder, v.p. ops. CareSys, Inc., New Brunswick, N.J., 1987-88, Lyndhurst, N.J., 1988—. Tutor Higher Achievement Program, Washington, 1986-87; vol. Big Sister-Big Bros., Inc., N.J., 1987—. Mem. Risk Ins. Mgmt. Soc., Gamma Phi Beta, Sierra Club, NAFE. Office: CareSys Co 1050 Wall St W Ste 140 Lyndhurst NJ 07071

GATES, DOROTHY LOUISE, educator; b. National City, Calif., Feb. 21, 1926; d. Harold Roger and Bertha Marjorie (Lippold) Gates; B.A., U. Calif., Santa Barbara, 1949; M.A., U. Hawaii, 1963, Ph.D., 1975; postdoctoral student U. Uppsala (Sweden), 1976, Bedford Coll., London, 1978, Cuban Ministry of Justice, 1979, Cambridge U., Eng., 1986. Dept. probation officer, Riverside County, Calif., 1950-54, 55-61; dir. La Morada, probation facility, Santa Barbara County, 1963-65; prof. sociology San Bernardino Valley Coll. (Calif.), 1965-87, prof. emeritus, 1987—; part-time tchr. criminology U. Redlands, Calif.; chmn. Riverside County Juvenile Justice and Delinquency Prevention Commn., 1971-88. Pres. Women's Equity Action League, Hawaii, 1972; mem. adv. group Riverside County Justice System, 1982. bd. dirs. San Bernardino County Mental Health Assn., Cooper Burkhart House, Riverside; mem. adv. council Ret. Sr. Vol. Program, San Bernardino; acad. pres. San Bernardino Valley Coll., 1986; pres., trustee Riverside Community Coll. Recipient Cert. of Recognition, Riverside YWCA; named Citizen of Achievement, San Bernardino LWV, 1985; NEH fellow U. Va., 1977; named Outstanding Prof. San Bernardino Valley Coll., 1987. Mem. Western Gerontology Assn., Am. Soc. Criminology, Calif. Probation, Parole and Correctional Assn. (award 1969), Women's Assn. Edn. and Rsch. (Calif. chpt.), LWV. Lodge: Kiwanis. Address: 4665 Braemar Pl #212 Riverside CA 92501

GATES, JOYCELYN, travel industry executive; b. Ind., Nov. 28, 1936; d. John J. and Florence Strawsma; m. Oscar N. Gates, Oct. 22, 1960; children: Sandra, Randall, Jere. Student, Patricia Stevens Finishing Sch, Chgo. Pres. Gold Tour and Travel Inc. Mem. Nat. Travel Assn., Am. Soc. Travel Agts., Lafayette C. of C., Women Bus. Owners Assn., Am. Assn. Ret. Persons. Address: 803 S 18th St Lafayette IN 47905

GATES, L. PATRICIA, advertising company executive; b. Los Angeles, Dec. 11, 1941; d. Harry Patrick Hoeye and Lily Maxine (Hulbert) Hazlewood. BA summa cum laude, Fordham U., 1989. Reg. stockbroker;. Asst. to pres. Marantette & Co., Detroit, 1969-72; asst. to br. mgr. William C. Roney & Co., Detroit, 1972-75; advt. dir. Thomson McKinnon Securities, N.Y., 1975-78; advt. dir., 1st v.p. Prudential-Bache Securities, N.Y., 1978-87; pres. Patricia Gates, N.Y., 1987--. Box office, set builder, Village Light Opera Group, N.Y., 1976-82; reading tchr. N.Y.C. Pub. Sch. Vol., 1987-88. Mem. Fin. Communications Soc., Fin. Advt. and Mktg. Assn., Alpha Sigma Lambda, YWCA (woman achiever of the year award 1982). Republican. Baptist.

GATES, MADI, interior designer; b. Salix, Iowa, Aug. 13, 1938; d. Ralph Fredrick Madison and Joyce Elaine (Rugger) King; m. James Roland Gates, Dec. 30, 1962; children: Kirsten Ann. BS in Nursing Edn., U. Minn., 1963; student interior design program, Calif. Poly. State U., 1983. Staff nurse Winnebago (Nebr.) Indian Reservation, 1959-60; intensive care nurse U. Minn. Hosp., Mpls., 1960-63; head nurse Sierra Vista Hosp., San Luis Obispo, Calif., 1963-64, "float" nurse, 1966-80; owner, designer Madi Gates Interiors, San Luis Obispo, Calif., 1983—. Mem./seamstress Altar Guild St. Stephen's Episc. Ch., San Luis Obispo, 1968-80; mem. Children's Home Soc., San Luis Obispo, 1971—; chmn. Achievement House Workshop for the Disabled, San Luis Obispo, 1980-81, bd. dirs.; pres. Rep. Women, San Luis Obispo, 1969-70; mem. Archtl. Rev. Commn. City of San Luis Obispo, 1988—; kitchen designer Showcase House San Luis Obispo, 1990. Recipient scholarship Sioux City (Iowa) Med. Aux., 1956-59; named Nurse of Yr., U. Minn., 1962. Mem. Cen. Coast Interior Designers, Am. Soc. Interior Designers (allied, cert. masters level), San Luis Obispo C. of C. Clubs: Ninety-nines (San Luis Obispo) (treas. 1979-80), Pharmacy Aux. (pres. 1963-64). Home and Office: 125 Serrano Heights San Luis Obispo CA 93405

GATES, MARILYN TAYLOR, school system administrator; b. Buffalo, N.Y., Aug. 15, 1942; d. Harry Newman and Dorothy (Cannon) Taylor; m. Richard W. Gates, Aug. 5, 1967 (div. Dec. 1988); children: Julie, Matthew. BA, Syracuse U., 1964; MA, U. Iowa, 1969. Cert. sch. administr. French tchr. Kenmore (N.Y.) Pub. Schs., 1964-67; teaching asst. U. Iowa, Iowa City, 1967-69; French instr. Kirkwood Community Coll., Cedar Rapids, Iowa, 1969-70; French tchr. Olean (N.Y.) City Schs., 1970-71; adj. faculty St. Bonaventure U., Olean, 1971-80, Alfred (N.Y.) U., 1979-81; tchr. of gifted, program adminstr. Bd. Coop. Ednl. Svcs., Olean, 1981-88; sr. program mgr. for curriculum B.O.C.E.S., Olean, 1988-89; asst. supt. schs. Pioneer Cen. Schs., Yorkshire, N.Y., 1989—; cons. distance learning Erie #1 Bd. Coop. Ednl. Svcs., Buffalo, 1985; state edn. adv. com. on evaluation N.Y. State Edn. Dept., Albany, N.Y., 1987; trainer Early Lit. Inservice Course, 1989—. Editor: Performance Based Assessment of K-2 Gifted Students, 1987. Cofounder and pres., bd. dirs. Olean Child Devel. Ctr., 1972-73; bd. dirs. Mental Health Assn. Cattaraugus County, Olean, 1984-87. Mem. Hanford Bay Club, Delta Kappa Gamma, Phi Delta Kappa (historian 1981-82, sec. 1982-84). Democrat. Home: 205 N Third St Olean NY 14760 Office: Pioneer Cen Sch Dist County Line Rd Yorkshire NY 14173

GATES, MARTINA MARIE, food products company executive; b. Mpls., Mar. 19, 1957; d. John Thomas and Colette Clara (Luetmer) G. BSBA in Mktg. Mgmt. cum laude, Coll. St. Thomas, 1984, MBA in Mktg., 1987. Tchrs. asst. Mpls. Area Vocat. Tech. Inst., Mpls., 1978-79; sec., regional sales mgr. Internat. Multifoods, Mpls., 1979, sec. bakery mix, mktg. mgr., 1979-80, sec., v.p. sales and new bus. devel., 1980, customer service rep. regional accounts, 1980-81, customer service rep. nat. accounts, 1981-82, credit coordinator indsl. foods div., 1982-85, asst. credit mgr. consumer foods div., 1985, advt./sales promotion mgr. indsl. foods div., 1985-86, asst. credit mgr. fast food and restaurant div., 1986-87, dir. devel. USA and Can. franchise area, 1987—. Vol. seamstress Guthrie Theater Costume Shop, Mpls., 1975—; alumni mem. New Coll. Student Adv. Council St. Thomas, St. Paul, 1984—; vol. Mpls. Aquatennial, 1987. Mem. Omicron Delta Epsilon.

GATES, MARY D., library director; b. Ft. Atkinson, Wis., Oct. 22, 1926; d. Clifford A. and Lucile (Curtis) Dexheimer; m. James Gates, Dec. 28, 1946 (dec.); children: Jane, Ann. BA, U. Wis., 1949, MA, 1974. Libr. dir. Dwight Foster Pub. Libr., Ft. Atkinson, 1974—. Active Ft. Atkinson Hist. Soc., 1970—. Mem. AAUW. Office: Dwight Foster Pub Libr 102 E Milwaukee Ave Fort Atkinson WI 53538

GATES, SIGNE SANDRA, lawyer; b. Washington, Dec. 19, 1949; d. Russell and Signe Eva (Nelson) G.; m. Peter Benjamin Knuck, Sept. 12, 1987. BA summa cum laude, Susquehanna U., 1971; JD, U. Mich., 1980. Bar: Conn. 1981, U.S. Dist. Ct. Conn. 1982. Mgmt. trainee Sears, Roebuck and Co., Alexandria, Va., 1971; mgmt. cons. Macro Systems, Inc., Silver Spring, Md., 1971-73; v.p. Program Resources, Inc., Annapolis, Md., 1973-78; assoc. Cummings & Lockwood, Stamford, Conn., 1980-83; corp. atty. Tetley Inc., Shelton, Conn., 1983-85; sr. atty. Gen. Signal Corp., Stamford, 1985—. Bd. dirs., sec. Norwalk, Conn., YMCA, Inc., 1985-88, Tri-State Employment Law Forum, N.Y.C., 1984-87; counsel, Infectious Disease Rev. Panel YMCA, Norwalk, 1988—; panelist Project to Increase Mastery of Math. and Sci., Conn., 1986, 87, 89. Named Outstanding Young Woman of Am., 1984. Mem. ABA, Conn. Bar Assn., Westchester-Fairfield Corp. Counsel Assn., Susquehanna U. Alumni-Parent Admissions Network (coord. 1989—). Democrat. Lutheran. Office: Gen Signal Corp High Ridge Pk Stamford CT 06904

GATES, THERESA ANN, air force officer; b. St. Paul, Jan. 13, 1959; d. James William and Eleanor June (Connaker) G. BA in Communications, Coll. St. Catherine, St. Paul, 1981. Commd. 2d lt. USAF, 1982, advanced through grades to capt., 1986; dep. pub. affairs officer USAF, Shaw AFB, S.C., 1982-86, dir. pub. affairs 9th Air Force, 1986-88; dir. pub. affairs 25th Air Force USAF, McChord AFB, Wash., 1988-90; dir. advt. and publicity 3535th Recruiting Squadron, Andrews AFB, Md., 1990—. Vol. coach St. Mathews High Sch., Sumter, S.C., 1987; pub. affairs vol. Am. Lung Assn., Sumter, 1988; media asst. Goodwill Games, Seattle, 1990. Recipient commedation medal, USAF, 1990. Mem. Air Force Assn., Women in Communications. Roman Catholic. Office: 25th Air Div Pub Affairs 3535 USAFRSQ (ATC) Andrews AFB MD 20331-5000

GATES-COHEN, LISA, small business owner, chef, caterer; b. Washington, July 11, 1955; d. Chester Robert and Peggy Jean (Dalton) Gates; m. Sergio Vivoli, Nov. 3, 1978 (div. Nov. 1, 1984); m. Mitchell Cohen, Sept. 21, 1987. AA, Fleming Coll., Florence, Italy, 1974. Dir. The Am. Sch. in Switzerland, Lugano, 1974-80; counter person Bar Gelateria Vivoli, Florence, 1978-80; costumer, choreographer, scene designer English Theatre of Florence, 1978; tchr. Dance Sch. Theatre, Florence, 1978-81; sec., treas. Vivoli Da Firenze, Inc., L.A., 1981-82; event coord. Calif. Catering Co., Beverly Hills, Calif., 1983; chef, sales rep. St. Germain To Go, West Hollywood, Calif., 1984; chef, cons. Posh Affair Catering Co., L.A., 1984-87; owner, chef, party planner Lisa Gates-Vivoli Catering, L.A., 1985—; catering mgr. Maple Drive Restaurant, Beverly Hills, 1990—. Mem. Mus. Contemporary Art, L.A., L.A. County Mus. Art, L.A. Theatre Ctr., NOW, L.A., Music Ctr. Unified Fund. Recipient Outstanding Achievement in Art award Bank of Am., Miraleste, Calif., 1972. Mem. NAFE, Am. Inst. Wine and Food, Da Camera Soc. (patron), Roundtable for Women in Foodsvc. Democrat. Home and Office: 1227 N Orange Grove Ave West Hollywood CA 90046

GATES-SPEARS, LORENE CYNTHIA, industrial designer; b. Fairview Park, Ohio, July 11, 1952; d. Lawrence Walter and Lillian Veronica (Stanek) Gates; m. Jackson E. Spears Jr., Sept. 30, 1989. BFA, Cleve. Inst. Art, 1976. Exterior and interior stylist Chrysler Corp., Detroit, 1977-82; sr. designer Volkswagen of Am., Troy, Mich., 1980-82; design exec. Zimmer Corp., Boca Raton, Fla., 1982-84, Collins & Aikman, Inc., N.Y.C., 1984—; commd. by Pres. Reagan to make presenation in Kiev, USSR, 1987. mem. Jr. League of Birmingham, Mich., 1981—; b. trustees Birmingham-Bloomfield Art Assn., 1988—. Scholarship Ford Motor Corp., 1973-76, GM, 1973-76, Chrysler Motor Corp., 1973-76. Mem. Color Mktg. Group, Winnetka Women's Club. Republican. Roman Catholic. Home: 111 Church St Winnetka IL 60093

GATHARD, MARY PAULA, healthcare administrator, director, nurse; b. Springfield, Ill., Oct. 12, 1939; d. Paul and Veva Maree (Salyer) Owings; m. George William Gathard, Jan. 10, 1959; children: Lisa Maree Gathard McGinnis, Debra Michele Gathard Benanti. Diploma in nursing, Meml. Hosp., 1965; BA in Psychology, Sangamon State U., 1973, MA, 1975, BA in Nursing, 1981. Staff nurse Meml. Hosp., Springfield, 1965-66; instr. Meml. Hosp. Sch. of Nursing, Springfield, 1966-70, St. John's Sch. of Nursing, Springfield, 1970-80; with staff devel. Meml. Med. Ctr., Springfield, 1980-83; dir. nursing McFarland Mental Health Ctr., Springfield, 1983—; instr. CPR, Am. Heart Assn., Springfield, 1980—; mem. community liaison com. dept. nursing MacMurray Coll., Jacksonville, Ill., 1984—. Mem. citizens for future Lincolnland Community Coll., Springfield, 1989—. Mem. Am. Nurses Assn., Ill. Nurses Assn. (sec. 1985-87, legis. com. dist. 9 1985—, mem. task force on access to health care 1986-88), Women in Mgmt. Republican. Office: McFarland Mental Health Ctr 901 Southwind Rd Springfield IL 62703

GATHERS, PATRICIA KATHLEEN, accountant; b. Johnstown, Pa., July 23, 1964; d. James Richard Jr. and Patricia Elizabeth (O'Connor) Chynoweth; m. Gerald Floyd Gathers, Dec. 24, 1985. BSBA, LaSalle U., 1986; postgrad., Villanova U., 1989—. CPA. Office clk. Somerset (Pa.) County Treas.'s Office, 1983; accts. payable clk. Blue Ribbon Svcs., Phila., 1984; intern Arthur Andersen & Co., Phila., 1985; staff acct. Brazina & Co., Bala Cynwyd, Pa., 1985-86, Arthur Andersen & Co., Phila., 1986-88; sr. acct. Crozer-Chester Med. Ctr., Chester, Pa., 1988-89; reimbursement acct. Children's Hosp. Phila., 1989-90; mgr. fin. svcs. Adult Communities Total Svcs., Inc., West Point, Pa., 1990—. Vol. Muscular Dystrophy Assn., Davidsville, Pa., 1973, Income Tax Assistance, Phila., 1983. Mem. NAFE, Pa. Inst. CPAs, Nat. League Postmasters (sec.-treas. Pa. chpt. 1982-83), Alpha Epsilon. Democrat. Roman Catholic. Home: 5515 Wissahickon Ave Apt D-203 Philadelphia PA 19144 Office: Adult Communities Total Svcs Inc 375 Morris Rd West Point PA 19486

GATIPON, BETTY BECKER, medical educator, consultant; b. New Orleans, Sept. 8, 1931; d. Elmore Paul and Theresa Caroline (Sendker) Becker; m. William B. Gatipon, Nov. 22, 1952 (dec. 1986); children: Suzanne, Ann Gatipon Sved, Lynn Gatipon Pashley. BS, Ursuline Coll., New Orleans, 1952; MEd, La. State U., 1975, PhD, 1983. Tchr. Diocese of Baton Rouge, 1960-74, edn. cons. to sch. bd., 1974-78; dir. Right to Read program Capital Area Consortium/Washington Parish Sch. Bd., Franklington, La., 1978-80; dir. basic skills edn. Capital Area Consortium/Ascension Parish Sch. Bd., Donaldsonville, La., 1980-82; instr. Coll. Edn. La. State U., Baton Rouge, 1982-84; evaluation cons. La. Dept. Edn., Baton Rouge, 1984-85; dir. basic skills edn. Capital Area Basic Skills/East Feliciana Parish Sch. Bd., Clinton, La., 1985-86; program coord. La. Bd. Elem. and Secondary Edn., New Orleans, 1987-89; asst. prof. Sch. Medicine La. State U. Med. Ctr., New Orleans, 1989—; evaluator East Feliciana Parish Schs., 1982-86; presenter math. methods workshops Ascension Parish Schs., 1980-84. Author curriculum materials, conf. papers; contbr. articles to edn. jours. Curatorial asst. La. State Mus., New Orleans, 1987—; soprano St. Louis Cathedral Concert Choir, New Orleans, 1988—; chmn. Symphony Store, New Orleans Symphony, 1990—; lector St. Angela Merici Ch. Mem. Am. Ednl. Rsch. Assn., Assn. Am. Med. Colls., La. Edn. Rsch. Assn., Soc. Tchrs. Family Medicine, New Orleans Film and Video Buffs, Phi Kappa Phi, Phi Delta Kappa. Roman Catholic. Home: 420 Old Hammond Hwy Apt 215 Metairie LA 70005 Office: LA State U Med Ctr Sch Medicine 1542 Tulane Ave New Orleans LA 70112

GATRELL, JOSELLE BERNSTEIN, government official; b. Long Branch, N.J., Sept. 7, 1942; d. Benjamin and Theresa Bernstein; m. Jacob W. Gatrell (div. Nov. 1982). BS, U. Md., 1964; cert. in stats. of health scis., Yale U., 1966; MS, Am. U., Washington, 1974. Statistician, programmer Nat. Ctr. for Health Stats., Rockville, Md., 1967-73; sect. chief Nat. Inst. Drug Abuse, Rockville, 1975-78, chief info. resources mgmt. br., 1978-82, asst. dir. Info. Resources Mgmt., 1982-83; chief data mng. br. Office Toxic Substances EPA, Washington, 1983-85, info. mgmt. specialist Info Resources Mgmt., 1985-86; statistician Nat. Inst. Mental Health, Rockville, 1965-67, chief info. mgmt. and analysis br., 1986-88; statistician FDA, Rockville, 1973-75, dir. div. regulatory info. systems, 1988—. Mem. Phi Kappa Phi. Home: 5503 Gunston Ln Camp Springs MD 20746 Office: FDA 5600 Fishers Ln (HFC-30) Rockville MD 20857

GAUB, MARGARET LUISE, anesthesiologist, educator; b. Guatemala City, Guatemala; d. William Henry and Margaret Rose (Lattelle) G. BS, U. Wash., 1954, MD, 1960. Diplomate Am. Bd. Anesthesiology. Anesthesiologist Miami Childrens Hosp., Miami, Fla., 1967-83, Orlando (Fla.) Regional Hosp., 1984, North Broward Hosp., Pompano Beach, Fla., 1984—; clin. prof. of anesthesiology U. Miami Sch. Medicine, 1970—. Mem. Am. Soc. Anesthesiologists, Am. Coll. Anesthesiology, Fla. Med. Assn., Broward County Med. Assn., Fla. Soc. Anesthesiologists. Office: 6833 Consolata St Boca Raton FL 33433

GAUBATZ, LYNN MARIE, musician, educator; b. Dallas, July 15, 1956; d. Frederick George and Estella Nelle (Weaver) Gaubatz. BMus, Boston U., 1978; MMus, Northwestern U., 1980. Prin. bassoonist Chgo. Civic Symphony, 1979-80; prof. bassoon Caracas Conservatory, Venezuela, 1981, Mozarteum Conservatory, Salzburg, Austria, 1982-84; prin. bassoonist Caracas Philharm., 1981, Chamber Orch., Albuquerque, 1984-85; prin. bassoon Md. Symphony, Hagerstown, 1986—; prof. bassoon Washington Conservatory, 1987—. Recipient Nat. Young Artist's award, 1979; named One of Am.'s Most Outstanding Young Working Women Glamour mag., 1988; Leonard Bernstein fellow, 1978. Home and Office: 7609 Lee Hwy #304 Falls Church VA 22042-2000

GAUDIANI, CLAIRE LYNN, academic administrator; b. Venice, Fla., Nov. 10, 1944; d. Vincent Augustus and Vera (Rossano) Gaudiani; m. David Graham Burnett; children: David Graham, Maria. BA, Conn. Coll., 1966; MA in French and Italian, Ind. U., 1969, PhD in French and Italian, 1975; PhD (hon.), Purdue U., 1989, Whitman Coll., 1989. Asst. prof. Purdue U., W. Lafayette, Ind., 1977-80, Emory U., Atlanta, 1980-81; sr. fellow in romance langs., acting assoc. dir. Joseph H. Lauder Inst. Mgmt. and Internat. Studies U. Pa., Phila., 1981-88; pres. Conn. Coll., New London, 1988—; mem. commn. internat. edn. Am. Coun. on Edn.; bd. dirs. So. New Eng. Telephone Co.; cons. Dana Found., Exxon Found., Rockefeller Found. Author: The Cabaret Poetry of Theophile de Viau: Texts and Traditions, 1980, Teaching Writing in the Foreign Language Curriculum, 1981, (with Carol Herron and others) Strategies for Development of Foreign Language and Literature Programs, 1984; author articles on 17th century French poetry, lang. acquisition and pedagogy, higher edn. mgmt. Chair assessment task force United Way, New London, 1988; hon. chair Summer Music Fund, New London, 1988; trustee Hazen Found.; bd. dirs. Eugene O'Neill Theatre Ctr. Recipient Coll. medal Conn. Coll., 1987; rsch. fellow Nat. Humanities Ctr., 1980-81, Am. Coun. Learned Socs., 1976-77. Mem. Am. Assn. Higher Edn. (bd. dirs. 1988—), MLA (adv. com. fgn. lang. programs 1988—), Conn. World Trade Assn. (bd. dirs.), Phi Beta Kappa. Roman Catholic. Home: 772 Williams St New London CT 06320 Office: Conn Coll Office of Pres Mohegan Ave New London CT 06320*

GAUDIERI, MILLICENT HALL, association executive; b. East Liverpool, Ohio, Jan. 26, 1941; d. John Thompson and Sara (Pollock) Hall; m. Alexander V.J. Gaudiere, June 10, 1967; 1 son, Alexandre Barclay Everson. A.A., Centenary Coll., Hackettstown, N.J., 1961; postgrad., U. Pitts., 1962. Polit. researcher U.S. embassy, Paris, 1964-65; asst. to pres. RTV Internat., Inc., N.Y.C., 1966-71; exec. dir. Assn. Art Mus. Dirs., Montreal, Que., Can., 1973—. Home 311 W York St Savannah GA 31401. Bd. dirs. Ga. Pub. Radio, Savannah, 1978-79. Mem. N.Y. Jr. League (dir. 1973-75 Vol. of Yr. award), Am. Assn. Mus. Republican. Presbyterian.

GAUDIO, MAXINE DIANE, biofeedback therapist, stress management consultant; b. Stamford, Conn., Oct. 7, 1939; d. Robert Fridolin and Doris (Altstadter) Goodman; m. Arthur Sebastian Gaudio, Oct. 7, 1962; 1 child, Dante Sebastian. Relaxation therapist The Biofeedback Clinic, New Canaan, Conn., 1970-73; chief EEG technologist St. Barnabas, Bronx, N.Y., 1973-75; biofeedback therapist Biofeedback Clinic, Stamford, Conn. and Winston-Salem, N.C., 1973—; clin. dir. Biofeedback Unltd. N.C., 1979—; clin. dir. Creative Mind Systems, Stamford, Conn., 1980—; tech. advisor Creative Mind Systems N.C., 1980-83; indsl. cons. major corps. U.S.A., 1976—; writer, creator stress video Hartley Prodns., Old Greenwich, Conn., 1984—; writer, creator, narrator Robert Gross Assocs., Stamford, Conn., 1984. Author, narrator video: Stress, 1984, Your Secret Energy Source, 1984; writer, dir. audio/visual package Captain Mind; creator, producer Stress and Relaxation, 1986-87; author, narrator book and tapes: Creative Union, 1980; author: Land Within the Shadow, 1980. Exec. dir. Friends of Children, Darien, Conn., 1985-87; dir. spl. projects Victim Svcs. Agy., N.Y.C.; bd. dirs. cons. Childhope, N.Y.C., 1987—. Mem. Am. Fedn. Press Women, Am. Soc. EEG Technologists, Am. Assn. Advancement Tension Control, Biofeedback Soc. Am., Biofeedback Soc. N.C., Internat. Platform Assn. Avocations: swimming; fencing; flying; metaphysics; astrology; piano. Club: Conn. Press. Home: 3 Hackett Circle Apt 2 Stamford CT 06905

GAUGER, MICHELE ROBERTA, photographer, studio administrator, corporate executive; b. Elkhorn, Wis., Feb. 28, 1949; d. Robert F. and Christiane J. (Guiffaut) Marszalek; m. Richard C. Gauger, May 3, 1969. Student U. Wis., Superior, 1967-69, U. Wis., Whitewater, 1978-80, Winona Sch. Profl. Photography-Chgo., 1984-89; Degree in Photographic Craftsmenship, 1990. Wedding photographer Fossum Studio, Elkhorn, 1973-78; owner Photography by Michele, Whitewater, 1978-81; pres., photographer, mgr., Michele Inc. of Wis., Whitewater, 1981—, Foxes Reg., 1987—; speaker Wedding Photographers Internat. Conv., Las Vegas, Nev., 1987, 89, Tenn. Profl. Photographers Assn., Nashville, 1987, Twin Cities Profl. Photographers, Mpls., 1987; lectr. Supra Color Seminar, Mpls., 1987, 89, San Francisco Profl. Photographers Assn., 1988, Monterey Profl. Photographers Assn., Nev. Profl. Photographers Assn., 1989, Mich. Profl. Photographers Assn., 1989. Contbr. articles to profl. jours.; works exhibited Chinese Nat. Gallery, Beijing, 1987, 88, 89. Mem. Nat. Arbor Found, Nebr., 1984—. Recipient 1st place Wedding Photography award Internat. Wedding Photography, 1983, 84, 87, 88 (two awards), 2nd place award, 1985, Grand award, 1988. Mem. Profl. Photographers Am. (Natl. Loan Collectional 1984), Exhibited Chinese Nat. Gallery, Beijing, China (2d place award 1988, Bronze medal 1989), Wis. Profl. Photographer Assn., Wedding Photographer Internat., Winona Sch. Profl. Photography Alumni Assn., Whitewater C. of C. Republican. Roman Catholic. Avocations: world travel, big game hunting, horseback riding, cooking. Home: Gauger Rd Rt 2 Whitewater WI 53190 Office: Michele Inc Rt 2 Whitewater Lake Whitewater WI 53190

GAUGHAN, JOANNE FRANCES, restaurant manager; b. Holyoke, Mass., Aug. 7, 1961; d. John Frances and Barbara Ann (Bosjolie) G. Assoc., Holyoke Community Coll., 1982. Lic. real estate saleswoman, Mass. Traveling waitperson trainer Denny's, Holyoke, 1980-83; salesperson Chatfield Paper, Springfield, Mass., 1983-84, Sonoda Real Estate, Holyoke, Mass., 1984-85; restaurant mgr. Fitzwilly's, Northampton, Mass., 1985—. Office: Fitzwilly's 23 Main St Northampton MA 01060

GAUL, KATHLEEN THERESA, forecast analyst; b. Paterson, N.J., Oct. 12, 1960; d. Joseph Bernard and Catherine Loretta (McCardle) G. Cert. in internat. mgmt., U. Copenhagen, 1985; BA, William Paterson Coll., 1987, MBA, 1990. Intern IBM, Montvale, N.J., 1986; bookkeeper Grand Union Co., Oakland, N.J., 1977-87; acctg. supr. Am. Cyanamid, Wayne, N.J., 1987—. Mem. NAFE, Omicron Delta Epsilon.

GAULDIN, DIANE MOTLEY, management; b. Danville, Va., June 30, 1959; d. Ocris Benjamin and Ruth (Parsons) M.; m. Drewry E. Gauldin. Certificate, Danville Community Coll. Researcher Dan River Inc., Danville, 1979-86; fitted sheet technician Dan River, Danville, 1988--; active mem., United Textile Workers, Danville, 1979-86. Author: Great American Poetry Anthology, 1988. Republican. Methodist.

GAULKE, MARY FLORENCE, library administrator; b. Johnson City, Tenn., Sept. 24, 1923; d. Gustus Thomas and Mary Belle (Bennett) Erickson; m. James Wymond Crowley, Dec. 1, 1939; 1 son, Grady Gaulke (name legally changed); m. 2d, Bud Gaulke, Sept. 1, 1945 (dec. Jan. 1978); m. 3d, Richard Lewis McNaughton, Mar. 21, 1983. B.S. in Home Econs., Oreg. State U., 1963; M.S. in L.S., U. Oreg., 1968, Ph.D. in Spl. Edn., 1970. Cert. standard personnel supr., standard handicapped learner, Oreg. Head dept. home econs. Riddle Sch. Dist. (Oreg.), 1963-66; library cons. Douglas County Intermediate Edn. Dist., Roseburg, Oreg., 1966-67; head resident, head counselor Prometheus Project, So. Oreg. Coll., Ashland, summers 1966-68; supr. librarians Medford Sch. Dist. (Oreg.), 1970-73; instr. in psychology So. Oreg. Coll., Ashland, 1970-73; library supr. Roseburg Sch. Dist., 1974—; resident psychologist Black Oaks Boys Sch., Medford, 1970-75; mem. Oreg. Gov.'s Council on Libraries, 1979. Author: Vo-Ed Course for Junior High, 1965; Library Handbook, 1967; Instructions for Preparation of Cards For All Materials Cataloged for Libraries, 1971; Handbook for Training Library Aides, 1972. Coordinator Laubach Lit. Workshops for High Sch. Tutors, Medford, 1972. Fellow Internat. Biog. Assn. (life); mem. So. Oreg. Library Fedn. (sec. 1971-73), ALA, Oreg. Library Assn., Pacific N.W. Library Assn., Am. Biog. Inst. (lifetime dep. gov.), Delta Kappa Gamma (pres. 1980-82), Phi Delta Kappa (historian, research rep.). Republican. Methodist. Clubs: Lodge: Order Eastern Star (worthy matron 1956-57). Home: 1625 Days Creek Rd Days Creek OR 97429 Office: Roseburg Pub Schs 1419 Valley View Dr Roseburg OR 97470

GAUSELMAN, OPAL L. M., accountant; b. Bladen, Ohio, Aug. 11, 1946; d. Leonard M. and Emma Lee Martin; m. Robert W. Gauselman, May 9, 1981. Student, U. Cin.; grad., So. Ohio Coll., 1969, Mt. St. Joseph Coll., 1984. Acct. John E. Shriver & Co., Cin., 1967-78; contr., treas. Mill End Shops of Cin., 1978-85, Vogely & Todd Inc., Nashville, 1986—. Recipient Good Citizen award DAR, Vol. award ARC. Mem. NAFE, Am. Soc. Women Accts. Mem. Ch. of Christ.

GAVIN, MARY C., rehabilitation services professional; b. Chgo., Mar. 5, 1934; d. Percy A. and Eileen (Rooney) Reed; divorced; children: John, Michael, Loretta, Peter, Margaret Anne. BS in Occupational Therapy, Mount Mary Coll., 1955; MS in Counseling, U. Wis., 1981. Occupational therapist Sherwood Nursing Home, Williams Bay, Wis., 1974-76, Lakeland Counseling Ctr., Elkorn, Wis., 1977-82; instr. occupational therapy dept. Univ. Wis., Milw., 1981-82; instr. occupational therapist dept. Elizabethtown (Pa.) Coll., 1982-85; mgr. psychiat. rehab. Swedish Am. Hosp., Rockford, Ill., 1985—; counselor M.K.G. Counseling Svc., Fontana, Wis., to date. Interviewer League of Women Voters, Rockford, 1988. Mem. Am. Occupational Therapy Assn., Ill. Occupational Therapy Assn., Wis. Occupational Therapy Assn., Assn. Guidance and Counseling, Internat. Psycho Geriatric Assn., Am. Soc. on Aging. Office: Swedish Am Hosp 1400 Charles Rockford IL 61104

GAVITT, PAULA CLAXTON, psychologist; b. Boston, Mar. 3, 1945; d. Charles Russell and Clara Maye (Thompson) Claxton; m. Jason A. Gavitt (div. Dec. 1977); 1 child, Brian E. Frysinger. Student, Lincoln U. (Pa.), 1965-69; BA, U. N.C., Asheville, 1971; MA, Western Carolina U., Cullowhee, N.C., 1972; EdS, Appalachian State U., Boone, N.C., 1989. Lic. psychol. assoc.; cert. sch. psychologist; cert. prin.; cert. supt. Sch. psychologist Graham Ctr., Charlotte (N.C)-Mecklenburg Schs., 1972-73; psychologist State Div. Social Svcs., Black Mountain, N.C., 1974-81, Black Mountain Ctr., 1981-84; sch. psychologist Lincoln County Schs., Lincolnton, N.C., 1984-86; BEH psychologist Harding High Sch. Upward Bound, Charlotte, 1986—; instr. computer sci. Johnson C. Smith U., Charlotte, 1990; psychologist/cons. Rutherford Juvenile Ct., Rutherfordton, N.C., 1985—; foster parent Gaston-Lincoln mental Health, Gastonia, N.C., 1988—. Vol. 4-H, Lincolnton, N.C., 1985-88. Mem. N.C. Sch. Psychology Assn. Democrat. Home: Rt 3 Box 460B Cherryville NC 28021 Office: Harding High Sch 2001 Alleghany St Charlotte NC 28208

GAWEHN, DOROTHY JEANNE, retail sales company executive; b. Omaha, Jan. 20, 1931; d. Robert Floyd and Margaret Marie (Sitzman) Sealock; m. Kenneth Emil Gawehn, Apr. 17, 1951 (div. Jan. 1985); children—Marilyn Gawehn Jeffries, Kenneth M., Eric M., Celeste Gawehn-Yates. Grad. high sch., Omaha, Nebr. Systems technician Nat. Welding Co., Richmond, Calif., 1926-63; lead data entry operator United Grocers Co., Fresno, Calif., 1964-68, data processing mgr., 1968-72, computer operator shift supr., Oakland, Calif., 1972-76, documentation specialist, 1976-82; mgr. adminstrv. systems Baddour, Inc., Memphis, 1983-89; with Fed. Express Corp., 1989—. Reader for the blind Sta. WTTL, Memphis, 1983—; vol. worker Crisis and Suicide Intervention, Memphis, 1985—, Docent for Ramesses exhibit, 1987. Recipient Key to Memphis. Mem. Internat. Tng. In Communication (club pres. 1989—), Data Processing Mgmt. Assn (Performance award 1973, Yosemite chpt.), Mensa (chmn. 1989—). Republican. Roman Catholic. Avocations: backpacking; reading; writing; travel; hiking. Home: 6644 Elkgate Rd Memphis TN 38115 Office: Fed Express Corp 3350 Miac Cove Memphis TN 38194

GAY, CAROL VIRGINIA, molecular biologist, educator; b. Belfast, ME, Apr. 8, 1940; d. Delmar Boynton and Charlotte Marium (Stuart) Lovejoy; m. Fred Dana Gay, Mar. 6, 1964; 1 child, Zachery Lewis. BA, U. Maine, 1962; MS, Pa. State U., 1967, PhD, 1972. Rsch. assoc. molecular and cell biology program Pa. State U., University Park, 1975-80, sr. rsch. assoc., 1980-88, assoc. prof. cell biology, 1988—, assoc. prof. poultry sci., 1988—; mem. study sect. NIH, Bethesda, Md., 1986-90. Editorial bd. Jour. Histochemistry and Cytochemistry, N.Y.C., 1976—; contbr. articles to profl. jours. Postdoctoral fellow NIH, 1973-75; recipient Rsch. Career Devel. award NIH, 1979-84. Mem. Am. Soc. Bone and Mineral Rsch., Am. Soc. Cell Biology, Am. Physiol. Soc., Royal Soc. Medicine.

GAY, CLAUDINE MOSS, physician; b. Alma, Ga., Nov. 30, 1915; d. Fred and Rosa (Mercer) Moss; B.S., Coll. William and Mary, 1935; M.D., U. Va., 1939; m. Lendall C. Gay, June 29, 1940 (dec. 1971); children—Gordon B., Spencer B.; m. J. Marion Bryant, 1974 (dec. 1986). Intern, Gallinger Mcpl. Hosp., Washington; practice medicine specializing in family practice, Washington, 1940—; mem. staff, exec. bd. Sibley Meml. and Capitol Hill Hosp., Washington; mem. Pres.'s Council on Malpractice, 1965; mem. health adv. commn. HEW, 1971-78; U.S. del. Med. Women's Internat. Congress, 5 times; del. Pres.'s Workshop on Non-Govtl. Orgn. Trustee Moss Charity Trust Fund, 1966—; adv. bd. Med. Coll. Pa., 1977; mem. president's council Coll. William and Mary. Recipient Capitol Hill Community Achievement award, 1986. Fellow Am. Acad. Family Practice (del. 1971-81; alt. del. to ho. dels. 1964-71); mem. Assn. Med. Women Internat. (del. 1966-72, councillor 1978-84), Royal Acad. Medicine, Pan Am. Med. Soc., D.C. Acad. Gen. Practice (pres.), Am. Med. Women's Assn. (councilor orgn. and mgmt. 1972-73, v.p. 1974, nat. pres. 1977, Blackwell medal 1988), D.C. Med. Women's Assn. (pres.), AMA, D.C. Med. Soc. (dir., exec. bd., past v.p., mem. nominating com. 1970, 81, relative value study com. 1970-72, constn. and constn. bylaws com., sec. family practice sect. 1966, 69, 78), DAR. Clubs: Women's Roundtable for Health Issues, Washington Forum (pres. 1987-88), Zonta (dir.). Home: 5030 Loughboro Rd NW Washington DC 20016 Office: 5000 Macomb St NW Washington DC 20016

GAY, PRISCILLA HALE, lawyer; b. Rochester, N.Y., Oct. 4, 1948; d. William Henry and Eleanor Randolph (Harper) G. BA, West Va. U., 1970; JD, WVU Coll. of Law, 1973. Atty. WV State Tax Dept., Charleston, W.Va., 1973-75; hearing examiner W.Va. State Tax Dept., Charleston, W.V., 1975-77; atty. Governor's Office of Health Affairs, Charlesotn, W.Va., 1977-78; atty. W.Va. State Tax Dept., Charleston, 1978-83, hearing examiner, 1983-85; sr. hearing examiner W.Va. State Tax Dept., 1985—; mediator U.S. Dist. Ct. No. Dist. W.Va., 1987—, arbitrator Am. Arbitration Assn., 1988—; adj. instr. Marshall U. Community Coll., Huntington, 1976—, W.Va. Coll. Grad. Studies, 1977. Author, Book, Administrative Practice W.Va. Tax Dept, 1988, Practice Before the W.Va. Tax Commissioner, 1977, editor, pamplet, Students Rights and Responsibilities, 1967. Bd. dirs. Cen. Child Care of W.Va., Inc., 1978-89, Shawnee Hills Commn. Mental Health Mental Retardation Ctr., 1980-88; organizer Fund for Arts, 1978. Mem. W.Va. State Bar (com. alternative dispute & resolution), Am. Arbitration Assn., Kanawha Bar Assn. Democrat. Episcopalian. Home: 60 Ninth Ave Saint Albans WV 25177 Office: WV State Tax Dept 1001 Lee St E PO Box 2389 Charleston WV 25328

GAY, VIRGINIA CAROLYN, educator; b. Moultrie, GA., Jan. 16, 1951; d. Wallace H. and Pauline (Murphy) G. BS, Ga. Southwestern Coll., 1973; MEd, Ga. Southwestern U., 1981. Tchr. Colquitt County Bd. Edn., Moultrie, 1973-81, Douglas County Bd. Edn., Douglasville, Ga., 1981—. Mem. Profl. Assn. Ga. Educators. Democrat. Baptist. Office: Chestnut Log Middle Sch Pope Rd Douglasville GA 30135

GAYE, KATHLEEN TIGHE, financial services marketing executive; b. Newark, June 9, 1953; d. Robert Edward and Marie (Schmidtz) Tighe; m. Donald James Gaye, Sept. 28, 1985. BA, Lycoming Coll., 1975. Advt. sales rep. Sta. WWPA Radio, Williamsport, Pa., 1976-78; account exec. Hutchins/Young and Rubican, Rochester, N.Y., 1978-81; v.p., advt. mgr. Chase Lincoln First Bank, Rochester, 1981-86; v.p., mktg. mgr. Citibank, Rochester, 1986—; instr. Am. Inst. of Banking, Rochester, N.Y., 1982, 83, 86; coord. Advt. Coun. of Rochester, 1988—. Fund raising corp. capt. Rochester Philharmonic Orch., 1988. Mem. Women in Communication Inc. (pres.-elect), Mktg. Communicators of Rochester. Home: 17 Nettlecreek Rd Fairport NY 14450 Office: Citibank 99 Garnsey Rd Pittsford NY 14534

GAYKEN, PATSY, accountant; b. Edinburg, Tex., Feb. 9, 1930; d. Wade Hampton and Lenore (Duran) Bliss; m. Donald P. Gayken,. BA, Pan Am. U., 1975, MBA, 1978. CPA. Ptnr. Bliss-Moore-Gayken, Edinburg, 1950-89; chief acct. Edinburg Gen. Hosp., 1983-84; internal auditor Hidalgo County, 1984--; grad. teaching asst. Pan Am. U., Edinburg, 1978; cons. McAllen (Tex.) and Upper Valley Arts Council, 1985--. Pres. Edinburg Jr. League, 1966-67, Girl Scout Council, 1958-59. Fellow AICPA, Tex. State Soc. CPA's; mem. AAUW (pres. local chpt. 1982-83), Tex. Assn. Assessing Officers, Kappa Delta Pi. Baptist. Home: 1721 Ann Edinburg TX 78539 Office: Hidalgo County 100 N Closner Edinburg TX 78540

GAYLOR, BETTIE MAY, communications specialist; b. Farmington, N.Mex., Nov. 6, 1959; d. David H. and Thelma Ruth (Monroe) G. Student, N.Mex. State U., 1979-80, San Juan Coll., 1985-86. Syndication account mgr. The Video Tape Co., North Hollywood, Calif., 1986-87; syndication mgr. Wold Communications, N.Y.C., 1987-89; owner Consolidated Communications, Astoria, N.Y., 1989—. Republican. Home: 32-31 35th St Astoria NY 11106

GAYLOR, DIANE MARIE, psychiatric social worker; b. Cleve., June 10, 1938; d. Albert Francis and Helen Catherine (Pietrazk) G. Student, Kent State U., 1956-60; BA in Sociology with honors, LaVerne U., 1967, MA in Teaching English, 1974; MSW, U. Iowa, 1979. Diplomate Am. Bd. Clin. Social Work, Am. Acad. Cert. Social Workers; lic. social worker, Iowa; life credential elem. edn., Calif.; life profl. cert. elem. edn., Iowa. Tchr. elem. schs. Cleve. Pub. Schs., 1958-64; tchr. elem. schs. Chino (Calif.) Pub. Schs., 1967-76, reading specialist, 1968-70, reading specialist upper elem. grades, 1970-76; social worker, chem. dependency unit Cherokee (Iowa) Mental Health Inst., 1977-78, social worker, children's unit, 1978-79; psychiat. social worker Keith Barnett, Psychiatrist, Sioux City, Iowa, 1979—. Mem. NEA, Nat. Assn. Social Workers, Acad. Cert. Social Workers, Iowa Mental Health Assn., Am. Bd. Examiners in Social Work, Great Books Found., Beta Sigma Phi. Home: 2021 Indian Hills Sioux City IA 51104 Office: PO Box 2018 Sioux City IA 51104

GAYLOR, MADELEINE, musician, conservationist; b. Somerville, Mass., May 30, 1901; d. Earl Leslie and Mary Violet (Dale) G. BS, Middlebury (Vt.) Coll., 1922; postgrad., Harvard U., Yale U., Princeton U. Head music dept. Crushing Acad., Ashburntian, Mass., 1927-52; music dir. First Parish Ch., Fitchburg, Mass., 1952—. Composer, researcher ch. music. Mem. Fitchburg Conservation Commn., 1969—, past chmn.; active mem. Nashua River Watershed Assn., town chmn. Boston Symphony Orch., music com. Fitchburg Library, 1972—; trustee Fitchburg Hist. Soc., 1989—; town chmn. for Boston Symphony Youth Concerts. Recipient Winged Victory award, Prof. and Bus. Women's Club, 1964, Fitchburg C. of C. Recognition award for Outstanding Citizen, 1983, Community Leadership award Fitchburg State Coll., 1984, The Counsel Cup award, Cushing Acad., 1984, Conservation award Nashua River Watershed Assn., 1989. Mem. AAUW, Quota Club, Middlebury Coll. Mortar Bd., Laurelwood Garden, Lexington Music Club, Fitchburg Art Museums, Intercollegiate Club. Home: 5 Prospect St Fitchburg MA 01420 Office: First Parish Ch Main St Upon Cameron Fitchburg MA 01420

GAYLORD, GLORIA L., state agency official; b. Warren, Ohio, Feb. 11, 1942; children: Katherine, Rebecca, Jennifer. BS, Edinboro (Pa.) U., 1964; MBA, St. Cloud (Minn.) U., 1986. CPA, Ohio. Acct. Peat Marwick Mitchell, Mpls., 1976-78; prof. acctg. Bowling Green (Ohio) State U., 1978-80, U. Toledo, 1980-83; commr. Pub. Utilities Commn. Ohio, Columbus, 1983—; mem. tech. adv. com., Ohio Coal Devel. Office. Author: Careers in Accounting, 1984. Bd. dirs., WOSU Pub. Radio and Television, Columbus, 1988. Mem. Nat. Regulatory Rsch. Inst. (bd. dirs. 1985—), Iowa State Regulatory Conf. (bd. dirs. 1988—), Ohio Soc. CPAs, Nat. Assn. Regulatory Utility Commrs. (communications com., v.p. Gt. Lakes Conf., 410(b) joint conf. for planning for future telecommunications network), Franklin County Pres. Club. Republican. Presbyterian. Office: Pub Utilities Commn Ohio 180 E Broad St Columbus OH 43266-0573

GAYLORD, KAREN WHITACRE, financial executive; b. Stuttgart, Fed. Republic of Germany, Dec. 25, 1951; d. Eugene Maxwell and Marion Eileen (Jones) W.; m. John William Gaylord; 1 child, Jeffrey Whitacre. BS in Acctg. cum laude, Pa. State U., 1973. CPA, N.J., CLU, chartered fin. cons. Auditor Peat, Marwick, Mitchell & Co., Trenton, N.J., 1973-75; chief mgmt. analyst N.J. Housing FIn. Agy., Mercerville, N.J., 1975-81; sales mgr., field underwriter Mut. of N.Y., North Brunswick, N.J., 1981-87; pres. P&R Fin. Svcs. and Tax Planning, East Windsor, N.J., 1984-87; sr. tng. cons. and asst. v.p. Merrill Lynch Pierce, Fenner and Smith, Princeton, N.J., 1987—; instr. Middlesex County Coll., Edison, N.J., 1983. Mem. NAFE, AICPA, N.J. Soc. CPAs, Am. Women's Soc. of CPAs. Home: 106 S Main St Allentown NJ 08501 Office: PO Box 9032 Princeton NJ 08543-9032

GAYNOR, LEAH, radio public relations writer, broadcaster; b. Irvington, N.J.; d. Jack and Sophia Kamish; AA, Miami Dade Community Coll., 1970; BA, Fla. Internat. U., 1975, postgrad., 1975—; m. Robert Merrill, Mar. 27, 1954 (div.); children: Michael David, Lisa Heidi, Tracy Lynn. Owner, operator Lee Gaynor Assos., pub. relations, Miami, Fla., 1970-72; exec. dir. Ft. Lauderdale (Fla.) Jaycees, 1970-71; host interview program Sta. WGMA, Hollywood, Fla., 1971-73, stas. WWOK and WIGL-FM, Fla., 1973-79; occupational specialist Lindsey Hopkins Edn. Ctr. Dade County Pub. Schs., publicity-pub. relations, Miami, 1971—, broadcaster talk show sta. WEDR-FM; host, producer weekly half-hour pub. service talk program, The Leah Gaynor Show, 1985—. Citizens Adv. Com. Career and Vocat. Edn., 1973—; mem. adv. com. North Miami Beach High Sch., 1977-79; communications com. Council Continuing Edn. Women Miami, 1972-79; mem. publicity Com. Ctr. Fine Arts, Mus. Sci. Mem. Women in Communications, Am. Women in Radio and TV (dir. publicity Goldcoast chpt. 1974-76), Alliance Career Edn. (publicity chmn.), United Tchrs. of Dade (legis. com.). Democrat. Home: 1255 NE 171 Terr North Miami Beach FL 33162 Office: 750 NW 20th St Miami FL 33127

GDOWSKI, DIANA, tax specialist; b. Utica, N.Y., Aug. 16, 1951; d. Michael and Frances Mary (Carzo) G. BA, U. San Diego, 1972; MA, U. So. Calif., 1979, MBA, 1981, M Bus. Taxation, 1986. CPA, Calif. Instr. French lang. Bishop Montgomery High Sch., Torrance, Calif., 1973-76, U. So. Calif., L.A., 1977-79; auditor Ernst & Whinney, L.A., 1981-82; instr. French lang. Torrance Unified Sch. Dist., 1988—; mgmt. cons. Ernst & Whinney, L.A., 1982-83; tax specialist Fox & Co., L.A., 1983-84; sr. tax specialist Kenneth Leventhal & Co., L.A., 1984-87; tax mgr. Deloitte, Haskins & Sells, Costa Mesa, Calif., 1987-88; mgr. tax acctg. Fluor Corp., Irvine, Calif., 1988—. Vice-pres., Village Ct. Homeowners' Assn., L.A., 1982. Mem. AICPA, Calif. Soc. CPAs. Republican. Roman Catholic. Office: Fluor Corp 3333 Michelson Dr Irvine CA 92730

GEALER, ELAINE GOLDEN, real estate professional; b. Detroit, Feb. 14, 1941; d. Saul B. and Helen E. Simkovitz; m. Michael Robert Edborg, May 5, 1973 (div. 1977). BA cum laude, USC, 1963, M of Social Work, 1970. children's services worker Los Angeles County, 1968-77; women's folk singing group RCA Records, 1962-65; city mgr. Art Seminar, 1981-84. Mem. Apt. Assn., Action, Santa Monica Hist. Soc., Santa Monica Bd. Realtors, Order of Knights of Micheal, The Archangel. Home: 1128 24th St Santa Monica CA 90403

GEANURACOS, ELSIE DA SILVA, foreign language educator; b. Bklyn., Dec. 29, 1922; d. John and Maria (Nascimento) Da Silva; m. George J. Geanuracos, Jan. 28, 1945; children: Constance, Patricia, James, Joan, John. BA, Hunter Coll., 1944; student Columbia U., 1944-47. 1st tchr. Portuguese lang. N.Y.C. Sch. System, 1945-50, Spanish tchr., 1945-50; prof. Spanish U. Bridgeport, Conn., 1969, 72, 73, Housatonic Community Coll., Bridgeport, 1970; founder, adviser Portuguese Scholarship Program, U. Bridgeport, 1973—, sec. Halsey Internat. Scholarship Program, 1974, mem. bd. assocs., instr. Spanish, Womens' Inst. U. Bridgeport; tutor Tutoring Ctr. Bridgeport. Com. mem. Womens' Aux. to Fairfield County Med. Assn., Am. Cancer Soc. Bridgeport chpt.; translator Bridgeport Hosp. Aux.; mem. bd. assoc. U. Bridgeport; mem. Bklyn. Hist. Soc., Bklyn.; mem. Greater Bridgeport Symphony Guild. Recipient citation for community service Am. Cancer Soc. Bridgeport chpt.; citation as an internationalist UN Assn., 1975; 10-yr. service plaque Portuguese Scholar Ship Program of HISP, 1983. Mem. AAUW (treas. Fairfield chpt.), UN Assn., Judeo-Christian Women's Assn. (mistress of ceremonies first awards luncheon 1974), Alpha Delta Pi. Avocations: swimming, reading, drapery making, knitting, traveling. Home: 102 Lu Manor Dr Fairfield CT 06432

GEAR, SARA MOREAU, state legislator; b. Burlington, Vt., Apr. 20, 1941; d. Omer Louis and Dorothy Mary (Martel) Moreau; m. Allen Frederick Gear, Aug. 10, 1963; children: Kristen, Amy, Heather. BS, U. Vt., 1963. Tchr. Montgomery County, Rockville, Md., 1963-64, Ethan Allen Nursery Sch., Burlington, 1972-74; interior decorator Impeccable Interiors, Burlington, 1976-83; pres. Gear Country Designs, Burlington, 1983-88; legislator Vt. Ho. of Reps., Montpelier, 1985—, asst. minority leader, 1987-88, majority leader, 1989-90. Commr. Burlington Police Dept. Mem. Legislature Leaders Assn., Am. Legislature Exch. Coun., Burlington Rotary. Home: 76 Crescent Beach Dr Burlington VT 05401 Office: Vt Ho of Reps 115 State St Montpelier VT 05602

GEARHART, MARILYN KAYE, mathematics educator; b. Tucson, Apr. 11, 1950; d. Raymond Fred and Joan Gazelle (White) Hagerty; m. Lon David Gearhart, Mar. 22, 1975; children: Amanda Kaye, Shannon Leigh. BA in Elem. Edn. with dis, Manchester Coll., 1972; MS in Elem Edn. summa cum, Ind. U., 1976; BS in Math. with high hon, Tri-State U., 1985; postgrad., Ind. U., 1983-89. Substitute tchr. South Bend (Ind.) Community Sch. Corp., 1971-72; tchr. DeKalb County Ea. Community Sch. Dist., Butler, Ind., 1972-77; founder, tchr. Pleasant View Christian Early Learning Ctr., Angola, Ind., 1981-85; also bd. dirs. Pleasant View Christian Early Learning Ctr., Angola; micro computer tchr. Purdue U., Ft. Wayne, Ind., 1984; substitute tchr. Met. Sch. Dist. Steuben County, Angola, 1985; math. tchr. DeKalb County Cen. United Sch. Dist., Auburn, Ind., 1985--. Author: (textbook) The Impossibility of Achieving and Maintaining an Utopia, 1971. Sponsor freshman class DeKalb High Sch., 1987-89, sophomore class, 1989—, Students Against Drunk Driving, Auburn, 1985—, Butler Elem. Little Hoosiers, 1973-77; attendance com. gifted and talented com. DeKalb High Sch., 1989—, coach acad. decathlon Hoosier Acad. Super Bowl, 1989—; leader Girl Scouts U.S., 1986—, product sales coord. Svc. Unit, 1989-90; active local PTA, various churches, Angola and Hamilton. Dir's. award Jr. Hist. Soc., 1981-85; maths. and sci. scholars Tri-State, 1985; grantee Tchrs. Retng. Fund. Ind.-State, 1983-85. Mem. NEA, AAUW (treas. 1987-89), Classie Lassies Home Extension, Beta Beta Beta Nat. Biol. Honor Soc. Home: RR 3 Box 185 Angola IN 46703 Office: DeKalb High Sch State Rd 427 Waterloo IN 46793

GEARHART, MARTHA SUSAN, veterinarian, freelance writer; b. Rochester, N.Y., Apr. 24, 1953; d. Richard Charles and Luttrelle Knapp (Patterson) G. AB cum laude with honors in Biology, Bryn Mawr Coll., 1975; DVM, Cornell U., 1979. Diplomate Am. Bd. Veterinary Practitioners (Splty. Companion Animal Practice). Pvt. practice, Macedon, N.Y., 1979-80, Honeoye Falls, N.Y., 1980-82, Kingston, N.Y., 1982-88, Red Hook, N.Y., 1989—; Congl. sci. and engring. fellow AVMA and AAAS, Washington, 1988-89; freelance writer on policy analysis and cons., agr., edn. and vet. medicine, 1989—; rsch. assoc. ecology field sta. Hudsonia, Ltd., Annandale, N.Y., 1989—; faculty assoc. Inst. for Teaching Math. and Sci. Simon's Rock of Bard Coll., Gt. Barrington, Mass., 1990—. Columnist Info. and Dialogue Exch. on Agr., 1989—. Mem. edn. com. Dutchess County Environ. Mgmt. Coun., 1990—. Harriet Judd Meml. scholar Bryn Mawr Coll., 1975-79. Mem. AVMA (polit. action com. policy bd. 1989—, legis. liaison N.Y. dists. 1-20, 1990—), N.Y. State Vet. Med. Soc. (govtl. rels. com. policy bd. 1989—), Am. Assn. Feline Practitioners, Am. Assn. Women Veterinarians, Am. Farmland Trust, Phi Zeta. Home and Office: 51 W Market St Red Hook NY 12571

GEBA, ELIZABETH C., real estate agent; b. N.Y.C., June 18, 1933; d. Peter and Anastazia (Slobodzian) Teleshesky; m. John Geba, June 9, 1951; children: Gregory, Donna, Linda. Student, Pohs Inst., N.Y.C., 1969. Cert. real estate broker, real estate appraiser. Mgr. Brownstones Unltd., N.Y.C., Martin Real Estate, Staten Island, N.Y.; pres. Geba Realty Assocs., Inc., Glen Spey, N.Y.; asst. dir. radio program, weekly bilingual commentator, 1982-85. Councilwoman, Rep. committeewoman Town of Lumberland, Sullivan County, N.Y.; sec. Zoning Commn.; mem. Environ. Coun.; mem. aux. Mercy Community Hosp., 1980-90; br. pres. Ukrainian Am. Womans League Am., 1981-82, membership chmn., 1990. Mem. NAFE, Sparrowbush C. of C., Nat. Assn. Realtors, N.Y. State Assn. Realtors, Sullivan County Bd. Realtors. Republican. Home: 259 Leers Rd Glen Spey NY 12737 Office: Rte 97 Sparrowbush NY 12780

GEBERT, SANDRA MARGOT, librarian; b. Amityville, N.Y., Apr. 8, 1961; d. Gerhard Otto and Margot Erika (Sindermann) G. BA, SUNY, Binghamton, 1986; MLS, So. Conn. State U., 1987. N.Y. state libr.'s cert. Home health care aide Comprehensive Home Care Svcs., Inc., Smithtown, N.Y., 1985; listener in children's rm. Kings Park (N.Y.) br. Smithtown Libr., 1986; English tutor So. Conn. State U., New Haven, 1987; children's libr. Middle Country Pub. Libr., Centereach, N.Y., 1987-88, West Islip (N.Y.) Pub. Libr., 1988; reference libr. Lindenhurst (N.Y.) Meml. Libr., 1989—. Libr. vol. Commack (N.Y.) High Sch. North; hosp vol. St. Johns Episc. Hosp., Smithtown. Mem. ALA, NAFE. Home: 141 Cornell Dr Commack NY 11725 Office: Lindenhurst Meml Libr One Lee Ave Lindenhurst NY 11757

GEDDES, BARBARA ELIZABETH, ombudsman program director; b. Lawrence, Kans., July 11, 1930; d. William Lewis and Hazel Mary (Douglas) Hartman; m. Clarke Robert Geddes, Nov. 13, 1946 (div. 1961); children: Douglas, Susan, Michele. Student, Washburn U., Topeka, 1950-51, Marietta (Ohio) Coll., 1960-61, U. Md., 1984-85, Ohio U., 1985-86. Coord. Children's Hosp., 1961-66; office mgr. Prescott and Co., Ohio, 1966-67; asst. dir. Tamblyn and Brown Inc., Ohio, 1967-68; regional dir. Internat. Svcs. Agy. Inc., 1968-73; pvt. What's Inna Name, Nyack, N.Y., 1973-74; dir. Ombudsman Program, Ohio, 1976-80; cons. Pvt., 1980-82; office svcs. mgr. Omni Pub., N.Y.C., 1982-83; freelance cons. Washington, 1983-85; administrator Ombudsman Program, W.Va., 1986--; cons. Resident's Rights, 1988--, guest lecturer, Med. Symnposium, W.Va., 1989, Sch. of Gerontology, W.Va. Univ., 1987--. Corporate Bd. mem., Vly. Mental Health, W.Va., advisor, W.Va. Family Councils of Nursing Home Residents, The Natl. Women's Political Caucus, former appointee by Governor of Ohio to the Commission on Prison Reform; campaign mgr. for presdl. candidate Shirley Chisholm, 1971-72. Mem. Natl. Welfare Conferences, Bus. and Prof. Womn's Orgn. Office: Agy on Aging Region VI 200 Adams St Fairmont WV 26554

GEDDES, JANE, professional golfer; b. E. Northport, N.Y., Feb. 5, 1960; d. Gerard George and Helen Evelyn (Zielinski) G. Student, Fla. State U., 1978-82. Profl. golfer, 1983—; Winner Boston 5 Classic, 1987, Jamie Farr Toledo Classic, 1987, GNA-Glendale (Calif.) Fedn. Classic, 1987, Women's Kemper Open, 1987, LPGA Championship, 1987, Women's Brit. Open, 1989. Champion U.S. Women's Open, 1986; named Most Improved Golfer, Golf Digest, 1986. Roman Catholic. *

GEDDES, SUSAN, infosystems specialist; b. Stoneham, Mass., Apr. 29, 1927; d. James Gardner and Katherine (Artz) G. BA, Tufts U., 1949. Programmer Lockheed Missile & Space, Sunnyvale, Calif., 1956-64; analyst Macy's, San Francisco, 1964-65; systems analyst Stanford (Calif.) U., 1965-69, Library of Congress, Washington, 1969-70; computer specialist Nat. Library Medicine, Bethesda, Md., 1970—. Mem. Am. Soc. Info. Sci. (chair spl. interest group on library automation 1973-74, pres. Potomac Valley chpt. 1976-77). Home: 7556 Spring Lake Dr Bethesda MD 20817

GEDEROS, MARY HANNA, college program director; b. Conde, S.D., Aug. 21, 1949; D. Robert Lee and Eldwin (Chaon) Taylor; m. Christopher James Gederos, Aug. 21, 1970; children: Holly, Mark, Julie. BS magna cum laude, No. State Coll., Aberdeen, S.D., 1970, M. magna cum laude, 1990. Elem. tchr. Northwestern Sch. Dist., Brentford, S.D., 1971-74; substitute tchr. Aberdeen Sch. Dist., 1974-79; learning disability tchr. Frederick (S.D.) Sch. Dist., 1979-81; cons. St. Lukes Hosp., Aberdeen, 1981; dir. Resource Ctr. for Women, Aberdeen, 1981-84; dir. planned giving Presentation Coll., Aberdeen, 1984-85, dir. devel., 1985—. Pres. S.D. Coalition Against Domestic Violence, 1982-84; stewardship chair Good Shepherd Luth. Ch., Aberdeen, 1988-90; bd. dirs. United Way, Aberdeen, 1989-90, AAUW, Aberdeen, 1986-88, Chamber of Congress, Aberdeen, 1987-90. Mem. S.D. Nat. Soc. Fundraising Execs. (sec.-treas. 1988-90), CASE (Bronze award 1988). Home: 1111 N Washington Aberdeen SD 57401 Office: Presentation Coll 1500 N Main Aberdeen SD 57401

GEE, IRENE, food products executive; b. N.Y.C., Aug. 17, 1950; d. Jimmy Set and Lin Fung (Ng) G.; B.A., Hunter Coll., 1971; M.S. in Family and Consumer Studies, Lehman Coll., 1974, M.S. in Guidance and Counseling, 1978; m. Oct. 17, 1981. Tchr., Olinville Jr. High Sch., Bronx, N.Y., 1971-75, Lehman Coll., Bronx, 1975-77, Harry Eiseman Jr. High Sch., Bklyn., 1978-80; food stylist, recipe developer Ladies Home Jour., 1977-78; food stylist, recipe developer Woman's Day Mag., 1979—, home economist, 1980—; owner, operator Irene's Catering, 1984—; food coordinator Evander Childs High Sch.; food cons. Corn Products Corp., 1978—; food stylist Nabisco, 1978, also Perdue Co.; reciper writer, judger natural food contsts Scholastic Mag.; judge nat. contests Choices mag.; developer recipe booklets various cos. including Progresso and Fla. Mushrooms; cons. food cos. and publs.; comml. model Mauna Loa Macadamia Nuts, Lewis & Neale; recipe developer Lipton Co. Food exhibitor Avant Grade Foods; contbr. articles to Forecast and Choices mags. Mem. Am. Home Econs. Assn., Home Economists in Bus., Am. Counseling Assn., Omicron Nu. Contbr. articles Woman's World mag.

GEE, NOLA FAYE, political consultant, rancher; b. Madison, W.Va., Mar. 9, 1934; d. Elmer Clyde and Gladys Macel (Miller) Ball; m. Burney F. Acton Jr., Nov. 5, 1955 (div. Aug. 1962); 1 child, Angela; m. Thomas Gibbs Gee, July 20, 1979 (div. May 1985). Student, Marshall U., 1950-52; cert. in teaching, U. Calif., Fresno, 1955. Cert. tchr., Calif. Tchr. Weaver Union Elem. Sch., Merced, Calif., 1952-53, 54-55, Wharton (W.Va.) Jr. High Sch., 1953-54, Fruit St. Elem. Sch., Bangor, Maine, 1956-57; exec. dir. Woman's Aux. to Tex. Med. Assn., Austin, 1957-63; spl. asst. state rep. to U.S. Senator John G. Tower Austin, 1967-72; statewide campaign mgr. reelection campaign Senator John G. Tower, 1972; staff asst. to pres. for exec. recruitment of Women for Presdl. Appointments The White House, Washington, 1973-74; regional campaign dir. Pres. Ford for Pres., Washington, 1975-76, chmn. del. operation in the western states, summer 1976; polit. cons., mgr. gearing up effort for campaign Senator John G. Tower Washington, 1977-78; co-owner Triple Creek Ranch, Austin, 1979—; mgr. statewide campaign Bill Clements for Gov., 1978; pvt. practice polit. cons., 1979—. Editor: newsletter Woman's Aux. to the Tex. Med. Assn., 1963-67; contbr. articles to profl. jours. Bd. dirs. Brackenridge Hosp., Austin, 1972-73; state com. woman Dist. 14 State Rep. Exec. Com., Austin, 1965-68; sec. Travis County Rep. Party, Austin, 1964-68; chmn. undecided voter program John G. Tower campaign for U.S. Senate, Austin, 1966; fin. dir. 14th Senatorial Dir., Austin, 1965-68; patron Performing Arts Ctr., U. Tex., 1987-89. Mem. Austin Lyric Opera Guild (pres.'s bd. 1987-88), Laguna Gloria Art Mus. Assn. of Am., Tex. Longhorn Breeder's Assn., Austin Club. Episcopalian. Home and Office: 16301 Fitzhugh Rd Austin TX 78736

GEER, EMILY APT, educator, historian; b. West Unity, Ohio, July 28, 1912; d. Norman J. and Pearl Winifred (Bayes) Apt; m. Stanley L. Fisher, Mar. 1934 (dec. 1945); m. Ralph H. Geer, Nov. 1, 1947 (dec. 1989); children: Constance (dec.), Norman. BS in Edn., Bowling Green (Ohio) State U., 1936, MA, 1952; PhD in History, Case Western Res. U., 1962. Elem. tchr. West Unity Pub. Schs., 1932-35; comparison shopper, staff asst. R.H. Macy, N.Y.C., 1937-42; owner, mgr. Fisher-Smith Archery Co., Bryan, Ohio, 1945-48; instr. history dept., asst. to dean edn. Bowling Green State U., 1952-62; from faculty mem. to prof. history U. Findlay (Ohio), 1964-77, chmn., div. social scis., 1966-77, prof. emerita, 1977—. Adv. bd.: Hayes Hist. Jour., 1976-83; contbr. articles to profl. jours; book revs.: Hayes Hist. Jour., The Register of the Ky. Hist. Soc., Pres. Studies Quar.; author: First Lady: The Life of Lucy Webb Hayes, 1984 (Ohioana Library Assn. award 1985). Pres. Shakespeare Round Table, Bowling Green, 1989—; pres. Bowling Green State U. Women, 1954-55. Recipient Disting. Service award, Ohio Acad. Hist., 1988. Fellow Ohio Acad. History (exec. coun. 1971-74), Ohio Hist. Soc. (bd. trustees 1985-88), Ohioana Library Assn., Hayes Hist. Soc., Ctr. for the Study of the Presidency, AAUW (legis. chmn. 1987—, past internat. relations chmn.). Democrat. Methodist. Home: 4 Parkwood Dr Bowling Green OH 43402

GEER, FRANCES PEARL, teacher; b. Shipman, Miss., Apr. 23, 1907; d. Joseph Leason and Amanda Caroline (Breland) Cockcroft; m. Vasco Rudolph GeerJr., Dec. 19, 1942; children: Judith Angela, Vasco Rudolph III. BA, Woman's Coll., Hattiesberg, Miss., 1930. Lic. tchr. Ala., Miss. Tchr. Moss Point (Miss.) Schs., 1934-39; tchr., prin. Bayou Cassat Sch., Pascagoula, Miss., 1947-48; tchr. South Sch., Pascagoula, 1947-48, various schs., Mobile, Ala., 1949-63; freelance artist Mobile, 1963—. Chmn. Mobile Arts and Crafts Fair, 1964; active in local activities to promote visual arts, 1963-72. Mem. AAUW (chmn. lit. group 1985-87), Azalea City Golf Club. Home: 170 Alverson Rd Mobile AL 36608

GEERTZ, HILDRED STOREY, anthropology educator; b. N.Y.C., Feb. 12, 1927; d. Walter Rendell and Helen (Anderson) Storey; m. Clifford Geertz, 1948 (div. 1979); children: Erika, Benjamin. BA, Antioch Coll., Yellow Springs, Ohio, 1948; PhD, Radcliffe Coll., 1956. Lectr. U. Chgo., 1963-68; from assoc. prof. to prof. anthropology Princeton (N.J.) U., 1970—; chmn. dept. anthropology Princeton U., 1972-77, 86, 88-89. Author: The Javanese Family, 1961, Kinship in Bali, 1974. Office: Princeton Univ Dept Anthropology Princeton NJ 08544

GEESEY, CYNTHIA JEAN, small business owner, fitness professional; b. Lebanon, Pa., Nov. 15, 1954; d. Eugene Ronald and Joann Elizabeth (Tarbert) G. BA, Lebanon Valley Coll., 1976. Dir. Ken Crest Svcs., Plymouth Meeting, Pa., 1980-87; instr. Haverford (Pa.) Coll., 1988—; owner, dir. Stretch Thru Stress, Phila., 1988—; researcher Inst. Survey Rsch., Phila., 1989—. Regional chair Heart at Work program Am. Heart Assn., Phila., 1989-90; bd. dirs. Phila. AIDS Relief, 1989-90. Named Mentor of Yr., Am. Heart Assn., Phila., 1989. Mem. NAFE, Delaware Valley Profl. Network (bd. dirs. 1987-90). Office: Stretch Thru Stress 741 S 9th St Philadelphia PA 19147

GEESLIN, SARA CHAMBERS, sales executive; b. Memphis, June 17, 1948; d. Macie Marion and Sarah (Hendrix) Chambers; m. Robert Dewey Knight, Aug. 17, 1969 (div. July 1981); children: Macy Marian, Robert Miles; m. Gary L. Geeslin, June 30, 1988. BBA in Banking and Fin. cum laude, U. Miss., 1970; grad., Inst. of Banking, 1972. Mgmt. trainee Deposit Guaranty Nat. Bank, Jackson, Miss., 1970-72; asst. tng. mgr. Deposit Guaranty Nat. Bank, Jackson, 1971-72; office mgr. Holiday Inn, Columbus, Miss., 1972-77, Old South Coors, Inc., Columbus, 1981-82; sales rep. J.L. Teel Co., Inc., Columbus, 1982-85; mgr. sales J.L. Teel Co., Inc., Columbus, Miss., 1985—. Mem. Columbus Jr. Aux., 1978—. Mem. Am. Bus. Women's Assn., U. Miss. Alumni Assn., Delta Gamma Alumni Assn. (pres. N.E. Miss. chpt. 1980, 81), Faulderal Soc., Presidents Club., Community Leaders of Am., Phi Kappa Phi, Beta Gamma Sigma, Krewe of Bacchus, Woodland Garden Club (Columbus), Northriver Yacht Club (Tuscaloosa, Ala.), Old Waverly Golf Club (West Point, Miss.), Columbus Country Club. Republican. Episcopalian. Home: 522 Huckleberry Hills Columbus MS 39701 Office: J L Teel Co Inc Highway 45 N Columbus MS 39701

GEFFEN, BETTY ADA, theatrical personal manager; b. Lachine, Que., Can., May 12, 1911; came to U.S., 1942, naturalized, 1945; d. Joseph and Minnie (Illievitz) Gottheil; student public schs., Montreal, Que.; m. Jacob N. Geffen, Dec. 23, 1944; 1 child, JoAnn Merle. Sec., Saul Cohen/Trustee in Bankruptcy, Montreal, 1926-28, Maxwell Cummings Real Estate, 1928-30, Monroe Abbey, Atty., 1930-31; with Tic-Toc, Stanley Grill and Chez Maurice, Montreal, 1931-41; sec. H.L. Green, N.Y.C., 1941-44; pvt. personal mgr., casting cons., N.Y.C., 1950—; cons. Consab Assos. Corp., N.Y.C., 1966—. Trustee Israel Cancer Research Fund.; vol. Floating Hosp. Mem. Nat. Acad. TV Arts and Scis., Women of the Motion Picture Industry, Motion Picture Pioneers, Internat. Platform Assn., The Nat. Mus. Women in the Arts (charter). Democrat. Clubs: Variety Women N.Y. (v.p. 1977-81, pres. 1982-86, chmn. bd. 1986-88), Brandeis U. Home and Office: 17 W 71st St Apt 7-A New York NY 10023

GEFFEN, FRANCES PEARL, teacher, consultant; b. Bklyn., Aug. 22, 1919; d. Elias and Sadie (Katz) Avram; (widowed 1974); children: Joan Louise Friedman, Bonnie Ann Ashman. BA, Hunter Coll., 1939; MA, Hofstra U., 1960. Cert. elem. tchr., N.Y. Tchr. elem. Oceanside (N.Y.) Pub. Sch., 1959-82, Bridgehampton (N.Y.) Sch., 1988—; reading cons. Oceanside Schs., 1982-85. Lectr. Ctr. for Creative Retirement, L.I. U., Southampton, 1988—; active E. Hampton (N.Y.) and Sag Harbor Meals on Wheels, 1988-89; active bus tours and mus. shop Guild Hall, E. Hampton, 1988-89. Mem. AAUW (recording sec. E. Hampton chpt. 1988-89), Hadassah (recording sec. E. Hampton chpt. 1988-89, Woman of the Yr. 1989). Republican. Home: 166 Gardiner Ave East Hampton NY 11937

GEFFNER, DONNA SUE, speech pathologist, audiologist, educator; b. N.Y.C.; d. Louis and Sally (Weiner) G. BA magna cum laude, Bklyn. Coll., 1967; MA, N.Y. U., 1968, PhD (NDEA fellow), 1970, postgrad., Advanced Inst. Analytic Psychotherapy, 1973-75. Asst. prof. Lehman Coll., 1971-76; assoc. prof. dept. speech St. John's U., 1976-81, prof., 1982—, dir. Speech and Hearing Ctr., 1976—, chmn. dept. speech communication scis. and theater, 1983—, developer M.A. program in speech pathology and audiology; pvt. practice, 1980—; cons. to corp. execs.; TV producer and hostess NBC, 1977-78, CBS, 1978-79. Contbr. articles to profl. jours. and textbooks; issue editor Jour. Topics in Lang. Disorders, 1980; editor ASHA monograph, 1987. Emmy nominee for Outstanding Instrnl. Program, 1978; recipient award Pres.'s Com. on Employment of Handicapped, Pres's. medal for Outstanding Faculty Achievement St. Johns U., 1987; N.Y. State Edn. Dept. grantee, 1976-78, CUNY Rsch. Found. grantee, 1972. Fellow Am. Speech, Lang. and Hearing Assn. (legis. councillor 1978-87, 90—); mem. N.Y. State Speech and Hearing Assn. (pres. 1978-80), Audiology Study Group N.Y. Office: St John's U Speech and Hearing Ctr Grand Central Pkwy Jamaica NY 11439

GEHL, ALICE ELVIRA, federal official; b. Washington, Feb. 11, 1936; d. Robert Benjamin Crump and Anita (Granai) Rinaldi; m. Edwin James Gehl, Jan. 12, 1958 (div. Jan. 1975); children: Elizabeth Jan, Rebecca Anne, Jeanne Marie, Donald Clifford. Student, Western Okla. State Coll., 1969-71, Air U., Gunter Air Force Sta., Ala., 1978-79. With Def. Lang. Inst., San Antonio, 1972-73, Wilford Hall USAF Med. Ctr., San Antonio, 1973-78; real estate assoc. Creative Realty, San Antonio, 1974-79; tng. clk. 3290th Tech. Tng. Group, San Antonio, 1978-79; clerical asst. U.S. Dept. Air Force, Washington, 1979-80, mgmt. asst., 1980-81; clerical asst. Office of Joint Chiefs of Staff, Washington, 1981-82; sec. health affairs Office of Sec. of Def., Washington, 1982-84; staff asst. Strategic Def. Initiative Orgn., Washington, 1984—. Cert. judge Miss. Am. Pageant, Washington, 1989—; tutor Operation Rescue, Washington, 1982-85; exec. sec. Mil. Aquabrats, San Antonio, 1976-77, Ptnrs. in Edn., Washington; chmn. ways and means com. Newburyport (Mass.) PTA, 1964-65. Recipient 1st pl. award Altus AFB Arts and Crafts Show, Ft. Clark Springs Photography Contest. Mem. NAFE, Federally Employed Women, Smithsonian. Republican. Lutheran. Home: 2213 N Van Dorn St #T2 Alexandria VA 22304

GEHRES, SISTER RUTH, academic administrator; b. Evansville, Ind., Apr. 4, 1933; d. Fay Alvin and Floretta Marie (Snyder) G. BA in English, Brescia Coll., 1962; PhD in English, St. Louis U., 1968. Elem. tchr. St. Joseph Sch., Nebraska City, Nebr., 1954-57; elem. prin. Our Lady of Mercy Sch., Hodgenville, Ky., 1957-58; jr. high sch. tchr. Sts. Joseph and Paul Sch., Owensboro, Ky., 1958-62; prof. English Brescia Coll., Owensboro, 1967—, chairperson Humanities Div. and English dept., 1969-77, alumni dir., 1977-79, pres., 1986—; tchr. English Gymnasium der Ursulinen, Straubing, Fed. Republic Germany, 1984-85. Bd. dirs. Owensboro Symphony Orch., Jr. Achievement, Owensboro, 1986—, Leadership Owensboro, 1986—; bd. dirs Ky. Ind. Coll. Fund, Louisville, 1986—; mem. bd. overseers St. Meinrad Seminary. Mem. MLA, Nat. Assn. Ind. Colls. and Univs., Assn. Cath. Colls. and Univs., Council Ind. Ky. Colls. and Univs., C. of C. Office: Brescia Coll 717 Frederica St Owensboro KY 42301

GEHRING, MARY ELLEN, group operations executive; b. Ishpeming, Mich., May 4, 1953; d. Llewellyn J. and Colleen E. (Parviainen) Pope; m. David C. Gehring, Apr. 3, 1983 (div.); 1 child, Mark Anthony. Student, North Mich. U., 1971-73. Lic. optician. Optician, dept. mgr. Cole Vision Corp., Columbus, Ohio, 1977-82, 85-87; groupn ops. mgr. Cole Vision Corp., Milw., 1982-85, Atlanta, 1987—. Mem. Am. Bd. Opticianry. Republican. Lutheran. Club: Atlanta Ski-Hi. Home and Office: 3109 Calumet Circle Kennesaw GA 30144

GEHRKE, KAREN MARIE, accountant; b. Gaylord, Minn., Apr. 12, 1940; d. Stanley Henry and Frieda Marie (Hammel) Ostermann; m. Orville Raymond Gehrke, Oct. 21, 1961; children: Kimberly, Karla, Kent. Grad. high sch., Gaylord, 1958. Inspector Fingerhut Mfg., Gaylord, 1959-60; rewinder 3M, Hutchinson, Minn., 1960-61; packer 3M, Hutchinson, 1971-72; sec. Boehmke Ins. Agy., Gaylord, 1961-63, Law Office of H.A. Knobel, Gaylord, 1964-68; teller First State Fed. Savs. and Loan, Hutchinson, 1969; sec. Wally's Tire Shop, Hutchinson, 1970, Lyle R. Jensen, CPA, Hutchinson, 1974-84; owner Jensen Acctg., Hutchinson, 1984—. Mem. Nat. Assn. Female Execs., Nat. Soc. Pub. Accts., Minn. Assn. Pub. Accts., Hutchinson Area C. of C. Office: Jensen Acctg 106 2d Ave SW Hutchinson MN 55350

GEIBEL, SISTER GRACE ANN, college president; b. Sept. 17, 1937. BA in Piano and Music Edn., Carlow Coll., 1961; MA in Music Edn., U. Rcohester, 1967, PhD in Music, 1975. Tchr. elem. and high schs., 1959-67, ch. musician, 1972-80; assoc. prof. and co-chmn. music dept. Carlow Coll., Pitts., 1981-82, acting acad. dean, 1982-83, dean, 1983-88, v.p. acad. affairs, 1984-88, pres., 1988—; mem. pres.'s coun. Pitts. Coun. on Higher Edn., numerous other ednl. orgns. Bd. dirs. Pitts. Rsch. Inst., Pitts. Youth Symphony Orch. Assn.; trustee Mercy Hosp., Pitts. Mem. Duquesne Club. Office: Carlow Coll 3333 Fifth Ave Pittsburgh PA 15213-3109*

GEIER, KATHLEEN ANN, telecommunications executive; b. Lynwood, Calif., Dec. 14, 1956; d. Charles Franklin and Betty Marie (Bennett) G. BA, Calif. State U., Long Beach, 1983; MBA, U. Phoenix, 1989. With ATT, 1981; acct. mgr. ATT, San Francisco, 1989—. Mem. Women in Telecommunications. Office: ATT 50 Fremont 5th Fl San Francisco CA 94105

GEIGER, BRENDA HOUSTON, audiologist, speech pathologist; b. Phila.; d. William Cooper and Sarah (Hand) Houston; children: Erin Leigh, Shawn Ian. BS, U. Southern Miss., 1965, MS, 1966, PhD, 1968. Asst. prof. U. So. Alabama, Mobile, Ala., 1968-74; chief, audiology speech pathology svc. VA Med. Ctr., Tuskegee, Ala., 1974—; adj. prof. Auburn U., Ala., 1976--. Baptist. Office: VA Med Ctr Hospital Rd Tuskegee AL 36083

GEIGER, KARLA MARY, health screening company executive, consultant; b. Milw., Oct. 14, 1964; d. Ilene Lois (Klein) Price; m. Christopher A. Geiger, Aug. 2, 1986. Student, Marquette U., 1986. Client svcs. rep. CBC, Oak Creek, Wis., 1982-85; office mgr. MEDIVAN, Inc., South Milwaukee, Wis., 1985-87; v.p. MEDIVAN, Inc., Cudahy, Wis., 1987—. Mem. Personnel-Indsl. Rels. Adminstrs. (safety com. 1989), Wis. Women Entrepreneurs, Job's Daus. Office: MEDIVAN 4602 S Packard Ave Cudahy WI 53110

GEIGER, LYNN ELLEN, psychologist; b. Syracuse, N.Y., Aug. 6, 1952; d. Carl Joseph and Jane Miriam (Easton) G.; m. Robert Edward Stevens, Aug. 12, 1979; children: Carl Stevens, Drew Stevens, Woody Stevens. BA in Spanish and Edn., Colgate U., 1974, MA in Counseling Psychology, 1975; MS in Clin. Psychology, Syracuse U., 1981, PhD in Clin. Psychology, 1982. Lic. psychologist, N.Y. Elem. sch. counselor Farmington (N.H.) Sch. Dist., 1975-78, project dir. Title I ESEA program, 1976-78; coord. psychology clinic Syracuse U., 1981-82; psychology intern Hutchings Psychiat. Ctr., Syracuse, 1982-83; supervising asst. psychologist St. Joseph's Hosp., Syracuse, 1983-88; clin. psychologist pvt. practice Fayetteville, N.Y., 1985—; adj. fculty Syracuse U., 1985—; asst. prof. Chapman Coll., Syracuse, 1982—; adj. instr. Whittemore Bus. Sch., U. N.H., Durham, 1976-78; cons.-trainer N.H. State Dept. Edn., Concord, 1977-78; lectr. child sexual abuse, 1987—. Mem. mental health task force N.H. Women's Meeting, Internat. Women's Yr., Concord, 1977; examiner N.H. Bd. Examiners, State Dept. Edn., Concord, 1977-78; mem. NOW, 1985—, Cen. N.Y. Orgn. for Women, 1986—. Mem. Cen. N.Y. Psychol. Assn. (chair ethics com. 1989—), Sexual Abuse Task Force, N.Y. State Pychol. Assn., Am. Psychol. Assn. Office: 6834 E Genesee St Fayetteville NY 13066

GEIGER, SHARON KAY, manufacturing executive; b. Wolf Lake, Ind., Sept. 7, 1945; d. Wilmer G. and Katherine I. (Deutsch) Nace; m. Joe L. Geiger, Sept. 2, 1966; 1 child, Jeffrey A. Student, Manchester (Ind.) Coll., 1965. Plant mgr. Viking, Inc., Columbia City, Ind., 1968—. Chmn. Arthritis Telethon, Fort Wayne, Ind., 1990, Cystic Fibrosis, Fort Wayne, 1990. Mem. NAFE, Am. Bus. Womens Assn. (com. 1989-90), Eagles Aux. (conductor 1989-90, pres. 1990—). Democrat. Baptist. Home: 3469 S St Rd 109 Albion IN 46701

GEIGER, TERESA MARIE, registered nurse; b. Valley Stream, N.Y., Oct. 17, 1964; d. Edward T. and Dorothy (Cermak) K. BSN, Molloy Coll., 1986. RN, N.Y. Nurse Schneider Children's Hosp. L.I. Jewish Med. Ctr., New Hyde Park, N.Y., 1986—; staff nurse Mercy Hosp., Rockville Ctr., N.Y.; mem. unit rep. patient classification com., L.I. Jewish Hosp. Med. Centre, New Hyde Pk., 1987-88, nursing rep. parent teaching group, 1989—. Republican. Roman Catholic. Home: 1007 Robin Rd Franklin Square NY 11010 Office: Mercy Hosp N Village Ave Rockville Centre NY 11570

GEIGER, VIVA ANN, customer service professional; b. New Eagle, Pa., July 20, 1964; d. James Donald MacDougall and Delores Mae (Nolder) Martin; m. John Joseph Geiger. AS, Pa. State Coll.-Behrend, 1984. Asst. mgr. Brooks Fashions, Erie, Pa., 1985-86; mgr. Dailey's Jewelers, Erie, 1986-87, Rentway, Inc., Erie, 1987-88; customer svc. rep. Kubinski Bus. Machines, Erie, 1988—; small bus. cons., Erie, 1987—; beauty cons., Mary Kay Cosmetics, Erie, 1988—. Mem. NAFE, Pa. State Alumni Soc., Hist. Preservation Soc., USGA, Theta Phi Alpha. Democrat. Home: 3201 Elmwood Ave Erie PA 16508 Office: Kubinski Bus Machines 4525 W Ridge Rd Erie PA 16506

GEISELMAN, DEBRA ANN, dentist; b. York, Pa., Sept. 7, 1955; d. Charles Henry and Estella Mae (Delp) G.; m. Michael Maskaly, Oct. 1, 1983; children: Matthew Michael, Natasha Ann. BA in Liberal Arts, Pa. State U., 1977; DDS, Temple U., 1981. Pvt. practice dentist York, Pa., 1982—. Mem. York County Dental Soc. (bd. dirs. 1986-89), Pa. Dental Assn. (mem. dental health planning com. 1989—), Am. Dental Assn. Republican. Lutheran. Office: 1900 East Market St York PA 17402

GEISELMAN, PAULA J., psychologist; b. Ohio, June 30, 1944; d. Paul and Rosemary (Dawson) Parsley. AB in Psychology with honors, Ohio U., 1971, MS in Exptl. Psychology, 1976; PhD in Physiol. Psychology, UCLA, 1983. Adj. asst. prof. UCLA, 1986—; dir. psychophysiol. rsch. UCLA Sch. Medicine, 1989—; lectr. in field. Reviewer for Sci. Jour., Am. Jour. Physiology, Physiology and Behavior, Brain Research Bulletin, Appetite: Determinants and Consequences of Eating and Drinking; contbr. numerous articles to profl. jours. Mem. Soc. Neurosci., AAAS, N.Am. Assn. Study of Obesity, Women in Neurosci., Assn. Acad. Women, Am. Psychol. Assn., Am. Psychol. Assn., Eastern Psychol. Assn., Western Psychol. Assn. (head of physiol. psychol., chair. Animal Feeding and Behavior paper session 1981), Assn. Advancement Psychology, Internat. Brain Research Orgn., World Fedn. Neuroscientists, Brit. Brain Research Assn. (hon.), European Brain and Behavior Soc. (hon.), N.Y. Acad. Scis., Sigma Xi, Psi Chi. Office: UCLA Dept Psychology Franz Hall 405 Hilgard Ave Los Angeles CA 90024-1563

GEISENDORFER, ESTHER LILLIAN, nurse; b. Ferryville, Wis., May 18, 1927; d. Peter C. and Christie G. (Quamme) Walker; student U. Wis.-LaCrosse, 1944-45; R.N., Fairview Hosp. Sch. Nursing, Mpls., 1948; m. James V. Geisendorfer, Sept. 23, 1949; children: Jane Geisendorfer Stokke, Karen Geisendorfer-Lindgren, Lois Geisendorfer Buchnis. Staff nurse Worthington (Minn.) Clinic, 1948-50; pvt. duty nurse, Sioux Falls, S.D., 1950-51; obstet. nurse Fairview Hosp., Mpls., 1951-53; staff nurse St. Anthony Hosp., Rock Island, Ill., 1953-54; obstet. nurse Fairview Hosp., Mpls., 1954-58, post anesthesia recovery nurse, 1958-62, emergency room nurse, 1962-66, obstet. nurse, 1966-68, head nurse obstetrics, 1968-76; staff devel. instr., clinician, Bellin Meml. Hosp., Green Bay, Wis., 1976—; instr. in prenatal and Lamaze classes Ob-Gyn Assocs. of Green Bay Ltd. Mem. Wis. Assn. Perinatal Care, Nordfjord Laget in Am., Wis. Nurses Assn. (Disting. Service award 1981), Nurses Assn. Am. Coll. Obstetrics and Gynecology (cert., founder Northeast Wis. chpt.), Wis. Acad. Scis., Arts and Letters, Nat. Perinatal Assn. Lutheran. Home: 1001 Shawano Ave Green Bay WI 54303 Office: 744 S Webster Ave Green Bay WI 54301

GEISLER, CAROL JOY, psychologist clinician, researcher, educator; b. N.Y., Mar. 3, 1948; d. Arthur H. and Sylvia (Bittner) G. BS in Math., MIT, 1968; MS in Math., NYU, 1970, MA in Psychology, 1973, PhD in Psychology, 1982. Lic. psychology, N.Y. Psychologist clinician, supr. Bklyn. Community Counseling Ctr., 1977—; pvt. practice psychologist N.Y.C., 1982—; researcher, educator, supr. Sch. of Social Work NYU, N.Y.C., 1983—; cons. in field. Mem. Am. Psychol. Assn., Am. Orthopsychiat. Assn., Soc. for Psychotherapy Rsch., N.Y. Soc. for Clin. Psychologists, Assn. for Psychoanalytic Self-Psychology. Democrat. Jewish. Office: NYU Sch of Social Work 3 Washington Sq N New York NY 10003 also: 150 W 13th St New York NY 10011

GEISLER, HARLYNNE, storyteller; b. Champaign, Ill., July 23, 1950; d. Asher Ossey and Betty Jean (McLaughlin) G.; m. Judson Francis Farrar, June 27, 1982. BS, U. Ill., 1972, MLS, 1973. Asst. librarian Prairie Elem. Sch., Urbana, Ill., 1973-75; librarian La Jolla (Calif.) Country Day Sch., 1975-80; part-time librarian San Diego Pub. Library, 1982-87; freelance profl. storyteller, 1980, cons. Gifted and Talented Edn., San Diego, 1981—; organizer, founder So. Calif. Storyswapping festival, San Clemente, Calif., San Juan Capistrano, 1984-85. Author: The Best of the Story Bag, 1988; editor Story Bag Newsletter. Mem. Nat. Assn. for the Preservation and Perpetuation of Storytelling (resource reviewer 1986—), Nat. Story League, Storytellers of San Diego. Democrat. Jewish.

GEISLER, LINDA WHITEHEAD, hospital administrator, nurse; b. Pitts., Aug. 2, 1953; d. Howard Roy and Myrtle Fidelty (Tomlinson) Whitehead; m. Gerald Louis Geisler, May 9, 1975; children: Susan Christina, Christopher Gerald, Daniel Louis. BSN, Carlow Coll., 1975; MS in Nursing Edn., U. Pitts., 1979. RN, N.Y., Ill. Head nurse Montefiore Hosp., Pitts., 1978-80; instr. Western Pa. Sch. Nursing, Pitts., 1980-81, San Jacinto Coll., Pasadena, Tex., 1981-83; with St. Therese Med. Ctr., Waukegan, Ill., 1983-88, asst. dir. nursing dept., 1985-86, v.p. patient svcs., 1986-88; dir. patient coordination Community Gen. Hosp., Syracuse, N.Y., 1988-90; v.p. nursing and patient care svcs. Community Gen. Hosp., 1990—; mem. adv. com. Coll. of Lake County, Chgo., 1986, Barat/Lake Forest Coll., Chgo., 1988. Bd. dirs. Emergency Med. Svcs. Bur. Adv. Commn., Syracuse, 1989—. Mem. Am. Coll. Healthcare Execs., Ill. Orgn. Nurse Execs., Hanlon Pool Club. Republican. Methodist. Home: 7579 Firebird Ln Manlius NY 13104 Office: Community Gen Hosp Broad Rd Syracuse NY 13215

GEISSERT, KATY, mayor; b. Wash., 1926; m. Bill Geissert; children: Bill Jr., Jack, Holly, Doug, Ann. BA in Journalism, Stanford U., 1948. Mem. Torrance (Calif.) City Council, 1974-86; mayor City of Torrance, 1986—; mem. Gov.'s Infrastructure Rev. Task Force, Calif. Past chmn. Torrance Park & Recreation Commn.; past mem. fin. adv. com. Torrance Sch.; past chmn. adv. bd. Calif. State U., Dominguez Hills, Torrance Salvation Army; mem. bond steering com. Torrance Library, 1967; chmn. local park bond issue steering com., 1971, Los Angeles County Sanitation Dist. Bd.; community cons. South Bay Harbor Vol. Bur.; mem. adv. bd. Torrance YWCA; bd. dirs. Switzer Ctr., region III United Way, Torrance LWV; mem. city selection com. Los Angeles County. Recipient PTA Hon. Service award, Woman of Distinction award Soroptimists, Community Service award Riviera Homeowners Assn., spl. citation Nat. Recreation & Park Assn.; named Disting. Citizen of Yr. Torrance Area C. of C., 1973, Woman of Yr. YWCA, Woman of Achievement award Redondo Marina Bus. & Profl. Women's Club. Mem. U.S. Conf. Mayors, League Calif. Cities (del., cities transp. com.), Calif. Elected Women's Assn. (bd. dirs.). Office: City of Torrance Office of Mayor 3031 Torrance Blvd Torrance CA 90503*

GEIST, KARIN RUTH TAMMEUS MCPHAIL, teacher, realtor, musician; b. Urbana, Ill., Nov. 23, 1938; d. Wilber Harold and Bertha Amanda Sofia (Helander) Tammeus; m. David Pendleton McPhail, Sept. 7, 1958 (div. 1972); children: Julia Elizabeth, Mark Andrew; m. John Charles Geist, June 4, 1989. BS, Juilliard Sch. Music, 1962; postgrad., Stanford U., 1983-84, L'Academia, Florence and Pistoia, Italy, 1984-85. Cert. tchr., Calif.; lic. real estate agt., Calif. Tchr. Woodstock Sch., Musoorie, India, 1957, Canadian, Tex., 1962-66; tchr. Head Royce Sch., Oakland, Calif., 1975-79, 87—, Sleepy Hollow Sch., Orinda, Calif., 1985—; realtor Freeholders, Berkeley, Calif., 1971-85, Northbrae Properties, Berkeley, 1985—; organist Kellogg Meml., Musoorie, 1956-57, Mills Coll. Chapel, Oakland, 1972—; cashier Trinity U., San Antonio, 1957-58; cen. records sec. Riverside Ch., N.Y.C., 1958-60; sec. Dr. Rollo May, N.Y.C., 1959-62, United Presbyn. Nat. Missions, N.Y.C., 1960, United Presbyn. Ecumenical Mission, N.Y.C., 1961, Nat. Coun. Chs., N.Y.C., 1962; choral dir. First Presbyn. Ch., Canadian, Tex., 1962-66; assoc. in music Montclair Presbyn. Ch., Oakland, 1972-88; site coord., artist, collaborator Calif. Arts Coun. Artist. Produced and performed major choral and orchestral works, 1972-88; producer Paradiso, Kronos Quartet, 1985. Grantee Orinda Union Sch. Dist., 1988. Mem. Choral Condrs. Guild, Berkeley Bd. Realtors, East Bay Regional Multiple Listing Svc., Calif. Tchrs. Assn., Commonwealth Club (San Francisco). Democrat. Home: 7360 Claremont Ave Berkeley CA 94705 Office: Northbrae Properties 1600 Hopkins Berkeley CA 94707

GEISWEIDT, LORILEE BARRICK, operations research analyst; b. Hanover, Pa., Aug. 4, 1960; d. Walter Sylvester and Josephine Lorena (Chronister) Barrick; m. Dale Robert, May 13, 1953. BS in Civil Engr. Tech., U. Pittsburgh, Johnstown, 1982; MBA in Ops. Rsch., U. Md., College Park, 1984. Operations research analyst Defense Systems Inc., McLean, Va., 1984-88, Naval Surface Warfare Ctr., Silver Spring, Md., 1988--. Mem. Operations Research Soc. of Am. Democrat. Lutheran. Home: 13621 Jacqueline Ct Silver Spring MD 20904

GEIWITZ, CYNTHIA ANN, lawyer; b. LaCrosse, Wis., Mar. 11, 1955; d. Gene Roy and Elsie Marie (Blessing) G.; m. Kenneth Albert Dube, Aug. 23, 1975; children: Destiny Anne, Christian Kenneth. BA, George Washington U., 1976; JD, Pepperdine U., 1979. Bar: Minn. 1980. Pvt. practice Rochester, Minn., 1980-82; v.p. 1st Bank S.D., Sioux Falls, 1982-89; staff atty. Dorsey & Whitney, Mpls., 1989—. Treas. Make-A-Wish Found. S.D., Sioux Falls, 1987-89; v.p. Estate Planning Coun., Sioux Falls, 1988, pres., 1989; dir. Killian Coll., Sioux Falls, 1989. Mem. Minn. State Bar Assn. Home: 9807 Tree Farm Rd Eden Prairie MN 55347

GEKAS, PAULA YVONNE, amdministrative executive; b. Adelaide, Australia, Mar. 12, 1966; d. Athanasios Kyria Kopoulos and Evgenia (Lintzeris)G. Student, Harrisburg Community Coll., 1989—. Student loan officer P.H.E.A.A., Harrisburg, Pa., 1984-85; sec. VITRO Govt. Contractor, Camp Hill, Pa., 1985-86; adminstrv. asst. The Commonwealth Found. for Pub. Policy Alternatives, Harrisburg, 1988--; pres. Future Bus. Leaders of Am., Mechanicsburg, Pa., 1982-84. Pres. Young Adult League, Camp Hill, 1987-88. Home: 4502 Chestnut Ave Camp Hill PA 17011 Office: 600 N Second St Ste 400 Harrisburg PA 17101

GELB, JUDITH ANNE, lawyer; b. N.Y.C., Apr. 5, 1935; d. Joseph and Sarah (Stein) G.; m. Howard S. Vogel, June 30, 1962; 1 child, Michael S. B.A., Bklyn. Coll., 1955; J.D., Columbia U., 1958. Bar: N.Y. 1959, U.S. Dist. Ct. (so. dist. and ea. dist.) N.Y. 1960, U.S. Ct. Appeals (2d cir.) 1960, U.S. Ct. Mil. Appeals 1962. Asst. to editor N.Y. Law Jour., N.Y.C., 1958-59; confidential asst. to U.S. atty. ea. dist. N.Y., Bklyn., 1959-61; assoc. Whitman & Ransom, N.Y.C., 1961-70, ptnr., 1971—. Mem. ABA (individual rights sect., real property & trust law sect.), Fed. Bar Counsel, N.Y. State Bar Assn. (trusts and estates com.), N.Y. State Dist. Attys. Assn., Assn. of Bar of City of N.Y., Columbia Law Sch. Alumni Assn. (bd. dirs.), Princeton Club, Assn. Ex-mem. Squadron A Club. Home: 169 E 69th St New York NY 10021 Office: Whitman & Ransom 200 Park Ave New York NY 10166

GELBACH, MARTHA HARVEY, genealogist; b. Hagerstown, Md., Feb. 21, 1913; d. George Gelbach and Carolyne Backer (Knode) Gelbach Schlagel. Student, Columbia U., 1943-45, U. Ill., Chgo., 1945-46; BS, Seton Hall U., 1950. Reporter Herald-Mail Pub. Co., Hagerstown, Md., 1929-33; rep. genealogist Flagstone of Chester, N.J., 1933-83; sr. pres. Children of the Am. Revolution, Ledgewood, N.J., 1950—; author, genealogist Brigade Hill Pub., Flemington, N.J., 1983-89, Penwell, Quincy, Pa., 1989—. Author: Prayers of the Amwell Valley, 1987, American Poetry Anthology, 1989, Best New Poets of 1989, 1989; contbr. articles to newspapers. Recipient Meritorious Svc. award Fed. Security Adminstrn., Washington, 1946, Eastern USA News Reporting award DAR, 1975, N.J. USA News Reporting award N.J. DAR, 1977; named Poet of Yr. Am. Poetry Assn., 1989. Mem. NRA, DAR (registrar 1937—), Am. Inst. Parliamentarians, Genealogical Soc. N.J., Hunterdon County Hist. Soc., Nat. Soc. U.S. Daus. of 1812 (registrar 1936—, regent 1980-83), Nat. Soc. Children Am. Revolution (sr. pres. 1983-88). Republican. Episcopalian. Clubs: Spring Brook, Chester Gun. Home and Office: 217 Village Rd Quincy PA 17247

GELBER RINALDO, SUZANNE, benefits consultant; b. Cin., June 16, 1945; d. Harold Martin and Annette (Witkin) Gelber; m. David Warren Rinaldo, Mar. 24, 1968; children: Rachel Ann, Lucinda. BA, Grinnell Coll., 1968; MA, U. Mass., 1969; MS, U. Mich., 1974, PhD, 1981. Asst. prof. Sociology Dept. Holy Cross, Worcester, Mass., 1979-83; adj. asst. prof. Harriman Sch. SUNY, Stony Brook, 1983-85; asst. dir. N.Y.C. Health & Hosps. Corp., 1985-86; network dir. Corp. Health Strategies, Met., N.Y.C., 1986-88; nat. accounts sales exec. Am. Psychology Mgmt., Arlington, Va., 1988-89; group benefits cons. Towers, Perrin, Forster and Crosby, 1988—; statistical cons. NIMH, Washington, 1985-87. Bd. dirs. Chappaqua N.Y. Children's Workshop, 1986-87; mem., allocations com. United Way, Wilton, Conn., 1988-. Mem. Nat. Assn. Female Execs. Democrat.

GELB-LIBERT, JOY Z., automobile executive; b. N.Y.C., July 13, 1931; d. Joseph R. and Evelyn (Goldman) Roth; m. Harold Libert, June 11, 1950 (div. 1981); children: Barry David, Jeffrey Alan, Gaye Libert Feinberg; m. Robert Gelb, Dec. 16, 1984 (div. 1986). BA, Finch Jr. Coll., N.Y.C., 1952, New Rochelle (N.Y.) Coll., 1981. V.p. Yonkers (N.Y.) Motors, 1950-84, Joy Pontiac-Datsun, Dumont, N.J., 1973-78; pres. Yonkers Motors Honda and Mazda, 1984—. Mem. Rep. Party Inner Circle, 1988-89; vol. worker White Plains (N.Y.) Hosp., 1968-75. Mem. Tamarack Country Club, Mayacoo Lakes Country Club. Home: 6 Colony Row Chappaqua NY 10514 Office: Yonkers Motors Corp 20 S Broadway Yonkers NY 10705

GELCI, GIANNA MARIA, financial accountant, computer consultant; b. Hoboken, N.J., Feb. 16, 1957; d. Ubaldo and Maria (Dimini) G. BS in Acctg., St. Peter's Coll., 1979. Lic. notary public, N.Y. Individual retirement account acct. Masters, Mates & Pilots Plans Individual Retirement Accounts, N.Y.C., 1980-83; corp. acct. Prudential Lines, Inc., N.Y.C., 1984-86; fin. reporter Securities Settlement Corp., N.Y.C., 1986-87; fin. acct. Robert Fleming, Inc., N.Y.C., 1987-89; sr. acct. Brown Bros. Harriman & Co., N.Y.C., 1989-90; with John Hancock Clearing Corp., N.Y.C., 1990—. Democrat. Roman Catholic. Home: 138 Palisade Ave Cliffside Park NJ 07010 Office: John Hancock Clearing Corp One World Fin Ctr New York NY 10281

GELENGER, LORRIE ANN, food products executive; b. Flint, Mich., Aug. 11, 1958; d. Malcolm Wright and Marjorie Arlene (Keith) Boughen; m. Stephen Martin Gelenger, Nov. 15, 1980; 1 child, Miranda Edith. BA, U. Mich., 1980. Cert. sanitation & food handling, Mich. Mgr. Denny's Corp., Saginaw, Mich., 1980-81, Burger Chef, Flint, 1981; mgr. various food svcs. Hyatt Regency, Flint, 1981-83; coffee shop mgr. Hyatt Regency, Dearborn, Mich., 1983-84; catering mgr. Fairlane Manor, Dearborn, 1984-85; gen. mgr. Stuart Anderson's, Southfield, Mich., 1985-88, Salvatore Scallopini, Southfield, 1988; catering sales mgr. Mich. Inn (now Sheraton Southfield), 1988—. Author: (tng. manuals) Stuart Anderson's, 1986, Kafay's-Hyatt Regency, Dearborn, 1983. State chmn. Mich. Jaycee Aux., 1980, pres., 1979; bd. dirs. Fair Winds coun. Girl Scouts U.S., 1976-78. Mem. Nat. Restaurant Assn. Home: 2036 N Vermont Royal Oak MI 48073

GELL, WENDY, Small business owner; b. N.Y.C., Mar. 20, 1948; d. Jock Gell and Edith Skolnick Manings; m. Hadley Mannings. Student, Roosevelt U., 1969, 71; Student, U. Wis., 1970. Prin. Wendy Gell Jewelry, N.Y.C., 1975—. Recipient numerous awards Editoral Credit in Fashion Jewelry. Office: Wendy Gell Jewelry 37 W 37th St New York NY 10016

GELLER, BARBARA JOHNSON, marketing professional; b. Duluth, Minn., Aug. 14, 1958; d. Adler Monroe and Phlaine Gertrude (Sonju) Johnson; m. Charles Edward Geller, Jan. 7, 1984. BA, Stephens Coll., 1980; MBA, U. Colo., 1985. Cert. mgmt. acct. Internal auditor Monsanto, Creve Coeur, Mo., 1980-83; internal controls analyst Monsanto, Creve Coeur, 1983-84; assoc. mktg. mgr. Container Corp. Am., Carol Stream, Ill., 1985-86; market analyst MCI, Chgo., 1987, product mgr., 1987-89; mgr. consumer mktg. MCI, St. Louis, 1989—.

GELLER, JANICE GRACE, nurse; b. Auburn, Ga., Feb. 25, 1938; d. Erby Ralph and Jewell Grace (Maughon) Clack; m. Joseph Jerome Geller, Dec. 23, 1973; 1 child, Elizabeth Joanne. Student, LaGrange Coll., 1955-57; BS in Nursing, Emory U., 1960; MS, Rutgers U., 1962. Psychiat. staff nurse dept. psychiatry Emory U., Atlanta, 1960; nurse educator Ill. State Psychiat. Inst., Chgo., 1961; clin. specialist in mental retardation nursing Northville, Mich., 1962; faculty Coll. Nursing Rutgers U., Newark, 1962-63, faculty Advanced Program in Psychiat. Nursing, 1964-66; faculty Coll. Nursing U. Mich., Ann Arbor, 1963-64; faculty, Teheran (Iran) Coll. for Women, 1967-69; clin. specialist psychiat. nursing Roosevelt Hosp., N.Y.C., 1969-70; faculty, guest lectr. Columbia U., N.Y.C., 1969-70; supr. Dept. Psychiat. Nursing Mt. Sinai Hosp., N.Y.C., 1970-72; pvt. practice psychotherapy N.Y.C., 1972-77, Ridgewood, N.J., 1977—; faculty, curriculum coord. in psychiat. nursing William Alanson White Inst. Psychiatry, Psychoanalysis and Psychology, N.Y.C., 1974-84; mem. U.S. del. of Community and Mental Health Nurses to People's Republic of China, 1983. Contbr. articles to profl. jours.; editorial bd. Perspectives in Psychiat. Care, 1971-74, 78-84; author: (with Anita Marie Werner) Instruments for Study of Nurse-Patient Interaction, 1964. Committeewoman Bergen County Rep. Com., 1989; mem. Rep. County Com., Bergen County, N.J. Recipient 10th Anniversary award Outstanding Clin. Specialist in psychiat.-mental health nursing in N.J., Soc. Cert. Clin. Specialists, 1982; Fed. Govt. grantee as career tchr. in psychiat. nursing, Rutgers U., 1962-63; cert. psychiat. nurse and clin. specialist, N.J., N.Y. Mem. AAAS, LWV, Am. Nurses Assn. (various certs.), N.J. State Nurses Assn. (chairperson), Soc. Cert. Clin. Specialists in Psychiat. Nursing, Coun. Specialists in Psychiat. Mental Health Nursing, Am. Group Psychotherapy Assn., Am. Assn. Mental Deficiency, World Fedn. Mental Health, Friends of the Hermitage, Soc. of Valley Hosp. of Ridgewood, AMA Aux., Bergen County Med. Soc. Aux., Sigma Theta Tau, Coll. Club. Address: 159 Fairmount Rd Ridgewood NJ 07450

GELLER, LINDA BERGER, software development corporation executive, financial executive; b. Bklyn., June 10, 1944; d. Nathan and Sylvia (Dombush) Berger; m. Richard Morton Geller, Sept. 4, 1966; children: Lisa, Deborah, Naomi. Student N.Y. U., 1962-64, New Sch. Social Research, 1964-65; BS, SUNY-Old Westbury, 1977; MA, N.Y. Inst. Tech., 1983; cert. advanced bus. mgmt. SUNY. Cert. tchr. N.Y. Bus. mgr. Tri-Tech., West Babylon, N.Y., 1967-72, treas., chief fin. officer, 1972-81, dir., 1981—; pres., chief exec. officer Am. Software Devel. Corp., West Babylon, 1981—. Chairperson Long Island Div. Israel Bonds, Hicksville, N.Y., 1984; v.p. Oyster Bay Jewish Ctr., N.Y., 1980; trustee Wantagh Jewish Ctr., N.Y., 1970-76; chairperson Parents Assn. Solomon Schechter, Jericho, N.Y., 1976-80. Ednl. grantee L.I. Regional Edn. Ctr. Econ. Devel., 1985. Mem. Women Econ. Devels. L.I. (bd. dirs. 1988—), Nat. Assn. Women Bus. Owners (founder Long Island chpt. 1985, officer 1985-88). Republican. Avocations: skiing, music, choir member. Office: Am Software Devel Corp 11 Farmingdale Rd West Babylon NY 11704

GELLER, MARGARET JOAN, astrophysicist; b. Ithaca, N.Y., Dec. 8, 1947; d. Seymour and Sarah (Levine) Geller. A.B., U. Calif.-Berkeley, 1970; M.A., Princeton U., 1972, Ph.D., 1975. Research fellow Center for Astrophysics, Cambridge, Mass., 1974-78; research assoc. Harvard Coll. Obs., Cambridge, 1978-80; sr. vis. fellow Inst. of Astronomy, Cambridge, Eng., 1978-82; asst. prof. Harvard U., 1980-83; astrophysicist Smithsonian Astrophys. Obs., Cambridge, 1983—. Contbr. articles to profl. jours. NSF fellow, 1970-73. Mem. Am. Astron. Soc. (councillor), Assoc. Univs. for Research in Astronomy (dir-at-large), AAAS, Internat. Astron. Union. Office: Ctr for Astrophysics 60 Garden St Cambridge MA 02138*

GELLER, NANCY LORCH, biostatistician; b. N.Y.C., Nov. 3, 1944; d. Theo Michel and Cynthia (Marquith) Lorch; m. Herbert M. Geller. BS, CCNY, 1965; MS, Case Inst., 1967; PhD, Case Western Res. U., 1972. Asst. prof. U. Rochester (N.Y.), 1970-72, U. Pa., Phila., 1972-78; assoc. prof. Med. Coll. Pa., Phila., 1978-79; asst. to assoc. mem. Meml. Sloan-Kettering Cancer Ctr., N.Y.C., 1979—. Contbr. articles to profl. publs. NIH grantee, 1987—. Office: Meml Sloan Kettering Cancer 1275 York Ave New York NY 10021

GELLERSTEDT, MARIE ADA, manufacturing company executive; b. Davenport, Iowa, Oct. 19, 1926; d. Charles Beecher and Marie Elizabeth (Pasvogel) Kaufmann; m. Keith Orval Gellerstedt, Mar. 16, 1957; children: Lori Beth Doroba, Keith Todd, Jon Erik, Cory Andrew. BBA, Augustana Coll., 1950. Gen. mgr., pres. Nixalite Co. Am., East Moline, Ill., 1957—. Life mem. Moline St. High Sch. PTA, also bd. dirs., 1973-76. Mem. Ill. Mfrs. Assn., Nat. Trade Show Exhibitors Assn., Internat. Exhibitors Assn., Nat. Pest Control Assn., Nat. Animal Damage Control Assn., Nat. Assn. Women Bus. Owners, Nat. Assn. Ind. Bus., East Moline Bus. Assn., Constrn. Specifier Inst. Republican. Lutheran. Clubs: Moline-Rock Island, Zonta (bd. dirs. 1980-84). Lodges: Daus. of Mokanna Zal Caldron, Daus. of Nile.

GELLMAN, GLORIA GAE SEEBURGER SCHICK, marketing professional; b. La Grange, Ill., Oct. 5, 1947; d. Robert Fred and Gloria Virginia (McQuiston) Seeburger; m. Peter Slate Schick, Sept. 25, 1978 (dec. 1980); 2 children; m. Irwin Frederick Gellman; 3 children. BA magna cum laude, Purdue U., 1969; student, Lee Strasberg Actors Studio; postgrad., UCLA, Irvine. Mem. mktg. staff Seemac, Inc. (formerly R.F. Seeburger Co.); v.p. V.I.P. Properties, Inc., Newport Beach, Calif. Profl. actress, singer; television and radio talk show hostess, Indpls., late 1960s; performer radio and television commls., 1960s—. Mem. Orange County Philharm. Soc., Orange County Master Chorale, Orange County Performing Arts Ctr., treas.; bd. dirs., v.p. membership, mem. acquisition coun., Newport Harbor (Calif.) Art Mus.; bd. dirs., mem. founders soc., Opera Pacific; patron Big Bros. Big sisters Starlight Found.; mem. Visionaries Newport Harbor Art Mus. Named one of Outstanding Young Women of Am., 1972. Mem. AAUW, AFTRA, Internat. Platform Assn., Screen Actors Guild, Actors Equity, U. Calif. Irvine Chancellor's Club, U. Calif. Irvine Humanities Assocs. (founder, pres., bd. dirs.), Mensa, Orange County Mental Health Assn., Alpha Lambda Delta, Delta Rho Kappa. Home: PO Box 1993 Newport Beach CA 92663

GELMAN, ELAINE EDITH, nurse; b. Bklyn., Feb. 16, 1927; d. Michael Levi and Shirley (Drezner) Rodkinson; m. David Graham Gelman, Apr. 6, 1952; children: Eric, Andrew, Amy. BS, CUNY, Queens, 1946; RN, NYU, 1948. Cert. pediatric nurse practitioner, N.Y., 1977. Operating room staff, supr. Queens Gen. Hosp., Bellevue, Beth-El Hosp., N.Y.C., 1948-61; labor and delivery room staff, supr. Georgetown Hosp., Washington, 1962-66; pub. health nurse N.Y.C. Dept. Pub. Health, 1966-72; pediatric nurse practitioner child and youth program Roosevelt Hosp., N.Y.C., 1972-82; pvt. practice N.Y.C., 1982—. Mem. Dem. County Com., N.Y.C., 1984—; apptd. to N.Y. State Bd. of Nursing, 1990. Fellow Nat. Assn. Pediatric Nurses Practitioners (legis. chmn. 1986-88), Coalition of Nurse Practitioners, Inc. (pres. 1984-85, 87-88). Jewish. Home: 229 W 78th St New York NY 10024 Office: Pediatric Practice 241 Central Park West New York NY 10024

GELMAN, RITA GOLDEN, author; b. Bridgeport, Conn., July 2, 1937; d. Albert and Frances (Friedman) G.; m. Steven Gelman, Dec. 11, 1960 (div. 1987); children: Mitchell, Jan. BA in English Lit., Brandeis U., 1958; MA in Anthropology, UCLA, 1983. Staff writer Young Am. mag., N.Y.C., 1958-60; editor Crowell-Collier Pub. Co., N.Y.C., 1960-61, Macmillan Pub. Co., N.Y.C., 1973-74; juvenile cons. Book-of-the-Month Club, 1972-76; guest lectr. UCLA, 1976-78; mem. faculty extension program Calif. State U., Northridge, 1978-79. Author over 75 books for juveniles, 1973—, including Why Can't I Fly, 1976; (with Susan Buxbaum), Splash! All About Baths, 1987 (best sci. book for children award Am. Physics Inst., 1987); Inside Nicaragua: Young People's Dreams and Fears, 1988 (award ALA 1988). Mem. PEN, Soc. Children's Book Writers. Office: Curtis-Brown care M Marlow 10 Astor Pl New York NY 10003

GELORMINO, JOAN ANN, educator; b. Torrington, Conn., Jan. 3, 1939; d. Erminio and Jennie Rose Gelormino; B.S., Western Conn. State Coll., Danbury, 1960; M.S., U. Hartford, 1966; Ed.D., Nova U., Ft. Lauderdale, Fla., 1975. Tchr., Conn., 1960-68, tchr., dir., resource tchr. Early Childhood Learning Center, adj. faculty U. Hartford, 1969-71; dir. Early Childhood Program Univ. Sch., Nova U., 1971—, assoc. dir. Sch. Center, 1973—; cons. Early Childhood Program, Waterbury, West Hartford, Farmington, Conn., Long Beach, N.Y., Half Hollow, N.Y., Merrick, N.Y., Learning Inst. N.C.; cons. migrant edn., Fla. Seminole Pre-Sch. Programs, Broward County, Fla., 1970-75; bd. dirs., v.p. United Way Child Care Centers, Broward County, 1975—, pres., 1976-78. Mem. Broward County Environ. Control Bd., 1979-80; pres. Kids in Distress, 1987-88. Mem. Nat. Assn. for Edn. Young Children, Assn. for Childhood Edn. Internat., Soc. for Research Child Devel., Fla. Assn. for Children Under Six (conf. chmn. Hollywood 1980). Author: Pre-Number and Mathematic Skill Sequence With Activities, 1969; Constructing Games for Early Childhood Classrooms, 1974; Transactional Analysis For Parents and Teachers of Young Children, 1975. Home: 9800 SW 4th St Fort Lauderdale FL 33324 Office: 7500 SW 36th St Fort Lauderdale FL 33314

GELSINGER, LINDA MAE, cardiac data systems research specialist, clinical scientist; b. Robesonia, Pa., Jan. 8, 1950; d. Clarence Daniel and Esther (Forry) G.; divorced. A, Pa. Jr. Coll. of Med. Arts, 1969; student, Ea. Coll., St. Davids, Pa., 1969-70; BA in Social Studies and Biology, St. Joseph's U., Phila., 1975. Supr. cardivascular research lab. Lankenau Hosp., Phila., 1970-76; sales rep. Med. Monitors, Inc., Wyncote, Pa., 1976-77, Data Med., Inc., Wynnewood, Pa., 1977-81; systems specialist Cardiac Data Corp., Inc., Bloomfield, Conn., 1980-81; mktg. rep. Cardio Data Systems, Haddonfield, N.J., 1981-82, nat. sales mgr., 1982-86, sr. research specialist, 1987-88; sr. clin. scientist Wyeth-Ayerst Research, Radnor, Pa., 1988—. Singer Kol Simcha Choral, Phila., 1973-90, Sweet Adelines Barbershop chorus, 1974. Mem. NAFE, Am. Soc. Profl. and Exec. Women, Am. Mktg. Assn., Assocs. Clin. Pharmacology, Sigma Eta Chi. Republican. Home: Box 1036 RD #2 Robesonia PA 19551 Office: Wyeth-Ayerst Rsch 145 King of Prussia Rd Radnor PA 19087

GEMBALLA, ELEANOR F., nurse; b. Pa., Nov. 8, 1928; d. Joseph and Marie (Stein) G. BS in Nursing, U. Pitts., 1960; MS in Nursing, U. Indiana (Pa.), 1986. Staff nurse Citizens Gen. Hosp., New Kensington, Pa., 1953-54, asst. head nurse, 1954-56, head nurse, 1956-58, clin. instr., 1958-61, supr., 1961-78, asst. dir. nursing, 1978-79, dir. nursing, 1979—. Mem. Am. Orgn. Nurse Execs., Sigma Theta Tau. Office: Citizens Gen Hosp New Kensington PA 15068

GEMMEL, TERRY, accounting educator; b. Delhi, N.Y., Jan. 16, 1932; d. Robert Elliott and Sarah Isabelle (Russell) G. AS, North Shore Community Coll., Beverly, Mass., 1971; ABA, Lowell Technol. Inst., 1973, BBA, 1974; MBA, Suffolk U., 1976. Rsch. asst. North Shore Community Coll., 1966-76, instr., asst. prof., assoc. prof. acctg., 1976-88, prof., 1989—. Dir. West Newbury (Mass.) CD, 1986—; program chmn. West Newbury Hist. Soc., 1989-90; sec. North Shore CD Coun., 1988—. Mem. Mass. Assn. Acctg. Profls. (b.p. 1988-89, pres. 1990-91). Episcopalian. Home: 60 Stewart St West Newbury MA 01985 Office: North Shore Community Coll 3 Essex St Beverly MA 01915

GENDA, ELLEN VAN WAGNER, lawyer, educator; b. Chgo., Dec. 10, 1942; d. Paul David and Eleanor (Sullivan) Van Wagner; m. Burton Neal Genda, Mar. 27, 1964 (separated); children: Kevin Paul, Kelly Elan. BA, U. Ariz., 1964; MA, Calif. State U., L.A., 1971; JD, U. La Verne, 1984. Bar: Calif. 1984, U.S. Dist. Ct. (cen. dist.) Calif. 1985, U.S. Ct. Appeals (9th cir.) 1985. Tchr., adminstr. Baldwin Park (Calif.) Sch. Dist., 1965-81; assoc. Rose, Klein & Marias, Pomona, Calif., 1985—; prof. U. La Verne (Calif.) Coll. Law, 1987—. Writer, asst. editor U. La Verne Law Rev., 1981-83, editor-in-chief, 1983-84. Chmn. youth activities commn. City of Baldwin Park, 1971-81. Recipient Humanitarian and Svc. awards L.A. Human Rels. Commn., 1976, 77. Mem. Calif. Bar Assn., L.A. County Bar Assn., Ea. County Bar Assn., Phi Delta Theta. Home: PO Box 351 Blue Jay CA 92317 Office: Rose Klein & Marias 281 S Thomas 3d Fl Pomona CA 91766

GENERAL, KATHRYN ELAINE, educator; b. Vernon, Tex., May 22, 1954; d. Carroll Eugene and Margaret Ann (Lankford) Baldwin; m. Dale A. General, Nov. 29, 1980. BS in Elem. Edn., U. North Tex., 1977. Individual program planner Denton (Tex.) State Sch., 1975-77; elem. tchr. Dallas Ind. Sch. Dist., 1979—, 4th grade level chmn., 1986—; supr. student tchrs. East Tex. State U., Commerce, 1987—; presenter in field. Participant United Way, Dallas, 1984-89, DAV, Mesquite, Tex., 1986—; program dir. Runyon Elem. Sch. PTA, Dallas, 1987-88. Named Tchr. of Yr., E.M. Pease Elem. Sch., 1983, Best of Best Tchr. award subdist. II, Dallas Ind. Sch. Dist., 1984. Mem. Dallas Mus. Art. Republican. Home: 6204 Yellowstone Dr Mesquite TX 75149

GENGOR, VIRGINIA ANDERSON, financial planning executive, educator; b. Lyons, N.Y., May 2, 1927; d. Axel Jennings and Marie Margaret (Mack) Anderson; m. Peter Gengor, Mar. 2, 1952 (dec.); children: Peter Randall, Daniel Neal, Susan Leigh. AB, Wheaton Coll., 1949; MA, U. No. Colo., Greeley, 1975, 77. Chief hosp. intake service County of San Diego, 1966-77, chief Kearny Mesa Dist. Office, 1977-79, chief Dependent Children of Ct., 1979-81, chief child protection services, 1981-82; registered rep. Am. Pacific Securities, San Diego, 1982-85; assoc. Pollock & Assocs., San Diego, 1985-86; pres. Gengor Fin. Advisors, 1986—; cons. instr. Nat. Ctr. for Fin. Edn., San Diego, 1986-88; instr. San Diego Community Coll., 1985-88. Mem. allocations panel United Way, San Diego, 1976-79; chmn. com. Child Abuse Coordinating Council, San Diego, 1979-83; pres. Friends of Casa de la Esperanza, San Diego, 1980-85, bd. dirs., 1980—; 1st v.p. The Big Sister League, San Diego, 1985-86, pres., 1987-89. Mem. Inst. Cert. Fin. Planners, Internat. Assn. Fin. Planning, Inland Soc. Tax Cons., AAUW (bd. dirs.), Nat. Assn. Securities Dealers (registered prin.), Nat. Ctr. Fin. Edn., Am. Bus. Women's Assn., Nat. Assn. Female Execs., Navy League, Freedoms Found. Valley Forge, Internat. Platform Assn. Presbyterian. Avocations: community service, travel, reading. Home: 6462 Spear St San Diego CA 92120 Office: Gengor Fin Advisors 4950 Waring Rd Ste 7 San Diego CA 92120

GENOVESE, C. ELEANOR, editor; b. Chatham, Ont., Can., Apr. 11, 1920; came to U.S., 1946; d. R. Douglas and Candace Mildred F. (Crafts) Moorhouse; m. Frank C. Genovese, June 17, 1944; children: Margaret Genovese Vanderhoof, Steven, Jeremy, Anne Genovese Burns, Michael. BA with honours, Victoria Coll., Toronto, Ont., 1942; tchr. cert., U. Toronto, 1943; cert. advanced study, Harvard U., 1977. Tchr. Chatham Sch., 1943-44; tchr. world affairs Appleton (Wis.) Pub. Schs.s, 1949; office mgr. Daily Cardinal, Madison, Wis., 1946-48; treas. Pleiad Corp., Wellesley, Mass., 1974-83; adminstrv. asst. Babson-Bernays Competition for Homemakers, Wellesley, 1977-79; rsch. assoc. Earthwatch, Belmont, Mass., 1978-80; mng. editor Am. Jour. Econs., Babson Park, Mass., 1989—. Mem. AAUW (pres. Framingham-Wellesley br. 1961-62, sec. Mass. div. 1966-72, del. Nat. Women's Conf. 1977, Leadership in Community Honor Roll award Mass. div. 1981), Can. Hist. Assn., Ont. Geneal. Soc., New Eng. Hist. Genealogy Soc. Democrat. Unitarian. Home: 21 Appleby Rd Wellesley MA 02181 Office: Babson Coll Babson Park MA 02157

GENS, HELEN DIANE, software company executive; b. Boston, May 15, 1934; d. Julius and Sarah Leah (Lipman) Pransky; m. Richard H. Gens, June 10, 1952; children: William E., Sara Gens Birenbaum, Julie Gens Rich, James A., Cory J., Noah B. Cert. paralegal, Mt. Ida Jr. Coll., 1980. Treas., dir. Med. Svcs. Corp. Am., Newton, Mass., 1963-71; pres., med. cons. Medicons., Inc., Boston, 1971-77; exec. v.p. Consulteo, Inc., Newton, 1977-83; pres. Substantive Software, Inc., Manchester, N.H., 1983-85, HDG Software, Inc., Sherborn, Mass., 1985—; cons. Concord Healthcare Corp., Nashville, 1986-87, Integrated Health Svcs., Cockeysville, Md., 1986-87. Author, editor (software) Legal Ease, 1986, Legal Ease Real Estate, 1986, Legal Ease Corporate, 1986. Mem. town meeting Town of Sherborn, 1983—. Mem. Nat. Office Products Assn., Artificial Intelligence Assn., NAFE. Republican. Jewish. Home and Office: 5070 Gulf of Mexico Dr Longboat Key FL 34228

GENTILE, ARLENE ROSE, teacher, intern/principal; b. Jersey City, Apr. 27, 1939; d. Nicholas Joseph and Anna Marie (Dempsey) De Stefano; m. Vincent Ralph Gentile, Oct. 28, 1956; children: Denise Ann, Doreen Ann, Debra Ann, Robert Jude. AA in Liberal Arts, Middlesex County Coll., Edison, N.J., 1985; BA in Elem. Edn., Kean Coll., 1985, MA in Edn. Adminstrn., 1989. Tchr. St. Boniface Sch., Jersey City, 1962-67, St. Mary's Sch., Plainfield, N.J., 1967-79; tchr. Jefferson Sch., Plainfield, 1985—, adminstrv. intern, 1988—; acting v.p. Emerson Sch., Plainfield, 1989. Roman Catholic. Home: 1275 Rock Ave Apt G-9 North Plainfield NJ 07060

GENTILE, GINA ANNE, healthcare manager; b. Tampa, Fla., Jan. 10, 1963; d. Mathew Nicholas and Mary Theresa (Perriello) G. BA, Ursuline Coll., Pepper Pike, Ohio, 1985. Bus. mgr. Univ. Hosps., Cleve.; mktg. dir. Manor Care Corp., North Olmstead, Ohio; coord. home health care S.W. Gen. Hosp., Parma Heights, Ohio. Mem. North Olmstead C. of C. (trustee). Roman Catholic. Home: 2720 Pease Dr Rocky River OH 44116 Office: 6975 W 130th St Parma Heights OH 44130

GENTILE, REGINA DOMINICA, optometrist; b. Norwich, Conn., June 7, 1951; d. Daniel Rocco and Elizabeth (Piacenza) Gentile; m. Thomas Raymond Johnston, July 14, 1979; children: Timothy Daniel, Elizabeth Ann. BS, Fairleigh Dickinson U., 1973, Pa. Coll. Optometry, 1977. Lic. optometrist. Assoc. Dr. Frank Castaldi, Stamford, Conn., 1978-82; owner, optometrist Vision Cons., Stamford, 1982—. Mem. Am. Optometric Soc., Conn. Optometric Assn., Phi Zeta Kappa. Roman Catholic. Home: 764 Cranberry Lane Orange CT 06477 Office: Vision Cons 1 Bank St Stamford CT 06901

GENTILE, SHARON ANN, marketing executive; b. Frostburg, Md., Nov. 4, 1953; d. Stanley Leo and Elizabeth Rose (Aldridge) Weimer; m. Albert Ronald Gentile, Apr. 29, 1977 (div. 1986; children: Kristina Marie. RN, Sinai Sch. Nursing, Balt., 1974. Staff nurse, dept. head Sinai Hosp./Hanover Hosp., Balt., 1974-83; staff nurse respiratory ICU Ft. Howard (Md.) VA Hosp., 1983; rehab. specialist Gen. Rehab. Svcs., Columbia, Md., Resource Opportunities, Inc., Glen Burnie, Md., Med. Rehab. Svcs., Balt., 1983-86; rehab. coord. City of Balt., 1986-90; mktg. rep. Learning Svcs., Inc., Manassas, Va., 1990—; co-chair Injured Workers Task Force, Balt., 1990—, chmn. med. svcs. coordination, 1989—, early referral com., 1987—. Mem. Md. Rehab. Assn., Chesapeake Assn. Rehab. Profls. in Pvt. Sector, Assn. Rehab. Nurses, Md. Self Insurer & Employers Compensation Assn. (sec. 1989—). Methodist. Home: 35 Hardwood Dr Baltimore MD 21237 Office: Learning Services Inc 9524 Fairview Ave Manassas VA 22110

GENTILIN, KAREN EILEEN, advertising agency official; b. Kew Gardens, N.Y., Aug. 5, 1963; d. Garth and Mary L. (Vaughan) G. BA, Adelphi U., 1983-85. Account coord.; account group asst. J.P. Lohman Real Estate Advt., Rockville Center, N.Y., 1980-85; acct. group asst. J.P. Lohman Comml. Real Estate Advt., N.Y.C., 1985-86; saleswoman H.K. Benjamin Realty, Woodside, N.Y., 1985-86; acct. coordinator Young & Rubicam, N.Y.C., 1986—. Vol. St. Agnes Cathedral, Rockville Centre, N.Y., 1985-87, Our Lady Queen of Martyrs Ch., Forest Hills, N.Y., 1987-88, Covenant House, N.Y.C., 1988, Epiphany Ch., Bklyn., 1988. Mem. Nat. Assn. Female Execs., Delta Mu Delta. Office: Young & Rubicam 285 Madison Ave New York NY 10017

GENTLEMAN, JULIA B., state senator; b. Des Moines, Aug. 24, 1931; d. John and Marguerite Brooks; B.S., Northwestern U., 1953; m. Gregor Gentleman, 1954; children: Karen L., Marcia M., Katherine B., J. Brooks, MacGregor III. Formerly mem. Iowa Ho. of Reps., 1975-78; mem Iowa Senate, 1979—. Republican. Office: Iowa State House Des Moines IA 50319*

GENTRY, BELYNDA, marketing and communications executive; b. Charlotte, N.C., Sept. 26, 1952; d. Isaac Anderson Sr. and Juanita Belk Chew; m. William George Gentry Jr.; children: William George III, Damian, DeNeen. Mgmt. asst. Bur. Land Mgmt., Alexandria, Va., 1979-80, records mgr., 1980-83; equal opportunity asst. Bur. Land Mgmt., Washington, 1983-84, equal opportunity specialist, 1984-87, employee devel. specialist, 1987-89; dir. mktg. Dept. of Labor Acad., Washington, 1989—, editor dept. newsletter, 1989-90. Editor govt.-wide publ. Fed. Women's Interagy. Bd., 1982-83. Asst. den leader Cub Scouts, Boy Scouts Am., Landover, Md., 1984; pres. United Voices Choir, Glenarden, Md., 1978—, editor newsletter, 1989; adviser Intermediate Choir, Glenarden, 1984—; Sunday Sch. tchr. First Bapt. Ch., Glenarden, 1988—. Mem. NAFE, Toastmasters Internat. (area gov. 1989—, Area Gov. of Yr. award 1990, club. pres. 1988-90). Democrat. Home: 9307 Alcona St Lanham MD 20706 Office: Dept of Labor Academy 200 Constitution Ave NW Washington DC 20210

GENTRY, CAROLYN ADELE, athletic facility executive, tennis teaching professional; b. Richmond, Va., Mar. 28, 1952; d. Elliott McCartney and Hilda (Yarid) G. BS in Edn., U. Va., 1974. Tennis teaching profl. Recreation Dept., Lynchburg, Va., 1968-74; elem. sch. tchr. Albemarle County Schs., Charlottesville, Va., 1974-76; asst. dir. tennis Pinehurst (N.C.) Inc., 1976-80; dir. Courtside Athletic Club, Lynchburg, Va., 1980-86; mgr., teaching pro Mid-Town Tennis Club, Rochester, N.Y., 1986-87, Potomac (Md.) Tennis Club, 1987—. Producer, narrator (TV program) Witness Fitness, 1982; improvisational actor, 1989. Sports coord. Kaleidoscope Festival, Lynchburg, 1982-84. Mem. USTA, U.S. Profl. Tennis Assn. Presbyterian.

GENTRY, CYNTHIA SUE, childhood education executive; b. Hattiesburg, Miss., Oct. 6, 1930; d. Hiram Edward and Amanda Norfleet (Cox) Liles; m. Timothy Peters Gentry, Nov. 28, 1953 (dec. Dec. 1985); children: Sandra Carol Case, Timothy Edward, Stephen Bradford, Karen Ruth Bradshaw. BS, U. Houston, 1952; MS, Corpus Christi State U., 1983. Cert. tchr., reading tchr., diagnostician, Tex. Tchr. Houston (Tex.) Ind. Schs., 1952-54, 54-57, Corpus Christi (Tex.) Ind. Sch. Dist., 1968-78; libr. First Bapt. Ch., Corpus Christi, 1988-89, dir. childhood edn., 1989—. Mem. AAUW, Tex. Assn. Bapt. Schs., Corpus Christi State U. Alumni Assn. Baptist. Office: First Baptist Sch 3115 Ocean Dr Corpus Christi TX 78404

GENTRY, JOANNE HESTER, educational administrator; b. Watsontown, Pa., Aug. 19, 1934; d. Louis Elwood and Marie Eileen (Groff) Hester; m. William Gordon Gentry, Aug. 16, 1958 (div. Apr. 1974); children: Cyndi Gentry Summers, Lori Gentry Brantley, Brian. BS in Edn., Bloomsburg (Pa.) State U., 1956; MEd, U. North Fla., 1979. Cert. bus. edn. tchr., prin., supr., adminstr., Fla. Elem. tchr. Oceanway Elem. Sch., Jacksonville, Fla., 1956-57; tchr. bus. edn. Englewood High Sch., Jacksonville, 1957-60, Fletcher Sr. High Sch., Jacksonville, 1960-61; tchr. English, Southside Jr. High Sch., Jacksonville, 1961-62; tchr. bus. edn. Terry Parker High Sch., Jacksonville, 1962-80, asst. prin. for instrn., 1980-84, vice prin., 1984—; instr. bus. edn., program facilitator adult edn. program Fla. Jr. Coll., Jacksonville, 1956—. Bd. dirs. Pier Point South Condo Assn., St. Augustine Beach, Fla., 1988, sec., 1989, treas., 1990. Mem. ASCD, Nat. Assn. Secondary Sch. Prins., Fla. Assn. Sch. Adminstrs., Fla. Vocat. Assn., Duval County Vice Prins. Coun. (chmn. 1986), Duval County Assn. Prins. Assn. (chmn. 1982), Duval County Bus. Edn. Coun. (pres. 1976), Duval County Assn. Secondary Sch. Adminstrs. (bd. dirs. 1982, 86), AAUW, Phi Delta Kappa. Democrat. Lutheran. Home: 2170 A1A S Unit 62 Saint Augustine Beach FL 32084 Office: Terry Parker High Sch 7301 Parker School Rd Jacksonville FL 32211

GENTRY, MARTHA IMOGEN, teacher, writer; b. San Francisco, Dec. 23, 1926; d. Guy Vernellon and Mary Edna Whaley; m. Herbert D. Nightingale, Sept. 10, 1951 (div. 1962); children: Carolyn Marie Schleif, David Edwin; m. Marvin C. Gentry, Mar. 12, 1972. Cert., Rudolph Schaeffer Sch. of Design, San Francisco, 1945-46; BA cum laude, Whitman Coll., Walla Walla, Wash., 1950; MFA, U. Wash., 1953; postgrad., UCLA, 1959-68. Cert. elem. and secondary tchr., Calif., Oreg. Tchr. L.A. City Schs., 1960-72; supr. tchr. tng. UCLA, 1961-72; writer L.A. City Schs., 1968; profl. tutor for exceptional children Grants Pass (Oreg.) City Schs., 1978-79; lectr. several orgns., Western U.S. and Can., 1984-85; researcher Flower Essence Soc., Nevada City, Calif., 1987; dir. edn. Ch. of Light and Love, Grants Pass, 1987—; pres., founder Universal Inst. of Philosophy and Rsch., Grants Pass, 1987-88. Group leader Camp Fire Girls, Pomona, Calif., 1942-43; patron Barnstormers Theatre, Grants Pass, 1979-80; vol. Lovejoy Hospice, Grants Pass, 1989—; practitioner The Flower Essence Soc., Nevada City, Calif., 1987; congl. mem. Astara, Inc., Upland, Calif., 1989. Mem. Internat. Platform Assn., Oreg. Assn. for Children with Learning Disabilities, Internat. Order of St. Luke the Physician, Grants Pass Camera Club (pres. 1976-77, Women's Club (pres. Sedro Woolley, Wash. 1956-57), Odd Fellows, Oreg. State Grange, Grants Pass Grange (chaplain), Women's Assn. (chairperson 1976-79), Knife and Fork Club, Delta Gamma. Republican.

GENTRY, PATRICIA WEBB, communications analyst; b. Sandston, Va., May 7, 1947; d. James G. and Sue (Campbell) Webb; widowed; children: Rodney, Scott. AA in Sci., Va. Commonwealth U., 1968. Cert. in info. processing. Svc. rep., communications rep. C&P Telephone Co., Richmond, Va., 1968-73; communications system rep. C&P Telephone Co., Richmond, 1973-79; Communications rep. C&P Telephone Co., 1979-83; systems cons. AT&T, Richmond, 1983-87; sr. tech. cons. Sovran Fin. Svcs., Richmond, 1987—. Address: Rte 2 Box 99A Mechanicsville VA 23111

GENYK, RUTH BEL, psychotherapist; b. Los Angeles, Apr. 5, 1955; d. John Douglas Bel and Ella Adiline (Lips) Medeiros; m. Carl J. Hattermann, June 11, 1977 (div. Dec. 1979); m. Edward A. Genyk, Aug. 8, 1983; children: Steven, Timothy, Devlon, Suzanne. Student, U. Copenhagen, 1975; BA, BSW, Whittier Coll., 1977; MA, U. Detroit, 1979; MSW, U. Mich., 1987. Social worker, community liaison Family Service, Whittier, Calif., 1976-77; social worker Children's Group Home, Detroit, 1977, Family Group Homes, Ann Arbor, Mich., 1977; probation officer Dept. Corrections, Detroit, 1978-86, cons., 1977-79; psychotherapist, cons., liaison Cath. Social Services, Jackson, Mich., 1986—. Mem. Jr. League. Mem. Am. Corrections Assn., Mich. Corrections Assn., Nat. Assn. Social Workers, Am. Assn. Univ. Women. Democrat. Unitarian. Office: Wildwood Franchice 505 Wildwood Jackson MI 49201

GENZ, HELEN DORIS, bookkeeper; b. Danbury, Conn., Jan. 20, 1944; d. Frederick E. Genz and Mary A. Loss. Grad. high sch., Danbury. With gen. office staff Omaha Beef Co., Danbury, 1962-66; accounts payable clk. Danbury Hosp., 1966-72; sales sec. The Fair Cadillac-Oldsmobile Co., Danbury, 1973-84; sec./bookkeeper Van Houten Motors Inc., Danbury, 1986—. Roman Catholic. Home: 13 North Dr New Fairfield CT 06812

GEO-KARIS, ADELINE JAY, state legislator; b. Tegeas, Greece, Mar. 29, 1918; student Northwestern U., Mt. Holyoke Coll.; LLB, DePaul U. Admitted to Ill. bar; founder Adeline J. Geo-Karis and Assocs., Zion, Ill.; former mcpl., legis. atty. Mundelein, Ill., Vernon Hills, Ill., Libertyville (Ill.) Twp., Long Grove (Ill.) Sch. Dist.; justice of peace; former asst. state's atty.; mem. Ill. Ho. of Reps., 1973-79; mem. Ill. Senate, 1979—, minority spokeswoman jud. com.; mayor, City of Zion, Ill. Served to lt. comdr. USNR.; comdr. Res. ret. Recipient Americanism medal DAR; named Woman of Yr. Daughters of Penelope, Outstanding Legislator Ill. Fedn. Ind. Colls. and Univs., 1975-78, Legis. award Ill. Assn. Park Dists., 1976. Sponsor Guilty but Mentally Ill Law. Greek Orthodox. Office: 2610 Sheridan Rd Ste 213 Zion IL 60099*

GEORGE, BARBARA ANN, health care administrator; b. Santa Barbara, Calif., May 23, 1932; d. Louis Richard and Pearl Bernice (Miller) Smith; m. Louis Frank, June 12, 1953 (div. 1981); children: Anthony Charles, Nicholas Michael. Nursing diploma, St. Francis Hosp. Sch. of Nurs, San Francisco, 1953; AS, Santa Rosa Jr. Coll., 1975. Staff nurse St. Francis Meml. Hosp., San Francisco, 1953-55; office nurse Emile Torre, M.D., San Francisco, 1955-59, Gregory Smith, M.D., San Francisco, 1959-60; supervising nurse Planned Parenthood, San Francisco; exec. dir. Planned Parenthood/Marin, San Rafael, Calif., 1966-75, Nat. Council on Alcohol, Calif., 1975-79; v.p. Lawrence & Assocs., Santa Rosa, Calif., 1978-83; training dir. Albuquerque Employee Asst., Albuquerque, 1983-84; C.E.O. exec. dir. Addiction Recovery Ctrs. Inc., Forest Knolls, Calif., 1984--; cons. Dept. Health Edn. and Welfare, Calif., 1975-77, U.S. Bur. Indian Affairs, N.Mex., 1983-84; lectr. John F. Kennedy U., Oakland, 1984-88; nat. surveyor Commn. on Accreditation of Rehab. Facilities. Treas. N.C.A. Sonoma County, Santa Rosa, 1974-75; Pres. Y.W.C.A. Sonoma County, Santa Rosa, 1975-76, Bd. of Trustees, Santa Rosa Ch. of Religious Sci., 1988-89. Mem. Nat. Coun. on Alcoholism, Calif. Labor Mgmt. Plan, St. Francis Hosp. Alumni Assn., Assn. Labor Mgmt. Adminstrs. and Cons. on Alcoholism, Inc., Nat. Assn. Addiction Treatment Providers, Sebastopol Golf Club, Soroptomists Internat. Democrat. Metaphysical. Home: 1144 Baywood Dr #88 Petaluma CA 94952 Office: Addiction Recovery Ctrs Inc 145 Tamal Rd Forest Knolls CA 94933

GEORGE, CLAUDIA K., public accountant; b. Meriden, Conn., Dec. 6, 1949; d. Eric A. and Dorothy (Allen) Kriebel; m. Eugene O. George, Dec. 6, 1970. BA with honors, U. Fla., 1971; MBA, U. South Fla., 1984. CPA, Fla. Asst. dir. devel. Meml. Hosp., Sarasota, Fla., 1976-81; ptnr. Arthur & Swearingen, CPAs, Sarasota, 1981-89, Piper, Hawkins & George, CPAs, Sarasota, 1989—. Editor: (newsletter) Alert, 1982-87; host cable talk show Bottom Line, 1988-89. Trustee Pine Shores (Fla.) Presbyn. Ch., 1988—, treas./sec., 1988—, elder, co-chmn. budget com., 1987—; treas. David G. Bowman for Sarasota County Hosp. Bd. campaign, 1984, 88; chmn. child advocacy com. Sarasota Jr. League, 1980. Named Best Pub. Rels. Effort Fla. Hosp. Assn., 1981. Mem. AICPA, Fla. Inst. CPAs (treas. Gulfcoast chpt. 1988—, dir. edn. 1987, 88, pub. rels. com. 1987-88, scholarship com. 1986-87, sec. 1989, pres. elect 1990, pres. 1991), Sarasota County C. of C., Field Club. Republican. Office: Piper Hawkins & George CPAs 330 S Pinapple Ave Sarasota FL 34236

GEORGE, DIANE E., librarian, educational technology, computer education educator; b. L.I., N.Y., July 12, 1952; d. Arnold J. and Jeanette A. (Hester) G. BS, So. Conn. State U., 1974, MS, 1977. Cert. intermediate adminstr., libr. media specialist K-12, elem. edn. 1-8, driver's edn. Libr. media specialist New Canaan (Conn.) Pub. Schs., North Haven (Conn.) Pub. Schs., Branford (Conn.) Pub. Schs.; ednl. cons. to SEED Project, New Haven; Conn. del. N.E. Regional Ednl. Leadership Conf., 1983; participant forum Linking Children with Nature, Roger Tory Peterson Inst., 1988. Recipient Faculty Excellence award Branford Intermediate Sch., 1985-86. Mem. Assn. for Supervision and Curriculum Devel., Conn. Educators Computer Assn. (bd. dirs. 1989—), Conn. Ednl. Media Assn. (bd. dirs. 1984-85, cert. of appreciation 1984). Office: Branford Intermediate Sch 185 Damascus Rd Branford CT 06405

GEORGE, EDIE, college administrator; b. Evanston, Wyoming, Apr. 8, 1940; d. Harold Glen and Phyllis Marie (Smith) G.; m. Herschel G. Hester III, Dec. 26, 1969 (div. 1982); children: Lee Forsgren, Shelleice Stokes, Kristin Coombs. BS, Weber State Coll., 1969; postgrad., U. Utah, 1979-81.

Adminstrv. asst. Sta. KLO Radio, Ogden, Utah, 1958-61; asst. dir. printing Boise (Idaho) Cascade Corp., 1962-65; news, publs. asst. Weber State Coll., Ogden, 1965-67, publs. dir., 1967-74, pub. rels. dir., 1974-80, exec. dir. alumni rels., spl. svcs., 1980—; pres. Edie Hester & Assocs., Ogden, 1979—. Chair The Chamber's Leaders in Bus. Conf., Ogden, 1990, The Chamber's Early Bird Com., Ogden, 1989; bd. dirs. Ogden Symphony Ballet Assn., 1980-82; exec. com. The Chamber's Women in Mgmt. Commn., Ogden, 1989-90. Named Women of Yr. Edn. YWCA, 1985. Mem. Coun. for Advancement and Support of Edn., Am. Assn. of U. Adminstrs. (regional rep. 1980-88), Am. Bus. Women's Assn. (pres. 1981-82, Woman of Yr. 1982). Office: Weber State U 3750 Harrison Blvd Ogden UT 84408-1011

GEORGE, ELIZABETH ANN, asset manager; b. Ft. Dodge, Iowa, Nov. 19, 1948; d. Berhardt Arnold and Helen Marie (Jacobson) Bangert; m. Stephen R. George, July 11, 1971 (div. Feb. 1981); 1 child, Daniel R. BA, Wartburg Coll., Waverly, Iowa, 1971. Cert. property mgr.; real property adminstr. Sec. GMAC, Bayside, N.Y., 1971-73; legal sec. Dominick A. DeRiso, Atty., Bayside, 1973-74; sec. Dayton Hudson Properties, Mpls., 1974-76; asst. property mgr. to sr. property mgr. United Properties, Mpls., 1977-87; asset mgr. Coldwell Banker, Mpls., 1987-88, Richard Ellis, Mpls., 1988-89, Shelard Group, Mpls., 1989—. Mem. Inst. Real Estate Mgmt. (pres. 1986), Mpls. Bldg. Owners and Mgrs. Assn. (bd. dirs.). Lutheran. Office: Shelard Group 11095 Viking Dr Eden Prairie MN 55344

GEORGE, ELWANDA, beauty salon owner; b. Bonifay, Fla., Jan. 22, 1933; d. Marvin J. and Altha Lois (Rigby) Brock; m. Donald W. George, Mar. 2, 1951; children: Gary, Stephen, Kimball, Karen. Cosmetology diploma, Washington-Holmes Vocat.-Tech., 1981. Lic. cosmetologist; cert. hair colorist, Fla. Owner, mgr., stylist Image Ctr. Beauty Salon, Chipley, Fla., 1984—. Mem. NAFE, Am. Entrepreneurs Assn., Assn. Fashion and Image Consultants, Chipley C. of C. Home: Rte 5 Box 723 Chipley FL 32428

GEORGE, MARY SHANNON, state senator; b. Seattle, May 27, 1916; d. William Day and Agnes (Lovejoy) Shannon; B.A. cum laude, U. Wash., 1937; postgrad. U. Mich., 1937, Columbia U., 1938; m. Flave Joseph George; children—Flave Joseph, Karen Liebermann, Christy, Shannon Lowrey. Prodn. asst., asst. news editor Pathe News, N.Y.C., 1938-42; mem. fgn. editions staff Readers Digest, Pleasantville, N.Y., 1942-46; columnist Caracas (Venezuela) Daily Jour., 1953-60; councilwoman City and County of Honolulu, 1969-74; senator State of Hawaii, 1974—, asst. minority leader, 1978-80, minority policy leader, 1983-84, minority floor leader, 1987, minority leader, 1987—, chmn. transp. com., 1981-82; mem. Nat. Air Quality Adv. Bd., 1974-75, Intergovtl. Policy Ady. Com. Trade, 1988—, White House Conf. Drug Free Am., 1988—. Vice chmn. 1st Hawaii Ethics Commn., 1968; co-founder Citizens Com. on Constl. Conv., 1968; vice-chmn. platform com. Republican Nat. Conv., 1976, co-chmn., 1980; bd. dirs. Hawaii Planned Parenthood, 1970-72, 79-86, Hawaii Med. Services Assn., 1972-86; mem. adv. bd. Hawaii chpt. Mothers Against Drunk Driving, 1984—. Recipient Jewish Men's Club Brotherhood award, 1974; Outstanding Legislator of Yr. award Nat. Rep. Legislators Assn., 1985; named Woman of Yr., Honolulu Press Club, 1969, Hawaii Fedn. Bus. and Profl. Women, 1970; Citizen of Yr., Hawaii Fed. Exec. Bd., 1973, 76. Mem. LWV (pres. Honolulu 1966-68), Mensa, Phi Beta Kappa, Kappa Alpha Theta. Episcopalian. Author: A Is for Abrazo, 1961. Home: 782-G N Kalaheo Ave Kailua HI 96734 Office: State Capitol Rm 222 Honolulu HI 96813

GEORGE, PAULA LOUISE, advertising agency executive; b. Huntington, W.Va., June 16, 1952; d. Emil Ralph and Helen Louise (Hensley) G. BBA in Mktg., Marshall U., 1974. Mktg. mgr. Access Matrix Corp., San Jose, Calif., 1982-83; v.p., dir. mktg. Altus Corp., San Jose, 1983-84; pres., founder The SoftAd Group, Sausalito, Calif., 1985—; guest lectr. Stanford U.; participant exec.-in-residence Marshall U., Huntington, W.Va.; keynote speaker Direct Mktg. Assn. Ann. Confs., New Orleans, Atlanta, Advt. Age Creative Workshop, N.Y.C., Montreux Direct Mktg. Symposium, Montreux, Switzerland. Office: The SoftAd Group 207 Second St Sausalito CA 94965

GEORGE, SHIRLEY H., state librarian; b. Elgin, Ill., Dec. 29, 1938; d. Edwin William and Nora (Wiese) Hattendorf; m. Melvin R. George; children: Catherine, Elizabeth. BA, Valparaiso U., 1960; MLS, U. Minn., 1969; MBA, U. Chgo., 1982. Ref. libr. Elmhurst (Ill.) Pub. Libr., 1971-73; head ref. dept. Helen M. Plum Meml. Libr., Lombard, Ill., 1973-75; adminstrv. libr. Maywood (Ill.) Pub. Libr., 1975-84; asst. state libr. State Libr. Oreg., Salem, 1985-87; state libr. State Libr. Iowa, Des Moines, 1987—; bd. dirs. Bibliographic Ctr. for Rsch., Denver. Mem. ALA, Iowa Libr. Assn. Episcopalian. Office: State Libr of Iowa E 12th and Grand Des Moines IA 50319

GEORGE-PERRY, SHARON JUANITA, management consultant; b. Modesto, Calif., Sept. 21, 1938; d. H. Edward and Beatrice C. (Wright) Melin; m. John L. George, Apr. 27, 1956 (div. 1974); children: Terri A., Tami L., Timothy J., Tobin E.; m. William E. Perry Jr., Apr. 19, 1980. BS in Edn. magna cum laude, Calif. State U., Hayward, 1965; MEd Guidance in Counseling, Hardin-Simmons U., 1976; MBA in Mgmt., Golden Gate U., 1980. Cert. elem. edn., Calif., elem., secondary counseling, Tex. Tchr. elem. Hayward (Calif) Unified Sch. Dist., 1965-73; tchr. diagnostics, group therapist Tex. Youth Coun., Brownwood, 1974-75; assoc. dir. New Directions Psychiat. Half Way House, Abilene, Tex., 1975-77; exec. dir. Mental Health Assn., Abilene, 1977-78, San Francisco, 1979-84; assoc. pres. Perry Assoc. Mgmt. Cons., San Francisco, 1983—; exec. dir. cons. Vision of Am. At Peace, Berkeley, Calif., 1984, Oakes Children's Ctr., San Francisco, 1985—; mktg. dir. Mental Health Providers of Calif., 1987—; sr. assoc. Behavioral Health Systems; founding exec. dir., v.p. adminstrn. Planet Live Earthbeat TV, Inc.; bd. dirs. PL Enterprises, Inc.; vis. lectr. McMurry Coll., Abilene, 1976-78; cons. Dyess AFB, Abilene, 1976-78, Abilene Youth Ctr., 1976-78; speaker in field, 1979—. Chair Commn. on Status of Women of Marin County, Calif., 1985—; mem. adv. com. Displaced Homemaker Project, Sacramento, 1985—; founder, Children's Mental Health Policy Bd., 1984—; pres. Artisans Gallery, Mill Valley, Calif., 1984—; mem. Children's Mental Health Policy Bd., 1984—. Grantee Fed. Dept. Justice, Brownwood, 1975, pvt. community founds., Calif., 1979-87. Mem. NAFE, Council of Calif. Mental Health Contractors, Am. Soc. Profl. Exec. Women. Avocations: travel, gourmet cooking, hiking, public speaking. Home: 17 Ethel Ave Mill Valley CA 94941 Office: 100 Shoreline Hwy Ste 2953 Mill Valley CA 94941

GEORGOPAPADAKOU, NAFSIKA HELEN, pharmaceutical company biochemist; b. Thessaloniki, Greece, Jan. 6, 1950; came to U.S., 1968; d. Tasos Michael and Elli Elizabeth (Deli) G. BA, Mills Coll., 1971; PhD, Yale U., 1975. Rsch. fellow Harvard U., Cambridge, Mass., 1976-77; rsch. investigator E.R. Squibb & Sons, Princeton, N.J., 1977-80, sr. rsch. investigator, 1980-84; rsch. group chief Hoffmann-La Roche Inc., Nutley, N.J., 1984—. Contbr. articles to profl. jours. Mem. AAAS, Am. Chem. Soc., Am. Soc. for Biol. Chemists, Am. Soc. for Microbiology, Am Mgmt. Assn., Phi Beta Kappa. Office: Hoffmann-LaRoche Inc 340 Kingsland St Nutley NJ 07110

GEORGOPOULOS, MARIA, architect; b. Moussata, Cefalonia, Greece, Apr. 2, 1949; came to U.S., 1973; d. Vassilios and Joulia Georgopoulos; m. Demetrios Georgopoulos (div. 1974). BArch, Nat. Poly. Sch. Greece, Athens, 1972; MS, Columbia U., 1976. Registered architect, N.Y., Greece. Project mgr. Architects Design Group, N.Y.C., 1976-79, Griswold, Heckel & Kelly, N.Y.C., 1979-80; project dir. Lehman Bros., Kuhn Loeb Inc., N.Y.C., 1980-85; v.p. L.F. Rothschild Inc., N.Y.C., 1985—. Mem. AIA, Am. Women Entrepreneurs, Greek Inst. Architects. Greek Orthodox. Club: Douglaston (N.Y.). Home: 14 Melrose Ln Douglaston NY 11363 Office: LF Rothschild Inc 222 Broadway New York NY 10038

GEPNER, MARSHA KAY, communications professional; b. Champaign/Urbana, Ill., May 3, 1947; d. Robert E. and Lois (Mason) G. Student, Ind. U. Dir. pub. info. County Music Assn., Nashville, 1977-82; producer, writer The Nashville Network, 1982-85; mgr. communications Whirlpool Corp., LaVergne, Tenn., 1987—. Writer, remote location producer Willie Nelson's FarmAid Concert, 1985; writer, producer TV series "Yesteryear in Nashville";, "Offstage", 1982-85; writer/producer consumer mkt. videos on greatest hits of country music, 1989. Mem. Ladies Heritage Assn., Assn. for Preservation of Tenn. Antiquities. Episcopalian. Office: Whirlpool Corp 1714 Heil Quaker Blvd LaVergne TN 37086

GEPPERT, KATHRYN ANN, health facility administrator, consultant; b. Sherman, Tex., Mar. 16, 1953; d. Richard Arlen and Mary Lee (Thebeau) Timmerberg; m. James Wallace Geppert, May 13, 1977; children: Jason, Jamie Lynn. RN, Jewish Hosp. Sch. Nursing, 1974; BA in Mgmt., Webster U., 1987; MBA, Fontbonne Coll., 1988. Staff nurse North Kansas City Meml. Hosp., Mo., 1974-75, Vets. Hosp., Kansas City, 1975-77; clin. instr. St. John's Mercy Med. Ctr., St. Louis, 1977-78, head nurse, 1978-83; dir. nursing Am. Surgery Ctr., St. Louis, 1983-86; patient care coord. Children's Hosp., St. Louis, 1986-88; exec. dir. West County Surgery Ctr., Chesterfield, Mo., 1988—; cons. Lerwick Clinic, St. Louis, 1986, Stone Treatment Ctr., St. Louis, 1990—. Mem. Assn. Operating Rm. Nurses (com. chmn. 1976-89), Chesterfield C. of C. Office: West County Surgery Ctr 1130 Town & Country Commons Chesterfield MO 63017

GERACE, SUSAN TERESE, product designer; b. Glen Ridge, N.J., Aug. 12, 1950; d. Salvatore E. and Augustine J. (Scolaro) Capozzi; m. Michael Francis Gerace, Apr. 27, 1974; children: Lucas Gonzalez, Carmen Bustamante. Student, Ohio U., 1968-69; BS in Fashion Design with honors, Drexel U., 1971. Designer asst. Giorgio Di Sant'Angelo, N.Y.C., 1971-72; designer Commonwealth Toys, Bklyn., 1972-74; dir. Barbizon Sch. Fashion, San Diego, 1975-77; display artist Impact Decorating, San Diego, 1977-78; design dir. Eden Toys, Inc., N.Y.C., 1978—. Recipient 1st Pl. Herbal Garden award Anne Arundel County, Annapolis, Md., 1988. Mem. Md. Fedn. Art, Latin Am. Parents Assn. (social chmn. nat. capital region). Democrat. Roman Catholic. Home: 311 Fairlea Dr Edgewater MD 21037 Office: Eden Toys Inc 812 Jersey Ave Jersey City NJ 07310-1109

GERACI, ANTONINA MARIE, editor; b. Chgo, Feb. 15, 1967; d. Joseph and Maria (Castelluzzo) G. BS in Media Studies, U. Ill., 1989. Sales assoc. Madigans, Norridge, Ill., 1986-89; pub. rels. intern Kuehn Communications, Chgo., 1988-89, Urbana (Ill.) C. of C., 1988-89; mgmt. trainee Marshall Field and Co., Chgo., 1989-90; asst. editor Nat. Assn. Bds. of Pharmacy, Park Ridge, Ill., 1990—. Mem. Women in Communications Inc. (pub. rels. com. 1987-88). Home: 5114 N Michigan Ave Schiller Park IL 60176

GERACI, DIANE, academic librarian; b. Buffalo, Apr. 3, 1952; d. Robert Andrew and Mary Mathilda (Devosich) G. BA, SUNY, Cortland, 1974; MLS, SUNY, Buffalo, 1984, MA in Anthropology, 1985. Inter-libr. loan libr. SUNY-Binghamton, 1984-85, social sci. bibliographer, 1985—. Contbr. articles to profl. publs. Grantee N.Y. State/United Univ. Profls., 1985, 87, 89. Mem. ALA, SUNY Libr. Assn. (co-chair publs. com. 1989-91), Am. Soc. Info. Sci., Am. Anthrop. Assn., Beta Phi Mu. Office: SUNY Binghamton Box 6012 Binghamton NY 13902-6012

GERAGHTY, MARGARET KARL, finance company excutive, portfolio manager; b. Bklyn., May 31, 1947; d. Edward H. and Margaret Honora (Miller) Karl; m. John Matthew Geraghty, Sept. 9, 1972. BA, Marymount Coll., Tarrytown, N.Y., 1969; MA, Hunter Coll., 1974; advanced profl. cert., NYU, 1978. Fin. analyst GM, N.Y.C., 1969-73; dir. fin. analysis Equitable, N.Y.C., 1973-77; asst. v.p. Equitable Life Holding Corp., N.Y.C., 1977-79, Equitable Life Assurance Soc., N.Y.C., 1979-84; v.p. Equitable Capital Mgmt. Corp., N.Y.C., 1984—. Trustee Marymount Coll., 1984—, Mt. St. Dominic Acad., Caldwell, N.J., 1987—; treas. Cath. Big. Bros., N.Y.C., 1989—. Recipient Gloria Gaines award Marymount Coll., 1979. Mem. Fin. Women's Assn., Coll. Club Ridgewood, Rep. Club. Home: 250 Palmer Ct Ridgewood NJ 07450 Office: Equitable Capital Mgmt Corp 1285 Avenue of Americas New York NY 10019

GERAN, LEONORA ANN, academic administrator, educator; b. N.Y.C., Aug. 30, 1939; d. Joseph and Marianna (Biondo) Curasi; m. Dennis Paul Geran, Apr. 30, 1966; children: Denise, Kerry Ann. BS in Edn., CUNY, 1961, MS in Edn., 1965; postgrad., Widener U., 1987—. Cert. bus. edn. tchr., N.Y., Del. Permanent tchr. Washington Irving High Sch., N.Y.C., 1961-68; with Goldey-Beacon Coll., Wilmington, Del., 1975—, assoc. prof., 1984-89, asst. to provost, dir. personnel, 1989—; speaker, presenter in field. Mem. tchr. cert. com. Del. Dept. Pub. Instruction, 1984. Mem. Am. Assembly Collegiate Schs. Bus., Assn. Am. Colls., Coll. and Univ. Personnel Assn., Middle Atlantic Assn. Coll. of Bus. Adminstrn., Nat. Bus. Edn. Assn., Nat. Ctr. for Higher Edn. Mgmt. Sys., AAUW. Home: 7 N Colts Neck Way Hockessin DE 19707 Office: Goldey Beacom Coll 4701 Limestone Rd Wilmington DE 19808

GERARD, JEAN BROWARD SHEVLIN, ambassador, lawyer; b. Portland, Oreg., Mar. 9, 1938; d. Edwin Leonard and Ella (Broward) Shevlin; m. James Watson Gerard, June 20, 1959 (dec. 1987); children: James W., Harriet C. AB, Vassar Coll., 1959; JD, Fordham U., 1977; LLD (hon.), U. S.C., 1983. Bar: N.Y. 1978, Fla. 1978, D.C. 1979, U.S. Dist. Ct. (ea. and so. dists.) N.Y. 1978. Atty. Cadawalader, Wickersham & Taft, N.Y.C., 1977-81; ambassador, permanent rep. of U.S. to UNESCO, Paris, 1981-85; U.S. ambassador to Luxembourg, 1985-89. Editor: Fordham Internat. Law Forum, 1977. Bd. govs. Women's Nat. Rep. Club, 1967-73, 74-80, pres., 1971-73; hon. del. Rep. Nat. Conv., N.Y.C., 1972; alt. del. 18th Congl. Dist. N.Y., N.Y.C., 1980. Recipient SAR medal, 1970, medal of honor VFW, 1982. Mem. N.Y. County Lawyers Assn., Assn. Bar City of N.Y. Presbyterian. Clubs: Colony; City Midday (N.Y.C.); Capitol Hill (D.C.); Cercle de l'Union Interalliee (Paris); Cercle Munster (Luxembourg).

GERARD, VALRIE ANN, marine biology educator, researcher, consultant; b. Amityville, N.Y., Feb. 21, 1948; d. Vernon Arthur and Margy (Hoffmann) G. BA, SUNY, Buffalo, 1970; MA, U. Calif., Santa Cruz, 1974, PhD, 1976. Killam postdoctoral fellow Dalhousie U., Halifax, N.S., Can., 1976-78; rsch. fellow Calif. Inst. Tech., Pasadena, 1978-83; asst. prof. marine biology SUNY, Stony Brook, 1983-88, assoc. prof., 1988—; cons. Marine Rev. Com., Santa Barbara, Calif., 1981-89, Applied Biomath., Stony Brook, 1986-87; mem. adv. bd. Jour. Applied Phycology, 1988—. NSF grantee, 1985—, N.Y. State Sea grantee, 1987-88. Mem. Phycological Soc. Am., Phi Beta Kappa. Office: SUNY Marine Scis Rsch Ctr Stony Brook NY 11794-5000

GERARDI, MARYROSE ACERRA, psychologist; b. Rockville Centre, N.Y., Jan. 25, 1959; d. Salvatore J. and Stella R. (Esposito) Acerra; m. Robert J. Gerardi, Nov. 9, 1985; 1 child, Gabriela. BA, Fairfield (Conn.) U., 1981; PhD, SUNY, Albany, 1987. Lic. psychologist, Mass. Intern McLean Hosp., Belmont, Mass., 1985-86, behavioral specialist, 1986-87, asst. attending psychologist, 1987—; pvt. practice Arlington, Mass., 1987—; Feedback giver Leadership Devel. program Ctr. for Creative Leadership, Hartford Grad. Ctr., 1989—. Contbr. articles to profl. jours. Mem. Am. Psychol. Assn., Assn. Advancement Behavior Therapy. Office: 22 Mill St Ste 405 Arlington MA 02174

GERARD-SHARP, MONICA FLEUR, communications executive; b. London, Oct. 4, 1951; came to U.S., 1975; d. John Hugh Gerard-Sharp and Doreen May (Kearney) Dewhurst; m. Ali Edward Wambold, Nov. 21, 1981; children: Marina, Daniela. BA in Philosophy and Lit. with honors, U. Warwick, Eng., 1973; MBA in Fin., Mktg. and Internat. Bus., Columbia U., 1980. Editor Inst. Chem. Engrs., London, 1973-74; sub-editor TV Times Ltd., London, 1974-75; press officer, editor UN, N.Y.C., 1975-78; bus. mgr. Time-Life Video, N.Y.C., 1980-81; mgr. fin. analysis Time-Life Films, N.Y.C., 1981; v.p. T.V.I.S., N.Y.C., 1982-83; dir. strategy and devel. video group Time Video Info. Svcs., N.Y.C., 1984-85; asst. treas., officer Time Inc., N.Y.C., 1985-87; pub. Travel Todays mags. Fairchild Pubs. subs. Capital Cities/ABC, N.Y.C., 1987-88; dir. video programming Fairchild Pubs., Capital Cities/ABC, N.Y.C., 1988-89; pub. Entrée and Home Fashions Mag., N.Y.C., 1988—; cons. UN Bus. Council, N.Y.C., 1979; bd. rep. U.S.A. Network, N.Y.C., 1983-85; bd. dirs. Maga-Link, Communications Bridge. Editor: Everyone's United Nations, 1977; contbg. editor Asia Pacific Forum, 1976-77; contbr. articles to profl. jours. and mags., 1973-78. Bronfman fellow, 1979-80. Mem. Nat. Acad. Cable Programming, Am. Film Inst., Beta Gamma Sigma. Roman Catholic. Home: Deer Park Sunset Hill Rd Pleasant Valley NY 12569 also: 46 Thurloe Sq, London SW7, England Office: Fairchild Pubs 7 E 12th St New York NY 10003

GERBER, DAHLIA KATZ, jewelry store executive; b. Pitts., Mar. 20, 1933; d. Samuel S. and Iris (Klahr) Katz; m. Gilbert M. Gerber, Dec. 19, 1954; children: Jessica Hope, Zara Faith, Joshua Matthew, David Adam. BS in Edn., U. Pitts., 1954. Cert. permanent tchr., Pitts. Tchr. Pitts. Pub. Schs., 1954-58; pres. Dahlia's Chinoiserie Jewelers (formerly Chinoiserie of Shadyside, Inc.), Pitts., 1980—. Organizer, pres. Children's Aid Home for Spl. People, Inc., Pitts., 1976-81, bd. dirs., 1981—. Recipient Social Assistance award Women's Am. Orgn. for Rehab. through Tng., Pitts., 1980. Mem. Phi Sigma Sigma. Democrat. Jewish. Office: Dahlia's Chinoiserie 5824-5826 Forbes Ave Pittsburgh PA 15217

GERBER, GWENDOLYN LORETTA, psychologist, professor; b. Calgary, Alberta, Can.; came to U.S., 1958; d. Ernest and Alma (Tesky) G. AB, UCLA, 1961, MA, 1964, PhD, 1967; cert. in psychoanalysis, NYU, 1970. Lic. psychologist, N.Y. Clin. psychologist Hillside Hosp., Glen Oaks, N.Y., 1970-73; asst. prof. psychology John Jay Coll. of Criminal Justice CUNY, N.Y.C., 1973-77, assoc. prof. psychology, 1977—; pvt. practice in psychotherapy N.Y.C., 1970—. Contbr. chpts. to books and numerous articles to profl. jours. Fellowship USPHS, 1962-63, 66-67, NIMH, 1967-69; grantee CUNY, 1989-91. Mem. Am. Psychol. Assn. (bd. dirs. div. 39 sect. III 1988-92, exec. com. div. 35 1989-90), N.Y. State Psychol. Assn. (pres. acad. div. 1989-90), N.Y. Acad. Scis. (vice chair, psychology adv. com. 1990-92), Phi Beta Kappa, Chi Delta Pi. Office: Dept Psychology John J Coll 445 W 59th St New York NY 10019

GERBER, LINDA MAXINE, epidemiology educator; b. N.Y.C., Apr. 12, 1953; d. Kenneth K. and Hilda (Butschowitz) S.; m. Michael Leit, Feb. 27, 1982; children: Benjamin Kenneth Leit, Rachel Joanna Leit. BA, SUNY, Binghamton, 1973; MA, U. Colo., 1976, PhD, 1978. Rsch. assoc. Inst. Behavioral Sci., U. Colo., Boulder, 1978; rsch. assoc. Cornell U. Med. Coll., N.Y.C., 1979-81, asst. prof. pub. health, 1982-84, 87—, preceptor dept. pub. health, 1980-84, 87—; rsch. scientist, epidemiologist Nassau County Dept. Health, Mineola, N.Y., 1984; clin. asst. prof. pub. health Cornell U. Med. Coll., N.Y.C., 1984-86; dir. office epidemiology Nassau County Dept. Health, Mineola, 1985-86; asst. prof. clin. community and preventive medicine SUNY Sch. Medicine, Stony Brook, 1985-87; asst. prof. epidemiology in medicine and pub. health Cornell U. Med. Coll., N.Y.C., 1987—; rsch. intern East-West Population Inst., East-West Ctr., Honolulu, 1976-77; cons. Inst. Behavioral Sci. U. Colo., Boulder, 1974;mem. institutional rev. bd. Fordham U., N.Y.C., 1980—. Author: Relationship of Body Fat Distribution to Blood Pressure Level, 1990; contbr. articles to profl. jours. Mem. N.Y. Heart Assn., N.Y.C., 1980-88. Post-doctoral fellow Pub. Health Svc., Cornell U. Med. Coll., 1979-81, Fleischmann fellow U. Colo., 1978, NIMH predoctoral fellow U. Colo., 1975-78. Fellow Am. Assn. Phys. Anthropologists (job placement & devel. com. 1984—), Human Biology Coun., Am. Heart Assn. (coun. on epidemiology); mem. Soc. for Med. Anthropology. Office: Cornell U Med Coll Cardiovascular Ctr 525 E 68th St New York NY 10021

GERBER, LUCILLE D., elementary school educator; b. Adrian, Mich., Nov. 22, 1952; d. William C. and V. Lucille (Wilson) Brooks; m. Gerald F. Gerber, Aug. 3, 1985. BS, Ea. Mich. U., 1976, postgrad. Tchr. Ypsilanti (Mich.) Pub. Schs. Mem. NEA, Mich. Edn. Assn. Address: 615 N Mansfield Ypsilanti MI 48197

GERBERDING, JOAN ELIZABETH, broadcasting company executive, small business owner; b. Rockville Center, N.Y., July 29, 1949; d. Henry William and Edith Louise (Perry) G. Student West Chester State U., 1967-69. Asst. pub. relations dir. Conn. Heart Assn., Hartford, 1970-71; publs. editor Hartford Steam Boiler Ins. Co., 1971-72; asst. account exec. Wilson Haight & Welch, Inc., Hartford, 1972; copywriter Internat. Silver Co., Meriden, Conn., 1973-74; acct. exec. WCOD FM, Hyannis, Mass., 1975-76, gen. sales mgr., 1976-79, v.p., gen. sales mgr., 1979-80; sales devel. mgr. Nassau Broadcasting Co., WHWH AM/WPST FM, Princeton, N.J., 1980-82, gen. sales mgr., 1982-83, v.p. sales, 1983-85, corp. v.p., 1985—; cons. Woman's Newspaper of Princeton, 1984—; lectr., cons. Am. Women in Radio and TV, 1980—; lectr. Princeton YWCA/Women programs, Princeton, 1984—; co-owner Burg Dairy Ice Cream Co., 1988—. Recipient YWCA TWIN award, Princeton, 1984. Mem. Am. Women in Radio and TV, N.J. Broadcasters Assn., Am. Bus. Assn., Inc., Princeton Bus. Assn., Radio Advt. Bur. Democrat. Episcopalian. Avocations: writing, music, running. Home: 3 Sunrise Ave Hopewell NJ 08525

GERBERG, JUDITH LEVINE, human resource company executive; b. N.Y.C., Mar. 21, 1940; d. Murray Joseph and Pearl (Berens) Levine; m. Mort Gerberg, Feb. 1, 1969; 1 child, Lilia Anya Berens. Student, St. John's Coll., Annapolis, Md., 1958-60; BA in Comparative Lit., Columbia U., 1963, postgrad. in organizational devel., 1989; MA in Psychology and Art, NYU, 1966. Registered art therapist; cert. clin. mental health counselor. Program dir. Women's Selling Game, N.Y.C., 1979-84; mem. faculty Parsons Sch. Design, N.Y.C., 1979-85; pres. Judith Gerberg Assocs., N.Y.C., 1984—; developer, condr. program in orgnl. devel., team bldg. and communicatons skills, stress mgmt. Powerhouse, 1st outplacement for creative profls. Coauthor: The New York Women's Directory, 1973; contbr. articles and book revs. to various publs. Chmn. pub. rels. Profl. Women's Caucus, 1972. N.Y. State scholar, 1960. Mem. Am. Art Therapy Assn. (life, bd. dirs. 1980-84), N.Y. Art Therapy Assn. (founding, v.p. 1975), The Forum at Stephan Weiss (co-chmn. 1986-87), Women's Club N.Y., Liberty Club (exec. com.), Fin. Women's Assn. Home: 35 W 82d St New York NY 10024 Office: 250 W 57th St Ste 1019 New York NY 10107

GERBRACHT, TERRY LYNNE, traffic manager; b. Burley, Idaho, Sept. 23, 1955; d. Wendell Ames and Janet Marilyn (McAllister) Styner; m. Roeland Pieter Gerbracht, Nov,. 26, 1977; 1 child, Peter Lynn. BBA, U. Oreg., 1977. Transp. dept. Crown Zellerbach Corp., San Francisco, 1977-78; coord. transp. svcs. Crown Zellerbach Corp., Portland, Oreg., 1978-82; analyst transp. Crown Zellerbach Corp., Portland, 1982-86; with James River Corp., 1986—; mgr. group traffic James River Corp., Berlin-Groveton, N.H., 1989—; sec., bd. dirs. Berlin (N.H.) Mills Ry., White Mountain Day Care Ctr., Berlin. Mem. Coun. Logistics Mgmt. Office: James River Corp 650 Main St Berlin NH 03570

GEREAUX, KATHLEEN MARGARET, dentist; b. Kankakee, Ill., Aug. 10, 1957; d. Marvin Jackand Marjorie Elizabeth (Bloch) G. BS cum laude, Ill. Benedictine Coll., 1979; DDS, U. Ill., 1983. Pvt. practice Manteno, Ill., 1983-84; assoc. Cortez Dental Clinic, Bradenton, Fla., 1984-86; pvt. practice Holmes Beach, Fla., 1987—; tchr. Valencia Community Coll. Hygiene Sch., Gainesville, Fla., 1984-85. State Rep. Christiansen scholar, 1980-81. Mem. Manatee Dental Soc., Anna Maria C. of C., Manatee C. of C., Acad. Gen. Dentistry. Democrat. Roman Catholic. Office: 3909 E Bay Dr Holmes Beach FL 34217

GEREN, BRENDA L., business educator; b. Cleve., Sept. 9, 1950; d. Benny L. and Betty R. (Still) Elmore; m. Gilbert L. Geren; children: Melissa, Kristi. BBA, U. Tenn., Chattanooga, 1987; MBA, U. Tenn., 1989; postgrad., U. Manchester Bus. Sch., Manchester, England, 1987. Small bus. owner Waterville Grocery, Cleveland, Tenn., 1973—; instr. bus. Cleveland State Community Coll., Cleveland, 1989, U. Tenn., Chattanooga, 1989. Mem. Creative Arts Guild, Cleveland; vol. Spl. Olympics, Cleveland; docent Hunter Art Museum, Chattanooga. Recipient Honorarium for Research U. Tenn. Knoxville, 1987, Letter of Merit U. Manchester (England) Bus. Sch., 1987. Mem. Soc. Advancement of Mgmt., Omicron Delta Epsilon, Beta Sigma Phi. Home: 3218 Little John Cleveland TN 37311

GERHARDT, ROSARIO ALEJANDRINA, materials scientist; b. Lima, Peru, May 20, 1953; d. Jacob K. and Tarcila (La Cruz) G.; m. Michael Paul Anderson, Sept. 27, 1980; children: Heidi Margaret, Kathleen Elizabeth. BA, Carroll Coll., 1976; MS, Columbia U., 1979, D Engring. Sci., 1983. Teaching asst. Columbia U., N.Y.C., 1978-79, grad. asst., 1979-83, research assoc., 1983-84; postdoctoral fellow Rutgers U., Piscataway, N.J., 1984-86, asst. research prof., 1986—; cons. in field. Contbr. articles to profl. jours. Mem. Am. Ceramic Soc., Am. Phys. Soc., N.Y. Acad. Sci., Electron Microscopy Soc. Am., Materials Research Soc., Sigma Xi. Roman Catholic. Club: Materials Sci. N.Y. (sec. 1988—). Home: 92 Long Hill Rd Gillette NJ 07933

GERHART, DOROTHY EVELYN, insurance executive, real estate professional; b. Monett, Mo., Apr. 20, 1932; d. Manford Thomas and Norma Grace (Barrett) Ethridge; m. Robert H. Gerhart, Apr. 11, 1952 (div. Dec.

1969); children: Sandra Gerhart Kreamer, Richard A., Diane Gerhart Lacey. Grad. high sch., Tucson; student, U. Ariz., 1950-53. Owner, pres. Gerhart Ins., Inc., Tucson, 1967-70, 89—; agt. Mahoney-O'Donnell Agy., Tucson, 1970-73, Gerhart & Mendelsoh Ins., Tucson, 1973-78; agt., mgr. personal lines dept. Tucson Realty and Trust, 1978-83; ins. agt. San Xavier Ins. Agy., Tucson, 1985-89; pres. Gerhart Ins., Inc., Tucson, 1989-. Vol. Palo Verde Psychiat. Hosp. Mem. Nat. Fedn. Ind. Bus., Ind. Ins. Agts. Tucson (bd. dirs. 1973, 74, v.p. 1975, pres. 1976, First Woman Pres.), Fed. Home Life Ins. Co. (Pres.'s Club award 1986), Nat. Fedn. Small Bus., Altrusa Club of Tucson (bd. dirs. 1984, membership chmn. 1985, fund raising chmn. 1986). Republican. Mailing Address: PO Box 13421 Tucson AZ 85732 Office: Gerhart Ins Inc 5442 E Fifth St Tucson AZ 85711

GERHART, GLENNA LEE, pharmacist; b. Houston, June 11, 1954; d. Henry Edwin and Gloria Mae (Mrnustik) G. BS in Pharmacy, U. Houston, 1977. Registered pharmacist, Tex. Staff pharmacist Meml. City Med. Ctr., Houston, 1977-84, asst. dir. pharmacy, 1984—. Mem. Am. Soc. Hosp. Pharmacists, Tex. Pharm. Assn., Harris County Pharm. Assn., U. Houston Alumni Orgn. (life), Houston Cat Club, Nat. Cougar Club, Slavonic Benevolent Order of Tex., Greentrails Ladies Club, Kappa Epsilon. Republican. Methodist. Home: 19811 Cardiff Park Ln Houston TX 77094 Office: Meml City Med Ctr 920 Frostwood Houston TX 77024

GERIKE, ANN ELIZABETH, psychologist; b. Casper, Wyo., Aug. 24, 1933; d. Marcus Gustav and Lillie Helene (Grobengieser) G.; m. John W. Robinson, Oct. 20, 1959 (div. Mar. 1978); children: David Gerike, Margaret Ann, Catherine Elizabeth. BA, U. Nebr., 1955, MA, 1956, PhD, 1983; postgrad., Glasgow U., 1957-60. Editor U. Nebr. Press, Lincoln, 1962-80; clin. psychologist Mental Health and Mental Retardation Authority Harris County, Houston, 1984-87; pvt. practice Mpls., 1985—; psychologist Pyramid Mental Health Ctr., Mpls., 1988—; aging specialist Employee Adv. Resource, Control Data Corp., Mpls., 1988-89. Pres. Older Women's League, Houston, 1986; bd. dirs. Twin Cities Gray Panthers, Mpls., 1988—. Mem. Am. Psychol. Assn., Gerontol. Soc. Am., Minn. Psychol. Assn., Minn. Gerontol. Soc., Minn. Women Psychologists, Nat. Women's Studies Assn. (convenor Aging & Ageism Caucus 1986—). Democrat. Unitarian. Home: 3215 Columbus Ave S Minneapolis MN 55407 Office: Lakewood Counseling & Career Ctr 4815 W 77th St Minneapolis MN 55435

GERKEN, JEANNE LYNN, educator; b. Britton, S.D., Aug. 18, 1943; d. Herbert H. and Viola E. (Sayer) Freudenthal; m. Gerald Allen Gerken, Aug. 4, 1962; children: Pamela Jeanne and Paul Herbert (twins), Michelle Ellen. BA in Bus. Edn., Augustana Coll., Sioux Falls, S.D., 1974. Cert. bus. and vocat. tchr., S.D.; lic. real estate agt., S.D. Substitute tchr. Sioux Falls Sch. System, 1974-75; tchr. bus. S.D. Sch. for Deaf, Sioux Falls, 1974; tchr. bus. and English Edison Jr. High Sch., Sioux Falls, 1975-81; tchr. bus. and vocat. edn. Washington Sr. High Sch., Sioux Falls, 1981—; tchr. bus. Stenotype Inst. S.D., Sioux Falls, summer 1987; asst. property mgr. Gerken Properties, Sioux Falls, 1977—; cons. Am. Inst. Banking, Sioux Falls, 1983, adult edn., 1983—, enrichment elem. program, 1988-90, Kilian Community Coll., Brandon, S.D., 1982; chief examiner GED Test Ctr., Am. Coun. on Edn., Washington, 1983—; mem. adv. bd. for office systems SE Vocat. Tech. Inst., Sioux Falls, 1990; advisor Future Bus. Leaders Am., 1980-84. Foster parent Luth. Social Svcs., Brandon, 1969-74; trustee Brandon Luth. Ch., 1982-83; nurse aide state exam proctor Sioux Falls Health Ctr., 1989—. Mem. NEA (polit. vol.), S.D. Edn. Assn. (conv. chmn. 1987-88, SEKota Leadership award 1988), S.D. Bus. and Office Edn. Assn. (treas. 1982-84), Sioux Falls Multi-Housing Renters Assn., AAUW (bridge chmn. 1982-86), Sioux Falls Mothers of Twins Club (v.p., pres., treas. 1972-75, nat. conv. del. 1975), Moose, Elks, Delta Kappa Gamma (2nd v.p. Omicron chpt. 1990—). Democrat. Home: 308 N Needles Dr Brandon SD 57005 Office: Washington Sr High 315 S Main Ave Sioux Falls SD 57102

GERLACH, JEANNE ELAINE, English educator; b. Charleston, W.Va., Oct. 20, 1946; d. Lafayette and Edith Lorraine (Robinson) Marcum; m. Roger Thomas Gerlach Sr., Dec. 30, 1966; children: Roger Thomas Jr., Kristen Elaine. BS, W.Va. State Coll., Institute, 1974; MA, W.Va. State Coll., 1979, EdD, 1985; postgrad., U. North Tex., 1987—. Lang. arts tchr. Ohio County Schs., Wheeling, W.Va., 1974-79; English instr. West Liberty (W.Va.) State Coll., 1979-82; continuing edn. instr. Seattle Pacific U., 1982-85; asst. prof. English W.Va. U., Morgantown, 1985-86, Tarrant County Jr. Coll., Ft. Worth, 1986-88; dir. Communications Unlimited, Dallas, Pitts., 1986—; assoc. prof. English edn. W.Va. U., Morgantown, 1989—; cons. to bus. and corps., 1986—; co-dir. advanced writing project W.Va. U., Morgantown, 1989, lang. arts camps, 1988, 89, 90, lang. arts camps, 1988, 89, 90, yount writers inst. Contbr. articles to profl. jours. Mem. LWV, W.Va., DAR, Young Republicans, W.Va. Faculty Devel. grantee W.Va. U., 1989; recipient 1st. place Creative Writing award W.Va. Women's Clubs, 1976. Mem. Nat. Coun. Tchrs. English (chair women's com. 1986—, chair nominating com. 1988-89), Am. Ednl. Rsch. Assn., AAUW, AAUP, W.Va. U. Alumni Assn. (sec. 1990), Nat. Women's Studies Assn., Nat. Soc. Daus. Am. Revolution. Republican. Methodist. Home: 110 Lakeview Dr Morgantown WV 26505 Office: WVa U 604 Allen Hall Morgantown WV 26506

GERLITZ, CONNIE MARIE, insurance company executive; b. Atlantic, Iowa, Jan. 11, 1943; d. Roland Kunze and Marjorie Marie (Jahnke) McCue; m. Dennis Eugene Gerlitz, Oct. 22, 1976; 1 child, Jordan Ashland. BA magna cum laude, U. Wash., 1964. Cert. tchr., Wash. Ins. coordinator AAA, Seattle, 1964-66; ins. agt. LaBow Hynes, Seattle, 1966-69; regional mgr. Safeco Ins. Co., Seattle, 1969-83; v.p. United Pacific Ins. Co., Federal Way, Wash., 1983-87; sr. v.p. Reliance/United Pacific, Federal Way, 1987—; chmn. Nev. Assigned Risk Plan, Federal Way, 1984—; bd. dirs. Wash. Ins. Coun., Seattle, 1988—. Contbr. article to mag., chpt. to book. Active Seattle Rep. Party, 1976-80. Mem. Phi Beta Kappa. Home: 2415 78th NE Bellevue WA 98004 Office: Reliance Ins Co 33405 8th Ave S C-3000 Federal Way WA 98003

GERMAN, JEAN WESLEY, federal agency training consultant; b. Austin, Tex., June 21, 1931; d. Marvin William and Lorena (Pharr) Wesley; m. Robert K. German, July 9, 1955; 1 child, Elizabeth Lynn. BA, U. Tex., 1952, MA, 1954. Field rep. Am. Cancer Soc., Austin, 1954-55, Girl Scouts U.S., Council Bluffs, Iowa, 1956; pub. affairs and field rep. Nat. Fedn. Bus. and Profl. Women, Inc., Washington, 1957-58; asst. dir., then dir. Overseas Briefing Ctr. Fgn. Svc. Inst., Dept. State, Washington, 1983-88; asst. for spl. projects Fgn. Svc. Inst., Dept. State, 1988-89. Author, editor, fgn. culture guide booklets. Mem. Soc. Intercultural Edn., Tng. and Rsch., Assn. Am. Fgn. Svc. Women, U. Tex. LAMP, Mortar Bd., Alpha Lambda Delta, Delta Delta Delta. Democrat. Episcopalian. Home: 1311 Ardenwood Rd Austin TX 78722

GERMAN, KATHERINE L., academic administrator; b. Reading, Pa., May 10, 1947; d. John Elmer and Mabel Berdula (Flick) G.; m. L. Denton Crews, Aug. 4, 1983. BA, Pa. State U., 1969; MEd, Bowling Green State U., 1971; CAS, Harvard U., 1985; PhD, U. Ill., 1981. Tchr., coord. Eastwood Jr. High sch., Lucky, Ohio, 1971; dir. communications ctr. North Shore community Coll., Beverly, Mass., 1971-74; div. chair North Shore community Coll., Beverly, 1974-79; asst. academic dean North Shore community Coll., Lynn, Mass., 1979-88; v.p. Endicott Coll., Beverly, 1988-89, Devel. Inst., Boston, 1989—; reader U.S. Dept. Edn., Washington, 1980—; speaker and cons. in field. Contbr. articles to profl. jours. Vol. YMCA, Beverly, 1978-83, Am. Cancer Soc., Boston, 1988-90, King's Chapel, Boston, 1982-90. Recipient Pride of Performance award Commonwealth of Mass., 1985. Mem. Internat. Reading Assn., Am. Ednl. Rsch. Assn., Am. Assn. Higher Edn., Mass. Women in Pub. Higher Edn. (area coord. 1986-88), Am. Soc. for Tng. and Devel., League Women Voters, Phi Delta Kappa. Home and Office: 4 Longfellow Pl 2008 Boston MA 02114

GEROLIMATOS, BARBARA, pharmaceutical company executive; b. N.Y.C., July 13, 1950; d. Constantine and Margaret Pauline (Shea) G. BS, Fordham U., 1972; MPhil, Columbia U., 1976, PhD, 1979. Saleswomen, rte. driver Good Humor Corp., N.Y.C., summers 1969-71; NIH pub. svc. trainee dept. ob-gyn, Coll. Physicians and Surgeons Columbia U., N.Y.C., 1979-83; med. writer Ayerst Internat., N.Y.C., 1983-86; monitor clin. rsch. Ayerst Labs., N.Y.C., 1986-88; mgr. clin. investigation Boehringer Ingelheim Pharms., Ridgefield, Conn., 1988-89; assoc. dir. sci. and clin. affairs, consumer product div. Pfizer, Inc., N.Y.C., 1989—. Counselor N.Y. Women Against Rape, 1972-76; co-founder, coord. rape crisis intervention program Columbia-Presbyn. Med. Ctr., 1976-78; chmn. career counseling Alumni Assn. Scholarship Winners of Elec. Industry, 1985—; friend N.Y.C. Commn. on Status of Women, 1989—. Mem. Nat. Assn. Women Sci. (chmn. nominating com. 1985), Assn. Women Sci. (v.p. Met. N.Y. chpt. 1984-85, pres. 1986-89), N.Y. Acad. Scis. (women in sci. com. 1986—). Home: 90 Park Terr E Apt 2B New York NY 10034 Office: Pfizer Inc 235 E 42d St 3d Fl New York NY 10017

GERONEMUS, DIANN FOX, social work consultant; b. Chgo., July 4, 1947; d. Herbert J. and Edith (Robbins) Fox; B.A. with high honors, Mich. State U., 1969; M.S.W., U. Ill., 1971; 1 dau., Heather Eileen. Lic. clin. social worker, marriage and family therapist, Fla. Social worker neurology, neurosurgery and medicine Hosp. of Albert Einstein Coll. Medicine, 1971-74; prin. social worker ob-gyn and newborn infant service Rush-Presbyn.-St. Luke's Med. Center, Chgo., 1974-75; social worker neurology, adminstr. Multiple Sclerosis Treatment Center, St. Barnabas Hosp., Bronx, N.Y., 1975-77, socio-med. researcher (Nat. Multiple Sclerosis Soc. grantee), dept. neurology and psychiatry, 1977-79, dir. social service, 1979-80; field work instr. Fordham U. Grad. Sch. Social Service, 1979-80; preceptor, social work program Fla. Atlantic U., Fla. Internat. U.; mem. edn. com., med. adv. bd., program cons. Nat. Multiple Sclerosis Soc., 1980-83, area service cons., 1983-86 ; pvt. practice psychotherapy; social work cons.; cons. in gerontology, rehab. and supervision. Mem. Acad. Cert. Social Workers, Nat. Assn. Social Workers (diplomate), Registered Clin. Soc. Hosp. Social Work Dirs., Am. Orthopsychiat. Assn. Jewish. Contbr. articles to profl. jours. Home: 833 NW 81st Way Plantation FL 33324

GERRINGER-BUSENBARK, ELIZABETH JACQUELINE (THE MARCHIONESS DE ROE DEVON), systems analyst, consultant; b. Edmund, Wis., Jan. 7, 1934; d. Clyde Elroy and Matilda Evangeline Knapp; m. Roe (Don Davis) Devon Gerringer-Busenbark, Sept. 30, 1968 (dec. Dec. 1972); student Madison Bus. Coll., 1952, San Francisco State Coll., 1953-54, Vivian Rich Sch. Fashion Design, 1955, Dale Carnegie Sch., 1956, Arthur Murray Dance Studio, 1956, Biscayne Acad. Music, 1957, L.A. City Coll., 1960-62, Santa Monica (Calif.) Jr. Coll., 1963; Hastings Coll. of Law, 1973, Wharton Sch., U. Pa., 1977, London Art Coll., 1979; Ph.D., 1979; attended Goethe Inst., 1985. Actress, Actors Workshop San Francisco, 1959, 65, Theatre of Arts Beverly Hills (Calif.), 1963, also radio; cons, and systems analyst for banks and pub. accounting agys.; artist, singer, songwriter, playwright, dress designer. Pres., tchr. Environ Improvement, Originals by Elizabeth, Dometrik's, JIT-MAP, San Francisco, 1973—; atty. The Assn. Trial Lawyers Am.; steering com. explorations in worship, ordained min. 1978. Author: Explorations in Worship, 1965, The Magic of Scents, 1967, New Highways, 1967, Happening - Impact-Mald, 1971, Seven Day Rainbow, 1972, Zachary's Adversaries, 1974, Fifteen from Wisconsin, 1977, Bart's White Elephant, 1978, Skid Row Minister, 1978, Points in Time, 1979, Special Appointment, A Clown in Town, 1979, Happenings, 1980, Votes from the Closet, 1984, Wait for Me, 1984, The Stairway, 1984, The River is a Rock, 1985, Happenings Revisted, 1986, Comparative Religion in the United States, 1986, Lumber in the Skies, 1986, The Fifth Season, 1987, Summer Thoughts, 1987, Toast Thoughts, 1988, A Thousand Points of Light, 1989. Mem. Assn. of Trial Lawyers of Am. Address: PO Box 13943 San Rafael CA 94913

GERRISH, CATHERINE RUGGLES, food company executive; b. Winona, Minn., July 10, 1911; d. Clyde O. and Frances (Holmes) Ruggles; A.B., Radcliffe Coll., 1932, A.M., 1934; Ph.D., Harvard U., 1937; m. Hollis G. Gerrish, Sept. 10, 1946. Research asst. Harvard U., 1937-39; instr., asst. prof. econs. U. Ill., 1939-42, assoc. prof., 1946. Economist Bur. Budget, Exec. Office President, 1943-45; asst. editor Quar. Jour. Econs., 1951-69; treas., v.p. Squirrel Brand Co., Cambridge, Mass., 1966—. Pres. The Cambridge Homes, 1990—. Mem. Am. Econ. Assn., Nat. Tax Assn., Coll. Club of Boston (pres. 1948-51), Radcliff Alumnae Assn. (pres. 1953-55). Home: 207 Grove St Cambridge MA 02138 Office: 17 Boardman St Cambridge MA 02139

GERRITSEN, MARY ELLEN, pharmacologist; b. Calgary, Alta., Can., Sept. 20, 1953; came to U.S., 1978; d. Thomas Clayton and Alice Irene (Minton) Cooper; m. Paul William Gerritsen, Mary 24, 1975 (div. 1977); m. Thomas Patrick Parks, Oct. 11, 1980; children: Kristen, Madelene. BSc summa cum laude, U. Calgary, 1975, PhD, 1978. Postdoctoral fellow U. Calif., San Diego, 1978-80; asst. prof. N.Y. Med. Coll., Valhalla, 1981-86, assoc. prof., 1986-90; sr. staff scientist Miles Pharms., West Haven, Conn., 1990—, also head leukocyte group, 1990—; cons. Insite Vision, Alameda, Calif., 1987-89, Boehringer Ingelheim Pharms., Ridgefield, Conn., 1985-88; adj. assoc. prof. N.Y. Med. Coll., 1990—. Mem. editorial bd. Microvascular Rsch., 1988—; contbr. articles to profl. jours. Vol., mem. peer rev. com. N.Y. State Heart Assn., Syracuse, 1986—. NIH grantee, 1987; J.W. Killam Found. fellow, 1976; Med. Rsch. Council Can. fellow, 1978; NIH fellow, 1981. Mem. Am. Soc. for Pharmacology and Exptl. Therapeutics, Am. Physiol. Soc., Assn. Rsch. on Vision and Ophthalmology, Microcirculatory Soc. (council 1989—, Mary Weideman award 1985, Young Investigator award 1984). Office: Miles Inc Inst Arthritis/Autoimmunity 400 Morgan Ln West Haven CT 06516

GERSCHBACHER, CORINE MARIE, computer and electronics manufacturing company executive; b. Whittier, Calif., Mar. 8, 1961; d. Frank Joseph Gerschbacher and Shirley Ann Stahl. BA in Mktg., Whittier Coll., 1983. Acctg. analyst Health Valley Foods, Montebello, Calif., 1982-84; mktg. coord. Bland Contracting Co., Whittier, 1984-85; project mktg. specialist rsch. and devel., Taxan Corp., City of Industry, Calif., 1985-87; microcomputer systems cons Creative Micro Systems Group, Whittier, 1985—, hi-tech industry analyst, 1987-89; dir. of corp. communications M&A div. Toyo Bus. Ptnrs., Inc., Torrance, Calif., 1989—; cons. computer systems, Whittier, 1985-87; lectr. Computer Trading Post, Civic Auditorium, Glendale, Calif., 1987—. Editorial corr., writer The Computer Inputer mag., 1987—; contbg. writer PC Mag.; contbg. editor Computer Graphics World mag., reader rev. bd., 1986-87; prodn. corr. nat. TV program: The Computer Show, 1986—; photojournalist, reporter Computer PR Advisor. Recipient cert. of appreciation Pi Sigma Epsilon, 1986; Milo Hunt Merit scholar Whittier Coll., 1980-83. Mem. MBA Assn. (local activities dir. 1983-84), Calif. Scholarship Fedn. (life), Alpha Pi Delta. Home: 612 S Catalina Ave #201 Redondo Beach CA 90277 Office: 1880 S Crenshaw Blvd Ste 106 Torrance CA 90501 also: 1907 Deerpark #482 Fullerton CA 92631

GERSCOVICH, DOLORES R., psychologist; b. Chgo., Sept. 5, 1942; d. John J. and Dolores Rubel; children: Mark, Gabrielle. BA, U. Cen. Fla., 1981, MS, 1985; D Psychology, Fla. Inst. Tech., 1987. Lic. psychologist, Fla. Pvt. practice Maitland, Fla. Mem. Am. Psychol. Assn., Fla. Psychol. Assn., Internat. Soc. Clin. Hypnosis, Am. Soc. Clin. Hypnosis, Fla. Soc. Clin. Hypnosis, Nat. Register Health Svc. Providers in Psychology, Psi Chi. Office: 2600 Lake Lucien Dr Ste 200 Maitland FL 32751

GERSHON, NINA, magistrate; b. Chgo., Oct. 16, 1940; d. David and Marie Gershon; m. Bernard J. Fried, May 15, 1983. BA, Cornell U., 1962; LLB, Yale U., 1965; postgrad., London Sch. Econs., 1965-66. Magistrate U.S. Courthouse, N.Y.C., currently. Fulbright scholar. Office: US Courthouse Foley Sq New York NY 10007

GERSHUNY, DIANNE LYNETTE, city official; b. Chgo., Sept. 30, 1952; d. Joshua W. and Mary F. (Pritchard) G. BA, U. Calif., Berkeley, 1974; MBA, UCLA, 1977. Control chemist McGaw Labs., Glendale, Calif., 1975, 76; rsch. asst. UCLA, 1976-77; adminstrv. aide Ventura (Calif.) Regional Sanitation Dist., 1978-79, mgmt. asst., 1979-82, sr. mgmt. asst., 1982-84; asst. city adminstr., fin. dir. City of San Carlos (Calif.), 1983-86; asst. city mgr., fin. dir. City of Los Altos (Calif.), 1986-90; city mgr., 1990—. Mem. Am. Soc. Pub. Adminstrs., Internat. City Mgrs. Assn., Mcpl. Mgmt. Assts. No. Calif. (regional chmn. 1987-88, Outstanding Mgmt. Asst. award 1988). Office: City of Los Altos One N San Antonio Rd Los Altos CA 94022

GERSKE, JANET FAY, lawyer; b. Chgo., Nov. 14, 1950; d. Bernard G. Gerske and L. Fay (Knight) Capron; m. James P. Chapman, Dec. 5, 1982. BS, Northwestern U., 1971; JD, U. Mich., 1978. Bar: Ill. 1978, U.S. Dist. Ct. (no. dist.) Ill. 1978. Pvt. practice, Chgo., 1978-80, 84—; assoc. Jerome H. Torshen Ltd., Chgo., 1980-84. Chpt. chmn. Ind. Voters Ill./Ind. Precinct Orgn., Chgo., 1982-84; co-chmn. Ill. Women's Agenda Com., 1985-88, fin. officer, 1987-88; dir. Chgo. Abused Women Coalition, 1986—, sec., treas., 1988—. Mem. ABA, Assn. Trial Lawyers Am. Women's Bar Assn. Ill. (co-chmn. rights of women com. 1985-86, dir. 1988—), Chgo. Bar Assn. (co-chmn. legal status of women com. young lawyers sect.), Nat. Assn. Social Security Claimants' Rep., Ill. State Bar Assn. Democrat. Home: 850 W Oakdale Ave Chicago IL 60657 Office: 39 S LaSalle St Chicago IL 60603

GERSON, JACKI ELLEN, human resources executive; b. Scranton, Pa., Oct. 16, 1949; d. Albert M. and Lois M. (Oram) G. BS, Syracuse U., 1974. Asst. dir. vols. Community Med. Ctr., Scranton, 1969-74, personnel asst., dir. pub. rels., 1974-76; dir. personnel svcs. Wentworth-Douglass Hosp., Dover, N.H., 1976-89; v.p. human resources Fidelity Health Alliance, Manchester, N.H., 1989—; bd. dirs. N.E. Fed. Credit Union, Portsmouth, N.H., Bus./Edn. Coalition, Manchester; mem. bus. adv. bd. Employment Connection Specialists, Manchester, 1990—. Bd. dirs. Strafford County Prenatal and Family Planning Clinic, Dover, 1983-89. Mem. Am. Compensation Assn. (cert.), Am. Soc. for Health Care Human Resources Adminstrs., N.H. Soc. for Health Care Personnel Adminstrs. (sec. 1977-78, v.p. 1978-79, pres. 1979-81, 88-89). Office: Fidelity Health Alliance 100 McGregor St Manchester NH 03102

GERSONI-EDELMAN, DIANE CLAIRE, author, editor; b. Bklyn., Apr. 16, 1947; d. James Arthur and Edna Bernice (Krinski) Gersoni; B.A. cum laude, Vassar Coll., 1967; m. James Neil Edelman, Oct. 5, 1975; children—Michael Lawrence, Sara Anne. Asst. editor, then asso. editor Sch. Library Jour. Book Rev., 1968-72; free lance writer, 1972-74, 77—; writer, editor Scholastic Mags., Inc., N.Y.C., 1974-77; author: Sexism and Youth, 1974; Work-Wise: Learning About the World of Work from Books, 1980; cons., speaker in field. Club: Vassar (N.Y.C.). Contbr. articles, book revs. to anthologies, newspapers, mags. Home: care Edelman 301 E 78th St New York NY 10021

GERST, ELIZABETH CARLSEN (MRS. PAUL H. GERST), university dean, researcher, educator; b. N.Y.C., June 10, 1929; d. Rolf and Gudrun (Wiborg) Carlsen; A.B. magna cum laude, Mt. Holyoke Coll., 1951; Ph.D., U. Pa., 1957; m. Paul H. Gerst, Aug. 3, 1957; children—Steven Richard, Jeffrey Carlton, Andrew Leigh. Instr. physiology Grad. Sch. Medicine, U. Pa., 1955-57, Cornell U. Med. Coll., N.Y.C., 1957-58; instr. Columbia Coll. Physicians and Surgeons, N.Y.C., 1959-61, asst. prof., 1961—, dir. Center Continuing Edn. in Health Scis., 1978-87, asst. dean continuing edn., 1984-87, dir. Office Med. Edn., N.Y. Acad. Med., 1987—; Authors: (with others) The Lung, Clinical Physiology and Pulmonary Function Tests, 1955, rev. edit., 1962. Pres. Citizen's Ednl. Council Tenafly, 1972-73; mem. Citizens Long-Range Planning Com., Tenafly Bd. Edn., 1973-77, chmn. supt. search, edn., tchr. hiring, personnel coms.; vice chmn. Tenafly Environ. Commn., 1972-77; trustee Tenafly Nature Center, 1972-80; bd. dirs., chmn. environ. quality Tenafly LWV, 1971-78; v.p. Bergen County LWV, 1973-75. Porter fellow Am. Physiol. Soc., 1956-57. Mem. Middle States Assn. Colls. and Schs. (team Commn. on higher edn., 1984—), Soc. Med. Coll. Dirs. of Continuing Med. Edn., Am. Physiol. Soc. (task force Women in Physiology 1973-75), N.Y. County Med. Soc. (com. on continuing med. edn. 1978—), Physiol. Soc. Phila., Harvey Soc., Biophys. Soc., Alliance Continuing Med. Edn., N.Y. Acad. Scis., AAAS, Phi Beta Kappa, Sigma Xi, Sigma Delta Epsilon. Unitarian. Home: 141 Tekening Dr Tenafly NJ 07670 Office: Office Med Edn NY Acad Med 2 E 103d St New York NY 10029

GERSTBAUER-HILL, LOUANN, county official; b. Mishawaka, Ind., July 4, 1956; d. Joseph N. and Irma (Raes) Gerstbauer; m. David Hill, Sept. 6, 1975 (div. 1983); 1 child, Jeannie Ann. Cert. in travel, Boyd Career Ctr., 1974; student, Ind. U., 1974. Clk. Prescription Shop, Mishawaka, 1973-75; home health care mgr. Gen. Med. Corp., Newport News, Va., 1975-77; sec. engrng. dept. St. Joseph County, South Bend, Ind., 1977-78; exec. sec. bd. of commrs. St. Joseph County, South Bend, 1978-86; purchasing mgr. St. Joseph County, South Bend, Ind., 1986—; bd. dirs. United Way Emergency Food and Shelter Program, County Pauper Cemetary, St. Joseph County; mem. Local Energy Mgmt., St. Joseph County, 1986—. Mem. Mishawaka-Penn Women's Dem. Club, 1978—, St. Joseph County Young Dem. Club, 1978—, St. Joseph County Women's Dem. Club, South Bend, 1978—; del. Ind. State Conv., St. Joseph. Mem. Commn. on Status of Women of St. Joseph County (v.p. 1987—), K.C. (women's aux. 1985-87). Roman Catholic.

GERSTEIN, ESTHER, sculptor; b. N.Y.C., May 20, 1924; d. Leon and Lillian (Peretz) Grizer; m. Leonard B. Gerstein, Mar. 31, 1946; children: Lee Steven, Laurie Susan. Student, Pratt Inst., 1941-42, NYU, 1942-43; pvt. study, various sculptors; student, Cooper Union, 1946-48. Asst. tchr. Art Students League, N.Y.C., 1944-46; painting tchr. pvt. sch. Great Neck, N.Y., 1961-63; founder, instr. sculpture and painting Studio 33, Westbury, N.Y., 1964-72; sculptor and painter pvt. studios, N.Y.C. and Boca Raton, Fla.; lectr. Norton Mus., Palm Beach, Fla., 1985. Exhibited shows including Hecksher Mus., Huntington, N.Y., Norton Mus., Kellenberg Gallery, C.W. Post Coll., L.I., Firehouse Gallery, Nassau Community Coll., L.I., Lever House, N.Y.C., Grace Bldg., N.Y.C., Hofstra U.; represented in numerous pvt. and corp. collections throughout U.S. Mem. Artists Guild Norton Mus., Contemporary Sculptors Guild, L.I. Craftsman's Guild, South Shore Art League (1st prize sculpture and painting 1972). Home: 2383 Halyard Dr Merrick NY 11566

GERSTING, JUDITH LEE, computer science educator, researcher; b. Springfield, Vt., Aug. 20, 1940; d. Harold H. and Dorothy V. (Kinney) MacKenzie; m. John M. Gersting, Jr., Aug. 17, 1962; children: Adam, Jason. BS, Stetson U., 1962; MA, Ariz. State U., 1964, PhD, 1969. Assoc. prof. math. U. Cen. Fla., Orlando, 1980-81; asst. prof. computer sci. Ind. U.-Purdue U., Indpls., 1970-73, assoc. prof., 1974-79, prof., 1981—; staff scientist Indpls. Ctr. for Advanced Rsch., 1982-84. Author: Mathematical Structures for Computer Science, 1987, The Computer, 1988, The Programming Process/Pascal, 1989; contbr. articles to computer sci. jours. Mem. Assn. for Computing Machinery, IEEE Computer Soc., North Cen. Soccer Club (sec.-treas. 1988—). Office: Ind U-Purdue U 1201 E 38th St Indianapolis IN 46205-2868

GERSTLEY, LINDA JEAN, psychologist; b. Phila., Aug. 24, 1955; d. Kiefer Newman and Jean Louise (Refowich) G. MS, Hahnemann U., Phila., 1981, PhD, 1988. Lic. psychologist, Pa., Del. Counselor Aldersgate Youth Svc. Bur., Willow Grove, Pa., 1977-78; social worker Carson Valley Sch., Flourtown, Pa., 1978; rsch. asst. Hahnemann U., 1979-81; rsch. cons. Acorn, Wayne, Pa., 1981; program evaluator Path, Inc., Phila., 1981-82; rsch. assoc. VAMC Addiction Rsch. Ctr. U. Pa., Phila., 1985-87, 88-89; psychology intern Devereux Found., Devon, Pa., 1987-88; pvt. practice Raskin Assocs., Wilmington, Del., 1988—; staff psychologist Med. Ctr. Del., Wilmington, 1988—. Contbr. articles to profl. jours. Bd. dirs. Eagleville (Pa.) Hosp., 1990. Mem. Am. Psychol. Assn., Psychologists for Social Responsibility, Sigma Xi. Democrat. Jewish. Office: Raskin Assocs 19C Trolley Sq Wilmington DE 19806

GERTRUDE, KATY See **WILHELM, KATE**

GERVAIS, CHERIE NADINE, small business owner; b. Marysville, Calif.; d. Victor H. and Gladys A. (Poissant) Fehr; m. Charles N. Lichten; 1 child, Dublin M. Ryan. Student, Yuba Coll., Coll. of Marin, 1977. Owner, operator Grandma's Trunk Doll Hosp., San Francisco, 1969-72, San Rafael, Calif., 1972—; model various local fashion shows, San Francisco and Marin County, Calif., 1973-87. Author numerous poems. Recipient many 1st, 2nd and 3rd place ribbons at doll shows; named Poet of Month, San Rafael (Calif.) Pointer News, 1975. Mem. Dolls from the Attic (pres. 1988—), 101 Doll Club (pres. 1975-76), San Francisco Doll Club (pres. 1976-77), Women of the Moose. Democrat. Episcopalian. Home and Office: Grandmas Trunk Doll Hosp 918 B St San Rafael CA 94901

GERVAIS, HEIDI DIANNE, real estate broker; b. Meriden, Conn., Apr. 20, 1956; d. Lewis Edwin and Ingeborg Margaret (Zuck) Budd. AS, Middlesex Community Coll., 1977. Cert. real estate broker. Real estate broker Lewis E. Budd Real Estate Agy., Meriden, 1974—; real estate agt. J.I. Sopher, N.Y.C., 1981. Committeeman Cen. Conn. Realtors Comml. Investment Div., Meriden, 1989. Republican. Roman Catholic. Home: 85

Harness Dr Meriden CT 06450 Office: Lewis E Budd Agy 95 E Main St Meriden CT 06450

GERVAIS, LUCILLE CATHERINE MAYER, business consultant, educator; b. Johnsburg, Wis.; d. Raymond and Marie (Thome) M.;. Course in real estate, Mid-State Tech. Inst., Wisconsin Rapids; BS in communications, U. Wis., Stevens Point, 1983, BSBA in Econs., 1984; MS, U. Wis., Madison, 1985. Dept. head First Nat. City Bank, Republic of Panama, 1967-72; broker Galecke Real Estate, Stevens Point, 1978-82; pres. Whiting-Plover Credit Union, Stevens Point, 1983-84; program coord., bus. instr. Mid-State Tech. Inst., 1984-85; area small bus. agent U. Wis.-extension, Rhinelander, Wis., 1985-88; exec. dir., coord. U. Cornell Extension, Canton, N.Y., 1988—; bd. dirs., treas. Sta. WXPR, Rhinelander, 1986—; treas., bd. dirs. Whiting-Plover Credit Union, Wis., 1983-84; grad. teaching/rsch. asst. U. Wis., 1983-85; regional coord. Gov.'s Conf. on Small Bus., 1987. Reg. coord. Gov.'s Conf. Bus. and Econ. Devel. Named Realtor of the Year, 1981; Univ. Wis. research grantee, 1984. Mem. ASTD, NAFE, Am. Soc. Tng. and Devel., Internat. Assn. Sml. Bus., State Assn. Sml. Bus. and Entrepreneurship, Mgmt. Forum, Northwise Network, Toastmasters (chpt. pres. 1986-87, div. lt. gov. 1987-88, pres. Masena, N.Y. chpt. 1988-89, pres. Rhinelande chpt. 1990—). lodges: Toastmasters (Rhinelander) (local pres. 1986-87, div. lt. gov. 1987-88). Home: 214 N Eastern Ave Rhinelander WI 54501 Office: Cornell U Coop Extension University Pla Canton NY 13617

GERWIN, BRENDA ISEN, research biochemist; b. Boston, May 2, 1939; d. Maurice Joshua and Jeannette (Hershon) Isen; m. Robert David Gerwin, Dec. 18, 1960; children: David, Daniel, Joel. BA, Radcliffe Coll., 1960; PhD, U. Chgo., 1964. Instr. biochemistry Rockefeller U., N.Y.C., 1964-66, Case-Western Res. U., Cleve., 1966-69; biochemist molecular anatomy program Oak Ridge Nat. Lab., Rockville, Md., 1969-71; sr. staff fellow Nat. Cancer Inst. NIH, Bethesda, Md., 1971-73, chemist Lab. of Tumor Virus Genetics, Nat. Cancer Inst., 1973-81, chemist Lab. of Molecular Oncology, Nat. Cancer Inst., 1981-83, rsch. chemist Lab. Human Carcinogenesis, Nat. Cancer Inst., 1983—. Contbr. articles to profl. jours. Mem. Am. Soc. Biochemistry and Molecular Biology, Am. Soc. Microbiology, AAAS, Sigma Xi. Jewish. Office: Nat Cancer Inst Bldg 37 Room 2C08 Bethesda MD 20892

GESSERT, AUTUMN ROBERTA, telecommunications administrator; b. Milw., Nov. 25, 1958; d. Sherman Albert and Nancy Ann (Darnold) G.; divorced; 1 child, Phillip Patrick. Student, Marquette U., 1982-83, Nat. Ctr. Degree Studies. Telex operator Aqua-Chem, Inc., Milw., 1981-82, translator French, 1982-83, project coord., 1983-85, coord. telecommunications, 1985-86; mgr. telecommunications Mark Travel Corp., Milw., 1986-87; instr. computer networks and literacy U.S. Fed. Govt., Yuma, Ariz., 1987-89, computer systems adminstr., 1988—. With U.S. Army, 1977-78. Mem. Wis. Telecommunications Assn., NAFE. Republican. Lutheran. Office: Info Systems Command Attn: ASNC-TYU-OA-T Yuma Proving Ground Yuma AZ 85365

GESSERT, LISE LYNNE, finance company executive; b. Milw., Apr. 24, 1954; d. Edmund Kurt and Lynne Carol (McCoy) Rieger; m. Robert Joseph Gessert, June 17, 1978; children: Justin Michael, Jamie Lynne. BA in Chemistry, Carthage Coll., 1975; MBA in Finance, Marquette U., 1984. Lab technician Indsl. Bio-Test, Decatur, Ill, 1976-77, A.F. Staley Mfg. Co., Decatur, 1978-81; asst. group leader Indsl. Bio-Test, Decatur, 1977-78; sr. account exec. Emjay Corp., Milw., 1985-86; asst. v.p. The Milw. Co., 1986-88; mktg. specialist Strong/Corneliuson Capital Mgmt., Inc., Milw., 1988—; sec., treas. Life Line Communications Inc., Milw., 1989—. Advisor Jr. Achievement, Milw., 1987. Mem. Investment Mgmt. Cons. Assn. Inc.

GETCHEL, NELLIE I., nursing administrator; b. Washington, Vt., Oct. 23, 1932; d. Ernest Clarence and Ivis Lydia (Beede) G. BS in Nursing, Wayne State U., 1956; MS in Nursing, Boston U., 1966, EdD, 1971; RN, N.H. Hosp., Concord, 1951. Cert. advanced nursing adminstr. Assoc. prof. rehab. nursing, dir. grad. studies, assoc. dean. various univs.; chief nurse, assoc. chief VA Med. Ctr., various locations; assoc. chief VA Med. Ctr., Pitts. Mem. Capital Area Consortium, 1984-87. USPHS predoctoral fellow. Mem. ANA, Pa. Nurses Assn. (com. long range planning dist. 6 1989—, com. fundraising 1988-90, bd. dirs. 1990—), Sigma Theta Tau, Pi Lambda Theta. Presbyterian. Address: 2812 Autumnwood Dr Glenshaw PA 15116 Office: VA Med Ctr University Dr C Pittsburgh PA 15240

GETMAN, SHERYL MARIE, artist; b. Kalispell, Mont., Dec. 31, 1947; d. Dannie E. Loutherback and Shirley Jean (Barry) Michaelson; m. Daniel William Getman, Jan. 21, 1952; children: Guy Young, Crescent. Student, Ea. Mont. State Coll., 1968, 69, Calif State Coll., Fullerton, 1970, Mont. State U., 1974, 75, 76, Flathead Coll., Kalispell Mt., 1977, 78, Art Student's League, N.Y.C., 1988. Artist Jorgensen Pottery & Art Studio, Coram, Mont., 1978-83; owner, mgr. Spruce Park Truck Stop, Coram, 1980-83; pres., artist Sky Jordan Graphics, Kalispell, 1983-86; pres. Sky Jordan Restaurant Inc., Kalispell Mt., 1983-86; pres., artist Artistic Urges, Inc., Lambertville, N.J., 1986—; v.p. Sky Deco Inc., 1989—; feature writer Penington (N.J.) Post, 1989, also freelance writer; pres. Sky Rice Inc., 1990, Sky East Inc., 1990; instr. Reevaluation Counseling, Creativity Seminars, 1989—. Vol. Siddha Meditation Ctr. Mem. Nat. League Am. Pen Women, North Star Watercolor Soc. (bd. dirs. 1987-88). Unitarian. Home and Office: 466 Valley Rd Lambertville NJ 08530

GETTELFINGER, NANCY, mental health services administrator; b. Montgomery, Ala.; d. Robert Jerome and Doris (Mieman) G. BS in English, Ind. U., 1970; MPA, Cen. Mich. U., 1977. Lic. nursing home adminstr., Wis. Asst. bur. chief div. pub. welfare N.J. Dept. Human Svcs., Trenton, 1974-75, adminstrv. planner Office Budget and Fiscal Analysis, 1975-76, supr. staff cons. div. pub. welfare, 1976-77, supr. program devel. div. mental health and hosps., 1977-80; dir. state mental health facilities Wis. Dept. Health and Social Svcs., Madison, 1980-82, dir. ops., 1982-84; chief exec. officer So. Wis. Ctr. for Devel. Disabled, Madison, 1984-86; dir. psychiat. svcs. Gaston Meml. Hosp., Gastonia, N.C., 1986-88; exec. dir. Multi-County Mental Health Ctr., Tullahoma, Tenn., 1988—. Mem. Tenn. Assn. Mental Health Ctrs. Home: 1307 Ovoca Rd Tullahoma TN 37388 Office: Multi-County MH Ctr 1803 N Jackson St Tullahoma TN 37388

GETTELMAN, ROBIN CLAIRE, media specialist; b. Milw., Jan. 6, 1952; d. Robert Otto and Virginia Mae (Proffit) G.; m. Ted Bayard Johnson, Sept. 25, 1976 (div. Jan. 1985). BS in Secondary Edn., U. Wis., 1974; MA in Librarianship, U. Denver, 1975. Dir. instructional material ctr. Cripple Creek (Colo.)-Victor Sch. Dist., 1975-81; dir. Franklin Ferguson Meml. Libr., Cripple Creek, 1975-81; dir. instructional materials ctr. D.C. Everest Jr. High Sch., Schofield, Wis., 1981—; dist. media coord. D.C. Everest Area Schs., Schofield, 1988—; reviewer Sch. Evaluation Consortium, Madison, Wis., 1986, Marshfield, Wis., 1987, reviewer, coord., Ashland, Wis., 1989; chair media com. D.C. Everest Area Schs., Schofield, 1988—. Recipient Svc. award of the Yr., Franklin Ferguson Meml. Libr., 1981. Mem. Wis. Sch. Libr. Media Assn. (chair profl. devel. com. 1983, chair 1984, 85 confs. exec. bd. 1985), Wis. Ednl. Media Assn., Wausau Area Jaycees (community dir. 1986-87, chair cancer ski-a-thon 1987, chair 4th of July concessions 1989, Project Chmn. of the Month 1987). Methodist. Home: 2405 Petunia Rd Wausau WI 54401 Office: DC Everest Jr High Sch 1000 Machmueller Schofield WI 54476

GETTY, CAROL PAVILACK, government official; b. Wilmington, Del., Apr. 9, 1938; d. Frank Clifton McGrew and Maxine (Remaly) Fogarty; m. Lawrence Lee Pavilack, Aug. 18, 1960 (div. 1980); children: Douglas Brooks, Joann Clements; m. James John Getty, May 8, 1985. B.A., Wellesley Coll., 1960; M.S. in Criminal Justice, Ariz. State U., 1978; postgrad. Phoenix Coll., 1974, U. Oreg., 1975. Tchr. math. Beaver County Day Sch., Chestnut Hill, Mass., 1960-62; engring. aide Air Research, Phoenix, 1960-63; computer analyst Motorola, Phoenix, 1963; tchr. math. Phoenix County Day Sch., 1964-69; mem. Ariz. Bd. Pardons and Paroles, Phoenix, 1978-83; commr. U.S. Parole Commn., Washington, 1983—; tech. adviser Maricopa County Alts. to Incarceration Commn., 1980-83. Chmn. Annual Reports, Ariz. Bd. Pardons and Paroles, 1979, 80, 81, co-chmn. Rule Book, 1980. Treas., asst. treas., sec., impact community action, admissions & fin. Jr. League, 1970—; docent, treas. Phoenix Art Mus. League, 1968-79; vice chmn. Criminal Justice Adv. Com., Phoenix, 1973-78. Mem. Exec. Women in Govt., Nat. Fedn. Rep. Women, Am. Correctional Assn., Am. Paroling Authority, Womens C. of C. (exec. com. fed. exec. bd.), Soroptimists, Wellesley Club. Unitarian. Home: 7709 NW Westside Dr Kansas City MO 64152 Office: US Parole Commn Dept of Justice 10920 Ambassador Dr Kansas City MO 64153

GETTY, ESTELLE, actress; b. N.Y.C., July 25, 1923; m. Arthur Gettleman, Dec. 21, 1947; children: Barry, Carl. Student, New Sch. for Social Rsch., Herbert Berghof Studios; studied with Gerald Russak. Appeared in numerous stage prodns. on and off Broadway including Death of a Salesman, The Glass Menagerie, All My Sons, 6 Rms Rv Vu, Blithe Spirit, Arsenic and Old Lace, I Don't Know Why I'm Screaming, Widows and Children, Torch Song Trilogy, 1981-83; film appearances include The Chosen, 1982, Tootsie, 1983, Mask, 1984, Proctocol, 1984, Mannequin, 1987; TV appearances include (series) The Golden Girls, 1987— (Emmy award as outstanding supporting actress in a comedy series 1988, Golden Globe award for best actress in a comedy), (TV movies) No Man's Land, 1984, Copacabana, 1985; author: If I Knew Then What I Know Now...So What?. Office: Harris & Goldberg Talent Agy 2121 Ave of the Stars Ste 950 Los Angeles CA 90067*

GETZENDANNER, SUSAN, lawyer, federal judge; b. Chgo., July 24, 1939; d. William B. and Carole S. (Muehling) O'Meara; children—Alexandra, Paul. B.B.A., Loyola U., 1966, J.D., 1966. Bar: Ill. bar 1966. Law clk. U.S. Dist. Ct., Chgo., 1966-68; assoc. Mayer, Brown & Platt, Chgo., 1968-74, ptnr., 1974-80; judge U.S. Dist. Ct., Chgo., 1980-87; ptnr. Skadden, Arps, Slate, Meagher & Flom, Chgo., 1987—. Recipient medal of excellence Loyola U. Law Alumni Assn., 1981. Mem. ABA, Chgo. Council Lawyers. Office: Skadden Arps Slate Meagher & Flom 333 W Wacker Dr Chicago IL 60606

GETZIN, PAULA MAYER, chemistry, science and technology educator; b. N.Y.C., Oct. 6, 1941; d. Henry and Jenny (Lewis) Mayer; m. Donald R. Getzin, July 25, 1965 (div. 1977); children: Jeffrey, Andrew. BA, Radcliffe Coll., 1961; MA, Columbia U., 1962, PhD, 1967; MS, Stevens Inst. Tech., 1986. Asst. prof. Kean Coll. of N.J., Union, 1969-77, assoc. prof., 1977—; faculty fellow Princeton U, 1989-90. Mem. Bd. Edn., Highland Park, N.J., 1980-87, pres. 1982-84; mem. Human Rights Commn., Highland Park, 1990—. Mem. Am. Chem. Soc., Nat. Assn. Sci. Tech. and Society, Human Rights Commn. Home: 423 Lincoln Ave Highland Park NJ 08904 Office: Kean College of NJ Union NJ 07083

GEVANTMAN, JUDITH, financial analyst, consultant; b. Pitts., May 25, 1949; d. Chaim and Charlotte Selma (Max) G. AB cum laude, Goucher Coll., Towson, Md., 1971; postgrad., NYU, 1971-74; MPA, Harvard U., 1977. Dep.dir. N.Y.C. Addiction Svcs. Agy., 1971-74; asst. v.p., supr. Moody's Investors Svc., N.Y.C., 1978-85; v.p., dir. mcpl. rsch. Wertheim, Schroder & Co., N.Y.C., 1986-87; v.p., mgr. fixed income rsch. Mabon, Nugent & Co., N.Y.C., 1988; ptnr. Rsch. Assocs., Bklyn., 1989—; chmn. bd. dirs. GemStone Investors Assurance Corp., 1990—; cons. Downstate Med. Sch., Bklyn.,1975, Harvard U. Med. Sch., Boston, 1976, Boston Mus. Sci., 1977. Bd. dirs. Bruekelen Owners Corp., Bklyn., 1982-83; alumni rep. Goucher Coll., 1985—; trustee Congregation Bnai Avraham, Brooklyn Heights, N.Y., 1988—. UN fellow U. Kans., 1970, Univ. fellow NYU, 1971-73; Senatorial scholar Md. Legislature, 1967-71; Urban Corp. grantee, 1970. Mem. Mcpl. Forum N.Y., Mcpl. Analyst Group N.Y., Harvard Club (N.Y.C.).

GEWIRTZ, GERRY, editor; b. N.Y.C., Dec. 22, 1920; d. Max and Minnie (Weiss) G.; m. Eugene W. Friedman, Nov. 11, 1945; children: John Henry, Robert James. B.A., Vassar Coll., 1941. Editor Package Store Mgmt., 1942-44, Jewelry Mag., 1945-53; freelance editor promotion dept. McCall's Mag., Esquire, 1953-56; free-lance fashion and gifts editor Jewelers Circular Keystone, N.Y.C., 1955-71; editor, pub. The Fashionables, 1971-74, The Forecast, 1974—, Nat. Jeweler, Ann. Fashion Guide, 1976-80; editor, assoc. pub. Exec. Jeweler, 1980-83; editor The Gerry Gewirtz Report, N.Y.C., 1983—, The Fashion Source (formerly Internat. Fashion Index), N.Y.C., 1984—. Mem. exec. com. Inner City Council of Cardinal Cooke, N.Y.; chairperson women's task force United Jewish Appeal Fedn.; former bd. govs. Israel Bonds; former trustee Israel Cancer Research Fund, Central Synagogue; bd. dirs. Double Image Theater; former pres. women's aux. Brandeis U. Honored guest Am. Jewish Com., 1978; Israel Cancer Research Fund, 1978-81; recipient Disting. Community Service award Brandeis U., 1987; named to Jewellry Hall Fame, 1988. Mem. N.Y. Fashion Group, Nat. Home Fashions League (former pres.), Women's Jewelry Assn. (pres. 1983-87 , named editor who has contbd. most to jewelry industry 1984), Phi Delta Epsilon. Clubs: N.Y, Vassar, Overseas Press. Home: 45 Sutton Pl S New York NY 10022 Office: Gerry Gewirtz Report 310 Madison Ave Suite 824 New York NY 10017

GEYER, GEORGIE ANNE, syndicated columnist, educator, author; b. Chgo., Apr. 2, 1935; d. Robert George and Georgie Hazel (Gervens) G. B.S., Northwestern U., 1956; postgrad. (Fulbright scholar), U. Vienna, Austria, 1956-57; Litt. D. (hon.), Lake Forest Coll., (Ill.), 1980, Chgo. State U., Linfield Coll., St. Mary's of Notre Dame, St. Mary-of-the-Woods Coll., Am. Univ., Wilson Coll. Reporter Southtown Economist, Chgo., 1958; soc. reporter Chgo. Daily News, 1959-60, gen. assignment reporter, 1960-64, Latin Am. corr., 1964-67, roving fgn. corr. and columnist, 1967-75; syndicated columnist Los Angeles Times Syndicate, 1975-80; columnist Universal Press Syndicate, 1980—; Lyle M. Spencer prof. journalism Syracuse U., 1976; regular news commentator PBS' Washington Week in Review; questioner on Presdl. debate, Oct., 1984; steering com. Aspen Inst. Latin Am. Governance Project, 1981-82; regular panelist TV news program Washington Week in Rev.; commentator on the BBC; regular panelist Voice of America; regular questioner Meet the Press; sent by Internat. Communication Agy. on 3 worldwide speaking tours on Am. journalism: Nigeria, Zambia, Tanzania and Somalia, 1979, Philippines and Indonesia, 1981, Iceland, Norway, Belgium and Portugal, 1982; panelist Presdl. Debates, Oct., 1984; rep. Fulbright scholar program 40th anniversary, New Zealand, 1987. Author: The New Latins, 1970, The New 100 Years War, 1972, The Young Russians, 1976; (autobiography) Buying the Night Flight, 1983; subjects of interviews include Prince Sihanouk of Cambodia, Yassar Arafat, Anwar Sadat, King Hussein of Jordan, Pres. Khaddafy of Libya, the Ayatollah Khomeini, Sultan Qaboos of Oman, Pres. Juan Peron of Argentina, Pres. Siad Barre of Somalia, Prime Minister Mauno Koivisto of Finland, Anastasio Somoza, Jerzy Urban, Janusz Onyszkiewicz, Prime Minister Edward Seaga of Jamaica, Pres. Ronald Reagan, Pres. George Bush, others; discovered and had first interview with second most-wanted Nazi, Walter Rauff in Tierra del Fuego, Chile, 1966; found Dominican pres. Juan Bosch in hiding in P.R. during Dominican revolution, 1965; held by Palestinians as Israeli spy, 1973; imprisoned in Angola for writing about revolutionary government, 1976. Active Orgn. for S.W. Community Chgo., 1960-64; trustee Am. U., Washington, 1981-86; Council. Fgn. Rels. Recipient 1st prize Am. Newspaper Guild, 1962; 2d prize Ill. Press Editors Assn., 1962; award for best writing on Latin Am. Overseas Press Club, 1966; Merit award Northwestern U., 1968; Nat. Headliner award Theta Sigma Phi, 1968; Maria Moors Cabot award Columbia U., 1970; Hannah Solomon award Nat. Council Jewish Women, 1973; Ill. Spl. Events Commn. Woman's award, 1975; Northwestern U. Alumnae award, 1981; Woodrow Wilson fellow Rollins Coll.,, Winter Park, Fla., 1982; Disting. fellow Mortar Bd. Nat. Sr. Honor Soc., Am. U., 1982. Mem. Mortar Bd., Women in Communications, Chgo. Council on Fgn. Relations (dir.), Inst. Internat. Edn. (dir.), Midland Authors, Internat. Inst. Strategic Studies, Internat. Soc. Polit. Psychology, Women's Inst. for Freedom of Press, Internat. Press Inst., Cosmos Club (first woman mem.), Tavern Club (first woman mem.), Sigma Delta Chi. Home and Office: Pla 800 25th St NW Washington DC 20037

GEYSER, MERYL JOYCE, lawyer; b. Phila., Aug. 12, 1943; d. Herbert S. and Harriet (Witten) Leviton; m. Michael Robert Geyser, June 18, 1963; children: Richard Marshall, Jeffrey Steven. Student, U. Colo., 1961-64; BA, U. Wash., 1965; postgrad., San Jose State U., 1967-68; JD, Ariz. State U., 1978. Bar: Ariz. 1978. Ptnr. Sacks, Tierney, Kasen & Kerrick, P.A., Phoenix, 1978-88; dep. chief of staff Gov. of Ariz., Phoenix, 1988—; gov.'s liaison Task Force on Seriously Mentally Ill, Phoenix, 1989-90. Del. Dem. Nat. Conv., Kansas City, Mo., 1974; bd. dirs., sec. Phoenix Hebrew Acad., 1985—; bd. dirs. Cen. Ariz. Shelter Svcs., Inc., Phoenix, 1989—; mem. Joint Legis. Health Care Cost Containment Com., Phoenix, 1989—. Mem. Ariz. State Bar Assn., Maricopa County Bar Assn. Office: Office of Gov 1700 W Washington St Phoenix AZ 85007

GHERARDI, DIANE PAULA, small business owner; b. Pen Argyl, Pa., Aug. 8, 1941; d. Thomas Dominick and Jennie (DeRenzis) Verona; m. Kenneth Fishman (div. 1984); children: Mark Andrew, Pamela Anne; m. Robert Gherardi; stepchildren: Phyllis, Robert, Denise, Jeanine. BA, Wilson Coll., Chambersburg, Pa., 1963; MA, Georgetown U., 1963, pre-doctoral studies, 1963-66. Writer, researcher Georgetown U., Washington, 1963-64; cataloguer Folger Shakespeare Library, Washington, 1963-64; editor Inst. for Def. Analysis, Washington, 1964-65, Sci. Mag., Washington, 1965-66, P.C. Holt, Rinehart & Winston Pubs., N.Y.C., 1966-68; assoc. editor Ingenue mag., N.Y.C., 1968-70; sales assoc. Country Heritage Real Estate, Stroudsburg, Pa., 1986-88; v.p. Taos Rendezvous, 1988—. Vol. Greenwich Sch. System, Conn., 1975-79, United Way, Conn., 1980-82. Mem. Taos C. of C., Pa. Bd. Realtors, Conn. Bd. Realtors, AAUW, Nat. Honor Soc., Silver Key Soc., Sigma Phi. Home: 1060 Woodlands Dr Box 804 Angel Fire NM 87710

GHILARDI, MELINDA CHRISTINA, lawyer; b. Scranton, Pa., June 13, 1958; d. Joseph Paul And Eleanor Delores (Gasparini) G. BA, U. Scranton, 1979; JD, U. Pitts., 1983. Bar: Pa. 1984, D.C. 1985, U.S. Dist. Ct. (mid. dist.) Pa. 1984, U.S. Ct. Appeals (3d cir.) 1986, U.S. Supreme Ct. 1987. Asst. dist. atty. Lackawanna County Dist. Atty.'s Office, Scranton, 1984-86; asst. fed. pub. defender mid. dist. Pa. Fed. Pub. Defender, Scranton, 1986—. Mem. ABA, Nat. Assn. Criminal Def. Lawyers, Bar Assn. D.C., Lackawanna County Bar Assn., Pa. Assn. Criminal Def. Lawyers, Pa. Bar Assn. Roman Catholic. Home: 1603 Clay Ave Dunmore PA 18509 Office: Fed Pub Defender Mid Dist Pa 404 Scranton Ctr 401 Adams Ave Scranton PA 18510

GHILERI, SIRLEEN JEAN, programmer analyst; b. Southgate, Calif., Mar. 7, 1943; d. Sirl and Dorothy Jean (Kaylor) Myhand; m. Richard Alan Wilson, Apr. 10, 1960 (div. 1972); children: Richard Alan Jr., Michael Dale; m. Norman Phillip Ghileri, Mar. 12, 1973. A.A., Golden West Jr. Coll., 1970. Peace Corps, vol., Ethiopia, 1971; eligibility worker Santa Cruz Co., Calif., 1972-76; rancher Ghigleri Ranch, San Juan Bautista, Calif., 1976-82; applications programmer Madic Corp., Santa Clara, Calif., 1983-85; sr. programmer analyst Skyway Systems, Santa Cruz, 1985—. Chairperson Santa Cruz County Grand Jury, 1977-78. Mem. Prime Users Group, Mensa, Santa Cruz Bonsai Kai (founder), Saturday Morning Quilting Ladies (founder). Avocations: bonsai, quilting, gardening.

GHIRALDINI, JOAN, financial executive; b. Bklyn., Mar. 31, 1951; d. Robert and Anne (Centineo) G.; B.A., Smith Coll., 1972; M.B.A., U. Pa., 1975. Intern, N.Y.C. Econ. Devel. Adminstrn., 1971; econ. specialist Western Electric Co., N.Y.C., 1975-76; sr. fin. analyst Internat. Paper Co., N.Y.C., 1976-78, mgr. strategic planning, 1978-81; dir. fin. planning Executone Inc., Jericho, N.Y., 1981-82, dir. strategic bus. planning, 1982-83; dir. corporate analysis Equitable Life Assurance, N.Y.C., 1983-84; asst. v.p. First Boston Corp., N.Y.C., 1985—. Mem. Fin. Women's Assn. N.Y., Planning Forum, Wharton Bus. Sch. Club (past v.p.), Smith Coll. Club N.Y. (bd. dirs.). Home: 155 E 38th St New York NY 10016 Office: First Boston Corp 5 World Trade Ctr New York NY 10048

GHNASSIA, JILL DIX, English language educator; b. Harrisburg, Pa., Oct. 19, 1947; d. Robert Clough and Sarah Elizabeth (Hottenstein) Dix; m. Maurice Jean-Henri Ghnassia, Dec. 18, 1980. AB cum laude, Bucknell U., 1969; MA, Duke U., 1972, PhD, 1983. Asst. prof. English U. Hartford, Conn., 1985—; adj. prof. N.C. Wesleyan Coll., Rocky Mount, N.C., 1983-85; reviewer cons. MacMillan Pub. Co., N.Y.C., 1986—. Scholar Duke U., 1972-74, fellow, 1974-76. Mem. AAUW, MLA, South Atlantic Modern Langs. Assn., New Eng. Modern Langs. Assn., Nat. Coun. Tchrs. of English, New Eng. Assn. Tchrs. of English, Conn. Coun. of Tchrs. of English, New Eng. Victorian Studies Assn. AAUW, Phi Beta Kappa (treas. Greater Hartford chpt. 1987-89), Kappa Delta Pi, Alpha Lambda Delta (sr. award). Democrat. Lutheran. Home: PO Box 1069 New Hartford CT 06057 Office: U Hartford Coll Basic Studies 200 Bloomfield Ave West Hartford CT 06117

GIANCOLA, HOLLY HARRINGTON, retail company executive; b. San Francisco, Feb. 1, 1961; d. Jonathan David and Coralie (Phelps) Harrington; m. Frank James Giancola, June 14, 1986; 1 child, Michael Andrew. AS, Marymount U., Arlington, Va., 1981, BS cum laude, 1984; postgrad., Georgetown U. Law Ctr., 1985-86. RN, Va., D.C. Nurse Fairfax Hosp., Falls Church, Va., 1981-83; nurse Georgetown Hosp., Washington, 1983-84, clin. practitioner, 1984-88; pres. Harrington-Giancola Wardrobes Inc., Centreville, Va., 1988—; retail buyer Gt. Expectations Maternity, Centreville, 1989—; realtor Shannon and Luchs Realtors, Centreville, 1986—; mktg. cons. Mercure Group, Clifton, Va., 1989—; new bus. cons. Larry D. Worden CPA, Clifton, 1989—. Co-author: (pamphlet) Patient Guide to Angioplasty, 1985. Mem. Cabells Mill Neighborhood Watch, Centreville, 1989—; mem. Poplar Tree Elem. Sch. PTA, 1990—. Mem. NAFE, No. Va. Assn. Realtors, Cen. Fairfax C. of C., Fairfax County C. of C., Centreville Square Mchts. Assn. (pres. 1990—), Sigma Theta Tau. Republican. Episcopalian. Office: Great Expectations 14200-C Centreville Sq Centreville VA 22020

GIANCURSIO, DEBRA ANN, computer professional. BA, Oberlin Coll., 1980; MS, Dartmouth Coll., 1987. Systems engr. Corning (N.Y.) Glass Works, 1980-85; sr. systems specialist Bank of Boston, 1985—. Mem. Assn. for Computing Machinery.

GIANINNO, SUSAN MCMANAMA, marketing executive, advertising agency executive; b. Boston, Dec. 25, 1948; d. John Carroll and Barbara (Frances) Magner; m. Lawrence John Gianinno, June 7, 1970; 1 child, Alexandra Christin. BA in English Lit. and Psychology cum laude, Boston Coll., 1970; MA in Ednl. Psychology, Northwestern U., 1973; postgrad. in behavioral scis., U. Chgo. Psychiat. asst. Quinn Psychiat., Pavilion St Elizabeth's Hosp., Brighton, Mass., 1967-70; research assoc. com. human devel., dept behavioral scis. U. Chgo., 1973-79; resident adv. U. Chgo. Housing Systems, from 1979; research assoc., then research supr. Needham, Harper and Steers Advt. Inc., Chgo., 1979-80; dir. life style rsch. Needham, Harper and Steers Advt. Inc., Chgo., Il, from 1981; v.p., dir. creative rsch. Young & Rubicam N.Y., then sr. and exec. v.p., dir. rsch. svcs., since 1982; now exec. v.p., dir. mktg. Young & Rubicam, Inc. Contbr. papers, reports to profl. jours. Univ. scholar U. Chgo., 1975-77. Home: 90 Coachlamp Ln Stamford CT 06902 Office: Young & Rubicam 285 Madison Ave New York NY 10017

GIANTURCO, PAOLA, advertising executive; b. Urbana, Ill., July 22, 1939; d. Cesare and Verna Bertha (Daily) Gianturco; m. David Sanderson Hill, Mar. 12, 1988; 1 child from previous marriage, Scott Sangster. BA, Stanford U., 1961; postgrad. U. So. Calif., 1971. Pub. relations dir. Joseph Magnin, San Francisco, 1961-67; pub. relations dir., account exec. Hall & Levine Advt. Agy., Los Angeles, 1968-73, v.p., account supr., 1973-76, sr. v.p., 1977-82; v.p. Dancer Fitzgerald Sample, 1982-87, v.p., mgmt. supr. Saatchi and Saatchi DFS, Inc., 1988—. Past bd. dirs. The Country Schs., Mem. Women in Communications, Stanford Profl. Women (past mem. bd. dirs.), Nat. Investor Rels. Inst., Internat. Assn. Bus. Communicators, Bus. and Profl. Advt. Assn. Home: 30 Cecily Ln Mill Valley CA 94941 Office: Saatchi & Saatchi DFS Corp Communications Group 1010 Battery St PO Box 7166 San Francisco CA 94120

GIBB, BEVERLY JEAN, mental health therapist; b. Spokane, Wash., Mar. 13, 1963; d. Scott Evans Gibb and Doris Jean Woodward. BA, Linfield Coll., 1984; MS, East Wash. U., 1986. Cert. mental health counselor, Wash. Behavioral therapist Sacred Heart Med. Ctr., Spokane, 1986-89; residential therapist Kerr Youth and Family Ctr., Portland, Oreg., 1989; behavioral mgr. Pacific Crest Rehab. Ctr., Portland, 1989, Southcrest Rehab. Ctr., Spokane, 1989-90; mental health profl. Community Mental Health Ctr., Spokane, 1990—. Mem. Am. Psychol. Assn. (assoc.), Wash. State Psychol. Assn. (assoc.), Nat. Spinal Cord Assn., Nat. Head Injury Found., Inland Spinal Cord Injury Assn. (treas. 1988-89). Democrat. Home: E 407 18th Spokane WA 99203 Office: Community Mental Health Ctr S 107 Division Spokane WA 99202

GIBB, LISA JO CHRISTENSON, speech and language pathologist; b. Moline, Ill., Dec. 17, 1961; d. Richard Alan and Joanne Allen (Atkinson) Christenson; m. Ronald Scott, Feb. 14, 1987. BS, U. Wis., Stevens Point, 1984, MS, 1986. Cert. speech-lang. pathologist, myofunctional therapist. Speech-lang. pathology clin. fellow Med. Ctr., Princeton, N.J., 1987-88, speech-lang. pathologist, 1988-89; mgr. speech-lang. pathology Riverside Med. Ctr., Mpls., 1989—; care staff orientator, inservice presentor Med. Ctr., Princeton, N.J., 1987-88, supr. stroke/aphasia support group, 1988—; panel mem. Conf. for Cognitive Defecits in Multiple Sclerosis Patients, 1990. Contbr. articles in field to community pubs. Mem. Am. Speech-Lang.-Hearing Assn., Myofunctional Therapy Assn. Am., N.J. Speech and Hearing Assn. (com. for ann. state conv.), Jr. League Mpls. Republican. Home: 6129 Abbott Ave S Edina MN 55410 Office: Riverside Med Ctr Riverside at 25th Ave S Minneapolis MN 55454

GIBBENS, MARGARET LOUISE, construction company executive; b. San Antonio, Mar. 18, 1933; d. Samuel Alexander and Eileen Mary (McCarthy) Thielepape; m. Jack Stanley Gibbens, Apr. 7, 1929; children: Rockne Shawn, Shannon Leigh, Morgan Shane, Tierne Michelle, Erin Kay. Student, U. St. Thomas, Houston, 1951-55. Reservationist Eastern Air Lines, Houston and New Orleans, 1955-56; clk., sec. Chilton Credit Reporting, Dallas, 1982-84; sec. to pres. Modern Exec. Svcs., Mesquite, Tex., 1984-85; office mgr. Cuff/Muse Mktg., Mesquite, 1985-88, Luther Constrn. Co. Inc., Rowlett, Tex., 1989—. sec. Southwestern Shoe Travelers Assn., 1989—; den mother Cub Scouts Am., Mesquite, 1972; leader Blue Birds, Camp Fire Girls, Mesquite, 1974; treas. Shands Elem. Sch., Mesquite, 1974-75; tchr. religion St. Pius X Ch., Dallas, 1961-65. Mem. St. Pius X Ladies Soc. (pres. 1976-77, circle hostess 1966, 70, 80), Met. Dallas Home Builders Aux. (historian 1970). Democrat. Roman Catholic.

GIBBONEY, MARILYN LOUISE, travel consultant; b. Noblesville, Ind., Jan. 16, 1933; d. Worth Arnold Stage and Helen (Dresher) Guimond; m. Ottis Hyrcanous Rasor, June 17, 1949 (div. Aug. 1950); m. Clarence Wendell Gibboney, Jan. 3, 1951; children: Sue Elaine Davidson, Carl Edward (dec.). Cashier Publix Super Market, Tequesta, Fla., 1965-68, Conway (N.H.) Foodliner, 1968; operator New Eng. Telephone Co., Conway, 1969-71; co-owner Valley Travel Svc., Conway, 1976-88, mgr., 1988—. Pres., v.p., sec., treas. United Meth. Women; sec. United Meth. Womens Leadership Team, 1971-78; mem. Mt. Washington Valley Stompers Sq. Dance Club. Home: Box 3274 North Conway NH 03860 Office: Valley Travel 140 Main St Conway NH 03818

GIBBONS, JULIA SMITH, federal judge; b. Pulaski, Tenn., Dec. 23, 1950; d. John Floyd and Julia Jackson (Abernathy) Smith; m. William Lockhart Gibbons, Aug. 11, 1973; children: Rebecca Carey, William Lockhart Jr. B.A., Vanderbilt U., 1972; J.D., U. Va., 1975. Bar: Tenn. 1975. Law clk. to judge U.S. Ct. Appeals, 1975-76; assoc. Farris, Hancock, Gilman, Branan, Lanier & Hellen, Memphis, 1976-79; legal advisor Gov. Lamar Alexander, Nashville, 1979-81; judge 15th Jud. Cir., Memphis, 1981-83, U.S. Dist. Ct. (we. dist.) Tenn., Memphis, 1983—. Fellow Am. Bar Found.; mem. ABA, Tenn. Bar Assn., Memphis and Shelby County Bar Assn., Nat. Assn. Women Judges, Am. Judicature Soc., Phi Beta Kappa, Order of Coif. Presbyterian. Office: US Dist Ct 167 N Main St 1157 Fed Bldg Memphis TN 38103

GIBBONS, MARY PEYSER, civic volunteer; b. N.Y.C., Dec. 15, 1936; d. Frederick Maurice and Catherine Mary (McKelvey) Peyser; m. John Martin Gibbons, Dec. 26, 1955; children: Catherine Way, Mary Sloan, John, Fredericka Witter, Myles. Ptnr. Gibbons & Bibow Assocs., Hartford, Conn., 1986—; pres. Sefton & Sheil Ltd., Hartford, 1988—. Regent U. Hartford, 1988—, bd. trustees Hartford Art Sch., 1985—; pres. women's com. Wadsworth Atheneum, Hartford, 1978-80, bd. trustees, 1981—; bd. dirs. The Hartford Ballet, 1981—, Vol. Coms. of Art Mus., U.S. and Can., 1982—. Mem. Am. Assn. Mus. Vols. (pres. 1986-88, bd. dirs. 1982—, pres. 1986-88, contbr. articles to orgn. publs. 1986-88), Hartford Club, Hartford Golf Club. Office: Sefton & Sheil Ltd 1130 Prospect Ave Hartford CT 06105

GIBBONS, SANDRA LEE See MCLAUGHLIN, SANDRA LEE

GIBBONS, SHEILA MARIE, aerospace company executive; b. N.Y.C., Mar. 31, 1931; d. Joseph Vincent and Edna Marie (McCarthy) MacAvoy; children: Laura Cecile Burns, Philip Damian, Sally Honora Mc Mahon. BA in Art, Queens Coll., CUNY, 1952; JD, St. John's U., 1976. Bar: N.Y. 1977, Calif. 1977. Assoc. Carnahan & Freeman, Woodland Hills, Calif., 1977; asst. sec. Northrop Corp., L.A., 1978-80, sec., 1980-83, v.p., sec., 1983—. Honoree Tribute to Women in Internat. Industry, Nat. Bd. YWCA, Houston, 1983. Mem. ABA, L.A. Bar Assn. (subcom. fed. securities law), Am. Soc. Corp. Secs. (securities law com. 1981-84, adv. com. 1981-88, pres. L.A. chpt. 1984-88, ad hoc com. on tender offers 1984-85, bd. dirs. 1985-88, securities industry com. 1985-89, chmn. 1989-90), Am.-Irish Hist. Soc. Office: Northrop Corp 1840 Century Park E Los Angeles CA 90067

GIBBS, BEATRICE ESTHER, librarian; b. Malden, Mass., Oct. 16, 1918; d. Joseph S. and Della N. (Rainen) G.; (dec. Aug. 1976); children: Paula, Bonnie, Marian, Ben. BA, Tufts U., 1969; MA, Glassboro State U., 1972. Tchr. Mid. Twp., Cape May Courthouse, N.J., 1964-75; libr. Cape May County Libr., Cape May Courthouse, 1975-84, Montgomery County Libr., Bethesda, Md., 1985—. Pres. PTA, Wildwood, N.J., 1964-70; leader Girl Scouts Am., Wildwood, 1964-70; dir. Coop Nursery, Wildwood, 1966-70. With USN, 1942-45. Mem. Cape May County Art League (v.p. 1960-65), ALA, Cape May County Hist. Soc. (sec. 1965-68), Tufts Alumni Assn., Women in the Arts Museum, NCJW. Home: 1111 University Blvd W Silver Spring MD 20902 Office: Montgomery County Library 5501 Massachusetts Ave Bethesda MD 20816

GIBBS, JUNE NESBITT, state senator; b. Newton, Mass., June 13, 1922; d. Samuel Frederick and Lulu (Glazier) Nesbitt; m. Donald T. Gibbs, Dec. 8, 1945; 1 child, Elizabeth. BA in Math., Wellesley Coll., 1943; MA in Math., Boston U., 1947; postgrad., U. R.I., 1981-84. Mem. Republican Nat. Com. from R.I., 1969-80; sec. Republican Nat. Com., 1977-80; mem. R.I. State Senate, 1985—; mem. def. adv. com. Women in Services, 1970-72, vice chmn., 1972. Mem. Middletown Town Council, 1974-80, 82-84, pres., 1978-80. Served to lt. (J.G.) USNR, 1943-46. Home: 163 Riverview Ave Middletown RI 02840 Office: RI State Senate Providence RI 02903

GIBBS, LAVETA JANE, infosystems specialist; b. Nov. 17, 1948; d. Orvin Edgar and Velva Opal (Raulston) Elkins. B in Bus. with honors, Calif. State U., Sacramento, 1969. Computer operator, programmer Pan Am. Airlines, San Francisco, 1969-70; mgr. data processing Fantasy Records/Films, Berkeley, Calif., 1970-76; programmer, analyst Levi Strauss & Co., San Francisco, 1976-80; mgr. data processing Bank of Am., San Francisco, 1980-81; programmer, analyst McKesson, San Francisco, 1981-84; mgr. management info. services, internat. support Apple Computer Co., Cupertino, Calif., 1984—; internat. assignment Levi Strauss & Co., Europe, 1976-80, Apple Computer Co., Toronto, Can., Australia and Europe, 1984-87. Recipient various tennis trophies from tournaments in Las Vegas, Monterry, Tahoe and No. Calif., 1972-80.

GIBBS, MARGARET CATHERINE, retired public administration educator; b. Hot Springs, Ark., Apr. 7, 1914; d. Leonard Everett and Kate (Ludwig) King; m. George Gibbs IV, June 27, 1942; children: George V., Thomas Ashley, Katherine Wellington Gibbs Gengoux, Sarah Randolph Gibbs Beetem. BA cum laude, U. So. Calif., 1936, MPA, 1941; PhD in Pub. Adminstrn., Claremont Grad. Sch., 1973. Exec. sec. Univ. Religious Conf., L.A., 1937-38; mng. editor Palos Verdes Estates (Calif.) Bull., 1941-42; tchr. English to Latin Am. diplomats Washington, 1942; tchr. L.A. City High Schs., 1945-49; corr. L.A. Times, Claremont, Calif., 1950-62; lectr. pub. adminstrn. U. So. Calif., L.A., 1973-81; emeritus prof., chmn. dept. pub. adminstrn. Calif. State U., San Bernardino, 1975-80; cons. undergrounding com. League Calif. Cities, 1969; del. 2d U.S.-Japan Computer Conf., Tokyo, 1975, Inst. Adminstrv. Svcis., Mex., 1974, Abidjan, 1977. Contbr. articles to profl. jours. Bd. dirs. League Calif. Cities, 1962-70; mem. Los Angeles County Com. for Coordinating Delinquency, 1964-66; trustee Citrus Community Coll., Azusa, Calif., 1974-81; mem. Claremont City Coun., 1962-70; mem. program adv. com. Calif. State U., San Bernardino, 1977—; bd. councillors Sch. Edn., U. So. Calif., L.A., 1985—; docent Rancho Santa Ana Botanic Garden, 1983—. Recipient Beautiful Activist award Broadway Dept. Store and Germaine Monteil, 1972, merit award U. So. Calif., 1987; grantee Western Electric Fund, 1979. Mem. LWV, Am. Soc. Pub. Adminstrn. (nat. coun. 1979-82, Outstanding Achievement award Inland chpt. 1982), Trojan League, Internat. Congress Adminstrv. Sci., L.A. Philharmonic Assocs., Alpha Kappa Psi. Democrat. Episcopalian. Home: 650 W Harrison St Claremont CA 91711

GIBBS, MARILYN SHISLER, speech pathologist; b. Akron, Ohio, Mar. 6, 1948; d. Wilbur Orlo and Lenore (Gaberel) Shisler; m. July 3, 1971 (div. Mar. 1989); children: Jennifer Jane, James Robert. BS, Ohio State U., 1970; MS, So. Conn. State U., 1981, postgrad., 1988—. Speech pathologist Southington (Conn.) Pub. Schs., 1970-71, Winchester Pub. Schs., Winsted, Conn., 1981—, Nova Care, Winsted and Torrington, Conn., 1990. Sunday sch. tchr., mem. adminstrv. bd., mem. pastor-parish rels. com. 1st United Meth. Ch., Torrington. Mem. Am. Speech-Lang. and Hearing Assn., Assn. for Supervision and Curriculum Devel., Conn. Speech-Lang-Hearing Coords. in Schs. Office: Winchester Pub Schs 2 Wetmore Ave Winsted CT 06098

GIBBS, MARY BRAMLETT, banker; b. Corona, Calif., Sept. 18, 1953; d. Kenneth Frank and Kathy Lee (Hill) Harris; m. Charles Merrill Gibbs, 1987; student U. Md., 1974-77, Southwestern Grad. Sch. Banking. Br. mgr. Peoples Nat. Bank of Md., Suitland, 1972-77; with Post Oak Bank, Houston, 1977-82, asst. v.p. ops. mgmt., 1980-82; v.p. loan ops. First City Nat. Bank Houston, 1982-89; sr. v.p. First Interstate Bank Tex., 1989—. Bd. dirs., life mem. Big Sisters-Big Bros. of Houston; mediator Neighborhood Justice Ctr., 1981; mem. Christ Ch. Cath.; bd. dirs. Tex. So. U. Found., Houston Met. Ministries, Houston Area Urban League; nat. conf. chmn. Community Leadership Conf., 1990. Named Outstanding Young Houstonian, 1985, Woman on the Move, 1987. Mem. Nat. Assn. Bank Women, Nat. Assn. for Community Leadership (conf. chmn. 1990), NOW, Houston C. of C. (chair leadership Houston policy council). Contbr. articles to profl. jours. Office: 1st Interstate Bank Tex 808 Travis 4th Fl-MS595 Houston TX 77002

GIBBS, ROSE L., interior designer; b. Waynesboro, Ga., July 15, 1940; d. James C. Sr. and Julie Mae (Ward) Lovett; m. Edward Mason Gibbs, Nov. 1967; children: Anthony Wayne, Robert Wesley. BS, U. Ga., 1960. Receptionist FBI, Atlanta; asst. store mgr. Franklin Simon, Atlanta; buyer, mgr. J.C. Penney Co., Atlanta; co-owner E. & R. Interiors, Riverdale, Ga. Mem. NAFE. Address: 7426 Hwy 85 Riverdale GA 30274

GIBBS, SHARON L., healthcare consultant; b. Burbank, Calif., Mar. 8, 1950; d. Stuart Franklin and Sarah Adella (Hayes) Lee; m. William J. Givvs, Mar. 7, 1980; 1 child, Robert Paul Lee. BS in Nursing, Ga. State U., 1985. Staff nurse surg. ICU Grady Meml. Hosp., Atlanta; mgr. program evaluations, ednl. svc. coord. Ga. Med. Care Found., Atlanta; dir. internal rev., quality interventions Ga. Med. Care Found., State Peer Rev. Orgn. for Ga., Atlanta; healthcare cons., med. rev. specialist Culley-Gibbs & Assocs., Atlanta; cons. medicare part B Foster Med. Supply, Roanoke, Va. Mem. Am. Nurses Assn., Mortar Board, Sigma Theta Tau, Phi Kappa Phi. Address: 2753 Summit Ridge Rd Roanoke VA 24012

GIBBY, MABEL ENID KUNCE, psychologist; b. St. Louis, Mar. 30, 1926; d. Ralph Waldo and Mabel Enid (Warren) Kunce; student Washington U., St. Louis, 1943-44, postgrad., 1955-56; B.A., Park Coll., 1945; M.A., McCormick Theol. Sem., 1947; postgrad. Columbia U., 1948, U. Kansas City, 1949, George Washington U., 1953; M.Ed., U. Mo., 1951, Ed.D., 1952; m. John Francis Gibby, Aug. 27, 1948; children—Janet Marie (Mrs. Kim Williams), Harold Steven, Helen Elizabeth, Diane Louise, John Andrew, Keith Sherridan, Daniel Jay. Dir. religious edn. Westport Presbyn. Ch. Kansas City, Mo., 1947-49; tchr. elementary schs., Kansas City, 1949-50; high sch. counselor Arlington (Va.) Pub. Schs., 1952-54; counselor adult counseling services Washington U., 1955-56; counseling psychologist Coral Gables (Fla.) VA Hosp., 1956—; counseling psychologist Miami (Fla.) VA Hosp., 1956—, chief counseling psychology sect., 1982-86; sr. psychologist Office Disability Determination Fla. Hdqrs., 1987—. Sec. bd. dirs. Fla. Vocat. Rehab. Found. Recipient Meritorious Service citation Fla. C. of C., 1965, President's Com. on Employment of Handicapped, 1965; commendation for meritorious service Com. on Employment of Physically Handicapped Dade County, 1965, 81, named outstanding rehab. profl., 1966, 81; named Profl. Fed. Employee of Year, Greater Miami Fed. Exec. Council, 1966; Outstanding Fed. Service award Greater Miami Fed. Exec. Council, 1966; Fed. Woman's award U.S. Civil Service Commn., 1968, Community Headliner award Theta Sigma Phi, 1968, Outstanding Alumni award Park Coll., 1968, Freedom award The Chosen Few, Korean War Vets. Assn., 1986; certificate of appreciation Bur. Customs, U.S. Treasury Dept., 1969, Fla. Dept. Health and Rehab. Services, 1970. Mem. Am., Dade County (past sec.) psychol. assns., Nat., Fla. (past dir. Dade County chpt.) rehab. assns., Nat. Rehab. Counseling Assn. (past sec.). Patentee in field. Home: 10260 SW 56th St Miami FL 33165

GIBEAU, MARIE, Canadian federal official; b. Montreal, Que., Can., July 11, 1950; d. Philippe and Marguerite (Delisle) G. BA, U. Montreal, 1970, MBA, 1977; bachelor's degree, U. Que., Montreal, 1971. Dir. gen. Hans Selye Internat. Inst. Stress, Montreal, 1977-79; assoc., sr. cons. Pierre J. Hogue & Assocs., Montreal, 1979-88; MP from Ottawa Ho. of Commons, 1988—; prof. U. Montreal, U. Sherbrooke, Que., Can., U. Que., Montreal, 1982-88. Past sec., v.p. Montreal YWCA, pres., bd. adminstrn., 1984-88. Office: Ho of Commons, Parliament Bldgs, Ottawa, ON Canada K1A 0A6

GIBLETT, ELOISE ROSALIE, hematology educator; b. Tacoma, Wash., Jan. 17, 1921; d. William Richard and Rose (Godfrey) G. B.S., U. Wash., 1942, M.S., 1947, M.D. with honors, 1951. Mem. faculty U. Wash. Sch. Medicine, 1957—, research prof., 1967-87, emeritus research prof., 1987—; asso. dir., head immunogenetics Puget Sound Blood Center, 1955-79, exec. dir., 1979-87, emeritus exec. dir., 1987—; former mem. several research coms. NIH. Author: Genetic Markers in Human Blood, 1969; Editorial bd. numerous jours. including Blood, Am. Jour. Human Genetics, Transfusion, Vox Sanguinis; Contbr. over 190 articles to profl. jours. Recipient fellowships, grants, Emily Cooley, Karl Landsteiner, Philip Levine and Alexander Wiener immunohematology awards, distinguished alumna award U. Wash. Sch. Med., 1987. Fellow AAAS; Mem. Nat. Acad. Scis., Am. Soc. Human Genetics (pres. 1973), Am. Soc. Hematology, Am. Assn. Immunologists, Brit. Soc. Immunology, Internat. Soc. Hematologists, Am. Fedn. Clin. Research, Western Assn. Physicians, Assn. Am. Physicians, Sigma Xi, Alpha Omega Alpha. Home: 6533 53rd St NE Seattle WA 98115 Office: Puget Sound Blood Ctr Terry and Madison Sts Seattle WA 98104

GIBNEY, KRISTEN ELAINE, hospital products executive; b. May 30, 1948; d. John Edward and Lela Jane (Allen) Wade. AS in Bus., Chandler Coll., 1968. With Baxter Healthcare Div., Deerfield, Ill., 1975—; gen. mgr. Baxter Healthcare Div., Deerfield, 1985-87; pres. prescription svc. div. Baxter Healthcare Div., Deerfield, Ill., 1987—. Office: Baxter Healthcare Corp 1 Overlook Point Lincolnshire IL 60069

GIBNEY, SHARON ANN, lawyer; b. Columbus, Ohio, Aug. 15, 1953; d. Kay Jerome and Margaret Ann (Campbell) G. BA cum laude, Wittenberg U., 1975; JD, Capital U., Columbus, 1980. Bar: Ohio 1980, Mich. 1989, U.S. Dist. Ct. (so. dist.) Ohio 1981. Atty. Ohio Dept. Taxation, Columbus, 1980-85, Wendy's Internat., Inc., Dublin, Ohio, 1985-88, Little Caesar Enterprises, Inc., Farmington Hills, Mich., 1988-89, Metromedia Steakhouses Inc. (formerly Ponderosa Inc.), Dayton, Ohio, 1989—. Trustee Directions for Youth, Columbus, 1987-88; participant Columbus area Leadership Program, 1985; vol. instr. Columbus YMCA, 1980-85. Mem. ABA (franchise forum com., bus. law sect.), Internat. Franchise Assn. (corp.), Ohio Bar Assn., Mich. Bar Assn., Dayton Bar Assn. (mem. corp. counsel com.), Am. Corp. Counsel Assn. Republican. Mem. Ch. of Christ. Office: Metromedia Steakhouse Inc PO Box 578 Dayton OH 45401-0578

GIBSON, ALTHEA, professional tennis player, golfer, state official; b. Silver, S.C., Aug. 25, 1927; d. Daniel and Annie B. (Washington) G.; m. William A. Darben, Oct. 17, 1965; m. Sydney Llewellyn, Apr. 11, 1983. B.S., Fla. A&M Coll., 1953; D. Pub. Service (hon.), Monmouth Coll., 1980; LittD (hon.), U. N.C., Wilmington, 1987; LHD (hon.), Upsala Coll., 1989. Amateur tennis player U.S., Europe, and S.Am., 1941-58; asst. instr. dept. health and phys. edn. Lincoln U., Jefferson City, Mo., 1953-55; made profl. tennis tour with Harlem Globetrotters, 1959; community rels. rep. Ward Baking Co., 1959; joined Ladies Profl. Golf Assn. as profl. golfer, 1963; apptd. to N.Y. State Recreation Council, 1964; staff mem. Essex County Park Commn., Newark, 1970; recreation supr. Essex County Park Commn., 1970-71; dir. tennis programs, profl. Valley View Racquet Club, Northvale, N.J., 1972; tennis pro Morven, 1973—; athletic commr. State of N.J., Trenton, 1975—; recreation mgr. City of East Orange, N.J., 1980; mem. N.J. State Athletic Control Bd., 1986; spl. cons. Gov.'s Coun. Phys. Fitness and Sports, N.J., 1988—; winner world profl. tennis championship, 1960, Wimbledon Women's Singles Championship, 1957, 58, Wimbledon Women's Doubles Championship, 1956-58, U.S. Women's Singles Championship, 1957, 58. Appeared in the movie The Horse Soldiers, 1958; author: I Always Wanted to Be Somebody, 1958. Named Woman Athlete of Yr. AP Poll, 1957-58; named to Lawn Tennis Hall of Fame and Tennis Mus., 1971; named to Black Athletes Hall of Fame, 1974; named to S.C. Hall of Fame, 1983; named to Fla. Sports Hall of Fame, 1984. Mem. Alpha Kappa Alpha. Home: PO Box 768 East Orange NJ 07019

GIBSON, ELEANOR JACK (MRS. JAMES J. GIBSON), psychology educator; b. Peoria, Ill., Dec. 7, 1910; d. William A. and Isabel (Grier) Jack; m. James J. Gibson, Sept. 17, 1932; children: James J., Jean Grier. BA, Smith Coll., 1931, MA, 1933, DSc (hon.), 1972; PhD, Yale U., 1938; DSc (hon.), Rutgers U., 1973, Trinity Coll., 1982, Bates Coll., 1985, U. S.C., 1987, Emory U., 1990; LHD (hon.), SUNY, Albany, 1984, Miami U., 1989, Miami U., 1989. Asst., instr., asst. prof. Smith Coll., 1931-49; research assoc. psychology Cornell U., Ithaca, N.Y., 1949-66; prof. Cornell U., 1972—, Susan Linn Sage prof. psychology, 1972—; fellow Inst. for Advanced Study, Princeton, 1959-60, Inst. for Advanced Study in Behavioral Scis., Stanford, Calif., 1963-64; vis. prof. Mass. Inst. Tech., 1973, Inst. Child Devel., U. Minn., 1980; vis. disting. prof. U. Calif., Davis, 1978; vis. scientist Salk Inst., La Jolla, Calif., 1979; vis. prof. U. Pa., 1984; Montgomery fellow Dartmouth Coll., 1986; Woodruff vis. prof. psychology Emory U., 1988-90. Author: Principles of Perceptual Learning and Development, 1967 (Century award), (with H. Levin) The Psychology of Reading, 1975. Recipient Wilbur Cross medal Yale U., 1973, Howard Crosby Warren medal, 1977, medal for disting. svc. Tchrs. Coll., Columbia U., 1983; Guggenheim fellow, 1972-73, William James fellow Am. Psychol. Soc., 1989. Fellow AAAS (div. chairperson 1983), Am. Psychol. Assn. (Disting. Scientist award 1968, G. Stanley Hall award 1970, pres. div. 3 1977, Gold medal award 1986); mem. NAS, Eastern Psychol. Assn. (pres. 1968), Soc. Exptl. Psychologists, Nat. Acad. Edn., Psychonomic Soc., Soc. Rsch. in Child Devel. (Disting. Sci. Contbn. award 1981), Am. Acad. Arts and Scis., Brit. Psychol. Soc. (hon.), N.Y. Acad. Scis. (hon.), Italian Soc. Rsch. in Child Devel. (hon.), Phi Beta Kappa, Sigma Xi. Home: RD1 Box 265A Middlebury VT 05753

GIBSON, ELISABETH JANE, principal; b. Salina, Kans., Apr. 28, 1937; d. Cloyce Wesley and Margaret Mae (Yost) Kasson; m. William Douglas Miles, Jr., Aug. 20, 1959 (div.); m. Harry Benton Gibson Jr., July 1, 1970. AB, Colo. State Coll., 1954-57; MA, San Francisco State Coll., 1967-68; EdD, U. No. Colo., 1978; postgrad. U. Denver, 1982. Cert. tchr., prin., Colo. Tchr. elem. schs., Santa Paula, Calif., 1957-58, Salina, Kans., 1958-63, Goose Bay, Labrador, 1963-64, Jefferson County, Colo., 1965-66, Topeka, 1966-67; diagnostic tchr. Cen. Kans. Diagnostic Remedial Edn. Ctr., Salina, 1968-70; instr. Loretto Heights Coll., Denver, 1970-72; co-owner Ednl. Cons. Enterprises, Inc., Greeley, Colo., 1974-77; resource coord. Region VIII Resource Access Project Head Start Mile High Consortium, Denver, 1976-77; exec. dir. Colo. Fedn. Coun. Exceptional Children, Denver, 1976-77; asst. prof. Met. State Coll., Denver, 1979; dir. spl. edn. N.E. Colo. Bd. Coop. Edn. Svcs., Haxtun, Colo., 1979-82; prin. elem. jr. high sch., Elizabeth, Colo., 1982-84; prin., spl. projects coord. Summit County Schs., Frisco, Colo., 1985—; prin. Frisco Elem. Sch., 1985—; cons. Montana Dept. Edn., 1978-79, Love Pub. Co., 1976-78, Colo. Dept. Inst., 1974-75; cons. Colo. Dept. Edn., 1984-85, mem. proposal reading com., 1987—; pres. Found. Exceptional Children, 1980-81; pres. bd. dirs. N.E. Colo. Svcs. Handicapped, 1981-82; bd. dirs. Dept. Ednl. Specialists, Colo. Assn. Sch. Execs., 1982-84; mem. Colo. Title IV Adv. Coun., 1980-82; mem. Mellon Found. grant steering com. Colo. Dept. Edn., 1984-85. Mem. Colo. Dept. Edn. Data Acquisition Reporting and Utilization Com., 1983, Denver City County Commn. for Disabled, 1978-81; chmn. regional edn. com. 1970 White House Conf. Children and Youth; bd. dirs. Advocates for Victims of Assault, 1986—; mem. adv. bd. Alpine Counseling Ctr., 1986—; mem. placement alternatives commn. Dept. Social Svcs., 1986—; mem. adv. com. Colo. North Cen. Assn., 1988—; mem. tchr. cert. task force Colo. State Bd. Edn., 1990—. Recipient Ann. Svc. award Colo. Fedn. Coun. Exceptional Children, 1981; San Francisco State Coll. fellow, 1967-68. Mem. Colo. Assn. Retarded Citizens, Assn. Supervision Curriculum Devel., Nat. Assn. Elem. Sch. Prins., North Cen. Assn. (state adv. com. 1988—), Kappa Delta Pi, Pi Lambda Theta, Phi Delta Kappa. Republican. Methodist. Club: Order Eastern Star. Author: (with H. Padzensky) Goal Guide: A minicourse in writing goals and behavioral objectives for special education, 1975; (with H. Padzensky and S. Sporn) Assaying Student Behavior: A minicourse in student assessment techniques, 1974; contbr. articles to profl. jours. Home: 2443 S Colorado Blvd Denver CO 80222 Office: Frisco Elem Sch PO Box 7 Frisco CO 80443

GIBSON, ELIZABETH HARRIS, retired educator, counselor and educational administrator; b. Buhl Tuscaloosa County, Ala.; d. Levi and Carrie (Craig) Harris; m. Alvernis Rochelle, Aug. 9, 1944 (div. 1966); children: Cyntheia, Karen D.; m. John Gibson Jr., Mar. 9, 1974. BA, Stillman Coll., Tuscaloosa, 1952; MEd, Wayne State U., 1960; Edn. Specialist degree, U. Ala., 1971. Cert. tchr., counselor, Ala. Tchr. Tuscaloosa City Schs., 1953-71; tchr., counselor City Pub. Schs., Tuscaloosa, 1965-71; dir., coordinator career counseling and placement Saginaw Valley State U., University Center, Mich., 1971-78; ret., 1978; summer freshman counselor U. Ala., 1968-70. Chmn. bd. dirs. Child Day Care Learning Ctr., Bethel A.M.E. Ch., Saginaw, 1979—, organizer, chmn., adviser quality of life outreach, 1982-83; sec., mem. exec. bd. Mitten Bay (Mich.) coun. Girl Scouts U.S., 1978—; mem., organizer, convenor, chmn. Saginaw Nat. Issues Forum, 1982. Recipient Educator of Yr. award United Sisterhood-Wolverine State Bapt. Assn., 1981, Outstanding Svc. award Nat. Issues Forum, Washington, 1986. Mem. AAUW, LWV (sec.), Top Ladies of Distinction, Zeta Phi Beta (Woman of Yr. 1985, named to Zeta Hall of Fame 1988). Methodist. Home: 5191 Gatesboro Dr S Saginaw MI 48603

GIBSON, HELENA CHRISTINE, financial executive; b. Great Falls, Mont., July 22, 1937; d. Albert Henry Birch and Edith Lillian (Kyhn) Barth; divorced; children: Forrest Christian, Sherwood Paul, Carolyn Diane. BS, Calif. State U., Sacramento, 1980, MS, MA, 1982. Cert. fin. planner; registered prin., registered investment advisor. Prin. Chris Gibson, Enrolled Agt., Sacramento, 1976—; pres. Gibson's Fin. Planning and Investment Svcs. Inc., Carmichael, Calif., 1982-90; prin., registered investment advisor 1st Affiliated Securities, Inc., Bellevue, Wash., 1990—; expert witness, securities. Vol. Boy Scouts Am., Sacramento and Roseville, Calif., 1969-76; publicity chmn. St. Jude's Cath. ch., Redmond, Wash., 1990—. Recipient Silver Bear award Boy Scouts Am., 1974. Mem. Inst. Cert. Fin. Planners, Internat. Assn. Fin. Planning (program chmn. 1988), Comstock Club, Sacramento Met. C. of C., Bellevue Met. C. of C. Office: 1st Affiliated Securities Inc 10500 NE 8th St Ste 1400 Bellevue WA 98004-4347

GIBSON, KARON WHITE, nurse, corporate executive; b. Chgo., Oct. 31, 1946; d. Ronald Dugald and Vilma (Sada) White; m. R. Gibson. Diploma, Mt. Sinai Hosp., 1967. RN, Ill. Nurse Mt. Sinai Med. Ctr., Chgo., Christ Hosp.; nurse, pres. Am. Nurse, Chgo., chief exec. officer; cons. Nurses Registry, New Orleans, 1988—. Pub. rels. chair Nawbo, Chgo. Named Bus. Owner of the Yr., Nat. Assn. Women Bus. Owners, 1982. Mem. Am. Assn. Occupational Health Nurses. Republican. Episcopalian. Office: Am Nurse 5446 S Archer Ave Chicago IL 60638

GIBSON, KATHLEEN RITA, anatomy and anthropology educator; b. Phila., Oct. 9, 1942; d. Keath Pope and Rita Irene (Shewell) G. BA, U. Mich., 1963; MA, U. Calif., Berkeley, 1969, PhD, 1970. Teaching assoc. U. Calif., Berkeley, 1965-69; lectr., adj. assoc. prof. Rice U., Houston, 1973—; asst. prof. U. Tex. Health Sci. Ctr., Houston, 1970-73, assoc. prof., 1973-80, prof., 1980—; mem. com. on parenting behavior Social Sci. Rsch. Coun.,

N.Y.C., 1980-89;. Editor: (with S. Parker) Language and Intelligence in Monkeys and Apes, 1990, (with A. Petersen) Brain Maturation and Cognitive Development, 1990; co-author: (with M. Thames and K. Molokon) Genealogy and Demography of the West Main Cries, 1989; contbr. articles, commentaries, and abstracts to profl. jours. Mem. publs. com. Am. Assn. Primatologists, 1987-89. Conf. grantee Wenner Gren Found., 1990, Sloan Found., 1985, travel grantee NSF, 1984, 86, travel grant brit. Soc. Devel. Biology, 1982. Fellow Am. Assn. Phys. Anthropologists, Am. Assn. Anthropologists; mem. Am. Assn. Anatomists, AAAS, Internat. Primatological Assn., Lang. Origins Soc. Office: U Tex Health Sci Ctr Dept Anatom Scis Houston TX 77225

GIBSON, MARY E., education; b. Paw Paw, Mich., Mar. 9, 1939; d. Max Wilbur and Evelyn W. (Moshier) Harris; children: Scott, Stacy, Kevin. BBS, Western Mich U., 1961. Pres. Mary Gibson and Assocs.; co-owner Ednl. Showcase. Mem. Mich. Assn. Edn. Rep., Mich. Tchr. ESL. Office: 1334 Wheaton Troy MI 48083

GIBSON, NANCY JONES, managerial; b. Island, Ky., May 8, 1955; d. Eliga and Margie Marie (Jones) Romans; m. Billie A. Gibson II, June 9, 1989. Sec. cert., Bowling Green Bus. Coll., 1975. Sec. to dir. of food svcs. Western Ky. U., Bowling Green, 1975-77; sales sec., shipping supr. Union Inc., Costa Mesa, Calif., 1977-78, 80-82; exec. sec., claims, customer svc. mgr. Beacon Bay Enterprises, Inc., Newport Beach, Calif., 1982-88; exec. sec. Weiser Lock, Hunting Beach, Calif., 1988-89; human resource asst. McDonnell Douglas Space Systems Co., Hunting Beach, 1989-90. Mem. rsch. bd. advisors, dep. gov. Am. Biog. Inst. Mem. NAFE, Big Sisters Am., Father Flanagan's Boys Town, Women's Inner Circle of Achievement. Home: 16701 Bartlett Ln #2 Huntington Beach CA 92647 Office: 5301 Bolsa Ave Huntington Beach CA 92647

GIBSON, PATRICIA ANN, library administrator; b. Joplin, Mo., Nov. 14, 1942; d. Arrell Morgan and Dorothy (Deitz) G. BA in English, U. Okla., 1963, MLS, 1966, PhD in Edn., 1977. English tchr. Norman (Okla.) Pub. Schs., 1963-65; pub. svcs. librarian U. Okla. Health Scis. Ctr., Oklahoma City, 1966-68, serials librarian, 1971-72, dir. media prodn., 1972-77; coord. library svcs. Okla. Regional Med. Program, 1968-70; head reference dept. Wichita State U., 1978-80; mgr. library devel. DataPhase Systems, Inc., Kansas City, Mo., 1980-82; v.p. info. systems, library dir. Am. Acad. Family Physicians Found., Kansas City, 1982—; cons. Am. Coll. Cardiology Library, 1986-87. Contbr. articles to profl. jours. Chmn. regional screening com. Am. Field Svc., Kansas City, 1987-89. Kellogg Found. grantee, 1987-88. Mem. Med. Library Assn. (cert. chmn. library rsch. sect. 1989-90, chmn. med. library edn. sect. 1985), Kansas City Met. Library Network (pres. 1986, sec. 1987-89—), U. Mo./Kansas City Women's Coun. Democrat. Presbyterian. Office: Am Acad Family Physicians Found 8880 Ward Pkwy PO Box 8418 Kansas City MO 64114-0418

GIBSON, PEGGY KATHRYN, marketing professional; b. Council Hill, Okla., Feb. 14, 1936; d. Elmer Earl and Christina Kathryn (Emmons) Sharp; m. Stanley T. Gibson, June 5, 1955; children: Coyne A., Kelly S. Student, Okla. State U., 1953-54, Houston Community Coll., 1974-76. Sec. Shanks Ins. Agy., Drumright, Okla., 1954-55, office mgr., 1955-56; underwriter Robert G. Perrine, Tulsa, Okla., 1956-58; office mgr. Girling Health Care, Austin, Tex., 1969-70; sr. sec. Hudson Engring., Houston, 1973-74, sr. supr., 1974-78; office mgr. Bell & Murphy & Assocs., Houston, 1978-81; exec. mgr. Girling Health Care, Houston, 1981-85; v.p., sec., treas., bd. dirs. Jofree Corp., Houston, 1985—. Bd. advisors Hosp. Vols., Austin, 1968; mem. Nat. Coun. on Aging, Houston, 1983. Mem. NAFE, Am. Bus. Womens Assn., Tex. Ind. Producers and Royalty Owners Assn. Republican. Office: Jofree Corp 1100 Louisiana Ste 3610 Houston TX 77002

GIBSON, ROBERTA MAXINE, manufacturing executive; b. Modesto, Calif., July 10, 1944; d. Ernest Milton Olson and Julia Pauline (Perkins) Crites; m. Tommie Gibson. Student, Modesto Jr. Coll., 1969. Operator Pacific Telephone, Modesto, Calif., 1966-68; mgr. Fashion Two Twenty Cosmetics, Modesto, 1968-74; salesperson Bob May Real Estate, Modesto, 1977-79; owner Oakdale (Calif.) Hobby Horse Ceramics, 1985--. Mem. Oakdale C. of C., Nat. Fed. Independent Bus., Calif. Assn. Republican. Office: Oakdale Hobby Horse Ceramic 10513 Pioneer Ave Oakdale CA 95361

GIBSON, ROBERTA SUZANNE, hospital nurse-executive; b. Ladysmith, Wis., Feb. 8, 1950; d. Robert Earl and Margaret Elizabeth (Holmes) Foizie; m. Bruce Harley Gibson, Nov. 18, 1972; children: Robin Dawn, Kimberly Margaret. Diploma in nursing, Madison Gen. Hosp., 1973; BS in Health Care Adminstrn., U. Minn., 1990. RN; cert. nurse adminstr. Staff nurse Divine Savior Hosp., Portage, Wis., 1973, U. Wis. Hosp., Madison, 1974; program dir., nurse Roseau (Minn.) Children's Home, 1975-76; supr. long term care unit Roseau Area Hosp., 1976-78, adminstr. asst., 1978-79, dir. nursing, 1979—. Bd. dirs., mem. adv. com. Northland Commnity Coll., Thief River Falls, Minn., 1989—. Maternal and child health grantee Quin County Bd. Health, 1984—. Mem. Minn. Orgn. Nurse Execs. (chmn. govt. affairs com. 1987-90, pres. Dist. A 1990), Am. Orgn. Nurse Execs. Home: Box 55 HCR 4 Roseau MN 56751 Office: Roseau Area Hosp 715 Delmore Dr Roseau MN 56751

GIBSON, VALERIE, emergency room and intensive care adminstrator, instructor; b. Grosse Point, Mich., July 15, 1957; d. Mario and Louise (Fiori) Bulgarelli; m. Mark Gibson, Apr. 25, 1987; 1 child, Briana Renee. BSN, Ea. Mich. U., 1980; MA, Cen. Mich. U., 1985. Cert. nursing asst., cert. nursing adminstr. 1988. Adminstrv. mgr. Hutzel Hosp., Detroit, critical care educator; clin. nurse educator St. John Hosp., Detroit, asst. mgr., preceptor, adminstr. emergency rm. and intensive care unit, 1985—. Author: Structured vs. Nonstructured Orientation Programs in a Critical Care Setting. Lt. Grosse Pointe Power Squadron. Mem. AACN, Sigma Iota Epsilon, Sigma Theta Tau. Home: 22484 Ardmore Pk Saint Clair Shores MI 48081 Office: 4707 St Antoine Detroit MI 48201

GIBSON, WANDA D., educational coordinator; b. Phoenixville, Pa., Oct. 5, 1948; d. Walter Norris and Cora Lee (Travis) Durden; m. Kenneth Gibson, Aug. 1, 1970; children: Wendy, Jeremy. BS, Ashland (Ohio) Coll., 1976; postgrad., Wright State U., current. Ednl. coor. DRET Schs., Inc., Miamisburg, Ohio; registrar dept. head, instr. DRET Schs., Inc., Springfield, Ohio; tchr. Pioneer Joint Vocat. Sch., Shelby, Ohio; sec. Robert W. Lett, Esq., Ashland, Ohio; Workshop leader on lesson plans devel. Mem. NAFE, Ohio Bus. Tchrs. Assn., Kappa Delta Pi. Home: 5417 Taywell Dr Springfield OH 45503

GIDDENS, ZELMA KIRK, broadcast executive; b. Lafayette, Ala.; d. James William and Eunice (Rice) Kirk; grad. So. Union Jr. Coll., 1932; student Auburn U., 1934-35; m. Kenneth R. Giddens, May 19, 1934; children: Annsley Giddens Green, Therese Giddens Greer, Sara Kay Glenday. With Sta. WKRG-AM, 1947-55; with Sta. WKRG-AM-FM-TV, Mobile, Ala., 1955—, vice chmn., treas., 1960—. Founder, Mus. for Women's Art, Washington; trustee, Nat. Symphony. Mem. Smithsonian Assos., Mobile C. of C., Nat. Gallery Art Circle, Friends of Kennedy Ctr., Nat. Press Club, Am. Newspaper Women's Assn. Home: 2555 N Delwood Dr Mobile AL 36606 Office: 555 Broadcast Dr Mobile AL 36616

GIDEON, SHARON LEE, educator; b. Roswell, N.Mex., Mar. 24, 1955; d. Talmage Dever and Maggie Lee (Payton) Dever Franklin. BA, Baylor U., 1977; MLA, So. Meth. U., 1985. Teaching cert., Tex. Tchr. Plano (Tex.) ISD, Klein ISD, Spring, Tex., Sulphur Springs (Tex.) ISD. Author: History and Relationship to it Environment. Mem. PEA (a.r. rep. chair external communication 1989, a.r. rep. chair, mem. chair 1990). Mem. TSTA, NEA, Plano Edn. Assn., Classical Assn. of the Middle and S. Am. Classical League, Tex. State Jr. Classical League, Eastern Star. Republican. Baptist. Home: 3618 Hilltop Ln Plano TX 75023 Office: Clark High Sch 529 Spring Creek Pkwy Plano TX 75023

GIDEON-HAWKE, PAMELA LAWRENCE, fine arts, small business owner; b. N.Y.C., Aug. 23, 1945; d. Lawrence Ian Verry and Lily S. (Stein) Gordon; m. Jarrett Redstone, June 27, 1964; 1 child, Justin Craig Hawke. Grad. high sch., Manhattan. Owner Gideon Gallery Ltd., L.A., 1975—; prin. Pamela L. Gideon-Hawke Pub. Rels., L.A., 1984—. Sec. Design Alliance to Combat Aids, L.A., 1986—; pres. San Fernando Valley West Point Parents Club, 1990—. Named Friend of Design Industry Designers West Mag., 1987. Mem. Am. Soc. Interior Designers (publicist), Internat. Soc. Interior Designers (trade liaison 1986-88), Network Exec. Women in Hosp. (hospitality chairwoman 1990—), Internat. Furnishings & Design Assn. (programs chmn.). Office: Gideon-Hawke Pub Rels 8748 Melrose Ave Los Angeles CA 90069 Also: 8748 Melrose Ave Los Angeles CA 90069

GIDWITZ, NANCY, marketing executive; b. Chgo., Mar. 30, 1948; d. Gerald Saul and Jane (Blumenthal) G.; m. John M. Gleason Jr. (div. 1986). BA, Brown U., 1970. Editorial asst. Am. Geog. Soc., N.Y.C., 1971-72; free lance various prodn. cos., N.Y.C., 1972; producer Joshua Tree Prodns., N.Y.C., 1973-74; prodn. mgr. Edward Deitch, N.Y.C., 1975; account exec. New Dimensions Mktg., Chgo., 1975-79, v.p., 1979-84, pres., 1984—. V.p., bd. dirs. Chgo. Acad. Scis., 1981-84, 86-90, sec. 1984-86; trustee Brown U., Providence, R.I., 1982-88; bd. dirs. Ill. Spl. Events Commn., Chgo., Springfield, 1977-84. Mem. NATAS, Publicity Club Chgo. Office: New Dimensions Mktg 213 W Institute Pl Chicago IL 60610

GIER, AUDRA MAY CALHOON, environmental chemist; b. Bella Vista, Peru, Aug. 21, 1940; came to U.S., 1944; d. Nathan Moore and Olivia Cleo (Hite) Calhoon; m. Delta Warren Gier, Apr. 4, 1968. BA, Austin Coll., 1962; MS in Chemistry, Kans. State Coll., 1964; MA in History of Sci., U. Wis., 1974; postgrad., York U., Toronto, Can., 1974-79. Food technologist Midwest Rsch. Inst., Kansas City, Mo., 1963-64; chemist Mobay (formerly Chemagro), Kansas City, 1964-67; instr. chemistry St. Andrews Presbyn. Coll., Laurinburg, N.C., 1967-68; chemist Cardinal Chem. Co., Columbia, S.C., 1968; asst. prof. chemistry Lea Coll., Albert Lea, Minn., 1969-72; psychology intern emergency unit Thistletown Regional Centre for Children & Adolescents, Toronto, Ontario, Can., 1975-77; assoc. prof. chemistry Cleveland Chiropractic Coll., Kansas City, 1979-84; adj. faculty Park Coll., Parkville, Mo., 1982—; environ. chemist, quality assurance specialist Ecology & Environ., Inc., Overland Park, Kans., 1987—; pres. Delta and Assocs., Inc., Kansas City, 1988—. Author: Highlights of Organic Chemistry, 1985; co-editor: (with D.W. Gier) History and Directory of Chemical Education, 1974, (with D.W. Gier) Peace is Something Speshl; co-inventor, co-patentee acetylenic ketones as herbicides. Adv. bd. Kansas City Interfaith Peace Alliance, 1980—, bd. dirs., 1982-85, pres. 1985-86; bd. dirs. Prairie Star Dist./Unitarian-Universalist Midwest (Upper), 1985—; co-chair Bragg Symposium on Humanism, Kansas City. 1980—; chair Social Responsibility Com. (Prairie Star dist. UUA), 1986—. Recipient Social Justice award Social Justice Com. Prairie Star Dist, 1985; named Woman of Yr., 1982, Humanist of Yr., 1987, All Souls Unitarian Ch., Kansas City. Mem. ACLU, DAR, Am. Chem. Soc., Am. Soc. for Quality Control, Inst. for Society, Ethics, and the Life Scis., Midwest Bioethics Ctr., Planned Parenthood, Nat. Abortion Rights Action League. Democrat. Home: 5828 Cherry Kansas City MO 64110

GIER, KARAN HANCOCK, counseling psychologist; b. Sedalia, Mo., Dec. 7, 1947; d. Ioda Clyde and Lorna (Campbell) Hancock; m. Thomas Robert Gier, Sept. 28, 1968. BA in Edn., U. Mo., Kansas City, 1971; MA Teaching in Math/Sci. Edn., Webster U., 1974; MA in Counseling Psychology, Western Colo. U., 1981; MEd Guidance and Counseling, U. Alaska, 1981; PhD in Counseling, Pacific Western U., 1989. Nat. cert. counselor. Instr. grades 5-8 Kansas City-St. Joseph Archdiocese, 1969-73; ednl. cons. Pan-Ednl. Inst., Kansas City, 1973-75; instr., counselor Bethel (Alaska) Regional High Sch., 1975-80; ednl. program coord. Western Regional Resource Ctr., Anchorage, 1980-81; counselor U. Alaska, Anchorage, 1982-83; coll. prep. instr. Alaska Native Found., Anchorage, 1982; counselor USAF, Anchorage, 1985-86; prof. U. Alaska, Anchorage, 1982—; dir. Omni Counseling Svcs., Anchorage, 1984—; prof. Chapman Coll., Anchorage, 1988—; workshop facilitator over 100 workshops on the topics of counseling techs., value clarification, non-traditional teaching approaches, peer-tutor tng. Co-author: Coping with College, 1984, Helping Others Learn, 1985; editor, co-author: A Student's Guide, 1983. Mem. Am. Bus. Women's Assn., Blue Springs, Mo., 1972-75, Ctr. for Environ. Edn., World Wildlife Fund, Beta Sigma Phi, Bethel, Alaska, 1976-81. Recipient 3rd place color photo Yukon-Kuskokwim State Fair, Bethel, 1978. Mem. Coll. Reading & Learning Assn. (peer tutor sig leader 1988—), Am. Assn. Counseling & Devel., Alaska Assn. Counseling & Devel. (pres. 1989-90), Alaska Career Devel. Assn. (pres.-elect 1989-90), Nat. Rehab. Assn., Nat. Rehab. Counselors, Greenpeace, Human Soc. of the U.S. Wolf Haven Am., Wolf Song of Alaska. Home: 8102 Harvest Circle Anchorage AK 99502 Office: Omni Counseling Svcs 8102 Harvest Circle Anchorage AK 99502

GIERLASINSKI, KATHY LYNN, accountant; b. Chewelah, Wash., May 21, 1951; d. John Edward and Margaret Irene (Seefeldt) Rail; m. Norman Joseph Gierlasinski, May 23, 1987. BBA, Gonzaga U., 1984. CPA, Wash. Legal sec. Redbook Pub. Co., N.Y.C., 1974-75, Howard Michaelson, Esquire, Spokane, Wash., 1975-76; sec. Burns Internat. Security Svcs., Spokane, 1977-79; sec. to contr. Gonzaga U., Spokane, 1979-81, acctg. asst., 1981-82; staff acct. Martin, Holland & Petersen, CPA's, Yakima, Wash., 1984-87; sr. staff acct. Strader Hallet & Co., P.S., Bellevue, Wash., 1988—; treas. White Pass Ski Patrol, Nat. Ski Patrol Systems, Wash., 1987—; editor, chmn. audit com. Mt. Spokane Ski Patrol, 1983-84. Mem. AICPA (charter), Am. Soc. Women Accts. (editor 1987), Nat. Assn. Accts., Wash. Soc. CPAs (sec. Sammamish Valley chpt. 1990—). Republican. Lutheran. Home: 21730 2d Ave SE Bothell WA 98021 Office: Strader Hallett & Co PS 2750 Northup Way Ste 400 Bellevue WA 98004

GIESLER, JEANETTE LOUISE, business owner, clothing executive; b. Cripple Creek, Colo., July 25, 1952; d. Harry John and Phyllis Etta (Akin) G.; m. George Edmund Ormsby, June 2, 1974 (div. June 1982); children: Zachary Edmund Montgomery, Elisabet Ney. Student, Clark County Community Coll., 1972-75, U. Nev., Las Vegas, 1974-75. Owner Pepis Casino Clothiers, Las Vegas, 1974-81, Western Bar Supply, Las Vegas, 1980-82, Shirt Lady & Co., Las Vegas, 1980-85; real estate acquisition rep. J.R. Biven's & Assoc., Denver, 1985-86; owner Profl. Clothing Co., Las Vegas, 1986—. Campaign coord. Gov.'s and State Treas.'s Race, Clark City; bd. dirs. Nev. Zool. Soc., Las Vegas, 1984-87. Mem. NAFE. Democrat. Episcopalian. Office: Profl Clothing Co 2590 State St Las Vegas NV 89109

GIFFIN, MARGARET ETHEL (PEGGY GUFFIB), management consultant; b. Cleve., Aug. 27, 1949; d. Arch Kenneth and Jeanne (Eggleton) G.; m. Robert Alan Wyman, Aug. 20, 1988; 1 child, Samantha Jean. BA in Psychology, U. Pacific, Stockton, Calif., 1971; MA in Psychology, Calif. State U., Long Beach, 1973; PhD in Quantitative Psychology, U. So. Calif., 1984. Psychometrist Auto Club So. Calif., Los Angeles, 1973-74; cons. Psychol. Services, Inc., Glendale, Calif., 1975-76, mgr., 1977-78, dir., 1979—; researcher Social Sci. Research Inst., U. So. Calif., Los Angeles, 1981; instr. Calif. State U., Long Beach, 1989—; mem. tech. adv. com. on testing Calif. Fair Employment and Housing Commn., 1974—, mem. steering com., 1978—. Mem. Am. Ednl. Rsch. Assn., Soc. Indsl. Organizational Psychology, Am. Psychol. Assn., Personnel Testing Coun. So. Calif. (pres. 1980, exec. dir. 1982, 88, bd. dirs. 1980—). Club: Athletic (Los Angeles). Home: 330 S Westmoreland Ave Los Angeles CA 90020 Office: 100 W Broadway #1100 Glendale CA 91210

GIFFORD, VIRGINIA SNODGRASS, music cataloger and bibliographer; b. Cottonwood, Idaho, June 15, 1936; d. John Howard and Virginia B. (Tibbs) S.; m. Guy A. Gifford, July 29, 1965 (div. Feb. 1973); 1 child, Stephen Jonathan. BA, Cen. Wash. U., 1957, MEd, 1959; MSLS, Cath. U. Am., 1969. Music cataloger Copyright Office, Washington, 1965-69; editor catalog publs. Libr. of Congress, Washington, 1969-73, music cataloger spl. materials cataloging div., 1983—; music libr. Vassar Coll., Poughkeepsie, N.Y., 1973-80; performing arts cataloger copyright office, 1980-83; adj. prof. sch. of libr. and info. sci. Cath. U. Am., 1990—. Author: Music for Oboe, Oboe d'amore, English Horn at the Libr. of Congress, 1983. Mem. Music. Libr. Assn. (chmn. N.Y.-Ont. chpt. 1975-77), Am. Fedn. Musicians, Internat. Double Reed Soc., Royal Scottish Country Dance Soc. Democrat. Methodist. Home: 714 9th St SE Apt 3 Washington DC 20003 Office: Libr of Congress Music Sect SMCD Madison Bldg Rm 547 Washington DC 20547

GIGGAR-JOHNSON, MONYA MARIE, financial services marketing professional; b. Lake Charles, La., Nov. 12, 1957; d. Leo Alfred and Margie Marie (Landry) Giggar; m. Robert Edward Johnson, Apr. 2, 1985. BBA, U. Ark., Little Rock, 1980; MBA, U. North Tex., Denton, 1982. Mktg. researcher Park Davis Appraisers, Dallas, 1982-83; mktg. coord. Dallas Postal Credit Union, 1983-84; pub. rels. support staff Page Hendricks Pub. Rels., Ft. Worth, 1984-85; mgmt. trainer Sunbelt Savs., Dallas, 1985-86; mgr. br. mktg. First Gibraltar Bank FSB, Dallas, 1986-90. Mem. Am. Soc. Tng. and Devel., Women in Communications, Mktg. Masters, 500 Inc. Home and Office: 3033 Cemetery Hill Rd Carrollton TX 75007

GIGLIETTI, PATRICE ANN, financial reporting accountant; b. New Haven, Mar. 22, 1964; d. Robert William and Kathleen Shea (McCormack) G. BSBA magna cum laude, Boston U., 1986. CPA, Mass. Sr. acct. Arthur Andersen & Co., Boston, 1986-89; fin. reporting acct. Thermo Electron Corp., Waltham, Mass., 1989—. Mem. AICPA, Mass. Soc. CPAs, Nat. Assn. Accts., Beta Gamma Sigma, Beta Alpha Psi. Republican. Roman Catholic. Office: Thermo Electron Corp 101 1st Ave PO Box 9046 Waltham MA 02254-9046

GIKAS, CAROL SOMMERFELDT, museum director; b. St. Louis; m. Ken Gikas. Student, U. Mo., 1968-70; BA in Studio Art, U. Ark., Little Rock, 1973; MA, U. Tex., 1977; postgrad. Mus. Mgmt. Inst., U. Calif., summer 1981. Asst. mus. registrar Ark. Arts Ctr., Little Rock, 1972-74; assoc. curator Leeds Gallery, U. Tex., Austin, 1977-80; exec. dir. La. Arts and Sci. Ctr., Baton Rouge, 1980—; mem. grants adv. panel So. Arts Fedn., 1981, Arts & Humanities Council Greater Baton Rouge, 1982, 83, div. arts La. State Arts Council, 1981, 85; mem. adv. bd. U.S.S. Kidd/La. Naval Mus., Baton Rouge, 1981, 84, La. Dept. Edn., 1981; state rep. to council S.E. Mus. Conf., 1984, 85. Sec. Gov.'s commn. for Anniversary of La. State Capitol, 1981, 82; active Baton Rouge C. of C. Goals Conf., 1984, 85, Leadership Greater Baton Rouge, C. of C., 1985, 86; trustee ARC, 1986—; mem. Mayor's Commn. for Bicentennial of U.S. Constn. Mem. Am. Assn. Mus., Art Mus. Assn. (regional rep. 1983—). Office: La Arts & Sci Ctr Inc PO Box 3373 Baton Rouge LA 70821*

GILB, CORINNE LATHROP, history educator; b. Lethbridge, Alta., Can., Feb. 19, 1925; d. Glen Hutchison and Vera (Passey) Lathrop; m. Tyrell Thompson Gilb, Aug. 19, 1945; children: Lesley Gilb Taplin, Tyra. BA, U. Wash., 1946; MA, U. Calif., Berkeley, 1951, law student, 1950-53; PhD, Harvard U., 1957. History lectr. Mills Coll., Oakland, 1957-61; prof. humanities San Francisco State U., 1964-68; rsch. assoc. U. Calif., Berkeley, 1953-68; prof. history Wayne State U., Detroit, 1968—; dir. planning City of Detroit, 1979-85; special cons. Calif. Legis., 1963, 64. Author: Conformity of State to Federal Income Tax, 1964, Hidden Hierarchies, 1966, numerous chpts. in books; contbr. articles to profl. jours. Guggenheim fellow, 1957; grantee Social Sci. Rsch. Coun. Mem. Internat. Soc. Comparative Study of Civilizations (governing council 1985—), No. Calif. World Affairs Council, various acad. assns. Presbyterian.

GILBANE, JEAN ANN (MRS. THOMAS F. GILBANE), construction company executive; b. Providence, Aug. 22, 1923; d. Vincent Thaddeus and Edna (Leary) Murphy; m. Thomas F. Gilbane, Sept. 12, 1946; children: Thomas, Robert, Richard, Jean, John, James. Student, Elmhurst Acad., 1941, Coll. New Rochelle, 1945. Sec. Gilbane Bldg. Co., Providence, 1950-81, treas., 1982—, also bd. dirs.; bd. dirs. Gilbane Properties, B.T. Equipment Co. Active Women's R.I. Hosp. Guild; mem. corp. Emma Bradley Hosp., Butler Hosp.; former trustee Coll. New Rochelle; bd. dirs. Women's Resource Ctr. South County; bd. dirs. So. County Hosp. Decorated lady Order Holy Sepulcher. Roman Catholic. Clubs: Dunes, Point Judith Country (bd. govs. 1985-88); Beach (Palm Beach); University, Wannamoisett. Home: 80 Don Ave Rumford RI 02916 Office: Gilbane Bldg Co 7 Jackson Walkway Providence RI 02940 also: 400 S Ocean Blvd Apt 402 N Palm Beach FL 33480

GILBERT, JOAN STULMAN, petroleum company executive; b. N.Y.C., May 10, 1934; student Conn. Coll. for Women, 1951-53; m. Phil E. Gilbert, Jr., Oct. 6, 1968; children: Linda Cooper, Dana, Patricia. Br. coord. Vol. Service Bur., Westchester, N.Y., 1970-72; public relations dir. Westchester Lighthouse, 1972-76; exec. dir. Westchester Heart Assn., 1976-77; mgr. community rels. Texaco Inc., White Plains, N.Y., 1977—. Bd. dirs. Lend-A-Hand, Coll. Careers, Westchester Edn. Coalition, The Westchester Lighthouse, New Orchestra of Westchester, Westchester Coalition, Youth Counseling League, Pvt. Industry Coun.; former trustee Westchester Coun. for the Arts, Choate-Rosemary Hall, United Way of Westchester, Teatown Lake Reservation. Mem. Met. Transit Authority (insp. gen. mgmt. adv. bd.), Pub. Relations Soc. Am. (chpt. pres. 1977), Advt. Club (dir.), Women in Communications, Sales and Mktg. Execs. Westchester (former dir.). Westchester County Assn. Home: The Croft Spring Valley Rd Ossining NY 10562 Office: 2000 Westchester Ave White Plains NY 10650

GILBERT, JUDITH ARLENE, lawyer; b. Los Angeles, Jan. 9, 1946; d. Beril B. and Dorothy Marilyn (Stern) Gilbert; student U. Calif.-Berkeley, 1963-64; AB in Econs. magna cum laude, UCLA, 1967; JD, Harvard U., 1970; m. Joel Philip Schiff; children: Lauren Michelle, Jared Daniel. Bar: Calif. 1971. Assoc. Rosenfeld, Meyer & Susman, 1970-72, Quittner, Stutman, Treister & Glatt, Los Angeles, 1972-74, Abeles & Markowitz, and predecessor, Beverly Hills Calif., 1974-76; Sr. Counsel legal dept, credit advice-N.Am. Div. Sect. Bank of Am. Nat. Trust & Savs Assn., 1977-88, of counsel Denton, Hall, Burgin & Warrens, 1988-90; contract ptnr. Lewis, D'Arrato, Brisbois & Bisgaard, 1990—; judge protem Mcpl. and Small Claims Ct.; mem. arbitration panel Los Angeles Superior Ct.; planning com. ann. meeting State Bar Calif., 1986-87, also host com. ann. meeting , 1987; bd. dirs. Pub. Counsel, 1986-89. Mem. Los Angeles County Com. Human Resources; active Girl Scouts U.S.A., Cystic Fibrosis, City of Hope; bd. govs. Arthritis Found., 1989; co-chair drugs in workplace task force Temple Emanuel, 1989—; mem. steering com. drugs in workplace program Temple Emanuel-Jewish Fedn. Coun. Mem. ABA (litigation and banking, corp. & comml. sects., comml. transactions litigation com., creditor's rights litigation com., others), Calif. State Bar Conf. (resolutions com. of state bar, 1988—, del. 1973—, vice chair com. living wills and right to die 1977, com. on rights and obligations of unmarried cohabitators 1978-80, and legal separation 1980-81), Los Angeles Bar Assn. (bd. trustees 1984-85, comml. law and bankruptcy, taxation and copyright sects. steering com., co-chair fund raising sub-com. 1986, com. to defeat Prop 6), Beverly Hills Bar Assn. (ex-officio mem. bd. govs., exec. com. pres. 1985-86, 86-87, del. to state bar conf. of dels. 1973—, vice chair, 1980, chair, 1982, 1986, atty. fee disputes panel, numerous other positions), Calif. Women Lawyers Assn., Women Lawyers Assn. Los Angeles, Fin. Lawyers Conf., Comml. Law League Am., Fed. Bar Assn., Thespians, Collegian Singers, Brick Muller Soc., UCLA Alumni Assn. (adv. bd., mem. scholarship bd.), Tower and Flame, Phi Beta Kappa, Gamma Delta Epsilon, Pi Gamma Mu, Omega Delta Epsilon, Phi Chi Theta, Delta Phi Epsilon. Clubs: Merchants, Sutherland (sec.-treas. 1968-69). Office: Lewis D'Amato Brisbois & Bisgaard 261 S Figueroa St Five Pk-Ste 300 Los Angeles CA 90012

GILBERT, JUDITH MAY, human relations executive; b. Miami, Fla., Dec. 2, 1934; d. Stanley C. and Martha (Scheinberg) Myers; children: Robert, Carolyn, Mark. Student, U. N.C., 1952-53; BA, U. Fla., 1956. Project coord. Miami Beach Redevel. Agy., Miami Beach, Fla., 1977-78, dir. community svcs., 1978-79; dir. victim/witness svcs. Office of State's Atty., 11th Judicial Cir. of Fla., Dade County, Miami, 1980; exec. dir. S.E. region Am. Jewish Congress, Miami, 1980-83; assoc. dir. community rels. Greater Miami Jewish Fedn., 1983-90, dir. community rels., 1990—. Bd. dirs. Stanley C. Myers Community Health Ctr. Inc., Miami Beach, 1988—, Dade-Monroe Mental Health Bd., 1982-84, High Sch. in Israel, Miami, 1978-80; mem. Fla. Ednl. Equity Act Adv. Group, Dade County Schs., 1986-88; pres. Nat. Council Jewish Women, Miami, 1974-77; v.p. So. Dist. Nat. Council Jewish Women, 1976-77. Recipient Vol. Activist award Germaine Monteil, 1972, Hannah G. Solomon award Nat. Council Jewish Women, 1978. Mem. AAUW, Nat. Community Relations Dirs. Assn., Human Relations Profls. of Greater Miami, Alpha Epsilon Phi. Office: Greater Miami Jewish Fedn 4200 Biscayne Blvd Miami FL 33137

GILBERT, LINDA CHERYL, food futurist, consultant; b. Panama City, Fla., Nov. 19, 1956; d. Ralf E. and Loretta M. (Greth) G.; m. Raymond W.

Wolf, Mar. 12, 1983; children: Brenna, Ben. BS in Agr. and Food Sci., U. Ariz., 1978. Dir. Rodale Press, Inc., Emmaus, Pa., 1979-88; v.p. Sweet Heat Spice Co., Emmaus, 1987—; pres. HealthFocus, Inc., Emmaus, 1988—. Office: HealthFocus Inc 216 N 4th St Emmaus PA 18049

GILBERT, RACHEL SHAW, state legislator, real estate broker; b. Ottawa, Kans.; d. Herbert M. and L.C. Ferris (Pile) Shaw; B.A., U. Nebr., 1956; M.A., Coll. of Idaho, 1969; children—Cheryl Allison Gilbert Brady, Kimberly Lynn. Sch. tchr., Nebr., 1952-57; broker Walker & Co. Real Estate, Boise, Idaho, 1969-71; broker-owner Gilbert & Assocs. Realtors, Boise, 1972-82; mem. Idaho Ho. of Reps., 1980-83, Idaho Senate, 1984—. Bd. dirs. United Way, Boise, 1963-68, Boise Philharm. Orch., 1966-68; chmn. Idaho Legis. Dist. 15, 1980. Mem. Nat. Assn. Realtors (dir. 1980-86), Idaho Assn. Realtors (dir. 1978-80), Idaho Assn. Commerce and Industry (dir.), Boise C. of C. (v.p. 1979). Republican. Home: 1111 Marshall St Boise ID 83706 Office: 1487 N Cole St Boise ID 83704

GILBERT, SUZANNE HARRIS, advertising executive; b. Chgo., Mar. 8, 1943; d. Lawrence W. and Dorothea (Wilde) Harris; children—Kerry, Elizabeth, Gregory. B.S., Marquette U., 1965; postgrad. U. Chgo., 1983-84. Fin. planner Sci. Research Assocs., Chgo., 1965-67; fin. analyst Leo Burnett Co., Chgo., 1967-70; sr. v.p. fin. adminstrn., sec.-treas. Clinton E. Frank Inc., Chgo., 1975-85; with Campbell-Ewald Co., Detroit, 1985—; formerly group sr. v.p., Lintas: Campbell-Ewald, Warren, Mich.; exec. v.p., chief fin. officer, Lintas: Campbell-Ewald, Warren, 1990—. Office: Lintas: Campbell Ewald 30400 Van Dyke Ave Warren MI 48093

GILBREATH, FREIDA CAROL, data processing executive; b. Huntsville, Ala., Oct. 26, 1949; d. Murray and Edna Merle (Smith) Dixon; m. Robert Keith Gilbreath, May 4, 1969; children: Scott McKinley, Emily Luanne. Student, N.E. Jr. Coll., Rainsville, Ala., 1967-69. Cashier Dunnavant's Dept. Store, Huntsville, 1968-69; sec. Pensacola (Fla.) Mill Supply Co., 1970-71; bookkeeper Arkay Trucking Co., Guntersville, Ala., 1971-72, Creswell Indsl. Supply, Guntersville, 1972; computer operator Guntersville Hosp., 1972-77, Housing Devel. Co., Huntsville, 1977-79; data systems coord. Bapt. Med. Ctr., Fort Payne, Ala., 1979-84, Centre, Ala., 1982-84; programmer-analyst Bapt. Med. Ctr., Birmingham, Ala., 1984—. Mem. Data Processing Mgmt. Assn., NAFE. Methodist. Office: Bapt Med Ctr 3201 4th Ave S Birmingham AL 35222

GILCHRIST, ANNE MARIE, computer scientist; b. Augusta, Ga., Apr. 23, 1960; d. Albert Waller and Agnes Marie (Gallaher) G.; 1 child Joanna Christine. BS in Info. and Computer Sci., Ga. Inst. Tech., 1982, MS in Info. and Computer Sci., 1988. Sr. software analyst Intergraph, Huntsville, Ala., 1982-84; software engring. mgr. Sales Technologies, Inc., Atlanta, 1989; rsch. scientist Ga. Tech. Rsch. Inst., Atlanta, 1984-89, 89—; software engring. mgr. Sales Techs., Inc., Atlanta, 1989. Mem. Assn. for Computing Machinery, Computer Soc. of IEEE. Home: 2417 Woodacres Rd NE Atlanta GA 30345 Office: Ga Tech GTRI/ECSL/CSTD Atlanta GA 30332

GILCHRIST, ELLEN LOUISE, writer; b. Vicksburg, Miss., Feb. 20, 1935; d. William Garth and Aurora (Alford) G.; children—Marshall Peteet Walker, Jr., Garth Gilchrist Walker, Pierre Gautier Walker. B.A. in Philosophy, Millsaps Coll., 1967; postgrad., U. Ark., 1976. Freelance writer, journalist; commentator, morning edit. of news Nat. Pub. Radio, Washington, 1984, 85. Author: The Land Surveyor's Daughter, 1979, In The Land of Dreamy Dreams, 1981, The Annunciation (Book of Month Club alternate in U.S. and Sweden), 1983, Victory Over Japan (Am. Book award 1984), 1984, Drunk With Love, 1986, Falling Through Space, 1987, The Anna Papers, 1988, Light Can Be Both Wave and Particle, 1989, (poems) Riding Out the Tropical Depression; contbr. short stories poems to literary publs. Recipient Poetry award U. Ark., 1976, Craft in Poetry award N.Y. Quar., 1978, Fiction award The Prairie Schooner, 1981, Poetry award Miss. Arts Festival, 1968, Saxifrage award, 1983, Fiction award Miss. Acad. Arts and Sci., 1982, 85, Am. Book award Victory Over Japan, 1984, J. William Fulbright prize U. Ark., 1985, Lit. award Miss. Inst. Arts and Letters, 1985; 2 Pushcart prizes; grantee NEA, 1979. Mem. Author's Guild.

GILE, MARY STUART, educational executive; b. Montreal, Que., Can., Mar. 24, 1936; d. William Gillies and Hazel Irene (Stuart) Sinclair; m. Robert Hall Gile, Mar. 29, 1974; children—D. Christopher, Julia Mary, John, Robertson Sinclair. BS, McGill U., 1957; MEd, U. N.H., 1971; EdD, Vanderbilt U., 1982. Specialist phys. edn. Protestant Sch. Bd. Greater Montreal, 1957-64, kindergarten tchr. White Mountains Sch. Bd., Littleton, N.H., 1965-67; dir. Open Door Kindergarten, Salem, N.H., 1967-69; coord. State Follow Through, State of N.H., 1969-80, N.H. Right to Read, 1973-74, U.S. Sec.'s Initiative in Excellence chpt. 1 Edn. Consol. and Improvement Act, 1983-84; sr. cons. edn. N.H. State Dept. Edn., Concord, 1969-85; v.p. edn. and devel. Acad. Applied Sci., Concord, 1985—; coord. early childhood cert. and degree programs N.H. Tech. Inst., Concord, 1989—; state dept. staff assoc. to U. N.H., Durham, 1970-74; mem. Gov.'s Task Force on Sexual Harassment, Concord, 1981-83; chair N.H. Trust Fund for Prevention of Child Abuse and Neglect, 1986, Commr.'s Com. on Alt. Work Schedules, Concord, 1982-84; commr.'s rep. State Day Care Adv. Com., Concord, 1984-85. Contbr. articles to profl. jours. Pres. Concord Parents and Children, 1977-82; chmn. Citizens Adv. Bd. to Community Devel., 1978-82; bd. govs. Merrimack County United Way, 1983-88; pres. N.H. Assn. for Mental Health, 1984-86. Recipient Appreciation cert. Maine Dept. Edn., 1984, cert. outstanding achievement N.H. State Bd. Edn., 1985, Imperial Oil Ltd. scholar, 1953; U. N.H. early childhood fellow, 1969. Mem. N.H. Assn. for Edn. Young Children, Phi Delta Kappa. Congregationalist. Avocations: skiing, music, theater, hiking.

GILES, JEAN HALL, retired corporate exececutive; b. Dallas, Mar. 30, 1908; d. C. D. and Ida (McIntyre) Overton; m. Alonzo Russell Hall, II, Jan. 23, 1923 (dec.); children: Marjorie (Mrs. Kenneth C. Hodges, Jr.), Alonzo Russell III; m. Harry E. Giles, Apr. 24, 1928 (div. 1937); 1 child, Janice Ruth; 1 adopted child, Marjean Giles. Student Colo. State Christian Coll., Hamilton State Univ. Capt., comdg. officer S.W. Los Angeles Women's Ambulance and Def. Corps., 1941-43; maj., nat. exec. officer Women's Ambulance and Def. Corps, 1944-45; capt., dir. field ops. Communications Corps of the U.S. Nat. Staff, 1951-52; dir. Recipe of the Month Club. Active Children's Hosp. Benefit, 1946; coord. War Chest Motor Corps, 1943-44; dir. Los Angeles Area War Chest Vol. Corps and Motor Corps, 1945-46; realtor Los Angeles Real Estate Exchange, 1948—, now ret.; also partner Tech. Contractors, Los Angeles. Bd. dirs. Tchr. Remembrance Day Found. Inc. Mem. Los Angeles C. of C. (women's div.), A.I.M., Los Angeles Art Assn., Hist. Soc. So. Calif., Opera Guild So. Calif., Assistance League So. Calif., Needlework Guild Am. (sect. pres. Los Angeles), First Century Families Calif., Internat. Platform Assn. Clubs: Athletic; Town Hall, The Garden (Los Angles); Pacific Coast. Home: P O Box 01-443 Long Beach CA 90801

GILES, JUDITH MARGARET, communication educator; b. Sonora, Calif., Nov. 20, 1939; d. James Wilson and Phyllis Sue (Stafford) G. BA, Calif. State U., 1982; MA, CBN U., Virginia Beach, Va., 1986; A. Ministry, Christ for the Nations, Dallas, 1974. Real estate broker Mason McDuffie, Berkeley, Calif., 1975-77, Taylor Realty, Sonora, Calif., 1978-82; adminstr., instr. Christ for the People, Pleasant Hill, Calif., 1975-77, Mt. Zion Ministries, Concord, Calif., 1977-88; instr. Calif. Assn. Realtors, Sacramento, 1980-82; adminstrv. asst., instr. Air Force Chaplaincy, Washington, 1983-84; asst. media/press coordinator Nat. Religious Broadcasters, Washington, 1983-86; grad. teaching asst. Christian Broadcasting Network U., Virginia Beach, Va., 1984-86; instr. Global Outreach Bible Inst., Modesto, Calif., 1987—; real estate broker Re/Max Real Estate Cen., Modesto, Calif., 1987—; lectr. in field; communications cons.; radio commentator; TV guest host. Author: A Historical Overview of the Women's Movement in America, 1986; producer, dir. TV documentary: The United Jewish Fedn., 1985, What's in a Name, 1985, Chiropractic, Lutheran Council, 1984. Mgr. pub. relations dir. South Lake Tahoe Community Choir, 1971. Named Assoc. of Yr., Recruiter of Yr. Century 21, 1987. Mem. Calif. Assn. Realtors, Nat. Assn. Realtors. Republican. Club: Women's. Lodges: Order Eastern Star, Rainbow Girls. Home: 1817 Scott Ave Modesto CA 95350

GILES, KAREN DENISE, air force officer; b. Jackson, Mich., Nov. 14, 1961; d. Harry Albert and Mary Louise (Hinck) Brunner; m. Steven Howard Coulson, Dec. 23, 1988. BS, U. Ill., Champaign, 1984; MS, Fla. Internat. U., 1989. Comd. 2d lt. USAF, 1985, advanced through grades to capt., 1989; billeting mgmt. and mortuary affairs instr. Air Force Inst. Tech./DEH, Wright-Patterson AFB, Ohio, 1989—; cons. in field. Decorated Air Force Commendation medal, Air Force Achievement Medal. Mem. NAFE, Assn. Death Edn. and Counseling, Svcs. Soc., Delta Delta Phi, Phi Kappa Phi. Office: United States Air Force AFIT DEH W-Patterson AFB OH 45433

GILES, LYNDA FERN, clinical psychologist; b. Detroit, May 18, 1943; d. Samuel and Shirley (Finkelstein) S.; m. David Reuven Schenk, Sept. 5, 1965 (div. July 1975); children: Jared, Jamie; m. Conrad Leslie Giles, Nov. 26, 1978. BA, U. Mich., 1965, PhD, 1989; MSW, Wayne State U., 1977; PhD in Edn.-Psychology, U. Mich., 1989. Cert. social worker, clin. social worker. Clin. psychologist Counseling Assocs. Inc., Southfield, Mich., 1977—. Mem. com. on identity and affiliation Jewish Welfare Fedn., Detroit, 1985-88, com. on univ. rels., 1987—, com. on edn., 1987—. Mem. Nat. Assn. Social Workers, Counseling Assocs. (chmn. Southfield gifted and talented program 1979-81), Mich. Soc. Clin. Social Workers. Democrat. Club: Franklin Country. Home: 6300 Westmoor Birmingham MI 48010 Office: Counseling Assocs Inc 25835 Southfield Rd Southfield MI 48075

GILES, PHYLLIS LENORE, retired educator; b. Fowler, Colo., Oct. 11, 1912; d. Odin Neil and Lillian Valeria (Deutschman) Williams; m. Albert E. Giles, 1943 (dec.); children: Richard Brian, Tyler William. BA, U. N.C., 1939; MA, Northwestern U., 1964. Elem. sch. tchr. Delearbon, Colo., 1933-34; elem. sch. tchr. La Veta, Colo., 1934-35, Colorado Springs, Colo., 1935-40; tchr. jr. high sch. Colorado Springs, 1940-43; elem. sch. tchr. Montgomery, Ala., 1943, Denver, 1947-48; tchr. Pocatello (Idaho) Jr. High, 1950-51; elem. sch. tchr. Salt Lake City, 1951-53, Park Ridge, Ill., 1953-78. Planner weekly classical music programs USO, 1941-42. Mem. AAUW (chair daytime bridge 1988-90, chair internat. rels. Des Plaines chpt. 1988—), PEO (former chaplain, 2d v.p. for unaffiliated, northwest sub. roundtable). Congregationalist.

GILKES, MARTHA JANE WATKINS, government consultant, scuba diving educator, underwater photographer, photojournalist; b. Aberdeen, Miss., Jan. 28, 1953; d. Robert McCluney and Martha Evelyn (Rye) Watkins; m. David Anthony Gilkes, June 1, 1981. B.A., Miss. State U., 1974, M.A., 1975. Served with U.S. Peace Corps, Grenada, 1975-77; cons. disaster relief Am. embassy, Barbados and Antigua, West Indies, 1977-88; free-lance scuba diving instr., 1979-90; owner, operator Fanta-Sea Island Divers and Fanta Sea Island Excursions, Antiqua, 1990; Contbr. articles to mags. Photographer underwater postcards. Pres. Eastern Caribbean Safe Diving Assn., Barbados, 1984-90, Barbuda/Antigua Diving Club, Antigua, 1984-85. Mem. Ams. Womens Club (pres. 1990), Alpha Zeta, Phi Mu. Republican. Baptist. Address: Dolphin View, Half Moon Bay Antigua also: PO Box 4680 Charlotte Amalie Saint Thomas VI 00801

GILL, ANNA PIETRANGELO, pharmaceutical company trademark specialist; b. S Polo Matese, Campobasso, Italy, Aug. 27, 1944; came to U.S.A., 1954; d. Lucianao F. and Angelina (Canzona) Pietrangelo; m. Phillip W. Gill, June 11, 1966; children: Michael, David. BS in Mgmt., Rutgers U., New Brunswick, N.J., 1983. Trademark adminstr. Johnson and Johnson, New Brunswick, N.J., 1977-82; mgr., trademark services Alcon Labs., Inc., Ft Worth, Tex., 1982--; mem. US Trademark Assn., N.Y, Pharmaceutical Trademarks Group, England, Pharmaceutical Mfrs. Assn., Wash., 1984--. Mem. AAUW. Republican. Home: Rte 1 Box 1429 Burleson TX 76028

GILL, CAROLE O'BRIEN, family therapist; b. Providence, R.I., Apr. 7, 1946; d. Charles Warren and Angelina (Carcieri) O'Brien; m. Frank Ralston Gill, Oct. 17, 1964, (div. 1975); children: Michael Patrick, Peter Ralston. BA in Edn., U. R.I., 1978, BA in Psychology, 1984, MS in Marriage and Family Therapy, 1986. Cert. tchr.; lic. marriage and family therapist. Tchr. East Greenwich Sch. System, R.I., 1978-79; counselor U. R.I., Providence, 1984; clin. asst., therapist Family Therapy Clinic, Kingston, R.I., 1984-86, family therapist, East Greenwich Ptnrs. in Psychotherapy, 1986-88, Children's Friend and Svc., 1988—; pvt. practice, East Greenwich, 1988—; supr. student-interns U. R.I., 1989—; vol. Hotline/Sympatico, Wakefield, R.I., 1984; coordinator Women's Connection U. R.I., 1984; co-facilitator women's abuse group Women's Resource Ctr., Wakefield, R.I., 1985-86. Mem. Friends of East Greenwich Pub. Libr., 1981—, R.I. Chpt. Nat. Com. for Prevention of Child Abuse. Mem. Nat. Coun. on Family Rels., Am. Assn. Female Execs., R.I. Marriage and Family Assn. (v.p. 1988—, pres. student assoc. orgn. 1987-88), Am. Assn. Marriage and Family Therapy, Am. Psychol. Assn., New Eng. Psychol. Assn., R.I. Psychol. Assn. Avocations: archeology, anthropology, photography, needlework, music. Office: Children's Friend and Service 2 Richmond St Providence RI 02903

GILL, DIANE L., psychology educator; b. Watertown, N.Y., Nov. 7, 1948; d. George R. and Betty J. (Reynolds) G. BS in Edn., SUNY, Cortland, N.Y., 1970; MS, U. Ill., 1974, PhD, 1976. Tchr. Greece Athena High Sch., Rochester, N.Y., 1970-72; asst. prof. U. Waterloo, Ont., Can., 1976-78; asst. prof. U. Iowa, Iowa City, 1979-81, assoc. prof., 1981-86; assoc. prof. U. N.C., Greensboro, 1987-89; prof. U. N.C., Greenboro, 1989—. Author: (book) Psychological Dynamics of Sports, 1986; editor Jour. of Sport and Exercise Psychology, 1985-90; editorial bd. Jour. of Applied Sport Psychology, 1988—; contbr. articles to profl. jours. Fellow Assn. for the Advancement of Applied Sport Psychology, Am. Alliance for Health, Phys. Edn., Recreation and Dance (pres. 1987-89); mem. N.Am. Soc. for the Psychology of Sport and Phys. Activity (pres. 1988-91), Am. Psychol. Assn. Democrat. Office: U NC Dept Exercise and Sport Sci Greensboro NC 27412

GILL, ELLEN WILDY, plastic company executive; b. Hemingford, Nebr., Jan. 21, 1915; d. Edward Samuel and Sylvene (Potmesil) Wildy; m. Merwyn C. Gill, May 21, 1939; children: Stephen E., Phillip C., Debaney D. BS in Commerce, U. So. Calif., L.A., 1938. Office mgr. Bluff's Creamery, Scottsbluff, Nebr., 1938-39; sec. to pres. Lanz of Calif., L.A., 1940-42; v.p. charge purchasing, treas. M.C. Gill Corp., El Monte, Calif., 1954-89. Treas. K.L. Carver Sch. P.T.A., San Marino, Calif., 1955-56. Named Western Plastics Woman of Yr., 1983. Home: 1385 El Mirador Dr Pasadena CA 91103 Office: 4056 Easy St El Monte CA 91731

GILL, EVALYN PIERPOINT, editor, publisher; b. Boulder, Colo.; d. Walter Lawrence and Lou Octavia Pierpoint; student Lindenwood Coll., B.A., U. Colo.; postgrad. U. Nebr., U. Alaska, M.A., Cen. Mich. U., 1968; m. John Glanville Gill, Nov. 10, 1943; children: Susan Pierpoint, Mary Louise Glanville. Lectr. humanities Saginaw Valley State Coll., University Center, Mich., 1968-72; mem. English faculty U. N.C., Greensboro, 1973-74; editor Internat. Poetry Rev., Greensboro, 1975—; pres. TransVerse Press, Greensboro, 1981—. Bd. dirs. Eastern Music Festival, Greensboro, 1981—, Greensboro Symphony, 1982—, Greensboro Opera Co., 1982—, Weatherspoon Assn.; chmn. O. Henry Festival, 1985. Mem. Am. Lit. Translators Assn., MLA, N.C. Poetry Soc., Phi Beta Kappa. Author: Poetry By French Women 1930-1980, 1980, Dialogue, 1985, Southeast of Here: Northwest of Now, 1986; editor: O. Henry Festival Stories, 1985, 87, Women of the Piedmont Triad: Poetry and Prose, 1989; contbr. poetry to numerous mags. Home: 1501 Kirkpatrick St Greensboro NC 27408 Office: PO Box 2047 Greensboro NC 27402

GILL, JOANNE CARLYNE, social worker; b. Alhambra, Calif., Feb. 28, 1933; d. Dallasy Roland and Queen Esther (Walker) Shields; divorced; children: Christine Lampe, Michael, Marla. Student, U. Calif., Berkeley, 1950-51; AA, Santa Ana Coll., 1961; BA, Calif. State Coll., Fullerton, 1971. Eligibility technician Social Svcs. County of Orange, Calif., 1966-71, eligibility supr., 1971-74, social worker II, 1974-81, sr. social worker, 1981—; mem. Case Load Forum com. Orange County, 1974—; stewart Orange County Employees Assn., 1968—, chairperson Coun. of Reps., 1974-75, bd. dirs., 1975—. Leader, bd. dirs. 4-H Coop. Extension, Orange County, 1967-77; coach, referee Am. Youth Soccer Orgn., Tustin, Calif., 1977-85; mem. camp and campaign coms., camp counselor YMCA, Santa Ana, 1982-86. Mem. Order Ea. Star (sentenal 1984-85). Republican. Office: County of Orange 1517 Braden Ct Orange CA 92668

GILL, LUNDA LUCINDA, family therapist; b. Oklahoma City, Nov. 12, 1959; d. James Russell and Lunda (Hoyle) G. BS in Psychology, BBA, So. Meth. U., 1983; MA in Psychology, Pepperdine U., 1986; postgrad., Calif. State U., Northridge, 1988-89. Mental health worker Timberlawn Psychiat. Hosp., 1983-84; adminstrv. asst. Fiber-Seal L.A., Inc., 1984-86; counselor II, admissions supr. Pride House, 1986-87; sr. family therapist Phoenix House-Tuum Est, 1987-88; family counselor, crisis worker Haven Hills, Canoga Park, Calif., 1988—. Mem. Jr. League L.A., Psi Chi, Delta Sigma Pi, Alpha Delta Pi. Republican. Episcopalian. Home: 1225 Vista Superba Glendale CA 91205

GILL, RAHEELA SAFDAR, bank executive; b. Chgo., Aug. 1, 1967; d. Safdar Ali and Parveen (Malik) G. BA, Northwestern U., 1987; postgrad, U. Chgo. Corp. trainer Skokie (Ill.) Fed. Savs. & Loan, 1987-89; comml. lender The No. Trust Co., Chgo., 1989—. Vol. Juvenile Diabetes Found., 1988-89, Girl Scouts Am., 1989. Mem. Am. Soc. Tng. and Devel. (editorial bd.), Northwestern Club Chgo., Chi Omega (active coord.). Republican. Islam. Home: 9107 Samoset Skokie IL 60076 Office: No Trust Co 50 S LaSalle Chicago IL 60675

GILL, RONNIE JOY, newspaper editor; b. Bklyn., Dec. 13, 1949; d. Robert and Frances (Noble) Ginsberg; m. Martin Harvey Gill, Nov. 24, 1971 (div. Nov. 1984). BA, Queens Coll., 1971. Adminstrv. asst. Technicolor, Inc., N.Y.C., 1971-72; daily TV listing editor Newsday, Inc., Melville, N.Y., 1972-74, TV book listing editor, 1974-79, editor, editing supr., 1979-87, editor, editing mgr., 1987-90, TV Plus editor, 1990—. Contbr. numerous articles to publs., 1973—. Mem. L.I. Press Club. Jewish. Office: Newsday 235 Pinelawn Rd Melville NY 11747

GILL, WINIFRED M., psychiatric nurse; b. Bklyn., Apr. 11, 1958; d. George J. and Winifred (Serridge) G. BS in Psychology, Fordham U., 1980; postgrad., Seton Hall U.; AAS in Nursing, County Coll. of Morris, 1984. RN, N.J.; cert. in ACLS, BLC, IV, coronary care and chemotherapy. RN Chilton Meml. Hosp., Pompton Plains, N.J., Newton (N.J.) Meml. Hosp.; staff RN Chilton Meml. Hosp., Pompton Plains. Home: PO Box 457 Sussex NJ 07461

GILLAM, JEAN CLARE, financial services specialist; b. Gadsden, Ala., Apr. 7, 1959; d. Henry Grady and Peggy Ann (Alldredge) G. BA, Samford U., 1981. Cet. gen. securities exam. series 7 Nat. Assn. Securities Dealers. Account exec. Merrill Lynch, Gadsden, 1981-83; client svcs. rep. Merrill Lynch, Birmingham, Ala., 1983—. Mem. Ala. Security Dealers Assn., AAUW (group leader night group 1985-86, program chair night group 1986-87, sec. night group 1987-88), Bal d'Or, Delta Zeta. Methodist. Home: 3027 Asbury Park Pl Birmingham AL 35243 Office: Merrill Lynch Am South Sonat Tower Ste 1000 Birmingham AL 35203

GILLE, ISABELLE MARIE-NOÔLLE AMELIE, psychologist; b. N.Y.C., Dec. 25, 1959; d. Gaston and Giséle (Corbière) G. BA magna cum laude, Barnard Coll., 1980; MA, Hofstra U., 1981, PhD, 1985; postdoctoral cert., Adelphi U., 1990. Lic. psychologist, N.Y. Sch. psychologist William Floyd Sch. Dist., Shirley and Mastic, N.Y., 1983-86; clin. psychologist South Shore Ctr. Psychotherapy, Merrick, N.Y., 1986-88; sch. psychologist Human Resources Sch., Albertson, N.Y., 1986-90; psychologist Hewlet-Woodmere Sch. Dist., N.Y., 1990—; pvt. practice Merrick, 1986—. Postdoctoral fellow Adelphi U., 1986—. Mem. APA, Nassau County Psychol. Assn., N.Y. State Psychol. Assn., Nassau County Mental Health Assn. Office: 124 N Merrick Ave Merrick NY 11566

GILLER, RUTH EDNA, business association executive; b. Hampstead, London, Eng., Nov. 5, 1929; came to U.S., 1952, permanent resident, 1956; d. George and Judith (Gunzburg) Bradlaw; m. Marshall Giller, Jan. 27, 1952; children: Paul Bradlaw, Sara. Student London U., 1946-50. Mgr., Children's Zoo Festival of Britain, 1950-52; mgr. Better Bus. div. Cape Kennedy Area C. of C., 1967-72; mgr. Trade Practice div. Better Bus. Bur., Eastern Pa., Phila., 1972-78; exec. dir. Better Bus. Bur. Western Mich., Grand Rapids, 1979—. Mem. Scottish Israelite Soc., Soc. Consumer Affairs Profls., West Mich. Women Execs., Women in Communications. Democrat. Jewish. Club: Torch. Office: Better Bus Bur Western Mich 620 Trust Bldg Grand Rapids MI 49503

GILLER, SUSAN ANN, infosystems specialist; b. White Hall, Ill., Nov. 15, 1946; d. Edward Bonfoy and Mildred Floranna (Schmidt) G. BS, U. Ill., 1969; postgrad., MIT, 1969-71. Mgr. sales Boulder (Colo.) Mountaineer, 1973-77; ski instr. Yosemite (Calif.) Mountaineering Sch., 1977-79; programmer Renaissance Computing Inc., Cambridge, Mass., 1982—. Mem. Assn. Computing Machinery, Am. Alpine Club (bd. dirs. 1982-88), Am. Mountain Found. (bd. dirs. 1989—), Am. Mountain Guide Assn. Home: 3762 Davidson Pl Boulder CO 80303

GILLERMAN, DAWN IRIS, food products company professional; b. Chgo., Aug. 5, 1956; d. Joseph and Elaine Blanche (Miller) G.,. BS in Microbiology, U. Ga., 1978. Lab. technician MacMillan Rsch., Marietta, Ga., 1978-80; quality control. supr. Golden State Foods, Conyers, Ga., 1980-83; baking/mixing supr. Nabisco, Atlanta, 1983-85, area mgr., 1985-88, baking specialist, 1988-89, mixing mgr., 1989, quality control mgr., 1989—. Recipient Van Der Heide award Buscuit and Cracker Mfrs. Assn., Washington, 1989. Mem. Inst. Food Technologists, Green Peace, World Wildlife Assn., Atlanta Zoo. Jewish. Office: Nabisco 1400 Murphy Ave SW Atlanta GA 30310

GILLESPIE, ANITA WRIGHT, nursing administrator; b. S.C., Jan. 3, 1953; d. Ernest L. and Thelma G. Wright; m. Howard Gillespie, Aug. 4, 1973; children: Christopher, Howard III. BSN, N.C. A&T State U., 1974. Cert. CPR instr., ACLS cert. Nursing instr. Norfolk (Va.) Community Hosp., 1975-76, staff nursr emergency dept., 1876-79; asst. nurse mgr. emergency dept. Mercy Hosp., Cin., 1979-83; evening dir. Mercy Hosp. Anderson, Cin., 1983—. Mem. ANA, NAFE, Nat. Coun. Negro Women, N.C. A&T Alumni Assn., Alpha Kappa Alpha. Home: 1611 Laval Dr Cincinnati OH 45255 Office: Mercy Hosp Anderson 7500 State Rd Cincinnati OH 45255

GILLESPIE, HELEN DAVYS, product communications manager; b. San Jose, Calif., Nov. 23, 1954; d. Robert Bruce and Helen Davys (Street) G.; m. Nigel George Haden, May 1, 1982 (div. June 1986). BA in English with honors, Calif. State U., Chico, 1976; postgrad. in English, U. Sheffield, Sheffield, England, 1976-77, Calif. State U., Chico, 1977-78. Bus. analyst Dun & Bradstreet, San Jose, 1978-80; personal asst. Times Computer Svcs., London, 1980; adminstr. Exec. Aviation, Palo Alto, Calif., 1981; sr. writer/editor Tymnet/McDonnell Douglas, San Jose, 1982-86; mgr. sales support Pactel Spectrum Svcs., Walnut Creek, Calif., 1987; mgr. product communications Varian Assocs., Inc., Sunnyvale, Calif., 1987—; owner Writing & Editing Svcs., San Jose, Calif., 1987—. Mem. Airline Owners & Pilots Assn., Writers Connection, Art Inst. Chgo., Mus. Soc. of San Diego, Bus. Profl. Advt. Assn. Office: Varian 220 Humboldt Ct Sunnyvale CA 94089

GILLESPIE, MARY KREMPA, psychologist, consultant; b. New Haven, Oct. 31, 1941; d. Albert Charles and Marye (Bemis) Krempa; m. J. Joseph Gillespie, Sept. 1, 1962 (div. 1979); children: Carolyn Gillespie Kottmeyer, James Joseph III (dec.). Assoc. in Fine Arts Music, Mount Aloysius, 1961; BA in Psychology cum laude, Immaculata (Pa.) Coll., 1973; MA in Clin. Psychology, West Chester (Pa.) U., 1974; postgrad., Temple U., 1976-80; PhD in Social Psychology, Walden U., 1988. Lic. psychologist Pa. Exec. dir. Open Door Counseling Ctr., West Chester, 1975-77; therapist Temple U. Community Counseling Clin., Phila., 1977-78; doctoral intern Coatesville (Pa.) Vets. Hosp., 1978-79; sr. psychologist Delaware Valley Psych Svcs., Phila., 1979-81; dir. Substance Abuse Programs Resource Spectrum, Phila., 1980-81; psychologist 1910 Barn Counseling Ctr., Phoenixville, Pa., 1982-85, Ambler (Pa.) Psychol. Svcs., 1980-84; dir. Eaglesmere Psychology Assocs., Malvern, Pa., 1983—; cons., bd. mem. Rape Crisis Coun., West Chester, 1974-77; expert witness in child custody matters, County Cts. of Phila., Chester and Bucks Counties, Pa., 1982—; rsch. cons., mem. clin. bd. MindsEye Ednl. Systems, Wayne Pa., 1989—; proprietress Eaglesmere Bed and Breakfast, Malvern, 1988—. Author: Outcome Study of an Innovative Paradoxical Treatment for Panic Attacks, 1988. Pub. speaker on psychol. issues, 1974—. Recipient Univ. fellowship Temple Univ., Phila., 1976-77. Mem. Am. Psychol. Assn., Pa. Psychol. Assn., Assn. for Applied

Psychophysiology and Biofeedback, Pa. Soc. Behavioral Medicine and Biofeedback, Phi Theta Kappa, Psi Chi. Home: RR 3 Box 2350 Malvern PA 19355-9712 Office: Eaglesmere Psychology Assoc 2350 Pheasant Hill Ln Malvern PA 19335-9712

GILLESPIE, NELLIE REDD, academic administrator; b. Brookhaven, Miss.; d. Zelmer Morris and Willie (Woods) Redd; divorced; 1 child, David Lauren. BS in Acctg., U. So. Miss., 1958; postgrad., Nat. Assn. Coll. Univs. Bus. Officer's Inst. Sr. auditor Fla. State U., Tallahassee, 1968-74, controller, 1974-76, asst. v.p. adminstrv. affairs, 1976-78, assoc. dir. student fin. affairs, 1978-82; administr. dept. revenue State of Fla., Tallahassee, 1982-83; dir. fin., adminstrn. City of Altamonte Spring, Fla., 1983-84; internal auditor Jackson (Miss.) State U., 1984—. Vol. Graham/Mixson gov. campaign, inaugural com., 1983, Ray Mabus gov. campaign, 1987; Gov.'s appointee Miss. Bd. Health and Human Services, 1988-92; div. leader United Way, Cancer Fund drives; mem. Leon High Sch. Choral Parent Assn., dist. adv. council Leon County Sch. Bd.; bd. dirs. Ctr. for Creative Employment. Mem. Assn. Coll. Univ. Auditors, Nat. Assn. Coll. Univ. Bus. Officers (so. chpt.), Am. Mgmt. Assn., Nat. Assn. Female Execs., Inst. Internal Auditors, AAUW (v.p. 1967—), Nat. Assn. Bds. Pharmacy (gov.'s com. Fla. bd. 1979-83), Am. Assn. Computer Profls. (audit com. dist. III), Fla. LWV, U. So. Miss. Alumni Assn., Tallahassee Ins. Women's Assn. (charter, treas. 1960-65), Sigma Sigma Sigma. Democrat. Mem. Ch. Christ. Club: Pilots (Anchor Club sponsor). Lodge: Civitan.

GILLETTE, CAROL MAY, medical technologist; b. Cleve., Nov. 30, 1940; d. Henry Blair and Grayce Phare (Davidson) Hubble; m. Donald Alfred Gillette, Feb. 26, 1958; children: Catherine, Anthony, Lucia, David, Carroll, Andrea, Lisa, Daniel, Rosemary. AS, Flint (Mich.) Jr. Coll., 1960; BA in Biology, U. Mich., Flint, 1963. Registered med. technologist. Lab. asst. Flint Osteo. Hosp., 1960-61; staff med. technologist Flint Gen. Hosp., 1961-62, 65-66; med. technologist Ballenger Highway Med. Lab., Flint, 1965-66; chief med. technologist Flint Med. X-ray and Lab., 1976-87; microbiologist Flint Med. Clinic, 1984-87; med. technologist St. Joseph Hosp., Flint, 1963—. Recipient 25 yr. svc. pin St. Joseph Hosp., 1988. Mem. Am. Soc. Clin. Pathologists, Mensa, Genesee Landlords Assn. Roman Catholic. Home: 9174 N Irish Rd Mount Morris MI 48458

GILLETTE, ETHEL MORROW, columnist; b. Oelwein, Iowa, Nov. 27, 1921; d. Charles Henry and Myrne Sarah (Law) Morrow; student Coe Coll., 1939-41; BA, Upper Iowa U., 1959; MA, Western State Coll., 1969; m. Roman A. Gillette, May 6, 1944; children: Melody Ann, Richard Alan, William Robert. Stenographer, Penick & Ford, Cedar Rapids, Iowa, 1941-43, FBI, Washington, 1943-44; tchr. Fayette (Iowa) High Sch., 1959-60, Jordan Jr. High Sch., Mpls., 1960-64, Montrose (Colo.) High Sch., 1964-68; family living, religion editor The News-Record, Gillette, Wyo., 1977-79, columnist Distaff Side, 1979-84. Mem. Western Writers Am. (assoc.), Nat. Writers Club. Contbr. articles to various mags. Home: 1804 E Locust St Montrose CO 81401

GILLETTE, SUSAN DOWNS, advertising executive; b. Phila., Mar. 4, 1950; d. George Woodrow and Ruth (McFarland) Downs; m. Raymond Gene Gillette, Oct. 6, 1979; children: Margaret Anne, Lindsay Ray. BA, No. Ill. U., 1972. Advt. asst. Wescom Inc., Downers Grove, Ill., 1972-73; copywriter Steven Walters Advt., Chgo., 1973-75; dir. creative services DDB Needham Worldwide, Chgo., 1975—, exec. v.p. Active Acquired Immune Deficiency Syndrome pub. info. com. Chgo. Dept. Pub. Health; tchr. local Sunday Sch. Recipient Gold Lion award Cannes Film Festival, 1978, Silver Lion award, 1987, Vol. award Am. Cancer Soc., 1986; named Creative Dir. of Yr., Ad Week mag., 1986, Advt. Woman of Yr., Women's Advt. Club Chgo., 1990. Clubs: Women's Ad, Chgo. Ad. Office: DDB Needham 303 E Wacker Dr Chicago IL 60601*

GILLIAM, LYNDA FAYE, telecommunications consultant; b. Cleve., Oct. 30, 1949; d. Warren and Vernice Octavia (White) G.; 1 child, Raven Vernice. BA in Bus., Kent (Ohio) State U., 1971; AA in Communications, Massey Inst., 1973. Ops. mgr. Tel Inc. Communications, L.A., 1974-77; asst. office mgr. BBDO/West Advt., L.A., 1977-80; project coord. AM West Telephone Co., L.A., 1980-82, Com Systems, Inc., L.A., 1982-84; sales mgr. Dencom Systems, Inc., L.A., 1984-85; free-lance telecommunications cons. L.A., 1985—; trainer, cons. AT&T Phone Co., Los Angeles, 1985-87. Vol. career guidance cons. Los Angeles Youth Guidance; counselor Young Dems., Los Angeles, 1985. Mem. Nat. Assn. Female Execs., Summit Orgn. Roman Catholic. Home and Office: Gilliam and Assocs 4532 W 16th Pl Los Angeles CA 90019

GILLIAM, MARY, travel executive; b. Pampa, Tex., Apr. 18, 1928; d. Roy and Hylda O. (Bertrand) Brown; divorced; 1 child, Terry K. AA, Amarillo (Tex.) Bus. Coll., 1949. Flight attendant Braniff Internat. Airways, Dallas, 1950-53; from reservation agt. to mgr. passenger sales Trans-World Airlines, various locations, 1953-81; exec. v.p. Lakewood (Colo.) Travel, 1981; mgmt. cons. Bank One Travel, Columbus, Ohio, 1981-82; pres. Icaria Travel, Inc., Tucson, Ariz., 1986—, Intensive Trainers Inst., Tucson, 1983—; examining team Accrediting Coun. for Continuing Edn. and Tng. Mem. Tucson Better Bus. Bur., 1983—, Ariz. Rep. Com., 1978—. Recipient Award of Excellence Trans-World Airlines, N.Y.C., 1972, Pres.' Hall of Fame award, 1973. Mem. Am. Soc. Travel Agts. (scholarship chmn., nat. schs. com., Industry Service award 1980), Inst. Cert. Travel Agts., Pacific Asia Travel Assn., Women in Travel, Soc. Travel and Tourism Educators. Republican. Methodist. Office: Intensive Trainers Inst 2700 W Broadway Tucson AZ 85745

GILLIAM, PAULA HUTTER, transportation company executive; b. N.Y.C.; d. Irving and Edna Phyllis (Manes) Hutter; m. Stanley Spencer Rolnick (div.); children: Jeffry Hutter Gilliam, Pamela Sara Bielory; m. Peter Gilliam, 1981. AA, Centenary Coll., 1961. Pres. Paula Rolnick Sales, N.Y.C., 1970-74; mdse. mgr. Kirby Block Internat., N.Y.C., 1974-78; pres. P.M.G. Internat. Ltd, N.Y.C., 1981—; dir. corp. sales Rical Air Express, Inc., N.Y.C., Rical Ocean Forwarding, N.Y.C.; ptnr. The Goldon Unicorn Restaurant, 20 Mott St. Restaurant. Producer (Broadway show) Stardust, 1987; exec. producer (plays) Long Days Journey Into the Night, 1988, Ah Wilderness. V.p. Murray Hill Com., N.Y.C., 1982—, chmn. block party, 1983—; bd. advisors 132 E 35th St., N.Y.C., 1984-86; vol. aide June Eisland Council Women, Riverdale, N.Y., 1979—; bd. dirs. Theater Off Park, 1983-88. Mem. Women in Internat. Trade. Democrat. Clubs: Women's Traffic, Met. Traffic. Home and Office: 132 E 35th St New York NY 10016

GILLIARD, JUDY ANN, sales professional; b. Ventura, Calif., Aug. 21, 1946; d. Sam Albert and Betty (Hardacre) G. A in Hotel and Restaurant Mgmt., Santa Barbara (Calif.) Community Coll., 1974. Supr. dining room Santa Barbara Biltmore, 1972-73; supr. food service, instr. dining room ops. Santa Barbara Community Coll., 1972-73; cons. J. Gilliard & Co., Santa Barbara, 1973-74; exec. mgr. Head of the Wolf Restaurant, Palm Springs, Calif., 1974-76; salesperson Indio (Calif.) Daily News, 1976-77; sales cons. Jurgensons Restaurant, Palm Springs, 1977-79; account exec. Sta. KPSI-FM, Palm Springs, 1978-84, gen. sales mgr., 1984-88, v.p., gen. mgr., 1988—. Co-author: The Guiltless Gourmet, 1983, The Guiltless Gourmet Goes Ethnic, 1990. Home: 696 N Hermosa Palm Springs CA 92262

GILLICE, SONDRA JUPIN (MRS. GARDNER RUSSELL BROWN), personnel executive; b. Urbana, Ill.; d. Earl Cranston and Laura Lorraine (Rose) Jupin; BS, Lindenwood Coll., 1958; MBA, Loyola Coll., 1982; m. Gardner Russell Brown, Jan. 12, 1980; 1 son, Thomas Alan Gillice. Div. tng. supr. Liberty Mut. Ins. Co., Chgo., N.Y.C., 1958-68; personnel officer N.Y. Citibank, 1968-70, 1st Nat. Bank of Chgo., 1970-72; mgr. human resources Potomac Electric Power Co., Washington, 1973-81; dir. personnel U.S. Synthetic Fuels Corp., Washington, 1981-86, v.p. human resources, Guest Services, Inc., 1987—. Mem. industry adv. bd. Behrand Coll., Pa. State U. Mem. Edison Electric Inst. (chmn. tng. and mgmt. devel. com.), AAUW (pres. Falls Church br. 1976-78), Washington Nat. Restaurant Assn., Am. Soc. Personnel Adminstrs., Washington Personnel Assn., Greater Met. Washington Bd. Trade, Loyola Coll. Bd. Govs., Nat. Bd. Med. Coll. of Pa., Soroptimists (pres. Washington chpt. 1979-80), DAR, Army Navy Country, Soc. Magna Charta Dames, Edgartown Yacht Club, Country Club of Culpeper, Inc. Republican.

GILLIES, ANN STEADRY, media services director; b. Chgo., Nov. 22, 1941; d. Frederick Oscar and Floy Lucille (Fetherston) Steadry; m. William Browne Gillies, III, June 27, 1964; children: Robert Coburn, David Carlson. BA in History, Carleton Coll., 1963; MA in Pub. Affairs, Sangamon State U., 1974. Tchr. Evanston (Ill.) Twp. High Sch., 1963-64, New Trier Twp. High Sch., Winnetka, Ill., 1964-66; reporter, anchorwoman WICS-TV, Springfield, Ill., 1974-89; ordained elder Presbyn. Ch., Springfield, 1979—; lay pastor Presbyn. Ch., Louisville, 1989—, dir. media svcs., 1989—; dean Lay Pastors Sch. Presbyn. Ch., Peoria, Ill., 1986-89; leadership devel. chair Presbyn Ch. Great Rivers, Peoria, 1983-86; communications & devel. chair Synod of Lincoln Trails, Indpls., 1988-89; com. on ministry Presbyn. of Great Rivers, Peoria, 1988-89; bd. mgrs. Nat. Coun. Chs., N.Y.C., 1989—. Lay minister Presbyn Ch. Mem. Religions Pub. Rels. Coun., Women in Communications, NAFE. Democrat. Presbyterian. Office: Presbyn Ch Rm 2218 100 Witherspoon St Louisville KY 40202-1396

GILLIKIN, VIRGINIA, lawyer; b. Providence, July 30, 1952; d. Durwood Earl and Theresa Marie (Goushakjian) G. BA cum laude, Providence Coll., 1974; MA, MEd, Columbia U., 1976; JD, Bklyn. Law Sch., 1982. Bar: N.Y. 1983, U.S. Dist. Ct. (so. and ea. dists.) N.Y. 1988. Assoc. Newman, Tannenbaum, Helpern, Syracuse & Hirschtritt, N.Y.C., 1982-83; assoc. Martin, Clearwater & Bell, N.Y.C., 1983-86, Berman, Paley, Goldstein & Berman, N.Y.C., 1987-88, Killarney, Brody & Fabiani, N.Y.C., 1988-89; pvt. practice N.Y.C., 1989—. Mem. ABA, Assn. of Bar of Bar of City of N.Y. Home: 200 E 27th St Apt 6T New York NY 10016

GILLILAND, MARION CHARLOTTE S., volunteer; b. Duluth, Minn., Dec. 29, 1918; d. John Oscar and Jenny Olympia (Wangberg) Spjut; m. Charles Herbert Gilliland, Mar. 6, 1942; children: Charles Herbert Jr., Marion Charlotte Jr., Patricia Ann, Norman Paul, Cynthia Eileen. BA in Anthropology with honors, U. Fla., 1963, MA in Anthropology, 1965. Author: The Material Culture of Key Marco, Florida, 1976, Key Marco's Buried Treasure, 1989; contbr. articles to newspaper and profl. jours. Pres. Alachua County (Fla.) Children's Com., 1959-61, Alachua County Scholarship and Loan Fund, 1960-62; v.p. govtl. rels. div. Gainesville (Fla.) C. of C., 1977-79; health com. Human Svcs. Planning coun., Gainesville, 1980-84; bd. dirs. Fla. Arts Celebration, Gainesville, 1984—. Recipient Peggy Wilcox Svc. award State of Fla., 1975. Mem. Fla. Med. Assn. Aux. (pres. 1969-70, bd. dirs. 1970-73), AMA Aux. (sec. 1975-76, v.p. so. regional 1976-78, historian 1978-79), Alachua County Med. Aux. (pres. 1960-61), So. Anthropol. Soc., Fla. Anthropol. Soc., Archael. Inst. Am., Nat. Assn. Underwater Investigators, Fla. Mus. Assocs., Fla. Women's Alliance (charter mem.), Mortar Bd. (hon.), Phi Kappa Phi. Home: 3031 SW 70th Ln Gainesville FL 32608

GILLIN, KATY ELIZABETH, public relations executive; b. Miles City, Mont., Jan. 22, 1964; d. William Francis and Dixie Lorene (Morse) G. B in Speech Communication, Mont. State U., 1986. Account exec. Joyce LeKas Pub. Relations, San Jose, Calif., 1987-89; account supr. PRX Advt. & Pub. Rels., San Jose, Calif., 1989—; bd. dirs. WOMA. Contbr. articles to profl. jours. Home: 1330 Crazy Pete's Woodside CA 94062

GILLIO, CAROLYN IRENE, psychotherapist; b. Wells, Minn., Jan. 1, 1931; d. William Frederick and Antonia Willemina (Augst) Moll; m. Cesar Padilla, June 28, 1953 (div. 1967); children: Paula, Mark, Julie; m. Frank Gillio, May 24, 1969. BA, Gustavus-Adolphus Coll., 1952; postgrad., U. Chgo., 1952-53; MSW, U. Calif., Berkeley, 1955. Psychotherapist Agnews St. Hosp., San Jose, Calif., 1955-56; supr. San Jose Family Svcs., 1956-68; psychotherapist Mid-Peninsula Psychotherapy Clinic, Sunnyvale, Calif., 1968-76; pvt. practice psychotherapy Sunnyvale, 1976—; adj. instr. U. Calif.-Santa Cruz Extension, Sunnyvale, 1979-80; cons. Santa Clara County (Calif.) Mental Health, 1975-78, other orgns. in field. Mem. Cen. Core Comprehensive Mental Health Planning Commn., Santa Clara, Calif., 1965-67; chmn. Sunnyvale Coordinating Coun., 1968; bd. dirs. No. County Social Planning Coun., Santa Clara, 1968-69. Recipient Disting. Svc. award Santa Clara County Family Svc., 1968; named Disting. Woman on Mid-Peninsula, Girls Club of the Mid-Peninsula, 1973. Fellow Nat. Assn. Social Workers (bd. dirs. 1970-71), Soc. Clin. Social Workers (legis. com. 1975-77), Soc. Clin. Social Work (bd. dirs. 1977-81); mem. AAUW (mem. com. 1986-87, book reviewer 1988), Alphas. Home: 435 Logan St Santa Cruz CA 95062 Office: 869 Cumberland Dr Sunnyvale CA 94087 also: 940 Saratoga Ave Ste 208 San Jose CA 95129

GILLIS, CHRISTINE DIEST-LORGION, financial planner, stockbroker; b. San Francisco; d. Evert Jan and Christine Helen (Radcliffe) Diest-Lorgion; B.S., U. Calif., Berkeley; M.S., U. So. Calif.; children—Barbara Gillis Pieper, Suzanne Gillis Seymour (twins). Cert. fin. planner. Account exec. Winslow, Cohu & Stetson, N.Y.C., 1962-63, Paine Webber, N.Y.C., 1964-65; sr. investment exec. Shearson Hammill, Beverly Hills, Calif., 1966-72; fin. planner, asst. v.p. EF Hutton, L.A., 1972-87; 2nd v.p. Shearson Lehman Hutton, Glendale, Calif., 1988; v.p. investments Dean Witter Reynolds, Glendale, 1988—. Mem. Inst. Cert. Fin. Planners, Town Hall of Calif. (life, corp. sec. 1974-75, dir., gov. 1976-80), Women Stockbrokers Assn. (founding pres. N.Y.C. 1963), Women of Wall Street West (pres. 1979-84), Navy League (life; dir.), Assistance League Pasadena, AAUW (life; trustee ednl. found.), Bus. and Profl. Women, U. Calif.-Berkeley Alumni Assn. (life), Town and Gown (life), Rotary (charter), DESCANSO, Sunrise Club, Phi Chi Theta (life). Episcopalian. Home: 959 Regent Park Dr La Canada Flintridge CA 91011 Office: 801 N Brand Blvd Ste 908 Glendale CA 91209

GILLISS, BARBARA ELLEN, educational company executive, educator, travel executive; b. Lewiston, Idaho, June 18, 1938; d. Albert Arnold Anderson and Dorothy Maude (Desso) Nobach; m. Harvey Eugene Keating, June 18, 1960 (div. Dec. 1976); children: Brian Elliot, Kimberly Ellen; m. Charles Maxwell Gilliss, Mar. 25, 1979. BS in Edn., West Oreg. State Coll., 1960; MEd, Adminstrn., U. Hawaii, 1972; postgrad., U. San Diego. Cert. tchr., supr., Hawaii, Oreg., Calif. Tchr. Parkrose Sch. Dist., Portland, Oreg., 1962-63, North Vancouver (B.C., Can.) Sch. Dist., 1964-66; adminstrv. asst., dissemination specialist Hawaii State Dept. Edn., U. Hawaii Curriculum Research & Devel. Group, Honolulu, 1967-77; curriculum coordinator, tchr. supr. Windward Dist. Hawaii State Dept. Edn., Kaneohe, 1978-82; resident instr. UCLA, Los Angeles, 1980; instr. Mt. San Jacinto (Calif.) Coll., 1982—; owner Automotive Service Ctr., Hemet, Calif., 1984-85; pres. Uniglobe Butterfield Travel, Inc., Rancho Californ, Calif, 1987—, Ednl. Materials Unltd., Rancho Californ, 1980—; cons. bilingual edn. Hawaii State Dept., 1975-77, Mgmt. Bank Hemet, Kaiser Devel. Co., 1984-85; comptr., ops. mgr. C.M. Gilliss Investments and Real Estate, Honolulu, Temecula, 1979—. Travel columnist Temecula Valley Bus. Jour.; contbr. articles to profl. jours. Mem., com. chair Homeowner's Assn., Rancho California, 1985—. Recipient Leadership award Hahaione PTA, 1975. Mem. Western Oreg. Coll. Alumni Assn., Am. Assn. of U. Women, Nat. Assn. Female Execs., Am. Mgmt. Assn. Democrat.

GILLISS, CATHERINE LYNCH, nurse, educator; b. New Britain, Conn., Apr. 18, 1949; d. James A. and Lorraine (Balocki) Lynch; m. Thomas P. Gilliss, June 6, 1970. BS in Nursing, Duke U., 1971; MS in Nursing, Cath. U. Am., Washington, 1974; D of Nursing Sci., U. Calif., 1983; cert. adult nurse practitioner, U. Rochester, 1979. Staff and charge nurse Duke U. Med. Ctr., Durham, 1971, VA Hosp., Washington, 1971-72; asst. prof. U. Md., Balt., 1974-76, The Cath. U. Am., 1976-79; assoc. prof. U. Portland, Oreg., 1979-83; lectr. in nursing Sonoma State U., Rohnert Park, Calif., 1983-84; assoc. prof. U. Calif., San Francisco, 1984-89, 1989—; bd. dirs. Nat. Council Family Relations, St. Paul. Co-author Toward a Science of Family Nursing, 1989; contbr. articles to profl. jours. Recipient NRSA award NIH, 1981-83, Pres. fellow U. Calif. Regents, 1983, Disting. Practitioner Nat. Acad. Practice, 1985; NIH rsch. grantee, 1986-89. Fellow Am. Acad Nursing; mem. Am. Nurses Assn., Am. Heart Assn., Nat. Coun. on Family Rels. Office: U Calif San Francisco Sch Nursing San Francisco CA 94143-0606

GILLMAN, FLORENCE MORGAN, education educator; b. Utica, NY, Apr. 27, 1947; d. Wesley B. and Ann (Malone) Morgan; m. John L. Gillman, Sept. 23, 1983; 1 child, Anne Marie. BA, Catholic U. Am., Wash., 1974; MA, Catholic U. Am., 1976; PhD, U. Louvain, Belgium, 1982, STD, 1984. Asst. prof. Gonzaga U., Spokane, Wa., 1982-84; adjunct asst. prof. Mundelein Coll., Chgo., 1984-86; assoc. prof. U. San Diego, 1986. Author: Women Who Knew Paul, 1991, Dying With Christ: Rom. 6:5, 1991; contbr. articles to profl. jours. Mem. Soc. Biblical Literature, Catholic Biblical Assn. Roman Catholic. Office: U San Diego Dept Religious Studies San Diego CA 92110

GILLMOR, KAREN LAKO, strategic planner; b. Cleve., Jan. 29, 1948; d. William M. and Charlotte (Sheldon) Lako; m. Paul E. Gillmor, Dec. 10, 1983; children: Linda D., Julie E. BA cum laude, Mich. State U., 1969; MA, Ohio State U., 1970, PhD, 1981. Asst. to v.p. Ohio State U., Columbus, 1972-77, spl. asst. dean law, 1979-81; asst. to pres. Ind. Cen. U., Indpls., 1977-78; rsch. asst. Burke Mktg. Rsch., Indpls., 1978-79; v.p. pub. affairs Huntington Nat. Bank, Columbus, 1981-82; fin. cons. Ohio Rep. Fin. Com., Columbus, 1982-83; chief mgmt. planning and rsch. Indsl. Commn. Ohio, Columbus, 1983-86; mgr. physician rels. Univ. Hosps., Columbus, 1987—; legis. liaison Huntington Bancshares, Ohio, Ohio State U., Columbus. Bd. dirs. Nat. Adv. Com. on Women's Health. Grantee Andrew W. Mellon Found. 1978, Carnegie Corp. 1978. Mem. Women in Mainstream, Women's Roundtable, Ohio Fedn. Rep. Women, Assn. Higher Edn., Coun. Advancement and Support Edn., DAR, Phi Delta Kappa. Methodist. Clubs: Capital, University (Columbus), Ohio State U. Faculty. Office: Univ Hosps 456 W Tenth Ave Columbus OH 43210

GILLSON, PAULINE MARGARET, publisher; b. Histon, Cambridge, Eng., July 8, 1943; d. Arthur Frank and Marjorie Edith (Fordham) Foster; m. Malcolm W. Gillson (div. Mar. 1988). Grad., Impington (Eng.) Village Coll., 1958. With Saxone Shoe Sales, London, 1960-62; tax and payroll marshall Cambridge (Eng.) Engring. Ltd., 1963-66; gen. mgr. Traders Post, Inc., Nashville, 1971—. Organizer Art Guild, Nashville, 1990—; organizer car shows and promotions, Nashville, 1990—. Office: Traders Post Inc 2740 Elm Hill Pike Nashville TN 37214

GILL THOMPSON, NORMA N., home health care executive; b. Akron, Ohio, June 26, 1920; d. Richard Nottingham and Esther (Mullennax) Day; m. Edward Grover Gill, Sept. 5, 1938 (dec. 1974); children: Marilyn A., David E.; m. Herbert George Thompson, Oct. 1, 1983; 1 child, Sally Thompson. Cert. enterostomal therapy, Cleve. Clinic Found., 1958. Dir. R.B. Turnbull Jr., M.D. Sch. Enterostomal Therapy Cleve. Clinic Found., 1961-78, coord. enterostomal therapy, 1978-81; pres., cons. Worldwide Home Health Care Ctr., Inc., Akron, 1981—; cons. Akron City Hosp., St. Thomas Hosp. Med. Ctr., Children's Hosp. Med. Ctr. Akron, Cuyahoga Falls (Ohio) Gen. Hosp., Akron Vis. Nurses' Assn. Stoma Care Team; lectr. on ostomy care; cons. in establishing enterostomal therapy schs., Eng., Australia, Germany, France, Sweden, India, Japan, Brazil, Argentina, Peru, Chile; 1st dir. Rupert B. Turnbull Sch. of Enterostomal Therapy, Cleve. Clinic Found., 1961-90. Author ednl. materials; contbr. numerous articles on ostomy-related topics to various publs. Mem. Akron Ostomy Assn., Am. Urological Assn., Internat. Ostomy Assn. (profl. adv. bd. 1980-83, 83-85), Internat. Assn. Enterostomal Therapy, United Ostomy Assn., World Coun. Enterostomal Therapists, Ileitis and Colitis Found., French Assn. Stoma Therapy (hon. pres.), Nat. Assn. Owners, Women's Network Akron, World Coun. Enterostomal Therapists (Norma N. Gill Found. established 1980), United Ostomy Assn., Internat. Assn. Enterostomal Therapy. Democrat. Methodist. Office: Worldwide Home Health Ctr 926 E Tallmadge Ave Akron OH 44310

GILLUM, ELSIE FELTS (JUDY GILLUM), engineering company executive; b. Jacksonville, Fla., June 16, 1930; d. Ethelbert Hayward and Elsie Maybeth (Gregory) Felts; m. Don Edwyn Massey, July 22, 1957 (div. Apr. 1966); m. Jimmie Corbett Gillum, June 30, 1968. Assoc. Sci., Hillsborough Community Coll., 1984. Cert. profl. sec. Sec., Rosenblum's, Jacksonville, Fla., 1948-50; exec. sec. Gibbs Corp., Jacksonville, 1950-60, Ryder Truck Lines, Jacksonville, 1960-62; asst. corp. sec. Greiner Engring. Scis., Inc., Tampa, Fla., 1962—. Mem. Profl. Secs. Internat. (pres. City Ctr. chpt. 1985-86, Sec. of Yr. 1985-86, Fla. div. Sec. of Yr. 1986-87), Exec. Women Internat. (sec. 1984), Greater Brandon C. of C. Roman Catholic. Avocations: needlework; reading; gardening. Home: 2205 Martin Rd Dover FL 33527 Office: Greiner Engring Scis Inc 7650 W Courtney Campbell Causeway PO Box 31646 Tampa FL 33630

GILMAN, ELLEN DEBORAH, psychiatrist; b. Newton, Mass., Oct. 18, 1940; d. Arthur and Ruth (Friedman) Stern; m. Michael Gilman, 1960; children:. Student, Radcliffe Coll., 1957-60, Tufts U., 1964. Attending psychiatrist Baystate Med. Ctr., Springfield, Mass., 1971—; instr. psychiatry Tufts U. Med. Sch., Boston, 1976—. Mem. Am. Psychiatric Assn., Mass. Med. Soc., Mass. Psychiatric Assn. Office: 780 Chestnut St Ste 27 Springfield MA 01107

GILMARTIN, KAREN BAUST, lawyer; b. Phila., May 22, 1961; d. Fred G. and Veronica L. (Pappas) Baust; m. Michael R. Gilmartin, Sept. 3, 1983; 1 child, Courtney Melissa. BA, U. Miami, Fla., 1983; JD, U. Miami, 1986. Bar: Fla. 1986. Assoc. Adams, Kelley, Kronenberg & Kelley, Miami, Fla., 1987—. Mem. ABA, Fla. Bar (rules com. of workers' compensation sect.), Dade County Bar Assn., Assn. Trial Lawyers Am. Democrat. Roman Catholic. Office: Adams Kelley Kronenberg & Kelley Pla Royale 15600 NW 67th Ave Ste 204 Miami Lakes FL 33014

GILMER, DEBORAH ANN, police officer; b. Schenectady, Apr. 1, 1951; d. Nelson Walter and Ruth (Morton) G. BA cum laude, Wittenberg U., Springfield, Ohio, 1973; MEd in Rehab. Counseling, U. Pitts., 1974. Addictions clinician Regional Mental Health Ctr., Howard Community Hosp., Kokomo, Ind., 1975-80; police officer Springfield (Oreg.) Police Dept., 1981-85, motor officer, 1985—. Recipient Medal of Valor, Springfield Police Dept., 1986. Mem. Oreg. Peace Officers Assn. Office: Springfield Police Dept 344 N A St Springfield OR 97477

GILMER, PENNY JANE, biochemist, educator; b. Hackensack, N.J., Aug. 19, 1943; d. Peter E. and Barbara D. (Joynt) G.; m. Sanford A. Safron, Sept. 9, 1980; children—Helena M., Nathaniel S. B.A. in Chemistry, Douglass Coll., 1965; M.A. in Organic Chemistry, Bryn Mawr Coll., 1967; Ph.D. in Biochemistry, U. Calif.-Berkeley, 1972. Bank Am.-Giannini postdoctoral fellow Stanford U. (Calif.), 1973-75, USPHS and NIH postdoctoral fellow, 1975-77, acting asst. prof. human biology, 1976-77; asst. prof. chemistry Fla. State U., Tallahassee, 1977-84, assoc. prof., 1984—, interim assoc. dean coll. arts and scis., 1990—; lectr. in field. Recipient Faculty Rsch. award Fla. State U., 1978, 84, 86, 90; grantee NIH, 1979-81, Research Corp., 1979-86, 1990—, Am. Cancer Soc., 1981-83, Nat. Sci. Found., 1990—, Jessie Ball duPont Fund, 1987-89. Mem. Fedn. Biol. Chemists, Am. Chem. Soc., AAAS, Sierra Club, Audubon Soc., Southeastern Immunology Conf. (dir. 1979-84, pres. 1982), Assn. Women in Sci., Sigma Xi. Democrat. Lodge: Zonta Internat. Contbr. numerous articles to profl. jours. Office: Fla State U Dept Chemistry Tallahassee FL 32306-3006

GILMORE, BARBARA, health and fitness executive; b. Pasadena, Calif., Aug. 31, 1954; d. C. A. and Alma Elizabeth (Wilson) G. BS in Microbiology with honors, Oreg. State U., 1976; Ms In Exercise Physiology with honors, U. Oreg., 1983. Exercise sci. and health instr. Lower Columbia Coll., Longview, Wash., 1985-89; dir. of health and fitness Weyerhauser Paper Co., Longview, 1989—; nutrition instr. Lower Columbia Coll., Longview, Wash., 1990—. Mem. Am. Coll. Sports Medicine. Office: Weyerhauser Paper Co 3401 Industrial Way Longview WA 98632

GILMORE, JUNE ELLEN, psychologist; b. Middletown, Ohio, Oct. 22, 1927; d. Linley Lawrence and Elizabeth Kathleen (Barker) Wetzel; m. John Lester Gilmore, July 6, 1945; children: John Lester Jr., Michael Edward. BS, Miami U., Oxford, 1961; MS, Miami U., 1964. Lic. psychologist, Ohio. Intern in psychology Hamilton (Ohio) City Schs., 1963-64; psychologist Talawanda, Shiloh, Trenton Schs., Butler County, Ohio, 1964-66, Franklin (Ohio) City Schs., 1966-72, Wapakoneta (Ohio) City Schs., 1972-76, Cin. City Schs., 1978-86; pvt. practice psychology, 1975—; planner, evaluator Warren/Clinton Counties Mental Health Bd., Ohio, 1986-88; adj. instr. Wright State U., Dayton, Ohio, 1989—. Co-author: Summer Children-Ready or not for School, 1986, The Rape of Childhood--No Time to be a Kid, 1990. Sec. Tri County Drug Council, Lima, Ohio, 1974; chmn. Auglaize County Social Services, Wapakoneta, Ohio, 1973-75. Mem. Ohio Sch. Psychologists Assn. (exec. bd. 1982-86), Southwestern Ohio Sch. Psychologist Assn. (pres.), Southwest Council Exceptional Children (Pres.), Nat. Assn. Sch. Psychologists, Ohio Psychol. Assn., Butler County 648

Mental Health Bd. (bd. dirs. 1978-86, pres. 1983-84). Republican. United Methodist. Home and Office: 6120 Michael Rd Middletown OH 45042

GILMORE, LOUISA RUTH, retired nurse, retired firefighter; b. Pitts., Oct. 31, 1930; d. Albert Leonard and Bertha Christina (Birch) Huber; m. William Norman Kemp, May 27, 1950 (div. 1975); children: Janyce Louise Kemp Lipson, Barbra Lea Kemp Bilharz, Robert William, Paul Lee, Charles Albert; m. Robert James Gilmore, Sept. 1, 1989. Diploma in nursing, San Bernardino Community Coll., Needles, Calif., 1983. Office nurse Santa Fe Clinic, Needles, 1953-57; spl. duty nurse Needles Communities Hosp., 1957-62; nurse supr. Santa Fe Clinic, 1962-79; staff nurse in surgery Needles Desert Communities Hosp., 1979-90, ret.; CPR instr. Needles Desert Communities Hosp., 1987-90; med. officer San Bernadino County Fire Dept., Needles, 1980-83, pub. info. officer 1983-90. Mem. Calif. State Fireman Assn., Needles Firefighters Assn. (treas. 1987, 88), Beta Sigma Phi-Zeta Gamma (treas. 1966, sec. 1967, v.p. 1968, pres. 1969, named Sweetheart Queen 1969), Order of Rose (life).

GILMORE, MARJORIE HAVENS, lawyer, civic worker; b. N.Y.C., Aug. 16, 1918; d. William Westerfield and Elsie (Medl) Havens; AB, Hunter Coll., 1938; JD, Columbia, 1941; m. Hugh Redland Gilmore, May 8, 1942; children: Douglas Hugh, Anne Charlotte Gilmore Decker, Joan Louise. Admitted to N.Y. State bar, 1941, Va. bar, 1968; rsch. asst. N.Y. Law Revision Commn., 1941-42; assoc. firm Spence, Windels, Walser, Hotchkiss & Angell, N.Y.C., 1942, Chadbourne, Wallace, Parke & Whiteside, N.Y.C., 1942-43; atty. U.S. Army, Washington, 1948-53. Sec., Thomas Jefferson Jr. High Sch. PTA, 1956-58; parliamentarian Wakefield High Sch. PTA, 1959-60, chmn. citizenship com., 1960-61; publicity chmn. Patrick Henry Sch. PTA, sec., 1964-65; parliamentarian Nottingham PTA, 1966-69; mem. extra-curricular activities com. Arlington County Sch. Bd.; area chmn. fund drive Cancer Soc., 1955-56; active Girl Scouts U.S.A., 1963-70; mem. '41 com. Columbia Law Sch. Fund. Recipient Constl. Law award Hunter Coll., 1938. Mem. Arlington Fedn. Women's Clubs (rec. sec. 1979-80), No. Dist. Va. Fedn. Women's Clubs (chmn. legis. com. 1986-88, chmn. pub. affairs No. dist. 1988-90), Columbia Law Sch. Alumni Assn., Alpha Sigma Rho. Presbyn. Club: Williamsburg Woman's of Arlington (corr. sec. 1970-72, 1st v.p. 1972-74, pres. 1974-76, chmn. communications 1981-82, chmn. legis. com. 1982-86, 90—). Home: 3020 N Nottingham St Arlington VA 22207

GILMORE, MILLICENT JONES, military career officer; b. Altoona, Pa., July 17, 1920; d. Harry Elvey and Sylvia Violet (Burk) Jones; m. Jack DeWolf Gilmore, Apr. 30, 1963 (div. May, 1967). BS in Edn., Millersville U., 1942; postgrad studies, Geo. Washington U., 1942-43 1945-47, U. Fla., 1948. Pub. relations staff Nat. Housing Agy., Washington, 1942-43; statistician British Ministry of Supply, Washington, 1943-44; economist Dept. of Labor, Washington, 1944-47; tchr. Dade County Bd. of Instruction, Miami, 1947-51; mgmt. analyst HQ Andrews AFB, Washington, 1951-52; personnel officer USAF, various cities, 1952-72; tutor Orange County Schs., Orlando, Fla., 1973-74. Author: History of Jones-Burk Family 1978. Major USAF, 1952-72. Mem. AAUW (pres. local chpt. 1989-91), Young Women's Community Club, USAF Women Officer's Assn., Retired Officers' Assn., Am. Legion. Democrat. Lutheran. Home: 8067 Woodduck Dr Orlando FL 32825

GILMORE, SUSAN ASTRID LYTLE, speech and language pathologist; b. Phila., July 12, 1942; d. Ford Bertrand and Astrid Elizabeth (Hammerstrom) Lytle; m. Stuart Irby Gilmore, June 6, 1970 (div. Dec. 1981); 1 child, Ford Lytle. BA, U. Pacific, 1964, MA, 1965; PhD, Ohio U., 1968. Cert. pub. sch. adminstr., elem. tchr., speech-lang. pathologist, Calif. Asst. prof. spl. edn., speech-lang. pathology La. State U., Baton Rouge, 1968-76, assoc. prof., 1976-79; supr. spl. edn. Sacramento City Unified Sch. Dist., 1979—, acting adminstrv. specialist Spl. Edn. Dept., 1988—; cons. State Dept Health, Baton Rouge, 1970-75, State Dept. Hosps., Baton Rouge, 1973-75; instr. U. Pacific, Stockton, Calif., 1979, ind. examiner Sacramento City Unified Sch. Dist., 1979; acting adminstrv. specialist Spl. Edn. Dept. Sacremento City Unified Sch. Dist., 1988—. Editor: (asst.) Lang., Speech and Hearing Services in Schs., 1983—; contbr. articles to profl. jours. Vestry mem. Trinity Episcopal Cathedral Ch., Sacramento, 1983-85, altar guild mem. 1980—; bd. dirs. Friends of People With Chronic Mental Illness, Sacramento, 1983-85. Mem. Assn. Calif. Sch. Adminstrs., Am. Speech-Lang.-Hearing Assn., Calif. Speech-Lang.-Hearing Assn. (cert. of appreciations 1985—), Council for Exceptional Children (sec.), Am. Assn. Mental Deficiency, Kappa Alpha Theta (pres. 1961-62), Phi Delta Kappa. Republican. Home: 6333 Driftwood St Sacramento CA 95831 Office: Sacramento City Unified Sch Dist 4701 Joaquin Way Sacramento CA 95822

GILNER, GRACE MARIE, physical therapy educator; b. Freeport, N.Y., July 16, 1961; d. Harold Francis and Marie Elizabeth (Gerdon) G.; m. Robert Charles Zick, Aug. 6, 1989. AS magna cum laude, Nassau Community Coll., Garden City, N.Y., 1981; BS with highest honors, SUNY, Stony Brook, 1984; MS, L.I. U., 1988. Cert. phys. therapist, N.Y. Phys. therapist Brookdale Hosp. Med. Ctr., Bklyn., 1984-87; pvt. practice Baldwin, N.Y., 1987—; lead phys. therapist Ctr. for Rehab., Floral Park, N.Y., 1987-88; phys. therapist Manhasset (N.Y.) Pediatric Rehab., 1988-89; instr. phys. therapy asst. program Nassau Community Coll., 1989—. Mem. Am. Phys. Therapy Assn., Phi Theta Kappa. Roman Catholic. Home: 650 Parsonage Pl Baldwin NY 11510 Office: Nassau Community Coll Stewart Ave Garden City NY 11530

GILROY, HOLLIE A., research director; b. Plainfield, N.J., Feb. 2, 1963; d. James Thomas and Geraldine Louise (Smalley) G. BA, Rutgers U., 1985. Rsch. dir. The Marcus Group, Inc., Secaucus, N.J.; legis. coord. The Marcus Group, Inc., Secaucus. Recipient Paul Tillett Pol. Sci. award, L'Hommedieu scholarship; named Stanton-Anthony scholar. Mem. NAFE, PRSA, Phi Theta Kappa, Psi Beta. Home: 25 Horizon Dr Edison NJ 08817 Office: 132 W State St Trenton NJ 08608

GILROY, PATRICIA ANNE, legislative staff member; b. Balt., Jan. 27, 1944; d. Ralph Charles and Catherine G. (Foley) G.; m. Ted McKinnies Russell, Feb. 25, 1979. BA, Vassar Coll., 1966; MA, U. Madrid, 1967. Legis. asst., corr. dir. Senator Christopher Dodd, Washington; legis. corr. dir. Senator John Culver, Washington; personal sec. Rep. Allard Lowenstein, Washington; mil. affairs specialist Senator Robert Kennedy, Washington. Home: 1414 17th St NW #814 Washington DC 20036

GILTNER, ALYCE SHARLENE, business educator; b. Cairo, Ill., Nov. 25, 1960; d. Arthur S. and Wanda H. (Bankson) Ervin; m. Bruce Neal Giltner, May 21, 1988. BS in Bus. Edn., Southeast Mo. State U., 1982, MAT, 1984. Bus. instr. Shawnee Community Coll., Ullin, Ill., 1986--; advisor, Phi Beta Lambda, Metropolis, Ill. 1986--. Mem. Southern Ill. Bus. Educators Assn. Office: Shawnee Coll Metro Ctr 10th Catherine Metropolis IL 62960

GIMBEL, PATRICIA A., lawyer; b. Bismarck, N.D., May 21, 1955; d. Albert and Verna Margaret (Scharf) G.; m. Dennis Michael Lothspeich, Aug. 5, 1989. BA cum laude, U. N.D., 1979, JD, 1987. Bar: Minn., N.D. Asst. to dir. U. N.D. Art Gallery, Grand Forks, 1977-80; clk. Burlington No., Grand Forks, 1981; mktg. coord. Columbia Mall Shopping Ctr., Grand Forks, 1981-84; assoc. John Winters Law Office, Crookston, Minn., 1987-89; mem. staff Legal Svcs. N.E. Minn., Brainerd, Minn., 1989-90; assoc. Collin W. Fritz & Assoc., Brainerd, Minn., 1990—. Bd. dirs. Friends of N.D. Mus. of Art, Grand Forks, 1988—; bd. dirs. Project Safe, Crookston, Minn., 1988-89. Recipient Disting. Svc. to Low Income Clients award N.W. Minn. Legal Svcs., 1989. Mem. ABA (bd. dirs. 1988-89), Acad. Family Law Mediators (assoc.), Minn. Women Lawyers, AAUW, Minn. Bar Assn., N.D. Bar Assn., Zonta Internat. Home: Star Rt Pequot Lakes MN 56472 Office: Collin W Fritz & Assoc PO Box 426 Brainerd MN 56401

GIMBUTAS, MARIJA, archaeologist, educator; b. Vilnius, Lithuania, Jan. 23, 1921; came to U.S., 1949, naturalized, 1955; d. Daniel and Veronica (Janulaitis) Alseika; m. Jurgis Gimbutas, 1942; children: Danute, Zivile, Rasa. M.A., U. Vilnius, 1942; Ph.D., U. Tubingen, Germany, 1946; postgrad., U. Heidelberg and Munich, Germany, 1947-49; PhD (hon.), Calif. Inst. Integral Studies, San Francisco, 1988. Research fellow Peabody Mus., Harvard U., Boston, 1955-63; lectr. dept. anthropology Peabody Mus., Harvard U., 1962-63; fellow Center for Advanced Study in Behavioral Scis., Stanford, Calif., 1961-62; prof. European archaeology and Indo-European studies UCLA, 1963—; fellow Netherlands Inst. for Advanced Studies, 1973-74; project dir. excavations of Neolithic S.E. Europe, Obre, Bosnia, 1967-68, excavations at Sitagroi, N.E. Greece, 1968-69, excavations at Anza, Central Macedonia, 1969-70, at Achilleion, Thessaly, Greece, 1973-74, at Scaloria, nr. Manfredonia, Italy, 1979-80. Author: Die Bestattung in Litauen in der vorgeschichtlichen Zeit, 1946, Prehistory of Eastern Europe, 1956, Ancient Symbolism in Lithuanian Folk Art, 1958, The Balts, 1963, The Bronze Age Cultures of Central and Eastern Europe, 1965, The Slavs, 1971, The Gods and Goddesses of Old Europe, 1974, Neolithic Macedonia, 1976, The Goddesses and Gods of Old Europe, 1982, Die Balten, 1983, Baltai priešistoriniais laikais, 1985; co-editor: (with Colin Renfrew and Ernestine Elster) Excavations at Sitagroi. A Prehistoric Village in Northeast Greece, 1986, The Language of the Goddess, 1989, Achilleion, a Neolithic Village in Northern Greece, 6400-5600 B.C. Monumenta Archaeologica, UCLA, 1989; editor: Jour. Indo-European Studies, 1973—, Monumenta Archaeologica, 1976—. Recipient Woman of Yr. award Los Angeles Times, 1968; NSF fellow, 1959-60, 68-69, 73-76; Smithsonian fellow, 1967-71; Nat. Endowment for Humanities grantee, 1967; Kress Found. fellow, 1967-72; subject of Festschrift Proto-Indo-European. The Archaeology of Linguistic Problems. Mem. Assn. Field Archaeologists, Assn. for Advancement Baltic Studies (pres. 1980-82), Council for Old World Archaeology, Am. Anthrop. Assn., Internat. Assn. for Promotion of Studies of Southeastern Europe, Inst. of Lithuanistics, Internat. Assn. Proto-and Prehistoric Religion, Internat. Soc. for Comparative Study of Civilization, Am. Inst. Archaeology. Home: 21434 W Entrada Rd Topanga CA 90290 Office: UCLA 115 Kinsey Hall 405 Hilgard Ave Los Angeles CA 90024

GINDES, MARION E., clinical psychologist, consultant; b. Bklyn., July 14, 1939; d. Robert I. and Minna Alterwein; (div.); 1 child, Jessica Hornstein; m. David S. Palermo, June 29, 1980. Student, Smith Coll., 1957-59; BA, Barnard Coll., 1961; MS, PhD, Columbia U., 1965. Lic. psychologist, N.Y., Pa. Staff psychologist, instr. Bronx Mcpl. Hosp. Ctr., Albert Einstein Coll. Medicine, 1965-67; dir. psychol. svcs. Coney Island Mental Health Ctr., Bklyn., 1967-69; asst. prof. Albert Einstein Coll. Medicine, 1970-72; asst. prof. psychology, 1972-80; dep. chairperson CUNY, Bklyn., 1973-76; vis. assoc. prof. Pa. State U., University Park, 1980-82; co-founder, bd. mem. Centre Valley Mgmt. Meadows Psychiat. Ctr., Centre Hall, Pa., 1981-85, cons. psychol. staff, 1985—; pvt. practice State College, Pa. and N.Y.C., 1969—; adj. assoc. prof. Pa. State U., 1982—; exec. com. Counseling Ministry of Christian Mission, State Coll., 1984-89; cons. Commonwealth Pa., 1989; conducted numerous psychol. workshops. Contbr. articles to profl. jours.; editor: Social Intervention, 1971; reviewer for maj. pub. cos. and profl. jours. Mem. Pa. Task Force on Women, N.Cen., 1986-87, Interdisciplinary Task Force on Alcoholism, State Coll., 1982-84; adv. bd. Parents Without Partners, State College, 1981-86; cons. Children & Youth Svcs., 1989. USPHS grantee, 1962-63, 64-65, NIMH grantee, 1969-70, Grant Found. grantee, 1970-75, CUNY grantee, 1977-79. Fellow Pa. Psychol. Assn., Cen. Pa. Psychol. Assn. (pres. 1989-90, exec. bd. 1986—);mem. AAUW (bd. dirs. 1987-89), Am. Psychol. Assn., Ea. Psychol. Assn., Mental Health Profl. Pa. (v.p. 1982-83, pres. 1983-86), Soc. Rsch. Child Devel., Am. Orthopsychiat. Assn., Am. Women Entrepreneurs, Sigma Xi, Kappa Delta Pi.

GINGERICH, FLORINE ROSE, lawyer; b. Lowville, N.Y., Nov. 25, 1951; d. Beryl J. and Marion A. (Jantzi) G.; m. Douglas W. Purcell, Nov. 26, 1988; 1 child, James. BA in History, Goshen Coll., 1973; JD, U. Mich., 1976. Bar: Wash. 1976, U.S. Dist. Ct. (we. dist.) Wash. 1976. Assoc. Davis, Wright & Jones, Seattle, 1976-83; v.p., corp. counsel Seattle Trust and Savs., 1983-85, v.p., sec., corp. counsel, 1985-87; assoc. Hiscock and Barclay, Seattle, 1987-88, ptnr., 1989—. Mem. planning and allocations conf. panel United Way of King-Seattle County, 1979-82; bd. dirs. Consumer Credit Counseling Svcs. of Seattle, 1982-83, Friends of Youth, Renton, Wash., 1986—, v.p., 1988—. Mem. ABA, Wash. State Bar Assn., Seattle-King County Bar Assn. Clubs: Seattle, Columbia Tower (Seattle). Office: Hiscock and Barclay 6400 Columbia Ctr 701 5th Ave Seattle WA 98104

GINGRICH, KAY M., hypnotherapist, beautician; b. Harrisburg, Pa., Nov. 18, 1945; d. John A. L. and Kathryn S. (Williams) Rothermel; m. Gerald I. Gingrich, Jan. 24, 1984; children: Jeri Williams, Annette Boyer, Gary. Student, Christian Internat. Coll., Phoenix; cert., Biblical Counseling Found., 1981; postgrad., Am. Inst. Hypnotherapy, Calif.; cert. paralegal, Nat. Edn. Corp., Pa. Cert. Nat. Guild Hypnotherapists; lic. cosmotologist. Beautician Manor Care Kingston Ct., York, Pa.; pvt. practice hypnotherapy York; store clk. Marietta Emporium, Marietta, Pa.; beautician White Hall Nursing and Rehab., Lancaster, Pa.; pvt. practice beautician Elizabethtown, Pa.; lectr. in field. Mem. NAFE, Associated Counselors and Hypnotherapists (v.p.), Am. Assn. Counseling and Devel., Am. Assn. Christian Counselors, Am. Assn. Mental Health Counselors, Nat. Guild Hypnotherapists (Hall of Fame 1990). Home: Rt. 11 Box 384 Kreutz Creek York PA 17406

GINGRICH-PETERSEN, CAROLYN ASHCRAFT, psychologist; b. Waxhaw, N.C.; d. J. Carl and Carolyn (Ray) Wolfe; m. Thomas L. Ashcraft (div. 1973); children: Anne C., Thomas Wolfe; m. Marvin E. Petersen, Nov. 14, 1982. BS, U. N.C.; MA, Vanderbilt U., PhD, 1963. Lic. psychologist, Tenn., Pa., Fla. Psychologist Peabody Child Study Ctr., Nashville, 1963-64; researcher U.S. Dept. Edn.-Peabody, Nashville, 1964-65; assoc. prof. Tenn. State U., Nashville, 1965-66; asst. prof. U. Tenn., Nashville, 1966-69, LaSalle Coll., Phila., 1970-72; adj. instr. U. Pa., Phila., 1970-73; clin. psychologist Overbrook Sch. for Blind, Phila., 1974-76, Fla. Sch. for Deaf and Blind, St. Augustine, 1976-78; asst. prof. psychology U. Tampa, Fla., 1979-82; assoc. and adj. prof. S.D. State U., Brookings, 1983-89, cons., teaching adjunct courses dept. psychology, 1989—; cons. Tenn. Dept. Edn., Cookeville, 1966-69, Charter Hosp., Tampa, 1979-82; organizer symposia for profl. meetings. Contbr. to profl. publs. Bd. dirs. Brookings Hosp. Aux., 1985-88; v.p. S.D. Art Mus. Guild, 1988-89. Fellow Am. Psychol. Soc., Pa. Psychol. Assn.; mem. Southeastern Psychol. Assn., Nat. Register Psychologists. Republican. Home: 1029 9th Ave Brookings SD 57006

GINN, SUSAN B., training and educational specialist; b. Troy, Ala., Aug. 21, 1950; d. Robert Henderson and Idaleen (Hudson) Barr; m. Jerry Wesley Ginn, Aug. 9, 1989; children: Patrick, John, Dana. BS in Edn., Troy State U., 1972, MS in Sch. Adminstrn., 1983. Tng. specialist Dept. of the Army, Ft. McPherson, Ga.; edn. specialist Dept. of the Army, Ft. Rucker, Ala.; force integration officer Dept. Army, Ft. Sheridan, Ill.; tchr. Dale City Bd. Edn., Ozark, Ala. Recipient nomination for Nat. Civil Svc. League Career award, Comdrs. award for excellence, 1989; named Army Aviation Ctr. Profl. Woman of Yr., 1988. Mem. AAUW, AAAA, Assn. U.S. Army (4th v.p. 1984-85), Federally Employed Women (v.p. local chpt. 1982-83), Beta Sigma Phi, Kappa Delta Pi, Gamma Beta Phi. Methodist. Home: 128 Logan Loop Fort Sheridan IL 60037 Office: Dept of US Army Fort Sheridan IL 60037

GINSBERG, EMILY SUZANNE, high technology executive; b. Horseheads, N.Y., Sept. 26, 1935; d. John and Anna (Nosko) Boor; m. David Lawrence Ginsberg, Dec. 30, 1969; children: Daniel, Laura. BA in Econs. and Math., Elmira Coll., 1956; MS in Computer Sci., Poly. U. N.Y., 1981. Sr. job analyst N.Y. Life Ins., N.Y.C., 1956-64, personnel researcher, 1977-78; mgr. commissions Mgmt. Assistance, Inc., N.Y.C., 1965-67, br. adminstrn. mgr., 1967-68; exec. asst. to pres. Programming Techniques, Inc., N.Y.C., 1968-69; teaching asst. Poly. U., White Plains, N.Y., 1980-81; mgr. verification systems Fingermatrix, Inc., North White Plains, N.Y., 1981-84, v.p., 1984—. co-inventor fingerprint verification method, 1986. Mem. Am. Soc. Indsl. Security, Assn. Computing Machinery, NOW, Phi Beta Kappa. Clubs: The Town, Old Scarsdale Assn. (N.Y.). Home: 18 Autenrieth Rd Scarsdale NY 10583 Office: Fingermatrix Inc 30 Virginia Rd North White Plains NY 10603

GINSBERG-FELLNER, FREDDA, pediatric endocrinologist, researcher; b. N.Y.C., Apr. 21, 1937; d. Nathanaiel and Bertha (Jagendorf) Ginsberg; m. Michael J. Fellner, Aug. 27, 1961; children: Jonathan R., Melinda B. AB, Cornell U., 1957; MD, NYU, 1961. Diplomate Am. Bd. Pediatrics, Am. Bd. Pediatric Endocrinology. Intern Albert Einstein Coll. Medicine, N.Y.C., 1961-62, fellow in pediatrics, 1962-63, 64-65, 66-67, resident in pediatrics, 1963-64, 65-66, clin. instr. pediatrics, 1967; assoc. in pediatrics Mt. Sinai Sch. Medicine, N.Y.C., 1967-69, asst. prof., 1969-75, assoc. prof., 1975-81, dir. div. pediatric endocrinology, 1977—, prof. pediatrics, 1981—. Mem. med. scis. rev. com. Juvenile Diabetes Found., 1985-88; mem. N.Y. State Coun. on Diabetes, Albany, 1988-89; chmn. Camp NYDA for Diabetic Children, Burlingham, 1977-89. Grantee NIH, 1977—, Am. Diabetes Assn., 1978, March of Dimes, 1983-87, Juvenile Diabetes Found., 1982-88, Wm. T. Grant Found., 1985-89. Fellow Am. Acad. Pediatrics; mem. Am. Diabetes Assn., Soc. Pediatric Rsch., Am. Pediatric Soc., Endocrine Soc., Lawson Wilkins Pediatric Endocrine Soc., N.Y. Diabetes Assn. (pres.-elect 1985-87, pres. 1987-89, Svc. award Camp NYDA 1989). Office: Mt Sinai Med Ctr 1 Gustave Levy Pl Box 1198 New York NY 10029

GINSBURG, ANN, biochemist, researcher; b. Porterville, Calif., Jan. 17, 1932; d. Maurice Wilcox and Ruth Francis (Harris) Forman; m. Victor Ginsburg, May 27, 1955; children: Mark, Lisa Ruth. BA, U. Calif., Berkeley, 1954, MA, 1956; PhD, George Washington U., 1964. Chemist NIAMD/NIH, Bethesda, Md., 1956-58, 63-64; fellow USPAS, Bethesda, 1960-63; chemist NIDR/NIH, Bethesda, 1964-66; rsch. chemist NHLBI/NIH, Bethesda, 1966-74, chief protein chemistry sect., 1974—. Exec. editor: Archives of Biochemistry and Biophysics, 1984—; co-editor: Current Topics in Cellular Metabolism, Vol. 26, 1985; contbr. numerous articles to jours. and chpts. to books. Mem. Am. Soc. Biochemists and Molecular Biologists, Am. Soc. Biol. Chemists, Am. Chem. Soc., Biophys. Soc., Calorimetry Conf. Office: NHLBI/NIH Bldg 3 Rm 208 Bethesda MD 20892

GINSBURG, IONA HOROWITZ, psychiatrist; b. N.Y.C., Dec. 2, 1931; d. A. Eugene and Gertrude (Seidman) Horowitz; m. Selig M. Ginsburg, Aug. 15, 1954 (div. 1984); children: Elizabeth, Jessica. AB, Vassar Coll., 1953; MD, Columbia U., 1957. Diplomate Am. Bd. Psychiatry and Neurology. Pvt. practice N.Y.C., 1961—; instr. psychiatry Columbia U., N.Y.C., 1961-81, asst. clin. prof. psychiatry, 1981—; psychiatrist student health svc. NYU, N.Y.C., 1978—; cons.-liaison psychiatrist dept. dermatology Columbia Presbyn. Med. Ctr., N.Y.C., 1982—. Contbr. articles to profl. jours. Mem. Am. Soc. for Adolescent Psychiatry, N.Y. Soc. Adolescent Psychiatry (pres. 1986, Cert. of Appreciation 1986), Am. Psychiat. Assn., Am. Psychosomatic Soc., Met. Coll. Mental Health Assn. (pres. 1980).

GINTER, EVELYN, social services organization executive; b. Hebron, N.Y., Dec. 12, 1932; d. Mark H. and Hazel (DeKalb) Glasier; m. Earle F. Ginter, June 1, 1952; children: John, David, Margaret. BS in Home Econs., Cornell U., 1953; M in Social Svc., Bryn Mawr Coll., 1983, MS in Law-Social Policy, 1984. Cert. elem. and nursery sch. tchr., N.J. Elem. tchr. Woodbury (N.J.) Pub. Schs., 1956-58; founder, head tchr., chmn. bd. dirs. Woodbury Child Devel. Ctr., 1968-76; Title XX coord. Human Svcs. Coalition Gloucester County, Woodbury, 1976-80; counselor Women in Transition, Phila., 1981-82; intern, legis. aide to Senator Ray Zane, N.J. Senate, Woodbury, 1982-83; exec. dir. People Against Spouse Abuse, Glassboro, N.J., 1984—; mem. adv. bd. RSVP, Gloucester County, 1985—, Gloucester County Probation Adv. Bd., 1986—, Rape Abuse Prevention Program, Glassboro, 1988—; co-chmn. Gloucester County Prosecutor's Working Group on Domestic Violence, 1986—. Del. White House Conf. on Family, Balt., 1980. Mem. Nat. Coalition Against Domestic Violence, N.J. Coalition for Battered Women (treas. 1984-86) AAUW (past pres. Gloucester County Br., fellowship created in her name 1975). Office: People Against Spouse Abuse POBox 755 Glassboro NJ 08028

GINTER, SALLY ANN, chemical company executive; b. Kalamazoo, Dec. 2, 1944; d. Hubert Clayton and Dorothy Lucille (McCallum) Pettengill; m. Ronald Francis Cornier, June 11, 1966 (div. Apr. 1973); 1 child, Nicole Lynn; m. Thomas O'Neal Ginter, Sept. 1, 1973; 1 child, Mark Allan. BA in Chemistry, Albion Coll., 1967. Chemist Dow Chem. Co., Midland, Mich., 1967-72, rsch. chemist, 1972-75, sr. rsch. chemist, 1975-78, rsch. specialist, 1978-82, rsch. leader, 1982-84, devel. assoc., 1984-86, mgr. tech. svc. and devel., 1986-87, devel. mgr. New Ventures Commercialization, 1987-88; rsch. mgr. applied organics and functional polymers rsch. Dow Chem. Co., Midland, 1988-89, sr. rsch mgr. applied organics and functional polymers rsch., 1989, lab. dir. chems. and metals tech. svc. and devel., 1989—; treas. Brominated Flame Retardant Industry Panel, Lancaster, Pa., 1986-87; adv. Nat. Acad. Fire Scis., Salt Lake City, 1986-87. Contbr. articles to profl. jours., 1971-84; patentee in field. Mem. Nat. Tax Limitation Com., Washington, 1980, Huepac, Midland, 1987. Mem. Am. Foundrymen's Soc., Fire Retardants Chem. Assn. (treas., bd. dirs. 1984-87), Soc. Plastics Industry, Phi Beta Kappa, Alpha Lambda Delta, Alpha Xi Delta. Republican. Methodist. Office: Dow Chem Co 2020 Bldg Midland MI 48674

GINZIG, CAROL A., treasurer and corporate secretary; b. Bklyn.; m. Randall Ginzig, Dec. 21, 1980. MBA in Corp. Fin., Pace U., 1982. Banking and planning supt. Rolls-Royce, Inc., N.Y.C., 1982-83; asst. treas. Rolls-Royce, Inc., 1983-86; asst. treas., asst. sec. Rolls-Royce, Inc., Greenwich, Conn., 1986-87; treas., asst. sec. Rolls-Royce, Inc., 1987-88, treas., corp. sec., 1988—. Fin. chair Jr. League Cen. Westchester, Westchester, N.Y. Office: Rolls Royce Inc 475 Steamboat Rd Greenwich CT 06836

GIOANNINI, THERESA LEE, educator; b. Galesburg, Ill., Nov. 21, 1949; d. Raymond Frank and JoAnn (Keefe) G.; m. Jerrold Paul Weiss, May 23, 1979; children: Gregory Martin, Douglas Peter. BS, St. Mary of the Woods (Ind.) Coll., 1971; MS, NYU, 1976, PhD, 1978. With NYU Med. Ctr., N.Y.C., 1978—, rsch. prof., 1985—; assoc. prof. CUNY, N.Y.C., 1990—. U.S. Dept. HHS/NIH fellow, 1980-83. Mem. AAAS, Am. Men and Women in Sci., Am. Chem. Soc. Home: 283 Avenue C Apt 7H New York NY 10009 Office: CUNY Baruch Coll New York NY 10010

GIORDANO, ANNE SHIRLEY, elementary educator; b. New Haven, Conn., Dec. 29, 1937; m. Charles B. Giordano, June 6, 1959; children: Catherine Elrod, Peter, David, Mark. BS in Elem. Edn., New Haven State Tchrs. Coll., 1959; MA, Catholic U., Wash. DC, 1970; postgrad., U. Md. Tchr. Reynoldsburg (Ohio) Pub. Sch., 1959-60, Columbus (Ohio) Pub. Sch., 1960-61; thcr. Prince George's County Sch., Upper Marlboro, Md., 1966-86; instructional support tchr. Prince George's County Sch., Upper Marlboro, 1986-87, elem. instructional specialist, 1987—; part-time instr. Strayer Coll., Washington, 1970-81, Trinity Coll., Washington, 1989—. Chairperson Assn. Sch. Adminstr. and Supt., 1986. Mem. Assn. Sch. Based Adminstrs. and Suprs. Prince George's County, Devel., Internat. Reading Assn., Prince George's County. Roman Catholic. Home: 2212 Hallow Ln Bowie MD 20716

GIORDANO, ANTOINETTE R., insurance agent; b. Bklyn., Jan. 21, 1948; d. James V. and Mildred (DeGia) Capalbo; m. Louis L. Giordano Jr., Apr. 27, 1968; children: Danielle, Denise, Dawn. AAS in Bus. Adminstrn., Suffolk Community Coll., 1985; BS in Bus. Mgmt., St. Joseph's Coll., Patchogue, N.Y., 1987. Registered ins. rep.; lic. life, health, property ins. agt., N.Y. Registered rep., ins. agt. Prudential Fin. Svc., Patchogue; policy advisor Union Savs. Bank, Patchogue; stockbroker Investors Ctr. Inc., Holtsville, N.Y.; fin. advisor Apple Bank for Savs., East Setauket, N.Y., 1990—.

GIORDANO, E. LYNN, advertising agency executive. Formerly with Foote Cone & Belding, N.W. Ayer; with Lintas: N.Y., N.Y.C., 1981—, exec. v.p., exec. creative dir., 1985—. Recipient numerous creative awards. Office: Lintas: NY 1 Dag Hammarskjold Pla New York NY 10017*

GIORDANO, PATRICIA SCHOPPE, interior decorator; b. Houston, Aug. 29, 1947; d. Conrad Joseph and Ellen Patricia (Condon) Schoppe; m. Natale Joseph Giordano, Apr. 17, 1971; children: Keith Joseph, Michael David, Ryan Peter, Todd Christopher. Student, U. Houston, 1965-67, NYU, 1969. Prin. Patricia S. Giordano Interiors, Ridgefield, Conn., 1975—; pub. speaker various floral design and horticulture workshops. Bd. dirs. Family and Children's Aid, Inc., Danbury, Conn., 1976-78, program rev. com., nominating com., 1978, head pub. rels., 1978-79, pres. aux., 1976-79; v.p. Twin Ridge Homewoners' Assn., Ridgefield, Conn., 1978-79, chmn., founder area beautification, 1978; pres. East Ridge Middle Sch. PTO, 1988-89. Recipient award of Excellence Fed. Garden Clubs Conn., 1984, Tricolor award Nat. Council State Garden Clubs, 1984, Aboreal award Nat. Council State Garden Clubs, 1984, Hort. Excellence award Nat. Council State Garden Clubs, 1984. Mem. Allied Bd. Trade, Caudatowa Garden Club (v.p. 1987-89, 90). Republican. Roman Catholic. Club: Caudatowa Garden (v.p. 1987-89, 90-91).

GIORDANO, TONI ANN, sales auditor; b. S.I., Dec. 5, 1962; d. Anthony Mario and Anita Marie (Tsea) G. BA, NYU, 1984. Field coordinator Merrill Lynch, N.Y.C., 1984-85; mgr. Rae Twin Cinema, S.I., 1981-87; sales auditor N.Y. Mets, Flushing, 1986—. NYU Merit scholar, 1980-84. Democrat. Roman Catholic. Home: 183 Prescott Ave Staten Island NY 10306

GIORGI, ELSIE AGNES, physician; b. N.Y.C., Mar. 8, 1911; d. Anacleto and Maria (Maserati) G. BA, Hunter Coll., 1931; MD, Columbia U., 1949. Diplomate Am. Bd. Internal Medicine. Intern Cornell 2d med. div. Bellevue Hosp., N.Y.C., 1949-50, asst. resident in medicine Cornell 2d med. div., 1950-52, chief resident in medicine Cornell 2d med. div., 1952-53, chief gen. med. clinics Cornell 2d med. div., 1953-59, assoc. attending physician Cornell 2d med. div., 1953-62, physician, specialist in internal medicine, 1953-61; physician, specialist in internal medicine L.A., 1962—; psychiat. trainee Cedars of Lebanon Hosp., Los Angeles, 1961-62, assoc. attending physician, 1962—; dir. div. home care and extended care, Cedars-Sinai Med. Ctr., Los Angeles, 1962-66; chief adolescent clinic, med. dir. clinics Mt. Sinai Hosp., Los Angeles, 1962-66, assoc. attending physician dept. medicine, 1962-69, attending physician, 1970—; med. dir., coordinator U. So. Calif. Family Neighborhood Health Services Ctr. for Watts, 1966-67; attending physician Los Angeles County Hosp., U. So. Calif. Med. Ctr., 1966-71; assoc. mem. dept. internal medicine Orange County Med. Ctr., Calif., 1969—, dir. ambulatory care services, 1969-72; staff St. John's Hosp., Santa Monica, Calif., 1970—; asst. prof. clin. medicine, attending sr. physician internal medicine Cornell U. Med. Coll., 1957-62; asst. prof. clin. medicine UCLA, 1962-66, guest lectr. Sch. Social Welfare, 1964—, assoc. clin. prof. medicine and community medicine Sch. Medicine, 1972—, PRIMEX, 1972-73; asst. prof. medicine Sch. Medicine, U. So. Calif., 1966-69, adj. prof. medicine, community medicine, family medicine Coll. Medicine, U. Calif., Irvine, 1969-72; cons. Martin E. Segal Co., 1969—, VA Hosp., Long Beach, Calif., 1972—, Washington, 1972—; cons. health care sect. Social Security Adminstrn., Balt., Los Angeles County Health Dept., Calif. Council for Health Plan Alternatives, Burlingame, Regional Med. Care Program, 1971-73, Tb and Health Assn. of Los Angeles; mem. nat. adv. bd. Nat. Council Sr. Citizens, Washington; mem. adv. com. USPHS, Calif. Dept. Pub. Health; mem. med. adv. com. Vis. Nurse Assn., Los Angeles, 1976; mem. adv. bd. Life Extension Inst., N.Y.C.; mem. edn. com. Am. Cancer Soc., San Francisco; cons. ednl. films. Author sect. in textbook; contbr. articles to profl. publs. Active Town Hall, Los Angeles; vol., bd. dirs. South Central Child Care Ctrs. for South Central Los Angeles; mem. nat. adv. bd. for legal research and services for elderly Nat. Council Sr. Citizens; mem. UCI-21 project com. U. Calif. Recipient Achievement award AAUW, 1968, Better Life award Am. Nursing Home Assn., 1974, lifetime commitment award Watts Health Found., 1987; named to Hall of Fame, Hunter Coll. Alumni Assn., 1976; feature This Is Your Life program TV Sta. KNBC, 1984. Mem. AMA, New York County Med. Assn., Calif. Med. Assn., Los Angeles County Med. Assn., Los Angeles County Soc. Internists, Am. Pub. Health Assn. (med. care sect.), Gerontol. Soc., Western Gerontology Assn., Comprehensive Health Planning Assn., Nat. Acad. Scis., Inst. Medicine. Home: 153 S Lasky Dr Ste 3 Beverly Hills CA 90212

GIOSEFFI, DANIELA, poet, author, educator; b. Orange, N.J., Feb. 12, 1941; d. Daniel Donato and Josephine (Buzevska) G.; m. Richard J. Kearney, Sept. 7, 1965 (div.); 1 child, Thea D.; m. Lionel B. Luttinger, June 6, 1986. BA, Montclair State Coll., 1963; MFA, Cath. U. of Am., 1966. Cons., poet N.Y. Poets-in-the-Schs., Inc., N.Y.C., 1972-85; freelance writer, lectr. at numerous univs. throughout U.S. and Europe, 1977—; honored speaker Internat. Feminist Bookfair, 1990; prof. speech and Communication arts, St. Francis Coll.; prof. speech., communication arts and writing Pace U., Bklyn. Coll., 1981—; prof. writing L.I. U.; author (novels) The Great American Belly, 1977, 4th edit., 1979; collection of poems: Eggs in the Lake, 1979; non-fiction: Earth Dancing; Mother Nature's Oldest Rite, 1981; Women on War and Survival: Global Voices for the Nuclear Age, 1988; Dust Disappears: translations of Carilda Oliver Labra of Latin America, 1989; contbr. poetry and fiction to numerous periodicals and anthologies; performer stage presentations of work throughout U.S. and Europe; plays produced Off-Off-Broadway include The Golden Daffodil Dwarf, Care of the Body, The Sea Hag in the Cave of Sleep, N.Y.C., 1988. Pres. Bklyn. Citizens for Sane Nuclear Policy, 1987-89; participant IV Feminist Internat. Bookfare, Barcelona, Spain, 1989; exec. bd., chair media watch com. Writers and Pubs. Alliance for Nuclear Disarmament, 1978—. Grantee N.Y. State Coun. on Arts, 1972, 77, grantee World Peach Edn. Ploughshares Fund, 1989, Womens' Leadership Devel.; recipient Poetry/Fiction award Creative Artists' Pub. Service Program, N.Y.C., 1971. Mem. PEN Am. Ctr., Actors' Equity Assn., Acad. Am. Poets, Nat. Book Critics Circle. Address: Earth Celebrations PO Box 197 Brooklyn Heights NY 11202

GIOVANNI, NIKKI, poet; b. Knoxville, Tenn., June 7, 1943; d. Jones and Yolande Cornelia (Watson) G.; 1 son, Thomas Watson. BA in History with honors, Fisk U., 1967; postgrad. in social work, U. Pa., 1967; LHD (hon.), Wilberforce U., 1972, Worcester U., 1972; DLitt (hon.), Ripon U., 1974, Smith Coll., 1975, Coll. Mt. St. Joseph on Ohio, 1983. Founder Nixtom Ltd., 1970; asst. prof. black studies Queens Coll., CCNY, 1968; assoc. prof. English Rutgers U., 1968-72; prof. creative writing Coll. Mt. St. Joseph on the Ohio, 1985; now prof. Va. Poly Inst. and State U., Blacksburg; vis. prof. English Ohio State U., 1984. Poet, writer, lectr.; author: Black Feeling, Black Talk, 1968, Black Judgement, 1969, Re-Creation, 1970, Broadside Poem of Angela Yvonne Davis, 1970, Night Comes Softly, 1970, Spin a Soft Black Song, 1971, Gemini, 1971, My House, 1972, A Dialogue: James Baldwin and Nikki Giovanni, 1973, Ego Tripping and Other Poems for Young Readers, 1973, A Poetic Equation: Conversations Between Nikki Giovanni and Margaret Walker, 1974, The Women and the Men, 1975, Vacationtime, 1980, Those Who Ride the Night Winds, 1983, Sacred Cows. . . and other Edibles, 1988; rec. artist: (album) Truth Is On Its Way, 1972, others; TV appearances include: Soul!, Nat. Ednl. TV network, numerous talk shows including the Tonight Show; participant Soul at the Center, Lincoln Center Performing Arts, N.Y.C., 1972. Vol. worker Nat. Council Negro Women, now life mem. Recipient Outstanding Achievement award Mademoiselle mag., 1971, Omega Psi Phi award, others; Ford Found. grantee, 1967. Address: care William Morrow & Co 105 Madison Ave New York NY 10016*

GIRALDI, WANDA WILLIAMSON, lawyer; b. El Dorado, Ark., Oct. 5, 1943; d. Lee Eugene and Mary Jane (Bogard) Williamson; m. Rodolfo G. Giraldi, Mar. 4, 1976; 1 child, Richard Anthony. BA, Newcomb Coll., 1964; MA, Tulane U., 1966; PhD, Ind. U., 1972; JD, John Marshall Law Sch., 1980. Bar: Ill. 1980, La. 1981, U.S. Dist. Ct. (ea. dist.) La. 1981, U.S. Ct. Appeals (5th cir.) 1981, U.S. Dist. Ct. (no. dist.) Ill. 1982. Assoc. Marshall J. Auerbach & Assocs., Ltd., Chgo., 1980-87; law clk. U.S. Jud. Dist. Ct., Houma, La., 1982; pvt. practice, New Orleans, 1987—. Active Spring Valley (Ill.) Park Bd., 1985. Recipient Hornbook award and Corpus Juris Secundum award West Pub. Co., 1980; John Marshall fellow, 1980. Mem. ABA, Fed. Bar Assn., Ill. Bar Assn., La. Bar Assn., Chgo. Bar Assn. (vol. legal svcs. 1982, chmn. travel com. 1983-84), Newcomers Club (pres. Spring Valley chpt. 1985). Democrat. Presbyterian.

GIRARD, ANDREA EATON, communication executive, consultant; b. N.Y.C., Oct. 16, 1946; d. Samuel Robert and Mimi (Eaton) G. Student, Syracuse U., 1964-66; BA cum laude, Finch Coll., 1968; MA, Columbia U., 1971. V.p. Charing Cross Press, N.Y., 1970-72; assoc. producer, talent dir.TV shows "To Tell the Truth" and "Snap Judgment" Goodson Todman Prodns., N.Y., 1972-80; programming exec. David Letterman-NBC, N.Y., 1980; dir. of talent, producer Daytime/Arts and Entertainment Networks (Hearst/ABC Video Enterprises), N.Y., 1981-84; dir. current programming acquisition, sr. producer Lifetime Network (Hearst/ABC/Viacom Entertainment Svcs.), N.Y., 1984-86; pres. Girard Communications, N.Y., 1986—, dir. med. communications advantage internat., 1990—; talent coord./prodn. asst. Guber-Ford-Gross Prodns., N.Y., 1968-70; judge Emmy awards Internat. Film and TV Festival; speaker pub. rels. coun. sch. of continuing edn. NYU; media cons. to med. industry, 1987—. Producer, writer (documentaries) Cave Dwellers of Crete, 1974, Sponge Divers of Kalymnos, 1979, Gypsies of the Camargue, 1983. Active fund raising bd. Jersey Wildlife Preservation Trust, N.Y.; active hospitality com. United Nations, N.Y., Big Apple com. for the benefit of the image of N.Y. Mem. NATAS, Women in Radio and TV, Women in Cable, Internat. Assn. of Cooking Profls., Le Club (N.Y.). Office: Girard Communications 201 E 77th St Ste #7F New York NY 10021

GIRARD, DEBORAH ANN, screenwriter; b. N.Y.C., Apr. 29, 1954; d. George Peter Arthur and Anastasia Rose (Bukauchis) G; m. Philip James Bosi. BA cum laude, Hunter Coll., 1976; postgrad., DePaul U., Chgo., 1989—. Assoc. producer Smith/Greenland Advt., N.Y.C., 1978-79, Sta. WOR-TV, N.Y.C., 1979-80; writer Warner-Amex, N.Y.C., 1981, Young & Rubicam Advt., N.Y.C., 1982; assoc. producer, writer Sta. WCBS-TV subs. CBS-TV News, N.Y.C., 1982-84; assoc. producer CBS-TV News, Los Angeles, 1984-85; writer Simon & Schuster Software, N.Y.C., 1986, The Travel Channel, N.Y.C., 1987—; writer screenplay Ailes Communications Inc., N.Y.C., 1987-88. Assoc. producer: Best TV Commercials :30, 1979 (Andy award 1979); writer: (variety series) Livewire, 1981 (Best Children's Cable Program award 1981). Recipient Best Exptl. Play award Playwright Ctr. Dramatist Contest, 1989. Mem. Internat. TV Assn. Republican. Roman Catholic.

GIRARD, LINDA WALVOORD, literature educator, poetry and children's author; b. Amsterdam, N.Y., Nov. 16, 1942; d. Christian H. and Marie (Verduin) Walvoord; m. Delmar W. Girard, Jan. 4, 1969; 1 child, Aaron. BA, Hope Coll., 1964; MA, U. Chgo., 1968, postgrad., 1968—; postgrad., U. Ill., 1971-74. Instr. Millikin U., Decatur, Ill., 1966-68; asst. prof. North Cen. Coll., Naperville, Ill., 1970-71; mem. faculty Inst. Children's Lit., Redding Ridge, Conn., 1988—; self-employed author and pub., 1980—. Author: You Were Born on Your Very First Birthday, 1983, My Body is Private, 1984, Who is a Stranger and What Should I Do?, 1985, Adoption is for Always, 1986, Jeremy's First Haircut, 1986, At Daddy's on Saturdays, 1987, We Adopted You, Benjamin Koo, 1989, Earth, Sea and Sky: The Work of Edmond Halley, 1985, Alex, The Kid With AIDS, 1990; contbr. articles, criticisms, revs., and poems to profl. jours. Fellow in poetry Ill. Arts Coun., 1985, Ford Found. fellow, 1964-65, U. Chgo. fellow, 1965-66, U.S. Office Edn. fellow, 1971-74; recipient 1st Place Book award in El/Hi div. Chgo. Women in Publishing, 1987, 88. Mem. Authors' Guild, MLA, Soc. Children's Book Writers, Children's Lit. Assn.

GIRARD, MARY SABEL, clinical counselor, retired personnel executive; b. Huntington, W.Va., Oct. 8, 1912; d. Isaac Herbert and Minnie Myrtle (McLaughlin) Sabel; m. Richard Anthony Girard, June 16, 1965. BA, Randolph-Macon Woman's Coll., 1934; MS, NYU, 1935; cert. in clin. counseling, Postgrad. Ctr. Mental Health, 1974. Personnel mgr. Ohrbach's, Newark, 1935-44; pers. corp. dir. Ohrbach's, N.Y.C., 1944-69, v.p. for personnel, 1969-72; ret., 1972, pvt. practice as clin. counselor, 1974—; personnel cons. Sears, Roebuck & Co., N.Y.C., 1973-77, Hosp. for Spl. Surgery, N.Y.C., 1974-75. Contbr. articles to profl. jours. Vice pres. Sun Cities Symphony Orch., 1983-84, pres., 1985-86; bd. dirs. Sundome Assn. for Performing Arts, Sun City West, Ariz., 1987-88. Recipient commencement citation Lab. Inst. Merchandising, 1972. Mem. Internat. Transactional Analysis Assn., Palmbrook Country Club, Eta Mu Pi, Tau Kappa Alpha, Zeta Tau Alpha. Republican. Mem. United Ch. of Christ.

GIRARD, NETTABELL, lawyer; b. Pocatello, Idaho, Feb. 24, 1938; d. George and Arranetta (Bell) Girard. Student, Idaho State U., 1957-58; BS, U. Wyo., 1959, JD, 1961. Bar: Wyo. 1961, D.C. 1969, U.S. Supreme Ct. 1969. Practiced in Riverton, 1963-69; atty.-adviser on gen. counsel's staff HUD; assigned Office Interstate Land Sales Registration, Washington, 1969-70; sect. chief interstate land sales Office Gen. Counsel, 1970-73; ptnr. Larson & Larson, Riverton, 1973-85; pvt. practice Riverton, 1985—; guest lectr. at high schs.; condr. seminar on law for layman Riverton br. A.A.U.W., 1965; condr. course on women and law; lectr. equal rights, job discrimination, land use planning. Editor: Wyoming Clubwoman, 1966-68; bd. editors Wyo. Law Jour, 1959-61; writer Obiter Dictum column Women Lawyers Jour; also articles in legal jours. Chmn. fund drive Wind River chpt. ARC, 1965; chmn. Citizens Com. for Better Hosp. Improvement, 1965; chmn. subcom. on polit., legal rights and responsibilities Gov.'s Commn. on Status Women, 1965-69, adv. mem., 1973—; rep. Nat. Conf. Govs. Commn., Washington, 1966; local chmn. Law Day, 1966, 67; mem. state bd. Wyo. Girl Scouts U.S., sec., 1974-89, mem. nat. bd., 1978-81; state vol. adviser Nat. Found., March of Dimes, 1967-69; legal counsel Wyo. Women's Conf., 1977; pres. Riverton Civic League, 1987-89. Recipient Spl. Achievement award HUD, 1972, Disting. Leadership award Girl Scouts U.S.A., 1973, Franklin D. Roosevelt award Wyo. chpt. March of Dimes, 1985, Thanks Badge award Girl Scout Coun., 1987, Women Helping Women award in recognition of effective advancement status of women Riverton Club of Soroptimist Internat. 1990; named Outstanding Woman, Wonder Woman and Girl Scouts U.S.A., 1982. Mem. Wyo. Bar Assn., Fremont County Bar Assn., D.C. Bar Assn., Women's Bar Assn. for D.C., Internat. Fedn. Women Lawyers, Am. Judicature Soc., Am. Trial Lawyers Assn., Nat. Assn. Women Lawyers (del. Wyo., nat. sec. 1969-70, v.p. 1970-71, pres. 1972-73), AAUW (br. pres.), Wyo. Fedn. Womens Clubs (state editor, pres. elect 1968-69, treas. 1974-76), Prog. Women's Club, Riverton Chautauqua Club (pres. 1965-67), Riverton Civil League (pres. 1987-89), Kappa Delta, Delta Kappa Gamma (hon. mem. state chpt.). Home: 224 W Sunset St PO Box 687 Riverton WY 82501 Office: 513 E Main St Riverton WY 82501

GIRDEN, LISA JAN, family and marriage therapist; b. Stamford, Conn., Aug. 28, 1959; d. Eugene Lawrence and Charlene Margot (Tobin) Girden. BA, Bucknell U., 1981; MS, U. Pa., 1982, 84. Cert. in marriage and family therapy. Tchr., Internat. Sch. Paris, 1980-81; mental health worker Ctr. for Autistic Children, Phila., 1983; asst. dir., acting dir. Old Pine Community Ctr., Phila., 1984-85; counselor Inst. for Learning, Phila., 1985—; pvt. practice psychology, family therapy, Phila., 1986—, Rittenhouse Counseling Assocs., Phila., 1985-86; dir. aftersch. program Old Pine Community Ctr., Phila., 1985-87; psychologist Downs Syndrome children Cooke Found., 1987-88. Mem. Am. Psychol. Assn., Assn. Humanistic Psychology, Am. Assn. Counseling and Devel. Avocations: skiing, horseback riding, needlepoint, gourmet cooking, travel.

GIRE, SHARON LEE, state legislator; b. Jan. 13, 1944; m. Dana A. Gire. BS in Edn., Ohio State U., 1965, postgrad. in counseling psychology, 1966; MSW, Wayne State U., 1975. Commr. Macomb County, 1984-86; chairperson budget com., pers. com., data processing subcom., bldg. and grounds subcom.; mem. fin. com., pers. and labor rels. com., health and human svcs. com., pub. works and transp. com., consumers com., econ. devel. com., pub. health com., senior citizen and retirement com., Macomb County Retirement Commn., Mich. Ho. of Reps., 1987—; chairwoman constn. and women's issues; mem. Mich. Assn. Counties Legis. Conf., Mich. Assn. Counties Ann. Conf., Mich. Assn. Counties Seminar County Govt., Mich. Mcpl. League State Legis. Confs., Mich. Mcpl. League Annual Confs., Mich. Mcpl. League Regional Meetings, Mich. Mcpl. League Workshops. Teen program cons. Cen. region YWCA, 1971-73; program dir. Macomb br. YWCA, 1969-71; mem. Mt. Clemens Bd. Zoning Appeals, 1977-83; commr. City of Mt. Clemens, 1977-84; mem. Mich. Women in Mcpl. Govt., 1978-84; mem. comml. and indsl. devel. com., 1978-84; city liaison for student govt. day, 1979-84; mayor pro-tem City of Mt. Clemens, 1979-84; vice chairwoman Mich. Mcpl. League Region 5, 1982; dir. N.E. Interfaith Ctr., 1977-84. Home: 37567 Radde Mount Clemens MI 48043

GIRGA, BARBARA ANN, psychotherapist, college counselor; b. Rayland, Ohio, Oct. 11, 1937; d. Virgil and Marjorie Fisher; children: Susan R., Robert E. BA, Bakersfield Coll., 1973; MA, Calif. State U., 1978; postgrad., Ky. Christian Coll., U. Calif., Santa Barbara, 1987. Lic. marriage, family, child counselor. With Water Assn. of Kern County, 1976-81; editor Bakersfield C. of C., 1977; diet counselor Nutra Systems, 1980; analyst Occidental Petroleum, 1981-86; psychotherapist, coll. counselor, 1986—; pvt. practice, clin. therapist Bakersfield (Calif.) Counseling Group, 1987-89; pvt. practice Bakersfield, 1989—; seminar leader, 1976—. Author numerous poems. Mem. AACD, Am. Assn. for Marriage and Family Therapy, Am. Businesswomen's Assn., Chi Sigma Iota. Home: 2401 San Ramon Ct Bakersfield CA 93304

GIRLANDO, REGINA MARIA, nurse; b. Addis Ababa, Ethiopia, Dec. 28, 1952; came to U.S., 1962; d. Frederick Ralph and Maria I. G. BS in Nursing, U. Md., 1975, MS in Nursing, 1982. RN. Commd. 1st lt. U.S. Army, 1971; advance through grades to maj. U.S. Army, Ft. Monmouth, N.J., 1985; clin. nurse Patterson Army Hosp., Ft. Monmouth, N.J., 1975-76; clin. nurse, charge Letterman Med. Ctr., Presidio of San Francisco, Calif., 1977-81; clin. nurse 121st Evacuation Hosp., Yongsan, Seoul, 1981-82; cardiovascular clin. specialist Walter Reed Army Med. Ctr., Washington, 1983-85, dir., intensive care nursing course, 1985-88; head nurse, surgical intensive care unit Womack Army Community Hosp., Ft. Bragg, N.C., 1988—. Recipient Phyllis J. Verhonick Rsch. award, U.S. Army Nurses Corp., Washington, 1988, Aileen Holmes award, Greater Washington Chpt. Am. Army Nurses Corp, 1987. Fellow Am. Assn. Critical-Care Nurses. Office: Walter Reed Army Med Ctr Washington DC 20307

GIROLAMO, MARYANNE M., psychotherapist; b. Newark, Sept. 9, 1945; d. William B. and Katherine (Doughan) Morley; m. Michael A. Girolamo, Aug. 14, 1971; children: Karen Elise, Jonathan Michael. BA, Annhurst Coll., 1967; cert. of advanced grad. studies, So. Conn. State U., 1984. Nat. cert. counselor. Psychotherapist Mercy High Sch., Middletown, Conn., Stress Mgmt. Assocs., Cromwell, Conn., Counseling Affiliates, Cromwell; workshop leader on employee assistance and preventive edn. programs. Mem. Am. Assn. For Counseling and Devel., Assn. for Specialists in Group Work. Home: 24 Iron Gate Ln Cromwell CT 06416

GIRON, VANESSA O., portfolio analyst; b. Havana, Cuba, Aug. 21, 1962; d. Arturo G. and Delia del Carmen (Galguera) G. AA in Bus., Miami-Dade Community Coll., 1983; BA in Fin., Fla. Internat. U., 1989. Sr. portfolio analyst Reserve Fin. Mgmt. Corp., Miami, Fla.; mgr. of investor acctg. Bankatlantic, Ft. Lauderdale, Fla.; investor reporting specialist Gen. Devel. Corp., Miami. Mem. NAFE, Miami Heart Inst., MBA, Coral Gables Jaycees. Home: 434 Vilabella Ave Coral Gables FL 33146

GIRONE, JOAN CHRISTINE CRUSE, communications executive, former county official; b. Kingston, Ont., Can., Aug. 30, 1927; naturalized U.S. citizen; d. Arthur William and Helen Wilson Cruse; m. Joseph Michael Girone, June 26, 1954; children: Susan, Richard, William. Buyer, Franklin Simon, Inc., N.Y.C., 1946-54; supr. Midlothian dist. Chesterfield County (Va.) Bd. Suprs., 1976-88, vice chmn., 1976-82; bd. dirs. Cen. Va. Ednl. Telecommunications Corp., 1989—. Founding mem. Capitol Area Agy. on Aging, 1973-89; commr., chmn. Richmond (Va.) Regional Planning Dist. Commn., 1976-88; chmn. community edn. adv. com. Va. Bd. of Edn., 1972-79; mem. Va. Gov.'s Adv. Bd. on Aging, 1980-82; chmn. Richmond Met. Transp. Planning Orgn., 1981-88; bd. visitors Va. State U., 1980-84; chmn. Chesterfield County Com. to elect John Warner and Paul Trible to U.S. Senate, 1979, 82, 84; Chesterfield chmn. Marshall Coleman for Gov., 1981—; chmn. Women for Reagan-Bush, 1984; state chmn. Va. Fedn. Rep. Women, mem. candidate recruitment com., 1985; mem. Central Va. River Basin com., 1985; evaluation task force United Way of Greater Richmond, 1985; bd. dirs. Maymont Found., 1982—, YMCA Greater Richmond, ARC Va. Capital chpt., Family and Children's Services, 1988. Recipient Good Govt. award Richmond First Club, 1985. Mem. Va. Assn. Counties (exec. bd. 1982-87), Richmond Metro C. of C. (bd. dirs. Chesterfield Bus. Coun. 1989—), Huguenot Rep. Woman's Club (Rep. Woman of Yr. 1983). Home: 2609 Dovershire Rd Bon Air VA 23235

GIROUARD, SHIRLEY ANN, nurse, policy analyst; b. New London, Conn., Jan. 16, 1947; d. Maxime Albert Girouard and Irene Barbara (Arnold) Reid. BA in Sociology, Ea. Conn. State Coll., 1972; MA in Sociology, U. Conn., 1974; MSN, Yale U., 1977; PhD in Policy Analysis, Brandeis U., 1988. Nurse Woodstock (Conn.) Pub. Health Assn., 1968-70; staff nurse Clinton (Conn.) Convalescent Ctr., 1970-72; ins. edn. coord. Middlesex Meml. Hosp., Middletown, Conn., 1973-75; clin. nurse specialist Dartmouth Hitchcock Med. Ctr., Hanover, N.H., 1977-83; staff nurse Dartmouth Hitchcock Med. Ctr., Hanover, 1983-84; legis. cons., lobbyist N.H. Nurses Assn., Concord, 1985-87; program officer Robert Wood Johnson Found., Princeton, N.J., 1987—; pvt. practice cons., 1983-87, Profl. Devel. Cons., Lebanon, N.H., 1983-87. Author: (chpt.) Health Policy and Nurse Services, 1989; mem. editorial bd. Clin. Nurses Specialist Jour., 1986—; contbr. articles to profl. jours. State rep. N.H. Legislature, Concord, 1982-84; counselor City of Lebanon Coun., 1984-87. Fellow Am. Acad. Nursing; mem. Am. Nurses Assn. (project dir. 1986), N.J. State Nurses Assn., Sigma Theta Tau. Democrat. Office: Robert Wood Johnson Found Rt 1 and College Rd Princeton NJ 08540

GISH, LILLIAN, actress; b. Springfield, Ohio; d. James Lee and Mary (Robinson) Gishi. AFD, Rollins Coll.; HHD, Mt. Holyoke Coll.; DFA (hon.), Bowling Green State U., 1976, Middlebury Coll. Debut on stage at 5; appeared in films including Birth of a Nation, Hearts of the World, Broken Blossoms, Way Down East, Orphans of the Storm, La Boheme, Scarlet Letter, Annie Laurie, The Wind, The Enemy, Night of the Hunter, Duel in the Sun, Portrait of Jennie, The Unforgiven, 1960, Follow Me Boys, 1966, The Comedians, 1967, A Wedding, 1978, Thin Ice (TV), 1980, Hambone and Hillie, 1984, Sweet Liberty, 1986, The Whales of August, 1987 (Nat. Bd. Rev. Film Award Best Actress 1987); movies made in Italy include The White Sister, Romola; appeared in plays including Crime and Punishment, 1948, Miss Mabel (title role), 1950, The Curious Savage, 1950, A Trip to Bountiful, Portrait of a Madonna, The Wreck of the 5:25, The Family Reunion (Pulitzer prize), All the Way Home, 1960-61, Romeo and Juliet (role of nurse), 1965, Anya, 1966, I Never Sang for My Father, 1967-68, Too True To Be Good, 1963, A Passage to India, 1963, Uncle Vanya, 1973, A Musical Jubilee, 1975, also TV plays including Twin Detectives, 1976, Sparrow, 1977, Hobson's Choice, 1983; appeared in TV series The Love Boat; toured Europe, Russia, U.S. as lectr. on art films, 1969, 71-73; TV documentary American Masters: Lillian Gish, 1988; Royal Command appearance, Queen Elizabeth the Queen Mother, 1980; author: The Movies, Mr. Griffith and Me, 1969, Dorothy and Lillian Gish, 1973, An Actor's Life for Me, 1987. Recipient hon. Acad. Award, 1971, Handel medallion City of N.Y., 1973, Kennedy Center honors City of N.Y., 1982, Life Achievement award Am. Film Inst., 1984, Dartmouth Film Soc. award, 1990; Dorothy and Lillian Gish Film Theatre on campus Bowling Green (Ohio) State Coll. Address: 430 E 57th St New York NY 10022

GISHLER, DARA L., chamber of commerce executive; b. Kalamazoo, May 29, 1953; d. Otis Edson Jr. and Mary O. (Hatfield) Bevins; m. Robert L. Gishler, June 7, 1989. BS in Profl. Aeros., Embry-Riddle Aero. U., Ft. Bragg, N.C., 1978; MBA in Mgmt., Western Mich. U., 1988, MA in Communication, 1989. News reporter, announcer Sta. WJIM, Lansing, Mich., 1973-74, Sta. WVIC, Lansing, 1974-75; air traffic contr. FAA, Wichita, Kans., 1979-81; svc. rep. Kalamazoo Fire Equipment div. Vanguard Fire & Supply Co., 1982-85; owner, v.p. No. Light Industries, Inc., Kalamazoo, 1983-86; machine operator Master Craft, Kalamazoo, 1985-87; personnel mgr. Summit Polymers, Inc., Kalamazoo, 1987-88; mktg. mgr. Three Rivers (Mich.) C. of C., 1989—. Contbr. poetry to various publs. Mem. various coms. Kalamazoo Women's Festival, 1983—; campaign worker Rep. Mary Brown, Kalamazoo, 1986; mem. mktg. com. Planned Parenthood, Kalamazoo, 1987-88. With U.S. Army, 1975-79, sgt. Mich. ANG, 1988—. Mem. Am. Soc. for Tng. and Devel. (communications com. Kalamazoo 1986—), Kalamazoo Network (features editor newsletter 1982—), Western Mich. U. Alumni Assn., Mt. Holyoke Coll. Club (Ann Arbor, Mich.). Office: Three Rivers Area C of C 140 W Michigan Ave Three Rivers MI 49093

GIST, SUZANNE, health educator, consultant; b. Effingham, Ill., Sept. 18, 1958; d. Albert Neal and Nancy Carolyn (Drake) G. Student, N. Tex. State U., 1977-79, Tex. Woman's U., 1979; BS in Nursing, U. Tex., Arlington, 1979-81; postgrad., Marymount U., 1987—. RN; cert. diabetes educator. Staff nurse Irving (Tex.) Community Hosp., 1981-82, charge nurse, 1982, nurse ICU, 1982-83; diabetes edn. cons. Becton Dickinson, Rochelle Park, N.J., 1983-85; mgr. ea. coast Becton Dickinson, Franklin Lakes, N.J., 1985-88; dir. advantage diabetes unit Capitol Hill Hosp., Washington, 1988-89; health cons. Am. Health Care Adv. Assn., Arlington, Va., 1989—; instr. CPR AHA, Irving, Tex., 1982-83; recruiter Irving Community Hosp., 1981-83. Mem. NAFE, Am. Diabetes Assn., Juvenile Diabetes Assn., Am. Assn. Diabetes Educators, Delta Zeta. Republican. Home: 4632 D S 28th Rd Arlington VA 22206 Office: 4632 D S 28th Rd Arlington VA 22206

GITNER, DEANNE, writer; b. Lyons, N.Y., Jan. 8, 1944; d. Myron and Mary (Kurland) Gebell; m. Gerald L. Gitner, June 24, 1968; children: Daniel Mark, Seth Michael. AB, Cornell U., 1966. Cert. English tchr. Tchr. English Gates (N.Y.) Chili Cen. Sch., 1966-68, Wantagh (N.Y.) Jr. and Sr. High Sch., 1968-70, F. Weiner Sch., Houston, 1980-81; writer Bellaire Texan,

Houston, 1980; rep. sales McDougal Littel & Co., Chgo., 1981-83; writer Millburn Short Hills Ind., New Providence, N.J., 1987—. Contbr. articles to profl. publs. Mem. Nat. Coun. Jewish Women (v.p. Houston sect. 1976-79, pres. 1980-81, v.p. Essex County, N.J. sect. 1983-88, pub. rels. com. 1981-90, chmn. nat. bull. subcom. 1990—, vol. award). Office: PO Box 336 Short Hills NJ 07078

GITTMAN, BETTY, educational research and program coordinator; b. N.Y.C., Mar. 15, 1945; d. Kallman and Rebecca (Santcroos) G.; m. Aug. 5, 1965 (div. 1977); children: Stephen Loeb, Leslie Loeb, Sherry Loeb; m. Victor Arnel, Mar. 5, 1981. BS, NYU, 1966; MS, CUNY, 1969; PhD, Hofstra U., 1979, Cert. Advanced Study, 1987. Cert. ednl. adminstr., N.Y. Tchr. N.Y.C. Bd. Edn., Kew Gardens, 1966-68; instr. New Sch. for Social Rsch., N.Y.C., 1980-81; ind. cons., 1981—; asst. coord. office instl. rsch. and evaluation Bd. Coop. Ednl. Svcs. of Nassau County, Westbury, N.Y., 1984—; adj. prof. L.I. U., Brookville, N.Y., 1987—. Cons. Office Substance Abuse Prevention NIH, HHS, 1990—; developer numerous social programs. Hofstra U. Doctoral fellow, 1976. Mem. Am. Ednl. Rsch. Assn., Northeastern Ednl. Research Assn., Am. Psychol. Assn., Nat. Coun. Adminstrv. Women in Edn., Nat. Coun. on Measurement in Edn., Mensa (rsch. dir. Greater N.Y. children's com. 1984-85), Kappa Delta Pi, Phi Delta Kappa (rsch. rep. 1990—). Republican. Jewish. Office: Bd Coop Ednl Svcs of Nassau County Office Instl Rsch and Evaluation Valentines and The Plain Rd Westbury NY 11590

GIUDICE, PATRICIA ANN, systems analyst; b. Bklyn., Nov. 1, 1942; d. Pasquale Joseph and Elena Victoria (Alfano) Ferrara; m. James Giudice, Sept. 28, 1963; children: Paula Marie, Pamela, Jennifer Lynn. AS, SUNY, Farmingdale, 1984; BS, Adelphi U., 1986. Systems analyst Grumman Corp., Bethpage, N.Y., 1980-86, estimator, 1986-87; human resource info. systems analyst NEC Am., Inc., Melville, N.Y., 1988—. Recipient Trustees' award Adelphi U., 1987. Office: NEC Am 8 Old Sod Farm Rd Melville NY 11747

GIULIANTI, MARA SELENA, former mayor, volunteer leader; b. N.Y.C., June 3, 1944; d. Leon and Bertha (Jablonky) Berman; m. Donald Giulianti, May 29, 1966; children: Stacey Alexander, Michael Alan. BA, Tulane U., 1966. Social worker L.A. County Social Svcs., 1966-68; adminstrv. asst. neurosurg. cons. D. Giulianti, MD, Hollywood, Fla., 1980-83; campaign mgr. City Commr. Suzanne Gunzburger, Hollywood, 1982; mayor City of Hollywood, 1986-90; vice chmn. Broward Employment and Tng. Adminstrn. Broward County, Fla., 1987-89, chmn., 1989-90; exec. bd. Fla. League Cities, Tallahassee, 1986-90, bd. dirs. 1990; econ. devel. task force Nat. League Cities, Washington, 1987-90; mem. Met. Planning Orgn., Broward County, 1986-90. Contbr. articles to local newspapers. V.p. CHARLEE Family Care Homes, Broward County, 1986-88, bd. dirs. 1988—; pres. Women in Distress, Broward County, 1982-83, bd. dirs. 1983-90; commr. Commn. on Status of Women, Broward County, 1984-86, Fla. Commn. on Drug and Alcohol Concerns, Tallahassee, 1984-85, Dem. Exec. Com., Broward County, 1984-88. Recipient Hannah G. Solomon award, 1983, Giraffe Stick Your Neck Out award Women's Advocacy - the Majority/Minority 1986, Leadership award Leadership Hollywood Alumni, 1987, City of Peace award Israel Bonds, Broward County, 1987, Broward County Woman of Yr., Am. Jewish Congress, 1988; Menorah award Histadrut, 1990; named Woman of Yr. Women in Communications Inc., 1990. Mem. Nat. Council Jewish Women (nat. bd. mem. 1985-89), Jewish Fedn. So. Broward (chair community relations com. 1981-82, bd. dirs. 1982-90), Broward County Med. Aux. (br. pres. 1977-78), Nat. Jewish Community Relation Adv. Council (exec. bd. 1985-87), Rotary. Democrat.

GIURGIU, ALEXANDRA MARIA, business executive, industrial engineer; b. N.Y.C., Mar. 28, 1958; d. Mircea Anthony and Lucia (Badescu) G.; m. Alessandro A. Piol. B.S., Sch. Engring. and Applied Sci. Columbia U., 1979, M.S., 1983. Sr. officer for project fin. and adminstrn. Chemtex, Inc., N.Y.C., 1979-84; dir. internat. ops. Intersoft Corp. (doing bus. as Lifeboat Assocs.), N.Y.C., 1984; dir. strategy and corporate devel. Ing. C. Olivetti & C.S.p.A., N.Y.C., 1986—; freelance writer Defis mag., Paris, 1983—. Office: Olivetti 535 Madison Ave 19th Fl New York NY 10022

GIVAN, PRISCILLA WHITE, marketing consultant; b. Greenwich, Conn., July 21, 1942; d. John Hazen and Mary Tefft (Schwarz) White; m. Curtis Varney Givan, June 22, 1963 (div. Feb. 1981); children: Amy Gwendolyn, Curtis Varney Jr. AA, Lasell Jr. Coll., 1962; BA in English, U. R.I., 1986. Pres., owner Pearson Travel Corp., Providence, R.I., 1974-80; mgr. product Taco Inc., Cranston, R.I., 1980-83, dir. mktg. services, 1983-84; mgr. UNIPAS div. Taco, Cranston, R.I., 1984-85; cons. mktg. & Mgmt. Priscilla White Givan and Assoc., Barrington, R.I., 1985—; owner, pres. Creative Packaging Unltd., Barrington, 1987—; lectr. Brown U. 1986, R.I. Sec. St. Women Bus. 1986. Mem. human resource com. R.I. Tech. Coun.; mem. Jr. League Providence, bd. dirs., 1975-79; mem. Barrington YMCA, bd. dirs., 1973-76); mem. vestry St. John's Episc. Ch., 1985—. Mem. NAFE, Advt. Club (bd. dirs.), Woman's Network (bd. dirs. 1986-89), Providence C. of C., Narragansett Bay Yachting Assn. (chairperson jr. sailing orgn. 1974-78). Republican. Home: 5 Anchorage Way Barrington RI 02806 Office: Priscilla White Givan and Assoc 5 Anchorage Way Barrington RI 02806

GIVENS, JANET EATON, writer; b. N.Y.C., July 5, 1932; d. Irving Daniel and Matilda (Schmelzle) E.; m. Richard Ayres Givens, Aug. 24, 1957; children—Susan Ruth, Jane Lucile. B.A., Queens Coll., 1953; M.A., Columbia U., 1955. Lic. tchr., N.Y. Tchr. pub. elem. schs., Silver Spring, Md., 1953-55, Mamaroneck, N.Y., 1955-59; supr. prospective tchrs., part-time lectr. Queens Coll., N.Y.C., 1959-68. Author: The Migrating Birds, 1964; Something Wonderful Happened, 1982; Just Two Wings, 1984; contbg. author: Tensions Our Children Live With, 1959. V.p. PTA, Pub. Sch. 219, Queens, N.Y., 1972-73, del. to United Parents Assn., 1971-72, editor PS 219 News, 1971-73. Home: 147-11 68th Rd Flushing NY 11367

GIVENS, JUDITH CHARLENE See **KELLEHER, JUDITH CHARLENE**

GIVENS JULIAN, LEISA IRENE, lawyer; b. Anderson, Ind., Jan. 26, 1959; d. Wayne DeRoyce and Alethea Nonda (Critser) Givens; m. Jay Therman Julian, May 22, 1982; children: Sarah Whitney, Spencer Mitchell. BS, Ball State U., 1980, MBA, 1983; JD, Ind. U., 1989. Bar: Ind., 1989. Grad. asst. Ball State U., Muncie, Ind., 1981-83; stockbroker K.J. Brown & Co., Inc., Muncie, 1983-86; prosecutor intern Marion County Prosecutor's Office, Indpls., 1988-89; dep. prosecutor Madison County Prosecutor's Office, Anderson, Ind., 1989—; pvt. practice Anderson, 1989—. Pres. Anderson (Ind.) Community Schs. Bd., 1988-89, v.p., 1987-88, asst. sec., 1986-87. Mem. ABA, Ind. Bar Assn. Democrat. Methodist. Home: 320 W 12th St Anderson IN 46016 Office: 2 W Eighth St Anderson IN 46016

GIVLER, DIANE BERYL, state government computer executive; b. Harrisburg, Pa., Feb. 27, 1953; d. George Edward and Beryl Rosalyn (Hicks) Usoff; children: Diane Beryl Givler II. BA, Elizabethtown Coll., 1974; MPA, Pennstate U. Capital Campus, 1978. Lead data analyst Probation and Parole Comm. Pa., Harrisburg, 1978-80; lead systems analyst Surveillance, Utilization Review, Comm. Pa., Harrisburg, 1980-82; computer systems analyst Integrated Cen. Systems Comm. Pa., Harrisburg, 1982-85; mgr. state acctg. tech. staff Bur. Fin. Mgmt., Harrisburg, Pa. asst. nursery Ch., 1982--, Sec. interfaith council, Middletown Area Churches, 1984-86, asst. leader Girl Scouts, 1988-90. Mem. Beaufort Hunt Inc., E-Star Legion. Republican. Methodist. Home: 511 Cattell St Middletown PA 17057 Office: Bur Fin Mgmt 931 N 7th St Harrisburg PA 17105

GJERSTAD, LIDDE MARIE, nutritionist; b. Skovby, Odense, Denmark; came to U.S., 1958; d. Christian and Henrietta (Thomsen) Hansen; m. Gunnar Gjerstad, Nov. 26, 1953 (div. June 20, 1968); 1 child, Erik Christian. BS, Suhr's Coll., Copenhagen, Denmark, 1943; MS, Purdue U., 1954; postgrad., Tex. Women's U., 1971. Asst. to dean Suhr's Coll. of Home Econs., Copenhagen, Denmark, 1946-57; instr. The Sch. Dietetics, Copenhagen, 1948-56; head dietician Seton Hosp., Austin, Tex., 1959-66; dietary cons. OEO, Austin, 1966-68, various hosps. in Cen. Tex., Austin, 1966-69; instr. home econs. South West Tex. State U., 1969-72; nutritionist Tex. Dept. Health, 1972-74; chief nutritional svcs. Profl Svcs. Div. Tex. Dept. Health, 1974—; lectr. in field. Author: Compositions & Processing -- The School of Dietetics, 1955. Recipient Fullbright Travel Grant, 1952, Purdue U. Grad. Fellow Grant, 1953. Mem. Am. Dietetic Assn. (gerontol. nutrition dietetic sec. 1985-86), Austin Dietetic Assn. (pres.s elect 1965-66, pres. 1966-67), Tex. Dietetic Assn. (chmn. gerontol. nutrition chmn. 1983-84, 84-85), Tex. State Nutrition Council (pres. elect, 1985-86, pres. 1986-88), Suhr's Alumni Assn. (pres. 1954-57), Altrusa (2nd v.p. 1983-84, 1st. v.p. 1984-85, pres. 1985-86). Republican. Lutheran. Home: 11903 Dove Haven Austin TX 78753 Office: Tex Dept Health 1100 W 49th St Austin TX 78756

GLACE, BETH WINIFRED, sports medicine and nutrition researcher; b. Newburgh, N.Y., Sept. 5, 1960; d. Walter Frederick and Shirley (Innis) G. AAS, Orange County Community Coll., Middletown, N.Y., 1980; BS in Nutrition, Marymount Coll., 1987; postgrad., NYU, 1988—. Registered lab. technician. Sr. technician, rsch. div. Avon Products, Suffern, N.Y., 1980-85; office mgr. Broadway Office of Chiropractic, Newburgh, 1985-87; dietitian Middletown Psychol. Ctr., 1987-90; sports medicine and nutrition researcher Nicholas Inst. Sports Medicine, N.Y.C., 1990—; nutrition cons. to women's basketball team Iona Coll., New Rochelle, N.Y., 1989—. Coach, Shawangunk Runners, New Paltz, N.Y., 1988—. Recipient award for scholastic excellence Am. Soc. Clin. Pathologists, 1980, award for excellence in food/nutrition Gen. Foods, 1985. Mem. Am. Dietetic Assn. (affiliate). Lutheran. Office: Nicholas Inst Sports Med 130 E 77th St New York NY 10013

GLACEL, BARBARA PATE, management consultant; b. Balt., Sept. 15, 1948; d. Jason Thomas Pate and Sarah Virginia (Forwood) Wetter; m. Robert Allan Glacel, Dec. 21, 1969; children: Jennifer Warren, Sarah Allane, Ashley Virginia. AB, Coll. William and Mary, 1970; MA, U. Okla., 1973, PhD, 1978. Tchr. Harford County (Md.) Schs., 1970-71; tchr. Dept. Def. Schs., W.Ger., 1971-73; ednl. counselor U.S. Army, W.Ger., 1973-74; lectr. U. Md., W.Ger., 1973-74; adj. prof. Suffolk U., Boston, 1975-77, C.W. Post Ctr., L.I. U., John Jay Coll. Criminal Justice, N.Y.C., 1979-80, St. Thomas Aquinas Coll., N.Y.C., 1981; acad. adviser Cen. Mich. U. 1981-82; adj. prof. St. Mary's Coll., Leavenworth, Kans., 1981, Anchorage Community Coll., 1982; asst. prof. U. Alaska-Anchorage, 1983-85; ptnr. Pracel Prints, Williamsburg, Va., 1981-85; sr. mgmt. tng. specialist Arco Alaska, Inc., 1984-85; mgmt. cons. Barbara Glacel & Assocs., Anchorage, 1980-86, Washington, 1986-88; gen. mgr. mgmt. programs Hay Systems, Inc., Washington, 1986-88; pres., mng. ptnr. Pace Cons. Group, Burke, Va., 1988—; 2d v.p., bd. dirs. Chesapeake Broadcasting Corp. Md.; mem. adj. faculty Ctr for Creative Leadership, 1986—; guest lectr. U.S. Mil. Acad. Chmn. 172d Inf. Brigade Family Council; mem. U.S. Army Sci. Bd., 1986-90. Recipient Comdr.'s award for pub. service U.S. Dept. Army, 1984. AAUW grantee, 1977-78. Mem. Am. Soc. Tng. and Devel. (bd. dirs. Anchorage chpt.), Am. Psychol. Assn., Soc. for Indsl. and Organizational Psychology. Author: Regional Transit Authorities, 1983; (with others) 1000 Army Families, 1983, The Army Community and Their Families, 1989. Home: 5617 Tilia Ct Burke VA 22015 Office: Pace Cons Group 5290 Lyngate Ct Burke VA 22015

GLACKEN, CYNTHIA, design and communication firm executive; b. Boston, Mar. 23, 1943; d. Francis X. and Dorothy A. (Marple) G. BA, Regis Coll., Weston, Mass., 1965; postgrad., Tufts U., Somerville, Mass., 1967, Boston U., 1968, Lee Strasberg Theatre Inst., NY, 1971-73. Tchr. East Jr. High Sch., Walpole, Mass., 1965-69; flight attendant TWA, 1969-80; writer, pres. Cynthia Glacken Assoc. Inc., NYC, 1981—; seminar dir. Werner Erhard and Assoc., San Francisco, 1986—. Exec. dir. Stewardesses for Women's Rights, N.Y.C., 1973-76. Office: Cynthia Glacken Assocs Inc 251 E 51st St New York NY 10022

GLACKIN, CAROLINE ELIZABETH W., marketing professional; b. Wilmington, Del., June 30, 1959; d. Howard T. and Maria E. (Boerstler) Wiedenman; m. Michael J. Glackin, Aug. 7, 1981; 1 child, Marie Elizabeth. AB magna cum laude, Bryn Mawr Coll., 1981; MBA, U. Pa., 1984. Systems analyst E.I. DuPont De Nemours, Wilmington, 1981-82; strategic planner AT&T, Parsippany, N.J., 1983; sr. bus. analyst Am. Mgmt. Systems, Arlington, Va., 1984-85; mktg. mgr. Speakman Co., Wilmington, 1985-88; pres. Wyndham Assocs., Wilmington, Del., 1988—; co-pub. De Valley Family Times; part-time instr. U. Del., Newark, spring 1989. Gloekner Bus. Plan award Univ. Pa. Wharton Sch., Phila., 1983. Mem. Am. Mktg. Assn. (bd. dirs. Del. chpt.), Wilmington Women in Bus. (chair publicity), Del. Saengerbund and Libr. Assn., Del. Entrepreneurs' Forum, Del. Indsl. Bus. Network, Del. State C. of C. Democrat. Lutheran. Home: 27 Winding Hill Dr Hockessin DE 19707

GLACKING, MARJORIE JOYCE STRAUB, teacher; b. Freeport, Ill., Sept. 6, 1936; d. Melvin Conrad and Dorothy Eltheda (Ferris) Straub; m. James Robert Glacking, Apr. 23, 1970. BS in Edn., No. Ill. U., 1958; student, U. Colo., 1960. Cert. elem. tchr. ILl. Tchr. Sterling (Ill.) Pub. Schs., 1958-66, Lake Forest (Ill.) Pub. Schs., 1966—. Bd. dirs. Liberty-Fremont Concert Soc.; mem. Friends of Cook Library, Ill. Prairie Pioneers. Mem. AAUW (bd. dirs. Mundelein-Libertyville Br.). Lutheran. Home: 1130 Dawes St Libertyville IL 60048 Office: Lake Forest Pub Schs 95 W Deerpath Rd Lake Forest IL 60045

GLADSTONE, JOYCE ANN, insurance agent; b. Bigstone, Va., Aug. 18, 1942; d. William R. and Mary A. (Hensley) Bailey; children: Tammy L., Michelle R.; m. George H. Rouse, Sept. 15, 1979. BS, East Tenn. State U., 1965; MS, Boston U., 1976; cert. advanced grad. studies, Va. Tech. U., 1982. Cert. tchr., Va. Tchr. Army Edn. Ctr., Ft. Sill, Okla., 1965-66, Ft. Carson, Colo., 1967-69, Penns Grove (N.J.) Pub. Sch., 1966-67; salesperson Salad Master Corp., Dallas, 1971-72; prin. U.S. Dependent Schs., Pisa, Italy, 1972-76; supr. alt. edn. Donald J. Howard Vocat. Sch., Winchester, Va., 1976-79; instr. Va. Tech. U., Blackburg, 1979-84; agt. State Farm Ins. Co., Vienna, Va., 1984—. Leader 4-H, Va., 1979-88; sec. Outstanding Virginian Day Com., Warrington, 1980-82; organizer No. Va. 4-H Ambassadors, 1981-86; chmn. Smithsonian Spring Celebration, 1982. Mem. Nat. Assn. Female Execs., AAUW, Va. Assn. 4-H Adult Leaders (speaker 1983), State Farm Millionaires Club, State Farm Legion of Honor, Am. Bus. Women, Phi Delta Kappa (program v.p. 1979-84, v.p. membership com., pres., nat. del., dist. del., speaker 1983, Pres.' award 1983). Office: State Farm Ins Co 374 Maple Ave E Suite 200 Vienna VA 22180

GLADSTONE, KIM DIANE, lawyer; b. Lansing, Mich., Nov. 4, 1957; d. Marvin Phillip and Maureen Delores (Pritz) G. BA, Mich. State U., 1980; JD, Thomas M. Cooley, 1988; postgrad., U. San Diego, 1990. Bar: Mich. 1988. Assoc. Law Office of R.J. Barton, Lansing, 1988; rsch. assoc. Neil, Dymott, Perkins, Brown & Frank, San Diego, 1989, Giomi, Smith & Woods, San Diego, 1989—. Bd. govs. Thomas M. Cooley Law Sch., 1988—. Recipient Outstanding Svc. award Thomas M. Cooley Law Sch., 1988. Mem. ABA, Mich. Bar Assn., Ingham County Bar Assn., Phi Alpha Delta. Home: 6546 Friars Rd #108 San Diego CA 92108

GLADSTONE, SUZANNE PINK, clinical psychologist; b. Bronx, N.Y., Sept. 20, 1935; d. Lester Winthrop and Beatrice (Meister) Pink; m. Mark Bernard Gladstone, Feb. 3, 1957; 1 child, Leslie. BS, Pa. State U., 1957; Postgrad., U. Paris, France, 1959; MS, Utah State U., 1962; PhD, U. Md., 1971. Lic. clin. psychologist, Md., D.C. Teaching asst. U. Md., College Park, 1965-66; psychology trainee VA Hosp., Balt., WAshington, 1966-70; instr. Montgomery Coll., Rockville, Md., 1975-79; supr., psychologist Dept. of Human Resources, Washington, 1971—; clinical psychologist Gaithersburg, Md., 1972—; co-dir. Assocs. in Marriage and Divorce Therapy, Gaithersburg, 1980—. Fellow Md. Psychol. Assn., D.C. Psychol. Assn.; mem. Am. Psychol. Assn., Am. Orthopsychiat. Assn., Nat. Registry Health Svc. Providers. Home: 7704 Westfield Dr Bethesda MD 20817 Office: 15924 Shady Grove Rd Gaithersburg MD 20877

GLAESSMANN, DORIS ANN, county official; b. Northampton, Pa., Feb. 18, 1940; d. Frank G. and Theresa (Fischl) Zwikl; m. Edward Glaessmann, Sept. 1, 1962; children: Edward Jr., Robert F. Grad. high sch., Northampton, 1958. Sec., bookkkeeper John F. Moore Agy., Inc., Allentown, Pa., 1958-64; ct. clk. Criminal div. Clk. of Cts. Office, Allentown, 1968-69, asst. dep. clk., 1969-76, chief dep. clk., 1976-82; clk. of cts. Lehigh County Criminal and Civil divs., Allentown, 1982—. Den mother, sec. Cub Scout Pack 140, Allentown, Pa., 1973-78; mem., past bd. dirs. Quota Club Allentown, 1983—; mem. coun. St. Peter's Evang. Luth. Ch., Allentown, 1984-89. Mem. Nat. Assn. County Recorders and Clks., Internat. Assn. Clks., Recorders, Election Ofcls. and Treas., Pa. Prothonotaries and Clks. Assn. (pres.), Pa. Elected Women's Assn. (past sec.-treas., past pres. Lehigh Valley chpt.). Democrat. Home: 945 E Lynnwood St Allentown PA 18103-5250 Office: Lehigh County 455 Hamilton St PO Box 1548 Allentown PA 18105-1548

GLANCY, DOROTHY JEAN, lawyer, educator; b. Glendale, Calif., Sept. 24, 1944; d. Walter Perry and Elva T. (Douglass) G.; m. Jon Tobias Anderson, June 8, 1979. BA, Wellesley Coll., 1967; JD, Harvard Law Sch., 1970. Bar: D.C. 1971, Calif. 1976, U.S. Dist. Ct. D.C. 1971, U.S. Ct. Appeals (D.C. cir.) 1972. Assoc. Hogan & Hartson, Wash., 1971-73; counsel U.S. Senate Judiciary Subcomm. on Constitutional Rights, Wash., 1973-74; fellow in Law & Humanities Harvard U., Cambridge, Mass., 1974-75; asst. to assoc. prof. law Santa Clara U., Calif., 1975-82, prof. law, 1984—; vis. prof. law U. Arizona, Tucson, 1979; asst. gen. counsel U.S. Dept. of Agr., 1982-83; cons. Commn. Fed. Paperwork, Wash., 1976.; dir. summer Law Study Program in Hong Kong, 1985—; advisor Restatement, Third, Property: Servitudes, 1986—. steering comm. Harvard Law Sch. Assn. Celebration 35, Cambridge, 1988. Fellow Wellesley Coll., Harvard U.; mem. ABA, Am. Law Inst., Calif. Women Lawyers, Soc. of Am. Law Tchrs., Phi Beta Kappa. Democrat. Office: Santa Clara U Sch Law Santa Clara CA 95053

GLANTZ, GINA, consultant; b. N.Y.C., Apr. 3, 1943; d. Nathan L. and Lillian (Rosenbaum) Stritzler; m. Ronald A. Glantz, Oct. 17, 1968; children—Amy Samantha, Peter Samuel. B.A., U. Calif.-Berkeley, 1965. Chief of staff County Exec. Peter Shapiro, County of Essex, N.J., 1978-82; owner, mgr. Gina Glantz Cons., Springfield, N.J., 1982-83; sr. cons. Mondale for Pres., Washington, 1984; nat. field dir. Mondale/Ferraro, Inc., Washington, 1984; ptnr. Martin & Glantz, San Francisco, 1985—. Chmn. nat. edn. and tng. council Democratic Nat. Com., Washington, 1981-84. Home: 96 Ave Del Norte San Anselmo CA 94960 Office: Martin & Glantz 100 Shoreline Hwy Mill Valley CA 94941

GLASBERG, PAULA DRILLMAN, advertising executive; b. Dusseldorf, Germany, Nov. 22, 1939; came to U.S., 1940, naturalized, 1942; d. Solomon and Regina (Rubin) Drillman; m. H. Mark Glasberg, June 19, 1960; children: Scot Bradley, Hilary Jennifer. B.A., Bklyn. Coll., 1957; M.A., New Sch. Social Research, 1959, Ph.D., 1962. Rsch. asst. McCann-Erickson, N.Y.C., 1962-64; v.p. Marplan, Inc., N.Y.C., 1964-70, Tinker/Pritchard Wood, Inc., N.Y.C., 1970-72; exec. v.p., chmn. exec. com. Rosenfeld, Sirowitz & Lawson, Inc., N.Y.C., 1972-78; exec. v.p., chmn. exec. com., dir. Marschalk Co. div. Interpublic Group of Cos., N.Y.C., 1978-1982; exec. v.p., dir., dir. strategic planning McCann-Erickson World Wide, Inc., 1983—; bd. dirs. Stern Coll. for Women; sponsor mem. Yeshiva U. Women's Orgn., 1985—. Mem. Am. Assn. Advt. Agys., Am. Mktg. Assn., Advt. Rsch. Found., AAAS, Am. Psychol. Assn., Internat. Platform Assn., N.Y. Acad. Scis. (fellow), Nat. Assn. Psychologists. Home: 14 E 73rd St New York NY 10021 Office: 750 3rd Ave New York NY 10017

GLASER, JOY HARRIET, pediatrician, educator; b. N.Y.C., June 17, 1941; d. David and Pauline (Eisen) Schildkraut; m. Jack Glaser, Aug. 4, 1963; children: Ellen, Wendy, Steven, Joel. BA, William Smith Coll., 1962; MD, NYU, 1965. Diplomate Am. Bd. Pediatrics. Internship Bellevue Hosp., 1965-66; resident Beth Israel Med. Ctr., N.Y.C., 1966-67, asst. attending staff, 1968-77; chief resident Pedo-Beth Israel, 1967-68; instr. Mt. Sinai Med. Sch., N.Y.C., 1970-77; fellow in infectious disease Montefiore Hosp., Bronx, N.Y., 1977-79; asst. prof. pediatrics Albert Einstein Coll. Medicine, Bronx, 1979-85, assoc. prof., 1985—; dir. pediatric infectious diseases Bronx Mcpl. Hosp. Ctr., 1987—. Contbr. articles to med. jours., chpts. to books. Recipient rsch. prize Am. Liver Found., 1985, teaching award dept. pediatrics Albert Einstein Coll. Medicine, 1988. Fellow Am. Acad. Pediatrics; mem. Am. Soc. for Microbiology, Pediatric Infectious Disease Soc., Phi Beta Kappa. Home: 17 Haverford Ave Scarsdale NY 10583 Office: Bronx Mcpl Hosp Ctr Pelham Pkwy Rm 803 Bronx NY 10461

GLASER, NANCY ELLEN, venture capitalist; b. Hawthorne, N.J., Apr. 24, 1945; d. John Joseph and Marie (Schilde) G. BS, Marshall U., 1967; MBA, Stanford U., 1985. Tchr. spl. edn. Quincy (Mass.) Sch. System, 1967-68; mgr. sales Macy's Dept. Store, Atlanta, 1968-71; group mgr. Daly City, Calif., 1971-73; buyer merchandising The Gap, Inc., San Bruno, Calif., 1973-75, dir. mdse. control, 1976-78; mng. dir. Lord & Taylor, Stamford, Conn., 1978-81; dir. retail and franchise Barton's Candy Corp., Bklyn., 1981-83; gen. ptnr. U.S. Venture Ptnrs., Menlo Park, Calif., 1985—; bd. dirs. Gymboree Corp., Burlingame, Calif. Mem. New Enterprise Forum Stanford (Calif.) U. Bus. Sch., 1986—, exec. mem. bd. alumni cons. team, 1987—; bd. dirs. Am. Field Svc., 1989—; bd. dirs. Exploratorium Mus., San Francisco, 1988—. Mem. Western Assn. Venture Capitalists. Republican. Home: 54 Cape Hatteras Ct Redwood City CA 94065 Office: US Venture Ptnrs 2180 Sand Hill Rd Ste 300 Menlo Park CA 94025

GLASGOW, NORMA FOREMAN, state official; b. Hollis, Okla., Nov. 3, 1927; d. Edd Terrell and Ruby (Battles) Holly; m. Maurice J. Foreman, Feb. 13, 1953 (dec. 1958); children: Kim Alan, Kerry Joan Foreman; m. Keith W. Glasgow, Aug. 9, 1980. BS in Edn., Southwestern State Coll., Weatherford, Okla., 1947; MS in Edn., U. So. Calif., 1951; postgrad. U. Mich., 1964; PhD, U. Tex., 1971. Project adminstr. Ednl. Testing Service, Los Angeles, 1947-50; asst. to prodn. mgr. Pacific Press, Inc., Los Angeles, 1950-52; tchr. journalism and English pub. schs., Mich. and Okla., 1958-60; dir. publs. Tascosa High Sch., Amarillo, Tex., 1960-64; asst. dir. news info services, instr. journalism West Tex. State U., Canyon, 1964-67; communications specialist S.W. Ednl. Devel. Lab., Austin, Tex., 1967-70; asst. to commr. higher edn. coordinating Bd. Tex. Coll. and Univ. System, 1971-77, asst. commr. sr. colls. and univs. coordinating bd., 1977-81; commr. higher edn. State of Conn., Hartford, 1981—; mem. New Eng. Bd. Higher Edn., 1984—, State Job Tng. Coordinating Council, 1983—, Gov.'s High Tech. Council, 1983; mem. Edn. Commn. of States, 1981—, mem. policy and priorities com., 1983—, mem. steering com., 1983-87; ex officio mem. Conn. Bd. Edn., 1981—; mem. Conn. Council on Edn. for Employment, 1981; bd. dirs. Conn. Student Loan Found., 1981—. Corporator Hartford Hosp., 1982—, Newington Children's Hosp., 1983—; bd. dirs. U. Conn. Ednl. Properties, Inc., 1982—. Mem. Am. Assn. for Higher Edn., State Higher Edn. Exec. Officers Assn. (exec. com. 1987—, pres. 1988-89). Democrat. Home: 3 Country Club Dr West Simsbury CT 06092 Office: Dept Higher Edn 61 Woodland St Hartford CT 06105

GLASGOW, WILLENE GRAYTHEN, abstractor, consultant; b. Vancouver, Wash., Mar. 10, 1939; d. William Louis and Zorah (Williams) Graythen; m. Ray Buck Glasgow, Feb. 8, 1964 (div. June 1969). BA in History, Centenary Coll., 1975; postgrad., La. State Law Sch., 1984, S.E. La. U., 1989. Tchr., educator St. Tam Parish Sch. Bd., Lacombe, La., 1964-65; abstractor St. Tam Parish Legal News, Covington, La., 1965-66, Kansas City Title Ins. Co., New Orleans, 1966-69, Lawyers Title Ins. Corp., New Orleans, 1975-77, Frawley, Wogan, Miller & Co., New Orleans, 1977-79; owner, mgr. Idea House and Sweet Home Antiques, Metairie, La., 1973-76; owner, mgr., abstractor Willene Glasgow & Assocs., Metairie, 1969-73, Covington, La., 1979—. Author: Decoupage and Related Crafts, 1972. Bd. dirs. Air, Water and Earth Inst., Covington, 1989; bd. dirs, pres. Pontchartrain Area Recycling Coun., Inc., Covington, 1989; mem. Citizens Adv. Com. on Solid Waste, 1988, 89; coord. Pontchartrain Area Recycling Conv., 1988; fund raiser March of Dimes, Am. Cancer Soc., Arthritis Found., also others, 1986—. Named hon. sec. state State of La., 1987. Mem. Petroleum Landman's Assn., Covington C. of C. (legis. chmn. 1988—, Mem. of Yr. award 1988), AAUW (conf. chmn. 1988-89, chmn. Ednl. Found. 1989—, Mem. of Yr. award Covington-Mandeville br. 1989). Home and Office: 447 S Vermont St Covington LA 70433

GLASHOW, ANDREA JEAN, accountant; b. White Plains, N.Y., May 10, 1961; d. Samuel and Audrey Ellen (Marks) G. BBA in Pub. Acctg., Pace U., 1983. CPA, N.Y. Acct., auditor Blonder, Seymour & Shapss, CPAs, N.Y.C., 1985-88, BDO Seidman, White Plains, 1988-89; pvt. practice White Plains, 1989—; cons., fin. adviser, White Plains, 1989—. Treas., bd. dirs. White Plains Hist. Soc., 1984-90. Home: 1 Landmark Sq #526 Port Chester NY 10573

GLASKEY, SUSAN M., implementation manager; b. Linden, N.J., Dec. 9, 1960; d. Daniel F. and Charlotte A. (Marsh) G. AAS, Middlesex County Coll., 1985; student, Thomas Edison Coll. Claims mgr. Home Life Ins., Piscataway, N.J., 1981-84, tng. claims, 1984-86; sr. user analyst Loyalty Life, Continental Ins., Piscataway, N.J., 1986-87; implementation mgr. Blue Cross and Blue Shield of N.J., Florham Park, 1987—. Mem. NAFE, Phi Theta Kappa. Home: 1132G Easton Ave Somerset NJ 08873 Office: Blue Cross/ Blue Shield NJ 15 Vreeland Rd Florham Park NJ 07932

GLASPIE, APRIL CATHERINE, diplomat; b. Vancouver, B.C., Can., Apr. 26, 1942. BA, Mills Coll., 1963; MA, Johns Hopkins U., 1965. With Foreign Service U.S. Dept. of State, 1966—; polit. officer U.S. Embassy, Cairo, 1973-77; asst. to Asst. Sec. State for Near Ea., S. Asian Affairs Washington, 1977-78; polit. officer U.S. Embassy, London, 1978-80, U.S. Mission to UN, N.Y.C., 1980-81; dir. lang. inst. U.S. Embassy, Tunis, Tunisia, 1981-83; polit. officer, dep. chief of mission U.S. Embassy, Damascus, Syria, 1983-85; dir., Office of Jordan, Lebanon, and Syrian Affairs U.S. Dept. of State, Washington, 1985-87; ambassador to Iraq, 1987—. Office: care State Dept US Amb to Iraq Washington DC 20520 also: Am Embassy, Alwiyah, PO Box 2447, Baghdad Iraq*

GLASS, CAROLYN BENNION, specialty advertising company executive; b. Jacksonville, Fla., Mar. 13, 1946; d. Thomas Raymond and Vivian Pauline (Thomas) Bennion; m. Theodore C. Glass, Jan. 23, 1965 (div. 1983); children: Lorilee, T. Scott, Michael C. Grad. high sch., Jacksonville. Sec. Jacksonville (Fla.) Splty. Advt. Co., 1975-80, sales rep., 1980-82, v.p., 1982-83, exec. v.p., 1983—. Mem. Jacksonville Advt. Fedn., Riverside Avondale Preservation Soc. Democrat. Baptist. Office: Jacksonville Splty Advt Co 6030 Arlington Expwy Jacksonville FL 32211

GLASS, MARTHA DAUGHTRY, information specialist; b. Martinsville, Va., Aug. 28, 1944; d. Harry Lee and Alice Glenwood (Goode) Daughtry; m. Edward Fontaine Colston (div. 1973); children: Lynne Fontaine Colston Coats, John Vaughan; m. Fred Stephen Glass, June 9, 1982; 1 stepchild, Elizabeth Foust. BA, Westhampton Coll., 1966; M in Pub. Affairs, N.C. State U., 1975. Edn. specialist div. emergency mgmt. State of N.C., Raleigh, 1975-78, edn. br. chief, div. emergency mgmt., crime control and pub. safety dept., 1978-81; with Carolina Power & Light Co., Raleigh, 1981—, sr. specialist energy info. Harris Nuclear Plant Visitors Ctr., 1985—, specialist on loan emergency mgmt. sect., 1984-85; profl. devel. co-chair women's program coun. Carolina Power & Light Co., 1988-90; organizer, past pres. New Hill (N.C.) Energy Info. Forum, 1989. Vol. N.C. Symphony, Raleigh, Friends of the Coll., Raleigh, Oakview Restoration Steering Com., Raleigh; adult trainer Philmont scout ranch Boy Scouts Am., Cimarron, N.Mex., 1982-84, 86-87; pres. Energy Info. Forum, Raleigh, 1985; mem. econ. devel. task force City of Raleigh, 1990; active N.C. Child Advocacy Com.; 2d v.p. Wake County Dem. Women, 1989—. Recipient Silver Beaver award Boy Scouts Am., 1984. Mem. Raleigh Pub. Rels. Soc. (sec. 1986, v.p. 1987, pres. 1988, 89), Am. Nuclear Soc. (vice chmn., chmn. elect Eastern Carolinas chpt. 1990—), N.C. Equity (women-elect Raleigh chpt.). Episcopalian. Home: 113 Whispering Pines Ct Cary NC 27511 Office: Carolina Power & Light Co Rt 1 Box 326 New Hill NC

GLASSETT, JANE, accounting professional; b. Blue Island, Ill., Nov. 28, 1960; d. John Edward and Dolores (Roth) Fialkowski; m. Kevin Lund Glassett, July 16, 1988. BBA, Washington U., St. Louis, 1982, MBA, 1983. CPA, Ill., Calif. Staff auditor Arthur Andersen & Co., Chgo., 1983-85, sr. auditor, 1985-88, mgr., 1988; sr. internal auditor Gt. Am. Bank, San Diego, 1988-89; acctg. mgr. BEI Motion Systems Co., Carlsbad, Calif., 1989—. Mem. AICPA, Am. Women's Soc. CPAs. Office: BEI Motion Systems Co 2111 Palomar Airport Rd Ste 250 Carlsbad CA 92009

GLASSMAN, CAROLINE DUBY, state supreme court justice; b. Baker, Oreg., Sept. 13, 1922; d. Charles Ferdinand and Caroline Marie (Colton) Duby; m. Harry Paul Glassman, May 21, 1953; 1 son, Max Avon. LLB summa cum laude, Williamette U., 1944. Bar: Oreg. 1944, Calif. 1952, Maine 1969. Atty. Title Ins. & Trust Co., Salem, Oreg., 1944-46; assoc. Belli, Ashe, Pinney & Melvin Belli, San Francisco, 1952-58; ptnr. Glassman & Potter, Portland, Maine, 1973-78, Glassman, Beagle & Ridge, Portland, 1978-83; justice Maine Supreme Judicial Ct., Portland, 1983—; lectr. Sch. Law, U. Maine, 1967-68, 80. Author: Legal Status of Homemakers in State of Maine, 1977. Mem. Am. Law Inst., Oreg. Bar Assn., Calif. Bar Assn., Maine Bar Assn., Maine Trial Law Assn. Roman Catholic. Home: 56 Thomas St Portland ME 04102 Office: Supreme Jud Ct 142 Federal St Portland ME 04112-0368

GLASSMAN, ELIZABETH JANE, foundation administrator, art historian, arts administrator; b. Houston, Mar. 13, 1949; d. Arthur Leonard and Lenore (Homonoff) G. Student, Inst. Art and Archaeology, Sorbonne, 1969-70; BA in Art History, Sweet Briar Coll., 1971; MA in Art History, U. N.Mex., 1977; MBA, U. St. Thomas, Houston, 1989. Asst. curator Tamarind Inst., Albuquerque, 1972-74; research asst. for prints and photographs Met. Mus. Art, N.Y.C., 1974; asst. to curator Alverthorpe Gallery, Phila., 1974-75; lectr. Glassell Sch. Art Mus. Fine Arts, Houston, 1976-77; adj. curator prints and photographs Menil Found., Houston, 1976-82; adj. prof. art history U. Houston, 1976-85; ptnr. Glassman & Lorenzo Cultural Planners, Houston, 1984—; spl. cons. graphic arts dept. Det. Inst. Arts, 1977, 80; bd. dirs. Rice Design Alliance, Houston, 1983—, pres., 1987—; bd. dirs. Tex. Accts and Lawyers for Arts, 1983—, Houston Ctr. for Photography, 1983—; lectr. in field. Author: Clicheverre: Hand-Drawn, Light Printed, 1980, Transfixed by Light, 1981, The Rowdy London of William Hogarth, 1984, Reading Prints: A Selection from the Menil Foundation Collection, 16th to 19th Centuries, 1985; contbr. articles to profl. publs.; curator exhbns., 1973—. Panel mem. Cultural Arts Coun. Houston, 1985; judge Bayou Show, Houston, 1985, 89. Tamarind Inst. fellow, N.Mex., 1972, Met. Mus. Art, 1974. Mem. Print Coun. Am., Phi Kappa Phi. Home: 3712 Lake St Houston TX 77098 Office: The Georgia O'Keeffe Found PO Box 40 Abiquiu NM 87510

GLASSMAN, GERALDINE JOAN, controller; b. Bronx, N.Y., Apr. 13, 1936; d. Louis Fuccillo and Doris Lane; m. Stanley B. Glassman, Feb. 23, 1958. Student, CUNY, 1954-55. Adminstrn. asst. computers Sleepwear Inc., N.Y.C., 1953-73; office mgr. Daniel D. Cole Inc., White Plains, N.Y., 1973-76; controller, v.p. fin. Paul Hardman Co., Mt. Vernon, N.Y., 1976—, also bd. dirs., 1987—. Republican. Jewish.

GLATMAN-STEIN, MARCIA, executive search company executive; b. N.Y.C., Feb. 28, 1944; d. Martin and Jean (Bykowsky) Eisenberg; m. Allan Glatman, June 27, 1965 (div. 1979); children: Jill, Kim; m. Seymour Stein, Nov. 22, 1983. BA, Hunter Coll., 1965, MA, 1969. Cert. tchr., N.Y. Tchr. N.Y.C. Bd. Edn., 1965-70; counselor Rockland Community Coll., Suffern, N.Y., 1976-77; acct. mgr. Alexander Ross Assoc., N.Y.C., 1978-80; sr. acct. mgr. Stevenson Group, N.Y.C., 1981-83; v.p. Richards Cons., N.Y.C., 1983-84, E.G. Todd Assocs., N.Y.C., 1984-88; pres. HRD Cons., Inc., Clark, N.J., 1989—. Mem. Am. Soc. Tng. and Devel., Am. Compensation Assn., Human Resource Planning Assn., Met. Assn. for Applied Psychologists, Nat. Assn. Corp. and Profl. Recruiters, Soc. for Human Resource Mgmt. Office: HRD Cons Inc 60 Walnut Ave Clark NJ 07066

GLATZMAIER, LISA ANN, systems analyst; b. Rochester, Minn., Jan. 19, 1962; d. C.I. and Delores Rose (Zeverino) G. BS, U. Wis., 1986. Systems analyst Ace Telephone Assn., Houston, Minn., Citizen's Security, Red Wing, Minn. Mem. IEEE, NAFE.

GLAZE, LYNN FERGUSON, development consultant; b. Oakland, Calif., May 24, 1933; d. Kenneth Loveland and Constance May (Pedder) Ferguson; m. Harry Smith Glaze, Jr., July 3, 1957; children: Catherine, Charles Richard. B.A., Stanford U., 1955, M.A., 1966. Devel. dir. Greenwich Acad., Conn., 1982-84; devel. cons. Del. Learning Ctr., Brandywine Mus., Opera Del., Ctr. for Creative Arts, 1984—; dir. devel. Am. Lung Assn. Del., Wilmington, 1987—. Pres. Darien-Norwalk YWCA, Conn., 1973-76; mem. St. Michael's Day Nursery, 1984—; sec. Darien Republican Town com., Darien, 1974-79; dist. chmn. Darien Rep. Meeting, 1974-76, mem. Rep. Nat. Conv. Platform Com., 1988; vestry St. Luke's Ch., Darien, 1979-82; justice of the peace, Darien, 1981-84; bd. dirs. Episc. Ch. Home, 1987; mem. Gov.'s Small Bus. Council, 1987; mem. Del. Rep. State Com., 1987—. Coro Found. fellow 1981. Mem. Nat. Soc. Fund Raising Execs. (Brandywine chpt.).

GLEASON, ALICE BRYANT, sales executive; b. Lynchburg, Va., Apr. 17, 1940; d. Samuel Albert and Alice (Tibbits) Bryant; m. Marion Massie Gleason, Feb. 18, 1957; children: Sharon, Marion Massie Jr., Frances, Michael, Mark, Marilyn, Melonie, Matthew. Lic. real estate agt., Va. Owner, mgr. 8 beauty shops, Waynesboro, Va., 1962-79; realtor Century 21-Chateau Realty, Vienna, Va., 1979-81; vertical market specialist Idea Systems, West Palm Beach, Fla., 1981; account mgr. Micro Brokers Inc., Arlington, Va., 1981-82; East Coast mgr. Am. Peripheral Systems, McLean, Va., 1982-83; div. v.p. PC Telemart Inc., Fairfax, Va., 1983-84; comml. account mgr. Molecular Computer, San Jose, Calif., 1984-85; corp. liaison person Computerland-101 Corp., Richmond, Va., 1985-86; exec. v.p. mktg. and sales Total Concept Inc., Richmond, 1986-87; cen. Fla. rep. CPU Corp., Tex., 1987-88; area sales mgr. Am. Distbrs., Marietta, Ga., 1988—, Mini Computer Assoc., Jacksonville, Fla.; bd. dirs. Millennia Group, Orlando, Fla., Star Quality Studios; cons. Paperless Office, WAshington, 1984, ITM, Walnut Creek, Calif., 1984. Compiler: The View from High Top, 1978. Organizer Nelson County Taxpayers Assn., 1974, Cen. Va. Geneal. Assn., Charlottesville, 1978; state advisor Peace Through Strength, 1983; chmn. Women for Reagan-Bush Campaign, Nelson County, Va., 1984. Republican. Mormon. Home: 8616 Lansmere Ln Orlando FL 32811 Office: Mini Computer Assoc 8031-8 Phillips Hwy Jacksonville FL 32256

GLEASON, BONNIE J., elementary education educator; b. Frederick, Okla., Oct. 18, 1929; d. Jim and Bertha Thomason; divorced; children: David, Stephen, John, Ruth, James. BS in Edn., So. Nazarene U., 1965; MEd, Memphis State U., 1970; PhD, Kans. State U., 1983. Prof. edn. K-8 State Dept. Edn., Tenn., 1965-70, Kans., 1969-84, Okla., 1984—; advisor Kappa Delta Pi, Phillips U., 1983—, sponsor Assn. Non-Traditional Students, 1989—; facilitator Project Wild, Okla., 1984—. Contbr. articles to profl. jours. 1st v.p. bd. dirs. YWCA, Enid, Okla., 1988-89; bd. dirs. N.W. Pastoral Care, 1989—. Recipient Heaton scholarship Kans. State U. Alumni, 1982; named Outstanding Alumni So. Nazarene U., 1987. Mem. AAUW, Nat. Sci. Tchrs. Assn., Assn. Coll. Tchrs. of Edn., Okla. Sci. Tchrs. Assn., Okla. Tchrs. of Math Assn., Phi Delta Kappa (pres. Cimmaron chpt. 1990—). Home: 1014 Freeland Dr Enid OK 73701 Office: Phillips U 102 University Blvd Enid OK 73702

GLEASON, JOANNA, actress; b. Toronto, Ont., Can., June 2, 1950; d. Monty and Marilyn (Plotell) Hall. Grad., UCLA. Broadway debut I Love My Wife, Ethel Barrymore Theatre, 1977; Broadway appearances include Hey! Look Me Over, 1981, The Real Thing, 1984, A Hell of a Town, 1984, A Day in the Death of Joe Egg, 1985, It's Only a Play, 1985, Social Security, 1986, Into the Woods, Old Globe Theatre, San Diego and Martin Beck Theatre, N.Y.C., 1987 (Marie Antoinette award for leading actress in a mus., N.Y. Outer Critics Circle award, Drama Desk award); appeared in films Heartburn, 1986, Hannah and Her Sisters, 1987; TV appearances include Why Us?, 1981, Great Day, 1983, Still the Beaver, 1983, series Hello, Larry, 1979-80. Mem. Actors' Equity Assn. Office: care Agy Performing Arts 888 7th Ave New York NY 10106*

GLEASON-FAY, HELEN WILL, executive placement manager; b. Pitts., Nov. 28, 1940; d. Adrian George and Gertrude Rose (Tulisiak) Will; m. Edwin David Gleason, Sept. 9, 1961 (div. Feb. 1976); children: Kurt, Kim, Adrian; m. Anthony Clement Fay, Mar. 21, 1986. BS, Pa. State U., State College, 1962. Account exec. Mgmt. Recruiters, Louisville, 1979-85, tech. recruiting mgr., 1985-89; owner and gen. mgr. Mgmt. Recruiters of North Pinellas County, Inc., Clearwater, Fla., 1989—. Mem. Am. Kennel Club (lic. judge of herding breeds 1985—, lic. profl. handler 1969-85, columnist AKC Gazette 1979-88), German Shepherd Dog Club of Am. (bd. dirs. 1980-89). Republican. Roman Catholic. Office: Management Recruiters 2963 Gulf to Bay Blvd #220 Clearwater FL 34619

GLEICH, CAROL S., health professions education executive; b. Kewanee, Ill., Jan. 18, 1935; d. Carl and Edna (Krause) Gleich; A.B., U. Iowa, 1958, M.S., 1967, Ph.D., 1972. Program dir. med. tech. program, asst. prof. dept. pathology U. Iowa, Iowa City, 1972-77; health manpower edn. officer Bur. Health Professions, Health Resources and Services Adminstrn., HHS, Rockville, Md., from 1977, allied health cons. to Egypt; dir. Geriatric Edn. Ctrs. of PHS; adj. assoc. prof. U. Md. Sch. Medicine; mem. Iowa Health Manpower Com., 1976—; cons. U. Wis. System Acad. Affairs, 1976; panelist and participant workshops. Cert. clin. chemistry technologist, Nat. Registry Clin. Chemistry. Mem. Am. Soc. Allied Health Professions, Nat. Council for Internat. Health, Am. Soc. Clin. Pathologists (assoc.; cert. med. technologist; sec. ASCP Bd. Registry, 1975-77), Am. Soc. Med. Tech., D.C. Soc. Med. Tech. (Outstanding Med. Technologist of Yr. 1975), Beta Beta Beta, Alpha Mu Tau. Assoc. editor Am. Jour. Med. Tech., 1974-83, Jour. Allied Health, 1982-85; contbr. articles to profl. publs., papers to confs. Home: 14800 Rocking Spring Dr Rockville MD 20853 Office: Parklawn Bldg Room 4C-04 5600 Fishers Ln Rockville MD 20857

GLEIS, LINDA HOOD, physician; b. Louisville, Jan. 28, 1952; d. Edgar Pete Hood and Joan Ray (Brenner) Hulsey; m. Gregory Eric Gleis, Aug. 18, 1973; children: Eric, Matthew, Kevin. BA, Bellarmine Coll., 1974; MD, U. Louisville, 1978; cert. in phys. med. and rehab., Frazier Rehab. Ctr., 1982. Diplomate Am. Acad. of Phys. Med. and Rehab. Dir. residency tng. Frazier Rehab. Ctr., Louisville, Ky., 1985-; asst. clin. prof. of medicine U. Louisville, Louisville, Ky., 1985-; chief Rehab. Medicine Svc.-VA, Louisville, Ky., 1986-; partner Rehab. Assoc.-PSC, Louisville, Ky., 1986-. Leadership Circle, Metro United Way, Louisville, Ky., 1988-. Recipient Outstanding Cath. Alumni award Archdiocese of Louisville, 1990. Fellow Am. Acad. Phys. Medicine and Rehab.; mem. Jefferson County Med. Soc. (pres. elect 1990—), U. Louis Med. Alumni Assn. (pres. 1989), Ky. Acad. Phys. Medicine and Rehab. (sec.-treas. 1988—). Catholic. Office: Rehab Assoc PSC 708 Medical Towers N Louisville KY 40202

GLEN, ALIDA MIXSON, psychologist; b. Danbury, Conn., Oct. 24, 1930; d. Gerard E. and Anna Mildred (Henderson) Mixson; m. Anatol Glen, June 5, 1971. BA in History, U. Mass., 1953; postgrad., Columbia U., 1954; MA in Personnel Adminstrn., Syracuse U., 1958; PhD in Psychology, Ohio State U., 1967. Lic. psychologist, Ohio, Fla. Psychologist VA Med Ctr., Cleve., 1966-79, Walter Afield MD Clinic, Tampa, Fla., 1979-80; psychologist in pvt. practice St. Petersburg, Fla., 1980—, VA Med. Ctr., Bay Pines, Fla., 1981—; bd. dirs. Nat. Coun. on Compulsive Gambling, N.Y.C., 1972—; conductor workshops in field; lectr. in field. Contbr. articles to profl. jours. Mem. Citizens adv. Bd., Western Res. Psychiatric Hosp., 1970-78; bd. dirs. Samaritan Counseling Ctr., Clearwater, Fla., 1985-88. Recipient Career Svc. Award for Profl. Excellence, Cleve. Fed. Exec. Bd., 1973, Gamblers Anonymous of Cleve. Award for Profl. Support and Merit, 1978, others. Mem. Am. Psychol. Assn., Fla. Psychol. Assn., League of Women Voters. Episcopalian.

GLENESK, GAIL BELLE, marketing educator; b. Goose Bay, Nfld., Can., May 14, 1955; came to U.S., 1980; d. Norman Andrew and Irene Marie Lorraine (Galluchon) G. BSc with honors, U. Toronto, 1978; MBA, Andrews U., 1982; PhD, U. S.C., 1988. Account examiner Ministry Housing, Toronto, Ont., Can., 1977-80; instr., rsch. asst. U. S.C., Columbia, 1983-85; asst. prof. mktg. Western Mich. U., Kalamazoo, 1986—; cons. William R. Biggs/Gilmore Assocs., Kalamazoo, 1989, Richard D. Irwin, Inc., Homewood, Ill., 1989, Dryden Press, Hinsdale, Ill., 1989, Houghton Mifflin Co., Boston, 1990. Contbr. articles to profl. jours. Recipient Best Paper award Tourism Svcs. Mktg. Conf., Cleve. 1986; Kenneth W. and Diane Bauer scholar Andrews U., 1981; fellow Am. Acad. Advt., 1988; internship Advt. Ednl. Found., N.Y.C., 1990. Mem. Acad. Mktg. Sci., Am. Advt. Assn., Am. Mktg. Assn., Assn. for Consumer Rsch., TV Bur. Advt., Beta Gamma Sigma, Delta Mu Delta. Office: Western Mi U Dept Mktg Haworth Coll Bus Kalamazoo MI 49008-3899

GLENN, ANDREA POUTASSE, editor; b. Cleve., Sept. 13, 1951; d. Eugene Francis Poutasse and Helen (Kingston) Ingram; m. Grant Matthew Glenn, Aug. 4, 1973; children: Alexander, Charles, Margaret. BS, Kans. State U., 1973. Advt. copywriter Emerson/Franzke Advt., Topeka, 1973-78; editor Kansas! mag. Kans. Dept. Commerce, Topeka, 1978—. Author, editor: Kansas In Color, 1981. Active Jr. League Topeka, 1981—; bd. dirs. Mulvane Art Ctr., Topeka, 1987—; bd. dirs. Hist. Topeka, Inc., 1985-88; co-chmn. Carousel Gala Opening, Topeka, 1989. Mem. Women In Communications (officer 1973-79), Regional Pubs. Assn. Episcopalian. Home: 7828 SW 37th Ave Topeka KS 66614 Office: Kans Dept Commerce 400 SW 8th Ave 5th Fl Topeka KS 66603

GLENN, BELINDA, construction engineer; b. Garden City, Kans., June 27, 1963; d. Everett Lee and Karin Kaye (Coerber) G. BS in Constrn. Sci., Kans. State U., 1986. Surveyor Coleman Indsl. Constrn. Co., Wichita, Kans., 1986-87, foreman, 1987; field engr. Herzog Contracting Corp., L.A., 1987-89; project engr. Herzog Contracting Corp., Long Beach, Calif., 1989—. Mem. NAFE, Kans. State U. Alumni Assn. Lutheran. Home: 10720 Lakewood Blvd Apt 123 Downey CA 90421 Office: Herzog Contracting Corp 853 Atlantic Ave Long Beach CA 90813

GLENN, DEBRA PAHAL, business educator; b. Monroe, La., Feb. 2, 1953; d. John Elmer and Ruby Mae (Parker) Pahal; m. Curtis Edwin Glenn, oct. 21, 1977; children: Stein Michael, Terah Grasty. BS, Northeast La. U., 1974; MS, La. Tech. U., 1980. Lic. vocat. instr., La. Social worker La. Dept. Pub. Welfare, Monroe, 1974-77; planning asst. City of Shreveport, La., 1977-78; tchr. bus. Claiborne Acad., Homer, La., 1980-83; post-grad. in English La. Tech. U., Ruston, 1981; tchr. bus. Bienville Acad., Bryceland, La., 1985-86; asst. libr. Claiborne Parish Libr., Homer, 1986-89; instr. bus. Claiborne Tech. Inst., Homer, 1989—. Asst. dir. children's choir 1st Bapt. Ch., Homer, 1988-89. Mem. La. Vocat. Assn., Northeast La. Librs. Network, Weight Watchers Internat. (counsellor, leader 1989-90), Nat. Collegiate Assn. Secs. (v.p. 1973-74), Nat. Hon. Fraternity Bus. Educators, La. Tech. U. Alumni Assn., Northeast La. U. Alumni Assn., Delta Pi Epsilon. Republican. Home: 725 North Main St Homer LA 71040 Office: Claiborne Tech Inst 3001 Minden Rd Homer LA 71040

GLENN, LINDA MACDONALD, lawyer; b. Perth Amboy, N.J., Sept. 29, 1955; d. John and Anna (Janocko) Stefanik; m. John Arch MacDonald, Sept. 17, 1983 (dec. Feb. 1984); m. Kim C. Glenn, Dec. 31, 1987. BA, Rutgers U., 1977; JD, Western New Eng. Law Sch., 1981. Assoc. Manning, West Santianiello and Pari, Providence, 1981-82; spl. asst. atty. gen.Atty. Gen.'s Office, Providence, 1982-87, sr. trial atty. civil div., 1988—; ptnr. Saunders, Dumas & Fleury, East Greenwich, R.I., 1987-88; ptnr. Dumas & MacDonald, 1988—; legal counsel R.I. House Com. on spl. Legislation, Health Edn. and Welfare Com.; asst. city solicitor, City of Warwick. Bd. dirs. YWCA, R.I., 1983, Leukemia Soc. R.I., 1983-85; mem. Cancer Support Group R.I., 1983-85. Named Outstanding Woman, YWCA, R.I., 1983, Outstanding Bd. Mem., Leukemia Soc. R.I., 1984, Warwick B.P.W. Woman of Yr., 1988. Mem. ABA, Assn. Trial Lawyers Am. R.I. Assn. Trial Lawyers, R.I. Bar Assn., R.I. Women's Network, LWV, Warwick Bus. and Profl. Women. Greek Catholic. Home: 26 Corey Ave Warwick RI 02818 Office: Dumas & MacDonald 139 Main St East Greenwich RI 02818

GLESS, SHARON, actress; b. Los Angeles. Student, Gonzaga U. Appeared in TV series Faraday and Company, 1973, Switch!, 1975-78, Turnabout, 1979, House Calls, 1981-82; star TV series Cagney and Lacey, 1982-88 (Emmy nomination 1983, Emmy award, 1986), The Trials of Rosie O'Neill, 1990—; appeared in TV miniseries The Immigrants, 1978, The Last Convertible, 1979; numerous other guest appearances in TV series; TV movies include All My Daughters, 1972, My Darling Daughters' Anniversary, 1973, Richie Brockelman: The Missing 24th Hours, 1976, The Islander, 1978, Crash, 1978, Hardhat and Legs, 1980, The Miracle of Kathy Miller, 1981, Letting Go, 1985, The Outside Woman, 1989; motion pictures include The Star Chamber, 1983. Recipient Emmy Award, 1986, 87 for best actress in a drama series (Cagney and Lacey). Office: care Creative Artists Agy 1888 Century Park E Suite 1400 Los Angeles CA 90067*

GLEVA, KAREN J., quality control executive; b. South Bend, Ind., July 29, 1952; d. Jack and Virginia M. (Lang) Palmer; m. John C. Gleva Sr., Nov. 10, 1979; children: John, Sarah, Lorrajean, Matthew, Mark, Steven. AA, Ind. Vocat. Tech. Coll., 1972. Quality control supr. H&R Block, Inc., Mishawaka, Ind.; bookkeeper Papczynski Constrn. Inc., Lakeville, Ind. Sec., treas. Citizen Info. Exch., Tues. Am. Beacon Cabarets, 1986-88. Lutheran. Home: 5039 W Packard Ave South Bend IN 46619

GLICK, CYNTHIA SUSAN, lawyer; b. Sturgis, Mich., Aug. 6, 1950; d. Elmer Joseph and Ruth Edna (McCally) G. AB, Ind. U., 1972; JD, Ind. U.-Inpls., 1978. Bar: Ind. 1978, U.S. Dist. Ct. (so. dist.) Ind. 1978, U.S. Dist. Ct. (no. dist.) Ind. 1981. Adminstrv. asst. Gov. Otis R. Bowen, Ind., 1973-76; dep. pros. atty. 35th Jud. Cir., LaGrange County, Ind., 1980-82, pros. atty., 1983—. Campaign aide Ind. Rep. State Cen. Com., Indpls., 1972-73. Named Hon. Speaker, Ind. Ho. of Reps., 1972, Sagamore of the Wabash, Gov. Ind., 1974. Fellow Ind. Bar Found.; mem. ABA, Ind. State Bar Assn., LaGrange County Bar Assn. (pres. 1983-86), DAR, Bus. and Profl. Women's Club, Phi Delta Phi, Delta Zeta. Republican. Methodist. Lodge: Eastern Star. Home: 113 W Spring St LaGrange IN 46761 Office: 113 W Spring St LaGrange IN 46761

GLICK, DEBORAH KELLY, accountant; b. Waterbury, Conn., Sept. 9, 1953; d. John Francis and Jeanne Doris (Weaving) Kelly; m. William Martin Glick Jr., June 30, 1973 (div. Oct. 1977); children: Kimberly, William III. BS, Post Coll., Waterbury, 1982; MS in Taxation, U. New Haven, 1990. CPA, Conn. Staff acct. DeAngelis Lombardi & Kelly CPA's, Waterbury, 1981-82, John J. Baldelli, CPA, Naugatuck, Conn., 1982-84; ptnr. Baldelli Glick & Co. CPA's, Naugatuck, 1984—. Mem. Am. Inst. CPA's, Conn. Soc. CPA's, Nat. Soc. Pub. Accts., Nat. Soc. Exec. Females. Democrat. Roman Catholic. Office: Cornerstone Profl Park PO Box 1129 Woodbury CT 06798-1129

GLICK, GINA PHILLIPS MORAN, physician; b. Chgo., Dec. 6, 1931; d. Edward Langan Moran and Virginia Louise Phillips; m. L. Michael Glick, Feb. 9, 1957; children: Mark Michael, Celeste Michele, Felicia Michele, Matthew Michael. Student, Mundelein Coll., Chgo., 1949-52; MD, Loyola U., Chgo., 1956. Diplomate Am. Bd. Anesthesiology. Intern Mercy Hosp., Chgo., 1956-57; resident in anesthesia Chgo. Wesley Mem. Hosp., 1957-59; pvt. practice anesthesia Cumberland, M.D., 1959-83; clin. instr. anesthesia U. Md., Balt.; chmn. dept. anesthesia Sacred Heart Hosp., Cumberland, 1967-83; asst. prof. anesthesia U. Tex. S.W. Med. Ctr., 1985—; dir. Jenkins Anesthesiology Libr. Recipient gold, silver and bronze medals Md. chpt. Am. Heart Assn., Community Achievement award Sta. WCBC, 1981, St. Benedict medal St. Scholastica High Sch., Chgo., 1978. Mem. Am. Soc. Anesthesiologists, Tex. Soc. Anesthesiologists, Dallas County Soc. Anesthesiologists, Dallas County Med. Soc., Md.-D.C. Soc. Anesthesiologists (pres. 1970-72). Roman Catholic. Office: U Tex Sci Med Ctr Dept Anesthesiology 5323 Harry Hines Blvd Dallas TX 75235

GLICK, JANE MILLS, biochemistry professor; b. Memphis, Nov. 26, 1943; d. Albert Axtell Jr. and Mary Louise (Baynes) Mills; m. John Harrison Glick, May 25, 1968; children: Katherine Anne, Sarah Stewart. AB, Randolph-Macon Woman's Coll., 1965; PhD, Columbia U., 1971. Postdoctoral trainee NIH, Bethesda, Md., 1971-73; postdoctoral fellow Sch. of Medicine Stanford (Calif.) U., 1973-74; rsch. asst. prof. biochemistry Sch. Dental Medicine U. Pa., Phila., 1974-77; asst. prof. biochemistry Med. Coll. of Pa., Phila., 1977-82, assoc. prof. biochemistry, 1982-90, prof. biochemistry, 1990—. Assoc. editor: Jour. Lipid Rsch., 1985-86, mem. editorial bd., 1987—; contbr. articles to profl. jours. Mem. bd. trustees Episcopal Acad., Merion, Pa., 1989—. Recipient Rsch. Svc. award NIH, 1975-77, Young Investigator award, 1980-83, Teaching award Lindback Found., 1985. Mem. AAAS, AAUP (sec. 1990—), Arteriosclerosis Coun. of Am. Heart Assn. (program com. 1990—), Am. Soc. Biol. Chemists, Phi Beta Kappa, Sigma Xi. Presbyterian. Office: Med Coll of Pa 3300 Henry Ave Philadelphia PA 19081

GLICK, KAREN ANDREA, lawyer; b. Santa Barbara, Calif., Apr. 3, 1962; d. Laurence Roger and Marilyn Frances (Davis) G. BA, U. Calif., Irvine, 1983; JD, U. So. Calif., L.A., 1986. Bar: Calif. 1986, U.S. Dist. Ct. Calif. 1986, U.S. Ct. Appeals (9th cir.) 1986. Assoc. Buchalter, Nemer, Fields & Younger, Newport Beach, Calif., 1986—. Mem. Orange County Bar Assn., Calif. Bar Assn., Orange County Bankruptcy Forum, Orange County Women Lawyers, Calif. Women Lawyers. Democrat. Jewish. Office:

Buchalter Nemer et al 660 Newport Ctr Dr Ste 1400 Newport Beach CA 92660

GLICK, NANCY JOAN, optician, small company owner; b. Washington, Oct. 2, 1932; d. William and Rae (Breakstone) Perau; m. Burton Glick, Apr. 1, 1950 (div. June 1986); children: Debra Helene, Marlene Ann. Student, Strayers Bus. Coll., 1950. Registered cert. optician. Optician, part-owner Glick Optician Inc., Silver Spring, Md., 1958-78; optician dispensing Montgomery Mall Opticians, Bethesda, Md., 1978-79, Watergate Opticians Inc., Washington, 1979—; optical rep. frames Berry Opticians Co., Marietta, Ga., 1979—; owner, optician Watergate Opticians, Inc., Washington, 1980—; cons. fashion eyewear. Fellow The Nat. Guild of Rx Opticians, The Washington Guild of Rx Opticians, The Acad. of Dispensing Opticians. Democrat. Jewish. Home: 5113 Wickett Terr Bethesda MD 20814

GLICK, RUTH BURTNICK, author, lecturer; b. Lexington, Ky., Apr. 27, 1942; d. Lester Leon and Beverly (Miller) Burtnick; m. Norman Stanley Glick, June 30, 1963; children: Elissa, Ethan. BA, George Washington U., 1964; MA, U. Md., 1967. bd. dirs. Columbia Literary Assocs., Ellicott City, Md., 1981—; lectr. S.W. Writers Conf., Houston, 1984, Nebr. Writers' Guild, Omaha, 1985, Bouchercon, Balt., 1986, Triangle Romance and Fiction Writers' Conf., Raleigh, 1988. Author: (with Nancy Baggett) Dollhouse Furniture You Can Make, 1977, Dollhouse Lamps and Chandeliers, 1979, Soup's On, 1985, Oat Bran Baking, 1989; (with Eileen Buckholtz, Carolyn Males and Louise Titchener) Love Is Elected, 1982 (named one of best romances 1982), Southern Persuasion, 1983; (with Titchener) In the Arms of Love, 1983 (Romance best seller list), Brian's Captive, 1983 (Romance best seller list), Reluctant Merger, 1983 (Romance best seller list), Summer Wine, 1984, Beginner's Luck, 1984, Mistaken Image, 1985, Hopelessly Devoted, 1985, Summer Stars, 1985, Stolen Passion, 1986, Indiscreet, 1988; (with Baggett and Gloria Kaufer Greene) Don't Tell 'Em It's Good for 'Em, 1984, Eat Your Vegetables!, 1985; (with Buckholtz) End of Illusion, 1984, Space Attack, 1984, Mission of the Secret Spy Squad, 1984, Mindbenders, 1984, Doom Stalker, 1985, Captain Kid and the Pirates, 1985, The Cats of Castle Mountain, 1985, Logical Choice, 1986, Great Expectations, 1987, A Place in Your Heart, 1988, Saber Dance, 1988, Postmark, 1988, Roller Coaster, 1989 (Young Adult Best Seller List), Silver Creek Challenge, 1989, Needlepoint, 1989, Life Line, 1990; (with Kathryn Jensen) The Big Score, 1989 (Young Adult Best Seller List), Night Stalker, 1989 (Young Adult Best Seller List); (Peregrine Connection series) Talons of the Falcon, 1986, Flight of the Raven, 1986, In Search of the Dove, 1986 (Lifetime Achievement award for romantic suspense series 1987); (not collaboration) Dollhouse Kitchen and Dining Room Accessories, 1979, Invasion of the Blue Lights, 1982, More Than Promises, 1985, The Closer We Get, 1989, others; contbr. articles to profl. jours. U. Md. Am. studies fellow, 1964-65. Mem. Wash. Ind. Writers, Author's Guild, Romance Writers of Am. (lectr. Detroit 1984, Atlanta 1985, Dallas 1987, Boston 1989), Wash. Romance Writers (bd. dirs.), Sisters in Crime.

GLICK-COLQUITT, KAREN LYNNE, college administrator; b. Bucyrus, Ohio, Sept. 2; d. Phillip Dole and Bernice Grace (Shasteen) Glick; B.S.J., Bowling Green State U., 1967, M.A., 1979; m. Michael Colquitt; children: M. Todd, K. Christine. Editor, Bowling Green (Ohio) State U., 1972-74; account exec. Howard E. Mitchell, Jr., Advt., Findlay, Ohio, 1974-77; asst. to dir. Student Devel. Program, Bowling Green State U., 1977-79; dir. pub. info. Bluffton (Ohio) Coll., 1980-83; asst. to v.p. for instl. advancement Findlay (Ohio) Coll., 1983-85; assoc. dir. devel. Bluffton Coll., 1985—. Mem.Council Advancement & Support Edn., Internat. Assn. Bus. Communicators. Anglican. Club: Bowling Green U. Press (charter mem. 1983). Office: Bluffton Coll Bluffton OH 45817

GLICKENHAUS, SARAH BRODY, speech therapist; b. Mpls., Mar. 8, 1919; d. Morris and Ethel (Silin) Brody; BS, U. Minn., 1940, MS, 1945; m. Seth Morton Glickenhaus, Oct. 23, 1944; children: James Morris, Nancy Pier. Speech therapist Davison Sch. Speech Correction, Atlanta, 1940-42; speech pathologist U. Minn., Mpls., 1945-46; speech therapist Queens Coll., N.Y.C., 1946-48; speech therapist VA, N.Y.C., 1949-50; pvt. practice, New Rochelle, N.Y., 1950-71; speech therapist Abbott Sch. United Free Sch. Dist. 13, Irvington, N.Y., 1971-79; pvt. practice, Scarsdale, N.Y., 1979—; tutor learning disabled children New Rochelle Public Schs., 1968-71. Mem. AAAS, Am. Speech Hearing & Lang. Assn., N.Y. State Speech &Hearing Assn., Westchester Speech & Hearing Assn. Club: Harvard (N.Y.C.). Jewish. Home and Office: 100 Dorchester Rd Scarsdale NY 10583

GLICKMAN, LAURA LEE, lawyer; b. Bklyn., Apr. 26, 1946; d. Daniel Bernard and Miriam K. (Friedman) G.; A.B. with honors, UCLA, 1967, J.D., 1970; m. James D. Leewong, Feb. 18, 1979; children: Andrea Jane, Hilary Anne. Bar: Calif., U.S. Supreme Ct., U.S. Ct. Appeals, U.S. Dist. Ct. Pvt. practice, Pacoima, Calif., 1971-72, L.A., 1972—; staff atty. San Fernando Valley Neighborhood Legal Svcs., Inc., Pacoima, 1971-72, directing atty., 1972; clin. supervising atty. Legal Aid Found. L.A., 1972-74; adj. clin. prof. Loyola U. Sch. Law, L.A., 1972-74. Chmn. young profl. leadership group Jewish Fedn. Council Greater L.A., 1977-78, also mem. community relations com., 1978, leadership devel. com., 1978; referee bd. retirement L.A. County Employees Retirement Assn., 1975—. Recipient Bancroft-Whitney award, 1968, Appellate Advocacy award UCLA Law Sch., 1970. Mem. State Bar Calif., L.A. County Bar Assn., Women Lawyers Assn. L.A., UCLA Law Alumni Assn. (dean's counsel), Calif. Women Lawyers Assn. Office: 3435 Wilshire Blvd Ste 1800 Los Angeles CA 90010

GLICKMAN, MARLENE, social organization administrator; b. Evansville, Ind., May 13, 1936; d. Morris Jack and Sarah (Krawll) Foreman; m. Marshall Levi Glickman, Jan. 9, 1956; children: Cynthia Anne, Joseph Leonard. Student, Ohio State U., 1954-56. Area dir. The Am. Jewish Com., Buffalo, 1982—. Pres. Human Rights Adv. Coun., Western N.Y., 1988—; bd. dirs. YMCA, Buffalo and Erie County, 1990—; mem. United Way Agy. Allocations Com.; chairwoman Towns and Villages div. United Way, 1981; pres. N.E. lakes coun. Union Am. Hebrew Congregations, 1982-86, Meals on Wheels of Buffalo and Erie County, 1981-83, Coun. of Congl. Pres.-Erie County, 1979-81, Temple Beth Am, 1978-80, Sisterhood Temple Beth Am., 1969-71, 76-77; vice chair gen. campaign United Jewish Appeal, 1980, chairwoman woman's div. 1979. Recipient Abraham Pugash Community Rels. award for establish Kosher Meals on Wheels, Jewish Family Svc., Buffalo and Erie County, N.Y., 1975, Hannah G. Solomon award Nat. Coun. Jewish Women, 1985. Mem. Union Am. Hebrew Congregations (bd. dirs. nat. camp commn. 1982—), Commn. on Synagogue Music, Nat. Cantorial Placement Commmn., Hadassah (life), Assn. Reform Zionists Am. (del. to Israel 1987), Brandeis Women's Com. Office: The Am Jewish Com 3407 Delaware Ave Kenmore NY 14217-1421

GLICKMAN, PAULA RIVLIN, public relations and development executive; b. N.Y.C.; d. Harry Nathaniel and Eugenie (Graciany) Rivlin; m. Ivan Melvin Glickman, Oct. . 21, 1962; children: Allison, Michael, Ellen. BS, Cornell U., 1958; postgrad., Harvard U., 1955. Editor The MacMillan Co., N.Y.C., 1961-66; dir. communications, pub. relations and sales Arista Imports, N.Y.C., 1968-72; editor Kraus-Thompson Orgn., Ltd., Millwood, N.Y., 1982-84; mgr. Companion of N.Y. a Mutual of Omaha Co., Rye, N.Y., 1984-88; dir. external affairs St. Vincent's Hosp. and Med. Ctr. of N.Y, Harrison, 1988—. Chmn. Cornell Tradition, Westchester, N.Y., 1986-88; area chairperson Cornell Alumni Admissions Ambassadors Network, Rye, Port Chester, N.Y., 1970—; bd. dirs. Am. Cancer Soc, Westchester, 1986-88. Mem. Pub. Rels. Soc. Am., Assn. Devel. Officers, Women in Communications, Cornell Club (bd. govs. 1983—). Home: 85 Allendale Dr Rye NY 10580 Office: St Vincents Hosp 240 North St Harrison NY 10528

GLIME, REBECCA LEE, management consultant; b. Detroit, Mar. 4, 1961; d. Raymond George and Anne Gretchen (Ross) G. BS in Psychology magna cum laude, Albion Coll., 1983; MS in Indsl./Organizational Psychology, Ill. State U., 1987. Social worker Mich. Human Svcs., Ann Arbor, 1983-85; cons. Arthur Young, Chgo., 1987-89; sr. cons. organizational cons. div. Laventhol and Horwath, Chgo., 1989—. Recipient honors Detroit News Writing Contest, Detroit News, 1975; Albion fellow Albion Coll., 1983. Mem. Am. Psychol. Assn. (assoc.), Am. Compensation Assn., Soc. for Indsl. and Organizational Psychologists, Phi Beta Kappa. Office: Laventhol and Horwath 300 S Riverside Pla Chicago IL 60606

GLINK, ILYCE RENÉE, writer; b. Chgo., July 13, 1964; d. Ronald Morton and Susanne Rae (Kraus) G.; m. Samuel J. Tamkin, Aug. 20, 1989. BA, U. Ill., 1986. Pub. rels. writer Falk Assocs., Chgo., 1986-87; mem. editorial acquisitions staff Contemporary Books, Chgo., 1987-88; freelance writer Chgo., 1988—. Contbr. articles to Chgo. Tribune, Crain's Chgo. Bus., Washington Post, numerous others. Mem. Chgo. Women in Pub. (freelance forum editor 1988-90). Office: 3500 N Lake Shore Dr Chicago IL 60657

GLITMAN, KAREN MICQUE, state legislator; b. Ottawa, Can., Feb. 23, 1963; d. Maynard Wayne and Christine (Anundsen) Slitman; m. Glenn Russell, July 27, 1985. BA, U. Vt., 1985. Mem. Vt. Legislature, Mount Pelier, 1985—, asst. minority leader, 1988—. Democrat. Home: 197 Archibald St Burlington VT 05401 Office: 197 Archibald St Burlington VT 05401

GLOBERMAN, LINDA MARILYN, dermatologist, educator; b. L.A., May 15, 1951; d. Alfred Abraham and Helene (Schulz) G.; m. Gary Hall Jackson, Aug. 19, 1984. BA in Psychobiology, UCLA, 1972; MD, U. So. Calif., 1976. Diplomate Am. Bd. Dermatology. Intern Mercy Hosp., San Diego, 1976-77; resident in dermatology U. Calif. Affiliated Hosps., Irvine, 1977-80, chief resident, 1980; pvt. practice Tarzana, Calif., 1980-84, Irvine, 1982—; clin. assoc. dermatology Calif. Coll. Medicine-U. Calif., Irvine, 1979-80, 85—; mem. staff Western Med. Ctr., Children's Hosp. Orange County, U. Calif. Med. Ctr., Irvine, Health Care Med. Ctr., Irvine Med. Ctr. Contbr. articles to med. jours. Bd. dirs., membership chmn. People for Irvine Community Health, 1987-89. Recipient Med. Woman of Yr. award Tarzana C. of C., 1982, Woman of Achievement award Irvine Bus. and Profl. Women, 1985; Rancho Los Amigos Interdisciplinary Program fellow, 1973. Mem. Am. Acad. Dermatology, Soc. for Investigative Dermatology, Am. Soc. for Dermatologic Surgery, Salerni Collegium, Am. Med. Women's Assn. (br. sec.-treas. 1979-80), Calif. Med. Assn., Orange County Med. Assn., Orange County Dermatol. Soc. (sec.-treas. 1987-88, v.p. 1989, pres. 1990), Irvine Med.-Dental Soc. (sec.-treas. 1986-88, bd. dirs. 1989—), Irvine C. of C., Phi Beta Kappa, Phi Delta Epsilon. Office: 4902 Irvine Center Dr Ste 105 Irvine CA 92714

GLODOWSKI, SHELLEY JEAN, office manager; b. Stoughton, Wis., Jan. 27, 1950; d. Rodney Keller and Janet Maude (Nelson) Peterson; m. Randolph Raymond Glodowski, July 31, 1976. BA, Hamline U., 1972. Cert. secondary English tchr. Substitute tchr. Stoughton (Wis.) Schs., 1973-74; office worker Wis. Pharm. Assn., Madison, 1973-74; legal sec. Howard Hippman, Oregon, Wis., 1974-76; typist 3 dept. psychiatry U. Wis., Madison, 1976-78, supr., specialist fiscal affairs, 1978-79, grad. sec. dept. sociology, 1979-82, program asst. sch. music, 1982-84, dept. sec. sch. music, 1984-85, adminstrv. sec. phys. scis. lab., 1985-87, office mgr. instructional materials ctr., 1987—; profl. musician Z.B.M. Band, Oregon, Wis., 1986—; sound engr. Midwest Book Rev. program, Madison, 1986-89. Book reviewer, 1975—; costume designer (musical prodn.) GODSPELL, Oregon Straw Hat Players, 1990. Canvasser Dem. party, Stoughton, Wis., 1968; mem., organizer WSEU 2412 Clerical Union, Madison, 1990; vol. Wis. Libr. Assn., Madison, 1987-90; coord. fundraising cabaret Unitarian Ch., Madison, 1984—; choir mem. Unitarian Universalist choir, Madison, 1979—; mem. AFSME Union. Mem. Madison Musicians Assn. Home: 137 Washington St Oregon WI 53575 Office: Instructional Materials Ctr 225 N Mills St Madison WI 53575

GLOGOWSKI, DOROTHY ANN, medical group official; b. Ellwood City, Pa., July 6, 1964; d. Henry Paul and Margaret Eleanor (Uebelacker) G. AA, Community Coll. Beaver County, Monica, Pa., 1984. Practice mgr. Bay Psychiat. Med. Group, Torrance, Calif., 1985—. Office: Bay Psychiat Med Group 22503 Kent Ave Ste A Torrance CA 90505

GLOSSER, CARYLE ROSEN, psychologist; b. Scranton, Pa., Oct. 6, 1946; d. Irving Roy and Minnie (Steckel) Rosen; m. Mark Louis Glosser, Sept. 5, 1976; children: Jennifer, Deborah. BS, Pa. State U., State College, 1968; MEd, Temple U., Phila., 1970; PhD, U. Pitts., 1978. Lic. psychologist. Aftercare coord. N.E. Community Mental Health/Mental Retardation Ctr., Phila., 1970; supr. counseling Rebecca Gratz Club, Phila., 1970-73; dir. Umbrella Program, New Kensington, Pa., 1973-74; psychotherapist No. Community Mental Health/Mental Retardation, Pitts., 1974-78; pvt. practice Pitts., 1978—; adj. asst. prof. U. Pitts. Sch. Dental Medicine, 1981-87; rsch. assoc. dept. anthropology U. Pitts., 1989-90. Mem. Am. Psychol. Assn., Pa. Psychol. Assn. Office: 401 Shady Ave Ste B107 Pittsburgh PA 15206

GLOSUP, LORENE See DEAN, DEAREST

GLOTZBACH, LOUISE MARIE DEITER, psychologist, nurse; b. Paxico, Kans., July 31, 1927; d. George Thomas and Golda Katherine (Davis) Deiter; m. Wilfrid Otto Glotzbach, Feb. 14, 1950; children: Jeanette Drisko, Jane Cummings, Robin, Bill, Ellen, Amy Migliazzo. RN, Sch. Nursing, Sabetha, Kans., 1948; BA in Psychology, Washburn U., 1969; MS in Adult Edn., Kans. State U., 1973; MS in Nursing, U. Kans., 1977; PhD in Psychology, U. Mo., 1984. RN, Kans., Mo.; cert. med. psychotherapist. Nurse Winter VA Hosp., Topeka, 1948-51, 56-58, Topeka State Hosp., 1953-55; nurse ICU St. Francis Hosp., Topeka, 1961-64; mem. faculty Stormont-Vail Sch. Nursing, Topeka, 1965-74, Penn Valley Jr. Coll. Sch. Nursing, Kansas City, Mo., 1974-78; nurse practitioner Kansas City, 1978-86, pvt. practice psychologist, 1978—; cons. to family-owned businesses, 1987—; pvt. practice workshop presenter, Kansas City, 1977-87; evaluator McGraw-Hill Pub., 1979-80. Mem. Am. Psychology Assn., Kansas City Assn. for Mental Health, Am. Assn. for Marriage and Family Therapists (clin.), Nat. Coun. on Alcoholism (mem. bd. trustees), Assn. Employee Assistance Profls., Kansas City Greater Psychol. Assn. (legis. affairs com. 1985-86), Family Firm Inst. Democrat. Roman Catholic. Home: 651 W 69th Terr Kansas City MO 64113 Office: Family Inst Assocs 8301 State Line Ste 216 Kansas City MO 64114

GLOVER, HILDA WEAVER, counselor, psychotherapist; b. Washington, Sept. 28, 1933; d. Frank Lowrie and Elisabeth (Wilson) Weaver; m. William Rudel Glover, July 12, 1958 (div. June 1976); children: Gail Glover Madha, Gina. BA in English, Miami U., Oxford, Ohio, 1956; MS in Clin. Psychology, Va. Commonwealth U., 1973. Tchr. English and music Quantico (Va.) Post High Sch., 1956-59; staff psychologist Tex. Rehab. Commn., Houston, 1971-77; dir. counseling Episcopal Ch. of the Epiphany, Houston, 1978-88; counselor Snowflake Counseling, Houston, 1988—. Singer Bay Area Chorus, Houston, 1989—. Mem. Am. Psychol. Assn., Tex. Psychol. Assn., Nat. Assn. Alcohol and Drug Abuse Counselors, Tex. Assn. Alcohol and Drug Abuse Counselors, Houston Assn. Alcohol and Drug Abuse Counselors, Clear Lake (Tex.) Assn. Alcohol and Drug Abuse Counselors. Democrat. Office: Snowflake Counseling 1720 Sunset Blvd Houston TX 77005

GLOVER, IMOGENE (IMOGENE DAVISON), media specialist, educator; b. Texhoma, Okla., Nov. 4, 1924; d. Gerald Olin and Vinita Olive (Riley) Davison; m. James William Westerfield, Apr. 30, 1944 (div. 1944); m. Wallen T. Glover, Nov. 17, 1951; children: Doris Jean, David Wayne and William Terry (twins). Student, Kans. U., summer 1943; BA, Panhandle State U., Goodwell, Okla., 1966; MEd, U. Okla., 1972. With advt. sales dept. Sta. KGYN, Guymon, Okla., 1958-62; sec., tchr. Guymon Pub. Schs., 1966-88; crew leader U.S. State Census Bur., Enid, Okla., 1990—. Co-editor: (hist. books) Panhandle Pioneers, 1989. Pres. Texhoma Hist. Soc., 1990—; bd. dirs. State Dept. of Librs., Oklahoma City, 1982-84; alt. del. Nat. Dem. Conv., N.Y.C., 1979; county chair Tex. County Dems., 1978-88, 90—. Mem. Okla. Libr. Assn., Okla. Ret. Edn. Assn. (legis. com. 1979-83, polit. action team, 1979-84), AAUW (past. pres. Goodwell chpt. 1990-91), Mystic Rebekah Lodge (past. dist. dep. Guymon chpt. 1988-90), Epsilon Sigma Alpha, Beta Tau (pres. 1964, 77, Sweetheart 1978). Mem. Christian Ch. Home: 217 S Canyon Guymon OK 73942 Office: Texhoma Hist Soc 212 W Main Texhoma OK 73949

GLOVER, LAURICE WHITE, psychoanalyst, musician; b. Los Angeles, Oct. 15, 1930; d. Lawrence Francis and Alice Violet (King) White; B.A., Occidental Coll., 1951; M.S. in Social Work, Columbia U., 1956; cert. in psychoanalysis and psychotherapy Postgrad. Ctr. Mental Health, N.Y.C., 1971, cert. in supervision of psychoanalysis, 1975; student pipe organ Norman Wright, Robert Owen, Virgil Fox; m. Norman James Glover, Aug. 18, 1956 (div. 1963), remarried, 1983; stepchildren—Valerie Scott, Norman James, Susan Charlotte, John Thomas. Pvt. practice psychoanalysis, N.Y.C., 1968—; faculty and sr. supr. psychoanalysis Postgrad. Ctr. Mental Health, N.Y.C., 1976—, asst. dean of tng., 1982—, tng. analyst, 1985—; asst. clin. prof. psychiatry Albert Einstein Coll. Medicine, Yeshiva, U., N.Y.C., 1975—; adj. asst. prof. psychology Bronx Community Coll., 1974; tng. analyst Nat. Psychol. Assn. for Psychoanalysis, 1974-76; psychoanalysis faculty Nat. Inst. Psychotherapies, 1978—; faculty, sr. supr. psychoanalysis, tng. analyst Tng. Inst. Mental Health Practitioners, 1979-84. Organist, choir dir. Throggs' Neck Lutheran Ch., Bronx, N.Y., 1964-67; jazz organist Hotel Barbizon for Women, 1965-66; organist, choir dir. 4th Ave. Meth. Ch., Bklyn., 1967—74. Mem. Soc. Clin. Social Workers, Nat. Assn. Social Workers, Am. Group Psychotherapy Assn., Am. Guild Organists, Am. Theatre Organists Soc., Am. Fedn. Musicians. Contbr. articles to profl. publs. Office: 271 Central Park W New York NY 10024

GLOVER, MARTY ANNE, construction manager; b. Danville, Ill., Oct. 24, 1958; d. Donald William and Jane Ellen (Blind) G. BA, DePauw U., 1980. Asst. mgr. K-Mart Corp., Plymouth, Mich., 1980-83, Lyttons, Chgo., 1984-85; project coord. Keno & Sons Constrn., Highland Park, Ill., 1985-88; constrn. mgr. Charles A. Stevens, Chgo., 1988-89, Schal Assocs., Inc., Chgo., 1989—. Mem. Coll. Reps., 1979-80, 43d Ward Reps. Mem. Nat. Assn. Women in Constrn. (bd. dirs. 1988—), Tri Kappa. Methodist. Office: Schal Assocs Inc 200 W Hubbard Chicago IL 60610

GLOWAC, LAURIE ANN, health facility administrator; b. Evanston, Ill., Aug. 6, 1947; d. Gregory Dorian and Suzanne (Adams) Huffaker; m. Ronald Joseph Glowac, Aug. 23, 1969; children: Todd Davis, Kimberly Ann. BA, U. Wis., 1969, MS, 1974. Research asst. Ogran Social & Tech. Innovation, Madison, Wis., 1971-72; adminstr. planning St. Mary's Hosp. Med. Ctr., Madison, 1973-78; project coord. Dept. Fam Practice U. Wis., Madison, 1979-81; adminstr. New Physicians for Wis., Madison; exec. dir. Wis. Inst. Family Med/, Madison, 1986-88; dir. med. staff relations Physicians Plus Med. Group, 1988--. Tchr. St. Patrick's Sunday Sch., Madison, 1982-84; parish coun., v.p., St. Patricks Ch., Madison, 1984—; pres. Lake View Sch., Madison, 1987-88. Roman Catholic. Home: 155 Lakewood Blvd Madison WI 53704 Office: Physicians Plus Med Group 345 Wash Ave Madison WI 53713

GLOWITZ, CHARLINE SILVIA, educational management consultant; b. N.Y.C., Oct. 8, 1951; d. Solomon Jacob and Claire Sara (Liker) G. Qualified dir. N.Y. State Edn. Dept. Human resources adminstr. Tech. Career Insts. (formerly RCA Insts.), N.Y.C., 1974-79; exec. dir. N.Y. State Assn. of Career Schs., N.Y.C., 1979-86; pvt. practice ednl. mgmt. consulting, N.Y.C., 1986—. Recipient Outstanding Achievement award N.Y. State Assn. Career Schs., 1985. Mem. Am. Soc. Assn. Execs., N.Y. Soc. Assn. Execs., Nat. Assn. Female Execs., N.Y.C. C. of C., Alpha Beta Kappa. Home: 175 W 87th St New York NY 10024

GLOYD, SUSAN VITALI, internist; b. Phila., Aug. 29, 1950; d. Daniel Francis and Barbara Jean (Vickers) Vitali; m. Park W. Gloyd, Jr., Sept. 22, 1973; children: Peter, Timothy, Matthew. BSc, Gwynedd Mercy Coll., Gwynedd Valley, Pa., 1972; MD, Temple U., 1976. Diplomate Am. Bd. Geriatric Medicine. Intern U. Tex. Health Sci. Ctr., San Antonio, 1976-77, resident in internal medicine, 1977-79; commd. officer USPHS, 1979, advanced through grades comdr., 1985; staff internist Chinle (Ariz.) Indian Health Svc. Hosp., 1979—; staff physician Chinle Nursing Home, 1979-85. Recipient achievement award USPHS, 1982, Isolated Hardship award, 1985; named Physician of Yr., Indian Health Svc., 1988. Mem. ACP, Assn. Mil. Surgeons U.S., Commd. Officers Assn., Alpha Delta Kappa. Office: Chinle USPHS Hosp PO Drawer PH Chinle AZ 86503

GLÜCK, LOUISE ELISABETH, poet; b. N.Y.C., Apr. 22, 1943; d. Daniel and Beatrice (Grosby) G.; m. Charles Hertz (div.); 1 child, Noah Benjamin; m. John Dranow, 1977. Student, Sarah Lawrence Coll., 1962, Columbia U., 1963-65. Vis. poet Goddard Coll., U. N.C., U. Va., U. Iowa; Elliston prof. U. Cin., 1978; vis. faculty Columbia U., 1979; faculty M.F.A. program Goddard Coll., also Warren Wilson Coll., Swannanoa, N.C.; Holloway lectr. U. Calif., Berkeley, 1982; vis. prof. U. Calif.-Davis, 1983; Scott prof. poetry Williams Coll., 1983, faculty, 1984—; Regents prof. poetry UCLA, 1985-88; Delivered poem Harvard U. commencement, 1990. Author: Firstborn, 1968, The House On Marshland, 1975, Descending Figure, 1980, The Triumph of Achilles, 1985, Ararat, 1990. Recipient Lit. award Am. Acad. and Inst. Arts and Letters, 1981, Nat. Book Critics Circle award in poetry, 1985, Melville Cane award Poetry Soc. Am., 1986, Sara Teasdale Meml. prize Wellesley Coll., 1986; grantee Rockefeller Found., NEA, 1969-70, 79-80, 88—, Guggenheim Found., 1975-76, 87-88.

GLUECK, HELEN IGLAUER, physician; b. Cin., Feb. 4, 1907; d. Samuel Iglauer and Helen R. Ransohoff; 1 child, Charles. BA, Wisc. U., 1929; MD, Cin. U., 1934. Instr. U. Cin. Dept. Med., 1945-59; asst. prof. U. Cin. Dept. Med. Hematol, 1959-65; prof. U. Cin. Dept. Med. Hematol., 1965-78; prof. emeritus U. Cin. Depts. Med. and Pathology, 1979—; dir. coagulation research; dir. research U. Cin., Dept. Pathologist, 1956--. Contbr. articles to profl. jours. Bd. mem. Hebrew Union Coll., Cin. 1972--. Fellow Am. Coll. Physicians, mem. Internat. Thrombosis and Hemostasis. Jewish. Office: U Cin Dept Pathology Med Sci Bldg Eden & Bethesda ML529 Cincinnati OH 45267

GLUECK, SYLVIA BLUMENFELD, writer; b. Tulsa, Dec. 23, 1925; d. Maurice and Sina (Turk) Blumenfeld; m. Norton Shushan Glueck, June 15, 1947; children: Nancy Eisen, Milton Glueck. BJ, U. Mo., Columbia, 1949. Publicity dir. Sta. WDSU, New Orleans, 1946-47; advt. copywriter Swiftway Direct Mail, New Orleans, 1961; freelance writer and author New Orleans and San Antonio, 1965—. Author book, 1990; contbr. mag. articles and newspaper features, 1984-85, (Golden Pro award 1986). Mem. Women in Communication, Austin Writers Guild, San Antonio Writers Guild (publicity chmn.), Alamo Writers, San Antonio Profl. Writers Group, Mensa, Am. Assn. Univ. Women. Home and Office: 309 W Magnolia #1 San Antonio TX 78212

GLYMPH, DIANNE TYLER, librarian; b. Burlington, N.C., Sept. 10, 1958; d. Earle Goodson and Mayme Alcora (Ellis) Tyler; m. Michael Joe Glymph, Sept. 26, 1981. BA cum laude, Presbyn. Coll., 1980; MLS, Univ. S.C., 1981. Head libr. Christ Ch. Episc. Sch., Greenville, S.C., 1981-83; reference libr. Greenvill County Libr., 1983—; ch. libr. Trinity Luth. Ch., Greenville, 1987—. Contbr. to profl. jours. Singer Greenville Chorale, 1982—; bd. dirs. Walter Johnson Club of Presbyn. Coll., 1987—, Pebble Ridge Homeowners Assn., 1989—. Mem. S.C. Libr. Assn. (sec. archives and spl. collections 1987-88), Piedmont Libr. Assn., Staff Assn. Greenville County Libr. (pres. 1987-88). Home: 3008 Chipping Ln Columbia SC 29223 Office: Greenville County Library 300 College St Greenville SC 29601

GMUER, CECILIA ANN, pathologist; b. N.Y.C., Apr. 9, 1953; d. Henry and Josephine Cecilia (Seyfert). BS in Biology, Rensselaer Polytechnic Inst., Troy, 1975; MD, Albany Med. Coll., 1977. Intern Mallory Inst. of Pathology, Boston, 1977-78, sr. asst. resident, 1978-79; resident in clin. pathology Boston VA Med. Ctr., 1979-81; asst. pathologist St. Joseph's Hosp., Providence, 1981, assoc. pathologist, 1982-87, assoc. dir., 1987—; chmn. blood usage com., St. Joseph Hosp., Providence, 1985—. Fellow Coll. of Am. Pathologists; mem. R.I. Soc. of Pathologists (pres.), Am. Assn. of Blood Banks.

GNIADEK, CHERYL LYNN, financial accountant; b. Chgo., Feb. 21, 1947; d. Theodore Edward and Elsie Amelia (Grasmick) Whiffen; m. Richard Lawrence Gniadek, Nov. 15, 1969 (dec. Feb. 1979). BSBA, Ill. State U., 1969. Prodn. sec. Universal Tng. Systems, Lincolnwood, Ill., 1969-71; exec. sec. Alliance Am. Insurers, Chgo., 1971-78; temp. sec. Kelly Svcs., Grand Rapids, Mich., 1978-79; sec. Honeywell, Inc., Grand Rapids, Mich., 1979-80, sales corr., 1980-81; adminstr. customer quality Honeywell, Inc., Ft. Washington, Pa., 1981-84; rep. customer service Honeywell, Inc., Valley Forge, Pa., 1984-88; fin. acct. Honeywell, Inc., Ft. Washington, 1987—. Mem. Am. Bus. Women's Assn. (New Directions Charter chpt., pres. 1986, Woman of Yr. 1985), Instrument Soc. Am. (treas. edn. com. Phila. sect., sec.), Nat. Assn. Female Execs. Democrat. Roman Catholic. Home: 857 Thoreau Ct Warminster PA 18974 Office: Honeywell Inc 1100 Virginia Dr Fort Washington PA 19034

GNOZZO, NANCY ANN, sales executive; b. Buffalo, Sept. 29, 1945; d. George and Lucille Mary (Lorenzo) Miserantino; m. Joseph Daniel Gnozzo, May 28, 1966 (div.); children: Jamie, Steven. BS, SUNY, Buffalo, 1967. Tchr. Bd. Coop. Ednl. Services, Umsville, N.Y., 1971-72; dir. Barbizon Sch. Modeling Services, Buffalo, 1978-80; account exec. Sta. WPhD, Buffalo, 1980-82; account exec., regional mgr. Sta. WHTT, Buffalo, 1982—; voice talent coordinator free lance, Buffalo, 1978-88. Mem. Am. Women in Radio and TV, Nat. Assn. Female Execs. Office: Sta WHTT Buffalo Hilton Hotel Church and Terrace Sts Buffalo NY 14202

GOAD, LINDA MAY, research scientist; b. Highland Park, Mich., Sept. 21, 1948; d. Donald and Alfreda (Flasinski) Sicko; m. Earl Glen Goad, June 1, 1974; 1 child, Aaron Michael. BS, Wayne State U., 1970; PhD, CUNY, 1974. Rsch. assoc. II U. Mich., Ann Arbor, 1974-76, asst. rsch. scientist, 1976-78, assoc. rsch. scientist, 1978-84, rsch. scientist, 1984—. Contbr. book chpts. and articles to profl. jours. Mem. Electron Microscopy Soc. Am., Phycol. Soc. Am., Am. Soc. Limnology and Oceanography, Internat. Soc. Stereology, Internat. Assn. Great Lakes Rsch. Office: U Mich Ctr for Aquatic Sci 2200 Bonisteel Blvd Ann Arbor MI 48109-2099

GOBAR, GAIL TAMARA, nurse; b. Bronx, N.Y., Nov. 4, 1940; d. Jack Arthur and Anne (Schussler) Ossin; m. Seymour Gobar, Nov. 10, 1962; children: Bonnie Deborah, Tammy Dana. RN, N.y. Med. Coll. and Flower and Fifth Ave. Hosp., 1961; EdD (hon.), Rhyme U., Buffalo, 1985. Head nurse of cardiology Flower and Fifth Ave. Hosp., N.Y.C., 1960-62; head nurse, supr. Jersey Shore Med. Ctr., Neptune, N.J., 1963-67; surg. asst. Dr. M. Levbarg DDS, Bricktown, N.J., 1978-81; adminstr. for handicapped programming Family YMCA's of Ocean County, Lakewood, N.J., 1981-87, also bd. dirs.; freelance writer Penfield, N.Y., 1987—; part-time nurse Jersey Shore Med. Ctr., Neptune, 1967-70; part-time staff nurse Medictr. of Am., Lakewood, 1968-70; govs. appointee Juvenile Alcohol Prevention Adv. Bd., Ocean County, 1982-84. Columnist for weekly newspaper, Ocean County, 1978-81; editor Flower-Fifth Ave. Hosp. Alumni Newspaper. Mem. Lakewood Bd. Edn., Ocean County Bd. of Elections, 1975-78, 84-86; pres. coord. Parents Against Forced Busing, Lakewood, 1972-75; troop leader Ocean County Girl Scouts, Lakewood, 1972-77; coord. Pop Warner Girls Activities, Lakewood, 1975-80; mayor's appointee Civil Defense Adv. Bd., 1977-79. Recipient Ocean County Girl Scouts Hidden Heroine award, 1976, Assistance to Handicapped award N.J. Dept. of Human Services, 1984. Mem. N.J. Sch. Bds. Assn., Sisterhood Ahavat, Shalom (bd. dirs. Lakewood 1964-70), FFAH Nursing Alumni Assn., Rotary (recipient Speakers award 1985, Lakewood). Republican. Jewish.

GOCKE, NEVA CULLEY, health care facility professional; b. Middlebourne, W.Va., Oct. 23, 1935; d. Fonzo A. and Rose Ann (Straight) Culley; m. Thomas V. Gocke Jr., June 6, 1959; children: Thomas V. III, John David, Meredith Ann. Diploma, St. Mary's Sch. Med. Tech., Clarksburg, W.Va., 1958; BA in Sociology cum laude, W.Va. U., 1981, MA in Sociology, 1985, MPA, 1987. Rsch. technician W.Va. U., Morgantown, 1963-87; adminstrv. aide VA Med. Ctr., Clarksburg, 1987—. Mem. NAFE, Am. Soc. Pub. Adminstrn., Am. Hosp. Assn., Svc. League Morgantown (com. chmn. 1972—), W.Va. U. Alumni Assn., Soc. for Women in Pub. Adminstrn., Aux. Monongalia Gen. Hosp., Am. Assn. Ret. Persons, Mortar Bd. Roman Catholic. Home: 479 Lawnview Dr Morgantown WV 26505

GOCKLEY, BARBARA JEAN, corporate professional; b. Pitts., July 26, 1951; d. William Ervin and Dorothy Marie (Wolf) Cain; m. William Lee Gockley, Mar. 29, 1975 (div. Aug. 1989); children: Ervin Cain, Marianne Cain, William Cain. Student, Ind. U. Pa., 1969-71, Thomas Edison State Coll., 1986—. Cert. Prodn. Inventory Mgmt., Purchasing Mgmt. Asst. materials mgr. Redman Mobile Homes, Ephrata, Pa., 1972-75; mgr. inventory control Gym-Kin, Inc., Reading, Pa., 1975-77; supr. prodn./inventory control Wyomissing Converting, Reading, 1979-82; mgr. prodn./inventory control Dorma Door Controls, Inc., Reamstown, Pa., 1982-85, project mgr., 1985-86; materials mgr. Powder Coatings Group div. Morton Internat., Reading, 1986—; dir. programs Congress for Progress Inc., 1984-88, vice chmn., 1988-89, chmn. 1989-90; instr. Berks campus Pa. State U., Reading, 1985-86. Dir. Reinholds (Pa.) PTA, 1978-81; bd. dirs. Cocalico Sch. Bd., Denver, Pa., 1985—. Recipient Internat. Vol. Service award Am. Prodn. and Inventory Control Soc., 1986. Mem. Am. Prodn. and Inventory Control Soc. (treas. Schuylkill Valley chpt. 1981-82, pres. 1982-84, dir. membership Region IX, 1985-86, asst. v.p. 1987, v.p. 1988-89), Nat. Assn. Purchasing Mgrs., Assn. Mfg. Excellence, NAFE, Am. Bus. Women's Assn., Soc. Mfg. Engrs., Mothers of Twins Club (nominating chmn. 1977-78)(Lancaster, Pa.). Republican. Presbyterian. Office: Morton Internat Powder Coatings Group PO Box 15640 PO Box 15640 Reading PA 19612

GODA, ELLEN MARIE KILLELEA, construction engineer; b. N.Y.C., Jan. 7, 1952; d. Joseph Richard and Lillian Ruth (Smith) Killelea; m. Jovan Goda, Apr. 6, 1990. BS in Architecture, Ga. Inst. Tech., 1974. Draftsman Sy Richards Architect Inc., Atlanta, 1974; layout engr. Westinghouse Elevator Co., Atlanta, 1974-77; asst. project engr. Turner Constrn. Co., Detroit, 1977-79, project engr., 1979-86, sr. engr., 1986-89, quality assurance mgr., territory safety dir., 1988-89; project engr. Turner Constrn. Co., Albany, N.Y., 1989-90; constrn. cons., 1990—; arbitrator Am. Arbitration Assn. Nat. Panel of Arbitrators for the Constrn. Industry, Detroit, 1987—. Mem. Mensa, Greenpeace, Sierra Club. Home: 2 Grant Hill Rd Clifton Park NY 12065

GODBEY, HELEN KAY, city official; b. Ft. Worth, Jan. 18, 1946; d. Paschal Lee and Ester Katherine (Williams) Godbey; children: Tammy Denise Thompson, Shelly Rae Thompson. AAS, Tarrant County Jr. Coll., 1985; B in Career Arts Dallas Bapt. U., 1987, postgrad. U. Tex., Arlington, 1988—. Cert. mcpl. clk., Tex. peace officer. Ct. clk. City of Ft. Worth, 1966-68; transcriber for ct. reporters, Dallas and Tarrant Counties, 1970-75; sec. City of Euless Police Dept., Tex., 1975-81; city sec. Euless, 1981-89; asst. city mgr., 1989—; speaker, instr. police report writing Tex. A&M U., Tarrant County Jr. Coll. Police Acad., 1979-81; speaker IBM, various computer groups, Tex., Calif., 1983—, North Tex. State U. Ctr. for Community Services, Denton, 1984, 87—. Recipient Disting. Service awards Euless Police Dept., 1976, 79. Mem. Internat. Inst. Mcpl. Clks. Advanced Acad. (co-chair 1989-90, com. on technol. devel. 1984—, constl. revisions), Tex. Mcpl. Clks. Assn. Inc. (trustee officer 1987—, treas. com. 1989, v.p. 1990), Bus. and Profl. Women, Internat. City Mgmt. Assn., Am. Soc. for Pub. Adminstrn., North Tex. City Mgmt. Assn., Tex. City Mgmt. Assn., North Tex. City Secs. Assn. (pres. 1986), Kiwanis (v.p. Mid-Cities chpt. 1989-90). Baptist. Avocations: reading, hiking. Home and Office: PO Box 1344 Euless TX 76039

GODBY, CAROLYN SUE, business education teacher; b. Taylorville, Ill., June 6, 1938; d. Harold Dean and Goldie (Elliott) Kuntzman; m. Russell Alfred Godby, June 20, 1964; 1 child, Edith Marie. BS in Edn., Ill. State U., 1959, MS, 1964. Cert. secondary tchr., Ill. Bus. tchr. Atlanta (Ill.) High Sch., 1959-60, Ill. Central Coll., East Peoria, 1967-68, 74-75, Pekin (Ill.) Community High Sch., 1960—. Contbr. articles to mags. Vol. Kickapoo coun. Girl Scouts U.S.A., 1976-84; lay counselor, newsletter editor Tazewell County Vol. Ct. Counselors, Pekin, 1971-76; teens advisor YWCA, Pekin, 1963-65, 68-70; active Our Savior Luth. Ch., Pekin, 1966-70. Fellow AAUW (2d v.p. Ill. state div. 1973, pres. local chpt. 1971, award 1973-75); Peoria Area Bus. Edn. Assn. (pres. 1977, award 1978), Pekin Tchrs.' Alliance, Nat. Bus. Edn. Assn., Ill. Bus. Edn. Assn., Ill. Assn. Bus. Profls. Am. (classroom educators adv. coun. 1987), Fish Club (sec. 1973-76). Home: 2438 Willow St Pekin IL 61554

GODDARD, CAROL ANN, newspaper editor; b. Chgo., Mar. 26, 1941; d. Robert Charles and Cecilia Margaret (Vonesh) Bosh; m. Joseph S. Goddard Jr., Feb. 9, 1966 (div. Mar. 1981); children: Laura Anne, Leslie Elizabeth. BA, DePauw U., 1063; postgrad., Northwestern U., 1964, U. Ill., 1979, No. Ill. U., 1980-81. Adminstrv. asst. A.G. Becker, Chgo., 1963-67; owner P&C Mktg., Hinsdale, Ill., 1975-79; reporter Doings newspaper, Hinsdale, 1979-82, assoc. editor, 1982-84, mng. editor, 1984-86; mng. editor Pioneer Press, Oak Park, Ill., 1986-90; exec. editor Pioneer Press, Park Ridge, Ill., 1990—. Chmn. Hinsdale Concert Com., 1989, Hinsdale Plan Commn. 1989—; bd. dirs. Sarah's Inn (abused women shelter), Oak Park, 1989—. Mem. Suburban Press Club Chgo. (bd. dirs. 1980—, treas. 1980-81, pres. 1986-87, editorial awards), Zonta. Roman Catholic. Home: 219 W Maple St Hinsdale IL 60521 Office: Pioneer Press 130 S Prospect Ave Park Ridge IL 60068

GODDARD, M. FAY, editor; b. Seattle, Aug. 6, 1931; d. Harold Fay and Muriel Isabel (Lundy) G. Student, Seattle Pacific Coll., 1949-50; diploma, Prairie Bible Inst., 1954. Field missionary Overseas Missionary Fellowship, Philippines, 1954-60; with mag. production Overseas Missionary Fellowship, Phila., 1961-74; editor East Asia's Millions Overseas Missionary Fellowship, Robesonia, Pa., 1975-90; dep. internat. editor Overseas Missionary Fellowship, Robesonia, Singapore, 1990—. Editor: Broken Snare, 1972, Born for Battle, 1981, To A Different Drum, 1984, A Boy's War, 1988. Republican. Presbyterian. Office: Overseas Missionary Fellowship 404 S Church St Robesonia PA 19551

GODDARD, SANDRA KAY, educator; b. Steubenville, Ohio, Oct. 31, 1947; d. Albert Leonard and Mildred Irene (Hill) G. BS in Edn., Miami U., Oxford, Ohio, 1969; MEd, Miami U., 1973. Elem. tchr. Edison Local Sch. Dist., Hammondsville, Ohio, 1969—, Gregg Elem. Sch., Bergholz, Ohio, 1969—; former mem. curriculum com. Jefferson County Sch., Steubenville. Publicity chmn., recording sec., box office chmn. Steubenville Players, 1981-83; mem. Edison Local Adv. Coun. on Drug Edn., 1987—; state judge Ashland Oil Tchr. Achievement awards, 1988—; mem. exec. com. Gregg Elem. PTA, 1990. Martha Holden Jennings scholar, 1972-73. Mem. NEA (del. to rep. assy. 1979, 85, 86, 87, 88), Ohio Edn. Assn. (mem. exec. com. 1983-89, pres's. cabinet 1985-87), Ea. Ohio Edn. Assn. (pres. 1978-79, mem. exec. com. 1983-89), Edison Local Edn. Assn. (pres. 1974-75, v.p. 1986-88, 89—), Ohio Valley Uniserv. Coun. (treas. 1986—), Delta Kappa Gamma (legis. chairperson 1990). Democrat. Methodist. Home: 200 Fernwood Rd #11 Wintersville OH 43952 Office: Gregg Elem Sch RD 1 Bergholz OH 43908

GODDESS, LYNN BARBARA, real estate broker; b. N.Y.C., Mar. 3, 1942; d. Eugene Daniel and Hazel Cecile (Kinzler) G.; divorced. BS, Columbia U., 1963, postgrad., 1964-66. Coord. John M. Burns Assembly Campaign, N.Y.C., 1963; dir. spl. events, projects Kenneth B. Keating Senatorial Campaign, N.Y.C., 1964; dist. dir. fund raising Muscular Dystrophy Assn. Am. Inc., N.Y.C., 1965-66; exec. acct. fund raising, pub. relations Victor Weingarten Co., N.Y.C., 1966-67, Oram Group (formerly Harold L. Oram Inc.), N.Y.C., 1967-70; dir. devel. City Ctr. Music Drama Inc., N.Y.C., 1970; sales person Whitbread-Nolan, N.Y.C., 1971-73; from asst. v.p. to sr. v.p. Cross and Brown Co., N.Y.C., 1973-1985; sr. v.p. Cushman & Wakefield, Inc., N.Y.C., 1985—. Trustee Young Adults. Mem. Nat. Soc. Fund Raisers, Assn. Fund Dirs., Real Estate Bd. N.Y. (named Most Ingenious Broker Yr. 1975). Office: Cushman & Wakefield Inc 1166 Avenue of Americas New York NY 10036

GODEK, KAREN DENISE, aerospace engineer; b. Tokyo, Dec. 21, 1956; (parents Am. citizens); BS in Aerospace Engring., U. Tex., 1978; MS in Systems Engring., U. Houston, 1985. Sr. engr. Lockheed Engr. and Mgmt. Svcs., Houston, 1978-86; aerospace engr. Johnson Space Ctr. NASA, Houston, 1986—. Vol. Clear Lake Emergency Med. Corps, Houston, 1979—. Recipient Youth Appreciation award Dallas Optimist Club, 1972. Mem. AIAA (sr., treas. Houston sect. 1983-84, vice-chmn. 1984-85, chmn. 1986-87), Alpha Chi, Tau Beta Pi, Sigma Gamma Tau. Office: NASA/ Johnson Space Ctr Houston TX 77058

GODERSTAD, SUSAN GRACE, accountant; b. Coeydon, Iowa, Nov. 20, 1959; d. Ronald L. and Dorothy M. (Finlay) Frazier; m. Todd Martin Aug. 8, 1981; children: Melinda Kay, Erik Todd. BS in Bus. and Econs., Culver-Stockton Coll., 1981. Acct. Builders Devel. and Fin., Wayzata, Minn., 1983—. Mem. Clean Water Action Project, Mpls., 1989-90. Mem. NAFE. Republican. Home: 16409 Hilltop Terr Minnetonka MN 55345 Office: Builders Devel & Fin Inc 1055 E Wayzata Blvd Wayzata MN 55391

GODEZ, SUSAN LYNN, teacher; b. Wheeling, W.Va., Sept. 9, 1953; d. Anton Martin and Helen (Mesojedick) G. BS in Biol. Scis., Ohio State U., 1975; tchr. cert., Muskingum Coll., 1977; MS Adminstrn.-Supervision, U. Dayton, 1983. Cert. chemistry, biol. scis., comprehensive sci. tchr., high sch. prin., sci. supr., Ohio. Tchr. Zanesville (Ohio) City Schs., 1977-84, Birch Walthen Sch., N.Y.C., 1984-85; tchr. sci., with attendance office Grandview Heights City Schs., Columbus, Ohio, 1985—, coord. partnerships in edn., 1987—. Recipient Gov.'s award for excellence in youth sci. opportunities Ohio Dept. Edn., 1988. Mem. Assn. for Sch. and Curriculum Devel., Nat. Sci. Tchrs. Assn., Sci. Educators Coun. Ohio, Ohio Assn. Secondary Sch. Adminstrs., Career Edn. Assn., AAUW (sec. Worthington, Ohio 1987-89), Phi Delta Kappa. Republican. Methodist. Office: Grandview Heights City Schs 1587 W 3d Ave Columbus OH 43212

GODFREY, JOLINE DUDLEY, business owner; b. Lincoln, Maine, Apr. 16, 1950; d. Leland and Gail (York) Dudley; m. David Pierce Godfrey, Mar. 25, 1972 (div. 1977). BS, U. Maine, 1972; MSW, Boston U., 1977; postgrad., Brandeis U., 1983. From clin. social worker to intrapreneur Polaroid Corp., Cambridge, Mass., 1977-86; founder, chmn. Odysseum, Inc., Boston, 1986—; bd. dirs. Corp. Design Found., Boston; mem. adv. bd. U. Mass. Coll. of Mgmt., Boston, 1987—. Contbr. articles to profl. jours. Coun. mem. Photographic Rseouce Ctr., 1989—. Kellogg Found. fellow, 1989—. Democrat. Office: 406 Lion St Ojai CA 93023

GODSEY, LINDA RUTH, data processing executive; b. Granite City, Ill., Jan. 13, 1950; d. Glen Ray and Lora Margaret (Robinson) Hollis; m. James Gordon Godsey, Mar. 24, 1982. Student, Southern Ill. U., 1968-71. Bank teller First Granite City Natl. Bank, Granite City, Ill., 1971-77; cash control agent Six Flags Over Mid Am., Eureka, Mo., 1977-80; teller supr. Mark Twain Natl. Bank, St. Louis, Mo., 1980-83; client svc. mgr. Automatic Data Processing, St. Louis, Mo. Office: Automatic Data Processing 9735 Landmark Pkwy Dr Saint Louis MO 63127

GODWIN, GAIL KATHLEEN, author; b. Birmingham, Ala., June 18, 1937; d. Mose Winston and Kathleen (Krahenbuhl) G. Student, Peace Jr. Coll., Raleigh, N.C., 1955-57; B.A. in Journalism, U. N.C., 1959; M.A. in English, U. Iowa, 1968, Ph.D., 1971. News reporter Miami Herald, 1959-60; rep., cons. U.S. Travel Service, London, 1961-65; editorial asst. Saturday Evening Post, 1966; lectr. Iowa Writers Workshop, 1972-73, Vassar Coll., 1977, Columbia U. Writing Program, 1978, 81. Author: novels including The Perfectionists, 1970, Glass People, 1972, The Odd Woman, 1974, Violet Clay, 1978, A Mother and Two Daughters, 1982, The Finishing School, 1985, A Southern Family, 1987; short stories Dream Children, 1976, Mr. Bedford and The Muses, 1983; (with Robert Starer) librettos The Last Lover, 1975, Apollonia, 1979, Anna Margarita's Will, 1981, Remembering Felix, 1987. Recipient Thomas Wolfe Meml. award Lipinsky Endowment of Western N.C. Hist. Assn., 1988, Janet Kafka award U. Rochester, 1988; fellow Center for Advanced Study, U. Ill., Urbana, 1971-72; Am. specialist USIS, 1976; Nat. Endowment Arts grantee, 1974-75; Guggenheim fellow, 1975-76; recipient award in lit. Am. Acad. and Inst. of Arts and Letters, 1981. Mem. P.E.N., Authors Guild, Authors League, Nat. Book Critics Circle, ASCAP. Home: PO Box 946 Woodstock NY 12498

GODWIN, JOAN MASSEY, special events coordinator; b. Selma, N.C., Jan. 13, 1931; d. Clayborne Ledbetter Massey and Eva (Blackman) Person; m. W. Frank Godwin, Feb. 14, 1954 (separated); children: Nan Massey Pridgen, W. Frank, Jr. Student U. N.C., Greensboro, 1949-50; AA, Peace Coll., Raleigh, N.C., 1951; Student, Meredith Coll., 1976-78. Exchange dir. for Fed. Republic Germany, Friendship Force Raleigh, 1981, for S.Am., 1982, for USSR, 1983, pres., 1984-85, bd. dirs., 1985-87; exchange dir. for people's Republic China, Friendship Force Internat., Atlanta, 1985; exchange dir. for Norway, Citizens for Understanding, Raleigh, 1989—. Co-coord., co-fundraiser 1st Internat. Festival Raleigh, Inc., 1985; mem. Sister Cities Ad Hoc Com., Raleigh, 1983-84; bd. dirs. Sister Cities Internat., 1983-86, Internat. Visitors Coun., Raleigh, 1984-86. Recipient Outstanding Svc. award Friendship Force Internat., 1980, Disting. Svc. award N.C. Friendship Force, 1984. Democrat. Home: 3700 Shadybrook Dr Raleigh NC 27609

GODWIN, MARY JO, editor; b. Tarboro, N.C., Jan. 31, 1949; d. Herman Esthol and Mamie Winifred (Felton) Pittman; m. Charles Benjamin Godwin, May 2, 1970. BA, N.C. Wesleyan Coll., 1971; MLS, East Carolina U., 1973. Cert. libr., N.C. From libr. asst. to asst. dir. Edgecombe County Meml. Library, Tarboro, 1970-76, dir., 1977-85; asst. editor Wilson Library Bull., Bronx, N.Y., 1985-89, editor, 1989—; mem. White House Conf. on Libraries and Info. Svcs. Task Force. Treas. Edgecombe United Way, Tarboro. Mem. ALA (3M/JMRT Profl. Devel. award 1981), N.C. Library Assn. (sec. 1981-83), Am. Soc. Mag. Editors. Democrat. Episcopalian. Office: Wilson Libr Bull 950 University Ave Bronx NY 10452

GODWIN, NANCY ELIZABETH, home economics supervisor; b. Ft. Bragg, N.C., Sept. 17, 1951; d. Nathan Harold and Opal Elizabeth (Hickox) G. AS, South Ga. Coll., 1971; BS, North Ga. Coll., 1973; MEd, Ga. So. Coll., 1978, edn. specialist, 1982. Tchr. Nicholls (Ga.) Pub. Sch., 1974-78; instr. Swainsboro (Ga.) Vocat. Sch., 1978-82; supr. Ga. Dept. Edn., Swainsboro, 1982—. Mem. Clean Community Commn., 1988-89, Arts Coun., 1987—. Mem. Ga. Assn. Future Homemakers Am. (hon.), Ga. Vocat. Assn., Am. Vocat. Assn., Nat. Assn. Suprs. Home Econs., Home Econs. Edn. Assn., Am. Home Econs. Assn., Ga. Home Econs. Assn. (chmn. area scholarship and legis. 1985 89), Swainsboro C. of C., Future Homemakers Am. Alumni Assn., Pilot Club (Found. rep. Emanuel County 1984-85, projects coord. 1985-86, pres.-elect. 1986-87, pres. 1987-88, bd. dirs. 1988-89, historian, area leader 1989-90, pub. rels. area leader 1990—, state outreach. coord. 1990—). Democrat. Baptist. Office: Ga Dept Edn Rte 3 Box 423 Swainsboro GA 30401

GODWIN, SARA, writer; b. St. Louis, Feb. 18, 1944; d. Robert Franklin II and Annabelle (Palkes) G.; divorced; children: Jane, Josh; m. Charles D. James, May 1, 1990. BA, Calif. State U., 1967; grad., UCLA, 1968-70, U. Calif., Berkeley, 1970-71, W.I. Inst. Fairleigh Dickinson U., St. Croix, V.I., 1971-72; MA, Dominican Coll., 1974. Writer, editor Standard Oil of Calif., San Francisco, 1975-77, Gannett Corp., San Rafael, Calif., 1977-79; sr. writer Shaklee Corp., San Francisco, 1979-88; freelance writer Marin County, Calif., 1988—. Author: Seals, 1990, Gorillas, 1990; contbg. editor Last Puff, 1990 (Lit. Guild selection); contbr. cover stories and feature articles to numerous U.S. and fgn. mags.; featured in radio show Ask the Gardener on Sta. KSFO, San Francisco, 1980-81. Recipient 1st prize Calif. Press Women, for travel writing, 1982, corp. communications, 1983, personal column, 1984. Fellow Royal Hort. Soc.; mem. Pacific Area Travel Assn., U. Calif. Alumni Assn., Internat. Platform Assn. Home: PO Box 1503 Ross CA 94957

GODWIN-AUSTEN, PAMELA, motion picture executive; b. Denver, June 9, 1952; d. Joseph Godwin and Helen Grace Godwin-Austen. BA, U. Calif., Santa Cruz, 1978. Asst. to v.p. mktg. Dino DeLaurentiis Corp., Beverly Hills, Calif., 1978-79; mgr. of advt. and publicity Lorimar Distrn. Internat., L.A., 1979-81; dir. publicity Producers Sales Orgn., L.A., 1981-85; dir. mktg. Interaccess Film Distbn., L.A., 1985-88; v.p. Dennis Davidson Assocs., Beverly Hills, 1988—. Office: Dennis Davidson Assocs 211 S Beverly Dr #200 Beverly Hills CA 90210

GOEBEL, BARBARA LEEPER, professor of psychology; b. Griggsville, Ill., July 27, 1921; d. Arthur Lowell and Helen (Brown) Leeper; m. William Mathers Goebel, Mar. 10, 1944; children: William Mathers Jr., Helen Elizabeth. AB, Ill Coll., 1943; MA, Ill. State U., 1965; PhD, U. Ill., 1973. Lic. psychologist, Ill. Instr. psychology Ill. State U., Normal, 1965-73, prof. emeritus, 1990—, asst. prof., 1974-80, assoc. prof., 1980-85, prof. of psychology, 1985-89; coord. devel. master's sequence in psychology Ill. State U.; med./profl. bd. dirs. Bloomington/Normal chpt. Alzheimer's Disease and Related Disorders Assn., Inc., 1987—; speaker in field. Contbr. numerous articles to profl. jours. Mem. numerous civic orgns. Mem. NEA, Ill. Edn. Assn., Ill. Assn. Higher Edn., Am. Psychol. Assn., Am. Ednl. Rsch. Assn., Am. Coun. on Measurement, Gerontol. Soc. Am., S.W. Psychol. Assn., Mid-Western Ednl. Rsch. Assn., Phi Kappa Phi, Kappa Delta Pi.

GOEBEL, MARISTELLA, clinical psychologist, educator; b. Racine, Wis., Sept. 10, 1915; d. James Nicholas and Henrietta Marie (Rademacher) Goebel. BS, Edgewood Coll., 1944; MA, Cath. U. Am., 1946, PhD, 1966. Diplomate Am. Bd. Clin. Biofeedback. Mem. Dominican Sisters; tchr. English Cathedral High Sch., Sioux Falls, S.D., 1946-47, Heart of Mary High Sch., Mobile, Ala., 1947-49; assoc. prof. edn. Rosary Coll., River Forest, Ill., 1949-61, prof. psychology, 1966—; clin. psychologist Hines VA Hosp., Ill., 1970—; cons. Sinsinawa Dominican Sisters, Wis., 1966—. Author, editor tchr. guides Southeastern Curriculum Com., vols. Kindergarten-grade 8. Contbr. numerous articles to profl. jours. Mem. task force ch. related project Chgo. Heart Assn., 1979—, NHLBI Hypertension Investigation Pooled Project, 1982—, Citizens Ambassador Del. to China, 1987. Recipient NIH awards, 1962-33, 65-66, 82-84, Outstanding Achievement in Psychol. Research, Ill. Psychol. Assn., 1982; Performance award Hines VA Hosp., 1983. Clin. fellow Am. Assn. Biofeedback Clinicians, Des Plaines, Ill., 1983. Mem. AAAS, Am. Psychol. Assn., Am. Assn. Biofeedback Clinicians (cert.), Assn. for Applied Psychophysiology and Biofeedback, Soc. Clin. and Exptl. Hypnosis, Biofeedback Soc. Ill. (bd. dirs.), Soc. Behavioral Medicine. Avocations: gardening, knitting, bicycling. Home: 7900 W Division River Forest IL 60305 Office: Hines VA Hosp Hines IL 60141

GOEDEKE, NANCY LYNN, marketing professional; b. St. Paul, Oct. 28, 1955; d. John Fred and Joyce Maree (Hiers) G. BA in Edn., Bethel Coll., 1977. Pub. rels. rep. U. Minn., Mpls., 1979-81; pub. rels. rep. clinic pub. rels. office U. Minn. Hosp., Mpls., 1981-83; mktg. adminstrv. asst., telemarketing coord. Med. Graphics Corp., St. Paul, 1983-86; from assoc. mktg. communicator to provider svcs. adminstr. Health Risk Mgmt., Edina, Minn., 1984-86; site analyst United Healthcare Corp., Minnetonka, Minn., 1986-87; mktg. communications mgr. U.S. Fed. Credit Union, Mpls., 1988—. Spokesperson pub. and media rels. vol. ARC, Minn., 1985—; facilitator Colonial Ch.'s Job Transition Workshop, Edina, 1988—; del. State IR Party, Eagan, Minn., 1990—. Recipient Bridge award Credit Union Nat. Assn., 1989. Mem. Women in Communications, Inc., Fin. Inst. Mktg. Assn., Midwest Direct Mktg. Assn. Mem. Christian Ch. Home: 3560 Blue Jay Way Eagan MN 55123 Office: US Fed Credit Union 2772 E 82d St Minneapolis MN 55425

GOEHNER, DONNA MARIE, university dean; b. Chgo., Mar. 9, 1941; d. Robert and Elizabeth (Cseke) Barra; m. George Louis Goehner, Dec. 16, 1961; 1 child, Michelle Renee. BS in English, So. Ill. U., 1963; MSLS, U. Ill., 1966, CAS in L.S., 1974; PhD in Edn., So. Ill. U., 1983. Rsch. assoc. U. Ill., Urbana, 1966-67; high sch. librarian St. Joseph-Ogden Sch. System, St. Joseph, Ill., 1967-68; curriculum lab librarian Western Ill. U., Macomb, 1968-73, periodicals librarian, 1974-76, coordinator for tech. svcs., 1977-78, acquisitions and collection devel. librarian, 1979-86, acting dir. library, 1986, dean library svcs., 1988—; assoc. Univ. librarian for tech. and adminstrv. svcs. Ill. State U., Normal, 1986-88. Contbr. articles to profl. jours. Mem. ALA, Assn. Coll. and Rsch. Libraries (chmn. univ. libraries sect. 1988-89), Ill. Assn. Coll. and Rsch. Libraries (pres. 1985-86), Ill. Library Assn. (A-cad.Librarian of Yr. 1989). Home: 121 Kurlene Dr Macomb IL 61455 Office: Western Ill U Univ Library Macomb IL 61455

GOEHRING, MAUDE COPE, business educator; b. Persia, Tenn., Jan. 5, 1915; d. James Lawrence and Bobbie C. (Ross) Cope; m. Harvey John Goehring Jr., Aug. 12, 1950. BS in Edn., Ind. U. of Pa., 1948; MEd, U. Pitts., 1950; student, Lebanon Valley Coll., 1944-45. Tchr. Penn Hills Sr. High Sch., Pitts., 1948-68; tchr. U. Pitts., 1959-60, ret., 1968; vol. chmn. ICU, operating rm. and info. desk Margaret R. Pardee Meml. Hosp., Hendersonville, N.C., 1990—; coord. Henderson County Ct. House Vols., Hendersonville, 1983-89; cons., counselor tax aid program Am. Assn. Ret. Persons, Hendersonville, 1981—. Neighborhood chmn. Girl Scouts U.S., Butler County, Pa., 1976-79; bd. dirs. ARC, Hendersonville, 1986—. Mem. AAUW (officer), Gideon Internat. Aux. (pres., sec. 1969), Delta Pi Epsilon (pres., sec., del. Pitts. chpt., life, nat. del. 1957). Republican. Lutheran. Home: 110 Castleton Ln Hendersonville NC 28739-9707

GOERDT, MARCIA FAE, hospital administrator; b. Waterloo, Iowa, Sept. 7, 1950; d. James William and Shirley Faye (Olson) Cech; m. Glen Joseph Goerdt, Mar. 3, 1983; 1 child, Alyssa Faye. AA in Accts., U. Kirkwood Community Coll., Cedar Rapids, Iowa, 1977; BA in Acctg., U. Iowa, 1980,

MA in Health and Hosp. Adminstrn., 1987. CPA. Staff acct. Braun & Bartlett CPAs, Tucson, 1986-87, St. Mary's Hosp., Tucson, 1987-88; chief fin. officer Copper Queen Hosp., Bisbee, Ariz., 1988—. Mem. Healthcare Fin. Mgmt. Assn. Home: 615 W Vista Bisbee AZ 85603

GOETTLING-KRAUSE, GISELA ERIKA WALTRAUD, singer, voice teacher; b. Berlin, Aug. 15, 1926; came to U.S., 1957; d. Gustar Reinhold and Gertrud (Weiberg) Krause; m. Woldemar Goettling, Feb. 4, 1956 (dec.); 1 child, Kira Xenia Honeycutt; m. Baldwin Ford, July 10, 1971 (dec .). Diploma in voice teaching, Staatliches Prufungsamt, Hamburg, Germany; diploma in opera singing, Deutsche Buhnengenossenschaft, Hamburg. Music tchr. Staatliche Jugendmusikschule, Hamburg, 1951-56, Staatliche Gewerbe und Hauswirtschaftsschule, Hamburg, 1956-57; voice tchr., dir. vocal repertoire Cosmopolitan Sch. Music, Chgo., 1960-63; sr. tchr. music dept. U. Chgo. Lab. Sch., 1964-; mem. faculty Am. Cons. Music, 1967-80; pvt. practice Chgo., 1963-67, 1980-; pvt. practice, Hamburg, 1950-57, Chgo., 1963-66; gen music tchr. Harris Sch., Chgo., 1961-64; tchr. in applied voice William Rainey Harper Coll., 1971-; participant Internat. Voice Tchrs. Conf., Strassbourg, France. Soloist in numerous concerts. Mem. Nat. Assn. Tchrs. Singing (regional contest judge), Music Tchrs. Nat. Assn. (div. contest judge), Soc. Am. Musicians, Internat. Platform Assn., Bundesverband Deutcher Gesangspadagogen, Chgo. Artists Assn. Home: 715 Ashley Ct Hoffman Estates IL 60195 Office: Fine Arts Bldg 410 S Michigan Ave Ste 608 Chicago IL 60605

GOETZ, BETTY BARRETT, health physicist; b. Atlanta, Jan. 8, 1943; d. Vose Matthew and Fay (Howard) Barrett; m. Charles David Goetz, Mar. 25, 1972; children: Lisa Fay, Gayle Catherine. BA, Emory U., 1963, M in Med. Sci, 1972; BS, U. Ga., 1965. Tchr. jr. high sci. City of Decatur (Ga.) Bd. of Edn., 1965-66; tech. specialist, radiology Emory U. Sch. of Medicine, Atlanta, 1967-72, sr. assoc. allied health professions, 1977-82, health physicist, 1973—, sr. assoc. community health, 1983—; cons. in field. Contbr. articles and papers to profl. jours. Mem. Decatur, Ga. Edn. Adv. com., 1987, St. Thomas More Parent's Club, Decatur, 1980—, St. Thomas More Bd. Edn., 1981-85, Internat. Platform Assn., 1989—, Ga. Conservancy, 1989—, Friends of Fernbank, 1989—. Mem. Health Physics Soc. (sec. Atlanta chpt. 1976-79), SE Chpt. Am. Assn. of Physicists in Medicine, Ga. Assn. Radio Physicists, SE U. Radiation Safety Officers. Republican. Methodist. Home: 3661 Canadian Way Tucker GA 30084 Office: Emory U Radiation Safety Office Atlanta GA 30322

GOETZ, CECELIA HELEN, judge; b. N.Y.C.; d. Isador and Sylvia (Cohen) G.; m. Jack I. Spiegel, Nov. 1, 1958; children—Matthew I. Spiegel, Robert Spiegel. B.A. cum laude, N.Y. U., 1940, LL.B., 1940, LL.M. in Taxation, 1957. Bar: N.Y. 1940, U.S. Dist. Ct. (so. and ea. dists.) N.Y. 1951, U.S. Ct. Appeals (2d cir.) 1958, U.S. Ct. Appeals (1st cir.) 1952, U.S. Ct. Appeals (9th cir.) 1967, U.S. Ct. Appeals (5th cir.) 1976. Atty. claims div. (now civil div.) Dept. Justice, Washington, 1943-46; assoc. counsel Office Chief of Counsel for War Crimes, Nuremberg, Ger., 1946-48; ptnr. Goetz & Goetz, N.Y.C., 1949-51; asst. chief counsel Office Price Stblzn., Washington, 1951-52; spl. asst. to atty. gen., tax div., Dept. Justice, Washington, 1952-53; assoc. Weisman, Celler, Allan, Spett & Sheinberg, N.Y.C., 1953-58, Kaye, Scholer, Fierman, Hays & Handler, N.Y.C., 1958-64; ptnr. Herzfeld & Rubin, P.C., N.Y.C., 1964-78; judge U.S. Bankruptcy Ct., Eastern Dist. N.Y., Bklyn., 1978—. Mem. Assn. Bar City N.Y., N.Y. State Bar Assn., ABA, N.Y. County Lawyers Assn., NYU Law Rev. Alumni Assn., N.Y. Women's Bar Assn., Women's Bar Assn. State N.Y. Nat. Conf. Bankruptcy Judges, Nat. Assn. Women Judges (founding), Assn. Women Judges State N.Y., Women's City Club N.Y. Office: US Bankruptcy Ct 601 Veterans Meml Hwy Hauppauge NY 11788

GOETZ, RUBY GAIL, educator; b. Chgo., Dec. 27, 1933; d. Ruben Dees and Burma Bess (Buckingham) McDaniel; m. Gilbert Goetz, Feb. 7, 1956 (div. May 1980); children: Blake Gilbert, Sally Dee, Scott David. BS, Murray State U., 1955; post grad., various insts., 1961-75; MA, U. San Francisco, 1981. Cert. elem tchr., learning specialist, resource specialist, adminstrv. svcs. Elem. tchr. Sch. Dist. #163, Park Forrest, Ill., 1955-57, Riverside (Calif.) City Schs., 1958-60, Simi Valley (Calif.) Sch. Dist., 1965-75; learning handicapped tchr. Happy Valley (Calif.) Sch. Dist., 1979-81; resource specialist Shasta County Office of Edn., Redding, Calif., 1981—; owner Palisades Paradise Bed and Breakfast, Redding, 1985—. Mem. Dem. Women, Redding, 1989. Mem. AAUW, Am. Assn. of Bed and Breakfast, Shasta Wheelman, C. of C. (greeters com. 1986—), Shasta County Educators Assn., Calif. Tchrs. Assn., NEA. Home: 1200 Palisades Ave Redding CA 96003 Office: Shasta County Office of Edn 1644 Magnolia Ave Redding CA 96001

GOETZKE, GLORIA LOUISE, medical social worker, income tax specialist; b. Monticello, Minn.; d. Wesley and Marvel (Kreidler) G. BA, U. Minn., 1964; MSW, U. Denver, 1966; MBA, Coll. St. Thomas, 1977. Med. social worker VA Med. Ctr., Los Angeles, 1980—; income tax preparer and instr. H&R Block, Santa Monica, Calif., 1980—; field instr. grad. social work students at UCLA and U. So. Calif. Mem. Nat. Assn. Social Workers (cert.), Nat. Assn. of Enrolled Agts. Lutheran.

GOFF, KATHLEEN ANN MURRAY, marketing director; b. Chattanooga, Apr. 12, 1960; d. Charles Gerald and Lois Ann (Schnurr) Murray; m. John Nathaniel Goff, Mar. 15, 1986. BA in Interior Design, Calif. State U., Long Beach, 1982. Sales rep. Innovative Components, Bell, Calif., 1983-84; showrm. mgr. La Cor Wicker, Laguna Miguel, Calif., 1984-85; sales rep. Elite Communications, Santa Ana, Calif., 1985; archtl. specialist Stratton Industries, Placentia, Calif., 1985-86; dir. client svcs. Reese, Lower, Patrick & Scott, Lancaster, Pa., 1986—. Mem. pub. rels. com. Am. Heart Assn., Lancaster, 1990—; acount rep. ann. campaign United Way, Lancaster, 1989; v.p. United Cerebral Palsy, Lancaster, 1988—; mem. Lancaster Twp. Zoning Hearing Bd., 1990. Mem. Soc. Mktg. Profl. Svcs. Republican. Roman Catholic. Office: Reese Lower Patrick & Scott 1910 Harrington Dr Lancaster PA 17601

GOFF, LILA JOHNSON, historical society administrator; b. Redwood Falls, Minn., Jan. 10, 1944; d. Byron Willard and Camilla (Henry) Johnson; m. Robert Eugene Goff, Apr. 24, 1974; children: Emily Lee, Matthew Byron. BA in History, U. Minn., 1965. Chief Oral History Office Minn. Hist. Soc., St. Paul, 1967-69, head Audio Visual Library, 1969-76, asst. dir. for library and mus. collections, 1976-85, asst. dir. for library and archives, 1985—; mem. Minn. Ind. Scholars Forum. Dep. coord. Minn. State Hist. Records Adv. Bd. Mem. Oral History Assn. (pres. 1989-90), Oral History Assn. Minn. (pres. 1985-87), Am. Assn. State & Local History, Orgn. Am. Historians. Home: 1151 E Orange Ave Saint Paul MN 55106 Office: Minn Hist Soc Libr & Archives Div 690 Cedar St Saint Paul MN 55101

GOFF, SHARON ROSE, travel agency executive; b. Red Bud, Ill., Dec. 10, 1943; d. Harry Herman and Ardell W.C. (Melching) Huebner. B in Music Edn., So. Ill. U., 1966, M in Vocal Music, 1970. Cert. tchr., Ill. Tchr. music Johnston City (Ill.) Schs., 1967-71; tour cons. Presley Tours, Inc., Makanda, Ill., 1971-77; co-owner, v.p. Manner Travel, Inc., Belleville, Ill., 1977-78; owner, pres. Sunshine Holidays, Belleville, 1978—; singer Robert Shaw Chorale, N.Y.C., 1967; cons., speaker to hotels, travel orgns. and various groups, 1977—. Sec. 622 Postal Coun. Bd., Belleville, 1985—; cons. Belleville Econ. Devel. Commn., 1989—. Mem. Nat. Tour Assn. (cert. tour profl., conv. vol. 1982—). Office: Sunshine Holidays 3125 W Main St Belleville IL 62223

GOFORTH, CAROLYN MAE, artist; b. Toledo, June 7, 1931; d. Herbert Ernest John and Frieda Elsie (Reeck) Graves; m. John William Goforth, Dec. 27, 1952; children: David J., Cynthia L. Goforth Sawyer, Mark W., Laurie A. Goforth Hullinger. BS in Edn., Bowling Green State U., 1953, MA, 1977. Cert. tchr., Ohio. Art tchr. Columbus (Ohio) Pub. Schs., 1953-55, Toledo Pub. Schs., 1955-86; mgr. and co-owner Prestige Studio and Gallery, Toledo, 1988—; art judge, 1980—. Exhibited watercolors in group shows: Toledo Mus. Art, Grandpa's Jug, 1988; First Nat. Bank, Garden Forms, 1986 (3rd place); Athena, Winter, 1987 (1st place), Specturm, Oak Creek Canyon, 1987 (Best of Show). Nominated to top 25 grads., Bowling Green State U., 1989; named Art Tchr. of Yr., Gov. award, Ohio, 1981, Outstanding Tchr., Toledo Pub. Schs., 1981; recipient award of Honor State Art Exhibit, 1989. Mem. Nat. League Am. Pen Women (art exhibit award of honor 1989), Athena, Spectrum (bd. dirs. 1986-88), Friends of Photography (edn. com. 1988—), Toledo Artist Club, Nat. Women in Arts, Ladies Oriental Shrine of N.Am., Ohio and Toledo League of Am. Pen Women. Home: 5730 Sloan Rd Toledo OH 43615

GOGGANS, ROBERTA DAILY, superintendent of education; b. Colbert Co., Ala., Jan. 11, 1926; d. Henry Delofton and Lou Ella (Taylor) Daily; m. Maurice Dow Goggans, Nov. 16, 1946; (wid. 1960); children: Martha Jane, Sheri Susan, Edsel, Dow, Maurice Daily. BS, Florence State Tchr., Florence, 1957; AA,MA, U. Ala., Tuscaloosa, 1964-81. Tchr. Colbert Co. Bd. Edn., Tuscumbia, Ala., 1949-52, Marion Co. Bd. Edn., Hamilton, Ala., 1954-66; prin. Byrd Jr. High Sch., Detroit, 1966-69; tchr. Marion County Bd. Edn., Hamilton, supt., 1985-89; clk. typist Office Scientific Research Wash., 1944-45; farmer Pvt. Practice Marion county, 1982-89. Mem. Gov. Council JTPA Alabama, 1982-86, TVA Commission Alabama, 1986-89, Shottsville United Methodist Ch. Alabama, 1958-89. Mem. AASA ,AEA, NEA, MCEA, Farm Bur., Forestry, Cattlemen's Assn., Co. Devel. Com. Co., Health Com., V.P. Alpha Delta Kappa, Phi Delta Kappa, BPW Hamilton, Fine Arts Hamilton. Democrat. Methodist. Home: Rt 5 Box 262 Hamilton AL 35570 Office: Marion Co Bd Edn PO Box 189 Hamilton AL 35570

GOGGIN, KATHLEEN MARY, publishing executive; b. Elgin, Ill., Mar. 31, 1956; d. James William and Virgene Reita (Ohrwall) G. BS in Edn., U. Ga., 1978; postgrad., Ga. State U., 1979-82. Flight attendant Delta Airlines, Atlanta, 1978-85; publisher Sports Atlanta, 1982-85; dist. mgr., Textile World McGraw-Hill, Atlanta, 1985-88; dist. mgr., Modern Plastics McGraw-Hill, Chgo., 1988—. Recipient cert., medal, N.Y. Road Runners, 1986, cert., medal Boston Athletic Cub, 1983, cert., medal Marine Corp., 1983, 85. Mem. Am. Textile Machinery Assn. (tech. com. 1985-88), Bus. Profl. Advt. Assn. (awards com. 1987-88), Am. Mgmt. Assn., Soc. Plastics Engrs., Buckhead Towne Club, Downtown Sports Club, Phi Kappa Phi. Roman Catholic. Office: 3M/Media Networks 401 N Michigan Ave Chicago IL 60611

GOGOLIN, MARILYN TOMPKINS, educational administrator, language pathologist; b. Pomona, Calif., Feb. 25, 1946; d. Roy Merle and Dorothy (Davidson) Tompkins; m. Robert Elton Gogolin, Mar. 29, 1969. BA, U. LaVerne, Calif., 1967; MA, U. Redlands, Calif., 1968; postgrad., U. Washington, 1968-69; MS, Calif. State U., Fullerton, 1976. Cert. clin. speech pathologist; cert. teaching and sch. adminstrn. Speech/lang. pathologist Rehab. Hosp., Pomona, 1969-71; diagnostic tchr. L.A. County Office of Edn., Downey, Calif., 1971-72, program specialist, 1972-75, cons. lang., 1975-76, cons. orgns. and mgmt., 1976-79, dir. administrv. affairs, asst. to supt., 1979—; cons. lang. sch. dists., Calif., 1975-79; cons. orgn. and mgmt. and profl. assns., Calif., 1976—; exec. dir. L.A. County Sch. Trustees Assn., 1979—. Founding patron Desert chpt. Kidney Found., Palm Desert, Calif., 1985. Doctoral fellow U. Washington, 1968; named One of Outstanding Young Women Am., 1977. Mem. Am. Mgmt. Assn., Am. Speech/Hearing Assn., Calif. Speech/Hearing Assn., Am. Edn. Research Assn. Baptist. Home: 15 Sweetwater Irvine CA 92715 Office: LA County Office Edn 9300 E Imperial Hwy Downey CA 90242

GOLA, SANDRA VALENTINA, graphic designer, educator; b. Passaic, N.J., Mar. 10, 1955; d. Henry Andrew and Ann (Skripak) G. BFA, Pratt Inst., 1978. Asst. Brodsky Graphics, N.Y.C., 1980-82; art dir. Cycles Peugeot, Carlstadt, N.J., 1982-83; owner, pres. Skylight Graphics, Hackensack, N.J., 1983—; instr. Art Ctr. of No. N.J., New Milford, 1983-85, Parsons Sch. of Design, N.Y.C., 1985-86. Designer: Challenge tire tube packaging (Creativity award 1983), Johnson & Jonnson Ultrasound sales kit (Art Dir. Club of N.J. award 1985), KLM stationery (Creativity award 1984), Letraset Sales Portfolio (DESI award 1987, Creativity award 1987). Mem. Art Dir.'s Club of N.J., NAFE, Mensa. Avocations: bicycling, aerobics, nautilus, skiing. Home: 466 Boulevard Garfield NJ 07026 Office: Skylight Graphics 397 Hudson St Hackensack NJ 07601

GOLASHESKY, CHRYSA ZOFIA, telecommunications company executive; b. Bayonne, N.J., Feb. 16, 1957; d. John Stanley and Margaret Walterine (Stanko) G. BS, Pa. State U., 1978; MBA, Rutgers U., 1980. Mktg. analyst ITT - Domestic Transmission Systems, Inc., N.Y.C., 1980-81; market rsch. analyst ITT - U.S. Transmission Systems, Inc., N.Y.C., 1981-82; project mgr., market researcher ITT - U.S. Transmission Systems, Inc., Secaucus, N.J., 1982-85, mktg. mgr., 1985-86; product mgr. Metromedia Long Distance, Inc., Secaucus, 1986-87, dir. product mgmt., 1987-88, dir. mktg., 1988-89; dir. product mktg. Metromedia/ITT Long Distance, Inc., Secaucus, 1989—. Mem. edn. com. OLA Parish, Bayonne, N.J., 1986—; mem. Christian Founds. for Ministry, Irvington, N.J., 1988-90. Roman Catholic. Home: 101 W 24th St Bayonne NJ 07002 Office: Metromedia/ITT Long Distance 100 Plaza Dr Secaucus NJ 07096

GOLBERT, GLORIA ESTHER, seminar leader; b. Washington, July 9, 1940; d. Arthur and Bella Fruma (Goldenberg) Finkelstein: m. Thomas M. Golbert, Mar. 9, 1963; children: Charles, Robert, Sharron. BA, George Washington U., 1962; MS, U. Wis., Milw., 1965. Sales rep. Internat. Med. Corp., Englewood, Colo.; dir. NSF Women in Computr Sci. Program U. Denver, 1980-88; seminar leader Prime Learning Internat., Alpine, Utah, 1987—; assoc. dir. Passages Displaced Homemaker Program, Denver, 1982-88. Recipient Woman at Work award, Gov. Colo., Denver, 1985. Mem. Nat. Speakers Assn., U. Denver Hillel Found. (1st v.p. 1989—), Phi Delta Kappa. Jewish. Office: Prime Learning Internat 255 Union Blvd Ste 120 Lakewood CO 80228

GOLD, BREENA FAY, advertising executive; b. Harrisburg, Pa., Aug. 12, 1956; d. Stanley M. and Edith C. (Goldberg) G. BA in Speech Communication and Radio/TV Broadcasting, Pa. State U., 1978. Asst. press sec. Pa. Office of Gov., Harrisburg, 1978-79; dep. press sec. Office Pa. State Sec. Commerce Dept. Commerce, Harrisburg, 1979-82; exec. Saatchi & Saatchi DFS/Pacific, Torrance, Calif., 1984—. Club: Advt. (Los Angeles). Office: Saatchi & Saatchi DFS/ Pacific 3501 Sepulveda Blvd Torrance CA 90505

GOLD, ERICA LOUISE, film editor; b. N.Y.C., June 30, 1959; d. Leo and Janet Guttman (Becker) G. BFA, N.Y.U., N.Y., 1982. Asst. editor Valkhn Films, N.Y.C., 1982-84; editor Big Fights, Inc., N.Y.C., 1984-85; editor/writer Videofashion, Inc., N.Y.C., 1985; editor CNN, N.Y.C.; tech. dir. Nippon TV Internat. Corp., N.Y.C., 1987-89; editor Worldwide TV News, 1989—, United Nations, 1989—. Editor: (narrative film) "Dot", 1982. Active N.Y. Acad. TV ARts & Scis., N.Y.C., 1981-85, Assn. of Hunterdon Devel. Ctr./Twigs, Hunterdon, N.J., 1986.

GOLD, PHRADIE KLING See KLING, PHRADIE

GOLD, SANDRA ORENBERG, counselor; b. New Brunswick, N.J., Apr. 17, 1937; d. Maxwell H. and Pauline P. (Mezey) Orenberg; BS, Temple U., 1957; MS, Rutgers U., 1960, EdD, Rutgers U., 1970; nat. cert. counselor, 1985; nat. cert. career counselor, 1985; m. Arnold P. Gold, Nov. 7, 1968; children: Amelia, Margaret; children by previous marriage: Jeffrey Silver, Stephen Silver, Jennifer Silver. Group worker Reed St. Neighborhood House, Phila., 1956-57; tchr. Irving Sch., Highland Park, N.J., 1957-58; chmn. English dept. Pub. Schs. East Brunswick (N.J.), 1958-60, guidance counselor, 1960-62; grad. asst. Counseling Inst., Rutgers U., New Brunswick, N.J., 1961-62, counseling practicum supr. trainee, 1965-66; cons., Englewood, N.J., 1962—; cons. in field. Bd. dirs. Jewish Community Center on the Palisades, Tenafly, N.J., 1972—, mem. exec. cabinet new bldg. campaign, 1972—, v.p., program chmn., 1975-84; v.p. Leadership Devel., 1984-88; founding chairperson Thurnauer Sch. of Music, 1985-88; pres., 1988—, trustee, 1985—. co-chmn. supt.'s adv. coun. Englewood Pub. Schs., N.J. 1971-74, mem. adv. bd. Title VII program, 1974-80; youth adv. United Jewish Fund, Englewood, 1973-78, bd. dirs., 1973-84, nat. leadership award, 1977; mem. walkathon com. United Jewish Appeal, 1973—, chmn. walkathon, 1985, mem. cabinet women's div., 1972—, v.p. women's div., 1976-77, bd. dirs., 1984; v.p. United Jewish Community Bergen Country, 1986—; chmn. United Jewish Community Bd. Com. for the Devel. of Group Homes, 1985-87, 1986; pres. United Jewish Community Assn. for the Developmentally Disabled, 1987-88, pres. emeritus, 1988—; bd. dirs. Coun. of Jewish Fedns., 1989—, mem. Task Force on the Disabled, 1985-88, chmn. com. Jewish Individuals with Disabilities, 1989—; Jewish Agy. del., Jerusalem, 1980-86; mem. benefit com. Babies Hosp., Columbia Presbyterian Med. Ctr., N.Y.C., 1975-85, mem. child Sch. PTO, com., 1976-78; chmn. ednl. needs com. Dwight Morrow High Sch. PTO, Englewood, 1978-81; mem. nat. new leadership com. Jewish Welfare Bd., N.Y.C., 1980—; chmn. nat. leadership devel. manual com., 1981—, mem. scholarship com., 1982—, nat. leadership award, 1980, bd. dirs. Florence G. Heller-Jewish Welfare Bd. Research Ctr., 1982—; bd. dirs. Nat. Jewish Welfare Bd., 1986—, founding mem. com. on disabilities; mem. biennial com. Jewish Welfare Bd., 1986—; mem. Gov.'s Adv. Council Holocaust Edn., 1982-86; mem. edn. com. Anti-Defamation League, 1984—, mem. N.J. bd., 1985—, mem. regional bd., 1985—; trustee Parents Assn. of Manhattan Sch. Music, 1985—; bd. dirs. Jewish Home and Rehab. Ctr., 1986—; pres. Columbia Grammar and Preparatory Sch. Parents Assn.-High Sch. Forum, 1987-88, 90-91; bd. dirs. Jewish Edn. Svc. N.Am., 1987—; pres. United Jewish Com. Community Advocacy Program, 1989—; mem. Myoclonus Research Bd.; mem. allocations rev. task force, fund distribution subcom. Bergen County United Way . Recipient Human Relations award Am. Jewish Com., Tenafly, 1982; named hon. dir. Friends of Lubavitch, 1983, recipient Community Leader award, 1984; Nat. Def. Edn. Act fellow, 1959-60. Mem. Nat. Vocat. Guidance Assn. (state chmn. 1959-65), N.J. Personnel and Guidance Assn. (mem. bd. govs. 1959-66), Am. Personnel and Guidance Assn. (mem. bd. govs. 1959-66), Nat. Sch. Counselors Assn., Am. Personnel and Guidance Assn. (mem. internat. com. 1974-75), LWV, Am. Assn. for Counseling and Devel., Nat. Council Jewish Women (life), Hadassah (life), Delta Kappa Pi. Contbr. to Pediatric Therapy (ed. Harry C. Shirkey), 1971, rev. edit., 1974; co-editor Jewish Welfare Bd. Leadership Devel. Manual, 1987. Home: 260 Lincoln St Englewood NJ 07631 Office: 330 Johnson St Englewood NJ 07631

GOLD, SHERYL ANN VAN ORDEN, publishing company administrator; b. Glen Ridge, N.J., June 9, 1962; d. Doris Ann (Jacobus) Van Orden; m. Darrell Philip Gold, Jan. 23, 1988; 1 stepchild, Phillip. BS in Bus. Mgmt., U. Hartford, 1984. Prodn. specialist Davis Printing Corp., Hackensack, N.J., 1984-85; mfg. asst. Macmillan Pub. Co., N.Y.C., 1985-86, jr. mfg. supr., 1986-87; buyer, analyst Field Publs., Middletown, Conn., 1987-89, sr. buyer, analyst, 1989—. Office: Field Publs 245 Long Hill Rd Middletown CT 06457

GOLD, SHIRLEY JEANNE, state legislator, labor relations specialist; b. N.Y.C., Oct. 2, 1925; d. Louis and Gussie (Lefkowitz) Diamondstein; BA in Music, Hunter Coll., 1945; MA in Behavioral Sci. (Crown-Zellerbach Corp. scholar), Reed Coll., 1962; m. David E. Gold, June 22, 1947; children: Andrew, Dana. Tchr., Portland (Oreg.) Public Schs., 1954-68; pres. Portland Fedn. Tchrs., Am. Fedn. Tchrs./AFL-CIO, 1965-72, pres. Oreg. Fedn. Tchrs., 1972-77; cons. labor relations to univs., coll., Portland, 1977-80; mem. Oreg. Ho. of Reps., Salem, 1980-88, majority leader, from 1985, chmn. legis. rules, ops. and reform, human resources com., 1983-84, revenue com., 1987—, policy and priorities, com. of edn., commn. of states, from 1987, campaign fin. reform com., from 1987; now state senator Oreg. Senate; mem. Oreg. Tchr. Tenure Rev. Bd., 1965-72; mem. Nat. Multi-State Consortium, 1974; mem. Speak Out Oreg. com. to White House and Congress, 1978; mem. Oreg. Task Force on Tax Reform; AFL-CIO scholar George Meany Inst., 3 times, 1976-77; commr. Edn. Commn. of States; mem. Oreg. Commn. on Women. Chairperson precinct com., conv. del. Oreg. Democratic Party, 1960-80, dist. leader, chairperson edn. com., 1978-80; charter mem., mem. exec. bd., v.p. Oreg. Council for Cts., 1977-80. Named to Hunter Coll. Hall of Fame, 1985, Citizen of Yr., 1985. Mem. Hunter Coll. Alumni Assn., Reed Coll. Alumni Assn., Pacific N.W. Labor History Assn., Portland Fedn. Tchrs., Oreg. Fedn. Tchrs., Oreg. Fedn. Dem. Women, Oreg. Coalition for Nat. Health Security, Oreg. Women's Polit. Caucus, Com. on Drug Abuse, Northwest Oreg. Health System, ACLU, Coalition Labor Union Women. Jewish. Contbr. articles on labor relations to Willamette Week newspaper, 1977-80; editor Oreg. Tchr. newspaper, 1970-72. Office: H295 State Capitol Salem OR 97310*

GOLD, SUSAN MORRISON, desktop publisher; b. Portland, Maine, Mar. 18, 1949; d. Edward Elias and Helyn Rose (Walton) Dudley; m. John Coopersmith Gold, Sept. 16, 1989; 1 child, Samuel Bowman Morrison. Student, Brandeis U., 1967-69, 70; BA in English, U. So. Maine, 1971. Reporter Biddeford-Saco Jour. (now Jour. Tribune), 1973-76; freelance writer for local and regional publs., 1976-87; editor, prodn. mgr. Munjoy Hill Observer, 1988—; owner, mgr. Custom Communications, desktop pub., Portland, 1989—; staff writer Bus. Digest, 1981-87; coord. Maine Fishermen's Forum, 1984-87. Author: Toxic Waste, Pharaohs' Curse, Passenger Pigeons, Shoes for Sport, The Alligator, Balls; contbg. editor Comml. Fisheries News, 1976-87; editor Maine Enterprise, 1987-89; producer, dir., writer video The 10th Year: Maine's Fishing Industry, 1976-1985, 1985. Del. Maine Dem. Conv., 1988; mem. Rape Crisis Ctr., Portland, 1990; mem., paper editor Munjoy Hill Neighborhood Orgn.; bd. dirs. Unitarian-Universalist Ch. Saco-Biddeford, 1990-91. Recipient 3d place award New Eng. Press Assn., 1975, bronze award, nat. Ozzie award, 1988. Mem. Nat. Press Women's Assn. (2d place nat. award book category 1985), Maine Media Women (1st place award for feature writing 1984), Maine Writers and Pubs. Alliance, Biddeford-Saco C. of C. and Industry (membership dir.). Office: Custom Communications PO Box 16036 Portland ME 04101

GOLD, VICTORIA, stockbroker; b. Tampa, Fla., Apr. 14, 1943; d. Maurice and Sylvia (Silverman) Levine; m. Stanley F. Gold (div. Jan. 1977); children: Michael, Ari. BA in Edn., U. Fla., 1964. Tchr. Dade County Schs., Miami, Fla., 1964-70; owner, mgr. Textile Outlet, Orlando, Fla., 1970-77, Victoria's Family Clothing Outlet, Tampa, 1977-82; realtor Merrill Lynch, Tampa, 1982-87; stockbroker Kober Fin., Tampa, 1987—. Jewish. Office: KobeFin 8400 E Prentice Ave Ste 1203 Englewood CO 80111

GOLDBERG, CARYN, publishing executive, consultant; b. Bklyn., Feb. 18, 1953; d. Sidney and Jean (Greenbaum) G. BA, Bklyn. Coll., 1974; postgrad., Columbia U., 1974-75. Account exec. J.C. Geever Inc. Fundraising Cons., N.Y.C., 1975-79; v.p. Coun. on Mcpl. Performance, N.Y.C., 1979-80; dir. devel. Richmondtown Restoration, S.I., N.Y., 1980-85; pres. Minds Over Matter-A Cons. Group, West Hollywood, Calif., 1988—; mng. editor Gay & Lesbian Community Yellow Pages, L.A., 1986—. Bd. dirs. Lesbian and Gay Pub. Awareness Project, L.A., 1987-89. Office: Mind Over Matter-A Cons Grp 7985 Santa Monica Blvd Ste 181 West Hollywood CA 90046

GOLDBERG, ESTELLE MAXINE, mathematics educator; b. Las Vegas, Nev., Apr. 19, 1934; d. Charles Platt and Ida Frances (Ehrlich) Fowler; m. Melvin Leonard Goldberg, July 25, 1954; children: David, Rachel. BA, UCLA, 1953; PhD, Columbia U., 1965. Prof. math. San Francisco State U., 1962-79, ret., 1979. Mem. Phi Beta Kappa. Home: 110 Pine Needle Ln Altamonte Springs FL 32714

GOLDBERG, GERALDINE ELIZABETH, biokinesiologist; b. Neptune, N.J., Mar. 22, 1939; d. Albert Voorhees and Katherine Irene (Mulholland) McCormick; m. Arthur Goldberg, July 1, 1961. BS cum laude, East Stroudsburg U., 1967; MA in Psychology, Fairleigh Dickinson U., 1971. Staff clin. psychologist Youth Devel. Clinic, Newark, 1971-75; psychotherapist in clin. psychology Mental Health Cons. Ctr., N.Y.C., 1975-85; human resources specialist AGE Corp., Livingston, N.J., 1979—; sec. bd. dirs. AGE Corp., Livingston, 1977—, v.p., 1980—. Mem. N.J. Assn. Profl. Psychologists (past pres.), Am. Psychol. Assn. (assoc.), N.J. Psychol. Assn. (assoc.).

GOLDBERG, JOCELYN HOPE SCHNIER, market research consultant; b. N.Y.C., Mar. 29, 1953; d. Alex and Eileen Rosalie (Firstenberg) Schnier. AB, Princeton U., 1974; MBA, Harvard U., 1977. Statis. technician John Hancock Inc., Boston, 1974-75; product mgr. Gen. Foods Corp., White Plains, N.Y., 1977-78; strategic/tactical bus. planning analyst Bausch & Lomb Corp., Rochester, N.Y., 1979-81; mgmt. assoc. Gordon S. Black Corp., Rochester, 1981-84; pres. Rochester Rsch. Group, N.Y., 1985—; bd. dir. Cen. Trust Co. (A Midlantic Bank). Mem. exec. bd. Boy Scouts Am. Coun.; bd. dirs. Cen. Trust Co. (Midlantic) of Rochester, N.Y. Contbr. articles to profl. jours. Recipient Achievement award Wall St. Jour., 1977. Mem. Profl. Ski Instrs. Am. (cert.). Clubs: Princeton (v.p. 1974 Princeton Class 1989—), Harvard U. Bus. Sch. (bd. dirs.). Home: 16 Ontario St Honeoye Falls NY 14472 Office: PO Box 22954 Rochester NY 14692

GOLDBERG, JODI LYNN, nurse; b. Hartford, Conn., Jan. 12, 1961; d. Lazarus and Selma (Rome) G. BS in Nursing, U. Miami, 1983. RN. Student nurse VA Hosp., West Haven, Conn., 1982, Miami, Fla., 1982-83; lic. practical nurse Coral Gables (FLa.) Hosp., 1983; RN in neurosurgery George Washington Hosp., Washington, 1984-86; nurse evaluator, markerter New Medico Assocs., Lynn, Mass., 1986—. Mem. Assn. Rehab. Nurses, Nat. Assn. Female Execs., Continuity Care Assn., No. Va. Head Injury Found., Md. Head Injury Found., D.C. Head Injury Found. Home and Office: 9847 Bristol Square Ln Bethesdal MD 20814

GOLDBERG, LEE WINICKI, furniture company executive; b. Laredo, Tex., Nov. 20, 1932; d. Frank and Goldie (Ostrowiak) Winicki; student San Diego State U., 1951-52; m. Frank M. Goldberg, Aug. 17, 1952; children: Susan Arlene, Edward Lewis, Anne Carri. With United Furniture Co., Inc., San Diego, 1953-83, corp. sec., dir., 1963-83, dir. environ. interiors, 1970-83; founder Drexel-Heritage store Edwards Interiors, subs. United Furniture, 1975; founding ptnr., v.p. FLJB Corp., 1976—, founding ptnr., sec. treas., Sea Fin., Inc., 1980, founding ptnr., First Nat. Bank San Diego, 1982. Den mother Boy Scouts Am., San Diego, 1965; vol. Am. Cancer Soc., San Diego, 1964-69; chmn. jr. matrons United Jewish Fedn., San Diego, 1958; del. So. Pacific Coast region Hadassah Conv., 1960, pres. Galilee group San Diego chpt., 1960-61; supporter Marc Chagall Nat. Mus., Nice, France, U. Calif. at San Diego Cancer Ctr. Found., Smithsonian Instn., L.A. County Mus., San Diego Mus. Contemporary Art, San Diego Mus. Art, San Diego Opera. Recipient Hadassah Service award San Diego chpt., 1958-59. Democrat. Jewish.

GOLDBERG, LESLIE REBECCA, foster care worker; b. Chgo., Sept. 8, 1959; d. Jerome Allan and Ina Joy (Lev) G. AA in Liberal Arts, Oakton Community Coll., Des Plaines, Ill., 1980; B of Social Work, Ill. State U., 1982; postgrad., Northeastern Ill. U., 1986-87. Christmas worker Salvation Army, Chgo., 1987-88; foster care worker Family Care Svcs., Chgo., 1988—. Mem. Woman's Am. Orgn. for Rehab. through Tng., Skokie, Ill., 1989. Democrat. Jewish. Office: Family Care Svcs 234 S Wabash Chicago IL 60604

GOLDBERG, PAMELA WINER, financial consultant; b. Boston, Oct. 14, 1955; d. Arthur Leonard and Marilyn (Miller) Winer; m. Marc Evan Goldberg, June 11, 1983; children: Frederick Warren, Alyssa Rachel. BA, Tufts U., 1977; MBA, Stanford U., 1981. Day care dir. Community Action Inc., Haverhill, Mass., 1977-79; lending assoc. Bankers Trust Co., N.Y.C., 1980-81; mgr., bank officer, corp. fin. dept. Citicorp, N.Y.C., 1981-82; assoc. dir., mergers and acquisitions group State Street Bank, Boston, 1983-85; ind. strategic cons. Wellesley, Mass., 1986—. Mem. exec. bd. Friends of Beth Israel Hosp., Boston, 1987—; pres. parent orgn. Temple Beth Elohim Nursery Sch., Wellesley, Mass., 1990—; trustee Recuperative Ctr., Boston, 1988—. Home and Office: 31 Lathrop Rd Wellesley MA 02181

GOLDBERG, SUSAN SOLOMON, library director; b. N.Y.C., Mar. 18, 1944; d. Elias and Minnie (Barnett) Solomon; m. Eric A. Goldberg, Mar. 27, 1966; children—Evan, Jessica, Joanna. B.A., Harpur Coll. SUNY-Binghamton, 1965; M.S., Columbia U., 1966. Librarian N.Y. Pub. Library, 1966-67, br. librarian, 1967-68; reference librarian Bklyn. Pub. Library, 1971-72; reference librarian Finkelstein Meml. Library, Spring Valley, N.Y., 1975-76; coordinator adult services Tucson Pub. Library, 1977-80, dep. dir., 1980-87; mng. dir. Ariz. Theatre Co., Tucson, from 1987; dir. Mpls. Pub. Libr., 1990—; mem. adj. faculty Pima Community Coll., Tucson, 1978, U. Ariz., Tucson, 1978-79; cons. Contbg. author: Critical Issues Conference 8, 1979; Public Librarianship, 1982; Reorganization in the Public Library, 1984. Vice pres. Cultural Alliance of Tucson, 1981-82; chmn. arts and culture com. Tucson Tomorrow, 1982-87; mem. Ariz. Commn. on Arts, Phoenix, 1983-87. Mem. ALA, Pub. Library Assn. (pres.), Library Adminstrn. and Mgmt. Assn., Ariz. Library Assn., NOW (pres. Rockland County br. 1974-76). Office: Mpls Pub Libr Office of Dir 300 Nicollet Mall Minneapolis MN 55401*

GOLDBERG, VICKI BELLE, service executive; b. Chgo., Oct. 21, 1945; d. Julius and Esther (Kennor) Comm; m. Sheldon Goldberg, Aug. 16, 1970; children: Felicia, Sharisse. BA in Psychology, Northeastern Ill. U., 1967. Lic. employment counselor, Ill.; cert. teacher, Ill. Elem. sch. tchr. Sch. Dist. 21, Wheeling, Ill., 1967-70; community svc. rep. Welcome Wagon, Memphis, 1977-80; mktg. rep. McDonald's Corp., Oakbrook, Ill., 1980-83; personnel cons. Debbie Temps, Niles, Ill., 1983-85; day care ctr. dir. Kinder Care, Palatine, Ill., 1985-86; office mgr. Casey Svcs. Inc., Des Plaines, Ill., 1986-89; regional mgr. TemPro Resources, Inc., Oakbrook Terrace, 1989—. Advisor Morton Grove (Ill.) Pk. Dist., 1981; columnist Vol. Svcs. of Skokie (Ill.) Valley, 1988—. Mem. Nat. Assn. Temporary Svcs., Ill. Assn. Personnel Cons., Oak Brook Assn. Commerce and Industry, DuPage Area C. of C. Office: TemPro Resources Inc 17 W 755 Butterfield Rd Oakbrook Terrace IL 60181

GOLDBERG, WHOOPI, actress; b. N.Y.C., Nov. 13, 1955; d. Robert and Emma (Harris) Johnson; 1 child, Alexandrea Martin. Mem. San Diego Repetory Theatre, 1975-80, Blake St. Hawkeyes, Berkeley, Calif., 1980-84. Appeared in one-person show Whoopi Goldberg on Broadway, 1984-85; films include The Color Purple, 1985, Jumping Jack Flash, 1986, Burglar, 1986, Telephone, 1987, Fatal Beauty, 1987, The Long Walk Home, 1989, Ghost, 1989; TV film: Kiss Shot, 1989, My Past Is My Own; TV series: Star Trek: The Next Generation, 1988, Bagdad Cafe; TV specials include: Tales From the Whoop: Hot Rod Brown, Class Clown, 1990. Address: care Creative Artists Agy Inc 9830 Wilshire Blvd Beverly Hills CA 90212

GOLDBERGER, BLANCHE RUBIN, sculptor, jeweler; b. N.Y.C., Feb. 2, 1914; d. David and Sarah (Israel) Rubin; m. Emanuel Goldberger, June 28, 1942; children—Richard N., Ary Louis. B.A., Hunter Coll., N.Y.C., 1934; M.A., Columbia U., 1936; Certificat d'Etudes, Sorbonne, Paris, 1936; postgrad. Westchester Arts Workshop Sculpture and Jewelry, White Plains, 1961-70, Silvermine Coll. Arts, 1962, Nat. Acad. Arts, N.Y.C., 1968. Tchr. French and Hebrew, N.Y.C. High Sch. System, Scarsdale Jr. and Sr. High Schs. One-woman shows include: Bloomingdale's, Eastchester, N.Y., 1975, Scarsdale Pub. Library, N.Y., 1976, Temple Israel, White Plains, N.Y., 1975, Greenwich Art Barn, Conn., 1972 Westlake Gallery, White Plains, N.Y., 1981; exhibited in group shows at Hudson River Mus., Yonkers, N.Y., 1978, Silvermine-New Eng. Ann., Silvermine, Conn., 1979; represented in permanent collection at Scarsdale High Sch. Library, N.Y.; sculpture commn. Jewish Community Ctr. White Plains, N.Y., 1988; also pvt. collections. Recipient award Beaux Arts of Westchester, White Plains, N.Y., 1967, First Prize, White Plains Art Show. Mem. Nat. Assn. Women Artists, Nat. Assn. Tchrs. French, Scarsdale Art Assn. (bd. dirs.; first prizes for sculpture). Jewish. Avocations: lecturing on sculpture, reading contemporary lit. in Hebrew, the violin, classical music concerts.

GOLDBERGER, NANCY RULE, psychologist, researcher; b. Canton, Ga., Oct. 25, 1934; d. James Clifford and Virginia (Doss) Rule; m. Leo Goldberger, Aug., 1970; 1 child, Jessica. BA, NYU, 1960, PhD, 1966. Lic. psychologist, N.Y., Mass. Rsch. scientist, mem. faculty Rsch. Ctr. for Mental Health NYU, N.Y.C., 1965-72; dir. evaluation Simon's Rock of Bard Coll., Great Barrington, Mass., 1972-82; staff psychologist Austin Riggs Ctr., Stockbridge, Mass., 1982-85; mem. faculty Fielding Inst., Santa Barbara, Calif., 1986—; cons. in field; assoc. Inst. for Teaching Math. & Scis., Simon's Rock of Bard Coll., 1988—. Author: (with others) Women's Ways of Knowing, 1986, 88 (Disting. Publ. award 1987, Critics Choice award 1988); contbr. articles to profl. jours. Mem. Am. Psychol. Assn., Am. Women in Psychology. Home: RFD#1 Box 34 Housatonic MA 01236 Office: 110 Bleecker St #10-B New York NY 10012

GOLD-BIKIN, LYNNE Z., lawyer; b. N.Y.C., Apr. 23, 1938; d. Herbert Benjamin Zapoleon and Muriel Claire (Wimpheimer) Sarnoff; m. Roy E. Gold, Aug. 20, 1956 (div. July 1976); children: Russell, Sheryl, Lisa, Michael; m. Martin H. Feldman, June 28, 1987. B.A. summa cum laude, Albright Coll., 1969-73; J.D., Villanova Law Sch., 1973-76. Bar: Pa. 1976, U.S. Dist. Ct. (ea. dist.) Pa. 1976, U.S. Supreme Ct. 1979. Assoc. Pechner, Dorfman, Wolffe, Rounick & Cabot, Norristown, Pa., 1976-81; ptnr. Olin, Neil, Frock & Gold-Bikin, Norristown, 1981-82; pres. Gold-Bikin Devlin & Assocs., Norristown, 1982—. Author: Pennsylvania Marital Agreements, 1984; contbg. editor, Fairshare Mag., 1987—; course planner for 12 manuals on continuing legal edn., 1978—. Mem. Albright Coll. Pres.'s Council, Reading, Pa., 1982—. Fellow Am. Acad. Matrimonial Lawyers, Internat. Acad. Matrimonial Lawyers, Pa. Bar Found.; mem. ABA (family law sect. council mem. 1981—), Pa. Bar Assn. (family law sect. council mem. 1980—), Montgomery County Bar Assn. (chmn. family law com. 1984-86), Pa. Trial Lawyers Assn. (chmn. family law sect. 1988-90). Office: Gold-Bikin Devlin & Assocs 516 Dekalb St PO Box 869 Norristown PA 19404

GOLDEN, BETH ROBINSON, psychologist; b. N.Y.C., Aug. 17, 1959; d. Harold Joseph and Silvia (Robinson) G. BA, SUNY, Binghamton, 1981; MS, Va. Commonwealth U., 1984, PhD, 1988. Rsch. assoc. dept. psychology Va. Commonwealth U., Richmond, 1987-88; staff psychologist counseling svcs. Lehigh U., Bethlehem, Pa., 1988-90, asst. dir. counseling svcs., 1990—; adj. asst. prof. dept. counseling psychology Lehigh U., 1988—. Contbr. articles to profl. jours. N.Y. State Regents scholar, 1977. Mem. Am. Psychol. Assn., Am. Group Psychotherapy Assn., NOW. Office: Lehigh U Johnson Hall #36 Univ Counseling Svcs Bethlehem PA 18015

GOLDEN, LESLIE BLACK, real estate agent; b. Dallas, Aug. 21, 1955; d. Aubrey C. Jr. and Martha (Cartwright) Black; m. G. Hawkins Golden II, Sept. 21, 1985; children: G. Hawkins III, John Houston. BBA, U. Tex., 1977. Advt. prodn. asst. Neiman Marcus, Dallas, 1977-78; group account exec. Registry Hotel, Dallas, 1978-80, sales mgr., 1982-83; sales mgr. Doubletree Inn., Dallas, 1980-82, Sheraton Park Cen., Dallas, 1983-85; real estate agt. Golden-King Properties, Dallas, 1985—. Mem. Jr. League Dallas, 1988—; chmn. arrangements and coloring book fundraiser Innovators Dallas Symphony, 1980-89, bd. dirs., 1986-89; chair phone com., auditor chmn. jr. group Dallas Garden Club, 1983—, bd. dirs., 1987-89; bd. dirs. Yellow Rose Gala com. Multiple Sclerosis, Dallas, 1985-89; hon. trustee Dallas Symphony Orch., 1988-89; chmn. Easter egg hunt Dallas So. Meml., 1987-89, bd. dirs. 1987-89; vol. Freedom Ride Found., 1987. Mem. Dallas Country Club, Park Cities Club, Kappa Alpha Theta Alumni. Office: Golden King Properties 8533 Ferndale Ste 202 Dallas TX 75238

GOLDEN, MARLENE PATRICIA, accountant, controller; b. Palisades Park, N.J., Sept. 21, 1955; d. Irwin Arthur and Louise (Gomez) Forman; m. Daniel Eugene Golden, May 6, 1984; 1 child, Victoria Nicole. BS, Montclair State Coll., 1977; postgrad., Fairleigh Dickinson U., 1981-83. Cashier, bookkeeper Atlantic & Pacific Tea Co., Palisades Park, 1972-76; gen. acct. Pub. Service Electric & Gas, Newark, 1976-77; asst. to controller Am. Leprosy Missions, Inc., Bloomfield, N.J., 1977-80, dir. data processing, 1980-83, controller, 1983—; cons. acct. McCarthy Landscapes, Palisades Park, 1980-81, Abbey Chiropractic Ctr., Bogota, N.J., 1984—. Mem. Assn. Female Execs., Christian Ministries Mgmt. Assn., Montclair State Coll. Alumni Assn., Phi Chi Theta Alumni Assn., Phi CHi Theta Undergrad. Alumni Assn. Roman Catholic. Home: 262 W Madison Ave Dumont NJ 07628 Office: ALM One Broadway Elmwood Park NJ 07407

GOLDEN, NANCY FELICE, sales professional; b. Long Beach, N.Y., Mar. 26, 1950; d. Romie James and Lucille Eleanor (Mehler) Rice. BA in Secondary Edn., Hofstra U., 1971. Dept. mgr., asst. buyer Forest Distributors Co., Garden City, N.Y., 1971-73; buyer Times Square Stores Inc., Bklyn., 1973-77, Caldor Inc., Norwalk, Conn., 1977-79, Lechmere Inc., Woburn, Mass., 1979-80; prin., pres. N. Golden Assocs., Salem, Mass., 1980—; ptnr. Tausey/Golden Sales Assocs., Salem, Stoughton, 1986—; v.p. In-Store Svcs. Inc, 1987—; ptnr. Fenway Sales, 1988—. Editor The New Englander newsletter, 1984-85, 87; copyrighted composer, lyricist, 1986—. Vol. Mondale/Ferraro campaign, 1984, United Way of Boston, 1987, Save the Children, 1988—, Help Hopitalized Vets., 1989; sponsor Boston Philharmonic, 1990. Hon. fellow John F. Kennedy Libr., 1989. Mem. DAV Commander Club, Box Project, Housewares Club New Eng. (pres., chmn. bd. dirs. 1985—), Greenpeace. Democrat. Jewish. Office: Tausey/Golden Sales Assocs 710 Turnpike St Stoughton MA 02072

GOLDEN, RENATA MICHELE, photographer, journalist; b. Chgo., Nov. 3, 1952; d. Michael Francis and Eileen Rose (Foley) G. Student, U. N.Mex., 1974-76; BS, Ariz. State U., 1978. Photojournalist The Mesa (Ariz.) Tribune, 1978-80; rsch. asst. Mus. for Contemporary Art, Chgo., 1981; darkroom printer for Olympics AP, L.A., 1984; instr. photography City of Phoenix, 1983-87; owner, photographer Renata Golden Photography, Phoenix, 1980—. One-woman photography exhibitions Phoenix Pub. Library, 1984, Austin Gallery, Scottsdale, Ariz., 1987, Tempe Fine Arts Ctr., 1988; exhibited in group shows at Tucson Art Mus., Scottsdale Ctr. for the Arts, Southwestern Invitational; author, photographer articles and pictures for numerous publs. including Scottsdale Progress, USA Today, U.S. News and World Report, Christian Science Monitor, N.Y. Photo Dist. News. Office: 1222 E Edgemont Phoenix AZ 85006

GOLDEN, SHERI DIANNE, bank officer; b. Oklahoma City, Oct. 24, 1960; d. Robert Fulton and Julianne (Bayles) G. Student, Corpus Christi State U., 1986. Team leader NCNB of Tx., Austin; ops. analyst M Bank, Corpus Christi; teller Ind. Am. S and L, Corpus Christi; asst. mgr. Warehouse Liquors, Corpus Christi; rsch. of pvt. and non-pvt. bus. for the SBA. Mem. NAFE. Home: 4513 Hebert Ln Corpus Christi TX 78413

GOLDENBERG, DEBRA ANN, lawyer; b. Washington, Dec. 25, 1959; d. Solomon Alcona and Betty June (Sragovitz) G. BS, Dickinson Coll., 1981; JD, Wake Forest U., 1984. Bar: Va. 1984, D.C. 1985, U.S. Dist. Ct. (ea. dist.) Va. 1985, U.S. Dist. Ct. (we. dist.) 1989, U.S. Ct. Appeals (4th cir.) 1989. Assoc. Tighe, Curhan & Piliero P.C., Washington, 1984-85; pvt. practice Arlington, Va., 1985—. Mem. Wake Forest U. Law Rev., 1982-84. Active Make-A-Wish Found., D.C. Mem. ABA, Arlington County Bar Assn. (cts. com. 1986—). Home: 3600 Launcelot Way Annandale VA 22003 Office: 2009 N 14th St Ste 510 Arlington VA 22201

GOLDFARB, JOANNE JACOB, architect; b. Detroit, Jan. 17, 1934; d. Saul Jacob and Ruth Blumberg; m. Ronald Lawrence Goldfarb, June 9, 1957; children: Jody Anne, Nicholas, Maximilian. BArch, Syracuse U., 1957. Lic. architect, Va., D.C. Pvt. practice architecture Alexandria, 1967-78; prin., ptnr. Design Plus Architects Inc., Alexandria, 1978-85; prin. Joanne Goldfarb Architect AIA, Alexandria, 1985—; vis. fellow Woodrow Wilson Vis. Fellows Program, 1975-78; lectr. Smithsonian Instn. Residence Assoc. program, Washington, 1985. V.p. Hollin Hills Civic Assn., Alexandria, 1980; juror Fairfax County Design Awards, Va., 1985. Mem. AIA (bd. dirs. North Va. chpt. 1979-81, 84-87, bd. dirs. VA Soc. 1990, chpt. sec. 1985, treas. 1986, pres. 1988, design award 1979, 80, 83), Assn. for Study of Man Environ. Rels. (bd. dirs. 1975—). Home: 7312 Rippon Rd Alexandria VA 22307 Office: 721 Gibbon St Alexandria VA 22314

GOLDFRANK, MRS. HERBERT J. See KAY, HELEN

GOLDHABER, GERTRUDE SCHARFF, physicist; b. Mannheim, Fed. Republic of Germany, July 14, 1911; came to U.S., 1939, naturalized, 1944; d. Otto and Nelly (Steinharter) Scharff; m. Maurice Goldhaber, May 24, 1939; children: Alfred Scharff, Michael Henry. Student, univs. Freiburg, Zurich, Berlin; Ph.D., U. Munich, 1935. Research assoc. Imperial Coll., London, Eng., 1935-39; research physicist U. Ill., 1939-48, asst. prof., 1948-50; assoc. physicist Brookhaven Nat. Lab., Upton, N.Y., 1950-58; physicist Brookhaven Nat. Lab., 1958-62, sr. physicist, 1962—; cons. nuclear data group NRC, Nat. Acad. Scis., AEC Labs. ACDA, 1974-77; adj. prof. Cornell U., 1980-82, Johns Hopkins U., 1983-86; Phi Beta Kappa vis. scholar, 1984-85; mem. sci. conf. Yamada Found., Japan, 1983; discovered pseudomagic nuclei, 1986, researched their level schemes and theoretical interpretation. Mem. editorial com. Ann. Rev. Nuclear Sci, 1973-77; N. Am. rep. bd. editors Jour. Physics G (Europhysics Jour.), 1978-80. Trustee-at-large Univ. Research Assn. governing Fermi Nat. Accelerator Lab., 1972-77; ednl. adv. com. N.Y. Acad. Scis., 1982—; Nat. Adv. Com. on Pre-Coll. Material Devel., 1984-88. Fellow Am. Phys. Soc. (council 1979-82, chmn. panel on improvement pre-coll. physics literacy 1979-82, chmn. audit com. 1980, mem. com. on profl. opportunities 1979-81, com. on history of physics, exec. com. 1983-84), AAAS (mem.-at-large sect. B physics com. 1986-88); mem. Nat. Acad. Scis. (mem. report rev. com. 1973-81, mem. acad. forum adv. com. 1974-81, mem. com. on edn. and employment of women in sci. and engring. 1978-83, commn. on human rights 1984-87), Sigma Xi. Home: 91 S Gillette Ave Bayport NY 11705 Office: Brookhaven Nat Lab #510A Upton NY 11973

GOLDIN, CLAUDIA DALE, economics educator; b. N.Y.C., May 14, 1946; d. Leon and Lucille (Rosansky) G. BA magna cum laude, Cornell U., 1967; MA, U. Chgo., 1969, PhD, 1972; MA (hon.), U. Pa., 1985. Asst. prof. econs. U. Wis., Madison, 1971-73; asst. prof. Princeton (N.J.) U., 1973-79, vis. fellow indsl. relations sec., 1987-88; vis. lectr. Harvard U., Cambridge, Mass., 1975-76, prof., 1990—; assoc. prof. U. Pa., Phila., 1979-85, prof., 1985-90; mem. Inst. Advanced Study, Princeton, 1982-83; rsch. assoc., project dir. Nat. Bur. Econ. Rsch., Cambridge, 1979—. Author: Urban Slavery in the American South, 1976, Understanding the Gender Gap, 1990; editor Jour. Econ. History; mem. editorial bd. Am. Econ. Rev., 1985—; contbr. articles to profl. jours. Guggenheim fellow, 1987-88; NSF award, 1975-77, 79-81, 81-82, 84-86, 87-89. Mem. Am. Econ. Assn., Econ. History Assn. (trustee 1984—, v.p. 1988-89). Office: Harvard U Littaner Ctr Dept Econs Cambridge MA 02138

GOLDING, PATRICIA JOYCE SURRATT, educator; b. Radford, Va., Mar. 11, 1948; d. Cleophus and Mary Frances (Entsminger) Surratt; m. Roger Alexander Golding, Sept. 1, 1967; children: Chad, Seth, Arynn. BS in Elem. Edn., Radford U., 1971; MA in Curriculum Instrn., Va. Poly. Inst. and State U., 1976, postgrad., 1976—. Tchr. mentally retarded Carroll County Schs. Fancy Gap Elem. (Va.), 1971-73; diagnostic prescriptive tchr. Project Score Carroll County Schs. and Galay City, Hillsville, Va., 1973-74; elem. tchr. Carroll County Schs., Fancy Gap Elem. (Va.), 1974-76; tchr. learning disabled students Hillsville Intermediate Sch., Carroll County Schs., 1976-78, Carroll County High Sch., Carroll County Schs., Hillsville, 1978-88; coord. talented and gifted Carroll County Schs., 1989—; coord. spl. edn. Woodlawn Intermediate Sch., 1989; supervisor of talented and gifted program, spl. edn. coord., 1989-90; southwest regional rep. Va. Coun. on Learning Disabilities, 1990-91; adj. faculty reading and verbal studies Wytheville (Va.) Community Coll., 1978-87; dept. chmn. spl. edn. dept. Carroll County High Sch., Hillsville, 1981-88, faculty coun., 1987-88; advisor spl. edn. learning disability adv. com. New River Community Coll., Dublin, Va., 1987—; cons. Va. State Task Force Secondary Learning Disabled, Richmond, Va., 1988—. Author: Learning Disability Handbook for Teachers, 1974, rev. edit., 1985. Bible sch. dir. First United Meth. Ch., Hillsville, 1974, 82, 83, 85, family life com., 1982-87. Mem. Nat. Coun. on Learning Disabilities, Va. Coun. on Learning Disabilities (southwest regional rep. 1989—), Blue Ridge Ladies Golf Assn. (tournament chmn. 1988-89). Home: 1212 Maple Dr PO Box 281 Hillsville VA 24343 Office: Carroll County Schs Hillsville VA 24343

GOLDMAN, ARLENE LESLIE, retail company executive; b. Paterson, N.J., July 7, 1956; d. Jacob and Bertha (Deck) G.; student Am. U., 1974. Asst. store mgr., asst. buyer Latt's Country Squire, Washington, 1976-77; ops. mgr. Complement, Washington, 1977-78; with Bidermann Industries, 1978-83, prodn. mgr. Jean-Paul Germain div., N.Y.C., 1979-80, dir. ops., 1980-81, v.p., 1981-83; nat. sales mgr. Ralph Lauren div., 1984-86; ind. cons., 1986; v.p. adminstrn. Summit Office Supply, N.Y.C., 1986—. Mem. Friend Whitney Mus., Met. Mus. Art (sustaining mem.), ORT. Home: 23 E 10th St Apt 608 New York NY 10003 Office: Summit Office Supply Co 303 W 10th St New York NY 10014

GOLDMAN, BARBARA DEREN, film producer, interior decorator; b. Bridgeport, Conn., Dec. 22, 1949; m. James Goldman, Oct. 25, 1975. BS, U. Bridgeport, 1971. Pres. Barbara Deren Assocs., N.Y.C., 1975—, Raoulfilm Inc., N.Y.C., 1979—; v.p. Trans-Internat. Revisions, 1980—. Co-author: Where to Eat in America, 1987; contbr. to book Feast of Wine and Food, 1987.

GOLDMAN, BARBARA S., editor, director, calligrapher; b. Pitts., Jan. 25, 1946; d. Albert H. and Ida G. (Koltin) Snyder; m. Harold L. Goldman, Aug. 20, 1967; children: Marc David, Robert Jay. Student, U. Pitts., 1964. Freelance calligrapher Pitts., 1975—; with pub. rels. dept. Winchester-Thurston Sch., Pitts., 1986-88; curriculum dir. pub. rels. Rodef Shalom Temple, Pitts., 1980—; with pub. rels. dept. Community Day Sch., Pitts., 1982-84; creator, editor children's newspaper Jewish Chronicle, Pitts., 1984-86; creator, producer Pitts. Cable TV, Pitts., 1988; creator, editor children's newspaper Pitts.'s Child Publ., 1989—. Creator: (boardgame) It's News To Me!, 1989. Mem. communications com. United Jewish Fedn. of Greater Pitts., 1987; assoc. mem. Greater Pitts. Commn. for Women, 1989. Recipient Bronze award Coun. Jewish Fedns., 1985; Coalition for Advances in Jewish Edn. grantee, 1986, Pitts. Community TV Programming Trust grantee, 1988. Mem. Am. Press Assn., Coalition for Advances in Jewish Edn., Women in Communications, Inc. Home: 1140 McCabe St Pittsburgh PA 15201 Office: Rodel Shalom Congregation Fifth & Morewood Aves Pittsburgh PA 15213

GOLDMAN, JANET PARKER, business administrator; b. Brookline, Mass., June 9, 1958; d. Robert Alan and Lucy (Thimann) P. BA, Cornell U., 1980. Lic. real estate. Sales rep. McGraw-Hill Co., Boston, 1981-82; office mgr. Chestnut Hill (Mass.) Psych. Assn., 1982-85; dir. adminstrv. svcs., internat. applied prof. edn. specialist The Parker Acad., Sudbury, Mass., 1985—. Producer, host children's TV show Cablevision Cable, Acton, 1987—. Vol. tchr. English as a 2d Language Cornell U., Ithaca, N.Y., 1980-81; story reader Children's Reading Program, Acton Sch., 1985—. Named one of Outstanding Young Women of Am., 1980. Mem. Am. Soc. Profl. and Exec. Women. Office: The Parker Acad 248 Concord Rd Sudbury MA 01776

GOLDMAN, JILL MINKOFF, pharmaceutical company information systems executive; b. Kansas City, Mo., July 12, 1953; d. Julius Burt and Eloise Joy (Shlensky) Minkoff; m. Barry Charles Goldman, Jan. 30, 1982; children: Joshua Scott, Elise Lynn. Certificat D'Assiduite, Université de Grenoble (France), 1968; B.A., Pomona Coll., 1974. Mktg. rep. IBM, Riverside, Calif., 1974-77, San Francisco, 1978-79; dir. store systems Neiman Marcus, Dallas, 1979-81; dir. end-user computing services. Marion Labs., Kansas City, Mo., 1982-89, dir. info. systems data and techs., 1989—; dir. corp. info. systems Marion Merrell Dow, Inc., 1989—. Sch. pres. ARC, Kansas City, Mo., 1966-67; v.p. chpt. B'nai B'rith Girls, Kansas City, 1968-69; active Menorah Hosp. Aux., March of Dimes. Mem. Nat. Coun. Jewish Women, Share, Inc., Guide Internat. Corp. Home: 5406 State Line Mission Hills KS 66208 Office: Marion Merrels Dow Inc 9300 Ward Pkwy Kansas City MO 64114

GOLDMAN, KATHRYN LOUISE, organizational consultant; b. N.Y.C., Mar. 15, 1946; d. George Samuel and Jeanne Gordon (Rosenbluth) G. BA magna cum laude, Goucher Coll., 1967; cert. in critical langs., Princeton U., 1967; M in Philosophy, Columbia U., 1973, PhD, 1980. Lic. clin. sociologist, Tex. Researcher Internat. Rsch. and Exchs. Bd., N.Y.C., 1973; profl. counselor Austin (Tex.) Community Coll., 1975-78, chair human devel. div., 1978-84; pvt. practice organizational cons. Carmel, Calif., 1980—; orgnl. devel. cons. Exxon Chem. Co., Linden, N.J., 1988-90; prof. mgmt. Monterey (Calif.) Inst. Internat. Studies, 1984—, Naval Postgrad. Sch., Monterey, 1984. Contbr. articles to profl. jours. Bd. dirs. Neighborhood Assn., Peninsula Concerned Neighbors, Pacific Grove, Calif., 1985. Fulbright fellow, 1967-78, Univ. fellow, 1970-73. Mem. Acad. Mgmt., Sociol. Practice Assn., Orgn. Devel. Network. Office: Strayer Cons Group 2099 Gateway Pl Ste 320 San Jose CA 95110

GOLDMAN, NANCY JOAN KRAMER, calligrapher, designer; b. Kew Gardens, N.Y., July 5, 1953; d. Franklin and Barbara (Richter) K.; m. Steven Craig Goldman, June 18, 1978; children: Allison, Eric. AB, Goucher Coll., 1975; MBA, Northeastern U., 1980. Owner, mgr., designer Notes Unltd., Randolph, Mass., 1984—; with Randolph Pub. Sch., 1985-86; calligraphy instr. M.E. Young P.T.O. Elem. Sch., Randolph, 1987—, Massasoit Community Coll., Brockton, Mass., 1988—. Reporter (Goucher quarterly) Class Rep., 1987—. Mem. AAUW (v.p. 1987—). Home: 8 Bonnie Ln Randolph MA 02368 Office: Notes Unltd Randolph MA 02368

GOLDMAN, ROSLYN BAKST, art appraiser and consultant; b. Bklyn., Apr. 14, 1938; d. Benjamin and Sylvia (Lubart) Bakst; m. John Lee Goldman, July 19, 1959; children: Michael E., Andrew L., Lawrence I. BS, Cornell U., 1959; MS, U. Rochester, 1978. Dir. Artworks at Sibley's,

Rochester, N.Y., 1979-85; ind. appraiser Rochester, N.Y., 1985—; pres. Rochester Assn. Art Dealers, 1984, Allofus Art Workshop, 1980-82, Arts for Greater Rochester, 1989—. Editor Catalog of Prints, Prints of Norman Kent, 1987, Columbia Banking Collection; contbr. articles to profl. jours. Mem. Appraisers Assn. Am., Pub. Art Com. Monroe County (chair). Home and office: 50 Pelham Rd Rochester NY 14610

GOLDMAN-SEFTON, MINDY SUSANNE, family therapist; b. Atlanta, July 16, 1959; d. Donald and Sarah Ann (Shymlock) Goldman; m. Michael Sean Sefton, Sept. 13, 1986; 1 child, James Michael Sefton. BA in Psychology, Calif. State U., Northridge, 1982; MA in Marriage and Family Therapy, U.S. Internat. U., 1984, Psychology D., 1989. Counselor Social Advocates for Youth, San Diego, 1983-84; group therapist Parents', Daus.' & Sons' United, Escondido, Calif., 1984; predoctoral intern North Shore Children's Hosp., Salem, Mass., 1985-86; therapist Glendale Adventist Med. Ctr., Glendale, Calif., 1986-87; family therapist Cypress (Calif.) Family Counseling Ctr., 1987-89; parenting skills instr. Active Parenting, Cypress, 1989—; family therapist Cypress Psychol. Svcs., 1990—; adj. faculty North Shore Community Coll., Beverly, Mass., 1985-86, Cypress Coll., 1990—; cons. La Petite Acad. Preschool, Huntington Beach, Calif., 1989-90, Mil. Base Child Devel. Ctrs., Tustin, Eltoro, Long Beach, Calif., 1987-90. Contbr. articles to profl. jours. Vol. counselor Huntington Beach High Sch., 1989-90, Lexington Jr. High Sch., Cypress, 1989-90. Mem. Child Sexual Abuse Network, Am. Psychol. Assn. (assoc.), Am. Assn. for Marriage & Family Therapy. Office: Cypress Psychol Svcs 5252 Orange Ave Ste 201 Cypress CA 90630

GOLDSCHMIDT, MILLICENT EDNA, microbiology educator; b. Erie, Pa., June 11, 1926; d. Isaac Jerry and Mary Tilly (Samuel) Cohen; m. Eugene P. Goldschmidt, Apr. 10, 1949 (dec. 1980); children: Richard, Carol Goldschmidt Warley. BA, Case-Western Res. U., 1947; MA, Purdue U., 1950, PhD, 1952. Instr. chemistry Hood Coll., Frederick, Md., 1958-60; asst. prof. medicine U. Md./U.S. Army Med. Unit, Frederick, 1960-61; NIH postdoctoral fellow U. Tex., Austin, 1961-63; rsch. instr. Baylor Med. Sch., Houston, 1963-67; assoc. microbiologist, acting chief microbiology sect. U. Tex.-M.D. Anderson Cancer Ctr., Houston, 1967-71; assoc. prof. U. Tex. Health Sci. Ctr., Houston, 1971-73, assoc. prof. clin. microbiology Med. Sch., 1973-76, NIH postdoctoral fellow dental br., 1977-78, assoc. prof. dental br., 1979—; dir. grad. program in microbiology U. Tex. Health Sci. Ctr., 1981-89; coord. Baylor Protocol to Help Plan Lunar Receiving Labs. at NASA, 1966-67; vis. prof. Kans. State U., 1980—; mem. evaluation panel in biomed. scis. NSF grad. fellowship program, Washington, 1989—. Author monographs, rsch. papers and abstracts. Mem. sci. rev. bd. Sci. and Engrng. Fair Houston, 1975—; host family Inst. Internat. Edn., Houston, 1975—; mem. adult edn. com. Temple Beth Israel, Houston, 1984—; treas. Houston Gt. Books Coun., 1988—. Recipient Tex. Woman's Achievement in Sci. award Woman's Hosp. System Tex., 1986. Fellow Am. Acad. Microbiology (bd. govs. 1985-87); mem. Am. Soc. Microbiology (coun. policy com. 1986-89, found. lectr. 1988—), Assn. for Women in Sci. (chpt. pres. 1985-86; named Outstanding Woman in Sci. Gulf Coast chpt. 1985-86), Houston Assn. Med. Microbiologists (pres. 1982-84), TEx. Soc. Microbiologists (pres. 1981-82), Internat. Assn. Dental Rsch., Sigma Xi (Tex. Med. Ctr. chpt. pres. 1985-86). Home: 3611 Cloverdale St Houston TX 77025 Office: U Tex HealthSciCtr Houston 6515 John Freeman Blvd Houston TX 77030

GOLDSMITH, ARLENE FRANCES, psychologist; b. Jersey City, May 23, 1941; d. Henry and Margaret Adele (Berman) Applebaum; m. Lee S. Goldsmith, June 10, 1962; children: Ian, Lani, Jordan. BA, NYU, 1962; MA, CUNY, 1964, PhD, 1969. Lic. clin. psychologist. Asst. psychologist Abbott House, Irvington, N.Y., 1964-66, Coll. Discovery, N.Y.C., 1965-68; assoc. psychologist Queensborough Community Coll., Bayside, N.Y., 1966-68, Fairleigh Dickinson U., Hackensack, N.J., 1969-70; staff psychologist Rockland Mental Health Clnic, Pomona, N.Y., 1969-76; cons. psychologist N.Y. Hosp., Nyack, 1977—; pvt. pracitce Pomona, N.Y., 1970—. Mem. religious sch. bd. Westchester Reform Temple, Scarsdale, N.Y., 1988—. Mem. Am. Psychol. Assn. Home: 1 Boulder Brook Rd Scarsdale NY 10583 Office: Summit Profl Bldg Rte 45 and Pomona Rd Pomona NY 10970

GOLDSMITH, CATHY ELLEN, special education teacher; b. N.Y.C., Feb. 18, 1947; d. Eli D. and Gertrude A. G. BS, NYU, 1968, MA in Elem. Edn., 1971, MA in Ednl. Psychology, 1974. Cert. phys. handicapped, K-6 elem. edn. tchr., N.Y. Tchr. trainable retarded children N.Y.C. (N.Y.) Bd. Edn., tchr. of learning disabled emotionally disturbed adolescents. Represented in permanent collections Bopst Libr. NYU. Bd. dirs. United Jewish Appeal. Recipient Charles Oscar Maas Essay award in Am. History, Disting. Alumni Svc. award NYU, 1987. Mem. NYU Alumni Leadership Coun. (past pres.), Nat. Profl. Assn. in Edn., Coun. for Exceptional Children, Coun. for Learning Disabilities, Found. for Exceptional Children, The Orton Dyslexia Soc., Assn. for Supervision and Curriculum Devel., N.Y. State-N.Y.C. Assn. Tchrs. of the Handicapped, Hillel Jewish for Coll., Youth, Fedn. Jewish Philanthropies, B'nai Brith, Pi Lambda Theta. Home: 3 Washington Sq Village 12J New York NY 10012

GOLDSMITH, KATHLEEN MAWHINNEY, accountant; b. Bklyn., July 16, 1957; d. James R. and Carmela (Ditria) Mawhinney; m. Marc Bruce Goldsmith, Oct. 7, 1979; 1 child, James Ryan. BS, Alfred U., 1979; MBA, U. Conn., 1986. CPA, Conn. Acct., Price Waterhouse, Stamford, Conn., 1979-83; controller OCE Bus. Systems Inc., Stamford, 1983-89; dir. planning and control Gestetner, Greenwich, Conn., 1989—. Adv., Jr. Achievement, 1980-81. Named Outstanding Young Women of Am. Mem. Am. Inst. CPAs, Conn. Soc. CPAs, Phi Kappa Phi, Delta Mu Delta. Home: 24 Lampost Dr West Redding CT 06896 Office: OCE Inc 1351 Washington Blvd Stamford CT 06902

GOLDSMITH, MAXINE IRIS, library administrator; b. Tarrytown, N.Y., Apr. 25, 1947; d. Abraham Herman and Florence (Levinsky) Kaplan; m. Brian P. Goldsmith, Apr. 3, 1971; children: Scott, Leslie. BS, Russell Sage Coll., 1969; MLS, Rugers U., 1970. Reference librarian McGraw-Hill, Inc., N.Y.C., 1970-71; periodicals librarian N.J. State Libr., Trenton, 1971-76; librarian N.J. Div. Criminal Justice, Trenton, 1976-77; libr. adminstr. N.J. Dept. Higher Edn., Trenton, 1978—; bd. dirs. adv. com. Sch. Communications, Info. & Libr. Svc., Rutgers U., New Brunswick, N.J. Editor: (index) Popular Periodicals Index, 1975—; author: (bibliography) Going to College in New Jersey, 1978, 80. Bd. dirs. after sch. program Hopewell Valley YMCA, Pennington, N.J., 1988—. Mem. Spl. Librs. Assn. (sec.-treas. edn. div. 1989-91, pres. Princeton Trenton chpt. 1985-86), Hadassah (fin. sec. Lawrence chpt. 1987—). Jewish. Home: 16 Brandon Rd Trenton NJ 08638 Office: NJ Dept of Higher Edn 20 W State St CN542 Trenton NJ 08625

GOLDSMITH, NANCY CARROL, nursing services director; b. Conemaugh, Pa., May 11, 1940; d. John and Mary (Appley) Stinich; m. Sidney Goldsmith, Apr. 2, 1966. RN, Temple U., 1961; BS in Health Care Mgmt. magna cum laude, Phila. Coll. Textiles and Sci., 1986; MA in Health Care Adminstrn. summa cum laude, Antioch U., Yellow Springs, Ohio, 1988; PhD in Health Care and Hosp. Adminstrn. summa cum laude, Southwest U., New Orleans, 1990. Nurse, head nurse to med. surg. supr. Temple U. Hosp., Phila., 1961-67; nursing rsch. assoc. Smith Klein & French, Inc. and Ames Med. Co., Phila. and Elkhart, Ind., 1967-69; sr. nursing rsch. assoc. NIH, Washington, 1969-75; adminstrv. supr. nursing svcs. Rolling Hill Hosp. and Diagnostic Ctr., Elkins Park, Pa., 1975-87, lectr. legal aspects nursing, 1980-90, dir. cost containment strategies, 1987-89, lectr. in nursing mgmt., 1989—, asst. dir. nursing svcs., 1988-89, exec. dir., 1989—; instr. med./surg. nursing Temple U. Sch. Nursing, 1964-67, chmn. ann. fund raising, 1978-86; cons. cost containment and strategies United Hosps., Inc., Phila., 1988—. Author 2 books. Inventor use of dextrostix in hypoglycemic range, 1972 (Rsch. award 1974); co-patentee multipurpose biopsy needle, 1972. Mem. Rep. Nat. Com., 1972—. Recipient Mayor's Liberty Bell award City of Phila., 1978, Legion of Honor award Chapel of Four Chaplains, Phila., 1981. Mem. Am. Hosp. Assn., Am. Mgmt. Assn., Temple U. Nurse's Alumni Assn. (bd. dirs., pres. 1980-84, dir. continuing edn. com. 1986—), Temple U. Gen. Alumni Assn. (bd. dirs. 1980-88, Disting. Svc. award 1984), Downtown Club Temple U., Phi Beta Kappa. Republican. Jewish. Office: Rolling Hill Hosp 60 E Township Line Rd Elkins Park PA 19117

GOLDSTEIN, BARBARA BLOCK, educator; b. Newport News, Va., Dec. 25, 1942; d. Irving Block and Rita Shirley (Sarfan) Spirn; m. Ralph Martin Goldstein, June 23, 1963; children: Irving Block, Beth Conn, Jay Alan. BA, Duke U., 1963; MA, Coll. William and Mary, 1984, postgrad., 1984—. Tchr. Newport News Sch. System, 1963-87, reading tchr., 1977-87, instrnl. specialist, 1987-89; prin., 1989—; bd. dirs. Newport News Reading Coun., 1977—. Mem. Tidewaters Assn. Early Childhood Devel. (bd. dirs.), Newport News Coun. Jewish Women (past treas.), Hadassah (officer), Delta Kappa Gamma (bd. dirs.). Home: 1 Lantern Circle Newport News VA 23606 Office: Riverside Elem Sch 1100 Country Club Ln Newport News VA 23606

GOLDSTEIN, BETH LISA, marketing manager; b. Bklyn., May 7, 1963; d. Arthur Melvin and Ruth Neddie (Ampel) G. BA, Brandeis U., 1985; student, Boston U., 1989. Organizational analyst New Medico Assocs., Lynn, Mass., 1985-86; asst. dir. mktg. New Medico Assocs., Lynn, 1986—. Mem. Am. Mktg. Assn. Office: New Medico Assocs 14 Central Ave Lynn MA 01901

GOLDSTEIN, CHARLOTTE L(IPSON), marketing professional, public relations executive; b. Boston, Aug. 1, 1929; d. George Lipson and Frances (Feldstein) L.; m. Norman R. Goldstein, Sept. 15, 1948; children—Sue, David, Julie. Student Mary Brooks Coll., 1945-47. Pres. Engineered Inspection System, Robbinsville, N.J., 1970—. Contbr. articles to profl. jours. Bd. dirs. Congregation Beth Chaim, 1977-82, Sunday Sch. tchr., 1952-69, adult edn. com., mem. bd. continuing edn., caring coms.; charter mem. West Windsor Library Commn., 1981-85; mem. West Windsor Twp. Commn. on Aging. Mem. Middlesex County (N.J.) Bd. Realtors (assoc.), Mercer County Bd. Realtors, Hunterdon County Bd. Realtors, So. Monmouth County Bd. Realtors, Somerset County Bd. Realtors, Burlington County Bd. Realtors, Pa.-Bucks County C. of C. Princeton C. of C., Mercer C of C. Republican. Jewish. Clubs: Hadassah (pres. 1952-53), B'nai B'rith (bd. dirs. 1968-70). Avocations: china painting, cooking, traveling, bridge, reading. Home: 10 Jeffrey Ln Princeton Junction NJ 08550 Office: Engineered Inspection System Inc 1200 Route 130 Robbinsville NJ 08691

GOLDSTEIN, CONSTANCE SUE, magazine editor; b. Pitts., Jan. 18, 1931; d. Sol and Lena (Levenson) Bornstein; m. Richard N. Goldstein, Aug. 5, 1952 (div. 1973); children: Judy Goldstein Richardson, Glen, Nancy. BA with honors in Journalism, U. Pa., 1951. Editor The Counselor mag., Langhorne, Pa., 1972-74; exec. editor Successful Meetings mag., Phila., 1974-81; v.p., account exec. United Travel, Jenkintown, Pa., 1981-82; editor Corp. Meetings and Incentives mag. Edgell Communications, N.Y.C., 1982—; discussion leader Gt. Books Found., Phila., 1970—. Contbr. articles to mags. Pres. PTA, Willow Grove, Pa., 1968; v.p. LWV, Jenkintown, 1970; sec. class of 1952, U. Pa., Phila., 1982. Mem. Soc. Incentive Travel Execs. (program chmn. ann. meeting, 1990), Meeting Planners Internat. (v.p. 1978-79), Soc. Am. Travel Writers. Democrat. Jewish. Office: Corp Meetings & Incentives 270 Madison Ave New York NY 10016

GOLDSTEIN, DEBRA EDELSON, lawyer; b. Stamford, Conn., Oct. 5, 1950; d. A. Herbert and Sylvia (Gordon) Edelson; m. Jeffrey S. Goldstein, Aug. 11, 1974; children: Jennifer Alyss, Lisa Nicole. BA, Wellesley Coll., 1972; JD, Georgetown U., 1975. Bar: N.Y. 1976. Atty. Ogilvy & Mather Advt., N.Y.C., 1975-79, v.p., atty., 1979-86, sr. v.p., assoc. gen. counsel, 1986—. Mem. Lawyers Pro-Choice, Planned Parenthood, N.Y.C., 1982—. Mem. Am. Assn. Advt. Agys. (legal affairs com. 1985—, chmn. 1988—), Am. Corp. Counsel Assn., Women in Law Depts., N.Y. State Bar Assn. (exec. com. corp. counsel sect. 1982—, sec. corp. counsel sect. 1984, pub. rels. com. 1983—). Democrat. Jewish. Office: Ogilvy & Mather Advt Worldwide Pla 309 W 49th St New York NY 10019

GOLDSTEIN, DORIS MUELLER, librarian, researcher; b. Somerville, N.J., Mar. 11, 1942; d. Henry Frederick and Sophie (Lages) Mueller; m. Steven Morris Goldstein, July 4, 1971. BA, U. Nebr., 1964, MA, 1966; cert., Goethe U., Frankfurt, Fed. Republic Germany, 1966; MLS, U. Md., 1973. Vol., instr. Peace Corps, Addis Abeba, Ethiopia, 1966-68; cataloger Libr. of Congress, Washington, 1968-69; instr. Bowie (Md.) State Coll., 1969-72; libr. Kennedy Inst. for Ethics Georgetown U., Washington, 1973-81, dir. libr. and info. svcs., 1981—, dir. Nat. Reference Ctr. for Bioethics Lit., 1984—; dons. dept. nursing George Mason U., Fairfax, Va., 1984-89; adj. faculty mem. in library sci. U. Md., 1990. Author: Bioethics: A Guide to Information Sources, 1982; editor Scope Note Series, 1985—; contbr. articles to profl. jours. Ford Found. grantee, 1964. Mem. Spl. Librs. Assn., Med. Libr. Assn., D.C. Libr. Assn., Phi Beta Kappa, Alpha Lambda Delta, Delta Phi Alpha, Beta Phi Mu (pres. Iota chpt. 1985-86). Office: Georgetown U Kennedy Inst Ethics Washington DC 20057

GOLDSTEIN, EVIE CARA, lawyer; b. N.Y.C., Mar. 12, 1959; d. Maurice and Bernice Phyliss (Raff) G. BA, U. Rochester, 1980; JD, Yale Law Sch., 1984. Bar: N.Y. 1985. Rsch. asst. and asst. to dir. of conf. White House Conf. for Children and Youth, Washington, 1980-81; assoc. Weil, Gotshal & Manges, N.Y.C., 1984—. Mem. N.Y. State Bar Assn. Office: Weil Gotshal & Manges 767 Fifth Ave New York NY 10153

GOLDSTEIN, FERN, fine artist, custom designer, design consultant; b. Chgo., Jan. 26, 1935; d. William and Esther G.; divorced. Student, U. Ill., Urbana, 1954, Art Inst. Chgo., 1966. Color separator Am. Decal, Chgo.; colorist, designer Chtham Fabrics, Chgo.; make up artist Adrien Arpel Cosmetics, Chgo.; started art dept. for learning disabled Assoc. Talmud Torahs, Chgo.; gave pvt. art lessons Chgo.; designer, maker handcrafted jewelry Gift Shop of Mus. Contemporary Art, Chgo.; designer jewelry and drawings for pvt. sale, designer drawing and painting combinations for pvt. sale; Cons. Dept. of Textiles, Art Inst. of Chgo., 1989, Assoc. Talmud Torahs, 1987-89; researcher in field. Artist in field, inventor; numerous one-woman shows at Northtown Libr.; exhibitor Antony's Restaurant, Evanston, Ill., Evanston Women's Club, Sales and Rental Gallery-Art Inst. of Chgo., Evanston Art Ctr., Lincolnwood Art Festival, Howard-Western Shopping Ctr. Art Festival, Highland Park Art Festival, Dept. of Textiles, Art. Inst. of Chgo. Philanthropy, Assoc. Talmud Torahs, Chgo., Friends of Refugees of Eastern Europe, 1986-87, Am. Com. for the Weizmann, Inst. Sci. Recipient Crown of Royalty Assoc. Talmud Torahs, 1987, First Daughter of Israel award Simon Wiesenthal Ctr., 1988. Mem. Art Inst. Chgo. (life, mem. Sustaining Fellows), Textile Soc. (life), Classical Art Soc., Terra Art Mus., Mus. Contemporary Art. Office: 3270 N Lakeshore Dr Apt 14C Chicago IL 60657

GOLDSTEIN, FRANCINE ELLEN, marketing professional; b. N.Y.C., May 28, 1952; d. Samuel Charles and Miriam (Peretz) G. BS, Syracuse U., N.Y., 1973; MS, N.Y. U., 1976. Buyer positions Abraham & Straus, N.Y.C., 1977-79, Alexanders, N.Y.C., 1979-82; mktg. analyst AMC, N.Y.C., 1982-84; dir. mktg. Bonnie Doon Hosiery, N.Y.C., 1984-85, v.p. mktg. and design, 1986-88, sr. v.p., 1988-89; merchandising mgr. E.G. Smith Hosiery, N.Y.C., 1989—. Office: EG Smith Hosiery 38 W 28th St New York NY 10001

GOLDSTEIN, JUDITH SHELLEY, reading and learning specialist; b. Bklyn., Mar. 5, 1935; d. Maurice and Mary (Goldstein) G. BA, Adelphi U., 1956; MA, Columbia U., 1957; EdD, Hofstra U., 1984. Cert. permanent tchr. in reading, spl. and elem. edn., N.Y. Early childhood tchr. N.Y.C. Sch. System, Bklyn., 1957-80; reading specialist Southampton (N.Y.) Unified Sch. Dist., 1981-87; spl. edn. tchr. Amagansett (N.Y.) Sch., 1987-88; mem. adj. faculty C.W. Post Campus, L.I. U., Brookville, N.Y., 1984-88; supr. clin. practice Southampton Campus L.I. U., 1988—; exec. dir. nursery sch. Jewish Ctr. of Hamptons, East Hampton, N.Y., 1988-89; bd. dirs. Alternatives East End Counseling Project, Southampton, 1989—; adj. assoc. prof. Southampton Campus L.I.U., 1989—; adj. asst. prof. Suffolk County Community Coll., 1989—; adj. assoc. prof. Dowling Coll., 1990—. Mem. Guild Hall, East Hampton, 1980—; v.p. edn. Hadassah, East Hampton, 1989—. Mem. Internat. Reading Assn., Assn. for Supervision and Curriculum Devel., AAUW (v.p. programming 1987-89). Democrat. Home and Office: 138 Windward East Hampton NY 11937

GOLDSTEIN, JUNE C., airlines media official; b. South Bend, Ind., May 14, 1935; d. Demar E. and Selma J. (Luzny) Borkowski; m. Leslie S. Goldstein, May 3, 1975. BA, Loyola U., Chgo., 1971. Sales and promotion exec. Sta. WNDU-TV, Sta. WSBT-TV, South Bend, 1955-58; adminstrv. asst. Sta. WGN-TV, Chgo., 1959-62; producer Sta. WBBM-TV, CBS Inc., Chgo., 1962-68; cons., producer Chgo. Bd. Edn., 1968-71; project mgr. Advanced Systems, Inc., Elk Grove, Ill., 1971-78; ind. producer Hawthorne Prodns., Chgo., 1978-80; project mgr. Systema Corp., Chgo., 1980-83; owner, ind. producer Hawthorne Assocs., Chgo., 1983—; sr. staff media specialist United Airlines, Chgo., 1989—. Producer video negotiations series, 1975 (award N.Y. Film Critics 1975); writer, producer video hosp. adminstrn. program, 1985 (award Internat. TV Assn. 1985). Mem. NAFE, Internat. Interactive Communications Soc., Nat. Soc. Performance & Instruction, Women Employed, Women United. Office: United Airlines 1200 Algonquin Rd Elk Grove IL 60006

GOLDSTEIN, MARSHA FEDER, tour company executive; b. Chgo., July 7, 1945; d. Charles S. and Geraldine (Shulman) Feder; m. Michael Warren Goldstein, Dec. 26, 1966; 1 child, Paul Goldstein. B.A., Roosevelt U., Chgo., 1967. Tchr. art Chgo. Pub. Schs., 1967-68; free-lance artist, Chgo., 1968-71; tchr. architecture Brandeis U., Northfield, Ill., 1974-80; tour guide My Kind of Town Tours, Highland Park, Ill., 1975-79, owner, 1979—; art cons. Randall Pub. Co., Inc., 1984—. Editor: Highland Park by Foot or Frame, 1980. Contbr. to book in field. Chmn., commr. Highland Park Hist. Preservation Commn.; bd. dirs. Next Theatre Co., Evanston, Ill.; charter mem. Nat. Mus. Women in the Arts. Recipient Cert. of Completion, Chgo. Arch. Found., 1975; Cert. of Appreciation, Machinery Dealers Nat. Assn., 1982. Mem. Nat. Assn. Women Bus. Owners (bd. dirs. Chgo. chpt., v.p.), Women's Exec. Network, Chgo. Assn. Commerce & Industry (active youth motivation program), Chgo. Conv. and Tourism Bd., Chgo. Soc. Assn. Execs., Milw. Conv. and Tourism Bd. Republican. Jewish. Club: Brandeis U. Nat. Women (bd. dirs., v.p. 1977-84). Home: 266 Aspen Ln Highland Park IL 60035 Office: My Kind of Town Tours PO Box 924 Ravinia Sta Highland Park IL 60035

GOLDSTEIN, NANCY BERNICE, lawyer, chemist; b. N.Y.C., Aug. 11, 1954; d. Michael and Jean Regina (Bryer) G.; m. Wesley Andrew Wildman, Oct. 24, 1987. BS in Chemistry, CUNY, 1976; JD, U. San Diego, 1983. Bar: Calif. 1984, U.S. Dist. Ct. (cen. dist.) Calif. 1985, U.S. Ct. Appeals 1985. Analytical chemist U.S. EPA, Edison, N.J., 1976-77; investigator, consumer safety officer U.S. FDA, N.Y.C., 1977-80, consumer affairs officer, 1980-81; pvt. practice law Beverly Hills, Calif., 1984-85; ptnr. Goldstein & Goldstein, Santa Monica, Calif., 1985-89; assoc. Schurmer & Drane, Santa Barbara, Calif., 1989—. Editor: FDA Consumer mag., 1976; photographer newspaper U. San Diego Law Sch. Paper, 1981-83. Atty. Hospice AIDS Project, L.A., 1986—, Domestic Violence Counseling Project, L.A., 1989—. Regents scholar NYU, 1972. Mem. Calif. Bar Assn., Santa Monica Bar Assn., L.A. County Bar Assn. (social com. 1986-88, settlement officer landlord and tenant com. 1986—), Conejo Ski Club. Democrat. Jewish. Office: Schurmer & Drane 801 Garden St 3d Fl Santa Barbara CA 93101

GOLDSTEIN, PHYLLIS ANN, art historian, educator; b. Chgo., Apr. 27, 1926; d. Frederick and Belle Florence (Hirsch) Jacoby; m. Seymour Goldstein, Nov. 19, 1947 (dec. 1980); children: Arthur Bruce, Kathy Susan Goldstein Maultasch. BA, Hunter Coll., 1948; MA, Hofstra U., 1985. Tchr. home econs. Cin. Pub. Schs., 1948-50; nutrition instr. Brandeis U. Nat. Women's Com., Westbury, N.Y., 1975-78; instr. art history Brandeis U. Nat. Women's Com., 1984—, Herricks Adult Community Edn. Program, 1990—. Camp counselor, troop leader Girl Scouts U.S.A., N.Y.C. and Cin., 1942-51; cub leader Boy Scouts Am., Westbury, 1960-62; leader 4-H Club, Westbury, 1963-64; active Sisterhood of Temple Beth Avodah, Westbury, 1958-70, pres., 1964-65; active Sisterhood Temple of Beth Am., Merrick, N.Y., 1980—. Mem. Modern Mus. Art, Jewis Mus N.Y., Met. Mus. Art, Williamsburg Mus. Democrat.

GOLDSTEIN, ROBIN ELLEN, health facility administrator, consultant; b. Boston, Jan. 31, 1958; d. Melvin Edward and Anna Louise (Levine) G. BA, U. Mass., 1980; MS, Fla. State U., 1982, PhD, 1985. Lic. psychologist, Mass. Clin. dir. Meadowbrook Ctr., Tyngsboro, Mass., 1985-86; clin. dir. adolescent unit McLean Hosp., Belmont, Mass., 1986-87, spl. projects cons., 1987-88; chief of psychology Waltham-Weston Hosp., Waltham, Mass., 1988—, dir. outpatient mental health, 1989—; adj. faculty Lesley Coll. Grad. Sch., Cambridge, Mass., 1987—; instr. in psychology dept. psychiatry Harvard U. Med. Sch., Cambridge, 1986—; cons. Levinson Inst., Inc., Belmont, 1988—. U. Mass. Alumni scholar, 1979. Mem. Am. Psychol. Assn., Mass. Psychol. Assn., Nat. Register Health Svc. Providers in Psychology, Phi Beta Kappa, Phi Kappa Phi. Office: Waltham-Weston Hosp Hope Ave Waltham MA 02254

GOLDSTEIN, SANDRA, consumer products importing company executive, designer and importer; b. Chgo., Dec. 7; d. Jack Julius and Esther Judith (Glickman) Gilbert; student U. Wis., U. Ill.; m. Seymour Leo Goldstein, Aug. 12, 1951; 1 child, Jennie S. Co-founder, sr. v.p., sales mgr. Jennie G. Sales Co., Inc., Lincolnwood, Ill., 1961—. Bd. dirs. Ill. Found. Dentistry for Handicapped. Mem. Nat. Assn. Convenience Stores, Nat. Oil Jobbers Assn., Ill. Petroleum Assn., Tex. Oil Marketers Assn., Intermountain Oil Jobbers Assn., Wis. Oil Jobbers Assn., Ind. Oil Jobbers Assn., Mich. Oil Jobbers Assn., Mo. Oil Jobbers Assn., Iowa Oil Jobbers Assn. Clubs: Carleton (Chgo.); Springs Country (Rancho Mirage, Calif.). Home: 6400 N Cicero Ave Lincolnwood IL 60646 Office: Jennie G Sales Co 3770 W Pratt Ave Lincolnwood IL 60645 Other: The Springs 23 Cornell Rancho Mirage CA 72290

GOLDSTEIN, SYLVIA BEATRICE, lawyer; b. N.Y.C., Feb. 21, 1919; d. Max David and Lillian Rose (Sheinick) Weitzman; m. Joseph Goldstein, Feb. 15, 1946 (dec. 1982). BA, L.I. U., 1940; JD, Bklyn. Law Sch., 1944. Bar: N.Y. 1944. Jr. sec. Boosey-Hawkes-Belwin Inc., N.Y.C., 1940-43; sec. Boosey & Hawkes Inc., N.Y.C., 1943-49, dept. head, 1949-84, v.p., corp. sec., 1984-89, corp. sec., 1984—. Mem. ABA, Nassau County Women's Bar Assn., Am. Women in Radio and TV (area v.p. 1978-82, bd. dirs. N.Y.C. chpt. 1983-84, nat. chairperson found. 1980-82), Copyright Soc. U.S. (trustee 1984-89), Tcherepnine Soc. (bd. dirs. 1984—). Home: 2758 Central Ave Baldwin NY 11510 Office: Boosey & Hawkes Inc 24 E 21st St New York NY 10010

GOLDSTON, BARBARA M. HARRAL, editor; b. Lubbock, Tex., Jan. 26, 1937; d. Leonard Paul and Olivette (Stuart) Harral; m. John Rowell Toman (div. 1963); 1 child, Stuart Rowell; m. Olan Glen Goldston, 1989. BE, Tex. Christian U., 1959; MLS, U. Hawaii, 1968; postgrad., Golden Gate U., 1980-82. Tchr. pub. elem. schs., various cities, Tex. and Hawaii, 1959-66; contracts abstractor, indexer Champlin Oil Co., Ft. Worth, 1963-64; adminstrv. asst. engring. Litton Industries, Lubbock, Tex., 1964-65; mgr. rsch. library Hawaii Employers' Coun., Honolulu, 1968-72; rsch. cons. Thailand Hotel Study, Touche-Ross Assocs., Honolulu, 1974; dir. med. library U. S.D.-Sacred Heart Hosp., Yankton, 1977-79; editor, adminstrv. coord. book div. ABC-Clio, Inc., Santa Barbara, Calif., 1981-88; free-lance rsch./editorial cons. Albuquerque, 1988-89; instr. Santa Fe Community Coll., 1989—; ptnr. Broome-Harral, Inc., Albuquerque, 1989—. Author, editor with others Hist. Periodical Dir., 5 vols., World Defense Forces compendium. Vol., contbr. Boy's Ranch, Amarillo, Tex., 1987—; mem. Lobero Theater Group, Santa Barbara, 1975-76; mem., treas. Yankton Med. Aux., 1977-79. Mem. ALA, Spl. Libraries Assn., Med. Libraries Assn., Am. Soc. Info., Sci., Albuquerque C. of C., Tex. Christian U. Alumni Assn., Delta Delta Delta. Republican. Episcopalian. Home: 9300 Seabrook NE Albuquerque NM 87111 Office: PO Box 3824 Albuquerque NM 87190-3824

GOLIA, MARY ANN, corporate management executive; b. Bronx, N.Y., Dec. 6, 1957; d. Joseph Anthony and Vivian (Fornatoro) G. Diploma, Sanford H. Calhoun, Merrick, Long Island, N.Y., 1975. Claims rep. Travelers Ins. Co., Garden City, N.Y., 1975-76, Nixon-Gallagner Ins. Agy., N.Y.C., 1977-80; corp. sec. Bishop's Service Inc., N.Y.C., 1980-86; computer systems adminstr., adminstrv. asst. mergers and acquisition dept. Lazard Freres & Co., N.Y.C., 1986—. Recipient Shorthand Cert. State N.Y. 1975. Home: 1699 Meadowbrook Rd North Merrick NY 11566

GOLIGHTLY, CECELIA KING, healthcare administrator, nurse; b. Orlando, Fla., July 8, 1936; d. Max Luie Bavar and Lillian (Wetherbee) King; m. Horace Hugh Golightly, Nov. 29, 1957; children: Donald Maxwell,

Thomas Michael, Amy Franncis. Diploma, Presbyn. Hosp., Charlotte, N.C., 1958; cert., U. Minn., 1976, BS, 1977, MPH, 1978. Dir. nursing St. Joseph's Home and Hosp., River Falls, Wis., 1969-75; assoc. dir. nursing St. Joseph's Hosp., St. Paul, Minn., 1975-77; dir. spl. projects St. Joseph's Hosp., St. Paul, 1978-79; dir. nursing Eitel Hosp., Mpls., 1979-82, assoc. adminstr., 1982-83, sr. adminstr., 1983-84; exec. dir. elderly svcs. Lifespan Corp., Mpls., 1984-87; cons. Good Neighbor Svcs., Inc., St. Paul, 1987-88; dir. nursing Med. Coll. Ga., Augusta, 1988-90; v.p. patient care Northside Hosp., Atlanta, 1990—; cons. Ganong Health Care Cons., Chapel Hill, N.C., 1978-84; pres. Presearch. Author: Help with Career Planning, 1979, Creative Problem Solving for Healthcare Professionals, 1981, Using Executive Search, 1988, Turnover At the Top, 1988. Bush leadership fellow Bush Found., 1977. Mem. Jour. of Nursing Adminstn. (bd. dirs. 1983-86), Affiliated Hosp. Svcs. (bd. dirs. 1982-87), Am. Coll. Healthcare Execs., Am. Orgn. of Nurse Execs., Womens Club of Mpls. Repubican. Episcopalian. Office: Northside Hosp 1000 Johnson Ferry Rd Atlanta GA 30342

GOLLER, SUE-GRAY, finance executive; b. Greenville, S.C., Aug. 26, 1951; d. Harold Poehlmann Jr. and Mary Alice (Gribble) G. BA magna cum laude, Randolph Macon Woman's Coll., 1973; MBA, U. Va., 1977. Strategy analyst Cost of Living Coun., Washington, 1973-74; environ. analyst Fed. Maritime Commn., Washington, 1975; corp. planning analyst Mfrs. Hanover Trust Co., N.Y., 1977-78, asst. sec., 1978-80, asst. v.p., 1980-82, v.p., 1982-85; v.p., teamleader Mfrs. Hanover Fin. Mgmt. Systems, N.Y., 1985-87; v.p., dist. mgr. Mfrs. Hanover Trust Co., N.Y., 1987—. Vol. St. Bartholomew's Shelter Feeding Program, N.Y., 1982-86. Mem. Cash Mgmt. Assn. of New Eng., N.Y. Jr. League (v.p. 1988—), Randolph-Macon Woman's Coll. Alumnae (v.p. 1979-82). Republican. Episcopalian. Home: 320 E 54th St #1F New York NY 10022 Office: Mfrs Hanover Trust Co 270 Park Ave New York NY 10017

GOLLIN, SUSANNE MERLE, cytogeneticist, cell biologist; b. Chgo., Sept. 22, 1953; d. Harvey A. and Pearl (Reiffel) G. BA in Biology, Northwestern U., 1974, MS, 1975, PhD, 1980. Diplomate Am. Bd. Med. Genetics, Clin. Cytogenetics. Postdoctoral fellow U. Rochester Med. Ctr. (N.Y.), 1979-81; rsch. assoc. in cell biology Baylor Coll. of Medicine, Houston, 1981-83, rsch. assoc. in genetics, 1983-84; asst. prof. dept. pathology and pediatrics U. Ark. Med. Scis., 1984-87; dir. cytogenetics lab. Ark. Children's Hosp., 1984-87; assoc. mem. Pitts. Cancer Inst., 1987—; asst. prof. human genetics U. Pitts., 1987—, dir. clin. cytogenetics lab., 1988—; mem. pediatric oncology group., mem. exec. com. Ark. Genetics Program. Vol. Lighthouse for the Blind, Houston, 1983; chmn. med. ethics and civil liberties com. ACLU/Pitts., 1989—. Mem. Am. Soc. Human Genetics, Am. Soc. Cell Biology, AAAS, Soc. Analytical Cytology, Pitts. Cancer Inst. (assoc.), Southwest Oncology Group (core com. cytogenetics), Sigma Xi. Avocations: gardening, photography, pulled thread embroidery. Contbr. articles to profl. jour. Office: U Pitts Dept of Human Genetics 130 DeSoto St Pittsburgh PA 15261

GOLLIS, ELAINE SANDRA, nurse; b. Fall River, Mass., Mar. 30, 1938; d. Harold and Esther (Packer) G.; m. Pasquale Margiotta, May 16, 1968 (div. Oct. 1986); children: Ellen, Mark. Nurse, Worcester City Hosp., 1959; BS, Post Coll., 1989; postgrad., Hartford Grad. Ctr., 1989—. Dir. nursing Hebrew Home and Hosp., Hartford, Conn., 1963-68, Jewish Home for Aged, San Francisco, 1968; clin. supr. Hebrew Home and Hosp., Hartford, 1971-81, coordinator patient care, 1981-82, clinic coordinator ambulatory care, 1982-84, ombudsman, 1984; acting dir. nursing Hebrew Home and Hosp., Hartfield, 1984-85, asst. dir. nursing, 1985—; clinical assoc. Dept. Restorative Dentistry Sch. Dental Med. U. Conn., Farmington, 1986—, geriodontic seminarian, 1986—. Mem. Conn. Orgn. Nurse Execs., Am. Nurses Assn. (cert. nurse adminstr.). Jewish. Office: Hebrew Home and Hosp 1 Abrahams Blvd West Hartford CT 06117

GOLLON, BARBARA ANN, infosystems specialist; b. N.Y.C., Feb. 11, 1944; d. Abraham and Sarah (Fried) G. BS, SUNY, Buffalo, 1965; MS, L.I. U., 1976; cert. in microcomputers, New Sch. Social Rsch., 1985. Tchr. Montgomery County Schs., Rockville, Md., 1965-70; elem. tchr. N.Y.C. Schs., 1970-73; bus. skills tchr. Lt. Joseph P. Kennedy Home, Bronx, N.Y., 1973-75; learning disabilities specialist Bklyn. Schs., 1975-76; psycho-ednl. diagnostician Manhattan, 1976-85; microcomputer tchr., trainer-software coordinator N.Y.C. Bd. Edn., 1985-86; ednl. computer cons., trainer B.G. Assocs., N.Y.C., 1986—; cons. in field. Contbr. articles to profl. publs. Bd. dirs. Mark Twain Owners' Corp., N.Y.C., 1989. Mem. Coun. for Exceptional Children, Am. Assn. Media Specialists, Assn. Computer Educators, Internat. Assn. Computers in Edn. Home: 133 I Seminary Dr Mill Valley CA 94941 Office: B G Assocs/Kidtech 100 W 12th St 2N New York NY 10011

GOLOMB, CLAIRE, psychology educator; b. Frankfurt am Main, Germany, Jan. 30, 1928; came to U.S., 1958; d. Chaskel and Fanny (Monderer) Schimmel; m. Dan S. Golomb, Feb. 24, 1954; children: Mayana, Anath. BA, Hebrew U., Jerusalem, 1954; MA, New Sch. for Social Rsch., 1959; PhD, Brandeis U., 1969. Instr. psychology Wellesley (Mass.) Coll., 1969-70; asst. prof. Brandeis U., Waltham, Mass., 1971-74; assoc. prof. psychology U. Mass., Boston, 1974-77, prof., 1977—. Author: Young Children's Sculpture and Drawing, 1974, The Child's Creation of a Pictorial World, 1990. Mem. Am. Psychol. Assn., Jean Piaget Soc. Office: U Mass Harbor Campus Boston MA 02125

GOLONKA, SHEILA LORRAINE, information systems analyst; b. Washington, Pa., Feb. 17, 1958; d. Walter Golonka and Mildred Matijevich. Assoc., Robert Morris Coll., Coraopolis, Pa., 1985; Bachelor, Robert Morris Coll., 1988. From clk. typist to sec. Washington (Pa.) County, 1977-79; from sec. I to supr. word processing Mobay Corp., Pitts., 1979—, info. system analyst, 1989—. Mem. NOW, Assn. Info. System Profls., NAFE, Women in Computing. Democrat. Roman Catholic. Office: Mobay Corp Mobay Rd Pittsburgh PA 15205

GOLUB, SHARON BRAMSON, psychologist, educator; b. N.Y.C., Mar. 25, 1937; m. Leon M. Golub, June 1, 1958; children: Lawrence E., David B. Diploma, Mt. Sinai Hosp. Sch. Nursing, 1957; BS, Columbia U., 1959, MA, 1966; PhD, Fordham U., 1974. Head nurse Mt. Sinai Hosp., N.Y.C., 1957-59; contbg. editor RN Mag., Oradell, N.J., 1967-74; asst. prof. psychology Coll. New Rochelle, N.Y., 1974-79, assoc. prof., 1979-86, prof., 1986—, dir. women's studies, 1978-79, chmn. dept. psychology, 1979-82; pvt. practice individual and group psychotherapy Harrison, N.Y., 1976—; adj. prof. psychiatry N.Y. Med. Coll., Valhalla, 1980—. Author: Periods: From Menarche to Menopause; editor: Menarche, 1983 (Assn. Women in Psychology Disting. Pub. award 1984, Book of Yr. award Am. Jour. Nursing 1984), Lifting the Curse of Menstruation, 1983, Health Care of the Female Adolescent, 1984, Health Needs of Women as They Age, 1984; (with Rita Jackaway Freedman) Psychology of Women: Resources for a Core Curriculum, 1987, Women and Health, 1982-86, mem. editorial bd., 1986—; mem. editorial bd. Psychology of Women Quar., 1989—. Grantee Nat. Libr. Medicine, 1983-84; NIH rsch. fellow, 1971-74. Fellow Am. Psychol. Assn. (chmn. task force on teaching psychology of women 1980-83), Soc. for Menstrual Cycle Research (pres. 1981-83, bd. dirs. 1981—), Assn. Women in Psychology, Am. Assn. Sex Educators, Counselors and Therapists, Ea. Psychol. Assn., Phi Beta Kappa, Sigma Xi, Psi Chi. Office: Coll New Rochelle Dept Psychology New Rochelle NY 10801

GOLZMAN, ITA HASS, cartoons and comic strips company executive; b. Bronx, N.Y., May 9, 1951; d. Jacob and Roza (Weissman) Hass; m. Larry Stanley Golzman; children: David, Risa, Talia. BA in English, Hunter Coll., N.Y.C., 1973; MA in Psychology, Queens Coll., Flushing, N.Y., 1975. Sec. N.Y.C., 1969-71; salesperson Hearst Corp./King Features, N.Y.C., 1971-76, asst. to dir., 1976-81, dir. licensing, 1981-90, sr. dir. licensing, 1990—. Office: Hearst Corp/King Features 235 E 45th St New York NY 10017

GOMEZ, CAROL VARTULI, communications executive, speech writer; b. Burlington, Vt., Dec. 21, 1950; d. Dominic and Lorraine (Courville) Vartuli; m. Fernando Gomez-Escallon, Oct. 29, 1972 (div. Jan. 1989); children: Kenton David and Christopher. BA in English, Art, Western Conn. U., 1973; MA in Journalism, Pub. Communications, Fordham U., 1982. Freelance writer Bedford, N.Y., 1974-84; mag. editor, communications specialist IBM Corp., White Plains, N.Y., 1984-86, U.S. newspaper editor, 1986-88; speech writer, sr. communications specialist IBM Corp., Somers, N.Y., 1988—. Contbr. articles to newspapers. Tutor, trainer, coord. Literacy Vols. Am., N. Westchester chpt., 1980-85. Mem. Women in Communications. Office: IBM Corp PO Box 100 Rte 100 Somers NY 10589

GOMEZ, JULIE, accountant; b. Havana, Cuba, Jan. 9, 1946; d. Jose Manuel and Maria Josefa (Rivera) G. A in Acctg., Northwestern U., Chgo., 1971; BS in Acctg., DePaul U., Chgo., 1983; MBA in Exec. Program, Northwestern U., Evanston, Ill., 1987. CPA, Ill. Treas., contr. Chesterfield Svc. Corp., Chgo., 1969-83; exec. v.p., treas. Medi-Data Svc. Ltd., 1983-87; asst. v.p. fin. svcs. Crum & Forster Mgrs. Corp., Chgo., 1987—. Mem. AICPA's, Ill. CPA Soc. Republican. Home: 3180 N Lake Shore Dr #9B Chicago IL 60657 Office: Crum & Forster Mgrs Corp 200 S Wacker Dr Chicago IL 60606

GOMEZ, MADELEINE YVONNE, clinical psychologist; b. Puerto Plata, Dominican Republic, Aug. 29, 1956; came to U.S., 1959; d. Evaristo and Madeleine (Dugué) Gomez; m. Thomas Patrick O'Callaghan; children: Michelle Marie Schenkelberg, Bianca Nicole O'Callaghan. BA magna cum laude, Case Western Res. U., 1978; PhD, Northwestern U., 1988. Diplomate in sex therapy Am. Bd. Sexology. Extern Evanston (Ill.) Hosp., 1979-81, Northwestern Meml. Hosp., Chgo., 1980-82; psychotherapist Pilsen-Little Village Community Mental Health Ctr., Chgo., 1980-83; intern Hines (Ill.) VA Hosp., 1982-83; asst. dir. mental health Chgo. Health Maintenance Orgn., 1983-86, assoc. dir. mental health, 1986-89; clin. assoc. Inst. Stress Mgmt., Chgo., 1987-89; dir. PsycHealth Ltd., Evanston, 1989—; chief mental health svcs. Chgo. Health Maintenance Orgn., 1989—; testing cons. Ill. Dept. Children and Family Svcs., 1984—; mem. communications com. Greater Chgo. Coun. for Nat. Com. for Prevention of Child Abuse, 1990—; mem. allied profl. staff Charter Barclay Hosp., Hartgrove Hosp. Guest on local TV programs; contbr. to profl. publs. Mem. Am. Psychol. Assn., Ill. Psychol. Assn. Office: Chgo HMO 540 N LaSalle St 4th Fl Chicago IL 60611

GOMEZ, VIRGINIA, pharmacist; b. N.Y.C., Sept. 5, 1934; d. Armando Gomez and Virginia Ramos; m. Nicolas Robert CAussade, Oct. 2, 1965 (div. Oct. 2, 1978); children: Nicolas Roberto, Armando Nicolas. BS in Pharmacy, U. Puerto Rico, 1960. Registered pharmacist, P.R., La. Adminstr. Farmacia Nueva, Barranquitas, P.R., 1960-62; dir. pharmacy svc. San Jorge Hosp., Santurce, P.R., 1962-81, DeDiego Hosp., Inc., Santurce, 1981-84; staff pharmacist VA Med. Ctr., New Orleans, 1984-87, Gainesville, Fla., 1987—. Mem. Colegio de farmaceuticos de P.R., Am. Soc. Hosp. Pharmacists, La. Soc. Hosp. Pharmacists, N.Cen. Fla. Soc. Hosp. Pharmacists, Alachua Pharmaicst Assn. Republican. Roman Catholic.

GONCE, NANCY CUMMINGS, librarian, educator, researcher; b. Birmingham, Ala., May 21, 1939; d. Truman and Mozelle (Brown) Cummings; m. Robert L. Gonce; children: Nancy Suzanne, Elizabeth Mozelle. BS in Library Sci., U. Ala., 1961; MS in Library Sci., George Peabody Coll., 1961. Area librarian Ala. Pub. Library Service, Tuscaloosa, Ala., 1961-62; area librarian Ala. Pub. Library Service, Florence, Ala., 1962-64, field rep., 1964-67; librarian Riverbend Ctr. Mental Health, Florence, 1972-78; program coord. U. North Ala. Coop. Campus Ministry, Florence, 1980-82; mem. steering com. U. North Ala. Coop. Campus Ministry, 1988-89, chmn. bd., 1989-90; libr. Muscle Shoals (Ala.) Bd. Edn., 1982-83, 1984-90; program devel. coord. Shoals, Inc., Florence, 1985-84; owner Gonce and Assocs., Florence, 1984—; del. Ala. Govs conf. on Librs., 1967, White House Conf. on Librs. and Info. Sci., 1979; adv. Ala. State Com. on Libr. Devel., 1973; mem. com. for regional confs. Ala. Govs. Conf. on Librs. and Info Svcs.; cons. Ala. Music Hall of Fame, Muscle Shoals, 1985—; officer mgr., cons. W.C. Handy Music Festival, Florence, 1985—; founding bd. dirs., grants writer Safeplace, Inc., Florence, 1985; columnist arts/cultural affairs-Fanfare Times Daily, 1989—. Author arts column, Times Daily Weekly., 1989—. Mem. founding mem. bd. Gingerbread Playhouse, Florence, 1976, Music Presentation Soc., Inc., 1980—; adv. bd. Kennedy Douglas Ctr. for Arts, Florence, 1980-82; bd. dirs. Florence Ballet Co., 1979-83; adv. com. WomanHealth, Birmingham, Ala., 1981-83 state conf. del. Nat. Conf., Internat. Women's Yr., Ala., 1978-79; mem. dept. of ch. and soc. Episcopal Dicoese, Birmingham, 1980-84, Ala. recruiter NBC Election Unit, 1980—; bd. dirs. Muscle Shoals Concerts, Inc., 1990—; sec.-treas. Muscle Shoals Concert Guild, 1990—. Mem. AAUW (Outstanding Service award 1981), Ala. Library Assn. (various state coms.), C. of C. of Shoals (co-chmn. edn. com. and cultural affairs comm.). Democrat. Home: 321 Palisade Dr Florence AL 35630 Office: Gonce and Assocs 115 1/2 E Mobile Florence AL 35630

GONCHAR, ROSALIE JAMES, retired wholesale food company executive; b. Savannah, Ga., Sept. 9, 1927; d. Thomas Patterson James and Catherine Mae (Crider) Roberts James; m. Gershon Alexander Gonchar, Dec. 27, 1952 (dec. Jan. 14, 1988). With IBM-code sect. Nat. Security Agy., Washington, 1943-45; computer operator So. States Iron-Roofing Co., Savannah, 1948-53; owner, pres. Gonchar Produce Co., Savannah, 1955-88. Democrat. Jewish. Lodges: B'nai B'rith, Hadassah. Avocation: artist.

GONCHER, SUSAN ELLEN, computer software executive; b. Herrin, Ill., Nov. 3, 1950; d. John and Doris Elaine (Cook) Grozik; m. Donald John Goncher, Oct. 20, 1973; children: Andrew Joseph, Katrina Elise. BS, So. Ill. U., 1972; MS, Nat. Coll. Edn., 1981. Tchr. English, Bloomingdale Sch. Dist., Ill., 1973-74; personnel asst. Chgo. Pneumatic Tool Co., Bensenville, Ill., 1974-75; exec. asst. Bus. Appraisal Co., Oak Brook, Ill., 1975-76, System Devel. Corp., Oak Brook, 1976-77; office services mgr. Advanced System Applications, Inc., Bloomingdale, Ill., 1977-80, mgr. personnel adminstrn., 1980-84; with CA Bus. Ptnrs., Bloomingdale, Ill., 1986-87; owner, pres., Statice Gro, West Chicago, Ill., 1987—. Contbr. articles to profl. jours. Ill. State scholar, 1968. Mem. Am. Soc. Personnel Adminstrn., Am. Mgmt. Assn., Alpha Omicron Pi. Russian Orthodox. Home: 1704 Jeanette Ave Saint Charles IL 60174 Office: Statice Gro PO Box 25 West Chicago IL 60185

GONGORA, MAEDALE, purchasing agent; b. Dewitt, Ark., Apr. 2, 1935; d. Homer Lee and Jessie L. (Stilley) Dillon; m. Frederick M. Isenberg, Nov. 30, 1956 (div. Feb. 1961); children: Vincent Luis Gongora, Valerie Gongora Hines. BS in Fashion Mdse., Woodbury U., 1955. Cert. purchasing mgr. Buyer L.A. Times/KTTV, 1961-68; purchasing mgr. KTTV-Channel 11, Hollywood, Calif., 1968-72; dir. material mgmt. Children's Hosp. of L.A., 1972-87; dir. purchasing Pomona (Calif.) Unified Sch. Dist., 1987—. Mem. Toastmasters Internat. (pres. L.A. chpt. 1985-86, Outstanding Toastmaster award 1984, 85, 88), Women in Mgmt. Home: 1250 Hill Dr Los Angeles CA 90041

GONNELLA, NINA CELESTE, biophysicist; b. Phila., Dec. 22, 1953; d. Anthony and Antoinette E. Gonnella. BA, Temple U., 1975; PhD, U. Pa., 1979; postdoctoral, Calif. Inst. Tech., 1979-81, Columbia U., 1981-83; research assoc., Yale U., 1984. Sr. rsch. scientist CIBA Geigy Pharm. Co., Summit, N.J., 1983-88, sr. staff scientist, 1989—; vis. scientist Yale U., 1984. Contbr. articles to profl. jours. NSF fellow, 1976-79. Mem. ACS, Soc. Magnetic Resonance in Medicine, Phi Lambda Upsilon. Office: CIBA GEIGY 556 Morris Ave Summit NJ 07901

GONNERMAN, CHARNEY LOUISE, organization executive; b. Luverne, Minn., Nov. 25, 1945; d. George William and Margaret Lucile (Arnold) Ziegahn; m. William Wallace Wilmot, June 7, 1967 (div. May 1976); children: Jason Lamar, Carina Louise; m. David Allen Gonnerman, Sept. 27, 1980; stepchildren: Melissa Diane, Paula Marie. BA, Augustana Coll., Sioux Falls, S.D., 1967. Dist. dir. Totem coun. Girl Scouts U.S.A., Seattle, 1967-70; presch. tchr. 1st Congl. Ch., Missoula, Mont., 1974-76, YWCA, Missoula, 1973-74; asst. state dir. S.D. Green Thumb, Sioux Falls, 1978-80; dir. Aging Svcs. Ctr., Sioux Falls, 1980; exec. dir. Vol. and Info. Ctr., Sioux Falls, 1980-83, YWCA, Sioux Falls, 1983—; co-owner, mgr. Small World, Missoula, 1975. Bd. dirs. YWCA, Missoula, 1971-73; organizer, dir. Isabella County Recycling, Mt. Pleasant, Mich., 1970-73; trainer, leader Girl Scouts U.S.A., Mt. Pleasant, 1970-73, leader, Brandon, S.D., 1982; bd. dirs. Interagy. Steering Com., Sioux Falls, 1981-83, Child Protection Coun., 1981-83, Valley Drive Recreation Ctr., 1984, Aging Svcs. Ctr., 1979, Family Violence Coalition, 1985, S.D. Office Volunteerism, 1984; mem. S.D. Nat. Abortion Rights Action League, 1990—, numerous others. Recipient Women Serving S.D. award S.D. Advocacy Network for Women, 1990. Mem. Nat. Assn. YWCA Execs., Nat. Assn. Fund Raising Execs., AAUW, Nat. Women's Polit. Caucus, Sioux Falls Pers. Assn., Nat. Parks and Conservation Assn., Badger Wilderness Assn., Brandon-Valley Booster Club, Cosmopolitan Club. Democrat. Methodist. Home: 409 Lakota Brandon SD 57005 Office: Sioux Falls YWCA 300 W 11th St Sioux Falls SD 57102

GONYA, PATRICE YEAGER, insurance company official; b. Bremen, Ga., Aug. 17, 1951; d. Forest William and Madge Moore (Cain) Yeager; B.S., U. Mo., Columbia, 1972, M.B.A., 1978; m. David E. Gonya. CPCU; CLU; Chartered Fin. Cons. Devel. trainee State Farm Ins. Co., Columbia, 1972-73, jr. acct., 1973-74, acct., 1974-77, asst. acctg. mgr., Springfield, Pa., 1977-79, acctg. supt., 1979-83, acctg. mgr., Rohnert Park, Calif., 1983-86, mgmt. asst., 1986-87, asst. div. mgr., 1987-88, div. mgr., Tulsa, 1988—. Vol. drives Heart Fund, 1975, 76; office co-chmn. United Way, 1979, chmn., 1980, mem. campaign effectiveness council, 1982; bd. dirs. Domestic Violecne Intervention Svcs., Inc.; mem. Sonoma County Transp. Com., 1980. Mem. NAFE, Nat. Assn. Accts. Office: State Farm Ins Co 12222 State Farm Blvd Tulsa OK 74146-5402

GONZALES, LUCILLE CONTRERAS, educational administrator; b. Colton. Calif., Nov. 30, 1937; d. Antonio Colunga and Ramona (Arroyo) Contreras; AA, San Bernardino Valley Coll., 1958; BA, U. Calif., Santa Barbara, 1960; MA, Claremont Grad. Sch., 1969; m. Enrique Gonzales, Aug. 27, 1960; children: Leticia Maria, Cecilia Maria. With Chino (Calif.) Public Schs., 1960-85, bilingual classroom tchr., 1970-74, bilingual coordinator, 1974-76, coordinator consol. application-intergroup relations, 1976-78, supr. spl. projects, 1978, adminstr. spl. projects, 1978-82, dir. spl. projects, 1982-85; dir. state and fed. programs Pomona Pub. Schs., Calif., 1985-88; edn. programs cons. Calif. Dept. Edn., 1988—; trainer State Dept. Edn. for Program Quality Review Trainers and Reviewers for Elem., Middle Grades, and Reviewers for Secondary in Edn., Master Trainers for Program Quality Rev.; mem. State Supts. Regional Adv. Hispanic Council, State Supts. Middle Grade Task Force, State Dept's. Middle Grades Program Quality Criteria Task Force, State's Supt. Adv. Com. on Gifted Edn. Mem. Migrant Regional Exec. Bd.; mem. Bilingual Dirs. Task Force; mem. Expanded Curriculum Cons. Steering Com.; rep. Calif. State Dept. Edn. Mem. NAFE, San Bernardino County Assn. Compensatory Edn. Dirs. (pres., v.p.), P.E.O., Assn. Secondary Spl. Projects, Assn. Calif. Sch. Adminstrs., Calif. Assn. of Adminstrs. of State and Fed. Ednl. Programs, Nat. Assn. Fed. Ednl. Program Adminstrs., Am. Assn. Sch. Adminstrs., Assn. State and Fed. Adminstrs. of Programs, Los Angeles County Bilingual Dirs., Large Urban Dirs., Assn. Large Urban Dirs., Pi Lambda Theta, Delta Kappa Gamma, Phi Delta Kappa. Lodge: Soroptimist. Home: 4955 Tyler St Chino CA 91710 Office: 721 Capitol Mall Sacramento CA 95814

GONZALES, PATRICIA BUCK, infosystems executive, educator; b. Cin., Sept. 23, 1940; d. John Henderson and Gladys Irene (Smith) Buck; m. Richard Lawrence; children: Michele, Rick, Carmen, Lisa. Student, Wroxton Coll., England, 1987; Purdue U., 1969, 70, 79. Programming WCIA-TV, Madison, Wis., 1959-60; media dir. Hall, Haerr, Peterson & Harney, Peoria, Ill., 1963-68; instr. Academy of Word Processing, Munster, Ind., 1986—; pres. Embedded Systems, Inc., Hammond, Ind. advisory com. Women's Conference Purdue Calumet, Internat. Women's Day Conference. mem. Folger Shakespeare Library, Nat. Museum of Women in the Arts, LWV, Purdue U. Women's Club. Democrat. Episcopalian.

GONZALEZ, DIANE KATHRYN, social worker; b. Cin., Aug. 20, 1947; d. Joseph Curtis and Kathryn Mary (Diskin) Gonzalez; BA in Social Work, U. Dayton, 1969; AM in Social Work, U. Chgo., 1973; m. Thomas Connolley Leibig, July 5, 1974; 1 child, Abigail. Social worker Hamilton County Welfare Dept., Cin., 1969-71; social worker obstetrics dept. and prenatal clinic social service dept. St. Francis Hosp., Evanston, Ill., 1973-78; rap group leader Teen Scene, Planned Parenthood Assn., Chgo., part-time, 1979-80; social worker Chgo. Comprehensive Care Ctr., 1980—; chmn. adv. com. Evanston Continuing Edn. Ctr., 1978-80. Mem. landmark dist. com. Old Town Triangle, 1983— (chmn. 1987-89); gen. co-chmn. Old Town Art Fair, 1984-85, gen. chmn. 1986-87. Mem. Nat. Assn. Social Workers (cert.), Acad. Cert. Soc. Workers, Old Town Triangle Assn. (bd. dirs.). Roman Catholic. Home: 218 W Menomonee St Chicago IL 60614

GONZALEZ, GISELA ALEXANDRA, financial services executive; b. Guines, Habana, Cuba, Apr. 24, 1949; came to U.S., 1954; d. Luis A. and Reina G. (Soler) G. BSBA, Washington U., St. Louis, 1971; MS in Indsl. Adminstrn., Carnegie Mellon U., 1973, postgrad., 1973-75. Fin. economist FDIC, Washington, 1976-78, sr. fin. economist, 1978-80; v.p. Kaplan Smith & Assocs., Washington, 1980-82, sr. v.p., 1983-84; v.p. Drexel Burnham Lambert, Chgo., 1984-86; sr. dir. Continental Bank Corp., Chgo., 1986-88; sr. v.p. Mich. Nat. Corp., Farmington Hills, 1989; dir. acquisitions Ford Fin. Svcs. Group, Dearborn, Mich., 1990—; adj. asst. prof. George Washington U., Washington, 1978-79. Cons. applied econs. program Jr. Achievement, 1990; foster parent Plan Internat., 1990. Mem. Econs. Club of Detroit, Columbia Yacht Club.

GONZALEZ, KIMBERLY REGINA, controller; b. Walnut Creek, Calif., Nov. 5, 1964; d. Earl Glenn and Marilynn Mae (Roberts) Kramar; m. George Gonzalez, May 30, 1987; children: Joshua Alan, Nathaniel James. BS in Internat. Bus. summa cum laude, Woodbury U., 1986. Controller Charisma Missions Inc., Los Angeles, 1985—, dir., treas., 1986—. Assoc. producer (TV program) Alabare, L.A., 1988—. Mem. NAFE, Am. Soc. Profl. and Exec. Women, Am. Mgmt. Assn., Cath. Communicators Assn. (elected vice chmn. 1990—). Republican. Roman Catholic. Home: 1069 Ave C Redondo Beach CA 90277 Office: Charisma in Missions Inc 1059 S Gage Ave Los Angeles CA 90023

GONZALEZ, LYNN AMMIRATO, supermarket executive; b. Paterson, N.J., Nov. 12, 1948; d. George Louis Ammirato and Barbara Alta (Rish) Modzelewski. BS in Edn., William Paterson Coll., 1970. Tchr. St. Boniface Sch., Paterson, N.J., 1969-73; customer svc. mgr. Supermarket Gen. Corp., Woodbridge, N.J., 1973-79, pers. recruiter, 1979-80, mgmt. recruiter, 1980-81, tech. recruiter, 1981-83, mgr. assoc. rels., 1983-84, mgr. human resources planning, 1984-85, dir. assoc. rels., 1985—; mem. adv. bd. Our House, Inc., Berkley Heights, N.J. Roman Catholic. Office: Supermarkets Gen Corp 301 Blair Rd Woodbridge NJ 07095

GONZALEZ, MARIA CHRISTINA, communications educator; b. Ft. Stockton, Tex., Mar. 15, 1957; d. Alejandro Ramon and Maria Senaida (Ureta) G. BS magna cum laude, U. N. Tex., 1978; MA, SUNY, Buffalo, 1982; PhD, U. Tex., 1986. Tchr. Rosemont Middle Sch., Ft. Worth, 1979-80; instr., dormitory dir. SUNY, Buffalo, 1980-82; instr. U. Tex., Austin, 1985-86; project dir. Gov.'s Office, Austin, 1984-86; lectr. U. Ill., Chgo., 1986; asst. prof. Rutgers U., New Brunswick, N.J., 1986-88; Fulbright prof. Facultad de Psicologia, Chihuahua, Mex., 1988-89; asst. prof. U. N. Tex., Denton, 1988—; cons. in field. Editor: Texas Child Abuse Prevention Handbook, 1985; contbr. articles to profl. publs. Leader, Girl Scouts U.S.A., New Brunswick, 1986-88; bd. dirs. Nat. Com. for Prevention of Child Abuse, Newark, 1987-88. Recipient award Tex. Migrant Coun., 1986; U. N. Tex. rsch. grantee, 1989. Mem. Speech Communication Assn., Internat. Communication Assn. (paper evaluatory reader 1987—), Phi Beta Phi. Democrat. Roman Catholic. Office: U N Tex Dept Communication Denton TX 76203

GONZÍLEZ, SISTER PAULA, biology educator, futurist; b. Albuquerque, Oct. 25, 1932; d. Hilario Chavez and Emilia Anna (Sanchez) G. BA, Coll. Mt. St. Joseph, Cin., 1952; MS, Cath. U. Am., 1962, PhD, 1966. Joined Sisters of Charity of Cin., Roman Cath. Ch. Instr. sci. Regina Sch. Nursing, Albuquerque, 1952-54; tchr. biology Seton High Sch., Cin., 1955-60; assoc. prof. biology Coll. Mt. St. Joseph, 1965-70, prof., 1970—; freelance futurist, educator, environmentalist, lectr., condr. workshops, cons. Fellow USPHS, 1961-65. Mem. Alt. Energy Assn. (pres. 1988—), Union Concerned Scientists, Inst. Noetic Scis. Democrat. Home: 5820 Bender Rd Cincinnati OH 45233 Office: Sister of Charity of Cin 5900 Delhi Rd Cincinnati OH 45051

GONZLIK, PAMELA JOAN, legal secretary; b. N.Y.C., Apr. 20, 1948; d. John Martin and Regina (Cohen) Gonzlik; secretarial diploma, A.O.S. acctg. degree, Taylor Bus. Inst., 1975; student in acctg. Pace U., 1975. Stock records clk. G. A. Saxton & Co., N.Y.C., 1970-71; sec., bookkeeper Acme Quilting Co., Inc., N.Y.C., 1971-73; acct., sec., office mgr. Alwyn Ptnrs., N.Y.C., 1975-77; treas. Independence Plaza Tenants Orgn. and Rent Strike Com., 1977-78; sec. Atalanta Corp., N.Y.C., 1978-80, exec. sec., adminstv. asst. splty. foods div., 1986-87; legal sec. City of M.Y. Law Dept., 1980-86; adminstrv. asst., office mgr. Sandy Soroush Designs, Inc., N.Y.C., 1987-88; legal sec. Eleanor Jackson Piel, N.Y.C., 1989—; polit. action vol. Mondale for Pres. campaign; cable TV vol., producer, host, performer Musical Interludes cable TV show Exptl. TV Coop., Inc., N.Y.C., 1978-82; performer cabaret showcase Dangerfield's, 1984; performer passenger talent shows aboard Cunard Countess, 1985-86, Queen Elizabeth II, 1986-88, 87, 90, Sagafjord, 1988; vol., adminstrv. asst. ETC Studios, 1978-82; developer cable TV game shows. Mem. Nat. Carousel Assn., Channel 13, and Channel 21 Pub. Broadcasting Service, WNYC-Pub. Radio, Phi Chi Theta (rec. sec. Gamma Xi chpt. 1976-77). Home: 40 Harrison St Apt 38E New York NY 10013

GOOCH, NANCY JANE, real estate company official, mortgage executive; b. Ann Arbor, Mich., Dec. 19, 1941; d. Donald B. and Marjorie (Gilchrist) G. BA, Western Mich. U., 1963; MA, Ea. Mich. U., 1987. Lic. real estate broker, Fla., Mich. Tchr. Broward County Schs., Ft. Lauderdale, Fla., 1968-73; v.p. Chinelly Real Estate, Inc., Miramar, Fla., 1973-83; closing exec. Cenville Devel. Co., Hollywood, Fla., 1983-86; mortgage originator Empire of Am., Southfield, Mich., 1987—; exec. dir. Ednl. Rsch. and Guidance Svcs., Ann Arbor, 1986—. Editor Bridlepath mag., 1983-84; contbr. numerous articles to various publs. Pres. Broadway Area Neighborhood Assn., Ann Arbor, 1985-86. Recipient honors S. Fla. Trail Riders Broward County, 1983. Mem. Wayne-Oakland Bd. Realtors, Am. Saddlehorse Assn. (Mich. bd. dirs. 1989—), Women's Econ. Club. Republican. Office: Empire of Am 33897 Five Mile Rd Livonia MI 48154

GOOCH, PATRICIA CAROLYN, cytogeneticist; b. Michie, Tenn., Mar. 28, 1935; d. James Lide and Mary Frances (Hyneman) G. BS, U. Tenn., Knoxville, 1957. Tchr. sci. Knoxville City Sch. System, 1957-58; biologist Oak Ridge Nat. Lab., 1958-70, 73—; research assoc. Grad. Sch. Biomed. Sci., U. Tex., Houston, 1970; sr. research analyst Northrop Corp., NASA-Johnson Space Ctr., Houston, 1970-72; organizing com. sci. confs. Contbr. articles to profl. jours. Named Outstanding Tenn. Woman, U. Tenn. Pan-Hellenic Assn., 1974, one of Outstanding Young Women of Am., 1968. Mem. Anderson County Dem. Women's Club (membership chmn. 1985-86). Mem. AAAS, Am. Genetic Assn., Genetics Soc. Am., Environ. Mutagen Soc., U. Tenn. Alumni Assn. (chpt. treas. 1980-81, chpt. sec. 1981-82, chpt. v.p. 1982-83, chpt. pres. 1983-84, nat. bd. govs. 1984-87), Oak Ridge Pan-Hellenic Assn. (benefit chmn. 1961), Delta Gamma Alumni Assn. (pres. Knoxville Area 1959-61, 67-69), Sigma Xi (chpt. admissions com. 1977-79). Mem. Ch. of Christ. Club: Big Orange (sec. 1978-80, 82-84). Home: 226 Tusculum Dr Oak Ridge TN 37830 Office: Oak Ridge Nat Lab Biology Div PO Box Y Oak Ridge TN 37830

GOOD, ANNE LEEPER (JOHN CARTER GOOD, MRS.), civic worker; b. Jackson, Tenn., Nov. 10, 1923; d. Robert Allen and Ola (Crittenden) Leeper; A.B., B.S. cum laude, Lambuth Coll., 1944; m. John Carter Good, Oct. 28, 1945; children—John Robert, Carter Crittenden, William Allen. Co-chmn. Introduction to Washington com. The Hospitality and Info. Service, 1968-71, treas., 1971-75, v.p., 1975-77, pres., 1977-79, chmn. fin. com., 1983-85, exec. com., 1985-86; trustee Meridian House Internat., 1977-79, counselor, 1980—; membership chmn. Spanish Portuguese Study Group, 1968-69, v.p., 1969-70, pres., 1970-71; mem. ladies' bd. House of Mercy, 1970—, treas., 1972-74, trustee, treas., 1986—. Bd. dirs. D.C. br. Nat. Capitol Area YWCA, 1971-78, 79-85, rec. sec., 1974, treas., 1974-76, 81-85; com. Hannah Harrison Career Sch., 1971-78, 79—, chmn., 1976-77, chmn. investment com., 1985-86; bd. dirs. Nat. Capital Area YWCA, 1973-79, fin. com., 1978—; chmn. YWCA Internat. Fair, 1983; bd. dirs. Rosemount Infant Day Care Ctr., 1972-82, v.p., 1974-76; bd. dirs. Washington chpt. Achievement Rewards for Coll. Scientists, 1971-72. Clubs: St. Albans Sch. Mothers (pres. Washington 1964-65), Air Force Officers Wives (mem. bd. Washington 1959-61).

GOOD, JOAN DUFFEY, artist; b. Irvington, N.J., Apr. 8, 1939; d. Joseph Edmund and Mary Kathleen Duffey; m. Robert Whitney Meyers, Feb. 19, 1960; children: Robert Whitney Jr., Mary Kathleen; step-children: Alison H., Forrester H.; m. Allen Hovey Good, June 12, 1976. Student, Rosemont Coll., 1958-59, Summit Art Ctr., 1973-78; BA in Psychology and Studio Art, Drew U., 1987. interior design house Maytime Festival of Homes, 1985; freelance interior design cons., 1987-89; bd. dirs. Atlantic Nat. Acquisition & Mergers, Inc., Summit, N.J.; curatorial assoc., gallery com. N.J. Ctr. for Visual Arts, Summit, 1989-90. Co-curator Constructed Reality, photogrpahy show, N.J. Ctr. for Visual Arts, 1990; one-woman show include World Trade Ctr., N.Y.C., 1988; exhibited in group shows at Madison (N.J.) Pub. Libr., 1986, Chatham (N.J.) Pub. Libr., 1987, Korn Gallery, Drew U., 1986, 87, 89, 90, N.J. Ctr. for Visual Arts, 1987, 88, 89, 90, Oak Knoll Sch. Alumnae Art Exhibit, 1989, 90; represented in numerous private collections, Mass., Fla., Tex., N.J., N.Y., Calif. V.p., pres., membership chmn. PTO, 1966-69; homecoming com. mem., 1989, 90, historian Oak Knoll Sch. Alumnae Bd., Summit, 1988-90. Mem. N.J. Ctr. for Visual Arts, The Drew Art Assn., Chatham Fish & Game Assn., Mantoloking Yacht Club, Summit Tennis Club. Republican. Roman Catholic. Home: 149 Kent Place Blvd Summit NJ 07901

GOOD, JUDITH MARIE, marketing executive; b. North Bend, Oreg., Jan. 16, 1955; d. Armand Allen and Doris Evelyn (Wilmot) Boyer; m. John Wilbert Good, June 8, 1984. BA, Oreg. State U., 1979, MBA, 1984. Sec.-treas. J.B. Good, Inc., Corvallis, Oreg., 1977—. Author brochure: Arboriculture, 1987, others. Active various charitable orgns. Mem. Internat. Soc. Arboriculture, Nat. Mail Order Assn., Nat. Assn. Female Execs., Global Releaf of the Am. Forestry Assn. Republican. Office: 5250 NE Hwy 20 Corvallis OR 97330

GOOD, LINDA LOU, educator; b. Zanesville, Ohio, May 30, 1941; d. John Robert and Alice Laura (Fulkerson) Moore; B.S. in Elem. Edn., Ohio U., 1964; m. Larry Alvin Good, Jan. 11, 1964; children—Jason (dec.), Alicia and Tricia (twins), Amy Jo. Tchr., West Muskingum Sch. Dist., 1962-64; 1st grade tchr., Bellevue, Ohio, 1964-68, 2d grade tchr., Zanesville Sch. System, 1970—; head tchr. Munson Sch., Zanesville. Co-chmn. Zane Trace Commemoration; pres. Munson-Garfield Schs. PTA; mem. Trinity Presbyn. Ch. Mem. NEA, Ohio Edn. Assn., Zanesville Edn. Assn., Eastern Ohio Tchrs. Assn. Presbyterian.

GOOD, MADELYN E., company executive; b. Chillicothe, Ohio, Aug. 21, 1931; d. Elmer William and Alice (Blair) Madden; m. William E. Good, June 15, 1968; children: Timothy, William Jr., Terry, Melissa. Student, Ohio U., Chillicothe Bus. Sch., 1950. Cert. fgn. real estate agt. V.p. bd. dirs., stock holder Pools and Things, Inc., Chillicothe; co-owner Good Enterprises, Chillicothe; dir. Mega-Trend, Inc., Lakeland, Fla.; owner Madelyn's Beauty Shop, Chillicothe. Recipient monetary award U.S. Govt., 1960; named Miss Armed Forces Ct., Wright-Patterson AFB, Dayton, Ohio. Mem. Sister Sorority, Internat. Traders, LWV (sec. 1967-68), NAFE. Democrat. Presbyterian. Home: 1380 Porter Dr Chillicothe OH 45601 Office: Pools & Things Inc 1575 N Bridge St Chillicothe OH 45601

GOOD, MARY LOWE (MRS. BILLY JEWEL GOOD), business executive, chemist; b. Grapevine, Tex., June 20, 1931; d. John W. and Winnie (Mercer) Lowe; m. Billy Jewel Good, May 17, 1952; children: Billy, James. BS, Ark. State Tchrs. Coll., 1950; MS, U. Ark., 1953, PhD, 1955, LLD (hon.), 1979; DSc (hon.), U. Ill., Chgo., 1983, Clarkson U., 1984, Ea. Mich. U., 1986, Duke U., 1987; hon. degree, St. Mary's Coll., 1988, Kenyon Coll., 1988, Stevens Inst. Tech., 1989, Lehigh U., 1989, Northeastern Ill. U., 1989. Instr. Ark. State Tchrs. Coll., Conway, summer 1949; instr. La. State U., Baton Rouge, 1954-56; asst. prof. La. State U., 1956-58; asso. prof. La. State U., New Orleans, 1958-63; prof. La. State U., 1963-80; Boyd prof. materials sci., div. engring. research La. State U., Baton Rouge, 1979-80; v.p., dir. research UOP, Inc., Des Plaines, Ill., 1980-84; pres. Signal Research Ctr. Inc., 1985-87; pres. engineered materials research div. Allied-Signal Inc., Des Plaines, Ill., 1986-88; sr. v.p.-tech., Allied-Signal Inc., Morristown, N.J., 1988—; chmn. Pres.'s Com. for Nat. Medal Sci., 1979-82; mem. Nat. Sci. Bd., 1980—, chmn., 1988-90; mem. adv. bd. NSF Chemistry Sect., 1972-76; mem. com. medicinal chemistry NIH, 1972-76, Office of USAF Rsch., 1974-78, chemist div. Brookhaven and Oak Ridge Nat. Labs., 1973-83, chem. tech. div. Oak Ridge Nat. Lab., catalysis program Lawrence-Berkeley Lab.; catalysis program coll. engring. La. State U.; vice chmn. Nat. Sci. Bd., 1984, chmn., 1988-90. Contbr. articles to profl. jours. Bd. dirs. Oak Ridge Assoc. Univs., Indsl. Research Inst.; trustee Renssalaer Polytech. Inst.; adv. bd. Mayor Byrne's Chgo. Task Force High Tech. Devel. Recipient Agnes Faye Morgan research award, 1969, Distinguished Alumni citation U. Ark., 1973, Scientist of Yr. award Indsl. R & D Mag., 1982, Delmer S. Fahrney medal Franklin Inst., 1988; AEC tng. grantee, 1967, NSF internat. travel grantee, 1968, NSF research grantee, 1969-80. Fellow AAAS, Am. Inst. Chemistry (Gold medal 1983), Chem. Soc. London; mem. Am. Chem. Soc. (1st woman dir. 1971-74, regional dir. 1972-80, chmn. bd. 1978, 80, pres. 1987, Garvan medal 1973, Herty medal 1975, award Fla. sect. 1979), Internat. Union Pure and Applied Chmistry (pres. inorganic div. 1980-85), Nat. Acad. Engring., Zonta (past pres. New Orleans club, chmn. dist. status of women com. and nominating com., chmn. internat. Amelia Earhart scholoarship com. 1978-88, pres. internat. Found. 1988-90, mem. internat. bd. 1988-90), Phi Beta Kappa, Sigma Xi, Iota Sigma Pi (regional dir. 1967—, hon. mem. 1983). Home: 21 Oak Park Dr Convent Station NJ 07961 Office: Allied-Signal Inc PO Box 1021R Morristown NJ 07960-1021

GOOD, NANCY SUSAN, university official; b. Detroit, Mar. 22, 1940; d. Stanley Edward and Sybyl Delores (Adams) G.; m. James Anthony Waters, Oct. 25, 1958 (div. Sept. 1985); children: James A., Dawn Lisa, Kathleen, Christine. BGS, Wayne State U., 1988. Rsch. coord. Cranbrook Ednl. Community, Birmingham, Mich., 1983-84; dir. devel. The Adventure Sch. (now Eaton Acad.), Birmingham, 1984-85; devel. officer Wayne State U. Sch. Medicine, Detroit, 1985-89; assoc. dir. devel. U. Detroit, 1989—; cons. Southeastern Mich. Hospice Found., Southfield, 1986, Wayne State U., 1989-90. Mem. NAFE, Am. Prospect Rsch. Assn. (bd. dirs. Mich. chpt., membership chmn. 1989—). Roman Catholic. Office: U Detroit 4001 W McNichols Rd Detroit MI 48221-3090

GOODALL, FRANCES LOUISE, nurse, civic worker; b. Gove, Kans., Apr. 30, 1915; d. Francis Mitchel and Ella Aurelia (Brown) Sutcliffe; m. Richard Fred Goodall, Feb. 22, 1946; children: Roy Richard, Gary Frederick. Student, U. Kans., 1932-33, Ft. Hays State Coll., 1933-34; BS in Nursing, U. Wash., 1939. RN, Wash. Nurse King County Hosp. System, Seattle, 1939-41; office nurse Dr. Cassius Hofrictor, Seattle, 1941-42. Pres. Hawthorne Elem. Sch. PTA, Seattle, 1960-61, Caspar Sharples Jr. High Sch. PTA, Seattle, 1967-68; historian Seattle Coun. PTA's, 1964-65, 68-69; den mother Boy Scouts Am., Seattle, 1963-67; active United Good Neighbors, Seattle, 1964-68; treas. Women's Overseas Svc. League, Seattle, 1970-74, treas., 1987—. 1st lt. Nurse Corps, AUS, 1942-46, PTO. Recipient vol. award King County Hosp. System, 1964, Acorn award Franklin High Sch. PTA, 1965. Mem. U. Wash. Alumni Assn (v.p. 1966-70), U. Wash. Nursing Alumni Assn., Seattle Mus. Art Soc. (assoc., social com., bd. dirs.), Fedn. Womens Clubs, Seattle Geneal. Soc., Lake City Emblem Club, Order Eastern Star, Sigma Sigma Sigma, Kappa Delta (pres. Seattle alumni 1954-55, sec. alumnae cooperation bd. 1963-82). Republican. Presbyterian. Home: 4111 51st St S Seattle WA 98118

GOODELL, CHRISTINA MARIE, human resources consultant; b. Pottstown, Pa., July 19, 1959; d. Chester Carl and Anna Marie (Savelloni) Maccarone; m. James Chandler Goodell, Sept. 5, 1987. AA, Goldey Beacom Coll., Wilmington, Del., 1979; BS, Goldey Beacom Coll., 1982. Human resources rep. Chem. Bank, Wilmington, Del., 1982-86; human resources adminstr. Scottish & York Internat. Ins., Inc., Wilmington, Del., 1986-91; freelance human resources cons. Langhorne, Pa., 1988—; mem. Del. Bus., Industry and Edn. Alliance, Del. Coun. on Workplace Wellness. Group leader Weight Watchers Internat., Wilmington, 1984-87, Bucks County, Pa., 1990—; assoc. mem. Big Bros./Big Sisters of Del., advisor Job Search Clinic, Ministry of Caring, 1985-86; mem. Del. C. of C., Lower Bucks County C. of C., Pa., 1989. Mem. NAFE, Am. Mgmt. Assn., Soc. Human Resource Mgmt., Goldey Beacom Coll. Alumni Assn. (founding bd. dirs., 1982-84). Republican. Roman Catholic. Home and Office: 1 Denton Circle Newtown PA 18940

GOODEN, GLENDA STEVENS, state official; b. Bluefield, W.Va., June 17, 1953; d. Theodore Malcolm and Rosalee (Shanklin) Stevens; m. Barry D. Gooden, Feb. 13, 1982; 1 child, Steven. BS, Bluefield State Coll., W.Va., 1974. Investigator W.Va. Human Rights Commn., Charleston, W.Va., 1975-77; sales rep. IBM, Ashland, Ky., 1977-79; ins. agt. Allstate Ins. Co., Charleston, 1979-80; legal unit mgr. W.Va. Human Rights Commn., Charleston, 1981—. Bd. dirs. New Steps & Movements, Charleston, 1985-87. Named Outstanding Young Woman of Am., 1986. Mem. Delta Sigma Theta (pres. 1989-91). Democrat. Baptist. Home: 202 Thurston Dr Charleston WV 25311

GOODENOUGH, JUDITH BEACH, poet; b. Berea, Ky., Oct. 25, 1942; d. Robert Fullerton and Eva (Ripley) Beach; m. John Byer Goodenough, Apr. 23, 1966; children: Anne, Elizabeth. BA, Radcliffe Coll., 1964. Author: Dower Land, 1984, Milking in Novermber, 1990; pub. poems, 1979—. Democratic. Unitarian. Home and Office: 300 Wildberry Rd Pittsburgh PA 15238

GOODENOUGH, JUDITH ELIZABETH, biologist, author; b. Geneva, N.Y., Sept. 28, 1948; d. Raymond Charles and Betty (Davis) Levrat; m. Stephen Michael Goodenough, Aug. 21, 1971; children: Aimee Elizabeth, Heather Michelle. BS, Wagner Coll., 1970; PhD, NYU, 1977. Lab. asst. Wagner Coll., 1970; grad. teaching asst. NYU, 1971-74, instr., 1974; grad. teaching asst. U. Mass., Amherst, 1974-75, lectr., staff asst., 1975-83, lectr., staff assoc., 1983—, instr. Sch. Continuing Edn., 1975. Author: Lab Studies in Introductory Zoology, 4th edit., 1984, 5th edit., 1988, Animal Communication, 1984, The Lab Collection, 1987, Lab Exerciese in Introductory Biology, 1987, Supplement to Lab Collection, 1988; contbr. articles to profl. jours. Mem. staff, bd. dirs. Pinecrest Lutheran Leadership Sch., Port Murray, N.J., 1974—; supt. Sunday Sch. Immanuel Lutheran Ch., Amherst, Mass., 1986—. Faculty growth grantee U. Mass., Amherst, 1976, faculty research grantee U. Mass., 1980, 82; recipient Disting. Teaching Award U. Mass., 1986. Mem. AAAS, Animal Behavior Soc., Sigma Xi. Lutheran. Avocations: needlecrafts; stained glass; camping. Home: 16 Brookwood Dr Florence MA 01060 Office: U Mass Dept Zoology Morrill Sci Ctr Amherst MA 01003

GOODEY, ILA MARIE, psychologist; b. Logan, Utah, Feb. 1, 1948; d. Vernal P. and Leona Marie (Williams) Goodey. BA with honors in English and Sociology, U. Utah, 1976; Grad. Cert. Criminology, U. Utah, 1976, MS in Counseling Psychology, 1984, PhD in Psychology, 1985. Speech writer for dean of students U. Utah, Salt Lake City, 1980-89, psychologist Univ. Counseling Ctr., 1984—; cons. Dept. Social Services, State of Utah, Salt Lake City, 1983—; pvt. practice psychology Consult West, Salt Lake City, 1985-86; pub. relations coordinator Univ. Counseling Ctr., 1985—; cons. Aids Project, U. Utah, 1985—; pvt. practice psychology, Inscapes Inst., Salt Lake City, 1987-88; writer civic news Salt Lake City Corp., 1980—; mem. Senator Orrin Hatch's Adv. Com. on Disability Oriented Legis., 1989—. Author book: Love for All Seasons, 1971; play: Validation, 1979; musical drama: One Step, 1984. Contbr. articles to profl. jours. Chmn. policy bd. Dept. State Social Service, Salt Lake City, 1986—; campaign writer Utah Dem. Party, 1985; appointed to Utah State Legis. Task Force on svcs. for people with disabilities, 1990. Recipient Creative Achievement award Utah Poetry Soc., 1974, English SAC, U. Utah, 1978, Leadership award YWCA, 1989, Golden Flame award J.C. Penny, 1989, Volunteerism award State of Utah, 1990. Mem. AAUW, Am. Psychol. Assn., Utah Psychol. Assn., Internat. Platform Assn., Mortar Board, Am. Soc. Clin. Hypnosis, Utah Soc. Clin. Hypnosis, Soc. Psychol. Study Social Issues, League of Women Voters, Phi Beta Kappa, Phi Kappa Phi, Alpha Lambda Delta. Mormon. Clubs: Mormon Theol. Symposium, Utah Poetry Assn. Avocations: theatrical activities, creative writing, travel, political activities. Office: U Utah Counseling Ctr 2450 SSB Salt Lake City UT 84112 also: Inscapes Inst 34 S 600 E Salt Lake City UT 84102

GOODFELLOW, JOAN BENNETT, building trade executive; b. Williamsport, Pa., Nov. 6, 1928; d. Kenneth Victor and Martha Emily (Covert) Bennett; m. John Goodfellow, May 30, 1955 (div. 1974); 1 child, John Charles, II. Student Ithaca Coll. Gen. mgr. Bennett Chem. Co., Hagaman, N.Y., 1948-65, Halifax Tile & Floor, Ormond Beach, Fla., 1967-70; office mgr. Service Paint & Glass, Daytona Beach, Fla., 1967; owner, pres. Halifax Tile & Floor Covering, Inc., Ormond Beach, 1970—; v.p. New Era, Inc., Ormond Beach, 1982—. Fellow Nat. Assn. Women in Construction (charter mem.), Nat. Assn. Home Builders Inc., Internat. Pilot Club, Inc., (internat. affairs dir.). Avocations: Golf; travel. Home: 2926 Anchor Dr Ormond Beach FL 32074 Office: Halifax Tile & Floor Covering Inc 275 Kenilworth Ave Ormond Beach FL 32074

GOODFELLOW, ROBIN IRENE, surgeon; b. Xenia, Ohio, Apr. 14, 1945; d. Willis Douglas and Irene Linna (Kirkland) G. B.A. summa cum laude, Western Res. U., Cleve., 1967; M.D. cum laude, Harvard U., 1971. Diplomate Am. Bd. Surgery. Intern, resident Peter Bent Brigham Hosp., Boston, 1971-76; staff surgeon Boston U., 1976-80, asst. prof. surgery, 1977-80; pvt. practice medicine specializing in surgery Jonesboro, La., 1980-81; practice medicine specializing in surgery Albion, Mich., 1984-87, Coldwater, Mich., 1987—. Bd. Overseers Case Western Res. U., 1977-82. AAUW fellow, 1970. Fellow ACS; mem. AMA, Phi Beta Kappa. Republican. Methodist.

GOODFRIEND, WENDY LEE, psychologist; b. N.Y.C., Nov. 17, 1959; d. Stephen Philip Goodfriend and Susan Louise (Turberg) Resnik. BFA, NYU, 1982; MA in Psychology, Yeshiva U., 1986, PhD in Clin. Psychology, 1990. Tchr., therapist autistic nursery Bellevue Hosp., N.Y.C., 1982-83; residential extern in psychology Children's Village, Dobbs Ferry, N.Y., 1984-85; extern in psychology psychiat. day treatment and outpatient dept. Harlem Hosp. Ctr., N.Y.C., 1985-86; intern in psychology adult chem. dependency unit Meml. Coastview, N.Y.C., Calif., 1988; intern in psychology Univ. Counseling Ctr. Calif. State U., Long Beach, 1987-88; intern in psychology Cannexxus, L.A., 1988-89; psychologist Daytop Village, Redwood City, Calif., 1989—. Mem. APA.

GOODHART, KAREN STEPHAN, sales executive; b. Bklyn., Jan. 14, 1947; d. Frank Herman and Bernadette (Brady) S.; m. James Stanley Goodhart, June 7, 1969 (div. Jan. 1983); children: Kristen Stephanie, Erika Lee. BA, Alvernia Coll., 1969. Elem. tchr. Schuylkill Valley Sch., Leesport, Pa., 1969-78; mgr. sales Radio Shack, Reading, Pa., 1978-84, The Computer Source, Reading, 1984; buyer Boscov's, Reading, 1985-86; with sales dept. Info. Mgmt., Blue Bell, Pa., 1986; mgr. sales Bio-Med Pa., Inc., Allentown, 1986-87, v.p. sales, 1987-88; v.p. sales Med. Disposal Services, Inc., Reading, 1988. Mem. Nat. Solid Waste Mgmt. Assn., Am. Soc. Health Care, Nat. Exec. Housekeeping, Assn. Practitioners Infection Control. Democrat. Roman Catholic. Office: Med Disposal Svcs Inc 1420 Clarion St Reading PA 19601

GOODHEART, DIANE LOUISE, accountant; b. Arcadia, Calif., Feb. 23, 1962; d. Clyde Raymond and Barbara Jean (Peterson) G. BA, North Park Coll., 1988. Sales asst. Merrill Lynch, Pierce, Fenner & Smith, Inc., Chgo., 1984-85; acct. Pizzeria Uno Restaurant Group, Chgo., 1988-90.

GOODHEART, KAREN, consultant; b. Evanston, Ill., Mar. 24, 1958; d. Clyde R. and Barbara J. (Peterson) G. BSBA magna cum laude, U. Fla., 1985. Lic. real estate broker. Pvt. practice cons. comml. loan asset mgmt. New Orleans; asset mgr. FSLIC, New Orleans, Citicorp Savs. of Ill., Chgo., BJF Devel. Ltd., New Orleans; cons. Laventhol and Horwath Real Estate Adv. Svcs., Orlando, Fla. Recipient numerous scholastic awards. Mem. NAFE, World Trade Ctr. New Orleans, Fin. Mgmt. Assn. Home: 400 Preston Blvd Apt 41 Bossier City LA 71111

GOODHUE, MARY BRIER, lawyer, state senator; b. London, 1921; naturalized, 1942; d. Ernest and Marion H. (Hawks) Brier; m. Francis A. Goodhue, Jr., May 15, 1948; 1 child, Francis A., III. BA, Vassar Coll., 1942; LLB, U. Mich., 1944. Bar: N.Y. 1945. Assoc. Root, Clark, Buckner & Ballantine, N.Y.C., 1945-48; asst. counsel N.Y. State Crime Commn., N.Y.C., 1951-53, Moreland Commn., N.Y.C., 1953-54; mem. firm Goodhue, Arons & Neary and predecessors, Mt. Kisco, 1955—; mem. N.Y. State Assembly from 93d Dist., 1975-78, N.Y. State Senate, 1979—. Trustee, Presbyn. Hosp., N.Y.C., Westchester Mental Health Assn.; N.Y. del. Nat. Women's Conf., Houston, 1977. Mem. ABA, West Bas Assn., No. Westchester Bar Assn. Office: 126 Barker St Mount Kisco NY 10549 also: McLain St Mount Kisco NY 10549 also: NY State Senate Albany NY 12224

GOODIN, JULIA C., medical examiner; b. Columbia, Ky., Mar. 10, 1957; d. Vitus Jack and Geneva (Burton) G. BS, Western Ky. U., 1979; MD, U. Ky., 1983. Diplomate Am. Bd. Clin. and Anatomic Pathology, Am. Bd. Forensic Pathology. Intern Vanderbilt U. Med. Ctr., Nashville, 1983, resident in anatomic and clin. pathology, 1984-87; fellow in forensic pathology Med. Examiner's Office, Balt., 1987-88; asst. med. examiner Office of Chief Med. Examiner, Balt., 1988-90; dep. chief med. examiner State of Tenn., 1990—; asst. med. examiner Nashville, 1990—; clin. prof. Balt. U. Med. Sch., 1988-90, Vanderbilt U. Med. Ctr., 1990—. Lt. comdr. USNR, 1985—. Mem. Am. Acad. Forensic Sci., Assn. Mil. Surgeons of U.S., Mid-Atlantic Forensic Pathology Assn., Md. Soc. Pathologists, Nat. Assn. Med. Examiners. Home: 2209 Natchez Trace Nashville TN 37212 Office: Office Med Examiner 84 Hermitage Ave Nashville TN 37210

GOODING, GRETCHEN ANN WAGNER, physician, educator; b. Columbus, Ohio, July 2, 1935; d. Edward Frederick and Margaret (List) Wagner; m. Charles A. Gooding, June 19, 1961; children: Gunnar Blaise, Justin Mathias, Britta Meghan. BA magna cum laude, St. Mary of the Springs Coll., Columbus, 1957; MD cum laude, Ohio State U., 1961. Diplomate Am. Bd. Diagnostic Radiology. Intern Univ. Hosps., Columbus, 1961-62; rsch. fellow Boston City Hosp., 1962-63, Boston U., 1963-65; with dept. radiology U. Calif., San Francisco, 1975—, assoc. prof. in radiology, 1981-85, prof., vice chmn., 1986—; asst. chief radiology VA Med. Ctr., San Francisco, 1978-87, chief radiology, 1987—, chief ultrasonography, 1975—; speaker in field. Mem. editorial bd. San Francisco Medicine, 1986-90, Applied Radiology, 1987-89; contbr. articles to profl. publs., chpts. to books. Fellow Am. Coll. Radiology, Am. Inst. Ultrasound in Medicine (bd. govs. 1981-84, chair convention program 1986-88, Presdl. Recognition award 1984); mem. RSNA (mem. com. 1984-88), Bay Area Ultrasound Soc. (pres. 1979-80), Soc. Radiologists, U.S., ARRS, CRA, AUR, CRS, Calif. Med. Assn., Am. Assn. Women Radiologists (pres. 1984-85). Roman Catholic. Office: VA Med Ctr Radiology Svc 4150 Clement St San Francisco CA 94121

GOODIN-GAUTIER, SANDIA JOYCELYN, marketing executive; b. Hampton, Va., Sept. 4, 1956; d. Roger Allen and Joyce Evelyn (Cunningham) Goodin; m. Douglas Vernon Gautier, Nov. 10, 1979 (div. Feb. 1988). AA, Miss. Gulf Coast Jr. Coll., 1976; BA, U. South Ala., 1984. Systems cons. Entre Computer Ctr., Gulfport, Miss., 1984-85; sr. sales rep. Bush Office Supply & Computer Co., Pascagoula, Miss., 1985-86; account exec. Mobile (Ala.) Mental Health Ctr., 1986-88, cons. employee assistance program, 1987-88; regional mktg. dir. Sunbelt Profl. Assocs., Inc., Mobile, 1986-88; mktg. cons. Bradford-Birmingham (Ala.) Adult Treatment Ctr., 1989—. Loan exec. United Way, Mobile, 1986, trainer, 1987; campaign mgr. Jackson County (Miss.) Election, 1987. Mem. Am. Mktg. Assn. (sec. 1988-89), Assn. Labor Mgmt. Adminstrs. and Cons. on Alcoholism, Mortar Bd., Am. Heart Assn. Guild of Birmingham, Birmingham Area C. of C., Irondale C. of C., Phi Theta Kappa, Omicron Delta Kappa. Republican. Baptist. Office: Bradford-Birmingham Adult Treatment Ctr 1221 Alton Dr Birmingham AL 35216

GOODKIN, DEBORAH GAY, internal management consultant; b. Oceanside, N.Y., Dec. 8, 1951; d. Harold and Rose (Mostkoff) G.; m. Glenn Richard; 1 child, Samuel Goodkin Richard. BA, Syracuse U., 1972; M. Urban Planning, NYU, 1977. Planner, Nassau-Suffolk Planning, Hauppauge, N.Y., 1972; asst. to treas. Nat. Assn. Savs. Banks, N.Y.C., 1973; planning aide Dept. City Planning, N.Y.C., 1973-79; planner, real property mgr. N.Y.C. Bd. Edn., 1979-81, dir. Capital Budget Bur., 1981-85; supervising mgmt. engr. Port Authority N.Y. & N.J., 1985-90, mgr. fin. systems, 1989—; cons. C Corp., L.A., 1983—. Security cons. Dem. Nat. Com., N.Y.C., 1980. Recipient C.F.O. Award of Excellence, 1987. Mem. Women in Govt. (guest lectr. 1983), Syracuse U. Alumni Assn., NYU Alumni Assn. Author: (zoning law) Bay Ridge Zoning Dist., 1978. Artist: Show of Selected Works, Sireuil,

France, 1983. Office: Port Authority One World Trade Ctr New York NY 10048

GOODMAN, BARBARA EASON, physiology educator; b. Hanover, N.H., Nov. 17, 1949; d. Robert Henry and Helen Esther (Mansfield) Eason; m. Douglas Robert Goodman, May 14, 1972; children: Rebekah Corey, Timothy DeForest Goodman. BA, Duke U., 1972; PhD, U. Minn., 1981. Postdoctoral fellow UCLA Sch. Medicine, L.A., 1980-83, rsch. faculty, 1983-86; asst. prof. U. S.D. Sch. Medicine, Vermillion, 1986—; sci. reviewer Am. Heart Assn. Great Plains region, Sioux Falla, S.D., 1990; cons. U. Calgary (Can.), 1990. Contbr. articles to profl. jours. Pres. Day Care Ctr. Bd., Vermillion, 1990, United Ministries, Vermillion, 1988—; leader Girl Scouts Am., Vermillion, 1987—. Grantee NIH, 1988-93, NSF/Experimental Program to Stimulate Competitive Rsch., 1989-92. Mem. Am. Physio. Soc., Am. Thoracic Sco., Am. Heart Assn. (cardiopulmonary coun. 1988—), NOW (pres. Vermillion chpt. 1987—). Democrat. Methodist. Office: U SD Sch of Medicine Phys Pharm Dept Vermillion SD 57069

GOODMAN, BONNIE ANN, physician; b. Richamond Ctr., Wis., Aug. 1, 0148; d. John Thomas and Mildred (Fox) LeVake; 1 child, Stacey Lynn. Postgrad., U. Wis., 1964; student, St. Xavier Coll., 1974, Chgo. Coll., 1978. Family physician Walter E. Olson Clinic, St. Germain, Wis., 1979-81; assoc. dir. of emergency medicine Louise Bung Hosp., Chgo., 1981-83; family physician Family Doctor, Phoenix, 1983-85; medical dir. & founder Ariz. Wellness Inst., Sun City; profl. advisory panel, Blue Cross Blue Shield of Wis., Eagle River, 1980-81; physician advisory panel Humana Health Plan, Phoenix, Ariz., 1988--. Team physician, H L Richards High Sch., Oaklawn, Ill., 1976-79, Eagle River Falcons Hockey Team, Wis., 1979-81; U.S. Men's Nat. Hockey Tournament, Eagle River, Wis., 1980. mem. Am. Osteopathic Assn., Ariz. Osteopathic Assn., Am. Coll. of Osteopathic Gen. Practice, Am. Geriatrics Soc., Northwest C. of C. Republican. Roman Catholic. Home: Ariz Wellness Inst 12301 W Bell Rd B106 Sun City AZ 85374

GOODMAN, BRENDA JOYCE, management consultant; b. Allentown, Pa., Jan. 30, 1955; d. Donald Baer and Jane Joyce (Rubenstein) Goodman. AB, Smith Coll., 1975; JD, Columbia Law Sch., 1978. Assoc. Coudert Brothers, N.Y., 1978-82; internat. attorney PepsiCo., Purchase, N.Y., 1982-83; pres. Evolutionary Strategies, Inc., N.Y., 1985--; adjunct prof. Coll. Human Services, N.Y., 1988--; bd. trustees Community Svc. Soc., Stamp Out AIDS; chmn. Community Svc. Soc. Empowerment Inst. Contbr. articles to jours. Campaign mgr. Judge Angela Mazzarelli, 1985. Mem. Bus. Profl. Women, Nat. Women's Pol. Caucus, Nat. Ogrn. Women, Women's City Club, World Future Soc.

GOODMAN, CAROL ROSLYN, family therapist; b. N.Y.C., Nov. 30, 1950; d. Bernard N. and Shirley (Greenberg) Hirshfield; m. Stephen R. Goodman, Aug. 15, 1971; children: Audra, Dena, Julie. BA, Hunter Coll., 1972; MA, New Sch. for Social Rsch., 1977; doctoral student, The Fielding Student, Santa Barbara, Calif., 1987—. Psychologist asst. Bernard Fineson Devel. Ctr., Howard Beach, N.Y., 1975-76; counselor Boerum Hill Rehab. Residence, Bklyn., 1976-77; founder, clin. dir. JESPY House, South Orange, N.J., 1978-85; founder Mothers' Ctr. of Cen. N.J., South Plains, 1978-84; founder, dir. Independence Ctr., L.A., 1986—; adj. prof. Montclair State Coll., Upper Montclair, N.J., 1979, 80. Contbr. articles to profl. jours. Mem. steering com. L.A. Coalition for Reproductive Freedom, 1989—. Mem. Am. Psychol. Assn. (assoc.), Learning Disabilities Assn. Office: Independence Center 3640 S Sepulveda Blvd #102 Los Angeles CA 90034

GOODMAN, ELLEN HOLTZ, journalist; b. Newton, Mass., Apr. 11, 1941; d. Jackson Jacob and Edith (Weinstein) Holtz; m. Robert Levey; 1 dau., Katherine Anne. B.A. cum laude, Radcliffe Coll., 1963; hon. degrees, Mt. Holyoke Coll., Amherst Coll., U. Pa., U. N.H. Researcher, reporter Newsweek Mag., 1963-65; feature writer Detroit Free Press, 1965-67; feature writer columnist Boston Globe, 1967-74, assoc. editor, 1986—; syndicated columnist Washington Post Writers Group, 1976—; radio commentator Spectrum, CBS, 1978-80, NBC, 1979-80; commentator NBC Today Show, 1979-81. Author: Close to Home, 1979, Turning Points, 1979, At Large, 1981, Keeping in Touch, 1985, Making Sense, 1989. Trustee Radcliff Coll. Named New Eng. Newspaper Woman of Year New Eng. Press Assn., 1968; recipient Catherine O'Brien award Stanley Home Products, 1971, Media award Mass. Commn. Status Women, 1974, Columnist of Year award New Eng. Women's Press Assn., 1975, Pulitzer Prize for Commentary, 1980, prize for column writing Am. Soc. Newspaper Editors, 1980, Hubert H. Humphrey Civil Rights award, 1988; Nieman fellow Harvard U., 1974. Office: Globe Newspapers Co 135 Morrissey Blvd Boston MA 02107

GOODMAN, GAIL BUSMAN, small business owner; b. N.Y.C., Feb. 8, 1953; d. Irving Laurence and Harriet (Topol) Busman; m. Laurence Goodman, June 17, 1979 (div. 1987). Student, Northwestern U., 1970-72; BS magna cum laude, Tufts U., 1975. Staff occupational therapist St. Joseph's Hosp., Yonkers, N.Y., 1975-77; sr. occupational therapist N.Y. Hosp., White Plains, 1977-79; chief occupational therapist Phelps Hosp., Tarrytown, N.Y., 1979-80; occupational therapy cons. Elmwood Manor Nursing Home, Nanuet, N.Y., 1982-83; v.p. tng. Facelifters, Bklyn., 1981-86; pres. Visual Impact, Rye, N.Y., 1987—, ConsulTel, Rye, 1988—; guest speaker Columbia U., N.Y.C., 1977, 78, 79, 82. Mem. Women In Sales (pres. Westchester chpt. 1989—). Democrat. Jewish.

GOODMAN, GERTRUDE AMELIA, civic worker; b. El Paso, Tex., Oct. 24, 1924; d. Karl Perry and Helen Sylvia (Pinkiert) G. BA, Mills Coll., 1945. Chmn. El Paso chpt. Tex. Social Welfare Assn., 1963-65, bd. dirs., 1965-70; dir. Pan-Am. Round Table El Paso, 1970-71, sec., 1973-74, Texc. PART bd. dirs., 1966—; founder, 1st chmn. El Paso Mus. Art Mems. Guild, 1966-68; bd. dirs. Mus. Art Assn., 1962-69, also v.p.; chmn., dir. El Paso C. of C. Woman's Dept., 1976-77; pres. bd. dirs. El Paso Pub. Libr., 1978-80; pres. El Paso County Hist. Soc., 1981-82, bd. dirs., 1986-87; mem. planning div. El Paso United Way, 1953—, chmn. agy. rels. com.*. Recipient Hall of Honor award El Paso County Hist. Soc., Nat. Human Rels. award NCCJ, 1981, numerous awards for civic vol. work. Home: 905 E Cincinnati Ave El Paso TX 79902

GOODMAN, LILA VIDA, teacher; b. Bklyn., Nov. 15, 1934; d. Abraham John and Martha (LeWinter) Silverman; m. Harold Ralph Sandler (div. 1977); children: Elisa Sandler Shafran, Pamela Sandler Greenbaum, Adam; m. Gerald Goodman, 1984. BA, Bklyn. Coll., 1955; MA, L.I. U., 1976. Cert. tchr., N.Y. Tchr. English John Dewey High Sch., 1955-57, 63—. Home: 977 E 80th St 2 Brooklyn NY 11236

GOODMAN, MARGUERITE RUTH, lawyer; b. Bklyn.; d. Samuel S. and Minnie (Blechschmidt) G.; children: Katherine Petty, Ethan Petty. BA, CUNY, 1961; postgrad., Oxford U., Eng., 1961; MA, Cornell U., 1963; JD, Dickinson Sch. Law, 1978. Bar: Pa. 1978, U.S. Dist. Ct. (ea. dist.) Pa. 1978, U.S. Ct. Appeals (3d cir.) 1979, U.S. Supreme Ct. 1988. Assoc. Pepper, Hamilton & Scheetz, Phila., 1978-81; ptnr. Kohn, Savett, Klein & Graf, P.C., Phila., 1986—; asst. city solicitor Phila. Law Dept., 1981, dep. city solicitor, 1981-83, div. dep. city solicitor, 1984-86; Won 1st Pl. Nat. Moot Ct. Competition, 1977. Mem. ABA, Phila. Bar Assn. Office: Kohn Savett Klein & Graf PC 1101 Market St 24th Floor Philadelphia PA 19107

GOODMAN, PATTI FRIEDLANDER, marketing executive; b. Newark, Apr. 4, 1955; d. Sol Louis and Shirley (Cohen) Friedlander; m. Robert Stewart Goodman, Feb. 26, 1977. BA magna cum laude, Georgetown U., 1977; MBA summa cum laude, Rutgers U., Newark, 1979. Employment supr. Kelly Svcs. Inc., Newark, 1977-78; market rsch. asst. Supermarkets Gen., Woodbridge, N.J., 1979; mktg. rsch. analyst Campbell Soup Co., Camden, N.J., 1980-8l, sr. market rsch. analyst, 198l, asst. mktg. mgr. beverage new products, 198l-83, mktg. mgr. beverages, 1983-85, sr. mktg. mgr. LeMenu Light Style, 1986-87, dir. mktg. Premium Meals, 1987—; dir. mktg. Traditional Meals, 1989—; mktg. cons.; guest lectr. Cherry Hill (N.J.) C. of C., SBA, 1989. Mem. NAFE, Beta Gamma Sigma. Democrat. Jewish. Home: 6 Oak Tree Ct Westampton NJ 08060 Office: Campbell Soup Co Campbell Pl Camden NJ 08101

GOODMAN, ROBIN FERN, therapist, psychologist, educator; b. Hartford, Conn., Dec. 3, 1955; d. Morris and Sarah Frances (Buchman) G. BA magna cum laude, Smith Coll., 1977; MA in Art Therapy, NYU, 1979; PhD in Clin. Psychology, Adelphi U., 1989. Tchg. asst. Smith Coll., 1976-77, Adelphi U., 1986-88; art therapist Edwin Gould Svcs., Bronx, N.Y., 1979-80, Bronx (N.Y.) Children's Psychiat. Hosp., 1979-82; child life specialist Mt. Sinai Hosp., N.Y.C., 1982-85; psychology clk. Interfaith Hosp., Bklyn., 1985-86; cons. Sheltering Arms, N.Y.C., 1987; instr. ADEG, Torino, Italy, 1988; intern Bellevue Hosp., N.Y.C., 1988-89; psychologist NYU Med. Ctr., N.Y.C., 1989—; adj. assoc. prof. NYU, 1982—; adj. faculty Vt. Coll., 1985—; vis. instr. A.D.E.G., Torino, Italy, 1988; acting dir. grad. art therapy program NYU, 1990. Exhibited graphics in group shows, 1974-79; published in field. Recipient rsch. prize Adelphi U., 1990. Mem. Am. Art Therapy Assn. (membership chmn. 1981-85, pres.-elect 1989—), N.Y. Art Therapy Assn. (bd. dirs., membership chmn. 1978-80, chmn. govt. affairs 1979-83), Phi Beta Kappa, Psi Chi.

GOODMAN, VALERIE DAWSON, psychiatric social worker; b. Bluefield, W.Va., Feb. 2, 1948; d. Francis Carl and Lesly (Collett) Dawson; m. David William Goodman, June 9, 1985; 1 child, Amanda Lynn. BS, W.Va. U., 1970, MS, 1972; MSW, U. Md., 1980. Lic. social worker. Social worker Md. Children's Aide Family Svcs. Soc., Balt., 1972-78; social worker III Montgomery County Dept. Social Svcs., Rockville, Md., 1980-81; clin. social worker Johns Hopkins Hosp., Balt., 1981-83; pvt. practice Balt., 1986—; supr. Johns Hopkins Hosp., 1983-86, chair Brogden com., 1984-85. Speaker in field. Mem. Kappa Delta. Home: 64 Hamlet Dr Owings Mills MD 21117

GOODNIGHT, MARIE LOUISE, retired biology educator; b. Blue Island, Ill., Aug. 27, 1916; d. Rudolph W. and Louise Sophia (Blatt) Ostendorf; m. Clarence J. Goodnight, Aug. 25, 1940 (dec.); m. Anne Marie Goodnight Bachnowski, Charles James. BS, Kans. State U., 1938; MS, U. Ill., 1939. Asst. in zoology U. Ill., Champaign, 1938-39; instr. biology Purdue U., West Lafayette, Ind., 1946-49, 58-65; ret., 1965. Co-author: Zoology, 1954, 2d edit., 1964, Biology, 1962; contbr. articles on taxonomy, distbn. and life histories of opiliones to sci. jours. Bd. dirs. Mich. Children's Aid Soc., Kalamazoo, 1968-70; com. mem. YWCA, Kalamazoo, 1989—; vol. Planned Parenthood, Kalamazoo, 1989—. Travel grantee Am. Philos. Soc., Chiapas, Mex., 1950. Mem. Am. Arachnological Soc., Am. Micros. Soc., Assn. for Tropical Biology, Am. Inst. Biol. Scis., AAUW (pres. Kalamazoo 1979-83, grantee 1968), Sigma Xi (travel grantee 1956), Phi Kappa Phi. Democrat. Unitarian. Home: 1633 Chevy Chase Blvd Kalamazoo MI 49008

GOODNOW, WILMA ELIZABETH, software publishing company executive, consultant; b. Lafayette, Ind., Jan. 2, 1944; d. Charles Hillis and Florence Elizabeth (Keirn) Rush; m. James Dorn Goodnow, June 11, 1966; 1 child, Charles James. BSME, Ind. U., 1965, BS in Mgmt., 1966; M in Music, U. Mich., 1968; EdD in Adult Edn., No. Ill. U., 1980; MS in Mktg., Ga. State U., 1983. Asst. prof. Millikin U., Decatur, Ill., 1980-81; asst. to v.p. Ga. Inst. Tech., Atlanta, 1982; pres. Bradley U./Market ACTION Rsch. Software Inc., Peoria, Ill., 1984—; account assoc. Winona Market Research Bur., Phoenix, 1986; mem. faculty Am. Grad. Sch. Internat. Mgmt., Glendale, Ariz., 1986-87; cons. Coca Cola USA, Atlanta, 1984, Advanced Research Corp., Tokyo, 1984-87, City Group, Atlanta, 1984, Nat. Linen Service, Atlanta, 1985. Author statis. software MAPWISE 2.01; contbr. articles to profl. jours. Reader 1st Ch. of Christ Scientist, Wheaton, Ill., 1979; concertmistress Scottsdale (Ariz.) Community Coll., 1987; bd. dirs. Paradise Valley Community Coll., Phoenix, 1987. Mem. Mensa, Beta Gamma Sigma, Phi Kappa Lambda. Republican. Home: 6421 N Post Oak Rd Peoria IL 61615 Office: Market ACTION Rsch Software Inc Clarendon Arms Ste 21 16 W 501 58th St Chicago IL 60514-1740

GOODRICH, GLORIA JEAN, federal agency administrator; b. Lima, Ohio, Feb. 21, 1934; d. Orville John and Lila Mae (Rigel) Mortimer; m. Merlin Virgil Goodrich, June 6, 1953; children: Sandra Kay, Gregory Lynn, Geoffrey Virgil. Student, Owosso Coll., 1952-55, 67-68, Muskegon (Mich.) Community Coll., 1971-73. Cert. legal asst., 1988. Estimator E.H. Sheldon & co., Muskegon, 1975-77; dep. clk. U.S. Fed. Ct., Tucson, 1977-81, supr., 1982—. Tchr. ch. sch., Ohio, Mich., Ariz., 1950—; leader Boy Scouts Am. and Girl Scouts U.S., Mich., 1966-71; mem. Tucson Clean and Beautiful. Mem. Ariz. Assn. for Ct. Mgmt., Tucson Assn. Legal Assts., Nat. Assn. for Female Execs. Avocations: walking, reading, sewing, teaching, needlework.

GOOD-SEPT, MARCIA KAY, attorney; b. Webster City, Iowa, Apr. 27, 1962; d. George Gerald and Faye Joann (Simms) Good; m. Darrell Lee Sept, June 14, 1980. AA, Dawson Comm. Coll., 1984; BS, Eastern Montana Coll., 1986; JD, U. Colo., 1989. Program asst. McCone County ASCS, Circle, Mont., 1980-84; primary caregiver Oakmont Daycare, Billings, Mont., 1984-86; law clerk Hill and Robbins PC, Denver, Colo., 1987-89; treas. Women's Law Caucus, Boulder, 1987-88. Interviewer, Legal Aid and Defender Clinic, Boulder, 1986-87, Volunteer, Boulder County Legal Services, 1987-88, Boulder County Safehouse, 1986-87, mem. Big Brothers and Sisters, Billings, 1984-86. Mem. ABA, Colo. Bar Assn., Phi. Alpha Delta. Democrat.

GOODSON, CAROLE EDITH MCKISSOCK, technology educator; b. Des Moine, Dec. 31, 1946; d. William Thompson and Edith (Johnson) McKissock; m. Robert Wayne Peterson, July 1978; 1 son, David Shelby Peterson. B.S., U. Houston, 1968, M.Ed., 1971, Ed.D., 1975. Tchr., Spring Branch Ind. Sch. Dist., Houston, 1968-69; mem. faculty Coll. Tech., U. Houston, 1972—, instr., 1972-75, asst. prof., coll. counselor, 1975-78, assoc. prof., coll. counselor, 1978-81, assoc. prof., chmn. related courses tech., 1981—, assoc. dean, assoc. prof. tech. math., 1982—; prof., 1988. Author: (with S.L. Miertschin) Technical Mathematics With Applications, 1983, 2d edit., 1986; Technical Mathematics with Calculus, 1985; Technical Algebra with Applications, 1985, Technical Trigonometry with Applications, 1985; contbr. articles to publs. Recipient Dow Outstanding Young Faculty award Am. Soc. Engring. Edn., 1982. Mem. Am. Soc. Engring. Edn. (vice chmn. 1985-86, chmn. 1987-89, sec.-treas. div. 1982-84, regional chair 1982-83, bd. dirs. 1989—), Nat. Coun. Tchrs. Math., Math. Assn. Am., Phi Kappa Phi (chpt. pres. 1985), Tex. Assn. of Sch. Engring. Tech. (sec. 1986—). Presbyterian. Office: U Houston Coll Tech 361-T2 Houston TX 77004

GOODSON, LINDA JANE KLECKLEY, educator; b. Lexington, S.C., Dec. 31, 1942; d. Walter A. and Alma (Keisler) Kleckley; 1 child, George A. BA, Newberry (S.C.) Coll., 1965; MEd, U. S.C., 1982, PhD, 1988. Child care caseworker Dept. Social Svcs., Greenville, S.C., 1965-67; tchr. Lexington Sch. Dist. 2, Cayce, S.C., 1967-73; tchr./adminstr. Lexington Sch. Dist. 1, 1973-84; dir. field experiences for elementary edn. Columbia (S.C.) Bible Coll. and Sem., 1984—; cons. spelling textbook series Assn. Christian Sch. Internat., 1989-90. Mem. Assn. Early Childhood Edn. Internat., Assn. Supervision and Curriculum Devel., S.C. Assn. Supervision and Curriculum Devel. Republican. Evangelical Ch. Home: 130 Stubblefield Lexington SC 29073 Office: Columbia Bible College PO Box 3122 Columbia SC 29230

GOODSPEED, BARBARA, artist; b. Gardner, Mass., Sept. 1, 1919; d. George Daniel and Bernice (Lucas) G. Diploma Stoneleigh Coll., 1939, Famous Artist Schs., Westport, Conn., 1955. Free-lance photographer, N.Y.C., 1941-52, Christmas card designer, Sherman, Conn., 1952-69, oil and watercolor, fine arts artist, Sherman, 1969—. Illustrator: Forever Flowers, 1979. Recipient Merit award Sheffield Art League, 1979, 81, 83, others; named Artist of Yr., Art League of Harlem Valley, 1981. Fellow Am. Artists Profl. League (John Dole Meml. award); mem. Salmagundi Club, Hudson Valley Art Assn., Acad. Artists, Nat League Am. Pen Women, Kent Art Assn., Inc. (pres. 1970-72, 80-83, 85-88, medal of Merit 1979, Grumbacher Gold medal 1988), Berkshire Watercolor Soc. (co-founder, sec. 1984—, Edgar A. Whitney award 1989), Housatonic Art League (v.p., bd. dirs. 1977-83). Avocations: camping, crafts. Home and Studio: Holiday Point Rd PO Box 406 Sherman CT 06784

GOODSTEIN, JEANETTE TREAT, consultant; b. Wooster, Ohio, Nov. 6, 1940; d. Ralph Baldwin and Eloise Rae (Wyman) Treat; m. Leonard D. Goodstein, Aug. 28, 1972. BA with honors, Coll. Wooster, 1962; MA, Tufts U., 1963; PhD, Ariz. State U., 1983. Mgmt. intern NASA, Washington, 1963-64; program mgr. Peace Corps, Washington, 1965-70, OEO, Washington, 1971-72; cons. faculty social medicine Vrije Univ., Amsterdam, The Netherlands, 1972-73; program dir. Ctr. Pub. Affairs, Tempe, 1974-79; exec. dir. Soc. Rsch. Child Devel., Washington, 1986-89; cons. Cin., San Diego, 1973-74, 80-85, Washington, 1990—; cons. Cathay Pacific Airways, LTD, Hong Kong, 1989—, Human Interaction Rsch. Inst., L.A., 1989—, various fgn. and domestic orgns., 1971—. Author: Explorations in Behavior, Motivation and Adjustment, 1975; editor: the Rural Poor: Unseen by Policymakers, 1978; contbr. articles to profl. jours. Mem. City of Poway (Calif.) Citizens Budget com., 1980; chmn. art show com. and mem. govt. com. San Diego Women's Opportunity Week, 1985. Recipient Faculty Women's Assn. scholarship Ariz. State U., 1977. Mem. Am. Psychol. Assn., Soc. for Rsch. in Child Devel., Am. Polit. Sci. Assn., Am. Soc. Pub. Adminstrn. (bd. dirs. Phoenix chpt., 1975-77), Phi Alpha Theta. Democrat. Presbyterian. Office: 1737 S St NW Washington DC 20009

GOODSTEIN, MADELINE PRAGER, science consultant; b. N.Y.C., Oct. 23, 1920; d. Julius and Henrietta (Goldfarb) Prager; m. Julian Goodstein, Jan. 12, 1947; children: Elaine Goodstein Robinson, Barbara, Ronald. BA, Bklyn. Coll., 1941; MS in Chemistry, Poly. Inst. N.Y., 1948; EdD in Chemistry, Columbia U., 1968. Chemist Trubek Labs., East Rutherford, N.J., 1941-49; lectr. Bklyn. Coll., 1959-62; part time asst. prof. U. Hartford, West Hartford, Conn., 1963-64; asst. prof. Cen. Conn. State U., New Britain, 1967-71, assoc. prof., 1971-77, prof., 1977-83; dir. Sci-Math Project, North Haven, Conn., 1983-87; cons. Sci-Math Project, San Francisco, 1987—. Author: Sci-Math Modules, 2 vols., 1983, Numbers in Science, 1987, (with M.V. Orna) Introduction to the Chemistry and Technology of Color, 1977; contbr. articles to profl. publs. Grantee NSF, 1972, 77-82, Nat. Diffusion Network, U.S. Dept. Edn., 1983-87; recipient Outstanding Educators Am. award, 1973, cert. of merit U.S. Dept. Edn., 1982. Mem. Am. Chem. Soc., New Eng. Assn. Chemistry Tchrs. (pres. 1979-81, hon. mem.), Conn. Sci. Tchrs. Assn. (cert. appreciation 1982, 83), Nat. Sci. Tchrs. Assn. (chmn. various coms., life), Textbook Authors Assn. Jewish. Home and Office: 6 Woodland Dr Woodbridge CT 06525

GOODSTONE, ROSEMARY ANN, photographer; b. Wauwatosa, Wis., Feb. 2, 1947; d. Mary Ann (Bielicki) Fryt; m. Alan M. Goodstone, Nov. 27, 1968; 1 child, Julie R. Grad. high sch., Franklin, Wis. Receptionist, bookkeeper Family Fin., Milw., 1966-67; credit investigator Mortgage Assocs., Milw., 1967-68; sec., word processor IBM Corp., Milw., 1968-73; color artist Goodstone Candids, Franklin, Wis., 1974-84; photographer Goodstone Photography, Franklin, 1984—. Mem. Franklin Sch. Bd. Coms., 1982—; leader Girl Scouts U.S.A., Franklin, 1985; bd. dirs. Childbirth Edn. Assn., Milw., 1973-78; pres., bd. dirs. Parent Tchr. Orgn., Milw. and Franklin, 1978-85. Mem. Profl. Photographers Am., Wis. Profl. Photographer's Assn. (membership svcs. 1988—, restraint trade com. 1988—, bd. dirs. 1989—, Scholarship 1987, Cert. Appreciation 1989), Southeastern Wis. Profl. Photographer's Assn. (editor newsletter 1990, reservations chair, program chair Milw. chpt. 1989—, membership chairperson 1988-89, print co-chairperson 1987-88, recipient competition ribbons), Wis. Bus. and Profl. Women. Roman Catholic. Office: 7121 B S 76th St Franklin WI 53132

GOODWILL, MARGARET JANE, artist; b. L.A., Sept. 27, 1950; d. David and Erna Pauline (Kremser) G.; m. James Vincent Erickson, Sept. 6, 1980. Student, U. Calif., Santa Barbara, 1968-70; BFA cum laude, Calif. Coll. Arts and Crafts, 1972. Graphic artist Proarts, Oakland, Calif., 1970-71; creative art dir. Am. Analysis Corp., San Francisco, 1974-76; dir. Lone Wolf Gallery, San Francisco, 1982-84; prin., artist Calif. and Hawaii, 1984—. One-woman show Lone Wolf Gallery, 1985, Wrubel Gallery, Berkeley, Calif., 1988; two-woman show St. Mary's Coll., Moraga, Calif., 1973; exhibited in group shows San Francisco Art Festival, 197l, 72, A Gallery, Palm Desert, Calif., 1986, Banaker Gallery, Walnut Creek, Calif., 1988; mural for Prevention Cruelty to Animals Hdqrs., San Francisco, 1980. Recipient lst prize Ossining (N.Y.) Women's Club, 1968, Poughkeepsie (N.Y.) Art Ctr., 1968, merit award Delta Art Show, Antioch, Calif., 197l; N.Y. State Regent's scholar, 1968, Walnut Creek Civic Arts scholar, 1970. Mem. Calif. Coll. Arts and Crafts Alumni Assn., Oakland Mus., Mus. Modern Art San Francisco, Nat. Geog. Soc., Smithsonian Assocs.

GOODWIN, BARBARA, nurse, military officer; b. Phila., Dec. 23, 1938. Diploma, Boston City Hosp. Sch. Nursing, 1959; BS, U. Pa., 1968; MS, U. Colo., 1972; grad., Sq. Officer Sch., 1973, Air Command & Staff Coll., 1974, Air War Coll., 1977. Commd. officer USAF, advanced through ranks to brig. gen., 1988, nurse, 1962—; staff nurse USAF, Otis AFB, Mass.; clinic nurse USAF, Naha AFB, Okinawa, Japan, 1963-65; clinic staff nurse USAF Hosp., Minot AFB, N.D., from 1965; flight nurse Aeromed. Evacuation, Rhein-Mein AFB, Frankfurt, Fed. Republic Germany, 1968-71; charge nurse USAF Med. Ctr., Scott AFB, Ill., 1972-73, asst. for nursing svcs., Hdqrs. Mil. Airlift Command, 1984-88; clin. nurse specialist Malcolm Grow USAF Med. Ctr., Andrews AFB, Md., 1973-74, coord. surg. nursing practice, from 1974; asst. chief nurse USAF Regional Hosp., Lakenheath, Eng., 1977-79; adminstrv. staff officer Office of Chief Air Force Nurse Corps, Bolling AFB, D.C., 1979-83; chmn. dept. nursing David Grant USAF Med. Ctr., Travis AFB, Calif., 1983-84; chief USAF Nurses Corps, Office of Surgeon Gen. USAF Hdqrs., Washington, 1988—. Decorated Legion of Merit with one oak leaf cluster. Mem. ANA, Aerospace Med. Assn., Assn. Mil. Surgeons of U.S., Air Force Assn., Sigma Theta Tau. Office: USAF Surgeon Gen Bldg 5681 Bolling AFB Washington DC 20332-6188*

GOODWIN, BRENDA GAYLE, marketing professional, insurance company executive; b. Chattanooga, Tenn., July 19, 1954; d. Claude and Jesse Marie (Cleghorn) Lasley; m. William Stanley Goodwin,. Student, Carson Newman Coll., 1973. V.p. mktg. AGA, Inc., Chattanooga, Tenn., 1974-84; mkgt. office mgr. Ins. Inc., Cleve., 1984-87; asst. v.p., mktg. mgr. Alexander & Alexander, Chattanooga, 1987--; instr. Ins. Women, Chattanooga, 1987--. Mem. Insurors Chattanooga, Soc. CPCU, Soc. CIC. Republican. Baptist. Office: Alexander & Alexander Osborne Office Ctr Ste 403 Chattanooga TN 37411

GOODWIN, ELIZABETH TANNER, dentist, researcher; b. Biddeford, Maine, May 15, 1957; d. Charles Victor and Shirley (Mewer) Tanner; m. Kurt Joseph Goodwin, July 5, 1980; children: Sarah Joy, Megan Elizabeth, Michael Patrick. BA in Zoology and BS in Chem. Engring., U. Maine, 1979; DMD, Tufts U., 1982. Researcher USPHS/Tufts U., Boston, 1979-82; gen. practice dentistry USPHS, Unalhaven, Maine, 1982-85; researcher USPHS, Boston, 1985—; dentist Dr. Norman Rogers, Methven, Mass., 1986—; research task team Pub. Health Service, Boston, 1986—; educator dentistry Mass. Edn. Dept., Georgetown, Mass., 1986—. Organizer Hotline: Rape, Suicide, Drugs, Alcohol, Orono, 1977-79, Adopt-a-Grandparent, Groveland, Mass., 1985—; pres. Health Council, Vinalhaven, 1983, 84-85; mem., sec. Mothers Against Drunk Driving, Georgetown, 1985—; mem. Mothers Against Nuclear War, Boston, 1986—. Mem. ADA, Am. Acad. Gen. Dentists, Acad. of Women Dentists (Woman Dentist of Yr. 1983-85), Mass. Dental Soc. of Merrimac Valley, Phi Beta Kappa, Phi Kappa Phi. Presbyterian. Club: Young Profls. with Children (Georgetown) (sec. 1985-86, pres. 1986—0. Lodge: Order of Eastern Star (Worthy Assoc. Matron 1983-85). Home: PO Box 193 Groveland MA 01834

GOODWIN, JEAN MCCLUNG, psychiatrist; b. Pueblo, Colo., Mar. 28, 1946; d. Paul Stanley and Geraldine (Smart) McClung; m. James Simeon Goodwin, Aug. 8, 1970; children: Laura (dec.), Amanda Harding Goodwin, Robert Caleb, Paul Joshua, Elizabeth Cronin Goodwin. BA in Anthropology summa cum laude, Radcliffe Coll., 1967; MD, Harvard U., 1971; MPH, UCLA, 1972. Diplomate Am. Bd. Psychiatry and Neurology, Am. Bd. Forensic Psychiatry. Resident in psychiatry Georgetown U. Hosp., 1972-74, U. N.Mex. Medicine, 1974-76; asst. dir., dir. psychiatric residents tng. U. N.Mex., 1979-85; prof. Med. Coll. Wis., 1985—; from inst. to assoc. prof. dept. psychiatry U. N.Mex. Sch. Medicine, 1976-85; cons. protective services Dept. Human Services, N.Mex., 1976-84; lectr. profl. groups. Author: (book) Effects of Hight Altitude on Human Birth, 1969, Sexual Abuse: Incest Victims and their Families, 1982, 2d edit. 1989; editorial bd. Jour. Psychosocial Stress, 1985—; contbr. numerous articles on child abuse to profl. jours. Chmn. work group on child sexual abuse Surgeon Gen.'s Violence and Pub. Health, Leesburg, Va., 1985. Recipient Saville Prize in Family Planning, UCLA Sch. Pub. Health, 1972, Esther Haar award Am. Acad. Psychoanalysis, 1990; Nat. Cen. Child Abuse and Neglect grantee, 1979-82, Nat. Inst. Aging grantee, 1980-85. Fellow Am. Psychiat. Assn. (dist. br. treas., sec. N.Mex. br. 1980-82, exhibits and programs subcoms. 1985—), Internat. Soc. Study Multiple Personality Dissociative Disorders (child abuse liason com. 1984), Am. Profl. Soc. Sexual Abuse Children (bd. dirs. 1986-90), Am. Med. Women's Assn. (state dir. 1978-80),. Democrat.

Roman Catholic. Home: 4015 N Lake Dr Milwaukee WI 53211 Office: Milw County Mental Health Complex 9455 Watertown Plank Rd Milwaukee WI 53226

GOODWIN, MARYELLEN, state legislator; b. Providence, Sept. 27, 1964. Student, R.I. Coll. mem. 12th Ward Dem. Com., R.I. Young Dems. Mem. state senate State of R.I., 1986—. Roman Catholic. Home: 325 Smith St Providence RI 02908 Office: R I State Senate Providence RI 02903*

GOODWIN, MIMI KATE MUNROE, office manager, singer; b. N.Y.C., Oct. 14, 1956; d. William Raymond and Silvia Virginia (Saydah) Munroe; m. William Bartley Goodwin, Mar. 7, 1986; children: Caitlin, Alexander. BA, U. So. Maine, 1980; MA, Aaron Copland Sch. of Music, Queens, N.Y., 1986. Office mgr. J.V.L. Assocs. Inc., New York, NY, 1985--. Mem. Am. Guild of Musical Artists, Natl. Assn. of Female Execs. Office: JVL Assoc Inc 1360 York Ave New York NY 10021

GOODWIN, PEGGY JANE, psychologist, consultant; b. Newton, Mass., Feb. 24, 1954; d. Delmar W. Goodwin and Tensie (Lovejoy) Cahill; m. Christopher J. Kiepper, Apr. 1, 1989; 1 child, Eamon. BA, Syracuse (N.Y.) U., 1976; MA, Tex. Tech. U., 1980; D in Psychology, Antioch/N.E. Grad. Sch., 1988. Lic. psychologist, N.H., Vt. After-care worker VA Day Treatment Ctr., Syracuse, 1975-76; psychometrist Goodwill Industries, Lubbock, Tex., 1977; counselor Rape Crisis Ctr., Lubbock, 1977; prin. psychologist Belchertown (Mass.) State Sch., 1980-81; pub. guardian Office of the Pub. Guardian, Concord, N.H., 1982-83; habilitation specialist Upper Valley Devel. & Tng. Ctr., Lebanon, N.H., 1984; behavioral medicine therapist Dartmouth Med. Sch., Hanover, N.H., 1985-89; pvt. practice clin. psychologist Norwich, Vt., 1989—; cons. psychologist Mt. Ascutney Psychiat. Assocs., Windsor, Vt., 1989—. Anderson Swenson Meml. scholar Tex. Tech U., 1976; Disting. Grad. Student award N.H. Psychol. Orgn., 1989. Mem. Am. Psychol. Assn., Assn. for the Advancement of Behavior Therapy. Home and Office: RFD 1 Box 9 East Thetford VT 05043

GOODWIN, ROSANNE, photographic sales official; b. San Diego, July 21, 1954; d. Donald Ira and Beverly (Stern) G. AB in Am. Social History, U. Calif., Berkeley, 1976; MA History Mus. Studies, Cooperstown Grad. Program, 1977. Grad. intern Colo. Hist. Soc., Denver, 1977-78; gen. mgr. Photo Imports Camera Exchange, San Diego, 1978-84; sales rep. Satter, Inc., Denver, 1985—. Author: The Coloradoans, 1978. Vol. Denver Art Mus., 1987-88; bd. dirs. Rocky Mountain Golden Bears, 1990. Nat. Mus. Act fellow, 1977-78. Mem. Photog. Mktg. Assn., Children of Photog. Industry (founder), Colo. Women Photog.-Video Reps. (pres. 1988). Democrat. Office: Satter Inc 4100 Dahlia St Denver CO 80207

GOODYEAR, HOLLY SUE, accounting administrator; b. Cleve., Dec. 19, 1942; d. Martin Henry and Marie Louise (Waite) Barabas; m. William A. Goodyear, Sept. 14, 1963 (div. July 1980). BA, Heidelberg Coll., 1963. Cost analyst U.S. Steel Corp., Lorain, Ohio, 1963-74, systems analyst, programmer, 1974-83, analyst rods and wire div., 1983-84, staff supr., acctg. and analysis tubular, 1984-87; supr. gen. acctg. appropriation control and accounts payable USX Corp., Lorain, 1987-89; coord. acctg. systems USS/Kobe Steel Co. (merger with USX Corp. and Kobe Steel), Lorain, 1989—; mem. Lorain City Schs. Acctg. and Computing Adv. Com., 1990—. Mem. Cleve. Pub. Radio Community Adv. Bd., 1984—, sec. 1989—. Mem. NAFE, Ohio Fedn. Bus. and Profl. Women (pres. 1988-89, trustee Ohio Florence Allen Endowment Fund 1988—, Ohio Retirement Living Found. 1986-90), U.S. Steel/Kobe Assocs. Club. Republican. Methodist. Office: USS/Kobe Steel Co 1807 E 28th St Lorain OH 44256

GOOGINS, SONYA FORBES, banker; b. New Haven, Nov. 9, 1936; d. Edward and Madeline Forbes; m. Robert Reville Googins, June 21, 1958; children: Shawn W. and Glen. R. BE, U. Conn., 1958; postgrad., Dartmouth Inst., 1978. Tchr. Manchester (Conn.) High Sch., 1958-61, Creative Nursery Sch., Glastonbury, Conn.; pres. Colonial Printing Co., Glastonbury, 1971-76; sales mgr. Glastonbury Stationers, 1977-81; br. mgr., lending officer to bank officer Conn. Nat. Bank, Hartford, 1982-89. Mayor Town of Glastonbury, 1983-85, 87-91; coun. mem. and majority leader Town Coun., 1979—; active Econ. Devel. Commn., Youth Svcs. Commn., LWV, Rep. Town Coms.; active policy bd. Capitol Region Coun. Govts., Hartford, 1983-85, 87-89, treas., 1987—, chmn. 1989-91. Recipient Outstanding Service award Friends of Glastonbury Youth, 1985. Mem. Glastonbury Bus. and Profl. Women (past pres. and founder, Woman of Yr. 1986), Glastonbury C. of C. (bd. dirs. 1975-80), Hartford Women's Network. Roman Catholic. Club: Glastonbury Jr. Woman's (past pres.). Home: 74 Forest Ln Glastonbury CT 06033

GOOLKASIAN, PAULA A., psychologist, educator; b. Methuen, Mass., Aug. 9, 1948; d. Paul K. and Sadie T. (Touma) G.; m. Francis C. Martin, July 29, 1978; 1 child, Christopher. BA, Emmanuel Coll., 1970; MS, Iowa State U., 1972, PhD, 1974. Asst. prof. U. N.C., Charlotte, 1974-79, assoc. prof., 1979-85, prof. psychology, 1985—, pres. faculty, 1989—; cons. in field. Contbr. articles to profl. jours. Nat. Def. Ednl. Act. fellow, 1971-74; grantee NSF, NIH, and numerous others. Mem. AAAS, Am. Psychol. Assn., Psychonomics Soc., Eastern Psychol. Assn., Internat. Soc. Psychophysics., Soc. Computers in Psychology (sec., treas. 1989-91), Sigma Xi, Phi Kappa Phi. Home: 7107 Preston Ct Charlotte NC 28215 Office: U NC Dept Psychology Charlotte NC 28223

GOOREY, NANCY JANE, dentist; b. Davenport, Iowa, May 8, 1922; d. Edgar Ray and Glenna Mae (Williams) Miller; m. Douglas B. Miller, Sept. 12, 1939 (div. 1951); children: Victoria Lee, Nikola Ellen, Douglas George, Melahna Marie; m. Louis Joseph Roseberry, Feb. 22, 1980. Student, Wooster (Ohio) Coll., 1939-40; DDS, Ohio State U., 1955, cert. dentistry, 1955-56. Mem. faculty coll. dentistry Ohio State U., Columbus, 1955-86, dir., chmn. div. dental hygiene coll. dentistry, 1969-86, asst. dean coll. dentistry, 1975-86, mem. grad. faculty colls. dentistry and medicine, 1980—, asst. dean, prof. emeritus colls. dentistry and medicine, 1986—; moderator, prodn. chmn. Lifesavers 35 Prodns, 1981—. Producer, video program Giving Your Mouth a Sporting Chance, 1990. Chmn. State Planning Com. for Health Edn. in Ohio, Columbus, 1976-77, 87-88; founder, chmn. Coun. on Health Info., Columbus, 1981-85, pres., 1985-86; trustee Mayor's Drug Edn. and Prevention Program, Columbus, 1990—. Named Nancy Goorey Vol. of Yr., Columbus Health Dept., 1988-89; recipient Nancy Goorey Dental Hygiene award Ohio State U., Columbus, 1988. Fellow Am. Coll. Dentists (pres.-elect 1989-90), Am. Soc. Dental Anesthesiology, Internat. Coll. Dentists; mem. Am. Assn. Dental Edn. (v.p., pres. 1972-77), ADA (nat. consumer advisor 1975-78), Ohio Dental Assn. (cons. 1979—, Ohio Disting. Dentist 1983), Columbus Dental Soc. (pres. bd. dirs. 1986-87, 89—), Ohio State U. Starling Womens Club (pres. 1982-83), Ohio State U. Faculty and Profl. Women's Club (pres. 1971-72), Omicron Kappa Upsilon (hon.). Republican. Episcopalian. Office: Ohio State U Coll Dentistry 305 W 12th Ave Columbus OH 43210

GOOSMAN, ELEANOR MCKEE, art therapist; b. Fairmont, W. Va., June 8, 1917; d. Cyrus John and Gertrude Gene (Kennedy) McKee; m. (dec. 1986); children: Lynn A. Page, Thomas W. Goosman. BFA, Wright State U., 1984, MAT, 1986. Registered art therapist. Dir. art therapy Villa Fairborn, Ohio, 1986-88; tchr., trainer art therapy interns Wright State U., Dayton, Ohio, 1986-89; dir. art therapy Greenwood Manor, Xenia, Ohio, 1989—, Crystal Manor, Fairborn, 1989—; cons. master of art therapy Villa Springfield, Ohio 1986—. Mem. Am. Art Therapy Assn., Inc., Miami Valley Art Therapy Assn., Buckeye Art Therapy Assn., Wright State Alumni Assn., Chi Sigma Iota., Ea. Star.

GOOTGELD, MARLA, electronics executive; b. Racine, Wis., July 8, 1954; d. Erwin Howard and Betty Jane (Gorsuch) Jacobi; m. Gary Lynn Gootgeld, Sept. 9, 1956; children: Shannon Marie, Jessica Ann. AS in Bus., West Valley Coll., 1974; BSBA, San Jose (Calif.) State U., 1976. Assoc. buyer Nat. Semiconductor, Sunnyvale, Calif., 1979-80; buyer NCR Micrographics, Mountain View, Calif., 1980-82; sr. buyer Calif. Microwave, Inc., Sunnyvale, 1982-87; purchasing mgr. XMR, Inc., Santa Clara, Calif., 1987—. Mem. Am. Prodn. and Inventory Control Soc., Assn. Purchasing Mgmt., Silicon Valley Group Purchasing Mgmt. Assn. Home: 3188 Cyrus Ave San Jose CA 95124 Office: XMR Inc 5403 Betsy Ross Dr Santa Clara CA 95054

GOOTMAN, PHYLLIS MYRNA, educator; b. N.Y.C., June 8, 1938; d. Albert and Ida (Krieger) Adler; m. Norman Gootman, June 1, 1958; children: Sharon Hillary, Craig Seth. BA cum laude, Barnard Coll., 1959; PhD, Yeshiva U., 1967. Research assoc., dept. physiology and biophysics U. Wash., Seattle, 1963; instr., dept. physiology Albert Einstein Coll. of Med., Bronx, N.Y., 1968-70; asst. prof. Albert Einstein Coll. of Med., Bronx, 1970-73; asst. prof. to prof., dept. physiology SUNY, Bklyn., 1973-75, assoc. prof., 1975-81, prof., 1981—; vis. asst. prof. dept. physiology, Albert Einstein Coll. Medicine, Bronx, 1973-76; cons. pediatrics, Schneider Children's Hosp., L.I. Jewish-Hillside Med. Ctr., SUNY, Stony Brook, New Hyde Park, N.Y., 1976—, Clin. Campus Albert Einstein Coll. Med., 1989—, participant in numerous symposia. Contbr. articles to profl. jours.; mem. editorial bd. Jour. of Developmental Physiology, 1986—. Recipient Hendel Family award, Brandeis U., 1957; John Miles Davidson fellow in physiology, Albert Einstein Coll. of Medicine, 1973; recipient numerous grants in field. Mem. AAAS, Soc. for Neurosciences, Biophysical Soc., Am. Physiological Soc., Am. Heart Assn., Am. Inst. Biological Scis., Microcirculatory Soc., Soc. for Experimental Biology and Medicine, Am. Assn. for Lab. Animal Sci., Internat. Soc. for Devel. Neurosciences, Royal Soc. of Medicine. Office: SUNY Health Sci Ctr Bklyn 450 Clarkson Ave Brooklyn NY 11203

GORAN, JUDITH H., data process executive; b. Boston, Mar. 28, 1952; d. Samuel Martin and Rosalind (Kahn) G.; m. Alan R. Gordon, Oct. 7, 1988. BA in Lit., The Am. U., 1973. Asst. buyer Jordan Marsh Co., Boston, 1973-77; sales rep. CFS, Inc., West Roxbury, Mass., 1977-83, Trac Line Software, Hicksville, N.Y., 1983; owner FORMAT, Dedham, Mass., 1984—. Mem. Nat. Bus. Forms Assn. Jewish. Home: 50/56 Broadlawn Pk #508 Chestnut Hill MA 02167 Office: FORMAT 19 Needham St Dedham MA 02026

GORDAN-FELLER, CARLA JANINE, religious psychologist, spiritual educator; b. Nettleton, Ark., July 4, 1936; d. Paul Martin and Corinne (Parrot) Neff; m. Frank Edward Gordan (div. 1975); children: Richard M., Shawn, Deborah; m. Richard A. Feller, 1975. DD, Coll. Divine Metaphysics, 1970, D Divine Metaphysics, 1972, D Religious Psychology, 1974. Assoc. minister Ch. of Universal Light, Staten Island, N.Y., 1972-75; pres. Inst. of Man, Cedar Rapids, Iowa, 1975-79, Gordan and Assocs., Dallas, 1979—; dir. curriculum Peace Valley Retreat Ctr., Caddo Gap, Ark., 1988—; pres. Soc. Universal Love, Dallas, 1988—. Author: The Prayer of Jesus, 1972, Meditation of Masters, 1973, Voice in the Wind, 1974, The Fear Factor, 1975, Benedictions of Life, 1976, A Soul Becoming, 1990; creator, narrator, lectr. audio and video tapes. Mem. Spiritual Frontier Fellowship (life). Office: Soc Universal Love 1407 Braeburn Dr Richardson TX 75082

GORDON, ALICE CLEORA JORDAN, retired educator; b. Overall, Tenn., Sept. 9, 1912; d. Sam Wyatt and Jennie (Williamson) Jordan; widowed, 1961. BS, Agrl. and Indsl. State U., Nashville, 1945; BA, Clark Coll., Atlanta, 1946; MEd, Middle Tenn. State U., 1969. Mem. Nat. Tchrs. Assn., Tenn. Tchrs. Assn., Rutherford County Tchrs. Assn., Nat. Ret. Tchrs. Assn., Tenn. Ret. tchrs. Assn., Rutherford County Ret. Tchrs. Assn. (past pres.), AAUW (life), Tenn. Libr. Assn. (life), Assoc. Country Women's Coun., Country Women's Coun., Nat. Extension Homemakers Coun., Tenn. Extension Homemakers Coun., Rutherford County Extension Homemakers Coun., Holloway Extension Homemakers Club, Gamma Beta Phi. Democrat. Baptist. Home: 610 Johnson St Murfreesboro TN 37130

GORDON, AUDREY KRAMEN, university administrator; b. Chgo., Nov. 18, 1935; d. Edward J. and Anne (Levin) K.; children: Bradley, Dale, Holly. BS with highest distinction, Northwestern U., 1965, MA, 1967, postgrad., 1971; MA, U. Chgo., 1970; postgrad., U. Ill., Chgo., 1988. Cert. in clin. pastoral edn. Lectr. Northwestern U., Evanston, Ill., 1966-74; high sch. dir. Beth Emet Synagogue, Evanston, 1962-77; vis. asst. prof. Beloit (Wis.) Coll., 1974-75; research specialist U. Ill., Chgo., 1983-86, dir. continuing edn., 1986—, lectr., 1989—; coord./counselor Jewish Hospice, Chgo., 1984-89; community prof. Govs. State U., Park Forest South, Ill., 1978-88; lectr. Loyola U. Strich Sch. Medicine, Maywood, Ill., 1982—; pres. Rainbow Hospice, Des Plaines, Ill., 1982-86, bd. dirs.; v.p. Ill. State Hospice Orgn., 1984—, pres. 1989-90; v.p. Hillel Governing bd. U. Ill., Chgo., 1988-89; prof. adv. bd. Horizon Hospice, Chgo, 1978-86. Co-author: They Need To Know: How To Teach Children about Death, 1979. Mem. Am. Pub. Health Assn., Ill. Pub. Health Assn., Assn. for Death Edn. and Counseling (co-chmn. ann. conv. 1983), Alpha Sigma Lambda, Alpha Kappa Lambda. Office: U Ill Sch Pub Health 2121 W Taylor Ave Chicago IL 60612

GORDON, BONNIE HEATHER, writer, editor; b. Phila., Oct. 18, 1952; d. Herman E. and Jean (Twersky) G.; m. Ed Kaplan, Apr. 2, 1978; 1 child, Philip Gordon Kaplan. BA in English, Temple U., 1975. Pub.'s rep. Columbia U. Press, N.Y.C., 1975-76; asst. editor mag. div. Dun-Donnelly Corp., N.Y.C., 1976-78; asst. editor High Times mag. Tixeon Inc., N.Y.C., 1978-79; staff editor Nat. League for Nursing, N.Y.C., 1981-82; freelance writer and editor N.Y.C., Cin., N.J., 1982—. Author: Thus May Be Figured in Numberless Ways, 1985; editor, pub. Sapiens, 1981; writer, producer (documentary video) Which is Why Poetry is Weightlifting, 1990. Mem. bus. and profl. br. Nat. Coun. Jewish Women, 1989-90. Mem. Editorial Freelancers Assn., Women in Communication, Phi Beta Kappa. Jewish.

GORDON, BRENDA CAMP, educator; b. Gainesville, Tex., Aug. 20, 1955; d. Richard O'Daniel and Mary Sue (Riley) C.; m. Charles K. Gordon, Mar. 16, 1974 (div. Feb. 1990); 1 child, Zachary Bryan. BS in Edn. summa cum laude, U. North Tex., 1976, postgrad., 1988. Cert. secondary tchr., Tex. Cashier/bookkeeper Krogers, Dallas, Denton, Tex., 1972-74, 74-76; sr. stenographer Continental Telephone, Dallas, 1974; math tchr. DeWitt Perry Jr. High, Carrollton, Tex., 1976-77, Bowie High Sch., Arlington, Tex., 1977-80; instr. U. Hawaii, Honolulu Community Coll., 1981; bookkeeper, writer Charles K. Gordon, DO, Bedford, Tex., 1986-88; loan adminstn. specialist Lomas Mortgage USA, Dallas, 1988; mng. editor Am. Lit. Review, Denton, 1989—; teaching fellow U. North Tex., Denton, 1988—; writer, designer Dept. English, U. North Tex., 1989—. Scholarship North Tex. State U., 1974, Marquis Meml. scholarship, 1975. Mem. Grad. Schs. of English (sec. 1989—), Nat. Coun. of Tchrs. of English, Phi Kappa Phi. Home: 3032 Hollandale Dallas TX 75234 Office: U North Tex Dept English Denton TX 76203

GORDON, DONNA GRACE, retired nurse, civic worker; b. Thomson Station, N.S., Can., Aug. 30, 1934; came to U.S., 1967; d. Hugh Ross and Doris Geneve (Smith) Patterson; m. John Edward Bourne, Apr. 30, 1956 (div. Aug. 1966); m. Steve Sol Gordon, June 6, 1967 (dec. Aug. 1980); children: Kathy Penelope (dec.), Kenneth David (dec.), Jeri Lynn (dec.), Kim Patricia, Robert Denys. Grad., Halifax Children's Hosp. Nursing Sch., 1955. RN, N.S., Calif. Staff nurse Halifax (N.S.) Children's Hosp., 1955-56, house supr., 1957-66; in-svc. dir., staff nurse Granada Hills (Calif.) Community Hosp., 1967-69; staff nurse infection control Encino (Calif.) Hosp., 1971-77; staff nurse Valley Presbyn. Hosp., Van Nuys, Calif., 1978; nat. dir. Nu-Med Systems, Inc., Van Nuys, 1980-83; fin. cons. Northridge, Calif., 1982-84, ret., 1984. Bd. dirs. San Fernando Teen Ctr., Van Nuys, 1977-83, acting exec. dir., 1983-84; bd. dirs. ARC, Redwood Empire, Calif., 1986—, chmn. vols., 1988—, chmn. disaster action team, 1986—, emergency mgmt. vol., 1986—; ruling elder St. Andrew Presbyn. Ch., also chmn. fellowship; coord. disaster vols. No. Calif. Floods, 1986; staffing officer L.A./Whittier Earthquake, 1987. Named Vol. of Yr. ARC, 1987-88; recipient Clara Barton award for outstanding svc. ARC, 1988.

GORDON, ELLEN RUBIN, candy company executive; d. William B. and Cele H. (Travis) Rubin; m. Melvin J. Gordon, June 25, 1950; children: Virginia, Karen, Wendy, Lisa. Student, Vassar Coll., 1948-50; B.A., Brandeis U., 1965; postgrad., Harvard U., 1968. With Tootsie Roll Industries, Inc., Chgo., 1968—, corp. sec., 1970-74, v.p. product devel., 1974-76, sr. v.p., 1976-78, pres., chief operating officer, 1978—, also dir.; v.p., dir. HDI Investment Corp. Mem. vis. com. Harvard U. Med. Sch. and Sch. Dentistry, com. univ. resources; pres. Cele H. and William B. Family Fund Inc. Recipient Kettle award, 1985. Mem. Nat. Confectioners Assn. (v.p., bd. dirs., exec. com. of bd. dirs., chmn. tade rels. com.), Nat. Confectioners Wholesale Assn. (chmn. trade rels. com.), Co. of 200 (immediate past pres., bd. dirs.). Home: PO Box 706 Mellon Rd Center Harbor NH 03226 Office: Tootsie Roll Industries Inc 7401 S Cicero Ave Chicago IL 60629

GORDON, FRANCINE E., personnel director; b. Bklyn., Nov. 12, 1948; d. Emil and Sylvia (Packer) G. BA in Psychology, Vassar Coll., 1969; MA in Organizational Behavior, Yale U., 1971, PhD in Organizational Behavior, 1974. Asst. prof. Grad. Sch. Bus. Stanford U., 1972-77; gen. mgr. Calif. Actors Theatre, Los Gatos, 1977-80; assoc. dir. career planning and placement San Jose (Calif.) State U., 1981; dir. new bus. devel. Pacific Bell, San Ramon, Calif., 1981-87; recruiting mgr. Tandem Computers, Cupertino, Calif., 1987-89; mgr. tng. and employment Ungermann-Bass, Santa Clara, Calif., 1989—; self employed, cons. 1973-81. Contbr. articles to profl. jours.; author: Bringing Women Into Management, 1974, Perspectives on Bringing Women Into Management, 1975. Recipient Mervin Haskel award Textile Vets; 1970. Mem. Am. Mgmt. Assn., Am. Psychol. Assn., Western Coll. Placement Assn. (committee chmn. 1985), Acad. Mgmt., Phi Beta Kappa. Office: Ungermann-Bass 3990 Freedom Circle Santa Clara CA 95051

GORDON, GERD STRAY, historian, educator, writer; b. Stavanger, Norway, Nov. 15, 1912; came to U.S., 1948; d. Johannes and Ella (Stray) Johansen; m. Johan Vogt (div.); children: Mette Wernøe, Gerd Ada Vogt, Christina Isaksen; m. Raymond Gordon; 1 child, Karen Allyn. Student, Oslo U., 1937-41; BA, Fla. State U., 1960; MA, U. Pitts., PhD, 1978. Cert. tchr., Fla., Pa. Accredited corr. Aftenposten-Norsk Dameblad, Oslo, 1948-55; tchr. Panama C.Z. Schs., Panama Episc. Sch., 1960-61, Am. Coop. Sch., Tunis, Tunisia, 1962-64; tchr. Am. Internat. Sch., Bangkok, 1965-68, Djakarta, Indonesia, 1968-69; tchr. Am. Sch., New Delhi, India, 1969-70, Pitts. Pub. Sch. System, 1970-83; freelance lectr., 1983—; lectr., Slippery Rock (Pa.) Coll., U. Kans., Lawrence, Vanderbilt U., Nashville; presenter, Symposium of Scandinavian Historians. Author: Kvinnen Idag (Woman Today), 1952; contbr. articles to numerous publs including Dictionary of Scandinavian History, 1986. Dem. ofcl., Denver, 1952-57, election judge, 1954-58; bd. dirs., rep., Planned Parenthood, Denver and Pitts., 1952-89; participant Citizen Day Com. signed S.P. Kinney II Denver Woman's Press Club, 1965, Senate of Pa., 1985. Resistance worker during German occupation of Norway, World War II. Recipient Outstanding Citizen award Norwegian Resistance; Ella Lyman Cabot Trust grantee U. Pitts. Mem. Denver Women's Press Club (bd. dirs. 1952—), Pitts. U. Historian Alumnae Orgn., Fla. State U. Alumnae Assn., AAUW (bd. dirs. Pitts. chpt. 1984—), LWV (past bd. dirs. Denver and Pitts. chpts.), Countryside Garden Club (bd. dirs. 1970—). Home: 224 Rockingham Rd Pittsburgh PA 15238

GORDON, JANET JEAN, veterinarian; b. Plymouth, Minn., Dec. 1, 1956; d. Irving Block and Gladys Elaine (Regnier) Sommers; m. Bradley James Gordon, Oct. 12, 1984 (separated May 1990). BS, Kans. State U., 1978, DVM, 1981. Veterinarian Rancho Segvoia Vet. Hosp., Simi Valley, Calif., 1981-82; veterinarian Gerald Gardner Equine Svcs., Thousand Oaks, Calif., 1981-82; veterinarian applied techs. and pharms. Sprayberry Animal Hosp., Marietta, Ga., 1982-86; veterinarian Raptor Ctr., U. Minn., St. Paul, 1986-87, Fitz Vet. Assn., St. Paul, 1987-88, Minn. Racing Commn., Mpls., 1987—, New Hope (Minn.) Animal Hosp., 1988—; Companion Bird Found., St. Paul, 1988-90. Illustrator (book) Field Guide to Equine Colic, 1986, articles to numerous profl. jours. Mem. Am. Vet. Med. Assn., Am. Animal Hosp. Assn., Assn. Avian Veterinarians, Audubon Soc., Friends of the Earth, Sierra Club. Office: New Hope Animal Hosp 3709 Winnetka Ave N New Hope MN 55428

GORDON, JANINE M., advertising agency executive; b. N.Y.C., Oct. 2, 1946; d. Moses Fortune and Emma (Leo) Mager. B.A., U. Pa., 1968. Asst. buyer Bloomingdale's, N.Y.C., 1968-69; fashion credits editor Harper's Bazaar, N.Y.C., 1969-72; asso. dir. pub. relations Cotton, Inc., N.Y.C., 1972-73; press officer Harrods Ltd., London, 1973-74; project mgr. J.C. Penney Co., Inc., N.Y.C., 1974-75; dir. pub. relations Bozell, Jacobs, Kenyon & Eckhardt, Inc., N.Y.C., 1975-77; exec. v.p. corp. communications Saatchi & Saatchi Advt., 1977—. Mem. Advt. Women N.Y. (oper. com.), Pub. Rels. Soc. Am., Pub. Club London. Club: Cosmopolitan. Office: Saatchi & Saatchi Advt 375 Hudson St New York NY 10014

GORDON, JULIE PEYTON, foundation administrator; b. Jacksonville, Fla., June 21, 1940; d. Robert Benoist Shields and Betty (Cavanaugh) Peyton; m. Robert James Gordon, June 22, 1963. BA, Boston U., 1963; MA, Harvard U., 1965, PhD, 1969. Asst. prof. English Ill. Inst. Tech., Chgo., 1968-75, assoc. prof., 1975-77, asst. dean students, 1975-78; asst. dean acad. affairs Northwestern U., Evanston, Ill., 1978-80, assoc. dean univ. coll., 1980-85, sec. Econometric Soc., 1975—, exec. dir. Econometric Soc., 1985—; mem. nat. adv. com. ALA, Chgo., 1983-86. Author: Seasons in the Contemporary American Family, 1984. Grantee NEH, 1971-73; project scholar NEH, 1983-86. Mem. Phi Beta Kappa. Home: 1039 Forest Ave Evanston IL 60202 Office: Northwestern U Dept Econs Econometric Soc Evanston IL 60208-2400

GORDON, JUNE, psychology educator, consultant, artist; b. Oshkosh, Wis., June 17, 1929; d. Felix and Harriet (Fero) Staerkel; m. Donald Emmanuel Gordon, Feb. 6, 1951; children: Bonita, Judy, Teresa, Thomas, Alexander, Philip. BS, Rollins Coll., 1971, MEd, 1974; EdS, U. Fla., 1976; EdD, Fla. State U., 1979; advanced study Jung Inst., Switzerland, 1982, U. Wis., 1984; imagery tng., London, 1985. Cert. sch. psychologist, Fla.; lic. mental health counselor. Freelance artist, Calif., Fla., Wis., Ala., 1958-74; coord. women's program Seminole Community Coll., Sanford, Fla., 1974-84; adj. prof. psychology Rollins Coll. and Seminole Community Coll., Winter Park, Fla., 1974—; pvt. practice counseling mental health svc., Sanford, 1984—; bd. dirs. Project Wedge, Cen. Fla. Ednl. Consortium for Women, Orlando; cons. in field. Artist: painting Mother, Mother, The CIA is Coming (Wis. Blue Ribbon 1967), The Skaters (Merit award, Oviedo, Fla. 1985); author: (with others) Divorce, 1977; Legal Rights, 1979; contbr. articles to profl. jours. Founder Cen. Fla. Commn. on Status of Women, 1975; pres. Seminole County Mental Health Ctr., Inc., Fla., 1980-81, bd. dirs., 1989—; bd. dirs. Met. Alcohol Coun., Orlando, 1981-83, Citrus coun. Girl Scouts U.S., 1984-88; committeewoman Dem. Exec. Com. of Seminole County, 1981-84; gov.'s appointee East Cen. Fla. Regional Planning Coun., 1983-86. Recipient Fannie Lou Hamers Human Rights award NOW, 1980, Best of Jewelry award Seminole Community Coll., Sanford, Fla., 1989. Mem. AAUW (pres. 1983-85, bd. dirs. Fla. state div. 1986-89), Nat. Wellness Assn., Jung Soc. North Fla., Fla. Assn. Community Colls., Future Soc. Avocations: all artistic and creative activities, designing, traveling, gardening. Home: 309 Idyllwilde Dr Sanford FL 32771

GORDON, KATHERINE, biotechnologist; b. Las Cruses, N.Mex., Sept. 20, 1954. PhD, Wesleyan U., Middletown, Conn., 1982. Postdoctoral fellow Yale U., New Haven, 1982-84; sr. scientist Integrated Genetics, Framingham, Mass., 1984-89; assoc. dir. Genzyme Corp., Framingham, 1989—. Office: Genzyme Corp 1 Mountain Rd Framingham MA 01701

GORDON, KRIS ROMSTAD, information systems specialist; b. Columbia, S.C., Sept. 8, 1945; d. Rolf Norman Romstad and Marion Elizabeth (Nutter) Whitenack; m. Donald E. Gordon; children: Scott, Brian, Erin. Student, Wake Forest U., 1963-66; BA, Augusta (Ga.) Coll., 1978, MBA, 1980; cert., U. Ga. Computer Sci. Inst., 1987. With Med. Coll. of Ga., Augusta, 1980—; assoc. prof. infosystems, computing resources coord. Med. Coll. Ga. Sch. Allied Health Scis., Augusta, 1989—; asst. prof. infosytems Med. Coll. of Ga., Augusta, 1984-89; cons. Jenkins County Hosp., Millen, Ga., 1986-88, Augusta Correctional Med. Inst., Augusta, 1987. Contbr. articles to profl. jours. Mem. Historic Augusta, 1989—. Recipient Disting. Svc. award Sch. Allied Health Scis., 1989. Mem. Assn. for Computer Educators, AAUW, Leadership Augusta, Augusta Coll. Alumni Assn. (v.p. for awards, bd. dirs. 1984-89). Home: 4178 Heathcliff Dr Martinez GA 30907 Office: Med Coll of Ga 1120 15th St Augusta GA 30912-0400

GORDON, LINNEA HAMMERSTEN, registered nurse; b. Boston, June 21, 1945; d. Vincent Nils and Shirley (Durr) Hammersten; m. Robert L. Gordon, June 3, 1978. AA, Colby Sawyer Coll., 1965; BSN, Cornell U., 1968; MS, Boston Coll., 1980. RN, Mass. From evening charge nurse to head nurse Payne Whitney Psychiatric Clinic, N.Y. Hosp., N.Y.C., 1968-71; evening charge nurse Chetwynde Nursing Home, West Newton, Mass., 1971; staff nurse Monroe (Mich.) County Health Dept., 1973-74; from community health nurse to supr. Blue Cross Coord. VNA of Upper Cape Cod, Falmouth, Mass., 1974-79; exec. dir. Health Resource Ctr., West Barnstable, Mass., 1981-88; nursing instr. Cape Cod Community Coll., 1983-86, 88; nursing mgmt., mktg. rep. Alternative Care, 1988-89; adminstr. All Cape

Health Care, 1989—. Author: Alzheimer's Disease: A Family Care Guide, 1987, For Your Health Seniors Cape Cod Forum. Bd. dirs. Elders Svcs. of Cape Cod, Mass., Erna Yaffee Found., 1987; adv. com. Ctr. on Aging, Cape Cod Community Coll., 1985; sec. Wood Rise Trust, 1986; steering com. Prospect Cape Cod Health, 1987. Named Woman of Yr., Bus. and Profl. Women's Club of Cape Cod, 1983. Mem. Am. Nurses Assn., Mass. Nurses Assn. (bd. dirs. 1983-85, Image of Profl. Nursing award, 1986, dist. III bd. dirs. pub. rels. com., Achievement award for Outstanding Service, 1985), Am. Pub. Health Assn., Cape and Islands Area Nursing Edn. (chairperson 1985-87), Mass. Health Planning and Devel. (bd. dirs. 1984-86, mgmt. com. 1980-86), Upper Cape Registered Nurses, League of Women Voters, Cape Cod Cornellians, Mass. Pub. Health Assn., Nat. League for Nursing, Sigma Phi Omega, Sigma Theta Tau.

GORDON, LYNNE A., counselor; b. Richland Ctr., Wis., June 7, 1939; d. Claude and Florence (Leone) Peacock; m. Gary Gordon, Aug. 20, 1961 (dec.); children: Susan, Scott. BS, U. Wis., 1961; postgrad., Western Mich. U., Grand Valley State U. Mgr. of pastoral svcs. Mercy Hosp., Muskegon, Mich.; tchr. Montague (Mich.) Area Schs.; pvt. practice Child Care Ctr., Montague. Mem. ADEC, CAPS, NACC, ACPE. Home: 2466 E Riverwood Dr Twinlake MI 49457 Office: 2466 E Riverwood Dr Twin Lake MI 49457

GORDON, MARIA T., account executive; b. Poughkeepsie, N.Y., Mar. 19, 1965; d. Francis Robert and Veronica (Higgins) G. BA magna cum laude, Marist Coll., 1987. Sr. account exec. G.S. Schwartz and Co., Inc., N.Y.C.; coord. of the annual fund Marist Coll., Poughkeepsie; communications specialist IBM East Fishkill, Hopewell Junction, N.Y. Active in civic orgns. Mem. NAFE, The Network Line, Alpha Chi. Home: 34-38 30th St Astoria NY 11102

GORDON, MARY CATHERINE, author; b. L.I., N.Y., Dec. 8, 1949; d. David and Anna (Gagliano) G.; m. James Brain, 1974; m. Arthur Cash, 1979; children—Anna Gordon, David Dess Gordon. BA, Barnard Coll., 1971; MA, Syracuse U., 1973. Tchr. English Dutchess Community Coll., Poughkeepsie, N.Y., 1974-78, Amherst (Mass.) Coll. Novels include Final Payments, 1978, The Company of Women, 1981, Men and Angels, 1985, The Other Side, 1989; (short stories) Temporary Shelter, 1987. Recipient Kafka prize for Fiction, 1979, 82. Roman Catholic. Address: care Random House Inc Publicity Dept 201 E 50th St New York NY 10022*

GORDON, MIRIAM POSEY, special education teacher; b. Jasper, Ala., Nov. 18, 1947; d. Milford Marlin and Ethel Mae (Hyche) Posey; m. Johnny James Gordon, May 26, 1972; children: Whitney Nicole, John Grant. Student, Walker Coll., Jasper, 1965-67; BS, U. Ala., 1972, MA, 1973. Cert. spl. edn. tchr., Ala. Libr. Carl Elliott Regional Libr., Jasper, 1968-70; spl. edn. tchr. Walker County Bd. Edn., Jasper, 1972—. Vol. Mothers' March of Dimes, 1990. Mem. NEA, AAUW, Jasper Classroom Tchrs., Ala. Edn. Assn., Walker County Edn. Assn. (past pres.), Kappa Delta Pi, Alpha Delta Kappa. Baptist. Home: Rte 9 Box 18 Jasper AL 35501

GORDON, NINA MARLENE, import company executive; b. Louisburg, N.C., Nov. 12, 1951; d. Billy Marlin Gordon and Edith Ruby (Moore) Gilliam. Student, N.C. State U., 1975. With sales Billy Gordon Datsun, Burlington, N.C., 1975-78, gen. mgr., 1978-82; ind. lease agt. Greensboro, N.C., 1982-84; sales mgr. Carl Johnson Automotive, New Bern, N.C., 1984-86; with sales Jack Pickard Imports, Greensboro, 1986-87, lease/bus. mgr., 1988—; lease/bus. mgr. Gate City Lincoln Mercury, Greensboro, 1987-88. Named All Am. Amateur Softball Assn., Chatanooga, 1975, Calif., 1978, Fla., 1979, York, Pa., 1980. Republican. Baptist. Home: 4336 A Edith Ln Greensboro NC 27409

GORDON, NINA ROBIN, graphic designer, owner; b. Canton, Ohio, Nov. 6, 1959; d. Irving Martin and Roberta (Levine) G. BA in English, Coll. Wooster, 1980; AA in Specialized Technology, Art. Inst. Pitts., 1983. Graphic desinger Advt. Brainstorms, Mpls., 1984-85; owner, creative dir. The Robin Group, Mpls., 1985—; show com. '90 Am. Inst. Graphic Arts, Mpls., 1990-91. Prin. works include "Take Advantage of Us" brochure, 1987 (Desi award for Excellence 1985), "St. Joseph Hospital" brochure, 1985 (IABC award for Excellence 1985), "Take Advantage of Us" brochure, 1985 (IABC award for Excellence 1985). Vol. phone crisis counselor Y.E.S., Mpls., 1990—; big sister Friend to a Child, Mpls., 1987-89. Mem. Art Dir./Copywriters Club. Office: The Robin Group 10 S 5th St Minneapolis MN 55401

GORDON, PAULA ROSSBACHER, musician, educator, producer, arts consultant; b. Fort Riley, Kans., Aug. 3, 1953; d. John Robert and Nancy (Fray) Rossbacher; m. Douglas Seth Gordon, June 19, 1976. BMus, Mansfield (Pa.) U., 1975, MS, 1980; postgrad., Pa. State U., Westminster Choir Coll. Cert. Yamaha music tchr. Grad. asst. Mansfield U., 1975-76; pers. and pub. rels. dir. McCarthy Ent., Williamsport, Pa., 1981; gen. mgr. Williamsport Symphony Orch., 1982-87; producer, exec. dir. Theatre by the Sea, Cape May, N.J., 1986-89; arts cons. N.Y., Pa., N.J., 1985—; owner, designer Gordon Graphics, Williamsport, 1988—; freelance performer/pianist, 1975—; arts cons., 1985—. Co-author: A History of Trinity Church, 1989. Bd. dirs. Coll./Community Arts Council, Mansfield, 1974, Williamsport Players, 1980. Republican. Lutheran. Home and Office: 1024 Packer St Williamsport PA 17701

GORDON, RITA SIMON, civic leader, former nurse, educator; b. Frederick, Md., Feb. 1, 1929; d. Jacob and Anna (Stein) Simon; m. Paul Perry Gordon, July 2, 1948; children—Stuart Yael, Hugh Ellis, Myla. R.N., Frederick Meml. Hosp., 1949. R.N., Md. Surg. staff nurse Prince Georges Gen. Hosp., 1949-50; pediatric staff nurse (part-time) Frederick Meml. Hosp., 1950-54; surg. office nurse, 1960-62; nurse blood program ARC 1954-83. Author: (with Paul P. Gordon) Textbook History of Frederick County. 1975. Mem. Frederick County Bd. Edn., 1975-85, pres., 1979-80, 83-84; mem. exec. com. Md. Assn. Bd. Edn., Annapolis, 1978-85, pres., 1983-84; bd. assocs. Hood Coll., Frederick, 1985—; mem. Md. Task Force on Ednl. Funding, Annapolis, 1983-84, Md. Values Edn. Com., Annapolis, 1979-83, Fed. Relations Network, Nat. Sch. Bd. Assn., 1978-82; bd. dirs. Community Commons, Frederick, 1983-85; area field rep. Am. Field Service, Frederick, 1970-75; assoc., mem. adv. com. Vocat. Tech. Edn., publicity com. 1973 Snow Ball, Frederick Meml. Hosp. Aux.; past bd. dirs., v.p. Beth Sholom Synagogue, 1982-83, pres., 1988—; historian, past pres. Beth Sholom Sisterhood; past bd. dirs. Nat. Council Jewish Women, Frederick; vol. aide Frederick Waverly Elem. Sch.; officer, chmn. fund raising North Market St. Sch.; active Girl Scouts U.S.A.; past pres., v.p. Frederick Improvement Found. Editor, Town Crier. Named Woman of Yr., Bus. and Profl. Woman's Club, 1975; Frederick's Outstanding Woman, Internat. Woman's Yr., 1975. Mem. Frederick Sect. Nat. Council Jewish Women (pres. 1986-88), C. of C. (Planned Growth-2000 com.), Md. Hist. Soc., Internat. Graphoanalysis Soc., Md. Jewish Hist. Soc., Frederick County Hist. Soc. Clubs: Woman's Civic (Frederick); Rotary Inner Wheel (Gaithersburg, Md.) (v.p. 1975). Avocation: hist. research. Home: 202 Meadowdale Ln Frederick MD 21701

GORDON, ROBIN GAIL, court investigator; b. Chgo., Oct. 15, 1937; d. Phillip Gordon and Ethel Fay (Robbins) London; stepdau. Jack London; m. Stephen Irving Forstein, June 9, 1957 (div. 1972); children: Leora Rachel, Micah Aaron. BA, U. Cin., 1963; MS, Kans. State U., 1980, postgrad., 1981-82. Art and activity therapist Topeka State Hosp., 1969-84; program mgr. Las Trampas Residential Sch. Developmentally Disabled Adults, Lafayette, Calif., 1984-86; activity, jobs and ednl. therapist Sunny Hills Children's Svcs., San Anselmo, 1986-88; ct. investigator Superior Ct. Calif. Alameda County, Oakland, 1988—; mem. Crack Babies/Grandmother Task Force, Oakland, 1989—; pres. Kans. Art Therapy Assn., 1977-80. Mem. Am. Art Therapy Assn., Calif. Assn. Ct. Investigators. Home: 2206 Acton St Berkeley CA 94702 Office: Ct Investigators Rm 20 1221 Oak St Oakland CA 94612

GORDON, ROSE MARIA ELIZABETH, counselor-therapist, consultant, lecturer; b. Camden, N.J., Aug. 27, 1931; d. Rocco and Mary Antonio Theresa (Sartarella) Locantore; m. Irving Gordon, Feb. 29, 1952 (div.); children: Rocky, Maia, Heidi, Aaron. B.S. in Secondary Edn. and Sociology, U. Nev.-Las Vegas, 1978, M.S. in Rehab. Counseling, 1981. Cert. Nev. Counselor-therapist Verdun Trione. Therapist care unit Community Hosp. North Las Vegas, 1984-85; owner, exec. dir. Nev. Growth Ctr., 1985-87; cons.-lectr. Raleigh Hills Hosp., Las Vegas, 1982-83; faculty Clark County Community Coll., 1984—; founder, exec. dir. The Counseling Ctr.; part-time thrapist care unit North Las Vegas Hosp., 1975-85; cons. in field. Rape crisis and vol. counselor-therapist Clark County Jail, Las Vegas, 1982-85; entrepreneur Maya Enterprises, 1990—; founder, bd. dirs. August Found., Cocaine Outreach Network, 1984-90; past pres. Counselors-Community Action Against Rape; expert in cocaine treatment; expert witness in cts. on chem. dependency. Mem. Am. Rehab. Assn., Am. Counseling & Devel., Nev. Rehab. Assn., Am. Psychol. Assn. (assoc.), Nev. Psychol. Assn. Office: 3609 W Charleston Blvd Las Vegas NV 89102

GORDON, SARA J., realtor; b. Chgo., Mar. 10, 1937; d. Samuel A. and Mary (Rumore) Mondello; m. John Raymond Gordon, Oct. 29, 1960; children: John R., Paul J., Robert M., James P. BA, Chgo. Tchrs. Coll., 1958; MA, Loyola U., Chgo., 1964. Tchr. Chgo. Pub. Schs., 1958-60, Peoria (Ill.) Pub. Schs., 1960-64; realtor lst United - Rich Port, Oak Brook, Ill., 1978-80, Adams & Meyers, Hinsdale, Ill., 1980-83; realtor, prin. Brush Hill Realtors, Hinsdale, 1983—. Pres. Peoria Jr. Women's Club, 1969, Oak Brook Women's Club, 1985-86. Mem. AAUW (v.p. Oak Brook chpt. 1989-90), DuPage Bd. Realtors, LaGrange Bd. Realtors. Office: Brush Hill Realtors 25 W Chicago Ave Hinsdale IL 60521

GORDON, TERESA PEALE, education educator; b. Luling, Tex., Feb. 12, 1948; d. Jack Roswald and Clara Elizabeth (Junek) G.; m. Jarvis Windom, Aug. 31, 1969 (div. 1973). Postgrad., Ambassador Coll., Pasadena, Calif., 1966-69; BA summa cum laude, Houston Baptist U., 1976, MBA, 1981; PhD, U. Houston, 1986. Lic. CPA, Tex., 1977. Sec., bookkeeper Electronic Modules, Inc., Pasadena, Calif., 1970-71; pub. acctg. dba Windoms Bus. Svc., Wheatland, Wy., 1971-73; controller Hayes Tools, Inc., Houston, 1976; staff acct. Griese and Kares, CPAs, Houston; dir. fin. Neighborhood Ctrs., Inc., Houston, 1977-82; controller Tex. Upsetting and Finishing, Inc., 1981-82, Health Internat., Inc., Houston, 1982; asst. prof. Houston Baptist U., 1982-86; grad. teaching fellow U. Houston, 1984-85; asst. prof. U. Idaho, 1986-. Bd. dirs. United Way of Latah County. Nat. Merit Scholar, 1966. Mem. AICPA, Am. Women's Soc. Cert. Pub. Accts., Am. Acctg. Assn. (Roderick M. Steele Disting. Professorship award 1989). Office: U Idaho Coll Bus and Econs Moscow ID 83843

GORDON-OMELKA, JUDITH MICHELE, middle school educator; b. Sioux City, Iowa, Oct. 4, 1947; d. Albert Asher and Lenore (Cohn) Gordon; m. Dennis Leon Omelka, June 13, 1981. BA magna cum laude, Metro State Coll., 1987. Cert. elem. tchr. Elem. tchr. lang. arts Denver Pub. Schs., 1988—; pres. Colo. Gifted and Talented Special Interest Council, Denver, 1989-90. Mem. Nat. Assn. Gifted Children, Colo. Assn. Gifted Children, Internat. Reading Assn., Nat. Assn. Tchrs. English, Phi Delta Kappa, Kappa Delta Pi (pres. Pi Nu chpt. 1986-88, sec. 1989-90). Jewish. Home: 610 S Ogden B Denver CO 80209

GORDY, ADRIENNE YVONNE, day care director; b. Chester, Pa., Sept. 6, 1958; d. John Edward Sr. and Minnie Doris (McNeil) G. BA in Afro-Am. Studies, Tougaloo (Miss.) Coll., 1981; MS in Elem. Edn. & Childhood Edn., Widener U., 1990. Cert. elem. edn. tchr., Pa. Substitute tchr. Concord Day Care Ctr., Chester, 1981-83; devel. tchr. Delaware County Head Start, Chester, 1983-88; dir. Mt. Pleasant Nursery Sch., Twin Oaks, Pa., 1988—. Pres. bd. dirs. Camp Cherith in Pa., 1988—. Recipient Cora Richardson award Mt. Pleasant Bapt. Ch., 1989. Mem. Delaware Valley Assn. for the Edn. of the Young Child, Nat. Coun. of Negro Women, Alpha Kappa Alpha. Home: 713 Kerlin St Chester PA 19013 Office: Mt Pleasant Nursery Sch 101 Washington Ave Twin Oaks PA 19014

GORDY, DENISE MARIE, healthcare administrator; b. Pitts., June 25, 1958; d. Edward John and Marian Frances (Louzil) Duda. BS, U. Pitts., 1980; postgrad., U. W.Va., 1985-86, Fairmont (W.Va.) State Coll., 1983-84. Asst. dir. med. records United Hosp. Ctr., Clarksburg, W.Va., 1980-81, dir. med. records, 1981-83, dir. med. data svcs., 1983-86; instr. art program Fairmont State Coll., 1982-85; cons. Heritage Convalescent Home, Bridgeport, W.Va., 1981-86; dir. health info. AMI Griffin (Ga.) Spalding Hosp., 1986-87, adminstrv. dir. devel., 1987—; instr. AMRA, Chgo., 1988-89; speaker W.Va. Med. Record Assn., Charleston, 1983-86, bd. dirs., pres. 1985-86. Bd. dirs. Am. Cancer Soc., Griffin, 1988-91, pres.-elect, 1990-91; bd. dirs.United Way-Spalding County, Griffin, 1988-89. Recipient Apprecation for Svc. award W.Va. Med. Record Assn., 1984, Cert. of Recognition Spalding County Older Ams., 1989. Mem. Am. Med. Record Assn. (coun. chair 1986-88), Ga. Med. Record Assn. Republican. Roman Catholic.

GORE, CYNTHIA DOLORES, sales official; b. Paris, Tenn., Oct. 27, 1962; d. William Rex and Scarlett Dolores (Gaddy) G. BS, U. Tenn., Martin, 1985. Sales mgr. Ramada Inn Downtown, Nashville, 1985-86; dir. sales Ramada Inn Opryland, Nashville, 1986-88; pharm. sales rep. Miles Pharm., West Haven, Conn., 1988—. Mem. Order of Ea. Star, Alpha Delta Pi (pledge advisor 1989—). Republican. Mem. Reorganized Ch. of Jesus Christ of Latter-day Sts. Home and Office: 39 Hickory Hollow Pl Antioch TN 37013

GORE, PATRICIA LYNN, educator; b. Kansas City, Kans., Oct. 28, 1946; d. Francis Clyde and Frances Gertrude (McNerney) G. BS in Edn., Cen. Mo. State u., 1968, MS in Edn., 1974. Tchr. R-7 Sch. Dist., Lee's Summit, Mo., 1968—. Lee's Summit C. of C. scholar, 1984. Mem. Internat. Reading Assn., AAUW (1st v.p. 1978-79, pres. 1979-81, treas. 1983-87), Lee's Summit Edn. Assn., Mo. Tchrs. Assn. (recording sec. 1988-89, parliamentarian 1989-90, pres.-elect 1990—), Phi Kappa Phi, Delta Kappa Gamma (corr. sec. 1984-86, pres. 1986-90, area coun. v.p. 1989-90). Republican. Methodist. Office: Greenwood Elem Sch 805 W Main Greenwood MO 64063

GOREE, BEA M., labor relations consultant; b. Bonn, Germany, Nov. 13, 1932; came to U.S., 1938; d. Herbert and Liselotte (Neisser) Dieckmann; m. Max Goree, Dec. 23, 1954 (div. Mar. 1976); children: Max Edward, Michael Stephen, Elizabeth Lynn Goree Soriano. BA, Washington U., St. Louis, 1954; M in Labor and Indsl. Rels., Mich. State U., 1978. Engring. draftsman State of Mich., Lansing, 1969-78, labor rels. adminstr., 1978-90; labor rels. cons. Goree Assocs., Lansing, 1990—. Various ofices All Saints Ch., East Lansing, Mich. Office: PO Box 1721 East Lansing MI 48826

GORHAM, LINDA JOANNE, investment banker; b. Boston, June 25, 1951; d. Joseph Leo and Rose (Avila) G. AS, Northeastern U., 1975, BS, 1976; MBA, Babson Coll., 1978; postgrad., Coll. Fin. Planning, Denver. Various positions Stop & Shop Co. Inc., Boston, 1974-83; sr. analyst Capital Fin. Planning, Needham, Mass., 1983-85; fin. cons. United Resources, Needham, 1985-86; mng. dir. Mingolelli Fin. Svcs., Framingham, Mass., 1986-88; v.p. Mingolelli & Assocs., Framingham, 1986-88; with Lyons Planning Group, Waltham, Mass., 1988-89; investment banker Carriage House Capital, Boston, 1989—; adj. faculty Northeastern U., 1988—. Mem. Inst. Cert. Fin. Planners, Am. Soc. Profl. and Exec. Women, Nat. Assn. Female Execs., Babson Coll. Women Alumni in Bus., Babson Women Investors Club, Babson Mentor Program (chairwoman 1986—), Babson Women in Bus., Sigma Epsilon Rho. Office: Carriage House Capital 225 Friend St Boston MA 02114

GORMAN, ANNE D., marketing professional; b. Nov. 9, 1950. Student, Clara Maass Meml. Sch. Nursing, 1971; BS in Mgmt., Mercy Coll., 1988; postgrad., L.I. U. Sales mgr. GV Med. Inc., Mpls.; imaging sales rep. Gen. Electric Med. Systems, Whippany, N.J.; ea. regional sales mgr., tech. sales rep. Matrix Instruments Inc., Orangeburg, N.Y.; coronary care/ICU nurse Clara Maass Meml. Hosp., Belleville, N.J., St. Michael's Med. Ctr., Newark; sales mgr. GV Med. Inc., Mpls. Mem. NAFE, Am. Assn. Critical Care Nurses, Radiologic Socs. Home: 32 Somerset Dr Suffern NY 10901 Office: 3750 Annapolis Ln Minneapolis MN 55447

GORMAN, KAREN MACHMER, optometrist; b. Poughkeepsie, N.Y., June 4, 1955; d. James Andrew and Joan (Benton) Machmer; m. D.L. McCartney III, Aug. 16, 1976 (div. June 1982); m. N. David Gorman, Oct. 16, 1985; l stepchild, Danette Y. Gorman. BS in Optometry, U. Houston, 1976, OD, 1978. Pvt. practice Dallas, 1978-83, 1984-85, Hurst, Tex., 1984-85, St. Joseph, Mo., 1986—. Contbr. poetry to lit. jour.; actress (play) Nove Care Back Innocent, Robidoux Resident Theater, St. Joseph, 1990. Vol. Dallas Humane Soc., 198l; patron Robidoux Resident Theater, St. Joseph, 1988-89; sponsor, coach, cheerleader and drill team Mo. Western State Coll., St. Joseph, 1985-86. Recipient Optometric Recognition awards, 1986-90; U. Houston scholar, 1972-76. Mem. U. Houston Alumni Assn, CWENS, Tau Sigma.

GORMAN, MARCIE SOTHERN, franchise executive; b. N.Y.C., Feb. 25, 1949; d. Jerry R. and Carole Edith (Frendel) Sothern; m. N. Scott Gorman, June 14, 1969 (div.); children: Michael Stephen, Mark Jason; m. Robert Borys, Apr. 22, 1989. AA, U. Fla., 1968; BS, Memphis State U., 1970. Tchr., Memphis City Sch. System, 1970-73; tng. dir. Weight Watchers of Palm Beach County and Weight Watchers So. Ala., Inc., West Palm Beach, Fla., 1973—, area dir., then pres., 1977—; pres. Markel Ads, Inc. Cubmaster Troop 130. Hon. lt. col. a.d.c. Ala. Militia. Mem. Women' Am. ORT (program chmn. 1975), Optometric Soc. (sec. 1973), Weight Watchers Franchise Assn. (chair mktg. com., mem. advt./mktg. coun., chairperson region IV bd. dirs., treas.), Nat. Orgn. Women, Exec. Women of the Palm Beaches, Am. Bus. Women's Assn., Nat. Assn. Female Execs., Zonta. Home: 429 N Country Club Dr Atlantis FL 33462 Office: 2459 S Congress Ave West Palm Beach FL 33406

GORMAN, SUSAN MARIE, marketing director; b. Seattle, Jan. 1, 1946; d. Francis Rex. and Gleda Arbutus (Miller) G.; m. James Patrick Jones; children: Bryan Patrick Jones, Darin Michael Jones; m. Scott Sutton Gratrix. BS in Secondary Edn., Emporia State U., 1967. Substitute tchr. Emporia Pub. Schs., Emporia, Kans., 1968-69; office mgr. M. Gene Ball, D.D.S., P.C., Lakewood, Colo., 1974-80; office mgr., mktg. coord. Lee Architects/Interior Designers, Lakewood, 1980-84; dir. mktg. Tandem Enterprises, Inc., Denver, 1984—. Mem. Speakers' Bur., Big Sisters Colo., Denver, 1985—; bd. dirs. Arapahoe Mental Health Ctr., Englewood, Colo., 1988—, pres., 1990. Mem. Soc. for Mktg. Profl. Svcs. (sec., v.p., pres., past pres., Mem. of Yr. award 1987), Cherry Creek Commerce Assn., NAFE, South Metro C. of C. (leadership program 1989-90). Roman Catholic. Office: Tandem Enterprises Inc 3665 Cherry Creek Dr N Ste 100 Denver CO 80209

GORMAN, WILMA ROSE, real estate company official; b. Youngstown, Ohio, Dec. 13, 1923; d. Emrick and Catherine (Merl) Gessler; m. Robert J Gorman, Aug. 17, 1946 (dec.); children: Michele, Catherine, David, Margaret. BS in Secondary Edn., Youngstown State U., 1946. Tchr. sci. Mineral Ridge (Ohio) High Sch., 1946-48; med. technician Dr. R.M. Kiskaddon, Youngstown, 1962-73; tchr. Youngstown Vocat. Sch., 1973-75; sales mgr. for 5 counties Ency Brit., Youngstown, 1975-78; sales agt. Burgan Real Estate, Ltd., Youngstown, 1979—. Pres. Children's Theatre, Youngstown, 1959-64, Youngstown Playhouse, 1973-78, Jr. Philharm., Youngstown, 1967-69; past regional bd. govs. Nat. Children's Theatre, Youngstown; v.p. RSVP, Youngstown, 1985. Recipient Outstanding Leadership award Mahoning Valley Camp Fire, 1957, 67, Camp Fire awards, 1964-69, Vol. award Youngstown Playhouse, 1976, Outstanding Svc. award, 1978, Best Daytome Vol. award, 1973. Mem. Youngstown Area Bd. Realtors, Mahoning County Watercolor Soc. (sec. 1987-90), Garden Forum (publicity sec. 1975-78), Ridgewood Garden Club. Home: 292 Brainard Dr Boardman OH 44512 Office: Burgan Real Estate Ltd 5335 Market St Boardman OH 44512

GORMLY, BARBARA DIESNER, financial consultant; b. Olmutz, Czechoslovakia, Dec. 3, 1943; came to U.S. 1961; d. Robert and Eva (Cooper) Diesner; m. William M. Gormly, Aug. 21, 1965; children: Kirsten Eve, Kellie Blaine. BA in French/Ger. w/hons., U. Tex., El Paso, 1967. Tchr. German/French Hinsdale South High Sch., Hinsdale, Ill., 1967-69, Newark High Sch., San Francisco, 1969-70; tchr. French Community Coll. of Allegheny County, Pitts., 1976-79; v.p. Cons. in Pub. Fin., Scottsdale, Ariz., 1982—, also bd. dirs.; bd. dirs. Women's Adv. Bd. of Great Western Bank, Phoenix, 1985-86, Citibank Adv. Bd., Phoenix, 1986-87. Mem. AAUW, Econ. Club of Phoenix. Republican. Methodist. Office: Cons in Pub Fin Ltd 8711 E Pinnacle Peak Rd Scottsdale AZ 85255

GORTNER, SUSAN REICHERT, nursing educator; b. San Francisco, Dec. 23, 1932; d. Frederick Leet and Erida Louise (Leuschner) R.; m. Willis Alway Gortner, Aug. 25, 1960; children: Catherine Willis, Frederick Aiken. AB, Stanford U., 1949; M Nursing, Western Res. U., 1957; PhD, U. Calif., Berkeley, 1964; postgrad., Stanford U., 1983. Staff nurse, instr., supr. Johns Hopkins Hosp. Sch. Nursing, Balt., 1957-58; instr. to asst. prof. Sch. Nursing U. Hawaii, Honolulu, 1958-64; staff scientist, rsch. adminstr. div. nursing USPHS, Bethesda, Md., 1966-78; assoc. dean, researcher Sch. Nursing, U. Calif., San Francisco, 1978-86, acting chmn. dept. family health, 1982, prof. dept. family health care nursing, 1978—; fellow, assoc. faculty mem. Inst. Health Policy U. Calif.-San Francisco, 1979—, affiliates faculty mem. Inst. for Aging and Health, 1981—, adj. prof. internal medicine dept. gen. medicine Sch. Medicine, 1989—, dir. cardiac recovery lab. Sch. Nursing, 1987—; Fulbright lectr., rsch. scholar Norwegian Fulbright Commn., Oslo, 1988. Contbr. articles, papers to profl. pubs., chpts. to books. Health advisor N. Fork Assn., Soda Springs, Calif., 1981-88. Disting. scholar Nat. Ctr. Nursing Rsch., 1990; named Disting. Alumna Frances Payne Bolton Sch. Nursing, 1983. Fellow Am. Acad. Nursing; mem. Am. Nurses Assn. (chair exec. com., coun. nurse rsch. com. 1976-80, cabinet on nursing rsch. 1984-86), Am. Heart Assn. (coun. cardiovascular nursing, exec. com. 1983—, coun. epidemiology 1989—), Soc. for Behavioral Medicine (program com. 1986—). Home: 470 Cervantes Rd Portola Valley CA 94028 Office: U Calif N411Y 4th and Parnassus San Francisco CA 94143-0606

GOSS, BARBARA CRAIG, pharmaceutical executive; b. Birmingham, Ala., May 14, 1945; d. William Jr. and Erma Mae (Buchanan) Craig; m. Theodore C. Goss, June 15, 1975 (div.); children: Aisha Miranda, Dalila Kesi. BS in Nursing, Med. Coll. Ga., 1974, MS in Nursing, 1976. RN, Ga. Nurse Grady Meml. Hosp., Atlanta, 1966-71; pub. health nurse Fulton County Health Dept., Atlanta, 1971-75, pub. health nurse supr., 1975-79; territory sales rep. Bristol Labs. of Bristol Myers, Griffin, Ga., 1980-82; hosp. sales rep. Bristol Labs. of Bristol Myers, Atlanta, 1982-84, hosp. sales territory mgr., 1984-88; hosp. sales territory mgr. Bristol Labs. of Bristol Myers, Birmingham, 1988—; cons., speaker in field. Patentee in field. Mem. Birmingham Urban League, Inc., 1988. Mem. Birmingham Area Pharm. Reps. (sec. 1988—), Ala. Soc. Hosp. Pharmacists, Atlanta Bus. Women Assn., Ga. Nurses Assn., Am. Nurses Assn., Birmingham Book Club (v.p. 1988). Democrat. Methodist. Home: 307 Chase Plantation Circle Birmingham AL 35244

GOSS, EILEEN ABEL, editor; b. Cleve., Nov. 12, 1942; d. Henry and Faye (Zelivyansky) Abel; m. Lawrence Allan, Dec. 20, 1964; children: Melissa, Deborah. BS, Ohio U., Athens, 1964. Tchr. Cleve. Bd. of Edn., 1964-68; substitute tchr. Cleve. U. Hts., 1968-72; tchr. Hebrew Acad., Cleve., 1972-77; prodn. editor Am. Metal Mkt. Metalworking News, Des Plaines, Ill.; asst. editor Shelby Report of the SE/SW, Atlanta, 1980-85; editor Leisure Times, 1985—; recorder Leads Inc., 1988; program chmn. Career Connections, 1988. Editor: Leisure Times, 1985—. Tutor Carlsbad Adult Learning Program, 1988--. Mem. Soroptimist Internat., Brandeis Women, B'nai B'rith Women, Rotary Internat. Home: 7320 Esfera St Carlsbad CA 92009 Office: 2382 Faraday Ave #300 Carlsbad CA 92008

GOSS, GEORGIA BULMAN, translator; b. N.Y.C., Dec. 1, 1939; d. James Cornelius and Marian Bright (McLaughlin) Bulman; m. Douglas Keith Goss, Dec. 21, 1957; children: Kristin Anne, David. BA, U. Mich., 1961. Libr., High Altitude Obs., Boulder, Colo., 1963-64, U.S. Bur. Standards, Boulder, 1964-65; cons. editor Spanish lang. pilots' tng. manual, 1981-82; freelance translator, Englewood, Colo., 1982—. Mem. Internat. Bus. Assn. of the Rockies, U. Mich. Alumni Assn., Phi Sigma Iota. Republican. Episcopalian. Home and Office: 5091 S Boston St Englewood CO 80111

GOSSETT, KIMBERLY A., nurse; b. Columbus, Ind., Sept. 22, 1960; d. David J. and Jane A. (Noblitt) Miller; m. Scott P. Gossett, Aug. 8, 1987. BS, Butler U., 1982; BSN, Elmhurst (Ill.) Coll., 1987. RN. Nurse Christ Hosp., Oak Lawn, Ill., 1987-88, Mercy Hosp. and Med. Ctr., Chgo.,

1988—. Mem. Sigma Theta Tau. Home: 3620 S Austin Blvd Cicero IL 60650

GOTCHER, JOAN ELAINE, nurse; b. Stephentown, July 21, 1935; d. Arthur Wheeler and E. Rita (Palmer) Wetherwax; m. Raymond Lee Smith Sr., Sept. 22, 1958 (div. Feb. 1970); children: Cynthia Jean, Nancy Jean, Raymond Lee Jr., David Lee; m. Harold E., Nov. 6, 1978. Nursing (diploma), St. Luke's Hosp. Sch. of Nursi, Pittsfield, 1956; AA Liberal Arts, San Bernardino Valley Coll., San Bernardino, 1976; BS in Health Science, Redlands U., Redlands, 1986; MBA in Mgmt., Redlands U., 1989. Oper. room staff nurse Redlands Community Hosp., 1957-60; head nurse San Bernardino County Med. Ctr., 1966-80; head nurse quality assurance coord. Kaiser Found. Hosp., Fontana, 1980—; chief rehab. nurse, San Bernardino County Med. Ctr., 1975-80. Mem. Am. Mgmt. Assn., So. Calif. Quality Assurance Nurse Profls., So. Calif. Nursing Diagnosis Assn. Republican. Roman Catholic. Home: 12374 Vivienda Avenue Grand Terrace CA 92324 Office: Kaiser Foundation Hospital 9966 Sierra Avenue Fontana CA 92335

GOTHARD, DONITA, psychologist, educator; b. Minden, La., June 9, 1932; d. Donald Elmer and Nita (Brunt) Gothard. BA, Northwestern State U. La., 1954, MEd, 1961; PhD, U. Ala., 1970. Tchr. Bossier (La.) Parish Schs., 1954-61, counselor, 1961-67; instr. Northwestern State U. La., 1967-68; dir. human relations Caddo (La.) Parish Schs., 1970-71; sch. psychologist Caddo (la.) Parrish Schs., 1971-73; asst. prof. psychology La. State U., Shreveport, 1973-76; assoc. prof., Shreveport, 1976-81; prof. prof., 1981-85, prof. emeritus, 1985, also coordinator specialist degree sch. psychology; founder, pres. West Park Psychol. Services, Inc. Mem. Am. Psychol. Assn., La. Psychol. Assn., Soc. Personality Assessment, Am. Registry Lic. Psychologists and Mental Health Profls. Home: 10126 Keatchie-Marshall Rd Keatchie LA 71046

GOTLIEB, JAQUELIN SMITH, pediatrician; b. Washington, Oct. 20, 1946; d. Turner Taliaferro and Lois Barbara (Fisk) Smith; m. Edward Marvin Gotlieb, June 25, 1970; children: Sarah Ruth, Aaron Franklin, David Jacob. BS in Zoology, Duke U., 1968; MD, Med. Coll. Va., 1972. Diplomate Am. Bd. Pediatrics. Rotating intern Med. Coll. Va. Hosps.-Va. Commonwealth U., Richmond, 1972-73, resident in pediatrics, 1973-74; pvt. practice Richmond, 1974-75, Stone Mountain, Ga., 1976-86, 87—; resident in pediatrics U. Colo., Denver, 1975-76; med. dir., cons. CIGNA Healthplan Ga., Atlanta, 1986-87; sch. physician Richmond City Schs., 1974-75. Troop leader Boy Scouts Am., Atlanta, 1988; bd. dirs. Ga. Health Found., Atlanta, 1985—. Fellow Am. Acad. Pediatrics; mem. Med. Assn. Ga., DeKalb Med. Soc. (com. chmn. 1976), Atlanta Women's Network. Office: Pediatric Ctr 5405-D Memorial Dr Stone Mountain GA 30083

GOTSOPOULOS, BARBARA LYNN, communications company executive; b. Paterson, N.J., Mar. 16, 1948; d. Albert Raymond and Vivian Betty (Polkoph) Parker; m. Nicholas Solon Gotsopoulos, Mar. 15, 1970. BS, Rensselaer Poly. Inst., 1969. Prin. in wholesale distbg. co. Hollywood, Fla., 1981-84; pvt. practice commodities trading cons. Hollywood, 1984-87; pres. Blue Springs Capital Corp., Hollywood, 1985-86, 1st Fla. Commodities, Inc., North Lauderdale, 1987; ptnr. Multinat. Svcs., Hollywood, 1986-87; br. office mgr. Ind. Brokers Group, Inc., North Lauderdale, 1987; asst. to sr. v.p. E.F. Hutton and Co., Inc., North Miami Beach, Fla., 1987-88, Prudential-Bache Securities, North Miami Beach, 1988; communications cons. Telus Communications, North Miami, 1988-89, Metagram Am., Inc., Hollywood, Fla., 1989—. Charter mem. Rep. Presdl. Task Force. Mem. Nat. Assn. Female Execs. (charter), United Greeks Am. (co-founder), Alpha Psi Omega. Home: PO Box 183 Hallandale FL 33008

GOTTESMAN, RITVA ANNELI, chiropractor; b. Oulu, Finland, Jan. 31, 1946; came to U.S. 1967; d. Arvi Jalmari and Kirsti (Mannermaa) Hurskainen; m. Howard Joseph Gottesman,Sept. 5, 1967; children: Tina Maria, Eric Simeon. AAS, Nassau Community Coll., Garden City, N.Y., 1980; BA, Hofstra U., Uniondale, N.Y., 1982; DC, N.Y. Chiropractic Coll., Greenvale, N.Y., 1986. Pvt. practice chiropractic East Islip, N.Y., 1986—. Corres. sec. Drug Abuse Stops Here, East Islip, 1988-89; vol. instr. YMCA, Bay Shore, N.Y., 1989; adv. bd. Fire Island Light House, 1988-89. Mem. Am. Chiropractic Assn., N.Y. Chiropractic Assn., AAUW, Lionesses (v.p. 1989—), Phi Theta Kappa, Phi Beta Kappa, Phi Chi Omega. Lutheran. Address: 23 Irish Ln East Islip NY 11730

GOTTFRIED, MARTHA ANN, real estate broker; b. Evansville, Ind., Apr. 21, 1937; d. Francis J. and Mildred E. (Schatz) Heines; student U. Evansville, 1958, Palm Beach Jr. Coll., 1971; m. Robert W. Gottfried, Nov. 13, 1970. Sec. production control Mead Johnson & Co., Evansville, 1956-61, sec., v.p. internat. div., 1961-63, sec., pres. internat. div., 1963-67, adminstrv. asst., chmn. bd., 1967-70; corp. sec.-treas., dir. Robert W. Gottfried, Inc., Palm Beach, Fla., 1970—; pres. Martha A. Gottfried, Inc., Real Estate, Palm Beach, 1977—; Mem. Internat. Fedn. Real Estate Fedn., Nat. Womens Council Realtors, Palm Beach Bd. Realtors, Palm Beach Civic Assn. Roman Catholic. Clubs: Poinciana, Govs. (Palm Beach). Home: 748 HiMount Palm Beach FL 33480 Office: 219 Worth Ave Palm Beach FL 33480

GOTTI, MARGARET R., academic administrator; b. Glasgow, Scotland; married; 2 children. Bachelor's, Hunter Coll.; PhD, Fordham U. Instr. Iona Coll., Lehman Coll., Westchester Community Coll.; assoc. prof., chmn. dept. pub. adminstrn. Pace U., 1981-87; v.p. Pace U., White Plains, N.Y., 1987—; mem. Westchester Edn. Coalition, Westchester 2000 Edn. Com.; pres. Tuckahoe Bd. Edn. Contbr. articles to profl. jours. Named Citizen of Yr., Bronxville Manor Assn., 1986. Office: Pace U-White Plains Campus 75 N Broadway White Plains NY 10603*

GOTTLIEB, JANE ELLEN, librarian; b. Bklyn., Dec. 8, 1954; d. Eli David Gottlieb and Edythe (Schwartz) Rosenberg. BA in Music, SUNY, Binghamton, 1976; MLS, Columbia U., 1978. Librarian Am. Music Ctr., N.Y.C., 1978-82; reference librarian Lincoln Ctr. Performing Arts, N.Y.C., 1982-83; head librarian Mannes Coll. Music, N.Y.C., 1983-86, The Juilliard Sch., N.Y.C., 1986—; judge Paul Revere Awards, Music Publishers Assn., 1987. Assoc. editor: The Musical Woman: An International Perspective, 1983—; contbr. articles to The New Grove Dictionary of American Music, 1986. Mem. Music Library Assn. Office: Juilliard Sch Lila Acheson Wallace Libr 144 W 66th St Lincoln Ctr New York NY 10023

GOTTLIEB, LESLIE E., public relations executive; b. N.Y.C., Sept. 21, 1944; d. Manuel and Doris (Sife) G. BA cum laude, Syracuse U., N.Y., 1962-66; MA, Am. U., Washington, 1966-68. Legis. aide Rep. Lester Wolff, Washington, 1967-68; acting legis. asst. Senator Alan Cranston, Washington, 1970-71; legis. aide Congl. Black Caucus, Washington, 1972-71; pub. relations dir. The Jewish Mus., N.Y.C., 1973-77; media specialist The Ford Found., N.Y.C., 1977-87; dir. communications Council on Econ. Priorities, N.Y.C., 1987; cons. U.S. Holocaust Meml. Council, N.Y.C., 1985, Religious Task Force, Bklyn., 1984, 87. Contbr. article to profl. jour. V.p. Lexington Dem., N.Y.C., 1984—; mem. N.Y. County Dem. Com., 1983—. Mem. Pub. Relations Soc. Am., Women in Communications, Communications Network Phila. (bd. dirs. 1986). Jewish.

GOTTLIEB, LUCILLE MONTROSE FOX, retired state official; b. Hartford, Conn., May 30, 1929; d. Louis Paul and Rose Tomasina (Vignone) Montrose; student Cambridge Sch. Bus. Sci., 1948, Hillyer Jr. Coll., 1950; m. Francis R. Fox, Jr., June 26, 1954; m. Ralph Gottlieb, Sept. 28, 1979. Adminstrv. fiscal mgmt. officer Conn. Hwy. Dept., Hartford, 1950-61, asst. pub. relations dir., 1961-65, personnel asst., 1965-70; liaison officer Conn. Dept. Transp., from 1970; v.p. TV 58, Shoreline Communications Inc., 1976—. Chmn. Rocky Hill Park Com., 1968, Pool and Teen Center Com., 1976-77, Park and Recreation Adv. Bd., 1969; mem. Govs. Environ. Policy Com., 1972-74; chmn. Park and Recreation Adv. Bd., 1970; v.p. Gov's. Environ. Policy Panel on Travel and Transp.; amb. Conn. World Trade Assn.; mem. Conn. Boys Town of Italy, Fla. Beaudoin Soc.-Nova U.; trustee Council 13 Original States, 1978. Mem. NCCJ, Antiquarian Landmarks Soc. Conn., Fedn. Bus. and Profl. Women (chmn. pub. relations), Pub. Personnel Assn. Greater Hartford (v.p.), Conn. Employees Assn., Nat. Resources Council Conn., Great Meadow Conservation Trust, Conn. Pub. Health Assn., Women in Communications (v.p. Conn. chpt. 1978), Conn. Hist. Com., Conn. Italian-Am. Cultural Assn. (pres. 1978), Smithsonian Inst., Met. Opera Guild, Ft. Lauderdale Symphony Soc., Ft. Lauderdale Opera Guild, Audubon Soc., Am. Mus. Natural History, Internat. Platform Assn., Fla. Holy Cross Aux. (life). Republican. Roman Catholic. Clubs: Lady Hilton VIP, Cosmopolitan Hartford, Officers of Conn. (sec.). Creator Gertie Glitter anti litter symbol. Home: 3500 Galt Ocean Dr Fort Lauderdale FL 33308 Also: 16 Judd Rd Wetherfield CT 06109

GOTTLIEB, MARISE SUSS, medical educator, epidemiologist; b. N.Y.C., July 16, 1938; d. Lester J. and Fannie (Freeman) Suss; m. A. Arthur Gottlieb, June 8, 1958; children: Mindy Cheryl, Joanne Meredith. AB, Barnard Coll., 1958; MD, NYU, 1962; MPH, Harvard U., 1966. Intern, Mass. Meml. Hosp., 1962-63; resident dept. epidemiology Harvard U., 1965-68, instr. dept. medicine, H.M., Boston, 1969-70, also resident, asst. in Medicine Peter Bent Brigham Hosp.; dir. chronic disease control N.J. Dept. Health, Trenton, 1970-75; asst. prof. Rutgers Med. Sch., Piscataway N.J., 1972-75; assoc. prof. Tulane U. Sch. Medicine, New Orleans, 1975—; assoc. prof. Sch. Pub. Health, 1975-80; chief chronic disease control, La. Dept. Health and Human Resources, New Orleans, 1975-85; dir. clin. and regulatory affairs, v.p. med. affairs Imreg Inc., New Orleans, 1985—; mem. epidemiology and disease control study sect. NIH, Bethesda, Md., 1982-85. NIH traineeship, 1965-66, spl research fellow Nat. Inst. Arthritis, Metabolism and Digestive Diseases, 1966-68. Diplomate Am. Bd. Preventive Medicine. Fellow Am. Coll. Preventive Medicine, Am. Coll. Epidemiology; mem. Am. Diabetes Assn., Soc. Epidemiol. Rsch., Am. Fedn. Clin. Rsch., Am. Pub. Health Assn., La. Health and Human Resources Assn. (dir. chronic disease control 1975-85). Contbr. articles to profl jours. Office: Imreg Inc 144 Elk Pl Ste 1400 New Orleans LA 70112

GOTTLIEB, SALLY ANN, computer company executive; b. Bethesda, Md., June 13, 1951; d. Paul Wolfgang and Elinor Mae (Pries) Shadle; m. Roger Martin Gottlieb, Dec. 18, 1976. BA, U. Calif., Berkeley, 1973; postgrad., San Jose State U., 1990—. Tech. asst. Pacific Gas & Electric Co., San Francisco, 1973-76, sr. analyst-programmer, 1976-78; supr. HRIS Human Resources Information Systems, San Francisco, 1979-84; supr. benefits adminstrn. Pacific Gas & Electric Co., San Francisco, 1985-89; benefits mgr. Apple Computer, Inc., Cupertino, Calif., 1989—; instr. cert. course Am. Compensation Assn., Scottsdale, Ariz., 1984—. Recipient 1st prize for total benefits communications Bus. Ins. mag., 1987. Mem. Am. Compensation Assn. Office: Apple Computer Inc 10725 N DeAnza Blvd M/S 39F Cupertino CA 95014

GOTTRY, KARLA MAE STYER, food products executive; b. Mankato, Minn., Aug. 10, 1951; d. Richard Ernest and Ione Agnetha (Miller) Styer; m. James Bilotti (div. 1980); m. Steven R. Gottry, Nov. 7, 1984; 1 child, Kalla Paige. Grad. high sch., Mankato, 1969. Sales person Continental Airlines, L.A.; sales sec. Western Airlines, Bloomington; sales rep. Kuehn Pearson Rufer, Bloomington, 1984—. Republican. Lutheran. Office: Kuehn Pearson Rufer 7825 Telegraph Rd Bloomington MN 55438

GOTTSCHALK, JANICE K., operations and financial executive; b. Racine, Wis., Feb. 23, 1951; d. James R. and Ruby Inez (Meininger) Glidden; m. Gene A. Gottschalk, Jan. 23, 1971. BS in Bus. Mgmt., U. Wis., Parkside, 1976; MBA, Marquette U., 1980. Cert. CPA, Minn. Chief operating officer, chief fin. officer ILBC Affiliates, Inc., Mpls.; corp. contr. The Confections Group, St. Paul; group acctg. mgr. Ward-Johnston, Inc., Milw. Mem. Minn. Soc. CPAs, Nat. Assn. Accts., World Wildlife Fund, Am. Amateur Racquetball Assn. Home: 14724 Southampton Dr Burnsville MN 55337

GOTWALT, NORMA JEAN, educational administrator; b. York, Pa., Oct. 8, 1930; d. Edwin Laverne and Alma Naomi (Allison) G. BS, Bucknell U., 1952, MS, 1956; postgrad. in ednl. adminstrn., Pa. State U., 1969. Tchr. Harrisburg (Pa.) Sch. Dist., 1952-61, head tchr., 1961-66, elem. prin., 1966-78, supr. elem. instrn. programs, 1978-84, dir. div. elem. edn., 1984—; mem. erly childhood edn. com. Harrisburg Area Community Coll., 1988-90; state c hmn. sch. site task force Am. Heart Assn., 1989-90. Com. mem. 2d century initiative Tri-County United Way, Harrisburg, 1988-89, Harrisburg Mayor's Census Task Force, 1989; mem. Mayor's Commn. on LIteracy, 1990; bd. dirs. Art Assn. Harrisburg, 1988—, Family and Children's Svcs., Harrisburg, 1989—; allocations panelist Allied Arts Fund, Inc., Harrisburg, 1989-90. Recipient edn. div. Salute of Women Who Work, Pomeroy's Dept. Store, 1983. Mem. Am. Assn. Sch. Adminstrs. (pres.-elect nat. women's caucus 1988-90, pres. 1990—, chairperson exec. com. 3d nat. literacy conf.), Nat. Assn. Elem. Sch. Prins., Assn. for Supervision and Curriculum Devel., Bus. and Profl. Women's Club (pres. Harrisburg 1963-65), Zonta (pres. Harrisburg-Hershey 1980-82), Phi Delta Kappa (pres. 1984-85). Home: 20 Round Hill Rd Apt 1 Camp Hill PA 17011 Office: Harrisburg Sch Dist 1201 N 6th St Harrisburg PA 17102

GOUDY, JOSEPHINE GRAY, social services administrator; b. Des Moines, Nov. 30, 1925; d. Gerald William and Myrtle Maria (Brooks) Gray; B.A., State U. Iowa, 1953, M.S.W., 1966; m. John Winston Goudy, June 5, 1948; children: Tracy Jean, Paula Rae. Lic. social worker, Iowa. Child welfare supr. Iowa Dept. Social Services, 1960-68; psychiat. social worker Community Mental Health Center Scott County (Iowa), 1966-71; social work instr. Palmer Jr. Coll., Davenport, Iowa, 1967-70; psychiat. social worker, chief social services Jacksonville (Ill.) State Mental Hosp., 1971-74; coordinator community mental health outpatient services McFarland Mental Health Center, Springfield, Ill., 1974; exec. dir. Macoupin County Mental Health Center, Carlinville, Ill., 1974—; chmn. Human Services Edn. Council, Springfield, 1979-81; bd. mem. Alzheimer's Disease and Related Disorders Assn., Springfield Ill. Area Chpt., past exec. Davenport Community Welfare Council. Mem. Nat. Assn. Social Workers (Social Worker of Yr. Central Ill. area 1983), Acad. Cert. Social Workers, Am. Personnel and Guidance Assn., AAUW (br. pres. 1964-66, mem. state bar 1966-68, br. grantee 1975), Internat. Fedn. U. Women, U. Iowa Alumni Assn., Bus. and Profl. Women (Woman of Yr. 1983), Delta Kappa Gamma, Kappa Delta Pi. Republican. Methodist. Club: Carlinville Women's (pres. 1975-77). Home: 364 W Tremont St Waverly IL 62692 Office: 100 N Side Sq Carlinville IL 62626

GOUGÉ, SUSAN CORNELIA JONES, microbiologist; b. Chgo., Apr. 18, 1924; d. Harry LeRoy and Gladys (Moon) Jones; student Am. U., Washington, 1942-43, La. Coll., 1944-45; BS, George Washington U., 1948; postgrad. Georgetown U., 1956-58, 66-69, Vt. Coll. of Norwich U., M.A. in Pub. Health, 1984; m. John Oscar Gougé , Aug. 7, 1943; children: John Ronald, Richard Michael (dec.), Claudia Renée Gougé Carr. Med. technician Children's Hosp. Research Lab., Washington, 1948-49; bacteriologist George Washington U. Research Lab., D.C. Gen. Hosp., 1950-53; med. microbiologist Walter Reed Army Inst. Research, Washington, 1953-61; research asst. Dental Research, Walter Reed Army Med. Ctr., 1961-62; microbiologist antibiotics div. FDA, 1962-63; supr. quality control John D. Copanos Co., Pharms., Balt., 1963-64; research tng. asst. infectious diseases and tropical medicine Howard U. Med. Sch., 1964-65; research assoc. Georgetown U. Lab. Infectious Diseases, D.C. Gen. Hosp., 1966-69; mycologist Georgetown U. Hosp. Lab., 1969-70; microbiologist Research Found. of Washington Hosp. Ctr., 1971-73; dir. quality control Bio-Medium Corp., Silver Spring, Md., 1973-76; microbiologist Alcolac, Inc., Balt., 1976-77; microbiologist div. labs., dept. human resources Community Health and Hosps. Adminstrn., Washington, 1978-79; microbiologist div. ophthalmic devices, Office Device Evaluation Ctr. for Devices and Radiol. Health, FDA, Rockville, Md., 1979—. Sec. to exec. bd. Bethesda Project Awareness, 1970-71; vol. lead poisoning detection testing project, D.C. Office Vols. Internat. Tech. Assistance, 1970-71; vol. Zacchaeus Free Clinic, Washington, 1979-84. Mem. Nat. Capital Harp Ensemble, 1941-65; mem. parish social concerns com. Roman Cath. Ch. Recipient medal community service; registered microbiologist Nat. Registry Microbiologists; specialist microbiologist Am. Acad. Microbiology. Mem. AAAS, VITA, Am. Soc. for Microbiology, Am. Inst. Biol. Scis., Am. Chem. Soc., Internat. Union Pure and Applied Chemistry, N.Y. Acad. Scis., Am. Pub. Heath Assn., Albertus Magnus Guild, Capital Bus. and Profl. Women's Club (rec. sec. 1973-74, 1st v.p. 1974-75, pres. 1975-76), Winchester Bus. and Profl. Women, World Affairs Council of Washington D.C., Toastmasters (sec. 1979-80), Pi Kappa Delta. Roman Catholic. Office: FDA Div Ophthalmic Devices Office Device Evaluation 1390 Piccard Dr Rockville MD 20850

GOUGH, MRS. HERBERT FREDERICK See GOUGH, JESSIE POST

GOUGH, JESSIE POST (MRS. HERBERT FREDERICK GOUGH), retired educator; b. Nakon Sri Tamaraj, Thailand, Jan. 26, 1907 (parents Am. citizens); d. Richard Walter and Mame (Stebbins) Post; B.A., Maryville Coll., 1927; M.A. in English, U. Chgo., 1928; Ed.D., U. Ga., 1965; m. Herbert Frederick Gough, June 30, 1934; children: Joan Acland (Mrs. Alexander Reed), Herbert Frederick. Tchr. English, Linden Hall, Lititz, Pa., 1930-32; tchr. Fairyland Sch., Lookout Mountain, Tenn., 1955-64; rsch. asst. English curriculum studies ctr. U. Ga., 1964-65; asso. prof. elem. edn. LaGrange (Ga.) Coll., 1965-73, prof., 1973-75; prof. N.W. Ga. area tchr. edn. svcs., 1969-71. Mem. Walker County (Ga.) Curriculum Coun., 1959-61, Walker County Ednl. Planning Bd., 1958-60. Mem. Am. Ednl. Rsch. Assn., Internat. Reading Assn., Nat., Ga. edn. assns., Delta Kappa Gamma. Home: 8111 Savannah Hills Dr Ooltewah TN 37363

GOUGH, JUDY S., municipal official; b. Charlottesville, Va., Dec. 7, 1945; d. Marcellus Bradley and Julia Ennis (Johnson) Sclater; m. Robert Houston Gough; children: Laura Ann, Robert Houston Jr. Sec. U. Va., Charlottesville, 1965-68; adminstrv. asst. Madison House-U. Va., 1968-73; fiscal asst. County of Albemarle, Charlottesville, 1973—. Bd. mem. Hearthstone Children's House (now Ronald McDonald House), Charlottesville, 1981-88, Dept. Volunteerism, Commonwealth of Va., Richmond, 1986-88; bd. mem., pres. Ctr. for Vol. Devel., Blacksburg, Va., 1983-88 (Achievement award 1988); pres. Henley Mid. Sch. Devel. Adv. Coun., 1985-87; sec. Western Albemarle Boosters Assn., 1985-88; pres., sec. Univ. Bapt. Ch., 1980-88, com. mem. and Sunday sch. tchr. Mem. Va. Fin. Officers Assn. (exec. sec. 1986-90), Va. Fed. Women's Club (pres. Shenandoah Dist. 1988-90, Charlottesville Jrs. 1970-83), Haviland Women's Club (pres. 1983-85). Baptist. Home: 3535 Brinnington Rd Charlottesville VA 22901 Office: County of Albemarle 401 McIntyre Rd Dept Fin Charlottesville VA 22901

GOUGH, KATHLEEN (ELEANOR KATHLEEN GOUGH ABERLE), research anthropologist; b. Hunsingore, Wetherby, Yorkshire, Eng., Aug. 16, 1925; arrived in Can., 1967; d. Albert and Eleanor (Umpleby) G.; m. Eric John Miller, July 5, 1947 (div. 1950); m. David Friend Aberle, Sept. 5, 1955; 1 child, Stephen Daniel. BA, Girton Coll., Cambridge, Eng., 1946, MA, 1949; PhD, U. Cambridge, 1950. Rsch. fellow Wenner-Gren Found. Anthropology Rsch. Radcliffe Coll., Harvard U., 1953-54; lectr. anthropology U. Manchester, Eng., 1954-55, rsch. assoc., 1960-61; vis. lectr. U. Calif., Berkeley, 1955-56, Wayne State U., Detroit, 1959-60; lectr., rsch. assoc. U. Mich., Ann Arbor, 1956-59; asst. prof. Brandeis U., Waltham, Mass., 1961-63; rsch. assoc. U. Oreg., Eugene, 1963-67; assoc. prof. then prof. Simon Fraser U., Burnaby, B.C., Can., 1967-70; rsch. assoc. U. B.C., Vancouver, Can., 1971—; field research in South India, 1947-49, 51-53, 64, 76, Socialist Republic of Vietnam, 1976, 82, People's Republic of Kampuchea, 1982; vis. prof. U. Toronto, Can, 1970. Author: Ten Times More Beautiful: the Rebuilding of Vietnam, 1978, Rural Society in Southeast India, 1981, Rural Change in Southeast India, 1950s to 1980s, 1989, Political Economy in Vietnam, 1989; co-author, editor: Matrilineal Kinship, 1961, reprinted 1973, 74, Imperialism and Revolution in South Asia, 1973; mem. editorial bd. Bull. of Concerned Asian Scholarsm 1969—; contbr. articles to profl. jours. Recipient Outstanding Rsch. award Am. Social Sci. Rsch. Coun., 1963; grantee Am. Soc. Sci. Rsch. Coun., 1954, 58, Social Scis. and Humanities Rsch. Coun. Can., 1974-81, 82-86. Fellow Am. Anthrop. Assn., Royal Anthrop. Inst. (Curl Bequest prize 1953), Royal Soc. Can.; mem. Canadian Assn. Sociology and Anthropology, Canadian Assn. Asian Studies. Home: 4518 Marine Dr, West Vancouver, BC Canada V7W 2N9

GOUGH, PAULINE BJERKE, magazine editor; b. Wadena, Minn., Jan. 7, 1935; d. Luther C. and Zita Pauline (Halbmaier) Bjerke; BA, U. Minn., Mpls., 1957; BS, Moorhead (Minn.) State Coll., 1970; MS, Ind. U., Bloomington, 1972, EdD, 1977; children: Mary Pauline, Sarah Elizabeth, Philip Clayton. Reporter women's page San Jose (Calif.) Mercury-News, 1957-58; with rsch. dept. Campbell-Mithun Advt., Mpls., 1958-60; tchr. Univ. Elem. Sch., Bloomington, 1970-79; freelance writer Agy. Instructional TV, Bloomington, 1974-80; mem. adj. faculty Ind. U.-Purdue U., Indpls., summers 1976, 77; asst. editor Phi Delta Kappan, Bloomington, 1980-81, mng. editor, 1981-88; editor, 1988—; mem. profl. staff Phi Delta Kappa, 1981—, also leader insts. on writing for publ. Recipient Disting. Alumna award Moorhead State U., 1982. Mem. Phi Beta Kappa, Phi Delta Kappa. Author articles in field. Home: 3570 Oakridge Dr Bloomington IN 47401 Office: Phi Delta Kappan 8th & Union St Box 789 Bloomington IN 47402

GOULD, EILEEN GORDON, interior designer; b. Atlanta, Nov. 5, 1948; d. Morris and Blanche (Moston) Gordon; m. Edward L. Gould, May 28, 1978 (div. Jan. 1988); 1 child, Taylor Gray. Student, U. Ga., NYU. Model, actress, pub. rels. Atlanta, N.Y.C., 1970-74; interior designer Atlanta, 1976—, profl. fundraiser, 1982—; TV producer Best of Atlanta, Video Mag., and Ga. Teleprodns.; dir. mktg. Jean-Claude Jitrois/Shockey Enterprises, 1989—; owner Designs of Sigmon-Gould Interiors, 1978—. Dir. entertainment, M.C. for Maynard Jackson campaign for mayor, Atlanta, 1989; fundraising dir. The Nat. Coll. Alumni Found., 1988, 89; dir. major donations The Link Counseling Ctr., 1990. Mem. Buckhead Bus. Assn. Home: 7155-56 Roswell Rd Atlanta GA 30328

GOULD, HELEN GRACE, business owner, educator; b. Chillicothe, Mo., Mar. 17, 1904; d. Louis Henry and Mary Hannah (Waterman) G. BA cum laude, U. Tex., 1937; postgrad., U. Colo., 1969, W. Tex. U., 1956. Cert. tchr., Tex. Sec. to pres. State Tchrs. Assn., Commerce, Tex., 1926; substitute tchr. Wichita Falls (Tex.) Jr. Coll., 1926-27; dean of girls, sr. counselor Wichita Falls High Sch., 1927-72; co-owner Gould Realty, Wichita Falls, 1944—. Author poems. Vol. Sr. Citizens Ctrs.'s Meals on Wheels, 1972-82; mem. Rep. Women Bicentennial Commn., Wichita Falls, 1976; pres. Episcopal Churchwomen, Ch. of Good Shepherd, 1976-78, mem. vestry, 1980-82. Mem. NEA, Tex. Deans and Counselors (life), Wichita Falls Bd. Realtors, Tex. Realtors Assn., Nat. Ret. Tchrs. Assn., Tex. Ret. Tchrs. Assn., Wichita Falls Ret. Tchrs. Assn., Nat. Realtors Assn., AAUW, DAR (vice regent 1970-72, regent 1972-74), Datson (pres. 1986-88), Daus. of the King (pres.), Alpha Delta Pi. Home and Office: 2404 Martin Wichita Falls TX 76308

GOULD, MARCIA RAE, county official; b. Grand Rapids, Mich., Oct. 3, 1937; d. John and Dorothy Jean (Stewart) Tiethof; m. Robert Allen Kelley, Aug. 17, 1957 (div. 1969); children: Patrick Kelley, Kathleen Kelley Heyrman, Michael Kelley, Sean Kelley, Ryan Kelley;l m. Larry Wayne Gould, June 12, 1948; 1 child, Lucia Gould. Student, Grand Rapids Jr. Coll. With Mich. Bell, Grand Rapids, 1955-58, Gen. Telephone, Mt. Pleasant, Mich., 1958-59, Woolworth Co., 1952-55; mem. Alger County Social Svcs. Bd., Munising, Mich., 1987-88; Winner dem. primary for U.S. Congress, 1990. Sec. Alger County Dem. Party, Munising, 1980-82, vice chmn., 1982-84, chmn., 1984-86, county commr., 1986-88; Dem. primary candidate for U.S. Congress, 1988. Democrat. Christian Ch. Home: Route 1 Box 87 Shingleton MI 49884

GOULD, MARTHA B., librarian; b. Claremont, N.H., Oct. 8, 1931. BA in Edn., U. Mich., 1953; MS in Library Sci., Simmons Coll., 1956; cert., U. Denver Library Sch. Community Analysis Research Inst., 1978. Childrens librarian N.Y. Pub. Library, 1956-58; adminstr. library services act demonstration regional library project Pawhuska, Okla., 1958-59; cons. N.Mex. State Library, 1959-60; childrens librarian then sr. childrens librarian Los Angeles Pub. Library, 1960-72; acctg. dir. pub. srvices, reference librarian Nev. State Library, 1972-74; pub. services librarian Washoe County (Nev.) Library, 1974-79, asst. county librarian, 1979-84, county librarian, 1984—. Contbr. articles to jours. Treas. United Jewish Appeal, 1981; bd. dirs. Temple Sinai; trustee RSVP, North Nevadans for ERA; mem. exec. bd. Biggest Little City Com., 1989—; No. Nev. chmn. Gov.'s Conf. on Librs., 1990; mem. bd. Champaign for Choice. Recipient Nev. State Library Letter of Commendation, 1973, Washoe County Bd. Commrs. Resolution of Appreciation, 1978, Freedom's Sake award AAUW, 1989, Hall of Fame award Nev. Women's Fund, 1989. Mem. ALA (bd. dirs. intellectual freedom round table 1977-79, intellectual freedom com. 1979-83, council 1983-86), Nev. Library Assn. (chmn. pub. info. com. 1972-73, intellectual freedom com. 1975-78, govt. relations com. 1978-79, v.p., pres.-elect 1980, pres. 1981, Spl. Citation 1978, 87), ACLU (bd. dirs., Civil Libertarian of Yr. Nev. chpt. 1988), NCCJ (chair No. div. govs. conf. for women 1989). Office: Washoe Country Libr 301 S Center St PO Box 2151 Reno NV 89505

GOULD, MAXINE LUBOW, lawyer, marketing professional, consultant; b. Bridgeton, N.J., Feb. 28, 1942; d. Louis A. and Bernice L. (Goldberg) Lubow; B.S., Temple U., 1962, J.D., 1968; m. Sam C. Gould, June 17, 1962 (div. Dec. 1984); children—Jack, Herman, David. Head resident dept. student personnel Temple U., 1962-66; dir., treas. Hilltop Interest Program, Inc., Los Angeles, 1973-74; law clk. law firms, Los Angeles, 1975-77; with Buffalo Resources Corp., Los Angeles, 1978-82, corp. sec., 1979-82; corp. sec., securities prin. Buffalo Securities Corp., Los Angeles, 1979-82; corp. sec. LaMaur Devel. Corp., Los Angeles, 1979-82; contracts analyst, land dept. Texaco Inc., Los Angeles, 1982-83; exec. dir. Sinai Temple, West Los Angeles, 1983-85; pres. Cutting Edge, Los Angeles, 1986; adminstr. law firm Robinson, Wolas & Diamant, Century City, 1986, acctg. firm Roth, Bookstein & Zaslow, Los Angeles, 1986-87; project coordinator Cipher, 1987; mktg. dir. Am. Bus. Capital, Beverly Hills, Calif., 1988—. Mem. Roscomare Valley Assn. Edn. Com., Bel Air, Calif., 1975-76; subcom. chmn. Roscomare Rd. Sch. Citizens Adv. Council, Bel Air; active various community drives. Recipient Joseph B. Wagner Oratory award B'nai B'rith, 1959, Voice of Democracy award, 1958-59, award Commentator Club, 1959. Mem. ABA (law office econs. sect.), Los Angeles County Bar Assn. (assoc., law office econs. sect., fee dispute arbitration panel), Nat. Assn. Legal Adminstrs. (Beverly Hills chpt.), NAFE (network dir.), Nat. Assn. Law Firm Mktg. Adminstrs., Calif. Women Lawyers, Women in Bus. (co-chmn. membership com.), Calif. CPA Soc. (adminstr. com.), Nat. Assn. Synagogue Adminstrs., Am. Assn. Petroleum Landmen, Los Angeles Assn. Petroleum Landmen, Textile Profl. Soc., Comml. Fin. Assn., Phi Alpha Theta, Alpha Lambda Delta. Jewish. Home: 2501 Roscomare Los Angeles CA 90077 Office: Am Bus Capital 400 S Beverly Dr #208 Beverly Hills CA 90212

GOULD, ROBERTA YVONNE, business owner, consultant, personnel executive; b. Grand Rapids, Mich., Dec. 15, 1932; d. Robert Lewis and Neva Mae (Caukin) Clark; m. Willard LeRoy Hawes, July 12, 1951 (dec. Feb. 1967); 1 child, Mark Leslie; m. Alfred Prince Gould, Aug. 16, 1969. Grad. high sch., Hastings, Mich. Gen. office positions Am. Linen, San Diego, 1967-76; with accounts receivable dept. Precision Metals Co., El Cajon, Calif., 1976-78; bookkeeper D&D Enterprises, El Cajon, 1978-80; cons., owner, mgr. Elite Personnel Agy., San Diego, 1981—. Mem. Calif. Personnel Assn., San Diego Employers Assn., El Cajon C. of C., San Diego C. of C., Order of Ea. Star. Republican. Office: Elite Pers Agy 3435 Camino Del Rio S #313-314 San Diego CA 92108

GOULDER, CAROLJEAN HEMPSTEAD, psychologist; b. Houston, Minn., Apr. 9, 1933; d. Orson George and Jean Helen (Lischer) Hempstead; m. L. Lynton Goulder, Jr., May 26, 1956 (div. 1978); children: Jean Virginia, David Thomas, Ann Rachel; m. John T. Blake, Apr. 12, 1986. BS, Hamline U., 1956; CAGS, R.I. Coll., 1975, MA in Sch. Psychology, 1972; postgrad., Nova U., 1977-78. Cert. psychologist, R.I.; nat. cert. sch. psychologist. Dept. head, instr. Highsmith Hosp., Fayetteville, N.C., 1956-57; instr. nursing New Eng. Deaconess Hosp., Boston, 1957-58; dir. psychol. svcs. Burrillville Sch. Dept., Harrisville, R.I., 1972-79, sch. psychologist, 1972—; coord. presch. handicapped, 1985-86; lectr. pediatric problems Sturdy Meml. Hosp., Attleboro, Mass., 1970-72; cons. Wheeler Sch., Providence, 1970-73. Chmn. 2d Congl. Ch. Sch., Attleboro, Mass., 1962-65, mem. religious edn. com., kindergarten com. and choir, 1965; active 1st Unitarian Ch., Providence, 1982—. Mem. R.I. Sch. Psychologists Assn., Nat. Assn. Sch. Psychology, Am. Psychol. Assn. (assoc.), Mass. Psychol. Assn. (assoc.), Coun. for Exceptional Children, Delta Kappa Gamma. Office: AT Levy Sch Spl Svcs Office Harrisville RI 02830

GOULDING, NORA See CLARK, SUSAN

GOULET, CYNTHIA WAGNER, lawyer; b. Dickinson, N.D., Aug. 25, 1957; d. Clarence H. Wagner and Muriel Ann (Allen) Kisse; m. Wallace R. Goulet Jr.; children: Matthew Wyatt, Michael Wallace. BS, N.D. State U., 1979; JD, U. N.D., 1985. Newspaper reporter Assoc. Printer, The Record, Grafton, N.D., 1981-82; assoc. DePuy Law Firm, Grafton, 1985-87, De Puy Law Firm, Grafton; ptnr. Goulet Law Firm, Grafton, 1987—; pvt. staff atty. Legal Aid of N.D., Bismarck, 1985; mem. Legal Svcs. Com., Bismarck, 1987, N.D. Gender Fairness in Judiciary Com., Bismarck, 1988—. Author: N.D. Law Review, 1985. Mem. St. Johns Cath. Ch., Grafton, 1981—. Mem. ABA, AAUW, N.D. Bar Assn., Walsh County Bar Assn. (treas., 1987-89), Fair Oaks Golf Club. Democrat. Roman Catholic. Office: Goulet Law Firm 16 W 10th St Box 431 Grafton ND 58237

GOULET, LORRIE, sculptor; b. Riverdale, N.Y., Aug. 17, 1925. Student, Inwood Potteries Studios, N.Y.C., 1932-36, Black Mountain Coll., N.C., 1943-44. One-woman shows Clay Club Sculpture Ctr., N.Y.C., 1948, 55, Cheney Libr., Hoosick Falls, N.Y., 1951, Contemporaries Gallery, N.Y.C., 1959, 62, 66, 68, Rye Art Ctr., N.Y., 1966, New Sch. Assocs., N.Y.C., 1968, Temple Emeth, Teaneck, N.J., 1969, Kennedy Galleries, N.Y.C., 1971, 73, 75, 78, 80, 82, 86, Carolyn Hill Gallery, N.Y.C., 1988, Caldwell (N.J.) Coll., 1989; group shows include Mus. Natural History, 1936, Whitney Mus. Am. Art, N.Y.C., 1948, 49, 50, 53, 55, Met. Mus. Art, N.Y.C., 1951, Detroit Inst. Arts, 1960, Pa. Acad., 1950, 51, 52, 54, 59, 64, NAD, N.Y.C., 1966, 75, 77, Corcoran Gallery, Washington, 1966; represented in permanent collections N.J. State Mus., Wichita Mus. Art, Hirschhorn Sculpture Mus., Washington, also pvt. collections. Tchr. Mus. Modern Art, 1957, 64, Scarsdale Studio Workshop, 1959, 61, New Sch., 1961-75, Art Students League, 1981, 82, 83, 84, 85, 86, 87, 89. Recipient numerous art awards, various commns. Mem. Artists Equity, Audubon Artists, Sculptors Guild, Visual Artists and Galleries Assocs., Nat. Sculpture Soc., Nat. Acad. Design.

GOULET, SUZANNE CLAIRE, ski area manager; b. Boston, July 2, 1965; d. Richard Arthur and Anita Marie (Cormier) G. BS, U. Maine, 1990; postgrad., U. N.H., 1990—. Asst. gen. mgr. Atlantic Forests Ski Area, Amesbury, Mass., 1987—. Vol. Homemakers Organized for More Employment, Orland, Maine, 1984-86; publicity vol. OXFAM, Orono, Maine, 1989; mem. Orono Peace and Social Justice Com., 1986-87, 89. Mem. Newburyport Art Assn., Sierra Club, Appalachian Trail Conf. (2,000 miler 1988), Green Mountain Club, Maine Island Trail Conf., Shredders-R-Us Snowboard Club (pres. 1988—), Nat. Art Edn. Assn. Home: 25 Phillips Dr Newburyport MA 01950 Office: Atlantic Forests Ski Area PO Box 452 Amesbury MA 01913

GOULSTON, MARILYN GWEN, teacher; b. Waterville, Maine, Jan. 8, 1949; d. Ralph and Rachel (Fine) G.; m. Robert Jos. Shurman, Nov. 25, 1972 (div. 1975). Student, Bertley Coll., Waltham, Mass., 1973; BA, U. Mass., Boston, 1988, postgrad., 1989. Cert. educator. Bus. mgr. Hadco Corp., Boston, 1971-80; cons. 190 Realty Corp., Revere, Mass., 1985-87; cons. The Family Ctr., Somerville, Mass., 1987-89, adminstrv. dir., 1987-89; instr. English composition U. Mass., Boston, 1989—; bd. mem. East Boston News, 1985. Contbr. articles to profl. jours. Mem. Friends of Bird Isle Flats, East Boston, 1988, Com. for Accuracy in Middle East Reporting, Boston, 1989, People for Ethical Treatment of Animals. Mem. Nat. Council Tchrs. of English. Democrat. Jewish.

GOUR, BETTY, dance instructor, choreographer; b. Chgo., July 10, 1914; d. Andre Anastus and Marie Luella (Weeden) G. Studies with George Balanchine, Edna McRae, Anatole Vilzak, others. Dancer Chgo. Civic Opera Ballet, 1929-34, Am. Ballet Co. and Met. Opera Ballet, 1935-36; dancer, capt. of touring group Chester Hale Tex. Comets, 1937-40; dancer Broadway prodn. Frederika Imperial Theatre, 1937; dancer Phila. Ballet, 1940-44, Am. Jubilee New York's World's Fair, N.Y.C., 1940; dancer Nat. Co. of Oklahoma, 1944-53, ballet mistress, 1946-53; instr., choreographer stage play "Oklahoma" West Berlin, Fed. Repubic Germany, 1951, Paris, 1955; instr. of choreography movie version of "Oklahoma", 1954, staged various prodns., 1953-58; instr., owner dance studio Chgo., 1958-64; ballet mistress Ruth Page's Chgo. Opera Ballet, 1957-59; instr. dance Butler U., Indpls., 1964-86, assoc. prof. emeritus, 1986—, choreographer "Oklahoma", 1990—; instr. ballet Dance Kaleidoscope, Indpls., 1987—; choreographer Chgo. Nat. Auto Show, 1957-58, Chgo. World's Fair of Music and Sound, 1962, Nat. Boat Show, 1963, 20 ballets for the Butler Ballet, 1964-86, Nat. Arts and Letters Competition, 1990. Home: 4710 Hinesley Ave Indianapolis IN 46208

GOURLEY, MARY MARGARET, clinical laboratory scientist; b. Pitts., Nov. 30, 1942; d. Andrew William and Margaret (Boros) Matta; m. John Patrick Gourley, Nov. 16, 1968; 1 child, Christine Denise. Student, Juniata Coll., 1960-63, Montefiore Hosp. Sch. Med. Tech., 1964. Chemistry technologist J.R. Sugarman Lab., Pitts., 1964-65; technologist St. Joseph's Hosp., Pitts., 1965-67, 72-77, chief technologist, 1968-72; supr. blook bank South Hills Health System, Pitts., 1977-79; chief technologist Med. Chek Labs., Pitts., 1979-82; mgr. lab. South Side Hosp., Pitts., 1982-89; lab. mgr. Podiatry Hosp., 1989—; lab. cons. MG & Assocs., Pitts., 1989—; presenter in field, 1979—. Deacon Swissvale (Pa.) Presbyn. Ch., 1987—. Mem. Nat. Certifying Agy. for Med. Lab. Pers. (cert. clin. lab. scientist, clin. lab. dir., clin. lab. supr.), Am. Soc. Clin. Pathologists (cert. med. technologist), Am. Soc. Med. Tech. (bd. dirs. 1987—), Pa. Soc. for Med. Tech. (pres. 1983-84, bd. dirs. 1983-88, recipient Dolbey award 1984, pres. SW chpt. 1972-73, 82-83, bd. dirs. 1970-77, 80-83), Clin. Lab. Mgmt. Assn. (bylaws com. 1987-88, bd. dirs. Western Pa. chpt. 1983-84, 87-88, pres. 1985-86, bylaws chair 1988-90), Am. Assn. Blood Banks, Alpha Mu Tau. Republican. Office: MG Assocs 4729 Stanton Ave Pittsburgh PA 15201-1655

GOUVEIA, JUDITH KATHLEEN BLAKE, business executive; b. Wahaiwa, Hawaii, Oct. 18, 1944; d. Floyd Gerald Blake and Margaret Leialoha (Solomon) Kaluna; m. Patrick Ross Gouveia Sr., Dec. 13, 1947; children: Sainna, Janjse, Patrick Jr. Student, Grace Downs Coll., 1964-66. Sales mgr. Hawaii Western Cabinets, Honolulu, 1969-77; owner Marge's Lunchwagon, Waianae, Hawaii, 1977-80; co-owner Waianae Texaco Sta., 1976-80; pres. Gouveia Sales, Inc., Honolulu, 1968-88; ptnr. MW Investors, Honolulu, 1981—, Melville & Blake, Honolulu, 1980—, Developers Four, Inc., Honolulu, 1988—; owner Gonveia Poultry Co., Waianae, 1973—; entertainer Heidi's Bistro, Honolulu, 1987-89, Arthur's Restaurant, Honolulu, 1989—; officer Telecheck Fed. Credit Union, Honolulu, 1968-70. Advisor 4H Am., Waianae, 1973-74; mem. Waianae Neighborhood Bd., 1984; entertainer Jerry Lewis Telethon at Waianae Shopping Mall, Muscular Dystrophy Assn., 1990. Recipient Good Citizen award Honolulu Channel 2 News, 1975. Mem. Bldg. Industry Assn., Gen. Contractors Assn., Profl. Singers Honolulu (sec. 1988). Republican. Baptist. Home: 87-746 Farrington Hwy Wainae HI 96792 Office: Melville & Blake 1188 Bishop St PH3610 Honolulu HI 96813

GOVIG, VALERIE COWLS, publisher, editor; b. Portland, Oreg., Sept. 4, 1934; d. Thomas Ewart and Charlene (Endecott) Cowls; B.A. (undergrad. poetry award 1956), U. Oreg., 1956; m. Melvin Emerson Govig, Sept. 4, 1954; children—Dana Hope Derry, Kari Joy Cress. Grad. asst. English dept. U. Oreg., 1956-57; advt. copywriter Hutzler's Dept. Store, Balt., also freelance copywriter, 1971-76; pub.-editor Kite Lines mag., Balt., 1977—; pres. Aeolus Press, Inc., 1977—. Founder Md. Kite Festival, 1967; publicity chmn. Liberty Rd. Recreation and Parks Council, 1971-73; mem. public relations com., editor newsletter Chesapeake council Camp Fire Girls, 1973-75. Recipient Ernest Thompson Seton award Camp Fire Girls, 1975. Mem. Balt. Pubs. Assn., Am. Kitefliers Assn. (founder 1978), Md. Kite Soc. (founder 1969). Office: KiteLines Mag PO Box 466 Randallstown MD 21133-0466

GOVIN, MARY-JANE C., public relations executive; b. Milw., June 30, 1943; d. James Francis and Jane Shirley (Prasser) Ircink; m. Albert R. Govin, Oct. 3, 1964; children: Terri J. Govin Wolf, Cheryl A., Linda M., Gregory A. BA, Mt. Mary Coll., 1987. Exec. sec. Joseph Schlitz Brewing Co., Milw., 1961-63, Milw. and Suburban Transport Co., Milw., 1963-65; dir. religious edn. St. Joan of Arc Parish, Okauchee, Wis., 1980-88; dir. communications Wis. Inst. of CPAs, Brookfield, Wis., 1988—. Mem. Internat. Assn. Bus. Communication, Am. Soc. Assn. Execs., Pub. Rels. Soc. of Am., Women in Communications, Inc. (prog com., speaker regional conf. 1990). Roman Catholic. Home: 417 Greenland Ave Oconomowoc WI 53066 Office: Wis Inst of CPAs 180 N Executive Dr Brookfield WI 53005

GOWANS, KATHY ELIZABETH, nurse, consultant; b. Kansas City, Mo., June 10, 1948; d. Walter Henry and Bettie (Rice) Ziegler; m. John J. Gowans (div. Feb. 1989); children: Jonathan, Jeremy. AD in Nursing, Kansas City Community Coll., 1983. RN, Kans., Mo.; cert. midwife. Cons., educator ACHI/FACT, Blue Springs, Mo., 1975-83; nurse U. Kans. Med. Ctr., Kansas City, 1983-85, Humana Hosp., Overland Park, Kans., 1985-89; pres., founder Materna Care, Kansas City, Mo., 1986—; officer Kansas City (Mo.) State U., 1975-79; dir., founder FACT, Kansas City, Mo., 1979-83. Author, editor: Birth with Confidence, 1979. Guest speaker Neil Poindexter Radio Show, Kansas City, Mo., 1977, Walt Bodine Radio Show, Kansas City, Mo., 1977. Mem. Nurses Assn. Ob-Gyn, Mo. Midwives Assn. Home and Office: 513 NE Newport Dr Lees Summit MO 64064

GOWANS, MRS. WILLIAM RORY See REMICK, LEE

GOWDY, MIRIAM BETTS, nutritionist; b. Nelsonville, Ohio, Jan. 9, 1928; d. Charles Donald and Lillian Mary (Linscott) B.; m. Robert Averill Gowdy, Oct. 12, 1950 (div. 1977); children: Carol Jo, Robert Jr., Bruce. BA in Home Econs., Ohio Wesleyan U., 1949; student, Duke U., 1949-50, Calif. State U., L.A., 1975-76. Registered dietitian. Dietitian L.A., 1977—; cons. Nat.-in-Home Health, Van Nuys, Calif., 1984-87. Mem. Am. Diabetes Assn. (cons. San Fernando Valley Unit 1976-80, bd. dirs. N.W. chpt. 1977-82), Consulting Nutritionists (chmn. elect. So. Calif. chpt. 1979-81), Calif. Dietetic Assn. (chmn. diabetes care practice 1979-81), Am. Heart Assn. (mem. gov. bd. N.W. chpt. 1988-89), Sierra Club, Nat. Audubon Soc. Republican. Episcopalian. Home and Office: 21900-268 Marylee St Woodland Hills CA 91367

GOWENS, VERNEETA VIOLA, journalist; b. South Holland, Ill., Mar. 19, 1913; d. William and Mary Cawthorne (Fowler) Gibson; ed. public schs., Bryant and Stratton Bus. Coll.; m. Albert Gowens, July 17, 1936; children—Victoria Ann Gowens Utke, Mary Ann Gowens Weiss. Clk., pub. relations worker Chgo. and Riverdale Lumber Co., Chgo., 1934-45; feature writer, women's editor Tribune Publs., Harvey, Ill., 1960-62; feature writer, women's editor Star-Tribune, Williams Press, Chicago Heights, Ill., 1963-78; freelance writer; script writer variety shows Ship Ahoy, 1963, Fair 'n' Square, 1964; contbr. to Internat. Altrusan, 1974, Church Herald, 1977. Sunday sch. tchr., youth leader 1st Ref. Ch., South Holland; mem. editorial council Ch. Herald, Ref. Ch. in Am., 1976-82; pres. Dist. 150 PTA, 1965-66; adv. com. program in ltd. occupation tng. Thornton High Sch., 1963-69; mem. South Holland Indsl. Commn., 1965-68; bd. dirs. Family Service and Mental Health Center of South Cook County, Ill., 1974-77; mem. South Holland unit Salvation Army, 1958—; judge Internat. Teen Pageant, 1969; mem. South Holland Community Chest, 1978—; adv. bd. Thornton Community Coll. nursing program, 1976-83; active South Holland Diamond Jubilee, 1969; mem. South Holland Cable Commn., 1984—. Recipient award South Holland C. of C., 1970, Genoa council K.C., 1974, Village of South Holland, 1969, 1st pl. in contest No. Ill. U., 1974, 75, award Suburban Press Found., 1969, 1st pl. award Ill. Press Assn., 1973, 50 other awards in writing. Mem. Ill. Women's Press Assn. (Woman of Yr. 1974, award 1978), Nat. Fedn. Press Women (1st pl. Sweepstakes award 1976). Home: 16830 S Park Ave South Holland IL 60473

GOWL, COLLEEN BUTLER, advertising agency executive. With FCB/Leber Katz Ptnrs., N.Y.C., 1986—, exec. v.p., 1988—. Office: FCB/Leber Katz Ptnrs GM Bldg 767 Fifth Ave New York NY 10153*

GOYKE, LOUISE RENEE, computer systems manager; b. South Holland, Ill., Dec. 11, 1966; d. Willard Anthony and Gloria Faye (Kern) G. Student, Thornton Community Coll., 1985-88, DePaul U., 1988—. Office asst. Basic Steel Corp., Riverdale, Ill., 1985-87, computer systems mgr., programmer, 1987—. Mem. Beta Gamma Sigma. Roman Catholic. Office: Basic Steel Corp 14100 Basic Steel Dr Riverdale IL 60627

GOYNES, ROXIE F., lawyer; b. Natchez, Miss., Nov. 15, 1957; d. Francis Robert and Flora Mae (Parker) Goynes. BA, La. Coll., Pineville, 1979; JD, So. U., 1983; student, La. Tech. U., Ruston, 1975-76. Law clk., legis. liaison Div. Adminstrn., State La., Baton Rouge, 1981-82, Gladney & Ponder, Baton Rouge, 1982-83, John Comish & Woodie Wyatt, Baton Rouge, 1983; pvt. practice law Baton Rouge, 1983-84, 87—; assoc. Reina & LeBlanc, Denham Spring, La., 1984-87; legal counsel Livingston Civitan, 1985-88, Capitol Area Rsch. & Devel. Coun., 1987-89. Mem. ABA, La. Bar Assn., Baton Rouge Bar Assn. (family law com., lawyers in classrom com.), Baton Rouge Bd. Realtors, Baton Rouge C. of C. Democrat. Baptist. Office: 11842 Justice Ave Suite A Baton Rouge LA 70816

GOZBERK, BARBARA ANN, accountant; b. Bronson, Tex., Apr. 1, 1941; d. Thomas Christopher and Anna Lela (Pitts) Stanton; m. Aydin Mehmet Gozberk, Nov. 11, 1966. BBA in Acctg., Stephen F. Austin State U., 1962. CPA, Tex. Gen. acct. Polyspede Electronics Inc., Dallas, 1963-70; asst. contr. Trinity Valley Foods, Dallas, 1970-77; mgr. gen. acctg. Fox & Jacobs, Dallas, 1977-78; mgr. gen. acctg. Mitsubishi Aircraft Internat. Inc., Dallas, 1979-84, dir. fin. and acctg., 1984-90; pvt. practice Dallas, 1990—. Mem. AICPA, Tex. Soc. CPA's (Dallas chpt.), Citizens for Sound Economy, English First, Ronald Reagan Presdl. Found., Stephen R. Austin State U. Alumni Assn., Sigma Kappa. Republican. Mem. Ch. of Christ.

GRABFIELD, DEBORAH DILLER, academic administrator, consultant; b. Greenport, N.Y., Oct. 26, 1954; d. Frank Joseph Diller and Jean (Newbold) Andrews; m. Philip White Grabfield, Feb. 14, 1988; 1 child, Alyssa Wells. BS, Am. U., 1976; MS, U. Pa., 1988. Asst. dir. admissions U. Pa., Phila., 1979-85, assoc. dir. grad. programs, 1985-88; freelance fin. svc. cons. Chgo., 1988—; dir. Vacation Bible Sch., Phila., 1986-88; tchr., cons. Winnetka (Ill.) Day Care Ctr., 1988-89; tutor Salem Christian Sch., Chgo., 1988-89; tchr. ESL Adult Literacy Program Oakton Community Coll., 1989-90. Press liaison campaign to elect Bill Green, Phila. Mem. LWV (voter registration com. Phila. chpt. 1984), Winnetka Yacht Club, Glenview (Ill.) Tennis Club. Home: 7 Bittersweet Ct Centerport NY 11721

GRABOWSKI, ELIZABETH, health care administrator; b. Laskowiec, Poland, July 24, 1940; came to U.S., 1948.; d. Stanley and Marianna (Tatko) Backiel; m. John A. Grabowski; children: Elizabeth C. Taylor, Julia M. Smith, John A., Emilia A. AAD in Nursing, Memphis State U., 1975; BS in Nursing, Elmhurst (Ill.) Coll., 1981; MS in Nursing, U. Louisville, 1988. Clin. dir., owner Diabetes Resource Ctr., Louisville; diabetes nurse clinician edn. dept. Humana Hosp. Audubon, Louisville; guest faculty, course presenter Allan and Donna Lansing Sch. of Nursing and Health Scis., Bellarmine Coll., Louisville. Contbr. articles to profl. jours. Mem. ARC, Oldham County 9chmn. adv.bd. 1989—), tech. adv. com. for nursing svcs. Medicaid programs, Ky. (chmn. 1987—), Ky. Nurse Recognition Banquet Com. (chmn. 1987—). Recipient Hoechst-Roussel Pharms. award for clin. excellence, academic scholarship Kiwanis Internat., Clairol Found., others. Mem. Am. Nurses Assn. (named Med.-Surg. Nurse of Yr. 1990), Ky. Nurses Assn., Ky. Nurses Assn. Dist. 1, Am. Assn. Diabetes Educators, Greater Louisville Assn. Diabetes Educators, Sigma Theta Tau, others. Home: 4010 Dana Rd Crestwood KY 40014 Office: Diabetes Resource Ctr Inc 4014 Dutchmans Ln Louisville KY 40207

GRABOWSKI, JANICE LYNN, school board executive, civic leader; b. Parma, Ohio, Dec. 28, 1948; d. Philip Edward and Marjorie (Woodrig) Konscak; m.Gary Michael Grabowski, June 23,1967; children: Michael John, Jennifer Lynn. Student, Cleve. State U., 1966-67. Pres. Brunwick City Bd. Edn., 1987-88, bd. mem., 1982—, legis. liaison, 1983—; bd. dirs. Medina County Career Ctr., 1982—, legis. liaison, 1983—, pres., 1984; del. Ohio Schs. Bd. Assn., 1982-89, exec. com. N.E. region, 1983—, treas., 1984, state policy and legis. com., 1984-86, 88—, moderator state conf., 1985-89, arrangement and hospitality com., 1986, trustee, 1987—, presenter, 1988-89; chmn. 13th Congrl. Dist. Nat. Sch. Bds. Assn., Fed. Relations Network, 1984-89; del. nat. cong. Houston, San Francisco, Anaheim Calif. 1983-85; presenter Ohio Assn. for Supervision and Curriculum Devel., 1987; Sunday sch. tchr., 1980. Mem. Nat. Audubon Soc. Home: 3968 Keller-Hanna Dr Brunswick OH 44212 Office: Brunswick City Schs Bd Edn 3643 Center Rd Brunswick OH 44212

GRACE, CORINNE BISSETTE, oil and gas company owner; b. Middlesex, N.C., Nov. 9, 1929; d. Oscar and Mary (Massey) Bissette; m. Michael Paul Grace II, Aprl 26, 1954 (div. 1987); children: Michael Paul III, Corinne Yvonne, Winston R., Janette Patrice, John Zacharias. BA, U. N.C., 1952. Ptnr. Grace Oil, Dallas and Carlsbad, N.Mex., 1961-83; owner Grace Oil, Carlsbad, 1983—. Sponsor various civic orgns.; mem. Centennial Planning Bd. and Spl. Events Com., U. N.C., Greensboro, 1988—. Mem. Carlsbad C. of C., N.Mex. Oil and Gas Engring. Com., Ind. Petroleum Assn. N.Mex., N.Mex. Geol. Soc., Riverside Country Club. Office: Grace Oil 3722 National Parks Hwy Carlsbad NM 88220

GRACE, JUDY DIANE, education educator; b. Los Angeles, Nov. 12, 1946; d. Thomas Logan and Mary Ellen (Armer) G. BA, Northeastern U., Boston, Mass., 1968, MA, 1970; MS, Old Dominion U., Norfolk, Va., 1976; PhD, U. Ariz., 1984. Instr. Norfolk (Va.) State U., 1970-74; assoc. prof. Tidewater Community Coll., Va. Beach, 1974-84; research asst. U. Ariz., Tucson, 1984-85, coord. acad. affairs; asst. prof. Iowa State U., Ames, 1986-87; adj. assoc. prof. Geo Washington U., 1986-88; dir. of rsch. Coun. for Advancement and Support of Edn., Washington, 1988—; cons. community colls., Nebr., Iowa, 1986-87. Mem. Assn. Study of Higher Edn., Am. Ednl. Research Assn. Office: Coun for Advancement & Support of Edn 11 Dupont Circle Ste 400 Washington DC 20036

GRACE, JULIANNE ALICE, manufacturing company executive; b. Riverdale, N.J., Oct. 29, 1937; d. Arthur Edward and Julia May (McCarthy) Thompson; m. Daniel Vincent Grace, July 2, 1960; children: Daniel Vincent III, Deirdre Elizabeth. BA, Marymount Manhattan Coll., 1959; MA, Fordham U., 1960. Dir. admissions Marymount Manhattan Coll., N.Y.C., 1966-72; mgr. human resources The Perkin-Elmer Corp., Norwalk, Conn., 1972-78, dir. human resources, 1978-81, asst. sr. v.p. semiconductor equipment, 1981-83, asst. pres., 1983-85, v.p., asst. to chief exec. officer, 1985-86; v.p. adminstrn. The Perkin-Elmer Corp., Norwalk, 1986—. Bd. dirs. Norwalk and Wilton chpts. ARC, 1975-85; bd. trustees Norwalk YMCA, 1986; active Norwalk Community Coll. Found., 1986—, Fairfield 2000; bd. dirs. Waveny (Conn.) Care Ctr. Woodrow Wilson Nat. Found. fellow, 1959-60. Mem. Econ. Soc. Conn., Nat. Investor Rels. Inst., Am. Soc. Personnel Adminstrn., Regional Plan Assn. Com., Sports Car Club of Am., Roton Point Club (Rowayton, Conn.), Econ. Club, Wolfpit Running Club. Home: 54 Louise's Ln New Canaan CT 06840 Office: Perkin-Elmer Corp 761 Main Ave Norwalk CT 06859-0315

GRACEN, BELINDA SUSAN, small business owner; b. San Bernardino, Calif., July 3, 1951; d. William James Terhorst and Alice (Wilson) Swanson; m. James Michale Gracen, Aug. 29, 1970; children: James Robert, Richard William, Jennifer Renee. Student, Denver Woman's Coll., 1970. Waitress Robinhood Restaurant, Englewood, Colo., 1967-69, Whitespot Restaurant, Denver, 1969-70; waitress, hostess Village Inn Pancake House, Boulder, Colo., 1970-71; grocery checker King Soopers, Boulder, Colo., 1971-72; grocery owner Community Mkt., Eugene, Oreg., 1973--; restaurant owner Dairy King Restaurant, Oreg., 1975-78; property mgr., owner RJB Properties Inc., Eugene, Oreg., 1980-83; grocery owner Miller's Grocery, Eugene, Oreg., 1982-85, Lawrence St. Grocery, Eugene, Oreg., 1984-87, Alder St. Mkt., Eugene, Oreg., 1986-88; grocery owner Amazon Mkt., 1988--, corp. sec. Lane Community Mkts. Inc., Eugene, Oreg., 1982--. Republican. Office: Lane Community Mkts Inc 1815 W 11th Ave Eugene OR 97402

GRADISON, HEATHER JANE, government official; b. Houston, Sept. 6, 1952; d. David Lowe Stirton and Dorothy Johanne (Flatt) Cox; m. Willis D. Gradison, Jr., Nov. 29, 1980; children: Maile Jo, Benjamin David, Logan Jane. BA, Radford U., 1975; postgrad., George Washington U., 1976, 78. Summer intern So. Ry. System, Washington, 1974, mgmt. trainee, market rsch. asst., asst. rate officer, rate officer, 1975-82; mem. ICC, Washington, 1982-90, vice chmn., 1985, chmn., 1985-90; asst. to pres. Am. Enterprise Inst., Washington, 1990—; cons. for pub. enterprise reform World Bank. Mem. Rep. Congl. Wives Club, Level IV Presdl. Appointees Orgn. Office: Am Enterprise Inst 1150 17th St NW Washington DC 20423

GRADOVILLE, KATHLEEN EVOY, nurse; b. Waukegan, Ill., June 1, 1962; d. James Edwin and Shirlee Mae (Rundquist) Evoy; m. Bernard Lawrence Gradoville, Mar. 17, 1990. BS in Nursing, U. Iowa, 1986. RN. Staff nurse Childrens Meml. Hosp., Chgo., 1986-88, clin. educator, 1988-89; staff nurse Iowa Meth. Med. Ctr., Des Moines, 1990, pediatric clin. instr., 1990—; acting night charge nurse Childrens Meml. Hosp., Chgo., 1986, quality assurance com. chmn., 1986-88, policy and procedure hosp. rep.,

1987-89, joint commn. on accredidation of hosps., visit coord., 1989, nurse recruiter cons., 1990; CPR instr. Am. Heart Assn., 1988—. Author: Evaluating Discharge Instructions in a Pediatric Setting. Mem. Iowa Nurses Assn. Methodist.

GRADY, ANN JACQUELINE, bank executive; b. Medford, Mass., Sept. 11, 1959; d. Thomas Francis and Patricia (Bowman) G. BA magna cum laude, Boston Coll., 1983, MA magna cum laude, 1984; postgrad., Harvard U., 1985. Editor Mass. Register Office of Sec. of State, Boston, 1983-85; dir. state census Office of Sec. of State, 1985-87; banking officer Bank of Boston, 1987-88, v.p. govt. banking, 1988—. Contbr. articles to profl. jours. Vice chmn Medfield Dem. Town Com., 1986-88, chmn., 1988-90; mem. platform com. Mass. Dem. State Com., Boston, 1982-86; exec. mem. Mass. Young Democrats, 1979—; pres. Grady Polit. Com., Medfield, Mass., 1983—; vol. nat. telethon Boston Coll. Recipient Disting. Alumni award Boston Coll., 1985. Mem. Greater Boston C. of C., NAFE, Boston Coll. Career Network (pres. 1988—), Boston Women's City Club, Boston Coll. Young Alumni Club (dir. communications 1988—). Roman Catholic. Home: PO Box 2703 Boston MA 02208 Home: 5 Hearthstone Dr Medfield MA 02052-2125

GRADY, KATHRYN FABER, marketing communications professional; b. Akron, Ohio, Sept. 17, 1960; d. James Arthur and Sharon Harriet (Ricker) Faber; m. Steven Vincent Grady, Aug. 1, 1981 (div. 1987). BS in Speech, Northwestern U., 1981. Mgmt. trainee, then sales promotion mgr. Bank New Orleans, 1981-82; retail product mgr. 1st Nat. Bank Commerce, New Orleans, 1983-84; liability product mgr. Conn. Nat. Bank, Hartford, 1984-85; asst. dir. sales promotion CIGNA Individual Fin. Svcs. Co., Hartford, 1986-89; dir. mktg. communications individual fin. svcs. div. CIGNA Corp., Hartford, 1989—. Adviser Jr. Achievement, New Orleans, 1981-82; bd. dirs. Asylum Hill Christian Community, Hartford, 1990—. Mem. Women in Communications. Republican. Congregationalist. Home: 237 B Farmington Ave Hartford CT 06105 Office: CIGNA Corp 900 cottage Grove Rd S 325 Bloomfield CT 06002

GRADY, MAUREEN FRANCES, lawyer; b. N.Y.C., Oct. 6, 1960; d. Frank J. and Pauline (Laberge) G. BA, Manhattan Coll., 1982; JD, Georgetown U., 1985. Bar: N.Y. 1986, U.S. Dist. Ct. (so. and ea. dists.) N.Y. 1987, U.S. Ct. Appeals (2d cir.) 1990. Assoc. Griffin, Scully & Savona, N.Y.C., 1985-87, Morris & Duffy, N.Y.C., 1987-88, Summit, Rovins & Feldesman, N.Y.C., 1988-89; asst. gen. counsel N.Y.C. Transit Authority, 1989—. Recipient Bur. Nat. Affairs award. Mem. Assn. of Bar of City of N.Y. (young lawyers com. 1987-90), Phi Beta Kappa, Epsilon Sigma Pi, Phi Alpha Theta. Republican. Roman Catholic.

GRAEB, THELMA SAVARD, registered representative, insurance agent; b. Rochester, N.Y., July 16, 1934; d. Basil Eugene and Thelma Lucile (Daus) Savard; BS, Syracuse U., 1956, PhD, 1974; MA, Northwestern U., 1958; ins. cert. Am. Coll., Bryn Mawr, Pa., 1986; m. Harold Sigfreid Graeb, Jr., July 19, 1958; children: Bruce, Jacqueline, Sharon, T. Randall. CLU, chartered fin. cons. Supr., Hearing and Speech Center, Yale Sch. Medicine, New Haven, 1956-57; pvt. practice speech pathology, Newport, R.I., 1959-62; supr. hearing and speech Suffolk Rehab. Center for the Physically Handicapped, Inc., Commack, N.Y., 1963-66; asst. prof. spl. edn. N.J. State Coll., Jersey City, 1966-67; cons. speech and hearing dept. Mountainside Hosp., Montclair, N.J., 1967-69; dir., div. audiology Hearing & Speech Center of Rochester (N.Y.), Inc., 1969-71; U.S. Office Edn. fellow Syracuse U., 1971-73, dir. BOCES, 1973-75; ednl. cons. Organizational Change & Staff Devel., Manlius, N.Y., 1976; prin. Rockwell Elem. Sch., Nedrow, N.Y., from 1976; agt. Donohue Mapstone Agy., Equitable Fin. Cos., Syracuse, N.Y., 1985—; dir. Environ. Tech., Inc., Buffalo. Mem. Am. Assn. Sch. Adminstrs., Nat. Council for Exceptional Children, Am. Speech and Hearing Assn., Assn. Profl. Women in Mgmt., Nat. Assn. Women Bus. Owners, Million Dollar Round Table, Nat. Assn. Life Underwriters, Greater Syracuse C. of C. (pres.' cabinet), Phi Delta Kappa, Pi Lambda Theta, Zeta Phi Eta, Kappa Alpha Theta. Contbr. articles to profl. jours. Home: 7619 Glencliffe Rd Manlius NY 13104 Office: Donohue Agy 500 S Salina St Ste 1200 Syracuse NY 13202

GRAEFE, ANN ELIZABETH, civic worker; b. Twin Falls, Idaho, May 23, 1935; d. Loyal Iliff and Mary Helen (Grant) Perry; m. Roger Allen Graefe, June 22, 1957; children: Roger Allen, Michael Anthony, Peter John, Robert Grant, Paul Christopher. BA in Dietetics, Holy Name Coll., Spokane, Wash., 1957; degree in secondary edn. and home econs., Idaho State U., 1970. Swimming tchr. YMCA, Sheboygan, Wis., 1957-62; bridal cons. Bon Marche, Twin Falls, Idaho, 1962-65; swimming tchr. Twin Falls City, 1965-75; tchr. home econs. Twin Falls Sch. Dist., 1969-70, Hansen (Idaho) Sch. Dist., 1970-71; bridal cons. Teresia's, Twin Falls, 1971-76; owner Teresia's, 1976-77; outreach and home delivered meals coord. Twin Falls Sr. Citizens Ctr., 1987—. Mem. AAUW (pro-life, pres. Twin Falls br.), Idaho Home Econs. Assn. (pres. 1965-66). Roman Catholic.

GRAF, DOROTHY ANN, business executive; b. Nashville, Mar. 21, 1935; d. Henry George and Martha Dunlap (Hill) Meek; student Montgomery Coll., 1979—; m. Peter Louis Graf, Oct. 28, 1971; children—Sidney E. Pollard, Deborah Lynn Pollard, Robert George Pollard, Michelle Joy Graf. Office mgr. Pa. Life Ins. Co., Miami and Dallas, 1957-72; exec. sec. to med. dir. Pitts. Children's Hosp., 1974; sec. GE./TEMPO, Washington, 1974-76; adminstrv. asst. to sr. v.p. Logistics Mgmt. Inst., Washington, 1976-81, dir. adminstrv. services, 1981—; dir. KHI Services, Inc. Mem. Washington Tech. Personnel Forum. Democrat. Baptist. Home: 20404 Remsbury Pl Gaithersburgh MD 20879 Office: 6400 Goldsboro Rd Bethesda MD 75886

GRAFELMAN, JUDY RAE, hospital department administrator; b. Peoria, Ill., Apr. 7, 1953; d. Raymond Chester Grafelman and Edna Louise (Belk) Brown; m. Terry W. Morovic, Aug 1, 1975 (div. Aug. 1979). RN, Luth. Hosp. Sch. Nursing, Moline, Ill., 1973; BS, Coll. St. Francis, Joliet, Ill., 1986; M in Health Adminstrn., Coll. St. Francis, 1989. Surgery staff nurse St. Francis Trauma Ctr., Peoria, 1973-74; surgery staff nurse Procter Community Hosp., Peoria, 1974-82, asst. coord. ambulatory surgery, 1982-87, dept. head ambulatory surgery/endoscopy, 1987—. Mem. Assn. Operating Room Nurses, Soc. for Ambulatory Care Profls., Ill. Assn. Quality Assurance Profls., Am. Coll. Health Care Execs., Soc. Gastroenterology Nurses and Assocs. Home: 6917 N Michele Ln Peoria IL 61614

GRAFFIS, KATHLEEN ANN, personnel executive; b. Pontiac, Mich., Oct. 19, 1953; d. William Paul and Florence (Black) McDermott; m. Keith Edward Graffis, July 11, 1981; children: Justin William, Megan Erin. Lit., Sci. and Arts, U. Mich., 1975. Investment banker Clayton Brown & Assocs., Sarasota, Fla., 1982-85, A.G. Edwards, Point Charlotte, Fla., 1985-89, Barnett Bank Inc., Sarasota, 1989-90; account coord. Estee Lauder, Sarasota, 1990—. Bd. dirs. Charlotte County Estate and Tax Planning Commn., Point Charlotte, 1986-89. With USMC, 1979-81. Mem. Am. Bus. Womens Assn. Republican. Roman Catholic.

GRAGG, SARA ELIZABETH, motel executive; b. Malvern, Ark., Mar. 28, 1930; d. Alymer James and Martha Thelma (Cross) Wells; m. Glen E. Keller, Dec. 18, 1949 (div. 1964); children: Michael, Kathryn, Kim; m. Paris R. Green, Sept. 15, 1968 (dec. 1969); m. Billy Max Gragg, May 14, 1970 (dec. 1987). BA, U. Ark., 1949, MA, 1950, PhD, 1971. Exec. asst. dept. psychiatry U. Ark. Med. Ctr., Little Rock, 1951-56; asst. prof. English Ark. State U., Jonesboro, 1962-66; instr. English dept. U. Ark.-Fayetteville, 1966-69; asst. prof. U. Mo.-Rolla, 1968; pres. Gragg Motels, Inc., Fayetteville, 1970-89; lectr. Tex. A&M, Galveston, Tex., 1988—. Author: The Artistic Unity of Carlyle's French Revolution, 1971. Pres. Ark. Med. Soc. Aux., Jonesboro, 1963-64; Republican county chmn., Jonesboro, 1962-63. Named Woman of Yr., Bus and Profl. Women, Mountain View, Ark., 1961. Mem. Ark. Motel Assn., Am. Hotel and Motel Assn., Ark. Retail Mchts. Assn., Internat. Platform Assn., Fayetteville C. of C., Coll. English Assn., Phi Beta Kappa, Lambda Tau, Psi Chi. Methodist. Avocations: writing, travelling. Home: Route 11 Smokehouse Rd Fayetteville AR 72701 Office: Tex A&M Dept Gen Academics PO Box 1675 Galveston TX 77553

GRAH, KAREN ELIZABETH, military officer; b. Phila., Mar. 10, 1953; d. Ernest and Margaret (Alper) G.; 1 child, Amanda Elizabeth. BA in Psychology, Columbia Coll., 1979; postgrad., Webster U., 1984-85. Enlisted USN, 1972, advanced through grades to lt., 1983; adminstrv. officer, asst. intelligence officer Strike Fighter Squadron, Lemoore, Calif., 1980-84; personnel officer Service Sch. Command, Great Lakes Naval Base, Ill., 1984-87; chief testing mgmt. El Paso (Tex.) Mil. Entrance Processing Sta., 1987-89; exec. officer Navy and Marine Corps Res. Readiness Ctr., El Paso, Tex., 1989—. Mem. Naval Res. Assn. Republican. Methodist. Home: 5852 Devontry El Paso TX 79934 Office: Naval & Marine Corps Res Readiness Ctr 4810 Pollard St El Paso TX 79930

GRAHAM, ALBERTA NEWSOME, personnel representative; b. Quitman, Ga., Sept. 1, 1955; d. Ted and Mamie (Newsome) Davis; m. Alfred Graham, Oct. 29, 1983; children: Tangela Adams, Rashaan Nicole. Cert., Valdosta State Coll., 1981, BBA in Mgmt., 1985. Clk. Ga. Power Co., Valdosta, 1981, sec., 1983-84, personnel specialist, 1984-89, personnel rep., 1989—. Chmn. United Way of Ga. Power Co., Valdosta, 1985-86; mem. Laurel St. Ch. of Christ, Quitman, Ga. Mem. Profl. Secretarial Internat., Women of Ga. Power (corr. sec. 1987—, 2nd v.p. 1988—, sunshine chmn. 1986-87), Ga. Power Fed. Credit Union (bd. dirs.), Am. Soc. for Personnel Adminstrn., Zeta Phi Beta. Democrat. Home: 908 Bethune St Valdosta GA 31601 Office: Ga Power Co 901 N Patterson St Valdosta GA 31601

GRAHAM, ANNA REGINA, pathologist, professor; b. Phila., Nov. 1, 1947; d. Eugene Nelson and Anna Beatrice (McGovern) Chadwick; m. Larry L. Graham, June 29, 1973; 1 child, Jason. BS in Chemistry, Ariz. State U., 1969, BS in Zoology, 1970; MD, U. Ariz., 1974. Diplomate Am. Bd. Pathology. With Coll. Medicine U. Ariz., Tucson, 1974—, asst. prof. pathology, 1978-84, assoc. prof. pathology, 1984—. Fellow Am. Soc. Clin. Pathologists, Am. Assn. Pathologists, Coll. Am. Pathologists; mem. AMA (pathology sect. coun. Chgo. chpt. 1988—), Ariz. Soc. Pathologists (pres. Phoenix chpt. 1989—), Am. Soc. Clin. Pathologists (chmn. adv. coun. Chgo. chpt. 1987—). Republican. Baptist. Home: 1489 W Chapala Dr Tucson AZ 85704 Office: Ariz Health Scis Ctr Dept Pathology Tucson AZ 85724

GRAHAM, ANNE, government official; b. Annapolis, Md., Dec. 28, 1949. Grad., Bradford Coll.; postgrad., Columbia U. Spl. asst. to dep. dir. for communications Republican Nat. Com., Washington, 1971; with White House News Summary Office, Washington, 1973, Office of Sec. of Treasury, 1974-75; press sec. to Senator Harrison Schmitt, Washington, 1976-79; asst. press sec. Reagan-Bush Campaign, 1980-81; dep. spl. asst. to Pres. for communications, Washington, 1981; asst. sec for legislation and pub. affairs Dept. Edn., Washington, 1981-85; mem. Consumer Product Safety Commn., 1985—. Office: Consumer Product Safety Commn 5401 Westbard Ave Bethesda MD 20816*

GRAHAM, AUDREY, management; b. Chgo., Nov. 3, 1953; d. Willie and Pearlene (Smith) G. AA, Cen. YMCA, Chgo., 1975; student, Roosevelt U., 1989—. Directory assistance, keypunch operator Ill. Bell Tel., Chgo., 1971-72; mental health trainee Thresholds, Chgo., 1973-74; fin. control clk. Ill. Pub. Aid, Chgo., 1974-75; phys. instr. Chgo. Park Dist., Chgo., 1975-78; human rights investigator State Ill., Chgo., 1978-85; equal opportunity specialist, sr. coutract compliance office City Chgo., 1985-87; dbe specialist Chgo. Transit Authority, Chgo., 1987--; mgr., DBE Program, Chgo. Transit Authority, 1989--; pres. Audrey N. Graham & Assocs. Mgmt. Consultants, 1988—; com. mem. CEDCO, Chgo. Regional Purchasing, 1987—, Conf. of Minority Transit Officials, Chgo., 1988—. Precinct capt. 15th Ward, 1977, election judge, 1978–, ward coordinator, Democratic Orgn., 1983, deputy registrar Pro-can, Chgo., 1987. Mem. NAFE, Am. Mgmt. Assn. Baptist. Home: 3001 S Michigan Ave Chicago IL 60616 Office: Chgo Transit Authority 350 N Orleans Merchandise Mart Pla Chicago IL 60654

GRAHAM, BARBARA JEANNETTE, foreign language educator, translator; b. Boston, Oct. 11, 1936; d. Edward L. and Rotha A. (Staples) G. BA, U. Vt., 1958; MA, U. Ark., 1960; PhD, U. Miami, 1969. Instr. Spanish, Drake U., Des Moines, 1960-64; prof. Spanish, English and humanities St. Thomas U., Miami, Fla., 1967—; freelance translator, Miami, 1977—; translator Greater Miami Opera, 1977-80; evaluator So. Assn. Schs. and Colls., Miami, 1990. Campaign worker for candidate Dade County Sch. Bd., Miami, 1989. Fulbright grantee, 1964; grad. fellow U. Miami, 1966-67. Mem. Am. Assn. Tchrs. Spanish and Portuguese, Am. Coun. on Teaching Fgn. Langs. Office: St Thomas U 16400 NW 32d Ave Miami FL 33054

GRAHAM, BRENDA J., nursing instructor; b. West Bend, Wis., July 30, 1944; d. Herman James and Dotha Lee (Owens) Johnson; 1 child, La Trelle Denise Jackson. AAS, Bronx Community Coll., 1971; BS, Savannah State Coll., 1987. Cert. RN, Ga., N.Y., S.C. Nursing instr. South Coll., Savannah; dir. of nursing Pleasantview Nursing Home, Metter, Ga.; collection supr. Am. Red Cross, Savannah; program coord. Savannah (Ga.) State Coll. Vol. Savannah Literacy Program, Teens Talking and Women's Christian Orgn. Mem. Am. Nurses Assn., Ga. Assn. Nurses in Long Term Care, Savannah Women's Network. Home: PO Box 2733 Athens GA 30612-0733

GRAHAM, CAROL ETHLYN, insurance company administrator; b. Guthrie, Okla., Nov. 28, 1941; d. Brance Alma Woodard and Rachel Ione (Brown) Meininger; m. Morton J. Graham Dec. 14, 1965 (div. Apr. 1985); children: Brance D., Kelly L., S. Robert, M. Jeff III. AS in Civil Tech., Okla. State U.-Tech. Inst., 1978; cert. in flood plain analysis, U. Okla., 1979. Cert. premium auditor, Okla. Factory worker Aero Comdr., Bethany, Okla., 1963-66; legal asst. Whit Ingram Atty., Oklahoma City, 1966-75; bookkeeper Joe Roselle Atty., Oklahoma City, 1966-78; hydraulic analyst Cunningham Cons. Inc., Oklahoma City, 1978-80; premium auditor loss control Atwell, Vogel and Sterling, Dallas, 1982-83; premium auditor Mid-Continent Casualty Co., Tulsa, 1983—. Mem. NAFE, Ins. Auditors Assn. of Oklahoma City (sec. 1985-86, pres. 1986-87, v.p. 1988-89, treas. 1989-90), Ins. Auditors Assn. of S.W., Women Execs. Cen. Okla., Nat. Soc. Ins. Premium Auditors. Democrat. Home: PO Box 1613 Guthrie OK 73044 Office: Mid-Continent Casualty Co 1646 S Boulder PO Box 1409 Tulsa OK 74101

GRAHAM, CORA JOYCE, nurse, educator; b. New Orleans, Aug. 20, 1948; d. Walter Albert and Elouise (Jones) G.; divorced; 1 child, Cutler R. Gultry. BS in Nursing, Dillard U., 1971; MS in Nursing, U. So. Miss., 1979; BRE, Christian Bible Coll., Kenner, La., 1980; grad., Stevenson Acad. Hair Design, New Orleans, 1984. RN, La. Staff nurse, acting head nurse, relief ICU supr. USPHS, New Orleans, 1970-77; ptnr., mgr. J.J. Fried Chicken-Big Bob's, New Orleans and Kenner, La., 1974-80; clin. instr. Charity Hosp. Sch. Nursing, New Orleans, 1980-81, New Orleans Skilled Tng. Ctr., 1987—; supr. Eye, Ear, Nose and Throat Hosp., New Orleans, 1981; employee health and relief supr. New Orleans Gen. Hosp., 1981-82; dir. nursing Luth. Nursing Home, New Orleans, 1982; co-owner, mgr. Magda & Cora's Salon, New Orleans, 1985; adminstr. Bayou State Home Health, Inc., New Orleans, 1985-87; clin. specialist, relief supr. Coliseum Med. Ctr., New Orleans, 1988—; pvt. duty nurse, New Orleans, 1982—; contract nurse, Personal Health Care, Inc., New Orleans, 1987—; clin. specialist, staff nurse DePaul Hosp., New Orleans, 1988-89. Mem. SCLC, Kenner, La. Mental Health Assn. grantee, 1977-79. Mem. Assn. for Practitioners Infection Control, Am. Nurses Assn., Christian Ministers Union Assn., La. Assn. for Home Health, La. Cosmetology Assn., Ebony Orchids Club. Democrat. Baptist. Home: 508 Compromise St Kenner LA 70062 Office: Coliseum Med Ctr 3601 Coliseum St New Orleans LA 70115

GRAHAM, FRANCES KEESLER (MRS. DAVID TREDWAY GRAHAM), psychologist, educator; b. Canastota, N.Y., Aug. 1, 1918; d. Clyde C. and Norma (Van Surdam) Keesler; m. David Tredway Graham, June 14, 1941; children: Norma, Andrew, Mary. B.A., Pa. State U., 1938; Ph.D., Yale U., 1942. Acting dir. St. Louis Psychiat. Clinic, 1942-44; instr. Barnard Coll., 1948-51; research assoc. Sch. Medicine, Washington U., St. Louis, 1942-48, 53-57, U. Wis., Madison, 1957-64; asso. prof. pediatrics and psychology U. Wis., 1964-68, prof., 1968-86, Hilldale research prof., 1980-86; prof. U. Del., Newark, 1986—; Cons. Nat. Inst. Neurol. Diseases and Blindness perinatal research br.; mem. exptl. psychology research review com. NIMH, 1970-74, NRC, 1971-74; mem. bd. sci. counselors NIMH, 1977-81, chmn., 1979-81; mem. Pres.'s Commn. for Study of Ethical Problems in Medicine and Biomed. and Behavioral Research, 1980-82. Mem. editorial bd. Jour. Exptl. Child Psychology, 1964-67, Child Devel., 1966-68, Jour. Exptl. Psychology, 1968-73, Psychophysiology, 1968-73; contbr. articles to profl. jours. Recipient Research Scientist award NIMH, 1964—, Disting. Alumna award Pa. State U., 1983. Mem. NAS, Am. Psychol. Assn. (coun. 1975-77, pres. div. physiol. and comparative psychology 1978-79, G. Stanley Hall award 1982, Disting. Scientist award 1990), Am. Psychol. Soc. (William James fellow 1990), Soc. Rsch. Child Devel. (council 1965-71, pres. 1975-77), Soc. Psychophysiol. Rsch. (dir. 1968-71, 72-75, pres. 1973-74, Disting. Contbns. award 1981), Soc. Exptl. Psychologists, Soc. Neurosci., Psychonomic Soc., Acoustical Soc. Am., Am. Psychol. Soc., Internat. Soc. Devel. Psychobiology, AAAS (chmn. sect. psychology 1979), Phi Beta Kappa, Sigma Xi. Home: 311 Dove Dr Newark DE 19713

GRAHAM, JENNIFER CECILE, interior designer; b. Bridgetown, Barbados, Apr. 30, 1963; d. Albert C. and Lorraine D. Graham; stepmother: Margaret L. (McCurdy) G. BFA in Interior Architecture with distinction, N.Y. Sch. Interior Design, 1985, Design diploma, 1984; student, Hunter Coll., 1984-85. Asst. mgr. designer Alleyne, Aguilar & Altman, Real Estate Developers, Barbados, 1981-82; designer Edmund Motyka Assocs., N.Y.C., 1983-85; project mgr. ITHA Internat., N.Y.C., 1985-85; designer Interior Resources Internat., N.Y.C., 1985-86; project mgr. Total Concept N.Y., Inc., N.Y.C., 1986—; cons. R. Protas Assocs., N.Y.C., 1986-89; coord. program Acad. Environ. Scis., N.Y.C., 1985. Recipoient Svc. award for promotion of interior design N.Y. Sch. Interior Design, 1984, 1st Place Profl. Office Design award Trading Floor, Designer Mag., 1990. Mem. Nat. Assn. Female Execs., Am. Soc. Interior Designers (asst. coordinator mentor program 1986). Mem. Anglican Ch. Club: Barbados Equestrian Assn. Home: 20 Waterside Pla New York NY 10010 Office: Total Concept NY Inc 12 East 49th St Tower 49 New York NY 10017

GRAHAM, JOANN, federal programs coordinator; b. Cin., July 19, 1956; d. Thomas Edgar and Mary Ellen (Mullen) G. Student, U. Cin., 1977—. Clk. typist U.S. Dept. Army, Cin., 1973-74, statis. clk., 1974-75; sec. Glenmary Home Missioners, Fairfield, Ohio, 1975-76; med. records technician USPHS, Cin., 1976-80; with U.S. Post Svc., 1980—; postmaster U.S. Post Svc., Mt. Olivet, Ky., 1985-86; affirmative action and EEO programs coord. U.S. Post Svc., Cin., 1986—; chairperson EEO com. Fed. Exec. Bd., Cin., 1988-89. Mem. ASTD, Nat. Career Devel. Assn., Am. Assn. for Counseling and Devel., Federally Employed Women. Democrat. Roman Catholic. Office: US Postal Svc 1591 Dalton Ave Rm 202T Cincinnati OH 45234-9431

GRAHAM, KATHARINE, newspaper executive; b. N.Y.C., June 16, 1917; d. Eugene and Agnes (Ernst) Meyer; m. Philip L. Graham, June 5, 1940 (dec. 1963); children: Elizabeth Morris Graham Weymouth, Donald Edward, William Welsh, Stephen Meyer. Student, Vassar Coll., 1934-36; AB, U. Chgo., 1938. Reporter San Francisco News, 1938-39; mem. editorial staff Washington Post, 1939-45, mem. Sunday, circulation and editorial depts., pub., 1969-79; pres. Washington Post Co., 1963-73, 77, chmn. bd., chief exec. officer, 1973—; co-chmn. Internat. Herald Tribune; bd. dirs. Bowater Mersey Paper Co., Ltd., Reuters Founders Share Co. Ltd., Urban Inst., Fed. City Council, Council for Aid to Edn. Life trustee, U. Chgo.; hon. trustee George Washington U.; mem. sr. adv. bd. of the Joan Shorenstein Barone Ctr. on the Press, Politics and Pub. Policy, Harvard U. Fellow Am. Acad. Arts and Scis.; mem. Am. Soc. Newspaper Editors, Nat. Press Club, Coun. Fgn. Rels., Overseas Devel. Coun., Met. Club, Cosmopolitan Club, 1925 F Street Club. Home: 2920 R St NW Washington DC 20007 Office: Washington Post Co 1150 15th St NW Washington DC 20071

GRAHAM, KATHERINE ELIZABETH, marketing executive; b. Bridgeport, Conn., Apr. 30, 1964; d. James Joseph and Karen Marie (Neal) G. BS in Communications, Boston U., 1986; postgrad., Harvard U., 1986—. Account exec. Sta. WVJV-TV, Framington, Mass., 1986-87, Sta. WEEI, Boston, 1987-89; acct. exec. Sta. WHDH-TV, Boston, 1989-90, retail mktg. mgr., 1990—. Office: Sta WHDH-TV 7 Bulfinch Pl Boston MA 02114

GRAHAM, KIRSTEN R., information service executive; b. Inglewood, Calif., July 20, 1946; d. Ray Selmer and Ella Louise (Carter) Newbury; m. Frank Sellers Graham, July 31, 1981. BS, U. Wis., Oshkosh, 1971; MS, U. Colo., 1980; postgrad., Army War Coll., 1987. Cert. Flight instr. Chief info. svc. Mont. State Dept. Labor and Industry, Helena, Mont.; dir., personal property and bus. lic. div. County of Fairfax, Va.; analyst officer U.S. Army Pentagon, Washington; battalion commdr. U.S. Army, Frankfurt, West Germany; assoc. prof. U.S. Army, West Point, N.Y. Mem. Nat. Ski Patrol. LTC, U.S. Army, 1964-88. Mem. Data Processing Mgr's Assn.

GRAHAM, LINDA DIANE See ALEXANDER, LINDA DIANE

GRAHAM, LOIS CHARLOTTE, retired educator; b. Denver, Mar. 20, 1917; d. James Washington Brewster and Martha Wilhemina (Raukohl) Plunkett; m. Milton Clinton Graham, June 30, 1940 (dec.); children: Charlotte, Milton, Charlene, James. AB, Ouachita Bapt. U., 1939; postgrad., U. Nev., Reno, 1953, 63, 68, Ark. State U., 1954, 59. Cert. tchr., Colo., Nev., Ark. Tchr. Fairmount Sch., Golden, Colo., 1939-40, Melbourne (Ark.) Sch., 1940-41, Blytheville (Ark.) Jr. High Sch., 1944-45, Hawthorne (Nev.) Elem. Sch., 1952-81; substitute tchr. Mineral County Sch. Dist., Hawthorne, 1988—; sr. resource cons. dept. geriatrics U. Nev.-Reno Med. Sch., 1988—, del. to Rural Health Conf., Hawthorne, 1990; officer Mineral County Tchrs. Assn., 1955-65; ad hoc com. Nev. State Tchrs., 1965. Asst. to pres. High Sch. PTA, Hawthorne, 1958, Elem. PTA, Hawthorne, 1961; pianist, choir dir., tchr. various churches, 1927—. Mem. AAUW (membership v.p. 1988-91), Delta Kappa Gamma. Republican. Baptist. Home: PO Box 1543 Hawthorne NV 89415

GRAHAM, LOLA AMANDA (MRS. JOHN JACKSON GRAHAM), poet, photographer, writer; b. nr. Bremen, Ga., Nov. 12, 1896; d. John Gainer and Nancy Caroline Idella (Reid) Beall; m. John Jackson Graham, Aug. 3, 1917 (dec.); children: Billy Duane, John Thomas, Helen (Mrs. D. Hall), Donald, Beverly (Mrs. Bob Forson). Student Florence Normal Sch., 1914. Tchr. elem. public sch., Centerdale, Ala., 1914, Eva, Ala., 1915; free lance photographer and writer, 1950—; editor poetry column Mobile Home News, 1968-69; designer jacket cover for Reader's Digest book Our Amazing World of Nature, designer ski sweaters sold to Catalina Mills and various pattern cos. Recipient numerous nat. prizes, 1950—; Crossroads of Tex. grand nat. in poetry for For Every Monkey Child, 1980; executed prize-winning Sioux Indian and heirloom photog. quilts. Mem. Nat. Poetry Soc. Ina Coolbrith Poetry Soc., Chapparal Poets. Author: (booklet) How to Recycle Ancestors and Grandcestors, (poetry) Recycling Center, 1988. Contbr. photographs to Ency. Brit., also numerous mags. and books; designer ski sweaters 1930s. Address: 225-93 Mount Hermon Rd Scotts Valley CA 95066

GRAHAM, MARGARET HELEN, information scientist, consultant; b. Dallas, Dec. 25, 1923; d. Talford Gillespie and Helen Gould (Holbrook) Smith; m. Ronald Arthur Graham, Apr. 25, 1950; children: Alan R., Brian Y., Cathy A. BS, Mary Washington Coll., U. Va., 1947. Lit. chemist Sharples Chem. Co., Wyandotte, Mich., 1947-50; supr. lit. searching Ethyl Corp., Ferndale, Mich., 1950-56; pvt. practice cons. Trenton, Mich., 1956-63; tech. librarian Gen. Motors Rsch. Labs., Warren, Mich., 1963-66; mgr. info. svcs. Exxon Rsch. and Engring., Florham Park, N.J., 1966-86; v.p. Jandec Corp., New Providence, N.J., 1986—; cons. UN Indsl. Devel. Orgn., Vienna, 1986—; bd. dirs. Engring. Info., N.Y.C.; mem. adv. bd. Chem. Abstracts Svc., Columbus, Ohio, 1978-82; chmn. com. tech. info. Am. Petroleum Inst., 1974-84; mem. coms. U.S. Nat. Commn. on Libraries and Info. Sci. Contbr. chpts. to books, articles to profl. jours. Fellow Am. Inst. Chemists; mem. Am. Chem. Soc., Am. Soc. Info. Sci., Spl. Libraries Assn. Home: 92 Pine Way New Providence NJ 07974

GRAHAM, MARTHA, dancer, choreographer; b. Pitts., May 11, 1894. Studied with Ruth St. Denis and Ted Shawn; LL.D., Mills Coll., Brandeis U., Smith Coll., Harvard, 1966, also numerous others. Faculty Eastman Sch., 1925. Soloist Denishawn Co., 1920, Greenwich Village Follies, 1923, debut as choreographer-dancer, 48th St. Theatre, N.Y.C., 1926; founder, artistic dir., Martha Graham Dance Co., 1926—, also Martha Graham Sch. Contemporary Dance; choreographer with music composed by Aaron Copland, Paul Hindemith, Carlos Chavez, Samuel Barber, Gian-Carlo Menotti, William Schuman, others of more than 170 works including Appalachian Spring, Cave of the Heart, Errand into the Maze, Clytemnestra, Frontier, Phaedra, Herodiade, Primitive Mysteries, Night Journey, Seraphic

Dialogue, Lamentation, Acts of Light, Rite of Spring, Judith, Heretic, Diversion of Angels, Witch of Endor, Cortege of Eagles, A Time of Snow, Plain of Prayer, Lady of the House of Sleep, Archaic Hours, Mendicants of Evening, Myth of a Voyage, Holy Jungle, Dream, Chronique, Lucifer, Scarlet Letter, Adorations, Point of Crossing; guest soloist leading U.S. orchs. in solos Judith, Triumph of St. Joan; fgn. tours with Martha Graham Dance Co., 1950, 54, 55-56, 60, 62-63, 67, 68; some under auspices U.S. Dept State; collaborated in over 25 set designs with Isamu Naguchi, also Alexander Calder; also designed costumes for many of her dances; Author: Notebooks of Martha Graham, 1973. Recipient Aspen award 1965, Creative Arts award Brandeis U., 1968, Disting. Service to the Arts award, Nat. Inst. Arts and Letters, 1970, Handel medallion City of N.Y., 1970, N.Y. State Council on Arts award, 1973, Presdl. Medal of Freedom, 1976, Kennedy Center honor, 1979, Samuel H. Scripps Am. Dance Festival award, 1981, Meadows award So. Meth. U., 1982, Gold Florin City of Florence, 1983, Paris Medal of Honor, 1985, Arnold Gingrich Memorial award N.Y. Arts and Bus. Council, 1985, Nat. Medal for Arts, 1985, Decorated knight Legion of Honor (France), 1983; Guggenheim fellow, 1932. Office: Martha Graham Dance Co 316 E 63rd St New York NY 10021*

GRAHAM, MAXENE OBERMAN, journalist; b. Corry, Pa., June 12; d. Aaron Harry and Mary Alice (Cohen) O.; 1 son, Aron Robert. AB in Journalism, U. Miami, Coral Gables, Fla. Editor, columnist The Miami (Fla.) Herald, 1977-82; columnist Community Newspapers, Miami, 1982-85; with personal invesment mgmt., 1987—. Vol. Miami Feeding Miami, 1987-89, Food Recovery Program, Miami, 1990; v.p. Dem. Women's Club of Dade County, Miami, 1985; co-chmn. Temple Beth Am Pennies for Soviet Jewry Campaign, Miami, 1990; vol. Internat. Book Fair. Recipient Publicity award Dem. Women's Club Fla., 1985. Mem. AAUW (bd. dirs. 1990—), Internat. Assn. Bus. Communicators (hospitality chmn. 1987-88), Greater South Dade C. of C. (county sub-com. chair 1988-89, Friends of Miami, Women's Com. of 100, Mortar Bd. Alumni Club, U. Miami Sch. Communication Alumnae Assn. (bd. dirs. 1988—), Alpha Epsilon Phi (pres. 1986—).

GRAHAM, RHEA LYDIA, engineering geologist, environmental auditor; b. Terre Haute, Ind., Aug. 11, 1952; d. Glenn and Audrey Maxine (Acton) G.; m. Clifford Neal Dahm, Aug. 30, 1980; children: Katharine, Kristina. AB, Bryn Mawr Coll., 1974; MA, Oreg. State U., 1977. Registered geologist, engrng. geologist, environ. assessor, Oreg., Calif. Geophysicist Exxon Co., U.S.A., Houston, 1977-78; engrng. geologist CH2M Hill, Inc., Portland, Oreg., 1978-83; geologist Forestry Scis. Lab., USDA, Corvallis, Oreg., 1983-84; mgr. environ. scis. Deuel & Assocs., Inc., Albuquerque, 1985-88; regulatory compliance officer Ponderosa Products, Inc., Albuquerque, 1988; sr. scientist Sci. Applications Internat. Corp., Albuquerque, 1988—; mem. com. for ground failure hazards NAS-NRC, 1986-87. Contbr. articles on engrng. geology and slope hazards to profl. jours. Mem. Am. Inst. Profl. Geologists (v.p. N.Mex. sect. 1988, pres. 1988-89), Geol. Soc. Am., Assn. Engrng. Geologists (editor newsletter Oreg. sect. 1983), N.Mex. Geol. Soc., N.Mex. Hazardous Waste Mgmt. Soc., Albuquerque Geol. Soc. (sec.-treas. 1985). Presbyterian. Office: SAIC 2109 Air Park Rd SE Albuquerque NM 87106

GRAHAM, SYLVIA SWORDS, educator; b. Atlanta, Nov. 15, 1935; d. Metz Jona and Christine (Gurley) Swords; m. Thomas A. Graham, Nov. 29, 1958 (div. 1970). BA, Mary Washington Coll., Fredericksburg, Va., 1957; MEd, W. Ga. Coll., Carrollton, 1980; SEd, W. Ga. Coll., 1981; postgrad., Coll. William and Mary, 1964-67. Tchr. Atlanta pub. schs., 1957-58, Newark County pub. schs., Newark, Calif., 1960-61; tchr. history Virginia Beach (Va.) pub. schs., 1964-75, Paulding County pub. schs., Dallas, Ga., 1976—; tour dr. Paulding High Sch. trips, Far East, 1985, Russia, 1989, Australia, 1988, 90. County chmn. Rep. Party, 1987-89, county chmn. for re-election of New Gingrich, 1982; mem. Gingrich edn. com., 1983, 88; 1st vice chmn. 6th Congl. Dist., 1989—; del. to Sixth Dist. Conv., 1981—, State Rep. Conv., 1981—, others. Named Star Tchr., Paulding County C. of C., Dallas, Ga., 1989. Mem. Dallas Woman's Club (pres. 1982-84, 1st v.p. 1986-88, pub. affairs chmn. 1986—, treas. for Civic Ctr. fund 1984—), Phi Kappa Phi. Republican. Baptist. Home: 204 Hart Cir Dallas GA 30132

GRAHN, BARBARA ASCHER, editor; b. Chgo., Mar. 26, 1929; d. Harry L. and Eleanor (Simon) Ascher; m. Robert D. Grahn, Dec. 23, 1952; children: Susan Grahn Gantz, Nancy Grahn, Wendy Grahn O'Brien. BA, Miami U., Oxford, Ohio, 1950. Promotion dir. George Williams Coll., Chgo., 1950-52; sales mgr. Chatham Mfg., Chgo., 1952-54; research asst. Standard Rate and Data Service, Skokie, Ill., 1968-70, adminstr. editorial services, 1970-75, asst. editor, 1975-77; editor Wilmette, Ill., 1977-87, mng. editor, 1987—. Precinct capt. Ill. Reps., 1956-58; pres. Community Club of Jewish Women, Skokie, 1958-60; bd. dirs., treas. North Shore Towers Condo Assn., Skokie, 1986-90. Mem. NAFE, Chgo. Ad Club, Alpha Epsilon Phi. Office: Standard Rate & Data Service 3004 Glenview Rd Wilmette IL 60091

GRALA, JANE MARIE, securities firm executive; b. Phila.; d. Stanley Frank and Anna Stephanie (Yurkiewicz) G. BS, Rutgers U., Camden, 1976; MBA, Winthrop Coll., 1979; postgrad., Am. Mgmt. Assn., N.Y.C., 1980-82, Am. Inst. Real Estate Appraisers, Chgo., 1985. Mgr. acctg. dept. NDI Engrng. Co., Pennsauken, N.J., 1968-72, project mgr., 1972-76; rep. sales Am. Cyanamid, Wayne, N.J., 1976-80; dist. mgr. Am. Appraisal Assocs., Phila., 1980-86; fin. advisor Prudential-Bache Securities, Clearwater, Fla., 1986—. Mem. Nat. Assn. Accts. (dir. advt. So. Jersey chpt. 1983-86), Assn. MBA Execs., Bus and Profl. Women's Assn., Nat. Assn. for Female Execs., Chi Delta, Phi Chi Theta. Republican. Office: Prudential-Bache Securities 28100 US Hwy 19 N Ste 100 Clearwater FL 34621

GRAMM, WENDY LEE, government official; d. Joshua and Angeline (AnChin) Lee; m. Phil Gramm, Nov. 2, 1970; children: Marshall Kenneth, Jefferson Philip. BA in Econs., Wellesley Coll., 1966; PhD in Econs., Northwestern U., 1971. Staff dept. quantitive methods U. Ill., 1969; asst. prof. Tex. A&M U., 1970-74, assoc. prof. dept. econs., 1975-79; research staff Inst. Def. Analyses, 1979-82; asst. dir. Bur. Econs. FTC, 1982-83, dir., 1983-85; adminstr. Office Info. and Regulatory Affairs, OMB, 1985-87; chmn. Commodity Futures Trading Commision, 1988—. Contbr. articles to profl. jours. Office: Commodity Futures Trading Commn 2033 K St NW Washington DC 20581*

GRAMS, ILEANA J., educator; b. Sierre, Valais, Switzerland, Sept. 12, 1945; came to U.S. 1948; d. Armand and Anna (Munster) Jacoubovitch; m. Bruce William Grams, June 27, 1964 (div. 1976); m. Robert Southwick Richmond, Sept. 7, 1980; 1 child, Miranda Susan Alice. BA, Goucher Coll., Towson, Md., 1964; PhD, Georgetown U., 1978. Instr. U. N.C.-Asheville, 1975-78, asst. prof., 1979-86, assoc. prof. philosophy, 1987—, dir. Ctr. for Jewish Studies, 1985-87. Woodrow Wilson fellow, 1966. Mem. Am. Philos. Assn., Phi Beta Kappa. Democrat. Jewish. Home: 332 Barnard Ave Asheville NC 28804 Office: Univ NC Dept Philosophy Asheville NC 28804

GRAN, CAROLINE MARY, Canadian provincial official; b. Saskatoon, Sask., Canada, Nov. 18, 1941; d. Charles Millard and Hilda Irene (Handbury) Masson; m. John Arvid Gran, Oct. 13, 1969; children: Blair Matthew, Corinne Mary. Grad. high sch. With advt. dept. various radio stas., Alta. and B.C., 1958-76; ministerial asst. to Provincial Govt. B.C., Victoria, Can., 1976-86; alderwoman Langley (B.C., Can.) Municipality, 1981-86; mem. Canadian Provincial Legis. Assembly, Victoria. Mem. Lions. Mem. Social Credit. Mennonite Brethren. Office: BC Legislature, Parliament Bldgs, 5718-B Glover Rd, Langley, BC Canada

GRANACKI, VICTORIA ANN, urban planning and development consultant; b. Chgo., Dec. 19, 1947; d. Leon and Myrtle Ann (Meyer) G.; m. Newton Lee Wesley, Sept. 17, 1977; children: Matthew Granacki Wesley, Monica Granacki Wesley. BA, Mundelein Coll., 1969; MS, U. Wis., 1975. Cert. planner. Dir. cen. area planning Dept. Planning City of Chgo., 1983-86; pres. Granacki Assocs., Chgo., 1986—; adj. lectr. U. Ill. Sch. of Urban Planning and Policy, Chgo., 1988—. Bd. dirs. Near North Montessori Sch. Mem. Landmarks Preservation Coun. Ill. (v.p. Chgo. programs, bd. dirs.), Am. Planning Assn., River West Assn., Land Econs. Soc., Lambda Alpha. Democrat. Roman Catholic. Office: 1105 W Chicago Ave Chicago IL 60622

GRANADOS, CANDACE MICHELE, physical therapist; b. Albuquerque, Nov. 5, 1958; d. Lewis Ray and Pristina (Chavez) G. BS in Phys. Therapy, U. N.Mex., 1981. Chief phys. therapist CHI, Albuquerque, 1981; adminstr. Sports Phys. Therapy & Rehab., Albuquerque, 1982-83; v.p. N.Mex. Phys. Therapist Inc., Albuquerque, 1983-88; v.p. Northeastern NMPT Inc.; mem. admissions com. U. N.Mex. Dept. Phys. Therapy, 1982-88, mem. clin. edn. staff, 1982—; com. Bernallilo County Sports Medicine Com., 1986-88; pvt. practice as physical therapist, 1988—; bd. dirs. N.Mex. Phys. Therapist Inc., Northeastern N.Mex. Phys. Therapist Inc. Mem. C. of C., Am. Phys. Therapy Assn., Nat. Assn. Female Execs., N.Mex. Phys. Therapy Assn., Albuquerque Medicine/Bus. Coalition, Am. Coll. Sports Medicine. Democrat. Roman Catholic. Avocations: water skiing, jogging, weight training, racquetball. Office: S Star Route Box 4088 Corrales NM 87048

GRANATH, KAY VIVIAN, management; b. Chgo., Oct. 26, 1949; d. Raymond D. and Vivian A. (Johnson) Granath; m. Mark J. Rodeghier, Mar. 1, 1979. BA, Eastern Ill. U., Charleston, 1971. Cert. Meeting Profl., Ill. Office adminstr. Nat. Accrediting Agy. Clinical Lab. Sci., Chgo., 1974-80; mgr. meeting planning Ill. CPA Soc., Chgo., 1980-84, DeVry Inc. A. Bell & Howell Co., Evanston, Ill., 1984-87; exec. dir. Meetings Mgmt. Inc., Chgo., 1987-89; adj. instr. Roosevelt U., Chgo., 1989; mem. MPI Mem. Relations Com., Dallas, 1989; dir. confs. and edn. Data Processing Mgmt. Assn., Park Ridge, Ill., 1989. Mem. Meeting Planners Internat. (Chgo. area chpt. pres. 1985-86, treas. 1981-82). Home: 6244 North Nordica Chicago IL 60631

GRANDE, PAULA GAIL, information specialist, librarian; b. N.Y.C., Mar. 1, 1949; d. Solomon Philip and Edna Esther (Corman) G. BA, Queens Coll., 1970, MLS, 1974. Claims rep. Social Security Adminstrn., Flushing, N.Y., 1970-72; asst. libr. William M. Mercer, Inc., N.Y.C., 1975-78; mgr. N.Y. office libr. Coopers & Lybrand, N.Y.C., 1978—. Indexer ins. periodicals, 1977—; contbr. abstracts to ins. and employee benefits lit., 1980—. Coord. Manhattan Vol. Support Group, Foster Parents Plan, Manhattan, N.Y., 1987—. Recipient Dunning Meml. award Foster Parents Plan, 1988. Mem. Spl. Librs. Assn. (treas. ins. employee benefits div. 1978-81, 88, sec. 1981-82, chmn. 1983-84, bd. dirs. 1984-85, Frances S. Cox award 1987). Democrat. Jewish. Home: 235 E 13th St Apt 2E New York NY 10003 Office: Coopers & Lybrand 1301 Ave of the Americas New York NY 10019

GRANDIN, TEMPLE, livestock equipment designer; b. Boston, Aug. 29, 1947; d. Richard McCurdy and Eustacia (Cutler) G. BA in Psychology, Franklin Pierce Coll., 1970; MS in Animal Sci., Arizona State U., 1975; PhD in Animal Sci., U. Ill., Urbana, 1989. Livestock editor Ariz. Farmer Ranchman, Phoenix, 1973-78; equipment designer Corral Industries, Phoenix, 1974-75; ind. cons. Grandin Livestock Systems, Urbana, 1975-90, Fort Collins, Colo., 1990—; lectr., asst. prof. animal sci. dept. Colo. Stte U., Fort Collins, 1990—; chmn. handing com. Livestock Conservation Inst., Madison, Wis., 1976—. Contbg. editor: Meat and Poultry Mag., Mill Valley, Calif., 1987—; author: Emergence Labelled Autistic, 1986; contbr. articles to profl. publs. Recipient Meritorious Svc. award, Livestock Conservation, Madison, Wis., 1986, Disting. Alumni award, Franklin Pierce Coll., 1989. Mem. Autism Soc. Am. (bd. dirs. 1988-89, Trammel Crow award 1989), Am. Soc. Animal Sci., Am. Soc. Agrl. Cons. (bd. dirs. 1981-83), Am. Soc. Agrl. Engrs., Am. Meat Inst. (supplier mem.), Am. Registry of Profl. Animal Scis. Republican. Episcopalian. Home: Grandin Livestock Systems 2918 Silver Plume Dr C-3 Fort Collins CO 80526 Office: Colo State U Animal Sci Dept Fort Collins CO 80523

GRANDPIERRE, SUSAN MORGANA, marketing professional; b. N.Y.C., Apr. 21, 1945; d. Kurt and Anne (Winter) G.; m. Richard P. Muller, Sept. 8, 1968 (div. 1976). BA in Internat. Trade, Hunter Coll., 1965. Rsch. asst. Conf. Bd., N.Y.C., 1965-68; economist IBM Corp., Armonk, N.Y., 1968-73; sr. economist Union Carbide Corp., N.Y.C., 1973-80; info. systems mgr. Linde div. Union Carbide Corp., Danbury, Conn., 1980-85; industry mktg. mgr. Digital Equipment Corp., Stow, Mass., 1986—. Editor: Nat. Assn. Bus. Economists News, 1978-81. Co-chmn. social concerns com. 1st and 2d Ch., Boston, 1988. Mem. Cedar Point Yacht Club. Unitarian. Home: 1151 Lowell Rd Schenectady NY 12306 Office: Digital Equipment Corp 40 Old Bolton Rd Stow MA 01775

GRANDY, NITA MARY, antique dealer, cosmetologist; b. Rexburg, Idaho, Aug. 28, 1915; d. David and Anna (Heinz) Heffel; m. Alex Kretekos, Jan. 25, 1931 (div. Apr. 1935); m. James Scott Grandy, Dec. 21, 1940. Grad. high sch., L.A. Pvt. practice cosmetology L.A., 1931-67; salesperson Richard Hudnut, San Francisco, 1941-42; technician Gibbs & Co. Beauty Supply, L.A., 1943-46; pvt. practice investments L.A., 1940—, pvt. practice antique appraising, 1978—, pvt. practice agt., 1978-80, pvt. practice antique dealer, 1978-86. Mem. Rep. Presdl. Task Force, Washington, 1983—. Home and Office: 6720 Spring Park Ave #18 Los Angeles CA 90056

GRANGE, JANET B., accountant; b. Salt Lake City, May 14, 1944; d. Ray Bernard Grange and Blanche (Afton) Hiddleson. Student, York (Nebr.) Coll., 1964-65, Harding Coll., 1965-66; BA in Edn., Boise (Idaho) State U., 1973; MPA, U. Alaska, 1986. Clk. Blake, Moffitt & Town, Boise, 1966-68; payroll clk. Pendleton Woolen Mills, Washaugal, Wash., 1968-69; rsch. clk. Blue Cross of So. Calif., L.A., 1969-70, Albertson's Inc., Boise, 1970-77; acct. City & Borough of Juneau, 1977-83; bookkeeper Juneau Elks Lodge, 1986-88; acct. Alaska Travel Adventures, Juneau, 1988-89, U. Alaska, Juneau, 1989—. Bd. dirs. Juneau Sports Assn., 1988-90. Mem. NAFE, Nat. Alumni Assn. of York Coll., U. Alaska Alumni Assn. Home: 2865 Mendenhall Loop Rd C-3 Juneau AK 99801

GRANNON-DEVINE, DEBRA LYNN, public information officer; b. Wash., Sept. 21, 1959; d. Elmer Eugene Devine and JoElla J. (Leonard) Nolley. Grad. high sch., Wash., 1977. Teller, loan clk. Otero Fed. Credit Union, Alamogordo, N.M., 1978-80; collateral, new acct. Grisson (Ind.) Fed. Credit Union, 1980-82; computer operator data processing Ft. Knox (Ky.) Fed. Credit Union, 1982-83; customer service rep. Myrtle Beach (S.C.) AFB Fed. Credit Union, 1983-87; adminstrv. sec. govtl. affairs Ind. Credit Union League, Indpls., 1988. Leader Gir Scouts, Inpls. 1988--. Mem. Exec. Females, Profl. Sec., YMCA. Roman Catholic. Home: PO Box 582 Bunker Hill IN 46914 Office: Ind Credit Union League 8200 Haverstick Ste 100 Indianapolis IN 46240

GRANOFF, JEAN KESSLER, personnel executive, business owner; b. Phila., Mar. 30, 1926; d. Louis and Sara (Gold) Kessler; m. Jerome Claymont Granoff (dec. Oct. 1973); children: Fern, Gail. BA, Temple U., 1948, MA, 1954. Pres., owner Powers Pers., Phila., 1975—. Home: Academy House 17N Philadelphia PA 19102 Office: Powers Pers 1530 Chestnut St Ste 310 Philadelphia PA 19102

GRANOWETTER, LINDA, physician, educator; b. N.Y.C., Aug. 13, 1951; d. Stanley and Claire (Teich) G. BA, SUNY, Old Westbury, 1972; BS, SUNY, Stony Brook, 1974, MD, 1978. Asst. prof. pediatrics, physician U. Pa., Phila., 1984-86; asst. prof. pediatrics, asst. attending physician Sch. George Washington U., Washington, 1986-87, Mt. Sinai Med. Ctr., N.Y.C., 1987—. Fellow Am. Acad. Pediatrics; mem. Am. Pediatrics Oncology Group, Pediatric Oncology Group., Am. Soc. Clin. Oncology. Democrat. Jewish. Office: Mt Sinai Med Ctr 1208 1 Gustave L Levy Pl New York NY 10029

GRANT, ALICIA BROWN, accountant; b. Dothan, Ala., Apr. 19, 1945; d. Rudolph and Grace (Tyus) B.; m. Paul A. Grant; children: Rodney, Christopher, Adam. BA, Fla. State U., 1970. CPA, Fla. Sr. auditor Peat, Marwick, Mitchell and Co., Tampa, Fla., 1970-73; internal auditor Home Fed. Savs. and Loan Assn., St. Petersburg, Fla., 1973-75; dir. internal audit, v.p. Duval Fed. Savs. and Loan Assn., Jacksonville, Fla., 1984-87; dir. internal audit Fla. Community Coll., Jacksonville, 1987-89. Chmn. Riverside Avondale Preservation, Inc., Jacksonville; mem. Mayor's Spl. Task Force on Recycling, Jacksonville; trustee Meml. Park Assn., Inc., Jacksonville. Mem. AICPA, Fla. Inst. CPA's, Inst. Internal Auditors (bd. govs. N.E. Fla. chpt.), Nat. Assn. Cert. Fraud Examiners, Civitan. Republican. Episcopalian. Office: Fla Community Coll 501 W State St Jacksonville FL 32202

GRANT, AMY, singer, songwriter; b. Augusta, Ga., 1961; d. Burton Grant; m. Gary Chapman; 1 child, Matthew Garrison Chapman. Student, Furman U., Vanderbilt U. Albums include Amy Grant, 1976, My Father's Eyes, 1977, Never Alone, 1978, Amy Grant in Concert, 1979, Amy Grant in Concert II, 1980, Age to Age (Grammy award), 1983, A Christmas Album, 1983, Straight Ahead, 1984, Unguarded (Grammy award), 1985, Lead Me On, 1988. Recipient 3 Dove awards Gospel Music Assn., Grammy award for contemporary gospel performance NARAS, 1982, for female gospel performance, 1983, 84, for female gospel vocal, 1985. Office: care A&M Records 1416 N LaBrea Los Angeles CA 90028*

GRANT, SISTER BARBARA LEE, hospital executive; b. Jackson, Miss., Aug. 13, 1946; d. Robert Emmett and Patricia (Horan) G. BS in Nursing, Marillac Coll., 1970; M of Health Adminstrn., Washington U., St. Louis, 1980. Staff nurse St. John's Mercy Med. Ctr., St. Louis, 1970-74; adminstrv. asst. St. Edward Mercy Med. Ctr., Ft. Smith, Ark., 1974-78; resident Mercy Health Svcs., Farmington Hills, Mich., 1980-81; asst. adminstr. Mercy Hosp., New Orleans, 1981-85, chief operating officer, 1985-87, chief exec. officer, 1987—. Bd. trustees Mercy Reg. Med. Ctr., Laredo, Tex., 1984-90, St. John's Mercy Med. Ctr., St. Louis, 1988-90; bd. dirs. St. Thomas Health Svcs., New Orleans, 1989—; sec. Met. Hosp. Coun., New Orleans, 1989, v.p., 1990—. Mem. La. Cath. Health Assn. (pres. 1989—). Office: Mercy Hosp 301 N Jefferson Davis Pkwy New Orleans LA 70119

GRANT, BETTY RUTH, educator; b. Alexandria, La., Apr. 14, 1937; d. Delila and Vonnie (Rogers) Nugent; m. Donald Eugene Grant, Mar. 28, 1958; children: David Nugent, Kenneth Don. BA, La. Coll., 1958; MA in Edn., Northwestern State U., Natchitoches, La., 1965; postgrad., East Tex. State U., 1975. Cert. elem. tchr., La., Tex. Classroom tchr. Woodland Elem. Sch., Pineville, La., 1958-66; 4th grade tchr. C.A. Tosch Elem. Sch., Mesquite, Tex., 1970—. Active Homeowners Assn., Mesquite, 1969—, Polit. Action Com., Mesquite, 1970-85. Mem. AAUW (pres. 1982), Mesquite Edn. Assn. (pres. 1977-78), Assn. Tex. Profl. Educators, PTA (treas. 1970, life), Alpha Delta Kappa (pres. 1984). Methodist. Home: 2537 Belhaven Mesquite TX 75150

GRANT, CAROL PHILLIPS, health facility activities administrator, nurse; b. Chester, S.C., June 6, 1956; d. William Rothell and Mary Elizabeth (Bennett) Phillips; divorced; 1 child, Allison Elizabeth. Student, U. S.C., Lancaster, 1979; BS in Nursing, Med. U. S.C., Charleston, 1982. RN, S.C. Staff charge nurse Chester County Hosp., 1979-82, Bapt. Med. Ctr., Columbia, S.C., 1982-84, Piedmont Med. Ctr., Rock Hill, S.C., 1984-85; med. svc. dir. Physicians Health Plan, Columbia, 1985-86; staff, charge nurse Richland Meml. Hosp., Columbia, 1986-88; dir. edn. and staff devel. Chester Co. Hosp., 1988—; ednl. cons. Chester County Fed. Lic. Practical Nurse's S.C., 1979-81. Mem. Speakers Bur. Chester County Hosp., 1988—. Mem. Am. Assn. Critical Care Nurses (cert., Midstone chpt.), Am. Lung Assn., Am. Heart Assn., S.C. Hosp. Assn., Soc. Educators, Med. Univ. S.C. Alumni Assn., Univ. S.C. Alumni Assn., Charleston Club, Columbia Club. Republican. Baptist. Office: Chester County Hosp Great Falls Hwy Chester SC 29706

GRANT, CHERYL, producer, television syndicator; b. Phoenix, Mar. 1, 1944; d. William Edward and Mary Louise (Weldon) Grant; m. Louis Tancredi, Nov. 27, 1976; children—John Francis, Jennifer Grant. Student U. Fribourg, Switzerland, 1963-64; B.A., Coll. of Notre Dame of Md., 1965; M.S., Syracuse U., 1966. Assoc. producer Girl Talk ABC Films, N.Y.C., 1968-70, New Jersey Speaker for Itself, WNDT-TV, N.Y.C., 1966-68, Communications and Education, WNDT-TV, N.Y.C., 1967, The Virginia Graham Show, RKO, Los Angeles, 1970-71, Manhattan Townhouse, Source Internat., N.Y.C., 1971-72, Collision Course, Wolper Prodns., Los Angeles, 1972, Living Easy with Dr. Joyce Brothers, Capricorn Prodns., N.Y.C., 1972-73, Mike Douglas Show, Westinghouse, Phila., 1974, Beverly & Vidal Sassoon, Sta. KCOP, Los Angeles, 1975, Dinah, 20th Century Fox, Los Angeles, 1975; hostess A.M. Miami, Sta. WPLG-TV, Miami, Fla., 1972; exec. producer/pres. Carter-Grant Prodns., Inc., Los Angeles, 1976—, Sherry Grant Enterprises, Inc., Los Angeles, 1982—. Programs have been honored by the Freedom Found. award, Internat. Film and TV Festival of N.Y. Gold Award and Calif. Motion Picture Assn. Golden Halo award. Mem. Acad. T.V. Arts and Sci., Women in Bus., Women in Film, Am. Women in Radio and TV, AFTRA, Women in Cable. Roman Catholic. Home: 18120 Sweet Elm Dr Encino CA 91316 Office: Sherry Grant Enterprises 17915 Ventura Blvd Ste 208 Encino CA 91316

GRANT, CYNTHIA ELIZABETH, museum director, teacher, consultant; b. Asheville, N.C., Oct. 4, 1948; d. Roger Alpine Grant, Jr. and Mary Elizabeth (Scott) Winterling; 1 child, Jonathan Worthington. B.A., Salem Coll., 1970; M.A. in History, Wake Forest U., 1986. Cert. tchr. social studies. Tchr. Asheville City Schs., 1970-71; buyer Navy Exchange, U.S. Navy, Roosevelt Roads, P.R., 1971-72; staff asst. Tulane U., New Orleans, 1972-74; ombudsman Am. Bankers Assn., Washington, 1977-78; mus. dir. City of Alexandria, Va., 1978-81; dir. Hist. Columbia (S.C.) Found., 1981-86; site mgr. Montgomery Place, Historic Hudson (N.Y.) Valley, Annandale, 1986—; cons. Kensington Plantation, Eastover, S.C., 1985-86, Hist. Beaufort Found., S.C., 1985; mem. resource com. Cultural Council, Columbia, 1983-86. Bd. dirs. Young Profls. of Columbia Mus., 1984-85; com. chmn. Leadership Columbia, 1983-86; event chmn. Champions of Children's Hosp., Columbia, 1984-86; mem. stewardship com. Shandon Presbyn. Ch., Columbia, 1983-86; mem. Reformed Ch. Rhinebeck; mem. granting rev. com. Dutchess County Arts Coun., 1987-89; mem. rev. com. IMS, 1984—. Recipient Pres.'s prize Salem Coll., 1970; John H. Stibbs award Tulane U., 1973. Mem. Am. Assn. Mus., Mid-Atlantic Assn. Mus., S.C. Fedn. Mus. (sec. 1983-84), Am. Assn. for State and Local History (award of merit for mus. 1984), Nat. Trust for Hist. Preservation, Redhook C. of C., N.Y. Preservation Alliance, Elmendorph Soc., Rhinebeck Hist. Soc., Columbia Forum, Rotary Internat., Red Hook (treas. 1989, sec. 1989-90). Democrat. Presbyterian. Avocations: photography, hiking, travel. Home: PO Box 21 Annandale-on-Hudson NY 12504-0021 Office: Hist Hudson Valley PO Box 32 Annandale-on-Hudson NY 12504

GRANT, DORIS LEONA, educator, consultant; b. Zanesville, Ohio, Aug. 30, 1915; d. Brooks Carey and Ida Mae (Hogan) Jackson; m. Arthur Lee Grant, Mar. 30, 1940; children: Anita, Arthur, Laureen. BS, Schauffler Coll., Cleve., 1937; MA, Case Western Res. U., 1956; postgrad., John Carroll U., 1970-71, Calif. Coast U., 1989—. Social worker Cleve. Welfare Dept., 1938-43; clk. Karamu House & Cedar YMCA, Cleve., 1943-46; tchr. Cleve. Bd. Edn., 1947-68; instr. Woodland Job Ctr., Cleve., 1968-70; adminstrv. intern Cleve. Bd. Edn., 1970-73, math. cons., 1973-75; math. instr., tutor Glenville Learning Devel. Ctr., Cleve., 1984--. Dean Regional Sch. Christian Mission, Sioux City, Iowa, 1982; treas. North Cen. Jurisdiction United Meth. Women, N.Y.C., 1984-88; chmn. religion & race com. Mt. Pleasant United Meth Ch., chmn. Lydia Cluster; trustee Flat Rock Children's Home, 1978-85, Ohio Literacy Network, Columbus, 1985—; tutor, trainer Interch. Coun., Cleve., 1985-86, mem. Ch. & Soc. Coun., 1983—; vols. coord. Greater Cleve. Project Resource Ctr., 1975-78, tng. specialist, 1978-82; workshop leader Parent Resource Ctr., Cleve., 1982-84; mem. Cleve. Literacy Coalition, 1985—; state chairperson Assault On Illiteracy Program, 1983—. Mem. NAACP, Nat. Council Negro Women, AAUW, Ohio Ret. Tchrs. Assn., Phillis Wheatley Assn. (trustee 1986--), Urban League Guild (co-chmn. 1986--), Ea. Star (co-chmn. 1987--), Alpha Kappa Alpha (chmn. 1983--), Nat. Phi Delta Kappa Inc. Democrat. Home and Office: 8923 Parmelee Ave Cleveland OH 44108

GRANT, ELAINE ELIZABETH, assistant dean; b. St. Louis, Sept. 17, 1941; d. John Thomas and Mabel Mary (Lutton) Rachel; m. Kerry E. Grant. BA, St. Louis U., 1963. Physician's asst. APT Found., New Haven, 1974-75; asst. dir. Methadone Maintenance Program, New Haven, 1975-76; asst. dir. Yale U., New Haven, 1976-78, exec. dir., 1978-88; asst. dean Physician Assoc. Program, New Haven, 1988—. Office: Physician Assoc Program PO Box 3333 382 Congress New Haven CT 06410

GRANT, ISABELLA HORTON, judge; b. Los Angeles, Sept. 24, 1924; d. John Daniel and Hannabelle (Horton) Grant. B.A., Swarthmore Coll., 1944; M.A., UCLA, 1946; J.D., Columbia U., 1950; LL.D. (hon.), Molloy Coll., 1976. Jr. profl. asst. OSS, Washington, 1944-45; economist Inst. Indsl. Relations, UCLA, 1946-47, Office Price Stblzn., Los Angeles, 1951-52; ptnr. Livingston, Grant, Stone & Kay, San Francisco, 1953-79; judge Mcpl. Ct., San Francisco, 1979-82, Superior Ct., San Francisco, 1982—. Bd. dirs. Advs.

for Women, San Francisco, 1980— . Fellow ABA; mem. San Francisco Bar Assn. (bd. dirs. 1978-79), Acad. Matrimonial Lawyers (pres. No. Calif. chpt. 1976), Assn. Family and Conciliation Cts. (pres. Calif. chpt. 1987-89), Nat. Coll. Probate Judges, Queen's Bench (pres. 1964), Calif. Tennis Club, Phi Beta Kappa. Office: Superior Ct City Hall San Francisco CA 94102

GRANT, JOANNE CATHERINE, auctioneer; b. Cornwall, N.Y., Nov. 25, 1940; d. Martin Emmett and Josephine Mary (Randazzo) Smith; m. Martin B. Grant, Jan. 11, 1964; children: Martin Andrew, Jennifer Allison. RN, Vassar Bros. Hosp. Sch. Nursing, 1961. RN Vassar Bros. Hosp., Poughkeepsie, N.Y., 1961-64, Dr. Morris Goldberger, N.Y.C., 1964-66, Dr. Martin Grant, New Windsor, N.Y., 1971-75; auctioneer Mid Hudson Galleries, Cornwall-on-Hudson, N.Y., 1976—, Guernseys, N.Y.C., 1984—. Author: The Painted Lamps of Handel, 1976, Price Guide to American Victorian Figural Napkin Rings, 1978. Bd. dirs. Orange County Assn. for Help of Retarded Children, Middletown, N.Y., 1973-84; mem. com. for spl. edn. Cornwall Sch. Dist., 1986-87. Mem. N.Y. State Auctioneers Assn., Appraisal Assn. Am. Office: Mid Hudson Galleries 1 Idlewild Ave PO Box 305 Cornwall-on-Hudson NY 12520

GRANT, JUANITA G., librarian; b. Princeton, W.Va., July 25, 1930; d. William Randle and Cora (Fitch) Grant; BS, Concord Coll., 1953; BS in Library Sci., U. N.C., 1955; M in Liberal Arts, Johns Hopkins U., 1970. Librarian, Spl. Services, U.S. Army, Germany, France, 1956-58; asst. librarian Carson Newman Coll., Jefferson City, Tenn., 1959-63; librarian Judson Coll., Marion, Ala., 1964-67; dir. Blount Library, Averett Coll., Danville, Va., 1967—; library adv. com. Va. Council Higher Edn., 1976-78; mem. adv. com. Danville Pub. Library, 1973-75; chmn. library com. Danville Mus. Fine Arts and History, 1976-80; mem. Louisa County Hist. Soc. Mem. ALA, Nat. Geneal. Soc., Va. Geneal. Soc., Va./N.C. Geneal. Soc., Southeastern Library Assn., Va. Library Assn., Am. Hist. Soc., Danville Hist. Soc., Book and Art Club, Wednesday Club, Phi Delta Kappa. Baptist. Home: 126 Primrose Ct Danville VA 24541

GRANT, KATHRYN ANN, registered nurse; b. Tooele, Utah, Feb. 11, 1946; d. Thomas Michael and Leone Kathryn (Olson) Keegan; m. Wayne A. Grant, III, Nov. 17, 1973 (div. 1986). Diploma, Luth. Deaconess Hosp. Sch. Nursing, 1969; BA, Park Coll., 1978; MA, Webster U., 1982. Cert. Psychiat. and Mental Health Nurse. Tchr. asst. Black Hills State Coll., Spearfish, S.D., 1964-65; nurse aide Lutheran Deaconess Hosp., Mpls., Minn., 1966-69; office mgr., peer counselor Washington Rape Crisis Ctr., 1974-76; registered nurse USAF and Air N.G., U.S. and Japan, 1970-76; direct sales rep. Avon Products, Inc., Fairview Heights, Ill., 1976-84; chiropractic asst. Faulkner Chiropractic Clinic, Ill., 1983-86; office mgr., chiropractic asst. Dr. Swiller's Chiropractic Office, Hartford, Conn., 1986; asst. head nurse Veterans Admin. Medical Ctr., Newington, Conn., 1986-89; asst. nurse mgr. inpatient psychiatry New Britain (Conn.) Gen. Hosp., 1989—. Author, Poems, "Thoughts", 1987. Sec. parish planning coun. Faith Luth. Ch., Fairview Heights, Ill., 1982-84; vol. nurse USAF Med. Ctr., Washington, 1975-76. Mem. Touch for Health Found. (instr. 1984—), Parker Chiropractic Rsch. Found., Am. Holistic Nurses Assn. Office: New Britain Gen Hosp 100 Grand St New Britain CT 06050

GRANT, MARGARET DAVIS, educator; b. Greenville, S.C., Aug. 15, 1944; d. Herbert Stowe and Mary Cornelia (Griffin) Davis; m. Francis Berry, Aug. 5, 1967; children: Lee Anne, Patrick David. BS in Edn., Fla. State U., Tallahassee, 1966. Cert. tchr., Ga., Fla., Ala. Tchr. Skyland Elem. Sch., Atlanta, 1966-67, Davis Elem. Sch., Montgomery, Ala., 1967-69, Seymca Pre-Sch., Montgomery, 1977-87, 1st United Meth. Pre Sch., Montgomery, 1987—. Vol. Jr. League of Montgomery 1978-89; mem. PTA. Mem. AEA, NEA, Jr. Woman's Club. Republican. Baptist. Home: 3424 Drexel Rd Montgomery AL 36106

GRANT, MARY KATHRYN, healthcare system executive; b. Bklyn., July 24, 1941; d. John T. and Mary L. (Guerin) G. BA, Mercy Coll., Detroit, 1964; MA, U. Notre Dame, 1969; PhD, Ind. U., 1974. Tchr. Sisters of Mercy Ednl. System, 1964-69; mem. faculty Mercy Coll., 1969-77; assoc. dean Mt. St. Mary's Coll., L.A., 1977-80; exec. dir. Mercy Health Conf., Farmington Hills, Mich., 1980-84; dir. sponsorship Cath. Health Assn., St. Louis, 1985-86; v.p., prin. Consol. Cath. Health Care, Westchester, Ill., 1987-89; dir. cons. Ministerial Devel. Svcs., Darien, Ill., 1989-90; sr. v.p. mission svcs. Holy Cross Health System Corp., South Bend, Ind., 1990—; chmn. ethics com. Mich. Cath. Hosp. Assn., Lansing, 1982-84; mem. adv. bd. Holy Cross Health System, South Bend, 1987—, Mission Advisor, Richmond, Va., 1988—. Author: A View of Unions in Mercy Healthcare Facilities, 1982, Quality of Worklife in Health Care Facilities: Approaches and Applications, 1985, Health Services for the Poor: A Challenge to Public Policy, 1984, The Congregation and the Corporation: Perspectives on the Critical Relationship, 1985, Health Ministry in Transition: A Planning Manual, 1989; contbr. articles to profl. publs. NSF grantee, 1979-80. Mem. Am. Coll. Health Care Execs. (nominee), Am. Hosp. Assn., Soc. Healthcare Planning, Long Beach Country Club. Democrat. Roman Catholic. Home: 4219 Thorndale Ave Chicago IL 60646 Office: Holy Cross Health System Corp 3606 E Jefferson Blvd South Bend IN 46615

GRANT, MIRIAM ROSENBLOUM, educator, journalist; b. Collinsville, Ala.; d. Harry M. and Rae (Rosenberg) Rosenbloum; m. Morton A. Grant, Nov. 17, 1952 (dec. 1967). AB, U. Ala., 1935; postgrad., U. Miami, 1968-69, Fla. Internat. U. Cert. tchr., Fla. Reporter Chattanooga Free Press., 1936-41, Birmingham (Ala.) Post, 1942; reporter, movie editor, drama critic Chattanooga News-Free Press, 1943-49; thcr., head journalism dept., newspaper and yearbook adviser North Miami (Fla.) Sr. High Sch., 1969-89. Recipient Golden Medallion Fla. Scholastic Press Assn., 1987, named life member, 1990, service award Coll. Fraternity Editors Assn., 1989. Mem. AAUW, U. Ala. Nat. Alumni Assn. (coun. mem. at large 1960-61), Ceramic League Miami (corr. sec. 1963-64), Women's Panhellenic Assn. Miami, Nat. Panhellenic Editors Conf. (vice-chmn. 1986-87, chmn. 1987-89), Sigma Delta Tau Alumnae League Greater Miami, Sigma Delta Tau (nat. pres. 1950-54, pres. Miami Housing Corp. 1957—, editor Torch 1968—, honor key, 1988), Theta Sigma Phi, Phi Lambda Pi, Rho Lambda.

GRANT, PENNY, pediatrician; b. N.Y.C., Dec. 19, 1959; d. Stanley Charles and Hilda (Kleinerman) G.; m. Lee Mark Cohen, Feb. 28, 1987. BA, Columbia U., 1980; MD, N.Y. Med. Coll., 1984. Diplomate Nat. Bd. Med. Examiners, Am. Bd. Pediatrics. Intern N.Y. Hosp. Cornell Med. Ctr., N.Y.C., 1984-86; resident Jackson Meml. Hosp., U. Miami, Fla., 1986-88, dir. pediatric care network, 1989-90; pediatrician Pediatric Assocs., P.A., Hollywood, Fla., 1988-89; asst. prof. dept pediatrics U. Miami, 1989—. Mem. Am. Acad. Pediatrics. Office: Child Protection Team 1150 NW 14th St Rm 212 Miami FL 33136

GRANT, PHYLLIS HUNT, hospital administrator; b. Biloxi, Miss., Dec. 15, 1951; d. Bartlo George and Mona Melissa (Hudson) Hunt; m. Warren C. Grant, Jr., June 7, 1980; 1 child, William Christopher. Student, U. So. Miss., Hattiesburg, 1971; B.S.N., U. Tenn., 1974; M.S.N., U. Ala., Birmingham, 1978, MS in Hosp. Adminstrn., 1989. Staff nurse pediatrics Meml. Hosp. Gulfport, Gulfport, Miss., 1974-75; staff nurse transport newborn intensive care Singing River Hosp., Pascagoula, Miss., 1975-76; staff nurse transport U. So. Ala. Med. Ctr., 1976-88; course coord. maternal-infant nursing U. So. Ala. Sch. Nursing, Mobile, 1979; neonatal outreach coord. U. So. Ala. Sch. Nursing, 1978-80; asst. dir. nursing maternal child svc. Glenn R. Frye Morial Hosp., Hickory, N.C., 1980-83; dir. nursing women/children's div. Bapt. Med. Ctr.-Montclair, Birmingham, Ala., 1983-86; v.p. nursing Bapt. Med. Ctr.-Montclair, 1986—. Contbr. articles to Jour. Obstetric Gynecologic & Neonatal Nursing, 1980, Am. Jour. Diseases Children, 1982. Named Outstanding Alumnus Coll. Nursing U. Tenn., 1988. Mem. Am. Coll. Health Care Execs. (nominee), Am. Orgn. Nurse Execs., Hoover C. of C., Birmingham East Kiwanis, Sigma Theta Tau. Roman Catholic. Office: Bapt Med Ctr Montclair 800 Montclair Rd Birmingham AL 35213

GRANT, RHODA, biomedical researcher, teacher, medical physiologist; b. Hopewell, N.S., Can., Jan. 12, 1902; d. James William and Marjorie Madelein (Cruickshank) G. BA with Hons. in Biology and Chemistry, McGill U., Montreal, 1924; MA in Biochemistry, McGill U., 1930, PhD in Exptl. Medicine cum laude, 1932. Biochemistry rsch. technician Med. Lab., Royal Victoria Hosp., McGill U., Montreal, 1925-29; demonstrator in physiology Banting & Best Med. Rsch. Inst., U. Toronto, Ont., Can., 1933-35; researcher on hearing Physiology Dept., McGill U., Montreal, 1936; asst. prof. physiology Med. Coll., Dalhousie U., Halifax, N.S., Can., 1937-38; teaching and rsch. faculty dept. physiology McGill U., 1939-47; rsch. assoc. clin. sci. med. Coll. U. Ill., Chgo., 1948-61; rsch. assoc. pathology med. Coll. U. Ill., 1961-66; participant in Internat. Symposium on Gastric Cancer, Nat. Cancer Inst./NSF, Japan, 1969. Contbr. articles to profl. jours., med. texts, physiol. handbooks. Mem. Can. Physiol. Soc., Am. Physiol. Soc. (affiliate), Royal Soc. Med. London, Sigma Xi. Home: 525 University Dr East Lansing MI 48823

GRANT, RUBY JAYNE JOHNSON, insurance executive; b. Glen Cove, N.Y., June 28; d. Alfred Lloyd and Ora Mae (Gibson) Pendleton; m. Nolan Eugene Floyd Grant; 1 child, Kristale Michelle. Grad. high sch., Glen Cove. Telephone operator N.Y. Phone Co., Roslyn, 1958-60; bookkeeper Town and Country, Roslyn, 1961-65; salesperson Parkview Realty, Westbury, N.Y., 1965-66; teller Meadowbrook Bank, Jericho, N.Y., 1966-67; cons. Met. Life Ins. Co., Hicksville, N.Y., 1968-73; agt. AllState Ins. Co., Glen Cove, 1973—. New Cassel Rep. Club, Westbury, N.Y., 1985—; pres. Glen Cove Youth Club, 1980-85, advisor, 1986—; chmn. insps. Nassau County Election Bd., 1987—. Mem. Nat. Assn. Negro Bus. and Profl. Women (life; rec. sec. 1985-87, chaplain 1987—), 100 Black Women L.I., Inc. Mem. Ch. of God in Christ, vice-chmn. trustee bd. Avocations: interior decorating, bicycling, roller skating. Home: 261 Brook St PO Box 10091 Westbury NY 11590 Office: Allstate Ins Co 821 Carman Ave Westbury NY 11590

GRANT, SANDRA MILLIKEN, physical therapist; b. Buffalo, Mar. 25, 1958; d. Elwood Ruthvin and Joyce Anita (Dyer) Milliken; m. Vernon Campbell Grant, May 27, 1989; stepchildren: Nicholas, Anne. BS in Phys. Therapy, Northeastern U., 1981. Registered phys. therapist, Nev., Maine. Staff phys. therapist Sunrise Hosp., Las Vegas, Nev., 1981-82; cons. phys. therapist Sandra L. Milliken, R.P.T., Ltd., Las Vegas, 1982-84; co-owner, pres., phys. therapist Sandra L. Milliken, R.P.T., Ltd., Scarborough, Maine, 1984—; co-owner, mgr., phys. therapist Milliken Phys. Therapy Ctr., Scarborough, 1984—, Biddeford, Maine, 1985—. Mem.Am. Phys. Therapy Assn. Republican. Home: PO Box 256 South Freeport ME 04078 Office: PO Box 1450 605 US Rte 1 Scarborough ME 04074

GRANT, SANDRA SWEARINGEN, long term care administrator; b. Columbia, Mo., July 28, 1944; d. Beverly Stone and Mildred (Hewitt) Swearingen; m. Stephen E. Grant, June 2, 1963 (div. May 1988); children: Darin Michael, Catherine Michelle. BGS, U. Mo., 1977; MA in Health Svcs., Webster U., 1983. Cert. nursing home adminstr. Purchasing asst. U. Mo. Med. Ctr., Columbia, 1964-66; sec. Jackson County Election Bd., Independence, Mo., 1976-77; adminstr. John Knox Village Care Ctr., Lee's Summit, Mo., 1977-89; dir. long term care Barnes Hosp., St. Louis, 1989—; bd. dirs. Mid-Am. Regional Council Long Term Care Ombudsman Program, 1987-88; instr., mem. long term care adv. bd. Kansas City (Kans.) Community Coll., 1987-89. Trustee Mid-West Health Congress, 1986-88. Mem. Am. Coll. Health Care Adminstrs. (pres. Mo. chpt. 1987-89, regional gov. 1989—), Mo. Health Care Assn. (pres. Dist I 1985-86, exec. bd.). Office: Barnes Hosp One Barnes Hospital Plaza Saint Louis MO 63110

GRANT, SARA CATHERINE, training and development specialist; b. Johnstown, Pa., Mar. 28, 1950; d. James Walter and Bernetta (Bewak) G. BS in English, Lock Haven U., 1973; MA in Adult Edn., Ind. U. of Pa., 1978; MA in Organizational Psychology, Columbia U., 1989. Tchr. English Williamsport (Pa.) Sch. Dist., 1973; adminstr. adult basic edn. Somerset (Pa.) Sch. Dist., 1973-77; dir. tng. Girl Scouts U.S. Council, Harrisburg, Pa., 1977-79, adult devel. cons., N.Y.C., 1979-82, dir. tng., N.Y.C., 1982-86; tng. and devel. specialist Tchrs. Ins. and Annuity Assn., Coll. Retirement Equities Fund, N.Y.C., 1986—. Contbr. articles to mags. Mem. ASTD. Democrat. Avocation: tennis. Home: 104-20 Queens Blvd Forest Hills NY 11375

GRANT, SUSAN, television executive; b. Boston, Dec. 23, 1954; d. Robert Nathan and Barbara (Weil) G.; m. Steven W. Korn, June 17, 1976 (div. Apr. 1982). AB, Vassar Coll., 1976. Rsch. asst. corp. devel. Cornell U., Ithaca, N.Y., 1976-78; asst. to v.p. fin. dept. Turner Broadcasting System, Atlanta, 1978-79; dir. pub. rels., regional sales mgr. Turner Cable News Network, 1979-81, dir regional sales and mktg., nat. sales mgr., 1982-85; v.p. sales Magnicom Systems, Inc., Stamford, Conn., 1985; dir. nat. accounts Intec Systems, West Palm Beach, Fla., 1985; account exec. Columbia Pictures TV, Atlanta, 1986-88, v.p. syndication S.E. region, 1989—. Mem. Atlanta chpt. Women in Cable (pres. 1980). Office: Columbia Pictures TV 1201 W Peachtree Ste 4820 Atlanta GA 30309

GRANT-LYNCH, CAROL LEE, director special services, psychologist; b. Passaic, N.J., Sept. 22, 1943; d. Joseph Louis and Ellen (Birish) Dobkowski; m. Carl R. Grant, Feb. 16, 1969 (div. july 1987); m. Mervin Dean Lynch, Aug. 13, 1989; 1 child, Eric Alexander. BA, William Paterson Coll., 1966; MA, NYU, 1970, D Psychology, 1984. Lic. psychologist, N.J., N.Y. Tchr. Bloomfield (N.J.) Pub. Schs., 1966-68, psychologist, 1970-87; dir. spl. svcs. Waldwick (N.J.) Pub. Schs., 1987—; adj. clin. prof. NYU, N.Y.C., 1983-86 adj. prof. Montclair (N.J.) State Coll., 1984-85. Mem. profl. alumni coun. Sch. Edn., Health and Nursing, NYU, 1989—. NYU fellow, 1981-82. Mem. Am. Psychol. Assn. (sch. psychol. task force 1989—), N.J. Psychol. Assn. (treas. 1985-88), N.J. Assn. Sch. Psychologists (pres. 1982-83), Nat. Assn. Sch. Psychologists (del. 1984-88), Eastern Ednl. Rsch. Assn. (2d v.p. 1989—), Bergen County Assn. Lic. Psychologists, NYU Sch. Psychology Alumni Assn. (founder 1988—). Home: 124 Frank Ct Mahwah NJ 07430 Office: Waldwick Pub Schs 155 Summit Ave Waldwick NJ 07463

GRANTUSKAS, PATRICIA MARY, educator; b. Irvington, N.J., Jan. 17, 1952; d. Albert Leonard and Mary Dolores (Gradeckis) G. BA summa cum laude, Kean Coll., 1973, MA, 1977. Cert. supr., reading specialist, reading tchr., elem. sch. tchr. Remedial reading tchr. Garwood (N.J.) Pub. Schs., 1973-77, reading specialist, test BSIP coord., 1977-89; reading instr. summer clinic Pingry Sch., N.J., 1977-82; reading clinician Kean Coll. Reading Clinic, Union, N.J., 1977-80; reading instr. summer program Newark Acad., Livingston, N.J., 1983—; reading specialist, basic skills coord. Harrington Park (N.J.) Sch., 1989—. Mem. YMCA. Mem. N.J. Reading Assn. (bd. sec. 1989-90), Suburban Reading Coun. (rec. sec. 1982-84, v.p. 1984-86, pres. 1986-88, Pres.'s award 1987, Club award 1988), Internat. Reading Assn., Delta Kappa Gamma, Kappa Delta Pi. Roman Catholic.

GRASSELLI, JEANETTE GECSY, university official; b. Cleve., Aug. 4, 1928; d. Nicholas W. and Veronica (Varga) Gecsy; m. Glenn R. Brown, Aug. 1, 1987. BS summa cum laude, Ohio U., 1950, DSc (hon.), 1978; MS, Western Res. U., 1958; DSc (hon.), Clarkson U., 1986, Mich. Tech. U., 1989. Project leader, assoc. Infrared Spectroscopist, Cleve., 1950-78; mgr. analytical sci. lab. Standard Oil (name changed to BP Am., Inc. 1985), Cleve., 1978-83, dir. technol. support dept., 1983-85, dir. corp. rsch. and analytical scis., 1985-88; Disting. vis. prof., dir. rsch. enhancement Ohio U., Athens, 1989—; bd. dirs. Nicolet Instrument Co., Madison, Wis.; vis. com. Nat. Inst. for Standards and Tech. Author, editor 8 books; editor: Vibrational Spectroscopy; contbr. numerous articles on molecular spectroscopy to profl. jours.; patentee naphthalene extraction process. Dir. N.E. Ohio Sci. & Engring. Fair, Cleve., 1977—; trustee Ohio U., Athens, 1985—, Holden Arboretum, Cleve., 1988—, Edison Biotech. Ctr., Cleve., 1988—; active corp. fund raising Rainbow Babies Children's Hosp., Cleve., 1987—. Recipient Disting. Svc. award Cleve. Tech. Soc. Coun., 1985; named Woman of Yr. YWCA, 1980; named to Ohio Women's Hall of Fame State of Ohio, 1989. Mem. Am. Chem. Soc. (Garvan medal 1986), Soc. for Applied Spectroscopy (pres. 1970, Dist. Svc. award 1983), Coblentz Soc. (bd. govs. 1968-71, William Wright award 1980), Phi Beta Kappa, Iota Sigma Pi (pres. fluorine chpt. 1957-60, nat. hon. mem. 1987). Republican. Roman Catholic. Home: 150 Greentree Rd Chagrin Falls OH 44022

GRASSO, DOREEN MARIE, art dealer; b. Pitts., Jan. 12, 1955; d. Frank Jules and Laverne (Damico) G.; 1 child, Sarah Elizabeth Dadisman. BA, U. Pitts., 1976. Dir. appraisal dept. Childs Gallery, Boston, 1977-78; asst. dir. painting dept. William Doyle Galleries Inc., N.Y.C., 1978-79, dir. print dept., 1983-84; dir. Dargate Fine Arts, Pitts., 1984-85; art dealer, appraiser Doreen M. Grasso Fine Paintings, Pitts., 1979-83, 85—; cons. Gallery G, Pitts., 1986-87, lectr. 1987; cons. Concept Art Gallery, Pitts., 1986; lectr. U. Pitts., 1985. Curator numerous exhbns. Fundraiser United Cerebral Palsy, 1989—, U. Pitts., 1990—. Mem. Nat. Soc. Fundraising Execs., Pa. Assn. Volunteerism. Office: 5850 Burchfield Ave Pittsburgh PA 15217

GRATES, CAROLE MARIE, state official, educator, consultant; b. Toledo, Jan. 22, 1939; d. Thomas Arthur and Gertrude Deliza (Wyllys) Harmon; m. Roger George Grates, Jan. 3, 1965; children: Eric John, Carole Marie. BA, Marygrove Coll., Detroit, 1961; MA, Wayne State U., 1965; MEd, Cen. Mich. U., 1979. Cert. tchr., Mich. Tchr. Spanish Livonia (Mich.) Pub. Schs., 1961-69; presch. tchr. Kinderhaus, Frankenmuth, Mich., 1971-73, Bridgeport (Mich.) Parent Coop. Presch., 1974-78; ednl. coord. Mich. Child Care Ctrs., Midland, 1978-79; licensing cons. div. child day care licensing Mich. Dept. Social Svcs., Saginaw, 1979—; mem. editorial staff, contbr. Better Homes and Ctrs. Mich. Dept. Social Svcs., Lansing, 1984—; instr. Cen. Mich. U., Mt. Pleasant, 1978—; pvt. program cons., 1988——; insvc. trainer, cons. Saginaw City Schs., 1988—, mem. family edn. svcs. com., 1978—. Co-chmn. Week of Young Child, Saginaw, Bay and Midland Counties, Mich., 1982-84, Children's Concerts, Saginaw, Bay and Midland Counties, 1988—; chmn. Saginaw County Child Abuse and Neglect Coun., 1989—. Mem. Nat. Assn. for Edn. Young Children, Assn. for Childhood Edn. Internat., Mid-Mich. Assn. for Edn. Young Children (program chmn., bd. dirs.), Community Coordinated Child Care Assn. (past chmn. Saginaw Valley region, Outstanding Contbn. to Children's Programs award 1990), AAUW (br. chmn. 1984-86), Kappa Gamma Pi. Office: Div Child Day Care Lic PO Box 5070 Saginaw MI 48605

GRAU, MARCY BEINISH, investment banking consultant; b. Bklyn., Aug. 7, 1950; d. Joseph Beinish and Gloria (Rosenbaum) Bennett; m. Bennett Grau, Nov. 19, 1978; 2 children. AB with high honors, U. Mich., 1971; postgrad., Columbia U., 1972, N.Y. Inst. Fin., 1973. Asst. to chmn. Bancroft Convertible Fund, N.Y.C., 1973-75; precious metals trader J. Aron & Co., N.Y.C., 1975-81, mgr. metals mktg., 1981-83; v.p. Goldman, Sachs & Co/J. Aron, N.Y.C., 1983-88; bus.-related translator Augustus Clothiers, N.Y.C., 1979—. Editor Precious Metals Rev. and Outlook, 1980—; contbr. article to profl. jours. Vol. worker, pediatrics dept. Lenox Hill Hosp., N.Y.C., 1978-79; asst. The Holiday Project, The Hunger Project, N.Y.C., 1978-83; vol. Yorkville Common Pantry, N.Y.C., 1984; tutor Yorkville Neighborhood Assn., N.Y.C., 1984; assoc. Child Devel. Ctr., N.Y.C.; trustee Congregation B'Nai Jeshurun, 1989—. Mem. Phi Beta Kappa. Democrat. Jewish. Home and Office: 300 W End Ave New York NY 10023

GRAU, SHIRLEY ANN (MRS. JAMES KERN FEIBLEMAN), writer; b. New Orleans, July 8, 1929; d. Adolph and Katherine (Onion) G.; m. James Kern Feibleman, Aug. 4, 1955; children—Ian, James, Nora Miranda, William, Katherine. B.A., Tulane U., 1950. Writer for Holiday, New Yorker, New World Writing, Mademoiselle, Sat. Eve. Post, Atlantic, The Reporter, 1954—; author: The Black Prince and Other Stories, 1955, The Hard Blue Sky, 1958, The House on Coliseum Street, 1961, The Keepers of the House, 1964 (Pulitzer prize for fiction 1965), The Condor Passes, 1971, The Wind Shifting West and Other Stories, 1973, Evidence of Love, 1977, Nine Women, 1986. Mem. Phi Beta Kappa. Office: 12 Nassau Dr Metairie LA 70005

GRAUE, DONNA MARIE, systems analyst; b. Queens, N.Y., Dec. 31, 1960; d. Robert Frederick and Mary Lou (Koffler) G. Diploma secretarial scis., Wood Sch., N.Y.C., 1982. Sec. Met. Life Ins. Co., N.Y.C., 1982-84, IBM Displaywriter system coord., 1984-85, jr. systems analyst, 1985—. Mem. NAFE, Queens Women's Ctr. Roman Catholic. Home: 114-45 120 St South Ozone Park NY 11420 Office: Met Life Ins Co One Madison Ave New York NY 10010

GRAVE, KATHERINE ANN, elementary educator; b. Springfield, Mo., Nov. 21, 1945; d. Verdon LeVerne and Mary Jane (McGregor) Derringer; m. Thomas Caswell Grave, June 28, 1975; children: Elaine Margaret, Michael David. BA, U. N.Mex., 1967; student, N.Mex. State U., 1964; postgrad., U. Calif., Berkeley, 1969, U. Calif., Santa Cruz, 1971. Cert. elem. tchr., Calif., sec. tchr., N.Mex. Tchr. Ukiah (Calif.) Unified Sch. Dist., 1968, Franklin-McKinley Sch. Dist., San Jose, Calif., 1968-75; substitute tchr. Reef-Sunset Elem. Sch. Dist., Avenal, Calif., 1976-80; substitute tchr. Merced (Calif.) City Sch. Dist., 1987-88, tchr., 1988—; piano tchr., N.Mex., Calif., 1968—, Hummingbird Music Camp, Jemez Springs, N.Mex., 1965—; presenter Arts Edn. Conf., Merced County Arts Council, 1989. Founder-dir. Artists-In-Schs. Program., ArTree, 1982—; program author, tchr. extra-curricular arts ESL project, 1989—. Bd. dirs. Merced County Regional Arts Council, 1981—, chmn. County Arts Festival, 1986-90; vol., com. chmn. Reading Is Fundamental, Avenal, 1977-81; troop leader Girl Scouts U.S., Merced, 1984-88; vol. Merced City Sch. Dist., 1982—. Named Arts Angel, Merced County Regional Arts Council, 1986. Mem. Jr. Woman's Club (various offices 1975-81, Jr. Citizen award 1979-80), AAUW (various offices 1975—, honored by named ednl. found. donation 1986). Democrat. Methodist. Home: 3256 Nancy Ct Merced CA 95340

GRAVES, ANNE CAROL FINGER, biological sciences educator; b. Ludlow, Miss., Nov. 29, 1933; d. Louis Albert and Maggie Beatrice (Trest) Finger; m. Robert Charles Graves, June 10, 1956; children: Robert William, Anita Ellen, Charles Louis. BS, Millsaps Coll., 1955; MS, Northwestern U., 1956; PhD, Bowling Green State U., 1982. Instr. Flint (Mich.) Community Coll., 1957-66; instr. Bowling Green (Ohio) State U., 1967-75, nonsvc. fellow, 1977-79, asst. prof, 1989—; asst. prof U. Toledo, 1983-86, rsch. asst. prof., 1986-88. Contbr. articles to profl. jours.; inventor techniques of plant cell transformation. Chairperson LWV, Bowling Green, 1985—; mem. Solid Waste Mgmt. Com., Wood County, Ohio, 1988-89, Water Quality Com., 1990, Regional and Wood County Environ. Health Com., 1970-76. Rsch. grant Eli Lilly Co., 1987, Upjohn Co., 1989; recipient Environ. Awareness award City of Bowling Green, 1974, Litter Prevention, 1990. Mem. AAAS, Am. Soc. for Microbiology, N.W. Ohio Electron Microscope Soc., Women in Sci., Sigma Xi. Presbyterian. Home: 627 Crestview Dr Bowling Green OH 43402 Office: Dept Biol Scis Bowling Green State U Bowling Green OH 43403

GRAVES, BARI CORDIA, commercial artist; b. Russellville, Ark., June 6, 1947; d. James Robert and Elizabeth Kerrol (Griffin) Williams; m. Edgar Dale Graves, Aug. 27, 1967; children: Philip Martin, Polly Jayne. AA, Allan Hancock Jr. Coll., Santa Maria, Calif., 1967. Self-employed piano instr. Lompoc, Calif., 1966-81, self-employed artist, 1976-82; self-employed artist Taylor, Austin, Tex., 1982-83; sec. Ch. of Christ, Morgantown, W. Va.; self-employed artist Morgantown, W. Va., 1985-89, Oreg., 1989-; judge for inmate art contest Fed. Prison Facility, Morgantown, W. Va., 1988, ballet set designer, El Reno Sch. of Ballet, Okla. 1984-85. Contbr. articles to profl. mags. supporter USA for Africa, El Reno, 1985. Republican. Church of Christ. Home: 15600 Willamina Creek Rd Willamina OR 97396

GRAVES, MRS. EDWARD S. See KILLEBREW, ELLEN JANE

GRAVES, MARY WARE, consultant dietitian; b. Franklin, Ind., Jan. 3, 1925; d. Noel C. and Fawnie Mary (Reed) Ware; m. Roscoe Graves, July 6, 1963; children:Larry David Myers, Virginia Ann Graves Tibbitt. BS, Purdue U., 1946; MBA, Ball State U., 1967. Registered dietitian. Dietetic intern Christ Hosp., Cin., 1947; food mgr. Purdue U., West Lafayette, Ind., 1947-50; asst. dir. dietetics Ball Meml. Hosp., Muncie, 1953-58; owner, mgr. Wingate Apts., Muncie, 1984—; adj. prof. for dietary food svc. course Ball State U.; cons. in field, Muncie, 1988—. Vol., capt. Minn. Cultural Ctr., 1988-90; pres. BF chpt. PEO Sisterhood, 1964-65, 76-77; active vol. in civic orgns. Recipient Woman in Achievement in the Professions award, 1982, Woman of Influence award, 1978, Disting. Health Care Food Svc. Adminstr. award, 1981 , Vol. Svc. award Minn. Cultural Ctr. award, 1989, 90. Mem. Am. Hosp. Assn. (pres. Hoosier Soc. Hosp. Food Svc. Adminstrn. 1981), Am. Dietetic Assn., Ball Meml. Hosp. Aux., Ind. Dietetic Assn. (pres. 1958-59), East Cen. Ind. Dietetic Assn. (pres. 1957-58), Internat. Tng. in Communication (past pres. Muncie club), Purdue Alumni Assn., Ball State U. Alumni Assn., Altrusa Club (pres. 1977-78), Purdue Club (pres. 1980-81), Toastmasters (Skilled Toastmistress award 1982). Republican. Methodist. Home: 410 N McKinley Ave Muncie IN 47303

GRAVES, MAUREEN ANN, counselor; b. Sioux City, Iowa, July 10, 1946; d. Jack Milford and Elizabeth Mildred (St. George) Dryden; m. Thomas Darrel Graves, Oct. 9, 1965; children: Michael James, Lorrie Michelle. Grad., Gestalt Inst. Iowa, 1980. Cert. drug and alcohol counselor, Nebr.; cert. profl. asst., U. S.D. Counselor Siouxland Coun. on Alcoholism and Drug Abuse, Sioux City, 1979-81; counselor, co-founder New Hope Alcohol and Addiction Ctr., South Sioux City, Nebr., 1981—; cons. St. Luke Hosp. Addiction Ctr., Sioux City, 1987—; trainer Va. Satir-Internat. Tng. Inst., Crested Butte, Colo., 1988-89. Vol., co-facilitator Siouxland Coun. on Alcoholism and Drug Abuse, Sioux City, 1976-78; mem. exec. team couple World Wide Marriage Encounter, Northeast Nebr., 1979-82. Mem. Avanta Network, Am. Mental Health Counselors Assn. Roman Catholic. Home: 424 W 16th St South Sioux City NE 68776 Office: New Hope Alcoholism and Addiction Ctr Inc PO Box 35 South Sioux City NE 68776

GRAVES, MAXINE ELIZABETH, personnel administration executive; b. Emporia, Va., Dec. 23, 1962; d. Bernard and Doris Marie (Woodley) Graves. BS, Old Dominion U., 1985. Library asst. Old Dominion U., Norfolk, Va., 1984-85; mental health therapist Community Mental Health and P.I., Norfolk, 1985-86; psychiatric technologist No. Va. Med. Health Inst., Falls Church, Va., 1986-87; personnel assoc. Britches of Georgetowne, Herndon, Va., 1986-89, personnel records supr., 1989—; profl. model Barone Modeling Agy., Alexandria, Va. Mem. Big Sisters Washington Met. Area, Inc.; participant community service program Venture in Voluntary Action. Mem. NAFE, NOW, Nat. Council Negro Women. Democrat. Baptist. Office: Britches of Georgetown 544 Herndon Pkwy Herndon VA 22070

GRAVES, NANCY STEVENSON, artist; b. Pittsfield, Mass., Dec. . BA, Vassar Coll., 1961; BFA, Yale U., 1961, MFA, 1964; PhD (hon.), Skidmore Coll. Numerous one-woman shows, including Whitney Mus. Am. Art, N.Y.C., 1969, Nat. Gallery Can., Ottawa, 1971, Neue Galerie der Stadt Aachen, Ger., 1971, Mus. Modern Art, N.Y.C., 1971, Inst. Contemporary Art, U. Pa., Phila., 1972, La Jolla (Calif.) Mus. Art, 1973, Art Mus. South Tex., Corpus Christi, 1973, André Emmerich Gallery, Inc., N.Y.C., 1974, 77, Janie E. Lee Gallery, Houston, 1977, 78, M. Knoedler & Co., 1979—, Bklyn. Mus., 1988; retrospective show travelled to Albright Knox Gallery, Buffalo, Akron (Ohio) Art Inst., Contemporary Arts Mus., Houston, 1980, Brooks Art Gallery, Memphis, Neuberger Mus., Purchase, N.Y., Des Moines Art Center, Walker Art Center, Mpls., 1981, Hirschorn Mus., 1986, Modern Mus. Ft. Worth, Santa Barbara Mus., Bklyn. Mus.; numerous group shows including Whitney Mus. Am. Art, N.Y.C., 1970, 76, Corcoran Gallery Art, Washington, 1971, 76, Parc Floral, Paris, 1971, Neue Galerie, Kassel, Germany, 1972, Serpentine Gallery, London, 1973, Project 74, Cologne, Germany, 1974, Berlin Nat. Galerie, 1976, Vancouver (B.C.) Art Gallery; represented in permanent collections, Mus. Modern Art, N.Y.C., Whitney Mus. Am. Art, N.Y.C., Ludwig Mus., Cologne, Nat. Gallery Can., Ottawa, Des Moines (Iowa) Art Center, La Jolla Mus. Contemporary Art, Art Mus. South Tex., Corpus Christi, Berkeley (Calif.) Mus. Art, Albright-Knox Art Gallery, Buffalo, N.Y., Chgo. Art Inst., Met. Mus. Art, N.Y.C., Hirschorn Mus., Nat. Gallery Art, Washington; was subject of numerous profl. publs., films. Vassar Coll. fellow, 1971-72; Fulbright-Hayes grantee, 1965-66; Paris Biennale grantee, 1971; Nat. Endowment for Arts grantee, 1972-73; Creative Artist Pub. Service grantee, 1974-75; recipient Skowhegan medal for Drawing and Graphics, 1980, Disting. Artistic Achievement award Yale U. 1985. Office: care Knoedler & Co Inc 19 E 70th St New York NY 10021

GRAVETT, LINDA SUE, legal administration; b. Greenfield, Ohio, Sept. 22, 1950; d. Lang Bolden and Vivian Ruth (Livingood) Laytart; m. Ronald S. Gravett, June 10, 1983. AA, Miami-Jacobs Jr. Coll., 1969; BBA, U. Cin., 1977, postgrad., 1988—. Cert. instr. Zenger-Miller Frontline Leadership. Asst. to pres. Hunkar Labs., Cin., 1977-81; pers. mgr. Frost and Jacobs Law Firm, Cin., 1981-85; adminstr. U.S. Ct. Appeals, Cin., 1985—; adj. faculty Fed. Jud. Ctr.; bd. advisors pers. and indsl. rels. program Xavier U.; instr. Am. Soc. for Pub. Adminstrn. study sessions for PAI. Mem. Am. Soc. for Pers. Adminstrn. (state coun. rep.), Soc. for Human Resource Mgmt., Greater Cin. Human Resources Assn. (bd. mem., past pres.). Home: 4054 Sandstone Ct Cincinnati OH 45245

GRAVLEY, NANCY CARROLL, state agency administrator; b. Dublin, Ga., Sept. 19, 1940; d. Otis Iverson and Rubye Louise (Hudson) Carroll; children: Vicki Chaffin Bennett, Bryan R. Chaffin, Jennifer Carroll Gravley. BS, North Tex. State U., 1975. Cert. tchr., Tex. Qualified mental retardation profl. Denton (Tex.) State Sch., 1975-79; supt. Edmond Oaks Ctr., Lewisville, Tex., 1979-84; program dir. Grand Junction (Colo.) Regional Ctr., 1985-86; supr. Pueblo (Colo.) Regional Ctr., 1986-88; adminstrv. dir. Idaho State Sch. and Hosp., Nampa, 1988—. Mem. Am. Assn. on Mental Deficiency (State Leadership award 1987), Nat. Assn. Supts., Pueblo C. of C. (com. 1986-87), The Twins Found. Democrat. Mem. Christian Ch. Lodge: Order Ea. Star. Office: Idaho State Sch and Hosp 3100 11th Ave N Nampa ID 83687

GRAY, ANN MAYNARD, broadcasting company executive; b. Boston, Aug. 22, 1945; d. Paul Maynard and Pauline Elizabeth MacFadyen; m. Richard R. Gray, Jr.; children: Richard R. Gray III, Dana Maynard. B.A., U. Mich., 1967; M.B.A., N.Y. U., 1971. With Chase Manhattan Bank, N.Y.C., 1967-68; with Chem. Bank, N.Y.C., 1968-73; asst. sec. Chem. Bank, 1971-73; asst. to treas., then asst. treas. ABC, Inc., 1974-76, treas., 1976-81, v.p. corp. planning, 1979-86; v.p. Capital Cities/ABC, Inc. (merged 1986), 1986—; sr. v.p. fin. ABC TV Network Group, 1988—; dir. Carteret Savs. Bank, Morristown, N.J., 1984-88. Trustee Martha Graham Ctr. of Contemporary Dance, N.Y.C., 1989—; mem. pub. affairs com. Cancer Care, N.Y.,1990—. Office: Capital Cities/ABC Inc 77 W 66th St New York NY 10023

GRAY, BARBARA L., management consulting executive; b. N.Y.C.. BA in Math., Hunter Coll. Cons. Auxton Computer Enterprises, N.Y.C., 1971-73, mktg. dir., v.p., 1973-78; pres., chief exec. officer Barron Systems Group, Ltd., N.Y.C., 1979-89, Barron Group, Ltd., N.Y.C., 1987—; dir. Mgmt. Devel. Lab., N.Y.U, 1989—. Author: Living An Empowered Life; creator seminar in creating choices. Founder Alt. Exec. Round Table, N.Y.C., 1980-84; chmn. exec. com. Tenants Assn., N.Y.C., 1984—; bd. dirs. Condominium Assn. N.J. Mem. Assn. for Rsch. and Enlightenment, Am. Mgmt. Assn. (coun. 1987—), Light Opera Manhattan, Garden State Ski Club, Vertical Club. Office: Barron Group Ltd 224 E 56th St New York NY 10022

GRAY, CAROL HICKSON, chemical engineer; b. Atlanta, Jan. 3, 1958; d. Ronald Allen and Charlotte Patricia (Blitch) Hickson; m. Randy Lee Gray, June 25, 1983; 1 child, Amanda Christine. BSChemE, Ga. Inst. Tech., 1979. Process engr. Air Products and Chems., Inc., Calvert City, Ky., 1979-83, sr. process engr., 1983-86, sr. prodn. engr., 1986-87, prin. prodn. engr., 1987-89; engring. supr. Air Products and Chems., Inc., Pasadena, Tex., 1990—. Mem. NAFE, Internat. Platform Assn. Office: Air Products Mfg Corp Box 3326 Pasadena TX 77501

GRAY, CONSTANCE ANN, professional public administrator; b. Brattleboro, Vt., May 31, 1937; d. Edwin William and Mabel Louise (Hawkes) G. BS, Simmons Coll., Boston, 1959; MAT, Harvard U., 1961. English tchr. Lexington (Mass.) Pub. Schs., 1961-64; buyer, mgr. Coll. House Pharmacies, Cambridge (Mass.) and Providence, 1964-84; field services program mgr. Div. Local Mandates State Auditor's Office, Boston, 1984-87; planning and profl. devel. coordinator Div. Local Mandates State Auditor's Office, 1987—. Mem. mgmt. rev. com. The Village Condo, Watertown, Mass., 1985, spl. projects David Finnegan for Mayor, Boston, 1983. Mem. Am. Mgmt. Assn., NAFE, Simmons Coll. Profl. Alumni Network (v.p. alumni exec. com. 1986—). Office: State Auditor's Office Div Local Mandates 100 Boylston St Room 950 Boston MA 02116

GRAY, DAHLI, accounting educator and administrator; b. Grand Junction, Colo., Dec. 28, 1948; d. Forrest Walter and Mary (Crockett) G.; m. Paul Victor Konka, Jan. 23, 1981; 1 child, Kimberly. BS, Ea. Oreg. State U., 1971; MBA, Portland (Oreg.) State U., 1976; D of Bus. Adminstrn., George Washington U., 1984. Instr. acctg. Portland State U., 1976-79, George Mason U., Fairfax, Va., 1980, George Washington U., Washington, 1981-82; asst. prof. Oreg. State U., Corvallis, 1983-86; research fellow U. Notre Dame, South Bend, Ind., 1986-88; assoc. prof. Am. U., Washington, 1988-90; chairperson, Walpert, Smullian & Blumenthal prof. Towson (Md.) State U., 1990—. Contbr. articles to profl. jours. Named Tchr. of Yr., Alpha Lambda Delta, 1986; Peat Marwick Mitchell & Co. fellow, 1986-88. Mem. Internat. Assn. Acctg. Research and Edn., Am. Inst. CPA's, Nat. Assn. Accts. (Andrew Barr award 1982, 84, Cert. Merit 1982), Am. Acctg. Assn., Inst. Cert. Mgmt. Accts. Democrat. Home: 12 Maymont Ct Timonium MD 21093 Office: Towson State U Sch Bus and Econs Acctg Dept Towson MD 21204-7097

GRAY, DARLENE AGNES, nurse; b. Prince Frederick, Md., June 10, 1957; d. Reynold Jerome Gray and Ellen (Madaglene) Cooke. AA, Charles County Community Coll., 1988; student, U. Md., Balt., 1982. Cert. med. asst.; lic. practical nurse. Secretarial aide U. Md. Ea. Shore, Princess Anne, Md., 1979-82; med. surg. technician Calvert Meml. Hosp., Prince Frederick, Md., 1982—; nurse Homecall, Prince George, Md., 1985—. Mem. NAACP, Md., 1987. Mem. Alpha Kappa Alpha.

GRAY, DAWN PLAMBECK, public relations executive; b. Chgo., Aug. 23, 1957; d. Raymond August and Eunice Eve (Fox) Plambeck; m. Richard Scott Gray, Apr. 13, 1985. BS, Northwestern U., 1979. Desk asst. Sta. WCFL, Chgo., 1979-80; writer UP Internat., Chgo., 1980; asignment editor Cable News Network, Chgo., 1980-81; account exec. Aaron Cushman and Assoc., Chgo., 1981-83; account exec. Ruder Finn & Rotman, Chgo., 1983-84, account supr., 1984-86, dir. consumer group, 1986-87; dir. pub. rels. Tassani Communications, Chgo., 1987-90; v.p. Marcy Monyek & Assoc., Chgo., 1990—. Mem. Ravinia Festival Assocs. Bd., Chgo., 1989—. Mem. Internat. Assn. Bus. Communicators (edni. rels. com. 1987-88, seminar chairperson 1988—, pres. 1990-91, Silver Quill award 1987, 88). Office: Marcy Monyek & Assocs 333 N Michigan Ste 1828 Chicago IL 60611

GRAY, DONNA MAE, agricultural products executive; b. Wing, Ill., Dec. 17, 1933; d. Sylvester Roy and Mary Henrietta (Watkins) Fosdick; m. Joyce Glenward Gray, June 1, 1952; children: Allen Keith, Glenda Mae, Cindy Lee, Terry Lynn. Nurses aid graduate, Fairbury Hosp.; student, Ill. State U., 1969-70, Winston Churchill Coll., Elec. Computor Programming Inst. Mgr., co-owner Glenn Donna Grocery Store, Fairbury, Ill., 1957; assembler Am. Screen Factory, Chatsworth, Ill., 1957; clk. Tull News Stand, Chatsworth, Ill., 1958; nurses aide Fairbury Hosp., 1959-65; supr. cost accounting Pontiac (Ill.) Chair Co., 1966-69; balancing clk. Mid Ill. Data Ctr., Pontiac, Ill., 1970-71; office mgr. Grant City Dept. Store, Pontiac, Ill., 1972-75; bookkeeper Pontiac (Ill.) Farm Store, 1976-77, mgr., v.p., 1977—. Tchr. illiteracy progarm. Mem. Small Bus. Conf., (delegate 1984-85), Retail Farm Equipment Assn., (pres. zone 4, 1978-80). Republican. Methodist. Office: Pontiac Farm Store Inc 1503 N Division Pontiac IL 61764

GRAY, EUNICE SULLIVAN, educator, writer, volunteer; b. Texico, N.Mex., Aug. 26, 1907; d. Samuel Houston and Mamie Law (Jones) Sullivan; m. Paxton H. Gray, Apr. 1, 1932. BJ, Tex. Woman's U., 1931; MEd, So. Meth. U., 1958. Tchr. Midway (Tex.) Pub. Schs., 1928-29, Chapel Hill (Tex.) Pub. Schs., 1929-30, Gladewater (Tex.) Pub. Schs., 1931-32, Sanger (Tex.) High Sch., 1943-45; history tchr. Highland Pk. Jr. High Sch., Dallas, 1954-69; dir. pub. info. Dallas County ARC, 1945-47; founder, vol. libr. Sanger Pub. Libr., 1970-86, also pres. bd. dirs., 1970-89; dir. Sanger Crisis Ctr., 1988—. Author: History of First Baptist Church, 90th Year, 1982, The Story of Sanger, 1986; columnist Now and Then Sanger Courier, 1970-89. Chmn. bd. dirs. Sullivan Sr. Ctr., Sanger, 1984-88; Dem. exec. com., Tex., 1943-45, precinct chmn., Sanger, 1970-84; bd. dirs. Denton County Hist. Commn., 1968—, Denton County Hist. Mus., 1973—. Recipient scholarship Trinity Coll., Dublin, Ireland, 1965, Poet Laureate award Pioneer Dist. Tex. Federated Womens Clubs, 1978, Outstanding Vol. award Tex. Fedn. Women's Clubs, 1984. Mem. AAUW, DAR (organizing regent John B. Denton chpt. 1980—), Hugueniot Soc. (nat. v.p. Founders of Manakin in Colony Va. 1962-64), Denton County Hist. Soc., Sanger C. of C. (bd. dirs. 1972-76, Outstanding Citizen of Sanger 1972), WednesdayStudy Club (pres. lit. dept. 1988—). Baptist. Home and Office: 808 N 6th St Sanger TX 76266

GRAY, FAY BETH, business educator; b. Memphis, Feb. 6, 1943; d. Lloyd V. and Ruth E. (Weaver) G. BBA, Memphis State U., 1964, MBA, 1966; PhD, Ga. State U., 1972. Cert. profl. sec. Admissions analyst Memphis State U., 1964-66; instr. Ark. State U., Jonesboro, 1966-69; adminstv. asst. Ga. State U., Atlanta, 1970-71; prof., chair CIS/ADMS dept. Ark. State U., Jonesboro, 1975—. Contbr. articles to profl. jours. Mem. Nat. Bus. Edn. Assn., So. Bus. Edn. Assn., Bus. and Profl. Women's Club, Delta Pi Epsilon, Delta Kappa Gamma. Baptist. Home and Office: Ark State U PO Box 188 Jonesboro AR 72467

GRAY, GLORIA JEAN, human services administrator; b. Des Moines, Sept. 27, 1948; d. Richard F. and Lois (Leak) G. BS, Iowa State U., 1969; MPA, Drake U., 1978, EdD, 1988. Caseworker Peoria (Ill.) County Dept. Pub. Aid, 1969-73; social worker Peoria Assn. Retarded Citizens, 1973-74; program supr., dept. dir., asst. dir. Iowa Children's and Family Svcs., Des Moines, 1975-88; exec. dir. Sunbeam Family Svcs., Oklahoma City, 1989—; peer reviewer Coun. on Accreditation Svcs. Families and Children, N.Y.C., 1986—; human svcs. instr. Des Moines Area Community Coll., 1978-88. Office: Sunbeam Family Svcs 616 NW 21st Oklahoma City OK 73103

GRAY, GWEN CASH, sales executive; b. Cowpens, S.C., Oct. 24, 1943; d. Woodrow C. and Marie (Hamrick) Cash; m. Charles H. Gray, Oct. 24, 1987 ; children: Dianne Marie Young, Teena Michele Bulman. BS, Limestone Coll., Gaffney, S.C., 1984. Broker assoc. Hammett-Miller Real Estate, Spartanburg, S.C., 1985—; bd. dirs. Citizens and So. Nat. Bank, Gaffney; lectr. in field. Contbr. articles to profl. jours. Advisor S.C. Peach Festival, Gaffney, 1977—, Clemson U. Extension Svc., 1987—. Named Woman of Yr. Bus. and Profl. Women, 1979, Woman of Yr. S.C. Rural Electric Coop., 1984. Mem. Am. Farm Bur., Nat. Peach Coun., Nat. Bd. Realtors, S.C. Farm Bur., S.C. Peach Coun., S.C. Bd. Realtors, S.C. Hort. Soc. (bd. dirs.), S.C. Assn. Agr. Agts. (Friend of Extension award 1986). Republican. Baptist. Home and Office: Hwy 110 Cowpens SC 29330

GRAY, HANNA HOLBORN, university president; b. Heidelberg, Germany, Oct. 25, 1930; d. Hajo and Annemarie (Bettmann) Holborn; m. Charles Montgomery Gray, June 19, 1954. AB, Bryn Mawr Coll., 1950; PhD, Harvard U., 1957; MA, Yale U., 1971, LLD, 1978; LittD (hon.), St. Lawrence U., 1974; HHD (hon.), St. Mary's Coll., 1974; LHD (hon.), Grinnell (Iowa) Coll., 1974, Lawrence U., 1974, Denison U., 1974; LLD (hon.), Union Coll., 1975, Regis Coll., 1976; LHD (hon.), Wheaton Coll., 1976; LLD (hon.), Dartmouth Coll., 1978, Trinity Coll., 1978, U. Bridgeport, 1978, Dickinson Coll., 1979, Brown U., 1979, Wittenburg U., 1979; LHD (hon.), Marlboro Coll., 1979, Rikkyo (Japan) U., 1979; LittD (hon.), Oxford (Eng.) U., 1979; LHD (hon.), Roosevelt U., 1980, Knox Coll., 1980; LLD (hon.), U. Rochester, 1980, U. Notre Dame, 1980, U. So. Calif., 1980, U. Mich., 1981; LHD (hon.), Coe Coll., 1981, Thomas Jefferson U., 1981, Duke U., 1982, New Sch. for Social Research, 1982, Clark U., 1982; LLD (hon.), Princeton U., 1982, Georgetown U., 1983; LHD (hon.), Brandeis U., 1983, Colgate U., 1983, Wayne State U., 1984, Miami U., Oxford, Ohio, 1984, So. Meth. U., Dallas, 1984; LLD (hon.), Marquette U., 1984, W.Va. Wesleyan U., 1985, Hamilton Coll., 1985; LHD (hon.), CUNY, 1985, U. Denver, 1985; LittD, Washington U., St. Louis, 1985; LHD (hon.), Am. Coll. Greece, 1986; LLD, Smith Coll., 1986, U. Miami, 1986; LLD (hon.), Columbia U., 1987; LHD (hon.), Muskingum Coll., 1987, Rush Presbyn. St. Lukes Med. Ctr., Chgo., 1987, N.Y.U., 1988; LHD, Rosemont Coll., 1988, Claremont U. Ctr. Grad Sch., 1989. Instr. Bryn Mawr Coll., 1953-54; teaching fellow Harvard, 1955-57, instr., 1957-59, asst. prof., 1959-60, vis. lectr., 1963-64; asst. prof. U. Chgo., 1961-64, asso. prof., 1964-72; dean, prof. Northwestern U., Evanston, Ill., 1972-74; provost, prof. history Yale U., 1974-78, acting pres., 1977-78; pres., prof. history U. Chgo., 1978—; bd. dirs. Cummins Engine Co., J.P. Morgan & Co., Morgan Guaranty Trust Co., Atlantic Richfield Co., Ameritech; fellow Center for Advanced Study in Behavioral Scis., 1966-67, vis. scholar, 1970-71; vis. prof. U. Calif., Berkeley, 1970-71. Editor: (with Charles Gray) Jour. Modern History, 1965-70; contbr. articles to profl. jours. Mem. Nat. Coun. on Humanities, 1972-78; trustee Yale Corp., 1971-74; bd. dirs. Chgo. Coun. Fgn. Rels., Andrew W. Mellon Found.; trustee Ctr. for Advanced Study in Behavioral Scis., Bryn Mawr Coll., Field Found., Ill., Howard Hughes Med. Inst.; bd. overseers Harvard U. Recipient Medal Liberty award, 1986; Fulbright scholar, 1950-52; U. Chgo. Newberry Library fellow, 1960-61; Phi Beta Kappa vis. scholar, 1971-72; hon. fellow St. Anne's Coll., Oxford U., 1978—. Fellow Am. Acad. Arts and Scis.; mem. Renaissance Soc. Am., Am. Philos. Soc., Nat. Acad. Edn., Phi Beta Kappa. Office: U Chgo 5801 S Ellis Ave Chicago IL 60637

GRAY, JENNIFER ANN, health care administrator; b. Santa Fe, N.Mex.; d. Daniel Sr. and Betty Sally (Russell) Torres. Cert. nursing, Adventist Med. Ctr., Glendale, Calif., 1973; student, UCLA, 1976, U. Calif., Fresno, 1980, U. Ariz., Tucson, 1983-87. Lic. nurse, Calif. Rsch. asst. Wilshire Industries, Inc., L.A.; unit supr. telemetry, staff nurse Monte Sano Hosp., L.A.; dir. planning West Coast Farms, Inc., Lakeview Terrace, Calif.; exec. program dir. Compu-Sat Ariz., Inc., Tucson; asst. exec. dir. Ctr. for Human Empowerment, Mt. Carmel Health, Columbus, Ohio, 1987—. Mem. Jr. League, Columbus, Ohio, 1988, Life Care Alliance, Columbus, 1988, AmeriFlora '92, Columbus, 1988, Calif. Task Force to Promote Self-Esteem; cochairperson Task Force on Domestic Violence; advisor Gov.'s Task Force on Edn., Phoenix, 1985. Recipient svc. award Life Care Alliance, 1989; grantee drop-out prevention program Joint Tng. Partnership Act, Tucson, 1986, adult edn. compter-assessed instruction in the GED program Pima County, Tucson, 1986. Mem. Nat. Coun. for Self-Esteem, NAFE. Home: 2201 Riverside Dr 309 Columbus OH 43221 Office: Mount Carmel Hosp 793 W State St Columbus OH 43222

GRAY, JOANNE MARIA, lawyer; b. Worcester, Mass., Dec. 29, 1958; d. Joseph Patrick and Jean Marie (Simonelli) G. AB, Coll. of Holy Cross, 1980; JD, Fordham U., 1983. Bar: N.Y. 1983. Assoc. Martin Clearwater & Bell, N.Y.C., 1983-84, Kopff Nardelli & Dopf, N.Y.C., 1984-87, Schneck & Weltman, N.Y.C., 1987—. Mem. ABA, Internat. Bar Assn., People for Am. Way. Office: Schneck & Weltman 666 Fifth Ave New York NY 10103

GRAY, JUDITH NEAPOLITAN, nurse; b. Chgo., Feb. 23, 1945; d. Raymond Joseph and Pauline Josephine (Filippi) Neapolitan; m. Frank Joseph Gray, Aug. 6, 1965; children: Frank, John. BS, Coll. St. Francis, Joliet, Ill., 1979; cert. sch. nurse practitioner, cert. pediatric nurse practitioner, U. Colo., 1990; MS, Nat. Coll., Evanston, Ill., 1989. RN, Ill. Staff nurse Holy Cross Hosp., Chgo., 1966-67; pvt. duty nurse Chgo., 1970-73; sch. nurse Dist. 135, Orland Park, Ill., 1973-75, Dist. 118, Palos Park, Ill., 1975-78; spl. edn. sch. nurse, coord. med./health svcs. South Met. Assn. for Low-Incidence Handicapped, Flossmoor, Ill., 1978—; mem. ad hoc com. for provision of safe health care for health-impaired students Ill. State Bd. Edn., Springfield, 1988—; mem. writing com. State of Ill. manual of health care procedures for health impaired students in sch. settings, Ill. Dept. Pub. Health, 1989-90. Co-author (tng. manual): Medical/Health Issues Affecting Children Ages Birth to Three, 1988; author (parent edn. curriculum): Nutrition: Health Habit of a Lifetime, 1989, Safety in No Accident. Mem. Orland Twp. Task Force on Youth, 1977; mem. and pro-tem chair SMA Human Rights Com., Floosmoor, 1978—; mem. Birth to Three Prevention/Intervention Interagency Coun., Flossmoor. Named Hearst scholar U. Colo., 1988. Mem. Nat. Assn. Sch. Nurses, Ill. Assn. Sch. Nurses, Ill. Assn. Sch. Health, Ill. Dept. Pub. Health Spl. Edn. Nurse Network, Coun. Exceptional Children, AAUW. Office: South Met Assn for Low-Incidence Handicapped 800 Governors Hwy Flossmoor IL 60422

GRAY, JUDY MARIE, administrative assistant; b. Fairview Heights, Ill., Nov. 2, 1964; d. J.D. Charles Herrington and Edith Gayle (Sharpe) Meadows; m. Tony Lane Gray, Aug. 18, 1984. Secretarial degree, Sparks Bus. Coll., Shelbyville, Ill., 1983. Clk. typist Franklin County Ct. House, Louisburg, N.C., 1983; dental asst. Spurgeon Eakes, DDS & Assocs., Franklinton, N.C., 1984; text editing technician Mallinckrodt Parenteral Plant, Raleigh, N.C., 1984-86; clk. typist III N.C. Dept. Ins., Raleigh, 1986-88, adminstrv. sec. IV, 1988—; part-time dealer Tupperware, 1988—. Field dir. Girl Scouts U.S.A.; Franklin County, N.C., 1985; pres. Franklinton Rescue and Emergency Med. Svcs. Aux., 1986, 87, sec., 1988; dir. children's choir Perry's Chapel Baptist Ch., Franklinton, 1987-89. Parents Without Ptnrs. grantee, 1982. Mem. NAFE. Democrat. Home: 502 Mitchell Ave Franklinton NC 27525-1661

GRAY, LOUISE ANN, music educator; b. Pitts., Aug. 31, 1953; d. Ronald James and Anna Mathilda (Kunich) G. BA, U. Pitts., 1975; postgrad., Duquesne U., 1976-77, M in Music Edn., 1985. Tchr. music St. Elizabeth Jr. High Sch., Pitts., 1978-79, St. Valentine Grade Sch., Bethel Pak, Pa., 1978-79, McNaugher Edni. Ctr., Pitts., 1979-82, Pioneer Edni. Ctr., Pitts., 1979-80, Columbus Traditional Acad., Pitts., 1982—; asst. to dir. All City Jr. Choir, Pitts., 1980-85; music libr. Ctrs. for the Musically Talented, Pitts., 1988—; tchr. arts propel program Pitts. Bd. of Edn., 1986—; instructional team leader Columbus Traditional Acad., 1988—. Allegheny Conf. on Community Devel. grantee, 1983, Pitts. Fund for Arts Edn. grantee, 1987. Mem. Music Tchr.'s Nat. Conf., Nat. Arts Edn. Rsch. Ctr. (tchr., researcher 1988—), Pa. Music Educator's Assn. Home: 5743 Kentucky Ave Pittsburgh PA 15232 Office: Frick Internat Studies Acad 107 Thackeray St Pittsburgh PA 15213

GRAY, MARGARET ANN, management educator, consultant; b. Junction City, Kans., Sept. 19, 1950; d. Carl Ray and Mayme Louise (Kopmeyer) G.; m. Dennis Wayne Stokes, June 9, 1973 (div. July 1981); m. Robert Frederick Carlson Jr., Nov. 21, 1987. BEd, Pittsburg State U., Kans., 1972; MBA, Wichita State U., 1981. Tchr., Sch. Dist. 1, Kansas City, Mo., 1972-73; tchr. Haysville Sch. Dist., Kans., 1974-81, dist. coord., 1979-81; instr. mgmt. Wichita State U., 1981-85; mgmt. devel. rep. Beech Aircraft Corp. a Raytheon Co., Wichita, 1985-87, mgr. mgmt. devel. and tng., 1988—; cons. Dartnell Inst., Chgo., 1983—; assoc. dir. Ctr. for Entrepreneurship, Wichita State U., 1984-85. Bd. dirs. Kans. Found. for partnerships in Edn., 1986—; mem. speaker's bur. United Way, 1986—, vol. tng. dir., 1987—, tng. com., 1987—, top leadership cabinet, 1989; bd. dirs. Kans. Literacy Group, 1989, Sedgwick County div. Am. Heart Assn., 1990; active Leadership 2000. Mem. ASTD (bd. dirs. Sunflower chpt.), Wichita C. of C. (bus. edn. success team 1988—), Beta Gamma Sigma. Democrat. Roman Catholic. Club: Turnip (Wichita). Avocations: ballet, cross country skiing, classical music, hot air balooning. Office: Beech Aircraft Corp 9709 E Central St Wichita KS 67206

GRAY, MARTHA HYNDMAN, nurse manager, nurse; b. N.Y.C., Aug. 14, 1939; d. Donald Earl and Genevieve Catherine (Schelling) Hyndman; m. Neil Gray, June 25, 1960 (div. Oct. 1982); children: Neil Gray Jr., Donald Hemmett, Jennifer Catherine. BS in Nursing, Simmons Coll., 1962. Staff nurse Vis. Nurse Assn. of Boston, 1962-64, New Eng. Bapt. Hosp., Boston, 1964-65; asst. head nurse Symmes Hosp., Arlington, Mass., 1965-81; clin. coord. Choate-Symmes Hosps., Inc., Arlington and Woburn, Mass., 1981-86; assoc. nurse mgr. Choate-Symmes Hosps., Inc., Woburn, 1986-87; staff nurse Sancta Maria Hosp., Cambridge, Mass., 1983-88, nurse mgr., 1988-89; nurse mgr. Hebrew Rehab. Ctr. for Aged, Roslindale, Mass., 1989—; treas. Nurse's Club of Simmons Coll., Boston, 1975—; cons., facilitator, trainer Voluntary Orgns., Mass., N.J. and Calif., 1973-81. Mem. Am. Nurses Assn. (cert. nursing adminstr.), Simmons Coll. Alumnae Assn. (pres. 1977-79), Jr. League of Boston (v.p. 1977-79), Simmons Club of Boston (pres. 1970-72). Republican. Home: 12 Coolidge Ave Lexington MA 02173

GRAY, MARY ELLEN, banker; b. Meriden, Conn., Mar. 15, 1948; d. Vincent Albert and Kathryn (Joyce) Aloia; m. Jeremy Warren Travis, June 3, 1970 (div. 1980); m. David Alan Gray, Aug. 28, 1982; children: Anthony Gale, Charles Vincent. AB in Philosophy, Vassar Coll., 1970; M Bus. Policy, Columbia U., 1982. Editorial asst. Doubleday & Co., N.Y.C., 1971-75; mgmt. trainee Chem. Bank, N.Y.C., 1976, real estate officer, 1977-81, v.p., 1981-88; sr. v.p. Chem. Bank N.J., Morristown, 1989, exec. v.p., 1990—. Mem. adv. bd. Sch. Fine and Performing Arts, Montclair (N.J.) State Coll., 1990—. Democrat. Office: Chem Bank NJ 2 Tower Ctr 18th Fl East Brunswick NJ 08816

GRAY, MICHELLE LEE, military officer; b. Denver, Jan. 20, 1963; d. John Hughes and Nancy Lee (Gouby) Anderson; m. Kevin Howard Gray, July 14, 1986; children: Michael William, Benjamin Hughes. BS cum laude, Emporia State U., 1985. Commd. 2d lt. U.S. Army, 1985, advanced through grades to 1st lt., 1986; morale support fund dir. U.S. Army, Fort Sheridan, Ill., 1985-86, fin. mgr. directorate of personnel and community activities, 1986-87, exec. officer community and family activities, 1987, chief fin. mgmt. personnel and community activities, 1987-88, adjutant S-1 Hdqtrs. Bn., 1988—; bus. mgr. F.W. Gray & Assoc., Ltd., Ottawa, Ill., 1990. Coordinator Ft. Sheridan Cub Scouts, 1985-88. Mem. Res. Officers Assn. (sec.

1987—, dept. jr. v.p., 1988-89), Assn. U.S. Army, NAFE, Garrison Wives Club Ft. Sheridan, Officers Wives Club. Democrat. Home: 2322 N 30th Rd Marseilles IL 61341 Office: 801 Canal St Ottawa IL 61350

GRAY, NANCY ANN OLIVER, school administrator; b. Dallas, Apr. 23, 1951; d. Howard Ross and Joan (Dawkins) Oliver; m. Doyle P. Gray, Nov. 24, 1973 (div. Jan. 1985); children: Paul, Jeff, Scott; m. David Nelson Maxson, Oct. 5, 1985. BA, Vanderbilt U., 1973; MEd, North Tex. State U., 1975; postgrad., Vanderbilt U., 1976-79. Cert. fund raising exec. Tchr. Highland Park High Sch., Dallas, 1973-75; chmn. drama dept. Harpeth Hall Sch., Nashville, 1975-77; assoc. dir. devel. Vanderbilt U., Nashville, 1977-78, assist. dean students, 1978-80; dir. spl. gifts U. Louisville, 1982-86; dir. major gifts Oberlin (Ohio) Coll., 1986-90; dir. capital programs The Lawrenceville (N.J.) Sch., 1990—; cons. United Way, Cleve., 1988-90, Oberlin Coll., 1990; guest lectr. Vanderbilt U., Nashville, 1987-88. Trustee Oberlin Libr. Bd. Trustees, 1989, Oberlin Sch. Endowment Bd., 1988-90, Oberlin Early Childhood Ctr., 1986-88, Vanderbilt U., Nashville, 1973-77; bd. dirs. Vanderbilt U. Alumni Assn., Nashville, 1984-85; mem. Jr. League, 1984-89, various coms. Named Outstanding Young Woman of Am., 1982, Outstanding Woman Achievement, Lorain County (Ohio) YWCA, 1988. Mem. Nat. Soc. Fund-Raising Execs. (pres. Louisville chpt. 1985-86), Coun. for Advancement Support to Edn. (conf. presenter). Home: 32 Laurel Wood Lawrenceville NJ 08648 Office: The Lawrenceville School Box 6125 Lawrenceville NJ 08648

GRAY, PAMELA, educator; b. Newark, Nov. 11, 1940; d. Irving William and Helen (Gail) G.; m. Robert Emil Kohn, Feb. 19, 1962 (div. 1978); children: Randall Evan Kohn, Andrew Robert Kohn, Cynthia Lee Kohn. BA, Upsala Coll., 1970; MA in Teaching, Seton Hall U., 1972, EdS, 1980, EdD, 1986. Cert. prin., supr., tchr., N.J. Tchr. 2d through 5th grade South Orange-Maplewood Bd. Edn., N.J., 1972-81, adminstv. and supervisory intern, 1980-81, tchr. of gifted, 1981; enrichment coordinator Mountainside (N.J.) Bd. Edn., 1982-85; coordinator, tchr. of gifted Livingston (N.J.) Bd. Edn., 1985-89; mem. adminstrv. com. Northeast Olympics of Mind, N.J., 1984-85; coord. gifted edn., staff developer, coord. grades 5 and 6, Springfield, N.J.; coord. gifted and talented assn., Union County, N.J. Author: Happy Birthday U.S.A., 1975, America Is Having A Birthday, 1976. Bd. dirs., treas., jour. chmn. Ruth Kohn Community Service, 1972-78. Boston U. scholar, 1979-80; State Dept. Gifted Edn. grantee, 1988-89. Mem. NEA, N.J. Ednl. Assn., Livingston Ednl. Assn., Nat. Assn. Gifted Children, Assn. for Supervision and Curriculum Devel., Kappa Delta Pi. Home: 138 Marion Dr West Orange NJ 07052

GRAY, PAMELA ANN, educator; b. W. Chester, Pa., May 18, 1948; d. John Pershing and Jean Anne (Beitler) Gray. BS, W. Chester U., 1971, W. Chester U., 1973; MEd., W. Chester U., 1976; doctoral studies, U. Cen. Fla., 1989—. Tchr. W. Chester Area Schs., 1970—; cons. to tchrs. and sch. dists. in sci. curriculum and edn. W. Chester Area Schs. Author: (curriculum guide) Science Laboratory in the Elementary School; co-author: (environ. curriculum guide) R.E.E.P., Regional Environmental Education Guide. Teaching English to Speakers Other Langs. scholar W. Chester U. Mem. Nat. Sci. Tchrs. Assn., Nat. Assn. Biology Tchrs., Pa. Sci. Tchrs. Assn., Pa. State Edn. Assn., Delaware Valley Assn. for Curriculum Devel. and Supervision, NEA, W. Chester Edn. Assn. (rep.), Green Peace, Sierra Club, Audubon Soc. Republican. Quaker. Home: PO Box 5728 Winter Park FL 32793-5728

GRAY, PATRICIA ELLEN, psychologist; b. Melrose, Mass., June 17, 1939; d. Howard Allan and Grace Ellen (Whitcomb) G. AA, Brevard Coll., 1959; BS, U. Mass., 1962; MS, Boston U., 1968; PhD, Boston Coll., 1982. Lic. psychologist, Mass.; RN, Mass. Head nurse Springfield (Mass.) Mental Health Clinic, 1962-63; pub. health nurse Vis. Nurse Assn. of Greater Lynn, Inc., Lynn, Mass., 1963-65, Vis. Nurse Assn. of Greater Boston, Inc., Boston, 1965-66; chief nurse Somerville (Mass.) Mental Health Clinic, 1968-88; pvt. practice psychologist Natick, Mass., 1976—; instr. major colls. and univs., Boston area, 1968-89; bd. advisors clin. Boston Gay and Lesbian Mental Health, 1986-88; cons. West-Ros-Park Mental Health Ctr., Roslindale, Mass., 1976-81, Cameron House, Somerville, 1976-82, Somerville Youth Svcs., 1968-86. Cons. Cambridge and Somerville Programs for Alcohol Referral and Edn. for Youth, Adv. Bd., Somerville, 1974-84, Mayor's Task Force on Drugs, Somerville, 1980-855, Full Circle Alternative High Sch., Somerville, 1973-84, Next Wave Alternative Jr. High Sch., Somerville, 1982-87. Tuition grantee NIMH, 1966-68.

GRAY, PENELOPE PARSONS, sports promotion agency executive; b. Washington; d. Vollie Earl and Mary (Pence) Parsons; 1 child, Richard R. Pooler. V.p. Sports Mgmt. Group, Charlotte, N.C. Office: Sports Mgmt Group 1901 Roxborough Rd Charlotte NC 28211

GRAY, SARAH ANN, prosthodontist, educator; b. Oceanside, Calif., Nov. 19, 1956; d. Roy Leonard and Martha Rose (Morris) Gibson; m. Glenn Joseph Gray, Aug. 23, 1977; children: Christopher, Lauren, Holly. BS, Pa. State U., 1977; DDS, Temple U., 1982, splty. cert. in prosthodontics, 1985. Dept. mgr. Gimbels, Phila., 1978; pvt. practice, Narberth, Pa., 1982—; instr. dept. prosthodontics Temple U. Sch. Dentistry, Phila., 1983-86, asst. prof., 1986—, asst. dean for admissions and student affairs, 1989—. Contbr. articles to profl. jours. Fellow Geriatric Edn. Ctr. Pa., 1988. Mem. Am. Coll. Prosthodontists, Pa. Prosthodontic Assn., Omicron Kappa Upsilon, Alpha Epsilon Delta. Home and Office: 219 Hampden Ave Narberth PA 19072 Office: Temple U Sch Dentistry 3223 N Broad St Philadelphia PA 19140

GRAY, SHEILA HAFTER, psychiatrist, psychoanalyst; b. N.Y.C., Oct. 19, 1930; m. Oscar Shalom Gray, Apr. 8, 1967. MD, Harvard U., 1958. cert. Washington Psychoanalytic Inst., 1969. Intern St. Elizabeths Hosp., Washington, 1958-59; resident McLean Hosp., Belmont, Mass., 1959-61; clin. and rsch. fellow Mass. Gen. Hosp., Boston, Mass., 1961-62; staff psychiatrist Chestnut Lodge, Inc., Rockville, Md., 1962-64; practice medicine, specializing in psychiatry and psychoanalysis Washington, 1964—; clin. asst. prof. psychiatry U. Md. Sch. Medicine, Balt., 1968-75, clin. assoc. prof., 1975-83, clin. prof., 1983—; instr. Washington Psychoanalytic Inst., 1971-75, teaching analyst, 1975—; mem. staff U. Md. Hosp., Balt.; physician mem. Commn. on Mental Health, Superior Ct. of D.C., 1972—; bd. govs. Nat. Capital Reciprocal Ins. Co., 1981—; cons. Walter Reed Army Med. Ctr., Washington, 1983—. Mem. Mayor's Adv. Com. on Mental Health Svcs. Reorgn., Washington, 1984; mem. adv. panel for Mayor's Environ. Design Awards Program, 1988-89; mem. exec. com. D.C. Fedn. Civic Assns., 1984—, asst. rec. sec., 1985, rec. sec., 1986-88, 2nd v.p., 1989—; v.p. programs Women's Equity Action League Met. D.C., 1986; commr. D.C. Adv. Neighborhood Commn., 1986-88. Fellow Am. Psychiat. Assn.; mem. Am. Psychoanalytic Assn. (diplomate Bd. of Profl. Standards), Washington Psychiat. Soc. (councillor 1981-83) Med. Soc. D.C. (exec. bd. 1982), Washington Psychoanalytic Soc. (dir. psychoanalytic clinic and councillor ex officio 1987-90), Palisades Citizens Assn. (bd. dirs. 1980—, treas. 1983-84, pres. 1984-86). Office: PO Box 40612 Palisades Sta Washington DC 20016

GRAY-FARMER, CHRISTAL LYNN, communications professional; b. Dayton, Ohio, Aug. 20, 1959; d. Robert Vincent and Rose Marie (Sams) Gray; m. Richard Craig Farmer, Feb. 27, 1982. Student, Wright State U., Dayton, 1977-81. Mktg. rep. Minute Man Printing, Dayton, 1978-79; advt. account exec. The Times, Kettering, Ohio, 1979-82; advt. coord. Ohio Communications, Kettering, 1983-84; advt. mgr. Ohio Communications, Dayton, 1984-86; corp. advt. mgr. Outdoor Sports Hdqrs., Dayton, 1986—. Recipient Excellence in Advt. award Shot Show, 1990. Mem. Am. Advt. Fedn. (Hermes excellence award 1987), Am. Mgrs. Assn., Nat. Sporting Goods Press Assn., Dayton Art Ctr., Dayton Advt. Club, Dayton Direct Mktg. Club. Republican. Lutheran. Home: 3013 Mohican Ave Kettering OH 45429 Office: Outdoor Sports Hdqrs 967 Watertower Ln Dayton OH 45449

GRAY-LITTLE, BERNADETTE, psychologist; b. Washington, N.C., Oct. 21, 1944; d. James and Rosalie (Lanier) Gray; m. Shade Keys Little, Nov. 21, 1971; children—Maura, Mark. Asst. prof. psychology, U. N.C.-Chapel Hill, 1971-76, assoc. prof., 1976-82, prof., 1982—. NIMH fellow, 1967-68; Fulbright fellow, 1970-71; NRC fellow, 1982-83. Mem. Am. Psychol. Assn., Phi Beta Kappa. Office: U NC Psychology Dept CB #3270 Chapel Hill NC 27599

GRAY-NIX, ELIZABETH W., occupational therapist; b. Milton, Mass., Apr. 9, 1956; d. Roland and Susan (Brooks) Gray; m. Ronald Harding Nix. BS, Utica Coll. of Syracuse U., N.Y., 1978. Reg. occupational therapist. Staff occupational therapist Walter E. Fernald State Sch., Waltham, Mass., 1978-82; head occupational therapist Walter E. Fernald State Sch., 1982-84, clin. supr., 1984—. Trustee Mass. Jaycees Charitable Trust, Mansfield, 1983—; dir.-at-large South End Hist. Soc., Boston, 1983-85, fundrasiing dir., 1985-87; alumni rep. Beaver Country Day Sch., Brookline, 1974—, alumni sec., 1988—. Recipient Baystater award #060, Mass. Jaycees, 1984, Armbruster Keyman award, 1981, Office of the Yr., 1987. Mem. Mass. O.T. Assn., State Employeed O.T. Assn. (union rep.), Am. O.T. Assn., Newton Jaycees (mem. coun. 1979-82), Riverside Jaycees (pres. 1983), Boston Ctr. for the Arts (mem. coun. 1979-84). Home: 48 Rutland Sq Boston MA 02118 Office: Walter E Fernald State Sch 200 Trapelo Rd Waltham MA 02154

GRAYSON, GRACE RIETHMULLER, teacher, consultant; b. Johannesburg, Transvaal, South Africa, Apr. 21, 1917; came to U.S., 1946; d. Frederick Edward Christian and Martha Johanna (Broodrijk) Riethmuller; m. Lincoln Blaisdell Grayson, Nov. 10, 1946; children: David Arthur, Guy. Student, Tchrs. Coll., 1934; cert. tchr., U. Calif., Berkeley, 1969; student, Diablo Valley Coll., Berkeley, 1978-83. Master judge flower shows and landscape design. Supr. revenue posting dept. NSW Tramways, Sydney, Australia, 1939-46; freelance writer Australia and U.S.A., 1945-57; columnist Cooma (Australia)-Monaro Express, 1953-57; corr. Australian Broadcasting Commn., Sydney, 1954-57; pvt. practice crafts instr. Pleasant Hill, Calif., 1962-64; class instr. floral design Woolworths, Walnut Creek, Calif., 1966-69; tchr. arts and crafts Mt. Diablo (Calif.) Unified Sch. Dist., 1965-73; ret., 1973; curator accessories Mus. Fashion, Lafayette, Calif., 1987—; cons. in field. Contbr. articles to profl. jours. Supporting mem. Berkeley Repertory Theatre, 1975—; fundraiser Alexander Mus. Natural History, Walnut Creek, 1981—; contbr. mem. Mus. Soc., San Francisco Mus. Fine Arts, 1984—. Fellow Royal Hort. Soc. London; mem. Costume Soc. Am., Monumental Brass Soc., Inst. Craft Edn., Fan Assn. N.Am. (pres. 1986-88, chmn. rsch. com. 1988—), Fan Circle Internat. (corr.), Diablo Women's Garden Club, East Bay Fan Guild, Walnut Creek Civic Arts Assn. Democrat. Episcopalian. Home: 2133 Pine Knoll Dr #16 Walnut Creek CA 94595

GREASER, CONSTANCE UDEAN, research organization executive; b. San Diego, Jan. 18, 1938; d. Lloyd Edward and Udean Greaser; B.A., San Diego State Coll., 1959; postgrad. U. Copenhagen Grad. Sch. Fgn. Students, 1963, Georgetown U. Sch. Fgn. Service, 1967; M.A., U. So. Calif., 1968; Exec. M.B.A., UCLA, 1981. Advt., publicity mgr. Crofton Co., San Diego, 1959-62; supr. Mercury Publs., Fullerton, Calif., 1962-64; supr. engring. support services div. Arcata Data Mgmt., Hawthorne, Calif., 1964-67; mgr. computerized typesetting dept. Continental Graphics, Los Angeles, 1967-70; v.p., editorial dir. Sage Publs., Inc., Beverly Hills, Calif., 1970-74; head publs. RAND Corp., Santa Monica, Calif., 1974—. Mem. nat. com. Million Minutes of Peace Appeal, 1986, Nat. Info. Standards Orgn., 1987—, nat. com. Global Cooperation for Better World, 1988. Recipient Berber award Graphic Arts Tech. Found., 1989. Mem. Women in Bus. (pres. 1977-78), Soc. for Scholarly Pubs. (nat. bd. dirs.), Women in Communication, Soc. Tech. Communication, Brahma Kumaris World Spiritual Orgn. Co-author: Quick Writer-Build Your Own Word Processing Users Guide, 1983; Quick Writer-Word Processing Center Operations Manual, 1984; editor: Urban Research News, 1970-74; mng. editor Comparative Polit. Studies, 1971-74; assoc. editor New Realities mag., 1988—; contbr. articles to various jours. Office: The Rand Corp 1700 Main St Santa Monica CA 90406

GREATHOUSE, PATRICIA DODD, psychometrist, counselor; b. Columbus, Ga., Apr. 26, 1935; d. John Allen and Patricia Ottis (Murphy) Dodd; m. Robert Otis Greathouse; children: Mark Andrew, Perry Allen. BS in Edn., Auburn (Ala.) U., 1959, M in Edn., 1966, AA in Counselor Edn., 1975. Cert. secondary tchr., Ala., Ga. Tchr. Columbus High Sch., 1959-61, Phenix City Bd. Edn., 1957-58; tchr. pub. schs. Russell County (Ala.) Bd. Edn., Phenix City and Seale, 1961-69, 71-80, 82-83, counselor pub. schs., 1969-82, 83—; psychometrist Russell County (Ala.) Bd. Edn., Seale, 1980-82; county psychometrist Russell County (Ala.) Bd. Edn., Phenix City, 1983—. Editor: (ann.) Tiger Tales, 1973 (award 1980). Treas. Ladonia PTA, Phenix City, 1966-68, parliamentarian, 1987-88; leader Ladonia chpt. 4-H Club, Phenix City, 1961-80; active March of Dimes, Am. Heart Assn.; rep. Mardi Gras; tchr. Sunday Sch., Vacation Bible Sch. N. Phenix Bapt. Ch.; vol. Reach to Recovery Am. Cancer Soc., 1980—. Named Mardi Gras Queen Phenix City Moose Club, 1987, hon. life mem. Ladonia PTA, 1967, Outstanding Tchr. of Yr., 1972; recipient Silver Clover award 4-H Club, 1966, Outstanding PTA Performance award 1986-87; nominated to Tchr. Hall of Fame, 1980-81, 81-82, 82-83. Mem. Russell County Edn. Assn. (pres.-elect 1973), Ala. Edn. Assn., NEA, Ala. Personnel and Guidance Assn., Ala. Assn. Counseling and Devel., Council Exceptional Children, Am. Bus. Women's Assn. (pres. Phenix City charter chpt. 1986-87, woman of yr. 1987, Perfect Attendance award), Delta Kappa Gamma (sec. 1979-80, pres. 1990-92), Kappa Iota. Democrat. Baptist. Lodge: Daus. of Nile (pres. Phenix City club 1984-85), Shrinettes (sec. Phenix City club 1980-81, 83-84, outstanding service award), Jetettes (v.p. Phenix City club 1976, 80), Jaycettes, Order Eastern Star (Worthy Matron 1981-82). Home: 1502 Nottingham Dr Phenix City AL 36867 Office: Ladonia Sch Rt 4 Box 982 Phenix City AL 36867

GREAVER, JOANNE HUTCHINS, mathematics educator, author; b. Louisville, Aug. 9, 1939; d. Alphonso Victor and Mary Louise (Sage) Hutchins; m. James William Greaver, Dec. 17, 1977; 1 child, Mary Elizabeth. BS in Chemistry, U. Louisville, 1961, MEd, 1971; MAT in Math., Purdue U., 1973. Cert. tchr. secondary edn. Specialist math Jefferson County (Ky.) pub. schs., 1962—; part-time faculty Bellarmine Coll., Louisville, 1982—, U. Louisville, 1985—; project reviewer NSF, 1983—; advisor Council on Higher Edn., Frankfort, Ky., 1983-86. Author: (workbook) Down Algebra Alley, 1984; co-author curriculum guides. Charter mem. Commonwealth Tchrs. Inst., 1984—; mem. Nat. Forum for Excellence in Edn., Indpls., 1983; metric edn. leader Fed. Metric Project, Louisville, 1979-82. Recipient Presdl. award for excellence in math. teaching, 1983; named Outstanding Citizen, SAR, 1984, mem. Hon. Order Ky. Cols.; grantee NSF, 1983, Louisville Community Found., 1984-86. Mem. Greater Louisville Council Tchrs. of Math. (pres. 1977-78, Outstanding Educator award 1987), Nat. Council Tchrs. of Math. (reviewer 1981—), Ky. Coun. Tchrs. of Math. (pres. 1990-91, Jeff County Tchr. of Yr. award 1985), Math. Assn. Am., Kappa Delta Pi, Zeta Tau Alpha. Republican. Presbyterian. Avocations: tropical fish; gardening; handicrafts; travel; tennis. Home: 11513 Tazwell Dr Louisville KY 40222 Office: J M Atherton High Sch 3000 Dundee Rd Louisville KY 40205

GREB, JACQUELINE KAY, museum administrator; b. Denver, Dec. 16, 1944; d. Arthur Ray and Marie Ethel (Leavell) G. BA, Colo. State Coll., 1967; MA, U. Northern Colo., 1973. Dept. head Todd County Independent Sch. Dist., Mission, S.D., 1969-74; staff mem. San Juan Community Coll., Farmington, N.Mex., 1975-76; insp. Peace Corp-Oman, Salalah, 1977-79; coord. Peace Corp Tng., Seeb, Oman, 1978-79; dept. head Sultan's Sch., Seeb, 1979-83; ref. staff U. N.Mex., Albuquerque, 1983-86, gen. coll., 1984-86; scholar-in-residence Cherokee Nat. Hist. Soc., Tahlequah, Okla., 1986-89; exec. dir. Children's Mus. Utah, Salt Lake City, 1989-90; cons. Bilingual Edn. Dept., Tahleguah, 1987-; Smithsonian Kellogg. Contbr. articles to profl. jours. Bd. dirs. Okla. Women in the Arts, Tulsa, Okla. Constitution 200. Mem. Okla. Mus. Assn., Am. Assn. State and Local History, Western History Assn. Office: Children's Mus Utah 840 N 300 W Salt Lake City UT 84103

GRECO, BARBARA RUTH GOMEZ, literacy organization administrator; b. Farifield, Calif., May 27, 1938; d. William Joseph and Ruth Marie (Fernandes) Gomez; m. Edward Fairfax Greco, Aug. 27, 1966; children: Michelle, William. B., James Madison U., 1987; Assoc. degree cum laude, Lord Fairfax Community Coll., 1985. Bd. dirs. Va. Literacy Coalition, Richmond, Region 4 Literacy Coordinating Com., Harrisonburg, Va.; pres. Literacy Vols. Am., Warren, 1988—; dir. mktg. and pub. rels. Wayside of Va. Inc., Strasburg, 1988; bus. cons. Wayside of Va., Inc., Strasburg, 1988, North Valley Bus. Jour., Winchester, 1989—, Echo Ridge Nursery, Winchester, 1990. Contbg. writer North Valley Bus. Jour., Winchester, Va. PTA chair County of Warren, 1974-78, mem. founding bd. coun. on domestic violence, 1980-88, vice-chair dem. com., 1981, pres. coun. on domestic violence, 1985-88, mem. crime commn.; mem. textbook adoption com. Warren County High Sch., 1985; bd. dirs. Va. chpt. Am. Lung Assn., 1980-82; bd. dirs. United Way, 1984; Warren County coord. Patterson for State Senate, 1979; campaign coord. William A. Hall for Clk. of Ct., 1981; supr. phone bank Charles Robb Campaign, 1981; campaign treas. Michael Kitts for Town Coun., 1984; campaign vol. Gerald Lee Baliles for Gov., 1986; troop leader Girl Scouts U.S., 1970-71, area coord., 1971-72. Mem. Shenandoah Valley Writer's Guild (past pres.), Phi Theta Kappa. Episcopalian. Home: PO Box 1188 Front Royal VA 22630

GRECO, JUDY WONG, educator; b. San Francisco, Apr. 30, 1950; d. Sun Ock and Mary Fay Fong (Hom) Wong; m. Dennis John Greco; 1 child, Julianne Lai Ming. BA in Edn., Nat. Coll. of Edn., 1972; MS in Spl. Edn., U. No. Colo., 1981. Cert. spl. edn. tchr., Ill., Colo. Educator Chgo. Pub. Schs., 1972-75, Englewood (Colo.) Pub. Schs., 1975-80, Jefferson County Pub. Schs., Lakewood, Colo., 1980—; mem. jr. high curriculum coun. Jefferson County Pub. Schs., 1984-87. Vol. Legal Aid of Denver, 1987-88, Colo. Initiative on Teen Pregnancy Pub. Edn., Denver, 1988-89; del. Colo. Dem. Party, Denver, 1984; instr. Handicap Program for Skiers, Winter Pk., Colo., 1985—. Mem. Englewood Educators (treas. 1977-80), Jefferson County Edn. Assn. (tchr. rights and activities com. 1986—, rep. 1987—, del. 1984—), Jr. League of Denver. Episcopalian. Home: 8127 Spring Creek Pass Littleton CO 80127 Office: Columbine High Sch 6201 S Pierce St Littleton CO 80123

GRECO, MARY CEBULSKI, teacher; b. Gainesville, Ga., Sept. 16, 1952; d. Henry Joseph and Angela Marie (Beltran) Cebulski; m. Joel Randy Blake, Nov. 1971 (div. Feb. 1975); 1 child, Jason; m. Steve Frank Greco, June 6, 1980. Student, DeKalb Community Coll., Ga. STate U., 1987. Cert. tchr., Ga. Day care worker Kiddie Kapers, Conyers, Ga.; tchr. aide J.H. House Elem. Sch., Conyers; youth worker UGA Cooperative Extension Service, Conyers; tchr. Flat Shoals Elem. Sch., Conyers, 1987—. Mem. Internat. Reading Assn.; campaign disg. orgn. County Sheriff, Rockdale County, 1984; staff Save the Children, Atlanta, 1984-86; mem. long range planning curriculum com. Rockdale County Bd. Edn.; sci. com. Rockdale County Bd. Edn.; v.p. Gwinnett County Concerned Citizens; grade chairperson K, Flat Shoals, 1989—. Mem. NEA (Student Tchr. of Yr. S.E. Region 1987), Ga. Edn. Assn., Internat. Reading Assn., Norris Lake Homeowners Assn. (sec.), Gwinnett Concerned Citizens (mem. com.). Roman Catholic. Home: 4345 Bowman Way Lithonia GA 30058 Office: Flat Shoals Elem Sch 1455 Flat Conyers GA 30208

GREEN, ADELE C., educator; b. Boston, Oct. 20, 1938; d. Benjamin and Leona (Rick) Cohen: m. Leonard N. Green, June 25, 1960; children: Lawrence Jeffrey, Stuart Avery, Joshua Steven. BE, Boston State Coll., 1960; MA, Hunter Coll., 1963; PhD, Kent State U., 1985. Instr. ESL Youngstown (Ohio) Internat. Inst., 1964-83, curriculum developer ESL, 1973-85; lectr., cons. ESL Yo (Ohio) Bd. Edn., 1985—; instr. psychology Youngstown State U., Yo, 1985—; presenter of papers conf. in ESL and newropsychology North America., 1978—. Author: Becoming Fluent in English, 1974; co-author Situational Exercises in Cross-Cultural Awareness; researcher/author chpts. in textbooks, reviewer. Trustee and founder Liberty Edn. Endowment, Inc. Liberty Twp., Ohio, 1979—, Youngstown Internat. Inst., women's div. Youngstown Jewish Fedn., v.p. 1979-81, Akiva Acad., Youngstown, 1986. Grantee cons. Youngstown State U. and U. Del., 1987—. Mem. Internat. Neuropsychol. Soc., Am. Psychol Assn., Am. Edn. Rsch. Assn., Tchrs. English to Speakers of Other Langs., Sigma Xi, Kappa Delta Pi. Office: Youngstown State U Psychology Dept DeBartolo Bldg Youngstown OH 44555

GREEN, ALLISON ANNE, educator; b. Flint, Mich., Oct. 5, 1936; d. Edwin Stanley and Ruth Allison (Simmons) James; m. Richard Gerring Green, Dec. 23, 1961 (div. Oct. 1969). BA, Albion Coll., 1959; MA, U. Mich., 1978. Cert. tchr., Mich. Tchr. phys. edn. Southwestern High Sch., Flint, 1959-62; tchr. math. Harry Hunt Jr. High Sch., Portsmouth, Va., 1962-63; receptionist Tempcon, Inc., Mpls., 1963-64; tchr. phys. edn. and math. Longfellow Jr. High Sch., Flint, 1964-81, tchr. math., 1981-87, 87—, tchr. lang. arts and social studies, 1986-87. Mem. Fair Winds council Girl Scouts U.S., 1943—, leader Lone Troop, Albion, Mich., 1957, sr. tchr. aide adviser, 1964-67; mem. Big Sisters Genesee and Lapeer Counties, 1964-68; mem. adminstrv. bd. Court St. United Methodist Ch.; treas. edn. work area, mission commn., sec. council on ministries, mem. worship com. United Meth. Women Soc. Christian Service, also chmn. meml. com. Mem. NEA, Mich. Edn. Assn., Mich. Assn. Mid. Sch. Educators, United Tchrs. Flint (bldg. rep.), Delta Kappa Gamma (treas. 1982-88, profl. affairs chmn. 1978-80, legis. chmn. 1980-82, pres. 1988-90), Alpha Xi Delta (pres. Flint, alumnae, v.p., treas., corp. pres. Albion Coll., alumnae dir. province 1972-77, Outstanding Sr. Albion Coll. 1959), Embroiderers Guild Am. (sec. 1977-80, maps rep. 1980-82), Phi Delta Kappa (historian 1985—). Home: 1002 Copeman Blvd Flint MI 48504 Office: 1255 N Chevrolet Ave Flint MI 48504

GREEN, BARBARA STRAWN, psychotherapist; b. Cleve., May 31, 1938; d. Charles Everard and Dorothy Haring (Strawn) G. BA, Pa. State U., 1960; MS, Columbia U., 1962; postgrad. in psychotherapy and psychoanalysis, Postgrad. Ctr. for Mental Health, N.Y.C., 1975. Cert. social worker, N.Y.; cert. Rutgers Summer Sch. Alcoholism Studies, 1982. Social worker VA, N.Y.C., 1962-66; sr. psychiat. social worker in child psychiat. Downstate Med. Ctr., Bklyn., 1966-71; staff therapist Inst. for Contemporary Psychotherapy, N.Y.C., 1971-73; social worker Lower East Side Service Ctr., N.Y.C., 1975-77; intake coordinator alcoholism program Postgrad. Ctr. for Mental Health, N.Y.C., 1981-82; program coordinator Bowery Residents Com., N.Y.C., 1984-86; pvt. practice psychotherapy N.Y.C., 1973—. Mem. Nat. Assn. Social Workers (sec. alcoholism com. N.Y.C. chpt. 1987-89), Social Workers Helping Social Workers (chmn. 1982-84).

GREEN, CAROL H., lawyer, educator, journalist; b. Seattle, Feb. 18, 1944; B.A. summa cum laude in History and Journalism, La. Tech. U., 1965; M.S.L. (Ford Found. fellow), Yale U., 1977; J.D., U. Denver, 1979. Intern, Shreveport (La.) Times, 1964, reporter, 1965-66; reporter Guam Daily News, 1966-67; city editor Pacific Jour., Agana, Guam, 1967-68; reporter, editorial writer, Denver Post, 1968-76, legal affairs reporter, 1977-79, asst. editor editorial page, 1979-81, house counsel, 1980-83, labor rels. mgr., 1981-83; assoc. Holme Roberts & Owen, 1983-85; v.p. human resources and legal affairs Denver Post, 1985-87; mgr. circulation sales and adminstrn. Newsday, 1988-90, mgr. circulation, 1990—; mem. corrections task force Colo. Criminal Justice Standards and Goals, 1985 speaker for USIA, India, Egypt. Bd. dirs. YWCA, Mile Hi Red Cross, Trans. Coun., Denver C. of C. Recipient McWilliams award for juvenile justice, Denver, 1971; award for interpretive reporting Denver Newspaper Guild, 1971-1979. Mem. ABA (forum on communications law), Colo. Bar Assn. (bd. govs. 1985-87, chairperson BAR-press com. 1980), Denver Bar Assn. (co-chairperson jud. selection and benefits com. 1982-85, 1st v.p. 1986), Alliance Profl. Women (exec. com.), Women's Forum, Leadership Denver. Clubs: Denver Press. Episcopalian. Office: Newsday 235 Pinelawn Rd Melville NY 11747

GREEN, CLAIRE MAGIDOVITCH, rabbi; b. Frankfurt, Federal Republic Germany, Dec. 7, 1953; d. Avshalom and Revelle Melva (Swadesh) Magidovitch; m. Steven Yale Green, June 21, 1986; children: Jacob Alexander, Daniel David. BA, Miami U., Oxford, Ohio, 1975; MHL, Reconstructionist Rabbinical, Wyncote, Pa., 1988. Ordained by Reconstructionist Rabbinical Coll., 1988. Rabbi Kol Emet Reconstructionist Congregation, Yardley, Pa., 1984-85; dir. Reconstructionist Creative Liturgy Ctr., Wyncote, 1984-85; edn. dir. Congregation Beth-El Suburban, Broomall, Pa., 1985-88; dir. spl. progs. Temple Beth Emeth, Wilmingtin, Del., 1989. Mem. Coalition for Alternatives in Jewish Edn., Am. Jewish Congress, Am. Jewish Com., Hadassah, Reconstructionist Rabbinical Assn., Delta Phi Alpha. Home: 554 Meadowbrook Dr Huntingdon Valley PA 19006

GREEN, DEBRA LYNN, educator; b. Mobile, Ala., Aug. 20, 1961; d. John Douglas Jr. and Maudie Ruth Green. BA, U. Fla., 1983; MA, U. South Fla., 1988. Cert. tchr. in early childhood edn., elem. edn., jr. high math., Fla. Tchr. sci., math. Marion County Sch. Bd., Ocala, Fla. Mem. NCTM,

Mu Alpha Theta, Kappa Delta Pi, Phi Eta Sigma, Phi Kappa Phi, Alpha Lambda Delta. Home: PO Box 1407 Belleview FL 32620

GREEN, ELAINE K., educator; b. N.Y.C., Aug. 3, 1932; d. Samuel and Rae (Siegel) Klenosky; m. George Green; children: Lauren Dee, Tammy Jane. BA, Queens Coll., 1954. Tchr. elem. N.Y.C. Bd. Edn., 1954-57. Sponsor bicycle safety legis., N.Y. State legis., 1962, 72; v.p. Oceanside (N.Y.) PTA, 1970, pres., 1972; v.p. Dem. Club Oceanside, 1974-76; pres. miami Salon Group, Fla., 1987—, Guild Greater Miami Opera, 1987—; co-chmn. Chopin Ball Com.; mem. March of Dimes Quest for Best Ball com. Recipient B'nai Brith Community Svc. award. Mem. Opera Guild Internat. (sec. SE region 1988—), Miami Opera Assn. (luncheon co-chmn.). Home: 19667 Turnberry Way North Miami FL 33180

GREEN, ERIKA ANA, medical writer, microbiologist; b. Lucenec, Czechoslavakia, May 27, 1928; came to U.S., 1955; d. Louis Roth and Elsa (Schwartz) Davidson; m. James Weston Green, July 8, 1961; children: James Philip, Stephen Henry. BS in Pharmacy, Universidad Central, Ecuador, 1955; MS in Physiology, CUNY, 1959; PhD in Microbiology, Rutgers U., 1971. Rsch. technician Sloan-Kettering Inst., N.Y.C., 1955-59; lit. scientist Johnson and Johnson, New Brunswick, N.J., 1959; rsch. assoc. Rutgers U., New Brunswick, 1959-61; med. abstractor Coun. Tobacco Rsch., N.Y.C., 1971-72; sci. editorial coord. Carter Wallace, Cranbury, N.Y., 1972-73; sr. lit. sci. Hoffman LaRoche, Nutley, N.Y., 1973-81; clin. rsch. sci. Hoffman LaRoche, Nutley, 1981-85; cons., med. writer J.L. Shapiro, Therades Inc., DuPont, 1985-88; med. writer Sandon Pharms., East Hanover, N.J., 1988 --. Author: Folate Antagonists, 1984; contbr. Am. Acad. Ency., 1978, articles to profl. jours. Mem. Am. Soc. Microbiology, Am. Med. Writers Assn., Theobold Smith Soc., Sigma Xi. Home: 409 Grant Ave Highland Park NJ 08904

GREEN, FLORA HUNGERFORD, lactation consultant, health educator; b. Mason City, Iowa, June 23, 1941; d. Mac Willard and Ethel Elizabeth (Hill) Hungerford; m. Ronald Eugene Green, Aug. 3, 1974; children: Elizabeth Jane, Marjorie Ann. Diploma, Meth-Kahler Sch. of Nursing, 1963; BS in Biology, Westmar Coll., 1964; BS in Nursing, Case Western Res. U., 1968; MA in Edn. Media, U. Minn., 1971. RN, Idaho, Calif., Iowa; cert. lactation cons., lamaze instr. Ednl. programmer U. Wis., Milw., 1970-72; asst. prof. nursing Idaho State U., Pocatello, 1972-76; dir. ins-svc. and patient edn. Bingham Meml. Hosp., Blackfoot, Idaho, 1976-77; staff nurse St. Agnes' Hosp., Fresno, Calif., 1979-81, Eden Hosp., Castro Valley, Calif., 1981-83; pvt. practice lactation cons. Fremont, Calif., 1985—; part-time mem. faculty Chabot Coll., Hayward Coll., Las Positas Coll., Livermore, Calif., 1987—; staff nurse high risk ob. dept. Stanford U. Hosp., 1989—; cons. media div. J.B. Lippincott Co., Phila., 1973-80; bd. dirs. Bay Area Lactation Assn., Daly City, Calif. Chmn. Blacow Sch. emergency and safety com., Fremont, 1987-88; bd. dirs. Bannock County ARC, Pocatello, 1976-77; emergency svcs. disaster cons. Idaho State U., Bannock County, Pocatello, Idaho, 1972-77. Mem. AAUW, IBCLC, So. Alameda ASPO (co-chairperson 1987-88, cert.), Internat. Lactation Cons. Assn., Internat. Childbirth Edn. Assn., German Lang. and Cultural Club, Sons of Norway, Sigma Theta Tau. Methodist.

GREEN, GAIL TERESA, corporate executive; b. N.Y.C., Feb. 19, 1953; d. Frank and Joan (Lyons) Sukana. BA in Psychology magna cum laude, Adelphi U., 1975. Account exec. Cunningham & Walsh (name change to N.W. Ayers), N.Y.C., 1980-81; paralegal Weil Gotshal & Manges, N.Y.C., 1981-83; account and sales exec. Albert Nipon Boutique, N.Y.C., 1984-85, Perry Ellis Ltd., N.Y.C., 1985-86, Div. Ten Pers., N.Y.C., 1986—; consulting Queens Community Coll. N.Y. 1987-89; advisor resumes Internat. Ctr. N.Y. 1987-89. Info. Person The Internat. Ctr. N.Y., 1988—, Spokesperson Gay Mens Health Ctr. N.Y., 1988—, Vol. N.Y. Cares, 1988—, Road Runners Club N.Y., 1988—, Telethon Channel 13 Pub. Broadcasting N.Y., 1978—. Recipient 100,000 sales club Roth Young 1987, 89. Mem. Nat. Assn Profl. Sales Women, Sierra Club (tchr. C.P.C. course for N.Y.C.). Democrat. Home: 10 Waterside Pla New York NY 10010

GREEN, GERTRUDE DORSEY, psychologist, author; b. Balt., Aug. 18, 1949; d. John Summerfield Green III and Gertrude Dixon (Dorsey) Wilson. AB, Dickinson Coll., 1971; MA, Bowling Green State U., 1972; PhD, U. Wash., 1981. Head resident Bowling Green (Ohio) State U., 1971-72; asst. dir. residence life Albion (Mich.) Coll., 1972-74; social worker Big Bros./Big Sisters, Lansing, Mich., 1975-77; pvt. practice as counselor Seattle, 1979-82, pvt. practice as psychologist, 1982—; cons. Hearing, Speech, Deafness Ctr., Seattle, 1987-88. Co-author: Lesbian Couples, 1988. Vol. regional com. Am. Friends Svc. Com., Seattle, 1981-; bd. dirs. Seattle Counseling Svc. for Sexual Minorities, 1981-84. Mem. Am. Psychol. Assn., Am. Assn. for Counseling and Devel., Feminist Therapy Assn., Assn. of Gay and Lesbian Psychologists. Mem. Soc. of Friends. Office: 521 19th E Seattle WA 98112

GREEN, IRENE MARTHA, education educator; b. Carroll County, Va., Mar. 22, 1928; d. James Festus and Nettie (Largen) Martin; m. Charles Frederick Green,. BS in Home Econs., Radford U., 1948; M in Adult Edn., Adminstr, U. Ill., 1981. Home econs. tchr. Bath County Sch Bd., Hot Springs, Va., 1948-49; home demonstrn. agt. Va. Coop. Extension Service, Whyhville, 1949-51; pres. Regional Assn., Roanoke, 1954-57; home demonstrn. Va. Coop. Extension Service, Roanoke, 1956-57; sci. tchr. Skokie (Ill.) Valley Jr. High, 1970-71; tchr. Evanston (Ill.) Twp. High Sch., 1971; home econs. adviser U. Ill. Coop. Extension Service, Grayslake, 1972—, advisor, 1980-84. Contbr. articles to mag. Bd. dirs. Lake Coounty Human Services Council, 1976-88; vice chmn. Chain Lakes Sr. Council, Lake County, 1982-85. Recipient Peer award, 1977; named Outstanding Woman of Achievement, Lake County YWCA, 1989. Mem. AAUW (v.p., membership chmn. Libertyville-Mundelein br., EFP gift honoree 1990), State Nat. Assn. Extension Home Economists (Disting. Svc. award, multi-county family life specialist), Epsilon Sigma Phi, Gamma Sigma Delta. Republican. Presbyterian. Home: 428 Arbor Ct Libertyville IL 60048 Office: U Ill Coop Extension 330320 N Hwy 45 Grayslake IL 60030

GREEN, JANE BURDEN, consultant; b. Knoxville, Tenn., Mar. 23, 1950; d. Jess W. and Leona (Patterson) Burden; m. Mar. 28, 1969 (1983); 1 child, Deanna Marie Green. Student, Middle Tenn. State U., Murfreesboro, 1968-69; BS magna cum laude, U. N.C., 1975. Cert. personnel cons., profl. sec. Adminstrv. asst. ind. hosiery div. Burlington No., 1970-73; indsl. co-op coord. Burlington City (N.C.) Sch., 1975-77; realtor assoc., broker Moser Real Estate, Graham, N.C., 1978-80; ops. cons. Pers. Placement, Inc., Burlington, N.C., 1980-85; sr. cons. Dunhill of Burlington, Inc., 1985-88; pres., owner Staffing Solutions, Inc., Greenville, S.C., 1988—. Alamance County 4-H Planning Com., Graham, N.C., mem. Tenn. 4-H All Stars, 1966. Named Counselor of the Year N.C. Assn. Person Cons., Pinehurst, 1986, Carolinas Region Cons. of the Year Dunhill, Charlotte, N.C., 1986, Data Processing Cons. of the Year, Dunhill, Charlotte, N.C., 1986, 1987.

GREEN, JOYCE HENS, federal judge; b. N.Y.C., Nov. 13, 1928; d. James S. and Hedy (Bucher) Hens; m. Samuel Green, Sept. 25, 1965 (dec.); children: Michael Timothy, June Heather, James Harry. B.A., U. Md., 1949; J.D., George Washington U., 1951. Bar: D.C. 1951, Va. 1956, U.S. Supreme Ct. 1956. Practice law Washington, 1951-68, Arlington, Va., 1956-68; ptnr. Green & Green, 1966-68; judge Superior Ct., D.C., 1968-79, U.S. Dist. Ct. for D.C., 1979—. Co-author: Dissolution of Marriage, 1986, supplements, 1987-89; contbr. supplements Marriage and Family Law Agreements, 1985-89. Trustee D.C. div. Am. Cancer Soc., 1963-76. Named Woman Lawyer of Yr., 1979. Fellow Am. Bar Found., Am. Acad. Matrimonial Lawyers; mem. Fed. Judges Assn. (bd. dirs.), ABA, Va. Bar Assn., Bar Assn. D.C., D.C. Bar, D.C. Women's Bar Assn. (pres. 1960-62), Exec. Women in Govt. (chmn. 1977), Kappa Beta Pi, Phi Delta Phi (hon.). Club: Nat. Lawyers (Washington). Office: US Dist Ct US Courthouse 3rd & Constitution Ave NW Washington DC 20001

GREEN, JUDITH MAXINE, small business owner; b. Bklyn., May 13, 1947; d. Nat and Faye (Sherr) Warman; m. Irwin Gerald, June 30, 1932 (div. 1986); children: Brooke Jennifer, Carrie Rebecca. Student, Bryant Coll., Providence, Rhode Island, 1965-66. Bookkeeper Dumont Camera, N.Y.C., 1966-71; motherhood N.Y.C., 1972; pres. Warman Prec. Products, N.Y.C., 1985—; v.p. Dumont Camera Corp., N.Y.C.; pres. Faye Warmen Enterprises, N.Y.C., 1985—. Mem., chmn. PTA, Searingtown, 1980, Hadassah, Searingtown, 1989; pres. Civic Assn., Roslyn, N.Y., 1979-89. Home: 42 Hickory Ln Roslyn NY 11577

GREEN, JUDY, mathematics educator; b. Bklyn., Sept. 6, 1943; d. Monroe J. and Rebecca (Shafran) Coven; m. Paul S. Green, June 19, 1964; children: Joanna Green DePorter, Seth. AB, Cornell U., 1964; MA, Yale U., 1966; PhD, U. Md., 1972. Instr. math. Howard U., Washington, 1966-67; asst. prof. math. Rutgers U., Camden, N.J., 1972-78, assoc. prof., 1978-89, chmn. dept. math. scis., 1978-89; prof. math. Marymount U., Arlington, Va., 1989—; hon. rsch. assoc. Smithsonian Instn. Museum Am. History, Washington, 1979—. Author: (with others) Women in American Mathematics, 1989, Contributors to American Mathematics, 1990; contbr. articles to profl. jours. Mem. AAUP (v.p. 1988-90), Am. Math. Soc., Assn. Symbolic Logic, Assn. Women Math. (v.p. 1977-78), History Sci. Soc., Math. Assn. Am. Home: 10106 Leder Rd Silver Spring MD 20902 Office: Marymount U 2807 N Glebe Rd Arlington VA 22207-4299

GREEN, JULIE JAYNE, photojournalist; b. Bartlesville, Okla.; d. Robert Carl and Beverly May Green. Student, Okla. State U., Bartlesville, Okla., 1974-78, N.Y. Inst. Photography, 1982. Photographer Explosive Records, Tulsa, 1984-86, Shyock Prodns., Tulsa, 1985, Jim Halsey Orgn., L.A., 1987-89, Atlantic Records, New York, 1989, Oak Ridge Boys Inc., Nasvhille, 1989—. Photojournalist Guitar Players Mag., Tulsa, 1986, Internat. Photographer, Washington, 1987-89, Okla. Eagle, Tulsa, 1987, The Am. Music Tchr. mag., 1990, Living Blues mag., 1989—, People mag., 1989—, Music Educators Jour., 1990, The Instrumentalist, 1990; author: Why I Sing the Blues, 1989; author jours. including Current Indian Problems, 1988, Visual Rock N Roll, 1989. Mem. The Human Soc. of U.S., Washington. Mem. Am. Film Inst., Tulsa Blues Soc. (editor 1989—), The Tulsa Blues Club (contbr.). Republican. Methodist. Home and Office: 6737 S Peoria 104A Tulsa OK 74136

GREEN, JUNE LAZENBY, federal judge; b. Arnold, Md., Jan. 23, 1914; d. Eugene H. and Jessie T. (Briggs) Lazenby; m. John Cawley Green, Sept. 5, 1936. JD, Am. U., 1941. Bar: Md. 1943, D.C. 1945. Claims adjuster Lumbermans Mut. Casualty Co., Washington, 1942-43, claims atty., 1943-47; pvt. practice Washington, 1947-68, Annapolis, Md., 1950-68; judge U.S. Dist. Ct. D.C., 1968—; mem. spl. ct. Regional Reorganization Act, 1987—; examiner bar, Washington, 1963-68. Named Woman Lawyer of Yr., 1965; recipient Lifetime Achievement award Alumni Assn. of Am. U., 1986. Mem. ABA, Md. Bar Assn., Bar Assn. D.C. (bd. dirs. 1966-68, cert. of appreciation 1984), Women's Bar Assn. D.C. (pres. 1955-57), Kappa Beta Pi. Club: Nat. Lawyers. Home: 464 W Joyce Ln Arnold MD 21012 also: 550 N St SW Washington DC 20024 Office: US Courthouse 3rd & Constitution Ave NW Washington DC 20001

GREEN, KAREN BLEIER, advertising agency executive; b. N.Y.C., Apr. 18, 1945; d. Benjamin and Sally (Karger) Bleier; m. Joseph H. Green, Sept. 3, 1966; children—Jessica, Adam. B.A., Simmons Coll., 1967; M.B.A, Harvard U., 1969. Media planner Ogilvy & Mather Inc., N.Y.C., 1969-71, asst. media dir., 1971-74, v.p., account supr., 1974-79, v.p., mgmt. supr., 1979-82, sr. v.p., mgmt. supr., 1982—. Office: Ogilvy & Mather Inc 309 W 49th St New York NY 10019

GREEN, KAREN INA MARGULIES, psychologist; b. N.Y.C., Jan. 27, 1939; d. Irwin Margulies and Roberta Rose (Goodbinder) Margulies-Varon; m. L.R. Green, Dec. 22, 1961 (div. June 1981); children: Garth Lorin, Allison Dawne. BA in Psychology with distinction, Duke U., 1959; MA, Boston U., 1960, postgrad., 1960-63; MA in Lit., Am. U., 1973. Lic. psychologist, D.C. Pvt. practice Green Assocs., Washington, 1968—; english tchr. Md. Sch. of Art & Design, Wheaton, Md., 1980; cons. psychologist Providence Hosp., Washington, 1981-82, New Ventures, Inc., Bowie, Md., 1984, Hood Coll., Frederick, Md., 1985; psychologist cons. Associated Health Practioners, Washington, 1987—, Behavioral Factors, Inc., Washington, 1986-89; sch. psychologist Pub. Schs. of D.C., Washington, 1967-68; rsch. psychologist Pres.' Commn. on Obscenity and Pornography, Washington, 1968-70; cons. psychologist Pub. Defender Svc., Washington, 1968-70. Playwright: These Dead Ladies Are My Friends, 1983 (winner of playwriting contest, 1983); dir. plays: Songs We've Never Sung, 1984, Where Has Love Gone, 1985; author (short story) Repetition, 1990. Mem. Am. Psychol. Assn. (assoc.), Internat. Coun. Psychologists, D.C. Psychol. Assn., Nat. Register Health Svc. Providers, Phi Beta Kappa. Home and Office: 1632 44th St NW Washington DC 20007

GREEN, LAQUITA STEPHENS, pharmaceutical company executive; b. Birmingham, Ala., Nov. 10, 1957; d. Roy Allen and Ouida (Camp) Stephens; m. John Alton Green, May 7, 1977 (div. Jan. 1981); m. Joseph Charles Zito, July 25, 1987. Student, Jefferson State Jr. Coll., Birmingham, Ala., 1976. Div. mgr. Tech. Products, Inc., Birmingham, Ala., 1979-81; pres., prin. Design Equipment, Inc., Birmingham, 1981-83; sales rep. ConvaTec div. E.R. Squibb & Sons, Princeton, N.J., 1983-87; regional mgr. ConvaTec div. Squibb Pharm., Princeton, 1987—. Pres. Vestavia Highlands Assn., Birmingham, 1984-87; adv. bd., Met. Devel., Birmingham, 1981-82, bd. dirs. City of Birmingham. Mem. Nat. Inst. Bus. Mgmt., Toastmaster Internat. Republican.

GREEN, LAURALEE MAYNARD, computer programmer, analyst; b. Glens Falls, N.Y., Dec. 11, 1959; d. George Clement and Joan Marie (Koch) Maynard; m. Stephen Fowler Green, Oct. 15, 1988. AS, Hesser Coll., Manchester, N.H., 1980; BS in Computer Programming, N.H. Coll., 1985. Computer programmer Servicing and Computing Tech., Manchester, 1981-83, N.H. Ball Bearings, Peterborough, 1985-86; MIS group leader Konica Bus. Machines USA Inc., Windsor, Conn., 1986—. Co-founder Ch. of God's Love, Manchester, Conn., 1990. Mem. NAFE. Home: 63 Elm St #305 Manchester CT 06040 Office: Konica Bus Machines USA 500 Day Hill Rd Windsor CT 06095

GREEN, LINDA LOU, logistics engineer; b. Cape Girardeau, Mo., Sept. 12, 1946; d. Barney Oldfield and Opal (Jeffries) G. BA, East Carolina U., 1967, MA, 1969; postgrad., U. Utah, 1969-70; grad., Naval War Coll., Newport, R.I., 1985, Command and Staff Coll., Ft. Leavenworth, Kans., 1990. Cert. in collegiate teaching. Asst. prof. history Jackson (Miss.) State U., 1970-72, Va. State U., Petersburg, 1972-74; commd. 1st lt. U.S. Army, 1974, advanced through grades to maj., 1983; logistics engr. land systems div. Gen. Dynamics Corp., Warren, Mich., 1983-84; systems analyst Raytheon Svc. Co., Huntsville, Ala., 1984-86; pres. Green & Assocs. Inc., Huntsville, 1985-86; logistics engr., cost analyst, br. mgr. Applied Rsch. Inc., Huntsville, 1986-90; sr. ILS analyst Native Am. Svcs. Inc., Huntsville, Ala., 1990; sr. systems analyst BDM Internat. Inc., 1990—; instr. U. Md., Fed. Republic of Germany, 1975-77, Calhoun Community Coll., Huntsville, 1990—. Author: Study Guides for American History, 1969, The Family Tree, 1989, Logistics Engineering, 1991. Mem. Rep. Nat. Com., Washington, 1986—. With USAR, 1983—. Mem. Soc. Logistics Engrs., Assn. U.S. Army (bd. dirs. Redstone, Huntsville chpt. 1988—), Res. Officers Assn., LWV. Baptist. Office: BDM Internat Inc 950 Explorer Blvd Huntsville AL 35807

GREEN, LINDA TERRY PROMO, clinical psychologist, school psychologist; b. Highland Park, Mich., Sept. 24, 1956; d. Gordon Edward and Ruth (Stark) Promo; div.; 1 child, Jeffrey Ryan Green. AA with high distinction, Schoolcraft Coll., Livonia, Mich., 1976; BA with distinction, U. Mich., Dearborn, 1978; MS, Eastern Mich. U., 1980; PsyD, Forest Inst., Wheeling, Ill., 1984. Lic. psychologist; cert. sch. psychologist. Staff psychologist St. Joseph Mercy Hosp., Pontiac, Mich., 1984-88, chief psychologist, 1988-89, dir. clin. tng., 1985-89, clin. supr. outpatient dept., 1988-89; sch. psychologist Clawson (Mich.) Bd. Edn., 1989—; pvt. practice Bloomfield Hills, Mich., 1984-88, Birmingham, Mich., 1989—. Mem. Am. Psychol. Assn., Mich. Psychol. Assn., Nat. Register. Home: 6600 W Dartmoor West Bloomfield MI 48322 Office: 1550 N Woodward Ste 210 Birmingham MI 48009

GREEN, LYNNE, producer, writer, director; b. Krsko, Yugoslavia, Oct. 16, 1944; came to U.S., 1949, naturalized, 1966; d. Robert and Albina (Schmuck) Prusak; m. Sam Robert Bass, Oct., 1974 (div. 1975). BFA with honors in Directing, Webster Coll. Conservatory of Theatre Arts, 1979. Intern Sta. KSDK-TV, 1987-88; producer-dir. videos Kurt Landberg, Architect and Seja Systems, 1987—. Dir. stage shows including Second Verse, N.Y.C., 1980, Button Button, N.Y.C., 1982, Atmosphere of Enforced Discipline, N.Y.C., 1981, Friend of a Friend, N.Y.C., 1982, The Other Woman: A Farce Closing Saturday Night, N.Y.C., 1983, Question Marks and Periods, 1981-83, Mrs. Michaelangelo, N.Y.C., 1983, Crimes of the Heart, Las Cruces, N.Mex., 1984, Antigone, St. Louis, 1985; ind. documentary Purse Strings, 1989-90. Invitational: New Faces, New Art YWCA's Women's Resource Ctr., 1990; video Its a Sin To Tell a Lie. Vol. Harriett Woods Com., St. Louis, 1986, Double Helix T.V., St. Louis. Recipient Best Dir. award Internat. Dirs. Festival, 1980. Mem. NOW, Ms. Found. for Women, Nat. Abortion Rights Action League. Democrat. Avocation: photography. Home: 4479 Weber Rd Saint Louis MO 63123

GREEN, MARGARET DELL, human services administrator; b. Melbourne, Ark., Aug. 6, 1952; d. Thomas James and Theo May (Finley) Harris; m. John E. Green, July 24, 1976 (div. Nov. 1985); 1 child, Amanda Marie. AA, So. Bapt. Coll., Walnut Ridge, Ark., 1972; BA, Ouachita Bapt. U., Arkadelphia, Ark., 1974; MS, Henderson State U., Arkadelphia, 1977. Lic. nursing home adminstr., Ark. Psychol. asst., adminstrv. asst. II, Human Devel. Ctr., Arkadelphia, 1974-80, acting supr., 1980, 86, coord. quality assurance, 1980-82, dir. residential living svcs., 1982-86; interim supt. SE Ark. Human Devel. Ctr., Warren, 1986-87, supt., 1987—; mem. quality assurance and programming com. Devel. Disabilities Svcs. Bd., Little Rock, 1989—, chmn. aggression mgmt. com., 1990. Asst. leader Brownie troop 174, Girl Scouts U.S.A., Arkadelphia, 1985-86; mem. vvocat. health occupations adv. coun. Warren Pub. Schs., 1986—, mem. millage steering com., 1990; bd. dirs. Bradley County Helping Hands, Warren, 1987—, Three Pines Riding Ctr., Pine Bluff, Ark., 1989—; mem. Warren Local Planning Group, 19890. Recipient plaque of appreciation and 5 yr. cert. Human Devel. Ctr., 1980, 10 yr. cert., 1986. Mem. Ark. Human Svcs. Employees Assn., Ark. Pub. Employees Assn. (Outstanding Pub. Employee award 1984), Am. Assn. on Mental Deficiency, Ark. Vol. Coords. Assn., SW Soc. on Aging, Ark. South Tourism Assn., Bradley County C. of C. (beautification com. 1990). Methodist. Office: SE Ark Human Devel Ctr Rte 3 1 Center Circle Warren AR 71671

GREEN, MARIA ANTOINETTE, employee benefits specialist; b. Washington, Apr. 24, 1964; d. John and Rosalie (Williams) G.; m. Kevin Stephen Hawkins, Aug. 11, 1990. BA in Sociology, Am. U., 1987. Counselor Community Svcs. for Autistic Adults, Rockville, Md., 1986-87; case mgr. D.C. Assn. Retarded Citizens, Washington, 1987-88, program coord., 1988-90; employee benefits specialist Georgetown U., Washington, 1990—; cons. D.C. Assn. Retarded Citizens, Washington, 1990. Vice-pres. Richard Allen Youth Coun., 1988—. Mem. NAFE, 4-F Found., Chi Rho Missionary Soc. Democrat. African Methodist Episcopal. Home: 703 Faraday Pl NE Washington DC 20017

GREEN, MARJORIE, automotive distribution, import and manufacturing company executive; b. N.Y.C., Sept. 27, 1943; d. Benjamin Maxon and Harriet (Weslock) Gruzen; m. Thomas Henry Green, May 31, 1964. Student Antioch Coll., 1961-63, CCNY, 1964-65. Adminstrv. asst. ednl. research U. Calif.-Berkeley, 1965-76; v.p., co-owner Automotion, Santa Clara, Calif., 1973—. Adv. bd. Import Car mag. Mem. Am. Fedn. State, County and Mcpl. Employees (pres. U. Calif. chpt. 1967), Porsche Club Am (v.p. Golden Gate region 1974, treas. region 1975). Home: 688 Cupples Ct Santa Clara CA 95051 Office: Automotion 3535 Kifer Rd Santa Clara CA 95051

GREEN, MARY HESTER, nurse; b. Oxford, N.C., May 6, 1941; d. Melvin and Martha Elizabeth (Bridges) Hester; m. Joe Lewis G., Dec. 24, 1962; children: Reginald, Renee G. Johnson, Terri Lynatta. AA in Applied Sci., SUNY, 1979; diploma in Christian Edn., Am. Bible Coll., 1984; BA in Christian Edn., City Univ., L.A., 1989; postgrad. in Christian Edn., N.C. Cen. U., 1985-86, City U. L.A., 1989—. Charge nurse Newark City Hosp., 1967-69, Lincoln Hosp., Durham, N.C., 1974-79; team leader Duke Med. Ctr., Durham, 1969—. Deaconess Pine Grove Ch., Creedmoor, N.C., 1971—, sunday sch. tchr., 1972-80, mem. choir, 1970—; mem. staff Bapt. Tng. Union, 1974—, mem. scholarship com.; leader Girl Scout U.S., 1976-78. Recipient Cert. Recognition YWCA, Durham, 1985, Disting. Service award Lincoln Hosp., 1976. Mem. NAFE, Am. Soc. Notaries, Internat. Platform Assn., Century Club Winston Salem U., Masons, Order Ea. Star. Democrat. Home: 5301 Whippoorwill St Durham NC 27704

GREEN, MEYRA JEANNE, banker; b. Cleve., Oct. 17, 1946; d. Meyrick Evans Green and Jeanne Bynon (Griffiths) Strauss; m. Frank W. Horn, Dec. 10, 1977 (dec. 1983); 1 stepchild, Donna; m. John Joseph Fleming, Aug. 29, 1987; 1 stepchild, Kerry. BA, Lake Erie Coll., 1968; MBA, NYU, 1973. Corp. planner Chem. Bank, N.Y.C., 1968-72, 1st Nat. City Bank, N.Y.C., 1972; security analyst Bank of N.Y., 1972-74; asst. treas. Credit Lyonnais, 1974-84; v.p. 1st Fidelity Bank, N.A., N.J., Newark, 1985—. Vol. Overlook Hosp. Hospice, Summit, N.J., 1985—. Mem. NYU Grad. Sch. Bus. Alumni. Republican. Home: 111 Woodland Rd Madison NJ 07940 Office: 1st Fidelity Bank NA NJ 550 Broad St Newark NJ 07192

GREEN, NANCY LOUGHRIDGE, publisher; b. Lexington, Ky.; d. William S. and Nancy O. (Green) Loughridge; BA in Journalism, U. Ky., 1964; MA in Journalism, Ball State U., 1971; postgrad. U. Ky., 1968, U. Minn., 1968. Tchr. English and publs. adv. Clark County High Sch., Winchester, Ky., 1965-66, Pleasure Ridge Park High Sch., Louisville, 1966-67, Clarksville (Ind.) High Sch., 1967-68, Charleston (W.Va.) High Sch., 1968-69; asst. publs. and pub. info. specialist W.Va. Dept. Edn., Charleston, 1969-70; tchr. journalism and publs. dir. Elmhurst High Sch., Ft. Wayne, Ind., 1970-71; adviser student publs. U. Ky., Lexington, 1971-82; gen. mgr. student publs. U. Tex., Austin, 1982-85; pres., pub. Palladium-Item, Richmond, Ind., 1985-89, News-Leader, Springfield, Mo., 1989—; dir. Harte-Hanks urban journalism program, 1984; pres. Media Cons., Inc., Lexington, 1980; dir. urban journalism workshop program Louisville and Lexington newspaper pubs., 1976-82; sec. Kernel Press, Inc., 1971-82. Contbr. articles to profl. jours. Bd. dirs. Jr. League, Lexington, 1980-82, Manchester Ctr., 1978-82, pres., 1979-82; chmn. Greater Richmond Progress Com., 1986-87, bd. dirs. 1986-89; pres. leadership Wayne County, 1986-87, bd. dirs., 1985-89; bd. dirs. Richmond Community Devel. Corp., 1987-89, United Way of the Ozards, 1990—, ARC, 1990—, Springfield Arts Coun., 1990—; mem. adv. bd. Ind. U. East, 1985-89, Richmond C. of C., 1987-89, Ind. Humanities Coun., 1988-89, Youth Communications Bd., 1988—. Recipient Coll. Media Advisers First Amendment award, 1987—, Carl Towley award Journalism Edn. Assn., 1988, Disting. Svc. award Assn. Edn. Journalism and Mass Communication, 1989; named to Ball State Journalism Hall of Fame, 1988. Mem. Student Press Law Ctr. (bd. dirs. 1975—, pres. 1985-87), Assoc. Collegiate Press, Journalism Edn. Assn., Nat. Council Coll. Publs. Advs. (pres. 1979-83, Disting. Newspaper Adv. 1976, Disting. Bus. Adviser, 1984). AP Mng. Editors, Columbia Scholastic Press Assn. (Gold Key 1980), So. Interscholastic Press Assn. (Disting. Service award 1983), Nat. Scholastic Press Assn. (Pioneer award 1982), Soc. Profl. Journalists. Home: 2222 E Berkeley Springfield MO 65804 Office: News-Leader 651 Boonville Ave Springfield MO 65801

GREEN, PAULA ANN, marketing and sales executive; b. Newark, Jan. 21, 1953; d. Frank and Lola (Raimo) G. Student, Upsala Coll., 1971-72, Thomas Edison State Coll. Account exec. TRW, Parsippany, N.J., 1977-87; sales account exec. EQUIFAX, Atlanta, Ga., 1987—. Chairperson Stone Run II Covenants com., Bedminster, N.J., 1987-89. Mem. NAFE, Consumer Credit Assn., Employees For Career Awareness and Devel. (nat. chairperson 1981-83). Office: EQUIFAX Credit Mktg 94 Church St New Brunswick NJ 08901

GREEN, PEGGY MEYERS, advertising agency executive; b. Detroit, June 9, 1943. BA, U. Mich., 1964; MA, Columbia U., 1966. V.p. Dancer Fitzgerald Sample, Inc. (now Saatchi & Saatchi Advt.), N.Y.C., sr. v.p., exec. v.p., 1988—. Office: Saatchi & Saatchi Advt 375 Hudson St New York NY 10014-3620*

GREEN, ROSE BASILE (MRS. RAYMOND S. GREEN), poet, author, educator; b. New Rochelle, N.Y., Dec. 19, 1914; d. Salvatore and Caroline (Galgano) Basile; BA, Coll. New Rochelle, 1935; MA, Columbia U., 1941; PhD, U. Pa., 1962; LHD (hon.), Gwynedd-Mercy Coll., 1979, Cabrini Coll.,

1982; m. Raymond S. Green, June 20, 1942; children: Carol-Rae Green, Raymond Ferguson St. John. Tchr., Torrington High Sch., Conn., 1936-42; writer, researcher Fed. Writers Project, 1935-36; free-lance script writer Cavalcade of Am., NBC, 1940-42; assoc. prof. English, univ. registrar Tampa U., Tampa, 1942-43; spl. instr. English, Temple U., Phila., 1953-57; prof. dept. English, Cabrini Coll., Radnor, Pa., 1957-70, chmn. dept., 1957-70. Exec. dir. Am. Inst. Italian Studies; dir. lit. com. Phila. Art Alliance; bd. dirs., trustee Free Library of Phila.; v.p., dir. Nat. Italian-Am. Found.; chair Nat. Adv. Council Ethnic Heritage Studies; adv. bd. Women for Greater Phila.; dir. Balch Inst. Phila. Decorated cavalier Republic of Italy; named Woman of Yr. Pa. Sons of Italy, 1975, Disting. Dau. of Pa., 1978; recipient Nat. Amita award for lit., 1976, Nat. Bicentennial award for poetry DAR, 1976, other awards for contbns. to lit. and edn. Fellow Royal Soc. Arts (London); mem. Am. Acad. Polit. and Social Sci., Acad. Am. Poets, Acad. Polit. Sci., Am. Studies Assn., Ethnic Studies Assn., AAUW (dir.-at-large), Nat. Council Tchrs. English, Am.-Italy Soc. (dir. 1952—), Eastern Pa. Coll. New Rochelle Alumnae (pres. 1951-54), Kappa Gamma Pi. Club: Cosmopolitan (Phila.). Author: Cabrinian Philosophy of Education, 1967; (poetry) To Reason Why, 1971, Primo Vino, 1974, 76 for Philadelphia, 1975, Century Four, 1981, Songs of Ourselves, 1982; (criticism) The Italian-American Novel, 1974; (poems) Woman, The Second Coming, 1977; Lauding the American Dream, 1980; The Life of Mother Frances Cabrini, 1984; Songs of Ourselves, 1982; (poems) The Pennsylvania People, 1984, Challenger Countdown, 1988; editor faculty jour. A-Zimuth, 1963-70. Home: 308 Manor Rd Philadelphia PA 19128

GREEN, RUTHANN, publishing executive; b. Streator, Ill., July 14, 1935; d. John Joseph and Edna Marie (Peters) G. BS in Edn., U. Ill., 1957. Elem. tchr. Jefferson Sch., Davenport, Iowa, 1957-59; tchr. Hinsdale (Ill.) Jr. High Sch., 1959-62; ednl. cons. Harcourt Brace & World, Chgo., 1962-63; exec. sec. Everpure, Inc., Oakbrook, Ill., 1963-68; ednl. cons. Houghton Mifflin Co., Europe, 1968-69, Palo Alto, Calif., 1969-77; sr. mktg. mgr. Houghton Mifflin Co., Boston, 1977-87; v.p., nat. sales mgr. Riverside Pub. Co., Chgo., 1987-89; v.p., dir. mktg. McDougal, Littell & Co., Evanston, Ill., 1990—. Author: WSIL: Why Should I Listen, 1987. Recipient Svc. award Am. Arbitration Assn., 1987, Golden Reel of Excellence Internat. TV Assn., 1983. Mem. Am. Mktg. Assn., Internat. Reading Assn., U.S. Bd. on Books for Young People, People for Am. Way, Common Cause, Am. Arbitration Assn. Home: 1310 Ritchie Ct Apt 21A Chicago IL 60610-2179 Office: McDougal Littell & Co PO Box 1667 Evanston IL 60204

GREEN, SARA EDMOND, office products company executive; b. Chgo., Mar. 10, 1954; d. David and Mary (Winton) G. AB, Washington U., St. Louis, 1976. Rsch. asst. U. Ill. Sch. Pub. Health/Cook County Hosp., Chgo., 1976-79; adminstrv. asst. Quartet Mfg. Co., Lincolnwood, Ill., 1979-80, purchasing mgr., 1980-84, customer rels. mgr., 1982-84, v.p. ops., 1984-87; v.p. Quartet Ovonics, Lincolnwood, 1986-87; exec. v.p. Quartet Mfg. Co., Quartet Ovonics, Skokie, Ill., 1987—, also bd. dirs. Mem. Nat. Office Products Assn., Wholesale Stationers Assn. (mfrs. com. 1988-90), Young Execs. Forum. Office: Quartet Mfg Co 5700 Old Orchard Rd Skokie IL 60077

GREEN, SHIA TOBY RINER, therapist; b. N.Y.C., July 1, 1937; d. Murray A. and Frances Riner; student CCNY, 1954-57; B.A., Antioch Coll., 1974, M.A., 1976; m. Gary S. Green, Sept. 4, 1957; children—Margot Laura, Vanessa Daryl, Garson Todd. Press. and legis. sec. U.S. Ho. of Reps., Washington, 1960-71; cons. Rehab. Services Adminstrn., Social and Rehab. Services, HEW, 1972-73; asst. dir. State of Md. Foster Care Impact Dmonstration Project, 1977-78; therapist Alexandria (Va.) Narcotics Treatment Program, 1979-84, Assocs. Psychotherapy Ctrs, Giburg, Md.; mem. treatment com. Alexandria Case Mgmt. and Treatment of Child Sexual Abuse. Mem. exec. bd. Children's Adoption Resource Exchange, Washington; vol. worker Girl Scouts U.S.A., also Boy Scouts Am., 1970-74. Mem. Am. Psychol. Assn., Md. Psychol. Assn., Am. Assn. Marriage and Family Therapy. Co-author: Permanent Planning in Maryland—A Manual for the Foster Care Worker. Home: One Lake Potomac Ct Potomac MD 20854 Office: 8915 Shady Grove Ct Gaithersburg MD 20877

GREEN, SHIRLEY MOORE, presidential assistant; b. Graham, Tex., Dec. 21, 1933; d. N. Edgar and Cora Day (Morrow) Moore; m. Paul M. Green, Aug. 26, 1967 (div. 1981); children: Ruth Lynn, Tracy Moore. Student, Midwestern U., Wichita Falls, Tex., 1952; BBA, U. Tex., 1956. Staff asst. Rep. Party, Austin, Tex., 1965-67; press asst. Bob Price U.S. Rep., Washington, 1967; coordinator Tex. and Ark. Bush for Pres. Campaign, Houston, 1979-80; dep. press sec. V.p. Bush, Washington, 1980-85, acting press sec., 1983; dir. pub. affairs NASA, Washington, 1985-86, dep. assoc. adminstr. communications, 1987-89; spl. asst. to the Pres. White House, Washington, 1989—; adv. bd. Office Personnel Mgmt., Washington. Local chmn. Jim Baker for Atty. Gen., 1978, Pres. Ford Com., San Antonio, 1976; trustee S.W. Found. Forum, San Antonio, 1974-78; bd. dirs. Child Welfare Bd. Bexar County, 1975-79. Recipient Exceptional Svc. medal NASA, 1989. Mem. Women in Communications, NAFE, Am. Newswomen's Club, Tex. Fedn. Rep. Women (editor Partyline mag. 1969-72, one of 10 Outstanding Rep. Women Tex. 1979). Presbyterian. Home: 1642 32nd NW Washington DC 20007 Office: NASA 400 Maryland Ave SW Washington DC 20546

GREEN, SUSAN RUTH, lawyer; b. Balt., Nov. 13, 1957; d. Allen Israel and Esther Ruth (Millstone) G. BA, U. Miami, Coral Gables, Fla., 1979; JD, U. Balt., 1983. Self employed lawyer Balt., 1983--. Mem. Fla. Bar Assn., D.C. Bar Assn., Md. Bar Assn., Fed. Bar Assn., Med. Criminal Def. Attys. Assn., Balt. City Bar Assn. Office: 225 W Read St Baltimore MD 21201

GREEN, WANDA LORIO, nurse; b. New Orleans, Sept. 30, 1954; d. Elton Warren and Ida Mae (Smith) L.; m. Alton Michael Green, June 4, 1977; children: Nicole, Uchenna, Ashley. AS, La. State U., 1979; BS in Nursing, Dillard U., 1989. RN, La. Staff nurse Charity Hosp., New Orleans, 1979-80; nursing supr. St. Claude Gen. Hosp., New Orleans, 1980-82; unit supr. DePaul Hosp., New Orleans, 1981-82; dir. nursing Quality Care, New Orleans, 1981; head nurse Charity Hosp., New Orleans, 1982-83; unit patient mgr. New Orleans Gen. Hosp., 1984-86; charge nurse St. Charles Gen. Hosp., New Orleans, 1986-89; quality assurance coord. Charity Hosp., New Orleans, 1989—; cons. and instr. in field. Pres. Ladies Unltd. Civic, New Orleans, 1981-86; nurse vol. Health Fair, New Orleans, 1983-85; parent vol. PTA. Mem. Nat. Black Nurses Assn., Nat. League for Nurses, Nat. C. of C. for Women, Santa Filomena Nursing Assn., New Orleans Assn. Quality Assurance Professions, La. Pub. Health Assn., Gamma Phi Delta (first Anti-Basileus 1989, v.p. 1989). Democrat. Baptist. Home: 4401 Werner Dr New Orleans LA 70126 Office: 3700 St Charles Ave New Orleans LA 70115

GREENAWALT, PEGGY TOMARKIN, advertising executive; b. Cleve., Apr. 27, 1942; d. Bernard H. and Gyta Elinor (Arsham) Freed; m. Gary Tomarkin, Aug. 7, 1966 (div. 1981); children: Craig William, Eric Lawrence; m. William Sloan Greenawalt, Oct. 31, 1987. BS, Simmons Coll., 1964. Asst. account exec. Howard Marks/Norman, Craig & Kummel, Inc., N.Y.C., 1964-66; account exec. Shaw Bros. Advt. Co., N.Y.C., 1966-67; copywriter Claire Advt. Co., N.Y.C., 1967; ptnr. Copywriters Coop., Hartsdale, N.Y., 1970-73; copy chief Howard Marks Advt., N.Y.C., 1973-80; sr. copywriter Wunderman, Ricotta & Kline, N.Y.C., 1980-82; v.p., assoc. creative dir. Ayer-Direct (N.W. Ayer), N.Y.C., 1982-84; sr. v.p., creative dir. D'Arcy Direct (D'Arcy, MacManus & Masius), N.Y.C., 1984-86; creative and mktg. cons., 1986-87; pres. Tomarkin/Greenawalt, Inc.; judge Clio Awards. Author: Kiss, The Real Story, 1980. Mem. Direct Mktg. Creative Guild, Direct Mktg. Assn., Direct Mktg. Club N.Y., Westchester Assn. Women Bus. Owners (bd. dirs.). Office: 45 E 30th St New York NY 10016

GREENAWALT, RUTH MARJORIE, librarian; b. Dunkirk, N.Y., Nov. 6, 1942; d. Vincent Prescott and Marjorie Mary (Kuhrt) Aldrich; m. Dale Elwood Greenawalt, July 27, 1976; children: Daniel Vincent, Trenton David. BS, SUNY, 1964; MLS, Syracuse U., 1965. Periodicals librarian SUNY, Fredonia, 1965-68; librarian James Madison U., Harrisonburg, Va., 1968-82; dir. library Bridgewater (Va.) Coll., 1984—. Contbr. articles to profl. jours. Mem. Va. Library Assn. Republican. Methodist. Home: RR 8 Box 101 Harrisonburg VA 22801 Office: Alexander Mack Meml Library Bridgewater Coll E College St Bridgewater VA 22812

GREENBAUM, CAROL ANN, librarian; b. N.Y.C., June 2, 1947; d. Charles P. and Agnes M. (Wise) Byrne; m. Peter A. Greenbaum, Feb. 10, 1968; children: Peter A., James B. AAS, Suffolk County Community Coll., 1983; BA, SUNY, Stony Brook, 1984; MLS, CW Post U., 1989. Cert. tchr., libr. Legal sec. James J. Frayne, Selden, N.Y., 1981-88; libr. Islip (N.Y.) Pub. Libr., 1987-89, Deer Park (N.Y.) Pub. Libr., 1989—; libr./tchr. Deer Park Schs., 1989—; liaison mem. Bd. Coop. Edn. Svcs. Libr., Lindenhurst, N.Y., 1989—. Co-author: Secondary School Library Media Curriculum, 1990; contbr. articles to libr. jours. Active WK Vanderbilt Hist. Soc., Oakdale, N.Y., 1979—, Dowling Coll. Restoration Com., Oakdale, 1986—, libr. div. Bd. Coop. Edn. Svcs., Lindenhurst, 1989—; high sch. coord./chairperson Human Understanding and Growth Seminar. Mem. L.I. Sch. Media Assocs., Inc., Sch. Libr. Media Specialists, Inc., Suffolk County Libr. Assn., Phi Theta Kappa, Alpha Beta Gamma. Democrat. Home: 171 Irish Lane Islip Terrace NY 11752 Office: Deer Park High Sch. 30 Rockaway Ave Deer Park NY 11729

GREENBERG, ARLINE FRANCINE, fabric designer firm executive; b. N.Y.C.; m. Sidney Greenberg. BA, Hunter Coll.; postgrad., NYU; AS, Parson Sch. Design, Pratt Inst. Ind. practice cons. firm in jewelry and design; v.p. Reliable Textile Co., N.Y.C.; dir. syling and creative svcs. Klopman Fabrics, N.Y.C., 1988—; guest lectr. AWED and F.I.T. Contbr. fashion articles to newspapers. Recipient Medal in Fine Arts; scholar NYU. Mem. Fashion Group, AATT, AWARE, Fashion News Workship, The Info. Exch.. Home: 555 Kappock St 15D Riverdale NY 10463

GREENBERG, BLU, author; b. Seattle, Jan. 21, 1936; d. Sam and Sylvia (Genser) Genquer; m. Irving Greenberg; children: Jeremy, David, Deborah, Jonathan, Judith. BA, Bklyn. Coll., 1957; BA in Religious Edn., Yeshiva U., 1958; MA in Clin. Psychol., City U., N.Y.C., 1967; MS in Jewish History, Yeshiva U., 1977. Instr. Dept. Religious Studies Coll. Mt. St. Vincent, N.Y.C., 1970-77; lectr. Pardes Inst., Jerusalem, 1974-75; guest lectr. Harvard U., Princeton U., Dartmouth U., U. Ind., and various other colls. Author: How to Run a Traditional Jewish Household, 1983, On Women and Judaism: A View from Tradition, 1982; (poetry) A Special Kind of Mother, 1990; mem. editorial bd. Lilith mag., Shofar, 1990—; contbr. articles to religious jours. Mem. exec. bd. Coalition for Soviet Jews, 1987—; trustees Jewish Found. for Christian Rescurers, 1990—; mem. steering com. Women of Faith in 80's, 1980—. Named Woman Yr. United Jewish Appeal-Bronx Div., 1984, Woman Valor Riverdale Jewish Ctr. 1971; recipient Myrtle Wreath Lit. award Hadassah 1976, Lit. award B'nai Brith women 1981, Svc. award Am. Jewish Com., 1990, Women of Achievement memoirist, 1990, Riverdale Jewish Community Coun. Svc. award, 1988. Mem. Sh'ma (mem.editorial bd. 1979—), Jewish Publ. Soc. (mem. editorial bd. 1985—), Hadassah Mag. (mem. editorial bd. 1984—), Jewish Women's Resource Ctr. (mem. adv. bd. 1982—), Jewish Book Council Am. (pres. 1983-86), Fedn. Commn. Synagogue Rels. (chmn. exec. bd. 1982-86), U.S.-Israel Women to Women (co-founder, mem. exec. bd. 1978—), Women Faith Eighties (mem. steering com. 1980—), Zionist Acad. Coun., B'nai B'rith Commn. Adult Edn. (mem. exec. bd.). Home and Office: 4620 Independence Ave Bronx NY 10471

GREENBERG, ELINOR MILLER, college administrator; b. Bklyn., Nov. 13, 1932; d. Ray and Susan (Weiss) Miller; m. Manuel Greenberg, Dec. 26, 1955; children: Andrea, Julie, Michael. BA, Mt. Holyoke Coll., 1953; MA, U. Wis.-Madison, 1954; EdD, U. No. Colo., 1981; LittD (hon.), St. Mary-of-the-Woods, Ind., 1983; LHD (hon.), Profl. Sch. Psychology, Calif., 1987. Exec. dir. Arapahoe Inst. for Community Devel., Littleton, Colo., 1969-71; founding dir. Univ. without Walls, Loretto Heights Coll., Denver, 1971-79, asst. acad. dean, 1982-84, asst. to pres., 1984-85; regional exec. officer Coun. for Adult and Experiential Learning, Chgo., 1979—; exec. dir. US West Communications CWA, Pathways to the Future, 1986—; cons. in field. Co-editor, contbr.: Educating Learners of All Ages, 1980; co-author: Designing Undergraduate Education, 1981, Widening Ripples, 1986, Leading Effectively, 1987; editor, contbr.: New Partnerships: Higher Education and the Nonprofit Sector, 1982; contbr. articles to profl. jours. Bd. dirs., exec. com. Anti Defamation League of B'nai B'rith, Denver, 1981—; vice chair Colo. State Bd. for Community Colls. and Occupational Edn., 1986-89; bd. dirs. Internat. Women's Forum, Griffith Ctr., Golden, Colo., 1982-86, Colo. Bd. Continuing Legal and Jud. Edn., 1984—; pres. Women's Forum of Colo., 1986; v.p. Women's Forum Colo. Found., 1987; mem. adv. bd. Anchor Ctr. Blind Child, Colo. Coalition Prevention Nuclear War; mem. Nat. Conf. on Edn. for Women's Devel., Community Adv. Bd. Colo. Woman News; co-chair Gov.'s Women's Econ. Devel. Taskforce, Women's Econ. Devel. Coun., 1988—; mem. bd. visitors U. Hosp., U. Colo., 1990—. Named Citizen of Yr., Omega Psi Phi, Denver, 1966, Woman of Decade Littleton Ind. Newspapers, 1970; grantee W. K. Kellogg Found., 1982, Weyerhaeuser Found., 1986, Fund for Improvement of Post Secondary Edn., 1977, 80; recipient Sesquicentennial award Mt. Holyoke Coll. Alumni Assn., 1987. Mem. Am. Assn. for Higher Edn., Assn. for Experiential Edn. (editorial bd. 1978-80), ACLU, Am. Coun. in Edn., Kappa Delta Pi. Democrat. Jewish. Home: 6725 S Adams Way Littleton CO 80122

GREENBERG, JUDITH HOROVITZ, genetics program director; b. Phila., Apr. 2, 1947; d. Monty B. and Evelyn (Cohen) Horovitz; m. Warren Greenberg, June 8, 1969; 1 child, Elyssa H. BS in Biology, U. Pitts., 1967; MA in Biology, Boston U., 1970; PhD in Biology, Bryn Mawr Coll., 1972. Rsch. assoc. ARC, Bethesda, Md., 1971-74; postdoctoral fellow NIH, Bethesda, 1974-75, sr. staff fellow, 1975-81, health scientist adminstr., 1981-88; dir. genetics program br. NIH, Nat. Inst. Gen. Med. Scis., Bethesda, 1988—. Mem. Soc. Devel. Biology, Am. Soc. Cell Biology, Am. Soc. Human Genetics, AAAS, Sigma Xi. Office: NIH 5333 Westbard Ave Westwood Bldg Rm 910 Bethesda MD 20892

GREENBERG, PEARL KATZ, college educator; b. N.Y.C., Jan. 29, 1927; d. Abe and Lucille (Berlin) Katz; m. Murray Greenberg, Sept. 12, 1947; 1 child, Kenneth. BS, NYU, 1958, MA, 1960; EdD, Columbia U., 1971; BFA, Cooper Union, 1981. Art educator Downtown Community Sch., N.Y.C., 1951-65, Kean Coll. of N.J., Union, 1965—; cons. in aging and art Bayonne (N.J.) Sr. Ctr., 1989. Author: Children's Experiences in Art: Drawing and Painting, 1966, Art and Ideas for Young People, 1970, Lifelong Learning and the Visual Arts: Developing Quality Programs, 1980, Vis. Arts and Older People, 1987. Founding mem., bd. dirs. U. Coun. for Art Edn., N.Y.C., 1965—; alumni bd. Cooper Union, N.Y.C., 1987—. Recipient Art Educator of N.J. Govs. award, 1985; spl. citation N.Y. Art Tchrs. Assn., 1987. Mem. Nat. Art Edn. Assn. (v.p. 1978-80, head high edn. eastern div. 1974-76, 84-87, chair, profl. materials com. 1980-83, Art Educator of Yr, 1984), Nat. Coun. on Aging. Home: 212 E Broadway New York NY 10002 Office: Kean College of NJ Morris Ave Union NJ 07083

GREENBERGER, BETTE JO, art teacher; b. Irwin, Penn., Apr. 28, 1937; d. William and Rose (Reisberg) Bergad; m. Howard Leroy Greenberger. BS, Chatham Coll., 1959; postgrad., Carnegie Mellon U., 1959-61; MS, Queens Coll., 1964. Cert. art tchr., N.Y. Elem. tchr. Pitts. Pub. Sch., 1959-61, Lawrence Pub. Sch., Woodmere, N.Y., 1961—; instr. N.Y. State Tchrs. Assn., 1983-89; critic for tchr. tng. program C.W. Post Coll., Molloy Coll., Adelphi U., Dowling Coll., N.Y. Inst. Tech., 1977-89. Recipient Gt. Tchr. award Lawrence Pub. Schs. PTA, 1974, Jenkins Meml. award N.Y. State PTA, 1976; Henry Clay Frick scholar, 1960. Mem. N.Y. State Art Tchrs. Assn., L.I. Art Tchrs. Assn., Early Am. Ind. Assn. Jewish. Home: 4 Washington Sq Village New York NY 10012 Office: Lawrence Pub Sch # 6 Sch Church Ave Woodmere NY 11598

GREENBERGER, MARSHA MOSES, industrial executive; b. Lakewood, N.J., Mar. 15, 1943; d. Bernard David and Ethel (Gordon) Moses; m. Paul Edward Greenberger (div. 1969); 1 child, Nathan Scott. Student, Kent (Ohio) State U., 1961-62. Mgr. gen. sales Ellison Products, Fairfield, N.J., 1972-79; gen. mgr. Indsl. Maintenance Corp., Cherry Hill, N.J., 1979-83; co-owner corp. sect. Ven-Mar Sales, Inc., Blairstown, N.J., 1983-89; pres. MGM Sales, 1989—. Mem. NE Fastner Assn. Office: MGM Sales 7 Comfort Ct Randolph NJ 07869

GREENBLATT, DEANA CHARLENE, teacher; b. Chgo., Mar. 13, 1948; d. Walter and Betty (Lamasky) Beisel; BEd., Chgo. State U., 1969; MA in Guidance and Counseling, Roosevelt U., 1973; m. Mark Greenblatt, June 22, 1975. Tchr., counselor Chgo. Pub. Schs., 1969-75, City Colls. of Chgo. GED-TV, 1976; tchr. Columbus (Ohio) Pub. Schs., 1976-86; participant learning exchange, Chgo. Active B'nai B'rith; vol. Right-to-Read, Columbus; mem. Community Learning Exchange, Acad. Yr. in U.S.A. Com. Counselor, 1989—. Columbus. Cert. tchr. K-9, Ill., Ohio; cert. personnel guidance, Ill., Ohio; cert. Chgo. Bd. Edn. Mem. Am. Personnel and Guidance Assn., Internat. Platform Assn., B'nai B'rith Women Club (chpt. v.p.). Democrat. Home: 4083 Vineshire Dr Columbus OH 43227

GREENBLATT, MIRIAM, author, editor, educator; b. Berlin; d. Gregory and Shifra (Zemach) Baraks; B.A. magna cum laude, Hunter Coll.; postgrad. U. Chgo., Spertus Coll.; m. Herbert Halbrecht (div. 1960); m. 2d, Howard Greenblatt, 1962 (div. 1978). Tchr., New Trier (Ill.) High Sch., 1978-81; editor Am. People's Ency., Chgo., 1957-58; editor Scott, Foresman & Co., Chgo., 1958-62; pres. Creative Textbooks, Evanston, Ill., 1972—. V.p. Chgo. Chpt. Am. Jewish Com., 1977-79, mem. nat. exec. council, 1980-84; treas. Glencoe Youth Services, 1981-83. Mem. Nat. Council Social Studies, Ill. Council Social Studies, Am. Hist. Assn., Chgo. Women in Publishing, Women in Mgmt. Jewish. Author: (with Chu) The Story of China, 1968, (with Cuban) Japan, 1971; The History of Itasca, 1976, (with others) The American People, 1986; James Knox Polk, 1988, Franklin Delano Roosevelt, 1989, (with Lemmo) Human Heritage, 1989, (with Jordan and Bowes) The Americans, 1989; John Quincy Adams, 1990; edit. cons. Peoples and Cultures Series, 1976-78; contbg. editor A World History, 1979. Address: 550 Sheridan Sq Evanston IL 60202

GREENE, ADELE S., management consultant; b. Newark; d. Adolph and Sara (Schubert) Shuminer; m. Alan Greene (div.); 1 child, Joshua. Student, Juilliard Sch. Music, 1942-44, NYU, 1942-44, New Sch. Social Research, 1944-47; diploma in mgmt., Harvard Bus. Sch., 1978. Account exec. Ruder and Finn Inc., N.Y.C., 1964-66, sr. assoc., 1966-68, v.p., 1968-72, sr. v.p., 1972-76; v.p. pub. affairs Corp. Pub. Broadcasting, Washington, 1976-78; pres., chief operating officer TV Program Group, Washington, 1978-80; pres. Greene and Assocs., N.Y.C., 1981—; instr. pub. relations and community affairs, NYU 1974-76; bd. dirs. Sci. Program Group, Washington 1976-81; treas., bd. dirs. Coliseum Park Apts. Co-author: Teen-Age Leadership, 1971. Advisor The Acting Co., Understudies, N.Y.C. 1987—; pres., chief operating officer Am. Craft Council 1980-81, trustee 1976-81; bd. dirs. Union Settlement, N.Y.C. 1987—; trustee Duke Ellington Sch. Arts, Washington, 1977-81. Mem. Pub. Relations Soc. Am. (silver anvil award 1971), Nat. Assn. Edn. Broadcasters, Am. Women Radio and TV. Home and Office: 30 W 60th St New York NY 10023 also: 31 Pond Dr W Rhinebeck NY 12572

GREENE, BARBARA ANN MARY, Canadian Parliament member; b. Pembroke, Ont., Can., Sept. 1, 1945; d. Aldred and Mary (Hutchinson) G.; 1 child, Caroline. BA in English, U. Toronto, Ont., 1966, postgrad., 1966-67, 86-87; MPA, Harvard U., 1981. Secondary tchr. English, media studies, dramatic arts North York (Ont.) Bd. Edn., Willowdale, Ont., 1967-72, 81-82, 1986-88. Elected contr. City of North York, 1972-80, 82-85; mem. Met. Toronto Coun., 1972-80, 82-85, exec. mem., budget subcom. mem., 1974-80, 82-85; dep. mayor North York, 1974-80; mem. Parliament Ottawa, Ont., 1988—. Office: House of Commons, Parliament Bldgs, Ottawa, ON Canada K1A 0A6

GREENE, BETSY KATHERINE, lawyer; b. Indpls., July 20, 1957; d. Harvey Allen and Beth (Vanvorst) G. BA, Ind. U., 1979, JD, 1982. Bar: Ind. 1982, U.S. Dist. Ct. (so. dist.) Ind. 1982, U.S. Ct. Appeals (7th cir.) Ind. 1989, U.S. Supreme Ct. 1989. Dep. prosecutor Morgan County Prosecutor's Office, Martinsville, Ind., 1983-85, chief dep. prosecutor, 1985-88; assoc. Nunn & Kelley Law Office, P.C., Bloomington, Ind., 1988—; adj. lectr. Ind. U. Sch. Law, Bloomington, 1982—; mem. Morgan County Child Protection Team, Martinsville, 1984-88. Campaign coord. Hoosiers for John Mutz, Morgan County, 1988. Mem. Ind. Trial Lawyers, Monroe County Bar Assn., Seventh Cir. Ct. Appeals Bar Assn. Office: Nunn & Kelley Law Office PC 123 S College Ave Bloomington IN 47403

GREENE, BEVERLY ANN, clinical psychologist; b. Orange, N.J., Aug. 14, 1950; d. Samuel and Thelma G. BA, NYU, 1973; postgrad. Marquette U., 1973-74; MA, Adelphi U., 1977, PhD, 1983. Lic. psychologist, N.Y., N.J. Fellow in psychology Mental Retardation Inst., N.Y. Med. Coll., Valhalla, N.Y., 1974-76; psychol. cons. Williamsburg Child Devel. Ctr., Bklyn., 1976-78; psychology intern East Orange VA Med. Ctr., 1978-79; rsch. asst. dept. neurosci. N.J. Coll. Medicine and Dentistry, Vet.'s Hosp., 1979-80; psychology trainee, Children's Partial Hospitalization Unit, Brookdale Hosp. and Med. Ctr., 1980; cert. sch. psychologist N.Y.C. Bd. Edn., 1980-82, staff psychologist, 1982-84; sr. psychologist, dir. inpatient child and adolescent psychol. svcs. King's County Psychiat. Hosp., 1984-89; supervising psychologist, clin. asst. prof. psychiatry U. Medicine and Dentistry N.J., 1989—; clin. instr. in psychiatry Downstate Med. Sch., 1982-85, clin asst. prof., 1985-89, acting dir. Children's Inpatient Unit, 1985-86; supervising psychologist, clin. asst. prof. dept. of psychiatry Community Mental Health Ctr. U. of Medicine and Dentistry of N.J., Newark, 1989—. Contbr. articles to profl. jours.; co-author books. Martin Luther King scholar, 1968-72, NIMH fellow, 1976-77. Mem. Inst. for Human Identity (bd. dirs. 1989-91), Am. Psychol. Assn. (chmn. subcom. ethnic minor women's div.), Internat. Neuropsychol. Soc., Nat. Assn. Black Psychologists, N.Y. Assn. Black Psychologists, Nat. Assn. Women in Psychology, N.Y. Assn. Women in Psychology, N.Y. Coalition of Hosp. and Instnl. Psychologists, Inst. for Human Identity (bd. dirs.). Office: 26 St Johns Pl Brooklyn NY 11217

GREENE, CAROLYN B., insurance executive; b. Gaston County, N.C., Apr. 4, 1948; d. William T. II and Louise C. Byers; m. Daniel M. Greene, Apr. 8, 1966; children: Daniel M., Casey Danyel. Charter property ins. woman. V.p. Prime Lines Ins. Agy. Inc., Lake Wylie, 1983-85; Br. mgr., agt. Watson Ins. of the Carolinas, Lake Wylie, S.C., 1985—. Mem. Past Pres. Gaston/Cleve. Assn. Ins. Women, CAPIA (chmn. S.C. ins. edn. coms. 1989, mem. various coms.). Presbyterian. Home: 2727 S Highway 161 York SC 29745 Office: PO Box 5243 Lake Wylie SC 59710

GREENE, CATHERINE ANTOINETTE, lawyer, educator; b. San Diego, Dec. 1, 1958; d. Robert Edwin and Gwenolyn M. (Chick) Greene. AA, MiraCosta Community Coll., Oceanside, Calif., 1978; BA in Eng., U. of Calif., Santa Barbara, 1981; JD, U. of the Pacific, 1984. Atty. pvt. practice, Oceanside, Calif., 1985-86; atty. pvt. practice, Vista, Calif., 1986-88, Encinitas, Calif., 1988—; instr. Mira Costa Community Coll., 1989—; legal referral panel, Community Resource Ctr., Encinitas, Calif., Women's Resource Ctr., Oceanside. Recipient Medal of Hon. Letters, Miracosta Community Coll., Oceanside, 1978. Mem. North County Bar Assn., Lawyers Club of S.D. Office: PO Box 2325 Leucadia CA 92024

GREENE, DEBORAH LYN, legislative analyst; b. Chgo., June 6, 1955; d. Martin and Eileen (Goldwach) G. AB, U. Mich., 1977, MSW, 1978. Asst. project coordinator Community Correction Resource Prog., Ann Arbor, Mich., 1977-78; asst. on evaluation projects Lenewee County Human Svcs., Adrian, Mich., 1978; project dir. RSVP of Tompkins County, Ithaca, N.Y., 1979-81; asst. and interim exec. dir. Human Svcs. Coalition, Ithaca, 1981-83; budget analyst Tex. Dept. Human Svcs., Austin, Tex., 1983-85; research dir. Tex. Health & Human Svcs. CoordinatingCouncil, Austin, 1985; higher edn. analyst Gov. Office of Budget & Planning, Austin, 1985-87; sr. policy analyst Senate Edn. Com., Austin, 1987; research/planning dir. United Way/Capital Area, Austin, 1987-89; legis. analyst, edn. com. Tex. Senate, Austin, 1989—; cons. Tex. Higher Edn. Coordinating Bd., Austin, 1988. Bd. dirs. Interim Planning Bd. for Homeless, Austin, 1987-88; comm. mem. Austin/Travis County AIDS Commn., Austin, 1989—; mem. Higher Edn. Formula Adv. Com., Austin, 1987—. Am. Field Svc. scholar, 1972-73. Home: 4603 Greystone Dr Austin TX 78731

GREENE, ELAINE F., clinical psychologist; b. Jersey City, Jan. 4, 1940; d. Harry and Reva L. (Drelich) G. BA, Brandeis U., 1961; MS, Columbia U., 1966, PhD, 1970. Lic. psychologist, N.Y. Pvt. practice psychologist; tchr. Rochester (N.Y.) Mus. and Sci. Ctr. Columnist in various newsletters. Rch. grantee Genesee Valley Psychol. Assn.; recipient Outstanding Psychologist award. Mem. Genesee Valley Psychol. Assn. (pres. 1983-88), N.Y. State Psychol. Assn., Alternatives for Battered Women Inc. Office: 304 Troy Rd Rochester NY 14618

GREENE, ELINORE ASCHAH, speech and drama professional, writer; b. Springfield, Mass., Oct. 14, 1928; d. Harry Joshua and Esther Gertrude (Cohen) Ziff; m. Kermit Greene, June 29, 1947; children: Clifford M., Laura L., William L. B Lit. Interpretation, Emerson Coll., Boston, 1949. Dramatic interpreter Margaret E. Richardson Lect. Agy., Boston, 1950s; dramatic interpreter Flora Frame Lect. Bureau, Boston, 1960s; speech tchr. Academie Moderne, Boston, early 1970s, pvt. practice, Newton, MA, 1975-87; speech cons. pvt. practice, Newton, 1985-89; writer Newton, 1989—. Author: children's stories, AIM, Lolli Pops, Happiness, 1970-80; poetry, Creative Urge. Mem. Aid to Speech Therapy Found. (pres. 1970s; bd. dirs. 1960s); Advocate Rose Award 1975), Mass. Communication of Boston, Am. Fedn. Theatre-Radio-TV Assn., Nat. Writers Orgn. (sr. mem.).

GREENE, ELIZABETH IVORY, real estate activist; b. N.Y.C., Jan. 17, 1929; d. Percy Van Eman Ivory and Elizabeth (Schofield) Post Price; m. James Benno Greene Jr. (dec.); children: Elizabeth Tylawsky, James Benno III, Edgar Charles Ivory. BA, Bennington Coll., 1952. Sculptor Hansen Lamps, N.Y.C., 1952-57; real estate agent Ely-Cruikshank Co., N.Y.C., 1968-70; prin. Greene Realty Ltd., N.Y.C., 1970—, Apocalyptic Holdings Ltd., N.Y.C., 1972—. Rep. candidate N.Y. State Assembly, 1986, 88, 90, Libertarian candidate, 1986; leader Rep. dist., N.Y.C., 1987—; dir. Community Rep. Club Greenwich Village; trustee City and Country Sch., N.Y.C., 1985, 89—; auxiliary Police City of N.Y. Recipient scholarship Bennington (Vt.) Coll., 1949-52. Mem. Small Property Owners Action Network (founder, pres. 1983—), Nat. Ctr. Neighborhood Enterprise, Village Visiting Neighbors (bd. dirs. 1987-89), DAR (John Jay chpt.), Greenwich Village C. of C. (bd. dirs.), Assn. Village Homewoners, N.Y. Mycological Soc. Home and Office: Small Prop Owners Action 279 W 12th St New York NY 10014

GREENE, EMILY BOYKIN, respiratory therapist; b. Mobile, Ala., Feb. 10, 1954; d. James Willis and Viola Rebecca (Dennis) Boykin; divorced, Sept. 1988; children: Jason, Ashley. BS in Biology, U. Ala., 1977; diploma in RRT/CRTT, U. Chgo. Hosp. and Clinic, 1980. Registerd respiratory therapist; cert. repiratory therapist. ACLS technician S.W. Tech. Sch., Mobile, 1989; respiratory therapist, supr., 1981—; BCLS Providence Hosp., Mobile, 1990. Mem. Delta Sigma Theta.

GREENE, FREDA, journalist, writer; b. London, Mar. 29, 1929; came to U.S., 1952; d. Philip and Stella (Teper) H.; 1 child from previous marriage, Sheryl. Degree (hon.), Regent St. Poly., London, 1947. Owner Images Internat., L.A., 1978—; cons. pub. rels. Nat. Ctr. on Deafness, L.A., 1979-83. Author: How To Get A Job In Los Angeles, 1985 (Women's Referral Svc. award 1990); editor Changing Homes, 1987-88. Bd. dirs. Women's Referral Svc., 1989—. Fellow World Literacy Acad.; mem. PEN (cons. L.A. chpt. 1979), Am. Soc. Journalists and Authors (v.p. 1987-88, cons. L.A. chpt. 1982), Women in Mgmt. (v.p. program 1989-90), Women's Nat. Book Assn. Office: Images Internat 6624 Newcastle Ave Reseda CA 91335

GREENE, JACQUELINE HOLLY, registrar; b. N.Y.C., Oct. 18, 1960; d. Allan Alfred and Anne (Gomez) Greene. AA, Coll. of the Canyons, Valencia, Calif., 1987—. Registrar United Coll. Bus., Downey, Calif., 1987—; ind. security cons. Recipient Collegiate award U.S. Achievement Acad., Adminstrn. of Justice, 1987. Mem. NAFE, Am. Soc. Indsl. Security.

GREENE, JANELLE LANGLEY, banker; b. Tarboro, N.C., July 27, 1940; d. Romey Roscoe and Stella Louise (Keene) Langley. Student, East Carolina U., 1958-61; cert., Chowan Coll., 1961, U. Ga., 1973, Appalachian U., 1977; diploma, Inst. Fin. Edn. Savs. & Loan, 1976; cert. diploma, Grad. Sch. Savs. and Loan U., 1979. Sec., receptionist Home Savs. & Loan, Rocky Mount, N.C., 1962-67, supr. services, acctg. teller ops., 1967-74, asst. sec., 1969-74, dept. head savs. and mktg., 1974-86, v.p., corp. sec., 1974—; dept. head non-traditional products, v.p., sec. Pioneer Savs. Bank (name formerly Home Savs. & Loan), Rocky Mount, 1986-88; sr. v.p., mgr. Pioneer Capital Investments, Rocky Mount, 1988—; v.p. bank subsidiaries Pioneer Capital Corp., Rocky Mount, 1988—; asst., sec., dir. HSL Investors, Inc., Rocky Mount, 1972-86; chmn. N.C. Savs. and Loan Conf., 1977. Mem. Rocky Mt. Zoning Bd., 1977-81, YMCA, Rocky Mt., 1976-80; alumni bd. Chowan Coll., Mufreesboro, N.C., 1985—, pres. 1989-90; mem. adv. council N.E.W. Performing Arts; mem. exec. com. N.C. Wesleyan Coll. Recipient Bronze medallion Am. Heart Assn., 1976. Mem. N.C. League Savs. Insts. (outstanding service plaque 1977), Am. Bus. Women's Assn. (Women of Yr. pres. 1976-77), Rocky Mount C. of C. (ambassador 1976-77, 88-89, Red Coat 1975-76, 88—), Pilot Club Internat. (lt. gov. N.C. dist., gov. 1986-87, coord. projects div. 1989-90, dir. 1989—), Lucheon Pilot Club (pres. Rocky Mt. chpt. 1977-78, Pilot of Yr. 1979-80, Pres. award 1982-83, Svcs. Unltd. award 1979-80), Beta Sigma Phi (pres. 1964-65). Democrat. Baptist. Home: 3004 Wellington Dr Rocky Mount NC 27803 Office: Pioneer Savs Bank 612 Sunset Ave Rocky Mount NC 27804

GREENE, KAREN SANDRA, singer, actress, educator; b. N.Y.C., Jan. 7, 1942; d. Nathan and Natalie (Barashick) Stein; m. Richard Greene, July 1, 1962 (div. 1980); children: Barry Randall, Lauren Jennifer. BA, U. Conn., 1988. Singer, Broadway actress N.Y.C., 1960-62; pres., educator Karen Greene Studios, Norwalk, Conn., 1962—; pres., dir. voice On Stage Acad., Bridgeport (Conn.) Jewish Ctr., 1985, dir. Norwalk Jewish Ctr., 1985, dir. Wilton (Conn.) Children's Theater, 1989-90; educator music and drama St. Luke's Sch., New Canaan, Conn., 1989—. Voiceover artist nat. performing tours; dir., vocalist soc. band Shades of Greene. Coord. Southwestern Conn. Women's Issues Conf., 1988; active women's equal rights, pro-choice. Mem. AFTRA, Actor's Equity Assn., Screen Actors Guild, Internat. Platform Assn. Home and Office: 4 Suburban Dr Norwalk CT 06851

GREENE, LINDA KAY, educator; b. Elk City, Okla., Nov. 8, 1943; d. Granville E. and Edna (Nicholson) G. BA, U. N.Mex., 1966, MA in Teaching of English, 1970. Cert. tchr. Calif., N.Mex. English tchr., English dept. chair Albuquerque Pub. Schs.; English tchr. Orange (Calif.) Unified Sch. Dist., Muroc Unified Sch. Dist., Edwards Air Force Base, Calif. Contbr. poems to profl. jours. Named Tchr. of Yr. (twice) Harrison Jr. High Sch., 1970's, Most Improved Bowler WIBC, early 1970's; recipient 3rd and 6th place N.Mex. Poet Soc. Contests, early 1970's. Mem. NEA (chair, co-chair), Albuquerque Press Club. Home: 6107 Del Campo Pl NE Chimney Ridge Albuquerque NM 87109-2529 Office: Albuquerque High Sch 800 Odelia NE Albuquerque NM 87102-1699

GREENE, LYNNE JEANNETTE, fashion designer; b. Albany, N.Y., Aug. 27, 1938; d. Zebulon Stevens and Helen Matilde (Maier) Robbins; m. Stanley E. Greene, Jan. 31, 1962 (dec. June 27, 1987); 1 child, Stuart Nathaniel. Student, Goucher Coll., 1956-57; BA, Parsons Sch. Design, 1960. Asst. designer Haymaker Sportswear (David Crystal), N.Y.C., 1959-61; designer Craig Craely Sportswear and Dresses, N.Y.C., 1961-63, Flair Lingerie, N.Y.C., 1964-66; designer, owner Kaleidoscope Lingerie, N.Y.C., 1966-67; head designer Contessa/Monique/Fisher Lingerie, N.Y.C., 1967-71; head designer, owner Lynne Greene Designs Retail, Montclair, N.J., 1972-74; designer, pres. Little Greene Apples Inc., Montville, N.J., 1971—; designer, dir. mktg. Lady Lynne Lingerie, Guy Laroche Lingerie, N.Y.C., 1973—; lingerie critic Pratt Inst., 1984—. Patentee in field; illustrator books and pamphlets in fashion field. Active participant Montville Soccer Assn, 1972-88, fund drives for Am. Heart Assn., Cancer Inc. Mem. The Fashion Group. Republican. Episcopalian.

GREENE, MARVA ROSALEE, counselor, educator; b. Salisbury, Md., Feb. 8, 1951; d. Fulton James and Lena May (Wilson) Williams; m. Lawrence Eugene Greene, Oct. 16, 1951 (div. Nov. 1976); m. Barry Purnell (div. June 1976); children: Purnell, Chandra L. Student, Towson State U., 1969-70; BA in Sociology, Salisbury State U., 1979, MEd Counseling-Guidance, 1982. Cert. mktg. cons. Lab. asst. Johns Hopkins U., Balt., 1971-72; coord. br. office Legg Mason Securities, Inc., Balt., 1972-74; supr. mut. funds Legg, Mason, Inc. div. 1st Regional Securities, Inc., Balt., 1974-76; receptionist Sta. WBOC-AM-TV, Salisbury, 1977-81, acct., 1982-83; coord. vol. activities Juvenile Svcs. Agy., Salisbury, 1983-86, sr. juvenile counselor, 1983—; adj. prof. U. Md. Eastern Shore, Princess Anne, 1987—, Wor-Wic Tech. Community Coll., Salisbury, 1989—; cons. Save the Youth, Salisbury, 1986—. Mem. Md. Commn. on Women, 1987, Foster Care Rev. Bd., 1987, Foster Grandparent Adv. Bd., 1987, Greater Salisbury Com., 1988-89; bd. dir. Lakeview Housing Authority, Mental Health Assn. Minority Affairs Scholarship Com. Worric Tech. Community Coll. Recipient svc. award Save the Youth, 1987-88. Mem. Am. Sociol. Assn., Am. Correctional Assn., Am. Probation and Parole Assn. (cert.), Nat. Coun. of Negro Women, Mid-Atlantic States Correctional Assn., Links, Alpha Kappa Alpha (grad. advisor 1987—, Grad. Advisor of Yr. award North Atlantic region 1989), Omicron Delta Kappa. Democrat. Baptist. Home: 630 Terrapin Ln Salisbury MD 21801 Office: Dept of Juvenile Svcs PO Box 625 Salisbury MD 21801

GREENE, MILDRED SARAH, education educator; b. Springfield, Mass., May 5, 1929; d. Meyer Kotchen and Kittie (Atkins) Epstein; m. Warren J. Greene, July 10, 1951 (dec. 1954); 1 child, Stephen A. BA, Wellesley Coll., 1951; MA, Harvard Radcliffe U., Cambridge, Mass., 1956, U. Mass., 1961; PhD, U. New Mex., 1965. Teaching fellow U. Mass., Amherst, 1957-59; teaching fellow U. New Mex., Albuquerque, 1960-61, instr., 1964-65; asst. prof. Ariz. State U., Tempe, 1966-76, assoc. prof., 1976-90, prof. emeritus, 1990—. Mem. MLA, Am. Soc. for 18th Century Studies, Rocky Mountain Modern Language, South Cen. 18th Century Studies, Phi Kappa Phi (pres. 1975-76), Harvard Club, Wellesley in Phoenix. Home: 7657 E Minnezona Scottsdale AZ 85251 Office: Ariz State U Dept Eng Tempe AZ 85287

GREENE, NANCY ELLEN, infosystems specialist, physicist; b. Worcester, Mass., Nov. 4, 1947; d. William Arthur II and Dorothy Goddard (Fuller) Green; m. Arthur Edward Greene, Sept. 12, 1970; 1 child, Ellen Dorothy. BS in Physics, Ohio State U., 1969, MS in Physics, 1971. Instr. physics U. Colo., Colorado Springs, 1971-73; physics programmer U. N.Mex., Albuquerque, 1973-76; data analyst Controlled Thermonuclear Reaction div. Los Alamos (N.Mex.) Sci. Lab., 1975-77, programmer, 1977-78, mem. staff, 1978-81; mem. staff Accelerator Tech. div. Los Alamos Sci. Lab., 1981-84, Adminstrv. Data Processing div. Los Alamos Sci. Lab., 1984-85; mem. staff Dynamic Testing div. Los Alamos Sci. Lab., 1985—, staff mem. supr., 1989—. Spkr. in field. Vol. Los Alamos Schs., 1980-88, Found. Valley Sch., Colo., 1990—. Nat. Merit scholar, Mich. State U., 1965, Nat. Defense Edn. Act Title IV fellow, Ohio State U., 1969. Mem. N.Mex. Digital Equipment Computer Users Soc. (exec. com. 1984-87, 88-90, registration chair computer conf. 1984-87, vice-chair 1988-89, publicity 1989-90), VAX Computer Local Users Group (chmn. 1981-82, sec. 1989—). Office: Los Alamos Nat Lab PO Box 1663 MS P940 Los Alamos NM 87545

GREENE, SARAH CAREY, real estate company executive and broker; b. Lansing, Mich., Dec. 6, 1941; d. Richard William and Clarice Helen (Gillison) Bigelow; m. Jerry Phillip Green, Feb. 25, 1984; children: Jerrol D. Carey Jr., Laura Joy Carey. Student, Lansing Community Coll.; Mich. State U.; postgrad., Fla. Keys Community Coll. Cert. CRB designee, instr. Success Series. Pres. Suncoast Unlimited, Inc., Big Pine Key, Fla.; broker-salesman Miley Real Estate, Big Pine Key; with acctg./revenue control Dept. Mgmt. and Budget, State of Mich., Lansing; bookkeeper fin. dept. City of Homestead (Fla.). Past dir. Real Estate Action Coun. Monroe County; bd. dirs., sec. Marathon and Lower Keys Bd. Realtors; pres. Women's Coun. Realtors, 1989. Recipient numerous honors. Mem. Lower Keys C. of C. (pres. 1987, 88), Rotary (bd. dirs. and sargeant-at-arms Big Pine and Lower Keys). Republican. Home: Rte 1 Box 600 Big Pine Key FL 33043 Office: PO Drawer 383 Big Pine Key FL 33043

GREENE, SARAH LOUISE, publisher; b. Lincoln, Nebr., July 24, 1952; d. William Henry and Helen (Kiesselbach) Greene; m. William Gordon Tucker, July 7, 1979; children: Kevan Theodore, Frederick Thomas, Karl Dylan. BS, No. Ariz. U., 1974; MS, Cornell U., 1980. Lab. technician City of Omaha, 1974-76; plant protection officer U.S. Dept. Agr., Westhampton Beach, N.Y., 1976-78; editorial asst. Plenum Pub. Co., N.Y.C., 1980-81; sr. editor Macmillan Pub. Co., N.Y.C., 1981-86; pres. Greene Pub. Asocs., Bklyn., 1986—; pub. Current Protocols Greene Pub. Asocs., 1986—. Editor: Introduction to Bryology, 1985, Current Protocols in Molecular biology, 1987-90, Current Protocols in Immunology, 1990. Mem. Am. Soc. for Microbiology. Office: Current Protocols 430 4th St Brooklyn NY 11215

GREENE, SHARON LOUISE, managing editor; b. Washington, Sept. 8, 1960; d. Gary Edward and Lorna Sybil (Herzog) G; m. Jeffrey D. Lally. Student U. Colo., 1980-82. Office mgr. Irving Kerner Literary Agy., Boulder, 1979-81; mgr. Alpha Micro Users Soc., Boulder, 1979-88 , editor, 1983—, meeting planner, 1984—, sec.-treas., 1983-86; exec. dir. Alpha Micro Users Soc., 1988—; cons. Club Mac, Boulder, 1984-85. Mem. NAFE. Am. Soc. Assn. Execs., Meeting Planners Internat. Democrat. Jewish. Avocations: fishing; camping; hiking; reading; sports. Office: Alpha Micro Users Soc 735 Walnut St Boulder CO 80302

GREENE, STEPHANIE HARRISON, marketing executive; b. Lake Forest, Ill., June 20, 1950; d. Howard Harrison and Gloria Juliet (Christensen) Greene. BA in Journalism and Advt., Syracuse U., 1972; MBA in Mktg., Cornell U., 1975. With Weeden & Co., Boston, 1972-73; product rep. Allis Chalmers, Matteson, Ill., 1975-76; asst. product mgr. Midwest Am./Am. Hosp. Supply, Des Plaines, Ill., 1976-77; product mgr. Borden, Inc., Columbus, Ohio, 1977-80; product line mgr. John Sexton & Co./Beatrice, Chgo., 1980-82; product mgr. non-foods PYA/Monarch/Sara Lee, Greenville, S.C., 1982-84; mktg. mgr. Fuller Brush/Sara Lee, Winston-Salem, 1984-89; pres. Corbett Harrison Greene, Mundelein, Ill., 1984—; mktg. mgr. The Greehill Corp., Libertyville, Ill., 1989—; bd. dirs. Career Pub., Mundelein. Editor: The Quotation Dictionary, 1968. Mem. Print Prodn. Club, Cornell U. Alumnae Assn. (pres. Class of '75), Pi Beta Phi. Republican. Episcopalian. Clubs: Holly Tree Garden (treas. 1983-84), Seredipity Garden (treas. 1978-79). Home: 408 Hampton Terr Libertyville IL 60048 Office: The Greehill Corp 15521 W Rockland Rd Libertyville IL 60048

GREENE, VIRGINIA CARVEL, chemist; b. Warrenton, Va., Jan. 8, 1934; d. Brooke Bartlett and Virginia Carvel (Hall) Chamblin; m. Edward Epes Winfield Bass, July 11, 1964 (div. 1972); m. Arthur Calhoun Greene, Nov. 20, 1977. AB, Sweet Briar Coll., 1955; MS, Tulane U., 1957; PhD, U. Va., 1963. Instr. Newcomb Coll., New Orleans, 1957-59; lab. dir. U. Va. Hosp., Charlottesville, 1965-67; assoc. prof. Longwood Coll., Farmville, Va., 1967-69; rsch. chemist FBI, Washington, 1969-77; instr., rsch. assoc. U. Va., Charlottesville, 1977-78; chemist Fgn. Sci. and Tech. Ctr., Charlottesville, 1979—. Contbr. articles to profl. jours. Sec. U. Va. Chemists Assn., Charlottesville, 1985-89; judge Piedmont Sci. Fair, Charlottesville, 1987-90; mem., bd. dirs. Family Svcs., Charlottesville, 1978-85, Charlottesville-Albemarle Symphony Orch., Charlottesville, 1979-83; vestry mem. St. Paul's Ch., Charlottesville, 1978-81, 84-86. Mem. Am. Chem. Soc., Va. Acad. Sci., Phi Beta Kappa. Democrat. Episcopalian. Home: 540 E Rio Rd Charlottesville VA 22901

GREENE, WENDY SEGAL, special education educator; b. New Rochelle, N.Y., Jan. 9, 1929; d. Louis Peter and Anne Henrietta (Kahan) Segal; m. Richard M. Greene Jr. (div. Mar. 1967); children: Christopher S., Kerry William, Karen Beth Greene Olson; m. Richard M. Greene Sr., Aug. 29, 1985 (dec. 1986). Student, Olivet Coll., 1946-48, Santa Monica Coll., 1967-70; BA in Child Devel., Calif. State U., Los Angeles, 1973, MA in Elem. Edn., 1975. Cert. tchr., Calif. Counselor Camp Watitoh, Becket, Mass., 1946-49; asst. tchr. Outdoor Play Group, New Rochelle, 1946-58; edn. sec. pediatrics Syracuse (N.Y.) Meml. Hosp., 1952-53; with St. John's Hosp., Santa Monica, Calif., 1962-63; head tchr. Head Start, L.A., 1966-77; tchr. spl. edn. L.A. Unified Sch. Dist., 1977—, Salvin Spl. Edn. Ctr., L.A., 1977-85, Perez Spl. Edn. Ctr., L.A., 1986-; rsch. instr. for motivational rsch. Anderson-Mconnell Agy., 1966. Contbr. to house organ of St. John's Hosp.; co-editor of newspaper for Salvin Sch., L.A. and The Eagle, Perez Sch., L.A., 1988—. Bd. dirs. Richland Ave. Youth House, L.A., 1960-63, Emotional Health Assn., L.A., 1961-66, Richland Ave. Sch. PTA, 1959-63; vol. Hospice of St. Joseph Hosp., Orange, Calif., 1985—. Mem. AAUW, So. Calif. Assn. Young Children, Olivet Coll. Alumni Assn. United Tchrs. Los Angeles, Kappa Delta Pi. Jewish. Club: Westside Singers (Los Angeles). Home: 14291 Prospect Ave Tustin CA 92680

GREENE-CURTIS, SALLY JANE, manufacturing company executive; b. Bedford, Ohio, June 25, 1953; d. Herman Joseph and Eileen Maude (Fenton) Greene; m. Howard Detroy Curtis Jr., Sept. 27, 1986; children: Marisa Anne, Emily Kathleen. BE, Ohio State U., 1975. Salesperson Scott and Assocs., Columbus, Ohio, 1975-77, Columbus Coated Fabrics, Columbus and Atlanta, 1977-81; mgr. product Columbus Coated Fabrics, Columbus, 1981-85; ptnr., pres. Chromagraphics Corp., Dallas, 1985—. Mem. Screenprinters Assoc. Internat. Office: Chromagraphics Corp 260 Bank St Southlake TX 76092

GREENEY, LAURA ANNE, editor, English educator; b. Bklyn., July 18, 1961; d. John H. and Florence E. (Taylor) G. BA in English, Fordham U., 1982; MA in English, NYU, 1985. Copy and prodn. editor Garland Pub., Inc., N.Y.C., 1983-86; devel. editor Paragon House Pubs., N.Y.C., 1986-88; sr. editor Brunner/Mazel Pubs., N.Y.C., 1989; adj. instr. English Fordham U., N.Y.C., 1988—; assoc. editor River Reporter literary supplement, Barryville, N.Y., 1990—; freelance editorial cons., 1989—. Contbr. articles to newspapers. Mem. Women's Nat. Book Assn., NAFE. Home: 294 11th St Brooklyn NY 11215 Office: Fordham U 113 W 60th St Room 924 New York NY 10023

GREENFIELD, CAROL NATHAN, psychotherapist; b. N.Y.C., Oct. 28, 1942; d. Arthur and Ida (Barkin) Nathan. BA, Boston U., 1964, EdM, 1965; MA, Antioch U., 1985. Lic. marriage, family, child therapist. Sch. psychologist BOCES, Ithaca, N.Y., 1965-71; therapist, caseworker, dir. outpatient family counseling Excelsior Youth Ctr., Denver, 1972-75; pvt. practice psychotherapy Denver, 1975-83; pvt. practice psychotherapy, marriage, family & child couns. Sacramento, Calif., 1985—; cons. Excelsior Youth Ctrs., 1985. NDEA fellow, 1966. Mem. Calif. Assn. Marriage and Family Therapists (legis. liaison Sacramento Valley chpt. 1988—), Am. Psychol. Assn. (assoc.). Jewish. Office: 945 University Ave #200 Sacramento CA 95825

GREENFIELD, HELEN MEYERS, real estate executive, publishing company executive, inspection and test service executive; b. Albany, N.Y., 1908; d. Stephen Ferencevich and Catherine (Bronkov) Meyers; m. Frank L. Greenfield, Apr. 1, 1929; children: Stuart Franklin, Val Shea. Grad., Baker's Bus. Sch., 1924. Accounts supr. George G. McCaskey Co., N.Y.C., 1924-29; spl. assignments purchasing dept. McCall's Pub. Co., N.Y.C., 1929, Fgn. Affairs Publs., Inc., N.Y.C., 1929-31; with purchasing dept. Glidden-Buick Corp., N.Y.C., 1931-32; interviewer Civil Works Adminstrn., N.Y.C., 1931-32; supr. filing and payroll systems Houston St. Project Ctr., N.Y.C., 1933-36; with dept. accounting Reuben H. Donnelley Co., N.Y.C., 1936-37; supr. layouts, makeup prins. of semi-monthly publs. Tide Publs., Inc., N.Y.C., 1939-41; asst. to purchasing agt., supr. maintenance perpetual inventory Hopeman Bros., N.Y.C., 1941-43; with money order div., corr. dept. U.S. Govt., P.O. Dept., N.Y.C., 1943-44, 1941-43; v.p. Frank L. Greenfield Co., Inc., N.Y.C., 1945-59, All Purpose Chair Corp., N.Y.C., 1950-55; pres. VAL Equipment, Inc., N.Y.C., 1950-62; v.p. Am. Testing Labs., Inc., N.Y.C., 1950-63; supr. personnel, purchases Irving Lampert Co., N.Y.C., 1951-52; account assignment coordinator, advt. contracts dept. Newsweek, N.Y.C., 1960-78; owner, operator Princess Helen Antiques; pres. Helen M. Greenfield Realty Corp., 1968-79; bus. cons., 1979—. Active New York Heart Assn.; founder, coord., show producer, dir. and hostess ann. banquet honor of Dr. Manuel Cabral, composer-dir. Mt. Laurel Ctr. Performing Arts, 1960-84; assoc. mem. Nat. Trust for Hist. Preservation; mem. Staten Island Hist. Soc., Staten Island Inst. of Arts and Scis.; mem. Statue of Liberty-Ellis Island Found. Inc. Named Hon. princess Cherokee Tribe by Chief Rising Sun of Richmond, Va. Mem. Internat. Platform Assn. Club: Order Eastern Star (past matron).

GREENFIELD, HELEN MUEHL, secondary education educator; b. Omaha, Jan. 20, 1910; d. John F. and Bertha Laura (Leesch) Muehl; m. Arthur Ludwig Greenfield, June 8, 1940. BS in Edn., U. S.D., 1956. Tchr. elem. Canistota (S.D.) Pub. Sch., 1930-34; primary tchr. Lennox (S.D.) Pub. Sch., 1934-40; rural sch. tchr. Miller Sch., Lennox, 1940-42; primary tchr. Jefferson Pub. Schs., Rapid City, S.C., 1945-47; primary tchr. Wilson Pub. Schs., Rapid City, 1947-73, ret., 1973; treas. Black Hills Tchrs. Scholarship Commn., Rapid City, 1983-90. Pres. history bd. First Congl. Ch., Rapid City, 1978-80. Mem. S.D. Edn. Assn. (life), Rapid City Concert Assn., Nat. Ret. Tchrs. Assn., Black Hills Ret. Tchrs. Assn. (state pres. 1986-88, Cert. of Appreciation 1988), Delta Kappa Gamma (parliamentarian 1983-90). Republican. Home: RR#8 Box 1510 Rapid City SD 57702

GREENFIELD, JOAN, direct marketing creative consultant; b. Pitts., Sept. 1, 1932; d. Sidney Arthur and Claudia (Isay) G. AB in English, U. Wis., 1953. Copywriter Montgomery Ward, N.Y.C., 1961-66; editor-in-chief Signet Club Plan, Cambridge, Mass., 1966-71; creative dir. Agawam Assocs., Rowley, Mass., 1976-80; v.p., assoc. creative dir. Kobs & Brady Advt., Chgo., 1980-86; exec. v.p., creative dir. Angela & Greenfield Advt., Chgo., 1986-87; sr. v.p., creative dir. Grey Direct Internat., 1987-89; direct mktg. creative cons. N.Y.C., 1989—. Contbr. articles to profl. jours. V.p. Women's Direct Response Group, Chgo., 1984-85. Mem. Direct Mktg. Assn., Direct Response Creative Guild (v.p.). Avocations: traveling, bridge, reading, entertaining, opera.

GREENFIELD, MEG, journalist; b. Seattle, Dec. 27, 1930; d. Lewis James and Lorraine (Nathan) G. B.A. summa cum laude, Smith Coll., 1952; Fulbright scholar, Newnham Coll., Cambridge (Eng.) U., 1952-53; D.H.L., Smith Coll., 1978, Georgetown U., 1979, Wesleyan U., 1982, Williams Coll., 1987. With Reporter mag., 1957-68, Washington editor, 1965-68; editorial writer Washington Post, 1968-70, dep. editorial page editor, 1970-79, editorial page editor, 1979—; columnist Newsweek, 1974—. Recipient Pulitzer prize for editorial writing 1978. Mem. Am. Soc. Newspaper Editors, Phi Beta Kappa. Home: 3318 R St NW Washington DC 20007 Office: Washington Post Co 1150 15th St NW Washington DC 20005

GREENFIELD, SUE MCCLAIN, business administration educator; b. Columbia, Tenn., Feb. 2, 1941; d. William Rex and Ann (McCain) McClain; m. David Wayne Greenfield; children: Anna Catherine, David Rex. BS, Vanderbilt U., 1961, MA, 1967; Ednl. Specialist, Tenn. Technol. U., 1976. Cert. tchr., Tenn. Tchr. bus. East Coweta High Sch., Senoia, Ga., 1961-62, Franklin (Tenn.) High Sch., 1962-63; tchr. bus. and English Maury County Sch. System, Columbia, Tenn., 1965-70; tchr. English Hay Long High Sch., Mt. Pleasant, Tenn., 1965-66; dir. fin. aid, instr. Vol. State Community Coll., Gallatin, Tenn., 1971-73; tchr. bus. Hendersonville (Tenn.) High Sch., 1973-76; dir. fin. aid and pub. rels. Columbia State Community Coll., 1970-71, assoc. prof. bus. and office adminstrn., 1976—. Mem. Maury County Bd. Edn., 1990-92. Named Outstanding Tech. Post Secondary Tchr. Tenn. Vocat. Assn., 1985, Tchr. of Yr. Tenn. Tech. Edn. Council, 1984-85. Mem. AAUW (pres. 1987-88), Bus. and Profl. Women, Tenn. Bus. Edn. Assn., Alpha Delta Kappa (sec. mid. Tenn. dist. 1987—), Delta Pi Epsilon (recording sec. 1987—). Presbyterian.

GREENFIELD, W. M, management consultant, educator; b. N.Y.C., Feb. 15, 1944; d. Tobin and Beatrice (Goldstein) G. BA with honors in History cum laude, Brandeis U., 1965; MBA, Harvard U., 1977. Mgr. internat. dept., internat. editor EDP Industry Report, Internat. Data Corp., Newton, Mass., 1965-69; asst. rsch. dir. Harbridge House, Inc., Boston, 1969-72; mgr. info. and devel. Blue Shield Mass., Inc., Boston, 1972-75; pres., founder W. M Greenfield Assocs., Boston, 1975—; lectr. mgmt. policy Boston U. Sch. Mgmt., 1977-84, 88—. Author: (with D. Curtin) Cash Flow Management, 1985; Accounting, 1986, Calculated Risk: A Guide to Entrepreneurship, 1986, 2d edit. pub. as Developing New Ventures, 1989, Successful Management Consulting: Building a Practice with Smaller Company Clients, 1987, Solve Your OWN Business Problems: Staying Sane while Staying Solvent, 1988; contbr. articles to profl. jours. Home: 455 Hope St Apt 4E Stamford CT 06906 Office: 37 Lawrence St Boston MA 02116

GREENGOLD, BONNIE BLUM, qualified pension administrator; b. N.Y.C., Sept. 14, 1955; d. Henry and Toby (Sklar) Blum; m. David G.

Greengold, July 31, 1977; 1 child, Laura Ann. BS in Applied Math., SUNY, Stonybrook, 1976. Pres., owner Pension Actuarial Consultants, Inc., Roslyn, N.Y., 1986—. Home and Office: 29 Dianas Trail Roslyn NY 11576

GREENHALGH, MARION LEE, petroleum company official; b. Syracuse, N.Y., Feb. 9, 1954; d. Russell Weaver and Jeanne Marion (Hughes) G. BS, Cornell U., 1976. Cert. hazzardous matls. mgr. Rsch. asst. biol. field sta. Cornell U., Bridgeport, N.Y., 1976; field ops. technician Nalco Environ. Scis., Syracuse, N.Y., 1976-78; sales engr. Dresser Magcobar, Victoria, Tex., 1978-80; sr. environ. engr. Magcobar div. Dresser Industries, Houston, 1980-84; staff environ. regulations analyst, coord. office safety Dames & Moore, Houston and Golden, Colo., 1984-86; environ. coord. Union Tex. Petroleum Corp., Houston, 1986—. Mem. Gulf Coast Environ. Affairs Group, Nat. Wildlife Fedn., Nat. Audubon Soc. Office: Union Tex Petroleum Corp 1330 Post Oak Blvd Houston TX 77056

GREENHILL, DIANE MARIE, real estate executive; b. Jamaica, N.Y., Dec. 8, 1960; d. Thomas Roland and Carol Jean (McKenna) G. BA, Fordham U., 1982. Exec. asst. real estate Div. Real Property, N.Y.C., 1982-85; sr. project mgr. real estate Met. Transp. Authority, N.Y.C., 1985-87; assoc. mgr. real estate Dun & Bradstreet Corp., N.Y.C., 1987—. Active Greenpeace, 1989—, Marine Conservatory, 1989—, N.Y.C. Ballet, 1984-86, Am. Ballet Theatre, 1987-88. Mem. Internat. Assn. Corp. Real Estate Execs., Real Estate Bd. N.Y., Comml. Real Estate Women. Roman Catholic. Office: Dun & Bradstreet Corp 299 Park Ave New York NY 10171

GREENHOUSE, LINDA JOYCE, journalist; b. N.Y.C., Jan. 9, 1947; d. Herman Robert and Dorothy Eleanor (Greenlick) G.; m. Eugene R. Fidell, Jan. 1, 1981; 1 child, Hannah Margalit Fidell. BA, Radcliffe Coll., 1968; M of Studies in Law, Yale U., 1978. Asst. to James Reston The N.Y. Times, N.Y.C., 1968-69, met. reporter, 1970-74, state polit. reporter, 1974-77; supreme ct. corr. The N.Y. Times, Washington, 1978-85, 88—, congl. corr., 1986-88. Bd. dirs. Yale Law Sch. Fund, New Haven, 1984—. Mem. Harvard Club of Washington (bd. dirs. 1989—). Office: The NY Times 1627 Eye St NW Washington DC 20006

GREENHUT, DEBORAH SCHNEIDER, management consultant; b. Yonkers, N.Y., Nov. 14, 1951; d. Howard and Virginia (Kelly) Schneider; m. Victor A. Greenhut, June 12, 1977; children: Adam, nathan. AB, Middlebury Coll., 1973; MA, Rutgers U., 1977, MPhil, 1979, PhD, 1985. Priority cons. East Brunswick, N.J., 1988—; community edn. faculty Raritan Valley Community Coll., Somerville, N.J., 1989—; cons. Inst. for Mgmt. and Tech. Devel., Edison, N.J., 1988—. Pub. Feminine Rhetorical Culture, 1988; author works on communications skills, computer tng., customer rels., video tng. program. Mem. MLA, NEMLA, STC, ASTD, Phi Beta Kappa. Home and Office: 35 Patton Dr East Brunswick NJ 08816

GREENOUGH, CAROL BOYER, cultural organization administrator; b. Geneva, N.Y., Jan. 1, 1930; d. Albert Langdon and Beulah Merle (Rose) Boyer; m. Robert Henderson Mowatt II, Oct. 15, 1949; (div. Nov. 1965); children: Robert III, Thomas, Rebecca; m. George Earl, July 8, 1967; (dec. Aug. 10, 1986). Student, East High Sch., Auburn, N.Y., 1947. Profl. photographer G and M Photos, Whitehall, N.Y., 1968—; bicentennial coordinator County Bd. Supervisors, Wash. County, N.Y., 1975-76; dir. Whitehall (N.Y.) Urban Cultural Park, 1980—; newspaper publisher Whitehall (N.Y.) Independent, Whitehall, N.Y., 1986-89; dir. Housing Rehab. Office, Whitehall, N.Y., 1989; mem. Historic Preservation Coun., 1976-88, NYS Coun. on the Arts Decent. Panel, Wash. County 1986-88. Trustee Skenesborough Mus., 1972—, chmn. mus. bd., 1989—; pres. Meals on Wheels, 1974-89, Hist. Soc. Whitehall, 1976, C. of C., 1977-79. Mem. Mettawee Valley Bus. and Profl. Women (pres. 1979-81), N.Y. State Bus. and Profl. Women (treas. 1983-87, 2nd v.p. 1987-88, 1st v.p. 1988-89), N.Y. State Urban Cultural Park Assn. Avocations: reading, knitting, gardening. Home: Box 238 Whitehall NY 12887 Office: Whitehall UCP 6 Williams St Whitehall NY 12887

GREENOUGH, MRS. PETER B. See SILLS, BEVERLY

GREENSPAN-MARGOLIS, JUNE RITA EDELMAN, psychiatrist; b. N.Y.C., June 28, 1934; d. Benjamin Robert and Theresa (Cooperstein) Edelman; divorced; 1 child, Alisa Greenspan; m. Gerald J. Margolis. AB, Bryn Mawr Coll., 1955; MD, Med. Coll. Pa., 1959; grad., Inst Phila Assn Psychoanalysis, Bala Cynwyd, 1975. Intern Albert Einstein Med. Ctr., Phila., 1959-60; pvt. practice medicine specializing in pediatrics Cinnaminson, N.J., 1961-67; psychiat. resident Hahnemann Med. Coll., Phila., 1967-71; practice medicine specializing in adult and child psychiatry, psychoanalysis Jenkintown, Pa., 1971—; instr. U. Pa. Sch. Medicine, Phila., 1975-77, clin. assoc. 1977-81, clin. asst. prof. 1981-85, clin. assoc. prof. 1985—; tng. and supervisory analyst Inst. of the Phila. Assn. Psychoanalysis, Bala Cynwyd, Pa., 1985—. Fellow Am. Coll. Psychoanalysis; mem. AMA, Am. Psychiat. Assn., Am. Psychoanalytic Assn. (cert. adult and child psychoanalysis), Am. Acad. Child Psychiatry, Ctr. for Advanced Psychoanalytic Studies (Princeton). Office: Benson East Suite 223-C Old York Rd Jenkintown PA 19046

GREENSTEIN, RITA RAPPOPORT, educator; b. Bronx, N.Y., July 4, 1928; d. Harry and Clara (Kuperman) Rappoport; m. Eli Greenstein, Dec. 26, 1948; children: Gail Ann Wade, Carol Joy Greenstein, Myra Ruth Cole. BS, NYU, 1950; MS, L.I. Univ., 1967. Music tchr. Hicksville, N.Y., 1956-58, Farmingdale (N.Y.) Sch. Dist., 1958-85; dir. Ctr. for Sr. Programs SUNY, Farmingdale, 1989; coach and accompanist N.Y. State Sch. Music Assn., 1963-89. Vol. Workmen's Circle Home for the Aged, Bronx, 1987-88, Am. Field Svc. Internat., N.Y., 1964-74; pres. Midway Jewish Ctr. Sisterhood, Syosset, 1954-56; leader Girl Scouts of Am., Queens, 1952, organizer, Hicksville, 1959-64; leader B'nai Brith Girls, Hempstead, 1968. Cert. of Honor B'nai Brith, 1968; cert. of merit Am. Field Svc. Internat., 1974. Mem. Am. Assn. of U. Women (pres. 1988—), N.Y. Choral Soc. (sect. leader 1988—). Democrat.

GREENWALT, SANDRA JOYCE, news director; b. San Jose, Calif., Dec. 5, 1962; d. Carl Albert and Margaret Laura (Kook) Early; m. Kenneth Dale Greenwalt, Sept. 10, 1983 (div. Apr. 1989); 1 child, Glenn Russell. BA in Communications, Wash. State U., Pullman, 1990. In-house announcer Ross Dress for Less, Silverdale, Wash., 1986-89, customer svc. clk., 1986-89; tech. crew asst. Beasley Performing Arts Colisuem, Pullman, 1989-90; TV comml. announcer Impact Prodns., Moscow, Idaho, 1990; TV news dir. CNN Headline News, Moscow, Idaho, 1989-90, TV anchor, reporter, 1989-90; radio anchor, reporter N.W. Pub. Radio, Pullman, 1990; radio news dir. Sta. KBRC, Mt. Vernon, Wash., 1990—. Bea Fry Meml. scholar Murrow Sch. of Communications, 1989. Mem. Women in Communications, Inc., Nat. Broadcast Soc., Radio-TV News Dirs. Assn. Office: Sta KBRC PO Box 250 Mount Vernon WA 98273

GREENWOOD, AUDREY GATES, librarian; b. Buffalo, Mar. 27, 1917; d. Marc Herbert and Genevieve Cecelia (Naab) Gates; B.A., D'Youville Coll., 1939; B.S. in Library Sci., Cath. U. Am., 1940, M.A., 1944; m. Clayton Edward Greenwood, Sept. 2, 1944; children—Mary Ellen, Nancy Jane, Susan Jean. Head librarian Gonzaga High Sch., Washington, 1940-45, Southeastern U. Evening Sch., 1941-45; reference librarian Cath. U. Am., evenings 1942-43; librarian St. Joseph's Collegiate Inst., Buffalo, 1945-46; head librarian Canisius High Sch., Buffalo, 1949-50; head librarian Eden (N.Y.) Central Schs., 1950-83, coordinator state and fed. funds, 1969-83, dir. adult edn., 1973-83. Mem. Eden Tchrs. Assn. (past pres.), Erie County Ednl. Assn. (past v.p.), NEA, N.Y. State Tchrs. Assn., N.Y. State United Tchrs. (state del., legis. chmn. Western zone, chmn. retirees of western N.Y. 1984-88, pres. 1989—, mem. ROC com. 1985-88, mem. editorial bd. The Active N.Y. State United Tchrs. Retiree, mem. Commn. 100), N.Y. State Retired Tchrs. Assn. (pres. Southtowns chpt. 1987—, legis. commn. 1987—), Am. Fedn. Tchrs. (nat. del.), Sch. Librarians Assn. Western N.Y. (past pres.), N.Y. Educators Assn., Delta Kappa Gamma. (state legis. chmn.), Beta Zeta (v.p. 1988—). Democrat. Roman Catholic. Home: 3688 Briarwood Ct Hamburg NY 14075

GREENWOOD, HARRIET LOIS, environmental consultant, researcher; b. Detroit, Oct. 4, 1950; d. Samuel H. and Elizabeth Ann (Bode) G.; m. Michael E. Carlson, Aug. 23, 1981 (div. Sept. 1986); m. Eric J. Halbeisen, Sept. 5, 1987; 1 child, Robin Faith. B.A. in Biology, Antioch Coll., 1972; M.S. in Teaching, Antioch Coll. of New Eng., 1975; postgrad. U. Mich., 1985-87. Dir. environ. studies Swanson Environ., Southfield, Mich., 1978-80; project mgr. ESEI, Ecol. Scis., Detroit, 1981-82; pres. Greenwood & Assocs., Detroit, 1982-83; mgr. environ. studies Environ. Rsch. Group, Ann Arbor, Mich., 1983-85; environ. policy specialist Clayton Environ., Southfield, 1985—. Rec. clk. Detroit Friends Meeting, 1985-88; bd. dirs., Friends Sch. Detroit, 1987—. U. Mich. fellow, 1985-86. Mem. Soc. Risk Analysis, Internat. Assn. Bus. Communicators, Cranbrook Inst. Sci., Mich. Assn. Environ. Profls., Nat. Assn. Environ. Profls. Quaker. Avocations: English country dancing, cross country skiing. Office: Clayton Environ Cons 22345 Roethel Dr Novi MI 48050

GREENWOOD, JANET KAE DALY, psychologist, educational administrator; b. Goldsboro, N.C., Dec. 9, 1943; d. Fulton Benton and Kelminy Ethel Esther (Ball) Daly; 1 child, Gerald Thompson. AA, Peace Coll., 1963; BS in English and Psychology, East Carolina U., 1965, EdM in Counseling, 1967; postgrad., N.C. State U., 1967-69, U. London, 1969; PhD in Counseling and Higher Ednl. Adminstrn., Fla. State U., 1972. Tchr. English Kinston (N.C.) City Schs., 1965-66, Goldsboro City Schs., 1966-67; counselor and psychometrist primary and secondary schs. County of Wake, N.C., 1967-69; coord. Am. Inst. for Fgn. Study, 1969; supr. student tours in Eng., France, Switzerland, Italy, and Capri, 1969; counselor Fla. State U., Tallahassee, 1969-72; asst. dir. counseling Rutgers U., New Brunswick, N.J., 1972-73; cons. to v.p. for student svcs. Rutgers U., New Brunswick, 1973-74, lectr. in counseling psychology, 1972-74; coord. and assoc. prof. counselor edn. U. Cin., 1974-77, adviser to grad. students, 1974—, vice provost student affairs, 1977—; cons. guidance South Plainfield Pub. Schs., 1973-76; adviser Parents Without Ptnrs., 1976; pres. Longwood Coll., Farmville, Va., 1981-87, U. Bridgeport, Conn., 1987—; bd. dirs. The Hydraulic Co., Gov.'s Partnership to Prevent Substance Abuse in the Workforce. Contbr. articles to profl. jours. Mem. Gov.'s Ad Hoc Edn. Com. on Tchr. Edn. and Counselor Edn., State of Ohio, 1975; mem. state planning commn. Nat. Identification of Women Project; chair Twin Rivers Tenants Rights Assn., 1972-74; bd. dirs. Bridgeport Hosp., Bridgeport Bus. Coun.; mem. adv. com. Bridgeport Pub. Edn. Fund; bd. dirs. Conn. Ballet Theatre, chair South End streeting com; mem. mgmt. adv. com. City of Bridgeport; mem. adv. com. United Way Tri-State; chair South End Steering Com; mem. The Schiavone Steering Com./Downtown Bridgeport Project, YWCA Bd., Champion/United Way, United Way Community Human Svcs. Planning Coun., Bridgeport Symphony Bd., Bridgeport Opera Bd., Bridgeport Area Coll./Univ. Consortium, Conn. Conf. Ind. Colls., The Newcomen Soc. of U.S., The United Way Ea. Fairfield County; mem. adv. bd. Sacred Heart/St. Anthony Sch., Roosevelt Sch; mem. ct. com. Regional Plan Assn.; bd. dirs. Conn. Ballet Theatre; chair The Bridgeport Regional Bus. Coun. Brass Ring Task Force on Leadership; bd. govs. Fairfield County Study; mem. hon. bd. dirs. Conn. Earth Day 20, Inc. Recipient Spl. award Black Arts Festival, Meritorious Svc. award Am. Assn. State Colls. and Univs. Mem. AAUP, Am. Coll. Pers. Assn. (editor and chair media bd. 1975—), Am. Pers. and Guidance Assn., Cin. Pers. and Guidance Assn., Ohio Psychol. Assn., Cin. Psychol. Assn., Organizational Behavior Assn., Am. Sch. Counselors Assn., Ohio Sch. Counselors Assn., Assn. for Women Faculty, Ohio Counselor Edn. and Supervision Assn., Kappa Delta Pi. Office: U Bridgeport 464 University Ave Bridgeport CT 06601

GREENWOOD, JOEN ELIZABETH, economist, consultant; b. Mineral Point, Wis., Aug. 29, 1934; d. John Edward and Lillian Laile (Rohr) G. BS, MA, U. Wis., 1956, 57; postgrad., Newnham Coll. Cambridge U., Eng., 1961-62; diploma in Advanced Mgmt. Program, Harvard U., 1983. Instr. econs. Wellesley (Mass.) Coll., 1962-68; sr. assoc. Charles River Assocs., Boston, 1968-79, v.p., 1979—; mem. bd. editors Energy Jour., 1979-83. Co-author: Folded, Spindled and Mutilated: Economic Analysis and U.S. v. IBM, 1983; contbr. to profl. publs. Mem. Commonwealth of Mass. Pub. Health Coun., Boston, 1973-79; vol. Hospice of Cambridge (Mass.). Earhart fellow U. Calif.-Berkeley, 1960-61; Fulbright scholar U.K., 1961-62. Mem. Internat. Assn. Energy Economists (v.p. 1978-84, exec. v.p. 1981-84), U. Wis. Alumni Assn. (bd. dirs. 1987—), Wis. Alumni Assn. Greater Boston (pres. 1987-89), Boston Club, Phi Beta Kappa. Home: 108 Chestnut St Cambridge MA 02139 Office: Charles River Assocs 200 Clarendon St Boston MA 02116

GREER, JEANETTE MULDER, broadcast executive, small business owner; b. Beaumont, Tex., Feb. 18, 1924; d. Herbert Thomas and Annie (Colichia) M.; m. Autry Micajah Greer, Dec. 31, 1971 (dec. 1979). Student, Dequesne U., 1941-42, Lamar U., 1947-50. Clk. Pure Oil Co., Nederland, Tex., 1942-43; billing clk. Norvell-Wilder Supply Co., Beaumont, Tex., 1943-45; traffic mgr. Beaumont Broadcasting Corp., 1945-47, acct., 1947-55; bus. mgr. Beaumont Broadcasting/TV Corp., 1955-63; asst. to mgr. Beaumont TV Corp., 1963-69; asst. sec., bus. mgr. Belo Broadcasting Corp., Beaumont, 1969-78, v.p., bus. mgr., 1978-84; bus. mgr. Sta. KFDM-TV div. Freedom-TV Sub, Inc., Beaumont, 1984-89; cons. broadcast bus., 1989—. Bd. dirs. Beaumont YWCA; active Beaumont Art Mus., Gallery Guild, 1985—. Mem. Pilot Club of Beaumont (pres. 1962-63), Am. Women in Radio and TV (sec.-treas. 1978-80, trustee 1987—), Beta Sigma Phi (bd. dirs. Beaumont chpt. 1980—). Roman Catholic. Home: 1440 Edson Dr Beaumont TX 77706 Office: Le Baubles and Beads 4325 Calder Beaumont TX 77706

GREER, JOANNE MARIE GREER, psychoanalyst, educator; b. New Orleans, Aug. 24, 1937; d. Carl Matthewson and Sydney (Comeaux) G.; m. Thomas Vernon Greer, Apr. 23, 1966; children: Marc Bernley, Carl Mathieu Cashen. BS, St. Mary's Dominican Coll., New Orleans, 1961; MEd, La. State U., Baton Rouge, 1966; PhD, U. Md., 1974; cert., Washington Psychoanalytic Inst, 1989. Lic. psychologist, Md. From tchr. to adminstr. Sisters of St. Joseph of Medaille, New Orleans, 1957-66; mem. measurement and stats. faculty U. Md., College Park, 1972-75; health statistician Office of Adminstr. Health Svcs. Adminstrn., Rockville, Md., 1975-77, chief spl. studies Office of Adminstr., 1977-80; assoc. dir. Rape Rsch. Ctr. NIMH, Rockville, 1980-81; dir. stats. U.S. Dept. HHS, Washington, 1981-87; dir. rsch., mem. pastoral cons. faculty Loyola Coll., Balt., 1989—; chmn., bd. dirs. Washington Psychoanalytic Clinic. Author: The Sexual Aggressor, 1982, Victims of Sexual Aggression, 1984, (film) Treatment of Rape Victims, 1981; contbg. author chpts. in books. NSF fellow U.S. Govt., 1965-69, NDEA fellow, 1969-72, State of Md. fellow U. Md., 1972-73. Fellow Md. Psychol. Assn.; mem. Am. Psychol. Assn., Am. Psychoanalytic Assn. (assoc.), Washington Psychoanalytic Soc., Am. Statis. Assn. Republican. Roman Catholic. Home: 12420 Kuhl Rd Silver Spring MD 20902

GREER, LINDA JEAN, nurse; b. Seattle, Sept. 6, 1950; d. Norman Joseph and Eileen Louise (Mullen) Foerstel; m. Stephen William Greer, Aug. 25, 1984; children: Amanda Lynne, Michael William James. BS in Nursing, U. Wash., 1972. Asst. head nurse U. Wash. Hosp., Seattle, 1975-79; RN staff Children's Hosp. Seattle, 1981-83; RN clinic Mollie Scott Clinic, Sun Valley, Idaho, 1984—; RN staff Moritz Community Hosp., Sun Valley, 1984—; sec., treas. Comme Les Filles, Sun Valley, 1987—; mem. audit com. U. Hosp., Seattle, 1976-79. Mem. Sun Valley C. of C., Alpha Xi Delta. Republican. Home: PO Box 602 Sun Valley ID 83353

GREER, ROBERTA LESLIE, tourism executive; b. Seattle, Nov. 14, 1935; d. Vanis Wells and Eleanor Clyde (Rossman) Elson; m. Glendon Alfred Greer, Mar. 22, 1957; children: Scott Allen, Eric Glen. BS in Adminstrn., Fin., City U., Seattle, 1980. Treas., ptnr. Jean's Fabrics, Kirkland, Wash., 1964-68; office mgr. various orgns., Kirkland, 1968-81; gen. ptnr. Land Devel. Co., Seattle, 1968-71; v.p. Seattle/King County Conv. and Vis. Bur., 1982-88; v.p. adminstrn./mktg. Tillicum Village Inc., Seattle, 1988—. Pres. Altrusa Internat., Kirkland, 1964, Kirkland Creative Arts Ctr., 1965; pres. Seattle Aquarium Soc., 1989-90; bd. dirs. Hearing, Speech, Deafness Ctr., 1987-90; vice chair region V Wash. State Tourism Devel., 1987-90. Club: Washington Athletic (Seattle). Office: 2200 6th Ave Ste 804 Seattle WA 98121

GREESON, JANET ROSEMARY, clinical director, psychotherapist; b. N.Y.C., May 28, 1943; d. Arthur Charles and Rosemary Margaret (Duffy) Durr; m. Eugene W. Boyle, Nov. 28, 1964 (div. 1969); children: Eugene, Jimmy; m. Charles W. Jowers, June 14, 1969 (div. Aug. 1977); 1 child, Rosemary; m. Alden N. Greeson, Apr. 21, 1984 (div. Mar. 1989). BA in Psychology, U. Cent. Fla., 1978; MA in Clin. Counseling, Rollins Coll., 1979; PhD, Columbia Pacific U., 1987. Cert. addictions, eating disorders, mental health counselor. Counselor alcoholism alcohol rehab. drydock USN, Orlando, Fla., 1978-79, program coordinator alcohol safety action program, 1979-82; assoc. prof. U. West Fla., Pensacola, 1981-82; psychotherapist Met. Alcohol Council Orlando, 1983-85; cons. eating disorders Brookwood Recovery Lodge, Birmingham, Ala., 1985; dir. Alcohol Rehab. Service div. Naval Hosp., Orlando, 1982-86; pvt. practice psychotherapy Orlando, 1981—; dir., founder Janet Greeson's New Life Ctr. For Depression, Anxiety, Orlando, 1986—; founding, chief exec. officer Janet Greeson's "A Place For Us" For Depression, Anxiety and Eating Disorders, Orlando, Daytona Beach, L.A. and Las Vegas, 1989—; founder, chief exec. officer Drug Free Cons., 1989; trustee exec. bd. Overeaters Anonymous Nat., Torrance, Calif., 1978-85; coordinator conf. on teenage alcohol abuse, Washington, 1983; supr. clin. practice site Rollins Coll., Winter Park, Fla., 1986-87. Mem. adv. bd. Profl. Counselor mag. Pres., treas., trustee Cen. Fla. Intergroup Alcoholics Anonymous, Winter Park, 1977—; bd. dirs. Grove, Altamonte Springs, Fla., 1981-82; mem. Chem. Dependency Network, Orlando, 1983—; founder, corp. dir. Freedom Walk, Inc., 1985; trustee exec. bd. dirs. Overeaters Anonymous, Torrance, Calif., 1978-85; organizer Superwoman Anonymous, cen. Fla., 1986—. Served with USN, 1961-64. Recipient Service to Mankind award Sertoma Club, 1979, appreciation award Lowell State Prison, 1979, cert. achievement U. Tex., 1986, award 30th Fla. Alcoholics Anonymous Conv., 1986. Mem. Internat. Assn. Eating Disorders (bd. dirs.), Am. Eating Disorders Assn. (cert.), Am. Mental Health Counselors (cert.), Am. Counseling and Devel. Assn., Nat. Assn. Alcoholism Counselors, Chem. Dependency Network, Fla. Alcohol and Drug Abuse Assn., Fla. Group Psychotherapy, Fla. Mental Health Counselors, Am. Labor Mgmt. Adminstrs. (sec., presenter conf. 1986-87), Nat. Assn. Female Execs., Am. Orthopsychiat. Assn. Republican. Roman Catholic. Clubs: Rebos (Casselberry, Fla.) (v.p. 1978-85, appreciation award 1983, pres., trustee), Alco-An (Orlando, Fla.). Home: 530 E Central Blvd Ste 1704 Orlando FL 32801 Office: Janet Greeson's A Place For Us PO Box 720895 Orlando FL 32872

GREGERSON, REBECCA OSTAR, accountant, business services consultant; b. Madison, Wis., Dec. 1, 1955; d. Allan William and Roberta (Hutchison) Ostar; m. James Charles Gregerson, Sept. 25, 1982; 1 child, Bryce James. BS in Bus. Adminstrn., Appalachian State U., 1977. Acct. Boker-Dick and Co., Silver Spring, Md., 1977-78, Fox and Co., Washington, 1978-80; sr. internal auditor Va. Poly. U., Blacksburg, Va., 1980-82; acct. Teepeedashary, Ltd., Wappingers Falls, N.Y., 1982-83, Leland G. Oathout, CPA, West Hurley, N.Y., 1983-84; owner Gregerson Bus. Services, Hyde Park, N.Y., 1984—. Mem. Hyde Park C. of C. Democrat. Home and Office: 29 Matuk Dr Hyde Park NY 12538

GREGG, DOROTHY ELIZABETH, marketing, opinion research and public relations executive; b. Tempe, Ariz.; d. Alfred Tennyson and Mamie Elizabeth (Walker) G.; B.A., U. Tex., 1944, M.A. (grad. fellow), 1945; Ph.D. (all-univ. grad. fellow), Columbia U., 1951, L.H.D. (hon.), 1967; m. Paul Hughling Scott, 1952; children—Kimerly, Gregg. Lectr., Columbia U., 1946-52, asst. prof. econs., 1952-54; asst. dir. public relations U.S. Steel Corp., N.Y.C., 1956-74; dir. corp. communications Celanese Corp., N.Y.C., 1974-75, corp. v.p. communications, 1975-81, corp. v.p. external affairs, 1981-83; exec. v.p. Research & Forecasts Inc., 1983-84; pres. D.E. Gregg Assocs., 1984—. Mem. civilian pub. relations adv. com. U.S. Mil. Acad.; mem. Gov. Cuomo's Com. on Productivity and Mgmt.; trustee Inst. for Future, WNYC Found. Mem. Found. Pub. Relations Research and Edn., Women in Communications (Nat. Headliner award 1980), Phi Beta Kappa, Pi Sigma Alpha. Clubs: Princeton, Zonta (N.Y.C.). Contbr. articles profl. mags., P.F. Collier & Son Ency. Office: 301 E 58th St New York NY 10022

GREGG, SUSAN J., radiology practice administrator; b. Oklahoma City; d. Owen Russell and Vera Evelyn Sampson; m. Robert L. Gregg III, July 1976; children: Kristin, Kerry, Robert. BA, Cen. State U., 1969; postgrad., Oklahoma City U. Adminstr. Radiology Group, Inc., Oklahoma City. Mem. Jr. Hospitality Club, Oklahoma City. Mem. NAFE, Med. Group Mgmt. Assn., Radiology Bus. Mgmt. Assn., Am. Mgmt. Assn., Oklahoma City C. of C. Republican. Methodist. Home: 8105 Magnolia Edmond OK 73034 Office: 1111 N Lee Ste 254 Oklahoma City OK 73103

GREGGAINS, JOANIE CATHERINE, media educator, producer; b. San Francisco, Feb. 18, 1944; d. Joseph John and Gilda Catherine (Lupertino) Ferro. BA in Phys. Edn., San Francisco State U., 1971, Cert. in Secondary Teaching, 1972. Cert. aerobic instr. Tchr. Roosevelt High Sch., San Francisco, 1972-79; fitness expert Sta. KGO-AM, San Francisco, host health talk show, 1986—; fitness expert Sta. KPIX, San Francisco, 1978-87, 1978-84; host, producer Morning Stretch, San Francisco, 1979—; cons. Calif. Prune Bd., 1981-83, Elaine Powers, Milw., 1982-85, Reebok Internat. Shoes, Canton, Mass., 1984-89; adv. bd. mem. Shape Mag., Woodland, Calif., 1983-88; host Crystal Light Nat. Aerobics competitions, 1986. Author: (book) Total Shape Up, 1984 (best seller); talent (video) Super Stomachs, 1985 (Gold award), J.G. One on One, 1988 (Gold and Platinum awards); producer, talent The Greggains Plan, 1989. Celebrity waiter Save High Sch. Sports, San Francisco, 1988; nat. spokesperson, creator City of Hope Friends for Life Benefit, 1989, 90. Named Healthy Am. Fitness Leader U.S. Jaycees and Pres. Coun. on Phys. Fitness, 1987, Legend of Aerobics City Sports Mag., Calif., 1985; recipient award for spl. support Am. Heart Assn., San Francisco, 1987. Mem. AFTRA, Internat. Dance and Exercise Assn., Aerobics and Fitness Assn. Am. Coll. of Sports Medicine, San Francisco State U. Alumnus Assn., Marin Humane Soc.,San Francisco Bay Club. Office: Joanne Greggains Prodns 201 Miller Ave Mill Valley CA 94941

GREGOR, DOROTHY DEBORAH, librarian; b. Dobbs Ferry, N.Y., Aug. 15, 1939; d. Richard Garrett Heckman and Marion Allen (Richmond) Stewart; m. A. James Gregor, June 22, 1963 (div. 1974). BA, Occidental Coll., 1961; MA, U. Hawaii, 1963; MLS, U. Tex., 1968; cert. in Library Mgmt., U. Calif., Berkeley, 1976. Reference librarian U. Calif., San Francisco, 1968-69; dept. librarian Pub. Health Library U. Calif., Berkeley, 1969-71, tech. services librarian, 1973-76; reference librarian Hamilton Library U. Hawaii, Honolulu, 1971-72; head serials dept. U. Calif., Berkeley, 1976-80, assoc. univ. librarian tech. services dept., 1980-84; chief Shared Cataloging div. Library of Congress, Washington, 1984-85; univ. librarian U. Calif.-San Diego, La Jolla, 1985—; instr. sch. library and info. studies U. Calif., Berkeley, 1975, 76, 83; cons. Nat. Library of Medicine, Bethesda, Md., 1985, Ohio Bd. Regents, Columbus, 1987. Mem. ALA, Library Info. Tech. Assn., Program Com. Ctr. for Research Libraries, Linked Systems Project Policy Com., OCLC (bd. trustees). Office: U Calif-San Diego Univ Librs Mail Code 0175G La Jolla CA 92093-0175

GREGOR, MARY JEANNE, educator; b. Portland, Oreg., Jan. 1, 1928; d. John Logan and Pauline (Hudson) Irish; m. Richard Gregor, May, 1953 (div. 1982); 1 child, Ian Nicholas. BA, Creighton U., 1949; MA, St. Louis U., 1952; PhD, U. Toronto, 1957. Fellow St. Louis U., 1949-50; lectr. overseas program U. Md., various countries, 1959-62; lectr. York U., Toronto, 1967-82; assoc. prof. San Diego State U., 1982-86, prof., 1986—. Editor, referee, cons. various philos. jours. including U. Chgo. Press, Princeton U. Press, Cambridge U. Press; author: Laws of Freedom, 1963; contbr. numerous articles on ethics, legal philosophy and aesthetics to profl. jours. Vol. various orgns., Toronto, San Diego. Susan Stebbing fellow, 1958-59, Margaret Snell fellow, 1959-60; named Henri Renard Lectr. Creighton U., 1984, Matchette Found. Lectr., 1981. Mem. Metaphys. Soc. Am., North Am. Kant Soc. (adv. bd. 1986—), Sierra Club. Republican. Roman Catholic. Home: 5708 Baltimore Dr #410 La Mesa CA 92042 Office: San Diego State U Dept Philosophy San Diego CA 92182

GREGORIUS, BEVERLY JUNE, obstetrician-gynecologist; b. Ottawa, Ill., June 21, 1915; d. Henry Godfrey and Arline (Barry) Pruette; m. Hans Harvey Gregorius, Apr. 6, 1939 (dec.); 1 child, Joan Gregorius Jones. BS, Madison (Tenn.) Coll., 1935; MD, Loma Linda (Calif.) U., 1946, MS, 1953. Intern, Los Angeles County Gen. Hosp., 1946-47; resident in ob-gyn, White Meml. Hosp., Los Angeles, 1949-52; practice medicine specializing in ob-gyn, Burbank, Calif., 1953-77; assoc. clin. prof. Loma Linda U. Med. Sch., also U. So. Calif. Med. Sch., 1956—; clin. prof. ob-gyn U. So. Calif. Med. Sch.,

1985—; program dir. ob-gyn residency program Glendale (Calif.) Adventist Med. Center, 1977-81, chmn. dept. ob-gyn, 1981-83, cons., 1983—. Bd. dirs. Arroyo Vista Family Health Found. Diplomate Am. Bd. Ob-Gyn. Fellow Am. Coll. Ob-Gyn, ACS, Internat. Coll. Surgeons; mem. Los Angeles Ob-Gyn Soc. (council 1979-86, pres. 1984-85). Adventist (mem. adminstrv. bd. dirs. 1985—). Home: 10635 Landale St North Hollywood CA 91602 Office: 1530 E Chevy Chase Suite 101 Glendale CA 91206

GREGORSKI, PEGGY WILK, nonprofit organization administrator; b. Chgo., June 15, 1959; d. Harry S. and Phyllis Rita (Kudlcaz) Wilk; m. David Layne Gregorski, Nov. 25, 1983; children: Laura Jean, Kathleen Mae. BA, Carthage Coll., 1981. Admissions rep. Carthage Coll., Kenosha, Wis., 1981-83, alumni dir., 1983-86; southeast area dir. Am. Heart Assn., Milw., 1986-87; dir. Kemper Ctr., Inc., Kenosha, 1987—. Mem. Coun. Nonprofit Orgns., Kenosha Lakeshore Hist. Places, Children's Svc. Soc. (bd. dirs. 1989—). Roman Catholic. Home: 7728 6th Ave Kenosha WI 53140 Office: Kemper Ctr Inc 6501 3rd Ave Kenosha WI 53140

GREGORY, ANN YOUNG, editor, publisher; b. Lexington, Ky., Apr. 28, 1935; d. David Marion and Pauline (Adams) Young; m. Allen Gregory, Jan. 29, 1957; children: David Young, Mary Peyton. BA with high distinction, U. Ky., 1956. Sec. Ky. edit. TV Guide, Louisville, summer 1956; traffic mgr. Sta. WVLK, Lexington, 1956-61; part time tchr. adult basic edn. Wise County (Va.) Sch. Bd., St. Paul, 1966-72; adminstrv. asst. Appalachian Field Services, Children's TV Workshop, St. Paul, 1971-74; editor, co-pub. Clinch Valley Times, 1974—; pres. Clinch Valley Pub. Co., Inc., St. Paul, 1974—. Editor, text writer: The Flood of '77 in the St. Paul Area, 1977; weekly newspaper columnist Of Shoes...and Ships...and Sealing Wax, 1974—. V.p. St. Paul PTA, 1970-73; trustee Lonesome Pine Regional Library Bd., 1972-80, chmn., 1978-80; chmn. com. to establish br. library in St. Paul, opened 1975; mem. adv. bd. Pro-Art, Wise County chpt. Va. Mus. Fine Arts, 1979-86; co-leader Brownie troop Girl Scouts U.S.A., 1971-76, bd. dirs. Appalachian council, 1st v.p. Appalachian Coun., 1985—; mem. adv. bd. Wise County YMCA, 1977-80; mem. Wise County Bd. Edn., 1975—, vice chmn., 1981—; pres. So. Region Sch. Bds. Assn., 1987-88; mem. Va. Edn. Block Grants Adv. Com., 1981-86, Region I State Literacy Coun., 1989—; mem. statewide planning coun. Va. Dept. Edn.; mem. Va. Coun. on Vocat. Edn., 1987—, chmn., 1989—; mem. exec. com. Va. High Sch. League, 1984-88; past pres. Wise County Humane Soc., Inc.; bd. dirs. Va. Sch. Bds. Assn., 1979-89, pres., 1985-86; bd. dirs. Va. Literacy Found., 1987-89. Named Outstanding Clubwoman of Yr., St. Paul Jr. Women's Club, 1964, 66, Outstanding Citizen, S.W. Va. dist. Va. Fedn. Women's Clubs, 1968, Woman of Yr. Wise County/ Norton Dem. Women's Club, 1986; recipient Rufus Beamer award Va. Poly. Inst., 1989; Ky. Broadcasters Assn. scholar, 1956. Mem. Va. Press Assn. (1st place award for editorial writing 1976), Nat. Press Women, Va. Press Women, Nat. Newspaper Assn., Women in Communications, Nat. Sch. Bds. Assn. (pub. relations com., nominating com. 1987), Mortar Bd., Delta Kappa Gamma (hon. mem. Alpha Psi chpt.), Phi Beta Kappa, Alpha Delta Pi. Democrat. Methodist. Home: PO Box 303 Longview Dr Saint Paul VA 24283 Office: PO Box 817 Russell St Saint Paul VA 24283

GREGORY, BONITA BELINDA, educator; b. Washington, Jan. 4, 1956; d. James Leon and Catheryn Evelyn (Albright) G.; adopted children: La Keisha Danielle, Latisha Michelle. BS in Spl. Edn., Brescia Coll., 1980. Cert. secondary tchr., Md. Spl. edn. tchr. Richmond County Schs., Warsaw, Va., 1981-85, Dallas Ind. Sch. Dist., 1985-86, Prince George County Schs., Clinton, Md., 1986—; cons. Gregory Day Camp, Silver Spring, Md., summers 1982—. Tchr. to mentally retarded Brescia Coll., Owensboro, Ky., 1978-80; vol. McKinney Hills Downs Syndrome Children, Silver Spring, 1975-76, Prince Georges County Spl. Olympics, 1987-88; severely handicapped tchr. Md. Nat. Capital Park and Planning Commn., Calverton, Md., 1986; sec. Clifton Park Citizens Assn. Recipient B award Brescia Coll., 1980. Mem. Prince Georges County Edn. Assn., Council for Exceptional Children. Democrat. Baptist. Home: 1206 Sarah Dr Silver Spring MD 20904

GREGORY, CYNTHIA KATHLEEN, ballerina; b. Los Angeles, July 8, 1946; d. Konstantin and Marcelle (Tremblay) G.; m. Terrence S. Orr, May 14, 1966 (div.); m. John Hemminger, 1976 (dec. 1984); m. Hilary B. Miller. Grad. high sch. Ford Found. scholar, San Francisco Ballet, 1961, soloist, 1962-65; principal, San Francisco Opera, 1964-65; with Am. Ballet Theatre, N.Y.C., 1965—, soloist, 1966, prin. dancer, 1967—, choreographer: Solo, 1979; created roles in Eliot Feld's Harbinger, At Midnight, Dennis Nahat's Brahams Quintet, Michael Smuin's The Eternal Idol, Gartenfest, Twyla Tharp's Bach Partita, John McFall's Interlude; dances leading female roles in classic repertory; guest artist with dance cos. including Zurich State Opera Ballet, Nat. Ballet of Cuba, Berlin State Opera Ballet, San Francisco Ballet, Ballet West, N.Y.C. Opera; permanent guest artist, Cleveland San Jose Ballet, 1986—; appeared on TV with San Francisco Opera, 1963-64; made TV appearance on The Edge of Night, 1981; author Ballet is the Best Exercise. Recipient Dance Magazine award 1975, Harkness Ballet Found. First Annual Dance award, 1978, Cyril Magnin award for outstanding achievement in the arts San Francisco C. of C., 1986. Office: Cleve San Jose Ballet 1 Playhouse Sq Ste 330 Cleveland OH 44115 also: Am Ballet Theatre 890 Broadway New York NY 10003*

GREGORY, HOLLY WANDA JANUSZKIEWICZ, lawyer; b. Rutland, Vt., May 14, 1956; d. Tadeusz and Marjorie Beatty (Martinson) Januszkiewicz; m. Joseph Henry Arguelles, June 17, 1978 (div. 1985); m. Robert Stephen Gregory, Aug. 23, 1987. BA with honors, SUNY, Purchase, 1979; JD summa cum laude, N.Y. Law Sch., 1986. Bar: N.Y. 1987. Law clk. to judge 2nd Cir. Ct. Appeals, Albany, N.Y. and N.Y.C., 1986-87; assoc. Weil, Gotshal & Manges, N.Y.C., 1987—; counsel WestFest, Inc., N.Y.C., 1988—. Editor: Journal of Proprietary Rights, 1989—; exec. editor: N.Y. Law Sch. Law Rev., 1985-86. Bd. mgrs., sec. Gatsby House Condominium, N.Y.C., 1989. Frederick C. Scholem scholar N.Y. Law Sch., 1983-86. Mem. ABA, N.Y. State Bar Assn. Soc. of Friends. Office: Weil Gotshal & Manges 767 Fifth Ave New York NY 10053

GREGORY, JEAN WINFREY, ecologist, educator; b. Richmond, Va., Feb. 13, 1947; d. Thomas Edloe and Kathryn (McFarlane) Winfrey; m. Ronald Alfred Gregory, Dec. 13, 1973. BS in Biology, Mary Washington Coll., 1969; MS in Biology, Va. Commonwealth U., 1975, postgrad. in pub. adminstrn., 1982—; MA in Environ. Sci., U. Va., 1983. Cert. ecologist, fisheries scientist. Lab. specialist A Cardiovascular Div. Med. Coll. Va., Richmond, 1969-70; pollution control specialist A State Water Control Bd., Richmond, 1970-77, pollution control specialist B, 1977-81, ecologist, 1981-85, ecology programs supr., 1985-88, environ. program mgr., 1988—; adj. faculty Va. Commonwealth U., Richmond, 1978—. Contbr. articles to profl. jours., 1972-88. Named One of Outstanding Young Women of Am., 1974; EPA fellow, Va., 1974-76. Mem. NOW, Am. Soc. Pub. Adminstrn., N.Am. Benthological Soc., Ecol. Soc. Am., Am. Soc. Limology and Oceanography, N.Am. Lake Mgmt. Soc. (bd. dirs. 1983-86), Am. Planning Assn., Virginia Lakes Assn. Democrat. Methodist. Office: State Water Control Bd Office Environ Rsch and Standards 2107 Hamilton St PO Box 11143 Richmond VA 23230

GREGORY, MARIAN FRANCES, educator, counselor; b. Gary, Ind., Apr. 24, 1919; d. August Robert and Agnes Mae (Sturgess) Kuhn; m. Robert Wayne Gregory. BS in Edn., Ind. U., 1941; MA in Counseling, Columbia U., 1960. Elem. tchr. Bremen (Ind.) Schs., 1941-46; elem. tchr. Gary Pub. Schs., 1947-56, tchr. remedial reading, 1956-68; elem. prin. Spaulding and Lincoln schs., Gary, 1968-74; student tchr. cons. Ind. U., Bloomington, 1974—. Author articles on genealogy. Mem., poll watcher LWV, Hammond, Ind., 1980-85; mem. Master Gardener Purdue U., Crown Point, Ind., 1977—; elder Presbyn. Ch. Mem. AAUW (pres. 1956-57), Bus. and Profl. Women's Club (pres. 1957-58), Nat. Soc. DAR, N.W. Ind. Woman's Club, Delta Kappa Gamma, Tri Kappa. Home: 2238 Ridge Rd Highland IN 46322

GREGORY, MARTHA ANN, librarian; b. Springfield, Mo., July 8, 1942; d. Ralph Winfred and Ruth (Clement) Pogue; m. Benjamin Ralph Gregory, Nov. 16, 1963; 1 child, Sarah. BS, U. Tulsa, 1972; MS, Okla. State U., 1989. Interlibrary loan libr. Tulsa City-County Libr., 1970-71, libr. asst., 1972-79, information II libr., 1979-86, econ. devel. information ctr. libr., 1986—; mem. Information and Rsch. Com., Met. Tulsa Econ. Devel. Found., 1988—; chmn. Okla. Online Users Group, Tulsa, 1980-86. Author: Tulsa Data Book, 1988. Mem. Special Librs. Assn. (program chmn. Okla. chpt. 1983-84), Am. Sociol. Assn., Southwestern Social Sci. Assn., Alpha Kappa Delta, Bus. and Profl. Women's Club (legis. chmn. 1985). Office: Tulsa City-County Library 400 Civic Ctr Tulsa OK 74103

GREGORY, VIRGIE MAE, state government audit specialist; b. Cin.; d. Virgil Lee and Helen L. (Coday) Terry; m. Sammy Dean Gregory, Nov. 3, 1964 (div. July 1970); children: Sammy Dean Jr., Tammy Kay. AA, So. State Community Coll., 1978; BS in Bus. Edn., Morehead State U., 1980. Sec. So. State Community Coll., Sardinia, Ohio, 1977-78, instr. bus., 1979-80; sec. Morehead (Ky.) State U., 1978, 79; substitute tchr. Ohio Valley Local Sch. Dist., West Union, 1979-80, Mason County Local Sch. Dist., Maysville, Ky., 1979-80; audit supr. Thomas E. Ferguson, Auditor of State, Columbus, Ohio, 1980—; tutor Zanes Trace Group Home, Winchester, Ohio, 1980; tchr. adult edn. program Ulysses S. Grant Joint Vocat. Sch., Bethel, Ohio, 1987, 88. Mem. Young Dems. Club Clermont County, Batavia, Ohio. Recipient Cert. of Award, Portsmouth, 1976, Diplomat award, Portsmouth, 1976, Exec. award, West Union, 1976; recipient Disting. Alumni award So. State Community Coll., Hillsboro, Ohio, 1989. Mem. Assn. Govtl. Accts., Ohio State Tchrs. Assn. Home: 279 S 4th St Williamsburg OH 45176 Office: Office of State Auditor 88 E Broad St Columbus OH 43213

GREGORY, WANDA JEAN, paralegal, court reporter, singer, musician, writer; b. Little Rock, Sept. 7, 1925; d. John Albert and Angie (Thompson) Deming; student Corpus Christie (Tex.) Jr. Coll.; m. G. C. Gregory, Jan. 15, 1945 (div.); 1 son, Rex Carleton. Ofcl. ct. reporter, Nueces County, Tex., 1959-76, 36th Jud. Dist. Ct., San Patricio, Live Oak, McMullen, Aransas and Bee Counties, Tex., 1979-82; freelance court reporter, Corpus Christi, 1976-78, 82-85, Honolulu, 1979. Vocalist with dance bands and jazz combos; pvt. tchr. jazz, pop singing and ballroom dancing; a founder Tex. Jazz Festival, 1960, appeared, 1961-82, 84-86, master of ceremonies, 1983; soloist Corpus Christi Interdenominational Choir. Mem. Tex. Jazz Festival Soc. (founder 1969, past pres.), Am. Fedn. Musicians. Democrat. Methodist. Home: 6440 Everhart Rd #2D Corpus Christi TX 78413 Office: 3751 S Alameda Corpus Christi TX 78411

GREGUS, LINDA ANNA, government official; b. Hartford, Conn., Mar. 24, 1956; d. Steven and Sylvia Christine (Ramunno) G. AB, Bowdoin Coll., Brunswick, Maine, 1978; MALD, The Fletcher Sch. Law and Dipl, Medford, Mass., 1985. Vol. VISTA, Phoenix, 1978-79; research asst. Econ. Research Assocs., Boston, 1979; ops adminstr. CRT Inc., Hartford, Conn., 1980-82; program officer U.S. Dept. of State, Wash. D.C., 1986-90; analyst CIA, Washington, 1990—. Recipient Milo Peck Scholarship Town of Windsor, Conn., 1984. Republican. Home: 1904 Wilson Ln McLean VA 22102

GREGUS, SHELLIE LYNN, home health care sales executive; b. L.A., Nov. 13, 1961; d. Edward Sr. and Antoinette Marie (Parziale) Levin; m. James Matthew Gregus, Aug. 9, 1986. Sec. Brunner Med. Equipment, Mentor, Ohio, 1982-84, cert. fitter and asst. mgr., 1982-84; home health care buyer, mktg. asst. Harris Wholesale Co., Solon, Ohio, 1985—, sales specialist, 1986—; dir. home health care Medic Drug, Inc., 1990—. Mem. Ohio Assn. of Durable Med. Equipment Cos. Home: 214 Briar Hill Dr Painesville OH 44077

GREIFELD, JULIA CONSIDINE, management consultant; b. New Brunswick, N.J., Mar. 1, 1957; d. William James and Elizabeth (Moore) C.; m. Robert Greifeld, July 18, 1957. BA, Iona Coll., 1979. Sales rep. Philip Morris USA, N.Y.C., 1979-84, Varta Batteries, Elmsford, N.Y., 1984-85; exec. recruiter Mgmt. Recruiters, Woodbury, N.Y., 1985-86; cons. The Whole Person Project, Elmont, N.Y., 1986-87; exec. recruiter Miragile Assocs., Northtport, N.Y., 1988-89, The Romark Group, Huntington, N.Y., 1989—. Mem. Huntington Club N.Y. Republican. Roman Catholic. Home: 28 Dunlop Rd Huntington NY 11743

GREIFF, CONSTANCE MANN, preservation consultant, author; b. N.Y.C., Oct. 4, 1929; d. Jacob and Evelyn (Weiss) Mann; m. Robert Greiff, Mar. 30, 1952; children: James Mann, Peter Raphael. BA, Vassar Coll., 1950; postgrad. in fine arts, NYU, 1950-54. Instr. Vassar Coll., Poughkeepsie, N.Y., 1951-52; copy editor, reporter Princeton (N.J.) Packet, 1967-69; cons. editor Pyne Press, Princeton, 1970-74; dir. Heritage Studies, Hopewell, N.J., 1970—; cons. Pa. State Capitol, Harrisburg, 1985-87, State Mus., Princeton, 1987-89; mem. N.J. Rev. Bd. for Hist. Preservation, 1979—. Co-author: Princeton Architecture, 1967 (award AASLH 1968); author: Lost America, 1970, John Notman, Architect, 1978, Independence, 1987. Vice pres. Hist. Soc. Princeton, 1968—; mem. Princeton Regional Planning Bd., 1972-80; pres. Preservation N.J., Belle Mead, 1978—; chmn. Borough of Rocky Hill (N.J.) Planning Bd., 1985—. Recipient citation N.J. Soc. Architects, 1981, ann. award N.J. Hist. Commn., 1986. Fellow Athenaeum Phila. (life); mem. Nat. Trust for Hist. Preservation (bd. advisors 1973-82), Hist. House Assn. Am. (bd. dirs.), Phi Beta Kappa. Office: Heritage Studies 20 Seminary Ave Hopewell NJ 08525

GREIMAN, APRIL, graphic designer; b. Rockville, N.Y., Mar. 22, 1948. BA, Kansas City (Mo.) Art Inst., 1970; studied design with Armin Hoffmann and Wolfgang Weingart, Algemeine Kunstgewerbeschule, Basel, Switzerland, 1970-71. Free-lance designer, 1971-75; asst. prof. Phila. Coll. Art, 1971-75; founder studio, L.A., 1976; design instr. Otis/Parsons Art Inst., L.A., 1981; dir. design program Calif. Inst. Arts, L.A., from 1982. Works exhibited at Phila. Coll. Art, 1974, 83, Albright Knox Gallery, Buffalo, 1979, UCLA, 1979, Tokyo Gallery, 1979, RISD, 1979, Cooper Hewitt Mus., N.Y.C., 1980, Mus. Modern Art, N.Y.C., 1980, Am. Inst. Graphic Arts, 1982, Kansas City Art Inst., 1983; work in collections Cooper Hewitt Mus., Walker Art Ctr., Mpls. Mem. Am. Inst. Graphic Arts, Soc. Typographic Arts. Home: 1570 Murray Circle Los Angeles CA 90026 Office: April Greiman Inc 620 Moulten Ave Los Angeles CA 90031*

GREIST, MARY COFFEY, dermatologist; b. Ft. Wayne, Ind., Jan. 31, 1947; d. George Alma and Irene Katherine (Zollinger) Coffey; m. Timothy William Greist, June 10, 1972; children: Heather Maria, Thomas, Timothy Michael. BA, Valparaiso (Ind.) U., 1969; MD, Ind. U., 1973. Intern in family medicine Duke U., Durham, N.C., 1973-74, resident in dermatology, 1973-77; asst. prof. dermatology sch. medicine Ind. U., Indpls., 1977-82, clin. asst. prof. dermatology sch. medicine, 1982—; pvt. practice Indpls., 1982—; dermatology cons. Eli Lilly and Co., Indpls., 1977-86, Elizabeth Arden and Co., Indpls., 1978-88, Medicare-Blue Cross/Blue Shield, Indpls., 1989—. Mem. Ind. State Dermatological Soc. (sec. 1985, v.p. 1986, pres. 1987-88). Democrat. Office: Greist/Ozols Dermatology 3850 Shore Dr Ste 311 Indianapolis IN 46254

GREMILLION, DENISE, restaurant manager; b. New Orleans, Nov. 2, 1955; d. E.C. and Lorraine (Armbruster) G. Assoc. degree, Del 9A00, New Orleans, 1984. Gen. mgr. TGI Fridays, Atlanta, asst. gen. mgr.; asst. gen. mgr. Houlihans, Atlanta; mgr. Houlihans, New Orleans. Mem. NAFE. Home: 1702 Cimarron Pkwy Dunwoody GA 30350

GREN, JOANN MARTHA, emergency medicine physician; b. Jackson, Mich., Nov. 6, 1956; d. Robert L. and Elizabeth (Afman) G. BS, Alma Coll., 1978; MD, Mich. State U., 1983. Rsch. asst. Upjohn Co., Kalamazoo, Mich., 1975-78 summers; visting lectr. Western Mich. U., Kalamazoo, 1984-87; resident internal medicine SMAMEC, Kalamazoo, 1983-86; flight physician Careflight Inc., Kalamazoo, 1986-87; physician Battle Creek (Mich.) Emergency Physicians, 1986-87; resident emergency medicine Boston City Hosp., 1987—; physician Melrose Wakefield Hosp. Melrose, Mass., 1988—; visiting lectr. Northeastern U., Boston, Mass., 1988—; pres. House Staff Orgn., Kalamazoo, Mich., 1985-86. Contbr. articles profl. jours., seminars. Mem. Am. Coll. Physicians, Am. Coll. Emergency Physicians, Emergency Medicine Residents Assn. Office: Emergency Dept Boston City Hosp 818 Harrison Ave Boston MA 02118

GRENSING, LINDA LEIGH, advertising executive; b. Milw., Aug. 17, 1959; d. John Lee and Delores Beatrice (Fenno) Richards; m. Gary Franklin Grensing, June 10, 1978 (div. 1989); 1 child, Justin Richard. BA, U. Wis., 1981. Advt. mgr. Profl. Edn. Systems, Inc., Eau Claire, Wis., 1982—; instr. Tech. Coll., Eau Claire, 1985—; owner Adworks, Eau Claire, 1987—. Author: A Small Business Guide to Employee Selection, 1986, Motivating Employees Through Non-Monetary Incentives, 1988; contbr. articles to profl. jours. Bd. dirs. Am. Heart Assn., 1988—, Am. Diabetes Assn., 1988—. Mem. Am. Soc. Journalists and Authors, Midwest Direct Mktg. Assn., NAFE, Toastmasters Club. Democrat. Lutheran. Home: 17889 Stillson Rd Chippewa Falls WI 54729

GRESHAM, KAREN CRAIG, legal secretary/paralegal; b. Andrews AFB, Md., Dec. 15, 1961; d. James Thomas and Twila Eleanora (Tinsman) Craig; m. David Wayne Pickering, Mar. 3, 1981 (div. Apr. 1983); Dustin David, Brandon James; m. Robert Anthony Gresham, June 21, 1986. Student, Carroll County Tech. Inst., 1985-86, Gwinnett Tech. Inst., 1986, Harris, Lanier, Atlanta, 1986. Consumer interviewer Consumer Network, Union City, Ga., 1982-83; newspaper carrier Gwinnett Daily News, Lawrenceville, Ga., 1984-85; evening supr. Kelly Svcs. Inc., Norcross, Ga., 1986; legal sec./paralegal C. Davis Bauman, P.C., Atlanta, 1986-89; adminstrv. asst. Stouffer Grand Beach Resort, St. Thomas, VI, 1989—. Vol. MADD, Atlanta, 1982-83. Mem. La Leche League (sec., mem.), Va. Genealogical Soc., Va. Genealogical Inst., Everton Internat. Genealogy Soc. Home: 3100 Sweetwater Rd Apt 2804 Lawrenceville GA 30244 Office: 24 Lenox Pointe NE Atlanta GA 30324

GRESHAM, PHYLLIS KILMER, nurse practitioner, educator; b. Arlington, Mass., Mar. 23, 1934; d. Everett Deane and Marjorie (Brigham) Kilmer; m. Glen Edward Gresham, Nov. 9, 1957; children: Stephen, David, Elizabeth, Jennifer. BS, Columbia U., 1956; MS, SUNY, Buffalo, 1985. RN, N.Y., Ohio; cert. sch. nurse tchr., N.Y. Staff nurse Vis. Staff Svc. N.Y., N.Y.C., 1956-58; field instr. Univ. Nursing Dist., Cleve., 1958-60; staff nurse Vis. Staff Svc., Cleve., 1962; data collector N.Y. State Long Term Home Care Evaluation Study, 1981-83; sch. nurse Coll. Learning Lab. SUNY, Buffalo, 1983—, instr., 1989, sch. nurse practitioner homeless project, 1989—; sch. nurse practitioner sch. health project G.B. Scrubbs, uffalo, 1985-88; mem., cons. task force Tech. Dependent Children, N.Y.C., 1989—. Chmn. child care bd. Amherst (N.Y.) Community Ch.; bd. dirs. Western N.Y. affiliate Am. Heart Assn., Buffalo. Recipient grad. faculty award for clin. excellence SUNY-Buffalo FAculty Nursing, 1986, program award of excellence Am. Heart Assn. Mem. Am. Nurses Assn. (cert. sch. nurse practitioner), N.Y. State Nurses Assn., Columbia-Presbyn. Alumnae Assn.

GRESKO, BERNETTA LIESER, special education educator, author; b. St. Martin, Minn., Sept. 17, 1938; d. Bernard Jacob and Caroline Martha Lieser; m. Laurence S. Gresko, Apr. 15, 1973. BS, Coll. of St. Teresa, Winona, Minn., 1959; MA, Calif. State U., Long Beach, 1971. Tchr. 2d grade Roseville (Minn.) Sch. Dist., 1959-61, Hudson Sch. Dist., La Puente, Calif., 1961-63; tchr. spl. edn. L.A. Unified Sch. Dist., Maywood, Calif., 1963-65, El Rancho Unified Sch. Dist., Pico Rivera, Calif., 1965—. Contbr. United Way, Foster Parent Plan, MADD, Sta. KCET Pub. TV. Mem. Am. Fedn. Tchrs., Calif. Assn. Resource Specialist, AAUW. Home and office: 157 Santa Ana Ave Long Beach CA 90803

GRETSCH, JUDITH CONSTANCE, electrical engineer; b. Washington, Feb. 1, 1963; d. William Rille and Alice (Parthemer) Gretsch. BSEE, Va. Poly. Inst. and State U., 1985. Engr. Sunhealth, Charlotte, N.C., 1986; elec. engr. Chas. T. Main, Inc., Charlotte, 1986—. Coach, Odessey of the Mind, Charlotte, 1989-90. Mem. Nat. Assn. for Female Execs., IEEE.

GREVE, MARILYN J., small business owner, interior decorator; b. Indpls., Jan. 13, 1943; d. Harry Winfred and Zylphia Ruth (Romeril) Dickerson; m. Wayne Gordon Greve, June 18, 1964; 1 child, Rodney Wayne. Interior decorator Ortonville, Mich., 1975-77; owner Frames by Marilyn, Ortonville, 1977-85, Flint, Mich., 1984—. Organist, Christ Community Nazarene Ch., Goodrich, Mich., 1972-86. Mem. Profl. Picture Framers Assn. (student 1986-87), Nat. Fedn. Ind. Bus., Ortonville C. of C. (sec. 1983-84, v.p. 1984-85). Republican. Home: 8295 Caribou Tr Clarkston MI 48348 Office: Frames by Marilyn G4215 Miller Rd Flint MI 48507

GREY, DEBORAH CLELAND, member Canadian parliament; b. Vancouver, B.C., Can., July 1, 1952; d. Mansell Caverhill Grey and Lilian Joyce (Russell) Levy. BA, U. Alta., Edmonton, Can., 1978, B of Edn., 1979. Tchr. Frog Lake (Alta.) Indian Res., 1979-80, Dewberry (Alta.) Sch., 1980-89; mem. parliament Canadian House of Commons, Ottawa, Ont., 1989—. Mem. Canadian Coun. Tchrs. English. Mem. Reform Party. Evangelical. Home: Gen Delivery, Heinsburg, AB Canada T0A 1X0 Office: House Commons, Parliament Bldgs, 709 Confederation Bldg, Ottawa, ON Canada K1A 0A6

GREY, MARGERY LYNN, editor; b. Norwalk, Conn., Jan. 19, 1960; d. Louis David and Betty Ruth (Horowitz) G. BA, Fairfield U., 1983. Asst. editor Conn. Mag., Bridgeport, 1982-85; mng. editor Fairfield (Conn.) Citizen-News, 1985-87, acting editor, 1988-89, dir. student internship program, 1985-89; mng. editor Accessories mag., Norwalk, Conn., 1989—; freelance editor, writer Cook's Mag., Bridgeport, 1985-87, Sports Mktg. Group, 1986-88, co-pres., 1895-89. Bd. dirs., chmn. pub. rels., co-pres. Literacy Vols. Am. Greater Bridgeport, 1987—; bd. mgrs., sec. Fairfield YMCA, 1988—. Recipient Herrick editorial award Nat. Newspaper Assn., 1988. Mem. Women in Communications (v.p. communications 1989—, job bank-chmn. 1988—, newsletter prodn. editor 1988-89). Democrat. Jewish. Home: 28 1/2 Pearl St Milford CT 06460 Office: Accesories Mag 50 Day St Norwalk CT 06854

GRIBBLE, CAROLE L., wholesale distributing executive; b. Toppenish, Wash., May 19, 1940; d. Harold Max and Gertrude Louisa (Spicer) Smith; m. Duane E. Clark, Aug. 1959 (div. 1963); 1 child, David Allen; m. Vance William Gribble, May 19, 1966 (div. 1989). Student, Seattle Pacific Coll. With B.F. Shearer, Seattle, 1959-60, Standard Oil, Seattle, 1960-62, Seattle Platen Co., 1962-70; ptnr. West Coast Platen, Los Angeles, 1970-87, Waldorf Towers Apts., Seattle, 1970—, Cascade Golf Course, North Bend, Wash., 1970-88; co-owner Pacific Wholesale Office Equipment, Seattle and L.A., 1972-87; owner Pacific Wholesale Office Equip., Seattle, L.A. and San Pablo, Calif., 1988—, Pac Electronic Service Ctr., Commerce and San Pablo, Calif., 1988—, Waldorf Mgmt. Co., 1988—. Republican. Methodist. Office: 1238 S Weller St Seattle WA 98144

GRIEDER, KAREN SUZANNE, radio producer; b. Paterson, N.J., Apr. 26, 1957; d. John Robert and Suzanne Jeanne (Ferrand) G.; m. Robert Tyrone DePriest, Sept. 24, 1988. AA with honors, Golden West Coll., Huntington Beach, Calif., 1982; student in Spl. Arts Studies, Richmond Coll., London, summer 1983; BA with distinction, Calif. State U., Long Beach, 1984. News and pub. affairs asst. Sta. KBIG, L.A., 1984; mktg. and fundraising asst. Sta. KLON, Long Beach, Calif., 1984-87; program coord., producer Sta. KABC and ABC Talkradio Network, L.A., 1987—. Mem. Nat. Assn. Broadcast Employees and Technicians. Office: KABC Radio 3321 S La Cienega Los Angeles CA 90016

GRIEM, SYLVIA FUDZINSKI, dermatology educator; b. West Allis, Wis., Feb. 24, 1929; d. Anton and Katherine (Janka) Fudzinski; m. Melvin L. Griem, Aug. 25, 1951; children: Katherine L., Robert C., Melanie E. BS, U. Wis., 1950, MD, 1953. Diplomate Am. Bd. Dermatology. Intern Kans. U. Med. Ctr., Kansas City, 1953-54; resident physician U. Chgo., 1954-57, asst. prof., 1954-80, assoc. prof., 1980—. Fellow Am. Acad. Dermatology; mem. Chgo. Dermatol. Soc. (pres. 1981-82), Wis. Med. Alumni Assn. (class rep. 1954—), Phi Beta Kappa, Alpha Omega Alpha. Democrat. Presbyterian. Home: 44 Sunset Trail Ogden Dunes IN 46368 Office: U Chgo 5841 S Maryland Ave Chicago IL 60637

GRIER, BARBARA G. (GENE DAMON), editor, lecturer, author; b. Cin., Nov. 4, 1933; d. Phillip Strang and Dorothy Vernon (Black) Grier; grad. high sch. Author: The Lesbian in Literature, 1967, (with others) 2d edit., 1975, 3d edit., 1981; The Least of These (in Sisterhood is Powerful), 1970; The Index, 1974; Lesbiana, 1976; The Lesbian Home Jour., 1976; The Lavender Herring, 1976; Lesbian Lives, 1976; pub. The Ladder mag., 1970-72, fiction and poetry editor, 1966-67, editor, 1968-72; dir. promotion Naiad Press, Reno, Nev., 1973—, treas., 1976—, v.p., gen. mgr., Tallahassee, Fla.,

1980—, chief exec. officer, 1987—. Democrat. Home: Rt 1 Box 3319 Havana FL 32333 Office: Naiad Press Inc PO Box 10543 Tallahassee FL 32302

GRIEST, DEBRA LYNN, government administrator; b. Columbus, Ohio, Feb. 7, 1959; d. Harry Lynn and Lura Mae (Purdin) G.; m. John Sturgis Clark, Nov. 25, 1938. BS, MS, Ohio State U., 1981; postgrad., Cleve. State U., 1989—, Case Western Reserve U., 1990—. Mgmt. intern Lewis Rsch. Ctr. NASA, Cleve., 1982-83; employee devel. specialist Lewis Rsch. Ctr. NASA, 1983-88, chief tng. and devel. Lewis Rsch. Ctr., 1988—; trainer Cleve. Mgmt. Devel. Consortium, 1988-89, Nat. Interpreters Assn., 1987-88. Contbr. articles to profl. jours. Cons. Bay Village (Ohio) Bd. Edn., 1988; leader Girl Scouts U.S., Cuyahoga County, Cleve., 1983-85. Mem. NAFE, Am. Soc. for Tng. and Devel., Acad. Mgmt., Bus. and Profl. Women (Young Career Woman of Ohio, Ohio fedn. 1985, v.p. NASA Lewis chpt. 1986). Presbyterian. Home: 626 Revere Dr Bay Village OH 44140 Office: NASA Lewis Research Ctr 21000 Brookpark Rd MS 15-4 Cleveland OH 44135

GRIFFEN, LUCILLE, protective services official; b. St. Louis, Nov. 10, 1954; d. Harold and Bessie (Motley) Williams; m. Walter Griffen, Sept. 23, 1941; children: La Grady, Josephine, Lashinda, Augustu. Student, St. Louis, 1982, Brodclay Coll., St. Louis, 1987-88. Social worker St. Clair County, St. Louis, 1982-83, Christ Ch. Homeless, Homeless Shelter, Mo., 1984-85.

GRIFFIN, BARBARA JANE, former county election official; b. Milw., Jan. 8, 1935; d. Ira Aaron and Marjorie Kathryn (Rheinfrank) Bickhart; m. John Acaster Ridley, June 7, 1958 (dec. July 1978); children: Deborah, Linda, Lisa; m. Donald S. Griffin, Apr. 18, 1987. BA in History, Duke U., 1957. Computer technician Bell Telephone Labs., Whippany, N.J., 1957-58; substitute tchr. B-R Edn. Assn., Bridgewater, N.J., 1970-75; mem. election bd. Somerset County, Bridgewater, 1975-86. Pres. Eisenhower PTA, Bridgewater, 1972, H.S. West PTA, Bridgewater, 1976-78, Coun. Sch. Assns., Bridgewater, 1974-76; chmn. $50,000.00 bldg. drive day care ctr., Bridgewater, 1980; chmn., mem. bd. dirs. Rolling Hills coun. Girl Scouts U.S., Bridgewater, 1976-83; area coord., chmn. Somerset County Spl. Olympics, Bridgewater, 1976-87; mem. woman's church assn., com. chmn., 1990; mem. Church Circle, leader-treas., 1989-90. Named Outstanding Vol. N.J. Spl. Olympics, 1981; recipient Community Patriot award, 1976, Thanks Badge Girl Scouts Am., 1979. Mem. Am. Field Svc. (treas. 1987-90). Republican. Presbyterian. Home: 208 Oakcrest Ln Pittsburgh PA 15236

GRIFFIN, DIANE EDMUND, research physician, virologist, educator; b. Iowa City, Ia., May 12, 1940; d. Rudolph William and Doris Irene (Swanson) Edmund; m. John Wesley Griffin, June 13, 1965; children: Christopher Todd, Erik Edmund. BA, Augustana Coll., Rock Island, Ill., 1962; MD, Stanford U., 1968, PhD, 1970. Diplomate Am. Bd. Internal Medicine, Am. Bd. Infectious Diseases. Resident in medicine Stanford (Calif.) U. Hosp., 1968-70; fellow Johns Hopkins U. Sch. Medicine, Balt., 1970-73, asst. prof., 1973-79, assoc. prof., 1979-86, prof., 1986—; investigator Howard Hughes Med. Inst., Balt., 1973-79; mem. virology study sect. NIH, 1982-86; mem. adv. com. Nat. Multiple Sclerosis Soc., 1986—; mem. microbiology and infectious diseases rsch. adv. com. NIH, 1989—. Author films and tapes; contbr. chpts. to books, articles to profl. jours. Grantee NIH, 1983—, Nat. Multiple Sclerosis Soc., 1986—. Fellow Infectious Diseases Soc. Am.; mem. Am. Soc. for Clin. Investigation, Am. Soc. for Virology (council 1987-89), Interurban Clin. Club. Democrat. Lutheran. Office: Johns Hopkins Sch Medicine 600 N Wolfe st Baltimore MD 21205

GRIFFIN, JANE FLANIGEN, research chemist structural; b. Buffalo, Mar. 26, 1933; d. Charles F. and Edith M. (O'Connor) Flanigen; m. Richard F. Griffin, Dec. 27, 1954; children: Richard F. Jr., Thomas More, Mary, Anne, Charles (dec.). BA in Chemistry, D'Youville Coll., Buffalo, 1950-54; PhD in Chemistry, SUNY, 1968-74. Indsl. lab. technician Linde Corp., 1952-53, jr. scientist rsch. lab., 1954-55; Danforth predoctoral fellow SUNY, Buffalo, 1967-72; from postdoctoral rsch. fellow to sr. rsch. scientist molecular biophysics dept. Med. Found. Buffalo, Inc., 1972-88, head Molecular Biophysics Dept., 1988—. Chmn. Pitts. Diffraction Conf., Buffalo, 1979, XI Internat. Congress of Biochemistry Satellite meeting on hormone: Molecular structure and protein interaction, 1979, nominating com. American Crystallographic Assn., 1979-80. Office: Med Found Buffalo 73 High St Buffalo NY 14203

GRIFFIN, (ALVA) JEAN, entertainer; b. Detroit, June 1, 1931; d. Henry Bethel White and Ruth Madelyn (Gowen) Durham; m. Francis Jay Griffin, July 8, 1958 (dec.); stepchildren: Patra, Rodney; 1 adopted child, Donald; children: Rhonda Jean, Sherree Lee. Student, Anderson Coll., 1952-53; DD (hon.), 1990. Ordained minister, 1990. Supr. Woolworth's, Detroit, 1945-46; operator, supr. Atlantic Bell Telephone Co., Detroit, 1947-51, Anderson, Ind., 1952-56; sec. to div. mgr. Food Basket-Lucky Stores, San Diego, 1957-58; owner, mgr. Jay's Country Boy Markets, Riverside, Calif., 1962-87; entertainer, producer, dir., singer Mae West & Co., 1980—; owner The Final Touch, Colorado Springs; tchr. art Grant Sch., Riverside, 1964-65; tchr., adviser Mental Retarded Sch., Riverside, 1976-77; instr. Touch for Health Found., Pasadena, Calif., 1975-79; cons., hypnotist, nutritionist, Riverside, 1976-79; mem., tchr. Psi field parapsychology. Mem. Rep. Presdl. Task Force, 1983. Recipient svc. award Rep. Presdl. Task Force, 1986. Mem. Parapsychology Assn. Riverside (pres. 1981-82). Mem. Ch. of Religious Science New Thought. Home: 201 Chapel Rd Sedona AZ 86336

GRIFFIN, JO ANN THOMAS, financial planner, tax specialist; b. b. Dallas, July 20, 1933; d. John Baxton and Joan Marion (Ament) Thomas; m. John Barrett Brown, June 29, 1963 (div. 1972); children: John Barrett Jr., Daniel Thomas; m. Thomas Reese Griffin, Jan. 25, 1976; stepchildren: Gregory Crawford, Kevin Bradley. BA, U. Miss., 1955; BS magna cum laude, Lamar U., 1964; MEd, U. Del., 1972. Cert. fin. planner. Site mgr. Motivational Ctr., Inc., Wilmington, Del., 1976-78; asst. dir. Indochinese scoial svcs. Associated Cath. Charities, New Orleans, 1978-79; dir. continuing edn. St. Mary's Dominican Coll., New Orleans, 1979-80; with fin. mgmt. U.S. Dept. Agr., New Orleans, 1981; tax auditor IRS, New Orleans, Phila., Del., 1981-86; revenue agt. IRS, Wilmington, Del., 1987—; tax specialist Horty & Horty, CPA's, Wilmington, 1986-87. Docent Winterthur, New Orleans Mus. Art, Wilmington and New Orleans, 1966-85; sustaining mem., advisor Jr. League of Wilmington, 1989—; lay reader, mem. outreach com. Episc. Ch. Diocese of Del., Wilmington, 1971—; regent Vieux Carre chpt. DAR, New Orleans, 1984; bd. dirs. Neighborhood Watch, New Orleans, 1983-85. Recipient Grad. Scholarship award AAUW, 1971, Sustained Superior Performance award IRS, New Orleans, 1984, Spl. Achievement award IRS, Wilmington, 1988, 89, Customer Svc. awards, 1989, 90. Mem. NAFE, Am. Soc. Women Accts. (sec. 1986-89), Wilmington Tax Group, Wilmington Women in Bus. Democrat. Episcopalian. Home: 900 N Broom St #16 Wilmington DE 19806 Office: IRS 844 King St Wilmington DE 19801

GRIFFIN, JOAN SOLOMON, banker; b. Washington, Feb. 26, 1958; d. Richard Allen and Elinor Ruth (Harris) Solomon; m. James I. Griffin IV, Oct. 10, 1988. BS, MIT; MBA, U. Pa. Registered civil engr. Cons. Charles River Assoc., Boston, 1980-81; fin. analyst Power Authority of N.Y., 1982; v.p. First Nat. Bank of Chgo., N.Y.C., 1983—. With N.Y.C. Foster Parents . Democrat. Jewish. Clubs: St. Barts Playhouse (program chair), Wharton (N.Y.C.). Office: First Nat Bank of Chgo 153 W 51st St New York NY 10019

GRIFFIN, LAURA M., educator; b. Woodland, Calif., Aug. 14, 1925; d. George Everette Ramsey and Bertha (Storz) Ramsey Lowe; m. Roy J. Griffin, Nov. 19, 1944; children: Robert Eugene, Dennis Charles, Kathleen Ann. AA in Social Sci., Sacramento City Coll., 1969; BA in Geography, Calif. State U., Sacramento, 1972. Cert. elem. and secondary tchr., Calif. Sec. Alameda Naval Air, Alameda, Calif., 1944-45, Cal-Western Life Ins., Sacramento, 1945-47, Pacific Sch. Dist., Sacramento, 1956-57; substitute tchr. Sacramento Unified Sch. Dist., 1974-75; tchr. Mt. Diablo Unified Sch. Dist., Concord, Calif., 1976—; pres. Heather Farm Garden Ctr., Walnut Creek, Calif., 1987-88, Walnut Creek Garden Club, 1983-84; sec. investment group AAUW, Walnut Creek, 1978-79. Guardian Jobs Daus.-Bethel 325, Walnut Creek, 1978-79; leader Girl Scouts Am., Sacramento, 1971-72; den mother Boy Scouts Am., Sacramento, 1957-60; publicity chmn. membership Northgate Music Boosters, Walnut Creek, 1976-77. Mem. Heather Farm Garden Ctr. (pres. 1987-88), Walnut Creek Garden Club (pres. 1983-84), Order of Eastern Star. Republican. Home: 637 Manhasset Ct Walnut Creek CA 94598

GRIFFIN, MARY FRANCES, retired library media consultant; b. Cross Hill, Laurens County, S.C., Aug. 24, 1925; d. James and Rosa Lee (Carter) G. AB, Benedict Coll., 1947; postgrad., S.C. State Coll., 1948-51, Atlanta U., 1953, Va. State Coll., 1961; MLS, Ind. U., 1957. Tchr.-librarian Johnston (S.C.) Tng. Sch., Edgefield County Sch. Dist., 1947-51; librarian Lee County Sch. Dist., Dennis High, Bishopville, S.C., 1951-52, Greenville County (S.C.) Sch. Dist., 1952-66; library cons. S.C. Dept. Edn., Columbia, 1966-87; vis. tchr. U. S.C., 1977; bd. dirs. Greater Columbia Lit. Coun.; mem. Richland County unit Assault on Illiteracy. Recipient Cert. of Living the Legacy award Nat. Council Negro Women, 1980. Mem. ALA, Assn. Ednl. Communications and Tech. S.C., Assn. Curriculum Devel., AAUW (pres. Columbia br. 1978-80), Southeastern Library Assn. (sec. 1978-80), S.C. Library Assn. (sec. 1979), S.C. Assn. Sch. Librarians, Nat. Assn. State Ednl. and Media Personnel. Baptist. Home: PO Box 1652 Columbia SC 29202 also: 1100 Skyland Dr Columbia SC 29210

GRIFFIN, MELANIE HUNT, accounting firm executive; b. Corpus Christi, Tex., Oct. 25, 1949; d. Roy Albert and Ola Emma (Hunt) G.; m. Robert Thompson; children: Maurice Dale, Donald Dwight, Merideth Thompson, Laura Thompson. BBA summa cum laude, Corpus Christi State U., 1977. CPA, Tex.; cert. fin. planner. Sec.-treas. Roy Hunt, Inc., Corpus Christi, 1970-78, dir., 1970-82; v.p. White, Sluyter & Co., Corpus Christi, 1978-80; pres. Whittington & Griffin, Corpus Christi, 1980-82, also dir.; sec.-treas., dir. Sand Express, Inc., Corpus Christi, 1975-82; prin. Melanie Hunt Griffin & Assocs., CPAs, Corpus Christi, 1982-84; ptnr. Fields, Nemec & Co., Corpus Christi, 1984—. Devel. chair Am. Heart Assn., chmn. bd. 1989-90, Leadership Corpus Christi Alumni, 1982—. Recipient Women in Careers award YWCA, 1989. Mem. Tex. Soc. CPAs (v.p. 1988-89, bd. dirs. 1987—, pres. Corpus Christi chpt. 1987-88), Corpus Christi State U. Alumni Assn. (bd. dirs. 1987-90), Tex. State CPAs Ednl. Found. (trustee), Exec. Women Internat. (chair philantrophy com. 1986-87), Internat. Assn. Cert. Fin. Planners, Internat. Assn. Fin. Planners, AICPA (personal fin. planning div., small bus. taxation com. 1990—), Bus. and Estate Planning Coun. Home: 10817 Stonewall St Corpus Christi TX 78410 Office: Fields Nemec & Co PO Box 23067 501 S Tancahua Corpus Christi TX 78403

GRIFFIN, PATRICIA ANNE, mathematics educator; b. Reidsville, N.C., May 27, 1941; d. Patrick Walton and Kathryn Stanfield (Johnson) G. BA, U. N.C., Greensboro, 1963, MA, 1969. Tchr. math. Fairfax County Schs., Vienna, Va., 1965-66, Greensboro City Schs., 1966-67; math. teaching asst. U. N.C., Greensboro, 1967-69, instr. math., 1969—. Mem. AAUP, Common Cause, ACLU, NOW, Phi Beta Kappa, Pi Mu Epsilon, Sierra Club. Democrat. Office: U NC Math Dept Bryan Bldg Greensboro NC 27412

GRIFFIN, SHARON L., lawyer; b. Toledo, June 14, 1939; d. Werner Gustave and Martha Lou (Doyle) Knauf; m. John Anthony Griffin, May 2l, 1963 (div. 1975); children: Simone Louise, Matthew Compton. BA, U. Mich., 196l; JD, U. Toledo, 1982. Bar: Ohio 1983, U.S. Dist. Ct. (no. dist.) Ohio 1985, U.S. Ct. Appeals (6th cir.) 1987, U.S. Supreme Ct. 1988. Editorial asst. Am. Jour. Comparative Law, U. Mich. Law Sch., Ann Arbor, 1962-64; adminstrv. asst. dept. edn. U. Melbourne (Australia), 1965; legal sec. Papua New Guinea, 1969-71; office mgr. engring. firm, Papua New Guinea, 1969-71; employment placement counselor Snelling and Snelling Pers., Toledo, 1972-74; adminstrv. asst. to dean U. Toledo Coll. Law, 1974-77; adminstrv. asst. Met. Toledo Consortium, 1977-83, acting program coord., 1983; litter control grant coord. dept. community devel. City of Toledo, 1984-85; pvt. practice Toledo, 1983—; mediator citizens settlement dispute program Toledo Mcpl. Ct. Vol. numerous local polit. campaigns; mem. legal svcs. com. Battered Women's Shelter, YWCA, Toledo; trustee YWCA, Toledo; mem. allocations com. United Way Greater Toledo, also team leader children svcs. panel; v.p. for fund raising, mem. adv. bd., past membership chmn. Democratic Women's Campaign Assn.; precinct chmn. Toledo Dem. Com., 1986—. Recipient cert. of participation United Way Greater Toledo, 1986, cert. of grateful appreciation, 1987; cert. of appreciation YWCA Battered Women's Shelter, 1986. Mem. ABA (family law com.), Ohio Bar Assn., Lucas County Bar Assn., Toledo Bar Assn. (pro bono program, citizens dispute settlement program com., family law com., cert. of commendation 1986), Toledo Law Assn., Women's Bar Assn. (pub. rels. com., newsletter com.), Ohio Acad. Trial Lawyers, ACLU (bd. dirs., legal com.), NOW (adv. counsel Toledo chpt.). Office: Gardner Bldg 500 Madison Ave Ste 540 Toledo OH 43604

GRIFFIN, SHERRY LUMBERT, stockbroker, financial planner; b. Wichita, Kans., Jan. 5, 1937; s. J. Delos and Volna (Liston) Lumbert; m. Ralph Stephens Griffin, June 4, 1955; children: James D., Ralph E. Diploma, Draughon's Coll., Lubbock, Tex., 1955. Cert. fin. planner. Ops. mgr. Goodbody & Co., Carlsbad, N.Mex., 1967-71; stockbroker Quinn & Co., Inc., Carlsbad, 1971-83; v.p., stockbroker, fin. planner Eppler, Guerin & Turner, Inc., Carlsbad, 1983—; bd. dirs., pres. Carlsbad Found. Pres. bd. dirs. Carlsbad Found., 1986-88. Mem. Inst. Cert. Fin. Planners Specializing in Retirement Planning and Investments, Carlsbad C. of C., Millionaires Club. Republican. Mem. LDS Church. Home: 802 Elma Dr Carlsbad NM 88220 Office: Eppler Guerin & Turner Inc 302 N Canyon PO Box 1898 Carlsbad NM 88220

GRIFFIN, SUSAN ANN, healthcare administrator; b. Barre, Vt., Aug. 12, 1946; d. Claude Loren and Celia Elizabeth (Taft) Lunt; m. Charles A. Griffin, June 14, 1967 (div. Apr. 1980); children: Mark Loren, Charles III. Diploma nursing, Elliott Community Hosp., Keene, N.H., 1967. RN, N.Y., Vt., Ariz. With Goodman Enterprises, Inc., Chgo., 1976-77, J. Milhening, Inc., Detroit, 1976-77; RN, float Scottsdale (Ariz.) Meml. Hosp., 1977; RN, back office James R. Bair, M.D., Scottsdale, 1977-83; med. adivce RN Cigna Health Plan, Scottsdale, 1983; supr. III, family practice, optometry, pediatrics, lab X-Ray Cigna Health Plan, Mesa, Ariz., 1983—. With U.S. Army, 1968-70. Mem. Am. Nursing Assn.

GRIFFIN, SUZANNE ELIZABETH, food products executive; b. Buffalo, May 10, 1963; d. Donald Edward Griffin and Susan Marie (Aaron) Schuler. BA in Psychology and Bus., SUNY, Albany, 1985; MBA in Mktg., Northeastern U., 1987. Promotion intern Gaines Foods, Tarrytown, N.Y., 1986; promotion asst. Richardson-Vicks USA (div. Procter & Gamble Co.), Wilton, Conn., 1987; product mgr. Perrier Group, Greenwich, Conn., 1988—. Northeastern U. scholar, 1987. Mem. Assn. MBA Execs. Republican. Roman Catholic. Office: The Perrier Group 777 W Putnam Ave Greenwich CT 06830

GRIFFIN, SYLVIA GAIL, reading specialist; b. Portland, Oreg., Dec. 13, 1935; d. Archie and Marguerite (Johnson) G. AA, Boise Jr. Coll., 1955; BS, Brigham Young U., 1957, MEd, 1967. Cert. advanced teaching, Idaho. Reading specialist Boise (Idaho) Pub. Schs., classroom tchr.; with Spanish for adults Boise Schs. Com. Edn.; lectr. in field; workshop leader. Author: Procedures Used by First Grade Teachers for Teaching Experience Readiness for Reading Comprehension, The Short Story of Vowels, A Note Worthy Way to Teach Reading. Advisor in developing a program for dyslexics Scottish Rite Masons of Idaho, Boise. Mem. NEA, Idaho Edn. Assn. (pub. rels. dir. 1970-72), Boise Edn. Assn. (pub. rels. dir. 1969-72, bd. dirs. ednl. polit. involvement com. 1983-89), Internat. Reading Assn., Orton Dyslexia Soc., Assn for Supervision and Curriculum Devel., Horizon Internat. Reading Assn., Alpha Delta Kappa.

GRIFFIN, VICKI ANN, automotive executive; b. Lafayette, Ind., Oct. 24, 1953; d. Richard Jerry and Mary Louisa (Smith) Stump; m. David Earl Griffin, Sept. 3, 1971. Student, U. No. Fla., 1985; Lic., Gold Coast Real Estate Sch., Ocala, Fla., 1981. Sec. Mercy Hosp., Orlando, Fla., 1973-74; v.p. Griffin Paint & Body, Orlando, 1974-78; asst. mgr. paint dept. Mark III Van Conversions, Ocala, 1978-81; corp. sec. Sherrod Vans, Inc., Jacksonville, Fla., 1981-85; graphic designer Orlando, 1985-88; pres. Crowne Motor Coach, Inc., Lakeland, Fla., 1988—. Republican. Roman Catholic. Office: Crowne Motor Coach Inc 1440 W Memorial Blvd Lakeland FL 33801

GRIFFIN, YVONNE MARIE, human resource development specialist; b. Harrodsburg, Ky., June 15, 1952; d. George Calvin and Emma Mae (Morgan) G. BA, Western Ky. U., 1975, MA, 1978; MEd, Vanderbilt U., 1985. Tchr. Harrodsburg City Sch. System, 1975-86; tech. writer (contract) GE, Columbia, Tenn., 1986-87; human resources devel. officer TVA, Chattanooga, 1987—. Mem. Am. Soc. Tng. and Devel., Ky. Edn. Assn., Cen. Ky. Edn. Assn. (bd. dirs.), Delta Sigma Theta. Republican. Methodist. Home: 1434 Stratman Circle Chattanooga TN 37421

GRIFFIN-HOLST, (BARBARA) JEAN, marketing professional; b. Pasadena, Calif., May 20, 1943; d. DeWitt James and Jean Marie (Donald) Griffin; m. Rodney C. Holst, Mar. 22, 1969 (div. May 1975); 1 child, Justin D. Griffin-Holst. BA cum laude, San Jose State U., 1967. Designer integrated cir. mask Fairchild Semicondr., Mountain View, Calif., 1967-69; sr. custom integrated cir. mask designer Nat. Semicondr., Santa Clara, Calif., 1969-71; sr. specialist Advanced Micro Devices, Sunnyvale, Calif., 1971-75; mgr. mask design and computer-aided design groups Precision Monolithics, Santa Clara, 1975-76; mgr. analog mask design and graphic services Signetics Corp., Sunnyvale, 1976-82; dist. mgr. tech. mktg. Computervision Corp., Santa Clara, 1982-84, dist. mgr. sales, 1984-85, mgr. distbr. sales, 1985-87; dir. U.S. field mktg. Sun Microsystems Inc., Mountain View, 1987—. Mem. NAFE, AAUW, Navy League U.S., San Francisco Mus. Modern Art, St. Francis Yacht Club (San Francisco), Commonwealth Club of San Francisco. Republican. Office: Sun Microsystems Inc 2550 Garcia Ave Mountain View CA 94043

GRIFFIS, KATHERINE MILLICENT, county agency administrator; b. Dallas, Feb. 20, 1954; d. Thomas Farr and Barbara Ann (Cloyd) G. BA, Birmingham-So. Coll., 1975; JD, Birmingham Sch. Law, 1981. Tax mapper Cole-Layer Trumble, Birmingham, Ala., 1975-76; sales assoc. Rich's, Inc., Birmingham, 1976-77; aide legal rsch., sec. John Lair, Atty. at Law, Birmingham, 1977-79; program coord. Ctr. for Labor Edn. & Rsch. U. Ala., Birmingham, 1979-84; contract adminstr. fed. job tng. Job Tng. Ptnrship. Act Adminstrv. Offices, City of Birmingham, 1984-90; adminstrv. analyst, Budget and Mgmt. Office Jefferson County Courthouse, Birmingham, Ala., 1990—; instr. labor/pers. law U. Ala.-Birmingham, 1986—, grant writing and adminstrn., 1989—; cons. women in employment Mayor's Commn. on Status of Women, Birmingham, 1986—; lectr. So. Coll., U. Ala., Birmingham, 1988. Editor (film) Work in Alabama: A Photographic Essay, 1983; cons. Ala. Pub. TV documentary on sexual harassment in the workplace. Cons. Ramesses II Exhbn., Memphis, 1987, Birmingham Mus. Art Egyptian Exhibit, 1988, Egyptian History and Culture Birmingham Festival of Arts, 1988; edn. com. BFA, 1988; exhbn. dir. Birmingham Festival Arts Internat. Fair, 1988; chmn. adv. bd. 70001, Inc. Mem. Am. Soc. Pers. Adminstrs., Southeastern Employment and Tng. Assn., NAFE (Network Birmingham), Earthwatch Expdns., Genius Loci (Baker St. Irregulars). Democrat. Lutheran. Office: Jefferson County Courthouse 716 N 21st St Rm 3 Birmingham AL 35203

GRIFFIS, SANDRA LEE, bookkeeper; b. Marks, Miss., Nov. 5, 1957; d. David William and Eunice Lee (Riddell) Cotten.; m. Rodney Keel Griffis, Dec. 10, 1976; children: Ginger Lee, Christopher Howard. Student, Northwest Miss. Jr. Coll., Senatobia, 1976--, Miss. Gulf Coast Jr. Coll., Gautier, 1974--; Strider Acad., Charleston, 1972-74; Student, ASI Computer Sch., Waterloo, 1987. Legal. sec. Alex B. Gates, Attorney at Law, Sumner, Miss., 1975-76; legal sec. Lawrence Magdovitz, Attorney at Law, Clarksdale, Miss., 1976-77; bookkeeper Nabors Chevrolet-Toyota, Inc., Clarksdale, 1977-84, K&R Specialty Advertising Co., Inc., Clarksdale, 1984-86; bookkeeper and office mgr. Ideas Unlimited, Inc., Memphis, Tenn., 1986—. Troop leader Girl Scouts Am., Southaven, Miss., 1988, 89, svc. unit dir., assn. chmn. and bd. dirs. Tenn-Ark-Miss. Girl Scouts of Am., 1989—. Rep. Presbyterian.

GRIFFITH, ELIZABETH ANN, business owner, consultant, nurse; b. Newton, N.J., Oct. 28, 1955; d. Walton Harris and Caroline Elizabeth (Manson) G.; m. Peter H. Vicinanza, Dec. 24, 1984 (div. Nov. 1988). BSN, U. San Francisco, 1976; AS in Software Engring., Norwalk State Tech. Coll., Conn., 1980. Med. svc. specialist USAF, 1976-79; project mgr. Comml. Computer Systems, Inc., Norwalk, 1979-83; spl. products mgr. Creative Output Inc., Milford, Conn., 1983-85; data processing mgr. Cornerstones Energy Group, Inc., Brunswick, Maine, 1985; owner, pres. OakWise, New Haven, 1984—; mktg. dir. EFT Corp., Inc., New Haven, 1989—. Mayor's appointee Solid Waste Mgmt. Commn., New Haven, 1988—; justice of the peace State of Conn., New Haven, 1989—; pres. New Haven Block Watch Assn., Inc., 1987, 88, 89. Republican. Episcopalian. Home and Office: 73 Lyon St New Haven CT 06511

GRIFFITH, KATHERINE SCOTT, communications executive; b. Atlanta, Jan. 16, 1942; d. Robert Sherrill and Emily Howell (Reynolds) G.; m. Henry Armand Terjen, Sept. 4, 1970 (div. Nov. 1979); 1 child, Henry Foster Terjen. AB, Sweet Briar Coll., 1964; Masters, Emory U., 1968. Editor South Today So. Regional Coun., Atlanta, 1969-72; editor Phoenix, Bklyn., 1972-73; dir. communications N.Y. C. of C. and Industry, N.Y.C., 1978-79; dir. pub. liaison N.Y.C. Dept. Ports. and Terminals, 1978-79; sr. pub. affairs officer Citicorp/Citibank, N.Y.C., 1981-84, asst. v.p., 1985-87; v.p. First Atlanta Corp., Atlanta, 1984; sr. mgr. Can. Imperial Bank of Commerce, N.Y.C., 1987-88, v.p. U.S. corp. communications, 1989—; pres. 150 Joralemon Street Corp., Bklyn., 1987-89. Pres. 78th Precinct Community Council, Bklyn., 1977-78; com. mem. Community Bd. 6, Bklyn., 1978-80; council mem. So. Regional Council, Atlanta, 1984—; bd. dirs.Atlanta Chamber Players, 1984. Mem. Pub. Rels. Soc. Am., Internat. Assn. Bus. Communications, Internat. Pub. Rels. Assn., N.Y. State Bankers Assn. (pub. rels. com. 1989-), Fin. Women's Assn. N.Y., Women Execs. in Pub. Rels., Jr. League, Beta Phi Mu. Democrat. Episcopalian. Office: Can Imperial Bank Commerce 425 Lexington Ave New York NY 10017

GRIFFITH, LEAH MARIE, librarian; b. Astoria, Oreg., Mar. 4, 1956; d. Frank Howard and Patricia (Kemmerer) G. BS in Social Scis., So. Oreg. State Coll., Ashland, 1978; MLS, Clarion (Pa.) U., 1987. Clk., libr. Multnomah County Libr., Portland, Oreg., 1979-83; libr. asst. Hillsboro (Oreg.) Pub. Libr., 1983; libr. dir. Cornelius (Oreg.) Pub. Libr., 1983-89; extension libr. Ohio Valley Area Librs., Wellston, Ohio, 1989—. Mem. ALA, Ohio Libr. Assn., Oreg. Libr. Assn. (chair pub. rels. com. 1985-86, founder small librs. round table). Democrat. Office: Ohio Valley Area Librs 252 W 13th St Wellston OH 45692

GRIFFITH, MARTHA H., controller; b. Brockton, Mass., Sept. 9, 1945; d. Ishmael Hayes and Jettie L. (Dudley) Davis; m. Jack C. Griffith, May 29, 1965 (dec. June 1984); Michael S., David M. Student, U. Ark., 1962-64; BA, Ball State U., 1967. Prin. Griffith Acctg. Co., Indpls., 1968-70; probate adminstr. Johnson & Weaver, Indpls., 1970-74; personnel adminstr. Hercules Inc., Houston, 1974-76; adminstr. Lapin Totz & Mayer, Houston, 1976-78, 76-80; bus. mgr. Pasadena (Tex.) Citizen, 1980-84; contr. Houston Community Newspapers, 1984-88, DCI Pub., Alexandria, Va., 1989—. Commr. Houston council Boy Scouts Am., 1983. Recipient Dist. Merit awards Boy Scouts Am., Houston, 1983. Mem. Internat. Newspaper Fin. Execs. (com. mem. 1986-89), Collier Jackson Users Group (moderator 1986-89), Nat. Assn. Female Execs. Democrat. Baptist.

GRIFFITH, MARY LOUISE KILPATRICK (MRS. EMLYN I. GRIFFITH), civic leader; b. Gadsden, Ala., Mar. 22, 1926; d. Lewis A. and Willie (Reid) Kilpatrick; m. Emlyn I. Griffith, Aug. 13, 1946; children: William L., James R. AB, Huntingdon Coll., 1947. Pres. Evergreen Twig, Rome, N.Y., 1966-67, Rome Home, 1973-75; mem. Bd. Edn. Rome City Sch. Dist., 1967-77; del. U.S.-China Joint Session on Trade and Law, Beijing, 1987, Soviet-Am. Conf. Comparative Edn., Moscow, 1988. Trustee Utica (N.Y.) Coll. Found., 1974-80, George Jr. Republic, 1974-78, Pub. Broadcasting Coun. Cen. N.Y., 1977-83, 1st Presbyn. Ch., Rome, 1979-85, Cen. N.Y. Assn. for the Blind and Visually Impaired, 1988—, Rome Coll. Found., 1988—; bd. dirs. Rome Art and Community Ctr., 1967-72, Rome chpt. Am. Field Svc., 1969-77, Utica Symphony Orch., 1989—. Recipient Rose for Living award Rotary Club, 1973, Civic award for conspicuous pub. service Colgate U., 1978. Mem. AAUW, PEO (pres. 1965-66), Nat. Soc. Lit. and Arts., Wednesday Morning Club (pres. Rome, N.Y. 1968-70). Home: Golf Course Rd Rome NY 13440

GRIFFITH, PATRICIA KING, retired nurse, civic and political worker; b. Des Moines, June 14, 1925; d. Eugene Arlo and Edith May (Yeager) King; m. Edwin Stewart Griffith, Jan. 31, 1948 (dec. Oct. 1964); children: Anne, Gail, Deborah, Spencer. Student, Mont. State Coll., 1943-44; BS in Nursing, U. Iowa, 1948; postgrad., SUNY, Cortland, 1965-72, Syracuse U., 1965-72. RN, N.Y.; cert. sch. nurse-tchr., N.Y. Sch. nurse, tchr. Jamesville-Dewitt (N.Y.) Cen. Schs., 1965-76; psychiat. nurse Hutchings Psychiat. Ctr., Syracuse, N.Y., 1976-87; ret., 1987. Committeewoman Syracuse Dem. Com., 1976—; com. mem. Cen. N.Y. Planned Parenthood, 1984—; program v.p. women's assn. Dewitt Community Ch., 1988—; bd. dirs. Syracuse Area Interreligious Commn., 1989—. Mem. AAUW (life, pres. Syracuse br. 1972, legis. chmn., 1974—; state chmn. Edn. Found. 1973-74), NOW (Unsung Heroine award Syracuse 1989), Common Cause, Nat. Wildlife Def. Fund, Save the River, Women's Polit. Caucus. Democrat. Home: 1169 Cumberland Ave Syracuse NY 13210

GRIFFITH, ROBERTA, art educator; b. Otego, N.Y., May 14, 1937; d. Roberta Charles Griffith and Jane Marie (Randolph) Griffith Elliott; m. Ray Schillmoeller, Mar. 26, 1966; children: David Robert, Raymond Mark. BFA, Chouinard Art Inst., 1960; MFA, So. Ill. U., 1962. Cert. tchr., N.Y. Tchr. art Am. Sch., Barcelona, Spain, spring, 1964; ceramic designer Design Technics, N.Y.C., 1965-66; Arkell Hall prof. art Hartwick Coll., Oneonta, N.Y., 1966—, chairperson art dept., 1974—. Contbr. articles to profl. jours. Sec., Upper Catskill Community coun. on Arts, 1974-78, v.p. 1978-79, pres. 1979-80; del.-at-lagrge Nat. coun. Edn. for Nat. Ceramic Arts, 1984-86, dir. publs., 1986; cons. in field. Recipient Young Am. 1962, Mus. Contemporary Crafts, Craftsmen USA 1966, Mu. Mem. AAUP (v.p. 1988-89, pres. 1989-90), Humanities Div. Hartwick Coll. (chairperson 1988-89). Republican. Episcopalian. Home: 32 Main St Otego NY 13825 Office: Hartwick Coll Oneonta NY 13820

GRIFFITHS, GEORGIA DOROTHY, systems and software engineer, consultant; b. Lynwood, Calif, June 27, 1951; d. Arthur and Dorothy (Schlafer) G. BA in Math. cum laude, Long Beach State U., 1973; MS in Computer Sci., U. So. Calif., 1977. Software engr. Hughes Aircraft, Fullerton, Calif., 1974-77; systems engr. TRW, L.A., 1977-81; lead digital designer Continental Controls, San Diego, 1981-83; lead software engr. Solar Turbines, San Diego, 1983-84, Compusec, San Diego, 1984-88; software engr., cons. Griffiths Assocs., Olivenhain, Calif., 1988—; tchr. U. Calif. San Diego, 1982-84. Contbr. articles to profl. jours. Mem. San Diego Career Women, Mortar Board (pres. 1973). Home and office: 2207 Sereno View Ln Olivenhain CA 92024

GRIFFITHS, MARTHA, lieutenant governor; b. Pierce City, Mo., Jan. 29, 1912; m. Hicks G. Griffiths. B.A., U. Mo.; J.D., U. Mich. Mem. Mich. Ho. of Reps., 1949-52; judge Recorders Ct., Detroit, 1953; U.S. rep. from Mich. Washington, 1955-75; lt. gov. State of Mich., 1983—; ptnr. Griffiths & Griffiths, Detroit. Democrat. Office: State Capitol Lansing MI 48913

GRIGG, BETTY ANN CARPENTER, medical corporation executive; b. Lincoln County, N.C., Nov. 23, 1932; d. Charles Frederick and Edna Elizabeth (Beck) Carpenter; m. Kenneth Andrew Grigg, Aug. 28, 1954; children: Kenneth Andrew Jr., Alexandra Grigg Beitz. BA, Wake Forest U., Winston-Salem, N.C., 1954; postgrad., George Washington U., 1969. Tchr. R.J. Reynolds High Sch., Winston-Salem, N.C., 1954-58; corp. sec. Kenneth A. Grigg, M.D., P.C., Washington, 1977—. Pres. Med. Officers Wives Club, Andrews AFB, Md., 1964-65; fundraiser Planned Parenthood Met. Washington, 1968-73; info. specialist breast cancer screening project Georgetown U. Hosp., 1973-77, mem. ladies bd., 1975—; group chmn. Meals on Wheels, Washington, 1975-77; bd. dirs. Sidwell Friends Sch. Parents Assn., Washington, 969-70, 76-77; mem. Parents Coun. Washington, 1975-76; polit. organizer numerous campaigns; bd. dirs. D.C. Polit. Action Com., 1974-75. Mem. Am. Psychiat. Assn. Aux., Med. Soc. Aux. D.C., AAUW (v.p. Washington br. 1976-77), Women's Nat. Dem. Club. Democrat. Home: 4832 Van Ness St NW Washington DC 20016 Office: 5225 Connecticut Ave NW Ste 616 Washington DC 20015

GRIGGS, PHYLLIS KAY, fast food chain executive; b. Grand Island, Nebr., Aug. 26, 1937; d. Fritz and Kathryn Rieger; m. Norman E. Griggs, Dec. 31, 1956 (div. 1971); 1 child, Tracy Kay. Grad., Nat. Sch. Bus., 1957. With Corner Constrn. Co., Rapid City, S.D., 1957-71; owner Mister Donut franchises, McAllen, Edinburgh and Brownsville, Tex., 1972—; chief exec. officer Ahora Que, Inc., McAllen, 1972—; owner Laundry Basket Laundromat, Weslaco, 1983—, Carousel Laundromats, McAllen, 1984—; mem. adv. council SBA, 1982—. Co-chmn. United Way, 1983; pres. McAllen Boy's Club, 1984—; assoc. mem. Boy's Club Am.; pres. Am. Heart Assn., 1987-88, 89-90; active Small Bus. Coun., Sr. Citizen's Adv. Bd.; bd. dirs. Firemen's Pensions Fund, Housing Svcs., McAllen Med. Ctr., 1990—; pres. bd. dirs. Humane Soc., 1990—; mem. Hidalgo County Elected Officials Assn.; commr. City of McAllen, 1986-90. Named Businessperson of Yr. for Tex. SBA, 1983, 5 State Region Businessperson ofYr., 1983. Mem. Orgn. Women Execs., Orgn. Outstanding Businesses (mem. steering com.), McAllen C. of C., Valley C. of C. (merit life mem.). Home: 1700 Fern St McAllen TX 78501 Office: 3616 N 23d #8 McAllen TX 78501

GRIGORIAN, MELINE, personnel service executive; b. Boston, Dec. 30, 1958; d. Carl Leon and Naomi Victoria (Basdekian) Zeytoonian; m. Avak Grigorian, May 2, 1987; 1 child, Ani Maral. BS in Mktg., Fla. State U., 1980. Pharmacy/store mgr. Rite Aid Corp., Medfield, Mass., 1980-81; sales rep. Am. Cablesystems, Arlington, Mass., 1981-83; personnel mgr. AAA Employment, Nashua, N.H., 1983-87; personnel mgr., sales rep. Ameribiz Employment, Bedford, N.H., 1983-87; v.p. Ameribiz Temps., Bedford, 1983-87; br. mgr. Olsten Corp., Framingham, Mass., 1987-88; v.p. ops., owner USA TEMPS, Ft. Lauderdale, Fla., 1988—; bus. cons. Jr. Achievement, Ft. Lauderdale, 1989-90. Vol. campaign Jim Smith Atty. Gen., Tallahassee, Fla., 1978; mem. Am. Mktg. Assn., Ft. Lauderdale, 1979-81. Mem. NAFE, Am. Bus. Women Am., Uptown Bus. Assn. (bd. dirs. 1989—), Ft. Lauderdale C. of C., Pompano Beach (Fla.) C. of C., Armenian Ch. Youth Orgn. Am. Armenian Apostolic. Office: USA TEMPS Inc 2700 W Cypress Creek Rd Fort Lauderdale FL 33309

GRIGSBY, MARGARET ELIZABETH, physician; b. Prairie View, Tex., Jan. 16, 1923; d. John Richard and Lee (Hankins) G. BS, Prairie View State Coll., 1943; MD, U. Mich., 1948. Diplomate: Nat. Bd. Med. Examiners, Am. Bd. Internal Medicine. Intern Homer G. Phillips Hosp., St. Louis, 1948-49, asst. resident medicine, 1949-50; asst. resident Freedmen's Hosp., Washington, 1950-51, asst. physician, 1952-56, attending physician, 1956; practice medicine specializing in internal medicine Washington, 1953-54; instr. medicine Howard U., Washington, 1952-57, asst. prof., 1957-60, assoc. prof., 1960-66, prof., 1966—, chief of infectious diseases, 1952-71, lectr. sch. social work, 1955-59, adminstrv. asst. dept. medicine sch. social work, 1961-63; epidemiologist USPHS, Ibadan, Nigeria, 1966-68; hon. vis. prof. preventive and social medicine U. Ibadan, 1967-68; cons. AID, Dept. State, 1970-71; mem. adv. com. anti-infective agents FDA, 1970-72. Contbr. articles to med. jours. Rockefeller Found. fellow Harvard U., 1951-52; research fellow Thorndike Meml. Lab., Boston City Hosp., 1951-52; China Med. Bd. fellow tropical medicine U. P.R., 1956; Commonwealth Fund Fellow U. London, 1962-63. Fellow ACP; mem. Nat. Med. Assn., Med. Soc. D.C., Royal Soc. Tripical Medicine and Hygiene, Am. Soc. Tropical Medicine and Hygiene, Medico-Chirug. Soc. D.C., Assn. Former Interns and Residents Freedman's Hosp., U. Mich. Alumni Assn., Prairie View Alumni Assn., Sigma Xi, Alpha Epsilon Iota, Alpha Kappa Alpha, Alpha Omega Alpha. Office: Howard U Dept Medicine 2041 Georgia Ave NW Washington DC 20060

GRIGSBY-STEPHENS, KLARON, corporate executive; b. East Prairie, Mo., Feb. 15, 1952; d. Klaron Grigsby and Sylvia Mae (Grigery) Oliver; m. Richard Earl Stephens, Aug. 13, 1986. Exec. asst. Quasar Petroleum Corp., Ft. Worth, 1974-80; sales mgr. ITT Life Ins. Corp., Ft. Worth, 1980-83; media buyer Boca Blue Star, Boca Raton, Fla., 1983-84; video editor Video Workshop, Pompano Beach, Fla., 1984-85; pres. Stephens Alfa Corp., Pompano Beach, 1985—; prin. Back In Times Antiques, Pompano Beach, 1990—. Author numerous poems. Sgt. USAF, 1970-74. Mem. Alfa Romeo Owners Club, Planetary Soc. Calif., Challenger Ctr. (Washington, hon.). Democrat. Office: Stephens Alfa Corp 1321 S Dixie Hwy W Pompano Beach FL 33060

GRIM, PATRICIA ANN, banker; b. Everett, Pa., Sept. 7, 1940; d. Harry Grant and Nellie Elizabeth (Koontz) Foor; m. James Woodrow Grim, Feb. 21, 1970. Student, Am. Inst. Banking, Rolling Meadows, Ill., Bank Adminstrn. Inst., The Bus. Women's Tng. Inst. Sec. William H. Snyder, Atty. at Law, Bedford, Pa., 1958-60; sec., loan teller First Nat. Bank of Everett, Pa., 1960-70; teller Orrstown (Pa.) Bank, 1970-81, asst. cashier, asst. sec., 1981-82, v.p., asst. sec., 1982—. Recipient Family Tng. Hour Leader of Yr. award Ch. of God State of Pa., Layman of Yr. award, 1979; nat. nominee Layperson of Yr., 1984. Mem. Ch. of God. Office: Orrstown Bank 3580 Orrstown Rd PO Box 60 Orrstown PA 17244-0060

GRIMAILA, PATRICIA PERPETUA, public health nurse; b. Wilkes-Barre, Pa., June 22, 1928; d. Joseph Adam and Anna Marie (Trimerka) G. BS Nursing, Georgetown U., 1954; MPH, Yale U., 1958; M. Higher Edn., U. Ariz., 1983. RN. Pub. health nurse Wyoming Valley Vis. Nurse Assn., Wilkes-Barre, 1949-52; dir. occupational health Georgetown U. Med. ctr., Washington, 1952-57; pub. health nurse-supr. USPHS, Fairfax, Va., 1958-60; researcher, cons. USPHS, Boston, 1960-64, Kansas City, Mo., 1964-65; cons., educator USPHS, Washington, 1965-69; cons. Indian Health Svc., Phoenix, 1969-74; researcher Indian Health Svc., Tucson, 1974-85; commd. nurse officer USPHS, 1958, advanced through grades to col., 1981, ret, 1985. Contbr. numerous papers on medicine and quality care in nursing homes in Quality Care Nursing Homes, 1965-69. Mem. D.C. League for Nursing (chairperson 1965-69, program chairperson 1965-69, pub. rels.), Am. Nurses Assn., Nat. League for Nursing. Roman Catholic.

GRIMES, CONNIE CARR, clothing retail executive; b. Luverne, Ala., Mar. 12, 1960; d. Samuel Millard and Lena Pearl (Mills) Carr; m. Adrian Fields Grimes, Sept. 4, 1982 (div. 1984). BS, Fashion Merchandising, Auburn U., 1982. Mgr. Brooks Fashion Stores, Inc., Montgomery and Auburn, Ala., 1983-85; area mgr. Brooks Fashion Stores, Inc., Huntsville, Ala., 1985-86; dist. mgr. Brooks Fashion Stores, Inc., Birmingham, Ala., 1986-88, One Price Clothing Stores, Inc., Birmingham, 1988—; field tng. cons. One Price Clothing Stores, Inc., 1989—. Republican. Baptist. Home: 3009 Alisa Way Birmingham AL 35243 Office: One Price Clothing Stores 1974 Forestdale Blvd Birmingham AL 35214

GRIMES, LENNA JUANITA, account executive; b. Norwich, Kans., Apr. 29, 1928; d. Emery Cleveland and Anna Maude (Stephens) Riley; m. James T. Grimes, June 12, 1949 (div. June 1971); children: Brenda Davis, James B., Jeff D., Jane Anne. Student, Colo. Woman's Coll., 1946-47; AA, Barton County Community Coll., Great Bend, Kans., 1973; BS, Sterling Coll., 1975. Realtor Don Dinning Gallery of Homes, Wichita, Kans., 1978-80; with Re/Max, Wichita, 1980-82; account exec. Wintrhop Pharms., div. Sterling Drugs, 1982—. Project leader Kab Clean Community System, Wichita, 1981; mem. Rep. Senatorial Inner Cir., Washington, 1984, Presdl. Roundtable, Washington, 1989. Mem. AAUW, Sedgwick County Rep. Women (publ. chmn. 1979-80), Phi Theta Kappa. Republican. Methodist. Home and Office: 8201 E Harry Townhouse 1903 Wichita KS 67207

GRIMES, MARGARET KATHERINE, English educator; b. Thomasville, N.C., May 5, 1955; d. Van Dolan and Edith Catherine (Bevan) G. BA, Catawba Coll., 1977; MA, U. N.C., 1978; postgrad., U. N.C., Greensboro, 1982-88. Instr. Western Piedmont Community Coll., Morganton, N.C., 1979-83; teaching fellow U. N.C., Greensboro, 1983-88; instr. English Louisburg (N.C.) Coll., 1988—. Contbr. book revs. Greensboro News & Record, 1986-87. Mem. various environ. and animal rights orgns. Mem. AAUW. Home: Rte 6 Box 477 Rocky Mount VA 24151 Office: Louisburg Coll 500 N Main St Louisburg NC 27549

GRIMES, MARTHA, author; b. Pittsburgh, Pa.; d. D.W. and June (Dunnington) G.; div.; 1 s.: Kent Van Holland. BA, MA, U. Md. Formerly instr. English U. Iowa, Iowa City; asst. prof. Frostburg State Coll., Frostburg, Md.; prof. Montgomery Coll., Takoma Park, Md., from 1970. Author: mystery novels The Man With a Load of Mischief, 1981, The Old Fox Deceiv'd, 1982, The Anodyne Necklace (Nero Wolfe Award for best mystery of yr.), 1983, The Dirty Duck, 1984, The Jerusalem Inn, 1984, Help the Poor Struggler, 1985, The Deer Leap, 1985, I Am the Only Running Footman, 1986, The Five Bells and Bladebone, 1987, The Old Silent, 1989. Address: care Little Brown & Co 34 Beacon St Boston MA 02106*

GRIMES, MARY ANNE, nurse; b. Kansas City, Kans., June 19, 1936; d. John Andy and Bertha Helen (Ball) G. R.N., St. Joseph's Hosp. Staff nurse St. Joseph's Hosp., Phoenix, 1957-61; office nurse Family Med. Clinic, Phoenix, 1961-62; pvt. duty nurse Central Registery, Phoenix, 1962-65; office nurse, mgr. Phoenix Urologic Clinic, 1965-79; sch. nurse Wilson Sch. Dist. 7, Phoenix, 1980-84, Balsz Sch. Dist. #31, 1984—. Primary fund raiser Classical Chorus Bach and Madrigal Soc., also sec., bd. dirs.; campaign worker Republican gubernatorial election, Phoenix, 1968, 70; patron Spreckels Organ Soc., San Diego. Mem. Am. Bus. Women's Assn. (pres. 1974-75), Nat. Assn. Sch. Nurses Inc., Ariz. Sch. Nurse Assn. Republican. Roman Catholic. Home: 1805 N 21st Pl Phoenix AZ 85006 Office: Balsz Sch Dist 31 4309 E Belleview Phoenix AZ 85008

GRIMES, PATRICIA STRAHOTA, architect, interior designer; b. Detroit, Sept. 27, 1951; d. Edward John and Theresa (Fodor) S.; m. Eugene Peter Grimes, Sept. 17, 1988. BS in Design, U. Mich., 1973. Registered architect, N.J. Draft person Hoad Engring., Ypsilanti, Mich., 1973; interior designer contract div. J.L. Hudson's, Detroit, 1973-74, John Steven's Assocs., Detroit, 1974, U. Mich., Ann Arbor, 1974-76, Ostgren Assocs., San Francisco, 1976-77; interior designer, architect Gensler & Assocs., San Francisco and N.Y.C., 1977-90; architect Cushman & Wakefield, Inc., N.Y.C., 1990—; guest lectr. N.Y. Sch. Interior Design, N.Y.C., 1984—. Mem. NOW, AIA (interiors subcom. 1988—). Office: Cushman & Wakfield 1166 Avenue of the Americas New York NY 10036-2766

GRIMES, RUTH ELAINE, city planner; b. Palo Alto, Calif., Mar. 4, 1949; d. Herbert George and Irene (Williams) Baker; m. Charles A. Grimes, July 19, 1969 (div. 1981); 1 child, Michael; m. Roger L. Sharpe, Mar. 20, 1984; 1 child, Teresa. AB summa cum laude, U. Calif.-Berkeley, 1970, M in City Planning, 1972. Research and evaluation coordinator Ctr. Ind. Living, Berkeley, 1972-74; planner City of Berkeley, 1974-76, sr. planner, 1983—, analyst, 1976-83; pres. Vets. Assistance Ctr., Berkeley, 1978—, also bd. dirs.; treas. Berkeley Design Advs., 1987—, also bd. dirs.; bd. dirs. Ctr. Ind. Living. Author: Berkeley Downtown Plan, 1988; contbr. numerous articles to profl. jours. and other publs. Honored by Calif. State Assembly Resolution, 1988; Edwin Frank Kraft scholar, 1966. Mem. Am. Inst. Cert. Planners, Am. Planning Assn., Am. Soc. Pub. Adminstrn., Mensa, Lake Merritt Joggers and Striders (sec. 1986—), Phi Beta Kappa. Home: 1330 Bonita Ave Berkeley CA 94709 Office: City of Berkeley 2180 Milvia St Berkeley CA 94704

GRIMLEY, CYNTHIA PATRIZI, rehabilitation consultant, special education teacher; b. Sharon, Pa., Mar. 29, 1958; d. James Donald and Delores Virginia (Maykowski) Patrizi; m. Kevin Neil Grimley, Apr. 11, 1987. BS, Youngstown (Ohio) State U., 1981; MS, Calif. State U., 1986. Lic. multiple subject tchr., spl. edn. and elem. tchr., severely handicapped edn. tchr., Ohio, Pa.; specialist credential, Calif. Residential program worker, supr., classroom tchr. Mercer County Assn. for the Retarded, Hermitage, Pa., 1980-82; tchr. spl. edn. Hermitage Sch. Dist., 1982-83; cons. property mgmt. Lorden Mgmt. Co., Covina, Calif., 1983-84; tchr. spl. edn. Fullerton (Calif.) Elem. Sch. Dist., 1984-87; vocat. rehab. cons. Profl. Rehab. Cons., Santa Ana, Calif., 1986-89, Pvt. Sector Rehab., Fullerton, 1989—i. Contbr. curriculum, articles in field. Coach spl. olympics, Fullerton, 1982-87; sec. So. Calif. Rehab. Exch., 1989, mem. at large, 1990—. Polish Art Club scholar, 1977. Mem. NEA, Nat. Assn. Rehab. Profls. in the Pvt. Sector, Calif. Nat. Assn. Rehab.Profls. in the Pvt. Sector, Assn. for Retarded Citizens. Democrat. Roman Catholic. Office: Pvt Sector Rehab 2555 E Chapman Ave Ste 300 Fullerton CA 92631

GRIMM, KATHLEEN, lawyer; b. Troy, N.Y., Mar. 21, 1946; d. Frederick Henry and Helen (Johnson) G. B.A., Manhattanville Coll., 1967; J.D. cum laude, N.Y. Law Sch., 1980; LL.M. in Taxation, NYU, 1984. Bar: N.Y. 1981. Tchr., Colegio de Vera Cruz, Cd. Obregon, Son., Mex., 1967-68; social worker, adminstr. Menorah Home & Hosp., Bklyn., 1969-78; atty. U.S. Dept. Treasury, IRS, N.Y.C., 1981-83; assoc. Parker, Duryee, Zunino, Malone & Carter, N.Y.C., 1983-85, 1st dep. Commr., N.Y.C. Dept. Fin., 1988—; dep. commr. audit and enforcement N.Y.C. Dept. Fin., 1985-88. Research coordinator casebook: Law, Medicine & Forensic Science, 1980. Mem. ABA, N.Y. State Bar Assn., Assn. of Bar of City of N.Y., N.Y. Law Sch. Alumni Assn. (bd. dirs.), Manhattanville Alumni Assn. (bd. dirs.). Roman Catholic. Club: Manhattanville of N.Y. (past pres.). Home: 333 E 69th St New York NY 10021 Office: NYC Dept Fin 1 Centre St New York NY 10007

GRIMM, PAULA, advertising executive, strategic planner; b. Troy, N.Y., Nov. 10, 1950; d. Frederick Henry and Helen Marie (Johnson) G. BA in Am. Studies, Manhattanville Coll., Purchase, N.Y., 1974. Rsch. assoc. Scali McCabe, Sloves, N.Y.C., 1974-79, assoc. rsch. dir., 1981-86; rsch. group head Dancer, Fitzgerald, Sample, N.Y., 1979-81; dir. of strategic planning and rsch. Saatchi & Saatchi DFS/Pacific, Torrance, Calif., 1986—. Mem. Townhall of L.A., 1989-90. Mem. Am. Mktg. Assn., Western States Advt. Agys., AEF Advt. Ednl. Found. Home: 6226 Colgate Ave Los Angeles CA 90036 Office: Saatchi & Saatchi DFS/Pacific 3501 Sepulveda Blvd Torrance CA 90505

GRIMMER, MARGOT, dancer, choreographer, director; b. Chgo., Apr. 5, 1944; d. Vernon and Ann (Radville) G.; m. Weymouth Kirkland; 1 child, Ashley Samantha Grimmer Kirkland; student Lake Forest; 1963, Northwestern U., 1964-68. Dancer, N.Y.C. Ballet prodn. of Nutcracker Chgo., 1956-57, Kansas City Starlight Theatre, 1958, St. Louis Mcpl. Theatre, 1959, Chgo. TentHouse-Music Theater, 1960-61, Lyric Opera Ballet, Chgo., 1961, 63-66, 68, Ballet Russe de Monte Carlo, N.Y.C., 1962, Ruth Page Internat. Ballet, Chgo., 1965-70; dancer-choreographer Am. Dance Co., Chgo., 1972—, artistic dir., 1972—; dancer, choreographer Bob Hope Show, Milw., 1975, Washington Bicentennial Performance, Kennedy Center, 1976, Woody Guthrie Benefit Concerts, 1976-77, Assyrian Cultural Found., Chgo., 1977-78, Iranian Consulate Performance, Chgo., 1978, Israeli Consulate Concert, Chgo., 1980 Chgo. Council Fine Arts Programs, 1978-87, U.S. Boating Indsl. Show, 1981—; dir.-tchr. Am. Dance Sch., 1971—; tchr. master classes U. Ill, 1975, 83, Anderson Hall, Occidental and Sebastopol Community Ctr., Calif., 1988, Park Point Club, Santa Rosa, Calif., 1988-89, Oakland (Calif.) Dance Collective, 1989—; appeared in TV commls. and indsl. films for Libbys Foods, Sears, Gen. Motors, others, 1963—, also in feature film Risky Business, 1982; soloist in ballet Repertory Workshop, CBS-TV, 1964, dance film Statics (Internat. Film award), 1967; soloist in concert Ravinia, 1973; important works include ballets In-A-Gadda-Da-Vida, 1972, The Waste Land, 1973, Rachmaninoff: Theme and Variations, 1973, Le Baiser de la Fee and Sonata, 1974, Four Quartets, 1974, Am. Export, 1975, Earth, Wind and Fire, 1976, Blood, Sand and Empire, 1977, Disco Fever, 1978, Pax Romana, Xanadu, 1979, Ishmael, 1980, Vertigo, 1982, Eye in the Sky, 1984, Frankie Goes to Hollywood, 1986, Power House Africano, 1987, others; dance critic Mail-Advertiser Publs., 1980-82; host cable TV show Spotlight, 1984-85, View-points, 1987. Ill. Arts Council Grantee, 1972-75, 78; Nat. Endowment Arts grantee, 1973-74. Mem. Actors Equity Assn., Screen Actors Guild, Am. Guild Mus. Artists. Home: 970 Vernon Ave Glencoe IL 60022 Office: 442 Central Ave Highland Park IL 60035

GRINDLE, BARBARA S., materials manager; b. Akron, Ohio, Dec. 5, 1955; d. George H. Jr. and Gloria (Lecroy) Shelton; m. Rickey F. Grindle, Dec. 21, 1976; children: Jason Andrew, Barbara Renee. BA, Ga. State U., 1989. Cert. effective time mgmt. Materials mgr. J. William Co. div. John H. Harland, Covington, Ga.; office mgr. TAJ Industries, Decatur, Ga.; sec. Glenn Rosser, Builder, Conyers, Ga.; clk. Liberty Nat. Life Ins., Gadsden, Ala. Mem. Nat. Assn. Purchasing Mgmt., Am. Purchasing Soc., NAFE. Home: 1190 Maggie Ln Conyers GA 30208 Office: 11194 Alcory Rd Covington GA 30209

GRISE, WILMA MARIE, small business owner; b. Kingfisher, Okla., Sept. 4, 1937; d. William and Martha (Brandt) Krittenbrink; m. Paul Grise, Aug. 23, 1956 (div. May 1962); children: Mary Monica MacMartin, Marti Gile. Founder, owner Wichita (Kans.) Auto Auction, 1966—. Democrat. Roman Catholic. Home: 4635 S Broadway Wichita KS 67216 Office: Wichita Auto Auction 3820 S Broadway Wichita KS 67216

GRISEUK, GAIL GENTRY, financial consultant; b. Providence, Jan. 24, 1948; d. Marvin Houghton and Gertrude Emma (Feather) Gentry; divorced; 1 child, Christina Deborah. Student (Fla. Power Corp. scholar), Fla. State U., 1966-70. Registry of Fin. Planning Practitioners. Cert. fin. ops. prin.; cert. gen. securities prin.; registered investment advisor. Asst. div. controller Mobile Home Industries, Tallahassee, 1968-70; owner, mgr. BDI Services, Tallahassee and Lake Charles, La., 1970-78; fin. cons. Aylesworth Fin., Inc., Clearwater, Fla., 1978-82; chmn. bd., chief exec. officer Gail Griseuk & Assocs. Inc., 1982-89, pres., chief exec. officer, 1989—; chief exec. officer GAI Internat. Investment Advisors, Inc., 1985—; instr., dir. vet. outreach Angelina Coll., Lufkin, Tex., 1975-76. Contbr. short stories to Redbook, McCall's, Christian Home. Vol., Sunland Tng. Center, 1970-72, George Criswell House, 1969-73. Mem. Inst. Cert. Fin. Planners, Internat. Platform Assn., Internat. Assn. Fin. Planners. Methodist. Home: 1024 Woodcrest Ave Clearwater FL 33516 Office: 5301 Central Ave Saint Petersburg FL 33710

GRISHAM, EDITH PEARL MOLES, librarian; b. Pinch, W.Va., Mar. 27, 1926; d. Edward Lawrence and Effie (Christy) Moles; m. Charles M. Grisham (div.). A.A., San Antonio Coll., 1958; B.B.A. cum laude, St. Mary's U., 1961; postgrad. Our Lady of the Lake, San Antonio, 1964; M.L.S., Tex. Woman's U., 1973. Billing, sales service asst. Uvalde Rock Asphalt Co., San Antonio, Tex., 1953-62; office mgr. Data Processing Ctr., Inc., San Antonio, 1962-64; serials librarian Houston Pub. Library, 1964-65, head lit. biography dept., 1966-68, head bus. and tech. dept., 1968-73; head Tech. Library Brown & Root, Inc., Houston, 1973-83; reference librarian Incarnate Word Coll., 1984—. Editor, compiler: Union List of Engineering Standards, Specifications, and Codes in Selected Texas Libraries, 1978. Served sgt. USAAF and USAF, 1944-53. Mem. Spl. Libraries Assn., Kappa Pi Sigma, Alpha Beta Alpha. Democrat. Lutheran.

GRISHAM, JUDITH ANN, nurse; b. Kansas City, Mo., Nov. 15, 1949; d. Joseph Edwin and Irene (Stump) Blough; m. Clarence Ray Black, Mar. 30, 1968 (div. 1984); children: Christina Lynn, Jennifer Ann, Carolyn Rae; m. Buford Glyn Grisham, May 2, 1987. Degree in nursing, Middle Tenn. State U., 1987. RN, Tenn., Fla. Stenographer Drs. Stern, Salky & Holloway, Memphis, 1971-72; staff nurse Lee Meml. Hosp., Ft. Myers, Fla., 1987—; asst. to instr. Lamaze childbirth classes, Memphis, 1974; com. mem. Profl. Practice Model Lee Meml. Hosp., 1989—. Vol. La Leche League Internat., Memphis, 1973-74; vol. Muscular Dystrophy Assn., Memphis, Nashville, 1979—, v.p. S. Suncoast chpt.; youth dir. Christ the King Luth. Ch., Memphis, 1982-83; chmn. Memphis Childbirth Edn. Assn., 1974-75; active in numerous booster clubs. Recipient award Muscular Dystrophy Assn., 1983. Mem. Gamma Beta Phi.

GRISPINO, MARIA GENEVIEVE, entrepreneur; b. Kingston, Pa., Jan. 10, 1954; d. Paul C. and Genevieve A. (Zyskowski) Sidloski; m. Anthony J. Grispino, May 26, 1985 (dec. Aug. 1989). AS in Bus. Adminstrn., Franklin U., Columbus, Ohio, 1981, BSBA, 1982, AS in Acctg., 1983. Installment loan clk. Northeastern Nat. Bank, Wilkes-Barre, Pa., 1971-73; clk. typist Naval Engring. Svc. Unit, Sigonella, Italy, 1977-78; word processing specialist Nat. Water Well Assn., Worthington, Ohio, 1980-81; contr. Donfast, Inc., Columbus, 1982-90, v.p., 1984-89; v.p. Gift of Gold Mktg., Inc., Dublin, Ohio, 1990, owner, 1990—; v.p. RPW & Assocs., Inc., Dayton, Ohio, 1987—; sec. DFD Inc., Dayton, 1985-88; treas. Thermal Devel. Corp., Columbus, 1988—. Author various handbooks. Asst. Vietnam Vets Am., Columbus, 1981-82. With USN, 1974-77. Mem. Franklin U. Alumni Assn., Investing in Earnest Ventures Investment Club, U.S. Golf Assn. (assoc.), Tau Pi Phi. Republican. Office: Gift of Gold Mktg Inc 6059 Frantz Rd Ste 202 Dublin OH 43017-3322

GRISSOM, BEVERLY MCMURTRY, college official; b. Lebanon, Ky., June 10, 1946; d. Fernn Vance and Leoda Maye (Clemens) McMurtry; divorced; 1 child, Tammaye Vanece. BA, U. Louisville, 1968; MA, Western Ky. U., 1976; postgrad. in edn., U. Fla., 1990. Coord. Louisville Ind. Schs., 1974-75; learning mgr. tng. and svcs. ctr. Daytona Beach (Fla.) Community

Coll., 1975-77, coord., 1977-82, dir. spl. programs, 1982, dir. adult edn., 1982-89, dean adult edn., 1989-90, dean adult edn. and lifelong learning, 1990—. Bd. dirs. Daytona Beach Leadership Coun., 1982-90, bd. dirs. 1982-85, 86-90, sec. 1982-85, pres., 1989, 90; mem., past chmn. adv. bd. Daytona Beach Community Correctional Ctr., 1983—; past pres. and sec. adv. com. Spruce Creek High Sch., Daytona Beach, 1985-87; mem. dist. adv. com. Volusia County Schs., 1987—; chair Fla. Continuing Edn. Standing Com., 1989—. Mem. Fla. Assn. Community Colls. (sec., pres. local chpt. 1983-84, bd. dirs. region III., 1984-85, cert. of outstanding svc. 1988), Am. Assn. for Adult and Continuing Edn. (dir. at large 1988—, exec. planning com. 1986 conf., mem. exec. bd., sec. 1990—), Commn. on Adult Basic Edn. (pres. 1987-88, cert. of outstanding svc. 1978, 82), Fla. Adult Edn. Assn. (Outstanding Svc. award 1988, pres. 1989—), Pilot Club of Halifax Area (bd. dirs.). Home: 70 Timberlake Ln Ormond Beach FL 32174 Office: Daytona Beach Community College 1200 Volusia Ave Daytona Beach FL 32115

GRISSOM, KIMBERLY DIANE, sales executive; b. Columbia, Tenn., Mar. 22, 1963; d. Arnold Lee and Ruth Elizabeth (Massey) G. BFA in Graphic Design, U. Tenn., Chattanooga, 1987. Graphics officer TVA, Chattanooga, 1987-88; sales rep. Reynolds & Reynolds (previously The Arnold Corp.), Chattanooga, 1988—. Mem. Chattanooga Jaycees (bd. dirs. 1988-89, v.p. ways and means com. 1989-90, v.p. chpt. mgmt. 1990—, Dir. of Yr. 1989). Republican. Mem. Ch. of Christ. Home: 848-A Oak St Chattanooga TN 37403 Office: Reynolds & Reynolds 1119 Dodds Ave Chattanooga TN 37404

GRISSOM, PATSY COLEEN, college administrator, English educator; b. Mt. Pleasant, Tex., Jan. 9, 1934; d. Thomas A. and Cleo (Jones) G. BA, East Tex. State U., 1955; MA, Syracuse U., 1957; PhD, U. Tex., 1966. Student dean, head resident Syracuse (N.Y.) U., 1955-57; head resident, instr. English Hanover (Ind.) Coll., 1957-58, Trinity U., San Antonio, 1958-61; teaching asst., assoc. dean of students U. Tex., Austin, 1961-64; assoc. dean of students, asst. prof. English Trinity U., San Antonio, 1964-72, v.p. student affairs, prof. English, 1972—. Named Outstanding Prof., Trinity U. chpt. Mortar Bd., 1976. Mem. AAUW, Nat. Assn. Student Personnel Adminstrs., Nat. Assn. Women Deans and Counselors. Democrat. Presbyterian. Office: Trinity Univ Box 99 715 Stadium Dr San Antonio TX 78284

GRISWOLD, VALERIE ANNE, deputy district attorney; b. Bennington, Vt., July 26, 1962; d. Thomas and Ernestine Anne (Stafford) G. BS, Iowa State U., 1985; JD, U. San Diego, 1988. Bar: Calif. 1988. Assoc. Hagenbaugh & Murphy, L.A., 1988; dep. dist. atty. Orange County D.A.'s Office, Santa Ana, Calif., 1989—. Mem. ABA, Calif. Bar Assn., Orange County Bar Assn., Orange County Dist. Atty. Assn., Women Prosecutors Calif., Zool. Soc. San Diego, World Wildlife Fund, Calif. Marine Mammal Ctr., Sierra Club. Office: Orange County Dist Atty Off 700 Civic Ctr Dr W Santa Ana CA 92701

GRITTON, PATRICIA BAUMAN, manufacturing executive; b. Cin., Sept. 10, 1916; d. Paul Albert and Elenor Marvela (Simpson) Bauman; m. Robert J. Gritton, Oct. 11, 1947 (dec. Jan. 1983). BS in Libr. Sci., Kent State U., 1945; postgrad., Akron U., 1956, 65, 72, 85. Children's librarian Taylor Meml. Pub. Libr., Cuyahoga Falls, Ohio, 1937-56; owner Bauman Steel Rule Cutting Dies, Cuyahoga Falls, 1957—. Bd. dirs., membership chmn. Taylor Libr. Friends, 1967—; bd. dirs. Cuyahoga Falls Hist. Soc., 1975—; active Akron Radio Hall of Fame, 1983—, membership com., bd. dirs. 1989—. Recipient Contribution to the Achievement of John H. Glenn Jr. award Ohio C. of C. Mem. Ohio Pub. Employee Retirees Inc. (life), DAR, Cuyahoga Falls Camping Club, Widow to Widow Breakfast Club, Beta Sigma Phi (life). Democrat. Presbyterian. Home and Office: Bauman Steel Rule Cutting Dies 2825 Vincent St Cuyahoga Falls OH 44221

GRIVALSKY, ELEANOR ANN, sales executive; b. Morristown, N.J., Nov. 10, 1944; d. Stephen G. and Mary C. (Migdol) G. BS cum laude, Fairleigh Dickinson U., 1986; AA magna cum laude, County Coll. of Morris, 1978. Sales adminstr. Warner-Lambert Co., Morris Plains, N.J., exec. sec. State of N.J. commr. to Town of Boonton (N.J.) Housing Authority, 1987—; mem. Town of Boonton Bd. Adjustment, 1988—; vol. to various town and charitable orgns. and local hosps.; reader ch. svcs. Mem. NAFE, Toastmasters Internat., Kiwanis (Boonton First Aid Squad 1965-83), Delta Mu Delta, Phi Omega Epsilon, Omicron Delta Kappa. Home: 141 N Main St Boonton NJ 07005-1257 Office: Warner-Lambert Co 201 Tabor Rd Morris Plains NJ 07950

GRIZZLE, MARY R., state senator; b. Lawrence County, Ohio, Aug. 19, 1921; ed. Portsmouth Interstate Bus. Coll.; m. Ben F. Grizzle (dec.); children—Henry, Polley, Lorena, Mary Alice, Betty, Jeanne; m. Charles H. Pearson. Mem. Fla. Ho. of Reps., 1963-78; mem. Fla. Senate, 1978—, chmn. Exec. Bus. Com., vice chmn. Natural Resources and Conservation Com., Appropriations Com. Past chmn. Fla. Commn. on Status of Women; govt. rep. Nat. Conf. Women Community Leaders for Hwy. Safety; active P.T.A.; mem. Pinellas County (Fla.) Civil Service Com., Pinellas County Planning Com. Former town commr.; past pres. Women's Rep. Com. Named One of Ten Outstanding Women, St. Petersburg Times, 1966; recipient Achievement award Fla. Rehab. Assn., 1979; hon. life mem. Pinellas County Sch. Food Services, 1979; Largo Jr. Women's Club Woman of Year, 1980. Mem. League Women Voters, Largo Bus. and Profl. Womens Club, Altrusa, Woman's Club, Nat. Soc. Arts and Letters, Delta Kappa Gamma (hon. Alpha Phi chpt.). Episcopalian. Author: (with others) Thimbleful of History. Office: 2601 Jewel Rd Ste C Belleair Bluffs FL 34640

GRIZZLE, RHONDA MEWBORN, educator; b. Anderson, S.C., Dec. 7, 1952; d. Charles Duncan Mewborn and Carolyn Rebecca Smith; m. Ronnie Neal Grizzle, Dec. 17, 1972; children: Eli Russell Duncan and Tyler Blaine. BS, U. Ga., Athens, 1975, MEd., 1977. Tchr. Douglas Co. Bd. Edn., Douglasville, Ga., 1978-89; data collector Douglas Co., MCESA, Atlanta, 1985-90; dir. kindergarten Austell (Ga.) Presbyn. Ch., 1990—; math chairperson Annette Winn Elem. Lithia Springs Ga., 1982-89, Math subcom. Douglas Co. Sch. System Douglasville, 1982-90; curriculum study com. Douglas Co. Sch. System Douglasville, 1987-90. Creator: Exhibit DCAE Instructional Fair/Math Materials ECE, 1983 (hon. mention 1983), Exhibit DCAE Instructional Fair, Flying into Readiness, 1986 (1st Place Winner 1986); creator, dir. Second Saturdays Grant Park, 1980. Exec. bd. mem. Annette Winn PTA Lithia Springs, 1988-90; administrv. bd. mem. First United Meth. Ch. Lithia Springs, 1986-89; chairperson United Way Annette Winn Douglasville, 1987; coord. Bike-A-Thon St. Judes Children's Rsch. Hosp., Lithia Springs, 1990. Recipient Tchr. Honoree Nomination Atlanta Jour. Constitution Atlanta, 1989, Highest Sch. Participation 100% United Way Douglasville, 1987; named Tchr. of the Day WPLO, Atlanta, 1981. Mem. Douglas County Assn. Educators (chmn. and exec. bd. 1981-89), Ga. Presch. Assn., Assn. of Classroom Tchrs., Ga. Assn. Educators, NEA, Ga. Council Tchrs. of Math. Dem. Methodist. Home: 2395 Justine Terr Lighia Springs GA 30057 Office: Austell Presbyn Ch 5895 Love St PO Box 68 Austell GA 30001

GROAH, LINDA KAY, nursing administrator and educator; b. Cedar Rapids, Iowa, Oct. 5, 1942; d. Joseph David and Irma Josephine (Zitek) Rozek; diploma St. Luke's Sch. Nursing, Cedar Rapids, 1963; student San Francisco City Coll., 1976-77; BA, St. Mary's Coll., Moraga, Calif., 1978; BS in Nursing, Calif. State U.; MS in Nursing, U. Calif.; m. Patrick Andrew Groah, Mar. 20, 1975; 1 child, Kimberly; stepchildren: Nadine, Maureen, Patrick, Marcus. Staff nurse to head nurse U. Iowa, 1963-67; clin. supr., dir. oper. and recovery room Michael Reese Hosp., Chgo., 1967-73; dir. oper. rooms Med. Ctr. Cen. Ga., Macon, 1973-74; dir. oper. and recovery rooms U. Calif. Hosps. and Clinics, San Francisco, 1974-89, asst. dir. hosps. and clinics, 1982-86; clin. instr. U. Calif. Sch. Nursing, San Francisco, 1975—; cons. to oper. room suprs., to div. ednl. resources and programs Assn. Am. Med. Colls., 1976—; condr. seminars. Mem. Nat. League for Nurses, Am. Nurses Assn. (vice chmn. operating room conf. group 1974-76), Assn. Oper. Room Nurses (com. on nominations 1979-84, treas. 1985-87, Award for Excellence in Preoperative Nursing 1989), Ctr. for Study Dem. Instns. Author: Perioperative Nursing Practice, 1983, 2d edit., 1990; contbr. articles on operating room techniques to profl. jours. and textbooks; author, producer audio-visual presentations; author computer software. Home: 5 Mateo Dr Tiburon CA 94920 Office: M423B 3020 Bridge Way Ste 299 Sausalito CA 94965

GROAT, ROBIN R., travel agency executive; b. Bronxville, N.Y., Oct. 7, 1930; d. George V. and Elizabeth L. (Chase) Robbins; m. William B. Groat III, June 28, 1952 (div. 1974); 1 child, Janet L. Student, Queens Coll., 1953-54. Cons. FNCB Travel Svcs., N.Y.C., 1967; owner Esq. Travel Svc., N.Y.C., 1969-73; mgr. Don Travel Svc., N.Y.C., 1973-83, Walco, Palm Springs, Calif., 1983, Anderson Travel Svc., LaQuinta, Calif., 1983—. Mem., usher McCullam Theatre, Palm Desert, Calif., 1988—; sec. Casa Sonora Homeowners Assn., Palm Springs, Calif., 1985—; active La Quinta Arts Found., La Quinta, Calif., 1983—; dir. La Quinta Classic Jazz Festival, 1987—. Mem. La Quinta C. of C. (bd. dirs. 1985-86, 2d v.p. 1986-87, sec. 1987-88, 1st v.p. 1988-90, vol. 1988), Soroptimist Internat. Republican. Episcopalian. Home: 1713 Capri Circle Palm Springs CA 92264

GROBELNY, LORI JO-ANN, manufacturing executive; b. New Brunswick, N.J., June 14, 1954; d. Stanley Joseph and Rose Marie (Toth) G. BA, Douglass Coll., 1976. Mgr. prod. N.Am. Container Corp., North Brunswick, N.J., 1976—; bd. dirs. Indsl. Capital Corp., Lawrenceville, Housing Capital Corp., New Hyde Park. Mem. Nat. Rep. Com. Mem. Douglass Coll. Alumnae Assn. Roman Catholic. Club: Douglass Coll. Alumnae Assn. Home: 1 Apple St Edison NJ 08817 Office: N Am Container Corp 501 Finnegans Ln North Brunswick NJ 08902

GROESBECK, ELISE DE BRANGES DE BOURICA, artist; b. Versailles, France, Jan. 31, 1936 (parents Am. citizens); d. Vicount Louis de Branges de Bourcia II and Diane (McDonald) de Branges de Bourcia; student Phila. Coll. Art, 1954-55; m. James Richard Groesbeck, Oct. 3, 1958 (div. June 1969); children: Gretchen Atlee, Genevieve de Branges. One-man shows The Agnes Irwin Sch., Rosemont, Pa., 1973, Phila. Cricket Club, Chestnut Hill, Pa., 1973. Recipient prize Rehoboth Beach Art League, 1944; Agnes Allen Art prize Agnes Irwin Sch., 1954. Repubican. Episcopalian. Home: 3204 Leigh Rd Pompano Beach FL 33062 Office: Box 58 Pompano Beach FL 33061

GROFF, JOANN, state legislator, banker; b. Ft. Leonardwood, Mo., Oct. 10, 1956; d. Barry T. Groff and Ann (Ferry) Ragsdale. Student Georgetown U., 1974-76; B.S. in Bus. Adminstrn., Babson Coll., Wellesley, Mass., 1978. Office mgr. Morgan Smith for Congress, Northglenn, Colo., 1978; fair and rodeo asst. Adams County Commrs., Brighton, Colo., 1979; mktg. devel. officer Columbine Title Co., Lakewood, Colo., 1979-80; express agt., loan officer Wells Fargo Credit Corp., Englewood, Colo., 1981-84; pub. banking rep. Cen. Bank of Denver, 1985-89; mem. Colo. Ho. of Reps., Denver, 1983-89, chmn. audit com., 1989, fin. com. Mem. Colo. State Democratic Com., 1980—, Colo. State Exec. Com., 1983—, del. Nat. Conv., 1980, 84, alternate del., 1976. Bd. dirs. Westminster (Colo.) Community Artist Series, Marycrest High Sch., Colo. Food Bank Coalition. Mem. Met. North C. of C. Roman Catholic. Office: Colorado Counties Inc 1177 Grant Denver CO 80203

GROGAN, ALICE WASHINGTON, lawyer; b. Richmond, Va., Jan. 25, 1956; d. Thomas Boyd Washington Jr. and Dorothy Jane (Smith) W.; m. Ralph Houston Grogan, Feb. 4, 1989. BS with honors, Va. Poly. Inst., 1978; JD, U. N.C., 1984. Bar: N.C. 1984, U.S. Supreme Ct. 1988. Corp. sec., atty. Piedmont Aviation, Inc., Winston-Salem, N.C., 1984-88; assoc. Womble Carlyle Sandridge & Rice, Winston-Salem, 1988-89; legal counsel Wachovia Bank & Trust Co., Winston-Salem, 1989—. Mem. ABA (sec. taxation, sect. bus. law, corp. counsel com., subcom. fin. and securities), N.C. Bar Assn. (corp. counsel sect., young lawyers div.), Forsyth County Bar Assn. (young lawyers div.), Forsyth County Employee Benefits Coun., Va. Tech. Alumni Assn., U. N.C. Gen. Alumni Assn., U. N.C. Ednl. Found., Phi Kappa Phi, U.S. Rowing Assn.

GROGAN, BETTE LOWERY, steel fastener distribution executive; b. Seminole, Okla., Nov. 18, 1931; d. C.J. and Martha C. (Eakin) Lowery; m. Morris Rowell, Feb. 8, 1947 (div. Oct. 1960); children—Ronald Michael, Kathy D. Rowell Burkard; m. John Kenneth Grogan, Oct. 28, 1967. Student Del Mar Coll., 1949-51, So. Meth. U., 1963-65. Sec., office mgr. Carrigan Realty, Orlando, Fla., 1958-61; dist. sec. Tektronics, Inc., Orlando, 1961-63; legal sec. Jenkens, Anson, Spradley & Gilchrist, Dallas, 1963-67; real estate broker, Dallas, 1967-77; v.p. Grogan & Co., Dallas, 1972-77; pres. Fla. Threaded Products Inc., Orlando, 1977—; dir. Women's Bus. Ednl. Council (pres. 1986, chmn. bd. 1987), Inc., Orlando, pres., 1986. Mem. Planning and Zoning Commn., Carrollton, Tex., 1972-74; bd. dirs. Jr. Achievement, Orlando, 1981-83. Named Cen. Fla. Small Bus. Person of the Yr., SBA-C. of C., 1981. Mem. Women's Bus. Ednl. Confs. Fla. (bd. dirs. 1984-85, exec. v.p. 1985-86, pres. 1986, chmn. bd. dirs. 1987), Nat. Fedn. Ind. Bus. (guardian adv. council), Fastener Assn. (bd. dirs. 1980-84), Central Fla. Leadership Council (bd. dirs. 1984—), Greater Orlando C. of C. (chairperspm N.W. regional coun. 1990), Nat. Fedn. Ind. Businesses (Guardian Adv. Council Fla. 1987), Fla. Exec. Women, Better Bus. Bur. Central Fla. (mem. exec. com., chmn. 1989, bd. dirs. 1989), Beta Sigma Phi (pres. Orlando 1957-59). Republican. Episcopalian. Avocations: tennis, golf, reading. Office: Fla Threaded Products Inc 3060 Clemson Rd Orlando FL 32808

GROGAN, RAE, sales executive; b. Chgo., May 1, 1954; d. Raymond P. and Therese (Skorupa) Ulatoski; divorced; children: Sean Michael, Rae Michele. Student, Joliet Jr. Coll., 1973; student, Coll. DuPage, 1974-75Cert. ie. Adminstrv. asst. Sears, Roebuck & Co., Chgo., 1972-78; with real estate sales Centex Corp., Chgo., 1975-77, Columbia Homes, Chgo., 1978-79; photo studio mgr. PCA Internat., Miami, Fla., 1979-80; pub. relations dir. Counterpulsation, Inc., Miami, 1981-83; graphic design co. pres. Rae's Custom Creations, Inc., Miami, 1981-85; wholesale sales and regional mgr. Miramar Mktg., Inc., Miami, 1984-85; owner Imagination, Unltd. Chain of Gift Concessions, Miami, 1984-86; v.p. sales nat. and internat. Nat. Theme Prodns., San Diego, 1983-89; v.p. sales Masquerade Internat., San Diego, 1990—; nat. media rep. for Nat. Theme Prodns., 1983-89; guest speaker career devel. Catholic Women's Guild, 1983-89. Pres. Christ the King Women's Club, Miami, 1986; mem., vol. Archdiocese Miami Respect Life, 1986-88. Mem. NAFE, Am. Mgmt. Assn., Nat. Retail Merchants Assn., Ohio Coop. Edn. Assn., Midwest Coop. Edn. Assn., San Diego C. of C., Toastmasters. Roman Catholic. Office: Masquerade Internat Direct 1843 Hotel Circle S San Diego CA 92108

GROH, LUCILLE SIDER, pastoral counselor and administrator; b. Ont., Can., June 29, 1946; d. James Peter and Ida Grace (Cline) Sider; m. Dennis E. Groh, Apr. 29, 1984; children: Jeremy, Sara, Soren Dayton. BA, Messiah Coll., 1967; postgrad., Yale U., 1969; MS, U. Ky., 1970; PhD, Northwestern U., 1981. Ordained minister Congregational Ch. Dir. The Samaritan Pastoral Counseling Ctr. Evanston/Wilmette, Evanston, Ill.; sr. staff psychotherapist Parkside Pastoral Counseling Ctr., Park Ridge, Ill.; founder, editor Daughters of Sarah, Chgo.; asst. dir. Urban Life Ctr., Chgo. Contbr. articles to profl. jours. Fellow Am. Assn. Pastoral Counselors (chairperson profl. concerns com. cen. region). Home: 2743 Meadowlark Ln Evanston IL 60201

GROHNKE, SUSAN KAY, human resources executive; b. Starbuck, Minn., Oct. 3, 1944; d. Gilman Burnett and Lola Mary (Chambers) Heegard; m. Randolph C. Grohnke, Sept. 18, 1971 (div. 1978); 1 child, Michael Scott Femrite. Student, Mpls. Vo-Tech., 1965, Lowthian Sch., Mpls., 1975. Customer svc. Herberger's Dept. store, Alexandria, Minn., 1966-69; office adminstr. Gen. Adjustment Bur., Mpls., 1970-72; office adminstr., cons. Roth Young Peronnel, Mpls., 1972-76; v.p. adminstrn. Roth Young Exec. Recruiters, Mpls., 1988—. Asst. dir. Matt Blair Football Sch., Mpls., 1981-84; supr. Pro-Choice for Minn., Mpls., 1989-90. Mem. NAFE (Twin Cities chpt.), Mpls. C. of C., Minn. Assn. Human Resource Cons.n Northland Fitness Club. Office: Roth Young Exec Recruiters 4530 W 77th St Edina MN 55435

GRONDIN, MARY L., healthcare company executive; b. Mich., Oct. 19, 1941; d. Nathan F. and Mae L. (Jimo) G. MBA, Wagner Coll., 1977. Lic. nursing home adminstr., Ill., N.Y. Vice chmn. Caremore Corp., Evanston; acting adminstr. The Saratoga of Highland Park, Ill.; chief operating officer Frank Cuneo Meml. Hosp., Chgo. Author: Providing Alcoholism Services in Acute Care. Bd. trustees Am. Cancer Soc., 1984-85; mem. Uptown-Edgewater Commn., 1988-89. Mem. Am. Acad. Med. Adminstrs., Am. Coll. Healthcare Execs. Republican. Home: 4740 N Hamilton St Chicago IL 60625 Office: Port Clinton Sq 600 Central Ave Ste 333 Highland Park IL 60035

GRONICK, PATRICIA ANN JACOBSEN, school system administrator; b. Madison, S.D., May 1, 1931; d. Jay C. and Lauretta (Lynch) Jacobsen; m. Joseph Gronick, Aug. 12, 1950; 1 child, Joseph Patrick Michael. BS, Pa. State U., 1952; MEd, Kent State U., 1970; postgrad., John Carroll U., 1972—. Home economist to dir. regional home econs. West Pa. Power Co., Pitts., 1952-61; dir. nat. home econs. Cleve. Range Co., 1961-70; coord. mktg. edn. Beachwood, Mayfield, Richmond Heights, Orange, Chagrin Falls, West Geauga, Aurora and Solon Sch. Systems, Ohio, 1969—; coord. distributive edn. Mayfield, Richmond Heights, Orange, Bratenahl, and Beachwood Sch. Systems, Ohio, 1970—; cons. photog. food layouts, 1960-61. Recipient Mktg. award Ohio State Dept., 1983, 88, Svc. award, Voc. Ednl. Plannint Dist., Mayfield, 1988, Award for Ednl. Excellence, 1988, VIP award, 1988. Mem. Cleve. Social Health and Welfare Assn., Am. Home Econs. Assn., AAUW, Elec. Women's Round Table, Internat. Fedn. Univ. Women, Cath. Daus. Am., Home Economists in Bus., Woman's Club (rec. sec. Cleve. 1962, parliamentarian 1965-66), Isabella Guild (officer 1985-89), Delta Kappa Gamma. Home: 1126 Winston Rd Cleveland OH 44122 Office: Beachwood High Sch 25100 Fairmont Blvd Cleveland OH 44122

GRONNIGER, KIMBERLY NEWTON, corporate communications officer; b. St. Joseph, Mo., Oct. 6, 1960; d. Otto Allen and Rosa Lee (Murphy) Newton; m. Daniel Joseph Gronniger, July 21, 1984. AA, Highland Community Coll., 1979; BA in English, Washburn U., 1981; MS in Journalism, U. Kans., 1983. Staff writer Tulsa Daily Bus. Jour., 1984; publs. editor Security Benefit Group of Cos., Topeka, 1984-85; pub. rels. mgr. Goodyear Tire and Rubber Co., Topeka, 1985-89; pub. info. officer Fed. Home Loan Bank of Topeka, 1989, corp. communications officer, 1989—. Adviser Jr. Achievement, Topeka, 1986; bd. dirs. Kaw Valley coun. Girl Scouts U.S., 1988-90. Mem. Pub. Rels. Soc. Topeka (past pres.), Women in Communication (v.p. fin. 1990—), Internat. Assn. Bus. Communicators (membership chair 1990), Phi Theta Kappa, Phi Kappa Phi, Kappa Tau Alpha. Roman Catholic. Home: 4225 NW 39th St Topeka KS 66618

GROOME, SALLY LUCYNTHIA, former army officer; b. Pelham, N.C., Oct. 9, 1936; d. John Whitlock and Addie Estelle (Vass) G. BA, Furman U., 1959; MPA, Shippensburg U., 1983; diploma Naval Coll. of Command and Staff, 1975, U.S. Army War Coll., 1981; post master's degree Old Dominion U. Commd. 2d lt. U.S. Army, 1960, advanced through grades to col., 1982; mil. asst. to sec. of army Dept. of Army, Washington, 1977-78; exec. officer personnel info. systems dir. U.S. Mil. Personnel Ctr., Alexandria, Va., 1978-79; chief personnel actions br., officer personnel mgmt. dir., 1979-80; dep. chief of staff U.S. Army War Coll., Carlisle, Pa., 1981-83; dir. nat. security studies dept. corr. studies, 1983-84; dir. tng. Hdqrs. U.S.A. ROTC Cadet Command. Ft. Monroe, Va., 1984-86. Mem. DAV, Assn. U.S. Army, Nat. Assn. Uniformed Svcs., Am. Soc. Pub. Adminstrn., The Ret. Officers Assn. Methodist. Avocations: animal welfare, animal conservation, travel, reading, music. Home: 354 Warrington Circle Hampton VA 23669

GROOMS, MARY ELLA HICKS, educator; b. Brighton, Pa., Aug. 1, 1926; d. Emmanuel Henderson and Ella Whitfield (Evans) Hicks; m. Milton Kinney Grooms, Jr., Dec. 29, 1949 (div. Apr. 1956); 1 child, Ninfa Eileen Grooms Osei. AB, Knoxville (Tenn.) Coll., 1948; MEd, Temple U., 1975. Cert. tchr., Pa., N.J. Caseworker St. Louis Dept. Welfare, 1953-56; bilingual tchr. Phila. Dept. Edn., 1956—; asst. zone supr. English Phila. Exchange Tchr. Program, Guayama, P.R., 1961-62; head dept. fgn. lang. Ben Franklin Evening High, Phila.; rsch. asst. Temple U., Phila., 1973-75; owner, pres. Grooms Assocs., 1988—; investor real estate Spania-Mail Order Assocs., Multicultural Cons. Internat. Inc. Composer: (lyrics) Henderson-Jones Family Reunion; author numerous poems. Fellow Temple U., 1975, 1980—, Bilingual Doctoral fellowship, 1979. Mem. Am. Assn. Sch. Administrs., Teaching English as Second Lang. (N.J. and Pa.), Am. Fedn. Tchrs., Modern Lang. Assn., Pa. State Modern Lang. Assn., Phila. Classical Soc., Assn. Bilingual Tchrs., Spanish Adv. Bd. (exec. bd.), Women in Edn., Black Women for Edn. (polit. com.) Knoxville Coll. Alumni Club, Temple U. Alumni Assn., Lower Bucks County, Alpha Kappa Alpha, Phi Delta Kappa, Phi Delta Gamma (rec. sec. 1986—). Home and Office: 4278 Concord Dr Trevose PA 19047

GROOMS, SUZANNE SIMMONS, music educator; b. New Orleans, Jan. 9, 1945; d. Claude Arthur and Mary Rachel (Pierce) Simmons; m. Barton Collins Grooms, May 12, 1973; children: David Barton, Michael Claude. BS, U. Tenn., 1966; M Music Edn., So. Ill. U., 1969. Cert. Suzuki tchr. instrumental music. Mem. violin sect. Knoxville (Tenn.) Symphony Orch., 1958-66; violinist St. Louis Philharmonic Orch., 1967-68; instr. Suzuki Inst., U. Wis., Stevens Point, 1970-73; violinist Amarillo (Tex.) Symphony Orch., 1973-77; dir., coordinator Suzuki string program Amarillo Coll., 1977—; violin tchr., co-founder Amarillo Area Youth Symphony. co-author: (Suzuki handbook) How To Make Your Twinkle Brighter, 1985. Bd. dirs. March of Dimes, Amarillo, 1977-79; mem. Amarillo Jr. League, 1977-84; circle chmn. Meth. Ch., Amarillo; liaison Art Force; mgr. Amarillo Symphony Youth Orch. Grantee Harrington Found., 1981. Mem. Suzuki Assn. of Ams., Internat. Suzuki Assn., Symphony Guild. Home: 4908 Erik Amarillo TX 79106 Office: Amarillo Coll PO Box 447 Amarillo TX 79178

GROSH, DORIS LLOYD, industrial engineering educator; b. Kansas City, Mo., Nov. 29, 1924; d. Samuel Gale and Blanche (Phinney) Lloyd; m. L. Eugene Grosh Jr., Aug. 26, 1950; children: Katherine, Barbara, Margaret. AA, Kansas City (Mo.) Jr. Coll., 1944; BA in Math., U.Chgo., 1946; MS, Kans. State U., 1949, PhD in Stats., 1969. From asst. prof. to prof. indsl. engring. Kans. State U., Manhattan, 1968—, acting head dept. indsl. engring., 1977-78. Author: Primer of Reliability Theory, 1989. Leader, Camp Fire Girls, Tulsa, 1960-68; precinct capt. Dem. Party, Manhattan, 1987—. Mem. Am. Soc. Quality Control, Soc. Women Engrs., AAUP (local sec., v.p., pres.), LWV. Unitarian. Office: Dept Indsl Engring. Durland Hall Kans State U Manhattan KS 66506

GROSHNER, MARIA STAR, nuclear engineer; b. Las Vegas, Nev., Aug. 31, 1961; d. Robert Leroy and Stepheny (Higby) G.; m. Robert Clay Singleterry Jr., May 18, 1984. BS in Nuclear Engring., U. Ariz., 1984. Reactor operator EG&G Idaho, Inc., Idaho Falls, 1985-89, engr., 1989—, export control reviewer power reactors, 1990—. Mem. Citizen Energy Alert Network, U.S. Coun. Energy Awareness, Lexington, Md., 1987—. Mem. Am. Nuclear Soc. (medial rels. chmn. Idaho chpt. 1990), Soc. Women Engrs. (chpt. sect. rep. 1990—, v.p. Southeastern Idaho chpt. 1989, coord, Young women's Conf. 1990), Instrument Soc. Am., Toastmasters Internat. (chpt. pres. 1990, adminstrv. v.p. Jack C. High unit 1989, winner awards 1988, 89). Home: 365 Carol Ave Idaho Falls ID 83401 Office: EG&G Idaho Inc PO Box 1625 TRA 647 MS 7121 Idaho Falls ID 83415

GROSHONG, CLAUDIA CLARK, speech, language and learning disabilities professional; b. Bakersfield, Calif., May 18, 1949; d. Norris James and Elizabeth Ann (Stine) C.; m. James Scott Groshong, Aug. 15, 1970; children: Lorin Clark, Heather Clark. BA in Linguistics, U. Calif., Riverside, 1970; MS in Communicative Disorders, U. Redlands (Calif.), 1971; PhD in Learning Disabilities, Northwestern U., Evanston, Ill., 1980. Cert. tchr., Oreg. Adj. prof. Calif. State U., Hayward, 1973-74; lang./remediation specialist Lang. Assocs., Orinda, Calif., 1973-75; vis. prof. U. Calif., Berkeley, 1975-76; adj. prof. So. Oreg. State Coll., Ashland, 1982-88; vis. prof. U. Oreg., Eugene, 1988; resource specialist Helman Sch., Ashland, 1986-87; speech/lang. specialist Medford Sch. Dist. 549C, Medford, Oreg., 1988—; rsch. cons. Helman Sch., Ashland, 1987-88; diagnostic cons. Humboldt County Schs., Eureka, Calif., Siskiyou County Schs., Yreka, Calif., 1975. Author: Ambiguity Detection, 1980, Teaching Group Participation Skills, 1988. Choir mem. Presbyn. Ch., Ashland, 1980. Mem. Learning Disabilities Assn., Oreg. Assn. Supervision and Curriculum Devel., Ashland Assn. for Edn. of Young Children, Phi Beta Kappa.

GROSS, BARBARA ELIZABETH RUDD, advertising executive; b. Chgo.; d. Alfred Lee Rudd and Elizabeth Odessa (Little) Thomas; m. James E. Gross, Aug. 13, 1983 (div. 1988). BA, So. Ill. U., 1970; MBA, Lake Forest (Ill.) Grad. Sch. Mgmt., 1987. Tchr. Chgo. Bd. of Edn., 1971; exec. trainee

Marshall Field and Co., Chgo., 1971-73; from buyer trainee to assoc. buyer Montgomery Ward, Chgo., 1973-80; sales rep. Johnson Pub. Co., Chgo., account exec., 1981-88; sr. account exec. Johnson Pub. Co., 1988-89, v.p., 1989—. Producer, copywriter Through the Pages of Ebony, What You Should Know About Ebony, Travel with Ebony, 1982. Recipient award of merit CEBA, 1983, Kizzy Image and Achievement award Black Women's Hall of Fame, Chgo., 1987. Mem. Women's Advt. Club of Chgo., Alpha Kappa Alpha. Presbyterian. Office: Johnson Pub Co 820 S Michigan Ave Chicago IL 60605

GROSS, CAROLINE LORD (MRS. MARTIN L. GROSS), state official; b. Laconia, N.H., May 5, 1940; d. William Shepard and Marion (Manns) Lord; m. Martin L. Gross, Nov. 5, 1960. AB, Radcliffe Coll., 1963; MAT, Harvard U., 1964. Rsch. asst. Supr. Schs., Concord, N.H., 1965-66, N.H. Legis. com. ann. sessions, Concord, 1966, N.H. Fiscal com. 1967-68; adminstrv. asst. N.H. gov., Concord, 1969-70; coord. N.H. fed. funds, Concord, 1971-72, supr. checklist, 1969-84; mem. com. on appropriations N.H. Ho. of Reps., 1983-89, clk., 1985-86, div. head, 1987-89, majority leader, 1989-90. Mem. N.H. Commn. Status Women, 1972-75; del. N.H. Rep. Conv., 1968, 70, 74, 76, 78, 80, 82, 84, 86, 88; legis. policy asst. N.H. Ho. of Reps., 1974-81; trustee Concord Libr., 1974-77, Granite State Pub. Radio, 1979-82; Rep. city chmn., Concord, 1980-84; Rep. candidate N.H. State Senate, 1980; mem. N.H. Fiscal Com., 1989—; bd. dirs. Cen. N.H. Community Mental Health Svcs., 1984-86. Mem. Concord Bus. & Profl. Women, Harvard-Radcliffe of N.H. Club (co-pres. 1981-84). Home: 15 Rumford St Concord NH 03301 Office: State House Rm 106 Concord NH 03301

GROSS, EVELYN ROSENBERG, editor; b. Greenwood, S.C., Sept. 30, 1926; d. Ernest Royal and Alyce (Kahn) Rosenberg; m. Leonard Gross, Aug. 31, 1950 (div. 1977); children: Gayle, Sally, Ernest. BA, Sophie Newcomb Coll., 1947; grad., Realtors Inst., Orlando, Fla., 1976. Caseworker Mt. Sinai Hosp., N.Y.C., 1947-49; ptnr., tchr. modeling sch. Oklahoma City, 1956-57; pvt. practice realtor Ft. Lauderdale, Fla., 1969—; v.p. Globe Span Real Estate Co., Ft. Lauderdale, 1973—; exec. dir. MCK Real Estate Edn. Ctrs., Ft. Lauderdale, 1977—; owner Real Estate Salesmanship Ctrs., Ft. Lauderdale, 1974-77; editor Exposition/Phoenix/Uhlan Press, Ft. Lauderdale, 1988—. Author: (with L. Gross) Real Estate for the New Practitioner, 1976. Trustee Ft. Lauderdale u., 1971-75, vice chmn., 1975. Mem. Nat. Assn. Realtors, Fla. Assn. Realtors, Ft. Lauderdale Bd. Realtors, Women's Coun. Realtors. Jewish. Home: 2609 NE 27th Ave Fort Lauderdale FL 33306 Office: 1881 NE 26 St Fort Lauderdale FL 33305

GROSS, HARRIET P. MARCUS, free-lance writer, religious educator; b. Pitts., July 15, 1934; d. Joseph William and Rose (Roth) Pincus; children: Sol Benjamin, Devra Lynn. AB magna cum laude, U. Pitts., 1954; MA U. Tex., 1990; cert. Religious Teaching, Spertus Coll. of Judaica, Chgo., 1962; 1972-73; Asso. editor Jewish Criterion of Pitts., 1955-56; publs. writer B'nai B'rith Vocat. Svc., 1956-57; leader recreation program for handicapped adults United Cerebral Palsy of Greater Chgo., 1957-58; group leader Jewish Community Ctrs. of Met. Chgo., 1958-63; columnist Star Publs., Chicago Heights, Ill., 1964-80; pub. info. specialist Operation ABLE, Chgo., 1980-81; dir. religious sch. Temple Emanu-El, Dallas, 1983-86; tchr. writing Homewood-Flossmoor (Il.) Park Dist., Brookhaven Jr. Coll., Dallas, U. Tex., Dallas; advisor journalism program Prairie State Coll., Chicago Heights, 1978-80; adv. bd. The Creative Woman quar. publ. Governors State U., Governors Park, Ill. Bd. dirs., sec. Family Svc. and Mental Health Ctr. of South Cook County, Ill., 1965-71; mem. Park Forest (Ill.) Commn. on Human Rels., 1969-80, chmn., 1974-76; bd. dirs. Ill. Theatre Ctr., 1977-80, Park Forest Bus. and Profl. Assn., 1979-80, Greater Dallas sect. Nat. Coun. Jewish Women, 1981-87, Jewish Family Svc. of Dallas, 1982—, exec. com., 1987—; mem. exec. com. Jewish Community Rels. Coun. Dallas, 1983-85. Recipient Fellowship for Action Humanitarian Achievements award, 1974; Anti-Defamation League of B'nai B'rith Honor award, 1978; Dr. Charles E. Gavin Found. Community Service award, 1978, 1st Ann. Leadership award Jewish Family Svc., 1990. Mem. Nat. Fedn. Press Women, Ill. Woman's Press Assn. (named Woman of Yr. 1978), Intertel (pres. Gateway Forum of Dallas 1984-85), Nat. Assn. Temple Educators, Mensa, Sigma Delta Chi, Phi Sigma Sigma. Jewish. Developed 1st community newspaper action line column, 1966. Address: 8560 Park Ln #23 Dallas TX 75231

GROSS, JEANNE BILGER, music educator; b. West Manchester, Ohio, June 16, 1925; d. Paul Leonard and Irene (Leas) Bilger; m. Virgil Dean, Dec. 28, 1947; children: Debra Jill, Richard Dean. B. Music Ed., Otterbein Coll., 1947; MA, Ohio State U., 1976, PhD, 1987. Cert. music educator, supr. and cons. Tchr. high sch. music vocal Worthington (Ohio) Schs., 1947-49; vocal music tchr. jr. high (7th, 8th and 9th grades) Columbus (Ohio) Pub. Schs., 1949-50; music educator Westerville (Ohio) City Sch., 1968-89; adj. prof. grad. edn. program Nova U., Ft. Lauderdale, Fla., summer 1989. Author: Benjamin Russel Hanby, Ohio Composer Educator, 1987. Dissertation honored in Music Edn. Coun. Rsch. in Music Edn's., 1987. Mem. AAUW, Ohio Hist. Soc., Westerville Hist. Soc., Ohio Edn Assn., Westerville Edn. Assn., Music Educators Nat. Conf. Ohio Music Educators Assn. (speaker, clinician), Assn. for Supervision and Curriculum Devel. (ednl. cons. state conv.), Pi Kappa Lambda, Phi Delta Kappa, Phi Delta Gamma.

GROSS, JULIA ANN, insurance company executive; b. Lebanon, Mo., May 10, 1957; d. J.C. and Sue Carolyn (Doggett) Benage; m. Gilbert Glen Adkins Jr., July 30, 1977 (div. 1988); children: Myranda Caroline, Emily Sarah; m. Darrell Eugene Gross, May 31, 1989. BS in Psychology and Sociology, Southwest Mo. State U., 1979. Life underwriter tng. coun. fellow. Spl. projects coordinator Am. Nat. Property and Casualty, Springfield, Mo., 1978-85; life/health ins. specialist United Insurers, Inc., Springfield, 1986-88; pres. Am. Risk Mgmt. Inc., Springfield, 1988—. Active Make-A-Wish Found. Mo., Springfield, 1984—, Mayflower Descendants Mo., 1957—. Named Kans. City Agt. of Yr. Ozark Empire Agy., Springfield, 1988, 89; mem. Pres.' Club Kans. City Life Ins. Co., 1989. Mem. Nat. Assn. Life Underwriters (nat. sales achievement award 1988, Nat. Quality award 1989), UDC. Democrat. Methodist. Office: Am Risk Mgmt Inc 1640 E Sunshine Springfield MO 65804

GROSS, LAURA ANN, marketing professional; b. Kew Gardens, N.Y., July 11, 1948; d. Melvin Fredericks and Harriette (Levy) G. BA, Boston U., 1970; MA, Columbia U., 1974. Staff writer Am. Banker, N.Y.C., 1974-82, assoc. editor, 1982-88; dir. fin. svcs., instns., communications Am. Express Travel/Related Svcs. Co., N.Y.C., 1988-89; dir. sales promotion and pub. rels. Am. Express Travelers Cheque Group/Am. Express Travel Svcs., N.Y.C., 1989—. Author, editor consumer surveys and articles; speaker in field. Recipient editorial awards Pannellkerr Forster, 1984, N.E. Bus. Press Editors, 1986, N.Y. Bus. Press. Editors, 1987. Mem. Bank Mktg. Assn., Promotion Mktg. Assn., Pub. Rels. Soc. Am. (Silver Anvil 1990). Home: 14 Horatio St New York NY 10014 Office: Am Express Travelers Group 100 Church St 14th Fl New York NY 10007

GROSS, LAURIE SUE, educator; b. Cleve., May 23, 1964; d. Robert Paul and Arlane Sue (Brondfield) Gross. BS, Ohio State U., 1987; MEd, Cleve. State U., 1988—. Counselor Jewish Community Ctr., Cleve., 1983-85; spl. needs counselor Jewish Community Ctr., 1987; tchr. presch. Emmanuel Presch., Cleve., 1987-89; head tchr. Emmanuel Presch., 1988-89; tchr. multihandicapped/early childhood program Univ. Heights City Sch. System, Cleveland Heights, Ohio, 1989—. Softball coach S. Euclid Softball League, 1982—; awds. vol. Cuyahoga County Bd. Mental Retardation, Cleve., 1988; bd. dirs. Juvenile Diabetes Found. Recipient REcognition award, Juvenile Diabetes Found., 1986. Mem. Alpha Epsilon Phi. Democrat. Jewish.

GROSS, LESLIE PAMELA, sales executive; b. N.Y., Aug. 23, 1952; d. Gerald Jay and Pearl (Meltzer) G.;. AB, Cornell U., 1976. Ins. agt. Equitable Life, San Francisco, 1976-79; sales assoc. Digital Equipment Corp., San Francisco, 1979-81; from sales rep. to sales exec. Digital Equipment Corp., Santa Clara, Calif., 1981-87; corp. acct. mgr. Digital Equipment Corp., San Francisco. Missionary The Ch. of Jesus Christ of Latter-day Saints, Boston, Mass., 1973-75; pres. Women's Relief Soc., Stanford, Calif., 1986; counselor, Palo Alto, Calif., 1987-88; sec. Channing Place Homeowners Assn., Palo Alto, Calif., 1987-88 pres. 1988-90, sec. 1990—. Recipient Equitable Prodn. Growth award, The Equitable Life Assurance Soc., San Francisco, 1978. Office: Digital Equipment Corp 455 Market St 7th Fl San Francisco CA 94105

GROSS, MARCY SHARON, systems analyst; b. Bronx, N.Y., May 13, 1963; d. Mayer M. and Ruth H. (Koppel) G. BA in Philosophy, NYU, 1984, real estate lic., 1987; BA in Paralegal Studies, Adelphi U., 1985. Lic. real estate saleswoman, N.Y. Systems mgr. Postner & Rubin, N.Y.C., 1984-86; word processing supr. Scudder, Stevens & Clark, N.Y.C., 1986; automation specialist Deloitte Haskins & Sells, N.Y.C., 1987-89; network analyst Helmsley-Spear, Inc., N.Y.C., 1989—; cons. on systems, N.Y.C.; beauty cons. Nu Skin, N.Y.C., 1990—. Author tech. manuals. State of N.Y. scholar, 1980-84. Mem. NAFE, N.Y. PC Group, Arista. Office: Helmsley-Spear Inc Lincoln Bldg New York NY 10165

GROSS, MERRYL JANE, software usability engineer; b. Bklyn., July 5, 1963; d. Martin and Pauline (Fruhlinger) G. BS, MIT, 1985; MS, Tufts U., Medford, Mass., 1990. Human factors engr. Telephonics Corp., Huntington, N.Y., 1985-87; teaching asst. Tufts U., Medford, 1987-88; human factors engr. DEC, Maynard, Mass., 1988-89; usability engr. IBM, Roanoke, Tex., 1989—. Mem. Human Factors Soc. Office: IBM 5 W Kirkwood Dr 02-02-40 Roanoke TX 76299

GROSS, PRIVA BAIDAFF, art historian, retired educator; b. Wieliczka, Poland, June 19, 1911; came to U.S., 1941, naturalized, 1955; d. Israel and Leopolda (Friedman) Baidaff; Ph.M., Jagellonian U., Cracow, Poland, 1937; postgrad. (N.Y. U. scholar 1945-47), N.Y. U. Inst. Fine Arts, 1945-48; m. Feliks Gross, July 25, 1937; 1 dau., Eva Helena Gross Friedman. Mem. faculty Queensborough Community Coll., CUNY, 1961-81, assoc. prof. art history, 1971-81, ret., 1981, co-chmn. art and music dept., 1966-68, chmn. art dept., 1968-74, dir. coll. gallery, 1968-77. SUNY grantee, 1967. Mem. AAUW (dir. 1972-76, 1980-82), Coll. Art Assn. Am., Soc. Archtl. Historians, Gallery Assn. N.Y. State (dir. 1972-73), N.Y. State Assn. Jr. Colls., AAUP, Polish Inst. Arts and Scis. Am., Council Gallery and Exhbn. Dirs. (dir. 1970-72). Contbr. articles, revs. to profl. publs. Home: 310 W 85th St New York NY 10024

GROSS, ROCHELLE, correctional officer; b. Freehold, N.J., Jan. 21, 1949; d. Roy and Allie Mae (Stafford) Campbell; m. Freeman Gross, Sept. 14, 1965 (div. Jan. 1969); children: Freeman Jr., Delmas Frenette. AA, Fla. Jr. Coll., 1980; BA, U. North Fla., 1982. Lic. pesticide applicator; cert. instr. first aid, CPR, adult basic edn., and gen. ednl. devel. Interviewer Legal Aid Soc., Jacksonville, Fla., 1982; correctional counselor Fla. Dept. Corrections, Jacksonville, 1982-86, correctional officer II, 1986—. Author poetry, 1979. instr. first aid, CPR, ARC, Jacksonville, 1982—; mem. Sister's United; panelist Am. Media Svcs., 1988, Consumer Svcs., 1986—; bd. dirs. Singles for Jesus Ministry, Inc. Fla. Jr. Coll. scholar, Jacksonville, 1979, U. North Fla. Acad. scholar, Jacksonville, 1980-82. Mem. NAFE, Am. Corrections Assn., Am. Assn. Notaries, Cultural Enrichment Vols., Phi Theta Kappa. Democrat. Mem. Pentecostal Ch. Home: 340 Cherokee St Jacksonville FL 32205

GROSS, RUTH TAUBENHAUS, physician; b. Bryan, Tex., June 24, 1920; d. Jacob and Esther (Hirshenson) Taubenhaus; B.A., Barnard Coll., 1941; M.D., Columbia U., 1944; m. Reuben H. Gross, Jr., Aug. 22, 1942) (div. June 1952); 1 son, Gary E. Intern, Charity Hosp., New Orleans, 1944; resident in pediatrics Tulane U., New Orleans, 1945, Columbia U., N.Y.C., 1946, 47; instr. Radcliffe Infirmary, Oxford, Eng., 1949-50; instr. pediatrics Stanford (Calif.) U., 1950-53, asst. prof., 1953-56, asso. prof., 1956-60, prof., 1973—, acting exec. pediatrics, 1957-59, assoc. dean student affairs, 1973-75, dir. div. gen. and ambulatory pediatrics, 1975-85, dir. Stanford-Children's Ambulatory Care Center, 1980-85, nat. study dir. Infant Health and Devel. Program, 1983—; assoc. prof. pediatrics, co-dir. div. human genetics Albert Einstein Coll. Medicine, Yeshiva U., N.Y.C., 1960-64, prof. pediatrics, 1964-66; clin. prof. pediatrics U. Calif. Med. Center, San Francisco, 1966-73; dir. dept. pediatrics Mt. Zion Hosp. and Med. Center, San Francisco, 1966-73. Commonwealth fellow human genetics Instituto de Genetica, Pavia, Italy, 1959-60. Mem. Inst. Medicine, Nat. Acad. Scis., Am. Fedn. Clin. Research, Am. Pediatric Soc., Soc. Pediatric Research, Am. Acad. Pediatrics, Ambulatory Pediatric Assn., Soc. Research in Child Devel., Phi Beta Kappa, Alpha Omega Alpha, Sigma Xi. Contbr. articles to profl. jours.

GROSS, SHIRLEY MARIE, farm manager, artist; b. Beardstown, Ill., Apr. 4, 1917; d. Robert Lee and Marie Elizabeth (Ellrich) Northcutt; A.A., Stephens Coll., 1936; B.A., Ill. Coll., 1938; m. Carl David Gross, Oct. 4, 1941; children—David Lee, Susan Jean Gross Conner. Med. technologist St. John's Hosp., Springfield, Ill., 1938-41, Schmidt Meml. Hosp., Beardstown, 1957-64; librarian Beardstown Public Library, 1970-76; pvt. practice farm mgmt., Beardstown, 1958—; bd. dirs. First State Bank Beardstown, Heart of Ill. Investment Clubs; exhibitor various art shows, Ill., 1969—. Bd. dirs. Beardstown Hosp., Head Start; trustee First Congregational Ch. Beardstown. Winner art awards various shows. Mem. Am. Soc. Clin. Pathologists (med. technologist), Beardstown Bus. and Profl. Women's Investment Club, Cass County Hist. Soc., Beardstown Restoration Soc. Jacksonville Area Artist League, Beardstown Hosp. Aux., Beardstown Woman's Club, Cass County Coun. for the Arts Club, Beardstown Bus. and Profl. Women's Club (pres. local chpt. 1968-70), Supreme Emblem Club. Democrat. Home: 1116 Jefferson Beardstown IL 62618

GROSSE, JACQUELINE WEAVER, educator; b. Rocksprings, Tex., Dec. 9, 1926; d. Barney William and Tommie Iola (Epperson) Weaver; m. Alex Howard Grosse, June 16, 1950; children: Charles Howard, Nancy Gay Andrews, Karla Kay Bearden. BS, SWTU, San Marcos, 1950; MA, OLLU, San Antonio, 1978. Tchr. Kinney ISD, Bracket, Tex., 1947-48, Edwards ISD, Rocksprings, 1948-49, Mason ISD, Mason, Tex., 1950; librarian Mason ISD, Mason. Mem. exec. bd. Hill Country Community Action, San Saba, Tex., 1972, Hill Country Action Mason, 1970-89, v.p., 1988-89; mem. exec. bd. San Antonio Area Library, 1973-74, Mason County Library Bd., 1970-74, Mason Grant Coord., 1974, Mason Hist. Soc., 1968-80, Hill County. Mem. ALA, Tex. Library Assn., Tex. Joint Coun. Tchrs. of English, Nat. Coun. Tchr.'s of English, Assembly on Lit. for Adolescents, San Angelo English Tchrs. Riata Study Club (pres. Mason chpt. 1970-72). Democrat. Home: Box 128 Mason TX 76856 Office: Mason Ind Sch Dist Rucker Rt Box 31C Mason TX 76856

GROSSET, JESSICA ARIANE, computer analyst; b. Paris, Aug. 31, 1952; came to U.S., 1970; d. Raymond Louis and Barbara Ann (Byrne) G.; m. Bruce Edward Kaskubar, May 23, 1986. AA, Berkshire Community Coll., Pittsfield, Mass., 1972; BS, SUNY, Potsdam, 1979; postgrad., Ariz. State U., 1980, U. Minn., 1980-81. Computer programmer Kay-Bee Toy and Hobby Shops, Lee, Mass., 1974-78; computer analyst Mayo Clinic, Rochester, Minn., 1981—. Mem. Nat. Assn. Female Execs. Office: Mayo Clinic 200 SW 1st St Rochester MN 55905

GROSSETETE, GINGER LEE, gerontology administrator, consultant; b. Riverside, Calif., Feb. 9, 1936; d. Lee Roy Taylor and Bonita (Beryl) Williams; m. Alec Paul Grossetete, June 8, 1954; children: Elizabeth Gay Blech, Teri Lee Zeni. BA in Recreation cum laude, U. N.Mex., 1974, M in Pub. Adminstrn., 1978. Sr. ctr. supr., Office of Sr. Affairs, City of Albuquerque, 1974-77, asst. dir. Office of Sr. Affairs, 1977—; conf. coordinator Nat. Consumers Assn., Albuquerque, 1978-79; region 6 del. Nat. Council on Aging, Washington, 1977-84; conf. chmn. Western Gerontol. Soc., Albuquerque, 1983; mem. Council on Phys. Fitness and Health. Contbr. articles to mags. Pres. Albuquerque Symphony Women's Assn., 1972; exec. com. mem. Jr. League Albuquerque, 1976; campaign dir. March of Dimes N.Mex., 1966-67. Recipient N.Mex. Disting. Pub. Service award N.Mex. Gov.'s Office, 1983, Disting. Woman on the Move award YWCA, 1986. Fellow Nat. Recreation and Park Assn. (bd. dirs. Southwest Regional Council, pres. N.Mex. chpt. 1983-84, Outstanding Profl. 1982); mem. U. N.Mex. Alumni Assn. (bd. dirs. 1978-80, Disting. Alumni award 1985), Southwest Soc. on Aging (pres. 1984-85, bd. dirs.), Am. Soc. Pub. Adminstrn. (pres. N.Mex. Council 1987-88), Las Amapolas Garden Club (pres. 1964), Pi Alpha Alpha, Chi Omega (pres. alumni 1959-60). Home: 517 La Veta NE Albuquerque NM 87108 Office: Office of Sr Affairs 714 7th St SW Albuquerque NM 87102

GROSSI, MARGARET THORNE, city official; b. Bablyn, N.Y., May 10, 1928; d. George and Margaret (Devlin) Thorne; m. Carlo E. Grossi, Dec. 11, 1954; children: Eugene, Mary, Elizabeth, Sarah. BA, U. Notre Dame, S.I., N.Y., 1949; MD, Georgetown U., 1953; MPH, Columbia U., 1967. Dep. commr. for prog. devel. and evaluation N.Y.C. Dept. Health, 1980-83; assoc. clin. prof. pediatrics Cornell U. Med. Coll., N.Y.C., 1970—; asst. commr. maternal and child health svcs. N.Y.C. Dept. Health, 1976-80, dep. commr. med. affairs, 1983—. Fellow Am. Acad. Pediatrics; mem. N.Y. County Med. Soc., N.Y. Acad. Medicine, Am. Pub. Health Assn. Home: 520 E 82nd St New York NY 10028 Office: Dept Health 125 Worth St New York NY 10013

GROSSMAN, ELIZABETH KORN, nursing administrator, retired college dean; b. S.I., N.Y., May 15, 1923; d. George and Ethel (Elliot) Korn; m. Thomas Grossman, Feb. 23, 1952 (dec. 1987); 1 child, Thomas. BA, Hunter Coll., 1944; MN, Western Res. U., 1947; MS in Nursing Edn., Ind. U., 1960, EdD, 1972. Researcher Columbia Carbon Corp., Bklyn., 1944; staff nurse, asst. head nurse, head nurse, supr. Univ. Hosp., Cleve., 1947-52; Instr. Mt. Sinai Hosp. Sch. Nursing, Cleve., 1952-53; supr. maternity nursing Meth. Hosp., Indpls., 1953-57; instr. maternity nursing, 1957-59; instr. DePauw U., Indpls., 1959-62; asst. prof., assoc. prof., grad. maternity Ind. U., Indpls., 1959-66, chairperson grad.-undergrad. maternity nursing, 1966-73, dean Sch. Nursing, 1973-88; civilian nat. cons. emeritus USAF Nurse Corps, 1983-86. Contbr. articles to profl. jours. Elected mem. Hunter Coll. Hall of Fame, 1973. Fellow Am. Acad. Nursing; mem. Am. Nurses Assn., Nat. League Nursing (Nurse of Yr.), Ind. Citizen League for Nursing, Am. Assn. Colls. Nursing (treas. 1981-85), Nurses Assn. of Am. Coll. Ob-Gyn (4th and 7th nat. program meeting com. 1987-88, chair com. on edn. 1980-82), Midwest Alliance Nursing (treas. 1979-81), Sigma Xi, Sigma Theta Tau (Disting. Service award 1977, co-chmn. campaign for Ctr. for Nursing Scholarship), Rotary (Altrusa), Delta Kappa Gamma, Alpha Xi Delta (Woman of Distinction 1988). Republican. Roman Catholic. Home: 11201 Westfield Blvd Carmel IN 46032 Office: Ind U Coll Nursing 610 Barnhill Dr Indianapolis IN 46223

GROSSMAN, FRANCES KAPLAN, psychologist; b. Newport News, May 28, 1929; d. Rubin H. and Beatrice (Fischlowitz) Kaplan; m. Henry Grossman, July 26, 1970; children: Jennifer, Benjamin. BA, Oberlin (Ohio) Coll., 1961; MS, PhD, Yale U., 1965. Diplomate Am. Bd. Profl. Psychology. Asst. prof. Yale U., New Haven, 1965-69; asst. prof. Boston U., 1969-71, assoc. prof. psychology, 1971-82, prof. psychology, 1982—. Author: Brothers and Sisters of Retarded Children, 1971, Pregnancy, Birth and Parenthood, 1980. Bd. trustees Oberlin Coll., 1990—. Recipient Cert. of Appreciation, Oberlin Coll. Alumni Assn., 1983. Mem. Oberlin Coll. Alumni Assn. (pres. 1979-80), Sigma Xi, Phi Delta Kappa. Jewish. Office: Boston Univ Dept Psychology 64 Cummington St Boston MA 02215

GROSSWASSER, LEONORA MARIA, lawyer; b. St. Louis, Dec. 18, 1961; d. Sol R. and Nelly (Magit) G. BA, St. Louis U., 1984; JD, Columbia U., 1987. Bar: Tex. 1987, Calif. 1989. Assoc. Gardere & Wynne, Dallas, 1987-88, Graham & James, L.A., 1989—. Mem. young lawyers div. Jewish Fedn., Dallas, 1988, L.A., 1989—. Mem. ABA, Calif. Bar Assn., Tex. Bar Assn., Phi Beta Kappa, Alpha Sigma Nu, Pi Sigma Alpha. Democrat.

GROSTICK, SARA STANFORD, health educator; b. Cullman, Ala., Jan. 4, 1946; d. Dale and Lillie (Cochran) Stanford; m. Alan Wesley Grostick, Mar. 6, 1976; children: Charles Dale, Laura Alan. BS, U. North Ala., 1968; MA, U. Ala., 1974. Registered record adminstr. Supr. med. record div. U. Ala. Hosps., Birmingham, 1970-71; dir. med. record div. Hillcress Hosp., Birmingham; coord. med. record tech. Jefferson State Coll., Birmingham, 1972-74; dir. med. record tech. program Sch. Community-Allied Health, U. Ala., Birmingham, 1974-79, dir. med. record div. Sch. Health Related Professions, 1979—; cons. Ambulatory Care Ctr., U. Ala., Huntsville, 1987, Henderson and Walton's Women's Clinic, Birmingham, 1988. Editor Jour. Allied Health, 1986. Grantee Ala. Dept. Allied Health, 1987. Mem. Am. Med. Record Assn. (chmn. coun. edn. 1982-83, panel accreditation surveyors 1983-91, editor newsletter 1975-76), Ala. Med. Record Assn. (pres. 1974, Disting. Mem. award 1981), Kappa Delta Pi, Alpha Eta. Office: U Ala 1679 University Blvd Birmingham AL 35294

GROTH, JOYCE LORRAINE, chemistry educator; b. Meriden, Conn., Feb. 3, 1935; d. Lester William and Florence Mary (Bower) Weaver; m. Richard Henry Groth, June 6, 1959; children: Eileen L., Kathleen J. BS, Cen. Conn. State U., 1957; MS, U. Conn., 1959, PhD, 1964. Postdoctoral assoc. Wesleyan U., Middletown, Conn., 1964; asst. prof. U. Conn., Waterbury, 1964-68; tchr. Platt High Sch., Meriden, 1968-69, New Britain (Conn.) High Sch., 1969—. Mem. Bd. Health, Meriden, 1968-72. Mem. U.S. Figure Skating Assn. (intermediate test judge 1974—, club dir. 1975-79). Home: 75 Coe Ave Meriden CT 06450 Office: New Britain High Sch Mill St New Britain CT 06051

GROTTA, SANDRA BROWN, interior designer; b. Detroit, June 7, 1934; m. Louis William Grotta, Sept. 8, 1955. Student U. Mich., 1952-55, N.Y. Sch. Interior Design, 1964. Pres. S.G. Interiors, New Vernon, N.J., 1964—. Mem. Am. Soc. Interior Designers.

GROTTENDIECK, VIRGINIA RANDOLPH, educational admissions officer; b. Clarksburg, W.Va., Sept. 29, 1945; d. Sandford Fitz and Virginia Elnora (Thompson) Randolph; m. William Joseph Grottendieck III, Sept. 16, 1969; 1 child, Virginia Ann. BA, W.Va. U., 1967, MA, 1970. Admissions and records officer Glenville (W.Va.) State Coll., 1981—; Glenville State Coll rep. to W.Va. Higher Edn. Bd. Dirs. and Adv. Coun. Classified Employees, Charleston, 1984—. Sec., treas. Lewis/Gilmer (W.Va.) Regional Solid Waste Authority, 1989-90; troop leader Black Diamond coun. Girls Scouts U.S.A., 1980. Mem. AAUW (chair legal advocacy fund 1990—, pres. Glenville br. 1988—), W.Va. Fedn. Women's Clubs (bd. dirs., conservation chmn. 1990—), Woman's Club Glenville (pres. 1988-90). Democrat. Methodist. Home: 212 Johnson St Glenville WV 26351 Office: Glenville State Coll 200 High St Glenville WV 26351

GROTZINGER, LAUREL ANN, university dean; b. Truman, Minn., Apr. 15, 1935; d. Edward F. and Marian Gertrude (Greeley) G. B.A., Carleton Coll., 1957; M.S., U. Ill., 1958, Ph.D., 1964. Instr., asst. librarian Ill. State U., 1958-62; asst. prof. Western Mich. U., Kalamazoo, 1964-66; assoc. prof. Western Mich. U., 1966-68, prof., 1968—, asst. dir. Sch. Librarianship, 1965-72, chief research officer, 1979-86, interim dir. Sch. Library and Info. Sci., 1982-86, dean grad. coll., 1979—. Author: The Power and the Dignity, Scarecrow, 1966; editorial bd.: Jour. Edn. for Librarianship, 1973-77, Dictionary Am. Library Biography, 1975-77; contbr. articles to profl. jours. Mem. AAUW, ALA (sec. treas. Library History Round Table 1973-74, vice chmn., chmn.-elect 1983-84, chmn. 1984-85), Assn. Library Info. Sci. Edn., Am. Assn. Higher Edn., Council Grad. Schs., Mich. Council Grad. Deans (chmn. 1983-84, 86), Nat. Council Research Adminstrs., Mich. Acad. Sci., Arts and Letters (mem.-at-large, exec. com. 1980-86, pres. 1983-85, exec. com. 1990—), Phi Beta Kappa (pres. SW Mich. chpt. 1977-78), Beta Phi Mu, Pi Delta Epsilon, Alpha Beta Alpha, Delta Kappa Gamma (pres. Alpha Psi chpt. 1988—), Phi Kappa Phi. Home: 2729 Mockingbird Dr Kalamazoo MI 49008

GROVE, CHERYL WADE, nurse; b. Harrisburg, Pa., Feb. 11, 1946; d. Emerson Franklin and Kathryn Mae (Edinger) Wade; m. Robert Caldwell, Dec. 26, 1971; children: Andrew, Lisa. BSPA, St. Joseph's Coll., Windham, Maine, 1985. RN. Obstetrics nurse Reading (Pa.) Hosp. & Med. Ctr., 1967-68; head nurse Polyclinic Med. Ctr., Harrisburg, Pa., 1969-71; utilization rev. examiner Capital Blue Cross, Harrisburg, Pa., 1971-84; med. policy coord. COMPI, Harrisburg, Pa., 1985-88; quality assesment cons. Capital Blue Cross, Pa., 1988--. Mem. Hosp. Assn. Pa., Quality Assurance Profs. Cen. Pa., Pa. Assn. Quality Assurance Profs., Nat. Assn. Quality Assurance Profs. Democrat. United Methodist. Home: 104 Fairway Dr Camp Hill PA 17011 Office: Capital Blue Cross 100 Pine St Harrisburg PA 17100

GROVE, HELEN HARRIET, historian, artist; b. South Bend, Ind.; d. Samuel Harold and LaVerne Mae (Drescher) Grove; grad. Bayle Sch. Design, Meinzinger Found., 1937-39, Washington U., 1940-42; spl. studies, Paris, France. Owner studios of historic research and illustration, St. Louis, Chgo., 1943—; dir. archives, bus. history research Sears, Roebuck & Co., 1951-67; commmns. art and research for Northwestern U., Chgo.-Sears Roebuck & Co., art Lawrence U., Appleton, Wis. Home: 6326 N Clark St Chicago IL 60626 Studio: 6328 N Clark St Chicago IL 60626

GROVE, JEAN DONNER (MRS. EDWARD R. GROVE), sculptor; b. Washington, May 15, 1912; d. Frederick Gregory and Georgia V. (Gartrell) Donner; m. Edward R. Grove, June 24, 1936; children: David Donner, Eric Donner. Student, Cornell U., 1932, Hill Sch. of Sculpture, 1934-35, Corcoran Sch. of Art, 1935-37, 42-44, Cath. U. Am., 1936-37, Phila. Mus. Art Sch., 1967; B.S., Wilson Tchrs. Coll., 1939. Exhibited one-man shows, Wilson Tchrs. Coll., Washington, 1939, Grove Family Exhbns., Cayuga Mus. History and Art, Auburn, N.Y., 1964, Episcopal Acad. Gallery, Phila., 1966, group shows, Pa. Acad. Fine Arts, Phila., 1947, 48, 51, 53, N.A.D., N.Y.C., 1949, 78, 81, 83, 85, 87, 89, Nat. Sculpture Soc. at Archtl. League, N.Y.C., Topeka, 1957, Lever House, N.Y.C., 1974, 75, 86, Port of History Mus., Phila., 1987, Grace Bldg. N.Y.C., 1988, Equitable Gallery, N.Y.C., 1976, 78, 83, Park Ave. Atrium, N.Y.C., 1985, Art U.S.A., Madison Sq. Garden, N.Y.C., 1958, Corcoran Gallery Art, Washington, 1943-47, Internat. Gallery, Washington, 1946, Phila. Mus. Art, 1955, 59, 62, Phila. Art Alliance, 1957, 60, 66, Phila. Civic Ctr., 1968, Flagler Art Ctr., West Palm Beach, Fla., 1972, Norton Gallery Art, West Palm Beach, 1974, 81, 83, Cathedral St. John the Divine, N.Y.C., 1990; represented in permanent collections, Rosenwald Collection, Phila., Ch. of Holy Comforter, Drexel Hill, Pa., Fine Arts Commn., City Hall, Phila., Palm Beach County Govt. Ctr., West Palm Beach, Fla., Port of History Mus., Philadelphia; sculptor numerous portrait commns., garden figures and fountains, 1940—; (with E.R. Grove) Am. Express Goldpiece, 1982, St. Francis Meml. Plaque, 1990. Mem. adv. coun. Nat. Biog. Centre, Cambridge, Eng., 1989—. Recipient 1st prize sculpture Nat. Mus. Washington, 1946, 1st prize Sculpture Arts Club, 1946, Portrait prize Sculpture Arts Club, 1947, Morris Goodman award John Herron Art Mus., Indpls., 1957, Competition prize for design and sculpture Artists Equity Phila., 1960, Humane award Animal Rescue League of Palm Beach, 1974, 80, 85, Tallix Foundry award NSS Bicentennial Exhbn. Equitable Gallery, N.Y.C., 1976, Gold medal Acad. of Italy, 1979, Golden Centaur award, 1982, Competition prize and commendation Palm Beach County Commn.'s Meml. Chambers portrait plaque, 1986. Mem. Nat. Sculpture Soc., Nat. Acad. Design (assoc.), Artists Equity Assn. (dir. Phila. chpt. 1964-66), Phila. Art Alliance, Soc. of Four Arts, Norton Gallery Art, Soc. Washington Artists, Am. Medallic Sculpture Assn. (edit. bd. jour.), Fedn. Internat. de Medaille, English Speaking Union, Animal Rescue League of Palm Beach (com. chmn. 1972—, dir. 1975—), St. Mary's Guild of Episcopal Ch. Women (v.p. 1974-76), Nat. Women's Bd. Northwood Inst. (exec. com.), Kappa Delta Pi. Home and Studio: Sea-Lake Studio 3215 S Flagler Dr West Palm Beach FL 33405

GROVE, MYRNA JEAN, educator; b. Bryan, Ohio, Oct. 24, 1949; d. Kedric Durward and N. Florence (Stombaugh) G. Student, Bowling Green State U., 1970-71; BA in Edn., Manchester Coll., 1971; postgrad., U. No. Colo., 1974-76, Purdue U., 1977, St. Francis Coll., Ft. Wayne, Ind., 1986, Coll. Mount St. Joseph, Ohio, 1986. Cert. elem. tchr., Ohio. Tchr. elem. sch. Bryan City Schs., 1972—. Editor newspaper column Education Today, 1975-82, newsletter Northwest Ohio Emphasis, 1981-83, (award 1981). Dir., violinist Bryan String Ensemble, 1981—; organist Trinity Episc. Ch., Bryan, 1979-89; trustee Bryan Area Cultural Assn., 1984-89; Williams County Community Concerts (bd. dirs.). Jennings scholar Martha Holden Jennings Found., Bowling Green State U., 1982-83. Mem. Bryan Edn. Assn. (exec. com., pres. 1985-86), Ohio Edn. Assn. (presenter 1984, del. global issues 1986), Nat. Edn. Assn. (Ohio del., state contact 1986, 87), Ohio Assn. Gifted Children, Bus. and Profl. Women Ohio (individual devel. com. 1986—, speaking skills cert. 1987), Northwest Ohio Tchrs. Uniserv (sec. 1975-78), Northwest Ohio Manchester Coll. Alumni Assn. (past pres.), Nat. Assn. Gifted Children, Alpha Delta Kappa, Alpha Mu, Alpha Delta Kappa.

GROVER, PHYLLIS FLORENCE BRADMAN, artist; b. Passaic, N.J., Jan. 11, 1924; d. Samuel And Sue Bradman; m. Saul Grover, July 5, 1923: children: Keith, Jennet. Student, Cooper Union Coll., 1941-43, New Sch. for Social Rsch., 1967-68. Designer Am. Export Airlines, N.Y.C., 1942-44; sr. draftsman City N.Y. Marine & Aviation, 1944-46; portraitist N.Y.C., 1948-58; painter, sculptor High View, Sante Fe, N.Y., N.Mex., 1958-90; art show judge N.Y., N.J., Pa., 1958-82; art cons. N.Y.C., 1974—; co-founder Art in the Home Gallery, Long Island, N.Y., 1960-62; art cons., N.Y.C., Sante Fe, 1974—. Author numerous poems. Capt. Women Strike for Peace, Wash., 1969; founding mem. Community Arts Coun., L.I., 1958. Recipient Best of Woman Art award, 1977, 78. Mem. NOW, Sch. Am. Rsch., Women's Interart Assn., Archeol. Rsch. Soc., N.Y. State Archeol. Soc. of Orange County, Santa Fe Hist. Soc., Women in the Arts Assn. Democrat. Home and Office: Rt 9-86 S Santa Fe NM 87505

GROVER, ROSALIND REDFERN, oil and gas company executive; b. Midland, Tex., Sept. 5, 1941; d. John Joseph and Rosalind (Kapps) Redfern; m. Arden Roy Grover, Apr. 10, 1982; 1 child, Rosson. BA in Edn. magna cum laude, U. Ariz., 1966, MA in History, 1982; postgrad. in law, So. Meth. U., Dallas. Libr. Gahr High Sch., Cerritos, Calif., 1969; pres. The Redfern Found., Midland, 1982—; ptnr. Redfern & Grover, Midland, 1986—; pres. Redfern Enterprises Inc., Midland, 1989—; chmn. bd. dirs. Flag-Redfern Oil Co., Midland. Sec. park and recreation commn. City of Midland, 1969-71, del. Objectives for Convocation, 1980; mem., past pres. women's aux. Midland Community Theatre, 1970, chmn. challenge grant bldg. fund, 1980, chmn. Tex. Yucca Hist. Landmark Renovation Project, 1983, trustee, 1983-88; chmn. publicity com. Midland Jr. League Midland, Inc., 1972, chmn. edn. com., 1976, corr. sec., 1978; 1st v.p. Midland Symphony Assn., 1975; chmn. Midland Charity Horse Show, 1975-76; mem. Midland Am. Revolution Bicentennial Commn., 1976; trustee Mus. S.W., 1977-80, pres. bd. dirs., 1979-80; co-chmn. Gov. Clements Fin. Com., Midland, 1978; mem. dist. com. State Bd. Law Examiners; trustee Midland Meml. Hosp., 1978-80, Permian Basin Petroleum Mus., Libr. and Hall of Fame, 1989—. Recipient HamHock award Midland Community Theatre, 1978. Mem. Ind. Petroleum Assn. Am., Tex. Ind. Producers and Royalty Owners Assn., Petroleum Club, Racquet Club (Midland), Horseshoe Bay (Tex.) Country Club, Phi Kappa Phi, Pi Lambda Theta. Republican. Home: 1906 Crescent Pl Midland TX 79705 Office: PO Box 2127 Midland TX 79702

GROVER-HASKIN, KIM ARLEEN, dance educator; b. Pocatello, Idaho, Feb. 8, 1960; d. Byron J. and Betty Lue (Rankin) Grover; m. Andy H. Haskin, June 29, 1985. Student, U. Idaho, 1978-80; BA, SUNY, Potsdam, 1982; postgrad., Colo. Coll., 1982; MS, U. Oreg., 1986; postgrad., Tex. Woman's U., 1987—. Grad. instr. and fellow U. Oreg., Eugene, 1984-86; instr., choreographer Ballet SW, Denton, Tex., 1988—; mem. libr. staff Tex. Woman's U., Denton, 1988-90. Mem. Denton Humane Soc., 1989—. Mem. AAHPER and Dance, Nat. Dance Assn., Am. Dance Guild, Congress on Rsch. in Dance, Cecchetti Coun. Am. (cert.). Office: Ballet SW 309 S Locust St Denton TX 76201

GROVES, LINDELL GRIFFITH, elementary school educator; b. Portland, Oreg., Mar. 31, 1939; d. William Davis Griffith and Jane (Cady) Touhey; m. Larry Earl Groves, May 30, 1958 (div. Mar. 1990); children: Laura Ann Groves Mason, Leslie Louise, Linda Sue Groves Ferrell. BS, Oreg. State U., 1971, EdM, 1972. Tchr. Lakeview Elem. Sch., Albany, Oreg., 1971-73, Tangent (Oreg.) Elem. Sch., 1973-87, Oak Elem. Sch., Albany, Oreg., 1987—. Mem. Greater Albany Edn. Assn. (v.p., sec., area rep., bldg. rep. bargaining team), Oreg. Coun. Tchrs. Math., Spring Hill Country Club, Phi Kappa Phi, Phi Delta Kappa. Democrat. Presbyterian. Office: Oak Elem Sch 3610 SE Oak St Albany OR 97321

GROVES, ROSALIND GANZEL, corporate communications specialist; b. Phila., Aug. 1, 1934; d. John Edward and Flora Edith (Shultz) Ganzel; m. Harold Eber Woodbridge, Dec. 7, 1951 (div. June 1966); children: John Arthur, Martin Alan, June Marie; m. Gary Wayne Groves, Aug. 7, 1975 (div. 1980). AA, Fla. Keys Community Coll., 1972; BA, U. North Fla., 1975. Cert. profl. Hypnotist, Fla.; registered ins. agt., Fla. Program analyst Officer-in-Charge Constrn. Trident USN, St. Marys, Ga., 1981-83; with acctg. dept. Officer-in-Charge Trident USN, St. Marys, 1983-84; with telecommunications dept. Naval Air Sta., Jacksonville, Fla., 1985—; ins. agt. Hill and Co., Jacksonville, 1986-89; freelance writer and editor; dir. Behavior Modification Ctr., Jacksonville, 1983—; cons. on hypnosis, Jacksonville, 1983—; alumni career cons. U. North Fla., 1990—. Counselor Vol. Jacksonville, 1975-76; tchr. Duval County Sch. System, 1984; mem. Key West Art and Hist. Soc., 1984-89, Jacksonville Symphony Assn., 1990—; speaker Naval Air Sta. Jacksonville Speakers Bur., 1985—; vol. Jacksonville Upbeat Program, 1986—. Named Hon. Fire Reservist Phila. Fire Dept. Mem. Inst. Advanced Hypnology (newsletter editor 1983-85, sec. 1983-85, v.p. 1986-87), Navy League U.S., Fla. Assn. Profl. Hypnosis (newsletter editor 1985-87), The Exec. Female, Assn. to Advance Ethical Hypnosis, So. Bell Large Users Coun. (steering com. 1988-89), Navy League, Jacksonville C. of C., Jacksonville Symphony Assn., Offshore Power Boat Racing Assn. Republican. Mem. Ch. of Christ. Club: Internat. Toastmistress (sponsored new club). Home: 7212 Cypress Cove Rd Jacksonville FL 32244

GROVIER, MIREILLE M., communications consultant; b. New Orleans, Jan. 18, 1939; d. Leo Stephen and Mireille (Reich) Modenbach; m. Edwin J. Grovier, June 24, 1961; children: Reich Hawthorne, Sean Thomas, Noyes Keller. BA in German, Tulane U., 1960. Statistician Shell Oil Co., New Orleans, 1960-61; fabric, china artist Artistry by Mireille Grovier, San Jose, Calif., 1976-85; communications cons. free lance, San Jose, 1985-89; freelance writer Foothill Coll., Los Altos Hills, Calif., 1989. Pub., Dental Newsletter. Sec. Prospect Homeowners Coalition, San Jose, 1985; pres. women's soc. Grace United Meth. Ch., Saratoga, Calif., 1976. Recipient Award of Excellence German Govt., 1959-60. Mem. The Kenna Club, Phi Beta Kappa. Democrat. Mem. Unity Ch. Home: 6427 Prospect Rd San Jose CA 95129

GROWE, JOAN ANDERSON, state official; b. Mpls., Sept. 28, 1935; d. Arthur F. and Lucille M. (Brown) Anderson; children: Michael, Colleen, David, Patrick. B.S., St. Cloud State U., 1956; cert. in spl. edn., U. Minn., 1964; exec. mgmt. program State and local govt., Harvard U., 1979. Tchr. elem. pub. schs. Bloomington, Minn., 1956-58; tchr. for exceptional children elem. pub. schs. St. Paul, 1964-65; spl. edn. tchr. St. Anthony Pub. Schs., Minn., 1965-66; mem. Minn. Ho. of Reps., 1973-74; sec. of state State of Minn., St. Paul, 1975—; mem. exec. council Minn. State Bd. Investment; bd. dirs. Women Execs. in State Govt. Mem. Women's Campaign Fund, Women's Polit. Caucus, Minn. Women's Econ. Roundtable; candidate U.S. Senate, 1984; bd. dirs. Greater Mpls. council Girl Scouts U.S., Wayside House, Epilepsy Support Program. Recipient Minn. Sch. Bell award, 1977, YMCA Outstanding Achievement award, 1978; Disting. Alumni award St. Cloud State U., 1979; Charlotte Striebel Long Distance Runner award Minn. NOW, 1985. Mem. Nat. Assn. Secs. of State (pres. 1979-80), Bus. and Profl. Women, Inc., Minn. Equal Rights Alliance, AAUW, LWV. Roman Catholic. Office: Sec of State's Office 180 State Office Bldg Saint Paul MN 55155

GRUBB, LINDA FERN, architect; b. Maryville, Mo., Nov. 22, 1944; d. Earl Jackson and Juanda Fern (Boatwright) Shoemaker; m. Stephen Leslie Grubb, Sept. 3, 1966; children: Cydney Katherine, Jack Christopher. BArch, Kans. State U., 1967. Registered architect, Ill. Intern Coffin & Scherschel, Barrington, Ill., 1969-72, architect, 1972-74; dir. devel. Village of Barrington, 1974; pvt. practice planning cons. Barrington, 1975-77, pvt. practice architect, 1975—. Bd. dirs. Elgin (Ill.) Acad., 1985—; mem. Village of Barrington Plan Commn., 1981-89; preservation commr. Barrington Area Hist. Soc., 1982—, mem. devel. com., 1986—, bd. dirs. 1990—. Recipient Excellence award Archtl. Woodwork Inst., 1982. Mem. AIA, Assn. Preservation Technology, Nat. Trust Hist. Preservation, P.E.O. Republican. Office: 102 N Cook St #23 Barrington IL 60010

GRUBB, PHYLLIS BOWMAN, substance abuse counselor; b. North Tazewell, Va., Aug. 24, 1934; d. Clarence Earl and Russie (White) Bowman; m. James N. Grubb, July 18, 1953 (div. 1983); 1 child, Phyllis Ann Grubb Brady. AA, Durham Tech. Inst, 1976; BA, Goddard Coll., 1980. Cert. substance abuse counselor, N.C. Sec., comptroller Duke U. Med. Ctr., Durham, N.C., 1963-69; substance abuse counselor Alcoholic Rehab. Ctr., Butner, N.C., 1969—; mem. faculty, N.C. Sch. Alcohol & Drugs, Wilmington, 1979; pres., owner, South Granville Counseling Svcs., Butner, 1980—, Men/Women in Crisis Counseling Svcs., Durham, 1981—, Triangle Home Health Care, Inc., Durham, 1986—; pres., PEM Ventures, Durham, 1985—. Collaborator on TV spl., Women and Alcohol, 1977. Mem. Alcoholism Profls. N.C. (exec. bd. 1970-72, regional v.p. 1984-86), State Employees Assn., N-Vestment Assn. (pres. 1985-87), South Granville Exchange (bd. dirs. 1986—). Democrat. Presbyterian. Home: 1601 Kirkwood Dr Durham NC 27705 Office: Men Women In Crisis Counsel 1318 Broad St Durham NC 27705

GRUBE, REBECCA SUE, elementary educator, consultant; b. Lancaster, Pa., June 27, 1945; d. Warren Landis and Ruth Rebecca (Hackman) Newcomer; m. Terry Wayne Grube, Aug. 27, 1966; children: T. David, Joy Lynn, Matthew Warren. Student Juniata Coll., 1963-65; BA, Franklin and Marshall Coll., 1976; MEd, Millersville U., 1979; postgrad. Temple U., Wright State U. Cert. spl. edn., neurolinguistic programmer. Grad. asst. Millersville U., Pa., 1978-79; tchr. gifted and learning disabled Sch. Dist. of Lancaster, Pa., 1979-80; tchr. pvt. sch., Lancaster, 1980-81; elem. tchr. Lancaster County Day Sch., 1981-85, tchr. resource room, 1985—, chmn. elem. lang. arts curriculum, 1985-88, mem. curriculum com., 1986-87, tchr. psychology, head lower sch., 1989-90, dir. spl. projects, 1990—; pvt. practice ednl. cons., tutor, Lancaster, 1981—; dir. program Teaching Talented and Outstanding Pupils for Success, 1987, 88—; instr. Performance Learning Systems, 1987—, Wilkes Coll., 1987—. Contbg. editor United Evang. 1975; contbr. articles to profl. quars.; author research report. Pres. bd. dirs. Contact Lancaster, 1986, chairperson support workers, 1987-88; bd. dirs. Listening Ear, Parents of Adoptive Children Orgn., 1981-85, Martin Luther King Scholarship Fund, Janus L.D. Sch.; mem. Leadership Lancaster, 1989, Leadership Pa., 1990. Fellow Christa McAuliffe U.S. Dept. Edn., 1988-89, Leadership Lancaster, 1989; recipient award Lancaster Assn. Retarded Citizens, 1978-79, Cert. of Appreciation, AFL-CIO Community Services, 1983, CONTACT award City of Lancaster, 1988, Literacy award for Teaching Talented and Outstanding Pupils for Success Lancaster-Lebanon Reading Coun., 1988. Mem. Assn. for Supervision and Curriculum, Orton Dyslexia Soc., Assn. for Children with Learning Disabilities (past bd. dirs. Lancaster Lebanon chpt.), Pa. Assn. for Gifted Children, Council Exceptional Children, Nat. Assn. for Gifted Children, Cen. Pa. Friends of Jazz, Pi Lambda Theta (chmn. Lehman Home Project 1984-86). Republican. Lutheran. Avocations: tennis, walking, piano, drums, reading. Home: 18 Gordon Rd Lancaster PA 17603

GRUBER, HELEN ELIZABETH, medical researcher; b. Wallace, Idaho, Nov. 6, 1946; d. Hugo J. and Margaret A. (Dorsey) G. BS, U. Idaho, 1969; MS, Oreg. State U., 1974, PhD, 1976. Research asst. Oreg. State U., Corvallis, 1974-76; NIH postdoctoral fellow U. Iowa, Iowa City, 1976-78; research instr. U. Wash., Seattle, Tacoma, 1978-81; assoc. researcher, research medicine U. So. Calif., Los Angeles, 1981-86; dir. skeletal dysplasia morphology lab., assoc. researcher Cedars-Sinai Med. Ctr., UCLA, Los Angeles, 1986—; vol. tchr. Los Angeles Schs., Griffin Ave., 1986; mem. Cedars-Sinai Med. Ctr. Research Com., 1987—; mem. Cedars-Sinai Biosci. Library Task Force, 1988—. Contbr. articles to profl. jours. Recipient Appreciation award Griffin Ave. Sch., Los Angeles, 1986. Mem. Soc. Exptl. Biology and Medicine (editorial bd. 1986—), AAAS, Am. Fedn. Clin. Research, Am. Soc. Bone and Mineral Research, Am. Soc. Cell Biology, Women in Cell Biology, So. Calif. Bone and Mineral Club. Roman Catholic. Office: Cedars Sinai Med Ctr Med Genetics Birth Defects Ctr ASB 3d Fl Los Angeles CA 90048

GRUBER, MARION ELIZABETH, non-profit organization administrator; b. Balt., Apr. 8, 1945; d. William A. and Ruth (Lehman) Brown; m. J. Richard Gruber, Apr. 11, 1975; children: Shen Adams, Kalen Adams. AA, Monmouth Coll., 1967, BA in Psychology, 1967. Child care worker Family and Children's Svcs., West Hartford, Conn., 1967-68; acting mgr. Estes Park (Colo.) Area C. of C., 1975-77; hotel rooms mgr., personnel dir. Stanley Sheraton Hotel, Estes Park, 1977-79; asst. v.p. Colorado Springs (Colo.) C. of C., 1979-81, v.p., 1981-83; personnel dir. Antlers Plaza Hotel, The Broadmoor, Colorado Springs, 1981; exec. dir. The Vol. Ctr. Memphis, 1984-89, Wichita (Kans.) Festivals Inc., 1989—; del., Inst. C. of C. Mgmt., Boulder, Colo., 1982-84, U.S. C. of C., Washington, 1983-84. Contbr. articles to vol. svc. publs. Bylaws chmn., Memphis Coalition for Homeless, 1984-87; mem. oper. com., Memphis Ptnrs. for Youth Devel., 1985—; chmn. Tenn. Vol. Homecoming '86; mem. Nat. Vol. Ctr. Adv. Bd. , 1989. Recipient certs. of appreciation Gov. Ned McWherter, Mayor William Morris, Shelby County Govt., Mayor Richard Hackett, City of Memphis. Mem. Tenn. Network Vol. Adminstrs. (co-founder, v.p. 1987—), United Way Exec.Dirs. Assn., Assn. Vol. Adminstrs., Memphis Area Assoc. Vol. Adminstrs., Membership Execs. of Colo. C. of C., Leadership Memphis, Exec. Women Internat., Forum for Exec. Women, Kans. Press Women, Wichita Press Women. Home: 918 Shadyway Wichita KS 67203 Office: Wichita River Festival Wichita KS

GRUCZA, NANCY MARCECA, sales executive; b. Warren, Pa., Jan. 14, 1955; d. Arthur Anthony and Rose (Toppo) Marceca; m. Marc A. Grucza (div. Feb. 1980). BA, Villa Maria Coll., Erie, Pa., 1976; postgrad., Mid-Fla. Tech., 1984; MBA, Crummer Sch. Bus., Rollins Col, Winter Park, Fla., 1989. Cert. tchr. Head service office Plumpton Buick, Inc., Erie, Pa., 1978-79; tchr. J.F. Kennedy Day Care Ctr., Erie, Pa., 1979-80; reservations, sales Walt Disney World, Lake Buena Vista, Fla., 1980-85; adminstrv. asst. Orlando (Fla.) Computer Corp.; dir. sales, front office mgr. Ramada Inn Orlando Westgate, Kissimmee, Fla., 1986-89; front office mgr. The Georgian Luxury Resort, Lake George, N.Y., 1989; dir. sales, mktg. Best Western, Leesburg, Va., 1990—. Author: Parents and their children, 1976. Mem. Am. Soc. Travel Agts., Nat. Assn. Female Execs., Ramada Mgmt. Assn., Ramada Mgmt Assn. Mktg. Com. Republican. Roman Catholic. Home: 1210 Summerfield Dr Herndon VA 22070

GRUEBER, CYNTHIA MARIE, health services facility administrator; b. Saginaw, Mich., Jan. 23, 1957; d. Roy George and Arlene Louise (Kube) G. BSc. in Sociology, Mich. State U., 1979; M in Health Svc. Adminstrn., U. Mich., 1981. Rsch. asst. Mich. State U., East Lansing, 1978-79, U. Mich., Ann Arbor, 1979-80; adminstrv. extern Samaritan Health Ctr., Detroit, 1980, program asst., exec. asst., 1982-85, v.p. profl. & support svcs., 1985-87; v.p. profl. svcs. Mercy Hosps. and Health Svcs. of Detroit, 1987-90; assoc. dir. profl. svcs. Med. Coll. Va. Hosps., Richmond, 1990—. Author/editor: Monograph On Health Care for the Uninsured, 1985; contbr. articles to profl. jours. Mem. Am. Coll. Health Care Execs. (nominee). Lutheran. Home: 13017 Silent Wood Pl Richmond VA 23233 Office: Med Coll Va Hosps PO Box 510 Richmond VA 23204

GRUEN, MARY HOAGLAND, service company executive; b. Liberty, N.Y., June 25, 1918; d. Henry Elmer and Edna Fay (Hardie) Hoagland; children: Dietrich Richard, William Hardie. BA, Swarthmore Coll., 1939; MS, Ohio State U., 1942. Cert. Med. Tech., 1940. Med. tech.dept. med. rsch. Ohio State U., Columbus, 1940-43; hosp. recreation overseas ARC, 1943-46; personnel asst. Atlantic Mutual Ins. Co., N.Y.C., 1946-49; substitute tchr. Pleasantville NY Schs.; treas. Bd. Edn., Pleasantville, N.Y., 1962-73; personnel dir. Liberian Svcs. Inc., 1975-84; personnel dir., v.p. Liberian Corp. Svcs., Reston, Va., 1977-84, cons., 1984-87, also bd. dirs. Mem. Phi Beta Kappa. Home: 174 Main St Orleans MA 02653

GRUHL, ANDREA MORRIS, librarian; b. Ponca City, Okla., Dec. 9, 1939; d. Luther Oscar and Hazel Evangeline (Anderson) Morris; m. Werner Mann Gruhl, July 10, 1965; children: Sonja Krista, Diana Krista. B.A., Wesleyan Coll., 1961; M.L.S., U. Md., 1968; postgrad., Johns Hopkins U., 1970-71, U. Md., 1968, 71-73. Tchr. Broward County, Fla., Dept. Def. Montgomery County (Md.), 1961-66; libr. Prince Georges County (Md.) Pub. Libr., 1966-68, 81-83, U. Md., College Park, 1970-72; art history researcher Joseph Alsop, Washington, 1972-74; libr. Howard County Pub. Libr., Columbia, Md., 1969-70, 74-79; European exch. staff Libr. of Congress, Washington, 1982-86; cataloger fed. documents GPO, Washington, 1986—; mem. women's program adv. com., processing dept. rep. Libr. of Congress, 1983-86, mem. ofcl. del. to Internat. Fedn. Libr. Assns. ann. conf., Munich, 1983, Chgo., 1985; state del. White House Conf. on Librs., 1978, 90. Indexer, editor: Learning Vacations, 3d edit., 1980; LCPA Index to Libr. of Congress Info. Bull., 1984. Trustee Howard County Community Coll., 1989—, Howard County Pub. Libr., Columbia, Md., 1979-87; publ. chmn. LWV of Howard County, Md., 1974; citizen's rep. for Howard County and exec. bd. Balt. Regional Planning Council Libr. Com., 1976-79; Friends of the Libr., Howard County, Md., pres., 1976; vol. Nat. Gallery of Art Libr., Washington, 1978-80. Mem. Art Librs. Soc. N.Am. (coord., mem.'s publ. exhbn. 1980-82), ALA (mem. trustee assn. 1982-87, resources and tech. svcs. div., cataloging sect. 1988—, govt. documents roundtable 1988—), Libr. of Congress Profl. Assn. (coord. ann. staff art show 1982, 83, chmn. spl. interest group on libr. sci. 1985-87), Libr. of Congress Am. Fedn. State County and Mcpl. Employees Union 2477 (program chmn. 1984-86), Md. Libr. Assn. (pres. trustee div. 1982-83), Assn. Community Coll. Trustees, Kappa Delta Epsilon, Beta Phi Mu. Democrat. Lutheran. Home: 5990 Jacob's Ladder Columbia MD 21045 Office: Govt Printing Office Washington DC 20401

GRUMET, PRISCILLA HECHT, fashion specialist, consultant, writer; b. Detroit, May 11, 1943; d. Lewis Maxwell and Helen Ruth (Miller) Hecht; m. Ross Frederick Grumet, Feb. 24, 1968; 1 child, Auden Lewis. AA, Stephens Coll., 1963; student, Ga. State Coll., 1983-85. Buyer Rich's Dept. Store, Atlanta, 1963-68; instr. fashion retail Fashion Inst. Am., Atlanta, 1968-71; pres., lectr., cons. Personally Priscilla Personal Shopping Svc., Atlanta, 1971—; retail and customer svc. cons. By Priscilla Grumet, Atlanta, 1989—; instr. Cont. Edn. Program Emory U., Atlanta, 1976—; fashion merch. coord. Park Pl. Shopping Ctr., Atlanta, 1979-83; writer Altanta Bus. Mag., 1984—; cons., buyer Greers-Regensteins Store, Atlanta, 1986-87; Guest lectr. Fashion Group of Am., Rancho La Puerta Resort, Tecate, Mex., 1985—, adv. bd. Bauder Fashion Coll., 1986—, fashion panel judge Weight Watchers Internat., 1981. Author: How to Dress Well, 1981; reporter, Women's Wear Daily, 1976—; columnist Altanta Scene Mag.; contbr. numerous articles to mags. including Seventeen, Nat. Jeweler's. Pub. rels. dir., Atlanta Jewish Home Aux., 1986-89; admissions advisor, Stephens Coll., 1979—. Mem. Fashion Group, Inc., Women in Communications, Nat. Coun. of Jewish Women, Atlanta Press Club, Temple Sisterhood (speaker, spl. events com. 1983—). Home: 2863 Careygate NW Atlanta GA 30305

GRUNDY, BETTY LOU BOTTOMS, anesthesiologist; b. Dothan, Ala., Jan. 3, 1940; d. Wilmer Rudolph and Marie Belle (Brandon) Bottoms; m. David Mather Grundy, June 3, 1963; children: Jennifer Marie, Thomas Mather. Postgrad., Huntington Coll., Montgomery, Ala., 1956-59; MD, U. Fla., 1963. Gen. med. practice Homestake Gold Mine, Lead, S.D., 1964-65; resident in anesthesiology Peter Bent Brigham Hosp., Boston, 1965-67; pvt. practice, anesthesiology St. Luke's Hosp., Saginaw, Mich., 1967-75; asst. prof. anesthesiology Mich. State U., Saginaw, Mich., Case Western Reserve U., Cleve., 1975-79, U. Pitts., 1979-82; prof., chmn. of anesthesiology Coll. of Medicine, Oral Roberts U., Tulsa, Okla., 1982-84; prof. of anesthesiology U. Fla., Gainesville, 1984—; chief, anesthesiology service Veterans Adminstrn. Med. Ctr., Gainesville, Fla., 1984—; assoc. examiner American bd. of Anesthesiology, Hartford, Conn., evoked potentials com. American Electroencephalographic Soc., Atlanta, vol. site visitor Residency Review Com. for Anesthesiology, Accreditation Council for grad. Med. Edn., 1982—. Editor: The Quality of Care in Anesthesia, 1982, Evoked Potentials Intraoperative and ICU Monitoring, 1988. Recipient Spl. award for New Investigators in Anesthesiology, Nat. Inst. of Health, 1979. Methodist. Home: 504 NW 89th St Gainesville FL 32607 Office: Univ Fla Box J 254 JHMHC Gainesville FL 32610-0254

GRUNEWALD, KATHARINE KLEVESAHL, nutritionist, educator; b. Bonduel, Wis., Oct. 4, 1952; d. Vilas Louis and Ardyce (Moeller) Klevesahl; m. Orlen C. Grunewald, Aug. 23, 1975. BS, U. Wis., Green Bay, 1974; MS, U. Ky., 1976, PhD, 1979. Registered dietitian. Asst. prof. dept. foods and nutrition Kans. State U., Manhattan, 1979-85, assoc. prof., 1986—. Contbr. articles to profl. jours. Mem. AAHPER, Am. Dietetic Assn., Am. Inst. Nutrition, Am. Coll. Sports Medicine, Scientists Inst. for Pub. Info. Office: Kans State U Dept Foods and Nutrition Manhattan KS 66506

GRUNKE, MARY ELLEN, psychology educator, college program administrator; b. New Richmond, Wis., Nov. 25, 1950; d. Marvin Gustav and Lorraine Louise (Grosshans) G.; m. Clare Duckworth Vlahos, June 13, 1981 (div. Apr. 1983). Student, Bonn U., Fed. Republic of Germany, 1970-71; BA, Wartburg Coll., 1972; MA, U. Iowa, 1974, PhD, 1977. Asst. prof. psychology Coll. of Charleston, S.C., 1979-81; instr. in psychology Kansas City (Kans.) Community Coll., 1981-90, dir. honors program, 1990—; mem. adv. bd. Dushkin Pub. Group, Conn., 1990—. Del. Dem. Party Congl. Dist. Conv., Johnson County, Kans., 1988; mem. local govt. task force, Kansas City, 1990—. NIMH Rsch. fellow, 1976-77, 77-79. Mem. Am. Psychol. Assn. (reviewer Washington chpt. 1990—), Kans. Edn. Assn., Greater Kansas City Psychol. Assn. Lutheran. Home: 624 N 80th Terr Kansas City

KS 66112 Office: Kansas City Community Coll 7250 State Ave Kansas City KS 66112

GRUNNER, JOCELYN SARI, broadcast executive; b. N.Y.C., Mar. 15, 1958; d. Bernard and Ruth Rosa (Jaslove) G. BA, CUNY, 1979. Advt. broadcast negotiator Sawdon & Bess Advt., N.Y.C., 1979-80, Marschalk Advt., N.Y.C., 1980-81, Wells, Rich & Green Advt., N.Y.C., 1981-83; broadcast dir. Media Gen. Broadcast, N.Y.C., 1983-86; nat. broadcast account mgr. Katz Communication, N.Y.C., 1986-89, NBC, N.Y.C., 1989—. Mem. Advt. Women of N.Y. Office: NBC 30 Rockefeller Pla New York NY 10112

GRUNWALDT, CONSTANCE JEAN, sales executive; b. Appleton, Wis., Oct. 26, 1963; d. David Carl and Diane (Cory) G. BA in Polit. Sci., U. Wis., 1986. Sales rep. Procter and Gamble Distbg. Co., Milw., 1987-88, dist. field rep., 1988-89; brand asst. advt. dept. Procter and Gamble Distbg. Co., Cin., 1989-90; unit mgr. Procter and Gamble Distbg. Co., Chgo., 1990—. Vol. Planned Parenthood, Milw., 1988—, Susan Engelister for Senate, Milw., 1988; mem. Children's Adv. Milw. Women's Refuge, 1989—. Named Panhellenic Woman of Yr. U. Wis., 1986. Mem. NAFE, NOW. Methodist. Office: Procter & Gamble Distbg Co 1801 S Meyers Rd Ste 500 Oakbrook Terrace IL 60657

GRUPE, AMY ELIZABETH, management; b. Pitts., Nov. 3, 1958; d. Richard Helling and Ann (Stoehr) G. BS magna cum laude, W.Va. U., 1980. Cert. aerobic instr. Asst. buyer Kaufmann's Dept. Store, Pitts., 1980-82; sales rep. McCloy's Office Supply, Pitts., 1982; sales cons. Liken Medicare Ctr., Wheeling, W.Va., 1982-83; profl. sales rep. Schering Corp., Wheeling, W.Va., 1983-87; dist. mgr. Schering Corp., Pitts., 1987-90, San Diego, 1990—. Bd. dirs. Am. Liver Found., San Diego. Mem. NAFE, Internat. Dance-Exercise Assn., Reebok Profl. Alliance, Jaycees, Phi Upsilon Omciron. Home: 27985 Via del Agua Laguna Niguel CA 92656

GRUSH, MARY ELLEN, computer company executive; b. Aurora, Ill., Oct. 28, 1947; d. Byron Edward and Olga Marion (Olson) Grush; m. Kenneth Takagi Takara, Oct. 25, 1981; 1 child, Stephanie Suzanne Grush. B.A., Ft. Wright Coll., 1971; M.A., U. Denver, 1975. Mgr. met. info. retrieval network Bibliog. Ctr. for Research, Denver, 1975-77; customer services rep. tng. Lockheed Dialog Info. Systems, Palo Alto, Calif., 1977-78, computer ops. supr., 1978—. Mem. ALA, Spl. Libraries Assn., Beta Phi Mu, Pi Delta Phi. Home: PO Box 1378 Los Altos CA 94023

GRUSKIN, FELICE RHODA, accountant; b. Newark, June 21, 1928; d. Max and Frederich (Markowitz) Berlot; m. Abe Gruskin, Oct. 7, 1950 (dec. May 1971); children: Mark, Jay. BBA, CCNY, 1949. Asst. acct. Columbia U., N.Y.C., 1961-63; acct. N.Y. Med. Coll., N.Y.C., 1964-66, N.Y.C., 1967—; exec. dir. Transit Riders in Pursuit, N.Y.C., 1982—. Dist. leader Dem. Party, N.Y.C., 1977-85; bd. trustees Henry George Sch. Social Sci., N.Y.C., 1985—; treas. Washington Heights Inwood Dev. Corp., 1987—. Office: Transit Riders in Pursuit PO Box 310 New York NY 10032

GRUTZMACHER, JUNE EDITH, ophthalmologist; b. Phila., July 23, 1956; d. Philip William Clark and Edith Damone (Hinkle) G. Student, Pa. State U., 1974-75, Holy Family Coll., 1975-76; BA, LaSalle U., 1976-78; MD, Temple U., 1982. Diplomate Am. Bd. Ophthalmology, Nat. Bd. Med. Examiners. Attending ophthalmologist Hunterdon Med. Ctr., Flemington, N.J., 1986—, Mercer Med. Ctr., Trenton, N.J., 1989—; pvt. practice Lambertville, N.J., 1988—. Recipient Scholastic Achievement award Am. Med. Women's Assn., 1982. Fellow Am. Acad. Ophthalmology; mem. AMA (Physician's Recognition 1986, 89), N.J. Med. Soc., Hunterdon County Med. Soc., Women in Ophthalmology, Inc., Assn. of Women Surgeons, Lambertville C. of C., Alpha Omega Alpha. Office: 173 N Union St Lambertville NJ 08530

GRYNIUK, KATHLEEN DIANNE, developer, fund raiser; b. Torrington, Conn., Apr. 9, 1957; d. Joseph John and Frances (Arnista) G. BS in Community Health Edn., Western Conn. State U., 1979. Pub. health program asst. Conn. State Dept. Health Svcs., Hartford, Conn., 1980; project dir. Nat. Health Screening Coun., Washington, 1980-82, regional dir., 1982-84, program devel. specialist, 1984; alumni affairs coord. Uni. Conn. Health Ctr., Farmington, Conn., 1984-87; children's cancer fund coord. Univ. Conn. Health Ctr., Farmington, 1986-87, asst. dir. devel., 1987-89, dir. devel., 1989. Adv. bd. Univ. Conn. Children's Cancer Fund, 1986—. Mem. Greater Hartford C. of C., Coun. for Advancement and Support Edn., Nat. Assn. Hosp. Devel., Nat. Soc. Fund Raising Exec., Univ. Conn. Health Ctr. Aux. Democrat. Office: U Conn Health Ctr 309 Farmington Ave Farmington CT 06032

GRYPMA, JANE PATRICIA, management specialist; b. Tarrytown, N.Y., Sept. 30, 1960; d. Christiaan Hubert and Swan Liem (Sie) Grypma. BBA, U. Ariz., 1982. Programmer analyst FMC Corp., San Jose, Calif., 1983-86; programmer, systems analyst Wiltron Co., Morgan Hill, Calif., 1986—; co-mgr., founder Team Calif. Racing, Morgan Hill, 1987—. Vol. Spl. Olympics, Morgan Hill, Calif. Named All Am., 1988. Mem. Exchange Club Morgan Hill Gilroy (charter mem., ednl. dir. 1988—, Ride to End Abuse to Children founder, chmn. 1989—). Democrat. Roman Catholic. Home: 229 Del Monte Ln Morgan Hill CA 95037 Office: Wiltron Co 490 Jarvis Dr Morgan Hill CA 95037

GUARD, MARY BETH, lawyer, small business owner; b. Carmi, Ill., Aug. 19, 1955; d. William Frank and Jacqueline Lee (Galloway) Sharp; m. Lynndon Michael Guard, May 28, 1978. AA, Kaskaskia Coll., 1975; BS, So. Ill. U., 1977, JD, 1980. Bar: Okla., U.S. Dist. Ct. (we. dist.) Okla., U.S. Ct. Appeals (10th cir.). Atty. oil and gas dept. Commrs. Land Office State of Okla., Oklahoma City, 1980-84; gen. counsel Banking Dept. State of Okla., Oklahoma City, 1984-89; v.p., gen. counsel, wellnes dir. Okla. Bankers Assn., Oklahoma City, 1989-; gen. ptnr. Sweatshirt Chic, Oklahoma City, 1987—; lectr. continuing legal edn. courses, Okla. 1981—; magician Oklahoma City, 1982—. Editor The Phys. Edge; contbr. articles to profl. jours. Vol. various orgns.; mentor Search Sch. for Gifted Children, Moore, Okla., 1986, 87; bd. dirs., 3d v.p. YWCA, Oklahoma City, 1985-88. Mem. ABA (local com.), Okla. Bar Assn. (com. post. 1982-85), Oklahoma City Magic Soc. (v.p. 1985-86), Soc. Am. Magicians, Internat. Brotherhood. Magicians, Bus. and Profl. Women's Club (pres. 1983-84, Outstanding Woman of Yr. 1982, Outstanding Young Careerist 1985), Order of the Barrister, Phi Alpha Delta (justice 1979-80). Democrat. Methodist. Home: 201 NW 33d St Oklahoma City OK 73118 Office: Oklahoma Bankers Assn PO Box 18246 Oklahoma City OK 73154

GUARDO, CAROL J., academic administrator; b. Hartford, Conn., Apr. 12, 1939; d. C. Fred and Marion (Biase) G. BA, St. Joseph Coll., 1961; MA, U. Detroit, 1963; PhD, U. Denver, 1966. Asst. prof. psychology Eastern Mich. U., Ypsilanti, 1966-68; assoc. prof., staff psychologist U. Denver, 1968-73; assoc. prof., dean coll. Utica Coll. of Syracuse U., Utica, N.Y., 1973-76; prof., dean Coll. Liberal Arts, Drake U., Des Moines, 1976-80; provost, prof. U. Hartford, 1980-85; pres. R.I. Coll., Providence, 1986-90, Great Lakes Colls. Assn., Ann Arbor, Mich., 1990—; mem. Iowa Humanities Bd., 1976-80, pres., 1978-80; bd. dirs. Am. Coun. Edn., People's Bank. Author: The Adolescent As Individual: Issues and Insights, 1975; contbr. articles to profl. jours. Trustee St. Joseph Coll., Monmouth Coll. NSF fellow, 1964, NIMH fellow, 1964-66. Mem. Am. Assn. Higher Edn., Assn. Am. Colls. (vice chair 1987, chair 1988), Am. Psychol. Assn., Assn. Gen. and Liberal Studies (pres. 1979-81), Soc. Rsch. in Child Devel., Greater Providence C. of C., Phi Beta Kappa. Office: Great Lakes Colls Assn 2929 Plymouth Rd Ste 207 Ann Arbor MI 48105

GUCKER, JANE GLEASON, architect; b. Morristown, N.J., Nov. 14, 1951; d. James Patrick and Jean (Michelotti) Gleason; m. Douglas Brent Gucker, July 5, 1975. BArch, Va. Polytech. Inst. and U., 1975. Registered architect, Ill. Intern De-Witt-Admal & Assocs., Decatur, Ill., 1975-77, Marvin D. Miller & Assocs., Monticello, Ill., 1978-81; architect Archtl. and Engring. Svc. Corp., Decatur, 1983-89; evaluating architect State of Ill. Capitol Devel. Bd., Springfield, 1989—. Tutor Project Read, Decatur, 1987-88; bd. dirs. YWCA, 1985-89, chair bldg. com. 1987-89; bd. dirs. Habitat for Humanity, Decatur, 1987-90. Mem. AIA, Constrn. Specifications Inst. (cert.), Nat. Coun. Archtl. Registration Bds. (cert.), CSI (v.p., chair tech. documents com. Cen. Ill. chpt. 1990—). Episcopalian. Office: State Ill Capitol Devel Bd 3rd Fl, Wm G Stratton Bldg 401 S Spring St Springfield IL 62706

GUDWER, ROSEANNE DENIG, accountant; b. Racine, Wis., Nov. 16, 1936; d. Anthony John and Rose Mary (Mueller) Denig; m. John H. Gudwer, Sept. 13, 1958 (div. Oct. 1979); 1 child, Susan Marie Gudwer Krupp. BS in Bus. Mgmt., U. Wis.-Parkside, Kenosha, 1978. CPA, Wis. Staff acct. Western Pub., Racine, 1978-81, mgr. acctg., 1981-84; dir. acctg. Runzheimer Internat., Rochester, Wis., 1984—. Editor Racine/Kenosha Parents Without Ptnrs., 1979. Mem. AAUW (com. 1984), Nat. Assn. Accts., Wis. Inst. CPAs (bd. dirs. Racine/Kenosha chpt. 1981-83). Office: Runzheimer Internat Runzheimer Park Rochester WI 53167

GUENTER, GAIL MARIE, computer engineer, researcher; b. Milw., Apr. 17, 1961; d. Theodore Edward and June Dolores (Carlson) G. BS in Computer Sci., U. Wis., Milw., 1985. Software engr. Norland Corp., Ft. Atkinson, Wis., 1986-87; software support engr. Heurikon Corp., Madison, Wis., 1987-89, tech. support mgr., 1989-90, software engr., 1990—. Mem. Greenpeace, World Wildlife Fund, Nat. Wildlife Fedn. Mem. IEEE, IEEE Computer Soc., Soc. Women Engrs., Assn. Computing Machines (software engring. interest group, siggraph, computer graphics interest group), NAFE, U. Wis. Milw. Alumni Assn. Office: Heurikon Corp 8310 Excelsior Dr Madison WI 53717

GUERNSEY, JANET BROWN, physicist, educator, retired; b. Germantown, Pa., May 2, 1913; d. Clarence Montgomery and Luella Emily (Conwell) Brown; m. William Guernsey, June 20, 1936; children: Richard, David, Michael, Robert, Madeleine. BA, Wellesley Coll., 1935; MA, Harvard U., 1948; PhD, MIT, 1955. From instr. to prof. and chmn. dept. physics Wellesley (Mass.) Coll., 1941-78; teaching asst. Baldwin Sch., Bryn Mawr, Pa., 1935-36. Contbr. articles to profl. jours. Mem. Am. Assn. Physics Tchrs. (pres. 1975-76, pres. New England chpt. 1968-69, 79-80). Republican. Episcopalian. Home: Sabrina Farm Wellesley MA 02181 Office: Wellesley College Wellesley MA 02181

GUERRA, EMMA MARIA, accountant; b. Las Martinas, Cuba, Nov. 11, 1956; came to U.S., 1962; d. Heberto and Maria Emma (Ledesma) Salgueiro; m. Alfredo Guerra, June 28, 1974; children: Alfred Michael, David Christopher. BSBA with highest honors, Fla. Internat. U., 1977. CPA, Fla. Sr. acct. Deloitte, Haskins & Sells, Miami, Fla., 1977-81; v.p., chief fin. officer Union Fed. Savs. and Loan, Miami, 1981; mgr. Am. Express Co., Miami, 1981-83; pvt. practice Miami, 1983—. Mem. Am. Inst. CPA's (Elijah Watt Sells award 1977), Fla. Inst. CPA's. Roman Catholic. Home and Office: 10010 SW 28th St Miami FL 33165

GUESON, EMERITA TORRES, obstetrician-gynecologist; b. Angeles City, Philippines, Jan. 4, 1942; came to U.S., 1964; d. Lina (Torres) Gueson. AA, U. Sto. Tomas, Manila, Philippines, 1958, MD, 1963. Resident Phila. Gen. Hosp., 1966-71; attending Nazareth Hosp., Phila., 1973—; physician Holy Redeemer Hosp., Phila., 1983—; bd. dirs. Physicians Who Care; lectr. healthcare issues to consumer groups, Phila. Author: Doctors Under Fire, 1989. Fellow Am. Coll. Obstetricians-Gynecologists; mem. Phila. County Med. Soc., Pa. Med. Soc., AMA, Prolife Obstetricians-Gynecologists (charter). Office: 3101 Yeltman Ave Philadelphia PA 19020

GUETTERMAN, STEPHANIE ANN, insurance producer; b. Lemore, Calif., Aug. 24, 1969; d. Scott Allen and Nancy Jo (Forcade) G. Student, McKendree Coll., Lebanon, Ill., 1987. Cert. ins. producer, Ill. File clk. Forcade Ins. Agy., Granite City, Ill., 1984-88, ins. producer, 1988—. Mem. Ind. Ins. Agts. Ill., Collinsville Jr. C. of C. Democrat. Roman Catholic. Office: Forcade Ins Agy 1822 State St Granite City IL 62040

GUEVARA-LACKI, NANETTE ROSE, electrical contractor; b. San Francisco, Feb. 25, 1953; d. Conrad Lombardo and Nancy Ann (Lim) Guevara; m. Stephen Herbert Lacki, Jan. 25, 1973; children: Jonathan, Alexander. BA in Polit. Sci., U. Calif., Santa Cruz, 1976; student, U. Calif., Berkeley, 1971-73. Sr. color photographer Wilson & Lund Photography, Rock Island, Ill., 1973-74; journeywoman Lacki Elec., Santa Cruz, 1974-85; journeyman electrician SL Elec., Watsonville, Calif., 1985-86; owner/operator NGL Elec., Watsonville, 1986—; cons. UCSC Women's Network, Santa Cruz, 1987—. Bd. dirs. Shakespeare Santa Cruz, 1983—, YWCA, Watsonville, 1985-89; v.p. Alumni Scholarship Com., U. Calif., Santa Cruz, 1983—, bd. dirs., treas. Alumni Coun., 1987—. Mem. Assoc. Bldrs. & Contrs., United Minority Bus. Entrepreneurs, Women in Bus., AAUW, Women's Network Santa Cruz, Notre Dame Women's Club. Republican. Roman Catholic. Office: NGL Electric PO Box 839 Freedom CA 95019

GUGGENHEIMER, ELINOR, civic leader, writer; b. N.Y.C., Apr. 11, 1912; d. Nathan and Lillian (Fox) Coleman; m. Randolph Guggenheimer, June 2, 1932; children: Charles, Randolph Jr. Student, Vassar Coll., 1929-31; BA, Barnard Coll., 1934; DHL, Marymount-Manhattan Coll., 1987. Dir. N.Y.C. Audio-Visual Tng. Office, 1943-44, Day Care Coun. of N.Y., N.Y.C., 1948-60; commr. City Planning, N.Y.C., 1960-67; on-air host, "Straight Talk" WOR-TV, N.Y.C., 1970-73; chmn. Def. Adv. Com. on Women in Svcs., Washington, 1963, 64; commr. N.Y.C. Dept. Consumer Affairs, 1974-78; dir. Coun. Sr. Ctrs. and Svcs., N.Y.C., 1978-83; dir., pres. Nat. Child Care Action Campaign, N.Y.C., 1983—; lectr. Ctr. for Urban Affairs, New Sch. for Social Rsch., N.Y., 1965-70; tchr. Tchrs. Coll., Columbia U., 1969. Author: Planning for Parks, 1968, The Pleasure of Your Company, 1990; lyricist: Potholes, 1982. Bd. dirs. Community Svc. Soc., 1953—, Jewish Assn. Svcs. to the Aged, 1968—. Recipient Finley award City Coll. Alumni, Spl. award City of N.Y. Human Resource Adminstrn., 1984; named one of 100 Most Important Women in U.S. Ladies Home Jour., 1980, 88, Louise Waterman Wise Woman of Yr. Nat. Coun. Jewish Women, 1974. Mem. Bus. & Profl. Women, Cosmopolitan Club, Women's City Club, City Club of N.Y. (bd. dirs.), Lexington Democratic Club, Internat. Women's Forum (bd. dirs., founder, former pres.). Jewish. Office: Child Care Action Campaign 330 Seventh Ave New York NY 10001

GUGLIUZZA, KRISTENE KOONTZ, transplant and general surgery educator; b. Siloam Springs, Ark., May 2, 1956; d. Lloyd Lawson Koontz Jr. and Helen Ruth (Camfield) Smith; m. Joseph Thomas Gugliuzza III, Sept. 3, 1989. AS, Lake Land Coll., Mattoon, Ill., 1977; BS with honors, Ea. Ill. U., Charleston, 1978; MD, U. Ill., Rockford, 1982. Diplomate Am. Bd. Surgery. Intern dept. surgery Tulane U. Med. Sch. and Affiliated Hosps., New Orleans, 1982-83, resident, 1983-87, fellow div. transplantation, 1987-89, instr. surgery, rsch. assoc. in surgery and transplantation, 1989-90; asst. prof. U. Tex. Med. Br., Galveston, 1990—; spl. fellow in pancreas transplantation U. Minn., Mpls., 1989; recovery surgeon La. Organ Procurement Agy., New Orleans, 1989-90; presenter in field. Contbr. articles to med. jours. Recipient cert. of recognition Touro Infirmary, 1984, Outstanding Alumnus of Yr. award Lake Land Coll., 1989. Fellow ACS (assoc.); mem. AMA, So. Med. Soc., La. Med. Soc., Orleans Parish Med. Soc., Am. Med. Women's Assn., Assn. Women Surgeons, Tulane Surg. Soc., Tex. Transplant Soc. Office: U Tex Med Br 301 University Blvd Galveston TX 77550

GUIDA, PAT, information broker; b. Highland Park, Mich., Aug. 30, 1929; d. Wilfred Bernard and Patricia Mary (Kelly) Graham; m. Alexander Herbert Bohr, May 25, 1948 (div. July 1965); m. Edward Silvio Guida, Aug. 29, 1965; children: Niels Graham, Eric Alexander. Student, Regis Coll., 1946-48; BS cum laude, Fairleigh Dickinson U., 1961. Asst. librarian Warner-Lambert Research Inst., Morris Plains, N.J., 1961-64; librarian Reaction Motors Div. Thiokol, Denville, N.J., 1964-69; mgr., info. ctr. Foster D. Snell Div., Booz Allen & Hamilton Inc., Florham Park, N.J., 1969-80; pres. Pat Guida Assocs., Fairfield, N.J.; mem. Sci. Adv. Bd. EPA. Washington, 1978-82, Library Com. Chemists Club, N.Y.C., 1983-89. Editor: Chemical Digest, 1971-74. Pres. PTA, Sparta, N.J., 1959-60. Mem. AAAS, Am. Chem. Soc., N.Y. Acad. of Sci., Assn. Ind. Info. Profls., Chemists Club. Office: 24 Spielman Rd Fairfield NJ 07004

GUIDI, DORIS FRASER, university provost, educator; b. Pittsfield, Mass., Sept. 14, 1934; d. Walter Frank and Ina Lawson (Fraser) Jordan; m. William Richard Guidi, June 16, 1956; children: Eric Jordan, Cynthia Fraser. BA, U. Rochester, 1956; student, Oxford (Eng.) U., 1958; MS, L.I. U., 1975; EdD, Fairleigh-Dickinson U., 1983. Acad. advisor C.W. Post Campus, L.I. U., 1975-77, instr., 1977-82, asst. prof., 1982-87, assoc. prof., 1987—, chairperson health scis. dept., 1982-85, asst. dean. Sch. Health Professions, 1985-86, provost, 1986—; summer intern The Hastings Ctr., Hasting-on-Hudson, N.Y., 1981; cons., evaluator Empire State Coll. SUNY, Old Westbury, 1977-81. Vice chairperson Nassau County HIV Commn., 1989—. Named Outstanding Alumna Sch. Health Professions L.I. U., 1987. Mem. Am. Soc. Clin. Pathologists (affiliate, cert.). Office: LI U CW Post Campus Brookville NY 11548

GUIDO, JUDITH COOPER, higher education administrator; b. Nyack, N.Y.; d. Russell Seabury and Marjorie May (Osborne) Cooper; m. Fred J. Guido, Nov. 30, 1974. BA cum laude, Dominican Coll., N.Y., 1973; MA with honors, Manhattanville Coll., N.Y., 1974. Asst. to supt. for bus. Nyack Pub. Schs., N.Y., 1970-74; asst. to dean bus. program Dominican Coll., Orangeburg, N.Y., 1970-72; treas., bus. mgr. Elizabeth Seton Coll., Yonkers, N.Y., 1974-79; v.p. for fin. and adminstrn., treas. Union Theol. Sem., N.Y.C., 1979-86; exec. v.p., treas. Manhattanville Coll., Purchase, N.Y., 1986—. Mem. friends com. Mus. Am. Folk Art, 1978—; founding mem. Friends Union Theol. Sem. Burke Libr., N.Y.C., 1982—; mem. Pelham (N.Y.) Art Ctr., 1984—; trustee fin. com. The College Bd., N.Y.C., 1985-88; mem. steering com. Friends of the Performing Arts, Wave Hill, Riverdale, N.Y., 1985-89; bd. dirs. Morningside Area Alliance, N.Y.C., 1981-85. Mem. Nat. Assn. Coll. and Univ. Bus. Officers (bd. dirs. 1984—), Ea. Assn. Coll. and Univ. Bus. Officers (bd. dirs. 1979-88), Mgmt. Inst. for Religious Orgns. (adv. bd. 1983-88), Am. Mgmt. Assn., Nat. Assn. Coll. Aux. Svcs., Am. Hist. Assn., N.Y. Geneaol. and Biog. Soc., Nat. Trust for Hist. Preservation, Preservation League N.Y. Office: Manhattanville Coll Purchase St Purchase NY 10577

GUIDO, SHAREON CHRISTINE, mechanical contractor; b. Washington, Aug. 5, 1946; d. James Harold and Edna Louise (Mills) McCullough; m. Frank Michael Guido, June 7, 1975; 1 child, Craig Scott. Diploma, George C. Marshall Sch., 1964. Asst. corp. sec. First Charter Land, Falls Church, Va., 1969-70; sec. to v.p. Liberty Loan Corp., Falls Church, 1970-71; gen. mgr. Richards A/C Co. Inc., Falls Church, 1971-83; founder, pres. Precision Air, Inc., Falls Church, 1983—; sponsor Va. Apprenticeship Program, Fairfax, 1983—. Contbr. articles to profl. jours. Bd. dirs. Boys Clubs of Am., Falls Church, Va., 1975-76; leader Boy Scouts Am. Falls Church, 1975-78; instr. religious edn. Diocese of Arlington, Va., 1976-77; counselor Telecommunications for the Deaf, 1982; mem. adv. coun. bd. Salvation Army; guest lectr. Am. Lung Assn., 1983; notary pub. Va., 1971—; ofcl. Nat. Assn. Stock Car Auto Racing, 1972-74. Recipient Outstanding Service award Am. Lung Assn., 1983. Mem. Air Conditioning Contractors of Am. (mgmt. edn. com. 1987—), Falls Ch. Preservation Soc., Western Eastern Roadracers Assn., Plumbing, Heating, Cooling Contractors Assn., Am. Motorcyclist Assn., Am. Soc. Notaries, Rotary (bd. dirs., treas. 1990—). Roman Catholic. Office: Precision Air Inc 6048 Glen Carlyn Dr Falls Church VA 22041

GUIDONI, T. LEE, floor-covering/interior finishes company executive; b. Billings, Mont., Oct. 10, 1946; d. Angelo and Matye Lenore Ferro; m. John Charles Guidoni, Aug. 19, 1978; children: Michael Wong, Angela Wong, Robb Wong, Donald James Wong Jr. Student U. Mont. Corp. sec. L. and L. Flooring and Home Furnishings, Inc., Butte, Mont.; sr. programmer analyst Mont. Power Co., Butte. Office: 303 E Park St Butte MT 59701

GUIDRY, KAREN LOUISE, information resources analyst; b. Riverside, Calif., Dec. 3, 1956; d. Arthur H. and Helen Louise (Fraser) Tufft; m. Donald R. Guidry, may 27, 1978. BSBA, Colo. State U., 1978; MBA, La. State U., 1985. Communications analyst Ethyl Corp., Baton Rouge, 1980-86, communications system coordinator, 1986-87; communications system coordinator Ethyl Corp., Richmond, Va., 1987-89, info. resources analyst, 1989—; jr. achievement coordinator Ethyl Corp., Baton Rouge, 1983-87. Fund raiser Jr. Achievement, Baton Rouge, 1983-86; chmn. telecommunications adv. com. J. Sargeant Reynolds Community Coll., 1989—. Mem. Va. Telecommunications Assn. (bd. dirs. 1988—, treas. 1989—), Internat. Communications Assn. (alt. voting com.), Ethyl Mgmt. Club (mem. chmn. 1986-87). Republican. Presbyterian. Office: Ethyl Corp 330 S 4th St Richmond VA 23219

GUIFFRE, JEAN ELLEN, shopping service company executive; b. Roseville, Va., July 15, 1942; d. Robert Nolan and Anna Mary (Kolarik) Fritter; m. LaBre Benedict Guiffre, June 20, 1959; children: Michael C., Suzette M., Anna C., Guy A. Ptnr. LaBre Assocs., College Park, Md., 1962-82; founder, pres. Top Banana Shopping Svc. Inc., Brandywine, Md., 1982—; resource contact Prince Georges Community Coll.; cons. S.-E./Top Banana. Inventor lightweight delivery cart system. Mem. Nat. Assn. Self Employed, NAFE, Prince Georges County Woman Bus. Owners. Home and Office: 16314 Baden Westwood Rd Brandywine MD 20613

GUILLAUME, GERMAINE GABRIELLE, physics educator, researcher; b. Brussels, Nov. 22, 1949; d. Alphonse and Helene Albine (Minne) Cornelissen; m. Francis M. Guillaume, Nov. 22, 1975. MEd, U. Brussels, 1971, MA in Physics, 1971, PhD in Physics, 1976. Tchr. Lycee Emile Max, Brussels, 1971-73; fellow Inst. de Recheerche Sci. dans l'Industrie et l'Agriculture, Brussels, 1974-76; vis. rsch. fellow U. Minn., Mpls., 1976-79, rsch. fellow, 1979-82, rsch. assoc., 1982—, asst. prof., 1987—, assoc. dir., 1987—; referee several jours. Contbr. over 300 articles to profl. jours. Recipient Chronobiology award Hoechst, 1983; grantee NIH, 1981-84, 88—. Mem. Internat. Soc. Chronobiology (bd. dirs. 1985—), Internat. Soc. Rsch. on Civilization Diseases and the Environ. (N.Am. bd. 1987—, scientific coun. 1987—), Sigma Xi. Home: 511 Ryan Ave W Roseville MN 55113 Office: U Minn 5-187 Lyon Labs 420 Washington Ave SE Minneapolis MN 55455

GUILLEMETTE, GLORIA VIVIAN, dressmaker, designer; b. North Attleboro, Mass., June 27, 1929; d. Wilfred Anthony Roy and Sylviana (Bonnoyer) King; student Nat. Sch. Dress Design, 1976; m. Thomas William Guillemette, Mar. 24, 1963; children: Sylvia Marie, Katherine Anne, John Thomas. Machine operator dress mfg. cos., 1945-60; asst. to dressmaker and designer, Windsor, Conn., 1960-63; owner Mrs. G's Studio, Enfield, Conn., 1963-87; dir. Fashion Show, 1973, 76. Cub Scout commr. Boy Scouts Am., 1979-85; mem. Enfield Fair Rent Commn., 1979-87; justice of peace Conn., 1979—; mem. Republican Town Com., 1976—; sec. United Meth. Women, 1977-82; mem. Enfield Fair Rent Commn., 1979-87, Presdl. Task Force, 1982-83. Club: Republican Women.

GUILLERMO, LINDA SUE, clinical social worker; b. Chgo., July 4, 1951; d. Triponio Pascua and Helen Elizabeth (Moskal) G.; B.A., U. Ill., Chgo., 1973, M.S.W., 1975, postgrad., 1980; postgrad. Jane Addams Coll. Social Work, 1980-82; Diplomate in clin. social work, 1987. Mktg. research interviewer Rabin Research Co., Chgo., 1970-73; mktg. research interviewer, coder Marcor Mktg. Research, Inc., Chgo., 1973-75; social work intern Child and Family Services, Chgo., 1973-74, Chgo. Bd. Edn., 1974-75; social worker, therapist child abuse and neglect, case investigator, case planning cons., social service program planner Ill. Dept. Children and Family Services, Chgo., 1975-78, social service program planner, contract negotiator, monitoring agt. Central Resources Contracts and Grants, 1978-79; real estate sales person Sentry Realty, Chgo., 1976—; social worker, therapist, program coordinator, casework supr. of child abuse assessment and intervention program, proposal writer Casa Central, Chgo., 1979-82, casework cons. of child abuse assessment and intervention program, proposal writer, program dir. and casework supr. of early intervention program, 1979-85; social worker, clin. supr. Chgo. Bd. Edn., 1985—; tng. specialist City Coll. of Chgo., 1980; adj. asso. researcher Asher Feren Law Office, Chgo., 1980-81. Treas. Greenleaf Condominium Assn., Chgo., 1980-81, sec., 1987-88, interim pres. 1988, regional rep. North Ill. Assn. of Sch. Social Workers, 1986-87, Lic. real estate salesperson, Ill. Mem. Nat. Assn. Social Workers (register clin. social workers), Acad. Cert. Social Workers, Ill. Cert. Clin. Social Workers, North Side Real Estate Bd. Home: 3550 N Lake Shore-Condo 402 Chicago IL 60657

GUILLORY, LINDA, management consultant; b. Lawtell, La., Jan. 4, 1950; d. Leo Joseph and Adeline (LeMelle) Semien; children: Tina Gail Guillory,

Ashley Fachon Guillory. BA in Psychology, U. Colo., 1985. Operator Southern Bell Telephone Co., Lake Charles, La., 1969-70; asst. mgr. employment office Mountain Bell Telephone Co., Tucson, 1970-73; mgr. Human Resources Mountain Bell Telephone Co., Denver, 1973-85; pres./owner Transformative Mgmt., Inc., Denver, 1985--. Author: Myth and Method, 1989. Recipient Pluralism award Pub. Svc. Co. of Colo., 1988. Mem. Colo. Black Profls. Assn. (v.p. 1988--), Colo. Black C. of C. (bd. dirs. 1987--), Denver C. of C. Democrat. Roman Catholic. Office: Transformative Mgmt Inc 3050 Richard Allen Ct Denver CO 80205

GUILMARTIN, JUDITH OHR, field administrator; b. Irvington, N.J., Nov. 9, 1939; d. Norman T. and Louise (Hartkopf) Ohr; m. John F. Guilmartin, Mar. 7, 1966 (div. June 1987); children: Lore, Eugenia. BA, U. Maine, 1961. Mem. staff Passaic Co. Probation Office, Paterson, N.J., 1962-64; pers. officer USAF Webb (Tex.) AFB, 1964-66; pub. info. USAF Eglin (Fla.) AFB, 1966-67; supr. Quality Control Svcs., Friendswood, Tex., 1983-84; field mgr. NORC, U. Chgo., 1985-89; field mgr. S.E. Houston office U.S. Census Bur., Pasadena, Tex., 1989-90; sr. field adminstr. Inst. for Survey Rsch. Temple U., Phila., 1990—. Pres. Autauga County Rep. Women, 1979-80; fin. chair Reagan-Bush Campaign, 1980; campaign chair Folmer Gov Campaign, 1982, Prattville, Ala.; v.p. Bay Area Rep. Women, 1985. Mem. Alumni Ambassador U. Maine. Methodist. Home: 89 Franklin Dr Voorhees NJ 08043-0341

GUINAN, MARY ELIZABETH, physician, health science administrator; b. N.Y.C., Sept. 23, 1939; d. Michael and Mary (Lyne) Guinan; m. Peter M. Schantz, July 19, 1979; children: Aimee, Erica, Brendan. BA, Hunter Coll., 1961; PhD, U. Tex., Galveston, 1969; MD, Johns Hopkins U., 1972. Rsch. scientist Ctrs. for Disease Control, Atlanta, 1978-86, asst. dir. for sci., 1986—. Contbr. articles to rsch. publs. Capt. USPHS, 1978—. Mem. Am. Med. Women's Assn., Infectious Disease Soc. Am. Home: 2569 Circlewood Rd Atlanta GA 30345 Office: HHS Ctrs Disease Control 1600 Clifton Rd NE Atlanta GA 30333

GUINN, JANET MARTIN, psychologist, consultant; b. Rapid City, S.D., Aug. 16, 1942; d. Verne Oliver and Carolyn Yetta (Clark) Martin; m. David Lee Guinn, Oct. 27, 1962 (div. June 1988); children: Cynthia Gail, Kevin Scott, Garrett Lee. BS in Psychology, U. Alaska, 1980, MS in Counseling Psychology, 1983; PhD in Clin. Psychology, Calif. Sch. Profl. Psychology, 1988. Lic. psychologist, Alaska, Nev. Pvt. practice Anchorage, 1988—; clinician Behavior Medicine Cons., 1983-84; pvt. practice clinician, 1983-84; supr. Southcentral Counseling Ctr., Anchorage, 1984-85; cons. City/Borough of Juneau, Alaska, 1988; psychologist youth treatment program Alaska Psychiat. Inst., Anchorage, 1989-90; cons. in field; cons. Alaska Small Bus. Coalition, Anchorage, 1990—; reviewer Blors Corp.; bd. dirs. Yukon Brewing and Bottling Co., Anchorage. Active politics; active mem. Alaska Small Bus. Coalition, Anchorage, 1990—. Mem. Am. Psychol. Assn., Alaska Psychol. Assn., Internat. Neuropsychol. Soc., Rotary, Psi Chi. Republican. Office: 2020 Abbott Rd Ste 3 Anchorage AK 99507

GUINN, NORMA JOANNE, nurse, writer; d. Robert Dale and Donna Jeanette (Heckert) Clough; m. Patrick Brent Guinn, May 18, 1974; children: Ryan Paul Wesley, Brent Tyler. Diploma in nursing, Mercy Sch. Nursing, 1966; BS, Eastern Mich. U., 1974. RN, Mich. Surg. nurse E.W. Sparrow Hosp., Lansing, Mich., 1974-77, McKee Med. Ctr., Loveland, Colo., 1982—. Contbr. numerous articles to profl. jours. Mem. Assn. Operating Room Nurses. Republican. Home: 1516 Rancho Way Loveland CO 80537

GUISEWITE, CATHY LEE, cartoonist; b. Dayton, Ohio, Sept. 5, 1950; d. William Lee and Anne (Duly) G. BA in English, U. Mich., 1972; LHD (hon.), R.I. Coll., 1979, Eastern Mich. U., 1981. Writer Campbell-Ewald Advt., Detroit, 1972-73; writer Norman Prady, Ltd., Detroit, 1973-74, W.B. Doner & Co., Advt., Southfield, Mich., 1974-75; group supr. W.B. Doner & Co., Advt., 1975-76, v.p., 1976-77; creator, writer, artist Cathy comic strip Universal Press Syndicate, Mission, Kans., 1976—. Author, artist: The Cathy Chronicles, 1978; What Do You Mean, I Still Don't Have Equal Rights??!!, 1980; What's a Nice Single Girl Doing with a Double Bed?!, 1981; I Think I'm Having a Relationship with a Blueberry Pie!, 1981; It Must Be Love, My Face Is Breaking Out, 1982; Another Saturday Night of Wild and Reckless Abandon, 1982; Cathy's Valentine's Day Survival Book, How to Live through Another February 14, 1982; How to Get Rich, Fall in Love, Lose Weight, and Solve all Your Problems by Saying "NO", 1983; Eat Your Way to a Better Relationship, 1983; A Mouthful of Breath Mints and No One to Kiss, 1983; Climb Every Mountain, Bounce Every Check, 1983; Men Should Come with Instruction Booklets, 1984; Wake Me Up When I'm a Size 5, 1985; Thin Thighs in Thirty Years, 1986, A Hand to Hold, An Opinion to Reject, 1987, Why Do the Right Words Always Come Out of the Wrong Mouth?, 1988, My Granddaughter Has Fleas, 1989. Office: Universal Press Syndicate 4900 Main St Kansas City MO 64112

GUITERMAN FREUND, LAURA MAYER, academic program administrator; b. N.Y.C., Sept. 15, 1925; d. Francis Randolph and Laura (Walker) Mayer; m. Franklin William Guiterman, May 14, 1949 (wid. Dec. 1974); children: Franklin William Jr., Eric Randolph; m. Paul D. Freund, Dec. 29, 1977 (dec. Nov. 1980). BA, Adelphi U., 1945; postgrad., N.Y.U., 1945. Pub. relations assoc. Hotel Pierre, N.Y.C., 1947-51; owner, mgr. E.Colony House Inn, E.Hampton, N.Y., 1953-56; pub. relations cons. Union News Co., N.Y.C., 1955; mgr. pub. relations Brass Rail Restaurants, N.Y.C., 1957-58; pub. relations cons. Jr. Leagues of Am. and Marymount Coll., 1961-64; alumni, devel. officer, freelance editor, mem. staff sch. social work Columbia U., 1964—. Vol. Dem. Orgn., N.Y.C., St. Lukes Hosp., N.Y.C., Community Council, N.Y.C.; mgr. community club St. Bartholomew's Ch., N.Y.C., 1958-61; mem. Council for the Advancement of Edn. Mem. Geneological Soc. Democrat. Episcopalian. Clubs: Regency, Columbia (N.Y.C.), Ocean. Home: 22 E 93rd St New York NY 10128 Office: Columbia U McVickar 622 W 113th St New York NY 10025

GUITON, BONNIE F., federal agency director, adviser; b. Springfield, Ill., Oct. 30, 1941; d. Henry Frank and Zola Elizabeth (Newman) Brazelton; BA, Mills Coll., 1974; MS, Calif. State U., Hayward, 1975; EdD U. Calif., Berkeley, 1985; 1 child, Nichele Monique. Adminstrv. asst. to pres.'s spl. asst. Mills Coll., Oakland, Calif., 1970-71, adminstrv. asst. to asst. v.p., 1972-73, student svcs. counselor, adv. to resuming students, 1973-74, asst. dean of students, interim dir. ethnic studies, lectr., 1975-76; exec. dir. Marcus A. Foster Ednl. Inst., Oakland, 1976-79; adminstrv. mgr. Kaiser Aluminum & Chem. Corp., Oakland, 1979-80, v.p., gen. mgr. Kaiser CTR Inc., 1980-84, vice chmn. Postal Rate Commn., Washington, 1985-87, asst. sec. for vocat. and adult edn. U.S. Dept. of Edn., 1987-89; spl. adviser to the Pres. for Consumer Affairs, dir. U.S. Office Consumer Affairs, 1989-90; pres., chief exec. officer Earth Conservation Corps, Washington, 1990—. Community adviser Jr. League Oakland East Bay, Inc., 1977-78; bd. dirs. Univ. YWCA, Berkeley, 1976-77, Oakland Symphony Orch. Assn., 1977-79,. Bay Area United Way, NCCJ, Nat. Urban Coalition, Pacific Children's Center/Pacific Child and Family Counseling Ctr., 1977-78. Bd. dirs. Nat. Mus. Women in the Arts; mem. Exec. Women in Govt., Independent Agy. Women. Office: U S Office Consumer Affairs 400 Maryland Ave Washington DC 20201

GUITON, THERESA ANNE, engineer; b. Johnson City, N.Y., Sept. 5, 1962; d. Martin Edward and Sandra Dawn (Taylor) G. BS, Pa. State U., 1984, MS, 1987, PhD in Ceramic Sci., 1990. Civil engring. intern DOT, State Pa., Dushore, 1981, 82; ceramic engr. IBM Corp., Endicott, N.Y., 1983; fluoride glass researcher Pa. State U., University Park, 1983-84; grad. rsch. asst. Pa. State U., 1985-86, 86-90; mfg. devel. engr. Gen. Dynamics, Pomona, Calif., 1984-85, 86; material scientist Diamond Matls. Inst., State College, Pa., 1989; sr. rsch. engr. Dow Chem., Midland, Mich., 1990—. Contbr. articles to profl. jours. Recipient Xerox Rsch. award, 1988; Corning Glass fellow, 1985-86; Harbison Walker Refractories scholar, 1983-84. Mem. Materials Rsch. Soc. (PSU pres. 1988), Am. Ceramic Soc. (PSU v.p. 1983-84), Keramos, ACS, Soc. Women Engrs. (PSU pres. 1983-84), Sigma Xi. Office: Dow Chem Cen Rsch Lab 1776 Bldg Advanced Ceramics Midland MI 48674

GUIVER, ABBY BERNSTEIN, community relations specialist; b. St. Paul, Nov. 28, 1942; d. Joseph Carl and Laia D. (Goldberg) Bernstein; m. Michael Leonard Guiver, Dec. 22, 1973. BA, U. Ariz., 1964. Buyer I. Magnin, L.A., 1966-70, Goldwaters, Phoenix, 1970-74, Liberty House-Rhodes, Phoenix, 1974-76; mdse. div. mgr. Bullocks, Phoenix, 1976-80; pres. Meditech Inc., Phoenix, 1986-90; ptnr. Rossi Ptnrs., Phoenix, 1990—. Exec. bd. Phoenix Sister Cities Comm., 1980-86; bd. dirs. Nat. coun. Alcoholism, 1985—; mem. Gov.'s coun. Health and Fitness, 1989—; trustee Humana Hosp., 1990—. Mem. Ariz. Club. Office: Rossi Ptnrs 8700 E Via De Ventura Scottsdale AZ 85258

GULIAN, JO-ANNE, court reporter; b. Elmira, N.Y., Sept. 10, 1943; d. Lincoln Hart and Marion Eaton (Green) Roberts; m. Robert R. Gulian, June 15, 1963 (dv. 1987); children: David Thomas, Christopher Ross. Cert. in ct. reporting, Sch. Machine Shorthand, Rochester, N.Y., 1975. Cert. shorthand reporter, N.Y. Sr. reporter Bailey Reporting Agy., Rochester, 1975-77; reporter Family Ct. State of N.Y., Rochester, 1977; ct. reporter Rochester City Ct., 1978-81; sr. ct. reporter N.Y. Supreme Ct., Rochester, 1981—. Counselor Area Youth Ministry, Rochester, 1965-70; campaigner Dem. candidates, Rochester, 1970-73; paraprofl. Monroe County Mental Health Orgn., Fairport, N.Y., 1971-73; resource vol. Hillside Children's Ctr., Rochester, 1988—. Fellow Acad. Profl. Reporters, bd. dirs. Nat. Shorthand Reporters Assn., N.Y. State Shorthand Reporters Assn. (Hall of Fame, 1990, chmn. 1980-81, v.p. 1981-83, pres. 1983-85), Vertical Users' Group, Excel Users' Group; mem. Thielen Users' Group, C.A.T.S. Internat. Users' Group (dir. 1990). Office: NY Supreme Ct Rm 24 99 Exchange St Rochester NY 14614

GULICK, DONNA MARIE, accountant; b. N.Y.C., Jan. 25, 1956; d. H.R. and M.G. Gulick. MBA, Fairleigh Dickinson U., 1981, MS, 1986. Programmer Wash. State U., Pullman, 1983; acctg. analyst IBM, Tarrytown, N.Y., 1983-89, program mgr., 1989—. Mem. Assn. MBA Execs., ACM, Inst. of IEEE, Nat. Assn. Unknown Players, Delta Mu Delta. Roman Catholic. Home: 395 Rte 28 Bridgewater NJ 08807

GULKO, KATHLEEN, pizza company executive; b. Antigo, Wis., Aug. 18, 1943; d. Anton and Carmen H. (Koch) Brejcha; children: Heather, Aiisa, Marc, Sarah. AAS, SUNY, 1962. Chief exec. officer Kid's Korner Fresh Pizza, Inc., Waukegan, Ill.; fashion buyer Halle Bros., Cleve. Named nominee Arthur Young Entrepreneur of Yr. Mem. Internat. Franchise Assn. (program/edn. com.). Office: PO Box 9288 Waukegan IL 60079

GULLEDGE, KAREN STONE, educator, consultant; b. Fayetteville, N.C., Feb. 3, 1941; d. Malcolm Clarence and Clara (Davis) Stone; m. Parker Lee Gulledge Jr, Oct. 17, 1964. BA, St. Andrews Presbyn. Coll., Laurinburg, N.C., 1963; MA, East Carolina U., 1979; EdD, Nova U., 1986. Social worker Lee County, Sanford, N.C., 1963-64; tchr. Asheboro (N.C.) City Schs., 1964-67, Winston-Salem (N.C.)/Forsyth County Schs., 1967-70; research analyst N.C. Dept. Pub. Instrn., Raleigh, 1971-76, sch. planning cons., 1976-89, chief cons., 1989—; mem. N.C. Elem. Commn. of So. Assn. Colls. and Schs., 1889—; leader profl. seminars; speaker in field. Vol. N.C. Cancer Soc., Raleigh, 1970—, Am. Heart Assn., Raleigh, 1970—, N.C. Cystic Fibrosis Assn., Raleigh, 1970—, Raleigh Rescue Mission, 1975—; mem. N.C. State Capitol Preservation Found., 1988—, N.C. Mus. Art, 1988—; mem. alumni coun. St. Andrews Coll. Mem. Women in State Govt., N.C. Assn. Sch. Adminstrs., Council Ednl. Facility Planners, Delta Kappa Gamma. Democrat. Home: 7405 Fiesta Way Raleigh NC 27615 Office: Div Sch Planning 217 W Jones St Edn Annex I Raleigh NC 27601-1712

GULLIVER, SUZY BIRD, clinical psychologist; b. Bourne, Mass., Sept. 24, 1961; d. Ashbel Green and Alice Marie (McGeehin) G.; m. Leonard Dalton White, June 7, 1980 (div. Dec. 1985); 1 child, Ashbel William. BS, Quinnipiac Coll., 1983; MA, Conn. Coll., 1985; PhD, U. Vt., 1990. Teaching asst. Conn. Coll., New London, Conn., 1983-87; rsch. asst. U. Vt., Burlington, Vt., 1985-87; clin. intern Behavior Therapy Ctr., Burlington, 1987-89, West Haven (Conn.) Vet's. Hosp., 1989-90. Contbr. articles (with others) to jours. Chairperson The Schoolhouse, Inc., Burlington, 1988-89. Mem. Am. Psychol. Assn. (assoc.), Soc. Behavior Medicine (student), Assn. for Advancement Behavior Therapy (student). Democrat. Roman Catholic. Office: West Haven VA West Haven CT 11634

GUM, DAWN ALICIA, architect, consultant; b. Norristown, Pa., May 29, 1956; d. Richard Ferguson and Evelyn Jane (Hiltner) G. BS, Ga. Inst. Tech., 1978, MArch, 1980. Registered architect, Ga. Draftswoman Clifford A. Nahser, Architect, Atlanta, 1978-80, project mgr., assoc., 1988—; designer, draftswoman James Patterson & Assocs., Atlanta, 1980-82; job capt. Hall, Norris & Marsh, Architects, Atlanta, 1982-83; assoc. Rabun, Hatch, Portman, McWhorter, Hatch & Rauh, Atlanta, 1983-84; project mgr., assoc. Whatley & Ptnrs., Architects, Atlanta, 1984-85; project mgr. Richard Rauh & Assocs., Atlanta, 1985-87; prin., owner, mgr. Dawn A. Gum, Architect, Atlanta, 1987—; cons. to interior design cos., Atlanta, 1987—; graphic design cons. Callanwolde Fine Arts Ctr., Atlanta, 1988. Actress Families First, Atlanta, 1988. Ga. Inst. Tech. grantee, 1979. Mem. Nat. Trust for Hist. Preservation, NAFE, Atlanta Bot. Garden, High Mus. Lutheran. Office: 841 Durant Pl NE Atlanta GA 30308

GUMERSON, JEAN GILDERHUS, health foundation executive; b. Hayfield, Minn., Mar. 19, 1923; d. Nordeen Palmer and Mable Jeannette (Scharberg) Gilderhus; m. William Dow Gumerson Sr., Mar. 5, 1943 (dec. Jan. 1978); children: William Dow Jr., Ted Lee, Jon David. Student, U. Minn., 1941-42, U. Okla., 1961-62. Adminstrv. asst. to Rep. state party chmn. Oklahoma City, 1976-77; campaign coord. 1st dist. Paula Unruh for Congress, Tulsa, 1978; dir. pub. rels. C.R. Anthony Co., Oklahoma City, 1979-87; dir. human rels. Wilson Agy., Mass. Mut. Ins. Co., Oklahoma City, 1987; adminstrv. dir. Okla. Art Ctr., Oklahoma City, 1988-89; dir. Children's Med. Rsch., Inc., Oklahoma City, 1989—; pres. Presbyn. Healh Found., Oklahoma City, 1989—. Exec. com. Pres.'s Com. on Mental Retardation, Washington, 1986—; mem. So. Govs. conf. on Infant Mortality, Washington, 1987—; chmn. City-County Health Dept. Bd., Oklahoma City, 1980—, Okla. Alliance Against Drugs, 1987—; gov. appointee steering com. Healthy Futures, Oklahoma City, 1988—; mem. 5 Who Care Bd. Govs., Oklahoma City, 1982—; bd. dirs. Myriad Gardens Obs., Westminister Presbyn. Found., St. Anthony Hosp. Found. Recipient Gov.'s Arts award for community svc. Okla. Arts Coun., Woman of Yr. award Okla. Mental Health Assn., Humanitarian award Opportunities Indsl. Ctr., Outstanding Vol. Fund Raiser award Okla. chpt. Nat. Soc. Fund Raising Execs., 1988. Mem. Exec. Women in Govt., The Forum, Charter 35, Econ. Club. Okla., Theta Sigma Phi. Presbyterian. Home: 6206 Waterford Blvd #50 Oklahoma City OK 73118

GUMIENNY, HELEN L., sales executive; b. Bklyn., Feb. 17, 1939; d. Richard Hart and Helen Frances (Considine) Wolfe; children: Juliana Mascatello, Joseph S. Gumienny. AS in Nursing, Passaic Community Coll., 1981; BA in Communications magna cum laude, William Paterson Coll., 1984. Cert. interior design. Pres. JHG Renovation and Restoration, Washington, Helen Gumienny Interiors, Washington; program dir. physician sales Alexandria (Va.) Hosp.; tchr., lectr. in field. Host, producer (TV show) The Contemporary Woman, Columbia Cablevision, Channel 3, Oakland, N.J., 1980-85; correspondent, feature writer for four newspapers. Active domestic violence support groups, The New Apostolic Ch. Named Woman of Yr., Mrs. Packanack Lake; recipient Outstanding Svc. award, Leadership award, statehood modeling awards. Mem. NAFE, Woman's Guild, Woman's Club (pres.). Republican. Office: 4320 Seminary Rd Alexandria VA 22304

GUMP, JUDITH LOUISE, marketing professional; b. Chgo., Sept. 11, 1944; d. Frederick Philip and Hester Almira (Larson) Harris; m. Gayland Gregg Gump, June 26, 1976; children: Piper Louise, Jeane Michele. BA, Linfield Coll., 1967; postgrad., Internat. Christian U., Tokyo, 1965-66, Portland State U., 1969, Seattle Pacific U., 1986—. Model various publs., Oreg. and Japan, 1960-68, 72-74; performer and singer Bruce Kelly's New Oreg. Singers, Portland, 1971-77; art, drama tchr. talented and gifted Oreg. State U., Corvallis and Redmond, Washington, 1983-88; various bus. and civic positions Oreg., Wash, 1962—; corp. asst. to pres. Mgmt./Mktg. Assn., Inc., Portland, 1989—. Entertainer, writer recs. TV and radio, Japan, 1957-66; founder, exec. dir., producer Puffin Players Children's Theater Group, Corvallis, Oreg. & Wash., Portland, 1984—; author children's plays, 1984-88; contbr. articles to various publs;, U.S.A. and Japan. Founder, exec. dir. Corvallis H.E.L.P. Group, 1983-86, HSV Counseling and Referral, Corvallis and Portland, 1986—; dir. Lilly House Day Care, 1981-84; owner Food and Flowers/Catering, 1982, Corvallis; bd. dirs. com. chair Crossroads Internat., Corvallis, 1983-86; originator Neighborhood Watch, Corvallis, 1984-86; adv. bd., drama tchr. Community Schs., Corvallis, 1984; com. chair Corvallis Hist. Soc., 1978-91; vol. Children of the Am. Revolution, 1986-88. Mem. AAUW, Nat. Assn. Profl. Organizers, Am. Bus. Women's Assn., Nat. Assn. for Gifted, Nat. PTA (com. chairperson 1987-88), Nat. Assn. Female Execs., Japan Am. Soc., Lake Washington Gifted Assn. (com. chairperson 1987), Redmond Arts Assn., Order Ea. Star, Lady Elks, Beta Sigma Phi, Alpha Psi Omega. Democrat. Home and Office: 16105 NE Multnomah Portland OR 97230

GUNDERSEN, ALICE MARSHALL, business executive; b. Groveton, N.H., Nov. 19, 1934; d. Daniel Weeks and Eleanor Marshall; student Fisher Jr. Coll., Boston, 1952-53, Boston U., 1956, Northeastern U., 1957-59, Madonna Coll., 1966; B.M., U. Mich., 1970; m. Carl A. Gundersen, Apr. 11, 1959; children—Daniel Carl, Scott M. Exec. sec. with New Eng. Colls. Fund, Boston, 1956-58, with John Hancock Mut. Life Ins. Co., Boston, 1958-59; office supr. dept. human genetics U. Mich., Ann Arbor, 1964-67; adminstrv. coordinator and mgr. brokerage adminstrn. Alexander Hamilton Life Ins. Co., Farmington, Mich., 1973-75; supr. data services Delta Dental Plan of Mich., Southfield, 1976-83; cons. Nat. Med. Mgmt. Systems, Flint, Mich.; music dir. St. Timothy Presbyn. Ch., Livonia, Mich., 1964-72, Trinity Episcopal Ch., Farmington, 1975-77; CESA cons. Presbytery of Detroit, 1975-77, mem. task force on women, 1978-80, chair budget div., 1987—; mem. Livonia City Council, 1980-86; cons. women re-entering work force; systems cons. Adv. com. Livonia Sch. Bd., 1967-68; campaign coordinator City Council Candidate, 1970; active Livonia Com. for Better Human Relations, 1965-74; mem. Madonna Coll. Bus. Adv. Council, 1987—; chair outcounty adv. council, bd. dirs. Family Service Detroit and Wayne County, 1987. Cert. systems profl. Mem. Assn. Systems Mgmt. (publicity chmn. 1978, membership chmn. 1979-80, officer 1980-81, v.p., 1981-82, pres. 1983-84), Micro Mgrs. Assn., Women's Econ. Club Detroit (membership com., 1976, program com., 1977), Mich. Women's Polit. Caucus (polit. action chmn. 1979-81, state chmn. 1981-83), Nat. Women's Polit. Caucus (adminstrv. com. 1981-83), Livonia Hist. Soc. (pres., chair fund raising com. 1987-88). Home: 15715 Southampton St Livonia MI 48154 Office: 17199 N Laurel Park Dr Livonia MI 48152

GUNDERSEN, ALLISON MAUREEN, computer software consulting company executive; b. Syracuse, N.Y., Oct. 14, 1959; d. Jerrold Paul and Rosemarie Noël (Harvey) G. AB, Cornell U., 1981; postgrad., NYU, 1982-83. Assoc. Morgan Stanley & Co., N.Y.C., 1981-84, sr. assoc., 1985-86; project mgr. Morgan Stanley Internat., Tokyo, 1987-88; cons. Computech Cons. Svcs., Winchester, N.J., 1989-90; pres. Woman About Globe, Ltd., N.Y.C., 1990—; cons. Nomura Rsch. Inst. Am., N.Y.C., 1989-90. Mem. NAFE, Internat. Feminists Japan (coord. 1987-88), Internat. Ctr. for Photography, NOW (dir. membership proessing N.Y.C. 1990). Democrat. Office: Woman About Globe Ltd 250 W 15th St New York NY 10011

GUNDERSON, JUDITH KEEFER, golf association executive; b. Charleroi, Pa., May 25, 1939; d. John R. and Irene G. (Gaskill) Keefer; student public schs., Uniontown, Pa.; m. Jerry L. Gunderson, Mar. 19, 1971; children: Jamie L., Jeff S.; stepchildren: Todd G. (dec.), Marc W.. Bookkeeper, Fayette Nat. Bank, 1957-59, gen. ledger bookkeeper, 1960-63; head bookkeeper First Nat. Bank Broward, 1963-64; bookkeeper Ruthenberg Homes, Inc., 1966-69; bookkeeper, asst. sec./treas. Pennisular Properties, Inc. subs. Investors Diversified Services Properties, Mpls., 1969-72; comptroller, pres. Am. Golf Fla., Inc., dba Golf and Tennis World, Deerfield Beach, 1972-89, now stockholder, dir.; former sec., treas. Internat. Golf, Inc., now stockholder, dir. County committeewoman, Broward County, Fla., 1965-66; ind. agt. personal and family devel. seminars Slight Edge Enterprises, Inc. Mem. Am. Biog. Inst. Rsch. Assn. (dep. gov., bd. gov.), Internat. Platform Assn., Nat. Golf Found., C. of C., Beta Sigma Phi.

GUNKEL, DEBRA MARIE, lawyer; b. Lamar, Colo., Feb. 9, 1958; d. Shirley and Zora Marie (Ralstin) G.; m. Samuel P. Ynzunza, Mar. 22, 1989. BA, Colo. Coll., 1980; MBA, U. Denver, 1986; JD, Southwestern U., L.A., 1989; student, Boston U., 1990—. Assoc. Dickson, Carlson & Campillo, Santa Monica, Calif.; extern Tax div. U.S. Atty.'s Office, L.A. Campaign treas. Colo. State Rep., 1986. Mem. Nat. Assn. MBA Execs., MBA/JD Execs., L.A. Athletic Club. Republican. Office: Dickson Carlson & Campillo 1401 Ocean Ave 2d Fl Santa Monica CA 90406-2122

GUNN, CHRISTY HOWARD, actuary; b. Evanston, Ill., Oct. 6, 1954; d. Coydel Sandford and Ethel Marie (Franklin) Howard; m. Raymond Flynn Gunn, Aug. 26. 1978; children: Raymond Christopher, Justin Howard. BA, Oberlin Coll., 1976; MS in Stats., Carnegie Mellon U., 1979, MS in Pub. Policy and Mgmt., 1979. Analyst CNA, Chgo., 1979-83, mgr. comml. property pricing, 1983-85, mgr. profl. liability res. and ops. analysis, 1985—. Fellow Casualty Actuarial Soc.; mem. Am. Acad. Actuaries. Office: CNA CNA Plaza Chicago IL 60685

GUNN, JANET PENELOPE, engineer; b. Worrester, U.K., Jan. 10, 1954; d. J.B. and Freda Elizabeth (Pilcher) G. BA in Math., Hampshire Coll., 1975; postgrad., U. N.C., 1975-79. Various positions IBM Research, Yorktown Heights, N.Y., 1972-77; community of interest visitor Bell Labs, West Long Branch, N.J., 1978; prin. engr. Network Analysis Corp. (became Centel), Fairfax, Va., 1979—. Mem. IEEE, Ops. Research Soc. of Am., Am. Assn. of Artificial Intelligence, Hunter Valley Riding Club (v.p. 1984-85), Commonwealth Dresage and Combined Tng. Assn. (treas. 1988—).

GUNN, KAREN SUE, psychologist; b. Detroit, May 7, 1951; d. Robert Leroy and Margaret Elizabeth (Glenn) G. BA, Oakland U., Rochester, Mich., 1974; PhD, U. Mich., 1979. Cert. community coll. instr., Calif. Pres. Gunn Cons. Group, L.A., 1984—; instr. Santa Monica Coll.; exec. asst., community mental health psychologist L.A. County Dept. of Mental Health, 1980-83; bd. dirs. Hollywood Sunset Community Clinic. Author numerous papers on substance abuse, mental health, community devel., and child abuse. Recipient County of L.A. Commendation for Dedicated Svcs, 1987, Cert. of Recognition for Outstanding Svc. to Community, 1984, Mayor's Cert. for Appreciation for Outstanding Efforts and Accomplishments, 1988, Profl. Achievement award, 1989, Cert. of Recognition, Calif. Legislature Assembly, 1988. Mem. NAFE, Assn. Black Psychologists. Democrat. Home: 408 S Venice Blvd #207 Venice CA 90291 Office: 3400 W 6th St Ste 204 Los Angeles CA 90020

GUNN, KAY LEE, investor; b. San Antonio, Sept. 29, 1932; d. Louis Alexander and Katie Belle Wrage; m. John B. Gunn, Jan. 5, 1952 (div. 1986). Student, Hockaday Sch., 1948-51. Donator Jeanne Kirkpatrick Campaign, Wash., 1988, Dallas Zoo. Mem. DAR, Jamestowne Soc., Colonial Dames, Kappa Alpha Theta. Home and Office: 4327 Westide Dr Dallas TX 75209

GUNN, MARY ELIZABETH, English language educator; b. Great Bend, Kans., July 21, 1914; d. Ernest E. and Elisabeth (Wesley) Eppstein; m. Charles Leonard Gunn, Sept. 13, 1936 (dec. Apr. 1985); 1 child, Charles Douglas. AB, Ft. Hays State U., 1935, BS in Edn., 1936, MA, 1967. Tchr. English Unified Sch. Dist. 428, Great Bend, 1963-80; tchr. English Barton County Community Coll., Great Bend, 1977-84, tchr. adult edn., 1985-87, tchr. English as 2d lang., 1988—. Mem. planning com. Japan Internat. Christian U. Mem. AAUW, Bus. and Profl. Women (Woman of Yr. 1974), Kans. Adult Edn. Assn. (Master Adult Educator 1986), NEA, Kans. Assn. Tchrs. English, PEO, Delta Kappa Gamma. Democrat. Mem. United Ch. of Christ. Home: 3009 16th St Great Bend KS 67530 Office: Ctr for Adult Edn Barton Co Community Coll 1901 Lakin Ave Great Bend KS 67530

GUNTER, KAREN JOHNSON, government official; b. Pensacola, Fla., Jan. 7, 1948; d. Erskine DeWitt and Grace (Crutchfield) Johnson; m. Thomas A. Gunter, Aug. 25, 1975 (div. Dec. 198l). BS, U. So. Miss., 1970; MS, Fla. State U., 1976. Social svc. worker Fla. Bur. Blind Svcs., Pensacola, 1970-74; supervising counselor Fla. Bur. Blind Svcs., Tallahassee, West Palm, 1974-75; M.D. examiner Office Disability Determinations, Social Security Adminstrn., Tallahassee, 1976-80, M.D. rev. examiner, 1980-8l, M.D. hearing examiner, 1981-82, M.D. examiner supr., 1982-86, area office program adminstr., 1986—. Recipient Director's citation Social Security Adminstrn., 1978, Commr.'s citation, 1988, Profl. Supr. of Quarter award Office Disability

Determination, 1987. Mem. Nat. Assn. Disability Examiners (treas. 1982-85, pres. 1988-89, pres. S.E. region 1985-86), Fla. Assn. Disability Examiners (pres. 1982, Examiner of Yr. award 1984), Order Eastern Star. Democrat. Baptist. Home: 812 Voncile Ave Tallahassee FL 32303 Office: 227 N Bronough St Ste 6101 Tallahassee FL 32399-2380

GUNTER, KATHERINE ANN STOUGH, education educator; b. Montgomery, Ala., Dec. 25, 1956; d. Carroll Henry and Marion Alice (Kimbrough) Stough; m. Tony Allen. BS in Edn., Auburn U., 1979, MA in Adminstrn. Supr, 1984. Pub. sch. tchr. Montgomery (Ill.) County Pub. Sch., 1979-88; community services coord. Auburn Univ., Div. Continuing Edn., Montgomery, 1988--. Mem. Alpha Delta Kappa. Methodist. Home: 6013 Neill Dr Montgomery AL 36117 Office: Div Continuing Edn Auburn Univ Montgomery AL 36193

GUNTER, LISA ANN, state official, automotive emmissions inspector; b. Fairfax, Va., Sept. 28, 1967; d. Ernest Melvin and Barbara Ann G. AAS in Automotive Tech., No. Va. Community Coll., Alexandria, 1988. Automotive technician Templeton Oldsmobile, Vienna, Va., 1986—. Recipient Herbert Earl McCartney Automotive Technology scholarship, 1987; named Student of Year Coop. Edn. Dept. of Community Coll., Alexandria, Va., 1988. Mem. Oldsmobile Svc. Guild (cert. silver level 1988), Nat. Inst. for Automotive Svc. Excellence (master technician 1989), Northern Va. Community Coll. Automotive Assn., (v.p. 1987-88). Home: 4227 Hunt Club Circle #1013 Fairfax VA 22033

GUNTER, TERESA DIANNE, pharmaceutical representative, researcher; b. Lincolnton, N.C., Nov. 15, 1963; d. Terry Lee and Judy Ford (Hager) G. BS, U. N.C., 1985; MS, U. Ala., 1988. Clin. lab. asst., fed. jr. fellow VA Med. Ctr., Fayetteville, N.C., 1981-85; microbiology lab. asst. N.C. Meml. Hosp., Chapel Hill, 1985; ops. mgr. Direct Response Advt., Birmingham, Ala., 1987-88; pharm. rep. Parke-Davis, Birmingham, 1988—; genetic rsch. asst. U. N.C., 1984-85. U.S. Govt. fellow, 1981-85; Holt and Turrentine scholar U. N.C., 1984-85. Home: 2703 Heatherbrooke Rd Birmingham AL 35242

GUNTER-GORE, AVA ELAINE, law enforcement official; b. Warsaw, Ind., Sept. 16, 1952; d. Everett Russell and Avis Beth (Kimes) G.; m. Leslie Thomas Gore Jr., June 11, 1988; 1 child, Avriana Jean Gore. BS, Ind. State U., 1974, MS, 1982. Dep. U.S. marshal U.S. Marshal's Service, N.Y.C., 1975-77; instr. U.S. Marshal's Service, Washington, 1977-78; insp. witness security U.S. Marshal's Service, N.Y.C., 1978-82, Miami, Fla., 1982-85; chief dep. U.S. marshal U.S. Marshal's Service, Providence, 1982-89; chief dep. U.S. Marshals Svc., Mobile, Ala., 1989—; chief dep. U.S. marshal U.S. Marshal's Svc., Mobile, Ala., 1989—. Mem. Internat. Assn. Women Police, Fed. Law Enforcement Officers Assn., Bus. and Profl. Women's Club, Lambda Alpha Epsilon (v.p. 1974-75, Robert G. Caldwell award 1982). Republican. Presbyterian. Home: 8811 Whittington Dr Mobile AL 36695 Office: US Marshal's Svc PO Box 343 Mobile AL 36601

GUPTON, MARCIA WALKER, marketing/communications manager; b. Boston, July 14, 1954; d. Charles E. and Barbara L. (Hesse) Walker; m. Larry Thomas Gupton. BS in Graphic Design, U. Cin., 1978. Advt. mgr. Aspen Ribbons, Inc., Lafayette, Colo., 1979-84, mktg./communications mgr., 1984—. Mem. Denver Advt. Fedn., Rocky Mountain Direct Mktg. Assn., Lafayette C. of C. (bd. dirs. 1985-89, pres. 1987). Presbyterian. Office: Aspen Ribbons Inc 555 Aspen Ridge Dr Lafayette CO 80026

GURAK, KATHLEEN THERESA, multimedia producer; b. Passaic, N.J., Oct. 25, 1943; d. Edward Thomas and Mary Theresa (Glowacki) G. Prodn. coord., programmer 1492 Prodns., Inc., N.Y.C., 1968-70; pvt. practice video prodn. N.Y.C., 1971-75; sec., treas., co-owner Media House Inc., N.Y.C., 1976-80; co-owner Gurak/Santry Studios, N.Y.C., 1977-81; producer Jim Sant'Andrea, Inc., N.Y.C., 1982; instr. DMA, Inc., N.Y.C., 1982—; pvt. practice multimedia prodn. N.Y.C., 1983—; judge Internat. Film and TV Festival N.Y., 1989, 90. Mem. adv. com. to vol. dept. Ea. State Sch. & Hosp. For The Emotionally Disturbed, 1983; vol. Cabrini Hospice, N.Y.C., 1985—; mem. Candlelight Childhood Cancer Found. Recipient Bronze award Internat. Film and TV Festival, 1974, Gold award Internat. Film and TV Festival, 1976, 83, Silver award Internat. Film and TV Festival, 1980, Cabrini Hospice Vol. Service Recognition award, 1986. Mem. Assn. for Multi-Image, Nat. Hospice Orgn., N.J. Hospice Orgn., N.Y. State Hospice Assn., Pa. Hospice Network, N.J. Media Network (co-founder).

GURIK, DIANE GREEN, personnel company executive; b. Mansfield, Ohio, Apr. 21, 1949; d. Charles Vernon and J. Pauline Green; m. John Carl Gurik, Mar. 13, 1942; children: Jason, Jennifer, Brian, Scott, Christine. Student, Olivet Coll., 1968-69; cert. in nursing, Mid-Ohio Nursing Program, 1972; postgrad., Mansfield Bus. Coll., 1975. Treas. Jet Mgmt. Corp., 1974-78; adminstr. Wee Care Day Care Ctr., Mansfield, 1974-78; dir. nursing Allied Pvt. Duty Nurses Registry, Mansfield, 1978-83; founder, pres., chief exec. officer North Cen. Pers., Inc., Mansfield, 1983—, also chmn. bd. dirs. Mem. Better Bus. Bur., Mansfield, 1985—. Recipient Tribute to Women in Industry award YWCA. Mem. Mansfield C. of C. Republican. Home: 1221 Wittmer Rd Mansfield OH 44903 Office: N Cen Pers Inc 491 Lexington Ave Mansfield OH 44907

GURKE, SHARON MCCUE, naval officer; b. Bklyn., Apr. 4, 1949; d. James Ambrose and Marion Denise (Coombs) McCue; B.A., Molloy Cath. Coll., 1970; M.S. in Systems Mgmt., U. So. Calif., 1977; m. Lee Samuel Gurke, Apr. 16, 1977; children—Marion Dawn, Leigh Elizabeth. Commd. ensign U.S. Navy, 1970; advanced through grades to comdr., 1979; aircraft maintenance duty officer Orgn.-Intermediate Maintenance Officer, Comdr. Naval Air Force U.S. Pacific Fleet, Naval Air Sta., North Island, San Diego, 1974-77; head quality assurance div. Intermediate Maintenance Dept. Supporting Aircraft, Naval Air Sta., Miramar, San Diego, 1977-78, avionics div. officer, 1978-80; officer in charge Naval Aviation Engring. Service Unit Pacific Naval Air Sta., North Island, 1980-82; aircraft Intermediate Maintenance officer Naval Air Sta., Alameda, Calif., 1982-84; aircraft Intermediate Maintenance officer Naval Sta., Rota, Spain, 1984-86, Naval Air Systems Command Aviation Maintenance Policy Br., 1986-88, asst. program mgr. NACOLMIS, 19876-88; dir. ops. Naval Aviation Depot, North Island, 1988-90, Dept. of Navy OP-514C, 1990—. Interviewed by S.D. TV fo Success Story. Decorated 2 Naval Commendation medals, 2 Meritorious Svc. medals. Lic. pilot; first female naval officer selected for aero. engring. tng.; recipient Capt. Winifred Q. Collins award USN, 1980. Mem. Ninety Nines, San Diego Naval Women Officers Network (chmn.).

GURLEY, GAIL C., probation officer; b. Salisbury, N.C., May 12, 1942; m. Edward Gurley III; 1 child, Denise. BA in Psychology, U. N.C., Greensboro, 1983, MEd, 1988; B.L.E.T., GTCC, J.C. Price Campus, Greensboro, 1989. Cert. reality therapist, cert. law enforcement officer. Probation officer Dept. of Corrections, Greensboro; program mgr. crime control and pub. safety Victim and Justice Svcs, High Point, N.C.; res. patrol officer Gibsonville Police Dept. Contbr. article and poems to jours. Companion, Sexual Assault Victims Advocacy, High Point; big sister Big Bros./Big Sisters, High Point; mem. High Point Coalition Against Child Sexual Assault, Guilford County Jail Com., WHERE Forum. Recipient Chmn.'s award for acad. achievement GTCC. Mem. AACD, POCA, NCCASA, NCACD, Chi Sigma Iota, Phi Theta Kappa. Home: 3112 Pine Needles Rd High Point NC 27260

GURLEY, GERALDINE MARIE, banker; b. Twin Falls, Idaho, Oct. 22, 1947; d. Arthur Lee and Marie (Gubser) G.; m. Joseph Lamonica, Sept. 14, 1974 (dec. Aug. 1988). BA, Coll. Idaho, 1969; B in Internat. Mgmt., Am. Grad. Sch. Internat. Mgmt., Phoenix, 1970; Cert. de Lingua, U. Madrid, 1971. Adminstrv. asst. to gen. mgr. Arthur J. Fritz, Houston, 1972-73; asst. cashier Bank Am. Internat. of Tex., Houston, 1973-79; v.p. Bank One Houston, 1980—; mem. Houston Letter of Credit Group, 1973—, pres. 198. Mem. Houston Letter of Credit Group, Am. Legion Aux. Office: Bank One Tex 910 Travis St Ste 450 Houston TX 77002

GURNE, PATRICIA DOROTHY, lawyer; b. Phila., May 25, 1941; d. George Albert and Dorothy (Hammett) G.; B.A., MacMurray Coll., 1965; J.D., George Washington U., 1969; postgrad. Nat. Inst. Trial Adv., 1974. Bar: D.C. 1971. Law clk. to Judge Joyce H. Green, Superior Ct. D.C., Washington, 1969-71; assoc. Jackson & Campbell, P.C., and predecessors, Washington, 1971-75, partner, 1975—; mem. D.C. Ct. Appeals Jud. Conf., 1977—, D.C. Circuit Jud. Conf., 1979—; mem. U.S. Dist. Ct. Grievance Com., 1983-88. Trustee, George Washington U., 1981—; bd. dirs. D.C. Women's Com. for Crime Prevention, 1978-79. Mem. ABA, Bar Assn. D.C. (exec. council young lawyers sect. 1974-77, vice chmn. young lawyers sect. 1976-77, dir. 1986—, Young Lawyer of Yr. award 1979), Women's Bar Assn. (pres. 1978-79, dir. 1980-83), Women's Bar Found. (dir. 1981—, pres. 1984—), D.C. Bar (sec., dir. 1978-79, ethics com. 1979-82, judicial evaluation com. 1986—), George Washington Law Alumnae Assn. (bd. dirs., pres. 87-88).

GURNEY, ELIZABETH TUCKER GUICE, biologist, educator; b. Berkeley, Calif., Apr. 5, 1941; d. C. Norman and Elizabeth (Eichbauer) Guice; m. Theodore Gurney Jr., June 18, 1966. AB, U. Chgo., 1962; MS, U. Calif., Berkeley, 1970, PhD, 1975. NIH postdoctoral fellow U. Utah, Salt Lake City, 1975-77, rsch. asst. prof., 1976-83, rsch. assoc. prof., 1983—, assoc. dir. undergrad. rsch. opportunities program, 1990—. Contbr. articles to profl. publs., chpts. to books. Grantee Am. Cancer Soc., NIH. Mem. AAAS, Am. Soc. Cell Biology, Am. Soc. Microbiology. Office: U Utah Dept Biology Salt Lake City UT 84112

GURNEY, SUSAN LEE, electronics company executive; b. Bellefonte, Pa., Jan. 28, 1958; d. George Bruce and Virginia (Halligan) G. BFA, Pa. State U., 1980. Apprentice coord., then tech. dir. Boal Barn Playhouse, Boalsburg, Pa., 1977, 78; scenic technician Opera Co. of Boston, 1979; elec. technician Festival Theatre, University Park, Pa., 1979; drafter Tuck Electronics, Camp Hill, Pa., 1980-81; designer, then supr. Olivetti R & D, Harrisburg, Pa., 1981-89; designer Applied Rsch. Lab./Pa. State U., University Park, 1989; pres. Leko Corp., State College, Pa., 1987—. Bd. dirs., State College Community Theatre, Boalsburg, 1979-80. Mem. Mid-Atlantic Racal-Redac Users Group (v.p. 1989), Surface Mount Technology Assn., Nat. Racal-Redac Users Group, NAFE. Republican. Office: Leko Corp 531 Marylyn Ave State College PA 16801

GURNSEY, KATHLEEN WALLACE, state legislator; b. Donnelly, Idaho; d. Robert G. and Thelma (Halferty) Wallace; m. Vern L. Gurnsey, May 7, 1950; children: Kristina Johnson, Steve, Scott. BA in Bus. Adminstn., Boise State U., 1976. Mem. Idaho Ho. of Reps., Boise, 1974—. Bd. dirs. YMCA, Boise; elder, pres. Women's Assn. Ferat Presbyn. Ch.; bd. dirs. Fundsy, St. Luke's Aux.; mem. Def. Adv. Com. Women in the Svc., Dept. Def., 1982-84. Named Disting. Citizen Idaho Statesman, Woman of Yr. Soroptimist, Woman Achievement Altrusa club. Mem. AAUW, Bus. and Prof. Women, Jobs Daughters (Bethel guardian, honored queen). Republican. Presbyterian. Home: 1111 W Highland View Dr Boise ID 83702

GURVITCH, GERALDINE WILMA, scientific societies executive; b. Trenton, N.J., Dec. 31, 1942; d. William and Jane (Bachman) Frees; m. Marc Garson Gurvitch, 1967 (div. 1972); 1 child, Joshua Eugene. BA, George Washington U., 1965; MA, U. Pa., 1966. Tchr. English, Holton-Arms Sch., Bethesda, Md., 1966-68; teaching asst. George Washington U., Washington, 1968-69; adminstrv. asst. Soc. for Neurosci., Bethesda, 1969-80, dir. programs and publs., 1980-83; exec. dir. Genetics Soc. Am., Bethesda, 1983—, Am. Soc. Human Genetics, Bethesda, 1983—, Am. Bd. Med. Genetics, Bethesda, 1984-86. Asst. editor: Soc. for Neurosci. Symposia, Vols. I-IV, 1976-79. Woodrow Wilson fellow, 1965-66. Mem. Coun. Engring. and Sci. Soc. Execs., Phi Beta Kappa. Home: 8-B Ridge Rd Greenbelt MD 20770 Office: Genetics Soc Am-ASHG 9650 Rockville Pike Bethesda MD 20814

GUSHEE, ALLISON TAYLOR, financial advisor; b. Hartford, Conn., Apr. 6, 1962; d. Stephen Hale and Anne (Taylor) G. BA in Mech. Engring. & Comparative Lit., Brown U., 1984; MBA, Insead, Fountainebleau, France, 1987. Assoc. Bankers Trust Co., N.Y.C., Paris, Milan, Italy, 1984-89; sr. assoc. UI-USA, Inc., N.Y.C., 1989-90, v.p., 1990—. Fulbright scholar U. Mohammed V, Rabat, Morocco, 1985. Mem. NAFE, Princeton Brown Club. Episcopalian. Office: UI-USA Inc 610 Fifth Ave Ste 306 New York NY 10020

GUSSAK, ELIZABETH EMMONS, consultant dietitian; b. DeWitt, Iowa, Mar. 17, 1919; d. Richard A. and Beulah A. (Brown) Emmons; m. John J. Gussak (dec.). BS, U. Iowa, 1940, MS, 1941. Registered dietitian. Therapeutic dietitian U. Iowa Hosps., Iowa City, 1942-43; dietitian Wesley Meml. Hosp., Chgo., 1948-52; therapeutic dieitian VA, Iowa City, 1952-54, Bklyn., 1954-56; asst. chief dietitian VA, Chgo., 1956-57; therapeutic dietitian Jane Lamb Hosp., Clinton, Iowa, 1971-80; cons. dietitian Clinton, 1980—. Capt. U.S. Army, M.C., 1943-46, CBI. Mem. Am. Dietetic Assn., Miss. Valley Dietetic Assn., Iowa Dietetic Assn., AAUW (br. pres. 1984-86), VFW (jr. vice com. 1987—), CBI Vets. Assn. (life, nat. comdr. China-Burma-India, Award of Merit 1988), U. Iowa Alumni Assn. (life), PEO (chpt. pres. 1988—). Republican. Congregationalist. Home: 561 6th Ave S Clinton IA 52732

GUSSOW, MICHELLE DENISE, organization executive; b. Lompoc, Calif., Nov. 3, 1963; d. Elliott Floyd and Rosalie Davida (Kaufman) G. BA in Jewish Studies, Marshall U., 1985, MA in Intelligence, 1985. Lt. OSIOS, Indpls., 1981-82, capt., 1982-85, maj., 1985—; consumer researcher Consumer Svc. div. OSIOS, 1982, 88-89. Vol., mem. Sunday sch. staff Beth-El Zedeck Temple, Indpls., 1988—. Democrat.

GUSTAFSON, BARBARA ANN HELTON, lawyer; b. Washington, Ill., Apr. 26, 1948; d. Charles Duncan Helton and Marilou (Buckles) Balogh; m. Lee Alan Gustafson, Dec. 20, 1969. MusB, So. Ill. U., 1970; M of Music Edn., Vandercook Coll., 1972; JD, U. Chgo., 1983. Bar: Ill. 1983, U.S. Ct. Appeals (5th and 10th cirs.), 1984, La. 1988. Instr. music Harrison Sch., Wonderlake, Ill., 1969-72, Cook County Dist. 125, Alsip, Ill., 1972-73; bd. dir. orch. Kankakee (Ill.) Dist. III, 1973-80; atty. MidCon Corp., Lombard, Ill., 1983—. Violinist Kankakee Symphony, 1977-80; musician Kankakee Valley Theater, 1976-80. Mem. ABA, Ill. State Bar Assn., Chgo. Bar Assn., AAUW, Mu Phi Epsilon (treas. 1968-69). Lutheran. Home: 176 Hickory Creek Dr Frankfort IL 60423 Office: MidCon Corp 701 E 22nd St Lombard IL 60148

GUSTAFSON, JEANNE, investment consulting company executive; b. Yankton, S.D., Jan. 11, 1946; d. Frank E. Duffy and Dorothy Ella (Gossard) Hawkins; m. James E. Gustafson, Sept. 2, 1967. BA in English, U. Nebr., 1968. CLU; chartered fin. analyst. Tchr. English, Northern High Sch., Lincoln, Nebr., 1968-69; programmer, analyst Tchrs. Ins. and Annuity Assn.-Coll. Retirement Equity Fund, N.Y.C., 1969-72; systems analyst Hartford (Conn.) Group, 1972-74, with ops.improvement dept., 1974-75; cons. Hewitt Assocs., Lincolnshire, Ill., 1975-78; v.p. Bankers Trust Co., N.Y.C., 1978-80; sr. mgr. Peat Marwick Mitchell, N.Y.C., 1980-86; sr. v.p. Evaluation Assocs., Norwalk, Conn., 1986—. Contbg. author: Investment Banking Handbook, 1988. Fellow Life Mgmt. Inst.; mem. Soc. CLUs, Inst. Chartered Fin. Analysts, Inst. for Quantitative Rsch. in Fin., N.Y. Soc. Security Analysts, Stanwich Golf Club. Democrat. Roman Catholic. Office: Evaluation Assocs 200 Connecticut Ave Norwalk CT 06903

GUSTAFSON, REBECCA SUSANNE, military officer; b. Knoxville, Tenn., Jan. 6, 1962; d. John Albert and Tamara Elizabeth (Day) Badders; m. Gregory Thomas Gustafson, May 25, 1987. BA, U. Fla., 1984; postgrad., Old Dominion U., 1988—, Naval War Coll., 1989—. Commd. ensign USN, 1984, advanced through grades to lt., 1988, oceanographic watch officer Navfac Brawdy Wales, 1984-86; command, control and assist surtass officer, plans and programs officer, instr. Comoceansyslant USN, Norfolk, Va., 1986-90, head dept. curriculum and instrn., 1990—; command, control and assist surtass officer, plans and programs officer, instr. Comoceansyslant Redtrafac Dam Neck, Virginia Beach, Va., 1990—; lectr. USN, Norfolk, Va., 1988-89; Amway distbr. Active Dystrophic Epidermolysis Bullosa Rsch. Am., N.Y., 1985—, Norfolk Jaycees. Mem. Naval Inst., Women's Profl. Network, Fleet Res. Assn., Order Rainbow. Republican. Episcopalian. Home: 4305 Colonial Ave Norfolk VA 23508 Office: Readiness Tng Facility Dam Neck Virginia Beach VA 23461-5573

GUSTAVSON, JOAN ELLEN CARLSON, psychologist; b. Bingham Canyon, Utah, Feb. 26, 1947; d. Leonard Alfred and Melba Ellen (Brown) Carlson; m. Carl Roger Gustavson, June 6, 1964; children: Andrew Roger, Eric Cris. BS, N.D. State U., Fargo, 1982. Interviewer coord. Galveston (Tex.) Family Health Mental Health Survey Project, 1986-87; asst. rsch. dir. Psychiat. Ethology Lab., U. Tex. Med. Br., Galveston, 1985-89; asst. rsch. dir. coyote control project, ctr. environ. studies Ariz. State U., Tempe, 1985—. Editor: Roses and Catails: A Collection of Readings in Human Sexuality, 1981; contbr. articles to profl. jours. Named One of the Outstanding Young Women of Am., 1982. Mem. Am. Inst. Biol. Sci., Animal Behavior Soc., N.Y. Acad. Sci., Am. Psychol. Soc., Sigma Xi, Phi Kappa Phi. Home: 900 W Grove Pkwy #2017 Tempe AZ 85283 Office: Ariz State U Ctr Environ Studies Tempe AZ 85287-1201

GUTENBERG, RHONDA LYNN, industrial psychologist, educator; b. Detroit, July 28, 1957; d. Harold and Arlene Dorothy Gutenberg. B.A. with honors, U. Calif.-Berkeley, 1978; M.A., U. Houston, 1980, Ph.D., 1982. Mgmt. cons. Jeanneret & Assocs., Inc., Houston, 1980-86; vis. prof. U. Minn., Mpls., 1986-87; mgmt. cons. Personnel Decisions Inc., St. Paul, 1987—. Mem. Am. Psychol. Assn., Acad. Mgmt., Twin Cities Personnel Assn. Avocations: tennis, running, biking, scuba diving, photography.

GUTHEIL, DAWN MIRIAM, special education educator; b. St. Louis, Apr. 11, 1963; d. Robert Herman Gutheil and Naomi Kathryn (Winter) Rauff. European studies cert., Sorbonne, U. Paris, 1984; BA in Communications, Muhlenberg Coll., 1985; elem. edn. teaching cert., U. Mass., Boston, 1989. Cert. elem. edn. tchr., child care worker. Pub. rels. asst. Mass. Soc. CPA's, Boston, 1985-86; counselor New Eng. Home for Little Wanderers, Boston, 1986-90; tchr. Haliar Home for Children, Boston, 1990—. Vol. Big Sister of Greater Boston, 1986— (Outstanding Vol. 1988). Mem. Mass. Assn. Childcare Workers. Democrat. Lutheran. Office: The Haliar Home for Children 1225 Centre St Boston MA 02130

GUTHRIE, CATHERINE S. NICHOLSON, research scientist; b. Jackson, Miss.; d. James Benjamin and Catherine Cornelia (Steele) Nicholson; m. George Drake Guthrie, May 5, 1961; 1 child, George Drake Jr. BS, Auburn U., 1957; MS, Fla. State U., 1960; PhD, Ind. U., 1972. Instr. Fla. State U., Tallahassee, 1960, Boston State Coll., 1963-64; rsch. asst. Calif. Inst. Tech., Pasadena, 1960-62, MIT, Cambridge, 1964-65; trainee NIH, 1967-71; vis. asst. prof. U. Evansville, Ind., 1972-73; profl. staff mem. com. sci. and tech. U.S. Ho. of Reps., Washington, 1981; instr. sch. medicine Ind. U., Indpls., 1974-86, adj. rsch. scientist sch. medicine, 1986—; cons. Mead Johnson Co., Evansville, Ind., 1976, com. on environment and pub. works U.S. Senate, Washington, 1981. Contbr. articles to profl. jours. Genetic counselor Deaconess Hosp., Evansville, 1975; state bd. dirs. Citizens Energy Coalition, Indpls., 1975-76; bd. dirs. Child Find Orgn., Evansville, 1985-86. Fellow AAAS, 1979; Sarah Berliner fellow AAUW, 1978-79. Mem. Genetics Soc. Am., Sigma Xi, Sigma Delta Epsilon. Home: 700 Drexel Dr Evansville IN 47712

GUTHRIE, DIANA FERN, nursing educator; b. N.Y.C., May 7, 1934; d. Floyd George and A. May (Moler) Worthington; m. Richard Alan Guthrie, Aug. 18, 1957; children: Laura, Joyce, Tammy. AA, Graceland Coll., 1953; RN, Independence (Mo.) Sanitorium, 1956; BS in Nursing, U. Mo., 1957; EdS, Wichita State U., 1969, MS in Pub. Health, 1969; PhD, Walden U., 1984. Instr. red cross U.S. Naval Sta., Sangley Point, Philippines, 1961-63; acting head nurse newborn nursery U. Mo., Columbia, 1963-64, birth defect nurse dept. pediatrics, 1964-65, nursing dir. clin. research ctr., 1965-67, research asst., 1967-73; asst. then assoc. prof. sch. medicine U. Kans., Wichita, 1974-86, prof. dept. pediatrics and psychiatry, 1986—; adj. prof. dept. nursing Wichita State U., 1982—; diabetes nurse cons. Mo. Regional MEd Program, Columbia, 1970-73; diabetes nurse specialist sch. medicine U. Kans., 1973—; nat. advisor Humana Diabetes Ctr. Excellence, Lexington, Ky., 1982—, Phoenix, 1983—; joint appt. Dept. Psychiatry Sch. Medicine U. Kans., 1988—. Author: Nursing Management of Diabetes, 1982; contbr. articles to profl. jours. Health adv. bd. Mid-Am. All Indian Ctr., Wichita, 1978-80; bd. dirs. Wichita Urban Indian Health Clinic, 1980-82. Fellow Am. Acad. Nursing; mem. Am. Diabetes Assn. (affiliate, bd. dirs. 1979-83, pres. 1980-81, Outstanding Educator award 1979), Am. Assn. Disting. Educators (Disting. Svc. award), Am. Nurses Assn., Am. Assn. Med. Psychotherapists (profl. adv. bd. 1985—), Am. Assn. Biofeedback Clinicians, Am. Pub. Health Assn. Democrat. Mormon. Office: U Kans Sch Medicine 1010 N Kansas Wichita KS 67214

GUTHRIE, HELEN A., nutrition educator, consultant; b. Sarnia, Ont., Can., Sept. 25, 1925; d. David and Helen (Sweet) Andrews; m. George Guthrie, June 4, 1949; children: Barbara, Jane, James. B.A., U. Western Ont., 1946, D.Sc. (hon.), 1982; M.S., Mich. State U., 1948; Ph.D., U. Hawaii, 1968. Cert. registered dietitian. From instr. to assoc. prof. Pa. State U., University Park, 1949-73, prof., head nutrition, 1974-89, endowed prof. nutrition, 1989—. Chmn. Bd. of Health, State College, Pa., 1977-82. Recipient Borden award Am. Home Econs. Assn., 1976, W.O. Atwater award USDA, 1989. Mem. Am. Inst. Nutrition (councillor 1982—, pres. 1987, Elvejhem award for pub. svc. 1989), Soc. Nutrition Edn. (pres. 1978-79), Am. Dietetics Assn., Am. Pub. Health Assn., Inst. Food Tech., Internat. Life Sci. Inst.-Nutrition Found. (bd. trustees, 1979—, v.p. nutrition, 1986-89). Home: 1316 S Garner St State College PA 16801 Office: Pa State U University Park PA 16802

GUTHRIE, MARY LEE, jewelry company executive; b. Sedalia, Mo., May 8, 1965; d. Clarence Lee and Marilynn Francis (Rice) G. BSBA, Central Mo. State U., 1988. Mgr. trainee Capitol Mktg. Assocs., Shawnee Mission, Kans., 1988; coord. cen. office, asst. advt. coord., exec. asst. to pres. Tivol Plaza, Inc., Kansas City, Mo., 1989—. Mem. Pers. Mgmt. Assn.

GUTHRIE, RANDEE RAE, electrical engineer; b. Atlanta, July 17, 1960; d. Edgar Manley and Barbara Annette (Anderson) G. Student, U. Ga., 1979-81; BSEE Tech., So. Coll. Tech., 1988. Asst. mgr. nursery Terminus Racquet Club, Atlanta, 1978-79; demonstrator for video disk Allen and Bean, Smyrna, Ga., 1980-81; tchr. Pine Crest Day Care Sch., Marietta, Ga., 1982-83; ops. specialist Chi Chi's Restaurant, Atlanta, 1984-85; area systems engr. Motorola Communications & Electronics, Maitland, Fla., 1988—; coop student flight control systems Dryden Flight Rsch. Facility NASA, Edwards, Calif., 1985, artificial intelligence, 1986. Mem. IEEE, Gamma Phi Beta. Home: 1010 Reflections Circle 108 Casselberry FL 32707 Office: Motorola Communications 670 N Orlando Ave Ste 104 Maitland FL 32751

GUTIERREZ, ELIA GARZA, elementary educatory; b. Corpus Christi, Tex., Oct. 30, 1932; d. J.M. and Maria (Garcia) Garza; m. Albert A. Gutierrez, June 1, 1958; children: Alynn Ann Riley, Alda Alia Thompson, Alban Albert, Alane Alexandra. BS, Tex. Women's U., 1957; MA, Tex. A&M U., 1980. Cert. elem. tchr., Tex.; cert. elem. prin., Tex. Tchr. Corpus Christi Ind. Sch. Dist., 1957—; educator specialist bilingual edn. and ESL Corpus Christi Ind. Sch. Dist., 1957—. Mem., vol., social chmn. Sts. Cyril and Methiodus Sch. Bd., 1978, 79; v.p. Corpus Christi Classroom Assn., 1980-82; pres. Corpus Christi Assn. Bilingual Edn., 1982-83, 88-89; mem. Friends of the Libr., 1958—; mem., vol. guide info. desk Tex. State Aguarium; vol. tutor Drop-out Program. Recipient Award of Distinction, Tex. Assn. Bilingual Edn., 1987; named Tchr. of Yr., Corpus Christi Classroom Assn., 1988. Mem. AAUW, NEA, Tex. State Tchr.'s Assn., Tex. Women's U. Alumnae Assn. (past. pres.), Sceptre Club (pres. 1971, 87), Nyeces County Hist. Soc., Schoenslatt Club, Town Club, Beta Sigma Phi (girl of yr. 1978, 79, 80). Home: 6233 Pebble Beach Corpus Christi TX 78413

GUTIERREZ, LINDA, lawyer; b. San Antonio, Aug. 11, 1955; d. Frank S. III and Adelina (Aguirre) G. BA, Randolph Macon Women Coll., 1977; JD, U. Tex. Law Sch., 1982. Exec. asst. Mex. Am. Unity Coun., San Antonio, 1979; pvt. practice Law Office of Linda Gutierrez, San Antonio, 1983—. bd. dirs. Bexar County Women's Bar Assn., Child Advocates San Antonio, Pro Bono Law Project; pres. Mex. Am. Bar Assn., 1987-89. Named Outstanding Young Lawyer Bexar County Women's Bar Assn., 1986, Attorney Coach Tex. High Sch. Mock Trial competition., 1985, Outstanding new Attorney Pro Bono Law Project, 1984. Office: EEOC 5410 Fredericksburg Rd #200 San Antonio TX 78204

GUTSHALL, PRISCILLA JEAN, photographer; b. Whittaker, Pa., Feb. 22, 1944; d. William McClellan and Althea Mae (Fraker) Covert; m. Barry Lee Gutshall, July 13, 1968; 1 child, Jeanne Marie (dec.). Cert., N.Y. Inst. Photography, N.Y.C. Stewart Amalgamated Clothing Workers Union, Huntingdon, Pa., 1981-83; factory worker Arrow Shirt Co., Huntingdon, Pa., 1964-78, Huntingdon Apparel, 1978-82; part-time sec. 1st United Meth. Ch., 1986, 89; adminstr. Huntingdon Area Food Bank, 1983—; owner, operator Photos by Jean, Huntingdon, 1984—. Mem. Internat. Freelance Photographers Assn., Assoc. Photographers Internat. Democrat. Methodist. Home and Office: 508 12th St Huntingdon PA 16652

GUTTERMAN-REINFELD, DEBRA ELLEN, physician, consultant; b. N.Y.C., Nov. 13, 1948; d. George and Nettie (Liss) Gutterman; m. Stuart Glenn Reinfeld, June 20, 1982; children: Alan Jeffrey, Naomi Rebecca. BS, R.N. magna cum laude, SUNY Downstate Med. Ctr., 1972; postgrad. U. Auton, Guadalajara Sch. Medicine (Mex.), 1973-75; M.D., Coll. Medicine and Dentistry N.J., 1977. Intern, Boston City Hosp., 1977-78; resident in medicine Maimonides Med. Ctr., Bklyn., 1978-79, 79-80, Mt. Sinai Med. Ctr., Miami Beach, Fla., 1982-83; fellow Jackson Meml. Hosp., Miami, Fla., 1980-82; internist, cons. infectious diseases, former chief dept. internal medicine, former assoc. med. dir. Maxicare/Health Am., Ft. Lauderdale, Fla.; med. dir. Humana/Health Am., Plantation, Fla., 1988—; chairperson AIDS Fla. Taskforce, Humana Med. Plans, also chairperson quality assurance com.

GUTTERRES, CHERYL SCOFIELD, nurse educator; b. Sandwich, Ill., Aug. 16, 1933; d. Tracey L. and Stella L. (Hollenback) Scofield; m. Warluy R. Gutterres, Jan. 6, 1973. BSN, U. Iowa, 1958; M.Nursing Edn., U. Pitts., 1963; RN, Evanston Hosp. Sch. Nursing, 1954. Staff nurse Children's Meml. Hosp., Chgo., 1954-55, U.. Children's Hosp. Sch., Chgo., 1955-56; camp nurse The Outing Assn. for Crippled Children, Chgo., Oconomowoc, Wis., summers 1955, 56; staff nurse Univ. Hosp., Iowa City, 1956-58; staff nurse, head nurse, instr. Evanston (Ill.) Hosp. Sch. Nursing, 1958-59, 59-62; instr. U. Wis., Madison, 1963-66; supr. The Henrietta Egleston Hosp. for Children, Atlanta, 1966-70, dir. nursing, 1970-77; instr. Grady Meml. Hosp. Sch. Nursing, Atlanta, 1977-78; asst. prof. Ga. State U., Atlanta, 1979-89; med. case mgr. VPS Case Mgmt. Svcs., Inc., Atlanta, 1989-90; staff nurse Hospice Atlanta, 1989—; adv. coun. Grady Hospice Prog., Atlanta, 1987-88, vol., 1986—. Contbr. articles to profl. jours. Mem. Coun. for Children, Atlanta. Ga. State U. continuing edn. grantee, 1986, 87. Mem. Assn. Pediatric Oncology Nurses, Am. Nurses Assn. (cert. child and adolescent nurse 1983—), Ga. Nurses Assn. (chair coun. on pediatric nursing, sec. 5th dist. 1986-90), Nurses for Rsch., Nurses in Bus. Assn., Sigma Theta Tau. Home and Office: 187 Vidal Blvd Decatur GA 30030

GUTTERSON, JANET MIRIAM, foundation administrator; b. Brockton, Mass., Mar. 9, 1939; d. Axel Harold and Jennie Alberta (Ellmes) Anderson; m. Donald E. Cooper, May 25, 1962 (dec. 1966); m. Lyman P. Gutterson Jr., May 4, 1968; children: Melody Gutterson-Russell, Freya Diane. BS, Bridgewater State Coll., 1961; MS, Stetson U., 1990. Tchr. Montverde (Fla.) Acad., 1961-62; with pers. office South Shore Nat. Bank, Quincy, Mass., 1964-72; program coord. Lake County Bd. Commrs., Tavares, Fla., 1977-81; counselor State of Fla., Eustis, 1982-85; area supr. Green Thumb Program, Jacksonville, Fla., 1985-86; exec. dir. Lake County Family Health Coun., Eustis, 1986—; bd. dirs. Haven Inc., Leesburg, Fla., 1983-89; founding dir. Lake County Child Adv. Coun., Tavares, 1987-88. Mem. Lake County Svc. League, Leesburg, 1986—; mem. adv. bd. Lake Sumter Community Coll., 1987-88. Recipient Service award Fla. Choices, 1985. Mem. LWV, Chi Sigma Iota. Democrat. Episcopalian. Club: U.S. Pony (Altoona, Fla.) (sec. 1980-86). Home: 2470 Eastland Rd Mount Dora FL 32757 Office: Lake County Family Health Coun Inc 20 S Eustis St Eustis FL 32726

GUTTMAN, HELENE NATHAN, research executive; b. N.Y.C., July 21, 1930; d. Arthur and Mollie (Bergovoy) Nathan. B.A., Bklyn. Coll., 1951; A.M. (Andelot fellow), Harvard U., 1956; M.A., Columbia U., 1958; Ph.D. (Rutgers scholar), Rutgers U., 1960. Chartered chemist Royal Soc. Chemistry; registered profl. animal scientist. Research technician Pub. Health Research Inst., N.Y.C., 1951-52; control bacteriologist Burroughs-Wellcome, Inc., Tuckahoe, N.Y., 1952-53; vol. researcher Haskins Labs., N.Y.C., 1952-53; research asst. Haskins Labs., 1953-56, research assoc., 1956-60, staff microbiologist, 1960-64; lectr. dept. biology Queens Coll., N.Y.C., 1956-57; research collaborator Brookhaven Nat. Labs., Upton, L.I., N.Y., 1958; guest investigator Botanisches Institut der Technisches Hochschule, Darmstadt, Germany, 1960; research assoc. dept. biol. scis. Goucher Coll., Towson, Md., 1960-62; vis. asst. research prof. dept. medicine Med. Coll. Va. Richmond, 1960-62; asst. prof., then assoc. prof. dept. biology NYU, 1962-67; from assoc. prof. to prof. dept. biol. scis. U. Ill.-Chgo., 1967-75, prof., 1969-75; prof. dept. microbiology U. Ill. Med. Sch., 1974-75; assoc. dir. for research Urban Systems Lab. U. Ill., 1975; expert Office of Dir. Nat. Heart, Lung and Blood Inst., NIH, Bethesda, Md., 1975-77; coordinator research resources Office Program Planning and Evaluation Nat. Heart, Lung and Blood Inst., NIH, 1977-79; dep. dir. Sci. Adv. Bd., Office of Adminstr., EPA, 1979-80; program coordinator, post-harvest tech., food safety and human nutrition, sci. and edn. adminstrn. USDA, 1980-83, assoc. dir. Beltsville Human Nutrition Research Ctr., Agrl. Research Service, 1983-89; pres. HNG Assocs., 1983—; animal care coord. Nat. Program Staff Agr. Rsch. Svc./USDA, Beltsville, Md., 1989—. Sr. author: Experiments in Cellular Biodynamics, 1972; editorial bd. Jour. Protozoology, 1972-75, Jour. Am. Med. Women's Assn., 1978-81; sr. editor: Science & Animals: Addressing Contemporary Issues, 1989; editor Guidelines for Use of Rodents in Research, 1990; contbr. articles to profl. jours. and books. Mem. edn. com. Ill. Commn. on Status Women, 1974-75; cons. EPA, sci. adv. bd., 1974-79; Bd. dirs. Du Page County Comprehensive Health Care Agy., 1974-75. Recipient Thomas Jefferson Murray prize Theobald Smith Soc., 1959; spl. award for work in Germany Deutscher Forschungs Gemeinschaft, 1960; Fellow Dazian Found., 1956; research grantee. Fellow AAAS, Am. Inst. Chemists (com. chmn.), Am. Acad. Microbiology, N.Y. Acad. Scis.; mem. Soc. Am. Bacteriologists (pres.'s fellow 1957), Tissue Culture Assn. (com. chmn. Nat. Capital Area br. 1988-90), Am. Soc. Neurochemistry, Am. Soc. Biol. Chemistry, Neurosci. Soc., Am. Soc. Microbiologists, Am. Soc. Cell Biology (past com. chmn.), Am. Soc. Clin. Nutrition, Am. Soc. Tropical Medicine and Hygiene, Soc. Gen. Microbiologists (Eng.), Soc. Protozoology (past mem. exec. com.), Soc. Exptl. Biology and Medicine, Assn. Women in Sci. (past mem. exec. bd., past com. chmn.), Fed. Orgn. Profl. Women (past task force chmn., past pres.), Univ. and Coll. Women Ill. (past v.p.), Am. Running and Fitness Assn. (bd. dirs., mem. editorial bd.), Sigma Xi, Sigma Delta Epsilon (past coord. regional ctrs.). Home: 5607 McLean Dr Bethesda MD 20814 Office: Nat Program Staff Agrl Rsch Svc USDA BARC W Bldg 002 Rm 105 Beltsville MD 20705

GUY, ELEANOR BRYENTON, writer; b. Pitts., Sept. 6, 1930; d. Lloyd Charles and Verda Eleanor (Hooper) Bryenton; m. Daniel Sowers Guy, Dec. 22, 1962; children: Stanley, Sharon. BA, Ohio Wesleyan U., 1953. Program dir. Cleve. Met. YWCA, Lakewood, Ohio, 1953-56, ctr. dir., 1956-57; residence dir., mem. faculty St. Luke's Hosp. Sch. Nursing, Shaker Heights, Ohio, 1957-59; pers. asst., counselor Acacia Mutual Life Ins. Co., Washington, 1959-62; admissions counselor Ohio No. U., Ada, 1963-64; freelance writer Kenton (Ohio) Times, 1984-88, Ada Herald, 1988—. Sec. bd. trustees, chmn. pub. rels. com. Ada Pub. Libr., 1982-86; mem. pub. rels. com., bd. dirs. Hardin County Alcohol and Drug Abuse Ctr., Kenton, 1989—; chmn. publicity Town and Gown Planning Com., Ada, 1988; tchr., mem. edn. coun. localch. Mem. AAUW (pres. local chpt. 1978-80), Twice Ten Art Club (pres. 1984-85, sec. 1988-89). Methodist.

GUY, L(EONA) RUTH, educator; b. Kemp, Tex., Mar. 17, 1913; d. Henry Luther and Minnie Elizabeth (Murphy) G. AB, Baylor U., 1934, MS, 1949; PhD, Stanford (Calif.) U., 1953. Rsch. fellow N000, 1951-53; teaching asst. Stanford U., 1951; with U. Tex. Southwestern Med. Sch., Dallas, 1962—, prof., 1972-78, prof. emeritus, 1982—; assoc. dir. Parkland Meml. Hosp. Blood Bank, Dallas, 1953-78; cons. VA Hosp., Dallas, 1960-80, Temple, 1964-80; vis. prof. to Far East, China Med. Bd. of N.Y., N.Y.C., 1969-70. Author: (with others) Modern Blood Banking and Transfusion Practices, 1982; editor: Technical Manual, 1966; contbr. numerous articles to profl. jours. Bd. dirs. Dallas Repertory Theater, Dallas, 1983-89. Inducted into Tex. Women's Hall of Fame, Gov.'s Commn. for Women, 1989. Mem. Bus. and Profl. Women's Club Dallas, Inc. (pres. 1970-71), Am. Soc. Clin. Pathologist (assoc., hon. fellow, Disting. Svc. award 1989), Zonta (pres. Dallas chpt. 1961-62). Baptist. Home: 5825 Birchwood Dr #107 Dallas TX 75206

GUY, MILDRED DOROTHY, educator; b. Brunswick, Ga.; d. John and Mamie Paul (Smith) Floyd; BA in Social Sci., Savannah State Coll., 1949; MA in Am. History, Atlanta U., 1952; postgrad. U. So. Calif., U. Colo.; m. Charles H. Guy, Aug. 18, 1956 (div. 1979); 1 child, Rhonda Lynn. Tchr. social studies L.S. Ingraham High Sch., Sparta, Ga.; tchr. English and social studies North Jr. High Sch., Colorado Springs, 1958-84; ret., 1984; cooperating tchr. Tchr. Edn. Program, Col. Coll., 1968-72. Fund raiser for Citizens for Theatre Auditorium, Colorado Springs, 1979; bd. dirs. Urban League, 1971-75; del. to County and State Dem. Conv., 1972, 76, 80, 84; mem. Pike's Peak Community Coll. Council, 1976-83; mem. council of 500, Colorado Springs Opera; mem. nominating com. Wagon Wheel council Girl Scouts U.S.A., 1985-87. Recipient Viking award North Jr. High Sch., 1973, Woman of Distinction award Girls Scouts Wagon Wheel Coun., 1989; Outstanding Black Woman of Colorado Springs award, 1975; named Pacesetter, Atlanta U., 1980-81, Outstanding Black Educator of Yr., Black Educators of Dist. II, Colorado Springs, 1981; Outstanding Achievement in Edn. award Negro Hist. Assn. of Colorado Springs, 1983, Outstanding Ednl. Service award Colo. Dept. and State Bd. Edn., 1983, Dedicated Service award Pikes Peak Community Coll., 1983; Outstanding Community Leadership award Alpha Phi Alpha, 1985; award Colo. Black Woman for Polit. Action, 1985, Sphinx award, 1986; named in recognition sect. Salute to Women, Colorado Springs Gazette Telegraph, 1986. Mem. NEA (life mem.), AAUW, Colo. Council of Social Studies, Assn. for Study of Afro-Am. Life and History, Colo. LWV, Friends of Pioneers Mus. (life mem.), NAACP, Alpha Delta Kappa, Alpha Kappa Alpha (chpt. pres. 1984-86, award 1986). Baptist. Home: 3132 Constitution Ave Colorado Springs CO 80909

GUY, SHARON KAYE, state agency executive; b. Nashville, Apr. 5, 1958; d. Dallas Hearold and Elizabeth Jean (Towns) Gregory; m. Bryant Duran Guy, Aug. 29, 1984; 1 child, Anthony Lee. Grad. high sch., Chgo. Clk. Pub. Health dept. State of Tenn., Nashville, 1979-84, office mgr. Health Facilities commn., 1984—; acct. Bryant Guy Constrn., Nashville, 1984—. Blood drive coordinator ARC, Nashville, 1984—; campaign vol. United Way, Nashville, 1984—. Baptist. Home: 1361 Madison Creek Rd Goodlettsville TN 37072 Office: Tenn Health Facilities Comm 500 James Robertson Pkwy Nashville TN 37219

GUYNES, KAREN LEA, management training administrator; b. Dallas, Feb. 19, 1960; d. Vernon Albert and Adrienne Ann (Leslie) Guynes Jr.; m. Roger Whitfield Christian, Oct. 1, 1980 (div. Feb. 1982). Sales dir. Lincoln Property Co., Dallas, 1980-86; tng. dir. Summit Mgmt. Co., Charlotte, N.C., 1986—. Actor theater and film, Dallas, 1973-81. Mem. Am. Soc. for Tng. and Devel. Office: Summit Mgmt Co 212 S Tryon St Suite 800 Charlotte NC 28281

GUZMAN, DEBRA LYNNE, publishing company executive; b. Pasadena, Calif., Oct. 22, 1951; d. Robert Allen Briehof and Betty Ann (Kenney) Blake; m. James Luis Erviti, Sept. 24, 1983 (div. 1987); m. Jaime R. Guzman, Aug. 5, 1989. BA in Art History, Calif. State U., Chico, 1977. Slide librarian San Francisco Mus. Modern ARt, 1982-87; rsch. coordinator Access Press, San Francisco, 1987; specialist Pacific Bell Dir., San Francisco, 1987—. Bd. dirs. North Beach Neighbors, San Francisco, 1987-88, v.p., 1988. Mem. Amnesty Internat. (case work coordinator 1988-89), City Guides San Francisco. Democratic. Jewish. Home: 15 Jansen St San Francisco CA 94133 Office: Pacific Bell Dir 101 Spear St 560 San Francisco CA 94105

GUZMAN, JUANITA ELIZABETH, systems analyst, communication specialist; b. Cochabamba, Bolivia, July 5, 1961; came to U.S., 1977; d. Mario and Irma (Cardenas) G. BBA, U. Wis., Eau Claire, 1985. Exec. sec. IDEM, Cochabamba, 1978-79; sec. Bank of La Paz, Cochabamba, 1979-80, Eagle Nat. Bank, Miami, Fla., 1980-81; sec. asst. U. Wis., Eau Claire, 1981-85; systems asst. PennWell, Houston, 1985-86; systems analyst CBI Na-Con, Inc., Houston, 1986—; cons., Houston, 1985—. Recipient scholarship Am. Field Svcs., 1977. Mem. Soc. for Info. Mgmt., Data Processing Mgmt. Assn.

GWINN, NAOMI JEAN, railroad quality control inspector; b. Greeneville, Tenn., May 10, 1952; d. Robert Walter and Ima Jean (Ferguson) G. Grad. high sch., Greeneville, Tenn., 1974. Cert. journeyman electrician. Supr. Midstate Electronics, Beech Grove, Ind., 1975-77; elec. apprentice Amtrak, Beech Grove, Ind., 1977-80, elec. technician, 1980-86, quality control insp., 1986—. Mem. editorial staff Amtrak co. news, 1985-89; contbr. articles to mags. Mem. Nat. Assn. R.R. Bus. Women (Circle City chpt. #74, v.p. 1990), Nat. Assn. Female Execs., Internat. Brotherhood Elec. Workers. Democrat. Office: AMTRAK 202 Garstang Beech Grove IN 46107

GWINUP, KIMBERLY SUE, executive secretary; b. Fremont, Ohio, Nov. 20, 1965; d. Richard Albert and Jeanette (Metcalf) G. Grad. high sch., Marshall, N.C., 1984. Sec. Madison High Sch., Marshall, N.C., 1983-84; clk. typist Farmers Home Adminstrn., Marshall, 1985-86; exec. sec. Hamlin-Chastain Assocs., Asheville, N.C., 1986—. Republican. Baptist. Office: Hamlin Chastain Assocs 990 Sweeten Creek Rd Asheville NC 28803

GWYNN, KAY SUE, secondary education educator, retired, volunteer; b. Riverton, Wyo., June 28, 1917; d. Michael James and Charlotte Jane (Welton) Engle; m. George Ronald Gwynn, Sept. 25, 1942 (div. 1958); children: Barbara Irene, Donald George (dec.), Craig Ronald. AS, Casper Coll., 1967; BS, U. Wyo., 1970, BA, 1973, postgrad., 1970-73; postgrad., U. Wyo., 1978, Colo. State Coll., Greely, 1975. Rsch. psychologist U. Wyo., Laramie, 1968-73; jr. high sch. tchr. U. Sch., Laramie, 1972; high sch. tchr. Natrona Sch. Dist. 1, Casper, Wyo., 1974-79. Worker Dem. Women, Casper and Laramie, 1968—, Crisis and Suicide Line, Casper, 1985—, Planned Parenthood, Casper, 1987—; worker in intensive care Hosp. Aux.; v.p. Lupus Help Line, Casper, 1984-86. Mem. AAUW (bylaw com. and parliamentarian 1987-88, historian 1988—), Wyo. Assn. Counseling & Devel. (bd. dirs. 1982-87). Baptist. Home: 344 N Jackson Casper WY 82601

GYETVAN, ANGELA WILSON, marketing executive; b. Newport News, Va., Oct. 13, 1962; d. Emory Earl and Patricia (Benton) W.; m. Michael Francis Gyetvan, May 28, 1988. BA in English, Duke U., 1984; MBA in Mktg., Coll. of William and Mary, 1986. Asst. prodn. mgr. Colonial Williamsburg (Va.) Found., 1986-88; mktg. coord. Brøderbund Software, Inc., San Rafael, Calif., 1988-89, mktg. exec., 1989—. Mem. Duke Club of No. Calif., Am. Film Inst., Jr. League of San Francisco. Roman Catholic. Office: Brøderbund Software Inc 17 Paul Dr San Rafael CA 94903

GYLLANDER, NIKKI K., human services administrator; b. East Chicago, Ind., Mar. 9, 1946; d. Nick and Olga (Karchut) Migas; children: Grant, Greg. BSSW, No. Mich. U., 1972; MPA, U. Wis., Oshkosh, 1988; postgrad., Wis. State U., Whitewater. Cert. adminstrv. cons., surveyor Commn. on the Accreditation of Rehab. Facilities. Human svcs. dir. LaCrosse County, LaCrosse, Wis.; dep. dir. Sheboygan County Unified Bd., Sheboygan, Wis.; program coord. Florence County Combined Svcs., Florence, Wis. Author: Preventive Programs for Youth. Mem. Wis. Cos. Human Svcs. Assn., LaCrosse C. of C., Avant, LeConnoisseurs, Rotary. Home: PO Box 4002 LaCrosse WI 54602

GYULAY, JO-EILEEN, grief counseling organization administrator; b. Kansas City, Kans., July 6, 1941; d. Joseph Jr. and Ellen Bernadette (McGuire) G. BS in Nursing, U. Kans., 1965; MS in Maternal Child Health Nursing, Boston U., 1968; MA, U. Kans., 1979, PhD in Devel. Child Psychology, 1981. Cert. nurse practitioner. Clin. dir., patient field coord., dir. edn. Hospice Care Mid-Am., Kansas City, Mo., 1980-87; cons. Trinity Luth. Hosp., Kansas City, Mo., 1988-89; founder, pres. The Grief Inst. Mid-Am. Inc., 1989—. Author: The Dying Child, 1978. Named Nursing Alumnus of Yr. U. Kans. Sch. Nursing, for Outstanding Vol. Svc. Am. Cancer Soc., Area Hosp. Assn., Kansas City Area Employee of Yr., U. Kans. Med. Med. Ctr. Employee of Yr. Mem. Assn. for Death Edn. and Counseling, Am. Nurses Assn., Mental Health Assn. Johnson County, Oncology Nursing Soc., Sigma Theta Tau, Beta Sigma Phi. Home: 1421 B East Martway Cir Olathe KS 66061

GYURICSKO, HOLLY ANN, nurse; b. Waterbury, Conn., Dec. 5, 1964; d. Frederick Ferdinand and Pamela Marion (Osborn) G. BS in Nursing, U. Conn., 1987. Cert. emergency nurse. Emergency staff nurse Bristol (Conn.) Hosp., 1987-88, asst. patient care mgr. emergency rm., 1988-89; emergency staff nurse Kaiser Permanente Hosp., San Francisco, 1989-90, Peninsula Hosp., Burlingame, Calif., 1990—. Recipient Advanced Cardiac Life Support award Am. Heart Assn., 1989. Mem. Emergency Nurses Assn., Calif. Nurses Assn. Home: 811 Ashbury St Apt #4 San Francisco CA 94117

HAAG, CAROL ANN, environmental service executive; b. Jamestown, N.D., May 22, 1947; d. Richard C. and Grace A. (Miller) Joyce; m. Roger T. Haag, Sept. 14, 1968; children: Staci, Kelly, Chad. BS in Edn., Valley City (N.D.) State Coll., 1969; MS in Edn., N.D. State U., 1972; cert. in adminstrn., Kans. State U., 1981. Fin. sec. Butler Machinery Co., Fargo, N.C., 1969; instr. Moorhead (Minn.) Vocat. Sch., 1969-72; coord., instr. Moorhead (Minn.) State U., 1973-74; corp. sec. Jet-Way, Inc., Moorhead, 1974-77; coord. Johnson County Community Colls., Overland Park, Kans., 1978; spl. edn. coord., high sch. counselor Unified Sch. Dist., Salina, Kans., 1978-81; instr. Lansing (Mich.) Community Coll., 1982-86; pres., chief exec. officer EnviroLand, Inc., Dewitt, Mich., 1985—; speaker small bus. mgmt. Mem. NAFE, City (Lansing) Club. Lutheran.

HAAG, CAROL ANN GUNDERSON, marketing professional, consultant; b. Mpls.; d. Glenn Alvin and Genevieve Esther (Knudson) Gunderson; m. Lawrence S. Haag, Aug. 30, 1969; 1 child, Maren Anne. BJ, U. Mo., 1969; postgrad., Roosevelt U., Chgo., 1975—. Pub. relations writer, advt. copywriter Am. Hosp. Supply Corp., Evanston, Ill., 1969-70; asst. dir. pub. relations Rush-Presbyn. St. Luke's Med. Ctr., Chgo., 1970-71; asst. mgr. pub. and employee communications Quaker Oats Co., Chgo., 1971-72, mgr. editorial communications, 1972-74, mgr. employee communications programs, 1974-77; dir. pub. relations Shaklee Corp., San Francisco, 1978-82; pres. CH & Assocs., San Francisco, 1982-84; dir corp. communications BRAE Corp., San Francisco, 1984; dir. mktg. St. Francis Meml. Hosp., San Francisco, 1985-89, dir. mktg. and planning svcs., 1989—; cons. in field. Bd. dirs. Calif. League Handicapped; mem. adv. bd. San Francisco Spl. Olympics; mem. pub. relations com. San Francisco Recreation and Parks Dept., San Francisco Vol. Bur. Recipient 1st Place cert. Printing Industry Am., 1972, 74, 1st Place Spl. Communication award Internat. Assn. Bus. Communicators, 1974, 1st Place citation Chgo. Assn. Bus. Communicators, 1974, Gold award Healthcare Mktg. Reports, 1989. Mem. NATAS, Indsl. Communication Coun., Pub. Rels. Soc. Am., San Francisco C. of C. Club: San Francisco Press. Home: 133 Fernwood Dr Moraga CA 94556 Office: St Francis Meml Hosp 900 Hyde St San Francisco CA 91409

HAAGA, CANDICE ANN FOGEL, clinical psychologist; b. Pueblo, Colo., Jan. 15, 1960; d. Timothy John and Margaret Ann (Reid) Fogel; m. David Andrew Haaga, June 7, 1987. BA in Human Biology, Stanford U., 1983; MA in Psychology, U. So. Calif., 1985, PhD in Psychology, 1988. Rsch. asst. psychology dept. U. So. Calif., L.A., 1983-84, tchg. asst., 1984-86; therapist-in-tng. U. So. Calif. Human Rels. Ctr., L.A., 1984-87, clinic student coord., 1986-87; clin. intern Sepulveda (Calif.) Vets. Hosp, 1987-88; postdoctoral clin. fellow Ctr. Cognitive Therapy, Phila., 1988-89; psychotherapist, researcher Cath. U. Counseling Ctr., Washington, 1989—; campus cons. and liaison Cath. U. Counseling Ctr., Washington, 1989-90; adj. lectr. psychology Cath. U. Psychology Grad. Program, Washington, 1990. Contbr. articles to profl. jours. Pre-sch. tchr., religious edn. instr. Unitarian Ch. Rockville, Md., 1990. Recipient Nat. Merit scholarship, 1978, Dean's scholarship U. So. Calif., 1986, Am. Psychol. Assn. Sci. Directorate Dissertation grant, 1988. Mem. AAUW, Am. Psychol. Assn. (also Psychology of Women div.), Assn. Advancement of Behavior Therapy (editor spl. interest group column The Behavior Therapist 1989-90). Democrat. Unitarian. Office: Cath U Counseling Ctr 126 O'Boyle Hall Washington DC 20064

HAAR, ANA MARIA FERNÁNDEZ, advertising and public relations executive; b. Oriente Province, Cuba, Mar. 25, 1951; came to U.S., 1960, naturalized, 1970; d. Gilberto and Esmeralda Emiliana (Díaz) Fernández. Grad., Miami Dade Community Coll., 1971; student, Barry Coll., 1972-78. Adminstrv. asst. thru asst. v.p. nat. accounts Flagship Bank, Miami Beach, Fla., 1971-77; v.p. comml. lending Jefferson Nat. Bank, Miami Beach, 1977-78; pres. IAC Advt. Group, Miami, 1978—; instr. Miami Dade Community Coll. Women in Mgmt. Program, 1980-81; hostess Sta. WPBT Program Viva. Mem. Dade County Commn. on Status of Women, 1979-82; chmn. Econ. Devel. Task Force of Commn. on Status of Women, 1979-82; bd. dirs. Downtown Miami Bus. Assn., 1979-82, Family Counseling Svcs., Miami; Internat. Ctr. of Fla., chmn. healthcare com.; mem. Dist. Export Coun.; hostess (program) Viva, WPBT-TV; mem. community Svcs. Cedars Med. Ctr. Recipient Gran Orden Martiana of Cuban Lyceum for excellence in community svc., 1976, Up and Comers award South Fla. Bus. Jour., 1988. Mem. Advt. Fedn. Greater Miami, Greater Miami Advt. Fedn. (bd. dirs.), Asociación de Publicitarios Latino-Americanos (v.p.), Miami Beach C. of C. (hon. life, trustee), Greater Miami C. of C., Hispanic Heritage Festival Com., Home: 2451 Brickell Ave Miami FL 33129 Office: IAC Advt Group 2725 SW 3d Ave Miami FL 33129

HAAS, CAROLYN BUHAI, writer, publisher, consultant; b. Chgo., Jan. 1, 1926; d. Michael and Tillie (Weiss) Buhai; m. Robert Green Haas, June 29, 1947 (dec. June 30, 1984); children—Andrew Robert, Mari Beth, Thomas Michael, Betsy Ann, Karen Sue. B.Ed., Smith Coll., Northampton, Mass., 1947; postgrad. Nat. Coll. Edn., Evanston, Ill., 1956-59; Art Inst. Chgo., 1958-59. Tchr., Francis W. Parker Sch., Chgo., 1947-49; tchr. art Glencoe Pub. Schs., Ill., 1967-68, substitute tchr., 1964-72; co-founder PAR Leadership Tng. Found., Northfield, Ill., 1969-81; pres., editor CBH Pub., Inc., Northfield, 1979—; cons., writer, adv. bd. The Learning Line; cons. presch. sci. program Mus. Sci. and Industry, Chgo.; adv. bd. My Own Mag.; cons. in field. Author: (with Ann Cole and Betty Weinberger) I Saw a Purple Cow, 1972; A Pumpkin In A Pear Tree, 1974; Children Are Children Are Children, 1976; Backyard Vacation, 1978; Purple Cow to the Rescue, 1982; Recipes for Fun and Learning, 1982; author: The Big Book of Recipes for Fun, 1979; Look At Me: Activities for Babies and Toddlers, 1985, The Big Book of Fun II, 1989; contbr. articles to profl. jours. Pres., West Sch. PTA, Glencoe; pres. Jr. Bd. Scholarship and Guidance, Chgo.; bd. dirs. Family Counseling Service of Glencoe, Glencoe Human Relations Com.; pres., sec., bd. dirs. Glencoe Pub. Library; pres. Friends of Glencoe Pub. Library; co-founder Glencoe Patriotic Days Com.; co-chmn. Frank Lloyd Wright Bridge Com., Glencoe; pres., bd. dirs. Chgo. League Smith Coll.; mem. women's bd. Northwestern U.; bd. dirs. Chgo. chpt. Am. Jewish Com.; mem. women's com. Chgo. Symphony Orch. Clubs; bd. dirs., Art Resources in Teaching. Mem. Soc. Children's Bookwriters, Children's Reading Roundtable, Nat. Assn. Edn. Young Children, Assn. Childhood Edn. Internat., IRA, NEA, Phi Delta Kappa. Democrat. Jewish. Club: Northmoor Country (Highland Park, Ill.); Monroe, Carlton (Chgo.). Avocations: art; reading; sports; travel. Office: CBH Pub Inc Box 11738 Chicago IL 60611

HAAS, ELEANOR A. (MRS. PETER RALPH HAAS), marketing and business development consultant; b. Jersey City, Mar. 12, 1932; d. Nicholas Mark and Eleanor (Cochran) Alter de Csanytelek; m. Peter Ralph Haas, Oct. 22, 1966. BA, Smith Coll., 1953; cert., N.Y. Sch. Interior Design, 1960. Exec. sec. MCA Artists, Ltd., N.Y.C., 1954-56, Young & Rubicam, Inc., N.Y.C., 1956-58, J. Walter Thompson Co., N.Y.C., 1958-59, Stanford Rsch. Inst., N.Y.C., 1959, Deafness Rsch. Found., N.Y.C., 1960, Earl Newsom & Co., N.Y.C., 1961-65; account exec. Ruder & Finn, Inc., N.Y.C., 1965-68; founder, pres. The Haas Group, Inc., N.Y.C., 1968-87, HTL Ventures, Inc., N.Y.C., 1986—; v.p., dir. HMG Planning The Howard Marlboro Group, N.Y.C., 1988—; adj. assoc. prof. dept. journalism NYU, 1980-83, lectr. Sch. Continuing Edn., 1981-83. Mem. Info. Industry Assn., Am. Mktg. Assn., NATAS, Advt. Women N.Y., Hajji Baba Club. Office: HTL Ventures Inc 475 10th Ave 12th Fl New York NY 10018-1198

HAAS, ELLEN ROBERTA, personnel officer; b. N.Y.C., Oct. 28, 1942; d. Nathan and Lillian (Minkoff) Charney; m. Bert Robert Haas, Mar. 11, 1967 (dec. Sept. 1983); children: Caroline Audrey, Paul Edward. B.A., Hunter Coll., 1965. Tchr. speech improvement N.Y. Bd. Edn., Bklyn., 1965-69; mgr. Parker Finch Assocs., N.Y.C., 1978-81; permanent div. mgr. Towne Pers., N.Y.C., 1981-82; office mgr. Harvey Marcus Pers., N.Y.C., 1982; employment cons. Payson Ruby Agy., N.Y.C., 1982-85, D.J. Hertz & Assocs.,

N.Y.C., 1985-87, dir. pers. Am. Jour. Nursing Co., 1987-88; asst. treas., pers. officer Credit Lyonnais, 1988—. Rep. Parents League, N.Y.C., Bentley Sch., N.Y.C., 1974-75, pres. parents assn., Rhodes Sch., 1976-78, 85-87; fund raising chmn. Rhodes Sch., N.Y.C., 1982-85, Baldwin Sch. co-chmn., 1987. Home: 315 E 86th St New York NY 10028 Office: Credit Lyonnais 95 Wall St New York NY 10005

HAAS, INGRID ELIZABETH, physician; b. Portland, Oreg., June 5, 1953; d. Fred F. and Anastasia Haas; m. Thomas Edward Hendricks, Oct. 16, 1976; children: Kristen, Lauren. BS, Oreg. State U., 1975; MD, U. Oreg., 1978. Physician CIGNA Healthplan, Phoenix, 1982-84, chief of staff, 1984-85; pvt. practice Scottsdale, Ariz., 1985—; chmn. ob.-gyn. dept. Scottsdale Meml. Hosp. North, 1987-88, chief of surgery, 1988-89, chmn. laser com., 1990—. Mem. adv. bd. Scottsdale Meml. Office of Community Health Edn., 1990—. Mem. Am. Bd. Ob.-Gyn., Am. Coll. Ob.-Gyn., Am. Assn. Gynecologic Laparoscopists, Phoenix Ob.-Gyn. Soc., Maricopa County Med. Soc. Republican. Lutheran. Home: 10561 E Windrose Scottsdale AZ 85259 Office: 10900 N Scottsdale Rd #303 Scottsdale AZ 85253

HAAS, YVETTE RENEE, financial rating company official; b. Sandusky, Ohio, Feb. 27, 1963; d. Duane E. Haas and Cynthia M. (McIntyre) Charville. BSBA, Ohio No. U., 1985. Asst. mgr. The Ltd., Inc., Toledo, 1985-87; office mgr. Flex-Temp Employment Svcs., Cleve., 1987; ops. asst. Dow Jones & Co., Inc., Cleve., 1987-89; ops. mgr. Dow Jones & Co., Inc., Indpls., 1989—. Mem. NAFE. Office: Dow Jones & Co Inc 9100 Keystone Crossing 135 Indianapolis IN 46240

HAASE, GRETCHEN ELIZABETH, librarian; b. Bronxville, N.Y., Nov. 5, 1951; d.Walter H. and EvelynHope (Stoll) H. BA, Bates Coll., Lewiston, Maine, 1972; MLS, Simmons Coll., Boston, 1973. Ref. librarian BBDO Inc., N.Y.C., 1973-76; library dir. Oppenheimer Wolff & Donnelly, St. Paul, 1977—. Mem. Minn. Assn. Law Libraries (named Outstanding Librarian 1988). Office: 1700 First Bank Bldg Saint Paul MN 55101

HAAS-WOLFSON, JODY MARIE, director research programs or activities; b. Chgo., May 28, 1952; d. Howard Green and Carolyn (Werbner) H.; m. Alan Ira Nusinow, 1972 (div. June 1982); children: Jennifer, Benjamin; m. Ross Howard, 1984; 1 child, Jeffrey. BA, Wash. U., St. Louis, 1974; MEd, Wash. U., 1975; MLS, U. Chgo., 1986. Educator Special Sch. Dist. of St. Louis, 1975-76; dir. rsch. Resource Tech. Assocs. Inc., Des Plaines, Ill., dir. ops., chief oper. officer, v.p., 1985—; pres. R.J.R. Assocs., Inc., Des Plaines; assoc. Resource Tech. Assn., Inc., Des Plaines, 1984—; pres. R.J.R. Assocs., Des Plaines, 1989—. Mem. ORT Sandstone, Spl. Libr. Assn., ALA, Inst. of Food Technologists, Soc. of Plastic Engrs., Am. Soc. of Quality Control, Jewish United Fund. Democrat. Jewish. Office: Resource Tech Assocs Inc 2720 River Rd Des Plaines IL 60018

HABA, MICHELE LYNN, registered nurse; b. Bridgeport, Conn., Mar. 21, 1956; d. Eugene Edward and Josephine Carol (Perkowski) H. BSN, U. Bridgeport, 1978; cert. mgmt. devel., Fairfield (Conn.) U., 1984. RN, Conn. Registered nurse operating room St. Vincent's Med. Ctr., Bridgeport, 1978—; sales rep. HI Industries, Inc., Monroe, Conn., 1986—; pvt. duty nurse Jacqueline's Svcs., Stratford, Conn., 1989—. Mem. Assn. Operating Room Nurses. Republican. Roman Catholic.

HABBESTAD, KATHRYN LOUISE, writer; b. Spokane, Wash., Sept. 29, 1949; d. Bernard Malvin and Gertrude Lucille (Westberg) H. BA, U. Wash., 1971; postgrad., Seattle U., 1981-82. Mgr. bus. Seattle Sun, 1974-75; analyst, dep. dir. Research and Planning Office, Seattle, 1975-83; account exec. Southmark Fin. Services, Seattle, 1983-84; stockbroker Interstate Securities, New Bern, N.C., 1985-86; co-founder, assoc. pub. Havelock (N.C.) News, 1986-87; owner ISIS Enterprises, Spokane, 1988—; writer Spokane; sec.-treas. Seattle Sun Pub. Co., 1974-75, Veritas Services, Seattle, 1978-83; chmn. Energy Com. Nat. Congress for Community Econ. Devel., Washington, 1979-82. Treas. Havelock Chili Festival, 1985-87. Mem. Havelock C. of C., Mensa, Nat. Assn. Female Execs. Home and Office: 10000 SE 6th Ave #A-3 Bellevue WA 98004 Office: PO Box 1795 Spokane WA 99210

HABEEB, PATRICIA ANN, small business owner; b. New Orleans, Nov. 18, 1947; d. Albert Frederick Willilam and Dorothy Malinda (Van Lue) H. BA in Sociology, La. State U., 1969. Lic. real estate agt. Sec. to dir. pub. relations Greater New Orleans Tourist & Conv. Commn., 1973-74; passenger sales and svc. agt. Delta Queen Steamboat Co., New Orleans, 1974-77; sr. conv. sales mgr. Custom Convs. (formerly Orleans Transp. Svc., Inc.), New Orleans, 1977-81; owner, pres. Convs. a la Carte, Inc., New Orleans, 1981—. Del. White House Conf. on Small Bus., 1986; bd. dirs. Internat. House, New Orleans, 1984; commr. Internat. Trade, Industry & Tourism, La., 1987; mem. Mayor's Bus. Adv. Com., New Orleans, 1983, Women's Bus. Enterprise Com., New Orleans, 1983; role model YWCA. Named Woman of Yr., New Orleans Bus. & Profl. Women, 1980, Woman Bus. Owner of Yr., Women's Bus. Owners' Assn., 1987, Hon. State Sen., La. State Senate, 1986, Hon. State Rep., La. State Ho. of Reps., 1986, Achiever Am. Coun. Career Women, 1988, La. Women's Voice by Women's Yellow Pages, 1990. Mem. Meeting Planners Internat., Soc. Incentive Travel Execs., U.S. C. of C., Hotel Mgmt. Assn., World Trade Ctr., Internat. Fdn. Women's Travel Orgns., Greater New Orleans Tourist And Conv. Commn., New Orleans and the River Region C. of C., Am. Coun. Career Women, PEO, Zeta Tau Alpha. Republican. Methodist. Home: 22 Farnham Pl Metairie LA 70005 Office: Convs a la Carte Inc 301 Camp St New Orleans LA 70130

HABEN, MARY KAY, marketing executive; b. Chgo., Apr. 12, 1956; d. Mitchell and Helen (Wrobleuski) Kretch; m. Edward Raymond Haben, Dec. 18, 1982; 1 child, Michael William. BSBA, U. Ill., 1977; MBA, U. Mich., 1979. Marktg. rsch asst. Kraft, Glenview, Ill., 1979-80, assoc. br. mgr., 1980-82, br. mgr., 1982-84, category mgr., 1984-88, v.p., 1988—. Named one of 100 Best and Brighest Women in Advtg. Advertising Age Mag., 1988, 100 Best Mgrs. in the U.S. Bus. Month Mag., 1989, 40 Women Under AO Savvy Mag., 40 Under 40 to Watch Crain's Chgo. Bus., 1990. Office: Kraft Inc Kraft Ct C3N Glenview IL 60025

HABERL, VALERIE ELIZABETH, physical education educator; b. N.Y.C., July 6, 1947; d. William Anthony and Rose Mary (Hoholecek) H. BS, So. Conn. State U., 1969, postgrad., 1979. Cert. elem. tchr., Conn. Physical edn. instr. West Haven (Conn.) Bd. Edn., 1969—; supr. West Haven Parks and Recreation, 1980—, bowling instr., 1980—. Mem. Conn. Assn. Health, Phys. Edn., Recreation and Dance. Republican. Roman Catholic. Home: 18 Linden St West Haven CT 06516-5620

HABERLE, JOAN BAKER, state official; b. Hunterdon County, N.J.; m. William Haberle. Student, Rutger U. With Gold Agy., 1960-68; owner, operator Joan Baker Agy. (real estate), 1968-77, Joan Haberle Agy., Lambertville, N.J.; dir. N.J. Real Estate Commn., 1977-82; sec. of state State of N.J., Trenton, 1990—; past chairperson N.J. License Law Ofcls.; past mem. State Counsel Govts. and State Systems Counsel; chair Exec. Commn. on Ethical Standards, 1979-82, mem., 1990—; mem. N.J. Realignment Com. Chairperson Hunterdon County Dem. Com., 1979-80; former commr. Hunterdon County Tax Bd.; active local theater groups including Bucks County (Pa.) Playhouse, New Hope, St. John's Terrill Music Circus, Lambertville; mem. Del. County Covered Bridge Commn. Mem. Nat. Assn. Realtors (Realtor of Yr. award 1989), N.J. State Assn. License Law, N.J. Hist. Soc., Lambertville C. of C. Office: State of NJ Office Sec of State CN300 Trenton NJ 08625

HABLUTZEL, MARGO LYNN, lawyer; b. St. Louis, Dec. 16, 1961; d. Philip Norman and Nancy Carol (Zimmerman) H. AB in English Lit., U. Chgo., 1983; JD, Ill. Inst. Tech./Chgo.-Kent, Coll. of Law, 1986. Bar: Ill. 1986. Computer cons. various orgns., Chgo., 1984-89; legal writing instr. U. Oreg. Sch. Law, Eugene, 1986-87; project coord. ABA/net, Chgo., 1987-89; appellate brief writer, copyright cons. Whitted & Spain, P.C., Chgo., 1988-89; hearing officer Ill. Dept. Rehab. Svcs., Chgo., 1989—; jud. clk. Ill. Appellate Ct., Chgo., 1989-90; pvt. practice, 1990—; panel atty. Chgo. Vol. Legal Svcs. Found., 1988—; copyright cons. Soc. for Creative Anachronism, Inc., Milpitas, Calif., 1987—. Contbr. articles to profl. jours. Mem. ABA (chmn. com. on delivery legal svcs. to disabled, young lawyers' div. 1989—, new products editor Law Practice Mgmt. Mag. 1990—), Ill. Bar Assn. (exec. coun. intellectual property sect. 1989—, co-chmn. computer law com. 1989—), Chgo. Bar Assn. (bd. dirs. young lawyers' sect. 1989—). Office: 135 S LaSalle St Ste 1760 Chicago IL 60603

HACK, CAROLE MAE, media generalist; b. Greensburg, Pa., Jan. 17, 1942; d. Gerald Steel and Agnes Mae (McColly) Silvis; m. J. Michael Templin, 1963 (div. 1972); 1 child, Philip Colton Templin; m. Erwin H. Foersterling, June 6, 1973 (dec. 1973); m. Rolf Heinrich Hack, Nov. 25, 1976; children: Samantha Mae, Konrad Kristof. BA, MacMurray Coll., Jacksonville, Ill., 1962; postgrad., Sangamon State U., Springfield, Ill. Art tchr. Jacksonville (Ill.) High Sch., 1962-63, Md. Park Jr. High Sch., Suitland, Md., 1963-64, Turner Jr. High Sch., Jacksonville, 1964-65; media specialist Ill. Sch. for Deaf, Jacksonville, 1968—; part-time sec. Colton Ins. Agy., Jacksonville, 1965-68; prodn. coordinator for lession guides Captioned Films/Videos for The Deaf, Modern Talking Picture Svc., St. Petersburg, Fla. Contbr. articles to profl. jours. Vol. interpreter Our Redeemer Luth. Ch., Jacksonville, 1988—. Mem. Ill. Assn. for Ednl. Communication and Tech., Women in Communication, Ill. Tchrs. of Hearing Impaired. Lutheran. Home: 715 S Main St Jacksonville IL 62650 Office: Illinois School for Deaf 125 Webster Jacksonville IL 62650

HACK, LILLIAN A., bank executive; b. New Buffalo, Mich., Dec. 31, 1935; d. Anton and Tillie (Rydecki) Kujawski; m. Alfred J. Hack, Feb. 27, 1954; 1 child, Michele R. Gold. AA, Ohlone Coll., 1985; B., St. Mary's Coll., Moraga, Calif., 1987. V.p. bus. devel. Comml. Bank of Fremont; dir. membership svc. Fremont (Calif.) C. of C.; vin. svc. officer Bank of Am., Fremont. Mem. impact fee adv. com. City of Fremont, appointee community adv. group Alameda County Transp. Plan; finalist to fill city coun. seat City of Fremont; Tri-City chmn. Daffadil Days fundraiser Am. Cancer Soc., 1990. Mem. Fremont C. of C. (trustee scholarship found. 1990, Outstanding Svc. award 1988), Rotary. Home: 4040 Ralston Common Fremont CA 94538

HACKBARTH, ELIZABETH MARGARET, insurance broker; b. Hartford, Conn., Nov. 4, 1957; d. William Henry and Evelyn Margaret (Carlson) Erwin;; m. Robert Alan Hackbarth (div.); 1 child, Kristi Anne. Diploma, Newington (Conn.) High Sch., 1975. Underwriting asst. Travelers Ins. Co., Hartford, 1980-82; acct. adminstr. Marsh & McLennan, Inc., Hartford, 1982-84; comml. underwriter Suncoast Insurors, Sarasota, Fla., 1984-86; comml. customer svc. rep. Lykes Ins., Inc., Tampa, Fla., 1986-89; account underwriter Arthur J. Gallagher & Co., Clearwater, Fla., 1989—. Mem. Tampa Assn. Ins. Women, Nat. Assn. Ins. Women. Office: Arthur J Gallagher & Co 2953 US 19 N Ste 300 Clearwater FL 34621

HACKETT, CAROL ANN HEDDEN, physician; b. Valdese, N.C., Dec. 18, 1939; d. Thomas Barnett and Zada Loray (Pope) Hedden; B.A., Duke, 1961; M.D., U. N.C., 1966; m. John Peter Hackett, July 27, 1968; children—John Hedden, Elizabeth Bentley, Susanne Rochet. Intern. Georgetown U. Hosp., Washington, 1966-67, resident, 1967-69; clinic physician DePaul Hosp., Norfolk, Va., 1969-71; chief spl. health services Arlington County Dept. Human Resources, Arlington, Va., 1971-72; gen. med. officer USPHS Hosp., Balt., 1974-75; pvt. practice family medicine, Seattle, 1975—; mem. staff, chmn. dept. family practice Overlake Hosp. Med. Ctr., 1985-86; clin. instr. U. Wash. Bd. dirs. Mercer Island (Wash.) Preschool Assn., 1977-78; coordinator 13th and 20th Ann. Inter-profl. Women's Dinner, 1978, 86; trustee Northwest Chamber Orch., 1984-85 . Mem. Wash. Med. Soc., King County Med. Soc. (chmn. com. TV violence), DAR, Bellevue C. of C., NW Women Physicians (v.p. 1978), Seattle Symphony League, Eastside Women Physicians (founder, pres.), Sigma Kappa. Episcopalian. Clubs: Wash Athletic, Lakes. Home: 4304 E Mercer Way Mercer Island WA 98040 Office: 1128 112th Ave NE Bellevue WA 98004

HACKETT, JANICE CLAIRE, insurance professional; b. Nashville, Oct. 21, 1953; d. Floyd Thomas and Ann Claire (Taylor) H. BS, Middle Tenn. State U., 1975; MS, U. Tenn., 1978. Dir. food svcs. Humana/McFarland Hosp., Lebanon, Tenn., 1976-77; sr. v.p. risk info. svcs. Corroon & Black Corp., Nashville, 1980-84; v.p., sr. cons. R&D div. Corroon & Black Corp., 1984-89, v.p. nat. accounts svcs. div., 1989—. Contbr. articles on risk mgmt. to various publs. Vol. Christmas Clearinghouse, Nashville, 1987, 88, Nature Conservancy, Nashville, 1989, Tenn. Conservation League, Nashville, 1989. Baptist. Office: Corroon & Black Corp 1500 Nashville TN 37239

HACKETT, JEAN BATES, counselor; b. Haverhill, N.H., Oct. 27, 1943; d. Guy Wilbur and Rowena Jeanette (Monette) Bates; m. Thomas Ross Hackett, Apr. 6, 1963 (div. Jan. 1984); children: Thomas Jeffrey, Timothy Ross, Todd Christopher; m. Emilio J. Rodriguez, Aug. 9, 1990. Assoc. in Bus. Sci. with honors, Champlain Coll., Burlington, Vt., 1964; BA with honors, Trinity Coll., Burlington, 1974; MS in Community Counseling, St. Michael's Coll., Winooski, Vt., 1977. Counselor Interfaith Counseling, Scottsdale, Ariz., 1980; assoc. United Campus Christian Ministry, Tempe, Ariz., 1979-82; pvt. practice counseling Scottsdale, 1982—; lectr. various workshops and retreats; speaker on food addiction Nat. Med. Conf., 1989. Speaker local and nat. TV and radio talk shows and medical conventions. Vol. Boy Scouts Am., Vt., 1973-79; mem. Phoenix Art Mus. Mem. Am. Assn. for Counseling and Devel., MADD, Nat. Disting. Svc. Registry for Counseling and Devel. Republican. Congregationalist. Clubs: P.E.O. (Scottsdale) (sec., chaplain). Office: 7119 E 1st Ave Scottsdale AZ 85251

HACKETT, LOUISE, personnel services company executive, consultant; b. Sheridan, Mont., Nov. 11, 1933; d. Paul Duncan and Freda A. (Dudley) Johnson; m. Lewis Edward Hackett, June 24, 1962; 1 child, Dell Paul. Student U. Oreg., 1959-61; BA, Calif. State U.-Sacramento, 1971. Legal sec. Samuel R. Friedman, Yreka, Calif., 1952-58, Barber & Cottrell, Eugene, Oreg., 1958-59; paralegal Elmer Sahlstrom, Eugene, 1959-62; legis. aide Calif. Legislature, Sacramento, 1962-72; owner Legal Personnel Services, Sacramento, 1973-78, corp. pres., 1979—; pres. Legalstaff, Inc., 1987—; curriculum adv. dept. bus. Am. River Coll., Sacramento, 1974-79; founder, adminstr. Pacific Coll. Legal Careers, Sacramento, 1973-84; cons. legal edn. Barclay Schs., Sacramento, 1984. Designer, pub. Sacramento/Yolo Attys. Directory, 1974—. Author operations manual and franchise training textbook; contbr. articles to profl. jours. Adv. bd. San Juan Sch. Dist., 1975-84. Mem. Sacramento Women's Network, Calif. Assn. Personnel Cons., Sacramento Council Pvt. Edn. (pres. 1976-77), Pi Omega Pi. Clubs: Sierra Sail and Trail, Soroptimist Internat. Lodge: Order of Rainbow. Avocations: skiing; sailing; sports car rallying. Office: Legal Personnel Svcs 1415 21st St Sacramento CA 95814 also: 353 Sacramento St #1520 San Francisco CA 94111 also: 2107 Landings Dr Mountain View CA 94041 also: 111 N Market St San Jose CA 95113

HACKETT, NORA ANN, patent agent; b. Abington, Pa., June 17, 1943; d. Frank and Kathryn Reed; m. Colin Edwin Hackett, Nov. 30, 1968; children: Catherine, Sarah, Rebecca. BS, Pa. State U., 1964; ScM, Brown U., 1967, PhD, 1969. Registered patent agt. U.S. Patent, Trademark and Copyright Office. Rsch. fellow biol. chemistry Harvard Med. Sch., Boston, 1968-69; rsch. fellow in medicine Miriam Hosp./Brown U., Providence, 1969-71; assoc. biologist Inhalation Toxicology Rsch. Inst., Albuquerque, 1975-79; ind. cons. Livermore, Calif., 1980-82; patent adviser office of pres. U. Calif., Berkeley, 1984-87; patent adviser Lawrence Livermore Nat. Lab., 1987—. Contbr. to refereed sci. jours., other publs. Mem. AAUW, Am. Physiol. Soc., Am. Thoracic Soc., Sigma Xi. Office: Lawrence Livermore Nat Lab Box 808 L 703 Livermore CA 94550

HACKL, MURIEL FORSTER, publishing company executive; b. N.Y.C., Feb. 11, 1924; d. Englebert Michael Forster and Johanna (Barish) Gregory Forster; m. Alphons John Hackl, Feb. 2, 1946; 1 child, John Raymond. Student, Hunter Coll., 1942-45, George Washington U., 1946-48; cert., Oxford (Eng.) U., 1975. Sec. Nat. Soft Drink Mfrs. Assn., Washington, 1946-48, C.V. Maudlin, lobbyist, Washington, 1948-50; exec. v.p., sec. Acropolis Books Ltd., Washington, 1950—. Com. mem. New Coll. Book Fair, Sarasota, Fla., 1990. Recipient White House Beautification award, 1971, Advt. Woman of Yr. award Am. Advt. Fedn., 1972. Republican. Home and Office: 415 Wood Duck Dr Bird Key Sarasota FL 34236

HACKMAN, HELEN ANNA HENRIETTE, social services administrator, retired home economist; b. New Melle, Mo., Oct. 8, 1908; d. John Henry and Lydia Eliza (Meier) Hackman; AB, Central Wesleyan Coll., Warrenton, Mo., 1929; BS, U. Mo., 1942, postgrad., 1942; postgrad. U. Wis., 1934, U. Colo., 1953, 75, U. Ariz., 1975, 77. Prin., Wright City High Sch., 1929; home econs. tchr., Cape Girardeau, Mo., 1930-42; sr. extension adviser home econs. U. Ill., Pittsfield, 1942-78; sec. Pike County Health and Social Services Coordinating Com. Dietitian, buyer Oshkosh Wis. Camp Fire Girls Camp, summers 1935, 36, 37; sec.-treas. Western Ill. 4-H Camp Assn., 1952-54; mem. Western Ill. Fair Bd. Com., Griggsville, 1946—; v.p. Tri-county Assn. for Crippled, 1960—; tech. cons. White House Conf., 1960, 70; pres. Pike County Heart Assn., 1969, organizer Family Planning Centers, Diabetic and Blood Pressure Clinics, Pike County Health Dept., 1971; sec. Illini Hosp. Aux., 1978; Bd. dirs. Pike County Mental Health. Recipient Distinguished Service award Nat. Home Demonstration Agts. Assn., 1952; Meritorious Service award Heart Assn., 1960, 61. Mem. Ill. Home Advisers Assn. (sec. 1948), Nat. Assn. Extension Home Economists (3d v.p. 1951-53, pub. relations chmn. 1951-53), Am. Home Econs. Assn. (sec. Ill. nutrition com. 1967-69), Pittsfield Hist. Soc. Epsilon Sigma Phi (chief 1962), Gamma Sigma Delta. Clubs: Pittsfield Woman's (pres. 1979, 80, 81, 82), Pike County Bus. and Profl. (pres. 1970-71). Home: 230 S Illinois St Pittsfield IL 62363 Office: Hwy 36 and 54th St E Po Box 227 Pittsfield IL 62363

HACKMAN, VICKI LOU, physician; b. Lancaster, Pa., Nov. 11, 1952; d. Harry Eugene and Marian Ruth (Miller) H.; m. James Roger Begley, June 3, 1989. BS, Lebanon Valley Coll., 1974; MD, Med. Coll. of Pa., 1978. Resident St. Margaret Hosp., Pitts., Pa., 1978-81; family practitioner group practice Norlanco Med. Assoc., Elizabethtown, Pa., 1981-84; physician Kron Med. Corp., Chapel Hill, N.C., 1984-88; hosp. based family practioner Mary Breckenridge Hosp., Hyden, Ky.; pvt. family practice Medway (Maine) Family Practice, 1990—; staff physician Regional Hosp., Millinocket, Maine, 1990—; cons. Elizabeth Hosp. and Rehab. Ctr., 1982-84, Hyden Manor Nursing Home, 1988-89. Mem. AMA, Am. Bd. Family Practice, Am. Acad. Family Practice, Ky. Med. Assn. Republican. Methodist. Home: PO Box 390 Medway ME 04460 Office: Medway Family Practice Medway ME 04460

HADAS, ELIZABETH CHAMBERLAYNE, publisher; b. Washington, May 12, 1946; d. Moses and Elizabeth (Chamberlayne) H.; m. Jeremy W. Heist, Jan. 25, 1970 (div. 1976); m. Peter Eller, Mar. 21, 1984. A.B., Radcliffe Coll., 1967; postgrad. Rutgers U., 1967-68; M.A., Washington U., St. Louis, 1970. Editor U. N.Mex. Press, Albuquerque, 1971-85; dir., 1985—. Mem. Am. Studies Assn., Western Lit. Assn. Democrat. Home: 2900 10th St NW Albuquerque NM 87107 Office: U N Mex Press 1720 Lomas NE Albuquerque NM 87131

HADDON, PHOEBE ANNIESE, law educator, consultant; b. Washington, Aug. 29, 1950; d. Wallace James and Ida (Bassette) H.; m. Thurman N. Northcross, Dec. 16, 1972 (div. Dec. 1983); m. Frank M. McClellan, Dec. 31, 1985. BA with honors, Smith Coll., 1972; JD cum laude, Duquesne U., 1977; LLM, Yale U., 1985. Bar: Pa. 1977, U.S. Dist. Ct. (we dist.) Pa. 1977, D.C. 1979, U.S. Ct. Appeals (3d cir.) 1979, U.S. Dist. Ct. (ea. dist.) Pa. 1983. Field examiner Nat. Labor Rels. Bd., Cin. and Pitts., 1972-74; law clk. to judge U.S. Ct. Appeals (3d cir.), Pitts., 1977-79; assoc. Wilmer, Cutler & Pickering, Washington, 1979-81; asst. prof. law Temple U., Phila., 1981-84, assoc. prof. law, 1984—; pres. Phila. Mortgage Assistance Corp., 1987—; bd. dirs. Del. Valley Community Reinvestment Fund; hearing examiner Water Commn., Phila., 1985; cons. Redevel. Authority, City of Phila., 1985—, chmn. mortgage com., 1987-88, dep. exec. dir., 1989. Editor in chief Duquesne Law Rev., 1977; editor Pitts. Legal Jour., 1978-79. Mem. Big Bros.-Big Sisters of Phila., 1984—; bd. dirs. YMCA, Germantown, 1988—, Delaware Valley Chpt. March of Dimes, 1989—. Mem. ABA, Pa. Bar Assn., Phila. Bar Assn., Soc. Am. Law Tchrs. (bd. govs. 1985-89), Am. Law Inst. (ABA com. on continuing profl. edn. 1989-92), Barristers Assn., Nat. Bar Assn. (women lawyers div.), Smith Coll. Alumnae Assn. (bd. dirs. 1986-89, bd. counselors 1973-88), 21st Century League of Phila., Am. Assn. U. Profs. (bd. dirs. 1987—), Girlfriends, Inc. (co-pres. 1985—), Phila. Club. Office: Temple Law Sch 1719 N Broad St Philadelphia PA 19122

HADFIELD, DEBRA S., management, writer; b. Ogden, Utah, June 14, 1953; d. Robert W. and Lucy May (Smith) Spong; m. Eugene R. Hadfield, dec. 21, 1972; Children: Varden, Nathan, Neldon, Tamra, Trisa, Tawna. AA, Brigham Young U., 1979, BA in Communications, 1984. Hostess Let's Get Smart programme KDOT Radio, Provo, Utah, 1982; dir. Latter-day Girls Sing, Highland, Utah, 1987-89, Latter-day Presch., Highland, 1987—; pres. Personal Success Enterprises, Highland, 1989; v.p. Techcrete Co., 1989—; speaker for various bus. and community groups, sales trainer, Living Scriptures, Ogden, Utah. Author: book, ABC's for Grade Success, 1980; magazine articles, 1970—; newspaper articles, 1970—; weekly columnist The Citizen, Am. Fork, Utah 1988-89. Leader, Boy Scouts Am. 1983-90, newsletter editor, Am. Mothers, Inc., Utah, 1984-87 (dist. chmn.). Named Young Honor Mother of Utah, Am. Mothers, 1987, Mary Egging Mem. Award, Am. Mothers, 1987, Young Alumni Achievement Award, Brigham Young U. (first female recipient) 1984, Magna Cum Laude, Brigham Young U., 1984. Republican. Mormon. Home and Office: 9822 N 5300 W Highland UT 84003

HADLEY, CANDICE ANN, advertising executive; b. Janesville, Wis., Nov. 22, 1957; d. Edward Horton Hadley and Nancy Jane (Cox) Mulford; m. Robert Steven Johnson, June 18, 1988. BS, No. Ill. U., 1979. Writer DeKalb (Ill.) Daily Chronicle, 1978-79; editorial asst., assoc. editor Appaloosa News, Moscow, Idaho, 1980-81; co-editor Moscow Mag., 1981-82; Midwest editor Back Stage, Chgo., 1982-87; pres. Hadley Enterprises, Chgo., 1984—. Bd. dirs. U.S. Festivals Assn., 1984—; mem. adv. bd. Chgo. Coalition, 1988-89. Mem. Women in Film (founding bd. dirs. 1984-88), Chgo. Film and Video Coun. (v.p. 1982-88), Advt. Photographers Am. Democrat. Lutheran. Office: 1608 N Milwaukee Ste 1108 Chicago IL 60647

HADLEY, CAROLYN BETH, physician, educator; b. Dallas, Nov. 22, 1945; d. Charles Franklin and Sadie Beth (Humphreys) Hadley; m. Richard G. Suchan, Dec. 28, 1985; children; Richard C., Stephen G. BA with honors in Microbiology, U. Kans., 1968; MS in Clin. Microbiology, Columbia U. Coll. Physicians and Surgeons, 1974; MD, U. Pa., 1981. Diplomate Am. Coll. Med. Examiners., Am. Bd. Ob-Gyn. Lab technologist St. Joseph Mercy Hosp., Ann Arbor, Mich., 1968-70; sr. technologist, diagnostic microbiology service Columbia Presbyn. Med. Ctr., N.Y.C., 1970-73, sr. asst. supr., 1973-75; asst. microbiologist Hosp. of U. Pa., Phila., 1975-77, resident in ob-gyn, 1981-85, fellow in maternal fetal medicine, 1985-87; teaching asst. in microbiology U. Kans., 1968; teaching fellow microbiology U. Mich. Med. Sch., 1969; asst. prof. Med. Coll. Pa., 1987—. Recipient Undergrad. Research award U. Kans., 1967; Phillip Williams prize in obstetrics, 1984; S. Leon Israel prize in obstetrics, 1985; Henrietta Ottinger/Huston MacFarlane scholar Med. Coll. Pa., 1978—. Fellow Am. Coll. Ob-Gyn (jr. fellow); mem. AMA, Am. Soc. Microbiology (specialist in microbiology), Am. Soc. Clin. Pathologists (specialist microbiologist), Phila. Perinatal Soc., Soc. for Perinatal Obstetricians (assoc.), DAR, U. Kans. Alumni Assn., Phila. Obstet. Soc., Phi Beta Kappa. Office: Med Coll Pa Dept Ob-Gyn 3300 Henry Ave Philadelphia PA 19129

HADLEY, CORNELIA Q. (CONNIE HADLEY), insurance agent; b. Dermott, Ark., Mar. 29, 1930; d. Benjamin James and Lillie Rosetta (Herron) Franklin; m. Robert Lawrence Hadley Sr., Sept. 3, 1950; children: Vanessa C. Hadley Cobbins, Robert L. Jr., Walter D. Student, U. Mo., Kansas City, 1967-69. Button maker, stone setter Mendels Garment Mfr., Kansas City, Mo., 1956-61; cashier, asst. mgr. Famco Resturant, Kansas City, 1961-62; bookkeeper Bonner Springs (Kans.) Sanitation Dept., 1962-63; telephone receptionist Leaders Clothing Co., Kansas City, Kans., 1963-66; powder press supr. Army Ammunition Plant, Desoto, Kans., 1966-67; exec. dir. Econ. Opportunity Found., Kansas City, 1967-84; program coordinator, adminstrv. asst. to city mgr. City of Bonner Springs, 1975-77; ins. agt. Farmers Ins. Group of Cos., L.A., 1984—; cons. Nat. Coun. on Aging, Denver, 1972, Kansas City 1973, Des Moines, Iowa, 1974. Fellow Life Underwriters Tng. Coun. Mem. Nat. Assn. Life Underwriters, Kans. City C. of C., Bonner Springs Bus. and Profl. Women (chair legis. com. 1987), Nat. Assn. Female Execs. Republican. Club: Equal Rights Investors Investment Club. Home: 1530 S 94 St Kansas City KS 66111 Office: Farmers Ins 8245 Neiman Rd Ste 114 Lenexa KS 66214

HADLEY, JANE BYINGTON, psychotherapist; b. N.Y.C., Apr. 24, 1929; d. David and Ruth (Johnson) Millar; m. Arthur Twining Hadley, Feb. 24, 1979; children: Elisabeth Danish, Caroline Thies. BA, U. Va., 1951; MA, Columbia U., 1967. Intern Queens Coll., 1969; pvt. practice psychotherapy N.Y.C., 1971—. Bd. dirs. Planned Parenthood of N.Y. Mem. Am. Psychol. Assn., Cosmopolitan Club, Doubles Club, Edgarton Yacht Club. Democrat. Episcopalian.

HADLEY, LEILA ELIOTT-BURTON (MRS. HENRY LUCE, III), author; b. N.Y.C., Sept. 22, 1925; d. Frank Vincent and Beatrice Boswell (Eliott) Burton; m. Arthur T. Hadley, II, Mar. 2, 1944 (div. Aug. 1946); 1 child, Arthur T. III; m. Yvor H. Smitter, Jan. 24, 1953 (div. Oct. 1969); children: Victoria C. Van D. Smitter Barlow, Matthew Smitter Eliott, Caroline Allison F.S. Nicholson; m. William C. Musham, May 1976 (div. July 1979); m. Henry Luce III, Jan. 1990. Student, U. Witwatersrand, Johannesburg, S. Africa, 1954-55. Author: Give Me the World, 1958, How to Travel with Children in Europe, 1963, Manners for Children, 1967, Fielding's Guide to Traveling with Children in Europe, 1972, rev., 1974, 84, Traveling with Children in the U.S.A., 1974, Tibet-20 Years After the Chinese Takeover, 1979, (with Theodore B. Van Itallie) The Best Spas: Where to Go for Weight Loss, Fitness Programs and Pure Pleasure in the U.S. and Around the World, 1988, rev., 1989; assoc. editor: Diplomat mag., N.Y.C., 1964-65, Saturday Evening Post, N.Y.C., 1965-67; editorial cons. TWYCH, N.Y.C., 1985-87; book reviewer Palm Beach Life, Fla., 1967-72; contbg. editor Spa Vacations mag., 1989—; contbr. articles to various newspapers, mags. Mem. Soc. Woman Geographers (exec. council 1984—), Authors Guild, Nat. Writers Union, Nat. Press Club, Explorers Club. Republican. Presbyterian. Home: 4 Sutton Pl New York NY 10022 Office: Sterling Lord Literistic One Madison Ave New York NY 10010

HADOW, KATHARINE LUNSFORD, sales administrator; b. N.Y.C., Mar. 11, 1963; d. Kenneth Macdonald Hadow and Elizabeth (Shvetzoff) Blake; m. Andrew Macbeth Shaw, June 30, 1990. BA in Econs., Polit. Sci., Yale U., 1986. Asst. to v.p. strategic planning Viking Penguin Inc., N.Y.C., 1986-88; sales exec. Francosteel, N.Y.C., 1988—. Harry Havemeyer scholar Yale U., 1981. Office: Francosteel 345 Hudson St New York NY 10014

HAEFLINGER, SHARON KAY, educator, writer; b. Dickinson, N.D., June 13, 1949; d. Paul and Perpetua Jean (Wandler) Jahner; m. Charles Stephen Haeflinger, Dec. 14, 1974. BA in Social Work, U. N.D., 1971; MS in Counseling and Guidance, Cen. Mo. State U., 1975. Cert. tchr., Ill., guidance and counseling, Ill. Recreation specialist Am. Nat. Red Cross, Korea, 1971-72; social worker Am. Nat. Red Cross, Ft. Leonard Wood, Mo., 1972-74; tchr. St. Angela Sch., Chgo., 1976-79; project editor The Econ. Co. div. McGraw-Hill, Glendale, Calif., 1981-86; freelance writer Chino Hills, Calif., 1986—; vocat. exploration instr. Nat. Football League, Thousand Oaks, Calif., 1980; cons. Concept Spelling Inc., Newport Beach, Calif., 1981. Author: (book) Medical Care, 1985; contbr. articles to pubs. Urgent action writer Amnesty Internat., 1983—; religion tchr. St. Paul the Apostle Parish, Chino Hills, 1987. Mem. Soc. of Children's Book Writers, Ind. Writers of So. Calif., Nat. Assn. for Femal Execs., So. Calif. Booksellers Assn., Am. Overseas Assn. Roman Catholic. Club: Married Couples (co-pres. 1987). Home: 15683 Tern St Chino Hills CA 91709

HAEGER, PHYLLIS MARIANNA, association management company executive; b. Chgo., May 20, 1928; d. Milton O. and Ethel M. H. B.A., Lawrence U., 1950; M.A., Northwestern U., 1952. Midwest editor TIDE mag., 1952-55; exec. v.p. Smith, Bucklin & Assos., Inc., Chgo., 1955-78; pres. P.M. Haeger & Assos., Inc., Chgo., 1978—. Mem. Am. Soc. Assn. Execs., Chgo. Soc. Assn. Execs., Inst. Assn. Mgmt. Cos., Nat. Assn. Women Bus. Owners, Com. of 200, Chgo. Network, Fin. Women Internat. (exec. v.p.).

HAEMMERLIE, FRANCES MONTGOMERY, psychology educator; b. Gainsville, Fla., Feb. 2, 1948; d. Henry John and Ruth Elizabeth (Collins) H.; Robert L. Montgomery, June 16, 1979. BA, U. Fla., 1972; MS, Fla. State U., 1976, PhD, 1978. Assoc. prof. U. Mo., Rolla, 1978—. Contbr. articles to profl. jours, chpts. to books. Sec. Rolla Jr. High Parent-Student-Tchr. Assn., 1989-90. Recipient teaching awards U. Mo., 1980-85, 87-90, Amoco teaching award, 1981-82, faculty excellence award, 1986-89, Reade Beard faculty excellence award 1989-90. Mem. Am. Psychol. Assn. (chmn. div. 12 sect. IV 1990—), Southwestern Psychol. Assn. (placement chmn. 1986, program chmn. 1988-89), Psi Chi (outstanding adv. award 1980, 86, profl. svc. award 1983). Home: Rte 4 Box 322 Rolla MO 65401 Office: U Mo Dept Psychology 110 HSS Bldg Rolla MO 65401

HAESSLY, JACQUELINE, peace education specialist, writer, family life education specialist, consultant; b. Milw., Feb. 18, 1937; d. Jerome Francis and Janice (Ball) Haessly; m. Daniel G. DiDomizio, July 8, 1972; children: Michael, Ernest, Randolph, Francis, Kristyn. LPN, Sacred Heart Sch. Practical Nursing, Milw., 1958; student Alverno Coll., 1958-67; BS in Edn. U. Wis., 1971, MS in Edn., 1976. Staff nurse various local hosps., Milw., 1959-72; founder, dir. Milw. Peace Edn. Resource Ctr., 1974—; founder, pres. Peacemaking Assocs., Milw., 1983—, Creative Playtime, Milw., 1985—; cons., facilitator bus. and profl. orgns., 1974—; organizer prodn. Peace Child, Milw., 1985; cons. U. Wis., Milw., 1983—. Author: Peacemaking: Family Activities for Justice and Peace, 1980. Editor: Peacemaking for Children mag., 1983—, publs. (books) Peacemaking: Family Activities for Justice and Peace, 1980, Peacemaking Activity Book for Children, 1984, Gentle Gifts, 1985, What Shall We Teach OUr Children?, 1986, Learning To Live Together, 1989. Contbr. numerous articles to profl. publs. Bd. dirs. Milw. Mental Health Agy., 1975-78; coordinator food policy conf. The Peace Ctr., Milw., 1975-77; mem. peace studies task force Milw. Pub. Schs., 1983—; chmn. peace studies com. Parent Tchr. Council, Milw., 1983-86, 85-86. Mem. Fellowship of Reconciliation (mem. bd., chmn. com. 1984-85), Nat. Speakers Assn., Wis. Speakers Assn., Parenting for Peace and Justice (mem. bd. 1981-84), Wis. Writer's Council, Nat. Writer's Club, Nat. Profl. Speakers Assn., Wis. Profl. Speakers Assn. Roman Catholic. Avocations: swimming, hiking, biking, knitting, reading. Office: Peacemaking Assocs 2437 N Grant Blvd Milwaukee WI 53210

HAFFNER, JEANNINE MARIE, business owner; b. Oak Lawn, Ill., Apr. 24, 1966; d. John Paul and Gloria Jean (Griffin) H. Grad., Elizabeth Anthony Sch. Tech., 1987. Nail technician Lenny & Friends, Chgo., 1988-90; jewelry designer Maxine, Chgo., 1989—; nail technician Mobile Nails by Jeannine, Chgo., 1990—. Mem. Animal Rights Groups, Chgo., 1988-90, People for the Ethical Treatment of Animals, Chgo., 1988-90. State of Ill. scholar, 1990. Mem. Women in Communications, iNc. Lutheran. Home and Office: 2544 N Hamlin #2R Chicago IL 60647

HAFFNER, MARLENE ELISABETH, internist, health care administrator; b. Cumberland, Md., Mar. 22, 1941. Student Western Res. U., 1958-61; M.D., George Washington U., 1965. Intern, George Washington U. Hosp., Washington, 1965-66; fellow in dermatology Columbia-Presbyn. Med. Ctr., N.Y.C., 1966-67; resident in internal medicine St. Luke's Hosp., N.Y.C., 1967-69; fellow in hematology. Albert Einstein Coll. Medicine, Bronx, 1969-71, asst. clin. prof. medicine, 1971-73; vis. asst. attending Bronx Mcpl. Hosp. Ctr. (N.Y.), 1969-71; clin. assoc. in family, community and emergency medicine U. N.Mex. Sch. Medicine, Albuquerque, 1974-83, clin. assoc. dept. medicine, 1974-83; acting clin. dir. Gallup Indian Med. Ctr. (N.Mex.), 1973-74, chief adult outpatient dept., 1971-74, chief dept. internal medicine, 1971-74; dir. Navajo Area Indian Health Service, Indian Health Service, Window Rock, Ariz., 1974-81; assoc. dir. for health affairs Bur. Med. Devices, FDA, Rockville, 1981-82, dir. Office Health Affairs, Ctr. for Devices and Radiol. Health, 1982-87; dir. office of orphan products devel. FDA, 1987—; asst. clin. prof. dept. medicine Uniformed Services Univ. of Health Scis., Bethesda, Md.; asst. surg. gen., rear admiral USPHS. Home and Office: Orphan Products Devel FDA 5600 Fishers Lane (HF-35) Rockville MD 20852

HAFFORD, PATRICIA ANN, electronic company executive; b. Springfield, Mass., Feb. 11, 1947; d. Arthur Charles and Sophie Louise (Piesyk) Rood; m. Jerry William Hafford, May 1, 1971; children: Mark Dutton, Lauren Melynn. BA in Liberal Arts and Scis., U. Conn., 1968. Elem. tchr. East Granby (Conn.) Schs., 1968-69; presch. tchr. RCA-Discovery Ctr., East Hartford, Conn., 1969-70; tng. specialist Travelers Ins. Co., Hartford, 1970-73; scriptwriter ednl. TV Ednl. Satellite Tech. Demonstration Fedn. of Rocky Mt. States, Denver, 1973; tech. writer, computer documentation writer Hewlett-Packard Corp., Ft. Collins, Colo., 1973-77, documentation mgr., 1977-82, market devel. engr., 1982-83, product mgr., 1983—. Editor: Writing and Designing Operator Manuals. Mem. Soc. for Tech. Communication (v.p. Rocky Mountain chpt. 1979-81, chmn. Art and Writing Competition 1980-81, dir.-sponsor on bd. dirs. Region 8 Washington 1981-84). Republican. Methodist. Office: Hewlett-Packard 3404 E Harmony Rd Fort Collins CO 80525

HAFT, MARILYN GEISLER, lawyer; b. N.Y.C, Aug. 1, 1943; d. Frank and Sarah (Engelsohn) Geisler; m. Kenneth W. Bowser; 1 child, Samantha Danielle. BA, Bklyn. Coll., 1965; JD, NYU, 1968. Bar: N.Y. 1969, U.S. Supreme Ct. 1973, D.C. 1978. Staff counsel ACLU Nat. Office, N.Y.C., 1970-76; dep. counsel govt. ops. com. U.S. Congress, Washington, 1976-77; assoc. dir. office of pub. liaison The White House, Washington, 1977-78, dep. counsel V.P. Walter Mondale, 1978-79; N.Y. Primary campaign dir. Re-election for Carter/Mondale, N.Y.C., 1979-80; U.S. rep. Mission to the U.N., N.Y.C., 1980-81; sole practice entertainment law N.Y.C., 1981-89; of counsel Summit, Rovins & Feldesman, Esqs., N.Y.C., 1989-90; ptnr. Fischbein & Badillo, N.Y.C., 1990—; film producer Barking Dog Prodns., N.Y.C., 1987—. Author: Time Without Work, 1984; author, editor: Prisoner's Rights Sourcebook, 1972, Rights of Gay People, 1973; producer (film) In a Shallow Grave, 1988, Preston Sturges: The Rise and Fall of an American Dreamer, 1989. Democrat. Jewish. Home: 111 E 10th St New York NY 10003 Office: Fischbein & Badillo Esqs 909 Third Ave New York NY 10022

HAGAN, EPSIE LEWIS, health science facility administrator; b. Sylacauga, Ala., Aug. 11, 1927; d. Julius Lee and Lela Herbert (Hickman) Morris; m. Virgil William Hagan, Oct. 8, 1946; children: Virgil William III, Kitty, Jill, Pam, Scott Morris. Grad., High Sch. Adminstrv. asst. Regional Alcoholism Coun., Sylacauga, Ala., 1976-79, dir., 1979-81; programs asst. addictive disease program Bapt. Med. Ctr., Montgomery, Ala., 1981-83, dir. addictive disease program, 1983; dir. addictive disease program Citizens Hosp., Talladega, Ala., 1984; dir. Self Discovery Elmore (Ala.) County Hosp., 1984—. Chmn, Advisory council, Caradale House, Sylacauga, Ala., 1983-84. Mem. Ala. Assn. of Addictions Counselor (past pres. 1988), Natl. Assn. of Alcoholism and Drug Abuse Counselors (award comm. 1985--), Al. Counselor Cert. Board (sec. 1984--). Methodist. Home: Rte 2 Box 152 Eclectic Lake AL 36024 Office: Self Discovery Inc 1201 Co St Wetumpka AL 36092

HAGAN, KATHERINE ELLEN, academic administrator; b. Athens, Ga., May 18, 1959; d. Forrest Lee and Marthella (Gordon) H. AB, Sweet Briar Coll., 1981; M.Ed., U. Va., 1983. Compensatory aide Commerce (Ga.) City Schs., Commerce, Ga., 1983-84; residence hall dir. Ga. So. Coll., Statesboro, 1984-86; asst. dir. admissions U. S.C. Beaufort, Hilton Head, 1986-88, counselor, 1986—, dir. admissions, 1988—. Mem., Leadership Hilton Head, 1987-88; v.p., Profl. Women Hilton Head,. Mem. Nat. Assn. Women Deans, AAUW (publicity chmn. 1987—), S.C. Coll. Pers. Assn., Ga. Coll. Pers. Assn., Zonta. Methodist. Home: 307 Forest Beach Villas Hilton Head SC 29928 Office: U SC 102 Executive Ctr Hilton Head SC 29928

HAGBERG, VIOLA WILGUS, lawyer; b. Salisbury, Md., July 3, 1952; d. William E. and Jean Shelton (Barlow) Wilgus; m. Chris Eric Hagberg, Feb. 19, 1978. BA, Furman U., Greenville, S.C., 1974; JD, U. S.C., 1978, U. Tulsa, 1978; DOD Army Logistics Sch. honor grad. basic mgmt. def. acquisition, def. small purchase, advanced fed. acquisition regulation, Fort Lee, Va., 1981-82. Bar: Okla. 1978, Va. 1979, U.S. Ct. Appeals (4th cir.). With Lawyers Com. for Civil Rights, Washington, 1979; pub. utility specialist Fed. Energy Regulatory Commn., Washington, 1979-80; contract specialist U.S. Army, C.E., Ft. Shafter, Hawaii, 1980-81; contract officer/supervisory contract specialist Tripler Army Med. Ctr., Hawaii 1981-83; supervisory procurement analyst and chief policy sect. Procurement Div. USCG, Washington, 1983; contract officer and chief Avionics Engring Br. sect. engring., 1984; procurement analyst office of sec. Dept. Transp., 1984-85; contracting officer Naval Regional Contracting Ctr., Long Beach, Calif., 1985-87; chief acquisition rev. and policy, Hdqrs. Def. Mapping Agy., Washington. Mem. ABA (law student div. liaison 1977-78), Nat. Contract Mgmt. Assn., Va. State Bar Assn., Okla. Bar Assn., Phi Alpha Delta, Kappa Delta Epsilon. Home: 9810 Meadow Valley Dr Vienna VA 22181 Office: Def Mapping Agy (CARSO) 8613 Lee Hwy Fairfax VA 22031-2137

HAGEDORN, DOROTHY LOUISE, librarian; b. McKeesport, Pa., Sept. 4, 1929; d. Emil and Catherine (Middlemiss) H. B.A., Seton Hill Coll., 1950; M.S., Fordham U., 1952, Columbia U., 1957. Tech. info specialist Lawrence Radiation Lab., Berkeley, Calif., 1961-64; libr. New Orleans Pub. Libr., 1964-71, Tulane U., New Orleans, 1971—. Mem. ALA, La. Library Assn. Office: Tulane U Howard-Tilton Meml Libr 7001 Freret St New Orleans LA 70118

HAGEMANN, DOLORES ANN, accounts receivable clerk; b. Parkston, S.D., June 5, 1935; d. Jacob George and Margaret Marie (Mayer) Schumacher; m. Norbert Bernard Hagemann, June 8, 1954; children: Douglas, Pamela, Susan Ferden. AS, Des Moines Community Coll., 1984. Cert. notary pub., Iowa. Sales rep. Stanley Home Products, Westfield, Mass., 1970-76; owner, mgr. Hagemann Gen. Store, Lidderdale, Iowa, 1974-77; motor rt. carrier Des Moines Register, 1977-82; accounts receivable clk. City Water Dept., Lidderdale, 1981—; owner, designer Dolores' Silk Flower Shop, Lidderdale, 1986—; bd. dirs. Lidderdale Apartments, Inc. Author: (with other) The Official Carroll County Democrat Cookbook, 1984. Com. person Carroll County Dems., 1970—, sec., 1984-86, 2d vice chair, 1989-90, 1st vice chair, 1990—, chmn. county chairs and vice chairs assn. 5th Congl. dist. Iowa 1990—); counselor Carroll Help Line, 1982-87. Mem. Am. Assn. Ret. Persons, Holy Family Parish Guild (chair person 1976), Des Moines Community Coll. Alumni, Stewart Meml. Community Hosp. Aux. Democrat. Roman Catholic. Home: PO Box 68 Lidderdale IA 51452

HAGEN, CELESTE LYNNE, nursing educator; b. Loma Linda, Calif., May 11, 1956; d. Weldon James and Marlene Dean (Varner) H.; m. Mark Beckner, Mar. 17, 1979 (div. 1984). ASN, Pacific Union Coll., 1977; BSN, Loma Linda U., 1979; MSN, Calif. State U., L.A., 1986. RN, Calif. Surg. nurse Loma Linda Community Hosp., 1977-79; charge nurse newborn nursery White Meml. Med. Ctr., L.A., 1981-86; perinatal per diem nurse Verdigo Hills Hosp., Glendale, Calif., 1986-88; asst. prof. Pacific Union Coll., Glendale, Calif., 1982-84, 85-88; perinatal nurse U. Calif. at Davis Med. Ctr., Sacramento, Calif., 1989-90, perinatal and neo-natal nurse outreach educator, 1990—; presenter Western Inst. of Nursing Conf., Tempe, Ariz., 1987, UCLA Ann. Grad. Students Rsch. Day, 1988. Mem. Nat. Assn. Ob.-Gyn. and Neo-natal Nurses, Calif. State Nursing Honor Soc. (pres. steering com. L.A. chpt. 1988). Adventist. Office: U Calif Davis Med Ctr 2315 Stockton Blvd Sacramento CA

HAGEN, KATHRYN EILEEN, hospital consultant, free lance writer; b. Mt. Clemens, Mich., Aug. 13, 1952; d. Harold Eugene and Mary Lou (Schrade) Nigh; m. Thomas Lynn Hagen, May 7, 1983. AA in Nursing Tech., Purdue U., 1974, BA in Psychology, 1976, postgrad., 1979-80; BA in Acctg., Regents Colls., Albany, N.Y., 1990. RN, Ind. Outpatient therapist Mental Health Ctr., Ft. Wayne, Ind., 1977-78, dir. rsch. and evaluation, 1978-79; teaching asst. Purdue U., West Lafayette, Ind., 1979-80; intensive care, coronary care nurse Caylor-Nickel Hosp., Bluffton, Ind., 1981-82, St. Joseph's Hosp., Ft. Wayne, 1982-85; allergy nurse Office John F. O'Brian, M.D., Ft. Wayne, 1984-85; intensive care staff nurse Luth. Hosp. Ind., Inc., Ft. Wayne, 1985-86, quality assurance specialist, 1986-89; cons. in field. Lay missionary Our Lady of Victory Missionary Sisters, Denver, 1980-81; sr. lit. tutor Laubach Lit. Found., Ft. Wayne, 1985-87; bd. dirs. Arthritis Found., Ft. Wayne and Kokomo, 1988—; mem. parish coun. St. Patrick's Ch., 1986-87; vol. Friends of Libr., Ft. Wayne, 1984—; mem. Mental Health Assn., 1989—. Mem. Am. Soc. Quality Control, Ind. Assn. Quality Assurance Profls. Republican. Roman Catholic. Home and Office: 1901 S Park Rd Apt F115 Kokomo IN 46902

HAGEN, SUSAN HIRT, conflict management consultant; b. Erie, Pa., June 30, 1935; d. Henry Orth and Ruth Louise (Peterson) Hirt; m. Thomas Bailey Hagen, May 31, 1957; children: Jonathan, Sarah. BA, Wittenberg U., 1957; MS, Gannon U., 1980. Conflict mgmt. cons. Ctr. for the Practice of Conflict Mgmt., Miami, Fla., 1972—; bd. dirs. Erie Indemnity Co., Erie Family Life Ins. Co., Erie Ins. Co. Bd. dirs. Pa. Humanities Coun., Phila., 1987—, United Way of Pa., Harrisburg, 1988—, Single Parent Task Force, Erie, 1984—, Erie County Dept. Human Svcs., 1981-87, Hospitality House for Women, Erie, 1981-83, others: trustee Wittenberg U., Springfield, Ohio, 1987—, Edinboro (Pa.) U., 1988—, Erie Community Found., 1979-89; fundraiser Chautauqua (N.Y.) Found., 1987—, Warner Theater Restoration Com., Erie, 1985; mem. numerous other civic projects/orgns. Named Woman of Yr., Zonta Club of Erie, 1975, Hall of Excellence, Ohio Found. Ind. Colls., 1988, First Woman Pres., United Way; recipient Alexis de Toqueville award United Way, 1990. Home and Office: 5727 Grubb Rd Erie PA 16506

HAGEN, UTA THYRA, actress; b. Göttingen, Germany, June 12, 1919; came to U.S., 1926; d. Oskar F. L. and Thyra A. (Leisner) H.; m. Herbert Berghof, Jan. 25, 1957; 1 child, Leticia. DFA (hon.), Smith Coll., 1978; LHD (hon.), De Paul U., 1981, Wooster Coll., 1982; DFA (hon.). Tchr. acting Herbert Berghof Studio, N.Y.C., 1947—. Appeared as Ophelia, Dennis, Mass., 1937, as Nina in Sea Gull, N.Y.C., 1938, Key Largo, 1939, Vicki, 1942, Othello, 1943-45, Masterbuilder, 1947, Faust, 1947, Angel Street, 1948, Street Car Named Desire, 1948, 50, Country Girl, 1950, G.B. Shaw's Saint Joan, 1951-52, Tovarich, City Center, 1952, In Any Language, 1952, The Deep Blue Sea, 1953, The Magic and the Loss, 1954, The Island of Goats, 1955, A Month in the Country, 1956, Good Woman of Setzuan, 1957, Who's Afraid of Virginia Woolf, 1962-64, The Cherry Orchard, 1968, Charlotte, 1980; also univ. tour 1981-82, Mrs. Warren's Profession, Roundabout Theatre, N.Y.C., 1985—, You Never Can Tell, Circle in the Square, 1986—; (films) The Other, 1972, The Boys from Brazil, 1978, Reversal of Fortunes, 1990, Havana, 1990; TV appearances include A Month in the Country, 1956, Out of Dust, 1959; appeared in numerous TV spls. and guest star appearances including Lou Grant, 1982, A Doctor's Story, 1984; author: Respect for Acting, 1973, Love for Cooking, 1976, Sources, a Memoire, 1983. Recipient Antoinette Perry award, 1951, 63; N.Y. Drama Critics award, 1951, 63; Donaldson award best actress, 1951; London Critics award for best actress, 1963-64 season; Outer Circle award; named to Theatre Hall of Fame, 1981; Mayor's Liberty Medal, 1986. Address: Herbert Berghof Studio 120 Bank St New York NY 10014

HAGER, ELIZABETH SEARS, state legislator; b. Washington, Oct. 31, 1944; d. Hess Thatcher and Elizabeth Grace (Harper) Sears; m. Dennis Sterling Hager, Sept. 3, 1966; children: Annie Elizabeth, Lucie Caroline. BA, Wellesley Coll., 1966; MPA, U. N.H., 1979. Prin. Philbrook Ctr., Concord, N.H., 1970-71; rep. N.H. Gen. Ct., Concord, 1973-76, 85—; del. N.H. Constitutional Conv., Concord, 1974, 84; campaign coord. Anderson for Pres. Rep. Primary, N.H., 1980; councilor Concord City Coun., 1982—; mayor Concord City, 1988-90; bd. dirs. Chubb Investment Funds, Concord, 1987—. Commr. N.H. Commn. on the Status of Women; pres. Greater Concord United Way, 1980-81; campaign chair United Way of Merrimack County, Concord, 1986. Republican. Episcopalian. Home: 5 Auburn St Concord NH 03301 Office: Five Auburn St Concord NH 03301

HAGER, KATHY ELAINE, financial planner; b. Haskell, Tex., Sept. 17, 1951; d. Walter Richard Jr. and Joyce A. (Grand) H. BBA, Tex. Tech. U., 1972; postgrad., West Tex. State U., 1981-82, Amarillo Coll., 1982. CPA, Tex. Staff acct. Edwin E. Merriman & Co. CPAs, Lubbock, Tex., 1973-77; asst. controller F-S-W Cattle Co., Wildorado, Tex., 1977-79; tax acct. Santa Fe Energy Co., Houston, 1980-81, supr. tax compliance, 1981-86, sr. fin. analyst, 1986-89, mgr. planning, 1990—. Mem. AICPA, Nat. Assn. Accts. (pres. Amarillo chpt. 1984-85, pres.-elect Tex. council 1988-89, pres. 1989—90 nat. bd. dirs. 1987-89, nat. com. 1985-87, 89—), Tex. Soc. CPAs. Republican. Methodist. Office: Santa Fe Energy Co 1616 S Voss Ste 700 Houston TX 77057

HAGERTY, BETTY LEE, corporate affairs executive; b. Paterson, N.J.; d. John J. and Bess (Taylor) Benkendorf; divorced; 2 children. BS, Rutgers U. Youth adminstr. Rutgers Extension Service, New Brunswick, N.J., 1959-62; assoc. dir. YWCA, New Brunswick, 1969-78; exec. v.p. Nat. Soc. to Prevent Blindness, New Brunswick, 1978-84, also bd. dirs., 1984—; v.p. pub. affairs Mut. Benefit Life Ins. Co., Newark, 1984-89; v.p. corp. affairs Mut. Benefit Life Ins. Co. Inc., Newark, 1989—. Office: Mut Benefit Life Ins Co 520 Broad St Newark NJ 07101

HAGERTY, POLLY MARTIEL, banker; b. Joliet, Ill., Aug. 17, 1946; d. George Albert and Gene Alice (Roush) Jerabek; m. Theodore John Hagerty, Feb. 12, 1972. BS in Elem. Edn., Midland Luth. Coll., 1968; MEd in Early Childhood Edn., U. Ill., 1977; MBA in Fin., U. Tex., 1986. Elem. tchr. Madison Heights (Mich.) Sch. Dist., 1968-70, Taft Sch. Dist., Lockport, Ill., 1970-72; systems clerk U.S. Army, The Pentagon, Washington, 1972-74; psychology aide Psychology Clinic U. Ill., Urbana, 1974-75; elem. tchr. Champaign (Ill.) Sch. Dist., 1975-77; with recruitment Standard Oil of Ohio, Cleve., 1977-78; v.p. NCNB Texas-Houston, 1981-88, Citibank (Ariz.), Tucson, 1988—. Pres. Christus Victor Luth. Ch., League City, Tex., 1985-88, Luth. Ch. of the Foothills, Tuscson, 1990. Mem. NAFE, U. Ill. Alumni Club, Longhorn Assn., Wildcat Club. Republican. Lutheran. Home: 5921 N Oracle #278 Tucson AZ 85704 Office: Citibank 1 S Church Tucson AZ 85701

HAGGAR, SARA THOMPSON, computer programmer; b. Cleve., Feb. 14, 1963; d. Jack Lewis and Mary Ann (Peterson) Thompson; m. Jeffrey Douglas Haggar, Sept. 17, 1988. BS in Computer Sci., Purdue U., 1985. System devel. programmer IBM, Poughkeepsie, N.Y., 1985—. Mem. Phi Beta Kappa.

HAGGARD, GERALDINE LANGFORD, educational administrator; b. Wellington, Tex., Dec. 12, 1929; d. Frank and Zelma Dell (Edmondson) Langford; m. W. Roy Haggard (June 9, 1949 (dec. July 1986); children: Colby, Sarah Haggard Eubanks, Mary Haggard Peterson. BS in Edn., Tex. State Coll. for Women, 1949, M.Ed. in Elem. Edn., 1953; EdD in Reading, Tex. Woman's U., 1980. Cert. reading tchr., reading specialist, mid-level mgr. Tchr. Denton County Schs., Denton, Tex., 1949-63; tchr. grad 4 and Chpt. I reading Plano (Tex.) Ind. Sch. Dist., 1963-72, now cons. lang. arts; dir. Chpt. I Head Start; adj. prof. Tex. Woman's U., Denton; tchr. trainer Reading Recovery, Plano, 1989-90. Author, tchr. manuals, computer programs; editor spelling program. Pianist, tchr. Los Rios Bapt. Ch., Plano; organizer Plano Adult Literacy Council, Plano, 1982. Recipient various teaching awards. Mem. Nat. Council Tchrs. English, Internat. Reading Assn. (supervision com.), Tex. Reading Suprs. (1st pres. 1981), Tex. State Reading Council (treas.), North Tex. Reading Council (past pres.), Delta Kappa Gamma, Alpha Delta Kappa, Phi Delta Kappa. Home: 2017 Meadowcreek Plano TX 75074 Office: Plano Ind Sch Dist 1517 Ave H Plano TX 75074

HAGGERTY, MARY ANN, social services professional; b. Orange, N.J., Dec. 23, 1945; d. Francis Anthony and Grace Mary (Cullen) H. BA, St. Joseph Coll., Emmitsburg, Md., 1967. Exec. dir. Child Advs. of Calif., San Luis Obispo; case mgr. Wiley House, Allentown, Pa.; spl. project asst. Wiley House, Bethlehem, Pa. Mem. NAFE. Address: RD #2 Box 602 Coopersburg PA 18036

HAGLER, LILLIE MAE, retired educational administrator, civic worker; b. Birmingham, Ala., May 26, 1916; d. Edward Telford and Catherine Ann (Jones) Owen; m. Harold Hagler (dec. Sept. 1987); children: Harold Owen, Edward Telford. BS in Elem. Edn., Samford U., 1956; M in Elem. Edn., U. Ala., 1958, postgrad., 1963, MPA, 1974. Cert. elem. tchr., Ala. Sec. Judge Hugh Locke & Assocs., Birmingham, 1934-41; tchr. Lakeview Sch., Birmingham, 1950-54, South Highland Sch., Birmingham, 1956-61; tchr. Putnam Sch., Birmingham, 1961-74, prin., 1974-82; prin. McElwain Sch., Birmingham, 1982-85. Tchr. adult couples Trinity United Meth. Ch., 1970—, substitute tchr. Ladies Bible Class, tchr.'s aide spl. class for handicapped, mem., sec. missions commn.; vol. Children's Hosp. Recipient Citation, Birmingham City Coun., 1980, Commendation of Performance, 1985. mem. AAUW (editor bull. Birmingham chpt. 1987—), NEA (life, del. 1962-85), Birmingham Ret. Tchrs., Ala. Ret. Tchrs., Ala. Edn. Assn., Birmingham Edn. Assn., Birmingham Classroom Tchrs. (past pres.), Birmingham Prins. Assn., Ala. Assn. Elem. Prins., Delta Kappa Gamma, Kappa Delta Epsilon, Phi Delta Kappa. Republican. Home: 4 Eastwood Circle Birmingham AL 35209

HAGLUND, MARLENE LINDA, registered record administrator; b. Warwick, R.I., June 8, 1959. BS in Biology, Colby Sawyer Coll., New London, N.H., 1981; postgrad., Northeastern U., Boston, 1983. Registered record adminstr. Cancer program coord. Brown U. Hosp., Providence, 1989—. Mem. Am. Med. Record Assn.

HAGUE, JANE FRANCES, county official; b. Medford, Oreg., Mar. 20, 1946; d. Donald Thomas and Martha (Wiesen) MacRae; m. Donald Scholes Hague, June 28, 1974; 1 child, David Andrew. BS, Western Mich. U., 1968. Contract adminstr. Aerophysics Rsch. Corp., Bellevue, Wash., 1974-79; treas. Aerophysics Rsch. Corp., 1980-85; div. mgr. King County Adminstrn., Seattle, 1986—; state sponsor Closeup Found.-Citizen Bee Program, Wash., 1987-89; sponsor, chmn. Citizen's Pride Honor Roll, King County, 1988; mem. Wash. State Election Code Task Force, 1987-89. Pub. Somerset Sun Community Newspaper, 1985-88. Mem. Bellevue (Wash.) Planning Commn., 1986-89, Bellevue City Coun., 1989—, Metro Citizens Water Quality Adv. Com., Seattle, 1986-87, King County Redistricting Com., Seattle, 1986; bd. dirs. King County Rep. Cen. Com., 1982-85; chmn. 41st Legis. Dist. Rep. Orgn., Wash., 1982-85; bd. dirs. Somerset Community Assn., Wash., 1986-88; mem. steering com. Wash. Drug Free Bus. Recipient Disting. Svc. award Am. Soc. Pub. Adminstrs., 1988, Nat. Achievement award Nat. Assn. County Ofcls., 1989, hon. mention William Olsten award for excellence in records mgmt. Mem. Wash. Assn. County Ofcls. (legis. chmn. 1987-89, v.p. 1988-89, pres.-elect 1989-90, chmn. edn.-cert. program 1988-89), Wash. Athletic Club, Rotary. Episcopalian. Office: King County Adminstrn 553 King County Adminstrn Bldg Seattle WA 98104

HAGY, SUSAN HALL WINSTEAD, cable television company executive; b. Alexandria, Va., May 17, 1960; d. Harold Henry and Anne (McLawhorn) H. BS, Va. Commonwealth U., 1982. Coordinator pub. relations Cen. Va. Safety Council, Richmond, 1981; adminstrv. asst. Office Overload, Richmond, 1982, profl. voice, camera talent, 1983—; customer service rep. Continental Cablevision, Richmond, 1983-84, lead customer service rep., 1984, regional mktg. adminstr., 1984-85, regional trainer, 1985, mgr. regional tng., 1985—, dir. spkr.'s bur., 1987—; profl. voice, camera talent Park Ave. Teleprodns., Richmond, 1986—. Mem. pub. relations com. Va. Spl. Olympics, Richmond, 1984—; tour guide Fan Dist. Assn., Richmond, 1985. Mem. Am. Soc. for Tng. and Devel., Nat. Assn. Female Execs., Internat. TV Assn., Internat. Thespian Soc., Lakewood Research Group. Presbyterian. Office: Continental Cable Vision Va 1520 W Main St Richmond VA 23220

HAGY, TERESA JANE, elementary educator; b. Bristol, Va., Nov. 1, 1950; d. Don Houston and Mary Garnett (Yeatts) Hagy. BA in Pre-Edn., Va. Intermont Coll., 1970, BA in Elem. Edn., 1972; MEd, U. Va., 1976. Cert. tchr., Va., Tenn. Tchr. 1st and 4th grades St. Anne's Demonstration Sch., Bristol, Va., 1972-75; tchr. 1st, 3d, 4th, 5th and 6th grades Washington Lee Elem. Sch., Bristol, 1975—; clin. instr. edn. Va. Intermont Coll., Bristol, 1972-75; coordinator gifted and talented program Bristol Schs., 1980-82; condr. workshops; developer tests to evaluate reading progress. Pres. women's circle Cen. Christian Ch., Bristol, Tenn., also v.p. women's fellowship, libr. chmn., mem. ch. choir, dir. music for Bible Sch., Sunday sch. tchr. 3rd and 4gh grades, 1979-88; active ARC; pres. Nat. Alumnae Assn. V.I. Coll., 1987-89. Recipient numerous edn. awards. Mem. NEA, AAUW (sec. 1975-78, v.p. 1981-86), Va. Edn. Assn., Bristol Edn. Assn. (sec. 1978-80), Va. State Reading Assn., U. Va. Alumnae Assn., U. Va. Alumni Assn., Va. Intermont Coll. Alumni Assn. (nat. pres. 1987-89), Va. Inst. Alumnae Assn. (nat. pres. 1987-79), Delta Kappa Gamma (chpt. pres. 1988—). Republican. Home: 820 Virginia Ave Bristol TN 37620 Office: Washington Lee Elem Sch Washington Lee Dr Bristol VA 24201

HAGYE, MELISSA MARIE, telemarketing consultant; b. Whitehall, Pa., July 16, 1952; d. Frederick Steven and Marie Catherine (Groller) Becks; m. Anthony P. Gutleber, Sept. 22, 1973 (div. 1979); m. Francis John Hagye, June 20, 1981. BA in Psychology and Art, Cedar Crest Coll., Allentown, Pa., 1973; postgrad., Keene State Coll., 1973. Art interpreter Nat. Parks, Cornish, N.H., 1974; caretaker historic mansion Soc. for Preservation New Eng. Antiquities, Portsmouth, N.H., 1975; sales cons. Jim Royer Realty, Atlanta, 1976-78; telemktg. mgr. Dial Am. Mktg., Atlanta, 1978-81, PCA Internat., Charlotte, N.C., 1981-83; pres., owner CommPlan Assocs., Greer, S.C., 1983—; cons. Blue Cross Assn., Chgo., 1989. Author: Telemarketing Supervisor's Manual, 1988. Bd. mem. Parents Anonymous of S.C.; vol. Friends of the Zoo, 1990. Recipient Svc. award Piedmont Coun. on Child Abuse, Greenville, S.C., 1988-89. Mem. Am. Telemktg. Assn., Bus. and the Arts Com., Greenville C. of C. (seminars chmn. 1988-89, cons. 1986-87), Audubon Soc. Republican. Roman Catholic. Home and Office: 30-B Sugar Creek Villas Greer SC 29650

HAHN, BESSIE KING, library administrator, lecturer; b. Shanghai, People's Republic of China, May 14, 1939; came to U.S., 1959; d. Jen Fong and Wei (Lok) King; m. Roger Carl Hahn, 1962 (dec. 1983); children: Angela Yee-mei, Michael King-yau, Belinda Shee-wei; m. David Ware Duhme, 1989. B.A., Mt. Marty Coll., Yankton, S.D., 1961; M.S.L.S., Syracuse U., 1972. Librarian Carrier Corp., Syracuse, N.Y., 1972; life sci. bibliographer Syracuse U. Libraries, 1973-75, head sci. and tech., 1975-78; asst. dir. reader services Johns Hopkins U. Library, Balt., 1978-81; dir. libraries Brandeis U., Waltham, Mass., 1981—; cons. Shanghai Jiao Tong U. Library, Shanghai, 1983—, hon. prof., 1984. Editor Jour. Ednl. Media and Library Scis., 1983—; contbr. articles to profl. jours. Bd. govs. Abraham Lincoln Brigade Archives, 1989. Recipient Golden Cup award Johns Hopkins U. Class of 1980, 1980. Mem. ALA, Chinese-Am. Librarians Assn. (pres. 1982-83), Brandeis U. Nat. Women's Com. (life, hon. benefactor 1986). Home: 148 Sudbury Rd Weston MA 02193 Office: Brandeis U Libr 415 South St Waltham MA 02254

HAHN, ELIZABETH F., sales executive; b. Russellville, Ala., Dec. 23, 1914; d. Robert E. and Lizzie C. (Glass) Farned; m. Edward L. Hahn, July 10, 1936. Student, SWTC, 1932, U. North Ala., 1934. Pres. Hahn Sales/Enstocko Inc., Baton Rouge; with payroll Gen. Tire & Rubber Co., Baytown, Tex.; tchr. Belgreen High Sch., Russellville, Ala. Recipient 1st Woman of Achievement award YWCA. Mem. Instrument Soc. Am. Home: 7209 Joliet Ave Baton Rouge LA 70806

HAHN, JHYNELDA MAE B., educator; b. Roscoe, Tex., Nov. 27, 1942; d. Erwin William and Freddie Mae (Nichols) Bredemeyer; m. Nicky Dewain Hahn, Oct. 15, 1961; children: Charles Dewain, James Richard. AS, Odessa Jr. Coll., 1973; BS in Edn., U. Tex., Odessa, 1982. Sub. tchr. Ector County Ind. Sch. Dist., Odessa, 1973-75, tchr's. aide, 1975-82; clk. Anthony's Dept. Store, Odessa, 1976-77; elem. tchr. Austin Elem. Sch., Odessa, 1983—. Den mother, pack com., treas. Buffalo Trail coun. Boy Scouts Am. , Odessa, 1970—; co-treas. Ector High Reunion Com., Odessa, 1988-89. Mem. AAUW (life), Juliet Soc. Great Globe of S.W. Odessa (treas. 1986-88), Alpha Delta Kappa (treas. Gamma Tau chpt.). Lutheran.

HAHN, JOAN CHRISTENSEN, drama educator, travel agent; b. Kemmerer, Wyo., May 9, 1933; d. Roy and Bernice (Pringle) Wainwright; m. Milton Angus Christensen, Dec. 29, 1952 (div. Oct. 1, 1971); children: Randall M., Carla J. Christensen Teasdale; m. Charles Henry Hahn, Nov. 15, 1972. BS, Brigham Young U., 1965. Profl. ballroom dancer, 1951-59; travel dir. E.T. World Travel, Salt Lake City, 1969—; tchr. drama Payson High Sch., Utah, 1965-71, Cottonwood High Sch., Salt Lake City, 1971—; dir. Performing European Tours, Salt Lake City, 1969-76; dir. Broadway theater tours, 1976—. Bd. dir. Salem City Salem Days, Utah, 1965-75; regional dir. dance Latter-day Saints Ch., 1954-72. Named Best Dir. High Sch. Musicals, Green Sheet Newspapers, 1977, 82, 84, 90; recipient 1st place award Utah State Drama Tournament, 1974, 77, 78, 89, 90; Tchr. of Yr. award Cottonwood High Sch., 1989-90; Limelight award, 1982; Exemplary Performance in teaching theater arts Granite Sch. Dist., Salt Lake City, 1982. Mem. Internat. Thespian Soc. (sponsor 1968—, internat. dir. 1982-84, trustee 1978-84), Utah Speech Arts Assn. (pres. 1976-78, 88-90), NEA, Utah Edn. Assn., Granite Edn. Assn., Profl. Travel Agts. Assn., Utah High Sch. Activities Assn. (drama rep. 1972-76), AAUW (pres. 1972-74). Republican. Mormon. Avocations: reading; travel; dancing. Home: 685 S 1st E Box 36 Salem UT 84653 Office: Cottonwood High Sch 5715 S 1300 E Salt Lake City UT 84121

HAHN, KAREN VIRGINIA, marketing executive; b. Detroit, Jan. 9, 1947; d. A. Kurt and Virginia (Claspill) H. m. R. Eugene Neal, Jr., May 29, 1965 (div. 1973); children—Patricia, David. A.S., Sacred Heart U., 1975; B.A., Sarah Lawrence Coll., 1979. Legal asst. chems. group Comml. Olin Corp., Stamford, Conn., 1980-82; asst. to pres. H.K. James Co., Westport, Conn., 1982; asst. sec. Moore & Munger, Inc. and subs., Shelton, Conn., 1983-85, dir. adminstrv. services, 1984—, sec. corp., 1985—. Mem. Choraliers (sec. 1982-83), Am. Soc. Corp Secs. Republican. Mem. United Ch. of Christ. Office: Moore & Munger Mktg 230 Long Hill Cross Rd Shelton CT 06484

HAHN, LITHIA B., finance executive; b. Troy, N.C., Nov. 2, 1951; d. Tom Stewart and Anne Grace (Ward) Brooks; 1 child, Leslie Grace Hahn. AS in Bus. Adminstrn. Acctg., Wingate U., 1972. Cert. Govtl. Acctg. and Fin. Reporting County Adminstrn., Acctg. and Fiscal Control, Budgeting and Fin. Planning. Finance dir. Brunswick County, Bolivia, N.C., Stanly County, Albemarle, N.C. Participant conf. Nat. Assn. Counties, Anaheim, Calif., 1988-89, Miami, Fla., 1990—, legis. conf. NACO, Washington, 1987-88. Mem. Govt. Fin. Officers Assn., N.C. Assn. County Finance Officers (sec.-treas. 1988-89, 2nd v.p. 1989-90, 1st v.p. 1990—), N.C. Cash Mgmt. Trust (chmn., adv. bd. 1987-88), NAFE, Nat. Assn. County Finance Officers and Treasurers, Carolinas Assn. Govt. Purchasers. Home: PO Box 249 Bolivia NC 28422

HAHN, LUCILLE DENISE, paper company executive; b. Stony Point, N.Y., Oct. 8, 1940; d. Raymond and Catherine (Nobert) Hoyt. Lab. asst. Champion Internat. (formerly St. Regis Paper Co.), West Nyack, N.Y., 1972-74, technician, 1974-77, tech. asst., 1977-79, rsch. asst., 1979-82, technologist, 1982-84, sr. technologist, 1984-86, assoc. testing coord., 1986-89, testing engr., 1989—. Author: Testing Guidebook, 1990. Mem. NAFE, TAPPI (sec. process and product quality div. 1987-88, vice-chair 1989-90). Office: Champion Internat West Nyack Rd West Nyack NY 10994

HAHN, SHARON LEE, city official; b. Kenosha, Wis., Sept. 22, 1939; d. Vincent B. and Mary Lee (Vaux) McCloskey; m. Robert W. Hahn, Jan. 1967 (div. June 1977); 1 child, John V. Calhoun. Student Kent State U., 1983. Cert. mcpl. clk., notary pub., Ohio. Sec., Simmons Bedding Co., Columbus, Ohio, 1960-61; exec. sec. Westinghouse, Columbus, 1962-68; legal sec. Bricker Law Firm, Columbus, 1969-70; asst. to prosecutor Whiteleather Law Firm, Columbia City, Ind., 1970-77; legal sec. Metz, Bailey & Spicer, Westerville, Ohio, 1977-80; clk. of council, sec. to city mgr. City of Westerville, 1981-87; clerk of council, records mgr. City of Westerville, 1981—. Mem. Ohio Mcpl. Clks. Assn. (bd. dirs. 1984-86), Internat. Inst. Mcpl. Clks. (CMC award 1984, records mgmt. com. 1986—), Am. Assn. Records Mgrs. and Adminstrs. Presbyterian. Avocations: golf; organ; rug hooking; interior decorating. Home: 356 MacIntosh Way Westerville OH 43081 Office: City of Westerville 21 S State St Westerville OH 43081

HAI, CAROL SUE, interior designer; b. Ithaca, N.Y., Sept. 16, 1938; d. Norman Charles and Edna (Voronoff) Epstein; m. Richard B. Hai, June 18, 1961 (div. Apr. 1984); children: Jill Ilene, Paul Bradley. BS, Cornell U., 1960, postgrad., 1960-61. Showroom asst. Jack Lenor Larsen, N.Y.C., 1960; teaching asst. Cornell U., 1960-61; sportswear sales mgr. Davison-Paxon Co., Columbus, Ga., 1962-63; owner, interior designer Carol Sue Hai Interiors, N.Y.C., Rochester, N.Y., 1964—. Trustee Soc. Preservation Landmarks Western N.Y, 1971-85, Temple B'rith Kodesh; bd. dirs. Opera Theatre Rochester, Girl Scouts of Genesee Valley, 1990—; mem. coun. Cornell U., Meml. Art Gallery, U. Rochester. Recipient Helen Bull Vandervort Alumni Achievement award Cornell U., 1987. Mem. Interior Design Soc., Am. Soc. Interior Designers, Nat. Assn. Women Bus. Owners. Home and Office: 172 Allens Creek Rd Rochester NY 14618

HAIGHT, ANNA LOUISE, pharmaceutical executive; b. Everett, Wash., Dec. 19, 1958; d. Charles James and Ruth Mae (Preston) H. BA in Internat. Rels., Brigham Young U., 1983. Cert. employee rels. law. With Otsuka Am. Pharm. Inc., Rockville, Md., 1983—, mgr. gen. affairs, corp. legal affairs, 1985-90; sr. mgr. gen. affairs corp. legal affairs Otsuka Am. Pharm. Inc., Rockville, 1990—; intern Embassy of Japan, Washington, 1983. Trustee Otsuka Am. 401 (k) Savs. Plan.; Md. C. of C., 1980—. Full-tuition scholar Komazawa U., Japan, 1981. Mem. Washington Pers. Assn., Drug Info. Assn., Internat. Foundn. Employee Benefit Plans, Am. Mgmt. Assn., Montgomery High Tech. Coun., Nat. Cherry Blossom Festival Com. Inc. Office: Otsuka Am Pharm Inc 1201 Third Ave Ste 5300 Seattle WA 98101

HAIGHT, CAROL BARBARA, lawyer; b. Buffalo, May 3, 1945; d. Robert H. Johnson and Betty R. (Walker) Hawkes; m. H. Granville Haight, May 28, 1978 (dec. Nov. 1983); chidren: David Michael, Kathleen Marie. BSW summa cum laude, Widener U., Chester, Pa., 1980, BA in Psychology summa cum laude, 1980; JD cum laude, Widener U., Wilmington, Del., 1984. Assoc. Pepper, Hamilton & Scheetz, Phila., 1985-88, Hodgson, Russ, Andrews, Woods & Goodyear, Buffalo, 1988—; lawyer pvt. practice, Boca Raton, Fla., 1990—; arbitrator Am. Abribration Assn., 1988—, mediator, 1989—, mediation instr. Contbr. article to profl. jours. Mem. ABA, Am. Judicature Soc., Fla. Bar Assn., South Palm Beach County Bar Assn., Phi Kappa Phi, Phi Alpha Delta (treas. 1981-83), Phi Gamma Mu (treas. 1979-80). Republican. Episcopalian. Home: 22485 Martella Ave Boca Raton FL 33433 Office: 370 W Camino Gardens Blvd Ste 300 Boca Raton FL 33432

HAIGLER-MILLS, EUNICE ESTELLE YOUNG, program coordinator; b. Wash., July 25, 1950; d. Theodre A. and Cora L. Hamm; m. David V. Haigler; children: Shea Young, Mark, David, Tajzsha; m. Calvin J. Mills, Dec. 23, 1987. Cert., Essex Coll. of Bus., 1976; AS, AAS, Essex County Coll., 1977-80; BA, Rutgers Arts Science Coll., 1982; postgrad., Rutgers Graduate Sch., 1982. Asst dir. Boys Clubs of Newark, Newark, N.J., 1975-74; resident coord., counselor Domestic Violence Ctr., Elizabeth, N.J., 1982-84; bursars asst. Essex County Coll., Newark, N.J., 1977-85; counselor Jespy House, South Orange, N.J.; dir. La Petite Acad., Fredericksburg, VA., 1986; program coord. Fredersburg Area Rape Crisis Program, 1988. Harambee 360, Fredericksburg, 1989-, Frederick Area Comm. Relations Orgn., cons. Friend, 1978, sponsor, Love, 1978, co-founder, Abuse, 1980. Mem. Stop Child Abuse Now, SENA, Virginia Aligned Against Domestic Violence, Virginia Aligned Against Sexual Assault (bd. dir.). Democratic. Baptist.

HAIKALIS, SUSAN W(ILLIAMS), social worker; b. Montclair, N.J., Oct. 20, 1941; d. Richard Sugden and Helen Faith (Fellows) Williams; m. Peter Dennis Haikalis, May 27, 1967; 1 child, Joanna. BA, U. Mich., 1963; MSW, NYU, 1965. Cert. social worker; lic. clin. social worker, Calif. Dir. social work Riverside (Calif.) Community Hosp., 1968-70; med. social work cons. Vis. Nurse Assn. Riverside County, Riverside, 1970-75; case mgmt. specialist Riverside County Assn. Retarded Citizens, Riverside, 1975-77; program dir. Assn. for the Advancement of Mentally Handicapped, Princeton, N.J., 1977-79; assoc. dir. social work Mt. Zion Med. Ctr. U. Calif., San Francisco, 1980-86, dir. social work, 1986—; med. social work cons. Riverside, 1970-77. Author: (with Epke and Meadows) How Discharge Planning Works and Can Work for You Under Prospective Payment, 1985, Ins and Outcomes of Quality Assurance, 1989, How to Sail through a JCAHO Site Visit, 1990. Pres. bd. dirs. East Bay Regional Ctr., 1986; v.p., bd. dirs. Berkeley (Calif.) Pub. Edn. Found., 1986—. Recipient O.E. Nelson Service award Am. Cancer Soc., Riverside, 1971. Mem. Am. Hosp. Assn. (Soc. Hosp. Social Work Dirs., pres. no. Calif. chpt. 1983, chmn. state polit. action com. 1984—, mem. nat. nominating com. 1986, mem. nat. bd. dirs. 1989—). Democrat. Episcopalian. Office: Mt Zion Med Ctr U Calif 1600 Divisadero St San Francisco CA 94115

HAIKO, GERALDINE MAE, auto damage appraiser; b. Hartford, Conn., Nov. 5, 1940; d. Frank Joseph and May Lillian (Brandt) Haiko; m. Douglas Allen Gallant, May 27, 1961 (div. Mar. 1965); 1 child, Douglas Allen. AA, Vt. Coll., 1960. Rating clk. Travelers Ins. Co., Hartford, 1961-65; teller, adminstrv. asst., Soc. for Savs., Wethersfield, 1965-69; teller, asst. head teller, customer svc. officer Coral Ridge Nat. Bank, Fort Lauderdale, Fla., 1970-74; with customer svc. dept. Bank Coral Springs, Fla., 1974-76; pres. Frank J. Haiko, Inc., Wethersfield, 1976—. Mem. Ind. Auto Damage Appraisers (sec. NE region 1981-89, treas. NE region 1981—, nat. sec. 1985—), Wethersfield C. of C., U.S. C. of C., Greater Hartford C. of C. Republican. Avocations: cross country skiing, singing, dancing, spectator sports, Alpine skiing and golf. Office: Frank J Haiko Inc 36 Silas Deane Hwy Wethersfield CT 06109

HAIN, PEGGY SUZANNE, communications executive, photographer; b. Grand Island, Nebr., Feb. 15, 1962; d. Keith Russell and Janice Joan (Nietfeld) Reichardt; m. Kenneth Joseph Hain, June 2, 1984; 1 child, Mitchell Joseph. BJ with distinction, U. Nebr., 1984. Fin. counselor 1st Fed. Lincoln, Nebr., 1984-85; with employee edn. and tng. dept. 1st Fed. Lincoln Savs. & Loan, 1985-86; communications dir. League Nebr. Mcpls., Lincoln, 1986—; pub. rels. cons. Community Child Abuse Prevention Coun., Lincoln, 1987—. Mem. Internat. Assn. Bus. Communicators (v.p. mem. com. 1988—), Alpha Chi Omega (pres. Lincoln alumnae chpt. 1988-89). Republican. Roman Catholic. Home: 2843 N 65th St Lincoln NE 68507 Office: League Nebr Mcpls 1335 L St Lincoln NE 68508

HAINES, DIANA COPELAND, veterinerian; b. Providence, R.I., Nov. 25, 1950; d. Donald Eugene and Marjorie Lucille (Groves) Copeland; m. Richard Haines; 1 child, Daniel Richard. BS in Biology, Tulane U., 1972; DVM, La. State U., 1977. guest speaker Nat. Capital Area Br., Am. Assn. of Lab. Animal Sci., Bethesda, Md., 1983, guest lectr. Pathologist NCI Frederick (Md.) Cancer Research Facility, 1981-83; sr. scientist Ethicon, Somerville, N.J., 1983-84; staff pathologist Pathology Assocs., Inc., Ijamsville, Md., 1984-87, Hazleton Labs, Rockville, Md., 1987—; guest speaker N.C.A.B., A.A.L.A.S., Nat. Capital Area Bar, Am. Assn. Lab Animal Scis., Bethesda, Md., 1983; guest lectr. Contbr. articles to profl. jours. Capt. U.S. Army, 1977-81. Mem. Am. Coll. Veterinary Pathologist, Soc. Toxicologic Pathologists.. Republican. Methodist. Home: 5926 Taneytown Pike Taneytown MD 21787 Office: Hazleton Labs Am 1330 B Piccard Dr Rockville MD 20850

HAINSWORTH-STRAUS, CHRISTINE LOUISE, commercial real estate broker; b. Alton, Ill., Oct. 29, 1962; d. Joseph Richard and Nola Jo (Harwood) Hainsworth; m. Michael Wolcott Straus, Aug. 31, 1985; 1 child, Christopher. BBA, Principia Coll., 1983, BA in English Lit., 1983. Leasing agt. Murdoch & Coll., Inc., St. Louis, 1983-84, mktg. mgr., 1984-86; comml. real estate broker William D. Feldman Assocs., Culver City, Calif., 1986-88; comml. real estate broker R.A. Rowan & Co., 1988-89; pvt. practice, 1989—; editor Praxis, 1982, bus. mgr., 1983. Mem. Citizens for Light Rail Transit, St. Louis, 1984, 85; mem. telecommunications task force L.A. Cen. City Assn.; pres. L.A. Women's Exch., 1987-88; bd. dirs. 1st Ch. of Christ Scientist South Pasadena, v.p., 1988-89. Author: Subleasing: How to Avoid a Lose: Lose Situation, 1988 (book rev.) Dow Jones On-line Service Trammell Crow, Master Builder, 1989. Mem. NAFE, L.A. Women's Exchange (pres. 1987-88), Comml. Real Estate Women, Am. Indsl. Real Estate Assn., Friends of Huntington Library, Principia Alumni Assn., Writer's Group (pres. 1989-90), L.A. Jr. C. of C. Christian Scientist. Avocations: tennis, soccer, skiing, Japanese art and French Impressionist art. Home: 1272 E Loma Alta Altadena CA 91001

HAIR, MARCIA ELIZABETH, corporate art consultant; b. Miami, Fla., Oct. 16, 1948; d. James Ralph Hair and Marie Louise (Shonter) Yorra; m. Keith Terence Kelley, Jan. 10, 1970 (div. Oct. 1975); children: Patrick Shonter Kelley, Benjamin James Kelley; m. Ronald Elias Hickman, Mar. 15, 1986. Student, U. Ga., 1966-70; BA, Ga. State U., 1981. Asst. dir. Apple Tree Sch., Atlanta, 1971-74; dir. Mini Sch., Atlanta, 1974-76, Kinder Care, Atlanta, 1976-77, A Learning Place, Decatur, Ga., 1977-78; with sales/design div. Framesworks Gallery, Marietta, Ga., 1978—, corp. cons., 1985—. Contbr. articles to profl. jours. Bd. dirs. Cobb County YWCA; founder Deer Atlanta Task Force, Atlanta's Table, Cobb County Humane Soc., auction host and com. chmn. Mem. NAFE, Profl. Picture Framers Assn., Atlanta Track Club, The Circle for Tallulah Falls Sch. Democrat. Roman Catholic. Club: Atlanta Track. Home: 3350 Bryant Ln Marietta GA 30066 Office: Frameworks Gallery 26 Mill St Marietta GA 30060

HAIRALD, MARY PAYNE, education educator; b. Tupelo, Miss., Feb. 25, 1936; d. Will Burney and Ivey Lee (Berryhill) Payne; m. Leroy Utley Hairald, May 31, 1958; 1 child, Burney LeShawn. BS in Commerce, U. Miss., 1957, M in Bus. Edn., 1963; postgrad., Miss. Coll., 1964, Miss. State U., 1970, U. So. Miss., 1986, 87, 88, 90. Bus. edn. tchr. John Rundle High Sch., Grenada, Miss., 1957-59; youth recreation leader City of Nettleton, Miss., summers 1960-61; tchr. social studies Nettleton Jr. High Sch., 1959-70; tchr.-coord. coop. vocat. edn. program Nettleton High Sch., 1970—; area mgr. World Book, Inc., Chgo., 1972—; bus. instr. Itawamba Community Coll., Tupelo, 1975-80; sponsor Coop. Vocational Edn. Club, Nettleton, 1970—; advisor Distributive Edn. Clubs Am., Nettleton, 1985—. Editor advisor State DECA Newsletter; contbr. articles on coop. edn. to newspapers. Co-organizer Nettleton Youth Recreation Booster Club; fundraiser Muscular Dystrophy Assn. Named Star Tchr., Miss. Econ. Coun., 1978; recipient Nat. State Newsletter award Distributive Edn. Clubs Am., 1988, 89, 1st place Nat. Newsletter award 1988, 89, 90, Dist. II Advisor of Yr., 1990. Mem. Am. Vocat. Assn. (Coop. Vocat. Edn. Educator of Yr. award 1985, Mktg. and Coop. Edn. Tchr. of Yr. award 1988), Coop. Work Experience Edn. Assn., Miss. Assn Vocat. Educators (dist. sec.), Miss. Assn. Coop. Vocat. Edn. Tchrs. (v.p. 1980-83, pres. 1983-84, Miss. Tchr. of Yr. award 1984, 87), Miss. Assn. Mktg. Educators, Mktg. Edn. Assn., AAUW (charter). Democrat. Methodist. Home: PO Box 166 Nettleton MS 38858

HAITKO, DEBORAH ANN, chemist; b. New Haven, Sept. 22, 1951; d. John and Dorothy (Ajello) H. BA, Albertus Magnus Coll., 1973; MS, Yale U., 1974, M.Phil., 1975, PhD, 1978. Postdoctoral fellow Princeton (N.J.) U., 1978, Ind. U., Bloomington, 1978-80; staff chemist GE Corp. Rsch. and Devel. Ctr., Schenectady, N.Y., 1980—. Contbr. 24 articles to profl. jours.; 11 patents in field. Conn. State scholar Conn. State Scholarship Com., 1974-77, Todd Found. scholar, 1969-73. Office: GE Corp Rsch & Devel Ctr 1 River Rd Bldg K-1 Rm 5A38 Schenectady NY 12301

HAIZLIP, SHIRLEE ANNE MORRIS TAYLOR, film industry executive; b. Stratford, Conn., Sept. 3, 1937; d. Julian Augustus and Margaret Pauline (Morris) Taylor; m. Harold C. Haizlip, 1959; children: Deirdre Taylor, Melissa Morris. BA, Wellesley (Mass.) Coll., 1959; MA, Harvard U., 1965. Gen. mgr. Sta. WBNB-TV, St. Thomas, V.I., 1976-81; corp. sec. Sta. WNET-TV, N.Y.C., 1981-87; chief exec. officer Taylor Made Assocs., New Haven, 1987-89; dir. Nat. Ctr. Film/Video Preservation at Am. Film Inst., L.A., Washington (D.C.), 1989—. Contbr. articles to local newspapers, 1986-88. Campaign mgr. Althea J. Tyson Campaign, New Haven, 1988; founding dir. Rainbow Coalition, New Haven, 1988; bd. dirs. JAT Scholarship Fund, Ansonia, Conn., 1982—, Shurbert Theatre, New Haven, 1984-88, Jazzmobile, N.Y.C., 1982-88, Opera Ebony, N.Y.C., 1985-88, Community Affairs Bd., New Haven Register, 1986-88. Mem. Women in Film, Motion Picture Acad., TV Acad. Arts and Scis., Nat. Program TV Execs., Am. Women in Film and TV., Links, Inc. (pres.), AKA. Home: 622 Lillian Way Los Angeles CA 90004 Office: Nat Ctr Film/Video Presentor Am Film Inst 2021 N Western Ave Los Angeles CA 90027

HAJJAR, JEANETTE, educator; b. Boston, Aug. 8, 1927; d. Elias Murad and Nabeeha Saleem (Moghabghab) H. BA magna cum laude, Boston Coll., 1967; MA, Brandeis U., 1969, PhD, 1981. Radio technician MIT Radiation Lab., Cambridge, Mass., 1944-45; emergency ward technician Mass. Gen. Hosp., Boston, 1954-59; hematology technician Children's Cancer Research Found., Boston, 1959-67; tchr., lectr. various schs. and colls., Boston, 1972-77; operating room scheduler Mass. Gen. Hosp., Boston, 1973-74; mgr. Little City Hall-South End, Boston, 1978-79; ESL tchr. Peace Corps, Morocco, 1983-85, local area schs., Boston, 1978—; advocate, spokesperson TV/radio South End/Inner City and Arabic community, Boston, 1965-82; cons., lectr. on the Middle East, TV/radio and local newspapers, Boston, 1965-82. Translator: The Book of the Lighted Pathway, 1980; editor: Middle East Customs & Traditions, 1976; contbr., author, editor of articles and stories on the Middle East, Boston Arabic community, Boston South End, and the Boston Inner City. Elected rep. South End Project Area Com., Boston, 1969-71, 73-75; bd. dirs. Boston YWCA, 1971-73; mem. Founding com. Boston Ctr. for the Arts, 1970-71, Villa Victoria Housing Devel., Boston, 1973-75, Blackstone Community Sch., Boston, 1973-75. Scholar Boston Coll., 1961-66, full tuition scholar Brandeis U., 1967-68; NDFL fellow Brandeis U., 1968-71. Mem. Assn. Arab-Am. Univ. Grads. Democrat. Greek Catholic.

HAKES, NELL (ELIZA)BETH, interior designer; b. Long Beach, Calif., Mar. 8, 1961; d. Frederick Edward and Kerry Margaret (McCutchen) Hitchcock; m. Howard Winford Hakes, Aug. 30, 1986; 1 child, Howard

Edward. BS in Interior Design, San Jose State U., 1984. Apprenticeship Contract Office Group, San Jose, 1982-83; space planner Old L.A. Co., L.A., 1984; interior designer Raymond M. Rooker AIA/ASID, Cupertino, Calif., 1984-85; pvt. interior designer San Jose, 1985-88; interior designer, pres. Beth Hakes Interiors, Inc., Granada Hills, Calif., 1988—; cons., designer Frank Lloyd Wright's Hollyhock House, L.A., 1988—, Pasadena (Calif.) Showcase House, 1990. Mem. Am. Soc. Interior Design, Nat. Trust for Hist. Preservation, L.A. Conservancy, NAFE, Inst. Bus. Designers. Office: Beth Hakes Interiors 17939 Chatsworth St Ste 504 Granada Hills CA 91344

HAKIMOGLU, GERALDINE ANN, electronics executive; b. Doylestown, Pa., May 16, 1950; d. Joseph James and Marion Gertrude (Haly) Crilley; m. Ayhan Hakimoglu, Nov. 19, 1982. BA in English, Pa. State U., 1972; postgrad., Temple U., 1978. Asst. to v.p. pub. affairs Children's TV Workshop, N.Y.C., 1972-76; asst. sec., dir. corp. communications Aydin Corp., Horsham, Pa., 1976—. Trustee Assembly Turkish Am.. Orgns., 1987—. Recipient Community Svc. award Fedn. Turkish-Am. Soc., Bus. Person's award Assembly Turkish-Am. Assns., 1989. Office: Aydin Corp 700 Dresher Rd Box 349 Horsham PA 19044

HALAS, CYNTHIA ANN, auditor, business owner; b. Norristown, Pa., July 24, 1961; d. George and Maria (Mitrik) H. Student, Temple U., 1979-80, Montgomery County Coll., Blue Bell, Pa., 1986—. Columnist, corr. The Recorder, Conshohocken, Pa., 1980-81; claims supr. Liberty Mut. Ins. Co., Blue Bell, 1980-84; claims svc. rep. Met. Property & Liability Ins. Co., Wayne, Pa., 1984-87; model Frank James Assocs., Phila., 1986-87; auditor Susquehanna Adminstrs., Inc., Wayne, 1987—. Active Nat. Arbor Day Found. Mem. U.S. Fencing Assn., Smithsonian Assocs., Bucks County Acad. Fencing. Byzantine Catholic. Office: SAI Inc 994 Old Eagle Sch Rd #1016 Wayne PA 19087

HALASZ, MARILYNN JEAN, information services manager; b. Chgo., Nov. 12, 1937; d. Frank John and Vera Josephine (Staab) Macku; m. John Ernest Halasz, May 21, 1981. B.A., Rosary Coll., 1959; M.A.L.S., 1977; student foreign study, Univ. Coll., Oxford, Eng., 1971; M.A., DePaul U., 1972. Tchr. elem., secondary, and collegiate levels in English, sci. and math., 1959-77; cons. resource manual Ill. State Bd. Edn., Triton Coll., River Grove, Ill., 1975-76; sci. librarian John Crerar Library, Chgo., 1977-78; assoc. librarian Portland Cement Assn., Skokie, Ill., 1978, librarian, 1978-80, mgr. info. services sect., 1980-85; supr. Tech. Info. Ctr., Inst. Gas Tech., 1988-89; sr. info. specialist, Corn Products CPC Internat., 1989— cons. in field. Contbr. articles to profl. jours. Recipient grad. asst. award Dale Carnegie & Assocs., 1984. Mem. Spl. Libraries Assn. Roman Catholic. Club: Am. Assn. Univ. Women, Lyric Opera. Home: 514 S Garfield Ave Hinsdale IL 60521 Office: Corn Products a Unit of CPC Internat 6500 S Archer Rd Argo IL 60501

HALCO, ANN MARIE, hospital administrator; b. Van Buren, Maine, Oct. 13, 1936; d. Alderic Antoine and Pearl Louise (Levesque) Masse'; m. Robert Henry Halco, June 11, 1955; children: Karen Ann, Mark Robert, Christopher Lee, Lisa Marie. Student, Coll. of Law, 1964-66. Asst. planner Bendix Corp., Sylmar, Calif., 1962-65; bus. mgr. Raleigh Medical Ctr., Memphis, Tenn., 1966-72; dir. purchasing and materials mgmt. West Texas Hosp., Lubbock, Tex., 1972-76; administr. asst., dir. of personnel Lubbock General Hosp., Lubbock, Tex., dir. purchasing, 1982-86; assoc. mgr. Langston Financial Hosp., Tex., 1986-87; dir. purchasing West Texas Hosp., Lubbock, 1987--; Bd. mem., Texas Hosp. Assn., Austin, 1984-86, pres. Lubbock Soc. Hosp. Personnel, 1983-84. Contbr. articles to prof. mags. Dir. Camp Fire Council Bd, Lubbock, 1984-86, Mayor's Coucil for Women, 1984-85, Task Force for Women Committee, 1984-85. Mem. Natl. Assn. of Hosp. Materials Mgmt., Lubbock Swim Club (dir. 1973-79). Republican. Roman Catholic. Home: 4504 19th St Lubbock TX 79407 Office: West Texas Hosp 1401 9th St Lubbock TX 79401

HALE, CHARLOTTE, author, publishing executive; b. Jacksonville, Fla., Jan. 6, 1928; d. Anthony W. and Eleanor (Cunningham) Hale; m. Norris TeBeau Pindar III, May 23, 1986; 1 child by previous marriage, Stanley R. Smith Jr. Student, Armstrong Jr. Coll., 1947-48. Copy writer Sta. WSAV, Savannah, Ga., 1948-49, copy dir., 1949-51; copy dir. Sta. WSAV-TV, 1955-57; with advt. dept. Savannah News-Press, 1957-59; staff writer Sunday mag. Atlanta Jour.-Constn., 1960-70; free-lance writer, 1969—; founder, owner Charlotte Hale Communiqué; founder, pres. Epiphany Press, Savannah; cons. U.S. CSC, 1976-79; guest speaker various colls., schs., chs., clubs, 1969—; founder Time of Your Life mgmt. seminar, 1978, Facing Forward motivational seminar and workshop on aging, 1982, Going First Class seminar, 1984; speech writer state polit. candidates, 1959-68; news writer U.S. Army, Ft. Stewart, Ga., 1951. Author: Full-Time Living, 1978, (with Layona Glenn) I Remember, I Remember, 1968; editor and writer various books by Anita Bryant and Bob Green, 1970-77; editor: The Super Years, 1984; contbr. book revs. to newspapers. Vol. Savannah Symphony, 1955-59; bd. dirs. Savannah Mental Health Assn., 1957-59; trustee Ga. Conservancy, Inc., 1968-70. Mem. Nat. Speakers Assn., Chatham Commerce Club. Home: 629 E 55th St Savannah GA 31405

HALE, GINA LASTELLE, judge; b. Atlanta, June 10, 1959; d. William Henri Harrison and Larzette (Golden) H. BA, Utah State U., 1980, MBA, 1986; JD, Willamette U., 1983. Bar: Utah 1985. Pvt. practice Logan, Utah, 1985-87; adminstrv. law judge Olympia (Wash.) Office Adminstrv. Hearings, 1987-88, Vancouver (Wash.) Office Adminstrv. Hearings, 1988—. Mem. AAUW, Nat. Assn. Women Judges, Wash. Adminstrv. Law Judge Assn., Alpha Kappa Alpha, Alpha Chi Omega. Democrat. Episcopalian. Home: 3214 NE 62d Ave Apt H3 Vancouver WA 98661 Office: Office Adminstrv Hearings 111 W 39th St Ste A Vancouver WA 98660

HALE, MARGARET SMITH, insurance company executive, educator; b. Browning, Mont., May 10, 1945; d. Stephen Howard and Evelyn Sarah (Beer) Smith; m. Lawrence L. Hale, Apr. 25, 1970 (div. Jan. 1984); children: Katherine Moore, Laura Ellen. BSBA, Boston U., 1967; AS in Risk Mgmt., Ins. Inst. Am., 1986. Underwriter Chubb & Son, Inc., N.Y.C., 1967-70; br. mgr., asst. v.p. Chubb & Son, Inc., Boston, 1970-80; asst. v.p., account exec. Marsh & McLennan Inc., Boston, 1980-84; sr. v.p. Frank B. Hall, Boston, 1984-87; resident v.p. Warwick Ins. Co., Needham, Mass., 1987-90; exec. v.p. Hatch-Anderson-O'Donnell Ins. Agy. Inc., Arlington, Mass., 1990—; lectr. Risk and Ins. Mgrs. Soc., Boston, 1975-85; instr. fin. div. Babson Coll., Wellesley, Mass., 1987—. Bd. dirs. Lupus Erythematosus Assn., Boston, 1975-78, Parker Hill Med. Ctr., Boston, 1978-80; tchr. Congl. Ch. Sch., Needham, Mass., 1982—; chmn. ins. adv. com. Town of Needham, 1982—. Mem. Ins. Mgrs. Assn. (treas. Boston 1971-80), Ins. Library Assn. (dir. 1980-82). Home: 530 Chestnut St Needham MA 02192 Office: Hatch-Anderson-O'Donnell Ins Agy 669 Massachusetts Ave Arlington MA 02174

HALE, MARILYN CARLENE, store owner, manager; b. Durango, Colo., Sept. 7, 1951; d. Roland Glen and Ethel Margaret (Carey) Vesper; m. Ryan J. Hale, Mar. 6, 1971; children: Melanie, Misty, Ryan Jay. Grad. real estate essentials, Link's Sch. of Bus., 1970; grad. in real estate, Idaho State U. Vocat.-Tech., 1988. Lic. real estate agt., Idaho. Operator date processing machines Continental Ins. Co., Boise, Idaho, 1970; sr. data processing operator Monsanto Co., Soda Springs, Idaho, 1970-78; co-owner, office mgr. Caribou Auto Supply, Soda Springs, 1978-87; co-owner, mgr. Video Shack-Radio Shack, Soda Springs, 1982-84; owner, mgr., mcht. Sears Catalog Store, Soda Springs, 1986—. Pres. Soda Springs Jr. High Sch. PTA. Mem. Soda Springs C. of C., Beta Sigma Phi. Republican. Office: Sears Authorized Catalog Store 132 S Main Soda Springs ID 83276

HALE, MARY CARTER, life insurance company executive; b. Pittsfield, Mass., May 21, 1928; d. Stephen Hilliard and Mary Emma (Bull) Carter; m. Donald Bruce Hale, Apr. 10, 1948; children—M. Christine Hale Bienvenue, A. Stephen Hale. Mktg. asst. Berkshire Life Ins. Co., Pittsfield, Mass., 1963—. Sec.-treas. Tyringham Landowners Assn. (Mass.), 1977—; selectman Town of Tyringham, 1980—; v.p. Berkshire County Adv. Bd., 1984—; pres. Berkshire County Selectmen's Assn., 1985-86; sec.-treas. Berkshire County Police Chief's Assn., 1984-87; chief of police Tyringham, 1982-87 ; 1st v.p. Mass. Selectmen's Assn., 1985—, pres., 1989-90; mem. Local Gov.'s Adv. Coun. 1985—; exec. bd. Mass. Mcpl. Assn., 1985—, pres., 1988-89. Episcopalian. Address: Main Rd Tyringham MA 01264

HALE, MARY HELEN PARKER, university administrator; b. Merryville, La., May 25, 1920; d. James Carroll and Mollie (Dear) Parker; BA in English (scholar), La. Coll., 1940, BA in Music, 1940; MA in English (fellow), La. State U., 1942; PhD in Fine Arts (hon.), U. Alaska, 1965; m. George Erwin Hale, June 12, 1942; children: John Parker, James Milton, Nancy Anne. Instr., dir choral music, Boston 1944-45, Albany, N.Y., 1945, Washington, 1946-49, Anchorage, 1949-50; dir. Anchorage Community Chorus, 1951-59; founder, dir. Alaska Festival of Music, 1956-62; vice chmn. N.Am. Assembly Arts Agys., 1968-70; coordinator arts and community affiliates office Anchorage Community Coll. and U. Alaska, Anchorage, 1970-86; dir. pub. services Anchorage Community Coll., 1977-81, asst. to pres., 1979-81. Founder Alaska Southcentral High Sch. Music Festival, 1950; mem. Alaska Centennial Commn., 1963-65; charter mem. Alaska State Council on Arts, 1966, chmn., 1967-71; founder, mem., sec. Alaska Humanities Forum, 1974-79; mem. adv. bd. No. TV, Inc., 1979—, trust com.Anchorage Sr. Ctr., 1987—; vice-chmn. citizens adv. council Anchorage Community Coll., 1981, mem. adv. council, 1981-86, founder Arts Fair and Women's Ctr. adv. com. Celebrating Alaska's Women, 1945-65, 86, 87; vice chmn. Coalition Community Colls. in Alaska, 1986-88. Recipient Mayor's Disting. Service award, Anchorage, 1965; 49'er award, elected to Hall of Fame, Alaska Press Club, 1970, 72; Outstanding Vol. award U. Alaska, Anchorage, 1976; Outstanding Alumni award La. Coll., 1979; President's citation Anchorage C. of C., 1979; Disting. Service award Anchorage Community Coll., 1983. Mem. Anchorage Arts Council (charter mem.), U. Alaska Anchorage Alumni Assocs., Internat. Platform Assn., LWV, AAUW, Nat. Assn. Women Deans, Adminstrs. and Counselors, Woman's Club, Soroptimists (hon., pres. Anchorage chpt. 1956), Republican Women's Club, Mu Phi Epsilon, Beta Sigma Phi (hon.). Presbyterian. Home: 11601 Birch Rd Anchorage AK 99516

HALE, RUTH ANN, public relations specialist; b. Memphis, Dec. 17, 1956; d. Evelyn Juanita (Graham) Hardin; m. Richard Alan Hale, July 19, 1985. BA in Journalism, Memphis State U., 1985. Pub. rels. asst. Le Bonheur Children's Med. Ctr., Memphis, 1985-87; editorial asst. Bapt. Meml. Hosp., Memphis, 1987-89; asst. pub. affairs officer Shelby County Mayor's Office, Memphis, 1989—. Mem. Women in Communications (pres. 1990-91), Pub. Rels. Soc. Am., Memphis State U. Journalism Alumni Assn. (bd. dirs. 1988-90). Office: Shelby County Govt 160 N Mid-America Mall Ste 850 Memphis TN 38103

HALE, SINA KAYE, elementary music educator; b. Houston, Jan. 6, 1951; d. William Norman Pendleton and Janie Lee (Gardner) Swan; m. Barry Michael Hale, June 16, 1973; 1 child, Christopher Michael. MusB, U. North Tex., 1972. Elem. music tchr. Pasadena (Tex.) Ind. Sch. Dist., 1973—. Dir. Cherub Choir Sunset United Meth. Ch., Pasadena, 1988—; dir., accompanist Sunrise Men's Quartet, Pasadena, 1979—. Mem. Tex. Music Educator's Assn., Kodaly Educators Tex., Gulf Coast Orff Assn. Office: Young Elem Pasadena ISD 4221 Fox Meadow Pasadena TX 77504

HALE-ROBINSON, LORRAINE AUGUSTA, musician; b. Balt., Md., Apr. 20, 1948; d. LeRoy Mitchell and Emma Augusta (Collenberg) H.; m. David Jacobs, Oct. 29, 1969; (div. June, 1974); 1 child, Karen Marcia; m. Johnie Graves, Aug. 31, 1979. Cert., Western Md. Coll., Balt., 1966; Student, We. Md., Westminster, 1969; BA, E Carolina U., Greenville, 1977; MA, Carolina U., Greenville, 1983. Nat. Guild of Piano Tchrs. Cert. Dir. music MCAS Chapel Cherry Point, Havelock, Tex., 1971-74; instr. English E. Carolina U., Greenville, 1977-79; dir. music Christ Episc. Ch., New Bern, N.C., 1974-81; English, music instr. Craven Community Coll., New Bern, N.C., 1987—; English instr. N.C. Wesleyan, New Bern, 1986; dir. music St. Andrew Luth. Ch., 1982-87; tchr. Arendell Parrott Acad., Kinston, N.C., 1988; music, English instr., 1974—; musician, actress Cabaret Players, New Bern, N.C., 1983-89; music editor Composers Music Co., New Bern, N.C., 1987—. Composer Various Handbell Music at Dir's. Workshop 1989; Contbr. Articles to The Sun Journal 1987-89. Sec. E. Carolina Chap. Am. Guild of Organists New Bern N.C. 1985-87; Active Craven County Bicentennial Com. New Bern N.C. 1985-88, Women's Forum New Bern N.C. 1988-. Teaching fellow English Dept. E. Carolina U. Greenville 1977-78. Mem. Delta Omicron Profl. Music Frat., Phi Kappa Phi, Sigma Tau Delta, Guild of Organists, N.C. Composers Alliance, Occasional Gourmet. Republican. Lutheran. Office: Lorraine Hale Music 212 Metcalf St New Bern NC 28562

HALES, LISA LINN HERMAN, educational administrator; b. Omaha, Nov. 25, 1961; d. Larry Lee and Judy Kaye (Ensminger) Herman; m. Ronnie Hales, June 25, 1988. BSBA, U. Fla., 1983. Cashier Publix Supermarkets, Gainesville and Lakeland, Fla., 1978-84; meat merchandiser Fleming Cos., Inc., Geneva, Ala., 1984-89; admissions officer Phoenix Ednl. Systems, Dothan, Ala., 1989—. Nat. Food Brokers Assn. scholar, 1983; George Jenkins Found. scholar Publix Supermarkets, Inc., 1980-83; Nat. Honor Soc. scholar, 1980. Mem. NAFE, Phi Chi Theta, Alpha Xi Delta. Office: 134 Westgate Pkwy Dothan AL 36303

HALES, ROBERTA LOUISE, respiratory care supervisor; b. Norristown, Pa., Feb. 21, 1962; d. Raymond R. and Mary Louise (Scheetz) Salamone; m. Thomas E. Hales, Sept. 6, 1986. BS, Ind. U. Pa., 1984. Respiratory technician Presbyn. Hosp., Pitts., 1982, Monte Fiore Hosp., Pitts., 1982-84; respiratory therapist Children's Hosp. Phila., 1984-86, supr. respiratory care, 1986—; instr. CPR Am. Heart Assn., Phila., 1984-86; preceptor, Children's Hosp. Phila., 1985-86. Mem. Am. Assn. for Respiratory Care. Home: 314 E Brown St Norristown PA 19401 Office: Children's Hosp Phila 34th and Civic Ctr Blvd Philadelphia PA 19104

HALEY, JOHNETTA RANDOLPH, musician, educator, university administrator; b. Alton, Ill., Mar. 19; d. John A. and Willye E. (Smith) Randolph; children from previous marriage: Karen, Michael. MusB in Edn., Lincoln U., 1945; MusM, So. Ill. U., 1972. Vocal and gen. music tchr. Lincoln High Sch., E. St. Louis, Ill., 1945-48; vocal music tchr., choral dir. Turner Sch., Kirkwood, Mo., 1950-55; vocal and gen. music tchr. Nipher Jr. High Sch., Kirkwood, 1955-71; prof. music Sch. Fine Arts, So. Ill. U., Edwardsville, 1972—, dir. East St. Louis Campus, 1982—; adjudicator music festivals; area music cons. Ill. Office Edn., 1977-78; program specialist St. Louis Human Devel. Corp., 1968; interim exec. dir. St. Louis Council Black People, summer 1970. Bd. dirs. YWCA, 1975-80, Artist Presentation Soc., St. Louis, 1975, United Negro Coll. Fund, 1976-78; bd. curators Lincoln U., Jefferson City, Mo., 1974—, pres., 1978—; chairperson Ill. Com. on Black Concerns in Higher Edn.; mem. Nat. Ministry on Urban Edn., Luth. Ch.-Mo. Synod, 1975-80; bd. dirs. Council Luth. Chs., Assn. of Governing Bds. of Univs. and Colls.; mem. adv. council Danforth Found. St. Louis Leadership Program, nat. chmn. Cleve. Job Corps, 1974-78; trustee Stillman Coll; pres. congregation St. Philips Luth. Ch.; bd. dirs. Target 2000. Named Woman of Achievement in Edn. award Elks, 1987, Disting. Citizen St. Louis Argus Newspaper, 1970; recipient Cotillion de Leon award for Outstanding Community Service, 1977, Woman of Achievement award Suburban Newspaper of Greater St. Louis and Sta. KMOX Radio, 1988; Disting. Alumnae award Lincoln U., 1977; Disting. Service award United Negro Coll. Fund, 1979, SCLC, 1981; Community Service award St. Louis Drifters, 1979; Disting. Service to Arts award Sigma Gamma Rho, Fred L. McDowell award, 1986, Nat. Negro Musicians award, 1981, Sci. Awareness award, 1984-85, Tri Del Federated award, 1985, Bus. and Profl. Women's Club award, 1985-86, vol. yr. Inroad's Inc., 1986; named Duchess of Paducah, 1973; received Key to City, Gary, Ind., 1973. Mem. Council Luth. Chs., AAUP, Coll. Music Soc., Music Educators Nat. Conf., Ill. Music Educators Assn., Nat. Choral Dirs. Assn., Assn. Tchr. Educators, Midwest Kodaly Music Educators, Nat. Assn. Negro Musicians, Jack and Jill Inc., Women of Achievement in Edn., Friends of St. Louis Art Mus., The Links, Inc., Las Amigas Social Club, Alpha Kappa Alpha (internat. parliamentarian), Mu Phi Epsilon, Pi Kappa Lambda. Lutheran. Home: 30 Plaza Sq Saint Louis MO 63103 Office: So Ill U Box 1200 Edwardsville IL 62026

HALEY, LYODENE BRANHAM, catering coordinator; b. Tuscola, Ill., Nov. 20, 1935; d. Melvin Erhwin and Virginia Beatrice (Bell) Branham; m. Arthur Raymond Haley, Nov. 20, 1955 (div. 1978); children: Shawn Denae, Robyn Denise, Erin Kathleen. Student, Elkhart (Ind.) U., 1956. Registered X-ray tech. X-ray tech. Crippled Childrens Hosp., Phoenix, 1956-57; co-owner Credible Edibles, Phoenix, 1975-80; catering dir. Alston & Bird Law Firm, Atlanta, 1980—; cons. Homeless Cafe, Atlanta, 1988; com. for food Friendship Force, Atlanta, 1990. Author: (play) Along Lifes Road, 1970. Active Campaign to Elect Julian Bond, Atlanta, 1988, Campaign to Elect Andrew Young, Atlanta, 1990. Presbyterian. Office: Alston & Bird IBM Tower 1201 W Peachtree Atlanta GA 30309

HALFORD, DONNA LANELLE, English educator; b. Wichita Falls, Tex., Feb. 4, 1942; d. James Austin and Julia Selma (Jones) Allard; m. Thomas Burt Perrault, June 16, 1961 (div. 1975); children: Barry Perrault, Tom Perrault, Kendra Perrault, Elaine Perrault; m. Bob Halford, Jan. 21, 1977. BA, Tex. Woman's U., 1981, MA, 1985, PhD, 1990. Asst. prof. English Cameron U., Lawton, Okla., 1988—. Recipient Rhetoric Rsch. award North Tex. Fedn., 1987, 88. Mem. South Cen. Modern Lang. Assn., Nat. Coun. Tchrs. English, Okla. Coun. Tchrs. English, Sigma Tau Delta (pres. Denton, Tex. chpt. 1985-86). Mem. Christian Ch. Home: 1801 NW 75th St Lawton OK 73505 Office: Cameron U Dept English 2800 Gore Lawton OK 73505

HALFVARSON, LUCILLE ROBERTSON, music educator; b. Petersburg, Ill., May 17, 1919; d. Harris Morton and Lucille (Fox) Robertson; m. Sten Gustaf Halfvarson, Aug. 8, 1946; children: Laura, Eric, Linnea, Mary. BA, Knox Coll., 1941; MusM, Am. Conservatory, 1969. Cert. tchr., Ill. Tchr. Music & Speech Freeman Elem. Sch., Aurora, Ill., 1941-44; choral dir. Galesburg (Ill.) Sr. High Sch., 1944-46; dir. of music Our Savior Luth. Ch., Aurora, Ill., 1950-63, Westminster Presbyn. Ch., Aurora, 1963-84; vocal instr. Merit Music Program, Chgo., 1982—; choir dir. 1st Meth. Ch., Galesburg, Ill., 1944-46; choral-vocal instr. Waubonsee Community Coll. Sugar Grove, Ill., 1967-79; organizer Jr. Coll. Music Fest. Waubonsee Coll., Sugar Grove, 1972-73; pvt. practice vocal instr., Aurora, 1979—. Conductor Messiah Concert Waubonsee Coll., Paramount Arts Ctr., 1968—. Co-chmn. Citizens' Adv. Com. Paramount Arts Ctr., Aurora, 1977-78; founder, pres. United Arts Bd. of Fox Valley, 1977-82, chmn. Paramount Celebration of Arts, 1985-86; residency dir. Met. Life Affiliate Artist, Aurora, 1982-83; bd. dirs. YWCA, 1984—. Recipient Disting. Svc. award Cosmopolitan Club, Aurora, Ill., 1983; named Woman of Year YWCA, Aurora, 1976, Disting. Alumni Knox Coll., Galesburg, Ill., 1984. Mem. AAUW, DAR, PEO, Music Educators Nat. Conf., Am. Choral Dirs. Assn., Phi Beta Kappa. Home: 1105 W Downer Pl Aurora IL 60506

HALIK, NANCY LICKERMAN, real estate manager; b. Michigan City, Ind., Nov. 2, 1954; d. Howard Wayne and Carolyn Ruth (Adler) L.; m. George Raymond Halik, July 28, 1979 (div. June 1989); 1 child, Andrew. BS in Archtl. Studies, U. Ill., 1976; MArch, U. Mich., 1979. Registered architect, Ill. Architect Harry Weese & Assocs., Chgo., 1979-87; project mgr. Stein & Co., Chgo., 1987—. Mem. Working Mom's Group, Winnetka, Ill. Mem. AIA. Jewish. Office: Stein & Co 227 W Monroe Chicago IL 60606

HALKA, KATHLEEN GRACE, pharmaceutical company medical director; b. Passaic, N.J., Apr. 21, 1953; d. Stanley Anthony Halka and Caroline (Nieradka) Alcorn. BA, Immaculata Coll., 1975; MD, Creighton U., 1980. Diplomate Am. Bd. Internal Medicine, Nat. Bd. Med. Examiners. Intern medicine U. Medicine and Dentistry N.J.-Rutgers U. Med. Sch., New Brunswick, N.J., 1980-81, resident medicine, 1981-83; fellow hematology Thomas Jefferson U., Phila., 1983-86; instr. medicine U. Medicine and Dentistry N.J.-N.J. Med. Sch., Newark, 1986-89; assoc. med. dir. Winthrop Pharms., N.Y.C., 1989—. Contbr. articles to profl. jours. NIH Tng. grantee, 1983-86. Mem. ACP, AAAS, Internat. Soc. Exptl. Hematology, Am. Soc. Hematology, N.Y. Acad. Sci. Home: 148 W 23rd St 10G New York NY 10011 Office: Winthrop Pharms 90 Park Ave New York NY 10016

HALKIN, ADELE DIANE, fundraising executive; b. Chgo., Nov. 5, 1931; d. Julius and Ida Anna (Michael) Jacobs; m. Charles Brohammer III, 1954 (div. 1955); m. Leslie Halkin, Feb. 24, 1956 (div. 1972); children: Alexandra Joan, Margaret Ruth. BFA, Art Inst., Chgo., 1954. Cert. fundraising exec. Exec. dir. Med. Com. for Human Rights, Chgo., 1970-72; mgr. Allied Edn. Council, Chgo., 1972-74; exec. sec. Ill. State Lottery Control Bd., Chgo., 1974-80; field coordinator U. Ill. Survey Rsch. Lab., Chgo., 1980-82; dir. devel. Portes Ctr., Chgo., 1982-84; assoc. dir. devel. Legal Assistance Found., Chgo., 1984-85; dir. devel. Chgo. Commons Assn., Chgo., 1985-88; regional dir., special gifts, events B'Nai B'rith Internat., 1988-90; v.p. devel. Goodwill Industries of Met. Chgo, 1990—. Bd. dirs. Arts Unltd., Chgo., 1985—, Am. Cancer Soc., Chgo. Unit, 1965-68; state pub. rels. chmn. III Women's Polit. Caucus, Chgo., 1975-79; chmn. Internat. Clearing House Women Strike For Peace, Glencoe, 1968-72, mail campaign Chgo. Found. for Women, 1990—. Mem. Nat. Soc. Fund Raising Execs. (bd. dirs. 1987—), Am. Propsect Rsch. Assn., Publicity Club Chgo., Chgo. Press Club (bd. dirs. 1985—). Jewish. Home: 707 W Barry Chicago IL 60657 Office: Goodwill Industries of Met Chgo 600 W Polk St Chicago IL 60607

HALL, ADRIENNE ANN, advertising agency executive; b. Los Angeles; d. Arthur E. and Adelina P. Kosches; m. Maurice Hall; children: Adam, Todd, Stefanie, Victoria. B.A., UCLA. Founding ptnr. Hall & Levine Advt., L.A., 1960-80; vice chmn. bd. Eisaman, Johns & Laws Advt. Inc., L.A., Houston, Chgo., N.Y.C., 1980—; bd. dirs. Calif. Mfrs. Assn. Svc. Corp., Inc.; chmn. Eric Bovy Inc., 1986-89. Trustee UCLA; bd. regents Loyola-Marymount U., Los Angeles; mem. Blue Ribbon of Music Ctr., Pres. Circle, Los Angeles County Mus. Art, Calif. Gov.'s Commn. on Econ. Devel.; bd. dirs. Wonder Women Found., N.Y.C.; mem. adv. council Girl's Clubs Am.; mem. adv. bd. Girl Scouts U.S., Asian Pacific Women's Network, fashion group, Downtown Women's Ctr. and Residence, Leadership Am., Washington; mem. exec. bd. Greater Los Angeles Partnership for Homeless, Los Angeles Shelter Partnership Bd.; mem. Nat. Network for Hispanic Women. Recipient Nat. Headliner award Women in Communications, 1982; recipient Profl. Achievement award UCLA Alumni, 1979; named Woman of Yr. Am Advt. Fedn., 1973, Ad Person of the West award Mktg. and Media Decisions, 1982; Bus. Woman of Yr. award Boy Scouts Am., 1983; Women Helping Women award Soroptimist Internat., 1984; Bullock's 1st ann. portfolio award for exec. women, 1985; Communicator of yr. award Ad Women, 1986; Leader award YWCA, 1986; named One of 20 Top Corp. Women, Savvy mag., 1983. Mem. Internat. Women's Forum (bd. dirs., Woman Who Made a Difference award 1987), Am. Assn. Advt. Agys. (bd. dirs., chmn. bd. govs. western region), Western States Advt. Agys. Assn. (pres.), Hollywood Radio and TV Soc. (dir.), Nat. Advt. Rev. Bd., Overseas Edn. Fund, Com. 200 (western chmn.), Women in Communications, Orgn. Women Execs., Calif. Women's Forum (founder, chmn. The Trusteeship), L.A. Area C. of C. (bd. dirs. 1987—), Rotary (L.A. 5 chpt.), Internat. Bus. Fellows (mem. adv. bd.), Women's Econ. Alliance, Nat. Assn. Women Bus. Owners (adv. bd.), Am. Heart Assn. (adv. bd.), The 2000 Partnership, L.A. Clubs: Calif. Yacht; Stock Exchange, Los Angeles Advt. (pres.) (Los Angeles). Lodge: Rotary.

HALL, AMANDA MCFARLAND, real estate broker; b. Van Nuys, Calif., Oct. 20, 1940; d. Robert Emmett and Virginia Winifred (Phillips) McF.; m. Edwin Lanier King, Jan. 25, 1957 (div. July 1958); 1 child, Keith McFarland; m. Archie A. Hall, Oct. 20, 1966. Student, Cedar Valley Jr. Coll., Lancaster, Tex., 1981-83, 89—. Sec. YMCA, Dallas, 1958-62; sec. Vought Corp. div. LTV, Dallas, 1963-65, adminstrv. sec., 1965-75, exec. sec., adminstrv. asst., 1975-84; owner, broker A&A Real Estate Services, Cedar Hill, Tex., 1984—; mem. bus. devel. bd. Duncanville (Tex.) Nat. Bank, 1985—, investigative rev. bd. Dallas Eye Inst., Duncanville, 1985—. Contbg. columnist Cedar Hill Chronicle, 1977-79. Mem. park bd. City of Cedar Hill, 1977-79; fin. chair First United Meth. Ch., Cedar Hill, 1987—, also active vol. work; del. 1984 Rep. Nat. Conv., Dallas; sec. S.W. Dallas County Reps., 1982-84, pres., 1984-85, 89—, v.p., 1987-88. Mem. Greater Dallas Bd. Realtors, Am. Bus. Women's Assn. (membership chmn. 1987, v.p. 1987-88, pres. 1988-90), Order Eastern Star. Home: 823 Cherlyne Dr Cedar Hill TX 75104 Office: A&A Real Estate Services PO Box 430 Cedar Hill TX 75104

HALL, ANNA CHRISTENE, government official; b. Tyler, Tex., Dec. 18, 1946; d. Willie B. and Mary Christene (Wood) H. BA in Polit. Sci., So. Meth. U., 1969. Clk.-stenographer Employment and Tng. Adminstrn., U.S. Dept. Labor, Dallas, 1970, fed. rep., 1970-80; program analyst U.S. Dept. Labor, Washington, 1980-84, div. chief, 1984-87, exec. asst., 1987-88; office dir. U.S. Dept. Labor, Dallas, 1988—. Recipient Outstanding Performance award U.S. Dept. Labor, 1972, 73, 74, 79, Meritorious Achievement award, 1986. Mem. Partnership for Employment and Tng., Nat. Honor Soc.

Democrat. Presbyterian. Home: 2304 Hunters Run Dr Dallas TX 75232 Office: US Dept Lab ETA 525 Griffin St Rm 315 Dallas TX 75202

HALL, BEVERLY ELAINE, television director; b. Port Arthur, Tex., Feb. 18, 1957; d. Milton Crawford and Jacqueline Ruth (Pevoto) H. BS in Mass Communications, Lamar U., 1979. Lic. real estate agt., Tex. Tech. dir. Port Arthur Cablevision, 1975-76; prodn. asst. Sta. KJAC-TV affiliate NBC, Port Arthur, 1976-80; word processor The Mansion on Turtle Creek, Dallas, 1980-81; prodn. asst. Sta. KBMT-TV affilate ABC, Beaumont, Tex., 1982; air dir. Sta. KFDM-TV affilate CBS, Beaumont, 1982—; coordinator TV talent Bum Phillips Celebrity Golf Tournament, Bob Hope Birthday Celebration, Port Arthur, 1980; real estate agt. Am. Real Estate, Port Neches, Tex., 1982. Producer, dir.: Life in America, 1982; author: (tng. jour.) Air Director's Manuel, 1987. Republican. Baptist. Home: 2714 S Kitchen Dr Port Neches TX 77651 Office: Sta KFDM-TV 2955 Interstate 10 E Beaumont TX 77706

HALL, BRENDA YVONNE, lawyer; b. Shelbyville, Tenn., Sept. 26, 1957; d. William G. and Alene (Russell) Hall; m. Gary L. McDonald, Sept. 4, 1982; children: Gary Lloyd Jr., Emily Ann. AS, Columbia (Tenn.) State Community Coll., 1976; BA, U. Tenn., 1978, JD, 1980. Bar: Tenn. 1981, U.S. Dist. Ct. (ea. dist.) Tenn. 1981. Student atty. U. Tenn. Legal Clinic, Knoxville, 1980; law clk. Meares and Meares P.C., Maryville, Tenn., 1981; ptnr. Gamble & Hall, Wartburg, Tenn., 1981-82; ptnr. McDonald & Hall, Kingston, Tenn., 1982—; adv. bd. to bd. dirs. Rural Legal Svcs. and Pub. Defenders Office, Oak Ridge, 1981-82. Rsch. editor Tenn. U. Law Rev. 1979-80. Area dir. Knoxville Opera Co., 1982. Mem. ABA, Am. Trial Lawyers Assn., Tenn. Bar Assn. (House of Del. 1987—, bd. dirs. Young Lawyers Conf. 1985—), Roane County Bar Assn. (sec., treas. 1985-87), Roane County Bar Assn., Internat. Platform Assn., Gamma Beta Phi, Phi Kappa Phi, Pi Delta Phi., Alpha Gamma Rho, Phi Delta Phi. Democrat. Mem. Ch. Christ. Office: McDonald & Hall 145 Court Sq Kingston TN 37763

HALL, CARYL R., training and support coordinator; b. N.Y.C., May 11, 1949; d. Jacob Sidney and Marian (Werner) Brod; m. Richard Wein, June 20, 1970 (div. 1981); m. Roger Wayne Hall, July 3, 1982; 1 child, Christy. A in Applied Sci., Fashion Inst. Tech., 1969; BA in Mgmt., U. Redlands, 1981. Supr. word processing Coldwell Banker Mgmt. Corp., Los Angeles, 1973-75; sr. text processing operator Jet Propulsion Lab., Pasadena, Calif., 1975-77; office automation analyst Union Oil Co., Los Angeles, 1977-79; supr. word processing Gen. Electric, El Monte, Calif., 1979-81; supr. sales support Wang Labs., Culver City, Calif., 1981-87; sr. systems cons. Wang Labs., Los Angeles, 1987-88, sr. mktg. specialist Western ops., 1988-90; tng. and support coord. western region Heitman Fin. Ltd., Beverly Hills, Calif., 1990—. Club: Toastmasters (Los Angeles).

HALL, CATHY JAYNE WRIGHT, psychology educator; b. Rome, Ga., May 11, 1951; d. Hoke S. and Delcia (Gilmore) Wright; m. Thomas Lee Hall, June 6, 1972; 1 child, Chris. BA, Emory U., 1972; MEd, U. Ga., 1974, EdS, 1977, PhD, 1982. Lic. psychologist. Sch. psychologist Oconee County Schs., Watkinsville, Ga., 1974-80; asst. prof. Ft. Hays State U., Hays, Kans., 1983-87, East Carolina U., Greenville, N.C., 1987—. Contbr. articles to profl. jours. Mem. Am. Psychol. Assn., Southeastern Psychol. Assn., Nat. Assn. Sch. Psychologist, Phi Delta Kappa. Office: East Carolina U Psychology Dept Greenville NC 27858

HALL, CHERYL ANN, data processing executive; b. San Diego, Sept. 29, 1954; d. Leo Franklin and Anita Lillian (Beuerlein) H. BA, U. Cin., 1979. Intern Lomark, Inc., Middletown, Ohio, 1974-78, mgmt. info. systems operator, 1978-79; dir. accounts Home Care, Inc., West Chester, Ohio, 1979-81; installation dir. SMS, Inc., Malvern, Pa., 1982-85, sr. installation dir., 1985-89; project mgr. western region SMS, Inc., Long Beach, Calif., 1989—. Patron Sta. WVXU-FM, Cin., 1984—; sustaining mem. Cin. Zool. Soc., 1984—; advisor youth commn. United Synagogue Youth, Hamilton, Ohio, 1985-88; mem. leadership coun. Jewish Fedn., Cin., 1985-89, Jewish Community Ctr., Cin.; trustee Congregation Beth Israel, Hamilton, 1985-89; bd. dirs. Temple Beth Zion Sinai, Lakewood, Calif., 1990—. Mem. Assn. for Systems Mgmt., Orgn. for Rehab. through Tng. (v.p. 1985-86). Jewish. Home: 100 Mountain View E Long Beach CA 90805 Office: SMS Inc 3901 Via Oro Ave #110 Long Beach CA 90810

HALL, CYNTHIA HOLCOMB, federal judge; b. Los Angeles, Feb. 19, 1929; d. Harold Romeyn and Mildred Gould (Kuck) Holcomb; m. John Harris Hall, June 6, 1970 (dec. Oct. 1980); 1 child, Harris Holcomb; 1 child by previous marriage, Desma Letitia. A.B., Stanford U., 1951, J.D., 1954; LL.M., NYU, 1960. Bar: Ariz. 1954, Calif. 1956. Law clk. to judge U.S. Ct. Appeals 9th Circuit, 1954-55; trial atty. tax div. Dept. Justice, 1960-64; atty.-adviser Office Tax Legis. Counsel, Treasury Dept., 1964-66; mem. firm Brawerman & Holcomb, Beverly Hills, Calif., 1966-72; judge U.S. Tax Ct., Washington, 1972-81, U.S. Dist. Ct. for central dist. Calif., Los Angeles, 1981-84; cir. judge U.S. Ct. Appeals (9th cir.), Pasadena, Calif., 1984—. Served to lt. (j.g.) USNR, 1951-53. Office: US Ct Appeals 125 S Grand PO Box 91510 Pasadena CA 91109-1510

HALL, ELIZABETH, writer; b. Bakersfield, Calif., Sept. 17, 1929; d. Edward Earl and Ethel Mae (Butner) H.; m. Fred Roy Mason; children: Susan Elizabeth Anderson, David Frederic Mason; m. Scott O'Dell. AB, Fresno State Coll., 1962. Br. librarian Kern County Free Library, Shafter, Calif., 1958-66; librarian U. Calif., Irvine, 1966-67; assoc. editor Psychology Today mag., Del Mar, Calif., 1967-68; asst. mng. editor Psychology Today mag., Del Mar, 1968-72, mng. editor, 1972-76; editor-in-chief Human Nature mag., N.Y.C., 1976-79; pvt. practice textbook author, writer Waccabuc, N.Y., 1979—; cons. Giunti Barbera Editore, Florence, Italy, 1985—; v.p., bd. dirs. Human Nature Inc., N.Y.C., 1976—. Author: Voltaire's Micromegas, 1967, Phoebe Snow, 1968, Stand Up, Lucy!, 1971, Why We Do What We Do, 1973 (nat. merit award 1974), From Pigeons to People, 1975 (nat. merit award 1976), Possible Impossibilities, 1977, Growing and Changing, 1987; co-author: (with others) Developmental Psychology Today, several edits., Child Psychology Today, 1982, 2d edit., 1986, Psychology Today: An Introduction, 5th edit., 1983, 6th edit., 1986, Sexuality, 1984, Adult Development and Aging, 1985, Principles of Psychology Today, 1987, Seasons of Life, 1990. Mem. AAAS, Soc. Rsch. Child Devel., Gerontological Soc. Am., Internat. Soc. Infant Studies, Fezziwigs, Textbook Authors Assn., Authors Guild. Democrat. Home and Office: Make Peace Hill Box 4 Waccabuc NY 10597

HALL, FRANCOISE PUVREZ, psychiatrist, consultant in preventive medicine; b. Rocourt, Liege, Belgium, Nov. 4, 1932; came to U.S., 1946; d. Paul Auguste and Marguerite Sophie (Wydemans) Puvrez; m. Thomas Livingston Hall, Dec. 22, 1955 (div. 1976); children: Eric Livingston, Tefel Alan, Rachel Francoise. B.Sc. in Physiology with honors, McGill U., 1953; MD, Harvard U., 1957; MPH, U. P.R., 1962. Diplomate Am. Bd. Preventive Medicine. Staff physician Castaner (P.R.) Gen. Hosp., 1958-60; rsch. assoc. U. P.R., San Juan, 1962-63; asst. prof. Johns Hopkins Sch. Hygiene, Balt., 1963-73; pvt. practice psychiatry Chapel Hill, N.C., 1977-84; cons. child psychiatry Shehar Mental Hosp., Taif, Saudi Arabia, 1984; v.p. Nat. Peace Inst. Found., Washington, 1985; pvt. practice psychiatry Sylva, N.C., 1986-88; assoc. prof. U. N.D., Fargo, 1988—; adj. sr. rsch. dir. Far West Lab., San Francisco, 1986; mem. community adv. bd. peace and conflict studies program U. Calif., Berkeley, 1985-86. Contbr. articles to profl. jours. Bd. dirs. Nuclear Age Peace Found., Santa Barbara, Calif., 1986. Milbank Meml. Fund grantee, 1963-64; N.W. Area Found. grantee, 1989—; Bush Found. grantee, 1989—. Democrat. Quaker. Office: U ND Med Edn Ctr 1919 Elm St N Fargo ND 58102

HALL, JANE ANNA, writer, model; b. New London, Conn., Apr. 4, 1959; d. John Leslie Jr. and Jane Dezzie (Green) H. Grad. model, Barbizon Sch., 1976. Model Barbizon Agy., New Haven, 1977; employed by dir. of career planning Wesleyan U., Middletown, Conn., 1985-86; free lance writer, poet, 1986—. Author: Cedar and Lace, 1986, Satin and Pinstripe, 1987, Fireworks and Diamonds, 1988, Stars and Daffodils, 1989; founder, editor: (newsletter) Poetry in Your Mailbox, 1989—; exhibited one-woman show Westbrook (Conn.) Pub. Library, 1989. Mem., tchr. Sunday Sch. First Congl. Ch., Westbrook, Conn., 1977-90, asst. supt., bd. dirs. Christian Edn., 1979-84; mem. poetry reading Congl. Ch., BroadBrook, Conn., 1988, group poetry reading, group poetry display Westbrook Pub. Libr., 1989. Recipient 2d prize Conn. Poetry Soc., 1983, Cert. Merit for Disting. Svc. to the Community, 1989, Cert. World Leadership, 1989. Mem. Internat. Platform Assn., Romance Writers Am. (Conn. chpt. 1989—), Conn. Poetry Soc. (pres. Old Saybrook chpt. 1989—, world poetry chmn. 1989, 2d prize winner 1986 poetry contest), Romance Writers Am. (mem. Conn. chpt.). Office: PO Box 629 Westbrook CT 06498

HALL, JANE DORY, artist, musician; b. L.A., Oct. 27, 1944; d. Irving and Ada Alvina (Gunderson) Helbling; m. Jesse Woodrow Hall, May 1989. AA, Pasadena City Coll., 1975; cert. nurse's aide, Fibrogen's Sch. Nursing. Nurses aide Convalescent Hosp., Pasadena, 1980-81; dir. of activities Joy Inn, Pasadena, 1984-88; artist Pasadena, piano and flute tchr., musical performer. One woman shows include Pasadena Pla., 1984, Family Home Savs. Bank, 1988, Pasadena Pub. Libr., 1989, Pasadena City Hall., 1989, Pace Art Show, 1987-89; exhibited in group shows at Pasadena Presbyn. Ch., 1981-85, Descanso Garden, 1980-85. Active Dem. Club, Pasadena. Home: 1070 N Lake Ave #119 Pasadena CA 91104

HALL, JOY LOUISE, business educator; b. Centerville, Ia., June 2, 1954; d. Byron and Ora Evelyn (McElderry) H. AA, Indian Hills Comm., Centerville, 1974; BA, U. Northern Ia., Cedar Falls, Iowa, 1976; MA, U. Northern Ia., 1985. Bus. edn. Eastern Allamakee Schs., Lansing, Ia., 1976-78, New Hampton (Ia.) Schs., 1978--; park attendant U.S. Army Corps. of Engrs., Centerville, Ia., 1979-80; adult edn. Northeast Ia. Tech., Calmar; instr. North Ia. Community Coll., Mason City, Ia., 1985; workshop tchr., computer cons., New Hampton Schs., 1985--. Vol. United Way, 1978--, Red Cross Bloodmobile, New Hampton, Ia., 1982--, 3rd dist. com. Ia. Democrats, Waterloo, 1988. Mem. New Hampton Edn. Assn. (treas. 1987-89), Iowa State Edn. Assn., Alpha Delta Kappa (treas. 1984-88, v.p. 1988-90, pres., 1990—). Home: 816 E Spring New Hampton IA 50659

HALL, JOYCE TURNER, utility company administrator; b. Atlanta, Sept. 1, 1948; d. Joseph C. and Hazel (Wilkins) Turner; m. Larry B. Hall, Aug. 16, 1969; children: Lamont D., Lisa D. BA in Spanish and Secondary Edn., Clark Coll., Atlanta, 1970. Mgmt. trainee Sears, Atlanta, 1970-71, dept. mgr., 1971-72, asst. mdse. mgr. so. terr., 1972-77; supr. Oglethorpe Power Corp., Tucker, Ga., 1979-88, buyer II, 1988—. Recipient Youth Motivation commendation Nat. Alliance Bus., 1983; Communication Techniques award Eileen M. Higgins & Assocs., 1983. Mem. Nat. Assn. Purchasing Mgmt., NAACP, Clark Coll. Alumni Assn. Democrat. Roman Catholic. Home: 3467 Blazing Pine Path Decatur GA 30034 Office: Oglethorpe Power Corp 2100 E Exchange Pl Tucker GA 30085

HALL, KATHERINE ANN, corporate communications specialist, consultant; b. Topeka, Aug. 23, 1963; d. John Lyman and Kathe (Gau) H. BS in Journalism, U. Kans., 1985. Pub. rels. asst. Falk Assocs./CONTACT, Chgo., 1987-88; communications asst. Am. Soc. for Aesthetic Plastic Surgery, Arlington Heights, Ill., 1988-89; communications assoc. Menninger Found., Topeka, 1989—; pub. rels. cons. Tic Tah Rock Band, Chgo., 1989. Chmn. publicity com. Shawnee coun. Camp Fire, Inc., Topeka, 1990—. Mem. Women in Communications, Inc. Office: Menninger Found Box 829 Topeka KS 66601-0829

HALL, KATHRYN EVANGELINE, author, lecturer; b. Biltmore, N.C.; d. Hugh Canada and Evangeline Haddon (Jenkins) Hall; B.A., U. N.C., M.A.; diploma Adams Sch. Music, Montreat, N.C.; postgrad. Yale, U. London, Fla. Atlantic U. Author: The Papal Tiara, History of the Episcopal Church of Bethesda-By-The-Sea, 1964, The Architecture and Times of Robert Adam, 1969, The Pictorial History of the Episcopal Church of Bethesda-By-The-Sea, 1970-71, 86, Joseph Wright of Derby, A Painter of Science, Industry, and Romanticism, 1974, A History of English Architecture, 1976-82; Sir John Vanbrugh's Palaces and the Drama of Baroque Architecture, 1982-84, History of the Episcopal Church of Bethesda-by-the Sea 1889-1989 The First One Hundred Years, 1990; lectr. history, art and architecture, U.S., Eng. and Scotland, 1961—. Vice pres. The Jr. Patronesses, Palm Beach, Fla., 1964. Mem. Nat. League Am. Pen Women (Owl award 1972, 76, 77, pres. Palm Beach chpt. 1975-80), Palm Beach Quills (historian), Palm Beach County Hist. Soc. (gov.), Internat. Platform Assn., Nat. Soc. Arts and Letters, Soc. Four Arts, Cum Laude Soc., Palm Beach Civic Assn. Episcopalian. Clubs: Everglades (Palm Beach); English Speaking Union (Palm Beach and London). Home: Acadie PO Box 648 Palm Beach FL 33480

HALL, LEE, artist, educator, design school president; b. Lexington, N.C., Dec. 15, 1934; d. Robert Lee and Florence (Fitzgerald) H. BFA, U. N.C., 1955; MA, N.Y. U., 1959, PhD, 1965; postgrad., Warburg Inst. U. London, 1965; DFA (hon.), U. N.C.-Greensboro, 1976. Asst. prof. N.Y. State U. Coll., Potsdam, 1958-60; assoc. prof., chmn. art dept. Keuka Coll., 1960-62; assoc. prof. art Winthrop Coll., 1962-65; asst. prof., chmn. art dept. Drew U., Madison, N.J., 1965-67; assoc. prof., chmn. art dept. Drew U., 1967-70, prof., chmn. art dept., 1970-74; dean visual arts State U. N.Y. Coll. at Purchase, 1974-75; pres. R.I. Sch. Design, Providence, 1975-83; sr. v.p. Acad. for Ednl. Devel., N.Y.C., 1984—, dir. div. arts and communications; dir. rsch. on Pres. Kennedy's image in recent art, John F. Kennedy Meml. Library; panelist NEH, 1972-80. Exhibited in group shows in London, N.Y.C., Winston-Salem, Eugene, Oreg., others; author: Wallace Herndon Smith: Paintings, 1987, Ale Ajay, 1989; contbr. articles to profl. jours. Recipient research grant Am. Philos. Soc., 1965, 68; Childe Hassam Purchase award Am. Acad. Arts and Letters, 1977; RISD Athena medal, 1983. Mem. Am. Soc. Aesthetics, Coll. Art Assn., Pi Lambda Theta. Office: Acad for Ednl Devel 100 Fifth Ave New York NY 10011

HALL, LESLIE CARLTON, artist, consultant; b. Rockville Centre, N.Y., May 14, 1952; d. Robert Wilson and Barbara Louise (Lyon) H. Student So. Conn. State Coll., 1970-72. BA in Psychology, U. Conn., 1975. Freelance artist PBC Advt. Co., New Canaan, Conn., 1978-80; graphics artist Stamford (Conn.) Weekly Mail, part-time 1978-80; art dir. Tru-Line Publs., Spring Valley, N.Y., 1974-80; owner Creative Intentions, Wilton, Conn., 1980—; cons. for creative design, logos. Editor: Pipeline, 1980-83; editor, pub. Dob Edition mag., 1989—; artist for cover Doberman World mag., 1985. Active Rescue and Placement of Abused or Stray Doberman Pinschers, Wilton, 1976—; frequent judge Doberman Sweepstakes, Match Shows. Mem. Internat. Platform Soc., Doberman Pinscher Club of Am., Doberman Pinscher Club of Tappan Zee (treas. 1976-82), Doberman Pinscher Club of Danbury (Conn.). Republican. Episcopalian. Home and Office: 341 Olmstead Hill Rd Wilton CT 06897

HALL, LORETTA J., apartment rentals company owner; b. Lewiston, Idaho, Aug. 13, 1932; d. Ralph and Stella Rosenberger; m. Jess G. Hall, June 11, 1950 (dec. Apr. 1988); children: Jess, Clinton, Stanley, Gary. Student, Kenai Peninsula Community Coll, Soldotna, Alaska. Cert. context associated-pursuit of excellence, office procedures, small bus. mgmt., computer ops., hotel/motel introductions. Owner, mgr. rental units Alora Ventures, Seward, Alaska; adminstrv. asst., bookkeeper Hall Quality Builders, Seward, Alaska; owner, mgr. Loretta's Interiors, Kenai, Alaska; adminstrv. asst., bookkeeper Hall Constrn., Inc., Kenai. Past den mother Cub Scouts; past sec., treas., bd. dirs. condominium; founder, pres., chmn. activities, pub. newsletter New 90's Singles, 1990—. Home: 1593 Sycamore Clarkston WA 99403

HALL, MADELON CAROL SYVERSON, music teacher; b. Kerkhoven, Minn., Dec. 27, 1937; d. Reuben C. and Hattie C. (Anderson) Syverson; m. Lewis D. Hall, June 13, 1959 (dec. 1984); children: Warren L., Charmaine D. BA, Trinity Bible Coll., Chgo., 1959; MEd, U.Cin., 1973. Cert. tchr., Ohio. Dir. admissions, asst. registrar Trinity Bible Coll., 1959-62; supr. elem. music edn. Dist. 80 Cook County Schs., Norridge, Ill., 1962-65; tchr. Rockford (Ill.) City Schs., 1966-67; tchr. music elem. grades Boone County Pub. Schs., Florence, Ky., 1970-72, Oak Hills Local Sch. Dist., Cin., 1972—. Named Tchr. of the Yr., Oak Hills Local Sch. Dist., 1990-91. Mem. NEA, Ohio Edn. Assn., Music Educators Nat. Conf., Career Edn. Assn. (Tchr. of Yr. Ohio unit 1989-90), World Future Soc., The Hunger Project. Methodist. Home: 456 Happy Dr Cincinnati OH 45238

HALL, MAMIE BARTON, retired home economics educator; b. Roanoke, Va., Apr. 22, 1928; d. Clifton Early and Annie Lee (Ayers) Barton; m. William Pembroke Hall, June 23, 1951; 1 child, Carolyn. BEd, James Madison u., 1949; postgrad., U. Va., Charlottesville, 1958, 66-67, U. Va., Roanoke, 1972-73, 77-78, 82-84. Chartered cert. home economist, Va. Asst. postmaster U.S. Post Office Dept., Hardy, Va., 1943-49; clerical sec. U.S. Treas; home econs. tchr. Clifton Forge (Va.) Sch. Bd., 1949-52, Alleghany County Sch. Bd., Covington, Va., 1952-53; home econs., catering, Eng. tchr. City of Covington Sch. Bd., 1954-88; ret.; adv. Future Homemakers Am., Clifton Forge and Covington, 1949-88. Cons. Fall Foliage Festival/Miss Alleghany Highlands Pageant, Clifton Forge, 1975-85; 1st runner-up Mrs. Virginia Pageant, 1957; organizer, leader Covington-Alleghany County March of Dimes, 1978-85; judge arts and crafts shows, Clifton Forge and Covington; adv. com. Alleghany Highlands Arts and Crafts, 1987—. Mem. AAUW, Am. Vocational Assn., Am. Home Econs. Assn., NEA (life mem.), Va. Edn. Assn. (life mem.), Ret. Tchrs. Assn., Rainbow Mt. Garden Club, Kappa Delta Pi, Delta Kappa Gamma (parliamentarian 1979-81, sec. 1981-83), Beta Sigma Phi. Baptist. Club: Clifton Forge Women's (various offices). Home: 1701 Ridgevue Ave Forest Hills Clifton Forge VA 24422

HALL, MARCIA JOY, non-profit organization administrator; b. Long Beach, Calif., June 24, 1947; d. Royal Waltz and Norine (Parker) Stanton; m. Stephen Christopher Hall, March 29, 1969; children: Geoffrey Michael, Christopher Stanton. AA, Foothill Coll., 1967; student, U. Oreg., 1967-68; BA, U. Washington, Seattle, 1969. Instr. aide Glen Yermo Sch., Mission Viejo, Calif., 1979-80; market rsch. interviewer Rsch. Data, Framingham, Mass., 1982-83; adult edn. instr. Community Sch. Use Program, Milford, Mass., 1982-83; career info. ctr. coord. Milford High Sch., 1983-86; corp. rels. dir. Sch. Vols. for Milford, Inc., 1985-86; NE area coord. YWCA of Annapolis and Anne Arundel County, Severna Park, Md. 1987-89; exec. dir. West Anne Arundel County C. of C., Odenton, Md., 1989—, 1989—. Pres. PTO, Mission Viejo, 1979-80, Milford, 1981-84; consumer assistance vol., Calif. Pub. Interest Rsch. Group, 1977-78. Mem. NAFE, Internat. Platform Assn., Toastmasters (treas. 1988—, pres. 1989—). Home: 507 Devonshire Ln Severna Park MD 21146

HALL, MARGARET O'CONNOR, educator; b. Jacksonville, Fla., Nov. 30, 1940; d. James Benson and Ida (Moricz) O'Connor; m. Robert Willis Hall, June 27, 1963; children: Robert Benson, Michael Patrick. BA, Barry Coll., Miami, Fla., 1962; MA, Fla. State U., 1965, EdS, 1990. Cert. tchr., Fla.; lic. real estate agt., Fla. Tchr. Latin, Leon County Sch. Dist., Tallahassee, 1970—, tng. coord., 1987—; chmn. fng. lang. dept. Leon High Sch., Tallahassee, 1985—; realtor Community Realty Group, Tallahassee, 1975-77; coord. Mgmt. Devel. Ctr., Tallahassee, 1988—. Bd. dirs. Hospice, Habitat for Humanity, Am. Lung Assn., Jr. Mus., Leon County Human Svcs., Cities in Schs.; mem. Fla. Gov.'s Coun. on Juvenile Justice; sec. Jr. League Tallahassee, 1983-84, v.p., 1984-85, pres., 1985-86, also bd. dirs.; mem. Leadership Tallahassee. Named Tchr. of Yr., Leon County Sch. Dist., 1985, Tchr. of Yr. Panhandle Region, State of Fla., 1985, Vol. of Yr., Tallahassee Women's Clubs, 1986, Tallahassee Dem. newspaper, 1986. Mem. ASDC, Classical Assn. Mid. West and South, Nat. Assn. Secondary Sch. Prins., Classical Assn. Fla. (pres. 1988-90, Latin Tchr. of Yr. award 1989), Phi Delta Kappa, Alpha Delta Kappa. Democrat. Roman Catholic.

HALL, MARIAN ELLA See ROBERTSON, MARIAN ELLA

HALL, MARIE, nurse; b. Vanceboro, N.C., Oct. 25, 1942; d. Jasper Lee and Elsie Mae (Justice) Beavers; m. John Hall, May 9, 1987; children: Celeste, Deanne, William. LPN, Norfolk Tech. Vocat. Ctr., Norfolk, Va., 1974; RN, Norfolk Gen. Sch Profl Nursing, 1984. RN. Relief supr. Humana Bayside Hosp., Virginia Beach; o.p. intravenous therapist Humana Bayside Hosp., Virginia Beach, Va.; emergency rm. RN Maryview Hosp., Portsmouth, Va.; RN neuro-surg. intensive care unit Norfolk Gen. Hosp.; relief supr. Camelot Hall Nursing Home, Chesapeake, Va.; owner Silk Forest, Virginia Beach. Home: 5645 Gates Landing Rd Virginia Beach VA 23464

HALL, MARY FIELDS, nurse, naval officer; b. Clear Ridge, Pa., Oct. 14, 1934; d. John Dewey and Lila Eleanor (Smith) Fields; m. Noel Orbia Hall, Nov. 28, 1964; children: Noel Orbia, David R. BSN, Boston U., 1966; MS in Nursing Administrn., U. Md., Balt., 1973. Commd. ensign USN, 1959, advanced through grades to rear adm., 1987; charge nurse USN Hosp., Bethesda, Md., 1959-62, St. Albans, N.Y., 1962-64; ednl. coord. USN Hosp., Guam, 1966-68; ambulatory care supr. USN Hosp., Camp LeJeune, N.C., 1968-71; patient care coor. USN Hosp., Portsmouth, Va., 1973-75; dir. nursing svcs. USN Hosp., Quantico, Va., 1975-78; head profl. nursing br. Div. Nurse Corps, Bur. Medicine and Surgery, Washington, 1978-81; dir. nursing svcs. USN, Newport, R.I., 1981-83; commanding officer USN, various, 1983-87; dir., Navy nurse corps Naval Med. Command (now USN Bur. Medicine & Surgery), Washington, 1987—; dep. commdr. for personnel mgmt. Naval Med. Command, Washington, 1987-89; asst. chief for personnel mgmt. USN Bur. Medicine & Surgery, Washington, 1989—. Decorated Navy Commendation medal, Legion of Merit. Mem. Nat. League for Nursing, Nat. Assn. Female Execs., Assn. Mil. Surgeons of U.S., Bus. and Profl. Womens Club, Navy Nurse Corps Assn., Sigma Theta Tau. Mem. Christian Ch. Office: US Dept Navy BUMED-05 The Pentagon Washington DC 20350*

HALL, MARY-JO, management educator; b. Durham, N.C., Jan. 5, 1947; d. Paul Thomas and Miriam Josephine (Burroughs) H.; m. Emmett E. Stobbs, Jr., July 19, 1975. BA in Tchg., High Point Coll., 1969; MEd, U. Md., 1972; MBA, L.I. U., 1980; DA in Edn., George Mason U., 1990. Elem. tchr. N.C., Md., Korea, Fed. Republic Germany, 1969-75; adminstr. U.S. Govt., Sacramento, 1976-78; counselor, trainer U.S. Mil. Acad., West Point, N.Y., 1978-81; contracts negotiator USN, Dahlgren, Va., 1981-82; contracts adminstr. USAF, McChord, Wash., 1982-83; leadership and evaluation officer ROTC, U.S. Army, Ft. Lewis, Wash., 1983-84; mgmt. analyst USN, Washington, 1984-88; chief Program Mgmt. Office U.S. Army Engr. Schs., Ft. Leonard Wood, Mo., 1988-89; prof. mgmt. Def. Systems Mgmt. Coll., Ft. Belvoir, Va., 1989—. Recipient achievement award U.S. Army, 1989. Mem. Acad. Mgmt., Am. Soc. Mil. Compts. (edn. award Ozark chpt. 1989). Lutheran. Home: 7708 Gromwell Ct Springfield VA 22152-3134 Office: Def Systems Mgmt Coll SE-P Fort Belvoir VA 22060-5426

HALL, PAMELA S., environmental consulting firm executive; b. Hartford, Conn., Sept. 4, 1944; d. LeRoy Warren and Frances May (Murray) Sheely; m. Stuart R. Hall, July 21, 1967. BA in Zoology, U. Conn., 1966; MS in Zoology, U. N.H., 1969, BBA summa cum laude, Whittemore Sch. Bus. and Econs., U. N.H., 1982; student spl. grad. studies program, Tufts U., 1986—. Curatorial asst. U. Conn., Storrs, 1966; rsch. asst. Field Mus. Natural History, Chgo., 1966-67; teaching asst. U. N.H., Durham, 1967-70; program mgr. Normandeau Assocs. Inc., Portsmouth, N.H., 1971-79, marine lab. dir., 1979-81, programs and ops. mgr., Bedford, N.H., 1981-83, v.p., 1983-85, sr. v.p., 1986-87, pres., 1987—. Mem. Conservation Commn., Portsmouth, 1977—, Wells, Estuarine Rsch. Res. Review Commn., 1986-88, Great Bay (N.H.) Estuarine Rsch. Res. Tech. Working Group, 1987-89; trustee Trust for N.H. Lands, 1990—. Graham Found. fellow, 1966; NDEA fellow, 1970-71. Mem. ASTM, Am. Mgmt. Assn., Water Pollution Control Fedn., Am. Fisheries Soc., Estuarine Rsch. Fedn., Nat. Assn. Environ. Profls., Sigma Xi. Home: 4 Pleasant Point Dr Portsmouth NH 03801 Office: Normandeau Assocs Inc 25 Nashua Rd Bedford NH 03201

HALL, PEGGIE ANN, municipal government official; b. Escanaba, Mich., May 29, 1947; d. Arnold Raymond and Mildred Eleanor (Larson) Ottensman; m. Robert Matthew Hall III, Nov. 28, 1970 (div. Jan. 1989); children: Tiffani Lee, Erika Rae. Grad. high sch., Escanaba, Mich., 1965. Cert. pub. housing mgr. Sec. Coleman Nee Co., Escanaba, Mich., 1964-65, Straubel Paper Co., Green Bay, Wis., 1965-68; from sec. to mgr. dept. billing Hein-Werner Corp., Waukesha, Wis., 1969-74; from sec. to asst. purchasing agent Green Bay Food Co., 1974-85; exec. dir. Housing Auth. City of New London (Wis.), 1985—. Active in PTO Lincoln Sch., New London, 1985-89; mem. various coms. City of New London, 1985—. Mem. Nat. Assn. Housing Auth. (dist. sec. 1988-90, dist. chmn. 1990—), New London Bus. and Profl. Women (pres. 1989-90), New London C. of C., Aid Assn. of Luths. (pres. local chpt. 1988—), Eastern Star. Office: Housing Auth City of New London 505 Division St New London WI 54961

HALL, PHOEBE POULTERER, lawyer, judge; b. Watertown, N.Y., Dec. 4, 1941; d. William Taylor, Jr., and Betty (Bennett) Poulterer; m. Franklin P. Hall, July 26, 1969; children—Kimberly Ann, Franklin P. B.A., U. Del.-Wilmington, 1963; J.D., Georgetown U., 1969. Bar: Va. Assoc., Hall & Hall, Richmond, Va., 1969—; substitute judge Gen. Dist. Cts., City of Richmond, 1983—, commr. in chancery, circuit cts., 1981—; founding dir., Cardinal Savs. & Loan Assn., Richmond, 1978—. Bd. trustees, Va. Mus. Fine Arts, 1983—; commr. Human Relations Commn., Richmond, 1972-73; dir. Family and Children's Services, Richmond, 1976-78; mem. worship com. 1st Presbyterian Ch., Richmond, 1983—; mem. state central com. Democratic Party, Va., 1974-80; pres. Women's Health Adv. Bd. Med. Coll. Va., 1989—; trustee Presbytery of the James, 1989—. Recipient Outstanding Citizenship award Urban League, Richmond, 1983; first woman pub. defender, City of Richmond, 1970; designer, instr. first course for paralegals, Va. State Bar, 1974. Mem. ABA, Richmond Bar Assn., Met. Richmond Women's Bar (founding 1971—), Va. Trial Lawyers Assn., Assn. Trial Lawyers Am., Def. Research Inst., Bus. and Profl. Women's Assn., Am. Bus. Women's Assn. Lodge Soroptimists. Home: 9006 Cherokee Rd Richmond VA 23235 Office: Hall and Hall Suite One 700 Bldg Richmond VA 23219

HALL, SARA FINNEY, accountant; b. Amory, Miss., Oct. 24, 1937; d. James Frank and Lilli Ann (Johnson) Finney; m. Lee Boyce Hall (dec.); children: James Randle, Sandra Leigh. AA, Itawamba Jr. Coll., Fulton, Miss., 1958; BS, U. N.C., 1977. Staff acct. Coopers Lybrand, Birmingham, Ala., 1966-71; comptroller J.B. Braswell Engrng. Co., Birmingham, 1972-77; dir. internal audit Carraway Meth. Med. Ctr., Birmingham, 1977-1988, mgr. acctg., 1988—. Mem. Healthcare Fin. Mgmt. Assn., Healthcare Internal Audit Group (charter), Inst. Internal Auditors Inc., Nat. Assn. Accts. Republican. Baptist. Home: 1509 August Cir Birmingham AL 35215

HALL, SUSAN BARTHOLOMEW, finance company executive; b. Grosse Pointe Farms, Mich., Mar. 22, 1943; d. Arthur Peck Jr. and Mary Elizabeth (Meyer) Bartholomew; m. Stephan E. Hall, Mar. 24, 1979; children: Elizabeth L. Krebs, William T. Krebs II. BA, U. Mich., 1964, MA, 1966; cert., Coll. Fin. Planning, 1983. Cert. fin. planner. Acct. exec. Merrill Lynch, Pierce, Fenner & Smith, Inc., Detroit, 1975-80; broker-dealer Mut. Svc. Corp., North Palm Beach, Fla., 1980—; pres. Birmingham (Mich.) Fin. Planning Corp., 1982—. Mem. Inst. Cert. Fin. Planners, Internat. Assn. Fin. Planning, Registry Fin. Planner (sec. S.E. Mich. chpt. 1983-84, bd. dirs. 1982-85), AAUW, Jr. League. Club: Women's Econ. (Detroit) (bd. dirs. 1980-83, treas. 1981-82). Office: Birmingham Fin Planning Corp 401 S Woodward Ste 441 Birmingham MI 48009

HALL, TELKA MOWERY ELIUM, educational administrator; b. Salisbury, N.C., July 22, 1936; d. James Lewis and Malissa (Fielder) Mowery; m. James Richard Elium III, June 20, 1954 (div. 1961); 1 child, W. Denise Elium Carr; m. Allen Sanders Hall, Apr. 15, 1967 (div. 1977). Student, Am. Inst. Banking, 1955-57; BA, Catawba Coll., Salisbury, 1967; MEd, Miss. U. for Women, Columbus, 1973; EdD, Appalachian State U., 1975, U. N.C., 1990; postgrad., U. N.C., 1990—. Cert. early childhood, intermediate lang. arts and social studies tchr., curriculum specialist, adminstr., supr., supt., N.C.; notary pub., N.C. Bookkeeper, teller Citizens & So. Bank, Spartanburg, S.C., 1955-56; bookkeeper 1st Nat. Bank, Killeen, Tex., 1956-58; bookkeeper, savs. teller Exchange Bank & Trust Co., Dallas, 1958-61; acct. Catawba Coll., 1961-65; floater teller bookkeeping and proof depts. Security Bank & Trust Co., Salisbury, 1965-68, 71; tchr. Rowan County Sch. System, Salisbury, 1967-70, 71-72, 73-81; asst. prin. North Rowan Elem. Sch., Spencer, N.C., 1981—; receptionist H & R Block, Salisbury, 1979-83; Chpt. I reading tchr. Nazareth Children's Home, Rockwell, N.C., 1979-81. Pianist Franklin Presbyn. Ch., Salisbury, 1952-55, choir dir., 1975-87; past pres. Women of Ch., Sunday Sch. tchr., deacon; cons. Dial HELP, Salisbury, 1977-79; vocalist Concert Choir, Salisbury, 1981-83; charter mem. bd. dirs. Old North Salisbury Assn., 1980—. Civitan Music scholar, 1954, Kiwanis Acad. scholar, 1966, Catawba Coll. Acad. scholar, 1965-67, Mary Morrow Ednl. scholar N.C. Assn. Educators, 1966. Mem. AAUW (v.p. 1985-87), N.C. Assn. Sch. Adminstrs., N.C. Prins.-Asst. Prins. Assn., Rowan County Prins. Assn., Kappa Delta Pi, Theta Phi. Home: 1626 N Main St Salisbury NC 28144 Office: North Rowan Primary Sch 600 Charles St Spencer NC 28159

HALL, TENNIEBEE MAY, editor; b. Bakersfield, Calif., May 21, 1940; d. William Elmer and Lillian May (Otis) Hall; m. Harold Robert Hall, Feb. 20, 1965. BA in Edn., Fresno State Coll., 1962; AA, Bakersfield Coll., 1960. Cert. tchr., Calif. Tchr. Edison (Calif.) Sch. Dist., 1963-65; substitute tchr. Marin and Oakland Counties (Calif.), Berkeley, 1965-66; engrng. asst. Pacific Coil Co., Inc., Bakersfield, 1974-81; editor United Ostomy Assn., Inc., Irvine, Calif., 1986—. Co-author: Treating IBD, 1989, Current Therapy in Gastroenterology, 1989; author, designer: Volunteer Leadership Training Manuals, 1982-84; contbr. articles to Ostomy Quar., 1973—. Mem. Pacific Beach Town Coun., San Diego, 1977—; campaign worker Maureen O'Connor (1st woman mayor of city), San Diego, 1986; mem. Nat. Digestive Diseases Adv. Bd. NIH, Washington, 1986—; various vol. activities, 1966-74, 81-86. Mem. Nat. Assn. Parliamentarians (unit v.p. 1988-90), United Ostomy Assn. Inc. (regional program dir. 1980-84, pres. 1984-86, Sam Dubin award 1983, Industry Adv. award 1987, local commendation San Diego chpt. 1978), Nat. Found. for Ileitis & Colitis (nat. trustee 1986—, nat. v.p. 1987—, local commendation San Diego chpt. 1988). Home: 5284 Dawes St San Diego CA 92109-1231 Office: United Ostomy Assn Inc 36 Executive Park Ste 120 Irvine CA 92714

HALL, TINA ANN, lawyer; b. Roanoke, Va., Nov. 6, 1957; d. Tommie W. and Nancy L. (Stanback) H. BA, Roanoke Coll., 1985; JD, Washington and Lee U., 1988. Bar: Md. 1988. Assoc. Cable, McDaniel, Bowie & Bond, Balt., 1988—. Mem. Md. Bar Assn., Phi Beta Kappa. Office: Cable McDaniel Bowie & Bond 333 S Beaudry Los Angeles CA 90017

HALL, WENDY JULIA, marketing executive; b. Queens, N.Y., May 23, 1951. BA in English Lit. and Edn., Hofstra U., 1973; postgrad., NYU, 1976-80. Dir. pub. rels. Environ. Rsch. & Devel., N.Y.C., 1978-79; mktg. coord. Neville Lewis Assocs., N.Y.C., 1981-84; office mgr. architecture dept. Dean Witter Reynolds, N.Y.C., 1984-85; mktg. dir. Walker Assocs. Inc., N.Y.C., 1985-87; dir. mktg. Descon Interiors Inc., N.Y.C., 1988-90, Planned Expansion Group Inc., White Plains, N.Y., 1990—. Mem. Comml. Real Estate Women, Soc. for Mktg. Profl. Svcs., Internat. Facilities Mgmt. Assn., Assn. Real Estate Women (pub. rels. com.), NAFE. Office: Planned Expansion Group Inc 30 Glenn St White Plains NY 10603

HALL, YONG OK, social worker; b. Korea, Apr. 20, 1950; d. Chang Kun Oh and Seong Sun (Shim) H. adopted father Gabe McConnie Hall. BA in Sociology and Psychology, U. Wash., 1973, MSW, 1974-76. Bilingual counselor City of Seattle, 1973; geriatric social worker Good Samaritan Hosp., Puyallup, Wash., 1974-75; med. social worker Seatoma Convalescent Ctr., Kent, Wash., 1974-76; geritatric mental health cons. Lutheran Community Services, Bremerton, Wash., 1977-78; ombudsman Dept. Social & Health Services, Olympia, Wash., 1978—; initiator and bd. dirs. nursing home visitation program Friend-to-Friends, 1974-77; instr. Highline Community Coll., Kent, Wash., 1976, S. Puget Sound Community Coll., Tumwater, 1977; faculty mem. U. Wash., Seattle, 1978, St. Martin's Abbey Coll, Lacey, 1986-87; founder, advisor Wash. State Nursing Home Family Council, 1982—; bd. dirs. Nat. Tardive Dyskinesia Assn. Vol. USO, Tacoma, 1984—. Fellow The Oregon Health Scis. U., 1989; Nat. Mental Health grantee, 1974-76; recipient Merit Appreciation Sr. Svcs. of Washington, 1986. Mem. Nat. Assn. Social Work, Am. Geriatric Soc., Nat. Assn. State Omubdsman Program (bd. dirs. 1984-86), Am. Assn. For Univ. Women (bd. dirs. 1981-82), N.Y. Acad. Scis. Office: Wash Dept Social and Health Svcs PO Box 7581 Olympia WA 98501

HALLANAN, ELIZABETH V., federal judge; b. Charleston, W.Va., Jan. 10, 1925; d. Walter Simms and Imogene (Burns) H. U. Charleston, 1946; JD, W.Va. U., 1951; postgrad. U. Mich., 1964. Atty. Crichton & Hallanan, Charleston, 1952-59; mem. W.Va. State Bd. Edn., Charleston, 1955-57, Ho. of Dels., W.Va. Legis., Charleston, 1957-58; asst. commr. pub. instns. Charleston, 1958-59; mem., chmn. W.Va. Pub. Service Commn., Charleston, 1969-75; atty. Lopinsky, Bland, Hallanan, Dodson, Deutsch & Hallanan, Charleston, 1975-84; judge U.S. Dist Ct. (so. dist.) W.Va., 1983—. Mem. ABA, W.Va. Bar Assn. Office: US Dist Ct PO Drawer 5009 Beckley WV 25801

HALLBAUER, ROSALIE CARLOTTA, business educator; b. Chgo., Dec. 8, 1939; d. Ernest Ludwig and Kathryn Marquerite (Ramm) H. BS, Rollins Coll., 1961; MBA, U. Chgo., 1963; PhD, U. Fla., 1973. CPA, Ill.; cert. mgmt. acct., cost analyst. Assoc. prof. bus. Fla. Internat. U., Miami, 1972—. Mem. AICPA, Am. Accounting Assn., Nat. Assn. Accts.,Am. Woman's Soc. CPAs, Ill. Soc. CPAs, Inst. Mgmt. Acctg., Beta Alpha Psi, Pi Gamma Mu. Office: Fla Internat Univ Tamiami Trail Miami FL 33199

HALLBERG, NANCY LEVY, advertising agency executive; b. Englewood, N.J., Nov. 13, 1951; d. Israel and Gloria (Cutler) Levy; m. Garth R. Hallberg, Mar. 23, 1984. BA, U. Mich., 1973; MA, U. Ill., Urbana, 1974; MBA, U. Pa., 1978. Properties supr. McCarter Theatre, Princeton, 1975-76; account exec. J. Walter Thompson, N.Y.C., 1978-80, v.p., 1980—, account supr., 1980-84, mgmt. supr., 1984-88, sr. v.p., account dir., 1988—. Democrat. Jewish. Office: J Walter Thompson 466 Lexington Ave New York NY 10017

HALL BRAULT, PHYLLIS, hospital equipment company executive; b. Lockport, N.Y., June 16, 1941; d. Raymond Silsby and Rachel (Davis) Pease; 1 child, Heather Hall. BA, Ohio State U., 1963. Sec.-treas. Northside Surg., Rochester, N.Y., 1966-87; pres., chief exec. officer Northside Surg., 1987—; treas. Southside Apothecary, Rochester, 1981—. Chmn. bd. dirs. Rochester Mental Health Ctr., 1983-87; sec. Rochester Health Care, Inc., 1987-88, Health Assn. Rochester, 1972-73. Mem. AAUW (pres.-treas. Rochester br. 1970-74, Bus. and Industry Woman of the Yr. award Rochester br. 1989), Nat. Assn. Med. Equip. Suppliers, Rochester Women's Network, Monroe County Minority and Women Owned Bus. (adv. bd. 1989-90), C. of C. (comml. small bus. council bd. dirs. 1988-89), Nat. Assn. Women Bus. Owners (pres. 1988—), Rochester C. of C. (bd. dirs. 1989—). Democrat. Home: 431 Thomas Ave Rochester NY 14617 Office: Northside Surgical 1165 Portland Ave Rochester NY 14621

HALLE, MARILYN ANNE, family therapist, educator; b. Dexter, Maine, Jan. 30, 1933; d. Charlie Everett and Leona Ruth (Peavy) Hall; m. Samuel William Rinn III, June 28, 1953 (div. 1977); children: Kathryn Ann, Nancy Hall, Marilyn Louise, M. Jane. BA in Polit. Sci., U. Pitts., 1976, MEd, 1976. Counselor Churchill High Sch., Pa., 1975-76; trainer, counselor Contact Teleministries, Inc., Pitts., 1972-75; quality control mgr. Nike, Inc., Exeter, N.H., 1980-81, internat. quality control mgr., 1982-83; owner Ameribiz Employment, Portsmouth, N.H., 1985-87; family, spiritual couselor. Coordinator, bd. dirs. Wilkinsburg Community Ministry, 1972-73. Mem. AACD, NAFE. Republican. Avocations: treasure hunting; study and practice of metaphysics. Home: 20B Ash St Dover NH 03820

HALLE KEYLOUN, SUSAN ANNE, fashion designer; b. Acushnet, Mass., Jan. 21, 1952; d. Maurice Alfred and Eleanor (Germain) Beauregard; m. Stanley E. Halle, Aug. 27, 1972 (div. 1977); m. Theodore E. Keyloun, June 29, 1988. BFA, Pratt Inst., 1974. Asst. designer Shutterbug, N.Y.C., 1973-74, Love Eileen, N.Y.C., 1974-75; designer Lomie Casuals, N.Y.C., 1975-77, 8/10 EOM, N.Y.C., 1977-78, Christian Dior, N.Y.C., 1986-87; head designer M.B.D., N.Y.C., 1978-79, Flair Lingerie, N.Y.C., 1979-86, St. Anna, N.Y.C., 1987—; head designer, owner W.A.S.P. Inc., Edgartown, Mass., 1987—. Mem. Martha's Vineyard (Mass.) Preservation Soc., 1985—. Mem. Fashion Group. Republican. Home: Off Chappaquiddick Rd PO Box 898 Edgartown MA 02539 Office: St. Anna 48 E 43d St New York NY 10017

HALLENBERG, NANCY LEE, school administrator; b. Toledo, Feb. 13, 1941; d. Wallace John and Elizabeth Jane (Manley) Corban; m. James Edward Hofferberth, Aug. 26, 1961 (div. 1984); children: Matthew James, Wendy Lee, John Edward; m. Harvey Raymond Hallenberg, Feb. 14, 1986. BS in Edn., Ohio State U., 1962; MEd in Reading, George Mason U., Fairfax, Va., 1977; postgrad., U. Md., 1978, Ohio State U., 1979, 84. Lectr./asst. George Mason U., Fairfax, 1976-77; tchr. St. Joseph Montessori Sch., Columbus, Ohio, 1979-80; lead tchr., Erdkinder project St. Joseph Montessori Sch., 1980-84; elem. prog. coordinator Inst. Advanced Montessori Studies, Silver Spring, Md., 1984-87; elem. intern coordinator Inst. Advanced Montessori Studies, 1984-87; reading specialist City of Manassas pub. schs., Va., 1985-86; Montessori ednl. cons. Hallenberg & Hallenberg Cons., Chantilly, Va., 1984—; lectr./tchr. trainer Inst. for Adv. Montessori Studies, Silver Spring, 1983—; co-dir. The Claremont Sch., Annandale, 1986—; researcher in field; writer, dir., tchr. Montessori programs for secondary level students. Contbr. articles to profl. jours. Vol. tchr. gifted children Fairfax County pub. schs., 1977-78. Grantee, The Washington Post, 1985-86. Mem. Am. Montessori Soc., Armfield Farm Civic Assn., Phi Delta Kappa, Kappa Delta Pi. Office: The Claremont School 4326-K Evergreen Ln Annandale VA 22003

HALLER, HAYDEN ABNEY, registered lobbyist; b. Oklahoma, Dec. 2, 1950; d. William Charles and Jean (Lowry) Abney; 1 child, Aryn Andrew. BA in Psychology, U. Okla., 1976. Health planner W. Contra Costa Community Health Care Corp., Richmond, Calif., 1977-79; prin. planner, analyst W. Contra Costa Community Health Care, Richmond, 1979-80; cons. rsch. grant writer Cosmetic Surgeon, Oklahoma City, 1980-81; mktg. rep. The Prudential, Oklahoma City, 1981, administrv. mgr., 1983-86, govt. rels. specialist, 1986—, registered lobbyist, 1988—. Mem. Okla. Health Planning Adv. Coun., Oklahoma City, 1987—; pres. bd. dirs. Community Health Ctr., 1988-89, v.p. bd. dirs., 1987-88. Recipient Okla. Debutante award Beaux Arts Soc. Okla., 1969-70. Mem. Okla. Assn. Health Maintenance Orgn. (v.p. Oklahoma City chpt. 1988, pres. 1988-89), Kappa Alpha Theta. Home: 115 Monticello San Francisco CA 94132

HALLETT, CAROL BOYD, diplomat; b. Oakland, Calif., Oct. 16, 1937; married. Student, U. Oreg.; student, San Francisco State Coll. Field office rep. Calif. State Assemblyman and State Senator, 1966; staff asst. U.S. Congressman, 1967-76; assemblywoman Calif. State Assembly, Sacramento, 1976-82, minority floor leader, 1979-82; cons., dir. Found. for Individual and Econ. Freedom, Sacramento, 1982-83; dir. of parks and recreation Calif., 1982-83; western regional dir. Citizens For Am., Sacramento, 1983-84; asst. to U.S. Sec. Interior, 1984-85; nat. field dir. Citizens For Am., Washington, 1985-86; amb. Am. embassy, Nassau, Bahamas, 1986-89; U.S. commr. of customs U.S. Customs Svc., Washington, 1989—. Office: US Customs Svc 1301 Constitution Ave NW Washington DC 20229

HALL-EWIG, LEONA MAXINE, educational consultant; b. Tahlequah, Okla., Feb. 24, 1934; d. Henry Paul and Alta Addie (James) Simpson; m. Ernest Carl Hall, Oct. 28, 1953 (div. 1985); children: Sherry Jean, Pamela Kay; m. Gerald A. Ewig, Dec. 27, 1987. BS in Edn., Cen. State U., 1955; MS in Edn., U. Okla., 1963; cert. in counseling, Southwest Tex. State U., 1975; cert., Values Realization Inst., Hadley, Mass. Tchr. Hazelwood Sch. Dist., Florissant, Mo., 1971-72; elem. sch. counselor Austin (Tex.) Ind. Sch. Dist., 1972-76; asst. dir. univ. extension Coll. Home Econs., Stillwater, Okla., 1977-80; tng. coord. Child Care Careers, Stillwater, 1980-82; exec. dir. Child Care Careers, 1982-87; pres. New Horizons Learning System, Toledo, 1988—; com. chair, Child Care Connections, Oklahoma City, 1983-85; mem. adv. bd., Okla. Child Devel. Assn., Oklahoma City, 1986-87, Rose State Coll., Oklahoma City, 1985-87. Mem. Values Realization Inst., Okla. Nat. Assn. for Edn. of Young Children, Okla. Assn. for Children Under Six. Democrat. Home and Office: 2733 Barrington St Toledo OH 73609

HALLIDAY, HARRIET HUDNUT (HOLLY HALLIDAY), free-lance editor; b. Springfield, Ill., Dec. 7, 1941; d. William Herbert and Elizabeth Allen (Kilborne) Hudnut; BA, Coll. Wooster, 1963; postgrad. McCormick Theol. Sem., Northwestern U., 1989—; m. Terence C. Halliday, June 14, 1980; children: Tyler Hudnut Colman, Richard Terence, Kimberly Anne, Alastair Charles. Exec. sec. women's bd. Presbyterian Med. Ctr., San Francisco, 1965-68; editor Am. Bar Found., Chgo., 1968-70, asst. dir. publs., 1970-75, mng. editor Am. Bar Found. Research Jour., 1975-80; research asst. dept. philosophy Australian Nat. U., Canberra, 1980-82; mng. editor Chiron Publs., 1983-86; acad. asst. to dean social scis. U. Chgo., 1986-87; dir. BCH Corp., 1985-87; freelance editor, 1988—; pres. bd. dirs. Women's Exchange, 1988—. Mem. exec. com. jr. governing bd. Chgo. Symphony Orch., 1969-70, 75-76; officer adv. bd. Unitarian Presch. Center, Chgo., 1974-77; mem. Assocs. Rush-Presbyn.-St. Luke's Med. Ctr., 1974-79; mem. alumni bd. Coll. Wooster, 1978-80, also chmn. pub. relations com., mem. nominating com., by-laws revision com.; pres. Women's Exchange, 1988—; bd. dirs. Children's Theatre of Winnetka, Ill., 1984-85; exec. com. Chgo. Bible Soc., 1983-86. Republican. Presbyterian. Home and Office: 955 Vernon Ave Winnetka IL 60093

HALLIN, GAYLE ANNETTE, public health administrator; b. Mpls., Apr. 8, 1948; d. Gene Douglas and Melvina Therina (Ose) Sanford; m. John Paul Hallin, June 6, 1969; children: Kjersten, Britta, Johan. BS, U. Minn., 1970, MPH, 1977. Med./surg. nurse St. Joseph Hosp., Lancaster, Pa., 1970-71; orthopedic nurse Fairview Southdale Hosp., Edina, Minn., 1971-72; pub. health nurse Anoka (Minn.) County, 1972-75; health coordinator City of Bloomington, Minn., 1977-86; health adminstr. City of Bloomington, 1986—. Trustee Healtheast, St. Paul, 1966—, Bethesda Med. Ctr., St. Paul, 1977—; pres. Metro Trustee Coun., Mpls.-St. Paul, 1990; bd. dirs. North Suburban Youth Health Clinic, Robbinsdale, Minn., 1976-81; pres.-elect Bloomington Heart Health, Inc., 1986—; bd. dirs. Bloomington Found., 1989—; youth leader St. Paul Luth. Ch., Minnetonka, Minn., 1976—. Mem. Minn. Pub. Health Assn. (pres. 1988-89), Am. Pub. Health Assn., Minn. Community Health Svcs. Adminstrs. Assn., Minn. Pub. Health Nursing Dirs. Assn. Lutheran. Home: 14805 Lloyds Dr Minnetonka MN 55345

HALLOCK-MULLER, PAMELA, oceanography educator, biogeologist, researcher; b. Pierre, S.D., June 2, 1948; d. Graydon B. and Marjorie L. (Millard) H.; m. Robert Glenn Muller, Aug. 22, 1969. BA in Zoology, U. Mont., 1969; MSc in Oceanography, U. Hawaii, 1972, PhD in Oceanography, 1977. Asst. prof. earth scis. U. Tex. of Permian Basin, Odessa, 1978-83; assoc. prof. marine sci. U. South Fla., St. Petersburg, 1983-88, prof., 1988—; bd. dirs. Cushman Found. for Foraminiferal Rsch., Washington, 1989—. Assoc. editor Jour. Foraminiferal Rsch., Washington, 1985—; mem. editorial bd. Marine Micropaleontology jour., 1990—; tech. editor field trip guidebooks, 1982, 83; contbr. articles to sci. jours., chpts. to books. Vol. speaker Pinellas County (Fla.) Schs. Vol. Speakers Bur., 1984—, U. South Fla.-St. Petersburg Speakers Bur., 1989-90; judge local, regional and state sci. fairs, Fla., 1989-90; vol. Pinellas County Democrats, St. Petersburg, 1988. Deutscher Akademischer Austanschdienst rsch. fellow, Kiel, Fed. Republic Germany, 1978; summer faculty fellow Nat. Aero. and Space Adminstrn., Goddard Space Flight Ctr., 1987; NSF rsch. grantee, 1981, 85, 87, 89. Fellow Cushman Found. Foraminiferal Rsch., Geol. Soc. Am.; mem. Paleontol. Soc., Assn. Women Geoscientists, Soc. Sedimentary Geology (v.p. Permian Basin sect. 1982-83), Am. Littoral Soc. (sci. advisor Coral Reefs 1988-89), N.Am. Micropaleontol. Soc. Democrat. Office: U South Fla Dept Marine Sci 140 7th Ave S Saint Petersburg FL 33701

HALONEN, MARILYN JEAN, immunologist, researcher; b. Duluth, Minn., July 8, 1941; d. George Uuno and Helmi Elaine (Aalto) Wainio; m. Robert John Halonen (div.); m. Michael Anthony Cusanovich; 1 child, Darren Anthony. B.S., U. Minn., 1963; M.S., Iowa State U., 1968; Ph.D., U. Ariz., 1974. Research technician U. Chgo., 1964-65; med. technologist Mercy Hosp., Des Moines, 1965-66; research asst. U. Ariz., Tucson, 1968-71, research assoc., 1975-77, adj. asst. prof., 1977-83, research assoc. prof. dept. medicine, 1983-87, assoc. prof. dept. pharmacology, 1987—. Contbr. chpts. to books, articles to profl. jours. Postdoctoral fellow Ariz.-Am. Heart Assn., 1974-75; recipient Young Investigators Pulmonary award NIH, 1975-77, NIH Career Devel. award, 1977-82, grantee, 1977—. Mem. Am. Assn. Immunologists, Internat. Soc. Immunopharmacology, Am. Thoracic Soc. Office: U Ariz Health Scis Ctr Dept of Pharmacology Tucson AZ 85724

HALPER, ANITA SOLOVY, speech-language pathologist; b. Chgo., Feb. 16, 1935; d. Maurice E. and Ruth (Chavkin) Solovy; m. Ira S. Halper, Aug. 28, 1956; 1 child, Amy Ruth. BS, Northwestern U., 1956, MA, 1959. Speech pathologist Ill. Children's Hosp. Sch., Chgo., 1956-60; dir. dept. communicative disorders Rehab. Inst. Chgo., 1960—; adj. instr. communicative disorders No. Ill. U., Dekalb, 1979—; clin. asst. prof. dept. communication scis. and disorders Northwestern U., Evanston, Ill., 1978—; from instr. to asst. prof. rehab. medicine Northwestern Med. Sch., Chgo., 1968—. Contbr. articles to profl. jours.; co-author: numerous book chpts., editor books, jours.; author books. Fellow Am. Speech Lang. Hearing Assn. (chair clin. cert. bd. 1985-87, award 1987); mem. Internat. Neuropsychology Soc., Am. Congress Rehab. Medicine, Acad. Aphasia (treas. 1987—), Nat. Aphasia Assn. (adv. bd.), N.Y., Ill. Speech, Lang., Hearing Assn., Chgo. Speech, Lang., Hearing Assn. Office: Rehab Inst Chgo 345 E Superior Chicago IL 60611

HALPER, JAROSLAVA, pathology educator; b. Prague, Czechoslovakia, Aug. 1, 1953; came to U.S., 1980; d. Karel and Susanne (Kulka) Tausinger; m. Edward Charles Halper, Aug. 19, 1979; children: Yehuda, Daniel, Aaron. Student, Charles U., Prague, 1972-76; MD, U. Toronto, 1980; PhD, U. Minn., Rochester, 1986. Diplomate Am. Bd. Pathology. Resident pathology Albert Einstein Coll. Medicine, Bronx, N.Y., 1980-81; postdoctoral fellow Mayo Clinic Found., Rochester, 1981-82, pathology resident, 1982-86; rsch. assoc. Vanderbilt U., Nashville, 1985-86; asst. prof. pathology U. Ga., Athens, 1986—; clinician-investigator Mayo Clinic Found., 1984-86. NIH postdoctoral fellow Mayo Clinic Found., 1981-82; NIH rsch. grantee U. Ga., 1987-91; recipient Biotech. award U. Ga., 1990. Mem. AAAS, Am. Soc. Cell Biology, Am. Assn. Pathology, Internat. Acad. Pathology. Jewish. Home: 126 Henderson Ave Athens GA 30605 Office: U Ga Dept Pathology Athens GA 30602

HALPER, JUNE ANN, human resource development consultant; b. N.Y.C., Dec. 13, 1949; d. Harold Herbert and Sophy (Cohen) H. BS in Edn. magna cum laude, Syracuse U., 1970; MA in Guidance and Counseling, Columbia U., 1971, MEd, 1973. Asst. mgmt. devel. and tng. Philip Morris, USA, N.Y.C., 1971-75; organizational devel. and tng. RCA Missile and Surface Radar, Moorestown, N.J., 1975-80; prin. cons. Ebasco Svcs., Inc., N.Y.C., 1980-86; prin. Halper & Assocs., N.Y.C., 1986—; adj. instr. Am. Mgmt. Assn. Mem. N.Y. Human Resource Planners, Nat. Orgn. Devel. Network, N.Y. Orgn. Devel. Network, Am. Soc. for Tng. and Devel.

HALPERIN, CORRINE SANDRA, trade association administrator; b. Providence, Feb. 8, 1936; d. Barney and Rose Ruth (Bilsky) Gordon; B.A., Mercyhurst Coll., 1980; postgrad., SUNY, Buffalo; m. Leo William Egan, Nov. 28, 1986; children: Karen Halperin Shor, Micheal Jay, Amy Marlene. Freelance market researcher, 1968-72; exec. dir. Coun. Vols. Erie County, 1971-78; exec. dir. YWCA, Erie, 1978-81; unit dir. Am. Cancer Soc., Erie, 1982; adj. faculty Mercyhurst Coll., dir. community edn., 1982-84, dir. spl. events, 1984-85; program dir. Northwest Pa. Area Labor Mgmt. Coun., Erie, 1985-86, exec. dir., 1986—; adviser Hospitality House for Women, 1975-78; bd. dirs. GROW, 1988—. Chmn. Erie County Commn. Drug and Alcohol Abuse, 1978-80; active Pa. Commn. for Women, 1990—. Recipient Community Service award, 1977, 498 Hardworking Women in Pa., 1987. Mem. Indsl. Rels. Rsch. Assn., AAUW, Nat. Council Jewish Women, The Erie Eighty (pres. 1985-87, treas. 1987—). Contbg. editor: Vol. Adminstrn., 1973-83. Home: 3756 Gable Court Dr Erie PA 16506 Office: NW Pa Area Labor Mgmt Coun 818 Peach St Erie PA 16501

HALPERIN, ESTHER WAITZ, clothing company executive; b. Allentown, Pa., Aug. 17, 1925; d. Abraham and Sadie (Ostrow) Waitz; m. Marvin Goldberg, 1947 (div. 1957); m. Bernard Halperin, June 15, 1963 (dec. 1964); children—Richard Goldberg, Jonathan Halperin; m. Abe Krantz, June 19, 1974 (div. dec. 1985). B.A., Moravian coll., 1948; M.S., Temple U., 1962. Pre-sch. tchr. Jewish Community Ctr., Allentown, 1955-63, summer camp tchr. 1955-63; kindergarten tchr. Jewish Day Sch., Allentown, 1962; pres. Halsen Products, Inc., Slatington, Pa., 1964—. Chmn. Allentown United Way, 1966-81; subscriber Met. Opera, N.Y.C., 1974—. Mem. Atlantic Apparel Assn., Lehigh Valley Needle Trades (bd. dirs. 1964-80, chmn. Pa. apparel week 1969), Pi Delta Epsilon. Republican. Clubs: Hadassah, ORT (Allentown). Lodge: Shriners. Avocations: opera; ballet; dancing; travel. Home: 3717 Congress St Allentown PA 18104 Office: Halsen Products Inc 216 Cherry St Slatington PA 18080

HALPERN, FRANCES JOY, journalist, author; b. N.Y.C., Aug. 20; d. Murray Isaacs and Raya (Hamilton) Isaacs; m. Theodor Herzl Halpern; children: Michael, Leslie, Evan. Student, Am. Acad. Dramatic Arts, 1945, NYU. Staff writer Palos Verdes Peninsula (Calif.) News, 1968-73; columnist L.A. Herald Examiner, 1982-87, L.A. Daily News, Woodland Hills, Calif., 1987—; talk show host Sta. KTMS-AM, Santa Barbara, Calif., 1988—; guest panelist on publ. confs.; cons. U. Calif., L.A., 1984-86; workshop leader Santa Barbara Writer's Conf., 1979—. Author: Writer's Guide to West

Coast Publishing, 1980, Writer's Guide to Publishing in the West, 1982, (with others) Complete Guide to Writing Nonfiction, 1985, Complete Guide to Writing Fiction, 1990; contbr. articles to nat. mags. and newspapers, 1970—. Pres. Friends of the Libr., Palos Verdes Peninsula, 1967; editor State Friends of Libr., Calif., 1968; precinct worker polit. campaigns, Calif., 1965-80. Mem. Am. Soc. Journalists and Authors (treas. So. Calif. chpt., panelist, moderator N.Y. 1990), Authors Guild, Soc. Profl. Journalists, P.E.N. Ctr. West, Am. Women in Radio & TV, Women in Communications, Inc., and others. Democrat. Office: The Daily News PO Box 5657 Montecito CA 93150

HALVORSEN, SUSAN MARIE, management consultant; b. Chgo., Mar. 30, 1955; d. George Walter and Evelyn Irene (Wodzin) H. AA, Moraine Valley Community Coll., 1974; BA, Gov.'s State U., 1976; MBA, Lewis U., Romeoville, Ill., 1982. CPA, Fla. Specialist stats. Nat. Tea Co., Rosemont, Ill., 1971-77; supr. warehouse Carson Pirie Scott and Co., Chgo., 1977-78; asst. v.p., controller Fasano Pie Co., Chgo., 1978-83; controller ctr. Distron, div. Burger King, Lakeland, Fla., 1983-88; mgr. mgmt. cons. svcs. Applied Tech. Ctr. Price Waterhouse, Tampa, Fla., 1988—. Pres. St. Anthony Parish Council, Lakeland, 1986-89. Mem. AICPA, Fla. Inst. CPA's. Office: Price Waterhouse 1410 N Westshore Blvd Tampa FL 33630

HALVORSON, JUDITH ANNE (DEVAUD), elementary school educator; b. Bethesda, Md., Apr. 28, 1943; d. Henri J. and Mary L. (Baumgart) Devaud; m. Peter L. Halvorson, Feb. 4, 1964; 1 child, Peter Chase. BS in Edn., U. Cin., 1965; MA in Edn., U. Conn., 1974, Cert. Advanced Grad. Study in Edn., 1980. Tchr. Greenhills (Ohio) Forest Park City Schs., 1965-67, Weld County Schs., Greeley, Colo., 1969-70, Chaplin (Conn.) Elem. Sch., 1970—; program mentor State of Conn. and Chaplin Elem. Sch., 1988—; supr. student tchrs. East Conn. State U., U. Conn., U. No. Colo., 1969—. Vice-chmn., past chmn., sec. Coventry (Conn.), Ed. Edn., 1981—; com. chmn. Coventry Sch. Bldg., 1981—; chmn. Coventry Parks and Recreation Commn, 1980-82; mem. Dem. Town Com., Coventry, 1973—. Recipient grant Nat. Sci. Edn. project, Chaplin, Eastern Conn. State U., 1977-78; named Outstanding Elem. Tchr. of Am., Washington, 1974. Mem. NEA, Conn. Edn. Assn., Chaplin Edn. Assn. (past pres., v.p., chmn. negotiations 1970), Pi Lambda Theta (past pres., v.p., chmn. membership local chpt. 1974—), Phi Delta Kappa. Episcopalian. Home: 90 David Dr Coventry CT 06238

HALYARD, REBECCA ANNE, biology educator; b. Memphis, 1944; d. James L. and Alice (Sanders) H.; m. Brooke M. Pridmore, Mar. 21, 1987. BA, Emory U., Atlanta, 1965, MS, 1967; EdD, U. Ga., 1976. Profr. Clayton State Coll., Morrow, Ga., 1969—; Contbr. articles to profl. jours. Mem. Community Relations Commn. Dekalb County, 1984—; Sec. Atlanta Branch AM. Assoc. U. Women Atlanta, 1985-87; Pres. Atlanta Branch Am. Assoc. U. Women Atlanta, 1987-89. Mem. Soc. Coll. Science Tchr., Nat. Science Tchr. Assoc., Counselor at Large Soc. Coll. Science Tchr. Baptist. Office: Clayton State Coll 5900 Lee St Morrow GA 30260

HAMBURG, BEATRIX ANN, medical educator, researcher; b. Jacksonville, Fla., Oct. 19, 1923; d. Francis Minor and Beatrix (Downs) McCleary; married, May 25, 1951; children: Eric N., Margaret A. A.B., Vassar Coll., 1944; M.D., Yale U., 1948. Diplomate: Nat. Bd. Med. Examiners. Intern Grace-New Haven Hosp., 1948-49; resident Yale Psychiat. Inst., New Haven, 1949-50; resident in pediatrics Children's Hosp., Cin., 1950-51; resident in psychiatry Inst. Juvenile Research, 1951-53; research assoc. Stanford U. Med. Sch. (Calif.), 1961-71, assoc. prof. psychiatry, 1976-80; assoc. prof. Harvard Med. Sch., Boston, 1980-83; exec. dir. Div. Health Policy Research, 1981-83; prof. psychiatry and pediatrics Mt. Sinai Med. Sch., N.Y.C., 1983—, dir. div. child and adolescent psychiatry, 1988—; assoc. dir. Lab. of Stress and Conflict, Stanford U. Med. Sch., 1974-76; sr. research psychiatrist NIMH, Bethesda, Md., 1978-80; dir. studies Pres.'s Commn. Mental Health, 1977-78; mem. vis. com. Sch. Pub. Health, Harvard U., 1977-80, commn. on behavior and soc., Nat. Acad. Scis., 1983—. Author: Behavioral and Psychosocial Issues in Diabetes, 1980, School Age Pregnancy and Parenthood, 1986; contbr. numerous sci. articles to profl. jours. Trustee W.T. Grant Found., 1978—; bd. dirs. New World Found., 1978-83, Bush Found., Revson Found., Greenwall Found., 1986—; mem. Pub. Health Coun. State of N.Y., 1978-80. Vis. scholar Ctr. Advanced Study Behavioral Scis., 1967-68; recipient Outstanding Achievement award Alcohol, Drug Abuse and Mental Health Adminstrn., 1980. Fellow Am. Acad. Child Psychiatry; mem. AAAS (bd. dirs. 1987—), Inst. of Medicine of Nat. Acad. Scis., Soc. Profs. Child Psychiatry (program com. 1972-74), Am. Acad. Child Psychiatry (adolescent com. 1977-81), Soc. Adolesent Medicine, Am. Pub. Health Assn. (adolesent com. 1978-80), Soc. Study of Social Biology, Acad. Research in Behavioral Medicine (exec. council 1980), Phi Beta Kappa. Office: Mt Sinai Med Ctr 1 Gustave L Levy Pl New York NY 10029

HAMBURGER, MARY ANN, medical management consultant; b. Newark, Aug. 25, 1939; d. Herman and Sylvia (Strauss) Marcus; div. June 1966; children: Bruce David, Marc Laurence. AA, U. Bridgeport (Conn.), 1960. Office mgr. Millburn, N.J., 1970-84; propr., mgr. Mary Ann Hamburger, Assocs., med. mgmt. cons. co., Maplewood, N.J., 1984-; tchr. adult edn. South Orange Maplewood Bd. Edn., 1975-83; cons. Wellcare of N.Y.; profl. physician recruiter, N.Y., N.J. Mem. NAFE. Democrat. Jewish. Home and Office: 74 Hudson Ave Maplewood NJ 07040

HAMBY, CAROLYNN SUE, nurse, author; b. Washington, Ind., Apr. 12, 1938; d. Elbert Glen and Laura Catherine (Osha) Yarbrough; m. Richard Russell Hamby, Mar. 2, 1957; 1 child, Russell Glen. ASN, Vincennes (Ind.) U., 1960; BA in Psychology, U. Cen. Fla.; MA in Counseling, Rollins Coll., 1980; PhD, Tex. A&M U., 1985. RN, Va., Tex., Ill., Fla. Staff nurse USPHS, Norfolk, Va., 1963-65; psychiat. nurse USPHS, Ft. Worth, 1965-67; English tchr. Bridgetown Tire Co., Yokosuka, Japan, 1968-70; head nurse Physician's and Surgeons Hosp., Corpus Christi, Tex., 1970-72; nursing coord. psychiat. dept. VA Hosp., Downey, Tex., 1973-74; psychiat. staff nurse Medicenter Hosp., Wichita Falls, Tex., 1974-75; nursing edn. instr. Sunland Tng. Ctr., Orlando, Fla., 1975-77; asst. dir. Orlando Gen. Hosp., 1977-80; assoc. chief nurse extended care dept. Olin E. Teague VA Med. Ctr., Temple, Tex., 1980—; women's vet. coord. VA Med. Ctr., Temple, 1984—, mgr. fed. women's program, 1987—. Co-author: The Road to Personal Success; contbr. articles to profl. jours. Pres. Tem-Bel Am. Heart Assn., Temple, 1989—; bd. dirs. Bell County DWI Task Force, Belton, Tex., 1985—, Leadership Temple, 1988—; mem. bd. trustees Temple Pub. Library, 1985-88. Named one of Outstanding Citizens, Temple Jaycees, 1987; recipient Citation award Vincennes U., 1988. Mem. AAUW (bd. dirs. Tex. chpt. 1987—, Leadership growth trainer, community rep. 1988—), Fed. Employed Women, Torch Club, Phi Delta Kappa, Pi Lamba Theta. Republican. Home: 4105 Hickory Temple TX 76502 Office: Olin E Teague VA Med Ctr 1901 S 1st Temple TX 76501

HAMBY, JEANNETTE, state legislator; b. Virginia, Minn., Mar. 15, 1933; d. John W. and Lydia M. (Soderholm) Johnson; m. Eugene Hamby, 1957; children—Taryn Rene, Tenya Ramine. BS, U. Minn., 1956; MS, U. Oreg., 1968, PhD, 1976. Vice chmn. Hillsboro High Sch. Dist. Bd., 1973-81; mem. Washington County Juvenile Services Com., 1980—; mem. suggested legis. com. Council State Govts., 1981—, Oreg. state rep., 1981-83; mem. Oreg. State Senate from 5th dist., 1983—. Mem. Oreg. Mental Health Assn., Am. Nurses Assn., Oreg. Nurses Assn., Am. Vocat. Assn., Oreg. Vocat. Assn., Oreg. Vocat./Career Adminstrs., Phi Kappa Phi, Phi Delta Kappa. Lutheran. Republican. Office: Oreg State Senate Salem OR 97310 Home: 952 Jackson School Rd Hillsboro OR 97123*

HAMED, MARTHA ELLEN, government administrator; b. Washington, Jan. 14, 1950; d. Rockford Norris and Dorothy Hope (Lough) H. Student George Washington U., 1972-87, AA, 1985, BA in Psychology, Sociology, 1989. Command fed. women's program mgr. U.S. Atlantic Fleet, Norfolk, Va., 1978-79; fed. women's program mgr. Naval Ordnance Sta., Indian Head, Md., 1979-80; personnel mgr., EEO course dir. Naval Civilian Personnel Command, Arlington, Va., 1980-83; dep. EEO officer, site mgr. Ship Research and Devel. Ctr., Bethesda, Md., 1983-85, Naval Surface Weapons Ctr., Silver Spring, Md., 1985; command fed. women's program mgr. Naval Sea Systems Command, Washington, 1985-87, mgr. command tng. programs, 1987—; asst. dir. awards and performance appraisal programs, 1987-89; asst. mgmt. analysis Office of Insp. Gen., 1989—; owner, prin. Sophisticated Silks of Annapolis Floral Co. Recipient Sustained Superior Performance award Naval Civilian Personnel Command, 1982, Spl. Achievement award, 1983, Sustained Superior Performance award Naval Surface Weapons Ctr., 1985, Performance Mgmt. award Naval Sea Systems, 1986, 87, 88, Outstanding Performance award, 1989, Navsea Medallion, 1989; named to Outstanding Young Women Am., U.S. Jaycees, 1983. Mem. Federally Employed Women, NOW. Democrat. Episcopalian. Avocations: natural history, cats, salt-water fishing. Office: Naval Sea Systems Command OON3 Washington DC 20362

HAMEISTER, LAVON LOUETTA, farm manager, social worker; b. Blairstown, Iowa, Nov. 27, 1922; d. George Frederick and Bertha (Anderson) Hameister; B.A., U. Iowa, 1944; postgrad. N.Y. Sch. Social Work, Columbia, 1945-46, U. Minn. Sch. Social Work, summer 1952; M.A., U. Chgo., 1959. Child welfare practitioner Fayette County Dept. Social Welfare, West Union, Iowa, 1946-56; dist. cons. services in child welfare and pub. assistance Iowa Dept. Social Welfare, Des Moines, 1956-58, dist. field rep., 1959-64, regional supr., 1964-65, supr., specialist supervision, adminstrn. Bur. Staff Devel., 1965-66, chief Bur. Staff Devel., 1966-68; chief div. staff devel. and tng. Office Dep. Commr., Iowa Dept. Social Services, 1968-72, asst. dir. Office Staff Devel., 1972-79, coordinator continuing edn., 1979-86; now co-mgr. Hameister Farm, Blairstown, Iowa. Active in drive to remodel, enlarge Oelwein (Iowa) Mercy Hosp., 1952; active in devel. mental health ctrs. in N.E. Iowa in 1950's. Mem. Bus. and Profl. Women's Club (chpt. sec. 1950-52), Am. Assn. U. Women, Nat. Assn. Social Workers (chpt. sec.-elect 1958-59), Am. Pub. Welfare Assn., Iowa Welfare Assn., Acad. Cert. Social Workers. Lutheran.

HAMEL, ALDONA MARY, marketing executive; b. Lowell, Mass., Oct. 17, 1946; d. Frederick E. and Aldona Mary (Pieslak) H.; m. Robert Louis Gomes, Feb. 1, 1969 (div. 1977); m. David Exton Devendorf, Aug. 12, 1978; children: Hilary Dandridge, Alexandra Exton. BA, Boston U., 1968. Lic. real estate salesman, Conn. Mgr. litigation dept. Pepsico Leasing Corp., Lexington, Mass., 1969-74; mgr. vendor programs Keybank Inc. Leasing, Waltham, Mass., 1974-77; mgr. nat. accounts Pitney Bowes Credit Corp., Norwalk, Conn., 1977-83; v.p. Citicorp N.Am., Harrison, N.Y, 1984—; sr. v.p. mktg. DPF Group Ltd., Woodcliff Lake, N.J., 1986—. Mem. Am. Assn. Equipment Lessors (programming com. 1988, operating lease com. 1989—), Women in Equipment Leasing (founder, chmn. 1987—). Republican. Office: DPF Group Ltd 50 Tice Blvd Woodcliff Lake NJ 07675

HAMEL, ELIZABETH CECIL, teacher, volunteer; b. Altoona, Pa., June 13, 1918; d. Francis Anthony and Charlotte Margaret (Devine) Murphy; m. William Rogers Hamel, Mar. 2, 1943; children: Michele Ferencsik, Deirdre, Anthony, Cecily Charlyn Houston. BArt, Villa Maria Coll., 1939; MA, Pa. State U., 1940; cert. approval, U. Cambridge, Eng., summer 1986. Tchr. English, head Spanish dept. East High Sch., Erie, Pa., 1940-43; prof. lit. Vernon Ct. Jr. Coll., Newport, R.I., 1966-69. Mem. Francestown (N.H.) Improvement Assn., 1958—, Peterborough (N.H.) Hist. Soc., 1987—, Art and Hist. Soc. E. Martello Tower Mus., Key West, Fla., 1987—, Founder's Soc., Tennessee Williams Fine Arts Ctr., Key West, 1986—, Old Island Restoration Found., Key West, 1980—; bd. dirs. Friends of Libr., 1985-87, sec., 1986-87; mem. White House Vol. Group, Washington, 1972-74; trustee Newport County Preservation Soc. Mem. Gen. Fedn. Women's Club (bd. dirs. Key West chpt. 1986—), Key West Woman's Club (bd. dirs., parlimentarian 1986—, del. state conv. 1988), Peterborough Woman's Club, Garden Club, Greenfield Woman's Club (pres. 1979-80). Republican. Roman Catholic. Home: 16 Hanley Farm Warren RI 02885

HAMEL, VERONICA, actress; b. Phila., Nov. 20, 1943. Student, Temple U. Model, 10 yrs. First stage role in The Big Knife, off-Broadway; appeared with road company in Cactus Flower; appeared in TV miniseries 79 Park Avenue, 1977, Jacqueline Susann's Valley of the Dolls, 1981, Kane and Abel, 1985; star TV series Hill Street Blues, 1981-87 (Emmy nomination 1981, 82, 83); TV movies include The Gathering, 1977, Ski Lift to Death, 1978, The Gathering, Part II, 1979, The Hustler of Muscle Beach, 1980, Sessions, 1983; films include Cannonball, 1976, Beyond the Poseidon Adventure, 1979, When Time Ran Out, 1980, A New Life, 1988; appeared on stage in The Miracle Worker, St. Louis, 1982. Office: Agy for Performing Arts 9000 Sunset Blvd Ste 1200 Los Angeles CA 90069*

HAMEL, VICKI OTTO, retirement services officer; b. Chgo., May 25, 1947; d. Earle W. and Paula Mae (Holman) Otto; m. Francis H. Hamel, July 7, 1969. Student Western Ill. U., 1965-66, Berlitz Sch. Langs., 1967, U. N.C., Wilmington, 1984-85, Brunswick Tech. Coll., N.C., 1986. Office mgr. Adm. Coated Products, Inc., Skokie, Ill., 1966-69; paralegal law firm, Southport, N.C., 1972-74; credit mgr. Augusta Furniture Co., Staunton, Va., 1976-78; trust/tax clk. Franklin-Lamoille Bank, St. Albans, Vt., 1978-80; customs teller U.S. Customs Service, St. Albans, 1980-82; mgmt. analyst Dept. Army, Mil. Ocean Terminal, Southport, 1982-86, retirement services officer, Ft. McCoy, Wis., 1986-89, fed. women's program mgr., 1983-86; asst. dist. mgr. staff adminstrn. Bur. of Land Mgmt., Rawlins, Wyo., 1989—. Mem. Boiling Spring Lakes Planning Bd., 1985-86. Named Woman of Yr. Southport Jr. Women's Club, 1975; recipient profl. awards U.S. Govt. Mem. Gen. Fedn. Women's Clubs, N.C. Fedn. Women's Clubs (dist. v.p. 1974-75), Am. Soc. Profl. and Exec. Women, Am. Bus. Women's Assn., NAFE. Republican. Roman Catholic. Clubs: Southport Jr. Women's (pres. 1975), Southport Women's (pub. affairs dept. 1984). Home: 809 E Murray St Rawlins WY 82301 Office: Bur Land Mgmt Rawlins WY 82301

HAMELINK, CRYSTAL MARY, human resources executive; b. Little Falls, N.Y., Dec. 6, 1947; d. Harold J. and Marian Louise (Hood) Settle; m. Drew R. Hamelink, Aug. 4, 1973; children—Craig A., Michael M. B.A., Wagner Coll., 1969; M.P.A., SUNY-Albany, 1984. Dir. employee advancement program N.Y. State Dept. Civil Service, Albany, 1984-87, dir. external program services div., 1988— . Treas., emergency med. technician Ballston Lake Emergency Squad, Ballston Lake, N.Y., 1979—. Mem. Internat. Personnel Mgmt. Assn., Pi Alpha Alpha. Unitarian. Home: 122 Westside Dr Ballston Lake NY 12019 Office: NY State Dept Civil Svc State Office Bldg Bldg 1 Albany NY 12239

HAMILL, JUDITH ELLEN, municipal government administrator; b. Chgo., Mar. 8, 1953; d. William Patrick and Dolores Jean (Lhamon) H. MusB, Roosevelt U., 1975; M of Urban Planning and Policy, U. Ill., Chgo., 1979; M of Pub. Adminstrn., Harvard U., 1982. Staff asst. Thomas H. Miner & Assocs., Chgo., 1972-75; project dir. Chgo. Council on Fine Arts, 1977-78; project planning city of Chgo. Dept. Planning, 1978-81; research staff Stevenson/Stern for Ill., Chgo., 1982; ind. cons. Chgo., 1982-86; city planner Dept. Aviation, Chgo., 1986-87; dir. noise abatement office Dept. of Aviation, Chgo., 1987—. Vice chairperson Ill. Women's Polit. Caucus, Chgo., 1975-82; active Women in Govt. Relations, Chgo., 1977-82, Ill. Dem. Women, Springfield, Ill., 1981—, Cook County Dem. Women, Chgo., 1982—; mem. jr. governing bd. Chgo. Symphony Orch., 1981-89, mem. Bus. and Profl. Assn. of Chgo. Symphony Orch., 1990—; bd. dirs. Rogers Park Community Coun., 1990. Harvard U. Scholar, Cambridge, Mass., 1981-82. Club: Harvard of Chgo. Home: 1847 W Touhy Ave Chicago IL 60626

HAMILL, MARY KAY, space systems analyst; b. Ancon, Canal Zone, June 21, 1956; d. Jimmy Mearl Hamill and Marion Louise (Ross) McCullough. BS, U. South Miss., 1978; postgrad., Pepperdine U., 1990—. Tech. staff Space Applications Corp., Sunnyvale, Calif., 1985-87; sr. analyst mgr. Tecolote Rsch. Corp., Manhattan Beach, Calif., 1987-89; prin. investigator Nichols Rsch. Corp., El Segundo, Calif., 1989—. Instr., counselor 1736 House for Abused Women and Children, Hermosa Beach, Calif., 1989-90. Capt. USAF, 1979-85. Mem. U.S. Space Found., Armed Forces Communications Electronics Assn., Air Force Assn., NAFE. Republican. Office: Nichols Rsch Corp 300 Continental Ste 330 El Segundo CA 90245

HAMILTON, ANGELA L., insurance claims examiner; b. El Paso, Tex., July 11, 1955; d. Henry Hiram and Blanche Naomi (Eades) Lyda; m. Michael Lee Hamilton, June 11, 1955. AS, Greenville Tech. Coll., 1975. Cert. CPIW, gen. ins., personal auto coverage, workers compensation, investigation and operation lace, notary pub. Ins. claims examiner Seibels Bruce, Greenville, S.C.; claims rep. Am. Mut. Fire Ins., Greenville; customer svc. rep. Carolina Ins. Cons., Greenville; ins. claims sec. Underwriters Adjusting Co., Greenville. Mem. Greenville Assn. Ins. Women, NAFE.

HAMILTON, ANNE LINNEA, accountant; b. Joliet, Ill., Nov. 16, 1949; d. Charles Theodore and Margaret Kathleen (O'Neill) H.; 1 child, Jennifer Anne. BSBA, U. Phoenix, Ariz., 1987, MA in Mgmt., 1988. With Pima County, Tucson, 1979—, sr. budget analyst, 1982-86, acctg. officer, 1986—. Chair Girl Scouts Troop 250, Tucson, 1979-80; tng. supr. Ariz. Sch. for deaf and Blind, Tucson, 1981. Recipient T. Abner Huff award, 1987, Clarion Salute, 1984. Mem. Am. Soc. for Pub. Adminstrn., Assn. Govt. Accts., Network for Profl. Devel. Home: 6701 E Cooper St Tucson AZ 85710

HAMILTON, BARBARA, minister, human services director, consultant; b. Hartford, Conn., Jan. 3, 1943; d. Harry and Rose Ida (Cohen) Karpman; m. Benjamin Theodore Sporn, Sept. 4, 1960 (div. 1967); children: Mindy Rebecca Sporn, Sarah Ann Sporn. BA, Eckerd Coll., 1983; MA, Norwich U., Vt., 1985. Ordained to ministry Assn. of Spirit of Gaiabriel, 1988. Asst. publicity mgr. Estee Lauder Inc., N.Y.C., 1972-74; owner, ptnr. Strongstarr Inc., N.Y.C., 1975-77; owner Barbara Hamilton Cons. Services, N.Y.C., 1977-81; co-founder The Life Ctr., Tampa, 1981-83; co-founder, co-dir. Project Rainbow, St. Petersburg, Fla., 1983-87; dir. project Rainbow Cons. Services, Inc., 1987—; mem. adv. bd. Suncoast Children's Dream Fund, St. Petersburg, 1986—; cons. Cancer/Clergy Residency, St. Petersburg, 1983-87. Mem. Eckerd Coll. Alumni Bd. Recipient Service to Mankind awards Sertoma Club, 1984-85. Mem. Coun. of Elders East Coast; bd. trustees Assn. of Spirit of Gaiabriel, 1987—. Mem. Assn. Care Children's Health, Forum Death Edn. and Counseling, Internat. Imagery Assn., Nat. Soc. Fund Raising Execs., Assn. Humanistic Psychology, Eckerd Coll. Alumni Bd. Avocations: meditation, crystals, holistic health. Home: 7529 1/2 3rd Ave N Saint Petersburg FL 33710

HAMILTON, BEATRICE, psychotherapist, counseling administrator; b. Macon, Miss., Dec. 2, 1947; d. Walter Henley and Tiller (Cotton) Henley. BS, Miles Coll., 1972; MA, Atlanta U., 1974; EdD, Vanderbilt U., 1986. Nat. cert. counselor; cert. profl. counselor. Researcher Iowa State U.; dir., asst. prof. counseling ctr. U. Md. Eastern Shore, Salisbury; pvt. practice counseling Salisbury; lectr. Salisbury State U.; mgr. budgeting and planning Collins Svcs., Huntsville, Ala.; dir. residence Ala. A&M Univ., Huntsville. Contbr. articles to profl. jours. V.p. PTA. Recipient Human Rels. award, 1986. Mem. NAPW (chair evaluation com.), ACPA (adminstrv. leadership com.). Home: 1007 Kent Ave Salisbury MD 21801

HAMILTON, CONSTANCE BETTE, real estate broker, property manager; b. Northampton, Mass, May 7, 1933; d. Roy A. and Loretta Gracie (Short) H. BM in nursing, Syracuse U., 1960, MS, 1962; postgrad., Long Beach City Coll., Calif., 1977-81, present. Head nurse emergency room, clin. instr., supr. various hosps., Mass., N.Y., Calif.; grad. asst.sch. edn., dept. Philosophy Syracuse U., 1960-62; instr. nursing Los Angeles County, U. So. Calif. Med. Ctr. Sch. Nursing, 1962-64; project coordinator Develop. Diploma programs, Calif., 1964-67, master tchr., 1964-67; guest faculty, staff mem., cons. death dying and crisis Research and Training Ctr. Research Methods Course, Calif., 1967-75; research review, critique U.S. Pub. Health Service, Nursing Research div., Nursing Review and patient Care Com., 1967-70; nursing research assoc. Los Angeles County, Rancho Los Anigos Hosp., Calif., 1967-70; assoc. dir. patient care, comunity services Martin Luter King Jr. Gen. Hosp., Los Angeles, 1970-72; nurse cons. Staff Builders Assn., James Evans Assocs., 1972-73; dir. health services Comprenetics, Beverly Hills, Calif., 1972—; assoc. dir. nursing, critical care Meml. Hosp. Med. Ctr., Long Beach, Calif., 1973-78; real estate seminar coordinator Women Investing Now, 1975; real estate assoc. Pacific Shore Realty, Long Beach, Calif., 1977-82; real estate broker Park Terrace, Long Beach, Calif., 1982-85, H&L Properties, Long Beach, Calif., 1985—; nursing rep. research subcom. phys. therapy, occupational therapy Rancho Los Anigos Hosp., 1967-79; nurse cons. Am. Coll. Surgeons and Trauma, U. Ala., 1972.; cons. WICHE Conf. Nursing Research-Patient Quality Care, 1972-73; faculty Annual Con. Clin. Application Hyperbaric Oxygen; cons. VA Hosp., Wadsworth, Calif., 1976-77, VA Nursing Service Dept., Wadsworths, Va., 1977-78. Active Community Nursing Adv. Council, Watts-Willowbrook, Calif.; mem. United Way (adv. com., region IV). Nat. Assn. Realtors, Calif. Assn. Realtors, Long Beach Dist. Bd. Realtor, Health Manpower Com. Comprehensive Health Planning Assn. Los Angeles County, Am. Hosp. Assn. Am. Bus. Woman's Assn., Calif. Nurses' Assn., Long Beach Dist. Bd. Realtors Equal Opportunity Com. (chmn.), Long Beach Dist. Bd. Reators, Sigma Theta Tau, Pi Lambda Theta. Republican. Episcopalian. lodges: Zonta, Zonta Internat. Office: H&L Properties 355 Redondo Ave Long Beach CA 90814

HAMILTON, DAGMAR STRANDBERG, lawyer, educator; b. Phila., Jan. 10, 1932; d. Eric Wilhelm and Anna Elizabeth (Sjöström) Strandberg; A.B., Swarthmore Coll., 1953; J.D., U. Chgo. Law Sch., 1956; J.D., Am. U., 1961; m. Robert W. Hamilton, June 26, 1953; children—Eric Clark, Robert Andrew Hale, Meredith Hope. Admitted to Tex. bar, 1972; atty., civil rights div. U.S. Dept. Justice, Washington, 1965-66; asst. instr. govt. U. Tex.-Austin, 1966-71; lectr. Law Sch. U. Ariz., Tucson, 1971-72; editor, researcher Assoc. Justice William O. Douglas, U.S. Supreme Ct., 1962-73, 75-76; editor, research Douglas autobiography Random House Co., 1972-73; staff counsel Judiciary Com., U.S. Ho. of Reps., 1973-74; asst. prof. L.B. Johnson Sch. Pub. Affairs, U. Tex., Austin, 1974-77, assoc. prof., 1977-83, prof., 1983—, assoc. dean, 1983-87; vis. prof. Washington U. Law Sch., St. Louis, 1982; vis. fellow Univ. London, 1987-88. Mem. Tex. Bar Assn., Am. Law Inst., Assn. Pub. Policy Analysis and Mgmt. (mem. policy council), Kappa Beta Phi (hon.), Phi Kappa Phi (hon.). Democrat. Quaker. Contbr. to various publs. Home: 403 Allegro Ln Austin TX 78746 Office: U Tex LBJ Sch Pub Affairs Austin TX 78712

HAMILTON, DIANE BRONKEMA, nursing educator; b. Fulton, Ill., Sept. 24, 1946; d. Peter and Blanche (Hoogheem) Bronkema. Diploma, Northwestern U. Sch. Nursing, 1967; BSN, West Tex. State U., 1978; MA, U. Iowa, 1980; PhD, U. Va., 1987. RN. Instr. Mt. Mercy Coll., Cedar Rapids, Iowa, 1980-82; asst. prof. nursing U. Va., Charlottesville, 1985-87, Med. U. S.C., Charleston, 1988—; cons. in field. Author: Pharmacology in Nursing, 1988; contbr. articles to profl. jours. and chpt. to book. Bd. dirs. Heritage Coun., Cedar Rapids, 1980-82. Capt. USAF, 1970-75. NIH grantee, 1982, DuPont scholar, 1984; recipient Nat. Rsch. Service award NIH, 1983. Mem. ANA, Am. Assn. History Medicine, Am. Assn. History Nursing, Women's Club, Sigma Theta Tau. Home: 1405 Brockman Cir Charleston SC 29412 Office: Med U SC 171 Ashley Ave Charleston SC 29405

HAMILTON, ELEANOR LEIGH, writer, therapist; b. Portland, Oreg., Oct. 6, 1909; d. Kenneth and Clara Belle (Cunningham) Poorman; m. Albert Edward Hamilton, Aug. 12, 1932, (wid. 1969); children: Heather, Mark, Wendy, April. AB, U. Oreg., 1930; MA, Columbia U., PhD. Marriage counselor, psychologist, sex educator and therapist. Dir. girl reserves YWCA, San Jose, Calif., 1930-32; dir., founder Hamilton Sch., Inc., N.Y.C., 1933-48, Sheffield, Mass., 1948-83; marriage counselor, sex therapist Hamilton Sch., Inc., N.Y.C. and Sheffield, 1955-83; dir., founder Inverness Ridge Counseling Ctr., Inverness, Calif., 1983—; Cons. Inst. for Advanced Study of Sex, San Francisco, 1979—, Pt. Reyes Light, Pt. Reyes Station, Calif., 1986—. Author: Partners In Love, 1961, Sex Before Marriage, 1969, Sex With Love: A Guide for Young People (ALA award 1979), Soc. Scientific Study of Sex (Achievement of Yr. award 1979). Fellow Am. Assn. Marriage and Family Therapists; diplomate Am. Coll. Sexology; mem. Soc. for Scientific Study of Sex, Am. Soc. Journalists and Authors, Am. Fedn. TV and Radio Artists, Soroptomist (v.p. Pt. Reyes Station chpt. 1988—), Garden Club. Home and Office: Inverness Ridge Counseling Ctr 50 E Robert Dr Box 765 Box 765 Inverness CA 94937

HAMILTON, EMILY REBECCA, teacher; b. Lubbock, Tex., Aug. 3, 1938; d. James Franklin and Emily Rebecca (Davis) Potts-Johnston; m. Bobby Joe Durham, June 24, 1956 (div. 1966); children: Dawn R. Hatley, DeRene Sutton, William F. Durham, John C. Hamilton, Jr.; m. John C. Hamilton (dec.). BS in Sec. Edn., Tex. Tech. U., Lubbock, 1970; MS in Edn. supr. & Adm., Tex. Tech. U., 1981; postgrad. Tex. A & M U. Coll., 1985, 89. Bookkeeper & sales J. w. Reue at J. C. Penney Co., Floydada, Tex., 1951-56; sec. Floydada Ind. Sch. Dist., Floydada, 1956-57; bookkeeper J. W. Reue at

C. of C., 1958-61, Wylie Grain, Floydada; receptionist Tex. Highway Dept., Floydada, 1966-67; math. tchr. Lubbock Ind. Sch. Dist., Tex., 1971-72; bookkeeper Zwygardt Enterprises, Burlington, Colo., 1973-74; math. & english tchr. Stratton Sch., Stratton, Colo., 1974-77; math. tchr. Seminole Ind. Sch. Dist., Seminole, Tex., 1977--; coach, Math. for Math Bowl, Hobbs, 1978-90;, sponsor/dist. advisor, Tex. Future Tchrs. Assn., Austin, 1983-89; fgn. exch. tchr., Internat. Teaching Fellowship, Melbourne, Australia, 1986; number sense and math. coach Univ. Interscholastic League, 1988—; bd. dirs., Seminole Educators Assn., Seminole, Tex. Choir, tchr., bd. First United Meth. Ch., Seminole, 1977-89; participator Meals on Wheels, Seminole; hostess Youth for Understanding fgn. exchange student, 1988-89. Recipient: Exch. Tchr. Fellowship, Internat. Teaching Flsp. Mem. Seminole Educators Assn. (bd. dirs.) Tex. Tchrs. Assn., NEA, Tex. Assn. Supr. Math., ACBL. Home: PO Box 77 Seminole TX 79360

HAMILTON, EUGENIA ELIZABETH, hospital administrator; b. Dallas, Dec. 30, 1949; d. Walter Fred and Jeanette Rose (Arn) Born; m. David K. Monroe, Jan. 3, 1979 (div. Nov. 1978); m. William Bruce Hamilton Jr., Jan. 1, 1985; stepson: William Bruce Hamilton III. Student, U. Chgo., 1968-70; BSN, State U. N.Y., Stonybrook, 1972; MHSA, U. Mich., 1978. Nurse coordinator Nassau Suffolk RMP CHP, Centerreach, N.Y., 1972-73; transplant coordinator Northshore U. Hosp., Manhasset, N.Y., 1973-76; administrv. assoc. U. Mass. Med. Ctr., Worcester, 1979; from asst. administr. to v.p. clin. program mgmt. Mary Hitchcock Meml. Hosp., Hanover, N.H., sr. v.p. clin. program planning mktg., 1988--. Bd. mem. Lebanon Coll., 1984-89. Mem. Soc. for Health Planning and Mktg. American Hosp. Assn., Group on Institutional Planning American Assn. Med. Colleges, U. Mich. Hosp. Administrn. Alumni Assn. (pres. 1987-88). Office: Mary Hitchcock Meml Hosp 2 Maynard St Hanover NH 03756

HAMILTON, JACQUELINE, art consultant; b. Tulsa, Mar. 28, 1942; d. James Merton and Nina Faye (Andrews) H.; m. Richard Sanford Piper, Jan. 2, 1968 (div. June 1976). BA, Tex. Christian U., 1965; grad., Stockholm U., 1967; postgrad., Harvard U., 1972-73, Tufts U., 1971, Rice U., 1982-83, Houston Community Coll., 1986-87. Pvt. practice art cons. Houston, 1979—. Contbr. articles to profl. publs. Active Cultural Arts Council of Houston. Mem. Assn. Corp Art Curators, Rice Design Alliance, Tex. Arts Alliance, The Houstonian Club, The Forum Club, L'Alliance Francaise, Swedish Club. Presbyterian. Office: PO Box 1483 Houston TX 77251-1483

HAMILTON, JANET VIRGINIA, chemistry educator; b. Decatur, Ill., Nov. 11, 1936; m. Walter Scott Hamilton, Aug. 27, 1960; children: Karen Ann, Susan Kay. AB in Chemistry, Millikin U., Decatur, 1958; PhD in Phys. Chemistry, Tulane U., 1963. Sr. rsch. engr. phys. chemistry group Rocketdyne, a div. of N.Am. Rockwell Corp., Canoga Park, Calif., 1963-66; prof. natural sci. Tarrant County Jr. Coll., Hurst, Tex., 1967—. Contbr. papers on thermochemistry to sci. publs. Mem. Am. Chem. Soc., Tex. Jr. Coll. Tchrs. Assn., Denton County Amateur Radio Club, Sigma Xi, Phi Kappa Phi. Roman Catholic. Home: Rte 1 Box 272 Sanger TX 76266 Office: Tarrant County Jr Coll NE 828 Harwood Rd Hurst TX 76054

HAMILTON, JOYCE KAY, consulting and training company executive; b. Indpls., Mar. 7, 1950; d. John Samuel and Agnes June (Stribling) McPheeters; m. Gary Roger Hamilton, Aug. 30, 1975 (div. 1981). BS, U. Tex., 1983; M in Liberal Arts, So. Meth. U., 1989. Tax payer asst. IRS, Dallas, 1979-80; tech. asst. Dallas Dept. Edn., 1980-81 exec. adminstv. asst. Mass. Mut., Dallas, 1981-82; v.p. Excalibur Mktg., 1983—; mgr. corp. services, Louis G. Reese Inc., Dallas, 1984-85; owner, prin. Creative Visions...Creative Results, Dallas, 1985-89; owner Target Growth, Inc., Dallas, 1989—; also seminar and workshop leader. Served with USAF, 1974-77. Mem. Nat. Exec. Women's Assn., Am. Bus. Women's Assn. Republican. Club: Toastmistress.

HAMILTON, KAREN JUDE, cement company executive; b. Hagerstown, Md., Nov. 1, 1962; d. Frank Joseph and Joan Marie (Flock) H. AA, Hagerstown Jr. Coll., 1984. Stores supr. Independent Cement Corp., Hagerstown; stores clk./lab. technician Lone Star Cement, Hagerstown; clk. Manpower Temp. Svcs., Hagerstown. Mem. ASPICS. Home: 145 Milestone Garden Apts Williamsport MD 21795

HAMILTON, KATHERINE LOUISE, psychologist; b. Washington, Nov. 30, 1957; d. Paul Eugene and Mary Margaret (Bourget) H.; m. Curtis Craig Gostanian, Nov. 25, 1989. BA, U. N.C., 1980; MA, U. Ky., 1983, PhD, 1988. Coord. Benjamin Rush Inst., Culver City, Calif., 1986-89; asst. prof. Calif. Sch. Profl. Psychology, L.A., 1988-89; asst. clin. coord. Cath. Charities Clin. Svcs., L.A., 1989, clin. program dir., 1990—. James Johnston scholar U. N.C., 1976-80; U. Ky. fellow, 1982. Mem. Am. Psychol. Assn., Phi Beta Kappa, Phi Eta Sigma. Office: Cath Charities Clin Svcs 2035 Seviers Rd #4 Oxnard CA 93033

HAMILTON, KIMBERLY DARLENE, diversified service company executive; b. Seminole, Okla., Jan. 16, 1960; d. Lynn Vaughn Eidson and Louetta Darlene (Allen) Vannoy; m. Zachary Hamilton, Feb. 28, 1981. Student, Brookhaven Coll., 1985-87. Mgr. graphic info. services Grace Energy Corp., Dallas, 1977—. Mem. Assn. Records Mgrs. Adminstrn., Assn. Info. Image Mgmt. (bd. dirs., editor newsletter The Spittin' Image), In-Plant Printing Mgmt. Assn. Republican. Home: Rte 2 Box 133C Roanoke TX 76262 Office: Grace Energy Corp Natural Resources Group 13455 Noel Rd #1500 Dallas TX 75240

HAMILTON, LAURA ANN, social worker; b. Cordele, Ga., Nov. 16, 1939; d. Herbert Williams and Janie LaVerne (Lumpkin) Hamilton; student Valdosta State Coll., 1957-58; B.S., Fla. State U., 1961, M.S.W., 1965; postgrad. U. Ga., 1961-62, U. Chgo., summer 1967, W. Ga. Coll., 1969, Ga. State U., 1970; postgrad. U. Tex.-Arlington, 1985-88; PhD, 1988. Vis. tchr. Crisp County Schs., Cordele, 1961-63; social service worker Social Service Dept., Milledgeville (Ga.) State Hosp., 1963; med. social worker Crippled Children's Svc., Birmingham, Ala., 1964; psychiat. social worker Fla. State Hosp., Chattahoochee, 1965, Milledgeville State Hosp., 1965-66; cons. for social work projects ESEA Title I, Ga. Dept. Edn., Atlanta, 1966-68, ESEA Title III, 1968-71; cons. program evaluations and audits Robert Davis Assos., Inc., Atlanta, 1971-72; chief Div. Planning, Evaluation, Monitoring & Analysis, S.C. Dept. Social Svcs., Columbia, 1973-76; regional dir. social svcs. Regions 01 and 02, Tex. Dept. Pub. Welfare, Lubbock, 1976-77; partner Kaye Fleming Boutique and Bridal Corner, Ft. Worth, 1978-83; pvt. practice social work, Ft. Worth, Tex., 1978—; dir. Tarrant County Dept. Human Services, Ft. Worth, 1985—; field supr. Kirschner Assos., Inc., Albuquerque, 1972, 73; evaluator for edn. professions devel. act project Waycross (Ga.) City Schs., 1972, W. Ga. Ednl. Service Center, Carrollton, 1972; program auditor Clarke County Schs., Atlanta, 1972; instr. Human Resource Center, U. Tex., Arlington, 1977-79; lectr. in field. Mem. Acad. Cert. Social Workers, Am. Pub. Welfare Assn., Am. Soc. Pub. Adminstrn., Nat. Assn. Social Workers. Address: 1611 Trailridge Dr Arlington TX 76012

HAMILTON, MARIAN ELOISE, housing authority official; b. Salt Lake City, Mar. 21, 1931; d. Frederic William and Kathryn Eloise (Core) Wrathall; m. Stanley Keith Hamilton, Feb. 2, 1951 (dec. 1983); children: Edmond Scott, Perri Collette, Deena Kathryn. Student U. Utah, 1949-51, U. Calif.-Santa Barbara, 1951-52, U. Mont., 1952-53. Cert. pub. housing mgr. Field exec. Cross Timbers Girl Scouts, Denton, Tex., 1971-76; camp dir. Camp Kadohadacho, Pottsboro, Tex., 1971-75; acting dir. Wesley Pre-Sch., Denton, 1976-78; field dir. 1st Tex. Council, Campfire, Ft. Worth, 1979-81; housing mgr. Denton Housing Authority, 1981-88, exec. dir., 1988—; cons. on shared housing Tex. Agy. on Aging, Austin, 1984—; area rep. City of Denton Land Use Com., 1986-88; chmn. Elderly Svc. Providers of Denton County. Editor Heritage Highlights, 1981-88. Recipient Fred Moore award Denton chpt. NAACP, 1990. Mem. Nat. Assn. Housing and Redevel. Ofcls. (3 Merit awards), Am. Assn. Homes for Aging, Nat. Coun. on Aging, Nat. Trust for Hist. Preservation, Nat. Assn. Female Execs., First Tex. Coun. of Camp Fire (bd. dirs. SuRaHa, Flame award), Kimbell Mus. Fine Arts, Ft. Worth Bot. Soc., MedCare Home Svcs. (mem. review com.), Austin Writer's League, Altrusa Internat. (v.p.). Democrat. Avocations: writing, travel, reading. Home: 900 Sierra Dr Denton TX 76201 Office: Denton Housing Authority 308 S Ruddell Denton TX 76205

HAMILTON, MARY LUCIA KERR, banker; b. Denver, Aug. 3, 1926; d. Henry Hamilton and Helen (Clancy) Kerr; m. William A. Hamilton, June 15, 1957 (dec. Feb. 1989); children: Lucia M., Henry K., John A., Peter D. BS, Simmons Coll., Boston, 1948; JD, U. Toledo, 1958. Bar: Ohio 1958, U.S. Dist. Ct. (no. dist.) Ohio 1959. Sec. United Airlines, Toledo, 1953-55; exec. dir. Toledo Bar Assn., 1955-58; staff atty. Legal Aid Soc., Toledo, 1958-60; assoc. Cobourn, Yager, Smith & Beck, Toledo, 1960-69; trust officer, v.p. Toledo Trust Co., 1969-79; v.p., trust officer First Nat. Bank Toledo, 1979-89, Fifth Third Bank Toledo, N.A. (formerly First Nat. Bank Toledo), 1989—. Bd. dirs. United Way of Toledo, 1987-90, Sight Ctr., 1987-88; trustee Ohio Bar Found., 1982-87. Mem. Ohio Bar Assn. (fellow, exec. com. 1987-90), Toledo Bar Assn. (pres. 1977-78), Toledo Auto Club (bd. dirs. 1982—), Zonta (pres. Toledo club 1986-87), Toledo Club. Roman Catholic. Home: 2647 Pemberton Dr Toledo OH 43606 Office: Fifth Third Bank Toledo NA 606 Madison Ave Toledo OH 43604

HAMILTON, MYKOL CECILIA, psychology educator; b. Redwood City, Calif., May 24, 1952; d. Edward Donald and Mildred Catherine (Truelove) H. BA, Stanford U., 1974; MA, San Jose State U., 1978, UCLA, 1982; PhD, UCLA, 1985. Vis. asst. prof. psychology UCLA, 1985-86; vis. asst. prof. U. Ky., Lexington, 1986-87; asst. prof. U. So. Maine, Portland, 1987-88, Centre Coll., Danville, Ky., 1988—; faculty sponsor Social Concerns Action Group, Centre Coll., 1988—; researcher sex bias in lang. Author: (with others) Beyond Sex Roles, 1985, New Directions in Feminist Psychology, 1990. Grad. grant NIMH, 1979-82. Mem. Assn. for Women in Psychology, Ky. Acad. Sci. (Psychology div. sec. 1989—), Soc. for the Psychol. Study of Social Issues, Am. Psychol. Soc., Soc. for the Advancement of Social Psychology. Democrat. Office: Centre Coll Young Sci Hall Danville KY 40422

HAMILTON, NANCY BETH, data processing administrator; b. Lakewood, Ohio, July 22, 1948; d. Edward Douglas and Gloria Jean (Blessing) Familo; m. Thomas Woolman Hamilton, June 10, 1970; children: Susan Elizabeth, Catherine Anne. BA, Denison U., 1970. Cert. secondary edn. tchr., Fla. Tchr. Orange County (Fla.) Bd. Edn., 1970-71; registrar Jones Coll., Orlando, Fla., 1971-72; mgr. service dept. Am. Lawyers Co., Cleve., 1972-79, mgr. data processing dept., 1980—. Trustee, treas. Westshore Montessori Assn., Rocky River, Ohio, 1984-88; bd. dirs. Holly Ln. Sch. PTA, Westlake, Ohio, 1988—. Mem. Comml. Law League Am. (chmn. pamphlet com. 1989—), Alpha Phi (pres. Cleve. Westshore chpt. alumnae 1986-88). Republican. Methodist. Clubs: Westwood Country, Cleve. Yachting (Rocky River). Office: Am Lawyers Co 853 Westpoint Pkwy Ste 710 Cleveland OH 44145

HAMILTON, RHODA LILLIAN ROSEN, educator, consultant; b. Chgo., May 8, 1915; d. Reinhold August and Olga (Peterson) Rosen; grad. Moser Coll., Chgo., 1932-33; B.S. in Edn., U. Wis., 1953, postgrad., 1976; M.A.T., Rollins Coll., 1967; postgrad. Ohio State U., 1959-60; postgrad. in clin. psychology Mich. State U., 1971, 76; postgrad. Yale U., 1972, Loma Linda U., 1972; postgrad. in computer mgmt. systems U. Okla., 1976; postgrad. in edn. U. Calif., Berkeley, 1980; m. Douglas Edward Hamilton, Jan. 23, 1936 (div. Feb. 1952); children: Perry Douglas, John Richard. Exec. sec. to pres. Ansul Chem. Co., Marinette, Wis., 1934-36; personnel counselor Burneice Larson's Med. Bur., Chgo., 1954-56 adminstrv. asst. to Ernst C. Schmidt, Lake Geneva, Wis., 1956-58; asso. prof. fin. aid Ohio State U., 1958-60; tchr. English to speakers of other langs., Istanbul, Turkey, 1960-65; counselor Groveland (Fla.) High Sch., 1965-68; guidance counselor and psychol. cons. early childhood edn. Dept. Def. Overseas Dependents Sch., Okinawa, 1968-85; pres. Hamilton Assocs., Inc., Groveland, Fla., 1985—; vis. lectr. Okla. State U., 1980; co-owner plumbing, heating bus., Marinette, 1943-49; journalist Rockford (Ill.) Morning Star, 1956-58, Istanbul AP, 1960.; lectr. Lake Sumter Community Coll., 1989—. Vol. instr. U.S. citizenship classes, Okinawa, 1971-72. Mem. Fla. Retired Educators, Nat. Assn. Retired Fed. Employees, Am. Personnel and Guidance Assn., Nat. Vocat. Guidance Assn., Assn. Measurement and Eval. in Guidance, Am. Fedn. Govt. Employees, Nat. Council Measurement in Edn., Am. Sch. Counselor Assn., Phi Delta Gamma. Episcopalian. Clubs: Order Eastern Star (organist Shuri chpt. 1); Ikebana Internat. Author poetry on Middle East, 1959-64; Career Awareness, 1978. Home and Office: Hamilton Assocs Cons 255 E Waldo St Groveland FL 32736

HAMILTON, SANDRA, psychologist; b. Santa Monica, Calif., Sept. 14, 1959; d. Anthony Robert and Theresa Victoria (Manarino) H.; m. Hugh Richard Henderson; 1 child, Alexandra Jacqueline. BS, U. Calif., Santa Barbara, 1981; MS, U. Ore., 1982, PhD, 1987. Lic. psychologist, Oreg. Clin. therapist Psychology Clinic U. Oreg., Eugene, 1981-85, instr. dept. psychology, 1982-85; family therapist Oreg. Rsch. Inst., Eugene, 1984-85; psychology intern VA, Sacred Heart Gen. Hosp., U. Oreg. Counseling Ctr., Eugene, 1985-87; resident psychology Eugene, 1987-88, pvt. practice, 1988—; adj. asst. prof. dept. psychology U. Oreg., Eugene, 1987; faculty affiliate Ctr. for Study Women in Society. Contbr. articles to psychology jours. Sec. Phi Beta Patrons, Eugene, 1986-87. Recipient Chairperson award dept. psychology U. Calif., Santa Barbara, 1981; Jane Grant dissertation fellow Ctr. for Study of Women in Soc., Eugene, 1984. Mem. Am. Psychol. Assn. (jour. reviewer 1988—), Oreg. Psychol. Assn. (jour. editor 1988, rsch. award 1985), Lane County Psychologists Assn., Mental Health Assn., Psi Uni. Office: 66 Club Rd Ste 100 Eugene OR 97401

HAMILTON, SARAH TUCKER, real estate professional; b. Leon County, Nov. 4, 1944; d. Luchion and Sophie Tucker; m. Warzen C. Hamilton, Aug. 25, 1972; children: Felicity, Latonya, Warzen, Nicole. Ind. practice real estate Ellenwood, Ga.; baker Nabisco, Atlanta, Morrison's Cafe, Tallahassee, Fla.; maid Holiday Inn, Tallahassee. Community worker helping young people purchase homes. Home: 2061 San Marco Dr Ellenwood GA 30049

HAMILTON, SHIRLEY SIEKMANN, arts administrator; b. South Bend, Ind., Aug. 31, 1928; d. George F. and Clarice B. (Rapp) Burdick; student St. Mary's Coll., 1946-47; m. Max R. Siekmann, June 23, 1951; children: Sheryl, Pamela, David; m. Keith L. Hamilton, Sept. 3, 1983. Student Mary's Coll., 1946-47; BA, DePauw U., 1950; postgrad. Ind. U., South Bend. Tchr. public schs., St. Joseph County, Ind., 1950-51, Greencastle, Ind., 1951-52, Ft. Lauderdale, Fla., 1952-53; exec. dir. Michiana Arts and Scis. Council, Inc., South Bend, Ind., 1973-86; tech. asst. cons., adv. panelist Ind. Arts Commn.; treas. Ind. Alliance Arts Councils, 1982. Mem. St. Joseph County Parks and Recreation Bd., 1971-81; pres. Mental Health Assn. of St. Joseph County, 1972; bd. dirs. Civic Ctr. Found., South Bend, 1974-89, St. Joseph County Scholarship Found., 1977-82; pres., bd. dirs. United Way St. Joseph County, 1981-82. Recipient Community Service award Michiana Arts and Scis. Council, 1968, Arts award, 1987, Arts Service award, Ind. Assembly of Local Arts Agys., 1987. Mem. Ind. Arts Advs., Ind. Alliance Arts Councils, Nat. Assn. Arts Councils. Club: Jr. League South Bend (pres.). Producer 13 week TV series: Inside Our Schools (Jr. League of South Bend Outstanding Community Service award 1964). Office: 120 S St Joseph St South Bend IN 46601

HAMILTON, VIRGINIA (MRS. ARNOLD ADOFF), author; b. Yellow Springs, Ohio, Mar. 12, 1936; d. Kenneth James and Etta Belle (Perry) H.; m. Arnold Adoff, Mar. 19, 1960; children: Leigh Hamilton, Jaime Levi. Student, Antioch Coll., 1952-55, Ohio State U., 1957-58, New Sch. for Social Research. Author: children's novels Zeely, 1967 (Nancy Block Meml. award Downtown Community Sch. Awards Com.), The House of Dies Drear, 1968 (Edgar Allan Poe award for best juvenile mystery 1969), The Time-Ago Tales of Jadhu, 1969, Planet of Junior Brown, 1971; W.E.B. Dubois: A Biography, 1972; children's novels Time-Ago Lost: More Tales of Jahdu, 1973, M.C. Higgins the Great (John Newbery medal 1974), 1974 (Nat. Book award 1975), Paul Robeson: The Life and Times of a Free Black Man, 1974, Arilla Sun Down, 1976, Illusion and Reality, 1976, The Justice Cycle: Justice and Her Brothers, 1978, Dustland, 1980, Gathering, 1980, Jahdu, 1980, Sweet Whispers, Brother Rush, 1982 (Boston Globe/Horn Book award 1983), The Magical Adventures of Pretty Pearl, 1984, A Little Love, 1984, Junius Over Far, 1985, The People Could Fly, 1985, The Mystery of Drear House, 1987, A White Romance, 1987; editor: Writings of W.E.B. Dubois, 1975, In the Beginning: Creation Stories from Around the World, 1988 (Newbery Honor Book award 1988), Anthony Burns: The Defeat and Triumph of a Fugitive Slave, 1988 (Boston Globe Horn Book award 1988). Recipient Ohioana Lit. award, 1969, 84, Ohioana Lit. award for body of work, 1981, Coretta Scott King award for Fiction, 1980, 85, Regina medal for body of work, 1989. Address: Box 293 Yellow Springs OH 45387

HAMLAR, PORTIA YVONNE TRENHOLM, lawyer, author; b. Montgomery, Ala.; d. Harper Councill Sr. and Portia Lee (Evans) Trenholm; 1 child, Eric Lafayette. AB, Ala. State U., Montgomery, 1951; MA, Mich. State U., 1953; JD, U. Detroit, 1972. Bar: Mich. 1974, Ill. 1988. Atty. Chrysler Corp., Highland Park, Mich., 1973-80; asst. prof. law Widener U., Wilmington, Del., 1980-82; pvt. practice Detroit, 1982—; editor DEOC Pub. Co., Rochester, Mich., 1977-81; mem. Orgn. Resources Counselors, Washington, 1974-80; exch. prof. Nat. Urban League, 1976-79. Author, editor: Defending the Employer in OSHA Contests, 1977-81; mem.: U. Detroit Law Rev., 1972-73; editor: Mich. Environ. Law Digests, 1990. Mem., v.p. bd. dirs. Rochester Symphony Orch., 1983-86. Mem. ABA (chair subcom. labor law sect. 1975-80), Mich. Women's Econ. Club (speaker), Alpha Kappa Mu, Mu Phi Epsilon, Kappa Beta Pi. Home and Office: 27370 Evergreen Rd Lathrup Village MI 48076

HAMLIN, CAROLE ADRIENNE, nurse; b. Paterson, N.J., Sept. 1, 1938; d. Adam Joseph and Henriette (Hodowalski) Hartmann; m. C. Judson Hamlin, Sept. 10, 1961 (div. 1982). BS in Nursing, Georgetown U., 1961. RN, N.J., N.Y. Staff-head nurse Manhatta VA Hosp., N.Y.C., 1961-63; staff nurse VNA of Middlesex County, New Brunswick, N.J., 1963-64, Robert Wood Johnson Hosp., New Brunswick, 1964-67, Middlesex County Juvenile Facility, N. New Brunswick, N.J., 1980-84; head nurse Middlesex County Adult Corrections and Juvenile Facilities, N. New Brunswick, 1984—; health instr. Middlesex County Police Tng. Acad., Edison, N.J., 1987—. Pres., Weber Parent Tchr. Orgn., East Brunswick, N.J., 1975, 76, v.p., 1977. Mem. Am. Corrections Assn., Nat. Corrections Health Care Assn. Democrat. Roman Catholic. Home: PO Box 214 Milltown NJ 08850 Office: Middlesex County Correction PO Box 266 New Brunswick NJ 08903

HAMLIN, SONYA B., communications specialist; b. N.Y.C.; d. Julius and Sarah (Saltzman) Borenstein; m. Bruce Hamlin (dec. 1977); children: Ross, Mark, David. BS, MA, N.Y.U.; LLD (hon.), Notre Dame Coll., 1970. Host arts program Sta. WHDH-TV, Boston, 1963-65; host, producer, writer Meet the Arts program Sta. WGBH-TV, Boston, 1965-68; cultural reporter Sta. WBZ-TV, Boston, 1968-71, TV host, producer The Sonya Hamlin Show, 1970-75; host, producer Sunday Open House program Sta. WCVB-TV, Boston, 1976-80; host, producer, writer Speak Up and Listen program Lifetime Cable Network, N.Y.C., 1982-84; pres. Sonya Hamlin Communications, Boston and N.Y.C., 1977—, Different Drum Prodns., N.Y.C., 1982-86; pvt. practice communications cons., U.S. and Can., 1977—; adj. lectr. Harvard Grad. Sch., Cambridge, Mass., 1974-76, Harvard Law Sch., 1977-81, Kennedy Sch. Govt., Harvard U., 1978-79; adj. asst. prof. Boston U. Med. Sch., 1977-80; mem faculty Nat. Inst. Trial Advocacy, South Bend, Ind., 1977—, U.S. Dept. Justice, Washington, 1979-87, ABA, Chgo., 1979—; chmn. Law/Video Co., N.Y.C. and Waltham, Mass., 1987—. Author: What Makes Juries Listen, 1985, How to Talk So People Listen, 1988; contbr. articles to profl. jours.; dir., writer (films) China: A Different Path, 1979 (Emmy nominee), Paul Revere: What Makes a Hero, 1976, others. Bd. dirs. Gov. Commn. Status of Women, Mass., 1973-83; campaign co-chair Mass. ERA Campaign, 1975-76; cons. Gov. Michael Dukakis, 1978, Dem. Nat. Party, Washington, 1979; mem. nat. vol. action com. United Way, Washington, 1986—. Recipient Best Program award Internat. Ednl. TV Assn., Tokyo, 1969, Ohio State Cultural Reporting award, 1970; named Outstanding Broadcaster New Eng. Broadcasters, Boston, 1973; Sonya Hamlin Day named in her honor Mayor of Boston, 1974.; archive of her works established Boston U. Library, 1983. Mem. Am. Fedn. TV and Radio Artists, Nat. Acad. TV Arts and Scis. (two Emmy nominations).

HAMM, FRANCES JAYNE, educator; b. Vernon, Tex., Nov. 11, 1935; d. Nevin and Lona May (Young) Mote; m. Ronald Eugene Hamm, July 23, 1960; children; Mitchell Kelly, Amy Kylene. BS in Edn., U. North Tex., 1957; student, Brevard Community Coll., Eau Gallie, Fla., 1972-78-81, U. Central Fla., 1976. Certified tchr. all levels, Tex. Layout artist Vernon (Tex.) Daily Record, 1952-53; tchr. Fort Worth City Schs., 1937-60, Santa Fe (N. Mex.) City Schs., 1960-63, Graham Country Day Sch., Denton, Tex., 1967-70, First Bapt. Ch. Day Care, Denton, 1970-71, Brevard County Sch. Bd., Satellite Beach, Fla., 1972-83, Northside Ind. Sch., Vernon, Tex., 1983-84, Vernon Ind. Schs., 1984—; co-sponsor Nat. Jr. Honor Soc., Satellite Beach, Fla., 1975-83, Nat. Art Honor Soc., Vernon, Tex., 1984—; tutor Vernon Ind. Schs.1985—; univ. interscholastic league spelling coach, Vernon Ind. Schs., 1985-89; adjunct faculty Vernon Regional Jr. Coll., 1987-89. Mem. Wibarger County Hist. Commn., 1989—; chmn. mailing, proofreading Wilbarger County Family History, 1986; Sunday sch. tchr. First Baptist Ch., Vernon, Tex. Mem. AAUW, Assn. of Tex. Profl. Educators (sec. 1985-86), Delta Kappa Gamma (internat. sec. 1990, mem. chmn. 1988-90), Delta Gamma. Democrat. Baptist. Office: Vernon High Sch 2102 Yucca Ln Vernon TX 76384

HAMM, SUZANNE MARGARET, psychologist; b. Port Washington, Wis., June 28, 1943; d. Raymond and Margaret (Ernster) Hubing; m. Fred Joseph Hamm, July 28, 1973. BA, Dominican Coll., Racine, Wis., 1966; MS, U. Wis., Whitewater, 1972; PhD, U. Denver, 1986. Nationally cert. sch. psychologist; lic. psychologist. Sch. tchr. St. Charles Elem. Sch., Burlington, Colo., 1966-71; sch. psychologist Denver Public Sch., 1972—; part-time pvt. practice Denver, 1987—. Counselor Shelter for Battered Women, Denver, 1986-88; psychologist Shelter for the Homeless, Denver, 1987—; advisor Schs. for Urban Neighborhoods, Denver, 1989—. Recipient Sch. Psychol. of the Year, Colo. Assoc of Sch. Psychol, 1990. Mem. Am. Psychol. Assn., Colo. Psychol. Assn., Nat. Assn. Sch. Psychologists, Colo. Assn. Sch. Psychologists, Western Psychol. Assn., Nat. Ednl. Assn. Roman Catholic. Home: 590 S Poplar Way Denver CO 80224 Office: 3540 S Poplar St Denver CO 80237

HAMMEL-GEIGER, MARY CELESTE, artistic director, choreographer, dance instructor; b. Detroit, Feb. 14, 1956; m. Dix W.L. Geiger. Student, Severo Sch. Ballet, Detroit, 1964-74, John Cranko Sch., Stuttgart, Federal Republic of Germany, 1975. Profl. dancer Mainz (Federal Republic of Germany) Theater, 1975-76, Scapino Ballet, Amsterdam, The Netherlands, 1976-78; demi-soloist Grand Theatre Geneva, 1978-80; soloist, prin. Royal Ballet Flanders, Antwerp, Belgium, 1980-84; instr. ballet Severo Sch. Ballet, Livonia, Mich., 1984; owner, dir., instr., choreographer Geiger Classic Ballet Acad., West Bloomfield, Mich., 1985—; guest instr. Western Mich. U., Kalamazoo, 1987, guest choreographer and dancer, 1988; guest instr. Sch. of Vesoul, France, 1989. Choreographer: (ballets) A Classic Case, 1987, Peter and the Wolf, 1987, The Nutcracker, 1987. Recipient hon. award for ballet achievement Ford Found., Am. Ballet Sch., 1968-74. Mem. Mich. Dance Assn. Office: Geiger Classic Ballet Acad 5526 Drake Rd West Bloomfield MI 48322

HAMMER, HALI DIANE, musician; b. Bklyn., Apr. 6, 1948; d. Louis and Sherry (Cohen) Lipsky; m. Stephen Hammer, June 8, 1969 (div.); m. Bryan G. McLane, July 16, 1977 (div.); children: Bonnie, Adam. BA, Queens Coll., 1969; MLS, SUNY, Stonybrook, N.Y., 1975. Cert. elem. educator. Musician various locations, 1969—; admissions advisor Ulster County Community Coll., Stone Ridge, N.Y., 1979-80; co-owner Quarter Moon Cabaret, Rosendale, N.Y., 1979-84; activities aide Ulster County Infirmary, Kingston, N.Y., 1981-83; substitute tchr. Berkeley (Calif.) Unified Sch. Dist., 1985—; pub., producer At Long Last Records, Oakland, Calif., 1988—. Author: Cirrus, 1985. Publisher: My Work Is Play Record Album, 1988. Singer Bread & Roses, Mill Valley, Calif., 1989, Freedom Song Network, East Bay, Calif., 1989; v.p. Rosendale Youth Commn., 1980-84; publicity chairperson Rosendale St. Festival Assn., 1978-80; den mother Boy Scouts Am., Rosendale, 1983-84. Recipient Cert. of Merit Am. Song Festival, 1979. Mem. Broadcast Music Inc., Berkeley Fedn. Tchrs., NAFE, San Francisco Folk Music Club. Democrat. Home: 1901 6th St Berkeley CA 94710 Office: PO Box 20431 Oakland CA 94620-0431

HAMMER, SUSAN BERMAN, public relations executive, business owner; b. Buffalo, Sept. 12, 1950; d. Leonard and Judith H. (Goldenberg) B.; m. Tony Hammer, Aug. 17, 1975; 1 child, Erik Jason. BA, Northwestern U., 1972, MS in Journalism, 1975. Pub. info. asst. Sta. WBBM-TV, Chgo., 1972; news asst. exec. trailer Dem. Nat. Conv. ABC-TV News, Miami, Fla., 1972;

writer Chgo. Conv. and Visitors Bur., 1973-75; Washington corr. Sta. WYEN, Des Plaines, Ill., 1975; sr. v.p. Herbert H. Rozoff Assocs., Inc., Chgo., 1976-82; pres., owner Susan L. Berman Assocs., Inc., Deerfield, Ill., 1982—; v.p. corp. communications Sheldon Good & Co., Chgo., 1988-89; chairperson Chgo. Communications/10, 1982-83; cons. in field. Asst. regional dir. Nat. Movement for the Student Vote, Chgo., 1972; bd. dirs. Chgo. Women in Broadcasting, 1972-76, Younger Set Jewish Fedn., Dallas, 1985-87, Tamarisk chpt. ORT, Deerfield, 1989—. Mem. Nat. Assn. Real Estate Editors, Chgo. Soc. Clubs, Multiplex, Alpha Lambda Delta. Office: 9 Tamarisk Deerfield IL 60015

HAMMES, SARA ELIZABETH, reporter; b. Madison, Wis., Apr. 21, 1964; d. Richard Robert and Frede Ruth (Schwartz) H. BA in Econs., U. Calif., Berkeley, 1986. Advt. mgr. Energy Auditor and Retrofitter, Berkeley, 1986; speech writer, advisor Ministry of Fgn. Affairs, Seoul, South Korea, 1988; reporter Fortune Mag., N.Y.C., 1989—. Office: Fortune Mag 1271 Ave of the Americas New York NY 10020

HAMMES, TERRY MARIE, advertising executive; b. Chgo., Mar. 27, 1955; d. Howard John and Lorna Marie (Jeans) H. BFA with honors, U. Miami, Coral Gables, Fla., 1976; postgrad., St. Thomas Univ., Miami, 1990—. Lic. real estate broker, Fla. Pres. Hammes Advt. Agy., Coral Gables, Fla., 1978—; pres., broker Hammes Realty Mgmt. Corp., Coral Gables, 1986—; bd. dirs. Coral Gables Bus. Leaders, First Fla. Savings Bank, Ponce de Leon Devel. Assn., Coral Gables, v.p., 1990—. One-woman show includes U. Miami, Fla., 1975; juried art show Lowe Art Mus., 1976. Bd. dirs. Young Dems., Dade County, 1982-86, Miami Youth Mus.; mem. Leadership Miami, 1988—; mem. Leadership Miami, 1988—, exec. com., co-chair communications , 1990—. Named Miss Minn. Council of State Socs., 1975; Valley Forge Freedom Found. scholar, 1971; recipient Fla. award for Mktg. Excellence in Best Print Campaign, Best Corp. Campaign, Best Print Ad, Best Spl. Event, Best Collateral, 1989. Mem. Nat. Assn. Women Bus. Owners (pub. relations chmn. 1986), Builders Assn. South Fla. (editor, publisher 1986-87), Advt. Fedn. Greater Miami, Coral Gables C. of C., Greater Miami C. of C., Orange Key, Alpha Lambda Delta. Democrat. Home: 9234 SW 132d St Miami FL 33176 Office: Hammes Advt Inc 896 S Dixie Hwy Coral Gables FL 33146-2674

HAMMON, PATRICIA JANE, art consultant, appraiser; b. Cleve., Oct. 21, 1946; d. Arthur James and Jane Mary (Price) McClaskey; m. William M. Hammon, Jan. 7, 1971. Cert., Yale-New Haven Sch. Nursing, 1967; BFA, U. Hawaii, 1981. Staff nurse VA Hosp., Washington, 1969-71; edn. program coord. Honolulu Emergency Med. Svcs., 1976-78; edn. coord. CPR program Hawaii Heart Assn., Honolulu, 1978-79; cons. Honolulu Acad. of Arts, 1979-81; owner, cons., appraiser The Fine Art Assocs. at The Artloft (formerly The Art Loft), Honolulu, 1981—; v.p. Arts Coun. Hawaii, Honolulu, 1984-88. Air evacuation nurse vol., Honolulu chpt. ARC, 1972-75; docent, Honolulu Acad. of Arts, 1975-81; bd. dirs. Spl. Olympics, Honolulu, 1981-84; chmn. bd. dirs. Hawaii Heart Assn., Honolulu, 1986-88; mem. allotment panel Aloha United Way, 1988; 1st lt. nurses corps, U.S. Army, 1966-69, Vietnam. Mem. Internat. Soc. Appraisers, Hawaii Mus. Assn., Am. Soc. Interior Design (chmn. industry found. 1987-89), Plaza Club, Maunalua Bay Club, Beaver Creek Club, Co. Office: Fine Art Assocs at The Artloft Bldg 4 1020 Auahi St Honolulu HI 96814

HAMMOND, ANNA DEAN, state auditor; b. Princeton, Ky., Jan. 21, 1940; d. Cecil Carl and Dorothy Lee (Gray) Hobby; m. Malchom Ray Hammond, June 2, 1958; children: Michael Hammond, Cecile Lee Mitchell. BS in Acctg., Murray State U., 1986. Auditor div. audits Office Insp. Gen., State of Ky., Paducah, 1986—. Bd. mem. Caldwell County Sch. System, Princeton, 1972—, bd. chmn., 1977-79, 88—; bd. dirs. Ky. State Sch. Bd. Assn., Frankfort, 1989-90. Mem. Bus. and Profl. Women. Democrat. Baptist. Home: 1107 N Jefferson Princeton KY 42445

HAMMOND, CAROL ANNE, entrepreneur; b. Gainesville, Tex., Jan. 4, 1940; d. Charles Harvey and Alma Gladys (Proffer) Woolfolk; student North Tex. State U., 1957-58; mgmt. cert. Tarrant County Jr. Coll., 1981; children: Vanessa, Jaime, Christopher. Asst. to gen. supr. purchasing dept. Bell Helicopter/Textron, 1964-67; exec. sec. Paul R. Ray & Co., Inc., Ft. Worth, 1968-70, mgr. records and research, 1970-77, asst. corp. v.p., 1977; v.p. Gray & Assos., Inc., Dallas, 1977-78; sr. v.p., corp. sec., chief adminstrv. officer SE Assos. Corp., Dallas, 1978-83; pres., owner CH Research Services, Dallas, 1983—; prin. Paradise Performance Group, 1988—. Loaned exec. United Way of Met. Tarrant County (Tex.); sr. troop leader Circle T council Girl Scouts U.S.A., 1973-76. Recipient Women in Bus. Adv. award for Dallas dist. and Tex., SBA, 1986, 87. Mem. Am. Bus. Women's Assn. (chpt. Woman of Yr. award 1980; pres. 1981, Bus. Assoc. of Yr. 1990), Assn. Women Entrepreneurs of Dallas (pres. 1986-87), Dallas Bus. Assn. (bd. dirs.), WP Support Network (moderator 1990), Greater Dallas C. of C. (ind. bus. coun.). Home: 112 Stonegate Ct Bedford TX 76022 Office: 8700 N Stemmons Ste 422 Dallas TX 75247

HAMMOND, DEANNA LINDBERG, linguist; b. Calgary, Alta., Can., May 31, 1942; d. Albin William and Emma Lou (Thompson) Lindberg; m. Jerome J. Hammond, 1968 (div. 1980). B.A., Wash. State U., 1964; M.A., Ohio U., 1968; Ph.D., Georgetown U., 1977; student summer sch., U. Ariz., Guadalajara, Portland State U. With Peace Corps., Colombia, 1964-66; prof. English Universidad Industrial, Bucaramanga, Colombia, 1966-67; tchr. English, Spanish Pullman High Sch., Wash., 1969-74; lectr. Georgetown U., Washington, 1974-77; dir. summer sch. program Georgetown U., Quito, Ecuador, 1977; head lang. services Congl. Research Services Library of Congress, Washington, 1977—, mem. adv. bd. Nat. Translations Ctr.; mem. adv. bd. traduction, terminologie, rédaction U. Que., Can.; adv. bd. Ctr. for Applied Linguistics, Washington; v.p. Interlingua Inst., Westchester, N.Y. Translator: Psychological Operations in Guerrilla Warfare. Recipient Community Service award Sec. Califano, 1978. Mem. Am. Translators Assn. (nat. pres., rep., mem. policy com. to joint nat. com. on langs., accreditation com.), Internat. Fedn. Translators (program chmn. regional congress 1986, del. 1987, 90, mem. steering com. Regional Ctr. for N.Am.), Nat. Capital Area Translators Assn., Am. Assn. Tchrs. Spanish and Portuguese, Phi Beta Kappa, Phi Kappa Phi. Democrat. Home: 3560 S George Mason Dr Alexandria VA 22302 Office: Congl Rsch Lang Svcs Libr of Congress Washington DC 20540

HAMMOND, DOROTHY LEE, author, publisher, columnist; b. Fairfax, Mo., Sept. 24, 1924; d. Lee O. and Ella E. (Brunk) Martin; B.S., Maryville (Mo.) State Tchrs. Coll., 1949; m. Robert Byron, Sept. 1, 1944; children—Robert K., Kristy R., Byron K. Syndicated columnist Antiques and Collectibles, Columbia Features, Inc., N.Y.C., 1967-80; assoc. editor Colonial Homes mag., 1980—; pres. Hammond Publs., Inc., pubs. The Country Calendar, Sporting Dogs, Lipton Tea Herbal, Better Homes and Garden Folk Art, The Nat. Wildlife Fedn.'s Wildflowers Calendar, 1978—; author 20 books in field including: Confusing Collectibles, I-III; Mustache Cups; Collectible Advertising; Price Guide to Country Collectibles; The Pictorial Price Guide, Vol. I-X; pub. E.P. Dutton, Hearst Pubs.; cons. Smithsonian Instn. Methodist. Office: PO Box 8212 Munger Sta Wichita KS 67208

HAMMOND, (MARY) ELIZABETH, pathologist; b. Salt Lake City, Jan. 5, 1942; d. Edward Girard and Ruth (Hansen) Hale; m. John Morgan Hammond, Dec. 30, 1964; children: Jonathan Hale, Thomas Hale, Kathleen Hale. BS, U. Utah, 1963, MD, 1967. Diplomate Am. Bd. Pathologists. Intern, U. Utah, Salt Lake City, 1967-68; resident in pathology Mass. Gen. Hosp., Boston, 1970-72, clin. and research fellow, 1972-74, asst. pathologist, 1974-77; pathologist LDS Hosp., Salt Lake City, 1977—, dir. EM lab., 1978—; instr., then asst. prof. Harvard U. Med. Sch., Boston, 1974-77; clin. assoc. prof. U. Utah Med. Sch., Salt Lake City, 1981-82, assoc. prof., 1983—; dir. cardiac transplant pathology Utah Cardiac, Salt Lake City, 1986—; lectr. in field; mem. adv. com. Utah Tumor Registry, 1984. Mem. editorial bd. Jour. Heart Transplants, Internat. Jour. Radiological Oncology, Jour. Applied Pathology; contbr. articles to profl. jours., chpts. to books. Bd. dirs. Desert Found., Utah, 1979—. Grantee Desert Found., Utah, 1977-78; NIH fellow Stockholm, 1968-69; recipient research scholar award Am. Cancer Soc., Mass., 1974-77. Mem. Utah State Med. Soc., Am. Soc. clin. Pathologists, Utah Soc. Pathologists (pres. 1982-85), Am. Assn. Immunologists, Am. Assn. Pathologists, Internat. Acad. Pathology, N.Y. Acad. Scis., Southwest Oncology Group, Radiation Therapy Oncology Group, Alpha Epsilon Delta, Phi Beta Kappa, Alpha Omega Alpha. Mormon. Office: LDS Hosp EM Lab 8th Ave and C St Salt Lake City UT 84143

HAMMOND, JOANN, speech and language pathologist; b. Idaho Falls, Idaho, Oct. 7, 1957; d. Wayne Cyril and Janice (Meikle) H. BS, Utah State U., 1979, MS, 1981. Pvt. practice speech and lang. pathology, Idaho Falls, 1981—; dir. speech pathology Ea. Idaho Regional Med. Ctr., Idaho Falls, 1985—; v.p., bd. dirs. Dist. VII Home Health, Idaho Falls, 1988—. Mem. Am. Speech and Hearing Assn., Idaho Speech and Hearing Assn., Nat. Aphasia Assn. Home and Office: 211 E 15th St Idaho Falls ID 83404

HAMMOND, JUDY OLIVER, nursing educator; b. Cleveland, Miss., Sept. 13, 1946; d. William Judd and Mary Terry (Stephens) Oliver; children: John, Leigh, Billie. BSN, Baylor U., 1968; MA, U. Tex., Tyler, 1980; postgrad., Tex. Women's U., 1980—. Cert. in maternal child nursing. Instr. obstetrics Meridian (Miss.) Jr. Coll., 1969-70; instr. obstetrics Tex. Ea. Sch. Nursing, Tyler, 1971, 81-84, instr. medicine and surgery, 1979-80; instr. ob-gyn Tyler Jr. Coll., 1983-89, instr. medicine and surgery, 1984—, instr. nursing nutrition, 1988—, instr. LVN transition, 1989—; speaker and presenter in field. Med. missionary Amegios Internationales, Belize, 1980, 84. Mem. Am. Coll. Obstetricians and Gynecologists (cert. inpatient obstetric nurse), Nat. Perinatal Assn., Am. Soc. Prophylaxis in Obstetrics, Orgn. for Advancement Assoc. Degree Nursing, Tex. Jr. Coll. Tchrs. Assn., Sigma Theta Tau, Alpha Chi. Republican. Baptist. Home: 8307 Southland Dr Tyler TX 75703 Office: Tyler Jr Coll Tyler TX 75703

HAMMOND, KAREN SMITH, marketing professional, paralegal; b. Baton Rouge, Dec. 20, 1954; d. James Wilbur Smith and Carolyn (May) Carper; m. Ralph Edwin Hammond, Dec. 17, 1985. Student, La. State U., 1973-75, Colo. Women's Coll., 1976; BJ, U. Colo., 1978; cert. paralegal, U. Tex., 1981. Newspaper reporter Lakewood (Colo.) Sentinel, 1978; U.S. atty. No. Dist. Tex.; sales rep. circulation dept. UTA News Svc., 1979, Arlington Citizen Jour. newspaper, 1979-80; legal asst. Oscar H. Mauzy Atty.-at-Law, Dallas, 1981; U.S. atty. U.S. Dist. Ct. (no. dist.) Tex., 1981; editor Ennis (Tex.) Press, 1981-82; sales rep. VEU Subscription TV, Dallas, 1983-84; comml. account rep. U.S. Telecom, Dallas, 1984; with The Movie Channel/Showtime, 1985; mktg. rep. Allnet Communications, Dallas, 1985-87; owner Smith, Hammond & Assocs., Dallas, 1986—; advt. sales rep. for legal asst. Today Mag., 1987; sales rep. Telecable Inc., Richardson, Tex., 1988—; account exec. Brewer Communications, Carrollton, Tex., 1988-89, Plano (Tex.) Cellular, 1989—; triex agt. Pkwy. Pontiac, Dallas, 1983-86. Bus. writer Mid-Cities Daily News, 1981. Campaign mgr. Mark Bielamowicz for Mayor, Cedar Hill, Tex., 1979; active campaigns Martin Frost for U.S. Congress, Dallas, 1978, Jimmy Carter for Pres., Ft. Worth, 1980, Ann Richards for Gov., Tex., 1990. Mem. Women in Communications (fin. com. 1979), Dallas Assn. Legal Assts., Soc. Profl. Journalist, Dallas C. of C., Plano C. of C., NAFE. Democrat. Home: 18809 Lina St #2102 Dallas TX 75252 Office: IBA Cellular 330 Melrose Ste G Bldg 150 Richardson TX 75080

HAMMOND, MARGARET ANN, family therapist, social services administrator; b. Burlington, Vt., June 19, 1947; d. Francis Henry and Bertha (Shanks) H.; children: Kristin, Joshua, Jennifer. BA, U. Vt., 1976; MSW, Adelphi U., 1980; cert. in family therapy, Phila Child Guidance Tng. Ctr., 1984. Social worker Vt. Regional Cancer Ctr., Med. Ctr. Hosp. Vt., Burlington, 1980-82; family therapist Del. Valley Psychol. Clinics, Phila., 1982-85, Northside Ctrs., Inc., Tampa, Fla., 1985-87; assoc. dir. Brandon (Fla.) Ctr. for Family Therapy, 1987—. Asst. leader Girl Scouts U.S., Brandon, 1984-88; vol. Hospice of Hillsborough, Tampa, 1986-88. Mem. Nat. Assn. Social Workers (diplomate award 1982), Am. Orthopsychiat. Assn., Tampa Bay Assn. Marriage and Family Therapists (treas. 1988—), Fla. Soc. Clin. Social Workers, Am. Assn. for Marriage and Family Therapy (clin. mem.). Democrat. Episcopalian. Home: 4503 Country Gate Ct Valrico FL 33594 Office: Brandon Ctr 407 N Parsons Ave #103 Brandon FL 33510

HAMMOND, MARJORIE WOODFORD, small business owner; b. Windsor, N.Y., Mar. 1, 1936; d. Percy Edwin and Beatrice Marjorie (Lamoreaux) Woodford; m. Charles Dawes Hammond, July 1, 1958; children: Daniel John, Charles David, Michael, Kelly Hammond Perice, Eric Ernest. Student, Deposit Cen., N.Y., 1953; AAS, SUNY, Delhi, N.Y., 1956; Grad., Cornell U., 1980. Dietician St. Francis Hosp., Port Jervis, N.Y., 1956-57; restaurant hostess Fowler Dept. Store, Binghamton, N.Y., 1965-79; substitute tchr. Fort Mill (S.C.) Schs., 1980-83; office mgr., sec. PERM-EX ROOFING & SIDING INC, Rock Hill, S.C., 1983—; ptnr. Hammond Leasing, Rock Hill, S.C., 1988—. Mem. Chmn. Newcomer's Rock Hill S.C., 1984; tel. chmn. Newcomer's, Rock. Mem. S.C. Amateur Boxing Fedn., Nat. Boxing Fedn., Bowling Club, Rock Hill C. of C. Methodist.

HAMMOND, PATRICIA FLOOD, lawyer; b. Racine, Wis., Aug. 29, 1948; d. Francis James Flood and Shirley (Osterholt) Erickson; children: Bradley D. Mortensen, Erin N. Mortensen. Student, Wis. State U., Oshkosh, 1966-69, Alverno Coll., West Allis, 1973-74. Bar: Va.1985, U.S. Dist. Ct. (ea. dist.) Va. 1988. Br. dir. Am. Heart Assn., Manassas, Va., 1977-85; attorney Manassas, Va., 1985--. Author: Contbr. articles to profl. jours., 1978-85. Mem. Culpeper Community Devel. Corp., Va. 1988--. Mem. ABA, Assn. Trial Lawyers Am., Va. State Bar Assn., Prince William County Bar Assn. (treas., pres.-elect). Democrat. Episcopalian. Office: 9116 Center St Manassas VA 22110

HAMMOND, ROSE MARIE, clinical research coordinator; b. Rochester, Pa., June 16, 1949; d. Joseph Elmer and Naomi Eleanor (Shaffer) H. Assoc. in Nursing, Community Coll. Beaver Co., Monaca, Pa., 1976; BSN, U. Pitts., 1983; MA, Carnegie-Mellon U., Pitts., 1985. RN. SICU-staff and charge nurse Allegheny Gen. Hosp., 1976-77; ICU-staff and charge nurse Beaver Co. Medical Ctr., Rochester, Pa., 1977-78; specialty staff and charge nurse Eye and Ear Hosp., Pitts., 1978-86; clin. research coord. Pitts. Cancer Inst. Co-author: Am. Soc. Clin. Oncology abstracts, 1986, 88, 90; author Pitts. Cancer Inst. Abstract Reference, 1987. Mem. Oncology Nursing Soc., Sigma Theta Tau. Republican. Lutheran. Home: PO Box 7 Beaver Falls PA 15010 Office: Pitts Cancer Inst 200 Meyran Ave Pittsburgh PA 15213

HAMMOND, TERESA LYNN, chemist; b. Bay City, Mich., Sept. 11, 1961; d. Ronald Stanley and Marjorie Grace (Hool) Janasik; m. Jeffrey Albert Hammond, June 10, 1989. Student, U. Munich, 1981-82; BS in Biology, U. Mich., 1983. Rsch. technician Wayne State U., Detroit, 1983-85, Automotive Chem. Corp., Detroit, 1986-87, Mortell Corp., Plymouth, Mich., 1987, BASF Corp., Wyandotte, Mich., 1987-89; sr. rsch. technician CIBA-GEIGY, Madison Heights, Mich., 1989; analytical chemist Wall-Colmonoy, Madison Heights, 1990; rsch. technician DuPont DeNemours & Co., Inc., Mt. Clemens, Mich., 1990—. Recipient Billy Mitchell award Civil Air Patrol, 1978; named West Point nominee U.S. Congress, 1979. Democrat. Home: 5060 Mansfield Apt 10 Royal Oak MI 48073

HAMMOND-KOMINSKY, CYNTHIA CECELIA, optometrist; b. Dearborn, Mich., Sept. 1, 1957; d. Andrew and Angeline (Laorno) Kominsky; m. Theodore Glen Hammond, Sept. 21, 1985. Student Oakland U., Rochester, Mich., 1976-77; OD magna cum laude, Ferris Coll. Optometry, 1981. Lic. optometrist, Mich. Intern, Optometric Inst. and Clinic of Detroit, 1980, Ferris State Coll., Big Rapids, Mich., 1980, Jackson Prison (Mich.), 1981; assoc. in pvt. practice, Warren, Mich., 1981-82; optometrist Pearle Vision Ctr., Sterling Heights, Mich., 1982-87, K-Mart Optical Ctr., Sterling Heights, 1982-87, Royal Optical, Sterling Heights, 1988—; provided eye care to nursing homes, Mt. Clemens, Mich. Inventer binocular low vision aid device. Avocations: music, sports, bicycling. Home: 47626 Cheryl Ct Utica MI 48087 Office: Royal Optical 14300 Lakeside Circle Lakeside Mall Sterling Heights MI 48078

HAMNER, CAROL, educational administrator; b. Altus, Okla., Sept. 23, 1942; d. F.W. and Eudora Ernestine (Stacy) Elmore; m. Robert Daniel Hamner, Aug. 24, 1963; children: Jared Robert, Ryan F. BA, Wayland Coll., Plainview, Tex., 1964; MLIS, U. Tex., 1981. Cert. elem. tchr., learning resources specialist, Tex. Elem. tchr. Austin (Tex.) Ind. Sch. Dist., 1964-66; libr. Del Valle Ind. Sch. Dist., Austin, 1966-68; libr. aide Wayland Coll., 1968-70; libr. asst. St. Edward's U., Austin, 1970-71; learning resources specialist Abilene (Tex.) Ind. Sch. Dist., 1979—. Named Tchr. of Month, Abilene Rotary Club, 1987. Mem. AAUW, NEA, Tex. State Tchrs. Assn., Tex. Libr. Assn. (mem. intellectual freedom com. 1988-91), Tex. Conf. on Librs. and Info. Svcs. (steering com. 1990), Abilene Area Libr. Assn. Democrat. Baptist. Home: 3726 Concord Abilene TX 79603 Office: Abilene High Sch 2800 N 6th St Abilene TX 79603

HAMNER, SUZANNE LEATH, history educator; b. Ft. Worth, Feb. 29, 1940; d. Roland Martin and Mabel Lois (Hall) Leath; m. W. Easley Hamner, June 18, 1961; children: Janine Suzanne, Michael Edward. BA summa cum laude, Meredith Coll., Raleigh, N.C., 1961; MA, Tulane U., New Orleans, 1964. Teaching asst. Tulane U., New Orleans, 1963-64, 65-66; instr. history Coll. Liberal Arts Northeastern U., Boston, 1966-71, lectr. history Univ. Coll., 1972-73, 74-75, lectr. history Coll. Arts and Scis. and Univ. Coll., 1985—. Contbg. editor Reclaiming Our Global Heritage, Vol. I and Vol. II, 1990. Mem. adv. com. Follow Through Program, Cambridge (Mass.) Sch. Dept., 1977-79; treas., v.p., adv. bd. Buckingham Browne & Nichols Sch., Cambridge, 1980-86; clk., bd. dirs. Cambridge Civic Assn., 1976—; treas. Alice Wolf Election Com., City Coun., Cambridge, 1979—; overseer Handel & Haydn Soc., Boston, 1989—. Woodrow Wilson Found. fellow, Princeton, N.J., 1961-62; Tulane U. scholar, 1962-64. Democrat. Home: 3 Ellery Square Cambridge MA 02138 Office: Northeastern U History Dept 360 Huntington Ave Boston MA 02115

HAMPTON, CAROL MCDONALD, educator, administrator, historian; b. Oklahoma City, Sept. 18, 1935; d. Denzil Vincent and Mildred Juanita (Cussen) McDonald; m. James Wilburn Hampton, Feb. 22, 1958; children: Jaime, Clayton, Diana, Neal. BA, U. Okla., 1957, MA, 1973, PhD, 1984. Teaching asst. U. Okla., Norman, 1976-81; instr. U. of Sci. and Arts of Okla., Chickasha, 1981-84; coord. Consortium for Grad. Opportunities for Am. Indians, U. Calif., Berkeley, 1985-86; trustee Ctr. of Am. Indian, Oklahoma City, 1981—; vice chmn. Nat. Com. on Indian Work, Episcopal Ch., 1986, field officer Native Am. Ministry, 1986—. Contbr. articles to profl. jours. Trustee Western History Collections, U. Okla., Okla. Found. for the Humanities, 1983-86; bd. dirs. Okla. State Regents for Higher Edn., mem. adv. com. on social justice; mem. World Coun. of Chs. Program to Cambat Racism, Geneva, 1985—; bd. dirs. Caddo Tribal Coun., Okla., 1976-82. Recipient Okla. State Human Rights award, 1987; Francis C. Allen fellow, Ctr. fot the History of Am. Indian, 1983. Mem. Western History Assn., Western Social Sci. Assn., Orgn. of Am. Historians, Am. Hist. Assn., Okla. Hist. Soc., Assn. Am. Indian Historians (founding mem. 1981—). Democrat. Episcopalian. Club: Jr. League (Oklahoma City). Avocation: travel. Home: 1414 N Hudson Oklahoma City OK 73103 Office: Episcopal Ch Am Indian and Eskimo Ministry 924 N Robinson Oklahoma City OK 73102

HAMPTON, JEAN ELIZABETH, philosophy educator; b. Bay Shore, N.Y., June 1, 1954; d. William Russell and Elizabeth Jean (Manahan) H.; m. Richard Andrew Healey, July 8, 1978; 1 child, Andrew Russell Hampton-Healey. BA, Wellesley Coll., 1976; MA, Harvard U., 1979, PhD, 1980. Asst. prof. philosophy UCLA, 1980-87; assoc. prof. philosophy U. Pitts., 1987-88, U. Calif., Davis, 1988—. Author: Hobbes and The Social Contract Tradition, 1986; (with Jeffrie Murphy) Forgiveness and Mercy, 1988; mem. editorial bd. Pub. Affairs Quar., 1987—, Econs. and Philosophy, 1989—; contbr. articles on polit. philosophy, ethics and philosophy of law to profl. jours. Vol. Davis Parent Nursery Sch., Davis, 1988—. Am. Coun. Learned Socs. fellow, 1988, NEH summer fellow, 1988. Mem. Am. Philos. Assn. (program com. Pacific div. 1989—), Soc. for Christian Philosophers. Democrat. Congregationalist. Office: U Calif Dept Philosophy Davis CA 95616

HAMPTON, LUCILE PAQUIN SMITH (MRS. LAWRENCE CHARLES HAMPTON), artist, educator; b. Dubuque, Iowa, Jan. 7, 1904; d. Albert Hugo and Lola (Lichtenberger) Smith; m. Lawrence Charles Hampton, Dec. 16, 1930 (dec. 1960); children: Lawrence Charles Jr., Nancy Jeanne (Mrs. Merle Willis Asper Jr.), Elizabeth Mary (Mrs. John Erskine). Diploma, Chgo. Acad. Fine Arts, 1923; postgrad., Pasadena (Calif.) City Coll., 1947-48, 64, 67-68, UCLA, 1965-66; BA in Art, Calif. State U., Los Angeles, 1973. Cert. tchr., Calif. Artist advt. dept. Union Lithographing Co., Little Rock, 1923-24; art dir. advt. dept. M. Rich & Bros. Co., Atlanta, 1924-25; head fashion layout artist advt. dept. May Co., Los Angeles, 1925-29; sr. artist advt. dept. David Jones, Ltd., Sydney, Australia, 1929-30; cover designer Women's Budget Mag., Sydney, Australia, 1929-30; fashion illustrator Home Mag., Sydney, 1930; free-lance artist Broadway Dept. Stores and J.W. Robinson & Co. Dept. Stores, Los Angeles, 1930-35; fashion illustrator Robinson Accents Mag., Los Angeles, 1935; freelance artist Lucile Hampton Greeting Cards, San Marino, Calif., 1960—; head dept. art, tchr. of art essentials and history of art Anoakia Sch. Girls, Arcadia, Calif., 1963-66; substitute tchr. San Marino Unified Sch. Dist., 1973—. Troop leader Girl Scouts U.S., San Marino, 1948-56; active Girl Scout Leaders' Club, San Marino, 1948-56; active San Marino PTA, 1941-61, exec. bd., 1944-46; mem. San Marino Rep. Women's Club Federated, Opera Guild L.A.; bd. dirs. Euterpe Opera Reading, L.A., 1956-59; guild leader San Marino Community Ch. Women. Mem. AAUW (bd. dirs. Newport Beach-Costa Mesa br. 1982-83), DAR (regent San Marino chpt. 1960-61), Children Am. Revolution (sr. advisor, sr. pres. El Molino Viejo chpt. 1958-64, social dir. Cotillion Ball 1958-59), P.E.O. (pres. chmn. 1955-56), Women's Athletic Club, Pacific Coast Club, San Marino Women's Club, Friday Morning Jrs. Club, Kappa Pi. Republican. Presbyterian. Address: 234 Sherwood Pl Costa Mesa CA 92627

HAMPTON, MARGARET JOSEPHINE, educator, decorating consultant; b. Princeton, Mo., Nov. 25, 1935; d. Leland Isaac and Margaret Ellen (Wendt) Heriford; m. Ronald Keith Hampton, July 20, 1957; children: Kevin Keith, Ronda René. BS, Samford U., 1957; MEd in Home Econs., U. Mo., 1974. Cert. vocat. home econs. tchr., Mo., Ala. Elem. tchr. Birmingham (Ala.) Pub. Schs., 1957; vocat. home econs. tchr. Licking (Mo.) High Sch., 1957-68; tchr. Pattonville High Sch., Maryland Heights, Mo., 1968—; cons. North Cen. Schs. Accreditation Team, Columbia, Mo., 1970—, interior decorating Home Interiors, Dallas, 1981—; cons. lighting, home economist Intercounty Electric, Licking, 1963-67; supervising tchr. U. Mo., Columbia, 1972—; ednl. adv. council J.C. Penny Stores, St. Louis, 1978-80; cons. to food editor St. Louis County Star News, 1982-86. Author (with others) Mo. Family Relations Curriculum Guide, 1961-63. Mem. adv. council Parkway Sch. Dist., St. Louis, 1979-80, Mo. Gov.'s Conf. on Health and Drug Abuse, Jefferson City, 1986—. Recipient Outstanding Svc. award Mo. Vocat. Assn., 1989. Mem. Nat. Assn. Vocat. Home Econs. Tchrs. (sec. 1983-85, pres. 1986-88, editor and pub. jour. 1983-85), Am. Home Econs. Assn. (Mo. conf. chmn. 1979-80), Am. Vocat. Assn. (exec. bd. 1986—), Mo. Home Econs. Tchrs. Assn. (pres. 1979-81, legis. chmn. 1989-90, Tchr. of Yr. 1985-86), St. Louis Suburban Home Econs. Tchrs. Assn. (pres. 1978-79), Future Homemakers Am. (advisor St. Louis chpt. 1957-86). Baptist. Home: 1514 Sugargrove Ct Creve Coeur MO 63146 Office: Pattonville High Sch 2497 Creve Coeur Mill Rd Maryland Heights MO 63043

HAMPTON, MARIA HOPP, educator; b. Balt., Dec. 24, 1949; m. Thurman Bruce Hampton, Oct. 16, 1977; 1 child, Kathryn Adair. BA, Davis and Elkins Coll., 1971; MS, N.C. A&T State U., 1983. Tchr. Anne Arundel County Schs., Annapolis, Md., 1971-73, 75-77, Chapel Hill (N.C.)-Carrboro Schs., 1977-80; dir. recreation ctr. City of Balt., 1973-74, Dept. Def., Seoul, 1974-75; tchr. Eden (N.C.) City Schs., 1983—. Precinct chmn., 1st vice chmn. Rockingham County Dem. Com.; bd. dirs. Eden Boys Club, Morehead Meml. Hosp. Aux., Eden, Nat. Black Theater Festival, Winston-Salem, N.C. Mem. N.C. Assn. Educators (pres. Eden 1986-87), County Assn. Rockingham Educators (chmn. writing contest 1988), AAUW. Roman Catholic. Home: Rte 1 Box 739 Eden NC 27288

HAMPTON, SUZANNE HARVEY, pharmaceutical executive; b. Ogdensberg, N.Y., Oct. 27, 1934; d. Clarence George and Kathryn (Mulvey) Harvey; m. John K. Hampton, Jr., July 1, 1961 (div. 1980). BA, Drew U., 1956; MS, Tulane U., 1959; PhD, U. Tex., 1971. Asst. mem. U. Tex. Dental Sci. Inst., Houston, 1971-73; asst. prof. York Coll. of CUNY, Jamaica, 1973-77, Barnard Coll., N.Y.C., 1980-84; regulatory asst. Ayerst Labs. Inc., N.Y.C., 1984-87; regulatory adminstr. Bertex Labs., Inc., Wayne, N.J., 1987—. Democrat. Home: 47 Tulip Ave Ringwood NJ 07456 Office: Berlex Labs Inc 300 Fairfield Rd Wayne NJ 07470

HAMPTON-KAUFFMAN, MARGARET FRANCES, corporate finance planning and banking consultant; b. Gainesville, Fla., May 12, 1947; d. William Wade and Carol Dorothy (Maples) Hampton; m. Kenneth L. Kauffman, May 12, 1973; 1 child, Robert Lee. B.A. in French summa cum laude, Fla. State U., 1969; postgrad. U. Nice (France), summer 1969; M.B.A. in Fin. (Alcoa Found. fellow), Columbia U., 1974. Fin. analyst, economist Bd. of Govs. of Fed. Res. System, Washington, 1974-75; v.p. corp. fin. Mfrs. Hanover Trust Co., N.Y.C., 1975-76; v.p., dir. corp. planning and fin., asset and liability mgmt. and strategic planning coms. Nat. Bank of Ga., Atlanta, 1976-81; sr. v.p. corp. planning and devel. Bank South Corp., Atlanta, 1981-85; mng. ptnr. Hampton Mgmt. Cons., Atlanta, 1985—; co-founder Order Counsel and Affinity Mktg., 1989; dir. Accent Enterprises, Inc., Atlanta, TOMAK, Inc., Atlanta. Nat. trustee Leukemia Soc. Am., 1986—; trustee Ga. chpt. Leukemia Soc., 1980—, treas., 1981-82, 1st v.p., 1982-84. Named Trustee of Yr., Leukemia Soc., 1982, 85. Mem. Planning Execs. Inst., Atlanta Venture Forum, Inst. of Mgmt. Scis., Am. Inst. Banking, Inst. of Fin. Edn., Am. Fin. Assn., Downtown Atlanta C. of C., (govt. affairs subcom. 1976-77) Atlanta C. of C. (high tech. task force 1982-83), Ga. Women's Forum (sec./treas., bd. dirs. 1985-86), Ga. Exec. Women's Network (sec. 1982-83, dir. 1982-84), Mortar Bd., Alliance Française, Kappa Sigma Little Sisters (pres., treas., sweetheart), Phi Beta Kappa, Beta Gamma Sigma, Phi Kappa Phi, Alpha Lambda Delta, Pi Delta Phi, Alpha Delta Pi. Episcopalian. Club: Women's Commerce (charter mem., steering com. 1985-86).

HANAK-HALL, ELAINE CHERYL, systems accountant; b. Jersey City, July 3, 1945; d. John P. Sr. and Isabelle (Andriani) Hanak; (div. Oct. 1981); 1 stepchild, Julie Reinking; m. Thomas Lee Hall, Apr. 9, 1988. BA, Montclair State Coll., 1967; postgrad., U. Northridge, Calif., 1970-71; BS, Met. State Coll., 1976; postgrad., U. Colo., 1981-82. Acct. United Parcel Svcs., Commerce City, Colo., 1976-78; auditor USDA, Denver, 1978-80; operating acct. Air Force Directorate of Security Assistance Acctg., Denver, 1980-84; systems acct. Air Force Acctg. and Fin. Ctr., Denver, 1984-87, project mgr. systems devel., 1987-88, chief debt mgmt. support br., 1988—. Mem. Assn. Govt. Accts. (Spl. Achievement award 1987), Am. Soc. Mil. Compts., Air Force Assn., AAUW (chair internat. rels. com. 1988—). Office: Air Force Acctg & Fin Ctr AFAFC/AJDS Lowry AFB Denver CO 80279-5000

HANBACK, HAZEL MARIE SMALLWOOD, management consultant; b. Washington, Sept. 19, 1918; d. Archibald Carlisle and Mary Louise (Mayhugh) Smallwood; m. William B. Hanback, Sept. 26, 1942; 1 child, Christopher Brecht. AB, George Washington U., 1940; MPA, Am. U., 1968. Archivist, U.S. Office Housing Expediter, 1948-50; mgmt. engr. U.S. Archives, 1950-51; spl. asst.-indsl. specialist Sec. Def., 1951-53; dir. documentation div. Naval Facilities Engring., Alexandria, Va., 1953-81; mgmt. cons., 1981—. Author: Military Color Book, 1960—, Status of Women in a Cybernetically Oriented Soc., 1968—, (newsletter) Worms Eye View, 1982—. Pres., West End Citizens Assn., Washington, 1956-58; trustee George Washington U., 1979—. Nominee Rockefeller Pub. Service award, 1969, Fed. Woman's award, 1969; recipient cert. of merit Dep. Def., 1965. Mem. Mortar Bd., Phi Delta Gamma, Sigma Kappa. Democrat. Episcopalian. Clubs: George Washington U. (chmn. bd. 1971-75), Columbian Women (pres. George Washington U. 1967-69), Order Ea. Star. Home: 2152 F St NW Washington DC 20037 Office: 2154 F St NW Washington DC 20037

HANCOCK, CYNTHIA CHAPMAN, public relations executive; b. Meriden, Conn., Dec. 15, 1936; d. Edward Markus Chapman and Hazel Florence (Curtis) Pisini; m. James Robert McGuffie, June 3, 1956 (div.1959); 1 child, Cheryl Ann McGuffie; m. Dane Reed Hancock, Nov. 20, 1970; 1 child, Scott Reed Hancock. AA, Daytona Community Coll., Daytona Beach, Fla., 1960; BA, Stetson U., 1963. Cert. tchr. Fla. Tchr. English Ft. Lauderdale (Fla.) High Sch., 1968-70; sr. editor Fla. Living Mag., Ft. Lauderdale, Fla., 1972-73; pub. rels. assoc. Mktg. Svcs. Corp., Ft. Lauderdale, 1973-75; advt. account exec. Cameron/Friedlander, Ft. Lauderdale, 1975-77; pub. rels. dir. Am. Learning Systems, Ft. Lauderdale, 1977-81; pvt. practice pub. rels. cons. Ft. Lauderdale, 1977-84; tchr. English and journalism Hallandale (Fla.) High Sch., 1985-88; pub. rels. mgr. Mus. of Art, Ft. Lauderdale, Fla., 1988—; co-founder, pres. Week of the Ocean, Inc., Ft. Lauderdale, Fla. 1977—. Author various newsletters, proposals in field. Recipient Woman of Vision award Nat. Marine Educators Assn., 1983, James Centerino award Nat. Marine Educators Assn., 1984. Mem. Women in Communications, Beta Sigma Phi, Xi Eta Pi. Office: Mus Art One E Las Olas Blvd Fort Lauderdale FL 33301

HANCOCK, ELLEN MARIE, communications executive; b. N.Y.C., Apr. 15, 1943; d. Peter Joseph and Helen Gertrude (Houlihan) Mooney; m. W. Jason Hancock, Sept. 17, 1971. BA, Coll. New Rochelle, 1965; MA, Fordham U., 1966. With IBM, 1966—; programmer IBM, Armonk, N.Y., 1966-81; dir. communications programming sect., communication products div., Raleigh, N.C., 1981-83; v.p. communications programming sect. of communication prodn. div. IBM, Raleigh, N.C., 1983-84; asst. group exec. systems devel. info. systems tech. group IBM, Armonk, N.Y., 1984-85, v.p. telecommunication systems communication prodn. div., 1985-86, pres. communications prodn. div., 1986-88; v.p., gen. mgr. communication systems IBM, Somers, N.Y., 1988—; bd. dirs. ARDIS Co., Lincolnshire, Ill., Colgate-Palmolive Co., N.Y.C., ROLM Co., Norwalk, Conn., ROLM Systems subs. Siemens Co., Santa Clara, Calif. Bd. dirs. Coll. of New Rochelle, N.Y., 1986—, Marist Coll., Poughkeepsie, 1988—. Roman Catholic. Home: 126 Limestone Rd Ridgefield CT 06877 Office: IBM Corp Rte 100 Somers NY 10589

HANCOCK, EMILY STONE, psychologist; b. Syracuse, N.Y., Nov. 18, 1945; d. Theodore McLennan and Eleanor Sackett (Stone) H.; m. Philip Yenawine, Aug. 28, 1965 (div. 1970); 1 child, Tad. BA, Syracuse U., 1971; MSW, Boston U., 1974; EdD, Harvard U., 1981. Lic. clin. social worker, Mass., Calif.; ACSW. Clin. social worker Children's Hosp., Boston, 1974-77; pvt. practice Mass., Calif., 1976—; co-founder, therapist Divorce Resource Ctr., Cambridge, 1976-78; teaching fellow Harvard U., 1978-79; counselor Alameda County Superior Ct., Oakland, 1982—; screening coord. U. Calif., San Francisco Dept. Pediatrics, 1982-85; faculty, chair, Ctr. for Psychol. Studies, Albany, Calif., 1982—; chairwoman Askwith Symposium and Colloquial, Cambridge, 1979. Author: The Girl Within, 1989; editor: Harvard Ednl. Rev., 1979-81; contbr. articles to numerous profl. jours. fellow HEW, 1972-74, Danforth Found., 1978-80, NIMH, 1981-82; grantee Radcliffe Coll., 1978, 80, Woodrow Wilson Found., 1980. Fellow Am. Orthopsychiatry Assn.; mem. Am. Psychol. Assn., Acad. Cert. Social Workers, Phi Beta Kappa, Phy Kappa Phi. Home and Office: 1230 Glen Ave Berkeley CA 94708

HANCOCK, KATHLEEN MARIE, advertising executive; b. Bloomsburg, Pa., Dec. 7, 1962; d. Clyde Arthur and Virginia Lee (Davis) Tanner. Artist Lithoid, Inc., East Brunswick, N.J., 1981-82; project mgr. Font Tastic, Somerset, N.J., 1982-85; prin. The Advt. Advantage, Englishtown, N.J., 1985—. Mem. NAFE, Western Monmouth C. of C. Office: The Advt Advantage 11 Carriage Ln Englishtown NJ 07726

HANCOCK, LONI, city mayor; b. N.Y.C., 1940; children: Leita, Mara. BA, Ithaca Coll.; MA, Wright Inst. Mem. Berkeley City Council, 1971-79, co-sponsor Fair Representation Ordinance, introduced affirmative action program, mem. subcom. for creation of Ohlone Park; mem. Berkeley's Waterfront Adv. Commn., 1984-86; mayor City of Berkeley, 1986—. Mem. Berkeley Parent Nursery Schs., 1964-68, Berkeley Citizens Action Com., 1975—; mem., past pres. New Dem. Forum, 1982—; mem. adv. bd. Working Assets, 1984—; bd. dirs., v.p. Berkeley Office of Econ. Opportunity, 1969-71, Local Gov. Commn., Literacy Vols. of Am., Youth Project; past regional dir. of ACTION; exec. dir. Shalan Found., San Francisco, 1981—; mem., co-founder LeConte Neighborhood Assn., 1969-71. Mem. Sierra Club, Nat. Women's Polit. Caucus. Office: City of Berkeley Office of Mayor 2180 Milvia St 5th Fl Berkeley CA 94704*

HANCOCK, PRISCILLA TEDESCO, teacher; b. Farmingdale, N.Y., Aug. 25, 1938; d. Peter John and Lillian (Guando) Tedesco; m. Robert G. Hancock, Aug. 6, 1960; children: Gregory, Kimberly, Glenn. BS, SUNY, Cortland, 1960. Cert. tchr. kindergarten through grade 8. Instr. arts and crafts Farmingdale Youth Coun., 1956-63; tchr. Farmingdale Pub. Schs., 1960-63, Bay Shore (N.Y.) Schs., 1982—; tchr. in-svc. courses to tchrs. Bay Shore Schs., 1986-87. Mem. Student Fin. Aid Fund, Bay Shore, 1974-75, Bay Shore Hist. Soc., 1985—, Friends for L.I. Heritage, 1986—; organized student exhibits Bay Shore Garden Club Shows, 1985-87; co-founder mother's aux. Boy Scouts Am., Bay Shore, 1976. Recipient Citizenship awards DAR, 1956. Mem. N.Y. State United Tchrs. Assn., Bay Shore Classroom Tchrs. Assn., AAUW (life, tchr. needlework workshops L.I. 1967-79, v.p., treas. membership bd. 1966-76), Music Sponsors of Bay Shore.

HANCOCK, SANDRA OLIVIA, educator; b. Jackson, Tenn., Oct. 22, 1947; d. Carthel Leon and Thelma (Thompson) Smith; m. Jerome Hancock, Aug. 1, 1969; children: Casey Colman, Mandy Maria. BS, U. Tenn., 1969, MS, 1973; grad. safety seminar, Universal Cheerleaders Assn., 1989. Cert. educator. Educator Lexington (Tenn.) High Sch., 1969-70, Clarksburg (Tenn.) High Sch., 1970-78, 1983-90. Contbr. poetry to various publs. Cub scout leader Boy Scouts Am., Clarksburg, 1982-84; assoc. mem. Nat. Wildlife Fedn., 1987-89, St. Labre Indian Sch. and Home Arrow Club, Ashland, Mont., 1988-89, Coun. for Exceptional Children, 1987-88. Recipient Golden Poet award, 1985-89. Mem. NEA, Tenn. Edn. Assn., Clarksburg Edn. Assn., U.S. Olympic Assn., Nat. Cheerleaders Assn. (Superior Advisor Performance award 1988), West Tenn. Promotions Songwriters Assn. (lyricist 1990—), Am. Assn. Cheerleading Coaches and Advisors, World Wildlife Fund, Sierra Club, Wilderness Soc., Nat. Arbor Day Found., Phi Delta Kappa. Republican. Methodist. Home and Office: 435 Timber Ln Huntingdon TN 38344

HANCOX, SUSAN CAROLINE, human resources executive; b. N.Y.C., Jan. 14, 1950; d. Robert Owen and Roberta Magdaline (Kepple) H. BA, Denison U., 1971; MBA, Western N.E. Coll., 1984. Personnel clk. Lawrence Meml. Hosp., Medford, Mass., 1971-72, benefits asst., 1972; with Emerson Hosp., Concord, Mass., 1972-80, coord. personnel div., 1976-77, dir. personnel dept., 1977-80; v.p. human resources Beverly (Mass.) Hosp., 1980-87, Univ. Hosp., Boston, 1987—; cons. N.E. Med. Mgmt. Svcs., Beverly, 1985-87. Author: Pay for Performance, 1985, (with others) Criteria Based Performance Appraisal, 1985. Mem. Amesbury (Mass.) Town Planning Bd., 1983. Mem. Am. Soc. Healthcare Human Resource Adminstrs., Mass. Soc. Healthcare Human Resource Adminstrs. (pres. 1985). Office: Univ Hosp 88 E Newton St Boston MA 02118

HAND, KATHLEEN MARGARET, registered nurse; b. Seattle, Mar. 29, 1947; d. Arthur Kolbjorn and Margaret May (Gallagher) Hassel; m. Philip Joseph Hand, Nov. 25, 1970; children: Erica Kathleen, Kristen Marie. BS in Nursing, Pacific Luth. U., 1970. RN. Staff nurse St. Joseph Hosp., Tacoma, 1970; camp nurse Pacific Peaks Girl Scout Coun., Olympia, Wash., 1970, 87; oper. rm. nurse Salem Meml. Hosp., Oreg., 1971-72, Northwest Community Hosp., Des Moines, 1972-75; asst. head nurse, oper. rm. nurse Meridian Park Hosp., Tualatin, Oreg., 1975—; vol. educator Woodburn (Oreg.) Pub. Sch., 1988, 89—; bd. dirs. Benedictine Nursing Ctr., 1984-90, sec. 1987-88, v.p. 1988-89. Co-author: booklet Surgical Patient Handbook, 1974. Troop leader, Girl Scouts Am., 1986—; mem. French Prairie Hist. Soc., 1976—. Recipient grand cross color Wash. Rainbow Girls, Port Angeles, 1986, various state and nat. awards Oreg. Jaycee Women, 1981-83. Mem. AAUW (sec. 1976-88), Assn. Oper. Rm. Nurses. Republican. Home: 313 McLaughlin Dr Woodburn OR 97171

HAND, SALLIE CATHERINE, financial executive; b. Lowell, Mass., Oct. 13, 1964; d. James Francis and Pauline Jane (Burgess) H. Grad. high sch., Lowell, Mass., 1982. Sales rep. 1400 Motors, Lowell, 1985-87, Clyde Garfield, Nashua, N.H., 1987-89; fin. mgr. Matthew Motor Co., Fitchburg, Mass., 1989—. Mem. Lobsters Internat. Democrat. Roman Catholic. Office: Matthew Motor Co 314 John Fitch Hwy Fitchburg MA 01420

HAND, SALLY CAROLYN, law librarian; b. Kingston, N.Y., July 15, 1959; d. Samuel Burton and Harriet Audrey (Ashkenazy) H. BA, U. Vt., 1981; MSLS, U. N.C., 1983. Asst. librarian U.S. Ct. Appeals (2nd cir.), N.Y.C., 1983-86, Shearman & Sterling, Citicorp, N.Y.C., 1986-87; tax librarian Le Boeuf, Lamb, Leiby & MacRae, N.Y.C., 1987—. Recipient Outstanding Volunteerism citation Mayor Dinkins, 1990. Mem. Am. Assn. Law Librarians, Law Librarians Assn. Greater N.Y. Office: Le Boeuf Lamb Leiby & MacRae 520 Madison Ave New York NY 10022

HANDBERG, IRENE DEAK, corporate executive; b. Jamaica, N.Y.; d. Paul and Irene (Dyroff) Deak; children: Roger B. III, Ryan Paul. BS, Fla. State U.; MEd, U. N.C., 1970. Cert. tchr. in reading and math., N.C. Lead tchr., reading specialist Chapel Hill (N.C.) City Schs., 1966-69; dir. learning lab. Seminole Community Coll., Sanford, Fla., 1974-78; basic skills cons. EDL/McGraw-Hill Book Co., Orlando, Fla., 1978-82; regional dir. EDL/Arista Pub., Orlando, 1982-84; mktg. mgr., product mgr. Arista/Regents/EDL-Hachette, N.Y.C., 1984-85; v.p. mktg. and sales Raintree Pubs., Milw., 1985, gen. mgr., pub., 1985-87; dir. spl. projects Simon & Schuster, Englewood Cliffs, N.J., 1987-88; v.p. corp. devel. Simon & Schuster, N.Y.C., 1988-90, sr. v.p., 1990—. Co-author: EDL/McGraw-Hill Teacher's Guide. Elected precinct woman com. Dem. County Com., Fla.; capt. Nat. Cancer So., Fla., chm. Sch. Adv. Com., Fla. NSF fellow U. N.C., 1969; recipient Svc. award Jr. Achievement. Mem. Chief Exec. Officers Group (coun. small bus. execs.), Sales and Mktg. Execs., Profl. Dimensions, Chief Exec. Officers Club. Lutheran. Home: 300 E 93d St Apt 29C New York NY 10128 Office: Simon & Schuster 1230 Ave of Americas New York NY 10020 also: Prentice Hall Bldg Englewood Cliffs NJ 07632

HANDELMAN, ALICE ROBERTA, public relations professional, freelance writer; b. Bklyn., Mar. 17, 1943; d. Ned Harlan and Margaret (Isaacs) Samuels; m. Howard Talbot Handelman, Aug. 29, 1965; children—Karen Leigh, Patricia Gail, Marjorie Lynn. B.J., U. Mo., 1965. Intern reporter Miami (Fla.) News, summer 1964; staff feature writer St. Louis Blues, 1968-77; freelance writer, St. Louis, 1967—; also community relations assoc. Jewish Ctr. for Aged of Greater St. Louis, Chesterfield, Mo., 1981-85, dir. community relations and devel., 1985—; instr. hockey for women Meramec Community Coll., St. Louis, 1976-77; pub. relations cons. Jewish Family and Children's Svc., St. Louis, 1983, 89; adv. com. vis. prof. program JCA Assocs., 1981-83, Gerontol. Inst., St. Louis, 1981-83. Author, photographer: LaSalle Street--A History of the St. Louis Wholesale Flower Market, 1987; freelance writer, contbr. to St. Louis Globe-Dem., St. Louis Post-Dispatch, St. Louis Jewish Light, Hockey News, Hockey World, Ladve News, Sporting News, Hockey Pictorial, Suburban Jour. Newspapers; writer copy for Knight's Catalogue, 1983. Pub. relations chmn. Nat. Council Jewish Women, 1981-83, publicity chmn. fashion sale, 1985; pres. Weber Sch. PTA, Creve Coeur, Mo., 1982; mem. Women's Am. ORT, 1965—; life mem. Jewish Hosp. Aux., 1965—, Jewish Ctr. for Aged, 1986—; pres. Young Women's Coun. on Edn. of Jewish Fedn. St. Louis, 1969; mem. central advancement team Pkwy. Central High Sch., 1985—. Recipient William Randolph Hearst award Hearst Found., Columbia, Mo., 1965, United Way Graphic Design award, 1986, United Way Photography award, 1987, Star Communicator Photography award, 1987, 89, 1st place award communications contest Nat. Fedn. Press Women, 1988, 3d place award photo feature, 1989, 2d place award Guide to Jewish Life in St. Louis photo contest, 1989, 2d place award Jewish Hosp. St. Louis Generations of Women photo contest, 1989; Besse Marks Meml. scholar, 1964-65. Mem. Jewish Ctr. for Aged Auxilliary, Fellows of Jewish Hosp., Mo. Press Women (1st place corp. newsletter category state feature writing communications contest, 1988), Mo. Assn. Homes for the Aging (publicity com., Outstanding 1st Place Newsletter award), Women in Communications (Ruth Philpott Collins award 1984). Jewish. Club: Meadowbrook Country (Ballwin, Mo.). Home: 12 Terryhill Ln Saint Louis MO 63131 Office: Jewish Ctr for Aged of Greater St Louis 13190 S Outer 40 Rd Chesterfield MO 63017

HANDELMAN, KAREN, foundation administrator; b. Chgo., Sept. 13, 1954; d. Richard D. and Susan (Kosmatka) H. Student, U. N.D., 1972-74, Embry-Riddle Aero. U., 1974-75; BA in Linguistics, N.E. Ill. U., 1987. Enlisted USMC, 1975, advanced through grades to staff sgt., 1984; adminstr. Werik Disabled Vets. Found., Baton Rouge, 1988-90, assoc. dir. fins., 1990—; guest speaker La. State U., Baton Rouge, 1989. Author: Beirut Sentry, 1990. Vol. S.E. Region VFW, Baton Rouge, 1989—. Decorated Purple Heart. Mem. NRA, Nat. Soc. Disabled Vets., Am. Legion, Amvets. Democrat. Home: 1835 Mile Point #20 Baton Rouge LA 70804 Office: Werik Found 651 Laurel Baton Rouge LA 70802

HANDLER, ARLENE FRANCES, nurse; b. Chgo., Mar. 25, 1943; d. Hyman and Sophie (Twersky) Fridkin; m. Raymond Morton Handler, Dec. 7, 1962; children—Jonathan Alan, David Aaron, Deborah Lynn. Grad. Michael Reese Hosp. Sch. Nursing, Chgo., 1963; B.A. in Applied Behavioral Sci., Nat. Coll. Edn., 1981; B.S.N., U. Without Walls, Cin. R.N., Ill.; MEd, Nat. Coll. Edn., 1988; cert. sch. nurse, Ill., marital and family therapist Family Inst. Chgo., 1990. Staff nurse Michael Reese Psychiat. Hosp., Chgo., 1963-65; vol. nurse U.S. Air Force Hosp., Rantoul, Ill., 1965-67; staff nurse Lakeshore Psychiat. Hosp., Chgo., 1971; substitute sch. nurse Sch. Dist. 27, Northbrook, Ill., 1978-87, Stevenson High Sch., Prairie View, Ill., 1982-87, Hawthorne Sch., Vernon Hills, Ill., 1981-87; sch. nurse, team leader Early Childhood Devel. Enrichment Ctr., Arlington Heights, Ill., 1985-89; pvt. practice, family and marital therapist, 1988; program coord. Family Involvement, Nurturing, Devel.-Parent Tng. Project, Hoffman Estates, 1990—. Chmn. health and safety Sch. Dist. 27 PTA, Northbrook, 1974-78; co-chairperson screening com. Northbrook Caucus, 1976-78; mem., chairperson operation smoke detector Northbrook Safety Commn., 1977—; pres. Sch. Dist. 27 Council PTAs, Northbrook, 1978-80; v.p.-sch. Congregation Beth Shalom, Northbrook, 1981-83; vice chmn., chmn. by-laws Northbrook Plan Commn., 1982-87. Co-honoree State of Israel Bonds, 1983. Mem. Michael Reese Nurses' Alumnae Assn., LWV, Ill. Assn. Sch. Nurses, Am. Sch. Health Assn., Nat. Assn. Edn. of Young Children. Home: 4022 Rutgers Ln Northbrook IL 60062 Office: Hillcrest Sch 500 Hillcrest Blvd Hoffman Estates IL 60195

HANDLER, BARBARA HERSHEY, computer analyst; b. Detroit, Sept. 10, 1939; d. William and Irene Ida (Goldstaff) Hershey; m. Leonard Handler, June 25, 1961; children: Charles Andrew, Amy Elisabeth. BS, Mich. State U., 1961, MA, 1964; EdD, U. Tenn., 1982. Tchr. Williamston (Mich.) High Sch., 1961-64, Farragut High Sch., Knoxville, 1964-65, Webb Sch. of Knoxville, 1969-70, U. Tenn., 1969-80, 82-85; faculty Maryville (Tenn.) Coll., 1980-83, State Tech. of Knoxville, 1983-85; rsch. assoc. Oak Ridge (Tenn.) Nat. Lab., 1985-87; computer analyst Martin Marietta Energy Systems, Inc, Oak Ridge, Tenn., 1985—; pvt. tutor. Contbr. articles to profl. jours., tech. manuals. Sec. Children's Internat. Summer Villages, Knoxville, 1966-68; bd. dirs. Arnstein Jewish Community Ctr., Knoxville, 1983-89. Mem. LWV (treas. 1969-70), Assn. for Devel. Computer-Based Instructional Systems, Nat. Council Tchrs. Math., Phi Delta Kappa, Phi Kappa Phi, Pi Lambda Theta. Democrat. Jewish. Home: 1800 Kinglet Ln Knoxville TN 37919 Office: Martin Marietta Energy Systems Inc PO Box 2003 Oak Ridge TN 37831-7171

HANDLER, ELISABETH HELEN, public relations executive; b. Greenwich, Conn., Aug. 10, 1944; d. Meyer Srednick and Helen Eulalah (Sennette) H.; m. Joseph Paul Ozawa, Mar. 18, 1968 (div. Sept. 1978); children: Alison Jane, Susan Hilary. BA, Radcliffe Coll., 1966. Adminstrv. asst. Office for Health Affairs, Office Econ. Opportunity, Washington, 1966-68; acting adminstrv. dir.community mental health service Mass. Mental Health Ctr., Boston, 1969-71; tech. writer Job Corps., Office Econ. Opportunity, Washington, 1972, Merle Norman Cosmetics, Los Angeles, 1973-74; account supr. Wallace Jamie Resource Group, Los Angeles, 1977-79; account supr., v.p. Berkhemer and Kline, Inc., Los Angeles, 1979-82; sr. v.p. Fleishman-Hillard, Inc., Los Angeles, 1982—; tchr. pub. relations The Ad Ctr., Los Angeles, 1985—. Contbr. article to profl. jour. Mem. Pub. Relations Soc. Am., Internat. Assn. Bus. Communicators. Democrat. Office: Fleishman-Hillard Inc 515 S Flower St 7th Fl Los Angeles CA 90091*

HANDLER, EVELYN ERIKA, university president; b. Budapest, Hungary, May 5, 1933; d. Donald D. and Ilona Sass; m. Eugene S. Handler; children: Jeffrey, Bradley. BA, CUNY, 1954; MSc, NYU, 1962, PhD, 1963; LHD (hon.), Rivier Coll., 1982; DSc (hon.), U. Pitts., 1987, Hunter Coll. of CUNY, 1988. Rsch. asst. Sloan Kettering Inst., N.Y.C., 1956-58; rsch. assoc. Merck Inst. Therapeutic Rsch., Rahway, N.J., 1958-60; mem. faculty, dept. biol. scis. Hunter Coll., CUNY, N.Y.C., 1962-77, dean div. scis. and math., 1977-80; pres. U. N.H., Durham, 1980-83, Brandeis U., Waltham, Mass., 1983-90; Mem. nat. adv. gen. med. sci. coun. NIH, 1981-84; mem. Am. Coun. Pharm. Edn., 1978-82; mem. exec. com. Nat. Assn. State Univs. and Land Grant Colls., 1981-83, mem. com. on policies and issues, 1981—. Contbr. articles and abstracts to profl. publs. Mem. New Eng. Bd. Higher Edn., 1980—; mem. New Eng. Coun. Pres., 1980-83, N.H. Coll. and Univ. Coun., 1980-83, Post-Secondary Edn. Commn., 1980—; corp. mem. Woods Hole Oceanographic Instn., 1983-89, trustee, 1988—; bd. dirs. The New Eng. Ins. Co., 1987—; mem. exec. com. New Eng. Colls. Fund, 1989—. Mem. Assn. Ind. Colls. and Univs. Mass. (exec. com. 1986—), Assn. Am. Univs. (sci. and rsch. com. 1985—), New Eng. Coun., Inc. (bd. dirs., 1983 chmn. edn., edn and tech. 1985-89). Office: Brandeis U Office of Pres 415 South St Waltham MA 02254

HANDLER, RUBY ANN, actress, editor, financial packager, author; b. Wenatchee, Wash., Mar. 28; d. Lundy and Emily LeMaster; m. Leonard Handler, Feb. 1, 1975 (div. 1980); 1 child, Aaron Asher. Student, U. Wash., Seattle; diploma, Weist Barron Sch. of TV, 1978. Assoc. Zenith Press, N.Y.C., 1973-74; head fin. dept. Vineyard Gazette, Martha's Vineyard, Mass., 1974-77; packager Cecco, Santa Monica, Calif., 1984-85; v.p. Fin. Svcs., Glendale, Calif., 1985-86; freelance fin. packager L.A., 1986—; editor Petite mag., L.A., 1989—; v.p. creative affairs div. Istar Corp., L.A., 1989—. Author: Mind and Body Magic, 1988; films include Lost Empire, The Boy Next Door; TV series include Sledgehammer, The Jeffersons, Fall Guy, Fantasy Island, All My Children: off-Broadway plays include Much Ado About Nothing, Blythe Spirit, South Pacific, Cabaret, Guys and Dolls, Man of La Mancha, Man Who Came to Dinner, Bedside Manners. Recipient Brown Belt, Beverly Hills Karate Acad., 1989. Mem. Magic Castle, Nat. Assn. R.R. Passengers, Internat. Brotherhood Magicians, Women in Show Bus., Greater L.A. Zoo Assn., Friends of the Observatory, Inc., Masquers, Oceanic Navigation Rsch. Soc., Inc., Sons of the Desert, MENSA. Film Welfare League, Round Table West Literary Club, AFTRA, SAG, Kappa Alpha Theta. Republican. Jewish.

HANDLEY, JEAN M., telephone company executive; b. Manchester, Conn., Aug. 28, 1926; d. Francis P. and Margaret (Ivers) H. B.A., Conn. Coll., 1948; M.A., Northwestern U., 1949. Pub. rels. asst. So. New Eng. Tel. Co., New Haven, 1960, advt. and employee info. staff, 1960-66, dist. mgr., 1966-72; dist. mgr. AT&T, N.Y.C., 1972-73; gen. info. mgr. So. New Eng. Tel. Co., 1973-75; press rels. dir. AT&T, N.Y.C., 1976-78; v.p. pub. rels. So. New Eng. Tel. Co., 1978-84, v.p. pers. and corp. rels., 1984—; vice chmn. Sci. Park Devel. Corp., New Haven. Chmn. bd. Conn. Coll., New London; vice-chmn. Conn. Pub. Expenditure Coun., Hartford; bd. dirs. New Haven Symphony Orch.; assoc. fellow Calhoun Coll., Yale U. Recipient Women in Leadership award YWCA of New Haven, 1979; Greater New Haven C. of C. Community Leadership award, 1984, Women Achievers award, YWCA of N.Y., 1984. Mem. Pub. Rels. Soc. Am., Pub. Rels. Soc. N.Y., Women in Communications, Inc., Am. Women in Radio and TV. Office: So New Eng Tel Co 227 Church St New Haven CT 06506

HANDLEY, MARGIE LEE, asphalt manufacturing company executive, real estate company executive, engineer; b. Bakersfield, Calif., Sept. 29, 1939; d. Robert E. and Jayne A. (Knoblock) Harrah; m. Gordon Daniel Lovell, Feb. 17, 1956 (div. Sept. 1973); children—Steven Daniel Lovell, David Robert Lovell, Ronald Eugene Lovell; m. Leon C. Handley, Sr., Oct. 28, 1975. Grad. high sch., Willits, Calif. With Firco, Inc., Willits, 1955-57; receptionist, typist Remco Hydraulics, Inc., Willits, 1958-62; owner, operator Shasta Pallet Co., Montague, 1969-70; owner, operator Lovell's Tack 'n Togs, Yreka, Calif., 1970-73; v.p. Microphor, Inc., Willits, 1974-81; pres. Harrah Industries, Inc., Willits, 1981—, Hot Rocks, Inc., Willits, 1983—. Sec. Willits Community Scholarships, Inc., 1962; trustee Montague Methodist Ch., 1966-73; candidate State Senate 2nd S.D.; sec. Montague PTA, 1969; clk. bd. trustees Montague Sch. Dist., 1970-73; del. Calif. State Conf. Small Bus., 1984; alt. del. Rep. Nat. Conv., Kansas City, Detroit, 1976, 80; 3d dist. chmn. Mendocino County Rep. Central Com., 1978-84; mem. Calif. State Rep. Central Com., 1985, 86, 87; Rep. nominee for State Senate Calif. 2nd Senate Dist., 1990; charter mem. Senatorial Inner Circle, 1980—; mem. Rep. Congl. Leadership Council, 1980-82; Mendocino County chmn. Reagan/Bush, 1980, 84; Mendocino County co-chmn. Deukmejian for Gov., 1982; mem. Region IX Small Bus. Adminstrn. Adv. Council, 1982—; mem. Gov.'s Adv. Council, 1983—; del., asst. sgt. of arms Rep. Nat. Conv., Dallas, 1984, del., New Orleans, 1988; vice chmn. Mendocino County Rep.

Central Com., 1985; mem. Willits C. of C. (hon.), Calif. Transp. Commn., 1986—; state dir. North Bay Dist. Hwy. Grading and Heavy Engring. div. 1986. Named Mendocino 12th Dist. Fair Woman of the Year, 1987. Mem. Assn. Gen. Contractors Calif., Soroptimist Internat. Home: PO Box 1309 Willits CA 95490 Office: Hot Rocks Inc 42 Madrone St Willits CA 95490

HANDY, ALICE WARNER, state agency administrator; b. Wilmington, Del., Apr. 17, 1948; d. Carleton Thomas and Ruth Francis (Lees) H.; m. Peter A. Stoudt; children: Nicholas Lyon Gerow, Jennifer Lees Gerow, Abigail Hurst Gerow. BA, Conn. Coll., 1970; postgrad., U. Va., 1975-78. Asst. investment officer Travelers Ins. Co., Hartford, Conn., 1970-74; investment officer U. Va., Charlottesville, 1974-81, asst. v.p., investment officer, 1981-88, univ. treas., 1988-90, 90—; treas. Commonwealth of Va., Richmond, 1988-90, U. Va., Charlottesville, 1990—; chmn. state coun. on local debt, state treasury bd.; commr. Va. Agrl. Devel. Authority, Va. Port Authority; treas. Va. Coll. Bldg. Authority; mem. Va. Edn. Loan Authority, Va. Resources Authority, Va. Small Bus. Financing Authority; sec.-treas. Va. Pub. Bldg. Authority, Va. Pub. Sch. Authority, all 1988-90; cons. various Va. U. Founds., 1985—. Trustee Va. Outdoors Found., 1988-90, Va. Hist. Preservation Found., 1989-90; troop leader Girl Scouts U.S.A., Charlottesville, 1985-88; bd. dirs. Va. Discovery Mus., Charlottesville, 1988; mem. fin. cam. Thomas Jefferson Ch., Charlottesville, 1987—; treas. Preservation Alliance, 1990—. Democrat. Unitarian. Office: Univ Va PO Box 9012 Charlottesville VA 22906 Office: U Va PO Box 9012 Carlottesville VA 22906

HANDY, CATHERINE MARIE, librarian; b. Holyoke, Mass., May 10, 1932; d. Cornelius Joseph and Mary Agnes (Collins) Hickey; m. Wallace H. Handy, Nov. 1955 (dec. Nov. 1961); children: Cornelia and Roberta (twins), Mary. BA, U. Mass., 1953; MS in LS, So. Conn. State Coll., 1965. Tchr. New Salem (Mass.) Acad., 1953-54, Londmeadow (Mass.) Jr. High Sch., 1954-56; libr. Wilson Jr. High Sch., Windsor, Conn., 1965-69; reference libr. Westfield (Mass.) State Coll., 1969—; abstractor Libr. Currents, 1984-86. Vol. Noble Hosp., Westfield, 1977-80. Mem. ALA (cert. sch. and acad. libr., reviewer RQ 1980—, Choice 1984—), Assn. Coll. and Rsch. Librs., New Eng. Libr. Assn., NEA, Mass. Tchrs. Assn., Mass. State Coll. Assn. Roman Catholic. Home: 27 Park Avenue Ct Apt 12B West Springfield MA 01089 Office: Westfield State Coll Libr Western Ave Westfield MA 01086

HANEBORG, LINDA C., national communications director; b. Chgo.; d. John Arnold and Kathleen Rosetta (Kelly) Tenborg; m. Steven B. Haneborg, Jan. 3, 1970; children: Julie Brooke, Douglas Jordan. BS, Colo. State U., 1969; postgrad., Creighton U., 1966, So. Meth. U., 1973. Customer rep. Xerox Corp., Denver, 1973-76; asst. dir. mktg. Medema Homes, Denver, 1976-77; v.p., gen. mgr. Okla. Living Mag., Oklahoma City, 1979-86; dir. pub. rels., mgr. promotions Sta. KGMC-TV, Oklahoma City, 1987-88; asst. dir. corp. communications Express Svcs. Temporary & Permanent Personnel, Oklahoma City, 1988-89, dir. corp. communications, 1989—. Creator, 1st chairperson youth vol. program W. Mentally Retarded Residents, Denver, 1976-77; bd. dirs. Oklahaven Children's Ctr., Oklahoma City, 1985—. Mem. Am. Women in Radio and TV, Women in Communications, Oklahoma City Orch. League, Allied Arts Found. (Disting. Sales award), Sales & Mktg. Execs. Internat., Rep. Women's Club, Greens Country Club (bd. dirs. 1989), Oklahoma City Advt. Club (Addy award of merit 1990), Sigma Phi Gamma (pres. 1988-89). Republican. Roman Catholic. Office: Express Svcs 6300 NW Expy Oklahoma City OK 73132

HANEK, PATRICIA ANN, claims representative; b. Cleve., July 25, 1951; d. Leonard William and Marjorie Alwilda (Fulton) Schultz; m. Gary W. Gifford, Sept. 8, 1973 (div. Feb. 1980); m. John Nicholas Hanek, Sept. 26, 1980; children: Nicholas, William, Joel. BA, Cleve. State U., 1973; postgrad., Miami U., Oxford, Ohio, 1976-77. Med. intake worker Butler County Welfare, Middletown, Ohio, 1974-77; head cashier Montgomery Ward, Akron, Ohio, 1977-78; claims approver John Hancock Ins., Shaker Heights, Ohio, 1978-79; claims rep. Social Security Adminstrn., Painesville, Ohio, 1979-81, Parma Heights, Ohio, 1981—. Office: Social Security Adminstrn 6325 York Rd Parma Heights OH 44130

HANES, DARLENE MARIE, finance company executive; b. St. Mary's, Pa., Mar. 24, 1956; d. Donald Frank and Martha Mary (Krug) H. CLU degree, Am. Coll., Bryn Mawr, Pa., 1986, Chartered Fin. Cons. degree, 1988. CLU. Underwriter N.Y. Life Ins. Co., Concord, Calif., 1980-87; v.p. East Bay Fin. Ctr., Concord, 1987—, v.p. agy. devel., 1988—. Pres. Am. Cancer Soc. League, 1985-86, bd. dirs. 1984—; bd. dirs. Airport Commn., St. Mary's, 1975. Named Person of Day, Am. Heart Assn., 1985. Mem. Nat. Assn. Life Underwriters (Nat. Quality award 1985, 86, 87, Pres.'s Trophy 1986), Mt. Diablo Assn. Life Underwriters (bd. dirs. 1982—, pres. 1986-87), East Bay CLU Soc. (v.p. 1989), Calif. Assn. Life Underwriters (regional coord. 1987—), Gen. Agts. and Mgrs. Assn., Hosp. Guild (sec. 1989-90). Republican. Roman Catholic. Office: East Bay Fin Ctr 3227 Clayton Rd Concord CA 94519

HANEX, TAYLOR ANNE, financial consultant; b. Washington, Mar. 30, 1953; d. John Joseph and Eileen Mildred (Diamondson) H. MusB, Peabody Conservatory of Music, Johns Hopkins U., 1975, MusM, 1978; MBA, Fordham U., 1980; postgrad., U. Nebr., 1975, Conservatorio Mcpl. de Musica, Barcelona (Spain), 1976. Performer, royalty sales rep. G. Schirmer Music Publs., N.Y.C., 1977-78; rsch. asst. Bill Communications, N.Y.C., 1978-79; account exec. Microband Corp. Am., N.Y.C., 1981-82, nat. accts. mgr., 1983-85; asst. v.p. for bus. ops. Irving Bank Corp., N.Y.C., 1986, asst. v.p., 1986-87; fin. cons. Merrill Lynch, N.Y.C., 1987—; guest lectr. Kean Coll., 1983, Fordham U. Grad. Sch. of Bus., 1989; solo concert pianist East and Midwest U.S. U. Nebr. teaching fellow, 1975; recipient Mabel H. Thomas award Peabody Conservatory of Music, Balt., 1970; Fordham U. grad. fellow, 1979; Joseph Mullan scholar Peabody Conservatory of Music, 1975. Mem. Am. Mktg. Assn., Johns Hopkins Alumni Assn. (bd. dirs. N.Y. chpt. 1989), Peabody Conservatory of Music Alumni Assn. (chmn. 1989), Toastmasters Internat., Money Marketeers of NYU. Republican. Roman Catholic. Home: 233 E 69th St New York NY 10021 Office: Merrill Lynch 717 Fifth Ave New York NY 10022

HANEY, MARCELLA HELEN, talent and model agent; b. St. Louis, June 7, 1922; d. Anthony Stephen and Mildred Dorothy (Rollberg) Fischl; m. Peter V. Leggatt, Spet. 26, 1941 (dec. Apr. 1954); m. Robert T. Haney, Aug. 26, 1955 (dec. Jan. 1981). Student, Marygrove Coll., Detroit, 1939-41. Mem. staff Himelhose Bros., Detroit, 1941-44, Wiebolts Dept. Stores, Chgo., 1945-49, D. J Healys, Detroit, 1949-55; Patricia Stevens Modeling and Finishing Sch., Chgo.; owner Marce Haney Assoc. Talen and Model Agy., Detroit, 1961--. Invented panty hose, new form of panty hose. Speaker United Founds., United Way, Detroit, 1975--. Mem. Women's Advt. Club (pres. 1984-85), Adcraft Club, Fashion Group, Grosse Pointe Yacht Club. Republican. Roman Catholic. Home: 203 Country Club Dr Saint Clair Shores MI 48082 Office: Marce Haney Assoc 1150 Griswold Detroit MI 48226

HANEY, SUE ELLEN, software sales executive; b. Pitts., Dec. 22, 1945; d. Fred W. and E. Jane (Rebele) Schneider. Student, Mary Washington Coll., 1963-65; BA in Psychology, Carnegie-Mellon U., 1967. Tchr. spl. edn. Lancaster (Pa.) County Sch. System, 1968-69; tchr. elem. edn. Sch. Dist. of Lancaster, 1969-79; cons. Scott Foresman Co., Glenview, Ill., 1979-81; med. rep. Lederle div. Am. Cyanamid, Pearl River, N.Y., 1981-85; sales rep. ednl. software div. Houghton Mifflin Co., Bloomingdale, Ill., 1985-89; dist. mgr. ednl. software div. Houghton Mifflin Co., Hanover, N.H., 1989—. Office: Houghton Mifflin Co Ste 304 101 Campus Dr Princeton NJ 08540

HANFT, RUTH S. SAMUELS (MRS. HERBERT HANFT), health care consultant, educator, economist; b. N.Y.C., July 12, 1929; d. Max Joseph and Ethel (Schechter) Samuels; m. Herbert Hanft, June 17, 1951; children: Marjorie Jane, Jonathan Mark. BS, Cornell U., 1949; MA, Hunter Coll., 1963; PhD, George Washington U., 1989. Cons. Urban Med. Econs. Project, Hunter Coll., N.Y.C. and D.C. Dept. Health, 1962-63; health economist Office of Research and Stats., Social Security Adminstrn., Washington, 1964-66; chief grants mgmt., health div. Office Econ. Opportunity, Washington, 1966-68; sr. health analyst Office of Asst. Sec. Planning and Evaluation, HEW, Washington, 1968-71; spl. asst., asst. sec. health Office of Asst. Sec. Planning and Evaluation, HEW, 1971-72, dep. asst. sec. for health policy, research and stats., 1977-79, dep. asst. sec. for health research, stats. and tech., 1979-81; health care cons., 1981-88; cons., research prof. dept. health services adminstrn. George Washington U., 1988—; vis. prof. Dartmouth Med. Sch., 1976—; sr. research asso. Inst. Medicine-Nat. Acad. Scis., Washington, 1972-76. Contbr. articles to profl. jours. Mem. Med. Assistance Service bd. Commonwealth Va. Fellow Hastings Ctr.; mem. Inst. of Medicine, Nat. Acad. Sci. Jewish. Home: 3609 Cameron Mills Rd Alexandria VA 22305 Office: 600 21st St NW Washington DC 20052

HANIN, LEDA TONI, university administrator; b. Bronx, N.Y., Mar. 11, 1940; d. Paul Leopold and Milah (Russin) Wermer; m. Israel Hanin, June 12, 1960; children: Adam Jeffrey, Dahlia Beth. BA in Sociology, UCLA, 1962; cert. mktg., U. Pitts., 1978, MEd, 1984. Dir. confs. Western Psychiat. Inst., Pitts., 1974-77; dir. publicity Carnegie Inst., Pitts., 1977-81; dir. pub. and alumni relations grad. sch. indsl. adminstrn. Carnegie-Mellon U., Pa., 1981-86; dir. pub. relations grad. sch. bus. U. Chgo., 1986-88; exec. dir. Community Chest, Oak Park and River Forest, Ill., 1988-90; assoc. v.p. u. rels. DePaul U., Chgo., 1990—; adv. bd. Oak Pk. River Forest Day Nursery. bd. dirs. Chgo. chpt. Nat. Council for Prevention of Child Abuse. Winner CASE silver medal, 1987; 2-time winner Matrix prize for Pub. Relations, Women in Communications. Mem. Am. Assembly Collegiate Schs. Bus. (cons.), Pub. Relations Soc. Am. (accredited, chpt. pres. 1984-86, recipient prizes 1986), Publicity Club Chgo. (recipient Silver Trumpet award 1987), United Mental Health Assn. (pres. 1984-86, mktg. prize Western region). Jewish. Home: 1132 N Kenilworth Ave Oak Park IL 60302

HANINGER, ELSIE BLALOCK, corporate professional; b. Raleigh, N.C., Jan. 2, 1934; d. John W. Lacy and Virginia M. (Stephens) Blalock; m. Glenn James Haninger, Mar. 15, 1975. Student, Sheffield Sch. Interior Design, N.Y.C.; grad., Rex Hosp. Sch. Nursing, Raleigh, N.C., 1955; postgrad., Duke U., 1957. RN, N.C., Va., Ohio. Caudal labor nurse Drs. Branaman & McElrath, Raleigh, 1955-58; head nurse, surgery Rex Hosp., Raleigh, 1958-60; staff nurse White Cross Hosp., Columbus, Ohio, 1960-61; head nurse Riverside White Cross Hosp., Columbus, 1961-62; scrub & office nurse Glenn J. Haninger, M.D., Columbus, 1962-70; office mgr. Haninger & Haninger M.D.'s, Inc., Columbus, 1970-85; corp. sec. Haninger & Haninger M.D.'s, Inc., Gahanna, Ohio, 1970—, also bd. dirs. Contbr. articles to profl. jours. Vol. Columbus area Homeless Persons, Humane Soc. Recipient Pres. Cup Porsche Club, 1976, Nat. Champion, 1976, 81, Driver of Yr. award Sports Car Club Am., 1980. Mem. Am. Bus. Women's Assn., Am. Nurses Assn., AMA Women's Aux. Republican. Roman Catholic. Home: 5955 Headley Rd Columbus OH 43230 Office: Haninger & Haninger MDs Inc 181 Granville St Gahanna OH 43230

HANINGTON, PAULA KAY, lawyer; b. Colquitt, Ga., May 20, 1956; d. Buford Lavon and India R. (Lofton) Taylor; m. John Foster Hanington, May 3, 1986. BA cum laude, Valdosta State Coll., 1978; JD, U. Ga., 1981. Bar: Ga., U.S. Dist. Ct. (mid. dist.) Ga., 1983, U.S. Ct. Appeals (11th cir.), 1983. Assoc. Law Offices of John H. Hayes, Albany, Ga., 1982-84, Gilberg & Kraselsky, Albany, 1984-85; sole practice Albany, 1985—; pub. defender City of Albany, 1984-88; spl. asst. atty. gen. Ga. Atty. Gen.'s Office, 1986—; assoc. judge Recorder's Ct. City of Albany, 1988—. Mem. ABA, Ga. Bar Assn., Dougherty County Bar Assn. (lectr. 1983—), Assn. Trial Lawyers Am., Assn. Ga. Trial Lawyers, Soc. Outstanding Youmng Women Am., Women in Network. Office: 510 Flint Ave Albany GA 31701

HANKIN, ELAINE KRIEGER, psychologist, researcher; b. Scranton, Pa., Oct. 17, 1938; d. Maurice and Beatrice (Blumberg) Krieger; m. Abbe Hankin, Dec. 22, 1957; children: Susan Hankin-Birke, Elyse Rae. BA, Temple U., 1979, MEd, 1980; PhD, Bryn Mawr Coll., 1984. Therapist Comac Youth Service Bur., Willow Grove, Pa., 1975-76; therapist, supr. of interns Aldersgate Youth Service Bur., Willow Grove, 1975-84; staff psychologist Buck's County Guidance Ctr., Doylestown, Pa., 1981-84; psychologist, ptnr., clin. dir. Abington (Pa.) Psychol. Assocs., 1984—; v.p., adminstr. dir. Corp. Devel. Systems, Abington, 1984—; adj. staff NW Inst. Psychiatry, Ft. Washington, Pa., 1986—, Eugenia Hosp., Ft. Washington, 1986—. Mem. AAUW, Am. Psychol. Assn., Nat. Council on Family Relations, World Fedn. for Mental Health, Assn. for Mental Health Affiliation, Pa. Psychol. Assn., Pa. Council on Family Relations, Pa. Soc. Behavioral Medicine, Phila. Folk Song Soc., Phi Beta Kappa, Psi Chi. Home: 242 Ironwood Cir Breyer Woods Elkins Park PA 19117 Office: Abington Psychol Assocs 500 Old York Rd Ste 100 Jenkintown PA 19046

HANKINS, E. CANDICE, sales professional; b. Queens, N.Y., Dec. 20, 1966; d. Victor and Dorothy M. Hankins. BA, SUNY, Buffalo, 1988. Sales asst. Internat. Creative Mgmt., Inc., N.Y.C., CBS, Inc., N.Y.C.; sales rep. Southwestern Pub. Co., Nashville, Fayva Shoes, Yonkers, N.Y., Thom McAn, Yonkers, NY; sales agent Pan Am. World Airways; writer/co-producer Buffalo State Coll.; writer-prodn. asst. Delaware North Cos., Buffalo; news desk asst. Sta. WGRZ-TV, Buffalo; corp. communications asst. NBC, Inc., N.Y.C.; on-air talent MTV Network, NYC; Pub. Svc. Announcement Series, Washington; photography asst., N.Y.C. Editor Quar. Newsletter for Tchrs. of Spanish and Portuguese in Western N.Y., 1985-86. Mem. Nat. Broadcasting Honor Soc., Alpha Epsilon Rho (chpt. officer). Home: 201 W 107th St Apt 17 New York NY 10025

HANKINS, SHIRLEY, state representative; b. Colby, Kans., Nov. 9, 1931; d. Mack Olif Williams and Florance (Wheaton) Williams Richard; m. Myron M. Hankins, Sr., Aug. 6, 1950 (dec.); children—Myron M., Jr., Shelley D., Sherrey A. Mem. Wash. State Senate; mem. acad. adv. bd. Pa. Power and Light; bd. advisors Inst. for Regulatory Sci. Mem. Richland Rep. Women; past chmn. Tri-City Tech. Council; mem. adv. bd. Far West Fed. Lab. Consortium, exec. com. Nat. Conf. State Legislatures. Mem. Richland Fedn. Women's Clubs, Richland Bus. and Profl. Women's Clubs, Health Physics Soc. (Columbia chpt.), Am. Nuclear Soc., Inc. (Ea. Washington sect.), Thomas County Hist. Soc., Am. Legion Aux. #71, U.S. Navy League (hon.), Washington Women, Rotary.

HANKS, GRACE MARY, vocational rehabilitation facility executive; b. Galveston, Tex., June 18, 1954; d. Sebastiano and Giovanna (Palumbo) Buzzurro; m. David Terry Hanks, Oct. 10, 1982; children: Austin, Jenna. BS with honors, Southwest Tex. State U., 1976, MEd, 1978. Project dir. St. Anthony's Spl. Edn. Sch., San Antonio, 1978-79; asst. to pvt. practice psychologist San Antonio, 1979; tng. coord., program specialist Mental Health Assn. Dallas County, 1979-82; head tchr., asst. dir. Nev. Easter Seals, Sparks, 1982; vocat. evaluation specialist North Tex. Rehab. Svcs., Garland, 1982-84; exec. dir. Metrocrest Area Rehab. Ctr., Carrollton, Tex., 1984—; cons., Bethpage Industries, Dallas, 1988—. Author, editor, Family Advocate Program, 1980. Advocate, lobbyist, Tex. Industries for Blind and Handicapped, 1989, Coalition for Texans with Disabilities, Austin, 1989. Grantee Civic League Found., Carrollton, 1985-87, Metrocrest Women's Orgn., 1988, Redmon Found., Dallas, 1985, Addison Bus. Assn., 1985, 89. Mem. Dallas Rehab. Assn., Tex. Rehab. Assn., Nat. Rehab. Assn., Dallas Psychol. Assn., Metrocrest Profl. Womens Assn., Leadership, Carrollton Jaycees. Republican. Episcopalian. Home: 2012 Hearthstone St Carrollton TX 75010 Office: Metrocrest Area Rehab Ctr 1467 Lemay Dr No 108 Carrollton TX 75007

HANLON, BETTY ELLEN, nurse; b. Oradell, N.J., Mar. 7, 1935; d. Otto Conrad and Berta Christine (Eckert) Sander; m. James H., May 21, 1960; children: James Otto, Lorna Lee. Student, White Plains Hosp. Sch. of Nur, 1957, Pace U., White Plains, 1976. Registered Nurse. RN Whit Plains (N.Y.) Hosp., 1957—, community outreach, 1977-85; Homeless Shelter, 1986; coord. Open Arms Shelter St. Bernard's Ch., 1989—. Geriatric Visitor Sr. Dept. White Plains Hosp., 1986; Aids Buddy ARC, 1988--; Community Outreach White Plains Hosp., 1987--. Mem. White Plains Hosp. Auxillary. Republican. Roman Catholic. Home: 62 Chatterton Pkwy White Plains NY 10606

HANLON, PAMELA IRENE (PAMELA IRENE KASKIW), marketing executive; b. Park Falls, Wis., Aug. 10, 1948; d. James and Irene Leah (Schwall) Katchis; m. E. Andrew Kaskiw, July 7, 1984; 1 child, Stacey Irene Hanlon. BS in Acctg. Mgmt., U. Evansville, 1983; MBA in Health Care Mgmt., U. Colo., 1986. Cert. Health Care Fin. Mgmt. Cost acct. Isothermics, Inc., Franklin, N.J., 1975-76; dir. fiscal services Benjamin Rush Ctr., Syracuse, N.Y., 1976-78; fin. analyst Mead Johnson, Evansville, Ind., 1978-81; dir. fin. planning St. Mary's Med. Ctr., Evansville, 1981-84; controller Luth. Med. Ctr., Wheat Ridge, Colo., 1984-86; v.p. hosp., physician networks Integrated Med. Systems, Golden, Colo., 1986—; lectr. various seminars. Contbr. articles to profl. jours. Active Title XX Rev. Bd., Sussex, N.J., 1975; bd. dirs. Argyle Sq. Park. Mem. Health Care Fin. Mgmt. Assn. (advanced, matrix com. 1982), Am. Coll. Health Care Execs., Nat. Assn. Female Execs., Soc. Hosp. Planning and Mktg., Colo. Healthcare Adminstrs. Forum. Clubs: Newburg Swim Team (pres., treas. 1980-82), Deer Blvd Corp. (treas. 1984-86). Home: 11861 Bryant Circle Denver CO 80234 Office: Integrated Med Systems 1500 W 6th Ave Golden CO 80401

HANLON, SUSAN DEASY, human resources specialist; b. Steubenville, Ohio, Nov. 6, 1941; d. John Kershaw and Jean (McDougal) Deasy; m. John Culbreth Hanlon, Aug. 4, 1969. BA in Human Rels., Rollins Coll., 1963; MS in Leisure Svcs. and Studies, Fla. State U., 1973. Acting program dir. Leisure Program Office Fla. State U., Tallahassee, 1973-74, asst. prof. leisure svcs. and studies, 1976-82, student devel. coord. Div. Student Affairs, 1983-84; exec. dir. Vol. Action Ctr., 1974-76; pvt. practice cons., 1982-83, 84-86; mgr. employee tng. and devel. The Printing House, Inc., Tallahassee, 1986—; asst. dir. Lafayette Arts and Crafts Ctr. Tallahassee Park and Recreation Dept., 1970-72; program dir. University Union La. State U., 1969-70; recreation therapist Am. Red Cross, Washington, 1963-69. Bd. dirs. Leon County Assn. for Mental Health, Foster Grandparents Program, 1975, Leon Sch. Vol. Program, Telephone Counseling and Referral Svc.; steering com. Leon Assn. Retarded Citizens/Citizens Advocacy Com.; active HRS Task Force on Volunteerism, 1975. Named Advisor of Yr., Fla. State U., 1982; recipient Oglesby Union award, Fla. State U., 1982. Mem. Fla. State U. Coll. Edn. Alumni Assn. (pres. 1977-78), Zonta Club of Tallahassee (pres. 1982-83), Sigma Lambda Sigma. Home: 1548 Marion Ave Tallahassee FL 32303

HANMER, REBECCA W., government program official; b. Farmville, Va., Apr. 13, 1941; d. Howard Herman and Glenna Mae (Ward) H.; m. William A. Nerenberg, July 13, 1968 (div. 1972). BA, Coll. William and Mary, 1963; MA, Am. U., 1966. Program analyst Dept. Health Edn. and Welfare, Washington, 1964-66; environ. analyst Fed. Water Pollution Control, Washington, 1966-70; fed. agy. liasion adminstr. U.S. Dept. Interior, Office Fed. Activities, EPA, Washington, 1971-75; dir. Office Fed. Activities, EPA, Washington, 1975-77; dep. regional adminstr. region I EPA, Boston, 1977-79; regional adminstr. region IV EPA, Atlanta, 1980-81; dep. asst. adminstr. for water EPA, Washington, 1982-84, 86—, acting asst. adminstr. for water, 1983-84, 88—, dir. office water, 1984-86. Contbr. articles to profl. jours. on environ. and water pollution control. Mem. Nature Conservancy. Democrat. Methodist. Home: 407 A St NE Washington DC 20002 Office: EPA Washington DC 20460

HANN, BARBARA JOANN, financial advisor; b. Gardner, Mass., Aug. 16, 1946; d. Frank and Cecelia (Corapinski) Swercewski; m. Alton L. Hann Jr., Aug. 8, 1966 (div. Dec. 1976); 1 child, Christopher L. BS, Salem Coll., 1968; MEd, Bridgewater Coll., 1975. Tchr. McLean (Va.) High Sch., 1968-69, W Bridgewater High Sch., 1969-75; sr. editor McGraw Hill Book Co., N.Y.C., 1975-78; account exec. AT&T, N.Y.C., 1978-80; new bus. officer Barclays Bank, N.Y.C., 1980-83; leveraged acquisition officer Citibank N.A., 1983; v.p. Biotech Venture Capital, N.Y.C., 1984-87; v.p. pvt. placements Gruntal and Co., N.Y.C., 1987; prin. Hawthorne Ptnrs., N.Y.C., 1987—; dir. HSC Inc., Valhalla, N.Y., 1984-87, Quest Bus. Agy., Houston, 1984-87, Med. Magnetics, Inc., N. Bergen, 1985-87, Am. Bionuclear Inc., San Francisco, 1985-87. Mem. The Planning Forum, Nat. Assn. of Small Bus. Companies, Conn. Venture Group. Office: Hawthorne Ptnrs Ltd 1186 Broadway Ste 833 New York NY 10001

HANNA, BETTY ELLIOTT, editor; b. Breckenridge, Tex., Feb. 13, 1921; d. Ross and Mattie (Liles) Elliott; m. Joe C. Hanna, May 19, 1920; children: Judith, Stephen Elliott, Mark Monroe. B in Journalism, U. Tex., Austin, 1942. Feature editor Breckenridge Am., Tex., 1962—; appointee Tex. Hist. Com., Austin, 1987—. Author 3 books. Recipient Margaret Caskeky award for journalist excellence, First Place awards for feature stores in Tex. Press Assn. Methodist. Home: 201 N Harding Breckenridge TX 76024

HANNA, NORA CLARE, retail store executive; b. Belfast, No. Ireland, May 13, 1959; came to U.S., 1961; d. Joseph Paschal and Nora Eileen (Flynn) H. Grad. high sch., South San Francisco, Calif. Buyer Emporium Capwell, San Francisco, 1983-86; product devel. mgr. Carter Hawley Hale, N.Y.C., 1986-88; merchandiser Accessory Lady, N.Y.C., 1988—. Roman Catholic. Office: Accessory Lady 990 Ave of Americas Ste 17R New York NY 10018

HANNA, PEGGY ANN (ROTH), educator; b. Alliance, Ohio, Jan. 21, 1931; d. Chester Franklin and Blanche Lucille (Martin) Roth; m. Harold Llyod Hanna, Sept. 9, 1950; children: Keith E. (dec.), Evonne L., H. Roth. BA, Mt. Union Coll., Alliance, 1970, postgrad., 1975; postgrad., U. Akron, 1970, 71, 72-73, 75, Youngstown State U., 1980, 87, Kent State U., 1982, 88. 4th grade tchr. West Branch Sch. Sys./Knox Elementary Sch., Alliance, 1970-76; 5th grade tchr. West Branch Sch. Sys./Knox Elementary Sch., 1976-88; jr. high reading tchr. Damascus (Ohio) Jr. High Sch., 1988—; mem. Project T.E.A.C.H., Coll. of Mt. St. Joseph on the Ohio, 1984. Designer lit.-based reading program to complement French, German and Spanish lang. studies. Mem. West Branch Edn. Assn. (bldg. rep.), AAUW, NEA, N.E. Ohio Tchrs. Assn. Baptist. Home: 2637 S Union Ave Alliance OH 44601

HANNA, ROBERTA JONES, graphologist; b. Houston, Apr. 10, 1925; d. Daniel Waymond and Mary Frances (Curry) Jones; m. Joe Stephen Hanna, Dec. 20, 1947 (div. May 1973); children: Joe Stephen, Jordan Waymond, Eleanor Charlotte. Student, U. Houston, 1942-45. Cert. questioned document examiner. Display artist Houston Display Assn., 1942-46; owner, mgr. Hanna Displays, Houston, 1947-73, Roberta's Studio, Houston, 1962-78; owner, pres. Creative Industries S.W., Houston, 1976-78; owner, broker R.J. Properties, Houston, 1982; owner, mgr. Personality Profiles, Houston, 1985—; instr. graphoanalysis Spring Branch Ind. Sch. Patentee stained glass field, method of preserving flowers in lucite. Bd. dirs. Women's Christian Mission, Houston, 1962-65, dir. occupational therapy, 1963-65. Mem. Internat. Graphoanalyst Assn. (cert., master), World Assn. Document Examiners, Tex. Soc. Graphoanalysis, Am. Assn. Bus. Women, Nat. Assn. Profl. Women, Hal PC Computer Club, Rotary. Baptist. Office: Personality Profiles Memorial City Pla 820 Gessner Ste 200 Houston TX 77024

HANNA, ROSE ELIZABETH, nurse; b. New Washington, Ohio, Dec. 11, 1934; d. Anthony Cornelius and Ruth Anna (Ehrat) McCarthy; m. Gerald Elias Hanna, Oct. 18, 1958; children: Jennifer L. Hanna McCreight, Mary R. Hanna Chapman, Rebecca J., Amy C. Hanna Kolb. Diploma, St. Vincent Hosp. Sch. Nursing, 1955; BS in Nursing, Defiance Coll., 1985. R.N., Ohio. Staff nurse St. Vincent Hosp., Toledo, 1955-56, Defiance (Ohio) Hosp., Inc., 1956-72; operating room supr./dir. nurses to asst. adminstr. nursing Bryan (Ohio) Community Hosp., 1972-86; v.p. patient care Community Hosps. Williams County, Bryan and Montpelier, Ohio, 1986—. Mem. Ohio Soc. Nurse Execs., Rural Northwest Ohio Dir. of Nursing, St. Vincent Hosp. Alumni, Marysdale Altar Soc. Democrat. Roman Catholic. Home: 19707 Schick Rd Rte 1 Defiance OH 43512-9801 Office: Community Hosps Williams Co 433 W High St Bryan OH 43506

HANNAN, BRADLEY, educational publishing consultant; b. Rochester, N.Y., Apr. 24, 1935; d. Jack Seymour MacArthur and Alice E. (Knapp) Staley; m. William J. Hannan, Jr., June 15, 1957 (div. 1976); children: Megan Lee, Timothy, Patrick, Moira. BA, Ariz. State U., 1957. Tchr. various sch. dists. Ariz., 1957-62; English language cons. Evanston (Ill.) Twp. High Sch., 1963-65; editor, then sr. editor Harper & Row Pubs., Evanston, 1965-75; sr. reading text editor Scott, Foresman & Co., Glenview, Ill., 1975-78, sr. editor lang. arts, 1982-87; dir. reading McDougal Littell & Co., Evanston, 1978-81; project dir. spelling Ednl. Challenges, Alexandria, Va., 1981-82; dir. curriculum and product mgmt. for reading and lang. arts texts Open Court Pub. Co., Chgo. and Peru, Ill., 1987-88; cons., project dir. lang. arts texts Harcourt, Brace, Jovanovich, Orlando, Fla., 1988-89; sr. mng. editor reading, lang. arts, social studies Sci. Rsch. Assocs., Chgo., 1989; cons. edl. pub. Chgo., 1989—; speaker Internat. Reading Assn., New Orleans, 1981, Chgo. Women in Publishing, 1981, Childrens' Reading Roundtable, Chgo., 1985; developer reading textbook series. Mem. Internat. Reading Assn., Nat. Council Tchrs. English, Chgo. Book Clinic. Home and Office: 8500 N Trumbull St Skokie IL 60076

HANNAWAY, PATRICIA HINMAN, art scholar, historian; b. Mpls., Jan. 25, 1929; d. Ira Perry and Florence Elizabeth (Montgomery) Hinman; m. Glen H. Altland, June 12, 1948 (div. 1968); children: David Lee, Roger Dean, Stanley William (dec.), Glenn H. III (dec.); m. Walter F. Hannaway, Feb. 7, 1972 (dec. 1985). Grad. high sch., Mpls., 1947. Freelance writer Mpls., 1953-59; advt. copywriter Boutell's Inc., Mpls., 1958-59, Colle McVoy, Mpls., 1959, Knox-Reeves Advt., Mpls., 1960-62; woman's page editor Key West (Fla.) Citizen, 1963-65; creative dir. Grant Advt., Miami, 1967-68; info. specialist Fla. Dept. Commerce, Tallahassee, 1968-69; creative dir. Daniels Rainey Advt., Clearwater, Fla., 1969-72, Profl. Bus. Assocs., Lutz, Fla., 1988-90. Author: Winslow Homer in the Tropics, 1974. Pres. Friends of Library, Clearwater, 1975-76, Friends of Tampa Hills Library. Mem. NAFE. Democrat. Lutheran. Office: Agape Unlimited PO Box 7112 Wesley Chapel FL 33543

HANNEMAN, ELAINE ESTHER, salesperson; b. Waupaca, Wis., Aug. 28, 1928; d. Martin Fred Strey and Laura Rucks; m. Alfred Adam Hanneman, Feb. 14, 1948; children: Karen, Dale, Sally, Sandra. High sch. grad., 1946. Acct. AAL Life Ins. Co., Appleton, Wis., 1946-48; sales Artex Paint, Milw., 1960-74, Car Ins. and Memberships, Appleton, Wis., 1974-78, Am. Family Life, Columbus, Ga. Mem. Gold Century Club, Pres. Club, Am. Family Life. Lutheran. Home: 103 W St Box 244 Weyauwega WI 54983 also: 1842 Edgewater Dr Amherst WI 54407

HANNEN, ADA LORELEI, marketing professional; b. High Point, N.C., Nov. 8, 1942; d. Pearl Clayton and Germaine Rose (Slover) Jones; m. Charles Floyd Hannen, Apr. 6, 1960; children: Kimberly Rose, Paula Tamala, Scott Kevin. Grad. high sch., Apopka, Fla. Operator directory assistance So. Bell Tel. & Tel. Co., Orlando, Fla., 1969-72; clk. service orders So. Bell Tel. & Tel. Co., Orlando, 1972-74; clk. customer service So. Tel.& Tel.Co., Orlando, 1974-75, clk. dist. office, 1975-79; sales rep. So. Bell Tel. & Tel. Co., Orlando, 1979-85; sales mgr. Bell South Advt. and Pub. Co., Orlando, 1985-88, staf mgr. trainer, 1988-90; ptnr. Ladies' Consignment Shop, Orlando. Mem. Nat. Assn. Female Execs. Office: 3670 Maguire Blvd Orlando FL 32803

HANNER, DAWNA MELANSON, nurse, anaylst; b. Boston, June 4, 1947; d. Frank O. and Patricia C. (Sears) Melanson; m. David M. Hanner, Sept. 1984; children: Daniel Thompson, Scott Thompson. RN Sch. Nursing, Cooley-Dickinson Hosp., Northampton, Mass., 1968. RN, Tex., Mass., N.Y. Staff nurse Columbia Presbyn. Hosp., N.Y.C., St. Elizabeth's Hosp., Boston; registered nurse Children's Med. Ctr., Austin, Tex.; staff/charge nurse S.E. Tex. Med. Ctr. Hosp., San Antonio; registered nurse Dr. Robert A. Wymer, M.D., San Antonio; internatl med. triage nurse, supr./mgr. Southboro (Mass.) Med. Group; unit coord. insvc. implementation, nurse mgr. HMO unit Austin Regional Clinic, 1983-84; nurse auditor cost containment svcs. TSSF, Austin, Tex., 1985-88; nurse IV analyst Recipient Utilization Control Tex. Dept. Human Svcs., Austin, 1988—. Mem. NAFE, Tex. Med. Auditors Assn., Exec. Women Tex. Govt. Home: 1004 Alegria Austin TX 78757 Office: Tex Dept of Human Svcs 11044 Research Blvd Bldg D PO Box 149030 MC 613-S Austin TX 78714-9030

HANNON, BEVERLY A., state legislator; b. Manchester, Iowa, Mar. 30, 1932; d. John J. and Kathryn (Robinson) Hahesy; m. David L. Hannon, 1961; 6 children. AA, Kirkland Community Coll., 1982. Mem. Iowa State Senate, 1985—; mem. Iowa Women's Polit. Caucus. Mem. Jones County Tourism Assn., Jones County Hist. Assn. Democrat. Office: RR 2 Anamosa IA 52205*

HANNON, KITTY SUE, airline pilot; b. San Antonio, Oct. 10, 1954; d. Stanley Edgar and Barbara Lea (Owens) H.; m. Candler Gerald Schaffer, June 10, 1976 (div. 1983). MusB, U. Miami, Coral Gables, Fla., 1976. Flight attendant Eastern Airlines, Miami, Fla., 1977-84; pilot, instr. Tibben Flight Lines, Cedar Rapids, Iowa, 1981, Watham Flying Service, Cedar Rapids, 1981; pilot Mid Continent Airlines, Dubuque, Iowa, 1981-83, Cav Air/Jimmy Jet, Ft. Lauderdale, Fla., 1983, Airlift Internat. Airlines, Miami, 1983-84, Larken, Inc., Cedar Rapids, 1984, Life Investors, Cedar Rapids, 1984; pilot, flight engr. Eastern Airlines, Miami, 1984-89, instr. Boeing 717, supr. pilots, 1985-89, co-pilot, 1986-89, check airman, 1987-89; pilot N.W. Airlines, Miami, 1989—, Northwest Airlines, 1989; speaker in field. Author, producer: Boeing 727 Emergency and Abnormal Training Video, 1988. Vol. pilot Spl. Olympics Fla., Miami, Tallahassee, Fla., 1988; career day guest speaker Miami Schs., 1986, 88. Music and Band Scholar U. Miami, 1972-76; named Honoree, YWCA, 1984. Mem. YWCA Women's Network, Airline Pilots Assn., Aircraft Owners and Pilots Assn., Orange Key, Smithsonian Air and Space, Mortar Bd., Phi Kappa Lambda, Mu Alpha Theta, Phi Kappa Phi, Alpha Lambda Delta. Republican. Lutheran. Home: 3420 Torremolinos Ave Miami FL 33178

HANRATTY, CARIN GALE, pediatric nurse practitioner; b. Dec. 31, 1953; d. Burton and Lillian Aleskowitz; m. Michael Patrick Hanratty, May 22, 1983. BS in Nursing, Russell Sage Coll., 1975; postgrad., U. Calif., San Diego, 1980. Cert. CPR instr. Mgr. employee health ctr. Abbott Labs., Irving, Tex.; clin. mgr. pediatrics Trinity Med. Ctr., Carrollton, Tex.; pediatric nurse practitioner day surgery unit Children's Med. Ctr., Dallas; pediatric nurse practioner newborn nursery, drug coordinator perinatal intervention team for substance abusing women Parkland Meml. Hosp., Dallas. Instr. stop smoking program Am. Lung Assn., CPR; rep. United Way, 1988. Mem. ARC (profl., life), Am. Assn. Occupational Health Nurses, Nat. Assn. Pediatric Nurse Practitioners (v.p. Dallas chpt. 1982-83), Tex. Nurses Assn. Office: Parkland Meml Hosp c/o Pediatric Nurse Practitioners 5201 Harry Hines Blvd Dallas TX 75235

HANSCHU, LISA D., incentive marketing company owner; b. Kansas City, Mo., Apr. 13, 1960; d. David Jr. and Mary Ann (LeMoine) H. BA with honors, U. Ariz., 1981; M. in Internat. Mgmt., Am. Grad. Sch. Internat. Mgmt., 1983. Owner Motivation Through Incentives, Inc., Overland Park, Kans.; trade specialist State of Mo., Jefferson City; freelance mktg. cons. Mexico City, Mex. Named one of Top 10 Women-owned Businesses in Kansas City. Mem. Mo. Coun. on Women's Econ. Devel., Jr. League of Kansas City, Kansas City C. of C. (internat. com., centurians leadership tng.), Whole Person, Internat. Trad. Club. Home: 7301 Belinder Prairie Village KS 66208

HANSELL, HEIDI NERWIN, cardiovascular clinical nurse specialist; b. Rochester, N.Y., Nov. 12, 1953; d. Hubert and Magdalena (Weingartner) Nerwin; m. Gregory L. Hansell, Aug. 23, 1975 (div. Jan. 4, 1987). BS in Nursing, Alfred U., 1975; MS, Boston U., 1982. Cert. critical care nurse. Staff nurse Faulkner Hosp. Critical Care Ctr., Jamaica Plains, Mass., 1976-77; staff nurse Brigham & Women's Hosp., Boston, 1977-78, critical care educator, 1978-80, per diem nurse, 1980-82; head nurse critical care unit U. Mich. Hosp., Ann Arbor, 1982-84; cardiovascular clin. nurse Westside Cardiology Assocs., Santa Monica, Calif., 1984-85; critical care nursing educator Kaiser Permanente, Woodland Hills, Calif., 1985-87; cardiovascular clin. nurse specialist San Francisco Heart Inst., Daly City, Calif., 1987—; speaker in field; adj. prof. UCLA Sch. Nursing, Los Angeles, 1986-87; item writer Am. Assn. Critical Care Nurses, Newport Beach, Calif., 1984-89. Mem. Am. Heart Assn., Am. Assn. Critical Care Nurses (chpt. treas. 1979-82, pres.-elect 1982, membership com. 1985-86, strategic planning com. 1984-85, program chmn. 1982-87). Home: Two Fallon Pl #17 San Francisco CA 94133 Office: San Francisco Heart Inst 1900 Sullivan Ave Daly City CA 94015

HANSEN, AIMEE ISAACS, government official; b. Phila., Sept. 4, 1961; d. Thomas Edward and Miriam Edna (Stewart) Isaacs; m. Lawrence Thomas Hansen, Oct. 23, 1988. Student, American U., 1979-80; BBA, U. Pa., 1982; M in Pub. Policy, Rutgers U., Camden, N.J., 1989. Contract negotiator Naval Regional Contracting Ctr., U.S. Dept. Navy, Phila., 1983—; EEO counselor, Naval Regional Contracting Ctr., 1987—. Presbyterian.

HANSEN, BARBARA CALEEN, scientist, physiology and psychology educator; b. Boston, Nov. 24, 1941; d. Reynold L. and Dorothy (Richardson) Caleen; m. Kenneth Dale Hansen, Oct. 8, 1976; 1 son, David Scott. B.S., UCLA, 1964, M.S., 1965; Ph.D., U. Wash., 1971. Asst. prof. then assoc. prof. U. Wash., Seattle, 1971-76; prof., assoc. dean U. Mich., Ann Arbor, 1977-82; assoc. v.p. acad. affairs and research, dean grad. sch. So. Ill. U., Carbondale, 1982-85; v.p. for grad. studies and research U. Md., Balt. and Baltimore County, 1985-90; prof. physiology and psychology U. Md., 1990—; mem. adv. com. to dir. NIH, Washington, 1979-83; mem. joint health policy com. Assn. Am. Univs., Nat. Assn. State Univs. and Land-Grant Colls., Am. Council on Edn., Washington, 1982-86; mem. nutrition study sect. NIH, 1979-83; mem. program com. Inst. Medicine-Nat. Acad. Scis., Washington, 1982-84. Contbr. articles to profl. jours.; editor: Controversies in Obesity, 1983; chpts. on physiology. Mem. adv. com. Am. Bur. Med. Advancement China, N.Y.C., 1982-85; mem. adv. com. Robert Wood Johnson Found., Princeton, N.J., 1982—. Fellow U. Pa. Inst. Neuroscis., 1966-68; fellow Am. Acad. Nursing, 1977; Arthur Patch McKinley scholar of Phi Beta Kappa, 1964. Mem. Am. Physiol. Soc., Inst. Medicine of Nat. Acad. Scis., Am. Inst. Nutrition, Am. Soc. for Clin. Nutrition, Internat. Assn. for Study Obesity (pres. 1986—), N.Am. Assn. for Study Obesity (pres. 1984-85, 1986-90), Nat. Assn. State Univs. and Land Grant Colls. (chairperson coun. on rsch. policy and grad. edn. 1986-87), Phi Beta Kappa. Republican. Presbyterian. Office: U Md Sch of Medicine 10 S Pine St MSTF6-00 Baltimore MD 21201

HANSEN, BONNIE JO, home economist, educator; b. Bellefontaine, Ohio, July 29, 1950; d. Joe Eldon and Ethel Mae (Hurley) Buchenroth; m. Dwight D. Hansen, July 10, 1971; children: Jeffrey Allen, Dennis Joe. Student, Ohio State U., 1968-71; BS, Bowling Green State U., 1973; postgrad., Wright State U., 1986, Wilmington (Ohio) Coll., 1986, Ohio State U., 1989-90. Vocat. home econs. tchr. Toledo Pub. Schs., 1975-78; co-owner, operator Alphabetics, Toledo, 1981; sales rep. Nelson's Fund Raising Co., Oklahoma City, 1982-83; activities dir./pub. rels. The Guest House, Shreveport, La., 1984; stock broker Edward D. Jones & Co., Wilmington, Ohio, 1984-85; dep. clk. Clinton County (Ohio) Bd. Commrs., Wilmington, 1986; consumer/homemaking tchr. Wilmington High Schs., 1986—; family life cons., adult edn. dir. home econs., Toledo Pub. Schs., 1976-78. Chmn. Clinton County Corn Festival, 1986; co-chmn., 1988; mem. Troop #154 com. Boy Scouts Am., 1989—; advisor Creative Bunch 4-H club, 1988--; mem. United Meth. Ch. choir, 1986--; active Future Homemakers Am. (master advisor 1989, hon. mem. 1989). Mem. Am. Home Econs. Assn., Ohio Home Econs. Assn., Clinton County Home Econs. Assn. (sec. 1989—), AAUW (v.p. program Wilmington chpt. 1986-88), Beta Sigma Phi, Order Eastern Star. Republican. Home: 3603 S Beechgrove Rd Wilmington OH 45177 Office: Wilmington City Schs 300 Richardson Pl Wilmington OH 45177

HANSEN, DEBORAH A., psychologist, lawyer; b. New Rochelle, N.Y., Aug. 8, 1957; d. Manuel D. and Catherine (Sawyer) H. BA, Marist Coll., 1981; MA, St. Bonaventure (N.Y.) U., 1983; JD, Villanova (Pa.) U., 1988; PhD, Hahnemann U., 1989. Bar: N.Y., N.J. Rsch. assoc. Litigation Scis., N.Y.C., 1989-90; psychologist Arms Acres, Carmel, N.Y., 1990—; cons. in field. Mem. Am. Psychol. Assn., ABA, N.Y. State Bar Assn., N.J. State Bar Assn. Home: 48 Park Dr Warwick NY 10990

HANSEN, DEBORAH ANN, corrections official; b. East Brunswick, N.J., July 25, 1950; d. Oscar and Julia (Keleman) H. Student, Worcester (Eng.) Coll., 1971-72; BS in Psychology, Trenton (N.J.) State Coll., 1972; MS in Criminal Justice, Rutgers U., 1980. Parole officer N.J. Dept. Corrections, Trenton, 1972-77, sr. parole officer, 1977-79, chief bur. interstate svcs., 1980-84, dep. compact administr., 1984—; cons. Washington, 1986, Maine Dept. Corrections, 1983, also trainer; trainer affirmative action N.J. Dept. Corrections, Trenton, 1985-86; trainer basic course N.J. Police Tng. Commn., 1989—; coord., project mgr. Nat. Commn. to Restructure the Interstate Compact for Parolees and Probations, 1985-89; nat. coord. tng. task force Interstate Parole and Probation Initiatives, 1989—. Contbr. articles to profl. jours. Twp. coord. Jim Courtier for Congress, East Brunswick, N.J. 1984; campaign writer, advisor Flemming/Bowen for State Assembly, East Brunswick, 1983; mem. Middlesex County (N.J.) Rep. Orgn. Recipient Proclamation N.J. Legis., 1987, Gov.'s award Outstanding Women in State Govt., 1988, Frederick's award Parole and Probation Compact Adminstrs. Assn., 1987. Fellow Coun. State Govts. (mem. com. on suggested state legis.); mem. Am. Parole and Probation Assn. (mem. nat. program com. 1985-88), Interstate Compact Assn. Info. Network (chairperson subcom. on nat. law enforcement networking 1989—), Parole and Probation Compact Adminstrs. Assn. (pres. 1986-87), Psi Chi. Roman Catholic. Office: NJ Dept Corrections Whittlesey Rd Trenton NJ 08625

HANSEN, DORIS ANNE, accountant; b. Council Bluffs, Iowa, June 16, 1937; d. Boyd Vernon and Elizabeth Theresa (Shepersky) Porter; m. Robert LeRoy Hansen, Jan. 23, 1954; children: Lee, Lisa, Lance, Lori, Lary. Student, U. Nebr., Omaha, 1974, Morningside Coll., 1975-78, Briar Cliff Coll., 1980-83. Staff acct. Ballenger Automotive, Council Bluffs, 1953-56, Nonpareil Newspaper, Council Bluffs, 1956-59, Interstate Electric Supply Co., Inc., Council Bluffs, 1959-64; prin. Ken Johnson & Co., Omaha, 1964-75; owner Doris A. Hansen Acctg., Sioux City, Iowa, 1975-86; prin. King, Reinsch, Prosser & Co., Sioux City, 1986—; program chairperson Tri-State Women's Bus. Conf., Sioux City, 1987, chairperson, 1988—; cons. U.S. SBA, Des Moines, 1987—; moderator State White Ho. Small Bus. Conf., Des Moines, 1986, Regional White Ho. Small Bus. Conf., Chgo., 1986, State Small Bus. Issues Conf., Des Moines, 1987. Active Gov.'s Small Bus. Coun., Des Moines, 1983—, Gov.'s Future Growth Com., Des Moines, 1985, Sch. Dist. Econs. Task Force, Sioux City, 1986; chairperson Coun. on Sexual Assault and Domestic Violence, Sioux City, 1983-85; chairperson, bd. dirs. Small Bus. Devel. Ctr. Iowa State U., Ames, 1983—. Recipient Gov.'s Vol. award State of Iowa, 1986, 88. Mem. Nat. Assn. Accts. (nat. dir. 1985-87, pres. 1981-82, mem. edn. com. 1983-85, regional coun. sec. 1982-83). Roman Catholic. Office: King Reinsch Prosser & Co 500 Security Nat Bank Bldg Sioux City IA 51101

HANSEN, ELISA MARIE, art historian; b. Sarasota, Fla., July 14, 1952; d. Gotfred and Barbara (Ham) Hansen; m. Flemming Sogaard, 1987; children: Inga Marie, Anna Sofia. BA in Art History, Fla. State U., 1974; MA in Art History, So. Meth. U., 1982; MLS, U. So. Fla., 1984. Edn. specialist Pinellas County Art Coun., Clearwater, Fla., 1977-78; curator of edn. Mus. Fine Arts, St. Petersburg, Fla., 1978-80; asst. prof. Eckerd Coll., St. Petersburg, 1985-88, adj. prof., 1986-89; dir. adult and acad. programs The John & Mable Ringling Mus. Art, Sarasota, 1989—. Contbr. articles and book reviews to profl. jours. Mem. Am. Assn. Mus., Soc. for Advancement of Scandinavian Study. Republican. Lutheran. Office: The John & Mable Ringling Mus of Art 5401 Bayshore Blvd Sarasota FL 34243

HANSEN, FLORENCE MARIE CONGIOLOSI (MRS. JAMES S. HANSEN), social worker; b. Middletown, N.Y., Jan. 7, 1934; d. Joseph James and Florence (Harrigan) Congiolosi; B.A., Coll. New Rochelle, 1955; M.S.W., Fla. State U., 1960; m. James S. Hansen, June 16, 1959; 1 dau., Florence M. Caseworker, Orange County Dept. Pub. Welfare, N.Y., 1955-57, Cath. Welfare Bur., Miami, Fla., 1957-58; supr. Cath. Family Service, Spokane, Wash., 1960, Cuban Children's Program, Spokane, 1962-66; founder, dir. social service dept. Sacred Heart Med. Ctr., 1968-85, dir. Kidney Ctr., 1967—. Asst. in program devel. St. Margaret's Hall, Spokane, 1961-62; trustee Family Counseling Service Spokane County, 1981—, also bd. dirs.; mem. budget allocation panel United Way, 1964-76, mem. planning com., 1968-77, mem. admissions com., 1969-70, chmn. projects com. 1972-73, active work with Cuban refugees; mem. kidney disease adv. com. Wash.-Alaska Regional Med. Program, 1970-73. Mem. Spokane Quality of Life Commn., 1974-75. Mem. Nat. Assn. Social Workers (chpt. pres. 1972-74), Acad. Cert. Social Workers (charter). Roman Catholic. Home: 5609 Northwest Blvd Spokane WA 99205 Office: Sacred Heart Med Ctr W 101 8th St Spokane WA 99204

HANSEN, JANINE SUE, dairy scientist; b. Yankton, S.D., Nov. 23, 1962; d. Allen Nels and Janet Lee (Foelker) H. BS in Dairy Sci., S.D. State U., 1985. Lic. environ. health practitioner, N.D. Quality control supr. dairy div. N.D. Dept. Agr., Bismarck, 1985—. Mem. Internat. Assn. Milk, Food and Environ Sanitarians, N.D. Environ. Health Assn., Nat. Environ. Health Assn., N.D. Dairy Women, Nat. Future Farmers Am. Alumni Assn., N.D. Future Farmers Am. Alumni Assn. (pres. 1988—), Bismarck Future Farmers Am. Alumni Assn. (pres. 1986—). Lutheran. Home: 423 Pitcher Pk Devils Lake ND 58301 Office: ND Dept Agr 600 East Blvd 6th Fl Capitol Bldg Bismarck ND 58505

HANSEN, JO-IDA CHARLOTTE, psychology educator, researcher; b. Washington, Oct. 2, 1947; d. Gordon Henry and Charlotte Lorraine (Helgeson) H.; m. John Paul Campbell. BA, U. Minn., 1969, MA, 1971, PhD, 1974. Asst. prof. psychology U. Minn., Mpls., 1974-78, assoc. prof., 1978-84, prof., 1984—, dir. Ctr. for Interest Measurement Rsch., 1974—, dir. counseling psychology program, 1987—. Author: User's Guide for the SII, 1984, Manual for the SII, 1985; contbr. numerous articles to profl. jours., chpts. to books. Recipient early career award U. Minn., 1982, E.K. Strong, Jr. gold medal Strong Exec. Bd., 1984. Fellow Am. Psychol. Assn. (coun. reps. 1990-93), Am. Psychol. Soc.; mem. Am. Assn. Counseling and Devel. (extended rsch. award 1990), Assn. for Measurement and Evaluation (pres. 1988-89, Exemplary Practice award 1987, 90). Office: U Minn Dept Psychology 75 E River Rd Minneapolis MN 55455

HANSEN, JOYCE KAY, accountant, tax consultant, educator; b. Cedar Springs, Mich., Sept. 26, 1946; d. Raymond A. and Mildred Ruth (Mc Intyre) Wesche; m. John Raymond Hansen, Sept. 3, 1966; children: James K., Jeffrey K. BS in Journalism and Edn., Cen. Mich. U., 1968, MA in Math., 1971. Instr. math Clare Pub. Schs., Mich., 1968-72; adj. prof. Davenport Coll., Grand Rapids, Mich., 1974-79; prof., head dept. Jordan Coll., Cedar Springs, 1978-79; founder, dir. Mich. Tax Cons., Lansing, 1979-83; adj. asst. prof. Aquinas Coll., Grand Rapids, 1979—; pres., acct. J & J Bus. Services, Inc., Cedar Springs, 1980—; owner, pres., prin. Ascii Systems Corp., 1986—, Four J Enterprises Inc., 1987—. Columnist Cedar Springs Clipper, 1979-80; sports writer Cedar Springs Post, 1989-90. Treas. Cedar Springs Econ. Devel. Corp., 1982-85; founder, pres. Citizens for A Better Community, 1988-89. Named 1st woman to 200 Club, Mich. Tax Cons., 1980. Mem. Nat. Assn. Enrolled Agts., Ind. Accts. Assn. Mich. (edn. co-chmn. 1985-86, edn. chairperson 1986-87, vice chmn., chmn. Grand Rapids chpt. 1985-88, chpt. chair 1989-90), Nat. Soc. Pub. Accts. (rules com. 1986), Accreditation Council for Accountancy, Cedar Springs Area C. of C. (co-founder 1980, bd. dirs., pres., v.p. 1980-87). Republican. Methodist. Club: West Mich. Bus. (Grand Rapids). Avocations: reading, camping, travel, movies. Home: 4171 Indian Lakes Rd Cedar Springs MI 49319 Office: J & J Bus Services Inc PO Box 560 20 E Beech St Cedar Springs MI 49319

HANSEN, KAREN THORNLEY, certified public accountant; b. Chgo., June 1, 1945; d. Charles Bruce and Arlene Ann (McHale) Thornley; m. Terry Lee Hansen, Aug. 17, 1968; 1 child, Charles Scott. BA, Marycrest Coll., Davenport, Iowa, 1967. CPA, N.Y.; cert. M.T. Med. staff tech. Mercy Hosp., Davenport, Iowa, 1967-68, St. Joseph Hosp., Chgo., 1968, Spl. Hematology, Wilford Hall, USAF Hosp., Lackland AFB, Tex., 1973-78; staff acct. Lewittes & Co., Poughkeepsie, N.Y., 1980-81; sr. acct. Urbach, Kahn & Werlin, Poughkeepsie, 1981-82; ptnr. Hansen & Dunn, CPA's, Poughkeepsie, 1982—. Bd. dirs., sec. bd. United Way of Dutchess County, Poughkeepsie, 1988—; bd. dirs. YMCA of Dutchess County, Girl Scouts U.S., 1983-87; active Jr. League of Poughkeepsie, 1979—; membership com. Poughkeepsie Partnership, Inc. Mem. AICPA's, N.Y. State Soc. CPA's, Greater Poughkeepsie Area C. of C. (bd. dirs. 1986—), Amrita Club (bd. dirs. 1982—, pres. 1990), Poughkeepsie Tennis Club. Republican. Roman Catholic. Office: Hansen & Dunn 309 Main Mall Poughkeepsie NY 12601

HANSEN, KAREN V., sociology educator; b. Chico, Calif., Apr. 23, 1955; d. Edwin L. and Esther C. (Kanten) H.; m. Andrew L. Bundy, Feb. 16, 1985; 1 child, Benjamin Lowell. BA, U. Calif., Santa Barbara, 1977, MA, 1979, PhD, 1989. Dir. project Foote, Cone, and Belding/Honig, San Francisco, 1980-81; rsch. assoc. URSA Inst., San Francisco, 1981-84; coord. European search Emma Goldman Papers U. Calif., Berkeley, 1985-86, teaching asst., 1985, grad. student instr., 1988; asst. prof. sociology Brandeis U., Waltham, Mass., 1989—. Contbr. articles to profl. jours.; co-editor: (with Ilene Philipson) Women, Class, and the Feminist Imagination, 1990. Recipient Gertrude Jaeger prize U. Calif., 1988; fellow Am. Antiquarian Soc., 1988, Regents, U. Calif., 198-89; Woodrow Wilson grantee, 1988. Mem. AAUW, Sociologists for Women in Soc., Am. Hist. Assn., Am. Sociol. Assn., Nat. Women's Studies Assn., Orgn. Am. Historians, Women in Hist. Profession (ccord. com.). Office: Brandeis Univ Dept Sociology Waltham MA 02254

HANSEN, KATHLEEN ANN, journalism educator, librarian, researcher; b. Kenosha, Wis., Oct. 4, 1954; d. Richard Arthur and Frances Geraldine (Gallo) H.; m. John Charles Busterna, Jan. 7, 1978. BA in English, U. Wis., Kenosha, 1976, MA in Libr. Sci., 1977; MA in English, U. Wis., Madison, 1979. Asst. librarian to librarian U. Wis. Journalism Libr., Madison, 1977-78; asst. acquisitions librarian U. Wis.-Milw. Libr., 1979-81; asst. prof. and Severeid librarian U. Minn. Sch. of Journalism and Mass Communication, Mpls., 1981-87, assoc. prof. and Sevareid libr., 1987—; faculty advisor Women in Communication Inc. Student Chpt., U. Minn., 1989—. Co-author: Search Strategies in Mass Communications, 1987; author: computer-assisted instrn. publs.; contbr. articles to profl. jours. and conf. papers. Mem. Citizens League, Mpls., 1981—. U. Minn. rsch. grantee, 1982-90, Dow Jones News/Retrieval tchg. grantee, 1983-85. Mem. Assn. for Edn. in Journalism and Mass Communications (various positions 1981—), ALA, Am. Soc. for Info. Sci., Women in Communications Inc., Beta Phi Mu. Office: U Minn Sch Journalism 111 Murphy Hall 206 Church St SE Minneapolis MN 55455

HANSEN, KATHRYN ANN, stage manager; b. Dinuba, Calif., Mar. 2, 1957; d. Ernest Lawrence and Mary (Terzian) H. AA, Reedley (Calif.) Jr. Coll., 1978; BA, Calif. State U., Fresno, 1980. Stage mgr. Cabaret Dinner Theatre, Visalia, Calif., 1981-82, San Diego Repertory Theatre, 1982-83, Gaslamp Quarter Theatre, San Diego, 1983; gen. mgr. Bowery Theatre, San Diego, 1984-88; prodn. stage mgr. N.Mex. State U., Las Cruces, 1988; stage mgr. Nat. Theatre for Children, San Diego, 1988—; prodn. mgr. Del Mar (Calif.) Theatre Ensemble, 1989—; acctg. clk. Manpower, San Diego, 1988—. Democrat. Home: 41811 Rd 114 Dinuba CA 93618

HANSEN, KATHRYN GERTRUDE, former state official, association editor; b. Gardner, Ill., May 24, 1912; d. Harry J. and Marguerite (Gaston) Hansen; BS with honors, U. Ill., 1934, MS, 1936. Personnel asst. U. Ill., Urbana, 1945-46, supr. tng. and activities, 1946-47, personnel officer, instr. psychology, 1947-52, exec. sec. U. Civil Service System Ill., also sec. for merit bd., 1952-61, adminstrv. officer, sec. merit bd., 1961-68, dir. system, 1968-72; lay asst. firm Webber, Balbach, Theis and Follmer, P.C., Urbana, Ill., 1972-74. Bd. dirs. U. YWCA, 1952-55, chmn., 1954-55; bd. dirs. Champaign-Urbana Symphony, 1978-81; sec. Presbyn. Women 1st Presbyn. Ch., Champaign, 1986-90, mem. coordinating team, 1986—. Mem. Coll. and Univ. Personnel Assn. (hon., life mem., editor jour. 1955-73, newsletter, internat. pres. 1967-68, nat. publs. award named in her honor 1987), Annuitants Assn. State Univs. Retirement System Ill. (state sec.-treas. 1974-75), Pres.'s Council U. Ill. (life), U. Ill. Alumni Assn. (life), Friends of the Library (bd. dirs. 1987—), U. Ill. Found., Campus Round Table U. Ill., Nat. League Am. Pen Women, AAUW (state 1st v.p. 1958-60, hon., life), Champaign-Urbana Symphony Guild, Secretariat U. Ill. (life), Grundy County Hist. Soc., Delta Kappa Gamma (state pres. 1961-63), Phi Mu (life), Kappa Delta Pi, Kappa Tau Alpha. Presbyterian. Clubs: Monday Writers, Fortnightly (Champaign-Urbana). Lodge: Order Eastern Star. Author: (with others) A Plan of Position Classification for Colleges and Universities; A Classification Plan for Staff Positions at Colleges and Universities, 1968; Grundy-Corners, 1982; Sarah, A Documentary of Her Life and Times, 1984, Ninety Years with Fortnightly, Vols. I and II, an historical compilation, 1986; editor: The Illini Worker, 1946-52; Campus Pathways, 1952-61; This is Your Civil Service Handbook, 1960-67; author, cons., editor publs. on personnel practices. Home: 1004 E Harding Dr Apt 307 Urbana IL 61801

HANSEN, LAURIE JO, government affairs official; b. Arcadia, Calif., Apr. 26, 1960; d. Mark Herman and Sally Jo (High) H. BA in Social Sci., Communications, U. So. Calif., 1982. Staff cons. Calif. State Senate, Sacramento, 1981, 1982; staff cons. Calif. State Assembly, Glendale, 1981; campaign cons. John Garamendi for Gov., Santa Ana, Calif., 1981-82; lobbyist, cons. Murdoch, Mockler & Assoc., Sacramento, 1982-85; exec. adminstr. Calif. State Sen. John Seymour, Sacramento, 1985-88; mgr. western region govt. affairs Coun. Solid Waste Solutions, Sacramento, 1988—. Mem. Nat. Charity League, Newport Beach, Calif. Mem. U. So. Calif. Scapa Preators (v.p. 1985-86). Republican. Lodge: Internat. Order of Jobs Daus. (honored queen 1977). Office: Coun Solid Waste Solutions 770 L St Ste 960 Sacramento CA 95814

HANSEN, LISA YOUNG, municipal agency administrator; b. Rexburg, Idaho, Apr. 28, 1957; d. Rulon Squires and Lucille Cole (Young) McCarrey; m. Darrel Chancy Hansen, Mar. 23, 1984. A, Ricks Coll., 1977; student, Harvard U., summers 1977, 78, Brigham Young U., 1980-82. Geneal. clk. Stevensons Geneal. Ctr., Provo, Utah, 1977; typesetter, news clk. Valley News, Rexburg, Idaho, 1977-78; credit clk. Credit Bur. Idaho Falls, 1982-83; adminstrv. asst. Bonneville County Civil Defense, Idaho Falls, 1983—; speaker in field; radiol. defense officer State of Idaho, Bureau of Disaster Services, 1984—; sec. Bonneville Tricentennial Commn., 1983—, Bonneville Flood Control Coordinatig com., 1983—, Bonneville Bicentennial of the Constn. com., 1983—. Contbr. articles to profl. jours. Rep. United Way, Idaho Falls, 1986; vote clerk Bonneville County Elections Dept., Idaho Falls, 1980, 81; mem. Bonneville County Centennial Com., Nat. Coordinating Coun. Emergency Mgmt. Mem. Am. Civil Def. Assn. (co-resolutions chmn. 1985-87), Idaho Civil Def. Assn., Bonneville County Employees Assn. (pres. 1989), Lamba Delta Sigma. Republican. Mormon. Home: 874 W Goldie St Idaho Falls ID 83402 Office: Bonneville County Civil Def 605 N Capital Ave Idaho Falls ID 83402

HANSEN, MARLEEN BERRY, educational administrator; b. Luray, Va., Sept. 28, 1945; d. Lee Griggs and Margaret May (Kibler) Berry; m. Vagn Keith Hansen, June 7, 1969; 1 child, Vagn Keith II. BA, Lynchburg (Va.) Coll., 1967; MA, U. Va., 1971; MLS, U. Ala., 1977. Libr. asst. Alderman Libr., U. Va., Charlottesville, 1969-70, Washington and Lee U. Libr., Lexington, Va., 1971-74; bibliographer Raven Systems and Rsch., Washington, 1980-81; adminstrv. asst. Delta State U., Cleveland, Miss., 1983-85, U. N.C., Greensboro, 1985—. Mem. stormwater utility adv. com. High Point, N.C., 1990. Mem. AAUW (pres. High Point br. 1990—), Carolina Viking Lodge (vice chmn. 1990—), Beta Phi Mu. Democrat. Methodist. Office: U NC Sch Nursing McIver St Greensboro NC 27412

HANSEN, NANCY RUTH, finance professional; b. Bklyn., Sept. 5, 1963; d. Martin Arthur and Ruth Madelline (Bensen) H. BS in Bus. Systems, Taylor U., 1985. Gen. acct. Midland-Ross, Livingston, N.J., 1985-86; sales pco. coord. Nabisco Brands, Parsippany, N.J., 1986-87; deal coord. RJR Nabisco Planters Life Saver Co., Winston-Salem, N.C., 1988-89, deal adminstrn. supr., 1989—. Vol. counselor Friendship Crisis Pregnancy Ctr., Morristown, N.J., 1987, Salem Pregnancy Support Ctr., Winston-Salem, 1988—. Republican. Baptist. Office: Planters Life Savers 1100 Reynolds Blvd Winston-Salem NC 27102

HANSEN, PHYLLIS JEAN, librarian; b. Ames, Iowa, Nov. 28, 1934; d. Elmer N. and Florence (Faust) H. AB with honors, U. Ill., 1960, MS, 1961; MA, Calif. Poly. State U., 1984. Librarian, Queens Borough Pub. Libr., N.Y.C., 1961, San Leandro Community Libr. (Calif.), 1962-63, Calif. Poly. State U., San Luis Obispo, 1963—. Author bibliographies: Vitamin C, 1980, rev., 1984, Sex Role Stereotyping and Career Aspirations of Junior High and High School Students, 1983, Sex Role Stereotyping in Career Literature, 1984. Mem. ALA, Calif. Libr. Assn., Calif. Soc. Librarians, AAUW, County Hist. Assn. San Luis Obispo, Delta Kappa Gamma, Alpha Lambda Delta. Republican. Presbyterian. Club: Business and Professional Women (v.p. 1984-85, 1990—) (San Luis Obispo). Home: 1241 Fredericks St San Luis Obispo CA 93405 Office: Calif Poly State U Libr San Luis Obispo CA 93407

HANSEN, SUSANA, real estate corporation officer, consultant; b. Montevideo, Uruguay, June 21, 1943; came to U.S., 1968; d. Jorge Valdemar and Paula (Maruri) H.; m. Federico Padovan (div. 1974); 1 child, Paola Padovan; m. Rodolfo Careri, 1983 (div. 1989). BS in French, Alliance Française, Montevideo, Uruguay, 1964; BS, Fla. Internat. U., 1977. Cert. soc. studies tchr., Fla. Internat. U. Special asst. to pres. Hornblower, Werks, Hemphill, Noyes, Beverly Hills, Calif., 1968-71; v.p. special services Alitalia Airlines, N.Y.C., 1971-74; special asst. to pres. Interterra Inc., Miami, Fla., 1976-78; v.p. Grove Isle Realty, Coconut Grove, Fla., 1979-82; pres., broker Turnberry Realty Corp., Miami Beach, Fla., 1982-88; with Marina Hansen Klein Realty Corp., Miami Beach; cons. Latin Am. Assn. Real Estate Profl., Buenos Aires, 1978—. Fundraiser Restoration Statue Liberty, N.Y.C., 1985. Mem. Internat. Exec. Women Assn., London, Exec. Women's Edn. Travel, N.Y.C. Roman Catholic. Home: 19355 Turnberry Way #3D Miami Beach FL 33180 Office: Marina Hansen Klein Realty Corp 20801 Biscayne Blvd #308 Miami Beach FL 33180

HANSON, BETTY LUCILE, retail owner; b. Battle Creek, Mich.; d. Richard Raymond and Betty Lucile (Bruce) Fulkerson; m. Carl D. Hanson, Aug. 5, 1951; children: Steven, Crystal, Valentina, Dana, Melissa. P-sychology Degree, Olivet Coll., Mich., 1978. With Wolverine Ins. Co., Battle Creek, 1950, Kellogg Co., Battle Creek, 1952-54; owner Betty's Bridal Boutique and Gift Shop, Battle Creek, 1979—. Mem. Mich. Music Tchrs. Assn., Battle Creek Music Tchrs. Assn., AAUW, Susammma Winslow Cir., Battle Creek Area C. of C., Scottish Soc. Congregationalist.

HANSON, DIANE CHARSKE, management consultant; b. Cleve., May 15, 1946; d. Howard Carl and Emma Katherine (Lange) Charske; m. William James Hanson, June 30, 1973. BS, Cornell U., 1968; MS, U. Pa., 1989. Home service rep. Rochester Gas and Electric, N.Y., 1968-70; home economist U. Conn., Storrs, 1970-72; job analyst personnel dept. State of Conn., Hartford, 1972-73; sales rep. Ayerst Labs., Waterbury, Conn., 1973-80, sales trainer, 1979-80; dist. sales mgr. Phila., 1980-87; pres. Creative Resource Devel., W. Chester, Pa., 1986—; developer, pres. Womens Referral Network, West Chester, 1987-89. Bd. dirs., chmn. spl. events devel. com., aux. pres. Chester County Soc. for Prevention Cruelty to Animals, 1986—; mem. Chester County Devel. Coun. Mem. West Chester C. of C., Pa. State Tech. Devel. Ctr. (bd. dirs.), Am. Soc. for Tng. and Devel., Greater Valley Forge Pers. Assn., Phila. Human Resource Planning Group, Phila. O.D. Network. Home and Office: 824 W Strasburg Rd West Chester PA 19382

HANSON, JEANNE CAROL, health care administrator; b. New Haven, May 3, 1947; d. John Fletcher and Jeanne (Huttlinger) H. Diploma, Bryn Mawr (Pa.) Sch. Nursing, 1968; BS in Psychology, Eastern Coll., 1978; MBA in Health and Med. Service, Widener U., 1986. RN. Staff nurse pediatric unit Bryn Mawr (Pa.) Hosp., 1968-69; staff nurse psychiat. unit Haverford (Pa.) State Hosp., 1969-71, head nurse psychiat. admissions unit, 1971-73, instr. psychiat. nursing, 1973-80, dir. nursing edn. dept., 1980-87; asst. adminstr. Kendal-Crosslands, Kennett Square, Pa., 1987—. Mem. Friends Com. on Aging, Religious Coun. West Chester; bd. dirs., v.p. Media (Pa.) Child Guidance and Community Mental Health Ctr. Mem. Pa. Nurses Assn., LWV, Widener Grad. Alumni Assn. (v.p. 1987-89). Republican. Mem. Soc. of Friends. Office: Kendal-Crosslands PO Box 100 Kennett Square PA 19348

HANSON, JILL ALANE, veterinarian; b. Kans. City, Mo., Apr. 1, 1949; d. Jack Browning and Doris (Stockstill) Endler; m. Timothy John Hanson, July 31, 1976; children: Buck, Wesley. DVM, U. Mo., 1974. Owner, operator Hanson Animal Hosp., Coos Bay, Oreg., 1977—; comedian Little Ole Opry, 1981—. Guest editor: Veterinary Forum, 1989-90; cartoonist: Veterinary Economics, 1989. Sec. Little Theatre, Coos Bay, 1980—; active Ambassadors, Coos Bay, 1990. Named Woman of Yr. Little Theatre, 1985. Mem. Oreg. Vet. Med. Assn., Mo. Vet. Med. Assn., S.D. Vet. Med. Assn., Coos Bay C. of C., Am. Bus. Women's Assn. (pres. Coos Bay chpt. 1982—, Woman of Yr. 1989, one of Top Ten Bus. Women 1989). Office: Hanson Animal Hosp 45 E Lockhart Coos Bay OR 97420

HANSON, LEE, education educator; b. Chgo., Sept. 19, 1937; d. Raymond George and Marie (Warner) Chamberlain; m. Larry Hanson, Aug. 31, 1963 (div. 1975); 1 child, Michelle Anne. BA, Pomona Coll., Claremont, Calif., 1958; MA, U. Redlands, Calif., 1979. Cert. Educator, Calif. Med. illus. U. Pa., 1959-62; scientific illus. U. Hawaii, Honolulu, 1962-73; tchr. Santa Clara, Beverly Hills, Glendale, 1963-77; multi-arts specialist Glendale Unified Sch. Dist.; curriculum coord. art and gifted edn. Chula Vista (Calif.) City Sch. Dist., 1978-86; art specialist Palo Alto Unified Sch. Dist., 1986—; dir. Fine Cultural Experience, San Diego 1981-82; curriculum chair Calif. Art Edn. Assn. 1985-87; conf. presenter Nat. Art Edn. Assn. World Conf. for Gifted Talented. Co-author: Early Childhood Art, 1990, Art in Action 1985; Author: Kit, Creative Expressions 1985; Co-Author: Book, Arts for the Gifted and Talented, 1981. Panelist Calif. Arts Coun. 1980-81; mem. adv. bd. Southwestern Coll. Coll. for Kids Program, Calif. 1981-85; bd. dirs. Palo Alto (Calif.) Parents and Profls. for Arts, 1986-, Ruth Jansen Fund, Calif., 1987—; Art Judge Calif. State Exposition. Recipient Outstanding Art Supervisor award, Calif. Art Edn. Assn., 1985, Outstanding Art Educator award, 1989. Mem. Calif. Art Edn. Assn., Nat. Art Edn. Assn., Citicorp State Art Scholarship, Nat. Scholastic Art Program. Democrat. Office: Palo Alto Unified Sch Dist 25 Churchill Ave Palo Alto CA 94306

HANSON, LEILA FRASER, banker; b. Chgo., May 26, 1942; d. Paul and Emily (Dzierzyck) Hucko; m. Joseph Hanson; 1 child, Alec. AB in Polit. Sci. with high distinction, U. Ill., 1964, MA, 1966, PhD, 1971. Teaching asst. Carleton U., Ottawa, Ont., Can., 1967-68; lectr. polit. sci. U. Ky., Lexington, 1970, asst. dir., then acting dir. Office Internat. Programs, 1970-72; staff assoc., then asst. to vice chancellor U. Wis., Milw., 1972-76, asst. vice chancellor, 1976-77, asst. to chancellor, 1977; chief adminstr. to mayor City of Milw., 1977-82; sr. v.p. Banc One Wis. Corp., Milw., 1982—. Mem. adv. com. on women and minorities Office Wis. Commr. Securities, 1976-80; mem. Gov.'s Commn. Wis. Strategic Devel., 1983-85; bd. dirs. Milw. Exposition, Conv. Ctr. and Arena, 1978-82; bd. dirs., chmn. mktg. com. Milw. County Research Park Bd., 1987—, United Performing Arts Fund, 1987—; bd. dirs., exec. com. treas. Milw. Symphony Orch., 1979— , World Festivals Inc., 1982—; bd. dirs. Milw. Urban League, 1988-89; mem. corp. bd. adv. com. Milw. Sch. Engring., 1983—; bd. dirs., past pres. Milw. Council Alcoholism, 1979—; bd. dirs., chmn. mktg. div. United Way Greater Milw., 1987—, mem. campaign cabinet, 1986-87; mem. adv. council Robert M. LaFollette Inst. Pub. Affairs U. Wis., Madison, 1984—; bd. dirs. exec. com. Forward Wis., 1985—, U. Wis., Milw. Found., 1986—; bd. dirs. Bus. Against Drunk Drivers, 1987—; mem. U. Ill. Bus. Adv. Council, 1987—; mem. Am. Council on Edn. Nat. Commn. on Higher Edn. Issues, 1981-83; telethon co-chmn. United Cerebral Palsy of Southeastern Wis., 1987-88; U.S. rep. 20th Gen. Conf. of UNESCO, Paris, 1978. Recipient Outstanding Achievement award 4th Dist. Wis. Fedn. Women's Clubs, 1978, YWCA of Greater Milw., 1986; fellow Am. Council Edn., 1976-77. Mem. Am. Bankers Assn. (edn1. policy and devel. council 1983-86), Am. Inst. Banking (bd. dirs. 1988—), Bank Mktg. Assn., Phi Beta Kappa, Phi Delta Kappa. Office: Banc One Wisconsin Corp 111 E Wisconsin Ave Milwaukee WI 53202

HANSON, MARY JANE SHIRAR, nurse, educator; b. Coaldale, Pa., Mar. 2, 1953; d. William C. and Loretta R. (Krum) Shirar; m. James D. Hanson, June 4, 1983. Cert., Allentown Hosp. Sch. X-Ray, 1973; BS in Nursing magna cum laude, Cedar Crest Coll., 1982; MS in Nursing summa cum laude, U. Pa., 1987. R.N., Pa. Radiologic technologist Allentown (Pa.) Hosp., 1973-80; staff nurse Gnaden Huetten Hosp., Lehighton, Pa., 1980-86; nursing quality assurance coord. Gnaden Huetten Hosp., 1986-87, dir. edn., 1987-88; asst. prof. Cedar Crest Coll., Allentown, 1988—; cons., lectr., Albert Einstein Med. Ctr., Phila., 1987, Temple U. Hosp., Phila., 1987, Med. Coll. Pa., Phila., 1987, West Jersey Health System, Camden, N.J., 1987, 89; sec. adv. bd., Lehigh County Community Coll., Schnecksville, Pa., 1987-88. Vol. nurse, ARC, Lehighton, 1982-83. Mem. Am. Assn. Critical Care Nurses, Am. Nurses Assn., Sigma Theta Tau. Republican. Lutheran. Home: 494 Knoll Dr Lehighton PA 18235 Office: Cedar Crest Coll Allentown PA 18104

HANSON, ROBIN ELAINE, accountant; b. Jacksonville, Fla., Oct. 19, 1956. BBA, U. North Fla., 1978, M in Acctg., 1986. CPA, Fla. Staff acct. Peter Suess and Co., CPA's, Jacksonville, 1979-80; tax acct. Peat, Marwick, Mitchell, CPA's, Jacksonville, 1980-83, tax mgr., 1983; tax acct. The Charter Co., Jacksonville, 1983-84; tax supr. Touche, Ross & Co., CPA's, Jacksonville, 1984-85; dir. tax Fla. Rock Industries, Inc., Jacksonville, 1985—. Mem. AICPA, Fla. Inst. CPA's. Office: Fla Rock Industries Inc 155 E 21st St Jacksonville FL 32206

HANSON, SANDRA J. MCKENZIE, educational administrator; b. Amery, Wis., Jan. 15, 1949; d. Earl Edward and Ariel Gloria (Benson) McKenzie; m. Craig W. Hanson, June 14, 1969; 1 child, Andrea McKenzie. B.A., U. Wis.-Eau Claire, 1970; M.P.A., U. Puget Sound, 1978. Instr. S.W. Wis. Tech. Inst., Fennimore, Wis., 1970-72; account exec. Ad Factors Advt., Spokane, Wash., 1972-74; dir. spl. projects Wash. Community Colls. of Spokane, 1974-76; instr., pubs. advisor Community Coll. Dist. 12, Olympia, Centralia, Wash., 1978-81; dir. coll. rels. South Puget Sound Community Coll., Olympia, Wash., 1981-85; dir. coll. rels. and devel. Pierce Coll. Tacoma, Wash., 1985— ; dist. rep. 2-yr. coll. com. CASE, 1982-83, 84-86; dir. Graphic Identity Program, 1984. Editor, creative dir. Admissions Brochure Series, 1984. Co-dir. N. Thurston Citizens for Schs., 1978-80. Recipient Award of Merit, Olympia Tech. Community Coll., 1980-81. Mem. Coun. for Advancement and Support of Edn., Wash. Community Coll. Adminstrs. Assn. (exec. bd. dirs., sec-treas.), Wash. Info. Council (Nat. Admissions/Mktg. Report awards 1986-88), Nat. Coun. for Mktg. and Pub. Rels (regionals conf. planning com. 1988-90), Wash. State Community Coll. Pub. Info. Com. (pres. 1989-90), Nat. Coun. for Resource Devel. (cons. publs), Nat. Conf. Planning Com. Avocations: writing, sailing, skiing. Office: Pierce Coll 9401 Farwest Dr SW Tacoma WA 98498

HANSON, SUSAN JANE, mortgage company executive; b. Columbus, Ohio, Dec. 21, 1958; d. Paul Edward and C. Jane (White) Hanson Van Hoose. BA, Capital U., 1980, MBA, 1986. Lic. mortgage broker, Fla. Staff acct. Vantage Properties Inc., Columbus, 1980-81, asst. controller, 1981-84, controller 1984-87; real estate specialist credit adminstrn. Huntington Nat. Bank, Columbus, 1987-88; mgr., spl. comml. real estate loan officer Huntington Mortgage Co., Naples, Fla., 1988—. Mem. NAFE, Am. Mgmt. Assn., Nat. Assn. Office and Indsl. Parks., Columbus Women in Real Estate, Robert Morris Assn. Republican. Methodist. Avocations: sewing, swimming, bowling, ceramics, travel. Home: 3014 Osgood Rd E Columbus OH 43232 Office: Huntington Mortgage Co 400 5th Ave S Ste 204 Naples FL 33940

HANSON, SUSAN RUTH, nurse; b. Berwyn, Ill., Sept. 3, 1953; d. Emery Harold and Vinetta Louise (Fjellman) H. BS in Nursing, U. Ill., 1977. RN, Ariz., Ill.; cert. profl. in quality assurance. Staff nurse Luth. Gen. Hosp., Park Ridge, Ill., 1977-78; clin. resource nurse Kino Community Hosp., Tucson, 1979, clin. educator, nursing quality assurance coord., adminstrv. dir., quality mgmt. svcs., 1983—; clin. faculty Pima Community Coll., Tucson; staff nurse Med. Pers. Pool, Evanston, Ill., 1978, Alpha Nursing Care, Tucson, 1979. Del. Ariz. Congress, 1986, state rep. to Congress, 1988. Mem. NAFE, Ariz. State Bd. Nursing (legal/internal affairs com., 1988—), Am. Soc. Healthcare Risk Mgmt., Nat. Assn. Quality Assurance Profls., Ariz. Assn. Quality Assurance Profls. (so. region rep. 1984, 85, 2nd v.p. and program chairperson 1986, pres. elect 1987, pres. 1988), So. Ariz. Assn. Quality Assurance Profls. (1st regional rep.).

HANSOTIA, HOOTY NOSHIR, manufacturing exective; b. Haregaon, India, June 24, 1949; d. Keki Shapurji and Dina Rustomji (Jamasji) Sagar; m. Noshir Louji Hansotia, May 4, 1969; children: Michelle, Mark. BS in Econs., U. Bombay, India, 1970. Accts. clk. Graham Mortgage Co., Detroit, 1970, Sealright Corp., Kansas City, Mo., 1975-76; co-owner, v.p. Cottman Transmission (now Better Transmission), Independence, Mo., 1976-88, Shawnee, Kans., 1977-88, Kansas City, 1981-88, St. Joseph, Mo., 1984-85, Gladstone, Mo., 1984-85; v.p., co-owner A&J Truck Equipment INc., Kansas City, 1988—. Mem. NAFE, Zoroastrian. Republican. Office: A&J Truck Equipment INc 6822 Kansas Ave Kansas City KS 66111

HANTKE, TERRI LEE CAIN, personnel specialist, business consultant; b. Aberdeen, Md., Oct. 16, 1951; d. Donald Ames and Billie (Dawn) Cain; m. James Russell Hantke, June 16, 1970; children: Christopher, Stephanie, William. Student, SW Tex. State U., 1970, Chaminade U., 1988-89, L.A. Community Coll. Recruiter, bus. cons. Davenport & Co., Honolulu; br. mgr. Adams and Assocs., Inc., Honolulu; office mgr. Family Svc. Clinic, Honolulu; edn. staff mem. Wahiawa Gen. Hosp., Hawaii. Contbr. articles to profl. jours. Mem. coun. Boy Scouts Am. Mem. NAFE, Nat. Assn. Personnel Cons. Home: 1334 C Wiliwili Circle Wahiawa HI 96786

HANWACKER, PATRICIA AILEEN LUDWIG, real estate consultant; b. Bklyn., Mar. 22, 1951; d. Henry Raymond and Margaret Adelaide (Binz) Ludwig; divorced; children—Jessica, Jarrod. B.S. in Math., St. John's U., 1971; M.S. in Computer Sci., Stevens Inst. Tech., 1974. Lic. real estate broker. Planning, equipment engr. N.Y. Telephone Co., N.Y.C., 1971-74; computer systems engr. AT&T, N.Y.C., 1974-76; staff supr. market research and forecasting AT&T Long Lines, Bedminster, N.J., 1976-78, dist. mgr. fin. planning, 1978-80, dist. mgr. tech. sales support, Somerset, N.J., 1980-82; nat. account mgr. for ABC, AT&T Communications, N.Y.C., 1982-84; v.p. mktg. and sales Dama Telecommunications Corp., Parsippany, N.J., 1985-86; sr. nat. acct. mgr. IBM, MCI Telecommunications, Rye Brook, N.Y., 1986-88; real estate cons. Kohere & Cohen, Iselin, N.J., 1988—; pres. Houston Assocs., Inc., Millburn, N.J., PLH Assocs., Millburn, N.J.; cons. Curriculum Concepts, N.Y.C., 1976; v.p. Quantum Investment Corp., Millburn, N.J., 1978—. Mem. Soc. Women Engrs., Internat. Radio and TV Soc., YWCA, Pi Mu Epsilon. Republican. Office: 555 Rt 1 So Iselin NJ 08830

HANZALEK, ASTRID TEICHER, public policy consultant; b. N.Y.C., Jan. 6, 1928; d. Arthur Albin and Luise Gertrude (Funke) Teicher; m. Frederick J. Hanzalek, Nov. 11, 1955. A, Concordia Coll., 1947; BA, U. Pa., 1949. Cons. Suffield, Conn., 1960—; state rep. Conn. Gen. Assembly, Hartford, 1970-80, asst. majority leader, 1973-74, asst. minority leader, 1975-80; corporator Newington (Conn.) Children's Hosp., 1986—; bd. dirs. Suffield Bank, Conn. Water Co., Clinton. Contbr. articles to profl. jours.; comment features Sta. WSFB-TV and Sta. CP-TV,Hartford, 1975—. Trustee Priscilla Maxwell Ednicott Scholarship Fund, 1972—; vice-chmn. Greater Hartford chpt. ARC, 1975-82, Conn. State Ethics Commn., Hartford, 1985—; mem. Conn. Inter Agy. Libr. Planning Com., Hartford, 1975-85, Conn. State Coun. Environ. Quality, Hartford, 1980—; chmn. Conn. River Watershed Coun., Easthampton, 1980—, Conn. Sr. Intern Program, Bridgeport, 1980-90; sec. Conn. Humanities Coun., Middletown, 1980—; trustee Conn. Energy Found., Hartford, 1986—. Recipient Man of Yr. award Conn. Jaycees, 1972, Panelist of Yr., Auto. Consumer Action Panel, 1975-85. Mem. Antiquarian and Landmarks Soc. (v.p. 1974—), Conn. Forest and Park Assn. (bd. dirs. 1975—), Conn. Coun. Environ. Quality, Suffield Land Conservancy (bd. dirs. 1965—, founder), Nat. Order Woman Legislatros. Republican. Lutheran. Home: 155 S Main St Suffield CT 06078

HAPKE, JOYCE ZELLINGER, rehabilitation specialist; b. Phillips, Wis., Nov. 23, 1932; d. Vincent James Zellinger and Thelma Irene Simpson; m. Bruce William Hapke, June 18, 1954; children: Kevin, Jeffrey, Cheryl. BS, U. Wis., 1954; MS, Carnigie-Mellon U., 1972; MEd, U. Pitts., 1977, post-grad., 1978-88. Cert. Commn. on Rehab. Counseling. Kindergarten tchr./adminstr. Private, White Sands, N.M., 1954-55; food service supr. Cornell U., Ithaca, N.Y., 1955-56; substitute tchr. Churchill Sch. Dist., Pitts., 1971-75, Craighouse and Allegheny Intermediate, Pitts.; rehab. counselor Coun. Ho. Inc., Pitts., 1977-82, Goodwill Industries, Calif., 1982-83; rehab. supr. Renaissance Ctr., Pitts., 1984—. Pres. PTA, Pitts., 1971; com. mem. LWV, Pitts., 1970-75, United Mental Health, Pitts., 1978-82. Mem. Nat. Rehab. Assn., Nat. Rehab. Counseling Assn., Pa. Rehab. Assn. Republican. Presbyterian. Office: Renaissance Ctr 910 Penn Ave Pittsburgh PA 15222

HAQUE, MALIKA HAKIM, pediatrician; b. Madras, India; came to U.S., 1967; d. Syed Abdul and Rahimunisa (Hussain) Hakim; MBBS, Madras Med. Coll., 1967; m. C. Azeez Haque, Feb. 5, 1967; children: Kifizeba, Masarath Nashr, Asim Zayd. Rotating intern Miriam Hosp., Brown U., Providence, 1967-68; resident in pediatrics Children's Hosp., N.J. Coll. Medicine, 1968-70; fellow in devel. disabilities Ohio State U., 1970-71; acting chief pediatrics Nisonger Ctr., 1973-74; staff pediatrician Children and Youth Project, Children's Hosp., Columbus, Ohio, also clin. asst. prof. pediatrics Ohio State U., 1974-80; clin. assoc. prof. pediatrics Ohio State U., 1981—; pediatrician in charge community pediatrics and adolescent svcs. clinics Columbus Children's Hosp., 1982—; cons. Central Ohio Head Start Program, 1974-79; v.p. A.M. Haque Internat., Columbus. Contbr. articles to profl. jours. and newspapers. Charter mem. Republican Presdl. Task Force, 1982—, Nat. Rep. Senatorial Com., 1985—, U.S. Senatorial Club; charter founder Ronald Reagan Rep. Ctr. Recipient Physician Recognition award AMA, 1971-86, 88-91, Gold medals in surgery, radiology, pediatrics and ob/gyn; Presdl. medal of Merit, 1982; diplomate Am. Bd. Pediatrics. Mem. Am. Acad. Pediatrics (Ohio chpt., Prep fellow 1986), Ambulatory Pediatric Assn., Cen. Ohio Pediatric Soc. Muslim. Research on enuresis. Home: 5995 Forestview Dr Columbus OH 43213 Office: 700 Children's Dr Columbus OH 43205

HARA-ISA, NANCY JEANNE, graphic designer; b. San Francisco, May 14, 1961; d. Toshiro and Masaye (Nakahira) Hara; m. Stanley Takeo Isa, June 15, 1985. Student, UCLA, 1979-82; BA in Art and Design, Calif. State U., Los Angeles, 1985. Salesperson May Co., L.A., 1981; svc. rep. Hallmark Cards Co., L.A., 1981-83; prodn. artist Calif. State U., Los Angeles, 1983, Audio-Stats Internat. Inc., Los Angeles, 1983; prodn. asst. Auto-Graphics Inc., Pomona, Calif., 1984-85, lead supr., 1985-86; art dir., contbg. staff writer CFW Enterprises, Burbank, Calif., 1987-88; graphic designer, prodn. mgr. Bonny Jularbal Graphics, Las Vegas, Nev., 1988—; free-lance designer Pan Metal Corp. Writer Action Pursuit Games mag. Parade asst., mem. carnival staff Nisei Week, L.A., 1980-84; asst., mem. Summit Orgn., L.A., 1987—. Mem. NAFE, Women in Profl. Graphic Svcs. (acting 1st v.p. 1990—). Republican. Presbyterian. Home: 367 Cavos Way Henderson NV 89014

HARAKAL, CONCETTA, pharmacology educator, researcher; b. Colle di Macine, Chieti, Italy, Nov. 25, 1923; came to U.S., 1932; d. Francesco and Maria (Gagliardi) De Leo; m. Michael Harakal, Oct. 16, 1948. BA, U. Pa., 1945; PhD, Temple U., Phila., 1962. Clin. chemist Hahnemann Med. Coll. and Hosp., Phila., 1946-51; rsch. asst. Temple U. Sch. Medicine, 1951-54, asst. instr. pharmacology, 1954-57, instr., 1957-64, asst. prof., 1964-68, assoc. prof., 1968-76, prof., 1976—; mem. admissions com. Temple U. Med. Sch., 1978—, course dir. pharmacology, 1985—, dental pharmacology, 1987—; cons. Ednl. Testing Svc., Princeton, N.J., 1978—. Contbr. articles to profl. jours. Eucharistic min. communion St. Donato Ch., Phila., 1989—. Recipient Golden Apple Teaching awards S.A.M.A., 1975, 77, 80, 83, 85, 87, 89, Humanitarian Svc. award Legion of Honor, Chapel of the Four Chaplains, Phila., 1977, Sowell Meml. award Temple U., 1979, Lindback Found. award, 1980. Mem. AAAS, AMA, Am. Soc. Pharmacology and Exptl. Therapeutics, N.Y. Acad. Sci., 25 Yr. Club Faculty Temple U., Sigma Xi. Roman Catholic. Office: Temple U Sch Medicine Dept Pharmacology Philadelphia PA 19140

HARALAMBIDIS, MAROULA, management consultant; b. N.Y.C., Aug. 31, 1959; d. Haralambos and Olympia (Kotanidis) H. BA in Economics, Berea Coll., 1981. Customer svc. rep. Godiva Chocolatier, N.Y.C., 1984-85, asst. mgr., asst. clk., 1985-86, retail acct., 1986-87; bus. cons. Pat's Pizzeria, Pennsville, N.J., 1987—. Democrat. Home: 41 Salem Dr Pennsville NJ 08070 Office: Pat's Pizzeria 102 S Broadway Pennsville NJ 08070

HARALSON, LINDA JANE, communications executive; b. St. Louis, Mar. 24, 1959; d. James Benjamin and Betty Jane (Myers) N.; married. BA summa cum laude William Woods Coll., 1981; MA, Webster U., 1982. Radio intern Stas.-KFAL/KKCA, Fulton, Mo., 1981; paralegal Herzog, Kral, Burroughs & Specter, St. Louis, 1981-82; staffing coordinator, then mktg. coordinator Spectrum Emergency Care, St. Louis, 1982-85, mktg. mgr., 1985-87; dir. mktg. and recruitment Carondelet Rehab. Ctrs. Am., Culver City, Calif., 1987—; mktg. dir. outpatient and corp. services Calif. Med. Ctr., Los Angeles, 1987-88; mktg. dir. Valley Meml. Hosp., Livermore, Calif., 1988-89; account exec. Laurel Communications, Medford, Oreg., 1989—. Party chmn. Heart Assn., St. Louis, 1982—. Recipient Flair award Advt. Fedn. St. Louis, 1984, Hosps. award Hagen Mktg. Research and Hospitals mag., 1984; presdl. acad. scholar William Woods Coll., Fulton, 1977-81. Mem. Am. Mktg. Assn., Internat. Assn. Bus. Communicators, NAFE, Alpha Phi Alumnae Assn. (pres. chpt. 1985-87). Republican. Presbyterian. Club: Bon Amis (program com. 1985—) (St. Louis). Avocations: running, travel, sports, French, needlepoint. Office: Laurel Communications 724 S Central Ste 101 Medford OR 97504

HARAMUNDANIS, KATHERINE LEONORA, computer/data processing company executive; b. Boston, Jan. 25, 1937; d. Sergei Illarionovich and Cecilia Helena (Payne) Gaposchkin; m. John Haramundanis, Mar. 6, 1958; children: George John, Sergei Edward. BA, Swarthmore Coll., 1958; post-grad., Boston U. Rsch. assoc. Smithsonian Astrophys. Obs., Cambridge, Mass., 1958-74; tech. writer Wang Labs., Lowell, Mass., 1974-77; supr. Digital Equipment Corp., Marlboro, Mass., 1977—. Contbr. articles to profl. jours. Mem. AAAS, IEEE Computer Soc., Assn. Computing

Machinery, Assn. Computing Linguistics, Linguistic Soc. Am., Am. Astron. Soc., Am. Archeol. Soc., Am. Sch. Oriental Rsch. Home: PO Box 1365 Westford MA 01886

HARB, CHARLENE ALICE, musician, educator; b. Knoxville, Tenn.; d. Wadie Joseph and Alice (Makla) H.; m. Barry Lyle McDonald, Dec. 19, 1967 (div. Nov. 1977); 1 child, Barry Lyle McDonald Jr. Student, Aspen Sch. Music, 1965; MusB, U. Tenn., 1966; MusM, Ind. U., 1968, MusD, 1978; postgrad., Franz Schubert Inst., 1981. Artist, piano tchr. Blair Sch. Music, Nashville, 1968-73; from instr. to assoc. prof. Tenn. State U., Nashville, 1974-84; adj. instr. Scarritt Grad. Sch., Nashville, 1977-85; artist in residence, 1985-88; artist, piano tchr. George Peabody Tchrs. Coll., Nashville, 1969-73; from adj. to assoc. prof. U. Tenn., Nashville, 1978-80; coach Mozarteum Acad., Salzburg, Austria, 1982; adj. instr. Vanderbilt U., Nashville, 1980-82, Fisk U., Nashville, 1985—; mem. faculty Govs. Sch. for Arts, Murfreesboro, Tenn., 1985, 89; keyboardist, bd. dirs. Nashville Symphony Orch., 1988—; adj. assoc. prof. piano Vanderbilt U., 1988—. Performer in field. Mem. music adv. panel Tenn. Arts Commn., 1980-88; chair, music adv. panel 1984-86. Grantee Tenn. arts Commn., 1977, 78. Mem. Coll. Music Soc. (bd. dirs. S.E. chpt. 1980-82), Music Tchrs. Nat. Assn., Nashville Entertainment Assn. (bd. dirs. 1983-85), Am. Fedn. Musicians, Phi Kappa Phi, Pi Kappa Lambda, Sigma Alpha Iota. Episcopalian. Home: 2223 Belmont Blvd Nashville TN 37212

HARBACH, BARBARA CAROL, musician, composer; b. Lock Haven, Pa., Feb. 14, 1946; d. Ralph Franklin and Madeline (Heltman) H.; m. Thomas F. George, Apr. 26, 1970. BA, Pa. State U., 1967; M in Mus. Arts, Yale U., 1970; diploma, Musikhochschule, Frankfurt, Fed. Republic of Germany, 1971; DMA, Eastman Sch. of Music, Rochester, N.Y., 1981. Asst. prof. Nazareth Coll., Rochester, 1974-85; dir. music Christ Ch., Pittsford, N.Y., 1974-85; lectr. SUNY, Buffalo, 1985—; dir. music St. Agnes, Buffalo, 1988-89; dir. musik St. Paul's Luth. Ch., Eggertsville, N.Y., 1989—; dir. Orchard Park Chorale, 1990—. Author: 10 choral anthems, 1990; performer solo compact discs on organ and harpsichord, 1989-90. Regional chair Music Tchrs. Nat. Assn. for Organ and Harpsichord, Rochester, 1981-84; bd. dirs. Future Trends, Buffalo, 1987-88. Nazareth Coll. grantee, 1984, Peter C. Cornell Trust grantee, 1987, Confs. in the Disciplines grantee, 1986, 87, 89. Mem. Am. Guild Organists (dean 1982-84), Coll. Music Soc., Sonneck Soc., Women in Music Symposia (bd. dirs. 1986-89), Pi Kappa Lambda. Office: SUNY 222 Baird Hall Buffalo NY 14260

HARBER, LORETTA MICHELE, company executive; b. Amarillo, Tex., Dec. 15, 1954; d. James Frank and Lillian Mildred (Meredith) H.; m. John Steven Midkiff; 1 child John Steven II; m. Franklin Douglas Harber, Jan. 9, 1980. High sch. diploma, Brandon High, 1972. Pres. Balloonies, Tampa, Fla., 1984—. Contbr. articles to profl. jours., 1987. founder Italian children cultural Group, Tampa, 1986; pres. Small Bus. Networking, Tampa, 1987-88; bd. dirs. L'Unione Italiana, Tampa, 1988—. Recipient appreciation Small Bus. Networking, 1987, Paolo Longo medal L'Unione Italiana, 1989. mem. Nat. Assn. of Balloon Artists, SBN (pres., 1987-88), Italian Club (dir. 1988-). Democrat. Roman Catholic. Home: PO Box 562 Valrico FL 33594

HARBERS, SUSAN ETHEL, executive recruiting company executive; b. Jersey City, Dec. 8, 1944; d. Herbert F. and Ethel A. (Vogeley) H. BA, Vassar Coll., 1966. Chartered fin. analyst. Ter. asst. MHTCo Internat., N.Y.C., 1966-68; utility analyst lst Boston Corp., N.Y.C., 1969-72; asst. v.p. energy lending Citibank, N.Y.C., 1973-79; v.p. Pru-Bache Corp. Fin., N.Y.C., 1980-83; pres. Brady Assocs. Internat. Inc., N.Y.C., 1984—. Contbr. articles to profl. publs. Mem. Inst. Chartered Fin. Analysts, N.Y. Soc. Security Analysts, Vassar Club. Office: Brady Assocs Internat Inc 310 Madison Ave Ste 423 New York NY 10017

HARBERT, PAMELA ANNETT, employment relations specialist; b. Dumas, Tex., Jan. 21, 1963; d. Robert Lewis and Constance Inez (Colston) H. BBA, North Tex. State U., 1986. Clk. North Tex. State U., Denton, 1983, 86; asst. mgr. Memory Lane of Tex., Denton, 1983-84; mgr. Edison Bros. Apparels, Denton, 1984-85; personnel adminstr. TTI, Inc., Ft. Worth, 1986-88; employee rels. rep. Parkland Meml. Hosp., Dallas, 1988—. Mem. NAFE, Ft. Worth Personnel Assn. (membership com.). Democrat. Methodist. Office: Parkland Meml Hosp 5201 Harry Hines Blvd Dallas TX 75235

HARBISON, LILLIAN V. GRAY, retired educator; b. Lancaster, Mo., Aug. 28, 1914; d. Archie and Galelia (Lasley) Gray; m. Herman Lee Harbison, Aug. 18, 1946. AE, Hannibal-La Grange Jr. Coll., 1938; BS in Edn., N.E. Mo. State Tchrs. Coll., 1941; MEd, U. Mo., 1946; postgrad., U. Iowa, 1947-74. Cert. elem. tchr., prin. and counselor, Mo., Iowa. Tchr. Pleasant Valley Rural Sch., Edina, Mo., 1938-42; elem. tchr. and prin. Edina Pub. Sch., 1942-44; elem. tchr. Vallejo (Calif.) Pub. Schs., 1944-45; grad. asst., instr. Lab. Sch., U. Mo., Columbia, 1945-46; jr. high sch. spl. edn. tchr. Iowa City Pub. Schs., 1946-49, elem. tchr., 1949-67, 71-77, asst. elem. prin., 1967-69, elem. counselor, 1969-71; ret., 1977. Mem. flower garden com. Mayflower Retirement Home, Grinnell, Iowa, 1989—; chmn. parish leaders, chmn. ad hoc com. to exec. adminstrn., mem. social task force of human resource coun., co-chmn. watermelon feast Foxwood Springs, Raymore, Md., 1985-86. Hannibal-La Grange Coll. Trustees scholar, 1937. Mem. Nat. Ret. Tchrs. Assn. (v.p. Grinnell 1987—), AAUW (sec. 1987—), Pi Lambda Theta (v.p. 1948-50), Four Seasons Garden Club (pres. 1981-82), Raymore Garden Club (pres. 1984-85), Iowa City Woman's Club (v.p. social studies div. 1983-84), Pi Lambda Theta (v.p., pres. 1948-50), Delta Kappa Gamma (v.p. 1968-70), Phi Delta Kappa. Baptist.

HARBOUR, NANCY CAINE, lawyer; b. Cleve., July 30, 1949; d. William Anthony and Bernadette (Frohnapple) Caine; m. Randall Lee Harbour, Sept. 29, 1979. B.A. magna cum laude, U. Detroit, 1970; J.D., Cleve. State U., 1978. Bar: Mich. 1978. Writer, Project Map, Inc., Washington, 1971-72; newspaper reporter Alexandria Gazette, Va., 1972-73, Times Herald Record, Goshen, N.Y., 1973-75; atty. Conklin, Benham, et al., Detroit, 1978-82, Miller, Cohen, Martens, and Ice, P.C., Detroit, 1982-90, ptnr., 1990—. Mem. Am. Trial Lawyers Assn., Mich. Trial Lawyers Assn., Mich. Bar Assn., State Bar Mich. (mem. compensation council 1983-85), Gamma Pi Epsilon. Democrat. Office: Miller Cohen Martens & Ice PC 1400 N Park Pla 17117 W Nine Mile Rd Southfield MI 48075

HARD, ELIZABETH JACKSON See HRADEL, ELIZABETH HARD

HARDAGE, PAGE TAYLOR, university administrator; b. Richmond, Va., June 27, 1944; d. George Peterson and Gladys Odell (Gordon) Taylor; m. Thomas Brantley, July 6, 1968; 1 child, Taylor Brantley. AA, Va. Intermont Coll., Bristol, 1964; BS, Richmond Profl. Inst., 1966; MPA, Va. Commonwealth U., Richmond, 1982. Cert. tchr. Competent toastmaster, dir. play therapy svcs. Med. Coll. Va. Hosps., Va. Commonwealth U., Richmond, 1970—; instr. dept. pub. adminstrn. Va. Commonwealth U., Richmond, 1986—; dir. Int. Women's Issues Va. Commonwealth U., U. Va., Richmond, 1986—; bd. dirs. Math. and Sci. Ctr. Found., Richmond, Emergency Med. Svcs. Adv. Bd., Richmond. bd. dirs. Richmond Black Student Found., Richmond YWCA, 1989—; group chmn. United Way Greater Richmond, 1987; treas. Richmond Leadership Met. Mem. Am. Soc. Pub. Adminstrn., Adminstrv. Mgmt. Soc., Nat. Assn. Female Execs., Internat. Mgmt. Coun. (exec. com.), Richmond Alumni Assn. Unitarian. Office: Med Coll Va Hosps Va Commonwealth U PO Box 202 Richmond VA 23298

HARDAWAY, BEVERLY LYNNE, public relations executive; b. Wichita, Kans., Mar. 7, 1961; d. Elmer Gene and Mary Joyce (Conrad) H. Student, N.Mex. State U., 1979-82; student, Calif. Poly. Tech., Pomona, 1986-87. Restaurant mgr. Karl Karcher Enterprises, Anaheim, Calif., 1984-85; exec. searcher Douglas, Campbell and Assocs., Orange, Calif., 1986; staff writer L.A. Fairplex, Pomona, 1986-87; emergency svcs. staff City of Irvine (Calif.), 1987; with retail mgmt. Woman's World, Orange, 1987; pub. rels. dir. Orange County 4-H, Anaheim, 1987—; cons. various non-profit orgns., Orange County, Calif., 1986—; pres., chief exec. officer Buzzard Flyers Enterprises, Fullerton, Calif., 1990. Editor (newspaper) Talking It Over, 1987-88, news editor (newspaper) Maurauder Times, 1983. V.p. N.Mex. Young Republicans, 1980; advisor Orange County 4-H Teen Coun., Anaheim, 1989-90; pres. Women in Communications, Pomona, 1986-87. Mem. L.A. Media Mktg. 4-H Assn., Orange County Pub. Info. Officer Assn. Baptist. Office: Orange County 4-H 1000 S Harbor Anaheim CA 92805

HARDEE, EVELYN ROCKER, retired teacher; b. Metter, Ga., Jan. 27, 1921; d. Albert Herman and LaVernia (Fordham) Rocker; m. Leon Alton Hardee, Mar. 18, 1939; children: Lynne Hardee Pridgen, Jean Hardee Drake. BS in Elem. Edn., Ga. Tchrs. Coll., 1953. Cert. tchr., Va. Tchr. Norfolk (Va.) City Sch. Bd., 1949-81; now ret. Mem. Philanthropic and Ednl. Orgn. (past chpt. pres.), Ch. Women United (v.p. 1988-90), United Meth. Women (coord. Christian social involvement Norfolk dist.), Aux. Gideons Internat., Norfolk Assn. Classroom Tchrs. (pres. 1976-77, 79-80, scholarship trustee 1981-90, AAUW, Alpha Delta Kappa (Sigma chpt.). Home: 5813 Townley Ave Norfolk VA 23518

HARDEN, ALICE V., state legislator; b. Magnolia, Miss., Apr. 17, 1948; m. Dennis Labert Harden. Student, Jackson State U. Tchr.; mem. Miss. State Senate; mem. Hinds County Dem. Women. Mem. NAACP, various ednl. assns. Baptist. Address: PO Box 2067 Jackson MS 39255*

HARDEN, JOAN PIPER, fundraiser; b. N.Y., Aug. 16, 1947; d. John Mason and Lorez (Taylor) H. BA, City Coll. N.Y., 1972; MPA, Baruch Coll., N.Y., 1989. Cert. Fund Raising Exec. Sales rep. Xerox Corp., N.Y., 1973-74; dist. sales mgr. Am. Express, N.Y., 1975-78; sr. develop specialist Girl Scouts U.S.A., N.Y., 1979-89; assoc. dir. devel. The Grad. Sch. and Univ. Ctr., CUNY, 1989—. Mem. Nat. Soc. Fund Raising Exec., Nat. Forum Black Pub. Adminstrn., Coalition of 100 Black Women. Home: 2569 7th Ave New York NY 10039

HARDENBURG, LINA, data processing executive; b. Schenectady, N.Y., Oct. 23, 1949; d. Allen Jeffers and Lulo Mae (Nelson) Peek; m. Mark Thomas Hardenburg, Sept. 27, 1969; 1 child, Marta Lynn. Student, Am. U., 1967-69; cert. computer programming, Chubb Inst., 1985. Cert. quality analyst. Quality control supr. Captive Plastics, Inc., Piscataway, N.J., 1975-85; EDP quality assurance dir. R.H. Macy & Co., Inc., N.Y.C., 1985-90; change coord. UPS, Paramus, N.J., 1990—; facilitator Quality Circle Inst., Red Bluff, Calif., 1984. Del. N.J. Dem. Party Convention, Atlantic City, 1980; corr. sec. Mcpl. Dem. Orgn., Piscataway; pres. Lady Vols. of Arbor Hose Co., Piscataway, 1983-85; trustee Piscataway Library, 1986—. Mem. NASPA, Info. Systems Security Assn., Quality Mgmt. Assn., Quality Assurance Inst., N.J. Quality Assn., Computer Soc. of IEEE, Phi Mu. Baptist. Home: 1838 Brunella Ave Piscataway NJ 08854 Office: UPS 640 Winters Ave Paramus NJ 07652

HARDER, MARILYN ANNE, nurse anesthetist; b. Red Wing, Minn., May 24, 1951; d. Lloyd Henry and Solveig Gunhild (Kaasa) Harder; m. Gary Howard Wilson, Aug. 17, 1974 (div. 1982). BS in Nursing, St. Olaf Coll., Northfield, Minn., 1973; diploma in anesthesia, VA Med. Ctr., Albany, N.Y., 1981; postgrad., United Theol. Sem., New Brighton, Minn., 1988—. RN, Minn., N.Y. Nurse's aide Sem. Nursing Home, Red Wing, 1970-71; nurse VA Med. Ctr., Mpls., 1973-74, Albany, 1974-79; nurse Von Rensellaer Manor Nursing Home, Troy, N.Y., 1979; nurse anesthetist Tri-City Anesthesia Svcs., Albany, 1981-83, Hennepin County Med. Ctr., Mpls., 1983, VA Med. Ctr., Mpls., 1983-90, Midway Hosp., St. Paul, 1990—. Chmn. worship com., congl. coun. St. Paul Reformation Luth. Ch., 1988-90. Home: 2300 23d Ave S Minneapolis MN 55404

HARDER, SARAH SNELL, university administrator; b. Chgo., Sept. 9, 1937; d. Frank Wen and Margaret Louise (Bryne) Snell; student U. Iowa, 1955-58; B.A., B.S. cum laude, U. Wis., LaCrosse, 1963; M.A., Bowling Green State U., 1966; m. Harry R. Harder, Feb. 7, 1964; children—Richard, Bentley, Jennifer, Aaron. Mem. faculty in English, Bowling Green State U., 1967-68; mem. faculty English, U. Wis., Eau Claire, 1968, adv. to older students, 1975-77, asst. to chancellor for affirmative action, 1975-78, asst. to chancellor for affirmative action and ednl. opportunity, 1978—; mem. U. Wis. regents' task forces on basic skills, status of women, minority/disadvantaged students; cons. women's employment and equity, non-traditional programs in higher edn. Co-chmn. Nat. Women's Conf. Com., 1979-85, 89—; trustee Eau Claire Pub. Libr., 1980-85, pres., 1984-85; mem. Overseas Devel. Coun., 1989—, Nat. Peace Inst. Found. Bd., 1989—; chmn. bd. dirs. Women for a Meaningful Summit/US, 1987, pres., 1988—; co-chair Soviet-Am. Women's Summit, 1990, Alliance for Our Common Future, 1989; mem. govs. coun. Bus./Edn. Ptnrships., 1984—; mem. Nat. Coun. Pres. and Women's Agenda, 1985—; convener State Network Leadership Summit, 1989; chmn. bd. dirs. AAUW Ednl. Found., 1985-89; founding bd. dirs. Wis. Women's Network; exec. Leadership Eau Claire, C. of C. Named one of 80 Leaders for the Eighties, Milw. Jour., 1979, Named one of 100 Most Important Women Ladies Home Jour., 1988; 1st Excellence in Service award U. Wis.-Eau Claire, 1984; Dept. Edn. grantee, 1978—; named Disting. Alumnae Alpha Delta Pi, 1989. Mem. AAUW (nat. pres. 1985-89, dir. women's com., dir. legis. program com. mem. 1975—), Internat. Fedn. U. Women (status of women com. 1989—), LWV, Nat. Women's Polit. Caucus (award Wis. br.), Wis. Women's Coun. (chairperson 1983-87), Delta Kappa Gamma (chpt. pres.), Alpha Lambda Delta. Democrat. Co-designer Beyond ERA—an Action Plan, 1982; contbr. articles to Redbook, Grad. Woman Outlook, Stateswoman, The Am. Women, 1989-90. Home: U Wis Eau Claire WI 54701 Office: U Wis Library 2058 Eau Claire WI 54701

HARDIMAN, THERESE ANNE, lawyer; b. Chestnut Hill, Pa., Mar. 2, 1956; d. Edward Joseph and Grace Joan (Shaw) Hardiman; m. David J.P. Malecki, Feb. 3, 1990. BA in History, BA in Psychology, Mt. St. Mary's Coll., 1978; JD, Thomas M. Cooley Law Sch., 1983. Bar: Pa. 1983. U.S. Dist. Ct. (ea. dist.) Pa. 1983, U.S. Ct. Appeals (3d cir.) 1984, U.S. Dist. Ct. (mid. dist.) Pa. 1989. Staff rsch. asst. Internat. Brotherhood of Teamsters, Washington, 1978-79; law clk. Richard R. Rashid, Atty. at Law, Lansing, Mich., 1981-82; law clk. Pearlstine, Salkin, Hardiman & Robinson, Landsdale, Pa., 1981; staff asst. Employment Rels. Bd., Mich. Dept. Civil Svc., Lansing, 1982; mem. Pearlstine, Salkin, Hardiman & Robinson, Landsdale, 1983-86; v.p. Edward J. Hardiman & Assocs. P.C., 1986—. Editor-in-chief Pridwin, 1978, layout editor, 1977. Recipient Golden Key award, Delta Theta Phi, 1981; Outstanding Student award Student Bar Assn., Thomas M. Cooley Law Sch., 1982. Mem. ABA, Assn. Trial Lawyers Am., Pa. Assn. Trial Lawyers, Pa. Bar Assn., Monroe County Bar Assn., Montgomery County Bar Assn., Delta Theta Phi. Republican. Roman Catholic. Office: PO Box 850 Rt 940 Pocono Pines PA 18350

HARDIN, ELIZABETH ANN, textile company official, health care consultant; b. Charlotte, N.C., Nov. 21, 1959; d. William Gregg and Ann (Astin) H. BBA magna cum laude, U. Ga., 1981; MBA, Harvard U., 1985. cons., developer adminstrv. policy guide Chelsea (Mass.) Pub. Schs., 1989-90. Spl. project coord. NCNB Corp., Charlotte, 1981-82, investment officer, 1982-83; cons. Booz, Allen & Hamilton, Atlanta, 1985-86; asst. placement dir. Harvard U. Bus. Sch., Boston, 1986-87, dir. MBA program adminstrn., 1987-89, acting placement dir., 1988-89; mgr. employment Sara Lee Hosiery Group, Winston-Salem, N.C., 1990—. Mem. Harvard Non-Profit Fellowship Adv. Bd., 1986—, chmn., 1990; chmn. Harvard Non-Profit Mgmt. Fellowship, 1990; mem. AIDS Action Com. Mass.; active All Saints Epis. Ch., Belmont, Mass. Fellow State Farm Co. Found., 1980, Delta Gamma Found., 1983. Mem. Harvard Bus. Sch. Assn., Phi Kappa Phi, Delta Gamma (pres. alumnae Charlote, 1982-83). Republican. Office: Sara Lee Hosiery Group PO Box 2495 Winston-Salem NC 27102

HARDIN, HILLIARD FRANCES, microbiologist; b. Columbia, S.C., Dec. 12, 1917; d. Lawrence Legare and Addria Eugenia (Chreitzberg) H. AB, Duke U., 1939, MA, 1949, PhD, 1953. Bacteriologist Bowman Gray Sch. of Medicine, Winston-Salem, N.C., 1941-42; instr. Med. Sch. Duke U., Durham, N.C., 1948-53; from instr. to asst. prof. Med. Sch. U. Ark., Little Rock, 1954-58, rsch. assoc. Sch. of Medicine, 1958-63; chief mycology tng. unit C.D.C., Atlanta, 1963-68; dir. microbiology dept. VA Hosp., Little Rock, 1968—. With USNR, 1942-45. Mem. N.Y. Acad. Scis., Med. Mycology Soc. Am., Am. Bus. Women's Assn. (v.p. 1986-87, pres. 1987-88, Top 10 of the Yr. 1988). Republican. Methodist. Home: 301 Kingsrow Dr #401 Little Rock AR 72207

HARDIN, SHERRIE ANN, industrial and commercial photographer; b. Saratoga Springs, N.Y., May 28, 1950; d. Edward Asfoury and Olivia Dorethea (Rehm) Melrose; m. Lin Hardin, Feb. 13, 1972. Student, Polk Community Coll., Winter Haven, Fla., 1968-69, 77, La Harbor Coll., Wilmington, Calif., 1984-85, El Camino Coll., Hawthorne, Calif., 1985-87. Photographer Nissan Motor Corp. in USA, Gardena, Calif., 1985-86; gen. mgr. Awards-Rex Group, Hawthorne, 1986-88; photog. coord. Meisel, Atlanta, 1988-89; owner, mgr. Sherrie Hardin, Photographer, Stone Mountain, Ga., 1985—. Mem. NAFE. Home and Office: 1736 Wood Bend Dr Stone Mountain GA 30083

HARDIN, SONDRA HIGDON, healthcare executive; b. Jackson, Miss., Nov. 3, 1958; d. Robert Paul and Lena (McGee) Higdon; m. Steven C. Hardin. BS, U. Miss., 1980; MEd in Profl. Counseling, Delta State U., 1990. Sales asst. A.G. Edwards & Sons, Inc., Jackson, 1983-85; dir. ops. and compliance of investments Allen Fin. Group, Jackson, 1985-88; investments analyst Miss. Pub. Retirement Systems, Jackson, 1988-89; medicaid waiver case mgr. Delta Mental Health Ctr., Greenville, Miss., 1989. Mem. Profl. Young Women in Am. Republican. Baptist. Home: PO Box 331 Stoneville MS 38776 Office: Community Counseling Ctr 850 McAlister Greenville MS 39701

HARDIN, TERRI LYNN, investment company executive; b. Lebanon, Ky., Mar. 15, 1950; d. Jack Douglas and Thelma Theresa (Mattingly) VanDyke; m. Robert George Sanders Jr., Sept. 25, 1971 (div. Oct. 1982); children: Tina Lynn, Lori Anne; m. William Murray Hardin Jr., Dec. 15, 1984; children: Mari Beth, Tami Kaye. Cert. in dental assistance, Jefferson County Sch. for Dental Assts., Louisville, 1971. Nurse's aide Mary Immaculate Hosp., Lebanon, 1966-68; asst. Barnes Med. Lab., Louisville, 1969-70; dental asst. Sch. Dentistry U. Louisville, 1971-75; receiving asst. Bacon's Retail Store, Louisville, 1976-85; researcher, real estate cons. Wm. Hardin & Assocs., Louisville, 1984-86; pres., researcher Terri Lynn Corp., Louisville, 1986—, also bd. dirs. Mem. Nat. Assn. Female Execs. Democrat. Roman Catholic. Office: Terri Lynn Corp PO Box 16157 Louisville KY 40216

HARDIN-CHEUNG, JUDY ANN, educator; b. Santa Rosa, Calif., Feb. 3, 1945; d. Robert Stephens and Edna Rozella (Kramer) H. BA, Calif. State U. at Sonoma, Rohnert Park, Calif., 1966; MA, U. San Francisco, 1981. Tchr. St. Thomas (Virgin Islands) Dept. Edn., 1967-71, Sonoma Devel. Ctr., Eldridge, Calif., 1971—; co-chairperson Ednl. Svcs. Profl. Practice Group, Eldridge, Calif., 1989—. Author, pub.: Acorn to Embers, 1987, Welcome to the Inside, 1984; author, photographer, pub. Captions, 1986. Pres. Ina Coolbrith Circle, Orinda, Calif., 1987—. Recipient awards Silver Pegasus, 1983, Poets of the Vineyard, 1986, 87, Ark. Writers Conf., 1988. Mem. Calif. Fedn. Chaparral Poets (pres. 1989—), Calif. Writers Club (treas. Redwood writers br. 1985-86), Bay Area Poets Coalition. Home and Office: 704 Brigham Ave Santa Rosa CA 95404-5245

HARDING, ETHEL M., state legislator; b. Fishtail, Mont., Oct. 19, 1927; m. Warren Harding; 2 children. Student, Heald's Bus. Coll. Clk., recorder Lake County, Mont., 1967-84; owner, operator Mission Valley Concrete, 1967-84; rep. State of Mont., 1985-86, senator, 1987—. Republican. Mem. Ch. of Nazarene. Office: PO Box 251 Polson MT 59860*

HARDING, FANN, health scientist, administrator; b. Henderson, Ky., Jan. 29, 1930; d. James Hilary and Lucy (Caldwell) H. Student, Western Coll., Oxford Ohio, 1947-48; A.B. in Biology, Coker Coll., Hartsville, S.C., 1951; M.S. in Anatomy, Med. U. S.C., Charleston, 1954, Ph.D., 1958. Research and teaching asst. dept. anatomy Med. U. S.C., 1951-53, teaching fellow, 1953-55, research fellow, 1955-58; analyst pub. health research program, research and tng. grants br. Nat. Heart Inst., Bethesda, Md., 1958-61; scientist adminstr. research and tng. grants br. Nat. Heart Inst., 1961-64, chmn. nat. adv. heart council statements com., 1961-64, sr. health scientist adminstr. research grants br. (sect. chief), 1964-69, sr. health scientist adminstr. thrombosis and hemorrhagic diseases br. (acting chief), extramural program, also arteriosclerosis program, 1969-72; mem. Nat. Heart Inst. (Fellowship Bd.), 1966-68; sr. health scientist adminstr. thrombosis and hemorrhagic diseases program (acting chief), div. blood diseases and resources Nat. Heart and Lung Inst. (name changed to Nat. Heart, Lung and Blood Inst. 1976), Bethesda, 1972-74; asst. to dir. div. blood diseases and resources Nat. Heart, Lung and Blood Inst., 1974—, program dir. extramural research tng. and career devel. in blood diseases and transfusion medicine, exec. sec. blood diseases and resources adv. com.; asst. coordinator U.S.-USSR Health Exchange Program, 1974—; mem. Women's Action Program Adv. Coun., HEW, 1971-72; cons. James H. Mitchell Found., Washington, 1962-67, Washington VA Hosp., 1968-70; environ. cons. Henderson (Ky.) Citizens Com., 1974-76; bd. dirs. Lupus Found. Am., 1985-88; initiated and implemented concept of transfusion medicine, 1982—. Organizer NIH Orgn. for Women, 1970; bd. dirs. Assn. Women in Sci. Edn. Found., 1973-77; bd. visitors Coker Coll., 1974-78; bd. dirs., sec., treas. Nat. Children's Choir, Washington, 1981—. Recipient Ruth Patrick award, 1951; NIH award for sustained performance, 1973, Nat. award for contbns. to public policy Fedn. Orgns. for Profl. Women, 1977, Disting. Svc. award for initiating and guiding devel. of transfusion medicine Acad. Award Program Am. Assn. Blood Banks, 1990. Fellow Sigma Delta Epsilon; mem. AAAS (panel on women in sci. 1973-77), Nat. Women's Polit. Caucus (charter), Assn. Women in Sci. (founding mem., exec. bd. 1973-75), Fedn. Orgn. Profl. Women (founding pres., exec. bd. 1972—), Nat. Woman's Party (mem. bd. 1981, corr. sec. 1989), Microcirculatory Soc. (charter), Reticuloendothelial Soc. (charter), Am. Assn. Blood Banks, Internat. Soc. Thrombosis and Haemostasis, Internat. Soc. Blood Transfusion. Home: 1870 Wyoming Ave NW Washington DC 20009 Office: Nat Heart Lung & Blood Inst NIH Div Blood Diseases & Resources Bethesda MD 20892

HARDING, JANICE KAY, hospital administrator; b. Lafayette, Ind., Dec. 30, 1956; d. Donald Lee and Alice Louise (Fleenor) Slopsema; m. Richard Daniel Harding, Oct. 27, 1984; stepchildren: Jade, Jared. BBA, U. Evansville, 1979. Registrar Lockyear Coll., Evansville, 1979-82; bridal cons. Kruckemeyer & Cohn, Evansville, 1982-83; bus. adminstr. Evansville State Hosp., 1983-88, asst. supt., 1988—. Mem. Am. Bus. Womens Assn. (recording sec. 1983-84). Methodist. Office: Evansville State Hosp 3400 Lincoln Ave Evansville IN 47715

HARDING, SANDRA ELLEN, government personnel executive; Kokomo, Ind., Sept. 15, 1944; d. Lloyd Bates and Rosella Bell (Anderson) Johnson; m. Michael Harding, Nov. 13, 1970 (div. 1975). BA in Psychology, Colo. Women's Coll., 1966. Resident mgr. Women's Job Corps Ctr., Omaha, 1966-68; flight attendant United Air Lines, San Francisco, 1968-70; travel agt. Carlisle (Eng.) Travel Agy., 1971-73; personnel asst. Sundstrand Tech., Denver, 1973-78; pers. adminstr. C.A. Norgren Co., Denver, 1978-80; employment mgr. The Denver Post, 1980-83; employment specialist Los Alamos (N.Mex.) Nat. Lab., 1984-86; human resources mgr. Time Mirror Cable TV, Phoenix, 1986-89; fed. investigator U.S. Office Pers. Mgmt., Lakewood, Colo., 1990—. Mem. Soc. For Human Resources Mgmt., Internat. Dance Exercise Assn., Am. Compensation Assn., Internat. Assn. Pers. Women (pres.-elect Denver chpt. 1982-83, pres. 1983-84). Office: U S Office Pers Mgmt 12345 W Alameda Pkwy Lakewood CO

HARDING, SHEILA ANN, underwriter; b. Chgo., Sept. 28, 1940; d. John Henry and Margaret Mary (Spear) H.; div.; children: Moira, Brian. BS in Edn., Chgo. State U., 1962; MA in English, DePaul U., Chgo., 1966. CPCU. Tchr. high sch. English South Shore High Sch., Chgo., 1962-69; substitute speech tchr. Joliet (Ill.) Jr. Coll., Joliet High Sch., 1971-77; tchr. high sch. English Minooka (Ill.) High Sch., 1977-81; casualty underwriter Hartford Ins. Co., Chgo., 1981-86; major accounts underwriter Crum & Forster Ins., Oakbrook, Ill., 1986-89; major accounts exec. Home Ins. Co., Chgo., 1989—; tchr. Ins. Sch. Chgo., 1988-89. Recipient Babbit-Sommer award Ins. Sch. Chgo., 1988, 89. Mem. Soc. CPCU, Delta Kappa Gamma (membership chair and advt. coms. 1971-72). Democrat. Roman Catholic. Home: 5621 N Christiana Chicago IL 60659

HARDINGER, ROWENA ADALINE, home economics educator; b. Little Rock, Jan. 31, 1926; d. Ben A. and Ruth (Myers) Lincoln; children: Ruth Ann, Jon Lincoln, David Loren. BS, Iowa State U., Ames, 1947, MS, 1974. Cert. home econs. tchr., Iowa. Tchr. Albia (Iowa) Community Schs., 1947-83; with Coll. of Family & Consumer Sci., Ames, 1984—, mem. adv. coun.,

1990—; master gardener Iowa State Extension, Ottumwa, 1984—, master food processor, 1988—; program chair Delta Kappa Gamma, Chariton, Iowa, 1988—. Sec. Monroe County Arts Coun., Albia, 1984-87, membership chair, 1987—; mem. Rep. Cen. Com., Albia, 1987-89; mem. dist. and local coun. on ministries Meth. Ch., 1970-90. Mem. NEA (life), AAUW (life, div. svcs. coord. 1987-89, legis. chair 1984-86, br. pres. 1987-89, div. pres. 1990—). Home and Office: 201 S Main Albia IA 52531

HARDRICK, MARIA DARSHELL, revenue agent; b. Milw., Feb. 5, 1966; d. Dorotha G. Hardrick. BS, Wilberforce U., 1988. Revenue agt. IRS, Cleve., 1988—. Mem. Nat. Assn. of Black Accts. Baptist. Home: 26209 Cambridge Ln #104 Warrensville Heights OH 44128 Office: IRS 1240 E 9th St Cleveland OH 44199

HARDY, ANNE DUNLAP, artist, educator; b. Birmingham, Ala., Jan. 15, 1910; d. James Thompson and Georgia Bailey (Dixon) D.; m. Charles Lambdin Hardy Sr., Nov. 18, 1936; children: Albert Sidney II, Charles Lambdin Jr., Georgia Hardy Luck. AB, Brenau Coll., Gainesville, Ga., 1931; postgrad., Mus. Modern Art, L.I., N.Y., 1965, North Ga. Coll., 1966, U. Ga., 1970. Supr. art schs., Dawsonville, Ga., 1963-72; pvt. instr. art, Gainesville, 1960—, Dallas, 1961-63. One women shows include Gainesville, 1960, Piedmont Interstate Fair, Spartanburg, S.C., 1977, Lake Lanier Islands (Ga.) Art Show, 1977; group shows include Telfair Mus., Savannah, Ga., 1952, Columbus Art Mus., 1960, Motorola Art Show, Chgo., 1962, U. Ga. Cortona, Italy, 1970; represented in numerous pvt. collections. Mem. Hall County Library Bd., 1951-61, Atlanta Symphony Orch. Bd., 1953-58; pres. Yonah council Girl Scouts U.S., 1955-57, exec. dir., 1958-61; mem. Gainesville Beautification Com., 1979-81. Mem. Assn. Ga. Artists (v.p. 1952-54), Gainesville Art Assn., Ga. Arts Council, Alpha Delta Pi. Democrat. Episcopalian. Club: Garden of Ga. (bd. dirs. 1948-60). Avocations: gardening, cooking. Home: 105 Macon Circle Ashland VA 23005

HARDY, DORCAS RUTH, management consultant, investment executive; b. Newark, N.J., July 18, 1946; d. Colburn and Ruth (Hart) H. B.A., Conn. Coll., 1964-68; M.B.A., Pepperdine U., 1976. Legis. rsch. asst. U.S. Senator Clifford P. Case, Washington, 1970; spl. asst. White House Conf. Children and Youth, Washington, 1970-71; exec. dir. Health Svcs. Industry Commn., Cost of Living Coun., Washington, 1971-73; asst. sec. Calif. Dept. Health, Sacramento, 1973-74; assoc. dir. U. So. Calif. Ctr. Health Svcs. Rsch., 1974-81; asst. sec. human devel. svcs. HHS, Washington, 1981-86; commr. Social Security HHS, Washington, DC, 1986-89; sr. counselor to the chmn. Wright Investors' Svc., Bridgeport, Conn., 1989—. Bd. dirs. Jr. League of Pasadena, Wolf Trap Found. for Performing Arts, The Wednesday's Child Found., Md.; former chmn. Pres.'s Task Force on Legal Equality for Women. Mem. Renaissance Women, Nat. Fedn. Republican Women, Rep. Women's Forum, Exec. Women in Govt., Girl Scouts U.S.A. Office: Wrights Investors Svc 2909 S Woodstock St Arlington VA 22206

HARDY, ELLEN MARIE, actuary; b. Salt Lake City, Mar. 30, 1964; d. James Robert Hardy and Kay Jeanne Anderson Brewer. BS, U. Wash., 1986. Actuarial asst. United Pacific Ins. Co., Federal Way, Wash., 1986-87; cons. actuary Coopers & Lybrand, Seattle/Phila., 1987—. Mem. Casualty Actuaries of the N.W., Delta Zeta (co-chmn. yearbook 1989—). Home: 2909 Hamilton Dr Voorhees NJ 08043 Office: Coopers & Lybrand 2400 Eleven Penn Center Philadelphia PA 19103

HARDY, GYME DUFAULT, social worker; b. Conway, N.H., July 25, 1952; d. Ernest John and Emma Eleanor (Potter) Dufault. B Social Work, U. N.H., 1975; MSHS, N.H. Coll., 1983; PhD, Columbia Pacific U., 1987. Cottage tchr. Spaulding Youth Ctr., Tilton, N.H., 1978-80; social worker Merrimack County Nursing Home, Boscawen, N.H., 1980-85; regional ombudsman State of N.H., Concord, 1985-87, acting state ombudsman, 1987, long term care ombudsman, 1987—; tchr. N.H. Tech. Inst., Concord, 1986, 89; cons. Greater Concord Gerontology Resource Group, Concord, 1988—. Mem. Nat. Assn. Social Workers, Gerontol. Soc. Am., Am. Soc. Law and Medicine, Zonta Internat., Nat. Citizens Coalition for Nursing Home Reform, Nat. Assn. State Long Term Care Ombudsmen, N.H. Residential Care Assn. (bd. dirs. 1988—). Office: Office of LTC Ombudsman 6 Hazen Dr Concord NH 03301-6508

HARDY, JANE ELIZABETH, communications educator; b. Fenelon Falls, Ont., Can., Mar. 27, 1930; came to U.S., 1956, naturalized, 1976; d. Charles Edward and Augusta Miriam (Lang) Little; m. Ernest E. Hardy, Sept. 3, 1955; children: Edward Harold, Robert Ernest. BS with distinction, Cornell U., 1953. Garden editor and writer Can. Homes Mag., Maclean-Hunter Pub. Co., Ltd., Toronto, Ont., 1954-55, 56-62; contbg. editor Can. Homes, Southam Pub. Co., Toronto, Ont., 1962-66; instr. Cornell U., 1966-73, sr. lectr. in communication, 1979—; mem. Cornell U. Provost's Adv. Com. on Status of Women, 1977-81; lectr., condr. workshops on writing. Contbr. numerous articles to mags.; author numerous other publs., including brochures, slide set scripts; editor pro tem Cornell Plantations Quar., 1981-82. Mem. Women in Communications, Inc. (faculty adv. Cornell chpt. 1977—, liaison 1986—, chair, ind. adv. mem. 1988-90), Garden Writers Assn. Am., Royal Hort. Soc., Ithaca Garden Club, Ithaca Women's Club, Pi Alpha Xi, Phi Kappa Phi, Alpha Omicron Pi. Home: 215 Enfield Falls Rd Ithaca NY 14850 Office: Cornell U Dept Communication 328 Kennedy Hall Ithaca NY 14853

HARDY, JUNE DORFLINGER, painter, photographer, interior designer; b. N.Y.C., Feb. 2, 1929; d. William Francis Dorflinger, Jr. and Katheryn (Hait) Dorflinger Manchee; m. John Alexander Hardy, Jr., May 26, 1956. Grad., Briarcliff Jr. Coll., 1949; student, Parsons Sch. Design, 1949-50, N.Y. Sch. Interior Design, 1953-54, 87-89, Nat. Acad. Art-Art Students League, 1966-85, Columbia U., 1963. Asst. tchr. Peck Sch., Morristown, N.J., 1950-51; with pers. dept. McGraw Hill, Inc., 1951-52; editorial asst., then asst. editor Better Homes and Gardens mag., 1951-52, 1952-57; editorial asst., then asst. editor Successful Farming mag., 1952-57; freelance portrait painter and photographer, 1969-89; tchr. drawing and pastel painting Onteora Club, N.Y., 1977; mem. Twilight Park Exhbn. Com., 1983-87. Nat. Home Fashions League scholar, 1953; recipient 1st prize portrait in oil Twilight Park Art Show, 1976, 79, first prize figurative painting-pastel portrait, 1989, 1st prize portrait photography, 1977, 2d prize pastel landscape, 1979, 2d prize for flower photography, 1982, 3d prize oil portrait, 1987; 1st prize for flower photography Onteora Garden Club Show, 1982, 1st and 2d prizes for photography Twilight Park Art Show, 1985, 1st prize a pastel portrait, 1989. Mem. Art Students League (life), Colony Club (chmn. entertainment 1979-84), Onteora Club, Naples Art Assn. Republican. Episcopalian. Address: 14 Sutton Pl S New York NY 10022 also: Lions Gate 2919 Gulf Shore Blvd N Naples FL 33940

HARDY, LOIS LYNN, educational seminar training company executive; b. Seattle, Aug. 20, 1928; d. Stanley Milton and Helen Bernice (Conner) Croonquist; m. John Weston Hardy, July 29, 1951 (div. 1974); children: Sarah Lynn, Laura Lynn; m. Joseph Freeman Smith, Jr., Apr. 18, 1981; stepchildren: Nancy Smith Willis, Martha Smith Dahlquist. BA, Stanford U., 1950, MA, 1952; postgrad., U. Calif., Berkeley, 1957-78, U. San Francisco, 1978-81. Cert. life secondary tchr., life counselor, adminstr., Calif.; lic. career and ednl. counselor, Calif. Tchr., counselor Eastside Union High Sch. Dist., San Jose, Calif., 1951-55; dir. Lois Lynn Hardy Music Studio, Danville, Calif., 1955-69; high sch. tchr. San Ramon Unified Sch. Dist., Danville, 1969-71, counselor, 1971-83; dir. Growth Dynamics Inst., Alamo, Calif., 1976—; instr. Fresno (Calif.) Pacific Coll., 1976-79, Dominican Coll., San Rafael, Calif., 1979—; cons., trainer Personal Dynamics Inst., Mpls., 1976—, Performax Internat., Mpls., 1979—, San Jose Unified Sch. Dist., 1986-86, Novato (Calif.) Unified Sch. Dist., 1985-86, IBM, San Francisco, 1984, corp. and ednl. cons., 1951—. Author: How To Study in High School, 1952, 3d edit., 1973; (with B. Santa) How To Use the Library, 1954; How To Learn Faster and Succeed: A How to Study Workbook For Grades 1-14, 1982, rev., 1985; author various seminars; contbr. numerous articles to profl. jours. Choir dir., organist Community Presbyn. Ch., Danville, 1966-68, elder, 1974-75; speaker to numerous orgns., 1955—. Named Musician of Yr., Contra Costa County, 1978, Counselor of Yr., No. Calif. Personnel and Guidance Assn., 1980; Olive S. Lathrop scholar, 1948, AAUW scholar, 1950; recipient Colonial Dames prize in Am. History, 1950. Mem. Am. Assn. Counseling and Devel., Calif. Assn. Counseling and Devel., Calif. Tchrs. Assn., Calif. Career Guidance Assn., Nat. Speakers Assn., Am. Guild Organists, Stanford U. Alumni Assn., Calif. Assn. for the Gifted, Delta Zeta. Democrat. Presbyterian. Office: Growth Dynamics Inst PO Box 1053 Alamo CA 94507

HARDY, MARY LYNN, banking executive; b. Eupora, Miss., Dec. 29, 1941; d. Lonnie Lee and Violet Marie (Watson) Fortner; m. John C. Hardy, May 29, 1960; children: Patti, Phil, Paula. Student, Wood Coll., 1960. Asst. cashier Nat. Bank of Commerce of Miss., Starkville, Miss., 1970-74; asst. v.p. Nat. Bank of Commerce of Miss., Starkville, 1974-85, v.p., 1985—. Treas. Pilot Club, Starkville, 1987, bd. dirs., 1983-85. Mem. Nat. Assn. Bank Women (state membership chair 1986-87). Republican. Baptist. Office: Nat Bank of Commerce Hwy 82 East Starkville MS 39759

HARDY, VICTORIA ELIZABETH, cultural organization consultant; b. Marion, N.C., Feb. 26, 1947; d. Milton Victor Roth and Bertha Jean (Norris) R.; m. Grant Thomas Holt Jr., Sept. 14, 1968 (div. 1977); m. Michael Carrington Hardy, June 19, 1983; 1 child, Christopher. BS in Edn., U. Mo., 1970; postgrad., So. Ill. U., 1974-75; postgrad. Mgmt. Devel. Program, Stanford U., 1980-81. Pub. sch. tchr. English and Theater, 1970-75; gen. mgr. Miss. River Festival, Edwardsville, Ill., 1975-77; dir. events and svcs. Stanford (Calif.) U., 1977-83; exec. dir. Williams Ctr. for the Arts, Rutherford, N.J., 1983-87; pres., chief exec. officer Music Hall Ctr. for the Arts, Detroit, 1987-89; prin. ArtSoft Mgmt. Svcs., Conn., 1989—; nat. adv. bd. Snowbird (Utah) Inst., 1977—; mem. faculty CUNY, 1986-88. Pres., bd. dirs. New Performance Gallery, San Francisco, 1977-83; bd. dirs. Bay Area Dance Coalition, San Francisco, 1986; mem. Wingspread Conf. Johnson Found., Milw., 1983; mem. USICA study team People's Republic of China, 1981, Mich. Advocates for the Arts (state bd. dirs.). Recipient Gold medal for Community Programs Coun. for Advancement and Support of Edn., Stanford, 1985; named in Creativity in Business Doubleday, 1986. Mem. League of Hist. Am. Theaters. (pres. bd. dirs. 1987-89), Ptnrs. for Livable Places, Nat. Trust for Hist. Preservation, Assn. of Coll. Univ. and Community Arts Adminstrs. (exec. bd. dirs. 1977-83). Democrat. Office: ArtSoft Mgmt Svcs 37 Soundview Rd Guilford CT 06437

HARE, DELORES PRITCHARD, retail executive; b. Hickory, N.C., Feb. 4, 1944; d. Preston Howard Pritchard and Clara Mae (Harris) Pritchard-Sain; m. Wade Elmer Hare, May 5, 1962; children: David Wade, Nancy Carol. BA, Lenoir-Rhyne Coll., 1987; postgrad., Caldwell Community Coll., 1988. Office mgr. Old Hickory Co., Inc., Hickory, 1964-70; mgr. tupperware div. Live Wire Sales, Charlotte, N.C., 1971-74; tchr. aide Hickory City schs., 1974-79; customer svc. rep. Fidelity Fed. Savs. & Loan, Hickory, 1979-80; mgr. customer svc. Forest City Tool, Hickory, 1980—; free-lance instr. various orgns. Troop leader Catawba Valley Girl Scouts U.S., 1975-83. Mem. NAFE. Home: 536 29th St Pl SW Hickory NC 28602

HARE, SANDRA FLORENCE, internist, public health consultant; b. Phila., Oct. 23, 1952; d. John Dalrymple Hare and Hortense Cecelia (Daniels) Morris; m. Walter John Drubka, May 30, 1984. BA, Clark U., 1974; postgrad. in medicine, Loyola U., Chgo., 1974-75; MPH, U. Ill., Chgo., 1978; MD, Chgo. Med. Sch., 1983. Diplomate Am. Bd. Internal Medicine, Nat. Bd. Med. Examiners. Tchr. chemistry and physics Wyoming Sem., Kingston, Pa., 1975-76; rsch. asst., assoc. U. Ill. Sch. Pub. Health, 1976-78, occupational medicine cons., 1983-84; preceptor Western Ala. Health Svcs., Eutaw, 1980; cons. Carnow, Conibear & Assocs., Chgo., 1983-84; resident in internal medicine Mercy Hosp. and Med. Ctr., Chgo., 1984-87; attending staff physician Nat. Health Svc. Corps of Pub. Health Svc., Chgo., 1987—; attending physician Cook County Hosp., Chgo., 1987—; clin. asst. in medicine U. Ill. Med. Ctr., Chgo., 1985-87. Chmn. Big Bro.-Big Sister Program, Worcester, Mass., 1972-74; bd. dirs. Sheridan Square Condominium Assn., Evanston, Ill., 1987-89. 1st lt. USPHS, 1978-79. AAUW scholar, 1970, Jonas Clark scholar, 1970-74, USPHS scholar, 1979-83. Mem. AMA (physician recognition award 1987), ACP, Ill. Med. Soc., Chgo. Med. Soc. Democrat. Roman Catholic. Office: Cermak Health Svcs 2800 S California Ave Chicago IL 60608

HARGRAVE, CECILLE TERRY, interior designer; b. Paris, Tex., July 23, 1917; d. Carl C. and Una Lila (Sealy) Terry. B.A., East Tex. State U., 1938; postgrad. So. Meth. U. Downtown Coll., 1952-53, Little Sch. of Fine Arts, 1953; m. Glenn M. Hargrave, Oct. 9, 1937 (dec. Dec. 1984). Interior designer, specifiers-interior cons. Garland (Tex.) City Hall, ret.; guest editor Tex. Contractor, 1954, Furniture Age, 1956. Recipient Instns. Mag.'s award for Sam Rayburn Meml. Student Center, 1964; named Disting. Alumna, East Tex. State U., 1975. Mem. K.T. Ednl. Found. (hon.), East Tex. State U. Alumni Assn. (pres. Dallas county chpt.), Women in Architecture, Dallas Council World Affairs, Southwest Homefurnishing Assn., AAUW, Alpha Alpha Gamma, Chi Omega. Episcopalian. Clubs: Park Cities Toastmistress (founder, past pres.) (Dallas), Merriman Park Women's (v.p., pres. 1985-86). Projects include Sam Rayburn Meml. Student Center, East Tex. State U. Commerce, Tex., Midway Park Elem. Sch., Euless, Tex., 1st Nat. Bank, Garland, 1st Security Nat. Bank Dallas, 1st Security Fin. Systems, Inc., Dallas, Parkdale State Bank, Corpus Christi, Tex., Dallas Mus. Fine Arts, Republic Bank Garland, Parkdale Bank, Corpus Christi. Home: 6938 Winchester St Dallas TX 75231

HARGRAVE, SARAH QUESENBERRY, marketing, public relations company executive; b. Mt. Airy, N.C., Dec. 11, 1944; d. Teddie W. and Lois Knight (Slusher) Quesenberry. Student, Radford Coll., 1963-64, Va. Poly. Inst. and State U., 1964-67. Mgmt. trainee Thalhimer Bros. Dept. Store, Richmond, Va., 1967-68; Cen. Va. fashion and publicity dir. Sears Roebuck & Co., Richmond, 1968-73; nat. decorating sch. coord. Sears Roebuck & Co., Chgo., 1973-74, nat. dir. bus. and profl. women's programs, 1974-76; v.p., treas., program dir. Sears-Roebuck Found., Chgo., 1976-87, program mgr. corp. contbns. and memberships, 1981-84, dir. corp. mktg. and pub. affairs, 1984-87; v.p. personal fin. svcs. and mktg. Northern Trust Co., Chgo., 1987-89, Hargrave Mktg./Pub. Rels., 1989—. Bd. dirs. Am. Assembly Collegiate Schs. Bus., 1979-82, mem. vis. com., 1979-82, mem. fin. and audit com., 1980-82, mem. task force on doctoral supply and demand, 1980-82; mem. Com. for Equal Opportunity for Women, 1976-81; chmn., 1978-79, 80-81; mem. bus. adv. coun. Walter E. Heller Coll. Bus. Adminstrn., Roosevelt U., 1979-89; co-dir. Ill. Internat. Women's Yr. Ctr., 1975. Named Outstanding Young Women of Yr. Ill., 1976; named Women of Achievement State Street Bus. and Profl. Woman's Club, 1978. Mem. Assn. Humanistic Psychology, Am. Home Econs. Assn., Fashion Group, Eddystone Condominium Assn. (v.p. 1978-86), Am. Mktg. Assn., Chgo. Artists Coalition, Profl. Women's Network. Home and Office: 34 Fairlawn Ave Daly City CA 94015

HARGUS, VICKY LYN, business and legal administrator; b. Shawnee, Okla., Oct. 23, 1962; d. James Edward and Elma (Dunsmore) Hargus. AA, Aims Community Coll., Greeley, Colo., 1982; BS, Colo. State U., 1986; MBA, Regis Coll., Denver, 1990. Exec. sec. Farr Feeders, Inc., Greeley, 1978-80; office mgr. High Plains Regional Library System, Greeley, 1983-84; MIS and billing mgr. Fischer, Brown, Huddleson & Gunn, Attys. at Law, Ft. Collins, Colo., 1984-86; adminstrv. asst. Foxhoven's, Inc., Sterling, Colo., 1987-89; owner Hargus, Ltd., Sterling, Colo., 1989—. Recipient various scholarships and grants. Mem. NAFE (bd. dirs. N.E. Colo. affiliate 1987—), AAUW, Am. Mgmt. Assn., Internat. Thespian Soc. (best supporting actress), Golden Key, Sigma Iota Epsilon. Republican. Roman Catholic. Office: Hargus Ltd PO Box 13 Sterling CO 80751-0013

HARKINS, KIMBERLY KAY, auditor; b. Monterrey, Tenn., June 25, 1959; d. Thurman M. and Sara Jo (Bowden) Stamps. BA in Polit. Sci., U. Tenn., 1989; postgrad., Calif. Western Sch. Law, 1989—. Mgr., auditor Days Inn, Knoxville, Tenn., 1985-89. Staff writer Calif. Western Law Rev., 1990—. Sec. West Knoxville Rep. Club, 1989. Sgt. USAF, 1977-81. Mem. ABA, So. Assn. Polit. Sci., Phi Beta Kappa, Phi Alpha Delta, Gamma Beta Phi, Phi Eta Sigma, Pi Sigma Alpha. Home: 13326 Community Rd Apt 57 Poway CA 92064 Office: 350 Cedar St San Diego CA 92101

HARKINS, LIDA E., state legislator, educator; b. Jersey City, Jan. 24, 1944; d. Paul Vincent and Lida Cecelia (Higgins) McMahon; children: Michael, Julie, Joseph; m. Arthur Edward Harkins. BA, Regis Coll., 1966; cert. in pub. policy mgmt., Boston Coll., 1986. Tchr. Mass. Pub. Schs., 1966-68; dir. sch. bus. tng. partnership The Edn. Co-op., Wellesley, Mass., 1988-89; state legislator 13th Norfolk Dist., Needham, Dover and Medfield, Mass., 1989—; bd. dirs. Charles River Workshop for Retarded Citizens, Needham, 1989. Mem. com. Needham Sch., 1976-82, chmn., 1979-80; mem. Needham Town Meeting, 1976—; chmn. Needham Dem. Town Com., 1983-85; bd. dirs. Needham area Boy Scouts Am., 1989. Recipient Alumnae Achievement award Boston Coll., 1989, Golden Donkey award Rendon Report Annual Polit. awards, 1989. Mem. Women Dems. of Dover and Needham (bd. dirs.). Roman Catholic. Home: 14 Hancock Rd Needham MA 02192 Office: State House Rm 473B Boston MA 02133

HARKNESS, MABEL GLEASON, retired librarian; b. Oil City, Pa., Jan. 20, 1913; d. Charles Wilcox and Mabel Amy (Fulton) Gleason; m. Benjamin Olney, Mar. 23, 1946 (dec. 1963); m. Bernard Emerson Harkness, Sept. 5, 1964 (dec. 1980). AB, U. Rochester, 1935, MA, 1962. Cert. libr., N.Y. Libr. Stromberg-Carlson Co., Rochester, N.Y., 1942-51, Garden Ctr. Rochester, 1953-67, Monroe County (N.Y.) Bookmobile, 1952-53; now ret.; vol. cataloger Geneva (N.Y.) Hist. Soc.; editor Gleam mag., Rochester Poetry Soc., 1945, Engr.'s Notebook, Stromberg-Carlson Co., 1946-50, Garden Ctr. Bull., 1955-67; co-founder, past pres. Western N.Y. chpt. Spl. Libr. Assn., 1945. Compiles: Harkness Seedlist Handbook, 1986 (Worth award for botan./horticultural writing Am. Rock Garden Soc.); contbr. articles on horticulture, local history to various publs. Trustee Keuka Coll., Keuka Park, N.Y., 1971-80, now emeritus. Mem. AAUW (life), Am. Rock Garden Soc. (life), Alpine Garden Soc. (Eng.), Scottish Rock Garden Club (life). Republican. Episcopalian. Home: 5169 Pre-Emption Rd Geneva NY 14456

HARLACHER, BETH ANN, financial analyst; b. E. Stroudsburg, Pa., May 19, 1962; d. Anthony charles and Elizabeth Ann (Naismith) H. BS, Georgetown U., 1984; MBA, Boston U., 1988. Cert. educator of English as Second Lang. Lang. cons. Japanese Ministry Edn., Saitama, 1984-85; adminstrv. asst. Overseas Econ. Cooperation Fund of Japan, Washington, 1985-86; educator, cons. Interac, Tokyo, Tokyo, Japan, 1986; sr. corp. fin. analyst Norton Co., Worcester, Mass., 1988—; bd. dirs. Worcester (Mass.) Children's Theatre, 1989. Mem. Am. Mgmt. Assn., Nat. Assn. Credit Mgmt. Republican. Lutheran. Home: 8 Greenview St Apt 108 Framingham MA 01701 Office: Norton Co 120 Front St Worcester MA 01608

HARLAN, ESTLE MAE, business consultant, legal assistant; b. Portland, Oreg., Aug. 7, 1939; d. Vaughn Estle and Mae Marie (VanHorn) A.; m. Robert T. Butler, June 21, 1957 (div. 1972); children: Randy, Cindy Butler Bieker; m. Dale Morgan Harlan, June 13, 1975; stepchildren: Janice Harlan Raisl, David, James, Nancy Harlan Henderson. AS, Clackamas Community Coll., Oreg., 1977; BS, Marylhurst Coll., 1984; MPA, Lewis and Clark Coll., 1988. Bar: Oreg 1978; cert. legal asst. Legal asst. Dale M. Harlan, P.C., Milwaukie, Oreg., 1958-; owner, mgr. Harlan Bus. Cons. Inc., Milwaukie, Oreg., 1982—. Contbr. articles to trade publs. Bd. dirs. Clackamas Community Coll., 1985—, chmn., 1989-90; active Milwaukie (Oreg.) Parks and Recreation Commn., 1982, bus. adv. task force North Clackamas Sch. Dist. 12, 1986-88; precinct committeewomen Clackamas County Dem. Com., 1982—; campaign chmn. for county commr., 1982, 86—; mem. solid waste adv. com. Met. Svc. Dist., Portland, 1986—, recycling adv. com. Portland Dept. Environ. Quality, 1986-88, Gresham (Oreg.) Solid Waste Citizens Adv. Com., 1988-89, Portland Solid Waste Oversight Com., 1988-89; organist Clackamas Park Friends Ch., 1972—. Mem. Oreg. San. Svc. Inst. (cons. 1982—), Clackamas County Legal Secs. Assn. (pres. 1977-79, legal sec. of yr. 1979), North Clackamas C. of C. (adminstrv. affairs com. 1982—), Am. Hist. Soc. Germans from Russia, Rotary (Paul Harris fellow 1988, organist Milwaukie chpt.). Democrat. Mem. Evangelical Ch. Office: Harlan Bus Cons Inc 2202 SE Lake Rd Milwaukie OR 97222

HARLAN, JANE ANN, lawyer; b. Newton, Iowa, Oct. 8, 1947; d. Ellis and Julia (Blount) H.; m. Adel Zahian Hanna, 1971 (div. 1981); children: Samuel, Laura, Magda. BA, Drake U., 1969; JD, DePaul U., 1974. Bar: Ill. 1975, Wis. 1978, Iowa 1984. Pvt. practice Chgo., 1975-78, Greendale, Wis., 1978-84, Newton, 1984—. Cooperating atty. Wis. Civil Liberties Union, Milw., 1978-84; chairperson S.W. Suburban Dems., Milwaukee County, Wis., 1982-83. Recipient Outstanding Svc. plaque, Milw. Dems., 1983, citation for outstanding contbns. Wis. State Assembly, 1984. Mem. Iowa Bar Assn., Assn. for Retarded Citizens, NOW, Nat. Child Rights Alliance. Office: 300 Midtown Bldg Newton IA 50208

HARLAN, JEAN DURGIN, psychologist, writer, consultant; b. Racine, Wis., Sept. 9, 1924; d. Elmer Ralph and Pearl (Trumbull) Durgin; m. William Harrell Harlan, Oct. 5, 1946 (div. 1975); children: Betsy, Anne, John, Susan, Julie. BS, U. Wis., 1945; MS, Ohio U., 1968, PhD, 1978. Lic. psychologist, Wis. Asst. prof. child devel. Ohio U., Athens, 1969-79; sr. researcher Ohio State U., Columbus, 1979-82; freelance cons., writer, Racine, 1982-84; psychologist Lighthouse Counseling Assocs., Racine, 1984—; editorial cons. Merrill Pub. Co., Columbus, 1977-84, Scott, Foresman Co., Glenview, Ill., 1981-88; contbg. editor Curriculum Innovations, Inc., Highland Park, Ill., 1986-88; sci. edn. cons. Sesame Street, Children's TV Workshop, N.Y.C., 1988. Author: Science Experiences for the Early Childhood Years, 1976, 4th edit., 1988, Kindergarten Science, 1988; contbr. articles to profl. jours., children's stories to various publs. Fulbright grantee, Punjab, India, 1963. Mem. Am. Psychol. Assn., Nat. Assn. for Edn. Young Children (editorial bd., cons. editor 1987—). Office: Lighthouse Counseling Assoc 5605 Washington Ave Racine WI 53406

HARLAN, ROMA CHRISTINE, portrait painter; b. Warsaw, Ind.; d. Charles William and Fern (McCormick) H. Student, Purdue U., Art Inst. Chgo. Art chmn. D.C. Fedn. Women's Clubs. One-man shows: Lake Shore Club, Chgo., Little Gallery of Esquire Theatre, Chgo., Purdue U., West Lafayette, Ind., Hoosier Salon, Indpls., All-Ill. Soc. Fine Arts, Chgo., Kaufmann's Galery, Chgo., Lafayette (Ind.) Art Assn., Arts Club, Washington, George Washington U., Washington; exhibited numerous group shows; represented in permanent collections at Dept. of Navy Naval Hist. Ctr., Washington, D.C. Fed. Ct. House, SEC, Nat. Presbyn. Ch., Va. Theol. Sem., Alexandria, Nat. Guard Bldg., St. Stephen's Sch., Alexandria, Washington Nat. Fedn. Bus. and Profl. Women's Clubs, Washington, Children's Hosp. Nat. Med. Ctr., Alexandria, Lakeshore Club, Chgo., Purdue U. Dau. Ind. scholar. Mem. DAR, Ind. State Art Assn., Arts Club (Washington). Presbyterian. Address: 1600 S Joyce St A1607 Arlington VA 22202

HARLAN, SUSAN NEGLEY, marketing representative; b. Indpls., Jan. 12, 1949; d. Harold Hoover and Helen (Davies) Negley; m. Wayne E. Harlan, June 27, 1981; 1 child, Timothy James. BA, Ind. U., 1976. Pub. info. asst. Office of the Mayor City of Indpls., 1978-80; cons. pub. rels. Indpls. and Nashua, N.H., 1981-85; pub. rels., mktg. cons. Nashua, 1986—. Mem. Nashua Long Range Planning Commn., 1984-86, Nashua Child Care Commn.; commr. N.H. Commn. on the Status of Women, Concord, N.J., 1986—; rep. dist. 25 N.H. Ho. of Reps., 1988—. Mem. Women Communications, Inc. (founder, pres. N.H. chpt. 1986), Nashua Coll. Club. Republican. Mem. Ch. of Christ. Home: 32 MacDonald Dr Nashua NH 03062

HARLAND, BARBARA FERGUSON, nutritionist, educator; b. Chgo., Apr. 16, 1925; d. Frank Cleveland and Dorothy Sargent (Brown) Ferguson; m. James Wallace Harland, Sept. 6, 1947; children: Joseph A., Jane, Janet. BS, Iowa State U., 1946; MS, U. Wash., 1949; PhD, U. Md., 1971. Registered dietitian, lic. dietitian, lic. nutritionist. Chief dietitian Lakeview Meml. Hosp., Stillwater, Minn., 1946-47; dietitian U. Wash., Seattle, 1947-49; nutrition instr. U. Ind., Jeffersonville, 1964-65; math., sci. substitute tchr. Montgomery County High Schs., Md., 1966-67; nutrition instr. U. Md., College Park, 1967-70; rsch. biologist nutrition div. FDA, Washington, 1971-84; assoc. prof. nutrition and food sch. human ecology Howard U., Washington, 1984—; referee for Phytate Assn. Official Analytical Chemists, Washington, 1980—; mem. Howard U. Instl. Animal Care and Use Com., Washington, 1984—. Sr. author: (book chpt.) World Review of Nutrition and Diets, 1987; co-author: (textbook) Minerals, Nutrition and Metabolism, 1989; contbr. articles to profl. jours. Chmn. adminstrv. coun. Concord-St. Andrews United Meth. Ch., Bethesda, Md., 1977-83, vice-chmn. 1988—, planning com. 1984-88, peace advocacy com., 1984-88. Faculty and corp. rsch. grantee Howard U., Washington, 1985-87, rsch. grantee Procter & Gamble, Cin., 1988. Mem. Am. Inst. Nutrition, Am. Dietetic Assn., Am. Chem. Soc., Soc. Exptl. Biology and Medicine, Soc. Nutrition Edn., Kappa Omicron Nu (advisor Howard U. chpt.), Congl. Country Club (chmn. tennis com. Potomac, Md. 1982-84, chmn. paddle tennis com. 1988—). Republican. Methodist. Home: 7929 Robison Rd Bethesda MD 20817 Office: Howard U Dept Human Nutrition & Food Sch Human Ecology Washington DC 20059

HARLAND, MARY KATHRYN HOLTAN, business and economics educator; b. Forest City, Iowa, Mar. 3, 1946; d. Hans Oscar and Ruth (Hermanson) Holtan; m. Thomas Robert Harland, May 4, 1974. A.A., Waldorf Coll., Forest City, 1966; B.A., Wartburg Coll., Waverly, Iowa, 1969; M.A., Mankato State U. (Minn.), 1981. Instr., Chicago Lakes Area Schs., Minn., 1970-72, Hennepin Tech. Inst., 1972-77, Albert Lea Area Vo-Tech Inst. (Minn.), 1977-80; asst. prof. bus. and econs. Waldorf Coll., 1980—, acad. chair faculty; adj. faculty mem. Mankato State U., Minn., 1984; mem. evaluation team North Cen. Assn. Colls. and Schs.; cons., lectr. in field. Author ednl. materials. Mem. NAFE, Assn. Supervision and Curriculum Devel., Delta Pi Epsilon. Republican. Lutheran. Avocations: needlework, reading, bicycling. Home: RR 1 Box 44 Forest City IA 50436

HARLASS, SHERRY ELLEN POOL, magazine editor; b. Bourne, Mass., Jan. 2, 1961; d. Sydney Smith and Shirley Ruth (Fisher) Pool; m. Mark Paul Harlass, July 17, 1982. Student, S.W. Tex. State U., 1979-80; BA in Journalism, Midwestern State U., Wichita Falls, Tex., 1982. Reporter Wichita Falls Record News, 1980-82, Wichita Falls Times, 1982-83; staff writer Branch-Smith, Inc., Ft. Worth, 1984-85, prodn. editor, 1986-88, mng. editor, 1988—. Contbr. articles to newspapers. Named one of the Notable Women of Tex., 1983. Mem. Women in Communications Inc., Soc. Profl. Journalists, Nat. Fedn. Press Women, Tex. Press Women, Nat. Assn. Women in Horiculture, Mary/Martha Soc. (sec. 1986-88), Texas Rangers Women's Club (sec. 1986-88). Lutheran. Home: 1708 Carla Ave Arlington TX 76014

HARLEY, NAOMI HALLDEN, radiation specialist, environmental medicine educator; b. N.Y.C., Aug. 4, 1932; d. Carl Edward and Ida Wilson (Palmer) Hallden; m. John Henry Harley, Sept. 11, 1964. B.S., Cooper Union, N.Y.C., 1959; M.S., NYU, 1967, Ph.D., 1971, A.P.C., 1983. Phys. scientist U.S. Atomic Energy Commn., N.Y.C., 1951-65; research prof. environ. medicine NYU, 1965—; council mem., sci. com. chmn. Nat. Council on Radiation Protection and Measurement, Washington, 1982—. Contbr. articles to profl. jours. USPHS fellow, 1965. Mem. Health Physics Soc., AAAS, N.Y. Acad. Sci. Democrat. Club: NYU Alumni. Office: NYU Sch of Medicine Dept Environ Medicine 550 1st Ave New York NY 10016

HARLIN, MARILYN MILER, marine botany educator, researcher, consultant; b. Oakland, Calif., May 30, 1934; d. George T. and Gertrude (Turula) Miler; m. John E. Harlin II, Oct. 25, 1955 (dec. Feb. 1966); children: John E. III, Andrea M. Harlin Cilento. AB, Stanford U., 1955, MA, 1956; PhD, U. Wash., 197l. Instr. Am. Coll. Switzerland and Leysin, 1964-66; asst. prof. Pacific Marine Sta., Dillon Beach, Calif., 1969; asst. prof. marine biology U. R.I., Kingston, 197l-75, assoc. prof., 1975-83, prof., 1983—; guest scientist Atlantic Regional Lab., Halifax, N.S., Can., 973-78; hon. vis. prof. LaTrobe U., Bundoora, Victoria, Australia, 1984; resource person R.I. Coastal Resource Mgmt. Coun., 1980—, R.I. Dept. Environ. Mgmt., 1980; cons. Applied Sci. Assocs., Narragansett, R.I., 1988—. Co-editor: Marine Ecology, 1976, Freshwater and Marine Plants of Rhode Island, 1988. Bd. dirs. Westminster Unitarian Ch., East Greenwich, R.I., 1987; bd. govs. Women's Ctr., Kingston, 1989—. Grantee NOAA, 1975-81, Dept. Environ. Mgmt./EPA, 1989-91. Mem. Internat. Phycological Soc., Phycological Soc. Am. (editor newsletter 1982-84, editorial bd. 1988—), N.E. Algal Soc. (exec. com.), Sigma Xi (pres., sec. 19779-82). Office: U RI Dept Botany Kingston RI 02881

HARLOW, LISA LAVOIE, psychometrics educator; b. Hartford, Conn., Dec. 3, 1951; d. Jean Paul and Mary Bernadine (Heslin) Lavoie; m. Gary Russell Harlow, June 10, 1978; 1 child, Rebecca Marie. BA, Calif. State U., Fullerton, 1979, MA, 1981; PhD, U. Calif., L.A., 1985. Teaching asst. Calif. State U., 1978-80, instr. statistics, 1980; rsch. teaching assoc. U. Calif., 1980-85; asst. prof. psychometrics U. R.I., Kingston, 1985—. Reviewer of jours.; contbr. articles to profl. jours.; cons. editor Jour. Personality and Social Psychology, 1989—. Researcher, cons. Brown U. AIDS Project, Providence, 1988—. Grantee Orton Soc., Oak Found., 1988, faculty U. R.I., 1986—. Mem. Soc. Multivariate Exptl. Psychology, Psychometric Soc., Am. Psychol. Assn., Am. Psychol. Soc., AAAS, Am. Ednl. Rsch. Assn., Eastern Psychol. Assn., New Eng. Psychol. Assn., Soc. Psychologists in Addictive Behaviors, Assn. Prof. Acad. Women, Sigma Xi. Democrat. Roman Catholic. Home: 59 Mill Pond Rd Slowm RI 02877 Office: Univ R I Dept Psychology Kingston RI 02881-0808

HARMAN, JULIE ANN, television producer, director; b. Covina, Calif., July 11, 1958; d. Julian Arthur and Patricia (Kozlowski) Lobosky; m. Edward W. Harbert III, June 16, 1979 (div. 1985); m. Paul David Harman, Oct. 6, 1988. BS magna cum laude, Boston U., 1979. Rsch. analyst Home Box Office, N.Y.C., 1979-81; program dir. Nat. Subscription TV, L.A., 1981-83; producer Alan Landsburg Prodns., L.A., 1983-85; producer, dir. Sta. KABC-TV, L.A.; dir. TV Programming Enterprises, N.Y.C., 1986-87; freelance dir., 1987; producer, dir. Fox TV, Washington, 1988—. Recipient Emmy award, 1988. Mem. Dirs. Guild of Am., Am. Film Inst. Democrat. Roman Catholic.

HARMAN, MARLA ZELENE, lawyer; b. Harrisonburg, Va., Jan. 9, 1957; d. John and Pauline (Ruddle) H. BA, Bridgewater Coll., 1979; JD, W.Va. U., Morgantown, 1982. Lic. real estate broker. Self-employed Franklin, W.Va., 1982--. Dist. chmn. UDC, Colonial Dames DAR; bd. dirs. Family Crisis Ctr. Mem. ABA, W.Va. Bar Assn. Presbyterian. Home: Reeds Creek Rd Franklin WV 26807 Office: 1 S Main St Franklin WV 26807

HARMEL, HILDA HERTA See PIERCE, HILDA RUBIN

HARMELL, PAMELA HERSH, psychologist; b. L.A., Dec. 20, 1947. BA, UCLA, 1983; MA, Calif. Sch. Profl. Psychology, L.A., 1985, PhD, 1987. Intern, trainee MidValley Community Mental Health, El Monte, Calif., 1983-84, Chabad Residential, L.A., 1984-85; intern Verdugo Mental Health, Glendale, Calif., 1985-86, Wright Inst., L.A., 1986-87; post-doctoral fellow Cedars-Sinai Med. Ctr., L.A., 1987-88; pvt. practice Santa Monica, Calif., 1989—; psychologist, case reviewer Managed Health Network, L.A., 1990—; instr. Santa Monica Coll., 1987—; lectr., cons. in field, 1989—. Mem. Am. Psychol. Assn., Calif. Psychol. Assn., L.A. County Psychol. Assn. Office: 2730 Wilshire Blvd Ste 350 Santa Monica CA 90403

HARMEN, WENDY SUSAN, homecare specialist; b. New Brunswick, N.J., Oct. 19, 1960; d. John Johnston and Elaine Mason (Oberkotter) H. BS in Nursing, Cedar Crest Coll., 1982. Registered nurse Pa., N.J. Staff nurse Allentown (Pa.) Osteopathic Hosp., 1982-84; staff nurse, ICU, CCU Mercer Med. Ctr., Trenton, N.J., 1984-86; emergency dept. staff nurse Helene Fuld Med. Ctr., Trenton, N.J., 1987-88; homecare supr. Alan Healthcare Svcs., Hamilton Sq., N.J., 1989—. Vol. emergency med. tech. Lawrence Twp. 1st Aid Squad, 1985—, pres., 1987, lt., 1988—, sec. 1988—; deacon, choir mem. Lawrence Rd. Presbyn. Ch. Recipient Outstanding Svc. award Lawrence Twp. 1st Aid Squad, 1987. Presbyterian. Home: 16 Daniell Ct Lawrenceville NJ 08648 Office: Alan Healthcare Svcs 1700 Whitehorse Hamilton Sq Rd Ste B-4 Hamilton Square NJ 08690

HARMENING, DENISE M., clinical laboratory science educator, consultant; b. Balt., Jan. 24, 1952; d. George and Catherine (Leimbach) H. BS in Med. Tech., U. Md., Balt., 1974, MS in Medicine and Med. Tech., 1976, PhD in Clin. Pathology, 1981. Clin. asst. prof. Georgetown U. Sch. Medicine, Washington, 1987-88; clin. assoc. prof. program in med. tech. Cath. U. Am., Washington, 1987-88; prof., chmn. dept. lab. sci. Thomas Jefferson U., Phila., 1987-90; asst. prof., asst. dir. program in med. tech. U. Md. Sch. Medicine, Balt., 1982-85, dir. continuing edn. program in med. tech., 1984-85, assoc. prof. dept. path., 1987-88, prof., chmn. dept. medicine and rsch. tech., 1990—; dir. ednl. svcs. Am. Assn. Blood Banks, Washington, 1982-84, insp. accrediation program, 1985-88. Author: Clinical Hematology and Fundamentals, 1987, Modern Blood Banking, 1989, (with I. Isbister) Clinical Hematology, 1988; patentee cellular preservation field. Recipient teaching award Pathology Bds. Study Group, Inc., 1984; Clay Adams rsch. grantee, 1979; fellow Wallace Internat.-RMIT, Melbourne, Australia, 1988. Mem. Am. Assn. Blood Banks, Am. Soc. Clin Pathologists (cert. med. technologist), Am. Soc. Hematology, Am. Soc. Med. Technologists (chmn. hematology-hemostasis-sci. sect. region II, 1985, 87, 89, editor-in-chief CLS jour. 1987-89, Outstanding Svc. award 1988), Md. Soc. Med. Technologists (pres. 1987-88), ISBT, ISTH, Phi Kappa Phi, Omicron Sigma. Office: U Md Dept Med and Rsch Tech 32 Green St Baltimore MD 20201

HARMEYER, MARYELLEN, writer; b. Oakland, Calif., Feb. 12, 1965; d. Joseph Robert and Mary Catherine (Martin) Harmeyer. BA in English, U. Pacific, 1987. Staff writer Neo-Life Co. Am., Fremont, Calif., 1988—, editor newsletter, 1989—. Contbr. articles to Counselor mag. Mem. NAFE, Profl. Businesswomen's Conf.

HARMON, ARTICE WARD, occupational therapist; b. Hughes, Ark., Oct. 2, 1940; d. William Oscar and Alice Williams (Turner) Ward; BS, Ind. U., 1973; MPH, U. Ill., 1975; m. Luther Harmon, Dec. 5, 1959. Occupational therapy intern St. Elizabeth's Hosp., Washington, 1973, Helen Hayes Rehab. Hosp., W. Haverstraw, N.Y., 1973; staff occupational therapist Mercy Hosp. and Med. Center, Chgo., 1973-76; dir. occupational therapy program Westside Parents Ctr., of Retarded Children United, Chgo., 1976-77; head occupational therapy dept. Americana Health Care Ctr., Champaign, Ill., 1977-81; dir. occupational therapy program Chgo. State U., 1981—, acting dean Coll. Allied Health, 1985-86, 89; program devel. specialist, 1986—; guest lectr. allied health curriculum U. Ill., Champaign, 1975, grad. teaching assoc. occupational therapy curriculum Coll. Assoc. Health Professions, 1978-80, instr., 1980-81; chmn. steering com. Ill. Coun. Occupational Therapy Edn.; coord. statewide internship program Ill. Bd. Govs. State Colls. and Univs., Springfield, Ill., 1986-87; cons. in field. Mem. 1st congl. dist. of Ill. Congl. Health Adv. Task Force, 1988—. Mem. Am. Occupational Therapy Assn. (accreditation evaluator 1989—), Ill. Occupational Therapy Assn., Am. Pub. Health Assn., Am. Vocat. Assn., Ill. Vocat. Assn., Am. Vocat. Ednl. Rsch. Assn., Am. Soc. Allied Health Professions, People United to Save Humanity, Phi Delta Kappa, Kappa Delta Pi. Roman Catholic. Home: 5020 S Lake Shore Dr #806-N Chicago IL 60615 Office: Chgo State U Coll Allied Health 95th St at King Dr Chicago IL 60628

HARMON, BARBARA NELLE, financial director; b. Marion, Ohio, Oct. 25, 1944; d. Charles Debusman and Marjory June (Potter) H.; m. James Nash, Dec. 27, 1974 (div. Dec. 1977). BA, Lake Erie Coll., 1966; MS in Acctg., Colo. State U., 1980. CPA. Sr. acct. Touche Ross & Co., Denver, 1980-84; fin. analyst Ideal Basic Industry, Denver, 1984-85; supr. acctg. and control Stearns Catalytic, Denver, 1985-86; from asst. controller to controller Wood Bros. Homes subs. MDC Holdings, Denver, 1986-87; controller MDC Land Co. and MDC Constrn. Co., Denver, 1986; fin. and acctg. dir. Byerly and Co., Denver, 1987—. Del. People to People Ambassador Program for Tax, Acctg. and Auditing to the Peoples Republic of China. Mem. AICPA, Colo. Soc. CPAs, Beta Alpha Psi (acctg. chpt.). Democrat.

HARMON, CHARLOTTE BUCHWALD, writer, news and commentary; b. N.Y.C., May 26, 1916; d. Ephraim and Jennie (Heyman) B.; m. Lewis Harmon, June 27, 1938; 1 child, Jill. Student, Columbia U., 1936-37. Radio commentator Sta. WMCA, WNEW, WNBC, N.Y.C., 1938-48; producer, dir. Chapel Playhouse, Guilford, Conn., 1946-50, Clinton Playhouse, 1950-58; editor Backstage Pubs, N.Y.C., 1960-77; writer New England Appraisers Newsletter, Ludlow, Vt., 1961-76, 81—. Author: Book Broadway In A Barn 1947, How to Break into The Theatre 1950, The Flea Market Entrepeneur 1988; freelance writer. Home: 205 West 57th New York NY 10019

HARMON, CYNTHIA ANN, associate producer TV; b. Pitts., Sept. 14, 1956; d. James Eldon and Barbara Jean (Blancho) H. BS, E. Tex. State U., 1986. Recreational therapist Walter E. Ferwald State Sch., Waltham, Mass., 1977-84; assoc. producer KOFW-TV, Dallas, 1986-90, Diamond P Sports/TNN, Nashville, 1990—; prodn. asst. Diamond P Sports, Nashville, 1986—. field producer/editor television show NHRA Today, 1990. Mem. Soc. Profl. Journalists, Alpha Epsilon Rho, Alpha Chi, Phi Theta Kappa. Democrat. Roman Catholic. Office: Diamond P Sports 107 Music City Circle 103 Nashville TN 37214

HARMON, EMMA LEE, architectural designer, business owner, councilwoman; b. Sharpsville, Pa., Apr. 29, 1939; d. James McKarney Supplee and Anne (Woods) Thompson; m. William Hayes Harmon, Sept. 1, 1962 (div. 1984); 1 child, James McKarney Harmon. BArch, Kent (Ohio) State U., 1962. Drafter W.H. Harmon Architects, Orlando, Fla., 1970-73; pres., owner The Plan Shop, Inc., Orlando and Palm Bay, Fla., 1973-87, The Plan Place, Inc., Palm Bay, 1987—; pres. Engring. & Design Concepts, Palm Bay, 1986—; vice chmn. substance abuse program Broken Glass, Valkaria, Fla. Mem. coun. City of Palm Bay, 1989—; mem. League of Citys, Brevard County, Fla., 1989—, East Cen. Fla. Planning Coun., Orlando, 1989—; mem. Federated Rep. Women, South Brevard County, 1989—; mem. exec. com. Brevard County Reps., 1990—. Mem. Home Builders and Contractors Brevard County (assoc., Assoc. of the Month 1989), Bldg. Ofcls. Assn. Brevard County (assoc., Assoc. of the Yr. 1989), South Brevard Profl. Women's Network, Drafter's Guild (organizer), Palm Bay C. of C., Greater South Brevard C. of C. (growth mgmt. com.), Exch. Club (chpt. pres., charter pres., charter pres. Yellow Umbrella child abuse prevention program for South Brevard 1988-89). Home: 1482 Meadowbrook Rd NE Palm Bay FL 32905 Office: The Plan Place 1398 Palm Bay Rd Palm Bay FL 32905

HARMON, GAIL MCGREEVY, lawyer; b. Kansas City, Kans., Mar. 15, 1943; d. Milton and Barbara (James) McGreevy; m. John W. Harmon, June 11, 1966; children: James, Eve. BA cum laude, Radcliffe Coll., 1965; JD cum laude, Columbia U., 1969. Bar: Mass. 1970, D.C. 1976, U.S. Dist. Ct. D.C. Assoc. Gaston Snow & Ely Bartlett, Boston, 1970-75, Steptoe & Johnson, Washington, 1975-76, Roisman, Kessler & Cashdan, Washington, 1976-77; ptnr. Harmon, Curran & Tousley, Washington, 1977—. Pres. Women's Legal Def. Fund, 1982-84. Democrat. Episcopalian.

HARMON, JUDITH TRIVETTE, public relations executive, counselor; b. Jonancy, Ky., Aug. 22, 1938; d. Charles Franklin and Helen (Hubbard) Trivette; m. Harold Gilbert Harmon; children: Nicole Diane, Hillary Lynn. BA, U. Ky., 1961. Women's editor Lexington (Ky.) Challenge, 1961-62; adminstrv. asst., pub. rels. spokesperson U. Ky. Med. Ctr., Lexington, 1962-64; sec. DeKalb Sch. of Graphic Arts, Atlanta, 1975-76; community rels. dir. Henrietta Egleston Hosp. for Children, Atlanta, 1976-79; communications mgr. pub. rels. and advt. dept. Blue Cross & Blue Shield of Ga., Atlanta, 1979-83; sr. account exec. Bowes/Hanlon/Yarbrough Pub. Rels., Inc., Atlanta, 1984-86; v.p., account supr. Ketchum Pub. Rels., Atlanta, 1986—. Mem. fin. devel. com. Met. Atlanta chpt. ARC, 1987—. Recipient Golden Flame award Internat. Assn. Bus. Communicators, 1988, 89; named One of 5 Pub. Rels. All Stars, Atlanta Bus. Chronicle, 1988. Mem. Pub. Rels. Soc. Am. (certs. of excellence 1988, 89), Internat. Assn. Culinary Profls. Republican. Presbyterian. Home: 2067 Amberwood Way Atlanta GA 30309 Office: Ketchum Pub Rels Inc 1360 Peachtree St Atlanta GA 30309

HARMON, MERRILEE LAFFERTY, lawyer; b. Brownwood, Tex., Sept. 16, 1952; d. Robert Lee and Ernestine (Bessire) Lafferty; m. Lynn W. Malone, Sept. 28, 1981. BS, Baylor U., 1975, JD, 1978. Bar: Tex. 1978. Asst. dist. atty. McLennan County Dist. Atty.'s Office, Waco, Tex., 1979-81; assoc. Clark, Gorin, McDonald, Ragland & Mangrum, Waco, 1981-82; ptnr. McDonald, Harmon & Malone, Waco, 1983—. Mem. Tex. Acad. Family Law Specialists, Tex. Criminal Def. Lawyers Assn. (bd. dirs. 1983-88), Tex. Assn. Bd. Cert. Specialists (bd. dirs. criminal law sect. 1987—), Tex. Criminal Def. Lawyers Ednl. Inst. (bd. dirs. 1988-89), Nat. Assn. Criminal Def. Lawyers. Democrat. Methodist. Office: McDonald Harmon & Malone 3302 W Waco Dr Waco TX 76710

HARMON, VICTORIA THAM, controller; b. Kuala Lumpur, Malaysia, Dec. 24, 1956; m. Paul R. Harmon, June 1, 1985. B. Commerce, McMaster U., Hamilton, Ont., Can., 1980. Cert. mgmt. acct. Controller CAD Software, Inc., Littleton, Mass.; staff acct. Seidman and Seidman/CPA, Boston; internal auditor MIT, Cambridge, Mass., Toronto Transit Commn. Recipient Cert. of Achievement, Mass. Soc. CPA's.

HARMONAY, MAUREEN, thoroughbred bloodstock consultant; b. Yonkers, N.Y., Nov. 1, 1950; d. S. Leo and Dorothy (Cronin) H. BA in English, Newton Coll. Sacred Heart, Mass., 1972. Editorial asst. Boston Mus. of Sci., 1972-74; editorial dir. Action for Children's TV, Newtonville, Mass., 1974-80, Times Mirror Cable TV, Boston, 1981-82; pres. Harmonay Thoroughbred Assocs., Boston, 1982—. Editor Promise and Performance: Children with Special Needs, 1977, Promise and Performance: The Arts, 1979; editor Re: ACT, 1977-79. Mem. Nat. Wildlife Fedn., Horseman's Benevolent and Protective Assn., Mass. Thoroughbred Breeders Assn. (dir. 1983-86). Office: Harmonay Thoroughbred Assoc 1 Faneuil Hall Marketplace Boston MA 02109

HARMON BROWN, VALARIE JEAN, hospital laboratory director, information systems executive; b. Peoria, Ill., June 21, 1948; d. Donald Joseph and Frances Elizabeth (Classen) Harmon; m. James Roger Brown, Aug. 21, 1982. BSMT, Northwestern U., Chgo., 1970. Med. tech. Evanston (Ill.) Hosp., 1970-71, chief tech., 1971-75; med. tech. II M.D. Anderson Hosp., Houston, 1975-76; dir. lab. Physicians Ref. Lab., Houston, 1978-81, Med. Ctr. Hosp., Conroe, Tex., 1981—; lab. cons. Texaco Chem. Wellness Prog., Conroe, 1989; health career sponsor Willis Ind. Sch. Dist., Tex., 1989, 90. Coord. blood drive Gulf Coast Region Blood Ctr., 1986—; sponsor colon cancer screening Montgomery County Health Fair, 1986; sponsor Camp Sunshine/Lions Club, 1988; sponsor cholesterol screening Med. Ctr. Hosp. Health Fair, 1989. Mem. NAFE, Am. Soc. Clin. Pathologists, Am. Soc. Med. Technicians, Clin. Lab. Mgmt. Assn. Republican. Roman Catholic. Home: 61 Stephen F Austin Conroe TX 77302 Office: Medical Center Hospital 504 Medical Center Blvd Conroe TX 77304

HARNACK, MRS. CURTIS See CALISHER, HORTENSE

HARNESK, PRISCILLA ANN, career consultant; b. Hartford, Conn., May 13, 1955; d. Eric Adolph and Ruth Irene (Jordan) H.; m. David Allen Sauer. BS cum laude, U. Hartford, 1977; MS, Cen. Conn. State U., 1979. Admissions counselor U. Hartford, West Hartford, 1977-79; career counselor YWCA, Hartford, 1979-80; tng. coord. G. Fox & Co., Hartford, 1980-83; field rep. Pvt. Industry Coun., New Britain, Conn., 1983-85; tng. specialist Hosp. of St. Raphael, New Haven, 1985-89; career cons. Jaye Roseborough Career Cons. Svcs., Hartford, 1989—. Author: Matchbook, 1979. Vol. Am. Cancer Soc., New Britain, 1984; vol. Spl. Olympics, New Haven, 1985. Mem. Am. Soc. Tng. and Devel., Internat. Platform Assn., Phi Delta Kappa. Democrat. Roman Catholic. Home: 98 Acorn Dr Middletown CT 06457

HARNETT, LILA, publisher; b. Bklyn., Oct. 4, 1926; d. Milton Samuel and Claire S. (Merahn) Mogan; m. Joel William Harnett. BA, Bklyn. Coll., 1946; postgrad., New School, 1950. Personnel exec. Walter Lowen Agy., N.Y.C., 1947-52; pub. Bus. Atomics Report, N.Y.C., 1953-63; weekly columnist N.Y. State Newspapers, 1964-74; fine arts editor Cue Mag., N.Y., 1975-80; founder, contbg. editor Phoenix Home & Garden mag., 1980—, assoc. pub., 1988—. Mem. N.Y. State Coun. on the Arts, Town Tennis Club. Home: 4523 E Clearwater Pkwy Scottsdale AZ 85253 Office: Phoenix Home & Garden 4041 N Central Ave Phoenix AZ 85012

HARNEY, DEBRA ANN, publishing executive; b. Mineola, N.Y., Aug. 20, 1962; d. Edward Patrick and Arline Frances (Duffy) H. BA, SUNY, Albany, 1984. Tchr. A.G. Berner High Sch., Massapequa, N.Y., 1984-85; mktg. asst. Instl. Investor, N.Y.C., 1985; domestic sales Bankers Trust Co., N.Y.C., 1985-87; assoc. pub. Investing, N.Y.C., 1987—; v.p. DMA Communications, Inc., N.Y.C., 1987—. Office: DMA Communications Inc 249 E 55th St New York NY 10022

HARNSBERGER, THERESE COSCARELLI, librarian; b. Muskegon, Mich.; d. Charles and Julia (Borrell) Coscarelli; B.A. cum laude, Marymount Coll., 1952; M.L.S., U. So. Calif., 1953; postgrad. Rosary Coll., River Forest, Ill., 1955-56, U. Calif., Los Angeles Extension, 1960-61; m. Frederick Owen Harnsberger, Dec. 24, 1962; 1 son, Lindsey Carleton. Free-lance writer, 1950—; librarian San Marino (Calif.) High Sch., 1953-56; cataloger, cons. San Marino Hall, South Pasadena, Calif., 1956-61; librarian Los Angeles State Coll., 1956-59; librarian dist. library Covina-Valley Unified Sch. Dist., Covina, Calif., 1959-67; librarian Los Angeles Trade Tech. Coll., 1972—; med. librarian, tumor registrar Alhambra (Calif.) Community Hosp., 1975-79; tumor registrar Huntington Meml. Hosp., 1979—; pres., dir. Research Unltd., 1980—; free lance reporter Los Angeles' Best Bargains, 1981—; med. library cons., 1979—. Chmn. spiritual values com. Covina Coordinating Council, 1964-66; chmn. Neighborhood Watch, 1976—. Mem. ALA, Calif. Assn. Sch. Librarians (chmn. legis. com.), Covina Tchrs. Assn., AAUW (historian 1972-73), U. So. Calif. Grad. Sch. Library Sci. (life), Am. Nutrition Soc. (chpt. Newsletter chmn.), Nat. Tumor Registrars Assn., So. Calif. Tumor Registrars Assn., Med. Library Assn., So. Calif. Librarians Assn., So. Calif. Assn. Law Libraries, Book Publicists So. Calif., Am. Fedn. Tchrs. Coll. Guild, Faculty Assn. Calif. Community Colls., Inc., Loyola, Marymount Alumnae Assn. (coordinator), Pi Lambda Theta. Author: (poetry) The Journal, 1982, To Julia: in Memoriam; contbr. articles to profl. jours. Office: 2809 W Hellman Ave Alhambra CA 91803

HARPER, DEBORAH ANN FLAMMER, infosystems specialist; b. Red Bank, N.J., Dec. 8, 1953; d. David William and Elizabeth (McMurty) Flammer; m. William Arthur Harper, (div. Nov. 1984); 1 child, John William. BA, Purdue U., 1975. Tchr. Tuppecanoe Sch. Dist., Lafayette, Ind., 1975; sales mgr. ITT Terryphone Corp., Harrisburg, Pa., 1976-78; v.p. Interconnect Installation Corp., Greenville, R.I., 1978-82; office mgr. John Marandola Plumbing and Heating Co., Warwick, R.I., 1983-84; inside ops. mgr. James L. Day Co., Inc., Victor, N.Y., 1985-86; project mgr. Eastern area US West Info. Systems, Denver, 1986-87; exec. search cons. Mgmt. Recruiters Internat. Inc., Rochester, N.Y., 1987—. Mem. NAFE, Rochester Area Profl. Saleswomen (bd. dirs.). Presbyterian. Club: Purdue (Rochester).

HARPER, DEBORAH MORSE, apparel designer; b. Cheshire, Conn., Jan. 15, 1954; d. Wesley White and Jane (Guilford) H. Assocs., Chamberlyne Jr. Coll., 1974; student, Fashion Inst. Tech., 1978. Designer Deborah Harper Designs Ltd., N.Y.C., 1983—. Designer: Vogue, 1986, Elle mag., 1986-87, Donna, Italy, 1987, Interview Mag., 1987, Taxi Mag., 1987, Harpers Bazaar, 1987, Foreign Intrique, N.Y.C., 1987-88, Bergdorf Goodman catalogues, 1987-90, Fashion Accessories Exhbn., N.Y.C., 1987, Omni Show, N.Y.C., 1987, Pret Show, N.Y.C., 1987, Adrienne Viititini, Bern Conrad, Mary Ann Restivo, N.Y. Mag., 1988, Womans Wear and Womens Wear Daily, 1986, 87, 88, 89, 90. Recipient Exclusivity award Bergdorf Goodman, 1987. Mem. Am. Womens Econ. Assn., Nat. Assn. Female Execs. Episcopalian. Office: PO Box 7077 New York NY 10163-6026

HARPER, DENISE C., accountant; b. Cleve., July 22, 1955; d. Fred and Maggie L. (Owens) Harper. BA, Baldwin Wallace Coll., 1985; AAB, Cuyahoga Community Coll., 1982. Acct. Argo Tech. Corp., Cleve.; acctg. asst. TRW Inc., Cleve., acctg. clk. Mem. Black Data Processing Assn., NAFE.

HARPER, DIANNE SWEAT, marketing director; b. Walterboro, S.C., Dec. 4, 1949; d. James Ellison and Doris Genevieve (Robertson) Sweat; m. Robert J. Harper, Oct. 18, 1969; (div. 1989); 1 child, Traci Eleanor. Honors, Beaufort High Sch., Beaufort, 1967; BA, Ga. Southern Coll., Statesboro, 1973. English tchr. Woodbridge (Va.) Sr. High Sch., 1973-80; pub. info. asst. Sta. WHYY-TV, PBS, Phila., 1983-84; devel. dir. Red Cross Camden Co., Camden, N.J., 1984; mktg. communications mgr. Schaevitz Engring., Pennsauken, N.J., 1984-87; advertising dir. Altemose Co., Valley Forge, Pa., 1987-88; mktg. dir. WNY Mgmt., N.J., 1988--; cons. REB Mt. Laurel, N.J., 1987—. Chmn. Camp Le Jeune, Girl Scouts Am., N.C., 1981-82. Mem. Nat. Assn. Female Exec., Nat. Orgn. Women, League of Women Voters Camden Co., (pub. rels. chmn. 1988). Office: WNY Mgmt 633 W Rittenhouse St Philadelphia PA 19144

HARPER, DYAN, educational director; b. East Chicago, Ind., Jan. 30, 1942; d. John Henry and Dorothy Ilene (Lidgard) Harper; children: R. Scot McNabb, Sean McNabb. BA in Sociology, Ind. U., 1982. Adminstr. Stanley H. Kaplan Ednl. Ctr., Bloomington, Ind., 1983-86; ctr. dir. Stanley H. Kaplan Ednl. Ctr., Durham, N.C., 1987—; profl. entertainer various locations, 1970-84. Bd. dirs. Network of Career Women, Bloomington, Ind., 1986; chmn. bd. dirs. Leadership Bloomington Alumni, 1986; mem. Pub. Edn. Task Force, Durham, 1987, 90, Leadership Durham, 1988. Mem.

NAFE. Democrat. Unitarian Universalist. Office: Kaplan Ednl Ctr 2634 Chapel Hill Blvd #112 Durham NC 27707

HARPER, ELISABETH, investment management executive; b. LaGrange, Ill., Sept. 12, 1957; d. Philip Strickland and Harriet (Pierce) H. BA in Econs., Williams Coll., Williamstown, Mass., 1979; MBA with distinction, Harvard U., 1984. Asst. treas. Bankers Trust and Co., N.Y.C., 1979-82; assoc. Kidder, Peabody and Co., N.Y.C., 1983; mgmt. cons. McKinsey and Co., N.Y.C., 1984-88; sr. v.p. new bus. devel. The Putnam Cos., Boston, 1988—; pro bono cons., N.Y.C., Boston, 1987—. Program com. Sherborn (Mass.) Community Ctr. Found., 1990; fundraising agt. Williams Coll., 1980—; career adviser Harvard Bus. Sch., Boston, 1986—. Mem. NOW, Harvard Bus. Sch. Club N.Y. Democrat. Mem. Christian Ch. Home: 28 Everett St Sherborn MA 01770

HARPER, GLADYS COFFEY, health services adviser; b. Pitts.; d. Clarence William and India Anna (James) Jackson; B.A., U. Pitts., 1970, M.P.A., 1972, M.S.H., 1973; m. Thomas A. Harper, Jan. 21, 1968. With Allegheny County (Pa.) Health Dept., 1958—, chief office tng. and edn. adminstr., 1975-76, adv. curriculum devel. and health adminstrn., 1976—; health technician specialist office health affairs OEO, Washington, 1965; vis. lectr. Grad. Sch. Public and Internat. Affairs, U. Pitts., 1970—; bd. dirs. Heritage Nat. Bank, 1988—; panelist Sta. WQED-TV White House Conf. Food, Nutrition and Health; trustee Mayview State Hosp., 1975—, v.p. bd. trustees, 1978, trustee clin. pastoral edn. program, 1979-80; bd. dirs. United Mental Health, Inc. Co-producer documentary: What's Buggin' The Blacks?, Sta. KDKA-TV, 1968; host Weekly News Notes, Sta. KDKA-Radio, 1989. Program chmn. Law Day, Heritage Nat. Bank, 1988, Allegheny County Assn. Lawyers' Wives, 1975, v.p., 1978, pres., 1980; program chmn. Pa. Bar Assn. Wives Program, 1978; trustee Louis Little Meml. Fund, Allegheny County Bar Assn., 1979; founder Judge Thomas A. Harper Meml. Scholarship, Howard U. Sch. Law, 1984. Active Allegheny County Bicentennial Com., 1987, Afro-Am. Heritage Day Parade Com., 1987; exec. v.p. Afro-Am. Heritage Parade Assn., chmn. judging com., 1988; v.p. Hist. Soc. of Western Pa., 1988. Named Woman of Yr., Greyhound Corp., 1967, 1 of 25 Outstanding Pittsburghers, Wayfarer Mag., Chrysler Corp., 1967, Health Services award Pitts, Club United, 1970, Harold B. Gardner award-Md. Citizen Health award, Allegheny County Med. Soc., 1973, Drug Edn. recognition Pitts. Press, 1971, citation for environ. health curriculum devel. and supervision Chatham Coll., 1976, award African Meth. Episcopal Zion Ch., 1984; crowned Bahamas Princess Christmas Queen, Freeport, 1976. Mem. Am. Pub. Health Assn., Royal Soc. Health, Am. Soc. Pub. Adminstrn., Conf. Minority Pub. Adminstrs., Legis. Council Western Pa. (dir., v.p. elect 1982), Western Pa. Genealogy Soc. (pres. 1983), Legis. Council Western Pa. (pres. 1983), League Community Health Workers, AAUW, NAACP (Isabel Strickland Youth Advisor award 1967, Daisy E. Lampkin Human Rights award 1969), Hist. Soc. Western Pa. (trustee 1984, v.p. bd. trustees 1988), U. Pitts. Alumnae Assn. (Bicentennial scholarship com.), Program to Aid Citizen Enterprises. Home: 5260 Centre Ave Coronada Apts 502 Pittsburgh PA 15232

HARPER, JANET SUTHERLIN LANE, writer; b. La Grange, Ga., Apr. 2, 1940; d. Clarence Wilner and Imogene (Thompson); m. William Sterling Lane, June 28, 1964, (div. Jan. 1981); children: David Alan, Jennifer Ruth; m. John F. Harper, June 9, 1990. BA in English and Applied Music, LaGrange Coll., 1961; postgrad., Auburn U., 1963; MA in Journalism, U. Ga., Athens, 1979. Music critic The Brunswick News, Brunswick, Ga., 1979—; info. asst. Glynn County Schs., Brunswick, 1979-82; adj. prof. Brunswick Coll., Ga., 1981-87; dir. pub. info. & publs. Glynn County Schs., Brunswick, 1982—; columnist The Harbor Sound, Brunswick, Ga., 1983—; media relations Ga. Assn. of Ednl. Leaders, 1983—. Editor/writer: GAEL Conference Journals, 1987-89. Organist St. Simons United Meth. Ch., 1981—. Recipient Award of Excellence in Sch., Community Relations Ga. Bd. of Edn., 1984; Edn. Leadership award, Ga., 1989. Mem. Nat. Sch. Pub. Rels. Assn. (Golden Achievement award 1985, (2) 1988, 90), Ga. Sch. Pub. Rels. Assn., Brunswick Golden Isles C. of C., Mozart Soc., Phi Delta Kappa, Phi Kappa Phi, Sigma Delta Chi. Office: Glynn County Schs 1313 Egmont St Brunswick GA 31521

HARPER, LAURA JANE, academic administrator, consultant; b. Jackson, Miss., Aug. 18, 1914; d. William Pinckney and Elnora Malinda (Collins) H. BS, Belhaven Coll., 1934; MS, U. Tenn., 1948; PhD, Mich. State U., East Lansing, 1956; DSc (hon.), U. Helsinki, Finland, 1990. With Va. Polytech. & State U., Blacksburg, 1949—, acad. dean, 1960-80, prof., dean emeritus, nutrition cons., 1980—; nutrition cons. Helwan Univ., Cairo, Egypt, 1980, FAD in Southeast Asia, 1980-86, AID, Chile and Equador, 1983-84; nutrition edn. cons. World Coun. of Chs., Dakar, Senegal, 1980, World Bank, Java, Indonesia, 1988. Contbr. articles to profl. jours. Recipient Disting. Alumni award Mich. State Univ. Dept. of Food Sci. and Nutrition, 1986. Fellow Royal Acad. Sci.; mem. Am. Fedn. Home Econs., Internat. Fedn. Home Econs., Va. Fedn. Home Econs., AAUW, Va. Assn. Univ. Women (rep.), Assn. Women in Devel., Phi Delta Kappa, Phi Kappa Phi, Omicron Nu, Sigma Xi, Phi Sigma, Phi Tau Sigma Epsilon, Sigma PHi, Phi Upsilon Omicron, Omicron Delta Kappa. Home and Office: 100 Sunset Blvd Blacksburg VA 24060

HARPER, MARY SADLER, banker; b. Farmville, Va., June 15, 1941; d. Edward Henry and Vivien Morris (Garrett) Sadler; m. Joseph Taylor Harper, Dec. 21, 1968; children by previous marriage: James E. Hatch III, Mary Ann Hatch Czajka. Cert. Fla. Trust Sch., U. Fla., 1976. Registered securities rep., Fla. Dep. clk. Polk County Cts., Bartow, Fla., 1964-67; rep. Allen & Co., Lakeland, Fla., 1967-71; with First Nat. Bank, Palm Beach, Fla., 1971-89, sr. v.p., 1984-86, sr. v.p. S.E. Bank N.A., Palm Beach, 1986-89; pres., chief exec. officer Palm Beach Capital Svcs., Inc., 1986-88, mng. dir. Investment Svcs., Palm Beach Capital Svcs. Div., 1988; v.p. investments J.M. Rubin Found., Palm Beach, 1983—; sr. v.p. investment div. Island Nat. Bank of Palm Beach, 1989—; pres., chief exec. officer Island Investment Svcs., Inc., Palm Beach, 1989—, also bd. dirs.; mem. adv. coun. Nuveen, 1987-90. Mem. adv. panel Palm Beach County YWCA, 1984—; Jupiter Hosp. Found. Mem. Nat. Assn. Securities Dealers (registered), Fin. Women Internat., Fla. Securities Dealers Assn., Exec. Women of Palm Beaches (mem. fin. com. 1985—), Internat. Soc. Palm Beach (treas. 1986—), Jupiter Hosp. Med. Assn. (pres.'s club 1989—), Loxahatchee Hist. Soc., Sebring, Fla. Hist. Soc., Jupiter/Tequesta C. of C. (assoc.), United Daus. of Confederacy, Gov.'s Club, Jonathans Golf Club, Rotary (Palm Beach found. com. 1990—). Democrat. Baptist. Avocations: reading, history. Home: 630 Ocean Dr Apt 103 Juno Beach FL 33408 Office: Island Investment Svcs Inc Island Nat Bank Palm Beach 440 Royal Palm Way Palm Beach FL 33480

HARPER, PATRICIA ANN, social services administrator; b. Muskegon, Mich., July 9, 1957; d. Alwain Kenneth and Arlene Ann (Knoll) H. AAS, Muskegon Community Coll., 1977; BBA, Grand Valley State U., 1980; MBA, Grand Valley State Coll., 1983. Office asst. Radiology Muskegon (Mich.) P.C., 1975-80; office mgr. Ottawa County, Grand Haven, Mich., 1980-87, asst. friend of the ct., 1987—; mem. adv. com. Mich. Child Support Enforcement System; mem. State Ct. Adminstrv. Office Forms Com. Bd. dirs. Southwestern Mich. Family Support Council, Grand Rapids, 1984—. Mem. Am. Mgmt. Assn., Nat. Assn. Female Execs., Bus. and Profl. Women (pres. 1984-86; named Young Careerist 1982), Friends of Ct. Assn., FOCUS Users Group (pres.), Mich. NCR User's Group. Office: Ottawa County Friend of Ct 414 Washington Ave Grand Haven MI 49417

HARPER, ROBIN KELLY, family nurse practitioner; b. Washington, Dec. 16, 1961; d. William Shelton and Barbara Jean (McCallum) Steed; m. Leonard Boyd Harper, May 21, 1983. BS in Biology, St. Mary's Coll., St. Mary's City, Md., 1983; BS in Nursing, Cath. U. Am., 1985; MS in Nursing, U. Tex., 1989. Chemotherapy cert., Harris Meth., Tx. Psychiat. RN St. Elizabeth's Hosp., Washington, 1985-86; cancer RN Harris Meth., Ft. Worth, 1986-88; med. surgical RN Olsten Health Care, Ft. Worth, 1988-89; clin. nurse mgr. St. Francis Hosp., Greenville, S.C., 1990; emergency care nurse St. Francis Hosp., Greenville, S.C., 1989; breast self-examination instr. Am. Cancer Soc. Tex. Republican. Baptist. Home: 405 Althea St Easley SC 29642

HARPIN, LORNA RAE, financial analyst; b. Fremont, Nebr., May 8, 1958; d. Rudolph Fredrick and Frances Henritta (Vetter) Penke; m. Wayne A., Jan. 12, 1980, (div. Dec. 1987); 1 child, Nicholas A. Diploma, Ashland-Greenwood, 1976, Grad. Sch. of Banking, Madison, 1987. Bookkeeper Jerrys Tire Service, Wahoo, Nebr., 1976-77; acct. clk. Security Mutual Life Ins. Co., Lincoln, Nebr., 1977; teller, cashier Ashland, State Bank, Ashland, Nebr., 1978-84; asst. v.p., cashier River City Nat. Bank, Omaha, Nebr., 1984-89; v.p., cashier Century Bank Fort Collins, Colo., 1989—; com. chmn. Nat. Assn. of Bank Women, 1987-89. Bd. dirs. Ft. Collins chpt. Multiple Sclerosis Soc. Colo.; organist Choir Am. Luth. Ch., Ashland, Nebr., 1980-89. Recipient 1st Place Fine Arts Festival Piano Solo Ashland Jr. Women's Club. Mem. Ashland Women Jaycees, Ashland Jr. Womens Club (pres., v.p., sec.). Republican. Home: 3440 Windmill Dr #5-4 Fort Collins CO 80526

HARRAL, HARRIET BRISCOE, city official, communications consultant; b. San Antonio, June 28, 1944; d. Joe Edmund and Gene Aubrey (Hargis) Briscoe; m. Paul K. Harral, Aug. 6, 1966; children: Huard Briscoe, April Briscoe. BA, Baylor U., 1966, MA, 1967; PhD, U. Colo., 1973. Dir. cultural enrichment program OEO, Waco, Tex., 1967; tchr. English, Dallas Ind. Sch. Dist., 1967-69; tchr. speech Jefferson County Pub. Schs., Arvada, Colo., 1969-70; teaching assoc. U. Colo., Boulder, 1970-72; asst. prof. U. Ill., Chgo., 1974-78; adj. prof. U. North Fla., Jacksonville, 1978-83; dir. tng. and staff devel. City of Jacksonville, 1983-86; dir. tng. and orgnl. devel. City of Ft. Worth, 1987—; communications cons., Jacksonville, Ft. Worth, 1978—; chmn. regional tng. adv. coun. North Tex. Coun. Govts., Arlington, 1988—. Contbr. articles to acad. jours. and mags. Television host Broadway Bapt. Ch., Ft. Worth, 1987; bd. dirs., treas. Goodwill Industries, Ft. Worth, 1988—; bd. dirs., v.p. community svcs. United Way Greater Tarrant County, Ft. Worth, 1989—; bd. dirs., program chmn. Forum Ft. Worth, 1989—. Mem. Am. Soc. for Tng. and Devel. (bd. dirs. Ft. Worth 1987—, Disting. Achievement award 1988), Internat. Personnel Mgmt. Assn. (human resource planning regional com. 1988—), Internat. City Mgmt. Assn. (local arrangements steering com. 1989—), Baylor U. Alumnae Assn. (pres. Ft. Worth 1988—). Home: 2102 Pembroke Dr Fort Worth TX 76110 Office: Ft Worth City Hall Tng-Dev 1000 Throckmorton St Fort Worth TX 76102

HARRELL, THERESA ANN, state internal auditor; b. Eldorado, Ill., July 12, 1953; d. Charles Lee and Virginia Marie (Foster) Ferrell. B. in Acctg., Sangamon State U., 1984. CPA, Ill. Acct. Sangamon State U., Springfield, Ill., 1984; auditor Ill. State Bd. Edn., Springfield, 1985—; tax acct., bookkeeper Springfield, 1986—. Treas. Farmersville (Ill.) Gym Com., 1986-89. Mem. AICPA, Ill. CPA Soc. (com. chmn. federally assisted programs, Disting. Svc. award), Inst. Internal Auditors, Assn. Govt. Accts. Office: Ill State Bd Edn 100 N 1st St Springfield IL 62777

HARRELSON, TERESA LYNN, pharmacist; b. Mt. Airy, N.C., Oct. 25, 1950; d. James and Wilma (Martin) H. AS, Paducah (Ky.) Community Coll., 1970; BS, U. Ky., 1973. pharmacist Wagner's Pharmacy, Louisville, 1973-76; pharmacy dir. Healthcare Louisville, 1976-78; pharmacy svc. dir. Christian Ch. Home, Louisville, 1978-83; gen. mgr. Healthcare Prescription Svcs., Louisville, 1983-86; ter. mgr. D & R Pharmacy, Louisville, 1986—. Mem. River City Bus. & Profl. Assn., Louisville, 1981-86, Third Century, Louisville, 1983—, Coun. Women Pres. (pres. 1981-86), Louisville Jaycees, 1978-83. Named Jefferson County Pharmacist of the Year Jefferson County Acad. Pharmacy, Louisville, 1981. Mem. Nat. Assn. Retail Druggists (third party com., legis. conf. 1970-81), Am. Pharmacist Assn. (edn. com., 1979-80), Am. Soc. Cond. Pharmacist (profl. affairs com.,1989—), Ky. Pharmacist Assn. (pres. elect, pres., bd. dirs., sec. 1978-80, treas. 1982-84), Jefferson County Acad. Pharmacy (pres. elect, pres., chmn., 1979-81). Home: 9205 Tangley Ln Louisville KY 40242

HARRIFF, SUZANNA ELIZABETH, advertising consultant; b. Vicksburg, Miss., Dec. 30, 1953; d. David S. and F. Suzanna (McElwee) Bahner; m. James R. Harriff, Sept. 10, 1977; 1 child, Michael James. B.A. summa cum laude, SUNY-Fredonia, 1976; postgrad. Cornell U. Law Sch., 1981; postgrad. Colgate Rochester Divinity Sch., 1988—. Media asst. Comstock Advt., Syracuse, N.Y., and Buffalo, 1976-77; media buyer/planner G. Andre Delporte, Syracuse, 1979-81; media dir. Roberts Advt., Syracuse, 1982; dir. media services Signet Advt., Syracuse, 1982-84; owner, pres. MediaMarCon, Syracuse, 1984—. Music dir., pianist Manlius United Methodist Ch., N.Y., 1983—, youth dir., 1983-85; vol. Sta. WCNY-TV pub. TV auction drive. Mem. Syracuse Advt. Club (dir. 1985—, program chair 1986-88, pres. 1988-89), Nat. Assn. Female Execs., Irish-Am. Cultural Inst. Syracuse, Phi Beta Kappa. Democrat. Avocations: music; theatre. Home: 8180 Bluffview Dr Manlius NY 13104

HARRIMAN, LUCY L., reporter; b. Jersey City, July 29, 1951; d. John Raymond and Anne M. (Gildea) Hetman; m. William Jay Harriman, May 28, 1988; children: Renee Elizabeth Shepherd, Gregg Michael Shepherd. Student, Boston U., 1972, Bridgewater State Coll., 1984. News corr. The Enterprise, Brockton, Mass.; reporter Sta. WATD, Marshfield, Mass., The Patriot Ledger, Quincy, Mass. Mem. Hwy. Safety Adv. Com., 1985-89, chmn., 1986-89. Recipient numerous journalism awards. Mem. NAFE, NOW, New Eng. Press Assn. Roman Catholic. Home: 145 Summer St Duxbury MA 02332 Office: 400 Crown Colony Dr Quincy MA 02269

HARRIMAN, PAMELA DIGBY CHURCHILL, political action committee administrator; b. Farnborough, Eng., Mar. 20, 1920; came to U.S., 1959, naturalized, 1971; d. Edward Kenelm and Constance Pamela Alice (Bruce) Digby; B. Domestic Sci.-Economy, Downham (Eng.) Coll., 1937; postgrad. Sorbonne, Paris, 1937-38; m. Randolph Churchill, 1939; 1 son, Winston Spencer; m. 2d, Leland Hayward, May 4, 1960; m. 3d, W. Averell Harriman, Sept. 27, 1971. With Ministry of Supply, London, 1942-43; with Churchill Club for Am. Servicemen, 1943-46; journalist Beaverbrook Press, Europe, 1946-49; chmn., founder Democrats for the 90's, 1980—; bd. dirs. Comn. on Presidential Debates; trustee Presidential and Democratic 1988 Victory Party Fund; trustee, mem. exec. com. Brookings Instn.; mem. Council on Fgn. Rels.; trustee Rockefeller U., Coun. Nat. Gallery Art, Winston Churchill Found. U.S.; adv. council W. Averell Harriman Inst. for Advanced Soviet Studies, World Rehabilitation Fund; adv. com. World Rehab. Fund.; mem. bd. friends Kennan Inst. for Advanced Russian Studies; bd. dirs. Atlantic Council, Mary W. Harriman Found., also various philanthropic founds. Named Dem. Woman of Yr., Woman's Nat. Dem. Club 1980. Roman Catholic. Office: 3032 N St NW Washington DC 20007

HARRIMAN-KUMOR, LISA JAYNE, city official; b. Kansas City, Mo., Jan. 29, 1959; d. George Wendall Harriman and Pearl Arline (Murray) Crawford; m. Kyle Allen Wheeler, Aug. 11, 1979 (div. 1984); children: Chad Aaron, Joshua Lance; m. Jan Warren Kumor, Oct. 28, 1989; 1 child, Jan Alexander. AA in Mktg. and Graphic Design, Stephens Coll., Columbia, Mo., 1979; student, Howard Coll., Big Spring, Tex., 1979-80, U. Tulsa, 1983-84, Regis Coll., Denver, 1990—. Adminstrv. asst. Edward D. Jones & Co., Big Springs, 1980-81; br. adminstr. Edward D. Jones & Co., Claremore, Okla., 1981-82; adminstrv. asst. stormwater mgmt. dept. City of Tulsa, 1985-86; rsch. analyst arts, tourism and cultural resource project Nat. Conf. State Legislatures, Denver, 1986-87; mem. internat. trade staff Office of Gov., State of Colo., Denver, 1987; internat. mktg. specialist McDonnell Douglas Communications Industry Systems, Englewood, Colo., 1988; mktg. dir. Colo. Ctr. for Software Engring., Littleton, 1989—; econ. devel. specialist bus. and indsl. affairs dept. City of Littleton, 1989—. Mem. Colo. Gov.'s Internat. Bus. Devel. Com., 1987. Mem. NAFE, Econ. Devel. Coun. Colo., Colo. Jaycees, South Metro Denver C. of C. (new bus. com. 1989-90), Colo. Issues Network, Metro Denver Network (mktg. subcom. 1989-90), Mothers with Careers. Democrat. Home: 15963 E Nassau Dr Aurora CO 80013 Office: City of Littleton 2255 W Berry Ave Littleton CO 80165

HARRING, BARBARA ALLEN, civic worker; b. Salem, Mass., Sept. 10, 1933; d. Henry Vaughn and Helen Barbara (Jenney) Allen; m. Cedric Frasier Harring Jr., June 20, 1959; children: Vaughn Frasier, Linda. BA, Mt. Holyoke Coll., 1955. Rsch. biologist Arthur D. Little, Inc., Cambridge, Mass., 1955-62. Water safety instr. ARC, 1952-87, mem. aquatic sch. faculty, 1955-58, bd. dirs. Greater Concord (Mass.) chpt. 1971-77, water safety chmn., 1973; mgr. officer's club pool White Sands Missile Range, 1963; mem. aux. Emerson Hosp., Concord, Mass., 1966-87, vol., 1968-87, bd. dirs. 1978-81, mem. ethics com. 1979-82, quality and delivery of care com. 1981-86, devel. com., 1983-84; vol. Channel 2 Auction, 1970-75, area chmn., 1973-75; bd. dirs. Concord Family Svc., 1984—, pres., 1988—. Mem. Mass. Hosp. Assn. (legis. chmn. vol. svcs. adv. coun. 1982, trustee 1983-87, strategic planning com. 1983, presdl. search com. 1984-85), New Eng. Healthcare Assembly (com. of auxilians 1983-90, chmn. 1987), Am. Hosp. Assn. (com. on vols. 1987—). Unitarian. Home: 81 Wood Ln Acton MA 01720

HARRINGTON, DIANE GAIL, retail executive; b. Miami, Fla., Aug. 5, 1963; d. James Thomas and Eva Mae (Stephens) H. BBA, U. Miami, 1985, MBA, 1987. Mktg. rep. John Hancock Mut. Life Ins. Co., Boston, 1985-86; pres. Fla. Gold Seal Inc., Miami, 1986—. Counselor New Testament Bapt. Ch., Hialeah, Fla., 1983. Mem. Nat. Assn. Female Execs., Nat. Assn. Life Underwriters, Nat. C. of C., Ctr. Fine Arts, Nat. Assn. Hist. Preservation, Smithsonian Inst., Am. Inst. Researchers. Republican. Baptist. Home: 2620 NW 111 St Miami FL 33167

HARRINGTON, KATHY, advertising agency executive. Copywriter Stern Walters/Earle Ludgin, Inc. (now Stern Walters Ptnrs.), Chgo., from 1981, v.p., sr. v.p., pres., creative dir., 1987—. Office: Stern Watters Ptnrs Inc 150 E Huron Chicago IL 60611*

HARRINGTON, MARJORIE ELAINE, food products executive; b. Houston, Feb. 12, 1928; d. Leonard Fredrick Giesecke and Annie Lorena (Jinks) Wiley; m. Jack E. Tipple, May 2, 1950 (wid. May 1968); 1 child, Ronald Price; m. Ned Harrington, Nov. 4, 1972 (div. June 1976). BS, Ea. Mich. U., 1963, MA, 1968; PhD, U. Mich., 1972. Cert. tchr., vocational adminstrn. cert., Mich. Office mgr. Tyner Furniture, Ypsilanti, Mich., 1957-60; tchr. Wayne-Westland Schs., Westland, Mich., 1963-74, food svc. dir., 1978-89; prin. Franklin Jr. High Sch., Wayne, Mich., 1974-78; food svc. cons., Canton, Mich., 1985-89. Contbr. articles to profl. jours. Com. chmn. U. Mich. Scholarship Fund, Plymouth, 1987-89. Mem. Am. Sch. Food Svc. Assn., Mich. Sch. Food Svc. Assn., NEA, Am. Assn. U. Women. Democrat. Congregational. Home: 228 Redfield Ct Canton MI 48188 Office: Wayne-Westland Schs 36455 Marquette Westland MI 48185

HARRINGTON, SISTER NORA, college official; b. Holyoke, Mass., July 3, 1921; d. Maurice John and Mary T. (Courtney) Harrington; B.S., Coll. of Our Lady of Elms, 1944; M.S. in Chemistry, Fordham U., 1960. Joined Sisters of St. Joseph, Roman Catholic Ch., 1939; tchr. Sister Joseph's High Sch., Pittsfield, Mass., 1944-50; faculty Our Lady of Elms, 1950—, now assoc. prof. chemistry and physics, acad. dean, 1973-79, v.p., 1979—; mem. Sisters Senate, 1971-78, pres., 1972-74. NSF grantee Oak Ridge Summer Inst., 1968, Rensselaer Poly. Inst., 1970. Recipient Disting. Alumna award Coll. Our Lady of Elms, 1977; Nora Harrington Chemistry lecture established 1983. Mem. AAUP, AAUW, Am. Chem. Soc. Home and Office: 291 Springfield St Chicopee MA 01013

HARRINGTON, SUSAN DIANE, human resources director; b. East Chicago, Ind., July 3, 1949; d. Stanley and Dorothy (Rakowski) Smaron; m. Peter Gombos, Mar., 1969 (div. May 1976); 1 child, Jan L. BSBA, Ind. U., 1978; postgrad., Keller Grad. Sch. Mgmt., 1987-88. Personnel adminstr. Guarantee Res. Life Ins., Calumet City, Ill., 1973-77; personnel dir. U.S. Home Corp., Burr Ridge, Ill., 1978-79; dir. human resources Urban Investment & Devel. Co., Chgo., 1979-85, Balcor Co., Skokie, Ill., 1985-86, Homart Devel. Co., Chgo., 1986-89; cons. MKM Cons., Inc., Chgo., 1990—. Author, producer: Developing Together, 1980. Mem. Human Resources Mgmt. Assn. (compensation and benefits com. 1988-89), Am. Compensation Assn., Am. Soc. for Personnel Adminstrn. Office: MKM Cons Inc 444 N Michigan Ave Ste 1900 Chicago IL 60611

HARRIS, ALICE EATON, musician, music educator; b. Milw., Aug. 5, 1924; d. Edgar Philip and Dorothy Ruth (Morgenthau) Eaton; m. David H. Harris, June 18, 1947 (div. 1983); 1 child, Jean Harris Haig. BA, Barnard Coll., 1944; profl. artist's cert., Westchester Conservatory Music, 1947. Faculty Westchester Conservatory Music, White Plains, N.Y., 1944—. Chairperson Music Educators League Westchester, Scarsdale, N.Y., 1980-82. Mem. Am. Musicological Soc., N.Y. State Music Tchrs. Assn., Music Tchrs. Coun. Westchester (treas., rec. sec., libr. 1968-83, pres. 1989—), Westchester Musicians Guild.

HARRIS, ALICIA LYNNE, small business executive; b. Portland, Oreg., Dec. 14, 1958; d. Robert Langager and Shirlee E. (Finley) H. Student, Ea. Conn. State, 1986-87. Asst. mgr. Wendys Internat., Hillsboro, Oreg., 1980-81, Radio Shack, Salem, Oreg., 1981; sales mgr. Rainbow Vending, Salem, 1981-82; prin. Alicia's Property Mgmt., Norwich, Conn., 1985—; programmer Ea. Conn. State U., Willimantic, 1986-87; pres., prin. Gibson-Harris, Inc., Mystic, Conn., 1987; tutor acctg. Ea. Conn. State U., 1986-87. Editor, advisor New Dimensions mag., 1986-87; contbr. poetry, stories to various pubs. Served with USN, 1976-80, 82-85. Mem. Am. Entrepreneurs Assn., So. Conn. C. of C., Norwich Area C. of C. Republican. Baptist. Home: 577 Bank St New London CT 06320 Office: Gibson-Harris Inc 581 Bank St New London CT 06320

HARRIS, ANITA LOUISE, civic worker; b. Jamestown, N.Y., Aug. 6, 1952; d. Andrew and Rose Constance (Lovecchio) Scalise; m. David Scott Harris, Sept. 28, 1974; children: Joshua Todd, Andrew Jay, Jay David. Student, Baldwin-Wallace Coll., 1970-72; BA in Psychology, SUNY, Fredonia, 1974. Adminstrv. asst., cons. to bd. Jamestown Youth Bur., 1976-77; teller Bankers Trust Co. Western N.Y., Jamestown, 1974-75, 79-81, 82-83, human rels. dir., 1975, with comml. credit-collatoral dept., 1975-76, teller trainer, 1983. Co-developer, co-dir. 1st Ann. Empire State Conf. for Youth, 1977; vol. counselor crisis intervention program Jefferson Help Ctr., Jamestown, 1973-74; vol. crisis aide Chautauqua County Coun. on Alcoholism, Jamestown, 1976-82; bd. dirs. YWCA, Jamestown, 1976-82, mem. exec. bd., 1979-80, 88; mem. aux. bd. Jamestown Gen. Hosp., 1984-87; campaign worker So. Chautauqua County United Way, 1976, 78, 88; mem. Women on Alcoholism Task Force, Chautauqua County, 1978; parent rep., mem. com. on spl. edn. Jamestown Pub. Sch. Mem. AAUW (chmn. fin. and publicity scholarship program fundraising event Jamestown 1979-80, program chmn. 1989—, chmn., implementer community awareness program 1990). Roman Catholic. Home: 109 Superior St Jamestown NY 14701

HARRIS, ANN MARIE, sports coordinator; b. Dearborn, Mich., Jan. 6, 1959; d. Lloyd Arhtur and Frances Ann (Abe) H. AA, Henry Ford Community Coll., 1980; BS, Cen. Mich. U., 1982. With City of Dearborn Heights, Mich., 1977—; sports coord. City of Dearborn Heights, 1983—. Athletic supr. Henry Ford Community Coll., Dearborn, Mich., 1977-80; softball coach Annapolis High Sch., Dearborn Heights, 1982. Mich. Competitive scholar, 1977. Mem. Mich. Recreation and Parks Assn., Southwestern Mich. Recreation Exec. Group, Dad's Club, St. Albert Booster Club, Jaycees (charter pres. 1987, v.p. 1988-89). Roman Catholic. Home: 4643 Deaborndale Dearborn Heights MI 48125 Office: City of Dearborn Heights 1801 N Beech Daly Dearborn Heights MI 48127

HARRIS, ANNE SINGER, psychology educator, writer; b. Calcutta, India, Oct. 11, 1928; came to U.S., 1930; d. Samuel Earle and Marthedith (Furnas) Stauffer; children: Elizabeth J., Susan E. AB, Syracuse (N.Y.) U., 1949, MA, 1959; PhD, Stanford (Calif.) U., 1971. Lic. psychologist, Calif. Asst. prof. psychology, lectr. NYU, N.Y.C., 1968-69, U. Calif., Riverside, 1969-71; staff psychologist Riverside County Mental Health Clinic, Indio, Calif., 1971-75, asst. chief, 1973-75; staff psychologist Kaiser-Permanente Psychiatry Dept., Vallejo, Calif., 1976-86, chief psychologist, 1978-84; assoc. prof. psychology Calif. Sch. Profl. Psychiatry, Alameda, Calif., 1986—. Author: (with others) Psychological Development in Children, 1969; author poems and children's stories. Fellow Am. Orthopsychiatry Assn.; mem. Am. Psychology Assn., AAUP, Psi Chi. Home: 552 Santa Clara Ave Alameda CA 94501 Office: Calif Sch Profl Psychology 1005 Atlantic Ave Alameda CA 94501

HARRIS, BARBARA BECK CZIKA, consulting firm executive; b. Cleve., Oct. 17, 1942; d. Charles William and Jeanne Anne (DeLeur) Beck; m. Jack H. Harris Jr., Jan. 1, 1983; children: Joseph C. Czika, Brad D. Czika, Jack H., William W., Thomas P. Student, Case Western Res. U. Pres., chief exec. officer, chmn. bd. dirs. The Harris Group, Inc., Reston, Va., 1985—; adminstr. Sci. Applications Internat. Corp., McLean, Va., 1976-85. Mem.

Women in Aerospace, Women in Govt. Rels., Am. Mgmt., Internat. Platform Assn., NAFE, Va. Assn. Female Execs., Childhelp USA (exec. v.p.), Profl. Svcs. Coun. (bd. dirs.). Home: 911 Challedon Rd Great Falls VA 22066 Office: Harris Group Inc 1801 Robert Fulton Dr Reston VA 22091

HARRIS, BARBARA C(LEMENTINE), bishop; b. Phila., 1930. Grad., Charles Morris Price Sch. Advt. and Journalism, Phila.; student, Villanova U., Urban Theology Unit, Sheffield, Eng.; D in Sacred Theology (hon.), Hobart and William Smith Colls., 1981; DD (hon.), Gen. Theol. Sem., 1989, Episc. Div. Sch., 1989, Amherst Coll., 1989. Pres. Joseph V. Baker Assocs., Phila., 1958—; sr. staff cons., mem. community rels. dept. Sun Oil Co.; ordained deacon Episc. Ch., 1979, priest, 1980, bishop, 1989; priest-in-charge St. Augustine of Hippo, Morristown, Pa.; interim rector Ch. of the Advocate, Phila.; exec. dir. Episc. Ch. Pub. Co., 1984—; suffragan bishop Diocese of Mass., Boston, 1989—; trustee Episc. Div. Sch. Office: Episc Diocese of Mass 138 Tremont St Boston MA 02111*

HARRIS, BARBARA JANE, non-profit organization administrator, accountant; b. Texarkana, Tex., Mar. 2, 1953; d. Earl Dempsey and Adela Matilda (Stuessy) Bookout; m. Richard Douglas Harris, June 18, 1971; children: Shane Alexander, Robin Leigh. Student, U. Tex., 1972-76, Tex. Wesleyan U., 1977-81. With payroll dept. U. Tex., Arlington, 1972-77; data process supr. Tex. Wesleyan U., Ft. Worth, 1977-80, asst. comptroller, 1980-81, adminstrv. asst. to v.p., 1981-83; comptroller Sr. Citizen Svcs., Ft. Worth, 1983-87, assoc. dir., 1987—. Mem. Postal Customer Adv. Coun., Ft. Worth, 1989-90, Leadership Ft. Worth, 1989-90; publicity chair Alice Ponder Elem. PTA, Mansfield, Tex., 1988-89, 89-90, pres., 1990—. Mem. Nat. Assn. Meal Programs (regional rep. 1988—), Nat. Soc. for Fundraising Execs., NAFE. Democrat. Methodist. Home: 513 Cagle Crow Mansfield TX 76063 Office: Sr Citizen Svcs 1000 Macon St Fort Worth TX 76102-4577

HARRIS, BELINDA KAY, association executive; b. McComb, Miss., July 18, 1952; d. Isaac Sr. and Millye Mae Shaw; m. James Harris Jr., Dec. 26, 1972 (div.); children: Dorian Ashon, Leslie Nicole, Jasmine Dionne. BS in English and Secondary Edn., U. So. Miss., 1974. With employee devel. dept. FAA, Anchorage, 1974-78; ctr. dir. Agr. and Labor Program, Inc., Ft. Meade, Fla., 1979-81; child dev. coord. Agr. and Labor Program, Inc., Frostproof and Winter Haven, Fla., 1981-83; exec. dir. Girl's Club of Lakeland (Fla.), Inc., 1983—; pres. Girl's Club of Fla., Lakeland, 1985-86. Mem. Community Alliance Orgn., Lakeland, 1985—; chmn. pub. relations Talbot House Ministries, Lakeland, 1986—; pres. Winston Elem. PTA, Lakeland, 1983—; mem., fundraising chmn. Neighborhood Svc. Ctr., Lakeland, 1984-85; chmn. United Way (1986—, sec. 1985-86, Outstanding Svc. award 1987); treas. Girls Club Am., So. Region, 1987—; treas. Winston Elem. Sch. PTA, 1987-88; mem. sch. age children task force Polk County Sch. Bd., 1987-88. Democrat. African Methodist Episcopalian. Office: Girls Club of Lakeland PO Box 1975 Lakeland FL 33802

HARRIS, BETSY LEE, nurse; b. Neptune, N.J., Nov. 5, 1937; d. Malvin Henry and Anna Elizabeth (Pickett) Giddings; m. Stanly D. Harris. BS in Nursing, U. Mass., 1986, postgrad. Med. staff nurse Boston City Hosp., 1972-73, mem. staff, 1973-76, staff nurse, 1976-77; nurse Boston VA Med. Ctr., 1977-86; head nurse Boston VA, 1986--. Mem. adv. bd. U.S. Commn. Civil Rights Mass., Wash., 1987, Mass. Bay, Mass. Bay Community Coll. Mem. Am. Nurses Assn., Mass. Nurses Assn., Nat. Black Nurses Assn. (bd. dirs., past pres. N.E. region). Home: 149 Glenway St Dorchester MA 02121

HARRIS, BEVERLY LORRAINE, data processing executive; b. Chgo., July 10, 1945; d. Earl and Eva (Williamson) Wallace; m. James Harris, Dec. 22, 1966 (div. Oct. 1967); 1 child, Dana Keith. BS, Chgo. State U., 1988. Data entry operator Burlington RR, Chgo., 1968-72, temp. agys., Chgo., 1972-78; data conversion operator Nat. Opinion Rsch. Ctr., Chgo., 1978-80; computer operator Nat. Opinion Rsch. Ctr., 1980-85, applications programmer, 1985-86, local area network adminstr., 1986—; instr. Am. Friends Svc. Com., Chgo., 1988-89, Dept. on Aging & Disability, Chgo., 1987-88; cons. Cares Secretarial Svc., Chgo., 1987—. Mem. Chgo. Assn. for Microcomputer Profls. Democrat. Roman Catholic. Office: Nat Opinion Research Ctr 1155 E 60th St Chicago IL 60637

HARRIS, CATHERINE GARDRINE, social worker; b. Northampton, Mass., Oct. 4, 1958; d. Lenard Eugene and Jeannette Gardrine (Davis) H. BA in Psychology, Simmons Coll., 1980; postgrad., U. Mass., 1988—. Vocat. rehab. counselor Mass. Rehab. Commn., Boston, 1980-81; rehab. counselor day activity program Roxbury (Mass.) Multi-Svc. Ctr., 1981-84; protective social worker area office Mass. Dept. Social Svcs., Quincy, 1984-85; adoption social worker regional office Mass. Dept. Social Svcs., Cambridge, 1985-88, foster care coord., 1988-89; case reviewer cen. office Mass. Dept. Social Svcs., Boston, 1989—; skin care cons. Lynell II. Bd. dirs., treas. Third World Alliance, Simmons Coll., Boston, 1980—. Recipient Outstanding Svc. award Roxbury Multi-Svc. Ctr., 1984; named young woman Am., 1984. Mem. Am. Adoption Congress, Mass. Assn. for Mental Health (bd. dirs. 1980-83), Mass. Assn. for Profl. Foster Care (liaison person 1988-90), Zeta Phi Beta. Democrat. Home: 17 Kensington St Apt 1 Roxbury MA 02119

HARRIS, DALE HUTTER, judge, lecturer; b. Lynchburg, Va., July 10, 1932; d. Quintus and Agnes (Adams) Hutter; m. Edward Richmond Harris Jr., July 24, 1954; children—Mary Fontaine, Frances Harris Russell, Jennifer Harris Haynie, Timothy Edward. BA, Sweet Briar Coll., 1953; MEd in Counseling and Guidance, Lynchburg Coll., 1970; JD, U. Va., 1978; LLD (hon.), Wilson Coll., 1988. Bar: Va. 1978, U.S. Dist. Ct. (we. dist.) Va. 1978, U.S. Ct. Appeals (4th cir.) 1978. Admissions asst. Sweet Briar Coll. (Va.), 1953-54; caseworker Winchester/Frederick Dept. Welfare, Va., 1954-55; vis. lectr. Lynchburg Coll. (Va.), 1971; assoc. Davies & Peters, Lynchburg, 1978-82; substitute judge 24th Dist. Gen. Dist. and Juvenile and Domestic Relations Dist. Cts. Va., 1980-82; judge Juvenile and Domestic Relations Dist. Ct., Lynchburg, 1982—; lectr. law U. Va. Law Sch., 1986—; apptd. mem. commn. on Future Va's. Jud. system, 1987—. Vice chmn. bd. dirs. Sweet Briar Coll., 1976-86; vol. coordinator vols. in probation with Juvenile and Domestic Ct., 1971-73; chmn. steering com. for establishment Youth Service Bur., Lynchburg, 1972-73; chmn. bd. dirs. Lynchburg Youth Services, 1973-75; mem. adv. bd. Juvenile Ct., 1957-60, 62-68, sec., 1966-68; bd. dirs. Family Service Lynchburg, 1967-69; Lynchburg Fine Arts Ctr., 1965-67, Seven Hills Sch., 1966-73, Greater Lynchburg United Fund, 1963-65, Lynchburg Assn. Mental Health, 1960-61, Miller Home, 1980-82, Lynchburg Gen.-Marshall Lodge Hosps., Inc., 1980-82; v.p. Lynchburg Mental Health Study Commn., 1966; bd. dirs. Lynchburg Sheltered Workshop for Mentally Retarded Young Adults, 1965-69; bd. dirs. Lynchburg Guidance Ctr., 1959-61, v.p., 1970, pres., 1961; bd. dirs. Hist. Rev. Bd. Lynchburg, 1978-82. Mem. Nat. Council Juvenile and Family Ct. Judges, ABA, Va. State Bar (bd. govs. criminal law sect. 1988—), Va. Trial Lawyers Assn., Va. Bar Assn., Lynchburg Bar Assn., Phi Beta Kappa. Home: 1309 Crenshaw Ct Lynchburg VA 24503 Office: Juvenile and Domestic Relations Dist Ct PO Box 757 Lynchburg VA 24505

HARRIS, DEBRA LYNNE, jewelry sales company executive; b. Columbus, Ohio, Oct. 26, 1956; d. Conrad London and Ruth Evelyn (Berggas) H. B.S. in Bus., Ind. U., 1978. Founder, owner Gold Connection, Inc., Chgo., 1978—. Mem. Jewelers Bd. of Trade, Jewelers of Am.

HARRIS, DIANA CLELLAND, interior designer, small business owner; b. Phila., Mar. 28, 1952; d. Louis Corner and Lillian Eleanor (Salvesen) Clelland; m. George Wayne Harris, Oct. 5, 1979; 1 child, Morgan Anders. BFA, More Coll. Art, Phila., 1974. Interior designer Comml. Bus. Supply, Phila., 1973-74; pres., interior designer At Home Interiors, Inc., Stone Harbor, N.J., 1971—. Bd. dirs. Rep. Club of Stone Harbor, 1984—. Mem. Am. Soc. Interior Designers. Lutheran. Club: Garden of Stone Harbor (bd. dirs. 1978-84). Home: 11611 2d Ave Stone Harbor NJ 08247 Office: At Home Interiors Inc 9720 3d Ave Stone Harbor NJ 08247

HARRIS, DIANA KOFFMAN, sociologist, educator; b. Memphis, Aug. 11, 1929; d. David Nathan and Helen Ethel (Rotter) Koffman; student U. Miami, 1947-48; BS, U. Wis., 1951; postgrad. Tulane U., New Orleans, 1951-52; MA, U. Tenn., 1967; postgrad. U. Oxford (Eng.), 1968-69; m. Lawrence A. Harris, June 24, 1951; children: Marla, Jennifer. Advt. and sales promotion mgr. Wallace Johnston Distbg. Co., Memphis, 1952-54; welfare worker Tenn. Dept. Pub. Welfare, Knoxville, 1954-56; instr. sociology Maryville (Tenn.) Coll., 1972-75; instr. sociology Fort Sanders Sch. Nursing, Knoxville, 1971-78; instr. sociology U. Tenn., Knoxville, 1967—; series editor Garland Pub., Inc. 1989—. Chmn. U. Tenn. Coun. on Aging, 1979—; organizer Knoxville chpt. Gray Panthers, 1978; mem. Gov.'s Task Force on Preretirement Programs for State Employers, 1973; mem. White House Conf. on Aging, 1981; bd. mem. Knoxville-Knox County Council on Aging, 1976, Sr. Citizens Info. and Referral, 1979, Sr. Citizens Home-Aide Svc., 1977; del. E. Tenn. Coun. on Aging, 1977. Recipient Meritorious award Nat. U. Continuing Edn. Assn., 1982. Mem. Am. Sociol. Assn., AAAS, Gerontol. Soc. Am., Popular Culture Assn., So. Sociol. Soc., So. Gerontol. Soc. (Pres.'s award 1984), N. Central Sociol. Assn. Clubs: London Competitor's; Nat. Contest Assn.; Knoxville Kontestars. Author: Readings in Social Gerontology, 1975, (with Cole) The Elderly in America, 1977, The Sociology of Aging, 1980, 2d edit., 1990; co-author: Sociology, 1984, Annotated Bibliography and Sourcebook: Sociology of Aging, 1985, 2d edit., 1990, Dictionary of Gerontology, 1988; series editor Garland Pub., Inc., 1989. contbr. articles to profl. jours. Home: PO Box 50546 Knoxville TN 37950-0546 Office: U Tenn Dept Sociology PO Box 50546 Knoxville TN 37950

HARRIS, DIANE, financial services executive; b. Chgo., June 3, 1947; d. Donald O. and Lena (Cardman) H. BA, U. Calif., Santa Barbara, 1969; MBA, U. Calif., L.A., 1987. Mgmt. trainee Citizens Savs. & Loan Assn., Santa Barbara, 1969-70; asst. contr. Liberty Savs. & Loan Assn., L.A., 1970-74, R.M. Loeffler Trustee for Equity Funding, L.A., 1974-77, Beneficial Standard Corp., L.A., 1977-80; v.p., contr. Fidelity Interstate Life Ins. Co., L.A., 1980-82; pvt. practice cons. L.A., 1982-88; v.p. planning and budgeting Metmor Fin., Inc., L.A., 1988-89; v.p. corp. planning and analysis Telecredit Inc., L.A., 1990—. Mem. L.A. Conservancy, 1987—, L.A. County Mus. Art, 1987—, L.A. Chamber Orch. Vol. Coun., 1989—. Mem. U. Calif.-Santa Barbara Alumni Assn., John F. Anderson Grad. Sch. Mgmt. Alumni Assn., L.A. World Affairs Coun., L.A. Jr. C. of C., Profls. for Planned Parenthood, L.A. Office: 6171 W Century Blvd Los Angeles CA 90067

HARRIS, DIANE CAROL, healthcare executive; b. Rockville Centre, N.Y., Dec. 25, 1942; d. Daniel Christopher and Laura Louise (Schmitt) Quigley; m. Wayne Manley Harris, Sept. 30, 1978. BA, Cath. U. Am., 1964; MS, Rensselaer Poly. Inst., 1967. With Bausch & Lomb, Rochester, N.Y., 1967—, dir. applications lab., 1972-74, dir. tech. mktg. analytical systems div., 1974-76, bus. line mgr., 1976-77, v.p. planning and bus. programs, 1977-78, v.p. planning and bus. devel. Soflens div., 1978-80, corp. dir. planning, 1980-81, v.p. corp. devel., 1981—; v.p. RID-N.Y. State, 1980-83; mem. adv. bd. Merger Mgmt. Report, 1986—; bd. dirs. Delta Labs., Inc. Contbr. articles to profl. jours. Pres. Rochester Against Intoxicated Driving, 1979-83, chmn. polit. action com., 1983, 86; bd. dirs., chmn. long-range planning com. Rochester area Nat. Council on Alcoholism, 1980-84; bd. dirs. Rochester Rehab. Ctr., 1982-84, Friends of Bristol Valley Playhouse Found., 1983-87; mem. Stop DWI Adv. panel to Monroe County Legislature, 1982-87, N.Y. State Coalition for Safety Belt Use, 1984-85. Recipient Disting. Citizen's award Monroe County, 1979, Tribute to Women in Industry and Service award YWCA, 1983; NSF grantee, 1963; selected as one of 50 Women to Watch in Corp. Am. Bus. Week mag., 1987, one of 100 Women Duns Bus. Rev., 1988. Mem. Am. Mgmt. Assn., Fin. Execs. Inst., Assn. Corp. Growth, C. of C. (pub. safety com. Rochester Area chpt., task force on hwy. safety and legis. 1981-86), Phi Beta Kappa, Sigma Xi, Delta Epsilon Sigma. Home: 60 Mendon Center Rd W Honeoye Falls NY 14472 Office: Bausch & Lomb Inc 1 Lincoln First Sq PO Box 54 Rochester NY 14601-0054

HARRIS, DOLORES M., continuing education program director; b. Camden, N.J., Aug. 5, 1930; d. Roland Henry Sr. and Frances Anna (Gatewood) Ellis; m. Morris E. Harris Jr., 1948 (div. 1987); children: Morris E. Jr., Sheila Rodman, Gregory M. Sr. BS, Glassboro (N.J.) State Coll., 1959, MA, 1966; EdD, Rutgers U., 1983. Tchr. and reading specialist Glassboro Bd. Edn., 1958-68, dir. aux. svcs., 1968-70; supr. adult edn. Camden Welfare Bd., summer 1968; head state dir. Glassboro SCOPE, summer 1969-70; assoc. dir. Jersey City State Coll., summer 1971; dir. adult edn. Glassboro State Coll., 1970-74, dir. continuing edn. dept., 1989-90, acting assoc. v.p. acad. affairs, 1989—; chmn. adv. bd. Women's Ednl. Equity Communications Network project, San Francisco, 1977-78; bd. dirs. Glassboro State Coll. Mgmt. Inst.; cons. crossroads project Temple U., Phila., 1977; cons. corrections project Va. Commonwealth U., Richmond; cons. Mich. State Dept. of Edn., Lansing, 1973; examiner N.Y. State Civil Svc. Commn., 1976—; mem., vice-chmn. comm. Accrediting Coun. for Continuing Edn. and Tng., Richmond, 1985-89, chmn., 1989—. Author: (with others) Black Studies for ABE and GED Programs in Correction, 1975; author: guide How to Establish ABE Programs, 1972; founding editor: newsletter For Adults Only, 1970; contbr. articles to profl. jours. Founder, mem. bd. trustees, chair bd. Glassboro Child Devel. Ctr., 1974-87; bd. dirs. Gloucester County (N.J.) United Way, 1977—, sec. bd., 1980, pres. bd., 1983-85; charter mem., bd. dirs. Glassboro Glass Mus., 1979-87; vice chair, chair, mem. Gloucester County Commn. on Women, 1983-87; mem., chair edn. subcom. Gloucester County REACH, 1987—. Recipient Disting. Svc. award Holly Shores Girl Scouts Am., 1979, Disting. Alumnae award Glassboro State Coll., 1971, Disting. Svc. award Camden County, 1974; named to Legion of Honor, Chapel of Four Chaplains, 1983; named Woman of Yr., Gloucester County Bus. and Profl. Women's Club, 1985; named Woman of Achievement, Gloucester County Commn. on Women, 1987; named one of Outstanding Citizens, Holly Shores Girl Scouts Am., 1987; named one of 100 Most Influential Black Ams., Ebony mag., 1989. Mem. NEA, AAUW (v.p. membership com. Gloucester County chpt. 1986-87), N.J. Assn. (life, pres. 1973-74), Soc. Docta (charter, bd. dirs. 1987—), N.J. Edn. Assn., N.J. State Fedn. Colored Women's Clubs (pres. 1976-80), Northeastern Fedn. Women's Clubs (v.p.-at-large 1983-85, parliamentarian 1985—), Nat. Assn. Colored Women's Clubs, Inc. (pres. 1988—), Links Club. Baptist. Office: Glassboro State Coll Adult Continuing Edn Glassboro NJ 08028

HARRIS, DONNA LEE, reinsurance claim executive, lawyer; b. Indpls., Nov. 10, 1949; d. William Keith and Deloris Maxine (Costello) Smithey; m. Nov., 1989. BS, Ball State U., 1970; JD, Lewis & Clark Coll., 1984. Bar: Wash. 1984. Adjuster, supr. direct ins. Unigard Ins. Group, 1971-82; asst. v.p. reinsurance assumed claims Unigard Ins. Group, Seattle, 1982-86; exec. reinsurance claims, asst. v.p. Gen. Reinsurance Corp., San Francisco, 1986—. Mem. ABA, Def. Rsch. Inst., Wash. State Bar Assn.

HARRIS, DOROTHY CLARK, interior architect/designer, design instructor; b. Atlanta, Aug. 1, 1949; d. Robert Harold and Ethel Martin (Gibson) Clark; m. Ronald Neil Harris, Nov. 27, 1976. B in Visual Arts, Ga. State U., 1972, postgrad., 1979, 80, 81. With Associated Space Design, Inc., Atlanta, 1972-74, 76-86, v.p., 1986-89; interior designer Thompson Ventulett Stainback & Assocs., Architects, Atlanta, 1974-76; instr. in interior design Art Inst. Atlanta, 1975-76, Ga. State U., 1978; dir. interior architecture and design Rosser Fabrap Internat., 1989—. Mem. Nat. Assn. Corp. Real Estate Execs. (v.p. programs Atlanta chpt. 1989-90, v.p. membership Atlanta chpt. 1990-91), Internat. Facilities Mgmt. Assn. (awards chmn. Atlanta chpt. 1989-90), Comml. Real Estate Women, Atlanta Bd. Realtors, Atlanta C. of C. (Southside devel. task force 1988-90). Baptist. Home: 105 Hidden Valley Rd Fayetteville GA 30214 Office: Rosser Fabrap Internat 100 Peachtree St NW Ste 400 Atlanta GA 30303

HARRIS, DOROTHY DIERKS, educator; b. Columbus, Ga., Aug. 19, 1935; d. Henry Edward and Margaret (Greene) D.; children: Gavin, Dylan. BFA, U. Colo., 1957; MA, Columbia U., 1960, EdD, 1984. Sec. Mus. Modern Art, N.Y.C., 1957-58; instr. Auburn U., 1959; supr. Pub. Schs., Kennett, Mo., 1960; art tchr. Pub. Schs., Pearl River, N.Y.; prof. Jersey City State Coll., 1962--, chmn., 1982--. One-woman shows include Viridian Gallery, N.Y.C., 1987, Montclair Art Mus., 1989; exhibited in group shows at Mussavi Gallery, Soho, 1988, St. Lifer Art Exchange, Summit Art Ctr., N.J., St. Louis Mus., The New Birmingham Mus., Columbus Mus., Seoul, Korea, others; represented in permanent collections Block Drug Co., Jersey City State Coll., Am. Assn. State Colls. and Univs., Hebrew Home for Aged, Jewish Assn. for Svcs. for Aged. Mem. Nat. Assn. Sch. Art and Design, Women's Caucus Arts. Office: Jersey City State Coll 2039 John F Kennedy Blvd Jersey City NJ 07305

HARRIS, ELIZABETH ANN, marketing research professional; b. Huntington, N.Y., Apr. 29, 1957; d. Gordon Israel and Sondra Roberta (Epstein) H. BA, SUNY, Albany, 1979; student, U. Besancon, France, 1979; MBA in Mktg., Pa. State U., 1983. Customer svc. rep. N.Y. office Credit Industriel et Comml., 1979-80; customer svc. rep. Daval Steel, N.Y.C., 1980-81; instr. mktg. Pa. State U., University Park, 1982-83; market analyst World Trade Ctr., N.Y.C., 1983-84, Nat. Gypsum Co., Dallas, 1984-86; mgr. market rsch. Hanley-Wood, Inc., Washington, 1986-88, Domtar Gypsum, Ann Arbor, Mich., 1988—. Mem. NAFE, Am. Mktg. Assn. Home: 2735 Windwood Dr Apt 93 Ann Arbor MI 48105 Office: Domtar Gypsum PO Box 543 Ann Arbor MI 48106

HARRIS, ELIZABETH HOLDER, research scientist; b. Winston-Salem, N.C., Oct. 1, 1944; d. Edward Maxwell and Elizabeth Pollard (Jerome) Holder; m. Albert Kenneth Harris Jr., June 24, 1965; children: Hannah Blair, Thomas Edward Holder, Frieda Elizabeth. BA, Swarthmore Coll., 1965; PhD, Yale U., 1971. Postdoctoral rsch. assoc. Duke U., Durham, N.C., 1972-74; sr. rsch. assoc. Duke U., Durham, 1974-83, sr. rsch. scientist, 1984—. Author: The Chlamydomonas Sourcebook, 1989; contbr. articles to profl. jours. Mem. Genetics Soc. Am., Phycol. Soc. Am., Assn. for Women in Sci. Office: Duke U Dept of Botany Durham NC 27706

HARRIS, ELLA MAE, technical writer; b. Ames, Iowa, Oct. 23, 1930; d. Fred and Fay (Wolfram) Robertson; m. Marvin Edward Whatley, Nov. 23, 1950 (div. Oct. 1960); children: Gail Whatley Holcomb, Mark David, Walter Joseph; m. Thomas R. Harris, June 12, 1969. BS, Iowa State U., 1951; MBA, U. Tenn., 1972. Systems analyst Sci. Games Corp., Atlanta, 1975-76; tech. info. specialist Nat. Med. Audiovisual Ctr., Atlanta, 1976-78; systems programmer Ctrs. for Disease Control, Atlanta, 1978-80, 1st Nat. Bank Atlanta, 1980-85, Ga. State U., Atlanta, 1985, St. Joseph's Hosp., Atlanta, 1987; data processing recruiter Computer Network Resources, 1987; sr. tech. writer Digital Communications Assn., Alpharetta, Ga., 1988; sr. publs. specialist Emory U., Atlanta, 1989—. Author: (user's guide and reference manual) IRMA LAN, 1988 (award for excellence Soc. for Tech. Communications 1988). Singer Atlanta Symphony Orch. Chorus, 1974-80, Atlanta Bach Choir, 1986—. Recipient superior performance award Ctrs. for Disease Control, 1980. Mem. Psi Chi, Pi Mu Epsilon, Sigma Alpha Iota. Office: Emory U 2004 Ridgewood Dr Atlanta GA 30322

HARRIS, EMMA EARL, nursing home executive; b. Viper, Ky., Nov. 6, 1936; d. Andrew Jackson and Zola (Hall) S.; m. Ret Haney Marten Henis Harris, June 5, 1981; children: Debra, Joseph, Wynona, Robert Walsh. Grad. St. Joseph Sch. Practical Nursing. Staff nurse St. Joseph Hosp., Bangor, Maine, 1973-75; office nurse Dr. Eugene Brown, Bangor, 1975-77; dir. nurses Fairborn Nursing Home, Ohio, 1977-78; staff nurse Hillhaven Hospice, Tucson, 1979-80; asst. head nurse, 1980; co-owner Nu-Life Elderly Guest Home, Tucson, 1980—. Author: Thoughts on Life. Vol. Heart Assn., Bangor, 1965-70, Cancer Assn., Bangor, 1965-70. Mem. NAFE, Assn. Sr. Resources (cons. 1983—). Democrat. Avocations: theatre, opera. Home: 1082 E Seneca Tucson AZ 85719

HARRIS, EMMYLOU, singer; b. Birmingham, Ala., Apr. 2, 1947; m. Brian Ahern; children: Hallie, Meghann; m. Paul Kennerley, 1985; 1 stepchild, Shannon. Student, U.N.C.-Greensboro. Country music performer, singer, 1967—; assisted Gram Parsons on albums GP, Grievous Angels, 1973; toured with Fallen Angel Band, performed across Europe and U.S.; rec. artist on albums Reprise Records, Warner Bros. Records; appeared in rock documentary The Last Waltz, 1978; albums include Gliding Bird, 1969, Pieces of the Sky, 1975, Elite Hotel, Luxury Liner, Quarter Moon in a Ten-Cent Town, Blue Kentucky Girl, 1979, Roses in the Snow, 1980, Cimarron, Last Date, A Light from the Stable, Evangeline, 1981, White Shoes, 1985, Thirteen, Trio (with Dolly Parton, Linda Ronstadt) 1986, Angel Band, 1987, Bluebird, 1989; co-writer, co-producer: (with Paul Kennerley) Ballad of Sally Rose, 1985; composer songs. Pres. Country Music Found., 1983—. Recipient Grammy awards, 1976, 77, 80, 81, 84, 87; named Female Vocalist of Yr., Country Music Assn., 1980; co-recipient (with Dolly Parton and Linda Ronstadt) Acad. Country Music award for album of the yr., 1987. Office: care Mark Rothbaum & Assocs Box 2689 Danbury CT 06813

HARRIS, FRANCES ALVORD (MRS. HUGH W. HARRIS), consultant, retired radio-TV broadcaster; b. Detroit, Apr. 19, 1909; d. William Roy and Edith (Vosburgh) Alvord; A.B., Grinnell Coll., 1929; L.H.D. (hon.), Ferris State Coll., 1980; m. Hugh William Harris, Sept. 24, 1932; children—Patricia Anne (Mrs. Floyd A. Metz), Hugh William, Robert Alvord. With advt. dept. Himelhoch Bros. & Co., Detroit, 1929-31; broadcaster as Julia Hayes, Robert P. Gust Co., 1931-34; tng. and personnel dept. Ernst Kern Co., 1935-36; broadcaster as Nancy Dixon, Young & Rubicam, Inc., 1939-42; women's editor Sta. WWJ, Detroit, 1943-64, Sta. WWJ-TV, 1947-64, spl. features coordinator Sta. WWJ-TV-AM-FM, 1964-74; treas. I.C. Harris & Co., Detroit 1963-82, pres., chief exec. officer, 1982-84, chmn. bd., 1984-85. Mem. exec. bd. Wayne County chpt. Mich. Soc. for Mental Health, 1953-63; chmn. Mental Health Week, 1958-59; mem. Wayne County Commn. on Aging, 1975—, chmn., 1976-77; publicity com. YWCA, 1945, 2d v.p., 1963; mem. publicity com. Tri-County League for Nursing, 1956-61; publicity chmn. Met. Detroit YWCA Bd. Dirs., 1961-66, exec. com., 1962-67; campaign dist. chmn. United Found., 1959, unit chmn., 1960-61, chmn. speakers bur., 1974; exec. bd. United Found. Women's Orgn., 1962-64; governing bd. United Community Services Women's Com., 1961-66; bd. dirs. United Community Services, 1964-67; bd. dirs. Homemaker Service Met. Detroit, pres., 1969-70; bd. dirs. Vis. Nurse Assn., pres., 1974-76; bd. dirs. Camp Fire Girls of Detroit, mem. nat. council, 1967-72, mem. nat. bd., exec. com., 1970-72, pres., 1978-80; bd. dirs. Well Being Service Aging, 1969-74, Sr. Center, 1971-76, Friends Detroit Pub. library, 1972-77, Friends Children's Museum, 1972-74, 83—; trustee Detroit Com. Alcoholism, 1961-64; mem. Mayor's Com. for Freedom Festival, 1959, chmn. women's activities, 1965; mem. Mayor's Com. for UN Week, 1959; mem. Gov.'s Comm. Status of Women, 1962-69, Mich. State Women's Commn., 1969-77; mem. nat. council Homemaker Service, 1970-73; mem. adv. com. to trustees Grinnell Coll.; mem. bd. control Ferris State Coll., 1968-78; mem. def. adv. com. Women in the Services, 1970-73, chmn., 1973; program chmn. Met. Detroit YMCA, 1973-75; sec.-treas. Mich. Assn. Governing Bds. State Colls. and Univs., 1975, v.p., 1976-77, pres., 1977-78; bd. dirs. United Community Services, Detroit, 1973—, mem. assembly, 1984-90. Recipient Grinnell Coll. Alumni award, 1959, Mental Health Soc. Mich. award, 1958, Theta Sigma Phi Headliner award for Mich., 1951, nat., 1952, Heart of Gold award, 1976, Women's Advt. Club of Detroit Civic award, 1957, Mich. Gov. award NATAS, 1987; named Advt. Woman of Year, Detroit, 1958, 73, Soroptimist Woman of Yr., 1965, Fran Harris Day in her honor, Detroit, 1960, Vol. State of Mich., 1975; inducted into the Mich. Journalism Hall Fame, 1986, Mich. Women's Hall of Fame, 1988; commendation service award Mich. Assn. Bus. Owners. Mem. Am. Women in Radio and TV (pres. Detroit chpt. 1957-58, gen. chmn. nat. conv. 1966, Outstanding Community Service award 1972), Women's Advt. Club of Detroit (pres. 1959-60, mem. bd. 1974-77), UN Assn. U.S.A. (dir. Detroit chpt. 1962-65, Mich. div. bd. 1963-65), Advt. Fedn. (nat. v.p. women's activities 1964-67), Nat. Fedn. Press Women (hon.), 1973, Women in Communications (pres. Detroit 1950-51; del. to Asian-Am. Women in Broadcasting Conf. 1966, nat. 1st v.p. 1968-71, nat. pres. 1971-73, chmn. Communications Conf. Ams., 1968, del. III World Congress Women Journalists 1973), Pi Epsilon Delta. Episcopalian (communications com. local congregation and Diocese of Mich. 1965-66). Club: Women's Econ. (charter mem.; dir. 1975—, membership chmn. 1975, program chmn. 1976, public relations co-chmn. 1977, treas. 1978, sec. 1979, 1st v.p. 1980, pres. 1981) (Detroit). Author, editor: Focus: Michigan Women, 1977. Home: 34601 Elmwood Apt 241 Westland MI 48185

HARRIS, FRANCESCA TREPPEDA, art director; b. White Plains, N.Y., Dec. 29, 1958; d. Frank J. and Gemma M. (Russo) T.; m. Daniel O. Harris, Aug. 10, 1985. AAS, Fashion Inst. of Tech., 1980; student, N.Y.U., 1986. Designer, art director Ziff Davis Publ. Inc., N.Y., 1981-85; art dir. Grey Direct Mktg. Inc., N.Y., 1985-86; assoc. creative dir. Ed Sobel & Assocs. Inc., N.Y., 1986-88; sr. art dir. Gross, Townsend, Frank, Hoffman, N.Y., 1988-90, S.J. Weinstein Assocs. Inc., N.Y.C., 1990—; creative cons. Advt. Women of N.Y., 1987, sr. art dir., 1988; sr. art dir. E.R. Squibb & Sons Inc., DuoDerm, 1988, Smith Kline Beecham, Massengill, 1989, Merck Sharp & Dome, Noroxin, 1990. Art dir. American Movie Classics Mag., Creative/AD: Berlitz Intern., 1986, DigitalNews Mag., 1986, Stray Cats, 1984.

Recipient Award of Excellence Grey Direct Mktg., N.Y., 1985, RX Club award, 1990. Mem. Trout Unltd., Theodore Gordon Fly Fishing, Salty Flyrodders, Caanan Pine Grove Assn., Am. Inst. of Graphic Arts, Fashion Inst. Tech. Alumni Assn. Democrat.

HARRIS, GAYLE THOMAS, library researcher, writer; b. Hannibal, Mo., May 5, 1938; d. William Henry and Veneta (Minteer) Thomas; m. Samuel O. Harris (div. 1974); 1 child, Elinda Anne. BA, Chatham Coll., 1960. Asst. to Senator Thomas H. Kuchel, U.S. Senate, Washington, 1961-62; lit. rights adminstr. NBC, N.Y.C., 1962-63; examiner, analyst in govt. and pub. adminstrn. Libr. of Congress, Washington, 1963—. Mem. Alexandria (Va.) Commn. on Arts, 1984-87; chmn. hist. ministries Christ Ch., Alexandria, 1988—. Recipient quality, spl. achievement and meritorious svc. awards Libr. of Congress, 1963—. Mem. DAR (chpt. treas., vice regent, regent, 1983—), Am. Soc. for Theatre Rsch., U.K. Soc. for Theatre Rsch., Lincoln Group, Pi Sigma Alpha. Episcopalian. Home: 3205 Sharon ChapelRd Alexandria VA 22310 Office: Libr of Congress Washington DC 20559

HARRIS, GENEVA DUKE, information scientist; b. Henderson, N.C., Apr. 27, 1946; d. James Lewis and Queen Esther (Wilburn) Duke; m. Fred Walter Harris; children: Donald Walter, Wanda Lynne. Grad. high sch., Henderson. Database analyst Rose's Stores, Inc., Henderson, 1964-86; sr. database analyst Hanes Knit Products, Winston-Salem, N.C., 1986-88; sr. database analyst, cons. Computer Intelligence, Inc., Raleigh, N.C., 1988-89; sr. info. systems analyst Carolina Power & Light, Raleigh, 1989—. Mem. NAFE. Democrat. Baptist. Home: Rte 1 Box 42 Henderson NC 27536

HARRIS, GRACE SALZMAN, lawyer, consultant; b. Pitts., July 12, 1929; d. Jacob Leon and Libby Esther (Siff) Salzman; m. Robert S. Harris, Oct. 3, 1953; children: Andrea Harris Cohen, Rachel Efrati, Jonathan W. AB, U. Pitts., 1951, JD, 1968. Bar: Pa. 1968. Asst. editor Redbook mag., N.Y.C., 1951-53; tchr. Pitts. Bd. Edn., 1953-64; pvt. practice, 1968—; adj. prof. Allegheny Community Coll., Pitts., 1969-71; city atty. City of Pitts., 1970-84. Hon. chmn. Cancer Awareness Day, 1989; hon. mem. bd. Cancer Support Group, 1989—. Mem. Pa. Bar Assn. (ho. of dels. 1976-90), Allegheny County Bar Assn. (bd. dirs. 1980-89), U. Pitts. Law Sch. Alumni Assn. (bd. govs. 1970-80, pres. 1979, 80), Pitts. Gen. Alumni Assn. (pres., exec. bd. 1986-89). Democrat. Jewish. Home: 6567 Bartlett St Pittsburgh PA 15217-1833 Office: 6567 Bartlett St Pittsburgh PA 15217-1833

HARRIS, JESSIE G., retired educational administrator; b. Athens, Ga., May 12, 1909; d. Wiley Jackson and Dora (Hilley) Ginn; BBA, U. Ga., 1956; AB, Ga. State U., 1960; m. Hubert Lamar Harris, Nov. 25, 1930 (dec.); children: Mary Ann (Mrs. William Holley), Hubert Lamar, Dorothy (Mrs. Ronald Zazworksy), Martha Susan (Mrs. R. R. McCue, Jr.). Various secretarial positions ins. and law offices, 1923-30; sec. div. gen. extension U. Ga., 1930-35, asst. dir. div. gen. extension, 1935-47; assisted with compilation survey Univ. System Ga., Atlanta, 1949-50, adminstrv. asst. to regents, 1951-63, asst. exec. sec., 1963-67, assoc. exec. sec., 1967-72, asst. vice chancellor personnel, 1972-74, emeritus, 1974—; cattle farmer, 1972—. Asst. exec. dir. Ga. Scholarship Commn., 1965-66; assoc. exec. sec. Ga. Med. Edn. Bd., 1952-72. Mem. AAUW (chmn. study group 1964-66, treas. 1972, 73), Atlanta Hist. Assn., So. Hist. Soc., Hist. Soc. Walton County (trustee, bd. dirs.), Ga. Trust Hist. Preservation, Crimson Key Honor Soc., Mortar Bd., Phi Chi Theta, Delta Mu Delta, Psi Chi. Club: Atlanta Writers. Home: Rosemont Rt 4 Box 274 Monroe GA 30655

HARRIS, JOAN BERNSTEIN, writer, editor, producer; b. N.Y.C.; d. Leo and Hope (North) Bernstein; m. Thomas A. Harris. BA summa cum laude, U. Rochester, 1976. Host, interviewer, producer Warner Cable TV, Somerville, Mass., 1977-78; researcher, writer Sta. WBZ-TV, Boston, 1978; newscaster, writer, reporter Sta. WERS-FM, Boston, 1979; news anchor, producer, reporter Sta. WLBZ-TV, Bangor, Maine, 1979, Sta. WCSH-TV, Portland, Maine, 1979; newscaster, producer, editor, reporter Sta. WGSM/WCTO, L.I., N.Y., 1980-83; stringer reporter The Associated Press, N.Y.C., 1981-83; newswriter, editor, producer Am. Broadcasting Co., Inc., N.Y.C., 1983—; actress, singer Springfield St. Dinner Theater, Cambridge, Mass., 1978; narrator, radio commls. , Huntington, N.Y., 1981-82; narrator, actress Vanderbilt Planetarium Centerport, N.Y., 1982-83, Hayden Planetarium, N.Y.C., 1984; tchr. English The Internat. Ctr. N.Y., Inc., 1986-88. Mem. Writers Guild Am., AFTRA, Phi Beta Kappa. Office: ABC Radio News 125 West End Ave New York NY 10023

HARRIS, JOYA RENEE, advertising executive; b. Detroit, June 26, 1961; d. Joseph Benjamin and Pauline Elizabeth (McKinney) H. BA in Journalism, Howard U., 1983; MS in Advt., U. Ill., 1986. Assoc. producer Howard Video Prodns., Washington, 1980-83; prodn. asst. Potomac News Svc., Washington, 1983; sales rep. C.A. Howell & Co., Inc., Detroit, 1983-84; sales rep. intern The Wall Sreet Jour., Chgo.; rsch. asst. U. Ill., Urbana-Champaign, 1985-86; mgmt. trainee Ross Roy, Inc., 1986-87; freelance cons. Detroit, 1987—; ind. cons., Detroit, 1988; assoc. acct. rep. J. Walter Thompson/U.S.A., Detroit, 1989—. Co-author: Estimating the Impact of Advertising Media Plans: Media Executives Describe Weighting and Timing Factors; contbr. articles to profl. jours. Vol. United Found., Detroit, 1986—, United Negro Coll. Fund, Detroit, 1986—. Mem. NAFE, Adcraft Club, Jr. League, Link. Democrat. Roman Catholic. Home: 9000 E Jefferson Ave Apt 4-4 Detroit MI 48214

HARRIS, JUDITH HILL, food company executive; b. Greenwich, Conn., Oct. 15, 1949; d. John R. and Hazel L. (Meadows) Gregory; m. R. Woodman Harris, May 23, 1987; 1 child, Ian Wesley Hill. Student, Chatham Coll., 1971. V.p. Magnetic Data Systems, Cos Cob, Conn., 1973-75, Saltwater Farm, Inc., Cos Cob, 1975-81; exec. v.p. Seafood Mgmt. Corp., Greenwich, 1981—. Editor: The Complete Book of Seafood; co-author: Surimi: The Explosive Blended Seafood Market, New Markets for Maximizing New England Fisheries By-Products Values, Potential Market Demand for Fish Hydrolysate as Agriculture Feed Ingredients. Mem. Inst. Food Tech., Am. Soc. Assn. Execs., NAFE, Nat. Fisheries Inst. Home: 89 Dingletown Rd Greenwich CT 06830 Office: 22 Lafayette Pl Greenwich CT 06830

HARRIS, KAREN KOSTOCK, manufacturing company executive; b. Chgo., Sept. 11, 1942; d. Kenneth P. and Elsie A. (Raffl) Kostock; student Mundelein Coll., 1979; m. Roy Lawrence Harris, Feb. 14, 1981. Clerk, loan dept. Evanston (Ill.) Fed. Savs. and Loan, 1960-63, mgr. collection dept., 1963-65; credit adminstr. Packaging Corp. Am., Evanston, 1965-72, adminstrv. asst. to v.p., 1972-74; credit mgr. trainee Am. Hosp. Supply Corp., McGaw Park, Ill., 1974-75; cash mgr. asst. to treas. Pullman Standard, Chgo., 1975-76; nat. credit adminstr. Gen. Binding Corp., Northbrook, Ill., 1976-77; treas. C. H. Hanson Co., Chgo., 1977-79, sec.-treas., 1980—, dir., 1980—, adminstr., trustee C. H. Hanson Co. Pension Plan, 1979—, Employees Savs. and Profit Sharing Trust, 1978—; owner Stock Enterprises, Highland Park, Ill., 1980-81; partner Harris Enterprises, 1981—; pres. Sirrah Enterprises, Inc., 1982-88; ptnr. Montana Co., 1984-88; pres. Cottage Keepers Inc., 1986-87; ptnr. Mont. Co., 1984—; cons. in field; lectr. Founder Mundelein Weekend Coll. Scholar Grant. Recipient Cert. of Merit Chgo. Assn. of Commerce and Industry, 1981, 85. Mem. Nat. Fedn. Rep. Women, Swedish Club Chgo. (sec. 1981-82, steering com. 1982), Venice-Nokomis Rep. Woman's Club. Office: C H Hanson Co 3630 N Wolf Rd Franklin Park IL 60131

HARRIS, KATHERINE LEIDEL, television and radio producer, writer; b. Vienna, Austria, June 28, 1954; came to U.S. 1956; d. Donald Charles and Beverly (Broy)Leidel; m. Michael David Harris, Apr. 3, 1981; 1 child, David Michael. Student, Santa Clara (Calif.) U., 1972-73, Inst. European Studies, Madrid, 1973, George Washington U., 1974. Mgr./developer The Country Store, Knoxville, 1976-77; cons. Southeastern Sight & Sound, Raleigh, 1977-79; dist. mgr. Datatrak Inc., Raleigh, 1979; producer Capitol Broadcasting Co., Raleigh, 1979-80; newsanchor Mann Media Broadcasting, Raleigh, 1980-81, Fairbanks Broadcasting, West Palm Beach, Fla., 1981-83; writer West Communications, Orlando, Fla., 1987-88; pres. Intercultural Telecommunications, North Palm Beach, 1988—; pub. relations staff Archbald Power Corp., 1988. Contbr. articles to profl. jours. Advisor Palm Beach County Film Liaison Com., West Palm Beach, 1988—. Recipient Working Women's award, The White House, 1980. Mem. Fla Motion Picture & TV Assn. (v.p. 1987-88, bd. dirs. 1988—, pres. 1990 Palm Beach Area chpt.). Home: 143 Lighthouse Dr North Palm Beach FL 33408 Office: ITC 143 Lighthouse Dr North Palm Beach FL 33408

HARRIS, LENORE ZOBEL, school nurse; b. Shoemaker, Calif., Nov. 1, 1944; d. Jerome Fremont and Louise Maxine (Purwin) Zobel; m. Robert Thomas Harris, June 19, 1966; children: Rebecca Louise, Grant Thomas. BS in Pub. Health Nursing, Stanford U., 1967; postgrad., Calif. State U., San Diego, 1969-72, Calif. State U., Northridge, 1980-87, Calif. State U.-Stanislaus, Turlock, 1990—. RN, Calif. Staff nurse Stanford (Calif.) Univ. Hosp., 1967-68; pediatric nurse to pvt. practice physician San Diego, 1968-73; sch. nurse Oak Park Unified Sch. Dist., Agoura, Calif., 1978-79, Simi Valley (Calif.) Unified Sch. Dist., 1975-85; camp nurse Kennolyn Camps, Aptos, Calif., 1982, 83, 84; sch. nurse Ventura (Calif.) Unified Sch. Dist., 1984-87; coord. health svcs., Lincoln Unified Sch. Dist., Stockton, Calif., 1987—; originator, chmn. Disaster Preparedness Com., 1985-87; chmn. health adv. com. Lincoln Unified Sch. Dist., 1987—, family life edn. adv. com., 1988—; organizer, adviser Middle Sch. "Just Say No" Club, 1988—. Troop leader San Diego and Ventura area Girl Scouts U.S., 1963, 78-81; officer Ventura Parent Coop. Nursery Sch., 1976-81; pres. Poinsettia PTA, Ventura, 1985-87; officer Pacific Middle Sch. PTSA, Stockton, 1988-90, Lincoln High Sch. PTSA, Stockton, 1990—. Mem. AAUW, Nat. Assn. Sch. Nurses, San Joaquin County Sch. Nurse Orgn. (chmn. 1990—), Calif. Sch. Nurse Orgn., San Joaquin County Health Edn. Com. Office: Lincoln Unified Sch Dist 2010 W Swain St Stockton CA 95207

HARRIS, LINDA FAYE BATES, tax specialist; b. San Antonio, Dec. 25, 1939; d. James Fuller Chandler and Linda Stehle Donnelly; m. Richard Curtis Bates, Feb. 8, 1958 (div. 1975); children: Glenda Anne Snider, Roy Glen, Monty Lee; m. Val Wendell Harris, Nov. 21, 1988. Student, So. Meth. U., 1980-81. Asst. buyer, adminstrv. sec. Esco Mfg. Co., Greenville, Tex., 1969-76; assoc. acctg. Exec. Aircraft Services Inc., Dallas, 1976-78; asst. plant mgr. NL Industries Inc., Dallas, 1978-79; supr. ADP, Dallas, 1979-81, specialist, mgr. unemployment tax, 1984—; dir., adminstrv. sec. Jack Hunter and Assocs., Arlington, Tex., 1981-83; dir., asst. mgr. plant Herbalife Internat., Irving, Tex., 1984-87; ADP mgr. unemployment compensation mgmt. I Tax Specialists, Dallas, 1987—; owner, chief exec. officer Bates Mgmt. Cons., Inc., Mond, Tex., 1987—. Playwright: Texas River Ministry, 1965. Dir. Youth Camp So. Bapt. Conv., 1960-69, 1960-75; chmn. by-laws com. EEO, 1960-69; vol. firefighter, Tye, Tex., 1965-69; active PTA, 1965-69, So. Bapt. Mission Assn., 1965-75; mem. Hendrick Home Children Exec. Assn., 1959—. Mem. NAFE, Tex. Notary Assn. (cert.). Democrat. Home and Office: 5220 Timbercreek Rd Flower Mound TX 75028

HARRIS, LINDA KAY, graphic designer; b. Tottenville, N.Y., Sept. 27, 1947; d. William Herbert and Edith Irene (Zimmerman) Beck; m. Rodger William Clark; stepchildren: Heather, Kristy. BS in Psychology, U. Ill., 1979, BFA in Graphic Design, 1979. Dir. graphic svcs. Burnham Hosp., Champaign, Ill., 1979-86; prodn. mgr. Am. Oil Chemists' Soc., Champaign, Ill., 1986-87; owner Harris & Clark Expedition, Champaign, Ill., 1987—. With USAF, 1965-70. Recipient Creative Inking award Hammermill Paper Co., 1985. Mem. Champaign-Urbana Ad Club, C. of C., Women's Bus. Coun., Exec. Club of Champaign County. Office: Harris & Clark Expdn 23 Ashley Ln Champaign IL 61820

HARRIS, LISA CAMPBELL, accountant; b. Lenoir, N.C., July 1, 1961; d. Rex Douglas and Billie Jean (Seagle) C. BS, Gardner-Webb Coll., Boilinng Springs, N.C., 1985. Cost acctg. clk. Butler Polymet, Inc., Lenoir, sr. acctg. clk., assoc. gen. acct., gen. acctg. supr. Mem. NAFE, Am. Mgmt. Assn., Am. Payroll Assn. Baptist. Office: PO Box 820 Lenoir NC 28645

HARRIS, LOUISE, writer; b. Warwick, R.I., 1903; d. Samuel P. and Faustine M. (Borden) H. AB, Brown U., 1926; pvt. study organ with T. Tertius Noble, N.Y.C., 1938-42. Sec. Samuel P. Harris, Inc., 1928-42; tchr. piano and organ, ch. organist, recitalist Providence, 1928-50; founder, curator C.A. Stephens Collection; researcher Youth's Companion. Author: A Comprehensive Bibliography of C.A. Stephens, 1965, None But the Best, 1966, A Chuckle and A Laugh, 1967, The Star of the Youth's Companion, 1969, The Flag Over the Schoolhouse, 1971, Our Great American Story-Teller, 1978, Old Glory-Long May She Wave, 1981, Time for the Truth, 1987; compiler: Under the Sea in the Salvador (C.A. Stephens), 1969, C.A. Stephens Looks at Norway, 1970, Charles Adams Tales (C.A. Stephens), 1973, Little Big Heart (C.A. Stephens), 1974. Mem. R.I. Hosp. Corp.; 1st founder Brown U. Med. Sch. Recipient Statue of World Culture, Italy, 1984. Mem. Nat. Archives Assocs., Am. Guild Organists, Hymn Soc. Am., Audubon Soc., Brown Alumnae Assn., Nat. Trust Historic Preservation, Am. Bicentennial Rsch. Inst., Am. Heritage Soc., Am. Mus. Natural History, Smithsonian Instn. Assocs., Nat., Western R.I. Home: 395 Angell St Apt 111 Providence RI 02906 Office: Brown U Box 1926 Providence RI 02912

HARRIS, LYNNE STALLINGS, volunteer; b. Brownsville, Tenn., July 19, 1943; d. Morris Humphrey and Elsie (Akin) Stallings; m. Roger R. Harris, Aug. 8, 1965; children: Allison Hope, Robert Morris. BA, Union U., 1965. Tchr. Apopka (Fla.) Meml. High Sch., 1965-67; sec. Stallings Implement Co., Halls, Tenn., 1977-79; mgr. H&H Pallet Co., Inc., Halls, 1980-88; ret., 1988; mem. com. Dyer-Lauderdale County Div. Tenn. Job Svc., Ripley, 1983-88. Mem. Halls Community Ctr., 1983-88, Dyer County C. of C., Dyersburg, Tenn., 1985-88, Lauderdale County C. of C., Ripley, 1987-88. Mem. Chi Omega Alumnae (v.p. Dyersburg chpt. 1984-85, pres. 1985-86). Republican. Baptist. Home: Hwy 88 W Rte 2 Box 29A Halls TN 38040

HARRIS, MARGARET, pianist, conductor, composer; b. Chgo., 1943; d. William and Clara Harris. BS, Juilliard Sch. Music, 1964, MS, 1965. Debut as pianist at age 3; toured as child prodigy; debut with Chgo. Symphony Orch., 1953; condr., pianist Black New World ballet prodn.; toured Europe twice as mus. dir. Black New World and Negro Ensemble Co. N.Y.; debut Town Hall, 1970; pianist, condr. prodn. Hair; musical dir., condr. Two Gentlemen of Verona; made debut as symphonic condr. with Grant Park and Chgo. Symphonies, 1971; soloist original piano concerto L.A. Philharmonic, 1972, 73; condr. St. Louis, Minn., San Diego, Detroit symphonies, L.A. Philharmonic, Wolf Trap Park, Opera Ebony, N.Y.C., 1977, Winston-Salem, N.C. Symphony, 1988; mus. dir. One More Time, Israel, Europe, N.Y.; mus. dir./pianist I Love New York, Europe, 1984; mus. dir. Amen Corner, Broadway, 1984; artist-in-residence Hillsborough Coll., Tampa, Fla., 1984; mus. dir., condr. nat. TV spls.; mus. dir., condr. Raisin on Broadway and nat. tour; exec./music dir. Newark Boys Chorus; panelist Nat. Endowment Arts, Nat. Opera Inst. Affiliate Artists, N.Y.C., Dame Knights of Malta; composer of musical (with Ruby Dee), 1988; former artistic dir., condr. N.Y. Boys Choir; vis. disting. prof. U. West Fla., 1989—; pres. Margaret R. Harris Enterprises. Office: 165 W End Ave New York NY 10023

HARRIS, MARION HOPKINS, government official; b. Washington, July 27, 1938; d. Dennis Cason and Georgia (Greenleaf) Hopkins; m. Charles E. Harris, July 1957 (div. 1964); 1 child, Alan E. M.P.A., U. Pitts., 1971; M.P.A., U. So. Calif., 1984, D.P.A., 1985. Dir. program planning Rochester Urban Renewal Agy., N.Y., 1971-72; exec. dir. Fairfax County Redevel. and Housing Authority, Fairfax, Va., 1972-73; dep. dir. housing mgmt. HUD, Detroit, 1973-75, sr. field officer for housing, Washington, 1979—; mng. auditor GAO, Washington, 1975-79. Bd. dirs. S.W. Neighborhood Assembly, Washington, 1979-80; commr. S.W. Adv. Neighborhood Commn., Washington, 1986; mem. pub. adv. com. Washington Council Govts., 1985—. Recipient Outstanding Performance award HUD, 1984; Carnegie-Mellon mid-career fellow, 1970; Ford Found. travel-study awardee, 1970. Mem. Am. Acad. Soc. and Polit. Sci., U. So. Calif. Doctoral Assn., LWV (exec. bd. Washington 1983-84). Roman Catholic. Avocations: cross-country skiing; foreign travel; swimming. Home: 12306 Sea Pearl Ct Laurel MD 20708

HARRIS, MARTHA JANE, librarian; b. Milton, W.Va., Dec. 29, 1926; d. Dolphus Marshall and Julia Esther (Seabright) Martin; m. Byron Stanley Harris Sr., Dec. 1, 1944; 1 child, Byron Stanley. Student, Indian River Community Coll., Ft. Pierce, Fla., 1972-73; BS, Fla. State U., 1974, MA, 1975. Cert. tchr., Fla. Libr. Henrico County Sch. Bd., Richmond, Va., 1959-64; children's libr. Martin County Pub. Libr., Stuart, Fla., 1964-65, St. Lucie-Okeechobee Regional Libr. System, Ft. Pierce, 1965-70; dir. youth svcs. St. Lucie County Libr., Ft. Pierce, 1975-76; high sch. libr. Sch. Bd. St. Lucie County, Ft. Pierce, 1976-90. Mem. AAUW (br. pres. 1982-84), ALA, Fla. Libr. Assn., Order Ea. Star (chaplain 1957-58), Beta Phi Mu. Methodist. Home: 6710 Samba St Fort Pierce FL 34945

HARRIS, MARY B., home economics educator; b. Vanceville, La., Dec. 27, 1933; d. John Sidney and Bettie Clara (Merritt) Barnes; m. Robert Edward Harris, Sr., Dec. 31, 1950; children: Robert Jr., John, George. BS, Northeast La. U., 1970, MEd, 1972; EdD, Okla. State U., 1975. Cert. home economist, provisional vocat. homemaking, Tex., job specific home economics, Tex., type B vocat. home economics, prin. Prof. Sam Houston State U., Huntsville, Tex., 1975—; home econs. tchr. Waterproof (La.) High Sch. Contbr. articles to profl. jours. Participant African/Am. Cross-Cultural Study Tour of Sierra Leone (West Africa, funded by AAUW). Sex Equity grantee, Teen Responsibility grantee, Title Twelve grantee. Mem. Am. Home Econs. Assn., Am. Vocat. Assn., Assn. for Supervision and Curriculum Devel., AAUW (v.p.), Tex. Home Econs. Assn., Tex. Vocat. Tchr. Educators Assn., Omicron Nu, Phi Delta Kappa. Democrat. Baptist. Home: 224 Westridge Dr Huntsville TX 77340 Office: Sam Houston State Univ Dept Consumer Svcs Fashion & Design Academic Bldg II Huntsville TX 77341

HARRIS, MICALYN SHAFER, lawyer; b. Chgo., Oct. 31, 1941; d. Erwin and Dorothy (Sampson) Shafer. AB, Wellesley Coll., 1963; JD, U. Chgo., 1966. Bar: Ill. 1966, Mo. 1967, U.S. Dist. Ct. (ea. dist.) 1967, U.S. Supreme Ct. 1972, U.S. Ct. Appeals (8th cir.) 1974, N.Y. 1981, N.J. 1988. Law clk. U.S. Dist. Ct., St. Louis, 1967-68; atty. The May Dept. Stores, St. Louis, 1968-70, Ralston-Purina Co., St. Louis, 1970-72; atty., asst. sec. Chromalloy Am. Corp., St. Louis, 1972-76; sole practice, St. Louis, 1976-78; gen. counsel S.B. Thomas, Inc.; div. counsel CPC N.Am., 1978-84; corp. counsel and asst. sec. CPC Internat., Englewood Cliffs, N.J., 1984-88; assoc. counsel Weil, Gotshal & Manges, N.Y.C., 1988—. Mem. ABA (co-chmn. subcom. counseling the mktg. function, securities law com., tender offers and proxy statements subcom.), Ill. Bar Assn., N.Y. State Bar Assn. (securities regulation com.), Bar Assn. Met. St. Louis (past chmn. TV com.), Mo. Bar Assn. (past chmn. internat. law com.), Am. Corp. Counsel Assn. N.J. (past bd. dirs. and chmn. bus. law com.). Address: 625 N Monroe Ridgewood NJ 07450

HARRIS, NATHOLYN DALTON, food science educator, researcher; b. Calvary, Ga., Feb. 26, 1939; d. Martin Luther and Elvie (Clinard) Dalton; m. Ronald A. Harris, June 15, 1967; children: Rhonda Lynn, Scott Eaton. BS, Berry Coll., Mt. Berry, Ga., 1961; MS, Ohio State U., 1962; PhD, U. Wis., 1967. Instr. Berry Coll., 1962-63; rsch. asst. U. Wis., Madison, 1963-66, lectr., 1966-71; asst. prof. food sci. Fla. State U., Tallahassee, 1971-74, assoc. prof., 1975-86, prof., 1986—. Co-author: Meal Management, 1984; contbr. rsch. articles to profl. jours. Named an Outstanding Young Woman Am., 1961; Helena Chamberlain fellow Ohio State U., 1961. Mem. Inst. Food Technologists, So. Assn. Agrl. Scientists (exec. bd. 1974-83), Fla. Assn. Milk, Food and Environ. Scientists (exec. bd. 1988—), Southeastern Tchrs. Food and Nutrition (pres. 1983-84), Springtime Tallahassee, Sigma Xi (pres local chpt. 1985-86), Alpha Chi. Democrat. Baptist. Office: Fla State U 413 Sandels Bldg Tallahassee FL 32306

HARRIS, PATRICIA LEA, state librarian; b. Hanau, Fed. Republic Germany, Oct. 2, 1952; came to U.S., 1954; d. Harvey J. and Laurielea A. (Huth) H. BS in Edn., Wright State U., 1973; MLS, La. State U., 1975. Reference libr. Greene County Dist. Libr., Xenia, Ohio, 1975-78; br. head Greene County Dist. Libr., Fairborn, Ohio, 1978-79; devel. cons. State Libr. of Ohio, Columbus, 1979-83; pub. libr. cons. La. State Libr., Baton Rouge, 1983-84; asst. dir. for devel. Va. State Libr., Richmond, 1984-87; state libr. N.D. State Libr., Bismarck, 1987—; sec. Ohio Coun. of Info. and Referral Providers, 1976-79. Mem. Citizens Adv. Coun. on Adult Basic Edn., Bismarck, 1988—, Westrn Coun. State Librs., 1987—; bd. dirs. N.D. Coalition on Adult Lit., 1987—, N.D. Hist. Archives Assn., 1987—, State Hist. Records Adv. Bd., Bismarck, 1987—; mem., chief officer State Libr. Agys., 1987—. Mem. Mountain Plains Libr. Assn., SE Libr. Assn., Va. Libr. Assn., N.D. Libr. Assn., State Hist. Soc. N.D. (bd. dirs. 1987—), Am. Libr. Assn. Democrat. Roman Catholic. Office: ND State Libr 604 East Blvd Capitol Grounds Bismarck ND 58505

HARRIS, R. ELEANOR M., educator; b. Cleve., July 28, 1936; d. Henry Edward and Annie Elizabeth (Watkins) Murden; m. Lawrence Leonard Harris, Jr., Aug. 5, 1961; 1 child, Loren L. BS in Elem. Edn., Bowie (Md.) State Coll., 1958, MEd in Reading, 1973; EdD in Adminstrn., Nova U., Ft. Lauderdale, Fla., 1985. Tchr. elem. schs. Anne Arundel County Pub. Schs., Annapolis, Md., 1958-73, adminstrv. trainee, 1973-74, asst. prin., 1974-75, coordinator, 1975-79, adminstrv. asst., 1979—; Mem. instructional TV task force Md. State Dept. Edn., Balt., 1976-80, nutrition adv. com., 1979-83. Contbr. articles to profl. publs. Mem. Foster Care Rev. Bd. Office of Gov. State of Md., 1980-84, City of Annapolis Human Relations Commn., 1987—; bd. dirs. Anne Arundel County YMCA/YWCA, 1984—, Banneker Douglas Mus. Found., Annapolis, 1977-79, Community Action Agy., Annapolis, 1975-85, Opportunities Industrialization Ctr., Annapolis, 1983—. Recipient Community Svc. award Community Action Agy., 1980, Disting. Alumni award Nat. Assn. for Equal Opportunity in Higher Edn., 1988, Community Svc. award Opportunities Industrialization Ctrs., 1989. Mem. Am. Assn. Sch. Adminstrs. (sec. women's caucus 1983, Profl. Devel. award 1989), Nat. Acad. Sch. Execs. (Excellence in Adminstrn. award 1984), NAFE, Williamsburg Found., Phi Delta Kappa (pres., treas., sec. 1963-70, Human Rels. award 1977). Democrat. Baptist. Clubs: Frontiers Club Internat. (aux. mem. Annapolis chpt., Civic Betterment award 1987), Links, Inc. (parliamentarian, treas. 1983—), Delicados Inc. (nat. pres. 1981-83). Home: 1999 Forest Dr Annapolis MD 21401 Office: Anne Arundel County Bd Edn 2644 Riva Rd Annapolis MD 21401

HARRIS, ROBERTA LUCAS, social worker; b. St. Louis, Nov. 13, 1916; d. Robert Joseph and Clara Louise (Mellor) Lucas; A.B., St. Louis U., 1955, M.S.W., 1964; m. William F. Sprengnether Jr., Aug. 21, 1937 (dec. 1951); children: Robert Lucas, Madelon Sprengnether Littlejohn, Ronald John; m. Victor B. Harris, Sept. 13, 1955 (dec. June 1960). Field instr. Sch. Social Work St. Louis U., 1967-70; chief of domestic rels. City of St. Louis, 1966-86. Dir., Citizens' Housing Coun., 1956-60; del. to Community Family Life Clinic, 1957; dir. Landmarks Assn., 1957-63; pres. Compton Heights Improvement Assn., 1973. NIMH grantee. Mem. Nat., Mo. assns. social workers, Assn. Family Conciliation Cts. (dir. 1968-86), Greater St. Louis Probation and Parole Assn. (sec. 1976), St. Louis U. Sch. Social Svc. Alumni Assn. (sec. 1973), LWV (dir. 1956-61), Wednesday Club. Methodist. Home: 3137 Longfellow St Saint Louis MO 63104

HARRIS, ROBERTA STUART, nurse; b. Hendersonville, N.C., Apr. 20, 1937; d. Thomas R. and Alice (Boyd) Stuart; m. Crawford B. Harris, June 1, 1955; children: Rita Harris McClain, Rachel Harris Critchley, Rebecca. Assoc. in Nursing, Gardner Webb Coll., Boiling Springs, N.C., 1983. Staff nurse-LPN Cleve. Meml. Hosp., Shelby, N.C., 1962-64; with Lamplighter-Harris Pub. Rels., Forest City, N.C., 1964-80; charge nurse Rutherford (N.C.) Co. Convalescent Ctr., 1983-84; charge nurse psychiatry Spartanburg Reg. Med. Ctr. (S.C.), 1984—; mem. Help Line, Rutherford County Mental Health, 1978-80. Clare Cosner scholar, 1981. Mem. Rutherford County Mental Health Assn., Spartanburg County Mental Health Assn. Home: Rt 1 Box 716 Rutherfordton NC 28139 Office: Spartanburg Regional Med Ctr 101 Woods St Spartanburg SC 29303

HARRIS, RUTH BERMAN, harpist, composer; b. New Haven; d. Benjamin and Pauline Berman; m. Sydney I. Harris, Oct. 6, 1946; children—Mark (dec.), Kenneth, Susan. Student Inst. of Musical Art (now Juilliard), 1934-37, SUNY-Purchase, 1978-81; harp student with Marie Miller, Carlos Salzedo, Lucile Lawrence, Casper Reardon; composition student with Ronald Herder, 1978-81. Free lance orchestral harpist and soloist, NBC, 1938-42; CBS, 1942-50; staff harpist, soloist ABC, 1950-53; free lance harpist and soloist TV, symphony, movie and rec. industries, 1953—; harp tchr. pvt. practice and Westchester Conservatory, 1969—; guest of ministry of edn. and culture 8th and 9th Internat. Harp Contest, Jerusalem, 1982, 85; sponsor concerts for composers, Aaron Copland Competition Young Composers. Compositions include: Requiem Mark Sumner Harris for chamber orch. and voices, 1981; String Quartet, 1982; Miniatures nos. 1, 2, 3, 1976, 77, 78; Collection of Harp Solos: O Holy Night (A. Adam), arranged with Sydney Harris, 1982; Passacaglia for Two Pianos,

1982. Active LWV, Jewish Community Center of White Plains. Recipient Madrigal award, 1933; Meet the Composer grantee, 1982, 84, 85, 86, 87; Mem. Am. Harp Soc., Internat. League Women Composers, Music Tchrs. Council of Westchester (treas. 1981-83), Purchase Music Ensemble (v.p. 1983-85, pres. 1985—), NARAS, N.Y. Women Composers.

HARRIS, RUTH CAMERON, pediatrician, educator; b. Mt. Vernon, N.Y., Apr. 23, 1916; d. Robert Dimond and Jessie Van Wyck (Terwilliger) H.; m. A. Eugene Adams, Oct. 11, 1952; children: Lois H., Roberta H. A.B., Barnard Coll., 1937; M.D., Columbia Coll. Physicians and Surgeons, 1943. Asst. in pediatrics Coll. Physicians and Surgeons, Columbia U., N.Y.C., 1947; instr. Coll. Physicians and Surgeons, Columbia U., 1948-51, assoc., 1951-55, asst. prof., 1955-72, assoc. prof., 1972-76; prof. and chmn. dept. pediatrics Marshall U. Sch. Medicine, Huntington, W.Va., 1976-81; prof. emeritus Marshall U., 1981—; asst. pediatrician Babies Hosp., and Vanderbilt Clinic, 1947-50; asst. attending pediatrician and cons. Babies Hosp., Vanderbilt Clinic, 1950-76; med. cons. Holt Adoption Program, Inc., 1972-85 ; med. adv. chmn. Children's Liver Found., 1975-85. Contbr. articles on pediatric liver problems to med. jours. Mem. Soc. Pediatric Research, Am. Pediatric Soc., Am. Assn. Study Liver Disease, Harvey Soc., N.Y. Acad. Sci., Am. Acad. Pediatrics, N.Am. Soc. Pediatric Gastroenterology, Am. Soc. Human Genetics, Am. Med. Women's Assn., AMA, Assn. Women in Sci.

HARRIS, RUTH MORRISON, lawyer, educator; b. Chgo.; d. Robert Sachs and Sylvia (Morrison) H. BS, Northwestern U., MA; JD, DePaul U., 1955; postgrad., U. Chgo., 1960. Guidance counselor Chgo. Bd. Edn., 1960-77; atty. U.S. C.E., N.Y.C., 1962-63; pvt. practice Chgo., 1956-77, San Diego, 1978—. Mem. Ill. Bar Assn., Calif. Bar Assn., Lawyer Club San Diego, Am. Women for Internation Understanding, Internat. Assn. Through Vol. Activity. Home: 5363 La Jolla Blvd #46 La Jolla CA 92037

HARRIS, SANDRA ARRINGTON, human resources specialist, beauty consultant; b. Humboldt, Tenn., Aug. 7, 1951; d. Cecil Caldwell and Virginia Nell (Looney) Arrington; m. Timothy G. Harris, Jan. 29, 1983; 1 child, Jeffrey C. Simmons. Student, Shelby State Community Coll. Employee devel. specialist IRS, Greensboro, N.C.; fed. women's program mgr., other positions VA, Nashville; beauty cons. Mary Kay Cosmetics. Mem. NAFE, Am. Bus. and Profl. Women's Club, Toastmasters Internat. Home: 7187 Smoke Rise Ln Kernersville NC 27284

HARRIS, SANDY ELLEN, retail executive; b. Hays, Kans., Jan. 28, 1956; d. Kenneth and Mabel (Owen) H.; m. Larry Ohmie (div. Aug. 1987); children: Brandon, Austin. Student, Career DEvel. Ctr., 1974, Colo. U., 1975; BS in Bus., Colo. U., 1979, BS in Mktg., 1979. Mgr. Zales Corp., Dallas, 1974-78; wholesale, import rep. Fine Lines, Denver, 1978-80; pres., chief exec. officer ACL, Inc., Denver, 1980-86, FFI, Inc., Boulder, Colo., 1986—; cons. sales Tindalls, Inc.; exec. sales, job coord. Madeira Beach, Fla., 1988—. Authors: Manufacturing Processes, 1973, Marketing and Consumer Purchasing, 1974. Republican. Home: 1705 14th St #292 Boulder CO 80302

HARRIS, SHARON MAE, anesthesiologist; b. Dayton, Ohio, July 14, 1957; d. Robert Carroll and Frances Mae (Schank) H.; m. James Walton Manz, June 30, 1990. BS in Chemistry, Wright State U., Dayton, Ohio, 1979, MD, 1983. Diplomate Am. Bd. Anesthesiology. Intern dept. internal medicine Med. Coll. Wis., Milw., 1983-84, resident anesthesiology, 1985-87, chief resident anesthesiology, 1987; staff physician Med. Access Urgent Care, Milw., 1984-85; staff anesthesiologist St. Joseph's Hosp., Milw., 1987—; asst. prof. dept. anesthesia Med. Coll. Wis., Milw., 1987—. Named Outstanding Jr. Resident Med. Coll. Wis., 1986, Outstanding Sr. Resident, 1987. Mem. AMA, Wis. State Med. Soc., Wis. Soc. Anesthesiologists, Milw. Soc. Anesthesiology (sec. 1988-89). Republican. Methodist.

HARRIS, SHELLEY FOLLANSBEE, account executive; b. Quantico, Va., Oct. 20, 1949; d. Lawrence Peyton and June Maynard (Trout) H. BS in fine arts, Towson State U., 1973. Surgeon's asst. Drs. Bennett, Johnson & Eaton, P.A., Balt., 1979-82; pers. adminstr., human resources specialist LEGENT Corp. (formerly Morino Assocs., Inc.), Vienna, Va., 1983-88; pers. cons. Snelling & Snelling, Vienna, 1988-89; acct. exec. Forbes Assocs., Inc., Annandale, Va., 1989—. Recipient Regional awards for paintings. Mem. Am. Soc. Pers. Adminstrs., Artist's Equity. Episcopalian. Home: 851 Dogwood Ct Herndon VA 22070

HARRIS, SHEREEN NINA, graphic designer, desktop publisher; b. Alameda, Calif., Mar. 4, 1961; d. Jerry Nathan and Virginia Mae (Triplett) H.; m. John Patrick Doyle, Mar. 12, 1988; children: Hilary Dawn Harris Doyle, Heather Diane Harris Doyle, Hannah Dayne Harris Doyle. Student journalism, Chabot Coll., 1978-81, bus. machines cert., 1983; cert. med. asst., JPTA Sch., Fremont, Calif., 1985. Exec. asst. Assoc. Profl. Engrs., Union City, Calif., 1984-85; computer operator Internat. Clin. Labs., Dublin, Calif., 1986-87; med. asst. Med. Arts Lab., San Leandro, Calif., 1987-88; owner, propr. Harris Info. Systems, Oakland, Calif., 1987-90; owner, artist Now! Graphic Design, Oakland, 1990—; pub., editor Assoc. Entrepreneurs, Oakland, 1988—. Author: Poetry by Shasta, 1987, The Perfect Present, 1988. Treas. East Bay Coun., 1989—. Mem. DAR, Calif. Consortium for Prevention Child Abuse, Descs. Mayflower, Assn. for Rsch. and Enlightenment, Search for God Study Group. Republican. Office: 5251 Broadway Ste 533 Oakland CA 94618

HARRIS, STACY, print and broadcast journalist; b. Mpls.; d. LLoyd and Francine H. Student, Coll. of Emporia, Kans., 1969, Vanderbilt U., 1972; BA, U. Md., 1973. Regular contbr. Country Song Roundup, Derby, Conn., 1976-78; interim Nashville editor Country Song Roundup, Derby, 1978-79, Newsweek mag., N.Y.C., 1983—; writer Sta. ABC Radio News, N.Y.C., 1986—, SDX Gridiron Show, Nashville, 1990—. Author: (children's books) Comedians of Country Music, 1978, The Carter Family, 1978; editor: Spotlight on Country, 1984-86; Nashville editor Country Spirit, 1990—; contbg. author, researcher Country Music Stars and The Supernatural, 1978-79; contbg. editor Inside Country Music, 1981-83; contbr. articles to Nashville Banner, US, Entertaiment Weekly and other newspapers. Arbitrator Better Bus. Bur., Nashville, 1988. Recipient Voice of Democracy award VFW, 1969, Outstanding Teenager award, 1970. Mem. Nat. Entertainment Journalists Assn. (pres. 1989), Country Music Assn., Music Country PC Uers Group, Williamson County Humane Assn. (vol. 1988—). Home and Office: The Windsor Tower 4215 Harding Rd Nashville TN 37205-2017

HARRIS, SUSAN, television producer; b. Mt. Vernon, N.Y.; m. Paul Junger Witt. Dir. various episodes Soap, All in the Family, Then Came Bronson; creator, writer, co-exec. producer The Golden Girls (NBC-TV), 1985— (Emmy awards for best comedy series, Acad. Television Arts and Scis, 1986, 1987). Office: Witt/Thomas/Harris Prodns 846 N Cahuenga Hollywood CA 90038*

HARRIS, SUSAN HUNT, development writer, journalist; b. Cleve., Nov. 5, 1959; d. Warren H. and Rose Marie (Fulkerson) H. BA, Miami U., 1982. Assoc. editor Herald Pub. Co., Barberton, Ohio, 1982-83; reporter News-Herald Newspapers, Wyandotte, Mich., 1983-84, Mellus Newspapers, Lincoln Park, Mich., 1984-86, fund raising exec. Children's Hosp., Detroit, 1986-87; sr. devel. writer, media rels. coord. Northeastern U., Boston, 1987-89; freelance photographer, 1982—; freelance writer, editor, 1984—. Pub. rels. advisor Heritage Soc., Canal Fulton, Ohio, 1981-82; vol. Adult Creative Activities Program, Lincoln Park, 1983, Mass. Pub. Interest Rsch. Group, Amherst Family Ctr.; bd. dirs. Community Care Svcs. Recipient Excellence in Media award Assn., first place enterprise feature award Mich. Press. Assn. Retarded Citizens. Mem Miami U. Alumni Assn., Phi Mu.

HARRIS, TRACI ALANE, data processing executive; b. Montgomery, Ala., Feb. 21, 1961; d. Charles Henry and Sandra (Guest) Cox; m. Lawrence Joseph Harris, Apr. 30, 1988. Student, U. Heidelberg, Fed. Republic Germany, summer 1981, U. Muenster, Fed. Republic Germany, 1983-84; grad., Berry Coll., 1983; M of Internat. Bus., U. S.C., 1986. Staff auditor Arthur Andersen & Co., Frankfurt, Fed. Republic Germany, 1985-86; fin. specialist NCR (Nat. Cash Register Corp.), Dayton, Ohio, 1986-88; product mgr. Peripheral Products div. NCR (Nat. Cash Register Corp.), Wichita, Kans., 1988—; chairperson recycling com. NCR, 1989—, chairperson customer listening com., 1990—. Active Citizens for Recycling, Wichita, 1989—. Rotary Club scholar U. Meunster, 1983-84. Mem. NAFE, Am. Mktg. Assn., Toastmasters (sec.-treas. NCR chpt. 1990—), Alpha Chi, Beta Gamma Sigma. Home: 7400 E 32nd St N #702 Wichita KS 67226 Office: NCR Peripheral Products Div 3718 N Rock Rd Wichita KS 67226

HARRIS, VALERIE COLEMAN, educational administrator; b. King William, Va., June 5, 1957; d. James Edward Sr. and Maude Ellen (Taylor) Coleman; m. Ronald Stevenson Harris Sr., Aug. 1, 1981; 1 child, Ronald Steven Harris Jr. Student, Va. Commonwealth U., 1982-88, J. Sargeant Rey Coll., 1978-86. Adminstr. Med. Coll. Va., Richmond, 1981-90. Mem. NAFE. Home: 3404 Hollow Ridge Ct Chesterfield VA 23832

HARRIS, VERA EVELYN, personnel recruiting and search firm executive; b. Watson, Sask., Can., Jan. 11, 1932; came to U.S., 1957; d. Timothy and Margaret (Popoff) H.; student U. B.C. (Can.), Vancouver; children—Colin Clifford Graham, Barbara Cusimano Page. Office mgr. Keglers, Inc., Morgan City, La., 1964-67; office mgr., acct. John L. Hopper & Assos., New Orleans, 1967-71; office mgr. Elite Homes, Inc., Metairie, La., 1971-73; comptroller Le Pavillon Hotel, New Orleans, 1973-74; controller Waguespack-Pratt, Inc., New Orleans, 1974-76; adminstrv. controller Sizzler Family Steak Houses of So. La., Inc., Metairie, 1976-79; dir. adminstrn. Sunbelt, Inc., New Orleans, 1979-82, sec., dir., 1980—; exec. v.p. Corp. Cons., Inc., 1980-83, pres., 1984-86; pres. Harris Personnel Resources, Arlington, Tex., 1986—, Harris Enterprises, Arlington, 1986—; exec. dir. Nat. Sizzler Franchise Assn., 1976-79. Mem. Am. Bus. Women's Assn., Nat. Assn. Female Execs., La. Assn. Personnel Consultants (treas. 1985-86). Home: 8702 Winding Ln Fort Worth TX 76120 Office: Harris Personnel Resources 2000 E Lamar Blvd Ste 600 Arlington TX 76006

HARRIS, YVONNE LEIGH, financial controller; b. Huntington, W.Va., Sept. 9, 1945; d. Wallace Bailey and Effie Afton (Wikel) H.; m. George Howell Starr, Mar. 10, 1966 (dec. Aug. 1972); 1 child, Kirk Howell; m. Robert Warren Harris, July 3, 1973. BBA, Marshall U., 1969. Cert. profl. fin. officer, Wash. Fin. Officers Assn. Acctg. supr. Biochem. Procedures, Inc., North Hollywood, Calif., 1969-72; cash mgmt. supr. Washington Iron Works, Inc., Seattle, 1973-77; corp. acct. Formac, Inc., Seattle, 1977-78; asst. controller Advanced Tech. Labs., Bellevue, Wash., 1978-79; cost and pricing mgr. Wash. Iron Works, Inc., Seattle, 1979-81, corp. acctg. mgr., 1981-83, controller, 1983-85; cons. K & H Trust, Seattle, 1985—; controller Woodinville (Wash.) Water Dist., 1986—. Mem. Wash. State Fin. Officers Assn., Am. Water Works Assn., Country Cousins Club (treas. 1978-79, pres. 1980-82). Republican. Presbyterian. Home: 14906 210th Ave NE Woodinville WA 98072 Office: Woodinville Water Dist 17238 Woodinville-Duvall Rd Woodinville WA 98072

HARRIS-BAIN, AMY L., office manager; b. Des Moines, Apr. 6, 1937; d. Willard George and Grace Alma (Penry) Meck; m. Wilton James Harris Jr., June 27, 1952; children: Terry Sue, David Lee. Student, Boyles Van-Sant, 1955. Office mgr. Tex. Sign Builders, Austin, Cox's Investments, Austin, Tex., S&A Delivery Svc., Kansas City, Mo., Simon's USA, Kansas City, Kans. Author: Austin's Outstanding Women Directory, It's A Boy/It's A Girl, Time Out-Kid Stuff. V.p. local PTA; pres. B.P.W., 1990; chmn. Jr. Miss Program. Named Woman of Yr.; recipient Aksarben Good Neighbor award. Mem. NAFE, Bus. and Profl. Women, Beta Sigma Phi (pres., v.p.).

HARRIS-HOLOWAY, GERALDINE, corrections officer; b. Rocky Mount, N.C., May 12, 1958; d. Lona Stone. BS in Psychology, Va. State U., 1980; postgrad., Va. Commonwealth U., 1980. Tng. statistician Cnesus Bur., Suitland, Md., summers 1976-80; correctional officer youth ctr. D.C. Dept. Corrections, Lorton, Va., 1981-86; sgt. detention D.C. Dept. Corrections, Washington, 1986-90; lt. occoquan D.C. Dept. Corrections, Lorton, Va., 1990—. Vol. One Am., Washington, 1988-89; mem. Nat. Coun. Negro Women, Washington, 1989. Baptist. Home: 174 Chesapeake St NW Washington DC 20032

HARRISON, ALINE M., organic chemistry educator; b. Lincoln, Nebr., Aug. 30, 1940; d. Albert Movius and Elvira Deloris (Bitzen) Limburg; m. Ernest Augustus Harrison, Aug. 27, 1966; 1 child, Stephen Ernest. BS in Chemistry, U. Mich., 1962; MS in Chemistry, U. Md., 1967, PhD in Chemistry, 1981; postgrad., U. Santa Monica, 1989-90. Chem. lab. instr. York Coll. Pa., 1968-69, organic chemistry instr., 1970; lab. instr. Pa. State U., York, 1970-72; organic lab. instr. U. Md., College Park, 1972-73, 75-76, NIH grantee, organic chemistry rsch. asst., 1976-78; asst. prof. chemistry Dickinson Coll., Carlisle, Pa., 1978-79; asst. instr. chemistry York Coll. Pa., 1979-81, asst. prof. organic chemistry, 1981-90, assoc. prof. organic chemistry, 1990—. Contbr. articles to sci. jours. Resource mgmt. cons., tng. presenter Contact York, 1987—. Mem. AAAS, AAUP, Am. Chem. Soc. (program chair 1986, chair 1987, editor 1977-83), Pa. Soc. Behavioral Medicine and Biofeedback, Inst. Advancement of Health, MidAtlantic Assn. Liberal Arts Colls., Nat. Assn. Advancement of Health Profls. Office: York Coll Pa Country Club Rd York PA 17403-3426

HARRISON, ANNA JANE, chemist, educator; b. Benton City, Mo., Dec. 23, 1912; d. Albert S.J. and Mary (Jones) H. Student, Lindenwood Coll., 1929-31, L.H.D. (hon.), 1977; A.B., U. Mo., 1933, B.S., 1935, M.A., 1937, Ph.D., 1940, D.Sc. (hon.), 1983; D.Sc. (hon.), Tulane U., 1975, Smith Coll., 1975, Williams Coll., 1978, Am. Internat. Coll., 1978, Vincennes U., 1978, Lehigh U., 1979, Hood Coll., 1979, Hartford U., 1979, Worcester Poly. Inst., 1979, Suffolk U., 1979, Eastern Mich. U., 1983, Russell Sage Coll., 1984, Mt. Holyoke Coll., 1984, Mills Coll., 1985; L.H.D. (hon.), Emmanuel Coll., 1983; D.H.L., St. Joseph Coll., 1985, Elms Coll., 1985, Rhodes Coll., 1990. Instr. chemistry Newcomb Coll., 1940-42, asst. prof., 1942-45; asst. prof. chemistry Mt. Holyoke Coll., 1945-47, asso. prof., 1947-50, prof., 1950-76, prof. emeritus, 1979—, chmn. dept., 1960-66, William R. Kenan, Jr. prof., 1976-79; Mem. Nat. Sci. Bd., 1972-78; Disting. Vis. prof. U.S. Naval Acad., 1980. Author: (textbook with Edwin S. Weaver) Chemistry: A Search to Understand, 1989; contbr. articles to profl. jours. Recipient Frank Forrest award Am. Ceramic Soc., 1949; James Flack Norris award in chem. edn. Northeastern sect. Am. Chem. Soc., 1977; AAUW Sarah Berliner fellow Cambridge U., Eng., 1952-53; Am. Chem. Soc. Petroleum Research Fund Internat. fellow NRC Can., 1959-60; recipient Coll. Chemistry Tchr. award Mfg. Chemists Assn., 1969. Mem. AAAS (dir. 1979-85, pres. 1983, chmn. bd. 1984-85), Am. Chem. Soc. (chmn. div. chem. edn. 1971, pres. 1978, dir. 1976-79, award in chem. edn. 1982), Internat. Union Pure and Applied Chemistry (U.S. nat. com. 1978-81), Vols. in Tech. Assistance (bd. dirs. 1990—), Sigma Xi (bd. dirs. 1988—). Address: Mt Holyoke Coll Dept Chemistry South Hadley MA 01075

HARRISON, ANNE ELIZABETH, government official; b. Santa Maria, Calif., May 12, 1941; d. William Lee and Mary Hampton (Beveridge) H. B.S. cum laude, U. Calif.-Davis, 1964; M.S., U. Mich., 1966. Forest naturalist Coronado Nat. Forest, Forest Service, USDA, Tucson, 1966-72, dir. women's activities, regional office, eastern region, Milw., 1972-73, dir. regional visitor info. service, 1973-77, pub. info. officer Cleveland Nat. Forest, San Diego, 1977-81, pub. affairs officer Rocky Mountain Forest and Range Expt. Sta., Fort Collins, Colo., 1981-85, Pacific S.W. Research Sta., Berkeley, Calif., 1985-87, dir. office of info., 1987—; mem. environ. edn. adv. com. Ohio State U., Columbus, 1975-76; regional dir. S.W. region Assn. Interpretive Naturalists, Derwood, Md., 1979-81; project coordinator Seneca Rocks Visitor Ctr., W.Va., 1974-77. Editor, producer 6 tech. transfer modules Silviculture of Rocky Mountain Species, 1981-85 (Nat. Assn. Govt. Communicators nat. 1st place award for one title 1985). Contbr. tech. papers to symposia procs, bot. jours., 1960-80. Conservation chmn. Greenfield Jr. Women's Club, Wis., 1974; chmn. regional conf. S.W. Wis. Interpreter's Assn., 1975; active Christian Women's Clubs, Calif. Recipient 1st place award for exhibit Colo. State Forest Service, 1981, spl. act award USDA Forest Service, 1985. Mem. Nat. Assn. Female Execs., Pub. Relations Soc. Am., Council Biology Editors. Avocations: weaving; hiking; camping; canoeing; cross-country skiing. Office: USDA Forest Service Pacific Research Sta 1960 Addison St Berkeley CA 94704

HARRISON, BEATRICE MARIE (BEATRICE MARIE BINION), educational, human resource consultant, small business owner; b. Detroit, Sept. 10, 1958; d. Lamar Clinton Sr. and Mildred Arretta (Blount) Binion; m. Albert Willard Harrison III, Feb. 7, 1981; 1 child, Sophia Marie. BA in Psychology, Mich. State U., 1980; postgrad., Wayne State U., 1980-81, U. Mich., Dearborn, 1982-83, Ea. Mich. U., 1988; MA in Human Resource Mgmt., Marygrove Coll., 1990. Cert. counselor. Bookkeeper City Nat. Bank, Detroit, 1977; asst. sec. Mich. State U., East Lansing, 1979; co-ptnr., asst. Cordove Rental Co., Holly, Mich., 1980-83; counselor CBN, 700 Club Inc., Royal Oak, Mich., 1985; substitute tchr. Pontiac (Mich.) Sch. Dist., 1985-86; admissions counselor, adminstr. Jordan Coll., Detroit, 1986-87; assoc. dir. undergrad. admissions Marygrove Coll., Detroit, 1988-89; mem. Echoes of Gt. Lakes Mutual Life Ins. Co., 1986—. Assoc. mem. Detroit Symphony, 1984—, Detroit Inst. Arts, 1985—, State of Liberty/Ellis Island Found., 1984—; block chief Southfield (Mich.) Neighborhood Watch, 1984-86; mem. Senator Jackie Vaughn III Re-election Com., Mich., 1986—; team capt. Alberta T. Williams For Congress, mem. fundraiser, campaign com., 1990; bd. dirs. downtown Detroit br. YWCA, 1988—, mem. nominating com., community and corp. affairs com., 1989—; vol. fundraiser Sta. WDIV-TV Easter Seal Telethon, 1988, March of Dimes, Directory Coms., 1989. Mem. NAFE, NAACP (life), Am. Psychol. Assn. (student affiliate 1985-82), Mich. Assn. Collegiate Registrars and Admissions Officers, Guidance Assn. Metro Detroit, Top Ladies of Distinction, Inc. Club (Cite'd'etroit chpt. 1985—, mem. Founders' Day com. Detroit chpt. 1987, 88), Scrap Book Club, Dinner Dance Club. Roman Catholic. Home: 5658 Drake Hollow Dr E West Bloomfield MI 48322 Office: Harrison & Harrison Designs Inc PO Box 240458 West Bloomfield MI 48033

HARRISON, BETTY CAROLYN COOK, vocational educator, administrator; b. Cale, Ark., Jan. 11, 1939; d. Denver G. and Minnie (Haddox) Cook; m. David B. Harrison, Dec. 31, 1956; children: Jerry David, Phyllis Lynley. BSE, Henderson State Tchrs. Coll., Arkadelphia, Ark., 1959; MS, U. Ark., 1971; PhD, Tex. Agrl. and Mech. U., 1975. Tchr. secondary schs., McCrory, Ark., 1962-64, Taylor, Ark., 1964-69, Shongaloo, La., 1969-73, Minden, La., 1974-76, 77-80; adminstrv. intern La. Dept. Edn., 1974; cooperating tchr., supr. student tchrs. Grambling (La.) State U., 1974-76, La. Tech. U., Ruston, 1974-76, 78-80; asst. prof. vocat. edn. Va. Poly. Inst. and State U., Blacksburg, 1976-77; asst. prof. vocat. edn. Coll. Agr., La. State U., Baton Rouge, 1980-85, assoc. prof. Sch. Vocat. Edn., 1985-90, prof. vocat. edn., 1990—, sect. leader home econs. edn., 1982-85, head dept. home econs. edn. and bus. edn., 1985-87, dir. La. Job Link Ctr., 1988—; dir. grants U.S. Office of Edn., La. Dept. of Edn., U.S. Dept. of Labor-Job Tng. Ptnrship. Act, La. Dept. of Employment and Tng., Va. Dept. of Edn. Contbr. articles to profl. jours. HEW fellow, 1973; grantee Future Homemakers Am., 1956, Coll. Acads., 1956, Ark. Edn. Assn., 1956-69, Internat. Paper Co., 1966-68, La. Dept. Edn., 1972. Mem. Am. Home Econs. Assn., La. Home Econs. Assn. (bd. dirs., pres.-elect), La. Vocat. Assn. (bd. dirs.), La. Assn. Vocat. Home Econs. Tchrs. (pres.), Nat. Assn. Vocat. Home Econs. Tchrs., Nat. Assn. Vocat. Home Econs. Tchr. Educators (newsletter editor), Home Econs. Edn. Assn. (regional dir., nat. v.p., editor and chair pubs. 1987—), NEA (nat. assembly del.), Family Relations Council La. (edn. chmn. officer), Phi Delta Kappa, Delta Kappa Gamma, Gamma Sigma Delta. Democrat. Baptist. Home: 2100 College Dr #157 Baton Rouge LA 70808 Office: La State U Sch Vocat Edn Baton Rouge LA 70803

HARRISON, CARLA ISLEY, educator; b. Burlington, N.C., Dec. 13, 1948; d. Frederick Palmer and Elizabeth (Phillips) Isley; m. William Glenn Harrison III, June 17, 1973; children: Allison Palmer, William Glenn IV. BS, Atlantic Christian Coll., 1971; MEd, Elon Coll., 1989. Tchr. Chatham County Schs., Pittsboro, N.C., 1971-74, Alamance County Schs., Graham, N.C., 1974—; tchr. trainer Tchr. Effectiveness Program Alamance County Schs., 1986-87; mem. support team ICP Tchrs., 1988; mentor tchr. 1988—. Treas. Haw River Elementary PTA, N.C., 1981-82; mem. Alamance County Arts Assn., Graham, N.C., 1982-86; precinct ofcl. Alamance County Bd. Elections, Graham, 1982-84; hon. mem. Service League Alamance County, Burlington, N.C., 1980; chmn. Haw River Sch. Based Making Team, 1989—. 1st runner up Tchr. of Yr. Alamance County, 1989. Mem. NEA, N.C. Assn. Sci. Tchrs. (presenter conv. 1986), NAFE, N.C. Assn. Educators (rep. Haw River 1989-90), Smithsonian Inst. (assoc.), Internat. Reading Assn. (presenter 1988), Alpha Delta Kappa, Phi Mu. Democrat. Methodist. Clubs: Burlington Jr. Women's (chmn. child identification project 1986) (N.C.); Brownies (food and entertainment dir. 1985-86) (Graham, N.C.). Lodge: Moose. Home: PO Box 381 Steelecrest Rd Graham NC 27253 Office: Alamance County Schs Haw River Elementary Route 2 Box 1 Haw River NC 27258

HARRISON, CHRISTINE DELANE, educational administrator; b. Dearborn, Mich., July 22, 1947; d. Walter Frederick and Marguerite Elaine (Champagne) Hancock; m. Charles Richard Bashawaty, Aug. 31, 1968 (div. 1972); 1 child, Brett Charles; m. Andrew David Harrison, June 14, 1980; 1 child, Andrew David, II. BS, Ea. Mich. U., 1969. Cert. early elem. tchr., Mich. Tchr. Westland Schs., Mich., 1969-71, Dept. Army, Ansbach, Germany, 1971-72; prin. sec. chemistry dept. U. Mich., Ann Arbor, 1973-78; word processing mgr. Great Copy Co., Ann Arbor, 1978-79; dir., v.p. Great Lakes Sch., Madison Heights, Mich., 1979—. Editorial asst. Herbal Extracts, 1984; Bull. of Thermodynamics and Thermochemistry, 1973-78. Bd. dirs. Perry Nursery Sch., Ann Arbor, 1976-77. Recipient Prodn. award and Dedication award Los Feliz Apple Sch. Mem. Mich. Assn. for Supervision and Curriculum Devel., Nat. Trust for Hist. Preservation, Clawson C. of C., Greenpeace, Sierra Club. Avocations: reading, bicycling, aerobics, sailing. Office: Great Lakes Sch 1431 E Twelve Mile Rd Madison Heights MI 48071

HARRISON, DEBORAH ANN, automotive industry executive; b. Bowling Green, Ky., Aug. 29, 1957; d. T. C. and Nancy Carol (Lyle) H. AS in Bus. Mgmt., Nat. Edn. Corp., 1989. Background vocals Doc's Recording Studio, Hendersonville, Tenn., 1973-75; service mgr. Lyles Toyota, Gallatin, Tenn., 1975-80; mgr. D.G.'s Automotive, Ft. Walton Bch., Fla., 1980-83; asst. mgr. James Equipment & Supply Co., Albany, Ga., 1983-86, Hentschel Motorcars, Albany, 1986-88; service adv. Fritz Automotive, 1988-89; mgr. trainee Kroger's, Gallatin, Tenn., 1989; cons. Fritz Automotive, Gallatin, 1988-89. Charter mem. Gift for Life Assn., Albany, 1984. Recipient Silver Merit award Distributive Edn. Clubs Am., 1975, Bronze Merit award Distributive Edn. Clubs Am., 1975. Mem. Nat. Orgn. Female Execs., DECA (v.p. 1973-75), Girl Scouts (v.p. 1963-75), Smithsonian Assn. Democrat. Roman Catholic. Home: 230 Haze Hyde Hollow Rd Bethpage TN 37022 Office: R R Donnelley 801 Steam Plant Rd Gallatin TN 37066

HARRISON, FRANCES MARIE, insurance agency administrator; b. New Braunfels, Tex., July 3, 1934; d. Erwin and Elsie Amanda (Kappelmann) Heimer; m. John Charles Copeland, Oct. 21, 1954 (dec. 1959); children: Michael Dennis (dec.), Karen Lynn; m. Norwick Benton Harrison, July 26, 1963 (div. 1982). Grad. high sch., San Antonio. With USAA, San Antonio, 1952—, computer programmer, 1959-70; systems analyst USAA, 1970-77, mgr. ins. data processing, 1977—. Mem. German Texan Heritage Soc., San Antonio Genealogy Soc., Beethoven Damenchor, German Am. Soc. Republican. Lutheran. Home: 118 William Classen Dr San Antonio TX 78232 Office: USAA USAA Bldg San Antonio TX 78288

HARRISON, GLORIA GIMMA, travel company executive; b. Bklyn., Mar. 19, 1928; d. Mario Vito and Rosaria Elena (Geraci) Gimma; m. A.T. Harrison Jr., Dec. 22, 1948 (div. Mar. 1956); children: Arthur Thomas III, John Gimma; m. Henry J. Babis (dec. Dec. 1978). BA in Merchandising and Mktg., Finch Coll., 1945; MA in Psychol. Scis., Mich. State U., 1947. Cert. travel cons. Sec., account exec. NBC, N.Y.C., 1947-48; sec. Coca-Cola USA, Atlanta, 1967-74; adminstrv. asst. to Superior Ct. Judge John S. Langford Fulton County, Atlanta, 1974-81; owner, founder Harrison Travel Ltd., Atlanta, 1980-87, pres.; dist. sales mgr. The Travel Channel, Cert. Travel Agy.; sales mgr. S.E. region Auto Europe; founder, pres. Travel Media Group Ltd., 1989. Trustees Ctr. Visually Impaired, Atlanta, 1985, Village St. Joseph, Atlanta, 1987, St. Joseph's Hosp., 1988; treas. Ga. Indigent Def. Coun., 1984-90. Mem. Travel Industry Assn. Ga., Inst. Cert. Travel Agents, Pacific Asia Travel Assn., Am. Soc. Travel Agts., Cruise Line Internat. Assn., Prost Exec. Women in Travel, Travel Industry Assn. Ga. (bd. dirs.), Com. of 200. Home: 54 Ivy Chase Atlanta GA 30342-4517

HARRISON, HELEN EILEEN CONNOLLY, horticulture educator; b. Annapolis, Md., Apr. 15, 1949; d. Walter Curtis and Crystle Geraldine (Tossey) Connolly; m. Richard Francis Harrison, May 28, 1977; children: Christopher Curtis, Peter Connolly, Jessi Eileen. BA, N.C. State U., 1971;

MS, Ohio State U., 1976; PhD, Pa. State U.., 1979. Assoc. prof. horticulture U. Wis., Madison, 1980—. Contbr. articles to profl. jours. Active Assn. of Retarded Citizens, Madison, Autism Soc., Madison. Mem. Am. Soc. Hort. Sci. (extension div. v.p. 1990—), Internat. Soc. Hort. Sci., Master Gardeners Internat., Coun. Agrl. Sci. and Tech., CAST, Phi Kappa Phi. Office: Univ Wisconsin Dept Horticulture 1575 Linden Dr Madison WI 53706

HARRISON, JACKITA, nurse, funeral director; b. Gary, Ind., Nov. 22, 1947; d. Edwin Griffin Moore and Luella (Johnson) Mitchell; m. Alan Dinand Harrison, Aug. 10, 1966 (dec. 1972); children: Gina Fine Harrison, Janien Derniere Harrison. AS, City Coll. San Francisco, 1978, San Francisco Coll. Mortuary Sci., 1980; BS, U. San Francisco, 1985, M in Pub. Adminstn., 1987. RN; lic. funeral director/embalmer; nat. cert. oper. room nurse. Lic. practical nurse Victory Meml. Hosp., Waukegan, Ill., 1968-73; vocat. nurse St. Luke's Hosp., San Francisco, 1973-76; operating room nurse San Francisco Gen. Hosp., 1976-78; fun. dir., embalmer Assoc. Funeral Services, Oakland, Calif., 1980-84; staff nurse surgery Seton Med. Ctr., Daly City, Calif., 1981-85, St. Francis Meml. Hosp., San Francisco, 1985-86; operating room nurse U. Calif., San Francisco, 1978—; asst. clin. supr. Perioperative Services, San Francisco, 1987-89; nurse Vet. Administrn., Martinez, Calif., 1989-90; perioperative supr. Kaiser-Martinez, 1990—. Parent adv. Community Alliance for Spl. Edn., San Francisco, 1978-89; parent advisor, prin. adv. bd. Mercy High Sch., San Francisco, 1982-86; mem. Parkmerced Resident's Orgn., San Francisco, 1978—, Stanford Parents Assn., 1986-90. Mem. Assn. Operating Room Nurses (del. to Congress 1986 chair scholarship 1986-90, nominating com., chair rsch. com. 1990—), Nat. Bd. Funeral Dirs. Democrat. Roman Catholic. Home: PO Box 305 Pinole CA 94564

HARRISON, JANET LEAH, physician, educator; b. Ste. Genevieve, Mo., Nov. 26, 1944; d. Wilmer Leonard and Dorothy Ludora (Resinger) B.; m. Philip Lynn Harrison, Aug. 16, 1975; children: Elinor Clare, Laura Alexandra, Meredith Elise. BSN, U. Mo., 1968, MD, 1978. Diplomate Am. Bd. Anesthesiology. Anesthesiologist Andrain Med. Ctr., Mexico, Mo., 1982—; clinical instr. U. Hosp. and Clinics, Columbia, Mo., 1982—; cons. Ellis Fischel State Cancer Hosp., Columbia, Mo., 1984—. Author: articles on medicine, 1982, 1986. Mem. Physicians for Soc. Responsibility, Columbia, Mo., 1986—, PTA Columbia, (sec. 1988—), Neofight Columbia, 1982—, W.A.N.D. Columbia, 1986—. Recipient Women Student Award, Am. Med. Women Assn., Columbia, 1978. Mem. Am. Soc. of Anesthesiologists, Alpha Omega Alpha. Democrat. Methodist. Office: Anesthesia Specialists Inc 116 S Jefferson St Mexico MO 65265

HARRISON, JOAN S(HIRLEY), college dean; b. Orange, N.J., Apr. 29, 1934; d. Harry and Rose (Marshak) Horowitz; m. David Harrison, Mar. 23, 1958; children: Andrew L., Rachel E. AB magna cum laude, Tufts U., 1956; AM, Radcliffe Coll., 1957; MS, Bank St. Coll., N.Y.C., 1982; PhD, Union Grad. Sch., Cin., 1987. Tchr. Weehawken (N.J.) Pub. Schs., 1959-60; faculty Farleigh Dickinson U., Teaneck, N.J., 1960-61, 64-65; program developer, adminstr. Englewood (N.J.) Pub. Schs., 1964-67; asst. dean studies Sarah Lawrence Coll., Bronxville, N.Y., 1973-81, assoc. dean studies, 1981—, acting assoc. dir. Ctr. for Continuing Edn., 1980-81; dissemination assoc. Englewood Title III Project, 1972; mem. adj. faculty Bank Street Coll., 1981-83, 89, Empire State Coll., 1989; cons. N.Y.C. Bd. Edn., 198-23-84. Contbr. articles to profl. jours. Mem. planning bd. met. region Nat. Identification project of Am. Council on Edn., 1980-85. Mem. Phi Beta Kappa. Home: 2 Oxford Rd Hastings-on-Hudson NY 10706

HARRISON, JUDY COFFIN, publisher; b. Geneva, Ill., Oct. 1, 1939; d. Charles Howlles and Louise (Brydon) Coffin; m. David Francis Harrison, Oct. 10, 1958; children: Nancy Ellen, Juliana, David Francis Jr. Cert. in respiratory therapy, Seattle Cen. Community Coll., 1976-78. Cert. respiratory therapist, Wash. Dir. homecare Linde Homecare Med. Systems, Redmond, Wash., 1980-84; pub. Canoe mag., Kirkland, Wash., 1984—, CKI News, Kirkland, 1986—. Author: Canoe Tripping with Children, 1978, 2d e dit., 1990, Becoming Your Industry's Voice, 1990. Bd. dirs. NW Masters Swimmers Assn., Seattle, 1980-87, pres., 1982-84. Mem. N.Am. Paddlesports Assn. (nat. bd. dirs. 1987—, nat. pres. 1987-89), NW Publs. Assn. (pres. 1985-87). Republican. Office: Canoe Am Assocs 10526 NE 68th St Ste 5 Kirkland WA 98033

HARRISON, LEISA DIONE, application engineer; b. L.A., June 16, 1962; d. Alphonse Manfred and Willie Mae (Mickels) H. BS in Computer Sci., Calif. State U., Northridge, 1986; cert. vocat. tng., UCLA, Long Beach, 1987; postgrad., El Camino Coll., Torrance, Calif, 1988. CAD application engr. Xerox Corp., El Segundo, Calif., 1986-89; CAD system adminstr., mem. tech. staff II Hughes Aircraft Co., El Segundo, 1989—; CAD cons. CDM and Assocs., Fox Hills, Calif., 1988—; instr. basic programming L.A. Coun. Black Profl. Engrs., Inglewood, Calif., 1986-89. Mem. Nat. Assn. Female Execs., L.A. Coun. Black Profl. Engrs. (v.p. programs 1989—, chmn. computer lab. 1987-89). Democrat. Home: 415 Tamarack Ave #1 Inglewood CA 90301 Office: Hughes Aircraft Co 19300 Gramercy Pl Torrance CA 90501

HARRISON, LOIS COWLES, civic worker; b. Des Moines, Iowa, June 23, 1934; d. Gardner and Lois (Thornburg) Cowles; B.A., Wellesley Coll., 1956; m. John Raymond Harrison, June 24, 1955; children—Mark, Pat, Lois; m. Homer E. Hooks, Nov. 27, 1981. Dir., Cowles Media Co. (formerly Mpls. Star and Tribune Co.), 1975-85. Commr. Gov.'s Commn. on Status of Women, 1973-77, Fla. Ethics Commn., 1974-78; mem. Commn. on Fla. Constl. Revision, 1977-78; mem. Fla. Women's Polit. Caucus, 1973-75; trustee Cowles Charitable Trust, 1955—; v.p. LWV Fla., 1973-77, pres., 1977-80, bd. dirs., 1982-83, dir. edn. fund, 1973-77, dir. LWV U.S. ERA chair, 1980-82; bd. dirs. ERAmerica, 1980-82; pres. Planned Parenthood Central Fla., 1982-85; pres. Fla. Assn. Planned Parenthood Affiliates, 1987-89; dir. Fla. Fine Arts Coun., 1972-80, So. Legal Coun., 1980—; mem. Mayor's Creative and Performing Arts Coun., Lakeland, Fla., 1972-75; mem. Am. Bar Commn. on Evaluation of Profl. Standards, 1978-80; pres. Polk Mus. Art, 1985-86, bd. govs., 1988—; pres. The Hooks Group, 1985—. Mem. Wellesley Coll. Alumnae Assn. (v.p. bd. dirs. 1989—). Episcopalian. Home: 2311 Nevada Rd Lakeland FL 33803

HARRISON, LOIS SMITH, hospital executive; b. Frederick, Md., May 13, 1924; d. Richard Paul and Henrietta Foust (Menges) S.; m. Richard Lee Harrison, June 23, 1951; children: Elizabeth Lee Boyce, Margaret Louise Wade, Richard Paul. BA, Hood Coll., 1945; MA, Columbia U., 1946. Counselor CCNY, 1945-46; founding adminstr., counselor, instr. psychology and sociology Hagerstown (Md.) Jr. Coll., 1946-51, registrar, 1946-51, 53-54, instr. psychology and orienta, 1954-56; registrar, instr. psychology, Balt. Jr. Coll., 1951-54; bus. mgr., acct. for pvt. med. practice Hagerstown, 1953—; trustee Washington County Hosp., Hagerstown, 1975—; chmn. bd. Washington County Hosp., 1986—; bd. dirs. Home Fed. Savs. Bank, Hagerstown, 1983—; speaker ednl. panels, convs. hosp. panels and seminars. Author: The Church Woman, 1960-65. Trustee Hood Coll., Frederick, 1972—, chmn. bd., 1979—; mem. Md. Gov.'s Commn. to Study Structure and Ednl. Devel. Commn., 1971-75; pres. Washington County Coun. Ch. Women, 1970-72; appointee Econ. Devel. Commn., County Impact Study Commn. Bd.; bd. dirs. Md. Hosp. Assn. Quality Coun. Bd., Md. Hosp. Edn. Inst., 1988—, vice chmn., 1989—, Md. Chs. United, 1975—. Recipient Alumnae Achievement award Hood Coll., 1975, Washington County Woman of Yr. award AAUW, 1984, Md. Woman of Yr. award, 1984, Md. Woman of Yr. award Francis Scott Key Commn. for Md.'s 350th Anniversary, 1984. Mem. Hagerstown C. of C. Democrat. Mem. United Ch. Christ. Home: 1640 Fountain Head Rd Hagerstown MD 21740 Office: Washington County Hosp Hagerstown MD 21740

HARRISON, MARJORIE JEANNE, infosystems specialist; b. Milw., Apr. 27, 1923; d. Joseph Ray and Margaret Katherine (Oettinger) Ryan; m. Charles Leslie Harrison, Oct. 1, 1941 (dec. 1974); children: Patrick Ryan, Michael Carter, Thomas Charles. Student, Northwestern U., 1940-41; cert., Ohio U., 1957. Cert. elem. tch., Ohio. Substitute tchr. Boys Indsl. Sch., Lancaster, Ohio, 1956-61, pre-voc. tchr., 1961-63; mgr. Coll. Classics, Inc., Columbus, Ohio, 1964-69; adminstrv. aide auditor's office State of Ohio, Columbus, 1969-71, grants budget rev. officer dept. econ. community devel., 1971-75, MIS ops. officer dept. econ. community devel., 1975-79, MIS coord. dept. devel., 1979-89; mem. Pres. Task Force, Washington, 1985-87. Bd. dirs. YWCA, Lancaster, 1960-61; active Child Conservation League, 1957-60, League Women Voters, 1987—. Law enforcement asst. adminstrn. grantee, 1980. Mem. NAFE, DAV (comdrs .club Cin. chpt. 1977—), Nat. Assn. Criminal Justice Planners, Federated Women's Club, Comdr.'s Club. Republican. Methodist. Home: 4202 Shamley Green Dr Toledo OH 43623

HARRISON, MARTHA ELAINE, computer programmer, civilian military employee; b. Bitburg, Fed. Republic of Germany, June 30, 1962; d. Zadoc Daniel Jr. and Selina Elizabeth (McLaughlin) H. Student, U. Tenn., Chattanooga, 1980. Register operator Wendy's Old Fashioned Hamburgers, Chattanooga, 1978-79; clk. Provident Life and Accident Ins., Chattanooga, 1980, programmer, 1985—; mgr. Massey Enterprises, Inc., Chattanooga, 1981-82; algebra tutor U. Tenn., Chattanooga, 1982-83; register operator Wendy's Old Fashioned Hamburgers, Chattanooga, 1983, 1984; printer operator TVA/Boandi Temp Service, Chattanooga, 1985; disbursement officer 3397th U.S. Army Garrison, Chattanooga, 1981—. Served as disbursement officer USAR, 1981—. Named one of Outstanding Young Women of Am., 1983. Mem. Nat. Assn. of Female Execs., Res. Officers Assn., DAR, Mil. Order of World Wars. Democrat. Episcopalian. Home: 3623 Fountain Ave Apt 97 East Ridge TN 37412-1834

HARRISON, MARY ANNE, lawyer; b. Syracuse, N.Y., Apr. 15, 1944; d. James Robertson and Ruth (O'Connor) Urquhart; m. Douglas L. Thorpe, Oct. 2, 1977. BA, U. So. Calif., 1966; JD, U. Calif., Berkeley, 1969. Bar: Calif. 1970. Dep. atty. gen. State of Calif., 1970-73; sr. atty. Pacific Lighting Corp., 1973-76; v.p., sec., gen. counsel Buena Vista Distbg. Co., Inc., Burbank, Calif., 1976-85; v.p., asst. gen. counsel Fox, Inc., Beverly Hills, Calif., 1985—. Bd. dirs. ofcl. salaries authority City of L.A., 1979-80. Mem. ABA, State Bar Calif., L.A. County Bar Assn., Calif. Women Lawyers, Women Lawyers Assn. L.A. Office: Fox Inc PO Box 900 Beverly Hills CA 90213*

HARRISON, MARY FRANCES NALL, consumer education educator; b. Georgiana, Ala., June 23, 1918; d. Joseph Leslie and Vita (McClure) Nall; m. George Merlyn Harrison, Dec. 7, 1942 (div. June 1962); children: George Leslie, Mark Nall, Merry Leigh Harrison Duffey. BS in Home Econs., Auburn (Ala.) U., 1940; MS in Edn., Tex. A&I U., 1955; postgrad., U. Fla., 1984-88. Home mgmt. supr. Farm Security Adminstrn., Dallas County and Selma, Ala., 1940-43, 45-46; tchr. Norfolk (Va.) Pub. Sch. Bd., 1943-45; adult edn. supr. Corpus Christi (Tex.) Pub. Schs., 1946-55; clothing designer Sarita Lyons Clothing Mfg., Corpus Christi, 1955-56; tchr. Clubbs Jr. High Sch., Escambia County Sch. System, Pensacola, Fla., 1956-63; extension home econ. agt. Fla. Coop. Extension Svc., Hilliard, Fla., 1963-67; asst. prof., consumer edn. specialist Fla. Coop. Extension U. Fla., Gainesville, 1967-72, assoc. prof., cons. edn. specialist Fla. Coop. Extension, 1972-80, prof., consumer edn. specialist, 1980—. Contbr. over 200 articles on consumer edn. to extension publs. Fla. Dept. Energy grantee, 1980-81, 82, Nat. Coop Bank grantee, 1983-84, Fla. Bur. Pub. Mgmt. grantee, 1985, 86, 87, 88, 89. Mem. Fla. Assn. Extension Profls., Am. Coun. Consumer Interest, Am. Home Econs. Assn. (various dist. offices), Gainesville Gem. and Mineral Assn. (pres., sec., treas.), Fla. LWV, Gamma Sigma Delta, Epsilon Sigma Phi (sec., treas.). Democrat. Baptist. Home: 4902 NW 18th Pl Gainesville FL 32605 Office: U Fla Coop Extension Svc 3025 McCarty Hall Gainesville FL 32611-0130

HARRISON, MARY KATHRYN, social services administrator; b. Winnsboro, Tex., May 25, 1952; d. Ferrell Eugene and Ruby Ellen (Underwood) Harrison. BS, East Tex. State U., Commerce, 1973, MS, 1977. Social svcs. worker Dept. Pub. Welfare, Quitman, Tex., 1974-79; promotions coord. Gospel Pub. House, Springfield, Mo., 1979-82; social worker Dept. Human Resources, Sulphur Springs, Tex., 1982-84; adult protective svcs. specialist Dept. Human Resources, Sulphur Springs, 1984-87; social svcs. supr. Dept. Human Svcs., Longview, Tex., 1987-88, supr. adult protective svcs., 1988—; part-time instr. Evangel Coll., Springfield, 1979-80. Writer, editor curriculum materials. Named Social Worker of Yr., Tex. Dept. Human Svcs., 1986. Mem. Assemblies of God. Office: Tex Dept Human Services 911 NW Loop 281 Longview TX 75604

HARRISON, MARY LU, hospital administrator, social services professional; b. Shawnee, Ohio, Jan. 22, 1942; d. Elias F. and Mary C. (Williams) Hatem; m. Richard O. Harrison, Nov. 1968 (dec. June 1978); 1 child, Mary Caroline. BA, Coll. St. Mary of the Springs, Columbus, Ohio, 1963; MSW, Cath. U. Am., 1965. Lic. ind. social worker. Child welfare caseworker Athens (Ohio) County Childrens Svcs., 1965-66; child welfare supr. Franklin County Childrens Svcs., Columbus, 1966-70, child abuse supr., 1974-75; med. social worker Ohio State Univ. Hosps., Columbus, 1970-74, supr., 1974-76, asst. dir. social svc., 1976-78, dir. social svc., 1978-84, dir. med./surg., psychiat. and rehab., 1984—; cons. Social Svc. dept. Fayette Meml. Hosp., Ohio, 1987—; mem. geriatric adv. bd. Coll. Medicine Ohio State U., 1978—. Author: (booklet) Living With Chronic Illness, 1980. Mem. adv. bd. Health dept. City of Columbus, 1984—, Cen. Ohio Parkinson Assn., Columbus, 1980—. Mem. Nat. Assn. Social Workers (Ohio chpt.), Soc. Hosp. Social Work Dirs., Ohio Soc. Hosp. Social Workers (bd. dirs. 1983—). Democrat. Roman Catholic. Home: 3046 Rightmire Blvd Columbus OH 43221 Office: Ohio State U Hosps 410 W 10th Ave Columbus OH 43210

HARRISON, NELSINE FRANCES, elementary educator; b. Washington, Aug. 24, 1941; d. Nelson Augustine and Helen Catherine (Cooper) Parker; m. Tommy Lee Harrison, June 15, 1963 (div. Oct. 1970; 1 child, Tommy L. BS, D.C. Tchrs. Coll., 1963; MA magna cum laude, Calif. State U., Dominguez Hills, 1974. Cert elem. tchr.; cert. lang. tng. in Spanish. Spl. summer program tchr. Compton (Calif.) Unified Sch. Dist., 1980, English as 2d lang. tchr., 1982-83, English as 2d lang. curriculum developer, 1983-85, facilitator adminstrs. and staff workshops, 1984, summer sch. tchr., 1985, reading com. curriculum developer, 1986-87, IBM Writing to Read program mgr., 1987-89, sci. program curriculum developer, 1989, bilingual-English as 2d lang. tchr., 1969—; v.p. Dehra Cons., Washington, 1963-69. Author: Compton English as a Second Language, 1985; author curriculum guide; also articles. Judge, Beulahland Bapt. Ch., Gardena, Calif., 1984; chmn. social com. 120th St. and Denver Ave. Block Club, L.A., 1988—. DAR scholar, 1960. Mem. NEA, Calif. Tchrs. Assn., Compton Edn. Assn., Assn. for Supervision and Curriculum Devel., Nat. Alliance Black Sch. Educators, Nat. Black Child Devel. Inst., Alpha Kappa Alpha. Democrat. Episcopal. Home: 644 W 120th St Los Angeles CA 90044-3903 Office: Bunche Elem Sch 16223 S Haskins Ln Carson CA 90746

HARRISON, PATRICIA GREENWOOD, historian; b. Monticello, Ark., Jan. 2, 1937; d. Howard Walter and Lorene (Stewart) Greenwood; m. Edward Lindsay Harrison, Aug. 7, 1960; children: Gregory Edward, Rebecca Lindsay, Laura Patricia. BS, Henderson State Coll., 1959; MA, So. Meth. U., 1964; postgrad., U. Wis., 1965-67. Instr. history Eastfield Coll., Dallas, 1968-73, Richland Coll., Dallas, 1972-74, U. South Ala., Mobile, 1977-86, Spring Hill (Ala.) Coll., 1979—; book rev. editor Gulf Coast Hist. Rev., Mobile, 1985-87. Author: Women in Mobile during World War II; The Development of Gulf Shores, Alabama: An Interview with Ernie Hall Meyer. So. Meth. U. fellow, 1962-64. Mem. AAUW, Am. Hist. Assn., So. Hist. Assn., Ala. Assn. Historians, So. Assn. Women Historians, Oral History Assn., Phi Alpha Theta. Methodist. Home: 6409 Sugar Creek Dr S Mobile AL 36695 Office: Spring Hill Coll Dept History Mobile AL 36608

HARRISON, PHYLLIS, management consultant; b. Portland, Oreg., Feb. 2, 1934; d. Philip and Mabel (Dennis) Morgan; m. Robert Harrison, Dec. 10, 1979; children: Linda, Lora, Dennis, Douglas, Lisa Marie. Student, Franklin, Portland, Oreg. Ind. cons.; guest lectr. culinary dept. Clark Community Coll., Vancouver, Wash. Del. to People's Republic of China sponsored by U.S. Exchanges and China Ministry of Sci. Mem. Inst. for Managerial and Profl. Women, NAFE, Lioness Orgn. Home: 1402 SW 26th Circle Troutdale OR 97060

HARRISON, ROSALIE THORNTON (MRS. PORTER HARMON HARRISON), retired educator; b. Birmingham, Ala., Jan. 24, 1917; d. John William and Zora (Whetstone) Thornton; m. Porter Harmon Harrison, Apr. 12, 1941; 1 child, Porter Harmon. AB, Samford U., 1937; MA, U. Ala., 1945; postgrad., Tchrs. Coll., Columbia U., 1945-46, 53, Cath. U. Am., 1956, 63-64, George Washington U., 1957-58, 59, Am. U., 1962, U. Md., 1964-65, U. D.C., 1967-69, 70. Tchr. Pinson (Ala.). Sch., 1937-41; tchr. Children's Sch., U. Ala., 1939-41; tchr., asst. prin. Avondale Estates (Ga.) Elem. Sch., 1941-45; asst. tchr. Horace Mann-Lincoln Sch. of Tchrs. Coll., Columbia U., 1946; instr. English, Samford U., 1948; tchr. Lakeview Sch., Birmingham, 1948-49, Hazelwood and McFerran Sch., Louisville, 1950-53; with pub. schs. of Dist. of Columbia, Washington, D.C., 1956-82; tchr. Congress Heights Elem. Sch., Washington, 1956-63; guidance counselor Barnard Elem. Sch., Washington, 1963-82; adminstr. D.C. Project Head Start, summers 1966-69, coord. parent program, summers 1968-69; prin. Congress Heights-Savoy Elem. Summer Sch., Washington, 1971, Blow-Bowen Elem. Summer Sch., Washington, 1972. Del. Congress of Bapt. World Alliance, Rio de Janeiro, Brazil, 1960, Miami, Fla., 1965; dir. D.C. Bapt. Conv. Summer Mission Camp Girls Aux., 1955, assembly officer Dept. Bapt. Women, 1967-71, 73-77; dir. Bapt. Tng. Union, Riverside Bapt. Ch., Washington, 1954-65, also mem. choir, council, mem. numerous coms., officer, 1953—; past pres. Ministers Wives, D.C. Bapt. Conv. Ky. Col. Mem. NEA (life), Am. Assn. for Counseling and Devel., D.C. Assn. Counseling and Devel., Am. Sch. Counselor Assn., D.C. Sch. Counselor Assn., D.C. Elem. Sch. Counselor Assn. (past v.p.), D.C. Career Devel. Assn. (past pres.), Nat. Career Devel. Assn., Assn. for Multicultural Counseling and Devel., D.C. Assn. for Multicultural Counseling and Devel., Assn. Specialists in Group Work, D.C. Assn. Specialists in Group Work (charter), Am. Mental Health Counselors Assn., D.C. Mental Health Counselors Assn.; also Internat. Platform Assn., Council for Exceptional Children, Nat. Trust Hist. Preservation, D.C. Ret. Tchrs. Assn., The Columbian Women of the George Washington U. (past 1st v.p.), Smithsonian Nat. Assocs., U.S. Capitol Hist. Soc., Concerned Citizens Council Washington (pres.), Washington City Bible Soc. (bd. dirs.), Alpha Delta Kappa (past state pres. Washington, past pres. Gamma chpt.). Home: 3828 17th Pl NE Washington DC 20018

HARRISON, SHELLEY BROWN, communications executive; b. Alma, Mich., May 16, 1951; d. Charles Ralph and Marion Jean (Walker) Brown; m. John Francis Phelan, Aug. 4, 1979 (div. 1983); m. Leslie Frank Harrison, Sept. 14, 1985; children: Katherine, Jonathan. BA, U. Mich., Ann Arbor, 1973. Sales engr. Shure Bros., Inc., Evanston, Ill., 1974-79; sales rep. Filmways Audio Group, North Hollywood, Calif., 1979-80; ptnr. Sunwest Mktg., Burbank, Calif., 1980-84; gen. sales dir. Rts Systems, Inc.,, Burbank, Calif.; charter mem. bd. ITVA TV Assn., Los Angeles 1979-81; mktg. cons. Hollywood Sound Systems B & B Systems, Los Angeles 1984; conv. chairperson Audio Engr. Soc., Los Angeles 1986. Editor: Book, Profl. Intercom: Ref. Book 1987. Pub. Relations Folks-Friends of Little Kids, Burbank Calif., 1988. Paul Harris fellow Rotary Internat. Mem. Internat. TV Assn. (Pub. Relations 1979—), Audio Engring. Soc. (vice chair 89th Audio Engring. Soc. Conv. 1990), Rotary Club Hollywood Calif. Democratic. Office: RTS Systems Inc 1100 W Chestnut St Burbank CA 91506

HARRISON-CLARK, ANNE, foundation administrator; b. N.Y.C., Oct. 24, 1938; d. Edward Webb and Elizabeth Enright (Nash) Harrison; children: Elisabeth Bayley Clark, Carter Harrison Clark. AB in Am. Studies, Smith Coll., 1960. Asst. dir. vols. Mus. of Sci., Boston, 1960-62; instr. Pakistani-Am. Cultural Ctr., Karachi, 1966-68; dir. Women's Lobby Women and Health Project, Washington, 1974-76; legis. dir. Nat. Consumers League, Washington, 1977-78; Washington rep. Population Resource Ctr. and Population Assn. Am., 1978-83; dir. constituency devel. John Glenn Presdl. Com., Inc., Washington, 1983-84; v.p. pub. affairs March of Dimes Birth Defects Found., Washington, 1985—; cons., fundraiser for population and environ. concerns, 1984-85; cons. office of consumer affairs Dept. Health, Edn. and Welfare, Washington, 1978, Ctr. for Displaced Homemakers, Balt., 1976. Bd. dirs. Coalition for Health Funding, Washington, Alliance Non-Profit Mailers, Washington; mem. pediatrics adv. panel U.S. Pharmacopeial Conv., Inc., Washington. Mem. Women in Govt. Relations. Home: 7200 Denton Rd Bethesda MD 20814 Office: March of Dimes Birth Defects Found 1725 K St NW Ste 814 Washington DC 20006

HARRISON-JOHNSON, YVONNE E., pharmacology researcher; b. Norfolk, Va., Apr. 29, 1939; d. Hugo Herman and Georgia Mae (Hall) Harrison; m. Melvin C. Johnson, Sept. 27, 1975. BS, Howard U., 1959, MS, 1970, PhD, 1972. Rsch. asst. Wellcome Rsch. Lab., Tuckahoe, N.Y., 1964-69; rsch. assoc. Howard U., Washington, 1970-72; from biol. rsch. coord. to asst. to v.p. Hoffmann - La Roche Inc., Nutley, N.J., 1972—; bd. dirs. Consumer Health Info Resource Ctr. N.Y.C. Contbr. articles to profl. jours. Recipient Black Achiever in Industry awd. N. Y. YMCA, 1974, Twin Tribute to Women in Industry awd., YMCA, 1975, Disting. Alumni awd. Nat. Assn. Equal Opportunity in Higher Edn., 1983. Mem. AAAS, Am. Mgmt. Assn., Am. Pharm. Assn. Acad. Pharm. Scis., Am. Physiol. Soc., Am. Soc. for Pharnacology and Experimental Therapeutics (nominating com. 1985, chmn. Affirmative Action com. 1985-87, chmn. Minorities com. 1988—, Profl. Affairs com. 1985—). Home: 101 Highland Ridge Rd Manalapan NJ 07728

HARRISON-MCCLAFFERTY, MONICA REGINA, real estate executive; b. Panama City, Panama, Sept. 18, 1964; came to U.S., 1968; d. Robert Edwin and Mireya de Rosario (Ingram) Harrison; married. BS in Econs., U. Del., 1986. Mktg. assoc. Equitec Properties, L.A., 1987-88; leasing agt. Forest City Enterprises, L.A., 1988-89; realtor, assoc. Coldwell Banker, L.A., 1989—; pres., owner Prima, L.A., 1987—. Roman Catholic. Home: 8560 Hillside Ave Los Angeles CA 90069

HARRIS-SMITH, JOAN A., educational administrator; b. Wilkes-Barre, Pa., Apr. 14, 1933; d. George Walter and Marjorie (Halstead) Quigley; m. Joseph Michael Melchiona, Nov. 16, 1952 (div. July 4, 1960); children: Joseph, Joan; m. Lynn Rynearson Harris, Apr. 14, 1962 (div. July 18, 1971); children: Kenton, Lynn R. Jr., Sean, Kelly; m. Charles T. Smith, Feb. 14, 1984. Actress, dancer N.Y.C., 1949-72; owner, tchr. KLS Enterprises, Inc., Edwardsville, Pa., 1967-72; program dir. Coll. for Kids, King's and Wilkes Coll., Wilkes-Barre, 1976-79; exec. dir. Kids on Campus, Wilkes-Barre, 1979-80; dir. Marywood Coll., Scranton, Pa., 1981; owner, tchr. Joan Harris Centre for Gifted and Talented, Edwardsville, 1982—, also bd. dirs.; program dir. Pa. State U., Luzerne County Community Coll., Misericordia Coll., Wanticoke Coll. Author (with others) Creative Dance, 1977; editor (books) The First of the Three R's: Reason, 1978, True Myths, 1978, vol. II, 1980, A Tribute to Water, 1979, The Wheel, 1979, Our Country, 1979, Philosopher's Index, 1981, Common Clay, 1981. Mem. Rep. Nat. Com. Recipient Youth Res. Fund Talent Contest 1st and 2d place awards, 1984, Small Bus. Devel. award Greater Wilkes-Barre C. of C., 1985, Cert. of Appreciation O.K. Heart, 1985. Mem. NAFE, Nat. Assn. for Gifted, Dance Educators Am. Home: 185 Terrace Ave Trucksville PA 18708 Office: Ctr for Gifted and Talented Narrows Shopping Ctr Edwardsville PA 18704

HARRO, BARBARA LEIGH, clinical psychologist; b. Galesburg, Ill., Aug. 10, 1928; d. B. Everett and Nelle Bonita (Shover) Leigh; m. Thomas Shoop Harro, June 27, 1950; children: Kathleen, Peggy, Stephen. BA cum laude, Wheaton Coll., 1950; MA, Roosevelt U., 1969; Psy.D., Ill. Sch. Profl. Psychology, Chgo., 1989. Spl. tchr. Kankakee (Ill.) State Hosp., 1964-65, psychologist, 1967-74; dir. psychiat. outpatient clin. Riverside Med. Ctr., Kankakee, 1974-78; psychotherapist Mental Health Ctr. of Kankakee County, 1978—; psychology intern Riverside Med. Ctr., Kankakee, 1986-88, psychol. cons., 1989—; pvt. practice psychotherapy and neuropsychology Oakside Clinic, Kankakee, 1989—. Mem. Am. Psychol. Assn. (assoc.). Office: Oakside Clinic 201 N Wall St Kankakee IL 60901

HARROWER, ANGELINE A., social worker; b. South Pittsburg, Tenn., Dec. 18, 1937; d. Phillips Hackworth and Mildred Ruth (Curtis) Albea; children: Angeline S. Harrower, Chiara C. Turner. BA, U. Chattanooga, 1959; MS Social Work, U. Tenn., 1980. Speech therapist Orange Grove Ctr., Chattanooga, 1959-61; clin. asst. Syracuse (N.Y.) U., 1961-62; speech therapist Walker County Dept. Edn., LaFayette, Ga., 1962-63; welfare worker Tenn. Dept. Human Svcs., Chattanooga, 1970-73; adminstr./social worker Cath. Social Svcs., Chattanooga, 1973-82; caseworker II, III Family and Children's Svcs., Chattanooga, 1982-85; social worker/patient care coord. Siskin Meml. Found., Chattanooga, 1985-89; dir. social svcs. Renaissance Rehab. & Diagnostic Hosp., Chattanooga, 1989—; cons. Marion County Speech Hearing Ctr., Jasper, Tenn., 1985-89, ResCare Home Health, Chattanooga, 1988—, Kimberly Quality Care Home Health, Chattanooga, 1989—, ABC Home Health, Chattanooga, 1990—. Bd. dirs. Mizpah Congregation (sec. 1988-90); pres. Home and School Assn., All Saints Acad.,

1977-78. Named Social Worker Year Tenn. Soc. Health Care Social Workers, SE Coun., 1988-89. Mem. Nat. Assn. Social Workers SE Branch (sec., 1980-81, Mem. chmn., 1977-79, Tenn. Soc. Health Care Social Workers, SE Coun. (pres. 1987-88, v.p., 1986-87),. Jewish. Office: Renaissance Rehab Hosp 2412 McCallie Ave Chattanooga TN 37404

HARRY, SUSAN ELAINE, computer scientist, desktop publisher; b. Fayetteville, Tenn., May 24, 1961; d. Jerry Albert and Martha Maybelle (Reese) H.; m. James Lee Clarkson, Sept. 20, 1980 (div. Dec. 1984); 1 child, Tarek Ryan Alexander. Student, Northlake Coll., 1985. Sr. systems analyst Zale Corp., Irving, Tex., 1982-85; sr. programmer analyst Rep. Bank Dallas, 1985-87; printing systems analyst Xerox, Dallas, 1987-89; owner Miz Publ., Nashville, 1989—; speaker Xplor-A Xerox Users Group Orgn., Dallas and Orlando, Fla., 1985-87. Fund raiser The Hunger Project, Dallas, 1987, Dallas C. of C., 1988. Mem. NAFE, World Runners, Nat. Assn. Women Bus. Owners. Unitarian. Home: 1507 Woodmont Blvd Nashville TN 37215 Office: 501 Great Circle Rd Nashville TN 37228

HARSDORF, SHEILA ELOISE, state legislator, farmer; b. St. Paul, July 25, 1956; d. Ervin Albert and Eloise Vivian (Sodergren) H.; m. Vernon Clark Bailey, Nov. 18, 1989. BS in Animal Sci., U. Minn., 1978; grad., Wis. Rural Leadership Program, 1986. Loan officer Prodn. Credit Assn. River Falls, Wis., 1978-80; dairy farmer, Beldenville, Wis., 1980-88; mem. Wis. Assembly, 1988—; part-time dairy farmer; mem. adv. coun. for small bus., agrl. and labor Fed. Res. Bank Minn., Mpls., 1988; mem. Wis. Agrl. Stblzn. and Conservation svc. Com., 1987-88. Mem., chairwoman Pierce County Dairy Promotion Com., 1986; mem. Congressman's Adv. Coun. on Agr., 1988—, First Covenant Ch., River Falls. Mem. Wis. Farm Bur. (co-treas. 1982-85, Discussion Meet winner 1986), Wis. Holstein Assn., Dairy Shrine. Republican. Home: Rte 4 Box 219 River Falls WI 54022

HARSNEY, JOHANNA MARIE OFFNER, nurse; b. Youngstown, Ohio, Oct. 15, 1914; d. Michael and Elizabeth (Untch) Offner; m. Theodore Harsney, Aug. 11, 1941; 1 son, Karl Michael. Grad. Youngstown Hosp. Sch. Nursing, 1939; B.A. in Fgn. Langs., Youngstown U., 1972. Staff nurse Youngstown Hosp., 1939-40; pvt. duty nurse Youngstown Profl. Nurse's Registry, Youngstown, 1940-84. Vol. Red Cross nurses. Mem. Am. Nurses Assn., Profl. Nurses Registry (dir.), Ohio Nurses Assn. (pres. pvt. duty sect. 1979-84), Am. Bus. Women Assn. (v.p. Gold Torch chpt. 1978, Nurse of Yr. Dist. 3, 1983), Phi Lambda Pi (sec. Kappa chpt. 1973-74, v.p. 1973-74, pres. 1975). Home: 2204 Cranbrook Dr Youngstown OH 44511 Office: Profl Nurses Registry 3119 Market St Ste 224 Youngstown OH 44507

HART, ALISON ANN, publishing executive; b. Kansas City, Kans., July 27, 1963; d. Richard Franklin Jr. and Nathalie (Faris) H. BS in Journalism, U. Kans., 1987. Asst. Internat. Prodn. Assocs., N.Y.C., summer 1987; prodn. coord. Family Media Inc., N.Y.C., 1987-88; special events mgr. Woman's Day, N.Y.C., 1988—. Recipient music scholarship in voice, U. Kans. Music Faculty, 1981-85. Mem. Women in Communications (pres. coll. chpt. 1985), Meeting Planners Internat., N.Y. Choral Soc., Nebr. Soc. of N.Y., Alpha Delta Sigma, Kappa Alpha Theta; provisional mem. Jr. League.

HART, BOOTS DALE, motion picture producer, writer, accountant; b. Mt. Kisco, N.Y., Feb. 23, 1954; d. Saul and Norma Jean (Ashley) David. Freelance pub. rels. writer, prodn. acct., film writer L.A., 1973—, ind. film producer,, 1980—; cons. pub. rels. writer World Pvt. Exercise, L.A. Author: (novel) Reality & Mind, 1976, (film scripts) Inner Intrigue, 1982, Blastron, 1983, G.O.D.S., 1990. Home and Office: 2407 Wilshire Blvd Apot 286 Santa Monica CA 90403

HART, CAROLE URCELL, purchasing administrator; b. Balt., Jan. 5, 1955; d. Franklin Carroll and Kathryn (Marable) Adams; m. Terry Stephan Hart, June 24, 1978; 1 child, Brian Steven. AA, Broward Community Coll., 1975; B of Profl. Studies, Barry U., 1989. Acctg. clk. Bendix, Ft. Lauderdale, Fla., 1975-77, purchasing expeditor, 1977-79; purchasing agreements coord. Bendix Nat. Electronics, 1980-89; purchasing specialist Bendix, Ft. Lauderdale, Fla., 1979-80, buyer, 1980-84; sr. buyer Allied-Signal div. Bendix, Ft. Lauderdale, 1984-86; purchasing supr. Avionics Div. Bendix-King Air Transport, Ft. Lauderdale, 1986—; coord. partnership agreements Avionics div. Bendix-King Air Transport, Ft. Lauderdale, 1989—. Mem. NAFE, Nat. Assn. Purchasing Mgmt. Republican. Methodist. Office: Bendix 2100 NW 62d St Fort Lauderdale FL 33310

HART, CHRISTINE E., minister of culture and communications; b. Halifax, N.S., Canada, Feb. 3, 1950; d. Gordon L.S. and Catherine (MacKinnon); m. W. John Mowat; children: Tara, Melanie. BA, Acadia U., Wolfville, N.S., Can., 1970; LLB, U. Toronto, 1973. Bar: Ont. 1975, N.S. 1978. Law clk. to chief justice Ont. Supreme Ct., Toronto, Can., 1975-76; counsel Inter City Truck Lines Ltd., Toronto, 1976-79; ptnr. Morris, Rose & Ledgett, Toronto, 1979-86; mem. Ont. Legislature, Toronto, 1986—. Office: Ont Parliament, Parliament Bldgs, Toronto, ON Canada M7A 1A2

HART, CYNTHIA LOUISE, finance company executive; b. Marshalltown, Iowa, Apr. 4, 1948; d. Robert Lee and Beverly Ione (Greenfield) M.; m. Stephen Lothaire Brandt, July 20, 1967 (div. 1977); m. Leo Oswald Hart, May 27, 1984; children: Sabrina, Kirsten, Jennie. Student, U. Calif., Fullerton, 1966-69; BSBA in Mgmt., U. Calif., Berkeley, 1988. Asst. v.p., br. mgr. Hibernia Bank, San Francisco, 1975-82; sr. v.p. comml. loan and credit dept. Eureka Fed. Savs. and Loan, San Carlos, Calif., 1983-86; assoc. dir. Fed. Home Loan Bank, San Francisco, 1986-88; v.p. loan mgmt. Am. Real Estate Group, Stockton, Calif., 1988—; guest speaker Office of Edn. Fed. Home Loan Bank, Dallas, 1985—; mem. curriculum com. Am. Inst. Banking Edn., San Francisco, 1983. Contbr. articles to mags. in field. Bd. dirs. Bayshore Childcare Ctr., San Mateo, Calif., 1985. Mem. Nat. Assn. Credit Mgrs., Nat. Assn. Bus. Women, Harvard Bus. and Profl. Women's Group, Credit Women's Internat., Nat. Assn. Female Execs., Commonwealth Club of San Francisco. Lutheran. Office: Am Real Estate Group 445 N San Joaquin St Stockton CA 95201

HART, EILEEN KELLY, contracting administrator; b. Cambridge, Mass., Nov. 9, 1947; d. John Charles and Helen Patricia (Bielaski) Kelly; m. Douglas Ryan Bliven, Jan. 6, 1967 (div. Nov. 1978); children: Christopher Bryan, Jennifer; m. Stephen Christopher Hart, Feb. 25, 1983; stepchildren: Jennifer Lynn, Brian Stephen. Student, Montgomery Coll. With USN, 1965-88; analyst cost and price USN, Laurel, Md., 1983-86, contracting officer, 1986-88; contract adminstr. Systemhouse Fed. Systems Inc., Arlington, Va., 1988—. Mem. Nat. Contract Mgmt. Assn. (pres. local chpt. 1986-88, cert. profl. contract mgr.). Roman Catholic. Home: 17400 Soper St Poolesville MD 20837 Office: Systemhouse Fed Systems Inc Arlington VA 22201-4717

HART, ELSIE FAYE, educator; b. Shelbyville, Ill., Oct. 15, 1920; d. James Ray and Maude May (Allison) Cain; m. Harold Delbert Bible, June 15, 1941 (div. Apr. 1948); children: Gary H. Bible, Rex E. Bible; m. Frederick Christopher Hart, July 28, 1950; children: Susan Hart Eichman, Pamela L. Hart. Elem. teaching cert., Ea. Ill. U., 1942; BS in Edn., No. Ill. U., 1968; postgrad., Rockford Coll., 1972-73. Cert. elem. tchr., Ill. Tchr. Findlay (Ill.) Elem. Sch., 1942-47; tchr. Winnebago County Schs., Rockford, Ill., 1948-52, Rockford Parochial Schs., 1957-63; tchr. Rockford Pub. Schs., 1964-82, substitute tchr., 1982—. Contbr. articles to profl. jours. Pres. Assn. for Childhood Edn. Internat., Rockford, 1968-76; sec.-treas. Ill. Assn. for Supervision & Curriculum Devel., Rockford, 1970-80; mem. NEA, Ill. Edn. Assn., Rockford Edn. Assn., 1964-82; mem. Rockford Art Assn., 1968, Beta Sigma Phi, Rockford, 1950, Rockford Creative Dramatics Assn., 1968, Mauh-Nah-Tee See Country Club, Rockford, 1982; vol. tchr. Rockford Parochial schs. Recipient Cert. of Commendation in recognition of meritorious svc. Ill. Supt. Pub. Instrn., 1974. Mem. AAUW (historian Rockford chpt. 1970—), Ill. Retired Tchr.'s Assn., Winnebago/Boone Retired Tchr.'s Assn., Women of the Moose, Holy Family Women's Guild, Rockford Woman's Club (sec. 1970, publicity 1971, membership 1972, ways/means 1988-91), Ostende Dance Club. Republican. Roman Catholic. Home: 1507 Al Crest Rd Rockford IL 61107

HART, HELEN P., construction executive; b. Fonda, Iowa, Feb. 20, 1927; d. William and Bessie B. (McGowan) Prendergast; m. John J. Hart, Sept. 6, 1947; children: Marcia B., J. Alexander, Andrew P., Katherine W. Student, Iowa State U., 1944-46, Mary Crest, Davenport, Iowa, 1946-47; BA, Drake U., Des Moines, 1982. Cert. Property Mgr., Iowa. Pvt. practice Des Moines, 1947-74; pres. The Hart Co., Des Moines, 1974--; devel. chmn. Master Builders, Des Moines 1985-87; Pres. Bus. Network, Des Moines 1987--; V.P. Assn. Women Contractors, Des Moines 1989. Bd. dirs., Cath. co-chmn. Nat. Council Christians & Jews, Des Moines, 1985—, Meth. Hill Child Care Ctr., Des Moines, 1985—, Wesley Retirement Svcs., Des Moines, 1985—. Mem. Nat. Assn. Women Bus. Owners (treas.). Republican. Roman Catholic. Home: 3663 Grand Ave #108 Des Moines IA 50312 Office: The Hart Co 1517 Second Ave Des Moines IA 50314

HART, JANE, optical company executive; b. Bellingham, Wash., Aug. 20, 1948; d. William Lee and Neta Jane (Raines) Hopper. Cert., Am. Bd. Opticinary, 1986. Cert. varilux fitting, silor fitting, ABO. Gen. mgr. Broome Optical Co., Amarillo; instr. Amarillo (Tex.) Coll. Mem. Tex. Republicans. Mem. NAFE, Nat. Acad. Opticinary, Southwest Opticians Assn. Home: 3131 Fleetwood Amarillo TX 79109

HART, KITTY CARLISLE, arts administrator; b. New Orleans, Sept. 3, 1917; d. Joseph and Hortence (Holtzman) Conn; m. Moss Hart, Aug. 10, 1946 (dec. 1961); children: Christopher, Cathy. Ed., London Sch. Econs., Royal Acad. Dramatic Arts; DFA (hon.), Coll. New Rochelle; DHL (hon.), Hartwick Coll.; LHD (hon.), Manhattan Coll., Amherst Coll. Chmn. N.Y. State Council on the Arts. Former panelist: TV show To Tell the Truth; actress on stage and in films including The Marx Brothers A Night at the Opera, 1936; Broadway theatre appearance in On Your Toes, 1983-84; singer, Met. Opera, TV moderator and interviewer; author: (autobiography) Kitty, 1988; contbr. book revs. to jours. Assoc. fellow Timothy Dwight Coll. of Yale U.; bd. dirs. Empire State Coll.; formerly spl. cons. to N.Y. Gov. on women's opportunities; mem. vis. com. for the arts MIT. Office: 915 Broadway New York NY 10010

HART, LYNN PATRICIA, lawyer; b. Schenectady, N.Y., Sept. 12, 1954; d. H. Philip Hart and M. Patricia (Dinsmore) Hart-Franco; m. Frederick T. Muto, Sept. 8, 1979; children: Daniel Frederick, Christopher Hart. BA cum laude, Westmont Coll., 1976; JD, U. Calif., Berkeley, 1979. Bar: Calif. 1979. Law clk. to presiding justice U.S. Dist. Ct., San Diego, 1979-80; assoc. Heller, Ehrman, White & McAuliffe, San Francisco, 1980-83, Howard, Rice, et al, San Francisco, 1983—; lectr. fin. and estate planning Stanford U. Law Sch., 1989—. Author: Property not Subject to Probate Administration, 1986, Decedent Estate Practice CEB, 1986, Disclaimers: A Gift to the Post-Mortem Planner, 1988. Mem. estate planning coun. of San Francisco and East Bay; bd. dirs. Dwight House, Berkeley, 1982. Mem. ABA (real property, probate and trust law sect., chair post-mortem tax probate com., disclaimer com., nominating com.), Calif. State Bar (exec. com. 1987-90, CEB joint adv. com., estate planning, trust, probate and trust sub-com. 1988-90, asst. editor respective newsletters 1987-90), San Francisco Bar Assn. (probate and trust law sect., outstanding pro bono atty. 1982, 83), Calif. Women Lawyers, Women Tax Lawyers. Democrat. Presbyterian. Office: Howard Rice et al 3 Embarcadero Ctr San Francisco CA 94611

HART, MARIAN GRIFFITH, retired educator; b. Bates City, Mo., Feb. 5, 1929; d. George Thomas Leon and Beulah Winiferd (Hackley) Griffith; m. Ashley Bruce Hart, Dec. 23, 1951; children: Ashley Bruce Hart II, Pamela Cherie Hart Gates. BS, Cen. Mo. State Coll., 1951; MA, No. Ariz. U., 1976. Title I-Chpt. I reading dir. Page (Ariz.) Sch. Dist.; Title I dir. Johnson O'Malley Preschool, Page Sch. Dist.; dist. reading dir. Page Sch. Dist. Contbr. articles to profl. jours. Sec. Friends of Page Pub. Libr.; vol. tutor basic skills, tchr. Page Community Adult Literacy, 1990—. Mem. Delta Kappa Gamma (pres. Tau chpt. 1986-90, historian 1990—, state com. scholarship 1987-89, nominations com. 1989-91), Xi Alpha Kappa (past v.p.). Republican. Home and Office: 66 S Navajo Dr PO Box 763 Page AZ 86040

HART, MICHELLE A., systems architect, engineer analyst, consultant; b. Indpls., Apr. 22, 1961; d. Kenneth E. and Sandra (Pope). BS in Computer Sci., Ga. State U. Cert. trainer VM and MUS systems, personal computers. Systems analyst/progammer, cons. State of Ind.; project mgr. systems, engring. and systems analyst, architect, cons. Delco Electronics; team leader, systems analyst, architect/engr. IBM Profl. Svcs. Rsch. Triangle Pk., Durham, N.C.; systems architect, engr. analyst Advanced Info. Systems, Indpls., AGS Info. Svcs., Cin., GTE Telecommunications, Indpls.; owner Midwest Info. Svcs., Indpls. Mem. NOW; active Big Sister, Little Sister Program. Recipient communications awards. Mem. NAFE (dir. Ind. region), Women Entrepreneurs, Data Processing Assns., Computer Clubs. Home: 6111 E 42nd St Indianapolis IN 46226

HART, SALLY MILLNER, corporate executive; b. Washington D.C., Jan. 21, 1953; d. Walter Dearing and Margaret Scherer (Culver) Millner; m. David Dickinson Hart, June 10, 1972; 1 child, Allison Millner. BS, U. Calif., 1977; MS, Am. U., 1986. From clin. dietitian to chief clin. nutritionist Saga Corp., Kalamazoo, Mich., 1979-83; regional staff dietition Saga Corp., Washington Crossing, Pa., 1983-84, dir. human resources, 1984-86; dir. clin. nutritionist Marriott Corp., Washington Crossing, Pa., 1986-87, dist. mgr., 1987—; co-chairperson Nutritional Care Practices Com., Mich., 1981-82. Mem. Am. Dietetic Assn., Soc. for Nutrition Edn., Internat. Order of Jobs Daughters Behthel #16. Office: Marriott Corp PO Box 602-0601 Washington Crossing PA 18977

HART, SUSAN RENEE, engineer; b. Yuba City, Calif., May 30, 1961; d. William Patrick and Diana Lynn (Lentz) H. BS, Montana State U., Bozeman, 1984. Devel. engr. Hewlett-Packard Co., McMinnville, Oreg., 1984—, lead engr., 1988—. Designer house, 1987, clothing, 1976--. Adv., Jr. Achievement, McMinnville, Oreg., 1984-85, stage artist, Gallery Players of Oreg. Winner numerous 1st place awards: San Mateo County Fair, 1981-89. Mem. Gen. Soc. Mayflower Descendants, Knights of the Vine, Alpha Gamma Delta.

HART, SYLVIA E., nursing educator; b. Milw., July 26, 1928; d. Peter Michael and Sylvia Christina (Streff) H. RN, Sacred Heart Sch. Nursing, 1949; BSN, Alverno Coll., 1952; MS in Nursing, Catholic U. Am., 1962; PhD, NYU, 1967. Staff nurse Waupun (Wis.) Meml. Hosp., 1952-54; med. pediatric supr. St. Joseph Hosp., Beaver Dam, Wis., 1954-60; chmn. nursing dept. Alverno Coll., Milw., 1962-64; asst. prof. nursing NYU, N.Y.C., 1966-69; assoc. prof. sch. nursing, assoc. dean U. N.Y., Buffalo, 1969-72; prof. and dean sch. nursing U. Tenn., Knoxville, 1972—. Office: U Tenn-Knoxville Coll Nursing 1200 Volunteer Blvd Knoxville TN 37996-0230*

HARTER, JEAN ANN, architect, graphic art consultant; b. Kansas City, Kans., Sept. 28, 1959; d. Donald Lee Harter and Beth Arland (Hobbs) Stanley. B.Interior Arch., Kans. State U., 1983. Designer Michael Fox, Inc., St. Louis, 1983-85; interior architect Pabst Design Group, St. Louis, 1985; archtl. designer Interior Space Inc., St. Louis, 1985-88; ind. contractor, 1988—; cons. Barnes Design Assocs., St. Louis, 1985—. Mem. Inst. Bus. Designers (profl. mem.). Democrat.

HARTGROVE, BEVERLY NEWMAN, personnel officer; b. Winston-Salem, N.C., May 23, 1944; d. Edwin Karl and Daisy Faircloth (Groner) N.; m. Robert Hughes Hartgrove, Sept. 3, 1966. BA in Elem. Edn., U. N.C., Greensboro, 1966. Personnel asst. N.C. Dept. Cultural Resources, Raleigh, 1972-77, personnel technician, 1977-84, personnel officer, 1984—. Democrat. Mem. Moravian Ch. Office: NC Dept Cultural Resources 109 E Jones St Raleigh NC 27611

HARTIG, JUDITH MARTIN, lawyer; b. Cleve., Mar. 17, 1938; d. John B. and Helen (Hickam) Martin; children: Stephen, Tracy. BS, U. Wis., 1963; JD, Marquette U., 1979. Bar: Wis. 1979, U.S. Dist. Ct. (ea. and we. dists.) Wis. 1979. Ptnr. Hartig, Bjelajac, Michaelson & Kivlin, Racine, Wis., 1981—; mem. Gov.'s Adv. Coun. on Jud. Selection, Wis., 1987—. Del. Rep. Party Nat. Convs., 1968, 76; mem. Wis. Lottery Bd., 1988—. Mem. Wis. Women Entrepreneurs State Bd. Republican. Home: 82 Woodfield Ct Racine WI 53402 Office: Hartig Bjelajac et al 601 Lake Ave PO Box 38 Racine WI 53401-0038

HARTLEY, GRACE VAN TINE, foundation administrator; b. San Francisco, Aug. 24, 1916; d. Ellis Charles and Nadine (Allen) Van Tine; m. Frank Brooke Hartley (div. 1974); children: Shirley Hartley Hill, Linda Hartley Sims, Brooke Hartley Hudson, Jessie Hartley Brady, Frank. Student, De Anza Coll., 1975-77, Coll. of Marin, 1985-86. V.p. Barron & Hartley Builders, Alameda, Calif., 1946-72; pres. Aurley Apt. Houses, Sunnyvale, Calif., 1974-86; exec. dir. George Demont Otis Found., San Francisco, 1974—; pres. Western Arts Acad. Found., San Rafael, Calif., 1982—, Grace Group of Calif., Inc., Corte Madera, Calif. and San Rafael, 1983—. Author, producer: (audio visual) American Artists National Parks, 1976 (Bicentennial award 1976); exhibited in group shows at Golden Gate Collection, 1974 (Soc. Western Artists award 1974), Otis Centennial, 1980 (Calif. History Ctr. award 1980). Pres. Rep. Women's Club, Alameda, 1960-62; active Rep. State Cen. Com., Alameda, 1964, Ronald Reagan Presdl. Task Force, Corte Madera, 1978-80. Recipient cert. Achievement Internat. Platform Assn., Washington, 1982, Presdl. Achievement award Rep. Party, Corte Madera, 1987. Presbyterian.

HARTLEY, KAREN JEANETTE, lawyer, mediator, counselor; b. Oakland, Calif., Aug. 2, 1950; d. Samuel Louis and Jean Iris (Beven) Ostrow; m. Terry Van Hook, Aug. 29, 1970 (div. Mar. 1976); m. William Headley, Jan. 22, 1977 (div. Mar. 1988). BA in Psychology with highest honors, UCLA, 1972; DMin, Sch. of Theology, Claremont, Calif., 1976; JD cum laude, U. San Diego, 1982. Bar: Calif. 1982, U.S. Dist. Ct. (9th cir.) 1983; ordained minister Meth. Ch., 1973. From intern to asst. United Meth. Ch., 1969-71; asst. minister St. Paul's United Meth. Ch., San Bernardino, Calif., 1973-74; assoc. minister Claremont United Meth. Ch., 1974-76; sr. minister Santee (Calif.) United Meth. Ch., 1977-79; clk. Calif. Supreme Ct., San Francisco, 1981; cons. Regional Dept. Edn., San Diego, 1979-81; assoc. atty. Duke, Gerstel, Shearer & Bregante, San Diego, 1983-84, Finley, Kumble, Wagner et al, San Diego, 1984-87; prin. atty. Hartley & Assocs., San Diego, 1987—; mediator Community Mediation Ctr., San Diego, 1990—. Mem. Dem. Party, 1969—. Mem. ABA, Calif. Bar Assn., San Diego Bar Assn., Lawyer's Club. Office: Hartley & Assocs 964 Fifth Ave Ste 500 San Diego CA 92101

HARTLEY, MARIETTE (MARIETTE HARTLEY BOYRIVEN), actress; b. N.Y.C., June 21, 1940; d. Paul Hembree and Mary Ickes (Watson) H.; m. Patrick Francois Boyriven, Aug. 13, 1976; children: Sean Paul, Justine Emilia. Student, Carnegie Tech. Inst., 1956-57; studied with Eva Le Gallienne. Co-host Today Show, June 9-27, 1980. Appeared with Shakespeare Festival, Stratford, Conn., 1957-60; appeared in: nat. tours of Winter's Tale, A Midsummer Night Dream; films Ride the High Country, 1961, Marooned, 1968, Skyjacked, Marine, Improper Channels, 1981, O'Hara's Wife, 1982, 1969, 1988; TV appearances include Incredible Hulk (Emmy award for best actress 1979), Mash, Star Trek; TV series include: The Hero, Goodnight, Beantown, 1983; numerous TV films including Genesis II, 1973, The Killer Who Wouldn't Die, 1976, Last Hurrah, 1977, The Secret War of Jackie's Girls, 1980, The Love Tapes, 1980, No Place to Hide, 1981, Drop Out Father, 1982, M.A.D.D.: Mothers Against Drunk Driving, 1983, Silences of the Heart, 1984, My Two Loves, 1986, One Terrific Guy, 1986, Calloway's Climb, The Halloween That Almost Wasn't, The Second Time Around, African Queen; author: (with Anne Commire) Breaking the Silence, 1990. Recipient Clio award, 1979, 80, 81, Golden Apple award Hollywood Women's Press Club, 1979. Mem. Acad. Motion Picture Arts and Scis. Office: care Triad Artists Inc 10100 Santa Monica blvd Los Angeles CA 90067*

HARTLEY-LINSE, BONNIE JEAN, nurse; b. Chgo., July 26, 1923; d. Frank and Anna Kathleen (Koutecky) Kadlec; m. Robert William Hartley, June 23, 1949 (div. Feb. 1961); children: Robert Greig, Franklin James; m. Howard Albert Linse, June 10, 1978 (dec. Nov. 1985); stepchildren: Michael Howard, Janet Stokes. BS in Nursing, St. Xavier Coll., Chgo., 1945; cert. edn. Portland State Coll., 1965; MS in Nursing Edn., U. Oreg., 1972; cert. coll. health nurse practitioner program Brigham Young U., 1976. R.N., Oreg. Mem. faculty nursing St. Xavier Coll., 1945-47; head nurse U. Chgo. Clinics, 1947-48; nurse research newborn neurology U. Oreg. Med. Sch., Portland, summer 1961; coordinator dental assistant program, instr. biology Portland Pub. Schs., Oreg., 1965-67; health service clinician, adminstr. Clackamas Community Coll., Oregon City, Oreg., 1970-84; cons. Health Services Community Colls. of Oreg., 1972-84; pres. Coll. Health Nurses, State of Oreg., 1976-78. Vol. Task Force for Medically Needy of Clackamas County, Oreg.; mem. svc. vol. environ. learning ctr., Clackamas Community Coll. Mem. N.W. Oreg. Health Systems, Clackamas County Sub-Area Council, Oregon City, 1980-86. Recipient Recognition for Outstanding Service award Clackamas Community Coll., 1984; USPHS grantee, 1968. Mem. Am. Nurses Assn., Oreg. Nurses Assn. (Clackamas County unit 26), Pacific Coast Coll. Health Assn. (ann. conf. program coordinator 1980), Oreg. Coll. Health Dirs. Assn., Oreg. Health Decisions. Avocations: travel, piano, choral singing, swimming. Home: 18633 Roundtree Dr Oregon City OR 97045

HARTLY, MICHELLE JEANNETTE, children's program administrator; b. Cottonwood, Idaho, May 15, 1959; d. Terrence Wayne and Jeannette M. (Sanders) Maki; m. Russell Scott Hartly; children: Mitchell Scott, Barrett Matthew, Evan Bruce. Student, Ricks Coll., 1977-78. Program dir. Music in Motion, Libby, Mont., 1983-88; producer Libby Children's Theatre, 1985-88; substitute tchr. Libby Pub. Schs., 1985-88; profl. accompanist Libby High Sch., 1985-87; profl. musician Ctr. Stage Entertainment, Libby, 1989—; program dir. Creative Music Acad., Libby, summer 1980—; prodn. asst. Jmblin Entertainment, L.A., summer 1989—; tour dir. Jazzin Dance Ensemble, Provo, Utah, 1986, Uptown Girls, Salt Lake City, 1986. Co-founder children's ctr. Mem. Mont. Music Tchrs. Assn., Lincoln County Music Tchrs. Assn., Libby C. of C. Republican. Mormon. Home: 43 Indian Head Rd Libby MT 59923

HARTMAN, CATHERINE RUDISILL, educator; b. Biscoe, N.C., Mar. 24, 1916; d. Jacob Andrew and Annie (Dietz) Rudisill; B.S., Appalachian State Tchrs. Coll., 1944; M.A., Columbia U., 1950, profl. diploma Tchrs. Coll., 1959; student U. London, Heidelberg U., summer 1953, NYU, summer 1954, UCLA, summer 1956; m. Harold R. Hartman, Dec. 26, 1962. Primary tchr. Park Grace Sch., Kings Mountain, N.C., 1936-39; elem., music tchr. Oakhurst Sch., Charlotte, N.C., 1939-44, Gary Sch., Tampa, Fla., 1945-47; elem. supr. schs. Gaston County Schs., Gastonia, N.C., 1947-55, dir. instrn., 1955-61, asst. supt. in charge instrn., 1961-63; assoc. prof. edn. William Paterson Coll. of N.J., Wayne, 1964-85, assoc. prof. emeritus, 1985—, chmn. gen. elem. program com. for curriculum revision, 1967-68, chmn. dept. secondary edn., 1972-78, chmn. dept. adminstrv., adult and secondary programs, 1979-85. Mem. Assn. Supervision and Curriculum Devel. of NEA (nat. dir. 1958-61), NCCJ (Carolinas regional dir. 1952-62), AAUW (dir. Charlotte 1953-55), Assn. Childhood Edn. (life, treas. N.C. 1955-57, adviser Gaston County br. 1955-63), Am. Assn. Sch. Adminstrs. (life), Kappa Delta Pi, Pi Lambda Theta. Presbyterian.

HARTMAN, DEBORAH STANTON, food company executive; b. Maringa, Parana, Brazil, May 10, 1956; came to U.S., 1960; d. Edward Earl and Dorothy Van Meter (Stanton) H. BS, U. Fla., 1978; MBA, Pepperdine U., 1990. Calf raiser and milker Twin Acres Farm, Brooksville, Fla., 1978-79; chemist Fla. Dept. Agriculture, White Springs, 1979-80; mgr. quality control Kraft Dairy Group, Tampa, Fla. and Memphis, 1980-82; mgr. loss control, prodn. coordinator Kraft Dairy Group, Jacksonville, Fla., 1982-83; fats and oils formulation technologist, cheese products customer rep. Kraft Indsl. Foods, Memphis, 1983-86; mgr. food tech. Kraft Food Ingredients Corp., Anaheim, Calif., 1986—. Docent Memphis Zoo, 1982; vol. Memphis Hemophilia Soc., 1983. Recipient Fla. State Team award of Excellence, 1979. Mem. Inst. Food Technologists, Council for Agrl. Sci. and Tech., Am. Inst. Baking. Evang. Christian. Clubs: Jazz Heritage (Los Angeles); Nat. Geog. Soc. Office: Kraft Food Ingredients Corp 125 W Cerritos St Suite 2-125 Anaheim CA 92805

HARTMAN, DOMENICA NICOLETTE SAMARGIN, lawyer; b. Dolton, Ill., Oct. 4, 1960; d. Frank and Diana Catherine (Ciochetti) Samargin; m. Gary Michael Hartman, July 19, 1986. BS in Materials Sci. Eng., Purdue U., 1981; JD, U. Mich., 1987. Bar: Mich. 1987, U.S. Dist. Ct. (ea. dist.) Mich. 1987, U.S. Patent Office 1987. Engr. Bendix Energy Control div. Allied Signal Co., South Bend, Ind., 1982-84; patent law intern GM, Detroit, 1985-87, patent atty., 1987-90; prin. law office of Domenica N.S. Hartman,

Plymouth, Mich., 1990—. Author numerous patents including automotive internal reference solid electrolyte lean oxygen sensor. Mem. ABA, Mich. Bar Assn., Am Intellectual Property Law Assn., Mich. Patent Law Assn. Roman Catholic. Office: 15071 Bradner Rd Plymouth MI 48170

HARTMAN, EMILY LOU, botanist, educator, researcher; b. Kansas City, Mo., Dec. 19, 1932; d. Walter Arthur and Emily Louise (Obrecht) Hartman. BA, U. Kans., 1953, MA, 1955, PhD, 1957; MA, U. Denver, 1962. Instr. Calif. State Poly. Coll. San Luis Obispo, 1957-58; asst. prof. Kans. State U., Emporia, 1958-61, S.W. Mo. State U., Springfield, 1965-66; from asst. prof. to prof. botany U. Colo., Denver, 1966—, also curator herbarium, 1970—; dir. Fremont County Mountain Rsch. Sta., Canon City, Colo., 1974—. Contbr. articles to profl. jours. Mem. Am. Soc. Plant Taxonomists, Am. Assn. Systematics Collections, Calif. Bot. Soc., Inst. Arctic and Alpine Rsch., Colo.-Wyo. Acad. Sci. Home: 6563 E Alcorn Parker CO 80134 Office: U Colo at Denver Dept Biology 1200 Larimer Denver CO 80204

HARTMAN, JEANNETTE MARIE, public relations specialist; b. Wichita Falls, Tex., Apr. 20, 1952; d. Jean F. and Betty J. (Logan) Hartman. BS in Journalism, U. Kans., 1974. Publs. specialist Caudill, Rowlett Scott, Houston, 1974-76; reporter Evening Outlook, Santa Monica, Calif., 1976-80; pub. info. officer Santa Monica Coll., 1980-87; sr. media relations specialist Blue Cross Calif., Woodland Hills, 1987-88, pub. relations supr., 1988-89, pub. relations mgr., 1989; news bur. mgr. Jewish Fedn. Council Greater L.A., 1989—. Recipient 2d place for newsletters Calif. Community and Jr. Coll. Assn., 1982; John Swett award Calif. Tchrs. Assn., 1978. Mem. Pub. Relations Soc. Am., Internat. Assn. Bus. Communications, Women in Communications. Office: 6505 Wilshire Blvd #915 Los Angeles CA 90048

HARTMAN, JOAN EDNA, English educator; b. Bklyn., N.Y.C., Oct. 5, 1930; d. H. Graham and Edna (Kuebler) H. Student, Mt. Holyoke Coll., 1951; postgrad., Duke U., Durham, 1952, Oxford U., 1958-59; PhD, Radcliffe Coll., Cambridge, 1960. Instr. Washington Coll., Chestertown, Md., 1952-54; instr. Wellesley Coll., 1959-62, asst. prof., 1962-63; asst. prof. Conn. Coll., New London, 1963-66, CUNY-Queens Coll., Flushing, 1967-70; asst. prof. CUNY-S.I. Community Coll., 1970-72, assoc. prof., 1972-76; prof. CUNY-Coll. S.I., 1976—. Editor: Books Women in Print I, II, 1982, The Norton Reader, 1988; contbr. articles to profl. jours. Fellow, Am. Assn. u. Women, Nat. Endowment for Humanities, Mellon. Mem. Modern Lang. Assn., Nat. Coun. Tchrs. English, Nat. Women's Studies Assn., Soc. for the Study Women in the Renaissance, Nat. Arts Club. Office: Coll of Staten Island Staten Island NY 10301

HARTMAN, LEE ANN WALRAFF, educator; b. Milw., Apr. 21, 1945; d. Emil Adolph and Mabelle Carolyn (Goetter) Walraff; m. Patrick James Hartman, Oct. 5, 1968; children: Elizabeth Marie, Suzanne Carolyn. BS, U. Wis., 1967; postgrad., U. R.I., 1972-73, Johns Hopkins U., 1990. Cert. Wis. state tchrs. Educator Port Wash. Bd. Edn., Wis., 1967-68; ballet instr. Young Womens Christian Assn., Wilmington, Del., 1977-78; tutor Md Study Skills Inst., Columbia, 1984-86, Columbia, Md., 1985—; educator Howard County Bd. Edn., Columbia, Md., 1985—. Contbr. articles to profl. jours. Bd. dirs. Columbia United Christian Ch., 1980-83; mem. Gifted Talented Com., Columbia Md., 1980-90, USCG Officers Wives Club, 1970-72, Hosp. Auxiliary, 1970-72, Bay St. Louis troop leader, Girl Scouts Am., 1980—. Mem. AAUW, Home Hosp. Tchrs. Assn. Md. Office: Howard County Bd Edn Rt #108 Columbia MD 21044

HARTMAN, NANCY LEE, physician; b. Philipsburg, Pa., July 29, 1951; d. Richard Lee and Ann Hartman. Grad. Barbizon Sch. Modeling, 1970; AA, Harcum Jr. Coll., 1969-71; BA, Lycoming Coll., 1974; MS, L.I. U., 1977; MD, Am. U. of Caribbean in Plymouth, Montserrat, W.I., 1981. Med. technologist Lock Haven (Pa.) Hosp., 1971-72, Williamsport (Pa.) Hosp., 1972-73, Renovo (Pa.) Hosp., 1974; microbiologist and med. technologist Jersey Shore (Pa.) Hosp., 1974; microbiologist N.Y. Hosp. and Cornell Med. Center, N.Y.C., 1974-75, Drekter and Heisler Labs., N.Y.C., 1975, North Shore Labs., Inc., Syosset, N.Y., 1976-78; lab. technician North Shore Hosp., Manhasset, N.Y., 1981-82, Nat. Health Labs. Inc., Bethpage, N.Y., 1982; resident internal medicine program Interfaith Med. Ctr., Bklyn., 1983-84; med. cons. Shapiro & Baines, Mineola, N.Y., 1985-88; resident pathology program Lenox Hill Hosp., N.Y.C., 1986-87; resident clin. pathology Beth Israel Med. Ctr., N.Y.C., 1988-89; resident internal medicine, Lenox Hill Hosp., 1990—; med. cons. Reichenbaum and Silberstein, Great Neck, N.Y., 1988—, Meiselman, Boland, Reilly and Pittoni, Mineola, 1988—, Law Offices of Sybil Shainwald, N.Y.C., 1989—. Author: The Pocket Handbook of Infectious Agents and Their Treatments, 1987; also articles. Mem. Rep. Presdl. Task Force. Recipient Allied Health Professions Traineeship grant, 1975-77. Mem. AMA, Am. Women's Med. Assn., Am. Soc. Clin. Pathologists (registered med. technologist), Internat. Platform Assn., Am. Soc. Microbiology. Home: PO Box 847 Glenwood Landing NY 11547

HARTMAN, RUTH ANN, educator; b. Galion, Ohio, Aug. 18, 1938; d. Richard Lewis and Florence Evelyn (Ireland) Campbell; m. Richard Louis Hartman, Jan. 14, 1956; children: Jeffery Lee, Marsha Elaine, Jerry Steven. BS, Ohio State U., 1970; MEd, U. LaVerne, 1976, postgrad., 1985—; postgrad., U. Akron, 1977-85. cert. tchr., Ohio. Tchr. Willard (Ohio) City Schs., 1964-65; educator Mansfield (Ohio) City Schs., 1966—, home tutor, 1971-81, educator, 1977—; cons. Ohio State U., Ashland (Ohio) Coll., Mt. Vernon (Ohio) Nazarene Coll., 1976—. Co-author: Handbook for Student Teachers, 1983; contbr. to Norde News. Mem NEA, Ohio Edn. Assn., North Cen. Ohio Tchrs. Assn., Mansfield Edn. Assn. Republican. Methodist. Home: Rt 1 Plymouth OH 44865 Office: Mansfield City Schs 1138 Springmill Rd Mansfield OH 44906

HARTMAN-ABRAMSON, ILENE, adult educator; b. Detroit, Mich., Nov. 8, 1950; d. Stuart Lester and Freda Vivian (Nash) Hartman; m. Victor Nikolai Abramson, Oct. 24, 1941. BA, U. Mich., 1972; MED, Wayne State U., 1980, postgrad., 1988—. Mich. Secondary Continuing Teaching Cert. Program developer and instr. William Beaumont Hosp., Royal Oak, Mich., 1972-74; vocational counselor for emigres Jewish Vocational Service and Community Workshop, Detroit, Mich., 1974-81; program developer and cons. Detroit psychiatric Clinic, Detroit, Mich., 1982; instr. for foreign students Oakland Community Coll., Farmington Hills, Mich.; advisory bd. mem. Mich. Dept. of Educ., Detroit, 1981, lecturer, Internat. Conference of Teachers of Emglish to Speakers of Other Languages, 1981. Contbr. articles to prof. jours. Am. Arabic and Jewish Friends, Detroit, 1988--, Orgn. for Rehabilitation Through Training, 1986--, Wayne State U., Alumni Assn., 1980--. Mem. Assn. for Women in Maths., Am. Anthropol. Assn., Math. Assn. Am., Tchrs. of English to Speakers of Other Languages, Nat. Assn. Fgn. Student Affairs, Mich. Council on Learning for Adults. Jewish. Office: Oakland Community Coll 27055 Orchard Lake Rd Farmington MI 48018

HARTMAN-GOLDSMITH, JOAN, art historian; b. Malden, Mass., June 3, 1933; d. Hyman and Ruth (Hadler) Lederman; m. Alan Hartman, Jan. 10, 1952 (div.); 1 dau., Hedy Hartman; m. 2d Robert Goldsmith, Aug. 12, 1976. Instr., coordinator, initiator art history program China Inst. in Am., N.Y.C., 1967-77; lectr. Sch. Continuing Edn. NYU, 1967-77; exec. officer Jewish Mus., N.Y.C., 1976-77, dir. pub. info., 1977-80; founder, dir. Inst. for Asian Studies, Inc., N.Y.C., 1981—; lectr. Cooper-Hewitt Mus. of Design (Smithsonian Inst.), 1976, 83; lectr. museums Los Angeles, St. Louis, Pitts., Indpls., Buffalo, Rochester, N.Y., Toronto, Can., Denver Art Mus., Seattle Art Mus., Asian Art Mus. San Francisco; lectr. museums Oriental Ceramic Soc., Tokyo, Hong Kong; spl. lectr. tour Archaeol. Inst. Am., 1977; condr. seminars on Chinese jade Met. Mus. Art, N.Y.C., 1977, 81, 83; fellow in perpetuity, mem. vis. com. slide and photograph library Met. Mus. Art; trustee Indpls. Mus. Art; mem. art com. China House Gallery, N.Y.C.; program chmn. ann. conf. MAR-Assn. Asian Studies, Buchnel U., 1974. Am. corr.: Oriental Art mag., London, 1963-81; contbr. feature articles to profl. publs.; guest curator, author catalogs; author: Chinese Jade of Five Centuries, 1969, slide survey Introduction to Chinese Art, 1973, Chinese Jade, 1986; contbr. book revs. to learned jours. Nat. Endowment grantee, vis. specialist Buffalo Mus. Sci., 1972, Indpls. Mus. Art, 1971; reviewer NEH div. pub. programs, 1978—. Mem. Am. Oriental Soc., Assn. for Asian Studies (founding mem. Mid-Atlantic Region 1972, sec.-treas. 1973, adv. council 1974-75), Oriental Club of N.Y., Oriental Ceramic Soc. Office: Inst for Asian Studies PO Box 1603 FDR Station New York NY 10022

HARTMANN, DARLENE MARIE, health sciences-environmental consulting official; b. Las Vegas, Nev., July 21, 1963; d. Kenneth Henry and Janet Elizabeth (Belasco) Hartmann. AAS, Middlesex County Coll., 1983. Restaurant supr. Somerset (N.J.) Marriott Hotel, 1980-83; server Somerset (N.J.) Hilton Hotel, 1983-84; dining room supr. J.B. Winberie Restaurant & Bar, Princeton, N.J., 1984-85; restaurant mgr. Somerset Hilton Hotel, 1985-87; gen. mgr. Le Peep Restaurant, Edison, N.J., 1987-88; exec. sec. ENVIRON, Princeton, 1988—. Mem. Profl. Secs. Internat. Home: 103 Rabbit Hill Rd Cranbury NJ 08512 Office: ENVIRON Corp 210 Carnegie Ctr Ste 201 Princeton NJ 08540

HARTMANN, JUDY ANNE, health facility administrator, nurse; b. Dubuque, Iowa, Apr. 29, 1955; d. Carl Joseph and Kathleen Mary (Bertjens) H. BSN, Marycrest Coll., 1978; MSN, Boston U., 1983. RN, Minn. Staff nurse St. Mary's Hosp.-Mayo Clinic, Rochester, Minn., 1978-79, head nurse, 1979-81; staff nurse New Eng. Med. Ctr., Boston, 1982-83; clin. nurse specialist U. Wis. Hosp. & Clinic, Madison, 1983-88; dir. nursing Kans. Rehab. Hosp., Topeka, 1988—. Contbg. author: Rehabilitation Nursing Scope of Practice: Process and Outcome Criteria for Selected Diagnosis, 1988. Named one of Outstanding Young Women in Am., 1978. Mem. Assn. Rehab. Nurses, Am. Nurses Assn., Kans. State Nurses Assn. (sec. Dist. 1 Topeka chpt. 1989—), Wis. Assn. Rehab. Nurses (program chair Madison chpt. 1983-85, pres. 1987-88), Sigma Theta Tau. Home: 4140 SW 6th Ave #206 Topeka KS 66606 Office: Kans Rehab Hosp 1504 SW 8th St Topeka KS 66606

HARTMANN, RUTH ANNEMARIE, health care education specialist; b. Naumburg, Saale, Germany, Mar. 16, 1936; came to U.S., 1957; d. Kurt and Anna (Jöesch) H.; m. Karl-Heinz Falatyk (div. 1983); children: Ulrich, Ute; m. Franklin J. Herzberg, 1987. Diploma in nursing, Medizinische Fachschule, Potsdam, German Dem. Republic, 1956; BA in German summa cum laude, U. Wis., Milw., 1978, MLS, 1979; EdD in Adult Edn., Nova U., 1987. Info. specialist Fluid Power Assn., Milw., 1980-81; asst. librarian Miller Brewing Co., Milw., 1979-82; patient edn. librarian VA Med. Ctr., Milw., 1982-85, health care edn. specialist, 1986—; adj. prof. (part-time) grad. health-care scis. Cardinal Stritch Coll. Contbr. articles to profl. jours. Bd. dirs. Concord Chamber Orch., Milw., 1982—; vol. Cancer Soc., Milw., 1985—; vol. instr. Literacy Svcs. Wis., 1987—; reviewing bd. for program certificatin Am. Diabetes Assn., 1990—. Mem. Am. Assn. Adult Continuing Edn., Spl. Library Assn. (treas. 1981-83), Library Community of Milw., U. Wis. Alumni Assn., Area Council of Health Educators (chairperson 1986—), Nat. Wellness Council, Soc. Pub. Health Edn. Inc., Am. Soc. Healthcare Edn. and Tng., Phi Kappa Phi. Office: Clement J Zablocki VA Med Ctr Milwaukee WI 53295

HARTNAGEL, BETTY CAROLYN, health services executive, nurse; b. Mineral Wells, Tex., Apr. 16, 1951; d. Lewis R. and Mary Helen (Scott) Crosier; children: Amy, Amanda. AD in Nursing, Midwestern U., 1972; BS in Nursing with highest honors, U. Tex., Arlington, 1988. Cert. inpatient obstet. nursing, neonatal resuscitation certification instr. Women's svcs. coord. Palo Pinto Gen. Hosp., Mineral Wells, unit mgr. obstetrics, charge nurse obstetrics. Bus. and Profl. Women's Orgn. scholar. Mem. NAACOG, ANA, Maternal Child Health Coun., TNA, Alpha Chi, Sigma Theta. Baptist. Home: 609 NE 9th St Mineral Wells TX 76067 Office: 400 SW 25th Ave Mineral Wells TX 76067

HARTNESS, SANDRA JEAN, venture capitalist; b. Jacksonville Fla., Aug. 19, 1944; d. Harold H. and Viola M. (House) H. AB, Ga. So. Coll., 1969; post-grad., San Francisco State Coll., 1970-71. Researcher Savannah (Ga.) Planning Commn., 1969, Environ. Analysis Group, San Francisco, 1970-71; dir. Mission Inn, Riverside, Calif., 1971-75; developer, venture capitalist Hartness Assocs., Laguna Beach, Calif., 1976—; ptnr. Western Neuro-Care Ctr., Tustin Calif., 1983-89; pres. Asset Svcs., Inc., 1981—; former edn. dir. Laguna Bd. Realtors, 1982. V.p., mem. bd. dirs. Evergreen Homes, Inc.; pres. Asset Svcs., Inc.; recipient numerous awards for community svc. Democrat. Club: Soroptimists (Riverside, Calif.). Office: Hartness Assocs 32612 Adriatic Dr Monarch Beach CA 92677

HARTNETT, JENNIFER LYNNE, company official; b. Bartlesville, Okla., July 7, 1964; d. Sylvester Tryon and Berneitta Ilene (McCormack) H. BBA, Wichita State U., 1986; MBA, Washington U., St. Louis, 1988. Grad. asst. Wichita (Kans.) State U., 1986; asst. mgr. copr. devel. Southwestern Bell Corp., St. Louis, 1987; material planner Hewlett Packard Co., Palo Alto, Calif., 1988, prodn. supr., 1989—; cons. Schnuck's, St. Louis, 1988. Discussion leader Peninsula Bible Ch. Singles Outreach, Sunnyvale, Calif., 1989—. Wichita State U. scholar, 1986, Washington U. scholar, 1986-88. Mem. Inst. Indsl. Engrs., Am. Prodn. and Inventory Control Soc., Mortar Bd., Beta Gamma Sigma. Home: 900 High Sch Way #2237 Mountain View CA 94041 Office: Hewlett Packard Co 974 Argues Ave Mls 72VA Sunnyvale CA 94086

HARTNETT, KATHERINE, geographer; b. Bridgeport, Conn., Apr. 22, 1951; d. John Francis and Mary Bondaruk; m. Susan Stroud. BA, Bryn Mawr Coll., 1973; MA, Columbia U., 1978. Rsch. assoc. McCormick and Assocs. Inc., 1973-75; regional program mgr. NYS Dept. environmental conservation, Stony Brook, N.Y., 1978-80; spl. projects mgr. Hazardous Materials Div., Linden, N.J., 1980-82; pres. Teak Assocs. Ltd., 1982-84; engr., tech. analyst engrng. dept. Bklyn. Union Gas Co., 1984-87; project mgr. Groundwater Protection Bur., N.H. Dept. Environ. Svcs., 1987—. Mem. Deerfield (N.H.) Conservation Commn. Mem. AAAS. Home: 46 Middle Rd Deerfield NH 03037 Office: NH Dept Environ Svcs Groundwater Protection Bur PO Box 95 6 Hazen Dr Concrod NH 03301

HARTOM-BOZE, BARBARA CHESLENE, agricultural company executive; b. Union City, Ind., May 23, 1953; d. Chelsey Owen and Anne Marie (Snyder) B. AA, U. Dayton, 1973. Lab. technician Cargill, Inc., Dayton, Ohio, 1974-75, lab. supr., 1975-76, finishing supr., 1976-81; lab. mgr. Cargill, Inc., Memphis, 1981-85; refinery supt. Cargill, Inc., Cedar Rapids, Iowa, 1985-87; terminal mgr. Cargill, Inc., Elizabeth, N.J., 1987—; chmn. IFT, Memphis, 1983. Mem. Nat. Woman's Network, Elizabeth C. of C. (com. mem. 1987—). Office: Cargill Inc 132 Corbin St Elizabeth NJ 07201

HARTSFIELD, STEPHANIE LAVERNE, electronics engineer; b. Atlanta, June 16, 1962; d. Laywood Hartsfield Sr. and Mary Lou (Dugger) McCrary). BEE, Tuskegee U., 1987. Weatherization specialist Atlanta Housing Authority, 1982; tchrs. aide Southside Daycare Inc., Atlanta, 1983; weatherization specialist Atlanta Housing Authority, 1984; cashier, asst. mgr. Majik Market Inc., Atlanta, 1985; with prodn. Bronner Bros., Atlanta, 1986; electronic engr. FAA, Atlanta, 1987—. Mem. Nat. Assn. for Female Execs., IEEE (pub. relations 1983-84). Democrat. Baptist. Home: 4522 Pine Dr Forest Park GA 30050

HARTSOCK, LINDA SUE, educational and management development executive; b. St. Joseph, Mo., Feb. 20, 1940; d. Waldo Emerson and Martha (Skelkop) H. B.S., Central Meth. Coll., Fayette, Mo., 1962; M.Ed., Pa. State U., 1965; Ed.D., 1971. Cert. assn. exec. Am. Soc. Assn. Execs. Tchr. Jr. High Sch. (North Kansas City (Mo.) Public Sch. System), 1962-63; sr. resident Pa. State U., 1963-64, asst. coordinator residence halls, 1964-65, residence hall coordinator, 1965-66, asst. dean women, 1966-68, asst. dean students, 1968-71; researcher Center for Study Higher Edn., 1971, dir. new student programs, 1971-72; nat. dir. program AAUW, 1972-76; exec. dir. Adult Edn. Assn., 1976-80; now chief exec. officer Integrated Options, Inc., assn., edn. and mgmt. devel., Alexandria, Va.; designer tng. and ednl. programs for various orgns. and assn; adj. faculty George Washington U., 1980-84; v.p. fin. Com. for Full Finding Edn., 1979; mem. first adv. panel convened future directions of a learning soc. project Coll. Entrance Exam. Bd., 1978, mem. planning group for course-by-newspaper exam. project, 1979; bd. dirs. Coalition Adult Edn. Orgns., 1976; mem. White House Conf. on Aging Planning, 1979; mem. nat. adv. bd. Nat. Center Higher Edn. Mgmt. System Project to Develop a Taxonomy for the Field of Adult Edn., 1978; nat. adv. council on adult edn. Futures and Amendments Project, 1977; adv. Collection of Census Data, Nat. Center Ednl. Stats., 1977; mem. public policy com., program com. chmn. Adv. Council Nat. Orgns. to Corp. for Public Broadcasting, 1976; adv. devel. New Mediated Programs, Office Instructional Resources, Miami Dade Community Coll., 1976; mem. innovative awards com. Nat. Univ. Extension Assn., 1977; field reader U.S. Dept. Edn., 1981-83. Editorial bd.: Off to Coll. mag, 1972-74 ; contbr. articles to profl. jours. Recipient Disting. Alumni award Central Meth. Coll., 1978. Mem. AAUW, Am. Soc. Assn. Execs. (individual membership council 1979-81, edn. com. 1985-88, Univ. affairs commn., 1989—), Washington Women's Forum (budget, program and exec. com. 1978-82), Am. Assn. Higher Edn., Alumni Soc. Coll. Edn. Pa. State U. (bd. dirs., Outstanding Alumni award, chair strategic planning com. 1986-89), Pi Lambda Theta. Office: Integrated Options Inc PO Box 10280 Alexandria VA 22310

HARTSUCK, JEAN ANN, chemist; b. Enid, Okla., July 18, 1939; d. Joel Elijah and Marcella (Nelson) Yarborough; m. James Malcolm Hartsuck, June 17, 1962; children: Rebecca, Mary, Katie. BS with distinction, U. Okla., 1960; AM, Radcliffe Coll., 1962; PhD, Harvard U., 1964. Postdoctoral fellow Harvard U., Cambridge, Mass., 1964-69; asst. to assoc. mem. Okla. Med. Rsch. Found., Oklahoma City, 1970—, from asst. prof. to assoc. prof. biochemistry, 1970—. Contbr. chpts. to books, articles to profl. jours. Treas., All Souls Ch., Oklahoma City, 1990—; treas. Ladies Music Club, Oklahoma City, 1989—. NSF fellow, 1961-62; NIH fellow, 1962-64, 64-65, 71-76. Mem. Am. Chem. Soc., Am. Crystallography Assn., Am. Soc. Biol. Chemistry, Sigma Xi. Republican. Episcopalian. Home: 6909 NW Grand Blvd Oklahoma City OK 73116 Office: Okla Med Rsch Found 825 NE 13th St Oklahoma City OK 73104

HARTUNG, MARGARET URSULA, insurance account executive; b. L.A., July 9, 1941; d. Hermann Ferdinand and Emma Magdalene (Froehlich) H. BA, Occidental Coll., 1963; MA, UCLA, 1967. Cert. tchr., Calif. Tchr. various sch. dists, Calif., 1964-65, 67-68; mgr. personal lines dept. Lawson Stewart & McCory, L.A., 1969-70; tchr. Beverly Hills (Calif.) High Sch., 1970-79; various positions Comml. Lines, L.A., 1980-89; account exec. Andreini & Co., Ventura, Calif., 1989—. Mem. Chartered Property and Casualty Underwriters (cert.). Republican. Mem. Foursquare Church. Office: Andreini & Co 5851 Thille St Ventura CA 93003

HARTUNG, MARY, state legislator; m. Morris Hartung; children: Elizabeth, Susan, David. Retailer; former rep. from dist. 10 Idaho Ho. of Reps.; state senator Idaho Senate, 1990—. Bd. dirs. Payette Libr. Named Outstanding County Chmn., Idaho Rep. Party, 1982-83; named to Idaho Rep. Hall of Fame. Mem. Payette C. of C. Home: PO Box 147 Payette ID 83661*

HARTWICK, NANCI J., interior designer; b. St. Louis, Jan. 3, 1945; d. Stanley M. Knopf and Virginia Knopf Potter; m. Peter J. Hartwick, Aug. 20, 1976; 1 child, Elizabeth Ashleigh. BA, U. Ariz., 1966; MA, Tex. Tech U., 1974. Pvt. practice interior design; owner Inside-Out Interiors. Mem. AAUW, NAFE, Nat. Assn. Women Bus. Owners. Home: 193 Preston Dr Gillette NJ 07933

HARTZ, LUETTA BERTHA, insurance agent; b. Stevens Point, Wis., Sept. 29, 1947; d. Alfred Bernard Carl and Bertha Martha (Stauffer) Janz; student Madison (Wis.) Bus. Coll., 1965-66; m. James Patrick Hartz, Dec. 31, 1975. With Employers Ins. of Wausau (Wis.), 1966-68; casualty rater Sentry Ins. Co., Stevens Point, Wis., 1968-70, casualty supr., 1970-71, casualty trainor, 1971-72, customer service cor., 1972-74, bur. technician, 1974-75, customer service and acctg. mgr., Concord, Mass., 1975-79, personal lines property processing mgr., 1979-81, personal lines casualty processing mgr., 1981-83, comml. lines underwriting services mgr., 1983-85, comml. lines ops. mgr., 1985-87; agent Lewis P. Bither Ins. Agy., Inc., Tewksbury and Tyngsboro, Mass., 1988—; Campaign treas. Republican Party county clk. candidate, Portage County, Wis., 1972. Mem. U.S. Golf Assn. (assoc.), Nat. Assn. Ins. Women, Mass. Assn. Ins. Women. (Middlesex chpt.). Lutheran. Clubs: Emblem (1st asst. marshall 1980-81, treas. 1981-83). (Concord, Mass.); Maynard Country (bd. govs. 1984-86) (Mass.). Home: 40 Drummer Rd Acton MA 01720

HARTZ, RENEE SEMO, cardiothoracic surgeon; b. Bessemer Twp., Mich., Dec. 7, 1946; d. Rita Ann Semo; children: Tyler Joseph, Colin Wilson. BA, Western Mich. U., 1969; MD, Northwestern U., 1974. Diplomate Am. Bd. Surgery, Am. Bd. Thoracic Surgery. Intern pediatrics Children's Meml. Hosp., Chgo., 1974-75; intern gen. surgery Northwestern Meml. Hosp., Chgo., 1975-76, resident gen. surgery, 1976-79; chief resident cardiothoracic surgery Northwestern Meml. Hosp., 1979-81; instr. dept. surgery Northwestern U. Med. Sch., Chgo., 1978-81, assoc. in surgery, 1981-85; asst. prof. surgery med. sch. Northwestern U., Chgo., 1985-87, assoc. prof. surgery med. sch., 1987—; appointed to Northwestern Meml. Hosp., Chgo., Children's Meml. Hosp., Chgo., VA Lakeside Hosp., Chgo., Evanston (Ill.) Hosp., Columbus Hosp., Chgo.; laser researcher Northwestern U. Med. Sch., 1984—; mem. VA Nat. Surgical Merit Rev. Bd., Washington, 1986-89. Contbr. articles to profl. jours.; contbr. chpts. to Perioperative Cardiac Dysfunction II, 1985, General Thoracic Surgery, 1989, New Technology in Vascular Surgery, 1988. Mem. Am. Coll. Chest Physicians, Am. Coll. Surgeons, Am. Heart Assn., Am. Women's Med. Assn., Am. Soc. for Laser Medicine and Surgery, Assn. for Acad. Surgery, Chgo. Heart Assn., Chgo. Surg. Soc., Ill. Surg. Soc., Laser Inst. Am., Midwest BioLaser Inst., Soc. Thoracic Surgeons, Soc. Univ. Surgeons, Sigma Xi. Office: Northwestern U Med Sch 303 E Chicago Ave WARD 9-105 Chicago IL 60611-3008

HARTZELL, IRENE JANOFSKY, psychologist; b. Los Angeles; Vor-Diplom, U. Munich, 1961. BA, U. Calif., Berkeley, 1963, MA, 1965; PhD, U. Oreg., 1970. Lic. psychologist, Calif., Oreg., Wash. Psychologist Lake Washington Sch. Dist., Kirkland, Wash., 1971-72; staff psychologist VA Hosp., Seattle, 1970-71, Long Beach, Calif., 1973-74; dir. parent edn. Children's Hosp., Orange, Calif., 1975-78; clin. psychologist Kaiser Permanente, Van Nuys, Calif., 1979—; clin. instr. dept. pediatrics U. Calif. Irvine Coll. Medicine, 1975-78. Author: The Study Skills Advantage, 1986; contbr. articles to profl. jours. Intern Oreg. Legislature, 1974-75. U. Oreg. fellow, 1966-67, 69. Mem. Am. Psychol. Assn., Pi Lambda Theta. Office: Kaiser Permanente 13746 Victory Blvd Van Nuys CA 91401

HARTZLER, CHERYL ELAINE, financial planner; b. Kokomo, Ind., Feb. 16, 1945; d. Lowell Jay and Juanita Monell (Gasaway) Somsel; m. Edward W. Hartzler, June 11, 1967 (div. June 1981); children: Bryan Joseph, Andrea Lisabeth. BA, Ind. U., 1968; MBA, So. Ill. U., 1985; postgrad., Pacific Luth. U., 1982-83, Seattle Cen. Community Coll., 1979, S.Seattle Community Coll., 1980, Highline Community Coll., 1980-82, U. Washington, 1978, 83, Coll. for Fin. Planning, 1987—. Boutique mgr., jr. asst. buyer trainee Block's, Indpls., 1967-68; tchr. Indpls. Pub. Schs., 1968-71; with sales and inventory dept. Frederick & Nelson's Dept. Store, Seattle, 1971-72; co-owner video store Video World, Inc., Seattle, 1978-81; fin. planner and account exec. Guardian Fin. Svcs./SunAm. Fin. Svcs., Bellevue, Wash., 1983-89; pres. C.E. Hartzler & Assocs., 1986—; instr. continuing edn. N. Seattle Community Coll., 1985—; coordinated reorgn. of pvt. med. practice, Seattle, 1976; registered rep. Sun Am., 1989—; distbr., supr. Km-Matol, 1988—. Mem. Seattle Repertory Orgn., 1973—; bd. dirs. Seattle Opera Guild, 1978-80; cultural chmn. Highline Sch. Dist. Parent Teachers Students Assn., Seattle, 1978-83. Mem. Internat. Assn. Fin. Planners, Wash. Women United, Women's Bus. Exch., Assn. MBA Execs., NAFE, Am. Soc. Women Accts., Internat. Platform Assn., Alpha Chi Omega Alumni. Clubs: Olympic View Swim (Seattle); Leads (mgmt. team South Seattle chpt.). Home: 718 SW 199th Pl Seattle WA 98166 Office: Guardian Fin Svcs SunAm Fin 1300 114th Ave SE Ste 232 Bellevue WA 98004

HARTZLER, SUSAN FRANCES, public relations executive; b. Beverly Hills, Calif., May 26, 1958; d. Richard William and Margaret A. (McGill) H. BA in Journalism, San Diego State U., 1980. News producer KFMB-TV (CBS Affiliate), San Diego, 1980-83; account exec. Clein and Feldman Pub. Rels. Inc., L.A., 1983-84; publicist Harmony Gold, L.A., 1984-85; account exec. Joan Luther and Assocs., Beverly Hills, 1985-87; v.p. The Ford Group Pub. Rels., Beverly Hills, 1987—. Democrat. Methodist. Office: The Ford Group 9250 Wilshire Blvd Beverly Hills CA 90212

HARVARD, BEVERLY JOYCE BAILEY, deputy chief of police; b. Macon, Ga., Dec. 22, 1950; d. Arcelious and Irene (Perkins) Bailey; m. Jimmy C. Harvard, 1972. BA, Morris Brown Coll., 1972; MS, Ga. State U., 1980. Cert. FBI Nat. Acad. Police officer Police Bur. City of Atlanta, crime analysis officer, exec. protection officer, dep. chief police; spl. asst. to commr.

Dept. Pub. Safety City of Atlanta, dir. pub. affairs. Mem. Leadership Atlanta, 1983—; adv. bd. dirs. Big Brothers/Big Sisters, 1986—, Atlanta Victim/Witness Assistance Program, 1985—. Named Outstanding Atlantan, 1983, Alumna Yr., Morris Brown Coll., 1985, Bronze Woman Yr., Iota Phi Lambda, 1986, Woman Achiever Atlanta YWCA; recipient Trailblazer award for Law Enforcement City of Atlanta. Mem. Internat. Assn. Chiefs Police (tng. com. Ga. chpt.), Nat. Orgn. Black Law Enforcement (chmn. program), Bus. System Planning Team, Ga. State U. Alumni Assn. (bd. dirs. Atlanta chpt.), Delta Sigma Theta (parliamentarian). Office: Atlanta Bur Police Services 175 Decatur St SE Atlanta GA 30335

HARVELL, DIANE LYNN, state official; b. Springfield, Ill., Dec. 12, 1957; d. Virgil Lester and Frances Rose (Conover) H. BS in Mass Communication, Ill. State U., 1979. Sec. Westin Hotel Regional Sales Office, Washington, 1979-80; adminstrv. asst., writer, researcher Am. Gas Assn., Arlington, Va., 1980-81, consumer affairs asst., 1981-84, exec. asst., 1984-85; mktg. support and community rels. mgr. Burlington (Vt.) Free Press, 1986-87; asst. pub. info. officer Ill. Commerce Commn., Springfield, 1987—. Mem. Jr. League Springfield. Mem. Women in Communications, Delta Sigma Theta.

HARVEY, DORIS CANNON, trust company executive, citrus grower; b. Lake Wales, Fla., Mar. 13, 1930; d. Charles Bertal and Sarah (Holbrook) Cannon; m. O.J. Harvey (dec.); children: Barbara Kay, Nancy Jean. Pres. O.J. Harvey Inc., Tampa; v.p. Elfers Citrus Growers Assn., Palm Harbor, Fla.; personal rep. Estate of O.J. Harvey, Tampa; trustee O.J. Harvey Trust, Tampa; trustee Elfers Citrus Liquidating Trust, Palm Harbor. Bd. dirs. Tampa Home Assn., 1982-84; trustee Doris C. Harvey Marital Trust, Tampa, 1988, Palma Ceia United Meth. Ch., Tampa. Democrat. Methodist. Clubs: Centre, Tampa Woman's, Tampa Yacht and Country, Sword of Hope, Rose Circle, Hearts of Gold. Home and Office: 1114 Culbreath Isles Dr Tampa FL 33629

HARVEY, ENID MARY, real estate broker; d. Jackson and Mary (Fong) Chin; divorced. Student, Durham Coll., 1962-64; cert. in acctg., Am. Banking Inst., Miami, Fla., 1979, H&R Block, Hollywood, Fla., 1988. Accounts clk., tel. operator Jamaica Co-op. Ins. Co., Kingston, Jamaica, 1964-67; accounts clk. Grace Kennedy Co., Kingston, 1967-72; sec., personnel officer Rose hall Devel. Co., Montego Bay, Jamaica, 1972-76; sec., bookkeeper Cast Inc., Hialeah, Fla., 1976-79; credit investigator NCNB Bank (formerly Yes Bank), Miami, 1979-81; real estate salesman Century 21-Frank Cooper Realty, Miami, 1981-83; owner, real estate broker Premiere Homes Realty, Inc., Hollywood, 1983—. Recipient award Lib. Econ. & Social Devel., Hollywood, 1986. Mem. Hollywood Bd. Realtors, Miami Bd. Realtors, Nat. Assn. Realtors (Million Dollar Club), Better Bus. Bur. Anglican. Home and office: Premiere Homes Realty Inc 5735 Pembroke Rd Hollywood FL 33023

HARVEY, JANE R., investment company executive; b. Tarrytown, N.Y., Oct. 13, 1945; d. Fred W. and Margaret (White) Rosenbauer. Student, U. Ariz., Iona Coll., Coll. Fin. Planning; grad., Pace U. Cert. reg. rep. Fin. Architects Securities Corp.; lic. ins. counselor, lic. real estate agt.; RFP. V.p. Harvey-Kauss Investment Assn., Inc., Tucson. Contbr. articles to profl. jours. Active Resources for Women. Mem. Internat. Assn. Fin. Planning (past bd. dirs.), Am. Bus. Women's Assn., Am. Assn. Individual Investors, NAFE, NAWBNO, Tucson C. of C., Acad. Family Mediators. Office: 2311 E Broadway Tucson AZ 85719

HARVEY, JOANNE H., genealogist; b. Flint, Mich., July 24, 1932; d. Wilbur Joseph and Helen Ethel (McDougall) Snell; m. Kenneth James Harvey, June 12, 1954; children: Laura Ellen Harvey Peterson, Mary R. BA, Western Mich. U., 1954; MA in LS, U. Mich., 1956; AS in Bus., Lansing Community Coll., 1980. Cert. genealogist Bd. Cert. for Genealogists. Reference libr. Lansing (Mich.) Pub. Libr., 1955-60, Mich. State Libr., Lansing, 1967-69, Lansing Community Coll. Libr., 1970-78; legal asst. Office of Gov., State of Mich., Lansing, 1970-71; genealogist Lansing, 1970—. Author: From Glasgow to Fargo, The Living Record, Yesterday's Handwriting; contbr. articles to geneal. mags. Active Cen. United Meth. Ch., Lansing; docent Potter Park Zoo. Mem. Assn. Profl. Genealogists, Mich. Geneal. Coun. Mid-Mich. Geneal. Soc., Ont. Geneal. Soc., AAUW, Nature Conservancy, Mich. Profl. Genealogists Roundtable, Lansing Woman's Club. Home: 2420 Newport Dr Lansing MI 48906

HARVEY, KAREN KAY, principal; b. Pueblo, Colo., June 19, 1950; d. Kenneth Eugene Sr. and Ruth Naomi (Easton) H. BA, U. So. Colo., 1972; MA, U. No. Colo., 1977; PhD, U. Denver, 1988. Cert. tchr., adminstr., supt., Colo. Elem. tchr. Sch. Dist. #8, Fountain, Colo., 1972-73, Sch. Dist. #70, Pueblo, Colo., 1973-77, Sch. Dist. #5, Englewood, Colo., 1977-86; prin. Sch. Dist. #1, Denver, 1986—; adj. prof. U. Phoenix. Recipient Thatcher Found. scholarship, Pueblo, Colo., 1968. Mem. Colo. Coun. Internat. Reading Assn., Colo. Assn. Sch. Execs., Denver Elem. Prin. Assn., Phi Delta Kappa. Office: Denver Pub Schs Univ Pk Elem 2300 S Saint Paul St Denver CO 80210

HARVEY, KATHERINE ABLER, civic worker; b. Chgo., May 17, 1946; d. Julius and Elizabeth (Engelman) Abler; student La Sorbonne, Paris, 1965-66; AAS, Bennett Coll., 1968; m. Julian Whitcomb Harvey, Sept. 7, 1974. Asst. librarian McDermott, Will & Emery, Chgo., 1969-70; librarian Chapman & Cutler, Chgo., 1970-73, Coudert Freres, Paris, 1973-74; adviser, organizer library Lincoln Park Zool. Soc. and Zoo, Chgo., 1977-79, mem. soc.'s women's bd., 1976—, chmn. library com., 1977-79, sec., 1979-81, mem. exec. com., 1977-81; mem. jr. bd. Alliance Francaise de Chgo., 1970-76, treas., mem. exec. com., 1971-73, 75-76, mem. women's bd., 1977-80; mem. Fred Harvey Fine Arts Found., 1976-78; hon. life mem. Chgo. Symphony Soc., 1975—; mem. Phillips Acad. Alumni Coun., Andover, Mass., 1977-81, mem. acad.'s bicentennial celebration com. class celebration leader, 1978, co-chmn. for Chgo. acad.'s bicentennial campaign, 1977-79, mem. student affairs and admissions com., 1980-81; mem. aux. bd. Art Inst. Chgo., 1978-88; mem. Know Your Chgo. com. U. Chgo. Extension, 1981-84; mem. guild Chgo. Hist. Soc., 1978—; mem. women's bd. Lyric Opera Chgo., 1979—, chmn. edn. com., 1980, mem. exec. com., 1980-84, 88—, treas. women's bd., 1983-84, 1st v.p. 1988—; mem. women's bd. Northwestern Meml. Hosp., 1979—, treas., chmn. fin. com., 1981-84, mem. exec. com., 1981-88; bd. dirs. Found. Art Scholarships, 1982-83; bd. dirs. Glen Ellyn (Ill.) Children's Chorus, 1983—, founding chmn. pres.'s com., 1983; mem. women's bd. Chgo. City Ballet, 1983-84; trustee Chgo. Acad. Scis., 1986-88; bd. dirs. Grant Park Concert Soc., 1986—; adv. coun. med. program for performing artists Northwestern Meml. Hosp., 1986—; pres., bd. dirs. William Ferris Chorale, 1988-89. Mem. Antiquarian Soc. of Art Inst. Chgo. (life); bd. dirs. Grant Park Concerts Soc., 1986—. Mem. Arts Club of Chgo., Friday Club (corr. sec. 1981-83), Casino Club (gov. 1982-88, sec. 1984-85, 1987-88, 1st v.p. 1985-86, 2d v.p. 1986-87), Cliff Dwellers CLub. Home: 1209 N Astor St Chicago IL 60610

HARVEY, LYNNE COOPER, broadcasting executive, civic worker; b. nr. St. Louis; d. William A. and Mattie (Kehr) Cooper; A.B., Washington U., St. Louis, 1939, M.A., 1940; m. Paul Harvey, June 4, 1940; 1 son, Paul Harvey Aurandt. Broadcaster ednl. program KXOK, St. Louis, 1940; broadcaster-writer women's news WAC Variety Show, Fort Custer, Mich., 1941-43; gen. mgr. Paul Harvey News, ABC, 1944—; pres. Paulynne Prodns., Ltd., Chgo., 1968—, exec. producer Paul Harvey Comments, 1968—; pres. Trots Corp., 1989—; editor, compiler The Rest of the Story. Pres. woman's bd. Mental Health Assn. Greater Chgo., 1967-71, v.p. bd. dirs., 1966—; pres. woman's aux. Infant Welfare Soc. Chgo., 1969-71, bd. dirs., 1969—; mem. Salvation Army Woman's Adv. Bd., 1967; reception chmn. Community Lectures; Woman's com. Chgo. Symphony, 1972—; pres. Mothers Council, River Forest, 1961-62; charter bd. mem. Gottlieb Meml. Hosp., Melrose Park, Ill.; mem. adv. bd. Nat. Christian Heritage Found., 1964—; mem. USO woman's bd., 1983, woman's bd. Ravinia Festival, 1972—; trustee John Brown U., 1980—; bd. dirs. Mus. Broadcast Communications, 1987—. Recipient Religious Heritage of Am. award, 1974, Little City Spirit of Love award, 1987, Salvation Army Others award, 1989. Mem. Phi Beta Kappa, Kappa Delta Pi, Phi Sigma Iota, Eta Sigma Phi. Clubs: Chicago Golf, Woman's Athletic, Nineteenth Century Woman's, Press (Chgo.); Oak Park Country. Home: 1035 Park Ave River Forest IL 60305 Office: Box 77 River Forest IL 60305

HARVEY, MICHELLE MAUTHE, foundation administrator; b. Bethesda, Md., Dec. 29, 1954; d. Bemjamin Camille and Lelia Anne (Webre) Mauthe; m. Don Warren Harvey, Mar. 31, 1979; 1 child: Elise Brandner. BS in Forestry, U. South, 1976; MBA, Duke U., 1989. Forester Internat. Paper Co. Inc., Natchez and Brandon, Miss., 1976-80; framer, mgr. Frame Workshop, Lexington, Ky., 1981-83; mgr., dir. Country Stitchery Frameshop, Raleigh, N.C., 1984; dir. found. rels., placement and internship Sch. Forestry & Environ. Studies Duke U., Durham, N.C., 1984-90; dir. Am. Forest Found., Washington, 1990—. Bd. dirs. Raleigh Civic Ballet, 1989—, Wake County Literacy Coun., Raleigh, 1984-88, Soc. Preservation Hist. Oakwood City Lights Ball, 1988; fundraiser N.C. Symphony, Raleigh, 1985-86; mem. Humane Assn. Greater Louisville (devel. dir. 1980). Mem. Soc. Am. Foresters (mem. nat. com. on women and minorities 1985-88, N.C. communications chair 1988—), N.C. Forestry Assn. (mem. communications com.), N.C. Placement Assn., Assn. Internat Practical Tng., (regional adv. com. 1985—), So. Coll. Placement Assn., Oakwood Garden Club (Raleigh). Democrat. Roman Catholic.

HARVEY, PATRICIA JEAN, educational association administrator; b. Newman, Calif., Oct. 27, 1931; d. Willard Monroe and Marjorie (Greenlee) Clougher; m. Richard Blake Harvey, Aug. 29, 1965; children: G. Scott Floden, Timothy P. Harvey. BA, Whittier Coll., 1966, MA, 1971. Resource specialist Monte Vista High Sch. and Whittier (Calif.) High Sch., 1977—; dept. chairperson spl. edn. Whittier (Calif.) High Sch., 1982—. Author: (tchrs. manual) The Dynamics of California Government and Politics, 1970, 90; co-author: Meeting The Needs of Special High School Students in Regular Education Classrooms, 1988. Active Whittier Fair Housing Com., 1972; pres. Women's Aux. Whittier Coll., 1972-73, sec., 1971-72; historian Docian Soc. Whittier Coll., 1963-64, pres. 1965-66. Democrat. Episcopalian. Home: 424 Avocado Crest Rd La Habra Heights CA 90631 Office: Whittier Union High Sch 12417 E Philadelphia St Whittier CA 90601

HARVIE, PEGGY ANN, counselor; b. Middletown, Ohio, Oct. 29, 1936. BA in Sociology, U. Ill., 1972; MA in Human Resource Leadership, Azusa Pacific U., 1988, MA in Marriage, Family Therapy, 1988. Mgr. personnel Edward C. Minas Co., Hammond, Ind., 1979-81, Wycliffe Bible Translators, Huntington Beach (Calif.) and Papua New Guinea, 1981-84, Glasrock Home Health Care, Tustin, Calif., 1985-86, Bristol Park Med. Group, Costa Mesa, Calif., 1987-88; counselor Grace Fellowship Ch., Lansing, Ill., 1989—. Mem. Am. Soc. Counseling & Devel. Office: Grace Fellowship Ch Lansing IL 60438

HARVIEUX, ANNE MARIE, psychotherapist; b. St. Paul, Sept. 5, 1945; d. Walter Wallace and Magdalene C. (Rauer) H. BA, Mt. Mary Coll., Milw., 1970; MSW, U. Wis., Milw., 1979. Cert. clin. social worker. Caseworker Washington County Dept. Social Svc., West Bend, Wis., 1970-72; social worker St. Michael's Hosp., Milw., 1972-74; adminstrv. asst. Family Hosp., Milw., 1974-82; dir. social svc. Beloit (Wis.) Meml. Hosp., 1982-87; dir. counseling svc. Beloit Clinic, 1987—; mem. adv. bd. Credible Care, Janesville, Wis., 1987—, Parkside Lodge Wis., Beloit, 1989—. Bd. dirs. Waukesha (Wis.) Mental Health Assn., 1980-82, mem. women's exch.; mem. Family Violence Coun., Beloit, 1983-85, Rock County Mental Health Assn., Janesville, Wis., 1986, Beloit Teen Pregnancy Task Force, 1988—; v.p. First Light Group Home, Beloit, 1984-87. Mem. Nat. Assn. Social Workers. Home: 2300 Broken Hill Rd Waukesha WI 53188 Office: Beloit Clinic 1905 Huebbe Pkwy Beloit WI 53511 also: Inst Mental Health 6917 W Oklahoma Ave Milwaukee WI 53219

HARWAY, MICHELE, psychology educator and researcher; b. Takoma Park, Md, Sept. 13, 1947; d. Maxwell and Georgette (Volcovici-Nadelar) H.; m. Bruce Eric Antman, Dec. 23, 1979; children: Sasha Antman, Alissa Antman. BS, Tufts U., 1969; MA, U. Maryland, 1971; PhD, U. Md., 1974. Asst. dean U. Calif., Irvine, 1974; rsch. psychologist Higher Edn. Rsch. Inst., UCLA, 1974-77; asst. rsch. prof. psychology U. So. Calif., L.A., 1978-81; assoc. prof. Calif. Grad. Inst., L.A.; prof., dir. rsch. Calif. Family Study Ctr., North Hollywood, Calif., 1987-; mem. rsch. faculty Fielding Inst., Calif., 1986—; cons. various orgns. including Hughes Aircraft, Met. Water Dist., U.S. Dept. State, others, 1978-87; mem. part-time faculty UCLA, Mt. St. Mary's Coll., Wright Inst., Calif. Sch. Profl. Psychology, Calif. State U., 1978-86. Editor: Handbook of Longitudinal Research, vol. 1, vol. 2; author: Sex Discrimination in Counseling. Fellow Am. Psychol. Assn. Home: PO Box 241865 Los Angeles CA 90024

HARWELL, ANNE L., transportation company executive; b. San Francisco, June 11, 1963; d. Billy D. and Shirley A. (Williamson) H. BS in BA, Okla. State U., 1985. Corp. auditor Union Pacific Corp., Omaha, 1985-88; mgr. exec. stock options Union Pacific Corp., Bethlehem, Pa., 1988-90; accountant gas projects Union Pacific Resources Co., Ft. Worth, 1990—. Mem. Nat. Assn. Female Execs., Beta Alpha Psi. Home: 2316 Misty Ridge Circle #142 Arlington TX 76011 Office: Union Pacific Resources Co 801 Cherry St MS2907 Fort Worth TX 76102

HARWIN, SHERRY BROADWATER, communications executive, dental hygienist; b. Fairmont, W.Va., Nov. 23, 1948; d. Ralph and Lydia Lois (McCormick) Broadwater; m. Cary Carl Harwin, May 3, 1986; children: Carl, Brett, Craig. BS, Ohio State U., 1970, cert. in dental hygiene, 1969. Registered dental hygienist, Calif. Pvt. practice Brentwood, Beverly Hills, Calif., 1971—; dir. communications Software 99, Marina Del Rey, Calif., 1983-85; dir. commuications Sterling Castle Software, Marina Del Rey, 1985—. Editor: Best Choice 3, 1989, Logic Gem, 1988, Forget Me Not, 1987, Manager, 1986. Mem. Am. Dental Hygienist Assn., Macintosh Users' Group L.A., Delta Delta Delta. Office: Sterling Castle Software 702 Washington St Marina del Rey CA 90292-5598

HARWOOD, ELEANOR CASH, librarian; b. Buckfield, Me., May 29, 1921; d. Leon Eugene and Ruth (Chick) Cash; B.A., Am. Internat. Coll., 1943; B.S., New Haven State Tchrs. Coll., 1955; m. Burton H. Harwood, Jr., June 21, 1944 (div. 1953); children—Ruth (Mrs. William R. Cline), Eleanor, James Burton. Librarian, Rathbun Meml. Library, East Haddam, Conn., 1955-56; asst. librarian Kent (Conn.) Sch., 1956-63; cons. to Chester (Conn.) Pub. Library, 1965-71. Served from ensign to lt. (j.g.) USNR, 1944-46. Mem. Am., Conn. library assns., Chester Hist. Soc. (trustee 1970-72), D.A.V., Am. Legion Aux., Soc. Mayflower Descs. Mem. United Ch. Author: (with John G. Park) The Independent School Library and the Gifted Child, 1956, The Age of Samuel Johnson, (essay) Remember When, 1987. Recipient The Commemorative medal of Honor Am. Biog. Inst., 1987; biog. tribute Dr. Katie Wilcox, 1975. Home: Maple St Chester CT 06412

HARWOOD, VIRGINIA ANN, nursing educator; b. Lawrenceville, Ohio, Nov. 5, 1925; d. Warren Leslie and Ruth Ann (Wilson) H.; m. Kenneth Dale Juillerat, Dec. 21, 1946 (div. 1972); children: Rozanne Augsburger, Vicki Sue Terry, Carol Mann, Karen Nichols. RN, City Hosp. Sch. Nursing, Springfield, Ohio, 1946; BSN, Ind. U., 1968; MS in Edn., Purdue U., 1973, PhD, 1982. RN; cert. psychiat/mental health nurse. Staff nurse various hosps., 1946-60; pub. health nursing supr. Whitely County Health Dept., Columbia City, Ind., 1960-65; nursing supr., coordinator staff devel. Ft. Wayne (Ind.) State Hosp., 1965-69; faculty sch. nursing Parkview Hosp., Ft. Wayne, 1969-74; faculty dept. nursing Ball State U., Muncie, Ind., 1974-77; dir. nursing program Thomas More Coll., Ft. Mitchell, Ky., 1977-79; faculty sch. nursing Purdue U., West Lafayette, Ind., 1979-80; dean sch. nursing Ashland (Ohio) Coll., 1980-83; charge nurse VA Med. Ctr., Marion, Ind., 1986—; cons. to nursing program Franklin U., Columbus, Ohio, 1981-82. Bd. dirs. Opera d'Lafayette, 1979-80, Am. Cancer Soc., Ashland, 1980-83, Kno-Ho-Ko Community Action Agy., Ashland, 1982-83; active Rep. Nat. Com., 1978—, U.S. Senatorial Club, 1984, Rep. Pres. Task Force, 1982—; stewardship com. Trinity Luth. Ch., Ashland, 1982-83; worship com. St. John Luth. Ch., Marion, 1988—. Fellow Acad. Psychiat. Nurse Specialists; mem. Am. Nurses Assn., Ky. Nurses Assn. (by-laws com.), Ohio Nurses Assn. (pres. Mohican dist. 1981-83), Ind. State Nurses Assn. (legis. com. 1979-80, program chmn. dist. 1 1970-71), Am. Nurses Found., Nat. League for Nursing (coun. baccalaureate and higher degree programs 1974-83), Ind. League for Nursing (chair edn. coun. 1972-73), Mensa (participant U.S.-Can. rondevous 1988, Cambridge, Eng. 1980, 90) Intertel, Sigma Theta Tau. Home: 115 E 50th St Marion IN 46953

HASELTINE, FLORENCE PAT, research administrator, obstetrician, gynecologist; b. Phila., Aug. 17, 1942; d. William R. and Jean Adele Haseltine; m. Frederick Cahn, Mar. 12, 1964 (div. 1969); m. Alan Chodos, Apr. 18, 1970; children: Anna, Elizabeth. BA in Biophysics, U. Calif., Berkeley, 1964; PhD in Biophysics, MIT, 1964-69; MD, Albert Einstein Coll. of Medicine, 1972. Diplomate Am. Bd. Ob-Gyn. Asst. prof. dept. ob-gyn. and pediatrics Yale U., New Haven, 1976-82, assoc. prof. dept. ob-gyn. and pediatrics, 1982-85; dir. Ctr. for Population Research, Nat. Inst. Child Health and Human Devel. NIH, Bethesda, Md., 1985—; Chmn. Woman's Council of the Am. Fertility Soc. Co-author: Woman Doctor, 1976, Magnetic Resonance of the Reproductive System, 1987; co-editor 6 other books in reproductive scis. Fellow Am. Coll. Obstetrics and Gynecology; mem. AAAS (bd. dirs.), Am. Fertility Soc., Soc. Gynecologic Investigation, Soc. Study of Reproduction, Endocrine Soc.,Soc. Reproductive Endocrinologists. Office: NIH 6130 Executive Blvd Rm 604 Bethesda MD 20892

HASKELL, BARBARA, curator; b. San Diego, Nov. 13, 1946; d. John N. and Barbara (Freeman) H.; m. Leon Botstein; 1 child, Clara Haskell Botstein. BA, UCLA, 1969. Dir. UCLA Exptl. Arts Festival, 1966; asst. registrar Pasadena (Calif.) Art Mus., 1969, curatorial asst., 1970, asst. curator, 1970, assoc. curator, 1970-72, curator painting and sculpture, 1972-74, dir. exhbns. and collections, 1974; curator painting and sculpture Whitney Mus. Am. Art, N.Y.C., 1975—. Author: Arthur Dove, 1974, Marsden Hartley, 1980, Milton Avery, 1982, Blam! The Explosion of Pop, Minimalism and Performance 1958-64, 1984, Georgia O'Keefe: Works on Paper, 1985, Ralston Crawford, 1985, Charles Demuth, 1987, Donald Judd, 1988, also collection catalogs. Named Woman of Yr., Mademoiselle mag., 1973. Office: Whitney Mus Am Art 945 Madison Ave New York NY 10021

HASKELL, KIM SHOPP, dentist; b. Harrisburg, Pa., Feb. 20, 1953; d. George Milton and Caroline Ardella (Culver) Shopp; m. William Ziegler Haskell, Dec. 17, 1977; children: Jonathan Lanham, William Ziegler II. BS, U. Md., 1974, DDS, 1982. Pvt. practice Upper Marlboro, Md., 1982—. Mem. ADA, Acad. Gen. Dentistry, Md. State Dental Assn., Greater Upper Marlboro C. of C. Democrat. Episcopalian. Office: 14414 Old Mill Rd Upper Marlboro MD 20772

HASKEW, JOYCE ANNETTE, engineering firm executive; b. Westerly, R.I., Mar. 7, 1942; d. John Victor and Isabella (MacGonegal) Biswurm, Sr.; m. Kenneth Lacy Haskew, Apr. 20, 1960; children—Kevin Dean, Scot Lacy. A.A., Am. River Coll., 1961. Delineator, State of Calif., Sacramento, 1961-66; engr. Kenneth L. Haskew, Ft. Bragg, Calif., and Ely, Nev., 1971-77; estimator, engr. Park Shah Abbas Co., Esfahan, Iran, 1977-78; civil drafter Pillsbury Engring., Reno, Nev., 1978-79; real estate saleswoman Preferred Equities, Reno, 1979-80; engr. Haskew Engring. Inc., Ely, Nev., 1979—; vice chmn. Regional Planning Commn., Ely, 1983-84; chmn. No. Nev. Pvt. Industry Council, Reno, 1983. sch. bd. trustee Seat A Esmeralda County, Nev., 1987—; health counselor Sch. Natural Health, Spanish Fork, Utah, 1986. Mem. Nat. Assn. Realtors, Ely C. of C. (co-chmn. legis. com. 1983). Republican. Baptist. Club: Sweet Adelines (Ely, Nev., and Valdez, Alaska). Office: 411 2d St Goldfield NV 89013

HASKINS, THERESA JOAN, association executive; b. Jersey City, May 18, 1945; d. Edward David and Helen Patricia (English) H. Student, No. Va. Community Coll., 1980-81. Cert. payroll profl. Clk. typist, sec. Pub. Svc. Electric and Gas Co., Newark, 1963-69; with Am. Chem. Soc., Washington, 1969—, credit union mgr., 1980-88, disbursements mgr., 1980—. Mem. Am. Payroll Assn., Nat. Assn. Accts. Republican. Roman Catholic. Office: Am Chem Soc 1155 16th St NW Ste 310 Washington DC 20036

HASLING, JILL FREEMAN, meteorologist; b. Bryan, Tex., June 8, 1952; d. John Clinton and Marjorie (Schaeffer) Freeman; m. David Patrick Hasling, Jan. 5, 1973; 1 child, Jacquelyn Christine. BA, U. St. Thomas, 1975. V.p. Inst. Storm Rsch., Houston, 1974-87; dir. ops. Weather Rsch. Ctr., Houston, 1987—. Coach St.John's High Sch., Houston, 1981 --. Mem. Am. Meteorological Soc. (sec. local chpt.). Office: Weather Rsch Ctr 3710 Mt Vernon St Houston TX 77006

HASNAS, SANDRA G., cable television production/programming director; b. N.Y.C., July 20, 1962; d. Irving and Doris (Bluestein) H. BA, U. Miami, Coral Gables, Fla., 1984; MA, N.Y. Inst. Tech., 1987. Owner SGH Prodns., Lynbrook, N.Y., 1987—; prodn./programming supr. Adams-Russell Cable, Lynbrook, 1987-88; prodn./programming dir. Cablevision Systems-L.I., Lynbrook, 1988—. Mem. Nat. Acad. Cable Programming, Alpha Epsilon Rho. Jewish. Office: Cablevision Systems LI 338 Ocean Ave Lynbrook NY 11563

HASSELBALCH, MARILYN JEAN, state official; b. Omaha, Jan. 2, 1930; d. Paul William and Helga Esther (Nodgaard) Campfield; m. Hal Burke Hasselbalch, June 13, 1954 (div. 1973); children: Kurt Campfield, Eric Burke, Peter Nels, Ane Catherine. BA with high distinction, U. Nebr., 1951. Cert. secondary tchr., Nebr. Pub. sch. tchr. Omaha and Long Beach, Calif., 1951-55; staff asst. U.S. Congressman Charles Thone, Lincoln, Nebr., 1973-78, Gov. of Nebr., Lincoln, 1978-82; exec. asst. Nebr. State Treas., Lincoln, 1983-86; sr. asst. Nebr. Gov. Kay A. Orr, Lincoln, 1987—. Mem. camp bd. dirs. YMCA, Nebr., 1969-70; mem. Nebr. Edn. Policies Commn., 1982; state convention del. Rep. Party Nebr., 1986, 88; gov.'s rep. Nebr. State Hist. Soc., Lincoln, 1987—; del. Edn. Commn. of States, Balt., 1988; participant strategic leadership for gubernatorial execs. Duke U., 1987. Named to Outstanding Young Women Am., 1961. Mem. Nat. Fedn. Rep. Women, Lancaster Couny Rep. Women (exec. bd. 1988), Am. Legion Auxiliary, Danish Sisterhood Am., Phi Beta Kappa, Theta Sigma Phi, Kappa Tau Alpha. Lutheran. Home: 4705 South St Lincoln NE 68506 Office: Gov's Office State Capitol Lincoln NE 68509

HASSETT, CAROL ALICE, psychologist; b. Bklyn., Apr. 19, 1947; d. Joseph and Anna (Portanova) Lusardi; B.S., St. John's U., 1968; M.Ed., Hofstra U., 1974, Ph.D. in Psychology (teaching asst.), 1981; m. John J. Hassett, June 29, 1968; 1 son, John J. Tchr. Day Elem. Sch., Bklyn., 1968-69; psychologist Nassau County Dept. Drug and Alcohol also Mental Health Assn. Nassau County, East Meadow, N.Y., 1981-84; chief supervising psychologist Queens Outreach Project, 1985—; pvt. practice clin. psychology, 1984—; from adj. asst. prof. to adj. assoc. prof. Hofstra U., 1980—. Trustee, v.p. Malverne (N.Y.) Pub. Libr., 1986—; vice chair, bd. dirs. Malverne Vol. Ambulance Corps, 1976—; bd. govs. Kings County Cadet Corps, 1966-72. Cert. advanced emergency med. technician, pre-hosp. critical care technician; permanently cert. tchr., N.Y. Mem. Am. Psychol. Assn., Nassau County Psychol. Assn. (mem. bd. dirs. 1986—). Republican. Roman Catholic. Contbr. articles profl. jours. Home: 105 Franklin Ave Malverne NY 11565 Office: 230 Hilton Ave Hempstead NY 11550

HASSLER, BONNIE BARHAM, fashion consultant; b. Stillwater, Okla., June 7, 1932; d. Walter Elmo and Hope Virginia (Grubbs) Barham; m. Ferdinand Rudolph Hassler, Dec. 27, 1953; children: June Hilary Hassler Allers, Harriet Caroline Clause. BS, Okla. State U., 1953; cert., Internat. Inst. Color, San Francisco, 1983. Adminstr. Ctr. Study Human Systems, Chevy Chase, Md., 1979-82; pres. Dyad Mgmt., Kensington, Md., 1980—; ptnr. Reflections, Kensington, 1985—; ind. fashion cons., color theory educator Kensington, 1982—; cons., Les Couleurs, Richmond, Va., 1983—. Mem. women's com., Nat. Symphony Orch., Washington, 1989. Mem. Toastmasters Internat., Capital Speakers Club (chpt. pres. 1989), Harvard Club, Phi Kappa Phi, Chi Omega. Democrat. Office: Dyad Mgmt 9614 Kensington Pkwy Kensington MD 20895

HAST, JOAN EILEEN, communication company planning manager; b. Denver, Jan. 6, 1955; d. Bernard Arthur and Erma Ann (Pospisil) H. Student, U. Denver, 1973-74, Goethe Inst., Munich, 1974-75; BA in Internat. Affairs, U. Colo., 1983, postgrad., 1983-85, MS in Telecommunications, 1985. Owner, mgr. Celebrity Slickers Custom Jackets, Boulder, Colo., 1978-80; monogram specialist Custom Monogramming, Denver, 1981; summer intern in telecommunications Horizon House Pub., Dedham, Mass., 1983; office mgr. Universal Fuels Oil Co., Denver, 1983-84; sr. engr. GTE-Midwestern Telephone Ops., Fort Wayne, Ind., 1985-86; network adminstr. GTE-Info. Bus., Indpls., 1987-88; adminstrv. mgr. engring. assoc. devel. program GTE Svc. Corp., Stamford, Conn., 1988-89, mgr. advanced network planning GTE Mobilnet, Houston, 1989—. Advisor Jr. Achievement, Fort Wayne, 1985-86; vol. Fort Wayne Zoo, 1985; active YMCA, Fort Wayne. Research grantee U. Colo. Dept. Telecommunications, Honolulu, 1984, Las Vegas, 1984. Avocations: horses, foreign languages, traveling, art, ballet. Office: GTE Mobilnet 616 FM 1960 W Houston TX 77090

HASTINGS, DEBORAH, bass guitarist; b. Evansville, Ind., May 11, 1959; d. Mortimer Winthrop Hastings and Margaret Hooper (Smith) Zimmerman. Student music, U. Wis. Bass guitarist N.Y.C. and Madison, Wis., 1975—; freelance photographer Madison, 1976-81; performed with Ron Wood, Bo Diddley, Chuck Berry, Jerry Lee Lewis, George Gobel, Little Anthony and the Imperials, Ben E. King, Sarah Dash and others; performed at 1989 Inauguration Pres. George Bush; performed with Billy Preston, Dr. John, Koko Taylor, Willie Dixon, Albert Collins, Joe Cocker, Carla Thomas, Eddie Floyd, Ron Wood, Steve Cropper (Blues Brothers), Bo Diddley, Chuck Berry, Joe Louis Walker, Sam Moore, Chuck Jackson; TV shows include Legends of Rock and Roll live from Rome performed with Bo Diddley, BB King, James Brown, Little Richard, Ray Charles, Fats Domino, others. Author: Photographers Market, 1981; bass player TV shows Joan Rivers, 1987, Classsics of Rock and Roll, 1988, Gunslingers tour Live from the Ritz with Ron Wood & Bo Diddley, 1988, Live from the Ritz, 1989, Legends of Rock and Roll (live from Australia); 89 tours in Europe, Australia and Japan. Fundraiser, bassist polit. campaigns, Madison; bass player Pres. Bush inauguration, 1989. Recipient numerous awards for pottery, award Arts Coun., Madison, Arts Coun., Ann Arbor, Mich. Mem. Musicians Union (local 802). Democrat. Office: Talent Cons Internat 200 W 57th St Ste 910 New York NY 10019

HASTINGS, EVELYN GRACE, educator; b. Seguin, Tex., May 25, 1938; d. Ed Howard Coleman and Mae Stella (King) Haywood; m. Marvin Hastings, Oct. 9, 1982. BS, Tex. Luth. Coll., 1960; MA, U. Tex., San Antonio, 1985. Cert. tchr., Tex. Tchr. Seguin (Tex.) Ind. Sch. Dist., 1962—; sec. Guadalupe County Tchr.'s Meeting, Seguin, 1962-65, Juan Seguin Sch. PTA, 1969. Historian, corr. sec. Tex. Women's Conv., Ch. of Our Lord Jesus Christ, Tex., 1961-69, treas. Tex. State Armor Bears Young Peoples Union, 1960-63, pres., 1963-65, 68-70, sec. Tex. State Sunday Sch. Assn., 1960-63, asst. supt., 1968-70, state supt., 1970-74, local missionary pres. and fin. sec. of Refuge Ch.; state missionary 2d v.p. Tex.-Okla. State Conv.; state v.p. Ch. of our Lord Jesus Christ, 1985—, state supr. Tex. Jr. Conv., 1970—, Sunday supr. Lighthouse Ch., 1975—. Recipient Cert. of Outstanding Svc. Nat. Youth Congress Ch. of Our Lord Jesus Christ, 1968, Cert. of Appreciation, Tex.-Okla. Conv.of the Ch. of Our Lord Jesus Christ of the Apostolic Faith, 1989, Outstanding Svc. Plaque, 1981. Mem. AAUW (sec. 1968-70), NEA, Tex. State Tchrs. Assn. (minority del. 1982) Seguin Educators Assn. Democrat. Home: 950 Elsik Seguin TX 78155

HASTINGS, SUSAN ANN, marketing professional; b. Balt., May 1, 1955; d. Richard Elwood and Helen Marie (Thiel) H. BA in History magna cum laude, Loyola Coll., Balt., 1977; MS in Pub. Rels., Am. U., Washington, 1987. Account exec. Windsor Publs., Inc., Woodland Hills, Calif., 1977-78; assessor State Dept. Assessments, Balt., 1978-79; officer pub. rels. Met. Balt. Health Care, Inc., 1979-80; asst. dir. Health Fair '81, Balt., 1980-81; dir. pub. rels. Theriault's, Annapolis, Md., 1981-84; mgr. advt. and mktg. The Rouse Co., Balt., 1984-85; dir. mktg. Homart Devel. Co., Washington, 1985-88; dir. mktg. retail div. Biskind Devel. Co., North Olmsted, Ohio, 1988—. Contbr. to Bawlamer mag., 1981; reporter Mt. Vernon Newsletter, 1981; editor: Nat. Cherry Blossom Festival Program, 1987. Vol. Md. Hist. Soc., 1976-77, Citizen's Planning and Housing Assn., 1981-85; mem. Holly Tour Publicity Com., 1980-81, Community Holiday Celebration Com., 1982, Speaker's Bur., 1983; active mentor program Goucher Coll., 1984-85. Recipient Merchandising award Playthings mag., 1983, Advt. Excellence award Retail Advt. Coun., 1986, Exterior Holiday Decor and Design award Bus. and Profl. Assn. Georgetown, 1986, MAXI Merit award Consumer Advt. mag., 1986. Mem. Internat. Assn. Bus. Communicators (dir. publicity 1982, bd. dirs. 1982-85, treas. 1983, co-chair regional communications conf. 1983-84, pres. Balt. chpt. 1984, asst. dir. internal activities 1985, Spl. Projects award 1983), Capital Area Mktg. Dirs., Balt. Pub. Rels. Coun., Bus. and Profl. Women's Assn. (Chesapeake chpt. Young Career Woman Yr. award, 1981, Phi Alpha Theta, Alpha Sigma Nu. Democrat. Roman Catholic. Home: 841 Hamlet Ln A-2A Westlake OH 44145 Office: Biskind Devel Co 4999 Great Northern Mall North Olmstead OH 44070

HASTINGS, SUSAN KAY, auditor, accountant, consultant; b. Mason City, Iowa, Mar. 25, 1952; d. Arnold E. and Mildred E. (Thiemann) Hoveland; m. Robert E. Hastings, June 12, 1971. AA, North Iowa Area Community Coll., Mason City, 1973; BS, Nat. Coll. Bus., 1975. CPA, S.D. Staff acct. McGladrey Hendrickson & Pullen, Rapid City, S.D., 1975-80, mgr., 1980-84, ptnr., 1984-87; v.p., cons. First Fed. Savs. Bank, Rapid City, 1987—; mem. acctg. adv. bd. Nat. Coll., Rapid City, 1985—. Treas., bd. dirs. Rapid City Arts Coun., 1987—, Rapid City Arts Found., 1988—; active YMCA, Rapid City, 1973—. Mem. am. Inst. CPA's, S.D. Soc. CPA's. Fin. Mgrs. Soc., Inst. Internal Auditors, Arrowhead Country Club (Rapid City) (treas., bd. dirs. 1986—). Office: First Fed Savs Bank 909 St Joe St PO Box 8170 Rapid City SD 57709

HATCH, JAMI MCCOWAN, corporate communications specialist; b. Hot Springs, Ark., May 25, 1960; d. James Edward and Wanda (Higgs) McC.; m. Kurt Edgar Hatch, Nov. 29, 1986. BBA in Mktg., U. Wis., 1982. With Mobile Communications Corp., 1982—; sales mgr. Mobile Communications Corp., Austin, Tex., 1986-88; gen. mgr. Mobile Communications Corp., Austin, 1988—. Mem. Nat. Assn. Profl. Sales Women, C. of C. Home: 6316 Sprucewood Cove Austin TX 78731

HATCH, LYNDA SYLVIA, educator of talented and gifted; b. Portland, Oreg., Feb. 19, 1950; d. Marley Elmo and Undine Sylvia (Crockard) Sims. BA, Wash. State U., 1972; MS, Portland State U., 1975; EdD, Oreg. State U., 1984. Cert. tchr., Oreg. Tchr. 5th grade, outdoor sch. specialist Clover Park Sch. Dist. 400, Tacoma, 1971-72; tchr. 6th grade, outdoor sch. specialist Hillsboro (Oreg.) elem. Dist. 7, 1972-78, Bend (Oreg.)-La Pine Sch. Dist., 1978=82; grad. teaching asst. Oreg. State U., Corvallis, 1982-84; elem. curriculum specialist Bend (Oreg.)-La Pine Sch. Dist., 1983-85, tchr. 4th grade gifted and talented, 1985—; ednl. cons., tchr. workshops, 1973—; coordinator Odyssey of the Mind, Bend, 1985-89, Tchr.-Mentor Program for 1st Yr. Tchrs., Beaverton, Oreg., 1982-83. Contbr. articles to profl. jours. Vol., leader, bd. dirs. Girl Scouts U.S.A., 1957—; elder First Presbyn. Ch., Bend, 1980—; vol. hist. interpretation High Desert Mus., Bend, 1987—. Recipient Excellence in Teaching award Bend Found., 1985-86, 86-87; named Oreg. Tchr. of Yr., Oreg. Dept. Edn., 1982; Geraldine Rockefeller Dodge found. grantee, 1989, 90. Mem. Nat. Council Tchrs. Math., Nat. Sci. Tchrs. Assn., NEA, Oreg. Council Tchrs. Math. (bd. dirs. 1981-82), Oreg. Council Tchrs. English (bd. dirs. 1981-82), Oreg. Reading Assn., Phi Delta Kappa, Delta Kappa Gamma, others. Home: 1480 University Heights Dr N Flagstaff AZ 86001

HATCH, MARY WENDELL VANDER POEL, interior decorator, nonprofit organization executive; b. N.Y.C., Feb. 6, 1919; d. William Halsted and Blanche Pauline (Billings) Vander Poel; m. George Montagu Miller, Apr. 5, 1940 (div. 1974); children: Wendell Miller Steavenson, Gretchen Miller Elkus; m. Sinclair Hatch, May 14, 1977 (dec. July 1989). Pres. Miller Richard, Inc., Interior Decorators, Glen Head, N.Y., 1972—; bd. dirs. Eye Bank Sight Restoration, N.Y.C., 1975—, pres., 1980-88, hon. chair, 1988—; bd. dirs. Manhattan Eye Ear and Throat Hosp., N.Y.C., 1966—, v.p., 1978-90; sec. Cold Spring Harbor Lab., N.Y., 1985-89; bd. dirs. Spring Harbor Lab., N.Y., 1985—. V.p. North Country Garden Club, Nassau County, N.Y., 1979-81, 1983-85; dir. Planned Parenthood Nassau County, Mineola, N.Y., 1982-84, Hutton House C.W. Post Coll., Greenvale, N.Y., 1982—. Mem. Colony Club (N.Y.C.), Church Club (N.Y.C.), Order St. John Jerusalem (N.Y.C.). Republican. Episcopalian. Home: Mill River Rd Box 330 Oyster Bay NY 11771

HATCH, REBECCA BLACKMON, stockbroker; b. Live Oak, Fla., Nov. 18, 1955; d. Donald James and Marilyn Webb (Blackmon) H. BA, Fla. State U., 1977. Asst. dir. Fla. House, Washington, D.C., 1977-78; sec. Sci. and Tech. Commn. U.S. Ho. Reps., Washington, 1978-79; loan originator Cameron Brown Co., Annandale, Va., 1979-81; salesperson, mgr. Dictaphone Corp., Alexandria, Va. and Cin., 1981-83; mktg. rep. Computer Consoles, Inc., Reston, Va., 1983-85; account exec. Dean Witter Reynolds, Inc., McLean, Va., 1985-88, Johnston, Lemon and Co., Alexandria, Va., 1988-89, Ferris, Baker, Watts, Washington, 1989—. Bd. dirs. Cardinal Forest Homeowners Assn., fin. com., 1989—, treas., 1990—; mem. Jaycees, Washington, 1989—; coun. on ministries Messiah Ch., 1989—. Mem. Prince William Bd. Realtors, Fla. State Soc., Washington Tennis Patrons, Fairfax C. of C., Fla. State U. Alumni Club (pres. 1978-79, treas. 1986-87, v.p. 1987—), Nat. Assn. Securities Dealers and Secs. (lic. stock broker, registered rep.), Wash. Ski Club (MAST com., budget and fin. com.), Delta Zeta Alumni Assn. Democrat. Methodist. Home: 5838 Rexford Dr Springfield VA 22152

HATCH, SANDRA LEE, magazine editor; b. Lincoln, Maine, Aug. 19, 1948; d. Joseph Glenn and Muriel Josephine (Waltz) Grover; m. Charles Randall Hatch, July 27, 1968; children: Joseph, Sarah. BS, U. Maine, 1970. Cert. home econs. tchr., Mass. Tchr. home econs. Town of Methuen, Mass., 1970-82; editor quilt mag. House of White Birches, Berne, Ind., 1981—; editor cross-stitch mag. House of White Birches, Inc., Berne, Ind., 1982-84; editor Stitch N Sew Quilts/Quilt World Stitch N Sew Quilts/ Quilt World/ Quick & Easy Quilting, Berne, Ind., 1984—. Co-author: Putting on the Glitz, 1990; contbr. articles to profl. jours. Mem. Coll. Club of Greater Lawrence, Mass., 1980-88. Mem. New Eng. Quilter's Guild, New Eng. Quilt Mus., Merrimack Valley Quilters (pres. 1984-85). Democrat. Home and Office: RR1 Box 137 Sweet Rd Lincoln Center ME 04458

HATCHER, MARILYN ANN, realtor, educator; b. Newark, Sept. 27, 1950; d. Charles George and Ann (Hencoski) K.; m. Creel David, Aug. 10, 1974; children: Deborah Ann, David Michael. BA in Bus. Edn., Montclair State Coll., 1972; MBA in Mgmt., Fairleigh Dickinson U., 1980. Cert. tchr. N.J.; lic. realtor, N.J. Instr. Ocean Twp. Adult Even Sch., Oakhurst, N.J., 1969; instr., counselor Katharine Gibbs Sch., N.Y.C., 1972-75; instr. The Berkeley Sch., Ridgewood, N.J., 1977, No. N.J. Civil Svc. Tng. Ctr., Newark, N.J., 1978-80, Middlesex County Coll., Edison, N.J., 1980-83, Brookdale Community Coll., Lincroft, N.J., 1980-84; realtor-assoc. Schlott Realtors, Matawan, N.J., 1987—; tchr. St. John Vianney High Sch., Holmdel, N.J.; tech. sec. A.L. Straubing & Assocs., South Orange, N.J. Counselor day camp YMCA, YWCA; active local PTO, 1988-89; mem. legis. com., strategic planning com. Monmouth County Bd. Realtors, Middletown, N.J., 1988, strategic planning com. Mem. Assn. MBA Execs., N.J. Assn. Realtors, N.J. Bd. Realtors (mem. Million Dollar Sales club 1988), Monmouth County Bd. Realtors, Nat. Assn. Realtors, Residential Coun., Hazlet (N.J.) Thunderetts (bd. dirs. 1987). Home: 220 Randolph Rd Freehold NJ 07728 Office: Schlott Realtors 132 Rte 34 Matawan NJ 07728

HATCHER, MARTHA OLIVIA TAYLOR (MRS. FRANK PRODGEN HATCHER, SR.), biologist, educator, educational consultant; b. Birmingham, Ala., Feb. 17, 1920; d. Sanford Allia and Mary (McCullough) Taylor; B.S., Howard Coll., 1936-40; M.Ed. in Sci. Edn., U. Ga., 1966, Ed.D., 1973; tchrs. cert. Brenau Coll., 1964; m. Frank Pridgen Hatcher, Sr., Nov. 7, 1941; children—Frank Pridgen, Martha Elizabeth, Nancy Louise. Chief bacteriologist veterinary div. Ga. Dept. Agr., Atlanta, 1943-45; supr. surg. pathology lab. Jefferson Hillman Hosp., Med. Coll. Ala., Birmingham, 1945-46, research asst. in pathology, 1945-46; mgr. offices Fran Mar Farms, Inc., Gainesville, Ga., 1957-66; instr. biology Gainesville Jr. Coll., 1966-67, asst. prof. biology, 1967-74, assoc. prof., 1974-77, prof., 1977-82, acting chmn. div. natural scis. and maths., 1968-74, chmn., 1974-82; prof. biology, adminstrv. asst. Brenau Coll., 1982-87, dean student devel., 1986-87; pres. Hatcher & Assocs., Gainesville; accompanist music dept. Brenau Coll., Gainesville, 1959-61. Chmn. Gray Ladies Vol. Services, Gainesville chpt. ARC, 1957-62; sec. Yohah council Girl Scouts U.S.A., 1959-61; bd. dirs. Community Concert Assn. Gainesville, 1968-70; active Ed Dodd Mark Trail Found., 1986—, Lanier Orchestra League, 1984—, Pro Musica, 1984—, City of Gainesville. NSF sci. faculty fellow in microbiology, 1970-71. Mem. AAUP, AAAS, Am. Guild Organists, Am. Inst. Biol. Scis., Nat. Assn. Biology Tchrs., Assn. S.E. Biologists, Nat. Assn. Research Sci. Teaching, Ga. Acad. Sci., Nat. Sci. Tchrs. Assn., Am. Legion Aux. (pres. 1948-50), Am. Soc. Zoologists, Southeastern Assn. Educators of Tchrs. Sci. (pres. 1983-84; editor Newsletter), UDC (chpt. pres. 1949-51), Am. Soc. Microbiology, AAUW, Kappa Delta Pi, Alpha Epsilon Delta, Delta Kappa Gamma, Phi Delta Kappa, Phi Theta Kappa, Delta Zeta. Clubs: Music (pres. 1950-52), Federated Music (sec. 1957-58), Phoenix Soc., Pilot Internat. (pres. 1983-84) (Gainesville). Home: 840 Memorial Dr NE Gainesville GA 30501 Office: Hatcher & Assocs PO Box 753 Gainesville GA 30501

HATFIELD, JANE STAUFF, educator; b. Milw., Aug. 9, 1911; d. Grover Andrew and Marie Louise (Vogt) Stauff; m. Henry C. Hatfield, Mar. 15, 1937; children: Robert, Barbara Hatfield Bazyn. BA, Northwestern U., 1932. Instr. English Mass. Dept. Edn., Quincy, Mass., 1964—; sec. Cambridge Editorial Rsch., Inc, 1960-70. Author study guides for various English courses, 1964—, including: The American Woman, 1974, Black History, 1972. Bd. dirs. Cambridge YWCA, 1972-78; active Cambridge Civic Assn.

HATHAWAY, JOAN BOYETTE, secondary school administrator; b. Wilson, N.C., Aug. 11, 1935; d. John Bunyon and Ruth (Fleming) B.; m. Richard Edward Hathaway, Sept. 1, 1956; children: Donna, Richard Edward. BA, Atlantic Christian Coll., Wilson, 1955-57; MEd., U. S.C., Columbia, 1977-78. Copy writer Sta. WGTM, Wilson, N.C., 1955-56; tchr. Jackson Sch., Newport News, Va., 1957-59; dir. First Presbyn. Ch. Sch., Lumberton, N.C., 1963-66; tchr. Kindergarten Pub. Sch., Milw.; tchr. Albermarle Acad., Elizabeth City, N.C., 1968-69; tutor, supr. Columbia (S.C.) Reading Found., 1972-75; tchr. Hammond Acad., Columbia, 1969-75; dir. Sandhills Acad., Columbia, 1975—; cons., Thomas Hart Acad., Hartsville, S.C., 1986-88, Heritage Hall Acad., Norway, S.C., 1987-89, Richland Sch. Dist., Columbia, S.C., 1988; evaluator, Sandhills Acad., Columbia, 1979—; pres. ACLD, S.C., 1979. Author/Presenter, S.C. Council for Exceptional Children, 1985, Orton Dyslexia Soc., 1988. Bd. mem. S.C. Literacy Assn., Columbia, 1982-88, Midlands Human Resources Devel. Commn.,Columbia, 1983-87; exec. com. S.C. Ind. Sch. Assn., Columbia, 1984-85; curriculum tech. adv. panel Gov.'s Initiative for Workforce Excellence, Columbia, 1988-. Rep. Presbyterian.

HATHCOCK, CATHY LYNN, pharmacist, sales executive; b. Corinth, Miss., Feb. 28, 1959; d. Charles Ervin and Doris Alene (Whitaker) H. BS in Pharmacy, U. Miss., 1983. Lic. pharmacist, Miss. Pharmacy asst. Super D Drugs, Corinth, 1981-83; staff pharamacist James Bennett Apothecary, Corinth, 1982-84, North Miss. Med. Ctr., Tupelo, 1983-84, Miss. Dept. Health, Jackson, 1985-88, Doctors Hosp., Jackson, 1984-88; sales rep. Eli Lilly & Co., Indpls., 1988—; relief pharmacist Harlan Drugs, Jackson, 1985-88. Active Bush Presdl. Campaign, Jackson, 1988, mayoral campaign, Jackson, 1988, county ct. judge campaign, Corinth, 1988. Mem. Miss. Soc. Hosp. Pharmacists, Miss. Soc. Pharmacists (state com. 1984—), Ole Miss Alumni Assn. (phone com. 1983-90), Miss. Club (bd. dirs. 1989-90), Kappa Delta. Republican. Baptist. Home: S Village Green Circle Jackson MS 39211 Office: Eli Lilly & Co Lilly Corp Ctr Indianapolis IN 46285

HATTAL, TACEY THOMAS, nursing administrator; b. Buffalo, Dec. 8, 1955; d. Howard H. and Yvonne (Thomas) H. BA, Smith Coll., Northampton, Mass., 1978; BS in Nursing, Columbia U., 1980; MS in Nursing, U. Pa., 1986, postgrad., 1986. Asst. dir. nursing specialty svcs. Germantown Hosp. and Med. Ctr., Phila.; adminstrv. asst. The Grad. Hosp., Phila.; head nurse Lehigh Valley Hosp. Ctr., Allentown, Pa. Mem. AACN, NLN, AONE, SEPONE, Sigma Theta Tau.

HAUBER, PATRICIA ANNE, educator; b. Phila., Feb. 16, 1953; d. Frederick Joseph and Dorothy Marie (Delaney) Hauber. AA, Montgomery County Community, Blue Bell, Pa., 1973; BS, Bloomsburg U., 1975; MEd, Lehigh U., 1985, elem. prin. cert., secondary prin. cert., 1990. Tchr. North Penn Sch. Dist., Lansdale, Pa., 1975-85; sci. coord., tchr. St. Jude Sch., Chalfont, Pa., 1985—. Instr., trainer ARC, CPR programs, Lansdale, Pa., 1979—. Mem. AAAS, Pa. Sci. Tchrs. Assn., Assn. for Supervision and Curriculum Devel., Pa. Assn. for Supervision and Curriculum Devel. Democrat. Roman Catholic. Home: 391 Huckleberry Ln Harleysville PA 19438 Office: St Jude Sch 323 W Butler Ave Chalfont PA 18914

HAUCK, CHRISTINE CLAIRE KRAUS, insurance executive; b. McKeesport, Pa., May 22, 1951; d. Lawrence Elmer and Anne Mae (Seinar) Kraus; m. David T. Hauck, Feb. 6, 1971 (div. April 1986); children: Benjamin David, Christopher Thomas, Andrew Lawrence. Student, Duquesne U., 1969-71, U. Pitts., 1972-78, U. Charleston, 1978-81; BA, Ohio State U., 1984. Cert. ins. counselor. Claims asst. John Hancock Ins., Pitts., 1971-73; underwriter Chubb Ins. Group, Pitts., 1973-76; account rep., ins. agt. Frank B. Hall, Columbus, Ohio, 1982-85; customer svc. rep., agt. Andrew Ins. Assocs., Columbus, 1986-88, sr. customer svc. rep., 1988—; pres., sec. Positively Successful, Columbus, 1988—. Author poetry. Mem. Welcome Wagon, Upper Arlington, Ohio, 1981-84, Barrington Sch. Assn., Upper Arlington, 1982-87, Tremont Sch. ASsn., Upper Arlington, 1987-90, Upper Arlington Civic Assn., 1986-90; instr. St. Agatha Dept. Religious Edn., Upper Arlington, 1983-87; foster parent, 1975—. Mem. NAFE, Parents Without Ptnrs. Club, Steps to Greatness Club, Phi Kappa Phi. Democrat. Roman Catholic. Club: Parents Without Ptnrs. Home: 2121 Jervis Rd Columbus OH 43221-2727 Office: Positively Successful 2121 Jervis Rd Columbus OH 43221-2727

HAUCK, DONNA JOANNE, marketing executive; b. Rochester, N.Y., June 23, 1960; d. Donald Joseph and Helen Marie (Carrison) Kridel; m. Michael Jonathan Hauck, Sept. 3, 1983; 1 child, Mason Joseph. BA in Communications, U. Colo., 1981. Freelance video producer Seattle, 1981-82; media dir. Leslie & Hoover Advt., El Paso, Tex., 1982-84; mktg. dir. Flynn Group Advt., Colorado Springs, Colo., 1984-86; v.p. Teller Mktg., Inc., Conifer, Colo., 1986—. Active campaign head Injury Found., Colorado Springs, 1985, 86, Pub. TV Sta., Pueblo, Colo., 1985, 86; creative campaign. dir. Pub. Radio Sta., Colorado Springs, 1985, 86. Mem. Mfrs. Agts. Nat. Assn.

HAUCK, ELAINE MARIE, nurse, air force officer; b. Yankton, S.D., Oct. 22, 1950; d. Alfred Andrew and Hazel Marie (Stark) H.; m. David Carlton Shaw, Apr. 4, 1987. Diploma, St. Vincent Sch. Nursing, Sioux City, Iowa, 1971; BA in Health Svc. Adminstrn., St. Mary's Coll., Moraga, Calif., 1982; BS in Nursing, Old Dominion U., 1987; MBA, Nat. U., 1989. Staff nurse St. Vincent Hosp., Sioux City, 1972; commd. 2d lt. USAF, 1972-73, advanced through grades to lt. col., 1988; staff nurse various USAF Hosp., Tex., P.R. and Eng., 1972-76; nurse recruitment officer Omaha, 1976-79; charge nurse ob-gyn clinic Mather AFB, Sacramento, 1979-82; charge nurse multi svc. unit Yokota AFB, Japan, 1982-85; dir. ambulatory svcs. Nellis AFB, Las Vegas, Nev., 1987—; coord. outpatient clinic Nellis AFB, Las Vegas. Mem. Am. Nurses Assn., Nat. League Nursing, Am. Hosp. Assn. Ambulatory Care Soc., NAFE, Lladro Collector Soc. Republican. Lutheran. Office: 554 Med Group SGHZ Nellis AFB NV 89191

HAUCK, MARGUERITE HALL, broadcasting executive, antique dealer; b. Bayside, N.Y., June 30, 1948; d. Carlyle Washington and Anzonette Marguerite (Asmussen) Hall. Student, Syracuse U., 1966-67; B.A. summa cum laude, Queens Coll., CUNY, 1974. Assoc. producer Animatic Prodns., Ltd., N.Y.C., 1968-72; mktg. analyst BBDO, Inc., N.Y.C., 1974-75; mktg. analyst CBS, Inc., N.Y.C., 1975-76, dir. mktg. and research FM nat. sales, Radio div., 1976-85; dir. mktg. and research Christal Radio Sales div. Katz Communications, 1985-87; pres. Lennon Hall Antiques, Inc., 1986—; v.p. research and mktg. Christal Radio Sales div. Katz Communications, 1987—. Author: The 321 Billion Dollar Market, 1981, The Mid-Day Myth Exploded, 1982; columnist, TV-Radio Age mag., 1982, 89. Bd. dirs. Queens Coll. Student Services Corp., 1973-74. Recipient Queens Coll. Disting. Service award, 1974. Home: 20 Continental Ave Forest Hills NY 11375 Office: Christal Radio Sales One Dag Hammarskjold Pla New York NY 10017 also: Lennon Hall Antiques Inc 5 Continental Ave Forest Hills NY 11325

HAUENSTEIN, CHRISTINA MARIE, banker; b. Elizabeth, N.J., July 25, 1964; d. Richard Albert and Mary (Leszczak) H. BS, Monmouth Coll., Long Branch, N.J., 1986. Credit analyst Core States/N.J. Nat. Bank, Pennington, 1986-87; loan rep. Core States/N.J. Nat. Bank, Neption, 1987-88; asst. cashier, comml. lender Midlantic Nat. Bank, Red Bank, N.J., 1988—. Mem. N.J. Assn. Women Bus. Owners, Optimists. Roman Catholic. Office: Midlantic Nat Bank 140 Broad St Red Bank NJ 07701

HAUENSTEIN, NANCY DEAN, development administrator; b. Long Beach, Calif., May 29, 1961; d. C. Thomas and Marjorie (Kennedy) Dean; m. James G. Hauenstein, Sept. 26, 1987. Student, U. So. Calif.; BA, U. Calif., Irvine, 1987. Program supr. Washoe Med. Ctr., Reno, Nev.; asst. dir. Meml. Med. Ctr., Long Beach, Calif.; organizational specialist Nev. State Edn. Assn., Carson City, Nev.; dir. ann. giving U. Nev. Reno Found. Mem. Jr. League of Reno; bd. dirs. Sierra Nev. chpt. ARC; mem. aux. Washoe Med. Ctr.; mem. Sierra Women's Ensemble, 1989—. Recipient Am. Hosp. Assn. award for vol. excellence program "Adopting Pediatrics," 1989. Mem. NAFE, Dirs. of Vols. in Agencies, Am. Soc. Dirs. Vol. Svcs., Delta Delta Delta. Republican. Presbyterian. Home: 13655 Edmands Dr Reno NV 89511

HAUER, JEANNE T., marketing and communications executive; b. Salem, Ohio, Nov. 24, 1951; d. James Eugene and Mary Margaret (Stanton) Torrence; m. Richard John Hauer, Jr., Aug. 18, 1973; children: Megan, Kathryn. BA, Cleve. State U., 1974; AA, Ursuline Coll., 1971. Editor Arby's, Inc., Youngstown, Ohio, 1975-78; pres. Freelance Communications, Cleve., 1978-85; dir. pub. rels. Cellular One, Cleve., 1985-87; dir. mktg./ communications Cragin-Lang, Inc., Cleve., 1987—. Benefit chmn. Cleve. Orch., 1985, jr. com., 1981-90. Mem. NAFE, Pub. Rels. Soc. Am., Nat. Assn. Indsl. and Office Parks (publicity chmn. 1990), Cleve. Advt. Club. Roman Catholic. Office: Cragin Lang Inc 1215 Superior Ave Cleveland OH 44114

HAUG, NANCY G., marketing professional, consultant; b. Portland, Nov. 3, 1944; d. Everard O. and Doris C. (Blomberg) Johnson; m. Darrol K. Haug, May 4, 1943; 1 child, Rebecca L. Student, Linfield Coll., 1964; BS in Speech and Psychology, Portland State U., 1967. Dir. publications Mt. Hood Community Coll., Gresham, Oreg., 1971-74; mktg. rep. Cone Heiden, Seattle, 1974-77; dir. advt. and promotions Princess Tours, Seattle, 1977-81, dir. client services, 1981-83; dir. mktg. Manus Direct Mktg., Seattle, 1984-87, Airborne Express, 1987—; tour escort travel groups Alaska, China, Mex., 1977-83; cons. Pacific Celebration 89, Seattle, 1986; mem. Rhodes Scholarship Com., Seattle, 1986; chair person Direct Mktg. Day, Seattle, 1986. Producer film Alaska The Great Land, 1980. Bd. dirs. Job Corp, Seattle, 1976-80; hostess Edmonds Art Festival, Wash., 1985-86. Mem. Mktg. Communications Execs. Internat. (incorporator, hostess 1979-81); Seattle Direct Mktg. Assns. (founder, sec. 1984-86, pres. 1989-90), Sales Mktg. Execs. Internat., Puget Sound Advt. Fedn., Alaska Visitors Assn. Republican. Club: Skiyente (Portland) (pres.1972-73).

HAUGEN, MARILYN ANNE, nurse practitioner, health center director; b. Colorado Springs, Jan. 11, 1932; d. Arnold H. and Juanita P. (Porter) Miller; m. Halver Herbert Haugen, June 13, 1953; children—Steven Lee, Karen Elaine. B.A., Denver U., 1953; B.S. in Nursing, Miami U., Ohio, 1980. Cert. pediatric nurse practitioner; R.N. Tchr., Denver Pub. Schs., 1953-57; pediatric nurse Middletown Regional Hosp., Ohio, 1973-76, educator, 1976-77, pediatric nurse practitioner, 1978-82, project dir. maternal child health ctr., 1982—. Mem. adv. bd. Miami Valley Child Devel. Ctr., 1983—; chmn. Child and Family Health Services Consortium, 1986—; mem. adv. bd. Butler County Mental Health Assn.; treas. adv. bd. Butler County Mental Health Assn. Mem. Nat. Assn. Pediatric Nurse Practitioners and Assocs. (treas., fin. chair 1982-86, treas. Ohio chpt. 1980-84, Henry K. Silver award 1986, Pediatric Nurse Practitioner of Yr. Ohio chpt. 1986), Am. Nurses Assn., Ohio Nurses Assn., Mortar Board, Kappa Delta. Home: 613 Regent Dr Middletown OH 45044 Office: Middletown Regional Hosp 105 McKnight Dr Middletown OH 45044

HAUGEN, SUSAN DAWN, accounting educator; b. Rice Lake, Wis., Aug. 9, 1951. BS, U. Wis., Eau Calire, 1972; MS, cert. internal audit., U. Wis., Stout, 1980; EdD, Okla. State U., 1982. Cert. Mgmt. Acct. Bus. Edn. Instr. Chetek Sr. High Sch., 1972-74; sr. acct. U. Wis.-Stout, Menomonie, 1974-80; teaching asst. Okla. State U., Stillwater, 1981-82; computer Info. systems educator Drake U., Des Moines, 1982-85; acctg. educator U. Wis.-Eau Claire, 1985—; v.p. Assn. for Computer Educators, Harrisburg, Va., 1984-86, pres. Assn. for Computer Edns., Harrisburg, 1986-88; rsch. chmn. Delta Pi Epsilon Beta Sigma Chpt., Eau Claire, 1987-88; bd. dirs. Midwest Acctg.

Soc., Chgo., 1988-90, Royal Credit Union, Eau Claire, 1990—; sec., treas. M.W. Acctg. Soc., 1990—. Contbr. articles to profl. jours. Mem. Nat. Assn. Accts., Am. Acctg. Assn., Assn. for Computer Educators (pres. 1988—), Inst. Internal Auditors, Phi Kappa Phi, Phi Delta Kappa, Beta Alpha Psi (faculty v.p. 1986—), Delta Pi Epsilon. Lutheran. Office: U Wis Dept Accountancy Eau Claire WI 54702

HAUGHTON-DENNISTON, PAMELA GAIL, advocate; b. Troy, N.Y., Sept. 2, 1951; d. Alan Palmer Haughton and Mildred Joan (Frey) Peck; m. Kenneth G. Barnett, Aug. 24, 1974 (div. 1987); m. Lyle William Denniston, Mar. 5, 1988. BA in Religion, St. Lawrence U., 1973; MDiv, Colgate Rochester Theol. Sem., 1977. Ordained to ministry Bapt. Ch., 1977. Adminstrv. and rsch. asst. Am. Bapt. Chs., USA, Washington, 1977-79; legis. dir. Religious Coalition for Abortion Rights, Washington, 1979-84, state affiliate dir., 1984—. Mem. Phi Beta Kappa. Democrat. Baptist. Office: Religious Coalition for Abortion Rights 100 Maryland Ave NE Washington DC 20002

HAUGLAND, BRYNHILD, state legislator, farmer; b. Ward County, N.D., July 28, 1905; d. Nels and Sigurda (Ringoen) H.; BA, Minot State Coll., 1956; LLD (hon.), N.D. State U., 1984. Mem. N.D. Ho. of Reps., 1939—, chmn. com. social services and vets. affairs, mem. com. industry, bus. and labor. Mem. Def. Adv. Com. Women in Services, 1955-58. Vice chmn. N.D. Gov.'s State Health Planning Com., 1944-75; mem. Ward County Zoning Commn., Minot City Planning Commn., N.D. Bicentennial Commn. Bd. dirs. Internat. Peace Garden, 1953—, Minot State Coll. Found., Minot Commn. on Aging. Named N.D.'s Outstanding Woman in Law, 1973; Outstanding Legislator, Nat. Assembly Govt. Employees, 1979; recipient Golden award for Outstanding Service, Minot State Coll. Alumni, 1968; Hon. Mem. Uniformed Fire Fighters N.D., 1976; recipient Milky Way award Dairy Industry N.D., 1977, Disting. Service award Western N.D. Health Systems Agy., 1977-78, N.D. Water Wheel N.D. Water Users Assn./N.D. Water Mgmt. Dists. Assn., 1981, Service to Mankind award Sertoma Clubs, 1983, Merit award Pub. Health Assn. N.D., 1983, Liberty Bell award State Bar Assn., 1983, Disting. Service award Mental Health Assn. N.D., 1983, award Minot Assn. Home Builders, 1984, Good Citizen Scouting award, 1984, Disting. Service award Am. Protestant Health Assn., 1985; recognized state conv. Rep. Party for Half Century of Dedicated Pub. Service, longest serving legislator in nation presently serving; numerous others; inducted into Scandinavian Hall of Fame, 1984. Mem. Bus. and Profl. Women's Club (named Woman of Yr. 1956, 71), Am. Assn. Ret. Persons, Nat. Ret. Tchrs. Assn., Farmers Union and Farm Bur., Minot State Coll. Alumni Assn. (dir.), Eureka Homemakers Club, Delta Kappa Gamma. Lutheran. Club: Quota. Home: Box 1684 Minot ND 58701

HAUKE, MARY ELIZABETH, retired educator; b. Saugatuck, Mich., Mar. 14, 1911; d. Otis Ogden and May Louise (Cole) H. BS, Coll. William and Mary, 1956; AM in Edn., George Washington U., 1965. Cert. tchr., Va. Tchr. Belle Bryan Day Nursery, Richmond, Va., 1948-52, Congl. Pvt. Sch., Arlington, Va., 1952-60, 62-65, Washington Grove Elem. Sch., Montgomery County, Md., 1960-61, Flint Hill Pvt. Sch., 1961-62, Southside Day Nursery, 1965-66, Green Elem. Sch., 1977-70, Reid Elem. Sch., 1971-75; camp counselor, instr. swimming, crafts, sports, Richmond, 1952-65. Republican. Lutheran. Home: 3248 Daffodil Dell Zephyrhills FL 33541

HAUN, L. MAXINE SHARPE, employee benefits executive; b. Omaha, Mar. 13, 1926; m. William M. Haun, May 24, 1947 (div. 1970). BA, U. Nebr., 1946; postgrad., U. Wis., Milw., 1949-50; cert. in indsl. relations, UCLA, 1957. Suggestion system adminstr. Ralston Purina Co., St. Louis, 1947-49; employment officer Hotpoint Inc., Milw., 1950-51; ho. mag. editor Link-Belt Co., Phila., 1951-54; employee counselor Autonetics/Rockwell Internat., Anaheim, Calif., 1954-75; mgr. benefits, svcs. and recreation ctr. Def. Electronics Systems div. Rockwell Internat., Anaheim, Calif., 1975—; cons. blood donor resources devel. ARC, Anaheim; speaker in field; mem. adv. com. Pres.' Com. on Gerontology, Calif. State U.-Fullerton, 1982-83. Recipient Individual award ARC, 1976, 1st Ann. Lifetime Achievement award ARC Blood Svcs., 1990; Maxine S. Haun award named in her honor ARC, 1990. Mem. Nat. Employee Svcs. and Recreation Assn. (v.p. local chpt. 1978-79), Internat. Assn. Pers. Women (pres. 1966-67), Nat. Mgmt. Assn., Nat. Notary Assn., Internat. Soc. Pre-Retirement Planners, U. Nebr.-Omaha Alumni Assn., Bald Eagles Club, Air Force Assn. Republican. Home: 1630 S Pomona Ave C-26 Fullerton CA 92632 Office: Autonetics Electronics Syst 3370 Miraloma Ave 061 HD01 Anaheim CA 92803

HAUPT, ADRIENNE LYNN, nurse supervisor; b. East St. Louis, Ill., Jan. 6, 1948; d. Dewey Kirk and Glenda Marvell (Barwell) Stafford; 1 child, Daniel. BS in Nursing, U. Md., Balt., 1970; MSEd, U. So. Calif., L.A.1983; postgrad., Southwest Tex. State U. Commd. 1st lt. U.S. Army, 1970, advanced through grades to lt. col.; asst. supr. community health nursing Darnall Army Hosp., Ft. Hood, Tex., Walter Reed Army Hosp., Washington; supr. community health nursing US Army Hosp., Seoul, Republic of Korea; chief nurse med. element Joint Task Force; ret. U.S. Army, 1989. Decorated Legion of Merit medal, Meritorious Svc. medal. Mem. Am. Nurses Assn. (cert. nurse adminstr. and community health nurse), Am. Pub. Health Assn. Home: 4940 Arrayo Chamisa Dr NE Albuquerque NM 87111

HAUPTLI, BARBARA BEATRICE, defense company executive; b. Glenwood Springs, Colo., Sept. 20, 1953; d. Frederick James and Evelyn June (Rood) H.; m. Daniel Dunbar Macmurphy, Sept. 1, 1979 (div. July 1989). BBA, Western State Coll., 1975. Contract specialist USA-TACOM, Warren, Mich., 1981-86; contract buyer Martin Marietta Orlando (Fla.) Aerospace, 1986; purchasing expediter Moog, Inc., Clearwater, Fla., 1986-89; subcontract adminstr. Olin Ordnance, St. Petersburg, Fla., 1989—. Mem. Nat. Contract Mgmt. Assn. Office: Olin Ordnance Div 10101 9th St N Saint Petersburg FL 33716

HAUSAMMANN, BEVERLY ANN, sales specialist; b. Muncy, Pa., Sept. 20, 1934; d. Kenneth Ray and Mary Benedict (Crist) Hill; m. Kurt Hausammann Sr., May 26, 1956; children: Kurt Jr., Chris Albert. Telemktg. mgr. OHD Thermacore, Inc., Williamsport, Pa., 1982-88; sales svc. specialist Data Papers, Inc., Muncy, 1988-89. Mem. Divine Providence Hosp. Aux.; pres. Lycoming-Tioga Diocesan Coun. Cath. Women; past pres. local PTA; sr. scout leader Girl Scouts U.S. Recipient Outstanding Census Taker award, 1970. Mem. NAFE. Home: Elm Hill Rd 3 Box 263 Muncy PA 17756

HAUSCH, MARY ELLEN, newspaper editor; b. Akron, Ohio, Sept. 6, 1949; d. Walter Richard and Anne Marie McKinniss) H.; m. Bob Coffin, 1986. B.S.J. cum laude, Ohio U., 1970. Reporter Gazette Telegraph, Colorado Springs, Colo., 1970-71; reporter Las Vegas (Nev.) Rev.-Jour., 1971-74, reporter, asst. city editor, 1975, city editor, 1976, mng. editor, 1977-88, assoc. editor, 1988—. Bd. dirs. HELP Ctr., Las Vegas, 1980—, pres., 1985-87; vice chmn. Nev. Pub. Radio, Las Vegas, 1984-87; bd. dirs. Planned Parenthood of So. Nev., Las Vegas, 1984-87. Mem. Las Vegas C. of C. (mem. bd. women's Coun. 1986-89), Sigma Delta Chi (pres. Las Vegas chpt. 1975-76). Club: Variety. Home: 1139 S 5th Pl Las Vegas NV 89104 Office: Las Vegas Rev-Jour PO Box 70 Las Vegas NV 89125

HAUSE, EDITH COLLINS, college administrator; b. Rock Hill, S.C., Dec. 11, 1933; d. Ernest O. and Violet (Smith) Collins; m. James Luke Hause, Sept. 3, 1955; children—Stephen Mark, Felicia Gaye Hause Friesen. B.A., Columbia Coll., S.C., 1956; postgrad. U. N.C.-Greensboro, 1967, U. S.C., 1971-75. Tchr. Richland Dist. II, Columbia, 1971-74; dir. alumnae affairs Columbia Coll., 1974-82, v.p. alumnae affairs, 1982-84, v.p. devel., 1984-89, v.p. alumnae rels., 1989—. Named Outstanding Tchr. of Yr., Richland Dist. II, 1974. Mem. Columbia Network for Female Execs., Council for Advancement and Support Edn., Nat. Soc. Fund Raising Execs. Republican. Methodist. Home: Rte 4 Box 760 Prosperity SC 29127 Office: Columbia Coll Alumnae Office Columbia SC 29203

HAUSER, JOYCE ROBERTA, marketing professional; b. N.Y.C.; d. Abraham and Helen (Lesser) Frankel; divorced; children: Mitchell, Mark, Ellen. BA, SUNY, 1976; PhD, Union Grad. Sch., 1987. Editor Art in Flowers, 1955-58; pres. Joyce Advt., 1958-65; ptnr. Hauser & Assocs., Pub. Rels., 1966-75; dir. broadcasting Bildersee Pub. Rels., 1973-75; pres. Hauser & Assocs., Inc., Pub. Rels., 1975-78, Hauser-Roberts, Inc., Pub. Rels./Mktg., N.Y.C., 1978-85, Mktg. Concepts & Communications Inc., N.Y.C., 1985—; moderator show Perceptions Sta. WEVD, 1975-77, Speaking of Health Sta. WNBC, 1977—, 97 Health Line, Sta. WYNY, 1980-83, Conversations with Joyce Hauser, Sta. WNBC, 1975-86, What's on Your Mind, Sta. WYNY, 1983-84, Talk-Net, 1983—; entertainment critic Sta. WNBC, 1986—; instr. Baruch Coll., CCNY, 1980-85; asst. prof. NYU, 1987—. Sr. editor Art & Leisure News Svc., 1988—; contbg. editor Alive, 1976-77. Mem. Citywide Health Adv. Coun. on Sch. Health, 1970—, treas., 1980—; mem. adv. bd. degree programs NYU Sch. Continuing Edn.; mediator/artitrator Victim Svcs. Agy., 1986-87, Inst. Mediation & Conflict Resolution, 1985-86. Named one of 10 Top Successful Women Cancer Soc., 1976; recipient Professionalism award Sta. WNBC, 1980. Mem. AFTRA, Am. Women in Radio and TV (corr. sec. 1973, chmn. coll. women in broadcasting 1974), Acad. Family Mediators, Soc. Profl. Dispute Resolutions. Home: 115 E 82nd St New York NY 10028

HAUSER, RITA ELEANORE ABRAMS, lawyer; b. N.Y.C., July 12, 1934; d. Nathan and Frieda (Litt) Abrams; m. Gustave M. Hauser, June 10, 1956; children: Glenvil Aubrey, Ana Patricia. A.B. magna cum laude, Hunter Coll., 1954; Dr. Polit. Economy with highest honors (Fulbright grantee), U. Strasbourg, France, 1955; Licence en Droit, U. Paris, 1958; student law sch., Harvard U., 1955-56; L.L.B. with honors, NYU, 1959; LL.D. (hon.), Seton Hall U., 1969, Finch Coll., 1969, U. Miami, Fla., 1971. Bar: D.C. 1959, N.Y. 1961, U.S. Supreme Ct. 1967. Atty. U.S. Dept. Justice, 1959-61; sole practice N.Y.C., 1961-67; ptnr. Moldover, Hauser, Strauss & Volin, 1968-72; sr. ptnr. Stroock & Stroock & Lavan, 1972—; Handmaker lectr. Louis Brandeis Lectr. Series, U. Ky. Law Sch.; lectr. on internat. law Naval War Coll. and Army War Coll.; Mitchell lectr. in Law SUNY Buffalo; USIA lectr. constl. law Egypt, India, Australia, New Zealand; bd. dirs. Berkshire Bank, N.Y.; U.S. chmn. Internat. Ctr. for Peace in Middle East, 1984—; U.S. pub. del. to Vienna Follow-up meeting of Conf. on Security and Cooperation in Europe, 1986-88; mem. adv. panel on internat. law U.S. Dept. of State, 1986—. Contbr. articles on internat. law to profl. jours. U.S. rep. to UN Commn. on Human Rights, 1969-72; mem. U.S. del. to Gen. Assembly UN, 1969; vice chmn. U.S. Adv. Com. on Internat. and Cultural Affairs, 1973-77; mem. N.Y.C. Bd. Higher Edn., 1974-76, Stanton Panel on internat. info., edn., cultural relations to reorganize USIA and Voice of Am., 1974-75, Mid. East Study Group Brookings Inst., 1975, 87-88, U.S. del. World Conf. Internat. Women's Yr., Mexico City, 1975; co-chmn. Com. for Re-election Pres., 1972; co-chair Presdl. Debates project LWV, 1976; adv. bd. Nat. News Council, 1977-79; bd. dirs. March of Dimes of N.Y., Bd. for Internat. Broadcasting, 1977-80; trustee N.Y. Philharm. Soc.; adv. bd. Ctr. for Law and Nat. Security, U. Va. Law Sch/. 1978-84; vis. com. Ctr. Internat. Affairs Harvard U., 1975-81; bd. of visitors Georgetown Sch. Fgn. Svc., 1989—; co-chmn. Coalition for Reagan/Bush; bd. govs.; Am. Jewish Com.; chmn. adv. panel Internat. Parliamentary Group for Human Rights in Soviet Union, 1984-86; mem. spl. refugee adv. panel Dept. State, 1981; former trustee Internat. Legal Ctr., Legal Aid Soc. N.Y., Freedom House. Intellectual Exchange fellow, Japan Soc. Fellow ABA (life, standing coms. on law and nat. security, 1979-85, on world order under law 1969-78, on judicial selection, tenure, compensation, 1977-79, council sect. on individual rights and responsibilities, 1970-73, adv., bd. jour., 1973-78); mem. Assn. of Bar of City of N.Y., Am. Soc. Internat. Law (v.p. 1988—, exec. com. 1971-76), Am. Fgn. Law Assn. (dir.), Am. Arbitration Assn. (past dir.), Ams. Soc. (bd. dirs. 1988—), Inst. East-West Security Studies (bd. dirs., exec. com.), Council on Fgn. Relations, Harvard Law Sch. Assn. N.Y.C. (trustee), Friends of The Hague Acad. Internat. Law (bd. dirs.), N.Y. Philharm. Symphony Soc. (bd. dirs., mem. exec. com.), Catalyst (bd. dirs.). Republican. Office: Stroock & Stroock & Lavan 7 Hanover Sq New York NY 10004

HAUSMAN, HELEN M., educator; b. N.Y.C., July 5, 1924; d. Harry and Anna (Einhorn) Mandlowitz; m. Arthur Herbert Hausman, Nov. 24, 1923; children: Susan (dec.), Kenneth, Catherine. BA, George Washington U., 1950. Tchr. Suitland (Md.) Elem. Dist., 1950-51; vol. Stanford Hosp. and Children's Hosp. Aux., 1965-84. Co-author: The Testing Puzzle, 1982. Active San Mateo County ARC, 1981—; adv. mem. Golden Gate chpt. ARC, San Francisco; internat. com. mem. Bay Area chpt. ARC, 1985—; Calif. State PTA Bd. Mgrs., L.A., 1979-88; trustee, pres. bd. trustees Sequoia Union High Sch. Dist., Redwood City, Calif., 1976-89; trustee San Mateo County Community Coll. Dist., 1989—. Recipient hon. and continuing svc. awards, PTA, 1971, 81, Disting. Women award, Girls Club of San Francisco Bay Area Mid-Peninsula, 1976. Mem. Community Coll. League Calif. Home: 55 Flood Circle Atherton CA 94027

HAUSTEN, LISA ANNE, lawyer; b. St. Charles, Ill., Dec. 20, 1956; d. David Roy and Mary Elizabeth H.; m. Kirk Andrew Stubbee, Nov. 1, 1986. BA in Gen. Sci., Coe Coll., 1979; JD, U. Chgo., 1983. Bar: Ill. 1983. Assoc. Sidley & Austin, Chgo., 1983—. Mem. Am. Heart Assn., Jr. Bd. for the Erie House, English Speaking Union. Mem. ABA, Fed. Trial Bar, Ill. Bar Assn., Chgo. Bar Assn. (state and local tax com. 1987), Chgo. Assn. Commerce and Industry (state and mcpl. rev. com.), Ill. C. of C. (taxation com.), Ill. Taxpayers Fedn. Office: Sidley & Austin One 1st Nat Pla Chicago IL 60603

HAVEN, MARY CLARE, clinical chemistry educator; b. Stuart, Nebr., Dec. 6, 1939; d. Clarence Sylvester and Nelle Ida (Gaughenbaugh) Gilg; m. Guy T. Haven, Dec. 30, 1961 (div. 1980); children: Guy T., Douglas (dec.), Michelle. Student, Creighton U., 1962, MS, 1964. Rsch. asst. Tidy House Products Co., Omaha, 1959-62; rsch. chemist VA Hosp., Omaha, 1962-68; instr. U. Nebr. Med. Ctr., Omaha, 1968-75, asst. prof. pathology, 1975-88, assoc. prof. pathology, 1988—; cons. Pathology and Lab. Medicine, Omaha, 1980—, Abbott Labs., North Chicago, Ill., 1987-88. Editor: Laboratory Instrumentation, 1987; contbr. articles to profl. jours. Recipient award Sch. Allied Health Professions, U. Nebr. Med. Ctr., Omaha, 1988. Mem. Am. Assn. Clin. Chemistry (pres. elect Midwest sect. 1989), Toastmasters Club (Outstanding Pres. 1987). Democrat. Roman Catholic. Office: U Nebr Med Ctr Pathology 42d and Dewey Omaha NE 68105

HAVENS, CANDACE JEAN, city official; b. Rochester, Minn., Sept. 13, 1952; d. Fred Z. and Barbara Jean (Stephenson) H.; m. Bruce Curtis Mercier, Feb. 22, 1975 (div. Apr. 1982); 1 child, Rachel; m. James Arthur Renning, Oct. 26, 1986; children: Kelsey, Sarah. Student, U. Calif., San Diego, Darmouth Coll., Am. U., Beirut, 1973-74; BA in Sociology, U. Calif., Riverside, 1977. Project coord. social svc. orgn. Grass Roots II, San Luis Obispo, Calif., 1976-77; planning enforcement technician City San Luis Obispo, 1977-81, asst. planner, 1981-83, assoc. planner, 1983-86, coord. parking program, 1986-88; city project mgr. constrn. and parking structures constrn. City-County Libr. Bldg. Commn., San Luis Obispo, 1985-89, spl. asst. to city adminstr., 1989—. Past pres. Nat. Charity League, Riverside; mem. San Luis Obispo Med. Aux., 1986—, San Luis Obispo Arts Coun., 1986—; pres. San Luis Obispo Children's Mus., 1990—. Mem. Calif. Pub. Parking Assn., Instn. & Mcpl. Parking Congress, AAUW, Cen. Coast Women's League Club, Toastmaster (sec. 1986-87, v.p. 1987-88, pres. 1989—). Office: City of San Luis Obispo 990 Palm St San Luis Obispo CA 93401

HAVENS, CANDACE SHERWOOD, infosystems specialist; b. Vestal, N.Y., May 11, 1957; d. Willett Benjamin and Ellen Ingrid (Delfs) S. BA in Biology, Hamilton Coll., 1979; MBA, U. Puget Sound, 1985. Retirement plans analyst No. Life Ins., Seattle, 1980-81, methods analyst trainee, 1981-82, methods analyst, 1982-84, programmer analyst, 1984-85; assoc. systems analyst Xerox Corp., Tukwila, Wash., 1985-86, systems analyst, 1986-89, sr. systems analyst, 1989—; adv. bd. dirs. systems tech. conference Xerox Corp., 1987-88. Mem. Eastside Coalition for Homeless, Bellevue, Wash., 1987—, social justice com., Bellevue, 1987. Democrat. Unitarian. Clubs: Mountaineers, Nastar Ski Team. Office: Xerox Corp 6400 Southcenter Blvd Tukwila WA 98188

HAVENS, PAMELA ANN, communications executive; b. Plattsburgh, N.Y., Nov. 30, 1956; d. Thomas L. and MaryAnn (Zalen) Romeo; m. Stephen L. Havens, Aug. 9, 1986. BA, Eisenhower Coll., 1978; MA, SUNY, Plattsburgh, 1987. VISTA vol. Retired Sr. Vol. Program, Plattsburgh, 1978-79; copywriter, newsperson Stas. WEAV-AM/WGFB-FM, Plattsburgh, 1979-83; traffic clk. Sta. WCFE-TV, Plattsburgh, 1983-84, pub. info. coord., 1984-85; coll. rels. officer Clinton Community Coll., Plattsburgh, 1985-89; dir. publs. and communications Cayuga Community Coll., Auburn, N.Y., 1989—. Mem. Auburn Players Community Theatre. Named Young Careerist Alternate Bus. and Profl. Women's Club, 1986. Mem. Eisenhower Coll. Alumni Assn. (bd. dirs. 1990), Women in Communications, Inc., Kiwanis. Office: Cayuga Community Coll Franklin St Auburn NY 13021

HAVERKAMPF, KATHLEEN LEA, economist; b. Elgin, Ill., Nov. 26, 1959; d. David Allen and Mary Louise (Warner) H. BS, U. Wis., Stevens Point, 1982. Legis. asst. Wis. State Assembly, Madison, 1983-86; asst. personnel dir. Govs. Transition Team, Madison, 1986; dir. constituent rels. Govs. Exec. Office, Madison, 1987-88; econ. development cons. Wis. Dept. Devel., Madison, 1988—. Vol. Wis. State and Senate Assembly Elections, 1984-88, Wis. Gubernatorial Election, Madison, 1986, U.S. Presdl. Election, Wis., 1984. Named to Outstanding Young Women of Am., 1986. Mem. NAFE, Wis. Econ. Devel. Assn., Wis. Downtown Action Council (assoc.), Am. Econ. Devel. Coun., Wis. Govs. Club. Republican. Roman Catholic. Home: 2913 Turbot Dr Madison WI 53713 Office: Wisconsin Dept Development 123 W Washington Madison WI 53702

HAVILAND, CAMILLA KLEIN, lawyer; b. Dodge City, Kans., Sept. 13, 1926; d. Robert Godfrey and Lelah (Luther) Klein; m. John Bodman Haviland, Sept. 7, 1957. A.A., Monticello Coll., 1946; B.A., Radcliffe Coll., 1948; J.D., Kans. U., 1955. Bar: Kans. 1955. Assoc. Calver & White, Wichita, Kans., 1955-56; sole practice, Dodge City, 1956—; probate, county and juvenile judge Ford County (Kans.), 1955-77; mem. Jud. Council Com. on Probate and Juvenile Law. Mem. adv. bd. Salvation Army, U. Kans. Sch. Religion. Recipient Nathan Burkan award ASCAP, 1955. Mem. Ford County Bar Assn. (pres. 1980), S.W. Kans. Bar Assn. (pres. 1968), Kans. Bar Assn., ABA, C. of C., Order of Coif, PEO, Phi Delta Delta. Democrat. Episcopalian. Clubs: Prairie Dunes Country (Hutchinson, Kans.); Soroptimists. Contbr. articles to profl. jours. Home: 2006 E Lane Dodge City KS 67801 Office: 203 W Spruce Box 17 Dodge City KS 67801

HAVILAND, LEONA, librarian; b. Stamford, Conn., Nov. 10, 1916; d. Howard Brush and Ada Grace (Jewell) Haviland; B.S., U. Ala., 1940; M.S., U. Ill., 1951; postgrad. Columbia U., 1943, 56-60; m. Warren John Burke, Sept. 10, 1973. Jr. asst. Ferguson Library, Stamford, 1936-37, summers 1938-39, sr. asst., 1940-44; student asst. U. Ala., 1937-40; asst. to cataloguer U.S. Nat. Mus. Library, Washington, 1944-48; librarian Arts and Industries Mus., Smithsonian Instn., Washington, 1948-50; reference librarian U.S. Mcht. Marine Acad., Kings Point, N.Y., 1952-77. Mem. council YWCA, Washington, 1945-47. Mem. A.L.A., Spl. Libraries Assn. (past group membership chmn.), L.I. Hist. Soc., N.Y. Geneal. and Biog. Soc., Smithsonian Assos., South Street Seaport Mus., Alpha Beta Alpha, Alpha Lambda Delta. Home: 809 Pennsylvania Ave Saint Cloud FL 34769

HAVIST, MARJORIE VICTORIA, librarian, educator; b. Johnstown, Pa., Nov. 6, 1931; d. Victor Dale and Lillie Mae (Bross) Mulhollen; m. George I. Melhorn, Aug. 8, 1953 (dec. Dec. 1962); children—Susan Lynn, Bradford George; m. Ewald Jack Havist, Aug. 7, 1969. B.S. in Edn., Bucknell U., 1953; M.L.S., U. Wash., 1966. Cert. librarian, Wash. Engr., Boeing Co., Seattle, 1955, 57-58; librarian Bellevue Community Coll., Wash., 1966-78; head librarian Seattle Central Community Coll., Seattle, 1978-80; assoc. dean library Skagit Valley Coll., Mt. Vernon, Wash., 1980—. Bd. dirs. ARC Skagit County, Mt. Vernon, 1982; loaned exec. United Way Skagit County, 1983-84. Mem. ALA, Community Coll. Librarians and Media Specialists (pres. 1977-78), Community Coll. Library Dirs. Council (pres. 1981-82), Phi Theta Kappa. Republican. Lutheran. Office: Skagit Valley Coll 2405 College Way Mount Vernon WA 98273

HAWBAKER, DIANA SUE, software analyst, consultant; b. Des Moines, Jan. 6, 1953; d. Duane William and Pearl Jean (Zimmerman) H.; m. Gary David Perrin, Nov. 18, 1972 (div. 1974). Systems analyst Gen. Growth Devel., Des Moines, 1976-81, cons., 1981-82; project mgr. Mgmt. Controls, Des Moines, 1981-82; pres. Integrated Bus. Systems, Des Moines, 1982-83; project mgr. Gen. Instrument Corp., Des Moines, 1983-85, programming mgr., Balt., 1985-86; product mgr. software services Scan-Optics, Inc., East Hartford, Conn., 1986-90; assoc. dir. life & health benefits mgmt. system Mass. Mutual Life Ins. Co., Springfield, 1990—; cons. Wallace-Homestead, Des Moines, 1982-84, Mental Health Assn.; Polk County, Des Moines, 1982-84, Miller Pub., Mpls., 1984-85. Author software packages. Mem. NOW, Am. Bus. Women's Assn. (pres. Challenge chpt. 1981-82), Digital Equipment Corp Users Soc., Nat. Assn. Female Execs. Jehovah's Witness. Avocations: reading; camping; gardening; crafts; tennis. Home: 205 Vernon Ave Apt 152 Vernon CT 06066 Office: Mass Mutual Life Ins Co 1295 State St Springfield MA 01111

HAWK, MARY RUTH, dance company manager, dancer; b. Gainesville, Fla., Feb. 1, 1963; d. Robert Allan and Zelda Louise (Jarman) Hawk. BFA in Dance, Fla. State U., 1983; BA in Journalism, Ga. State U., 1989. Prodn. coordinator Smith/Garner Comml. Photography, Atlanta, 1984-86, Studio Graphics Commercial Photography, Atlanta, 1986-87; dancer Lee Harper & Dancers, Atlanta, 1984—, Several Dancers Core, Decatur, Ga., 1987-89; co. mgr. Several Dancers Core, Decatur and Houston, 1989—; pub. relations advisor Lee Harper & Dancers, Atlanta, 1985—; dancer, guest performer Several Dancers Core with Tanzfabirk, Berlin, 1988; guest star Gainesville (Fla.) Ballet Theatre, 1987; KTRK-TV crew asst. Dem. Nat. Conv., Atlanta, 1988. Mem. Women in Communications Inc., Image Film/Video, Phi Kappa Phi, Golden Key, Mortar Board. Home: care Zelda Hawk 4411 NW 14th Pl Gainesville FL 32605

HAWKEN, PATTY LYNN, nursing educator, dean of faculty; b. Wheaton, Ill., July 13, 1932; d. Leonard William and Betty (Stock) H. BSN, U. Mich., 1956; MSN, Case Western Res. U., 1962, PhD, 1970. Instr. U. Mich., Ann Arbor, 1956-57, Highland Hosp., Oakland, Calif., 1957-59; instr. Case Western Res. U., Cleve., 1960-63, asst. prof., 1963-67, assoc. prof., 1967-69, assoc. prof., assoc. in adminstrn., 1969-71; assoc. prof. Emory U., Atlanta, 1971-72, prof., dir., 1972-74; dean, prof. U. Tex. Health Sci. Ctr. Sch. Nursing, San Antonio, 1974—. Contbr. articles to nursing jours. Bd. dirs. Wesley Community Ctr., San Antonio, 1986, 89; mem. United Way Allocation Com., San Antonio, 1987; mem. adv. com. Trinity U. Health Care Adminstrn., San Antonio, 1984—, VA Dean's Com., San antonio, 1982—. Recipient Nurse of Yr. award Tex. Nursing Assn., San Antonio Chpt., 1985; named to Women's Hall of Fame, Mayor's Commn. on women, San Antonio, 1987. Fellow Am. Acad. Nursing; mem. Nat. League for Nursing (pres. 1989-91, pres.-elect 1987-89), Am. Assn. Colls. of Nursing (com. on edn. 1986-88), Commn. Grads. Fgn. Nursing Schs. (bd. trustees, pres. 1983-85), Am. Nurses Assn. (cabinet on edn. 1986-88), U. Tex. Health Sci. Ctr. Club (San Antonio), San Antonio 100 Club, Internat. Women's Forum (San Antonio). Home: 3042 Charter Crest San Antonio TX 78230 Office: U Tex Health Sci Ctr 7703 Floyd Curl Dr San Antonio TX 78284-7942

HAWKES, ELIZABETH LAWRENCE (BONNIE HAWKES), health services management consultant; b. Bryn Mawr, Pa., May 28, 1944; d. Edward Bettle and Anna Correy (Keen) Scull; m. Geoffrey Neale Hawkes, Aug. 12, 1972. BA in Chemistry, Hood Coll., 1966; cert. in occupational therapy, U. Pa., 1968; cert. in health care mgmt., B.C. Inst. Tech., Can., 1981; MS in Health Care Mgmt., U. B.C., 1988. Therapist Mary Bridge Children's Hosp., Tacoma, 1968-72; staff occupational therapist Pearson Hosp., Vancouver, B.C., 1972-74; staff occupational therapist Lions Gate Hosp., North Vancouver, B.C., 1974-76, sr. occupational therapist, 1976-78, supr. occupational therapy, 1978-82; researcher med. engring. Dept. Surgery U. B.C., Vancouver, 1983-84; lectr. U. B.C., Vancouver, 1981-86; clin. instr. U. B.C., North Vancouver, 1981—; cons. health services North Vancouver, 1983—; bd. dirs. Lions Gate Med. Rsch. Found., 1988-89. Contbr. articles to profl. jours. Bd. dirs. First Aid Ski Patrol, (coordinator 1977-79) (patrol 1973-80); first aid instr. St. John Ambulance, 1977-80, CPR instr. 1978. Mem. Can. Assn. Occupational Therapists (bd. dirs., com. chair 1982-87), B.C. Soc. Occupational Therapists, World Fedn. Occupational Therapists, Can. Council Health Service Execs., Am. Coll. Health Care Execs. Home: 1397 Harold Rd, North Vancouver, BC Canada V7J 1W9 Office: Vancouver Gen Hosp, 855 W 12th Ave, Vancouver, BC Canada V5Z1M9

HAWKEY, PENELOPE J., advertising agency executive; b. Morristown, N.J., Sept. 17, 1942; d. William R. and Jeanne Elizabeth (Haas) Sharp; m. William Stevenson Hawkey, May 26, 1968; children: Adam Stewart, Robin

Davidge, Renn McConnell, Timothy Schuyler, Molly Driscoll; stepchildren: Elizabeth Martin, William Stevenson. BA, Ohio U., Athens, 1964; MA, NYU, 1973. Jr. writer Grey Advt., N.Y.C., 1966; jr. writer, then v.p. J. Walter Thompson Co., N.Y.C., 1966-73; v.p., assoc. creative dir. McCann-Erickson, N.Y.C., 1973-74, sr. v.p., group creative dir., 1975-85; ptnr., exec. v.p. Dillon, Gordon, Hawkey, Short, N.Y.C., 1974-75; pres., exec. creative dir. The Bloom Agy., N.Y.C., 1985—. Office: Bloom Agy 304 E 45th St New York NY 10017*

HAWKINS, ALTONNETTE DENISE, telecommunications executive; b. Bklyn., Sept. 25, 1958; d. Ruben Alton and Lula Mae (Taylor) H. BA in Communications, Rutgers U., 1980; MPS in Telecommunications, NYU, 1986. Communications technician network ops. AT&T, Camden, N.J., 1981-83; staff asst. teleprocessing, data ctr. ops. AT&T, Piscataway, N.J., 1983-84, network design assoc. mgr. interactive network design, 1984-85, technical support mgr. data communications mgmt. ctr., 1985-86; project mgr. network ops. project mgmt. AT&T, Piscataway, 1986-87; quality cons. data processing corp. telecommunications AT&T, South Plainfield, NJ, 1987-88; systems cons. bus. mtkg. AT&T, Washington, 1988—; network dir. Career-Link, Piscataway, 1987. Named one of Most Outstanding Young Women Am., 1987. Mem. Alliance Black Telecommunications Employees (nat. chpt. liaison chairperson 1986-89), NAFE, Am. Soc. Quality Control, Am. Soc. Tng. and Devel. Office: AT&T 5000 Hadley Rd South Plainfield NJ 07080

HAWKINS, ANNIE LUCY, fitness counselor; b. Ft. Walton Beach, Fla., Aug. 12, 1955; d. Frank and Ruby M. (Agee) Riley; m. Larry A. Hawkins, June 13, 1955; children: Stacy, Todd, Jermaine. AA, City Coll. Chgo., Heidelberg, Fed. Republic Germany, 1987. Fitness counselor USA, Alexandria, Va.; aerobic instr. Spa Lady, Alexandria; enlisted U.S. Army, 1981. Recipient recognitions, Pres. of U.S., U.S. Sec. of Army, U.S. Sec. of Def. Home: 2315 Mary Baldwin Dr Alexandria VA 22307

HAWKINS, ELINOR DIXON (MRS. CARROLL WOODARD HAWKINS), librarian; b. Masontown, W.Va., Sept. 25, 1927; d. Thomas Fitchie and Susan (Reed) Dixon; A.B., Fairmont State Coll., 1949; B.S. in L.S., U. N.C., 1950; m. Carroll Woodard Hawkins, June 24, 1951; 1 son, John Carroll. Children's librarian Enoch Pratt Free Library, Balt., 1950-51; head circulation dept. Greensboro (N.C.) Pub. Library, 1951-56; librarian Craven-Pamlico Library Service, New Bern, N.C., 1958-62; dir. Craven-Pamlico-Carteret Regional Library, 1962—; storyteller children's TV program Tele-Story Time, 1952-58, 63—; bd. dirs. New East Bank of New Bern. Mem. New Bern Hist. Soc., 1973—, Tryon Palace Commn., 1974—; mem. adv. bd. Salvation Army; bd. dirs. Craven County Tourism Devel. Authority. Mem. N.C. Assn. Retarded Children, N.C. Library Assn. Baptist. Club: Pilot (pres. 1957-58, v.p. 1962-63). Home: PO Box 57 Cove City NC 28523 Office: 400 Johnson St New Bern NC 28560

HAWKINS, GERI SUE, interior designer, realtor; b. Kansas City, Mo., Sept. 4, 1940; d. William S. McCune and Verla J. (Kempter) McCune Stoll; m. LeRay D. Long, Oct. 12, 1958 (div. Dec. 1961); 1 child, Lori Diane Long Seidl; m. Ray Eldon Hawkins, Oct. 9, 1964; children: Lynn M., John Ted; stepchildren: Celeste, Steve. Student Kansas City Bus. Coll., 1961-62, U. Mo., Kansas City, 1974-75; AA, Maple Woods Coll., 1974. Interior designer Carpenter Bros. Inc., Kansas City, 1975-77; pres., designer Gerry Hawkins Interiors, Kansas City, 1977-81; interior designer R. D. Mann Inc., Kansas City, 1981-83; owner-designer Designs By Geri, Kansas City, 1983-89, Interior Designs by Geri Inc., Parkville, Mo., 1989—; realtor assoc. ERA Martin House, Platte City, Mo., 1984-85; interior designer Martin House Design, Platte City, 1984-85; sales rep. Ron Wood Real Estate, 1987-88; with J.D. Reece Realtors, 1988—. Local theatrical appearances, 1972-73. Leader Winding River council Girl Scouts U.S., 1966-71; mem. Grace Notes Singing Ensemble, Kansas City, 1980—; trustee Park Hill Bapt. Ch., Parkville, Mo., 1983-85. Mem. Platte County Bus. and Profl. Assn. (bd. dirs. 1980-81), Am. Soc. Interior Designers, Nat. Assn. Women Bus. Owners, Greater Kansas City C. of C., Platte County Women's Exch., Women in Bus., Patrician Club. Republican. Baptist. Avocations: tennis, swimming, golf, theatre, gardening. Home: 106 Main St Parkville MO 64152

HAWKINS, GINA GAYLE, guidance counselor; b. St. Louis, Mo., Sept. 10, 1963; d. Dewey Elisha and Mary Elaine (Fleenor) H. BA, Lincoln Christian Coll., 1985; MA, U. South Fla., 1987. Fla. Tchr. Cert. Guidance and Counseling. Guidance counselor Marissa (Ill.) Jr. Sr. High Sch., 1987-88; edn. coord. Care Unit of South Fla., Tampa, 1988; guidance counselor Hernando County Community High Sch., Brooksville, Fla., 1988-89, Graham Elem. Sch., Tampa, 1989—; intervention specialist Hernando County Sch. Bd., Brooksville, 1988—. Mem. Fla. Assn. for Counseling and Devel., Nat. Assn. for Counseling and Devel., Hernando County Assn. of Counseling and Devel., Ill. Assn. of Drug Abuse Counselors (student coun. chmn.). Republican. Office: Graham Elementary School 2915 Massachusetts Ave Tampa FL 33602

HAWKINS, IDA FAYE, educator; b. Ft. Worth, Dec. 28, 1928; d. Christopher Columbus and Nannie Idella (Hughes) Hall; m. Gene Hamilton Hawkins, Dec. 22, 1952; children: Gene Agner, Jane Hall. Student Midwestern U., 1946-48; BS, N. Tex. State U., 1951; student Lamar U., 1968-70; MS, McNeese State U., 1973.Tchr. DeQueen Elem. Sch., Port Arthur, Tex., 1950-54, Tyrrell Elem. Sch., Port Arthur, 1955-56, Roy Hatton Elem. Sch., Bridge City, Tex., 1967-68, Oak Forest Elem. Sch., Vidor, Tex., 1968—. 2d v.p. Travis Elem. PTA, 1965-66, 1st v.p., 1966-67; corr. sec. Port Arthur City coun. PTA, 1966-67; Sunday sch. tchr. Presbyn. Ch., 1951-53, 60-66. Named Tchr. of Yr., Oak Forest Elem., 1984-85. Mem. NEA, Tex. State Tchrs. Assn., Classroom Tchrs. Assn., Am. Psychol. Assn., McNeese State U. Alumni Assn. Home: 4075 Laurel Apt 8 Beaumont TX 77707 Office: Oak Forest Elem Sch 2400 Hwy 12 Vidor TX 77662

HAWKINS, JACQUELYN, educator; b. Russell Springs, Ky., Apr. 30, 1943; d. J.T. Hawkins and Maudie Bell Crew. BS, Andrews U., 1969; MEd, Xavier U., 1976. Cert. elem. tchr., Ohio, reading tchr. elem. and high sch., Ohio. Tchr. Cin. Pub. Schs., 1969—, Cummins Sch., Cin., 1971-81; tchr. Windsor Sch., Cin., 1982-83; tchr. Windsor Sch., 1983-89, acting contact tchr. chpt. 1 reading program, 1989—; rep. Cin. Coun. Educators Cin., 1986-89, also mem. book com.; mem. sch. improvement program Windsor Sch., 1982-84; mem. Sch. Improvement Program Cin., Cin. Coun. Educators. Chairperson United Way at Windsor Sch. Cin., 1986-89, United Negro Coll. Fund Cin., 1986-89, ARC, Windsor Sch., Cin., 1986-89; rep. Fine Arts Fund Cin., 1986-88; co-leader 4-H Club, Cin., 1987-88; leader Girl Scouts U.S., Cin., 1988-90; tutor Tabernacle Bapt. Ch., 1989; mem. Girl Scouts U.S., Cin., 1988-90. Recipient Cert. Achievement Cummins Sch. Cin., 1978. Democrat.

HAWKINS, JOELLEN MARGARET, educator; b. Harvey, N.D., Dec. 15, 1941; d. Charles Joel and Gertrude Adelaide (Waits) Beck; m. Charles Albert Watson, June 27, 1964 (div. 1978); children: John Charles, Andrew Bruce; m. David Gene Hawkins, Oct. 4, 1978. Student, Oberlin Coll., 1959-61; BS in Nursing, Northwestern U., Chgo., 1964; MS, Boston Coll., 1969, PhD, 1977. Cert. obstetric/gynecol. nurse practitioner. Staff nurse Sheboygan (Wis.) Meml. Hosp., 1964-65; instr., staff Boston Lying in Hosp., 1965-66, 68-69; staff nurse Guy's Hosp., London, Enland, 1968; campus nurse Roger Williams Coll., Bristol, R.I., 1969-70; instr. Salve Regina Coll., Newport, R.I., 1970-74; faculty mem. Roger Williams Coll., Bristol, 1974-75; assoc. prof. Boston Coll., Chestnut Hill, Mass., 1975-78; prof. U. Conn., Storrs, Conn., 1978-83, Boston Coll., Chestnut Hill, 1983—. Author, co-author 20 books; editor: Linking Nursing Education and Practice, 1987 (Book of Yr. award Am. Jour. Nursing 1988), Dictionary of American Nursing Biography, 1988; contbr. numerous articles to profl. jours. Recipient Disting. Alumni award North High Sch., 1989, Mentor award Sigma Theta Tau, 1988, Disting. Nurse Researcher Mass. Nurses Assn., 1984; named Fellow of the Am. Acad. Nursing Am. Nurses Assn., 1982. Mem. Am. Nurses Assn., Mass. Nurses Assn., Sigma Theta Tau, Internat. Women's Health Council, Am. Assn. for the History of Nursing (nominating chair 1989). Democrat. Unitarian. Home: 151 Stanton Ave Newton MA 02166 Office: Boston Coll Chestnut Hill MA 02167

HAWKINS, KATHERINE ANN, hematologist; b. Teaneck, N.J., Oct. 25, 1947; d. Howard Robert and Helen Ann (Foley) Hawkins; m. Paul Jonathan Chrzanowski, June 29, 1974; children: Eric, Brian. AB, Manhattanville Coll., Purchase, N.Y., 1969; MD, Columbia U., 1973. Intern Presbyn. Hosp., N.Y.C., 1973; intern Roosevelt Hosp., N.Y.C., 1974-75, resident, 1975-77; fellow NYU, 1977-79; attending hematologist Sickle Cell Ctr. St. Luke's Hosp., N.Y.C., 1985-87; assoc. attending physician St. Luke's - Roosevelt Hosp. Ctr., N.Y.C., 1989; asst. prof. clin. medicine Columbia U., N.Y.C., 1987—; mem. courtesy staff Drs. Hosp., 1989—. Contbr. articles to profl. jours. Mem. ACP, Am. Soc. Hematology, AMA, Am. Med. Women's Assn. Roman Catholic. Office: 20070 86th St New York NY 10024

HAWKINS, LINDA PARROTT, business educator; b. Florence, S.C., June 23, 1947; d. Obie Lindberg Parrott and Mary Francis (Lee) Evans; m. Larry Eugene Hawkins, Jan. 5, 1946; 1 child, Heather Nichole. BS, U. S.C., 1969; MS, Francis Marion Coll., 1978; postgrad. in edn1. adminstrn., U. S.C., 1985-90. Tchr. J.C. Lynch High Sch., Coward, S.C., 1973-80, Lake City (S.C.) High Sch., 1980—; Mem. Williamsburg Tech. Adv. Coun., Kingstree, S.C., 1985-90, Florence-Darlington (S.C.) Tech. Adv. Coun., 1981-87; speaker, presenter leadership workshops. Editor: Parliamentary Procedure Made Easy, 1983; contbr. articles to profl. jours. State advisor Future Bus. Leaders of Am., Columbia, S.C., 1978-86; treas. S.C. State Woman's Aux., 1983—. Named Outstanding Advisor S.C. Future Bus. Leaders of Am., 1985, Tchr. of Yr., S.C. Bus. Edn. Assn., 1988-89, Secondary Tchr. of Yr., Nat. Bus. Edn. Assn., 1989-90. Mem. Profl. Secs. Internat., Nat. Bus. Assn. (S.C. chpt., membership dir. 1986-89, so. region membership dir. 1989-92), S.C. Bus. Edn. Assn. (pres. 1989-90, treas. 1987-88, v.p. for membership 1986-87, jour. editor 1985-86), Am. Vocat. Assn., S.C. Vocat. Assn. (parliamentarian 1985-86, v.p. 1989-90), Internat. Soc. Bus. Educators, Lake City C. of C. (sec.-treas.), J.C. Lynch Elem. Sch. PTO. Democrat. Baptist. Home: Rte 1 Box 225 Coward SC 29530 Office: Lake City High Sch PO Box 1157 Lake City SC 29560

HAWKINS, MARY ELLEN, state legislator, public relations consultant; b. Birmingham, Ala.; student U. Ala., Tuscaloosa, 1945-47; m. James H. Hawkins, Feb. 13, 1960 (div., 1971); children—Andrew Higgins, Elizabeth, Peter Hixon. Congl. aide to several mems. U.S. Ho. Reps., 1950-60; art instr. Sumter County Schs., Americus, Ga., 1971-72; staff writer Naples (Fla.) Daily News, 1972-74; prin. Daniels-Hawkins, Naples, 1982-84; mem. Fla. Ho. of Reps., Tallahassee, 1974—; vice chmn. BancFloriad Corp., Naples, 1979—, also bd. dirs. Columnist, contbr. articles to local newspapers. V.p. Naples/Marco Philharmonic, 1984—; numerous offices Rep. Party of Ga., Americus, 1965-71. Recipient numerous awards for work in Fla. Legislature. Mem. Zonta Internat. Avocation: painting. Office: Fla Ho Reps The Capitol Tallahassee FL 32399 Other: 212 Naples City Hall 735 8th St S Naples FL 33940

HAWKINS, MARY RUTH REYNOLDS, educator, psychologist, researcher; b. Stuart, Va., June 8, 1944; d. Jesse Fay and Ruth Staples (Shockley) Reynolds; m. Dr. Richard Franklin Hawkins Jr., Mar. 23, 1967; children: Richard Franklin III, Mary Ellen, James. BS in Elem. Edn., Longwood Coll., Farmville, Va., 1966; MS in Psychology, Radford U., 1983, EdS. in Sch. Psych., 1986; postgrad., Polytechnic Inst. & State U., Blacksburg, Va., 1984—. Cert. sch. psychologist, tchr., Va. Elem. tchr. Patrick County Schs., Stuart, Va., 1967-68; elem. tchr. Henrico County Schs., Richmond, Va., 1968-71; pvt. tutor for learning disabled students U. Richmond, Richmond, 1974-75, Carlisle Sch., Martinsville, Va., 1977-78; sch. psych. practicum Wythe County Schs., Wytheville, Va., 1984; lectr. Wytheville Community Coll., 1984-89; sch. psychologist Smyth County Pub. Schs., Marion, Va., 1984—; Del. and mem. State Adv. Com for Gifted Edn., 1982-84; participant Va. Assembly on Policy for Elem. & Sec. Edn., Wintergreen, Va., 1984. Presenter: research, Creativity in Young Children, Va. Conf. 1985, Playfulness in Children, Va. Tech. Grad. Student Forum, 1987, Children's Play Human Devel. Conf. U. of Fla. 1988; workshop, Enhancing Playfulness, Va. Assn. for Early Childhood Edn. Conf. 1988. Co-founder, Supporters of Enriched End. and Knowledge, Support Group for Enriched Edn. Gifted, Smyth County, Va., 1981; vol. coach, Olympics of the Mind Team, Marion (Va.) Middle Sch., 1984; mentor Edn. for Ministry , Abingdon, Va., 1969. Mem. Smyth Counth Br. AAUW (pres. 1984-87), Va. Assn. of Sch. Psychologists, Nat. Assn. of Sch. Psychologists, Smyth County Mental Health Assn. (bd. dirs. 1985-89), Smyth County C. of C., Appalachian Peace Edn Ctr., Va. Assn. for Edn. of the Gifted (treas. 1981-82). Democrat. Episcopalian. Home: 109 Spottswood Pl Marion VA 24354

HAWKINS, MYLAN BARIN, computer consulting company executive; b. Chgo., Sept. 25, 1940; d. Harry Lewis Barin and Ruth (Kromelow) Lesser; m. Henry Roloff, July 26, 1959 (div. Sept. 1981); m. Prince Ashton Hawkins, June 27, 1982; children: Ari L., Kevin Barin. BA, U. Chgo., 1960. Div. dir. United Way Dade County, Miami, Fla., 1975-76; campaign mgr. Equality NOW, Reno, Nev., 1977-79; no. dir. March of Dimes, Reno, 1981-82; v.p. Interface Computer Cons., Reno, 1982-89; with Hawkins, Folsum & Clark, Reno, 1989—; cons. AT&T Liaison Program, Reno, 1983—, PBS, Reno, 1984-86. Editor (newsletter) Diabetes Edn. Ctr., 1980—; contbr. articles to profl. jours. Founder, chmn. Project Survival, Miami, 1969-75; bd. dirs. Nevadians for ERA, Reno, 1977-79; lobbyist ACLU, Now, Reno, 1977-79; adminstr. Diabetes Edn. Ctr., Reno, 1981—; acting coord. Coalition for Choice, 1989—; campaign mgr. Nev. Campaign For Choice, 1990. Home: 4465 Boca Way Apt 5 Reno NV 89502

HAWKINS, PAULA (MRS. WALTER E. HAWKINS), former senator; b. Salt Lake City; m. Walter Eugene Hawkins; children: Genean, Kevin Brent, Kelley Ann. Student, Utah State U., 1944-47, HHD (hon.), 1982; hon. doctorate, Nova U., St. Thomas Villa Nova, Rollins Coll. Dir. Southeast 1st Nat. Bank, Maitland, Fla., 1972-76; del. Republican Nat. Conv., Miami, 1968, 72, 76, 80, 84; mem. rules com. Republican Nat. Conv., 1972, co-chmn. rules com., 1980, co-chmn. platform com., 1984; bd. dirs. Fla. Fedn. Rep. Women, from 1968; elected mem. Fla. Pub. Svc. Commn., Tallahassee, 1972-79, chmn., 1977-79; mem. Rep. Nat. Com. for Fla., 1968-87, mem. rule 29 com., 1973-75; mem. U. S. Senate from Fla., 1981-87, mem. labor and human resources com., agriculture com., banking com., fgn. rels. com., drug free school com., chmn. subcom. on drug abuse, chmn. family and children subcom., 1982-86, chmn. drug enforcement caucus, 1981-87; apptd. permanent subcom. on narcotics control and terrorism OAS, 1981-87; U.S. del. to UN Narcotics Conv. Vienna, Austria, 1987; now with Paula Hawkins and Assocs., Winter Park, Fla.; v.p. Air Fla., 1979-80; bd. dirs. Philip Crosby Assocs., Alexander Proudfoot. Author: Children at Risk, 1986. Mem. Maitland Civic Center, 1965-76; charter mem. bd. dirs. Fla. Americans Constl. Action Com. of 100, 1966-68, sec.-treas., 1966-68; mem. Central Fla. Museum Speakers Bur., 1967-68, Fla. Gov.'s Commn. Status Women, 1968-71; mem. Pres.'s Commn. White House Fellowships, 1975; bd. dirs. Freedom Found., 1981—. Recipient citation for service Fla. Rep. Party, 1966-67, award for legis. work Child Fund Inc, 1982, Israel Peace medal, 1983, Tree of Life award Jewish Nat. Found, 1985, Mother of Yr. award, 1984, Grandmother of Yr.award, 1985, Albert Einstein Good Govt. award, 1986, Good Govt. award Maitland Jaycees, 1976, Outstanding award Am. Acad. Pediatricians, 1986; named Guardian of Small Bus. Nat. Fedn. Ind. Bus., 1982, Rep. Woman of Yr. Women's Nat. Rep. Club, 1981, Outstanding Woman of Yr. in Govt. Orlando C. of C., 1977, Woman of Yr., KC, 1973. Mem. Maitland C. of C. (chmn. congl. action com. 1967). Mem. Ch. Jesus Christ of Latter-day Saints (pres. Relief Soc., Orlando Stake 1960-64, Sunday sch. tchr. 1964-80). Club: Capitol Hill (Washington), Interlaken Country Club (Winter Pk.). Office: PO Box 193 Winter Park FL 32790

HAWKS, CAROL PITTS, librarian; b. New Orleans, Mar. 8, 1958; d. Leland Bascom and Mae Nell (Harper) Pitts. BA, Baylor U., 1980; M of Libr. and Info. Sci., U. Tex., 1981. Serials cataloger U. Houston Librs., 1981-82, head acquisition dept., 1982-87; head acquisition dept. Ohio State U. Librs., Columbus, 1987—; Mem. editorial bd. Libr. Acquisitions: Practice & Theory, 1989—. Contbr. articles to profl. jours. Mem. ALA (chairperson discussion group, com. mem.), N.Am. Serials Interest group, INNOVATIVE Users' Group (com. mem.). Office: Ohio State U Librs 1858 Neil Ave Mall Columbus OH 43210

HAWLEY, ANNE, museum director; b. Iowa City, Iowa, Nov. 3, 1943; d. Marshall Newton and Leone Ardith (Wilson) Hawley; m. Bruce Ivor McPherson, Sept. 4, 1977; 1 child, Katherine Black. BA, U. Iowa, 1966; MA, George Washington U., 1969; LHD (hon.), Lesley Coll, 1987; LHD (hon.), Williams Coll., 1989, Babson Coll., 1990. Intern in edn., Washington, 1967-69; research assoc. Nat. Urban League, Washington, 1969-71, Ford Found. Study Leadership in Pub. Edn., Washington, 1971-73; exec. dir. Cultural Edn. Collaborative, Boston, 1974-77, Mass. Council Arts/Humanities, Boston, 1977-89; mus. dir. Isabella Stewart Gardner Mus., Boston, 1989—. Bd. dirs. New Eng. Found. for Arts, 1978-89, Nat. Assembly/State Arts Agencies, Washington, 1981-83, Greater Boston Arts Fund, 1984-89, Boston Archtl. Found., Nat. Art Stabilization Fund. Fulbright scholar, 1986; recipient Design Travel Grant, Women's Travel Club, Boston, Mass., 1982, Art award Mass. Coll. Art, 1987, Lyman Ziegler award Commonwealth of Mass., 1988. Mem. Nat. Endowment for Arts (mus. panel 1978-81, dance panel 1982-84, design panel 1978-81, 88—), Boston Soc. Architecture (hon. mem. 1989). Office: Isabella Stewart Gardner Mus 2 Palace Rd Boston MA 02115

HAWLEY, JEAN GANNETT, publisher; b. Augusta, Maine, Jan. 16, 1924; d. Guy Patterson and Anne (Macomber) G.; m. Roger Chilton Williams, Oct. 11, 1945 (div. 1952); children: Roger Chilton Jr. (dec.), Guy G., Timothy A.; m. Sumner A. Hawley, Dec. 2l, 1970. Student, Bradford Jr. Coll., 1942-43; DBA (hon.), Portland U., 1958; LHD (hon.), Colby Coll., 1959, Nasson Coll., 1959; LLD (hon.), Bates Coll., 1980. Exec. v.p., mgr. nat. advtg. Guy Gannett Pub. Co., Portland, Maine, 1953, pres., 1954, pres., pub., 1959—. Recipient Deborah Morton award Westbrook Coll., 1965. Office: Guy Gannett Pub Co 1 City Ctr PO Box 15277 Portland ME 04101

HAWLEY, NANCI ELIZABETH, public relations and communications professional; b. Detroit, Mar. 18, 1942; d. Arthur Theodore and Elizabeth Agnes (Fylling) Smisek; m. Joseph Michael Hawley, Aug. 28, 1958; children: Michael, Ronald, Patrick, Julie Anne. Pres. Tempo 21 Nursing Svcs., Inc., Covina, Calif., 1973-75; v.p. Profl. Nurses Bur., Inc., L.A., 1975-83; cons. Hawley & Assocs., Covina, 1983-87; exec. v.p. Glendora (Calif.) C. of C., 1984-85; dir. membership West Covina (Calif.) C. of C., 1985-87; exec. dir. San Dimas (Calif.) C. of C., 1987-88; mgr. pub. rels. Soc. for Advancement of Material and Process Engrs., Covina, 1988—. Recipient Youth Motivation award Foothill Edn. Com., Glendora, 1987. Mem. NAFE, Pub. Rels. Soc. Am., Kiwanis Internat. (sec. 1989-90, Kiwanian of Yr. 1989), Soc. Nat. Assn. Publs., Am. Soc. Assn. Execs., Nat. Assn. Membership Dirs. Office: Soc Advancement Material & Process Engrs 1161 Parkview Dr Covina CA 91724

HAWLEY, SANDRA SUE, electrical engineer; b. Spirit Lake, Iowa, May 7, 1948; d. Byrnard Leroy and Dorothy Virginia (Fischbeck) Smith; m. Michael John Hawley, June 7, 1970; 1 child, Alexander Tristin. B.S. in Elec. Engring., U. Dayton, 1981; B.S. in Math. and Statis., Iowa State U., 1970; M.S. in Statis., U. Del., 1975. Research analyst State of Wis., Madison, 1970-71; research asst. Del. State Coll., Dover, 1972-73; asst. prof. math. and statis. Wesley Coll., Dover, 1974-81, chmn. dept. math. and computer sci., 1978-80; elec. engr. Control Data Corp., Bloomington, Minn., 1982-85; sr. elec. engr. Custom Integrated Circuits, 1985-89; sr. lead engr. Cardiac Pacemakers, Inc., 1989—. Contbr. articles to profl. jours. Elder, Presbyn. Ch. U.S.A., 1975—, mem. session Oak Grove Presbyn. Ch., Bloomington, 1985-88, chair united action, 1989—. NSF scholar U. Dayton, 1981. Mem. IEEE, Assn. Women in Sci., Soc. Women Engrs., Am. Statis. Assn. Home: 7724 W 85th St Circle Bloomington MN 55438 Office: Rosemount Inc 12001 Technology Dr Eden Prairie MN 55344

HAWN, GOLDIE, actress; b. Washington, Nov. 21, 1945; d. Edward Rutledge and Laura (Steinhoff) H.; m. Gus Trinkonis, May 16, 1969 (div.); m. Bill Hudson (div.); children: Oliver, Kate Garry, Wyatt Russell. Student, Am. U. Profl. dancer, 1965; profl. acting debut in Good Morning, World, 1967-68; mem. company TV series Laugh-In, 1968-70; appeared in TV spl. Pure Goldie, 1971; films include: Cactus Flower, 1969 (Acad. award best supporting actress), There's A Girl In My Soup, 1970, Dollars, 1971, Butterflies Are Free, 1971, The Sugarland Express, 1974, The Girl from Petrovka, 1974, Shampoo, 1975, The Duchess and the Dirtwater Fox, 1976, Foul Play, 1978, Seems Like Old Times, 1980, Best Friends, 1982, Swing-shift, 1984, Overboard, 1987, Bird on a Wire, 1989; exec. producer and star films Private Benjamin, 1980, Protocol, 1984, Wildcats, 1986; host TV spl. Goldie and Kids: Listen to Us!, 1982. Office: care Creative Artists Agy 1888 Century Pk E Ste 1400 Los Angeles CA 90067*

HAWORTH, ARLENE WILKINSON, financial services executive; b. Cleveland, Tenn., May 29, 1959; d. Grover Irvil and Elizabeth Ada Lou (Tilley) Wilkinson; m. Lowell Anthony Haworth, Oct. 9, 1982. BS, Freed-Hardeman Coll., 1981. Supr. bookeeping Liberty Studio, Inc., Cleveland, Tenn., Joseph Decosimo and Co., Chattanooga; ptnr. ABsolute Bookkeeping and Tax Svc., Chattanooga. Mem. Am. Inst. Profl. Bookkeeping. Address: 100 Cherokee Blvd Ste 103 Chattanooga TN 37405

HAWORTH, JOAN GUSTAFSON, economist, consultant; b. Deadwood, S.D., Nov. 10, 1938; d. Harold Edwin and Wilma Helen (Pranger) Gustafson; m. Charles Taylor Haworth, Apr. 10, 1960; children: Charles Stuart, John David, Ann Margaret. AB, Stanford U., 1960; MA, U. Oreg., 1965, PhD, 1970. Asst. prof. dept. econs. Fla. State U., Tallahassee, 1969-75, cons. Computer Ctr., 1969-72, assoc. prof. dept. econs., 1975-89; vis. assoc. prof. dept. econs. George Mason U., Fairfax, Va., 1975-76; pres. Economic Rsch. Svcs. Inc., Tallahassee, 1981—; cons. U.S. Commn. on Civil Rights, Washington, 1975-76, 81, Fla. Gov.'s Com. on Law Enforcement, Tallahassee, 1972-73; del. U.S.-USSR Sci. Exchange, Washington, 1979-80; speaker Am. Bar Assn., 1981—. Editor: Data Items, First Count, 1970; contbr. chpt. to book, articles to profl. jours. Sustaining mem. LeMoyne Art Ctr., 1985—, Fla. Econs. Club, 1989—. Margaret Byrnes honor scholar, 1956-60; NSF fellow, 1962-63; grantee U.S. Dept. Commerce, 1972-75, U.S. Dept. Agr., 1978=82. Mem. Am. Econ. Assn. (com. on status of women, bd. dirs., membership sec.), Am. Statis. Assn., Am. Mgmt. Assn., Fla. C. of C. (human rels. com.). Office: Econ Rsch Svc 4901 Tower Ct Tallahassee FL 32303

HAWORTH, PATRICIA ANNE, health physicist; b. West Union, Iowa, June 7, 1951; d. William John and Shirley Anne (Coglan) Schmelzer; m. Jay Michael, Oct. 28, 1989; 1 adopted child, Joshua Christopher Schmelzer; 1 stepchild, John Edward. BS, U. Iowa, 1976. Lab. asst. U. Iowa, Iowa City, 1974-78, lab. technician, 1978-82, chemist, 1982-84; health physicist Iowa Elec. Light & Power, Cedar Rapids, 1984-87, ALARA coord., 1987-88; radiol. engr. Detroit Edison, 1988—. Foster parent Dept. Human Svcs., Iowa City, 1987-88; vol. Dept. Corrections, Cedar Rapids, 1982, 83. Mem. Health Physics Soc. Democrat. Roman Catholic. Office: Enrico Fermi II Nuclear Power Plant Detroit Edison 6400 N Dixie Hwy Newport MI 48166

HAWPE, NANCY THOMAS, educator; b. Auburn, Ala., Dec. 16, 1946; d. Truman Edward and Virginia (Corcoran) Thomas; m. Edward C. Hawpe, July 1, 1967; 1 child, Jennifer R. BS, U. Del., 1973; MEd, Salisbury (Md.) State Coll., 1984; postgrad., U. Md., 1988—. Tchr. 2d grade Dover (Del.) Spl. Sch. Dist., 1967-68; tchr. kindergarten Milford (Del.) Sch. Dist., 1968-85, tchr. 1st grade, 1985—; mem. Gov.'s Early Childhood Com., Dover, 1987-88. Author: Trade Secrets mag., 1985; co-author: Kindergarten Guidelines, 1985. Mem. Sanctuary Choir Meth. Ch., Milford, 1979—; holiday booth chmn. Hosp. Fair Aux., Milford, 1976; bd. dirs. Second St. Players, Milford, 1988; dir. Cherub Choir Meth. Ch., Milford, 1980. Named Tchr. of the Yr., Milford Sch. Dist., 1989, Outstanding Del. Educator, U. Del., 1990. Mem. NEA, Internat. Reading Assn., Am. Ednl. Rsch. Assn., Phi Delta Kappa. Office: Ross Elem Sch 310 Lover's Ln Milford DE 19963

HAWTHORNE, JEWELL ANN, municipal administrator; b. Marshalltown, Iowa, Feb. 16, 1952; d. Arthur and Miriam Mae (Kreuger) Anselme; m. Richard Lowane Hawthorne, Mar. 16, 1973 (div. 1977); 1 child, Matthew Nathaniel. BS, Ariz. State U., 1974, MS, 1984. Specialist dept. econ. security State of Ariz., Phoenix, 1975-76; adminstrv. aide dept. human resources City of Phoenix, 1977-79, adminstrv. asst. police dept., 1979-80, sytems and procedures analyst police dept., 1980-81, rsch. analyst police dept., 1981-89, adminstrv. asst. dept. human resources, 1989-90, adminstrv. asst. II Dept. Neighborhood Improvement and Housing, 1990—. Editor Phoenix Police Dept. Ann. Report, 1986, 87. Sports dir. Theodore Roosevelt Council Boy Scouts Am., Phoenix, 1986-87, asst. den leader 1985-86. Mem. Nat. Assn. Police Planners, Am. Fedn. State County Mcpl. Employees (bd. dirs. local 2960 1978-79), Am. Soc. Pub. Adminstrn., Ariz. Mcpl. Mgmt. Assts. Assn. Office: Neighborhood Improvement and Housing Dept 920 E Madison Phoenix AZ 85034-2298

HAY, BETTY JO, civic worker; b. McAlester, Okla., June 6, 1931; d. Duncan and Kathryn Myrtle (Albert) Peacock; m. Jess Thomas Hay, Aug. 3, 1951; children—Deborah Hay Spradley, Patricia Lynn Daibert. B.A., So. Meth. U., 1952. Bd. dirs. White House Preservation Fund, 1980-87; bd. dirs. Nat. Mental Health Assn., 1978-87, pres., 1986, mem. fin. com. and child adolescent com., 1978-79, mem. resource devel. com., 1980-83; v.p. fundraising Mental Health Assn. Tex., 1980, bd. dirs., 1974—, pres., 1983-84; bd. dirs. Community Council Dallas, 1984—, bd. dirs. Mental Health Assn., Dallas County, 1972-88, pres., 1981-82; bd. dirs. United Way Met. Dallas, 1983—, treas., 1989; bd. dirs. Assn. Higher Edn. North Tex., 1980-82, vice chmn., 1982-83, chmn., 1984-85; mem. adv. bd. Sch. Social Work, U. Tex., Arlington, 1983—; mem. Nat. Commn. on Children, 1989-90, Dallas Council on World Affairs, Woman's Div., Dallas Symphony Orch. League, Historic Preservation League, March of Dimes Aux., 1982—; bd. dirs. Baylor Coll. Dentistry, 1987—. mem. exec. com., 1989, many past involvements in charitable orgns. Address: 7236 Lupton Circle Dallas TX 75225

HAY, ELIZABETH DEXTER, embryology researcher, educator; b. St. Augustine, Fla., Apr. 2, 1927; d. Isaac Morris and Lucille (Lynn) H. AB, Smith Coll., 1948; MA (hon.), Harvard U., 1964; ScD (hon.), Smith Coll., 1973, Trinity Coll., 1989; MD, Johns Hopkins U., 1952, LHD (hon.), 1990. Intern in internal medicine Johns Hopkins Hosp., Balt., 1952-53; instr. anatomy Johns Hopkins U. Med. Sch., Balt., 1953-56, asst. prof., 1956-57; asst. prof. Cornell U. Med. Sch., N.Y.C., 1957-60; asst. prof. Harvard Med. Sch., Boston, 1960-64, Louise Foote Pfeiffer assoc. prof., 1964-69, Louise Foote Pfeiffer prof. embryology, 1969—, chmn. dept. anatomy and cellular biology, 1975—; cons. cell biology sect. NIH, 1965-69; mem. adv. council Nat. Inst. Gen. Med. Sci., NIH, 1978-81; mem. sci. adv. bd. Whitney Marine Lab., U. Fla., 1982-86; mem. adv. council Johns Hopkins Sch. Medicine, 1982—; chairperson bd. sci. counselors Nat. Inst. Dental Research, NIH, 1984-86. Author: Regeneration, 1966; (with J.P. Revel) Fine Structure of the Developing Avian Cornea, 1969; editor: Cell Biology of Extracellular Matrix, 1981; editor-in-chief Developmental Biology Jour., 1971-75; contbr. articles to profl. jours. Mem. Scientists Task Force of Congressman Barney Frank, Massach, 1982—. Recipient Disting. Achievement award N.Y. Hosp.-Cornell Med. Ctr. Alumni Council, 1985, award for vision research Alcon, 1988. Mem. Soc. Devel. Biology (pres. 1973-74), Am. Soc. Cell Biology (pres. 1976-77, legis. alert com. 1982—, E.B. Wilson award 1989), Am. Assn. Anatomists (pres. 1981-82, legis. alert com. 1982—, Centennial award 1987), Am. Acad. Arts and Scis., Johns Hopkins Soc. Scholars, Nat. Acad. Sci., Inst. Medicine, Internat. Soc. Devel. Biologists (exec. bd. 1977), Boston Mycol. Club. Home: 14 Aberdeen Rd Weston MA 02193 Office: Harvard Med Sch Dept Anatomy & Cellular Biology 25 Shattuck St Boston MA 02115

HAY, JUDY THOMPSON, residential interior designer; b. Phoenix, Mar. 16, 1932; d. Cecil Clifford and Nadine Mary (Larimer) Cook; m. Robert Frank Pochini, Sept. 18, 1983. BA, U. Calif., Santa Barbara, 1953; M Journalism, U. Calif., Berkeley, 1965. Trade publs. editor Sunset Mag., 1966-73; owner, interior designer Lifestyle West, 1974-79; interior designer Berman's Drexel, 1979-85, Suburban House Drexel, 1986-87; ptnr., interior designer Judy Hay Interiors, Lafayette, Calif., 1987—; panelist Nat. consumer Action Panel, Carpet and Rug Industry, 1973-75; weekly columnist Furniture Today, 1974-75. Contbr. articles to profl. jours. and newspapers. Mem. Women in Communications, Internat. Furniture and Design Assn., ASID, Chi Omega. Republican. Mem. Unity Ch. Office: 47 Lafayette Circle Ste 167 Lafayette CA 94549

HAY, PAMELA CAMP, biology educator, researcher; b. Conway, Ark., Nov. 24, 1954; d. Edward Earl and Alice Virginia (Herrin) Camp; m. Herrick Richards Hay, May 19, 1989. BA, Hendrix Coll., 1976; MS, U. Ark., 1978; PhD, N.C. State U., Raleigh, 1982. Vis. lectr. U. N.C., Chapel Hill, 1982; postdoctoral assoc. U. Mo., Columbia, 1982-84, U. Dayton, Ohio, 1984-85; asst. prof. biology Davidson (N.C.) Coll., 1985—. Contbr. articles to profl. jours. Dana fellow Davidson Coll., 1985. Mem. Am. Soc. Plant Physiologists, Am. Soc. for Biochemistry and Molecular Biology. Office: Davidson Coll Dept Biology Davidson NC 28036

HAYASHI, LESLIE ANN, lawyer; b. Tokyo, Aug. 3, 1954; d. Warren Shizuo Hayashi and Gerde Ilse (Wilhelm) Smejkal; m. Alan Van Etten, May 10, 1986; 1 child, Justin Ken Van Etten. BA with distinction, Stanford U., 1976; JD, Georgetown U., 1979. Bar: Ill. 1980, Hawaii 1981, U.S. Dist. Ct. (no dist.) Ill. 1980, U.S. Dist. Ct. Hawaii 1981, U.S. Ct. Appeals (7th cir.) 1980, U.S. Ct. Appeals (9th cir.) 1982. Vis. fellow Am. Judicature Soc., Chgo., 1979-80, staff atty., 1980; assoc. Hamilton, Gibson, Nickelson, Rush & Moore, Honolulu, 1980-86; ptnr. now Rush, Moore, Craven, Kim & Stricklin, Honolulu, 1987-88; exec. dir. Hawaii Lawyers Care, Honolulu, 1988-89; per diem judge Honolulu, 1989—. Appt. ct. arbitrator Hawaii Supreme Ct., 1985—. Named Hawaii's Jr. Miss, 1972. Mem. Hawaii State Bar Assn. (dir. young lawyers div. 1987-88, v.p./pres. elect 1989), Hawaii Supreme Ct. (chmn. ad hoc com. on gender bias 1987—), Hawaii Women Lawyers (bd. dirs. 1986-87, pres. 1986-87), The Hawaii Women Lawyers Found. (bd. dirs. 1986—), Hawaii Women's Consortium (co-founder, dir. 1985). Democrat. Home: 1033 Hunakai St Honolulu HI 96816

HAYCOCK, KATHRYN PROFFITT, communications company executive; b. Hillsboro, Ore., Jan. 10, 1951; d. Willis Raymond Proffitt and Phyllis Josephine Hall; m. Paul Wadley Haycock, Sept. 10, 1973; children: Korbin Hal, Hollie Elizabeth, Garron Shepherd, Rachelle Dawn. Cert. dental hygiene, U. Ore., 1972. Staff dental hygienist Farm Workers Family Health Ctr., Toppenich, Wash., 1972-73; acting dir. dental hygiene Sch. Dental Hygiene Yakima (Wash.) Valley Coll., 1973-74; clin. instr. Sch. Dental Hygiene Phoenix Coll., 1975-80; pres., chief exec. officer Call-Am. Long Distance Phone Co., Phoenix, 1982—; chmn. bd. dirs. KLP Inc., Mesa, 1983—; bd. dirs. CompTel, Select Ocean Salmon. Mem. Altel of Ariz. (v.p. 1990—, lobbyist 1985), U.S. West Carrier Focus Group. Republican. Adventist. Office: Call-Am 1201 S Alma School Rd Ste 3950 Mesa AZ 95210

HAYDEN, ANNE ELIZABETH, insurance company executive; b. Kansas City, Mo., Aug. 17, 1948; d. Harvey Lee and Shirley Lee (Childs) Nichols; m. Robert Francis Hayden, June 27, 1975 (dec. 1989). BA with honors, U. Mo., 1969. With Met. Life Ins. Co., N.Y.C., 1970—, mgr. manpower resources, 1977-80, mgr. manpower planning, 1980-81, dir. employee rels., planning and devel., 1981-85, asst. v.p., 1985-88, v.p. employee rels., recruiting, communications, devel., 1988—; mem. exec. adv. bd. Fin. Employee Rels. Group, The Wharton Sch., U. Pa., Phila., 1984-85; mem. nat. adv. bd. Inst. Mgmt. Studies, San Francisco, 1985-86. Mem. adv. task force N.Y.C. Partnership/Mgmt. Assistance Com., 1989-90; mgmt. edn. adviser N.Y.C. C. of C., 1990; mem. bus. adv. group Gov.'s Adv. Com. on Child Care, 1990. Mem. Labor Policy Assn., U. Mo. Alumni Assn.

HAYEK, CAROLYN JEAN, judge; b. Portland, Oreg., Aug. 17, 1948; d. Robert A. and Marion L. (DeKoning) H.; m. Steven M. Rosen, July 21, 1974; children: Jonathan David, Laura Elizabeth. BA in Psychology, Carleton Coll., 1970; JD, U. Chgo., 1973. Bar: Wash. 1973. Assoc. firm Jones, Grey & Bayley, Seattle, 1973-77; sole practice law, Federal Way, Wash., 1977-82; judge Federal Way Dist. Ct., 1982—. Task force mem. Alternatives for Wash., 1973-75; mem. Wash. State Ecol. Commn., 1975-77; bd. dirs. 1st Unitarian Ch. Seattle, 1986-89, vice chair 1987-88, pres., 1988-89; den leader Cub Scouts Mt. Ranier coun. Boy Scouts Am., 1987-88, scouting coord., 1988-89; bd. dirs. Twin Lakes Elem. Sch. PTA. Mem. ABA, Wash. Women Lawyers, Wash. State Bar Assn., AAUW (br. pres. 1978-80, chmn. state level conf. com. 1986-87), King County Dist. Ct. Judges Assn. (treas., exec. com., com. chmn.), Elected Wash. Women (dir. 1983-87), Nat. Assn. Women Judges (nat. bd. dirs., dist. bd. dirs. 1984-86, chmn. rules com. 1988—), Women's Profl. and Managerial Network, Fed. Way Women's Network (bd. dirs. 1984-87, 88—, pres. 1985, program co-chair 1989—), Greater Fed. Way C. of C. (dir. 1978-82, sec. 1980-81, v.p. 1981-82). Republican. Office: Federal Way Dist Ct 33506 10th Pl S Federal Way WA 98003

HAYEK, GRACE MOLLY, editor; b. Madison, Wis., May 10, 1962; d. John W. and Patricia M. (Hess) H. BA, U. Wis., Madison, 1984; MLS, U. Wis., 1986. Archivist Chgo. Pub. Library Cultural Ctr., 1986-87; editor Am. Inst. Real Estate Appraisers, Chgo., 1987—. Office: Am Inst Real Estate Appraisers 430 N Michigan Ave Chicago IL 60611-4088

HAYEK, LEE-ANN COLLINS, statistician; b. Boston, Dec. 27, 1943; d. Harold L. and Rita (Omar) Collins; m. Elias Hayek, Sept. 8, 1970; children: Aron C., Katherine A., Natthew N., Christine B. AB, Emmanuel Coll., 1965; MS, Cath. U. Am., 1967; PhD, U. Md., 1978. Mathematician USAF Cambridge Rsch. Labs., Boston; chief analyst, quality control div. Blue Cross Western Pa., Pitts.; lectr. math. statistics Point Pk. Coll., Pitts.; chief statistician Consol. Natural Gas Svc. Co., Pitts.; assoc. prof. math sci. dept. Beaver County Coll., Monaca, Pa.; cons. govt. agcys., pvt. concerns; chief math. statistician Smithsonian Institution, Washington, 1973—; cons. various groups in field. Contbr. articles to profl. jours. Recipient grants NSF, NIH, AAAS, Outstanding Performance awd. Smithsonian Institution. Mem. Am. Statistical Assn., Am. Ednl. Rsch. Assn., Nat. Assn. Measurement in Edn., Nat. Hist. Soc., Soc. Systematic Zoology, Washington Statistical Soc., Psychometric Soc., Biometric Soc., ENAR. Office: Smithsonian Institution NHB E116 The Mall Washington DC 20560

HAYES, ALBERTA PHYLLIS WILDRICK, retired health service executive; b. Blakeslee, Pa., May 31, 1918; d. William and Maude (Robbins) Wildrick; diploma Wilkes Barre Gen. Hosp. Sch. Nursing, 1938-41; student Wilkes Coll., 1953-54, Pa. State U., 1969—; m. Glenmore Burton Hayes, Oct. 9, 1942; children—Glenmore Rolland, William Bruce. Nurse, Monroe County Gen. Hosp., East Stroudsburg, Pa., 1941-44; pvt. duty nurse, 1944-56; with White Haven (Pa.) Center, 1956-82, dir. residential services, 1966-82, ret., 1982. Pres. Tobyhanna Twp. Sch. PTA, 1948-49, Top-o-Pocono Women of Rotary, 1975-76; nurse ARC, 1955; adv. council Luzerne County Foster Grandparent Program, 1977—, Health Services Keystone Job Corps, Drums, Pa., 1977—. Mem. Am. Assn. Mental Deficiency, Am. Legion Aux. (unit pres. 1946-47). Club: Pocono Mountains Women's (Blakeslee). Home: PO Box 11 Blakeslee PA 18610

HAYES, ALEXANDRIA LYNN, education company executive; b. Washington, Oct. 16, 1957; d. James Noyes Orton and Rosemary Margaret (Corbin) Miller. BBA, Loyola Coll., Balt., 1985; postgrad., Boston U., 1989. Bus. analyst Martin Marietta Corp., Balt., 1978-85; prin. Alexanni Assocs., Nashua, N.H., 1985-86, cons., 1986—; mgr. navy program mktg. Raytheon MSD, Bedford, Mass., 1986-88; dir. catalog dept. Delta Edn., Inc., Hudson, N.H., 1988—. Author: (report) The Machine Vision Industry, 1984, (with others/catalog) Hands-On-Science, 1989, (catalog) Hands-On Math, 1990. Mem. NAFE, Am. Mensa, Toastmasters (sec. Bedford, Mass., club 1987), Phi Kappa Phi. Republican. Home: PO Box 7952 Nashua NH 03060 Office: Delta Edn Inc PO Box 915 Nashua NH 03051

HAYES, ALICE BOURKE, biologist, educator, university administrator; b. Chgo., Dec. 31, 1937; d. William Joseph and Mary Alice (Cawley) Bourke; m. John J. Hayes, Sept. 2, 1961 (dec. July 1981). B.S., Mundelein Coll., Chgo., 1959; M.S., U. Ill., 1960; Ph.D., Northwestern U., 1972. Researcher Mcpl. Tb San., Chgo., 1960-62; faculty Loyola U., Chgo., 1962—, chmn. dept., 1968-77, dean natural scis. div., 1977-80, asso. acad. v.p., 1980-87, v.p. acad. affairs, 1987-89; provost, exec. v.p. St. Louis U., 1989—; mem. NASA Space Biology program, 1980-86; mem. adv. panel NSF, 1977-81, Parmly Hearing Inst., 1986—; del. Botanical Del. to S. Africa, 1984; del. Botanical Del. to China, 1988; reviewer Coll. Bd. and Mellon Found. Nat. Hispanic Scholar award, 1985-86. Co-author books; contbr. articles to profl. publs. Campaign mem. Mental Health Assn. Ill., Chgo., 1973-89; trustee Chgo.-No. Ill. div. Nat. Multiple Sclerosis Soc., 1981-89, bd. dirs. 1980-88, com. chair , sec. to bd. dirs., vice-chmn. bd. dirs.; trustee Regina Dominican Acad., 1984-89; trustee Civitas Dei Found., 1984—; trustee St. Ignatius Coll. Prep., bd. dirs. 1984-89, sec., vice-chmn.; bd. dirs. Urban League, Met. St. Louis. Named to Teachers' Hall of Fame Blue Key Soc.; fellow in botany U. Ill., 1959-60; fellow in botany NSF, 1969-71; grantee Am. Orchid Soc., 1967; grantee HEW, 1969, 76; grantee NSF, 1975; grantee NASA, 1980-85. Mem. Am. Assn. for Higher Edn., Am. Assn. Univ. Adminstrs. (mem. program com. nat. meeting 1988), Am. Soc. Gravitational and Space Biology, Assn. Midwest Coll. Biology Teachers, Am. Soc. Plant Physiology, Bot. Soc. Am., AAAS, Am. Inst. Biol. Scis. Acad., Chgo. Network, Soc. Ill. Microbiologists (edn. com. 1969-70, Pasteur award com. 1975, pub. rels. com. 1974, chair speakers' bur. 1974-79), Chgo. Assn. Tech. Socs. (acad. liaison 1982-85, awards com. 1984—), AAUW (corp. rep. 1980—), Am. Council on Edn. (corp. rep. higher edn. panel), Ctr. Rsch. Librs.(nominating com. 1986), North Cen. Assn. Colls. and Schs. (cons., evaluator Commn. on Higher Edn., 1984—, commr.-at-large, 1988—), Sigma Xi, Delta Sigma Rho, Sigma Delta Epsilon, Phi Beta Kappa, Alpha Sigma Nu. Democrat. Roman Catholic. Club: Chgo. Network. Office: St Louis Univ 221 N Grand Saint Louis MO 63103

HAYES, ALLENE VALERIE FARMER, information specialist, government executive; b. Washington, Sept. 23, 1958; d. Thomas Jonathan and Allena V. (Joyner) Farmer; m. Thomas Gary Hayes; 1 child, Tommia Chanel. Student, Richmond Coll., London, 1980; BA, Clark U., 1980; cert., U. Oxford, Eng., 1981; M.L.S., U. Md., 1986. Libr. asst. NUS Corp., Gaithersburg, Md., 1981-82; cataloger Libr. of Congress, Washington, 1982-84, copyright specialist, 1984-85; congl. fellow Ho. of Reps. Com. on D.C., Washington, 1985—; English tutor, writer Natural Motion, Washington, 1983-84; intern, archivist Howard U., Washington, 1985. Compiler; Single Mother's Resource Directory, 1984. Compiler, editor: Policy Research, 1985. Author booklet: D.C. Statehood Issue, 1986. Mem. U. Md. College Park Black Women's Coun., 1984, NAACP; vol. Congl. Black Caucus Found., Washington, 1985. Recipient Fgn. Study award Am. Inst. for Fgn. Study, 1981; Congl. Black Caucus fellow, 1985. Mem. ALA, Libr. of Congress Profls. Assn., Daniel A.P. Murray Afro-Am. Culture Assn. of Libr. of Congress, Delta Sigma Theta (tutor 1986). Avocations: travel; writing; dance; drama; tennis. Home: 1120 K St NE Washington DC 20002 Office: Congress of US Ho of Reps Com on DC 2135 Rayburn House Washington DC 20515

HAYES, BERNARDINE FRANCES, computer systems analyst; b. Boston, June 29, 1939; d. Robert Emmett and Mary Agnes (Tague) H. BA in Edn., St. Joseph Coll., 1967; MA in Urban Affairs and Pub. Policy, U. Del., 1973, PhD in Pub. Policy, 1978. Joined Daus. of Charity of St. Vincent de Paul, 1957, laicized, 1971. Elem. tchr. St. Dominick Sch., Balt., 1960-63; tchr. sci., math. and art St. Mary's Sch., Troy, N.Y., 1963-65, Our Lady Queen of Peace Sch., Washington, 1965-68, St. Patrick Sch., Richmond, Va., 1968-69, St. Peter Cathedral Sch., Wilmington, Del., 1969-71; planner health and social svcs. Model Cities Program, Wilmington, 1971-72; dir. rsch. Del. State Dept. Mental Health, Wilmington, 1972-75; dir. planning and evaluation Mental Health, Mental Retardation Svcs., West Chester, Pa., 1976-78; instr. Boston U., 1978; div. dir. Systems Architects, Inc., Randolph, Mass., 1979-81; group mgr. Unisys Corp., Cambridge, Mass., 1981—; cons. in field; pres. and founder Hayes Assocs., a communication firm, 1989—. Contbr. numerous articles to profl. jours. Bd. sec. Model Cities, 1969-70; chairperson bd. State Service Ctr., Wilmington, 1972-75; mem. Human Rels. Commn., Washington, 1965-68; co-chmn. State-wide Coalition for Human Svcs., Del., 1972-74; activist Vietnam protest, Del., 1970-74, Civil Rights Movement, 1965—. numerous polit. campaigns, 1972—; alt. del. Mass. Dem. Conv., 1985; bd. v.p. Women's Action for Nuclear Disarmament, Arlington, Mass., 1982—, fin. com. chmn., 1983-85, 88—, treas., 1988—, chmn. polit. action com., 1983-84, dir. nat. voter registration campaign, 1984.; active Mondale for Pres., 1984, John Kerry for Senator campaign, Mass., 1984; del. Com. for an Enduring Peace, Soviet Peace Commn., Moscow, 1987; mem. Daughter of Charity of St. Vincent DePaul, 1957-71; bd. trustees Mass. Assn. for the Blind, 1989—; mem. NAACP. Fellow NSF, 1966. Mem. NOW, Women's Inst. Housing and Econ. Devel. (bd. dirs. 1985-88), Boston Computer Soc., Boston Mus. Fine Arts. Roman Catholic. Home: 49 Crane Rd Adams Shore Quincy MA 02169

HAYES, BREE AUDREY, educator, consultant; b. Newark, Apr. 27, 1945; d. Harvey and Gerry (Soroka) Botkin; m. Robert M. Levin, Sept. 5, 1965 (div. June 1977); children: Jon M., Ali; m. Richard Lee Hayes, Aug. 18, 1977; 1 child, Gillian Rachael. BS, Boston U., 1967, MEd, 1973, EdD, 1987. Lic. psychologist; cert. tchr. Tchr. English Zama (Japan) Machi High Sch., 1968-70; counselor Wayland (Mass.) High Sch., 1973-74, The High Sch., Brookline, Mass., 1974-75; psychologist Hamilton (N.Y.) Cen. Sch., 1977-79; lectr. in edn. Colgate U., Hamilton, 1979, vis. instr., 1980; dir. consultation and edn. Human Svc. Ctr., Peoria, Ill., 1980-83; pres. Resource Mgmt. Svcs., Inc., Peoria, 1983-88; asst. prof. U. Ga., Athens, 1988—. Mem. com. Greater Peoria C. of C., 1983-88; bd. dirs. Parents Anonymous, Peoria, 1980-83. Recipient Pres.'s award Assn. for Specialists in Group Work, 1989. Mem. Nat. Bd. Cert. Counselors (bd. dirs., sec., treas. 1990—), Assn. for Humanistic Edn. and Devel. (v.p. for rsch. 1990—), Am. Assn. for Counseling and Devel., Am. Psychol. Assn., Phi Delta Kappa, Pi Lambda Theta. Office: U Ga Dept of Counseling 402 Aderhold Hall Athens GA 30602

HAYES, EILEEN PATRICIA, opera theater executive; b. Tillamook, Oreg.; d. Clemens and Martha Dandridge (Maddox) H.; m. Gale Southard Martin, Dec. 28, 1985. BS, U. Oreg., 1968; BA, U. Nev., Las Vegas, 1985. Cert. tchr., Oreg.; cert. orch. mgr. Asst. to dir. L.A. Athletic Club, 1969-73; tchr. drama, music Tillamook Pub. Schs., 1973-74; mus. artist Portland Opera Co., Oreg., 1975-80, Oreg. Light Opera Co., 1977-78; mng. dir. Las Vegas Chamber Players, Las Vegas Symphony Orch., 1982-84; exec. dir. Nev. Opera Theatre, Las Vegas, 1985—; cons. theater arts dept. U. Nev., Las Vegas, 1983; pub. rels. dir. So. Nev. Mus. Arts Meml. Concert, Las Vegas, 1984; Columbia Artists Mgmt. Artist community concerts, 1988—. Newspaper writer, 1983; editor concert series program booklet, 1982-84; performance dir., artist Tribute to Vietnam Vets., 1975, Mus. Portrait (Nat. Endowment for Arts), 1986, 87. Patron Charleston Heights Art Ctr., Las Vegas, 1983—; com. mem. St. Rose de Lima Hosp. Aux., Henderson, Nev., 1983—; mem. Rep. Women of Clark County, 1985—, ball com. Nev. Gov.'s Inauguration, 1987; mgmt. artist for community concert series Columbia Artists, 1988-89; mem. St. Jude's Aux.; chmn. Western States Opera Conf., 1990—. Recipient Internat. Thespian award Drama Dir. Tillamook, 1973, Woman of Achievement award Las Vegas C. of C., 1989. Mem. Am. Guild Mus. Artists, NAFE, Met. Opera Guild, Internat. Assn. Bus. Communicators, Nev. Alliance for the Arts (bd. dirs. 1988—), Am. Symphony Orch. League, Assn. Calif. Symphony Orchs., Las Vegas C. of C. (nominating com. 1984, Woman of Achievement award in the arts 1989, women's coun.), L.A. Athletic Club, Order of Rainbow (worthy advisor 1963). Avocations: collecting antiques, swimming, dancing. Office: Nev Opera Theatre 3430 E Flamingo Rd Las Vegas NV 89119

HAYES, GLADYS LUCILLE ALLEN, community care organization official, poet, writer; b. Havelock, Nebr., Nov. 29, 1913; d. Harry Arthur and Louis (Vogel) Allen; m. James Franklin Hayes, Oct. 5, 1943; children: J. Allen, Warren Andrew. Secretarial diploma, Lincoln (Nebr.) Sch. Commerce, 1932; student, Santa Clara U., 1950-60; BS in Media Studies, Sacred Heart U., Fairfield, Conn., 1989, postgrad., 1989—. Cert. profl. religion tchr. Archdiocese of San Francisco. Exec. tech. sec. McCormick-Selph div. Teledyne Corp., Hollister, Calif., 1960-65; adminstrv. asst. to v.p. and contr. Greater Bridgeport (Conn.) Regional Narcotics Program, Inc., 1979-81; adminstrv. asst. to scientists and engrs. CBS Lab. div. CBS Inc., Stamford, Conn., 1968-76; sec. to Nobel laureate and physicist Dennis Gabor, Dsc, FRS U. London, U.S., 1979; corp. sec. Automated Power Systems, Inc., Bridgeport, 1976—; owner, mgr. GA Secretarial Svc., Stratford, Conn., 1980—; secretarial asst. Conn. Community Care, Inc., Stratford, Conn., 1986—; radio broadcaster Fairfield U., 1985—. Recipient Excellence in Aging award Conn. Community Care, Inc., 1989, Prize for Photography, City of Bridgeport, 1987, Pope Pius X medal, Diocese of San Francisco, 1959, Excellence in Aging, Conn. Community Care, Inc., 1989. Former residential fund raising chmn. ARC, Gilroy, Calif.; former motion picture chmn. St. Mary's Sch., Gilroy, also past pres. Mothers' Guild, former mem. Edn. Commn.; former fundraiser March of Dimes; mem. various choirs and choral groups, Calif., Conn.; mem. Nat. Coun. on Aging; tchr. religion Archdioces of San Francisco, Diocese of Lincoln, 1933-67. Recipient Excellence in Aging award Conn. Community Care, Inc., 1989, prize for photograph City of Bridgeport, 1987, Pope Pius X Medal of Honor, 1959. Mem. Nat. Honor Soc. Republican. Roman Catholic. Office: Conn Community Care Inc 2505 Main St Stratford CT 06497

HAYES, HELEN, actress; b. Washington, Oct. 10, 1900; d. Francis Van Arnum and Catherine Estell (Hayes) Brown; m. Charles MacArthur, Aug. 17, 1928 (dec. Apr. 1956); 1 child, James. Grad., Sacred Heart Acad., Washington, 1917; L.H.D., Hamilton Coll., Clinton, N.Y., 1939, Smith Coll., 1940, Elmira (N.Y.) Coll.; Litt.D., Columbia U., 1949, U. Denver, 1952; D.F.A., Princeton U., St. Mary's Coll. First appeared on stage, age six; mem. Columbia Players, Washington, 4 seasons; toured with Lew Fields and John Drew; mem. A.P.A. Phoenix Repertory Co., from 1966. Stage appearances include Old Dutch, Prodigal Husband, Pollyanna, Penrod, Dear Brutus, Clarence, Bab, To The Ladies, We Moderns, Dancing Mothers, Caesar and Cleopatra, What Every Woman Knows, Coquette, Mr. Gilhooley, Mary of Scotland, 1934, Victoria Regina, 1937-38, Ladies and Gentlemen, 1939-40, Twelfth Night, 1940-41, Candle in the Wind, 1941-42, Harriet, 1943-45, Happy Birthday, 1948, The Glass Menagerie, London, 1948, Farewell to Arms, 1950, Vanessa, 1950, The Wisteria Trees, 1950, Mrs. McThing, 1952, Mainstreet to Broadway, 1953, Skin of Our Teeth, Europe and U.S., 1955, Harvey, Long Days Journey Into Night, 1971; motion pictures include The Sin of Madelon, Claudet (Acad. award 1932), Arrowsmith, My Son John, 1951, Anastasia, 1956, Airport, 1970 (Acad. award Best Supporting Actress 1971), Herbie Rides Again, 1974, Helen Hayes: Portrait of an American Actress, 1974, One of Our Dinosaurs is Missing, 1975, Candleshoe, 1978, Hopper's Silence, 1981; TV shows The Snoop Sisters, 1972-74, played Mrs. Derth in TV revival Barrie's Dear Brutus, 1956, Twelve Pound Look, Mary of Scotland, Skin of Our Teeth, Christmas Tie, Drugstore on a Sunday Afternoon, Omnibus, A Caribbean Mystery, Murder With Mirrors, others; author: (novels) Our Best Years, 1986, Where The Truth Lies, 1988; (autobiography) My Life in Three Acts, 1990. Pres. Am. Nat. Theatre and Acad.; hon. pres. Am. Theatre Wing; 2d v.p. Actors Fund, from 1975—; chmn. women's activities Nat. Found. for Infantile Paralysis. Recipient best actress award Motion Pictures Acad. Arts and Scis., 1932; recipient Emmy award, 1954, Antoniette Perry award for best actress in Time Remembered, 1958, Medal of City of N.Y., Medal of Arts Finland, Am. Exemplar medal Freedoms Found., 1978, Laetare medal U. Notre Dame, 1979. Republican. Roman Catholic. *

HAYES, JACQUELINE CREMENT, real estate broker and developer; b. Chgo., Aug. 12, 1941; d. John and Lottie (Czech) Crement; m. Larry G. Hayes, Mar. 4, 1972 (div. Dec. 1978). BA in Mgmt., DePaul U., 1977. Lic. real estate broker, Ill. Bldg. mgr. LaSalle Bank Bldg., Chgo., 1978-80; v.p., gen. mgr. The Hayman Co., Chgo., 1981-83; propr. Jacqueline Hayes & Assoc., Chgo., 1983-86; ptnr. The Retail Group, Chgo., 1986—; panelist retail planning seminar Dept. Planning, City of Chgo., 1988, steering com. River North urban design plan, 1987-89, pedestrian count, 1989, Streeterville urban design plan. Docent Chgo. Archtl. Found.; mem. Burnham Pk. Planning Bd., Chgo.; bd. dirs., sec., chmn. Western chpt., chmn. membership, zoning and planning Greater North Michigan Ave. Assn., Chgo., 1986—; mem. adv. coun. Friends of Downtown, 1987-89; bd. dirs. Cactus Theatre. Named Broker of Yr. Chgo. Sun Times, 1986. Mem. Internat. Coun. Shopping Ctrs., Comml. Real Estate Orgn. (bd. dirs., v.p., chmn. membership 1986-89), Chgo. Office Leasing Brokers, River North Assn., Chgo. Assn. Commerce and Industry, Chgo. Real Estate Exec., Lambda Alpha (Ely chpt.). Office: The Retail Group 215 W Huron 3rd Fl Chicago IL 60610

HAYES, JENNIFER LYNN, advertising specialist; b. South Bend, Ind., Mar. 4, 1965; d. Lawrence Arthur and Sandra Lea (Stephenson) H. Degree in bus., Ind. U., 1987. Deli mgr. Pak-n-Shop, Osceola, Ind., 1981-87; sales rep. Encom, Elkhart, Ind., 1987-88; advt. coord. Pro-Tech Respirators, Buchanan, Mich., 1988—; grad. asst. Dale Carnegie Inst., South Bend, 1990—. Mem. Mich. Alive with Pride Com., 1990—. Mem. Am. Mktg. Assn., Sales and Advt. Exec.'s Club. Republican. Roman Catholic. Office: Pro Tech Respirators Inc 107 E Alexander St Buchanan MI 49107

HAYES, KATHE PENNEY, mental health administrator; b. Mineola, N.Y., June 21, 1949; d. Milton Arthur and Myrtle Viola (Antoinette) Penney; m. William Peter Hayes, Oct. 14, 1978; children: Jesse Michael, Adam Lee. BA, CUNY, S.I., 1971; MA in Community Psychology, Mansfield U., 1979. Recreation therapist Robert Packer Hosp., Sayre, Pa., 1973-75; psychiat. caseworker Robert Packer Hosp., Sayre, 1975-78; psychologist Elmira (N.Y.) Psychiat. Ctr., 1978-83, treatment team leader childrens svcs., 1983-90, chief of children and youth svcs., 1990—; regional rep. Human Svc. Com., Corning, N.Y., 1980-90; children and youth rep. Regional Planning Adv. Coms., Genessee, N.Y., 1989—; regional rep. Mental Health Community Children and Youth Task Force, Albany, N.Y., 1989—. Mem. PTA, Watkins Glen, N.Y., 1985—, Clemens Ctr. for Arts, Elmira, 1980—, Arnot

Art Mus., 1985-90. Mem. Nat. Assn. Rural Mental Health (treas. 1987-89, pres. elect. 1989-90, pres. 1990—), Nat. Rural Health Assn., Am. Assn. Mental Health Adminstrs. Democrat. Lutheran. Home: 2495 Old Corning Rd Watkins Glen NY 14891 Office: Elmira Psychiat Ctr 1000 Washington St Elmira NY 14902

HAYES, KATHLEEN ZIMMERMAN, retail store executive; b. Hammond, Ind., May 9, 1944; d. Warren Lee and Irene Rose (Glass) Zimmerman; B.S., Purdue U., 1967; M.B.A., U. Chgo., 1970; postgrad. in taxation DePaul U., 1979—. Pharmacist, various cos., Indpls. and Chgo., 1967-70; revenue agt. IRS, Des Moines, 1971-72; tax specialist McGladrey, Hendrickson & Co., Des Moines, 1972-75; tax mgr. Clow Corp., Oak Brook, Ill., 1975-79; tax compliance mgr. U.S. Gypsum Co., Chgo., 1979-82; tax mgr. Global Marine Inc., Houston, 1982-86; owner retail store, Houston. Pres. bd. Woman's Hosp. of Tex. Research and Edn. Found., 1986. C.P.A., Iowa, Ill. Mem. Tax Execs. Inst. (treas. Houston chpt., dir., chmn. internat. tax com.), Am. Inst. C.P.A.s, Iowa Soc. C.P.A.s, Ill. C.P.A. Found., Am. Women's Soc. C.P.A.s, Beta Alpha Psi. Home: 18203 Heaton Dr Houston TX 77084 Office: 78 Woodlake Sq Houston TX 77042

HAYES, LISA SANDERS, advertising executive; b. Manchester, Tenn., Feb. 29, 1960; d. Eugene Johnson and Anna Jane (Myers) Sanders; m. William Mark Todd, July 7, 1979 (div. Aug. 1985); m. William Robert Hayes, Aug. 23, 1986; 1 child, Dean Oliver. BFA, Mid. Tenn. State U., 1982. Dir. art The Art Office, Nashville, 1982; prin. Ad Arts Advt. Agy., Tullahoma, Tenn., 1983—. Bd. dirs. United Givers Fund, Tullahoma, 1988, pub. rels. officer, 1989, pub. rels. officer Tullahoma Hist. Preservation Soc., Inc., 1988-89. Mem. Nashville Advt. Fedn., Nat. Exchange Club, Kiwanis Club, Tullahoma C. of C. (bd. dirs. 1990-93). Home: 408 N Atlantic St Tullahoma TN 37388 Office: Ad Arts Advt Agy 111 S Anderson St Tullahoma TN 37388

HAYES, LISABETH ANN, advertising sales executive; b. Phila., Apr. 24, 1958; d. Hadley Lewis and Betty Jean (Aubertin) Conn; m. Michael Christopher Hayes, May 8, 1982 (div. May 1987). Student, Harvard U., 1980; BS, Trinity Coll., Hartford, Conn., 1980. Media planner Benton & Bowles, N.Y.C., 1980-81; merchant sales rep. Chem. Bank, N.Y.C., 1981-82; account exec. USA Network, Chgo., 1982-84; v.p., dir. advt. sales MTV Networks, Chgo., 1984—. Mem. Broadcast Advt. Club, Chgo. Advt. Club, Chgo. Cable Mgrs. Assn. (sec. 1990—), Jr. League Chgo., Multiple Schlerosis Soc., Phi Beta Kappa.

HAYES, MARIAN MERCER, newspaper advertising professional; b. Wilmington, N.C., June 27, 1963; d. Garvin Marion Mercer and Myra Louise (Price) Hines; m. William Arthur Russ, Sept. 28, 1980 (div. July 1987); m. Terry Dale Hayes, Aug. 5, 1988; 1 child, April Louise Russ. Grad. high sch., Southport, N.C., 1981. Receptionist The State Port Pilot, Southport, 1984-85, classified advt. mgr., 1985-87, advt. sales mgr., 1987-88; advt. sales The News Reporter Co., Inc., Whiteville, N.C., 1988—. Choir mem. Cherry Grove Bapt. Ch., Cerro Gordo, N.C., 1989-90, Girls in Action tchr., 1990, tchr. Sunday sch., 1990. Mem. NAFE. Democrat. Baptist. Home: Rte 1 Box 253-A Cerro Gordo NC 28430 Office: The News Reporter Co Inc 127 W Columbus St Whiteville NC 28472

HAYES, MARY ESHBAUGH, newspaper editor; b. Rochester, N.Y., Sept. 27, 1928; d. William Paul and Eleanor Maude (Seivert) Eshbaugh; B.A. in English and Journalism, Syracuse (N.Y.) U., 1950; m. James Leon Hayes, Apr. 18, 1953; children—Pauli, Eli, Lauri Le June, Clayton, Merri Jess Bates. With Livingston County Republican, Geneseo, N.Y., summers, 1947-50, mng. editor, 1949-50; reporter Aurora (Colo.) Advocate, 1950-52; reporter-photographer Aspen (Colo.) Times, 1952-53, columnist, 1956—, reporter, 1972-77, asso. editor, 1977—; tchr. Colo. Mountain Coll., 1979. Mem. Nat. Fedn. Press Women (1st prizes in writing and editing 1976-80), Colo. Press Women's Assn. (writing award 1974, 75, 78-85, sweepstakes award for writing 1977, 78, 84, 85, also 2d place award 1976, 79, 82, 83, Woman of Achievement 1986). Mem. Aspen Community Ch. Photographer, editor: Aspen Potpourri, 1968. Home: PO Box 497 Aspen CO 81611 Office: Box E Aspen CO 81611

HAYES, MARY PHYLLIS, savings and loan association executive; b. New Castle, Ind., Apr. 30, 1921; d. Clarence Edward and Edna Gertrude (Burgess) Scott; m. John Clifford Hayes, Jan. 1, 1942 (div. Oct. 1952); 1 child, R. Scott. Student, Ball State U., 1957-64, Ind. U. East, Richmond, 1963; diploma, Inst. Fin. Edn., 1956, 72, 76. Teller Henry County Savs. and Loan, New Castle, 1939-41, loan officer, teller, 1950-62, asst. sec., treas., 1962-69, sec., treas., 1969-73, corp. sec., 1973-84; v.p., sec. Ameriana Savs. Bank (formerly Henry County Savs. and Loan), New Castle, 1984—; exec. sec. Am. Nat. Bank, Nashville, 1943-44; v.p., sec. Ameriana Bancorp., New Castle, 1989—; corp. sec., Ameriana Fin. Svcs., 1984—; bd. dirs. Ameriana Ins. Co. Treas. Henry County Chpt. Am. Heart Assn., New Castle, 1965-67, 76-87, vol. Indpls. chpt. 1980—; membership sec. Henry County Hist. Soc., New Castle, 1975—; sec. Henry County Chpt. ARC, New Castle, 1976—. Recipient Gold medallian Am. Heart Assn., 1973, diploma of merit Inst. Fin. Edn., 1984, 20-Yr. award, 1983, 25-Yr. award Ind. affiliate Am. Heart Assn., 1987, 40-Yr. award Ind. League of Savs. Instns., 1988, NAPN award Am. Heart Assn., 1989, 15 Yr. Svcs. award Inst. Fin. Edn. Adminstrn., 1989. Mem. Inst. Fin. Edn. (sec., treas. East Cen. Ind. chpt. 1973—), Ind. League Savs. Insts. (25 Yrs. award 1975, 40 Yrs. Cert. award 1988), Henry County Hist. Soc. (membership sec.), Altrusa (past officer, bd. dirs. New Castle chpt.), PEO (past chaplain, sec.), Psi Iota Xi (past sec., treas.). Mem. Christian Ch. Office: Ameriana Savs Bank 2118 Bundy Ave New Castle IN 47362

HAYES, MARY REGINA, nurse; b. NYC, Oct. 13, 1953; d. John Robert and Rosemary Ann (White) Gillen; m. Thomas Anthony Hayes, Sept. 14, 1953. AAS, Kingsborough Community Coll., NY, 1976; Molloy Coll., Moltey Coll., NY, 1982; MS in Nursing, Lehman Coll., NY, 1988. Cert. emergency nurse. Staff nurse Peninsula Hosp. Ctr., NYC, 1976-80, staff nurse emergency dept., 1981-88, nurse educator, 1989—; staff nurse Maimonides Hosp., NYC; nurse educator Bklyn. Caledonian Hosp., 1988-89. Mem. Emergency Nurse Assn., American Irish Nurses Assn., Sigma Theta Tau.

HAYES, MYRA NELL, educator; b. Prattville, Ala., Jan. 22, 1943; d. William McKinley and Iva Lorraine (Hand) H. AB in Art History with honors, Samford U., 1965; M Art History, Ohio State U., 1972. Cert. tchr., Ga. Tchr. history Brevard County Schs., Titusville, Ga., 1965-70, DeKalb County Schs., Decatur, Ga., 1974—; also chmn. social studies dept. Walker High Sch., DeKalb County; mem. curriculum revision bd., Brevard County Schs., 1970, course guide revision and book selection com., DeKalb County Schs., 1980; developer humanities course, Walker High Sch., 1983-86; presenter seminars on art history. Mem. recreational com. Titusville City Coun., 1969-70. Mem. NEA, Ga. Edn. Assn., Orgn. DeKalb Educators, High Mus. Art, Pi Alpha Theta, Pi Gamma Mu. Home: 2390 G Lawrenceville Hwy Decatur GA 30033

HAYES, PATRICIA ANN, university president; b. Binghamton, N.Y., Jan. 14, 1944; d. Robert L. and Gertrude (Congdon) H. BA in English, Coll. of St. Rose, 1968; PhD in Philosophy, Georgetown U., 1974. Tchr. Cardinal McCloskey High Sch., Albany, N.Y., 1966-68; teaching asst. Georgetown U., Washington, 1968-71; instr. philosophy Coll. of St. Rose, Albany, 1973-75, instr. bus., spring 1981, adminstrv. intern to acad. v.p., 1973-74, dir. admissions, 1974-78, dir. adminstrn. and planning, 1978-81, v.p. adminstrn. and fin., treas., 1981-84; pres. St. Edward's U., Austin, Tex., 1984—; mem. adv. bd. NCNB Tex. Bd. dirs. United Way; mem. exec. bd. Capitol Area Coun. Boy Scouts Am.; mem. Seton Fin. Coun., Nat. Commn. on Migrant Edn. Mem. Nat. Assn. Ind. Colls. and Univs. (pub. rels. com.), Ind. Colls. and Univs. Tex., So. Assn. Colls. and Schs. (commn. on colls.), Tex. C. of C. (bd. dirs.). Roman Catholic. Office: St Edwards U 3001 S Congress Austin TX 78704

HAYES, SANDRA ECHOLS, city official; b. Buffalo, Nov. 4, 1944; d. Walter Montgomery and Vonceil Evelyn (Anderson) Echols; m. Lewyn M. Hayes, Jr., Nov. 29, 1969 (div. Apr. 1977); 1 child, Lewyn M. III. BS in Archtl. Engring., N.C. A&T State U., 1975; postgrad. in civil engring., N.C. State U., 1978. Regional planner Triangle J Coun. Govts., Research Triangle Park, N.C., 1970-74; transp. planner N.C. Dept. Transp., Raleigh, 1974-79; mgr. transp. East West Gateway Coun., St. Louis, 1980-83; mgr. capital budget N.J. Transit Corp., Newark, 1983-85; dir. data mgmt. budget N.Y.C. Transit Authority, Bklyn., 1985-87; dir. N.Y. Met. Transp. Coun., N.Y.C., 1987—. Mem. Bipartisan Women's Coalition, N.J., 1989. Mem. Transp. Rsch. Bd. (steering com. 1989—), Women's Transp. Seminar, Conf. Minority Transp. Ofcls. (N.J. bd. dirs. 1984-85), Nat. Forum Black Pub. Adminstrs. Democrat. Presbyterian. Office: NY Met Transp Coun One World Trade Ctr Ste 82E New York NY 10048

HAYES, THELMA ANN, state official; b. Cleve., Dec. 4, 1918; d. Eugene and Beatrice (Thomas) Roberts; m. James Andrew Hayes, Mar. 27, 1963; children by previous marriage—K. Machuma Bondele, Yvonne Parker, Eugene Kilgore, Fabienne Goins. Student Franklin U., 1952. Dep. clk. supr. Cleve. Mcpl. Ct., 1966-79; sec. Zion Chapel Bapt. Ch., 1966—; audit cons. State of Ohio, 1979—. Mem. NAACP, Nat. Council Negro Women. Democrat. Baptist. Avocation: bowling. Home: 694 E 120 Cleveland OH 44108 Office: Zion Chapel Bapt Ch 4234 Lee Rd Cleveland OH 44128

HAYKO, DIANNE, clinical nurse specialist; b. Omaha, Feb. 1, 1949; d. David Milton and Betty (Wallace) Carson; m. David George Hayko, Mar. 8, 1969; children: Douglas, Dawnielle. RN, Bishop Clarkson Sch. Nursing, Omaha, 1971; BSN, Bishop Clarkson Coll., 1984; MSN, Creighton U., Omaha, 1990. Staff RN Luth. Med. Ctr., Omaha, 1971-73; head nurse Luth. Med. Ctr., 1973-84; instr. Bishop Clarkson Coll., Omaha, 1984-86; coord. advanced placement Bishop Clarkson Coll., 1986-88; asst. dir. clin. progs. Bishop Clarkson Hosp., 1988-89; clin. nurse specialist St. Joseph Hosp., Omaha, 1989—; lectr. Coll. St. Mary, Omaha, 1989—; cons. Quality Assurance/Ednl. Resources, Omaha, 1988—. Editorial bd. Jour. Nursing Quality Assurance, 1989—. Recipient Nursing Excellence Award, Nebr. Nurses Assn., 1989. Mem. Am. Nurses Assn. (Nat. Disting. Svc. Registry), Midwest Nursing Rsch. Soc., AAUW, N. Am. Nursing Diagnosis Assn., Reg. Nursing Quality Assurance Orgn. (pres. 1989-90), Nebr. Nursing Diagnosis Interest Group (treas. 1989-90), Sigma Theta Tau. Home: 2517 N 68th St Omaha NE 68104

HAYLETT, MARGARET WENDY, television director, engineer; b. Ravenna, Ohio, Jan. 11, 1953; d. James Edward and Edith Marie (Campbell) H. Tech. cert., WIXY Sch. Broadcasting, Cleve., 1973; student, Empire State Coll., 1988—. FCC 1st class/gen. radio telephone lic. Engr. Sta. WJKW-TV, Cleve., 1973-81; engr. Sta. WOKR-TV, Rochester, N.Y., 1981-87, dir., 1987—. Home: 26 Harvest Rd Fairport NY 14450

HAYMAN, ROBYNE MARIE, strategic planning executive; b. St. Louis, Aug. 10, 1961; d. Robert Burns Edgar and Edna Jean (Burton) H. BA, Brown U., 1983; M Mgmt., Northwestern U., 1989. Saleswoman Harvard Coop. Soc., Cambridge, Mass., 1983-84; field rep. Marketeam Assocs., St. Louis, 1984; claim rep. Allstate Ins. Co., St. Louis, 1984-87, unit claim mgr., 1987; market rsch. analyst Merck Sharp & Dohme, West Point, Pa., 1988; dir. planning Accredited Premium Acceptance Corp. div. Mark Twain Bancshares, St. Louis, 1989—, bd. dirs., 1989-90. Interviewer nat. alumni schs. program Brown U., St. Louis, 1984-87. Mem. Brown U. Club (treas. 1984-87). Democrat. Home: 1371 Westmeade Dr Chesterfield MO 63017 Office: Mark Twain Bancshares APAC Div Chesterfield MO 63017

HAYMOND, PAULA J., psychologist, diagnostician; b. Warsaw, Ind., Sept. 29, 1949; d. George Milton and Phyllis (Freeman) H. BA, Butler U., 1971, MS, 1973; EdD, Ind. U., 1982. Lic. psychometrist, Ind.; lic. profl. counselor, Tex.; lic. psychologist, Tex. Sr. asst. psychology dept. Butler U., Indpls., 1970-71; behavioral clinician I psychology dept. Ind. Boys Sch., Plainfield, 1973-75, behavioral clinician II diagnostic unit, 1975-78; behavioral clinician II diagnostic unit Ind. Girls Sch., Indpls., 1978-80; human factors cons. Lund Cons. Inc., N.Y.C., 1981-82; adminstr. DePelchin Children Ctr./Bayou Pl., Houston, 1982-85; diagnostician Larry Ppollock PhD & Assoc., Houston, 1985-88; ptnr. Montrose Psychotherapy P.C., Houston, 1988—; biofeedback therapist, Teresa A. Atkinson RPT, Houston, 1989—; psychology supr. Larry Pollock PhD & Assoc., Houston, 1990—. Presenter S.W. Womens Conf. U. Tex. Dental Sch., Houston, 1990—. Mem. Am. Psychol. Assn., AACD, Delta Delta Delta, Kappa Kappa Kappa Phi. Office: Montrose Psychotherapy P C 716 Chelsea Pl Houston TX 77006

HAYNE, CAROLE HIXSON, psychologist; b. Grants Pass, Oreg., Nov. 11, 1942; d. Boyd George and Helen (Lenin) H.; children: Mary, Catherine, Julie. BS, U. Wash., Seattle, 1965; MA, U. N.D., 1980, PhD, 1983. Clin. psychologist Grant-Blackford Mental Health, Marion, Ind., 1983-85, VA, White City, Oreg., 1985—. Bd. dirs. Goodwill Industries, Jackson-Josephine County, Oreg., 1986—, Family Friends, Grants Pass, 1989—. Mem. Am. Psychol. Assn., AAUW. Office: Dept Vets Affairs White City OR 97503

HAYNE, HARRIET ANN, state legislator, rancher; b. Puget Island, Washington, Sept. 11, 1922; d. Albert Greger and Angeline Marie (Benjaminsen) Danielsen; m. Jack McVicar Hayne, Apr. 3, 1946; children: Mary Joan, John David, Alice Sue, Nancy Ann. Student, Healds Bus. Coll., San Francisco, 1941-42, Wash. State U., 1946-47. Rep. Mont. Legis. Assembly, 1979-80, 84-85;, 86-87, 88-89. Precinct, then state committeewoman, vice-chmn., active various campaigns Mont. Reps., Pondera County, 1964. Served as staff sgt. USMC, 1943-45. Mem. Am. Nat. Cattlewomen, Nat. Order Women Legislators, Am. Farm Bur., Am. Legion (aux.), Women Marines Assn., Nat. Fedn. Rep. Women. Lutheran.

HAYNER, JEANNETTE CLARE, state legislator; b. Jan. 22, 1919; m. Herman H. Hayner, 1942; children: Stephen A., James K., Judith A. BA, U. Oreg., 1940, JD, 1942. Atty. Bonneville Power Co., Portland, Oreg., 1943-47; mem. Wash. Ho. of Reps., 1972-76, Wash. Senate from Dist. 16, 1977—, minority leader, 1979-80, 83-86, majority leader, 1971-82, 87—; dist. chmn. White House Conf. on Children and Youth, 1970; dir. Standard Ins. Co. Portland, 1974—. Mem. Walla Walla Dist. 140 Sch. Bd., 1956-63, chmn. bd., 1959-61; mem. adv. bd. Walla Walla Youth and Family Svc. Assn., 1968-72; active YWCA, 1968-72; chmn. Walla Walla County Mental Health Bd., 1970-72; former mem. Wash. Coun. on Crime and Delinquency, Nuclear Energy Coun., Bonneville Power Regional Adv. Coun., State Wash. Organized Crime Intelligence Adv. Bd.; mem. Coun. State Govts. Governing Bd.; former asst. whip Republican Caucus. Mem. Wash. State Centennial Commn. Recipient Merit award Walla Walla C. of C., Pres's. award Pacific Luth. Univ., 1982, Pioneer award U. Oreg., 1988; named Legislator of Yr. Nat. Rep. Legislators' Assn., 1986, Chairman's award, 1989, Wash. Young Rep. Citizen of Yr., 1987, Legislator of Yr. Nat. Rep. Legislators Assn., 1989. Mem. Oreg. Bar Assn., Delta Kappa Gamma (hon.), Kappa Kappa Gamma. Lutheran. Office: State Senate State Capitol Olympia WA 98504 also: PO Box 454 Walla Walla WA 99362

HAYNES, GWENDOLYN MARY DUHON, educator; b. Lafayette, La., Feb. 24, 1963; d. Rose M. Duhon; m. Alton Raleigh Haynes, Apr. 25, 1987; 1 child, Grace Altonette. BA in Econs. and Fin., McNeese U., 1985; cert. in elem. edn., Houston Community Coll., 1985-86; MA in Guidance and Counse, Tex. So. U., 1987—. Cert. elem. tchr., Tex. Tchr., elem. youth enrichment program Tex. So. U., Houston, 1985-86, Houston Ind. Sch. Dist., 1985—. Tutor handicapped students spl. svcs. div. McNeese U., Lake Charles, La., 1984-85. Mem. Houston Assn. Black Psychologists. Democrat. Roman Catholic. Home: 3402 Southmore Blvd Houston TX 77004 Office: Turner Elem Sch 3200 Rosedale Houston TX 77004

HAYNES, JANICE BEHELER, banker; b. Salem, Va., Apr. 14, 1955; d. Robert Lacy Beheler and Frieda Mae (Underwood) Hall; m. John Barry Hall, June 9, 1972 (div. Dec. 1983) 1 child, Amy Michelle; m. Tracy Layne Haynes, Apr. 15, 1989. Grad. high sch., Shawsville, Va. Teller, bookkeeper Bank of Shawsville, 1973-75; office mgr. Hall's Construction Corp., Salem, 1975-77; bookkeeper First Nat. Bank, Christiansburg, Va., 1977-78; mgr. Old Dominion Savs. & Loan, Christiansburg, 1978-85, Jefferson Nat. Bank, Christiansburg, 1978-85; v.p. Blue Ridge Bank, Christiansburg, 1985—; co-owner Top Rail Restaurant and Country Lounge, Salem, Va., 1990—. Mem. Nat. Assn. Banking Women. Home: 191 Union Valley Rd Riner VA 24149 Office: Blue Ridge Bank 200 College St NW Christiansburg VA 24073

HAYNES, JEAN REED, lawyer; b. Miami, Fla., Apr. 6, 1949; d. Oswald Birnam and Arleen (Wiedman) Dow; m. William Rutherford Reed, Apr. 15, 1974 (div. Sept. 1981); m. Thomas Beranek Haynes, Aug. 7, 1982. AB with honors, Pembroke Coll., 1971; MA, Brown U., 1971; JD, U. Chgo., 1981. Bar: Ill. 1981, U.S. Dist. Ct. (no. dist.) Ill. 1983, U.S. Ct. Appeals (7th cir.) 1982. Tchr. grades 1-4 Abbie Tuller Sch., Providence, 1971-72; tchr./facilitator St. Mary's Acad., Riverside, R.I., 1972-74; tchr./head lower sch. St. Francis Sch., Goshen, Ky., 1974-78; law clk. U.S. Ct. Appeals (7th cir.), Chgo., 1981-83; assoc. Kirkland & Ellis, Chgo., 1983-87, ptnr., 1987—. Governing mem. Art Inst. Chgo., 1982-90, mem. aux. bd. 1986-90, membership com. aux. bd., 1987-90, v.p. for devel., 1988-90; vis. com. U. Chgo. Law Sch., 1990—. Mem. ABA (litigation sect., com. on affordable justice 1988—), Chgo. Bar Assn., Ill. Bar Assn. (life), Am. Judicature Soc. (life, membership policy com. 1988-89), Vertical Club, Law Club Chgo., International Club, Mid-Am. Club. Home: 30 Sutton Pl New York NY 10022-2365 Office: Kirkland & Ellis 200 E Randolph Dr Chicago IL 60601

HAYNES, MARCIA MARGARET, insurance agent; b. Bay City, Mich., June 28, 1931; d. Frederick O. and Margaret M. (Oakes) Rouse; m. N. Fred Haynes, July 20, 1957;children: Carol M. Krashen, David F. Haynes, Julie A. Haynes. BA, Denison U., Granville, Ohio, 1953. With advt.-sales dept. Birmingham (Mich.) Eccentric, 1953-55; tchr. Port Huron (Mich.) Area Schs., 1955-58; student tchr. coord. Mich. State U., Port Huron, Mich., 1967-70; insurance agent Northwestern Mut. Life Ins. Co., Port Huron, Mich., 1981—. Leader, Girl Scout U.S., Port Huron, 1956-57; treas. and bus. mgr., Port Huron Little Theater, Port Huron, 1959-1961; sec., v.p., and pres., Mus. of Arts and History, 1968-69, 74-80; sec., v.p. bd. dirs., Port Huron Hosp. Aux., 1960-70; trustee, Hist. Soc. of Mich., Ann Arbor, 1975-81; coordinator of preservation Round Island Lighthouse, Straits Mackinac, Mich., 1972-76; chmn. Horizons, Port Huron Bicentennial Com., Port Huron, 1976; active in Rep. State Bicentennial Com, Lansing, Mich. 1976; trustee, St. Clair County Community Coll., Port Huron, 1981—, vice chmn., 1985—; bd. dirs., Stuart House Mus., Mackinac Island, Mich., 1978, Internat. Symphony, Port Huron and Sarnia, Ont., Canada, 1983-86; sec., treas., and bd. dirs., Blue Water Area Tourism Bureau, Port Huron, 1985-87; adv. bd., Community Found. of St. Clair County, Port Huron, 1986-90. Mem. Nat. Life Underwriters, Port Huron Life Underwriters, Port Huron Estate Planning Coun. (pres. 1985-86), Mich. Mus. Assn. (bd. dirs. 1984-86), Rotary, Port Huron Golf Club. Episcopalian. Home: 813 Lakeview Ave Port Huron MI 48060

HAYNES, MARTHA PATRICIA, astronomer; b. Boston, Apr. 24, 1951; d. William Veech and Louise Mary (Healy) Haynes; BA, Wellesley Coll., 1973; M.A., Ind. U., 1975, Ph.D., 1978. Assoc. instr. Ind. U., 1974-76; jr. research assoc. Nat. Radio Astronomy Obs., Charlottesville, Va., 1976-78, asst. dir. Green Bank (W.Va.) Ops., 1981-83; instr. Piedmont Va. Community Coll., 1978; postdoctoral fellow Nat. Astronomy and Ionosphere Center, Arecibo Obs., P.R., 1978-80, staff research assoc., 1981; asst. prof. dept. astronomy Cornell U., Ithaca, N.Y., 1983-86, assoc. prof., 1986—; Co-recipient Henry Draper medal, NAS, 1989. Mem. Am. Astron. Soc., AAAS, Internat. Astron. Union, Internat. Union Radio Sci., N.Y. Acad. Scis., Sigma Xi. Office: Cornell U Space Scis Bldg Ithaca NY 14853*

HAYNES, MARTI (MARY ELIZABETH HAYNES), real estate agent; b. St. Louis, June 28, 1947; d. Elmer Ellsworth and Doris Elizabeth (Turner) H. BA in Polit. Sci., Roanoke Coll., 1968. Substitute tchr. city and county schs. Roanoke, Va., 1969-71; teller Colonial Am. Nat. Bank, Roanoke, 1971-73; realtor Peery Flora Realtors, Roanoke, 1973-75, Mastin & Assocs., Roanoke, 1975-78, Lugar Inc. Realtors, Roanoke, 1978-80, Mastin, Kirkland, Bolling, Realtors, Roanoke, 1980-88, Owens & Co., Roanoke, 1988—. Mem. Roanoke Valley Bd. Realtors (membership and advt. com. 1989, realtor's polit. action com. 1988, Silver Sales award 1986, Gold Sales award 1987, 88). Republican. Baptist. Home: 3807 Brandon Ave Ste 450 Roanoke VA 24018 Office: Owens & Co Realtors 4216 Brambleton Ave Roanoke VA 24018

HAYNES, MARY L., city clerk; b. Peoria Heights, Ill., July 17, 1942; d. Silas and Lydia Ann (Steiner) H.; m. Ronald Lee Haynes, June 11, 1961 (div. 1981); children: Eric Ronald, Kristine Ann. Student, U. Ill., 1986-87, No. Ill. U., 1988. Registered clk., 1988; cert. mcpl. clk., 1988. With Univ. Nat. Bank, Peoria, Ill., 1960-62; adminstrv. asst. Caterpillar Tractor Co., Peoria, Ill., 1962-70; pvt. practice Lincoln Heritage Life Ins., Peoria, Ill., 1978—; with City Clerk's Office, Peoria, Ill., 1980, deputy city clerk, 1981-85, city clerk and co-terminus town clerk, 1985—. Editor: Newsletter, The Elephant's Trunkline 1985—; Author: Book in Progress, Friendships and Feelings 1987. Fin. officer Peoria County I Search Unit Ill., 1985—; bd. sec., trustee Fireman's Pension Fund, Peoria, 1985—; mem. Peoria County Rep. Women, Ill., LWV. Mem. Cen. Ill. Mcpl. Clks. Orgn. (co-founder, pres. 1988—), Mcpl. Clks. Ill. (dist. dir. 1985-87, mem. elections and resolutions coms. 1987—, sec. 1988-89, v.p. 1989-90, 25th com. scholarship 1989-90), Ill. Women in Govt., LWV (pub. info. com. 111th Mcpl. League 1988), Internat. Inst. Mcpl. Clks. (profl. status com. 1988, edn. com. 1990—, Internat. 1990-91).

HAYNES, MARY RAPSTINE, county commissioner; b. Coral Gables, Fla., Jan. 16, 1945; d. B. Frank and Louise (Schulze) Rapstine; m. Christopher Alan Haynes, 1967; 1 child, Amy Christine. Student, Tex. Tech U., 1963-66; BA, U. Tex., 1967, MA, 1975. Rsch. asst. Inst. Biomed. Rsch., Austin, Tex., 1969; sci. tchr. Austin Pub. Schs., 1969-70, St. Clement's Sch., El Paso, Tex., 1971-74; teaching asst., dean edn. U. Tex., Austin, 1975; tchr., insvc. leader El Paso Pub. Schs., 1976-78; county chmn. Dem. Party, El Paso, 1978-80; farm mgr. Pecan Farm Joint Venture, El Paso, 1980-84; county commr. County of El Paso, 1983-89. Contbr. articles to profl. publs.; editor Individualized Science, 1972-74. Vice chmn. steering com. El Paso Urban Transp. Study, 1983-89; bd. dirs. Tex. Regional Rev. Com., Tex. Community Devel. Program, Tex. Com. of 100 on Merit Selection of Judges; del., chmn. fundraising County Dem. Party, 1972-74, chmn., El Paso, 1978-79; sec. El Paso Educator Polit. Action Com., 1978-80; co-chmn. Gov. Task Force for El Paso, 1978-80; bd. dirs. Keep El Paso Beautiful, 1984-89. Recipient Faceless Children's award Child Welfard Bd.; named Outstanding Elem. Sci. Tchr. award Tex. Edn. Agy., Women of Yr. in Politics award El Paso Women's Polit. Caucus. Mem. West Tex. County Judges and Commrs. Assn. (bd. dirs.), Jr. League (advisor 1987-88). Roman Catholic. Home: 221 Silverwood El Paso TX 79922

HAYNES, S. JANICE, corporate secretary; b. Peoria, Ill., Sept. 22, 1940; d. Edward Elsworth and Maxine Irene (Johns) Blue; children: Debra Jean, Terry Allen, Richard Scott. Cert. notary pub., Hawaii, computer tng., workers compensation. Corp. sec. Railings, Inc., Aiea, Hawaii; personnel mgr. Daiai, Inc., Aiea, Hawaii; asst. mgr. Shorty's Restaurant, Wichita, Kans., 11th Frame, Wichita. Bd. dirs. publicity membership, 1st v.p. Linwood Elem. Sch. PTA, Wichita, 1967-70, pres., 1970-72; troop leader Girl Scouts U.S.A., Wichita, 1968-73, troop organizer, 1969-73. Mem. NAFE, Nat. Assn. Women in Constrn., Am. Mgmt. Assn., Am. Soc. Notaries. Republican. Home: PO Box 30847 Honolulu HI 96820 Office: PO Box 818 Aiea HI 96701

HAYNES, SUSAN HENLEIN, hospital administrator, nurse; b. Louisville, Apr. 15, 1962; d. Carl Arthur and Patsy Jane (Cheatham) Henlein; m. Robert William Haynes, May 30, 1987. BSN, DePauw U., 1985; MHA, Duke U., 1987. Nurse Ind. U. Hosp., Indpls., 1984-85, Durham (N.C.) Care Ctr., 1985-86; adminstrv. resident Vanderbilt U. Hosp., Nashville, 1987-88, asst. adminstr., 1988—. Rep. United Way, Nashville, 1987—. Named Outstanding Young Careerist, Davidson County, Nashville. Mem. Am. Coll. Healthcare Execs., Middle Tenn. Healthcar Execs. Assn., Sigma Theta Tau, Jr. C. of C. Republican. Presbyterian. Home: 5230 Williamsburg Rd Brentwood TN 37027 Office: Vanderbilt U Hosp 1161 21s Ave S Nashville TN 37232

HAYNES-JONES, PATRICIA, librarian; b. N.Y.C., Sept. 19, 1949; d. Clifford Nathaniel and Martha Carsue (Ford) Haynes; m. Rodney S. Haynes-Jones. BA, Bernard M. Baruch Coll., 1981; MLS, Columbia U., 1984. With Carlysle & Jacquelyn, N.Y.C., 1967-68; files asst. Carnegie Corp N.Y., N.Y.C., 1969-77, head of files, 1977-78, adminstrv. asst., 1978-84, supr. files and archives, 1985-88, records mgr., 1988—. Former mem. Bronx Teen Pregnancy Network,Child Study Children's Book Com.; recording sec.

N.Y. Coalition of 100 Black Women. Mem. NAFE, Consortium of Found. Librs. (chmn. 1981-87), INFORMED (treas. 1983-84, sec. 1984-85, chmn. 1985-86), ALA, N.Y. State Libr. Assn., Spl. Libr. Assn., Assn. Records Mgrs. and Adminstrs., Soc. Am. Archivists. Home: 2954 Marion Ave Bronx NY 10458 Office: Carnegie Corp NY 437 Madison Ave New York NY 10022

HAYNOR, PATRICIA MANZI, nurse, hospital administrator; children: Kelly Christine, Craig. Diploma in nursing, Grasslands Hosp., Valhalla, N.Y.; BS in Nursing, Fairleigh Dickinsn U., 1967; MSN in Nursiing Adminstrn., U. Pa., 1969; DNSc, Widener U., 1989. RN, Pa., N.J., N.Y. Asst. dir. surg. nursing Thomas Jefferson U. Hosp., Phila., 1972-74; asst. dir. nursing care depts. Our Lady of Lourdes Hosp., Camden, N.J., 1974-76; assoc. dir. nursing West Jersey Hosp., Camden, 1976-79; dir. nursing West Jersey Health System, Camden, 1979-81, corp. dir. nursing, 1981-82; v.p. nursing Crozer-Chester (Pa.) Med. Ctr., 1982-85; coord. nursing adminstrn. program, asst. prof. Widener U., Chester, 1985-87; v.p. for nursing St. Francis Med. Ctr., Trenton, N.J., 1987—; cons. Nurse Assocs., Haddonfield, N.J., 1985—; clin. assoc. Villanova U. Sch. Nursing, Phila.; guest lectr. nursing svc. adminstrn. U. Pa. Sch. Nursing; preceptor grad. students in nursing svc. adminstr. Wiedener U., Villanova U., U. Del., 1982-85; speaker in field; mem. nursing adv. com. Delaware Valley Hosp. Coun., Inc., 1983-85; reviewer J.B. Lippincott Co. Contbr. articles to profl. publs. Bd. mgrs., chmn. fund raising com. Camden County unit Am. Cancer Soc.; bd. dirs., mem. fin. com. Delaware County Home Health Svcs.; bd. dirs., mem. personnel com. Family Planning Coun. Southeastern Pa. Mem. Am. Orgn. Nurse Execs., Acad. for Nursing Svc. Adminstrs. (candidate), Nat. League for Nursing, N.J. Soc. Nursing Svc. Adminstrs., Mgmt. Inst., Southeastern Pa. League for Nursing, Conf. Group for Nursing Svc. and Nursing Edn. Adminstrs., Nat. Forum for Adminstrs. Nursing Svc., AAUP, Mid-Atlantic Regional Nursing Assn. (pres. 1988). Home: 201 9th Ave Haddon Heights NJ 08035 Office: Univ of Delaware Coll of Nursing Newark DE 19713

HAYS, DIANA JOYCE WATKINS, consumer products company executive; b. Riverside, Calif., Aug. 29, 1945; d. Donald Richard and Evelyn Christine (Kolvoord) Watkins; m. Gerald N. Hays, Jan 30, 1964 (div. Jan. 1970), 1 child, Tad Damon. BA, U. Minn., 1975, MBA, 1982. Dir. environ./phys. sci. Sci. Mus. Minn., St. Paul, 1972-76; dir. mktg. rsch. No. Natural Gas Co., Omaha, 1977-78; mktg. asst., asst. product mgr. Gen. Mills, Inc., Mpls., 1978-81; product mgr. ortho pharms. Consumer Products div. Johnson & Johnson, Raritan, N.J., 1981-82, product dir. home diagnostics, 1982-86; mktg. dir. new market devel. Consumer Products div. Becton Dickinson & Co., Franklin Lakes, N.J., 1986-90; dir. home diagnostics worldwide program Becton Dickinson Advanced Diagnostics Div. Becton Dickinson & Co., Balt., 1990—; chmn. energy exhibit com. Assn. Sci.-Tech. Ctrs., Washington, 1974-75. Producer Ecologenie, 1975. Recipient Tribute to Women and Industry award YWCA, 1989. Mem. Am. Mktg. Assn., NAFE, Twin Mgmt. Forum (bd. dirs.), Am. Assn. of Health Svcs. Mktg., Beta Gamma Sigma (life). Republican. Roman Catholic. Office: Becton Dickinson & Co Advanced Diagnostic Div 225 International Circle Cockeryville MD 21030

HAYS, HOLLY MARY, editor, freelance photojournalist; b. L.A., Nov. 28, 1952; d. Herschel Martin and Mary Catherine (Miller) H. Cert. art history, Fla. State U., 1971; cert. computer sci., Fla. Atlantic U., 1979; BS in Journalism, U. Fla., 1974. Layout editor Ind. Fla. Alligator, Gainesville, 1974; reporter Gainesville Sun, 1974; computer specialist Gilbert Law Printing, Gardena, Calif., 1975; copy editor Hartford (Conn.) Courant, 1976-78; mech. artist CRC Press, Inc., Boca Raton, Fla., 1980-85; asst. editor Fla. Living mag., Ga. Living mag., Gainesville, 1986—; writer Womans World Mag., Englewood, N.J., 1987-89; writer, photographer Fla. Sportsman Mag., Miami, 1988—. Vol. Marjorie K. Rawlings State Hist. Site, Cross Creek, Fla., 1987—. Mem. Outdoor Writers Am. Republican. Home: PO Box 96 Lochloosa FL 32662 Office: North Florida Pub 102 NE 10th Ave Ste 1 Gainesville FL 32601

HAYS, MARILYN PATRICIA, lawyer, rancher, real estate executive; b. Yarrow, Mo., Sept. 19, 1935; d. John Dewey and Ruth (McKim) H.; m. Harold Clifton Ledbetter, Dec. 13, 1953 (div. 1972); children: Latricia Lyn, Lisa Ledbetter Cerio, David Clifton, Laura Lizanne; Harold Clifton, Jr.; m. Dean Leon Fortney, July 21, 1978. BS, N.E. Mo. State U., 1958; broker cert. U. Fla., 1976; MA, U. Mo., 1983; JD, Washburn U., 1987. Lic. real estate broker, Mo., Kans., Fla. Grad. Realtors Inst. Fashion coord. Ashells, Regina's Co., Kirksville, Mo., 1951-54; instr. pub. schs., Crocker, Novinger, Kirksville and University City, Mo., 1954-61; real estate salesstaff Goldman's Assocs., Daytona Beach, Fla., 1975-76; real estate broker Kellogg Century 21, Daytona Beach, 1976-78; pres. M.P. Hays Co., Olathe, Kans., 1978-82, Bucyrus, Kans., 1982—; cons. Goldman, Kellogg, Daytona Beach, 1975-78. Contbr. articles on real estate edn. to profl. jours. Pres. Fla. Osteopathic Med. Assn. Aux., Dist. IV, 1964-65, 73-74, pres.-elect, 1967-68; major chmn. Assn. of Jr. League, Daytona Beach, 1968-69, 72-73; Pan Hellenic del., 1972-78; adviser Ormond Beach Hosp. Guild, Fla., 1972-74; tchr. CCD Holy Rosary Cath. Ch., Bucyrus, 1987-88; mem. Altar Soc. Scholar, Mo. Coun. PTAs, 1953, KC, 1954; recipient Outstanding Sales Achievement award Kellogg Century 21, 1977. Mem. ABA, AAUW, Kans. Bar Assn., Miami County Bd. Realtors, Johnson County Bd. Realtors, Nat. Assn. Realtors, Kans. Assn. Realtors, Kans. Farm Bur., Women's Legal Forum, Fla. Osteo. Med. Assn. (pres.-elect 1967-68, aux., pres. dist. IV 1964-65, 73-74), Am. Quarterhorse Assn., Alpha Sigma Alpha, Phi Delta Phi. Republican. Clubs: Ormond Beach Woman's, Oceanside Country. Avocations: photography, cooking, horseback riding, antiquing. Office: 223d St and State Line Rd Rte 1 Box 161 Bucyrus KS 66013

HAYS, MARY KATHERINE JACKSON (MRS. DONALD OSBORNE HAYS), civic worker; b. Flora, Miss.; d. Rufus Lafayette and Ada (Collum) Jackson; student U. Miss., 1925-26, Millsaps Coll., 1926-27, 43-44; grad. Clark Bus. Sch., 1934; student Columbia U., 1935, Strayer Bus. Coll., 1951; m. Halbert Puffer Oliver, Aug. 9, 1927 (dec. 1934); m. 2d, Donald Osborne Hays, Aug. 30, 1937. Sec. to pres. McCullough Box and Crate Co., Pharr, Tex., 1934-36; sec. to field supr. Miss. Unemployment Compensatio Commn., 1936-37; rep. Homes of Tomorrow, 1940 N.Y. World's Fair; sec. to head interior design Lord & Taylor, N.Y.C., 1940; sales dept. Knabe Piano Co., N.Y.C., 1941-43. Active, Little Theatre, Wilkes Barre, Pa., 1937-39; charter mem. and incorporator Conf. State Socs., Washington, 1952; vol. worker Am. Cancer Soc., Washington, 1957; mem. Center City Residents Assn., Phila., 1956; mem. women's com. Nat. Symphony Assn., vol. worker USO, 1945-48, symphony sustaining com. drives, 1957; mem. women's com. Corcoran Gallery Art, Washington, 1957-62; mem. Pierce-Warwick Adoption Assn. of Washington Home for Foundlings; vol. Washington Heart Assn., 1959-66; mem. Nat. Capital Area chpt. United Ch. Women, 1957-72; mem. D.C. Episcopal Home for Children, 1961-86, D.C. Salvation Army Aux., 1962—. Mem. Miss. State Soc. D.C. (sec. 1950-53), Miss. Women's Club D.C., DAR (vice regent chpt. 1970-72, regent chpt. 1972-74, vice chmn. D.C. com. celebration Washington's birthday 1972-76, state librarian 1974-76), chpt. chmn. DAR Service for Vet. Patients Com., 1986-88, UDC (chpt. historian 1982-84, 86—, chaplain 1984-86), Johnstone Clan Am. (exec. council 1976-81), First Families of Miss. Episcopalian. Club: The Washington. Home: 4000 Massachusetts Ave NW Washington DC 20016

HAYS, TREVA NADEJA, small business owner; b. Knoxville, Iowa, Nov. 29, 1937; d. Cleveland Douglas and Zella Mae (Maddy) Simmons; m. Ronald Jean Hays, Feb. 14, 1960; children: Douglas, Ronalea, Yon. Grad. high sch., Attica, Iowa. Clk. Banker's Life Ins. Co. (name now The Principal), Des Moines, 1956-69; part owner R & T Svcs., Marshalltown, Iowa, 1974—, Ron's Auto, Marshalltown, 1984—. Mem. Ladies Aux. Shrine Hosp., Order Eastern Star. Republican. Lutheran. Home: 812 W Nevada St Marshalltown IA 50158 Office: Rons Auto 411 1/2 S 9th St Marshalltown IA 50158

HAYTER, KAREN JOHNSON, television producer; b. Dallas, Dec. 13, 1943; d. Chreston Julius (dec.) and Mary Nell (Biggerstaff) Johnson; m. Lonnie. BA, Baylor U., 1966; postgrad., North Tex. State U., 1968; MA, Baylor U., 1975, D of Edn., 1983. Lic. prof. counseling;. Teaching supr. Baylor Univ., Waco, Tex., 1977-82; clin. psychologist Tex. Dept. Correctional, Gatesville, 1982-84; lic. counselor Cons. & Counseling, Ft. Worth, 1984-86; producer, host cope COPE Acts Cable TV, Ft. Worth, 1986--. Author: How to Cope with Grief, 1986; contbr. articles to mags. Bd. dirs. Big Bros./Big Sisters, Ft. Worth; vol. March of Dimes,. Mem. Am. Psychol. Assn., Tex. Psychol. Assn., Tex. Assn. Counseling and. Baptist. Home: 2619 River Oaks Arlington TX 76006 Office: RTVC Acts 6350 W Freeway Fort Worth TX 76150

HAYWARD, MARGARET MCGEE, payroll accountant; b. Columbus, Miss., Dec. 14, 1959; d. Louis Calvin and Betty Joyce (Wallace) McGee; m. Michael Edward Hayward, May 16, 1981. BS, Miss. U. for Women, 1982, Miss. U. for Women, 1988. Payroll acct. Miss. U. for Women, Columbus, 1988—. Mem. AAUW (newsletter editor), Am. Soc. Women Accts., Office Personnel Assn. (parliamentarian), Wesley Found. (bd. dirs.), Miss. U. for Women Alumni Assn. Republican. Methodist. Office: Miss Univ for Women W Box 1604 Columbus MS 39701

HAYWARD, SALLY JANE, office designer, artist, calligrapher; b. Santa Monica, Calif., June 21, 1960; d. John Sidney and June Daphne (Downard) H. Grad. high schs., Woodland Hills, Calif. With various temp. cos. Woodland Hills, 1978-79; clk. Litton Industries, Canoga Park, Calif., 1979-80; prumatic technician The Prudential, Woodland Hills, 1980-82, graphic artist, 1982-84, office designer, 1984-86, sr. office designer, 1986—. Author, editor, designer newsletter The Rover, 1980-84; exhibited in group shows, 1978—. Episcopalian. Home: 6216 Ellenview Ave West Hills CA 91307-2711 Office: The Prudential 5800 Canoga Ave Woodland Hills CA 91367

HAYWARD, TERESA CALCAGNO, educator; b. N.Y.C., Jan. 28, 1907; d. Vito and Rosalie (Amato) Calcagno; m. Peter Hayward, Feb. 6, 1932; children: Nancy, Peter. BA, Hunter Coll., 1929; MA, Columbia U., 1931. Tchr. romance langs. Jr. High Sch. 164, N.Y.C., 1936-57, Jr. High Sch. 141, Riverdale, N.Y., 1957-71; tchr. English to Japanese women Nichibei Fujinkai, Riverdale, 1972—, chmn. Riverdale chpt., 1976-90. Bd. dirs. Riverdale chpt. UN Assn., 1973-90; mem. Hunger and Social Outreach com. Christ Ch., Riverdale. Democrat. Episcopalian. Avocations: concerts, piano, art lectures, travel.

HAYWOOD, ANNE MOWBRAY, pediatrics, virology, and biochemistry educator; b. Balt., Feb. 5, 1935; d. Richard Mansfield and Margaret (Mowbray) H. BA in Chemistry, Bryn Mawr Coll., 1955; MD, Harvard U., 1959. Cert. Am. Bd. Pediatrics. Intern pediatrics U. Calif. Med. Ctr., San Francisco, 1959-60; postdoctoral fellow biochemistry dept. Columbia U., N.Y.C., 1961-62; postdoctoral fellow div. biology Calif. Inst. Tech., Pasadena, 1960-61, 62-64; asst. prof. microbiology, microbiology dept. Northwestern U. Med. Sch., Chgo., 1964-66, Yale U. Med. Sch., New Haven, 1966-73; resident pediatrics U. Wash., Seattle, 1974-75, pediatric infectious disease fellow, 1975-76; pediatric infectious disease fellow Vanderbilt U., Nashville, 1976-77; assoc. prof. pediatrics and microbiology U. Rochester (N.Y.), 1977-85, assoc. prof. pediatrics, microbiology, medicine, 1985—; vis. asst. prof. Rockefeller U., N.Y.C., 1971-72; vis. scientist biophysics unit Agrl. Rsch. Coun., Cambridge, Eng., 1972-74, Inst. for Immunology and Virology, U. Zürich (Switzerland), 1987; vis. assoc. prof. dept. zoology U. Calif., Davis, 1986. Contbr. articles to profl. jours.; co-author: Infections in Children, 1982, Liposome Letters, 1983, Practice of Pediatrics, 1987, Molecular Mechanisms of Membrane Fusion, 1988, Practice of Pediatrics, 1977. Fogarty Internat. Ctr. Sr. fellow NIH, 1987, European Molecular Biology Orgn. fellow, 1973-74, NIH Spl. fellow, 1971-73, Am. Cancer Soc. Postdoctoral fellow, 1960-62; Harvard Med. Sch. scholar, 1955-59, Harriet Judd Sartain scholar, 1955-59, N.Y. Alumnae scholar Bryn Mawr Coll., 1951-55. Mem. Biophys. Soc., Am. Soc. for Biol. Chemists, Infectious Diseases Soc. Am. Democrat. Office: U Rochester Med Ctr PO Box 777 Rochester NY 14642

HAYWOOD, B(ETTY) J(EAN), anesthesiologist; b. Boston, June 1, 1942; d. Oliver Garfield and Helen Elizabeth (Salisbury) H.; m. Lynn Brandt Moon, Aug. 29, 1969 (div. Aug. 1986); children: Kim Lynn, Kris Lee, Kelly, Kasy R. BSc, Tufts U., 1964; MD, U. Colo., 1968. Intern Wilford Hall AFB, San Antonio, Tex., 1968-69; resident in pediatrics U. Ariz., Tucson, 1971-72, resident in anesthesiology, 1972-74; dir. Anesthesia dept. Pima City Hosp., Tucson, 1975-76; staff anesthesiologist South Community Hosp., Okla. City, 1977—; staff anesthesiologist Moore (Okla.) Mclp. Hosp., 1981-90, chief of anesthesia, 1990—; staff anesthesiologist St. Anthony Hosp., Okla. City, 1982—. Bd. dirs. N.Am. South Devin Assn., Lynnville, Iowa, 1978-86. Capt. USAF, 1968-69. Mem. AMA, World South Devin Assn. (U.S. rep., 1985—), Tufts U. Alumni Assn. (rep.), Chi Omega (treas. 1963-64). Republican. Presbyterian. Home: 1619 Westminister Pl Oklahoma City OK 73120

HAZARD, MERLE PABST, nurse, insurance company specialist; b. Syracuse, N.Y., Apr. 15, 1935; d. Merle William and Eunice Irene (Mosier) Pabst; m. Sherrill John Hazard, Jr., Sept. 3, 1955; children: Sherrill John III, Stephen Joel. RN, Gen. Hosp. Syracuse, 1955; BS in Psychology, Univ. of State of N.Y., Albany, 1979. Coord. geriatric health maintenance, discharge planning Vis. Nurse Assn., Pittsfield, Mass., 1977-82; mktg. rep. Vis. Nurse Assn. Met. Atlanta, 1984-86; community health supr. Peoria (Ill.) City-County Health Dept., 1986-87; dir. home care and hospice Vis. Nurse Assn., Neenah-Menasha, Wis., 1987-88; sales assoc. Century 21 Rollie Winter, Appleton, Wis., 1989; managed care supr. Employers' Health Ins. Co., Green Bay, Wis., 1989—. Contbr. articles to profl. jours. Organizer Newcomers Club, Suffield, Conn., 1965; committeewoman Rep. Town Com., Suffield, 1967; active various civic and religious orgns. Block grantee, Pittsfield, 1979-81. Mem. AAUW, Nat. League Am. Penwomen, PEO. Home: 1017 Woodcrest Dr Appleton WI 54915

HAZARD, ROBERTA LOUISE, naval officer; b. Boston, Nov. 8, 1934; d. Robert Louis and Louise Marie (Bourget) H. BS, Boston Coll., 1956, MA, 1957. Commd. ensign USN, advanced through grades to rear adm., 1988; adminstrv. asst. to chief naval ops. USN, Washington, 1970-74, dir. women's career policy & guidance, 1978-80; comdg. officer Naval Tech. Tng. Command USN, San Francisco, 1980-82; comdg. officer Naval Tng. Sta. USN, San Diego, 1983-85; comdr. Gt. Lakes Naval Tng. Ctr. USN, North Chicago, Ill., 1985-87; dir. manpower & pers. for Joint Chiefs Staff USN, Washington, 1987-89, dir. Navy personal readiness and community support, 1989—; First USN female officer selected to rear admiral (upper half). Bd. dirs. Armed Forces YMCA, Springfield, Va., 1988—; trustee Boston Coll., 1984—. Decorated Def. D.S.M.; recipient Alumni Disting. Pub. Svc. award Boston Coll., 1983, Calif. Women in Govt. award, 1984, Disting. Svc. award Lake County (Ill.) YWCA, 1986, John Paul Jones Disting. Leadership award Navy League, 1987, J.B. Hancock Leadership award, 1987. Mem. Alpha Omega. Republican. Roman Catholic. Office: Dir Navy Personal Readiness and Community Support Navy Annex Washington DC 20350

HAZARIAN, TINA LOLA REBECCA, art gallery owner; b. N.Y.C.; d. Haroutune Parsegh and Marguerite (Abroyan) H. Degree in Theater, Sch. Performing Arts, N.Y.C., Carnegie-Mellon U. Prodn. editor Hair Do and Beauty mag., N.Y.C., 1970-71; editor Dell Purse Books, N.Y.C., 1971-72; copy and prodn. editor textbooks McGraw-Hill Pubs., N.Y.C., 1972-73; free lance editor Macmillan, Inc., Dell Pub. Co. and McGraw-Hill Pubs., N.Y.C., 1973-74; svc. rep. Social Security Adminstrn., N.Y.C., 1974-75; med. records dir. Interboro Gen. Hosp., N.Y.C., 1975-77; mgr. East-West Natural Foods Restaurant, Woodstock, N.Y., 1978; program creator, counselor for immigrants Am. Gen. Benevolent Union, N.Y.C., 1978-79; assoc. curator Armenian Mus., N.Y.C., 1979-81; coord. Armenian earthquake relief med. vol. office Columbia Presbyn. Hosp., N.Y.C., 1989; owner, mgr. Hazarian Collection (Armenian Christian art), 1981—. Various starring roles off-off Broadway prodns., N.Y.C., 1975—; contbr. articles to profl. jours. Mem. Internat. Women's Writing Guild, Greenpeace, Amnesty Internat. Democrat. Armenian Orthodox. Office: care Taraian 153 Seaman Ave New York NY 10034

HAZEL, DIANE HUNTER, account executive; b. N.Y.C., Jan. 28, 1949; d. Samuel and Aileen (Samuels) Hunter; m. Frederick Hazel, Oct. 14, 1973; children: F. Douglas II, Courtney C. BBA, Adelphi U., 1969. Account exec. United Airlines, Newark Internat. Airport, N.J.; computer programmer Texaco, Inc., N.Y.C. Mem. Black Profl. Orgn. (pres. N.Y. chpt. 1983-84, v.p. nat. orgn. 1990—). Home: Six S Delaware Dr Central Nyack NY 10960

HAZELRIG, JANE B., biomathematics educator, researcher; b. Chattanooga, May 29, 1937; d. William Russell and Elizabeth Cecil (Marquet) Brownlee; m. Cooper Green Hazelrig, Aug. 31, 1958; children: William Russell, Susan Jane. BS, U. Ala.-Tuscaloosa, 1958; MS, U. Minn., 1965; PhD, U. Ala., Birmingham, 1976. Assoc. physicist, So. Research Inst., Birmingham, Ala., 1958-62; math. instr. U. Ala., Birmingham, 1959-62, instr. biomath., 1967-77, asst. prof., 1977-80, assoc. prof., 1980-82, assoc. prof. biostats. and biomath., 1982—; biophysics technician Mayo Clinic, Rochester, Minn., 1962-67; mem. biotech. resources rev. com. Div. Research Resources, Washington, 1985-87. Contbr. articles to sci. publs. Site visitor NIH. Mem. AAAS, Soc. for Math. Biology (bd. dirs. 1980-84), Soc. Indsl. and Applied Math., Mortar Bd., Sigma Xi, Phi Beta Kappa, Pi Mu Epsilon, Sigma Pi Sigma. Avocation: music. Office: U Ala Dept Biostats and Biomath University Sta Birmingham AL 35294

HAZELTINE, JOYCE, state official; b. Pierre, S.D.; m. Dave Hazeltine; children: Derek, Tara, Kirk. Student, Huron (S.D.) Coll., No. State Coll., Aberdeen, S.D., Black Hills State Coll., Spearfish, S.D. Former asst. chief clk. S.D. Ho. of Reps.; former sec. S.D. State Senate; sec. of state State of S.D., Pierre, 1987—. Adminstrv. asst. Pres. Ford Campaign, S.D.; Rep. com. chmn. Hughes County, S.D. Office: Sec of State's Office 500 E Capitol Pierre SD 57501

HAZELTON, NANCY TOLER, banker; b. Long Beach, Calif., July 11, 1949; d. Albert Eugene and Mary Olive (Fager) Toler; m. Charles Y. Hazelton, Mar. 1, 1969; children—Patricia, Christopher. Student Memphis State U., 1967-69, Sullivan Jr. Coll., 1983-84; diploma Inst. Fin. Edn., Chgo., 1977, cert., 1985. Mgmt. trainee Aristar, Inc., Memphis, 1968-76; loan officer Home Fed., Memphis, 1976-79; loan originator Future Fed. Savs. Bank, Louisville, 1979-85, v.p., dir. residential lending/secondary mktg., 1985—. Adult edn. guest speaker Jefferson Community Coll., Louisville, 1984; active Jeffersontown Booster Club, Ky. Mem. Women's Council Realtors, Mortgage Bankers Assn., Louisville Bd. Realtors (assoc.), Homebuilders Assn. Louisville (assoc.), Ky. Assn. Profl. Mortgage Women (program chmn. 1985-86), Mortgage Bankers Assn. Louisville (sec. 1988, v.p. 1989). Republican. Roman Catholic. Home: 3603 Pirogue Rd Jeffersontown KY 40299

HAZEN, BARBARA SHOOK, freelance writer; b. Dayton, Ohio, Feb. 4, 1930; d. Charles Harmon and Elizabeth Ann (Foster) Shook; m. Brackett Hazen (div. 1967); 1 child, Brackett Jr. BA, Smith Coll., 1951; MA, Columbia U., 1952. Editor Ladies' Home Jour., N.Y.C., 1952-57, Western Pub., N.Y.C., 1957-60; freelance writer N.Y.C., 1960—; writer on Andy and the Petbots and Kingdom Chums, ABC-TV, 1984-87; cons., writer CBS Children's Records, 1968-74; cons. Sesame St. mag., 1973-75;. Author over 40 children's books including: The Gorilla Did It, Tight Times, The Knight Who Was Afraid of the Dark and eight adult books. Mem. Am. Soc. Journalism and Authors, Authors League of Am., Authors Guild, Bank St. Writers Lab., Drama League of N.Y., Coffee House Club. Republican. Presbyterian. Home and Office: 108 E 82d St New York NY 10028

HAZLETT, D. MARLENE, retail store owner; b. Dublin, Ga., Dec. 6, 1948; d. Ralph Lewis and Dorothy Blanche (Perkins) H. BA in English, U. Ga., 1970. Cert. Ga. Bd. Realtors. Owner Goldseekers Jewelers, Dublin; local coun. coord. PEACH/JOBS Laurens County Dept. Family and Children Svcs., Dublin; eligibility specialist II Laurens County Dept. Family and Children Svc., Dublin; pers. mgr. PL Garment Finishers, Dublin; mgr. Jiffy's, Athens, Ga.; personnel asst. Rich-Sea Pak Corp., St. Simons Island, Ga.; claims examiner Dept. of Labor State of Ga. Field rep. Am. Cancer Soc., nominating com. Mem. NAFE, AAUW, Women in Bus. (bd. dirs.), Dublin Ladies' Golf Assn., Young Coun. Realtors, Laurens 2000 Com., Dublin/Laurens C. of C., Delta Gamma Alumnae Assn. Home: PO Box 2096 Dublin GA 31040 Office: PO Box 68 Dublin GA 31040

HAZLITT, JOAN QUITER, art dealer; b. Albion, Nebr., Sept. 20, 1936; d. Anthony Paul and Evelyn Mary (Husemann) Quiter; m. Gordon J. Hazlitt, July 13, 1968; children: Michael, Christopher. Student, Chouinard Art Inst., 1959-60, UCLA, 1960-63. Gallery asst. Frank Perls Art Dealer, Beverly Hills, Calif., 1960-75; pvt. art dealer Pasadena, Calif., 1975—; exhbn. asst. Matisse Retrospective, UCLA, 1966, Picasso Retrospective, L.A. County Mus., 1966-67. Mem. L.A. County Mus., Mus. Contemporary Art L.A.

HAZZARD, SHIRLEY, author; b. Sydney, Australia, Jan. 30, 1931; d. Reginald and Catherine (Stein) H.; m. Francis Steegmuller, Dec. 22, 1963. Ed., Queenwood Sch., Sydney, to 1946. With Combined Services Intelligence, Hong Kong, 1947-48, U.K. High Commr.'s Office, Wellington, N.Z., 1949-51, UN (Gen. Service Category), N.Y.C., 1952-62; Boyer lectr., Australia, 1984, 88. Author: Cliffs of Fall and Other Stories, 1963; novel The Evening of the Holiday, 1966; fiction People in Glass Houses, 1967; novel The Bay of Noon, 1970; History Defeat of an Ideal: A Study of the Self-Destruction of the United Nations, 1973; novel The Transit of Venus, 1980, History Countenance of Truth, 1990; contbr. short stories to New Yorker mag. Trustee N.Y. Soc. Library. Recipient 1st prize O. Henry Short Story awards, 1976, Lit. award Nat. Inst. Arts and Letters, 1966; Guggenheim fellow, 1974; recipient Nat. Book Critics Circle award for Fiction, 1981. Mem. Nat. Inst. Arts and Letters. Address: 200 E 66th St New York NY 10021

HEACOCK, GRACE ANNE, educator; b. Elgin, Tex., Jan. 3, 1943; d. James Frank and Emily Rebecca (Davis) Potts Johnston; m. James Irvin Badgett (div. 1977); children: Kay Lynne, Jamie Lee; m. Richard Knowles Heacock Jr., May 21, 1977. BS, Tex. Tech U., 1965, MS, 1966; cert. in bilingual and early childhood edn., U. Houston, 1975, 79; postgrad. in elem. edn., U. Alaska, 1983. Cert. vocat. and elem. educator, Tex., Alaska. Tchr. nutrition and early childhood Meth. Hosp. Sch. Nursing, Lubbock, Tex., 1965-66; instr. home econs. Wayland Bapt. Coll., Plainview, Tex., 1966-67; elem. tchr. Port Lavaca (Tex.) Ind. Sch. Dist., 1967-68; tchr. ABC Pvt. Kindergarten, Port Lavaca, 1969-70; vocat. tchr. Downtown Skill Learning Ctr., Pitts. Pub. Schs., 1973-74; early childhood tchr. Port Lavaca (Tex.) Ind. Sch. Dist., 1975-77; kindergarten tchr. Goliad (Tex.) Ind. Sch. Dist., 1978-80; tchr. Fairbanks (Alaska) North Star Borough Sch. Dist., 1980-83; tchr. Weller Elem. Sch. Fairbanks (Alaska) NSB, 1983—, vice prin. Weller Elem. Sch., 1990; presenter Alaska State Writing Consortium, 1986—; mem. adv. bd. Ctr. for Rsch. and Devel. Law Related Edn., 1988—, Alaska Law Related Edn., 1988—; edn. rep. comn. on fgn. trade Alaska Ho. of Reps., 1988-89. Contbr. articles to profl. jours. Founder, chmn. Interior Alaska Ecumenical Peace with Justice Coun., Fairbanks, 1985-88; organizer Strong Economy Needs Solid Edn., Fairbanks, 1987; founder, trainer Elem. Conflict Mgr. Program, Fairbanks, 1987—. Recipient community vol. award State of Alaska, 1985, appreciation award Alaska Native Edn., 1986, Martin Luther King Jr. Edn. award Martin Luther King Jr. Community Orgn., 1987, Weller Elem. Educator of Yr., PTA, 1988, Fairbanks Community Educator of Yr. award, Fairbanks Community Orgn., 1988, NOW award in recognition of contbn. to women as a Courageous Voice Echoing in our Lives, 1990. Mem. NEA, Nat. Coun. Social Studies, Alaska Coun. Social Studies (Tchr. of Yr. 1989), Alaska Edn. Assn., Fairbanks Edn. Assn., Nat. Coun. Geographic Edn. Democrat. Methodist. Home: 3012 Riverview Dr Fairbanks AK 99709 Office: Weller Elem Sch Elementary Dr Fairbanks AK 99712

HEAD, MARSHA MARIE, secretary; b. Christopher, Ill., Aug. 31, 1951; d. Stanley Lewis and Dorothy Delorse (Kuzminski) H. Student, Mt. San Antonio Coll., 1969-70, Rio Hondo Coll., 1972-73. Asst. to pres. DOW Radio Ind., Pasadena, Calif., 1973-82; sec. Internat. Window Corp., South Gate, Calif., 1982-86; purchasing agt. Patient Care Med. Sales, Santa Fe Springs, Calif., 1986-88; sec. to purchasing agt. U.S. Mfg., Pasadena, 1988; sec., gal Friday South East Concrete Assn., South El Monte, Calif., 1988—. Home: 5089 Coney Ave Covina CA 91722 Office: SE Concrete Products 11029 E Weaver Ave South El Monte CA 91733

HEAD, VIOLET BERYL, psychologist; b. Picton, Ont., Can., Mar. 30, 1922; d. Andrew Burton and Claribel (Miller) H. BA, Queen's U., Kingston, 1958; AM, U. Chicago, 1963, PhD, 1963. Reg. psychologist, Ont. Bd. Examiners Psychology. Elem. tchr. Ont., 1941-46; various positions in bus. Toronto, Ont., 1946-56; coordinator group services Internat. Inst. Met. Toronto, Ont., 1956-60; psychologist Toronto Psychiat. Hosp., 1963-65; coordinator group psychotherpy Addiction Research Found., Toronto, 1965-70; psychologist The Donwood Inst., Toronto, 1970-87, cons., 1987—; pvt.

practice psychology Toronto, Ont., Can., 1980—; cons. Project Turnabout: Ont. Nurses Assistance Prog. Inc., Toronto, 1987—. Contbr. articles to profl. jours. Mem. Ont. Psychol. Assn., Can. Group Psychotherapy Assn., (fellow, pres. 1977-79, bd. dirs. 1980-84), Am. Group Psychotherapy Assn. (bd. dirs. 1977-79, int. aspects com, 1980—), Internat. Assn. Group Psychotherapy, Royal Ont. Mus., Art Gallery Ont. Liberal. Clubs: Toronto Lawn Tennis, U. Chgo. Toronto. Home: 34 Standish Ave, Toronto, ON Canada M4W3B1 Office: 216 St Clair Ave W, Toronto, ON Canada M4V1R2

HEADDING, LILLIAN SUSAN (SALLY HEADDING), writer; b. Milw., Jan. 1, 1944; d. David Morton and Mary Davis (Berry) Coleman; m. James K. Hill (div. 1976); children: Amy Denise; m. John Murray Headding (div. 1987). BA, U. Nev., 1975; MA, U. Pacific, 1976. With Gimbels, Milw., 1963-65; retail mgr. Frandisco Corp., N.Y.C., 1965-66; store mgr. Anita Shops, Los Angeles, 1966-68, Clothes Closet, Sunnyvale, Calif., 1969-70; owner Lillian Headding Interiors & Comml. Design, Pittsburg, Calif., 1976-88; mfrs. rep. and assoc. J.G. West, San Francisco, 1989—; karate instr. Sch. of the Tiger, Pleasant Hill, Calif., 1988—, 1st degree black belt, 1973—. Author (as Sara Davis): When Gods Fall; short stories. Bd. dirs. Community Action Against Rape, Las Vegas, Nev., 1972-75; self-def. expert Las Vegas Met. Police Dept., 1972-75, North Las Vegas (Nev.) Police Dept.; co. supr. Family & Children's Services, Contra Costa County, Calif., 1985-86. Mem. Walnut Creek Writers Group (pres.), Philippine Hawaiian Black Belters Assn. Republican. Jewish. Office: 5333 Park Highlands Blvd #33 Concord CA 94521

HEAGARTY, MARGARET CAROLINE, pediatric physician; b. Charleston, W.Va., Sept. 8, 1934; d. John Patrick and Margaret Caroline (Walsh) H. BA, Seton Hill Coll., 1957; BS, W.Va. Sch. Medicine, 1959; MD, U. Pa., 1961; DSc honoris causa, Iona Coll., 1989. Diplomate: Am. Bd. Pediatrics. Intern Phila. Gen. Hosp., 1961-62; resident in pediatrics St. Christopher's Hosp. for Children, Phila., 1962-64; dir. pediatric ambulatory care services N.Y. Hosp.-Cornell Med. Ctr., N.Y.C., 1969-78; dir. pediatrics Harlem Hosp. Ctr. Columbia U., N.Y.C., 1978—, prof. pediatrics Coll. Physicians & Surgeons, 1987—; cons. Dept. HEW Promotion of Child Health, Washington; mem. Com. Community Oriented Primary Care Inst. Medicine, Washington; mem. Robert Wood Johnson Found. Program for Prepaid Managed Health Care, 1984; mem. governing council Inst. Medicine, Nat. Acad. Scis., 1986. Author: Changing the Medical Car System-Report of an Experiment, 1974, Medical Sociology: A Systems Approach, 1975, Child Health: Basics for Primary Care, 1980. Grantee Commonwealth Found., 1981, Robert Wood Johnson Found., 1983, Ctr. for Disease Control, 1985, Health Rsch. and Svc. Adminstrn., 1988, Nat. Inst. Allergy/Infectious Disease, 1988. Fellow Inst. Medicine (steering group for nat. forum on future of children and their families 1987—); mem. Ambulatory Pediatric Assn. (pres. 1976-77), Soc. Pediatric Research, Am. Pediatric Soc., Am. Acad. Pediatrics (com. on hosp. care 1988—), Assn. Pediatric Program Dirs., Nat. Bd. Med. Examiners. Home: 2520 Kingsland Ave Bronx NY 10469 Office: Columbia U-Harlem Hosp Ctr 506 Lenox Ave New York NY 10037

HEAGY, LORRAINE MARY, office manager; b. Lancaster, Pa., Aug. 19, 1935; d. Ralph Long and Ella Ruth Shreiner; m. John Franklin Heagy, Oct. 15, 1960 (dec. 1979); children: John Franklin III, Loralie Leslie, Michael David. Grad. high sch., Lititz, Pa. Clk. typist Woodstream Corp., Lititz, 1953-54, Lititz Mut. Ins. Co., 1955-56; sec. Warner Lambert Co., Lititz, 1956-61; adminstrv. asst. Elam G. Stoltzfus, Jr., Lancaster, Pa., 1973-84; mgr. office support dept. Lancaster Labs., 1984—. Democrat. Office: Lancaster Labs 2425 New Holland Pike Lancaster PA 17601

HEALD, EMILY EASTHAM, civic worker; b. Lawrence, Mass., July 14, 1917; d. Ernest Eugene and Elsie (Eastham) H. Grad. Katharine Gibbs Sch., Boston, 1935. With Mass. Electric Co., 1935-81; ret., 1981; trustee First Essex Savs. Bank, Lawrence, 1977-87 . Mem. Girl Scout Council Greater Lawrence Inc., 1935-63, pres. leaders assn., 1938-42, adviser sr. Girl Scouts planning bd., 1949-51, dir., 1951-63, sec. bd. dirs., 1952-53, v.p., 1957-61, pres., 1961-63, nat. council mem. 1949-51, 63-69, dir., pres. Merrimack River Girl Scout Council, Inc., 1963-70; dir. Methuen chpt. ARC, 1952-54, chmn., 1953-54, dir. Greater Lawrence chpt., 1954-81, sec., 1957-60, 1st vice chmn., 1961-63, chmn., 1963-65; sec. dist. 1 Mass. regional blood program, 1960-63, exec. com., 1963-66; chmn. Methuen div. Community Chest Drive, 1951; mem. budget com. United Fund, Lawrence, 1954-56, chmn. spl. gifts, Methuen, 1960; chmn. social action com. Greater Lawrence Council of Chs., 1959-61; sec. bd. dirs. Greater Lawrence Guidance Center; trustee Methuen Meml. Music Hall, Inc., 1949-81, sec., 1949-53, 55-56, 60-63, clk., 1951-55, 60-66, v.p., 1966-69, pres., 1969-73; pres. Gt. Harbors Residents Assn., East Falmouth, Mass., 1985-87 ; vestryman Grace Epis. Ch., Lawrence, Mass., 1972-75, sr. warder, 1976-78, St. Barnabas Meml. Episcopalian Ch., Falmouth, Mass., 1985-88, clk. vestry, 1988—. Clubs: Quota (Lawrence); Appalachian Mountain (Boston). Home: 54 Striper Lane East Falmouth MA 02536

HEALD, MELINDA MERLE, audiologist; b. Tokyo, July 29, 1962; d. Jack Mahoney and Cynthia Ann (Hall) H. BS, U. Ariz., 1984, MS, 1988. Audiologist intern Tucson, 1988; audiologist per diem Tucson Med. Ctr., 1988, Carondelet Health Svcs., Tucson, 1989—; audiologist, cons. Sunnyside Pub. Schs., Tucson, 1988—; audiologist/researcher U. Ariz., Tucson, 1989—; audiologist Amphitheatre pub. schs., Tucson, 1988-89, Tucson Med. Ctr., 1989—; cons. in field; lectr. in field; author in field. Recipient Jean R. Guloien award, U. Ariz., 1987, others. Mem. Alexander Graham Bell Assn., Ariz. Speech, Lang., Hearing Assn. (chmn. internat. rels./sci. affairs com.), Tucson Audiology Soc. (chmn.), Am. Auditory Soc., Am. Speech, Lang. and Hearing Assn. (recipient New Investigators award 1988), Nat. Disting. Svc. Registry. Home: 7952-164 E Colette Circle Tucson AZ 85710

HEALEY, ANN RUSTON, permanent deacons training program director; b. Havana, Cuba, Dec. 29, 1939; d. Homer Max and Elizabeth Dillon (Rea) H. BA in Spanish, French, Ohio Wesleyan U., 1961; MA in Religious Studies, Mundelein Coll., 1975; cert. pastoral leadership, St. Louis U., 1982; MDiv, Assn. for Clin. Pastoral Edn., Atlanta, 1983; postgrad., Columbia Pacific U., 1990—. Cert. social worker, Ill. Mental health social worker Dept. Mental Health, Chgo., 1964-68; hosp. social worker St. Joseph Hosp., Chgo., 1968-73; social work progam dir. Sr. Ctrs. Met. Chgo., 1973-75; retreat and spiritual dir. Cenacle Retreat House, Chgo., 1975-80; hosp. chaplain Barnes Hosp., St. Louis, 1981-82, Mercy Med. Ctr., Bakersfield, Calif., 1982-83; chaplain tng. supr. Immanuel Med. Ctr., Omaha, 1983-84; program dir. permanent deacon formation program Catholic Diocese Ft. Worth, 1984—; resident in clin. pastoral edn. Assn. for Clin. Pastoral Edn., Atlanta, 1981-82, 83-84; bd. dirs. S.W. Career Devel. Ctr., Arlington, Tex., v.p. 1990—; mem. adj. faculty Inst. for Pastoral Life, Kansas City, Kans., 1989—, Inst. for Religious and Pastoral Studies, U. Dallas, 1989-90; chmn. 2d Ecumenical Consultation on Deacons and Diaconate, Nat. Coun. Chs., Ft. Worth, 1988; retreat and spiritual dir., Tex., La., Kans., 1982—; dir. Twelve Step Journey to Wholeness Workshop, 1988—; mem. Bishop's Task Force on Women's Concerns, 1987—; mem. Tex. Cath. Conf. Task Force for Priest Shortage, 1984-85. Mem. Nat. Assn. Permanent Diaconate Dirs. (sec. 1987-89, region X rep. 1990—), Nat. Assn. Cath. Chaplains (cert.), Assn. for Clin. Pastoral Edn. (clin.), Midwest Assn. Spiritual Dirs. (assoc.), Coll. Chaplains (assoc.), Am. Assn. Pastoral Counselors (profl. affiliate 1990—), Charles A. Lindbergh N-X-211 Collectors' Soc. (curator 1988-90, archivist 1990—), Serra Club. Democrat. Home: 210 Mountainview Dr Hurst TX 76054 Office: The Catholic Center 800 W Loop 820 South Fort Worth TX 76108

HEALEY, LOIS ANN, designer, senior project manager; b. Newark, May 5, 1958; d. Edward Stanley and Sophie Barbara S. Student, Fashion Inst. Tech., 1976-77; BA, Kean Coll., Union, N.J., 1981; postgrad., Rutgers U., 1983-86. Cert. interior designer. Jr. draftsman F.J. Stiene Group, Ft. Lee, N.J., 1981-82; interior designer Drexel Burnham Lambert, N.Y.C., 1982-83, Bellemead Devel. Corp., Roseland, N.J., 1983-85; project architect Chase Manhattan Bank, N.Y.C., 1985-86; asst. v.p. Shearson Lehman Bros., N.Y.C., 1986—. Mem. Am. Soc. Interior Designers, Inst. Bus. Designers (various offices 1984—). Democrat. Roman Catholic. Office: Shearson Lehman Bros 2 World Trade Ctr 105 Fl New York NY 10048

HEALEY, LYNNE KOVER, editor, broadcaster, writer, educator; b. L.I., N.Y.; d. Richard Frederick Bascom and Margaret Harriet (Fuchs); div.; children: Christine Josepha, Lauren Teresa. AA in Journalism/Psychology, Middlesex County Coll., 1979; BA in Communication, Rutgers U., 1983; MA in English, Drew U., 1987. Editor A.M. Best Co., Oldwick, N.J., 1985—; free-lance cons. Sea-Land Corp., Menlo Park, N.J., 1984-85; free-lance writer, 1977-85; adj. prof. English Middlesex County Coll., Edison, N.J. Mem. Meeting Planners Internat. (bd. dirs. N.J. chpt., co-chairperson com. for Give Kids the World project), Rutgers U. Alumni Assn. (exec. com.), Alpha Sigma Lambda (grad. sch. scholar 1986, bd. dirs. Rutgers chpt.). Office: AM Best Co Ambest Rd Oldwick NJ 08858

HEALY, BARBARA ANNE, insurance company executive, financial planner; b. Chgo., May 21, 1951; d. William James Healy and Eileen Mary (Dooley) Dashiell; m. Gerald Lally Angst, June 9, 1973 (div. Sept. 1977). BA, No. Ill. U., 1973; MBA, DePaul U., 1976. Cert. fin. planner. Dept. head, instr. St. Benedict High Sch., Chgo., 1973-76; account rep. Xerox Corp., Chgo., 1976-78, mktg. specialist, 1978-79, high volume sr. sales exec., 1979-81; western dist. mgr. McGraw Hill, N.Y.C., 1981-82; fin. planner United Resources Ins. Service, Torrance, Calif., 1982-83, sales mgr., 1983-85, exec. v.p., 1985-86; regional v.p. United Resources Ins. Service, Foster City, Calif., 1986-89; v.p., nat. mktg. dir. Met. Life Resources (formerly United Resources Ins. Svcs.), Phoenix, 1990—; instr. Trenton Coll., Riverside, Ill., City Coll. Chgo., Northeastern Ill. U., Chgo., Prairie State Coll., Chicago Heights, 1976-81. Author: Financial Planning for Educators, 1987; contbr. articles to prof. jours.; speaker in field. Mem. Internat. Assn. Fin. Planners, Inst. Cert. Fin. Planners, Registry Fin. Planning Practitioners, Nat. Council Fin. Edn. Republican. Roman Catholic. Home: 10301 N 48th Pl Paradise Valley AZ 85253 Office: MetLife Resources A Div of Met Life 432 N 44th St Ste 354 Phoenix AZ 85008

HEALY, BERNADINE P., cardiologist, educator; b. N.Y.C., Aug. 2, 1944; d. Michael J. and Violet (McGrath) Healy; m. Floyd Loop, Aug. 17, 1985; children: Bartlett Anne Bulkley, Marie McGrath Loop. AB summa cum laude, Vassar Coll., 1965; MD cum laude Harvard Med. Sch., 1970. Diplomate Am. Bd. Med. Examiners, Am. Bd. Cardiology, Am. Bd. Internal Medicine (bd. dirs. 1983-87); lic. physician, Md., Ohio. Intern in medicine Johns Hopkins Hosp., Balt., 1970-71, asst. resident, 1971-72; staff fellow sect. pathology Nat. Heart, Blood & Lung Inst., NIH, Bethesda, Md., 1972-74; fellow cardiovascular div. dept. medicine Johns Hopkins U. Sch. Medicine, Balt., 1974-76, fellow dept. pathology, 1975-76, asst. prof. medicine and pathology, 1976-81, assoc. prof. medicine, 1977-82, asst. dean for postdoctoral programs and faculty devel., 1979-84, assoc. prof. pathology, 1981-84, prof. medicine, 1982-84; active staff medicine and pathology Johns Hopkins Hosp., from 1976, dir. CCU, 1977-84; dep. dir. Office Sci. and Tech. Policy, Exec. Office of Pres. White House, Washington, 1984-85; vice chmn. Pres.' Coun. Advisers on Sci. and Tech., 1990—; mem. Spl. Med. Adv. Group, Dept. Veterans Affairs, 1990—, chmn. adv. panel for Basic Rsch. for 1990's, Office Tech. Assessment, 1990—, mem. NHLBI Task Force on Atherosclerosis, 1990; chmn. Rsch. Inst. Cleve. Clinic Found., Ohio, 1985—; mem. Vis. Com. Bd. Overseers Harvard Med. Sch. and Sch. of Dental Medicine, Boston, 1986-89; councillor Harvard Med. Alumni Assn., 1987-90; mem. Nat. Adv. Bd. Johns Hopkins Ctr. for Hosp. Fin. and Mgmt., 1987—; mem. Bd. Overseers Harvard Coll., 1989—; chmn. Office of Tech. Assessment Panel New Devels. in Biotech., U.S. Congress, 1986-87; mem. U.S.-Brazil Panel on Sci. and Tech., 1987; mem. White House Sci. Council, 1988—; cons. Nat. Heart, Lung and Blood Inst., NIH, 1976—, mem. Adv. Com. to Dir., NIH, 1986—; chmn. steering com. Post-CABG Clin. Trial, 1987—; bd. dirs. Medtronic, Inc., Mpls., Nat. City Corp., Cleve., Nova Pharms., Balt.; mem. adv. bd. Bayer Fund for Cardiovascular Rsch., N.Y.C., 1987-89; trustee Edison BioTech. Ctr., Cleve., 1990—; chmn. Ohio Coun. on Rsch. and Econ. Devel., 1989—. Editorial cons. numerous jours.; abstract reviewer; editorial bd. Jour. Cardiovascular Medicine, 1980—, Am. Jour. Medicine, 1976—, Am. Jour. Cardiology, 1981-82, Circulation, 1981—, Jour. Am. Coll. Cardiology, 1982—. Contbr. articles to profl. jours. Matthew Vassar scholar, 1962-65, Harvard Nat. scholar, 1965-70; Eloise Ellery fellow, 1965-66, Stetler Research fellow, 1976-77; recipient Nat. Bd. Ann. award for Medicine, Med. Coll. Pa., 1983. Mem. Am. Fedn. Clin. Research (pres. 1983-84), Am. Heart Assn. (award 1983-84, 90, pres. 1988-89, fellow Coun. on Clin. Cardiology, Coun. on Circulation, dir. 1983-84), Am. Coll. Cardiology (bd. govs. 1979-82), ACP, Assn. Am. Med. Colls., Internat. Acad. Pathology, Am. Med. Women's Assn., Assn. for Women in Sci., Am. Soc. Clin. Investigation, Am. Bd. Internal Medicine (bd. govs. 1986—), Inst. Medicine, NAS, Johns Hopkins U. Soc. Scholars, Inst. Medicine NAS, Phi Beta Kappa, Alpha Omega Alpha. Office: Cleve Clinic Found Rsch Inst One Clinic Ctr 9500 Euclid Ave Cleveland OH 44195-5210*

HEALY, JANE ELIZABETH, newspaper editor; b. Washington, May 9, 1949; d. Paul Francis and Connie (Maas) H.; m. James Covington Clark, June 4, 1977; children: Randall, Kevin. BS, U. Md., 1971. Copy clk. N.Y. Daily News, Washington, 1971-73; met. reporter Orlando (Fla.) Sentinel, 1973-81, editorial writer, 1981-83, chief editorial writer, 1983-85, assoc. editor, 1985—. Recipient Pulitzer Prize, Columbia U., 1988, Sigma Delta Chi Disting. Service award, 1988. Mem. Am. Soc. Newspaper Editors (bd. dirs.), Nat. Conf. Editorial Writers. Office: care Orlando Sentinel 633 N Orange Ave Orlando FL 32801

HEAP, SYLVIA STUBER, civic worker; b. Clifton Springs, N.Y., Sept. 25, 1929; d. Stanley Irving and Helen (Hill) Stuber; B.A. cum laude, Bates Coll., 1950; postgrad. U. Conn. Sch. Social Work, 1952-54, Boston U. Sch. Social Work, 1953-54, SUNY, Brockport, 1979, SUNY-Potsdam, 1980, M.S. in Adult Edn., Syracuse U., 1989; m. Walker Ratcliffe Heap, June 9, 1951; children—Heidi Anne, Cynthia Joan, Walker Ratcliffe III. Dir. Y-Teens, YWCA, Holyoke, Mass., 1950-51; social group worker West Haven (Conn.) Community House, 1951-54; program dir. YWCA, Ann Arbor, 1954-55, part-time, 1955-59; mem. adv. bd. div. continuing edn. Jefferson Community Coll., 1965—, chmn. adv. bd., 1968—; pres. Jefferson County Med. Soc. Aux., 1971-72; bd. dirs. St. Lawrence Valley Ednl. TV, 1973-83, sec., 1976-80, treas., 1980-82; v.p., 1982-83, dir. Chem. People Project, 1983; bd. dirs. Watertown Lyric Theatre, 1973-83; bd. dirs. N.Y. State Med. Soc. Aux., 1974-85, 2d v.p. bd., 1979-80; fitness instr. Jefferson Community Coll., Watertown, 1977-86; chmn. health projects N.Y. State Med. Soc. Aux., 1981-85. Named Citizen of Yr. Greater Watertown C. of C., 1975, Friend of Community Colls. N.Y. State Bd. Trustees, 1988. Mem. Friends of Public TV, AAUW, Coll. Women's Club Jefferson County, Phi Beta Kappa. Unitarian Universalist. (UN office envoy 1978—).

HEAPHY, EILEEN MICHELE, diplomat; b. Ansonia, Conn., Oct. 1, 1945; d. Michael Joseph and Helen Emma (Schultz) H.; children: Jacqueline M., Ann H. BA, St. Joseph Coll., 1967; MA, Am. U., 1972. Consul U. S. Consulate, Bilbao, Spain, 1982-85; labor attache U.S. Embassy, Copenhagen, 1986-89; dep. dir. for No. Europe Dept. of State, Washington, 1989-90, dir. for No. Europe, 1990—. Editor: Open Forum Jour., 1981-82; contbr. articles to jours. Roman Catholic. Home: 3631 39th St NW Washington DC 20016

HEARD, CHAUNCY LEE, market research executive; b. Santa Barbara, Calif., Dec. 11, 1950; d. James D. and Constance (Campbell) Andros; children: Chauncy Richard, Shawn Richard. Student, Brookhaven Coll., Mt. View Coll., Richard Coll. Adminstrv. asst. Adia, Dallas, 1981-83, 86; with sales and telemktg. Hawaiian Caribbean Resorts, Dallas, 1985-87; with outbound sales U.S. Sprint-Advanced Telemktg., Irving, Tex., 1988-89; assoc. rsch. dir. Bus. Insights, Dallas, 1984—. Mem. Am. Film Inst., Nat. Museum of Women, Nat. Notary Assn. Home: 18040 Midway Villa 193 Box 7 Dallas TX 75287

HEARD, CHERYL VYETTE, education educator; b. Nov. 27, 1956; d. L.C. and Edith Louise (Nelms) H. BA, McKendree Coll., Lebanon, Ill., 1978; MS in Edn., So. Ill. U., Edwardsville, 1980. Presch. tchr. Gay's Kiddie Haven, East St. Louis, Ill., 1976-77; instr. reading So. Ill. U., 1978—; instr. State Community Coll., East St. Louis, 1987—; cons. Providence Enhancement Program, St. Louis, 1986-87. Mem. Nat. Assn. Devel. Edn., Internat. Reading Assn. (conf. program presenter 1990), Ill. Reading Coun., Urban League, NAACP. Democrat. Home: 4216 E Margaretta Ave Apt 2W Saint Louis MO 63115 Office: So Ill U Box 1630 Edwardsville IL 62026

HEARD, JOHNY CAROL, accountant, loan specialist; b. Banner, Va., Dec. 17, 1942; d. James Orbin and Juanita (Young) Hamm; m. William B. Heard, Dec. 24, 1960; children: William B., Rodney D. Student, Kansas City (Kans.) Community Coll. Loan specialist-realty U.S. Dept. HUD, Kansas City, Mo., 1979—, regional coordinator computer homes underwriting mgmt. systems, 1984—; acct., co-owner Heard Constrn. Co., Tonganoxie, Kans., 1983—. Recipient Outstanding Performance award U.S. Dept. HUD, 1983, 86, Spl. Achievement award U.S. Dept. HUD, 1984, 88, 89, Productivity award for idea published in HUD Handbook, 1989. Mem. Nat. Assn. Female Execs., Nat. Campers and Hikers Assn. (chpt. pres. 1982-83), Tonganoxie Genealogy Soc. (pres. 1986-87). Democrat. Presbyterian. Home: 1417 E 2nd St Tonganoxie KS 66086 Office: US Dept HUD 1103 Grand Kansas City MO 64106

HEARD, MARY FRANCES SUFFECOOL, federal agency administrator; b. Ft. Belvoir, Va., Nov. 1, 1948; d. Wilson Leroy and Frances Leola (Moore) Suffecool; m. Rodney Dale Heard, Sept. 22, 1972 (div. 1977). BS, Va. Poly. Inst. and State U., Blacksburg, 1970; MBA, Va. Poly. Inst. and State U., Reston, 1979. Systems analyst U.S. Dept. Def., Alexandria, Va., 1970-74; computer specialist U.S. Dept. Def., Washington, 1974-77; supervisory computer systems analyst U.S. Dept. Agrl., Hyattsville, Md., 1977-84; supervisory auditor U.S. Dept. Labor, Washington, 1984-85, asst. regional gen. insp., 1985-87, asst. office dir., 1987-90; audit mgr. U.S. Dept. State, Washington, 1990—. Active Potomac Hosp. Aux., Woodbridge, Va., 1977—. Recipient Spl. Achievement award U.S. Dept. Labor, 1985, Cert. Achievement Am. Soc. Profl. and Exec. Women, 1987. Mem. Assn. Govt. Accts., Data Processing Mgmt. Assn. (exec. v.p. 1985—), Nat. Assn. Female Execs., Fedn. Govt. Info. Processing Councils. Methodist. Clubs: Dale City Arts & Crafts, Friends of Potomac Library (v.p. 1983—) (Woodbridge). Home: 14402 Brandon Ct Woodbridge VA 22193 Office: US Dept State/OIG/AUD/IM 2401 C St NW Rm 6817 Washington DC 20520

HEARD, PATRICIA LOADER, art gallery director; b. Ashbourne, Derbyshire, Sept. 7, 1930; d. George Edinmore Gather and Kathleen (Littler); m. Arthur Marston Heard, June 15, 1929; children: Jonathan, Adam, Meredith. BA, Nottingham U., England, 1948-51. Dir./owner Gallery on the Green, Lexington, 1980—. Author: The American China Trade 1783-1843, 1974; From Wharf to Waterfall, 1977; Albert Gallatin Holt, 1983. Trustee, The N. H. Historial Soc., Concord, 1980, v.p., The N. H. Historial Soc., Concord, 1984-88, overseer, Strawbery Banke, Portsmouth, 1987. Democrat. Episcopalian. Home: 6 Doran Farm Ln Lexington MA 02173 Office: Gallery on the Green 1837 Massachusetts Ave Lexington MA 02173

HEAREY TAFFET, MICHELE, occupational therapist; b. Philadelphia, Aug. 15, 1959; d. Charles DeLisle and Michelene Mary (Pilch) Hearey; m. Robert Taffet, July 1, 1984. BS in Occupational Therapy, U. Pa., 1981. Registered occupational therapist. Dept. head occupational therapy Cooper River Convalescent Ctr., Pennsauken, N.J., 1982-84; staff therapist New Rochelle (N.Y.) Hosp. Med. Ctr., 1984-88, sr. therapist, chief, 1988—; with contract home care New Rochelle Hosp. Med. Ctr., 1984—; pvt. practice hand therapist. Mem. Am. Occupational Therapy Assn., N.Y. Occupational Therapy Assn. (Westchester chpt.), N.Y. Soc. Hand Therapy. Democrat. Roman Catholic.

HEARN, JOYCE CAMP, retired educator, state legislator; b. Cedartown, Ga., d. J.C. and Carolyn (Carter) Camp; m. Thomas Harry Hearn (dec.); children: Theresa Hearn Potts Bailey, Kimberly Ann Johnson, Carolyn Lee Becker. Student, U. Ga.; BA, Ohio State U., 1957; postgrad, U. S.C. Former high sch. tchr.; dist. mgr. U.S. Census, 2d Congl. Dist., 1970; mem. S.C. Ho. of Reps., 1975-89, asst. minority leader, 1976-78, 86— ; chmn. commn. alcohol beverage control, 1989—. Mem. Richland County Planning Commn.; bd. dirs. Meml. Youth Ctr. and Stage South; chmn. Nat. Adv. Com. on Occupational Safety and Health, 1982—; chmn. Sexual Assault Awareness Week; vice chmn. Dist. Republican Com., 1968; Rep. chmn. 2d Congl. Dist., 1969; Rep. chmn. Richland County, 1972; del., platform com. Rep. Nat. Conv., 1980, 84; moderator Kathwood Bapt. Ch., 1979-80, former asst. Sunday Sch. tchr.; bd. dirs. Small Bus. Devel. Ctr. S.C., Columbia Coll. Bd. Vis., Columbia Urban League, Fedn. of Blind; trustee Columbia Mus. Art; apptd. to Alcohol Beverage Control Bd., 1989, apptd. chmn. commn., 1990. Recipient Outstanding Citizen award Columbia Rape Coalition, 1977, Disting. Service award Claims Mgmt. Assn. S.C., 1977, Nat. Fedn. Blind S.C., 1978, Columbia Urban League, 1983, MADD, 1985, Outstanding Legislator of Yr. award Alcohol and Drug Abuse Assn., 1980, Retarded Citizens Assn., 1982, S.C. Rehab. Assn., 1984, S.C. Assn. of Deaf, 1987, Legislator of Yr., Fedn. of Blind, 1988, Disting. Legislator, DAV, 1989; Honoree, Easter Seals, 1989; numerous other awards. Mem. Nat. Order of Women Legislators (treas., v.p.), Order of the Palmetto, S.C. Women's Club, Columbia Women's Club (bd. dirs.), Larkspar Garden Club.

HEARN, KATHLEEN K. (KATHLEEN KLOTZ CROSHAL), lawyer; b. Sandusky, Ohio, Mar. 21, 1947; d. Earl A. and Mary W. (Donahue) Klotz; m. Dane P. Winters, Nov. 14, 1964 (div. Feb. 1972); children: Lisa C. Winters, Timothy D. Winters; m. Bruce L. Hearn, Apr. 18, 1981 (div. Dec. 1986); 1 child: Cassandra; m.James M. Croshal, May 3, 1987. BA Communications and Theatre, U. Colo., 1973, JD, 1979. Gen. mgr. Goldenrod Showboat, St. Louis, 1975; asst. mgr. box office, adminstrv. asst. Heritage Sq. Opera House, Golden, Colo., 1974-75, box office mgr., bus. mgr., 1976, bookkeeper, adminstrv. asst., 1975-76; bookkeeper Internat. Sports Distbrs., Golden, 1978-79; student atty. Legal Aid and Defender Program, 1977-78; dep. dist. atty. 10th Jud. Ct., Pueblo, Colo., 1979-81; assoc. J.E. Losavio Jr., Pueblo, 1981; pvt. practice Pueblo, 1981-87; asst. to county atty. Pueblo County Dept. Social Svcs., 1982-88; assoc. Petersen & Fonda, P.C., Pueblo, Colo., 1987—. Mem. ABA, Colo. Bar Assn., Pueblo County Bar Assn. (exec. com.), Colo. Trial Lawyers Assn., Pueblo C. of C.; Kiwanis Internat. Club., Phi Delta Phi (outstanding grad. region X), others. Office: Petersen & Fonda P C 650 Thatcher Bldg Pueblo CO 81003

HEARN, PAULA CLARICE, telecommunications industry executive, real estate; b. St. Louis, Sept. 16, 1955; d. Nathaniel and Mary (Griffin) Smith; m. Roger Wendell Hearn, Aug. 7, 1975; 1 child, Brandon Coryell. BA, U. Mo., 1977; MA, Webster U., 1990. CRT operator Western Union, Bridgeton, Mo., 1980—; sr. supr. Western Union, Bridgeton, 1980-84, ops. mgr., 1984—; real estate agent United Realtors, Belridge, 1986—. Home: 12833 Polo Parc Creve Coeur MO 63146 Office: Western Union 13022 Hollenberg Dr Bridgeton MO 63044

HEARN, ROSAMOND ERNST, music service executive; b. Boston, Sept. 17, 1924; d. Harry Benjamin and Mary (Downey) E.; divorced; children: Robert D., Diane G., Mary R., Kathleen Anne. Student, Boston U., 1940-42, Longy Sch. Music, 1947-49, Am. Conservatory Music, 1966-71, 74-77; music fellow, U. Colo., 1974-75. Lab. technician Consol. Rendering Co., Boston, 1942-52; organist, choir dir. Mass., Conn. and Ill., 1948-72; asst. condr., accompanist Am. Conservatory of Music, Chgo., 1970-73; organist, choir dir. Sacred Heart Ch., Lombard, Ill., 1973-78; mgr. music store Manhattan Sch. Music, 1978-79; organist Colesville Presbyn. Ch., Silver Spring, Md., 1979—; gen. ptnr., mgr. Allegro Music Service, Silver Spring, 1985—; mgr. choral music dept. Lyon Healy Co., Chgo., 1975-78; mgr. choral, vocal, organ depts. Harris Music Co., Rockville, Md., 1979-85. Columnist Mitzi's Merit Series, 1984—. Mem. Am. Guild Organists (bd. dirs. 1967-70), Am. Choral Dirs. Assn. (workshop coordinator), Music Educators Nat. Conf., Choristers Guild, Music Industry Council, Silver Spring C. of C., Delta Omicron (Outstanding Service to Music Profession 1968). Office: Allegro Music Service 1398 Lamberton Dr Silver Spring MD 20902

HEARN, ROSEMARY, English educator; b. Indpls., May 1, 1929; d. Oscar Thomas and Mabel Lee (Ward) H. BA, Howard U., 1951; MA, Ind. U., 1958, PhD, 1973. Mem. dept. English Lincoln U., Jefferson City, Mo., 1958-62, prof. English, 1962-64; dir. hon. program Lincoln U., Jefferson City, 1968-72, exec. dean acad. affairs, 1982-85, asst. to pres., 1985-87, exec. asst. to pres., 1987—, dean coll. arts & scis., 1989—; cons. HEW, Washington, 1977-78, Nat. Endowment for Humanities, Washington, 1980-81. Mem. adv. bd. Sta. KBIA Nat. Pub. Radio, Columbia, Mo., 1979-82, Mo. State Planning Commn., Mo. Coun. Arts. Recipient Community Svc. award Jefferson City United Way, 1983—, Second Bapt. Ch. Mem. Nat. Coun. Tchrs. English, Coll. Lang. Assn., AAUW, Am. Coun. Edn. Home: 811 E Dunklin St Jefferson City MO 65101 Office: Lincoln U Jefferson City MO 65101

HEARN, RUBY PURYEAR, foundation executive; b. Winston-Salem, N.C., Apr. 13, 1940; c. Mahlon Tasher H. and Ruby Mae (Hamilton) Puryear; m. Robert W. Hearn, Dec. 30, 1961; children: Janna E., Jennifer L. B.A., Skidmore Coll., 1960; M.S., Yale U., 1964, Ph.D., 1969. Postdoctoral research assoc. Yale U., New Haven, 1968-69; dir. content devel. Children's TV Workshop, 1972-76; program officer Robert Wood Johnson Found., Princeton, N.J., 1976-80, sr. program officer, 1980-82, v.p., 1983—. Trustee Meharry Med. Coll., 1981—; bd. overseers Dartmouth Med. Sch., 1986—. Recipient Outstanding Alumnae award Skidmore Coll., 1972. Mem. Inst. Medicine, Ambulatory Pediatric Assn., AAAS, ABA (pub. mem. accreditation com. 1980-82), Periclean Honor Soc. Democrat. Home: 7 St Johns Rd Baltimore MD 21210 Office: Robert Wood Johnson Found PO Box 2316 Princeton NJ 08543*

HEARN, SHARON SKLAMBA, lawyer; b. New Orleans, Aug. 15, 1956; d. Carl John and Marjorie C. (Wimberly) Sklamba; m. Curtis R. Hearn. BA magna cum laude, Loyola U., New Orleans, 1977; JD cum laude, Tulane U., 1980. Bar: La. 1980, Tex. 1982; cert. tax specialist. Law clk. to presiding judge U.S. Ct. Appeals Fed. Cir., Washington, 1980-81; assoc. Johnson & Swanson, Dallas, 1981-84, Kullman Inman Bee & Downing, New Orleans, 1984—. Recipient Am. Legion award, 1970. Mem. ABA, La. State Bar Assn., Tex. State Bar Assn., Dallas Women Lawyers Assn. Democrat. Roman Catholic. Home: 44 Swallow Ln New Orleans LA 70124 Office: Kullman Inman Bee & Downing 615 Howard Ave New Orleans LA 70130

HEARNE, GERARDETTE A., newswriter; b. Bklyn., Sept. 11, 1957; d. Thomas Joseph and Ann (Brown) H. Bachelor's, L.I. U., 1981; Master's, U. Mo., 1983. News reporter Sta. WTHI-TV, Terre Haute, Ind., 1985-88; newswriter Sta. WBBM-AM-TV, Chgo., 1987-88, WFLD-TV, Chgo., 1988—; reporter (TV documentary) Dioxin: The Deadly Dilemma (UPI award 1983), (TV news report) Jeff Hacker (UPI award 1987), (TV specials) The Miller Story (UPI award 1988). Author: The Texas Trivia Quiz Book, 1985. Mem. Writers Guild Am. Home: 452 W Aldine #305 Chicago IL 60657

HEARNE, NIKKI JO, aerospace company official; b. Topeka, May 21, 1951; d. Ernest Costello and Maxine (Irby) Turner; m. Lee Z. Hearne; children: Anjelique, Veleecia. Student, Cen. State U., 1969-70, Oscar Rose Coll., 1975, Tulsa (Kans.) Jr. Coll., 1981—. Personnel clk., prin. sec. N.E. High Sch., Oklahoma City, 1968-73; sec., clk. stenographer various orgns., Oklahoma City, 1973-77; clk. stenographer U.S. Army Corps. Engrs., Tulsa, 1977-78; prodn. control clk. McDonnell Douglas Corp., Tulsa, 1978-80, asst. foreman, systems analyst, 1980-82, sr. engr., 1982-83; data base control supr., 1983-84, sect. mgr., 1984-86, gen. foreman, 1986—.

HEARST, AUSTINE MCDONNELL, newspaper reporter, free-lance feature writer, columnist; b. Warrenton, Va., Nov. 22, 1928; d. Austin and Mary (Belt) McDonnell; m. William Randolph Hearst, Jr., 1948; children—William Randolph III, John Augustine Chilton. Ed. Warrenton County schs., Convent Notre Dame, Md., King-Smith Jr. Coll. Columnist Washington Times-Herald, 1946-56; syndicated columnist King Features Syndicate; radio commentator CBS, 1946-56. Clubs: Nat. Press (Washington), Sulgrave (Washington); Cosmopolitan. Office: Hearst Corp 959 8th Ave New York NY 10019

HEARST, BELLA RACHAEL, physician, researcher, artist; b. Pitts.; d. Aba and Bertha (Alpern) H. B.M., Chgo. Med. Sch., 1949, M.D., 1950; postgrad., Johns Hopkins U., 1952-53, Art Inst. Chgo., 1958-68. Rotating intern Norwegian Am. Hosp., Chgo., 1949-50; jr. asst. pathologist Cook County Hosp, Chgo., 1950-52; fellow med. legal pathology U. Md., 1953-54; sr. pathology resident Charity Hosp., New Orleans, 1955-56; spl. cardiac researcher Armed Forces Inst. Pathology, Washington, 1956-57; dir., coordinator pathology dept Hosp. O'Horan Menda Yucatan, Mexico, 1957-58; founder Bertha Hearts Found., Inc., 1958, exec. dir., 1958-63; founder Diabetic Inst. Am., Inc., Chgo., 1959, exec. dir., 1959-63; founder Internat. Diabetic Inst., Inc., Chgo., 1963, exec. dir, 1963—; dist. med. dir. compensation U.S. Dept. Labor, Chgo., 1968—; with Chgo. Dept. Health, 1977—, Uptown Neighborhood Health Ctr., 1977-78, Copernicus Multipurpose Ctr., 1978-79, Lakeview Neighborhood Health Ctr., Chgo., 1979—; research dir. Fed. Safety and Fire Council, Chgo.; research assoc. microbiology Stritch Sch. Medicine, Loyola U., Chgo.; staff physician Western Ill. U., 1971-72, assoc. prof., 1971-72. Author: Diabetes and Juvenile Delinquency, 1964, Diabetes and Fitness, 1964, Diabetic Statistical Research Survey, 1961-65, Diabetes and Blood Groups, 1965, Diabetes and Aging, 1965, Diabetes and Newborns; contbr. articles to various publs., art exhibit, Shuster Art Gallery, N.Y., 1966, Internat. Dermatology Congress, Munich, 1967. Recipient 3d prize AMA Conv., Chgo., 1962; recipient testimonial plaque for work sr. citizens Chelsea House, Chgo. Fellow Am. Coll. Angiology, Internat. Coll. Angiology, Am. Geriatric Soc., Royal Soc. Pub. Health; mem. Internat. Acad. Pathology, Am. Women's Med. Assn., Am. Soc. Microbiology, Am. Assn. for Study Neoplastic Diseases, Reticuloendothelial Soc. Office: 8 S Michigan Blvd Chicago IL 60603 also: PO Box A3579 Chicago IL 60690

HEARST, GLADYS WHITLEY HENDERSON, writer; b. Wolfe City, Tex.; d. William Henry and Helen (Butler) Whitley; student Trinity U., 1924-26; B.A., U. Tex., 1928, M. Journalism, 1928, postgrad., 1938-40; m. Robert David Henderson, May 17, 1933 (dec. 1941); m. Charles Joseph Hearst, Oct. 30, 1943 (dec. Nov. 1980). Editor, Future Farmer News, Austin, Tex., 1930-33; dir. Service Bur., Tex. Congress Parents and Tchrs., Austin, 1933-36; dir. Student Union, U. Tex., 1939-42; freelance writer, 1945—; instr. U. No. Iowa, 1946-47. Instr. writing Waterloo YWCA, 1966-69. Vice chmn. Black Hawk County Democratic party, 1945-57; mem. County Extension Program Planning Com., 1965-68; past deaconess United Ch. of Christ, chmn. long-range planning com., 1975-79; sec. Westminster Manor Residents Assn., 1983-85. Served to lt. WAVES, USN, 1942-45. Mem. AAUW (life, Iowa chmn. Status of Women 1954-56, past pres. Cedar Falls br.), Women in Communications (nat. pres., Disting. Service award 1962, 73, nat. chmn. by laws 1969-74, nat. citation 1969, Task Force Long-Range Planning Com. 1973-74; charter mem., v.p. NE Iowa chpt. 1978, grantee Austin chpt. 1986-87., 88-89), PEO, Readers Guild, Ret. Faculty-Staff Assn. (U. Tex.), Zeta Tau Alpha, Kappa Tau Delta, Sigma Delta Chi (scholarship award). Clubs: U. Tex. Faculty Woman's Capital Gains Investment (past pres., treas. 1970-73, cert. 1989) (Cedar Falls); Univ. Ladies. A writer Cedar Falls Centennial Pageant, 1952; writer, editor hist. book Cedar Falls Naval Station 1942-45, Anthology Family Histories Northeast Iowa (Iowa Arts Council grant), 1978. Presbyterian. Address: 4100 Jackson St Apt 230 A Austin TX 78731

HEASLEY, KATHARINE ZIEGLER, civic volunteer; b. Phila., Jan. 10, 1909; d. Samuel Lewis and May (Weston) Ziegler; widowed; children: Diane H. Van Dyke, David C. Heasley, Carolyn H. Hedrick, Sheila H. Gates, Douglas W. Heasley. AB, Vassar, 1931. Officer Federated Garden Clubs of N.Y. State, 1954-64, bd. dirs., 1965-90; chair Wildflower Symposiums, 1984, 86, Herb Symposium, 1988, Rock Garden Symposium, 1989; pres. Corner Community Ctr., Ithaca, N.Y., 1973-80; bd. dirs. Ithaca Garden Clubs. Beautification com. Mayor of Ithaca, 1988. Mem. Country Club of Ithaca, Nat. Coun. Garden Clubs, Ikebana Internat., Horticulture Soc., N.Y. Horticulture Soc., Pa. Horticulture Soc., Garden Club of Am. (mem.-at-large). Republican. Episcopalian. Home: 707 The Parkway Ithaca NY 14850

HEASTER, ARLENE LOUISE, chemical engineer; b. Chgo., May 13, 1958; d. Raymond R. and Marjorie J. (Buschek) Pult; m. Donald R. Heaster, Apr. 14, 1984. BS, U. Wis., Stevens Point, 1981; MS, Inst. Paper Chem., Appleton, Wis., 1985. Research scientist Weyerhaeuser Co., Tacoma, Wash., 1981-82; project engr. Weyerhaeuser Co., Columbus, Miss., 1982-83; grad. student The Inst. of Paper Chemistry, Appleton, Wis., 1983-85; devel. rep. Thilmany Pulp and Paper Co., Kaukauna, Wis., research scientist, 1987-88; process engr. Harris Group Inc., Wis., 1988--; adv. Jr. achievement, Appleton, Wis., 1986--, Engring Explorer post, Seattle, Wash., 1982-83, v.p. Women in Mgmt., Appleton, Wis., 1988. Panelist Future Focus Coalition, Appleton, Wis., 1987-88, panel leader Future Focus Task Force, Appleton, Wis., 1988--, planning Com., 1988--. Recipient Leadership award Paper Industry Mgmt. Assn., N. Cen. Chpt., 1981. Mem. Tech. Assn. of Pulp and Paper Ind., Paper Industry Mgmt. Assn., Lake States TAPPI. Office: Harris Group Inc 6161 W College Ave Appleton WI 54915

HEATH, BETSY ROBBINS, advertising executive, art director; b. W. Palm Beach, Fla., Sept. 11, 1953; d. Edward Alexander and Margaret Louise (Hardy) Robbins; m. Ben Ross Heath Jr., May 10, 1980; children: Kimberly Aileen, Ben Ross III. Student, Syracuse (N.Y.) U., 1971-72, Palm Beach (Fla.) Jr. Coll., 1972-73; BA, U. S. Fla., 1975. Designer, owner BETS, W. Palm Beach, 1980-83; account exec. Sta. WAMR-WCTQ, Venice, Fla., 1983-85; co-founder, pres. Results Unltd. Group, Inc., Venice, 1985—. Bd. dirs. Big Bros./Big Sistes of S. Sarasota County, Venice, 1989—. Mem. Sertoma. Methodist. Office: Results Unltd Group Inc 907 S Tamiami Trail Nokomis FL 34275

HEATH, CYNTHIA MARIE, science educator; b. Belhaven, N.C., Jan. 27, 1947; d. Julia M. (Heath) Ward. BS, A&T State U., 1968; MA in Edn., East Carolina U., 1984, postgrad., 1985; postgrad., East Carolina U., 1989. Sci. tchr. Aurora (N.C.) High Sch., 1968-72, Pantego (N.C.) High Sch., 1972-81, J.A. Wilkinson High Sch., Belhaven, 1981-89; sci. tchr. Northside High Sch., Pinetown, fall 1989, sci. dept. chair, 1990—; tchr. adv. coun. Merrill Pub. Co. Active Beaufort County Mental Health Assn., Washington, 1989—. Rep. Howard Chapin grantee, 1985, 88. Mem. N.C. Assn. Educators, NEA, Nat. Assn. Biology Tchrs., N.C. Sci. Tchrs. Assn., Nat. Sci. Tchrs. Assn., Assn. Suprs. and Curriculum Devel., Belhaven Alumni Assn. (pres. 1973—). Democrat. Baptist. Home: PO Box 121 Belhaven NC 27810

HEATH, MARIWYN DWYER, legislative issues consultant; b. Chgo., May 1, 1935; d. Thomas Leo and Winifred (Brennan) Dwyer; B. in Journalism, U. Mo., 1956; m. Eugene R. Heath, Sept. 3, 1956; children: Philip Clayton, Jeffrey Thomas. Mng. editor Chemung Valley Reporter, Horseheads, N.Y., 1956-57; self-employed freelance writer, platform speaker, editor Tech. Transls., Dayton, Ohio, 1966—; cons. Internat. Women's Commn., 1975-76; ERA coordinator Nat. Fedn. Bus. and Profl. Women's Clubs, 1974-82; mem. polit. and mgmt. coms. ERAmerica, 1976-82, exec. dir., 1982-88; pres. Miami Valley Regional Transit Authority, 1986-88, bd. dirs. 1984—. Mem. Gov. Ohio Task Force Credit for Women, 1973; mem. Midwest regional adv. com. SBA, 1976-82; pres. Dayton Pres.'s Club, 1973-74; chmn. Ohio Coalition ERA Implementation, 1974-75; appt. joint civilian orientation conf., U.S. Dept. Def., 1988. Recipient Legion of Honor award Dayton Pres.'s Club, 1987, Keeper of Flame award Ohio Sec. of State, 1990; named One of 10 Outstanding Women of World Soroptimist Internat., 1982. Mem. AAUW (dir. Dayton 1965-72, Woman of Year award Dayton 1974), Nat. Fedn. Bus. and Profl. Women's Clubs (pres. Dayton 1967-69, Ohio 1976-77, nat. politic. action com. 1985—, chmn. 1988—, Woman of Year award Dayton 1974, Ohio 1974, 83), Ohio Women (v.p. 1983-86, bd. dirs. 1977-89), Assn. Women Execs., Women in Communications. Republican. Roman Catholic. Address: 10 Wisteria Dr Dayton OH 45419

HEATLEY, CONNIE FRANCES, association executive; b. Bronx, N.Y., Oct. 10, 1942; d. Salvatore Charles and Mary Moscatiello LaMotta; m. Michael H. Heatley; children: Ray, Peter, David. BA, SUNY, Albany, 1969; postgrad., Fordham U., 1974. Activities coord. San Diego Assn. for the Retarded, 1970-72; edn. program dir. Edn. Ctrs. of Newark Archdiocese, 1973-79; dir. communications tng. Riverside Eating Disorder Clinic, Secaucus, N.J., 1979-84; communications coord. Sun Chem. Corp., N.Y.C., 1984-86; pub. relations dir. Nat. Coffee Assn., N.Y.C., 1986-87; v.p. pub. rels. Direct Mktg. Assn., N.Y.C., 1987-90, sr. v.p. pub. rels., 1988—. Recipient Silver-Mercury award Nat. Media Conf., 1988, finalist Mercury award, 1989, cert. of Merit IABC, cert. of Excellence. Mem. Pub. Relations Soc. of Am., Women in Communications, Am. Soc. Assn. Execs. Episcopalian. Office: Direct Mktg Assn 11 W 42d St New York NY 10036-8096

HEATON, MELINDA ANN, medical record administration educator; b. Tulia, Tex., Sept. 21, 1960; d. Don Kelly and Clara Ann (Neves) Jennings; m. Steven Thomas Heaton, Aug. 13, 1983; children: Amber Lane, Michael Steven. BS in Med. Record Adminstrn., Southwestern Okla. State U., Weatherford, 1983, MEd, 1988. Registered record adminstr. Office mgr. Dr. Gary Lawrence, Weatherford, 1983-84; dir. med. record dept. Southwestern Meml. Hosp., Weatherford, 1984-88; program dir., health info. mgmt. program Ark. Tech. U., Russellville, Ark., 1988--; pres. ad. com. Med. Record Program, Southwestern Okla. State U., 1984-88; pres. Employee Assn. Southwestern Meml. Hosp., 1985-86. Chairperson Christian Women's Fellowship-Lydia Circle, Weatherford, 1988. Mem. Am. Med. Record Assn., Okla. Med. Record Assn., Ark. Med. Record Assn. (chmn. archives com. 1989—, co-chmn. edn. com. 1989-90). Democrat. Presbyterian. Home: PO Box 1415 Russellville AR 72801

HEBB, CAROLINE RAUT, real estate professional; b. St. Louis, Dec. 8, 1919; d. Alfred and Nora Lee (Silger) Raut; m. Edwin E. Hebb, Aug. 11, 1956; children: Nancy, David. BS, U. Ill., 1939; PhD, Washington U., 1948. Cert. residential specialist. Position classifier U.S. Civil Svc. Com., Washington, 1940-45; teaching asst. Cornell U., Ithaca, N.Y., 1945-46; rsch. asst. Washington U., St. Louis, 1946-48; asst. prof. So. Ill. U., Carbondale, 1948-50; asst. prof. Coll. Medicine Wayne State U., Detroit, 1950-58; rsch. assoc. Detroit Inst. Cancer Rsch., 1950-58; realtor assoc. Real Estate One, Dearborn Heights, Mich., 1979—. Contbr. articles to profl. jours.

HEBENSTREIT, JEAN ESTILL STARK, religious educator, practitioner; d. Charles Dickey and Blanche (Hervey) Stark; student Conservatory of Music, U. Mo. at Kansas City, 1933-34; AB, U. Kans., 1936; m. William J. Hebenstreit, Sept. 4, 1942; children: James B., Mark W. Authorized C.S. practitioner, Kansas City, 1955—; chmn. bd., pres. 3d Ch., Kansas City, 1952-55, reader, 1959-62; authorized C.S. tchr., C.S.B., 1964—; bd. dirs. First Ch. of Christ Scientist, Boston, 1977-83, chmn. bd., 1981-82; mem. Christian Sci. Bd. of Lectureship, Christian Sci. Bd. Edn. Bd. trustees The Christian Sci. Pub. Soc. Mem. Art of Assembly Parliamentarians (charter, 1st pres.), Internat. Platform Assn., Pi Epsilon Delta, Alpha Chi Omega (past pres.), Carriage Club. Contbr. articles to C.S. lit. Home: 310 W 49th St Kansas City MO 64112 Office: 4849 Wornall Rd Suite 104 Kansas City MO 64112

HEBERT, MARY OLIVIA, librarian; b. St. Louis, Nov. 11, 1921; d. Arthur Frederick and Clara Marie (Golden) Meyer; certificate librarianship, Washington U., St. Louis, 1972; m. N. Hal Hebert, Sept. 9, 1943 (dec. Mar. 1969); children—Olivia, Stephen (dec.), Christina, Deborah, Beth, John, James. Secretarial positions in advt., 1942-43; v.p. Hebert Advt. Co., 1955-66; adminstrv. asst. communications Blue Cross, St. Louis, 1966-69, librarian, 1969—. Mem. Spl. Libraries Assn. (pres. St. Louis Metro chpt. 1984), St. Louis Med. Librs., St. Louis Regional Libr. Network (coun. 1986-89). Roman Catholic. Office: 4444 Forest Park Blvd Saint Louis MO 63108

HECHT, ANITA GESSLER, communications company executive; b. Prague, Czechoslovakia, Jan. 5, 1938; d. Alfred and Truda (Lengsfeld) Gessler; m. Melvin Salberg, Jan. 24, 1987. Student, Chatham Coll., Pitts., 1956-59; BA in Psychology, Hofstra U., 1960. Vocat. counselor N.Y. State Employment Service, N.Y.C., 1960-64; personnel mgr. Thomas Y. Crowell Co., N.Y.C., 1964-67; employment supr. Olivetti Corp. of Am., N.Y.C., 1967-68, mgr. employee benefits, 1968-74; employee relations advisor Mobil Corp., N.Y.C., 1974-76; dir. personnel Bantam Books Inc., N.Y.C., 1976-78; dir. employee benefits ABC, N.Y.C., 1978-81, dir. personnel-hdqrs., 1981-85; v.p. personnel Capital Cities/ABC Inc., N.Y.C., 1985—; mem. adv. bd. Hofstra U. Sch. Communications, 1985—. Mem. Murray Hill Assn., N.Y., 1970—. Mem. Am. Women in Radio & TV, Am. Soc. Personnel Adminstrn. Office: Capital Cities/ABC Inc 77 W 66th St New York NY 10023*

HECHT, ETHEL MORELL, construction administrator; b. N.Y.C.; d. Louis and Lillie Morell; m. Al Hecht (dec. 1981); children: Randy, Kenneth, Eric. Cert. women bus. enterprise, N.Y. Pres. Sands & Hecht Constrn. Corp., N.Y.C., 1968—. Constrn projects include NYU, Consolidated Edison N.Y., United Cerebral Palsy N.Y., ABE Stark Skating Rink Dept. Parks City N.Y., Mt. Sinai Hosp. Mem. Nat. Assn. Women Bus. Owners. Avocations: writing poetry; tennis; golf; bridge. Office: Sands & Hecht Constrn Corp 445 Northern Blvd Great Neck NY 11021

HECHT, IRENE WINCHESTER D., academic administrator; b. Manila, Oct. 17, 1932; arrived in U.S., 1945; d. Nevin Harland (Jim) and Rosalind (Winchester) Duckworth; m. Aug. 29, 1953 (div.); children: Tobias, Frederick, Matthew, Maude; m. Jerome Ron Saroff, June 18, 1980; stepchildren: Stephen, Matthew, Daniel. BA in Medieval History, Radcliffe Coll., 1957; MA, U. Rochester, N.Y., 1961; PhD in History, U. Wash., 1969. Assoc. prof. history Lewis and Clark Coll., Portland, Oreg., 1966-82, asst. dean faculty, 1972-73, assoc. dean faculty, 1973-82; dean Mary Baldwin Coll., Staunton, Va., 1982-85; dean Sch. Liberal Arts and Scis. Sangamon State U., Springfield, Ill., 1985-88; pres. Wells Coll., Aurora, N.Y., 1988—; bd. dirs. Pub. Leadership Edn. Network, Commn. on Women in Higher Edn. Contbr articles to profl. jours. Interviewer admissions office Radcliffe Coll., 1975-80;bd. dirs. Planned Parenthood, Portland, 1976-80, Neveh Shalom Synagogue, Portland, 1979-80, Temple Israel, Springfield, 1987-88, Auburn (N.Y.) Meml. Hosp., 1988—. Mem. Women's Coll. Coalition, Am. Assn. Higher Edn., AAUW, Assn. Colls. and Univs. of State of N.Y. (bd. dirs.), Am. Coun. Edn. Office: Wells Coll Office of Pres Aurora NY 13026

HECHT, MARIE BERGENFELD, educator, author; b. N.Y.C., Oct. 21, 1918; d. Frank Falle and Marie (Trommer) Bergenfeld; B.A., Goucher Coll., 1939; M.A., New Sch. for Social Research, 1971; m. Morton Hecht, Jr., Dec. 17, 1937 (div.); children—Ann (Mrs. David Bloomfield), Margaret, Laurence, Andrew. Tchr. Am. history Mineola High Sch., Garden City Park, N.Y., 1960-80. Mem. Am. Hist. Assn., Orgn. Am. Historians. Author (with Herbert S. Parmet): Aaron Burr: Portrait of an Ambitious Man, 1967; Never Again: A President Runs for a Third Term, 1968; John Quincy Adams: A Personal History of An Independent Man, 1972; The Women, Yes, 1973; Beyond the Presidency: The Residues of Power, 1976; Odd Destiny: The Life of Alexander Hamilton, 1982, The Church on the Hill, 1987. Address: 5 Hewlett Pl Great Neck NY 11024

HECK, KATHLEEN, sports medicine and clinical researcher; b. Bethesda, Md., Jan. 3, 1954; d. Joseph James and Inez Adelaide (Clerici) H. BS cum laude, James Madison U., 1975; MEd, U. Va., 1976; MBA, Xavier U., 1987. Cert. athletic trainer. Head women's athletic trainer Dartmouth Coll., Hanover, N.H., 1976-78; head women's athletic trainer, instr. Mich. State U., East Lansing, 1978-83; clin. rsch. assoc. Merrell Dow Rsch. Inst., Cin., 1984—; instr. fitness and conditioning Dartmouth Coll., Hanover, 1976-78, in sports medicine numerous sports medicine clinics and seminars, 1976-84; rsch. coord. sports medicine rsch. projects div. athletic medicine Mich. State U., 1980-84; presenter, speaker sports medicine meetings and workshops, 1976-84. Co-author: Athletic Training and Sports Medicine, 1983; contbr. sports medicine articles to profl. jours. Blood donor Hoxworth Blood Ctr. ARC, Cin., 1984—; mem. World Wildlife Fund, Washington, 1986—. Named one of Outstanding Young Women of Am., 1980. Mem. Nat. Athletic Trainers Assn. (editorial bd. jour. com., 1984—, bd. certification, nat. certification examiner 1978—), Drug Info. Assn., Assocs. Clin. Pharmacology. Office: Merrell Dow Rsch Inst 2110 E Galbraith Rd Cincinnati OH 45215

HECKART, EILEEN, actress; b. Columbus, Ohio, Mar. 29, 1919; d. Leo Herbert and Esther (Stark) Purcell; m. John Harrison Yankee Jr., June 26, 1943; children: Mark Kelly, Philip Craig, Luke Brian. BA, Ohio State U., 1942, LHD (hon.), 1981; postgrad., Am. Theatre Wing, 1944-48; LLD, Sacred Heart U., Bridgeport, Conn., 1973; DFA (hon.), Niagara U., 1981. Broadway plays include Voice of the Turtle, 1944, Brighten the Corner, 1946, They Knew What They Wanted, 1948, Stars Weep, 1949, The Traitor, 1950, Hilda Crane, 1951, In Any Language, 1953, Picnic, 1953, Bad Seed, 1955, A View From the Bridge, 1956, Dark at the Top of the Stairs, 1958, Invitation to a March, 1960, Everybody Loves Opal, 1961, Family Affair, 1962, Too True To Be Good, 1963, And Things That Go Bump in the Night, 1965, Barefoot in the Park, 1965-66, You Know I Can't Hear You When the Water's Running, 1967, The Mother Lover, 1968, Butterflies Are Free, 1969, Veronica's Room, 1973, The Effect of Gamma Rays on Man-in-the-Moon Marigolds, 1971, Remember Me, 1975, Mother Courage and Her Children, 1975, Mrs. Gibbs in Our Town, 1976; one-woman shows Eleanor, 1976, Ladies at the Alamo, 1977, Margaret Sanger-Unfinished Business, 1989; movies include Miracle in the Rain, Bad Seed, Bus Stop, Hot Spell, My Six Loves, 1962, Up the Down Staircase, 1966, No Way To Treat A Lady, 1968, Butterflies Are Free, 1972, Zandy's Bride, 1974, The Hiding Place, 1975, Burnt Offerings, 1975, Wedding Band, 1975, Heartbreak Ridge, 1986, Eleemosynary, 1989, The Cemetery Club, 1990; TV movies, 1947—; TV series Trauma Center, Annie McGuire, 1988-89; Oscar nomination, Film Daily citation 1956, Variety Poll of N.Y. Drama Critics award 1958, Save Me A Place at Forest Lawn 1967, (N.Y. Emmy), Butterflies Are Free 1973 (Acad. award, Straw Hat award 1973, 75, 77), Wedding Band, 1973 (Emmy nomination), Mary Tyler Moore Show, 1976, 77, Rock Stairs at the White House, 1979, FDR's Last Year, 1987, The Cosby Show, 1987, (dayime show) One Life to Live, 1987. Recipient Outer Circle award, 1953, Daniel Blum award, 1953, Sylvania TV award, 1954, Donaldson award, 1955, Hollywood Fgn. Press award, 1956, March Dimes award, 1970, Aegis award, 1970, Ohio State U. Centennial award, 1970, Gov.'s award of Ohio, 1977, Ohiana Libr. award, 1978. Mem. Pi Beta Phi.

HECKER, ANNE, professional society administrator; b. Dallas, Oreg., July 6, 1924; d. Elwyn Gordon and Dorothy Ida (Dick) Craven; m. Robert F. Hecker, Sept. 28, 1946; children: Sandra, Barbara, Nancy. BA, U. Oreg., 1945. Staff correspondent UPI, Portland, Oreg., Madison, Wis., 1945-46; publ. editor Nat. Aeronautics Assn., Washington, 1947; dept. editor Pacific Builder & Engr., Seattle, 1951-53; mng. editor NW Medicine, Seattle, 1953-54; contbg. editor Argus, Seattle, 1961-65; dir. pub. relations Wash. State Dental Assn., Seattle, 1965-77, asst. exec. dir., 1977-85, cons. pub. relations, 1985-87, exec. dir., 1987—. Bd. dirs. Camp Fire Inc., Kansas City, 1980-81, Seattle, King County, 1980-84, 86—. Mem. Am. Soc. Assn. Execs., Women in Communications (pres. 1977-78, Disting. Service award 1986). Democrat. Home: 13065 15th Ave NE Seattle WA 98125 Office: Wash State Dental Assn 2033 Sixth Ave #333 UAL Bldg Seattle WA 98121

HECKER, DEBRA ANN, beverage company executive; b. Kirkwood, Mo., June 10, 1963; d. Russell Charles and Emmi Marie (Schmidt) H. BA in Acctg./BA, Drury Coll., Springfield, Mo., 1985. CPA, Mo. Audit asst. Mo. Auditors Office, Jefferson City, 1985-87; internal auditor Anheuser Busch Cos., St. Louis, 1985-88; adminstrv. mgr. Anheuser Busch Inc., Denver, 1988—. Republican. Office: Anheuser Busch Inc 1455 E 62nd Ave Denver CO 80216

HECKER, SHARON RUTH, agricultural economist; b. Indpls., Sept. 26, 1958; d. Fred Carl and Alice Maia (Stevens) H. BS in Internat. Agronomy, Purdue U., 1980. Sales rep. Eli Lilly & Co., Indpls., 1980-83; market reporter USDA Mktg. Svc., Washington, 1983-86; broker C.H. Robinson Co., Boston, 1986-88; cons. UN Internat. Trade Ctr., Boston, 1988—; cons., Costa Rican Growers Assn., 1988; speaker in field. Mem. Produce Mktg. Assn., United Fresh Fruit and Vegetable Assn., NAFE, Boston Big Sister Assn., Purdue Alumnae, Delta Gamma Alumnae. Office: UN 112 Water St Boston MA 02109

HECKERLING, AMY, film director; b. Bronx. Grad., NYU, 1975; fellow, Am. Film Inst. directing program, 1975. Dir. films including (short film) High Finance, Getting It Over With, Fast Times at Ridgemont High, 1982, Johnny Dangerously, 1984, National Lampoon's European Vacation, 1985, Look Who's Talking, 1989 (also screenwriter); film appearance in Into the Night, 1985. Address: Gersh Agy 222 N Canon Dr Beverly Hills CA 90210*

HECKLER, MARGARET MARY, former ambassador; b. Flushing, N.Y., June 21, 1931; d. John and Bridget (McKeon) O'Shaughnessy; children—Belinda West, Alison Anne, John M. BA, Albertus Magnus Coll., 1953; LLB, Boston Coll., 1956; student, U. Leiden, Holland, 1952; numerous hon. degrees. Bar: Mass. 1956, also U.S. Supreme Ct. 1956. Mem. 90th to 97th Congresses, 10th Dist. Mass.; founder co-chmn. Congl. Women's Caucus; sec. HHS, 1983-85; ambassador to Ireland, 1985-89; mem. Mass. Gov.'s Coun., 1963-66; Alternate del. Rep. Nat. Conv., 1964, del., 1968, 72, 80, 84. Named Outstanding Mother of Year in Politics, 1984; Prince Henry the Navigator award (Portugal). Home and Office: Am Embassy care US Dept State Washington DC 20520

HECKMAN, CAROL A., biology educator; b. East Stroudsburg, Pa., Oct. 18, 1944; d. Wilbur Thomas and Doris (Betts) H. BA, Beloit (Wis.) Coll., 1966; PhD, U. Mass., Amherst, 1972. Rsch. assoc. Yale U. Sch. Medicine, New Haven, 1973-75; staff mem. Oak Ridge (Tenn.) Nat. Lab., 1975-82; adj.

assoc. prof. U. Tenn.-Oak Ridge Biomed. Grad. Sch., 1980-82; assoc. prof. Bowling Green (Ohio) State U., 1982-86, prof. biology, 1986—; cons. NSF, Washington, 1977-80; dir. EM facility Bowling Green State U., 1982—; NSF trainee, Amherst, 1967-70. Contbr. articles to profl. jours., chpts. to books. Internat. Cancer Rsch. Tech. fellow Internat. Union Against Cancer, Lyon, France, 1980, Heritage Found. fellow, Calgary, Can., 1982, guest rsch. fellow, Uppsala, Sweden, 1990-92; grantee NSF, 1981-84, 90-92, grantee NIH, 1987-88. Mem. AAAS, Am. Soc. Cell Biology, Electron Microscopy Soc. Am., N.W. Ohio Electron Microscopy (sec.-treas. 1986-90), Tissue Culture Assn., Ohio Acad. Sci., Sigma Xi. Episcopalian. Home: 861 Ferndale Ct Bowling Green OH 43402 Office: Bowling Green State U Dept Biol Scis Bowling Green OH 43403-0212

HECKMAN, JOANN, small business owner; b. Newton, N.J., Feb. 23, 1950; d. James Richard and Frances Margaret (Bertram) H. A.S. in Communications, Centenary Coll., 1982, B.A. cum laude in Communications and Journalism, 1984. Freelance reporter, editorial asst. Daily Advance, Roxbury Twp., N.J., 1979-81; asst. mgr., pressperson Jag-Ton Print World, Hackettstown, N.J., 1985; owner, operator Words-Worth Word Processing Services, Budd Lake, N.J., 1984—; word processor MetLife Security Ins. Co., East Hanover, N.J., 1985-87; co-owner, pres. The Crystal Works, Hackettstown, N.J., 1987—. Mem. Nat. Assn. Female Execs., AAUW, Phi Theta Kappa (Merit cert. 1982), Alpha Chi. Republican. Baha'i. Avocations: photography, graphic art and design, freelance writing, crafting. Home: 313 Shore Rd PO Box 114 Budd Lake NJ 07828 Office: The Crystal Works PO Box 7101 Hackettstown NJ 07840

HECTOR-HARRIS, CAROL ANN, journalist; b. Boston, July 10, 1950; d. Harold Raphael and Matilda Rachel (Robinson) Hector; m. William Edward Harris, Jr., Apr. 14, 1973; children: Jān, Sharif. BA, Ohio State U., 1978, MA in Polit. Sci., 1981. Freelance reporter Columbus, 1977; campus reporter Sta. WOSU, WOSR, Columbus, 1978; asst. ops. mgr. Sta. WOSU, Columbus, 1977-78, reporter, producer, 1978-80; freelance reporter Nat. Pub. Radio, Wash., 1980-81; health reporter, producer Sta. WFBE, Flint, Mich., 1981-82; intern Leg. Services Com., Columbus, 1983-84; dir. Office Pub. Info., Ohio Dept. Human Svcs., Columbus, 1984—. Bd. dirs. Friends of the Homeless, Columbus, Kathryn's Day Care, Columbus; Rainbow Coalition-Jackson for Pres., Columbus. Mem. Women in Communications, Inc., Nat. Assn. Black Journalists. Democrat. Episcopalian. Home: 45 Franklin Park W Columbus OH 43205 Office: Ohio Dept Human Svcs 30 E Broad St 32nd Fl Columbus OH 43215

HEDBACK, BRENDA LEE, elementary school educator; b. Indpls., Apr. 21, 1940; d. Earl Temple and Dallas Louise (Newman) Williamson; m. Ronald Collier Esterline, Mar. 14, 1939 (div. 1976); children: Laura Lee, Jennifer Lynn; m. James Philip Hedback, Apr. 7, 1940; children: Lisa, Jeff, Karen. BA, Ball State U., 1962; MS, Butler U., 1969. Cert. tchr., Ind. Tchr. Pike Twp. Schs., Indpls., Ind., 1962-66, Washington Twp. Schs., Indpls., Ind., 1970-74, Orchard Country Day Sch., Ind., 1976-88; owner, mgr. The Gold Dust Emporium, Indpls., 1988-89; 4th grade tchr. St. Richard's Sch., Indpls., 1990—; leader ednl. tour Europe Am. Coun. for Internat. Studies, 1980, 85, 87; outdoor edn. experiences overnights Gnaw Bone Camp, Nashville, Ind., 1976-87. Sponsor Africa Christian Children's Fund, 1987—. Mem. Psi Iota Xi. Republican. Office: St Richard's Sch Indianapolis IN 46220

HEDDEN, LUCY MARGARET, medical records administrator; b. Charleston, S.C., Dec. 28, 1949; d. Julius Clyde and Elizabeth Eugenia (McKee) H. Student, Coll. of Charleston, 1968-70; BS in Med. Record Adminstrnv., Med. U. S.C., 1972. Dir. med. records Greenville (S.C.) Meml. Hosp., 1972-78, St. Margaret's Hosp., Montgomery, Ala., 1978-81, St. Vincent's Med. Ctr., Jacksonville, Fla., 1981—; med. record cons. various nursing homes, 1986—. Mem. Am. Med. Record Assn. Home: 7824 Fawn Valley Ln Jacksonville FL 32256 Office: St Vincent's Med Ctr 1800 Barrs St Jacksonville FL 32204

HEDGE, JEANNE COLLEEN, health physicist; b. Scottsburg, Ind., May 30, 1960; d. Paul Russell and Barbara Jean (Belshaw) H. BS in Environ. Health, Purdue U., 1983. Chemistry and health physics technician Marble Hill Nuclear Generating Sta., Pub. Service Ind., Madison, 1983-84; radiation protection asst. Hope Creek Generating Sta., Pub. Service Electric & Gas Co., Hancock's Bridge, N.J., 1984-85, radiation protection technician, 1985-89; engr. Pub. Svc. Electric & Gas Co., Hancock's Bridge, 1989-90, lead engr., 1990—; mem. People to People Internat. Citizen Ambassador Exchange, People's Republic China, 1988. Recipient 6th Kup Yellow Belt Am. Freestyle Tae Kwan Do award, 1990. Mem. AAAS, NOW, Am. Nuclear Soc., Health Physics Soc., Am. Pub. Health Assn., N.Y. Acad. Scis., Tau Beta Sigma. Democrat. Methodist.

HEDGE, MARY GELHAUS, librarian; b. Hardin County, Iowa, Nov. 20, 1952; d. Eitel Frederick and Hazel Doris (Reed) Gelhaus.; m. William Edward Hedge, Sept. 18, 1976. BA, Elmhurst Coll., 1975; MLS, Ind. U., 1981. Dir. Christian edn. St. John's United Ch. of Christ, Michigan City, Ind., 1975-80; libr. La Porte County (Ind.) Pub. Libr., 1982—. Mem. LaPorte Literacy Coalition. Mem. ALA, AAUW, Ind. Libr. Assn., Friends Libr., Beta Phi Mu. Democrat. Office: La Porte County Pub Libr 904 Indiana Ave La Porte IN 46350

HEDGECOCK, DIXIE LEE, sales executive; b. Colorado Springs, Colo., Sept. 22, 1962; d. Jimmie Hardin and Lois Ann Vander (Hamm) Barbour; m. Craig Alan Hedgecock, June 7, 1986. BBA in Mktg., U. Iowa, 1985. Sec.-receptionist Corn States Hybrid Svc., Des Moines, 1982, 83, 84; retail account mgr., sales rep. I and II NCR Corp., Irving, Tex., 1985-88; account mgr. INFO-MART, Dallas, 1988-90; account exec. BEHAVIORTECH, 1990—. Mem. Nat. Retail Merchants Assn., U. Iowa Alumni Assn. Home: 1326 Pickwick Ln Irving TX 75060

HEDGES, JEAN KYLE, educator; b. Big Stone Gap, Va., Jan. 11, 1930; d. Robert Swanson and Vera Sue (Hampton) K.; m. Lewis Charles Hedges, Sept. 11, 1954; children: L. Kyle, S. Blair, Susan H., R. Hampton. BA, Mary Baldwin Coll., 1951; postgrad. studies, U. Va., 1970. Cert. tchr., Va. Tchr. Fairfax County Schs., Falls Church, Va., 1951-53, Alexandria, Va., 1953-54; subst. tchr. Arlington County Schs., Arlington, Va., 1972-75; sect. supr. County Treas. Office, Arlington, 1975-87; substitute tchr. Arlington County Schs., Arlington, 1987—. Mem. Ashton Heights Civic Assn., 1965—, English Curriculum Adv. Com., 1968-75; pres. Matthew Maury Sch. PTA, Arlington, Va., 1970-71; v.p. Ashton Heights Civic Assn., Arlington, 1973-74; asst. chief election officer Ashton Heights Precinct, Arlington, 1987—; treas. Women's Com. for Arlington Symphony, 1990; coord. FISH, North Arlington, 1989—. Mem. AAUW, DAR. Republican. Methodist. Home: 415 N Monroe St Arlington VA 22201

HEDGES, LORRETTE JEAN, management consultant; b. Saline County, Nebr.; d. John Jack and Bertha Bernice (Kunce) Kubicek; m. David V. Hedges; 1 child, Kathryn Ann. BS in Mgmt., U. Nebr., 1977. Exec. sec. Crete (Nebr.) Mills, 1949-57; office sec. John P. Burrell & Co., Lincoln, Nebr., 1957-58; asst. to agy. mgr. Equitable Life Assurance Soc. N.Y., Lincoln, 1959-61; office sec., cashier Northwestern Metal Co., Lincoln, 1961-82; bus. mgr. The Golden Carrot, Inc., Lincoln, 1982-89; cons. Lincoln, 1989—; adminstrv. asst. Kollmorgan and Assocs., Lincoln, 1990—; mgmt. cons. Lincoln, 1990—. Pub.: Uniquely Naphis: A Cookbook from Naphis Temple, 1980. Bd. dirs., pres. Izaac Walton League, Crete, 1957, Lincoln (Nebr.) coun. Campfire, Inc., budget chmn., 1975, bd. chmn., pres., 1979; bd. dirs., mem. residential chmn. Lancaster County Civic, Am. Cancer Soc., Lincoln, 1972-77; residential co-chmn. Leo Hill Regent Com., Lincoln, 1976. Recipient Luther Halsey Gulick award, Coun. Campfire, Lincoln, 1981, John Collier award, 1975; named Vol. of Yr. Lincoln Coun. Campfire, 1975. Mem. NAFE, Bus. and Profl. Women's Club (bd. dirs., state recording sec. 1960-61), Jobs Daus. (pres. Mothers Club 1979-80, Guardian sec. 1990). Democrat.

HEDGES, MARYLYNN JARRARD, health care company executive; b. Eastman, Ga., Jan. 5, 1951; d. Rudyard Kipling and Juanita Wimberley (Bledsoe) Jarrard; m. Grady Colson Barnhill, Feb. 26, 1971 (div. 1978); children: Briana Veda Barnhill, Brett Colson Barnhill; m. Thomas Michael, Feb. 19, 1980 (dec.). AA, DeKalb Community Coll., 1970, AS, 1977; BS summa cum laude, U. So. Miss., 1982, MS, 1986. RN. Charge nurse Peachford Hosp., Atlanta, 1977-78; charge nurse Piedmont Hosp., Atlanta, 1978-79; asst. dir. nursing Singing River Hosp. Systems, Pascagoula, Miss., 1980-85; shift supr. C.P.C. Parkwood Hosp., Atlanta, 1985-87; psychiat. rev. mgr. Am. Psychiat. Assn., Washington, Atlanta, 1987-89; dir. ops. Parkside Health Mgmt. Corp., Atlanta, Chgo., 1989-90; dir. nursing, dir. quality assurance Laurel Heights Hosp., Atlanta. Citizen ambassador to China (healthcare) People to People Internat., Spokane, 1989, 90. Mem. ANA, NAFE, Atlanta C. of C. (bus. mem.), Sigma Theta Tau, Kappa Delta Pi. Home: 5973 Wintergreen Rd Norcross GA 30093

HEDGES, MOLLIE ELLEN, elementary school educator; b. Columbus, Ohio, Oct. 14, 1952; d. Tracy Wheat and Maxine (Christy) Peters; m. Robert William Frampton, Sept. 15, 1973 (div. Feb. 1980); m. Charles Richard Hedges, Dec. 20, 1981; 1 child, Colin Harrison. BS in Elem. Edn., Kent State U., 1974; MA in Guidance and Counseling, Ohio State U., 1979. Cert. tchr., Ohio. Substitute thcr. Columbus Pub.Schs., 1974-76; tchr. 5th grade Circleville (Ohio) City Schs., 1976-77, tchr. 4th grade, 1977—. Deacon, Presbyn. Ch. of Circleville, 1990—. Mem. AAUW. Republican.

HEDGESPETH, JOANNE, psychologist, professor; b. Balt., July 15, 1954; d. James Rodman and Betty Jean (Ockenhouse) H. BA, Covenant Coll., 1977; MA, Rosemead Sch. of Psychology, 1979, PhD, 1982. Lic. psychologist. Postdoctoral fellow Reiss Davis Child Study Ctr., L.A., 1983-84; clin. psychologist USAF, Dayton, Ohio, 1984-86; pvt. practice psychology Beverly Hills, Calif., 1986—; asst. prof. psychology Pepperdine U., L.A., 1986—. Mem. Am. Psychol. Assn., Calif. State Psychol. Assn. Republican. Office: Pepperdine U GSEP 400 Corporate Pointe Culver City CA 92030

HEDICKER, MARIANNE, travel agency executive; b. E. Chicago, Ill., Nov. 4, 1946; d. Willaim C. and Eve (Constance) Slingerland; m. Daniel Jepperson (div.); children: Robyn L. Jepperson, Kelly D. Jepperson; m. William A. Moore (div.); children: Sara A. Moore, Olivia M. Moore. Student, U. Cin., 1969; student, S.O.C., 1982-84. Buyer McAlpins, Cin., 1969-75; owner Century Constrn., Cin., 1976-84; placement dir. Tri-State Travel Sch., Cin., 1984-85; travel agt. Tri-State Travel Sch., 1984-85; mgr. Accent on Travel, Cin., 1986-87, Blue Ash Exec. Travel, Cin., 1987; gen. mgr. Executravel, Cin., 1987-88; v.p. Executravel, Ft. Mitchell, Ky., 1988—. Home: 2338 Harrison Ave Cincinnati OH 45211 Office: Executravel 211 Grandview Dr Fort Mitchell KY 41017

HEDLEY-WHYTE, ELIZABETH TESSA, neuropathologist; b. London, Jan. 17, 1937; came to U.S., 1960; d. George Stanley and Elizabeth Margery (Hacking) Waller; m. John Hedley-Whyte, Sept. 19, 1959. MB, BS, Durham (U.K.) U., 1960; MD, U. Newcastle Upon Tyne (U.K.), 1976. Diplomate Am. Bd. Pathology, Examiner neuropathology. Resident pathology Children's New Eng. Deaconess and Peter Bent Brigham Hosps., Boston, 1960-65; fellow Cerebral Palsy Fedn., 1965-66; asst. neuropathologist Children's Hosp., 1966-68; instr., asst. prof., assoc. prof. pathology Harvard Med. Sch., Boston, 1968—; assoc. neuropathologist Mass. Gen. Hosp., Boston, 1981-83, neuropathologist, 1983—, dir. pathology residency tng., 1987—; cons. NIH, 1976-81. Contbr. articles to profl. jours. Welcome Trust fellow, 1984-85. Mem. NINCDS (chair program project com. 1979-81), Am. Assn. Neuropathologists (v.p., chair coms. 1976—), New Eng. Soc. Pathologists (sec., treas., pres. 1980-86). Office: Mass Gen Hosp 55 Fruit St Boston MA 02114

HEDLING, SUSAN ECKSTROM, newspaper editor; b. Buffalo, Mar. 16, 1946; d. Albert Wallace and Marguerite (Jefferson) Eckstrom; m. William George, Apr. 22, 1967, (div. May 1980); 1 child, Kristen; m. Thomas David Evans, Apr. 1, 1989. BA, Allegheny Coll., Meadville, 1967. Reporter Courier Express, Buffalo, 1967-69; polit. writer Norwalk (Conn.) Hour, 1970-72; editor Pitts. Bd. of Edn., 1972-77; cons. Booz, Allen & Hamilton, Washington; reporter, editor, columnist The Montgomery Jour., Rockville, Md., 1979—; Mem. steering com. Montgomery Leadership, Rockville, 1988—. Pres. Grosvenor Park Condo Assn., Rockville, 1981-82, Grosvenor Homeowners Assn., Rockville, 1982-85. Recipient Best Govt. Coverage Del. D.C. Press Assn., 1987, Best Series Del. D.C. Press Assn., 1988, Best Colum Del. D.C. Press. Assn., 1988. Mem. Montgomery County Press Assn. (pres.). Home: 7940 Brink Rd Gaithersburg MD 20879 Office: The Montgomery Jour 2 Research Ct Rockville MD 20850

HEDMAN, JANICE LEE, business executive; b. Elmhurst, Ill., Feb. 7, 1938; d. George Marion Hickman and Vera Beryl (Olsen) Sample; m. Daryl F. Hedman, Aug. 29, 1971 (div. Aug. 1983); children: Kevin G., Gregory Scott, Danny L., Shelly L.. Wolanski. Student, U. Puget Sound, 1970, Tacoma (Wash.) Community Coll., 1980. Head teller Puget Sound Nat. Bank, Tacoma, 1970-75; real estate agt. Shorewood Realty, Gig Harbor, Wash., 1975-80; mktg. rep. Western Fin. Planning, Inc., Tacoma, 1981-83; co-owner Schatz Avant Garde, Gig Harbor, 1984-86; asst. mgr. Classic Restaurant, Gig Harbor, 1984; co-owner, mgr. Hedman Enterprises, Gig Harbor, 1976—; v.p. adminstrn. Teardrop Am., Inc., Wenatchee, Wash., 1986—; pres. Teardrop N.W. Inc., Wenatchee, 1988—; co-owner J&R Mktg., Wenatchee, 1989—. Asst. Woman's Task Force, Tacoma, 1980, 81. Mem. C. of C. (ambasador), Epsilon Sigma Alfa (pres. 1980-81, v.p. 1981-82). Home: 803 82d St Ct E Tacoma WA 98404 Office: John L Scott Inc Gig Harbor Br 4801 Point Fosdick Dr NW Gig Harbor WA 98335

HEDTKE, BARBARA ANN, medical center executive; b. Tigerton, Wis., Feb. 5, 1956; d. Robert E. and Dorothy M. (Block) H. BS Social Work/Psychology, U. Wis., Oshkosh, 1977; MBA, U. Wis., Milw., 1983. Social worker, coord. Waupaca County Dept. Social Svcs./Unified Health Svcs., Wis., 1977-80; counselor II SLIC, St. Paul, 1980-81; exec. curriculum and rsch. asst. Bus. and Econs. Depts., U. Wis., Milw., 1982-83; asst. to v.p. Nicholas Co., Milw., 1983-84; cons. Stevens and Assocs., St. Paul, 1984; fin. mgr. MELD, Mpls., 1984-85; bus. mgr. Riverside Med. Ctr., Waupaca, Wis., 1986-90; trainer Nashville, 1987-90; asst. mgr. Bellin Hosp., Green Bay, Wis., 1990—. Researcher: (book) Economy of Chile, 1983. Bd. dirs. Waupaca Jaycees, 1987, mgmt. v.p., 1989, pres., 1989. Recipient Dir.'s Award for Outstanding Svc. Crisis Intervention Svcs. Winnebago County, Wis., 1976; Wis. State Honor scholar, 1974, Melvin Laird scholar, 1974. Mem. NAFE, Wis. Med. Credit Assn., Wis. Assn. Hosp. Admitting Mgrs., Cheyenne Shuffle Dance Club. Home: 1711 Libal St Green Bay WI 54301 Office: Bellin Hosp 744 S Webster Ave Green Bay WI 54305

HEEKIN, VALERIE ANNE, telecommunications technician; b. Santa Monica, Calif., Nov. 7, 1953; d. Edward Raphael and Jane Eileen (Potter) H. AA, L.A. Valley Coll., 1980; BS magna cum laude, Calif. Baptist Coll., 1987. Telecommunications technician Pacific Bell Co., Canoga Park, Calif., 1971—; pres. Odyssey Adventures, Inc., Sylmar, Calif., 1987—. Pres. Parkwood Sylmar Homeowners Assn., 1981-89; activist civil rights. Republican. Roman Catholic. Office: Pacific Bell Co 7222 Remmet Ave Canoga Park CA 91303

HEERE, KAREN R., astrophysicist; b. Teaneck, N.J., Apr. 9, 1944; d. Peter N. and Alice E. (Hall) Heere; m. Gary L. Villere, Aug. 28, 1967 (div. Feb. 1988). BA, U. Pa., 1965; MA, U. Calif., Berkeley, 1968; PhD, U. Calif., Santa Cruz, 1976. Research assoc. Nat. Research Council NASA Ames Research Ctr., Moffett Field, Calif., 1977-79; research astronomer U. Calif., Santa Cruz and NASA/Ames, 1979-86; assoc. prof. San Francisco State U., 1986-87; scientist Science Applications Internat. Corp., Los Altos, Calif., 1974-76, 1987—; vis. scientist TATA Inst. for Fundamental Rsch., Bombay, India, 1984; adj. prof. San Francisco State U., 1987—. Author numerous articles in field. Mem. Am. Astron. Soc. Home: 226 Flynn Ave Mountain View CA 94043 Office: Sci Applications Internat Corp 5150 El Camino Real Ste B-31 Los Altos CA 94022

HEFFER, JANET CASSANDRA, skating choreographer, writer; b. Ogden, Utah, Jan. 24, 1947; d. Ward Harris Smith and Florence E. (Empy) Powers; m. James Edward Heffer, June 8, 1968 (div. Apr. 1987); children: Clinton Edward, Kelly Cassandra. Student, U. Colo. Skating soloist and choreographer Sun Valley Ice Skating Club, Idaho, 1965; legal sec. Prieve, Gerlach & Meyer, Milw., 1968-69; skating profl. Denver U., 1969-73; skating profl. and choreographer Denver Country Club, 1969-74; prin. Creative Concepts in Advt., Denver, 1984—; cons. to Denver Civic Ballet, Symphony Guild, Cen. City Opera Assn., golf and tennis assns. Choreographer, dir. numerous skating shows, Sun Valley, U. Colo., 1965-71; writer TV show The Waterproof Duck. Rep. committeewoman, Denver, 1971-74; mem. Am. Biog. Inst. Adv. Bd., Colo. Barre Assn., Chancellors Soc.-Denver U. Libr. Assn. Recipient gold medal U.S. Figure Skating Assn., 1962. Mem. NAFE, U.S. Figure Skating Assn., U.S. Golf Assn. (assoc.), D.C. Women's Libr. Assn., Performing Arts Alliance, Internat. Platform Assn., Kappa Kappa Gamma. Mormon. Clubs: Cherry Hills Country, Glenmoor Country (Denver). Home: 4505 S Yosemite #117 Denver CO 80237 Office: Birko Corp PO Box 127 Westminster CO 80030

HEFFERNAN, CAROL GAMBLE, marketing professional; b. Wilmington, Del., Apr. 8, 1969; d. Radford Graham and Joyce Gail (Sampson) Gamble; m. Dennis Nelson Heffernan, Aug. 11, 1989. BS in Math., BA in English, King's Coll., Wilkes Barre, Pa., 1980. Mktg. support supr. Market Vision, N.Y.C., 1980-83; product mgr. Sanyo Bus. Systems, Moonachie, N.J., 1983-86; market planning mgr. Princeton (N.J.) Graphic Systems, 1986-88; mktg. dir. USNI Mil. Database, Arlington, Va., 1988-89, SCAN C2C Inc., Washington, 1989—. Active Bus. Vols. to Arts, Washington Cultural Alliance. Mem. Bus./Profl. Advertisers Assn., Info. Industry Assn., Chem. Mgmt. & Resources Assn. Office: SCAN C2C Inc 500 E St SW Washington DC 20024

HEFFERNAN, PATRICIA CONNER, management consultant; b. N.Y.C., Oct. 11, 1946; d. Arthur S. and Catherine (Center) Conner; B.A., U. Va., 1968; M.B.A., Suffolk U., 1980; m. John Joseph Heffernan, Sept. 13, 1969. Cert. mgmt. cons. office mgr. Wobbly Barn, Killington, Vt., 1968-72; bus. mgr. Woodstock Country Sch., Vt., 1972-74; treas., assoc. dean Vt. Law Sch., Royalton, Vt., 1974-83; mgmt. cons. Heffernan & Assocs., Killington, 1982-87; mgmt. cons., v.p. Sandage Inc., Burlington, Vt., 1987—. Vt. del. White House Conf. on Small Bus.; mem. region 1 adv. coun. U.S. Small Bus. Adminstrn.; mem. Gov.'s Commn. on Women; bd. dirs. Rutland div. Chittenden Bank, Rutland Regional Med. Ctr. Trustee, pres. Killington Mountain Sch., 1978-85; mem. Killington Planning Commn., 1975, vice chmn., 1976, chmn., 1977-79, 83-87; mem. Killington Zoning Bd., 1979-84, Vt. Epilepsy Assn., 1977—, Vt. Telecommunications Commn., Vt. Econ. Devel. Adv. Coun.; mem. Vt. steering com. for ACE Nat. Identification Program for Women in Higher Edn., 1978-83. Named Outstanding Leader Vt. YWCA, 1985, Woman of Yr. Vt. Bus. and Profl. Women Found., 1986. Mem. Inst. Mgmt. Cons. (v.p. New Eng. region), Women Bus. Owners Vt. (dir. 1983—, founder, pres. 1984-86), Nat. Assn. Women Bus. Owners. Office: Sandage Inc 215 College St Burlington VT 05401

HEFNER, CHRISTIE ANN, international media and marketing executive; b. Chgo., Nov. 8, 1952; d. Hugh Marston and Mildred Marie (Williams) H. BA summa cum laude in English and Am. Lit., Brandeis U., 1974. Freelance journalist, Boston, 1974-75; spl. asst. to chmn. Playboy Enterprises, Inc., Chgo., 1975-78, v.p., 1978-82, bd. dirs., 1979—, vice chmn., 1986-88, pres. 1982-88, chief oper. officer, 1984-88, chmn., chief exec. officer, 1988—; bd. dirs. Playboy Found.-Playboy Enterprises, Inc., Ill. chpt. ACLU, Mag. Pubs. Assn. Recipient Agness Underwood award L.A. chpt. Women in Communications, 1984, Founders award Midwest Women's Ctr., 1986, Human Rights award Am. Jewish Com., 1987, Harry Kalven Freedom of Expression award ACLU, Ill., 1987, Spirit of Life award City of Hope, 1988. Mem. Brandeis Nat. Women's Com. (life), Com. of 200, Young. Pres. Orgn., Chgo. Network, Voters for Choice, Dem. Nat. Com. Fin. Coun., Goodman Theatre, Phi Beta Kappa. Democrat. Office: Playboy Enterprises Inc 680 N Lake Shore Dr Chicago IL 60611

HEFNER, JERRIE LOU, personnel management specialist; b. Caro, Mich., Feb. 22, 1957; d. Donald Keith and Louise Marie (Benfield) Long; m. Johnny Stephen Hefner, Dec. 22, 1976; 1 child, Keith Michael. BBA, Drury Coll., 1983; M in Human Relations, Webster Coll., St. Louis, 1985; M in Mgmt., Webster Coll., 1985. Bus. mgr. Drury Coll., Ft. Leonard Wood, Mo., 1983-87; personnel mgmt. specialist civilian personnel office U.S. Dept. of Army, Ft. Leonard Wood, 1987—; instr. Tarkio Coll., Rolla, Mo., 1986—. Sgt. AUS, 1975-78. Named Outstanding Young Woman of Am., 1983. Mem. Am. Soc. Mil. Comptrollers, AAUW (1st v.p. 1986-87, pres. 1988-90). Home: 52 Rolla Gardens Dr Rolla MO 65401 Office: Civilian Personnel Office Bldg 315 Fort Leonard MO 65473

HEGEL, CAROLYN MARIE, farmer, farm bureau executive; b. Lagro, Ind., Apr. 19, 1940; d. Ralph H. and Mary Lucile (Rudig) Lynn; m. Tom Lee Hegel, June 3, 1962. Student pub. schs., Columbia City, Ind. Bookkeeper Huntington County Farm Bur. Co-op, Inc. (Ind.), 1959-67; office mgr., 1967-70; twp. woman leader Wabash County Farm Bur., Inc. (Ind.), 1970-73, county woman leader, 1973-76; dist. woman leader Ind. Farm Bur., Inc., Indpls., 1976-80, 2d v.p., 1980—, chmn. women's com., 1980—, exec. com. 1988—; farmer, Andrews, Ind., 1962—; dir. Farm Bur. Ins. Co., Indpls., 1980—, exec. com., 1988; mem. rural task force Great Lakes States Econ. Devel. Commn., 1987-88, Ind. Farm Bur. Svc. Co., 1980—, bd. dirs. Ind. Farm Bur. Found., Indpls., 1980—, Ind. Inst. Agr., Food and Nutrition, Indpls., 1982—, Ind. 4-H Found., Lafayette, 1983-86; com. mem. Hoosier Homestead Award Cert. Com., Indpls., 1980—; speaker in field. Women in the Field columnist Hoosier Farmer mag., 1980—. Named one of Outstanding Farm Woman of Yr. County Woman Mag., 1987. Organizer farm div. Wabash County Am. Cancer Soc. Fund Dr. (Ind.), 1974; Sunday sch. tchr., bd. dir. childrens' activities Bethel United Meth. Ch., 1965—, pres. Bethel United Methodist Women, Lagro, 1975-81; bd. dirs. N.E. Ind. Kidney Found., 1984—, Nat. Kidney Found. of Ind., 1985-89, v.p., 1986—. Recipient State 4-H Home Econs. ward Ind. 4-H, 1960; named Farm Woman of 1987 Country Woman mags. Mem. Leadership Am. Program, Women in Communication, Inc., Ind. Agrl. Mktg. Assn. (bd. dirs. 1980—), Producers Mktg. Assn. (bd. dirs. 1980—), Am. Farm Bur. Fedn. (midwest rep. to women's com. 1986—). Republican. Home: RR 1 Andrews IN 46702 Office: Ind Farm Bur Inc 130 E Washington St PO Box 1290 Indianapolis IN 46206

HEGENDERFER, JONITA SUSAN, public relations executive; b. Chgo., Mar. 18, 1944; d. Clifford Lincoln and Cornelia Anna (Larson) Hazzard; m. Gary William Hegenderfer, Mar. 12, 1971 (dec. 1978). BA, Purdue U., 1965; postgrad. Calif. State U.-Long Beach, 1966-67, Northwestern U., 1969-70. Tchr. English, Long Beach schs., Calif., 1965-68; editorial asst. Playboy Mag., Chgo., 1968-70; communications specialist Am. Med. Assn., Chgo., 1970-72; v.p. Home Data, Hinsdale, Ill., 1972-75; mktg. mgr. Olympic Savs. & Loan, Berwyn, Ill., 1975-79; sr. v.p. Golin/Harris Communications, Chgo., 1979-89; pres. JSH & A, Chgo., 1989; bd. dirs. Chgo. Internat. Film Festival, 1989, 90. Editor directory, Fin. Info. Nat. Directory, 1972; author: Slim Guide to Spas, 1984; contbr. articles to profl. jours. Co-chmn. pub. rels. com. Am. Cancer Soc., Chgo., 1984; com. mem. March of Dimes, Chgo., 1986; mem. pub. rels. com. Girl Scouts Chgo., 1989-90. Recipient 3 Golden Trumpet awards Publicity Club Chgo., 1983, 86, Silver Trumpet awards, 1984, 86, 88, Spectra awards Internat. Assn. Bus. Communicators, 1984, 85, 87, Gold Quill award, 1985, Bronze Anvil award Pub. Rels. Soc. Am., 1985. Mem. Am. Mktg. Assn., Publicity Club of Chgo., Pub. Rels. Soc. Am., Chgo. Women in Pub. Clubs: Council on Fgn. Relations, Art Inst. Chgo., Cinema Chgo. (bd. dirs.). Avocations: travel, photography. Office: JSH & A 3961 Fairview Downers Grove IL 60515

HEGHINIAN, ELIZABETH ALBAN TRUMBOWER, artist, educator; b. N.Y.C., Jan. 11, 1917; d. Eli Cadwallader and Maria Lucas (Coyle) Trumbower; course in indsl. design Pratt Inst., 1938; B.S. magna cum laude, N.Y. U., 1950, M.A., 1952, Ph.D., 1957; postgrad. Bklyn. Inst. Arts and Scis., 1963-66, Bklyn. Mus. Art Sch., L.I. U., 1963-66, Fairleigh Dickinson U., 1970; studied under Richard Mayhew, Geogiana Brown Harbeson, Edith Fetterolf, Katheryn I. Young, Howard W. Arnold, I.-Ching Ku; m. Aram Lincoln Heghinian, Aug. 24, 1957; children—Elizabeth Alban, Marie Hunazant. Indsl. designer Belle Kogan Assos., 1938-40; art dir. Norscross Pubs., 1940-42; buyer for battle damaged U.S. naval vessels and equipment Arma Corp., 1942-45; dir. arts and crafts YWCA Camp Program, 1946; designer Cosmopolitan Crafts, Camp Fire Outfitting Co., 1946-47; faculty N.Y. U., 1947-61, asst. prof. edn., 1957-61; specialist consultation services nat. arts and crafts com. Boys' Clubs Am., 1949-65; research and practicum in remedial reading techniques N.Y.C. Pub. Sch., Bklyn., 1966-68; exhibited in group shows Pratt Inst., 1936-38, N.Y. U., 1948-52; represented in permanent collection Bklyn. Mus. Art Sch., pvt. collections. Mem. nat. adv. com. on recreation programs and activities arts and crafts sect. Nat. Recreation Assn., 1958-62; pres. Camp Jefferson, Inc., N.Y.C.; dir. Camp Jefferson, Palisades Interstate Park, N.Y., 1945-86 ; active town wide camping and sch. year program Girl Scouts U.S.A., 1969-73; mem. N.Y. Assn. for Brain Injured Children, 1963-86 . Recipient Founders Day certificate, N.Y. U., 1950. Mem. Am. Watercolor Soc. (asso.), AAUW, Nat. Congress Parents and Tchrs., Tenafly Nature Center Assn., Palisades Interstate Park Camp Dirs.' Assn., Pi Lambda Theta, Kappa Delta Pi, Epsilon Pi Tau. Author: The Contribution of Craft Activities to the Philosophy and Objectives of Boys Clubs of America, 1957; (monograph) Crafts in Boys' Clubs, 1958. Address: 52 Howard Park Dr Tenafly NJ 07670

HEGINBOTHAM, JAN STURZA, sculptor; b. Flushing, N.Y., Dec. 8, 1954; d. Herman Louis and Evelyn Shirley (Cantor) Sturza; m. Donald Wesley Heginbotham, Aug. 3, 1975. BA in Secondary Art Edn., U. Md., 1975; pvt. study with, Boris Blai, Phila., 1976-78. Sculpture, workshops Landen Sch., Bethesda, Md., 1985, 87, 89, Columbia Union Coll., Takoma Park, Md., 1987; workshop coord. Arlington (Va.) Art Ctr., 1986-90; self-employed sculptor Falls Church, Va., 1976—; conductor workshops in field; works in pub. collection at Burtonsville High Sch., Montgomery, Md. Prin. works exhibited at Acad. of the Arts, Easton, Md., 1986, 90, Staunton (Va.) Fine Art Assn., 1989, Three Rivers. Arts Festival, Pitts., 1989, Audobon Artist's Annuals, Nat. Arts Club, N.Y.C., 1984, 89, Allied Artist's Am., Nat. Arts Club, N.Y.C., 1982, 86, 88, Artist's Equity, M.L. King Jr. Libr., Washington, 1988, Essex (Md.) Community Coll., Cockpit Gallery, 1986, Arlington Art Ctr. Membership, 1986, Holy Family Coll., Phila., 1985, Landon Sch., Bethesda, 1985, Pen & Brush, N.Y.C., 1985, McGillis Gardens Gallery, Bethesda, 1990; pub. commn. Montgomery County Pub. Schs., 1988. Merit scholar Scottsdale (Ariz.) Artist's Sch., 1987; recipient Members and Assocs. award Allied Artists of Am., 1986, Orion Nova award, 1982, Cert. of Award, Mayor and Mrs. Marion Barry of Washington, 1981; fellow Am. U., Washington, 1990. Mem. Artists Equity, Internat. Sculpture Ctr., Arlington Arts Ctr., Montgomery County Arts Coun. Home: 6123 Brook Dr Falls Church VA 22044

HEIDELBERG, HELEN SUSAN HATVANI, dentist; b. Greenville, Pa., July 30, 1957; d. Balazs Robert and Ilona Borbala (Nemeth) Hatvani; m. David Raymond Heidelberg, June 4, 1983; children: David William, Laura Shari, Lisa Nicole. AA, Cuyahoga Community Coll., 1977; BS in Biology magna cum laude, Cleve. State U., 1979; DDS, Case Western Reserve U., 1983. Resident in dentistry North Chicago (Ill.) VA Med. Hosp., 1983-84; assoc. dentist Steven D. Miller, DDS, Vernon Hills, Ill., 1984-85; gen. practice dentistry Norwalk, Ohio, 1986—. Mem. ADA, Ohio Dental Assn., N. Cen. Ohio Dental Soc., Great Lakes Dental Soc. (v.p. 1984), Norwalk C. of C. Home: 4 Victoria Cir Norwalk OH 44857 Office: Fisher-Titus Med Pk 266 Benedict Ave Norwalk OH 44857

HEIFETZ, SONIA, retired pharmacist; b. Rowne, Poland; d. Zise and Toiba (Ehrlich) Heifetz; came to U.S., 1929, naturalized, 1934; Ph.G., Temple U., 1933. Asst. chief pharmacist Grad. Hosp. U. Pa., Phila., 1937-49, dir. pharmacy services, 1949-77; formerly pharmacist-mgr. Rite-Aide Corp., now ret. Cert. tchr. of Russian, Phila. Bd. of Edn. div. sch. extension; asst. dir. pharmacy Eastern State Sch. and Hosp., Trevose, Pa., 1987—. Mem. Am. Soc. Hosp. Pharmacists, Del. Soc. Hosp. Pharmacists (hon.), Pa. Soc. Hosp. Pharmacists (hon.), Phila. Guild Hosp. Pharmacists (v.p. 1966, treas. 1967-77), AAUW. Home: 2665 Willits Rd Apt 324 Philadelphia PA 19114

HEIGHT, DOROTHY EPHRATES, insurance company executive; b. Albion, Mich., Feb. 23, 1950; d. Woodrow and Lillie Bell (Simpson) Wilson; m. Elbert L. Gibson, Aug. 6, 1968 (div. 1984); children: Illya, Erika; m. Jim F. Height. AA, Kellog's Community Coll., 1982; BA, Eastern Mich. U., 1985. Sr. agency adminstrn. specialist IV State Farm Ins. Co., Marshall, Mich., 1971-84, supr. II, 1984-88, supr. III, sr. agy. adminstrn. specialist, 1988—. Speaker Call Someone Concern, Inc., Albion, 1985-86; chmn. State Farm campaign United Way, 1988, active bd. of Greater Battle Creek; vol. Black History program Albion Pub. Schs., 1987; chmn. hospitality com. Albion Community Theater, 1981-84; mem. Table for Black Women, Battle Creek, Mich., 1985; grad. Project Blueprint, 1989; active Mid County Consortium Exec. Bd. Scholar Am. Bus. Women Assn., 1984, Miller Found., 1982, Eastern Star, 1982; recipient Nat. Stephen Buffon award Am. Bus. Women Assn., 1985. Mem. Nat. Assn. Female Execs., Sch. Social Work Assn., Nat. Mgmt. Assn. (bd. dirs. 1988), NAACP (bd. dirs. 1985-86). Democrat. Baptist.

HEIGHTON, GLADYS EHRENREICH, banker; b. Medina, N.Y., Aug. 2, 1932; d. Wilbur J. and Ada (Amos) Ehrenreich; m. George J. Heighton, June 14, 1958. Student, Am. Inst. Banking, U. Mass. Various positions to note teller Marine Midland Bank, Medina, 1950-75; asst. br. mgr. Lockport Savs. Bank, Medina, 1975-76, br. mgr., 1976-79, asst. sec., br. mgr., 1979-89, banking officer, br. mgr., 1989—. Former fin. sec. United Meth. Ch.; former rep. Gateway Home for Children, Williamsville, N.Y.; former county treas., sec. Salvation Army; former country treas. Am. Heart Assn.; former treas. Save Children Found.; former mem. adv. bd. Orleans County Nutrition for Aging; fund campaigner United Way; bd. dirs. Am. Cancer Soc., 1989—. Mem. Medina C. of C., Medina Women's Orgn., Medina Bus. and Profl. Women's Club), Order Eastern Star, Women of Moose. Home: 138 Chadwick St Medina NY 14103 Office: Lockport Savs Bank 55 East Ave Lockport NY 14103

HEILBRON, SUSAN M., publishing company executive, lawyer. BA magna cum laude, Syracuse U., 1966, MPA with highest honors, 1968; JD, Yale U., 1977. Rsch. analyst for chief exec. Nassau County, N.Y., 1966-67; pers. intern U.S. Govt., 1968-69; spl. asst. to pres. Am. Paper Inst., 1969-72; dir. planning, rsch. and evaluation, Office of Neighborhood Govt. Office of Mayor, N.Y.C., 1973-74, mayor's legis. rep. to city coun., 1979; assoc. Cravath, Swaine & Moore, N.Y.C., 1977-79, 80-84; commr. Dept. Ports and Terminals, N.Y.C., 1979-80; sr. v.p., gen. counsel N.Y. State Urban Devel. Corp., 1984-86; exec. v.p., supr. legal affairs The Trump Orgn., N.Y.C., from 1986; now v.p., gen. counsel Macmillan Pergammon Communication and Pub. Group, N.Y.C. Mem. N.Y. staff Robert Kennedy for Pres., 1968. Fellow Yale Law Sch., 1977. Mem. ABA, Assn. of Bar of City of N.Y., Phi Beta Kappa. Office: Macmillan Inc 866 3d Ave New York NY 10022*

HEILBRUN, CAROLYN GOLD, English literature educator; b. East Orange, N.J., Jan. 13, 1926; d. Archibald and Estelle (Roemer) Gold; m. James Heilbrun, Feb. 20, 1945; children: Emily, Margaret, Robert. B.A., Wellesley Coll., 1947; M.A., Columbia U., 1951, Ph.D., 1959; D.H.L., U. Pa., 1984, Bucknell U., 1985, Russell Sage Coll., 1987, Smith Coll., 1989; D.F.A., Rivier Coll., 1986. Instr. Bklyn. Coll., 1959-60; instr. Columbia U., N.Y.C., 1960-62, asst. prof., 1962-67, assoc. prof., 1967-72, prof. English lit., 1972—; Avalon Found. prof. humanities Columbia U., 1986—; vis. prof. U. Calif., Santa Cruz, 1979, Princeton U., N.J., 1981. Author: The Garnett Family 1961, Christopher Isherwood, 1970, Towards Androgyny, 1973, Reinventing Womanhood, 1979, Writing a Woman's Life, 1988, Hamlet's Mother and Other Women, 1990; 10 novels as Amanda Cross, 1964— (recipient Nero Wolfe award 1981). Guggenheim fellow, 1966; Rockefeller fellow, 1976; recipient Alumnae Achievement award Wellesley Coll., 1984, award of excellence Grad. Faculty of Columbia Alumni, 1984. Mem. MLA (pres. 1984), Mystery Writers Am. (exec. bd. 1982-84), Phi Beta Kappa. Club: Cosmopolitan (N.Y.C.). Office: Columbia U Grad Dept English 615 Philosophy Hall New York NY 10027

HEILIG, MARGARET CRAMER, nurse; b. Lancaster, Pa., Jan. 17, 1914; d. William Stuart and Margaret White (Snader) Cramer; m. David Heilig, June 1, 1942; children: Judith, Bonnie, Barbara. BAin Psychology, Wilson Coll., 1935; MSW, U. Pa., 1940; AAS in Nursing Delaware County Community Coll., 1970. Registered nurse. Caseworker Children's Bur., Lancaster, Pa., 1935-37, 39-42; group worker Ho. of Industry Settlement Ho., Phila., 1937-39; curriculum chmn. Upper Darby Adult Sch. (Pa.), 1958-68; health asst., camp mother Paradise Farm Camp, Downington, Pa., 1960-70, camp nurse, 1970-78, infirmary dir., 1978-86; med. surg. nurse Crozer-Chester Med. Ctr., Chester, Pa., 1970; out-patient nurse Maternal Infant Care, Chester, 1971; coll. nurse Delaware County Community Coll., Media, Pa., 1971-76, dir. health svcs., 1976-84, health cons., 1984—, Health Svcs., 1988—; cons. Coll. Health Svc. for Middle States Evaluation, 1988; writer coll. health newsletter, 1973—, mem. speaker's bur., dir. health fair, 1979—. Author: First Aid Booklet, 1976; also articles and columns in health field. Nurse for health screening children's program Tyler Arboretum, Media, 1982—, Update on Personal Health, Broadmeadows Women's Prison, 1973, 82; former leader Delaware County Council Girl Scouts U.S.; clk. Lansowne Friends Meeting, 1986-89; mem. Upper Darby Recreation Bd., 1956-58, Upper Darby Adult Sch. Bd., 1956-68, curriculum chmn., 1958-68; provider host home for fgn. exchange students, 1965-75; participant Audubon Ann. Bird Count, 1970—; coordinator, dir. Ann. Soc. of Friends Ch. Retreat, 1970—; ARC Speakers' Bur.-AIDS; tchr. Beginning Birding course Del. County Community Coll. Recipient Ollie B. Moten award Am. Coll. Health Assn., 1987; inducted into Legion of Honor Chapel of Four Chaplains, 1980. Mem. Am. Nurses Assn., Pa. Nurses Assn., Delaware County Nurses Assn. (membership chmn. 1977-78), Southeastern Pa. Coll. Health Nurses Assn. (co-founder, pres. 1983-85), Middle Atlantic Coll. Health Assn., Delaware Valley Soc. for Adolescent Health, Family Svc. Assn. Delaware County (bd. dirs. 1989—), LWV, Women's Internat. League for Peace and Freedom, Brandywine Conservance. Quaker. Avocations: piano and choral music, nature walking, handicrafts (craft participant Pa. Renaissance Faire 1985—). Home: 605 Mason Ave Drexel Hill PA 19026 Office: Del County Community Coll Media PA 19063

HEIM, KATHRYN MARIE, nurse, author; b. Milw., Sept. 29, 1952; d. Lester Sheldon Wilcox and Laura Dora (Corpie) Wilcox Sears; m. Vincent Robert Gouthro, June 30, 1970 (div. 1976); 1 child, Robert Vincent; m. George John Heim, Sept. 17, 1977 (div. 1988). AS in Nursing, Milw. Area Tech. Coll., 1983; BS in Nursing, NYU, 1986; MS in Mgmt., Cardinal Stritch Coll., 1988. RN. Staff geriatric nurse Clement Manor, Greenfield, Wis., 1983; nurse, health educator Milw. Boys Club, 1983-84; nurse mgr. Milw. County Mental Health Complex, Milw., 1984—, mem. gero-psychiat. inpatient adv. com., 1986-87; mem. nursing research com. Milwaukee County Mental Health Complex, 1986—; researching Loneliness as relates to mental health, 1989—. Mem. wellness task force Milw. County Mental Health Complex, 1988-89, chairperson sensory deficit com. Geropsychiatry, 1989-90; active Boy Scouts Am., Milw., 1978-80. Mem. Am. Nurses Assn. (cert. gerontol. nurse), Nat. Assn. Female Execs. (network dir. Milw. chpt.), Wis. Nurses Assn., NYU Alumni Assn., Cardinal Stritch Alumni Assn. (class rep. 1986-88), Milw. Area Tech. Coll. Alumni Assn. Clubs: South Shore Yacht, Cornucopie Yacht. Home: 351 N 62d St Milwaukee WI 53213 Office: Milw County Mental Health 9455 Watertown Plank Rd Wauwatosa WI 53226

HEIM, TONYA SUE, nurse, small business owner; b. Huntingburg, Ind., Nov. 9, 1948; d. Harold William and Marjorie Elouise (Buse) Rothert; m. James Frederick Heim, Sept. 6, 1969; children: Brian Christopher, Andrea Christine. Diploma, Deaconness Sch. Nursing, Evansville, Ind., 1969. RN, Ind. Oper. rm. staff nurse St. Joseph's Hosp., Huntingburg, 1969-71, emergency rm. staff nurse, 1969-71, staff nurse obstetrics dept., 1971-73, supr. obstetrics dept., 1973-85, dir. obstetrics oper. rm., 1985-88, dir. nursing, 1988-89, dir. obstetrics, oper. rm., infection control sterilizing, 1989—; owner, operator Holland (Ind.) Toning and Tanning Ctr., 1987—; co-owner Heim Hardware, 1989—. Instr., trainer ARC So. Ind., 1970—; chmn. health profl. adv. com., mem. exec. com. So. Ind./Ill. chpt. March of Dimes, 1978—; v.p., chmn. program com., bd. dirs. So. Hills Counseling Ctr., Jasper, Ind., 1988—; event coord. Hoosiers for Safety Belts, Dale, Ind., 1987; troop co-leader Girl Scouts Am., Holland, 1986-88; active Southridge Band Boosters, Huntingburg, 1986—; mem. AIDS coun. S.W. Dubois County Sch. Corp., 1988—; mem. adv. coun. Prenatal Substance Use Prevention Program, 1989—. Mem. Am. Nurses Assn. (bd. dirs.), Assn. Operating Rm. Nurses, Nurses Assn. Am. Coll. Obstetricians and Gynecologists, Huntingburg C. of C., Beta Sigma Phi (v.p.). Republican. Lutheran. Home: 403 2nd Ave Holland IN 47541 Office: St Josephs Hosp Leland Heights Huntingburg IN 47542

HEIMANN, JANET BARBARA, trail consultant; b. Santa Cruz, Calif., Dec. 18, 1931; d. John Louis and Charlotte Lucina (Burns) Grinnell; m. Richard Frank Gustav, July 10, 1953; children: David Robert, Gary Alan, Kathleen Janet. BS, U. Calif., Berkeley, 1954. Pres. Folsom Freedom Trails, Placer County, Calif., 1980-83; chmn. Adopt-a-Trail, Folsom Lake Trail Patrol, Placer County, 1986-88; bd. dirs. Loomis Basin Horseman Assn., Placer County, 1986-87. Mem. AAUW. Republican. Home: 11565 McCarthy Rd Carmel Valley CA 93924

HEIMBOLD, MARGARET BYRNE, publisher, educator, consultant; b. Tullamore, Ireland, June 24; came to U.S., 1966, naturalized, 1973; d. John Christopher and Anne (Troy) Byrne; m. Arthur Heimbold, Feb. 26, 1984; 1 child, Eric Thomas Gordon. BA, Queens Coll. Recipient cert. Dale Carnegie, 1977, Psychol. Corp. Am., 1981, Wharton Sch., 1983, Stanford U., 1989. Group advt. mgr. N.Y. Times, N.Y.C., 1978-85; pub. Am. Film, Washington, 1985-86, v.p., pub. Nat. Trust for Hist. Preservation, Washington, 1986-90; pres. Summerville Pub., Inc., Wasington, 1990—; advisor Mag. Pubs. Bd. dirs. Anchor Ctrs. Ireland. Am. Mem. NAFE, Women's Econ. Alliance, Soc. Nat. Assn. Publs. (chmn. editorial com., bd. dirs.). Avocations: golf, writing.

HEIMLICH, ELLEN KRAMER, lawyer; b. Evansville, Ind., Aug. 28, 1942; d. Morton Helper and Ann (Gordon) Kramer; m. Barry Noah Heimlich, Jan. 4, 1981; children: Amy, Mark. AA, Fashion Inst. Tech., 1965; BA cum laude, U. Miami, 1964; JD, Nova U., 1978. Bar: Fla. 1978, U.S. Dist. Ct. (so. dist.) Fla. 1979, U.S. Ct. Appeals, (11th cir.) 1981. Atty. Beyer & Lerner, Ft. Lauderdale, Fla., 1978-79; asst. atty. City of North Miami Beach, 1979-82; assoc. Kopelwitz, Pearlman, Atlas & Tropp, Ft. Lauderdale, 1985-86; corp. atty. Himedics, Inc., Hollywood, Fla., 1986—. Pres. South Fla. chpt. Stepfamily Assn. Am., North Miami Beach, 1985-88; mem. Diabetes Rsch. Inst., Broward County, Fla., 1987-88. Mem. ABA, Broward County Bar Assn., Phi Delta Phi. Democrat. Office: Himedics Inc 3800 N 29th Ave Hollywood FL 33020-1008

HEINE, MARY ELIZABETH, executive director; b. Evanston, Ill., Jan. 1, 1961; d. Donald Henry and Barbara Anne (Stanton) H. BA, Ill. Wesleyan U., Bloomington, 1983; MA, Eastern Ill. U., Charleston, 1984. Asst. coordinator Jamestown Yorktown Found., Williamsburg, Va., 1985-86; archivist Colonial Williamsburg Found., Williamsburg, 1986-87; exec. dir. Williamsburg Hotel, Motel Assoc., Williamsburg, 1987--. Coordinator Special Olympics Williamsburg, 1986--. Recipient Phi Alpha Theta, 1983. Mem. Am. Soc. Assn. Exec., Sigma Alpha Iota (Profl. music Soc.). Dem. Williamsburg. Home: PO Box 1023 Williamsburg VA 23187

HEINE, URSULA INGRID, biologist, researcher; b. Berlin, Feb. 19, 1926; came to U.S., 1959; Diploma in biology, Humboldt U., Berlin, 1950, Dr. rer. nat., 1953. Staff fellow Inst. for Cancer Rsch., Berlin, 1950-53; sr. scientist German Acad. Scis., Berlin, 1953-59; assoc. Duke U. Med. Ctr., Durham, N.C., 1959-68; scientist, sect. head div. cancer etiology DCE, Nat. Cancer Inst. NIH, Bethesda, Md., 1968-89; sr. scientist Program Resources Inc., Nat. Cancer Inst. NIH, Frederick, Md., 1989—; vis. scientist Coll. de France, Paris, 1971, Acad. Scis., Moscow, 1979, U. Cologne, Fed. Republic Germany, 1982-83. Contbr. chpts. to books, articles to profl. jours. Mem. Am. Assn. Cancer Rsch. (emeritus), Am. Soc. Cell Biology (emeritus).

HEINEMANN, KATHERINE (KAKI HEINEMANN), author; b. St. Louis; d. Herbert N. and Elsa S. (Straus) Arnstein; BS, Washington U., St. Louis, 1950, MA (Arts and Scis. Faculty award 1950), 1956; m. Morton D. May, 1937; children: David A., Philip F.; m. Sol Heinemann, July 8, 1950; 1 child, Kate Heinemann Taucher. Freelance writer, poet, 1960—; prof. English, U. Tex., El Paso, 1968-74; condr. poetry readings, workshops, 1968—; mem. El Paso Art Resources Dept. Bd., 1980-81; author: Brandings, 1968; Some Inhuman Familiars, 1983; taping for Poetry Collection of Library of Congress, 1982. Mem. PEN, Nat. Soc. Arts and Letters. Clubs: Coronado Country, El Paso Tennis, Sunset Heights Garden. Home: 4252 Ridge Crest Dr El Paso TX 79902

HEINEMAN RANSOM, KAREN BENVIN, food products executive; b. Tarrytown, N.Y., Apr. 27, 1953; d. Domenick John and Mary (Jelich) Benvin; m. Peter John Heineman, Nov. 20, 1976 (div. 1984); m. Robert Asa Ransom III, Oct. 1, 1988; 1 child, Ross Philip Walter. Student, Manhattanville Coll., 1971-74. Sales and decorating positions various orgns., 1971-76; co-founder, co-owner Homarus Inc., Mt. Kisco, N.Y., 1976—. Named Woman of Yr., Ctr. Food and Hotel Mgmt., NYU, 1983, 85; recipient Castle Entrepreneurial Achievement award Manhattanville Coll., Purchase, N.Y., 1989. Mem. Les Dames d'Escoffier (bd. dirs. 1989—). Roman Catholic. Office: Homarus Inc 76 Kisco Ave Mount Kisco NY 10549

HEINEN, GLORIA JEAN, business owner, real estate associate; b. Springfield, Mo., Oct. 27, 1942; d. Alfred Arthur and Doris Teresa (Busse) Engel; m. Dennis Dean Engelkens, Apr. 21, 1961 (dec. Aug. 1971); children: Laurie Jo, Julie Rae, Dennis Dean Jr., Kelly Ann, Brett Alan; m. Raymond LeRoy Heinen, June 30, 1972; children: Randolph Paul, Melinda Marie, Melanie Marie, Lisa Ann. Grad. high sch., Comfrey, Minn. Sec. State Farm Ins. Agy., Mankato, Minn., 1965-69; sec., agt. Apollo Ins. Agy., St. Cloud, Minn., 1969-72; real estate agt. Menzel Realty, Princeton, Minn., 1976-79; ins. agt. Nat. Farmers Union Ins. Agy., Princeton, 1978—; real estate agt. Centur 21, Princeton, 1979-84; broker, owner Riverside Pla. Realty, Princeton, 1984—, Zimmerman, Minn., 1987—. Mem. E. Cen. Bd. Realtors, Minn. Assn. Realtors. Democrat. Lutheran. Office: Riverside Pla Realty Riverside Pla PO Box 416 Princeton MN 55371

HEINRICH, BONNIE, state legislator; m. Willis Heinrich; 1 child. Student, Valley City (N.D.) State Coll. Writer, polit. cons.; mem. N.D. State Senate. Chmn. Dem. Com. dist. 32, N.D. Home: 1606 E Bowen Ave Bismarck ND 58504*

HEINRICH, DONNA TRAUSCHT, optometrist, educator; b. Oak Park, Ill., Apr. 14, 1960; d. Donald Charles and Arlene (Younker) Trauscht; m. Joseph Gerard Heinrich, June 6, 1987; 1 child, Timothy Joseph. BS in Biology, St. Mary's Coll., Notre Dame, Ind., 1982; OD, Ill. Coll. of Optometry, 1987; postgrad., So. Calif. Coll. of Optometry, 1987-88. Asst. instr. So. Calif. Coll. of Optometry, Fullerton, 1988—; prin. San Juan Family Optometry, San Juan Capistrano, Calif., 1989—; liaison Parents Active for Vision Edn., San Diego and Huntington Beach, Calif., 1989; vision screener Vision Cons., Yorba Linda, Calif., 1989—. Mem. Am. Optometric Assn., Calif. Optometric Assn., Orange County Optometric Soc., Coll. of Optometrists in Vision Devel. (assoc.). Republican. Roman Catholic. Home: 180 City Blvd W 2-106 Orange CA 92668 Office: San Juan Family Optometry 30220 Rancho Viejo Rd Ste D San Juan Capistrano CA 92675

HEINRICH, DOROTHEA JOSEPHINE, social services administrator; b. Chgo., May 25, 1917; d. Joseph and Josephine (Kallal) Brod; m. George A. Heinrich; children: Jerrold Joseph, Joel George. BA in Mgmt., DePaul U., 1978; grad. social therapist program, Forest Inst., 1979; MA in Psychology, Govs. State U., 1980; postgrad. in psychology, Kensington U., 1989. Exec. sec. to plant comptroller Douglas Aircraft Co., Park Ridge, Ill., 1940-45; exec. dir. The Ctr. of Concern, Park Ridge, 1978—. Mem. Met. Chgo. Coalition on Aging, Park Ridge C. of C. Lodge: Soroptimists. Home: 616 N Dee Rd Park Ridge IL 60068 Office: The Ctr of Concern S 223 1580 N Northwest Hwy Park Ridge IL 60068

HEINRICHS, MARY ANN, university dean; b. Toledo, Mar. 28, 1930; m. Paul Warren Heinrichs, Jan. 26, 1952; children—Paul, John, Nancy, James. Ph.D., U. Toledo, 1973. Prof. English, U. Toledo, Ohio, 1965-77, dean, 1977—. Contbr. articles to profl. jours. Mem. Community Planning Council Research Project Employed Women, Ohio, 1982-84; mem. Council Family Violence, Toledo, 1981—; com. chmn. St. Joseph Sch. Bd., Toledo, 1976-79. Recipient Outstanding Scholarship award U. Toledo, 1965; AAUW scholar, 1984; named One of Foremost Women 20th Century, 1987. Mem. Internat. Tech. Communications Soc. (chmn. 1979-80), Pi Lambda Theta (chpt. pres. and del. 1974-76), Phi Kappa Phi (chpt. pres. and del. 1969), AAUW (corp. rep. 1978-84). Roman Catholic. Lodge: Zonta. Avocations: hiking. Office: U Toledo 2801 W Bancroft Toledo OH 43606-3390

HEINTZ, CAROLINEA CABANISS, home economics educator, retired; b. Roanoke, Va., Jan. 19, 1920; d. Luther Bertie and Emblyn Bird (Jennings) Cabaniss; m. Howard Elmer Smith, Dec. 19, 1942 (div. Aug. 1975); children: Emblyn Davis, Cynthia Shannon, Cheryl Peterson, Melyssa Sexton; m. Raymond Walter Heintz, May 21, 1977; 1 stepchild, James. BS in Home Econ. Edn., U. Ala., Tuscaloosa, 1941; vocat. home econ. degree, Montevallo Coll., 1941. Cert. vocat. home econs. tchr. Swimming instr. Camp Mudjekeewis, Centerlovel, Maine, summer 1940; home econs. tchr. Roanoke Pub. Schs., 1941-43; dietitian U. Va., Charlottesville, 1943; nutrition edn. specialist Liberty Health Ctr. Svcs., Liberty Center, Ohio, 1974-80; home economist Dayton Hudson Dept. Store, Toledo, 1980-84; splty . food instr., continuing edn. U. Toledo, 1984-85; pres., mem. Greater Toledo Nutrition Coun., 1966-90. Speaker United Way, Toledo, 1965-90 (Outstanding Community Service award 1987); founder, pres. Mobile Meals of Toledo, Inc., 1968-71, adv. bd., 1988-90; affiliate mem. Arts Commn., Toledo, 1976-77; chmn. Sapphire Ball, Toledo Symphony Orch., Toledo Opera, 1978; adminstrv. coord. Feed Your Neighbor Program, Met. Chs. United, Toledo, 1979-86; deacon Collingwood Presbyn. Ch., 1969-71, elder, 1972-74, 77-79, trustee, 1984-86. Recipient Woman of Toledo award St. Vincent Hosp. & Med. Ctr. Guild, 1967, 80. Mem. AAUW (bd. dirs. 1974-76, chmn. and mem. gourmet group, 1972), Ohio State Med. Aux. (1st v.p. 1973-74, chmn. gourmet group 1967-90), Aux. to Acad. of Medicine (pres. 1967-68, Health Care award 1974), Toledo Opera Guild (pres. 1976-78), Sigma Kappa Alumni Assn. (various offices 1947-90). Republican. Home: 3407 Bentley Blvd Toledo OH 43606

HEINTZ, MARY ANN, financial executive, analyst; b. Chgo., May 28, 1956; d. Martin Henry and Antonina Ann (Calamai) H. BA in Acctg., Mich. State U., 1977; MBA in Fin., U. Chgo., 1980. Staff acct. Swift & Co., Chgo., 1978-79, fin. analyst, 1979-80, sr. fin. analyst, 1980-81, mgr. fin. analysis, 1981-82; sr. ops. analyst Kearney-Nat. Inc., Des Plaines, Ill., 1982-85; sr. fin. analyst Sara Lee Corp., Chgo., 1985-88, mgr. fin. analysis domestic, 1988-89, mgr. fin. analysis internat., 1989—. Coach high sch. volleyball. Home: 884 S Park Terr Chicago IL 60605 Office: Sara Lee Corp 3 First National Plz Chicago IL 60602

HEINTZELMAN, CAROL ANN, credit manager; b. Lehighton, Pa., Apr. 18, 1942; d. Franklin W. and Betty A. (Eckman) Heintzelman. Student, Greenville Tech. Coll., 1981, Am. Acad. of Drama, N.Y.C., 1962. Cert. collector. Gen. mgr. Traendly Buick, Inc., Poughkeepsie, N.Y., 1968-78; asst. br. mgr. Fishkill (N.Y.) Nat. Bank, 1965-68; corp. credit mgr. GBS Lumber, Inc., Maudlin, S.C., 1981—. Mem. Credit Profls. (pres. local chpt., CP State Credit Prof. of Yr. 1988, presenter workshop), Nat. Assn. Credit Mgrs. (local chmn., cert. credit and collections), Phi Theta Kappa. Republican. Home: 311 Goldsmith Rd 12 Simpsonville SC 29681

HEINTZLEMAN, MARY STRICKLER, property and casualty claims company executive; b. Fayetteville, Pa., May 3, 1921; d. Fred Stouffer and Mary Erma McKenzie (Strickler); children: Ida Mary, Richard Frederick, Rachel Louise. BS, Shippensburg State Coll., 1943; MA, Columbia U., 1949; student, Duke U., 1945. Cert. bus. edn. tchr., Pa. Sec.-treas. Nat. Property and Casualty Claims Rsch. Svcs., Inc., Chambersburg; bus. edn. tchr., supr. student tchrs. Shippensburg (Pa.) U.; lic. ins. agent, sec., with acctg. Strickler Agy., Inc., Chambersburg, Pa.; med. secretarial, legal and bus. tchr. Penn Hall Jr. Coll., Chambersburg. Mem. aux. Chambersburg Hosp. Mem. NAFE, Pa. Bus. Edn. Assn., Philanthropic Edn. Orgn. (treas. 1974—), Pa. Club (treas. 1947-48, pres. 1949), Order of Ea. Star, Delta Pi Epsilon, Beta Sigma Phi (pres. 1952). Republican. Lutheran. Home: 541 E Catherine St Chambersburg PA 17201

HEINZ, JOY MARIE, jeweler; b. N.Y.C., Oct. 10, 1964; d. Charles and Gladys Heinz; 1 child, Amanda. Student, Queens Borough Coll., 1985, Gemological Inst., N.Y.C., 1986. Cert. diamonds, colored stones, pearls, jewelry display, jewelry sales. Owner Joy Jewels, Flushing, N.Y.; with Greenwald Jewelers, Inc., N.Y.C.; supr. Malic Jewelers, N.Y.C., Albert Malic, Astoria, N.Y. Mem. Coun. Against Pub. Smoking. Mem. NAFE, Big Apple Caps. Home: 45-50 149th St Flushing NY 11355

HEINZE, LINDA HOLLI, promotion agency executive, lecturer; b. N.Y.C., Dec. 31, 1939; d. Rudolf Ley and Jessica Mary (Babcock) H. A.A., N.Y.C. Community Coll., 1959; student in bus. adminstrn. Pace Coll., 1964-68, New Sch. Social Research, 1969, Baruch Coll. CCNY, 1970. Asst. mgr. advt. makeup Look mag., N.Y.C., 1959-64; prodn. mgr. McCall mag., N.Y.C.,

1964-70; asst. promotion mgr. treasury div. J.C. Penney Co., N.Y.C., 1970-72; pres. Robert Brian Assocs., N.Y.C., 1972—. Mem. bus. games com. L.I. U.; bd. dirs. N.Y. chpt. Medic Alert, 1984-89. Mem. Am. Advt. Fedn. (Silver medal 1971), Advt. Women N.Y. (ELA award 1972). Office: Robert Brian Assocs 200 Park Ave # 303E New York NY 10166

HEINZMAN, PATRICIA ANN, nurse; b. Wurtzburg, Fed. Republic Germany, Feb. 10, 1957; (parents U.S. citizens) d. Peter and Georgia Christina (Hoffman) H. BS in Nursing, U. No. Colo., 1979. Lic. facial specialist Icenhower U. Beauty Arts, Houston, 1982. Nurse The Meth. Hosp.-Tex. Med. Cen., Houston, 1978-83; clin. nurse mgr. Truman Med. Cen., Kansas City, Mo., 1983; orthopaedic nurse clinician & office mgr. Roger W. Hood, MD, Overland Park, Kans., 1983—; lectr. The Back Cen. & Phys. Therapy Clin., Overland Park, 1987; co-lectr. Humana Hosp. Overland Park, 1987. Co-author: (manuals) Total Hip Replacement, 1984, Total Knee Replacement, 1984. Vol. Hist. Kansas City Found.; preview party chmn. Nat. Wildlife Art Show Ducks Unltd., Kansas City, 1989; mem. chmn., mdse. dir. Muskies Inc. (Pomme de Terre chpt.), Hermitage, Mo., 1989. Mem. Am. Acad. Orthopaedic Surgeons (planning com. 1984), Nat. Assn. Orthopaedic Nurses, Am. Assn. Oper. Rm. Nurses, Women's C. of C. (Am. Royal co-chmn.), Zonta (bd. dirs. 1986-88, Kansas City chpt., fin. chmn. 1986-88, chmn. status of women com. 1989-90, 90—) Sigma Theta Tau (charter). Home: 12934 W 108th St Overland Park KS 66210 Office: Roger W Hood MD 8300 College Blvd Ste 105 Overland Park KS 66210

HEISE, MARILYN BEARDSLEY, public relations company executive; b. Cedar Rapids, Iowa, Feb. 26, 1935; d. Lee Roy and Angeline Myrtle (Knudson) Beardsley; m. John W. Heise, July 9, 1960; children: William Earnshaw, Steven James, Kathryn Kay. BA, Drake U., 1957. Account exec. The Beveridge Orgn., Chgo., 1958-60; editor, pub. The Working Craftsman mag., Northbrook, Ill., 1971-78; columnist Chgo. Sun-Times, 1973-78; pres. Craft Books, Inc., Northbrook, 1978-84; v.p. Sheila King Pub. Rels., Chgo., 1984-87, Aaron D. Cushman, Inc., Chgo., 1987-88; pres. Creative Cons. Assocs., Inc., Glencoe, Ill., 1989—; mem. adv. panel Nat. Crafts Project, Ft. Collins, Colo., 1977; mem. adv. panel and com. Nat. Endowment for Arts, Washington, 1977; mem. adv. bd. The Crafts Report, Seattle, 1978-86. Recipient achievement award Women in Mgmt., 1978. Mem. Pub. Rels. Soc. Am. (accredited). Office: Creative Cons Assocs Inc 854 Grove St Glencoe IL 60022

HEISLER, JEANNE MICHELLE, insurance agency owner; b. N.Y.C., Mar. 24, 1954; d. Kenneth F. and Therese (DeRosier) Ronan; m. William J. Heisler, Aug. 10, 1974; William Jr., Christopher, Robert. Grad., Stuart Bus. Sch., 1973. CPCU, CLU, cert. ins. counselor, cert. profl. ins. woman. Sr. v.p., corp. treas., owner The Ronan Agy., Inc., Brick, N.J., 1972—; adv. council Norfolk and Dedham Ins. Co., Mass., 1983-85, Harleysville (Pa.) Ins. Co., 1984—. Team mother Toms River (N.J.) Little League, 1984—; com. chmn. Monsignor Donovan Alumni Assn., Toms River, N.J., 1987—. Recipient Vol. Achievement award N.J. Assn. of Assn. Execs., 1985, Presdl. Citation Ind. Ins. Agts. of Am., 1985. Mem. Ind. Ins. Agts. of N.J. (chmn. 1981-82, Young Agt. of Yr. 1981, faculty mem., edn. com. 1983, chmn. young agts. com. 1984-85, chmn. edn. and agy. service com. 1987—, presdl. citation 1982, Ins. Man of Yr. 1986), Ind. Ins. Agts. of Ocean County (pres. 1982-83, Agt. of Yr. 1980), DDANJ (exec. com. 1986—). Republican. Roman Catholic. Office: 35 Beaverson Blvd Brick NJ 08723

HEISSERMAN, THERESA ANN, transportation executive; b. Washington, Oct. 29, 1951; d. Robert Franklin Matchett and Shirley Francis (Malone) England; m. Keith Edwin Heisserman, July 17, 1982. Student, Mt. Diablo Valley Coll., 1970-72, Clark County Community Coll., 1983—. Acct. Perfect Parts Inc., Carlstadt, N.J., 1970-73; credit mgr. ES Levy of Galveston (Tex.) Island, 1973-75; acct. XL Controls Inc., Las Vegas, 1977-80, Nev. Airlines, Las Vegas, 1980-82, Air Cortez Internat. Airlines, Ontario, Calif., 1982-86; gen. mgr., sec., treas. Pub. Domain Software Group, Las Vegas, 1986-87; pres. Sierra Nev. Airways Inc., Las Vegas, 1987—. Vol., bd. dirs. Am. Cancer Soc. Mem. Am. Bus. Women's Assn. Republican. Methodist. Office: Sierra Nev Airways Inc 4990 Paradise Rd Las Vegas NV 89119

HEITKAMP, MARIE, school and clinical psychologist; b. Dayton, Ohio, Nov. 28, 1924; d. Clement and Matilda (Niekamp) H. BA, U. Dayton, 1961; MEd, Xavier U., Cin., 1969; MA, Specialist, U. Detroit, 1982; PhD, Wayne State U., 1978. Joined Franciscan Sisters of Poor, Roman Cath. Ch., 1941; lic. clin. psychologist, Mich. Social work asst. Cath. Charities, various cities, Ohio, 1944-50; adminstr. Mt. Carmel High Sch., Cin., 1950-59; recruitment dir. Franciscan Sisters of Poor, Cin., 1961-65; nat. lectr. Movement for Better World, Washington, 1965-69; adminstrv. sec., sch. psychologist Archdiocesan Spl. Edn. Office, Detroit, 1969-73; rsch. asst., teaching scholar, instr. Wayne State U., Detroit, 1973-76; sch. psychologist Hazel Park (Mich.) Schs., 1976-86, sch. and clin. psychologist, 1986—; sch. and clin. psychologist outpatient clinic, Birmingham, Mich., 1986—. Mem. Am. Psychol. Assn., Nat. Assn. Sch. Psychologists (cert.), Mich. Assn. Sch. Psychologists. Democrat. Home: 2251 E Outer Dr Detroit MI 48234

HEITKAMP, MARY KATHRYN (HEIDI HEITKAMP), commissioner, lawyer; b. Breckenridge, Minn., Oct. 30, 1955; d. Raymond Bernard and Doreen LaVonne (Berg) H.; m. Darwin K. Lange, June 9, 1984; children: Alethea Ruth, Nathan Dennis. BA, U. N.D., 1977; JD, Lewis and Clark Law Sch., 1980. Bar: N.D., U.S. Dist. Ct. N.D. Exec. dir. N.W. Environ. Def. Ctr., Portland, Oreg., 1978-79; rsch. asst. Natural Resources Law Inst., Portland, Oreg., 1979; atty. enforcement div. EPA, Washington, 1980-81; asst. atty. gen. Office N.D. State Tax Commr., Bismarck, N.D., 1981-85; adminstrv. counsel Office N.D. State Tax Commn., Bismarck, 1985-86; tax commr. State of N.D., Bismarck, 1986—; vice-chmn. Multistate Tax Commn., 1987-88, chmn. 1988-89. Crusade chairperson Am. Cancer Soc., N.D., 1988, 89, 90. Toll fellow Coun. State Govts., 1986; recipient Young Achiever award Nat. Coun. Women, 1987. Mem. Fedn. Tax Adminstrs., Midwestern States Assn. Tax Adminstrs., N.D. Bar Assn. Democrat. Roman Catholic. Office: Tax Dept State Capitol 600 E Boulevard Ave 8th Fl Bismarck ND 58505-0599

HEIZER, IDA ANN, real estate broker; b. Oxford, Colo., Mar. 14, 1919; d. Albert Henry and Ella (Engbrook) Ordener; m. Donald Heizer, Apr. 7, 1947; children—Robert John. Diploma, Brown's Bus. Coll., 1939; student Otero Jr. Coll., 1946-47, U. So. Colo., 1962; grad. Realtors Inst., Nat. Assn. Real Estate Bds., 1972. Cert. closer real estate, cert. residential specialist. Clk., Montgomery Ward Co., LaJunta, Colo., 1935-37; bookkeeper Colo. Bank & Trust Co., LaJunta, 1937-38; cashier/bookkeeper Fox Theatre, LaJunta, 1939-40; clk. Civil Service, LaJunta, 1940-45; stenoabstractor Deaf Smith Abstract Office, Hereford, Tex., 1948-50; sec. Otero County Agt. Office, Rocky Ford, Colo., 1953-55; real estate broker Pueblo Realty & Service Co., Inc., Colo., 1958-86; ret., 1988. Mem. Pueblo Bd. Realtors, Nat. Assn. Real Estate Appraisers, Nat. Assn. Realtors, Colo. Assn. Realtors, Women's Council Realtors, Daus. of the Republic Tex., Beta Sigma Phi. Lodge: Quota Internat. Home and Office: 331 Van Buren St Pueblo CO 81004

HELBERG, SHIRLEY ADELAIDE HOLDEN, artist; b. Solvay, N.Y., Mar. 9; d. Isaac Edgar and Gladys Evelyn (Tucker) Holden; student Syracuse U.; BE, Johns Hopkins U., 1969; MFA, Md. Inst. Art, 1975; m. Burton Edward Helberg; children: Keir Holm, Kristin Vaughan, Kecia Tucker, Kandace Holden, Kraig Brownlee. Tchr. various schs. in N.J. and Pa.; tchr. Manchester (Pa.) Pub. Schs., 1965-84, Balt. City Schs., 1988—; one-woman art show U. Va., Charlottesville, 1974, Cayuga Mus. Art and History, Auburn, N.Y., 1974, Hist. Soc. York Mus., Pa., 1977, York Coll., 1984, Country Club of York; Bd. dirs. York (Pa.) Arts Council, 1964-66. Mem. Nat. League Am. Pen Women (Pa. State art chmn. 1972-74, pres. Pa. orgn. 1974-76, nat. scholarship chair 1976-88, 88-90, 90—, v.p. 1988—, Disting. service award 1978, 80, 82, 84, 86, 88, 90, Disting. Achievement award 1988), NEA, Pa. State Edn. Assn., Nat. League Am. Pen Women (registrar 1986-88), Internat. Platform Assn., Harrisburg, York Art Assns., Pa. Watercolor Soc., Johns Hopkins Faculty Club. Republican. Methodist. Home: RD #4 Spring Grove PA 17362 also: 727 S Ann St Baltimore MD 21231

HELD, LILA M., art appraiser; b. Cleve., Oct. 5, 1925; d. Mark and Edythe H. (Dobrin) Bloomberg; m. Jacob Herzfeld, Oct. 20, 1946 (div. 1964); children: Garson, Michael; m. Merle Donald Held, Feb. 19, 1966; children: Joanne, Barbara. Student, Coll. William and Mary, 1945-46, Ohio State U., 1943-44, Case Western Reserve U., 1944-45; postgrad., Case Western Reserve U., 1962-66; student, Akron U., 1960-61; BS in Art Edn., Kent State U., 1961-62; M in Valuation Sci., Lindenwood Coll., 1989. Instr. art Canton (Ohio) YMCA, 1965, Beachwood (Ohio) Bd. Recreation, 1967-68; substitute tchr. art, art history Cleveland Heights, Ohio, 1967-68; freelance artist, writer, researcher, 1940—; art cons., appraiser Art Consultants Assocs., Englewood, Colo., 1985—; curatorial aid Denver Art Mus., 1985-89; fine arts appraiser, Cleve. Works exhibited in museums and galleries in Cleve., Akron, Richmond, Va., St. Louis; speaker in field; judge at numerous art shows. Mem. AAUW, Am. Soc. Appraisers (sr. mem., cert. in fine arts), Am. Art Soc., Denver Mus. Contemporary Art Soc., Denver Mus., Cleve. Mus. Art, Cleve. Ctr. for Contemporary Art (vol.), Cleve. Soc. for Contemporary Art, Nat. Coun. Jewish Women, Cleveland Women's City Club. Home and Office: 3330 Warrensville Center Rd Shaker Heights OH 44122

HELDENBRAND, MARILYN LOUISE, township governmental official; b. Detroit, Jan. 4, 1939; d. Edwin Forest and Laura Evelyn (Helmer) Tompsett; m. Robert L. Heldenbrand, Apr. 11, 1938; children: Deborah, Robert. Student, Schoolcraft, Livonia, Mich., 1973, Mich. State U., 1989. Notary public. Parks commr. Redford (Mich.) Twp., 1976-78, trustee, 1978-88, twp. clk., 1988—; sales, svc. acct. rep. Clevite, Troy, Mich., 1966-88. V.p. NRDCO community orgn., Redford, 1987—; sec. Volney Smith PTA, PTO, Redford, 1967-74; com. chmn. Boy Scouts Am., Redford, 1972-74; chmn. bd. dirs. Redford Community Hosp., 1983-88; sec. Hazardous Toxic Waste Commn., Redford, 1984-87; commr. Redford Zoning Bd. Appeals, 1978-80. Recipient Citizen of Yr. award Redford Rotary, 1988, Notable Women in Pub. Office award State of Mich., 1983. Mem. VFW, Redford Bus. and Profl. Women (pres. 1982, Woman of Yr. 1984), Purchasing Mgmt. Assn., Am. Legion, Elks (Am. award 1987), Redford Suburban League, Friends of Libr. Lutheran. Home: 19158 Lexington Redford MI 48240

HELDRICH, ELEANOR MAAR, publisher; b. Hagerstown, Md, Nov. 4, 1929; d. Richard and Sara (Mish) Maar; m. Frederick Joseph Heldrich; children: Sarah, Susan, Frederick, Philip. Grad. high sch., Balt. Editor Federated Garden Clubs of Md., Balt., 1975—; pub., founder Prospect Hill, Balt., 1981—. Pres. Beautiful Balt., Inc., 1985-87. Recipient of Publication Award Nat. Council of State Garden Clubs, 1984, 86. Mem. Pub. Mktg. Assn., Balt. Pubs. Assn., Internat. Assn. Ind. Pub. (Com. Small Mag. Editors and Pubs.). Office: Prospect Hill 216 Wendover Rd Baltimore MD 21218

HELF, JUDITH, marketing executive; b. N.Y.C., Nov. 30, 1951; d. Mortimer and Anita (Borkow) Pfeffer; m. Benjamin Pettinato, Jan. 31, 1982; children: Michael Steven, Samuel Jordan. Advt. dir. Lillian Vernon Corp., Mt. Vernon, N.Y., 1973-76; v.p. Ahrend Assocs., N.Y.C., 1976-82; v.p., pres., chief exec. officer Respond Direct Mktg. div. Ted Bates Internat., N.Y.C., 1982-85; prin. Judith Helf Direct Mktg., Bklyn., 1985—. Co-author: Industry Textbook Cataloger's Catalog 1980; contbr. articles to profl. jours. Mem. Direct Mktg. Assn., Direct Mktg. Club N.Y. Office: Judith Helf Direct Mktg 750 Carroll St Brooklyn NY 11215

HELFINSTINE, KELLY ANN (KELLY ANN BIEWENER), financial planner, securities company executive; b. Salt Lake City, Nov. 4, 1957; d. James William Helfinstine and Jan Elaine (Bragg) Marshall; m. James P. Biewener, Apr. 16, 1988. BA, U. Ariz., 1979. Cert. fin. planner. Mgmt. trainee The Ariz. Bank, Phoenix, 1980-81; mktg. rep. The Ariz. Lottery, Phoenix, 1981; pvt. practice fin. planning Phoenix, 1983-86; divisional v.p. Jones Internat. Securities, Phoenix, 1986—. Mem. Internat. Assn. Fin. Planners, Inst. Cert. Fin. Planners (cert.). Home: 2423 E Taxidea Way Phoenix AZ 85044 Office: Jones Internat Securities 9697 E Mineral Ave Englewood CO 80112

HELFMAN, BARBARA BROOK, interior plantscaping company executive; b. Cin., Dec. 18, 1941; d. Meyer Charles and Rose (Austrian) Brook; m. Edwin L. Helfman, Aug. 11, 1960 (div. 1980); children: Marc David, Eve M. BA in Psychology, Miami U., Oxford, Ohio, 1975. Pres., ptnr. Something Different Interior Plantscaping, Cin., 1975—; pres. Topsiders Inc., Cin., 1984—. Editor: Container Resource Directory, 1982; contbr. articles, columnist to Interiorscape mag., 1984—. Mem. Assn. Landscape Contractors Am. (bd. dirs. interior plantscape div. 1986—), Nat. Coun. Interior Hort. Cert. (cert., bd. govs. 1986-90). Republican. Jewish. Home: 3109 Shadow Hill Rd Middletown OH 45042 Office: Topsiders Inc 11345 Reed Hartman Ste 120 Cincinnati OH 45242

HELIOFF, ANNE GRAILE, painter; b. Liverpool, Eng.; d. Max and Frances Elizabeth (Beilenson) H.; student Columbia U., Art Students League, N.Y.C.; m. Benjamin Michael Hirschberg. One-woman exhbns. include: Capricorn Gallery, N.Y.C., 1966-69, Phoenix Gallery, N.Y.C., 1972, 74, 76, 82, 85, Woodstock (N.Y.) Artists Assn., 1988; group exhbns. include Milch Gallery, N.Y.C., 1940, Pepsi-Cola Nat., travelling show, maj. museums, U.S., 1947, Nat. Gallery Art, Washington, Pa. Acad. Ann., Art U.S.A., also bicentennial exhbn., 6 Americans in France, traveling show, 1976, museums in Florence and Naples, Italy; mem. U.S. del. 5th Congress Internat. Assn. Art, Tokyo, 1966; dir. exhbns. including 50 Yrs. of Woodstock Art (N.Y.), N.Y. State Tri-Centennial, 1959. Recipient Silver medal Albany (N.Y.) Mus. Art and Sci., 1957; Homer Boss scholar, 1939; Y. Kuniyoshi scholar, 1940-45. Mem. Woodstock Artists Assn. (life, past dir.), Art Students League (past dir.), Am. Soc. Contemporary Artists (past dir.; awards in oil, watercolor and acrylic), Nat. Assn. Women Artists, N.Y. Soc. Women Artists (past dir.), Archives of Am. Art, Smithsonian Mus. Home: 14 Neher St Woodstock NY 12498 Office: 340 W 28th St New York NY 10001

HELKE, CINDA JANE, pharmacology educator, researcher; b. Waterloo, Iowa, Feb. 27, 1951; d. Gerald and Lorna (Smith) Pieres; m. Joel Edward Helke, Aug. 10, 1974. BS in Pharmacy, Creighton U., 1974; PhD, Georgetown U., 1978. Staff fellow NIH, Bethesda, Md., 1978-80; asst. prof. dept. pharmacology Uniformed Svcs. Univ. of the Health Scis., Bethesda, 1980-85, assoc. prof. dept. pharmacology, 1985-88, prof. dept. pharmacology, 1988—; mem. adv. panel NIH, Bethesda, 1987—. Author chpts. in books; contbr. numerous articles to profl. jours. NIH grantee, 1981—. Mem. AAS, Am. Soc. Pharmacology and Exptl. Therapeutics, Soc. for Neurosci., Women in Sci., Women in Neurosci., Potomac chpt. Soc. for Neurosci. (sec., treas. Washington chpt. 1985-87). Democrat. Unitarian. Office: Uniformed Svcs U Health Sci 4301 Jones Bridge Rd Bethesda MD 20814

HELLAND, PATRICIA ANNE, college administrator; b. Green Bay, Wis., Mar. 24, 1964; d. Daniel Joseph and Constance Anne (Corrigan) H. BA in Biology, Cornell Coll., Mt. Vernon, Iowa, 1986. Assoc., cons. Don Elliott & Assocs., Nashville, 1986-88; assoc dir. of ann. giving Cornell Coll., Mt. Vernon, Iowa, 1988—. Mem. United Way, Green Bay, Wis., 1981-82; advisor Miltonian Literary Soc., Cornell Coll., 1988—. Recipient Gov's. Youth award Gov. of Wis., 1982; CASE Dist. VI grantee, 1988. Mem. Coun. for the Advancement and Support of Edn., Cedar Rapids C. of C., Beta Beta Beta. Democrat. Roman Catholic. Home: 1726 Woodside Ct NW Cedar Rapids IA 52405 Office: Cornell Coll Mount Vernon IA 52404

HELLER, AMY ANNE, film distribution company executive; b. N.Y.C., Nov. 10, 1957; d. Marvin and Ida (Melnitsky) H.; m. Dennis Robert Doros, June 10, 1990. BA in History summa cum laude, NYU, 1982; MA in History, Yale U., 1987. Asst. book editor Glamour mag., N.Y.C., 1981-83; asst. coord. Nuclear Weapons Freeze, N.Y.C., 1983; sales rep. First Run Features, N.Y.C., 1985-86; asst. gen. mgr. New Yorker Films, N.Y.C., 1986-87, dir. print and ednl. video sales, 1987—; pres. Milestone Film Video, N.Y.C., 1989—; cons. Women Make News, Leonia, N.J., 1986-87, Ann Slavit's The Red Shoes, Bklyn., 1986-87, Community Cinema Cons., N.Y.C., 1988-89. Contbr. articles to profl. publs. Mem. Phi Beta Kappa. Jewish. Office: Milestone Film & Video 275 W 96th St Ste 28C New York NY 10025

HELLER, BARBARA RUTH, statistician, educator; b. Milw., May 15, 1931; m. Alfred Heller, July 22, 1956; 1 child, Daniel. BS, Roosevelt U., 1953; MS, U. Chgo., 1965, PhD, 1979. Assoc. prof. Ill. Inst. Tech., Chgo., 1980—. Mem. Inst. for Math. Stats., Am. Statis. Assn., Am. Math. Soc., SIAM. Office: Ill Inst Tech Chicago IL 60616

HELLER, CHERYL CHRISTINE, advertising executive; b. Pitts., May 8, 1950; d. Robert B. and Adele (Dorazio) Yahner; m. Edwin H. Heller, Apr. 20, 1970 (div. 1972); m. 2d, Gary Nathan Scheft, Nov. 29, 1974. Student Boston Mus. Sch., 1972-73; B.F.A., magna cum laude Ohio Wesleyan U., 1972. Studio mgr. Giardin/Russell Agy., Watertown, Mass., 1972-74; design assoc. Gunn Assocs., Boston, 1974-80; v.p. design dir. Humphrey, Browning and MacDougall Agy., Boston, 1980-87; chmn., creative dir. Heller Breene, Boston, 1987—. Recipient numerous design awards. Mem. Am. Inst. Graphic Arts, Am. Soc. Typog. Arts. Democrat. Home: 191 Commonwealth Ave Boston MA 02116 Office: Heller Breene 101 Arch St Boston MA 02110*

HELLER, ELLEN DISTILLER, educator; b. Balt., Dec. 31, 1942; d. E. Melvin and Florence (Fox) Distiller; m. Drew Lee Heller, Aug. 19, 1943 (div. 1976); children: Dana Beth, William Morris. BA, Western Md. Coll., 1963; MS, Nova U., 1982. Tchr. English and creative writing Dade County Schs., Miami, 1963-66, 78—, Altoona (Pa.) Schs., 1966-68; lectr. and workshop presenter Dade County Schs. and other orgns., Miami, 1983—; ednl. rsch. and dissemination local site coord. AFT, Miami, 1987—. Vol. Campaign to Elect Dante Fascell, Miami, 1963-90, Kennedy Libr. exhibit, Miami, 1965, Campaigns to Elect Johnson, Carter, Dukakis, Miami; sec. Young Dems., Miami, 1964-65; active Dade County Reading Coun. Recipient Impact II award; NDEA fellow U. Ky., 1965. Mem. Nat. Coun. Tchrs. English, Fla. Coun. Tchrs. English, Dade County Coun. Tchrs. English, Tchrs. and Writers Collaborative, Univ. Miami Writing Inst. (assoc.), Book Rev. Club (pres. 1988-89), Stitchers of the Night, Phi Delta Kappa (bd. dirs. 1988—), Alpha Delta Kappa (sgt. at arms 1986-88, historian 1988—, corresponding sec. 1990—), Delta Kappa Gamma. Jewish. Home: 10808 SW 72d St Unit 133 Miami FL 33173 Office: Homestead Sr High Sch 2351 SE 12th Ave Homestead FL 33034

HELLER, KAREN LENORE, non-profit organization administrator; b. N.Y.C., Aug. 18, 1961; d. Marvin and Ida (Melnitsky) Heller; m. Steve J. Key, June 28, 1987. BA summa cum laude, Barnard Coll., 1983. Rsch. asst. Office for Disability Svcs., Barnard Coll., N.Y.C., 1981-83; freelance legal researcher Untapped Resources, Inc., N.Y.C., 1982-87; program coord. Nuclear Weapons Freeze Campaign, 15th Congl. Dist., N.Y.C., 1983-84; pub. benefits advocate, vol. trainer The Legal Aid Soc., N.Y.C., 1984-86; coord. health svcs. vols. ARC in Greater N.Y., N.Y.C., 1987-88, dir. vol. resources, 1988-90; sr. assoc. for volunteerism United Way of Am., Alexnadria, Va., 1990—; bd. dirs. Riverdale-Yonkers Soc. for Ethical Culture, Riverdale, N.Y., 1988-90. Vol. coord., co-founder Uptown Coffeehouse, Riverdale, 1987-90. Sr. scholar Barnard Coll., 1982-83. Mem. Assn. Vol. Adminstrn., Assn. Dirs. Vol. Svcs. in Health Care Facilities (assoc.), Phi Beta Kappa. Office: Unied Way Am 701 N Fairfax St Alexandria VA 22314

HELLER, LOIS JANE, physiologist, educator, researcher; b. Detroit, Jan. 4, 1942; d. John and Lona Elizabeth (Stockmeyer) Skagerberg; m. Robert Eugene Heller, May 21, 1966; children: John Robert, Suzanne Elizabeth. BA, Albion Coll., 1964; MS, U. Mich., 1966; PhD, U. Ill., Chgo., 1970. Instr. med ctr. U. Ill., Chgo., 1969-70, asst. prof., 1970-71; asst. prof. U. Minn., Duluth, 1972-77, assoc. prof., 1977-89, prof., 1989—; bd. dirs. Polinsky Med. Rehab. Ctr., Duluth. Author: Cardiovascular Physiology, 3d edition, 1989; contbr. numerous articles to profl. jours. Mem. Am. Physiol. Soc. (edn. com. 1989—), Am. Heart Assn. (bd. dirs. Minn. affiliate 1975-85, chair 1983-84), Soc. Exptl. Biology and Medicine, Sigma Xi (pres. Duluth club 1979-81. Home: 311 Halsey St Duluth MN 55803 Office: Univ Minn Sch of Medicine Duluth MN 55812

HELLER, MERYL A., speech-language pathologist; b. N.Y.C., June 8, 1952; d. Joseph A. and Bernice (Wand) Heller. BA, CUNY, Flushing, 1973; MS, U. Mich., 1974; postgrad., U. Mass., Boston. Speech/lang. pathologist Newington Children's Hosp., Conn., 1975-85; clin. supr. lang., speech and hearing dept. North Shore Children's Hosp., Salem, Mass., 1985-87; asst. dir. lang., speech and hearing dept. North Shore Children's Hosp., 1987—. Horace H. Rackham grantee, 1973-74. Mem. Am. Speech, Lang., Hearing Assn., Conn. Assn. for Children with Learning Disabilities (profl. adv. bd. 1983-85). Office: North Shore Children's Hosp 57 Highland Ave Salem MA 01970

HELLMANN, NORMA JANELLE, cytotechnologist; b. Honolulu, Jan. 21, 1949; d. Norman Louis and Margaret Janelle (Baker) Hellmann; BA, Carthage Coll., 1971; cert. Johns Hopkins Hosp. Sch. Cytotech., 1972. Asso. cytotechnologist Johns Hopkins Hosp., Balt., 1972-74; supr. cytology lab. Clin. Labs. of Nashville, 1974; ednl. coordinator Sch. Cytotech. Vanderbilt U., Nashville, 1974-76; supr. cytology lab. Clin. Labs. of Black Hills, Rapid City, S.D., 1976—; program coordinator CDC Workshops on Cytology, Rapid City, 1978. Mem. CAP, 1976-84, squadron comdr., 1982-83, dir. blood flight program S.D., 1976-83; exec. sec. Wonderland Homes Water and Service Co., 1979-80; founder, chmn. Literacy Council of Black Hills, 1984—; bd. dirs. Piedmont (S.D.) Vol. Fire Dept., 1985-87; mem. adv. council on community edn. Rapid City Schs. Mem. Am. Soc. Cytology, Am. Soc. Clin. Pathologists (assoc., cert. cytotechnologist), Internat. Acad. Cytology (cert.), Am. Soc. Cytotech., AAUW (S.D. v.p. program 1984-86, Woman of Worth award 1982), S.D. Advocacy Network for Women, Aircraft Owners and Pilots Assn., 99s (S.D. chmn. 1984-87), Exptl. Aircraft Assn., Beta Beta Beta, Alpha Mu Gamma. Republican. Lutheran. Home: 12205 Rena'ta Dr Black Hawk SD 57718 Office: PO Box 238 Rapid City SD 57709

HELLUMS, BONNIE CRANE, lawyer; b. Chgo., June 12, 1943; d. Newton Storey Blackford and Lorraine (Plachota) Crane; m. Nathan John Hellums, Dec. 30, 1967 (div. 1988); children: Gretchen Diane, John Sherwood; m. Carel Lewis Stith, July 21, 1990. BA, So. Meth. U., 1965; MEd, U. Ill., 1966; JD, South Tex. Coll. Law, 1981. Bar: Tex. 1983, U.S. Dist. Ct. (so. dist.) Tex. 1983, U.S. Supreme Ct. 1988. Women's counselor U. Houston, 1966-69; asst. dean students Rice U., Houston, 1969-74, dir. student activities and counseling, fgn. student advisor, 1974-84; pvt. practice Houston, 1984—; bd. dirs. Hellums Cons. Svc., Houston. Mem. adminstrv. bd. St. Luke's United Meth. Ch., Houston, 1980—, Houston Jr. Forum, 1984-88; pres. Women's Exec. Forum, Houston, 1988; bd. dirs. St. Agnes Acad., Houston, Covenant House, Ronald McDonald House. Mem. Nat. Assn. Women Deans, Adminstrs. and Counselors (pres. 1989-90). Republican. Home: 3763 Rice Blvd Houston TX 77005 Office: 3816 W Alabama St Ste 212 Houston TX 77027

HELLYER, CONSTANCE ANNE, writer, publication manager; b. Puyallup, Wash., Apr. 22, 1937; d. David Tirrell and Constance (Hopkins) H.; m. Peter A. Corning, Dec. 30, 1963 (div. 1977); children: Anne Arundel, Stephanie Deak; m. Don W. Conway, Oct. 12, 1980. BA with honors, Mills Coll., 1959. Grader, researcher Harvard U., Cambridge, Mass., 1959-60; reporter, researcher Newsweek mag., N.Y.C., 1960-63; author's asst. Theodore H. White and others, N.Y.C., 1964-69; freelance writer, editor Colo., Calif., 1969-75; writer, editor Stanford (Calif.) U. Med. Ctr., 1975-79; communications dir. No. Calif. Cancer Program, Palo Alto, 1979-82; pubs. dir. Stanford Law Sch., Palo Alto, 1982—. Founding editor (newsletter) Insight, 1978-80, Synergy, 1980-82; editor (mag.) Stanford Lawyer, 1982—; contbr. articles to profl. jours. and mags. Recipient Silver Medal award Council Advancement and Support of Edn., 1985, 89. Mem. No. Calif. Sci. Writers Assn. (co-founder, bd. dirs. 1979—), Nat. Sci. Writers Assn. (assoc.), Phi Beta Kappa. Democrat. Home: 2080 Louis Rd Palo Alto CA 94303 Office: Stanford Law Sch Stanford CA 94305-8610

HELM, CAROLE ANN, mayor; b. Los Angeles, Oct. 1, 1943; d. Robert Harry and Glenda Marie (Weaver) Horn; m. Ronald Roy Helm, June 5, 1965 (div. July 1988); children: Scott Eric, Heather Marie, Hilary Renee. BS magna cum laude, Wash. State U., Pullman, 1965. Research techician Baylor Coll. of Medicine, Houston, 1965-66; research chemist Inst. for Research, Houston, 1966-69; office mgr. U. Cities Woman's Clinic, P.S., Moscow, Idaho, 1982-86; mayor City of Pullman, Wash.; bd. mem. Assn. of Wash. Cities Bd. dirs., Olympia, 1986—, State of Wash. Fire Protection Policy Bd., Olympia, 1986--, v. chair, State Wash. Rail Devel. Comm.,

Olympia, 1987--, mem. State of Wash. Dept. of Ecology 2010 Com., Olympia, 1989, chair person Pullman Moscow Regional Airport Bd., 1986--. Mem. Phi Beta Kappa, Phi Kappa Phi, Beta Gamma Sigma. Office: City of Pullman PO Box 249 Pullman WA 99163

HELM, JOAN MARY, financial planner; b. Springfield, Ill., June 30, 1934; d. Elwood R. and Juanita (Nash) Ressler. Student, Northwestern U., 1972. Cert. fin. planner; registered fin. planning practitioner. With mgmt. engring. dept. Ill. Bell Tel. Co. and So. Bell, 1956-74; agt. Mut. of Omaha, 1974-78; gen. agt. Lafayette Life, 1977-84; prin. Linsco Pvt. Ledger, 1981—; pres. Helm Fin. Group, Inc., Boca Raton, Fla., 1981—; moderator radio show Sta. WSBR, 1972-73. Active Rep. Party, Chgo., 1986—. Mem. Internat. Assn. Fin. Planners (pres. Gold chpt. 1986-88, mem. Southeast coun. 1986-88), Estate Planning Coun., Inst. Cert. Fin. Planners, Internat. Platform Assn., Boca Hotel & Club, Jourdan's Bridge Club. Republican. Office: Helm Fin Group 400 S Dixie Hwy Ste 411 Boca Raton FL 33432

HELMINSKI, CAMILLE ADAMS, publisher; b. Jacksonville, Fla., Oct. 16, 1951; d. Moulton Lee and Mildred (Stockton) Adams; m. Edmund (Kabir) Richard Helminski, Oct. 19, 1974; children: Matthew, Shams, Cara. BA, Smith Coll., 1973. Co-dir. Threshold Books, Putney and Brattleboro, Vt., 1981—. Co-translator: Rumi Daylight, 1990, Happiness Without Death, 1991. Mem. NAFE, Nat. Mus. Women in the Arts, Wilderness Soc., NOW, Audubon Soc., Amnesty Internat., Threshold Soc. (co-dir., sec. 1985—).

HELMS, MARY ANN, nurse; b. Compton, Calif., Jan. 7, 1935; d. Raymond Whitfield and Amanda Zelpha (Hancock) Spencer; AA in Nursing, El Camino Coll., 1971; BS in Nursing, Calif. State U., Los Angeles, 1976; MA in Mgmt., St. Mary's Coll., 1978; MS in Nursing, Ariz. State U., 1985; postgrad., Columbia Pacific U., 1988—; cert. clin. specialist; m. Willard Ford Helms, Mar. 15, 1958; children: Michael Steven, Steven Allen. Med. sec., bookkeeper Palm Springs (Calif.) Med. Clinic, 1956-61; office mgr. William R. Stevens Ins. Agy., Santa Ana, Calif., 1961-63, I.J. Weinrot & Son Ins. Agy., Los Angeles, 1963-67; staff nurse Kaiser Found. Hosp., Harbor City, Calif., 1971-76; supr., coord. pediatrics Maricopa County Gen. Hosp., Phoenix, 1976-80; critical care nurse Phoenix Baptist Hosp., 1980-81, critical care mgr., 1981-89, clin. nurse specialist, 1989—, critical care cons., 1986—. Mem. Am. Nurses Assn., Am. Soc. Women Accts., Natural History Mus., Met. Mus. Art, Smithsonian Instn., Phoenix Zoo, Phoenix Art Mus., Cousteau Soc., Calif. State U. Alumni Assn., KAET Public Broadcasting System, Am. Assn. Critical Care Nurses, Ariz. Nurses Assn. Nat. League Nursing, Ariz. State U. Alumni Assn., Phi Kappa Phi, Alpha Gamma Sigma, Sigma Theta Tau. Mormon. Research on noise pollution on phys. and mental health of citizenry, phenylketonuria testing in Los Angeles, measurement of attitudes toward children in pediatric nurses, nursing practice, physiological changes with back massage, incidence of prolonged Q-T internal in critically ill patients, assessment of artierial circulation in vascular surgery patients; use of autotransfusion in hip and knee surgery patients. Home: 1007 E Michelle Dr Phoenix AZ 85022 Office: 6025 N 20th Ave Phoenix AZ 85015

HELMSIN, ELIZABETH POTH, finance executive, accountant, property manager; b. Clarksburg, W.Va., Dec. 27, 1925; d. Pieter and Catherina Anna (Donker) Poth; m. Guy Raymond Helmsin, Jan. 10, 1959. Student, Ohio State U., 1945-48, North Cen. Tech. Sch., Mansfield, Ohio, 1981-83. Bookkeeper Simon & Haas, Columbus, Ohio, 1948-61; contr. Grant Hosp., Columbus, 1961-71; v.p. fin. Samaritan Hosp., Ashland, Ohio, 1971—. Treas. Coun. on Aging, Ashland, 1981—. Mem. Healthcare Fin. Mgmt. Assn. (sec. Cen. Ohio chpt. 1963-65, treas., 1965-67, William G. Follmer award 1971, Robert Reeves award 1977, Frederick T. Muncie award 1982, Founders metal of Honor 1987), Altrusa Club Ashland (pres. 1985-86). Democrat. Methodist. Home: 11 Morgan Ave Ashland OH 44805 Office: Samaritan Hosp 1025 Center St Ashland OH 44805

HELMSLEY, LEONA MINDY, hotel executive; b. N.Y.C.; m. Harry B. Helmsley, Apr. 8, 1972. Vice pres. Pease & Elliman, N.Y.C., 1962-69; pres. Sutton & Towne Residential, N.Y.C., 1967-70; sr. v.p. Helmsley Spear, N.Y.C., 1970-72, Brown, Harris, Stevens, N.Y.C., 1970-72; pres. Helmsley Hotels, Inc., N.Y.C., 1980—. Named Woman of Yr. N.Y. Council Civic Affairs, 1970; named Woman of Yr. Town & Country Condos & Coops., 1981; recipient Service award Ort Sch. Engring., 1981, Profl. Excellence award Les Dames d'Escoffier, 1981, Spl. Achievement award Sales Execs. Club N.Y., 1981, Woman of Yr. award Internat. Hotel Industry, 1982. Home: 36 Central Pk S New York NY 10019 Office: Helmsley Hotels Helmsley Palace Hotel 455 Madison Ave New York NY 10022*

HELMS-VANSTONE, MARY WALLACE, anthropology educator; b. Allentown, Pa., Apr. 15, 1938; d. Samuel Leidich and Mary (Wallace) Helms; divorced. BA, Pa. State U., State College, 1960; MA, U. Mich., 1962, PhD, 1967. Instr. Wayne State U., Detroit, 1965-67; asst. prof. Syracuse (N.Y.) U., 1967-68; lectr. Northwestern U., Evanston and Chgo., Ill., 1969-79; prof. U. N.C., Greensboro, 1979—, head dept. anthropology, 1979-85. Author: Asang: A Miskito Community, 1971, Middle America, 1975, Ancient Panama, 1979, Ulysses' Sail, 1988; contbr. articles to profl. jours. Fellow Am. Anthrop. Assn.; mem. Am. Soc. Ethnohistory (pres. 1976), Am. Ethnological Soc., So. Anthrop. Soc. (pres. 1980-81, proceedings editor 1982—). Office: Univ NC Dept Anthropology Greensboro NC 27412

HELOISE, columnist, lecturer, broadcaster, author; b. Waco, Tex., Apr. 15, 1951; d. Marshal H. and Heloise K. (Bowles) Cruse; m. David L. Evans, Feb. 13, 1981. B.S. in Math. and Bus, S.W. Tex. State U., 1974. Owner, pres. Heloise, Inc. Asst. to columnist mother, Heloise, 1974-77, upon her death took over internationally syndicated column, 1977; author: Hints From Heloise, 1980, Help From Heloise, 1981, Heloise's Beauty Book, 1985, All-New Hints From Heloise, 1989, Heloise: Hints for a Healthy Planet, 1990; contbg. editor Good Housekeeping mag., 1981, Speaker for the House; co-founder, 1st co-pilot Mile Pie in the Sky Balloon Club. Mem. Good Neighbor Coun. Tex.-Mex. Mem. AFTRA, SAG, Women in Communication, Tex. Press Women, Internat. Women's Forum, Women in Radio and TV, Confrerie de la Chaine des Rotisseurs (bailli San Antonio chpt.), Ordre Mondial des Gourmets De'Gustateurd de U.S.A. Club: Death Valley Yacht and Racket. Lodge: Zonta. Home: PO Box 795000 San Antonio TX 78279 Office: care King Features Syndicate 235 E 45th St New York NY 10017

HELPHINGSTINE, CYNTHIA JEANETTE GOODSON, healthcare marketing executive; b. Kansas City, Mo., June 27, 1949; d. Louis Hoffman and Dorothy (Hoffman) Goodson; m. Stephen Ralph Helphingstine; children: Melissa, Matthew. BA, U. Mo., 1971, PhD, 1977; MBA, Lake Forest Grad. Sch. Mgmt., 1983. Dir. Baxter Healthcare Corp., Deerfield, Ill., 1977-86; pres. The Biotron Group, Highland Park, Ill., 1986—. Exec. com. MIT Enterprise Forum, Chgo., 1989; mem. pres.'s coun. Lake Forest (Ill.) Grad. Sch. Mgmt., 1988—. Recipient Midwest Med. Student Rsch. award, 1977. Mem. AAAS, Am. Hosp. Assn., Am. Assn. Clin. Chemistry, Am. Soc. Microbiology, Assn. Women in Sci., Tissue Culture Assn., Med.-Surg. Mktg. Rsch. Assn., Chgo. High Tech. Assn. Office: The Biotron Group 600 Central Ave Ste 333 Highland Park IL 60035

HELTON, LUCILLE HENRY HANRATTIE, academic administrator; b. Ft. Worth, Mar. 2, 1942; d. P.D. and Virginia (Clark) Henry; m. Wayne Hanrattie, June 26, 1965 (div. Apr. 1986); children: Clark, Chris; m. William M. Helton, Jr., Mar. 19, 1988. BA, So. Meth. U., 1964; MEd, U. Pitts., 1968; cert. in adminstrn., William Paterson Coll., 1984; cert. in mid-mgmt., Tex. Christian U., 1987. Cert. elem. tchr. N.J., Pa., Tex. Nat. field sec. Kappa Kappa Gamma Sorority, Columbus, Ohio, 1964-65; elem. tchr. Pitts. Bd. Edn., 1965-69; co-dir, chmn. dept. maths. Assn. Children with Learning Disabilities Sch., Pitts., 1969-72; tchr. elem., secondary, gifted and talented and home instrn. programs West Milford (N.J.) Bd. Edn., 1976-84; sch. dir., prin. Hill Sch., Ft. Worth, 1984—. Mem. adminstrv. bd. First Meth. Ch., Ft. Worth, 1987—, Council of Ministries of First Meth. Ch., 1986-87; bd. dirs. Community Psychiat. Ctr. Oak Bend Hosp., Ft. Worth, 1987—. Mem. Networking for Exec. Women, Tex. Ind. Sch. Consortium, Commn. on Status and Role of Women, Assn. for Children with Learning Disabilities, DAR, Delta Kappa Gamma, Phi Delta Gamma. Democrat. Methodist. Office: Hill Sch 3109 Lubbock Fort Worth TX 76109

HELTON, MELANIE HARDER, marketing executive; b. Dallas, Nov. 29, 1958; d. Donald Clifton and Jo Anne (Thompson) Harder; m. Ronald Kerr Helton, May 19, 1985. BS in Mktg., Miami U., Oxford, Ohio, 1980. Recruiter/supr. Culver Personnel Agy., San Diego, 1980-82; sales rep. Allergan Pharm., San Diego, 1982-84, Ethicon, Inc., San Francisco/San Diego, 1984-86; field mktg. specialist We. region Snyder Labs./Zimmer Patient Care, San Diego, 1986-88; product mgr. Zimmer Arthroscopy Systems, Denver, 1989-90, Concept/Bristol-Myers Squibb, Largo, Fla., 1990—. Mem. NAFE, Miami U. Alumni Assn., Pi Sigma Epsilon. Republican. Methodist. Office: Concept/Bristol-Myers Squibb 11311 Concept Blvd Largo FL 34643

HELTZEL, MARLENE SUE, nurse; b. Wauseon, Oh., July 15, 1934; d. Milton Corwin and Wilma Gladys (Meier) Burkholder; m. Robert Lincoln Heltzel, Apr. 3, 1953 (div. 1978); children: Robin Sue, Robert Lincoln. Dip., Wauseon High Sch., 1952, Toledo Hosp. Sch. Nursing, 1955. RN. Nurse Ohio State U., Columbus, 1955-60, Newark Hosp., 1960-61, Dr. Warren Koontz, Newark, 1961-62, Cleve. Clinic, 1962-65, McKeesport Hosp., Pa., 1965-71, Whetstone Convalescent Ctr., 1972-78, NW Pediatrics, Columbus, 1978-82; nurse specialist Ohio Dept. Human Svcs., Columbus, 1982--. Vol. Pennswood Unite Meth. Ch., Irwin; mem. Linworth Unite Meth. Ch., 1972—, trustee, 1982-83, nominating com., 1987-89, mission com., 1989—, vol. at open church, mem. Linworth United Meth. women. Named Girl of the Year Exchange Club Wauseon, 1952. Mem. Am. Nurses' Assn., Pa. Nurses Assn., Linworth Nurses Assn., Pennswood Woman Soc. Christian Svc. (pres. 1967-69). Republican. Home: 135 Heischman Ave Worthington OH 43085

HEMBY, DOROTHY JEAN, college counselor; b. Greenville, N.C., Aug. 21; d. Samul Emanuel and Queenie Ester Hemby; student Essex County Coll., 1971, Montclair State Coll., 1973-75, Kean Coll. N.J., 1975-77. Clk.-typist Remco Industries, Newark, IRS, Newark, 1963-66, VA Hosp., East Orange, N.J., 1966-71; part-time tchr. Newark Bd. Edn., 1973-76; coll. counselor/academic adviser Kean Coll. N.J., Union, 1976-77; vol. job evaluator N.J. Vol. Employment Service Team, Newark, 1977-78; coll. counselor/adviser Passaic County Community Coll., Paterson, N.J., 1978—, mem. tenure faculty review com, 1986—; chmn. H.O.P.E. com. Clk., East Orange Bd. Elections, 1971-72; v.p. Econ. Consumer's Community Aid., 1971-73; active local polit. orgn., 1973—; adv. Passaic County Gospel Choir and Christian Club; chairperson Passaic County Coll. Student Life Com., 1983-84; publicity coordinator Crispus Attucks Scholarship Found., 1986-87. Mem. N.J. Assn. Black Educators, Assn. Black Women in Higher Edn., Am. Personnel and Guidance Assn., Am. Counseling Personel Assn., N.J. Social Workers Assn., N.J. Behavioral Sci. Soc., Passaic County Acad. Council, Am. Assn. Counseling and Devel., N.J. Black Issues Assn. Clubs: 700, PTL. Office: Passaic County Community Coll College Blvd Paterson NJ 07509

HEMINGWAY, BETH ROWLETT, author, columnist, lecturer; b. Richmond, Va., May 6, 1913; d. Robert Archer and Evelyn Lucille (Doggett) Rowlett; B.Mus., Hollins Coll., 1934; m. Harold Hemingway, Apr. 2, 1938; children—Ruth Hartley, Martha Scott. Writer, Richmond-Lifestyle mag.; columnist Artistry in Bloom, Richmond Times-Dispatch; author: A Second Treasury of Christmas Decorations, 1961; Flower Arrangement with Antiques, 1965; Christmas Decorations Say Welcome, 1972; Antiques Accented by Flowers, 1975; Beth Hemingway's No Kin to Ernest, 1980; Holidays with Hemingway, 1985; lectr. numerous states, also Australia, 1966, Eng., 1977. Vol., Hermitage Meth. Home, 1977-79. Mem. Nat. League Am. Pen Women, Va. Writers Club, Richmond Hort. Assn., Va. Fedn. Garden Clubs (book rev. chmn.), Richmond Council Garden Clubs (flower arrangement chmn.), Clay Spring Garden Club (pres. 1953-55), Barton Garden Club (pres. 1959-61, 74). Republican. Methodist. Home: 1604 Derek Ln Richmond VA 23229

HEMLER, ELIZABETH ANN, nurse midwife; b. Lancaster, Pa., Oct. 10, 1956; d. Paul Martin and Elizabeth Taylor (Bouchelle) H.; m. William Stewart Mann, July 10, 1987. BS in Nursing, Georgetown U., 1978; MS in Nursing, Emory U., 1985. Cert. nurse midwife, RN. Staff nurse Georgetown U., Washington, 1978-79; vol. Peace Corps., Niger, 1979-82; staff nurse United Hosp., Grand Forks, N.D., 1982-83, childbirth instr., 1982-84; clin. nurse family ctr. U. N.D., Grand Forks, 1983-84, clin. instr. med. sch., 1984, 87-88; fellow Basset Hosp., Cooperstown, N.Y., 1987; rsch. instr. coll. nursing U. N.D., Grand Forks, 1986-88, clin. instr. coll. nursing, 1982-84, 86—; nurse midwife Valley Med. Assn., Grand Forks, 1987—; bd. dirs. Valley Family Planning, Grand Forks, 1989—, WIC, 1989—. Named Nurse of Yr. March of Dimes, Bismarck, N.D., 1988, one of Outstanding Young Women of Am., 1986. Mem. ANA,ICEA, NAACOG, Am. Coll. Nurse Midwives (chpt. chair 1988—, mem. div. of rsch. 1987—, mem. publicity, pub. rels. com. 1989—), N.D. Nurses Assn. Home: RR1 Box 219 Grand Forks ND 58201 Office: 1380 S Columbia Rd Grand Forks ND 58201

HEMLEY, JUDITH KEMP, retired public relations professional, civic leader; b. L.A., May 6, 1941; d. Norman Kemp McPhail and Ruth Taylor (Heineman) Condie; m. Phillip Robertson Sledge, Dec. 28, 1963 (div. 1974); 1 child, Darcy; m. M. Rogue Hemley, Nov. 26, 1982; stepchildren: Brandon, Bryan. BS, San Jose State U., 1962. Cert. secondary tchr., Calif. Prin. Robertson Sledge Co., Palo Alto, Calif., 1964-73; mgr. pub. rels. Cromwell-McKay Advt./Pub. Rels., Irvine, Calif., 1981-83; pvt. practice Orange County, Calif., 1983-86. Contbr. articles to various publs. Active Red Ribbon adv. coun. ARC, 1988—; mem. Ho. Ear Inst., 1986—, Chancellor's Club, U. Calif., Irvine, 1987—, mem. arboretum, mem. humanities assocs., Angels of Arts; mem. fundraising activities Newport Harbor Art Mus., Newport Beach, Calif., 1978—, trustee, 1979-80, mem. founder's circle, 1987—; trustee Assessment and Treatment Svcs. Ctr., Orange County, 1988—; pres. Sales and Rental Coun., Newport Beach, 1979-80; co-chairperson Fine Arts Patrons Coun., Newport Beach, 1980-81, gala Orange County Centennial, Inc., 1988, Newport Beach Concours d'Elegance, 1989; co-founder Grad. Night Found., 1987, Visionaries, Orange County, 1989; founder Opera Pacific. Mem. Newport Harbor Yacht Club, Ctr. Club, Peninsula Point Racquet Club. Home: 2254 Channel Rd Balboa CA 92661

HEMMINGS, MADELEINE BLANCHET, association administrator; b. Bryn Mawr, Pa., Aug. 14, 1942; d. Wilfred Loyola and Feroline (Sissenere) Blanchet; m. Richard Bagot Hemmings, Mar. 14, 1970; 1 child, Laurie Cornwall Hemmings. Cert. lang. and linguistics, U. Fribourg, Switzerland, 1961; BS, Cornell U., 1976. Owner Hallmark of Pa., Harrisberg, Pa., 1964-70; assoc. dir. human resources Cornell U., Ithaca, N.Y., 1972-77; policy dir. benefits NAM, Washington, 1977-79; policy dir. edn. C. of C. of the U.S., Washington, 1979-83; v.p. policy Nat. Alliance of Bus., Washington, 1983-85; pres. West Va. Roundtable, Charleston, W.Va., 1985-87; exec. dir. Nat. Assn. of State Dirs. of Vocat. Edn., Washington, 1987—; cons. Edn. Policy, Washington, 1979—; bd. dirs. Aslan Farms, Brookeville, Md. Author: The New Job Training Partnership Act, 1982. Campaign mgr. Connie Cook for Congress, Ithaca, N.Y., 1984; sponsor U.S. Pony Club, Olney, Md., 1987—. Mem. U.S. C. of C. (edn. com.), Cornell Pres. Club, Am. Society of Assn. Execs. (mem. chief exec. officer's com. 1989—). Republican. Roman Catholic. Home: 3600 Sundown Rd Brookville MD 20833 Office: 1420 16th St NW Ste 301 Washington DC 20036

HEMMINGSEN, BARBARA BRUFF, microbiology educator; b. Whittier, Calif., Mar. 25, 1941; d. Stephen Cartland and Susanna Jane (Alexander) Bruff; m. Edward Alfred Hemmingsen, Aug. 5, 1967; 1 child, Grete. BA, U. Calif., Berkeley, 1962, MA, 1964; PhD, U. Calif., San Diego, 1971. Lectr. San Diego State U., 1973-77, asst. prof., 1977-81, assoc. prof., 1981-88, prof., 1988—; vis. asst. prof. Aarhus U., Denmark, 1971-72; cons. Automated Microbiology, Inc., San Diego, 1984-85, Woodward-Clyde Cons., 1985, 87—. Author: (with others) Microbial Ecology, 1972; contbr. articles to profl. jours. Mem. Planned Parenthood, San Diego. Mem. Am. Soc. Microbiology, Soc. Protozoology, Soc. Gen. Microbiology, AAAS, Am. Women in Sci. (San Diego chpt.), Sigma Xi, Phi Beta Kappa (pres. Nu chpt. 1986-88). Democrat. Office: San Diego State U Dept Biology San Diego CA 92182-0057

HEMPEL, KATHLEEN JANE, paper company executive; b. Monroe, Wis., Nov. 10, 1950; d. Francis H. and Mary Joan (Martin) Mottley; m. Rolf R. Hempel, Aug. 1, 1970; children: Michelle, Patricia. Student, U. Wis., Platteville; grad., U. Wis., Stevens Point, 1972; MBA, Ariz. State U., Tempe, 1984. V.p. Ft. Howard Corp., Green Bay, Wis., 1973-82, 1st v.p., 1986-87, also bd. dirs.; sr. exec. v.p. Ft. Howard Corp., Green Bay, 1988—; cons. Hewitt Assocs., Phoenix, 1985-86; bd. dirs. Ft. Howard Found., Green Bay. Mem. County Exec. Ad Hoc Orgnl. Panel, Green Bay, 1987. Office: Ft Howard Corp 1919 S Broadway Green Bay WI 54304

HEMPFLING, LINDA LEE, nurse; b. Indpls., July 28, 1947; d. Paul Roy and Myrtle Pearl (Ward) H. Diploma Meth. Hosp. Ind. Sch. Nursing, 1968; postgrad. St. Joseph's Coll. Charge nurse Meth. Hosp., Indpl., 1968; staff nurse operating room Silver Cross Hosp., Joliet, Ill., 1969; charge nurse operating room Huntington (N.Y.) Hosp., 1969-73; night supr. oper. rm. Hermann Hosp., Houston, 1973-76; unit. mgr., purchasing coord. oper. rms., 1976-83; RN med. auditor, quality assurance and tng. coord. Nat. Healthcare Rev., Inc., Houston, 1984—. Future Nurses Am. scholar, 1965, Nat. Merit scholar, 1965. Mem. Nat. League Nursing, Am. Nurses Assn., Assn. Oper. Rm. Nurses, Tex. Med. Auditors Assn. Office: 1130 Earle Houston TX 77030

HEMPHILL, HELEN BERNETA, retired educator, civic worker; b. Keystone, Iowa, Jan. 9, 1912; d. George Irvin and Anna Maria (Fielman) Benzing; m. Marvel Woodrow Hemphill, Aug. 10, 1941; children: Cheryl Ann Hemphill Grills, David Daniel. Student, Iowa State U., 1935, 36, U. So. Calif., 1938; BA, U. No. Iowa, 1940; postgrad., Drake U. Cert. elem. and secondary tchr, Iowa. Tchr. Harcourt (Iowa) Sch., 1930-34, Keswick (Iowa) Sch., 1934-35, Owasa (Iowa) Sch., 1935-39, Ida Grove (Iowa) Sch., 1939-41, What Cheer (Iowa) Sch., 1943, Ft. Dodge (Iowa) Sch., 1960-77; unit control clk. Sears, Roebuck & Co., St. Louis and Boise, Idaho, 1941-42, 43-44; ret., 1977. Former leader, organizer Girl Scouts U.S.A.; vol. tchr. English to Vietnamese, Ft. Dodge, 1979; vol. Trinity Regional Hosp. Aux., Ft. Dodge, 1977—; mem. Older Iowans Legislature, 1977-82; chmn. group United Meth. Women, 1987-89; mem. adv. coun. Iowa Dept. Elder Affairs, 1989—. Recipient Leader in Edn. award Iowa Edn. Assn., 1965. Mem. AAUW (legis. chmn., treas. 1985), Am. Assn. Ret. Persons (sec. joint state legis. com. AARP-Iowa Ret. Tchrs. Assn. 1977-81). Home: 1636 11th Ave N Fort Dodge IA 50501

HEMPHILL, (NORMA) JO, special event and tour operating company executive; b. Enid, Okla., Nov. 25, 1930; d. Wyatt Warren and Wanda Markes (Parker) Stout; m. Benjamin Robert Hemphill, June 21, 1952; children: Susan Colleen, Robert Gary. Student, Okla. State U.; BA, U. Calif., Berkeley, 1955. Former acct. Better Bus. Bookkeeping, Lafayette, Calif.; tchr., Head Start tchr. Chino (Calif.) Elem. Sch., 1966-68; pres., founder Calif. Carousel and Carousel Tours, Lafayette, 1972—; speaker in field; cons., dir. various orgns. Former mem. bd. dirs. PTA, Moraga, Calif., Lafayette; bd. dirs. Children's Home Soc., Upland, Calif., 1965-69; past demonstration tchr. Presbytery of Bay Area, San Francisco; past supt. 1st Presbyn. Ch., Oakland, Calif., elder, 1977—, trustee, 1980; mem. hon. bd. adv. com. Festival of Lake, Oakland, 1982; bd. govs. Goodwill Industries, 1978-79. Named Person of Yr. award Advt.-Mktg. Assn. East Bay, 1978. Mem. Lake Merritt Breakfast Club (Oakland, spl. events com.), Pi Beta Phi (bd. dirs., spl. events com. Contra Costa County chpt.). Office: Calif Carousel & Tours PO Box 537 Lafayette CA 94549

HEMPHILL, MAUREEN LUCILLE, Canadian government official; b. Grand Forks, B.C., Jan. 26, 1937; d. Jim Leroy and Elaine Agnes Miller; children—Carol, Jim, Ross, Susan. R.N., Vancouver Gen. Hosp. Nurse, Vancouver Gen. Hosp., N. Vancouver Hosp., Good Samaritan Nursing Home, Edmonton; mem. Man. Legis. Assembly for Logan, 1981—. Minister of Edn., Govt. of Man., 1984—, minister Housing, 1986, minister Bus. Devel. and Tourism, 1986, minister Community Services, 1987. Address: Legis Bldg Rm 123, Winnipeg, MB Canada R3C 0V8

HEMSWORTH, KATHLEEN GARRIGAN, packaging executive; b. South Orange, N.J., Sept. 21, 1961; d. John Joseph and Kathleen (Valli) Garrigan; divorced. BS in Mktg. and Mgmt., Seton Hall U., 1983. Account mgr. Shell Packaging Group, Springfield, N.J., 1983-85, Accurate Box Co., Paterson, N.J., 1985-86; prin., dir. sales and marketing Source Packaging, Hackensack, N.J., 1986—. Roman Catholic. Office: Source Packaging 279 Huyler St South Hackensack NJ 07606

HENARD, ELIZABETH ANN, controller; b. Providence, Oct. 9, 1947; d. Anthony Joseph and Grace Johanna (Lokay) Zorbach; m. Patrick Edward Mann, Dec. 18, 1970 (div. July 1972); m. John Bruce Henard Jr., Oct. 19, 1974; children: Scott Michael, Christopher Andrew. Student, Jacksonville (Fla.) U., 1966. Sec. So. Bell Tel.&Tel., Jacksonville, 1964-69; office mgr. Gunther F. Reis Assocs., Tampa, Fla., 1969-71; exec. sec. Ernst & Ernst, Tampa, 1971-72; exec. sec. to pres. Lamalie Assocs., Tampa, 1972-74; exec. sec. Arthur Young & Co., Chgo., 1975; adminstrv. asst. Irving J. Markin, Chgo., 1975; contr., v.p., corp. sec. Henard Assocs., Inc., Dallas, 1983—. Mem. Dallas Investors Group (treas. 1986—), Bent Tree Country Club, Stonebriar Country Club, Hidden Hills Club (Austin). Republican. Roman Catholic. Home: 5706 Thames Ct Dallas TX 75252 Office: Henard Assocs Inc 15303 Dallas Pkwy Dallas TX 75248

HENDERSHOT, CAROL MILLER, physical therapist; b. Lancaster, Pa., July 24, 1959; d. Richard Horace and Joan Marie (Nonnenmocher) M. BS in Physical Therapy, Quinnipiac Coll., 1981. Staff phys. therapist Easter Seal Rehab. Ctr., Lancaster, 1981-85, phys. therapy dept. head, 1986-89; staff phys. therapist Community Hosp. of Lancaster, 1985-86, Spokane (Wash.) Guild's Sch. & Neuromuscular Ctr., 1990—. Dir. publicity and pub. rels. Lancaster Dist. United Meth. Women, 1988-89; vice chmn. coun. on ministries Covenant United Meth. Ch., Lancaster, 1988-90, chmn. ch. and society com., 1987, 88, mem. chancel choir, 1981-89, mem. adminstrv. bd., 1975-88; mem. trustee bd., chancel choir Audubon Pk. United Meth. Ch., 1990—. Mem. Neuro-Devel. Treatment Assn., Visiting Nurse Assn. (profl. adv. com. 1987-89), Beta Beta Beta. Democrat. Methodist. Home: 6007 Hopi Ct Spokane WA 99208

HENDERSHOTT LOVE, ARLES JUNE, television news director; b. Rockford, Ill., Oct. 22, 1956; d. Eugene Bourden and Rose Marie (Erickson) Hendershott; m. Joseph William Love, Sept. 20, 1986. BS with high honors, Ill. State U., 1979. Reporter Sta. WTVO-TV, Rockford, 1979-82, news producer, 1982-83; news assignment editor Sta. WIFR-TV, Rockford, 1983-86, news dir., 1986—; speaker Rockford Pub. Schs., 1980-83. Producer news story Pee Wee Explosion, 1985 (AP award 1986). Mem. com. YWCA, Rockford, 1987, Westminister Presbyn. Ch., Rockford, also tchr. Sunday Sch.; bd. dirs. No. Ill. chpt. March of Dimes, 1980-84, NW Ill. chpt. Spl. Olympics, Rockford, 1986—, Discovery Ctr. Mus., Rockford, 1987—. Recipient Leadership award Ken-Rock Community Ctr., Rockford, 1980. Mem. AAUW (bd. dirs. 1982-84), NAFE, Radio-TV News Dirs. Assn. (TV state coord. for Ill. 1989—), Ill. News Broadcasters Assn., Soc. Profl. Journalists, Am. Mgmt. Assn., Archeology Inst. Am., Univ. Chgo. Oriental Inst., Ill. Assoc. Press (exec. com. 1989—). Clubs: Lens & Shutter (pres. 1983-85, others), Zonta. Office: Sta WIFR-TV 2523 Meridian Rd Rockford IL 61105

HENDERSON, BARBARA B., hospital assistant administrator; b. Roanoke Rapids, N.C., Aug. 7, 1935; d. Ottis Summerel and Flossie Ann (Cox) Boyd; m. Edward Carlton Henderson, Sept. 15, 1957; children: Tanya, Edward Carlton, Jr. Grad. high sch., Roanoke Rapids, N.C. Benefits adminstr./personnel Airmold, W.R. Grace Co., Roanoke Rapids, N.C., 1975-78; sec., adminstr. Scotland Meml. Hosp., Laurinburg, N.C., 1979-87; asst. adminstr. Scotland Meml. Hosp., Laurinburg, 1987—. Mem. Interagency Council, Laurinburg, 1989; dir. United Way Scotland County, Laurinburg, 1987-89; pres. City PTA Council, Roanoke Rapids, 1969-70; dir. Halifax Mental Health Assn., Roanoke Rapids, 1969-70; leader Girl Scouts Am., Roanoke Rapids, 1965-71. Mem. N.C. Chpt. Assn. Risk Mgrs., Am. Soc. Healthcare Risk Mgmt., N.C. Pub. Rels. Assn., Pilot Club of Laurinburg (dir. 1985-87, past gov. award 1985), Jaycettes, C. of C. Democrat. Presbyterian. Home: 1205 Charles Dr Laurinburg NC 28352 Office: Scotland Meml Hosp 500 Lauchwood Dr Laurinburg NC 28352

HENDERSON, BERTHA ROBERTS, nursing administrator; b. Mobile, Ala., July 24, 1940; d. Willie and Ora (Johnson) Roberts; m. James B. Henderson, Dec. 21, 1959; children: Valerie Henderson Weatherspoon, James B. Jr., David S., Patrina D., Iris C. AS in Social Sci., Brookdale Community

Coll., Lincroft, N.J., 1976, AS in Nursing, 1981; BS Health Care Adminstrn., St. Joseph's Coll., Windham, Maine, 1989. RN, N.J.; cert. psychiat. nurse, N.J. Practical nurse N.J. Nurses Assn., Maplewood, 1980-82; head nurse Marlboro (N.J.) State Psychiat. Hosp., 1986-89, supr. nursing svcs., 1989—; chief exec. officer Dale Constrn. Co., 1990—; pvt. practice, Neptune, 1986—; cons. N.J. League for Nursing; entrepreneur Diabetic Cons. Ctr., Neptune, 1989. Contbr. articles to profl. jours. Block mem. Take Bite Out of Crime, Neptune, 1988—; organizer neighborhood diabetic support group, Neptune, 1989—; vol. Am. Heart Assn., 1990—. Mem. Am. Nurses Assn., Am. Diabetic Assn., Brookdale Community Coll. Alumni Assn., NAFE. Democrat. Baptist. Home: 4 Dale Pl Neptune NJ 07753 Office: Marlboro Psychiat Hosp State Hwy 520 Marlboro NJ 07748

HENDERSON, CAROL LEE, marketing professional; b. Marshalltown, Iowa, Apr. 6, 1957; d. Carl Frank and Georgiana (Kubik) Uchytil; m. Mark Ray Henderson, Apr. 23, 1982. BA in Polit.Sic. and Spanish, Iowa State U., Ames, 1979. Mtkg. mgr. Keosippi (Iowa) Mall, 1980-82, Eastfield Mall, Springfield, Mass., 1982-84, The Shops at Tabor Ctr., Denver, 1984-86, Bayside Marketplace (The Rouse Co.), Miami, Fla., 1986-89; mtkg. mgr. mall locations The Rouse Co., Columbia, Md., 1980-89; south Fla. regional mktg. mgr. Walt Disney Attractions, Miami, 1989—; co-mem. Superbowl Host Com., Miami, 1989; co-chmn. Superbowl Extravaganza Com., Miami, 1989. Mem. com. Dade Heritage Trust Gala for Freedom Tower, Miami, 1989; bd. dirs. Light Up Miami, 1988-89, Keep Dade Beautiful, Dade County, Fla., 1988-89, Hispanic Heritage Com., 1988-90; treas. Quincentennial Com., Inc., 1989-90. Mem. Women in Communications, Inc., Toastmasters Internat., Greater Miami C. of C. (trustee 1990—).

HENDERSON, DEIRDRE HEALY, decorating company executive; b. Chgo., Nov. 10, 1942; d. Laurin Hall and Patricia (Kelly) H.; m. Duncan Yeandle, Sept. 27, 1969; children: Allison Dow, Duncan Dylan. AA, Briarcliff Coll., 1962; BA, Conn. Coll., New London, 1964. Editorial asst. Commerce Clearing House, San Francisco, 1964-65; tchr. Harris Sch., Chgo., 1966-67; stockbroker Dominick and Dominick, E.F. Hutton, Chgo., 1968-70; ptnr. Park West Interiors, Chgo., 1976-88; founder, pres. Franklin and Copley, Ltd., Chgo., 1987—; V.p., bd. mem., Com. for Handgun Control, Chgo., 1976-84, organizer G.A. Ranney for U.S. Senate, Donald Haider for Mayor, Chgo., 1985-87. Officer, bd. dirs. Women's Bd. Rehab. Inst., Chgo., 1973-85, Women's Bd. Rush Presbyn., St. Luke's Hosp., Chgo., 1973-84; mem. U. Chgo. Women's Bd., Field Mus. Women's Bd., Antiquarian Soc. of the Art Inst. Mem. Chgo. Historical Soc. Guild (officer, bd. dirs.), Chgo. Acad. of Scis. (bd. dirs.), Chgo Found. for Edn. (bd. dirs.), Friends of Lincoln Park (bd. dirs.), Seven Seas Cruising Assn. (transatlantic sailor, officer bd. dirs.), Woman's Athletic Club (officer bd. dirs.), Friday Club. Episcopalian.

HENDERSON, DENISE LAUREEN, college official; b. Ft. Lee, Va., Nov. 7, 1952; d. Robert Carl and Levera Adele (Wells) H. AA, Richard Bland Coll., Petersburg, Va., 1973; BA, Coll. William and Mary, 1975; MA, Cath. U. Am., 1983. Cert. tchr., Va. Edn. specialist U.S. Army Engr. Sch., Ft. Belvoir, Va., 1980-85, 85-86; mgmt. analyst Navy Facilities Engring. Command, Alexandria, Va., 1985; occupation analyst Nat. Capital region Soldier Support Ctr., Alexandria, 1986; edn. specialist Army Mgmt. Staff Coll., Ft. Belvoir, 1986—; instr. Presdl. Classroom for Young Ams., Alexandria, 1982. Mem. Fed. Edn. Tech. Assn., Nat. Soc. for Performance and Instrn. Methodist. Home: 7357 Springleigh Way Alexandria VA 22310 Office: Army Mgmt Staff Coll Attention DAPE-CP-C Fort Belvoir VA 22060-5893

HENDERSON, DIANA ELIZABETH, English educator; b. Washington, Nov. 26, 1957; d. Donald Graham and Alaine (Marsh) H. BA, Coll. William and Mary, 1979; MA, Columbia U., 1980, MPhil, 1983, PhD, 1989. Instr. humanities Columbia Coll., N.Y.C., 1985-86; instr. English Middlebury (Vt.) Coll., 1986-89, asst. prof. English, 1989—, co-coord. women's studies, 1987-89; mem. editorial bd. Bread Loaf Writers' Conf., Ripton, Vt., 1989—. Contbr. articles to ednl. publs. Mem. AAUW, MLA, NOW, Nat. Women's Studies Assn., Amnesty Internat., Phi Beta Kappa. Democrat. Office: Middlebury Coll 119 Munroe Hall Middlebury VT 05753

HENDERSON, GERALDINE THOMAS, retired social security official, educator; b. Luling, Tex., Jan. 7, 1924; d. Cornelius Thomas and Maggie (Keyes) Thomas; m. James E. Henderson, Feb. 9, 1942 (dec. Apr. 1978); children—Geraldine, Jessica, Jennifer. B.S., Fayetteville State U., 1967. Tchr. Cumberland County Schs., Fayetteville, N.C., 1966-67, Fayetteville City Schs., 1967-68; with Social Security Adminstrn., Fayetteville, 1968-87; substitute tchr. Cumberland County Sch. System, 1987—; claims rep. Pres. Fayetteville State U. Found., 1981-82, NAACP, Fayetteville br., 1983— ; bd. dirs. Fayetteville Art Coun., 1984—, Cumberland County United Way, 1983—, chmn. div. corp. mission Fayetteville Presbytery, 1986, mem. personnel review bd. City of Fayetteville, 1987—; mem. LWV; inductee Nat. Black Coll. Alumni Hall of Fame, 1988; bd. dirs. Habitat for Humanity, Fayetteville, N.C., 1989. Nafeo Disting. Alumni, 1989. Mem. Legion Aux. (treas. 1981-83), Zeta Phi Zeta (Woman of Yr. 1984), Omega Psi Phi (Citizen of Yr. 1985). Democrat. Presbyterian. Avocations: creative dress design; gardening; travel.

HENDERSON, JANA L., federal agency administrator, infosystems specialist; b. Anamosa, Iowa, Feb. 19, 1944; d. H. Dean and Rosetta I. (Lyon) H.; m. Steven J. Reinking, June 18, 1966 (div. June 1971). BA cum laude, U. Iowa, 1966, MBA, 1975. Cert. secondary edn. tchr., math. Systems analyst Iowa Nat. Mut. Ins. Co., Cedar Rapids, 1966-73; sr. systems analyst Westinghouse Learning Corp. div. Westinghouse Corp., Iowa City, Iowa, 1973-77, sr. computer specialist, 1977-88; sr. program mgr. U.S. Dept. Edn., Washington, 1988—, also cons., 1976. Mem. NAFE, Beta Gamma Sigma. Methodist. Lodge: Order Eastern Star. Office: US Dept Edn 400 Maryland Ave SW ROB3 #4636 Washington DC 20202

HENDERSON, JANE WHALEN, travel company executive; b. Fort Dodge, Iowa, June 24, 1913; d. William L. and Blanche (Tremaine) Whalen; m. Lon St. Clair Henderson, Oct. 16, 1946 (div.); children: Thomas, Clare, Anne. Student Fort Dodge Jr. Coll., Iowa, 1931-32, Fort Dodge Bus. Coll., 1932-33, Armstrong Coll., 1937-38. Travel cons. Capwells Travel, 1938-42, Peck Judah Travel Bur., San Francisco, 1942-48; mgr. World Travel Bur., Anaheim, Calif., 1955-56, Fullerton, Calif., 1958-60; mgr. Travel Advisers, Santa Ana, Calif., 1964-65; internat. travel adviser Anaheim Travel, 1960-64; v.p. sales Orange Empire Travel Bur., Anaheim, 1965-70; owner, pres. Jane Henderson Travel, Orange, Calif., 1970—; cons N.Am. Sch. Travel, Newport Beach, Calif., 1968—; mem. adv. bd. Orange Nat. Bank, PanAm. Airways, Traveling Times, Valencia, Calif. Gold sponsor Miss Orange Pageant, 1976-86; mem. street naming com. City of Orange, 1985—, mem. sister city program, 1985—. Named Orange Citizen of Yr., 1983. Mem. Am. Soc. Travel Agts., Assn. Retail Travel Agts., Pacific Area Travel Assn., Orange County Travel Agts. (pres. 1978), Cruise Lines Internat., Orange C. of C. (bd. dirs.). Roman Catholic. Lodge: Soroptimists Internat. Office: Jane Henderson Travel 1876 N Tustin Ave Orange CA 92665

HENDERSON, KAREN LECRAFT, judge; b. 1944. BA, Duke U., 1966; JD, U. N.C., 1969. Ptnr. Wright & Henderson, Chapel Hill, N.C., 1969-70, Sinkler, Gibbs & Simons, P.A., Columbia, S.C., 1983-86; asst. atty. gen. Columbia, 1973-78; sr. asst. atty. gen., dir. of spl. litigation sect., 1978-82, deputy atty. gen., dir. of criminal div., 1982; judge U.S. Dist. Ct. S.C., Columbia, 1986-90, U.S. Ct. Appeals (D.C. cir.), Washington, 1990—. Apptd. Dist. Ct. Adv. Com. Mem. ABA (litigation sect. and urban, state and local government law sect.), N.C. Bar Assn., S.C. Bar (government law sect., trial and appellate practice sect., fed. judges assn.). Office: US Ct Appeals DC Cir US Courthouse PO Box 867 Washington DC 20002*

HENDERSON, L(EONA) HARRIETTE, retired social work administrator, consultant; b. Phila., Mar. 8, 1934; d. Luther and Leona (Wilson) Highsmith; m. Victor Parks Henderson, 1961 (div. 1978); 1 child, Craig Lamarr. BA, Fisk U., 1955; MS in Edn., Temple U., 1958; MSW, Adelphi U., 1973. Lic. social worker, N.Y. Caseworker HRS/D.S.S., N.Y.C., 1961-64, supr. I, 1964-68, supr. II, 1968-78, dir. home care, 1978-81, dir. children's spl. svcs., 1981-84, dep. dir. med. assistance program, 1984-85, 1st asst. dep. family svcs., 1985-86, dep. commr. family svcs., 1986-89; ret., 1989; social work cons. region 2 Head Start, N.Y.C., 1990—. Trustee Fisk U., Nashville, 1984-87, recruiter, 1984—; music dir. children's choir Good Shepherd Ch., West Hempstead, N.Y., 1970—; alto Carr-Hill Singers, 1983—. Recipient pub. svc. award Fund for City N.Y., 1985, spl. recognition HRA-Women's Advisors, 1989. Mem. Managerial Assn. N.Y.C., Social Work Mgrs. Nat. Network (Exemplar award 1988), NAACP (Social Svc. award 1987), Delta Sigma Theta. Home: 37 Melvin Ave West Hempstead NY 11552

HENDERSON, LINDA SHLATZ, pharmaceutical company executive; b. Johnson City, N.Y., Feb. 21, 1946; s. Myron and Anna (Maslak) Shlatz; m. George Richard Henderson, June 18, 1977; children—Lauren Ashley, Kristen Lane. B.S., St. Lawrence U., 1967; Ph.D., U. Rochester, 1972. Postdoctoral fellow Mt. Sinai Sch. Medicine, N.Y.C., 1971-74; instr. U. Mass. Sch. Medicine, Worcester, 1974-75; asst. prof. medicine U. Rochester, N.Y., 1975-77; asst. prof. biochemistry Med. Coll. Ohio, Toledo, 1977-83; mgr. Smith Kline & French Lab., Phila., 1984-89; asst. dir. SmithKline Beecham Pharmaceuticals, 1989—. Author: (with others) Mechanisms of Intestinal Secretion, 1979, Secretory Diarrhea, 1980, Hydrogen Ion Transport in Epithelia, 1984. Pres. Westmoreland Neighborhood Assn., Toledo, 1982-83; mem. Lower Merion Edn. Coun., Gladwyne, Pa., 1990. Mem. AAAS, N.Y. Acad. Sci., Drug Info. Assn., Am. Med. Writers Assn., Phi Beta Kappa, Sigma Xi. Presbyterian. Avocations: gardening; needlework; swimming.

HENDERSON, MARILYN ANN, communications company executive; b. Scranton, Pa., Aug. 3, 1949; d. William Joseph and Mary Ann (Banick) Delorey; m. William Edgar Henderson, Oct. 23, 1971. Student U. Scranton, 1968; BS, Pa. State U., 1970; MBA, Fairleigh Dickinson U., 1977. With AT&T, 1970-84, dist. mgr., various N.J. locations, 1977-83, div. mgr., Piscataway, N.J., 1983-84; div. mgr. Bell Communications Research, Piscataway, 1984—. Editorial bd. EXCHANGE Mag., 1986—; contbr. articles to profl. jours. Recipient various corp. awards and recognitions, 1976-85, Clements award Clements Found., 1967, 68, 69, 70. Mem. AAUW, Am. Mgmt. Assn., Assn. Computing Machinery, Tel. Pioneers Am. (v.p. Cen. State council 1987-88, pres. 1988-89), Women's Info. Network, Morris Mus., Morris County Hist. Soc., Frelinghuysen Arboretum, Hist. Speedwell, Pa. State Alumni Assn., Omicron Nu. Roman Catholic. Avocations: power boating, cats, golfing, historical preservation. Home: Ten Pond Hill Rd Convent Station NJ 07961 Office: Bell Communications Rsch 33 Knightsbridge Rd Piscataway NJ 08854

HENDERSON, MARY LYNN CRAWFORD, nurse; b. Columbus, Ga., Mar. 20, 1955; d. Andrew Clifford and Mae Nell (Billingsley) Crawford; m. Harold Henderson Jr., Apr. 2, 1983. BS in Nursing, Miss. Coll., Clinton, 1977; postgrad., U. South Fla., Ga. So. Coll. Cert. nurse examiner Fla. Rape Crisis Ctr., CPR/ARC first aid instr.; RN/ARNP family nurse practitioner. Dir. nursing Tallahassee Devel. Ctr.; family nurse practitioner Fla. State U. Student Ctr., Tallahassee; RN, house supr. Screven County Hosp., Sylvania, Ga.; health care cons. Voice of Calvary Ministries, Jackson, Miss.; sr. community health nurse Leon County Health Dept., Tallahassee. Mem. Fla. Nurses Assn. Home: 6832 Tomy Lee Trail Tallahassee FL 32308

HENDERSON, MAUREEN MCGRATH, medical educator; b. Tynemouth, Eng., May 11, 1926; came to U.S., 1960; d. Leo E. and Helen (McGrath) H. MB BS, U. Durham, Eng., 1949, DPH, 1956. Prof. preventive medicine U. Md. Med. Sch., 1968-75, chmn. dept. social and preventive medicine, 1971-75; assoc. epidemiology Johns Hopkins U. Sch. Hygiene and Pub. Health, 1970-75; assoc. v.p. health scis., 1975-81; prof. epidemiology and medicine U. Wash. Med. Sch., 1975—, head cancer prevention research program Fred Hutchinson Cancer Research Ctr., 1983—; chmn. epidemiology and disease control study sect. NIH, 1969-72; chmn. clin. trials rev. com. Nat. Heart, Lung and Blood Inst., 1975-79; mem. Nat. Cancer Adv. Bd., 1979-84; mem. bd. Robert Wood Johnson Health Policy Fellowship, 1989—. Assoc. editor jour. Cancer Research, 1987-88; mem. editorial bd. Jour. Nat. Cancer Inst., 1988—. Recipient John Snow award, 1990; Luke-Armstrong scholar, 1956-57; John and Mary Markle scholar acad. medicine, 1963-68. Mem. Inst. Medicine (coun. 1981-85), Am. Coll. Epidemiology, Assn. Tchrs. Preventive Medicine (pres. 1972-73), Soc. Epidemiol. Research (chmn. 1969-70), Internat. Epidemiol. Assn. (exec. officer 1971-76), Am. Epidemiol. Soc. (pres. 1989—), Coun. Cancer Rsch. (sci. adv. bd. 1989—), Am. Assn. for Cancer Rsch. Home: 5309 NE 85th St Seattle WA 98115 Office: Fred Hutchinson Cancer Ctr Cancer Prevention Rsch Program 1124 Columbia St Seattle WA 98104

HENDERSON, MAXINE OLIVE BOOK (MRS. WILLIAM HENDERSON, III), association executive; b. Rush, Colo., Apr. 22, 1924; d. Jesse Frank and Olive (Booth) Book; B.A., U. Colo., 1945; m. William Henderson III, Apr. 10, 1948; children—William IV, Meredith. Personnel adminstr. Gen. Electric Co., Schenectady and N.Y.C., 1945-54; asst. dir. placement Katherine Gibbs Sch., N.Y.C., 1967-70; v.p., dir. William Henderson Cons., Inc., N.Y.C., 1969-83, pres., dir., 1983-86; dir. recruitment Girl Scouts U.S.A., N.Y.C., 1973-78, dir. human resources, 1978-82, dir. career devel., 1982—. Pres., Goddard-Riverside-Trinity Sch. Thrift Shop, N.Y.C., 1964-65, Trinity Sch. Mothers' Orgn., N.Y.C., 1965-66; treas. Brearley Sch. Parents Assn., N.Y.C., 1966-67; mem. Whitney Mus., 1989—. Mem. Am. Portuguese Soc., 1983—. Episcopalian. Clubs: North Suffolk Garden, Nissequoque Beach, Nissequogue Platform Tennis Assn. (St. James, L.I., N.Y.). Home: 606 W 116th St New York NY 10027 also: Nissequogue River Rd Saint James NY 11780 Office: 830 3rd Ave New York NY 10022

HENDERSON, MELODY LYNN, health facility administrator; b. Norman, Okla., June 5, 1954; d. Harland Laverne and Dovie (LaVirda) H. ADN, Okla. State U. Tech. Inst., 1982; BA in polit. scie., U. Okla., 1976, MPH, 1988. RN, Okla. Asst. head nurse Presbyn. Hosp., Oklahoma City; charge nurse in neonatal ICU Children's Hosp. of Okla., Oklahoma City; mgmt. analyst Okla. Med. Ctr., Oklahoma City; clin. supr. Hillcrest Health Ctr., Oklahoma City. Mem. Am. Coll. of Health Care Execs., Nurses Assn. of Am. Coll. of Obstetricians and Gynecologists, Nat. Assn. of Female Execs.

HENDERSON, NANCY GRACE, marketing and systems executive; b. Berkeley, Calif., Oct. 23, 1947; d. John Harry and Lorraine Ruth (Johnson) H. BA, U. Calif., Santa Barbara, 1969; MBA, U. Houston, 1985; teaching credential, U. Calif., L.A., 1971. Chartered fin. analyst. Tchr. Keppel Union Sch. Dist., Littlerock, Calif., 1969-72, Internat. Sch. Prague, Czechoslovakia, 1972-74, Sunland Luth. Sch., Freeport, Bahamas, 1974-75; tchr., dept. head Internat. Sch. Assn., Bangkok, Thailand, 1975-79; exec. search Diversified Human Resources Group, Houston, Tex., 1979-82; data processing analyst Am. Gen. Corp., Houston, 1982-83, personnel and benefits dept., 1983-85, investment analyst, 1985-86, equity security analyst/quantitative portfolio analyst, 1986-87; v.p. mktg. and communications Vestek Systems Inc., San Francisco, 1987—; tchr. English as Second Language program Houston Metro. Ministries, 1980-81. Pres., bd. dirs. Home Owners Assn., Walnut Creek, Calif., 1988—; tchr. English to refugees, Houston Metro Ministries, 1982; exec. dir. Internat. Child Abuse Prevention Found.; ch. choir, coun., fundraising and com. chmn. Presbyn. Ch. Named a Notable Woman of Tex., 1984-85. Mem. Fin. Analysts Fedn. (assoc. for investment mgmt. and rsch.), Toastmasters (pres. Houston chpt. 1983, v.p. 1982-83). Office: Vestek Systems 388 Market St Ste 700 San Francisco CA 94111

HENDERSON, PATRICIA MCGOVERN, state human rights agency executive; b. Mobile, Ala., Aug. 6, 1940; d. Thomas Joseph and Babe Hope (Lowery) McGovern; children—Thomas Bain III, Patrick Sean. Student, Loretto Coll., Nerinx, Ky., 1958-61; B.A. in Psychology, Hawaii Pacific Coll., 1976; M.A., in Psychology, Antioch U., Honolulu, 1981. Cert. mgmt. Queen's Med. Ctr., 1977; cert. U. Ala. Sch. Medicine, 1979; cert. Neuropsychiat. Inst., UCLA, 1980. Dir., exec. sec. Mission and Youth Office for Catholic Diocese and Charities, Mobile, 1961-64; spl. edn. tchr. Ala. State Dept. Pub. Edn., Mobile, 1966-69; spl. edn. tchr., adminstr., social worker St. Peter Claver Sch. and Ctr., Tampa, Fla., 1970-72; chief adminstr., dir., prin., ednl. dir., social worker Salvation Army Kauluwela Corps, Kula Kokua Therapeutic Sch., The Self Ctr., Malama Makua Rehab. Ctr., 1973-77; exec. dir., chief exec. officer Protection and Advocacy Agy. of Hawaii and State Client Assistance Agy. of Hawaii, Honolulu, 1977—, pres., 1988—; cons. in field. Author: A Self Advocate-You Have the Right to Speak for Yourself, 1978. Co-author, co-editor The Answer Book for Parents on the Right to Education for the Handicapped Child, 1983. Bd. dirs. State Dept. Health Adv. Com., Honolulu, 1979—, Gov.'s State Planning Council on Developmental Disabilities, 1986—; chmn. human rights com. State Dept. Health, 1982—; co-chmn. Mayor's City and County Transp. for Handicapped/Elderly Task Force, 1984—. Recipient Disting. Service award Salvation Army, 1977; Keen, Dedicated, Outstanding Profl., Highest Calibre award Salvation Army, 1977; Spl. Contbns. Internat. Yr. of Disabled Persons award State Hawaii and Internat. Yr. Disabled Persons Council, 1981; Promotion and Advancement of Women award Hawaiian Telephone Co., 1984; Disting. American award Am. Biog. Inst., 1985; Quality Advocacy Service award Nat. Assn. Protection and Advocacy Systems, 1987. Mem. Nat. Tourette Syndrome Assn. (NW regional dir. 1984—), Nat. Assn. Protection and Advocacy Systems (exec. bd. dirs., officer 1987—), Nat. Client Assistance Orgn. (exec. bd. dirs., officer 1987—). Avocations: travel; theater; music; art collecting; photography. Home: Oahu 2240 Kuhio Ave #2101 Honolulu HI 96815

HENDERSON, ROSEMARY MILLER, state agency administrator; b. Waynesboro, Va., Jan. 25, 1940; d. George Bowers and Amanda Almeda (Lindley) Miller; m. Willian Christian Henderson, Nov. 10, 1967; children: Amanda Louise, Katherine Christian. BA, Pfeiffer Coll., 1961. Tchr. Albemarle (N.C.) City Schs., 1961-63; prodn. cost analyst Klann Inc., Waynesboro, Va., 1963-65; asst. rsch. scientist Philip Morris, Inc., Richmond, Va., 1965-68; programmer Union Camp, Inc., Savannah, Ga., 1968-69; programmer Va. Div. Motor Vehicles, Richmond, 1969-71, systems analyst, 1971-75, mgr., drivers svc., 1975-77; cons.. Viar & Co., Alexandria, Va., 1978-82; utility engr. Va. State Corp. Commn., Richmond, 1978—. Mem. Women Execs. Am., Eastern Star. Methodist. Home: 9316 Woodcrest Rd Richmond VA 23229 Office: Va State Corp Commn Governor and Bank Sts Richmond VA 23209

HENDERSON, SUZANNE, county government official; b. Dallas, Jan. 8, 1943; d. Arthur Lee and Pearle (Morgan) McDonald; m. Aubrey Don Henderson (div. 1971); children: Aubrey Don Jr., Jennifer Dawn. AAS in Legal Assistantship, 1984. Cert. legal asst., Tex.; lic. real estate broker, Tex. Asst. to adminstr. grant money Tarrant County Auditor's Office, Ft. Worth, 1972-84; paralegal asst. internat. sect. Hunt Oil Co., Dallas, 1985-86; county clk. County of Tarrant, Ft. Worth, 1987—; chmn. Tarrant County Child Care Com., Ft. Worth, 1989—. Active Circle T coun. Girl Scouts U.S., 1987; bd. dirs. Silver Star dist. Boy Scouts Am., 1989; past pres. Tarrant County Pachyderm Club, 1989; active Ft. Worth Civic Leaders; bd. dirs. Ft. Worth Founders Lions Club, 1987. Mem. NAFE, Nat. Notary Assn., Internat. Assn. County Clks. and Recorders, Tex. Assn. County and Dist. Clks., Smithsonian Assocs., Women's Policy Forum, Women Ofcls. in Nat. Assn. Counties. Office: County Clk Tarrant County Courthouse 100 W Weatherford St Fort Worth TX 76196-0401

HENDERSON-PIERCE, SHIRLEY ANNE, educational consultant; b. Niagara Falls, N.Y., May 23, 1943; d. Hubert J. Jamieson and Luella (Anderson) De Graves; m. Richard A. Pierce; children: Reneé L., John D. Henderson. BA in Acctg., Southeastern U., 1966; AA in Mgmt., Coll. DuPage, 1984; postgrad., Ill. Benedictine Coll., 1986—, George Williams coll. Technician FBI, Washington, 1963-64; mgr. data processing AT&T Long Lines, Washington, 1964-66; system analyst IBM, Washington, 1966-68; adult edn. instr. Lewiston-Porter High Sch., Youngstown, N.Y., 1974; owner Creative Svcs., Youngstown, 1975-78; mgr. Midwest region Comptek Research, Chgo., 1978-80; ednl. designer Multigraphics, Mt. Prospect, Ill., 1980-81, mgr. service publs., 1981-86, mgr. graphic services, 1986-89; mgr. pub. and mailing svcs. United Airlines, 1989—; pres. Pierce & Assocs., 1988—. Mem. Internat. Plant Mgmt. Assn., Nat. Soc. Performance and Instrn., Soc. Tech. Communication. Episcopalian. Home: 6329 New Albany Rd Lisle IL 60532

HENDLEY, EDITH DI PASQUALE, physiology and neuroscience educator; b. N.Y.C., Sept. 5, 1927; d. Michael and Rose (Parillo) Di Pasquale; m. Daniel Dees Hendley, Apr. 21, 1952; children: Jane Alice, Joyce Louise, Paul Daniel. AB, Hunter Coll. City N.Y., 1948; MS, Ohio State U., 1950; PhD, U. Ill., Chgo., 1954. Instr. U. Chgo., 1954-56; asst. lectr. U. Sheffield (Eng.), 1956-57; instr., rsch. assoc. Johns Hopkins U. Sch. Medicine, Balt., 1963-72; sr. investigator Friends Med. Sci. Rsch. Ctr., Balt., 1972-73; assoc. prof. U. Vt. Coll. Medicine, Burlington, 1973-83, prof., 1983—. Contbr. 36 papers to refereed jours.; co-author 4 books and one textbook of physiology for med. students. Rsch. grantee NIH, 1974—, NSF, 1986-89, Vt. affiliate Am. Heart Assn., 1982-83, The Sugar Assn. Inc., 1984-85. Mem. Am. Physiol. Soc., Am. Soc. Pharmacology & Exptl. Therapeutics, Soc. for Neurosci. (exec. com., treas. Vt. chpt. 1978—), Assn. for Women In Sci. (treas. 1972-74, exec. com. and long-range planning com. 1974-76), Women in Neurosci. (chair annual meeting 1982), AAAS. Home: 10 Highland Terr South Burlington VT 05403 Office: U Vt Coll Medicine Dept Physiology and Biophysics Burlington VT 05405

HENDLEY, ESSIE KIRKLAND, educator; b. Valdosta, Ga.; d. John Allyne and Linia Castilla (Showers) Kirkland; m. Barney Maxwell Hendley, May 11, 1946; children: Elleanor Jean, Marsha Dianne Hendley Hill. BS, Savannah State Coll., 1950; MA, Kean Coll., 1974. Tchr. Daisy Elem. Sch., Claxton, Ga., 1950-52; tchr. Jersey City Pub. Schs., 1953-61, Edison (N.J.) Twp. Bd. Edn., 1961-78; cons. State Dept. Edn., Trenton, 1974. Author: So You Want To Be A Teacher, 1974 (journalism award), (play) The First Thanksgiving, 1966. Fundraiser Muhlenberg Hosp., Plainfield, N.J., 1983-87; bd. dirs. YWCA, Plainfield, 1965-67, The Mayor's Task Force for Aged, Plainfield, 1982-83, United Way of Plainfield, 1989-92; mem. deacon bd. Bethel Presbyn. Ch., treas., 1987—. Recipient Community Svc. award Mayor and City of Plainfield, 1983, Jefferson Community Svc. Cup, Muhlenberg Hosp., Plainfield, 1987. Mem. AAUW, Nat. Assn. Univ. Women (pres. 1979-81, Woman of the Yr. 1984, Journalism award 1975), NAFE, Nat. Coun. Negro Women (life, Svc. to Youth award 1975), Phi Delta Kappa (fashion show chmn., Edn. Achievement award 1974, citation 1976). Home: 1324 Sunnyside Pl Plainfield NJ 07060

HENDON, LEA ALPHA, insurance company specialist; b. Hartford, Conn., Mar. 27, 1953; d. Charles Arthur and Willie Mae (Wilcox) Martin. BA in Edn., Boston Coll., Chestnut Hill, Mass., 1975; MA in Psychology, E. N.Mex. U., 1979. Cert. secondary edn. tchr., Mass. High Sch. Tchr. Boston Pub. Schs., 1975-77; coord student ref. prog. Eastern N.Mex. U., Portales, N.Mex., 1978-79; supr. Allstate Ins. Co., Farmington, Conn., 1979-80; bus./analyst AEtna Ins. Co., Hartford, Conn., 1980-83; office automation cons. Hartford (Conn.) Ins. Group, 1983-85; AEtna life & casualty adminstr. Aetna, Hartford, 1986—; pres. Black Data Processing Assn., Hartford, Conn., 1989-90; mem. adv. bd. Post Coll., Waterbury, Conn., 1987, nat. elections chairperson, 1989-90. Mentor, Conn. Minorities in Higher Edn., Hartford, 1985; adv. Jr. Achievement, Hartford, 1988-89. Mem. NAFE, Soc. for Human Resource Mgmt., Delta Sigma Theta, Psi Chi. Office: AEtna Life & Casualty 151 Framington Ave Hartford CT 06156

HENDREN, MERLYN CHURCHILL, investment company executive; b. Gooding, Idaho, Oct. 16, 1926; d. Herbert Winston and Annie Averett Churchill; student U. Idaho, 1944-47; B.A., Coll. of Idaho, 1986. m. Robert Lee Hendren, June 14, 1947; children—Robert Lee, Anne Aleen. With Hendren's Furniture Co., Boise, 1947-69; co-owner, v.p. Hendren's Inc., Boise, 1969-87, pres. 1987—. Bd. dirs. Idaho Law Found., 1978-84; chmn. Coll. of Idaho Symposium, 1977-78, mem. adv. bd., 1981—; bd. dirs. SW Idaho Pvt. Industry Council, 1984-87; pres. Boise Council on Aging, 1959-60, mem. adv. bd., 1986—; mem. Gov.'s Commn. on Aging, 1960, Idaho del. to White House Conf. Aging, 1961; trustee St. Luke's Regional Hosp., 1981—; mem. adv. bd. dirs. Boise Philharm. Assn., Inc., 1981—; bd. dirs. Children's Home Soc. Idaho, 1988. Mem. Boise C. of C. (bd. dirs. 1984-87). Republican. Episcopalian. Home: 3504 Hillcrest Dr Boise ID 83705 Office: 516 S 9th St Boise ID 83706

HENDRICK, KATE MARIE, sales manager; b. Schaumburg, Ill., Nov. 6, 1957; d. Philip Stanley Hendrick and Mary Lou Hoiss. BS in Bus. Adminstrn., U. N.C., 1980. Advt. sales rep. Chapel Hill (N.C.) Newspaper, 1980-81; schs. sales rep. Aanacomp Inc., Indpls., 1981-83; comml. markets sales rep. Motorola, Inc., Schaumburg, 1983-87, comml. markets sales mgr., 1987-90, telecom systems midwest and southeastern sales mgr. in charge of indirect distbn., 1988—; comml. bus. broker UR Bus. Brokers, 1990—; cons., program dir. Motorola, Schaumburg, 1988-89. Dir. United Way

Campaign, Chapel Hill, 1982. Mem. NAFE, Raleigh (N.C.) Ski & Outing Club, Great Raleigh (N.C.) Road Runners. Democrat. Roman Catholic. Home: 2556 Bark Wood Rd #202 Schaumburg IL 60175 Office: Motorola C & E Schaumburg IL 60196

HENDRICKS, ANGELA TUTONE, financial executive; b. Bklyn., Apr. 27, 1944; d. Sam and Mary (LaTorre) Tutone; m. Brian Michael Hendricks, June 23, 1973; 1 child, Jeanine Marie. BA in Econs., Ramapo Coll., 1990. Registered rep. N.Y. Stock Exchange. Account exec. Hirsch & Co., N.Y.C., 1962-70, Fahnestock & Co., N.Y.C., 1970-78. Tchr. St. Joseph Roman Cath. Ch., Bogota, N.J., 1987. Mem. Omicron Delta Epsilon, Delta Mu Delta. Republican. Home: 336 Van Buren Ave Teaneck NJ 07666

HENDRICKS, BARBARA, opera singer, recitalist; b. Stephens, Ark., Nov. 20, 1948; m. Martin Engstrom, 1978; children: Sebastian, Jennie. Studied with Jennie Tourel; grad., U. Nebr., 1969; student, Juilliard Sch., 1969—. Staged opera debut with San Francisco Opera in L'Incoronazione di Poppea, 1976, since has performed with maj. opera companies in U.S. and Europe, including Boston Opera, St. Paul Opera, Santa Fe Opera, Deutsche Oper, Berlin, Aix-en-Provence Festival, Salzburg Festival, Houston Opera, De Nederlandse Operastichting, Glyndebourne Festival Opera; Metropolitan Opera debut as Sophie in Der Rosenkavalier, 1986; recital debut at Town Hall, N.Y.C., Nov. 14, 1976; sang in world premiere of Final Alice (David del Tredici), 1976; appearances with symphony orchs., including Boston Symphony Orch., N.Y. Philharm., Los Angeles Philharm., Cleve. Symphony Orch., Phila. Orch., Chgo. Symphony, Berlin Philharm., Vienna Philharm., London Symphony Orch., Orchestre de Paris, Orchestre Nationale de France; appeared in film La Boheme, 1988; numerous recordings include Porgy and Bess, 1975, Negro Spirituals, 1983, Mozart Opera and Concert Arias, 1984, Bachianas Brasileiras, 1986, Schubert Lieder, 1986, Mozart Sacred Arias, 1988. Goodwill ambassador for refugees at UN, 1987. Recipient 1st prixe Internat. Concours de Paris, 1972, Grand Prix due Disque, 1976; named Winner, Geneva Internat. Competition, 1971, Commandeur des Arts et des Lettres, 1986. Office: care Harrison/Parrot Ltd, 12 Penzancl Pl, London W11 4PA, England*

HENDRICKS, CAROLYN SUE, communications company executive; b. Sheridan, Ark., Aug. 29, 1935; d. Burleigh Delpho and Elsie Lee (Trout) Moore; m. James Pearson Cathey; stepchildren: Lesa Handly, Traci. Grad. high sch., Little Rock. Dir. sales clk. Southwestern Bell Telephone Co., Little Rock, 1953-57, yellow pages telephone sales staff mem., 1957-69, supr. bus. office, 1969-70, edn. relations supr., 1970-78, acad. and community relations mgr., 1978-83, area mgr. external relations, 1983—. Bd. dirs. Pine Bluff Clean and Beautiful, Ark.; pres. Pine Bluff Sister Cities Inc., 1988—; bd. dirs., personnel chmn. Pine Bluff Symphony; bd. dirs. Literacy Coun., Pine Bluff; mem. profl. women's adv. bd. Nat. Bank Commerce, Pine Bluff. Mem. Ark. Fedn. Press Women, Bus. and Profl. Women's Club (Woman of Yr. award 1977, 87), Synergy (Pine Bluff). Office: Southwestern Bell Telephone Co 720 Beech St Pine Bluff AR 71601

HENDRICKS, DONNA DARLENE DENNEY, company executive; b. Lebanon, Tenn., Sept. 24, 1951; d. Verlon Monroe Denney and Virgie Mai Stubblefield. Student, U. Tenn., Nashville, 1969-72. Auditor Genesco, Nashville, 1969-72; pers. recruiter Darrell Walker Pers., Nashville, 1979-82; sales rep. Olsten Corp., Nashville, 1982-84; mgmt. recruiter Jane Jones Enterprises, Nashville, 1984-85, mktg. rep., 1985-86; br. mgr. Jane Jones Enterprises, Smyrna, Tenn., 1986—. Bd. dirs. Music City Golf Classic; bd. dirs., fundraiser DreamMakers, Inc.; fundraiser Children's Hosp. Vanderbilt, Am. Cancer Soc. Named Future Bus. Leader of Am. Home: 111 Highland Villa Dr Nashville TN 37211 Office: Jane Jones Enterprises 5 S Lowry St Smyrna TN 37167

HENDRICKS, GERTRUDE ELIZABETH, retired educator; b. Worthington, Ohio, Feb. 23, 1907; d. Caleb Fuller and Kathryn May (Rogers) Potter; m. Oscar William Hendricks, Aug. 1, 1932 (dec. 1935); children: William Hulin, Robert Clyde. BSc, Ohio State U., 1928, MSc, 1931. Life cert. home econs. tchr., Ohio. State supr. women's projects Works Projects Adminstrn., Columbuus, Ohio, 1935-40; dist. home mgmt. supt. Farm Security Adminstrn., Mansfield, Ohio, 1940; regional specialist home mgmt. and nutrition Farm Security Adminstrn., Indpls., 1940-42; dir. Child Care Ctrs., Youngstown, Ohio, 1943-46; tchr. home econs. Youngstown Pub. Schs., 1942, dir. family life edn., 1947-72; ret., 1972; instr. marriage psychology Youngstown State U., 1947-75; cons. health edn. workshops Kent (Ohio) State U., 1950-68; dir. pilot program for tng. child care aides U.S. Office Edn., Washington, 1967, mem. taxk force on poverty, Pa., 1968; mem. task force on consumer edn. Ohio Dept. Vocat Edn., 1969; mem. task force Curriculum Manual for Consumer Edn., 1970. Cons. Mahoning County Coun. on Aging and Nutrition, Youngstown, 1972—; precinct worker Mahoning Bd. Elections, 1972—. Recipient award Mahoning chpt. Nat. Coun. Cath. Women, 1966, Centennial award Ohio State U., 1970, award AARP, 1990; Gertrude E. Hendricks scholarship established at Youngstown State U., 1970. Mem. Mahoning Ret. Tchrs. Assn. (pres. 1982-83), AAUW (v.p. 1975-77), Youngstown Area Fedn. Women's Clubs (pres. 1980-82, community svc. award 1964, 67, 80, Woman of Yr. award 1986), Marion B. Roth Past Officers Club (pres. 1972-74, 87-88), Quota Club (pres. Youngstown 1966-68, Woman of Yr. award 1989).

HENDRICKS, PAIGE KELLY, public relations executive; b. New Orleans, Aug. 23, 1949; d. Gordon Brooks and Joan (Perkins) Kelly; m. G. David Hendricks, Jr., Feb. 13, 1971; children: Jeffrey Kyle, Erin Elizabeth. Student, Mt. Vernon Coll., 1967-68; BA, Tex. Christian U., 1970; postgrad. in English, North Tex. State U., 1977-80. Dir. student pub. relations Tex. Christian U., 1970; advt. designer, layout, copywriter, salesman Selma (Ala.) Times Jour., 1971-72; advt. designer, layout, copywriter Clinton Courier, Courier County News, Rome (N.Y.) Daily Sentinel, 1973; dir. pub. relations Utica (N.Y.) Community Trust Fund, 1974; theatre producer, upstate N.Y., 1973-76; owner Paige Hendricks Pub. Relations, Dallas/Ft. Worth, 1980—. Editor, publisher Greater Fort Worth Private School Directory, 1987, 88; creative, exec. dir. Summerarts, 1989. V.p. bd. dirs. Ft. Worth Theatre, 1986-88; Monticello Neighborhood Assn., 1986-88; mem. Jr. League, Forum Ft. Worth; chmn. bd. Kids & Co., Inc. Recipient Bronze Quill award Ft. Worth chpt. Internat. Assn. Bus. Communicators, 1987. Mem. Pub. Relations Soc. Am. (chartered mem. Ft. Worth chpt., mem. Counselor's Acad.), Women in Communications, Inc. (grantee 1979-80), Ft. Worth C. of C., KERA, Kappa Kappa Gamma Alumni Assn. Episcopalian. Office: 3537 W 7th St Ste 5 Fort Worth TX 76107

HENDRICKS, PAULETTE JANE, small business owner; b. Toledo, Oct. 6, 1941; d. Paul Heyman and Betty Jean (Kramer) Croll; m. J. Michael Hendricks, Feb. 18, 1960 (div.); 1 child, Michelle Annette. Student, Bowling Green State U., 1970, 84. Owner Freedom Designs, Port Clinton, Ohio, 1987—. Home: PO Box 528179 Port Clinton OH 43452 Office: Freedom Designs PO Box 528179 Port Clinton OH 43452

HENDRICKS, STACY ANN, physical therapist; b. Syracuse, N.Y., June 22, 1960; d. Dean Francis and Vivian Marie (Eagleton) H. BS in Physical Therapy, Russell Sage Coll., 1983. Staff physical therapist Munson Med. Ctr., Traverse City, Mich., 1983; staff psyical therapist St. Camillus Rehab. &Health Ctr., Syracuse, 1983-87; coord. outpatient svcs. St. Camillus Rehab. &Health Ctr., 1987—. Mem. Am. Physical Therapy Assn. (nominating com. 1987-89), Neuro Devel. Treatment Assn. Republican. Roman Catholic. Office: St Camillus Health & Rehab Ctr 813 Fay Rd Syracuse NY 13219

HENDRICKSON, CONSTANCE MARIE M., chemist, consultant; b. Baton Rouge, June 7, 1949; d. Clifton Eugene and Evelyn Marie (Watson) McRight; m. William Harwell Hendrickson, Dec. 28, 1971; children: Charles Douglas (dec.), David Gillis, Emily Elizabeth Marie. BA, La. Tech. U., 1971; PhD, La. State U., 1975; MEd, U. North Tex., 1984. Cert. profl. chemist. NIH rsch. fellow Johns Hopkins U., Balt., 1975-78; clin. chemistry fellow Sch. Medicine U. Ala., Birmingham, 1978-79; temporary asst. prof. Tex. Wesleyan Coll., Ft. Worth, 1980-81; chief chemist Rockwood Systems Corp., Dallas, 1981-82; dir., owner Ar'Kon Cons., Dallas, 1982—. Inventor high expansion foams. Fellow Am. Inst. Chemists; mem. Am. Chem. Soc. (local chair 1987-88, treas. chem. mktg. and econs. div. 1990), N.Y. Acad. Scis., Nat. Panel Consumer Arbitrators (sr.). Democrat. Home: 802 S Jefferson Irving TX 75060 Office: Ar'Kon Cons 2915 LBJ Ste 161 Dallas TX 75234

HENDRICKSON, MONA LYNN, financial consultant; b. Spokane, Wash., Apr. 3, 1951; d. Arthur Edward and Ermona E. (Maxwell) Rees; m. George Michael Hendrickson, May 1, 1971; 1 child, Wade Michael. AA, Charles S. Mott Community Coll., 1975; BA in Econs., U. Mich., Flint, 1978. Sr. supr. New Land Products, Flint., 1976-78; account exec. Merrill Lynch, Flint., 1978-83; fin. cons. Shearson Lehman Hutton, Flint., 1983—. Com. mem. Fairwinds Girl Scouts U.S., Flint, 1984, United Way Priority, 1989; tr eas. Warwick Pointe PTA, 1988-89; mem. Jr. League Flint, 1989; treas. and bd. dirs. YWCA Greater Flint, 1986—; bd. dirs. Goodwill Industries Flint, 1988—. Sgt. USAF, 1970-72. Mem. Zonta Club (treas., pres.-elect Flint II chpt. 1979-83, treas. Flint I chpt. 1987-88, asst. treas. 1988-89), Beta Sigma Phi. Democrat. Baptist. Home: 6455 Rustic Ridge Trail Grand Blanc MI 48439 Office: Shearson Lehman Hutton 2353 S Linden Rd Flint MI 48532

HENDRICKSON, VANESSA M., state court official; b. Morristown, N.J., Sept. 2, 1959; d. H. DeWitt and Loretta (Alexander) Hendrickson. BA, Rutgers U., 1981. Cert. team leadership. Customer svc. mgr. Bradlees Dept. Store, West Caldwell, N.J., 1981-83; probation officer Essex County Probation Dept., Newark, 1985-88; track coord. Superior Ct. N.J., Newark, 1988—; arbitration adminstr. Superior Ct. of N.J., Newark; chairperson Conf. of Arbitration Adminstrs., 1990—. Mem. NAFE. Home: 147 Cleveland St Apr A18 Orange NJ 07050

HENDRIE, ELAINE, public relations executive; b. Bklyn., d. David and Pearl (Saltzhauer) Kostell; m. Joseph Mallam Hendrie, July 9, 1949; children: Susan, Barbara. Asst. account exec. Benjamin Sonnenberg Public Relations firm, N.Y.C., 1953-57; pub. relations cons., writer, editor, 1957-72; dir. pub. relations and media Religious Heritage of Am., Washington, 1973-75; producer, interviewer Woman to Woman radio program, sta. WRIV and stas. WALK-AM and -FM, L.I., N.J., Westchester County, N.Y., Conn., 1974-77; exec. dir. Women in New Directions, Inc., Suffolk County, N.Y., 1974-77, cons. 1978—; nat. media coordinator NOW, Washington, 1978; media dir. Am. Speech-Lang.-Hearing Assn., Washington, 1979-80; pub. info. officer, head media and mktg. Dept. Navy, Washington, 1980-81; pres. Triangle Enterprises, 1982, Hendrie & Pendzick, 1982—; resource person for media Nat. Commn. on Observance of Internat. Women's Yr., 1977—; cons. Multi-Media Prodns. Inc., N.Y.C., 1978—, Women in New Directions, Inc., 1981—. Mem. adv. bd. Women's Ctr., SUNY-Farmingdale; mem. exec. bd. Energy Edn. Exponents, 1983—; chmn. Bellport (N.Y.) Bd. Archtl. Review, 1986—; mem. exec. bd. L.I. chpt. Am. Nuclear Soc. Club: Bellport Bay Yacht. Home: 50 Bellport Ln Bellport NY 11713

HENDRIX, SUSAN CLELIA DERRICK, civic worker; b. McClellanville, S.C., Jan. 19, 1920; d. Theodore Elbridge and Susan Regina (Bauknight) Derrick; m. Henry Gardner Hendrix, June 5, 1943; children: Susan Hendrix Redmond, Marilyn Hendrix Shedlock. BA, Columbia Coll., 1941; MA, Furman U., 1961; EdD (hon.) Columbia Coll., 1985. Cert. tchr., S.C. Tchr. Whitmire Pub. Schs., 1941-43, Greenville Pub. Schs., S.C., 1944-46, 58-63, dir. Reading clinic, 1965-68; counselor Greenville Pub. Schs., 1963-65; supr. Greenville County Sch. Dist., S.C., 1965-68, dir. pub. relations, 1968-83; grad. instr. Furman U., 1967-69; cons. Nat. Seminar on Desegregation, 1973. Author: (with James P. Mahaffey) Teaching Secondary Reading, 1966; Communicating With the Community, 1979; editor: Communique, 1968-83. Contbr. articles to profl. jours. and mags. Chmn. bd. trustees Columbia Coll., 1969-70; chmn. Greenville County Rehab. Bd., S.C., 1974-76; vice chmn. bd. Jr. Achievement, Greenville, 1978-79; chmn. S.C. Commn. on Women, Columbia, 1982-88; pres. United Methodist Women, Buncombe St. Ch., Greenville, 1956-57; mem. adminstrv. bd. Buncombe St. Ch., 1968—, bd. trustees, 1980-88; mem. United Meth. Ch. Southeastern Jurisdictional Council on Ministries, 1984-88; chmn. S.C. Conf. Council on Ministries United Meth. Ch., 1980-88, del. gen. conf., 1980, 84, 88; mem. Bd. Global Ministries United Meth. Ch., 1972-80, mem. Commn. Study of Ministry, 1984—, mem. gen. ch. coun. ministries, 1988—, researcher missions project, West Africa, 1986. Recipient Medallion Columbia Coll., 1980, Alumnae Disting. Svc. award Columbia Coll., 1983, Disting. Achievement award Women's History Week, Greenville, 1984, S.C. Woman of Achievement award, 1988. Mem. S.C. PTA (life), Alpha Delta Kappa (pres. 1970-72), Columbia Coll. Alumnae Assn., Democratic Women, S.C. Women in Govt. (bd. dirs. 1985-87). Home: 309 Arundel Rd Greenville SC 29615 Office: SC Commn on Women 2221 Devine St Columbia SC 29205

HENDRIX-WARD, NANCY KATHERINE, editor; b. Russellville, Ala., Nov. 28, 1944; d. Raymond Clyde and Mattye Lou (Kimbrough) Smith; m. Adrian Dale Hendrix, Jan. 8, 1963 (div. Mar. 1982); children: David Wayne, Amy Kathleen, Susan Gayle; m. Robert Lawrence, Feb. 22, 1986. AA, Draughon's Bus. Coll., Jackson, Miss., 1963; student, East Miss. Jr. Coll., Scoobe, 1978-79; AA, Anchorage Community Coll., 1981; student, U. Alaska, 1982-84. Dir. Retired Sr. Vol. Program, Big Springs, Tex., 1974-76; adminstr. USAF, Adana, Turkey, 1977-79; environ. specialist Minerals Mgmt. Svc. Dept. of Interior, Anchorage, 1980-85; tech. editor Intelligence and Threat Analysis Ctr. U.S. Army, Washington, 1985-87; editor Inst. Def. Analyses, Alexandria, Va., 1987-89; writer, editor minerals mgmt. svc. U.S. Dept. Interior, Herndon, Va., 1989—; coordinator Equal Opportunity com., Anchorage, 1983-85. Vol. counselor The Women's Ctr., Vienna, Va., 1987, Parent's Aid, Child Advocacy com., Anchorage, 1981-85; counselor Suicide Prevention Ctr., Anchorage, 1982-85. Mem. NAFE, LWV, Soc. for Tech. Communication, Federally Employed Women.

HENDRY, JEAN SHARON, psychopharmacologist; b. Hanover, Pa., June 2, 1947; d. Clarence Richard and Frances Lee (Manger) Shaver; m. Andrew Delaney Hendry, Jan. 17, 1970; 1 child, Robert Andrew. BA, Hunter Coll., 1976; MA, Princeton U., 1978; PhD, 1980. Rsch. asst. Hunter Coll., N.Y.C., 1974-75; asst. instr. Princeton U., Princeton, N.J., 1976-78; post doctoral fellow Med. Coll. Va., Richmond, 1979-82; psychology instr. U. Richmond, 1985-86, Pa. State U., Media, Pa., 1987-88; guest reviewer various psychological and pharmacological jours. Contbr. numerous articles to profl. jours. Nat. Trust for Hist. Preservation, Colonial Williamsburg Found., World Wildlife Assn., Greenpeace, Radnor Hist. Soc. Mem. Am. Psychol. Assn., Am. Psychol. Soc., Soc. for Stimulus Properties of Drugs, Smithsonian Instn., Assn. Princeton Grad. Alumni, Phila. Mus. Art, Am. Horseshow Assn. Home: 1271 Karen Ln Radnor PA 19087

HENE, SONYA JOHANNA, management; b. Chgo., Oct. 25, 1962; d. Erich and Gloria Patricia (Desio) H. BA, DePaul U., Chgo., 1985; M City & Regional Planni, Rutgers U., New Brunswick, N.J., 1987. Summer intern Village of Schaumburg, Ill., 1986; student intern City of New Brunswick, N.J., 1986-87; freelance, 1987-88; research analyst Broadacre Mgmt. Co., Chgo., 1988—; mem. planning and urban design com. Friends Downtown, Chgo. 1987--. Tutor Montgomery Ward/Caprini Green Tutoring Program, Chgo. 1988--; Adv. Com. Mem. Met. Planning Council, CHgo. 1988--. Recipient Cert. Participation in Real Estate Investment Workshop Harvard. Mem. Am. Planning Assn., Local Chap. Am. Planning Assn.

HENELY, JOANN HOUSH, real estate company owner; b. Sparta, Wis., May 29, 1928; d. Herman F. and Mekle E. (Owen) Housh; m. Michael Floyd Henely, Sept. 9, 1947; children: Michael William, John R., Robert M., Donald R. Student, Drake U., 1945-47; Grad., Hawaii Pacific U., 1981. Owner Henely Wholesale, Omaha, 1965-67; owner Red Carpet Real Estate, Danville, Alamo, Calif., 1968-73, Henely Assocs., San Diego, Honolulu, 1973—. Contbr. travel and real estate articles to publs. Pres., founder State of Hawaii Independent Travel Agts., Honolulu, 1986-88; past pres. Little League, Pony League, Newcomers, Hosp. Guild, Woman's Club, Church Woman's Guild, Omaha, 1958-64, Newcomers, Woman's Club, Hosp. Guild, Orinda, Calif., 1964-67; mem. Republican Women, Honolulu, LWV, Honolulu, A.S.H., abortion rights-pro-choice groups, Honolulu; ways and means chair Honolulu Symphony, 1987-88. Mem. AAUW (treas. Hawaii chpt. 1987-88, chmn. Friends Around the World Hawaii chpt. 1986-88, DAR (chpt. chair and TV movie com. Calif. 1988-95, state officer and TV movie com. chmn. Hawaii 1987, officer and membership com. Hawaii 1988, Hawaii del. to nat. conv. 1987). Republican. Unity. Home: 2727 De Anza Rd SD6 San Diego CA 92109 Office: Henely Assocs 2161 Kalia Rd 1212 Honolulu HI 96815

HENG, SIANG GEK, communications executive; b. Singapore, Singapore, Dec. 4, 1960; came to U.S., 1984.; BSEE with honors, Nat. U. Singapore, 1983; MSEE in Computer Engring., U. So. Calif., 1985. Rsch. engr. Nat. Univ. Singapore, 1983-84; systems mgr. LinCom Corp., L.A., 1985-87; fin. planner N.Y. Life Ins. Co., L.A., 1987-88; systems engr. Bell Labs. AT&T, N.J., 1988—; lectr. Singapore Poly. Inst., 1983-84; free-lance computer/communications cons., N.J. and L.A., 1987—. Contbr. articles to profl. jours. Mem. IEEE, NAFE (com. bd. mem. North Jersey affiliate). Office: AT&T Bell Labs Crawfords Corner Rd Rm 2B-618A Holmdel NJ 07733

HENIFF, MARILYN ROSE, teacher, mathematical sciences; b. Pierceton, Ind., July 14, 1939; d. Leslie Wilson Wiseman and Evelyn Pauline Richardson; m. Thomas Michael Heniff, July 12, 1969 (div.); 1 child, Thomas Robert Heniff. AB, Morehead (Ky.) State Coll., 1961; MA, Ind. State U., 1968. Cert. Sec. Edn. Math tchr. Monroe (Ohio) High Sch., 1961-62, Cromwell (Ohio) High Sch., 1962-64, Ossian (Ind.) High Sch., 1964-68; Math instr. Ind. State U., Terre Haute, Ind., 1968-69, Joliet (Ill.) Jr. Coll., 1969-71, 1974—; mem. Master Planning Action Com., Joliet (Ill.) Jr. Coll., 1988-89. Coach/mgr. Troy Softball, Shorewood, Ill., 1985-88; mem./treas. Troy Baseball Ladies Aux., Shorewood, 1984-88; mem. Troy Homeowners Assn., Shorewood, 1984-89, v.p., 1988-89; staff writer Insight, Homeowners' paper, Shorewood, 1986-89. Mem. Ill. Fedn. of Tchrs. (dist. sec. 1986-89), Ill. Com. Colls., Am. Mathematical Assn. of Two Yr. Colls., Mathematical Assn. of Am. Democrat. Office: Joliet Jr Coll 1216 Houbolt Ave Joliet IL 60436

HENKE, ANA MARI, education educator; b. Albuquerque, Apr. 21, 1954; d. David Ernest and Mary Anne (Gallegos) Sanchez; m. Michael John Henke, Aug. 14, 1976; children: Kristin Mari, Michelle Lee. BA in Spl. Edn., U. N.Mex., 1976, MA in Spl. Edn., 1983. Cert. elem. and secondary spl. edn. tchr., N.Mex.; cert. elem. and secondary phys. edn. tchr., N.Mex.; cert. elem. and secondary behavior disorder tchr., N.Mex. Tchr., supr. Perceptual Motor Learning Sch. U. N.Mex., Albuquerque, 1976, 82, tchr. phys. edn., 1980-82; tchr. phys. edn. Nat. Youth Sports Program, Albuquerque and San Diego, 1976-82; tchr. multihandicapped Chula Vista (Calif.) Pub. Schs., 1976-77; tchr. adaptive phys. edn. San Diego City Schs., 1977-78; lab. asst. Presbyn. Hosp., Albuquerque, 1979-80; tchr. Hermosa Jr. High Sch., Farmington, N.Mex., 1983-85, Heights Jr. High Sch., Farmington, 1985—; mem. Leadership & Risk-Taking, Nat. Summit for Hispanic Women, Albuquerque, 1989; in-svc. exercise therapist Four Corners Reg. Ednl. Conf., Farmington, 1985-86; supr. parents workshop Intervention/Awareness for Substance Abuse, Heights Jr. High Sch., 1985-86; instr. workshop Farmington Schs., 1986; active nat. youth sports prog. Leaders Are in Demand, NCAA-U. N.Mex., 1989; active progs. Bldg. Self Esteem by Taking Risks-AWAREL, 1989, Leadership/Self-Esteem Multicultural Settings workshop, dir. new tchr. tng. Coord. New Educator Support Program, 1989; mem. Leadership San Juan, 1990—. Named Young Career Woman of San Juan County Nat. Fedn. Bus. & Profl. Women, 1988-89. Mem. Phi Delta Kappa (sec. 1987—, v.p. 1988-89). Republican. Roman Catholic. Home: 4406 N Dustin Ave Farmington NM 87401

HENKE, JANICE CARINE, teacher; b. Hunter, N.D., Jan. 28, 1938; d. John Leonard and Adeline (Hagen) Hanson; m. Lawrence Robert Henke, May 5, 1962 (div. 1973); children: Toni L., Tom L., Tracy L.; m. Marlon Oscar Haugen, July 10, 1982. BS, U. Minn., 1965; postgrad., misc. schs., 1969—. Cert. elem. tchr., Minn., Iowa. Tchr. dance, 1953-56; tchr. kindergarten Des Moines Pub. Schs., 1964-65; tchr. elem. Ind. Sch. Dist. 284, Wayzata, Minn., 1969—; pvt. bus. history Wayzata, 1978—; marketer, promoter health enhancement Jeri Jacobus Cosmetics, Am. Choice Nutrition, Multiway, KM Matol, Wayzata, 1978—; developer ednl. software, marketer of software Computer Aided Teaching Concepts, Excelsior, Minn., 1983—; developer, author drug edn. curriculum, Wayzata, 1970-71; mem. programs com. Health and Wellness, Wayzata, 1988—; mem. Staff Devel. Adv. Bd., Wayzata, 1988; coach Odyssey of Mind, 1989—. Author, developer computer software; contbr. articles to newspapers. Fundraiser Ind. Reps. Wayzata, 1976-79; mem. pub. rels. com. Lake Minnetonka (Minn.) Dist. Ind. Reps., 1979-81, fundraising chmn., 1981-82; chmn. Wayzata Ind. Reps., 1981-82; sec. PTO, Wayzata, 1981-82. Mem. NEA, Minn. Edn. Assn., Wayzata Edn. Assn. (bd. mem., ins. chairperson). Lutheran. Office: Computer Aided Teaching 20380 Excelsior Blvd Excelsior MN 53331

HENKE, SUE ELLEN, corporate communications specialist; b. Herington, Kans., Feb. 19, 1951; d. Elden Herman and Margaret Emile (Maurer) H. BS, Kans. State U., 1973. Editor employee publs. Kans. Power and Light Co., Topeka, 1973-78, supr. pub. info., 1978-84, supr. co. publs., 1984-88, mgr. co. publs., 1988-90, dir. corp. communications, 1990—. Mem. communications com. United Way Greater Topeka, 1987-90; mem. exec. coun. Our Savior's Luth. Ch., Topeka, 1987-90. Recipient 2d place ann. report competition Reddy Communications, 1987, 1st place, 1988. Mem. Women in Communications (v.p. adminstrn. Topeka profl. chpt. 1975-77, v.p. programming 1982-83, pres.-elect 1987-88, pres. 1988-89, writing awards 1985—), Kans. Press Women (bd. dirs., sec. 1980-82, 1st v.p. 1982-84, pres. 1984-86, writing awards 1975—, Communicator of Achievement award 1988), Women in Energy (bd. dirs. Kans. 1979-80, programming chmn. 1986-87, pres. Topeka chpt. 1987-89), Topeka Press Women (sec.-treas. 1975-77, v.p. 1975-78, pres. 1978-80), Topeka Pub. Rels Soc. Republican. Home: 1305 MacVicar Ave Topeka KS 66604 Office: Kans Power and Light Co 818 Kansas Ave Topeka KS 66612

HENKEL, ELOISE ELIZABETH, writer, information specialist, educator; b. Chgo., Apr. 23, 1923; d. Milford Franklin and Eloise Elizabeth (Lewis) H. BS in Journalism, Northwestern U., Evanston, Ill., 1944; MA in English, U. Chgo., 1964. Reporter, Battle Creek Enquirer-News (Mich.), 1944-45; pub. relations writer Office of Mil. Govt. U.S., Berlin, 1946-47; reporter, rewriter UP, Chgo. and Omaha, 1948; corr. Women's News Service, Paris, 1949; pub. relations officer Internat. Refugee Orgn., Bremen, W.Ger., 1950-51; fgn. corr. Worldwide Press Service, Europe, North Africa, Near East., 1952-54; test constructor Navy Project U. Chgo., 1955; freelance writer, India, Afghanistan, 1956-58, Tibet, China, 1983; tchr. English Chgo. Bd. Edn., 1959-66, 72-75, 84-89; freelance corr., Vietnam, 1967-69; reporter Hammond Times (Ind.), 1971-72; media specialist U. Chgo., 1976-79, Ill. Inst. Tech., Chgo., 1980; developer Rainbow Condominium Assn., Chgo., 1981-82, Hollywood Condominium Assn., Chgo., 1987-89. Author: (with Dick Jones) How to Save Money in Paris, 1950. Recipient Best Feature Story award Ind. AP Mng. Editors, 1971, Best News Story award UPI Mng. Editors (Ind.), 1971, Stick-O-Type award for best feature story Chgo. Newspaper Guild, 1972. Mem. YWCA, YMCA; U.S. China Peoples Friendship Assn. Quaker. Club: Overseas Press. Home: 1454 W Hollywood Chicago IL 60660

HENKIN, PATRICIA, sales executive, customer service professional; b. Abington, Pa., Jan. 23, 1947; d. Arthur I. and Dorothy V. (Bergin) Huey; m. Allen J. Henkin.; 1 child, Andrea J. Student, Temple U. Lic. real estate agt. Tech. data processor Philco Ford Corp., Willow Grove, Pa.; tech. recruiter Keystone Pers., Ft. Washington, Pa.; supr. customer svc. Exide Battery, Horsham, Pa.; mgr. customer svc. Keystone Lighting, Spokane, Wash. Mem. Am. Prodn. and Inventory Control Soc. (past v.p. Buck-Mont chpt., mem. various programs). Address: TA Box 2787 Spokane WA 99220

HENKIN, ROXANNE LEE, educator, writing and reading consultant; b. Chgo., Jan. 4, 1951; d. Edwin and Audrey (Broady) H. BS magna cum laude, No. Ill. U., 1972, MS in Edn., 1983, postgrad., 1987—. Tchr. River Valley Sch. Dist., Sawyer, Mich., 1972-74; primary tchr. Barrington (Ill.) Sch. Dist. 220, 1974-88; writing coord. Elmhurst (Ill.) Sch. Dist. 205, 1988—; writing cons. Ill. Writing Project, 1985—; condr. numerous workhops on reading and literacy; pub. speaker, cons. in field. Contbr. articles to profl. jours. Recipient Ill. Master Tchr. award, 1984. Mem. Nat. Coun. Tchrs. English (elem. sect. com. 1989—), Assn. for Supervision and Curriculum Devel., Internat. Reading Assn., Ill. Reading Coun., No. Ill. Reading Coun. (parents and reading com. 1984-86), Lang. Experience Spl. Interest Coun. (publicity chmn. 1985, newsletter editor 1985-87), Phi Delta Kappa, Kappa Delta Pi. Home: 223 Country Dr Bartlett IL 60103 Office: Elmhurst Sch Dist 205 Elmhurst IL 60000

HENKLE, TERESA, writer; b. Baker, Oreg., Mar. 13, 1955; d. Ray and Ida Mae (Hall) Winn; children: Katy Lynn, Maxwell James. Student U. Oreg., 1973-75. Writer, co-founder Writers Assocs., Eugene, Oreg., 1975-77; writer

KASH-KSND, Eugene, 1976-78; writer, creative dir. Brockett Real Estate, Eugene, 1978-82; creative dir. Sta. KVMT, Vail, Colo., 1982—; writer Colle McVoy Advt., Denver, 1984-87; sr. writer Ireland Communications, Denver, 1985-87; writer Moses Anshell Advt., Phoenix, 1987—; editor URSUS Quar. Jour. N.Am. Bear Soc., 1990—; writer, cons. to local companies. Author: Inside A Storm, 1981. Contbr. articles and poetry to various publs. Formerly active PTA, also Gifted Children Orgn., Eugene; pub. relations, advt. chmn. Jim Hale for County Commr., Eugene, 1982; hon. mem. Friends of the Library; mem. Pub. Service Com., Greater Yellowstone Coalition. Mem. Denver Advt. Fedn., Ariz. Bear Soc. Avocations: environmental writing, hiking, running, reading. Home: 11026 N 28th Dr #24 Phoenix AZ 85029

HENLE, MARY, emeritus psychology educator; b. Cleve., July 14, 1913; d. Leo and Pearl (Hahn) H. A.B., Smith Coll., 1934, A.M., 1935; Ph.D., Bryn Mawr Coll., 1939; L.H.D. (hon.), New Sch. Social Research, 1983. Research assoc. Swarthmore Coll., Pa., 1939-41; instr. U. Del., Newark, 1941-42, Bryn Mawr Coll., Pa., 1942-44; mem. faculty Sarah Lawrence Coll., Bronxville, N.Y., 1944-46; from asst. prof. to assoc. prof. psychology New Sch. Social Research, N.Y.C., 1946-54, prof., 1954-83, prof. emeritus, 1983—; cons. Ednl. Services, Cambridge, Mass., 1965-67. Author: 1879 and All That, 1986; also articles, chpts. Editor books, including: Documents of Gestalt Psychology, 1961; Selected Papers of W. Köhler, 1971. J.S. Guggenheim Meml. Found. fellow, 1951-52, 60-61; research fellow Harvard U., Cambridge, 1963-64; sr. scholar Ednl. Services, Cambridge, 1964-65; vis. prof. Cornell U., fall 1981. Fellow Am. Psychol. Assn. (pres. div. 26 1971-72, pres. div. 24, 1974-75), AAAS; mem. EA. Psychol. Assn. (pres. 1981-82), Cheiron Soc. Democrat. Avocations: old houses; reading. Home: 3300 Darby Rd Apt 5212 Haverford PA 19041

HENLEY, BETH, playwright, actress; b. Jackson, Miss., May 8, 1952; d. Charles and Lydy H. B.F.A., So. Meth. U., 1974; postgrad. U. Ill., 1975-76. Performed with Dallas Minority Repertory Theater, pageant Gt. American People Show, New Salem State Park, Ill., 1976; author plays: Crimes of the Heart (Broadway), 1981, The Wake of Jamey Foster (Broadway), 1982, Am I Blue, 1982, The Miss Firecracker Contest (off Broadway), 1984, The Debutante Ball (world premiere South Coast Repertory Theatre), 1985, The Lucky Spot (produced Manhattan Theatre Club), 1987, Abundance (world premiere South Coast Repertory Theatre), 1989; co-screenwriter: True Stories, 1986; screenwriter: Nobody's Fool, 1986, Crimes of the Heart, 1986, Miss Firecracker, 1989. Recipient awards for Crimes of the Heart including Pulitzer prize for drama, 1981, N.Y. Drama Critics Circle Best Play award, 1981, George Oppenheimer/Newsday Playwriting award, 1980-81. Address: care Gilbert Parker William Morrris Agy 1350 Ave of the Americas New York NY 10019

HENLEY, CHERYL CHRIS, psychologist; b. Charlevoix, Mich.; d. Walter and Jean (Card) H.; m. children: Matthew Karl, Laura Eizabeth. BS, U. Dayton, 1970; MS, N.D. State U., 1985. tchr. Arrowhead Community Coll., Duluth, 1986—; lectr. Program to Aid Victims of Sexual Abuse, Duluth, 1988—; bd. dirs. Minn. Lic. Psychologists. Therapist Village Family Svcs., Fargo, N.D., 1984-86; psychologist Arrowhead Psychol. Assn., Duluth, Minn., 1986—; tchr. Arrowhead Community Coll., Duluth, 1986—; lectr. Program to Aid Victims of Sexual abuse, Duluth, 1988—. Participant Sexual Abuse Consortium, Duluth, 1986—, Eating Disorder Consortium, Duluth, 1986—; bd. dirs. Sexual Abuse Program, Fargo, 1985-86. Mem. Am. Psychol. Assn. (assoc.), Minn. Women Psychologists. Office: Arrowhead Psychol Clinic 324 W Superior St Ste 829 Duluth MN 55802

HENLEY, LILA MARY, government aide; b. Hinsdale, N.H., May 21, 1926; d. Arthur Paul and Delia Emmaline (Stewart) Bouchie; m. Nicholas John Rompon, May 3, 1945 (div. 1959); children: Sylvia Evelyn McDevitt, Donald Barry, John Stewart; m. Robert Wright Henley, Dec. 19, 1962; children: Robert Edward, Edith Elizabeth, Melinda Fell. AB, Bixby Bus. Coll., St. Petersburg, Fla., 1963; B in Ind. Studies, U. South Fla., 1988. Office mgr. Rompon & Assoc. Surveyors, Clearwater, Fla., 1946-53; investigative aide Pinellas County Constable, Clearwater, 1963; aide Pinellas County Legis. Del., Clearwater, 1963-69; legis. aide Fla. Ho. of Reps., Clearwater and Tallahassee, 1969-78, legis. aide IV, 1978—; mem. Gov.'s Commn. Status of Women-State of Fla., 1969-72; dir. Total Profl. Health Care, Clearwater, 1982—; mem. adv. com. Day Care and Early Childhood Devel.-Juvenile Welfare Bd., 1982-87, Joint Com. on Reapportionment, 1982, Joint Task Force on Howard Frankland Bridge, 1984-85, Joint Legis. Commn. on Blood Supplies, 1978, Spl. Com. on Child Day Care Facilites and Licensing, 1976, Gov.'s Task Force on Edn., 1972-73. Bd. dirs. Pinellas Emergency Mental Health Svcs., Clearwater, 1988—; mem. Nat. Rep. com., 1963—. Mem. Fla. Sheriff's Assn., Pinellas County Hist. Soc., Pinellas County Sch. Food Svc. Assn. (life), Tiger Bay Club, Beta Sigma Phi.

HENN, BARBARA JEANNE, academic librarian; b. Indpls., Aug. 2, 1936; d. George Louis and Kathryn Frances (Stewart) H. BS in Edn., Concordia Tchrs. Coll., 1958; MLS, Ind. U., 1967. Reference librarian Purdue U., W. Lafayette, Ind., 1967-68; with Ind. U., Bloomington, 1968—, asst. acquisitions librarian, 1980-85, head acquisitions sect., 1986—. Author: chpt. Advances in Library Administration and Organization, 1989. Mem. ALA (com. chair 1986-87, speaker San Francisco conf. 1987), Ind. Libr. Assn. (div. chair 1984-85), Ohio Valley Group of Tech. Svc. Librs., Ind. Consortium for Internat. Progress (speaker Indpls. chpt. 1986), Beta Phi Mu (pres. Chi chpt. 1973-74). Democrat. Methodist. Home: 4407 Kinser Dr Bloomington IN 47408 Office: Ind U Librs Main Libr E350 Bloomington IN 47405

HENNECY, BOBBIE BOBO, English language educator; b. Tignall, Ga., Aug. 11, 1922; d. John Ebb and Lois Helen (Gulledge) Bobo; AB summa cum laude, Mercer U., Macon, Ga., 1950; postgrad. Oxford (Eng.) U., 1961 English-Speaking Union Scholar; MA, Emory U., 1962; postgrad. Cambridge U., Eng., 1987; m. James Howell Hennecy, Dec. 28, 1963; 1 child, Erin. Adminstrv. asst. to pres., instr. Mercer U., 1950-61, instr. English, 1961-76, asst. prof., 1976-89, emeritus assoc. prof., 1989—; founder Tattnall Sq. Acad., Macon, 1968, sec. acad. corp., 1968-73, dir., 1968-78; Bobbie Bobo Hennecy scholarship named in her hon. Tattnall Sq. Acad., Mercer U.; NDEA fellow Emory U., 1962. Mem. AAUW (chpt. pres. 1964), MLA, S. Atlantic MLA, So. Comparative Lit. Assn., Am. Comparative Lit. Assn., Internat. Comparative Lit. Assn., Nat. Assn. Tchrs. English, Ga. Assn. Tchrs. English, English Speaking Union, LWV, Pres. Club of Mercer U., YWCA (life), Nat. Soc. So. Dames, Nat. Soc. Magna Charta, DAR (registrar 1980-82), Daus. of 1812, Descendants, Colonial Clergy, Daus. of Am. Colonists, Jamestowne Soc., UDC, Colonial Dames XVII Century (chpt. 1st v.p. 1988—), Colonial Order of the Crown (descendents of Charlemagne), Mid. Ga. Hist. Soc., Cardinal Key, Sigma Tau Delta, Sigma Mu (past pres.), Phi Kappa Phi, Alpha Psi Omega, Chi Omega (alumnae advisor). Baptist. Home: 1347-B Adams St Macon GA 31201

HENNEFER, NANCY WHITE, pharmaceutical company executive; b. Charleston, W.Va., June 28, 1958; d. Edward Roderick and Mary Lou (Himmler) White; m. Robert William Hennefer, Mar. 24, 1979; children: Robert Edward, Bradford Thomas. BSBA, Drexel U., 1980. CPA. Mgr. internat. currency risk SmithKline Beecham Corp., Phila.; supervising sr. acct. Peat, Marwick, Phila. Mem. AICPA, PICPA. Home: 1115 Yardley Rd Cherry Hill NJ 08034

HENNESSEY, ALICE ELIZABETH, forest products company executive; b. Havenhill, Mass., May 24, 1936; d. H. Nelson and Elizabeth E. (Johnson) Pingree; A.B. with honors, U. Colo., 1957; cert. with distinction Harvard-Radcliffe Program in Bus. Adminstrn., 1958; m. Thomas M. Hennessey, June 13, 1959; children—Shannon, Sheila, Thomas N. With Boise Cascade Corp. (Idaho), 1958—, sec. to pres., 1958-60, adminstrv. asst. to pres., 1960-61, 65-71, corp. sec., 1971—, v.p., 1974-82, sr. v.p., 1982—. Dir. First Interstate Bank of Idaho. Bd. dirs. Boise Pub. Libr. Found., U. Idaho Found.; sustaining mem. Boise Jr. League; mem. exec. bd. U S WEST Communications, Idaho. Mem. Am. Soc. of Corp. Secs., Nat. Investor Relations Inst., Pub. Relations Soc. of Am., Phi Beta Kappa, Alpha Chi Omega. Office: Boise Cascade Corp 1 Jefferson Sq Boise ID 83728

HENNESSEY, AUDREY KATHLEEN, academic administrator; b. Anchorage, Apr. 4, 1936; d. Lawrence Christopher and Olga Virginia (Strandberg) Doheny; m. Gerard Hennessey, Mar. 10, 1963; children: Brian, Kate. BA, Stanford U., 1957; HSA, U. Toronto, Ont., Can., 1968; PhD, U. Lancaster, Manchester, Eng., 1982. Asst. dir. European sales Univ. Soc., Heidelberg, Fed. Republic Germany, 1959-61; landman's asst. Union Oil Co. Calif., Anchorage, 1962-63; adminstr. group pension Mfgs. Life Ins., Toronto, 1963-65; instr. office systems Adult Edn. Ctr., Toronto, 1965-68; lectr. office systems Salford Coll. Tech., Lancashire, Eng., 1968-70; st. lectr. data processing Manchester Polytechnic, Eng., 1970-79; lectr. computation U. Manchester, Eng., 1979-82; assoc. prof. Tex. Tech. U., computer sci., Lubbock, 1982-86; assoc. prof. Tec. Tech. U., bus. adminstrn., Lubbock, 1987—, dir., 1987—; vis. instr. Fed. Law Enforcement Tng. Ctr., Glynco, Ga., 1984—. Author: Computer Applications Project, 1982; contbr. articles to profl. jours. Organizer Explore Scouts Computer Applications, Lubbock, 1983-85. Recipient various awards Tex. Instruments, 1982-86, Xerox Corp., 1985, Halliburton, 1986, Systems Exploration, 1987, State Tex., 1988—. Mem. Data Processing Mgmt. Assn. (pres. chpt. 1989), Soc. Mfg. Engrs., Assn. Computing Machinery. Office: ISOA-Tex Tech U MS 2101 Lubbock TX 79409

HENNESSEY, CAROL LUDWICK, former teacher; b. Pottstown, Pa., Mar. 12, 1949; d. John G. and Catherine (Besherwor) Ludwick; m. Timothy F. Hennessey, Dec. 28, 1974; children: Katie, Tim, Elizabeth. BS, Shippensburg Coll., 1971. Cert. tchr., Pa. Tchr. elem. sch. Pottsgrove Sch. Dist., Pottstown, 1971-76. North Coventry, Chester County Rep. committeewoman; bd. dirs. Pottstown Symphony Orch.; v.p. Pottstown Meml. Med. Ctr. Aux., 1989—. Mem. AAUW, Jr. Svc. League (pres. 1985-86), Pottstown Hist. Soc. (bd. dirs.). Roman Catholic. Home: 1178 Foxview Rd Pottstown PA 19464

HENNESSY, CHARLENE KOEHLER, executive, owner graphic design firm; b. Washington, Mar. 16, 1945; d. George Frampton and Doris (Ferguson) Koehler; m. John Garret Hennessy, July 3, 1966; children: Stephen P., Aaron Koehler. BS, U. Md., 1986. Paste-up, prodn. designer, sr. designer, advt. design dir. Columbia (Md.) Flier, Patuxent Pub. Co., 1975-80; graphics supr. Aspen Systems Corp., Rockville, Md., 1980-86; owner, pres. Iron Gate Graphics, Frederick, Md., 1986—; chairperson bus. exhibits Frederick County Women's Fair, 1988-89. Mem. pvt. industry coun. Job Tng. Agy., Frederick, 1988-89, Tourism Coun., 1988—; bd. dirs. Women's Ctr. Coun., 1987—, YMCA, 1989—. Mem. Advt. Fedn., Pro Net (pres. 1988-89), Met. Washington Art Dirs. Club, Frederick County Builders Assn., Frederick Bus. Exchange (v.p. 1989), Frederick C. of C., Toastmasters. Office: IronGate Graphics 7627 Iron Gate Ln Frederick MD 21702

HENNESSY, MARGARET B., health care executive; b. Oak Park, Ill., Apr. 10, 1952; d. Bernard Leo and Frances (Madigan) H. BA in Sociology and Psychology, St. Norbert Coll., DePere, Wis., 1974; MS, Rush U., Chgo. Communications specialist Ill. Cancer Coun., Chgo., 1983-84; adminstrv. asst. Rush-Presbyn./St. Luke's Med. Ctr., Chgo., 1984-85; adminstrv. intern Cook County Hosp., Chgo., 1985-86; fin. analyst Loyola U. Med. Ctr., Maywood, Ill., 1986-89; operating officer Howard Brown Meml. Clinic, Chgo., 1989—; guest lectr. Loyola U. Law Sch., 1989. Contbr. articles to profl. jours. Tchr. English as a second lang. World Relief Orgn., Chgo., 1989; cons. United Charities Camps, Chgo., 1989. Recipient Foster G. McGaw scholar, Am. Coll. health Care Execs., 1985. Mem. Rush U. Alumni Assn. (pres.-elect), Chgo. health Execs. Forum, Am. Coll. Healthcare Execs., Assn. of Ambulatory Care Adminstrs. Office: Howard Brown Meml Clinic 945 W George St Chicago IL 60657

HENNESSY, SUSAN MARGARET, university administrator; b. Bronx, N.Y., June 11, 1961; d. Thomas Francis and Joan Catherine (Leppert) Hennessy. BA in Edn., SUNY, Oswego, 1985; MA in Counseling, L.I. U., 1988. Cert. secondary edn. and sch. counseling. Residence hall coordinator L.I.U./C.W. Post Residence Life/Housing, Brookville, N.Y., 1985-89, quad dir., 1988, asst. student/staff devel., 1986-88, asst. dir., 1989—; skills trainer L.I. U./C.W. Post, 1985—, part-time tchr., 1989—; guidance counselor Mineola High Sch., 1986; crisis counselor Nassau County Coalition Against Domestic Violence, 1987. Editor freshman handbook and campus calendar. Mem. Assn. Coll. and Univ. Housing Officers Internat., Northeastern Assn. Coll. and Univ. Housing Officers, Nat. Assn. Female Execs., NOW, Greenpeace, Earthwatch, K.C.-Columbiettes. Home: LI U/CW Post PO Box 131 Brookville NY 11548 Office: LI U at CW Post Northern Blvd Brookville NY 11548

HENNEY, DAGMAR RENATE, mathematician, educator, researcher, consultant; b. Berlin; came to U.S., 1951; d. G. Albert and Margot (Philipp) Kirchner; m. Alan G. Henney, Aug. 16, 1953; 1 child, Alan G. Jr. Abitur, Lyceum, Hamburg, Federal Republic of Germany, 1951; BS, MS in Physics, Math., Miami U., Fla., 1956; PhD in Math., U. Md., 1965. came to U.S., 1951;. Instr. U. Md., 1956-65; prof. dept. math. George Washington U., Washington, 1965—; rsch. supr. U. Md., George Washington U., 1956—. Author of one book; contbr. numerous articles to profl. jours. Liaison between Congress and Scientific Community; advisor Pres.'s Com. Advancement of Women Scientists and other Minority Groups; mem. Pres.'s Com. Women in Policy Making Positions. Mem. APS, TIME (pres., faculty advisor), Am. Math. Assn., Am. Math. Soc., Nat. Assn. Sci. Workers, Nat. Fedn. Bus. and Profl. Women, Nat. Assn. Sci. Writers, Math Honor Soc., B'nai B'rith (scholarship), Phi Beta Kappa, Sigma Xi, Tri-Delta (scholarship). Home: 6912 Prince Georges Ave Takoma Park MD 20912

HENNING, EMILIE ANNE, college dean, nursing educator; b. Scotrun, Pa., Dec. 4, 1930; d. Lester Dimmick and Ada (Warner) Detrick. Diploma Methodist Hosp., N.Y.C., 1951; B.S. in Nursng, Seton Hall U., 1962; M.Ed. in Nursing Edn., Columbia U., 1965, Ed.D. in Nursing Edn., 1974. Cons. Newark Maternal/Infant Care Project, 1965-66; from instr. to asst. prof. Rutgers U., Newark, 1966-71, chmn., assoc. prof., 1973-76; dean and prof. Fla. State U., Tallahassee, 1976-82, East Carolina U., Greenville, N.C., 1982—; curriculum and accreditation cons. univ. schs. of nursing, 1971—. Contbr. chpt. to book, articles to profl. jours. Chmn. Capitol Adv. Council, Fla. Panhandle Health Systems Agy., 1981-82; active in polit. campaigns. Recipient honor cords Sigma Theta Tau, 1985. Mem. N.C. Nurses Assn. (chmn. baccalaureate and higher degree forum 1983-87, edn. com. 1983-87), Nat. League for Nursing (bd. rev. 1980-86, task force 1988—), N.C. Deans and Dirs. (sec.-treas. 1983-85), N.J. State Nurses Assn. (bd. dirs. 1975-76), Nat. Assn. Women Deans, Adminstrs. and Counselors, N.C. Assn. Women Deans, Adminstrs. and Counselors. Avocation: travel. Home: 1874A Quail Ridge Rd Greenville NC 27858 Office: E Carolina U Sch Nursing PO Box 2753 Greenville NC 27858-4353

HENNING, RONDA REGINA, computer security analyst, writer; b. Pitts., Oct. 9, 1957; d. Ronald Roy and Julia Ann (Butch) H.; m. Steven Eric Rose, Oct. 2, 1982. BA magna cum laude, U. Pitts., 1978; MS, Johns Hopkins U., 1986; MBA, Fla. Inst. Tech., 1990. Info. ctr. mgr. Dept. Def., Ft. Meade, Md., 1979-82; mgr. user software applications Nat. Computer Security Ctr., Ft. Meade, 1982-86, dep. chief database security research, 1986-87; staff engr. computer security Harris Corp., Melbourne, Fla., 1987—; program com. 4th Aeorspace Computer Security Application Conf., 11-13th Nat. Computer Security Conf., 5th-6th Ann. Computer Security Applications Conf. Sec. Waning Moon Community Assn., Columbia, Md., 1985-87; troop leader Girl Scouts Am. of Southwestern Pa., Pitts, 1975-79; mem. Ashley Manor Assn. Homeowners, Friends Nat. Zoo, Washington. Mem. IEEE (tech. com. 1987—), Honeywell Large System User's Assn., Internat. Fedn. of Info. Processing Socs. Working Group, Cen. Brevard Horseman's Assn. (exec. com.), Nat. Geog. Soc. Democrat. Roman Catholic. Office: Harris Corp/Govt Info Systems Div Mail Stop WI/7742 PO Box 98000 Melbourne FL 32902

HENNING, SUSAN JUNE, biomedical researcher; b. Griffith, N.S.W., Australia, June 6, 1946; came to U.S. 1971; d. William James Brett and Gwen (Hurle) Goddard; m. Graydon Read Henning, Jan. 6, 1968 (div. 1974); m. Mannige Vikram Rao, Aug. 17, 1974; children: Justin, Colin, Mitchell. BS, U. Melbourne, 1967, PhD, 1971. Instr. biology Stanford (Calif.) U., 1973-74; asst. prof. Temple U., Phila., 1975-79; assoc. prof. U. Houston, 1979-84, prof., 1984-89; vis. prof. Baylor Coll. Medicine, Houston, 1987-88; prof. dept. pediatrics Baylor Coll. Medicine, 1989—; cons. in field. Editorial bd. Biology of the Neonate, Basel, Switzerland, 1983—, Am. Jour. Physiology, Bethesda, Md., 1984—; contbr. articles to profl. jours., chpts. in books. Walter J. Gores awardee, Stanford U., 1974; Wellcome Found. fellow, 1975; NIH grantee, 1976-89, merit award, 1989. Mem. Soc. Exptl. Biology and Medicine, Endocrine Soc., Soc. for Pediatric Rsch., Am. Gastroenterol. Assn., Internat. Soc. Developmental Psychobiology, Soc. for Developmental Biology, Soc. Toxicology. Office: Baylor Coll Medicine One Baylor Plaza Houston TX 77030

HENNINGER, ANN LOUISE, biology educator; b. Chambersburg, Pa., Apr. 13, 1946; d. Clay Foster and Dorothy Annette (Knouse) H.; m. Mark Francis Trax, Mar. 3, 1973. AB, Wilson Coll., 1968; PhD, U. Mich., 1973. From asst. prof. to assoc. prof. biology Lebanon Valley Coll., Annville, Pa., 1973-83; dir. spl. programming and registrar Wartburg Coll., Waverly, Iowa, 1983-86, assoc. prof. biology and registrar, 1986-89, assoc. prof. biology, 1989—. Bd. dirs., officer Lebanon (Pa.) Family Planning, 1975-80, Am. Cancer Soc., Waverly, 1989—. Mem. Nat. Sci. Tchrs. Assn., Am. Physiol. Soc. (assoc.), Iowa Acad. Sci., AAUW (treas. 85-88, corp. rep. 1989—), Soc. Coll. Sci. Tchrs., Phi Beta Kappa, Beta Beta Beta, Sigma Xi. Lutheran. Office: Wartburg Coll 222 9th St NW Waverly IA 50677

HENNINGS, DEIRDRE ELLEN, copywriter; b. Oakland, Calif., Sept. 6, 1951; d. Robert Edward and Nancy (Wensley) H. Student, Oberlin (Ohio) Coll., 1969-71; BA, U. Minn., 1974; cert. in copy writing, NYU, 1987. Account and broadcast coord. Rapp & Collins Direct Response Advt., N.Y.C., 1979-82; writer, editor Nat. Assn. Purchasing Mgmt., N.Y.C. and Oradell, N.J., 1982-86; copywriter, account exec. AB Isacson Assocs., N.Y.C., 1986-89; copywriter Empire Blue Cross/Blue Shield, N.Y.C., 1989-90; freelance direct response copywriter L.A., 1990—. Mem. The Direct Mktg. Club So. Calif., Direct Mktg. Creative Guild L.A., L.A. Crative Club, Sierra Club. Democrat.

HENNION, CAROLYN LAIRD (LYN HENNION), mutual fund executive; b. Orange, Calif., July 27, 1943; d. George James and Jane (Porter) Laird; m. Reeve L. Hennion, Sept. 12, 1964; children—Jeffrey Reeve, Douglas Laird. B.A., Stanford U., 1965. Cert. fin. planner; lic. ins. agt.; registered gen. securities prin. Portfolio analyst Schwabacher & Co., San Francisco, 1965-66; adminstrv. coordinator Bicentennial Commn., San Mateo County Calif., 1972-73; dir. devel. Crystal Springs Uplands Sch., Hillsborough, Calif., 1973-84; tax preparer Household Fin. Corp., Foster City, Calif., 1982, freelance, 1983-87; sales promotion mgr. Franklin Distbrs., Inc., San Mateo, 1984-86, regional sales mgr., 1986—, v.p., 1988—; v.p. Viatech, Inc., 1986—. Editor: Lest We Forget, 1975. Pres. South Hillsborough Sch. Parents' Group, Calif., 1974-75; sec. Vol. Bur. of San Mateo County, Burlingame, Calif., 1975; chmn. Community Info. Com., Town of Hillsborough, 1984-86; mem., subcom. chmn. fin. adv. com., Town of Hillsborough, 1984-86. Recipient awards Council for Advancement and Support of Edn., 1981, Exemplary Direct Mail Appeals Fund Raising Inst., 1982, Wholesaler of Yr. Shearson Lehman Hutton N.W Region, 1989. Mem. Securities Industry Assn. (chmn. state membership 1989—), Internat. Assn. Fin. Planners (sec. Oreg. chpt. 1988-89, bd. dirs.), Inst. Cert. Fin. Planners, Ashland Shakespeare Festival, Jr. League, Rogue Valley Country Club. Republican. Home: 148 Greenway Cir Medford OR 97504 Office: Franklin Distbrs 130 E Main St #282 Medford OR 97501

HENNUM, LAURA ALFERD, communications executive, cable TV consultant; b. Portland, Oreg., Dec. 14, 1964; d. Roland Yarl and Elizabeth Edwina (Bellinger) Alferd; m. Eric Lawrence Hennum, Dec. 3, 1988. BA, Wash. State U., 1987. Press rels. officer St. Vincent Hosp. & Med. Ctr., Portland, 1987; account coord. Bacon & Hunt Pub. Rels., Portland, 1987-89; communications project mgr. Providence Med. Ctr., Portland, 1989—; cons. Evergreen Sch. Dist., Vancouver, 1989-90, Paragon Cable Co., Portland, 1990—. Mem. Pub. Rels. Soc. Am. (Award of Merit 1989), Women in Communications (v.p. 1989-90, named Outstanding New Mem. 1989), Wash. State U. Alumni Assn. Methodist. Home: 14004 NE 14th Cir Vancouver WA 98684 Office: Providence Medical Center 4805 NE Glisan Portland OR 97213

HENNUM, SUSANNA S., educator; b. Iquique, Chile, Jan. 14, 1928; came to U.S., 1935; d. William A. and Geneva E. (Lewis) Shelly; m. Paul R. Hennum, May 15, 1955; children: Ruth Eileen Hennum Fowler, Eric Lawrence. BA, DePauw U., 1950; MA, Wichita (Kans.) State U., 1970. Registrar, curatorial asst. to dir. Wichita Art Mus., 1970-74; instr. art history and women's studies Clark Coll., Vancouver, Wash., 1977-89, dir. index gallery, 1980-81; instr. art history Marylhurst (Oreg.) Coll., 1988—; lectr. art history Tabor Coll., Hillsboro, Kans., 1970, Wichita State U., 1969-70; docent Portland Art Inst., 1989—. Mem. mayor's com. Pick Out Art for City Hall, Vancouver, 1985; mem. women's com. Reed Coll., Portland, 1983-87; arts panel moderator Evergreen State Coll., Vancouver, 1980; docent trainer Nihonga Art Exhibit, Vancouver, 1985-86; bd. dirs. Columbia Bus. Commn. for the Arts, Vancouver, 1983-86. Recipient Commendation, Assn. Students Clark Coll. Bd. Commrs., 1983. Mem. AAUW (pres. Vancouver br. 1983-85, Grantee 1985). Home: 2800 NE 113th St Vancouver WA 98686

HENRI, LISE MARIE, production company administrator; b. Phila., Dec. 16, 1962; d. Edward Mark and Joan Ethel (Keller) H. BA in TV/Film, Temple U., 1984. Asst. to lit. agt. Triad Artists, L.A., 1986; asst. to producer Ponti Prodns., Santa Monica, Calif., 1986—. Mem. NOW, Women in Film, Women in Communications, Inc., Environ. Media Assn. Office: Ponti Prodns. Inc. 100 Wilshire Blvd #1050 Santa Monica CA 90401

HENRICH, LEANN JEAN, basketball coach; b. Storm Lake, Iowa, Nov. 8, 1957; d. Charles Dale and Gwendolyn Mae (Meseck) H. BA in Physical Edn., Buena Vista Coll., Storm Lake, 1976-80; MS in Physical Edn., Washington State U., Pullman, 1980-81. Graduate asst. Washington State U., Pullman, 1980-81; head basketball coach Calif. State U.-Stanislaus, Turlock, 1981—; bd. dirs. Warrior Girls Basketball Camp, Turlock, ASA Softball Umpire, Amateur Softball Assn., Turlock, NCAA, Kansas City, Basketball camps, Calif., 1982-88. Author: (Masters' Thesis) Comparison of Racquetball Grips, 1981. Fundraiser, Am. Cancer Soc., Turlock, 1987. Named Converse Basketball Coach of Yr., 1989. Mem. Womens Basketball Coaches Assn., Northern Calif. Athletic Conference Coaches Assn. (chmn.), Arrowhead Club. Republican. Methodist. Office: Calif State U Stanisl 801 W Monte Vista Turlock CA 95380

HENRICKSEN, ANNE E., public relations executive. Grad., Colo. State U. Gen. mgr. Hunt's Interior Design, Marquette, Mich., 1973-80; dir. corp. devel., v.p. mktg. Star Line Corp., Williamston, Mich., 1980-85; v.p. membership and devel. Chgo. Conv. and Visitors Bur., 1987-88; dir. corp. sales and nat. pub. rels. Star Line Corp., Livonia, Mich., 1989—. Mem. Domestic Violence Prevention and Treatment Bd., State of Mich., 1978-84; legis. rsch. analyst Mich. Ho. of Reps., Lansing. Home: 233 E Wacker Dr #2802 Chicago IL 60601 Office: Star Line Corp 38705 Seven Mile Rd Ste 445 Livonia MI 48152

HENRIKSON, KATHERINE POINTER, research scientist; b. Erie, Pa., Oct. 4, 1939; d. Leon Royce and Katherine (Hermen) Pointer; m. Ray C. Henrikson, Oct. 29, 1966; children: Charles, Andrew. BA in Chemistry, U. Rochester, 1961; MA in Med. Scis., Harvard U., 1962, PhD in Biol. Chemistry, 1967. Rsch. scientist Commonwealth Scientific and Indsl. Rsch. Orgn., Sydney, Australia, 1967-69; postdoctoral fellow Pathology dept. Columbia U., N.Y.C., 1970-71; asst. prof., biochemistry Fairleigh Dickinson Sch. Dentistry, Hackensack, N.J., 1974; rsch. assoc. to asst. prof. Albany (N.Y.) Med. Coll., 1976-79; rsch. scientist Wadsworth Ctr., State Health Dept., Albany, 1979—; asst. prof. SUNY Sch. Pub. Health, Albany, 1986—; ad hoc reviewer NSF, Washington, 1989; speaker in field. Mem. AAAS, Am. Soc. Biochemistry and Molecular Biology, Endocrine Soc., Am. Soc. for Microbiology, N.Y. Acad. Scis., Phi Beta Kappa. Home: 4 Oldox Rd Delmar NY 12054 Office: Wadsworth Ctr Lab & Rsch NY State Health Dept Albany NY 12201

HENRIKSON, LOIS ELIZABETH, photojournalist; b. Lytton, Iowa, Nov. 10, 1921; d. Daniel Raymond and Cora Elizabeth (Thomson) Wessling; m. Arthur Allen Henrikson, July 3, 1943; children: Diane Elizabeth Henrikson Slider, Janet Christine, Michele Charlene Henrikson Smetana. BS, Northwestern U., 1943. Adminstrv. asst. to v.p., dir. ops. bus. communications div. ITT Telecommunications Corp., Des Plaines, Ill., 1980-82; adminstrv. asst. to exec. v.p. Wholesale Stationers' Assn., Des Plaines, 1982-84, membership svcs. coord., editor membership roster, 1984-88; field editor

Office World News Bus./Indsl. div., FM Bus. Publs., Inc., Garden City, N.Y., 1988—. Contbg. editor Home World Bus. ICD Publs. chair safety com. Cumberland Sch. PTA, Des Plaines, 1957-58, chair publicity, 1960-61; bd. dirs. Maine West High Sch. Music Boosters, Des Plaines, 1967-69; capt. fin. drive YMCA, Des Plaines, 1964; mem. diaconate bd., visitation coord. First Congl. Ch., Des Plaines. Mem. NAFE, Am. Soc. Assn. Execs. (cert. membership mktg. 1986), Chgo. Soc. Assn. Execs. (registrar 1984-85), Am. Soc. of Profl. and Exec. Women, AAUW (chair social com. 1983-84, editor newsletter 1984-85, 88—), Am. Assn. Editorial Cartoonists (aux.), Soc. Profl. Journalists, Soc. Am. Bus. Editors and Writers, Nat. Soc. Magna Charta Dames (life), Am. of Royal Descent (life), DAR, Found. for Christian Living, Art Inst. Chgo., Alpha Gamma Delta. Republican. Home: 27 N Meyer Ct Des Plaines IL 60016 Office: Office World News FM Bus Publs Inc 1225 Franklin Ave Garden City NY 11530

HENRIQUES, PATRICIA ANN, management consultant; b. New Haven, Dec. 9, 1949; d. Walter Edward and Leontine Elizabeth (Marcus) Smith; m. Vico Emanuel Henriques, Jan. 12, 1981. B.A., Conn. Coll., 1971. Exec. asst. Bank of Am., Brussels and London, 1971-73; account exec. Cunningham & Walsh Advt., N.Y.C., 1973-76; dir. adminstrn. Computer & Bus. Mfrs. Assn., Washington, 1977-80; legal adminstr. Melrod, Redman & Gartlan, Washington, 1980-83; pres. Mgmt. Alternatives, Inc., Washington, 1983—. Mem. ABA, AMA (bd. of trade), Comml. Real Estate Women (treas.), Mentors, Inc. Republican. Home: 1708 23d St S Arlington VA 22202 Office: 1420 K St NW Ste 500 Washington DC 20005

HENRIQUEZ-FREEMAN, HILDA JOSEFINA, fashion design executive; b. Palmarito de Cauto, Oriente, Cuba, June 18, 1938; came to U.S., 1960; d. Matias and Isabel Beatrice (Freeman) Henriquez. BA, Bethune-Cookman Coll., 1963; postgrad., Tchrs. Coll., 1965-66, Roosevelt U., 1966, Northwestern U., 1969-70; cert., No. Ill. U., 1975; postgrad., Loop Coll., 1972-84. Modiste/couturier Fina Modas, Habana, Cuba, 1952-59; instr. English Habana Pub. Sch., Cuba, 1956-58; ct. reporter Govt. La Cabana, Habana, Cuba, 1959-60; language instr. Ft. Lauderdale Sch. Dist., Fla., 1963-64; custom design Freeman's Fashion Atelier, Chgo., 1965-68; pres. dir. Freeman's Fashion Acad., Chgo., 1968—; head designer Eur-Am. Creations, Chgo., 1978-81; cons. Freeman's Enterprise, Chgo., 1982—. Mentor Spanish coalition, Youth Career Awareness Program, Chgo., 1987. Mem. Cuban C. of C., Cuban Liceo, Ill. Assn. Trade and Tech. Schs., NAFE. Office: Freeman's Fashion Acad 410 S Michigan Ave Chicago IL 60605

HENRY, ANNE MARSHALL, mathematics educator; b. Oakland, Calif., Oct. 6, 1944; d. Charles Delaskie Marshall and Margaret Wilson (Fisher) Marshall James; m. Richard Lenert Henry, June 25, 1966; children: Margaret Elisabeth, Marion Curtiss Wilson, John Knox Marshall Henry. AB, Smith Coll., Northampton, Mass., 1966; MEd, Cabrini Coll., Radnor, Pa. Tchr. Milton (Mass.) Acad., 1966-67; tchr., pub. health Peace Corps, Nabeul, Tunisia, 1967-69; tchr. Springside Sch., Phila., 1971-74, Agnes Irwin Sch., Rosemont, Pa., 1972-87; housemaster, dir. of studies Lawrenceville (N.J.) Sch., 1987—; mem. assn. Tchrs. of Math. of Phila. and Vicinity, Phila., 1972-87. Mem. St. David's Ch., 1970—; chmn. bd. dirs. St. David's Nursery Sch., Wayne, 1980-87; chmn. com. Jr. League Phila., 1970-78. Mem. Nat. Coun. Tchrs. of Math., Milldam Club. Episcopalian. Home: PO Box 6763 Lawrenceville NJ 08648

HENRY, BARBARA A., newspaper editor; b. Oshkosh, Wis., July 23, 1952; d. Robert Edward and Barbara Frances (Aylesworth) H. BJ, U. Nev. Reporter Reno Newspapers, 1974-78, city editor, 1978-80, mng. editor, 1980-82; asst. nat. editor USA Today, Washington, 1982-83; exec. editor Reno Gazette-Jour., 1981-86; editor, dir. Gannett Rochester Newspapers, Rochester, N.Y., 1986—. Mem. Soc. Profl. Journalists, Associated Press Mng. Editors, Am. Soc. Newspaper Editors, Calif.-Nev. Soc. Newspaper Editors (bd. dirs.). Office: Dem & Chronicle 55 Exchange Blvd Rochester NY 14614*

HENRY, CLAUDETTE, state official; b. Oklahoma City, Mar. 13, 1947; d. Ray William and Janette (Edwards) Craig; m. B. Jack Henry. Student, Rose State Coll. Formerly revenue officer U.S. Dept. Treasury; formerly Okla. state rep., Okla. state treas., 1991—. Mem. LDS Ch. Republican. Address: Office of Treas 217 Capitol Bldg Oklahoma City OK 73105*

HENRY, DONNA EDWARDS, educator; b. Washington, Oct. 1, 1949; d. Conard Paul and Jean Marie (Kemp) E. BS, D.C. Tchrs. Coll., 1971; MA, Columbia U., 1974. Cert. tchr., Md. Tchr. Binghamton (N.Y.) Sch. System, 1971-73; group tchr., supr., acting dir. N.Y.C. Coll., 1974-76; tchr., supr. student tchrs. Balt. City Schs., 1976-87; tchr., supr. student tchrs. Prince George's County Schs., New Carrollton, Md., 1987-90, Laurel, Md., 1990—; asst. volley-ball coach Binghamton Sch. System, 1973; project dir. Fund for Ednl. Excellence, Balt., 1986-87 (ednl. grant). Contbr. articles and photographs to mags., 1973-74. Coach Balt. City Volleyball League, 1979-80; vol. Balt. Neighborhoods, Inc., 1980—. Mem. NAFE, NEA (vol. conv. communications com.).

HENRY, FRANCES ANN, journalist; b. Denver, July 23, 1939; d. Lewis Byford and Betsy Mae (Lancaster); m. Charles Larry, June 28, 1963, (div. May, 1981); children: Charles Kevin, Tracy Diane. BA in English, Carleton Coll., Northfield, Minn., 1960; MA in Social Sci., Colo. U., Denver, 1988; MA in Journalism, Memphis State U., 1989. Cert. tchr. Lang. arts tchr. Rolla Pub. Schs., Rolla, Mo., 1963-66; substitute tchr. Arapahoe County Pub. Schs., Littleton, Colo., 1973-76; journalism tchr. Douglas County Pub. Schs., Castle Rock, Colo., 1976-; mng. editor Douglas County News-Press, Castle Rock, Colo., 1986-87; editor Daily Helmsman Memphis State Univ., 1988--; editor Fourth World Bulletin, 1988; sec. Colo. High Sch. Press Assn., Boulder, 1981-83; pres. Colo. High Sch. Press Assn., Boulder, 1983-87; bd. dirs. Colo. High Sch. Press Assn., Boulder; delegate First Amendment Congress, Denver, 1984. Contbr. articles to profl. jours. Named Colo. Journalism Tchr. of the Year, Colo. High Sch. Press Assn., Boulder, 1985. Mem. AAUW, Colo Prress Women, Soc. Profl. Journalists, Greenpeace Wilderness Soc., Mensa, Kappa Tau Alpha. Democrat. Episcopal. Home: PO Box 781 Quincy FL 32351 Office: Douglas County High Sch 2842 Front St Castle Rock CO 80104

HENRY, JANE STINNETT, pharmacist; b. Winfield, Kans., May 2, 1952; d. Fagan C. and Ruth T. (Thornton) S.; m. David W. Henry, June 30, 1979. BS in Pharmacy, U. Kans., 1975, MBA, 1986. Pharmacy intern U. Kans. Med. Ctr., Kansas City, 1973-75; staff pharmacist Olathe (Kans.) Community Hosp., 1975-80, dir. pharmacy, 1980—. Recipient Leadership award Ciba Geigy, 1988, award Squibb Co., 1988, Harold N. Godwin Lecture award, 1989. Mem. Am. Soc. Hosp. Pharmacists (mem. coun. on adminstrv. affairs 1989-90, del. 1988, 89, 90), Am. Pharmacists Assn., Kans. Soc. Hosp. Pharmacists (pres. 1988, bd. dirs. 1986-87), Kans. Pharmacists Assn. (bd. dirs. 1988, chmn. long range planning com. 1987), Hosp. Pharmacists Greater Kansas City (treas. 1982), Purchasing Svc. Kansas City (chmn. 1983-84), Humane Soc. of Olathe. Republican. Presbyterian.

HENRY, JEAN SHELLEY JENNINGS, retired educator; b. Oct. 30, 1913; d. Walter Perry and Mary Arabella (McFarland) Jennings; m. Henry Patrick Jr., Feb. 18, 1936 (div. May 1983); children: Patrick Gillespie, Mary Gail. BA, Tex. Tech U., 1933; MA, Tex. Christian U., 1938. Tchr. English Lorenzo (Tex.) High Sch., 1933-34; tchr. social studies Palinview (Tex.) Independent Sch. Dist., 1934-36; educator Tex. Christian U., Ft. Worth, 1937-38, So. Meth. U., Dallas, 1950's; tchr. English The Hockaday Sch., Dallas, 1959-64; presenter in field. Mem. local and global svc. projects Church Women United, Arlington, Tex. 1983—; trustee Tex. Conf. of Chs., Christian Ch., 1985—; bd. govs. Internat. Inst., Renewal of Gospel Studies, 1983—; former bd. dirs. Coun. on Christian Unity, Indpls., Dallas UN Assn., Dallas Area Assn. Christian Chs., adminstrv. com. World Conf. Chs. of Christ, Area Christian Women's Fellowship, Greater Dallas Community of Chs., Women's Dialogue NCCJ; bd. elders Northwest Christian Ch., Arlington. Mem. AAUW (vol.), Nat. Benevolent Assn. (exec. com. 1990-92, trustee 1986-92), Arlington Woman's Club. Home: 1617 Fremman Ct Arlington TX 76013

HENRY, JUDY MARLOWE, broadcast programming administrator; b. Newnan, Ga., Mar. 13, 1948; d. Sawyer Davis and Mattie Louise (Holland) Marlowe; divorced; 1 child, Lisa Marlowe. Student, U. Ga., 1966-68, Oglethorpe U., 1987. Editorial dept. TV Guide mag., Atlanta, 1967-68; dir. KinderCare Learning Ctrs., Atlanta, 1972-76; corp. administrator Turner Broadcast System, Atlanta, 1977-83; assoc. dir. sports Sta. WTBS-TV, 1977—, producer Upclose, 1978-83, producer Good News, 1986—; asst. dir. ESPN, 1983—; program coordinator Cable News Network, Atlanta, 1983-89, producer Nuclear Arms Conf. at Emory U., 1985, producer Showbiz, 1986—, unit mgr. Reagan Years, 1988; cons. Very Spl. Arts Festival, Greenville, S.C., 1984—, Veratec Industries, Tucker, Ga., 1984—. Recipient Emmy award NATAS, Atlanta, 1978, Tetrahedron Presdl. citation, 1986. Mem. Am. Women in Radio and TV (Woman of Achievement 1990). Home: 1646 Esquire Pl Norcross GA 30093 Office: Cable News Network One CNN Ctr PO Box 105366 Atlanta GA 30348

HENRY, KATHLEEN MARIE, marketing executive; b. Stillwater, Okla., Sept. 24, 1950; d. Irl Wayne and Hulda Mary (Duncan) H. BS, Cen. State U., Okla., 1972. Community relations dir./account exec. Lowe Runkle Advt., Oklahoma City, 1972-74, account coordinator, 1975; sales promotion cons. McDonald's Corp., Houston, 1974; regional advt. supr. McDonald's Southfield (Mich.), 1975, regional advt. mgr., 1976-78, local store mktg. mgr., Oak Brook, Ill., 1978-80, staff dir., store mktg./sales promotion, 1980-82, home office dir. store mktg./sales promotion, 1982-83, dir. nat. sales promotion, 1983-84, internat. mktg. dir., 1984-85, mktg. dir. McDonald's System of France, 1985-86—, McDonald's System of Europe, 1985-88, v.p. mktg., 1988—. Publicity chmn. Keep Okla. Beautiful, 1973-74; publicity chmn. Muscular Dystrophy Assn. Am., Okla. chpt., 1973-74; bd. dirs. Southfield Arts Council, 1976-78. Recipient Pres.'s award, McDonald's Corp., 1978; Chgo. YWCA Leadership award, 1978; Disting. Former Student award, Cen. State U., 1979; named Outstanding Sr. Woman Cen. State U., 1972, Outstanding Greek Woman, 1972. Mem. Cen. State U. Alumni Assn. (dir. 1974) Cen. State U. Centennial Commn., Sigma Kappa. Office: McDonald's Corp McDonald's Pla Oak Brook IL 60521

HENRY, NANCY ROSE, school nurse; b. N.Y.C., Feb. 19, 1938; d. August George and Florence May (Kinder) Timmannn; m. Douglas W. Henry, Oct. 22, 1960 (div. 1987); children: Robert Douglas, Michael Wayne. BS, SUNY, Plattsburgh, 1960; postgrad., Ea. Wash. U., Cheney, 1972-73,75-80, Ea. Wash. U., 1986—; MEd, Whitworth Coll., Spokane, 1981. RN. Camp nurse United Meth. Ch., Brantingham, N.Y., 1960; staff nurse Physician's Hosp., Plattsburgh, 1964; instr. Champlain Valley Sch. of Nursing, Plattsburgh, 1964-65; sch. nurse Cheney (Wash.) pub. schs., 1973—. Editor newsletter, The Big Apple, 1978-80, Wellness - Your Move, 1988—. Pres. Cheney Community Svc. Coun., 1986, United Meth. Women, Cheney, 1981-83. Mem. AAUW (br. corr. sec. 1984-85, br. treas. 1990-91), Sch. Nurse Orgn. Wash., NEA, Wash. Edn. Assn., Cheney Edn. Assn., Alpha Delta Kappa. Office: Cheney Public Schools 520 4th St Cheney WA 99004

HENRY, ROSEANN, editor; b. Bronx, N.Y., Nov. 16, 1958; d. John J. and Anne E. (Henchy) H. BA, Hofstra U., 1980. Vol. VISTA Legal Services Corp., Burlington, Iowa, 1980-81; forms analyst Uniform Printing, N.Y.C., 1981-83; prodn. coordinator CBS mags., N.Y.C., 1983-85; prodn. editor Sci. Digest mag., N.Y.C., 1985-86; mng. editor Computers in Banking mag., N.Y.C., 1986-87, Discover mag., N.Y.C., 1987—. Mem. ACLU, NOW, Am. Soc. Mag. Editors. Democrat.

HENRY, SANDRA KEDNOCKER, civic worker and fundraiser, small business investment corporation executive; m. Charles J. Henry; children: Brendan Allan Hasenstab, Garratt Hill Hasenstab. BA, U. N.C., 1959; postgrad., U. Cin., 1966-67; grad. fin. forum, The Harris Bank, Chgo. Pres. Intervest Group, 1984-85. Past bd. dirs. North Shore Country Day Sch., Illinois Club, House of the Good Shepherd, Consular Bal-Libr. Internat. Rels.; bd. dirs. USO; div. bd. dirs., Ill. del. Am. Cancer Soc.; mem. woman's bd. Children's Home and Aid Soc. Ill.; mem. benefit com., bd. dirs. English Speaking Union of Chgo.; bd. dirs. Goodman Theatre; mem. women's bd. Japan Am. Soc. Chgo.; mem. benefit com. Brookfield Zoo, Apparel Industry of Chgo.; mem. Angel Ball com. Mundelein Coll.; mem. woman's bd., benefit chmn., exec. com. Am. Heart Assn.; mem. woman's bd., exec. com., benefit com. Five Hosp. Found.; pres. Intervest Group; vice chmn. bd. dirs., exec. com. Shakespeare Globe Ctr., midwest div. benefit chmn., 1988-90. Mem. NAFE, Internat. Platform Assn., Am. Biog. Inst. Rsch. Assn. (bd. govs.).

HENRY-THIEL, LOIS HOLLENDER, human resources executive; b. Phila., Jan. 19, 1941; d. Edward Hubert and Frances Lois (Nesler) Hollender; m. Charles L. Henry, Oct. 24, 1964 (div. 1971); children—Deborah Lee, Randell Huitt, Andrew Edward; m. Brian L. Thiel, Jan. 1, 1989. B.A., Thomas A. Edison Coll., 1979; M.S.W., Fordham U., 1981. Cert. social worker, N.Y., N.J.; lic. service profl., Ariz. Personnel asst., sec. IBM, Paterson, N.J. and St. Louis, 1964-66; minister's asst. Grace Luth. Ch., St. Cloud, Fla., 1966-68; adminstr./tchr. Fla. Finishing Acad., St. Cloud, 1968-70; adminstrv. asst. Newark Book Ctr., 1972-77; intern, med. social worker Jersey City Med. Ctr., 1979-80; intern, psychiatric/med. social worker VA Med. Ctr., Lyons, N.J., 1980-81; sch. social worker Lakeview Learning Ctr., Budd Lake, N.J., 1981-82; mgr. human resources Terak Corp., Scottsdale, Ariz., 1982-85; v.p. counseling and bus. devel. Murro & Assocs., Phoenix, 1985-88, exec. v.p. cons., 1988—; career cons., individual/family counselor/psychotherapist, speaker, Scottsdale, 1982; mem. employers com. Ariz. Dept. Econ. Security; cons. in field. Coordinator-vol. Job-A-Thon, Phoenix, 1983. Mem. Human Resources Council for Am. Electronics Assn., Am. Orthopsychiat. Assn., Nat. Assn. Social Workers, Am. Soc. Personnel Adminstrs., Phoenix Personnel Mgmt. Assn., Am. Compensation Assn., Ariz. Affirmative Action Assn. Home: 8628 E Granada Rd Scottsdale AZ 85257

HENSELMEIER, SANDRA NADINE, training and development consulting firm executive; b. Indpls., Nov. 20, 1937; d. Frederick Rost Henselmeier and Beatrice Nadine (Barnes) Henselmeier Enright; m. David Albert Funk, Oct. 2, 1976; children: William H. Stolz, Jr., Harry Phillip Stolz II, Sandra Ann Stolz. AB, Purdue U., 1971; MAT, Ind. U., 1975. Exec. sec. to dean Ind. U. Sch. Law, Indpls., 1977-78; adminstrv. asst. Ind. U.-Purdue U., Indpls., 1978-80, assoc. archivist, 1980-81; program and communication coordinator Midwest Alliance in Nursing, Indpls., 1981-82; tng. coordinator Coll./Univ. Cos., Indpls., 1982-83; pres. Better Bus. Communications, Indpls., 1983—; adj. lectr. Ind. U.-Purdue U. at Indpls., 1971—, U. Indpls. Center Continuing Mgmt. Devel. and Edn., Indpls., 1984—. Author: Successful Customer Service Writing, Winning with Effective Business Grammar, Successful Telephone Communication and Etiquette; contbr. articles to profl. jours. Mem. ASTD, Assn. Bus. Communication, Nat. Assn. Profl. Saleswomen, Greater Indpls. Literacy League, Indpls. C. of C., Assn. Profl. Writing Cons. Republican. Presbyterian. Avocations: traveling, walking, reading, learning new ideas. Office: Better Bus Communications 6208 N Delaware St Indianapolis IN 46220

HENSEN, DEIRDRE MUNISTERI, veterinarian; b. Bklyn, Apr. 10, 1954; d. Philip Xavier Munsteri and Marion May Murtha; m. David Roy Hensen, Nov. 8, 1987. BS, Cornell U., Ithaca, 1976; U. Pa., U. Pennsylvania, Phila., 1982. Vet. Medicine. Veterinarian Shirley Vet. Hosp., Shirley, N.Y., 1982-88, Miller Place (N.Y.) Animal Hosp.; sec. L.I. Vet. Med. Assn., L.I., N.Y., 1989, treas., 1996—; bus. mgr. L.I. Vet. Ultrasound Svcs., Shirley, N.Y. Author: Vet. Corner, 1988. Mem. Am. Vet. Med. Assn., N.Y. State Vet. Med. Assn., L.I. Vet. Med. Assn., Assn. of Avian Vets., Phi Kappa Phi. Office: Miller Pl Animal Hosp 815 Route 25A Miller Place NY 11764

HENSINGER, JANET PAULA MAUPIN, health facility administrator; b. Lexington, Ky., May 25, 1944; d. Paul Bryant and Lucile Jean (Holmes) Maupin; m. Lawrence W. Hensinger (div. May 1989). Student, U. Ky., 1962-65, Ky. State U., 1980. Cert. med. asst., adminstrv. Receptionist Drs. Burkhart & Burkhart, Lexington, 1965-74, office mgr., 1974-88; adminstr. Commonwealth Family Physicians, Lexington, 1988—; adv. bd. Ea. Ky. Univ. Med. Assisting Tech., Richmond, 1978-86; chmn. adv. bd. Fugazzi Coll. Med. Assisting Program, Lexington, 1979-85. Editor: (newsletter) The Forum, 1977 (1st place award), 1979 (2d place award). Mem. Am. Assn. Med. Assts. (pres. 1983-84, Outstanding Svc. award 1984), Ky. Med. Group Mgrs. Assn., Ky. Soc. Med. Assts. (life), Republican Women's Club. Mem. Christian Ch. Office: Commonwealth Family Phys 2370 Nicholasville Rd #203 Lexington KY 40503

HENSINGER, MARGARET ELIZABETH, horticultural, agricultural advertising and marketing executive; b. Jackson, Mich., Aug. 31, 1950; d. John Kenneth and Inez Estelle (McVay) H.; m. William C. Pixley, Apr. 26, 1985; children: William Christopher, Patrick Edward. BS, Eastern Mich. U., 1973. Salesperson Hunter Pub. Co., Winston-Salem, N.C., 1974-76, Josten's-Am., Topeka, 1976-77; editorial asst. Mich. Dept. Agriculture, Lansing, 1977-80, U. Fla., Apopka, 1981-82; pres. Country Carousel, Inc., Mt. Dora, Fla., 1983—; editor, pres. Green Pages Ltd., Mt. Dora, 1984-88; owner, pres. Sunbelt Mktg. Services, Inc., Mt. Dora, 1982—; pub. Fax-It-Green The Hort Fax Directory, 1987—; v.p., treas. Duragreen Mktg., Inc., Mt. Dora, Atlanta, 1990—. Mem. Leadership Am., Fairfax, Va., 1990. Mem. Tex. Assn. Nurserymen, Nat. Assn. Women in Horticulture (v.p., past pres., organizer), Am. Soc. of Advt. Promotion, Fla. Foliage Assn., Fla. Nurserymen and Growers Assn., Mt. Dora C. of C. (exec. bd., bd. dirs., sec. 1988-89, v.p. 1989—), Golden Triangle Reps. Women's Club. (pres.). Republican. Episcopalian. Home: PO Box 908 Zellwood FL 32798 Office: Sunbelt Mktg Svcs Box 1485 Mount Dora FL 32757

HENSLEY, ANNETTE ELAINE, teacher; b. Englewood, N.J., Aug. 12, 1964; d. William Skouras and Maria (Calamaras) Adams; m. Jeffrey Alan Hensley, July 19, 1987. AAS, Waubonsee Community Coll., Sugar Grove, Ill., 1985; BA, Aurora U., 1987; postgrad., Nat. Coll. Edn., 1988-90. Cert. tchr., Ill. Tchr. kindergarten Hillcrest Sch., Hoffman Estates, Ill., 1989—. Mem. Nat. Assn. for the Edn. of Young Children, Assn. for Childhood Edn. Internat. Home: 192 S Waters Edge Dr Glendale Heights IL 60139 Office: 500 Hillcrest Blvd Hoffman Estates IL 60195

HENSLEY, MARGARET ANN, swimming pools distributing company official; b. Knoxville, Tenn., May 6, 1941; d. Herman Geissler and Carrie Lucille (Wilmoth) Ballard; children—Dennis Keith Logan, David Wayne Logan, John Ballard Pecora, Felicia Ann Pecora. Student, Dale Carnegie Sch., 1969, Watterson Coll., Ft. Lauderdale, 1988—. Head subscriptions New Woman mag., Fort Lauderdale, Fla., 1974-75; med. asst. Medi Lab Systems, Fort Lauderdale, 1975-76; mgr. Swimming Pool Owners Assn., Fort Lauderdale, 1976-78; accts. receivable clk. Outdoor World Distbrs., Fort Lauderdale, 1978-81, purchasing agt., 1984, asst. mgr., 1986; credit mgr. Miller Assocs., Miami, Fla., 1981-83, adminstrv. mgr., Miller Miami Br., 1986-87; with Safety Plus, Inc., Louisville, 1987-88; rep. customer svc. Pool Water Products, 1988; br. mgr. Miller Assocs., 1988-89; coord. inside sales swimming pool div. Gorman Co., Inc., Ocala, Fla., 1989—. Named to Hon. Order of Ky. Cols., Gov. of Ky., 1986-87. Mem. Nat. Assn. Female Execs., Gold Coast Women in Credit. Avocations: golfing, bowling, art.

HENSLEY, MARY LYNNE FLOYD, health services administrator; b. Covington, Ky., June 6, 1952; d. Robert Forsythe and Maysie McDowell (Williams) Floyd; m. Carl Evans Hensley II, Apr. 15, 1972; children: Carl Evans III, John Thomas, James Michael. Student, Am. U., Washington, D.C., 1970-71; AS, N.Y. State U., Albany, 1983; BBA with high distinction, U. Iowa, 1985; postgrad., U. Iowa Advanced Mgmt. Inst., 1990. Acctg. technician R&D VA Med. Ctr., Iowa City, 1982-86; adminstr. Dept. Neurology, U. Iowa, Iowa City, 1986—; mem. adv. com. Kirkwood Community Coll., Cedar Rapids, Iowa, 1986—. Mem. PTA, Iowa City, 1982—, found. rep., 1989-90; pack com. chmn. ts, Boy Scouts Am., 1987-88, pack treas., 1988-89, den leader, 1986-89, troop merit badge instr., 1989—. Am. U. scholar, 1970-71, E. Lester Williams scholar, U. Iowa, 1984-85, Ponder Fund scholar U. Iowa, 1985. Mem. Nat. Assn. Accts., Med. Group Mgmt. Assn., Iowa Med. Group Mgmt. Assn, Assn. Profl. and Faculty Women, Am. Coll. Healthcare Execs., Healthcare Fin. Mgmt. Assn., Mortar Board, Omicron Delta Kappa, Beta Alpha Psi, Alpha Sigma Lambda, Beta Gamma Sigma, Phi Eta Sigma. Democrat. Methodist. Office: U Iowa Dept Neurology 2153 RCP Iowa City IA 52242

HENSON, ANNA MIRIAM MORGAN, educator; b. Springfield, Mo., Nov. 7, 1935; d. Bert Emerson and Esther Miriam (Crank) Morgan; m. O'Dell Williams Henson Jr., Aug. 1, 1964; 1 child, Phillip William. AB, Park Coll., 1957; MA, Smith Coll., 1959; postgrad., Australian Nat. U., Canberra, 1959-60; PhD, Yale U., 1967. Instr. Smith Coll., Northampton, Mass., 1960-61; rsch. assoc. Yale U., New Haven, 1968-74; with U. N.C., Chapel Hill, 1975—, rsch. assoc. prof. Sch. of Medicine, 1981-84, rsch. prof. Sch. of Medicine, 1984—. Office: U NC Dept Surg DivOtolaryngology Chapel Hill NC 27599

HENSON, CYNTHIA LYNN, systems analyst; b. Columbus, Miss., Mar. 19, 1958; d. Harlan Everett and Barbara Ann (Crocker) H. AS in Bus., Nat. U., 1982, BBA in Bus., 1983, MBA in Bus., 1985. Electronics asst. Serr Vendors, San Diego, 1974-77; prodn. control scheduler Topaz Inc., 1977-83; with Gen. Dynamics, San Diego, 1983-87, mgr. info. systems electronics div., 1987-89, mgr. total quality electronics div., 1989—. Vice chmn. corp. U.S. Savs. Bond Dr., 1990—; bd. dirs. Easter Seal Soc. San Diego County, 1990—. YWCA Tribute to Women in Industry Svc. award, 1988. Mem. Nat. Mgmt. Assn. (v.p. 1987-88). Office: Gen Dynamics Electronics 9601 Ridgehaven Ct MZ8282C San Diego CA 92123

HENSON, GENE ETHRIDGE, legal administrator; b. Lawrenceville, Ga., Sept. 26, 1924; d. Fred Golden and Cora Jewell (Smith) Ethridge; student public schs., Lawrenceville; m. James Arthur Henson, May 2, 1948 (dec.); 1 dau., Gena Arlene. With Smith, Currie & Hancock, Atlanta, 1959—, adminstr., 1965—. Ofcl. hostess for State of Ga., So. Gov.'s Conf., Atlanta, 1971; past adult tchr. First Bapt. Ch., Lawrenceville; mem. adv. council Center for Profl. Edn., Ga. State U., 1980-84. Mem. Am. Bar Assn. (assoc.), Assn. Legal Adminstrs. (nat. v.p. 1979—, dir. 1979-83), Atlanta Assn. Legal Execs. (1st pres. 1975), Assn. Legal Adminstrs. (v.p. Atlanta chpt., pres.-elect 1986-87, pres. 1987-88). Home: 74 Scenic Hwy Lawrenceville GA 30245 Office: Smith Currie & Hancock Harris Tower 2600 Peachtree Ctr Atlanta GA 30043

HENTZ, ANN LOUISE, English educator; b. Phila., June 23, 1921; d. Robert Alexander and Elizabeth (Jones) H. BA with high honors, U. Rochester, 1950; MA, Ohio State U., Columbus, 1951, PhD, 1956. Instr. Lake Forest (Ill.) Coll., 1956-58; asst. prof. Lake Forest (Ill.) Coll., 1958-65, assoc. prof., 1965-81, prof., 1981-86, prof. emerita, 1986—. Contbr. articles to profl. jours. Mem. Phi Sigma Iota, Phi Beta Kappa. Democrat. Mem. Society of Friends. Home: 870 Woodbine Ln Lake Forest IL 60045

HENTZ, MARIE EVA, real estate investor and developer; b. Detroit, Sept. 27, 1920; d. Charles and Eva (Follman) Hentz. Student Detroit Bus. U., Wayne State U. Draftsman, Cadillac Motor Co., Detroit, 1941-44; stenographer Great Lakes Steel Co., River Rouge, Mich., 1945-46, Can. Nat. R.R., Detroit, 1946-49; sec. UNOCAL, L.A., 1950-72; real estate investor, mgr., developer, Coto de Caza, Calif., 1950—; gen. ptnr. Hentz & Christensen, Ltd., South El Monte, Calif., 1953-86, Hentz Properties, Ltd., Burbank, 1971—. Mem. Union Oil Alumni, Coto Valley Country Club, Women's League of Coto de Caza. Republican. Avocations: gardening, reading, travel.

HEPBURN, KATHARINE HOUGHTON, actress; b. Hartford, Conn., Nov. 8, 1909; d. Thomas N. and Katharine (Houghton) H.; m. Ludlow Ogden Smith (div.). Student, Bryn Mawr Coll, 1928. Actress: (films) A Bill of Divorcement, 1932, Christopher Strong, 1933, Morning Glory, 1933 (Acad. award for best performance by actress 1934), Little Women, 1933, Spitfire, 1934, The Little Minister, 1934, Alice Adams, 1935, Break of Hearts, 1935, Sylvia Scarlett, 1936, Mary of Scotland, 1936, A Woman Rebels, 1936, Quality Street, 1937, Stage Door, 1937, Bringing up Baby, 1938, Holiday, 1938, The Philadelphia Story, 1940 (N.Y. Critic's award 1940), Woman of the Year, 1941, Keeper of the Flame, 1942, Stage Door Canteen, 1943, Dragon Seed, 1944, Undercurrent, 1946, Sea of Grass, 1946, Song of Love, 1947, State of the Union, 1948, Adam's Rib, 1949, The African Queen, 1951, Pat and Mike, 1952, Summertime, 1955, The Rainmaker, 1956, The Iron Petticoat, 1956, The Desk Set, 1957, Suddenly Last Summer, 1959, Long Day's Journey into Night, 1962, Guess Who's Coming to Dinner, 1967, (Acad. award for best actress 1968),The Lion in Winter, 1968 (Acad. award for best actress 1969), Madwoman of Chaillot, 1969, Trojan Women, 1971, A Delicate Balance, 1973, Rooster Cogburn, 1975, Olly, Olly, Oxen Free, 1978, On Golden Pond, 1981 (Acad. award for best actress 1981), The Ultimate Solution of Grace Quigley, 1985, (plays) The Czarina, 1928, The Big Pond, 1928, Night Hostess, 1928, These Days,

1928, Death Takes a Holiday, 1929, A Month in the Country, 1930, Art and Mrs. Bottle, 1930, The Warrior's Husband, 1932, Lysistrata, 1932, The Lake, 1933, Jane Eyre, 1937, The Philadelphia Story, 1939, Without Love, 1942, As You Like It, 1950, The Millionairess, Eng. and U.S.A., 1952, The Taming of the Shrew, The Merchant of Venice, Measure for Measure,, Eng. and Australia, 1955, Merchant of Venice, Much Ado about Nothing, Am. Shakespeare Festival, 1957, toured later, 1958, Twelfth Night, Antony and Cleopatra, Am. Shakespeare Festival, 1960, Coco, 1969-70, toured, 1971, The Taming of the Shrew, 1970, A Matter of Gravity, 1976-78, West Side Waltz, 1981, (TV movies) The Glass Menagerie, 1973, Love among the Ruins, 1975, The Corn Is Green, 1979, Mrs. Delafield Wants to Marry, 1986; Laura Lansing Slept Here, 1988; author: The Making of the African Queen, 1987. Recipient gold medal as world's best motion picture actress Internat. Motion Picture Expn., Venice, Italy, 1934; ann. award Shakespeare Club, N.Y.C., 1950; award Whistler Soc., 1957; Woman of Yr. award Hasty Pudding Club, 1958; outstanding achievement award for fostering finest ideals of acting profession, 1980; lifetime achievement award Council Fashion Designers Am., 1986. Office: William Morris Agy 151 El Camino Beverly Hills CA 90212 also: PO Box 17-154 West Hartford CT 06117*

HEPBURN, TRACY L., secretary; b. Augusta, Maine, Apr. 8, 1962; d. Harry C. and Marlene L. Everett; m. William Hepburn, Sept. 5, 1987. Student, U. South Maine. Cert. image and communication, personal lines ins. Former owner Hepburn Cleaning, Bath, Maine; med. sec. Brunswick (Maine) Manor; office mgr. Roebuck Real Estate, Bath; personal lines asst. underwriter Northern MGA, Fairfield, Maine. Leader church orgns. Mem. Nat. Exec. Housekeepers Assn., NAFE, Women's Bus. Devel. Corp. Republican. Baptist. Home: 30A High St Bath ME 04530

HEPPNER, GLORIA HILL, science foundation administrator, researcher; b. Gt. Falls, Mont., May 30, 1940; d. Eugene Merrill and Georgia M. (Swanson) Hill; m. Frank Henry Heppner, June 6, 1964 (div. 1975); 1 child, Michael Berkeley. BA, U. Calif., Berkeley, 1962, MA, 1964, PhD, 1967. Damon Runyon postdoctoral fellow U. Wash., Seattle, 1967-69; asst. and assoc. prof. Brown U., Providence, 1969-79, Herbert Fanger meml. lectr., 1988; chmn. dept. immunology, dir. labs., sr. v.p. Mich. Cancer Found., Detroit, 1979—; mem. external adv. com. basic sci. program M.D. Anderson Hosp. and Tumor Clinic, Houston, 1984—; mem. external adv. com. Case Western Res. U. Cancer Ctr., Cleve., 1988—; Sarah Stewart meml. lectr. Georgetown U., Washington, 1988. Editor: Macrophages and Cancer, 1988; mem. editorial bd. Cancer Rsch., 1989—, Jour. Nat. Cancer Inst., 1988, Sci., 1988—; contbr. over 200 articles to sci. jours. Recipient Mich. Sci. Trail-Blazer award State of Mich., 1987; fellow Damon Runyon-Walter Winchell Found., 1967-69. Mem. AAAS, Am. Assn. for Cancer Rsch. (bd. dirs. 1983-86, chmn. long range planning com. 1989—), Am. Assn. Immunologists, Metastasis Rsch. Soc. (bd. dirs. 1985-89), Women in Cancer Rsch. (nat. pres.), Internat. Differentiation Soc. (v.p. 1990—), LWV (bd. dirs. Grosse Pointe, Mich. 1989—). Democrat. Office: Mich Cancer Found 110 E Warren Ave Detroit MI 48201

HERALD, CHERRY LOU, research educator, research director; b. Beeville, Tex., Dec. 23, 1940; d. Edwin Sherley and Margaret Lucille (Caron) Bell; m. Delbert Leon Herald, Jr., July 31, 1964; children: Heather Amanda, Delbert Leon, III. BS, Ariz. State U., 1962, MS, 1965, PhD, 1968. Faculty rsch. assoc. Cancer Rsch. Inst. Ariz. State U., Tempe, 1973-74, sr. rsch. chemist Cancer Rsch. Inst., 1974-77, asst. to dir. and sr. rsch. chemist Cancer Rsch. Inst., 1977-83, asst. dir., assoc. rsch. prof. Cancer Rsch. Inst., 1984-88, assoc. dir., rsch. prof. Cancer Rsch. Inst., 1988—. Co-author: Biosynthetic Products for Cancer Chemotherapy, vols. 4, 5, & 6, 1984, 85, 87, sci. jours. Mem. Am. Soc. Pharmacognosy, Am. Chem. Soc. Office: Ariz State U Cancer Rsch Inst Tempe AZ 85287-2404

HERALD-SOWERS, ANITA ANN, business educator; b. Williamson, W.Va., Feb. 11, 1959; d. Edward Eugene and Rena Faye (Maynard) Herald; m. Frank Robertson Sowers Jr., Mar. 20, 1982; children: Brittni Renee and Brandon Edward. AS with honors, Bluefield State, 1979; BS in Bus. Edn., Concord Coll., 1981, BSBA summa cum laude, 1981; MS in Bus., Va. Tech., 1982. Asst. to inventory and receiving dir. Bluefield (W.Va.) State Coll., 1980; bus. instr. Bluefield HIgh Sch., 1981; asst. to pres., inventory mgr., personnel dir. Priss Prints Inc., Bluefield, 1983-84; computer operator, customer svc. rep. First Fed. Savs. & Loan, Princeton, W.Va., 1984-85; ops. asst., computer operator Flat Top Nat. Bank Trust Dept., Bluefield, 1985-86; customer svc. rep. credit dept. JcPenney Co., Bluefield, 1978-84. Mem. Nat. Bus. Edn. Assn., Alpha Chi, Phi Beta Lambda, Delta Pi Epsilon. Home: 1284 Brandl Dr Marietta GA 30060

HERBEIN, BONNIE FLEMING, purchasing consultant, former casino-hotel company executive; b. Morristown, N.J., Mar. 27, 1955; d. Douglas Haig and Mildred Lillian (Lachenauer) F.; m. Frank J. Herbein, Feb. 7, 1987; BA, Stockton State Coll., Pomona, N.J., 1977; student Susquehanna U., Selinsgrove, Pa., 1973-75. Exec. trainee, Montgomery Ward's, Johnson City, N.Y., 1977-79; systems analyst Reese Pally-Zipp Ltd., Atlantic City, 1979-80; retail shop mgr. Holiday Inn Harrahs Casino, Atlantic City, 1980; asst. dir. purchasing Ramada Tropicana Casino, Atlantic City, 1980-82; dir. purchasing Del Webb Claridge Casino, Atlantic City, 1982-86; pres. B.F. Inc., 1986—; v.p. purchasing Bertram Constrn. div. Perlman Properties, 1987-89, Viking Constrn., 1988-89. Vice chairperson N.J.-Pa.-Del. Regional Minority Council, Phila., 1985-86. Mem. Atlantic City Purchasing Assn. (pres. 1986-87), NAFE. Republican. Episcopalian. Home: 112 Roosevelt Ave Northfield NJ 08225 Office: Rainbow Constn 112 Roosevelt Ave Northfield NJ 08225

HERBENER, PATRICIA WENDY, risk management executive; b. Portland, Oreg., Dec. 23, 1945; d. Nels Bernhardt Jr. and Diana Dorothy (Hoogstraat) Palmquist. BA in History, North Park Coll., 1969. Claims rep. CNA Ins. Co., Los Alamitos, Calif., 1969-72; mgr. claims Ins. Co. N.Am., Los Angeles, 1972-80; regional supr. Crown Zellerbach Corp., Los Angeles, 1980-82; asst. v.p. Alexsis Risk Mgmt. Services Inc. subs. Alexander and Alexander, West Covina, Calif., 1982—. Mem. Calif. Self-Ins. Assn., Californians for Compensation Reform Policy Com., Calif. Assn. Svc. Orgns. (legis. chmn.). Republican. Office: Alexsis Risk Mgmt Svcs Inc 1501 W Cameron Ave #C-300 West Covina CA 91790

HERBERT, CLAIRE DONALDSON, account executive; b. London, Feb. 19, 1960; d. Henry S. and Joan S. (Wilkinson) Donaldson; m. John A. Herbert, Aug. 30, 1986. BJ, U. Tex., 1981. Advt. sales mgr. U. Tex. Publs., Arlington, 1981-83; E.D. DBG&H Advt. Agy., Dallas, 1983-84; advt./promo mgr. Siemens Med. Systems, Union, N.J., 1984-86; corp. account mgr. Market Source, Cranbury, N.J., 1986-89, Nat. Creative Mktg. Internat., Inc., Monmouth Beach, N.J., 1989—. Bd. trustees Huntington's Disease Found., N.J. Mem. Tex. Execs., PMAA. Democrat. Methodist. Office: Nat Creative Mktg Internat Inc PO Box 85 Monmouth Beach NJ 07750

HERBERT, MARILYNNE, public relations executive, freelance photographer; b. Columbus, Ga., Aug. 12, 1944; d. Herbert Paul and Victoria (Raskin) Gruber; m. Victor Daniel Herbert, June 23, 1968 (div. 1990); children: Alissa, Laura. BA, Colo. Woman's Coll., 1966. Adminstrv. asst. pub. rels. dept. Mt. Sinai Med. Ctr., N.Y.C., 1966-68; freelance photographer N.Y.C., 1977—; pub. rels. account exec. Ruder-Finn, Inc., N.Y.C., 1986—. Bd. dirs. Women of Westchester, White Plains, N.Y., 1977—, Byrdcliffe Performing Arts Orgn., New Rochelle, N.Y., 1987—, Nat. Women's Polit. Caucus, Westchester County, 1988—, Sr. Personnel Placement Bur., Inc., 1989—; bd. dirs., sec. New Rochelle Community Fund, 1986—. Recipient Spl. Recognition award Nat. Women's Polit. Caucus, 1989. Mem. Am. Soc. Mag. Photographer's, Silvermine Guild Artists. Jewish. Home: 88 Walworth Ave Scarsdale NY 10583 Office: Ruder-Finn Inc 301 E 57th St New York NY 10022

HERBERT, MARY E., personnel director; b. Pontypool, Wales, Mar. 27, 1945; d. Haywood and Catherine Olwyn (Snook) Robinson; m. John T. Herbert Jr., May 5, 1984; children: Stephanie, Travis, Suzanne, Jason. BA, Glassboro State Coll., 1967; MA, Cen. Mich. U., 1978. V.p. personnel Pitney Bowes, Inc., Stamford, Conn., dir. employee rels., mgr. sales tng. Home: 6 Gaxton Rd Stamford CT 06905

HERBERT, MARY KATHERINE ATWELL, free-lance writer; b. Grove City, Pa., Dec. 9, 1945; d. Perry Stewart and Luella Irene (Brown) Atwell; m. Roland Marcus Herbert, July 20, 1963; children: Stephen Todd, Amy Elizabeth, Jill Anne. BA, Ariz. State U., 1968, MA, 1973; film cert., U. So. Calif., 1978. Dir. promotion and advt. Maricopa County Fair, Phoenix, 1976; film writer Scottsdale Daily Progress, 1976-79; dir. pub. relations Phoenix Little Theatre, 1980-85; script analyst, 1985-86; exec. asst. to v.p. prodn. DeLaurentiis Entertainment Group, 1986; producer's assoc. film TRAXX, 1986-87; devel. assoc. Debin/DeVore Prodns., 1988-89; free-lance writer Glendale, Calif., 1989—. script writer TV shows Trial By Jury, Dick Clark Prodn., Green Eyes, Dry Heat, others. Mem. Encanto Homeowners Assn., Phoenix, 1976-80. Mem. Women in Communications, AAUW, Kappa Delta Pi, Pi Lambda Theta.

HERBIN, REECE A., family therapist; b. Greensboro, N.C., Oct. 27, 1946; d. Howard and Mary Louise (Headen) H. BA, U. D.C., 1973; MS, Nova U., 1982. Cert. LSWA. Soc. worker D.C. Pub. Defender Svc., Washington, 1972-76; social worker Yadkin-Surry County Mental Health, Yadkinville, N.C., 1982-83; family therapist Washington Assessment and Therapy Svcs., 1986-89, Focus/Home Intervention Program, Washington, 1986-88, Change Inc., Washington, 1989-90, Beal & Assocs., Atlanta, 1990—. Mem. NAFE, DC Mental Health Assn., Am. Assn. for Counseling and Devel., Am. Mental Health Counselor Assn., Nat. Black Social Workers, Nat. Black Child Devel. Inst. Mem. A.M.E. Ch. Home and Office: 2306 Old Gate Ct Fort Washington MD 20744

HERBISON, ROBIN J., consultant; b. Sidney, Oct. 24, 1961; d. Robert John and Emma S. (Miller) H. AB, Brown U., 1979-83; postgrad., Johns Hopkins U., 1988. Self-employed independent cons. Providence, R.I., 1981-85; cons. Databasics, Inc., Providence, R.I., 1985-86; info. systems analyst JHU Applied Physics Lab, Laurel, Md., 1986-88; sr. analyst JYACC, Inc., NYC; mem. Computers in Medicine seminar, China, 1986. Mem. Assn. for Computing Machinery, Nat. Assn. Emergency Med. Technicians.

HERBOLD-WOOTTEN, HEIDI, academic councilman; b. Oberndorf, Fed. Republic Germany, Dec. 24, 1936; came to U.S., 1978; d. Wolfgang Konrad Jakob and Ottilie Sophie (Küster) Herbold; m. Thomas Franklin Wootten, Apr. 12, 1978. Cert. in psychology, U. Cologne, Fed. Republic Germany, 1962, PhD, 1965. Lic. psychologist, Va. Asst. prof. U. Cologne, Fed. Republic Germany, 1962-78; pres. Inst. Applied Polygraph Sci., Virginia Beach, Va., 1979—; adj. prof. St. Leo Coll., Norfolk, Va., 1979—. Contbr. articles to profl. jours. Recipient study visit award NATO, 1968, Deutsche Forschungsgemeinschaft, 1976. Mem. AAAS, Am. Psychol. Assn., Am. Polygraph Assn. (chmn. com. rsch. and info. 1986-87), Va. Polygraph Assn. (v.p. 1983), Soc. Psychophysiological Rsch., Soc. Psychol. Study of Social Issues. Office: Inst Applied Polygraph Sci PO Box 5664 Virginia Beach VA 23455

HERBST, DELLA, state legislator; b. Wheeler, Minn., Feb. 26, 1935; d. Raymond C. and Lillian S. Wilson; m. John Lowell Herbst, 1954; children: John Lowell Jr., Perry L., Matthew. State rep. from Sheridan County Wyo. Ho. of Reps., 1983-86; state senator Wyo. Senate, Cheyenne, 1987—; chmn. Sheridan County Dem. Com., 1981-83, com. mem., 1987—. Democrat. Lutheran. Home: 353 W Mountain View Dr Sheridan WY 82801 Office: State Senate Cheyenne WY 82002*

HERBST, MARIE ANTOINETTE, state senator; m. Paul Herbst. BA, Albany State Tchr.'s Coll.; Masters, Columbia U.; postgrad. secondary sch. adminstrn., U. Conn. Former pub. sch. tchr. East Windsor, Conn.; now mem. Conn. State Senate from 35th Dist.; in 4th term as mayor Town of Vernon; chmn. pub. safety com.; asst. majority leader, 1989—; mem. fin., revenue, bonding com., 1989; mem. edn. com. Lector, Sacred Heart Ch.; past chmn. High Sch. CCD Sch.; past mem. Ladies of Sacred Heart; mem. Tri-Town Disabled Com., Vernon Town Council, 1975-79; past mem. Vernon Bd. Edn.; mem. Adult Edn. Adv. Commn., 1985; treas. Capitol Region Council of Govts., 1985. Mem. Internat. Edn. Assn., Nat. Edn. Assn., Conn. Edn. Assn., Phi Delta Kappa, Gamma Kappa Rho. Democrat. Roman Catholic. Home: 245 Brandy Hill Rd Vernon CT 06066 Office: Legis Office Bldg Capitol Ave Hartford CT 06106*

HERD, CHARMIAN JUNE, educator, singer, actress; b. Waterville, Maine, June 1, 1930; d. Samuel Braid and Jennie May (Lang) Herd; B.A., Colby Coll., 1950; postgrad. Boston U., 1951, EdM, U. Maine, 1965; edni. cert. No. Conservatory, Bangor, Maine, 1954; also study voice with Roger A. Nye. Dir. music State Sch. for Girls, Hallowell, Maine, 1950-51; head English, French, dramatics depts. St. George High Sch., Tenants Harbor, 1951-52; dir. music pub. schs. Albion and Unity, 1952-54, Troy, Freedom, Maine, 1953-54; dir. music pub. sch. system Belgrade, Maine, Waterville Jr. High Sch., 1954-55; dir. vocal music Waterville Jr. and Sr. high schs., 1954-58; head English and dramatics depts. Besse High Sch., Albion, 1959-62; tchr. French, Skowhegan Jr. High Sch., 1962-63; tchr. French, English, Skowhegan Sr. High Sch., 1963-69; tchr. French, Lawrence Sr. High Sch., Fairfield, Maine, 1969-71, chmn. drama and speech dept., 1972-79; instr. dramatics U. Maine, Farmington, 1969-70; tchr. conversational French, Skowhegan Adult Edn. Sch., 1963-69, drama instr., 1965-69; dance asst. Plaza Studio; producer, appeared in role of Vera, Mame, Waterville; soloist various churches, Maine, 1951—; mus. dir. children's sect., performing mem. Theater at Monmouth, Maine, 1970—, mem. exec. bd., 1976—, sec. bd. trustees, 1977—; performing mem. Augusta Players, Camden Civic Theatre, Portland Lyric Theatre, Waterville Players, Titipu Choral Soc., Waterville Community Ballet, Choral Arts Soc., Portland, Maine, 1980—, Riverside Theatre Co., Vero Beach, Indian River Ctr. for Arts; theatre chmn. ann. Maine Festival Arts, Bowdoin Coll., 1978—; soloist Vero Beach Chorale Soc., numerous club, ch., conv., coll. concerts, oratorios; performing mem. Vero Beach Solo Gates, Encore Alley Theatre, Esprit des Amis, Vero Beach, Ft. Pierce City Ballet, Fla.; treas. Coast Opera Co., Ft. Pierce, Fla., 1986—. Bd. dirs. Opera New Eng., 1980—, Portland Lyric Theatre, 1982—Mem. Waterville Friends Music, DAR, Waterville Theatre Guild (charter mem., pres. 1967—), Vero Beach Theatre Guild (Fla.), Encore Alley Theatre, Vero Beach, Waterville Bus. and Profl. Women's Club (program chmn. 1957-58, v.p. 1958-59, pres. 1959-61, chmn. drama dept. 1961, drama and music chmn. 1961—), Fla. Profl. Theatre Assn., Ednl. Speech and Theatre Assn. Maine (mem. exec. bd., pres. 1972-74), Maine Profl.-Community Theatre Assn. (mem. organizing com.), Actors Equity Assn., Albion-Burnham Tchrs. Club (sec. 1960-61), NEA, Maine Tchrs. Assn., New Eng. Theatre Conf. (exec. bd. 1976—, 1st v.p. 1976-77, conf. chmn. 1977), Theatre Assn. Maine (membership chmn. 1972-73, 2d v.p. 1973-74, exec. bd. 1972—, exec. sec. 1975—, state pres. 1976—), Internat. Platform Assn., Nat. Assn. Tchrs. of Singing (sec. Maine chpt. 1980—), Pine Tree Post Card Club (exec. bd., Spring show chmn. 1979-80, pres. 1982-84), Maine Hist. Soc., Bay State Post Card Club, R.I. Post Card Club. Club: Cecilia (Augusta, Maine). Composer sacred music: Babylon, 1959, The Greatest of These is Love, 1961, Pan; Keep Not Thy Silence, O God, Remember Now Thy Creator, Slow, Slow, Fresh Fount, A Witch's Charm, Hymn to God the Father. Avocations: acting, singing, oil painting, collecting opera and operetta scores. Home and Office: PO Box 714 Roseland FL 32957

HERFORTH, SANDRA LEE, engineering company executive; b. Omaha, Dec. 27, 1951; d. Samuel and Marion Elaine (Otte) H.; m. Leonard Christian Hebbert, Oct. 11, 1981; children: Jason Paul Herforth-Hebbert, Lisa Marie Herforth-Hebbert. Student, Boston U. Musician Mpls. and St. Paul Civic Orchs., 1970-71, various recording studios, Mpls., 1971-72; opening mgr. Formaggio, Inc., Cambridge, Mass., 1976-77; owner, gen mgr. Herforth Motors, Boston, 1972-87; regional sales adminstr. FOR-A Corp. Am., Newton, Mass., 1987-89; branch office mgr. Landy Assocs., Inc., Waltham, Mass., 1989—. Performed with renowned blues musician Sam Chapman (formerly of The Miss. Sheiks), 1974. Musician Lincoln (Nebr.) Youth Symphony, 1965-70; mem. Sci. Mus., Boston, 1989—; sec. coun. Faith Luth. Ch., Cambridge, 1981-85. Music scholar Augsburg Coll., Mpls., 1971. Mem. NAFE. Democrat. Home: 25 Wilson Park Brighton MA 02135 Office: Landy Assocs Inc 330 Bear Hill Rd Waltham MA 02154

HERGENHAN, JOYCE, public relations executive; b. Mt. Kisco, N.Y., Dec. 30, 1941; d. John Christopher and Goldie (Wago) H. B.A., Syracuse U., 1963; M.B.A., Columbia U., 1978. Reporter White Plains Reporter Dispatch, 1963-64; asst. to Rep. Ogden R. Reid Washington, 1964-68; reporter Gannett Newspapers, 1968-72; with Consol. Edison Co. of N.Y., Inc., N.Y.C., 1972-82, v.p., 1977-79, sr. v.p. pub. affairs, 1979-82; v.p. corp. pub. relations General Electric Co., Fairfield, Conn., 1982—. Office: GE 3135 Easton Turnpike Fairfield CT 06431

HERIS, TONI, psychologist, psychotherapist; b. Chgo., Feb. 28, 1932; d. Nicholas John and Mildred (Mangani) H.; m. Stan Harrison, Aug. 25, 1972. BA, Queens Coll., N.Y.C., 1954; MA, NYU, 1981, PhD, 1987, post-grad. Lic. psychologist, N.Y. Advt. cons./writer N.Y.C., 1971-86; career counselor NYU, N.Y.C., 1979-88; staff psychotherapist Ctr. for Marital & Family Therapy, N.Y.C., 1985-88; asst. prof. Baruch Coll. of City of N.Y., 1988—; pvt. practice psychology N.Y.C., 1987—; dir. career devel. Nat. Inst. for the Psychotherapies, N.Y.C., 1987—. Mem. Am. Psychol. Assn., Am. Assn. for Counseling & Devel., Kappa Delta Pi. Office: 9 E 68th St 34 New York NY 10021

HERITAGE, SHARON K., medical technologist; b. Muncie, Ind., Aug. 8, 1955. BS, Ball State U., 1977; MBA, Ind. Wesleyan U., 1990. Mgr. quality assurance SciCor, Inc., Indpls., lab. mgr.; asst. supr. chemistry Ball Meml. Hosp., Muncie, Ind. Mem. NAFE, Am. Soc. for Clin. Pathologists, Am. Soc. for Med. Technologists. Office: SciCor Inc 8200 SciCor Dr Indianapolis IN 46234

HERMAN, ANDREA MAXINE, newspaper editor; b. Chgo., Oct. 22, 1938; d. Maurice H. and Mae (Baron) H.; m. Joseph Schmidt, Oct. 28, 1962. BJ, U. Mo., 1960. Feature writer Chgo.'s American, 1960-63; daily columnist News American, Balt., 1963-67; feature writer Mainichi Daily News, Tokyo, 1967-69; columnist Iowa City Press-Citizen, 1969-76; music and drama critic San Diego Tribune, 1976-84; asst. mng. editor features UPI, Washington, 1984-86, asst. mng. editor news devel., 1986-87; mng. editor features L.A. Herald Examiner, 1987—. Recipient 1st and 2d prizes for features in arts James S. Copley Ring of Truth Awards, 1st prize for journalism Press Club San Diego. Mem. Soc. Profl. Journalists, Am. Soc. Newspaper Editors, AP Mng. Editors, Women in Communications. Office: LA Herald Examiner 1111 S Broadway Los Angeles CA 90015

HERMAN, BARBARA F., psychologist; b. Chgo., June 11, 1941; d. Nathan Herbert and Ruth (Hollander) Cohen; m. Avrum Herman, June 24, 1938 (div. Apr. 1984); children: Leslie, Marcia, Ellie. BA, U. Wash., 1962; MS, Butler U., 1976; PhD, Ind. State U., 1981. Registered psychologist; cert. tchr., Ind. Intern Riley Hosp. for Children, 1979-80, Butler U. Counseling Ctr., Indpls., 1978, Ind. State U. Counselor Edn., Terre Haute, 1979; counseling psychologist MetroHealth, 1981-85, assoc. dir. mental health svcs., 1985-86, dir. mental health svcs., 1986—; elem. and secondary tchr. various, Indpls., Seattle, Chgo., 1959-75; adj. prof. grad. div., counseling and psyhometrics, Butler U., 1982—; presenter seminars in field. Mem. gov.'s task force on Alzheimer's Disease and Related Dementias; bd. dirs. Jewish Family and Children's Svcs., Congregation Beth-El Zedeck; vol. Dem. cand. for gov. of Ind., Indpls., 1983, others. Democrat. Mem. Am. Psychol. Assn., Ind. Psychol. Assn., Am. Assn. Counseling and Devel., Mental Health Assn., Ind. State Mental Health Assn. (pub. policy com.). Office: MetroHealth 7160 Shadeland Station Way Indianapolis IN 46256

HERMAN, CAROL KORNGUT, advertising agency executive; b. Atlantic City, Oct. 14, 1952; d. Richard F. and Regina (Kornblau) Korngut; m. Henry Lewis Herman, Dec. 30, 1972; children—Matthew, Gregory. B.A., U. Pa., 1972. Asst. account exec. Honig-Cooper and Harrington Advt., N.Y.C., 1973-74; asst. account exec. Grey Advt., N.Y.C., 1974-75, account exec., 1976-78, account supr., 1978-80, v.p., mgmt. supr., 1981-84, v.p., group mgmt. supr., 1985-87, sr. v.p., 1987—. Office: Grey Advt Inc 777 3rd Ave New York NY 10017

HERMAN, CHLOE ANNA, broker manager; b. Chgo., Dec. 8, 1937; d. Robert Marius and Hope Manolatos; m. Ben Howse Herman, Oct. 16, 1960; children: Holly, Benjamin Andrew, Robert. BA, Northwestern U., 1959. Broker-assoc. Kole Real Estate, DesPlaines, Ill., 1972-76; broker-mgr. Century 21 Northwest, DesPlaines, 1976-77; broker-assoc. Wm. L. Kunkel & Co., DesPlaines, 1978-88; broker-mgr. Re/Max Suburban, Inc., Arlington Heights, Ill., 1988—; pres. AAUW N.W. Suburban br., 1984-86. Past pres. Three Hierarchs, St. John The Baptist Ch.; dir. Holy Family Planned Gift Adv. Coun., 1986, United Way, DesPlaines, 1990—. Mem. Womens Coun. Realtors (pres. elect 1989-90), N.W. Suburban Assn. Realtors (various coms. 1972—), Cert. Residential Specialists (charter), Cert. Real Estate Appraisers (sr. designated), Kiwanis. Office: Re/Max Suburban Inc 330 E Northwest Hwy Mount Prospect IL 60056

HERMAN, EDITH CAROL, public relations executive; b. Edgewood, Md., July 1, 1944; d. Herbert R. and Thirza E. (Simmons) H.; m. Leonard Wiener. B.A., Purdue U., 1966. Reporter Hollister Newspaper Chain, Wilmette, Ill., 1966-68; reporter Chgo. Tribune Newspaper, 1968-79, edn. editor, 1971-74, feature writer, 1976-79; sr. editor TV Digest Inc., 1980-83; pub. relations mgr. Am. Tel. & Tel., 1983—. Recipient Journalism award Ill. Edn. Assn., 1969-70; Editorial award Ill. Automatic Merchandising Council, 1977. Mem. Sigma Delta Chi. Home: 5501 Burling Ct Bethesda MD 20817

HERMAN, GRACE GALES, physician, poet; b. Lawrence, N.Y., May 12, 1926; d. Samuel Gales and Frances (Gleberman) Roberts; m. Roland Barry Herman, July 22, 1945 (div. Oct. 1981); children: Gail Ellen, Joan Elizabeth. BA, Cornell U., 1945; MD, Columbia U., 1949. Intern Mt. Sinai Hosp., N.Y.C., 1949-50; resident White Plains Hosp., N.Y., 1950-51; cancer researcher, gynecologist Columbia Coll. of Physician and Surgeon, N.Y.C., 1957-62; gynecologist Mt. Sinai Hosp., N.Y.C., 1962-69; examining physician Met. Life Ins. Co, N.Y., 1969-88. Contbr. articles to profl. jours.; poetry pub. in Colo. Quar., Minn. Rev., Poetry Rev. of Poetry Soc. Am., Purchase (N.Y.) Poetry Rev., Pembroke Mag., Embers, others. Dist. leader White Plains Democratic City Com. 1950-52. Mem. Poetry Soc. of Am., White Plains Democratic Club, Phi Beta Kappa, Alpha Omega Alpha, Phi Kappa Phi. Jewish. Home: 370 First Ave Apt 9c New York NY 10010

HERMAN, LAIL LEWIS, clinical psychologist; b. Chgo., May 3, 1934; d. Robert Leonard and Helen (Lanoff) Lewis; m. Stephen Mark Herman, Aug. 26, 1956; children: Ellen, William, Thomas, Jane. BA, Northwestern U., 1956; MA in Teaching, Harvard U., 1957; PhD, Northwestern U., 1986. Lic. clin. psychologist. English tchr. Leyden High Sch., Franklin Park, Ill., 1957-59, Glenbrook Schs., Northbrook, Ill., 1974-86; psychotherapist, clin. psychologist Roth Group, Northbrook, 1986-88; clin. psychologist Herman Frazier Assocs., Northbrook, 1988—; cons. AT&T, Naperville, Ill., 1986—; with dept. psychiatry U. Chgo., 1989—. Bd. dirs. Alliance for Mentally Ill, Chgo., 1986-90. Office: Herman Frazier Assocs 910 Skokie Blvd 207B Northbrook IL 60062

HERMAN, LYDIA BEATRICE, environmental services company executive; b. N.Y.C., Oct. 31, 1959; d. Bertrand Ian and Judith (Axelrood) H. BA, Dartmouth Coll., 198l; MA, Columbia U., 1985. Rsch. analyst Ctr. for Biology Natural Systems, Queens, N.Y., 198l-83; cons. Urban Resource Systems, Inc., Mexico City, 1983; mgr. tech. svcs. Energy Conservation and Facilities Mgmt. Corp., N.Y.C., 1984-86; exec. asst. to 1st asst. commr. N.Y.C. Div. Pub. Structures, 1986-87, dir. Office Planning and Mgmt. Analysis, 1987-89; exec. asst. to pres. Waste Mgmt. Internat., London, 1989-90; mgr. corp., pub. affairs Waste Mgmt. Europe, London, 1990—. Contbr. articles to profl. jours.

HERMAN, MARY MARGARET, pathologist, educator; b. Plymouth, Wis., July 26, 1935; d. Elmer Fredelein and Esther Lydia (Bross) H.; m. Lucien Jules Rubinstein, Jan. 31, 1969. BS in Med. Sci., U. Wis., 1957, MD, 1960. Diplomate Nat. Bd. Med. Examiners, Am. Bd. Anatomic Pathology, Am. Bd. Neuropathology. Rotating intern Mary Hitchcock Meml. Hosp., Hanover, N.H., 1960-61; resident neurology U. Wis. Hosps., 1961-62; intern pathology Yale U., New Haven, 1962-63, asst. resident in pathology, 1963-64, fellow neuropathology, 1964-65, rsch. assoc. pathology, 1967-68; fellow neuropathology Stanford U., Palo Alto, Calif., 1965-66, fellow, acting instr. neuropathology, 1966-67, asst. prof. pathology, 1967-74, assoc. prof. with tenure pathology, 1974-81; prof., co-dir. div. neuropathology U. Va. Sch. Medicine, Charlottesville, 1981—; vis. asst. prof. Albert Einstein Coll.

Medicine, Bronx, N.Y., 1971-72; mem. Nat. Inst. Neurol. and Communicative Diseases, NIH, program project rev. com., 1973-77; cons. lab. svc. VA Hosp., Salem, Va., 1982—; ad hoc mem. Pathology A Study Section, 1986—. Mem. editorial bd. Jour. Neuropathology and Exptl. Neurology; contbr. about 100 articles to profl. jours. Recipient Rsch. Career Devel. award NIH, 1967-72. Mem. AAAS, Am. Assn. Neuropathologists (Weil award 1974), Am. Assn. Pathologists, Am. Soc. Cell Biology, Internat. Acad. Pathology, Am. Tissue Culture Assn. Home: 303 Rookwood Dr Charlottesville VA 22901 Office: U Va Sch Medicine Dept Pathology Jefferson Park Ave Charlottesville VA 22901

HERMANN, GABRIELLE J., advertising agency executive. BS in Math. and Physics, U. Vienna, Austria; M in Physics, Hunter Coll. Formerly v.p. and gen. mgr. dry package desserts div. Gen. Foods U.S.A., White Plains, N.Y.; sr. v.p. Young & Rubicam N.Y., N.Y.C. Office: Young & Rubicam NY 285 Madison Ave New York NY 10017*

HERMANN, IRENE IRMA, manufacturing executive; b. N.Y.C., Sept. 25, 1914; d. Julius Bruno and Anuska (Gabris) Roesch; m. Marzell Roming, June 1935 (dec. 1957); children: Irene Roming Michaels, Marzell Roming Jr.; m. August Gustav Hermann, Mar. 24, 1960 (dec. 1983). Student, Secretarial Sch., N.Y.C., 1930-32. Sec. William Prym, Inc., N.Y.C., 1932-37; owner, Butcher Shop, Catskill, N.Y., 1937-42; owner Butcher Shop, Saugerties, N.Y., 1942-58; pres., chief exec. officer Methods Tooling and Mfg. Inc., Mt. Marion, N.Y., 1963—. Active in past various civic orgns. and projects. Mem. Saugerties C. of C. (v.p. 1953-57), Profl. Bus. Womens Assn., Kingston Mannerchor, Capitol Hill Club (Washington). Republican. Lutheran. Home: 11 Roming Lane Saugerties NY 12477 Office: Methods Tooling/Mfg Inc PO Box 400 Glasco Tpk Mount Marion NY 12456

HERMANN, MARGARET GLADDEN, political science educator; b. Rogersville, Pa., July 11, 1938; d. James W. and Cynthia E. (Hales) Gladden; m. Charles F. Hermann, June 4, 1960; children: Chris, Karen. BA, DePauw U., 1960; MA, Northwestern U., Evanston, Ill., 1963, PhD, 1965. Postdoctoral fellow Ednl. Testing Svc., Princeton, N.J., 1965-67; rsch. assoc. Mershon Ctr. Ohio State U., Columbus, 1970-86, rsch. scientist Mershon Ctr., 1986—, assoc. prof. polit. sci., 1988-90, prof. polit. sci., 1990—; cons. various govt. agys., 1973—, Worthington (Ohio) Pub. Schs., 1983-86. Editor: A Psychological Examination of Political Leaders, 1977, Political Psychology, 1986; co-author: Foreign Policy Behavior, 1982; editor Polit. Psychology jour., 1980-82; contbr. articles to profl. jours. Trustee, treas. Columbus Met. Women's Ctr., 1980-83; adv. com. Ctr. for Leadership and Change, Urban League, Columbus, 1980-86, Ohio Displaced Homemaker Network, 1986; co-dir. Leadership for the 90s, Columbus, 1988—. Recipient Woodrow Wilson fellowship, 1960-62, NIMH postdoctoral fellowship Edn. Testing Svc., 1965-67, award AAUW, 1985. Mem. Internat. Studies Assn. (v.p., chmn. publs. com. 1982, 89—), Internat. Soc. Polit. Psychology (pres. 1987-88, Outstanding Svc. award 1990), Am. Polit. Sci. Assn. (several coms.) Am. Psychol. Assn. Home: 7035 Rieber St Worthington OH 43085 Office: Mershon Ctr/Ohio State Univ 199 W 10th Ave Columbus OH 43201

HERMANN, NAOMI BASEL, librarian, interior decorator; b. N.Y.C., Feb. 12, 1918; d. Alexander and Rebecca (Deinard) Basel; m. Henry I. Almour, June 26, 1938 (dec.); 1 child, Jay Alexander; m. Stanford Leland Hermann, Dec. 20, 1951. BS in Edn., NYU, 1937; MLS, Columbia U., 1963; postgrad., Vassar Coll., Cornell U., Hunter Coll. Tchr. gifted children N.Y.C. Schs., 1946-58; libr. supr. 22 elem., jr. and sr. high schs., N.Y.C., 1958-72; libr. Brandeis High Sch., 1972-75; interior decorator, pvt. practice, N.Y.C., 1946—; instr. Children's Literature, N.Y.C. Bd. Edn., 1969-73; libr. examiner, N.Y.C. Bd. of Edn., 1967-72. Pres. Hadassah (life mem.), N.Y.C., 1939-41; mem. Coun. Jewish Women (life mem.), 1974—; charter mem. Eleanor Roosevelt Fund for Women and Girls. Mem. AAUW (pres. Boca Raton chpt. 1987-89), Boca Raton Noontime Ladies Club (pres.). Home: 550 S Ocean Blvd Boca Raton FL 33432

HERMANOFF, SANDRA MARLENE, public relations executive; b. Canton, Ohio; d. Max and Sylvia (Levin) Weisbrod; m. Michael Joel Hermanoff, Nov. 27, 1976; 1 child, Jeffrey Howard. BA in Journalism, Pub. Rels., Ohio State U., 1965. With Ont. Brewers Inst., Toronto, 1965; copywriter Miller Advt., Columbus, Ohio, 1965; asst. pub. rels. dir. Huntington Nat. Bank, Columbus, 1965; pub. rels. dir. Sta. CFTO-TV, Toronto, 1968-69; instr. pub. rels., journalism Humber Coll., Toronto, 1969-71; pub. rels. adminstr. Liza Minnelli-Desi Arnaz Celebrity Tennis Tournament for Children's Asthma Rsch. Inst. and Hosp., Denver, 1971; with Investor Rels., Toronto, 1972; with Continental Pub. Rels., Toronto, 1975-76; pub. rels. dir. W.B. Doner and Co., Southfield, Mich., 1982-85; pres. Hermanoff & Assocs., Inc., 1985—; past spl. events chair United Found. Mem. Pub. Rels. Soc. Am. (accredited), Pub. Rels. Soc. Am. Counselors Acad. (past pres.), Women in Communications, The Fashion Group, Detroit Econs. Club, Detroit Press Club, Detroit Club. Office: Hermanoff & Assocs 31500 W 13 Mile Rd #135 Farmington Hills MI 48018

HERMANSON, CAROL DIANE, nurse; b. Ortonville, Minn., Aug. 31, 1951; d. Willard Kenneth and Ardis Luverne (Kropuenske) Sogge; m. Durwin Duane Hermanson, Sept. 9, 1972; children: Eric, Mark, Scot. BS in Nursing, Mankato State Coll., 1973; postgrad., Mankato State U. Cert. gerontol. nurse ANA. Charge nurse Oaklawn Health Care Ctr., Mankato, Minn.; utilization rev. nurse, cons. Harry Meyering Ctr., Mankato; dir. nursing, charge nurse Waterville (Minn.) Care Ctr.; staff nurse Trimont (Minn.) Community Hosp.; adj. clin. faculty Mankato State U.; presenter continuing edn. workshops. Author: On PRN Medication Cards. Dir. Lighthouse Singers, 1985—; leader Vision Harvesters, 1985—. Home: 136 Sandpiper Dr Mankato MN 56001

HERMSEN, GAIL MARIE, company executive; b. Green Bay, Wis., Mar. 19, 1951; d. Russell Christian and Muriel Antonette (Jarvis) H.; m. Gregory James Hill, Jan. 30, 1976 (div. Nov. 1979); m. Kurt Mathew Keeley, Oct. 24, 1987; stepchildren, Travis, Kendra. BS in Environ. Sci. & Regional Planning, U. Wis., 1973; M in Urban & Regional Planning, U. Colo., 1979. Assoc. county planner Brown County Planning Comm., Green Bay, 1973-76; planner III Denver Regional Council of Govt., Denver, 1976-81; environmental planner Colo. Sch. of Mines Research Inst., Golden, 1981-82; project scientist Woodward Clyde Cons., Denver; pres. Hermsen Cons., Littleton, 1983--. Author: profl. paper, North American Lake Management Society, 1988. Pres. Montclair Community Assn., Denver, 1985-86; chmn. Denver Water Bd. Citizens Adv. Com., 1988—. mem. Am. Planning Assn., Assn. of Wis. Planners, Am. Planning Assn. Colo. Chptr., Colo. Wildlife Soc., Nature conservancy. Democrat. Roman Catholic.

HERN, KAREN SUE, communications manager; b. Parkersburg, W.Va., Aug. 29, 1949; d. Francis Eugene and Josephine (Salser) Boice; m. Edward Monroe III Nelson, Oct. 10, 1975 (div. 1988); m. John David Hern, Mar. 16, 1990. BS in Journalism Advt., W.Va. U., 1972. Claims rep. U.S. Health and Human Svcs., SSA, Wheeling, W.Va., 1973-74, Bridgeport, Ohio, 1974-75, Parkersburg, 1975-78; field rep. U.S. Health and Human Svcs., SSA, Marietta, Ohio, 1978-83; dir. pub. rels. Selby Gen. Hosp., Marietta, 1983-85; pub. rels. specialist, account exec. Lockney and Assoc. Advt., Parkersburg, 1985-86; mktg. communications specialist Forma Sci., Marietta, 1986-87; pub. rels. specialist Borg-Warner Chems., Internat. Ctr., Parkersburg, 1987-88; mgr. communications and pub. rels. GE Plastics, Parkersburg, 1988—. V.p., bd. dirs. Mid-Ohio Valley Fellowship Home, Parkersburg, 1990; past bd. dirs. Jr. League Parkersburg; campaign chmn. Wood County Heart Assn., 1978; adv. bd. Washington County Easter Seal Soc., 1983-85, Friends and Parents of the Hearing Impaired, Washington County, Ohio, 1983-84, I Can Cope Am. Cancer Soc., Washington County, 1983-84; mem. auction com. Easter Seal Soc., Wood County, 1989-90. Mem. NAFE, Am. Mktg. Assn. (v.p. 1986-87), Jr. League Parkersburg (chmn. state pub. affairs com. 1982-83, sec.-treas. com. 1989-90), Altrusa Internat., Greater Parkersburg C. of C. (pres. 1988—). Gen. Fedn. Women's Clubs (pres. Parkersburg jr. dept. 1978-79, rec. sec. 1979-80, chmn. state pub. affairs W.Va. jr. dept. 1980-82). Republican. Episcopalian. Office: GE Plastics 5th & Avery Sts Parkersburg WV 26101

HERNANDEZ, ANTONIA, lawyer; b. Torreon, Coahuila, Mexico, May 30, 1948; came to U.S., 1956; d. Manuel and Nicolasa (Martinez) H.; m. Michael Stern, Oct. 8, 1977; children: Benjamin, Marisa, Michael. BA, UCLA, 1971, JD, 1974. Bar: Calif. 1974, D.C. 1979. Staff atty. East Los Angeles Ctr. Law and Justice, 1974-77; directing atty. Legal Aid Found., Lincoln Heights, Calif., 1977-78; staff counsel U.S. Senate Com., Washington, 1979-80; assoc. counsel Mexican Am. Legal Def. Ednl. Fund, Washington, 1981-83; v.p. Mexican Am. Legal Def. Ednl. Fund, Los Angeles, 1984-85, pres., gen. counsel, 1985—; bd. dirs. Fed. Immigration Law Reporter, Washington, Oxfam Am., Boston, The Alan Guttmacher Inst., N.Y.C. Contbr. articles to profl. jours. Co-chmn. enriching diversity com. Los Angeles 2000; mem. Nat. Competition on the Constn., Hon. Com. on 75th Anniversary Dept. Labor. AAUW fellow, 1973-74. Fellow AAUW; mem. Calif. Bar Assn., Washington D.C. Bar Assn. Roman Catholic. Office: Mexican Am Legal Def Fund 634 S Spring St Ste 1100 Los Angeles CA 90014

HERNANDEZ, CELIDA ALCARAZ, accountant, benefits coordinator; b. Mexico City, Mar. 26, 1953; came to U.S., 1955; d. Jesus Maldonado and Maria (Alcaraz) Hernandez. BA, Tex. Tech U., 1976. CPA, Tex. Staff acct. Plains Cotton Coop. Assn., Lubbock, Tex., 1976-78, asst. acctg. mgr., 1978-80, acctg. mgr., 1980-87, accounts receivable supr., 1987-89, benefits coordinator, 1990—. Mem. Am. Inst. CPAs, Am. Women's Soc. CPAs (pres Lubbock chpt. 1987-88, treas. 1986-87), Tex. Soc.CPAs, Hispanic Assn. Women, Hispanic Women's Network Tex., Am. Bus. Women's Assn. (exec. focus, treas. 1989-90), Altrusa. Office: Plains Cotton Coop Assn 3301 E 50th St Lubbock TX 79404

HERNÁNDEZ, LINDA LOUISE (LINDA LOUISE CLARKE), educator, researcher; b. Wakefield, Mass., May 21, 1952; d. Robert H. and Helen B. (Barker) Clarke; m. William A. Dolan IV, Feb. 5, 1972 (div. May 1974); m. Miguel Hernández, Jan. 31, 1975; 1 child, Michael Robert. BS, U. Fla., 1973; MA, U. S.C., 1978, PhD, 1981. Rsch. psychologist WJB Dorn Dept. Vets. Affairs Hosp., Columbia, S.C., 1981—; asst. prof. psychology U. S.C., Columbia, 1982-87, assoc. prof. psychology, 1987—; ad hoc reviewer Psychopharmacology, NIH, NSF, DVA. Contbr. numerous articles to profl. jours. Recipient New Investigator Rsch. award Nat. Inst. Alcoholism and Alcohol Abuse, 1986-88; U.S. Dept. Vets. Affairs Rsch. grantee, 1984—, Nat. Inst. Drug Abuse, 1990—. Fellow Am. Psychol. Assn. (psychopharmacology divs.); mem. AAAS, Am. Psychol. Soc., N.Y. Acad. Scis., S.C. Acad. Sci., Soc. for Neurosci. (pres. S.C. chpt. 1986-87, councillor 1982-85), Sigma Xi (v.p. U. S.C. chpt. 1989-90). Office: WJB Dorn Dpt Vets Affrs Hsp Neuroscience Rsch 151A Columbia SC 29201

HERNANDEZ, MARJORIE RAY, financial planner; b. Hemingway, S.C., Mar. 6, 1927; d. James Earl Ray and Maybelle Jordan; divorced; 1 child, Roberta Jill Sharp. AB in English and History, U. Calif., Berkeley, 1962, MLS, 1965; teaching degree, U. Ill., 1966. Lic. real estate agt., Conn. Dir. profl. svcs. Weston (Conn.) Woods Film Studios, 1968-69; asst. dir. Danbury (Conn.) Pub. Libr., 1970-73, Westport (Conn.) Pub. Libr., 1973-74; assoc. state libr. Conn. State Libr., Hartford, 1974-79; broker rep. P&I Equities, White Plains, N.Y., 1980-82, MHA Fin. Corp., Braintree, Mass., 1983-84; broker rep. Townsley Assocs. & Co., Inc., Corning, N.Y., 1984-89, v.p. corp. devel., 1985-89; fin. officer Planned Mgmt. Co. Savs. Bank Rockville, Conn., 1989—; cons., propr. Colmar, Glastonbury, Conn., 1985—. Mem. Internat. Assn. Fin. Planning (bd. dirs. Hartford 1983-84, Disting. Svc. award 1984), Glastonbury Bus. and Profl. Women. Republican. Congregationalist.

HERNANDEZ, MINERVA, government official; b. Dallas, Oct. 18, 1959; d. Tony and Otalia (Ayala) H. B.Criminal Justice, So. Meth. U., 1982, MPA, 1986. Intern, housing dept. City of Dallas, 1982-84, agenda coordinator, budget & rsch., 1984-85, coun. asst. mayor and coun. office, 1985, adminstrv. asst. city mgr. office, 1985-86, 88-89, field rep. Office Minority Bus. Opportunity, 1989-90, budget analyst pub. works, 1990; adminstr. M/WBE Minority Affairs Office DART, Dallas, 1990—. Mem. Urban Mgmt. Assts. N.Tex., AAUW (interbr. coun. rep. 1985-87, dist. coordinator Tex. div. 1987-88), ACAL de Mex., Dallas Hispanic C. of C., Mundo Cultural Sociedad de Amigos de la Cultura Mexicana. Republican. Methodist. Office: DART Minority Affaris Office 601 Pacific Ave Dallas TX 75202

HERNANDEZ, SONIA CARIDAD, public relations executive; b. Havana, Cuba, July 19, 1954; came to U.S., 1966; d. Carlos P. Hernandez Avila and Ofelia Menendez Cespedes de Hernandez. Student, Barbizon Modeling Sch., 1980; AA, Miami-Dade Community Coll., 1986; student, Fla. Internat. U., 1988. Cert. customer service rep. Rep. ins. LaBella Ins. Agy., Port Chester, N.Y., 1972-76; adminstrv. asst. Avon Products Co., Rye, N.Y., 1977-80; adminstrv. asst. Sun Bank/Miami (Fla.) N.A., 1984-86, rep. customer service, 1986, officer customer service, 1987—. Mem. Internat. Jaycees. Office: Sun Bank/Miami NA 777 Brickell Ave Miami FL 33131

HERNANDEZ, WANDA GRACE, rehabilitation counselor, sales manager; b. Detroit, Apr. 23, 1942; d. Harry Lee and Lillian Delores (Williams) Williams; m. Ignacio Heriberto Hernandez, Nov. 25, 1969 (div. April 1979); 1 child, Heriberto Alejandro. BS, Wayne State U., 1973, MA, 1977. Substance abuse counselor Boniface Community Action Corp., Detroit, 1972-73; vocations rehab. counselor Mich. Rehab. Svcs., Detroit, 1974—. Named Disting. Rehab. Profl., Nat. Disting. Service Registry Library of Congress, 1987. Fellow Nat. Rehab. Assn.; mem. The Smithsonian Assocs. Jehovah Witness. Home: 9056 Patton Detroit MI 48228 Office: Mich Rehab Services 30 E Canfield Detroit MI 48201

HERNANDEZ-CHERNYS, GRISELLE CLAUDIA, hospital administrator, health care consultant; b. Havana, Cuba, May 18, 1953; d. Sabino and Maria (Vigoa) Hernandez. A.A., Miami Dade Jr. Coll., 1974; B.S., Fla. Internat. U., 1977; B.Pub. Adminstrn., Biscayne Coll., 1979. Ednl. services rep. Blue Cross of Fla., Miami, 1971-75, profl. relations rep., 1975-79; with fin. services dept. Mt. Sinai Med. Ctr., Miami Beach, Fla., 1979-83, asst dir. mktg., 1983—; cons. to various physicians, Miami, 1980—; cons. Humana Corp., Miami, 1980, Centro Medico de los Andes, Bogota, Colombia, 1983; guest educator Mil. Hosp., Bogota, 1983. Contbr. articles to profl. jours. Tchr. dance and cooking summer program YWCA, Miami, 1973, 74. Ford Found. scholar, 1968-70. Mem. Hosp. Fin. Mgmt. Assn., Nat. Assn. Female Execs., Profl. Women's Assn. Democrat. Home: 641 Sabal Palm Rd Miami FL 33137-3353 Office: Mt Sinai Med Ctr 4300 Alton Rd Miami Beach FL 33140

HERNDON, ROSEMARY VAN VLEET, educator; b. Driscoll, N.D., Feb. 24, 1931; d. Allen L. and Bertha Marie (Wilke) Van Vleet; m. Richard L. Helm, June 27, 1953 (div. 1971); children: Heidi Chin, Jonathan Heim; m. John Elliott Herndon, Feb. 11, 1972. AA, Stockton (Calif) Coll., 1950; BA, Calif. State U., San Jose, 1952; MA, Calif. State U., Turlock, 1979. 6th grade tchr. Alum Rock Union Sch. Dist., San Jose, 1952-55; tchr. gifted Sch. Dist. #88, Cook County, Bellwood, Ill., 1956-59; lectr. edn. Calif. SAtate U., Stanislaus, Turlock, 1971-87; reading specialist Livingston Union Sch. Dist., 1971-79; reading specialist Turlock Elementary Sch. Dist., 1979-90, cons., 1990—; lectr. in field. Contbg. author: Annotated Recommended Readings in Literature, 1988, Celebrating the National Reading Initiative, 1988. Literacy vol., 1990—. Mem. AaUW (moderator 1990, br. sec. 1987-90), Internat. Reading Assn. (Literacy award 1990), Stanislaus Reading Coun. (pres. 1986-87), Phi Delta Kappa. Republican. Evangelical Covenant Ch. Home: 1050 Lockhart Gulch Rd Scotts Valley CA 95066

HERON, JANE DATTARO, hospital administrator; b. Mt. Vernon, N.Y.; d. Guido and Teresa J. (Scally) Dattaro; m. Matthew D. Heron, Sept. 14, 1985. BS in Nursing, Columbia U., 1977; MBA, Southwest Mo. State U., 1989. RN, Washington, Va., Mo.; cert. advanced cardiac life support. Trauma coord. St. John's Hosp., Springfield, Mo.; asst. dir. Upjohn Healthcare Svcs., Springfield; staff nurse St. John's Hosp., Springfield; advice nurse Kaiser Permanente, Springfield, Va.; staff nurse II George Washington U. Hosp., Washington. Columbia U. scholar, N.Y. State Regents scholar; recipient Dale Carnegie Sales Course Human Rels. award. Mem. NAFE, Columbia U. Alumni Assn. Office: St John's Regional Health Ctr Emergency Trauma Ctr 1235 E Cherokee Springfield MO 65807

HERON, JEAN ELLEN, entrepeneur; b. Webster, Mass., Nov. 22, 1942; d. Peter Francis and Hedwidge (Teresa) H.; m. Girard Briant Connick, Oct. 19, 1985. BA, Regis Coll., 1964; MBA, Northeastern, Boston, 1970; postgrad., U. Mass. cert. fin. planner. With EG.G, Bedford, Mass., 1964-69; dir. mktg. IBD, Boston, 1969-70, MHA, Burlington, Mass., 1970-79; broker Jean Ellen Heron Real Estate, Nantucket, 1971—; account exec. SMS, Boston, 1979-83; regional sale mgr. CMI, Cambridge, Mass., 1983-85; pres. Island Inn, Nantucket, Mass., 1984—; salesman Martha Guttfied Real Estate, Palm Beach, Fla., 1987—; exec. dir. First Palm Beach Trust, Palm Beach, Fla., 1987—; experimenter experiment internat. living, Germany, 1962—; chmn. endowment com. St. Edwards, Palm Beach, 1989—. Mem. IBCFP, HFMA, Am. Coll. Health Care Exec. (pres. Mass. chpt. 1975-76), Palm Beach C. of C., Nantucket C. of C., New Eng. Innkeepers Assn., Palm Beach Bd. of Realtors (budget com. 1989—). Roman Catholic. Home: 232 Australian Ave Palm Beach FL 33480 Office: PO Box 2973 Palm Beach FL 33480

HERON, JOANNE ELIZABETH, financial planner; b. Boston, July 6, 1944; d. Peter Francis and Hedwidge Teresa (Sampson) H. BA, Regis Coll., 1966; MBA, U. Pa., 1974. Cert. fin. planner, stock broker, ins. broker, real estate broker, designer. Tchr., social worker Lay Apostulate Program, Kaimuki, Hawaii, 1966-67; fixed income mgr. and trader Putnam Mgmt. Co., Boston, 1967-73; fin. cons., bus. planner Ford Motor Co., Dearborn, Mich., 1974-77; mgr. ops., strategic planner Insilco, Meriden, Conn., 1977-79; pres. Refracted Mood Ltd., Lynnfield, Mass., 1978—, also chmn. bd. dirs.; exec. designer, pres. Jo Jo of Nantucket, Lynnfield, 1978—; real estate broker J.E. Heron Agy., Lynnfield, 1980—, ins. broker, 1988—, stock broker, 1988—. Active Historic Soc., Lynnfield, 1978—. Named Experimenter of Yr. Experiment in Internat. Living, 1965. Mem. Inst. Cert. Fin. Planners, Nantucket C. of C. Roman Catholic. Office: PO Box 1001 Lynnfield MA 01940 also: PO Box 3364 Palm Beach FL 33480

HERR, BONITA LOUISE BOWER, pharmacist, administrator; b. Indpls., Nov. 1, 1945; d. David William and Gladys Maria (Tollinche) Bower; m. Phillip James Herr, Aug. 23, 1969 (div. Aug. 1989); children: Phillip Michael, John Stephen. BS magna cum laude, U. Tex., 1970, MS in Pharmacy, 1974. Lic. pharmacist, Tex. Staff pharmacist Brackenridge Hosp., Austin, Tex., 1970, Holy Cross Hosp., Austin, 1970-71; hosp. pharmacy resident Harris Meth. Hosp., Ft. Worth, 1971-72; chief pharmacist St. Paul Med. Ctr., Dallas, 1972-76; dir. pharmacy South Arlington (Tex.) Med Ctr. Hosp. Corp. Am., 1976—; mem. tech. adv. bd., Hosp. Corp. Am., Nashville, 1979-82; pharm. adv. coun., U. Tex., Austin, 1984-87; hosp. adv. bd., McKesson Corp., San Francisco, 1985-87; bd. dirs., Rsch. and Edn. Found., Tex. Soc. Hosp. Pharmacists, Austin, 1983-87. Health occupational edn. mem., sec., Arlington Ind. Sch. System Bd., 1976—. Mem. Am. Soc. Hosp. Pharmacists, Tex. Soc. Hosp. Pharmacists, North Cen. Tex. Soc. Hosp. Pharmacists, Am. Pharm. Assn., Rho Chi, Phi Kappa Phi. Republican. Episcopalian. Office: HCA South Arlington Med Ctr 3301 Matlock Rd Arlington TX 76015

HERR, JUDY ANN, early childhood education educator; b. Valders, Wis., Nov. 12, 1941; d. Charles and Melba (Larson) Rolland; m. James Francis Herr, June 23, 1962; children: John, Mark. Student, U. Wis.-Stout, Menomonie, Wis., 1959-62, BS in Home Econs. Edn., 1965, MEd, 1967; EdD, U. Minn., 1982. Elem tchr. Virginia Beach (Va.) Pub. Sch. System, 1962-64; instr. child study dept. Stephens Coll., Columbia, Mo., 1966-69; instr. child devel. and family life dept. U. Wis.-Stout, Menomonie, 1967, prof., 1969—; project advisor Nat. Office Child Devel. for Parent-Child Ctrs., 1972-77; sec., bd. dirs. Tanglewood Corp., Menomonie, 1977-83; supr. Wis. Early Childhood Assn. Pub. Info. Project, 1978; tech. rev. com. Wis. Nutrition Edn. and Tng. Program, 1979-85; manuscript reviewer Jour. Tchr. Edn., Jour. Home Econs., Harcourt, Brace & Janvonovich, Merrill Pub. Co., 1983—; cons. Project Headstart, 1968-69, Social Dynamics, Pacific T&TA, Kirschner Assocs. Author: Working With Young Children, 1990; co-author: Creating Innovative Classroom Materials for Teachers of Young Children, 1979, Creative Resources for Early Childhood Classrooms, 1990, Creative Teacher Made Classroom Materials, 1990; contbr. articles to profl. jours. Advisor Menomonie Assn. for Edn. of Young Children, 1969—; adv. bd. Stout Found. U. Wis., 1978-84; mem. State Day Care Rules Implementation Coms., 1980, Child Welfare Adv. com., 1982, 83, Wis. State Day Care Adv. com. div. Health and Social Svcs., 1981-85, edn. subcom. vice chairperson 1981, chairperson 1982-83. Named to Dahlgren professorship Bd. Regents U. Wis., 1988; recipient numerous grants for child care rsch., 1976—. Mem. World Orgn. for Early Childhood Edn., Nat. Assn. for Edn. of Young Children, Nat. Assn. Early Childhood Tchr. Educators (bd. dirs. 1984-86), Am. Home Econs. Assn. (sec.-treas. child devel.-family life sect. 1987-88), Midwest Assn. for Edn. of Young Children (treas. 1982-85, pres. 1985-87, Shirley Dean award), Wis. Home Econs. Assn. (sec. 1983-85), Phi Kappa Phi, Phi Delta Kappa. Office: U Wis-Stout Menomonie WI 54751

HERR, RUTH SMITH, financial printing customer service representative; b. Lancaster, Pa., Apr. 7, 1965; d. Richard Carl Jr. and Lenore (Young) Smith; m. C. Jeffrey Herr, Aug. 20, 1988. AB in German and Policy and Mgmt. Studies magna cum laude, Dickinson Coll., 1987. Tchr., dorm parent Linden Hall Sch. for Girls, Lititz, Pa., 1987-89; customer svc. rep. R.R. Donnelley & Sons Fin. Printing, Lancaster, 1989—. Writer, editor Parents Guide to Dickinson Coll., 1986; contbr. articles to Lancaster Newspapers, Inc. Sunday sch. supt. Community United Meth. Ch., Lancaster, 1989—. Mem. Phi Beta Kappa, Kappa Alpha Theta, Omicron Delta Kappa. Republican. Home: 1125 W New St Lancaster PA 17603

HERRERA, MARY CARDENAS, teacher, music minister; b. Sugar Land, Tex., Feb. 21, 1938; d. Jose Chavez and Juanita (Lira) Cardenas; m. Saragosa Martin Herrera, Sept. 20, 1960; children: Michael, Patricia Ann, Aaron Martin Herrera, Katherine Ann. Grad., Patricia Stevens Bus. Sch., 1960. Sec. William Penn Hotel, Houston, 1959-66; payroll clk. Peakload, Inc., Houston, 1967-69; acctg. clk. Am. Gen., Inc., Houston, 1970-73; nurse asst. Ft. Bend Ind. Sch. Dist., Stafford, Tex., 1973-87, tchr.'s asst., 1987—; Numerous offices Holy Family Cath. Ch., Missouri City, Tex., 1982—, Hispanic choir dir., 1982-89; Hispanic del. Galveston-Houston Diocesis, 1987—; regional del. Encuentro Dioceseno Conf., San Antonio, 1983, 84, 85; dir., coord. Diocesen Hispanic Choir, 1982-86, music workshops, 1982-88. Songwriter in field. Mem., tchr. PTO, 1973—; mem. Holy Family Hispanic Com. Mem. Women's Aglow (praise and worship music minister Pasadena chpt. 1988—), Nat. Assn. Pastoral Musicians. Democrat. Home and Office: 4506 Ludwig Stafford TX 77477

HERRERA, SANDRA JOHNSON, school system administrator; b. Riverside, Calif., June 21, 1944; d. William Emory Johnson and Mildred Alice (Alford) Wimer; m. Wynn Neal Huffman, Feb. 19, 1962 (div. May 1967); 1 child, Kristen Lee; m. Steven Jack Herrera, June 21, 1985. AA in Purchasing Mgmt., Fullerton Coll., 1983; BSBA, U. Redlands, 1985, MA in Mgmt., 1988. Sr. purchasing clk Fullerton (Calif.) Union High Sch. Dist., 1969-77, buyer, 1977-79, coord. budgets and fiscal affairs, 1979-83; asst. dir. fin. svcs. Downey (Calif.) Unified Sch. Dist., 1983-85; dir. acctg. Whittier (Calif.) Union High Sch. Dist., 1985-89; asst. supt. bus. Whittier City Sch. Dist., 1989—; cons. Heritage Dental Lab., El Toro, Calif, 1981—. Spl. dep. sheriff Santa Barbara (Calif.) County Sheriff's Mounted Posse, 1986—; spl. dep. marshal U.S. Marshals Posse, Los Angeles, 1987—. Mem. Calif. Assn. Sch. Bus. Ofcls. (treas. S.E. sect. 1985, mem. acct. R & D com. 1983-89, mem. chief bus. officials com. 1989—), So. Calif. Paraders Assn. (exec. sec. 1976—), Calif. State Horsemens Assn. (regional v.p. 1986-87, sec. 1988), Alpha Gamma Sigma. Home: 18503 Sordello St Rowland Heights CA 91748 Office: Whittier City Sch Dist 7211 S Whittier Ave Whittier CA 90602

HERRERA, SHIRLEY MAE, personnel and security executive; b. Lynn, Mass., Apr. 5, 1942; d. John Baptiste and Edith Mae Lagasse; m. Christian Yanez Herrera, Apr. 30, 1975; children: Karen, Gary, Ivan, Iwonne. AS in Bus., Burdette Bus. Coll., Lynn, 1960; student, Wright State U., 1975-78. Cert. facility security officer, med. asst. in pediatrics. Med. asst. Christian Y. Herrera, M.D., Stoneham, Mass., 1972-74; human resource adminstr. MTL Systems, Inc., Dayton, Ohio, 1976-79; dir. pers. and security Tracor GIE, Inc., Provo, Utah, 1979—; cons. on family dynamics family enrichment program Hill AFB, Utah, 1980-82; cons. on health care mgmt. Guam 7th Day Adventist Clinic, 1983; cons. on basic life support and CPR, Projecto Corazon, Monterrey, Mex., 1987—. Chmn. women's aux. YMCA Counselling Svcs., Woburn, Mass., 1970; chmn. youth vols. ARC, Wright-Patterson AFB, Dayton, 1974-76; trustee Quail Valley Homeowner's Assn., Provo, 1988-89; rep. A Spl. Wish Found., Provo, 1989. Recipient James S. Cogswell award Def. Investigative Svc., Dept. Def., 1987. Mem. Soc. for Human Resource Mgmt., Inst. for Reality Therapy (cert.), Pers. Assn. Cen. Utah,

Internat. Platform Assn. Republican. Home: 3824 N Little Rock Dr W Provo UT 84604

HERRERÍAS, CATALINA, social work educator; b. N.Y.C., June 14, 1948; d. Guillermo Herrerias de Gongora and Monserrate (Colon) H.; m. Raymond E. Greenidge, Feb. 10, 1968 (dec. 1972); 1 child, Danielle Josette; m. Charles Wayne Unsell, Mar. 16, 1973 (div. 1979); 1 child, Jennifer Lynn. AA, Rose Jr. Coll., Midwest City, Okla., 1975-78; BA, U. Okla., 1980, MSW, 1981; PhD in Social Work, U. Tex., 1984. Lic. social worker, Pa. Sec. U.S. Dept. Def., Okla., Va., 1969-74, FAA, Okla. City, 1974-77; tax service rep. IRS, Okla. City, 1977-78; tchr. Montessori Day Sch., Del City, Okla., 1978-80; rsch. asst. sch. social work U. Okla., Norman, 1980-81; rsch. asst. sch. social work U. Tex., Austin, 1982-83, asst. instr., 1983-84; asst. prof. U. Mich., Ann Arbor, 1984-87, U. Pa., Phila., 1987—; cons. Big Bros./Big Sisters Am., Phila., 1987—, Dept. Human Services, Phila., 1989—, Children's Aid Soc., Detroit, 1984-87, Inst. Human Services, Columbus, Ohio, 1986—. Speaker pregnant teen program United Way, Germantown, Phila., Pa., 1989, So. Homes Foster Care Program, Phila., 1988; trainer Parent/Tchrs./Daughters Assn., Phila., 1988, Voyage House Program for Runaways, Phila., 1988. With USN, 1966-67. Woodrow Wilson Nat. fellow, 1984; named Mental Health Advocate Mich. Hispanic Mental Health Assn., 1987, one of Outstanding Young Women Am., 1983, 85; recipient Dissertation Rsch. award Am. Psychol. Assn., 1984, Clairol Take Charge award, 1989; recognized for vol. service Mich. Dept. Mental Health, 1987. Mem. Phila. Citizens for Children and Youth (bd. dirs. 1989—), Nat. Coalition Hispanic Mental Health Orgns. (adv. bd. 1985—), Nat. Assn. Social Workers, Nat. Coun. Family Relations, Nat. Corp. Puerto Rican Women, Am. Legion. Democrat. Roman Catholic. Home: 5204 Rorer St Philadelphia PA 19120 Office: U Pa Social Work 3701 Locust Walk Philadelphia PA 19104-6214

HERRICK, KATHLEEN MAGARA, social worker; b. Mpls., Oct. 18, 1943; d. William Frank and Mary Genevieve (Gill) Magara; m. John Middlemist Herrick, Feb. 5, 1966; children: Elizabeth Jane, Kathryn Mary. BA in Social Work and French, Coll. St. Benedict, St. Joseph, Minn., 1965; MSW (Mildred B. Erickson fellow 1975), Mich. State U., E. Lansing, 1976. Social worker II, Carver County Social Services, Chaska, Minn., 1965-70; therapist St. Lawrence Community Mental Health Center, Lansing, Mich., 1974-75; sch. social worker Ingham Intermediate Sch. Dist., Mason, Mich., 1975-76; home/sch. coordinator Eaton Intermediate Sch. Dist., Charlotte, Mich., 1976-81; caseworker St. Vincent Home for Children, Lansing, 1979-80; tchr. cons. for severely emotionally impaired, 1981-83; behavior disorder cons., 1983-85; sch. social work cons., 1985—. Chairperson bd. dirs. Eaton County Child Abuse and Neglect Prevention Council, 1986—; Democratic precinct del.; bd. dirs. Catholic Social Services, Lansing; specialist substance abuse prevention region XIII SAPE, 1987—. Mem. NEA, Nat. Platform Assn., Mich. Edn. Assn., Okemos High Sch. Parent Orgn., Kinawa Parent Orgn., Nat. Assn. Social Workers, Nat. Assn. Retarded Citizens, Am. Orthopsychiat. Assn., Mich. Assn. Sch. Social Workers, Mich. Assn. Emotionally Disturbed Children, Eaton County Assn. Retarded Citizens, Fegiold Assn. SE Mich., Nat. Platform Assn., NOW, Nat. Women's Health Network, Amnesty Internat., Phi Kappa Phi, Phi Alpha. Democrat. Roman Catholic. Home: 2330 Shawnee Trail Okemos MI 48864 Office: 1790 E Packard Hwy Charlotte MI 48813

HERRICK, SONJA JANE, healthcare administration executive; b. Willits, Calif., Mar. 30, 1949; d. Clifton Eugene and Eleanor Jane (Steinmeyer) Snider; m. Greg Herrick, May 18, 1986. Student, Pacific Union Coll., 1967-70, Moorpark (Calif.) Coll., 1973-76. Nursing staff scheduler Simi Valley (Calif.) Adventist Hosp., 1969-72, asst. pers. dir., 1973-76; data processing dir. Sini Valley (Calif.) Adventist Hosp., 1977-79; ops. mgr. info. systems St. Joseph's Med. Ctr., Burbank, Calif., 1979-82; data ctr. mgr. St. John's Hosp. & Health Ctr., Santa Monica, Calif., 1982-85; dir. data processing St. Joseph Hosp., Orange, Calif., 1985-88, dir. patient svc. contracts, 1987-90; assoc. Contract Payer Rev. Mem. Healthcare Mgmt. Assn., Info. Ctr. Mgmt. Assn. Republican. Home: POB 9459 Glendale CA 91226 Office: 3409 Wonder View Dr Los Angeles CA 90068

HERRICK, SUSAN LYNN, hospital offical, medical records consultant; b. Glens Falls, N.Y., Nov. 9, 1959; d. Robert Harlan and Marilyn Margaret (Schneider) H. BS magna cum laude, Colby-Sawyer Coll., New London, N.H., 1981. Registered records adminstr. Coder, supr. med. records Nashoba Community Hosp., Ayer, Mass., 1982-83; asst. dir. med. records, tumor registrar Portsmouth (N.H.) Hosp., 1983-86; dir. med. data svcs. Glens Falls Hosp., 1986—. Office: Glens Falls Hosp 100 Park St Glens Falls NY 12801

HERRING, CAROLYN LEIGH, cable television producer, director; b. Princeton, W.Va., Apr. 4, 1959; d. Herbert Clark andd Marien Elizabeth (Bentzel) H. BFA, N.Y. Inst. Tech., 1981; postgrad., NYU, 1987. Cablecaster TKR Cable Co., Warren, N.J., 1981-83, prodn. asst., 1983-85, asst. program mgr., 1985-90; freelance camera person C-Span Cable Network, Washington, 1988-89; instr. The Cen. for the Media Arts, N.Y.C., 1990—. Mem. The Nature Conservancy, 1989—. Recipient Ernie award N.Y. Inst. Tech., 1981, CAPE award Cable TV Network of N.J., 1986. Mem. Nat. Acad. Cable Programming (ACE award 1988), Am. Film Inst., Amnesty Internat. U.S.A., Greenpeace. Democrat. Methodist. Office: Ctr for Media Arts 26 W 26th St New York NY 10010

HERRING, NANCY L., registered nurse; b. Newport, R. I., Apr. 12, 1956; d. Wesley and Virginia Rita (Armstrong) H. BS, U. Ill., 1977, MPH, 1989. Acting head nurse Luth. Gen. Hosp., Pk. Ridge, Ill., 1977-82; mgr. clin. research Clintec Nutrition Co., Deerfield, Ill., 1982-88; nurse clinician New Eng. Critical Care, Inc., Wood Dale, Ill., 1988—. Vol. Dukakis Presdl. Campaign, Wheeling, Ill., 1988. Mem. Oncology Nursing Soc., Am. Pub. Health Assn., Am. Soc. Parenteral and Enteral Nutrition. Democrat. Roman Catholic. Home: 631 Portsmouth Pl Wheeling IL 60090

HERRING, PATRICIA LEBLANC, paper company executive; b. Cambridge, N.Y., Mar. 22, 1944; d. Frederick James and Alvera Ann (Alecknavic) LeBlanc; m. Kenneth Winton Herring, Aug. 23, 1965; 1 child, Trevor Patrick. BS in BA, So. Vt. Coll., Bennington, 1975; MEd in Human Resource Devel., U. Mass., 1984. With Sprague Electric Co., North Adams, Mass., 1963-76; adminstrv. coord. mktg. and sales Sprague Electric Co., 1976-78, manpower contr. analyst, 1978-84, human resource cons. MIS, 1984-85; supr. human resource devel. Internat. Paper Co., Augusta, Maine, 1985—. Editor Nor' Easter newsletter. Vice pres. communications Kennebec Valley United Way, Augusta, 1988—, bd. dirs., 1985—; mem. Maine Human Resource Policy Rev. Bd., Augusta, 1987—, U. Maine Community Prog. Adv. Council, 1987—. Recipient Outstanding Community Svc. award, City of North Adams, 1985. Mem. Am. Soc. Tng. and Devel. (prs. Maine chpt. 1989—), Personnel Assn. Kennebec Valley. Home: 28 W Hill Rd Gardiner ME 04345 Office: Internat Paper Co 9 Green St Augusta ME 04330

HERRING, SUSAN WELLER, anatomist; b. Pitts., Mar. 25, 1947; d. Sol W. and Miriam (Damick) Weller); m. Stephen E. Herring, Nov. 18, 1967 (div. Oct. 1983). BS in Zoology, U. Chgo., 1967, PhD in Anatomy, 1971. NIH postdoctoral fellow U. Ill., Chgo., 1971-72, from asst. prof. to prof. oral anatomy and anatomy, 1972-90; prof. orthodontics U. Wash., Seattle, 1990—; vis. assoc. prof. biol. sci. U. Mich., Ann Arbor, 1981; cons. NIH study sect., Washington, D.C., 1987-89; sci. gov. Chgo. Acad. Sci., 1982-90; mem. pub. bd. Growth Pub. Inc., Bar Harbor, Maine, 1982—. Mem. editorial bd. Acta Anatomica, 1989 --; contbr. articles to profl. jours. Woodrow Wilson fellow, 1967; NSF predoctoral fellow, 1967-71; NIH rsch. grantee, 1975; Muscular Dystrophy Found. rsch. grantee, 1975-78, 1981-92. Mem. Internat. Assn. Dental Rsch., Am. Soc. Zoologists (chmn. vertebrate zoology 1983-84, exec. com. 1986-88), Am. Assn. Anatomists (chmn. Basmajian com. 1988-90), Soc. Vertebrate Paleontology, Am. Soc. Mammalogists, Sigma Xi. Office: U Wash Dept Orthodontics SM-46 Seattle WA 98195

HERRINGTON-BORRE, FRANCES JUNE, state government human services executive; b. Austin, Tex., June 14, 1935; d. George Wilmas Neill and Mildred Lucille (Alexander) Williamson; m. Harold M. Herrington, June 6, 1953 (dec. Dec. 1978); children: Harold M. (dec.), Cheryl Anne Herrington; m. Thomas Raymond Borre, Apr. 5, 1985. Student, U. Tex., 1967-71. With Tex. Dept. Human Services, Austin, 1961—, adminstrv. technician, 1967-71, field rep., 1971-81, asst. personnel dir., 1981-88, labor relations dir., 1988-89, judge adminstrv. law, 1989—; free-lance profl. interpreter for deaf, 1964—; dir. Austin Sign Lang. Sch., 1964—; cons. in field; project dir. Gov.'s Office, 1980. Gov.'s appointee Joint Adv. Com. on Ednl. Services to Deaf, Austin, 1976-78; chmn. Tex. Commn. for Deaf Bd. Eval. of Interpreters, 1981-84; chmn. Tex. State Agy. Liaisons to Gov.'s Comm. for Women, 1985. Recipient Tex. Rehab. Commn. Merit award, 1977, Gov.'s citation, 1978; named An Outstanding Woman Central Tex., AAUW, 1982, Significant and Meritorious Service to Mankind award Capitol Sertoma Club, 1976, Disting. Service as Adv. and Interpretar award Dal-Tar Lions Club, 1977. Mem. Nat. Assn. of Deaf (Golden Hand award 1987), Tex. Assn. of Deaf (Service citation 1967, Vol. Service award 1971, Interpreter of Decade award 1981, Prsdl. citation for Outstanding Svc. to symposium on deafness 1989), Nat. Registry Interpreters for Deaf, Tex. Soc. Interpreters for Deaf (pres. 1969-70), Austin Interpreters for Deaf. Mem. Ch. of Christ. Home: 2404 Laramie Trail Austin TX 78745 Office: Tex Dept Human Services 701 W 51st St Austin TX 78769

HERRIOTT, BERNADINE SHRIVER, social services administrator; b. Zanesville, Ohio, Jan. 22, 1948; d. Howard and Mildred (Henderson) S.; m. Scott Huston Herriott, Dec. 24, 1969 (div. Dec. 1979); m. Carl Richard Stitak, June 6, 1982. BA in Sociology, Ohio State U., 1976; postgrad., DePaul U., Chgo., 1979; MPA, U. Toledo, 1989. Residential case mgr. Ohio Dept. of Mental, Retardation Devel. Disabilities, Columbus, Ohio, 1977-79; residential services mgr. Assn. for Devel. Disabilities, Columbus, Ohio, 1979-82; exec. dir. resident Homes, Inc., Newark, 1983-87; pvt. cons.; project dir. Josina Lott FDN, Toledo, 1987--; cons. Contemporary Psychological Services, Columbus, Ohio, 1983, Thompson Homes, Ltd., Reynoldsburg, 1985-86, Health Care and Retirement, 1987, Behrin's Homes, Toledo, 1989. Chairperson Ohio Pub. Awareness Campaign Adv. Com., 1985-86. Mem. Ohio Pvt. Residential Assn. (bd. trustees 1984-86, sec., 1986-87).

HERRMANN, CAROL, academic administrator; b. Mt. Kisco, N.Y., Dec. 23, 1944; d. Eugene C. and Anne M. McGuire; m. Robert O. Herrmann; children: John Martin II, Nell Elizabeth. AB, Bucknell U., 1966; MA, Pa. State U., 1970. Bus. editor, writer Centre Daily Times Newspaper, State College, Pa., 1980-82; with Pa. State U., University Park, 1982—, exec. asst. to pres. for adminstrn., 1986-88, v.p. for adminstrn., 1988—. Mem. Centre Regional Planning Commn., State College, 1973-80, chmn., 1974-76; media coord. Common Cause 23d Congl. Dist., 1977-80; bd. dirs. United Way, Centre County, Pa., 1989—. Mem. Women in Communications, AAUW, Kappa Tau Alpha. Home: 568 Ridge Ave State College PA 16803 Office: Pa State U Rm 205 Old Main University Park PA 16802

HERRMANN, KATHERINE SCOTT, geophysicist; b. Balt., Feb. 7, 1959; d. Louis Grebb and Rose Marie (Hurt) H. BS in Geophysics, Va. Poly. Inst. and State U., 1981. Exploration geophysicist ARCO Exploration Co., Dallas, 1981-85; explorationist Exxon Corp. U.S.A., Houston, 1985-90, fin. analyst computing dept., 1990—. Mem. NAFE, Am. Assn. Petroleum Geologists, Houston Jr. C. of C. (sec. 1987, bd. dirs. 1986). Republican. Home: 1519 Plumwood Dr Houston TX 77014 Office: EXXON Co PO Box 4279 Houston TX 77210

HERRON, CAROLIVIA, English educator; b. Washington, July 22, 1947; d. Oscar Smith and Georgia Carol (Johnson) H. AB in English Lit., Ea. Bapt. Coll., 1969; MA in English Lit., Viallanova (Pa.) U., 1973; MA, PhD, U. Pa., 1985. Asst. prof. Afro-Am. studies and comparative lit. Harvard U., Cambridge, Mass., 1986-90; assoc. prof. English Mt. Holyoke Coll., South Hadley, Mass., 1990—; bd. dirs. curriculum devel. program NEH, Cambridge, Study Group in Afro-Asiatic Roots of Classical Civilization, Cambridge; vis. fellow Folger Shakespeare Libr., Washington, 1989—; Benedict vis. prof. Carleton Coll., Northfield, Minn., 1989—; dir. Epicenter for the Study of Epic Lit. Mt. Holyoke Coll. Author: (novel) Thereafter Johnnie, 1990, (scholarly books) African American Epic Tradition, 1991, Selected Works of Angelina Weld Grimké, 1990; contbr. articles to profl. jours. Fulbright scholarship, 1985-86; Bunting fellow Radcliffe Coll., 1988—. Mem. Classical Assn. New Eng., MLA, Renaissance Soc. Am., African Lit. Assn., Latin Am. Studies Assn.

HERRON, ELLEN PATRICIA, retired judge; b. Auburn, N.Y., July 30, 1927; d. David Martin and Grace Josephine (Berner) Herron; A.B. Trinity Coll., 1949; M.A., Cath. U. Am., 1954; J.D., U. Calif.-Berkeley, 1964. Asst. dean Cath. U. Am., 1952-54; instr. East High Sch., Auburn, 1955-57; asst. dean Wells Coll., Aurora, N.Y., 1957-58; instr. psychology and history Contra Costa Coll., 1958-60; dir. row Stanford, 1960-61; assoc. Knox & Kretzmer, Richmond, Calif., 1964-65; admitted to Calif. bar, 1965; ptnr. Knox & Herron, 1965-74, Knox, Herron and Masterson, 1974-77 (both Richmond, Calif.); judge Superior Ct. State of Calif., 1977-87; gen. ptnr. Real Estate Syndicates, Calif., 1967-77; owner, mgr. The Barricia Vineyards, 1978—. Active numerous civic orgns.; bd. dirs. Rhonoh Sch., Richmond, YWCA, Econ. Devel. Council Richmond; alumnae bd. dirs. Boalt Hall, U. Calif.-Berkeley, 1980-84. Mem. ABA, Contra Costa Bar Assn. (exec. com. 1969-74), State Bar Calif., Calif. Trial Lawyers, Nat. Assn. Women Lawyers, Nat. Assn. Women Judges, Calif. Women Lawyers, Applicants Attys. Assn., Calif. Judges Assn. (ethics com. 1977-79, criminal law procedure com. 1979-80), Queen's Bench, Juvenile Ct. Judges Assn. Democrat. Home: 51 Western Dr Point Richmond CA 94801

HERRON, PATSY LUDGOOD, organization executive; b. Mobile, Ala., Sept. 15, 1953; d. Frank Lenell Ludgood and Marva (Mitchell) Brown; m. Gary Lavorn Herron, Aug. 26, 1977; 1 child, Cary Lashon. AA, Bishop State Jr. Coll., Mobile, 1973; BA, Ala. A&M U., 1975. Mgr. fund raising Deep South coun. Girls Scouts U.S.A., Mobile, 1975-85, tng. dir., 1975-81, 85-86, program dir., 1975-79, field dir., 1979—, interim dir. field svcs., 1986. Recipient appreciation cert. Deep South coun. Girl Scouts U.S.A., 1981, appreciation pin, 1982, appreciation plaque, 1985, Thanks Badge, 1987; appreciation plaque Little Brownie Bakers, Louisville, 1985. Mem. Assn. Girl Scout Exec. Staff, NAFE, Alpha Kappa Alpha (chmn. nominating com. Mobile 1984—), Kappa Apha Psi. Baptist. Home: 3406 Maureen Dr Mobile AL 36605 Office: Deep South Coun Girl Scouts 3483 Springhill Ave Mobile AL 36608

HERRON, WENDY WATTS, wine consultant; b. York, Pa., Oct. 9, 1952; d. Alphonso Irving and Daphne Jean (Gainsford) Watts; m. Frederic Joseph Bonnie, (div. 1986); m. Kenneth Scott Herron, Feb. 14, 1987. BS, U. Cin., 1975. Store mgr. The Grapevine, Inc., Birmingham, Ala., 1978-81; sales rep. Supreme Beverage Co., Birmingham, 1981-84, Internat. Wines Co., Birmingham, 1984-90; nat. sales exec. Kermit Lynch Wine Mcht., Berkeley, Calif., 1990—; speaker, instr. various groups, Birmingham; co-chmn. Sonoma Wine Tour of Birmingham, 1987-88, chmn. 1989-90; chmn. Wine Tour of France, Birmingham, 1988-89; mem. exec. com. Multiple Sclerosis Wine Auction, 1990—. Mem. Wine Educator's Soc., Tuesday Tasting Group. Democrat. Mem. United Ch. Christ.

HERSBERGER, JILL ANN GOSMA, software design engineer; b. Kokomo, Ind., July 25, 1954; d. John William and Ruth Gene (Ostrander) Gosma; m. Robert Scott Hersberger, Jan. 28, 1984; stepchildren: Whitney Elaine, Dana Michelle. BSME, Gen. Motors Inst., Flint, Mich., 1978; MS in Computer Sci., U. Calif., Berkeley, 1978. Co-op student Delco Radio, Gen. Motors Corp., Kokomo, Ind., 1972-77; quality control engr. Delco Electronics, Gen. Motors, Kokomo, 1978-82, software design engr., 1982—. Inventor: Method and Apparatus for Detecting Rotational Speed, 1989, Antilock Brake Controller with Brake Mode Filter, 1989, Method and Apparatus for Low Speed Estimation, 1989. Adviser Jr. Achievment, Kokomo, Ind., 1978-80. Recipient Gen. Motors Fellowship, Univ. Calif., Berkeley, 1976. Mem. AAUW (membership chmn. local chpt. 1989-91), Kokomo Engring Soc. (treas. 1984-85), Soc. Women Engrs., Gen. Motors Inst. Alumni, U. Calif. Berkeley Alumni, U. Calif. Berkeley Engring. Alumni. Methodist and Unitarian. Office: Delco Electronics 1 Corp Ctr CT3A Kokomo IN 46904-9005

HERTE, MARY CHARLOTTE, plastic surgeon; b. Milw., May 31, 1951; d. Clarence H. and Bernadette E. (Storch) H. BS, Mt. Mary Coll., Milw., 1973; MD, U. Wis., 1977. Diplomate Am. Bd. Plastic Surgery. Research fellow in plastic surgery Grad. Sch. Medicine Ea. Va. U., Norfolk, 1978; gen. surgery resident Univ. Hosps., Madison, Wis., 1978-81; plastic surgery resident Univ. Hosps., Madison, 1981-83; practice medicine specializing in plastic surgery Las Vegas, Nev., 1983—; chief of surgery Humana Hosp. Sunrise, Las Vegas, 1989; chief plastic surgery Humana Children's Hosp., Las Vegas, 1990—. Recipient Woman of Promise award Good Housekeeping Mag., 1985. Fellow Am. Coll. Surgeons, Am. Acad. Pediatrics; mem. Am. Cleft Palate Assn., Am. Soc. Plastic and Reconstructive Surgeons, Nev. State Med. Soc. (del. 1986-88), Clark County Med. Soc. (trustee 1986-88). Lodge: Soroptimist Internat. (treas./fin. sec. Greater Las Vegas chpt. 1985-87). Office: 3006 S Maryland Pkwy Ste 415 Las Vegas NV 89109

HERTEL, SUZANNE MARIE, education educator; b. Hastings, Neb., Aug. 8, 1937; d. Louis C. Hertel and W. Lenore (Cross) Budd. BA, Doane Coll., Crete, Neb., 1959; MSM, Union Theol. Sem., 1961; postgrad., U. Hartford, 1966, U. Conn., 1975; MA, Merrill Palmer Inst., 1977; EdD, Boston U., 1982. Music tchr. Pub. Sch., Wethersfield, Conn., 1962-63; serials libr. Hartford (Conn.)Sem. Found., 1963-64; elem. tchr. Pub. Sch., Glastonbury, Conn., 1965-79; asst. prof. Univ. Northern Iowa, Cedar Falls, Iowa, 1979-81; training mgr. Focus Research Systems Inc., W. Hartford, Conn., 1982-89; pers. adminstr. City of Hartford, 1989—. Mem. Am. Soc. Training and Devel., Am. Guild Organists. Democrat. Office: City of Hartford Mcpl Bldg 550 Main St Hartford CT 06103

HERTLE, MARILYN IONE, educator; b. Austin, Minn., Nov. 15, 1931; d. Raymond Harold and Florence O. (Benson) Bray; m. Clinton C. Hertle, Oct. 6, 1951 (div. June 1976); children: Sherri Maloney, Lori Charlson, Barbara Beattie (dec.). BS, Winona State U., 1971; MS in Elem. Edn., Mankato State U., 1978. Tchr. Mower County Rural Sch., Austin, 1950-51, 55-56; substitute tchr. Dist. 492 Pub. Schs., Austin, 1958-71, classroom tchr., 1971—. Mem. NEA, Minn. Edn. Assn., Austin Edn. Assn. Methodist. Home: 403 1st Ave NW Apt 1 Austin MN 55912

HERTWECK, ALMA LOUISE, sociology and child development educator; b. Moline, Ill., Feb. 6, 1937; d. Jacob Ray and Sylvia Ethel (Whitt) Street; m. E. Romayne Hertweck, Dec. 16, 1955; 1 child, William Scott. A.A., Mira Costa Coll., 1969; B.A. in Sociology summa cum laude, U. Calif.-San Diego, 1975, M.A., 1977, Ph.D., 1982. Cert. sociology instr., multiple subjects teaching credential grades kindergarten-12, Calif. Staff research assoc. U. Calif.-San Diego, 1978-81; instr. sociology Chapman Coll., Orange, Calif., 1982-87; instr. child devel. MiraCosta Coll., Oceanside, Calif., 1983-87, 88-89; instr. sociology U.S. Internat. U., San Diego, 1985—; exec. dir., v.p. El Camino Preschools, Inc., Oceanside, 1985—. Author: Constructing the Truth and Consequences: Educators' Attributions of Perceived Failure in School, 1982; co-author: Handicapping the Handicapped, 1985. Mem. Am. Sociol. Assn., Am. Ednl. Research Assn., Nat. Council Family Relations, Nat. Assn. Edn. Young Children, Alpha Gamma Sigma (life). Avocations: foreign travel; sailing; bicycling. Home: 2024 Oceanview Rd Oceanside CA 92056 Office: El Camino Preschs Inc 2002 California St Oceanside CA 92054

HERWIG, JANE S., publishers representative; b. Phila., Jan. 21, 1937; d. Paul E. and Kathryn W. (Weidner) Scheifele; m. Louis W. Herwig; children: Richard Louis, Bruce David. BS in Edn., Bucknell U., 1958; MEd, Temple U., 1962. Classroom tchr. Abington Twp. Pub. Schs., Abington, Pa., 1958-65; dir. advt. Talmage Assocs., Willow Grove, Pa., 1978-87; dir. sales and mktg. Travel Agt. mag., N.Y.C., 1987-89; pres. JH Mktg., Maple Glen, Pa., 1989—; instr. pub. rels. Chestnut Hill Coll., Phila. Assoc. editor Tour Operator Directory, 1978-87; coord. Directory for Boat Operators, 1986-89, Directory for Dinner Theatres, 1988-90. Founder, Child Care of Montgomery County, Abington, 1977, program dir., 1988—; dir. pub. relations Upper Dublin Library Bldg. Commn., Dresher, Pa., 1989—; co-founder Women's Ctr. of Montgomery County, Jenkintown, Pa., 1976. Mem. AAUW (tour operator 1980—, pres.), Phila. Pub. Rels. Assn., Valley Forge Conv. and Vis. Bur., Pocono Mountains Visitors Bur., Am. Bus Assn. Republican. Home: 1820 Thornbury Dr Maple Glen PA 19002

HERZ, SARA MOSS, clinical psychologist; b. N.Y.C., Sept. 16, 1940; d. Arthur Edward and Naomi (Fischer) Moss; m. Jack L. Herz, May 24, 1964; children: Stephen Evan, Allison Moss. BA, Syracuse (N.Y.) U., 1962; PhD, Yeshiva U., 1980. Lic. clin. psychologist. Psychology assoc. West Haven (Conn.) VA Med. Ctr., 1979-81; pvt. practice clin. psychology Westport, Conn., 1981—. Interviewer video archives for Holocaust studies Yale U., New Haven, 1985—; pres. bd. dirs. Conn. Renaissance, Norwalk, 1986-88; bd. dirs. So. Fairfield (Conn.) chpt. Am. Cancer Soc., 1981—, chmn. ethics com. Mem. Am. Psychol. Assn., Conn. Psychol. Assn., Conn. Soc. Psychoanalytic Psychologists, Fairfield County Psychologists. Office: 4 Whitney St Extension Westport CT 06880 also: 1200 E Putnam Ave Riverside CT 06878

HERZBERG, MARGARET ANN, nurse, researcher; b. Bellmore, N.Y., Dec. 11, 1957; d. Ernest Frederick and Ann Dorothy (Meehan) H. BS cum laude, Adelphi U., 1980. RN, N.Y. Nurse, office mgr. East Side Sports Medicine Ctr., N.Y.C., 1980-81; staff nurse Nassau County Med. Ctr., East Meadow, N.Y., 1981-83; surg. nurse, office mgr. Otolaryngology/Cosmetic Surg. Ctr., Wantagh, N.Y., 1987-88; nurse, office mgr. Phys. Therapy Office, Merrick, N.Y., 1987-88; pvt. practice orthopedic nurse researcher North Bellmore, N.Y., 1988—; dir. program devel. PRO-FORM Sports Medicine, P.C., St. James, N.Y., 1988—; pvt. practice med. and legal cons. North Bellmore, 1989—. Mem. Nat. Assn. Orthopaedic Nurses, Nat. Athletic Trainers Assn. (assoc.), Sigma Theta Tau (exec. bd. Alpha Omega chpt., newsletter editor 1982-87, charter Kappa Gamma chpt., newsletter editor 1988-89), Nat. Assn. Strength and Fitness Profls. (nat. sec. 1990—). Republican. Roman Catholic. Office: PRO FORM Sports Medicine PC 556-08 N Country Rd Saint James NY 11780

HERZBERG, SYDELLE SHULMAN, lawyer, accountant; b. N.Y.C., July 24, 1933; d. Hyman and Rose (Green) S.; m. Norman Joseph Herzberg, June 23, 1962; 1 child, Gilbert. BS, NYU, 1955; JD, Bklyn. Law Sch., 1957. Bar: N.Y. 1958; CPA, N.Y. Pub. acct. M. Sharlach & Co, N.Y.C., 1955-62; pvt. practice acctg. and law New Rochelle, N.Y., 1962—. Mem. bd. edn. Solomon Schechter Sch. of Westchester, White Plains, N.Y., 1975-78, bd. dirs. PTA, 1975-78; pres. PTA bd. Westchester Hebrew High Sch., Mamaroneck, N.Y., 1980-82; mem. budget adv. bd. City of New Rochelle, N.Y., 1975. Mem. AICPA, N.Y. State Soc. CPAs, ABA, N.Y. State Bar Assn., Westchester Women's Bar Assn., Huquenot-Thomas Paine Hist. Assn. (treas. 1987—, trustee 1987—), LWV (pres. New Rochelle chpt. 1983-85, treas. Westchester chpt. 1989—, budget chair N.Y. 1989—). Jewish. Home: 46 Longue Vue Ave New Rochelle NY 10804 Office: 519 Main St New Rochelle NY 10801

HERZECA, LOIS FRIEDMAN, lawyer; b. N.Y.C., July 7, 1954; d. Martin and Elaine Shirley (Rapoport) Friedman; m. Christian Stefan Herzeca, Aug. 15, 1980; 1 child, Jane Leslie. B.A. Harpur Coll., SUNY-Binghamton, 1976; J.D., Boston U., 1979. Bar: N.Y. 1980, U.S. Dist. Ct. (so. and ea. dist.) N.Y. 1980. Atty. antitrust div. U.S. Dept. Justice, Washington, 1979-80; assoc. Fried, Frank, Harris, Shriver & Jacobson, N.Y.C., 1980-86, ptnr., 1986—. Editor Am. Jour. Law and Medicine, 1978-79. Mem. ABA, N.Y.C. Bar Assn. Office: Fried Frank Harris Shriver & Jacobson 1 New York Pla New York NY 10004

HERZENBERG, CAROLINE LITTLEJOHN, physicist; b. East Orange, N.J., Mar. 25, 1932; d. Charles Frederick and Caroline Dorothea (Schulze) L.; m. Leonardo Herzenberg, July 29, 1961; children: Karen Ann, Catherine Stuart. SB, MIT, 1953; SM, U. Chgo., 1955, PhD, 1958. Asst. prof. Ill. Inst. Tech., Chgo., 1961-66, research physicist ITT Research Inst., 1967-70, sr. physicist, 1970-71; lectr. Calif. State U., Fresno, 1975-76; physicist Argonne Nat. Lab., Ill., 1977—; prin. investigator NASA Apollo Returned Lunar Sample Analysis Program, 1967-71; producer and host TV sci. series Camera on Sci. Author: Women Scientists from Antiquity to the Present: An Index, 1986. Contbr. articles to profl. jours. Candidate for alderman, Freeport, Ill., 1975; past chmn. NOW chpt., Freeport. Am. Phys. Soc. Congl. Scientist fellow finalist, 1976-77; recipient award in sci. Chgo. Women's Hall of Fame, 1989. Fellow Am. Phys. Soc. (past chmn. com.), AAAS; mem. Assn. Women in Sci. (nat. sec. 1982-84, pres. 1988-90), Sigma

Xi. Home: 1814 Valley View Dr Freeport IL 61032 Office: Argonne Nat Lab Argonne IL 60439

HERZLINGER, REGINA, educator; b. Tel Aviv, Dec. 5, 1943; came to U.S. 1952; d. Alexander and Ella (Joffe) E.; m. George Herzlinger, Jan. 27, 1966; children: Susan, Alexander. BA, MIT, 1965; PhD, Harvard Bus. Sch., 1971. Economist FPC, Washington, 1966-67; v.p. Various Cons. Firms, Cambridge, 1967-71; asst. sec. Gov. Commonwealth Mass., 1971; prof. Harvard Bus. Sch., Boston, 1971—; bd. dirs. Addiction Recovery Ctrs. Inc., Allegheny Power System, Health and Rehab. Properties Trust, Salick Health Care Inc. Trustee Bowdoin Coll. Brigham and Women's Hosp., 1985, MIT, 1986. Avocations:art, literature, tennis, aerobics. Office: Harvard Bus Sch Soldier's Field Baker Library 232 Cambridge MA 02163

HERZOG, BEVERLY LEAH, hydrogeologist; b. Fond du Lac, Wis., Aug. 27, 1954; d. Charles Victor and Helen Jean (Gutsch) H.; m. Craig Warren Cutbirth, June 2, 1979. BS in Geology, U. Wis., Oshkosh, Wis., 1976; MS in Hydrology, Stanford U., 1978. Cert. groundwater profl., profl. geologist. Asst. hydrogeologist Donohue & Assocs., Sheboygan, Wis., 1977; cons. Hydrocomp Internat., Palo Alto, Calif., 1977-78; asst. hydrogeologist Camp, Dresser & McKee, Champaign, Ill., 1978-79; asst. geologist Ill. State Geol. Survey, Champaign, 1980-84, assoc. hydrogeologist, 1985-90, hydrologist, 1990—. Co-author: Ground Water Sampling, 1990; contbr. numerous articles on groundwater to profl. jours; mem. editorial bd. Ground Water, 1986—, Ground Water Monitoring Rev., 1989—. Bd. dirs. DeWitt County chpt. ARC, Clinton, Ill., 1984-90, CPR and first aid instr. Champaign County chpt. ARC, 1978—; camp counselor Fox River Area coun. Girl Scout U.S., Appleton, Wis., 1972, 73, 76. Named Outstanding Vol., Champaign County chpt. ARC, 1987; recipient Best Paper award Ground Water Monitoring Rev., 1988, Disting. Achievement award Ill. State Geol. Survey, 1989. Mem. Assn. Ground Water Scientists & Engrs., Am. Geophys. Union, Am. Soc. for Testing & Materials, Am. Water Resources Assn., Sigma Xi. Home: 512 S Washington St Farmer City IL 61842 Office: Ill State Geol Survey 615 E Peabody Dr Champaign IL 61820

HERZOG, JOAN DOROTHY, healthcare executive; b. Chgo., July 5, 1938; d. Zigmund and Josephine (Kiras) Zaharski; m. Frederick Jarvis Herzog; children: Gregory Scott, Leslie Ellen, Allison Lynn. BS in Nursing, Loyola U., Chgo., 1961; MS in Health Services Adminstrn., Coll. St. Francis, 1985. RN, Ill. Staff nurse Cook County Dept. Pub. Health, Chgo., 1960-61; clinic nurse Norwood Med. Ctr., Chgo., 1965-70; office nurse Thaddeus Poremski, MD, Chgo., 1974-79; supr., audit/utilization rev. Thorek Hosp. and Med. Ctr., Chgo., 1980-81; dir. quality assurance St. Elizabeth's Hosp., Chgo., 1981-83; cons. Blue Cross & Blue Shield Assn., Chgo., 1983-84; mgr. utilization mgmt. CNA Ins. Cos., Chgo., 1984—; mem. adv. bd. Norell Home Health Care, Northbrook, Ill., 1984, Regional Strategic Planning and Mktg. Com., Alexian Bros. Med. Ctr., Elk Grove Village, Ill., 1988—; mem. profl. affairs com. Ancilla Systems, Elk Grove Village, 1985-87. With pub. relations Cavaliers Drum & Bugle Corps, Park Ridge, Ill., 1977-78; bd. dirs. Council Cath. Women, Park Ridge, Ill., 1974-75. Mem. Ill. Assn. Quality Assurance Profls. (regional rep. 1984), Am. Coll. Utilization Rev. Physicians (affiliate), Women's Health Exec. Network. Home: 615 S Lincoln Ln Arlington Heights IL 60005 Office: CNA Ins Cos CNA Plaza Chicago IL 60685

HERZOG, KATHRYN ROSE, health care administrator, hospice consultant; b. Des Moines, Nov. 10, 1955; d. Herman J. and Evelyn K. (Kempker) Wedel; m. Benjamin David Herzog, May 16, 1981; children: Sarah, Kate. BSN, U. Iowa, 1978; MSN, U. Tex., 1980. Staff nurse U. Iowa Hosp., Iowa City, 1977-79; head nurse, supr. Seton Med. Ctr., Austin, Tex., 1980-83; asst. dir. nursing Sacred Heart Med. Ctr., Chester, Pa., 1983-84; Nat. Standard Seminar Instr., hospice surveyer Joint Commn. on Accreditation of Hosps., Chgo., 1983—; exec. dir. Del. Hospice, Wilmington, 1984-85; dir. nursing Bapt. Hosp., Beaumont, Tex., 1986-89; guest lectr. Lamar U., 1988-89; dir. cancer programs Humana Hosp.-Clear Lake, 1989—. Author of monthly continuing edn. program for nurses, Cancer Awareness, 1983; rsch. presentation at Nat. Conf. on Nursing Adminstrn. Rsch., 1981; manuscript reviewer; contbr. articles to profl. jours. Co-faciliator "I Can Cope" program, Am. Cancer Soc., Austin, 1981-83, instr. self breast exam Austin, Wilmington, Del., Houston, 1980—; CPR Instructor Am. Heart Assn., Austin, Wilmington, Houston, 1979—; lecturer on women and cancer to local hosp. and community groups, Austin, Wilmington, Houston, 1980—. Nominated for Outstanding Young Alumnus U. Iowa, 1983. Mem. Tex. Nurses Assn. (dist. 5 first v.p. 1981-82), Oncology Nursing Soc. (convention del. 1982), Del. State Hospice Orgn. (state rep. 1984—), Nat. Hospice Orgn. (nat. convention workshop instr. 1983—), Am. Heart Assn., Am. Nurses Assn., Wilmington Women in Bus., Young Exec. Club, Phi Kappa Phi, Sigma Theta Tau. Avocations: china painting, reading, swimming. Home: 14307 Hillside Hickory Ct Houston TX 77062 Office: Humana Hosp-Clear Lake 500 Medical Center Blvd Webster TX 77598

HERZOG, RENEE BARBARA, production manager; b. N.Y.C., Feb. 27, 1947; d. Milton and Helen (Mohr) Semes; m. Ci Herzog, Oct 5, 1975; 1 child, Jennifer. BFA, NYU, 1967; postgrad., Queensboro Community Coll., 1985. Cert. in data processing. Asst. v.p. FA Components, Elmhurst, N.Y., 1985-87; asst. pub. CMP Publ., Manahasset, N.Y., 1987; prodn. mgr. ACS Communications, Great Neck, N.Y., 1987—. Appeared in plays Candide, 1973-76, Fiddler on the Roof, 1968-72. Sec. Concerned Citizens for the Edn. of the Gifted and Talented, Queens, N.Y., 1989. Mem. Nat. Assn. Female Execs., Alpha Beta Gamma, Actor's Equity Assn., Screen Actor's Guild. Office: ACS Communications 55 Northern Blvd Great Neck NY 11021

HESELTON, PATRICIA LA ROCK, child psychologist; b. Sault Ste Marie, Mich., Dec. 18, 1946; d. John Edward and Beatrice Mary (Carlin) La Rock; m. Frank Richmond Heselton, Jr., June 19, 1965 (Dec. 1981); children: Laura Kay, Karen Amanda. BA summa cum laude, U. Md., 1972; MA, U. Md., Balt., 1976; postgrad., U. Md., 1976-80. Limited lic. psychologist, Mich. Teaching asst. U. Md. Baltimore County, Balt., 1974-76, U. Md., College Park, 1976-78; doctoral intern Walter P. Carler Mental Health, Balt., 1979-80, Towson (Md.) State U., 1978-80; counseling coord. Chippewa County Domestic Violence Shelter, Sault Ste. Marie, 1980; family counselor Family Svcs. Ctr., Sault Ste. Marie, Ont., Can., 1981-83; psychologist Monroe County Youth Ctr., Monroe, Mich., 1983-88; evaluation and admissions psychologist Monroe County Community Mental Health, Monroe, 1988—; mem. Child Protection Team, Monroe, 1983-88. Contbr. articles to Jour. Personalized Instrn. Mem., bd. dirs. Rape Crisis Ctr., Monroe, 1985-87, Shelter, Inc., Monroe, 1986-87, Halfway House for Recovering Alcoholics, Sault Ste. Marie, Mich., 1981-83; vol. coord., tng. dir. Howard County (Md.) Rape Crisis Ctr., Columbia, 1974-80. Named one of Outstanding Young Women Am., 1978; univ. grantee U. Md., College Park, 1979, 80. Mem. Am. Psychol. Assn., Mich. Psychol. Assn., Phi Beta Kappa, Psi Chi, Phi Kappa Phi. Democrat. Episcopalian. Home: 6355 Ave C LaSalle MI 48145 Office: Monroe County Community Mental Health 1001 S Raisinville Rd Monroe MI 48161

HESS, DEBRA, attorney; b. Murray, Utah, Oct. 24, 1953; d. Odean Lot and Louise (Petersen) H. BA in English, U. Utah, 1984; JD, Whittier Coll., 1989. Sales ZCMI, Salt Lake City, 1972-79, Arthur Frank, Inc., Salt Lake City, 1986-89; law clk. South Bay Jud. Dist., Torrance, Calif., 1989—. Vol. counselor Salt Lake Rape Crisis Ctr., 1984-85, Utah Women's Clinic, Salt Lake City, 1984-85. Mem. ABA (natural resources sect., internat. law sect.). Home: PO Box 70467 West Valley City UT 84170

HESS, HARRIET SCHNEIDER, nursing consultant; b. Elizabeth, N.J., Jan. 27, 1927; d. Harry and Frances (Weiner) Schneider; m. William E. Hess, Aug. 14, 1980. BS in Edn., Hunter Coll., 1957; MA, Columbia U., 1958, MEd, 1970, EdD, 1974. RN, N.Y., Miss. Staff nurse various hosps., N.Y.C. and Buffalo, 1948, 49, Alton Road Hosp., Miami Beach, Fla., 1949; staff nurse, head nurse, pediatric supr. Queens Hosp. Ctr., Jamaica, N.Y., 1950-56; supr. Elmhurst (N.Y.) City Hosp., 1962; prof. nursing Univ. Med. Ctr., Jackson, 1978, sec. faculty senate, 1982; pvt. duty nurse Alba Registry for Nurses, Bklyn., 1948-50; asst. prof. maternal-child health Alfred (N.Y.) U., 1958-62; asst. prof. maternal-child nursing SUNY Downstate Med. Ctr. Coll. Nursing, Bklyn., 1968-69; presenter in field, 1963—; cons. numerous workshops and confs., 1966—; cons. U. Wyo., 1981, Delta State U., 1981, also others; mem. planning com. Deans and Dirs. Coun. of Schs. Nursing in Miss., 1978—; mem. accrediation rev. Bd. Trustees of State Instns. Higher Edn., Miss., 1979-81. Contbr. articles to profl. jours. Bd. dirs. Nurses House, Inc., 1977-79. Recipient Tchr. of Yr. award for grad. studies Univ. Med. Ctr., 1979, Spl. Faculty award, 1982; grantee N.Y. State Dept. Health, 1958-59. Mem. AAUP, ANA, Am. Ednl. Rsch. Assn., Miss. Nurses Assn., Nat. Coun. on Measurement in Edn., Nat. League for Nursing, Bellevue Schs. Nursing Alumnae Assn., Columbia U. Tchrs. Coll. Dept. Nursing Alumnae Assn. (life), Guardian Soc. (U. Miss.), Sigma Theta Tau. Jewish. Home: 548 Majorca Ct Satellite Beach FL 32937

HESS, HAZEL ELIZABETH, healthcare administrator; b. Olcott, W.Va., Nov. 2, 1929; d. Lloyd Forrest and Ethel Hazel (Turley) Akers; m. Kenneth Reed Hess Sr., Oct. 29, 1948; children: Kenneth Reed Jr., Susan Renee Conner. Grad. high sch., South Charleston, W.Va. Receptionist Valley Convalescent Hosp., Charleston, W.Va., 1952-55; with Highland Hosp., Charleston, W.Va., 1955—, acting adminstr., 1987-88, asst. adminstr., 1988—. Mem. Internat. Credit Assn. (bd. dirs. St. Louis chpt. 1980—, pres. 1983-84), CWI-Credit Profls. (bd. dirs. 1983—, pres. 1988-89, Credit Profl. of Yr. 1976-77, Woman of the Yr. 1984-85). Democrat. Home: Rt 7 Box 276B South Charleston WV 25309 Office: Highland Hosp 300-56th St PO Box 4107 Charleston WV 25364

HESS, IRMA, academic program director, translator; b. Frankfurt, Germany, Feb. 5, 1939; came to U.S., 1957, naturalized, 1960; d. Frederick and Martha (Mahlert) Alban; 1 child, Harold Alban Hess. B.A., New Sch. for Social Research, 1977; B.S., SUNY-Albany, 1976; M.A., NYU, 1979, M.P.A., 1984, advanced profl. cert., grad. of bus., 1986. Asst. to spl. psychol. testing Bd. Edn., Mt. Vernon, N.Y., 1959-65, health chmn., 1959-66; ind. practice bookkeeping, 1959-65; translator N.Y.C. cts. and agys., 1959—, interpreter, 1959-77; counselor Family Ct., Criminal Ct. Youth Div., N.Y.C., 1976-78; tchr. New Rochell Bd. Edn., 1976-78; adminstr. NYU, N.Y.C., 1978—. Vice pres. PTA, Mt. Vernon, 1968-70; chmn. Mt. Vernon Community Chest, 1971-73; sec. N.Y.C. br. ARC, 1975-77. Recipient Mayor of N.Y. accomplishment cert., 1978; scholar State of N.Y., 1976, NYU, 1978. Mem. Am. Soc. Pub. Adminstrs., U.S. Exec. Women, Am. Translators Assn., Am. Pub. Health Adminstrs., Am. Polit. Sci. Assn., N.Y. Acad. Scis., New Sch. for Social Research Alumni Assn., NYU Alumni Assn. Avocations: golf; ballet; tennis; folk music. Office: NYU D'Agostino Hall 110 W 3rd St New York NY 10012

HESS, KAREN MATISON, author; b. Austin, Minn, Apr. 11, 1939; d. George Wilbur and Marie Regina (Barnitz) M.; m. Sheldon T. Hess, July. BS, U . Minnesota, 1961; BA, U. Minn., 1961; MA, U. Minn, 1963; PhD, U. Minn., 1968. Instr. Hopkins Sr. High Sch., Hopkins, Minn., 1961-65; rsch. assoc. Upper Midwest Regional Edn. Lab., Bloomington, Minn., 1968-75; instr. Normandale Community Coll., Bloomington, 1968—; chief exec. officer Innovative Programming Systems, Inc., Bloomington, 1971—, Info. Age Communication, Bloomington, 1987—, Institute for Profl. Devel., Bloomington, 1987—. Contbr. articles to profl. jours. Adv. Council Chair-Community Edn., Bloomington, Minn.; mem. various coms. Recipient: Phi Beta Kappa, U. Minnesota, Minn., 1960: Named: Outstanding. Mem. Nat. Coun. of Tchrs. of English, Phi Delta Kappa, American Assn. Republican Lutheran. Office: 9001 Poplar Bridge Rd Bloomington MN 55437

HESS, MARCIA WANDA, educational assistant; b. Cin., Mar. 15, 1934; d. Edward Frederick Lipka and Rose (Wirtle) Lipka Stanley; m. Edward Emanuel Grenier, Aug. 9, 1952 (div.); m. Thomas Benton Hess, Mar. 25, 1960; children: Kathleen Ann, Cynthia Jean, Thomas Allen. Grad. high sch., Cin. Instr. asst. Cin. Pub. Schs., 1970—, also mem. staff desegregation workshop and unified K-12 reading communication arts program staff tng. com., tchr. instr. assts. handbook. Mem. Winton Place Vets of World War II Women's Aux. (pres. 1982-84, bd. dirs. 1982-84, 89—). Republican. Roman Catholic. Home: 765 Derby Ave Cincinnati OH 45232

HESS, MARGARET JOHNSTON, religious writer, educator; b. Ames. Iowa, Feb. 22, 1915; d. Howard Wright and Jane Edith (Stevenson) Johnston; B.A., Coe Coll., 1937; m. Bartlett Leonard Hess, July 31, 1937; children—Daniel, Deborah, John, Janet. Bible tchr. Community Bible Classes Ward Presbyn. Ch., Livonia, Mich., 1959—, Christ Ch. Cranbrook (Episcopalian), Bloomfield Hills, Mich., 1980—. Co-author: (with B.L. Hess) How to Have a Giving Church, 1974, The Power of a Loving Church, 1977, How Does Your Marriage Grow?, 1983, Never Say Old, 1984; author: Love Knows No Barriers, 1979; Esther: Courage in Crisis, 1980; Unconventional Women, 1981, The Triumph of Love, 1987; contbr. articles to religious jours. Home: 16845 Riverside Dr Livonia MI 48154

HESSE, GRETE ANNA ERNA, psychologist; b. Botersen, Kreis, Rotenburg, Federal Republic of Germany, Aug. 2, 1933; came to the U.S, 1955; d. Adolf Friedrich and Katharina Margarete (Dierks) H. BA in Psychology, Rutgers U., 1970; MA in Clin. Psychology, Fairleigh Dickinson U., 1972; PhD in Clin. Psychology, Union Inst., 1989; MS in Interdisciplinary Studies in Human Devel., U. Pa., 1989. Intern psychology N. J. Dept. Inst. and Agencies, Trenton, 1972-73; psychologist Cumberland County Guidance Ctr., Millville, 1974-80, Ancora Psychiatric Hosp., Hammonton, 1980—. Mem. Zonta (bd. dirs.). Lutheran. Home: 1 Marilyn Ave Vineland NJ 08360 Office: Ancora Psychiatric Hosp Spring Garden Rd Hammonton NJ 08037

HESSE, MARTHA O., executive; b. Hattiesburg, Miss., Aug. 14, 1942; d. John William and Geraldine Elaine (Ossian) H. B.S., U. Iowa, 1964; postgrad., Northwestern U., 1972-76; M.B.A., U. Chgo., 1979. Research analyst Blue Shield, 1964-66; dir. div. data mgmt. Am. Hosp. Assn., 1966-69; dir., chief operating officer SEI Info. Tech., Chgo., 1969-80; assoc. dep. sec. Dept. of Commerce, Washington, 1981-82; exec. dir. Pres.' Task Force on Mgmt. Reform, 1982; asst. sec. mgmt. and adminstrn. Dept. of Energy, Washington, 1982-86; chmn. FERC, Washington, 1986-89; sr. v.p. 1st Chgo. Corp., 1990; pres. Dolan Energy Corp., 1990—; bd. dirs. Am. Nat. Resources Co. (subs. of The Coastal Corp.); vice-chmn. Dean's fund, U. Chgo., 1981-85. Home: 999 Lake Shore Dr Chicago IL 60611

HESSELBEIN, FRANCES RICHARDS, foundation executive, consultant; b. South Fork, Pa.; d. Burgess Harmon and Anne Luke (Wicks) Richards; widowed, 1978; 1 child, John Richards. Student, U. Pitts.; DHL (hon.), Buena Vista Coll., 1987, Juniata Coll., 1990; D Mgmt. (hon.), GM Inst., 1990. Co-owner Hesselbein Studios, Johnstown, Pa., 1950-70; chief exec. officer Talus Rock Girl Scout Council, Johnstown, 1970-74, Penn Laurel Girl Scout Coun., York, Pa., 1974-76, Girl Scouts U.S., N.Y.C., 1976-90; prin. Frances Hesselbein Assocs., N.Y.C., 1990—; pres., chief exec. officer Peter F. Drucker Found. Nonprofit Mgmt., N.Y.C., 1990—; bd. dirs. Mut. of Am. Ins. Co., N.Y.C., Ind. Sector, Washington; mem. nat. bd. visitors Peter F. Drucker Grad. Mgmt. Ctr., Claremont (Calif.) Grad. Sch., 1987—; chmn. bd. govs. Josephson Ethics Inst.; mem. adv. com. to bd. dirs. N.Y. Stock Exchange, 1988—. Mem. edit. adv. bd. Nonprofit Mgmt. and Leadership. Dir. Youth for Understanding, Washington, 1984—; trustee Juniata Coll., Huntingdon, Pa., 1988—, Allentown (Pa.) Coll., 1988—; mem. Pres.'s Adv. Com. on the Points of Light Initiative Found., 1989—. Recipient Outstanding Achievement award Inter-Service Club Council, Johnstown, 1976, Entrepreneurial Woman award Women Bus. Owners of N.Y., 1984, Nat. Leadership award United Way of Am., Washington, 1985, Disting. Community Service award Mut. of Am. Ins. Co., 1985, Dir.'s Choice award Nat. Women's Econ. Alliance, 1988, Excellence in Leadership award Nat. Women's Econ. Alliance, 1989; named Outstanding Exec., Savvy Mag., 1985. Mem. Sky Club, Cosmopolitan Club, Pa. Soc. Club (N.Y.C.), Marco Polo Club. Office: Peter F Drucker Found Nonprofit Mgmt 666 Fifth Ave 19th Fl New York NY 10103

HESSER, DANIELLE ELAN, aerospace company executive; b. Bklyn., May 19, 1949; d. William and Marie (Nelson) DiBella. Student Prince George's Community Coll., 1981-85. Jr. electronics technician Enviromarine, Inc., Laurel, Md., 1978-80; computer operator Bendix Field Engring. Corp., Columbia, Md., 1980-81; computer operator Ford Aerospace Co., College Park, Md., 1981-83, with command mgmt., 1983-84; satellite controller, obs. engr. OAO Corp., Greenbelt, Md., 1985—. Mem. Assn. for Humanistic Psychology. Republican. Avocations: movies, theater, yachting, flying, metaphysics.

HESSER, MELANIE JEAN, mental health counselor; b. DuBois, Pa., Dec. 27, 1962; d. Matthew John and Violet T. (Krawczyk) H. BS in Rehab. Edn., Pa. State U., 1986; postgrad., Pitt U., Pitts., 1987—. Salesperson Sylvester's, Ocean City, Md., 1982; ride operator Jolly Roger Amusement Park, Ocean City, 1983; registry companion Intracorp Home Health Agy., State College, Pa., 1985; resident counselor Turtle Creek Mental Health/Mental Rehab., Inc., Munhall, Pa., 1986—; intern Rehab. Inst. Pitts., 1986, Westenr Psychiat. Inst. and Clinic, Pitts., 1989; practicum Brighton Woods Treatment Ctr., Pitts., 1988; vol. counselor Oasis Help Ctr., State College, 1985. Home: 170 Merrimac St Pittsburgh PA 15211 Office: Turtle Creek Valley MH/MR 905 Dickson St Ste 102 Munhall PA 15120

HESTAND, CYNTHIA ANN, actress; b. Sherman, Tex., June 15, 1955; d. Howard Anthony Jr. and Mary Janice (Cole) Hestand; m. Haskell Edmond Hestand Jr., Sept. 15, 1978. BA, Austin Coll., 1977, MA, 1979. Represented by Peggy Taylor Talent Agy., Dallas, 1980-83; adminstrv. asst. Stage #1, Dallas, 1982-84; performer State #1, Dallas, 1983, 84, New Arts Theatre, 1984, 86; founder, performer Rosser Sq. Prodns., Dallas, 1983-88, adminstrv. asst., 1986-87; represented by Joy Wyse Agy., Dallas, 1984-88, Harold Bock Agy., Dallas, 1988-89, J and D Talent Agy., Dallas, 1989—; founder, producer, performer, dir. The Open Stage, Dallas, 1988—; performer Theatre Three Main Stage, Dallas, 1982-87, Grimm Magician Players, Dallas, 1982-87; performer, mem. playreading com. Addison Centre Theater, Dallas, 1983-84; cons., Stage #1, 1984-85; performer Teen Children's Theater, Dallas Theater Ctr., Dallas, 1988, tchr., summer and fall 1989. Appeared in plays Light Up the Sky, 1987, Ghosts, 1987; films include Papa Was a Preacher, 1985, Circle Game, 1988. Vol., performer Garland (Tex.) Civic Theatre, 1981-82; supporter Operation Kindness, Dallas, 1989; vol. ASPCA, Dallas., 1981-82; mem. Red River Hist. Mus., Sherman, Tex.; active Dallas Zool. Soc., 1986—. Mem. Actors' Equity Assn., Dallas Theater Caucus, Chimera, Soc. for Theatrical Artist's Guidance and Enhancement, Women in Film, Kappa Gamma Chi Alumni. Episcopalian. Home and Office: The Open Stage 4034 Rosser Sq Dallas TX 75244

HESTENES, ROBERTA RAE, college president, minister; b. Huntington, Calif., Aug. 5, 1939; d. Robert James and Besse Rae (Nipp) Louis; m. John D. Hestenes; children: Joan Hestenes Lehnen, Eric Magnus, Stephen Eastvold. BA, U. Calif., Santa Barbara; M in Divinity, Fuller Theol. Sem., 1979, DD, 1983. Ordained to ministry Presbyn. Ch., 1979. Dir. adult edn. and small group ministries United Presbyn. Ch., Seattle, 1967-74; assoc. in ministry LaCanada (Calif.) Presbyn. Ch., 1974-84; assoc. prof., dir. Christian Formation and Discipleship program Fuller Theol. Sem., Pasadena, Calif., 1975-87; bd. dirs., chmn. strategic planning com. World Vision U.S., 1980—; bd. dirs. World Vision Internat., 1982—, chmn. bd. dirs., 1985—; pres. Eastern Coll., St. Davids, Pa., 1987—; cons. numerous Presbyn. orgns.; minister Kenya, Australia, South Africa, Singapore, Hong Kong, South Korea, Philippines, Cen. am. Author: (books) Using the Bible in Groups, 1985, Discovering II Corinthians/Galatians, 1986, (taped courses) Building Christian Community Through Small Groups, 1985, Helping Christians Grow: Adult Formation and Discipleship in the Local Church, 1987; co-editor: Women and the Ministries of Christ, 1979; contbr. articles to profl. jours.;. Fellow Case Methods Inst.; mem. Am. Acad. Religion, Religious Edn. Assn., Nat. Assn. of Profs. of Christian Edn. Office: Ea Coll Fairview Dr Saint Davids PA 19087

HESTER, BETTY PARRISH, health science association administrator; b. Ocilla, Ga., Jan. 26, 1936; d. Henry Wesley Sr. and Ruby (Snellgrove) Parrish; m. James F. Hester Sr., Apr. 17, 1957; (div. July 1984); children: James F. Jr., Susan Renee Hester Pitts, Joey Glenn. Student, Fitzgerald High Sch., 1955; studetn, Nat. Tumor Registrars Assn., 1988. Cert. Tumor registrar. Med. asst. Robert E Jones, M.D., Tifton, Ga., 1969-73, Carlton F. Flemming, M.D., Tifton, Ga., 1973-74; tumor registrar Tift Gen. Hosp., Tifton, Ga., 1975-82; office mgr. Bruce Sampson, M.D., Perry, Ga., F. Morris Davis, M.D., Tifton, Ga., 1983-84; tumor registrar Tift Gen. Hosp., Ga., 1984-85; medicare b clk. Blue Cross, Blue Shield, Jacksonville, Fla., 1985-86; tumor registrar S Ga. Med. Ctr., Valdosta, Ga., 1986—; Bd. dirs. Am. Cancer Soc., Tifton 1978-82. Den mother Brownies Girl Scouts U.S., 1970, mem. polio vacc drive Jaycettes, Tifton, Ga., 1970. Mem. Ga. Tumor Registrars Assn. (chmn. nominating com., 1981), Nat. Tumor Registrars Assn., Rosewood Garden Club (sec. 1984-85), Shriners (pres. marching patrol aux. 1982). Baptist. Home: 152 Blue Pool Dr Valdosta GA 31602

HESTER, CAROLYN LAVAR, hospital administrator; b. Memphis, July 30, 1948; d. James Bateman and Boneta Elmaida (LeBeau) Fite; m. Jimmy Noel Hester, May 22, 1980; 1 child, Matthew James. Student Technol. Inst. Monterrey, Nuevo Leon, Mex., 1968-69; B.S., Okla. State U., 1970. Social worker Okla. Dept. Welfare, Oklahoma City, 1970-72; instr. Pan Am. Airlines, Miami, Fla., 1972-74, Happy Time Sch., Richardson, Tex., 1975-77; sr. account exec. Fite-Davis Inc., Oklahoma City, 1977-80; dir. pub. relations Okla. State U. Tech. Inst., Oklahoma City, 1980-86; dir. pub. relations South Community Hosp., 1986—; dir. Fite-Hester Inc., Oklahoma City; advt. cons. Burl Holmes Ford, Oklahoma City, 1984—, Dodsons Cafeterias, Oklahoma City, 1984—, Sleepe Shoppe, Oklahoma City, 1984—. Author: Mary Lou Likes Blue, 1977, Stop Drop and Roll; also song lyrics, poetry. Active cub scouting, local Boy Scouts Am.; hon. police officer, Chickasaw, Okla.; bd. dirs. Okla. Children's Theatre, March of Dimes. Recipient Appreciation plaque Oklahoma City Hort. Ctr., 1984, Hon. Police Officer Chickasaw, Okla. Mem. PTA (membership chmn. 1983, carnival chmn. 1984, Helping Hands award 1985), Okla. Hosp. Assn., Am. Hosp. Assn., Oklahoma City Power Squadron (pub. relations officer 1985—), Oklahoma City Pub. Relations Assn., Nat. Clown and Laughter Hall of Fame (founder, chmn. bd. dirs.), Oklahoma City Running Club (bd. dirs. 1985), Oklahoma City C. of C., Kid Safe Assn. Democrat. Methodist. Club: Variety. Lodge: Lions (bd. dirs. local chpt.). Avocations: sailing, camping, writing. Office: South Community Hosp 1001 SW 44th St Oklahoma City OK 73109

HESTER, ELIZABETH JAMES, editor; b. Memphis, May 28, 1963; d. James Ernest and Jeanette Condra (Drew) Blindauer; m. Wayne Alan, Dec. 5, 1987. BA, U. Ala., Birmingham, 1987. Research asst. U. Ala., Birmingham, 1987-88; editorial asst. So. Living Mag., Birmingham, Ala., 1988—. Vol. So. Progress Corp., Birmingham, Ala., 1988-89, Birmingham Hist. Soc.; Docent Birmingham Mus. of Art, 1988-90, Jr. Patron Birmingham Mus. of Art, 1988-90. Recipient 1 Semester Scholarship Mobile-Worms Sister City Soc. Mem. Am. Assn. of Tchrs. of German, The Club. Republican. Methodist. Office: So Living Mag 2100 Lakeshore Dr Birmingham AL 35209

HESTER, MARYLEE BABENDREIER, educational administrator; b. Clarksburg, W.Va., Mar. 6, 1935; d. Charles Albert and Clarabel (Taylor) Babendreier; m. James David Hester, Feb. 7, 1953 (div. 1978); children: Catherine M. Wiesener, James David Jr., Deborah A. James, Michael F., Gregory R. Grad. high sch., Washington; student, Salem Coll., 1990—. Med. sec. dept. medicine Bowman Gray Sch. Medicine, Winston-Salem, N.C., 1970-75, asst. to chmn. dept. pediatrics, 1977—; adminstrv. sec. v.p. for profl. affairs N.C. Hosp., Winston-Salem, 1975-77. Mem. NAFE, Assn. Adminstrs. in Acad. Pediatrics. Republican. Roman Catholic. Home: 6533 Benson Ln Pfafftown NC 27040 Office: 300 S Hawthorne Rd Winston-Salem NC 27103

HESTER, NANCY ELIZABETH, county government administrator; b. Miami, Fla., Jan. 20, 1950; d. George Temple and Lorraine Patricia (Cluney) Hester; B.A., Bucknell U., 1972; M.I.A., Columbia U., 1974; M.B.A., Fla. Internat. U., 1979. Treasury rep. Westinghouse Elec. Co., N.Y.C., 1974-76; adminstrv. officer serving in bldg. and zoning, gen. services, and corrections and rehab. depts. Metro Dade County, Fla., 1979—, bur. comdr. corrections and rehab. dept., 1990—; adj. prof. Fla. Internat. U., Miami, 1980-83; realtor-assoc. Keyes Co., 1985-87; broker Keyes Nat. Referrals, 1988—. Asst. sec. bd. dirs. YWCA Greater Miami. Mem. Zool. Soc. Fla., Miami City Ballet Guild.

HETHERINGTON, MARY ELIZABETH, programmer analyst, economics consultant; b. Watertown, Mass., Sept. 5, 1962; d. William Francis and Helen Marie (Cassidy) H.; m. Jonathan Guy Gummer. BA in Psychology, Boston Coll., 1984. Mgr. Paperback Booksmith, Watertown, 1984-85, Royal Bookstore, Brookline, Mass., 1985-86; instr. Joy of Movement, Watertown,

1987—; programmer The New Eng., Boston, 1987—; personal trainer, 1989—. Big sister Big Sister Assn., Boston, 1989—. Mem. Excellence Excercise Assn., Aerobics and Fitness Assn. Am., ARC, The Alliance, Internat. Dance and Exercise Assn. Home: 39 Strathmore Rd Brookline MA 02146 Office: The New Eng 501 Boylston St Boston MA 02101

HETRICK, MICHELLE, truck parts company executive; b. Columbus, Ohio, Sept. 25, 1958; d. Saverio and Domenica Margaret (Zappia) Caruso; m. Lynn Paul Hetrick, Apr. 12, 1980; 1 dau., Vanessa Lynn. A.A., Stark Tech. Coll., Canton, Ohio, 1978. Vice-pres. Lynn Truck Parts Corp., Massillon, Ohio, 1979—. Mem. Massillon C. of C., Nat. Assn. Female Execs., Stark Tech. Alumni Assn., Internat. Truck Parts Assn. Republican. Roman Catholic. Clubs: Canton Jr. Woman's, Arboretum Garden, Timken Mercy Service League (Canton). Avocations: skiing; tennis; snowmobiling. Office: Lynn Truck Parts Corp 739 3d St SE Massillon OH 44646

HETRICK, SUZANNE H., mental health administrator; b. Harrisburg, Pa., June 25, 1943; d. Harold C. Hollingsworth and Anne H. (Zarfoss) Oakum; m. John A. Hetrick, Dec. 17, 1966; children: Brenton H., Joel Andrew. AB, Lebanon Valley Coll., 1965; MA, Kent State U., 1967, PhD, 1969. Licensed psychologist; cert. mental health adminstr. Counseling specialist Kent (Ohio) State U., 1969-71; exec. dir. Portage County Bd. Alcohol, Drug Addiction & Mental Health, Kent, 1971—; psychologist, adminstrv. ptnr. Western Reserve Psychol. Assocs., Stow, Ohio, 1974—; adj. asst. prof. Kent State U., Northeastern Ohio Univs. Coll. Medicine. Contbr. articles to profl. jours. Voter svc. chmn. Tallmadge (Ohio) League of Women Voters, 1987, pres., 1983-88; pres. Community Health Rsch. Group, Portage/Summit Counties, Ohio, 1989—; vice-moderator Kent United Ch. Christ. Recipient Fellowship NIMH, 1966-68, Outstanding Young Women Am. award, 1970. Mem. Kent Rotary, Ravenna C. of C., Aurora C. of C., Ohio Assn. Alcohol, Drug Addiction & Mental Health Svcs. (pres. 1984-85). Office: Portage Co Bd Mental Health PO Box 743 Kent OH 44240

HETTIGER, LORIN J., temporary employment agency executive; b. Milw., July 7, 1956; d. Elden M. and Doris M. (Larson) H.; m. Jeffrey L. Jacobs, July 6, 1990. BA in Communications, U. Wis., Green Bay, 1978; MS, U. Wis., Milw., 1984. Br. mgr. Kelly Temp Svcs., Casper, Wyo.; account rep. Kelly Temp Svcs., Janesville, Wis.; community svc. dir. Americana Healthcare Ctr., Green Bay; activity dir. Good Shepherd Home, Seymour, Wis.; regional mktg. dir. nursing home Hillhaven Corp., 1989ú. Mem., bd. dirs., program chair Am. Heart Assn. Mem. Am. Soc. Personnel Assn., Bus. and Profl. Women (bd. dirs.), Casper C. of C. Home: 700 S Forest Casper WY 82609

HETTLER, MADELINE THERESE, data processing company executive; b. Phila., Feb. 3, 1949; d. Francis Joseph and Cecilia (Freisburg) H. B.S., U. Pa., 1986. With tech. support dept. Martin Marietta, Phila., 1976-84, Sundata, Phila., 1984-85; system support disaster recovery coordinator Nat. Liberties Corp., Frazer, Pa., 1985-87; tech. cons. Micro Tempus Corp., Trerose, Pa., 1987—, Vanguard Group of Investment Cos., Chesterbrook, Pa. Home: 2217 Bond Ave Drexel HI-1 PA 19026 Office: Vanguard Group 1041 W Valley Rd Wayne PA 19087

HEUER, MARGARET B., data processing professional; b. Juneau, Alaska, Sept. 12, 1935; d. William George and Flora (Rusk) Allen; m. Joseph Louis Heuer; children: Leilani, Joseph, Daniel, Suzanne, Karen, Mark, Jerina. AA, San Bernardino Valley Coll., 1980. Cert. data processing, computer repair and maintenance, microcomputer support specialist. Coord. microcomputers lab Oakton Community Coll., Des Plaines, Ill. Office: 7701 N Lincoln Skokie IL 60077

HEUERTZ, SARAH JANE, dentist; b. Springfield, Mo., Aug. 28, 1950; d. Joseph Aloyuius and Josephine (Campbell) H. BS in Edn., S.W. Mo. State U., 1972; DMD, So. Ill. U., 1985. Switch bd. operator Mercy Villa Nursing Home, Springfield, 1966-70; typist, lab asst. S.W. Mo. State U., Springfield, 1970-72; tchr. math. and physics Sch. of the Osage, Lake Ozark, Mo., 1972-73; libr. Billings (Mo.) R.I. Sch., 1973-75; ref. libr. to children's dept. head Joliet (Ill.) Pub. Libr., 1975-77; instructional media coord. Summit Hill Sch. Dist., Frankfort, Ill., 1977-81; computer operator, database editor Joliet (Ill.) Pub. Libr., 1980-87; gen. dentist Dr. Joseph Propati, Evergreen Park, Ill., 1986-87; pvt. practice Alton, Ill., 1987—; computer operator, database editor Lewis & Clark Libr. System, Edwardsville, 1990—. Named Young Careerist Bus. and Profl. Women, 1977. Mem. ADA, Ill. State Dental Soc., Madison County Dental Soc., Zonta Internat. (sec. 1989-91), DAR, Sigma Pi Sigma, Kappa Pi Epsilon. Office: 901 Brown St Alton IL 62002

HEUMAN, DONNA RENA, lawyer; b. Seattle, May 27, 1949; d. Russell George and Edna Inez (Armstrong) H. BA in Psychology, UCLA, 1972; JD, U. Calif., San Francisco, 1985. Cert. shorthand reporter, 1978—; owner, Heuman & Assocs., San Francisco, 1978-86; real estate broker, Calif., 1990—. Mem. Hastings Internat. and Comparative Law Rev., 1984-85; bd. dirs. Saddleback, 1987-89. Jessup Internat. Moot Ct. Competition, 1985. Mem. ABA, NAFE, Nat. Shorthand Reporters Assn., Women Entrepreneurs, Calif. Shorthand Reporters Assn., Calif. State Bar Assn., Nat. Mus. of Women in the Arts, Calif. Lawyers for the Arts, San Francisco Bar Assn., Assn. Trial Lawyers Am., Commonwealth Club, World Affairs Council, Zonta (bd. dirs.). Home: 611 Cedar Ct Daly City CA 94014 Office: Superior Ct Calif Hall of Justice Redwood City CA 94063

HEUSCHELE, SHARON JO, college dean; b. Toledo, Ohio, July 12, 1936; 1 child, Brent Philip. BE, U. Toledo, 1965, MEd, 1969, PhD, 1973. Cert. elem., secondary tchr., Ohio. Asst. prof. Ohio Dominican Coll., Columbus, 1970-73, St. Cloud U., Minn., 1973-74; assoc. prof. Ohio State U., Columbus, 1974-79; dean instl. planning Lourdes Coll., Sylvania, Ohio, 1980—; cons. U. Hawaii, 1979, others. Bd. dirs. Trinity-St. Paul Inner City Program, Toledo, 1968; cons. Ohio Civil Rights Commn., 1972; active Democratic campaigns. U. Toledo fellow, 1967-69; recipient Citation, U. Toledo, 1979, Journalistic Excellence award Columbia Press Assn., N.Y.C., 1954. Mem. Am. Council Edn., Ohio Conf. Coll. and Univ. Planning, Soc. Coll. and Univ. Planning (com. 1984-85), Phi Theta Kappa, Phi Kappa Phi (Citation 1973), U. Toledo Alumni Assn., U.S. Coast Guard Aux. Lutheran. Avocations: fossil and mineral collecting, poetry, novel writing, horseback riding. Office: Lourdes Coll 6832 Convent Blvd Sylvania OH 43560

HEVENER, BARBARA COOLEY, accountant; b. Lansing, Mich., Apr. 22, 1945; d. Kenneth Donald and Mary Jane (Atwell) Cooley; m. Richard Neil Hevener Jr., Sept. 27, 1976; 1 stepchild, Carrollee Hevener. BA with honors, U. Fla., 1966; M in Acctg., U. S.C., 1981. CPA, S.C. Staff acct. S.C. State Auditor's Office, Columbia, 1981-82; dir. acctg. S.C. Comptroller's Office, Columbia, 1983-86, asst. comptroller gen. fin. reporting, 1986—. J. Hillis Miller Meml. scholar U. Fla., 1964; Olson Meml. fellow U. S.C., 1980; recipient Hon. Mention, Woodrow Wilson Found., 1966, CPA Exam award S.C. Assn. CPAs, 1981. Mem. AICPA, Assn. Govt. Accts., Beta Gamma Sigma, Phi Beta Kappa, Alpha Lambda Delta. Office: SC Comptroller Gen's Office PO Box 11228 Columbia SC 29211

HEWA, CYNTHIA LYNNE, health care organization executive; b. St. Louis, June 20, 1966; d. Donald Joseph and Jerilyn Lee (Scott) B. BSBA in Ops. Mgmt., U. Mo., 1988. Regional staffing coord. Spectrum Emergency Care, Inc., St. Louis, 1988-89; prodn. control planner Raytheon Co., Bristol, Tenn., 1989; physician recruiter Bristol Regional Med. Ctr., 1989—. Mem. NAFE, U. Mo. Alumni Assn., Phi Chi Theta, Zeta Tau Alpha Alumni Assn. Republican. Methodist. Home: 390 Grandview Ct Kingsport TN 37664 Office: Raytheon Co 100 Vance Tank Rd Bristol TN 37620

HEWETT, JOANNE LEA, physics educator; b. Boulder, Colo., Mar. 15, 1960; d. Robert Woody and Jean Marie (Hubbard) H.; m. Thomas Gerard Rizzo, June 7, 1985. BS, Iowa State U., 1982; MS, U. Calif., Irvine, 1984; PhD, Iowa State U., 1988. Vis. asst. prof. physics dept. U. Wis., Madison, 1988—. Mem. Am. Phys. Soc. Office: U Wis Physics Dept 1150 University Ave Madison WI 53706

HEWITT, DICKIE M., corporate executive; b. Florence, Ala., Dec. 12, 1938; d. Kenneth F. Sr. and Virginia L. (Goss) Stamps; m. Jerry A. Hewitt Sr., June 21; children: Jerry A., Charles T., Penny S. BBA, Stetson U., 1961; postgrad., West Chester U., Montgomery County Coll. Mgr. ops. Garrett Group, Inc., Bloomfield Hills, Mich.; dir. ops. James K. Stitcher Co., Lanham, Md.; v.p. ops. Friedman, Fuller, Blewitt, Inc., Tysons Corner, Va. Contbr. articles to trade jours. and newsletters. Recipient Outstanding Women Leadership award; named Hon. Col. Mem. NAFE, NAM, Nat. Assn. Wholesalers, Acctg. Firms Internat., Prince George's Women Bus. Owners, Va. Assn. Female Execs., NCO Wive's Club (pres.). Address: 166 Weedon Ct West Chester PA 19380

HEWITT, MARILYN PATRICIA, graphic artist, exhibits designer; b. Norfolk, Va., June 14, 1947; d. John Arthur Owens and Thelma (Small) Berlin; married, Aug. 14, 1972 (div. Nov. 1975). Student, Old Dominion U., 1970-72. Projection and sound equipment operator Naval Amphibious Sch., Norfolk, 1966-68, office draftsman, 1968-73; topography artist Hammon, Jensen and Wallen, Oakland, Calif., 1973-74; illustrator Comdr. Naval Surface Force, Norfolk, 1974-76, visual info. specialist, 1976-80, dir. graphic arts, 1980—, dep. EEO officer, 1982-85; owner Dynamic Hair & Nail, Norfolk, 1984-86, Abra-Cadabra Nails and Tan Salon, Norfolk, 1982—. Vol. artist Animal Assistance League, Virginia Beach, 1982, Am. Soc. Prevention Cruelty to Animals, Norfolk, 1980—. Recipient Superior Civilian Service medal Comdr.-in-Chief Harry Train, 1982. Mem. Am. Bus. Women Assn. (treas. Tidewater chpt. 1984-85, v.p. 1985-86, mem. Hallmark chpt.). Lutheran. Home: 4908 Preakness Way Virginia Beach VA 23464 Office: Comdr Naval Surface Force CINCLANTFLT Compound Norfolk VA 23511

HEWLETT, VALERIE BALCIK, physician's assistant; b. Weisbaden, Fed. Republic Germany, Aug. 19, 1963; came to U.S., 1974; d. Frank Eugene and Gudrun Anna (Grundig) B.; m. Joseph Alan Hewlett, Apr. 9, 1988. BA, Tenn. Temple U., 1985; BS, Trevecca Nazarene Coll., 1987. Cert. physician asst. Nat. Bd. Med. Examiners; cert. neonatal advanced life support instr. Am. Acad. Pediatrics. Rsch. asst. Memphis Physicians Group, 1986; mental health assoc. Parthenon Pavillion Psychiat. Hosp., Nashville, 1986-88; clin. clerkship Raleigh Fitkin Hosp., Ch. of Nazarene, Manzini, Swaziland, 1987; physician asst. resident neonatal dept. Los Angeles County-U. So. Calif. Women's Hosp., L.A., 1987-88, physician asst. staff newborn svc., 1988—. Mem. Am. Acad. Physician Assts., Nat. Wildlife Found., Pro-Life. Republican. Mem. Evangelical Ch. Home: 1417 Manhattan Beach Blvd Manhattan Beach CA 90266 Office: LAC-U So Calif Women's Hosp 1240 Mission Rd Los Angeles CA 90033

HEWSON, DONNA WALTERS, real estate executive; b. Columbia, S.C., Mar. 28, 1947; d. Jerry William and Rosa (Bryant) Walters; 1 child, Robert Alton Smith Jr.; m. James Robert Hewson, Oct. 1983 (div. 1986). Student, Hollins Coll., 1971-72, Va. Western Coll., 1972, Va. Polytech. and State U., 1972-73, U. S.C., 1978-79, 84, 85. Lic. residential and comml. real estate broker. Sales rep. Russell-Jeffcoat Realtors, Columbia, S.C., 1969-71; broker Russell-Jeffcoat Realtors, Columbia, 1971-72; adminstrv. asst. Roanoke (Va.) Valley Psych. Ctr., 1975-76; sales rep. Moore Bus. Forms, Columbia, 1976-79; project sales mgr. Continental Mortgage Investors, Columbia, 1979-80; broker, project sales mgr. Tom Jenkins Realty, Columbia, 1980-81; sales mgr., broker in charge RELM, Inc., Columbia, 1982-83; sales mgr. So. U.S. Realty/U.S. Shelter, Columbia, 1983-84; pres. WaltersHewson Co., Inc., Columbia, 1984—; v.p. Park Circle Properties, Inc., 1988-89, pres. 1989—. Pub. rels. chmn., bd. dirs. Women's Symphony Assn., 1988; pres. Philharm. Orchestra League; mem. Trinity Episcopal Cathedral, Hist. Columbia Found., Met. Opera Guild. Mem. NOW, Columbia C. of C. (com. chmn. 1987—), Nat. Assn. Real Estate Appraisers (sr. mem., cert., treas. 1990—), Columbia Bd. Realtors (mem. Million Dollar Club, 1981, 84, 86, Grievance com. mem. 1986-88), S.C. Assn. Realtors (Profl. Standards Com. 1986, polit. affairs com. 1987), Palmetto Real Estate Educators. Episcopalian. Office: Walters Hewson Co Inc PO Box 967 Columbia SC 29202

HEXT, KATHLEEN FLORENCE, corporate auditor; b. Bellingham, Wash., Oct. 7, 1941; d. Benjamin Byron and Sarah Debell (Youngquist) Gross.; m. George Ronald Hext, June 13, 1964 (div. 1972). BA magna cum laude, Lewis & Clark Coll., Portland, Oreg., 1963; MA, Stanford U., 1964; MBA, UCLA, 1979. CPA; chartered bank auditor; cert. info. systems auditor. Chief exec. officer Internat. Lang. Ctr., Rome, 1970-77; sr. auditor Peat, Marwick, Mitchell & Co., Los Angeles, 1979-81; mgr. fin. audit Lloyds Bank, Los Angeles, 1981-83, mgr. EDP audit, 1983-85; dir. corp. audit First Interstate Bancorp, Los Angeles, 1985-89, sr. v.p., gen. auditor, 1989—; treas., Arcadia H.O. Assoc., El Monte, Calif., 1982-84, 86-88, pres., 1985. Recipient Edward W. Carter award UCLA, 1979. Mem. AICPA, Inst. Internal Auditors, Calif. Soc. CPA. Republican. Episcopalian. Avocations: photography, microcomputers, reading. Home: 1226 Upland Hills Dr S Upland CA 91786 Office: First Interstate Bancorp 707 Wilshire Blvd Los Angeles CA 90017

HEYCK, GERTRUDE PAINE DALY, social club administrator; b. Houston, Nov. 30, 1910; d. David and Gertrude (Paine) Daly; m. Theodore R. Heyck, May 1, 1935; children: Jane Peel (Mrs. Donald H. Gaucher), Theodore Daly. Student, Wellesley Coll., 1929; BA, Brown U., 1934. Bd. dirs. Union Stock Yards, San Antonio, 1961-64. Mem. Jr. League. Clubs: Wellesley, Brown-Pembroke (v.p. 1950-60), Brown (Houston); Brown Faculty (Providence). Home: 1907 Bolsover Rd Houston TX 77005

HEYDE, MARTHA BENNETT (MRS. ERNEST R. HEYDE), psychologist; b. New Bern, N.C., Jan. 31, 1920; d. George Spotswood and Katherine (McIntosh) Bennett; AB, Barnard Coll., 1941; MA, Columbia, 1949, PhD, 1959; m. Ernest R. Heyde, Aug. 17, 1946. Instr. psychol. founds. and services Tchrs. Coll., Columbia U., N.Y.C., 1953-60, research asst., career pattern study Horace Mann-Lincoln Inst., Tchrs. Coll. Columbia U., 1957-59, research assoc., 1960-70, cons., 1970-73. Mem. Barnard Coll. Alumnae Council, 1956-61, 69—, pres. class, 1956-61. Trustee, Barnard Coll., 1974-78, hon. vice-chmn. Barnard Coll. Centennial, 1987-89. Mem. Am. Psychol. Assn., Am. Personnel and Guidance Assn., Sigma Xi, Kappa Delta Pi, Pi Lambda Theta. Contbr. to research monograph The Vocational Maturity of Ninth Grade Boys, 1960, Floundering and Trial After High Sch, 1967; coauthor: Vocational Maturity During the High School Years, 1979. Home: 140 Cabrini Blvd Apt 109 New York NY 10033

HEYE, JACQUELINE VITO COOPER, public relations executive, event planning consultant; b. Jackson Hole, Wy., May 12, 1940; d. Louis Vito; adopted d. Herbert Melbourne and Katherine Marie (Mailman) Cooper, 2944; m. Donald Ray Heye, Sept. 13, 1959 (div. 1969); children: Kelley Dawn, Kraig Donald. Student, S.D. State Coll., 1958-60, Nat. U., San Diego, 1988-89. Promotion dir. Retlaw Broadcasting Co., San Diego, 1967-79; prodn. asst. A. & G. Prodns., San Diego, 1980-81; dir. edn. resource mgmt. The Exec. Com., San Diego, 1981-88; dir. TEC Ext., San Diego; owner, pres. The Internat. Ctr. for Bus. Edn., San Diego, 1988—; cons. Young President's Orgn., The Exec. Com., 1981--, World Bus. Council, 1985-88, The Internat. Ctr., 1988--.

HEYER, ANNA HARRIET, retired music librarian; b. Little Rock, Aug. 30, 1909; d. Arthur Wesley and Harriet Anna (Gage) H. A.B., B.Mus., Tex. Christian U., 1930; B.S. in L.S., U. Ill., 1933; M.S. in L.S., Columbia U., 1939; M.Mus. in Musicology, U. Mich., 1943. Elem. sch. music tchr. Ft. Worth Pub. Schs., 1931-32; high sch. librarian, 1934-38; cataloguer library, U. Tex.-Austin, 1939-40; music librarian, asst. prof. L.S., N. Tex. State U. (name now U. N. Tex.), Denton, 1940-65, librarian emeritus, 1976; cons. music library materials Tex. Christian U., Ft. Worth, 1965-79; ret., 1979. Author: A Check-List of Publications of Music, 1944; A Bibliography of Contemporary Music in the Music Library, North Texas State College, 1955; Historical Sets, Collected Editions and Monuments of Music: A Guide to Their Contents, 1957, 2d edit., 1969, 3d rev. edit., 1980; contbr. articles to profl. pubis. Recipient citations for contbn. to music librarianship Music Library Assn., 1980, to music librarianship in Tex., 1983. Mem. ALA, Tex. Library Assn., Music Library Assn., AAUW, DAR. Mem. Disciples of Christ Ch. Clubs: Altrusa, Woman's Club Ft. Worth, Colonial Country. Home: 5334 Premier Ct Fort Worth TX 76132

HEYMAN, JUDITH ANN, public relations consultant; b. Chgo., Apr. 29, 1938; d. Ray Carl and Jeanette (Rosenblatt) Greenberg; m. Glenn Robert Heyman, Dec. 18, 1960; children: Scott, Rachel, Joanne. BS in Journalism, Northwestern U., Evanston, Ill., 1961. Press sec. U.S. Rep. John E. Porter, 10th Dist. Ill., 1981-82; reporter, copy editor, columnist Lerner Newspapers, Skokie, Ill., 1969-81; pub. rels. cons. In the Black Inc., Lincolnwood, Ill., 1982—; freelance editor and writer; campaign cons. numerous polit. campaigns. Mem. campaign staff State Senator Bob Kusta, Des Plaines, Ill., 1982, 84. Recipient First Pl. awards Suburban Newspapers Am., 1981, Lerner Newspapers Con test, 1980. Mem. Women in Communications, Publicity Club Chgo., Suburban Press Club Chgo. (Journalist of Yr. 1981). Jewish. Home: 4401 Morse Lincolnwood IL 60646 Office: In the Black Inc 4401 Morse Lincolnwood IL 60646

HEYMAN, JULIANE MARION, educator; b. Free City Danzig (Gdansk), Poland, Mar. 25, 1925; came to U.S., 1942; d. Fred S. and Martha Helen (Franck) H. BA, Barnard Coll., 1946; MA, U. Calif., Berkeley, 1948, MLS, 1949. Library advisor Govt. of Vietnam, 1957-59; info. cons. Mich. State U., Pakistan, 1960-61; tng. officer Peace Corps, Washington, 1961-66; dep. project dir. ALA, Washington, 1968-70; library advisor USAID, El Salvador, San Salvador, 1970-71; cons. USAID, Mauritania, 1978-79; asst. project dir. Devel. Assocs., Washington, 1975-77; dep. dir. Am. Home Econs. Assn., Washington, 1980-81; v.p. Flagship Travel Inc., Kent, Wash., 1984-88; prof. Radio for Peace Internat., San Jose, Costa Rica, 1989—; instr. Santa Barbara (Calif.) City Coll., 1983-86; cons. to various internat. orgns., Washington, 1975-83, Aspen (Colo.) Inst. for Humanistic Studies, 1972-73; tchr. Aspen Country Day Sch., 1972-75. Contbr. articles to profl. jours. Program v.p. League Women Voters, Aspen, 1973-74, bd. dirs., Santa Barbara, 1983-84, Sierra Club, Santa Barbara, 1985-87. Mem. Soc. for Internat. Devel. (v.p. 1980-82), Assn. for Asian Studies, Colo. Mountain Club (hike leader). Democrat. Jewish. Home and Office: 853 Cieneguitas Santa Barbara CA 93110

HEYMANN, MONICA GOLDA, graphic designer; b. Caracas, Venezuela, Jan. 4, 1959; d. George Daniel and Dorothy (Noe) H. BA in Psycho-Biology cum laude, Boston U., 1978; postgrad., Harvard U., 1979-80, Art Inst. Boston, 1980-82; BFA, The Cooper Union Sch. Art, 1984. Cons., exhibition, catalogue designer Rose Art Mus., Waltham, Mass., 1981; creative dir. Triad Press, Boston, 1980-82, Mallory Factor & Assocs., Inc., N.Y.C., 1984-85; art dir. Creative Dirs., Inc., N.Y.C., 1985-86; design dir. Dura Archtl. Signage Corp., L.I., 1986-87; pres. Heymann & Ptnrs., Advt. & Design Group, N.Y.C., 1987—; design cons. various corps., N.Y.C., 1980—. Art dir., editorial cons.: Ancient American Art: An Aesthetic View, 1981, PreColumbian Art, 1980; cons. holographic design, various corps.; designs published in Am. Corp.-Identity 4, Trademarks & Logotypes--world edit., Menu Designs I, Art Direction Mag., Typography Mag. Recipient Am. Corp. Identity design award. Mem. Am. Inst. Graphic Arts, Graphic Artists Guild. Office: 151 Lexington Ave Ste 2E New York NY 10016

HEYN, EILEEN LEONE, aerospace company executive; b. Moose Lake, Minn., Mar. 9, 1945. A.A., Highline Coll., Des Moines, Wash., 1983; BSBA City U., Bellevue, Wash., 1989. Asst. br. mgr. Cascade Savs. & Loan Assn., Lynnwood, Wash., 1971-72; assoc. br. mgr. Avco Fin. Services, Everett, Wash., 1972-74; quality assurance tech. aide Boeing Co., Seattle, 1975-82; retrofit rev. bd. coordinator Boeing, Seattle, 1982-84, exec. placement specialist, 1984-85, integrated employee records systems analyst, 1985-87, internal auditor, 1987-88, engring. data mgr., 1988—; cons. and lectr. in field. Author-editor: (Bulletin) Illuminations, 1981-82; contbg. editor: Advisor, 1982. Mem. Seattle Repertory Orgn., 1981—, Zonta Internat. ,1982; v.p. Lake Heights Community Club, Bellevue, Wash., 1985-86, pres., 1986-88, trustee 1988-90; vol. Spl. Olympics, 1987-89. Recipient Extra Mile award Boy Scouts Am., Seattle, 1979; Boeing awards, 1980, 82, 89. Mem. Am. Bus. Women's Assn. (pres. 1982-83, Member of Yr., 1982, Nat. Bus. Woman of Yr., 1983), Internat. Tng. in Communications Council (v.p. 1984-85), Seattle Profl. and Managerial Women's Network (bd. dirs. 1986-88), Inst. Internal Auditors, Am. Soc. Quality Control, Assn. Records Mgrs. Adminstrs. Avocations: speaking; hiking; traveling; theatre-going.

HEYUM, RENEE, anthropologist, curator emeritus; b. 1917. Formerly bibliographer Pacifica books Musee des Hommes, Paris; curator Pacifica Collection Ctr. Pacific Islands Studies, U. Hawaii Libr., from 1969, now curator emeritus. Decorated chevalier Civil Order (France). Office: U Hawaii Ctr Pacific Islands Studies Moore Hall 215 Honolulu HI 96822

HIBNER, RAE ANNE, nurse; b. Libertyville, Ill., Jan. 31, 1956; d. Richard Douglas and Raelene Ann (Warner) Lyons; m. John Paul Hibner, June 21, 1986; 1 child, Kevin John. Diploma, Luth. Gen. Hosp. Sch. Nursing, Park Ridge, Ill., 1979; BS in Nursing, U. Ill., Chgo., 1984; MS, No. Ill. U., 1987. RN. Staff nurse Cardiac Telemetry Luth. Gen. Hosp., 1979-81, staff nurse CCU, 1981-82; staff nurse CICU U. Ill. Hosp., Chgo., 1982-83, asst. head nurse CICU, 1983-86, head nurse CICU, 1986-88, staff nurse CICU-MICU, 1989—. Mem. Am. Assn. Critical Care Nurses, Am. Heart Assn. Republican. Roman Catholic.

HIBSCHWEILER, BARBARA MARY, wholesale distribution executive; b. Buffalo, Aug. 3, 1945; d. Alvin Jacob and Magdalen Anna (Troidl) H. BA, D'Youville Coll., 1967; MS, Canisius Coll., 1972. Cert. tchr., N.Y. Tchr. St. William's Sch., West Seneca, N.Y., 1968-70, St. Matthew's Sch., Buffalo, 1973-75; mgr. Sterling Bag & Supply Co, Inc., Lackawanna, N.Y., 1976—. Democrat. Roman Catholic. Office: Sterling Bag & Supply Co Inc Foot of Fisher Rd Lackawanna NY 14218

HICKAM, NANCY DIXON, public relations and personnel director; b. Galax, Va., Feb. 27, 1955; d. Glenn W. and Pearl M. (McKnight) Dixon; children: Kathryn, Jessica, Elizabeth. B in Social Work, Va. Internat. Coll., 1977; postgrad. in social work, Va. Commonwealth U., 1987—. Security officer Millers, Inc., Britol, Va., 1977-78, Bristol, 1978; med. social worker Twin County Home Health. Mem. NAFE, Nat. Assn. Social Workers, Jaycees, PTA . Baptist. Office: Twin County Home Health 152 Boyer Rd Galax VA 24333

HICKEY, BONNIE ANNE, purchasing manager; b. Bronx, Mar. 25, 1945; d. Daniel James and Elizabeth Bernice (Spengeman) H. Grad. high sch., Bayside, N.Y. Supr. Pan-Am. World Airways, Inc., N.Y.C., 1962-72, buyer, 1972-85; buyer N.Y.C. Transit Authority, Bklyn., 1985-88, purchasing supr., 1988-89, purchasing mgr., 1989—; mem. chem. com. N.Y.C. Transit Authority, Bklyn., 1986-87. Mem. Am. Mgmt. Assn. (Cert. 1986, 88, 89). Republican. Lutheran.

HICKEY, WINIFRED E(SPY), state senator, social worker; b. Rawlins, Wyo.; d. David P. and Eugenia (Blake) Espy; children—John David, Paul Joseph. B.A., Loretto Heights Coll., 1933; postgrad. U. Utah, 1934, Sch. Social Service, U. Chgo., 1936. Dir. Carbon County Welfare Dept., 1935-36; field rep. Wyo. Dept. Welfare, 1937-38; dir. Red Cross Club, Europe, 1942-45; commr. Laramie County, Wyo., 1973-80; mem. Wyo. Senate, 1980—; dir. United Savs. & Loan, Cheyenne. Pres., bd. dirs. U. Wyo. Found., 1986-87; pres. Meml. Hosp. of Laramie County, 1986-88; chmn. adv. council div. community programs Wyo. Dept. Health and Social Services; pres. county and state mental health assn., 1959-63; trustee, U. Wyo., 1967-71; active Nat. Council Cath. Women. Named Outstanding Alumna, Loretto Heights Coll., 1959, Woman of Yr. Commn. for Women, 1988, Legislator of Yr. Wyo. Psychologists Assn., 1988. Democrat. Club: Altrusa (Cheyenne). Pub. Where the Deer and the Antelope Play, 1967.

HICKMAN, DARCY J., state agency training officer; b. Seoul, Korea, Nov. 12, 1955; came to U.S., 1956; d. Norman William and Janis Vern (Baumbach) H. BA, Oreg. State U., 1977. Lic. investigator Oreg. Liquor Control Commn., Portland, Oreg., 1978-88, exec. asst., 1986-87, tng. and spl. projects coord., 1989—; contbr. Oreg. Liquor Control Commn., Portland, 1988-89; task force mem. DUII Countermeasure Task Force, Salem, Oreg., 1989—; committeeperson Alcohol Policy VII Nat. Conf., Portland, 1989—; mem. Clackamas County Criminal Justice Coun. Tng. Com., Portland, 1989—. Mem. Soc. Govt. Meeting Planners, Am. Soc. Tng. and Devel. Democrat. Home: 9617 SW Arikara Dr Tualatin OR 97062 Office: Oreg Liquor Control Commn 2525 SW 3d Ste 350 Portland OR 97201

HICKMAN, EDNA L., executive secretary; b. Clinton, La., Dec. 12, 1944; d. Ed and Leola (Parker) Brown; m. Leon Hickman, Aug. 17, 1968; 1 child, Adrian. BS, So. Univ., Baton Rouge, 1965. Exec. sec. Tex. So. Univ.,

Houston; owner Mr. Postman, Houston; with Houston Pub. Libr. Conductor workshops on personnel. Home: 6610 Trigate Missouri City TX 77489

HICKMAN, GRACE MARGUERITE, artist; b. Reno, Nev., Nov. 7, 1921; d. Charles Franklin and Jeannie (McPhee) Wolcott; m. Robert Frederick Hickman, Apr. 10, 1943; children—John Charles, Carol Ann Hickman Harp, David Paul. Student Emily Griffiths Opportunity Sch., Denver, 1968-71, Red Rocks Community Coll., Golden, Colo., 1974-75, Loretto Heights Coll., Denver, 1983-85. Tchr. art Aurora Parks & Recreation, Colo., 1979-81; instr. paint workshop Marine Resource Ctr., Atlantic Beach, N.C., 1981, 82; lectr. color theory Aurora Artists Club, 1985; instr. creative color Acapulco Art Workshops, 1987, 88. One woman shows: Internat. House, Denver, 1974, Foothills Art Ctr., Golden, Colo., 1975, Greek Market Place, Denver, 1976, Marine Resource Ctr., Atlantic Beach, N.C., 1983, Depot Art Ctr., Littleton, Colo., 1984, Sheraton DTC, Women's Bank Denver, 1986, NYU Sch. Environmental Medicine, Tuxedo, 1987, Studio Paul Kontny, Denver, 1988. group shows include: Wellshire Presbyn. Ch., Denver, 1975, Brass Cheque Gallery, Denver, 1978, Colo. Women in Arts, Denver, 1979, Garelick's Gallery, Scottsdale, Ariz., 1982; Bold Expressions, Littleton, Colo., 1983. represented in permanent collections: Augustana Luth. Ch., Denver, South Shores Ins. Agy., Huntington Beach, Calif., Texon Gen. Partnership, Englewood, Colo., others. Coordinator figure study Bicentennial Art Ctr., Aurora, 1986; pres. Depot Art Ctr., Littleton, Colo., 1980-82. Mem. Nat. Mus. for Women in the Arts, Artists Equity Assn., Colo. Artists Equity Assn. (chmn. publicity Colo. 1% for Art 1976-77), Pastel Soc. Am., Littleton Fine Arts Guild (pres. 1976-77), Art Students League, Colo. Speakers Bur. (coordinator), Nat. Mus. Women in Arts. Democrat. Lutheran. Club: Aurora Athletic. Avocations: swimming; reading; art history. Home: 12361 E Bates Circle Aurora CO 80014

HICKMAN, JOLENE KAY, banker; b. Omaha, Sept. 5, 1954; d. Thomas Earl and Bernice Leona (McCoy) H. B.A., Otterbein Coll., 1977. Teller Bancohio Nat. Bank, Columbus, Ohio, 1976-77, auditor, 1977-81; audit supr. Huntington Nat. Bank, Columbus, 1981-85, asst. v.p., mgr., 1985-87, mem. conversion team, 1986-87, mgr. quality assurance, 1987—. Mem. Victorian Village Soc., Columbus, 1983, Up Downtowners, Columbus, 1986. Mem. Nat. Assn. Bank Women (chmn. edn. and tng. 1986-87, Ohio state conf., chmn. Looking at Leadership series 1985-86), Nat. Inst. Auditors, NAFE. Republican. Methodist. Avocations: softball, racquetball. Home: 358 Blenheim Rd Columbus OH 43214 Office: Huntington Trust Co NA 41 S High St 10th Fl Columbus OH 43287

HICKMAN, LINDA MARIE, nurse; b. Ada, Okla., Nov. 10, 1953; d. Charlie Lewis and Bertha Mae (Vinson) Phelps; m. Ronnie Clarence Hickman, May 26, 1972; 1 child, Dustin Jake. RN, Cushing (Okla.) Mcpl. Hosp., 1974-75; AS, Okla. State U. Tech. Inst., 1974; student Cen. State U., Edmond, Okla., 1986—. Staff nurse Cushing Mcpl. Hosp., 1974-75; pub. health nurse Payne County Health, Cushing, 1975-78, 84-88; nurse cons. Care Manor, Stroud, Okla., 1982-83; house supr. Cushing Regional Hosp., 1982-83, asst. dir. home health service, 1983-84; communicable disease nurse Payne County Health Dept., Cushing, 1985-88. Author: Cushing Regional Hospital Home Health Service Policy and Procedure Manual, 1984. Self breast exam. instr. Am. Cancer Soc., 1984—. Cushing Bus. and Profl. Women's Club sr. scholar, 1972, named Career Woman of Yr., 1976. Mem. Okla. Pub. Health Assn. Democrat. Avocations: boating, skiing, camping, ceramics, woodworking. Home: Rt 4 Box 300 Cushing OK 74023

HICKMAN, LUCILLE, physical therapist; b. Chgo., July 21, 1949; d. Louis Melvin and Edna (Edwards) H. BA in Sociology, Lake Forest Coll., 1972; BS in Physical Therapy, Chgo. Med. Sch., 1975; M in Health Sci., Gov.'s State U., 1985. Staff phys. therapist Michael Reese Hosp., Chgo., 1975-79; dir. phys. therapy Provident Med. Ctr., Chgo., 1979-83; instr. phys. therapy Chgo. State U., 1983-87; pres. adminstrv. dir. R.O.C. Phys. Therapy Services, Chgo., 1985—; founder, pres. PhysioCare Ltd., Chgo., 1988—; pvt. practice therapy cons., Chgo., 1983—. Mem. Am. Phys. Therapy Assn., Nat. Soc. Allied Health. Democrat. Episcopalian. Office: ROC Phys Therapy Svcs 7057 S Stony Island Chicago IL 60649

HICKMAN, MARJORIE RUTH, company owner; b. Hastings, Nebr., Feb. 10, 1918; d. August John and Rachel Brock (Andrus) Anderson; widowed; chidren: Janice Annette, Dianne Kay. BA, Hastings Coll., 1942. Tchr. Adams County Schs., Kearney and Harvard, Nebr., 1936-40; sec. USAF, Washington, 1942-45, Internat. Monetary Fund, Washington, 1946-50; tchr. Hastings Pub. Schs., 1955-57, Littleton (Colo.) Pub. Schs., 1957-79; owner, pres., chmn. bd. Taste of the Rockies, Inc., Littleton, 1972—. Vol. Jr. Red Cross, Littleton, 1960-68; past Sunday sch. tchr. 1st Presbyn. Ch., Littleton. Mem. NEA, Nebr. Edn. Assn., Colo. Edn. Assn., Hastings Tchrs. Assn., Littleton Tchrs. Assn., Nat. Ret. Tchrs., Zonta Internat. (bd. dirs.), Alpha Delta Kappa (chaplain 1988-90). Republican. Home: 5983 S Fairfield St Littleton CO 80120

HICKMAN, PAULA DIANE, lawyer; b. Miami, Fla., July 24, 1947; d. Paul William Hickman and Eva Lena (McCampbell) Melvin. Student Longwood Coll., 1965-67; B.A. with honors, U. Tenn., 1969. Bar: Pa. 1980, N.H. 1981, Maine 1981, N.J. 1983, Fla. 1986. Flight attendant Pan Am. World Airways, N.Y.C., 1972-77; law clk. N.J. Superior Ct., Burlington, N.J., 1979-80; atty. Pub. Defender Program, Exeter, N.H., 1981-83; dep. clk. Rockingham County Superior Ct., Exeter, 1983-86; sole practice, Marathon, Fla., 1986; assoc. Spear & Deuschle, P.A., Ft. Lauderdale, Fla., 1988; with The Keyes Co., Ft. Lauderdale, 1989; instr. McIntosh Coll., Dover, N.H., 1984-85. Past treas. bd. dirs. Rockingham Family Planning. Mem. ABA, N.H. Bar Assn., Rockingham County Bar Assn. (past v.p., past sec./treas.). Office: PO Box 290155 Fort Lauderdale FL 33329-0155

HICKS, ALICE BLACKMORE, investment advisor; b. Winston-Salem, N.C., Dec. 19, 1946; d. Willie Franklin and Eleanor Gray (CAin) Blackmore; m. James Byron Hicks, Apr. 16, 1977; children: James Byron Jr., Daniel Franklin. BA in Math. and Econs., Duke U., 1969; MBA in Fin., NYU, 1973. V.p. Irving Trust Co., N.Y.C., 1969-78; ptnr. David J. Greene & Co., N.Y.C., 1978-85; dir., v.p. Delafield Asset Mgmt., N.Y.C., 1985-89; gen. ptnr. Delphi Asset Mgmt., New York, 1990—. Bd. dirs. YWCA Retirement Fund, N.Y.C., Greater N.Y. Fund, N.Y.C., 1984-85, East Side House Settlement, N.Y.C., Wilson Coll., Chambersberg, Pa., 1983-86. Mem. Fin. Analysts Fedn., Fin. Women's Assn., N.Y. Security Analysts, Lake Waramaug Country (Kent, Conn., mem. bd. 1979-88), Cosmopolitan Club. Democrat. Presbyterian. Home: 103 E 84th St New York NY 10028 Office: Delphi Asset Mgmt 485 Madison Ave New York NY 10022

HICKS, AUDREY MARION GRABFIELD, mathematics educator; b. N.Y.C., Oct. 20, 1957; d. Philip Robertson and Joanne Geneva (White) Grabfield; m. Matthew Barrington Hicks, May 17, 1986. AB in Math., Smith Coll., 1980; MA in Math., Wesleyan U., 1986. Tchr. math., equestrian coach Berkshire Sch., Sheffield, Mass., 1981-83; tchr.'s asst. Wesleyan U., 1983-85; adj. instr. math. Adirondack Community Coll., Glens Falls, N.Y., 1986, Castleton (Vt.) State Coll., 1986-88; instr. math. Green Mountain Coll., Poultney, Vt., 1987—; asst. dir. Camp Catherine Capers, Inc., Wells, Vt., summers 1980-86. Mem. Granville (N.Y.) Bd. Edn., 1989—. Republican. Episcopalian. Home: 9 Pine St Granville NY 12832 Office: Green Mountain Coll Poultney VT 05764

HICKS, BETHANY GRIBBEN, lawyer; b. N.Y., Sept. 8, 1951; d. Robert and DeSales Gribben; m. William A. Hicks III, May 21, 1982; children: Alexandra Elizabeth, Samantha Katherine. AB, Vassar Coll., 1973; MEd, Boston U., 1975; JD, Ariz. State U., 1984. Bar: Ariz. 1984. Sole practice Scottsdale and Paradise Valley, Ariz., 1984—. Mem. Jr. League of Phoenix, 1984—; bd. dirs. Phoenix Children's Theatre, 1988—; parliamentarian Girls Club of Scottsdale, Ariz., 1985-87, 89—, bd. dirs. 1988—. Mem. ABA (family law sect.), State Bar Ariz. (family law sect.), Maricopa County Bar Assn. (family law com.). Republican. Episcopalian. Club: Paradise Valley Country. Office: 4824 E Sparkling Ln Paradise Valley AZ 85253

HICKS, BRENDA JOY, communications specialist; b. Parsons, Tenn., July 22, 1943; d. Curtis Lloyd and Mary Ila (Rollings) Mosley; m. Leon Richard Hicks, Jr., Sept. 27, 1974; children: Samantha Erin, Zachary McBain. BS, U. Tulsa, 1976. Flight attendant and instr. TWA, Kansas City, Mo., 1965-72; interim pub. info. officer Tulsa City-County Libr. System, 1975-76; exec. dir. Honolulu Coun. Navy League of U.S., 1976-79; mgr. corp. communications C. Brewer and Co., Ltd., Honolulu, 1983-87; dir. pub. relations Chaminade U., Honolulu, 1987-88; devel. dir. Hawaii Bapt. Acad., Honolulu, 1988—; instr. in communications Chaminade U. of Honolulu, 1988-89. Editor newsletter Ka Leo Na Hui Ulumoku, 1977-78 (Award of Excellence 1977), C. Brewer Today, 1983-86 (Best Newsletter 1984). Mem. adv. group Mufi Hannemann for Congress, 1986; mem. publicity com. Hawaiian Sugar Planters Assn., 1985, A Million Trees of Aloha, 1985. Mem. Pub. Relations Soc. Am. (treas., bd. dirs. 1989—), Navy League U.S. (chmn. winter meeting 1985, bd. dirs. Honolulu coun. 1989—). Baptist.

HICKS, FRANCES ROSS, psychology educator; b. Middleton, Ill., July 23, 1900; d. Alonzo and Grace Amelia (Heaton) Ross; (widowed 1970); 1 foster child, Howard S. Brumbaugh. BA, Sterling Coll., 1922; MA, U. Colo., 1926; PhD, Peabody-Vanderbilt U., 1933; D of Pedagogy (hon.), Sterling Coll., 1957. Lic. psychologist, Ga. Vis. prof. U. Ga., Athens, summer 1948; prof. psychology Ga. Coll., Milledgeville, 1948-58, head psychology dept., 1958-68; Sterling Coll. Author: Be Alive As Long As You Live, 1969; contbr. articles to profl. jours. Mem. Ga. PTA. Murray (Ky.) State U. scholar, 1948. Mem. Ga. Psychol. Assn., Internat. Christian Univ. of Tokyo (womens com.), Ga. Coun. Moral and Social Concerns (trustee), AAUW (past pres.), Sigma Alpha Iota. Methodist. Home: 130 N Clark Milledgeville GA 31061

HICKS, JANET MARIE, banker; b. Bardstown, Ky., Jan. 3, 1955; d. John Adolph and Elizabeth Sueanna (Hayden) H. Diploma in Gen. Banking, The Am. Inst. Banking, 1984; AAS in Gen. Bus. Mgmt., Elizabethtown Community Coll., 1984, AAS in Banking Mgmt., 1985. Cert. bank examiner. Bookkeeper Farmers Bank and Trust Co., Bardstown, 1974-79; bank examiner Commonwealth of Ky., Frankfort, 1979—; instr. Ednl. Found. of State Bank Suprs., Washington, 1989—. Recipient Outstanding Scholastic Achievement award Ky. Bank Mgmt. Inst., 1987, 88, 89. Mem. NAFE, Soc. Fin. Examiners. Democrat. Roman Catholic. Home: 201 Honeysuckle Ln Bardstown KY 40004 Office: Ky Dept Fin Instns 911 Leawood Dr Frankfort KY 40601-3392

HICKS, JULIE BRASEL, public relations consultant; b. Springfield, Mo., Aug. 15, 1950; d. Kenneth Lee and Harriett Louise (Westland) Brasel; m. Bruce E. Hicks, Jan. 2, 1971 (div. 1985); 1 child, Jennifer Prescott. BA, U. Houston, 1972. Tchr. C.E. King High Sch., Houston, 1972-75; news editor Ft. Bend Mirror, Missouri City, Tex., 1978-81, mng. editor, 1981-83; owner JBH Ink, Missouri City, 1983-88; features copy desk Houston Chronicle, 1988-89; communications specialist Baylor Coll. of Medicine, 1989—. Weekly newspaper columnist, 1978-89. Cons. various polit. campaigns, Ft. Bend County; communications and pub. relations com. Ft. Bend Texans War on Drugs, 1983-88. Mem. Soc. Profl. Journalists, Ft. Bend C. of C., Mo. City Bus. Assn. (v.p. 1988), Tex. Pub. Rels. Assn., Kappa Delta (nat. dir. pub. rels 1987-88, dir. conf. communications 1988, assoc. editor Angelos mag.). Office: Baylor Coll Medicine One Baylor Pla Houston TX 77030

HICKS, KAREN KAY, banker; b. Orrville, Ohio, Aug. 21, 1953; d. George Irvin Haueter and Evelyn Eileen (Cunningham) Kiener; m. Randall Gene Hicks, Oct. 24, 1970; children: Cassandra Gene, Randall George, Amanda Jane. Stenography cert., Wayne County Jt. Vocat. Sch., 1971; student, Akron U., 1979—. Mgr. dist. office United Meth. Ch., Wooster, Ohio, 1972-73; with J.M. Smucker Co., Orrville, 1974-77; data entry operator 1st Nat. Bank, Orrville, 1977-81, ops. officer, 1981—. Vol. Kids In Safety Seats, 1984—; bd. dirs. Jaycees, 1988. Mem. Am. Inst. Banking, Nat. Assn. Bank Women (sec. 1988-89, v.p. 1989—, scholarship Northshore Group 1989, Buckeye Group 1989). Democrat. Methodist. Home: 6203 Dalton Fox Lake Rd North Lawrence OH 44666 Office: 1st Nat Bank 112 W Market St PO Box 57 Orrville OH 44667

HICKS, KIMA RENE, documentation analyst; b. July 2, 1960. BA in Journalism, Ohio State U., 1982. Sec. temp. agys., Dayton, Ohio, 1982-84; exec. sec. Unity State Bank, 1984-85; account exec. Sta. WDAO, 1985; editor BDM Corp., 1985-86; tech. writer Krug Internat., 1986-87; planning asst. NCR, 1987-88; adminstrv. sec. Mead Data Cen., Miamisburg, Ohio, 1987-88, documentation analyst, 1988—; announcer, broadcast technician Mt. Enon Bapt. Ch., 1983—; freelance writer, reporter Downtowner newspaper, 1983-85. Mem. women's aux. Ohio Bapt. Gen. Conv. Mem. NAFE, Soc. Tech. Communication, Women in Communications, Northwestern 2d Dist. Assn., Gospel Music Workshop Am., Jr. League Dayton, Dayton Urban League, NAACP, SCLC, Toastmasters. Home: 753 Kildare Pl Trotwood OH 45426

HICKS, LINDA JOYCE See BOYD, LINDA JOYCE

HICKS, LUCILE P., state legislator; b. Greenwood, Miss., May 11, 1938; m. William Hicks, 1960. BS, Millsaps Coll. High sch. sch. tchr.; mem. Mass. Ho. of Reps., until 1990, Mass. Senate, 1990—; mem. Wayland Rep. Town Com. Mem. LWV, Jr. League Boston, Kappa Delta Epsilon. Home: 5 Wildwood Rd Wayland MA 01778 Office: State House Boston MA 02133*

HICKS, M. ELIZABETH, pharmacist; b. Shawnee, Okla., Aug. 16, 1944; d. Joseph Robert and Betty Ruth (Thomas) Coughlin; m. Frank Jack Hicks, July 16, 1965 (dec. 1978); 1 child, Felicia Jeanette. BS, Okla. U., 1967. Lic. pharmacist. Pharmacy intern Liberty Drug, Chickasha, Okla., 1967-68; pharmacist St. Francis Hosp., Wichita, Kans., 1968, Hart Drug, Wichita, 1968-70; pharmacist, dir. Home Drug/PrePrep Med. Div., Wichita, 1970-82; pharmacist, mgr. Revco Drug, Wichita, 1982-87; pharmacist Gessler's Drug, Wichita, 1987—; author, presentor continuing edn. programs for nursing home adminstrs., dental technicians and nurses, 1967—. Mem. Commn. on the Status of Women, Wichita, 1985-87, bd. housing commrs. Wichita Housing Authority, 1989—; precinct committeewoman Dem. Cen. Com., Sedgwick, Kans., 1984—; co-chair Woman Fair, Wichita, 1985; chair Sedgwick County Coun. on Aging, Wichita, 1982-83. Mem. Wichita Acad. Pharmacists (pres. 1983-84), Kans. Pharmacists Assn. (chair PAC 1986-89), Am. Pharm. Assn., NOW (pres. Wichita chpt. 1981-82, state coord. 1988—). Home: 5233 W 1st Wichita KS 67212

HICKS, MARGARET ANN, laboratory manager; b. Richwood, W.Va., Jan. 27, 1954; d. Benjamin Franklin and Anna Marie (Kyer) Rader; m. Edward Allen Hicks, July 27, 1973; children: Brandi Elizabeth, Brett Edward. Degree in Med. Tech., Thomas Meml. Hosp. Sch. Med.T., 1973; student, Glenville (W.Va.) State Coll. Lab mgr., chief med. technologist Summersville (W.Va.) Meml. Hosp., 1973—. Deaconess, Summersville Bapt. Ch., 1988—. Mem. Am. Med. Tech. Assn. Democrat. Baptist. Home: St Rt 2 Box 172 Canvas WV 26662 Office: Summersville Meml Hosp Fairview Heights WV 26651

HICKS, MARYELLEN WHITLOCK, lawyer, judge; b. Odessa, Tex., Mar. 10, 1949; d. Albert Gannett Whitlock and Kathleen (Durham) Butler; m. Arvid Hicks, Oct., 1945 (dec. 1974); 1 child, Kathleen. BA, Tex. Woman's U., 1970, postgrad., 1971; JD, Tex. Tech. U., 1974. Bar: Tex. 1974. Assoc. Mitchell and Bonner, Ft. Worth, 1974-75; ptnr. Bonner and Hicks, Ft. Worth, 1975-77; judge mcpl. ct. City of Ft. Worth, 1977-78, chief judge, 1978-82; dist. judge 231st Dist. Ct., Ft. Worth, 1983—. Vice chmn. Sojourner Truth Theater, Ft. Worth, 1987-88. Nat. Acad. Arts and Scis. grantee Golden Gate Law Sch., 1979. Fellow Tex. Bar Found., Coll. State Bar Tex.; mem. Nat. Bar Assn., Tex. State Bar Assn., Tarrant County Bar Assn., Ft. Worth Black Bar Assn. (pres. 1987-88), Black Women Lawyers Tarrant County (co-founder), Positively Sisters (pres. 1987-88), Girlfriends Club, Rotary, Delta Sigma Theta. Democrat. Roman Catholic. Office: 231st Dist Ct 100 N Houston St Fort Worth TX 76119

HICKS, MILDRED WALKER, nurse, educator; b. Shivers, Miss.; d. Frank and Willie Walker; m. John B. Hicks; children: Millicent, John Jr., Lola, Ervin, Gloria. ASN, Miami-Dade Community Coll., 1973; BS in Health Adminstrn., Fla. Internat. U., 1980; M in Health Mgmt., St. Thomas U., 1987. Nurse adminstrn. coord. Victoria Hosp., Miami, Fla.; nurse supr. U. Miami; out-patient head nurse mgr. Mt. Sinai Med. Ctr., Miami Beach, Fla., 1970-87; nursing instr. Miami Lakes Health Occupation dept. Dade County Sch. Bd., Fla., 1989—. Dir. young adult usher bd. New Bethany/Bapt. Ch. Mem. Fla. Nursing Assn., Sigma Theta Tau, Chi Eta Phi. Baptist.

HICKS, PAULINE ELLIS, librarian; b. Tallahassee, May 20, 1947; d. Noah and Pauline (Dixon) Ellis; m. Leon N. Hicks, Jan. 5, 1980. BS, Fla. A&M U., 1968; MSLS, Western Mich. U., 1973. Libr. Jackson County Sch. Tng., Marianna, Fla., 1968-70, Marianna Mid. Sch., 1970-71, Vernon (Fla.) High Sch., 1971-72; libr. Fla. A&M U., Tallahassee, 1973-79, br. libr. Coll. of Pharmacy, 1979—, head libr., 1981—. Active St. Louis Pub. Sch. Role Model Program, 1988-89. Grantee NIH, 1985-90. Mem. Am. Assn. Colls. Pharmacy (chmn. awards com. 1987—), Fla. Health Sci. Libr. Assn. (reporter 1988—), North Fla. Libr. Assn. (sec. 1986-87). Democrat. Methodist. Home: 4019 Roberts Ave Tallahassee FL 32310 Office: Fla A&M U PO Box 367 Tallahassee FL 32307

HICKS, SANDY LEE, occupational engineer; b. Paterson, N.J., Oct. 27, 1959; d. William Trevalyn and Lois (Kearney) H. BS in Nursing, Ariz. State U., 1982, BS in Engring., 1987. RN, Ariz. Nurse technician St. Luke's Med. Ctr., Phoenix, 1981-82; field worker, nurse Maricopa County Dept. Health, Phoenix, 1983; clin. engr. Dyna-Cor/Entech, Phoenix, 1985, 86; engr. AT&T Nassau Metals, Gaston, S.C., 1988-89; occupational engr. AT&T Techs., Phoenix, 1989—. Mem. Soc. Women Engrs. Republican. Presbyterian. Office: AT&T 505 N 51st Ave Phoenix AZ 85043

HICKS, SUSAN LYNN BOWMAN, small business owner; b. Flint, Mich., Mar. 24, 1952; d. Richard and Carol Joanne (Haney) Bowman; m. Duane James Hicks, Aug. 6, 1977. BA, U. Mich., Flint, 1975; MA, Cen. Mich. U., 1981. Med. social worker Flint Osteo. Hosp., 1974-77; dir. med. social work and patient rels. Crittenton Hosp., Rochester, Mich., 1978—; owner, Susan Hicks Enterprises, 1988—; mgmt. tng. and devel. cons. Buick, Oldsmobile, Cadillac div. GM, Grand Blanc, Mich., 1985. Bd. dirs., chmn. com. Rochester Area Youth Guidance, Mich., 1986, chmn., 1988. Mem. Soc. for Hosp. Social Work Dirs. (Recognition award 1984, 85, pres.-elect 1985-86, pres. 1986-87, chmn. polit. and social action com. 1988—), Nat. Assn. Social Workers, NAFE, Soc. Patient Representatives. Methodist. Avocations: tap dancing, writing. Home and Office: 20483 Fox Detroit MI 48240-1207

HICKS-MOORE, PEGGY ANN, special event coordination company executive; b. L.A., Jan. 9, 1959; d. John Stipp and Virginia Marie (Grace) Hicks; m. John C. Moore, Nov. 30, 1985. AA in Communications, Harbor Coll., 1979; BA in Sociology, U. Calif., Santa Barbara, 1982. Publicist, asst. scheduler 1984 Olympics, L.A., 1984; account exec. The Lorsch Group Advt. Agy., L.A., Hollywood, Calif., 1984-85; exec. dir. Peace Resource Ctr., Santa Barbara, Calif., 1985-86; pres. PHM Communications, Santa Barbara, 1986—; freelance features writer Santa Barbara News Press, 1990; desktop pub. PHM Communications, 1988-90. Producer, dir. (documentary)Water Reclamation: The Wave of the Future, 1990; radio, TV announcer. Event coord., advance person Mondale for Pres., 1984; event coord., fundraiser Gary K. Hart for Congress, Santa Barbara, 1988, event coord. Dukakis for Pres., 1988, dep. campaign mgr. Landecker for City Coun., Santa Barbara, 1989; campaign mgr. Geis for County Auditor-Controller, Santa Barbara, 1990; actress Ensemble Theatre Co., Santa Barbara. Named Best Actress, Chapman Coll., 1978. Mem. Pub. Rels. Soc. Am., Women in Communications Inc., Summer Solstice Celebration (bd. dirs.). Democrat. Congregationalist. Home: 7602 Hollister Ave 302 Goleta CA 93117 Office: PHM Communications 7602 Hollister 302 Goleta CA 93117

HICKSON, EILEEN HASSETT, retired library clerk; b. Bronx, N.Y., June 3, 1916; d. John Charles and Eileen Marie (FitzGerald) Hassett; m. William Alexander Hickson, Jr., Jan. 2, 1944; children: Geoffrey Lawrence, Kevin Alexander. Student, Northwestern U., 1934-36; BA in Communication-Performing, SUNY, Old Westbury, 1988. Sec. J. Walter Thompson, N.Y.C., 1940-44; tchr. Adult Edn. Pub. Speaking, Port Washington, N.Y., 1952-57; prin. libr. clk. Port Washington (N.Y.) Pub. Libr., 1959-81; dir. Theatre Workshop, Port Washington, 1950's; clerical head Nassau County Libr. Assn., 1970; organized first adminstrv., clerical, support staff ACSS com., N.Y. Libr. Assn., 1975. Trustee Port Washington (N.Y.) Pub. Libr., 1984, 89; candidate for N.Y. State Gov.'s Commn. on Librs., 1990. Mem. AAUW, Northwestern Alumni Assn., SUNY Alumni Assn., Play Troupe Port Washington, Port Singers, Nat. Trust for Hist. Preservation, Zeta Phi Eta. Republican. Roman Catholic. Home: 4 Lincoln Pl Port Washington NY 11050

HIEATT, CONSTANCE BARTLETT, English language educator; b. Boston, Feb. 11, 1928; d. Arthur Charles and Eleonora (Very) Bartlett; m. Allen Kent Hieatt, Oct. 25, 1958. Student, Smith Coll., 1945-47; A.B., Hunter Coll., 1953, A.M., 1957; Ph.D., Yale U., 1959. Lectr. City Coll., CUNY, 1959-60; from asst. prof. to asso. prof. English Queensborough Community Coll., CUNY, 1960-65; asso. prof. St. John's U., Jamaica, N.Y., 1965-69; prof. English U. Western Ont. (Can.) London, 1969—. Author: The Canterbury Tales of Geoffrey Chaucer, 1964, rev. edit., 1981, The Realism of Dream Visions, 1967, Beowulf and Other Old English Poems, 1967, rev. edit., 1983, Essentials of Old English, 1968, The Miller's Tale by Geoffrey Chaucer, 1970, Spenser: Selected Poetry, 1970, (with Sharon Butler) Pleyn Delit: Medieval Cookery for Modern Cooks, 1976, rev. edit., 1979, Karlamagnus Saga, Vols. I and II, 1975, 1975, Vol. III, 1980, (with Sharon Butler) Curye on Inglysch, 1985, An Ordinance of Pottage, 1988; also children's books: (with A.K. Hieatt) The Canterbury Tales of Geoffrey Chaucer, 1961, Sir Gawain and the Green Knight, 1967, The Knight of the Lion, 1968, The Knight of the Cart, 1969, The Joy of the Court, 1971, The Sword and the Grail, 1972, The Castle of Ladies, 1973, The Minstrel Knight, 1974. Contbr. Yale U. fellow, and Lewis-Farmington fellow, 1957-59; Can. Council and Social Sci. and Humanities Rsch. Coun. grantee; Yale U. vis. fellow, 1985-86, 89—. Fellow Royal Soc. Can.; mem. MLA, Medieval Acad. Am., Internat. Arthurian Assn., Early English Text Soc., Internat. Saga Assn., Internat. Soc. Anglo-Saxonists, Children's Lit. Assn., Soc. Advancement of Scandinavian Studies, Assn. Can. Univ. Tchrs. English, New Chaucer Soc., Anglo-Norman Text Soc. Anglican. Home: 304 River Rd Deep River CT 06417 Office: U Western Ont, Dept English, London, ON Canada N6A 3K7

HIEBERT, ELIZABETH BLAKE, civic worker; b. Mpls., July 18, 1910; d. Henry Seavey and Grace (Riebeth) Blake; student Washburn U., 1926-30; B.S., U. Tex. 1933; m. Homer L. Hiebert, Aug. 29, 1935; children—Grace Elizabeth (Mrs. John E. Beam), Mary Sue (Mrs. Donald Wester), John Blake, Henry Leonard, David Mark. Sec. Topeka Regional Sci. Fair, 1958-60, bd. dirs., 1964—; bd. dirs. YMCA 1968-74, Topeka (Kans.) Friends of the 300; water safety instr. and swimming tchr. of handicapped; freelance writer; mem. adv. com. Kans. Ctr.; former mem. Shawnee County Advocacy Council on Aging; Shawnee County chmn. Arthritis Found. Hon. fellow Harry S. Truman Library; recipient Paul Harris award Rotary, 1985. Mem. D.A.R., Daus. Am. Colonists, AAUW (dir. 1944-62, 65—), N.E. Hist. and Geneal. Soc., Tex. U. Alumni, Am. Home Econs. Assn., Shawnee County Med. Aux. (past pres.), Nat. Audubon, Met. Mus. Art, Nelson Atkins Mus. of Art, P.E.O. (past local pres. coop. bd.), Topeka Art Guild, Nat. Soc. Ancient and Hon. Arty., Nat. Trust Historic Preservation, Internat. Oceanographic Found., Nat. League Am. Pen Women (pres. Topeka 1970-72), Washburn Alumnae Assn., Am. Assn. State and Local History, Colo. Hist. Assn., Shawnee County Hist. Soc., Mont., Minn., Kans. hist. socs., Smithsonian Assos., Oceanic Soc., Internat. Platform Assn., Topeka Friends of the Library, Cousteau Soc., Am. Assn. Zookeepers, Nat. Assn. for Mature People, Am. Assn. Ret. Persons, K.U. Spencer Mus. Art, Conn. Soc. Genealogists, Nat., New Eng. geneal. socs., Topeka Beautification Assn. (sec.), People to People, Archives Assos., Am. Space Found., Mus. Fine Arts Boston, Kans. Reading Assn., Am. Assn. Museums, San Diego Zool. Soc., Nat. Space Inst., Oriental Inst., Delta Kappa Gamma (hon.), Delta Gamma, others. Club: Topeka Knife and Fork. Editor children's page Household mag., 1934-39. Methodist. Home: 1517 Randolph Topeka KS 66604

HIENTON, DIANE DEBROSSE, lawyer; b. Fayetteville, Ark., Jan. 30, 1948; d. Joseph Denis and Opal Ruvena (Pitts) DeBrosse; m. James Robert Hienton, July 23, 1977. B.A., U. Hawaii, 1971; J.D., Ariz. State U., 1975. Bar: Ariz. 1975. Asst. chief counsel Ariz. Atty. Gen., Phoenix, 1976-78, 84—; staff atty. Ariz. Ct. Appeals, 1978-81, 82-84; assoc. Jennings, Kepner & Haug, Phoenix, 1981-82. Contbr. articles to profl. jours. Mem. 1984 Phoenix Citizens Bond Com., Ariz. Theatre Guilde, Phoenix, 1982-84; founding life mem. Ariz. Mus. Sci. and Tech., 1984; bd. dirs. Ariz. Women's

Town Hall. Mem. ABA, State Bar Ariz., Maricopa County Bar Assn. (pres. pub. lawyers sect. 1988), Jr. League Phoenix, Soroptimist (pres. 1988-89, editor Phoenix SOL Bull 1983-84). Republican. Office: Office of Atty Gen Dept Law 1275 W Washington Phoenix AZ 85007

HIGBEE, FLORENCE SALICK, librarian; b. Milw.; d. Otto Thomas and Mary (Reiter) Salick; B.A., U. Wis., 1933; M.S. in Library Sci., Cath. U. Am., 1965; 1 dau., Joan Florence. Reference librarian Shirlington br. of Arlington County Public Libraries, Arlington, Va., 1965-67; br. librarian Glencarlyn br. Arlington County Public Libraries, Arlington, 1967, Columbia Pike br., 1967-73; translator, archivist. Mem. nominating com. Literacy Council No. Va., Inc., 1973-74. State of Va. Grad. fellow, 1964-65. Recipient Humanitarian award Montgomery County (Md.) Humane Soc. Inc., 1990. Mem. ALA, Am. Malacological Union. Home: 13 N Bedford Arlington VA 22201

HIGBEE, JOAN FLORENCE, librarian; b. Washington, Jan. 1, 1945; d. Florence Salick H. Student, U. Sorbonne, 1962-63, U. Nancy, 1967-68; BA in French, George Washington U., 1967; MA and PhD in Romance Langs., Johns Hopkins U., 1975; MLS, Cath. U. Am., 1976. Libr. Collection Svcs. Dept., Libr. of Congress, Washington, 1976—; collections specialist Woodrow Wilson Internat. Ctr. Scholars, Smithsonian Inst., 1981—; instr. Johns Hopkins U., 1968-72; asst. d'anglais, Lycée Frédéric Chopin, Nancy, France, 1967-68. Author: Southwest European Studies, 1989; contbr. articles to profl. jours. Mem. ALA (councilor at large 1980-88, founding coordinator Library Union Task Force, past mem. policy monitoring com., resolutions com., com. profl. standards), Assn. Coll. and Research Libraries (past chair Western European specialists sect.). Office: Libr of Congress 1st and Independence Ave SE Washington DC 20003

HIGDON, BARBARA J., college president; b. Independence, Mo., May 18, 1930; m. 1950; 3 children. B.A., U. Mo., 1951, M.A., 1952, Ph.D. in Speech, 1961. Assoc. prof. English, speech, Tex. So. U., 1958-62; prof. Graceland Coll., Lamoni, Iowa, 1962-75, pres., 1984—; dean, v.p. acad. affairs Park Coll., 1975-84. Office: Graceland Coll Lamoni IA 50140

HIGDON, BERNICE COWAN, retired teacher; b. Sylva, N.C., Feb. 26, 1918; d. Royston Duffield and Margaret Cordelia (Hall) Cowan; m. Roscoe John Higdon, Aug. 12, 1945; children: Ronald Keith, Rodrick Knox, Krista Dean. BS, Western Carolina U., 1941; cert. tchr., So. Oreg. Coll., 1967; student, Chapman Coll., 1971. Cert. tchr., Calif. Prin., tchr. Dorsey Sch., Bryson City, N.C., 1941-42; expeditor Glenn L. Martin Aircraft Co., Balt., 1942-45; tchr. elem. sch. Seneca, S.C., 1945-46, Piedmont, S.C., 1946-47; tchr. elem. sch. Columbia, S.C., 1950-51, Manteca, Calif., 1967-68; kindergarten tchr. 1st Bapt. Ch., Medford, Oreg., 1965-67; tchr. elem. sch. Marysville (Calif.) Unified Sch. Dist., 1968-83; tchr. Headstart, Manteca, 1968. Former counselor Youth Svc. Bur., Yuba City, Calif.; troop leader Girl Scouts U.S.A., Medford, 1962-63; past Sunday sch. tchr. 1st Bapt. Ch., Medford; bd. dirs. Christian Assistance Network, Yuba City, 1984-85; aux. vol. Fremont Med. Ctr., Yuba City, 1984—. Recipient cert. of appreciation Marysville Unified Sch. Dist., 1983, Christian Assistance Network, 1985; cert. of recognition Ella Elem. Sch., Marysville, 1983. Mem. Calif. Ret. Tchrs. Assn., Nat. Ret. Tchrs. Assn., Sutter Hist. Soc., AAUW, Am. Assn. Ret. Persons. Home: 1264 Charlotte Ave Yuba City CA 95991

HIGDON, POLLY SUSANNE, judge; b. Goodland, Kans., May 1, 1942; d. William and Pauline Higdon; m. John P. Wilhardt (div. May 1988); 1 child, Liesl. BA, Vassar Coll., 1964; postgrad., Cornell U., 1967; JD, Washburn U., 1975; LLM, NYU, 1980. Bar: Kans. 1975, Oreg. 1980. Assoc. Corley & Assocs., Garden City, Kans., 1975-79, Kendrick M. Mercer Law Offices, Eugene, Oreg., 1980-82; pvt. practice law Eugene, 1983; judge U.S. Bankruptcy Ct., Eugene, 1983—. Active U.S. Peace Corps, Tanzania, East Africa, 1965-66. Mem. Am. Bankruptcy Inst., Nat. Conf. Bankruptcy Judges, Nat. Assn. Women Judges. Office: US Bankruptcy Ct 211 E 7th Rm 404 PO Box 1335 Eugene OR 97440

HIGGINS, BARBARA LOUISA, education educator; b. San Diego, Oct. 24, 1945; d. William Henry and Juanita (Wesley) Green; m. David Zook Higgins, Aug., 1974. BA, San Diego State U., 1968; postgrad., U. Calif., 1973; Calif. Poly., 1977; postgrad., U. Calif., Irvine, 1989. Tchr. San Diego City Schs., 1969-71, Solana Beach (Calif.) Sch. Dist., 1972-73, Atascadero (Calif.) Sch. Dist., 1975-77; tchr., developer Old Mission Sch., San Luis Obispo, Calif., 1982-84; dir., tchr. Montessori Child Devel. Ctr., Huntington, Calif., 1986-87; tchr., special education Juvenile Ct. Sch. Intensive Care Facility, Orange, Calif., 1987--; advisor Sathya Sai Baba, Tustin, Calif., 1987—. Author: Edn. Materials. Gold mem. Museum of 20th Century Arts, Laguna Beach, Calif, 1989. Mem. Calif. Tchrs. Assn., Nat. Edn. Assn., Phi Lambda Theta. Democrat. Office: Intensive Care Facility 483 S City Dr Orange CA 92668

HIGGINS, DOROTHY MARIE, academic dean; b. Lawrence, Mass., May 1, 1930; d. John Daniel and Mary Jane (Herbertson) H. AB, Emmanuel Coll., 1951; MS, Cath. U., 1961; PhD, Boston Coll., 1966. Assoc. prof. chemistry Emmanuel Coll., Boston, 1966-88, chair chemistry dept., 1974-85; div. chair math., sci., tech. Roxbury Community Coll., Roxbury Crossing, Mass., 1988-90; dean arts and scis. Teikyo-Post U., Waterbury, Conn., 1990—; grant cons. N.E. coll. Optometry, Boston, 1986; faculty cons. Zymark Corp., Hopkinton, Mass., 1982; rsch. assoc. U. Mass., Boston, 1975-84. Editor: (workbook) Geometry: Development Students, 1989; editor sci. newsletter, 1989; editorial adv. bd. Jour. Coll. Sci. Teaching, 1984-88. Instrumentation grantee NSF, 1985, Chautauqua grantee NSF, 1981-82, Instrumentation grantee George Alden Trust, 1985, Boston Globe Found., 1985, Extramural Assoc. grantee NIH, 1984. Mem. Am. Chem. Soc., New Eng. Chem. Tchrs., North Sci. Tchrs. Assn., Soc. Coll. Sci. Teaching, Sigma Xi. Democrat. Roman Catholic. Office: Teikyo Post U 800 Country Club Rd Waterbury CT 06723-2540

HIGGINS, ISABELLE JEANETTE, librarian; b. Evanston, Ill., Dec. 13, 1919; d. Frank LeRoy and Ada Louise (Wilcox) Heck; m. George Alfred Higgins, Jan. 23, 1945; children: Alfred Clinton, Donald Quentin, Heather Higgins Aanes, Laura Higgins Palmer, Carol. BS, Northwestern U., 1940; MLS, U. Md., 1971. Cert. tchr., Md. With Liebermann Waelchli Co., Tokyo, 1940-41, Shanghai (People's Republic of China) Evening Post, 1941-42; editorial asst. Newsweek mag., N.Y.C., 1944; wire editor FCC, Washington, 1944-46; rsch. and analysis China desk CIA, Washington, 1946-49; supr. library vols. Westbrook Sch., Bethesda, Md., 1965-69; reference librarian Montgomery County Pub. Libraries, Bethesda, 1969-83; librarian Brooks Inst. Photography, Santa Barbara, Calif., 1984—; treas. Friends of Santa Barbara Pub. Library, 1987-88. Mem. Spl. Libraries Assn., Calif. Library Assn., Md. Library Assn., AAUW (bd. dirs. Santa Barbara chpt. 1988—, del. nat. conv. 1989), Santa Barbara Little Gardens (pres. 1987-89), The Floriade Garden (v.p. 1987-88, pres. 1990—). Congregationalist. Home: 1128 Garcia Rd Santa Barbara CA 93103 Office: Brooks Inst Photography 801 Alston Rd Santa Barbara CA 93108

HIGGINS, JOAN MARIE, freelance writer, producer; b. Shamokin, Pa.; d. Leon Francis and Anna (Kiewlak) H. Student, Middlesex County Coll., Edison, N.J., 1971-73, The New Sch. for Social Rsch., N.Y.C. Adminstrv. asst. Middlesex County Coll., Edison, N.J., 1971-72; mem. staff Eyewitness News/ABC-TV, N.Y.C., 1972-86; planning unit editor, field producer Eyewitness News/ABC-TV, 1985-86; freelance producer, writer, publicist N.Y.C., 1986-87, Children's Television Workshop, N.Y.C., 1986-87; producer, publicist Dino DeLaurentis Entertainment Co., N.Y.C., 1987, Zarem Pub. Rels., N.Y.C., 1987, Self Mag., 1986-87; sr. publicist Avon Books/The Hearst Corp., N.Y.C., 1987-89; ptnr. Gale & Higgins Communications. Recipient Emmy award cert. of recognition for rsch. on TV spl., NATAS, 1981. Mem. Writers Guild Am. Home: 301 Saint James Ave Woodbridge NJ 07095

HIGGINS, PATRICIA ANN, communications executive; b. Woodbury, N.J., June 27, 1951; d. John David and Louise Helen (Brooks) H.; 1 child, Jesse. BS in Pub. Communications, Syracuse U., 1973. Newspaper reporter Times Herald-Record, Middletown, N.Y., 1973-74; advt. copywriter Advt. Div., Inc., Chgo., 1974-75, freelance journalist, 1975-77, 79-83; newspaper reporter Suburban Trib Chgo. Tribune, 1977-79; dir. communications The Contemporary Quilt, Chgo., 1980-83; sr. account supr. Hill and Knowlton, Inc., Chgo., 1984-87; sr. dir. corp. communications World Book, Inc., Chgo., 1987—; lectr. in field. Media relations supr. United Airlines Silver Wings, 1986, "Mikey" reintro. Quaker Life Cereal, 1986 (Golden Trumpet award 1986), 1988 World Book Ency. Mem. Irish Children's Fund, Downers Grove, Ill., 1982; sponsor Save the Children, Conn., 1983—; mem. adv. bd. Reflections program Nat. PTA, Chgo., 1988—; bd. dirs. U.S. Acad. Decathlon, L.A., 1988-89. Co-recipient Silver Anvil award Pub. Relations Soc. Am., 1984, co-recipient 2 Silver Trumpet awards Publicity Club Chgo., 1986. Mem. Direct Selling Assn. (communications com. 1989—), Soc. Profl. Journalists, Women in Communications (bd. dirs. Chgo. chpt. 1990—), Syracuse U. Newhouse Sch. Alumni Assn., Chgo. Headline Club, Chgo. Syracuse U. Alumni Club, Evergreen Bath and Tennis Club. Methodist. Office: World Book Inc 101 NW Point Blvd Elk Grove Village IL 60007

HIGGINS, SISTER THERESE, college president; b. Winthrop, Mass., Sept. 29, 1925; d. James C. and Margaret M. (Lennon) H. A.B. cum laude, Regis Coll., 1947; M.A., Boston Coll.; Ph.D., U. Wis.; D.H.L., Emmanuel Coll.; postgrad. in lit. and theology, Harvard U.; LL.D. (hon.), Northeastern U. Joined Congregation of Sisters of St. Joseph, Roman Cath. Ch., 1947; instr. Regis Coll., Weston, Mass., 1963-65; asst. prof. Regis Coll., 1965-67, asso. prof., 1968—, pres., 1974—, also trustee. Book reviewer: Boston Globe, 1965—. Trustee Waltham (Mass.) Hosp., 1978-85, Cardinal Spellman Philatelic Mus., 1976—; mem. Mass. Gov.'s Commn. on Status Women, 1977-79, Nat. Com. Ecclesial Role Women. U. Wis. research grantee Eng. Mem. Nat. Cath. Ednl. Assn., AAUW, MLA, AAUP, Assn. Ind. Colls. and Univs. Mass. (exec. com.), New Eng. Colls. Fund, NEASC (commn.). Office: Regis Coll 235 Wellesley St Weston MA 02193*

HIGGINS-STAHULAK, ELIZABETH JEAN, artist, calligrapher; b. Chgo., Oct. 13, 1950; d. James Theodore and Celia Sylvia (Schwartz) Patterson; m. Philip Arthur Higgins, Sept. 26, 1970 (div.); children: Timothy James, Brian Philip; m. Paul John Stahulak, Sept. 20, 1986. Grad., Loop Jr. Coll., Chgo., 1970; student, Art Inst. Chgo., summers 1964-66. Freelance calligrapher Palos Heights, Ill., 1983—; clients include Gleneagles Country Club, Lemont, Ill., Midway Airlines, Chgo., Gold Coast Air Fair, Chgo., MIT, Inc., Oakbrook, Ill., Northwestern U. Dental Sch., No. Trust Bank, Heritage Bank, Tinley Park, Ill.; calligraphy portraits of people's names and articles with airbrush illustration. Artist pictures, 1983. Picture lady Sch. Dist. 218, Palos Heights, 1984—. Mem. Ancient Mystical Order Rosea Crusis (sororal, artist 1984), Chgo. Calligraphy Collective.

HIGGS, ELIZABETH JO, savings and loan association executive; b. Chestertown, Md., June 30, 1960; d. Charles Arnold and Mary Elizabeth (Hawkins) Downey; m. Elwood Glenn Higgs, Jr., Aug. 1978; 1 child, Stephanie Lynn. Ed. pub. schs., Centreville, Md. Teller Sudlersville (Md.) Bank, 1978-79; bookkeeper, then proof operator Peoples Bank of Kent County, Chestertown, 1979-80, from new accounts clk. to supr. loan dept., 1980-85; asst. mgr. 2d Nat. Fed. Savs., Salisbury, Md., 1985—; sr. asst. bank mgr., computer trainer 2d Nat. Fed. Savs., Salisbury, 1987—; programmer, bookkeeper P. Patrick McClary Real Estate, Golts, Md., 1987-89; asst. v.p., br. mgr., 1989—. Treas. Sudlersville Elem. Sch. PTA, 1985-87; leader Chesapeake Bay coun. Girl Scouts U.S., 1987—; mem. Sudlersville Vol. Fire Co., 1986—; rep. Queen Anne's County Coun., Centreville, 1987-88. Methodist. Lodge: Moose. Home: Rt 1 Box 182-EF Millington MD 21651 Office: Second Nat Fed Savs 790 Ritchie Hwy Severna Park MD 21146

HIGH, DOROTHY HELEN FRANK, city recreation administrator; b. Lincoln, Nebr., Feb 3, 1935; d. Theodore Ludwig and Lillian Winifred (Schellberg) F.; m. Duane High, Nov. 18, 1955; children—Ted Frank, Catherine Nadine. B.S. in Edn., U. Nebr., 1956; M.S. in Edn., Chadron State Coll., 1967. Instr. phys. edn. Lincoln Pub. Schs., Nebr., 1956-58, Alliance City Schs., Nebr., 1964-67, Scottsbluff Pub. Schs., Nebr., 1967-69, Hiram Scott Coll., Scottsbluff, 1969-71; asst. prof. edn., Tarkio Coll., Mo., 1971; recreation supr. City of Scottsbluff, 1973—. Mem. adv. bd. Nebr. Council Ednl. TV, Lincoln, 1968-70, Nebr. Dept. Edn., 1970; bd. dirs. Southeast Recreation Ctr., Scottsbluff, 1975-80, Jaycee Sr. Ctr., Scottsbluff, 1978-82; mem. adv. bd. Foster Grandparent Program, Scottsbluff, 1983—; sec., bd. dirs. North Platte Valley chpt. ARC, 1989. Mem. Am. Assn. Leisure and Recreation (pres.-elect 1985-86, pres. 1986-87), Am. Alliance Health, Phys. Edn., Recreation and Dance (bd. govs. 1986-87, pres. central dist. 1982-84, Honor award 1975), Nebr. Assn. Health, Phys. Edn., Recreation and Dance (pres. 1972-73, Honor award 1970), Am. Soc. Aging., Soroptimist Internat. (pres. Scotts Bluff County chpt. pres. 1978-79). Republican. Lutheran. Avocations: tennis; swimming. Home: 2210 7th Ave Scottsbluff NE 69361 Office: City of Scottsbluff 1818 Ave A Scottsbluff NE 69361

HIGH, MONIQUE RAPHEL, writer; b. N.Y.C., May 3, 1949; d. David and Dina (Cornfield) Raphel; m. Robert Duncan High, June 6, 1969 (div. 1981); 1 child, Nathalie Danielle High; m. Grigori Raiport, Nov. 8, 1985 (div. 1987); m. Ben Walter Pesta II, Dec. 7, 1987. BA, Barnard Coll., 1969. Asst. pub. rels. dir. Thomas More Coll., Fort Mitchell, Ky., 1969-70; lectr. in field. Author: The Four Winds of Heaven, 1980, Encore, 1981, The Eleventh Year, 1983, The Keeper of the Walls, 1985, Thy Father's House, 1987, Between Two Worlds, 1989; author(With Grigori Raiport), Red Gold, 1988; contbr. articles to profl. jours. including Men's Look, Men's Fitness, Shape, Muscle and Fitness, Moxie. Mem. L.A. Commn. on Assaults Against Women. Mem. The Authors Guild, Alliance Francaise, Barnard Club. Democrat. Jewish. Home: 431 S Rexford Dr Beverly Hills CA 90212

HIGH, SHAROLYN PARKER, travel consultant; b. Sept. 28, 1945; d. Llewlyn Homer and Myrtle (Holcomb) Parker; m. Harry J. High; children: Joseph, Christina, Patricia. BS, Pa. State U., 1966, MEd, 1969. Tchr. Balt. Co. Bd. Edn., Towson, Md., 1967-69; supr. Child Nutrition Progams State Md., 1969-83; travel cons. Roeder Travel Ltd., Cokeysville, Md., 1987—. Mem. Am. Soc. Travel Agts., Assn. Sch. Bus. Offcl., Parents of Multiples (pres.), Summer Hill Club. Home: 13903 Sunnybrook Rd Phoenix MD 21131 Office: Roeder Travel Ltd 9805 York Rd Cockeysville MD 21030

HIGHSMITH, CAROL MCKINNEY, photographer; b. Leaksville, N.C., May 18, 1946; d. Luther Carlton and Ruth (Carter) McKinney; m. Mark Steven Highsmith, Dec. 1966 (dec. June 1969); m. Theodore Landphair, June 1988. BA in Photography, Am. U., 1986. Audience promotion mgr. Sta. WPHL-TV, Phila., 1967-71; account exec. Sta. KYW, Phila., 1974-76, Sta. WMAL, Washington, 1976-84; owner, prin. Carol M. Highsmith Photography, Washington, 1984—; Contbr. photography to Time mag., Smithsonian mag., Life mag., Fortune mag., others; one-woman show includes AIA traveling exhibit, 1987—; photog. chronicler hist. renovation projects. Author, photographer Pennsylvania Avenue: America's Main Street, Union Station: A Decorative History of Washington's Grand Terminal. Bd. dirs. Columbia Hosp. for Women, Washington, 1981—. Mem. Am. Soc. Mag. Photographers Washington Bd. Trade (sgt.-at-arms 1980-81). Home: 7501 Carroll Ave Takoma Park MD 20912 Office: 3299 K St NW Ste 404 Washington DC 20007

HIGHSMITH, LINDA YVONNE, business manager; b. Anaheim, Calif., Nov. 8, 1949; d. Louis Le Saout and Martha J. (Line) Nichols; m. Sammy A. Highsmith, Dec. 1, 1967; children: Carey Y., Sammie A. Jr. BBA, U. Tex., San Antonio, 1981. CPA, Tex. With Kerrville (Tex.) State Hosp., 1969—. Sec. credit com., sec. loan com. Hilco Fed. Credit Union, Kerrville, 1989-90; vol. income tax assistance IRSA, Kerrville, 1989-90. Mem. AICPAs, Am. Women's Soc. CPAs, Tex. Soc. CPAs, Tex. Pub. Employees Assn., Nat. Exch. Club (sec., treas. 1990—), Kerrville Exch. Club (sec., treas. 1990—), Beta Gamma Sigma. Republican. Methodist. Home: 22 Elm Way Kerrville TX 78028 Office: Kerrville State Hosp 721 Thompson Dr Kerrville TX 78028

HIGHSMITH, WANDA LAW, association executive; b. Cleveland, Mo., Oct. 25, 1928; d. Lloyd B. and Nan (Sisk) Law; student U. Mo., 1954-56; 1 dau., Holly. Legal sec., firms in Mo. and D.C., until 1960; various staff positions Am. Coll. Osteopathic Surgeons, 1960-72, asst. exec. dir., conv. mgr., Alexandria, Va., 1974—. Mem. Profl. Conv. Mgmt. Assn., Washington Soc. Assn. Execs., Am. Soc. Assn. Execs., NAFE. Republican. Methodist. Home: 400 15th St S Apt #1305 Arlington VA 22202 Office: Am Coll Osteopathic Surgeons 123 N Henry St Alexandria VA 22314

HIGHTOWER, ARLENE JANICE, nursing administrator; b. St. Albans, N.Y., Mar. 7, 1949; d. Ernest Charles and Dolores Agnes (Hendel) Krebs; children: Meredith Lynn, Courtney Elizabeth. BS in Nursing, Salve Regina Coll., 1970; MS in Nursing, U. R.I., 1981. Clin. instr. Salve Regina Coll., Newport, R.I., 1977-79, U. R.I., Kingston, 1979-81; supr. maternal child nursing Good Samaritan Hosp., West Islip, N.Y., 1981-85, dir. maternal child nursing services, 1985—. Active Suffolk Perinatal Coalition, Hauppauge, N.Y., 1986—; sch. bd. Our Lady of Lourdes Sch., West Islip, 1986—. Served to lt. USN, 1970-76, comdr. res., 1986—. Mem. Nurses Assn. Am. Coll. Ob/Gyn (cert.), Naval Reserve Assn., Assn. Mil. Surgeons U.S., Am. Soc. Psychoprophylaxis in Obstetrics. Roman Catholic. Home: 207 Cooper Rd North Babylon NY 11703 Office: Good Samaritan Hosp 1000 Montauk Hwy West Islip NY 11795

HIGHTOWER, MARY ANN, data processing professional, real estate agent; b. Preston, Ga., Jan. 27, 1945; d. Len Edward and Bertha (Williams) Allen; children: Mark, Gregory Jr. BS, U. Conn., West Hartford, 1987. Lic. real estate agt., Conn. Data processing coord. Town of Bloomfield; accounts clk. Town of Bloomfield (Conn.); bookkeeper Westwood Auto Leasing, Wethersfield, Conn.; psychiat. nurse technician Inst. of Living, Hartford, Conn. Mem. Data Processing Mgmt. Assn., Govt. Mgmt. Info. Scis. (cert., past pres. Conn. chpt.), Nat. Assn. Realtors, Conn. Assn. Realtors, Greater Hartford Assn. Realtors, Adminstrs. User Group, Alpha Sigma Lambda.

HIGINBOTHAM, BETTY LOUISE WILSON, botanist, consultant; b. Louisville, July 5, 1910; d. Samuel Gould Wilson and Stella Jane (Robbins) McCracken; m. Noe Higinbotham, Apr. 3, 1937 (dec. Feb. 1980). BA, Butler U., 1932, MA, 1935. Soc. editor New Albany (Ind.) Daily Ledger, 1935-37; editor Williams & Wilkins, Pubs., Balt., 1937-38; botanical writer Columbia Ency., N.Y.C., 1938-41; editor Washington State Inst. of Tech., 1950; head editorial dept. Washington State U. Press, Pullman, 1951-52; assoc. editor N.W. Sci., Pullman, 1952-56; bryological cons. Northrup Space Labs., 1967, Battelle N.W., Richland, Wash., 1968-71; instr. plants Orcas Island U. Washington, Seattle, 1981; instr. plants San Juan Islands U. Washington, Friday Harbor, 1982-84, Skagit Valley Coll., Friday Harbor, 1985-86; botanical writer Internat. Encyclopedia, N.Y.C., 1938-51, study program Ency. Brittanica, N.Y.C., 1938-41; cons. Nat. Park Svc., Friday Harbor, 1986-87. Freelance writer nature mags.; discovered (with Noe Higinbotham) new species of moss; contbr. papers to sci. jours. Mem. Am. Bryological and Lichenological Soc. (v.p. 1960-61, pres. 1961-62), Am. Radio Relay League, Amateur Radio Emergency Svcs., Young Ladies Relay League, Delta Zeta, Theta Sigma Phi (hon.), Phi Kappa Phi, Kappa Tau Alpha.

HIGMAN, SALLY LEE, company executive; b. Hinsdale, Ill., Sept. 12, 1945; d. Lee Fulton and Freda Margaret (Doehle) H. AB in Social Scis., Shimer Coll., Mt. Carroll, Ill., 1967; MA in Govt., Claremont (Calif.) Grad. Sch., 1969; M of Planning, U. So. Calif., 1973; Cert. in Higher Studies in Ekistics, Athens Tech. Orgn., Athens Ctr. of Ekistics, 1970. Cons. Doxiadis Assocs., Athens, Greece, 1971; rsch. asst. U. So. Calif., 1971-72; cons. Republic of Ecuador, Quito, 1973-75, UN Devel. Prog., Quito, 1975-76; environ. analyst Tetra Tech Inc., Pasadena, Calif., 1976-78; sr. environ. planner Nus Corp., Sherman Oaks, Calif., 1978-81; project mgr. ACT, Inc., Westminster, Calif., 1981-87; owner Higman Doehle Environ. Cons., L.A., 1987-88; pres. Higman Doehle Inc., L.A., 1988—. Contbr. articles to profl. jours. Ford Found. scholar U. So. Calif., 1971-73, jr. rsch. fellow Athens Ctr. of Ekistics, 1969-71; intern Social Sci. Rsch. Coun., Ford Found., 1973-75. Mem. Internat. Right-of-Way Assn., Shimer Coll. Scholastic Soc. Democrat. Episcopalian.

HILARY, SANDRA MARIE, councilwoman; b. Mpls., Jan. 9, 1938; d. Frank and Aurora Martha (Hager) Paar; m. Thomas J. Hilary (div.); 1 child, Michael Christopher. Student, North Hennepin Jr. Coll., Brooklyn Park, Minn., 1974-76, U. Minn., 1976-78. Clk. Northwestern Nat. Bank, Mpls., 1954-57; cashier Gateley's Dept. Store, Mpls., 1957-60; assembler, welder Honeywell Co., Mpls., 1960-62; waitress Little Jack's Restaurant, Mpls., 1962-80; vol. dir. Queen Nursing Home, Mpls., dir. social svc., 1980-84; chmn. Inner City Ward Caucus; mem. Criminal Justice Coordinating Bd., Com. on Urban Environ. Conv. and Visitor's Bd., Downtown Mgmt. Com., Mpls. Community Devel. Agy. Bd., Regional Transit Bd., Light Rail Transit Adv. Bd., Transp. Adv. Bd.; del. Nat. League Cities. Mem. Hennepin County Task Force on Hazardous Waste, Coalition for Def. Neighborhood Priorities, Minn. Freeze, East Side Neighborhood Svcs., Congress Neighborhood Task Forces, Jordan Area Community Coun., Hennepin County Women's Polit. Caucus, Minn. Women's Polit. Caucus, Minn. Women's Consortium; advisor Urban Concerns Workshop; past pres. Hawthorne Area Community Coun.; bd. dirs. MarBe Sr. Citizens Ceramic Workshop; campaign vol. John F. Kennedy for Pres., also local campaigns; others. Mem. Minn. Women Elected Ofcls., LWV, NOW, Mpls. Urban League, MADD, NAACP. Mem. Democrat-Farmer-Labor Party. Roman Catholic. Home: 2306 Fremont Ave N Minneapolis MN 55411 Office: City of Mpls City Hall Rm 307 Minneapolis MN 55415

HILBERT, ANGELIA H., elementary guidance counselor; b. Columbia, Mo., Nov. 26, 1949; d. Ernest Wayland and Opal Elizabeth (Gruebbel) Smith; m. Thomas Daniel Hilbert, Aug. 3, 1974; 1 child, Alicia Danielle. AA, Christian Coll., Columbia, Mo., 1969; BS Edn., Cen. Meth. Coll., 1971; MEd, U. Mo., 1975. Tchr. Warren County R III Sch., Warrenton, Mo., 1971-74, elem. guidance counselor, 1974—. Pres. Four County Mental Health Coun., 1987-89. Mem. AAUW, Am. Bus. Women's Assn., Nat. Assn. Edn. Young Children, Mo. Sch. Counselor Assn., Warren County Hist. Soc. (v.p. 1990), Delta Kappa Gamma (pres. 1988-90). Mem. United Ch. Christ. Office: Warren County R III Sch 302 Kuhl Warrenton MO 63383

HILBERT, VIRGINIA LOIS, computer consultant and training executive; b. Detroit, June 4, 1935; d. Howard G. and Lois (Garner) Swaggerty; m. James R. Hilbert, Nov. 24, 1958; children: James Jr., Jennifer, Douglas, Alexandra. BA with honors, U. Mich., 1957. Govt. analyst personnel dept. City of Detroit, 1957-60; owner, dir. Profl./Tech. Devel., Inc. (doing bus. as Lansing (Mich.) Computer Assn. and Lansing Computer Inst.), 1978—. Sec. Tennis Patrons Bd., Lansing, 1984—, Pro Symphony, 1984—; active Lansing Art Gallery, 1978-84. Mem. Lansing C. of C. (small bus. coun., cochairperson info. and seminar S.B.E.), Women Bus. Owners Assn., Am. Soc. Tng. and Devel., Mich. Tech. Coun., Nat. Bus. Edn. Assn., Gov.'s Small Bus. Conf. (del., gov.'s work group), Mich. Opportunity Card., Nat. Assn. Trade and Tech. Sch. (key 1989—), Mich. Orgn. of Pvt. Vocat. Sch., Alpha Phi (pres. heart equipment fund bd. 1975-86). Episcopalian. Home: 938 Wildwood East Lansing MI 48823 Office: Lansing Computer Inst 501 N Marshall St Lansing MI 48912

HILDEBRAND, CAROL ILENE, librarian; b. Presho, S.D., Feb. 15, 1943; d. Arnum Vance and Ethel Grace (Cole) Stoops; m. Duane D. Hildebrand, Mar. 21, 1970. BA, Dakota Wesleyan U., Mitchell, S.D., 1965; M.Librarianship, U. Wash., 1968. Tchr. Watertown (S.D.) High Sch., 1965-67; library dir. Chippewa County Library, Montevideo, Minn., 1968-70, The Dalles-Wasco County Library, The Dalles, Oreg., 1970-72; librarian Salem (Oreg.) Pub. Library, 1972-73; library dir. Lake Oswego (Oreg.) Pub. Library, 1973-82; asst. city librarian Eugene (Oreg.) Pub. Library, 1982—; cons. in field; conductor workshops in field. Vice chmn. League Women Voters, Lane County, 1987; bd. dirs. Oreg. Libr. PAC, 1986—; sec. Citizens for Lane County Library, 1985-88. Mem. ALA (chpt. councilor 1990—), AAUW (bd. dirs. 1986), Pacific N.W. Library Assn. (pres. 1989-98), Oreg. Library Assn. (pres. 1976-77), Rotary (bd. dirs. 1989—), Phi Kappa Phi. Methodist. Office: Eugene Public Library 100 W 13th Ave Eugene OR 97401

HILDEBRANDT, CLAUDIA JOAN, banker; b. Inglewood, Calif., Feb. 12, 1942; d. Charles Samuel and Clara Claudia (Palumbo) H. B.B.A., U. Colo. Head teller First Colo. Bank & Trust, Denver, 1969-70; asst. cashier First Nat. Bank, Englewood, Colo., 1975-79, asst. v.p., 1979-83, v.p., 1983—; owner CJH Enterprises, Inc., Breckenridge, Colo., 1980—. Mem. Nat. Assn. Bank Women, Fin. Women Internat. (pres. elect. 1989—), Am. Soc. for Personnel Adminstrn., Am. Inst. Banking, Mile High Group. Roman Catholic. Home: 6602 E Cornell Ave Denver CO 80224 Office: First Nat Bank 333 W Hampden Ave Englewood CO 80110

HILFSTEIN, ERNA, science historian, educator; b. Kraków, Poland; came to U.S., 1949, naturalized, 1954; d. Leon and Anna (Schonfeld) Kluger; B.A., CCNY, 1967, M.A., 1971, Ph.D., City U. N.Y., 1978; m. Max Hilfstein; children: Leon, Simone Juliana. Tchr. secondary schs., N.Y.C., 1968-84, 86—; vis. prof. Queens Coll., 1973; affiliate Grad. Sch./Univ. Center, City U. N.Y. NEH grantee, 1984-85; recipient Merit Silver medal, Rector's medal U. N. Copernicus, Torun, 1989, Order of Merit medal Republic of Poland, 1990. Mem. History Sci. Soc., Polish Inst. Arts and Scis. in Am., N.Y. Acad. Scis., United Fedn. of Tchrs. (chpt. chmn. 1978-84, 86—, del. 1980—). Democrat. Jewish. Author: Starowolski's Biographies of Copernicus, 1980; collaborator English version of Nicholas Copernicus Complete Works, vol. 1, 1972, vol. 2, 1978, vol. 3, 1985; contbr. articles and revs. to profl. jours. Editor: Science and History, 1978. Home: 1523 Dwight Pl Bronx NY 10465

HILGENBERG, EVE BRANTLY HANDY, government official; b. Balt., Mar. 3, 1942; d. Sydney Speiden and Evelyn Harned (Crady) Handy; m. Thomas Rodney Twells, June 21, 1963 (div. Mar. 1971); 1 child, Thomas Rodney; m. John Christian Hilgenberg, Apr. 3, 1971; 1 child, Elizabeth Crady. BA, Goucher Coll., 1963. Sr. exec. svc. assoc. commr. U.S. Social Security Adminstrn., Balt., 1979—. Recipient Superior Achievement award Dept. Human Svcs., 1978. Home: 38 Warrenton Rd Baltimore MD 21210

HILL, ADRIENNE NICOLE, clinical therapist, psychometrist, researcher; b. San Francisco, Sept. 8, 1964; d. David J. and Barbara J. (Bayone) McKinney; m. Jerry Laron Hill, Dec. 26, 1987. BS, U. Wash., 1986; MA, Chapman Coll., 1989. Mental health specialist Highline Evaluation & Treatment Facility, Seattle, 1988-89; pvt. practice Seattle, 1989—; psychometrist U. Wash., Seattle, 1989—; intern Cen. Area Community Mental Health Ctr., Seattle, 1988. U. Wash. acad. scholar, 1985. Mem. Am. Psychol. Assn. (assoc.), Alpha Kappa Alpha (dean of pledges 1985, leadership fellow 1985). Home: 15110 Macadam Rd S #A203 Tukwila WA 98188 Office: Adrienne N Hill MA PO Box 68266 Seattle WA 98168

HILL, AGNES LAVONE LYLES, educator; b. Spartanburg, S.C., Dec. 23, 1953; d. Joseph and Ernestine E. (Stephens) Lyles; m. Allan A. Hill; children: Alethea L., Allison L. BS, Winthrop Coll., 1975; MEd, Converse Coll., 1979; postgrad., U. S.C., 1977-87. Tchr. Pacolet (S.C.) Elem., 1975-87, Cannons Elem., Spartanburg, 1987-90. Mem. S.C. Edn. Assn., Delta Sigma Theta. Baptist. Home: 302 Chelsea St Moore SC 29369

HILL, ANITA CARRAWAY, state legislator; b. Chatfield, Tex., Aug. 13, 1928; d. Archie Clark and Martha (Butler) Carraway; B.A. in Journalism, Tex. Woman's U., 1950; m. Harris Hill, Sept. 20, 1952; children—Stephen Victor, Virginia Evelyn. Reporter Garland (Tex.) Daily News, 1950-51; ednl. dir. First Meth. Ch., Garland, 1951-53; chemist Kraft Foods Co., Garland, 1953-56; legis. aide, Tex. Legislature, 1975-77; mem. Tex. Ho. of Reps., 1977—, mem. mcpl. bond and revenue sharing coms., 1971-74. Awards chmn. City of Garland Environ. Council; mem. City of Garland Park and Recreation Bd., 1971-77, chmn., 1976-77; life mem. PTA. Named Disting. Alumna, Tex. Woman's U., 1981. Mem. Garland C. of C., Rowlett C. of C., Bus. and Profl. Women's Club (Garland Woman of Year, 1980), AAUW, Tex. Assn. Elected Women. Republican. Methodist. Office: 203 Republic Bank Bldg 705 W Ave B Garland TX 75040

HILL, ANITA RAE, art galler operator; b. O'Donnell, Tex., Apr. 29, 1928; d. August William and Carrie E. (Hilliard) Meynig; m. Robert Dean Hill, Aug. 22, 1959. BA in Comml. Art, Tex. Technol. U., 1951. Sec., clk. Sun Oil Co., Snyder, Tex., 1951-52; clk., draftsman Sun Oil Co., Midland, Tex., 1952-54, Humble Oil Co., Midland, 1954-59; juror, judge, tchr. pvt. art classes, various locations, N.Mex., 1959-70, Dallas, 1970-80; owner, operator Anita Meynig Creations, Dallas, 1980—; comml. artist Hunter Art Svc., Dallas, 1975-80; lectr., demonstrator art socs., Tex., N.Mex., 1960—. Writer, illustrator: Magic Moonbeam, 1964; illustrator booklet: Christmas Story, 1983. Vol. Hobbs (N.Mex.) Med. Hosp., 1962-65, Summer Arts and Crafts, Roswell, N.Mex., 1962-65, Roswell Summer Camp for Children, 1966. Winner Best of Show award N.Mex. Watercolor Soc., 1970, Southeast N.Mex. State Fair, Roswell, 1970, Plano (Tex.) Art Soc., 1975; winner 1st pl. Artists and Craftsmen Assn., Dallas, 1976. Mem. Southwestern Watercolor Soc. (pres. 1980-81), Allied Artists Am., Knickerbocker Artists, Allied Artists Am., Women Artists of West. Republican. Baptist. Home and Office: Anita Meynig Creations 6335 Brookshire Dr Dallas TX 75230

HILL, ANNA MARIE, manufacturing executive; b. Great Falls, Mont., Nov. 6, 1938; d. Paul Joseph and Alexina Rose (Doyon) Ghekiere. AA, Oakland Jr. Coll., 1959; student, U. Calif., Berkeley, 1960-62. Mgr. ops. OSM, Soquel, Calif., 1963-81; purchasing agt. Arrow Huss, Scotts Valley, Calif., 1981-82; sr. buyer Fairchild Test Systems, San Jose, Calif., 1982-83; materials mgr. Basic Test Systems, San Jose, 1983-86; purchasing mgr. Beta Tech., Santa Cruz, Calif., 1986-87; mgr. purchasing ICON Rev., Carmel, Calif., 1987-88; materials mgr. Integrated Components Test System, Sunnyvale, Calif., 1988-89; mfg. mgr. Forte Communications, Sunnyvale, 1989—; cons., No. Calif., 1976—. Counselor Teens Against Drugs, San Jose, 1970, 1/2 Orgn., Santa Cruz, 1975-76. Mem. Am. Prodn. Invention Control, Nat. Assn. Female Execs., Nat. Assn. Purchasing Mgmt., Porsche Club Am., Am. Radio Relay League. Democrat. Club: Young Ladies Radio League. Home: 2922 Park Ave Soquel CA 95073 Office: Forte Communications 680 W Maude Ave Sunnyvale CA 94086

HILL, BARBARA MAE, librarian; b. Keene, N.H., Sept. 19, 1924; d. Gale Earl and Gertrude Wiseman (Reed) Hill; B.E., Keene Tchrs. Coll., 1946; M.S., Simmons Coll., 1952. Tchr. sci. and math. Thayer High Sch., Winchester, N.H., 1946-47; children's librarian Keene Pub. Library, 1947-52; asst. librarian Mass. Coll. Pharmacy and Allied Health Scis., Boston, 1952-58, assoc. librarian, 1958-69, librarian, 1969—; bd. dirs. Fenway Library Consortium, 1975—, coordinator, 1982-84; bd. dirs. Fenway Libraries Online, Inc., 1987—. Mem. Am. Assn. Univ. Profs., Drug Info. Assn., Am. Assn. Colls. Pharmacy (ho. of dels. 1979-80, chmn.-elect libraries-ednl. resources sect. 1981-82, chmn. 1982-83), Med. Library Assn. (chmn. pharmacy group 1965-66, chmn. pharmacy and drug info. sect. 1985-86), Spl. Libraries Assn. (vice chmn. pharm. div. 1972-73, chmn. 1973-74), Kappa Delta Pi, Rho Chi. Office: Mass Coll of Pharmacy and Allied Health Scis 179 Longwood Ave Boston MA 02115

HILL, BETTY JEAN, academic administator; b. Ishpeming, Mich., Nov. 27, 1937; d. Azarius William and Evelyn (Herring) Parsons; m. Edwin E. Hill, Nov. 27, 1959 (dec. 1979); children: Cheryl, Kenneth; m. Harold Ralph Pawley, June 27, 1981. B in Nursing, No. Mich. U., Marquette, 1972, MEd, 1974; M in Nursing, Wayne State U., 1977, PhD, 1979. RN, Mich. Staff nurse St. Luke's Hosp., Marquette, 1958-60; supr. Meadowbrook Hosp., Bellaire, Mich., 1959-60; head nurse St. Luke's Hosp., Marquette, 1960-62, clin. instr., 1868-70; asst. prof. No. Mich. U., Marquette, 1972-75, assoc. prof., 1978-80, asst. dean, 1980-82, dean, 1982—. Contbr. articles to jours.; author: (with others) Theory Construction, 1981. Fund Chairperson Hospice, Marquette, 1988. Mem. Mich. and Nat. League for Nursing, Mich. Assn. Colls. of Nursing (treas. 1986-90), Midwest Alliance in Nursing, Mich. and Am. Assn. of Colls. of Nursing, Marquette Econ. Club (pres. 1989-90), Rotary Club, Planned Parenthood, Sigma Theta Tau. Methodist. Home: 1510 Garfield Marquette MI 49855 Office: No Mich U Coll Sch Nursing Magers Hall Marquette MI 49855

HILL, CLARA EDITH, psychology educator; b. Shivers, Miss., Sept. 13, 1948; d. Fletcher Von and Anna (Teich) H.; m. Jim Gormally, May 25, 1974; children: Kevin, Katherine. BA, So. Ill. U., 1970, MA, 1972, PhD, 1974. Lic. psychologist, Md. Asst. prof. dept. psychology U. Md., College Park, 1974-78, assoc. prof. dept. psychology, 1978-85, prof. dept. psychology, 85—. Author: Therapist Techniques and Client Outcomes, 1989; contbr. articles to profl. jours. Grantee NIMH, 1983-90. Mem. Soc. Psycotherapy Rsch. (pres. North Am. chpt., 1990); fellow Am. Psychol. Assn. Office: U Maryland Dept Psychology College Park MD 20742

HILL, CLAUDIA ADAMS, tax consultant; b. Long Beach, Calif., Oct. 14, 1949; d. Claude T. Adams and Geraldine (Jones) Crosby; m. W. Eugene Hill, Sept. 14, 1968 (div. Oct. 1983); children: Stacia Heather, Jonathan Eugene; m. Larry C. Enoksen, June 4, 1988. BA, Calif. State U., Fullerton, 1972; MBA, San Jose State U., 1978. Systems analyst quality assurance group United Technology Ctr., 1972-73; with Commrs. Adv. Group IRS, 1987; prin., owner Tax Mam, Inc., 1974—; noted lectr. in field of taxation. Chmn. editorial rev. com. The Calif. Enrolled Agt.; contbr. articles to profl. jours. Mem. Nat. Assn. Enrolled Agts., Calif. Soc. Enrolled Agts. (mission chpt., chmn. IRS/Franchise Tax Bd., Tax Bur. liaison com.). Republican. Office: TAX MAM Inc 10680 S DeAnza Blvd Cupertino CA 95014

HILL, CYNTHIA ANN, advocate; b. San Angelo, Tex., Oct. 17, 1953; d. Manford E. Underwood and Betty J. (Capps) Ellis; m. Jacky D. Hill, Nov. 7, 1971 (div. 1974); 1 child, Jennifer M. BS, Howard Payne U., 1980. Communications officer Brady (Tex.) City Police Dept., 1976-80; chief juvenile probation officer 198th Jud. Dist. Juvenile Probation Dept., Brady, 1980—; liason officer Brady Ind. Sch. Dist., 1985, Menard and Junction (Tex.) Ind. Sch. Dist., 1985. V.P. Child Welfare Bd., Brady, 1980. Named one of Outstanding Young Women of Am., 1980. Mem. Kiwanis(1st woman mem.). Democrat. Baptist. Home: 1301 S High Brady TX 76825 Office: 198th Jud Dist Juvenile Probation Dept PO Box 548 Brady TX 76825

HILL, CYNTHIA LEIGH, food products executive; b. Muskegon, Mich., Nov. 13, 1957; d. Edward J. and Phyllis J. (Lyons) Doll; m. LaMar A. Hill, June 6, 1979; children: Nicole M., Adam P., Erica L. BS in Food Science and Human Nutrition, Mich. State U., 1979. Quality control technician Ralphs Grocery Co., L.A., 1979-80, quality control mgr., 1980-81, prodn. mgr., 1981-86; dir. technical svcs. VandeKamps Bakery, L.A., 1986-88; dir. quality assurance and R&D GF Baking Div. Freihofers, Albany, N.Y., 1988 --. Mem. Inst. Food Technologists. Office: Charles Freihofer Baking Co Prospect Rd Albany NY 12206

HILL, DEANN GAIL, construction executive; b. Holyoke, Mass., Apr. 25, 1953; d. Cecil Arthur and Drema Aldene (Mundy) H. BA in Sociology, W.Va. State Coll., 1975; MA in Counseling and Guidance, W.Va. U., 1976; postgrad., W.Va. Coll. of Grad. Studies, 1980-85. Case worker Charleston (W.Va.) Guidance Clinic, 1975-77; social worker W.Va. Dept. Mental Health, Huntington, 1977; office mgr. C/D Hill & Son, St. Albans, W.Va., 1978-83, pres. mktg., 1986—; dep. clk. Kanawha County Circuit Ct., Charleston, 1984-86. Co-exec. dir. Kanawha Dem. Club, Charleston, 1987—; active W.Va. Symphony League, Charleston, 1987—, co-chair League, 1987—, Symphony Sunday, 1989; active St. Francis Hosp. Aux., chair fundraising com., 1986-87. Mem. Contractors Assn. W.Va. (program com., legis. com., exposition com. 1988—), NAFE, W.Va. U. Alumni Assn. (sec. 1989—), Charleston Regional C. of C. (mem. legis. com.). Roman Catholic. Home: Coal River Rd PO Box 226 Saint Albans WV 25177 Office: PO Box 99 Dawes WV 25059

HILL, DIANA JOAN, religious organization administrator; b. Pleasant Corner, Pa., June 17, 1936; d. Lawrence Edwin Aaron and Arlene (Wessner) Hausman; m. Bruce Handwerk Hill, June 22, 1957; children: Adrian Bruce, Anita Diann. BS in Edn., Kutztown U., 1958; postgrad., Temple U., 1958-61. Elem. tchr. Cheltenham (Pa.) Twp. Schs., 1958-62, Rockford (Ill.) City Schs., 1965-66; caseworker Lehigh County Children-Youth Services, Allentown, Pa., 1975-85; dist. rep. Luth. Brotherhood, Allentown, 1985—. Publicity chmn. LVW Rockford, 1965-66, human resources chair, Oyster Bay, N.Y. 1968-73; precinct capt. Dem. Party, Massapequa, N.Y., 1973-74. Mem. Lehigh Valley Assn. Life Underwriters. Democrat. Lutheran. Office: Luth Brotherhood 1013 Brookside Rd PO Box 3402 Allentown PA 18106-3402

HILL, DIANE SELDON, psychologist; b. Mpls., Sept. 17, 1943; d. Earl William and Geraldine (Le Veille) Seldon; m. David Reuben Hill, May 14, 1986 (div. Feb. 1988); children: Anna Marion, Jason David. BA, Mt. Holyoke Coll., 1965; MA in Psychology, U. Minn., 1968, PhD in Psychology, 1974. Lic. psychologist, Colo; diplomate in clin. psychology Am. Bd. Profl. Psychologists. Instr., counselor Student Counseling Bur. U. Minn., Mpls., 1968-70, advisor women's programs, Student Activities Bur., 1970-71; instr. psychology Augsburg Coll., Mpls., 1970-71; counselor, tchr. humanities Emma Willard Sch., Troy, N.Y., 1972-75; dir. counseling and reengagement Colo. Women's Coll., Denver, 1976-77; clin. field supr., Sch. Profl. Psychology U. Denver, 1977—; pvt. practice Denver, 1979-89; mgmt. and organizational cons. Somerville and Co., Inc., Denver, 1989—; asst. clin. prof. psychology U. Colo. Health Scis. Ctr., Denver, 1979—; staff affiliate Ctr. for Creative Leadership, Colorado Springs, Colo., 1986—; presenter at profl. meetings; expert witness on psychology ethics in civil litigation case in Colo., 1988; presenter testimony before Colo. legis. hearing coms. and Colo. Ins. Commn. Named NDEA IV fellow U. Minn., 1967-68. Fellow Am. Psychol. Assn. (subcom. on sexual exploitation of clients by therapists div. psychology of women 1985—); mem. Colo. Psychol. Assn. (bd. dirs. 1979-82, dir. polit. action com.), Rocky Mountain Psychol. Assn., Am. Assn. State Psychology Bds. (mem.-at-large exec. com. 1983, pres. 1988—, del. 1982-83), Colo. Bd. Psychologists Examiners (bd. dirs. 1981—, vice chmn., 1982-83, chmn., 1983-85), Women's Forum Colo. (mem. com. 1979—), Vail Racquet Club. Episcopalian. Home: 2052 Bellaire St Denver CO 80207 Office: Somerville & Co Inc 1625 Broadway Denver CO 80202

HILL, DONNA MARIE, communications executive; b. Amesbury, Mass., July 25, 1957; d. Robert and Marie Doris (Lucier) Menzigan; m. Douglas Everett Hill, July 5, 1986. BS in Math., U. Lowell, 1979, MBA in Ops., 1983. Material control analyst AVCO Corp., Wilmington, Mass., 1979-81; ops. analyst Blue Cross & Blue Shield, Boston, 1981-83, risk analyst, 1983-84; systems analyst Bell Atlantic, Bethesda, Md., 1984-86; cons. internal Bell Atlantic, Bethesda, 1986-89, project mgr., 1989—. inventor (software) User-assisted Adhoc Reporting, 1988, Natural English Report Access, 1988. Vol. Montgomery County Vol. Assn., Montgomery Md., 1983—, PALS, Montgomery County, Md., 1984—, Kennedy Ctr. for the Arts, Washington, 1985—; bd. dirs. Youth Activities Commn., Amesbury Mass., 1984. Mem. Ops. Rsch. Soc., Intelligent Computer Rsch. Inst., NAFE, Focus User Group (co-chair artificial intelligence group 1989). Republican. Roman Catholic. Office: Bell Atlantic 6701 Democracy Blvd Bethesda MD 20817-1586

HILL, DOROTHY BELLE, teacher; b. Drexel Hill, Pa., Mar. 28, 1936; d. George Elza and Eleanor (Murray) H.; 1 child, Peter Scott. Postgrad., U. Ariz., 1956-57; BS, West Chester State U., 1958; postgrad., Temple U., 1962-65, Penn. State U., 1964-65. Tchr. Rose Tree Media Sch. Dist, 1958-59, Upper Darby Sch. Dist., Drexel Hill, Pa., 1961--; social studies com. for long range planning, Upper Darby Sch. Dist., 1985--. Author: History of 5 Original Families in Upper Darby Township, 1986; publ. editor, writer local hist. soc. newsletter. Com. person Rep. Group, 1984—; cong. chairperson Del. County Rep. Woman, 1966, v.p. Upper Darty Hist. Soc., 1987-89, pres., 1989—, chmn. bd. dirs. to date; alt. del. 1988 Rep. Nat. Conv.; pres. Multiple Sclerosis, 1989—; co-chairperson Heart Fund; vol. Friends of the Luken's, dir. Friends of the Swedish Cabin. Episcopalian. Home: Mansion and Marvine Rds Drexel Hill PA 19026 Office: Upper Darby Sch Dist Bond and Roberts Ave Drexel Hill PA 19026

HILL, EARLENE HOOPER, state legislator; b. Balt., Oct. 22; d. Otis Barnett Hooper and Thelma E. (Richardson) Young; m. Thomas C. Hill Jr., Mar. 9, 1966; 1 child, Charisse E. BA, Norfolk State U., 1967; MSW, Adelphi U., 1976. Mgr. N.Y. State Dept. Social Svcs., N.Y.C., 1979-88; mem. N.Y. State Assembly, 1988—; mem. women's program, shop steward Pub. Employees Fedn., 1980-88, mem. exec. bd. Mem. exec. bd. Jack & Jill of Am., Inc., Nassau County, N.Y., 1985—; mem. Nat. Women's Polit. Caucus, N.Y.C., 1987—. Mem. Negro Bus. and Profl. Women (Cen. Nassau chpt.), Delta Sigma Theta. Democrat. Office: NY State Legislature Legis Office Bldg #433 Albany NY 12248

HILL, ELIZABETH TREZISE, economics educator; b. DuBois, Pa., Mar. 26, 1936; d. William H. and Ethel L. (Lyons) Trezise; m. Richard A. Hill, May 30, 1958 (dec. Sept. 1981); children: Joan H. Smeltzer, David R. BSBA, Pa. State U., University Park, 1958; MA in Econs., U. Del., 1974; PhD in Econs., U. Md., 1985. Instr. in econs. Pa. State U., York, 1976-78; economist Pa. Milrite Coun., Harrisburg, 1982-84; asst. prof. econs. Pa. State U., Mont Alto, 1985—. Treas. Reinhardt Found., York, 1986—. Mem. Am. Econ. Assn., Ea. Econ. Assn., Nat. Assn. Bus. Economists, Pa. Econ. Assn. (bd. dirs. 1989—), Com. on the Status of Women in the Econs. Profession, Am. Bus. Women's Assn. Office: Pa State U Mont Alto Campus Mont Alto PA 17237

HILL, ELLEN BROWN, rehabilitation and emergency medicine nurse; b. Pitts., Dec. 21, 1944; d. F. Gordon and Muriel Edith (Dunkerley) Brown. Diploma in nursing, St. Francis Gen. Hosp., Pitts., 1969; AA magna cum laude, Butler County Community Coll., Butler, Pa., 1982; BSN, La Roche Coll., Pitts., 1986; postgrad., Slippery Rock (Pa.) U., 1987. RN, Pa.; cert. EMT, pre hosp. trauma technician. Sch. nurse Mars (Pa.) Area Sch. Dist., head athletic trainer; gerontology staff nurse St. Barnabas Free Home, Gibsonia, Pa.; staff nurse emergency medicine dept. Norrell Health Care, Mars. Chmn. disaster health svcs. ARC. Recipient Thanks for Helping award ARC, 1983. Mem. Emergency Nurses Assn., St. Francis Gen. Hosp. Alumni Assn., Phi Theta Kappa. Home: 20 Butler St Extension Valencia PA 16059

HILL, EMITA BRADY, academic administrator; b. Balt., Jan. 31, 1936; d. Leo and Lucy McCormick (Jewett) Brady; children: Julie Beck, Christopher, Madeleine. BA, Cornell U., 1957; MA, Middlebury Coll., 1958; PhD, Harvard U., 1967. Instr. Harvard U., 1961-63; asst. prof. Western Reserve U., 1967-69; from asst. prof. to v.p. Lehman Coll. CUNY, Bronx, N.Y., 1970--. Mem. Am. Assn. Higher Edn., Assn. Am. Coll., Am. Soc. for 18th Century Studies, Internat. Soc. for 18th Century Studies, Phi Beta Kappa. Office: Lehman Coll CUNY Bronx NY 10468

HILL, EMMA LEE, educator; b. Crane, Tex., Jan. 13, 1949; d. Howard Lee and Eddie Marie (Gill) H. BS, Hardin-Simmons. U., 1970, MEd, Abilene Christian U., 1974, postgrad., 1979. Cert. provisional elem. mentally retarded, lang./learning disabilities, bilingual tchr., profl. supr., profl. midmgmt., tchr. appraiser, Tex. Tchr. Kileen (Tex.) Ind. Sch. Dist., Harker Heights, 1970-71, Winters (Tex.) Ind. Sch. Dist., 1971-73, Abilene (Tex.) Ind. Sch. Dist., 1973—; bldg. rep. Supt.'s Task Force on Schs. 5-Yr. Plan, Abilene, 1990-91. Illustrator: (book) Richard the Great, 1967. Mem. local election com. Tex. Tchrs. for Gov., Abilene, 1988; sec. Abilene PTA, 1980-82, Tex. PTA, 1980-82. Scholar Abilene C. of C., 1967-69. Mem. Assn. for Supervision and Curriculum Devel., Internat. Reading Assn., Tex. Assn. Bilingual Educators (pres. Abilene 1988-89), Tex. Classroom Tchrs. Assn., Assn. Tex. Profl. Educators (bldg. rep. 1980—, Outstanding Tchr. award 1989), AAUW, Nat. Honor Soc., Delta Kappa Gamma (treas. Abilene 1990-91). Home: Rte One Tye TX 79563 Office: Abilene Pub Schs 625 S 8th St Abilene TX 79602

HILL, EMMA WILLIS, security analyst; b. Washington, Oct. 7, 1952; d. Dumond Peck and Elizabeth (Willis) H.; m. Michael Kent Minter, Apr. 4, 1981; children: Michael Murat, William Peck. Student, Colo. Coll., 1970-72; BS in Econs., Tufts U., 1974; MBA, U. Va., 1978. Jr. analyst Dean Witter Reynolds, N.Y.C., 1978-81; assoc. mng. dir. Wertheim Schroder & Co., N.Y.C., 1981—. Mem. Fin. Analysis Fedn., N.Y. Soc. of Security Analysts. Club: Bronxville Field. Home: 10 North Rd Bronxville NY 10708 Office: Wertheim Schroder & Co 787 7th Ave New York NY 10019

HILL, EULA VERTNER, state government official; b. Americus, Ga., Aug. 16, 1928; d. Oscar Thomas and Eula Vertner (Forrest) Harrell; m. Jefferson Perry Hill, Nov. 28, 1946 (dec. Oct. 1985); 1 child, Robert Perry. Ed. Southwestern Coll., Americus, Ga. Cert. tchr., Ga. 6th and 7th grade tchr. Plains (Ga.) Sch., 1946-47; buyer, office mgr. Belk's Dept. Store, Americus, 1949-60; field service mgr. Ga. Dept. Labor, Americus, 1961—. V.p., organizer Inter-Agy. Council, 1970—; active Ga. Council on Aging, 1964-74; organizer Americus unit Ga. Heart Assn., 1975; adv. bd. Ga. Dept. Human Resources, 1976-78; chmn. bd. advisors for bus. edn. South Ga. Tech. Inst., 1973—; mem. career devel. bd. Ga. Southwestern Coll., Americus. Recipient Cert. of Appreciation Kiwanis Club of Americus, 1985. Mem. Nat. Assn. Female Execs., Acad. Women in Mgmt., Internat. Assn. Personnel in Employment Security (chmn. profl. standards com. 1986-87, Ga. chpt. activities chmn. 1987-88, exec. com. 1987—), Americus-Sumter County Bus. and Profl. Women (founder), others. Democrat. Methodist. Home: Rt 4 Vienna Rd Americus GA 31709 Office: Ga Dept Labor 120 W Church St Americus GA 31709

HILL, EVELYN ANN, sales and marketing professional; b. Covington, Ky., May 29, 1942; d. Frederick Holroyd and Evelyn Ann (Thomson) Eastabrooks; m. Rexford Lee Hill III, Sept. 12, 1964 (div. 1983); children: Eric Douglas, Rexford Alan, Gerald Alexander, Andrew David. BS in Design, U. Cin., 1965. Office mgr. United Ch. of Christ, St. Louis, 1983-84; program coord. Acme Premium Supply, St. Louis, 1984-86, mgr., 1986—; freelance artist St. Louis, 1960—. Illustrator: Life Through Time, 1975. Coord./advisor Guardian Angels N.Y., St. Louis, 1981-82; advisor Pres.'s Commn. on Continuing Edn., Eden Sem., St. Louis, 1982-83; advisor Ecumenical Task Force on Hunger, 1982; cons. Women's Task Force on Employment, 1975-76; cons. Nat. Bd. Homeland Ministries, United Ch. of Christ, 1982, mem. St. Louis Assn. United Ch. of Christ, pres., 1981-82. Best of Show award Siegfried Reinhardt County Artists, 1976. Mem. NAFE, Direct Mktg. Assn., Sierra Club. Home: 1137 Olivaire Saint Louis MO 63132 Office: Acme Premium Supply 4100 Forest Park Ave Saint Louis MO 63108

HILL, I. KATHRYN, professional society administrator; b. Phila., Apr. 6, 1950; d. Joseph Anthony and Irma Lorraine (Walther) Piehs; m. John Patrick McElwain, May 17, 1969 (div. Aug. 1979); children: John Charles, Brian Patrick; m. David Terence Hill, Sept. 27, 1980. BA, Widener Coll., 1979; MEd, Temple U., 1982. Cert. secondary tchr., Pa. Translator, transcriber Sci-Tech, Inc., Phila., 1970-77; tchr. West Chester East High Sch., West Chester, Pa., 1978, Garnet Valley Jr., Sr. High Sch., Concordville, Pa., 1979; asst. sec. to dir. Allied Health Programs. Nat. Bd. Med. Examiners, Phila., 1980-81, evaluation program asst., 1981-82, evaluation program assoc., 1982-84, sr. program assoc., 1984-85; asst. exec. v.p. Fed. of State Med. Bds., Fort Worth, 1985-86, asst. exec. v.p. and exec. dir. of the FLEX bd., 1986—. Editor: (FLEX Guidelines, 1985, 87, FLEX Info. Bull., 1987-89; co-editor Fedn. Exchange, 1986-89; contbr. articles to profl. jours. Mem. Am. Ednl. Rsch. Assn., Nat. Coun. on Measurement in Edn., Assn. of Am. Med. Colls. Republican. Lutheran. Office: Fed of State Med Bds 6000 Western Pl Ste 707 Fort Worth TX 76107-4168

HILL, JUDITH DEEGAN, lawyer; b. Chgo., Dec. 13, 1940; d. William James and Ida May (Scott) Deegan; m. Dennis M. Havens, June 28, 1986; children by previous marriage: Colette M., Cristina M. BA, Western Mich. U., 1960; cert. U. Paris, Sorbonne, 1962; JD, Marquette U., 1971. Bar: Wis. 1971, Ill. 1973, Nev. 1976, D.C. 1979. Tchr., Kalamazoo (Mich.) Bd. Edn., 1960-62, Maple Heights (Ohio), 1963-64, Shorewood (Wis.) Bd. Edn., 1964-68; corp. atty. Fort Howard Paper Co., Green Bay, Wis., 1971-72; sr. trust adminstr. Continental Ill. Nat. Bank & Trust, Chgo., 1972-76; atty. Morse, Foley & Wadsworth Law Firm, Las Vegas, 1976-77; dep. dist. atty., criminal prosecutor Clark County Atty., Las Vegas, 1977-83; atty. civil and criminal law Edward S. Coleman Profl. Law Corp., Las Vegas, 1983-84; pvt. practice law, 1984-85; atty. criminal div. Office of City Atty., City of Las Vegas, 1985-89, pvt. practive law, 1989—. Bd. dirs. Nev. Legal Services, Carson City, 1980-87, state chmn., 1984-87; bd. dirs. Clark County Legal Services, Las Vegas, 1980-87; mem. Star Aux. for Handicapped Children, Las Vegas, 1986—; Greater Las Vegas Women's League; jud. candidate Las Vegas Mcpl. Ct, 1987. Recipient Scholarship, Auto Specialties, St. Joseph, Mich., 1957-60, St. Thomas More Scholarship, Marquette U. Law Sch., Milw., 1968-69; juvenile law internship grantee Marquette U. Law Sch., 1970. Mem. ABA, Nev. Bar Assn., Woman's Bar Assn. of Ill., So. Nev. Assn. Women Attys., Ill. Bar Assn., Washington Bar Assn. Democrat. Club: Children's Village (pres. 1980) (Las Vegas, Nev.). Home: 1110 S 5th Pl Las Vegas NV 89104 Office: 726 S Casino Center Blvd Ste 211 Las Vegas NV 89104

HILL, JUDITH SWIGOST, business analyst, information systems designer; b. Harvey, Ill., Dec. 31, 1942; d. J.W. and M.J. (Kuczaik) Swigost; m. Wallace H. Hill, May 16, 1982; stepchildren: Scott, Amy, Molly, Elizabeth. BA in English/Theater, U. Ill., 1964; postgrad., Am. U., 1967-69, New Sch. for Social Research, N.Y.C., 1977-82, 83-85. Vol. U.S. Peace Corps, Philippines, 1964-66; recruiter U.S. Peace Corps, Washington, 1966-67; program mgr. U.S. Peace Corps, Micronesia, 1968; dir. corr. U.S. Peace Corps, Washington, 1969; editor, prin. Congl. Monitor, Inc., Washington, 1970-76; legis. analyst Philip Morris, Inc., N.Y.C., 1976-77; tech. analyst, writer Jesco, Inc., N.Y.C., 1978-79; assoc. pub. Thomas Pub. Co., N.Y.C., 1980-84; bus. analyst AGS, Inc. Ind. Cons., N.Y.C., 1984—; ind. cons. on expert systems design and devel., N.Y.C., 1987—. Contbr. articles to profl. jours. Active Murray Hill Com., N.Y.C., 1986—. Mem. Assn. Systems Mgmt., Am. Assn. Artificial Intelligence, Assn. Computing Machinery, Spl. Interest Group Artificial Intelligence, World Future Soc., Nat. Assn. Returned Peace Corps Vols., Returned Peace Corps Vols. of Greater N.Y. (by-laws com. 1985-86. speakers bur. 1987-88). Republican. Jewish. Home: 155 E 34th St Apt 12-C New York NY 10016

HILL, KAREN WATERSTRAUSS, retirement housing administrator; b. Salt Lake City, May 2, 1946; d. James Jr. and Mary Josephine (Allen) Riley; children: Kelly, Michael, John. AS, U. Utah, 1976. Lic. real estate salesperson, Calif.; cert. occupancy specialist. Mgr. Homestead Builders, West Los Angeles, Calif.; affordable housing asst. Casden Co., Beverly Hills, Calif.; HUD housing insp. Davis County Housing Authority, Farmington, Utah; adminstr. Retirement Housing Found., Los Angeles. Recipient commendation for outstanding work with sr. citizens. Mem. NAFE, Am. Assn. Homes for Aging, Calif. Assn. Homes for Aging. Home: 4803 River Grass Rd Tampa FL 33617

HILL, KATHY LYNN, pharmacy representative; b. Columbia, Mo., Jan. 9, 1955; d. Charles Edward Hill and Carol (McShane) Hill Peters. AA in Bus. Adminstrn., Sierra Community Coll., 1975; BS in Mktg., Calif. State U., Sacramento, 1979. Sales rep. Burrough's Corp., Sacramento, 1979-81; territory rep. Sandoz, East Hanover, N.J., 1981-82; profl. territory rep. McNeil Pharm. subs. Johnson & Johnson, Springhouse, Pa., 1982-87; pharmacy svc. rep., field sales trainer Syncor Internat. Corp., Chatsworth, Calif., 1987—. Mem. Sierra Valley Nuclear Medicine Assn. (membership chmn. 1989—), Nat. Soc. Sales Tng. Execs.

HILL, LA JOYCE CARMICHAEL, marketing professional; b. Tifton, Ga., Nov. 14, 1952; d. Ralph Eugene and Vista Eloise (Dooley) Carmichael; m. Bobby Wayne Hill, Jan. 1, 1972. AS, Abraham Baldwin Agri. Coll., Tifton, 1971. With R.E. Carmichael Co. Inc., 1970-89, sec./treas., 1978-88, pres., chmn. bd., 1988-89; v.p. J & B Power Equipment, Inc., 1989—. Mem. Chula Charge United Meth. Women, (sec. treas. 1986—). Methodist. Home: PO Box 947 Tifton GA 31793

HILL, LARKIN PAYNE, real estate company data processing executive; b. El Paso, Tex., Oct. 30, 1954; d. Max Lloyd and Jane Olivia (Evatt) H.; m. J. Franklin Graves, July 12, 1975 (div. July 1979). Student Coll. Charleston, 1972-73, U. N.C., 1973. Lic. real estate broker, N.C. Sec., property mgr. Max L. Hill Co., Inc., Charleston, S.C., 1973-75, sec., data processor, 1979-82, v.p. adminstrn., 1982—; resident mgr. Carolina Apts., Carrboro, N.C., 1975-77; sales assoc., Realtor, Southland Assocs., Chapel Hill, N.C., 1977-78; cons. specifications com. Charleston Trident Multiple Listing Service, 1985. Mem. NAFE, Royal Oak Found., Scottish Soc. Charleston (bd. dirs. 1989—), Preservation Soc., Charleston Computer Users Group, N.C. Assn. Realtors, Spoleto Festival USA (chmn. auction catalog com. 1990). Republican. Methodist. Avocations: reading, crossword puzzles, furniture restoration, T'ai Chi. Home: 7 Riverside Dr Charleston SC 29403 Office: Max L Hill Co Inc 632 Saint Andrews Blvd Charleston SC 29407

HILL, LAURA JO, educator; b. Roswell, New Mex., July 9, 1959; d. Daniel Lavator and Shirley (Whitehead) H. BA, Tex. Tech. U., 1981, MA, 1984. Supr. Tex. Tech U. Food Service, Lubbock, 1979-82; French tchr. Tex. Tech U., Lubbock, 1981-82, 1983-84; Englih tchr. Internat. Edn. Services, Tokyo, Japan, 1984-86; recreation supr. City Longview (Tex.) Parks & Leisure Services, 1986--; con. in Aquatics, Northeast, Tex., 1986--; cert. operator Nat. Swimming. Author: Business English for Chemists, 1983. Mem. Am. Legion Auxiliary, Longview, 1986--, Tex. Tech Ex-student Assn.,. Mem. Nat. Recreation and Parks Assn., Tex. Recreation and Parks Soc. Republican. Presbyterian. Home: 630 Green Oak Longview TX 75604

HILL, LENORA MAE, astrologer; b. Harper, W.Va., June 2, 1937; d. Ibra Sepheus Fancher and Hazel Rebecca (Shunk) Mauger; m. Donald Charles Ludwig, Feb. 22, 1958 (div. Oct. 1972); children: Audrey Lynn Christ, Donald Charles Jr.; m. Arthur Richard Hill, June 25, 1976. Student, Pa. State U., Reading, 1968-69. Asst. librarian Pa. State U., Reading, 1965-70; research librarian Kawecki Berylco Industries, Reading, 1972-76; proprietor The Galaxy, Birdsboro, Pa., 1976—; mem. faculty Australian Fedn. Astrologers Internat. Conf., 1980, 82, New Zealand Fedn. Astrologers Internat. Conf., 1980, 82, Ramapo (N.J.) Community Coll. Metaphysical Conf., 1979-81; mem. Huna Research, Inc.; speaker in field; featured on radio, tv talk shows. Author: Astrology? Metaphysics?, 1984; contbr. articles to profl. jours. Chair numerous local scholarships funds; active Barry Goldwater for Pres. Mem. Am. Fedn. Astrologers Network. Home and Office: Box 172 R#4 Birdsboro PA 19508

HILL, LINDA LEE, rehabilitation services professional; b. Howell, Mich., Oct. 24, 1947; d. Charles and Mildred June (Myers) Hill; m. Wendell Hagg (div. 1974); 1 child, Stacy Lynn. BA with honors, Mich. State U., East Lansing, 1979, MA, 1981. V.p., dir. Recovery Unlimited, Okemos, Mich., 1974—. Vol. counselor Coun. Against Domestic Assault, Lansing, Mich., 1987-89. Mem. Nat. Assn. Rehab. Profls. in the Pvt. Sector, Nat. Rehab. Assn. Home: 840 King Ct East Lansing MI 48823

HILL, LOUISE B., paramedical aesthetician; b. Augusta, Maine, May 28, 1952; d. Armand B. and Rita (Gaboury) Laliberte; m. Brian A. Hill, Nov. 20, 1985 (dec. Dec. 1986). Student, U. Fla., 1972-73, U. Maine, Farmington, 1978-80; cert., M.G. Westmore Acad., 1985-86. Med. aesthetics Dr. Brian Hill, Gardiner, Maine, 1982-86; ptnr. Electrolysis & Skin Care Ctr. (now Kosmetikos), Bangor, Maine, 1989—; cons. Downeast Plastic Surgery, Bangor, 1987—; staff Preneleges Mass., Eye/Ear Hosp., Boston. Mem. NAFE, Woman in Bus., Nat. Cancer Soc., Cen. Maine Health Assts. (pres. 1984—). Office: Kosmetikos Evergreen Woods 700 Mt Hope Ave Bangor ME 04401

HILL, MARILYN J., training and career develoment executive; b. Oshkosh, Wis., June 26, 1929; d. Kenneth Leonard and Grace Evelyn (Jones) Thompson; m. Richard E. Hill, June 5, 1951; children: Mark, Kenneth, Richard, Joy, Sarah. BA, Carroll Coll., 1951; MA, Marquette U., 1973; ABD, U. Minn., St. Paul, 1977. Devel./tng. mgr. Donohue Engring. and Architects, Sheboygan, Wis., 1978-89; pres. Thompson/Hill Group Profl. Tng. Svcs., 1990—. Bush Leadership fellow, 1976. Mem. Am. Soc. Tng. and Devel., Wis. Sociol. Assn., Planned Parenthood. Republican. Presbyterian. Home: 47 Point Elkhart Elkhart Lake WI 53020

HILL, MARION THELMA, elementary school teacher; b. Chgo., Sept. 21, 1937; d. Herbert and Helen E. (Robinson) Hill. BEd, Chgo. Tchrs. Coll., 1963; MEd, Roosevelt U., 1971. Account clk. USDA, Chgo., 1957-58; ward clk. Cook County Hosp., Chgo., 1959-60; postal clk. U.S. P.O., Chgo., 1960-63; tchr. Chgo. Pub. Sch. System, 1963—. vol. tutor Salvation Army, Chgo., 1973; VBS tchr. Antioch-Bapt. Ch., Chgo., 1981-88; program coord. Roots Com. Orgn., Chgo. 1989. Mem. Chgo. Bd. of Realtors, South Suburban Bd. of Realtors, Phi Delta. Democratic. Protestant.

HILL, MARY ANN, marketing executive; b. Binghamton, N.Y.; d. Charles Louis and Mary (Roscoe) H.; m. Edward F. Meehan. MusB, Syracuse U., MusM. Spl. asst. U.S. Dept. Energy, Washington, 1978-79; mktg. account mgr. IBM, N.Y.C., 1973-78, mktg. mgr., 1976-78; v.p. mktg. staff Office Products div. IBM, Franklin Lakes, N.J., 1979-82; mktg. practices advisor IBM, White Plains, N.Y., 1982-84; cons. corp. hdqrs. IBM, Armonk, N.Y., 1984-86; program mgr. work sta. product mktg. IBM, Atlanta, 1986-89, health industry mktg., 1989—; alumni mem. President's Commn. on Exec. Exchange, 1979—; mem. Echo Health Conf., 1989—. Soprano soloist Blue Hill Troupe, N.Y.C., 1976-89; bd. dirs. Atlanta Community Concerts, 1989—. Mem. Nat. Assn. Exec. Women, Pre-Mozart Soc., Atlanta Music Club. Home: 3812 Glen Arbor Ct Atlanta GA 30319 Office: IBM H10H01 4111 Northside Pkwy Atlanta GA 30327

HILL, MARY CHRISTINA, executive assistant, marketing executive; b. Uniontown, Pa., June 30, 1949; d. Andrew William and Helen Veronica (Vrabel) Sabol; m. Eric B. Hill, Aug. 19, 1984. BS, Westminster Coll., New Wilmington, Pa., 1971. Office mgr. Aurora Assocs., Inc., Washington, 1979, project dir., mgmt. info. coord., 1979-81, dir. conf. and travel svcs., 1981-83, coord. office ops., 1984, coord. Job Corps Ctr., 1985-86, mktg. coord. Job Corps Ctr., 1986-88; mgr. adminstrv. support HCX, Inc., Washington, 1988-89, mktg. coord., 1989, exec. asst., 1989—. Mem. NAFE. Democrat. Home: 8751 Contee Rd 404 Laurel MD 20708

HILL, MARY LOU, small business consultant; b. Phila., July 8, 1936; d. Norman Findlay and Gladys Louise (Weigand) Tompkins; m. Ernest Clarke Hill Jr., Mar. 15, 1958; children: Sally, Holly, Randy, Chuck, Jim. Student, U. Miami, 1954-55, U. Okla., 1955-57; BBA, Portland State U., 1979, M in Taxation, 1982. CPA, Oreg. Staff acct. Fordham & Fordham, Hillsboro, Oreg., 1982-84; instr. Portland (Oreg.) State U., 1984-85; owner The Bookshelf, Sunriver, Oreg., 1985-88; instr. Cen. Oreg. Community Coll., Bend, 1986, 88—; small bus. cons., 1988—. Mem. Oreg. Soc. CPAs, Kappa Kappa Gamma. Democrat. Christian Scientist. Home: PO Box 4574 Sunriver OR 97707 Office: PO Box 4574 Sunriver OR 97707

HILL, MARY RAE, geologist, educator, writer; b. Great Falls, Mont., Sept. 2, 1923; d. Raymond Ernest and Mary Caroline (Brantly) H.; m. Edwin Weber, Aug. 13, 1948 (div.). BA, U. Colo., 1944; MA, San Francisco State U., 1970; postgrad., U. Colo., 1947-48, U. Ill., 1945-46. Jr. geologist Phillips Petroleum Co., Bartlesville, Okla., 1944-45; rsch. asst. Ill. State Geol. Survey, Urbana, 1945-46; grad. asst. U. Colo., Boulder, 1947-48; geologist, sr. geologist Calif. Div. Mines and Geology, San Francisco, 1949-75; western info. officer, geologist U.S. Geol. Survey, Menlo Park, Calif., 1975-80; adj. prof. geology San Francisco State U., 1977—; freelance writer Santa Fe; v.p., sec. Santa Fe Internat. Enterprises, Inc., 1990—. Author: Geology of Sierra Nevada, 1975, California Landscape, 1984; editor Calif. Geology mag., 1956-74; filmmaker, Barrier Beach, 1970, others. Mem. Assn. Earth Sci. Editors (life, pres. 1973). Home: Rte 7 Box 124-MU Santa Fe NM 87505

HILL, MAUREEN KELLEY, teacher; b. Chattanooga, Apr. 2, 1951; d. Joseph Henery and Bessie Mae (Waterhouse) Kelley; m. M.C. Commander Jr., Sept. 22, 1973; 1 child M.C. Commander III (Trey); m. David Jeffrey Hill, Oct. 6, 1979; children: Ellyn Cara, Andrew Kelley, Bethany Anne. Cert. of secretarial adminstrn., U. Tenn., 1971; Assoc. Degree in Early Childhood Edn., Chattanooga State Tech. Community Coll., 1988. Exec. sec. Selox, Inc., Chattanooga, 1971-73, GAF, Chattanooga, 1973-76, Criminal Ct. Judge, Chattanooga, 1977-79; tchr. presch. Christ Acad., Chattanooga, 1985—. Coord., dir. of many musicals and plays Christ United Methodist Ch., Victims' Rights Los Angeles and Chattanooga, 1987. Mem. Tenn. Assn. of Young Children, Chattanooga Assn. of Young Children, Student Educators Club, Phi Theta Kappa, Pi Beta Phi, Boosters. Republican. Methodist. Home: 514 Picture Ridge Dr Chattanooga TN 37421 Office: Christ Acad 8645 E Brainerd Rd Chattanooga TN 37421

HILL, NOLANDA SUE, broadcast executive; b. Dallas, June 16, 1944; d. Nolan R. and Francile (Morrison) Butler; m. Sheldon K. Turner, Jr., Feb. 14, 1971 (div. 1975); m. 2d, Billy B. Hill, Jr., June 25, 1976; 1 son, Andrew Butler. B.A., B.S., Stephen F. Austin U., Nacogdoches, Tex., 1966. Exec. producer Doubleday Broadcasting, Dallas, 1968-70; pres. U.V. Sports, Los Angeles, 1970-71; chief exec. officer, chief fin. officer Nat. Bus. Network, Dallas, 1972-74; pres. Handel Pub., Dallas, 1974-76; chief exec. officer, chief fin. officer Nat. Bus. Network, Dallas, 1976-84; pres., chief exec. officer Corridor Broadcasting Corp., Dallas, 1984—; mem. bd. Tex. Bd. Archtl. Examiners, Austin, 1983-86; moderator FCC/White House Symosium for Women Ownership in Telecommunications, 1983. Editor: National Directory of Performing Arts and Civic Centers, 1974, 75, 76; National Directory Arts/Canada, 1976. Mem. Speakers' Club Ho. of Reps., 1983; mem. Dallas March of Dimes, Dallas Mus. Art, Leadership Tex., 1985. Mem. Nat. Assn. Broadcasters. Democrat. Home: 3507 Mc Farlin St Dallas TX 75205

HILL, PAMELA, television executive; b. Winchester, Ind., Aug. 18, 1938; d. Paul and Mary Frances (Hollis) Abel; m. Tom Wicker, Mar. 9, 1974; 1 son, Christopher; stepchildren—Cameron Wicker, Grey Wicker, Lisa Freed, Kayce Freed. B.A., Bennington Coll., 1960; postgrad., Universidad Autonoma de Mexico, 1961, U. Glasgow, 1958-59. Fgn. affairs analyst Nelson A. Rockefeller Presdl. Campaign, 1961-64; researcher, assoc. producer, dir., producer NBC News, 1965-73, dir. White Paper series, 1969-72, producer Edwin Newman's Comment, 1972; producer Edwin Newman's Comment Closeup Documentary series ABC News, N.Y.C., 1973-78; exec. producer Closeup Documentary series ABC News, 1978-89; v.p. ABC News, 1979-89; v.p., exec. producer spl. assignments investigations Cable News Network, N.Y.C., 1989—. Author: United States Foreign Policy, 1945-65, 1968; Contbr. photographs to Catching Up With America, 1969. Trustee Bennington Coll. Recipient Christopher award, 1979, 80, Pinnacle award Am. Women in Radio and TV, 1984, Overseas Press Club Citation for Excellence, Matrix award, 1980; also Ms. Hill and Closeup have received 20 Emmy awards, 10 duPont-Columbia awards, 2 George Foster Peabody awards, 5 Ohio State awards, 7 Christopher awards, 3 Overseas Press Club awards, 9 Clarion awards, 17 CINE awards, others. Mem. Dirs. Guild, Writers Guild, Nat. Acad. Television Arts and Scis. Office: Cable News Network 5 Penn Pla 24th Fl New York NY 10009

HILL, PATRICIA ARNOLD, management consultant, realtor, former government official; b. Balt., Oct. 29, 1936; d. George Henry and Mildred Mae (Kress) Arnold; student No. Va. Community Coll., part time 1966-76; m. Richard Denzil Hill, Oct. 24, 1970; children: Terry Marlene Fomby, Debra Michelle Hill. Sec. firm McEwan & Walker, Chattanooga, 1955; clk.-typist Bur. Aeros., Washington, 1956-58, security clk., 1958, security asst., 1959-62, security specialist Bur. Aeros. and Naval Weapons Washington, 1962-66; security specialist Bur. Naval Weapons, 1962-66, Naval Ordnance Systems Command, 1966-74; security specialist Naval Sea Systems Command, Washington, 1974-75, head classification mgmt. br., asst. dir. security div., 1975-80, dep. dir., head info. security br. security div., 1980-83, security mgr. and dir. security div., 1983-86; realtor, Town and Country Properties; cons. in mgmt., adminstrn. and security, Alexandria, Va., 1986— . Mem. NAFE, Nat. Classification Mgmt. Soc., Ind. Sec. Assn., Va. State Soc., Profl. Bus. Women, Nat. Assn. Realtors, Va. Assoc. Realtors, No. Va. Assn. Realtors, Conservative Network. Baptist. Home: 1003 Collingwood Rd Alexandria VA 22308

HILL, PATRICIA FRANCINE, business consultant; b. Buffalo, Jan. 9, 1955; d. Walter W. and M. Phyllis (Jones) H. BA in Math., Swarthmore Coll., 1977, BS in Engring., 1977; MS in Computer Engring., U. Mich., 1980; MBA, Harvard U., 1990. Mem. tech. staff AT&T Bells Labs., Middletown, N.J., 1980-86; sr. systems analyst Internat. MarketNet (IMNET), N.Y.C., 1986, Marine Midland Bank, N.Y.C., 1987-88; sr. bus. cons. Kraft Gen. Foods, Skokie, Ill., 1989—; lectr. in field. Active various charitable orgns. Mem. Nat. Assn. Negro Bus. and Profl. Women, Nat. Tech. Assn. Democrat. Episcopalian.

HILL, PATRICIA LISPENARD, insurance educator; b. N.Y.C., June 25, 1937; d. George Joseph and Elizabeth (Lispenard) H.; children: George, Christopher, Susan, Daniel, Frederic, Elizabeth. Student Barnard Coll., 1954-55, Pace U., 1972-74, Coll. of Ins., 1980. Lic. ins. broker, 1961—; owner, dir. Hill Sch. of Ins., N.Y.C., 1978—; also ptnr. Hill & Co. Ins. Brokers. Office: 139 Fulton St New York NY 10038

HILL, REGINA EILEEN, civil engineer; b. Atlanta, Aug. 4, 1962; d. Thomas and Lillie M. (Callahan) Weaver; m. Joshua A. Hill, Jr. BSCE, Tenn. State U., 1986. Civil engr. U.S. Army Corp. Engrs., Nashville, 1987; environ. engr. Tenn. Dept. Health and Environ., Nashville, 1988—. Author: Advantages of a Refuse Heat Plant over a Coal Heat Plant, 1985, Highway Drainage, 1986. Mem. Nat. Tech. Assn., NAFE, ASCE, Alpha Kappa Alpha. Home: 628 Malta Dr Nashville TN 37207

HILL, ROBYN LESLEY, artist, designer; b. Sydney, Australia, Apr. 28, 1942; d. Frank Bragg and Florence Margorie (Turnham) H. Grad., Nat. Art Sch., Sydney, 1962; studied with Edward Betts, Claude Croney, Fred Leach, Maxine Masterfield, 1969-85. Art mistress S.C.E.G.G.S., Sydney, 1963-66; art dir. Am. Greetings, Cleve., 1967-78; sr. program dir. Those Characters From Cleve., 1978-90. Creative, designer (TV program) The Special Magic of Herself the Elf (Can. Emmy award 1982); exhibited at Catherine Lorillard Wolfe Nat. Exhbn., N.Y., Massillon Mus. Invitational, Ohio, Adirondacks Nat. Show, N.Y., Artists Soc. Internat., San Francisco,. Mem. Nat. Watercolor Soc. (signature), Nat. Watercolor USA Hon. Soc. (award Springfield Art Mus. 1984, signature), Ohio Watercolor Soc. (So. Ohio Bank award 1983, signature), North Coast Collage Soc. (signature), Ky. Watercolor Soc. (exhibiting mem.). Episcopalian. Home: 2770 Wildflower Dr Rocky River OH 44116 Office: Those Characters from Cleve 10500 American Rd Cleveland OH 44144

HILL, RUBYE ROBINSON, home economist; b. Richmond, Va., Sept. 10, 1926; d. Clarence Roosevelt and Mary Eugertha (Knight) Robinson; m. Robert Henry Hill, July 9, 1949; children: Michael R., Marsha A. Hill Prah, Marvin L. BS, Va. State U., Petersburg, 1947, MS, 1948. Tchr. vocat. home econs. Hoffman-Boston Jr. & Sr. High Sch., Arlington, Va., 1948-53; tchr. vocat. home econs. Thomson (Ill.) Community High Sch. #301, 1962-84, ret., 1984; substitute tchr. Carroll County Schs., Ill., 1984—; state sponsor Future Homemakers of Am., Ill., 1968-71. Contbr. articles in profl. jours. Bd. dirs., dist. chmn. Green Hills Girl Scout Am. coun., Freeport, Ill., 1984—; chmn. Dorothy Foofilf Scholarship Com., Mt. Carroll, Ill., 1990—. Named Tchr. of the Yr., State of Ill. Bd. of Pub. Instruction, 1973; recipient Appreciation award Local Future Farmers of Am., 1976, Ill. Future Homemakers of Am., 1984. Mem. NEA (life), Am. Vocat. Assn., Am. Home Econs. Assn., Ill. Home Econs. Assn., Ill. Vocat. Home Econs. Tchr.'s Assn. (pres. elect 1981-84, Outstanding Mem.), Ill. Vocat. Assn. (bd. dirs. 1981-84), Home Econs. Edn. Assn., Delta Kappa Gamma (pres. Carroll County chpt. 1988—). Baptist. Home: Rural Rte 1 Box 43 Thomson IL 61285

HILL, RUTH FOELL, language consultant; b. Houston, Sept. 13, 1931; d. Ernest William and Florence Margaret (Kane) Foell; children: Linden Ruth, Andrea Grace. Student, Principia Coll., 1950; BA, U. Calif., Berkeley, 1952; postgrad., San Diego State, 1955, Cen. Piedmont, 1981. Cert. tchr., Calif. Owner, dir. Art Gallery of Chapel Hill (N.C.), 1966-75; ecumenical bd. Campus Ministry, Charlotte; with referral svc. Charlotte (N.C.) Bed and Breakfast Registry, 1980-90; lang. cons. Berlitz Internat., Raleigh, N.C., 1988—; cert. cons. Performax Internat.; rep. UN decade for women conf. NGO Forum, Nairobi, Kenya, 1985, Woman and Global Security Conf., 1985, emerging issues forum N.C. So. U., 1987-89. Mem., bd. dirs. LWV, chmn. natural resources com.; USIA grant region 6 coord. Internat. Exch. Network; mem. N.C. Leadership Forum, N.C. Citizen's Assembly, 1989; chmn. Wk. Edn. Pub. Forum on Energy, Union Concerned Scientists, 1990. Hewlett Found. scholar; recipient award-outstanding athlete Women's Athletic Assn. Mem. AAUW (v.p. membership com., bd. dirs.) Ams. for Legal Reform (adv. bd.), Am. Farm Land Trust, Carolina Coun. on World Affairs, Chapel Hill/Carrboro Sch. Art Guild (pres.), M.W. Acad., World Wide Women in Environment. Republican. Christian Scientist. Office: PO Box 220802 Charlotte NC 28222

HILL, SARA FRANCES, nurse; b. Suffolk, Va., Sept. 25, 1953; d. Edward Holland and Sara Leigh (Whitley) H. Student, Chowan Coll., Murfreesboro, N.C., 1971-72; diploma, Louise Obici Sch. Nursing, Suffolk, 1975; student, U. N.C., 1977-80, N.C. State U., 1981-82. RN, N.C.; nat. cert. in perioperative nursing. Oper. rm. staff nurse, mem. cardiac surgery team Duke U. Med. Ctr., 1975-84; asst. head nurse operating room Pitt County Meml. Hosp.-East Carolina U., Greenville, N.C., 1984-85, asst. supr. operating room, 1985, clin. nurse specialist operating room, 1985-88, staff nurse operating room, 1989—; cardiovascular patient care coord. U. Ky. Med. Ctr. and VA Med. Ctr., Lexington, 1988-89; visitor Munich Heart Inst., 1978, Max Planck Inst., Bad Nauheim, Fed. Republic Germany, 1981, Columbia-Presbyn. Med. Ctr., N.Y.C., 1984, Great Ormond Street Hosp. for Sick Children, London, 1986, Boston Children's Hosp., 1987. Mem. Assn. Operating Room Nurses, Southeastern Surg. Nurses Assn., Am. Heart Assn., Mended Hearts. Baptist. Home: 101 Laura Ln Apt C-2 Greenville NC 27858 Office: Pitt County Meml Hosp 200 Stantonsburg Rd Greenville NC 27834

HILL, SHIRLEY ALINE, cable network executive; b. Perry, Fla., Dec. 1, 1956; d. William Harlen and Laura Maryjane (Lockman) Pritchett; m. Gary Leonard Hill, Apr. 2, 1983; 1 child, Jessica; stepchildren: Dan, Lori, Cheri, David, Trisha. BA in Bus., Taylor U., 1979. Acct. GM, Marion, Ind., 1978-79, payroll auditor, 1979-80; N.E. mktg. coord. Continental Cablevision, Findlay, Ohio, 1980-81, state mktg. mgr., 1981-82; mktg. rep. Sta. ESPN, Chgo., 1982-83; affiliate rels. mgr. CBN Cable Network, Chgo., 1983-89; v.p., western dir. affiliate rels. The Family Channel, Chgo., 1989—. Mem. Women in Cable (bd. dirs. Chgo. chpt. 1989—), Ill. Cable TV Assn., Cable TV Adminstrv. and Mktg. Assn. (chpt. bd. dirs. 1989—), Nat. Cable Acad. Cable Programming. Republican. Office: The Family Channel 1301 W 22nd St Ste 902 Oak Brook IL 60521

HILL, SHIRLEY ANN, mathematics educator; b. Kansas City, Mo., Aug. 26, 1927; d. George Haddon and Lena (Oberdiek) H. BA, U. Mo., 1948; MA, U. Kansas City, 1956; PhD, Stanford U., 1961; LHD (hon.), U. Nebr., Omaha, 1984. Tchr. Kansas City Sch. Dist., 1956-58, Jefferson Union Dist., Santa Clara, Calif., 1958-60; research assoc. Stanford (Calif.) U., 1960-63; prof. U. Mo., Kansas City, 1963—, Curator's prof., 1987—. Author: (with others) Introduction to Logic, 1964, Elementary Geometry, 1976; editor: Education in the 80s: Mathematics, 1982.. Mem. Nat. Coun. Tchrs. Math. (pres. 1978-80), Math. Scis. Edn. Bd. (chmn. 1985-90), U.S. Commn. on Math. Instrn. (chmn. 1976-80), Nat. Bd. Profl. Teaching Standards (bd. dirs. 1988—), Phi Beta Kappa.

HILL, SUE ANNETTE, bookkeeper, secretary; b. Union County, Miss., Nov. 26, 1964; d. John Wayne and Janie Sue (Azlin) H. BS, Blue Mountain Coll., 1986. Cert. in computer literacy, Miss. Sec. Pugh Tackle Co., Inc., New Albany, 1981; libr. asst. Blue Mountain (Miss.) Coll., 1982; radiologist asst. Union County Gen. Hosp., New Albany, 1984; office mgr. Radiologist and Billing Office, New Albany, Miss., 1987; clk., bookkeeper dept. human svcs. State of Miss., New Albany, 1990—. Sunday sch. tchr., soloist local Bapt. ch. Mem. NAFE, Psi Chi (v.p.). Home: Rte 1 Box 39 Etta MS 38627

HILL, SUSAN SLOAN, safety engineer; b. Quincy, Mass., June 1, 1952; d. Ralph Arnold and Grace Elenore (Sloan) Crosby; m. William Loyd Hill, Dec. 16, 1973 (div. July 1982); m. William Joseph Graham, Sept. 10, 1983 (div. Feb. 1985). Assoc. Sci. in Gen. Engring., Motlow State Community Coll., Tullahoma, Tenn., 1976; BS in Indsl. Engring., Tenn. Technol. U., 1978. Intern, safety engr. Intern Tng. Ctr., U.S. Army, Red River Army Depot, Tex., 1978-79, Field Safety Activity, Charlestown, Ind., 1979, system safety engr. Communications-Electronics Command, Ft. Monmouth, N.J., 1979-84, gen. engr., 1984-85; chief system safety Arnold Air Force Sta., USAF, Tullahoma, 1984; system safety engr. U.S. Army Safety Ctr., Ft. Rucker, Ala., 1985—. Recipient 5 letters of appreciation U.S. Army, 1982. Mem. Assn. Fed. Safety and Health Profls. (regional v.p. 1980-84), Soc. Women Engrs., Nat. Safety Mgmt. Soc., Am. Soc. Safety Engrs., System Safety Soc., Nat. Assn. Female Execs., Order Engr. Republican. Episcopalian. Avocations: bowling, needlework, sewing, cooking, golf. Home: 115 Liveoak Dr Enterprise AL 36330 Office: US Army Safety Ctr Attn CSSC-SE Fort Rucker AL 36362

HILL, TRACEY, civic organization administrative director; b. Madison, N.J., June 12, 1946; d. Walter and Sally (Brewer) H. BS in Polit. Sci., Rutgers U., 1973. Cert. Am. Cons. League. Dir. ACLU of N.J., Newark, 1970—; pres. bus. and fin. mgmt. Tracelin Assn., Rahway, N.J., 1983—; profl. grants writer Scanlon and Newhouse, N.Y.C., 1984, Soc. for Preservation of Natural Music, Kingsbridge, N.Y., 1984-85, Inst. for Devel., Enhancement and Advancement of Women, Plainfield, N.J., 1984, Save the Children Found., Neward, 1984; cons. grantswriting and tech. assistance N.J. Women and AIDS Network, New Brunswick, 1989; assoc. producer pub. affairs spls. WBGO-AM, 1978-80. Author: The Business Plan Write-Guide: A Layman's Guide to Writing a Business Plan, 1990. Recipient Legal Assts. in Svc. Tng. award, 1986, Am. Biog. Inst. award, 1988. Mem. NAFE, Am. Cons. League, Bus. and Profl. Women USA, Nat. Writers Club, Internat. Platform Assn., Rep. Progressive Assn. Home and Office: PO Box 1822 Rahway NJ 07065

HILL, VALERIE CHARLOTTE, nurse, real estate salesperson; b. Shaftsbury, Vt., Dec. 2, 1932; d. William Henry Harrison and Angeline Margaret

Stella (Fuller) Hill; m. Edward Joseph Klanit (dec. July 1984); 1 child, Joyce Ellen Klanit Artadi. Grad., The Mount Sinai Hosp. Sch. of Nursing, 1955. RN, N.Y. Staff nurse The Jack Martin Respiratory Ctr. of The Mt. Sinai Hosp., N.Y.C., 1955-57; v.p. Chauffeurs Unlimited, Inc., N.Y.C., 1957-77; staff nurse Rusk Inst., N.Y.C., 1957-58, Beth Israel Med. Ctr., N.Y.C., 1978-79; owner, mgr. Powers Fish Market, Inc., N.Y.C., 1977-84; tchr. Techs. for Creating, Albany, N.Y., 1983—; staff nurse Doctors Hosp., N.Y.C., 1984-86; pvt. duty nurse Personal Health Care Services, Albany, N.Y., 1987-88; nurse Albany Med. Ctr. Hosp., 1988—; real estate sales assoc. Century 21-Stanley Major Ltd., West Sand Lake, N.Y., 1988, Century-21 Home Towne Properties, Albany, 1989—. Author numerous poems. Recipient Outstanding Service to Community award Mayor Koch City of N.Y., 1983. Mem. Alumnae Assn. of Mt. Sinai Hosp. Sch. Nursing (various coms. 1965-77, bd. dirs. 1968), Nat. Bd. Realtors, N.Y. State Assn. Realtors, Inc., Albany County Bd. Realtors, Women's Coun. Realtors. Democrat. Clubs: Empire State Girls Bowling. Home: 70 Second St Albany NY 12210 Office: Albany Med Ctr Hosp 43 New Scotland Ave Albany NY 12208 also: Century 21-Home Towne Properties 1167 Central Ave Albany NY 12205

HILL, WENDY PAULEN, hospital administrator; b. Monroeville, Ala., Dec. 30, 1952; d. Arnold Julian and Jean (Dailey) P.; m. James Miles Hill III, Mar. 9, 1974. BA, Trinity U., 1975, MS, 1986. Claims clk. II Grady Meml. Hosp., Atlanta, 1975-76; outpatient ins. supr. Guadalupe Valley Hosp., Seguin, Tex., 1977-79, asst. adminstr., 1985—; bus. mgr. Guadalupe Valley Radiology, Seguin, 1979-85; exec. dir. Guadalupe County Med. Soc., Seguin, 1984—; cons. W.P. Hill, Seguin, 1984—. Mem. bd. dirs. Am. Heart Assn., Seguin, 1983—, communications chmn., 1985—, bd. dirs. community coun., v.p. 1986, pres. 1987—; active Nat. Affiliate Pub. Affairs Network, Washington, 1987—. Ted Sparling scholar, Trinity U., 1986. Mem. Am. Hosp. Assn., Tex. Hosp. Assn., Am. Coll. Health Care Execs., Trinity U. Alumni Assn. (chmn. membership 1986—, mem. exec. bd. 1988—), Guadalupe County Med. Soc. (exec. dir. 1984—). Republican. Office: Guadalupe Valley Hosp 1215 E Court St Seguin TX 78155

HILL-DONISCH, KARLA, management consultant; b. St. Paul, Minn., June 26, 1959; d. Robert Vernon and Venera Bernadette (Finocchiaro) Hill; m. David Arthur Donisch, Aug. 13, 1983. BS, U. Minn., 1981; MA, St. Mary's Coll., 1987. Trainer/cons. Heitzinger & Assocs., Madison, Wis., 1982-84; tng. program specialist Hazelden Found., Mpls., 1984-90; tng. entrepreneur Mpls., 1990—; cons. Graphic Unltd., Mpls., 1989—, The Travel Co., Mpls., 1990, Universal Tradewinds, 1990. Author: (pamphlet) Women in Sports and Chemical Use, 1987. Recipient sports letters U. Utah and Minn. Athletics, Salt Lake, Mpls., 1977-81. Mem. NAFE, Nat. Assn. for the Self-Employed, Women's Sports Found. (adv. bd. 1988-90), NOW. Home and Office: 3524 Aldrich Ave South Minneapolis MN 55408

HILLDRUP, MARY EILEEN, interior designer; b. Wilkes-Barre, Pa., Aug. 9, 1946; d. Patrick Edward and Ruth (Garber) Hosey; m. Merle Bolen (div. 1969); m. E. Gordon Hilldrup Jr.; 1 child, Kimberly Gail. Degree, Johnston-Willis Hosp. Sch. Nsg, 1974; BS with distinction, George Mason U., 1978; postgrad., N.Y. Sch. Interior Design. RN, Va.; lic. real estate agt., Va. Charge nurse Mary Washington Hosp., Fredericksburg, Va., 1974-78, radiology nurse, 1988—; realtor assoc. Freeman Assocs., Fredericksburg, 1978-79; pub. health nurse Rappahannock Area Health Dept., Fredericksburg, 1979-86; office mgr., nurse Pratt Med. Ctr., Fredericksburg, 1986-88, support staff nurse, 1988; founder Edghill Concepts, Inc., 1989—. Editor: White German Shepherd Book, 1982. Mem. Nat. Fedn. Ind. Bus., Allied Bd. Trade, Fredericksburg Country Club, Sigma Theta Tau. Republican. Episcopalian. Home and Office: 11711 Catharpin Rd Spotsylvania VA 22533

HILLEGASS, CHRISTINE ANN, psychologist; b. Lancaster, Pa., July 13, 1952; d. Michael and Ann Christine (Wolf) H.; m. E. Cornelius Kocsis, Aug. 6, 1983. BA, Bard Coll., 1975; MA in Forensic Psychol., John Jay Coll. Criminal Justice, 1979; postgrad., Rutgers U., 1986—. Staff psychologist Dept. Corrections, Adult Diagnostic Treatment Ctr., Avenel, N.J., 1979-84; dir. Monmouth County Sexual Abuse Treatment and Prevention Program, Ocean, N.J., 1984-87; cons., trainer, therapist various mental health, social svc., correctional and law enforcement agys., 1981—; mem. Monmouth County Sexual Abuse Com., West Long Branch, N.J., 1983—, chair, 1986-87, co-chair, 1987-88; mem. N.J. Statewide Sexual Abuse Network, 1984-89, Monmouth Prosecutor's Task Force on Child Abuse, Freehold, N.J., 1985-86. Recipient Woman of Achievement award Monmouth County Adv. Commn. on Status of Women, 1987. Mem. Am. Psychol. Assn., N.J. Psychol. Assn., Am. Assn. Sex Educators, Counselors and Therapists, Am. Profl. Soc. on Abuse of Children.

HILLEMAN, JERYL LYNN, biopharmaceutical executive; b. Washington, Sept. 27, 1957; d. Maurice R. and Lorraine (Witmer) H.; m. William A. Albright, Jr. BA, Brown U., 1979; MBA, U. Pa., 1982. Analyst Merck, Sharp & Dohme, Holland, 1979-80; mgr., direct mail Am. Express, N.Y.C., 1982-84; dir. br. mktg. Fidelity Investments, Boston, 1984-86; chief fin. officer Cytel Corp., La Jolla, Calif., 1987—; bd. dirs. Glytec, Inc., La Jolla. Mem. U. Calif. San diego Connect, Athena, Wharton Club (officer). Office: Cytel Corp 11099 N Toney Pines Rd La Jolla CA 92037

HILLER, DAGMAR C., office manager; b. Newark, Mar. 30, 1962; d. Werner and Helga Marianne (Maile) H. BS, Boston Coll., 1984. Office mgr. Gen. Spice, Inc., South Plainfield, N.J. Mem. NAFE.

HILLER, PHYLLIS LILLIAN, child and family therapist, composer; b. Petaluma, Calif.; d. Carl Ivan and Lilly Florence (Riewerts) Unger; divorced; children: Julie, David, Daniel, Jonathan. AA, U. Calif., Berkeley, 1946; AB, San Francisco State U., 1949; MS, Peabody Vanderbilt U., 1976. Tchr. Novato (Calif.) Unified Sch. Dist., 1949-64, music curriculum specialist, 1965-67; composer Ramo Song Story/Oak Hill Music Pub. Co., Nashville, 1970—; media producer Oak Hill Music Pub. Co., Novato, 1981; grant coord. NCCJ, Nashville, 1976-78; child and family therapist, psychol. counselor Rebound, Inc., Gallatin, Tenn., 1985—; pvt. practice child and family counselor Nashville, 1989—; Composer: Choices, 1981, My Name is Fibby, 1980, God is a Suprise, 1974, Stages of Being. Mem. ASCAP, Sane Nuclear Policy, Internat. Transactional Analysis Assn., Nashville Psychotherapy Inst., Nashville Assn. Education for Young Children. Democrat. Unitarian. Home and Office: Po Box 120068 Nashville TN 37212

HILLERT, GLORIA BONNIN, anatomist, educator; b. Brownton, Minn., Jan. 25, 1930; d. Edward Henry and Lydia Magdalene (Luebker) Bonnin; m. Richard Hillert, Aug. 20, 1960; children: Kathryn, Virginia, Jonathan. BS, Valparaiso (Ind.) U., 1953; MA, U. Mich., 1958. Instr. Springfield (Ill.) Jr. Coll., 1953-57; teaching asst. U. Mich., Ann Arbor, 1957-58; instr., dept. head St. John's Coll., Winfield, Kans., 1958-59; asst. prof. Concordia Coll., River Forest, Ill., 1959-63; vis. instr. Wright Jr. Coll., Chgo., 1974-76, Ill. Benedictine Coll., Lisle, 1977-78, Rosary Coll., River Forest, 1976-81; prof. anatomy and physiology Triton Coll., River Grove, 1982—; advisor Springfield Jr. Coll. Sci. Club, 1953-57, Concordia Coll. Cultural Group, 1959-62; program dir. Triton Coll. Sci. Lectr. Series, 1983—. Dem. campaign asst., Maywood, Ill., 1972 and 1988; vol. Mental Health Orgn., Chgo., 1969-73. Mem. AAUW, Ill. Assn. Community Coll. Biol. Tchrs., Nat. Assn. Biol. Tchrs. Lutheran. Home: 1620 Clay Ct Melrose Park IL 60160 Office: Triton Coll 2000 N 5th Ave River Grove IL 60171

HILLERY, MARY JANE LARATO, producer, television host, editor, columnist, reserve army officer; b. Boston, Sept. 15, 1931; d. Donato and Porzia (Avellis) Larato; Asso. Sci. (scholar), Northeastern U., 1950; BS, U. Mass. Harvard Extension, 1962; grad. Command and Gen. Staff Coll., 1982; m. Thomas H. Hillery, Feb. 25, 1961; 1 son, Thomas H. Sales agt., linguist Pan Am. Airways, Boston, 1955-61; interpreter Internat. Conf. Fire Chiefs, Boston, 1966; tchr. Spanish, YWCA, Natick, Mass., 1966-67; community rels. cons., adv. bd. dirs., lectr. for migrant edn. project div. Mass. Dept. Community Affairs, Boston, 1967-69; editor-in-chief Sudbury (Mass.) Citizen, 1967-76; assoc. editor The Beacon, 1976-79, contbg. editor, 1979-83; area editorial adviser Beacon Pub. Co., Acton, Mass., 1970-80, editor, 1976-80; columnist Town Crier, 1987—; contbg. editor Towne Talk, 1975-79, Citizens' Forum, 1975-81; dir. pub. affairs Mass. Dept. Environ. Quality Engring., 1981-83; producer, host TV interview show For the Record. Mem. Bus. Adv. Com., 1972-77, Sudbury Sch. Com., 1976-77; mem. Meml. Day Celebration Com., 1972—, master of ceremonies, 1973-90; mem. Sudbury Town Report, 1967-72, 85-88, chmn., 1969-72; chmn. Sudbury Vets. Adv. Com., 1986—; panelist Internat. Women's Year Symposium, 1975, Women in Politics, 1987, Women In Mil., 1987; mem. congl. 5th dist. Mass. nomination bd. USMA West Point, 1985—. Served with USN, 1950-54; lt. col. USAR; liaison officer U.S. Mil. Acad., 1976-89; pub. affairs officer 94th USAR Command, 1982-83 (meritorious svc. medal 1985), Office of Sec. of Def., The Pentagon, Washington, 1989—; mem. Congl. Nominating bd. USMA, 1985—; editor Hansconian, 1983-85. Decorated Meritorious Service medal. Named Editor of Year, Beacon Pub. Co., 1970; recipient medal of appreciation Internat. Order DeMolay, 1969, certificates of appreciation U.S. Def. Civil Preparedness Agency, 1975, Mass. Bicentennial Commn., 1976, Res. Officers Assn., 1986; citations Mass. State Senate, 1979, 82; Newswriting award Media Contest, Air Force Systems Command, 1984. Mem. Nat. Editorial Assn., Nat. Newspaper Assn., New Eng. Press Assn., Bus. and Profl. Women's Club (1st v.p. 1973-74, pres. 1974-76, parliamentarian 1978-88, state bylaws com. 1977-78, 79-81, 1986-88, state legis. chmn. 1979-81, 86-88, State Polit. Action Com. Chmn., 1988-89, Woman of Yr. 1979, Woman of Achievement 1982), LWV (dir. 1964-68), Nat. League Am. Pen Women (exec. bd. Boston 1974-76, 78-88, pres. 1976-78, publicity chmn. 1979-80, chmn. bylaws com. 1979-80, 86-88, parliamentarian 1978-80, 82-88, auditor 1980-82, 84-88, 1st v.p. 1988—), Res. Officers Assn. (life; state sec. 1978-79, pres. Boston chpt. 1986-88, army coun. rep. 1989-90, budget com., 1990—, state publicity chmn. 1988-90, Outstanding Svc. award 1978-79), Omega Sigma. Home: 66 Willow Rd Sudbury MA 01776

HILLGREN, SONJA DOROTHY, journalist; b. Sioux Falls, S.D., May 17, 1948; d. Ralph Oliver and Priscilla Adeline (Mannes) Hillgren; m. Ralph Lee Hill (dec.). BJ, U. Mo., 1970, MA, 1972; postgrad. (Nieman fellow), Harvard U., 1982-83. Washington corr. Ohio-Washington News Svc., 1972-73; reporter UPI, Annapolis, Md., 1974-76; reporter/editor UPI, Washington, 1976-78; farm editor UPI, 1978-88; Washington corr. Knight-Ridder, Washington, 1988-90; Washington editor Farm Jour., 1990—; radio broacaster UPI, 1978-88. Recipient J.R. Russell award, Newspaper Farm Editors of Am., 1985, Reuben Brigham award, Agrl. Communicators in Edn., 1988. Mem. Nat. Assn. Agrl. Journalists (pres. 1987-88), Nat. Press Club, Soc. Profl. Journalists, Coun. on Fgn. Rels., Congl. Country Club, Pi Beta Phi. Episcopalian. Home: 2800 29th Pl NW Washington DC 20008 Office: Farm Jour 941 National Press Bldg Washington DC 20045

HILLIARD, SHAREN ANNE, school program adminstrator; b. Mpls., May 13, 1942; d. Paul Ezetic and Maxene Fern (Carlson) DuFresne; m. Gary Leslie Hilliard, Nov. 16, 1963; children: Wendy, Lynn. BS, U. Minn., 1964; MA, Coll. St. Thomas, St. Paul, Minn., 1986; postgrad., Coll. St. Thomas, St. Paul. Tchr. Mpls. Pub. Schs., 1964-68; tchr. Wayzata (Minn.) Pub. Schs., 1978-85, coord. programs for gifted and talented children, 1985—; lectr. in field. Co-author: (handbook) Nuts and Bolts-A Guide to Beginning an Enrichment Triad, 1987. Recipient Excellence in Edn. award Minn. Assn. Commerce and Industry, 1986; Twincities area Writer's Project fellow, 1981—. Mem. Minn. Educators of Gifted and Talented (pres. 1988-89), Delta Kappa Gamma, Phi Delta Kappa. Presbyterian. Home: 4805 Ithaca Ln Plymouth MN 55446 Office: 305 Vicksburg Ln Plymouth MN 55447

HILLIER, JUDITH A., elementary counselor; b. Mayville, N.D., Apr. 18, 1951; d. Melvin O. and Elizabeth (Dekker) Gunderson; m. William I. Hillier, May 28, 1973. BS in Elem./Special Edn., U. N.D., 1973, MS in Guidance/Counseling, 1980. Cert. tchr., guidance counselor, N.D. Basic skills - math tchr. Thompson (N.D.) Pub. Schs., 1973-74; 5th and 6th grade tchr. Unity Pub. Sch., Petersburg, N.D., 1974-76; elem. counselor Valley City (N.D.) Pub. Sch., 1981—; trainer, cons. Nurturing Program for Parents and Children, Valley City, 1988—, co-facilitator, 1987—; facilitator Systematic Tng. for Effective Parenting, Valley City, 1981-87. Bd. Dirs. After Sch. Program - Latch Key, Valley City, 1986—, Abused Persons Outreach Ctr., Valley City, 1984—. Recipient Ruth Meiers Svc. to Children award, Outstanding Vol., 1987. Mem. Valley City Edn. Assn. (pres. 1988-90), N.D. Sch. Counselors (bd. dirs. 1984-90), AAUW (pres. 1982-85), NEA, N.D. Educators Assn., Am. Assn. Counseling Devel., Pi Lambda Theta, Delta Kappa Gamma (v.p. 1986-88), Phi Delta Kappa. Home: 214 6th St NW Valley City ND 58072

HILLIS, LLEWELLYA W., marine biology educator; b. Windsor, Ont., Can., Jan. 17, 1930; d. Llewellyn and Pearl Evelina (Williams) H.; m. Paul a. Colinvaux, June 17, 1961; children: Catherine M., Roger P. A.R.C.T., Toronto Conservatory Music, Ont., Can., 1948; BA with honor, Queen's U., Kingston, Can., 1952; MS, U. Mich., 1953, PhD, 1957. Postdoctoral fellow Nat. Rsch. Coun. of Can., U. New Brunswick, Frederickton, 1957-59; asst. prof. U. Victoria (Can.), 1959-61; vis. prof. botany Duke U., Durham, N.C., 1961-62, Queen's U., Belfast, Northern Ireland, 1962-63; sr. scientist Internat. Indian Ocean Expedition on Te Vega, 1963; guest investigator biology Yale U., New Haven, 1964; asst. prof., rsch. assoc. botany Ohio State U., Columbus, 1964-71; founders fellow AAUW, London, 1971-72; asst. prof. zoology Ohio State U., Columbus, 1972-79; assoc. prof. zoology Sch. Natural Resources, Ohio State U., Columbus, 1979—; guest investigator Woods Hole (Mass.) Oceanographic Inst., 1987—; assoc. Univ Herbaria, Harvard U., Cambrigde, Mass., 1987; vis. investigator Australian Inst. Marine Sci., Townsville, Australia, 1988; councillor Queen's U. Can., Kingston, 1985-91; advisor Nat. Acad. Com. on Internat. Coop., People's Republic China, Washington, 1986; cons. taxonomy o fcoral reef organisms; vis. scholar Green Coll. U., Oxford, Eng., 1986. Contbr. articles to profl. jours. Sustaining bd. Pro Musica, Columbus, 1988—; active workshops Am. Women in Sci. Columbus. Bunting Inst. Sci. fellow, rsch. scholar Radcliffe Coll., 1985-87. Mem. Marine Biol. Assn. UK, Internat. Soc. for Reef Studies, Oceanographic Soc., Biominerology Assn., Internat. Phycological Soc., Am. Phycological Soc., Brit. Phycological Soc., Am. Women in Sci., AAUW, AAUP, Friends of the Farlow Harvard U. Home: 319 S Columbia Ave Columbus OH 43209 Office: Ohio State U Dept Zoology 1735 Neil Ave Columbus OH 43210

HILLIS, MARGARET, conductor, musician; b. Kokomo, Ind., Oct. 1, 1921; d. Glen R. and Bernice (Haynes) H. BA, Ind. U., 1947; grad. student choral conducting, Juilliard Sch. Music, 1947-49; D.Mus. (hon.), Temple U., 1967, Ind. U., 1972, Carthage Coll., 1979, Wartburg Coll., 1981; DFA (hon.), St. Mary's Coll., 1977, Lake Forest Coll., 1980; DHL (hon.), St. Xavier Coll., 1988; D.Mus. (hon.), Adrian Coll., 1990. Dir., Met. Youth Chorale, Bklyn., 1948-51; asst. condr., Collegiate Choral, N.Y.C., 1952-53; mus. dir., condr., Am. Concert Choir, N.Y.C. from 1950, Am. Concert Orch. from 1950; condr., instr., Union Theol. Sem., 1950-60, Juilliard Sch. Music, 1951-53; dir. choral dept., Third St. Music Sch. Settlement, 1953-54; founder, music dir., Am. Choral Found., Inc., from 1954; choral dir., N.Y.C. Opera Co., 1955-56, Chgo. Mus. Coll. of Roosevelt U., 1961-62; condr., choral dir., Santa Fe Opera Co., 1958-59, Chgo. Symphony Chorus, 1957—; music dir., N.Y. Chamber Soloists, 1956-60; choral condr., Am. Opera Soc., N.Y.C., 1952-68; mus. asst. to music dir., Chgo. Symphony Orch., 1966-68; music dir., condr., Kenosha Symphony Orch., 1961-68; condr., choral dir., Cleve. Orch. Chorus, 1969-71; prof. conducting, dir. choral orgns., Northwestern U. Sch. Music, 1970-77; vis. prof. conducting, Ind. U. from 1978; resident condr. Chgo. Civic Orch. from 1967; music dir. Choral Inst., 1968-70, 75; mus. dir., condr., Elgin (Ill.) Symphony Orch., 1971-85; condr. Chgo.'s Do-It-Yourself Messiah, 1976—; dir. choral activities San Francisco Symphony Orch., 1982-83; guest condr., Chgo. Symphony, Cleve. Orch., Minn. Orch., Nat. Symphony Orch., others. Artists' adviser Nat. Fedn. Music Clubs Youth Auditions, 1966-70; mem. vis. com. dept. music U. Chgo., from 1971; chmn. choral panel Nat. Endowment for Arts, 1974-82 ; hon. mem. Roosevelt U. Coun. of 100, from 1976; adv. bd. Cathedral Choral Soc. Washington Cathedral, from 1976; mem. Nat. Coun. Arts, 1985—. Civilian flight instr. USN CAA, WTS, World War II. Recipient Grammy awards for best choral performances: Verdi's Requiem, 1978, Beethoven's Missa Solemnis, 1979, Brahm's Ein Deutsches Requiem, 1980, Berlioz' La Damnation de Faust, 1983, Haydn's Creation, 1984, Brahm's Ein Deutsches Requiem, 1985, Orff's Carmina Burana, 1987; recipient Grand Prix du Disque for Berlioz' La Damnation de Faust, 1982; recipient Golden Plate award Am. Acad. Achievement, 1967, Alumnus of Year award Ind. U. Sch. Music Alumni, 1969, Steinway award, 1969, Chgo. YWCA Leader Luncheon I award, 1972, Friends of Lit. award, 1973, SAI Found. Circle of 15 award, 1974, Woman of Yr. in Classical Music award Ladies Home Jour., 1978, Leadership for Freedom award Women's Scholarship Assn. Roosevelt U., 1978. Mem. Nat. Fedn. Music Clubs (hon., citation for contbns. to musical life of nation 1981), Am. Choral Dirs. Assn., Assn. Choral Condrs., Am. Music Center, P.E.O., Sigma Alpha Iota (hon.), Pi Kappa Lambda (hon.), Kappa Kappa Gamma (Alumni Achievement award 1978), Chorus America (formerly Assn. Profl. Vocal Ensembles), Am. Symphony Orch. League, Nat. Soc. Lit. and Arts. Office: Chgo Symphony Orch 220 S Michigan Ave Chicago IL 60604

HILLMAN, CAROL BARBARA, manufacturing consultant; b. N.Y.C., Sept. 6, 1940; d. Joseph Hoppenfeld and Elsa (Spiegel) Hoppenfeld Resika; m. Howard D. Hillman, May 25, 1969. BA with honors, U. Wis., 1961; Fulbright scholar U. Lyon (France), 1961-62; MA, Cornell U., Ithaca, N.Y., 1966. Asst. editor Holt Rinehart & Winston, Pubs., 1965-66; staff assoc. pub. rels. Ea. Airlines, N.Y.C., 1966-74; pub. affairs mgr. Squibb Corp., N.Y.C., 1974-75; asst. dir. corp. pub. rels. Burlington Industries, N.Y.C., 1975-77, dir. corp. pub. rels., 1977-80, v.p. pub. rels., 1980-82; v.p. corp. communications Norton Co., Worcester, Mass., 1982-89, sr. cons. 1989-90; sr. v.p. communications Dun & Bradstreet Bus. Credit Svcs., Murray Hill, N.J., 1990—; mem. Pub. Affairs Coun., Machinery & Allied Products Inst., 1982-89; mem. dep. policy com., agenda com. Mass. Bus. Roundtable, 1982-89; bd. dirs. Mass. Econ. Stabilization Trust, 1987—. Mem. Cornell Coun., Ithaca, 1981-85, pub. rels. com. 1981-88; mem. adv. coun. Coll. Human Ecology, Cornell U., Ithaca, 1982-84; mem. adv. bd. Ct. Apptd. Spl. Advocates, Worcester, 1983-87; voting mem. Wis. Union Trustees, U. Wis., Madison, 1982—; mem. Clark U. Assocs., Worcester, 1983-89; bd. dirs. Planned Parenthood League Mass., 1986—; trustee Quinsigamond Community Coll., Worcester, 1987—. Cornell Grad. fellow Cornell U., 1962. Mem. Pub. Rels. Soc. Am., Women's Econ. Forum, Worcester C. of C. (bd. dirs. 1984-87), Pub. Rels. Seminar (com. mem. 1981-89), Phi Beta Kappa, Phi Kappa Phi, Cornell. Home: 299 Belknap Rd Framingham MA 01701 Office: Dun & Bradstreet 1 Diamond Hill Rd Murray Hill NJ 07974-0027

HILLMAN, DEBORAH JEANNE, consumer products professional; b. Bristol, Pa., Oct. 19, 1962; d. Richard Austin and Barbara (Woods) H. BSBA, Bucknell U., 1984. Sales rep. Procter & Gamble, Phila., 1984-85, unit mgr., 1986-88, account sales mgr., 1988—. Mem. Bryn Mawr Presbyn. Ch. Home: 1025 David's Run Phoenixville PA 19460

HILLMAN, JULIE RENAE, education and construction executive; b. Springhill, La., Mar. 17, 1962; d. William Edward and W. Jean (Oliver) H.; m. Steven J. Kinelski. B Music Edn. and Piano Pedagogy, Queens Coll., 1985, MEd, 1988. Cert. tchr., N.C. Legis. asst. U.S. Ho. of Reps., Washington, 1983; mktg. asst. Troutman Industries, Charlotte, N.C., 1985-86; tutor Learning Founds., Charlotte, 1981-87, sec. of corp., 1988—, also bd. dirs.; fin. mgr. Harmon Constrn. Co., Charlotte, 1986—; cons. Learning Found. Raleigh, 1986—, Mayland Community Coll., Spruce Pine, N.C., 1987—. Named Queens and Dana scholar Queens Coll., 1980-85. Mem. NAFE, Oratorio Singers of Charlotte. Republican. Home: 228 E Kingston Ave Charlotte NC 28203 Office: Learning Founds 1700 Abbey Pl Charlotte NC 28209

HILLMAN, RITA, investor; b. N.Y.C., May 16, 1912; d. Rudolf and Bertha (Goodman) Kanarek; m. Alex L. Hillman, Aug. 23, 1932 (dec. 1968); children: Richard Alan (dec.), Alex L. Student NYU, 1929-32. Mem. Met. Mus. Art (mem. vis. com. 20th century art dept.), Am. Friends Israel Mus. (exec. com.), Bklyn. Acad. Music (vice chmn.), Internat. Ctr. Photography (chmn.), Alex Hillman Family Found. (pres.). Home: 895 Park Ave New York NY 10021 Office: 630 Fifth Ave New York NY 10111

HILLMAN-JONES, GLADYS CORNELIA, educational administrator; b. Albany, N.Y., Jan. 15, 1938; d. Thomas Benjamin and Minnie Geneva (Colclough) Brooks; m. Harold Jones, Apr. 19, 1980; 1 son by previous marriage, George I. Hillman III. BS, SUNY, Oneonta, 1960; MA, Kean Coll. (formerly Newark State Coll.), Oneonta, 1970. Tchr. public schs. Albany, N.Y., 1960-64, Newark, N.Y., 1964-69; vice prin. Chancellor Ave. Sch., Newark, N.Y., 1969-76; prin. Marcus Garvey Sch., Newark, N.Y., 1976-78, George Washington Carver Elem. Sch., Newark, N.Y., 1978-81, Mt. Vernon Sch., Newark, N.Y., 1984—; dep. exec. supt. Newark Public Schs., 1981-84; mgr. Cernitin Am. Inc.; instructional cons. Barnell Loft Pub. Co. Chmn. bldg. fund com. local Bapt. Ch., Newark. Recipient Disting. Alumnus award SUNY-Oneonta, 1983, Outstanding Accomplishments award Essex County Civic Club, 1987, Adminstrv. Leadership award Benedetto Croce Ednl. Soc., Woman-on-the-Move award Bethany Bapt. Ch., 1988, Outstanding Achievement award Centennial Commn. of Orange, N.J., 1988. Mem. NAACP (life), Am. Assn. Sch. Adminstrs., Internat. Reading Assn., Assn. Supervision and Curriculum Devel., United Coun. Negro Women, N.J. Reading Assn., Essex County Coun. Sch. Adminstrs., Delta Sigma Theta (chmn. scholarship com. 1973-77), Delta Pi chpt. Phi Delta Kappa, Inc. (Outstanding Leadership award 1989). Baptist (chmn. Black coll. com. 1978-81, chmn. bd. Christian edn. 1982-85). Office: 142 Mt Vernon Pl Newark NJ 07106

HILLNER, KATHLEEN ANHALT, speech and language pathologist; b. Evanston, Ill., Dec. 18, 1956; d. Robert Theodore and Milberna Bernice (McWhiney) Anhalt; m. Norman Edgar Hillner, July 26, 1986; 1 child, Jonathan Robert. BS, Northwestern U., 1979; MS, U. Wis., Madison, 1981. Speech pathologist Community Consol. Sch. Dist. 54, Schaumburg, Ill., 1981—, speech chairperson, 1986—; mem. in-svc. com. N.W. Suburban Spl. Edn. Orgn., Mt. Prospect, Ill., 1988—; mem. computer software preview com. Schaumburg Sch. Dist. 54, 1987—; mem. S/L criteria com. N.W. Suburban Spl. Edn. Com., 1986—. Named to Hall of Fame, Schaumburg Edn. Assn., 1988. Mem. Am. Speech-Lang. Hearing Assn., Northwest Suburban Speech-Lang. Hearing Assn., Schaumburg Edn. Assn. Home: 717 Bayside Ct Wheeling IL 60090

HILLS, CARLA ANDERSON, federal official, lawyer; b. Los Angeles, Jan. 3, 1934; d. Carl H. and Edith (Hume) Anderson; m. Roderick Maltman Hills, Sept. 27, 1958; children: Laura Hume, Roderick Maltman, Megan Elizabeth, Alison Macbeth. A.B. cum laude, Stanford U., 1955; student, St. Hilda's Coll., Oxford (Eng.) U., 1954; LL.B., Yale U., 1958; hon. degrees, Pepperdine U., 1975, Washington U., 1977, Mills Coll., 1977, Lake Forest Coll., 1978, Williams Coll., 1981. Bar: Calif. 1959, U.S. Supreme Ct. 1965. Asst. U.S. atty. civil div. Los Angeles, 1958-61; partner firm Munger, Tolles, Hills & Rickershauser, Los Angeles, 1962-74, Latham, Watkins & Hills, Washington, 1978-86, Weil, Gotshal & Manges, Washington, 1986—; asst. atty. gen. civil div. Justice Dept., Washington, 1974-75; sec. HUD, 1975-77; U.S. trade rep. Exec. Office of the Pres., 1989—; dir. IBM, Corning Glass Works, Am. Airlines, Fed. Nat. Mortgage Assn., The Henley Group, Chevron Corp.; adj. prof. Sch. Law, UCLA, 1972; mem. Trilateral Commn., 1977-82, Am. Com. on East-West Accord, 1977-79, Internat. Found. for Cultural Cooperation and Devel., 1977—, Fed. Acctg. Standards Adv. Council, 1978-80; bd. dirs. Internat. Exec. Service Corps.; mem. corrections task force Los Angeles County Sub-Regional; adv. bd. Calif. Council on Criminal Justice, 1969-71; mem. standing com. discipline U.S. Dist. Ct. for Central Calif., 1970-73; mem. Adminstrv. Conf. U.S., 1972-74; mem. exec. com. law and free soc. State Bar Calif., 1973; bd. councillors U. So. Calif. Law Center, 1972-74; trustee Pomona Coll., 1974-79, U. So. Calif., Brookings Instn.; mem. at large exec. com. Yale Law Sch., 1973-78; mem. com. on Law Sch. Yale Univ. Council; Gordon Grand fellow Yale U., 1978; mem. Sloan Commn. on Govt. and Higher Edn., 1977-79; mem. advisory com. Princeton U., Woodrow Wilson Sch. of Pub. and Internat. Affairs, 1977-80; trustee Am. Productivity and Quality Ctr., 1988—. Co-author: Federal Civil Practice, 1961; co-author, editor: Antitrust Adviser, 1971, 3d edit., 1985; contbg. editor: Legal Times, 1978—; mem. editorial bd.: Nat. Law Jour, 1978—. Trustee U. So. Calif., 1977-79, Norton Simon Mus. Art, Pasadena, Calif., 1976-80, Lawyers Com. for Civil Rights under Law, 1978-84; trustee Urban Inst., 1978-80, chmn., 1983—; co-chmn. Alliance To Save Energy, 1977—; vice chmn. adv. council on legal policy Am. Enterprise Inst., 1977-84; bd. visitors, exec. com. Stanford U. Law Sch., 1978-81; bd. dirs. Am. Council for Capital Formation, 1978—; mem. adv. com. M.I.T.-Harvard U. Joint Center for Urban Studies, 1978-82. Fellow Am. Bar Found.; mem. Los Angeles Women Lawyers Assn. (pres. 1964), ABA (chmn. publs. com. antitrust sect. 1972-74, council 1974, 77-84, chmn. 1982-83), Fed. Bar Assn. (pres. Los Angeles chpt. 1963), Los Angeles County Bar Assn. (mem. fed. rules and practice com. 1963-72, chmn. issues and survey 1963-72, chmn. sub-com. revision local rules for fed. cts. 1966-72, mem. jud. qualifications com. 1971-72), Am. Bar Inst. Clubs: Yale of So. Calif. (dir. 1972-74); Yale (Washington). Office: US Trade Rep 600 17th St NW Washington DC 20506*

HILLS, PATTI LYNN, human resources specialist; b. Kennewick, Wash., Apr. 21, 1953; d. Lyle Harry and Ellene Lavonne (McGrath) Morgan; m. John Dale Hills, July 1, 1972 (div. Mar. 1983). AS, El Paso Community Coll., Colorado Springs, Colo., 1972; BS, Regis Coll., Denver, 1982; post-grad., Webster U., Kansas City, Mo., 1989—. Sec. Adams County Sch. Dist., Thornton, Colo., 1972-73; sec. Montgomery Ward & Co., Denver, 1973-77, computer operator, 1977-79, sec., 1979-83, personnel supr., 1983-84; personnel mgr. Montgomery Ward & Co., Shawnee Mission, Kans., 1984-86; govt. funds coord. Montgomery Ward & Co., Kansas City, Mo., 1986; div. tng. mgr. Montgomery Ward & Co., Kansas City, 1986-88; regional human resource mgr. KFC Nat. Mgmt. Co., Irving, Tex., 1988-90; human resource mgr. Businessland, Inc., Lenexa, Kans., 1990—; mem. adv. bd. Full Employment Coun./Pioneer Project, Kansas City, 1987-88. Big sister Big Sisters Am., Denver, 1984. Mem. Am. Soc. Quality Control, S.W. Placement Assn. Republican. Home: 10704 W 116th St Overland Park KS 66210 Office: Businessland 8273 Melrose Dr Lenexa KS 66214

HILLSON, JAN LESLIE, rheumatology educator; b. Norwich, Conn., Oct. 3, 1952; d. Joseph Stanley and Muriel Anne (Veckerelli) H.; m. David Robert Haynor, June 18, 1983; children: Samuel Joseph, Benjamin Paul. BS, Mich. State U., 1973; MS, Scripps Inst. Oceanography, 1976, Calif. Inst. Tech., 1976; MD, Stanford U., 1980. Diplomate Am. Bd. Internal Medicine, 1983. Resident in internal medicine U. Wash. Med. Ctr., Seattle, 1980-83, acting instr. medicine, 1984-85, fellow biochemistry and rheumatology, 1985-89, acting asst. prof. rheumatology, 1989—; attending physician U. Wash.; speaker in field. Contbr. sci. articles to profl. jours. NIH fellow, 1986-89, recipient Furst award, 1989. Mem. AAAS, ACLU, Am. Coll. Rheumatology, Amnesty Internat., Sigma Xi. Democrat. Home: 2446 Warren St N Seattle WA 98109 Office: U Wash Med Ctr 1400 Pacific St Seattle WA 98195

HILPERT, BRUNETTE KATHLEEN POWERS (MRS. ELMER ERNEST HILPERT), civic worker; b. Baton Rouge; d. Edward Oliver and Orvilla (Nettles) Powers; AB, La. State U., 1930, BS in Libr. Sci., 1933; postgrad. Columbia U., 1937; m. Elmer Ernest Hilpert, Aug. 1, 1938; children—Margaret Ray, Elmer Ernest II. Cataloguer, La. State U. Libr., Baton Rouge, 1930-36, La. State U. Law Sch. Libr., 1936-38; libr. Washington U. Law Sch. Libr., St. Louis, 1940-42; reference libr. Washington U. Libr., St. Louis, 1952-54. Drive capt. United Fund, St. Louis, 1956; del. White House Conf. on Edn., St. Louis, 1962; trustee John Burroughs Sch., 1959-63; bd. dirs. Grace Hill Settlement House, 1957-63, v.p., 1960-62; bd. dirs. Internat. Inst., 1964-68; bd. dirs. Neighborhood Health Ctr., 1964-67, sec., 1964; dir. Arts and Edn. Council, 1967-87; pres., dir. Women's Assn. St. Louis Symphony Soc., 1969-71; exec. com., bd. dir. St. Louis Symphony Soc., 1969—; bd. dirs. Miss. River Festival, 1969-74; dir. women's adv. bd. Continental Bank & Trust Co., 1970-77, 79-80; bd. dirs. St. Louis Inst. Music, 1971-75; bd. dirs. St. Louis String Quartet, 1971-77, pres., 1975-77; bd. dirs. Community Music Sch., 1973-75, Little Symphony Concerts Assn., 1975-78, St. Louis Conservatory and Schs. for Arts, 1975-84, Dance Concert Soc., 1977-81, Women's Aux. Bd. Bethesda Gen. Hosp., 1981—. Recipient Woman of Achievement award St. Louis Globe Democrat, 1967. Mem. Nat. Soc. Arts. and Letters (bd. dirs. 1964-65, 80-82, 87—). Delta Zeta. Republican. Presbyterian. Clubs: Wednesday (rec. sec. 1963-64), Univ. Home: 630 Francis Pl Apt 1-N Saint Louis MO 63105

HILT, DIANE ELAINE, educator; b. Gadsden, Ala., Jan. 3, 1944; d. William Edward and Adele Helen (Plasman) Frantz; m. James Hines Hilt, Mar. 13, 1968. BS, Jacksonville (Ala.) State U., 1965; MEd, Ga. State U., 1972. Cert. adminstr., supr., tchr. math, Ala., Ga. Actuarial clk. Life Ins. Co. Ala., Gadsden, 1965-66; tchr. Trinity Pvt. Sch., Columbus, Ga., 1968-69, Phenix City (Ala.) Sch. System, 1969-71; tchr. to computer resource tchr. Post Dependent Schs., Ft. Benning, Ga., 1971—, chairperson dept. math., 1973-85, coord. curriculum, 1980-84, instr. staff devel., 1985—; owner computer bus., 1984-85; active Tchr. In Space Program, NASA, 1985; sch. system rep. to survey Rand Corp., 1987; pres. Fla. Instructional Computing Conf., Orlando, 1988; speaker La. Conf. for Computer Using Educators, 1988, North Cook Ednl. Svc. Ctr., St. Charles, Ill., 1990, Ga. Tech. Conf., Columbus. Contbr. to curriculum guide, 1969. Sec. PTA, 1979-80, Columbus Community Concerts, 1983; usher Springer Theater, Columbus, 1984. Mem. NEA (del. 1978-79), Nat. Coun. Tchrs. Math. (guest speaker 1970), Profl. Assn. Ga. Educators, Benning Edn. Assn. (sec. 1973-77), Assn. for Supervision and Curriculum Devel. Methodist. Lodge: Rotary (pres. Columbus chpt. 1975-76). Home: 3301 Tewson Dr Columbus GA 31909

HILTON, ARLEEN ANTOINETTE, military officer; b. Phila., Aug. 21, 1961; d. Edward William and Arleen Antoinette (Milosek) H.; m. Justice Stanley Stewart, Mar. 24, 1984 (div. 1988); m. James P. Coates, Oct. 27, 1989. BA in Foreign Svc., Pa. State U., 1983; postgrad., U.S. Army Command & Gen. Coll., Ft. Leavenworth, Kans., 1986. Commd. 2nd lt. U.S. Army, 1983, advanced through grades to capt.; served as tactical surveillance officer and platoon leader U.S. Army, Germany, 1983-86; mgr. collection requirements U.S. Army, Ft. Bragg, NC, 1986—. Republican. Roman Catholic. Home: Haus 76, 8801 Ottenhofen Federal Republic Germany Office: 312th Spt Ctr APO New York NY 09326

HILTON, EVA MAE (EVE HILTON), banker; b. Long Beach, Calif., Jan. 19, 1950; d. Albert Martin Wennekamp and Eva Geraldine (Hughes) Wennekamp Johnson; m. Charles H. Hilton, Jr., Nov. 30, 1968 (Div. 1982). Sr. teller Bank of Hawaii, Kailua, 1969-70; asst. mgr. ops. Ariz. Bank, Tucson, 1970-79; teller Valley Nat. Bank, Salome, Ariz., 1979-80; asst. v.p., sr. project analyst Citibank (Ariz.), Phoenix, 1980—; instr. Am. Inst. Banking, Tucson, 1981. Mem. NAFE. Avocations: racquetball, water sports, reading. Home: 13233 N 25th Dr Phoenix AZ 85029 Office: Citibank (Ariz) 10888 N 19th Ave Phoenix AZ 85029

HILTZ, DAWN PAPP, children's shoe manfacturing executive; b. Norwalk, Conn., Nov. 30, 1959; d. Frank Stephen and Elizabeth Madeline (Mola) Millard; m. Ellis Andrew Hiltz, Jr., Sept. 11, 1982. Student, Norwalk State Tech. Coll., Sacred Heart U., Am. Inst. Banking. Clk. Union Trust Co., Norwalk, 1978-82; asst. mgr. Matthew's, Westport, Conn., 1982; asst. to pres. ISP, Inc., Norwalk, 1982-86; asst. to pres. Pure Water Techs., Inc., Westport, 1986-89; R&D asst. to v.p. Toddler Univ., 1989—. Vol. Norwalk Seaport Assn., 1985, 86. Mem. NAFE, South Norwalk Boat Club Aux. (sec. 1989, 90). Republican. Roman Catholic. Avocations: skiing, scuba diving, photography. Home: 92 Barlow Plain Dr Fairfield CT 06430-5102 Office: Toddler U 257 Riverside Ave Westport CT 06880

HILZENDEGER, CONNIE COLLEEN, executive secretary; b. Bismarck, N.D., Jan. 14, 1950; d. John and Bertha Beatrice (Freuer) Mertz; m. Lawrence Ben Hilzendeger, Nov. 29, 1969; children: Renee Lynn, Shannon Lee. Student, Interstate Bus. Co., 1968, Ea. Mont. Coll., part-time 1988—. Sec. Soil Conservation Svc. USDA, Bismarck, 1970-77, sec. plant protection and quarantine, 1977-78; sec. plant protection and quarantine USDA, Billings, Mont., 1978-86; field contact rep. IRS, Billings, 1986-90; exec. sec. Western area power adminstrn. U.S. Dept. Energy, Billings, 1990—. Vol. Girl Scouts U.S, Bismarck and Billings, 1976-81, Yellowstone County 4-H Club, Billings, 1980-86; Sunday sch. tchr. Luth. Ch. of Good Shepherd, Billings, 1978-86. Mem. NAFE, Beta Sigma Phi (fellow). Home: 1008 Maywood Dr Billings MT 59102

HIMEL, ELIZABETH GRACE, mechanical artist; b. Thibodaux, La., Mar. 16, 1960; d. Warren Joseph and Lucille (Miller) H. Student, Nicholls State U., Thibodaux, 1980. Printer Nicholls State U., 1978-79, Thibodaux Printing and Pub., 1981-84; graphic artist Foxworth-Galbraith, Dallas, 1984-85; typesetter Typeworks of Dallas, 1985-87; pvt. practice typesetting and graphic art Dallas, 1987-88; typsetter, mech. artist Neiman Marcus, Dallas, 1989—. Active in U.S.-China Friendship Assn., Dallas, 1986-87; vol. The Sci. Place, Dallas, 1986; exec. mem. The 500, Inc., Dallas, 1987-89; mem. Dallas Mus. Art, 1986—, Met. Mus. Art, 1985—. Mem. NOW, Compugraphic Integrator and Modular Composition System Application Group Exch., Smithsonian Assocs. Office: Neiman Marcus 1618 Main St Dallas TX 75201

HIMELSTEIN, PEGGY DONN, marriage and family therapist; b. Beacon, N.Y., Sept. 21, 1932; d. Leon and Sophie Donn; m. Philip Himelstein, June 1, 1952; children: Steven, Carol, Roger. BS, U. Tex., 1954; MA, U. Tex., El Paso, 1971; PhD, Fla. Inst. Tech., 1983. Lic. counselor, Tex.; cert. psychologist, Tex. Dir. Ednl. Devel. Ctr., El Paso, 1971-75; marriage and family therapist El Paso Psychiat. Clinic, 1976-78; instr. in psychology El Paso Community Coll., 1979-82; psychology intern El Paso Ctr. for Mental Health/Mental Retardation Svcs., 1981-82; marriage and family therapist Jewish Family & Children's Svcs., El Paso, 1986-88; pvt. practice El Paso, 1978—. Mem. Am. Psychol. Assn., Am. Assn. Marriage and Family Therapy (clin.), Soc. for Clin. and Exptl. Hypnosis, El Paso Psychol. Assn. (pres. 1981-82), El Paso Assn. for Marriage and Family Therapy (pres. 1989-90), Tex. Psychol. Assn., Southwestern Psychol. Assn. Home: 331 Rainbow Circle El Paso TX 79912 Office: 1810 Murchison Dr Ste 308 El Paso TX 79902

HIMES, JANE ANN, public relations executive; b. Johnstown, Pa., June 20, 1923; d. Joseph George and Anna (Berg) Dupin; m. William E. Himes, Dec. 29, 1943 (div. Mar. 1977); children: Douglas D., Gregory T. Student, Memphis State U., 1977-86. Sec. Nat. Radiator Co., Johnstown, 1940-44; student loan officer 1st Nat. Bank Mercer County, Sharon, Pa., 1970-76; adminstrv. asst. trust div. Nat. Bank Commerce, Memphis, 1976-78; adminstrv. asst. to chmn. bd. Buckman Labs. Internat., Inc., Memphis, 1978-79, dir. pub. rels., 1979—, editor Bu-Lines/By-Lines, 1980—; mem. profl. adv. bd. Sch. Journalism, Memphis State U., 1986—. Mem. adv. bd. Adopt-A-Sch., Memphis, 1983-86, 88—; chmn. bd. dirs. Crime Stoppers Memphis, 1987-88, 89—; mem. adv. bd. arts in schs. Memphis Arts Coun., 1989—; v.p. bd. dirs. Home Health Care Found., Memphis, 1989—; bd. dirs. communications chmn. Tenn. chpt. Am. Heart Assn., Memphis and Nashville; elder Prsbyn. Ch., Memphis; mem. adv. bd. Porter Leath Children's Ctr. Recipient Vol. of Yr. award Am. Heart Assn., Memphis, 1985. Mem. Pub. Rels. Soc. Am. (bd. dirs. Memphis 1985—, pres. 1988, Profl. of Yr. award 1988, nat. presdl. citation 1988), Optimists, Rotary. Republican. Office: Buckman Labs Internat Inc 1256 N McLean Memphis TN 38108

HIMMELBAUER, LINDA DIANNE, water quality analyst; b. Inglewood, Calif., Jan. 21, 1965; d. John Emmrich and Velma Linda (Petrecue) H. Student in chemistry, Met. State Coll., Denver, 1986-90. Cert. water quality analyst, Colo. Chem. analyst Environ. Sci. and Engring., Englewood, Colo., 1987-88; water quality analyst City of Westminster, Col., 1988—; part time instr. Red Rocks (Colo.) Community Coll., 1990—. Mem. Am. Chem. Soc., Rocky Mt. Water Quality Analyst Cert. Coun. (test com.), Colo. Water Quality Analyst Assn. Office: Big Dry Creek City of Westminster 13150 N Huron St Westminster CO 80234

HIMMELSTEIN, CAROLE SHAPIRO, marketing executive; b. Phila.; m. Stephen A. Himmelstein, Apr. 17, 1962; children: Hope S., Scott A., Stuart K. BA in Chemistry, Trenton State Coll., 1979; MS in Biomed. Engring., Drexel U., 1982. Asst. product mgr. Air-Shields Vickers, Hatboro, Pa., 1984-86, product mgr., 1986-89; product mgr. Edward Weck, Inc., A Squibb Co., Princeton, N.J., 1989—. Trustee Deborah Heart and Lung Ctr. Found. and Rsch. Inst., Browns Mills, N.J., 1982-86, 88—; chmn. bd. trustees Deborah Rsch. Inst., 1984-86; regional chmn. Deborah Hosp. Found. Mem. Am. Mktg. Assn., Phila. Assn. Med. Instrumentation.

HIMMS-HAGEN, JEAN MARGARET, biochemist; b. Oxford, Eng., Dec. 18, 1933; d. Frederick Hubert and Margaret Mary (Deadman) H.; m. Paul Hagen, Sept. 29, 1956; children: Anna, Nina. B.Sc., U. London, 1955; Ph.D., Oxford U., 1958. Postdoctoral fellow Harvard U., 1958-59; asst. prof. physiology U. Man., 1959-64; assoc. prof. biochemistry Queen's U., 1964-67; assoc. prof. biochemistry U. Ottawa, 1967-71, prof., 1971—, acting chmn. dept., 1975-77, 87, chmn. dept., 1977-82. Assoc. editor Can. Jour. Biochemistry, 1967-71, Can. Jour. Physiology & Pharmacology, 1971-75, Am. Jour. Physiology, 1979-88; mem. editorial bd. Proceedings Experimental Biology & Medicine, 1984-90; council mem. Med. Research Council of Can., 1970-75 (exec. 1970-73); mem. five grants coms. Med. Research Council since 1969; chmn. metabolism grants com., 1972-75; mem. Can. Council Animal Care, 1970-78; author numerous research publs. and sci. rev. articles (mostly book chpts.). Recipient research grants Med. Research Council, 1960—, career award, 1968-77, Bond award Am. Oil Chemists Soc., 1972. Fellow Royal Soc. Can.; mem. Canadian Biochem. Soc. (Ayerst award 1973), Am. Soc. Pharmacology and Exptl. Therapeutics, Am. Inst. Nutrition, Biochem. Soc. U.K. Home: 233 Tudor Pl, Ottawa, ON Canada K1L 7Y1 Office: U Ottawa Dept Biochemistry, 451 Smyth Rd, Ottawa, ON Canada K1H 8M5

HINCHEY, PATRICIA ANN, health care executive; b. Fall River, Mass., Nov. 16, 1952; d. Paul Thomas and Dorothy Teresa (Lyons) Hinchey; m. William Joseph Wooldridge, Apr. 7, 1984; stepchildren: Teresa, Sandra, Christina. BA in secondary Edn./English, R.I. Coll., 1976; postgrad., U. New Haven, 1984. Prog. rep. Hosp. Assn. R.I., Providence, 1976-79; group purchasing coordinator Conn. Hosp. Assn., Wallingford, 1979-80; dir. group purchasing prog. Conn. Hosp. Assn., 1980-83; assoc. v.p. shared svcs. home health div. MedEcon Svcs., Inc., Louisville, 1983-84; dir. group progs. MedEcon Svcs., Inc., 1985-87, group v.p., 1987-90, exec. v.p., 1990—; bd. dirs. Group Purchasing Group, treas., 1987; bd. dirs. MedEcon. Mem. Am. Soc. Hosp. Pharmacists, Am. Soc. Hosp. Materials Mgmt.

HINCHLIFFE, GWENDOLYN ANN, family service organization official; b. Bristol, Pa., June 26, 1948; d. William and Jane Marie (McElroy) H. AA, Bucks County Community Coll., 1968. Office worker Prudential Ins. Co., Langhorne, Pa., 1968-69; asst. travel mgr. Auto Club Cen. N.J., Trenton, 1969-72; asst. compaid coordinator comp. engring. div. Rohm & Haas Co., Bristol, 1974-82; electronics engring. aide Chessell Corp., Newtown, Pa., 1983-84; communications coordinator G.R. Murray Ins., Princeton, N.J., 1985-87; adminstrv. mgr. S.D. Catalano, Inc., Langhorne, 1988-89; office mgr. Jewish Family Svc. Delaware Valley, Ewing, N.J., 1989—. Mem. Nat. Assn. Female Execs., Bucks County Community Coll. Alumni Assn., Nat. Geographic Soc. Democrat. Roman Catholic. Home: 2809 Bath Rd Bristol PA 19007 Office: Jewish Family Svc Delaware Valley 51 Walter St Ewing NJ 08628

HINCKLEY, DAWN MARGARET, state government investigator; b. Maywood, Calif., Oct. 31, 1949; d. William Lovejoy and Margaret Hinckley; divorced; children: Robert Sterling, Heather Audrey. AA in Real Estate, Cerritos (Calif.) Coll.; AA in Criminal Justice, Calif. State U., Long Beach, 1984; BA in Sociology; postgrad. in law, Pacific Coast U. Assoc. Bell (Calif.) Realty Co., 1972-83; dep. commr. Calif. Dept. Real Estate, Los Angeles, 1984—; owner apt. bldg. Republican. Roman Catholic. Clubs: Citizens for Downey, Exec. Women, Corvette U.S.A.

HINDE, BOBBIE TORLA, city official, consultant; b. San Diego, May 24, 1946; d. Charles Carroll and Dazel Pauline (Russell) H.; m. Vincent O. Akhimie, Mar. 10, 1972; children: Patricia O., Vincent O. II. BA, U. Wash., 1968. Lic. realtor. Dir. community planning and mgmt. City of Ann Arbor, Mich., 1974-77, asst. city adminstr., 1974-77; dir. econ. devel. City of Louisville, 1977-80, asst. cabinet dir., community devel., 1980-84; exec. dir. Louisville Indsl. Devel. Authority, 1979-83; dir. planning and econ. devel. City of Bellingham, Wash., 1984-85; exec. dir. C. of C. Greater Fed. Way, Wash., 1985-87; dir. code adminstrn. Town of New Canaan, Conn., 1987-90; sr. assoc. Akhimie and Kask, Inc., Engrs., Planners & Econs., Seattle, 1985—. Founding mem. bd. dirs. Louisville Econ. Devel. Corp., Louisville, 1978. Mem. Bldg. Ofcls. and Code Adminstrs. (cert. bldg. ofcl.), Internat. City Mgmt. Assn. (host com. 1982), New Canaan C. of C. (bd. dirs. 1988—), Lions (speaker, chmn. 1988—). Episcopalian. Home: One Strawberry Hill #14B Stamford CT 06902

HINDLE, PAULA ALICE, nurse; b. Cambridge, Mass., Feb. 26, 1952; d. Edward Adam and Geraldine Ann (Donahue) H. BS in Nursing, Fitchburg State Coll., 1974; MS in Nursing, Duke U., 1980; MBA, Simmons Coll., 1988. Staff nurse Mt. Auburn Hosp., Cambridge, Mass., 1974-75; staff nurse U. Hosp., Boston, 1975-77, head nurse, 1977-79; staff nurse Duke U. Med. Ctr., Durham, N.C., 1979-80, clin. instr., 1980-81, area mgr., 1981; nurse leader, clin. dir. New Eng. Med. Ctr., Boston, 1981-87; cons. Ctr. for Nursing Case Mgmt., Boston, 1984-87; v.p. nursing Faulkner Hosp., Boston, 1987—. Active Am. Heart Assn. Mem. Am. Assn. Critical Care Nurses, Mass. Orgn. Nurse Execs. (legis. com.), Am. Orgn. Nurse Execs. (fin. com.), Statewide Women's Legislative Network, Sigma Theta Tau. Democrat. Roman Catholic. Home: 147 Kelton St Apt 507 Brighton MA 02134 Office: Faulkner Hosp Allandale at Centre St Boston MA 02130

HINDMAN, LESLIE SUSAN, auctioneer; b. Hinsdale, Ill., Dec. 1, 1954; d. Don J. and Patricia (de Forest) H. Student, Pine Manor Coll., 1972-74, U. Paris, 1974-75, Ind. U., 1975-76. Mgr. Sotheby Parke Bernet, Chgo., 1978-82; pres. Leslie Hindman Auctioneers, Chgo., 1982—, Salvage One Archtl. Artifacts, Chgo., 1986—; co-owner Chgo. Antiques Ctr., 1990—. Mem. Com. of 200, Internat. Women's Forum, Young Pres's. Orgn., Arts Club Chgo. Club: Women's Athletic (Chgo.) (bd. dirs. 1988—). Home: 1440 N Lake Shore Dr Chicago IL 60610 Office: Leslie Hindman Auctioneers 215 W Ohio Chicago IL 60610

HINDS, ANN M., programmer, systems analyst; b. Denver, Oct. 4, 1949; m. Robert Hinds, Aug. 26, 1976; 1 child, Michelle. BBA/Bus. Info. Systems with honors, Eastern N.Mex. U., 1982. Sr. programmer, analyst CrediCard Systems Inc., Amarillo, Tex.; programmer, analyst AMI Investment Corp., Amarillo; programmer Pioneer Corp., Amarillo; programmer analyst Amarillo Hardware Co. Advisor student chpt. Eastern N.Mex. Univ., 1983-84, chmn. fund raising, social chmn., 1989-90. Mem. DPMA. Home: 4918 Princeton Amarillo TX 79109 Office: Amarillo Hardware Co PO Box 1891 Amarillo TX 79172

HINDS, BARBARA MARIE, corporate secretary; b. Lynwood, Calif., Jan. 17, 1949; d. Tildo and Louise Maxine (Duff) Bartoletti; m. Hubert H. Hinds Jr., Apr. 16, 1976 (div. June 1989). Grad. high sch., South Gate, Calif. Various positions Atlantic Richfield Co., L.A., 1969-77, asst. corp. sec., 1977—. Mem. Am. Soc. Corp. Secs. Republican. Office: Atlantic Richfield Co 515 S Flower St Rm 4589 Los Angeles CA 90071

HINE, DARLENE CLARK, history educator, administrator; b. Morley, Mo., Feb. 7, 1947; d. Levester and Lottie May (Thompson) Clark; m. William C. Hine, Aug. 21, 1970 (div. 1975); m. Johnny Earl Brown, July 25, 1981 (div. Aug. 1986); 1 child, Robbie Davine. BA in Am. History, Roosevelt U., 1968; MA, Kent State U., 1970, PhD in Afro-Am. History, 1975. Teaching asst. Kent State U., Ohio, 1968-71; asst. prof. history, coordinator Black studies, S.C. State Coll., Orangeburg, 1972-74; asst. prof. Purdue U., West Lafayette, Ind., 1974-79, assoc. prof., 1980—, interim dir. African Studies and Research Ctr., 1978-79, vice provost, 1981-86; John A. Hannah Prof. History, Mich. State U., East Lansing, 1986—; mem. Ind. Com. for Humanities, 1983-85; invited lectr. colls. and univs. including Harvard U., 1975, U. Ill., Chgo., 1981, St. Olaf Coll., 1981, Ind. U., 1982, U. Tex., Austin, 1983, So. Meth. U., 1983; grant rev. panelist NEH, 1979-80, Ford Found., NRC, 1980, 81, 82. Author: Black Victory, 1979, When the Truth is Told: A History of Black Women's Culture and Community in Indiana, 1875-1950, 1981, Black Women in the Nursing Profession: A Documentary History, 1984, Black Women in White: Racial Conflict and Cooperation in the Nursing Profession 1890-1950, 1989; contbr. chpts. to books, articles to publs., book revs. to jours. Mem. Ind. Com. for Humanities, Indpls., 1982—. Alumni fellow Kent State U., 1971-72, Nat. Humanities Ctr. fellow, 1986, Am. Council Learned Socs. fellow, 1986; research awardee Africana Studies and Research Ctr., 1975, 78; faculty devel. grantee Purdue U., 1978-79; research awardee Rockefeller Archive Ctr., 1978; Rockefeller Found. fellow for minority group scholars, 1980; research grantee Eleanor Roosevelt Inst., 1980-81; project grantee Fund for Improvement of Post-Secondary Edn., 1980-82; NEH grantee, 1982-83; 1st place essay award Degolyer Inst., 1982, Disting. Alumni award Roosevelt U., 1988. Mem. Assn. for Study of Negro Life and History (exec. council 1979, 2d v.p. 1985-88), Orgn. Am. Historians, So. Hist. Assn., So. Assn. Women Historians (v.p. 1983—), Am. Hist. Assn., Assn. Black Women Historians, Phi Alpha Theta. Democrat. Baptist. Home: 2357 Burcham Dr East Lansing MI 48823 Office: Mich State U Dept History East Lansing MI 48824-1036

HINEMAN, NANCY LEE, protective services official; b. West Chester, Pa., Mar. 23, 1951; d. Leon Joseph and Nancy Josephine (Bruno) Mascaro; 1 child, Marty Hineman. Grad. high sch., Concordville, Pa. Lic. cosmetologist, Del. and Pa.; pvt. detective, Pa.; cert. in sci. crime detection, Pa. Pvt. practice cosmetology Wilmington, Del. and Media, Pa., 1969-74; detective criminal investigation div. Delaware County Dist. Atty., Media, Pa., 1975-78; polygraphist Criminal Investigation div. Delaware County, 1975-78; v.p., co-owner Urella's Detective Bur., Media, 1978—. Recipient Spl. Commendation award U.S. Monetary War Coll., San Diego, 1988. Mem. NAFE, Pa. Polygraph Assn., Nat. Detective Assn. Republican. Roman Catholic. Office: Urella's Detective Bur 160 Paxon Hollow Rd Media PA 19063

HINER, LESLIE DAVIS, business owner, lawyer; b. Canton, Ohio, Sept. 30, 1957; d. Wendell Hughes and Margaret Alvina (Klebaum) Davis; m. Ward Christopher Hiner, July 23, 1983; children: Elaine Margaret, Travis Davis. BA, Coll. of Wooster, Ohio, 1980; JD, U. Akron, Ohio, 1985. Bar: In. 1985. Intern Legis. Svcs. Agy., Indpls., 1984; assoc. Ecklund, Frutkin & Grant, Indpls., 1985-87; v.p. Hiner Van & Storage, Kokomo, Ind., 1987—; mem. adj. faculty U. Indpls., 1986-87. Alto Indpls. Symphonic Choir, 1984-86; allocations coun. United Way, Kokomo, 1987—, vice chair, 1988-89, chairperson 1989—, bd. dirs., 1989—, exec. com., 1989—; atty. Legal Aid Kokomo, 1987-89; bd. dirs. Montessori Children's House, Kokomo, 1989—; bd. dirs., vice chairperson Lantern Hills Conservancy Dist. 1986-87; co-chairperson Steve Johnson for State Senate Re-election Campaign, 1990—. Mem. Ind. Bar Assn. (pub. rels. com. 1986-89, corp. counsel sect. 1988—), Howard County Bar Assn., Altrusa, Kokomo C. of C. (legis. affairs com. 1987—, chairperson 1989—, bd. dirs. 1990—, transp. com. 1990—), Phi Alpha Delta. Republican. Lutheran. Office: Hiner Van & Storage 1106 S Dixon Rd Kokomo IN 46902

HINERFELD, RUTH J., civic organization executive; b. Boston, Sept. 18, 1930; m. Norman Hinerfeld, children: Lee, Thomas, Joshua. A.B., Vassar Coll., 1951; grad., Program in Bus. Adminstrn., Harvard-Radcliffe Coll., 1952. With LWV, 1954—, UN observer, 1969-72, chairperson internat. relations com., 1972-76, 1st v.p. in charge legis. activities, 1976-78, pres., 1978-82; dir. LWV Overseas Edn. Fund., 1975-76, trustee, 1975-86; chairperson LWV Edn. Fund, 1978-82; mem. White House Adv. Com. for Trade Negotiations, 1975-82; sec. UN Assn. of U.S., 1975-78, vice chmn., 1983—, bd. govs., bd. dirs., 1975—; mem. econ. policy coun.; vice chair Overseas Devel. Coun.; mem. U.S. del. auspices of Nat. Com. on U.S.-China Relations and Chinese People's Inst. Fgn. Affairs, 1978. Mem. coun. Nat. Mcpl. League, 1977-80, 83-86. del.-at-large Internat. Women's Year Conf., Houston, 1977; mem. exec. com. Leadership Conf. on Civil Rights, 1978-82; trustee Citizens Research Found., 1978—; mem. Nat. Petroleum Coun., 1979-82; mem. U.S. del. to World Conf. on UN Decade for Women, 1980; mem. adv. com. Nat. Inst. for Citizen Edn. in the Law, 1981—; mem. North South Roundtable, 1978-88; mem. nat. gov. bd. Common Cause, 1984-90; vice chmn. U.S. com. UNICEF, 1986-90, treas., 1990—; mem. vis. com. Harvard U. Bus. Sch., 1984-90; mem. Bretton Woods Com. Recipient Disting. Citizen award Nat. Mcpl. League, 1978; Outstanding Mother award Nat. Mother's Day Com., 1981; Aspen Inst. Presdl. fellow, 1981. Mem. Council on Fgn. Relations, Phi Beta Kappa. Office: 11 Oak Ln Larchmont NY 10538

HINES, DAISY MARIE, writer; b. Hanna City, Ill., Dec. 31, 1913; d. Frank W. and Edith Earl (Folger) Humphrey; m. Herbert Waldo Hines, Jr., Dec. 20, 1958; children—Grace Consuelo, Ruby Marie. Student Western Ill. U., 1955-57, So. Ill. U., 1956. Mem. staff advt. dept. Macomb Daily Jour. (Ill.), 1943-47; writer, exec., dir., promoter McDonough County Tb Assn., 1949-58; sec. U.S. Dept. Agr., Macomb, 1955-58; researcher, writer 1st Nat. Bank, Springfield, 1963; adminstrv. asst. to state legislator, 1964-69; newspaper columnist, free-lance writer, mem. survey staff Prairie Farmer Pub. Co., Oak Brook, Ill., 1965-79, Successful Farming, Des Moines, 1982; Springfield corr. Automotive News. Active Altar Soc. Blessed Sacrament Cath. Ch., Springfield; chmn. Illiopolis unit Univ. Ill. Home Extension; pub. relations dir. Springfield chpt. Am. Cancer Soc., 1961-68; 2d v.p. Ill. Conf. Tb Workers, 1952-53; mem. Sangamon County Farm Bur., St. John's Hosp. Auxiliary. Mem. Nat. League Am. Pen Women (pres. Springfield chpt. 1972-73, sec. Ill. br. 1974), Western Ill. U. Alumni Council (sec.; Disting. Alumni award 1982; com. mem. Coll. Applied Scis. Agr. rep. Alumni Council), Ill. Press Assn. USAF Air Def. Team (hon. life), Ill. Women for Agr., Civil War Round Table, Sangamon County Hist. Soc. Club: Republican Women's. Address: 2504 S Holmes Ave Springfield IL 62704

HINES, JUDITH DUNBAR, chef, culinary consultant; b. Indpls., Mar. 25, 1947; d. Andrew Marvin and Hilda (Michel) Dunbar; (div. 1976). Student, U. Ill., 1965-67; AS, Roosevelt U., 1969, Dumas Pere Sch. for Chefs, 1977. Cert. cooking tchr., Ill., Calif. Showrm. mgr. Chromcraft Corp., Chgo., 1974-79, 83; prodn. mgr. Taico Design, Chgo., 1976-79; owner, mgr. What's Cookin Cookware Store & Sch., Brownwood, Tex., 1979-81; promotions and tng. mgr. Joy of Cooking, Manchester, N.H., 1981-83; owner, events dir. Judith Dunbar Hines Culinary Svcs., Chgo., 1983—; owner Demo-Pros, Ltd., Chgo., 1984—, Yan Can Internat. Cooking Sch., 1989—; culinary events dir. Carson Pirie Scott, Chgo., 1985-89; cons., trainer Lentrade, Houston, 1983—. Editor column Lincoln Park News, 1983-85. Named Top Tchr. of Chgo. Chgo. Tribune, 1988. Mem. Women's Food Svc. Network (bd. dirs.), Les Dames D'Escoffier Chgo., Internat. Assn. Cooking Profls. (bd. dirs. 1985-87), Cooking Advancement Rsch. and Edn. Found. (auction chmn. 1987-88, 89-90). Home: 840 Sea Spray Foster City CA 94404 Office: Yan Can Internat Cooking 1064-G Shell Foster City CA 94404

HINES, LINDA MARIE, educational and community service agency executive; b. Denver, Dec. 20, 1940; d. Laurence Gerald and Betty Marie (Fish) Arnold; m. Donald Merrill Hines, June 10, 1961; children: Warren Donald, Eric Daniel, Alan Bennett. BA summa cum laude, Lewis & Clark Coll., 1962; MA, Ind. U., 1967. Tchr. Eisenhower High Sch., Yakima, Wash., 1962-65; teaching assoc. Ind. U., Bloomington, 1965-67; rsch. assoc. Wash. State U., Pullman, 1973-74, editor Coll. Vet. Med., 1974-76, dir. Info. & Rsch. Svcs., 1977-79, dir. Vet. Pub. Rels. & Devel., 1979-83; exec. dir. The Delta Soc., Renton, Wash., 1983—; cons. sci. & tech. com. Holden Village, Chelan, Wash., 1978-83; planning com. mem. NIH Workshop, Bethesda, Md., 1987. Co-author: Guidelines: Animals in Nursing Homes, 1983; co-editor: Phi Kappa Phi jour., 1986. Co-founder Fish Vols., Pullman, 1970-72; bd. dirs. Elderhostel Planning Com., Pullman, 1977-79, N.Am. Riding for Handicapped, Denver, 1980-81; cons. Seattle Housing Authority-Pets, 1984; co-founder People-Pet Partnership, Pullman, 1979-83; sec. Internat. Assn. Human-Animal Interaction Orgns., 1989—; mem. social concerns com. Luth. Ch. Recipient Recognition award Seattle Kennel Club, 1988; grantee SAFECO, 1982, Charles Engelhard Found., 1983-90. Mem. Am. Soc. Assn. Execs., AAUW, Wash. Soc. Assn. Execs., Am. Luth. Ch. Women (pres., libr.), Book Club, Issaquah Alpa Trail Club. Office: The Delta Soc 321 Burnett Ave S 3d Fl Renton WA 98055

HINES, MARION LOUISE See DEXHEIMER, MARION LOUISE

HINES, MARY JANE, teacher; b. Reading, Pa., May 14, 1934; d. Charles Henry and Anna Margaret (Mattingly) Rowe; m. Ronald Calvin Hines, Aug. 19, 1961. BS magna cum laude, Bob Jones U., 1957; MA, Saginaw (Mich.) Valley Coll., 1976. Cert. elem. tchr., Fla., Mich. Sec. Orange County Bank, Paoli, Ind., 1952-53; tchr. Pensacola (Fla.) Christian Sch., 1957-61, 63-64; substitute tchr. Hazel Park (Mich) Schs., 1961-63; tchr. Warren (Mich.) Consol. Schs., 1964—. Mem. Detroit Zool. Soc., Royal Oak, 1987—. Bob Jones U. scholar, 1957. Mem. NEA, ASCPA, Mich. Edn. Assn., Warren Edn. Assn., Nat. Wildlife Fedn., World Wildlife Fund, Wilderness Soc., Sierra Club, Greenpeace, Natural Resources Def. Coun., Nat. Arbor Day Found., Nat. Parks and Conservation Assn., Environ. Def. Fund, African Wildlife Found., People for Ethical Treatment of Animals. Baptist. Office: Warner Elem Sch 2791 Koper Sterling Heights MI 48310

HINES, PATRICIA, social worker; b. Watertown, N.Y., Nov. 4, 1947; d. Arthur and Bella (O'Neil) Hines; BS, SUNY, Oswego, 1969; MSW, SUNY, Buffalo, 1975; M in Pub. Adminstrn., Fairleigh Dickinson U., 1982. Supr. social work Ocean County Bd. Social Services, Toms River, N.J., 1973-77, adminstrv. supr. social work, 1977-83, dep. dir., 1983—; social work cons. Medictr. and Rainbow Day Care, Lakewood, N.J., 1975—, Ocean County Vis. Homemaker Service, Inc., Toms River, 1975-80, Community Meml. Hosp., Toms River, 1978-79, Medictr., Summit, Manchester Manor, Green Acres Manor, Laurelton Village, Belle Reve, Country Manor, Bartley Manor Convalescent Ctr., Ocean Convalescent Ctr., Barnegat Nursing Facility, Burnt Tavern Convalescent Ctr., Jackson Health Care Ctr., Harrogate Life Care Community, Green Acres Manor, Whiting Healthcare, Crestwood Manor Life Care; prin. in Sr. Care Planning Assocs.; instr. social work Georgian Court Coll., Lakewood, 1975—. Chmn. Ocean County Title XX Coalition, 1977-82; bd. dirs. Ocean County Family Planning Program, Toms River, 1969-73, Mental Health Bd., 1983-84; mem. exec. bd. United Way, 1983-90; mem. Aging Network Service. Cert., Dr. Thomas Gordon Parent Effectiveness Trainer. Mem. Acad. Cert. Social Workers, Nat. Assn. Social Workers (nat. register clin. social workers). Home: 13 Bay Harbor Blvd Brick NJ 08723 Office: 1027 Hooper Ave Toms River NJ 08753

HINES, RUTH ANN, municipal clerk; b. Sandusky, Mich., July 7, 1958; d. Robert Richard and June Ann (Duncan) Hazen; children: Eric Richard, Aaron Raymond, Michelle Renee. AAS, Grand Rapids Bapt. Coll., Mich., 1980. From dep. clk. to office coord. Charter Twp. of Springfield, Davisburg, Mich., 1978-86, trustee, 1986-88; clk., treas. Village of Holly, Mich., 1988—; recording sec. Charter Twp. of Springfield, 1978—. Mem. Internat. Inst. Mcpl. Clks., Mich. Mcpl. Clks. Assn., Oakland County Clks. Assn., Oakland County Treas. Assn., Mich. Mcpl. Treas. Assn. Baptist. Office: Village of Holly 202 S Saginaw Holly MI 48442

HINES, VONCILE, special education educator; b. Detroit, Dec. 1, 1945; d. Raymond and Cleo (Smith) H. AA, Highland Park Community Coll., 1967; BEd, Wayne State U., 1971, MEd, 1975; MA, U. Detroit, 1978. Tchr. primary unit Detroit Bd. Edn., 1971-79, spl. educator, 1979—; tchr. trainee Feuerstein's Instrumental Enrichment, 1988—; cons. Queen's Community Workers, Detroit, 1977—; evaluator Teen Profl. Parenting Project, New Detroit Inc., 1986-87; guest educator, critic "Express Yourself", Sta. WQBH 1400 AM, 1989. Author: I Chose Planet Earth, 1988; inventor in field. Recipient Cert. of Merit State of Mich., 1978, 88, Cert. Appreciation Queen's Community Workers, 1980, Award of Recognition Detroit City Council, 1984. Mem. Assn. for Children and Adults with Learning Disabilities (cert. of appreciation 1988), Assn. Supervision and Curriculum Devel., Nat. Thinking Skills Network, NAFE, Nat. Council Negro Women (presenter 1987), Met. Detroit Alliance of Black Sch. Educators. Democrat. Office: Ednl Co-Creations PO Box 03869 Detroit MI 48203

HINES, YVONNE MARIA, grain company executive; b. Bklyn., July 8, 1953; d. Thomas William and Phyllis Sarah (Scoon) H.; 1 child, Alanna Therese. Diploma high sch., Middle Village, N.Y., 1971. Acctg. sec. Knight, Vale & Gregory, Tacoma, 1972-74; legal sec. Eisenhower, Carlson, Newlands, Reha, Elliott & Henriot, Tacoma, 1974-76; rsch. asst. Continental Grain Co., N.Y.C., 1976-77, adminstrv. asst., 1977-80; merchandiser Continental Grain Co., Taylorville, Ill., 1980-81; gen. mgr. Continental Grain Co., Tupelo, Miss., 1981—. Mem. agr. com. Community Devel. Found., Tupelo, 1981—; vol. Shelter and Assistance in Family Emergencies, Inc. Named Vol. of the Yr., Shelter and Assistance in Family Emergencies. Mem. NAFE, Miss. Feed & Grain Assn. (bd. dirs. 1987—, pres. 1990), Nat. Grain & Feed Assn. (bd. dirs. 1987—). Home: 105 Ann Circle Tupelo MS 38801 Office: Continental Grain Co 400 S Broadway Tupelo MS 38801

HINKELMAN, RUTH AMIDON, insurance company executive; b. Streator, Ill., June 4, 1949; d. Olin Arthur and Marjorie Annabeth (Wright) Amidon; m. Allen Joseph Hinkelman, Jr., Oct. 28, 1972; children: Anne Elizabeth, Allen Joseph III. AB in Econs., U. Ill., 1971. Underwriter Kemper Ins. Group, Chgo., 1971-75; acct. exec. Near North Ins. Agy., Chgo., 1975-76; underwriter Gen. Reinsurance Corp., Chgo., 1976-78, asst. sec., 1978-79, asst. v.p., 1979-83, 2nd v.p., 1983-87, v.p., 1987—. Home: 133 Linden Ave Wilmette IL 60091 Office: Gen Reinsurance Corp 300 S Riverside Plaza 2000N Chicago IL 60606

HINKFUSS, ROSEMARY, legislator; b. Lima, Ohio, Sept. 30, 1931; d. William Adrian and Marie Catherine (Steinemann) Walsh; m. William Hinkfuss; children: Eileen, Timothy, Paul, Mary, Anne, Christopher. BS, Cardinal Stritch Coll., 1954; postgrad., Cath. U., Washington, U. Wis., Green Bay, St. Norbert Coll. Alderperson Green Bay City Council, 1974-82; supr. Brown County Bd., Green Bay, 1974-82; tchr. elem. and middle schs. Ohio, Md. and Wis.; assessor Wis. Dept. Industry, Labor, Human Relations, Greenbay; legislator Wis. State Assembly, Madison. Bd. dirs. Green Bay Packers, Inc., 1980—, Premontre High Sch., Green Bay, 1983—; mem. United Way Human Svcs. Found., Green Bay, 1984—; dir. Girl Scouts of Am., Green Bay, 1984—; mem. Dem. Party Wis. Named Woman of Yr. Green Bay-DePere Profl. Women's Club, 1980; recipient First Place Essay award Am. Legion, Community Svc. award Cardinal Stritch Coll., 1987. Roman Catholic. Office: Wis State Assembly State Capitol Madison WI 53702

HINKLE, BETTY RUTH, educational administrator; b. Atchison Kans., Mar. 18, 1930; d. Arch W. and Ruth (Baker) Hunt; m. Charles L. Hinkle, Dec. 25, 1950 (div.); children—Karl, Eric. B.A., U. Corpus Christi, 1950; M.S., Baylor U., 1956; M.A., U. North Colo., 1972, Ed.D., 1979. Cert. tchr. Tex., 1950, Mass., 1961, Colo., 1966; cert. adminstr., Colo., 1976. Mem. faculty Alice (Tex.) Independent Sch. Dist., 1950, Waco (Tex.) Ind. Sch. Dist., 1951-52, 1953-58; Hawaii Pub. Schs., Oahu, 1952-53, Newton Pub. Schs., Newtonville, Mass., 1962-63; Colorado Springs (Colo.) Pub. Schs., 1966-78; cons., exec. dir. spl. projects unit Colo. State Dept. Edn., Denver, 1978—; mem. technology com. Colorado Dept. Edn.; alt. foreman Denver Grand Jury, 1983. Recipient Dept. of Edn. Specialists award Colo. Assn. Sch. Execs., 1979, Employee Yr. award Colo. Dept. Edn., 1986, Fed. Ednl. Program Adminstrv. Coun. Ann. award for Distinctive Svc. to Colo. Children, 1988. Mem. Am. Assn. School Adminstrs, Colo. Assn. Sch. Execs (coordinating council, 1976-79, v.p. dept. of edn. specialists 1974-75, pres. 1975-76), Assn. for Supervision and Curriculum Devel., Phi Delta Kappa. Republican. Home: 550 E 12th Ave Apt 903 Denver CO 80203 Office: Colo Dept Edn 201 E Colfax Denver CO 80203

HINKLE, MURIEL RUTH NELSON, naval warfare analysis company executive; b. Bayonne, N.J., Mar. 17, 1929; d. Andrew and Florence Martha Ida (Nuber) Nelson; student Md. Coll. for Women, 1947-49; B.A., U. Md., 1951; m. David Randall Hinkle, June 5, 1954; children—Valerie Nelson, Janet Lee, Sally Ann. Mgr., Wildacres Thoroughbred Horse Farm, Waterford, Conn., 1960-70; illustrator Naval Warfare Predictions/Computer Simulated Naval Engagements, Analysis & Tech., Inc., North Stonington, Conn., 1970-73; pres. Sonalysts, Inc., Waterford, 1973-88, chmn., chief exec. officer, 1973—, also founder, past dir. Command Engring. & Tech. Services Co.; pres., chief exec. officer, chmn. Stonington Farms Inc. (now Mystic Valley Hunt Club), 1983—, Conn. Nat. Bank Adv. Bd., 1988—; chmn., chief exec. officer Angiers Assocs., 1989—, S.I. Devel. Corp., 1989—; cons. anti-submarine warfare cruise missile weapon systems Gen. Electric Co., 1974-76; cons. Def. Nuclear Agy. for Tactical Nuclear Effects in anti-submarine warfare, 1974-75; spl. edn. substitute tchr. Waterford Pub. Schs., 1968-74. Bd. trustees Thames Sci. Center, 1979-82. Recipient commendation for services to submarine force Comdr. Submarine Squadron Ten, 1973, SBA New Eng. Contractor of Yr. award, 1986, SBA Adminstr.'s award for excellence, 1985, 86. Mem. Am. Horse Shows Assn., Nat. Audubon Soc., Submarine Devel. Group Two Wives Club (pres. 1968), Sigma Kappa (pres. Senesk chpt. 1987-89), Navy Wives Club. Republican. Baptist. Co-author: Scope of Acoustic Communications Systems in Naval Tactical Warfare, 1974; Non-Acoustic Anti Submarine Warfare, 1974; Nuclear Weapons Effects in Anti Submarine Warfare, 1974; Measures of Effectiveness, Naval Tactical Communications, 1975; co-author: Destroyer ASW Barrier, 1977. Home: RD 1 Box 168-A Stonington CT 06378 Office: Sonalysts Inc 215 Parkway N PO Box 280 Waterford CT 06385

HINMAN, ELAINE MARIE, aerospace engineer; b. Lincoln Park, Mich., Nov. 18, 1960; d. John Edward and Florence Emelie (Langouse) H. BS in Aero. Engring., U. Mich., 1983; MS in Aerospace Engring., U. Tenn., 1989. Engr. Marshall (Ala.) Space Flight Ctr. NASA, 1983—. Chmn. Robotics Informal Working Group of Marshall Space Flight Ctr., 1986-87; test diver Neutral Bouyancy Simulator, Extravehicular Mobility Unit suit, 1987. Recipient Performance award NASA, 1987, Tech. Innovation award, 1989, Cert. of Appreciation, 1988. Mem. AIAA (Outstanding Young Aero Engr. of the Yr. 1986), NOW, Soc. Mfg. Engrs. Robotics Internat. (chpt. chmn. 1989-90, sec. 1987, Outstanding Engr. 1988), Von Braun Astron. Soc., N. Ala. Sci. Fiction Assn. (bd. dirs. 1985-87). Home: 124 Waters Edge Ln Madison AL 35758 Office: NASA Marshall Space Flight Ctr Marshall AL 35812

HINMAN, MYRA MAHLOW, English educator; b. Saginaw County, Mich., Jan. 11, 1926; d. Henry and Cynthia (Mims) Mahlow; B.S., Columbia U., 1946; M.A., U. Fla., 1954, Ph.D., 1959; m. George E. Olstead, 1948 (div. 1967); 1 son, Christopher Eric; m. Charlton Hinman, 1968 (dec. 1977); 1 stepdau., Barbara. Asst. prof. Memphis State U., 1959-61; instr. U. Kans., Lawrence, 1961-63, asst. prof., 1963-68, asso. prof. English lit., 1968—. Travel grantee Am. Council Learned Socs., 1966. Mem. MLA, Internat. Arthurian Soc. (conf. speaker), Shakespeare Assn. Am. (conf. presenter), U. Va. Bibliog. Soc., AAUP, Midwest MLA, S. Atlantic MLA, United Burmese Cat Fanciers, Am. Shorthair Cat Assn., Phi Kappa Phi. Assoc editor: Hinman Text, Complete Works of Shakespeare; mem. editorial bd. Computer-Assisted Composition jour.; contbr. articles to profl. jours. Home: 1932 Maine St Lawrence KS 66046 Office: U Kans Wescoe Hall Lawrence KS 66045

HINNANT, HILARI ANNE, educator; b. Coral Gables, Fla., Mar. 23, 1953; d. William Walker and Margaret Elizabeth (Ennis) H.; m. M. Greg Miller. BS in Edn., U. Ga., 1974; MS in Edn., Fla. Internat. U., 1976. Art tchr. Banyan Elem. Sch. Dade County, Miami, 1974-79; tchr. Hilliard (Fla.) Sr. High Sch., 1979-80, Callahan (Fla.) Jr. High Sch., 1980-81; tchr. Duval County Pub. Schs., Jacksonville, Fla., 1981-83, Jacksonville, 1982-83; tchr. The Am. Sch., Hamburg, West Germany, 1983-84, Brevard County Pub. Schs., Rockledge, Fla., 1984-86; clin. experience facilitator U. Wis., LaCrosse, 1987-88; tchr. Sarasota County Pub. Sch., Sarasota, Fla., 1988-90; asst. dir., exploratorium specialist Ednl. Rsch. Ctr. for Child Devel. U. South Fla., Tampa, 1990—; illustrator, writer Brevard County Maths. Curriculum Guide Rockledge,. Author of poems. Selby grantee, 1989. Mem. Nat. Assn. for Edn. Young Children, Internat. Reading Assn., So. Assn. for Children Under Six, Fla. Assn. for Children Under Six (conf. presenter 1990), Manasota Track Club, Kappa Delta Pi (presenter internat. convocation 1988), Phi Delta Kappa (pres. chpt. 1989), Delta Gamma. Democrat. Roman Catholic. Home: 4419 Vieux Carre Circle Tampa FL 33613-3053

HINSCH, GERTRUDE WILMA, biology educator; b. Chgo., Oct. 20, 1932; d. Hans Rudolph and Gertrude (Kalb) H. BSEd, No. Ill. U., 1953; MS, Iowa State U., 1955, PhD, 1957. Instr. Mt. Holyoke Coll., South Hadley, Mass., 1957-60; asst. prof., then assoc. prof. Mt. Union Coll., Alliance, Ohio, 1960-67; assoc. prof. U. Miami (Fla.), 1966-74; prof. U. S. Fla., Tampa, 1974—. Office: U S Fla Dept Biology Tampa FL 33620

HINTON, S(USAN) E(LOISE), author; b. Tulsa, 1948; m. David Inhofe, 1970. Grad., U. Tulsa, 1970. Author teen-age fiction; books include The Outsiders, 1967, That Was Then, This Is Now, 1971, Rumble Fish, 1975, Tex, 1979, Taming the Star Runner, 1988; screen play Rumble Fish, 1983. Recipient Media and Methods Maxi award, 1975; Nat. Book award nominee, 1981. Office: care Press Rels Delacorte Press 1 Dag Hammarskjold Pla New York NY 10017*

HINTZ, MONICA E., transportation company executive; b. South Milwaukee, Wis., Aug. 8, 1947; d. Arnold Stanley and Phyllis Ruth (Rootes) Kaczanowski; 1 child, Michael D. Student, Spencerian Bus. Coll., 1965, LaSalle U., 1968-69. Sec. George J. Meyer Mfg., Cudahy, Wis., 1965-70; export coord. Vilter Export Corp., Milw., 1970-80, Schenkers Internat. Forwarders, Milw., 1980-82, Fritz Cos., Inc., Milw., 1982-88; br. mgr. World Cargo, Inc., Milw., 1988, Pan Am. Container Corp., Milw., 1988—. Mem. NAFE, Wis. Internat. Transp. Assn., Milw. World Trade Assn. (edn. com. speaker, program coord. 1985—), Delta Nu Alpha. Roman Catholic. Home: 3723 S Chicago Apt 1 South Milwaukee WI 53172

HINZ, MITTIE DEAN, nursing manager; b. Cumberland, Md., Feb. 27, 1941; d. Wilson Ice and Juanita K. (Coffield) Poling; m. Reinhold Hans Hinz, Feb. 23, 1963; children: Michael Shawn, Kristian Wolfram. Diploma in Nursing, Meth. Sch. Nursing, Dallas, 1962; BSN, Incarnate Word Coll., 1973; MSN, U. Tex., 1978; postgrad., U. Ala., Birmingham, 1985—. Cert. childbirth educator. Staff nurse Meth. Hosp. Dallas, 1962-63; staff nurse 97th Gen. Army Hosp., Frankfurt am Main, Fed. Republic of Germany, 1964-65; asst. area dir. ob-gyn. nursing Santa Rosa Med. Ctr., San Antonio, 1972-75; instr. nursing Meth. Hosp. Sch. Nursing, Lubbock, Tex., 1976-81; asst. prof. nursing sch. nursing Tex. Tech U. Health Sci. Ctr., Lubbock, 1983-89; perinatal coord. St. Anthony Hosp., Oklahoma City, 1989; relief charge nurse perinatal unit Univ. Med. Ctr., Lubbock, Tex., 1990—; cons. Equifax Corp., Lubbock, 1980-88, Borning Corp., Spokane, Wash., 1985-87. Co-author: Clinical Application of Nursing Diagnosis, 1989. Vol. Young Parent Svcs., Lubbock, 1987-88; mem. adv. bd. S. Plains Health Agy., Lubbock, 1979-80, Vis. Nurse Svc., Lubbock, 1980-85. Med. Ctr. Grad. Sch. fellow U. Ala., Birmingham, 1985. Mem. Nurses Assn. for Gynecologic, Obstetric and Neonatal Nursing (sec Antonio chpt. 1973-75, coord. Lubbock chpt. 1975-78, chmn. Tex. sect. 1979-85, nat. nominating com. 1983, nat. bylaws com. 1986-87, rep. to Am. Coll. Obstetricians and Gynecologists nat. com. on OB tech. bulls. 1987-90, nat. ad hoc com. electric fetal monitoring statement 1988, ad hoc adv. bd. contraceptive edn. program 1989, dist. VII chmn. 1990—), Nurses Assn. of Am. Coll. Obstetricians and Gynecologists (cert. in-patient obsteric nurse, mem. exec. bd. 1990—), Am. Nurses Assn., Tex. Nurses Assn., Internat. Childbirth Edn. Assn., Am. Assn. Psychoprophylaxis in Childbirth. Methodist. Home: 2825 22d St Lubbock TX 79410-1619

HIPSLEY, JANE FRANCES, nurse; b. Balt., Aug. 9, 1926; d. William Russell and Marquerite Eugenia (Cecil) Gardiner; m. Daniel. RN, Mercy Hosp., 1947; BS, St. Joseph's Coll., 1985; MS, Loyola U., 1988. Office mgr. agt. Hipsley Ins. Agy., Balt., 1948-68; staff Mercy Hosp., Balt., 1969-73; office nurse mgr. Edward L. Frey Jr., Balt., 1973-74; staff Mercy Hosp., Balt., 1975-77, obstetric clinic mgr., 1978; staff nurse Sheppard Pratt Hosp., Towson, Md., 1988—; co-leader self awareness group, recruitment and retention com. Sheppard Pratt Hosp. Mem. Mercy Hosp. Alumnae, St. Joseph's Alumnae, Psi Chi. Republican. Roman Catholic. Home: 519 Penny Ln Cockeysville MD 21030 Office: Sheppard & Enoch Pratt Baltimore MD 21204

HIRANO, JUNE YAMADA, education center administrator; b. Honolulu, Aug. 27, 1943; d. Harry Taketo and Aiko (Endo) Yamada; m. Michael James Hirano, Mar. 31, 1973. BEd, U. Hawaii, 1965, MA, 1967. Instr., assoc. dir. for tng. Speech Communications Ctr., U. Hawaii, Honolulu, 1967-69, asst. to dir., grad./undergrad. coordinator univ. dept. speech communications, 1969-70; asst. coordinator for participant activities East-West Ctr., Honolulu, 1970-73, selections adminstr., 1973-79, award service officer, 1979—. Co-author: (learning manuals) Speech Communication Learning System, vol. I and II, 1st edit., 1968, 3d edit., 1970, Speech Power Learning System, 1969. Mem. Am. Assn. Collegiate Registrars and Admissions Officers (rep. Nat. Council on Evaluation of Fgn. Ednl. Credentials 1985-88), Nat. Assn. for Fgn. Student Affairs, Phi Kappa Phi. Avocations: Oriental art, contemporary prints, ceramics. Office: East-West Ctr 1777 East-West Rd Honolulu HI 96848

HIRN, DORIS DREYER, health service administrator; b. N.Y.C., Dec. 3, 1933; d. James Howard and Dorothy Van Nostrand (Young) Dreyer; student Colby Jr. Coll., 1950-51, Hofstra U., 1953-56; m. John D. Hirn, Oct. 27, 1956; children—Deborah Lynn, Robert William. Owner, Dutchlands Farm, Albany, N.Y., 1957-62, Hickory Hill Farm, Galena, Ill., 1965-75; adminstr. Home Health Service, Chgo., 1972-74, exec. dir. Suburban Home Health Service, 1974-87; exec. dir. Home Health Svc. Chgo. North, 1987—; ptnr. Candor Assocs.; dir. Nat. Health Delivery Systems, Serengeti Prodns., Inc.; bd. dirs. Lifeline Pilots, Inc., NAHC, Fin. Mgrs. Forum, Ill. Long Term Task Force, Ill. Homecare Coun., BBH Assocs., Inc., Caregivers, Inc. Author: Survey Process in Home Health Manual; contbr. nat. seminars on quality assurance, reimbursement legislation; also articles to various periodicals. Served with WAVES, 1951-52. Recipient Ill. Govs. award for Excellence Home Care Agy., 1989. Mem. Nat. Assn. Home Care. Clubs: Chgo. Yacht. Home: 5747 N Sheridan Chicago IL 60660

HIRONIMUS, SHARON LYNN, management; b. Berwyn, Ill., Aug. 19, 1936; d. Frederick Henry and Olga Catherine (Jeschke) Garner; m. Ronald Lee Hironimus, July 31, 1954; children: William, Deborah, Ann. Student, Am. Inst. Banking, Chgo., 1972, Coll. San Mateo, Calif., 1975-81, Nat. Inst. Credit, San Francisco, 1975-80. Credit analyst Wauconda Nat. Bank, Ill., 1965-67, First Nat. Bank Mundelein, Ill., 1967-72, Cen. Bank, San Mateo, Calif., 1972-73; credit correspondent Ampex Corp., Redwood City, Calif., 1973-74, credit analyst, 1974-76; credit rep. Ampex Corp., Calif., 1976-79; asst. division credit mgr. Ampex Corp., Redwood City, Calif., 1979-82, division credit mgr., 1982--; bd. dirs. Nat. Assn. Credit Mgmt., San Francisco 1979. Home: 1820 Chula Vista Dr Belmont CA 94002 Office: Ampex Corp 401 Broadway Redwood City CA 94063-3199

HIRONO, MAZIE KEIKO, state legislator; b. Fukushima, Japan, Nov. 3, 1947; came to U.S., 1955, naturalized, 1957; d. Laura Chie (Sato) H. B.A., U. Hawaii, 1970; J.D., Georgetown U., 1978. Dep. atty. gen., Honolulu, 1978-80; house counsel INDEVCO, Honolulu, 1982-83; sole practice, Honolulu, 1983-84, Shim, Tam, Kirimitsu & Naito, 1984-88; mem. Hawaii Ho. of Reps., Honolulu, 1980—. Del., State Democratic Party Conv., Honolulu, 1972-82; bd. dirs. Nuuanu YMCA, Honolulu, 1982-84, Moiliili Community Ctr., Honolulu, 1984, Mem. U.S. Supreme Ct. Bar, Hawaii Bar Assn., Phi Beta Kappa. Democrat. Office: Ho of Reps Rm 331 Honolulu HI 96813

HIRSCH, IRMA LOU KOLTERMAN, nurse, association administrator; b. Clay Center, Kans., June 11, 1934; d. Arthur Henry and Mildred (Peterson) Kolterman; m. William A. Hirsch, June 8, 1958; children—David William, Brian Duane. B.S. in Nursing, U. Kans., 1957; M.Nursing, U. Washington, Seattle, 1961. R.N. Mo. Instr. Duke U., Durham, N.C., 1961-64; nurse clinician U. Kans. Med. Ctr., Kansas City, 1968-70; project dir., cons. Mo. Regional Med. Program, Kansas City, 1970-74; project dir., program coordinator Am. Nurses' Assn., Kansas City, 1974-79; supr. VA Med. Ctr., Kansas City, 1979-81; dept. dir., 1981-83, policy devel., 1983—; cons. nursing edn. Joint Commn. on Accreditation of Hosps., Chgo., 1973; cons. for project devel. Am. Nurses Found., Kansas City, 1974; cons. nursing standards Health Standards Directorate, Ottawa, Ont., Can., 1978; trustee Presbyterian Manors of Mid-Am., Newton, Kans., 1979-86. Editor: Guidelines for Review of Nursing Care at the Local Level, 1976, Nursing Quality Assurance Management/Learning System, 1982, Peer Review in Nursing, 1982, Issues in Professional Practice, 1985, Classification Systems for Describing Nursing Practice, 1989. Mem. Friends of Art, Kansas City, 1975—, Internat. Relations Council, Kansas City, 1980—, Historic Kansas City Found., 1982—; chpt. pres. Am. Field Services, Kansas City, 1978-79. Mem. Am. Nurses Assn., Mo. Nurses' Assn. (pres. Mo. dist. 1980-81), Kans. U. Nurses Alumni Assn. (pres. 1964-66), N.Am. Nursing Diagnosis Assn. (mem. task force 1973-77), Sigma Theta Tau. Club: P.E.O. (Kansas City). Avocations: home and financial management; walking; skiing. Home: 1035 W 57th Terr Kansas City MO 64113 Office: Am Nurses' Assn 2420 Pershing Rd Kansas City MO 64108

HIRSCH, JUNE SCHAUT, architectural firm administrator; b. Green Bay, Wis., Sept. 30, 1925; d. Clifford Charles and Eleanor Josephine (Arts) Schaut; m. Marshall E. Gilette, Jan. 23, 1946 (div. 1974); children: Ronald Leigh, Patrick Allen, Vicki Jeanne Baumann; m. Hubert L. Hirsch, Nov. 7, 1975. Student, St. Mary's Sch. Nursing, Rochester, Minn., 1943-45, U. Wis., Sheboygan, 1974-75. Cert. med. asst., 1966. Med. asst. James W. Faulkner, M.D., Phoenix, 1953-56; med. office mgr. Edward E. Houfek, M.D., Sheboygan, Wis., 1956-75; med. office cons. Profl. Mgmt. Inc., Milw., 1975-77; office mgr., adminstrv. asst. Schroeder & Holt Architects Ltd., Milw., 1977—; instr. med. asst. program Lake Shore Tech., 1975-76. Mem. Am. Assn. Med. Assts. (nat. trustee 1963-66), Wis. Soc. Med. Assts. (life mem., mem. exec. bd. 1960-81), Greater Milw. Med. Assts. (mem. exec. bd. 1975-89), Lake Shore Med. Assts. (mem. exec. bd. 1959-75). Republican. Roman Catholic. Home: 10200 W Bluemound Rd #918 Wausatosa WI 53226 Office: Schroeder & Holt Architects 212 W Wisconsin Ave Milwaukee WI 53203

HIRSCH, PAULA JEAN, computer trainer/analyst; b. Wichita, Kans., Nov. 9, 1944; d. Paul Gotlieb and Charlotte Ella (Dale) Heide; m. Roland Felix Hirsch, July 11, 1971; children: Elizabeth, Sallie, Paul. AA, Cottey Coll., 1964; BS in Elem. Edn., U. Kans., 1966; Cert. in Computer Applications, Montgomery Coll., 1988. Tchr. Ontario-Montclair Sch. Dist., Calif., 1966-68, Bellevue (Wash.) Pub. Schs., 1968-70; sec. to regional v.p. Castrol Oils, Inc., Hackensack, N.J., 1970-71; asst. to dir. complaints City of Orange, N.J., 1980-81, v.p. planning bd., 1982-83; sec., dir. of nat. sales QEI,

Inc., Springfield, N.J., 1981-83, sec., dir., 1981-83; computer trainer/analyst Computer Data Systems, Inc., Rockville, Md., 1988—. V.p. LWV, Orange, 1978-79; v.p., bd. dirs. YWCA of Essex and West Hudson, Orange, 1980-84. Mem. Am. Soc. Tng. and Devel., Balt.-Washington Info. Systems Educators, Inc., AAUW (chmn. coun. Montgomery County 1989-90), Montgomery County Youth Orch. Assn. (chmn. bd. 1990-91), Eastern Star. Home: 20458 Waters Point Ln Germantown MD 20874 Office: Computer Data Systems Inc 1 Curie Blvd Rockville MD 20850

HIRSCHBERG, VERA HILDA, writer; b. N.Y.C., Sept. 19, 1929; d. Bernard and Minnie (Margolis) Lieberman; m. Peter Hirschberg, Aug. 21, 1949; children: Karen Hirschberg Tuso, Paul. BJ, Hunter Coll., 1950. Staff writer Pacific Stars and Stripes, Tokyo, 1956-64; corr. Newsweek, Guatemala, 1964-65; transp. staff writer N.Y. Jour. Commerce, Washington, 1969-70; transp. editor Nat. Jour. Mag., Washington, 1970-72; dir. women's programs, presdl. speechwriter The White House, Washington, 1972-74; dir. tech. transfer HUD, Washington, 1974-75; dep. spl. asst. to Sec. Pub. Affairs Dept. Treasury, Washington, 1975-77; press. sec. U.S. Sen. William Roth, Jr., Washington, Jan. to Dec. 1977; editorial cons. various govt. and non-govt. clients, 1977-78; pub. affairs dir. White House Conf. on Libr. and Info. Svcs., Washington, 1978-80; sr. writer, adminstr.'s speechwriter NASA, Washington, 1980—. Editor: Israel at the Polls, 1977; author numerous newspaper and mag. articles. Recipient Outstanding Svc. citation The White House, 1973, Meritorious Svc. award Dept. Treasury, 1977, Exceptional Performance award NASA, 1982, Exceptional Svc. medal, 1988. Mem. Exec. Women in Govt. (founding mem. 1973), Zionist Orgn. Am. Republican. Jewish. Office: NASA Hdqrs Code PM 400 Maryland Ave SW Washington DC 20546

HIRSCHENFANG, GAIL, cantor; b. N.Y.C., July 29, 1954; d. Seymour and Leah (Solomon) H. BA in Math., SUNY, Plattsburg, 1975; B Sacred Music, Hebrew Union Coll., N.Y.C., 1981, M Sacred Music, 1988. Cantor Balt. Hebrew Congregation, 1981-82, Temple Beth Zion, Buffalo, 1983-89, Temple Beth-El, Birmingham, Mich., 1989—. Soprano soloist Buffalo Philharm. Orch., 1984-89. Mem. Black-Jewish Leadership Dialogue, Buffalo, 1987-89. Mem. Am. Conf. Cantors (bd. dirs. 1981-89). Democrat. Office: Temple Beth-El 7400 Telegraph Rd Birmingham MI 48010

HIRSCHFELD, ARLENE F., civic worker, homemaker; b. Denver, Apr. 6, 1944; d. Hyman and Gertrude (Schwartz) Friedman; m. A. Barry Hirschfeld, Dec. 17, 1966; 2 children. Student, U. Mich., 1962-64; BA, U. Denver, 1966. English tchr. Abraham Lincoln High Sch., Denver, 1966-70. Advisor to pres. Jr. League of Denver, 1987—, sustaining advisor ways and means coun., 1989-90, pres., chmn. bd. dirs., 1986-87, v.p. ways and means, 1985-86, v.p. mktg., 1981-82, chmn. Holiday Mart, fin. coun. mem. 1980-81, chmn. Colo. Cache mktg. com., 1978-79, bd. dirs., 1981-82, 1985-87, participant in Nat. Jr. League Mktg. Conf.; trustee Graland Country Day Sch., 1988—, bd. sec. 1990—, chmn. edn. com., 1989—, chmn. parent coun. nominating com., 1984-85, pres. parent coun., 1982-83, auction chmn., 1980, 81; bd. dirs. Allied Jewish Fedn., 1988—, various positions women's campaign, 1982—; co-chmn. collector's choice event Denver Art Mus., 1989; devel. com. Women's Found. of Colo., 1987—, mem. bd., 1987-89; co-chmn. benefit luncheon Pub. Edn. Coalition, 1990, mini grants selection com., 1985-87; mem. bd. Minoru Yasui Community Vol. award, 1986-87; mem. Greater Denver C. of C. Leadership Denver, class of 1987-88. Named Humanitarian of Yr. Nat. Jewish Ctr., 1988; named to Colo. Women's Edcn. Devel. Coun. by Gov. of Colo., 1989—. Office: 5200 Smith Rd Denver CO 80216

HIRSCHFELD, LINDA EVELYN, purchasing executive; b. Celina, Ohio, Sept. 11, 1947; d. Dale Fredrick and Evelyn Elsie (Harmeyer) Grimes; m. Lynn Virgil, Jan. 1, 1966; children: Randall Brian, Kimberly Ardyn. Post-grad., Indiana U., 1969; BS in Edn. (cum laude), Ohio Northern U., 1965-68. cert. Purchase mgr. 3rd grade tchr. St. Marys City Schs., Ohio, 1968-69; 1st grade tchr. Bath Local Schs., Lima, Ohio, 1969-71; co-owner GH Ceramic Supply, New Knoxville, Ohio, 1971-82, GHS, St. Marys, Ohio; purchasing agent Koneta Rubber Co. (Lancaster Colony Corp.), Wapakoneta, Ohio, 1982--, LRV-Easco (Lancaster Colony Corp.), Ohio, 1987--; pres. Ceramic Distbrs. of Am., Chgo., 1978-79; bd. dirs. Ceramic Distbrs. of Am., Chgo., 1973-80. Contbr. articles to profl. jours. Asst. dir. music 1st United Ch. of Christ, New Knoxville, Ohio, 1985—; pres. 1st U.C.C. Women's Guild, 1988-89, New Knoxville, 1985-86. Mem. Nat. Assn. Purchasing Mgmt. (sec. 1984-86, sec. Lima, Ohio chpt. 1988-89, 1st v.p. 1989—), New Knoxville Music Boosters (v.p. 1988-89, pres. 1989—). Republican. Home: 9639 Botkins Angle Rd New Knoxville OH 45871 Office: Koneta Rubber Co 700 Lunar Dr Wapakoneta OH 45895

HIRSCHFELD, SUE ELLEN, geological sciences educator; b. Ossining, N.Y., Jan. 12, 1941; d. Ira Bertram and Helen Caroline (Rieser) H. BS, U. Fla., 1963, MS, 1965; PhD, U. Calif., Berkeley, 1971. Prof. Calif. State U., Hayward, 1971—, chair dept. geol. scis., 1988—. Contbr. articles to profl. jours.; co-author videotape in field, 1985. Grantee Calif. State U., 1976, 78. Mem. AAAS, Geol. Soc. Am., Paleontolog. Soc., Soc. for Econ. Paleontologists and Mineralogists, Assn. for Women Geoscientists (founder). Home: 4244 Gem Ave Castro Valley CA 94546 Office: Calif State U Hayward CA 94542

HIRSCH-FIKEJS, JUDITH ANN, minister; b. Macon, Ga., Aug. 17, 1939; d. Alvin and E. Jo (Vaughn) Hirsch; m. George Arthur Fikejs, Mar. 20, 1959; children: Ann-Laureen, Jeffrey, Allison, Tracy. BA, Stephens Coll., 1982; MDiv, Fuller Theol. Seminary, Pasadena, Calif., 1985. Ordained to ministry, Presbyn. Ch. (USA), 1986. Studio musician Word, Sacred and RCA Records, Chgo., 1958-65; nursing asst. Good Samaritan Hosp., San Jose, Calif., 1966-69; pvt. music instr. various, 1966-82; high sch. tchr. Linfield Sch., Temecula, Calif., 1977-82; jr. high tchr. Pacific Christian High Sch., L.A., 1983-85; interim dir., Christian edn. Pasadena Presbyn. Ch., 1984-85; pastor Community Presbyn. Ch., Acton, Calif., 1985—; mission study coordiantor Presbytery of San Fernando and L.A., 1986—; chair Sta. Clarita New Ch. devel. steering com., 1989—; chaplain Antelope Valley Rehab. Ctrs., Acton and Castiac, Calif., 1987—; vol. chaplain VA Hosp., Sepulveda, Calif., 1989—. Author religious column, Acton News, 1985—; conf. reviewer, The Presbyterian, 1987. Bd. dirs. Antelope Valley Rehab. Ctrs., L.A. County, 1988-89; bd. dirs., pres. Agape Home for Women Alcoholics, Lancaster, Calif., 1986-89; chmn. Com. for Nat. Am. Ministries, L.A., 1987-88. Recipient Vol. award, L.A. Assessor, Acton Rehab. Ctr., 1988. Mem. Nat. Assn. Female Execs., Rotary. Democrat. Home: 23137 Magnolia Glen Dr Valencia CA 91354 Office: Community Presbyn Church 32142 Crown Valley PO Box 177 Acton CA 93510

HIRSCHHORN, JOYCE DONEN, speech communication educator; b. Rye, N.Y., June 29, 1926; d. Isaac and Edith (Koosis) Donen; m. Adrian Hirschhorn, Aug. 27, 1950; children: Robert Z., Nancy. AB, U. Mich., 1946; MA, Columbia U., 1947. Prof. speech communication South Cen. Community Coll., New Haven, Conn., 1970—. Editor Communitas, 1983; contbr. articles to Communitas, jour. of Community Colls. of Conn., 1981-89. Bd. dirs. Am. Lung Assn. Conn., New Haven, 1975—. Mem. Speech Communication Am., Internat. Listening Assn., Internat. Semantic Soc., AAUP, Ctr. for Independent Study. Democrat. Office: South Cen Community Coll 60 Sargent Dr New Haven CT 06511

HIRSH, CYNTHIA O'CONNOR, bank executive; b. Oswego, N.Y., June 16, 1943; d. William Joseph and Lucy Anna (Coe) O'Connor; married; children: Cynthia, Maria, Maureen, Jonathan. Asst. v.p., sales mgr. Norstar Bank Cen. N.Y., Fulton; customer svc. rep. Norstar Bank Cen. N.Y., Central Square; mgr. Oneida Savings Bank, Hamilton, N.Y., Oswego County Savings Bank, Fulton. Hon. chair Greater Fulton United Way Fund Driver, 1989-90; mem. Fulton Local Devel. Corp.; bd. dirs. Oswego County Opportunities. Mem. NAFE, Internat. Mgmt. Coun., Three Rivers Bus. and Profl. Women, Greater Fulton C. of C., Optimist Club, Kiwanis Club. Home: RR 55 Box 69 Lanning Rd Fulton NY 13069

HIRSHBERG, MARCIE SUE, nurse; b. Cin., Feb. 4, 1959; d. Charles Snyder and Dorothy Karlin (Wolman) H. Student, Vanderbilt U., Nashville, 1977-81; MN, Emory U., Atlanta, 1983-85. Inpatient Obstetric Nurse/NAACOG Certification Corp. Camp nurse Camp Kawaga for Boys, Minocqua, Wis., 1981; staff nurse II Michael Reese Hosp., Chgo., 1981-83; pediatric office nurse Charles Hirshberg, MD, Nashville, 1983—; RN/home health Pediatric Svcs. Am., Decatur, Ga.; staff nurse Henrietta Egleston Hosp., Atlanta, 1983-85, Jackson Meml. Hosp., 1985-86; maternal child clin. coordinator Broward Gen. Med. Center, Ft. Lauderdale, 1986-88; nurse mgr., obstetrics Mt. Sinai Med. Center, Miami, 1988-89; labor, delivery, recovery, postpartum/neonatal ICU nurse St. Francis Hosp., Miami Beach, Fla., 1989-90; specialist ob-gyn svcs. Warner-Lambert Co. div. Parke-Davis, Miami, N.J., 1990—; lectr. Bnai Brith Youth Orgn. Atlanta 1984-85, Emory U. Atlanta 1987. Vol. Jewish Fedn. of Greater Miami, 1985—, Bnai Brith Youth Orgn. Atlanta, 1984; guardian ad litem 11th Jud. Cir. Ct. Fla., 1989—. Mem. Nurses' Assn. Am. Coll. Obstetricians & Gynecologists, B'nai B'rith (advisor youth orgn. Miami chpt. 1990—), Sigma Theta Tau, Om Delta Kappa, Gamma Phi Beta (v.p. 1980-81). Republican. Jewish. Home and Office: 2025 Brickell Ave #904 Miami FL 33129

HIRSH-PASEK, KATHRYN ANN, psychology educator; b. Williamsport, Pa., Mar. 10, 1953; d. Morton and Joan (Cramer) Hirsh; m. Jeffrey Ivan Pasek, Aug. 17, 1975; children: Joshua, Benjamin, Michael. Student, Manchester Coll., Oxford, Eng., 1973-74; BS in Psychology-Music summa cum laude, U. Pitts., 1975; PhD in Human Devel.-Psycholinguistics, U. Pa., 1981. Cons. rsch. psychologist on software ease-of-use Sperry Univac, Inc., Blue Bell, Pa., 1980-84; asst. prof. psychiatry Med. Coll. N.J., Rutgers U., Newark, 1981-85; asst. prof. psychology, dir. Infant Speech Perception Lab., Swarthmore (Pa.) Coll., 1982-84; asst. prof., dir. Infant Lang. and Perception Lab. Haverford (Pa.) Coll., 1984-87, Temple U., Phila., 1987—; pres. Spl. Things Distbg. Co., Inc., Ardmore, Pa., 1983—; cons. Head Start and get set program Sch. Dist. Phila., 1989; cons. on reading Katzenbach Sch. for Deaf, West Trenton, N.J., 1981-85; cons. on lang. comprehension in pygmy chimpanzee Yerkes Primate Ctr., Atlanta, 1989; ad hoc reviewer Jour. Child Lang., Devel. Psychology, Child Devel., Jour. Ednl. Psychology, Jour. Applied Psychology, Freeman Press; presenter papers at profl. meetings. Contbr. articles to profl. jours.; composer, lyricist, performer : (children's mus. cassettes) Jumpin' in a Puddle, 1987, Staying Up, 1988, Hugs and Kisses, 1990. Condr. workshops for community groups; bd. dirs. Kaiserman br. Jewish Community Ctr., 1988—; mem. exec. bd. young leadership coun. Fedn. Jewish Agys., 1980-84; co-chmn. psychol. svcs. div. Fedn. Allied Jewish Appeal, 1985-87; v.p. JCC Camps, 1982-84. Dean's scholar U. Pitts., 1976; grantee NINH, 1979-80, 82-84, 89—, Pew Meml. Trust, 1985-87, Temple U., 1988-90, Spencer Found., 1986-89. Mem. Am. Psychol. Assn. (ad hoc reviewer div. 7), Soc. for Rsch. in Child Devel. (ad hoc reviewer), Piaget Soc. (ad hoc reviewer), Sigma Xi, Pi Lambda Theta, Omicron Delta Kappa. Office: Temple U Psychology Dept Philadelphia PA 19122

HIRSON, ESTELLE, retired educator; b. Bayonne, N.J.; d. Morris and Bertha (Rubinstein) Hirson; student UCLA, U. So. Calif., summers 1949-59, San Francisco, summer 1955, U. Hawaii, 1955; B.E., San Francisco State U., 1965. Tchr. High St. Homes Sch., Oakland, Calif., 1949-54, Prescott Sch., 1955-60, Ralph Bunche Sch., 1960-72; owner Puzzle-Gram Co., Los Angeles, 1946-49; pres. Major Automobile Co., 1948-60. Chpt. v.p. City of Hope, San Francisco, 1962-63; bd. dirs. Sinai-Duarte Nat. Med. Center, 1946-50, also parliamentarian, life mem. Mem. NEA, Calif., Oakland, Los Angeles tchrs. assns., Sigma Delta Tau. Democrat. Mem. Order Eastern Star; Scottish Rite Women's Assn. (v.p. L.A. 1982, fin. sec. 1989). Rights to ednl. arithmetic game Find the Answer 1948, 51. Home: 8670 Burton Way Apt 328 Los Angeles CA 90048

HIRST, WILMA ELIZABETH, psychologist; b. Shenandoah, Iowa; d. James H. and Lena (Donahue) Ellis; m. Clyde Henry Hirst (dec. Nov. 1969); 1 dau., Donna Jean (Mrs. Alan Robert Goss). AB in Elementary Edn., Colo. State Coll., 1948, EdD in Ednl. Psychology, 1954; MA in Psychology, U. Wyo., 1951. Elem. tchr., Cheyenne, Wyo., 1945-49, remedial reading instr., 1949-54; assoc. prof. edn., dir. campus sch. Nebr. State Tchrs. Coll., Kearney, 1954-56; sch. psychologist, head dept. spl. edn. Cheyenne (Wyo.) pub. schs., 1956-57, sch. psychologist, guidance coordinator, 1957-66, dir. rsch. and spl. projects, 1966-76, also pupil personnel, 1973-84; pvt. cons., 1984—; vis. asst. prof. U. So. Calif., summer 1957, Omaha U., summer 1958, U. Okla., summers 1959, 60; vis. assoc. prof. U. Nebr., 1961, U. Wyo., summer 1962, 64, extension div., Kabul, Afghanistan, 1970, Catholic U., Goias, Brazil, 1974; investigator HEW, 1965-69; prin. investigator effectiveness of spl. edn., 1983—; participant seminar Russian Press Women and Am. Fedn. Press Women, Moscow and Leningrad, 1973. Sec.-treas. Laramie County Council Community Services, 1962; mem. speakers bur., mental health orgn.; active Little Theatre, 1936-60, Girl Scout Leaders Assn., 1943-50; mem. Adv. Council on Retardation to Gov.'s Commn.; mem., past sec. Wyo. Bd. Psychologist Examiners, vice chmn., 1965-74; chmn. Mayor's v.p. Model Cities Program, 1969; mem. Gov.'s Com. Jud. Reform, 1972; adv. council Div. Exceptional Children, Wyo. Dept. Edn., 1974; mem. transit adv. group City of Cheyenne, 1974; bd. dirs. Wyo. Children's Home Soc., treas., 1978-84, sec. 1984—; sec. rsch. on women's prisons State of Wyo., 1989; del. Internat. Conv. Ptnrs. of Ams., Jamaica, 1987; bd. dirs. Goodwill Industries Wyo., chmn., 1981-83; mem. Wyo. exec. com. Partners of Americas, 1970-86; del., moderator pers. com. Presbytery of Wyo., 1987; Friendship Force ambassador to Honduras, 1988; chmn. bd. SE Wyo. Mental Health Center; elder 1st Presbyn. Ch., Cheyenne, 1978—, also bd. dirs.; chmn. adv. assessment com. Wyo. State Office Handicapped Children, 1980, 81; mem. allocations com. United Way of Laramie County. Named Woman of Year, Cheyenne Bus. and Profl. Women, 1974. Diplomate Am. Bd. Profl. Psychology. Mem. Internat. Council Psychologists (chmn. Wyo. div. 1980-85), AAUP, Am. Assn. State Psychology Bds. (sec.-treas. 1970-73), Wyo. Psychol. Assn. (pres. 1962-63), Laramie County Mental Health Assn. (bd. mem., corr. sec. 1963-69, pres.), Wyo. Mental Health Assn. (bd. mem.), Internat. Platform Assn., Am. Ednl. Research Assn., Assn. Supervision and Curriculum Devel., Assn. for Gifted (Wyo. pres. 1964-65), Am. Personnel and Guidance Assn., Am. Assn. Sch. Adminstrs., NEA (life, participant seminar to China 1978), AAUW, Cheyenne Assn. Spl. Personnel and Prins. (pres. 1964-65, mem. exec. bd. 1972-76), Nat. Fedn. Press Women (dir. 1979-85), DAR (vice regent Cheyenne chpt. 1975-77), AARP (state coordinator 1988—, preretirement planning specialist 1986—, leadership coun., state del. nat. conv. 1990), Psi Chi, Kappa Delta Pi, Pi Lambda Theta, Alpha Delta Kappa (pres. Wyo. Alpha 1965-66). Presbyn. Lodge Soc. Colonial Dames XVII Century, Order Eastern Star, Daus. of Nile. Clubs: Wyo. Press Women, Zonta (pres. Cheyenne 1965-66, treas. dist. 12 1974). Author: Know Your School Psychologist, 1963; Effective School Psychology for School Administrators, 1980. Home and Office: 3458 Green Valley Rd Cheyenne WY 82001

HIRYOK, KATHRYN ANN, fundraising organizer; b. Warren, Ohio, June 10, 1942; d. Edward J. and Mary K. (Namton) Lukco; m. Paul Joseph Hiryok, June 16, 1961 (dec. Apr. 1971); children: Janine Marie, Daniel Paul. Student Kent State U., 1978—. Office mgr. Warren Otologic Group, Ohio, 1963-71, exec. asst., 1971-74, fin. dir., 1975-88; property mgr. Northmar Ctr., Warren, 1984-88; asst. nat. dir. Israel Tennis Ctrs., N.Y.C., 1975—. Founder/organizer Warren Women's Network, 1981-85; bd. dirs. Warren Family Svc. Assn., 1984-87, chmn. pub. rels., 1985, v.p., 1986; trustee Trumbull County United Way, 1986-87. Mem. NAFE, Am. Assn. Editorial Cartoonists (hon.). Jewish. Home: 333 Rector Pl Apt 9Q New York NY 10280 Office: Israel Tennis Ctrs Assn 928 Broadway #900 New York NY 10010

HISHINUMA, KATHLEEN K., telephone company executive; b. Honolulu, Aug. 26, 1954; d. Tokuichi and Alice (Arakaki) Hayashi; m. Robin A. Hishinuma, Nov. 24, 1979. BBA, U. Hawaii, 1976. CPA, Hawaii. Ast. treas. Grace Bros. Ltd., Honolulu, 1976-80; svc. cost specialist GTE Hawaiian Telephone, Honolulu, 1980-81; revenues and earnings adminstr. GTE Hawaiian Telephone, 1981-83, rates and tariff mgr., 1983-85; staff mgr. revenue rsch. GTE Svc. Corp., Stamford, Conn., 1985-86; revenue planning mgr. GTE Svc. Corp., 1986-88; dir. regulatory conformance GTE Telephone Ops., Irving, Tex., 1988—. Recipient GTE Outstanding Achievement award, 1986, 88. Mem. AICPAs, Hawaii Soc. CPAs, NAFE, Am. Soc. Women CPAs. Office: GTE Telephone Operations PO Box 152092 WO8IO2 Irving TX 75015-2092

HISIGER, KERRI ILEEN, police officer; b. N.Y.C., Dec. 29, 1955; d. Jack and Delilah (Pyken) H. BA, John Jay Coll., 1984, MPA, 1987; postgrad., N.Y. Law Sch., 1989—. Officer N.Y. Police Dept., N.Y.C., 1980—. Scholar Mobil Co., 1985, N.Y. Law Sch., 1989. Mem. N.Y. Police Dept. Patrolmen Benevolent Assn., Shomrim Soc. Democrat. Jewish. Home: 219-38 75th Ave Bayside NY 11364 Office: NY Police Dept 24 Precinct 151 W 100th St New York NY 10025

HITCHCOCK, CONNIE GINEVRA, nurse; b. El Campo, Tex., Dec. 11, 1954; d. Michael Lawrence and Adah Lavonne (Torrey) Ginevra; m. James R. King, Aug. 26, 1977 (div. 1980); 1 child, Kelly; children: Brandon, Michael. Lic. vocat. nurse, Hill Country Meml. Hosp., Fredericksburg, Tex., 1975; student, Bapt. Meml. Hosp. Staff nurse Sid Peterson Meml. Hosp., Kerrville, Tex., 1975-79, N.E. Bapt. Hosp., San Antonio, 1980; dir. nurses Casa De Amistad, San Antonio, 1980-82; charge nurse Four Seasns Northwest, San Antonio, 1982-84; asst. dir. nurses Manor Care Inc., San Antonio, 1984-89; part time nurse trainee Manor Care, Inc. Leader, San Antonio coun. Girls Scouts U.S., 1986-88; mem. St. Brigid's Athletic Assn. Mem. Nat. Student Nurses Assn. Democrat. Roman Catholic. Home: 6764 Spring Front San Antonio TX 78249 Office: Manor Care Inc Four Season NW 8300 Wurzbach San Antonio TX 78229

HITCHCOCK, GEORGIA MAGDALENE, retired educator, civic worker; b. Frenchcreek, N.Y., Apr. 8, 1904; d. James Emmett and Florence Alys (Morrison) H.; 2 children. BS, Pa. State U., 1926; MA, Columbia U., 1932, PhD, 1940. Cert. tchr., Pa., N.Y. Tchr. pub. schs., Millville, Pa., 1927-28, Girard, Pa., 1928-29; tchr. N.Y.C. Sch. System, 1931-60; dietician Schraft Co., N.Y.C., 1930-31; ret., 1960. Columnist Around and About, North East (Pa.) Breeze, 1975—. Active numerous civic orgns., including past sec., mem. Permanent Com. for Prevention Juvenile Delinquency, N.Y.C.; formerly active ARC, N.Y.C.; vol. Hamot Hosp., Erie, Pa., 1974-75, Meals on Wheels, North East; past pres. North East Woman's Club; mem. Erie County Flower Guild, North East Libr. Bd., North East Community Fair Assn.; past bd. dirs. New Eng. Woman's Soc.; formerly active Girl Scouts U.S.A.; mem. Camp Fire Girls, 1918-20. Recipient numerous awards for civic work, including ARC, USN. Mem. Am. Assn. Retired Persons, DAR (past bd. dirs. N.Y. State, past regent Triangle chpt.-Northfield, Pa. and North East) Magna Charta Dames, Pa. Garden Club (master accredited judge), AAUU (life), North East Garden Club (past pres.), Lawrence Park Garden Club, Westfield Garden Club, also others. Democrat. Roman Catholic.

HITCHCOCK, KAREN RUTH, biology educator, university dean; b. Mineola, N.Y., Feb. 10, 1943; d. Roy Clinton and Ruth (Wardell) H. BS in Biology, St. Lawrence U., 1964; PhD in Anatomy, U. Rochester, 1968. Postdoctoral fellow in pulmonary cell biology, Webb-Waring Inst. Med. Rsch., 1968-70; asst. prof. dept. anatomy Tufts U. Sch. Medicine, Boston, 1970-75, assoc. prof. dept. anatomy, 1975-80, assoc. prof., acting chmn. dept. anatomy, 1976-78, assoc. prof., chmn. dept. anatomy, 1978-80, prof., chmn. dept. anatomy and cellular biology, 1980-82, George A. Bates prof. histology, chmn. dept. anatomy and cellular biology, 1982-85; prof. dept. cell biology and anatomy Tex. Tech U. Health Scis. Ctr., assoc. dean Tex. Tech U. Sch. Medicine, Lubbock, 1985-87; vice chancellor rsch., dean grad. coll., prof. cell biology,anatomy and biol. scis. U. Ill., Chgo., 1987—; mem. adv. com. NIH, Nat. Bd. Med. Examiners, 1983-85. Mem. Am. Assn. Anatomy (chmn., exec. council 1979-81), Am. Assn. Anatomists (exec. com. 1981-85, v.p. 1986-88, pres. 1990-91), Nat. Bd. of Med. Examiners, Nat. Assn. for Biomed. Rsch. (bd. dirs. 1990), Ill. Soc. Med. Rsch. (pres. 1990). Home: 505 N Lake Shore Dr Chicago IL 60611 Office: U Ill Chgo Grad Coll Chicago IL 60680

HITCHCOCK, LILLIAN DOROTHY STAW, educator, actress, musician; b. Detroit, Dec. 19, 1922; d. Charles Stawowczyk And Mary Waligora; m. Richard Elmer Hitchcock, June 28, 1952; children: Charles, Harriet, Roger, Stephen. BA in Edn., Wayne State U., 1946, MA in Interpretative Speech, 1952; postgrad., U. Wis., 1948; cert. in art, Inst. for Am. Univs., Avignon, France, 1981; cert. in French, Cath. U. Paris, 1983. Speech and English tchr. Lakeview High Sch., St. Claire Shores, Mich., 1947-49; speech and journalism tchr. Mercy Coll., Detroit, 1949-52; speech and English tchr. Birmingham (Mich.) Pub. Schs., 1960-88, Bloomfield Hills (Mich.) Pub. Schs., Detroit Pub. Schs., 1960-70; French tchr. Montessori, Bloomfield Hills, 1988—. Performer, dir. Civic Theatre, Wayne U., Cath. Theatre, Detroit, 1943-46; chmn. Detroit Theatre Olympiade for World Community Theatre, 1979; del. to People's Republic of China, People to People-Health Care, 1984; mem. St. Dunstan's Theatre, Bloomfield Hills; docent Cranbrook Mus. Modern Art, Bloomfield Hills, 1988—. Mem. AAUW (bd. dirs. children's theatre Birmingham 1960-80), UN rep. and del. 1970-73), Tuesday Musicale. Roman Catholic. Home: 6140 Westmoor Rd Birmingham MI 48010

HITE, CATHARINE LEAVEY, orchestra manager; b. Boston, Oct. 1, 1924; d. Edmond Harrison and Ruth Farrington Leavey; B.A., Coll. William and Mary, 1945; m. Robert Atkinson Hite, Aug. 28, 1948; children—Charles Harrison, Patricia Hite Barton, Catharine Hite Dunn. Restoration guide Williamsburg Restoration, 1944-45; asst. edn. dept. Honolulu Acad. Arts, 1945-46; sec., tour guide edn. dept. office chief curator Nat. Gallery Art, 1946-48; opera liason/coord. Honolulu Symphony, 1972-73, asst. to gen. mgr., 1973-75, community devel. dir./opera coord., 1975-77, dir. ops./opera prodn. coord., 1977-79, orch. mgr., 1979-84, mem. exec. com., 1965-69, pres. women's assn., 1965-66; com. chmn., opera assn. chmn. Hawaii Opera Theatre, 1966-69. Mem. W. R. Farrington Scholarship Com., 1977-82, chmn., 1982-89; mem. community arts panel State Found. Culture and the Arts, 1982, State Found. Music and Opera, 1984; docent Iolani Palace, 1990. Mem. Jr. League, Phi Beta Kappa. Episcopalian.

HITE, SHERE D., author, cultural historian; b. St. Joseph, Mo., Nov. 2, 1942; m. Friedrich Horicke. B.A. cum laude, U. Fla., 1964, M.A., 1968; postgrad., Columbia U., 1968-69. Dir. feminist sexuality project NOW, N.Y.C., 1972-78; dir. Hite Rsch. Internat., N.Y.C., 1978—; instr. female sexuality NYU, 1977—; lectr. Harvard U., McGill U., Columbia U., Cambridge U. (Eng.), The Sorbonne, Paris, also numerous women's groups, internat. lectr., 1977-90; mem. adv. bd. Am. Found. Gender and Genital Medicine, Johns Hopkins U. Author: The Hite Report: A Nationwide Study of Female Sexuality, 1976, The Hite Report on Male Sexuality, 1981, Women and Love: A Cultural Revolution in Progress, 1987; cons. editor: Jour. Sex Edn. and Therapy, Jour. Sexuality and Disability. Mem. NOW, AAAS, Am. Hist. Assn., Am. Sociol. Assn., Acad. Polit. Sci., Soc. for Women in Philosophy, Internat. Women Writer's Orgn. (v.p.). Office: PO Box 5282 FDR Sta New York NY 10022

HITE, SHIRLEY L., real estate company executive and owner; b. Blackwell, Okla., May 11, 1935; d. Clarence Clifford and Rosetta Ethyle Davison; m. Ralph E. Hite, June 13, 1954; children: Ralph E. III, Deborah L., Terry L. AA, Coffeyville Coll., 1954; grad., Realtor Inst. Cert. relocation specialist. Pres., broker-owner KC Classic, Inc., Realtors, Overland Park; broker mgr. Showcase of Homes, Inc., Realtors, Overland Park; sales exec. Real Estate 100, Inc., Overland Park. Bd. trustees Cen. United Meth. Ch. Mem. NAFE, Women's Coun. Realtors, Johnson County Bd. Realtors, Kans. Assoc. Realtors, Nat. Assn. Realtors. Home: 25220 W 71st St Shawnee Mission KS 66227 Office: 7295 W 97th St Overland Park KS 66212

HITT, IOLA HALEY, dietitian, consultant; b. Absorokee, Mont., Jan. 4, 1919; d. John Perry and Dorothea Marion (Haggerty) Haley; m. Wright Hitt, June 21, 1947; children: Samuel, Jeffrey, Robert, Douglas, Julie Anne. BS, Oreg. State U., 1941; postgrad., U. Calif., 1946. Intern Mass. Gen. Hosp., Boston, 1941-42; dietitian U. Calif. Hosp., San Francisco, 1942-43; clin. dietitian U.S. Marine Hosp., Detroit, 1947; out-patient dietitian City Hosp., Detroit, 1947-48; clin. dietitian Wayne County Hosp., Eloise, Mich., 1948-54; asst. dir. dietetics dept. William Beaumont Hosp., Royal Oak, Mich., 1957-60; sch. lunch dir. Troy (Mich.) Bd. Edn., 1961-63; dir. food svc. Paterson (N.J.) Gen. Hosp., 1965-70; dir. dept. dietetics Chilton Meml. Hosp., Pompton Plains, N.J., 1970-86; cons., instr. Morris County Schs., Denville and Cedar Grove, N.J., 1975—; Nutrition advisor Mt. Lakes (N.J.) Bd. Edn., 1987—. Chairperson mayor's com. UN Weekend, Mt. Lakes, 1965-86; social chmn. St. Peters Episcopal Ch., Mt. Lakes. 1st lt. M.C. U.S. Army, 1943-46. Winner in running since 1983 (17 trophies); recipient Pres.'s award in swimming, 1980. Mem. Am. Dietetic Assn. (pres. N.J. chpt. 1987-88), AAUW (scholarship chmn. 1970-71), N.J. Dietetic Assn. (adminstrn. chmn. 1968-72), Am. Hosp. Food Svc. Adminstrs. (chmn. 1982-83), Cosmos Club, Lake Arrowhead Club. Home: 1 Lakewood Dr Mountain Lakes NJ 07046

HIXSON, SHEILA ELLIS, state legislator; b. L'Anse, Mich., Feb. 9, 1933; divorced; children: Denise, Lynn, Andy, Todd. AB, No. Mich. U., 1953. Tchr. Head Start; campaign mgr., aide Congressman William Ford, Mich., 1963-64; adminstrv. aide to state senator, 1965-66, legal aide to sec. of Dem. Nat. Conv., 1966-76; mem. Md. Ho. of Dels., Annapolis, 1976—, mem. ways and means. Chair task force on child abuse and neglect, joint com. on fed.-state relations, lottery com.; mem. Montgomery County Dem. State Cen. Com. Mem. Nat. Assn. Sunday Sch. Instrs., Nat. Profl. and Bus. Women's Orgn., Women's Polit. Caucus, Plowmen and Fishermen, NOW. Home: 1008 Broadmore Circle Silver Spring MD 20904 Office: Md Ho of Dels Room 221 Annapolis MD 21401

HJELLE, MARY ANN, educator; b. Grand Forks, N.D., May 7, 1930; d. Andrew George and Stella (Curry) Omlid; m. Roger D. Hjelle, July 21, 1951. BA with honors, U. N.D., 1951. Cert. home econs. tchr., Minn. Home econs. tchr. Osseo (Minn.) Pub. Schs., 1953-54, Waconia (Minn.) Pub. Schs., 1955-56, Spring Lake Pk. (Minn.) Pub. Schs., 1956-57, St. Louis Pk. (Minn.) Pub. Schs., 1962-63; substitute tchr. Pub. Schs. in Mpls., St. Louis Pk., Minnetonka, Minn., 1954-70; ret.; advisor Future Homemakers Am., Waconia, 1955-56. Vol. Reps. Golden Valley, Minn., 1963, 65, Leukemia Soc. Am., Deephaven, 1980—, Minnetonka Sr. Ctr., 1987. Mem. AAUW (membership v.p. Minnetonka br. 1981-82, historian 1989-90, Outstanding Achievement award 1982), Delta Gamma, Phi Upsilon Omicron, Minnetonka Country Club. Lutheran. Home: 3935 Walden Rd Deephaven MN 55391

HLAVA, DIANE ELIZABETH, preservation planner; b. Glendale, Calif., July 9, 1948; d. Robert Norman and Dorothy (Muro) Williams; m. Edward Rudolf Hlava, Mar. 21 1970 (div. 1990). BA, Calif. State U., L.A., 1973, MA, 1988. Cert. elem. tchr., Calif. Tchr. L.A. Unified Sch. Dist., 1975-76, Rosemead (Calif.) Sch. Dist., 1976-77; resource tchr. Pasadena (Calif.) Unified Sch. Dist., 1977-78; editorial asst. L.A. Times, 1978-80, copyeditor, feature writer, 1980-83; cons. Sierra Madre, Calif., 1983—; assoc. planner Environ. Planning Assocs., L.A., 1989; asst. planner City of Burbank, Calif., 1989—; instr. Cerritos Community Coll., Norwalk, Calif., 1990—. Bd. dirs. Pasadena Heritage, 1984-90, sec. bd. dirs., 1985-86; mem. steering com. Pasadena Resident in Def. of the Environ., 1988—; reader Henry G. Huntington Libr. and Art Gallery, 1985—. Mem. Assn. for Women in Architecture, L.A. Conservancy, Am. Planning Assn., Assn. Environ. Profls., Soc. of Architectl. Historians (bd. dirs. So. Calif. chpt. 1989—), Sierra Club. Democrat. Office: PO Box 1057 Sierra Madre CA 91025

HLAVAC, PHYLLIS JOAN IDLE, nurse; b. Lima, Ohio, Nov. 28, 1949; d. Fred Raymond and Ruth Avis (Hurley) Idle. BS in Nursing, Ohio State U., 1971; M. Nursing, Emory U., 1981. Staff devel. instr. St. John Hosp., Cleve., 1974-79; asst. clin. coord. Cobb Gen. Hosp., Austell, Ga., 1979-80; clin. assoc. Nell Hodgson Woodruff Sch. Nursing, Emory U., Atlanta, 1984-90; dir. maternal-child nursing Anderson Meml. Hosp., Anderson, S.C., 1989-90; clin. nurse specialist Northside Hosp., Atlanta, 1990—. Recipient Fed. Traineeship for grad. study. Mem. ANA, GNA, NANN, GANN, NPA, SPA, GPA, NAACOG (cert. RNC in neonatal nursing, cert. neonatal nurse practitioner), Sigma Theta Tau. Home: 1803 Riverview Dr Marietta GA 30067 Office: Northside Hosp 1000 Johnson Ferry Rd NE Atlanta GA 30342

HLOZEK, CAROLE DIANE QUAST, business executive; b. Dallas, Apr. 17, 1959; d. Robert E. and Bonnie (Wootton) Quast. BS, Tex. A&M U., 1982, BBA, 1982. Internal auditor Brown & Root Inc., Houston, 1982-84; asst. contr. Wilson Supply Co., Houston, 1984-86, sr. acctg. supr., Hydro Conduit Corp., Houston, 1986-87; fin. analyst Am. Capital, Houston, 1989—. Mem. MENSA, Houston Zool. Soc., Nat. Wildlife Assn., Houston Livestock Show and Rodeo. Lutheran. Home: 8034 Log Hollow Houston TX 77040 Office: Am Capital PO Box 3121 Houston TX 77253-3121

HMIELESKI, CAROL LYDIA, local government official; b. Perth Amboy, N.J., June 7, 1950; d. Alexander and Rose (Brozozowski) Shumny; 1 child, R.J. BA, Rider Coll., 1972; MA, Rutgers U., 1984. Tchr., South Amboy Bd. Edn., N.J., 1972-73, St. Stephens Sch., Perth Amboy, N.J., 1974-76, St. Theresa's Sch., Linden, N.J., 1976-80; registered pub. purchasing official; ins. analyst The Children's Pl., Pinebrook, N.J., 1980-83; purchasing agt. Borough of Carteret, N.J., 1983—; notary public, State of N.J., 1983—; continuing edn. tchr. Woodbridge Bd. Edn., N.J., 1979—. Mem. Nat. Inst. Govtl. Purchasing (treas. 1984—), Govtl. Purchasing Assn., Carteret Police Athletic League. Roman Catholic. Avocation: antique collecting.

HO, WEIFAN L., retail buyer; b. N.Y.C., Mar. 11, 1951; d. Ho chee and Kwan Fong Lui. Student, Middlebury Coll.; BA, CCNY, 1972. Buyer Bloomingdales, N.Y.C.; sr. buyer Carson Pirie Scott, Chgo.; buyer Gimbels, N.Y.C. Mem. NAFE. Office: 1000 Third Ave New York NY 10022

HOADLEY, IRENE BRADEN (MRS. EDWARD HOADLEY), librarian; b. Hondo, Tex., Sept. 26, 1938; d. Andrew Henry and Theresa Lillian (Lebold) Braden; m. Edward Hoadley, Feb. 21, 1970. B.A., U. Tex., 1960; A.M.L.S., U. Mich., 1961, Ph.D., 1967; M.A., Kans. State U., 1965. Cataloger Sam Houston State Tchrs. Coll. Library, Huntsville, Tex., 1961-62; head circulation dept. Kans. State U. Library, Manhattan, 1962-64; grad. asst. U. Mich. Dept. of Library Sci., 1964-66; librarian gen. adminstrn. and research Ohio State U. Libraries, Columbus, 1966-73; asst. dir. libraries adminstrv. services Ohio State U. Libraries, 1973-74; dir. of libraries Tex. A. and M. U. Library, College Station, Tex., 1974—; dir. Higher Edn. Act Inst. Quantitative Methods in Librarianship, Ohio State U., summer 1969; instr. inst. U. Calif. at San Diego, 1970, summer; Mem. steering com. Gov's. Conf. on Library and Info. Services, Ohio, 1973-74, joint chairperson, 1974; mem. adv. com. Library Services and Constrn. Act Cuyahoga County Pub. Library, Cleve., 1973. Author: (with others) Physiological Factors Relating to Terrestrial Altitutes: A Bibliography, 1968; Editor: (with Alice S. Clark) Quantitative Methods in Librarianship: Standards, Research, Management, 1972; Contbr. (with Alice S. Clark) articles to profl. jours. Recipient Scarecrow Press award for library lit., 1971; Distinguished Alumnus award Sch. Library Sci., U. Mich., 1976. Mem. ALA, Ohio Libr. Assn. (chmn. constn. com. 1967-68, chmn. election tellers com. 1969, asst. gen. chmn. local conf. com. 1969-70, sec. 1970-71, v.p., pres.-elect 1971-72, chmn. budget advisory com. 1971-72, pres. 1972-73, bd. dirs. 1970-75), Tex. Libr. Assn. (com. on White House conf. 1975-77, vice chmn., chmn. coll. and univ. div. 1977-78, exec. bd. 1978-81, legis. com. 1987-89, Tex. Libr. of Yr.), Assn. Rsch. Librs. (bd. dirs. 1978-81, search com. for exec. dir. 1980), Midwest Fedn. Libr. Assns. (exec. bd. 1973-74, chairperson program com. 1974), Online Computer Libr. Ctr. (pres. User's Council 1983-84, 84-85, trustee 1984—, chmn. pers. and compensation com. 1987-89), Tex. Conf. Librs. and Info. Svcs. (co-chair program com.), Phi Kappa Phi, Phi Alpha Theta, Pi Lambda Theta, Beta Phi Mu, Phi Delta Gamma. Home: Route 5 Box 1048 College Station TX 77840

HOAG, SHARON KAY, software engineer; b. Adrian, Mich., Jan. 9, 1963; d. John J. and Bonita L. (Bunge) H. BS, Ea. Mich. U., 1985. Software engr. CText, Ann Arbor, Schlumberger, Ann Arbor, Mich. Mem. NAFE.

HOANG, JOY GONZALES, special event planning executive; b. Carmel, Calif., Dec. 30, 1949; d. Jose Quijano and Caridad Rodriquez (Martinez) Gonzales; m. Jack Minh Hoang, July 16, 1968 (dec. Aug. 1987); children: Jolene, Mario, Jack, Cherie, Elizabeth. Student pvt. schs., Carmel and Monterey, Calif. Front desk mgr. Royal Inn, Monterey, 1972-74; asst. reservations mgr. Hyatt Hotel, Monterey, 1977-78; catering services rep. Casa Munras Hotel, Monterey, 1977-78; reservations mgr. Doubletree Hotel, Monterey, 1980-82, front office mgr., 1982-84, dir. catering, 1984-87, rooms div. mgr., 1987, dir. human resources, 1987-89; conf. and spl. event planning mgmt. exec. Outrageous Occasions, Monterey, Calif., 1989—. Chmn. parent adv. council Monterey Sch. Dist., 1984-86; active Leadership Monterey Peninsula; bd. dirs. local YWCA. Mem. NAFE, Cen. Coast Pers. Network, Nat. Assn. Catering Execs., Am. Soc. Assn. Execs., Profl. Conv. Mgmt. Assn., Internat. Platform Assn., Soroptimist. Democrat. Roman Catholic. Home: 590 Harcourt Ave Seaside CA 93955 Office: Outrageous Occasions 1015 Cass St Ste #1 Monterey CA 93940

HOBACK, FLORENCE KUNST, psychiatrist; b. Grafton, Wv., Oct. 26, 1922; d. G H A and Mary (Conaway) Kunst; M. John Holland Hoback, Oct. 27, 1945; children: Holly Hoback Clark, Conaway K. AB, W.Va. U., 1944; postgrad., U. Md., Balt., 1948. Pvt. practice medicine Huntington, W.Va., 1950-55; psychiatrist VA Hosp., Huntington, 1955-60; instr. psychiatry Tng. Med. Coll. VA, Richmond, 1960-65; pvt. practice psychiatry Huntington; cons. Social Security, Huntington, Wv., 1987. Police commn. City of Huntington, 1975-77. Fellow Am. Psychiatric Assn. (pres. 1975-76), mem. AMA, W.Va. Med. Assn., Am. Women's Med. Assn. Home and Office: 2658 3d Ave Huntington WV 25702

HOBAN, LILLIAN, author, illustrator; b. Phila., May 18; d. Jules and Fanny (Godwin) Aberman; m. Russell Conwell Hoban (div.); children: Phoebe, Abrom, Esmé, Julia. Student, Phila. Mus. Sch., 1944-48, Hanya Holm Sch. Dance, N.Y.C., 1945-55, Martha Graham Sch. Dance. Author, illustrator: (children's books) I Can Read, Arthur Series, 1972—; illustrator: (children's books) Frances Series, 1964— (Notable Book award), First Grade Series, 1967—, Jim Books, Charlie the Tramp (Christopher award). Mem. PEN, Authors Guild, Soc. Children's Book Writers. Democrat. Jewish.

HOBBIE, SUSAN JANET, banker; b. Englewood, N.J., Jan. 11, 1943; d. Caleb K. and Janet (Brown) H.; m. George M. Bennett Jr., June 9, 1973 (div. Mar. 1987). BA, Pa. State U., 1965; MBA, U. Conn., 1982, postgrad., 1983. Aide to Sen. Gaylord Nelson U.S. Senate, Washington, 1966-68; aide to Rep. Thomas J. Meskill U.S. Ho. Reps., Washington, 1968-70; spl. asst. to Gov. Thomas J. Meskill State of Conn., Hartford, 1971; dep. commr. Conn. Dept. Community Affairs, Hartford, 1972, commr., 1973-74; dir. ho. Republican office Conn. Ho. Reps., Hartford, 1975-81; acad. advisor Grad. Sch. Bus. U. Conn., Hartford, 1982-83; govt. rels. officer Conn. Mut. Life Ins. Co., Hartford, 1983-84; v.p. area mgr. community banking The Conn. Bank and Trust Co., N.A., Hartford, 1985, v.p. regional mgr., 1985-86; pres., gen. mgr. Bank of New England Life Ins. Co., Boston, 1987—; dir. Conn. Housing Fin. Authority, Hartford, 1972-74; mem. Canton Housing Authority, Canton, 1974-75; vice chmn., commr. State Elections Enforcement Commn., Hartford, 1982-83. Del. Rep. Nat. Conv., Dallas, 1984, alt., New Orleans, 1988; fin. com. to U.S. Rep. Nancy L. Johnson, Conn., 1985—; mem. state fin. com. Conn. Republicans, Hartford, 1986—; advisor Julie Belaga for Gov. Com., Westport, 1986; corporator Newington Children's Hosp., 1986—; bd. dirs. Greater Hartford Architecture Conservancy, Hartford, 1984-87, chair nominations, 1985, 86, 87; bd. dirs. Nat. Rep. Legis. Campaign Com., Washington, 1986—. Named Disting. Women of Conn. UN Internat Woman's Year, 1970. Home: 215 Tunxis Rd West Hartford CT 06107 Office: Bank New Eng Life Ins Co 28 State St Boston MA 02109

HOBBS, ANN TODD, sales executive; b. Forrest City, Ark., Nov. 25, 1926; d. William Joe and Maudie (McGee) Todd; m. James Robert Hobbs, Mar. 29, 1948; children: Bardara Ray, Sandra Lynn Davis Hobbs, Brenda Onstott Hobbs. Student, Memphis U., 1948. Bookkeeper Forrest City (Ark.) Wholesale Grocery, 1949-51, Kimdell Wholesale Grocery, Ft. Worth, Tex., 1951-58, A. Brandt & Co., Ft. Worth, 1958-64; saleswoman A.L. Randall Co., Prairie View, Ill., 1964—; Speaker Richland Coll., Dallas, 1986-87. Vol. Al-Anon Drug Program, Ft. Worth, 1986-87; tchr. Beckspur Baptist Ch., Forrest City, 1949-51. Mem. Am. Acad. Florists, Tex. State Florists Assn. (wholesale dir. 1982-84, chair wholesale com., 1983-84, chair membership 1983-84, fin. com. 1986—, chair credit union 1981-87, chair convention 1987, pres. 1987-88), Ft. Worth Florists Assn. (sec. 1982-84). Republican. Baptist. Home: PO Box 211 Hurst TX 76053

HOBBS, JEWELL ELIZABETH, educator; b. Washington, Sept. 10, 1945; d. Jewel Edgar Hobbs and Norma Long. BA, Howard U., 1968; MA, Trinity Coll., Washington, 1975; postgrad., Union Inst. Program dir. YWCA, Rochester, N.Y., 1968-69; Head Start tchr. D.C. Pub. Schs., Washington, 1969—. Producer for pub.-access TV. Named one of Outstanding Young Women of Am.; recipient Cert. for Community Svc. Mem. NAFE, D.C. TV, Assn. for Childhood Edn. Internat., Washington Scholastic Press Ann., D.C. Assn. for Adult Devel. and Aging, Nat. Guild of Hypnotists, Phi Delta Kappa. Democrat. Baptist. Home: 2158 30th St NE Washington DC 20018

HOBBS, JOAN PIZZO, data processing executive; b. Providence, Oct. 11, 1957; d. Ralph Edmund and Albina Margaret (Walsh) Pizzo; m. Walter Romeo Hobbs III, Nov. 22, 1979; children: Kelsey Mackensie, Spencer William. BS, BA, R.I. Coll., 1979; cert., Blake Programming Inst., 1980; MBA, Providence Coll., 1988. Lic. real estate broker, R.I. Substitute tchr., pub. schs. R.I., 1979-80; billing clk. Femic Inc., North Providence, R.I., 1980-81; software cons. I.P.L., Inc., Providence, R.I., 1981-84; programmer, analyst A.S.E. Services Inc., Woonsocket, R.I., 1984-85; mgr. data processing Builders Specialties, Pawtucket, R.I., 1985—. Elem. sch. computer edn. vol. Mem. NAFE. Home: 1049 Smithfield Ave Lincoln RI 02865 Office: Builders Specialties Co 258 Pine St Pawtucket RI 02865

HOBBS, PATRICIA ANN, educator; b. Sullivan, Ind., Sept. 5, 1934; d. Charles Roland and Hester May (Asdell) Thudium; m. Lee Charles Siple, May, 1956 (div. Mar. 1975); children: Mark Christopher, John Nelson; m. Howard Walter Hobbs, June 19, 1976. BS, U. Ill., 1957. Sec. Colo. State U., Ft. Collins, 1965-77; owner pre-sch. Children's House, Lamar, Colo., 1978-82; dir. Lamar Community Day Care Ctr., Lamar, 1982-88; head tchr. Head Start, Lamar, 1988—. Home: 410 E Parmenter St Lamar CO 81052

HOBEN, SISTER MARIAN WILLIAM, college president; b. Coaldale, Pa. BA in English, Immaculata Coll., 1955; MA in English, Villanova U., 1961; PhD in English, U. Pa., 1968. Joined Servants of Immaculate Heart of Mary, Roman Cath. Ch. Elem. tchr. various schs., 1944-55; secondary tchr. various schs., 1955-60; faculty Immaculata (Pa.) Coll., 1960—, chmn. dept. English, 1971-74, dean coll. devel., 1973-78, acad. dean, 1978-82, pres., 1982—. Chair Gov.'s Citizen's Adv. Com., Pa., 1983-85. Recipient Outstanding Grad. English Dept. medal Villanova U. Grad. Sch., 1982, scroll Newcomen Soc., 1987. Mem. AAUW, Commn. for Ind. Colls. and Univs. (exec. and instl. research coms. 1983—), Pa. Assn. Colls. and Univs. (chair student relations com. 1984—), Nat. Council Tchrs. English, Alpha Sigma Lambda (Iota Kappa chpt.). Office: Immaculata Coll Immaculata PA 19345-0901*

HOBOR, NANCY ALLEN, management; b. Chgo., Aug. 18, 1846; d. John Selden and Jane (Rinder) Coulson; m. Michael Joseph Hobor, Apr. 29, 1972; children: Aquinas Adam, Justinian Ram. BA, U. Chgo., 1968, MA, PhD, 1973; MBA, Northwestern U., Evanston, Ill., 1977. Pub. affairs analyst Standard Oil, Chgo., 1973-77; v.p. pub. affairs Am. Hosp. Supply Corp., Evanston, Ill., 1978-86;, 1986-88; dir. investor relations UAL Inc., Chgo., Ill., 1986-88; dir. communications and investor rels. Morton Internat., Ill., 1988-; dir. AHSC Employee Credit Union, Evanston, Ill., 1984-86; mem. Chgo. Fin. Exchange, 1988—. Fellow: Ford Found., U. Chgo. 1972-73. Office: Morton Internat 110 North Wacker Dr Chicago IL 60606

HOBSON, CYNTHIA REGINA, civil service administrator; b. Chgo., Mar. 27, 1940; d. Johnny Austin and Lillian (Cole) Austin Brewer; m. Lawrence Earl Hobson, July 17, 1960; children: Bryan, Craig, Christopher. AA, Kennedy/King Jr. Coll., Chgo., 1958; BS in Human Relations/Orgn. Behavior, U. San Francisco, 1979. Cert. in labor relations U. Calif., Davis. Tchrs. aide Head Start Program, Sacramento, 1966; clk. Motor Vehicle Dept., Sacramento, 1968; equal employment cons. Dept. Corrections, Sacramento, 1971-76; assoc. personnel analyst State Personnel Bd., Sacramento, 1976-79; assoc. budget analyst Gen. Svcs., Sacramento, 1979-81; chief adminstrv. svcs. Health and Welfare Data Ctr., Sacramento, 1981-86; dep. div. chief Calif. Energy Commn., Sacramento, 1986—; cons. conf. planning, Sacramento; career counselor. Bd. dirs. YWCA, Sacramento, 1989—; mem. adv. bd. Consumnes River Coll., Sacramento, 1976—. Recipient Outstanding Women's award YWCA, 1989; Return to the Source award Calif. Black State Educators, 1980. Mem. Sacramento Black Women's Network (life; founder, pres. 1979-82, Spl. Recognition 1989), NAACP (life), Black Advocates in State Svc. (treas. 1975). Democrat. Roman Catholic.

HOBSON, GINGER KAY, public information officer; b. Meadville, Pa., May 7, 1959; d. George Earl and Barbara Elaine (Garvin) Jacobs; m. Andrew James Hobson, June 11, 1983. BS, Westminster Coll., New Wilmington, Pa., 1981; MBA, Babson Coll., Wellesley, Mass., 1989. From internat. auditor to fin. analyst Gen. Electric Co., Schenectady, NY, 1981-83; investment analyst Gen. Electric Co., N.Y.C., 1983-85; contract adminstrv. Gen. Electric Co., Wilmington, Mass., 1985-87; contract compl. auditor Gen. Electric Co., Lynn, Mass.; gov. acctg. mgr. BBN Communications Corp., Cambridge, Mass., 1988-89; govt. compiance mgr. Metcalf & Eddy Cos. Inc., Wakefield, Mass., 1989—. Republican. Methodist.

HOBSON, LOIS REN(É)E, foundation administrator; b. Salisbury, N.C., Sept. 14, 1949; d. Rufus and Mary (Kerr) H.; 1 child, Kevin. BA, Livingstone Coll., 1971; Student, Trinity Coll., 1982, Prince Georges Community Coll., 1983. Exec. dir. Child Care Systems, Washington, 1974-85; case mgr., recruiter Big Bros. Inc., Washington, 1984—; cons. in field. Tchr., ARC, 1982, Positive Energy, 1989. Recipient Outstanding Svc. award D.C. Gov., 1981. Mem. NAACP, NAFE, Bus. Women Assn. Am. Methodist. Office: Child Care Resources 1730 K St NW Ste 304 Washington DC

HOCHMEISTER, ANGELA BETH, lawyer; b. Evansville, Ind., Apr. 9, 1958; d. John Louis and Ruth Mae (Kirsch) H. BS, James Madison U., 1980; JD, U. Richmond, 1983. Bar: Va. 1983, U.S. Dist. Ct. (ea. dist.) Va. 1983, U.S. Dist. Ct. (we. dist.) Va. 1984. Assoc. James D. Parker, Hampton, Va., 1983-84, Hatmaker & Dinsmore, Harrisonburg, Va., 1984-85, Law Office David J. Hatmaker, Harrisonburg, 1985-87; pvt. practice Harrisonburg, 1987—; spl. justice for commitment hearings Gen. Dist. Ct., Harrisonburg, 1986—; adj. prof. James Madison U., Harrisonburg, 1984-85, Blue Ridge Community Coll., Weyers Cave, Va., 1988—. Bd. dirs. Big Bros./Big Sisters, Harrisonburg, 1984, com. chmn., 1985-87, sec. 1987-88; treas. Area C Reherd Acres Homeowner's Assn., Harrisonburg, 1984-89; bd. dirs. Blue Ridge Legal Aid Svcs., 1989—; pres. Area C Reherd Acres Homeowner's Assn., Harrisonburg, 1990—. Mem. ABA, Va. State Bar, Harrisonburg/Rockingham County Bar Assn. (sec.-treas. 1987-88), Assn. Trial Lawyers Am., Va. Trial Lawyers Assn., Working Women's Forum. Home: 874 Vine St Harrisonburg VA 22801 Office: 306 Sovran Bank Bldg Harrisonburg VA 22801

HOCHRON, BERYL JUDITH, marketing and advertising consultant; b. N.Y.C., Jan. 2, 1947; d. Nathan and Marion (Freedman) Sadowsky; m. Joel Hochron, Jan. 2, 1981; 1 child, Matthew Noah. BBA cum laude, CCNY, 1968; MBA, Baruch Coll., 1972. Staff acct. Haskins & Sells, N.Y.C., 1963-65; grad. asst. Baruch Coll., 1968-69; project dir. Batten, Barton, Durstine & Osborn Advt., N.Y.C., 1969-71; sr. project dir. AHF Mktg. Rsch. Co., N.Y.C., 1971-74; mgr. RCA, N.Y.C., 1974-76; sr. rsch. mgr. Clairol Inc., N.Y.C., 1976-83; group mgr. Lever Bros., N.Y.C., 1983-85; cons. mktg. rsch., 1985—. Mem. Am. Mktg. Assn. (asst. sec. N.Y. chpt. 1980-81, sec. 1981-82), Nat. Assn. Female Execs. Home: 248 Harriman Rd Irvington-on-Hudson NY 10533

HOCHSCHILD, CARROLL SHEPHERD, company administrator, educator; b. Whittier, Calif., Mar. 31, 1935; d. Vernon Vero and Effie Corinne (Hollingsworth) Shepherd; m. Richard Hochschild, July 25, 1959; children: Christopher Paul, Stephen Shepherd. BA in Internat. Rels., Pomona Coll., 1956; Teaching credential U. Calif., Berkeley, 1957; MBA, Pepperdine U., 1985; cert. in fitness instrn., U. Calif., Irvine, 1988. Cert. elem. tchr., Calif. elem. tchr. Oakland Pub. Schs. (Calif.), 1957-58, San Lorenzo Pub. Schs. (Calif.), 1958-59, Pasadena Pub. Schs. (Calif.), 1959-60, Huntington Beach Pub. Schs. (Calif.), 1961-63, 67-68; adminstrv. asst. Microwave Instruments, Corona del Mar, Calif., 1968-74; co-owner Hoch Co., Corona del Mar, 1978—. Rep. Calif. Tchrs. Assn., Huntington Beach, 1962-63. Mem. AAUW, P.E.O. (projects chmn. 1990—), Internat. Dance-Exercise Found., NAFE, Am. Soc. for Tng. and Devel. (Orange County chpt.), Republican. Presbyterian. Clubs: Toastmistress (corr. sec. 1983), Jr. Ebell (fine arts chmn. Newport Beach 1966-67).

HOCHSTADT, JOY, biomedical research scientist, scientific and research director; b. N.Y.C., May 6, 1939; d. Julius Louis and Edith (Tabatchnick) H.; m. Harvey Leon Ozer, Feb. 3, 1960; 1 child, Juliane Natasha Hochstadt-Ozer. A.B. in Zoology, Barnard Coll., 1960; A.M. in Biologic Scis. (grad. fellow 1961-62), Stanford U., 1963; vis. fellow in tumor biology, Karolinska Inst., Stockholm, 1964-65; research fellow in biol. chemistry, Harvard U., 1965-66; Ph.D. in Microbiology, Georgetown U., 1968; postdoctoral fellow NIH, 1968-70. Diplomate Am. Bd. Clin. Chemistry. Instr. biology Coll. San Mateo, Calif., 1962-63; teaching asst. microbiology Georgetown Med. Sch., 1967-68; established investigator Am. Heart Assn.; lab. biochemistry Nat. Heart and Lung Inst., Bethesda, Md., 1970-72; sr. scientist Worcester Found. Exptl. Biology, Shrewsbury, Mass., 1972-76; adj. prof. biochemistry Central New Eng. Coll., Worcester, Mass., 1974-75; vis. prof. membrane research Weizmann Inst. Sci., Rehovot, Israel, 1976; vis. prof. biochemistry and biophysics U. R.I., Kingston, 1976-77; research prof. microbiology N.Y. Med. Coll., Valhalla, 1977-81; dir. Div. Clin. Biochemistry and Basic Research in Pathology, Cath. Med. Center, Queens, 1981-88; prof. clin. microbiology Cornell U. Med. Sch., 1986—; v.p., scientific dir. Hercon Labs. Corp. subs. Health Chem Corp., N.Y.C., 1988-90; sr. v.p. Biomed. Techs. div. Princeton Polymer Labs., Plainsboro, N.J., 1989—; predoctoral trainee USPHS, 1966-67, spl. trainee, 1973; investigator Am. Heart Assn., 1970-75; mem. NSF postdoctoral fellowship evaluation panel in biology NRC, 1975—; mem. postdoctoral fellowship evaluation panel NATO, 1978—; mem. cell biology study sect. NIH, 1979—, mem. biomed. scis. fellowship com., 1979—. Editorial bd. Jour. Bacteriology, 1975-80; contbr. research papers, methods articles and monographs to profl. lit. Mem. nat. policy com. Profl. Women's Caucus, 1970-73; mem. alumnae council Barnard Coll., 1975—; mem. com. revision biochemistry and biotech. div. U.S. Pharmacoprial Conv., 1990—. Cancer Internat. Rsch. Coop. Snall scholar, 1965; fellow USPHS, 1967-70; grantee NIH, 1973, NSF, 1978-80; travel award Am. Soc. Biol. Chemists, Stockholm, 1973, Hamburg, 1976, Am. Soc. Microbiology, Jerusalem, 1973. Fellow Am. Acad. Microbiology, Am. Inst. Chemists (profl. opportunities com., legis. com.), Nat. Acad. Clin. Biochemistry; mem. Am. Heart Assn. (basic sci. council), Am. Soc. Microbiology (status of women com. 1970-73, sec. physiology div. 1972-74, mem. divisional nominating com. 1973), Am. Soc. Biol. Chemists, Am. Assn. Clin. Chemists, AAAS, Am. Soc. Clin. Rsch., Am. Chem. Soc., Genetics Soc. Am., Harvey Soc., Am. Assn. Cancer Rsch., N.Y. Acad. Scis., Fedn. Am. Scientists, Assn. Women in Sci. (affirmative goals and actions com. 1973-75), Tissue Culture Assn. (Northeast planning com. 1986—), Am. Soc. for Cell Biology. Home: 300 Central Park W New York NY 10024 also: 1347 Cambridge Ct Saw Creek Bushkill PA 18324 also: 21 Spur Rd Roaring Brook Lake Putnam Valley NY 10579 Office: Princeton Polymer Labs 501 Plainsboro Rd Plainsboro NJ 08036

HOCKEBORN, MARGARET LANKFORD, nurse; b. Suffolk, Va., Mar. 1, 1959; d. Joel Dellie and Margaret Elizabeth (Weaver) Lankford. BS in Nursing, Old Dominion U., 1982, MS in Nursing, 1985. RN, Va. RN staff nurse I Children's Hosp. of the King's Daus., Norfolk, Va., 1982, RN staff nurse II, 1982-84, staff nurse float pool, 1984-85; nursing coord. Children's Health System, Inc., Norfolk, 1985-88; clin. nurse specialist for women's svcs. Maryview Med. Ctr., Portsmouth, Va., 1988-89; dir. women's and children's svcs. Maryview Med. Ctr., 1989—; hospice nurse, cons. EDMARC, Suffolk, Va., 1984-88; instr. Norfolk State U., 1986-8; cons. 1987—; family nurse practitioner NAVCARE Clinic, Va. Beach, 1987—; adj. faculty Old Dominion U., 1988. Advisor Wesleyan Found., Old Dominion U., 1985. Mem. Am. Nurses Assn., Va. Nurses Assn. (pres. 1989), Va. Soc. for Profl. Nursing, Am. Acad. of Nurse Practitioners, Tidewater Nurse Practitioner Assn., Sigma Theta Tau. Home: 1907 Gatewood Ct Chesapeake VA 23320 Office: Maryview Medical Center 3636 High Street Portsmouth VA 23707

HODES, BARBARA, management consultant; b. Chgo., Nov. 30, 1941; d. David and Tybe Zisook; children from previous marriage: Brian, Valery; m. A. Bruce Schimberg, Dec. 29, 1984. BS, Northwestern U., 1962. Ptnr. Just Causes, cons. not-for-profit orgns., Chgo., 1978-86; cons. in philanthropy, community involvement, and organizational devel., 1987—; Chgo. cons. Population Resource Ctr., 1978-82. Woman's bd. dirs. Mus. Contemporary Art; bd. dirs., vice chmn. Med. Rsch. Inst. Coun., Michael Reese Med. Ctr.; bd. dirs., chmn. Midwest Women's Ctr.; trustee Francis W. Parker Sch.; mem. adv. com. ACLU. Office: 209 E Lake Shore Dr Chicago IL 60611

HODGE, ANNE HARKNESS, sales executive; b. Knoxville, Tenn., July 21, 1951; d. Alexander Jones and Mary Belle (Lothrop) Harkness; m. David S. Egerton, Apr. 21, 1972 (div. 1979); children: David, Mary; m. Floyd R. Hodge, June 3, 1989. Student, Agnes Scott Coll., Decatur, Ga., 1969-71, U. Tenn., 1971-73. Mktg., advt. mgr. Volunteer Realty, Knoxville, 1975-77; adminstrv. asst. nat. sales Creative Displays, Knoxville, 1977-81; salesperson WEZK Radio, Knoxville, 1981-86, sales mgr., 1988—; sales and mktg. mgr. Cellular One, Knoxville, 1986-87; cons. nat. outdoor advt., Berkline Corp., Morristown, Tenn., 1978-81, U. Tenn., Knoxville C. of C.; speaker nat. convs. Contbr. articles to profl. jours. Bd. dirs. Knoxville Polit. Action Com., 1983—, Knoxville Arts Coun., 1981-83, Knoxville Beautification Bd., 1978-83, Boy Scouts Fin. Com., 1988—; com. mem. Dogwood Arts Festival, 1982—, United Way, 1977-81. Mem. Ad Club (bd. dirs. 1978-81). Republican. Presbyterian. Home: 538 Broome Rd Knoxville TN 37909 Office: WEZK 825 Central Knoxville TN 37917

HODGE, KIMBERLEY SUE, organizer; b. Clarion, Pa., Sept. 21, 1957; d. Merle Clyde and Hazel (Wedekind) H. BA in German, Chatham Coll., Pitts., 1980. Community organizer ACORN, Memphis and Pitts., 1980-83; union organizer Svc. Employees Internat. Union, Washington, 1985—. Democrat. Home: P O Box 2076 Covington KY 41012-2076 Office: Service Employees Internat 1216 E McMillan #306 Cincinnati OH 45206

HODGE, MARY GRETCHEN FARNAM, manufacturing company manager; b. DeFuniak Springs, Fla., Sept. 24, 1943; d. Thomas Dewey and Mary Catherine (Mixon) Farnam; m. Spessard L. Hodge, Apr. 28, 1962; children: Jennifer Robin, Monica Leigh, Stephanie, Lea. Student, Orlando Coll. Adminstrv. asst. The Cameron and Barkley Co., Orlando, Fla., 1961-68, office mgr. Machine Tool div., 1975-76; mgr. Frazer Machinery and Supply Co., Orlando, 1976—. Pioneered effort to establish parent support groups for gifted edn., Seminole County, 1979; sec. Parent of Gifted Edn., Seminole County, 1980-87; mem. adv. bd. Exceptional Student Edn., Seminole City, Fla., 1980—; chairperson Maitland (Fla.) Centennial Founders Bd., 1985; tour guide Orlando Opera Guild, Winter Park, Fla., 1985; celebrity waitress Leukemia Soc. Am., Orlando, 1986; co-chairperson Project Graduation Lyman High Sch., Seminole County, 1986—; chairperson Alzheimers Resource Auction Dinner, Winter Park, 1987 88; bd. dirs. Maitland Civic Ctr., 1983-86, v.p. bd. dirs. 1987-88, pres., bd. dirs. 1988-89, ex-officio bd. dirs. 1989-90. Recipient appreciation plaque Dividends, Seminole City, 1974-75, cert. appreciation Maitland Civic Ctr., 1986, Alzheimer Resource Ctr., Winter Park, 1987, Pres.'s Gavel, 1989. Mem. Am. Machine Tool Distbrs., Soc. Mfg. Engrs. Democrat. Methodist. Club: Maitland Woman's (several offices 1976—). Home: 95 Lake Destiny Trail Altamonte Springs FL 32714 Office: 6217 Edgewater Dr Orlando FL 32810

HODGE, MARY JO, health facility administrator; b. Talladega, Ala., June 15, 1935; d. John Bowling and Martha Allene (Royal) McKinney; B.S., Auburn U., 1956; M.S. (fellow), U. Miss., 1958; D.Pub. Adminstrn., N.Y. U., 1978; m. Charles Cedric Hodge, Aug. 6, 1955; children—Donna, Holly. Psychometrist, Student Guidance Center, Auburn U., 1956-58; psychologist McGuffey Reading Clinic U. Va., Charlottesville, 1962-64, U. Va. Hosp., 1964-65; psychologist St. Lawrence Psychiat. Center, Ogdensburg, N.Y., 1966-73, mental hygiene treatment team leader, 1973-78; dir. Instn. Edn. and Tng., Gowanda Psychiat. Center, Helmuth, N.Y., 1978, dir. treatment services, 1979—. Bd. dirs. N.Y. Regional Geriatric Ctr., 1983-85. Mem. Am., Eastern psychol. assns., Am. Coll. Healthcare Execs., Assn. Mental Health Adminstrs. (treas. N.Y. chpt. 1985-87, mem. editorial bd. chpt. newsletter 1989—), Am. Soc. Pub. Adminstrn. (chair membership Niagara frontier chpt. 1988-89), Assn. for Rural Mental Health, Kappa Delta Pi, Chi Delta Phi, Pi Tau Chi. Avocation: quiltmaking. Home: PO Box 112 Helmuth NY 14079 Office: Gowanda Psychiat Ctr Helmuth NY 14079

HODGE, PEARL MCDONALD, sports manager; b. Baker, Fla., Mar. 4, 1950; d. Alexander Baggett and Dorothy Hodge. BA, Jersey City State Coll., 1971, MA, 1972. Assoc. dir. Jersey City State Coll., Jersey City, N.J., 1973-76; career counselor Calif. State U., Long Beach, Calif., 1977-79; counseling coordinator Long Beach City Coll., Long Beach., 1979-81; pres. World Class Mgmt., Long Beach. Mem. Nat. Assoc. Female Exec., Am. Mgmt. Assoc. Office: World Class Mgmt PO Box 21053 Long Beach CA 90801

HODGES, ANN E., marketing consultant; b. L.A., June 20, 1931; d. Rex Lucien and Bess Myrtle (Johnson) Hodges. BA, Principia Coll., 1951; MF, State U. Iowa, 1955. Owner Acad. Matching Svc., Long Beach, Calif.; mktg. cons. ind. practice Long Beach; sales mgr. Chambers Pub. Svc., Santa Fe Springs, Calif. Named Sales Woman of Yr. Mem. NAFE.

HODGES, CAROL ANN, education educator; b. St. Louis, Mar. 28, 1942; d. Violet E. (Hantak) H.; m. James L. Wardrop, June 13, 1964 (div. 1973); children: Lara J., Amy J.; m. Hugh G. Petrie, Aug. 26, 1978. AB in Liberal Arts, Washington U., 1963; MS in Edn., U. Ill., 1976, PhD in Edn., 1978. Cert. elem. edn., Mo., N.Y., reading specialist, N.Y. Elem. tchr. Brentwood (Mo.) Pub Sch., 1963-66; asst. prof. U. Ill., Champaign, 1978-81, Buffalo State Coll., 1981-83; adminstr. Park Sch. of Buffalo, 1983-86; asst. prof. Buffalo State Coll., 1986-90, assoc. prof., 1990—. Editorial bd. Reading Psychology, 1981—; co-author: Perspectives on Early Childhood, 1990; contbr. articles to profl. jours. Bd. dirs. Effective Parenting Info. for Children, Buffalo, 1986—. Mem. Am. Ednl. Rsch. Assn., Internat. Reading Assn., Nat. Reading Conf., Coll. Reading Assn., Niagara Frontier Reading Assn. (v.p., bd. dirs.), Phi Beta Kappa, Kappa Delta Pi, Phi Delta Kappa. Office: Buffalo State Coll 1300 Elmwood Ave Buffalo NY 14222

HODGES, GAYLA DIANNE, professional speaker; b. Lyndonville, Vt., Apr. 27, 1950; d. Edgar Francis Field and Velma Phyllis (Brown) F.; m. Timothy Richard Hodges Sr., Dec. 24, 1977; 1 child, Timothy Richard Jr.; stepchildren: Rebekah, Paris. BA in Psychology, Ottawa U., Phoenix, 1989. Dir. mktg. Ariz. Limousines, Phoenix, 1985-87; dir. sales and mktg. Arrangements & Tours, Phoenix, 1987-88; owner, pres. PowerPlay, Phoenix, 1988—; instr. community edn. Noricopa Community Coll. Dist. Dep. registrar Rep. party, Phoenix, 1988-89. Recipient Young Careerist award Ariz. State Bus. and Profl. Women, 1977, winner Individual Devel. Program Speakoff, 1989. Mem. ASTD, Ariz. State Bus. and Profl. Women, Midtowners Bus. and Profl. Women's Club (pres. 1988-89, Woman of Achievement award 1977, 88-89) Toastmasters. Office: PowerPlay Motivational Workshops 3729 W Bloomfield Rd Phoenix AZ 85029

HODGES, JOLYNE C., food company executive; b. Montebello, Calif., May 22, 1948; d. William A. and Irene V. (Hull) Madison; m. Kimberly Hodges. BS, U. Ark., Fayetteville, 1981. Plant mgr. Ark. Dehydrated Foods, Springdale; dept. sec. U. Ark., Fayetteville; adminstrv. asst.; plant mgr. Ark. Dehydrated Foods, DeQueen. Contbr. articles to profl. jours. Mem. NAFE, BPW. Home: 240 W Sycamore Box 57 Fayetteville AR 72703 Office: PO Box 107 Springdale AR 72764

HODGES, LINDA SUSAN, banking officer, branch manager; b. Phila., Jan. 6, 1961; d. Donald F. and Jane E. (LeVan) H. BA magna cum laude, Lafayette Coll., 1983; postgrad., Villanova U., 1987—. Asst. mgr., acting branch mgr. Mellon Bank, Haverford, Pa., 1983-86; banking officer, branch mgr. Mellon Bank, Wayne, Pa., 1986-90; banking officer, br. mgr. Bryn Mawr (Pa.) Trust Co., 1990—. Mem. Main Line C. of C. (recruiting), Delaware County C. of C., Wayne Bus. Assn. (recruiting), St. Davids Park Condominium Assn. (sec.), Lafayette Coll. Alumni Club (events com. Phila chpt.), Pi Beta Phi (treas., membership com. Mainline/Phila. chpt.). Office: Mellon Bank c/o Manager 366 W Lancaster Ave Wayne PA 19087

HODGES, MARGARET ANN, television editor, newspaper columnist; b. McCamey, Tex., Sept. 7, 1928; d. Ernest Cornelius and Margaret Isabel (Wood) Haynes; m. Cecil Ray Hodges, July 2, 1954 (div. Nov. 1974); children—Craig McNeley, Elizabeth Ann. B.J., U. Tex., 1948. Reporter, Houston Chronicle, 1948-51; society editor The News, Mexico City, 1951-52; reporter Houston Chronicle, 1952-54, TV editor, columnist, 1962—; radio critic Sta. KIKK, Houston, 1981—. Mem. Critics Consensus (dir. 1965-75), TV Critics Assn. (founder, exec. bd., v.p., pres.). Club: Houston Press (pres. 1967-68). Office: Houston Chronicle Texas and Travis Sts Houston TX 77002

HODGES, PAULINE RUTH, librarian, information specialist; b. Exeter, N.H., Feb. 4, 1944; d. Deane Llewllyn and Abbie Minerva (Ford) H.; m. Rodney W. Bean, Sept. 23, 1966 (div. 1978); 1 child, Leonard; m. Robert L. Justus, May 12, 1990. BA, Antioch Coll., 1967; MLS, U. Pitts., 1977. Info. specialist Ohio State U. Librs., Columbus, 1978-82; assoc. libr. Chem. Abstracts Svc., Columbus, 1982-87, team leader, 1987—. Contbr. articles to profl. jours. Mem. coun. and long range planning com. 1st Community Ch., Columbus, 1982-86. Mem. Am. Soc. Info. Sci. (newsletter editor Columbus chpt. 1980-82, chmn. 1985), Ohionet (chmn. adv. coun. 1988-90). Office: Chem Abstracts Svc 2540 Olentangy River Rd Columbus OH 43202

HODGES, PRISCILLA B., office manager; b. Eden, N.C., Feb. 25, 1940; d. Willie Albert and Flora Hannah (Bryant) Berry; m. James Willie Hodges, Aug. 26, 1960. BA in Bus. Adminstrn., Western Carolina Coll., 1960; BA in Bus. Law/Acctg., Tri City Coll., 1958. Cert. admitting mgr., N.C. and nat. Ins.-admissions mgr. Humana Hosp., Greensboro, N.C.; bus. office mgr. Charter Hosp. Greensboro. Mem. ABWA, HFMA, Am. Guild of Patent Account Mgmt., N.C. Assn. Healthcare and Admitting Mgrs. (pres.). Office: PO Box 10399 Greensboro NC 27404

HODGSON, WINFRED HUDSON, writer; b. Rappahannock County, Va., June 11, 1920; d. Robert Ray and Annie Mary (Jasper) Hudson; m. Alfred S. Hodgson, June 13, 1942; children: John Alfred, James William. BS, Mary Washington Coll., 1940. Cert. secondary tchr., Va. Tchr. High Sch., White Stone, Va., 1940-41; clerical tng. officer U.S. Govt., Washington, 1941-44; substitute tchr. various high schs., Fairfax County, Va., 1955-68. Author: (short story) Hicall, 1978; contbr. articles to mags. Campaign chair McLean-Fairfax County (Va.) Democratic Com., 1952-77. Mem. AAUW, Friends of Arts and Scis., Solo Theatre Guild (bd. dirs. 1984-87), Solo Soc. Lifetime Angels, Sarasota Opera Guild. Democrat. Presbyterian. Home: 5300 Ocean Blvd 201 Sarasota FL 34242

HODNETT, DIANNE MARIE, risk management executive; b. Neptune, N.J., July 30, 1947; d. Theodore and Betty Jane (Trotta) Griffin; m. Phillip Barry Hodnett, Dec. 31, 1968; children: Phillip Barry, Theodore James. Student, Temple U., 1965-66. Asst. personnel dir. CARE, Inc., N.Y.C., 1969-79; v.p. human resources NICO, Inc., N.Y.C., 1979-87; v.p. risk mgmt. The LVI Group, Inc., 1987—; cons. ICCC, Neptune, 1980—. Treas. Coalition for Better Govt., Wyandranch, N.Y., 1983-86; v.p. Wyandranch PTA/PTSA Council, 1985-86. Mem. NAFE, Am. Soc. for Personnel Adminstrn., RIMS. Democrat. Methodist. Home: 93 Ridge Rd Wheatley Heights NY 11798 Office: The LVI Group Inc 345 Hudson St New York NY 10014

HODNETT, EARNESTINE, personnel management specialist; b. Virginia Beach, Va., Feb. 1, 1949; d. David and Mary Elizabeth (Scott) H. B.S. in Bus. Adminstrn., Norfolk State U., 1978; MBA in Pub. Adminstrn. Valdosta State Coll., 1988. Employee rels. clk. Navy Pub. Works Ctr., Norfolk, 1967-76; acctg. tech., 1976-78; personnel mgmt. specialist, 1978-80, personnel staffing specialist, 1980-82, employee rels. specialist, 1982-84; employee rels. specialist Naval Submarine Base, Kings Bay, Ga., 1984-85, personnel mgmt. specialist, 1985-86, supervisory labor rels. specialist, 1986-88, labor rels. specialist Eighth Army CPO, Seoul, Republic of Korea, 1988-90, supervisory pers. mgmt. specialist, 1990—. Bd. dirs. United Way, Camden County, Ga., 1985. Mem. Black Profl. Women Club Inc. (chairperson scholarship com. 1983-84), Soc. Labor Rels. Profls., Federally Employed Women, Personnel Mgmt. Soc., Phi Delta Kappa, NAACP. Democrat. Avocations: reading, golf, aerobics, camping. Office: Office Civilian Pers Dir Eighth US Army Attn: CPJ-SES APO San Francisco CA 96301

HODSON, JANET DAWN, small business owner; b. Fort Riley, Kans., Nov. 26, 1947; d. James Albert and Henrietta H. BA, U. Calif., Berkeley, 1969; MA, Calif. State U., Fresno, 1980. Adminstrv. aide SSI Trailer Corp., Emeryville, Calif., 1969-71; counselor Calif. Rehab. Ctr., Patton, 1972-74; health educator County Health Dept., Riverside, Calif., 1975; pub. relations staff United Way, Fresno, Calif., 1976-77; dir. of planning and allocations United Way, Ventura, Calif., 1978-82; adminstrv. aide County of Fresno, Calif., 1977-78; owner, operator J.D. Hodson & Assocs., Ventura, Calif., 1982—; owner Pregaphone Inc., Ventura, Calif., 1986—; instr. Oxnard (Calif.) Jr. Coll. , 1985-86, 88-89. Inventor: Pregaphone, 1988. Chmn. Local Agy. Formation Commn., Ventura, 1984-88, Ventura Coll. Bus. Adv. Com., 1986-88; mem. AB90 Com., Ventura, 1977. Mem. Consult/Net (founder), Profl. Women's Network (bd. dirs.), Toastmasters (bd. dirs. Ventura chpt. 1985-86). Office: JD Hodson & Assocs 3875 Telegraph Rd Ste A-160 Ventura CA 93003

HOEFLING, JUDY ELAINE, educator; b. Saginaw, Mich., Sept. 14, 1946; d. Sinclair George and Elaine (Duncan) H. BA, Cen. Mich. U., 1968, MA in Guidance and Counseling, 1969. Cert. elem. tchr. Tchr.'s aide Head Start, Riverdale, Mich., 1968; tchr. 2nd grade Owosso (Mich.) Pub. Schs., 1969-74, tchr. 3rd grade, 1975-78, tchr. 4th grade, 1979—; sch. rep. communications com. Owosso Pub. Schs., 1988-90; mem. health-social studies, libr. coms., 1978-90; cooperating tchr. edn. dept. Mich. State U., East Lansing, 1987-90. Vol. Coun. on Aging, Owosso, 1990. Mem. Mich. Edn. Assn., Owosso Edn. Assn. Office: Central Sch 600 W Oliver Owosso MI 48867

HOEFLING, VIRGINIA ANN, lawyer; b. N.Y.C., Aug. 1, 1931; d. Amerigo and Lucy S. (Mauriello) De Vito; m. Vincent R., Aug. 12, 1951; children: Richard, Raymond, Charles, Francis, Stephen, Jeannine. BA in Urban Studies, Bradford Coll., 1976; JD cum laude, Suffolk U., 1980. Bar: Mass. 1980, U.S. Dist. Ct. Mass. 1981, U.S. Ct. Appeals (1st cir.) 1981, U.S. Supreme Ct. 1988. Pvt. practice, Boston, 1981-82; law clk. to presiding justices Mass. Superior Ct., Boston, 1981, 82-83, chief law clk. to presiding justice, 1983-84; asst. atty. gen. State of Mass., Boston, 1985—. Editor Suffolk Transnational Law Jour., 1979-80; also contbr. articles to profl. jours. Pres. St. John Neumann Guild, Roxbury, Mass., 1966-86; mem. Town Meeting, Winchester, Mass., 1976—, Gov.'s Task Force on Presumptive Sentencing, 1984-85; liaison senate and house criminal justice coms., Superior Ct. Task Force, 1984-85; assoc. mem. Winchester Zoning Bd. Appeals, 1985-87, vice chmn. 1988-89, chmn. 1989—; mem. Supreme Judicial Ct. Gender Bias Study Com.; mem. Fee Generating Work Group, Gender in the Cts., 1988-89; mem. patient care assessment adv. com. Bd. Registration in Medicine, 1987—. Recipient St. John Neumann award, St. John Neumann Ctr., Phila., 1980. Mem. ABA (conf. medigap ins. issues 1989), Mass. Bar Assn. (justice task force 1984-85, chem. dependency com. 1985-88), Boston Bar Assn. (speaker continuation ins. coverage for divorced spouses 1990), Mass. Assn. Women Lawyers (asst. treas. 1983-84, treas. 1984-85, asst. corr. sec. 1985-86, corr. sec. 1986-87, recording sec. 1987-88, v.p. 1988-89), Mass. Assn. Women Lawyers Scholarship Found. (exec. bd. mem. 1983—), Boston Bar Assn.,Phi Delta Phi. Democrat. Roman Catholic. Home: 156 Forest St Winchester MA 01890 Office: Dept Atty Gen One Ashburton Pl Boston MA 02108

HOEFT, ELIZABETH BAYLESS, speech/language pathologist; b. Dayton, Ohio, Aug. 18, 1942; d. G. Harold and Elsie Dorthea (Rigg) Bayless; m. Douglas Laton Hoeft, Aug. 29, 1964; children: Brian, Amy. BA, Denison U., Granville, Ohio, 1964; MA, No. Ill. U., DeKalb, Ill., 1970; postgrad., U. Ill., Chgo., 1988—. Speech/lang. pathologist Sch. Dist. U-46, Elgin, Ill., 1966-69, Elgin Easter Seal Ctr., 1969-76, Bartlett (Ill.) Learning Ctr., 1977-79, Sch. Dist. U-46, Elgin, 1979—; grad. asst. Ill. Inst. Developmental Disabilities, Chgo., 1988-89; cons. in field; lectr. in field. Rsch. Incentive grantee, Sch. Dist. U-46, 1986, AAUW Ednl. Found. grantee, 1990. Mem. Ill. Speech, Lang., Hearing Assn., Am. Speech, Lang., Hearing Assn., Elgin Tchrs. Assn., Ill. Edn. Assn., NEA, AAUW, Delta Delta Delta. Lutheran. Home: 614 Center St Elgin IL 60120

HOEL, SONJA LESLIE, venture capitalist; b. Pitts., July 6, 1966; d. Lester Arneman and Unni Sonja (Blegen) H. BS with distinction, U. Va., 1988. Fin. asst. London Stock Exchange, 1988; investment analyst TA Assocs., Boston, 1989—; teaching asst. U. Va., Charlottesville, 1987, computer cons., 1987-88, computer analyst, 1987-88, lab. cons., 1988-89. Big sister, Madison House, Charlottesville, 1985-89; area com. chmn. Multiple Sclerosis Rehab. Rsch. Benefit, Charlottesville, 1988; tutor, Madison House, Charlottesville, 1985-86; mem. fundraising com., shelter vol. Women's Lunch Pl., 1989—. Mem. Nat. Venture Capital Assn., New Eng. Venture Capital Assn., Nat. Bus. Incubation Assn., Beta Gamma Sigma, Nat. Honor Soc., Kappa Delt. Republican. Presbyterian. Home: 127 Myrtle St Apt 5 Boston MA 02114 Office: TA Assocs 45 Milk St Boston MA 02109

HOELKER, LOUISE CATHERINE, human services administrator; b. Rochester, N.Y., Oct. 25, 1962; d. Joseph Paul and Catherine Francis (Petro) Licata; m. Joseph E. Hoelker. BS in Nursing, Wright State U., 1985; postgrad., U. S.C., 1985-86, Xavier U., 1990—. RN, Ohio. Youth specialist ARC, Cin., 1986-88; dir. vols. and communications Shriners Burn Inst., Cin., 1988—. Mem. Pub. Rels. Soc. of Am., Am. Soc. of Dirs. and Vols., Women in Communications Inc., Ohio Soc. of Dirs. and Vols. Roman Catholic. Office: Shriners Burns Inst 202 Goodman St Cincinnati OH 45219

HOELTERHOFF, MANUELA VALI, newspaper editor, critic; b. Hamburg, Federal Republic of Germany, Apr. 6, 1949; came to U.S., 1957; d. Heinz Alfons and Olga Christine (Goertz) H. B.A., Hofstra U., 1971; M.A., NYU, 1973. Assoc. editor Arete Pub. Co., Princeton, N.J., 1977-80; editor-in-chief Art and Auction Mag., N.Y.C., 1979-81; arts editor Wall Street Jour., N.Y.C., 1981-89, books editor, 1989—. Recipient Pulitzer prize Columbia U., 1983; recipient citation for disting. commentary Am. Soc. Newspaper Editors, 1982, 83. Office: Wall St Jour 200 Liberty St New York NY 10281*

HOEMAN, SHIRLEY POLLOCK, educator, administrator and consultant; b. St. Charles, Mo., Oct. 15, 1942; d. Laurence J. and Bernadine (Beumer) Pollock; m. Richard D. Hoeman; children: Christopher, Timothy, Jonathan. BS in Nursing, U. Mo., 1964; MPH, U. Minn., 1974; MA, Rutgers U., 1982, PhD, 1984. Dir. nursing Sister Kenny Inst., Mpls., 1970-72; asst. prof. nursing U. Minn., Mpls., 1974-75; supr., cons. Minn. Dept. Health, Mpls., 1974-76; asst. prof. community Creighton U., Omaha, 1976-78; asst. prof. community health Rutgers U., Newark, 1978-81; dir. home health agy. Middlesex Hosp., New Brunswick, N.J., 1981-82; dir. rsch. and edn. Kessler Inst. for Rehab., West Orange, N.J., 1983-88; assoc. prof. pediatric rehab. Thomas Jefferson U., Phila., 1988-90; pres., cons. Health Systems Consultations, Long Valley, N.J., 1983-90—; cons. Project HOPE Armenia, USSR, 1989—, Nursing Rsch. West Ctr. Project, N.J., Pa., 1989—; adminstrv. dir. ctr. for human devel. and rehab. Morristown (N.J.) Meml. Hosp.; numerous nat. and internat. presentations. Author: Rehabilitation/Restorative Care in Community, 1990; contbr. articles to profl. jours. Vol. Homeless Shelter, Morristown, N.J., 1988—; mem. profl. adv. com. Hospice Morris County, 1988—; chmn. nat. rsch. com. Rehab. Nursing Found., Skokie, Ill., 1986—. Scholar NSF, 1960-64; USPHS Title II trainee, 1972-74, numerous other grants for projects and rsch., 1980—. Mem. Am. Pub. Health Assn., Assn. Rehab. Nurses, Am. Nurses Assn., Am. Congress Rehab. Medicine (chmn. pediatric rehab. task force), Am. Anthrop. Assn., Coun. on Nursing and Anthropology, Soc. for Med. Anthropology. Home and Office: 6 Camp Washington Rd Long Valley NJ 07853

HOERBER, MARY ELIZABETH, lawyer; b. Libertyville, Ill., Oct. 28, 1960; d. John Leonard and Julia Yolanda (Raia) H. BA in English and Prelaw magna cum laude, Barry U., 1982; JD cum laude, U. Miami, 1985. Bar: Fla. 1985, U.S. Dist. Ct. (so. dist.) Fla. 1986, U.S. Dist. Ct. (mid. dist.) Fla. 1989. Assoc. Anderson, Moss, Parks & Russo, Miami, Fla., 1985—; cons. Dade County Sch. Bd., Miami, 1986-87. Contbr. Nat. Rep. Party, Washington, 1984—, Covenant House, Ft. Lauderdale, Fla., N.Y.C., 1988—, Paralyzed Vets. Am., Wilton, N.H., 1984—; mem. Miami Right-to-Life, Miami, 1982—; sponsor Compassion, Internat., Colorado Springs, Colo., 1982—. Mem. ABA (litigation sect. 1985—), Am. Judicature Soc., Assn. Trial Lawyers Am., Acad. Fla. Trial Lawyers, Dade Couny Bar Assn. (young lawyers sect. 1986—, vol. lawyer 1988—), Def. Rsch. Inst., Dade County Trial Lawyers Assn., Fla. Assn. Women Lawyers. Republican. Roman Catholic. Home: 6870 SW 45 Ln #8 Miami FL 33155 Office: Anderson Moss Parks et al 100 N Biscayne Blvd #2500 Miami FL 33132

HOEY, RITA MARIE, public relations executive; b. Chgo., Nov. 4, 1950; d. Louis D. and Edith M. (Finnemann) Hoey; m. Joseph John Dragonette, Sept. 4, 1982. BA in English and History, No. Ill. U., 1972. Asst. dir. Nat. Assn. Housing and Human Devel., Chgo., 1975; public relations account exec. Weber Cohn & Riley, Chgo., 1975-76; publicity coordinator U.S. Gypsum Co., Chgo., 1976-77; with Daniel J. Edelman, Inc., Chgo., 1977-84, sr. v.p., 1981-84; exec. v.p. Dragonette, Inc., Chgo., 1984—. Mem. Pub. Relations Soc. Am., Women in Communications. Home: 3416 S Cherry Valley Woodstock IL 60098 Office: Dragonette Inc 303 E Wacker Dr Ste 218 Chicago IL 60601

HOF, LISELOTTE BERTHA, biochemist; b. Cologne, Germany, Jan. 1, 1937; came to U.S., 1967; d. Heinrich and Hedwig (Boemann) Hof; m. Peter B. Weber, Oct. 5, 1972. MS, U. Cologne, 1963, PhD, 1965. Postdoctoral fellow mental health rsch. inst. U. Mich., Ann Arbor, 1967-68; NIH postdoctoral fellow dept. pediatrics U. Chgo., 1968-70; asst. prof. dept. physiol. chemistry U. Bochum (Fed. Republic Germany), Germany, 1970-72; asst. prof. dept. biochemistry Albany (N.Y.) Med. Coll., 1972-78, assoc. prof. dept. biochemistry, 1978—; assoc. prof. biomed. sci., sch. pub. health SUNY, Albany, 1988—; women's liaison officer Albany Med. Coll., 1978—. Contbr. articles to profl. jours. V.p. faculty orgn. Albany Med. Coll., 1984-90. Grantee Sigma Delta Epsilon, rsch. grantee NIH, 1977, 78, 88, Nat. Multiple Sclerosis Soc., 1983. Mem. Am. Chem. Soc. (alternate councilor 1985-89, mem. exec. coun. Eastern N.Y. chpt. 1985-88, pub. rels. chair. Eastern N.Y. chpt. 1987-89), Am. Soc. Biochem. Molecular Biology, Am. Soc. Neurochemistry (pub. affairs com. 1987-89), AAAS, Soc. Complex Carbohydrates, N.Y. Acad. Scis., Assn. Women in Sci. Office: Albany Med Coll A-10 47 New Scotland Ave Albany NY 12208

HOFBAUER, RITA ANNE, non-profit fundraising organization administrator; b. N.Y.C., Oct. 21, 1936; d. George Clement and Margaret Gertrude (McDonnell) H. BA cum laude, D'Youville Coll., 1966; MA, Villanova U., 1967. Cert. in ednl. adminstrn. Tchr. Parochial Sch. System, Atlanta, 1959-64, ednl. adminstr., 1967-69; tchr. Parochial Sch. System, Phila., 1964-66, ednl. adminstr., 1969-71; dir. tng. Grey Nuns of the Sacred Heart, Yardley, Pa., 1971-75, v.p., 1975-79; asst. dir. Leadership Conf. of Women Religious, Silver Spring, Md., 1979-86; exec. dir. Support Our Aging Religious, Silver Spring, 1987—; mem. adv. bd. Assn. Cath. Colls. and Univs., Washington, 1979-85; cons. Bon Secours Health Corp., Columbia, Md., 1985, Hosp. for Sick Children, Washington, 1986. Co-author: Making Social Analysis Work, 1982; editor: Taking a Corporate Stand, 1980, Women in Ministry, 1981, An Old Voice in a New Age, 1983. Chmn. Rachael's Women's Ctr., Washington, 1989—; bd. dirs. D'Youville Coll., Buffalo, 1975-83. Mem. NAFE, Nat. Assn. Fundraising Execs., Beethoven Soc., Smithsonian Assn. Democrat. Roman Catholic. Office: Support Our Aging Religious 8820 Cameron St Silver Spring MD 20910

HOFER, JUDITH K., retail company executive. b. Feb. 16, 1940, Hillsboro, Oreg. d. Frank E. Hofer and Helen K. Cook. BA Oreg. State. U., 1959, BS, Portland State U., 1961. Trainee, buyer, Meier & Frank Dept. Store, Portland, Oreg., 1961-65; v.p., gen. mgr., Clark Jr., Portland, 1966-72; v.p., gen. merchandising mgr. Meier & Frank, Portland, 1972-76; gen. mgr. Emporium-Capwell, San Francisco, 1976-78; exec. v.p. Famous-Barr Stores (subs. The May Co.), 1978-81; pres., chief exec. officer Meier & Frank, Portland, Oreg., 1981-83; pres., chief exec. officer, May Co., L.A., 1983-86, Famous-Barr Co. (div. May Department Stores Co.), St. Louis, 1986-87, Meier & Frank (div. May Department Stores Co.), Portland, 1988—; bd. dirs. Greyhound Corp., Phoenix, Key Bank of Oreg., Portland. Bd. dirs. Assn. Portland Progress, 1988—, Boy Scouts Am., St. Louis, 1986-88, Downtown St. Louis, 1986-88; trustee Nat. Jewish Hosp. & Asthma Ctr., Denver, 1983-87, City of Hope Hosp., Duarte, Calif., 1984-88; bd. counselors Sch. Bus. Adminstrn. U. So. Calif., L.A., 1984-86. Named one of ten Women of Achievement City of St. Louis, 1980; recipient Spirit of LIfe award City of Hope, L.A., 1985. Mem. Nat. Women's Forum, Fashion Group, Com. of 200, Assn. U. Women, Young Pres.' Orgn. Avocation: antique doll collecting. Office: Meier & Frank 621 SW 5th Ave Portland OR 97204

HOFF, JULIENNE NORA, college dean, nurse; b. Detroit, Aug. 10, 1939; d. Basil and Laura Julia (McKenna) Howell; m. William R. Hoff, June 16, 1979. BSN, Mercy Coll., 1963; MEd in Nursing Edn., Columbia U., 1968;

PhD, U. Mich., 1984. RN. Staff nurse, asst. head nurse St. Mary's Hosp., Grand Rapids, Mich., 1963-64; nursing supr. Mercy Hosp., Bay City, Mich., 1964-66; asst. prof. nursing Mercy Coll., Detroit, 1968-72, 1976-80, dir., dean of nursing, 1980-86; dean, div. of nursing and health Madonna Coll., Livonia, Mich., 1987—. Co-author: Role of Liberal Arts in Nursing, 1987. Recipient acad. achievement scholarship Mercy Coll., 1957-58. Contbn. to Advancement of Nursing award, Mich. Soc. Hosp. Adminstrs., 1984. Mem. Mich. Nurses Assn., Detroit Nurses Assn. (chmn. nominating com. 1987-88), Mich. Assn. Colls. of Nursing (v.p. 1989-90), Sigma Theta Tau. Home: 18235 University Park Rd Livonia MI 48152 Office: Madonna Coll-Div Nursing 36600 Schoolcraft Rd Livonia MI 48150

HOFF, KATHLEEN PATRICIA (PATRICIA LOWRY), educator; b. Chgo., Apr. 29, 1927; d. Robert Beardsley Fredrick and Kathleen Cleola (Heilman) Hardy; B.A., Ball State U., 1951, M.A., 1964, Ed.D., 1968; postgrad. Bowling Green State U., Sam Houston State U., Tex. A&M; m. Victor John Hoff, Oct. 15, 1988; children from previous marriage: Fredrick Robert Hugh Lowry, Patricia Marjorie Lowry. Tchr. English and social studies various elem. and high schs., Ind., Ohio, and Tex.; now mem. faculty Coll. of Edn., Sam Houston State U., Huntsville, Tex.; poetry judge, ednl. cons., lectr. in field. Leader Girl Scouts U.S., 4-H, Campfire Girls; bd dirs. Deep East Tex. Coun. Govts., Huntsville Leadership Inst.; mem. citizens rev. com. Huntsville Item; asst. chaplain Tex. Dept. Corrections. Recipient Outstanding Alumnus award Ball State U./Kappa Delta Pi, 1977. Mem. AAUW, AAUP, Internat. Reading Assn., Assn. Supervision and Curriculum Devel., Early Reading Rsch. Coun., Tex. Assn. Profs. of Reading, NEA, Internat. Congress on Arts and Communication, Tex. Assn. Tchr. Educators, Tex. Assn. for Improvement Reading, NOW, Tex. Women for ERA, Am. Quarterhorse Assn., Am. Poultrymen, Bulldog Club Am., Audubon Soc., Delta Sigma Theta, Phi Delta Kappa, Delta Kappa Gammma. Christian Scientist. Clubs: Order Eastern Star, Bus. and Profl. Women. Author: Handbook for Parents of Kindergartners, 1964; Teacher Evaluation, 1968; contbr. articles to profl. jours.; author reports on literacy edn. in Indonesia, others. Office: Sam Houston State Univ Coll Edn Huntsville TX 77341

HOFF, MARY KATHRYN, judge, lawyer; b. St. Louis, Jan. 5, 1953; d. Walter B. and Dolores M. (Schoendienst) H.; m. Peter M. Stragand, Oct. ll, 1986; l child, Samuel H. BA, U. Mo., 1974; JD, St. Louis U., 1978. Bar: Mo. 1978. Asst. pub. defender State of Mo., St. Louis, 1978-82; assoc. Leonard Buckley, Inc., St. Louis, 1982-86; of counsel Schuchat, Cook & Werner, St. Louis, 1986-89; judge 22d Jud. Cir. Ct., St. Louis, 1989—. Mem. Nat. Assn. Women Judges, Mo. Bar Assn., Met. Bar Assn. St. Louis, Women Lawyers Assn. St. Louis (pres. 1986-87). Office: 22d Jud Cir Ct 1320 Market St Saint Louis MO 63103

HOFF, SHIRLEY ARLENE, insurance agent, financial planner; b. Hanover, Pa., July 12, 1934; d. Samuel David and Miriam May (Kroh) H. BS, Western Md. Coll., 1960, MEd, 1964; postgrad., U. No. Iowa, 197l. Cert. tchr. math., Md.; lic. Nat. Assn. Security Dealers; LUTCF. Bookkeeper, saleswoman Singer Sewing Ctr., Westminster, Md., 1956; cost record clk. Balt. Gas & Electric Co., 1957-58; tchr. math. and sci. Baltimore County Bd. Edn., Towson, Md., 1960-65; tchr. math. Carroll County Bd. Edn., Westminster, 1965-76; sales rep. Met. Ins. Co., Pikesville, Md., 1977-82; ins. agt. Frederick (Md.) Underwriters, Inc., 1982-83; ind. ins. agt. Westminster, 1983-84; life underwriter Mut. N.Y., Towson, 1984-85; owner, mgr. S.A. Hoff Agy., Westminster, 1985—; charter v.p. Balt. chpt. Women's Life Underwriters Conf., 1983-86. Vice pres. women Grace Ch., Westminster, 1988-89, pres., 1966, 89—, choir mem., 1966—, mem. evangelism com., 1982—, Sunday sch. tchr. Fellow Life Underwriter Tng. Coun.; mem. Am. Soc. CLU and Chartered Fin. Cons., Carroll County Assn. Life Underwriters (sec. 1980-82, state committeewoman 1986-88), Balt. Health Underwriters Assn. (dir. membership 1988-89), Md. Assn. Health Underwriters (dir. membership 1988-89), Carroll County C. of C., Carroll County Bus. and Profl. Women (pres. 1982-83, Woman of Yr. 1985), AAUW (treas. Carroll br. 1979-83), NAFE, Phi Delta Gamma (pres. Psi chpt. 1969-71, 85-87, del. biennial convs. 1968-86). Democrat. Home and Office: 14 Kemper Ave Westminster MD 21157

HOFFBAUER, DIANE KAYE, education educator; b. Zumbrota, Minn., Jan. 19, 1955; d. John Henry and Norma Carol (Wordes) H.; m. Brian Walter DeMarcus; 2 children. EdD in Curriculum-Instrn., U. S.C., 1988. Tchr. Kulingen Daghem, Karlstad, Sweden, 1974-75, Wilson Community Sch., Mankato, Minn., 1977-78; tchr. reading Morris (N.Y.) Pub. Schs., 1978; early childwood specialist Oneonta (N.Y.) State U., 1978-83; instr. reading Isothermal Community Coll., Spindale, N.C., 1983-85; dir. spl. svcs. Western Carolina U., Cullowhee, N.C., 1985-88; asst. prof. curriculum and instrn. dept. Mankato State U., 1988—. Bd. dirs. Planned Parenthood, Oneonta, 1978-83, PATH, home for battered women, Spindale, 1983-85, Children's House, Mankato, 1988-89; vol. to Thailand, Am. Refugee Com., Ban Vanai Camp, 1980. Recipient Outstanding Educator award Physically Challenged, Inc., 1988, Group Study Exchange award Rotary Found., 1988. Mem. Assn. Children with Learning Disabilities, Am. Edn. Rsch. Assn., Coun. for Exceptional Children, Assn. Handicapped Student Svc. Programs Postsecondary Edn. (trainer, cons. 1988—). Lutheran. Home: 512 Sherman St North Mankato MN 56001 Office: Mankato State U Box 52 Mankato MN 56002

HOFFEE, PATRICIA ANNE, molecular genetics educator; b. Columbiana, Ohio, Oct. 1, 1937; d. Wilbur L. and Alberta H. (Smith) H. BS, U. Pitts., 1959, MS, 1960, PhD, 1963. Asst. prof. molecular biology Albert Einstein Coll. Medicine, Bronx, N.Y., 1966-67; asst. prof. microbiology U. Pitts. Sch. Medicine, 1967-70; vis. prof. U. Parana, Brazil, 1972-73; assoc. prof. microbiology U. Pitts. Sch. Medicine, 1970-78, prof. molecular genetics, 1978—; vis. prof. U. N.C., Chapel Hill, 1982-83; cons. NIH, Bethesda, Md., 1971-76, VA, Washington, 1978-81; co-dir. MD/PhD Program, Pitts., 1985-90. Editor: Purine and Pyrimidine Metabolism, 1978; contbr. articles to profl. jours. Judge, Buhl Sci. Fair, Pitts., 1980-88. Grantee NIH, 1968-1992, ACS, 1976-78. Fellow Nat. Acad. Microbiology; mem. Am. Soc. Microbiology, Am. Soc. Advanced Sci., Am. Soc. Molecular Biology and Biochemistry. Office: U Pitts Sch Medicine Dept Molecular Genetics and Biochemistry Pittsburgh PA 15261

HOFFER, ALMA JEANNE, nursing education educator; b. Dalhart, Tex., Sept. 15, 1932; d. James A. and Mildred (Zimlich) Koehler; m. John L. Hoffer, Oct. 7, 1954; children: John Jr., James Leo, Joseph V., Jerome P. BS, Bradley U., 1970; MA, W. Va. Coll. Grad. Study Inst., 1975; EdD, Ball State U., 1981, MA, 1986. Reg. Nurse. Staff nurse St Joseph Hosp., South Bend, Ind., 1958-59, Holy Cross Cen. Sch., St Joseph Hosp., South Bend, Ind., 1959-63; sch. nurse South Bend (Ind.) Sch. Corp., 1970-72; faculty staff Morris Harvey Coll., Charleston, W. Va., W. Va. Inst. of Tech., Montgomery, 1975-76; asst. prof. Ball State U., Ind., 1976-77, Ind. U.-Purdue U., Ft. Wayne, 1977-81; assoc. prof. The U. Akron, Ohio, 1981-83, asst. dean, grad. edn., 1983—; bd. trustees Akron Child Guidance, 1983-88, Chair Planning Com., 1988, nursing cons. Blick Clin., Akron, 1988, research cons. St. Joseph Hosp., Ohio, 1989. Author: Family Communication in Family Health Promotion Theories, Assessment, 1989. Researcher, funded project, Family Nursing of the Elderly in Acute Care Hospitals, 1988--. Task force mem. Gov. Celeste's Employee Assistance Program for State U. Campuses, Ohio 1983-84, del. People to People Citizen Ambassador Program to Europe, 1988. Mem. Am. Nurses Assn., Nat. League for Nursing, Midwest Nursing Research Soc., Transcultural Nursing, Sigma Theta Tau, Portage Country Club. Republican. Roman Catholic. Office: U Akron Mary Gladwin Hall Akron OH 44325

HOFFER, M(ARY) JANE, freelance photographer; b. Montreal, Quebec, Canada, Oct. 27, 1947; d. Arthur and Wynne (Malkinson) H. BA in Art History, McGill U., Montreal, Canada, 1968; MA in Art & Edn., Columbia U. Tchrs. Coll., 1971, EdD in Art & Edn., 1983. Photography instr. John Jay Coll. Criminal Justice, N.Y.C., 1972-76; photographer Hunter Coll. Tchr. Corps, N.Y.C., 1979-82; freelance photographer N.Y.C., 1974—. Exhibited in group shows at Gallery 1199, 1977, Gallery of Camera Art, 1976, Camera Club N.Y., 1975, Donnell Libr., 1975, NOW Conf., 1975, Macy Gallery, 1975, Internat. Photo Optical Show Assn., 1974, Lower East Side Print Shop, 1973-75, Met. Mus., 1973-75, Donnell Libr., 1973-75, Cork Gallery of Avery Fisher Hall, 1973-75, Soho Photo Gallery, 1973, 75, Ziegfeld Gallery, 1972-73, M.U.S.E.U.M. Gallery, 1970; one-woman show Wall Gallery, John Jay Coll. Criminal Justice, 1988, 89. Mem. Am. Assn. Profl. Photographers. Home and Office: 509 W 110th St Apt 5D New York NY 10025

HOFFER, SHARON KAY RIFE, educator; b. Huntington, W.Va., Sept. 8, 1944; d. Benjamin Harrison and Kathleen (Estes) Rife; m. Harry Ernest Hoffer, Dec. 26, 1965; children: Kathleen Rife, Harry Ernest Jr., Deirdre Elaine. BA, Marshall U., 1966; postgrad., Ohio State U., 1989—. Cert. tchr., Ohio. Tchr. Cabell County Schs., Huntington, 1966-68; tchr. history, fgn. lang. Teays Valley Local Sch. Dist., Ashville, Ohio, 1979—. Mem. AAUW, NEA, Ohio Edn. Assn., Phi Alpha Theta. Democrat. Presbyterian. Home: 7311 Stout Rd Circleville OH 43113

HOFFMAN, ANN FLEISHER, labor union official, lawyer; b. Phila., June 1, 1942; d. Willis Jr. and Mary (Leffler) Fleisher; m. Charles Stuart Hoffman Jr., June 7, 1964 (div. 1979); m. Arnold Perry Rubin, Jan. 1, 1985. BA, Barnard Coll., 1964; JD, U. Md., 1972. Bar: Md., 1972, N.Y., 1978. Reporter, producer Sta. WBAL-TV, Balt., 1965-68; assignment editor, producer Sta. WJZ-TV, Balt., 1968-69; assoc. Edelman, Levy and Rubenstein, Balt., 1972-77; assoc. gen. counsel Internat. Ladies' Garment Workers Union, N.Y.C., 1977-79; dir. Profl. And Clerical Employees div. Profl. And Clerical Employees div., N.Y.C., 1987—; exec. asst. to Atty Gen. U.S. Dept. Justice, Washington, 1979-81; counsel Dist. 1 Communications Workers Am., N.Y.C., 1981-85; adminstrv. asst. to v.p. Communications Workers Am., N.Y.C. and Cranford, N.J., 1985-87; lectr. U. Md. Sch. of Law, Balt., 1972-77; adj. faculty Cornell U. Trade Union Women's Studies Program, N.Y.C., 1979-85; trustee Botto House Am. Labor Mus., Haledon, N.J., 1986-89. Author: (with others) Legal Status of Homemakers in Maryland, 1978, Bargaining for Child Care, 1985, 2d. ed. 1990. Founding mem. Women's Law Ctr., Balt., 1971-77; mem. Balt. City Charter Review Commn., 1973-76; bd. dirs. ACLU Md. Chpt., Balt., 1975-77, Campfire Girls Chesapeake Council, Balt., 1976-77; co-chair Sachs for Atty. Gen., Md., 1976-77; pub. mem. N.Y. State Banking Bd., N.Y.C., 1984-85. Mem. ABA, Coalition of Labor Union Women (treas. N.Y.C. chpt. 1981-83), Nat. Network of Women Union Lawyers (founder), Lawyers and Legal Workers for Working Women (founder), Cornell U. Adj. Faculty Fedn., Order of Coif. Home: 253 Friar Ln Mountainside NJ 07092 Office: Internat Ladies' Garment Workers' Union 1710 Broadway New York NY 10019

HOFFMAN, ARLENE FAUN, podiatric medicine educator, physiologist; b. N.Y.C., Nov. 23, 1941; d. Abraham S. and Pearl Tootsie (Weiss) H. BS, CUNY, 1962; PhD in Physiology, SUNY, Bklyn., 1966; D of Podiatric Medicine, Calif. Coll. Podiatric Medicine, San Francisco, 1976. Instr. CUNY, N.Y.C., 1964-66; assoc. prof. basic scis. Calif. Coll. Podiatric Medicine, 1967-68, prof., 1969—, asst. dir. basic scis., 1967-69, dir., 1969-75, assoc. dean curricular affairs, 1972-75, assoc. prof. podiatric medicine, 1978-81, prof., 1981—; postdoctoral fellow immunophysiology Stanford U. Med. Sch., Palo Alto, Calif., 1966-67; mem. physiology sect. Nat. Bd. Podiatry Examiners, 1967-76; mem. tng. grant rev. com., heart and cardiovascular sect. Nat. Heart, Lung and Blood Inst., 1976-77; cons. Vascular Evaluation Cos., 1986—; mem. Bd. Podiatric Medicine, 1985—. Editor: Yearbook of Podiatric Medicine & Surgery, 1979—; editor, mem. adv. bd. Jour. Am. Podiatric Med. Edn., 1971-75; author: The Podiatry Curriculum, 1970; contbr. articles to profl. jours. Bd. dirs. Lyon-Martin Womens Alternative Med. Svcs., San Francisco, 1980-82, Nat. Ctr. for Lesbian Rights, San Francisco, 1989—. USPHS fellow, 1962-66. Fellow Am. Assn. Podiatric Dermatology, Am. Soc. Podiatric Medicine, Nat. Acad. Practice; mem. Am. Podiatric Med. Assn. (editor jour. 1970—). Office: Calif Coll Podiatric Medicine 1835 Ellis St San Francisco CA 94115

HOFFMAN, BARBARA A., state legislator; b. Balt., Mar. 8, 1940; d. Sidney Wolf and Eve (Simonoff) Marks; m. Donald Edwin Hoffman, 1960; children—Alan Samuel, Michael Stuart, Carolyn Mara. B.S., Towson State U., 1960; M.A., Johns Hopkins U., 1966. Secondary sch. tchr., Balt., 1960-63; supr. student tchrs. Morgan U., Balt., 1968-73; exec. dir. Md. Democratic party, 1979-84; mem. Md. State Senate from 42d Dist., 1983—. Bd. dirs. Kennedy Inst. for Handicapped Children. Co-author: Journeys in English, 1968. Recipient Outstanding Contbns. to Party award Md. Dem. party, 1984. Mem. Md. Assn. Elected Women (exec. bd. 1985), Nat. Order Women Legislators, Balt. Blews Coalition Blacks and Jews, Md. Com. for Children (pres. 1983), Hadassah (group pres. 1980-82). Jewish. Office: Md State Capitol Bldg Annapolis MD 21401 Other: 2905 W Strathmore Ave Baltimore MD 21209

HOFFMAN, BARBARA ALLEN, giftware company executive, consultant; b. Racine, Wis., May 11, 1943; d. James A. Tree and Lois E. (Jensen) Levy; m. W.H. Hoffman; children: Mark, Andrew, Nikki; 1 stepchild, Joseph. BA, Carthage Coll., Kenosha, Wis., 1965; MS, Cardinal Stritch Coll., Milw., 1989. Tchr. Racine Unified Sch. Dist., 1965-71, Watertown (Wis.) Unified Sch. Dist., 1971-76; ptnr., mgr. County Road Stencils, Watertown, 1982—; cons., tchr. Small Bus. Devel. Ctr., Whitewater, Wis., 1988—. Bd. dirs. Watertown Meml. Hosp., 1976—, YMCA, Watertown, 1988—. Mem. Women Bus. Owners, NAFE, Wis. Women Entrepreneurs, Rotary. Home and Office: 1309 Neenah St Watertown WI 53094

HOFFMAN, BERNADINE M., mathematics and psychology educator; b. Chgo., Jan. 18, 1947; d. Alexander J. and Bernadine M. (Strumski) Blattner; m. Alan G. Hoffman, June 8, 1968; children: Karen, Kevin. BS, Mich. State U., 1968, MA, 1969; supr. cert., U. Cen. Ark., 1986; elem. prin. cert., Henderson State U., 1988. Cert. elem. prin., elem. instr., mid. sch. math. instr., spl. edn. instr., spl. edn. supr. Tchr. math. and computer sci., dept. chair/tchr. spl. edn. Hot Springs (Ark.) Jr. High Sch.; tchr. spl. edn. Attwood Elem. Sch., Lansing, Mich.; instr. math. and psychology Garland County Community Coll., Hot Springs; supr. chpt. 2 programs Dept. Edn. State of Ark.; conductor numerous inservice workshops for tchrs. and adminstrs. Bd. dirs. St. John's Parochial Sch., 1979-82, chmn. bd., 1982-82; leader Girl Scouts U.S., 1980-82. Recipient Gov.'s Award for Vol. Svc., Meritorious Award for Achievements in Svc. to Southwest Jr. High Sch., Spl. Recognition for Vol. Time Weeken Communication Tng. Workshops. Mem. Assn. for Supervision and Curriculum Devel., Ark. Assn. Ednl. Adminstrs., Nat. Coun. Tchr. Math., Ark. Coun. Tchr. Math. Home: 401 Darrel Dr Hot Springs AR 71913 Office: Ark State Dept Edn 4 Capital Mall Rm 204B Little Rock AR 72203

HOFFMAN, BETH LYNN, lawyer; b. Buffalo, July 27, 1943; d. Abraham and Bernice (Revo) Rapport; m. Sanford R. Hoffman, June 21, 1964; children: Kevin, Rebecca. BE, SUNY, Buffalo, 1965, JD, 1974. Bar: N.Y. 1975, U.S. Dist. Ct. (we. dist.) N.Y. 1975; cert. elem. tchr., N.Y. Tchr. Kenmore (N.Y.) Schs., 1965-66, Skokie (Ill.) Schs., 1966-67, New Hyde Park (N.Y.) Schs., 1967-70; assoc. Cohen Swados, Buffalo, 1974-76; trial lawyer, ptnr. Bouvier, O'Connor, Cegielski & Levine, Buffalo, 1976—. Active Women for Downtown, Buffalo, 1984—; citizens' ambassador People to People, Eng., Hungary and Fed. Republic Germany, 1985; bd. dirs. Dream Machine Mus., Buffalo, 1984-87, Amherst Y-U, 1988—. Mem. Women Lawyers Western N.Y., Internat. Assn. Def. Counsel (faculty, editor newsletter, vice chmn. products liability, 1987, chmn. automobile ins. com. 1988—), N.Y. State Bar Assn. (tort reparations com. 1986-88), Erie County Bar Assn. (chmn. negligence com. 1984-85), We. N.Y. Assn. Def. Attys. (sec. 1989-90). Office: 1200 Liberty Bldg Buffalo NY 14202

HOFFMAN, BETTY JANE, circuit court clerk; b. Mayville, Wis., Apr. 7, 1933; d. Theodore Henry and Henrietta Elizabeth (Luebke) Machmueller; m. Lyle Eugene Cole, May 12, 1956 (dec. Sept. 1977); children—David Allen, Nanette Rae Cole Mlodzik, Ritchie Brian; m. Clarence Carl Hoffman, May 30, 1981; stepchildren—Judith Ann Aldrich, Clarence Allen Hoffman. Student pub. schs., Ripon, Wis. Cashier Thorp Fin. Corp., Ripon, 1951-56; dep. clk. cir. ct. Green Lake County, Green Lake, Wis., 1968-78, clk. cir. ct., 1979—. Mem. Green Lake County Republican party, 1970—, Wis. Rep. party, 1979—, Green Lake County Rep. Women, 1975—, v.p. elect 1987. Mem. Wis. Clk. of Cts. Assn., Nat. Assn. Ct. Mgmt., Tri-County Officers Assn. Lutheran. Avocations: sewing; cooking; travel. Home: 446 Scott St Green Lake WI 54941 Office: Clk of Cir Ct Courthouse 492 Hill St Green Lake WI 54941

HOFFMAN, CANDY LYNN, banker; b. Bronx, N.Y., Dec. 9, 1957; d. Robert and Beverly (Kronick) Berman; m. Bruce Ira Hoffman, June 5, 1983; 1 child, Marissa Robyn. AAS, Nassau Community Coll., 1978; BS, NYU, 1980. Asst. mgr. Citibank, NA, N.Y.C., 1978-86; sales mgr. Marine Midland Bank, NA, N.Y.C., 1986-89; asst. v.p., br. mgr. Nat. Community Bank, Maywood, N.J., 1989—. Mem. Mercer County C. of C. Home: 16 Snowbell Ct East Brunswick NJ 08816

HOFFMAN, CAROL KNIGHT, data processing executive, consultant; b. Lexington, Ky., Feb. 3, 1943; d. Walter E. and Lina K. (Baldauf) Knight; m. John C. Williams; 1 child, Susan. BS in Math. and Secondary Edn., Syracuse (N.Y.) U., 1965; MS in Computer Sci., Rutgers U., 1980. Programmer Litton Industries, Orange, N.J., 1968-70; programmer, analyst Norcross, Inc., N.Y.C., 1971-73; sr. programmer, analyst Ednl. Testing Service, Princeton, N.J., 1974-78; sr. analyst Houston Industries, 1980-83; cons. Computer Horizons, Parsippany, N.J., 1983-85; staff mgr. AT&T, N.J., 1985-87; pres. Hoff-Will Corp., Princeton, 1987—; tchr. Sch. Bus. Partnership, Houston, 1981-83. Photographer Friendswood (Tex.) Soccer Assn., 1983; coach's asst. Princeton Soccer Assn., 1984-85. Mem. IEEE, Mensa, Ind. Mgmt. Cons. Network of Princeton, Student Parents Orgn., Duchesne Parents Orgn. Presbyterian.

HOFFMAN, CATHERINE MARY, educator; b. Herrin, Ill., Nov. 12, 1946; d. Edward Herman and Minnie (Montani) Kitze; m. Edward Francis Hoffman Jr., Aug. 10, 1968; children: Christine Suzanne, Carolyn Elizabeth. BA in Chemistry, Rosary Coll., 1968; MA in Elem. Edn., Nat. Coll. Edn., 1987. Cert. secondary edn. tchr., Ill. Rsch. chemist Hines VA Hosp., Maywood, Ill., 1968-73; substitute tchr. Sch. Dists. 203 and 204, Naperville, Ill., 1987—. Mem. AAUW (treas. 1978-80, publicity 1976-78, newsletter 1982-85), Coun. Cath. Women (publicity chair Naperville chpt.). Democrat. Roman Catholic. Home: 232 James Ln Naperville IL 60540

HOFFMAN, DARLEANE CHRISTIAN, chemistry educator; b. Terril, Iowa, Nov. 8, 1926; d. Carl Benjamin and Elverna (Kuhlman) Christian; m. Marvin Morrison Hoffman, Dec. 26, 1951; children: Maureane R., Daryl K. BS in Chemistry, Iowa State U., 1948, PhD in Nuclear Chemistry, 1951. Chemist Oak Ridge (Tenn.) Nat. Lab., 1952-53; mem. staff radiochemistry group Los Alamos (N.Mex.) Sci. Lab., 1953-71, assoc. leader chemistry-nuclear group, 1971-79, div. leader chem.-nuclear chem. div., 1979-82, div. leader isotope and nuclear chem. div., 1982-84; prof. chemistry U. Calif., Berkeley, 1984—; faculty sr. scientist Lawrence Berkeley (Calif.) Lab., 1984—; panel leader, speaker Los Alamos Women in Sci., 1975, 79, 82; mem. subcom. on nuclear and radiochemistry NAS-NRC, 1978-81, chmn. subcom. on nuclear and radiochemistry, 1982-84; mem. commn. on radiochem. and nuclear techniques Internat. Union of Pure and Applied Chem., 1983-87, chmn., 1987—; mem. com. 2d Internat. Symposium on Nuclear and Radiochemistry, 1988; planning panel Workshop on Tng. Requirements for Chemists in Nuclear Medicine, Nuclear Industry, and Related Fields, 1988, radionuclide migration peer rev. com., Las Vegas, 1986-87, steering com. Advanced Steady State Neutron Source, 1986—, steering com., panelist Workshop on Opportunities and Challenges in Research with Transplutonium Elements, Washington, 1983. Contbr. numerous articles in field to profl. jours. Recipient Alumni Citation of Merit Coll. Scis. and Humanities, Iowa State U., 1978, Disting. Achievement award Iowa State U., 1986; fellow NSF, 1964-65, Guggenheim Found., 1978-79. Fellow Am. Inst. Chemists (pres. N.Mex. chpt. 1976-78), Am. Phys. Soc., AAAS; mem: Am. Chem. Soc. (chmn. nuclear chemistry and technology div. 1978-79, com. in sci. 1986-88, exec. com. div. nuclear chem. and tech. 1987—, John Dustin Clark award Cen. N.Mex. sect. 1976, Nuclear Chemistry award 1983, Garvan medal 1990), Am. Nuclear Soc. (co-chmn. internat. conf. Methods and Applications of Radioanalytical Chemistry 1987), Norwegian Acad. Arts and Scis, Sigma Xi, Phi Kappa Phi, Iota Sigma Pi, Pi Mu Epsilon, Sigma Delta Epsilon, Alpha Chi Sigma. Methodist. Home: 2277 Manzanita Dr Oakland CA 94611 Office: Lawrence Berkeley Lab MS70A-3307 NSD Berkeley CA 94720

HOFFMAN, DONNA COY, educator; b. Cin., Apr. 18, 1940; d. Clifford Donovan and Dorothy (Roessler) Coy; m. Donald Edward Hoffman, June 17, 1961; children: David Clifford, Dawn Susan Hoffman Osha. BS in Edn., Miami U., Oxford, Ohio, 1961; MEd, Xavier U., 1989. Cert. profl. tchr., Ohio, N.J. English tchr. Oak Hills Local Sch. Dist., Cin., 1961-62; vis. tchr. Westfield (N.J.) Sch. Dist., 1974-77; teaching staff Fair Oaks Hosp., Summit, N.J., 1974-77; learning disabilities resource tchr. Finneytown Local Sch. Dist., Cin., 1979—; staff devel. com. Finneytown Schs., Cin., 1988-91; in-svc. com. Hamilton County Schs., Cin., 1988, 90. Deacon, chmn. Presbyn. Ch. of Wyoming, Cin., 1989-92; pres. Jr. Woman's Club Western Cin., 1966; founder, advisor Oak Hills Jr. Woman's Club, Cin., 1967. Named Outstanding Educator, Spl. Edn. Regional Resource Ctr. of Southwest Ohio, 1988. Mem. Coun. for Exceptional Children, Orton Dyslexia Soc., Assn. for Supervision and Curriculum Devel., Assn. on Handicapped Student Svcs. Programs in Post-Secondary Edn., Transition and Communication Consortium on Learning Disabilities (state planning com. Ohio 1990-92). Republican. Office: Finneytown High Sch 8916 Fontainebleau Terr Cincinnati OH 45231

HOFFMAN, GRETEL BONNEVAL HOLCOMB, communications company executive; b. Silver Spring, Md., Mar. 9, 1962; d. William Spencer and Marietta Sue (Duncan) Holcomb; m. John Allen Hoffman, July 2, 1988. BS, Auburn U., 1984. Cert. gen. contractor, Fla. Project mgr. BCB Co., Atlanta, 1984-85; constrn. mgr. BellSouth Mobility, Atlanta, 1985-87, gen. mgr., 1987—; adj. prof. U. North Fla., 1990—. Mem. NAFE, Internat. Assn. Corp. Real Estate Execs. Democrat. Episcopalian. Office: 7077 Bonneual Rd Ste 110 Jacksonville FL 32216

HOFFMAN, JENNIFER ISOBEL, librarian; b. Washington, Sept. 13, 1948; d. Robert Gustavos and Maureen (May) Moll; m. Melvin Jacob Hoffman, Aug. 21, 1971; children: Robert, William. BA in English, SUNY, 1971, MS in Edn., 1973, M in Library Sci., 1978. Librarian Buffalo & Erie Co. Pub. Library Extension Services Br. Libra, 1981-88, Buffalo & Erie Co. Pub Library Contracting Libraries Elma Pu, 1988—. Ward chmn. Am. Cancer Soc., Erie County. Mem. Am. Library Assn. Democrat. Episcopalian. Office: Elma Pub Libr 1830 Bowen Rd Elma NY 14059

HOFFMAN, JUDY GREENBLATT, preschool director; b. Chgo., June 12, 1932; d. Edward Abraham and Clara (Morrill) Greenblatt; m. Morton Hoffman, Mar. 16, 1950 (div. Jan. 1983); children: Michael, Alan, Clare. BA summa cum laude, Met. State Coll., Denver, 1972; MA, U. No. Colo., 1976. Cert. tchr., Colo. Pre-sch. dir. B.M.H. Synagogue, Denver, 1968-70, Temple Emanuel, Denver, 1970-85, Congregation Rodef Shalom, Denver, 1985-88; tchr. Denver Pub. Schs., 1988—; bilingual tchr. adults in amnesty edn. Denver Pub. Schs., 1989-90. Author: I Live in Israel, 1979, Joseph and Me, 1980 (Gamoran award). Coordinator Douglas Mountain Therapeutic Riding Ctr. for Handicapped, Golden, Colo., 1985—; dir. Mountain Ranch Summer Day Camp for Denver Pub. Schs., 1989—. Mem. Nat. Assn. Temple Educators. Democrat.

HOFFMAN, LINDA R., foundation executive; b. New Haven, Conn., July 23, 1940; d. Bernard Harry and Sylvia (Paul) Rosenfield; m. Peter A. Hoffman, Sept. 25, 1965; 1 child, Tracie Lee. BA, Russell Sage Coll., 1962; MSW, Columbia U., 1968. Cert. social worker, N.Y. Case worker Conn. Dept. Welfare, New Haven, 1962-63; case worker N.Y.C. Bur. Child Welfare, 1963-65, supr., 1965-66; asst. to commr. program planning N.Y.C. Dept. Social Svcs., 1968-70; spl. asst. to commr. N.Y.C. Spl. Svcs. for Children, 1972-79; exec. dir. N.Y. Found. Sr. Citizens, N.Y.C., 1979—; cons. USIA, Teheran, Iran, summer 1975; adj. prof., mem. adv. coun. Columbia Sch. Social Work. Mem. Community Bd. #8, N.Y.C., 1981—, legis. com. N.Y.C. Commn. Status of Women, 1981—, adv. com. Brookdale Inst. Aging, Columbia U., 1981—, exec. com. policy on aging N.Y. Community Trust's Ctr.; mem. pub. programs and policy com., chmn. aging task force United Jewish Appeal Fedn. N.Y., N.Y.C., 1982—. Recipient Presidential Recognition award for Community Service, 1983. Mem. Nat. Assn. Social Workers (cert.). Home: 55 E 87th St New York NY 10128 Office: New York Found Sr Citizens 150 Nassau St Suite 1730 New York NY 10038

HOFFMAN, MARY CATHERINE, nurse anesthetist; b. Winamac, Ind., July 14, 1923; d. Harmon William Whitney and Dessie Maude (Neely) H.; R.N., Methodist Hosp., Indpls., 1945; cert. obstet. analgesia and anesthesia, Johns Hopkins Hosp., 1949, grad. U. Hosp. of Cleve. Sch. Anesthesia, 1952; Staff nurse Meth. Hosp., 1945-49; research asst., then staff anesthetist Johns

Hopkins Hosp., 1949-62; staff anesthetist Meth. Hosp., 1962-64, U. Chgo. Hosps., 1964-66; chief nurse anesthetist Paris (Ill.) Community Hosp., 1966-80; staff anesthetist Hendricks County Hosp., Danville, Ind., Ball Meml. Hosp., Muncie, Ind., 1981-86; instr.-trainer CPR, 1975-81; mem. Terr. 08 CPR Coordinating Com., 1975-80. Mem. Am. Assn. Nurse Anesthetists, Am. Heart Assn., Ind. Fedn. Bus. and Profl. Women's Clubs (Ill. dist. chmn. 1977-78, state found. chmn. 1978-79; found. award 1979). Republican. Presbyterian. Home: 1700 N Maddox Dr Muncie IN 47304

HOFFMAN, MERLE HOLLY, social psychologist, political activist, author; b. Phila., Mar. 6, 1946; d. Jack Rheins and Ruth (Dubow) H.; m. Martin Gold, June 30, 1979. BA magna cum laude in Psychology, Queens Coll., 1972; postgrad., CUNY, 1972-75. Founder, pres. Choices Women's Med. Ctr., Forest Hills, N.Y., 1971—; family planning cons. Health Ins. Plan, N.Y.C., 1973—; founder, pres. Ctr. for Comprehensive Breast Svcs., N.Y.C., 1979—, Merle Hoffman Enterprises, N.Y.C., 1986—; speaker, debator on women's rights and polit. issues; founder, pres. Nat. Liberty Com., 1981. Cons. editor Female Health Topics and Diagnostic Reporter, 1979-81; editor, pub. ednl. jour. On The Issues; contbr. articles in field to various publs.; producer documentary film Abortion A Different Light; founder N.Y. Pro-Choice Coalition; host cable TV series MH: On the Issues, 1986. Mem. Nat. Assn. Abortion Facilities (co-founder, pres. 1976-77), Nat. Abortion Fedn. (co-founder, sec. 1977-78), Phi Beta Kappa. Office: Choices Women's Med Ctr Inc 97-77 Queens Blvd Forest Hills NY 11374

HOFFMAN, RAMONA KAY, marketing executive; b. Jasper, Ind., Dec. 22, 1956; d. Raymond B. and Lucille P. (Becher) Knies; m. Bert A. Hoffman, Oct. 13, 1979; 1 child, Calley Ray. AA, Watterson Coll., Louisville, 1977. Pres. Patoka Bay, Inc., Jasper, 1979-89; customer svc. rep. Jasper Seating Co., 1988, mktg. dir., 1988—; pres. 3-D Merchants Assn., Jasper, 1982-84, 86. Sec., bd. dirs. Jasper C. of C., 1983-85. Mem. Am. Mgmt. Assn. Republican. Roman Catholic. Office: Jasper Seating Co 932 Mill St Jasper IN 47546

HOFFMAN, ROBIN RHOADES MENGE, speech pathologist; b. Providence, Dec. 13, 1952; d. Charles Montrose and Ruth Louise (Rhoades) Menge; m. Donald Allen. BA, Allegheny Coll., Meadville, Pa., 1975; MA, Wash. State U., Pullman, 1978. Speech-lang. specialist Tulare County Dept. Edn., Visalia, Calif., 1978—. Vol. Nat. Rep. Com., Visalia Tulare Co. Calif., 1988--. Mem. Calif. Speech-Language Hearing Assn., Am. Speech Language Assn. Republican. Lutheran. Home: 924 S Jennie Dr Visalia CA 93277 Office: Tulare County Dept Edn County Civic Ctr Visalia CA 93291

HOFFMAN, SUE ELLEN, elementary teacher; b. Dayton, Ohio, Aug. 23, 1945; d. Cyril Vernon and Sarah Ellen (Sherer) Stephan; m. Lawrence Wayne Hoffman, Oct. 28, 1967. BS in Edn., U. Dayton, 1967; postgrad., Loyolla Coll., 1977, Ea. Mich. U., 1980; MEd, Wright State U., 1988. Cert. reading specialist and elem. tchr., Ohio. 5th grade tchr. St. Anthony Sch., Dayton, Ohio, 1967-68, West Huntsville (Ala.) Elem. Sch., 1968-71; 6th grade tchr. Ranchland Hills Pub. Sch., El Paso, Tex., 1973-74; 3rd grade tchr. Emerson Pub. Sch., Westerville, Ohio, 1976, St. Joan of Arc Sch., Aberdeen, Md., 1976-78, Our Lady of Good Counsel, Plymouth, Mich., 1979-80; 5th grade tchr. St. Helen Sch., Dayton, 1980—. Selected for membership Kappa Delta Pi, 1988. Mem. Internat. Reading Assn., Nat. Cath. Edn. Assn. Roman Catholic. Home: 2174 Green Springs Dr Kettering OH 45440 Office: St Helen Sch 5086 Burkhardt Rd Dayton OH 45431

HOFFMAN, TERESA ESTHER, speech and language pathologist, hospital official; b. Pitts., Apr. 24, 1957; d. Frank David Salimando and Shirley Anne (Ward) Pagac; m. Dean M. Shaver, Sept. 29, 1979 (div. Aug. 1986); 1 child, Stephanie Anne; m. Robert Allen Hoffman, July 2, 1988. BS in Speech Pathology and Audiology, California U. Pa., 1979, MEd in Speech Pathology and Audiology, 1981. Cert. speech and hearing pathologist, Pa. Speech therapist Easter Seal Soc., Somerset, Pa., 1979; grad. asst. Calif. U. Pa., 1980-81; speech therapist, then dir. Somerset Ctr., United Cerebral Palsy So. Alleghenies Region, Johnstown, Pa., 1979-80, 81; speech and hearing specialist II, Somerset (Pa.) Habilitation Ctr., 1981-84; speech-lang. pathologist Crossroads, Speech and Hearing, Inc., McMurray, Pa., 1984-86; pre-sch. speech-lang. pathologist Intermediate Unit 08, Ebensburg, Pa., 1986-87; dir. head injury program Rehab. Hosp. Altoona, Pa., 1987—, dir. speech-lang. pathology, 1988—; presenter in field. Recipient spl. award Tribute to Women in Bus. and Industry, 1989. Mem. Am. Speech-Lang.-Hearing Assn. (cert.), Pa. Speech and Hearing Assn., Acad. Neurologic Communications Disorders, Am. Coll. Healthcare Execs., Soroptomists. Home: 200 N Phaney St Ebensburg PA 15931 Office: Rehab Hosp Altoona 2005 Valley View Blvd Altoona PA 16602

HOFFMAN, VALERIE JANE, lawyer; b. Lowville, N.Y., Oct. 27, 1953; d. Russell Francis and Jane Marie (Fowler) H. Student, U. Edinburgh, Scotland, 1973-74; BA summa cum laude, Union Coll., 1975; JD, Boston Coll., 1978. Bar: Ill. 1978, U.S. Dist. Ct. (no. dist.) Ill. 1978, U.S. Ct. Appeals (3rd cir.) 1981, U.S. Ct. Appeals (7th cir.) 1983. Assoc. Seyfarth, Shaw, Fairweather & Geraldson, Chgo., 1978-87, ptnr., 1987—. Author: Cases and Materials; Arts, Entertainment and Media Management Law, 1985; Affirmative Action and the Regulation of Federal Contractors, 1989. Dir. Remains Theatre, Chgo., 1981—. Mem. ABA, Chgo. Bar Assn., Lawyers for Creative Arts, Chgo. Yacht Club, Univ. Club Chgo. (dir. 1984-87), Phi Beta Kappa. Office: Seyfarth Shaw Fairweather & Geraldson 55 E Monroe # 4200 Chicago IL 60603

HOFFMANN, CAROL TOMB, computer software developer, financial planner; b. Balt., Nov. 3, 1952; d. Richard John and Doris Elaine (Shoemaker) Tomb; m. Michael R. Hoffmann, July 29, 1973; children: Kurt M., Kristen E., Kevin R. Student, Drake U., 1972; AS, Harcum Jr. Coll., 1973; cert., Inst. Cert. Fin. Planners, 1988. Various retailing positions N.Y. and Iowa, 1973-76; store opening area supr. Brandeis, Des Moines, 1976-77, Peterson, Harned Von Maur, Des Moines, 1977-78; adminstrv. asst. Clk. Iowa Supreme Ct., Des Moines, 1978-79; retirement fund advisor Jones, Hoffmann and Davison, Des Moines, 1978-83; fin. advisor Michael R. Hoffmann, P.C., Des Moines, 1983—; pres. Nouveau Riche, Ltd., Des Moines, 1986—. Mem. Internat. Bd. Standards and Practices for Cert. Fin. Planners, Internat. Assn. for Fin. Planning, Am. Assn. Individual Investors, Blank Park Zoo, Nat. Rifle Assn., Des Moines Art Ctr., Des Moines Sci. Ctr., Friends Iowa Pub. Television. Office: Nouveau Riche Ltd 3708 75th St Breakwater Bldg Des Moines IA 50322

HOFFMANN, CONSTANCE WELLINGS, city manager; b. Pitts., Dec. 11, 1950; d. William John and Marjorie Wellings; m. Stephen Hoffmann, Apr. 10, 1971. BA in Polit. Sci., Fla. Atlantic U., 1971, MA in Polit. Sci., 1972. Research asst. Fla. Atlantic U., Boca Raton, 1970-73; with City of Fort Lauderdale, Fla., 1974—, dep. city mgr., 1979-80, city mgr., 1980—. Recipient Outstanding Young Leader award Ft. Lauderdale Jaycees, 1981; named Woman of Yr./Broward County Atlantic-Fla. chpt. Women in Communications, 1981, Woman of Yr. South Fla. Bus. & Profl. Women, 1985. Mem. Internat. City Mgrs. Assn., Nat. Trust for Hist. Preservation, Fla. City and County Mgr. Assn. (bd. dirs. 1983-86). Office: City of Fort Lauderdale PO Box 14250 Fort Lauderdale FL 33302

HOFFMANN, JOAN CAROL, academic dean; b. Cedarburg, Wis., Feb. 20, 1934; d. Frank Ernst and Althea Wilhelmina (Behm) H. Nursing diploma Michael Reese Hosp., 1955; BS in Zoology, U. Wis., Madison, 1959; PhD in Physiology, U. Ill., Chgo., 1965. RN. Sci. instr. Michael Reese Hosp., Chgo., 1959-62; USPHS trainee U. Ill., Chgo., 1962-64; NSF postdoctoral fellow Coll. de France, Paris, 1964-65; asst. prof. U. Rochester, N.Y., 1965-70; assoc. prof., prof. U. Hawaii, Honolulu, 1970-83; dean of students U. Mass. Med. Sch., Worcester, 1983—; chmn. anatomy U. Hawaii, 1973-80. Contbr. articles to sci. jours. NIH rsch. grantee, 1966-75. Mem. Endocrine Soc., Soc. for Study of Reprodn., Am. Physiol. Soc., Am. Assn. Anatomists, Women in Endocrinology (sec. 1978-79, pres. 1987-88), Phi Beta Kappa, Sigma Xi. Avocations: gardening, needlework, furniture building/refinishing, reading. Home: 30 Russell Rd Wellesley MA 02181 Office: U Mass Med Sch Office 55 Lake Ave N Worcester MA 01655

HOFFMANN, NANCY LARRAINE, state legislator; b. Needham, Mass., Sept. 22, 1947; m. Mark Hoffmann, 1971; children: Eva, Anna, Gustav. B.A., Syracuse U.; M.S., U. Md. Former polit. organizer, Tenn., Miss., city councilor Syracuse, N.Y., 1980-84; mem. N.Y. State Senate from 48th Dist., 1984—, mem. agr., crime and correction, fin., environ. conservation, local govt., tourism, recreation and sports coms. Mem. Gov.'s Council on Fiscal and Econ. Priorities. Democrat. Presbyterian. Home: PO Box 268 De Witt NY 13214 Office: N Y State Senate Albany NY 12224*

HOFFMASTER, STEPHANIE JOAN, counselor; b. Somers Point, N.J., Mar. 1, 1953; d. Lynwood Carlton and Irma Joan (Hulse) Smith; m. Apr. 12, 1975 (div. July 1985); 1 child, Stephanie Joy. AAS in Community Svc. and Social Welfare, Cumberland County Coll., 1986; student, Thomas A. Edison State Coll., 1986—. Resident mgr., leasing agt. Leonard Real Estate Mgmt. Co., Charlotte, N.C., 1982-83; dir. food and clothing distbn. ctr. New Testament Fellowship Ch., Charlotte, 1983-84; social svc. asst. Vineland (N.J.) Devel. Ctr., 1985; job counselor, social svc. asst. Rural Devel. Corp., Port Norris, N.J., 1986; extended employment counselor Jersey Cape Diagnostic Tng. and Opportunity Ctr., Cape May Court House, N.J., 1986—; chairperson forms com. Jersey Cape Diagnostic Tng. and Opportunity Ctr., 1987—. Mem. PTA, 1986—, Mariners Bible Study Class, 1989—; mem. Eve circle United Meth. Women, 1989—; devel., supr. clothing and furniture dr. Cambodian Refugees in N.C., 1982; elem. tutor Spanish-Am. students, 1974; tchr., tchr. aid various ch. youth programs in N.J. and Pa., 1971-75; couns., resident advisor Summer Outreach Program for Teenagers, 1971-74. Mem. NAFE, Ocean City Cultural Arts Ctr. Office: Jersey Cape Diagnostic Tng and Opportunity Ctr Crest Haven Rd Cape May Court House NJ 08210 Address: PO Box 512 Marmora NJ 08223

HOFFMEIER, KATHY ANN, management; b. Sioux City, Dec. 28, 1956; d. Shirlee (Kennelly) Erlemeier; m. Craig Alan Hoffmeier, June 20, 1956. Student, Iowa State U., 1979; B in Edn., U. New Orleans, 1983. Tchr. Orleans Parish Sch., New Orleans, La., 1980-82; high sch. relations dir. Phllips Jr. Coll., New Orleans, 1982-83; regional mgr., v.p. Stafco, Inc., Durham, N.C., 1983--; bd. dirs. Profl. Staffing, New Orleans, 1987--. Vol. New Orleans Zoo, 1980-84. Mem. Durham C. of C., Durham Jr. Women's League, Bus. profl. Women, Women in Mgmt. Office: Stafco Inc 1000 Park Forty Plaza Ste 170 Durham NC 27713

HOFFMEISTER, JANA MARIE, cardiologist. MD, SUNY Upstate Med. Ctr., Syracuse, 1976. Diplomate Am. Bd. Internal Medicine. Intern Albany (N.Y.) Med. Ctr., 1976-78, asst. resident, 1978-79, resident, 1979-80, fellow div. cardiology, 1981-83; fellow div. cardiology Emory U., Atlanta, 1984; fellow coronary angioplasty and interventional cardiology Emory U. Hosp., 1985-86; presenter numerous cardiology confs. Contbr. numerous articles to profl. jours. Mem. AMA, Cardiac Soc. Upstate N.Y., N.Y. State Soc. Internal Medicine, Syracuse Med. Alumni Assn., Pres's. Club, Lamplighters Soc. of Emory U. Home: 7 Reddy Ln Loudonville NY 12211

HOFFNER, MARILYN, university administrator; b. N.Y.C., Nov. 16, 1929; d. Daniel and Elsie (Schulz) H.; B.F.A., Cooper Union; m. Albert Greenberg, May 29, 1949; children—Doren Roe, Peter Cooper. Art dir. Printers' Ink mag., N.Y.C., 1953-63; art dir. Print mag., N.Y.C., 1960-62; corp. art dir. Vision, Inc., Latin Am., 1963-75; dir. alumni relations Cooper Union, 1975-82, dir. devel., 1982—. Bd. dirs. Art Dirs. Club N.Y., 1973-75, 79-82, exec. sec., 1973-75, exec. treas., 1979-82; mem. Citizens Adv. Cultural Arts Com. Dutchess County, 1978-80. Named Alumnus of Yr., Cooper Union, 1968; recipient Gold medal Art Dirs. Club, 1979. Mem. Cooper Union Alumni Assn. (editor-in-chief 1971-74, 1st v.p. 1974-75), Council Advancement and Support of Edn., Type Dirs. Club (numerous awards), Nat. Arts Club (exhbn. com.). Contbg. editor Print mag., 1960-62, Art Direction, 1959-64, Graphics mag., 1959-62; designer mags., advt., books. Home: 51 Fifth Ave New York NY 10003 Office: 41 Cooper Sq New York NY 10003

HOFFNUNG, AUDREY SONIA, speech and language pathologist, educator; b. N.Y.C., Mar. 15, 1928; d. Nathan and Gussie (Karp) Smith; B.A. cum laude, Bklyn. Coll., 1949; M.A., Columbia U., 1950; Ph.D., City U. N.Y., 1974. Cert. and lic. speech pathologist, N.Y.; m. Joseph Hoffnung, Nov. 26, 1950; children—Bonnie Fern, Tami Lynn. Rehab. therapist Ridgewood Cerebral Palsy Center, 1949-50; dir. speech therapy Kingsbrook Med. Center, Bklyn., 1950-55; therapist and cons. Morris J. Solomon Clinic, Bklyn., 1956-58; therapist Speech and Hearing Center Bklyn. Coll., 1958-62, 63-64; pvt. practice speech therapy Hewlett (N.Y.) Med. Center, 1961-63; pvt. practice speech therapy, Oceanside, N.Y., 1964-71; cons. on staff for aphasic patients Phys. Medicine and Rehab. Center, South Nassau Communities Hosp., 1964-65; part-time lectr. Speech and Hearing Center, Queens (N.Y.) Coll., 1970-72; adj. lectr. dept. speech Bklyn. Coll., 1973-74, asst. prof. speech pathology, 1974-77; asst. prof. dept. speech communication and theatre St. John's U., Jamaica, N.Y., 1977-80, asso. prof., 1980—; guest lectr. N.Y. Orton Soc., 1979, Brookdale Med. Center, 1978; mem. profl. adv. bd. Vis. Home Health Services of Nassau County, 1973—. Author: (with Valletutti and McKnight) Facilitating communication in young children with handicapping conditions. Mem. Am. Speech and Hearing Assn., N.Y.C. Speech, Hearing and Lang. Assn., N.Y. State Speech and Hearing Assn. (chairperson student activities 1978-79), L.I. Speech and Hearing Assn., Nat. Student Speech-Lang.-Hearing Assn. (hon. advisor 1988), Aphasia Study Group of N.Y.C., N.Y. Acad. Scis. Contbr. articles on speech pathology to profl. jours. Home: 3282 Woodward St Oceanside NY 11572 Office: St John's U Dept Speech Communication Utopia and Grand Central Pkwys Jamaica NY 11439

HOFFORD, SUZANNE, marketing and sales management executive; b. Annapolis, Md., July 17, 1957; d. John Labbee and Grace Helen (George) Hofford; m. H. Jack McCall, Jr., July 20, 1985. BS, Clemson U., 1978, MS, 1980; postgrad., Colgate Darden U., 1987. Mktg. mgr. Milliken and Co., Spartanburg, S.C.; pres. Hofford McCall Enterprises, Greenville, S.C. Mem. Spartanburg C. of C. Home: 25 Byrd Blvd Greenville SC 29605 Office: 1200 E Main St Spartanburg SC 29304

HOFMANN, ADELE DELLENBAUGH, pediatrician; b. Boston, Oct. 12, 1926; d. Frederick Samuel and Anne Celestine (Goddard) Dellenbaugh; m. Frederick G. Hofmann, July 26, 1957 (div. 1982); children: Peter, Anne. BA, Smith Coll., 1948; MD, U. Rochester, 1952. Diplomate Am. Bd. Pediatrics. Intern U. Minn. Hosp., Mpls., 1952-53; resident in pediatrics Babies' Hosp., N.Y.C., 1953-55; Nat. Fedn. fellow Presbyn. Hosp., N.Y.C., 1955-57; chief ambulatory pediatrics St. Luke's Hosp., N.Y.C., 1957-63; assoc. dir. adolescent medicine Beth Israel Hosp., N.Y.C., 1963-70; dir. adolescent medicine NYU Med. Ctr./Bellevue Hosp., N.Y.C., 1970-82; dir. student health UCLA, 1983; med. dir. ambulatory pediatrics Children's Hosp. Orange County, Orange, Calif., 1984-90; dir. adolescent medicine U. Calif.-Irvine, Orange, 1990—; cons. WHO, 1976-84; bd. dirs. Huntington Beach (Calif.) Community Clinic, others. Author: The Hospitalized Adolescent, 1976 (Am. Nurses Assn. award 1988), Consent and Confidentiality in Child and Adolescent Health Care, 1984; author, editor: Adolescent Medicine, 1986, 2d edit., 1989 (Am. Coll. Internal Medicine award 1987). Recipient recognition award CAFAM, Bogota, Colombia, 1989, Collegio de Medicos, Venezuela, 1988, others. Fellow Am. Acad. Pediatrics (chair sect. adolescent health 1978-79; sect. award in adolescent health 1984), Soc. Adolescent Medicine (pres. 1976-77; disting. svc. award 1981); mem. Western Soc. Pediatric Rsch., Internat. Soc. Adolescent Medicine. Democrat. Home: 1551 Tahiti Ave Laguna Beach CA 92651 Office: Dept Pediatrics Univ Calif Irvine Med Ctr 101 The City Dr Orange CA 92668

HOFSTETTER, GEORGENE LOUISE WEIGEL, real estate broker; b. St Louis, July 3, 1954; d. Robert Lewis and Georgene Nancy (Walbancke) Weigel. Student, Real Estate Appraisal Course, Union, 1983, Career Edn. System, St Charles, 1984. V.p. Weigel Screen Process, Eureka, Mo., 1972-81; salesperson Countryside Brokers, Inc., Augusta, Mo., 1982-87, broker, co-owner, 1988-89, owner, 1989—. Campaign Coordinator for State Rep. Craig Kilby, 21st Dist. 1986. Mem. Nat. Assn. Ind. Fee Appraisers (designated appraiser; v.p. Tri-County, 1988, pres. 1989, bd. dirs. St. Louis Metro., 1989, 1990—). Republican. Episcopalian. Home: Rt 1 Box 322 Marthasville MO 63357

HOFT, LYNNE ANN, educator, remedial specialist; b. Carroll, Iowa, Mar. 1, 1945; d. Norman North and Dorothy Mae (Dean) Hoft. BA, Briar Cliff Coll., 1971; MA in Spl. Edn., Ariz. State U., 1979; postgrad., U. Minn. Cert. elem. and spl. edn. tchr., Ariz., Minn. Tchr. St. Edward Sch., Waterloo, Iowa, 1968-70; tchr. Chino Valley Sch., Ariz., 1971-77, program developer, 1974-76; spl. edn. tchr. Tuba City Pub. Jr. High Sch., Ariz., 1978-82; spl. edn. tchr., dept. chmn. Tuba City High Sch., 1983-86, curriculum developer, 1984-85; remedial specialist Eagles' Nest Mid-Sch., 1986-88; spl. edn. coord. chpt. 1 epsilon program Hopkins (Minn.) Pub. Schs., Hennepin County Home Sch., 1988—; founder, pres. Unltd. Learning Enterprises, Inc., Tuba City, 1983-85; trainer Developing Capable People. Probation aide Waterloo Juvenile Ct., 1970-71; vol. instr. Prescott Spl. Olympics 1977-78; local coord. Tuba City Spl. Olympics, 1978-80. Mem. NEA, Minn. Edn. Assn., Hopkins Edn. Assn., Tuba City Unified Edn. Assn. (pres. 1985-86), Internat. Platform Assn., Delta Kappa Gamma. Democrat. Avocations: reading, piano, camping, hiking, writing.

HOFTIEZER, HELEN LOUISE, director of acute/ambulatory care; b. Clear Lake, S.D., Nov. 8, 1950; d. William Howard and Charlotte Lauretta (Seablom) Tvedt; m. Thomas Edward Hoftiezer, Oct. 10, 1970; children: Tasha, Shantel, Jessica, Joshua. BS, S.D. State U., 1986; postgrad., U. Minn., 1989—. With St. Ann's Hosp., Watertown, S.D., 1971—; staff RN med. St. Ann's Hosp., 1972, staff RN OR, 1972-76; asst. supr. OR St. Anne's Hosp., 1976-81, mgr. OR, 1981-83, dir. nursing, 1983-86; dir. acute care Priarie Lakes Health Care Ctr., Watertown, 1986-87; dir. acute/ambulatory care Priarie Lakes Health Care Ctr., 1987—; coord. Paramedic Program, Watertown, 81 hour EMT Program, Watertown, 1981; pres. LAVTI Adv. Bd., Watertown, 1985-89, Multi-Dist. Career Ctr. Adv., Watertown, 1985-89. Mem. Luth. Ch., Watertown, 1983—, mgmt. com., 1989; mem. Child Protection Team, Watertown, 1985-89, prins. adv. com. Jr. High Sch., Watertown, 1986-89. Mem. Am. Orgn. of Nurse Execs., S.D. Hosp. Assn. (coun. on profl. practice 1989), S.D. Orgn. of Nurse Execs. (program chmn. 1986-88), Am. Coll. Healthcare Execs. Republican. Lutheran. Office: Prairie Lakes Health Care 400 10th Ave Northwest Watertown SD 57201

HOGAN, BARBARA JANE, personnel professional, lawyer; b. Durham, England, Jan. 3, 1939; d. Arthur and Maud Jane (Smith) Gillett; m. David J. Powell, July 14, 1960 (div. 1968); m. Walter H. Hogan, June 19, 1971 (dec.). Student, Durham U., 1957-58; BA, Wellesley (Mass.) Coll., 1977; JD, Suffolk U., Boston, 1980. Bar: Mass. 1980, U.S. Dist. Ct. Mass. 1981. Adminstrv. asst. Arthur D. Little, Inc., Cambridge, Mass., 1964-69, pers. asst., 1969-70, pers. rep., 1970-72, pers. mgr., 1972-81; dir. human resources Gen. Cinema Corp., Chestnut Hill, Mass., 1981-87; v.p. human resources Winchester (Mass.) Hosp., 1987—; pvt. practice law Rockport, Mass., 1981—. Mem. Mass. Bar Assn., Mass. Health Care Human Resources Assn. (sec. 1989-90).

HOGAN, CHARLENE JO, telecommunications executive; b. Pitts., Dec. 23, 1948; d. George F. and Imogene (O'Neill) Howland; m. Edward M. Hogan, Oct. 8, 1988; stepchild, Allison. BA, U. Va., Fredericksburg, 1970. Asst. mgr. AT&T Treasury, Piscataway, N.J., 1970-71; from. mem. programming staff to dist. mgr. corp. budget Controller's dept. AT&T, Piscataway, N.J., 1971-84; dist. mgr., chief fin. officer orgn. Controller's dept. AT&T, Morristown, N.J., 1984-89; dist. mgr. AT&T Consumer Mktg., Basking Ridge, N.J., 1989—. Mem. NAFE, Franklin Greens Ski Club. Republican. Presbyterian. Home: 19 Heritage Dr Warren NJ 07059 Office: AT&T Consumer Mktg 295 N Maple Ave Basking Ridge NJ 07920

HOGAN, KRISTINA A., sales professional; b. Boulder, Colo., May 8, 1948; d. Francis D. and Juanita Ruth (Butler) Armstrong. BA, Fla. State U., 1970; MSCJ, Rollins, 1977; cert., U. Denver, 1982. Asst. dir. Guardian Technologies, Denver; dir. Colo. Dept. of Health/ADAD, Denver; regional coord. Colo. Dept. Hwys./Hwy. Safety, Denver; govt. affairs rep. BI, Inc., Boulder. Mem. Am. Correctional Assn., Am. Soc. for Pub. Adminstrn., Criminal Justice Planner, Colo. Correctional Assn., Women's Mgmt. Group, Injury Prevention Network, Friendship Program, Alpha Xi Delta. Home: 27465 Spruce Ln Evergreen CO 80439

HOGAN, SHEILA JOAN, financial analyst; b. Torrance, Calif., May 2, 1965; d. James Donald and Joan Ruth (Frintz) H. BA, Harvard U.-Radcliffe Coll., 1987. Fin. analyst Drexel Burnham Lambert, Beverly Hills, Calif., 1987—. Mem. NAFE, NOW, Sierra Club. Democrat. Home: 4903 Rolling Meadows Rd Rolling Hills Estates CA 90274 Office: Drexel Burnham Lambert 131 S Rodeo Dr Beverly Hills CA 90212

HOGE, GERALDINE RAJACICH, teacher; b. Eveleth, Minn., Apr. 8, 1937; d. Robert and Dora (Tassi) Rajacich; m. Gregg LeRoy Hoge, Sept. 15, 1963 (div. Feb. 1972); 1 child, Sheryl Maurine. BS, U. Minn., 1959; MA with honors, Pepperdine U. Cert. elem. tchr., Calif. Tchr. Chaska (Minn.) Pub. Schs., 1959-60, Minnetonka (Minn.) Pub. Schs., 1960-62, Norwalk (Calif.) La Mirada Pub. Schs., 1962-64, Culver City (Calif.) Unified Sch. Dist., 1966—. Fellow mem. Culver City Guidance Clinic Guild, 1981-89, Calif. State Rep. Cen. Com., Sacramento, 1986-88, L.A. County Rep. Cen. Com., 1987—; vice chmn. 49th Assembly Dist. Cen. Rep. Com., Culver City, 1988—. Named Tchr. of the Yr. Elks Lodge, 1982; grantee, 1988-89. Fellow Am. Fedn. Tchrs., Calif. Fedn. Tchrs., Culver City Fedn. Tchrs. (v.p. 1978-79), Alpha Delta Pi (historian 1956-59). Republican. Office: Culver City Unified Sch 4034 Irving Pl Culver City CA 90232

HOGEBOOM, PATRICIA ANN SCHRACK, high school guidance counselor; b. Buffalo, Feb. 17, 1937; d. Royal Elmer and Jeannette (O'Toole) Schrack; m. Willard Leroy Hogeboom, Sept. 17, 1960; children: Christopher John, Matthew Patrick. BS, Syracuse U., 1959; MS, L.I. U., 1981. Cert. guidance counselor. English tchr. South Park High Sch., Buffalo, 1960-62, North Babylon (N.Y.) High Sch., 1963-64, Islip (N.Y.) Jr. Highh Sch., 1969-70; career counselor Suffolk County Libr., 1973-76; owner, tchr. Loaves of Love Baking Sch., Oakdale, N.Y., 1973-79; cons. Islip (N.Y.) Div. Sr. Citizens Svcs., 1979-84; instr. St. Joseph's Coll., Patchogue, N.Y., 1983-86; guidance counselor Riverhead (N.Y.) High Sch., 1986-87, McKenna Jr. High Sch., Massapequa, N.Y., 1987—; bd. dirs. Pat Hogeboom Presents Workshops in Human Devel., Oakdale, 1984—; cons. Suffolk County Office for Aging, Smithtown, N.Y., 1984-86. Contbr. articles on elderly to Suffolk County News, 1983; contbr. essays to Newsday and N.Y. Times, 1980-84. Vestrymember St. Mark's Episc. Ch., Islip, 1984-87, chalice bearer, lay reader. Mem. AAUW (pres. N.Y. State div. 1990—, gift honoree Islip br. 1982, Project Renew grantee 1980), Am. Soc. Tng. and Devel., N.Y. State Counselor's Assn., Nassau County Counselor's Assn., Personnel and Guidance Assn. Home: 55 W Shore Dr Oakdale NY 11769

HOGG, MARY JEAN, marketing executive; b. Cottonwood Falls, Kans., Mar. 5, 1926; d. Clarence F. and Vicotrine Cooweesta (Fry) Gladfelter; children: Christine, Linda, Kathrine. BS, Kans. State Tchrs. Coll., 1947; postgrad., State U. Iowa, San Diego State U. Tchr. Allen (Kans.) High Sch., 1948, Garnett (Kans.) Jr. High Sch., 1948-50, Iowa City Jr. High Sch., 1950; lab. instr. Coll. Medicine State U. Iowa, 1950-53; exec. Suzy Zoo Greeting Cards, San Diego, 1971—. Active YMCA, San Diego; U.S. Del. to the Second Joint Session on Trade, Industry and Econ. Devel., Beijing, 1989. Mem. PEO Sisterhood, Nat. Greeting Card Assn., Nat. Assn. Sch. Supply Dealers, San Diego Opera Assn., San Diego State U. Women's Assn. (pres. 1990), Alpha Sigma Alpha. Office: 9401 Waples Ste 150 San Diego CA 92121

HOGG, ROZALIA CRUISE, genealogist; b. Bluefield, W.Va., Dec. 31, 1931; d. George Mortimer and Beulah Grove (Fleshman) Cruise; m. Edward Welford Hogg, Jr., June 20, 1953 (dec. 1972); children: Gayle Hogg Wells, Alice Ann Hogg Conaty, Nancy Hogg Pingry. Student, Madison Coll., Harrisonburg, Va., 1951-53; BA in History, Mary Baldwin Coll., 1978. Kindergarten tchr. Ft. Meade, Md., 1953-54; tour guide Woodrow Wilson Birthplace, Staunton, Va., 1978-80, P. Buckley Moss Mus., Waynesboro, Va., 1990; genealogist Patrick County, Va., 1985—. Bd. dirs. Augusta County (Va.) Hist. Soc., 1987—; vice chmn. hist. commn. City of Waynesboro, 1986—. Mem. Women of the Ch.-1st Presbyn., Rosecliff Garden Club (pres. 1973-74), Va. Mus. Fine Arts, Sigma Sigma Sigma, Phi Alpha Theta. Home: 10 Pelham Greene West Waynesboro VA 22980

HOGGATT, CLELA ALLPHIN, English educator; b. Des Moines, Sept. 9, 1932; d. Addison Edgar and Frances (Buckallew) Philleo; m. Charles

Allphin; children: Beverly, Valerie, Clark, Arthur, Frances; m. John Hoggatt. AA, Grand View Jr. Coll., 1952; BA summa cum laude, U. No. Iowa, 1954; MA, Tex A&I U., 1961. Cert. life tchr. Iowa, Tex.; permanent life community coll. credential, Calif. Tchr. social studies Los Fresnos (Tex.) Jr. High Sch., 1954-55; tchr. English Cummings Jr. High Sch., Brownsville, Tex., 1956-59, Fickett Jr. High Sch., Tucson, 1963-66, Portola Jr. High Sch., L.A., 1956-59; instr. speech Tex. Southmost Jr. Coll., Bronsville, 1959; tchr. history and English Ysleta High Sch., El Paso, Tex., 1963-66; prof. English L.A. Trade-Tech. Coll., 1969-75, L.A. Mission Coll., 1975—. Author: Women in the Plays of Henrik Ibsen, 1975, The Writing Cycle, 1986, Good News for Writers, 1990; contbr. to Words, Words, Words, 1981. V.p. Friends West Valley Library, Reseda, Calif., 1984—. Grand View Jr. Coll. scholar, 1951-52, U. No. Iowa scholar, 1953-54. Mem. Nat. Coun. Tchrs. English, Am. Mensa, Pi Gamma Mu. Democrat. Office: LA Mission Coll 1212 San Fernando Rd San Fernando CA 91340

HOGH, DAWN MARIE, system test engineer; b. Flint, Mich., Feb. 6, 1962; d. Don Dee and Joan Marjorie (Polsgrove) Woodard; m. Christian Peter Hogh, Aug. 18, 1984. BA in Econs., U. Mich., 1984, MS in Indsl. Ops. Engring, 1985. Customer liaison Buick Motor Div., Flint, 1984; project mgr. AT&T Bell Labs., Holmdel, N.J., 1986-89, system test supr., 1989—. Mem., liaison Future Pioneers Am., AT&T, Holmdel, 1986—. Mem. Project Mgmt. Inst., Operations Research Soc. of Am., Holmdel Volleyball Club (vice-chairperson 1987-89). Democrat. Presbyterian. Home: 19 Emory Dr Lincroft NJ 07738 Office: AT&T Bell Labs Rm 3F-301 Crawfords Corner Holmdel NJ 07733

HOGLE, CHERYL MAE, academic administrator; b. Plattsburgh, N.Y., July 20, 1945; d. George Matthew and Hilda Mae (Armstrong) H. BA in History, SUNY, Plattsburgh, 1968, MS in Counseling, 1972. House dir. Middlebury (Vt.) Coll., 1968-69; resident counselor Coll. Tech. SUNY, Canton, 1969-74; personnel coord. residence halls SUNY, Plattsburgh, 1974-79, assoc. dir. campus life, 1979—, coord. Freshman Experience Program, 1988—; sec. bd. dirs. Coll. Aux. Svc., Plattsburgh, 1983-89, pres., 1989—. Recipient Chancellor's award for excellence in profl. svc. SUNY, 1987, N.Y. State Excellence award United Univ. Profls, 1990. Mem. Nat. Orientation Dirs. Assn., Omicron Delta Kappa (faculty dir. province I, 1988—). Democrat. Methodist. Home: 6 N Beekman St Plattsburgh NY 12901 Office: SUNY Angell Ctr 110 Plattsburgh NY 12901

HOGSETTE, SARAH MARGARET, lawyer; b. Atlanta, May 18, 1948; d. Daniel Lawrence and Dorothy (Hayes) H. B.S., U. Ga., 1970; J.D., Emory U., 1981. Bar: Ga. 1981. Law clk. DeKalb Superior Ct., Decatur, Ga., 1981-83, Supreme Ct. of Ga., Atlanta, 1983-84; atty. Life Ins. Co. of Ga., Atlanta, 1984—. Bd. dirs. The Joel Chandler Harris Assn., 1987—, Greater Atlanta chpt. Lupus Found. Am., 1986—. Recipient award Bur. Nat. Affairs, 1981; Douglas Lee Peabody Meml. award, 1981. Mem. ABA, State Bar Ga., Atlanta Bar Assn., The Lawyers Club of Atlanta (bd. dirs., sec./treas. 1988—), Corp. Counsel Assn. Greater Atlanta, Atlanta Pub. Affairs Council. Episcopalian. Office: Life Ins Co of Ga 5780 Powers Ferry Rd NW Atlanta GA 30365

HOGUE, CAROL J. ROWLAND, epidemiologist; b. Springfield, Mo., Dec. 11, 1945; d. Perry Albright and Lois Virginia (Spencer) Rowland; m. L. Lynn Hogue, May 28, 1966; 1 child, Elizabeth Rowland. AB summa cum laude, William Jewell Coll., Liberty, Mo., 1966; MPH, U. N.C., 1971, PhD, 1973. Rsch. assoc. Sch. Pub. Health U. N.C., Chapel Hill, 1969-73, asst. prof. Sch. Pub. Health, 1974-77; assoc. prof., dir. epidemiology program, div. biometry U. Ark. for Med. Scis., Little Rock, 1977-82; br. chief pregnancy epidemiology br. Ctrs. Disease Control, Atlanta, 1983-88, dir. div. reproductive health, 1988—, vis. scientist, 1982-83; cons. FDA, Washington, 1978-80, EPA, Washington, 1980-81; fellow Environ. Health Inst., Pittsfield, Mass., 1990—. Contbr. articles to profl. jours., chpts. to books. Mem. nat. perinatal health promotion com. March of Dimes, White Plains, N.Y., 1990—; priority one adv. coun. Kiwanis Internat., 1990—. Fellow Am. Coll. Epidemiology; me. Soc. Epidemiologic Rsch. (pres. 1987-90), Am. Epidemiological Soc., Am. Pub. Health Assn. (program devel. bd. 1976-78), Population Assn. Am., Internat. Epidemiol. Assn., Nat. Med. Com., Planned Parenthood Fedn. Am. Democrat. Episcopalian. Office: Ctrs for Disease Control 1600 Clifton Rd RN Atlanta GA 30333

HOGUE, VIOLA MAYE, infosystems specialist; b. Fredericksburg, Va., Dec. 7, 1948; d. James Fenton Armstrong and Alma (Baird) English; m. Lonnie Gregory Hogue. AAS, No. Va. Community Coll., 1982, AA, 1984; BS in Computer Sci., Mary Washington Coll., 1985. Programmer Mailing List Systems Ltd., Lorton, Va., 1981-83; programmer/analyst Unisys Corp., Dahlgren, Va., 1983-88; sr. programmer Syscon Corp., Dahlgren, 1988-90; sr. programmer, analayst Ensco, Inc., Manassas, Va., 1990—; instr., lectr. No. Va. Community Coll., Woodbridge, 1982—; cons. in field. Mem. Hist. Fredericksburg Found., Inc., 1988—. Mem. NAFE, Phi Theta Kappa. Seventh Day Adventist. Home: 11183 Hamlet Ct Fredericksburg VA 22401 Office: Ensco Inc Manassas VA 22110

HOGYA, MARY GOLDING, government official; b. Essex County, N.J., June 16, 1946; d. Wesley Irwin and Florence Grace (Smith) Golding. Cert., Universite de Grenoble, France, 1967; B.A, Lake Erie Coll., 1968. Editor, writer Bur. Labor Stats., Washington, 1968-72; analyst Employment and Tng. Adminstrn., Dept. Labor, Washington, 1972-78; budget, fiscal officer Interstate Commerce Commn., Washington, 1978-88; dir. adminstrn. U.S. Sentencing Commn., Washington, 1988—. Editor, author lit. jour. Nota Bene, 1967, Monthly Labor Rev., 1968-72. Recipient Outstanding Performance awards Dept. Labor, 1974, 78; Spl. Achievement Awards, Interstate Commerce Commn., 1983, 85. Avocations: writing poetry and short stories. Office: US Sentencing Commn 1331 Pennsylvania Ave NW Suite 1400 Washington DC 20004

HOHN, JAYNE MARIE, optometrist; b. Parkston, S.D., May 12, 1957; d. Marlin W. and Wilma A. (Schoenfelder) H. BS, Pacific U., 1979, OD, 1983. Optometrist Dr. J.W. Hanley, Aberdeen, S.D., 1983; pvt. practice optometry Rapid City, S.D., 1984—. Tutor Laubach Literacy Coun., Rapid City, 1986—; lector, extraordinary eucharistic minister Cathedral of Our Lady of Perpetual Help; sec. World Apostolate of Fatima, Diocese of Rapid City, 1989-90. Named Rossman scholar Pacific U., 1978. Mem. Am. Optometric Assn., S.D. Optometric Soc., Laubach Literacy Coun., Hadassah. Republican. Roman Catholic. Office: 501 Kansas City St Rapid City SD 57701

HOINKES, MARY ELIZABETH, lawyer, government official; b. Washington, Aug. 13, 1940; d. Howard Egger and Elizabeth Mae (Lucas) Wahrenbrock; m. H. Dieter Hoinkes, July 24, 1965. BA, Randolph-Macon Women's Coll., 1962; postgrad. Sch. of Law, U. Va., 1962-63; JD, George Washington U., 1965. Bar: D.C. 1965, U.S. Ct. Appeals (D.C. cir.), U.S. Supreme Ct. Assoc. Clifford & Miller (now Clifford & Warnke), Washington, 1965-68; adminstrv. ofcl. Internat. Labor Office (UN specialized agy.), Geneva, 1969-70, asst. dir. Washington office, 1970-76; atty. adv. U.S. Dept. State, Washington, 1976-77, asst. legal adv. for oceans, environment and sci. affairs, 1977-80, dep. asst. sec. of state for environment, health and natural resources, 1980-81; dep. asst. dir. for multilateral affairs ACDA, Washington, 1981-85, dep. gen. counsel, 1985—; mem. bd. appellate rev. U.S. Dept. State, Washington, 1982—; chmn. sr. advisers on environment UN Econ. Commn. for Europe, Geneva, 1980-82; vice-chmn. com. on environment Orgn. for Econ. Coop. and Devel., Paris, 1980-81. Bd. trustees Randolph-Macon Woman's Coll. Mem. Coun. on Fgn. Rels. Office: US Arms Control and Disarmament Agy 320 21st St Washington DC 20451

HOIT-THETFORD, ELIZABETH, college administrator; b. Selma, Ala., Sept. 7, 1948; d. James Hamilton and Geraldine Helen (Gardner) Hoit; m. James D. Campbell (div. 1969); 1 child, James D. Jr.; m. Richard Rust Thetford, Aug. 10, 1979. BS, East Tenn. State U., Johnson City, 1972, EdD, 1986; MEd, William Carey Coll., Hattiesburg, Miss., 1982, EdS, 1984. Secondary tchr. St. John High Sch., Gulfport, Miss., 1972-73; owner Fireside Handcrafts, Starkville, Miss., 1973-76; project dir. Miss. Arts Commn., Jackson, 1974-76; secondary tchr. St. Martin Attendance Ctr., Biloxi, Miss., 1977-84; doctoral fellow East Tenn. State U., Johnson City, 1984-86; instr. Hawaii Pacific Coll., Honolulu, 1986-88; program specialist U. Hawaii, Kapidani Community Coll., Honolulu, 1988-89; continuing edn. coord. Tech. Coll. Lowcountry, Hilton Head Island, S.C., 1990—. Author play: And If They Are Not, 1970; editor: Development Across the Life Span, A Study Guide to Accompany Human, 1985; editor Hawaii Pacific Rev., 1987; newsletter editor Tenn. Audiovisual Assn., 1985-86, Hawaii Coun. Tchrs. English, 1987-88. Dir. adminstrn. Hugh O'Brian Youth Found. State Leadership Seminar, Hawaii, 1988, vice-chair, 1989. East Tenn. State U. doctoral fellow, 1984-86. Mem. Am. Soc. Tng. and Devel., Nat. Coun. Tchrs. English, South Atlantic Philosophy of Edn. Soc., Women in Acad. Adminstrn., Women in Communications, Inc., Alphs Psi Omega, Phi Delta Kappa (newsletter editor 1985-86), Kappa Delta Pi. Presbyterian. Home: 130 E 54th St Savannah GA 31405 Office: Tech Coll Lowcountry PO Box 5976 Hilton Head Island SC 29938

HOKE, EUGENA LOUISE, educator; b. Chgo., Feb. 26, 1949; d. Edward LaMar and Edna Lucille (Weikert) H. BS, Bowling Green State U., 1971; MEd, U. Maine, Orono, 1977. Cert. educator. Tchr. educable mentally retarded Marion Local Schs., Maria Stein, Ohio, 1971-73, Tri-Valley Local Sch., Dresden, Ohio, 1973-74; tchr. Edgewood Local Schs., Trenton, Ohio, 1974-78; learning disabilities tchr. Oak Hills Local Sch. Dist., Cin., 1978—; mem. prin.'s adv. com. C.O. Harrison Elem. Sch., Cin., 1987—, mem. tchr. asst. team, 1988—. Mem. Vol. in the Parks, Hamilton County, Ohio, 1981-88; vol. Cin. Symphony Assn., 1988—; PTA. Mem. NEA, Ohio Education Assn., Oak Hill Education Assn.,. Methodist. Home: 5566 Biscayne Cincinnati OH 45248

HOLADAY, SUSAN MIRLES, editor; b. Batavia, N.Y., Nov. 2, 1938; d. Norman and Sada Jule (Jacobson) Goldberg; m. William C. Holaday, Dec. 25, 1968 (dec. Feb. 1977). BA, Syracuse U., 1960; MA, U. Chgo., 1963. Equipment editor Instns. Mag., Chgo., 1964-65; co. editor Wyman-Gordon Co., Worcester, Mass., 1968-69; writer Profile Communications, Maynard, Mass., 1969-71; assoc. editor Lodging & Food-Service News, Boston, 1972-75, mng. editor, 1975-83; editor Foodservice East (formerly Lodging & Food Svc. East), Boston, 1983—. Club: Alfa Owners NE (Boston) (founder, sec. 1970-77). Office: Food Svc East 545 Boylston St #605 Boston MA 02116

HOLAMON, GLADYS MARIE AVERY, accountant; b. Halfway, Tex., Dec. 26, 1927; d. Samuel A. and Nova Ethel (Dudley) Avery; m. James Otis Holamon Sr., May 19, 1951; 1 child, James Otis Jr. Cert., Durham Bus. Coll., Ft. Worth, 1950, Internat. Inst. Natural Health Scis., Huntington Beach, Calif., 1980, Donsbach Herbal Inst., Huntington Beach, 1983. Journalist, Brady Standard, Brady, Tex., 1947-49; real estate broker, Ft. Worth, 1963-79; oil and gas acct. R.T. Roark, Ft. Worth, 1975—; owner health food store, Arlington, Tex., 1979-84; cons. and lectr. in field. Contbr. articles to profl. jours. Pres., North Tex. Herb Club, Dallas, 1986, cofounder Greater Ft. Worth Herb Soc., 1985; founder Herb Soc. of North & Cen. Tex., 1988; bd. dirs. The Herb Soc. Am., 1989; mem. Ft. Worth Bot. Soc. Inc., 1986. Recipient Cert., Ctr. for Bldg. Better Health Naturally, 1981. Mem. Nature Conservancy. Baptist. Clubs: Desk and Derrick (Ft. Worth) (bd. dirs.), Los Amigos Del Mesquite, Ft. Worth Cactus and Succulent Soc., Native Plant Soc. of Tex., Friends of Ft. Worth Ctr. and Refuge, Desk and Derrick (bd. dirs. oil and gas group local chpt.), Coun. Petroleum Accounts Soc. Avocations: health rsch., collecting rare books and papers on herbs and health, herb rsch. Home: 1712 Robin Rd Arlington TX 76013

HOLAN, JERRI-ANN, architect; b. Madison, Wis., May 17, 1959; d. Edward Raymond and Gail J. (Wold) H. BArch with high honors, U. Fla., 1980; MArch with honors, U. Calif., Berkeley, 1983. Lic. architect, Calif. Fellow Arkitekturhøgskolen, Oslo, 1983-84; author Rizzoli Internat. Publs., N.Y.C., 1987—; project mgr. R.H. Lee & Assocs., Larkspur, Calif., 1985-87, Rosekrans & Assocs., San Francisco, 1988; architect Christopherson & Graff, Architects, Berkeley, 1988—. Author: Norwegian Wood-A Tradition of Building, 1990. Fulbright grantee, 1983-84, Marshall Fund scholar Marshall Assn., Washington, 1984, Am. Scandinavian fellow Am. Scandinavian Assn., N.Y.C., 1983-84. Mem. AIA (vol. 1987—, photography award, 1990), Fulbright Assn. Alumni, U. Calif.-Berkeley Alumni. Democrat. Home: 1823 Curtis St Berkeley CA 94702 Office: Christopherson & Graff 2921 Adeline St Berkeley CA 94703

HOLBERT, JANICE HUGHES, financial professional; b. Corpus Christi, Tex., June 26, 1952; d. Jack A. and Dorothy M. (Dyer) Hughes; m. Bruce R. Holbert, May 29, 1969 (div. 1975); 1 child, Richard W. Cert., Am. Inst. Banking, Beaumont, Tex., 1985. With Comml. Nat. Bank, Nacogdoches, Tex., 1972-78; mem. loan dept. staff Citizens Nat. Bank, Beaumont, 1978-83; loan sec. Allied Bank Beaumont, 1983, First City Tex., Beaumont, 1983-84; loan sec., asst. cashier, v.p. Beaumont Bank N.A., 1984-89; fin. mgr. Eagle Auto Sales, Beaumont, 1989—. Mem. Am. Inst. Banking (v.p. edn. Southeast Tex. chpt. 1985-86, sec. bd. dirs. 1986-88, office adminstr.). Office: Eagle Auto Sales Rte 9 Box 1373A Beaumont TX 77713

HOLBERT, SUE ELISABETH, archivist; b. Denver, Jan. 24, 1935; d. Roger Dean and Beth Helen (Bryant) Ramey; children: Virginia S., Roger Frederick. BA, U. Nebr., 1956; postgrad., U. Minn., 1975-79. Editor Nebr. Edn. News Nebr. Edn. Assn., Lincoln, 1956-58; advt. asst. Augsburg Pub. House, Mpls., 1961-62; edit. asst. publs. div. Minn. Hist. Soc., St. Paul, 1965-69, asst. curator manuscripts, 1972-75, curator, 1975-76, dep. state archivist, 1976-79, state archivist, 1979—; grants officer Macalester Coll., St. Paul, 1969-72. Author: (with June D. Holmquist) A History Tour of 50 Twin City Landmarks, 1966, Archives and Manuscripts: Reference and Access, 1977; compiler: (with June D. Holmquist and Dorothy D. Perry) History Along the Highways, 1967; contbr. Women in Minnesota, 1977; contbr. articles to profl. jours. Mem. Women Historians of Midwest, Soc. Am. Archivists (pres. 1988), Midwest Archives Conf. Democrat. Unitarian. Home: 807 St. Clair #3 Saint Paul MN 55105 Office: Minn Hist Soc 1500 Mississippi St Saint Paul MN 55101

HOLBROOK, BARBARA CARR SAN, advertising agency executive; b. Roanoke, Va.; d. Louis James and Eleanor (Brophy) San; m. John Pinckney Holbrook, May 29, 1956 (dec. 1989); children—David Carr, Priscilla Mann. B.A., U. N.C. Copywriter Doherty, Clifford, Steers, Shenfield, N.Y.C., 1954-56, Doyle, Dane, Bernbach, N.Y.C., 1956-58, Ogilvy & Mather, N.Y.C., 1958-59; copy group head Benton & Bowles, N.Y.C., 1959-70; v.p., assoc. creative dir. Grey Advt. Inc., N.Y.C., 1970-89, creative dir., 1989—. Bd. dirs. Nat. Assn. for Visually Handicapped. Named to Clio Hall of Fame, 1955; recipient Clio award, 1977, Hollywood Internat. Broadcast award, 1970, Andy award, 1970, 83, Grey Advt. Pres.'s award, 1985, 88; Bus. Bldg. award Procter & Gamble, 1989, World Class Advt. award, 1990. Democrat. Episcopalian. Office: Grey Advt Inc 777 3d Ave New York NY 10017

HOLBROOK, JOAN, artist; b. Dillwyn, Va., Nov. 24, 1934; d. Clayton Irving and Elma Benning (Pearson) Poole; m. David James, Jr., Aug. 18, 1966; 1 child, Suzette Bardill. Postgrad., Westhampton Coll., Richmond, 1955; AB in Zoology, U. N.C., Chapel Hill, 1957; postgrad., Dept. of Art U. N.C., Chapel Hill, 1988. Research asst. Dept. of Surgery, U. N.C, Chapel Hill, 1957-59; biologist U.S. Fish & Wildlife Labs., Beaumont, N.C., 1959-60; research analyst Dept. of Biochemistry, U. N.C., Chapel Hill, 1961-80; media artist Self-Employed, Chapel Hill, N.C.; juror Waterworks Gallery, Salisbury, N.C., 1983; artist A Section of Nat. Peace Ribbon, Chgo., 1985; dir. of exhibitions Ctr. Gallery, Carrboro, N.C., 1984. Contbr. articles to profl. jours. Recipient Purchase award N.C. Arts Soc., Raleigh, 1980, First Prize Graphics Rocky Mt. Art Ctr., 1981, 1985, Jury award UNC Sch. of Pub. Health, Chapel Hill, 1977. Mem. Ctr. Gallery, Southeastern Women's Art Caucus, Durham Art Guild, Delta Phi Alpha. Democrat. Home: 757 Old Rd Chapel Hill NC 27514

HOLBROOK, NORMA JEANNETTE, nursing educator; b. Napton, Mo., Oct. 26, 1939; d. R. Milton and Thelma M. (Miller) Cochran; m. Ralph E. Holbrook, June 30, 1961; children: Tamara M., Jennifer L. BS in Nursing, Cen. Mo. State U., 1965; M of Nursing, Kans. U., 1982. Staff nurse Menorah Med. Ctr., Kansas City, Mo., 1965-66, head nurse, 1966-67; instr. nursing Met. Community Coll., Kansas City, 1967-68; staff nurse Independence (Mo.) Med. Ctr., 1971-73; staff nurse St. Francis Hosp., Topeka, 1975-80, 84—, mem. continuing edn. com., 1988—; instr. nursing Washburn U., Topeka, 1981-85, asst. prof., 1986-89; edn. coord. St. Francis Hosp. and Med. Ctr., 1989—; mem. nursing quality assurance com. Stormont Vail Regional Med. Ctr., Topeka, 1982-83, mem. task force for improved implementation nursing care plans, 1983. Mem. nursing adv. com. ARC, Capital City chpt., Topeka, 1980—, chmn. 1982-83, 88-89. Presentor ednl. programs on nursing process and care planning, goal setting, values clarification and ethics in care of the elderly. Mem. editorial bd. Kansas Nurse, 1990; contbr. articles to profl. jours. Mem. Am. Nurses Assn. (served on coun. of continuing edn. Kansas State Nurses Assn. 1987-89, editorial bd. Kansas Nurse 1990—), Sigma Theta Tau (pres. 1987-90, pres. elect Eta Kappa chpt. 1990—). Republican. Methodist. Office: Washburn U 1700 College St Topeka KS 66621

HOLCOMB, ALICE WILLARD POWER, diversified investments executive; b. Franklin County, Ga., Sept. 11, 1922; d. William McKinley and Flora Sarah (Cash) Cantrell; m. Fleming Mitchell Power, May 6, 1941 (dec. Sept. 1967); children: Susan Cantrell, Fleming Michael; m. George Waymon Holcomb, June 4, 1982. Student, Toccoa (Ga.) Falls Coll., 1939-40; BS, Perry Bus. Sch., 1941. Owner Power Poultry Co., Toccoa, 1950-61, Fleming Mitchell Power Properties, Toccoa and Athens, Ga., 1962—, Power's (retail shops), Athens, 1968-85; ptnr. Power Constrn. Co., Athens, 1972—, Athens Indsl. Electric, Athens, 1973—. Mem. Athens Hist. Soc. Mem. DAR. Republican. Baptist. Home and Office: 199 Avalon Dr Athens GA 30606

HOLCOMB, CARAMINE KELLAM, volunteer worker; b. Painter, Va., Jan. 23, 1941; d. Emerson Polk and Amine (Cosby) Kellam; m. Isaac Somers White, Nov. 25, 1961 (div. 1975); children: Marie Kellam, Caramine, Virginia Somers; m. Harry Sherman Holcomb III, May 12, 1979. AA, St. Mary's Coll., Raleigh, 1960; Cert., Richmond Bus. Coll., Va., 1961. Bd. dirs. Kellam Energy, Inc., Belle Haven, Va., 1980—, Auto Plus, Inc., Belle Haven, 1980—, Shore Stop, Inc., Belle Haven, 1981—. Contbr. articles to profl. jours. Trustee Northampton-Accomack Meml. Hosp., Nassawadox, Va., 1986—, v.p. aux., 1986-88, pres. aux. 1988-90, sec. bd. trustees, 1989-91; bd. dirs. Ea. Shore Hist. Soc., Onancock, Va., 1987—; bd. dirs. Med. Soc. Va. Aux., Richmond, 1984—, v.p., 1989-91. Mem. Garden Club Ea. Shore (pres. 1973-75, 85-87). Home: PO Box 40 Warehouse Franktown VA 23354

HOLCOMB, CONSTANCE L., sales and marketing management executive; b. St. Paul, Oct. 28, 1942; d. John E. Holcomb and Lucille A. (Westerdahl) Hope. BS, U. Minn., 1965; MA in Intercultural Edn., U. of the Americas, Puebla, Mex., 1975. Rsch. analyst U.S. Dept. Def., Washington, 1965-66; br. gen. mgr. Berlitz Lang. Schs., Mexico City, 1966-68; pres., gen. mgr. Centro Lingüistico, Puebla, 1968-72; gen. mgr., prof. Lang. Ctr. Am. Sch. Found., Puebla, 1972-74; assoc. prof., dir. lang. programs U. of the Americas, Puebla, 1974-76; prof., dean faculty of langs. Nat. Autonomous U. Mex., Mexico City, 1976-78; dir. sales & mktg. Longman Pub. Co., N.Y.C., 1978-80, dir. internat. sales & mktg., 1980-84; mng. dir. ESL Pub. Div. McGraw-Hill Book Co., N.Y.C., 1984-85; dir. mktg. mgmt. McGraw-Hill Tng. Systems and Book Co., N.Y.C., 1985-86; dir. mktg. electronic bus. McGraw-Hill Book Co., N.Y.C., 1986-87; info. industry mgmt. cons., ind. contractor, N.Y.C., 1987—; v.p. MexTESOL, Mexico City, 1977-78. Editor: English Teaching in Mexico, 1975; contrb. articles to profl. jours. Mem. Assn. Am. Pubs. (com. chmn. internat. div. 1980-84, exec. com. 1980-84), Info. Industry Assn., Nat. Assn. Women Cons., Am. Soc. Profl. and Exec. Women. Office: 66 Madison Ave Ste 9E New York NY 10016

HOLDEN, LINDA ANNE, construction company executive; b. Boston, Aug. 13, 1939; d. Ernest Carl and Margaret (McGarry) Fleischer; m. Howard Thomas Olnowich, Aug. 19, 1961 (div. Dec. 1978); children: Gayle Diana Chamberlain, Gary Duane Olnowich; m. Walter Glenn Holden, May 24, 1980. BA in Social Psychology, SUNY, Binghamton, 1979. Sales mgr. Stein Builders, Binghamton, N.Y., 1970-75; exec. officer So. Tier Home Builders, Binghamton, 1975-80; pres. The Linda Constrn. Co., Charlotte, N.C., 1980—. Mem. Cabarrus Newcomers Club, Concord, N.C., 1980—, pres. 1983. mem. Cabarrus County Home Builders Assn. (treas. 1982, v.p. 1983), Women in Constrn. Republican. Methodist. Office: The Linda Constrn Co 6024 McDaniel Ln Charlotte NC 28213

HOLDEN, SANDRA S(UE), insurance executive; b. Hannibal, Mo., Mar. 22, 1938; d. John Thomas and Mary Louise (Rouse) Massey; m. Robert Henry Dumit, 1958 (div. Sept. 1963); m. Sidney K. Holden, Apr. 16, 1966; 1 child, Michael Andrew. Student, U. Mo., 1956-58; BS in Mgmt., Ariz. State U., 1963; cert. teaching, U. Mo., 1969, postgrad., 1980. Sec. Ariz. Title & Trust Co., Phoenix, 1958-60; data entry clk. Ariz. Pub. Svc., Phoenix, 1960-63; rsch. staff agr.-econs. dept. U. Mo., Columbia, 1963-64; adminstrv. asst. electronics dept. Monsanto Co., St. Louis, 1964-69; substitute tchr. Pinellas County Schs., Clearwater, Fla., 1975-79; tchr., coop. edn. coord. Boone County R4 Schs., Hallsville, Mo., 1979-81; asst. credit mgr. Philips & Co. (Wholesale Electric and Plumbing), Columbia, Mo., 1981-82; asst. v.p. Boone County Abstract Co., Columbia, 1982-88; pres. Guaranty Land Title Ins. of Columbia, 1988—. Mem. Muleskinners Local Dems., Columbia, 1989—; trustee Daniel Boone Regional Library Bd., Columbia, 1987—. Personnel Mgmt. Soc. scholar, 1962. Mem. Am. Land Title Assn., Columbia Mo. Bd. Realtors, Women's Coun. Realtors (mem. governing bd. Columbia chpt. 1987—), Mo. Land Title Assn. (chairperson com. Mexico, Mo. chpt. 1986-88), Women's Network of Columbia C. of C., Bus. Women Owners (women's network). Office: Guaranty Land Title Ins 15 N 4th St Columbia MO 65201

HOLDER, ANGELA RODDEY, lawyer, educator; b. Rock Hill, S.C., Mar. 13, 1938; d. John T. and Angela M. (Fisher) Roddey; 1 child, John Thomas Roddey Holder. Student, Radcliffe Coll., 1955-56; B.A., Newcomb Coll., 1958; postgrad., Faculty of Law-King's Coll., London, 1957-58; J.D., Tulane U., 1960; LL.M., Yale U., 1975. Bar: La. 1961, S.C. 1960, Conn. 1981. Counsel Roddey, Sumwalt & Carpenter, Rock Hill, S.C., 1960—; atty. criminal div. New Orleans Legal Aid Bur., 1961-62; counsel York County Family Ct., S.C., 1962-64; asst. prof. polit. sci. Winthrop Coll., Rock Hill, 1964-74; research assoc. Yale Law Sch., 1975-77, exec. dir. program in law, sci. and medicine, 1976-77; lectr. dept. pediatrics Yale Med. Sch., 1975-77, asst. clin. prof. pediatrics and law, 1977-79, assoc. clin. prof., 1979-83, clin. prof., 1983—; counsel for medicolegal affairs Yale-New Haven Hosp. and Yale Med. Sch., 1977-89. Author: The Meaning of the Constitution, 1968, 2d edit., 1987, Medical Malpractice Law, 1975, 2d edit. 1978, Legal Issues in Pediatrics and Adolescent Medicine, 1977, 2d edit., 1985; contbg. editor: Prism mag.; contbg. editor., AMA; mem. editorial bd.: IRB; Law, Medicine and Health Care, Jour. Philosophy and Medicine; contbr. articles to profl. jours. Mem. Rock Hill Sch. Bd., 1967-68; bd. dirs. Family Planning Clinic, chmn., 1970-73; bd. trustees Ednl. Commn. for Fgn. Med. Grads., 1990—. Mem. ABA, S.C. Bar Assn. (medico-legal com. 1973—), La. Bar Assn., Soc. Med. Jurisprudence, Am. Soc. Hosp. Attys., Am. Soc. Law and Medicine (treas. 1981-83, sec. 1983-85, pres. 1986-87). Democrat. Episcopalian. Home: 23 Eld St New Haven CT 06511 Office: Yale U School of Medicine 333 Cedar St New Haven CT 06510

HOLDER, ELAINE EDITH, psychologist, educator; b. Boulder, Co., July 9, 1926; d. Joseph C. and Ethel M. (Woodhouse) Jones; m. Wayne B. Holder, Nov. 28, 1947 (div. 1981); children: Wayne B. Jr., Elaine J. Zieroth, Steven A., Lynda M. BA cum laude, U. Colo., 1948; MA, New Mexico State U., 1951; PhD, U. Mo., 1956. Lect. Calif. State Univ., Fresno, 1964-79, Calif. Poly State Univ., San Luis Obispo, 1979-83; assoc. prof. Calif. Poly. State Univ., San Luis Obispo, 1984-88; prof. Calif. Poly. State Univ., San Luis, 1988-89; ret., 1989. contbr. articles to profl. jours. Mem. Mothers for Peace, San Luis, 1981—; sec. bd. dirs. Hospice of San Luis Obispo County. Mem. Am. Psychol. Assn., Phi Beta Kappa, Pi Gamma Mu, Sigma Xi. Democrat. Home: 931 West St San Luis Obispo CA 93401

HOLDER, GAIL JILLIAN, physical therapist; b. Trinidad, West Indies, Feb. 16, 1953; came to U.S., 1986; d. Wilbert and Ilene Sheila (Moseley) DeCoteau; m. Ronald A. Holder (div. Apr. 1985); children: Ian, Jillian. Diploma in phys. therapy, U. W.I., Mona Jamaica, 1976; MS in Exercise Physiology, L.I. U., 1985. Phys. therapist P.O.S. Gen. Hosp., Trinidad, 1976-83; pvt. practice Trinidad, 1985-86; sr. phys. therapist Goldwater Meml. Hosp., N.Y.C., 1986-88; pvt. practice Bklyn., 1988—; phys. therapist ob-gyn. Ministry of Health, Trinidad, 1979, YMCA, Bklyn., 1985; sports phys. therapist Women's Nat. Basketball Team, Trinidad, 1985-86. Mem. Am. Phys. Therapy Assn. Home: 516 E 29th St Brooklyn NY 11210

HOLDER, HOLLY IRENE, lawyer; b. Albuquerque, May 16, 1952; d. Howard George and Dorothy Evelyn (Doll) Holzum; m. William B. Holder Jr., June 4, 1974; 1 child, Eric James. BA with honors, U. Colo., 1974; JD with honors, U. Denver, 1980. Bar: Colo. 1980, U.S. Ct. Appeals (10th cir.) 1980. Chemist Indsl. Labs., Denver, 1974-76; law clk. to presiding justice Colo. Supreme Ct., Denver, 1979; assoc. Calkins, Kramer, Grimshaw and Harring, Denver, 1980-82, 84-88, McKenna, Conner & Cuneo, Denver, 1988-90, Saunders, Snyder, Ross & Dickson, Denver, 1990—. Mem. adv. com. Regional Coun. Govts. Water Resources Mgmt., 1984—; chmn. Chatfield Basin Assn., Denver, 1987, Chatfield Basin Master Plan Task Force, Denver, 1986—. Recipient Disting. Svc. award Denver Regional Coun. Govts., 1987. Mem. Colo. Bar Assn., Denver Bar Assn., Mensa. Republican. Office: Saunders Snyder Ross & Dickson 707 17th St #3500 Denver CO 80202

HOLDER, JANICE MARIE, lawyer; b. Canonsburg, Pa., Aug. 29, 1949; d. Louis V. and Sylvia (Abraham) H.; m. George W. Loveland II, June 5, 1976 (div. Mar. 1987). Student, Allegheny Coll., 1967-68, Sorbonne, 1970; BS summa cum laude, U. Pitts., 1971; JD, Duquesne U., 1975. Bar: Pa. 1975, Tenn. 1979, D.C. 1988. Sr. law clk. to chief judge U.S. Dist. Ct. for Western Dist. Pa., Pitts., 1975-77; assoc. Catalano & Catalano, P.C., Pitts., 1977-79, Holt, Batchelor, Spicer & Ryan, Memphis, 1980-82; pvt. practice Memphis, 1983-87; assoc. James S. Cox & Assocs., Memphis, 1987-89; pvt. practice law Memphis, 1989—; solicitor Borough of McDonald (Pa.), 1978-79. Bd. dirs. Alliance for Blind and Visually Impaired, Memphis, 1984—. Mem. ABA, Tenn. Bar Assn., Memphis Bar Assn. (bd. dirs. 1985-87, editor Bar Forum 1987—), Assn. for Women Attys. (treas. 1989). Home: 1955 Oliver Ave Memphis TN 38104 Office: Morgan Keegan Tower #950 50 North Front St Memphis TN 38103

HOLDER, JOYCE FIORELLA, horticulturist, business owner; b. Pharr, Tex., Sept. 21, 1926; d. Del and Helen (Forgy) Fiorella; m. Marx M. Holder (div. 1977); children: David E., Leslie L., Allison P. BA, U. Tex., 1950. Owner Tropical Nursery, Del Ray Beach, Fla., 1980—. Recipient Beautification award Del Ray City, 1985. Mem. Everglades Country Club, Met. Club N.Y.C. Home: 2202 Falcon Hill Dr Austin TX 78745

HOLDER, PATRICIA WENZEL, teacher, educator; b. Milw., Mar. 1, 1925; d. Edwin Henry and Amanda (Edmann) Wenzel; m. Roy Ingvold Satre (div. 1970); children: Helen, Rodrick, Brian, Bruce; m. Hugh William Holder. BA, Carthage (Ill.) Coll., 1945; MS Edn, SUNY, Geneseo, 1964. Cert. elem. tchr., N.Y. Elem. tchr. Carthage (Ill.) Schs., 1944-45; tchr. Caledonia-Mumford (N.Y.) Schs., 1960-64, Lewiston-Porter Sch., Youngstown, N.Y., 1964-67; tchr. for emotionally disturbed Canandaigua (N.Y.) Sch., 1968-69; tchr. Bloomfield Cen., Holcomb, N.Y., 1970-86; tchr. bilingual edn. Bloomfield Cen., Holcomb, 1970-86. Artist: paintings and dolls, 1970-89. Vol. Home for Disabled, Victor, 1988-89; bd. dirs. YWCA, 1965-66. Mem. AAUW (exhibitor art show 1989), Victor Garden Club (sec. 1987, beautification com. 1987-89), VFW, Dance Internat. (Rochester), Niagara Falls Coll. Club, Beta Beta Beta. Republican. Home: Sweet Water Golf & Tennis Club 249 Ramsgate Way Haines City FL 33844

HOLDER, RUTH ELSIE, publishing executive; b. Phoenixville, Pa., Nov. 23, 1953; d. Jay Edwin and Clara Ruth (Hamm) H. BA, Ursinus Coll., 1975. Bookkeeper, reporter Carbondale (Pa.) News, 1975-76; editor Triboro Banner, Old Forge, Pa., 1976-77; pub., owner Triboro Banner, Taylor, Pa., 1977—. Mem. White Haven (Pa.) Coun., 1977-85; sec. Lower Luzerne County Solid Waste Authority, Hazleton, Pa., 1979-88; elder Presbyn. Ch. White Haven, 1984—. Mem. Greater Scranton (Pa.) C. of C., Greater Scranton Jaycees. Republican. Office: Triboro Banner 105 S Main St Taylor PA 18517

HOLDER, SANDRA SUE, learning disabilities researcher; b. Washington, Nebr., July 17, 1938; d. Myron William Melton and Verona Lucille (Nelsen) Melton-Klipp; m. N. Gaylord Holder, Feb. 13, 1960; children: Stacey, Jennifer, Debra, Steven, Kirk. AA, Aims Community Coll., 1988; BA in Psychology, U. No. Colo., 1990, postgrad., 1990—. Staff X-ray tech. St. Lukes Hosp., Denver, 1958-61; office nurse, X-ray tech. Drs. Monty & Chisholm, Denver, 1962-65; staff X-ray tech. St. Anthony North Hosp., Westminster, Colo., 1970-74; reading aide Sch. Dist. 27J, Brighton, Colo.; computer entry clk. Sch. Dist. 27J, Brighton, 1978-79; co-owner maid svc., 1979-81; ins. agt. Oestman Ins. Agy., Brighton, 1982-84; food svc. worker United Air Lines, Denver, 1984-86; vol. library aide Sch. Dist. 27J, Brighton, 1974-76; vol. reading program Sch. Dist. 27J, 1975-76. Mem. Budget Com. Sch. Dist. 27J, Brighton, 1974, Goals Com., 1974; chmn. Parent Adv. Coun., Brighton, 1975; organizer Community Resource File, Brighton, 1976. Mem. Am. Registry of X-Ray Technologists. Episcopalian. Home: 734 S 1st Ave Brighton CO 80601

HOLDER, SUSAN MCCASKILL, business analyst; b. Tulsa, July 8, 1956; d. Allan Murdock McCaskill and Kathryn Irene (Padgett) Dolan; m. Robert Newton Holder, Jr., Nov. 30, 1985; children: Tara Susan, Abigail Megan. BA in Bus. Mgmt., Upsala Coll., East Orange, N.J., 1978; MBA in Fin., Fairleigh Dickinson U., 1985. Comml. underwriter State Farm Ins. Cos., Wayne, N.J., 1978-81, svc. supr., 1981-83; adminstrn. mgr. Digital Equipment Corp., Piscataway, N.J., 1983-85; project mgr. Digital Equipment Corp., Princeton, N.J., 1985-87, area adminstrv. svcs. mgr., 1987-88, area adminstrv. support mgr., 1988-89; bus. analyst U.S. Hdqrs. Digital Equipment Corp., Alpharetta, Ga., 1989—, Westboro, Mass., 1989—. Mem. pastor-parish rels. com., mem. nurture com., Sunday sch. tchr. presch. class Christ United Meth. Ch., Roswell, Ga., 1990—. Mem. AAUW (br. sec. Point Pleasant, N.J. 1986-89). Home: 1810 Azalea Springs Trail Roswell GA 30075 Office: Digital Equipment Corp 5555 Windward Pkwy W Alpharetta GA 30201

HOLDER, VIRGINIA MARY, community television executive; b. St. Paul, Aug. 31, 1942; d. Nicholas Peter and Virginia Mary (Bennett) Yarusso; children: Tammy Jean, Andrea Rachelle Holder Carpenter. BA in Speech, Theater Arts, U. Minn., 1972. Cert. adult vocat. edn. tchr., Minn. Program coord., traffic mgr., prodn. mgr. KAVT-TV, Austin, Minn., 1972-75; instr. TV prodn. Austin Tech. Coll., 1972-75, 83-87; dir. devel. KSMQ-TV, Austin, 1980-87; telecommunications specialist Austin Tech. Coll., 1987; exec. dir. Suburban Community Channels, St. Paul, 1987—; pres. Cable TV Adv. Com., Austin, 1985; mem. telecommunications adv. bd. Minn. state Bd. Vocat. Tech. Edn., St. Paul, 1986-87; chair pub. rels. Austin C. of C., 1986-87; presenter seminars. Producer TV program Come for Coffee, White Bear Lake, Minn., 1989-90; author tng. materials. Pres. Southeastern Minn. Arts Coun., Rochester, 1983. Recipient awards Pub. Broadcasting System, 1981, 85, Minn. Cable Communications Bd., 1981, Minn. Edn. Assn., 1983,. Mem. Minn. Assn. Cable TV Adminstrs., Nat. Fedn. Local Cable programmers, Suburban Area C. of C. (bd. dirs. 1990—), White Bear Lake C. of C. Home: 2085 Dotte Dr Apt 305 White Bear Lake MN 55110 Office: Suburban Community Channels 1902 E County Rd B Saint Paul MN 55109

HOLDERBAUM, LINDA SUE, association executive; b. Albion, Mich., Dec. 10, 1951; d. Jack VanNess and Betty E. (Yeomans) Poirier; m. Robert S. Holderbaum, Feb. 14, 1985; 1 child, Joshua Robert. BS in Art Edn., Western Mich. U., 1974. Instr., coordinator Am. Indian Program, Battle Creek (Mich.) Schs., 1979-85; curator exhibits Art Ctr. Battle Creek, 1977-87; free lance writer Doll Castle News Mag., N.J., 1984—, Doll Reader Mag., Fredericksburg, Md., 1984—; guest curator Krasl Art Ctr., St. Joseph, Mich., 1988—; downtown event promotions mgr. Downtown Battle Creek Assn., 1987-89; exec. officer Battle Creek Assn. Home Builders, 1987—; exhibit curator Davidson Bldg. of Visual and Performing Arts, Kellogg Community Coll., Battle Creek, 1988—; cons. Detroit Antique Toy Mus., 1988—, Carlton Park Hist. Mus., Hastings, Mich., 1977-80. Contbr. articles to profl. jours. Mem. United Fedn. Doll Clubs, Battle Creek Area Doll Clubs (pres. 1985-87). Home: 107 N 32d St Battle Creek MI 49015

HOLDERNESS, CHERYL ANN, accountant; b. Steubenville, Ohio, Jan. 22, 1959; d. Clarence Edwin and Shirley Mayota (Stacy) Ross; m. Alan Eugene Holderness, July 29, 1978 (div. Oct. 1986); children: Cassandra Ann, Ashley Elizabeth. BS, Milligan Coll., 1981. Acct. Milligan Food Svc., Milligan College, Tenn., 1980-81; NCR posting clk. Publix Foods, Johnson City, Tenn., 1983-84; acct. United Oil, Johnson City, 1986; asst. to owner So Happy Craft Shop, Elizabethton, Tenn., 1986-88; staff acct. Thor Power Tools, Virginia Beach, Va., 1988-89, First Hosp. Corp. Choice, Norfolk, Va., 1989—. Worth advisor Internat. Order Rainbow Girls, Galion, 1976—; mem. Circle K., Johnson City, 1977-79. Recipient Recognition, 2000 Notable Am. Women, 1990. Mem. NAFE. Republican.

HOLDERNESS, SUSAN RUTHERFORD, religious education administrator, convention planner, tour guide; b. Cherokee, Iowa, Nov. 5, 1941; d. Parker William and Ruth Elvera (Peterson) Rutherford; m. Michael Aaron Holderness, Aug. 12, 1961; children: Lauren, Lisa, Jennifer, Joshua. BA in Edn., Wayne State U., Nebr., 1964; student, Iowa State U., 1960-61, Vocat. Cert., 1973. Tchr. various high schs. including Norwalk (Iowa) High Sch., 1968-78; hist. site interpreter Salisbury House, Des Moines, 1971-78, 84-88, Minn. State Hist. Soc., St. Paul, 1978-84; cons. Profl. Match Cons., Des Moines, 1985-90; tour guide and conv. planner Des Moines Tour and Conv. Svcs., 1987—; also dir. Christian edn. Douglas Ave. Presbyn. Ch., Des Moines. Vice pres. fund raising Des Moines Symphony Guild, 1990—; bd. dirs., treas. Greenwood Sch. PTA, Des Moines, 1987-89; co-chmn. Civic Music Assn., Des Moines, 1987; pres., v.p., tour dir. St. Paul New Residents, 1980-83, others in past. Mem. Iowa Victorian Soc., Compass Club (internat. pres. 1986-87), Kappa Delta Phi, Gamma Phi Beta. Republican. Presbyterian. Home: Owl's Head Hist Dist 2900 Forest Dr Des Moines IA 50312 Office: Douglas Ave Presbyn Ch 4601 Douglas Ave Des Moines IA 50310

HOLDSWORTH, JANET NOTT, nurse, educator; b. Evanston, Ill., Dec. 25, 1941; d. William Alfred and Elizabeth Inez (Kelly) Nott; children: James William, Kelly Elizabeth, John David. B.S. in Nursing with high distinction, U. Iowa, 1963; M.Nursing, U. Wash., 1966; postgrad. U. Colo., 1981, U. No. Colo., 1982. Registered nurse, Colo. Staff nurse U. Colo. Hosp., Denver, 1963-64, Presbyn. Hosp., Denver, 1964-65, Grand Canyon Hosp., Ariz., 1965; asst. prof. U. Colo. Sch. Nursing, Denver, 1966-71; counseling nurse Boulder PolyDrug Treatment Ctr., Boulder, 1971-77; pvt. duty nurse Nurses' Official Registry, Denver, 1973-82; cons. nurse, tchr. parenting and child devel. Teenage Parent Program, Boulder Valley Schs., Boulder, 1980-88; bd. dirs., treas. Nott's Travel, Aurora, Colo., 1980—; instr., nursing coord. ARC, Boulder, 1979—, instr., nursing tng. specialist, 1980-82. Mem. adv. bd. Boulder County LaMaz Inc., 1980-88 ; mem. adv. com. Child Find and Parent-Family, Boulder, 1981—; del. Rep. County State Congl. Convs., 1972-88, sec. 17th Dist. Senatorial Com., Boulder, 1982—; vol. chmn. Mesa Sch. Parent Tchr. Orgn., Boulder, 1982—, bd. dirs., 1982—, v.p., 1983—; elder Presbyn. ch. Mem. Am. Nurses Assn., Colo. Nurses Assn. (bd. dirs. 1975-76, human rights com. 1981-83, dist. pres. 1974-76), Soc. Adolescent Medicine, Coun. High Risk Prenatal Nurses, Coun. Intracultural Nurses, Sigma Theta Tau. Republican. Home: 1550 Findlay Way Boulder CO 80303 Office: Teenage Parent Program 3740 Martin Dr Boulder CO 80303

HOLEY, MERCEDES GARRIGA, educator; b. Pensacola, Fla., Sept. 9, 1918; d. James Estañol and Mary (Carreras) Garriga; m. Thomas J. Holey, Sept. 6, 1952. BS, Fla. State U., 1938; MA, Seton Hall U., 1958; PhD, Hunter Coll., 1969. Cert. instr., N.J. Staff asst. ARC, 1941-45; pres. Garriga Export Co., Century, Fla., 1945-52; instr. Wall Twp. Pub. Schs., N.J., 1952-61, Anaconda Copper Mining Co., Chuquicamata, Chile, 1962, Oradell Pub. Schs., Oradell, N.J., 1962-79; dir. vols. Philharmonic Ctr. for the Arts, Naples, Fla., 1987—; bd. dirs. Naples/Marco Philharmonic League, Naples. Co-author: Let's Speak French, 1969. Pres. Oradell Edn. Assn., 1975-77; vol. Marco Island (Fla.) Hosp. Aux., 1985-88; asst. vol. Marco Island Pub. Libr., 1985-88. Grantee NDEA Lang. Inst., Iona Coll., 1963. Mem. NEA (del. 1975, 77), AAUW (v.p. 1982-84), Woman's Club (Marco Island, parliamentarian 1981-88). Republican. Roman Catholic. Home: 570 Bay Villas Ln Naples FL 33963

HOLFORTY, PEARL MARTHA, accountant; b. Detroit, Oct. 31, 1928; d. Johannes and Martha Mary (Francoys) Kramer; m. Clifford W. Holforty, Mar. 27, 1948; children: Kathleen Diane, David Alan, Wendy Lauren, Michael Todd. Student, Mich. State U., 1945-47; BS, Wayne State U., 1970, MBA, 1973. Controller Sta. WPON, Pontiac, Mich., 1958-60; bus. mgr. Holforty, Widrig & O'Neill Assocs., Inc., Troy, Mich., 1960-69; staff acct. Plante & Moran, CPAs, Southfield, Mich., 1970-77, ptnr., 1977—; founding mem., chair, pres., chief exec. officer Liberty BIDCO Investment Corp., 1988—; part-time faculty Wayne State U., 1974-77; mem. small bus. adv. coun. Fed. Res. Bank Chgo., 1985-87; del. White House Conf. on Small Bus., 1986. Bd. dir. met. Detroit YMCA; commr. Govs. Entrepreneurial and Small Bus. Commn., mem. employability skills task force for State of Mich.; trustee Mich. Accountancy Found., Wayne County Intermediate Sch. Dist.-Found. for Excellence. Recipient Edward G. Erickson award, 1970, Elijah Watts Sells award, 1971, Headliners award Wayne State U., 1983; Phi Gamma Mu scholar, 1970; named Woman Advocate of Yr. SBA Mich., 1986. Mem. Am. Inst. CPAs, Nat. Assn. Accts. (pres. chpt. 1979), Mich. Assn. CPAs, Assn. Sch. Bus. Ofcls., Nat. Assn. Women Bus. Owners (chpt. pres. 1986-87), Women's Econ. Club (pres. 1989-90), Fairlane Club, Beta Gamma. Presbyterian. Home: 5000 Town Center Apt 2803 Southfield MI 48075 Office: Plante & Moran PO Box 307 Southfield MI 48037

HOLIAN, KATHERINE STOVER, academic administrator; b. Modesto, Calif., Oct. 14, 1947; d. Lee and Della (Kopperud) Stover; m. Brad Lee Holian, Dec. 28, 1968 (div. May, 1984); children: Joshua, Matthew. Student, Whitter Coll., 1965-67, Pitzer Coll., 1967-68; BA, U. Calif., 1969; MBA, U. Nebr., 1987. Research, adminstrv. asst. U. Calif. Physics Dept., Berkeley, 1969-72; adminstrv. sec. Los Alamos (N.Mex.) Nat. Lab., 1980-84; grad. research asst. Dept. Mgmt. and Econs., Omaha, 1986-87; fin. analyst Majers Corp., Omaha, Nebr.; program coord. Met. Community Coll., Omaha, Nebr., 1987--. Mem. Supt. Adv. Com. and Gifted Edn. Com., Los Alamos, 1981-84; various ch. coms. at local and synod levels, Omaha, 1988—; vol. senate campaign for Bob Kerry, Omaha, 1988; mem. parent adv. com. of gifted edn. Millard Pub. Schs., 1989—. Mem. AAUW, Beta Gamma Sigma. Democrat. Lutheran. Office: Met Community Coll PO Box 3777 Omaha NE 68103

HOLIDAY, EDITH ELIZABETH, lawyer, federal official; b. Middletown, Ohio, Feb. 14, 1952; d. Harry Jr. and Kathlyn (Watson) H.; m. Terrence B. Adamson, June 8, 1985; 1 child, Kathlyn Holiday Adamson; 1 stepchild, Terrence Morgan Adamson. Student, Miami U., Oxford, Ohio, 1970-71; BS with honors, U. Fla., 1974, JD, 1977. Assoc. Read Smith Shaw & McClay, Washington, 1977-83, Dow Lohnes & Albertson, Atlanta, 1983-84; exec. dir. Commn. on Exec. Legis. and Jud. Salaries, Washington, 1984-85; spl. counsel polit. action com. Fund for Am. Future, Washington, 1985-87; dir. ops. George Bush for Pres., Inc., Washington, 1987-88; chief counsel, nat. fin. and ops. dir. Bush-Quayle 88, Washington, 1988; with legal svcs. staff George Bush for Pres. Compliance Com., Washington, 1988; asst. sec. for pub. affairs and pub. liaison, counselor to sec. Departmental Offices, U.S. Dept. Treasury, Washington, 1988; gen. counsel U.S. Dept. Treasury, Washington, 1989—; legis. asst. to U.S. Senator Nicholas F. Brady, Washington, 1982-83. Recipient spl. citation John Marshall Bar Assn. Mem. Phi Delta Phi, Kappa Tau Alpha. Office: The White House 1600 Pensylvania Ave NW Washington DC 20500

HOLLADAY, WILHELMINA COLE, real estate, interior design and museum executive; b. Elmira, N.Y., Oct. 10, 1922; d. Chauncy E. and Claire Elizabeth (Strong) Cole; m. Wallace Fitzhugh Holladay, Sept. 27, 1946; children: Wallace Fitzhugh, Scott Cole. BA, Elmira Coll., 1944; postgrad. art history, U. Paris, 1953-54, U. Va., 1960-61; PhD (hon.), Moore Coll. Art, 1988, Mt. Vernon Coll., 1988, Elmira Coll., 1989. Exec. sec. Howard Ludington, Rochester, N.Y., 1944-45, Chinese Embassy, Washington, 1945-48; staff Nat. Gallery of Art, Washington, 1957-59; dir. interior design div. Holladay Corp., Washington, 1970—; dir. Holladay-Tyler Printing Corp., 1982-86; dir. Adams Nat. Bank, 1978-86, chmn. 1978-86; pres., bd. dir. Nat. Mus. Women in the Arts, 1982—; pres. First Corp.-WNB, 1980-86. Founder archival libr. of periodicals, books, exhbn. catalogs on women's art for rsch. purposes; bd. dirs. Am. Field Svc., 1964-80, Internat. Student House, 1973—, Leeds Castle Found.; mem. coun. Friends of Folger Shakespeare Libr., 1978-82; mem. world svc. coun. YMCA; trustee Corcoran Gallery of Art, 1980—; pres. Holladay Found., 1980—; mem. profl. adv. com. interior design Mt. Vernon Coll.; mem. Mayor's Blue Ribbon Com. Recipient Horizon's Theatre award, 1986, Anti-Defamation award, 1987, Thomas Jefferson award Am. Soc. Interior Designers, Disting. Woman's award Northwood Inst., 1987, Disting. Achievement award Nat. League Am. Pen Women, 1988; named Woman of Achievement, Washington Ednl. TV Assn., 1984, Woman of Distinction Coun. Ind. Colls., 1987, Washingtonian of Yr., Washingtonian Mag., 1987. Mem. Am. Assn. Mus., Am. Fedn. Art, Women's Caucus for Arts, Met. Mus. Art, Mus. Modern Art, Art Libraries of N.Am., Archives Am. Art, Golden Circle of Kennedy Center, Arttable, Smithson Soc., Internat. Women's Forum, Nat. Women's Econ. Alliance (dir. 1984—, Soaring Eagle award 1988), Phillips Gallery Art (patron). Episcopalian. Home: 3215 R St NW Washington DC 20007 Office: Nat Mus Women Arts 1250 New York Ave Washington DC 20005

HOLLAND, BETH, actress; b. N.Y.C.; d. Samson and Florence (Liebman) Hollander; m. Louis L. Friedman, Aug. 28, 1954; children: Ellen Lynn, Cathy Jayne. Pvt. studies in acting, voice tng. Arts funding cons. N.Y. State Senate, 1974-89. Appeared in various roles on TV, film and theatre, also comedy video Your Favorite Jokes, 1988. Mem. AFTRA (pres. N.Y. chpt. 1989—, bd. dirs., trustee Health and Retirement Funds, past treas.), SAG, N.Y. TV Acad. (past bd. dirs.), Actors Equity Assn., Twelfth Night Club (bd. dirs.), Episcopal Actors Guild, Cath. Actors Guild, Players Club. Office: AFTRA 260 Madison Ave New York NY 10016*

HOLLAND, CHRISTIE ANNA, biochemist, virologist; b. Newport News, Va., Aug. 25, 1950; d. Charles Everett and Helen (Bailey) Holland; m. Robert Keith Walty, June 24, 1989; 1 child, Joshua. BS, U. Richmond, 1972; PhD, U. Tenn., 1977. Postdoctoral fellow Worcester Found. for Exptl. Biology, Shrewsbury, Mass., 1977-79, Ctr. for Cancer Rsch.-MIT, Cambridge, Mass., 1979-84; asst. prof. dept. radiation oncology U. Mass. Med. Ctr., Worcester, 1985-89, assoc. prof. dept. pharmacology, 1990—. Mem. AAAS, Internat. Soc. Exptl. Hematology, Am. Soc. Cell Biology, Am. Soc. Virology. Office: U Mass Med Sch Dept Pharmacology 55 Lake Ave N Worcester MA 01605

HOLLAND, GAY WILLMAN, art educator; b. Urbana, Ill., Jan. 30, 1941; d. Harold Bowen and Martha Evangeline (Righter) Willman; m. Morris K. Holland, Feb. 1, 1962 (div. 1969); 1 child, Laura Gay Holland. BFA, Calif. State U., 1974; MFA, U. Ariz., 1984. Asst. prof. Frostburg (Md.) State U., 1984-89; assoc. prof. So. Utah State Coll., Cedar City, 1990—. Illustrator Macmillan Pub. Co., N.Y.C., 1984—, McDougal, Littell & Co., Evanston, Ill., 1989, Addison-Wesley Pub., San Francisco, 1989, numerous illustrations for children's books, 1984-90; work included in annual Best Am. Illustration, Am. Illustration, Inc., N.Y.C., 1984, 85; works exhibited at Soc. Illustrators Student Exhbn., N.Y.C., 1984. Mem. Coll. Art Assn., Met. Mus. Art N.Y. Home: 117 South 100 West 5 Cedar City UT 84720 Office: So Utah State Coll Art Dept Cedar City UT 84720

HOLLAND, GENE GRIGSBY (SCOTTY HOLLAND), artist; b. Hazard, Ky., June 30, 1928; d. Edward and Virginia Lee (Watson) Grigsby; m. George William Holland, Sept. 22, 1950; 3 children. BA, U. S. Fla., 1968; pupil of Ruth Allison, Talequah, Okla., 1947-48, Ralph Smith, Washington, 1977, Clint Carter, Atlanta, 1977, R. Jordan, Winter Park, Fla., 1979, Cedric Baldwin Egeli Workshop, Charleston, S.C., 1984. Various clerical and secretarial positions, 1948-52; news reporter, photographer Bryan (Tex.) Daily News, 1952; clk. Fogarty Bros. Moving and Transfer, Tampa and Miami, Fla., 1954-57; tchr. elem. Schs., Hillsborough County, Fla., 1968-72; salesperson, assoc. real estate, 1984—; owner, operator antique store, 1982-87. One-woman and group shows include Tampa Woman's Clubhouse, 1973, Cor Jesu, Tampa, 1973, bank, Monks Corner, S.C., 1977, Summerville Artists Guild, 1977-78, Apopka (Fla.) Art and Foliage Festival, 1980, 81, 82, Fla. Fedn. Women's Clubs, 1980, 81, 82; numerous group shows, latest being: Island Gifts, Tampa, 1980-82, Brandon (Fla.) Station, 1980-81, Holland Originals, Orlando, Fla.; represented in permanent collections including Combank, Apopka, also pvt. collections. Vol. ARC, Tampa, 1965-69, United Fund Campaign, 1975-76; pres. Mango (Fla.) Elem. Sch. PTA, 1966-67; pres. Tampa Civic Assn., 1974-75; vol. Easter Seal Fund Campaign, 1962-63; art chmn. Apopka Art & Foliage Festival, 1990. Recipient numerous art awards, 1978-82. Mem. Internat. Soc. of Artists, Coun. of Arts and Scis. for Cen. Fla., Fedn. of Women's Clubs (pres. Hillsborough County 1974-75, v.p. Tampa 1974-75), Meth. Women's Soc. (sec. 1976-77), Nat. Trust for Historic Preservation, Nat. Hist. Soc., Cen. Fla. Geneal. and Hist. Soc., Am. Guild Flower Arrangers, Internat. Inner Wheel Club (past chmn. dist. 696, pres. Tampa 1972-73), Musicale Club (1st v.p. bd. incorporators Tampa 1974-75), Apopka Woman's Club (pres. 1981-82, bd. dir. 1983-85), Apopka Tennis Over 50's Group Club (pres. 1988-90). Home: 1080 Errol Pkwy Apopka FL 32712 Office: PO Box 700 Plymouth FL 32768

HOLLAND, IRIS KAUFMAN, state legislator; b. Springfield, Mass., Sept. 30, 1920; d. Leo and Sadie Kaufman; grad. Rider Coll., Trenton, N.J.; m. Gilbert S. Holland, Jan. 1, 1941; children—Judy, Richard, Donald. Mem. Mass. Ho. of Reps. from 2d Hampden Dist., 1973—, Republican whip, 1979-82, asst. Republican floor leader, 1983-87, mem. Ho. Com. on Ways and Means, 1987—; columnist Your State Ombudsman; guest lectr. Mt. Holyoke, Smith, Springfield, Am. Internat., Western New Eng. colls.; Robert A. Taft lectr. Tufts U., U. Mass. Bd. corporator Baystate Med. Center, Springfield Day Nursery; chmn. spl. commn. Help for Homeless; adv. bd. Am. Internat. Coll.; trustee Bay Path Jr. Coll.; bd. dirs. Friends of the Homeless, Goodwill Industries, Coalition for the Homeless, Carew Hill Girls Clubs, Western Mass. Radio Reading Service for the Blind; mem. spl. com. Pres. John F. Kennedy Meml. Named Woman of Yr., Women's Div., Greater Springfield C. of C.; recipient Woman of Achievement award Mass. Fedn. Bus. and Profl. Women's Clubs; Outstanding Legislator of Yr. award Mass. League Cities and Towns; Disting. Citizen award Rep. Club of Mass. Mem. LWV, Mass. Caucus Women Legislators (founder). Club: Zonta Internat.

HOLLAND, JOY, health care facility executive; b. N.Y.C., Oct. 24, 1946; d. Harry Walson and Edna May (Simmons) H.; d. Ida Alberta Clark, (stepmother) H.; m. Chesley Roderick Richardson, Sept. 21, 1985; children: Carl Allen Fields, Craig Anthony Fields. AA in Nursing, Olive-Harvey Coll., 1972; BS, St. Joseph Coll., Bklyn., 1976; M in Health Adminstrn., C.W. Post Coll., 1978. Staff nurse U. Chgo. Hosp. and Clinics, Chgo., 1972; head nurse N.Y. Hosp., N.Y.C., 1972; clinic adminstr. Morrisania-Montefiore Hosp., Bronx, N.Y., 1973; head nurse, supr. Pilgrim Psychiat. Hosp., Brentwood, N.Y., 1974, assoc. dir. staff devel., 1974-76, dir. nursing, 1976-78; surveyor, cons Joint Commn. on Accrediation of Hosps., Chgo., 1978-82; dir. Ypsilanti (Mich.) Regional Psychiat. Hosp., 1986-90, Clinton Valley Ctr., Pontiac, Mich., 1990—; dep. commr. dept. mental health State of Ohio, 1980-82; cons. Joint Commn. Accreditation of Hosps.; adj. lectr. Sch. Nursing, U. Mich.; cons. specialist, bd. dirs. Holland-Richardson Assocs., Detroit. Contbr. author (book) Guide to J.C.A.H. Nursing Standards, 1985, 86 edits. Bd. dirs. Women in Crisis, Inc., N.Y.C., Washtenaw County (Mich.) ARC; bd. dirs. psychiatry dept. Chelsea (Mich.) Hosp. Mem. N.Y. Acad. Sci. (life), Bus. and Profl. Women, Inc., Masons, Order Ea. Star. Republican. Office: Clinton Valley Ctr 140 Elizabeth Lake Rd Pontiac MI 48341-1000

HOLLAND, KELLY GILL, poet, consultant; b. Salem, Oreg., July 26, 1934; d. John Peter and Dorothy Marie (Bishop) Gottfried; m. Robert Harry Gill, Oct. 1, 1960 (div. 1972); children: Denise Nielle, Lisa Maria, Holliday Trina, Anna Lloyd; m. Lewis Ross Holland, July 7, 1986. Student, Willamette U., 1953, Portland State U., 1965, Oreg. Coll. of Edn., 1966. Writer, announcer Sta. KOCO, Salem, 1951-53, Sta. KMED, Medford, Oreg., 1953-54; writer, announcer pub. rels. Sta. KRCO, Prineville, Oreg., 1954-55; writer pub. rels. Sta. KOIN, Portland, Oreg., 1955-56; prodn. asst. Sta. KGW-TV, Portland, 1958-61; owner, producer GMG Prodns., Portland, 1961-66; free-lance writer Portland, 1966-76; tchr. humanities pvt. sch., Willamette Valley, Oreg., 1976-81; gallery mgr. Delphian Gallery, Sheridan, Oreg., 1976-81; artist rep. Portland, 1981-87; chief exec. officer Art Resources and Tech., Portland, 1987—. Author poetry; actress. Pvt. tchr. ESL, Sheridan, 1980-81. Recipient Voice of Democracy award State of Oreg., Salem, 1952. Mem. N.W. Regional Artist Guild (pres. 1983—), Portland C. of C. (committeewoman 1978-84). Office: Art Resources and Tech PO Box 408 Lake Oswego OR 97034

HOLLAND, LISA ANN, real estate broker; b. Houston, Nov. 11, 1959; d. Robert Gene and Shirley Ann (Collins) H. B.B.A., S.W. Tex. State U., 1982. Sr. property mgr. Century 21, San Marcos, Tex., 1980-83; v.p. Heritage Mgmt., Houston, 1983-84; exec. property mgr., broker U.S.A. Mgmt., Houston, 1984-86; pres. Waterford Mgmt., Houston, 1986—. Mem. Gulf Coast AAU, Profl. Assn. Diving Instrs., Community Assn. Inst., Inst. Real Estate Mgmt., Am. Soc. Constrn. Anaylsts (officer). Office: 3400 Timmons St #1 Houston TX 77027

HOLLAND, MARGARET MCPHERON, retired mathematics educator; b. Kansas City, Mo., Jan. 19, 1906; d. William Jerome and Ettie May (Stevenson) McPheron; m. Preuit Irwin Holland, Mar. 27, 1947 (dec. 1970); children: Wanda Holland Foote, Mollie Holland Curlee, Preuit Irwin Jr.; m. Charles Murdock Graves, Aug. 26, 1989 (dec. 1989). Diploma, Florence State Normal Coll., 1924; BS, Birmingham So. U., 1928; MA, Peabody Coll., 1931; AA, U. Ala., 1972. Cert. tchr., sch. adminstr., Ala. Tchr., dept. head math. various high schs., Ala., 1924-38, Woodlawn High Sch., Birmingham, Ala., 1938-64; supr. math. Birmingham Secondary Schs., 1964-76; ret., 1976; inst. dir., NSF, Samford U., U. Ala., Birmingham City Schs., all Birmingham, 1964-76. New products editor, The Math. Tchr., 1976-85; contbr. to numerous publs. Bd. dirs., Birmingham Credit Union, 1942-90; pres. Mt. Royal Towers, 1985-89, bd. dirs., 1985-90; com. chair Birmingham Festival of Arts, 1981. Mem. Cosmopolitan Club Birmingham (pres. 1989-90), LWV (v.p. 1972), Ala. Coun. Tchrs. Math. (past officer), Nat. Coun. Tchrs. Math. (regional dir. Southeastern states 1973-76), Profl. Panhellenic Assn., Birmingham Ret. Tchrs. Assn. (treas. 1977-79), Boni Amici Garden Club (sec. 1988-89), Daffodil Garden Club, AAUW, Kappa Delta Epsilon (nat. pres. 1964-68, nat. treas. 1990—). Methodist.

HOLLAND, MERLE SUSAN, psychologist; b. Phila., June 23, 1945; d. Salem Harris and Anne (Goldstein) Lumish; m. Peter M. Holland, May 26, 1968; children: Matthew David, John Michael. BA, U. Pa., 1967; MA, NYU, 1968; EdD, U. Houston, 1985. Lic. psychologist, Tex. Pvt. practice Houston, 1987—; cons. River Oaks Bapt. Sch., Houston, 1987—; mem. med. staff Baywood Hosp., Webster, Tex., 1987—, Belle Park Hosp., Houston, 1987—. Mem. adv. coun. Kesher, Houston, 1988—. Mem. Am. Psychol. Assn., Tex. Psychol. Assn., Houston Psychol. Assn., Orton Dyslexia Soc. (Houston chpt. exec. bd. 1988—, v.p. 1990—). Home: 3319 Plumb Houston TX 77005 Office: 4615 Post Oak Pl Ste 201 Houston TX 77027

HOLLAND, NANCY HINKLE, physician; b. Paris, Ky., July 10, 1921; d. Charles Thomas and Sue Clay (Buncker) Hinkle; m. Charles Phillip Holland, July 3, 1961. BS, U. Denver, 1949; MD, U. Louisville, 1954. Asst. prof. pediatrics U. Cin., 1962-64; asst. prof. pediatrics U. Ky., 1964-67, assoc. prof. pediatrics, 1967-72, prof. pediatrics, 1972—; resident Cin. Childrens Hosp., 1955-57, fellow in immunology, 1957-60; bd. dirs. Nat. Sub-bd. Pediatric Nephrology, 1976-82. Contbr. articles to profl. jours. Bd. dirs. Hendle Contracting Corp., Paris, 1960—. 2d lt. U.S. Army, 1643-45. Mem. Am. Acad. Pediatrics, Am. Soc. Pediatric Nephrology, Am. Pediatric Soc., Internat. Soc. Nephrology, Soc. Pediatric Rsch. Home: Clifton Farm Stamping Ground KY 40379 Office: U Ky Med Ctr Dept Pediatrics Lexington KY 40536

HOLLAND, NANCY MARIE, insurance agency executive; b. Chgo., May 5, 1948; d. Thomas George and Frances Mary (Fister) H. Student, Morraine Valley Community Coll., Ins. Inst. Ill., Chgo. Bd. Underwriters, 1978—. Acctg. clk. Wineman Bros. Ins., Chgo., 1967-72; asst. account exec. Frank B. Hall & Co., Chgo., 1972-78; account exec., v.p. Bayly, Martin & Fay, Inc., Des Plaines, Ill., 1978-83; pres. Holland Ins. Agy., Inc., Willow Springs, Ill., 1983—; cons. Roller Skating Rink Operators Assn., Lincoln, Nebr., 1981—. Mem. Ams. for Legal Reform, Am. Congress Real Estate, Found. Christian Living, Common Cause, Moral Majority, Am. Mus. Natural History. Republican. Home: 39 Ottawa Ct Justice IL 60458 Office: Holland Ins Agy Inc PO Box 128 Willow Springs IL 60480

HOLLAND, PATRICIA ANN, residential real estate broker and executive; b. Port Arthur, Tex., Sept. 21, 1951; d. John Edward and Maye (Gray) Whittington; m. Denton Roy Holland, Sept. 19, 1975; children: Jocelyn Dianne, Kimberly Joanne. Student, Tex. Women's U., Denton, Tex., 1969-70; assoc., Eastfield Jr. Coll., Mesquite, Tex., 1976. Lic. real estate broker. Independent real estate agt. Mesquite, 1981-84; Real estate agt. Waters & Moore Assocs., Dallas, 1984-85; pres., broker Waters & Moore Assocs., 1985—. Editor: (directory) Meadowglen Neighborhood Association, 1984. Organizer, elected pres. Meadowglen Neighborhood Crime Watch Assn., Mesquite, 1984—; mem. Parent/Tchrs. Assn., Mesquite, 1983—. Mem. Greater Dallas Bd. Realtors, Tex. Assn. Realtors, Nat. Assn. Realtors, NAFE. Republican. Baptist. Home: 1602 Meadowglen Ln Mesquite TX 75150 Office: Waters & Moore Assocs Inc 5485 Belt Line Rd Ste 375 Dallas TX 75240

HOLLAND, SANDRA GUNTER, businesswoman, journalist; b. Mount Airy, N.C., Jan. 12, 1952; d. Joseph Bernard and Rondalene Geralda (Stanley) Gunter; m. Gasper O. Holland, Feb. 14, 1981; children: Abraham Justus, Noah Jonah. BS in Journalism, Va. Commonwealth U., Richmond, 1973; postgrad., U. Tex., Austin, 1974, U. North Texas (formerly North Tex. State U.), Denton, 1975-78. Report writer Va. Dept. Hwys., 1973; newsletter editor Tex. Employment Commn., Austin, 1977-80; former tchr. English, journalism and ESL, 1981-82; part-time reporter Sta. KBOP, 1985-87; columnist, bus. newspaper, 1987-88; owner Holland Secretarial Svcs. , 1982—; part-time reporter Sta. KBOP, 1985-87. Pub. (mags.) Austin, Go, Income Opportunities, Lady's Circle, Women's Circle, Woman's World, (newspapers) Grit, San Antonio Light, Pleasanton Express, Brush Country Advertiser, Wilson County News, Medina Valley Times, Devine News, Floresville Chronicle-Jour. Mem. Pleasanton Friends of Libr., San Antonio Zool. Soc., Friends of Sta. KLRN-TV, Longhorn Mus. Soc., Nat. Arbor Day Found.; mgr. fundraiser bike-a-thon, Cystic Fibrosis, 1987-89; chmn. Atascosa County chpt. ARC, 1987-88; media contact congl. candidate, 1980, office mgr., election coord. Rep. Com. of Atascosa County, 1986, 88, cofounder and charter pres. Atascosa County Rep. Women's Club, 1986-87, publicity chmn. 1986-88, sec. 1988; ch. clk. com. chmn. Bapt. ch., 1989—; mem. Atascosa County Hist. Commn., 1989-90; bd. dirs. Atascosa (RHI) Health Clinic, Inc., 1988-91, vice chmn. of bd., 1989, com. chmn. With USAR, 1977-90. Recipient letter of Appreciation USAR, 1982, cert. of Commendation Tex. Com. for Employer Support of Guard and Res., 1982, U.S. 5th Army Minaret award, 1982, Danforth award, 1973, Freedom Found. awards, 1980, 82. Mem. Mensa, UDC, Pleasanton C. of C., Nat. Soc. Notaries. Baptist. Home and Office: 529 Oakhaven Dr Pleasanton TX 78064

HOLLAND-JONES, PAULA ELAINE, educational administrator; b. Brenham, Tex., Oct. 6, 1955; d. Hugh Elmer and Frankie Dois (Miles) Holland; m. Gregory David Jones, Jan. 2, 1955 (div. 1988); children: Clay, Chase. BSEd, Abilene Christian U., 1978. Cert. tchr., Tex.; cert. alcohol and drug abuse counselor, Tex. Edn. technician Austin (Tex.) State Sch., 1978; tchr., coach Brownfield (Tex.) Middle Sch., 1982-84; aerobic instr. Nautilus Fitness Ctr., Lubbock, Tex., 1985-88; tchr. phys. edn. Brownfield Intermediate Sch., 1986-88; dir. student svcs. Slaton (Tex.) Ind. Sch. Dist., 1988—; presenter at profl. confs.; facilitator self-esteem support groups for children, Brownfield, 1984-87, intervention group Terry County Juvenile Probation, Brownfield, 1984-87. Referral coord. Project Life, Brownfield, 1984-87; v.p. Family Network, Brownfield, 1984-86; coord. Jump Rope for Heart, Brownfield, 1986-88; vol. Brownfield unit Am. Cancer Soc., 1986. Mem. Tex. Assn. Alcohol and Drug Abuse Counselor, Nat. Assn. Alcohol and Drug Abuse Counselors, Slaton Classroom Tchrs. Assn. (mem. west AIDS edn. com.), Slaton Jaycees, Slaton Lions Club. Democrat. Home: 700 S 18th St Slaton TX 79364 Office: Slaton Ind Sch Dist 300 S 9th St Slaton TX 79364

HOLLEIN, HELEN CONWAY, chemical engineer, educator; b. Fort Bragg, N.C., Mar. 21, 1943; d. Arthur Conway and Helen Vann (Parker) Faris; m. Leo Bernard Hollein, Sept. 10, 1966; children: Mary, Kathleen, Michael. BS Chem. Engring., U. S.C., 1965; MS, N.J. Inst. Tech., 1979, D Engring. Sci., 1982. Registered profl. engr., N.J. Process engr. Exxon Rsch. and Engring. Co., Florham Park, N.J., 1965-67; tchr. Livingston (N.J.) High Sch., 1967-69; substitute tchr. Singapore Am. High Sch., 1970-71; teaching asst. N.J. Inst. Tech., Newark, 1977-78, adj. intr., 1978-81; asst. prof. chem. engring. dept. Manhattan Coll., Riverdale, N.Y., 1982-88, assoc. prof., 1988—, head dept. chem. engring., 1989—. Contbr. articles to profl. publs., chpt. to book. Recipient Teetor Ednl. award SAE, 1984; NSF grantee, 1983-88. Mem. Soc. Women Engrs. (sr.), Am Soc. Engring. Edn., Am. Inst. Chem. Engrs., Nat. Soc. Profl. Engrs., Sigma Xi (pres. Manhattan Coll. chpt. 1989-90). Office: Manhattan Coll Chem Engring Dept Riverdale NY 10471

HOLLEMAN, SANDY LEE, religious organization administrator; b. Celina, Tex., June 6, 1940; d. Guy Lee and Gustine (Kirby-Sheets) Luna; m. Allen Craig Holleman, June 5, 1959. Cert., Eastfield Coll., 1979. With Annuity Bd., So. Bapt. Conv., Dallas, 1958—; mgr. personnel So. Bapt. Conv., Dallas, 1983-85, dir. human resources, 1985—. Mem. Am. Mgmt. Soc. (dir. salary surveys local chpt. 1986—, v.p. chpt. svs. 1987—), Soc. Human Resource Mgmt., Dallas Personnel Assn., Diversity Club Dallas (program chmn. 1976, v.p. 1977), Order Ea. Star, Daus. of Nile. Baptist. Home: 4524 Sarazen Dr Mesquite TX 75150 Office: Annuity Bd So Bapt Conv 2401 Cedar Springs Rd Dallas TX 75221-2190

HOLLEN, PATRICIA JEAN, nurse educator; b. San Francisco, May 18, 1945; d. William H. and Bonnie P. (Jones) Monger; m. David K. Hollen, June 18, 1966 (div.); 1 child, Elizabeth J. BSN, U. Va., 1967, cert. pediatric nurse practitioner, 1971; MS, Wright State U., 1980; PhD, U. Rochester, N.Y., 1986. Team leader Children & Youth Project, Charlottesville, Va., 1967-69; pediatric nurse practitioner, team supr. Cen. Va. Community Health Ctr., New Canton, Va., 1972; pediatric nurse practitioner Pediatric Assocs., Huntsville, Ala., 1972-73, Elmira, N.Y., 1974-77; from instr. to asst. prof. Elmira Coll., 1980-87; asst. prof. U. Rochester, 1987—. Contbr. articles to profl. jours. Mem. grad. nursing program com. Wright State U., Dayton, Ohio, 1979-80; mem. grievance com. and grad. studies com. Elmira Coll., 1986-87; mem. adv. com. Planned Parenthood So. Tier, Elmira, 1982-83, mem. pub. affairs legis. com., 1984-85, bd. dirs., 1984-85; mem. adv. bd. Profl. Nursing Edn. for Chemung County, Elmira, 1985-87. Nat. Rsch. Svc. Award fellow, 1984-86. Mem. Sigma Theta Tau, Delta Kappa Gamma. Democrat. Presbyterian. Home: 1 Bramblewood Ln Penfield NY 14526 Office: U Rochester 601 Elmwood Ave Rochester NY 14626

HOLLENBACH, SISTER RUTH F., college president. Student, Sch. Sisters U. Notre Dame; BS in Math. and Sci., Webster Coll., 1952; MA in Philosophy, U. Notre Dame, 1958, PhD, 1960; postgrad., Cath. U., 1964, U. Notre Dame, 1971. Tchr. math., sci. St. Joseph High Sch., Conway, Ark., 1952-55; chairperson dept. philosophy Notre Dame Coll., St. Louis, 1958-65; prof. Am. studies Nanzan U., Nagoya, Japan, 1966-78, adminstr. internat. div., 1974-78; fin. dir., dir. devel. Maria Ctr., St. Louis, 1978-84; adminstr. St. Mary's Spl. Sch., St. Louis, 1984-87; pres. Mt. Mary Coll., Milw., 1987—. Office: Mt Mary Coll 2900 N Menomonee River Pkwy Milwaukee WI 53222

HOLLENBECK, MARYNELL, municipal government official; b. Nashville, May 2, 1939; d. Lee B. and Beulah B. (Bradley) Reifel; children: Braeson, Danelle. BA, Iowa State U., 1976, MS, 1980; PhD, ABD, 1981. Cert. regulatory mgr. EPA, DOT, OSHA regulation. Dir. environ. svcs. Bd. Pub. Utilities, Kansas City, Kans.; prof. Southwest Mo. State U., Springfield, Mo.; instr. Iowa State U., Ames; profl. cons. to Springfield Newspapers, Inc., Victims of Domestic Violence, Springfield Health Dept., 1984-86, Southwest Ctr. for Ind. Living, 1986-88. Contbr. articles to profl. jours. Advisor Gamma Sigma Sigma, 1984-86; mem. Hazardous Materials Ctrl. Rsch. Inst., Kansas City (Kans.) Hazardous Materials Adv. Bd.; mem. Greene County Cen. Dem. Com., 1981-86, Story County Cen. Dem. Com., 1977-81; v.p. bd. dirs. Battered Women's Program, 1985-86. Recipient Bus. and Profl. Women award for Leadership and Service, 1976. Mem. Air & Waste Mgmt. Assn. (dir. midwest sect.), Nat. Assn. Hazardous Waste Generators, Gamma Sigma Delta, Phi Kappa Phi, Alpha Kappa Delta, Sigma Xi (recipient E.A. Ross award for scientific research 1977, Von Tungeln award for leadership, research and service 1980). Unitarian. Office: 1211 N 8th St Kansas City KS 66101

HOLLERAN, PAULA RIZZO, psychology and counseling educator, researcher, consultant; b. N.Y.C.; d. A.M. and Jean T. Rizzo; m. Brian Patrick Holleran, Aug. 22, 1970; children: Tracy Lynn, Brett Daniel. BA, Bklyn. Coll., 1959; MA, U. Conn., 1963; PhD, U. Mass., 1969. Tchr. Shell Bank Jr. High Sch., Bklyn., 1960-62; instr. psychology SUNY, Oneonta, 1963-67, assoc. prof., 1969-70, prof. psychology and counseling, mem. grad. faculty, women's studies faculty, chair dept., 1970—, spl. asst. to assoc. commr. U.S. Office Edn., Washington, 1967-68; cons., specialist Headstart and Followthrough Projects, 1968-71; v.p. Rainbow Assocs./Cons., Oneonta, 1979—; presenter at nat. and regional confs. Contbr. numerous articles to profl. jours.; co-author Nat. Assessment of Women's Studies Programs in Higher Edn.; co-developer Couples Communication Workshop and Gender Summit Game for Marriage Counselors. Officer Oneonta Taxpayers Assn. 1978-79; bd. dirs. Goodyear Lake Assn., Md., N.Y., 1984—; co-dir. Hillside Homeowner's Assn., 1987—. U.S. Office Edn. fellow HEW, 1967-68, rsch. grantee Commonwealth Mass. Bur. Rsch., 1969-70, Walter B. Ford Faculty grantee, 1988—, PDQ grantee SUNY, 1990. Mem. Am. Assn. Counseling and Devel., Am. Ednl. Rsch. Assn., Assn. for Women in Psychology, New Eng. Ednl. Rsch. Orgn (best paper award 1981, 87), N.E. Ednl. Rsch. Assn. Office: SUNY Dept Psychology and Counseling Oneonta NY 13820

HOLLERAN, SHEILA, development officer; b. Irvington, N.J., May 1, 1939; d. Thomas Jerome and Loretta Dorothea (Griffin) Holleran. BA, Dunbarton Coll. Holy Cross, Washington, 1961; MA, Jersey City State Coll., 1969. Joined Sisters of Charity of St. Elizabeth, 1961; cert. sch. adminstr., N.J. Tchr. Sisters of Charity of St. Elizabeth, Convent Station, N.J., 1963-68, Ridgewood, N.J., 1968-70; elem. sch. prin. Sisters of Charity of St. Elizabeth, Tenafly, N.J., 1970-78, Montclair, N.J., 1978-86; grant dir. for aged Sisters of Charity of St. Elizabeth, Convent Station, N.J., 1986—, spl. events dir. for maj. fund raisers, 1986—, dir. direct mail program, 1990—. Mem. Nat. Cath. Devel. Conf., N.J. Soc. Fund Raising Execs. Home: 158 High St Passaic NJ 07055 Office: Sisters of Charity Convent Station NJ 07961

HOLLESEN, HOLLIE MARIE, mechanical engineer; b. Chgo., Jan. 21, 1959; d. Sivert Charles and Helen Adele (Burns) H. BS in Mech. Engring., Ill. Inst. Tech., 1986. Draftsman Dormeyer Industries, Chgo., 1980-82; engring. tech. Appleton Electric Co., Chgo., 1982-83; Co-op Gen. Motors Packard Electric Div., Warren, Ohio, 1983-86; field engr. Gen. Electric-Power Generation, Oak Brook, Ill., 1987—. Mem. ASME (pres. 1984, 86). Home: 3853 N Ravenswood Ave Chicago IL 60613 Office: 2015 Spring Rd Rm 409 Oak Brook IL 60521

HOLLEY, AUDREY RODGERS, lawyer; b. N.Y.C., Jan. 18, 1939; d. Mortimer W. and Susan K. Rodgers; m. George M. Holley Jr., July 30, 1964 (dec. Oct. 1983); 1 child, Stephen C.R. BA, Radcliffe Coll., 1961; JD, U. Detroit, 1981. Bar: Mich. 1982, U.S. Dist. Ct. (ea. dist.) Mich. 1982. Assoc. Rickel & Baun, P.C., Detroit, 1985-90, David M. Thomas, P.C., Detroit, 1990—. Mem. ABA, Fed. Bar Assn., Mich. Bar Assn., Detroit Bar Assn. Office: David M Thomas PC 400 Renaissance Ctr Ste 950 Detroit MI 48243

HOLLEY, BARBARA LEE, county tax collector; b. Milton, Fla., Feb. 6, 1940; d. Theodore L. and Naomi (Echols) Lee; m. Millard D. Holley, June 19, 1959; 1 child, Karen. Grad. high sch., Milton, Fla. Cert. tax collector, Fla. Sec. to sch. prin. Canal St. Sch., Milton, Fla., 1958-59; clk. County Tax Collector's Office, Milton, 1959-82; interim tax collector County of Santa Rosa, Milton, 1982, tax collector, 1982—. Sunday sch. tchr. Pineview United Meth. Ch., fin. sec. 1983-89. Named 1976 Farm Family, County C. of C., Milton. Mem. Pilot Club of Milton (rec. sec. 1988-90). Home: 1324 Pineview Ch Rd Jay FL 32565 Office: Santa Rosa County 801 Caroline St Milton FL 32570

HOLLEY, LAUREN ALLANA, psychologist, family therapist; b. Balt., Oct. 9, 1948; d. Winston Willouby and Mary Elizabeth (Hart) Holley; B.S., Morgan State U., 1976; M.A., Antioch U., 1978. Night communications staff ARC, Balt.; behavioral cons. Walter P. Carter Ctr., Interdisciplinary Behavior Mgmt. Program, Balt.; dir., psychologist assoc. Community Team. Mem. multi-cultural com. Bryn Mawr Sch., 1989. Recipient Merit award Voter Registration Com., 1980, award outstanding achievement Jobs Project, Morris Goldseker Found., 1979-80. Mem. NAACP. also: Walter P Carter Ctr 630 W Fayette St Baltimore MD 21201

HOLLIDAY, ANNE ELAINE, accountant; b. Liverpool, N.Y., May 9, 1962; d. John Charles and Virginia Mae (Yates) H. BA in Acctg. with honors, U. N.H., 1984; student, Fla. State U., 1980-81, Palm Beach Atlantic Coll., 1981-82; BS in Acctg. cum laude, N.H. Coll., 1987. CPA, N.H. Bookkeeper Leighton Chevrolet, York, Maine, 1982-83; comptr. Resource Analysts, Inc., Hampton, N.H., 1983-86; staff acct. RC Montville & Co., CPAs, Greenland, N.H., 1986-89; owner, mgr. Holliday & Assocs., CPAs, Greenland, N.H., 1989—; bd. dirs., sec. Rolling Meadow Pet Cemetery, Stratham, N.H., 1989—. Bd. dirs. Richie McFarland Children's Ctr., Stratham, 1988-89; bd. dirs., sec. N.H. Soc. for Prevention Cruelty to Animals, Stratham, 1989—; vol. Pro Portsmouth, N.H., 1988—. Mem. AICPA, N.H. Soc. CPA's. Republican. Home: 64 Breakfast Hill Rd Greenland NH 03840 Office: 1 Bayside Rd Greenland NH 03840

HOLLIDAY, JENNIFER YVETTE, singer, actress; b. Houston, Oct. 19, 1960; d. O.L. Holliday and Jennie V. Eaton. Began singing career in gospel music with Houston Bapt. Ch. choirs; appeared in Don't Bother Me, I Can't Cope, Houston, 1978, Your Arms Too Short to Box with God, Broadway debut, 1979-81, Dream Girls, Broadway, 1981-83, Los Angeles, 1983-84, Sing, Mahalia, Sing, 1985; recs. include Feel My Soul, 1983, Say You Love Me, 1985, Get Close to My Love, 1987. Recipient Grammy award (Rhythm and blues vocal) for And I Am Telling You I'm Not Going, 1982; Tony award for Best Actress in Muscial, Dream Girls, 1982; Ace award for Best Performance in a Cable TV Musical Spl., 1988. Address: care Mike Keller Inc 1133 Broadway #911 New York NY 10010*

HOLLIDAY, KAREN KAHLER, public relations consultant; b. Lindenhurst, N.Y., Dec. 12, 1959; d. Robert Raymond and Emily Barbara (Kmetz) Kahler; m. John Mark Holliday, June 25, 1983; 1 child, Courtney Anne. BA magna cum laude, U. Miss., 1982; M in Journalism, La. State U., 1987. Bus., fin. reporter Northeast Miss. Daily Jour., Tupelo, Miss., 1982-83; fin. columnist New Orleans Bus. Newspaper, 1983-84; dir. pub. relations First Commerce Corp., New Orleans, 1984-86; pub. rels. cons. New Orleans and Belden, Miss., 1986—; instr. Pub. Relations, Loyola U., New Orleans, 1988. Mem. task force United Way Corp. Campaign, New Orleans, 1986, Leadership Lee; bd. dirs. Friends of Lee County Libr., N.E. Miss. Habitat for Humanity. Rhodes Scholar semi-finalist, 1981; named Outstanding Journalism Grad., U. Miss., 1982. Mem. Pub. Relations Soc. Am., Community Devel. Found., U. Miss. Alumni, Kappa Kappa Gamma. Republican. Methodist.

HOLLIDAY, LINDA L., lawyer; b. Baton Rouge, Feb. 22, 1951; d. J. Sidney Sr. and Ione Grace (McKay) H. BS, La. State U., 1972, MEd in Adminstrn., 1975, JD, 1983. Bar: La. Pvt. practice law Baton Rouge; dir. handicap program La. State U., Baton Rouge; data processing/telecommunications cons. La. State Cts., Baton Rouge; paralegal instr. La. State U., Baton Rouge. Contbr. articles to profl. jours. Bd. dirs. Audubon Girl Scouts, 1990—. Named Woman of Achievement nominee YWCA-Baton Rouge. Mem. ABA, Am. Trial Lawyers Assn., La. Bar Assn., Baton Rouge Bar Assn., Data Processors Assn., Data Processing Mgr's. Assn. (pres. BR chpt. 1988). Democrat. Roman Catholic. Home: 614 Wiltz Dr Baton Rouge LA 70806 Office: 228 Napolean St Baton Rouge LA 70801

HOLLIEN, PATRICIA ANN, small business owner, scientist; b. N.Y.C., May 11, 1938; d. Leon and Sophia (Biernacki) Milanowski; m. Harry Hollien, Aug. 26, 1969; children: Brian, Stephanie, Christine. AA, Sante Fe Jr. Coll., 1969; ScD (hon), Marian Coll., 1983; student, U. Fla., 1977—. Rsch. asst. Marineland Rsch. Labs., 1965-69; co-owner, exec. v.p. Hollien Assocs., 1969—; owner, dir. Forensic Communication Assocs., Gainesville, Fla., 1981—; vis. assoc. Royal Inst. Spl. Transmission Lab., Stockholm, 1970, Wroclaw Tech. U., Poland, 1974; asst. in research Inst. Advanced Study Communication Scis. U. Fla., 1977-83, assoc. in research, 1983—; adj. asst. prof. Communication Sci. Lab., N.Y., 1982—. Co-author: Current Issues in the Phonetic Scis., 1979; contbr. articles to profl. jours. bd. dirs. Ann. Retirement Village, Waldo, Fla., 1981—. Mem. Internat. Soc. Phonetic Scis. (council reps. 1983—), Am. Assn. Phonetic Scis., Acad. Forensic Application of the Communication Scis., Am. Acad. Forensic Scis. Home: 229 SW 43 Terrace Gainesville FL 32607 Office: Forensic Communication Assocs PO Box 12323 Gainesville FL 32604

HOLLIES, LINDA HALL, pastor, educator, consultant; b. Gary, Ind., Mar. 29, 1943; d. James Donald and Doretha Robinson (Mosley) Adams; m. Charles H. Hollies, Oct. 14, 1962; children—Gregory Raymond, Grelon Renard, Grian Eunyke. B.S. in Adminstrn., Ind. U., 1975; M.A. in Communications, Gov. State U., 1980; M.Div., Garrett-Evang. Theol. Sem., 1986—. Tchr. Hammond Public Schs., Ind., 1975-77; supr. Gen. Motors Corp., Willow Springs, Ill., 1977-79; gen. supr. Ford Motor Co., East Chicago Heights, Ill., 1979-82; coordinator Women in Ministry Evangelical Theol. Sem., Evanston, Ill., 1984-86; pastor New Life Community Fellowship United Methodist Ch., Lansing, Mich., 1983-86; clin. pastoral edn. intern supr., 1986-88; sr. pastor Richards St. United Meth. Ch., 1988—; founder, dir., cons. Church Aflame Workshops, Inc., Chgo., 1982—, Woman to Woman Ministries, Inc. Trustee Garrett Evang. Theol. Sem., 1984-86; appointee Mayor's Commn. on Role and Status of Women, Gary, 1982-83. Ford fellow, 1975, Benjamin E. Mays fellow, 1984; Crusade scholar United Meth. Ch., 1984; Lucy Ryder Myer scholar, 1985-86, Dr. Martin L. King scholar, 1989. Mem. Bus. and Profl. Women Assn., Nat. Assn. Pastoral Educators, Urban League, NAACP, Internat. Toastmistress Club (pres. 1976-77). Democrat. Avocations; reading; preaching; creative writing; latch hook. Home: 212 Sherman St Joliet IL 60433 Office: The Richards St United Meth Ch 212 Richards St Joliet IL 60433

HOLLIMAN, BECKY SELLERS, health plan company executive; b. Thomasville, Ga., May 6, 1954; d. Robert and Helen (Beall) Sellers; children: Virginia, Leigh. BS in Sociology, Auburn U., 1976; MS in Hosp. & Health, U. Ala., Birmingham, 1978. Adminstrv. intern Lee County Hosp., Opelika, Ala., 1975; admistrv. resident U. Ala., Birmingham, 1977-78; health cons. Franklin Meml. Health Ctr., Mobile, Ala., 1978; asst. adminstr. U. So. Ala. Med. Ctr., Mobile, 1978-85; exec. dir. Mobile Health Plan/PrimeHealth, Mobile, 1985—. Active Mobile United, Leadership Mobile, ARC. Mem. Am. Coll. Hosp. Adminstrn. Home: 516 Springpark Dr E Mobile AL 36608 Office: PrimeHealth 124 S University Blvd Mobile AL 36608

HOLLIN, BETTY A., sales executive; b. St. Leon, Ind., Dec. 4, 1956; d. Lawrence A. and Doris J. (Hahn) Frey; 1 child, Matthew. Studetn, IUPUI, Indianapolis. Account exec. Westfield (Ind.) Decorator Fashions; dist. dir., sales mgr. Decorating Den, Indpls.; regional pricing analyst Super X Drug Stores, Carmel, Ind. Active local PTA; religious edn. aide. Named Mktg. Exec. of Yr., Internat. Franchise Assn. Mem. NAFE. Democrat. Roman Catholic. Home: 2575 Chaseway Ct Indianapolis IN 46268

HOLLINGER, PAULA COLODNY, state senator; b. Washington, Dec. 30, 1940; d. Samuel and Ethel (Levy) Colodny; m. Pal Hollinger, Sept. 16, 1962; children: Ilene, Marcy, David. RN, Mt. Sinai Hosp., N.Y.C., 1961. Mem. Md. Ho. of Dels., 1978-86; mem. Md. Ho. of Dels. Md. State Senate, Annapolis, 1987—, chmn. health subcom. of econ. and environ. affairs com., 1987—; mem. Gov.'s Adv. Coun. on AIDS adminstrv. exec., legis. rev. com.; mem. Joint Com. on Health Care Cost Containment, Gov.'s Task Force to Study Nursing Crisis; vice-chair health com. Nat. Conf. of State Legislatures, 1990, past chair sci. and resource tech. com.; adv. com. Mental Health Laws; Senate chair Joint Commn. on Fed. Rels.; chmn. Acid Rain Workgroup, Orgn. Rehab. Tng. Bd. dirs. Nat. Coun. Jewish Women, Safety First; vice chair health com. Nat. Conf. of State Legislatures, 1990; mem. Gov.'s Tastk Force to Study Nursing Crisis; past pres. Women Legislators of Md., 1986, 87, 88. Recipient Murry Guggenheim award, 1961, Edith Rosen Strauss award, 1987, Verda Welcome award for outstanding polit. achievements and pub. svc., 1989, Legislator of Yr. award Md. Nurse's Assn., 1984. Mem. Women Legislators of Md. (v.p. 1985, pres. 1986, 87, 88), B'nai Brith Women. Office: Md State Senate Annapolis MD 21401-1991

HOLLINGSWORTH, CORNELIA ANN, food scientist; b. Carrollton, Ga., Mar. 6, 1957; d. Robert Allen Jr. and Peggy (Carroll) H. BS, Auburn U., 1979; MS, U. Nebr., 1981, PhD, 1984. Rsch. scientist Armour Food Co., Scottsdale, Ariz., 1984-88; mgr. rsch. and devel. Bil Mar Foods, Inc., Zeeland, Mich., 1988—. Co-author book chpt.; contbr. abstracts to profl. jours. Mem. Jr. League, Holland. Mem. Inst. Food Technologists (profl.), Am. Meat Sci. Assn. (profl.), Phi Tau Sigma (bd. dirs. 1988-91), Gamma Sigma Delta, Delta Gamma. Baptist. Home: 636 Appletree Dr Holland MI 49423 Office: Bil Mar Foods Inc 8300 96th Ave Zeeland MI 49464

HOLLINGSWORTH, MARGARET CAMILLE, financial services administrator, consultant; b. Washington, Feb. 20, 1929; d. Harvey Alvin and Margaret Estelle (Head) Jacob; m. Robert Edgar Hollingsworth, July 14, 1960 (div. July 1980); children: William Lee, Robert Edgar Hollingsworth Jr., Barbara Camille, Bradford Damion. AA, Va. Intermont Coll., 1949. Bookkeeper Fred A. Smith Real Estate, Washington, 1949-53; adminstrv. mgr. Airtronic, Inc., Bethesda, Md., 1953-61; pers. mgr. Sears Roebuck, Washington, 1973-74; adminstrv. mgr., communication mgr. Garvin GuyButler Corp., San Francisco, 1980-88, exec. sec., mgr., 1989—; assoc. Robert Hollingsworth Nuclear Cons., Walnut Creek, Calif., 1975-79. Mem., bd. dirs. Civic Arts, Walnut Creek, 1975—. Recipient Spl. Recognition award AEC, 1974. Mem. Commonwealth Club, Beta Sigma Phi (pres. 1954). Democrat. Presbyterian. Home: 1108 Lime Ridge Dr Concord CA 94518 Office: Garvin GuyButler Corp 456 Montgomery St #1900 San Francisco CA 94104

HOLLINGSWORTH, MARTHA LYNETTE, educator; b. Waco, Tex., Oct. 9, 1951; d. Willie Frederick and Georgia Cuddell (Bryant) J.; m. Roy David Hollingsworth, Dec. 31, 1971; children—Richard Avery, Justin Brian. A.A., McLennan Community Coll., 1972; B.B.A., Baylor U., 1974. Tchr., Connally Ind. Sch. Dist., Waco, 1974—; with Adult Edn. Night Sch., 1974-78; chairperson for Area III leadership conf. Vocat. Office Careers Clubs Tex., Waco, 1985—; active Lakeview Little League Booster Club, 1985—. Mem. PTA (hon. life), Vocat. Office Edn. Tchr.'s Assn. Tex., Assn. Tex. Profl. Educators (v.p. local chpt. 1988—), Future Homemakers Am. Area VIII (hon.), Tex. Future Farmers Am. (hon.), Delta Kappa Gamma. Baptist. Office: Connally Vocat Dept 715 Rita Waco TX 76705

HOLLINGSWORTH, MEREDITH BEATON, nurse; b. Danvers, Mass., Oct. 5, 1941; d. Allan Cameron and Arlene Margaret (Jerue) Beaton; m. William Paul Hollingsworth, Nov. 19, 1983; stepchild, Brendon R. Diploma, R.I. Hosp. Sch. Nursing, Providence, 1968; BS in Nursing, U. Ariz., 1976; MS in Human Resource Mgmt., Golden Gate U., 1984; enterostomal therapy nursing program, U. Tex., 1988; postgrad., U. N.Mex. Cert. enterostomal therapy nurse. Commd. ensign USN, 1968, advanced through grades to lt. comdr., 1979; charge nurse USN, USA, PTO, 1968-88; command ostomy nurse, head ostomy clinic Naval Hosp. Portsmouth, Va., 1985-88; pres., chief exec. officer Enterostomal Therapy Nursing Edn. and Tng. Cons. (ETNetc), Rio Rancho, N.Mex., 1989-90; mgr. clin. svcs. we. area support systems Internat., Inc., Charleston, S.C., 1990—; pres. PAUMER Assocs., Virginia Beach, Va., 1988-89. Mem. adminstrv. bd. Baylake United Meth. Ch., Virginia Beach, 1980-83; deacon St. Paul's United Ch., Rio Rancho; active Am. Cancer Soc. Mem. Internat. Assn. Enterostomal Therapy (govt. affairs nat. com., govt. affairs com. Rocky Mountain region, pub. rels. com., pres. Rocky Mountain region), United Ostomy Assn., World Coun. Enterostomal Therapists, N.Mex. Soc. Healthcare Edn. and Tng. of Am. Hosp. Assn., N.Mex. Assn. for Continuity of Care, N.Mex. Health Care Assn., N.Mex. Assn. for Home Care, N.Mex. Hosp. Assn., N.Mex. Chpt. Nurses Assn., Care Star Network. Republican. Office: 3213 May Circle Rio Rancho NM 87124-2027

HOLLINSHEAD, MARY HANTON, educator; b. Cameron, S.C., Sept. 24, 1940; d. Louis and Nina L. (Seaberry) Hanton; m. William L. Hollinshead, June 8, 1963; 1 child, Derek Keith. BA, S.C. State Coll., 1962; postgrad., Ga. State U., 1983, 88. Cert. early childhood edn. with emphasis in reading and lang. arts., adminstrn. and supervision. Instructional resource tchr. Fulton County Bd. Edn., Atlanta, tchr., asst. prin. Mem. NEA, Ga. Assn. Edn., Fulton County Assn. Educators, Nat. Coun. Elem. Tchrs., Assn. for Supervision and Curriculum Devel.

HOLLINSHEAD, MAY BLOCK, anatomist, educator; b. N.Y.C., Nov. 28, 1913; d. Abraham and Pauline (Markle) Block; m. Merrill Taylor Hollinshead, May 10, 1942; 1 child, Richard Clark. AB, Hunter Coll., 1936; PhD, Columbia U., 1951. Rsch. asst. Vanderbilt U. Sch. Medicine, Nashville, 1942; lab. asst. Stat. Hosp./Army Air Field, Amarillo Shepard Field, Tex., 1943; asst. in anatomy Bowman Gray Sch. Medicine/U. N.C. Med. Sch., Winston-Salem/Chapel Hill, N.C., 1943, U. So. Calif. Sch. Medicine, L.A., 1945, Columbia U. Coll. of Physicians and Surgeons, N.Y.C., 1949-51; instr. in anatomy NYU Coll of Medicine, N.Y.C., 1951-56; asst. prof. anatomy Seton Hall Coll. Medicine and Dentistry, Jersey City, N.J., 1956-61; assoc. prof. anatomy N.J. Coll. Medicine and Dentistry, Jersey City/Newark, 1961-72; prof. anatomy U. of Medicine and Dentistry, N.J. Med. Sch., Newark, 1972—. Contbr. articles to profl. jours.; contbg. author to books in field. Recipient grant-in-aid Columbia U., NYU, 1941, Curtis Scholarship, 1948; named Woman of the Yr., Am. Med. Women's Assn. (br. 4, N.J.), 1979. Mem. Am. Assn. Anatomists, AAAS, CAJAL Club, N.Y. Soc. Electron Microscopists, Union of Concerned Scientists, NOW, Nat. Women's Health Network, Gray Panthers, Amnesty Internat., Sigma Xi. Home: 2 Winthrop Pl Leonia NJ 07605 Office: Univ of Medicine/Dentistry NJ Med Sch/185 S Orange Ave Newark NJ 07103-2757

HOLLIS, ELEANOR HANNAH, controller, treasurer; b. Scranton, Pa., Dec. 29, 1931; d. Arthur Henry and Evelyn Aleta (Sisco) Jones; m. John C. Jones, Mar. 3, 1951 (div. 1977); m. Warren T. Hollis III, May 26, 1978; children: Henry, Douglas Jones, Kathleen Early, David, Gordon. Student, Drakes Bus. Coll., Newark, 1951, Tampa (Fla.) Bay Tech. Sch., 1973. Cert. notary-at-large, Fla. Exec. sec. Firemens Ins. Co., Newark, 1949-51; income tax preparer Edison, N.J., 1951-55; exec. sec., acct. U.S. Envelope Co., Edison, N.J., 1955-60; exec. sec., contr. YMCA, New Brunswick, N.J., 1960-70; contr., purchasing agt. Yale Indsl. Trucks, Tampa, Fla., 1970-72; contr., office mgr. Teleprompter Cable TV, Brandon, Fla., 1972-75; comptr., office mgr. Plant City (Fla.) Newspapers, 1975-78; acct. Ins. Svc. Fla., Sarasota, 1978-81; contr., pers. dir., office mgr. Sta. WGUL-AM-FM, New Port Richey, Fla., 1981-84; contr., treas. Sta. WTMP-AM, Tampa, 1984—; owner Eleanor's Acctg. and Income Tax Svc., Tampa, 1951—. Scout leader Girl Scouts U.S., 1947-49, 55-70; den mother, area rep. Boy Scouts Am., 1959-65; advisor Rainbow Girls, 1970-75; advisor, treas. Job's Dau., 1970-76, other civic activities. Mem. Am. Women in Radio and TV (treas., hospitality chair, bd. dirs. 1986—, named Exec. of Yr. 1987), Order of Amaranth (royal matron, grand officer, grand lectr. 1970-78). Republican. Baptist. Home: PO Box 3388 Spring Hill FL 34626 Office: Sta WTMP 5207 Washington Blvd Tampa FL 33619

HOLLIS, KATHLEEN SUE, accountant, auditor, state official, naval reserve officer; b. Champaign, Ill., Sept. 18, 1955; d. James R. and Ellen Louise (Woods) H. Student, DePaul U., 1978-79; BA, U. Ill., Chgo., 1982; student, Columbia Pacific U., 1989—. Acct. Champaign Nat. Bank, 1978; supr. aircraft services Dept. Def., Chgo., 1978-83; methods and procedures analyst Alexander Proudfoot Co., Chgo., 1983-84; security cons. Excalibur & Assocs., Bridgeview, Ill., 1984-86; examiner Ill. Dept. Fin. Instns., Chgo., 1986—. Contbr. articles to profl. publs. With USAF, 1974-78, lt. USNR, 1984—, Ill. Air NG, 1978-84. Ill. Air NG scholar, 1979-82. Mem. Soc. Fin. Examiners, Ill. Soc. Fin. Examiners, Nat. Assn. Female Execs., U.S. Naval Inst., Air Force Assn., Naval Res. Assn., Am. Mgmt. Assn., Ill. NG Assn. (legis. comm. 1979-83, membership com. 1981-83), Internat. Platform Assn. Republican. Episcopalian. Office: Ill Dept Fin Instns 100 W Randolph St Ste 15-700 Chicago IL 60601

HOLLIS-ALLBRITTON, CHERYL DAWN, retail paper supply store executive; b. Elgin, Ill., Feb. 15, 1959; d. L.T. and Florence (Elder) Saylors; m. Thomas Allbritton, Aug. 10, 1985. BS in Phys. Edn., Brigham Young U., 1981; cosmetologist Sch. Beauty Culture, Berwyn, Ill., 1981. Retail sales clk. Bee Discount, North Riverside, Ill., 1981-82, retail store mgr., Downers Grove, Ill., 1982, Oaklawn, Ill., 1982-83, St. Louis, 1983; retail tng. mgr. Arvey Paper & Supplies, Chgo., 1984, retail store mgr., Columbus, Ohio, 1985—. Mem. Nat. Assn. Female Execs. Republican. Mormon. Avocations: cosmetology, reading, travel. Office: Arvey Paper & Supplies 431 E Livingston Columbus OH 43215

HOLLISTER, CHARLOTTE ANN, computer systems design-implementation consultant; b. Santa Fe, Jan. 2, 1940; d. Bertram Keats and Sara Evelyn (Vaughn) H.; m. Donald Carl Clagett, June 22, 1968; children: Jennifer, Sarah, Emma. BA, Vassar Coll., 1961; PhD, Yale U., 1965. Rsch. asst. NYU, N.Y.C., 1965-68; programmer Harvard U. Observatory, Cambridge, Mass., 1969; sr. applications scientist Bolt Beranek and Newman, Inc., Cambridge, 1969-78, sr. scientist, 1980-84; product planner GE, Schenectady, 1979-80; dep. mgr. Bolt Beranek & Newman Labs., Inc., Cambridge, Mass., 1980-84, sr. mgr., 1985—. Contbr. articles on computer systems to profl. jours. Vol. Berkshire Ballet, Pittsfield, Mass., 1984-86. Mem. Assn. for Computing Machinery, Am. Chem. Soc. (com. chmn. N.E. sect. 1975-77, sec. 1977-79, svc. award 1979). Democrat. Episcopalian. Home: 193 Bartlett Ave Pittsfield MA 01201 Office: Bolt Beranek & Newman Inc 33 Moulton St Cambridge MA 02138

HOLLISTER, LYNDA JEANNE (ROSE HOLLISTER), corporate training specialist, behaviorist; b. Erie, Pa., Sept. 10, 1960; d. Herbert Alan and Carolyn (Homer) H. BA in Interpersonal and Pub. Communication, Bowling Green (Ohio) State U., 1982, MEd in Guidance and Counseling, 1984. Mgr. residence hall Bowling Green State U., 1982-84; dir. campus life Coll. of St. Francis, Joliet, Ill., 1984-87; clin. behaviorist Health Care Inst., Chgo., 1987-89; trainer, orgn. devel. specialst U. Chgo. Hosps., 1990—; dir. tng. John M. Ruh, Inc., Chgo., 1987—; assoc. Performax/Carlson Learning Cos., 1987—; cons. Interviewing Cons.'s Inc., Chgo., 1987—. Chmn. svc. com. Soaring Twenties, Christ Ch. Oak Brook, Ill., 1989, hospitality com., 1988-89, bd. dirs., 1989-90. Recipient Award of Merit Nat. Assn. Sch. Personnel Adminstrs., 1985. Mem. Nat. Assn. Female Execs. Office: Univ Chgo Hosps 1025 E 57th St Culver Hall Rm 305 Chicago IL 60637

HOLLOWAY, BARBARA JEAN CHAMBERS, educator; b. Pensacola, Fla., June 23, 1938; d. Colon and Annie Bell (Mickles) Chambers; m. John Frederick Holloway Jr., May 11, 1962; Frederick Dwayne, Deloris Jeanette. BS, Bishop Coll., 1960; MEd, Cleve. State U., 1979; student, Kent State U., 1980-81. Sec. Horace Mann Jr. High Sch., Omaha, 1960-62; service rep. Northeastern Bell Telephone Co., Omaha, 1963-65; tchr. Pennsauken (N.J.) High Sch., 1969-72, Sawyer Bus. Coll., Cleve., 1972, John Adams High Sch., Cleve., 1972-73; tchr., coordinator Bedford (Ohio) High Sch., 1973—, chmn. bus. edn. dept., 1983—; part-time tchr. Cuyahoga Community Coll., Warrensville, Ohio, 1975-85; speaker Vocat. Edn. Div. Ohio Edn. Dept., 1978-79, Kent (Ohio) State Bus. Edn. Conf., 1979, AM Cleve. Talk Show, 1979, Bedford Rotary, 1979; bd. dirs. Saunder Office and Computer Products, Inc., Solon, Ohio, Datalink Systems, Chagrin Falls, Ohio. Mem. Jay-cettes, Willingboro, N.J., 1971-72, Orange Bd. Edn. Task Force, Orange Village, Ohio, 1982-83; coordinator Vocat. Bus. Edn. Drive-In Conf. Cleve. State U., 1974-75. Recipient Disting. Service award Cory United Methodist Ch., 1980. Mem. N.E. Ohio Bus. Tchrs. Assn. (Tchr. of Yr. 1979, 86), Cleve. Area Bus. Tchrs. (bd. dirs., sec. 1978-80), Ohio Office Edn. Assn. (regional advisor 1975-78), Pi Lambda Theta, Alpha Kappa Alpha, Phi Delta Kappa. Clubs: Couples, Funchasers Camping. Home: 4809 Lander Rd Chagrin Falls OH 44022 Office: Bedford Sch Dist 475 Northfield Rd Bedford OH 44146

HOLLOWAY, CINDY, mortgage company executive; b. Queens, N.Y., Aug. 8, 1960; d. Richard Stephen and Beverly Bunny (Harris) Tannenbaum; m. David Milton Holloway (div. Mar. 1986); 1 child, Benjamin Jerome. BA, Calif. State U., Fullerton, 1981. Lic. real estate broker. Waitress Bob's Big Boy, San Bernardino, Calif., 1984-85; receptionist RNG Mortgage Co., San Bernardino, 1985; loan processor Quality Mortgage Co., Colton, Calif., 1985-88, loan officer, 1988—. Mem. San Bernardino Bd. Realtors (spl. events com. 1988—, communications com. 1990), Nat. Trust for Hist. Preservation. Home: PO Box 3187 Crestline CA 92325 Office: Quality Mortgage Co 1060 E Washington Ste 125 Colton CA 92324

HOLLOWAY, EDNA LARUE, real estate sales agent; b. Hanover, Pa., July 28, 1942; d. Maurice Edward and Helen Viola (Smith) Wisner; m. Donald LeRoy Holloway, Dec. 29, 1963. BA, Towson State U., 1964, MEd, 1972; cert. in vol. mgmt. U. Colo., 1981. Cert. Grad. Realtors Inst., 1989. Tchr. Balt. County Pub. Schs., Towson, 1964-74; bookkeeping asst. Gen. Bus. Systems, Parkton, Md., 1974-76; bookkeeper sec. Ret. Sr. Vol. Program, Grand Rapids, Mich., 1976-77, dir., 1977-79; vol. resources coordinator DeKalb County Health Dept., Decatur, Ga., 1981-87; agt. Northside Realty, Snellville, Ga., 1987—; cons., liaison vol. DeKalb, Ga. and Atlanta, 1980-81; cons., trainer First Bapt. Ch. Atlanta, 1983; asst. conv. coordinator Balt. Life Ins. Co., 1974-76; sec., receptionist State Farm Ins. Co., 1980-81. Mem. Nat. Bd. Realtors, Gwinnett Bd. Realtors, Council Vol. Adminstrs. (bd. dirs. 1982-86), Ret. Sr. Vol. Program (v.p. adv. coun. 1980-86), Assn. Vol. Adminstrn. (regional liaison nat. assn.), Charg II. Republican. Club: Rivermist Women's (Lilburn, Ga.). Avocations: piano, tennis, gardening. Home: 3704 Shawnee Run Lilburn GA 30247 Office: Bob Wood Realty 5344 Five Forks Trickum Rd Lilburn GA 30247

HOLLOWAY, JULIA BOLTON, university professor; b. London, England, Apr. 14, 1937; Arrived in US Dec. 1953.; d. John Robert Glorney and Sybil Margaret (Rutherford) B.; m. Halbert Harold, (separated 1967); children: Richard, Colin, Jonathan. BA in English, San Jose State, Calif., 1954-57; MA in English, U. Calif., Berkeley, 1966-67; PhD in English, U. Calif., 1974. Asst. tchr. U. Calif., Berkeley, 1967-71; asst. prof. Quincy Coll., Ill., 1971-74; assoc. master Princeton Inn Coll., N.J., 1974-76; asst. prof. Princeton U., 1974-81, U. Colo., Boulder, 1981-87; vis. prof. So. Meth. U., 1987-91; assoc. prof. U. Colo., Boulder, 1987; acting curator Casa Quidi, Florence, Italy, 1987-88; dir. Medieval Studies U. Colo., Boulder, 1988—. Author Book Bibliography of Latini, The Pilgrim and the Book: Dante, Chaucer, 1986; Editor, Translator Book Latini, II Tesoretto, 1981; contbr. articles to profl. jours. Bd. dirs. Colo. Endowment for the Humanities, 1983-86, Rocky Mountain Peace Ctr., 1983-86; mem. Quaker Del. to Heads of State, 1980; vice-chmn. Colo. Women's Agenda, 1988. Recipient Summer Seminar, Summer Stipend awards NEH; AAUW Founders fellow, 1987-88. Mem. Chair Com TEAMS, Early English Text Soc., Medieval Acad., New Chaucer Soc., Bronte Soc., James Joyce Found., Browning Inst., Modern Lang. Assn. Democrat. Office: U Colo Dept Medieval Studies CB 226 Boulder CO 80309

HOLLOWAY, LISABETH MARIE, librarian; b. Mitchell, S.D., May 5, 1926; d. Ernest Nelson and Leila Marie (Seastrand) Feind; m. George Martin Holloway, June 16, 1951; children: George Nelson, James Burton. BA, U. Pa. Coll. for Women, 1945; MLS, Drexel Inst., 1950. Assoc. curator, curator hist. coll. Coll. Physicians of Phila., 1964-76; archivist, editor Germantown Hist. Soc., Phila., 1981—; dir. Ctr. for History of Foot Care Pa. Coll. of Podiatric Medicine, Phila., 1981—; editor The Watermark Assn. of Librarians in the History of the Health Scis., 1977-87. Co-editor: Standard History of the Medical Profession of Philadelphia, 1977; Medical Obituaries: American Physicians' Biographical Notices in Selected Medical Journals Before 1907, 1981; A Fast Pace Forward: Chronicles of American Podiatry, 1987. Mem. Am. Assn. for the History of Medicine, Assn. of Librarians in the History of the Health Scis. (chmn. 1975-77), Germantown Hist. Soc. (v.p. 1986—). Office: Pa Coll of Podiatric Medicine Eighth at Race Philadelphia PA 19107

HOLLOWAY, MURIEL D., state legislator; b. Haverhill, Mass.; d. Carl and Martha (Wilson) Dinsmore; m. H. Douglas Holloway, 1948; children: Elizabeth, Cathy. State rep. Maine Ho. of Reps.; now senator from dist. 20 Maine State Senate, Augusta. Past program dir. YWCA. Mem. Nat. Orgn. Women Legislators, Bus. and Profl. Women, Boothbay Harbor C. of C. Republican. Home: Shore Rd Box 560 North Edgecomb ME 04556 Office: Maine State Senate Augusta ME 04330*

HOLM, CAROL ELIZABETH SACHS, psychologist; b. Chgo., Sept. 18, 1932; d. Edward Charles and Esther Elizabeth (Kuhn) Sachs; m. Richard John Holm, Dec. 18, 1955 (div. 1980); children: Karen Marie, David Scott, Lynn Elizabeth, D'Anne Barbara. BA, Carthage Coll., 1956; MA, U. Minn., 1975, PhD, 1986. Tchr. Spanish El Paso (Tex.) City Schs., 1955-56, Bloomington (Minn.) Pk. Dept., 1960-62; youth dir. Mpls. Hearing Soc., 1971-76; psychologist deaf svcs. Courage Ctr., Golden Valley, Minn., 1977-79; counselor hearing impaired support svcs. U. Minn., Mpls., 1979-84; psychologist deaf svcs. for the hearing impaired Family Mental Health Ctr., Tulsa, 1985-88, dir. svcs. for the deaf and hearing impaired, 1988—; mem. Okla. Adv. Commn. on Svcs. to Deaf, Oklahoma City, 1985-88, Okla. Adv. Bd. on Mental Health to Deaf, Oklahoma City, 1986—; sec. bd. dirs. Tulsa Self Achievement Ctr., 1985-89. Author: MN Importance Questionnaire: Adaptation for Hearing Impaired People, 1989. Mem. Senate Subcom. for Equal Opportunities for Women, U. Minn., 1981-84; mem. adv. com. Spl. Svcs. for the Handicapped, Bloomington, 1976-78. Nat. Inst. for Handicapped Rsch. fellow, 1982; named Deaf Woman of the Yr., Quota Club, 1981, Disabled Profl. Woman of the Yr., Pilot Club of Tulsa, 1988. Mem. Am. Psychol. Assn., Okla. Deafness and Rehab. Assn. (chair planning com. 1986-87), Nat. Assn. of the Deaf, Okla. Coun. for the Hearing Impaired, Phi Beta Kappa. Republican. Lutheran. Home: 7718 S 68th E Ave Tulsa OK 74133 Office: Family Mental Health Ctr 2725 E Skelly Dr Tulsa OK 74112

HOLM, HANYA, choreographer, dancer, dance educator; b. Worms-am-Rhine, Germany; came to U.S., 1931, naturalized, 1939; d. Valentin and Marie (Moerschel) Eckert; divorced; 1 child, Klaus Holm. Ed. pvt. schs., Germany; student of music, Hoch Conservatory and Dalcroze Inst., Frankfurt-am- Main; grad., Dalcroze Inst., Hellerau; dance diploma, Mary Wigman Central Inst., Dresden, Germany; D.F.A. (hon.), Colo. Coll., 1960, Adelphi U., 1969. Chief instr., co-dir. Wigman Inst., Dresden, 10 yrs; dir. dance dept. Mus. Theatre Acad., N.Y.C., 1962—; dir. own sch. N.Y.C., until 1968; dir. summer sessions in dance Colo. Coll., 1941-83; mem. staff Alwin Nikolais/Murray Louis Dance Theatre Lab., N.Y.C., 1972—, Juilliard Sch., N.Y.C., 1975—; tchr., lectr. Bretton Coll., Eng., 1979; pioneer Labanotation for copyright on dance scores musicals Kiss Me, Kate, 1948, My Darlin' Aida, 1952, My Fair Lady, 1956. Mem. original Wigman Co., performer, dance dir., choreographer, Europe, until 1931, under auspices Sol Hurok, founder, dir., N.Y. Wigman Sch. Dance, 1931, which later became Hanya Holm Sch. Dance; began Am. concert career, 1936; major prodns. Trend, 1937 (N.Y. Times award from John Martin as best dance composition of year), Metropolitan Daily, 1938, Tragic Exodus, 1938 (Dance Mag. award for best group choreography in modern dance); choreographer: Eccentricities of Davey Crockett, 1948, Kiss Me, Kate (Cole Porter), 1948 (best choreographer N.Y. Drama Critics award), Eng. prodn., 1951, Out of this World (C. Porter), 1950, My Darlin Aida, 1952; choreographer, dir.: The Golden Apple, 1954 (Critics Circle citation best musical); Reuben- Reuben, 1955; staged dances for re-make of film Vagabond King, 1956; choreography and mus. numbers My Fair Lady, 1955-56 (Tony nominee), Israeli prodn., 1964, Where's Charley, My Fair Lady; English prodns., 1958; choreography and mus. numbers Camelot, 1960; Christine, 1960-61, Anya, 1965; staged dances television show Pinocchio, 1957, Dinner with the President, 1963, Metropolitan Daily; 1st dance prodn. on TV, 1939; dir., choreographer world premiere opera The Ballad of Baby Doe, Central City, Colo. opera house, 1956; appeared on Am. Cancer Soc. series Tactic, NBC, 1959; dir., choreographer opera Orpheus and Euridice (Gluck), Vancouver Internat. Festival, 1959. Recipient Capezio award, 1978, award Fedn. Jewish Philanthropies, 1959, Colo. Centennial award and Gov.'s award, 1973, 74, Heritage Honor award Nat. Dance Assn., 1976, award and medal of distinction in fine arts City of Colorado Springs, 1978, Samuel H. Scripps Am. Dance Festival award, 1984; subject of film Hanya Holm, Portrait of an Artist/Teacher, 1983; Samuel H. Scripps Am. Dance Festival award, 1984, Astaire award (spl. citation for lifetime achievement) 1987, Dance Mag. award 1990. Mem. Am. Arbitration Assn. (nat. panel arbitrators), Soc. Stage Dirs. and Choreographers (v.p.). Address: care Selma Tamber 45 W 54th St New York NY 10019

HOLMAN, BETTY ANN, manufacturing executive; b. Omaha, Oct. 13, 1937; d. Michael John and Alice Belle (Kelly) Murray; m. Keith David Holman, Oct. 28, 1961; children: Madonna Holman Wilt, Lisa Marie, Michael Keith, Julie Holman Benedetti, Nancy Holman Welch. BSBA, Creighton U., 1959; postgrad., U. Va., Falls Church, 1969, George Mason U., 1969, 78, No. Va. Community Coll., 1980-85. Pres. KABS Bowling Assocs., Vienna, Va., 1976-79; owner, designer House of Quilts, Vienna, Va., 1979-80; mgr. banquets Evans Farm Inn, McLean, Va., 1980; mgr. reservations, asst. front officer Ramada Inn, Bethesda, Md., 1981-82; mgr. reservations, tour/travel Ramada Cen. Hotel, Washington, 1982-83; dir. sales Wellington Hotel, Washington, 1983-84; broker VR Bus. Brokers, Vienna, 1984-86; dir. sales and mktg. hotel div. Stuart A. Bernstein Co., Washington, 1986; pres., chief exec. officer Evergreen Products, Moneta, Va., 1980—; owner, designer Mountain Mama Toy-Craft Co., Moneta, 1989—, Mountain Mama Toy Co., 1981—; cons. in field; bd. dirs. Holman Enterprises, Moneta. Mem. Isle of Pine Assn., Moneta, 1972—, James Madison's Vols., Vienna, 1978-81, St. Leo's Vols., Fairfax, Va., Smith Mountain Lake Assn., Moneta, 1980—; del. Fairfax Reps., Vienna, 1986, Va. Reps., Vienna, 1986. Mem. Hotel Sales and Mktg. Assn., Govt. Meeting Planners, Delta Zeta. Roman Catholic. Office: Evergreen Products Rt 1 Box 294 Moneta VA 24121

HOLMAN, KAREN MARIE, university official; b. Anchorage, Sept. 6, 1962; d. Joseph Willie and Rose Millicent (Watson) Anderson; m. Robert L. Holman Jr., Nov. 27, 1982. AA in Bus. Adminstrn., Anchorage Community Coll., 1984; student, Alaska Pacific U., 1989. Sr. office clk. Bur. of the Census, Anchorage, 1980; premium audit clk. Providence Wash. Ins., Anchorage, 1981-82; info. systems clk. G.A Ltd., Anchorage, 1982-83; purchasing agt. State of Alaska, Anchorage, 1984-88; purchasing buyer U. Alaska, Anchorage, 1988-89. Del. Dem. Group State Caucuses, Anchorage; mem. Greater Friendly Temple Ch. of God in Christ; bd. dir. Alaska Women's Resource Ctr. Mem. Internat. Order Foresters. Home: 3722 Randolph St Anchorage AK 99508

HOLMBERG, GEORGIA MCKEE, historian, educator, writer, researcher; b. Pitts., Nov. 3, 1946; d. George Waite and Eleanor Bessie (Smith) McK.; m. James C. Holmberg PhD, Aug. 8, 1970. BA in Pol. Sci., Chatham Coll., Pitts., 1968; MA in History, U. Pitts., 1969, PhD in History, 1979. Cert. D'Etudes Francaises, Universite de Poitiers. Lectr. in Am. studies Chatham Coll., Pitts., 1972; teaching asst. U. Pitts., 1969-71, teaching fellow, 1972-73, lectr. in history, 1981—; guest lectr. U. Pitts. Informal Program, 1987, U.S. Constitution Bicentennial, Historical Soc. of Western Pa., Pitts. 1987, Soc. of Mayflower Descendants, Pitts., 1989. Author, editor: Colonial America, 1988, The American Revolution and Federal Period, 1990; researcher, author mus. program curriculum Frontier Democracy, 1987-88. Chmn. alumnae scholarship com. Winchester-Thurston Sch., Pitts., 1987-88; area chpt. Am. Cancer Soc., Mt. Lebanon, Pa., 1981-90. Nat. essay contest winner, Textron, Inc., Providence, 1976. Mem. Inst. Early Am. History and Culture, AAUW, Fedn. Ind. Schs., Chatham Coll. Alumnae Assn. (corr. sec. 1968—, columnist alumnae mag. 1968—). Office: Dept of History Forbes Quadrangle U Pitts Pittsburgh PA 15260

HOLMBERG, JOYCE, state legislator; b. Rockford, Ill., July 19, 1930; m. Eugene Holmberg, Apr. 12, 1952; children: Gail, Polly. BS, No. Ill. U., 1952, MA, Alfred Adler Inst., Chgo., 1979. Tchr. Rockford Ill. Pub. Schs., 1952-55, adminstr., 1967-82; mem. Ill. State Senate from 34th Dist., 1983—; chmn. senate local govt. com. Democrat. Office: Ill State Capitol Bldg 200 S Wyman St Rockford IL 61107

HOLMES, BARBARA ANN KRAJKOSKI, educator; b. Evansville, Ind., Mar. 21, 1946; d. Frank Joseph and Estella Marie (DeWeese) Krajkoski; m. David Leo Holmes, Aug. 21, 1971; 1 child, Susan Ann Sky. BS, Ind. State U., 1968, MS, 1969, specialist cert., 1976; postgrad. U. Nev., 1976-78. Acad. counselor Ind. State U., 1968-69, halls dir., 1969-73; dir. residence halls U. Utah, 1973-76; sales assoc. Fidelity Realty, Las Vegas, Nev., 1977-82. cert. analyst Nev. Dept. Edn., 1981-82; tchr. Clark County Sch. Dist., 1982-87, computer cons., dir. instructional mgmt. systems, 1987-90, chair computer conf., 1990, adminstrv. specialist K-6, 1990—. Named Outstanding Sr. Class Woman, Ind. State U., 1969; recipient Dir's. award U. Utah Residence Halls, 1973, Outstanding Sales Assoc., 1977; Tchr. of Month award, 1983, Dist. Outstanding Tchr. award, 1984, Dist. Excellence in Edn. award, 1984, 86, 87, 88. Mem. Nev. Assn. Realtors, AAUW, Am. Assn. Women Deans, Adminstrs. and Counselors, Am. Personnel and Guidance Assn., Am. Coll. Personnel Assn., Nevadans for Equal Rights Amendment, Alumnae Chi Omega (treas. Terre Haute chpt. 1971-73, pres., bd. officer Las Vegas 1977—), Clark County Panhellenic Alumnae Assn. (pres. 1978-79), Computer Using Educators So. Nev. (sec. 1983-86, pres.-elect 1986-87, pres. 1987-88, state chmn. 1988-89, conf. chmn. 1989—), Job's Daus. Club, Order Ea. Star. Developed personal awareness program U. Utah, 1973-76. Home: 2531 E Oquendo Rd Las Vegas NV 89120 Office: Clark County Sch Dist Div Curriculum and Instrn 601 N Ninth St Las Vegas NV 89101

HOLMES, CAROLYN COGGIN, museum director; b. Raleigh, N.C., Jan. 6, 1939; d. Robert Clifton and Nola (Henley) Coggin; m. David Lynn Holmes; children: Henley Madden, Catesby Coggin. BA, Wake Forest U., 1961; MAT, Duke U., 1962. Tchr. of French Needham Broughton Sr. High Sch., Raleigh, N.C., 1961-64, Washington-Lee R. High Sch., Arlington, Va., 1964-66; asst. prof. East Carolina U., Greenville, 1966-67, Campbell Coll.,

Buie's Creek, N.C., 1967-68; tchr. of French Tidewater Acad., Wakefield, Va., 1968-74; restoration contractor, cons. Smithfield, Va., 1972-75; exec. dir. Ash Lawn-Highland (home of James Monroe), Charlottesville, Va., 1975—; cons. on restoration, Charlottesville, 1972—. Commr. Isle of Wight (Va.) Planning Com., 1973-77. Mem. Am. Assn. Museums, Va. Assn. Museums (sec., coun. mem. 1985-89), Va. Assn. Presdl. Houses and Museums (sec., treas., pres. 1984—), Nat. Trust for Hist. Preservation. Democrat. Episcopalian. Office: Ash Lawn-Highland Rte 6 Box 37 Charlottesville VA 22901

HOLMES, CYNTHIA MISAO BELL, health services administrator; b. Yokohama, Japan, June 5, 1949; d. Isaac Walter Bell and Chihoko (Adachi) Bell Parker; m. Edward Theodore Holmes, Dec. 21, 1967 (div. Mar. 1973); children: Kenya K., Larik D. BA, Columbia U., 1975; MBA, CUNY, 1977. Teller, N.Y. Bank for Savs., N.Y.C., 1968-69; sec., adminstrv. asst. Columbia U., N.Y.C., 1970-75; asst. day ctr. dir. N.Y. State Dept. Mental Hygiene, N.Y.C., 1976-77; planner, cons. Hosp. Affiliates, Inc., Nashville, 1977-79; program adminstr. Marion County Health Dept., Indpls., 1979—. Bd. dirs. Ind. Black Expo, Inc., 1981, 82; bd. dirs. chmn. Actors Ink Theatre Prodn. Co., Indpls., 1982-86; organizer Health Fair, Ind. Black Expo, 1981, 82; mem. evaluation com. United Way Greater Indpls. Assoc. U. Programs in Health Administrn. scholar, 1975, 76. Mem. Met. Health Council Indpls. (bd. dirs., sec. 1980—), Ind. Primary Health Care Assn. (bd. dirs., treas. 1982-86), Nat. Assn. Community Health Ctrs., Nat. Assn. Securities Dealers. Avocations: theater production, financial planning, business consulting, sweepstaking, real estate investment. Office: Marion County Health Dept 222 E Ohio St Indianapolis IN 46204

HOLMES, FRANKIE ANN, internist, educator; b. Honolulu, Mar. 3, 1950. BS in Chemistry, Coll. William and Mary, 1972; MD, Med. Coll. Va., 1976. Diplomate Am. Bd. Internal Medicine, Am. Bd. Med. Oncology, Nat. Bd. Med. Examiners. Med. intern Hartford (Conn.) Hosp., 1976-77, resident in medicine, 1977-79; emergency room physician Windham Community Hosp., Williamantic, Conn., 1979-81; fellow in med. oncology U. Tex. M.D. Anderson Hosp. and Tumor Inst., Houston, 1981-83, asst. internist, 1983-88, assoc. internist, 1988—, instr. clin. medicine, 1983-87, asst. prof. medicine, 1987-88, assoc. prof., 1988—; presenter, lectr. profl. meetings, 1984—. Contbr. articles and abstracts to med. jours., chpts. to books. Mead Johnson Pharm. Co. grantee, 1985—. Mem. AMA, ACP, AAAS, Am. Assn. for Cancer Rsch., Am. Med. Women's Med. Assn., Am. Soc. Clin. Oncology, So. Assn. for Oncology, So. Med. Assn., Tex. Med. Assn., Tex. Soc. Med. Onccologists, Harris County Med. Assn., Houston Soc. Internal Medicine, Phi Beta Kappa. Home: 7447 Brompton Houston TX 77025 Office: U Tex MD Anderson Hosp Box 78 1515 Holcombe Blvd Houston TX 77030

HOLMES, HELEN BEQUAERT, researcher; b. Boston, Sept. 6, 1929; d. Joseph Charles and Frances Alice (Brown) Bequaert; m. Francis William Holmes, June 7, 1953; children: Peter Alan, Sarah Ruth, Joseph Mark. AB, Oberlin Coll., 1951; MS, Cornell U., 1953; PhD, U. Mass., 1970. Cert. secondary tchr., Mass. Sci. tchr. Northampton (Mass.) Sch. for Girls, 1965-67; asst. prof. biology Springfield (Mass.) Tech. Community Coll., 1971-73, Russell Sage Coll., Troy, N.Y., 1976-78; vis. lectr. genetics Tufts U., Medford, Mass., 1978-80; rsch. assoc. Fedn. of Orgns. for Profl. Women, Washington, 1978-82; vis. scholar Spelman Coll., Atlanta, 1982-83; vis. scientist U. Groningen, The Netherlands, 1984-85; scholar assoc. Women's Rsch. Inst. Hartford (Conn.) Coll. for Women, 1986-88; assoc. fellow Inst. for Advanced Study in Humanities U. Mass., Amherst, Mass., 1988—; con. U.S. Congress Office of Tech. Assessment, Washington, 1987. Editorial bd. Bioethics, 1986—, Hypatia, 1987—; editor: Birth Control and Controlling Birth, 1980, The Custom Made Child, 1981; contbr. articles to profl. jours. Mem. Pub. Transp. Com., Amherst, Mass., 1989—. Grantee NSF, 1978-81, 82-83; recipient Fulbright award Coun. for Internat. Exchange of Scholars, U. Waikato, 1986-87. Mem. Nat. Women's Studies Assn. (sci. and tech. task force), Feminist Internat. Network on the New Reproductive Technologies, Soc. for Women in Philosophy (organizer, regional conf. 1989), Phi Beta Kappa, Sigma Xi. Mem. Soc. of Friends. Home: 24 Berkshire Terr Amherst MA 01002

HOLMES, JACQUELIN ANN, equal employment opportunity administrator; b. Balt., Sept. 5, 1947; d. Paul Chester and Ethel Marie (Parker) Bianchi; m. Larry Lee Lockman, Nov. 29, 1963 (div. Oct. 1972); children: Carole Jean, Gregory Stephen; m. John Stephen Holmes, July 27, 1974. AA in Psychology, Community Coll. of Denver, 1975; BBA, Regis Coll., 1988. Cert. personnel classification, examinations and rules interpretation, Colo.; lic. claims adjuster. With staff support/counseling div. Community Coll. of Denver North Campus, 1973-74, asst. to dir. community services div., 1974-77; claims adjuster State Compensation Ins. Fund, Denver, 1978-80, 82-84; owner day care ctr. Littleton, Colo., 1980-82; personnel analyst Colo. Dept. Labor & Employment, Denver, 1984-88; adminstrv. officer III Colo. Dept. Natural Resources, Denver, 1988—. Student govt. rep. Community Coll. of Denver, 1973-74; organizer Classified Employees Council, Denver, 1975; vol. orgn. support Arapahoe County Family Day Care, Littleton, 1981-82; coach Teen Quiz Team (Champions 79-83), Littleton, 1979-83; marriage enrichment cons. Littleton Ch. of the Nazarene, 1986-87; Sunday sch. tchr., 1980-87. Named an Outstanding Employee Gov.'s Office Colo. State Govt., 1986. Mem. Internat. Personnel Mgrs. Assn., Colo. Equal Opportunity/Affirmative Action Coalition, Inc., Colo. Coun. Mediators Assn., Pilot Club Internat. (denver). Home: 6746 S Dahlia Ct Littleton CO 80122 Office: Colo Div Labor Spl Funds 1120 Lincoln St #1403 Denver CO 80203

HOLMES, JERI, fashion designer, small business owner; b. Phila., Feb. 22, 1910; d. Max and Sophie (Greenberg) Smiler; m. Manuel La Porte, Feb. 18, 1934 (div. Feb. 1944); m. Willard Gordon Staley Holmes, Sept. 19, 1946 (dec. 1984). Grad. high sch., Phila. Asst. buyer suit and coat dept. Bonwit Teller, Phila., 1934; from salesperson to asst. buyer Bonwit Teller, N.Y.C.; buyer Rich's, Atlanta, Saks Fifth Ave., N.Y.C.; owner, operator Holmes of Calif., L.A., 1947-55, Jeri Holmes for Jantzen Internat., Portland, Oreg., 1956-61; instr. and merchandiser for models and various designers Govt. of Italy, Rome, 1961; designer lines J. G. Knits for Anne Klein Jrs., Arkin Orgn., others, N.Y.C.; designer with Bill Holmes Pre-Cut Knit Kits, Calif.; owner, operator Unique Boutique, Newport Beach and Laguna, Calif.; condr. fashion and color-coordinating seminars aboard cruise ships. Contbr. articles on fashion to various publs.; featured designer mags. and TV programs including Today Show with Dave Garroway, 1954. Named Designer of Yr., Calif. Apparel News, 1949, Macy's San Francisco, 1951; recipient Cert. of Merit, Woolknit Assn., 1954, Prestige award French Lace Fedn., 1965; honoree several orgns. and assns. Mem. Am. Women Entrepreneurs, Fashion Group Internat., Internat. Women's Writing Guild. Home: 41 Park Ave New York NY 10016

HOLMES, PATRICIA ANNE, nursing director; b. Youngstown, Ohio, July 26, 1927; d. Ford Proctor and Alma Florence (Lamb) Agey; m. Edward Joseph Holmes, June 1, 1949 (dec. 1973); children: Douglas, Christine. Student, St. Elizabeth Hosp. Med. Ctr., 1948. Certified Restorative Rehab. Nurse. Staff nurse Youngstown Hosp. Assoc., Ohio, 1949-50, St. Elizabeth Hosp. Med. Ctr., Ohio, 1954-56; dir. nursing Peaceful Acres Nursing Home, North Lima, Ohio, 1963-72; nursing dir. Colonial Manor N.H., Youngstown, Ohio; dir. nursing, asst. adminstr. Assumption N.H., Youngstown, Ohio, 1975-78; dir. nursing Desert Valley Med. Ctr., 1978—; asst. adminstr., cons. Desert Vly. Med. Ctr., Scottsdale, Ariz., 1986—. Mem. NAFE. Republican. Lutheran. Office: Westwood Rehab Med Ctr 748 Boardman Canfield Rd Youngstown OH 44512

HOLMES, SUSAN G., educator; b. Kansas City, Mo., Mar. 7, 1955; d. Burton E. and Gloria A. (Spencer) H. BA, U. Kans., Lawrence, 1980. Cert. music therapy, education. Tchr. Dade Coutny Schs., Miami, Fla.; entertainment coord. And More Music Corp., Miami, Fla.; music therapist, tchr. ESOL Miami; tchr. ESOL Miami Correctional Ctr. Tchr. ESOL to newly-arrived immigrants. Recipient Honor for TV series CBS News. Mem. Nat. Orgn. for Exec. Women. Office: Met Correctional Ctr 15801 SW 137th Ave Miami FL 33177

HOLO, SELMA REUBEN, museum director, educator; b. Chgo., May 21, 1943; d. Samuel and Ghita (Hurwitz) Reuben; m. Sanford Holo, June 14, 1964 (div. 1981); children: Robert, Joshua; m. Fred Croton, June 18, 1989. BA, Northwestern U., 1965; MA, Hunter Coll., 1972; PhD, U. Calif., Santa Barbara, 1980. Lectr. Art Ctr. Coll. of Design, Pasadena, Calif., 1973-77; curator of acquisitions Norton Simon Mus., Pasadena, 1977-81; dir. Fisher Gallery and mus. MA art history/mus. studies program U. So. Calif., L.A., 1981—; guest curator, cons. Getty Mus., Malibu, Calif., 1975-76, 81; guest curator Isetan Mus., Tokyo, 1982; cons. Nat. Mus. for Women in Arts, Washington, 1984; reviewer grants Inst. Mus. Svcs., Washington, 1986, 87, Getty Grant Program, 1988-89; panel chmn. Internat. Com. on Exhbn. Exch., Washington, 1984; panelist NEA, Washington, 1985; mem. admission panel Mus. Mgmt. Inst., 1990; hon. curator Tokyo Fuj Mus. Author: (catalogues) Goya: Los Disparates, 1976; co-author: La Tauromaquia: Goya, Picasso and the Bullfight, 1986; editor: Keepers of the Flame, The Unofficial Artists of Leningrad, 1990; contbr. articles to profl. jours. Disting. Scholar fellow La Napoule Art Found., 1988; Kress Found. grantee, N.Y., 1979, Internationes Fed. Republic of Germany grantee, 1985; recipient Fuj Fine Art Award, 1990. Mem. Coll. Art Assn. (survey com. mus. studies programs 1986), Am. Assn. Mus., Art Table. Office: U So Calif Fisher Gallery 823 Exposition Blvd Los Angeles CA 90089-0292

HOLSINGER, FRAN, small business owner; b. Boise, Idaho, Sept. 4, 1938; d. Vearl Glenn and Mary Frances (Charters) Kirby; m. Robert Eugene Holsinger, Apr. 8, 1961; children: Gregory, Julie, Pamala, Christopher. BA, Cen. Wash. State, 1960; postgrad., Willamette Coll. of Law. Owner Rusumes Plus, Beaverton, Oreg.; job developer, mktg. Pacific Bus. and Futures, Portland, Oreg.; sales rep. Bobbs Merrill Edn. Pub., Spokane, Wash.; sales assoc. Century 21 Real Estate, Spokane. Author: Packaging Yourself for the Job Market. Mem. Beaverton Area C. of C., Ambassadors Com., Small Bus. Com. Mem. Beta Sigma Phi (pres. Beaverton coun.). Republican. Roman Catholic. Home: 14540 SW Downing Beaverton OR 97006 Office: 9800 SW Beaverton-Hillsdale Hwy 203 Beaverton OR 97005

HOLSTEIN, CHARLOTTE GARELICK, civic worker; b. Rochester, N.Y., Sept. 1, 1925; d. Morris M. and Esther B. (Hoffenberg) Garelick; m. Alexander Edwin Holstein Jr., June 12, 1946; children: Carol Holstein Killian, David Alan, Philip Lester, Elizabeth Holstein Sardelli. BS in Edn., SUNY, Brockport, 1946. Tchr. Syracuse (N.Y.) City Sch. Dist., 1946-51; civil svc. examiner N.Y. State Civil Svc., 1975-77; field reader U.S. HHS, 1980-81; chmn. Loretto Geriatric Ctr., Syracuse, 1979-90; founder, exec. dir. Leadership Greater Syracuse, 1990—; project dir. Women in Community Svc., Syracuse, 1965-67; founder, pres. Meals on Wheels, Syracuse, 1959-63; bd. mem. Community Found., Syracuse and Onondaga County, 1970-76; founder, mem., vice-chmn. Welfare Rsch., Inc., 1973-86; chmn. Nat. Com. Role Women, 1975-80; chmn Pay Equity Task Force, 1985-86. Bd. govs. Am. Jewish Com., 1972—, v.p., 1984-87; chmn. Jewish Communal Affairs Commn., 1988—; chmn. bd. visitors Syracuse U. Coll. for Human Devel., 1986-90; bd. mem. United Way Central N.Y., Syracuse, 1981-87; chmn., founder Syracuse Commn. for Women, 1986-90; advisor, mem. Pres. Adv. Com. for White House Conf. on Families, 1979-81; presentor, del. UN NGO Forum, Conf. for Women, Nairobi, Kenya, 1985; mem. Syracuse Housing Partnership, 1989; co-chmn. Am. Jewish Com., Latin Am. Human Rights, 1987. Recipient Community Svc. award Rotary Club, Syracuse, 1960, Woman of Achievement for Vol. Leadership award Syracuse Post Standard Newspaper, 1961; Hannah Solomon award for leadership Nat. Coun. Jewish Women, Syracuse, 1975, Mayor's Achievement award Mayor City of Syracuse, 1989. Democrat. Home: 314 Kimber Rd Syracuse NY 13224 Office: Leadership Greater Syracuse 217 Montgomery St Syracuse NY 13202

HOLSTON, SHARON SMITH, government official; b. Cleve., Dec. 15, 1945; d. Charles Coolidge and Eva Mae (Hall) Smith; m. Joseph Holston, Jr., Dec. 22, 1973; children: Joseph Ikaweba, Eve Denise. AB, Columbia U., 1967; M in Pub. Adminstrn., Harvard U., 1986. Personnel mgmt. specialist U.S. Commn. Civil Rights, 1967-70, HEW, 1970-72; EEO officer FDA, Rockville, Md., 1972-74, personnel mgmt. specialist, 1975-77, acting exec. officer, 1977-79, spl. asst. to assoc. commr. mgmt. and ops., 1979-80, dep. assoc. commr. mgmt. and ops., 1980-88, acting assoc. commr. mgmt. and ops., 1986-88. Recipient Award of Merit, FDA, 1982, 87, also commr.'s spl. citation, 1985; Sr. Mgmt. citation HHS, 1988. Fin. sec., mem. Jack & Jill of Am.; active Mt. Calvary Bapt. Ch. Office: FDA Mgmt and Ops 5600 Fishers Ln Rockville MD 20857

HOLT, BARBARA BERTANY, management consultant; b. Bridgeport, Conn., Nov. 4, 1940; d. Stephen Edward and Mary G. Bertany; student Regis Coll., 1958-59; BA in English, U. Bridgeport, 1962; m. Robert Holt, Dec. 5, 1971; children: Pamela Maren, Laura Kimbel, Mary Brooke. Instr. speech and theatre, U. Bridgeport (Conn.), 1962-69; gen. mgr. BFL Assos., Exec. Recruitment, N.Y.C., 1969-72; founder, pres. Barbara Holt Assos., mgmt. cons., N.Y.C., 1972—; mem. faculty New Sch. for Social Rsch. Chmn. bd. advisers Fine Arts Acad. Fairfield; v.p., bd. dirs. Stamford Chamber Orch. Decorated dame Order of St. John. Mem. N.Y. Fashion Group, Women in Mgmt. Club: Atrium (N.Y.C.). Developer, producer video career mgmt. series for public TV, 1976. Office: Barbara Holt Assocs Box 713 Southport CT 06490

HOLT, BERTHA MERRILL, state legislator; b. Eufaula, Ala., Aug. 16, 1916; d. William Hoadley and Bertha Harden (Moore) Merrill; m. Winfield Clary Holt, Mar. 14, 1941; children: Harriet Wharton Holt Whitley, William Merrill, Winfield Jefferson. AB, Agnes Scott Coll, 1938; LLB, U. Ala., 1941. Bar: Ala., 1941. With Treasury Dept., Washington, 1941-42, Dept. Interior, Washington, 1942-43; mem. N.C. Ho. of Reps. from 22d Dist., 1975-80, 25th Dist., 1980—, chmn. select com. govtl. ethics, 1979-80, chmn. constl. amendments com., 1981, 83, mem. joint commn. govtl. ops., 1982-88, chmn. appropriation com. justice and pub. safety, 1985-88 . Pres., Democratic Women of Alamance, 1962, chmn. hdqrs., 1964, 68; mem. N.C. Dem. Exec. Com., 1964-75; pres. Episcopal Ch. Women, 1968; mem. coun. N.C. Episcopal Diocese, 1972-74, 84-87 , chmn. budget com. 1987; chmn. fin. dept., 1973-75, parish grant com., 1973-80, mem. standing com., 1975-78; chmn. Alamance County Social Svcs. Bd., 1970; mem. N.C. Bd. Sci. and Tech., 1979-83; past bd. dirs. Hospice N.C.; bd. dirs. State Coun. Social Legis., State Conf. Social Work, N.C. Epilepsy Assn., N.C. Pub. Sch. Forum, 1989, U. N.C. Sch. Pub. Health Adv. Bd., Salvation Army Alamance County, N.C., Nursing Found, 1989, Epilepsy Found., 1989; bd. Alternatives for Status Offenders Burlington, N.C., Sch. Pub. Health Adv. Bd. Recipient Outstanding Alumna award Agnes Scott Coll., 1978, Legis. award for svc. to elderly Non-Profit Rest Home Assn., 1985, health, 1986, ARC, 1987, Faith Active in Pub. Affairs award N.C. Coun. of Chs., 1987, Ellen B. Winston award State Coun. For Social Legis., 1989. Mem. N.C. Women's Forums, Law Alumni Assn. U. N.C. Chapel Hill (bd. dir. 1978-81), N.C. Bar Assn., NOW, English Speaking Union, N.C. Hist. Soc., Les Amis du Vin, AAUW, Pi Beta Phi, Phi Kappa Gamma (hon.), Century Club. Address: PO Box 1111 Burlington NC 27215

HOLT, BEVERLY ELAINE (BEVERLY ELAINE COX), educator; b. Little Rock, Aug. 27, 1945; d. Carl Bernard and Artie Mae (Huffman) Cox; 1 child, Dena Elaine. BS in English and Bus. Edn. with honors, Henderson State U., 1966, MS in English, 1969; postgrad., U. Houston, 1981, East Tex. State U., 1981-85. Lang. arts tchr. Helena-West Helena (Ark.) Ind. Sch. Dist., 1966-67; English tchr. Hughes (Ark.) Ind. Sch. Dist., 1967-69; adult bus. edn. tchr. Arkadelphia (Ark.) Ind. Sch. Dist., 1969-70; English tchr. Bismarck (Ark.) Ind. Sch. Dist., 1970-71; tchr. English, bus. Lee Acad., Auburn, Ala., 1976-77; lang. arts tchr. Longview (Tex.) Ind. Sch. Dist., 1977-78; tchr. bus. Kilgore (Tex.) Coll., 1978-79; chmn. English dept., audio-visual dir. Kilgore Ind. Sch. Dist., 1979-85; media specialist Spring Hill Ind. Sch. Dist., Longview, 1985—; teaching specialization panel U. Tex., Tyler, 1983-84; mem. adv. bd. Region VII Edn. Service Ctr., Kilgore, 1984-85; com. mem. Tex. Edn., So. Assn. Study, Kilgore, 1984-85. Mem. Tex. Assn. for Gifted/Talented, Tex. Joint Council Tchrs. English, Tex. Library Assn., Tex. Assn. Supervision and Curriculum Devel., Tex. Edn. Assn. (adv. com. 1984-85), Alpha Chi., Phi Beta Lambda, Delta Kappa Gamma. Home: 2902 Ruidosa Longview TX 75605

HOLT, GEORGINA L., ceramic artist; b. Kansas City, Dec. 18, 1934; d. George Allen and Rose (Voos) Miller; m. Richard H. Holt, Aug. 17, 1957; children: Mark, David, Timothy, Theresa. BA, Loretto Coll., Denver, 1956; postgradx., U. Mo., Kansas City, 1968-70, Art Inst. Kansas City, 1970-72. Layout artist Hallmark Card Co., Kansas City, Mo., 1956-57; tchr. art Notre Dame de Sion High Sch., Kansas City, 1967-76; installation artist Jacksonville (Fla.) Mus. Art and Sci., 1982-84; ind. ceramic artist Jacksonville, 1978—; docent tchr. Jacksonville Art Mus., 1978-88; show curator U. N. Fla., Jacksonville, 1988—; juror Duval County Art Dept., Jacksonville, 1987—; ledctr. Jacksonville Art Mus., Am. procelains, 1986-89. Author: Koger Collection, 1986, American Crafts for the Home (book I & II). Recipient Spl. Commendation, Mayor's Office for Vol. Docent at Jacksonville Museum of Arts & Sci., 1982. Mem. Am. Crafts Council, Fla. Craftsmen Inc., Jacksonville Coalition of Visual Arts, Jacksonville Art Mus., Crown Craftsmen Inc. (gallery installation dir. 1985-87). Republican. Home: 3737 Cove Ct Jacksonville FL 32211

HOLT, HELEN KEIL, physicist; b. West Palm Beach, Fla., Mar. 23, 1937; d. John Arthur and Katharine (Rickards) Keil; m. Lawrence Galles Holt, Dec. 28, 1958; children: Daphne Jane, Leslie Elizabeth. BA, Barnard Coll., 1958; MS, Yale U., 1960, PhD, 1965. Physicist Nat. Bur. Standards, Washington, 1965-86. Contbr. articles on electron-atom scattering, atomic physics and lasers to profl. jours. Recipient Sustained Superior Performance award Nat. Bur. Standards, 1968; Woodrow Wilson fellow, 1958. Fellow Am. Phys. Soc.; mem. Sigma Xi. Home: 6740 Melody Ln Bethesda MD 20817

HOLT, JUDITH ANN, motel owner; b. Portland, Oreg., Dec. 25, 1940; d. Austin Lee and Mildred Sarah (Robison) Stevens; m. Francis Lloyd Frazier, Aug. 4, 1962 (div. 1974); children: Kimbra Leanne, Jennifer Stevens; m. Bruce Douglas Holt, Nov. 14, 1975. Student, U. Oreg., 1959-60; BS, Portland State U., 1963, postgrad., 1974. Social worker State of Oreg., Portland, 1963-65; cost analyst Rocket Rsch., Redmond, Wash., 1976-79; co-owner, mgr. Beachfront Motel, Lincoln City, Oreg., 1981—; pvt. practice tax. cons., Lincoln City, 1983—. Chmn. Citizens Rev. Bd., Newport, 1982—; mem. Juvenile Svcs. Commn., Newport, 1982—; bd. dirs. Victims Offenders Reconciliation, Lincoln City, 1987—. Mem. Oreg. Soc. Tax Cons. (sec. 1983-84), AAUW (pres. Lincoln City chpt. 1986-89). Home: 3313 NW Inlet Ave Lincoln City OR 97367 Office: Beachfront Motel 3313 NW Inlet Ave Lincoln City OR 97367

HOLT, MARGARET MARY, nursing coordinator; b. Chgo., Jan. 16, 1935; d. Mary (Buzy) Moore; (div. July 1988); children: Robert, Sally, Mary. BS, U. Mich., 1957; MS, Case Western Reserve U., 1972, MA in Sociology, 1980. RN, Ohio. Staff nurse pediatrics The Queens Hosp., Honolulu, 1957; staff nurse obstetrics Doctors Hosp., Seattle, 1957-58; staff nurse pediatrics U. Mich. Hosp., Ann Arbor, 1959-60; instr. Fairview Gen. Sch. Nursing, Cleve., 1961-67; prof. Lorain County Community Coll., Elyria, Ohio, 1967—; instr. Huron-Road Sch. Nursing, Cleve., 1987-88, Cuyahoga Community Coll., Cleve., 1989-90. Mem. Bowman for County Commr. Com., Elyria, 1986. Mem. Elyria Quota Club (pres. elect 1990), Western Reserve Assn. (coun. mem. 1984), Nat. League for Nursing (accreditation visitor bd. rev. 1979—), Am. Nurses Assn. (peer assistance program 1972—), Lorain County Dist. Nurses Assn. (treas. 1989-90). Office: Lorain County Coll 1005 N Abbe Rd Elyria OH 44055

HOLT, MARJORIE SEWELL, lawyer, retired congresswoman; b. Birmingham, Ala., Sept. 17, 1920; d. Edward Rol and Juanita (Felts) Sewell; m. Duncan McKay Holt, Dec. 26, 1946; children: Rachel (Mrs. Kenneth Hall Tschantre), Edward, Victoria (Mrs. Robert Schumaker). Grad., Jacksonville U., 1945; J.D., U. Fla., 1949. Bar: Fla. 1949, Md. 1962. Practiced in Annapolis Md., 1962; clk. Anne Arundel County Circuit Ct., 1966-72; mem. 93d-99th Congresses from 4th Dist. of Md., 1973-86; mem. armed services com.; vice chmn. Office Tech. Assessment, 1977; chmn. Republican Study com., 1975-76; of counsel Smith, Somerville & Case, Balt., 1986-90; supr. elections Anne Arundel County, 1963-65; del. to Rep. Nat. Conv., 1968, 76, 80, 84, 88; mem. Pres.'s Commn. on Arms Control and Disarmament. Co-author: Case Against The Reckless Congress, 1976, Can You Afford This House, 1978. Recipient; Distinguished Alumna award U. Fla., 1975. Mem. Am., Md., Anne Arundel bar assns., Phi Kappa Phi, Phi Delta Delta. Presbyterian (elder 1959). Home: 151 Boone Trail Severna Park MD 21146

HOLT, PAMELA GAIL, arts commission administrator; b. Balt., Jan. 26, 1958; d. Edward Eugene and Charlotte (Coleman) H. MusB, Howard U., 1979; MA, Am. U., 1983; postgrad., U. Minn., 1988, Georgetown U., 1989. Comml. property analyst Aetna Casualty and Surety Co. Inc., Balt., 1979-81; cons. Office Mayor's Advisor for Cultural Affairs, Washington, 1982-83; program coord., legis. grants officer D.C. Commn. on Arts, Washington, 1984-87, dep. dir., 1987—; cons. Holt and Assocs., Washington, 1981—; site evaluator expansion arts program Nat. Endowment for Arts, Washington, 1990. Mem. planning com. Charter Day, Howard U., Washington, 1984-89; rescue aide ARC, Washington; mem. Coalition 100 Black Women, Washington, 1987-90; mem. arts dist. team D.C. Downtown Partnership, 1989-90; bd. rep. Com. To Promote Washington, 1987-90. Recipient Outstanding Performance award Govt. of D.C., 1988; scholar Howard U., 1975-78. Mem. Assn. Am. Cultures (vice chmn. 1989-90), Alpha Kappa Alpha (Svc. and Acad. Achievement award 1979). Home: 810 Tewkesbury Pl NW Washington DC 20012

HOLTE, DEBRA LEAH, investment advisory firm executive, chartered finanical anaylst; b. Madison, Wis., July 16, 1952; d. Daniel Kennseth and Marian Anne (Stemme) Reitan; m. Peter A. Holte, Apr. 28, 1973 (div. 1981). BA, Concordia Coll., Moorhead, Minn., 1973. Tchr. Grove City (Minn.) Pub. Schs., 1973-74; with pub. relations dept. Mont. Dakota Utilities, Bismarck, N.D., 1974-77; rep. Abbot Labs., Mpls., 1977-79; capital markets specialist 1st Bank Mpls., 1981-83; v.p. Allison-Williams Co., Mpls., 1983-86, Nelson, Benson & Zellmer, Denver, 1986-90; exec. v.p. Wagner & Hamil, Denver, 1990—; bd. dirs., v.p., treas., chairperson fin. com. Denver Children's Home, 1987—. Active Denver Jr. League, Western Pension Com., 1987—; bd. dirs. Denver Children's Home, 1987—, v.p., treas., chairperson fin. com.; bd. dirs. Minn. Vocat. Edn., Mpls., 1984-86. Mem. Fin. Analysts Fedn., Denver Soc. Security Analysts (bd. dirs., chairperson ethics and bylaws com. 1987, chairperson edn. com. 1988, chairperson membership com. 1989), Colo. Ballet (bd. dirs.). Republican. Lutheran. Office: Wagner & Hamil 410 17th St Ste 840 Denver CO 80202

HOLTEN, VIRGINIA LOIS ZEWE, college administrator; b. McKeesport, Pa., Mar. 29, 1938; d. Albert J. and Virginia Kathryn (Minnick) Zewe; m. Darold Duane Holten, Dec. 29, 1962; 1 child, Peggy. B.A., Carlow Coll., 1960; M.S., U. N.D., 1962, Ph.D., 1965; diploma U. Glasgow, Scotland, 1975. Researcher Oak Ridge Nat. Lab., 1965-67; assoc. prof. Riverside City Coll., Calif., 1968-78; dean natural sci., 1978-82; v.p. instrn. Victor Valley Coll., Victorville, Calif., 1982-86; supt., pres. Lassen Coll., 1986—. Contbr. articles to profl. jours. Am. Cancer Soc. postdoctoral fellow, Oak Ridge, 1965-67; named Outstanding Student, Brit. Inst. Mgmt., Glasgow, 1975. Mem. AAUW, Lassen County C. of C., Assn. Calif. Community Coll. Adminstrs., Soroptomists. Home: 760 Washu Ln Susanville CA 96130 Office: Lassen Coll P O Box 3000 Susanville CA 96130

HOLTON, ANNE LYSBETH, magazine publisher; b. Pitts., June 10, 1950; d. James Leo and Ruth Anna (Homan) H. BS in Psychology, U. Bridgeport, 1972; postgrad. NYU. Legis. aide to Congressman Henry Helstoski of N.J., 1973-74; asst. to advt. dir. New Times Mag., N.Y.C., 1974-75, sales rep., 1975; advt. sales rep. Rolling Stone mag., N.Y.C., 1975-77; advt. sales rep. Ms. mag., N.Y.C., 1977-78, N.Y. adv. mgr., 1978-79, nat. advt. mgr., 1979, advt. dir., 1979-82; mktg. dir. Gentlemen's Quar. Mag., 1982-85; v.p., advt. dir. Parade Mag., 1985-87; pub., US Mag., 1987—. Mem. Mag. Pubs. Assn., Nat. Women's Polit. Party. Republican. Office: US Magazine 1 Dag Hammarskjold Plaza 10th Floor New York NY 10017

HOLTON, SUSAN A., educator; b. Columbus, Ohio, Apr. 24, 1948; d. William C. and Mary (Floyd) H.; 1 child, Christopher L. Holton-Jablonski. BS, Miami U., Oxford, Ohio, 1970; MA, Case Western Res. U., 1973, PhD, 1976. Dir. Gabriel Ames Assocs., Framingham, Mass., 1975—; asst. prof. Bridgewater (Mass.) State Coll., 1984-88, dept. chair., assoc. prof., 1988—; bd. dirs. Profl. Orgn. in Higher Edn.; coord. Mass. Faculty Devel. Consortium, 1988—; chair., nominating com. Unitarian Universalis Assn., Boston, 1987—. Author: The Mad Madonna, 1987, Under the Influence of Life; contbr. articles to profl. jours. Dir. Ch. the Larger Fellowship, Boston, 1987—; founder FOCUS on Gifted and Talented, Framingham, Mass. Mem. Speech Communication Assn., Boston Area Assn. Psychol. Type (founder), N.E. Assn. Psychol. Type, AAUW, Ea. Communications Assn., Communications Assn. Mass., Alban Inst., AAUP, Am. Assn. for Higher Edn. Office: Bridgewater State Coll Rondileau Campus Ctr Bridgewater MA 02324

HOLTSCLAW, GWENDOLYN PHEAGIN, academic administrator; b. Franklin, N.C., July 15, 1945; d. James Thomas and Martha (Elliott) P.; m. Timothy Allen Holtsclaw, May 20, 1989; children: James Mason, Melissa Scott. BA, Meth. Coll., Fayetteville, N.C., 1968. Cert. tchr., N.C. Tchr. journalism Cumberland County Schs., Fayetteville, 1968-77; founder, dir. East Coast Cheerleading Camp, Fayetteville, 1970-88; dir. publs. Meth. Coll., Fayetteville, 1977-85, cheerleading and dance coach, 1979-88, dir. spl. projects, 1985-88, pres. Gwynco products, 1986-88; pres. Internat. Cheer Ltd., Inc., Fayetteville, 1988—; cons. N.C. Dept. Pub. Instrn., Raleigh, 1985—; exec. coord. Nat. Cheerleading Coaches' Confs., Fayetteville, 1986—. Editor: (newsletter) N.C. AE Assn. Educators Polit. Action Com. Edn., 1973-76; columnist N.C. Scholastic Sports mag.; contbr. articles to profl. jours. Named Outstanding Young Women of Am., 1975, Tchr. of Yr., Pine Forest High Sch., Fayetteville, 1976. Mem. Nat. Assn. Dance/Exercise Instrs., Nat. Assn. Cheerleading Coaches (mem. planning bd. 1986-88), N.C. Cheerleading Coaches Assn. (bd. dirs. 1985-88), Meth. Coll. Alumni Assn. (sec. 1970-72, pres. 1973-76, bd. dirs. 1976-80, Alumnus of Yr. 1977), Alpha Xi Delta. Democrat. Episcopalian. Home: 444 Morningside Dr Fayetteville NC 28311 Office: Internat Cheer LTD Inc 5847 Ramsey St Fayetteville NC 28311

HOLTZ, GAIL RAMAGNANO PINTO, medical association administrator; b. Bklyn., Sept. 20, 1947; d. Anthony Ramagnano and Helen Griebel; m. Nicholas Pinto, Oct. 13; m. Alex Holtz, Nov. 30, 1985; children: Lisa, James, Rebecca, Melissa. AAS, Ulster County Community Coll., Stone Ridge, N.Y., 1976; BS in Nursing, SUNY Regents Coll., Albany, 1980; MS in Nursing, SUNY Regents Coll., 1985; postgrad., Adelphi U. Charge nurse, team leader Mountainside Hosp., Montclair, N.J., 1977-79; nursing supr. Sands Point Skilled Nursing Facility, Port Wash., N.Y., 1979; clinician, staff nurse State U. Hosp., Stony Brook, N.Y., 1979-81; asst. dir. nursing Cobble Hill (SNF), Bklyn., 1981-83; chairperson New Eng. Inst. Technol., Fla., 1984; asst. prof. nursing Elizabeth Seton Coll., Yonkers, N.Y., 1985-87; tchr. Lewis Wislon Tech. Ctr., Northport, N.Y., 1985-87; dir. nursing svcs. Surfside Nursing Home, Far Rockaway, N.Y., 1987-88; adminstrv. nursing supr. Coll. Medicine dept. nursing Albert Einstein Hosp., 1988—; pvt. practice, 1988—. Home: 299 Bow Dr Hauppauge NY 11788

HOLTZAPFEL, PATRICIA KELLY, health facility executive; b. Madison, Wis., Jan. 29, 1948; d. Raymond Michael and Laura Margaret (Stegner) Kelly; m. Robert Adrian Bunker, Oct. 4, 1975 (div. June 1979); children: Donald, Theresa, Nicole, Douglas; m. Raymond Paul Holtzapfel, Mar. 12, 1983; children: David, Richard. RN; cert. pub. health nurse. Staff nurse Madison Gen. Hosp., 1970-72; bloodmobile staff nurse ARC, Madison, 1972-73; pub. health nurse Dane County Pub. Health Dept., Madison, 1973-75; field health nurse CIGNA Health Plan, Phoenix, 1975-84; dir. nursing Olsten Health Care, Phoenix, 1984-85; mgr. bus. Holtzapfel Phys. Therapy and Pain Control Clinic, Phoenix, 1985-89, bus. cons., 1989—; supr. CIGNA Healthplan Ariz., Phoenix, 1989—. Bd. dirs. Deer Valley Vocat. Arts Adv. Coun., Phoenix, 1986-89. Mem. The Exec. Female Assn., Ariz. Networking Council. Office: Holtzapfel Phys Therapy and Pain Control Clinic 4025 W Bell Rd Ste #2 Phoenix AZ 85023

HOLTZCLAW, DIANE SMITH, educator; b. Buffalo, May 26, 1936; d. John Nelson and Beatrice M. (Salisbury) Smith; m. John Victor Holtzclaw, June 27, 1959; children: Kathryn Diane, John Bryan. BS in Edn. magna cum laude, SUNY, Brockport, 1957, MS with honors, 1961; postgrad., SUNY, 1960-65, Canisus Coll., 1979, Nazareth Coll., 1981-82. Tchr. Greece Cen. Sch., Rochester, N.Y., 1957-60; supr. SUNY, Brockport, 1960-64, assoc. prof. edn., 1960-64; dir. Early Childhood Ctr., Fairport, N.Y., 1968-80; tchr. Fairport Cen. Schs., 1971—; cons. in field. Ch. music dir., Rochester, N.Y., 1983—; pres. bd. dirs. Downtown Day Care Ctr., Rochester, 1974-83; mem. exec. bd. Rochester Theatre Organ Soc., 1988—. Mem. Fairport Edn. Assn. (exec. bd. 1982-83, del. 1983), N.Y. State United Tchrs., AAUW (exec. bd. 1973-74, 77-79, 83-84, pres. Fairport br. 1971-73), Internat. Platform Assn., Kappa Delta Pi. Home: 1455 Ayrault Rd Fairport NY 14450 Office: Fairport Cen Schs 38 W Church St Fairport NY 14450

HOLTZER, MARILYN EMERSON, physical chemist, educator; b. Belleville, Ill., July 22, 1938; d. Robert August and Ethel Ruth (Hodges) Emerson; m. Alfred Melvin Holtzer, June 24, 1969; children: Rachel, Dan. AB in Math., Washington U., St. Louis, 1960, AM in Chemistry, 1963, PhD in Chemistry, 1966. Instr. Washington U., 1972-80, rsch. asst. prof., 1990—; asst. prof. Webster U., Webster Groves, Mo., 1967-69; instr. John Burroughs Sch., St. Louis, 1969-70; vis. asst. prof. U. Mo., St. Louis, 1971-72. Contbr. articles to profl. jours.; exhibited fiber art in various shows including St. Louis Artist Guild, 1984. Shell fellow, 1964; recipient Du Pont Rsch. award, 1963. Mem. Biophys. Soc., Protein Soc., St. Louis Weavers' Guild (sec., treas., exhibit chmn.), St. Louis Artists' Guild (Arachne prize 1977, 79, Crawford prize 1980, 83), Handweavers' Guild Am., Midwest Weavers' Conf. Office: Washington U Dept Chemistry 1134 One Brookings Dr Saint Louis MO 63130

HOLTZMAN, ELIZABETH, lawyer, municipal official; b. Bklyn., Aug. 11, 1941; d. Sidney and Filia Holtzman. A.B. magna cum laude, Radcliffe Coll., 1962; J.D., Harvard U., 1965; L.D.S., Regis Coll., 1975, Skidmore Coll., 1980, Simmons Coll., 1981, Smith Coll., 1982. Bar: N.Y. Assoc. Wachtell, Lipton, Rosen, Kalz & Kern, N.Y.C., 1965-67; asst. to mayor N.Y.C., 1968-69; assoc. Paul, Weiss, Rifkind, Wharton & Garrison, 1970-72; mem. 93d-96th Congresses from 16th dist., N.Y.; vis. prof. Law Sch. and Grad. Sch. Pub. Adminstrn. NYU, 1981; dist. atty. Kings County, Bklyn., 1982-89; comptr. City of N.Y., 1990—. N.Y. State Dem. committeewoman, 1970-72; del. Dem. Nat. Conv., 1972; mem. Select Commn. Immigration Policy, 1979-80; mem. Pres.'s Nat. Commn. on U.S. Observance Internat. Women's Yr.; Dem. nominee U.S. Senate, 1980; mem. Am. Jewish Commn. Holocaust; bd. overseers Harvard U., 1976-82; mem. Helsinki Watch Com., 1981—. Lawyers Com. Internat. Human Rights, 1981-88. Recipient Nat. Coun. Jewish Women's Faith and Humanity award, YWCA Elizabeth Cutter Morrow award, Maccabean award N.Y. Bd. Rabbis, Alumni recognition award Radcliffe Coll. Alumnae Assn., 1973, N.J. and L.A. ACLU awards for contbns. to def. of Constn. and preservation of civil liberties, 1981, Athena award N.Y.C. Commn. on Status of Women, 1985, Woman of Yr. award N.Y. League Bus. and Profl. Women, 1985, Jan Korzak award 5th Ann. Kent State Holocaust Conf., 1986, Outstanding and Meritorious Svc. award Jewish War Vets. of U.S., 1986, Award of Remembrance Warsaw Ghetto Resistance Orgn., 1987, Gates of Freedom award State of Israel Bonds, 1987, Award of Honor United Jewish Appeal, 1988. Fellow N.Y. Inst. Humanities; mem. Nat. Women's Polit. Caucus (Outstanding Svc. award 1987), Bar Assn. of City of N.Y., Phi Beta Kappa. Office: 1 Centre St New York NY 10007

HOLUM-HARDEGEN, LAURA LYNN, budget analyst; b. St. Paul, May 31, 1956; d. Donald Loyd and Helen Edna (McQuiston) Holum; m. Neil J. Hardegen, July 17, 1977. BA, U. Md., 1978; MS, Gallaudet U., 1980. Program analyst, audiologist, mgmt. analyst Walter Reed Army Med. Ctr., Washington, 1981-87, mgmt. analyst, 1985-87; program analyst U.S. Mil. Dist. of Washington (D.C.), 1987-89; budget analyst Naval Data Automation Command, Washington, 1989-90, Office of Sec., Dept. of Commerce, Washington, 1990—. Contbr. articles to profl. jours. Elizabeth E. Benson scholar Gallaudet U. Mem. Am. Soc. Mil. Comptrollers, NAFE, U.S. Dressage Fedn., Phi Beta Kappa, Phi Kappa Phi. Home: 241 Carriage Ln Huntingtown MD 20639

HOLZAPFEL, CHRISTINA MARIE, biologist; b. Balt., Jan. 24, 1942; d. Carl Martin and Ruby (Carlson) Holzapfel; m. William Emmons Bradshaw, May 10, 1971; 1 child, Pilar Antonia Bradshaw. BA, Goucher Coll., 1964; MS, U. Mich., 1968, PhD, 1970; postdoctoral fellow, Harvard U., 1970-71. Grad. research fellow U. Mich., Ann Arbor, 1964-70, lectr., 1970; research asst. Canary Islands, Spain, 1965-66; research fellow Harvard U., Cambridge, Mass., 1970-71; research assoc. U. Oreg., Eugene, 1971—, Tall Timbers Research Sta., Tallahassee, 1977-78, Imperial Coll., Silwood Park, Ascot, U.K., 1986. Contbr. articles to profl. jours. Bd. dirs. Eugene City Planning Com., 1980-81, Eugene Youth Symphony, 1980-84. Fellow Woods Hole Marine Biol. Labs., 1963. Mem. Ecol. Soc. Am., Soc. for Study of Evolution, Sigma Xi. Lutheran. Office: U Oreg Dept Biology Eugene OR 97403

HOLZBERGER, SHEILA MARIE, marketing consultant; b. Davenport, Iowa, Nov. 29, 1960; d. Paul James and Dorothy Ann (Barto) O'Donnell; m. Charles Holzberger, Feb. 12, 1958; 1 child, Jessica Marie. BA In English, U. Md., 1982, MA in Instructional Tech., 1989. Assoc. editor Amecom div. Litton Industries, College Park, Md., 1982-83, tech. editor Amecom div., 1983; text writer Indsl. Tng. Corp., Herndon, Va., 1983-84, instructional technologist, 1984-85, mgr. communications, 1985-87; dir. communications Gen. Bus. Svcs., Germantown, Md., 1987-88; sr. mktg. mgr. Indsl. Tng. Corp., Herndon, Va., 1988-89; pvt. practice mktg. cons., 1989—. Editor: 1988 Tax Tips, 1987; staff writer Diversions mag., Frederick, Md., 1987—; contbr. articles to profl. jours. Phi Beta Kappa. Mem. NAFE, Phi Beta Kappa. Roman Catholic. Home: 229 Diamond Dr Walkersville MD 21793

HOLZENDORF, BETTY SMITH, state representative; b. Jacksonville, Fla., Apr. 5, 1939; d. Fannie Holmes; m. King Holzendorf II; children: Kim, King III, Kevin, Kessler. BS in Biology, Edward Waters Coll., Jacksonville, 1965; MS in Biochemistry, Atlanta U., 1971; MEd, U. Fla., 1973. Tchr. Duval County Sch. Bd., Jacksonville, 1965-70; asst. prof. Edward Waters Coll., Jacksonville, 1971-72, dir. rsch., 1972-74, dir. fin. aid, 1974-75; with affirmative action com. City of Jacksonville, 1975-78; adminstrv. aide Mayor's Office, Jacksonville, 1979-87; field rep. Dept. Transp., Jacksonville, 1987-88; state rep. State of Fla., Jacksonville, 1988—. Recipient Outstanding Educator award, 1972. Mem. Nat. Coun. Negro Women (life), Nat. Conf. Black State Legis., Fla. Coun. Black State Legis., Alpha Kappa Alpha (life). Democrat. Mem. African Meth. Episcopal Ch. Office: 5045 Soutel Dr #60 Jacksonville FL 32208

HOMAN, MARY CAROLYN, family physician; b. Mpls., Jan. 30, 1958; d. Charles Joseph and Frances (Sinnaeve) H. BA, Coll. of St. Catherine, St. Paul, 1980; MD, U. Chgo., 1985. Diplomate Am. Bd. Family Practice. Researcher 3M Co., St. Paul, 1980-81; resident in family practice St. Paul-Ramsey Med. Ctr., 1985-88, assoc. staff emergency room, 1987-90; pvt. practice Mpls., 1988—; rsch. in cardiology U. Minn., Mpls., 1987—. Instr. water safety, com. mem. ARC, St. Paul, 1980-85. Jaycees Coll. Ct. Honors scholar, 1980. Mem. Am. Acad. Family Practice, Hennepin County Med. Soc., Phi Beta Kappa, Iota Sigma Pi. Roman Catholic. Home: 4078 Beffin Bay N Eagan MN 55403 Office: Family Med Clinic 3809 42d Ave S Minneapolis MN 55406

HOMAYSSI, RUBY LEE, small business owner; b. Jan. 14, 1945; d. Raymond and Elmira (Carter) K. BS in Food & Nutrition, So. U., Baton Rouge, 1967; MA, Pepperdine U., 1981; A.Hosp. Dietetics, Tuskegee Inst., Ala., 1969. Staff dietitian Nat. Naval Med. Ctr., Bethesda, Md., 1969-70; chief clin. nutrition and dietitian dept. Naval Hosp. Chelsea, Mass., 1970-74; chief dietitian, asst. food mgmt. officer Naval Submarine Med. Ctr., Groton, Conn., 1974-78; chief clin. nutrition Naval Hosp. Portsmouth, Va., 1978-83; chief clin. nutrition and dietetics Naval Hosp. Orlando, Fla., 1983-88; pres. Elmira's P.A.N.T.R.Y., Inc., Orlando, 1988—; cons. in field. Contbr. articles to profl. jours. Dir. Vol. Ctr. of Seminole County; 3rd v.p. Civic Theatre of Cen. Fla., Orlando, 1989, 2d v.p. 1990—; 1st v.p. Orlad Opera Co., 1987-88; bd. dirs. Maitland Arts Coun.; pub. edn. chmn. Am. Cancer Soc., Orlando,, 1987-90; prodn. chmn. March of Dimes, 1988—; bd. dirs. HOSPIC; mem. community advisors bd. TV-24; chmn. Seminole Chamber-Community Rels., Symphony Orch. Assocs. Bd., 1991 Symphony Ball. Named Woman of the Yr., Am. Bus. Women's Assn., 1987, Women of Achievement in Arts Downtown Exec. Women's Coun., 1989; recipient Angle award, 1989. Mem. Am. Dietetic Assn., Fla. Dietetic Assn., AAUW, Am. Bus. Women's Assn. (pres. 1987), Nat. Assn. Female Execs., Girl Friends Club, Torch Club. Republican. Baptist. Home: 1409 Pylewood St Fern Park FL 32730

HOMBS, MARGARET MAVOURNEEN, teacher; b. Evanston, Ill., May 17, 1934; d. Pat and Eloise (Taylor) O'Brien; m. Max David Garten, June 27, 1957 (div. 1968); m. John Hayden Hombs, Dec. 7, 1969 (div. 1990); children: Eric, Lisa, Kurt; stepchildren: Stacy, Karin. BA in Music, Marymount Coll., 1955; MA in Edn., Loyola U., Westchester, Calif., 1956; postgrad. in library sci., Calif. State U., Los Angeles, 1984. Tchr. Baldwin (Calif.) Park Sch. Dist., 1956-57, Garden Grove (Calif.) Union Sch. Dist., 1961-74; tchr. Morongo Union Sch. Dist., Morongo Basin, Calif., 1974—, tchr. dist. curriculum and instruction, 1979—; tchr. county lang. arts and county media Morongo Union Sch. Dist., Morongo Basin, 1981-84; secondary chair Morongo Union Sch. Dist., Morongo Basin, Calif., 1985-86; mentor tchr., developer dist. curriculum Morongo Union Sch. Dist., Morongo Basin, 1986-89; coord. Writing Celebration, San Bernardino, Calif., 1979-81, 1986-88; com. mem. Garden Grove Union Sch. Dist., 1964-70; CJSF advisor Garden Grove and Morongo Sch. dists., 1960—; chair site dept., 1964-69, 79-81, 87-88, libr., 1981-84; cons. Prentice-Hall, 1989—. Contbr. numerous articles to profl. jours.; editor English textbook, 1965. Soloist, choir dir., St. Christopher's Cath. Ch., Joshua Tree, Calif., 1978—, dir., soloist Hi Desert Cultural Ctr., 1978—; actress, stage mgr., Playhous Guild, Joshua Tree, 1978—. Named Best Director H. Desert Playhouse Guild, Joshua Tree. Mem. Nat. Coun. Tchrs. of English, Libr. Media Specialists, Morongo Tchrs. Assn., Calif. Media Libr. Educators Assn., Calif. Tchrs. Assn., NEA, Assn. Supervision and Curriculum Development, 4-H Club (leader 1973-78), Alpha Mu Gamma. Republican. Home: PO Box 158 Joshua Tree CA 92252 Office: La Contenta Jr High Sch PO Box 1779 Yucca Valley CA 92252

HOMER, AGNES MABEL NARNEY, teacher; b. Cleve., Ohio, Oct. 18, 1946; d. Lilo Edward and Anna Mary (Burke) N.; m. Robert Dewaine, Sept. 22, 1979. BS, Bowling Green St. U., Ohio, 1970. Profl. Cert. Spl. Edn., Social Studies, Tchr. Legal sec. Cuyahoga County Prosecutor, Cleve., 1964-65; customer svc. Ohio Bell Telephone, Cleve., 1968; tchr. Cleve. Pub. Schs., 1970-. Mem. Cleve. Tchrs. Union, Weight Watchers Club. Democrat. Roman Catholic. Home: 17610 Valley View Ave Cleveland OH 44135

HOMER, TAMARA KUKRYCKA, advertising executive; b. Warsaw, Poland, Feb. 23, 1932; came to U.S., 1949, naturalized, 1953; d. Basil and Alexandra (Masiuk) Kukrycka; m. Edward John Homer, Sept. 6, 1954. BA, Hunter Coll., 1954; postgrad. New Sch. for Social Sci., 1956-58. Pres. Sunwear, Inc., N.Y.C., 1964-66; exec. v.p. Allerton, Berman & Dean, N.Y.C., 1966-73; founder, pres. Homer & Durham Advt., Ltd., N.Y.C., 1973—. Author travel guides for European countries. Trustee New Eyes for the Needy, Short Hills, N.J., 1982—; bd. dirs. Nat. Assn. to Prevent Blindness, March of Dimes, N.Y.C., 1983—. The Network Mus. Recipient Matrix award Women Execs. in Communication, 1983, Extraordinary Service to Nation's Tourism, Republic of Ireland, 1976, Leadership award March of Dimes, 1987; named to Hall of Fame, Hunter Coll., 1983. Mem. Advt. Women of N.Y. (bd. dirs.; pres. 1983-85), Women Execs. in Pub. Relations, Fin. Women's Assn. N.Y., Fashion Group, Am. Advt. Fedn. (com. chmn. 1985—), Fin. Women's Assn. N.Y. Republican. Ukrainian Orthodox. Avocations: painting; tennis; fresh water fishing. Home: 2 Joanna Way Short Hills NJ 07078 Office: Homer & Durham Advt Ltd 115 Fifth Ave New York NY 10003

HOMESTEAD, SUSAN, psychotherapist; b. Bklyn., Sept. 20, 1937; d. Cy Simon and Katherine (Haas) Eichelbaum; m. Robert Bruce Randall, 1956 (div. 1960); 1 child, Bruce David; m. George Gilbert Zanetti, Dec. 13, 1962 (div. 1972); m. Ronald Eric Homestead, Jan. 16, 1973 (div. 1980). BA, U. Miami-Fla., 1960; MSW, Tulane U., 1967. Lic. clin. social worker, Va., Calif. Pvt. practice, cons., Richmond, Va., 1971—; psychotherapist, cons. Family and Children's Svcs., Richmond, 1981—, Richmond Pain Clinic, 1983-84; cons. Health Internat. Va., P.C., Lynchburg, 1984-86, Santa Clara DSS, Calif., 1986-88, Franklin St. Psychotherapy & Edn. Ctr, Santa Clara, 1988-90; pvt. practice, Santa Clara, 1973-75, 88—; co-dir. asthma program Va. Lung Assn., Richmond, 1975-79, Loma Prieta Regional Ctr.; chief clin. social worker Med. Coll. Va., Va. Commonwealth U., 1974-79; field supr. 1980 Census, 1981-87. Contbr. articles to profl. jours. Active Peninsula Children's Ctr., Morgan Ctr., Coun. for Community Action Planning, Community Assn. for Retarded, Comprehensive Health Planning Assn. Santa Clara, Mental Health Commn., Children and Adolescent Target Group Calif., Women's Com. Richmond Symphony, Va. Mus. Theatre, mem. fin. com. Robb for Gov.; mem. adv. com. Lung Assn.; mem. steering com. Am. Cancer Soc. Va. div. Epilepsy Found., Am. Heart Assn., Cen. Va. Guild for Infant Survival. Mem. Va. Soc. Clin. Social Work, Inc. (charter mem., sec. 1975-78), Nat. Assn. Social Workers, Soc. for Psychoanalytic Psychotherapy, Am. Acad. Psychotherapists, Internat. Soc. for the Study of Personality and Dissociation, Acad. Cert. Social Workers, Am. Assn. Psychiatric Svcs. for Children, Soc. Study Multiple Personality and Dissociation. Jewish. Home: 950 Berry Ave Los Altos CA 94024

HOMMELL, ADRIENNE ELIZABETH, educator; b. Englewood, N.J., Aug. 4, 1934; d. Adrien B. and Adele Jessie (Thomass) H. BA, Tusculum Coll., 1956. Cert. elem. tchr., N.J. Media specialist Eastampton Twp. Elem. Sch., Mt. Holly, N.J., 1968—. Vice-chair person Eastampton Twp. Zoning Bd. Adjustment, 1981—. Mem. AAUW, N.J. Edn. Assn., NEA, Eastampton Twp. Edn. Assn. Home: 27D Hunters Cir Mount Holly NJ 08060

HOMRICH-HENDERSON, JEAN MARIE, marketing executive; b. Kalamazoo, May 12, 1964; d. James George and Mary Ann (Perlick) Homrich; m. Terral Robert Henderson, Feb. 1, 1986; 1 stepchild, Julie. Student, Western Mich. U., 1982-83, Kalamazoo Valley Community Coll., 1984. Adminstrv. asst. Enterprise Food Svcs., Inc., Kalamazoo, 1982-84, mktg. asst., 1984-86, dir. mktg., 1986-89, v.p., 1989—, mktg. cons., 1990—. Editor newsletter the Press! Press!, 1990. Recruiter CROP Walk 90, Church World Svc., Kalamazoo, 1990; chmn. vendor com. YMCA Olympics, Kalamazoo, 1989. Mem. Women In Communications. Office: Enterprise Food Svcs Inc 520 Picadilly Rd Kalamazoo MI 49007

HONADLE, BETH WALTER, economist; b. Elmira, N.Y., Mar. 9, 1954; d. T. John and Nancy E. (Fink) Walter; m. George Holmes Honadle, July 30, 1977. BA in Polit. Sci., Syracuse (N.Y.) U., 1975, MPA, 1976, MA in Econs., 1977, PhD in Pub. Adminstrn., 1979. Manuscript and rsch. asst. Maxwell tng. and devel. programs Syracuse U., 1976, adminstrv. asst. pub. adminstrn. dept., 1976-77, rsch. asst. Met. studies program, 1977-79; instr. in pub. adminstrn. Onondaga Community Coll., Syracuse, 1978; economist econ. rsch. svc. div. USDA, 1979-83; leader orgn. and delivery local svcs. project USDA, Washington, 1983-85, nat. program leader for econ. devel., 1985—; adj. prof. pub. adminstrn. Am. U., 1986-87. Author: Public Administration and Public Employee Compensation: A Guide to the Literature, 1983, Prospectives on Management Capacity Building, 1986; contbr. articles to profl. jours.; author chpts. in books. Mem. Community Devel. Soc. (rsch. com. 1983-84, membership com. 1985-88, bd. dirs., chair community econ. devel. sect. 1987-88, nominating com., 1988—), Am. Soc. for Pub. Adminstrn. (chair sect. on intergovtl. adminstrn. and mgmt. 1982-83, bd. dirs. nat. chpt. 1983-86, ann. meeting chair 1984, 85, co-chair monthly luncheons 1985-86, selection com. for James Webb award 1987, Spl. Recognition award 1985), Syracuse U. Alumni Assn. (bd. dirs. Washington chpt. 1983-84). Home: Hidden Creek Farm 39844 Poor Farm Rd North Branch MN 55056 Office: Univ of Minnesota 240 F Coffey Hall 1420 Eckles Ave Saint Paul MN 55108

HONEYCHECK, LINDA JEAN, lawyer; b. Passaic, N.J., Dec. 6, 1949; d. Julius E. and Jeanette C. (Pypec) Kinsky. BS magna cum laude, Fairleigh Dickinson U., 1981; JD, Seton Hall U., 1985. Bar: N.J., U.S. Dist. Ct. N.J. With Hoffmann-La Roche Inc., Nutley, N.J., 1967—, mgr. drug reg. aff., 1984-86, atty., 1986-88; gen. atty. Hoffmann-La Roche Inc., Nutley, 1988—; bd. dirs. Good Govt. Com. Hoffmann-La Roche Inc., Nutley, 1986—. Bd. dirs. Women's Polit. Action Com. of N.J., 1987—. Recipient Tribute to Women and Industry, YWCA of Ridgewood, 1989. Mem. ABA, N.J. Bar Assn., Essex County Bar Assn. Home: 2 Ann St S-217 Clifton NJ 07013 Office: Hoffmann-La Roche Inc 340 Kingsland St Nutley NJ 07110

HONEYCHURCH, DOROTHY ANNE, retired educator; b. Arnegard, N.D., Apr. 1, 1925; d. Olaf and Anna (Stenehjem) Drovdal; m. Fred A. Honeychurch, Dec. 27, 1950; children: Sandra, J. Robert, Susan Honeychurch Stephens. BS in Edn., St. Olaf Coll., 1946; MEd, Western Mont. Coll., 1969, postgrad., 1973; postgrad., Mont. State U. Tchr. sci. and home econs. Plentywood (Mont.) High Sch., 1947-48; tchr. home econs. Poplar (Mont.) High Sch., 1948-50, Missoula County High Sch., Missoula, Mont, 1950-51, Butte (Mont.) High Sch., 1953; tchr. home econs. East Jr. High Sch., Butte, 1967-79, dean girls, 1979-83; ret., 1983; tchr. home econs. Libby (Mont.) High Sch., 1989; owner, operator Butte Floral Shop, 1951-77. Treas. Butte Symphony, 1985—; mem. coun. Episcopal Diocese of Mont., Helena, 1987—; bd. dirs. Big Bros. and Sisters, Butte, 1988—. Mem. AAUW, Am. Assn. Ret. Persons, Butte Jr. League, Butte Exec. Club (treas. 1988—), P.E.O. (pres. Butte 1958), Daus. Norway (nat. pres. 1960-62), Rotana (pres. Butte 1960), Alpha Delta Kappa (pres. Butte 1975). Republican.

HONG BAILAR, THERESA YUMEE, marketing professional, freelance journalist; b. Seoul, Republic of Korea, Feb. 19, 1964; came to U.S., 1969; d. Sung Chull and Chung Ok (Lee) Hong; m. Gregor Scott Bailar, Apr. 4, 1987. BA, Dartmouth Coll., 1986. Copywriter Coakley Heagerty, Santa Clara, Calif., 1986-87, Bernard Hodes Advt., Palo Alto, Calif., 1987-88; freelance journalist Palo Alto, 1986—; mktg. copywriter Intuit, Palo Alto, 1988, mktg. communications mgr., 1989—. Contbr. numerous articles to nat. and internat. publs.; copywriter pub. svc. announcement United Way (Joey award 1988, Addy award 1989). Publicist, cons. Asian Heritage Coun., Mountain View, Calif., 1988; vol. Korean Cultural Svcs. Ctr., San Francisco, 1988. Humanities predoctoral fellow U. Calif., Santa Cruz, 1989—. Mem. Nat. Asian Am. Telecommunications Com., Asian Am. Journalists Assn.

HONNER, B. JOAN, advertising executive; b. N.Y.C., Oct. 23, 1952; d. William John and Mary Patricia (Edwards) H.; m. Donald J. Sutherland, Oct. 3, 1987; 1 child, Chelsea Lauren. Student, Endicott Coll., 1970-71. Art dir. Kerrigan Studio, Darien, Conn., 1971-73, Foote Cone and Belding, Phoenix, 1973-77; sr. art dir. Foote Cone and Belding, Chgo., 1977-81; v.p., assoc. creative dir. J. Walter Thompson, Chgo., 1982-86; v.p., exec. art dir. BBDO Chgo., 1986—; cons. J. Walter Thompson, Toronto and San Francisco, 1983-84; owner Fla. Antiques, Geneva, Ill., 1986-89. Recipient 1st Place TV local campaign WGN 6th dist. ADDY, 1980, Best Internat. TV campiagn Pepsi Clio, 1985. Roman Catholic. Home: 1969 N Lincoln Ave Chicago IL 60614

HONNOLD, KATHRYN S., executive secretary; b. Pataska, Ohio, Nov. 10, 1936; d. Harold S. and Stella E. (Slack) Williams; m. Robert I. Honnold, Aug. 18, 1956; children: Jayne, Robin. Student, Franklin U., N.Y. Sch. Modeling. Sales assoc. Realty World Bruce J. Baird Realty, Pataskala, Ohio; adminstrv. asst., office mgr., sec. Monsanto, Columbus, Ohio; coun. mem. Pataskala Village; exec. sec. Banc One Asset Mgmt., Columbus, Ohio. Mem. Pataskala Village Coun.; appointed mem. Licking County Sr. Citizen's Levy Adv. Bd., 1989; model for periodic fashion shows. Named Sec. of Yr., 1987. Mem. NAFE, Profl. Secs. Internat., Nat., State and County Real Estate Assocs.. Home: 295 Laurel Ln Pataskala OH 43062 Office: Bankone 100 E Broad St Columbus OH 43271-0163

HONORÉ, CARLA A., educator; b. Seattle, July 8, 1959; d. Raymond Michael and Annie Lila (Leonard) H. BA in Psychology, U. Calif., Irvine, 1981. Teaching credential, Calif. Tchr. L.A. Unified Sch. Dist., 1982—; lifeguard L.A. City Recreation and Parks, 1977—. Mem. Sub-Pacific Divers Club (treas. 1985-87). Office: 255 N Clarence St Los Angeles CA 90033

HONZIK, MARJORIE KNICKERBOCKER PYLES, psychologist emeritus, educator emeritus; b. Johannesburg, Transvaal, Republic South Africa, May 14, 1908; came to U.S., 1927; d. Jay Franklin and Maude Ethel (Knickerbocker) Pyles; m. Charles H. Honzik, Aug. 7, 1935 (dec. 1969); children: Eleanor, Elizabeth. BA, U. Calif., Berkeley, 1930, MA, 1933, PhD, 1936. Research asst. Inst. Child Welfare, Berkeley, 1932-65; lectr. child devel. Mills Coll., Oakland, Calif., 1952-60; lectr. psychology U. Calif., Berkeley, 1954-75, research psychologist Inst. Human Devel., 1965-75, research psychologist IV, lectr. emeritus, 1975—. Gen. Edn. Bd. fellow, Honolulu, 1938-40; NSF, Inst. Aging, Nat. Inst. Neurol. Diseases and Blindness, USPHS grantee, 1958-82. Fellow Am. Psychol. Assn. (G. Stanley Hall award 1983), Am. Assn. Advancement Sci.; mem. LWV. Democrat. Unitarian. Office: U Calif Inst Human Devel Berkeley CA 94720

HOOD, OLLIE RUTH, health facilities executive; b. San Francisco, Nov. 26, 1947; d. Rodger Brown and Lucile Brooks (Reid); m. McKinley Hood, Aug. 27, 1969 (div. 1987); children: Antoinette Brown, Kirk Stewart, Seancy Hood. BA, San Francisco State U., 1971. Asst. sec., v.p. Weyerhauser Mortgage Co., L.A., 1971-80; asst. supr. Plaza Mortgage Co., L.A., 1980-84; data entry supr. Western Standard Truck, L.A., 1984-85; mgr. Kaiser Hosp., San Francisco, 1985—. Patentee in field. Mem. Calif. Assn. Hosp. Admitting Mgrs., Nat. Assn. Hosp. Admitting Mgrs., NAFE, Kaiser Permanente Club (2d v.p. 1987), Nat. Assn. Women (v.p. 1989—). Jehovah's Witness. Home: 27766 Manon Ave #117 Hayward CA 94544

HOOD, VIRGINIA FORD (MRS. FREDERICK REDDING HOOD), civic worker; b. Vinita, Okla., May 1, 1905; d. William Thomas and Demmeria (Byrd) Ford; student Northeastern State Tchrs. Coll., 1920-21, 21-22; A.B., U. Okla., 1924; m. Frederick Redding Hood, Dec. 7, 1924; children—Frederick Redding, William Richard, Virginia Carol (Mrs. Kenneth Lee Pierce). Pres., Ladies Aux. Oklahoma County Med. Soc., 1937, co-chmn. Oklahoma City conv. So. Med. Conv., 1938, chmn. state conv. Okla. Med. Soc., 1950. Dist. chmn. Big One Drive, United Fund, Oklahoma City, 1953; chmn. Okla. Art Center Drive, 1957; capt. spl. gifts div. United Appeal, 1960-69, gen. chmn. Kappa Alpha Theta Found. Drive, 1964-65; chmn. Heritage Hills Hist. Home Tour, 1970-72; pres. Mothers Assn. U. Okla., 1957-58, Okla. Art League, 1960-61, Heritage Hills Aux., 1972-73; mem. Modern Classics, Oklahoma City; dir. YWCA, 1939-41, 66-72, met. bd. dirs., 1969-72, v.p., 1966-69, chmn. personnel com. 1966-68, 70-72, mem. dept. campus Christian life Okla. Assn. Christian Chs., 1964-68; pres. Heritage Hills Women's Com. of Hist. Preservation, 1973—. Mem. Kappa Alpha Theta (Okla. chmn. 1928-31, pres. Oklahoma City alumnae chpt. 1948-51, corp. bd. Alpha Omicron chpt. at U. Okla. 1954-57, 77-83, alumnae dist. pres. 1957-60, grand council 1960-64, v.p. service 1966-70, mem. bd. trustees found. 1966-70 Virginia Ford Hood Scholarship Fund created in her honor by Oklahoma City mems. 1984). Mem. Christian Ch. (deaconess bd. Oklahoma City 1954-57, 65-68, 72-75, 78-81, past chmn.; pres. Christian Women's fellowship Crown Heights Christian Ch., 1960-61, 61-62, tchr. bus. women's class, sponsor young married class, vice chmn. gen. bd. 1979-80, chmn. gen. bd. 1980-81, elder 1984-87). Club: Coterie Study (Oklahoma City).

HOOK, JULIA JANE, health organization administrator; b. Pasadena, Calif., Feb. 25, 1955; d. Ralph Adam and Kate Ellen (Beisel) King; m. Steven K. Hook, Aug. 31, 1974 (div. 1985); children: Jill Jane, Lisa Marie. BS, U. Laverne, 1989. Nutrition asst. San Dimas (Calif.) Community Hosp., 1972-73; admitting rep. Foothill Presbyn. Hosp., Glendora, Calif., 1973-75; EEG technician Pomona (Calif.) Valley Hosp., 1975-83; med. practice mgr. Office of Dr.'s M. Ali and R. Soudmand, San Dimas, 1983, Office Dr.'s David R. Rice and Richard L. Matthews, Pomona, 1983-87; coord. provider rels. pvt. practice plan CIGNA, San Bernandino, Calif., 1987-88; mgr. provider rels. corp. hdqtrs. health plan CIGNA, Glendale, Calif., 1988; mgr. med. affairs health plans CIGNA, Glendale, 1988-89; dir. managed care svcs., chief exec. officer St. Mary Med. Ctr., Physicians of Greater Long Beach, Calif., 1989—; med. practice mgmt. cons., 1983-88. Mem. Calif. Med. Assts. Assn. (rec. sec. 1987-88, chaplain 1985-86, chairperson reservation com. 1986-87), Am. Soc. Electroneurographic Technologists, NAFE, Women in Health Care Adminstrn., San Antonio Liaison Secs. (exec. com. 1984-86). Republican. Episcopalian. Home: 998 Bidwell Rd San Dimas CA 91773 Office: 999 Alantic Ste 205 Long Beach CA 90813

HOOK, VIRGINIA MAY, marketing executive; b. Balt., Mar. 11, 1932; d. Arthur M. Monroe McClelland and Margaret (Shipley) McClelland Warfield; m. Donald F. Hook, Aug. 25, 1951 (dec. Dec. 1978); children: Donald F., Jr., Donna J. Hook Kellner. Grad. high sch. Teller, Cen. Savs. Bank, Balt., 1950-68, tng. dir., 1968-71; ops. mgr. Mature Temps, Inc., Balt., 1971-81; pres. VMH Mktg. Ltd., Glen Burnie, Md., 1982—. Mem. adv. coun., sr. aides program D.C. Dept. Labor, 1980-81; active local Democratic party. Mem. Bank Pers. Assn. Md. (sec. 1969-71), Pers. Assn. Md. (sec. 1979-80), Exec. Women's Network, Market Rsch. Assn., Am. Mktg. Assn., Nat. Assn. Women Bus. Owners, Nat. Assn. Demonstration Cos. Methodist. Lodge: Order Eastern Star. Home: 3 Southerly Ct Towson MD 21204 Office: 8566 Laureldale Dr Laurel MD 20707

HOOKE, ANNE MORRIS, microbiologist, educator; b. Sydney, N.S.W., Australia, July 15, 1939; came to U.S., 1968; d. Elwyn Lindsay and Mona (Naylor) Morris; m. Augustus William Hooke, Aug. 21, 1959 (div. Dec. 1979); children: Alison, Elizabeth, Meredith. BS, George Mason U., 1972; PhD, Georgetown U., 1979; student, Sydney U., 1957-59. From rsch. assoc. to asst. prof. pediatrics Med. Sch. Georgetown U., Washington, 1979-87; assoc. prof. microbiology Miami U., Oxford, Ohio, 1987—. Contbr. articles to profl. jours. Mem. Am. Soc. for Microbiology (chair com. on status of women in microbiology 1986—), Fedn. Orgns. for Profl. Women (pres. 1986). Office: Miami U Dept of Microbiology Oxford OH 45056

HOOKER, ALICE LOUISE INGRAM, civic leader; m. Henry Williamson Hooker; children: Bradford Williamson, Lisa Hooker Campbell, Timothy Ingram. BA in Am. Culture, Vassar Coll., Poughkeepsie, N.Y., 1955. Mem. Centennial Club Nashville; rep. St. Timothy's Area Admissions, 1985-89, trustee, 1985-90, Balt., past chmn. Ann. Giving Campaign, 1983-84, trustee, 1985—; past co-chmn. 1983 Lawn and Garden Fair, Nashville; past trustee, past vice chmn. Ensworth Sch. Bd., Nashville, bd. dirs., 1985—, chmn. devel. com., 1989—; past bd. dirs., past mem. exec. com. Canby Robinson Soc.; past chmn. bd. dirs. Children's Hosp. of Vanderbilt U., Nashville, bd. dirs., 1987-90; past bd. dirs. Nashville Symphony Assn., United Way of Nashville; sustaining mem. Jr. League of Nashville, 1985—, past co-chmn. cookbook com., past chmn. admissions com.; mem. exec. com. of med. ctr. bd. dirs. Vanderbilt U. Hosp., 1985—; bd. dirs. Project Pencil, Nashville, 1985—, Meml. Found., 1988—, Leadership Nashville, 1989—, Nashville Meml. Hosp., Meml. Found., 1988—; ongoing hon. chmn. Iroquois Meml. Steeplechase Nashville; past chmn. fin. com., past bd. dirs. Hist. Travelers Rest. Mem. Nat. Soc. Colonial Dames Am. (state treas. 1989—, chmn. finance com.). Clubs: Tenn. Pony (past dist. commr.), Garden of Nashville (bd. gardeners), Colonial Dames. Home and Office: 370 Vaughn Rd Nashville TN 37221

HOOKER, KAREN ANN, psychology educator; b. Cleve., Sept. 8, 1955; d. Kent Albert and Judith Ann (Tucker) H.; m. Kenneth Paul Provencher, Mar. 7, 1981; 1 child, Christopher. BS, Denison U., Granville, Ohio, 1978; MA, Coll. William and Mary, Williamsburg, Va., 1981; PhD, Pa. State U., State College, 1985. Nat. Inst. Aging. postdoctoral fellow Duke U., Durham, N.C., 1984-86; asst. prof. psychology Syracuse (N.Y.) U., 1987—; fellow All-Univ. Gerontology Ctr., Syracuse, 1989—. Contbr. articles to profl. jours., chpt. to book. Ednl. Testing Svc. summer fellow, Princeton, N.J., 1980; Nat. Inst. Aging. predoctoral fellow, 1982-84. Mem. Am. Psychol. Assn., Gerontol. Soc. Am., Soc. Rsch. in Child Devel., Soc. Behavioral Medicine, AAAS, Psi Chi. Office: Syracuse U 430 Huntington Hall Syracuse NY 13244

HOOK-HAYGOOD, MARSHA, personnel director/human resources specialist; b. N.Y.C.; d. Malachi and Elverso H.; m. Donald Haygood; children: Hart, Gregory, Kenneth, Shawn. BA, Herbert Lehman Coll., 1977. Recruiter Western Union Internat., N.Y.C., 1977-78; recruiter Bulova Watch Co., Astoria, N.Y., 1978, employment supr., 1980; pers. mgr. Loews Corp., N.Y.C., 1980-82; asst. pers. dir. Orion Pictures Corp., N.Y.C., 1984-85, pers. dir., 1985-89, v.p. human resources, 1989—. Mem. Am. Mgmt. Assn., Soc. for Human Resource Mgmt. Office: Orion Pictures Corp 711 Fifth Ave New York NY 10022

HOOKS, VANDALYN LAWRENCE, educator; b. Dyersburg, Tenn., Feb. 26, 1935; d. James Bridges and Mary Lucille (Anderson) Lawrence; m. Floyd Lester Hooks, June 15, 1952; children—Lawrence James, Steven Lester. BA, Ky. Wesleyan U., 1967; MA, Western Ky. U., 1970, Edn. Specialist, 1976; postgrad. U. Tenn., 1975. Tchr., Owensboro Bd. Edn., Ky., 1967-71, adminstr., 1976—; dir. career experience Western Ky. U., Bowling Green, 1971-73; dir. career edn. Owensboro Daviess County Sch. Dist., 1973-76; curriculum developer Career Experience Voc. Edn., Frankfort, Ky., 1971-76; cons. Motivation Workshop, Bowling Green, 1971-76, Decision and Goal Setting, 1971-76. Editor; Ky. Assn. Elem. Prin. Jour., 1977-81. Contbr. articles to profl. jours. Organizer, Ky. Council for Better Edn., Owensboro, 1984; legis. advisor Eagle Forum, leadership forum, Washington, 1985, 86-87; Rep. legis. researcher. Recipient Presdl. award, Ky. Wesleyan Coll., 1966. Mem. Concerned Edn. of Am., Nat. Council for Better Edn., Heritage Found., Pro Family Forum, Eagle Forum, Plymouth Rock Found., Nat. Council Christian Educators. Republican. Baptist. Address: 1302 Waverly Pl Owensboro KY 42301

HOOPER, ANNE DODGE, pathologist, educator; b. Groton, Mass., July 16, 1926; d. Carroll William and Bertha Sanford (Wiener) Dodge; m. William Dale Hooper, June 17, 1952; children: Elizabeth Anne, Hoan Elaine, Caroline Mae. AB, Washington U., St. Louis, 1947, MD, 1952. With forensic pathology dept. Med. Examiners Office, Phila., 1958-60; from pathologist to acting chief lab svc. VA Hosp., Coatesville, Pa., 1960-66, St. Albans (Vt.) Hosp., 1966-69; dir. lab. Kerbs Hosp., St. Albans, 1966-71, Williamson Appalachian Regional Hosp., South Williamson, Ky., 1971-73, Beckley (W.Va.) Appalachian Regional Hosp., 1974-76; asst. prof. pathology W.Va. Sch. Osteo. Medicine, Lewisburg, 1977, assoc. prof. pathology, 1978—. Contbr. articles to profl. jours. Pres. local elem. sch. PTA, St. Albans, 1967-68; pres. Greenbrier unit Am. Cancer Soc., Lewisburg, 1989—, bd. dirs. W.Va. div., Charleston, 1987—, profl. edn. com. W.Va. div., 1982—. Fellow Coll. Am. Pathologists, Am. Acad. Forensic Scis.; mem. AMA, W.Va. Med. Soc., Raleigh County Med. Soc., Am. Soc. Clin. Pathologists (cert.), Internat. Acad. Pathologists, Nat. Assn. Med. Examiners, Coll. Osteo. Pathologists (assoc.). Office: WVa Sch Osteo Medicine 400 N Lee St Lewisburg WV 24901

HOOPER, JANE ANN, mechanical engineer; b. Cin., Sept. 26, 1964. BSME, Case Western Res. U., 1987. Cert. engr.-in-tng., Ohio. Coop. engr. Standard Oil Ohio, Cleve., 1984-86; product tech. engr. Procter & Gamble Co., Cin., 1987—. Advisor Jr. Achievement, Cin., 1988-89; v.p. Wyoming (Ohio) Players Community Theatre, 1988-89, pres., 1989—. Mem. ASME, Ohio Soc. Profl. Engrs. Office: Procter & Gamble Co 6105 Centerhill Rd PE2W20 Cincinnati OH 45254

HOOPER, LOIS, school photography company executive; b. Denver, Apr. 13, 1947; d. Archie Henry and Daisy Elizabeth (Burgess) Yetter; m. John Hooper, June 9, 1967 (div. Apr. 1987); children: Jeff, Crystal. Student, Rockmont Coll., 1967. Nat. sales dir., nat. conv. mgr., retail gen. mgr. Portrai World Inc., Anaheim, Calif.; pres., chief exec. officer The Picture Lady, Inc., Broomfield, Colo.; mem. amb. team Jostens All-Products Group, 1990—. Recipient Disting. Sales award, 1983, Cert. of Achievement, 1989. Mem. Sales and Mktg. Execs., Am. Bus. Women's Assn., Salesman With A Purpose. Republican. Office: 11575 N Wadsworth Blvd Bloomfield CO 80020

HOOPS, DIANE KINUKO, management information systems professional, consultant; b. Medford, Oreg., Feb. 18, 1961; d. Harold S. and Thelma K. (Okita) Sekiguchi; m. Thomas D. Hoops, June 23, 1984. BS, U. Nev., 1982. Programmer Sage Computer Tech., Reno, Nev., 1983-85; sta. mgr. Hertz Corp., Reno, 1985-87; MIS coord. Owen Distbn. Co., Sparks, Nev., 1987—; instr. part-time Truckee Meadows Community Coll., Reno, 1986; tech. writing cons. Perpetual Data Systems, Inc., Reno, 1987—. Vol. YWCA, Reno, 1988. Mem. NAFE, Am. Bus. Women's Assn. (pub. rels. chmn. 1988-89, enrollment chmn. 1989-90), U. Nev. Alumni Assn., Reno/Sparks C. of C. Episcopalian. Office: Owen Distbn Co 450 Lillard Dr Sparks NV 89431

HOOSIN, JANICE LAUTT, social worker; b. Chgo., June 22, 1942; d. Herbert and Ruth Jean (Rubenstein) Lapine; B.A., U. Ill., 1964; M.S.W., Jane Addams Grad. Sch. Social Work, 1966; postgrad. U. Utah, summer, 1977. Cert. mental health adminstr., psychiat. social worker, Ill. Psychiat. social worker New Trier Twp. High Sch., East Winnetka, Ill., 1966-70; dir. day hosp. St. Vincent's Hosp., N.Y.C., 1970-73; psychotherapist (part-time) New Trier East High Sch., Winnetka, 1973-74; dir. psychiat. day hosp. dept. psychiatry Evanston (Ill.) Hosp., 1974-78, dir. partial hospitalization, 1978-88; pvt. practice, 1988—; clin. assoc., field work supr. U. Chgo. Sch. Social Svc. Adminstrn., 1974—; cons. in field; pvt. practice marital and individual psychotherapy, specializing in co-dependency and chem. dependency, 1975—. NIMH fellow, 1964-66; cert. psychiat. social worker, Ill. Mem. Nat. Assn. Social Workers, Assn. Mental Health Adminstrs. Jewish. Home: 2638 N Burling St Chicago IL 60614 Office: 636 Church St Ste 715 Evanston IL 60201

HOOVER, BETTY-BRUCE HOWARD, educator; b. Wake County, N.C., Mar. 20, 1939; d. Bruce Ruffin and Mary Elizabeth (Brown) Howard; m. Herbert Charles Marsh Hoover, Sept. 3, 1961; children—David Andrew, Howard Webster, Lorraine VanSiclen. B.A., Wake Forest U., 1961; M.A., U. S. Fla., 1978. Tchr. English, Greensboro Sr. High Sch., N.C., 1961-62, Lindley Jr. High Sch., Greensboro, 1963, Berkeley Prep. Sch., Tampa, Fla., 1976—, chmn. English dept., 1977-85, dir., dean upper div., 1984—, chmn. curriculum com., 1982-86. Pres., Suncoast Midshipmen Parents Club, Tampa Bay Area, 1983-84. Mem. Assn. Supervision Curriculum Devel., Nat. Council Tchrs. English, Wake Forest U. Alumni Assn., DAR, Hillsborough County Bar Aux., Cum Laude Soc. (sec. 1981—), Nat. Honor Soc., Phi Beta Kappa, Phi Sigma Iota, Sigma Tau Delta. Republican. Episcopalian. Avocations: sewing; gardening. Home: 4504 Beachway Dr Tampa FL 33609 Office: Berkeley Preparatory Sch 4811 Kelly Rd Tampa FL 33615

HOOVER, CYNTHIA JANE, pediatrician; b. Pitts., Aug. 31, 1953; d. William Wilson Jr. and Anne Pauline (Lawson) H. BA with distinction, U. Rochester, N.Y., 1974; MD, U. Pitts., 1978; MA in Religious Studies, Cen. Bapt. Theol. Sem., 1983. Diplomate Am. Bd. Pediatrics., Am. Bd. Med. Examiners. Intern, then resident in pediatrics Children's Mercy Hosp., Kansas City, Mo., 1978-81; asst. prof. pediatrics, pediatric emergency physician Children's Mercy Hosp., Kansas City, 1983-86; asst. prof. pediatrics U. Kans. Med. Ctr., Kansas City, 1981-82, fellow in ambulatory pediatrics, 1982-83; pvt. practice Londonderry (N.H.) Pediatrics, 1986—; pediatrician Derry (N.H.) Sch. Based Clinic, 1987—; pediatric cons. N.H. PTA, Manchester, 1988—; bd. dirs. Derry Vis. Nurse Assn. Mem. coun. Bethany Covenant Ch., Bedford, N.H., 1988—. Fellow Am. Acad. Pediatrics; mem. Christian Med. Soc., N.H. Med. Soc., N.H. Pediatric Soc., Parkland Med. Ctr. Med. Staff, Granite State Wheelmen. Republican. Mem. Evang. Covenant Ch. Home: 91 Winterwood Dr Londonderry NH 03053 Office: Londonderry Pediatrics 184 Mammoth Rd Londonderry NH 03053

HOOVER, JUDITH ANN, college administrator; b. Ann Arbor, Mich., Sept. 11, 1941; d. Gene Dallas and Jewel Mary (Stommel) Maybee; m. Kenneth Ray Hoover; children: Andrew Lee, Erin Elizabeth. BA in English, History, Beloit Coll., 1963; MAT in Sociology, Coll. Wooster, 1973. Coord. programs, grants City of Wooster (Ohio), 1972-76, mgr. budget, research, 1976-78; coord. mental health edn. Community Mental Health, Retardation Bd., Wooster, 1978-80; dist. dir. home office U.S. Rep. Les Aspin, Racine, Wis., 1980-87; owner, pres. Communication Resources, Racine, 1987—; asst. to pres. Whatcom Community Coll., Bellingham, Wash., 1989—. Bd. dirs. Women's Resource Ctr., Racine, 1982-87, United Way, Wooster, 1975-78, United Way of Whatcom County, 1989—; pres. Wayne County Health, Edn., Welfare Assn., Wooster, 1979-80 (HEW award 1980), treas. Wayne County Legal Aid Soc., Wooster, 1977-80. Recipient Cert. Appreciation UAW Local 180, Racine, 1987. Mem. Phi Beta Kappa. Democrat. Episcopalian. Home: 507 16th St Bellingham WA 98225 Office: Whatcom Community Coll 237 W Kellogg Rd Bellingham WA 98226

HOOVER, JULIE TARACHOW, corporate executive. BA, Bryn Mawr Coll. V.p. corp. project Capital Cities/ABC, Inc., N.Y., 1984—. Office: Capital Cities/ABC Inc 77 W 66th St 20th Fl New York NY 10023

HOOVER, LOLA MAE, communications company executive; b. Monticello, Ark., Apr. 1, 1947; d. Victor Arthur and Essie (Humphries) Piper; divorced; 1 child, Larry Wayne. With prodn. dept. AT&T, West Chgo., 1965-78, 1st level shop mgr., 1978-83, warehouse mgr., 1983-84, office mgr., 1984-86; with Mfg. Resource Planning project, 1986-87, leader Mfg. Resource Planning project, 1987-88, mgr. script planning and prodn. control, 1988—. devel. quality excellence program, 1986. Baptist. Home: 207 Briar Ln North Aurora IL 60542 Office: AT&T Info Systems 1700 Hawthorne Ln Chicago IL 60185

HOOVER, MARY SUE MILLEN, harbinger ombudsman; b. Kansas City, Mo., Dec. 18, 1929; d. George Frederick and Ruby Lee (Bray) Millen; m. Homer Halbert Hoover, Sept. 1, 1950; children: Frederick Andrew, Anthony Eric, Rebecca Sue. BS in Phsy. Edn., U. Mo., 1952. Tchr. K.C. Mo. Sch. Dist., 1952-57, 1958-66; homemaker Baghdad, Iraq, 1957-58; homemaker, tchr. Raytown, Mo., 1958-60; homemaker, thcr., ombudsman Kansas City, 1960-67; harbinger ombudsman Nat. Order Simple Majority, Kansas City, Mo., 1967-90; with SPTA, 1978-90, Acquarian Genesis, Kansas City, 1988-90. Home: 8804 Manchester Kansas City MO 64138

HOOVER, MOLLY ANN, automobile sales executive, speaker, consultant; b. The Dallas, Oreg., May 17, 1948; d. Lile Wendell Hoover and Margaret Ernestine (Howard) Trullinger; m. Denny W. Homer, Mar. 28, 1970 (div. 1977). BS, Oreg. State U., 1970, EdM, 1975. Tchr. bus. Aloha High Sch., Beaverton, Oreg., 1971-75; dental office mgr., Bridgeport, Wash., 1975-77; dist. sales mgr. Chrysler Corp., Portland, 1978-81; leasing mgr. Teague Motor Co., Salem, Oreg., 1981-83; nat. project mgr. A.D.P. Dealer Services, Portland, 1984-85; mng. dir. StyleRight Seminars, Portland, 1985-86; founder, pres. M. Hoover & Assocs. Automotive Mktg., Portland, 1986—; word processing cons. Far West Fed., Portland, 1977; leasing cons. Pacific Coast Leasing, 1984. Comdr., Angel Flight ROTC Women's Aux., Corvallis, Oreg., 1968-70; treas., bd. dirs. Douglas Fed. Credit Union, Bridgeport, Wash., 1976-77; exhibit hall chmn. Small Bus. Adminstrn. Women's Conf., 1984. Named Salem Woman of 80's, Salem Spokesman Rev., 1982. Mem. Inst. Managerial and Profl. Women (v.p. 1985-86, conf. dir. 1986), Nat. Assn. Female Execs., Zonta Internat., Kappa Alpha Theta, Phi Beta Lambda. Avocations: cross country skiing, painting, needlepoint, travel. Home: 2187 Crown Point Hwy Troutdale OR 97060 Office: PO Box 5515 Portland OR 97228

HOOVER, RENA VIRGINIA, retired educator; b. Dundee, Miss., July 11, 1925; d. Eli and Mary Etta (Spratlin) Bailey; m. Norman Clark Hoover, Dec. 18, 1953 (dec. 1981); children: Mary Etta, Norman David. AA, Wood Jr. Coll., 1947; BS, Delta State Tchrs. Coll., Cleveland, Miss., 1949; MS, U. Wis., 1956. Thcr. math. Clarksdale (Miss.) High Sch., 1949-54, Fresno (Calif.) High Sch., 1954-56, Tappan Jr. High Sch., Ann Arbor, Mich., 1956-58; thcr. math. Sacramento High Sch., 1959-61, 63-89, dept. chmn., 1963-87; tchr. math. Am. River Coll., Sacramento, 1961-63; ret., 1989. Mem. Calif. Math. Coun., Nat. Coun. Tchrs. Math., NEA, Calif. Tchrs. Assn., Sacramento Tchrs. Assn. Republican.

HOPE, AMMIE DELORIS, computer programmer, systems analyst; b. Washington, Nov. 28, 1946; d. Amos Alexander and Amanda Irene (Moore) H. BA cum laude, Howard U., 1976; postgrad., Am. U., 1983. Adminstrv. asst. Coun. of D.C., Washington; Cath. sch. tchr. St. Benedict the Moor Cath. Sch., Washington; police officer Met. Police Dept., Washington; computer programmer/analyst IRS, Washington. Contbr. articles on adminstrn. of justice, computer applications, and systems devel. to profl. jours. Recipient Spanish award, Spl. Achievement award; Pub. Svc. scholar; named Civil Assn. honoree; trustees scholar; pub. svc. fellow; Civic Assn. honoree. Mem. Alpha Kappa Delta. Home: 1904 D St NE Washington DC 20002

HOPE, GERRI DANETTE, telecommunications executive; b. North Highlands, Calif., Feb. 28, 1956; d. Albert Gerald and Beulah Rae (Bane) Hope. AS, Sierra Coll., Calif., 1977; postgrad. Okla. State U., 1977-79. Sr. admissions clk. Bass Meml. Hosp., Enid, Okla., 1978-79; instructional asst. San Juan Sch. Dist., Carmichael, Calif., 1979-82; telecommunications supr. Delta Dental Svc. of Calif., San Francisco, 1982-85; telecommunications coordinator Farmers Savs. Bank, Davis, Calif., 1985-87; telecommunications mgr. Sacramento Savs. Bank, 1987—; cons. and lectr. in field. Mem. Telecommunications Assn. Republican. Avocations: writing, computers, ceramics, animal behavior, participating in Christian ministry. Home: 3025 U St North Highlands CA 95660

HOPE, MARGARET LAUTEN, civic worker; b. N.Y.C., Dec. 17; privately educated; m. Paul C. Debry, Jr., Nov. 9, 1943; m. 2d, Fred H. Hope, Jr., Mar. 30, 1959; 1 son, Frederick H., III. Bd. dirs. Nat. Leukemia Soc., 1974—; co-chmn. giftcom. Heart Ball, Palm Beach, Fla., 1967; mem. ball coms. various charity fund raising events. Mem. Jr. League N.Y.C. Clubs: Everglades, Sailfish (Palm Beach); Women's Nat. Republican (N.Y.C.); St. James (London, Eng.). Address: 236 Dunbar Rd PO Box 601 Palm Beach FL 33480

HOPKINS, BRIDGET ANN, veterinarian; b. New Orleans, Oct. 7, 1960; d. James Albert Hopkins and Gayle Ann Rimbolt. BS, Nicholls State U., Thibodaux, 1982; DVM, L.A. State U., Baton Rouge, 1987. Animal health technician L.A. Dept. of Agriculture, Thibodaux, La., 1982-83; tchr. ED White Catholic High Sch., Thibodaux, 1983; sr. camp counselor Saddle Rock Camp for Girls, Mentone, Ala., 1980-84; vet. fellow Bowman Gray Sch. of Medicine, Winston-Salem, N.C.; veterinarian/owner Summerville Vet. Clinic, Summerville, Ga., 1987--. Recipient: Outstanding Student Award, LSU Sch. of Vet. Medicine & Louisiana Vet. Med. Assn., 1986, Scholarship Award, IAMS Pet Foods, 1987,. Mem. Am. Vet. Med. Assn., L.A. Vet. Med. Assn., Ga. Vet. Med. Assn., Northwest Ga. Vet. Med. Assn., Optimist Internat. Dem. Roman Catholic.

HOPKINS, CECILIA ANN, educator; b. Havre, Mont., Feb. 17, 1922; d. Kost L. and Mary (Manaras) Sofos; B.S., Mont. State Coll., 1944; M.A., San Francisco State Coll., 1958, M.A., 1967; postgrad. Stanford U.; Ph.D., Calif. Western U., 1977; m. Henry E. Hopkins, Sept. 7, 1944. Bus. tchr. Havre (Mont.) High Sch., Mateo, Calif., 1942-44; sec. George P. Gorham, Realtor, San Mateo, 1944-45; escrow sec. Fox & Cars 1945-50; escrow officer Calif. Pacific Title Ins. Co., 1950-57; bus. tchr. Westmoor High Sch., Daly City, Calif., 1958-59; bus. tchr. Coll. of San Mateo, 1959—, chmn. real estate-ins. dept., 1963-76, dir. div. bus., 1976-86, coord. real estate dept., 1986—; cons. to commr. Calif. Div. Real Estate, 1963—, mem. periodic rev. exam. com.; chmn. Community Coll. Adv. Com., 1971-72, mem. com., 1975—; projector direction Calif. State Chancellor's Career Awareness Consortium, mem. endowment fund adv. com., community coll. real estate edn. com., state community coll. adv. com.; mem. No. Calif. adv. bd. to Glendale Fed. Savs. and Loan Assn.; mem. bd. advisors San Mateo County Bd. Suprs., 1981-82; mem. real estate edn. and rsch. com. to Calif. Commr. Real Estate, 1983—; mem. edn., membership, and profl. exchange coms. Am. chpt. Internat. Real Estate Fedn., 1985—. Recipient Citizen of Day award KABL, Outstanding Contbns. award Redwood City-San Carlos-Belmont Bd. Realtors; named Woman of Achievement, San Mateo-Burlingame br. Soroptimist Internat., 1979. Mem. AAUW, Calif. Assn. Real Estate Tchrs. (state pres. 1964-65, hon. dir. 1962—, outstanding real estate educator of yr. 1978-79), Real Estate Cert. Inst. (Disting. Merit award 1982), Calif. Bus. Edn. Assn. (certificate of commendation 1979), San Francisco State Coll., Guidance and Counseling Alumni, CREEA (dir. emeritus), Theta Alpha Delta, Pi Lambda Theta, Delta Pi Epsilon (nat. dir. interchpt. rels. 1962-65, nat. historian 1966-67, nat. sec. 1968-69), Alpha Gamma Delta. Co-author: California Real Estate Principles; contbr. articles to profl. jours. Home: 504 Colgate Way San Mateo CA 94402

HOPKINS, CHARLENE MARTHA, entrepreneur; b. Alma, Ark., Oct. 17, 1934; d. William Henry and Lettie Luticia (Robinson) Turknett; m. Dexter G. Hopkins, Aug. 17, 1951 (dec. 1980); children: Stephen Glenn, Kelly G. BS in Edn., N.Mex. State U., 1970; MS in Edn., Ea. N.Mex. U., 1975. Cert. tchr., N.Mex. Tchr. Carlsbad (N.Mex.) Mcpl. Schs., 1971-81; pvt. investor various businesses, 1981—. Democrat. Baptist. Office: Recreation rentals Inc Hwy 82 Downtown Cloudcroft NM 88317

HOPKINS, EDWINA WEISKITTEL, graphic designer; b. Cin., June 7, 1947; d. Edwin and Moody (Bowling) Campbell; m. Michael J. Weiskittel, May 1966 (dec. May 1970); 1 son, Todd Michael; m. Franklin Hopkins, June 1973 (div. June 1977). Student, U. Cin., 1965-66. Asst. to art dir. World Library Publs., Cin., 1965-68; comml. artist Campbell & Assocs. Art Studio, Cin., 1969-73; prodn. mgr. William Wilson Advt. Agy., Palos Verdes, Calif., 1973-74; ptnr. Hopkins & Hopkins Design Studio, Redondo Beach, Calif., 1975-76; owner, graphic designer Winnissa Comml. Art Studio, Rolling

Hills, Calif., 1976-81; pres. Winnissa Inc., Redondo Beach, 1981—. U. Cin. hon. scholar, 1965. Mem. NAFE, Nat. Assn. Women Bus. Owners, Redondo Beach C. of C. Home and Office: 718 Ave D Redondo Beach CA 90277

HOPKINS, JEANNE SULICK, accountant; b. Fair Lawn, N.J., Oct. 14, 1952; d. Peter and Margaret (McLaughlin) Sulick; m. Ronald T. Hopkins, Aug. 23, 1975. B.S., Syracuse U., 1974, M.B.A., 1975. With Price Waterhouse, Syracuse, 1975-83, staff acct., 1975-78, sr. acct., 1978-80, audit mgr., 1980-83; mgr. cost acctg. United Technologies/Carrier Corp., Syracuse, 1983-85; owner J.S. Hopkins & Co., CPA's, 1985-87, ptnr. Dannible & McKee, CPAs, 1987—; instr. in field. Mem. fund raising com. Syracuse Symphony Orch.; mem. Nat. Assn. Panhellenics. Mem. Am. Inst. C.P.A.s, Planning Execs. Inst., Hosp. Fin. Mgmt. Assn., N.Y. State Soc. C.P.A.s, Syracuse U. Alumni Assn., Delta Delta Delta. Club: Zonta. Office: Dannible & McKee 499 S Warren St Syracuse NY 13202

HOPKINS, JUDITH OWEN, oncologist; b. Norfolk, Va., Sept. 6, 1952; d. Austin and Edythe Owen; m. Marbry Benjamin Hopkins, III; 1 child, Benjamin Owen Hopkins. BS magna cum laude, Westhampton Coll., 1974; D of Medicine, U. Va., 1977. Diplomate Am. Bd. Internal Medicine, Am. Bd. Oncology. Resident in internal medicine Bowman Gray Sch. Medicine, N.C. Baptist Hosp., Winston-Salem, 1977-80, oncology fellowship, 1980-82; pvt. practice Winston-Salem, 1984—; clin. asst. prof. medicine Bowman Gray Sch. Medicine, Winston-Salem, 1984—, asst. prof. medicine, 1982-84; cons. physician various hosps., presenter workshops and exhibits, including Am. Cancer Soc. Indsl. Cancer Prevention Series, 1980, Clin. Oncology Confs. and others. Contbg. author: Tumors of the Central Nervous System, 1982; contbr. articles to profl. jours and abstracts. Bd. dirs. Hospice of Winston-Salem/Forsyth County, 1988—, profl. adv. com. 1982—; preceptor for alt. curriculum, Bowman Gray Sch. Medicine, 1988; speakers bur., Am. Cancer Soc., 1982—, chmn. profl. edn. com., 1982-85; mem. long-range planning com. Forsyth-Stokes-Davie County Med. Soc. and others. Mem. Am. Coll. Physicians, Am. Soc. Internal Medicine, N.C. Soc. Internal Medicine, Forsyth-Davie-Stokes County Med. Soc., Am. Soc. Clin. Oncology, Gynecologic Oncology Group, Piedmont Oncology Assn., Southeastern Cancer Control Consortium, Alpha Omega Alpha, Phi Beta Kappa. Episcopalian. Home: 313 Susanna St Kernersville NC 27284 Office: 2825 Lyndhurst Ave Ste 103 Winston-Salem NC 27103

HOPKINS, LINDA ANN, school psychologist; b. Bristol, Va., Aug. 23, 1937; d. James Robert and Trula Mae (Mink) Broce; A.B., King Coll., 1959; M.A., East Tenn. State U., 1977, postgrad., 1977-79; postgrad. Radford U., 1978-79; m. James Edwin Hopkins, Oct. 8, 1960; children: James Edwin, David Lawrence. Social worker Washington County Welfare Dept., Abingdon, Va., 1959-61; social worker Bristol (Va.) Welfare Dept., 1963-65, Washington County Welfare Dept., 1965-68, Bristol Meml. Hosp., 1968-72; psychologist Washington County Public Schs., Abingdon, 1978-87; pvt. practice sch. psychology, Abingdon, 1987—; clin. coordinator Critical Incident Stress Debriefing team; adj. prof. East Tenn. State U., 1989—. Mem. Bristol Preservation Soc., Soc. for Preservation of Bristol's Older Homes. Mem. Nat. Assn. Sch. Psychologists, Va. Psychol. Assn., Va. Assn. Sch. Psychologists, Phi Kappa Phi. Methodist. Home: 423 Pennsylvania Ave Bristol TN 37620 Office: The Oaks P O Box 2077 Abingdon VA 24210

HOPKINS, MARY EVELYN, business educator, management consultant; b. Erie county, Pa., May 21, 1919; d. Harrison C. and Harriet V. (Sisson) H. AB magna cum laude, U. Pa., 1940; student U. Md., 1942. MA in Indsl. Psychology, Case Western Res. U., 1958, PhD, 1963. Cert. indsl. psychologist, Hawaii. With U.S. Employment Svc., Pa.; owner Pers. Mgmt. Svcs., Erie, Pa., 1952-56; Indsl. Rels. dir. Ajax Iron Works, 1945-52; staffing dir. Nat. City Bank, Cleve., 1956-60; asst. prof. mgmt. Calif. Western U., San Diego, 1960-63, U. Tex.-El Paso, 1965-66; from asst. prof. to assoc. prof. mgmt. U. Hawaii-Manoa, 1963-65, 66-86; cons. indsl. psychologist, 1986—. Contbr. articles to profl. jours. Mem. Am. Psychol. Assn., Acad. Mgmt., Am. Soc. Personnel Adminstrn. (1st hon. mem. Hawaii chpt., founding officer, original sec. dir. nat.). Home: 1556 Piikoi St Apt 2004 Honolulu HI 96822

HOPKINS, SUZANNE, industrial engineer; b. Aiken, S.C., Aug. 26, 1964; d. Donald Gene and Emma Ruth (Trahan) H. AAS, Lamar U., BS, 1986. Drafter Austin Industries, Beaumont, Tex.; indsl. engr. LTV Aerospace, Dallas, Circuit City Stores, Walnut, Calif. Mem. NAFE, Inst. Indsl. Engring., Lamar U. Alumni Assn., Profl. Assn. Diving Instrs., Orange County Ski Club. Office: 680 S Lemon Ave Walnut CA 91789

HOPKINSON, JOAN E., petroleum company executive; b. Rawlins, Wyo., Mar. 5, 1934; d. Robert Stephen and Bramlet Clarkey (Wade) Ault. Student, Lakewood Jr. Coll. Mgr. Petro, Inc., Eloy, Ariz.; mgr., asst. mgr. T.G.Y., Phoenix. Home: 5133 Keresan Phoenix AZ 85044

HOPKINSON, SHIRLEY LOIS, library science educator; b. Boone, Iowa, Aug 25, 1924; d. Arthur Perry and Zora (Smith) Hopkinson; student Coe Coll., 1942-43; A.B. cum laude (Phi Beta Kappa scholar 1944), U. Colo., 1945; B.L.S., U. Calif., 1949; M.A. (Honnold Honor scholar 1945-46), Claremont Grad. Sch., 1951; Ed.M., U. Okla., 1952, Ed.D., 1957 Tchr. pub. sch. Stigler, Okla., 1946-47, Palo Verde High Sch., Jr. Coll., Blythe, Calif., 1947-48; asst. librarian Modesto (Calif.) Jr. Coll., 1949-51; tchr., librarian Fresno, Calif., 1951-52, La Mesa, Cal., 1953-55; asst. prof. librarianship, instructional materials dir. Chaffey Coll., Ontario, Calif., 1955-59; asst. prof. librarian ship, San Jose (Calif.) State Coll., 1959-64; assoc. prof., 1964-69, prof., 1969—. Dir. NDEA Inst. Sch. Librarians, summer 1966; mem. Santa Clara County Civil Service Bd. Examiners. Mem. ALA, Calif. Library Assn., Audio-Visual Assn. Calif., NEA, AAUP, AAUW (dir. 1957-58), Bus. Profl. Women's Club, Sch. Librarians Assn. Calif. (com. mem., treas. No. sect. 1951-52), San Diego County Sch. Librarians Assn. (sec. 1945-55), Calif. Tchrs. Assn., LVW (bd. dirs. 1950-51, publs. chmn.), Phi Beta Kappa, Alpha Lambda Delta, Alpha Beta Alpha, Kappa Delta Pi, Phi Kappa Phi (disting. acad. achievement award 1981), Delta Kappa Gamma. Author: Descriptive Cataloging of Library Materials; Instructional Materials for Teaching the Use of the Library. Contbr. to profl. publs. Editor: Calif. Sch. Libraries, 1963-64; asst. editor: Sch. Library Assn. of Calif. Bull., 1961-63. Office: San Jose State U Rm LN-608 San Jose CA 95192

HOPPA, MARY ANN, software engineer; b. Pitts., Oct. 24, 1959; d. Edward Michael and Mary (Sevanich) Malloy; m. Robert Valentine Hoppa, Mar. 15, 1987. BA in French, BS in Applied Math., Auburn U., 1981; MS in Computer Sci., George Mason U., 1985; postgrad., Old Dominion U., 1988—. Mem. tech. staff Locus, Inc., Alexandria, Va., 1981-85; sr. software engr. CACI, Inc.-Fed., Fairfax, Va., 1985-87; mem. tech. staff The MITRE Corp., Langley AFB, Va., 1987—. Fellow George Mason U., 1983. Mem. Assn. for Computing Machinery, HSL-32 Officers Wives Club (sec. 1988, chmn. newsletter 1989). Republican. Roman Catholic. Office: The MITRE Corp Box 716 Langley AFB VA 23665

HOPPER, ANITA KLEIN, molecular genetics educator; b. Chgo., Sept. 24, 1945; d. Irving and Rose (Warshawsky) Klein; m. James Ernest Hopper, Jan. 3, 1971; 1 child, Julie Victoria. BS, U. Ill., Chgo., 1967; PhD, U. Ill., 1972. Postdoctoral researcher genetics U. Wash., Seattle, 1971-75; asst. prof. microbiology U. Mass. Med. Sch., Worcester, 1975-78, assoc. prof. microbiology, 1978-79; assoc. prof. biochemistry Hershey Med. Sch., Pa. State U., Hershey, 1979-87, prof. biochemistry, 1987—; genetic biology panel NSF, Washington, 1981-85; mem. genetic study sect. NIH, Bethesda, 1985-89; organizer RNA processing Cold Spring Harbor meetings, 1989, 90; co-chmn. 5th Summer Symposium in Molecular Biology: The Nucleus, Pa. State U., 1986. Editor Molecular & Cellular Biology, 1989—, editorial bd., 1986-90; contbr. articles and symposium papers to profl. jours. Grantee NIH, 1979—, NIH U. Louisville Med. Sch., 1989, NSF, 1988-91; postdoctoral fellow NIH, 1971-73. Mem. Am. Soc. Microbiology (chair-elect genetics & molecular biology div. 1987, chair genetics & molecular biology div. 1988), Am. Assn. Biochemists, AAAS. Office: Pa State U Med Sch Dept Biochemistry Hershey PA 17033

HOPPER, GRACE M., mathematician; b. N.Y.C., Dec. 9, 1906; d. Walter Fletcher and Mary Campbell (Van Horne) Murray; m. Vincent Foster Hopper, June 15, 1930 (div. 1945). BA, Vassar Coll., 1928; MA (Vassar fellow, Sterling scholar), Yale U., 1930, PhD, 1934; postgrad. (Vassar faculty fellow), NYU, 1941-42; DEng (hon.), Newark Coll. Engring., 1972; DSc (hon.), C.W. Post Coll. L.I. U., 1973, Pratt Inst., 1976, Linkoping (Sweden) U., 1980, Bucknell U., 1980, Acadia (Can.) U., 1980, So. Ill. U., 1981, Loyola U., Chgo., 1981; LLD (hon.), U. Pa., 1974; D Pub. Service (hon.), George Washington U., 1981. From instr. to assoc. prof. math. Vassar Coll., Poughkeepsie, N.Y., 1931-44; asst. prof. math Barnard Coll., N.Y.C., summer 1943; research fellow engring. scis., applied physics computation lab Harvard U., Cambridge, Mass., 1946-49; sr. mathematician Eckert-Mauchly Computer Corp., Phila., 1949-50; sr. programmer Eckert-Mauchly div. Remington Rand, 1950-59; systems engr., dir. automatic programming devel. UNIVAC div. Sperry Rand Corp., Phila., 1959-64, staff scientist systems programming, 1964-71; vis. lectr. Moore Sch. Elec. Engring., U. Pa., 1959-63, vis. assoc. prof. elec. engring., 1963-74, adj. prof., 1974; professorial lectr. George Washington U. from 1971. Contbr. articles to profl. jours. Served to comdr WAVES, 1944-46, from 1967, capt. USNR, 1973; later served active duty NAVDAC. Decorated Legion of Merit, Meritorious Service award; recipient Naval Ordnance Devel. award, 1946, Connelly Meml. award, 1968, Wilbur L. Cross medal Yale U., 1972, Sci. Achievement award Am. Mother's Com., 1970, others. Fellow Brit. Computer Soc. (disting.), Assn. Computer Programmers and Analysts, IEEE (McDowell award 1979, Piore award 1988), AAAS; mem. Nat. Acad. Engring., Assn. Computing Machinery, Data Processing Mgmt. Assn. (Man of Yr. award 1969), Am. Fedn. Info. Processing Socs. (Harry Goode Meml. award 1970), Soc. Women Engrs (Achievement award 1964, Franklin Inst., U.S. Naval Inst., Internat. Oceanographic Found., DAR, Dames Loyal Legion, Hist. Soc. Pa., Geneal. Soc. Pa., N.H. Hist. Soc., New Eng. Hist. Geneal. Soc., Valley Forge Hist. Assn., Ret. Officers Assn., Huguenot Soc. Pa., Nat., N.Y. geneal. socs., Pechin Soc., Phi Beta Kappa, Sigma Xi. Home: 1400 S Joyce St Arlington VA 22202*

HOPPER, SALLY, state legislator; widowed; children: Nancy, Joan, Caroline, Anne. BA, U. Wyo., 1956. Mem. Colo. Senate, Denver, 1987—, chmn. health, environ., welfare and instns. com.; chmn. bd. dirs. Spalding Rehab. Hosp. Mem. nat. bd. Physically Challenged Access to the Woods; bd. dirs. Vols. for Outdoor Colo. Mem. Kappa Kappa Gamma. Republican. Episcopalian. Home: 21649 Cabrini Blvd Golden CO 80401

HOPPER, SHEILA MARIE, industrial engineer; b. Fukuoka, Japan, Dec. 1, 1962. BS in Indsl. Engring., Calif. Polytech. U., 1985. Indsl. engr. Apple Computer, Inc., Garden Grove, Calif., 1984-85; systems analyst Aaron-Ross Corp., Glendora, Calif., 1985-87; indsl. engr. II Alps Electric (U.S.A.), Inc., Garden Grove, 1987—. Mem. Inst. Indsl. Engrs. (chpt. devel. com. 1986-87). Home: 16425 Vasquez Ave Victorville CA 92392 Office: Alps Electric USA Inc 7301 Orangewood Ave Garden Grove CA 92641

HOPPER, SHERRY LEIGH, communications executive; b. Cin., Mar. 26, 1954; d. Troy and Marie (Napier) Morris; m. John Edward Hopper Jr., Apr. 29, 1983; stepchildren: Jill Christine Hopper Neal, John Eric Hopper III. BS, Bowling Green State U., 1976. Mng. editor Youth Take-home Papers Standard Pub. Co., Cin., 1976-79; dir. publs. and pub. info. U. Cin. Found., Cin., 1979-83; asst. mgr. B. Dalton Booksellers, Orange Park, Fla., 1983-84; dir. communications U. Cin. Found., 1984—. Editor, writer (recruiting) McMicken Society Brochure, 1988 (cert. of excellence 1989), (annual report) U. Cin. Devel. Report, 1989 (award of excellence 1990); contbr. more than 500 short stories and poems to mags. Recipient Journalism Scholarship award Scripps Howard, 1974. Mem. Cin. Editors Assn. (profl.), Coun. for Advancement/Support of Edn., Nat. Writers Club (profl., manuscript critic 1988—), Pub. Rels. Soc. Am. (profl.) Women in Communications Inc. (profl.), The Cousteau Soc., Environ. Def. Fund. Home: 4613 Brookview Dr Batavia OH 45103 Office: U Cin Found 425 Oak St Cincinnati OH 45219

HOPPMANN, BARBARA ELSIE, lawyer; b. N.Y.C., Feb. 3, 1953; d. William Walter and Catherine (Keim) Hoppmann; m. Ronald James D'Angelo, May 16, 1987. BA in English, Fordham U., 1975, JD, 1978. Bar: N.Y. 1979, U.S. Supreme Ct. 1984, U.S. Dist. (ea. and so. dist.) N.Y. 1985, U.S. Tax Ct. 1986. Ptnr. Albert W. Cornachio P.C., N.Y.C., 1979-80; asst. assoc. prof. Fordham U., N.Y.C., 1980-81; pvt. practice, N.Y.C., 1980—. Mem. Bronx County Bar Assn., ABA, N.Y. State Bar Assn., Met. Women's Bar Assn. (v.p. 1989—), Women's Bar Assn. of State of N.Y. (bd. dirs. 1985—), Bronx Women's Bar Assn. Democrat. Roman Catholic. Office: 2300 86th St Brooklyn NY 11214

HOPTA, ANNA MARIE, financial analyst; b. Sewickley, Pa., Feb. 8, 1961; d. Mike and Audrey Mae (Walker) H. AA magna cum laude, Robert Morris Coll., 1981, BSBA magna cum laude, 1982, MBA summa cum laude, 1989. Mktg. asst. Pappan's Family Restaurant, Bridgewater, Pa., 1983-84; cost acct. Sewickley Valley Hosp., 1984-90; sr. fin. analyst Allegheny Gen. Hosp., Pitts., 1990—; mem. tech. adminstrv. svcs. com. Hosp. Coun. of Western Pa., Warrendale, 1986-88; 1st v.p. Sewickley Valley Hosp. Credit Union, 1987-90. Robert Morris Coll. scholar, 1979. Mem. Hosp. Fin. Mgmt. Assn. Republican. Lutheran.

HORAITIS, ANGELICA POLITO, business machines company official; b. Youngstown, Ohio, Dec. 2, 1952; d. Nick and Mary (Esposito) Polito; m. Michael G. Horaitis, Feb. 20, 1982; 1 child, Ariana. BS in History and Secondary Edn., Youngstown State U., 1974. Adv. sales rep. nat. accounts div. IBM, Columbus, Ohio, 1978-83; bus. practices advisor nat. distbn. div. IBM, Boca Raton, Fla., 1983-86; mktg. mgr. IBM, Boston, 1986-89; adminstrv. asst. to v.p. IBM, Montvale, N.J., 1989—. Democrat. Roman Catholic. Home: 46 Old Kings Hwy Wilton CT 06897

HORAKOVA, ZDENKA ZAHUTOVA, toxicologist, pharmacologist; b. Jindrichuv Hradec, Czechoslovakia, Apr. 6, 1925; came to U.S., 1968, naturalized, 1974; d. Josef and Aloisie (Sohajova) Zahut; m. Vaclav Horak, Sept. 26, 1949; 1 child, David. M Pharmacy, Charles U., Prague, Czechoslovakia, 1949, D of Natural Scis., 1952; PhD in Pharmacology, Czechoslovakian Acad. Scis., Prague, Czechoslovakia, 1962. Sustantant pharmacy Kostelec Nad Orlici, Czechoslovakia, 1945-47; teaching asst. dept. pharmacology med. faculty Charles U., Prague, 1949-50; rsch. pharmacologist, head pharmacology dept. Rsch. Inst. Pharmacy and Biochemistry, Prague, 1950-68; rsch. pharmacologist exptl. therapeutics br. Nat. Heart and Lung Inst., NIH, Bethesda, Md., 1969-74; rsch. pharmacologist sect. on molecular pharmacology Nat. Heart, Lung and Blood Inst., NIH, Bethesda, 1974-77; rsch. pharmacologist Lab. Cellular Metabolism Nat. Heart, Lund and Blood Inst., NIH, Bethesda, 1977-78; toxicologist residue evaluation and surveillance div. Food Safety and Quality Svc., U.S. Dept. Agr., Washington, 1978-81; toxicologist residue evaluation and planning div. Sci., Food Safety and Inspection Svc., U.S. Dept. Agr., Washington, 1981-87; toxicologist forest pest mgmt. Forest Svc., U.S. Dept. Agr., Washington, 1987—; vis. guest Zambon Pharm. Rsch. Inst., Bresso-Milano, Italy, 1968. Contbr. articles to profl. jours. Recipient award Patent and Invention Office, Prague, 1960; WHO fellow Milan, Rome, 1961. Mem. Am. Soc. Pharmacology and Exptl. Therapeutics, Soc. Toxicology, Internat. Union Pharmacology, Internat. Soc. for Study Xenobiotics, Internat. Soc. Biochem. Pharmacology, Internat. Inflammation Club, European Biol. Rsch. Assn., Inflammation Rsch. Assn., Soc. Exptl. Biology and Medicine, Cell and Molecular Biology in Space, Toxicology Forum, Immunotoxicology Discussion Group, Archeol. Inst. Am., Czechoslovak Soc. Arts and Scis., Internat. Assn. Med. Assistance to Travelers, Smithsonian Assocs. Democrat. Roman Catholic. Home: 5508 Oakmont Ave Bethesda MD 20817

HORDEMAN, AGNES MARIE, real estate professional, investment company executive; b. Phila., May 19, 1929; d. Hector and Victoria (Charais) Hill; m. Walter George Hordeman, Sept. 28, 1947 (dec. Jan. 1990); children: Phyllis, Kim, Henry, Rex, Gary. BA in Social Sci., Thomas Edison U., 1978. Relief dir. New Chgo. Trustee's Office, Hobart Twp., Ind., 1962-64; exec. sec. Real Estate Office, Pine Beach, N.J., 1964-65; office mgr. Crestwood Village, Whiting, N.J., 1965-67; reporter Ocean County Daily Times, Lakewood, 1967-69; real estate agt. De-Bow Agy., Lakewood, 1972-73, Century 21 Sullivan Agy. and Centurion and Rimm Howell, 1973-79; dir. Counteract Agy. for Children, Jackson, N.J., 1974-75; pres. Blue Sky Realty, Jackson, 1979-89; appraiser Garden State Bank, Jackson, 1986-87; pres. Brassica Inc., Jackson, 1986-87. Contbr. articles to profl. jours. Mem. com. Jackson Twp. Rep. Orgn., 1964-76; rep. to People's Republic China amb. program SBA. Named Woman of Yr. Girl Scouts U.S., 1975. Mem. Nat. Assn. Real Estate Appraisers, Ocean County Bd. Realtors, Monmouth County Bd. Realtors, N.J. Bd. Realtors, Nat. Bd. Realtors, NAFE, Jackson C. of C. (v.p., directory chmn., pres. 1989, map chmn.). Republican. Roman Catholic. Clubs: Legion Mary (v.p. 1962-64) (New Chgo.); Rosary Sodality (v.p. 1967) (Jackson). Home: 315 Edwards Ln Vancouver WA 98661

HORE, MARLENE CAROLE, advertising company executive; b. Montreal, Que., Can., Aug. 7, 1944; d. Stan Sam and Mollie (Kushner) Abelson; m. Ron J. Hore, July 1968 (dec. Apr. 1985); children: Seanna, Melissa. EdB, Mc Gill U., Montreal. Promotion writer CFCF Radio and TV, Montreal, 1966-68, copy writer, 1969-70; copy writer Vickers and Benson, Montreal, 1970-71; copy writer J. Walter Thompson Co., Ltd., Montreal, 1971-73, v.p. group, creative dir., 1973-78; creative dir. J. Walter Thompson Co., Ltd., 1978-83; nat. creative dir. J. Walter Thompson Co., Ltd., Montreal, 1984—, exec. v.p., 1986—, vice chmn. nat. creative dir., 1987—. Mem. Agy. Creative Dirs. Assn. (founding mem.), Art Dirs. Club of Toronto (bd. dirs.). Office: J Walter Thompson, 160 Bloor St E, Toronto, ON Canada M4W 3P7*

HOREL, LISA STANDER, planning and allocations specialist; b. Syracuse, N.Y., June 10, 1955; d. Karl and Anne G. (Forman) Stander; m. Timothy Horel, July 30, 1972; children: Anne, Corinne. BA, SUNY, Buffalo, 1981; MEd in Rural Family Devel., U. Vt., 1989. Peer tutor edn. opportunity program SUNY, Buffalo, 1981; bank teller Merchants Bank, Burlington, 1981-83; homevisitor CVOEO Head Start, Burlington, Vt., 1983-85; exec. dir. Milton (Vt.) Family Community Ctr., 1985-88; lectr. U. Vt., Burlington, 1988-90; planning and allocations specialist United Way of Santa Clara County, Calif., 1990—; cons. to non-profit orgns., 1986—; fed. grant reviewer, Health and Human Svcs. Head Start Bur., 1987, 89; state grant reviewer, Dept. of Edn. and Agy. of Human Svcs., 1987—; book reviewer Children Today, 1989. Contbr. articles to profl. jours. Mem. Children and Family Coun. for Prevention, 1988—; parent support group Hiawatha Elem. Sch.; participant Leadership Chittenden; vol., participant leadership program United Way of Santa Clara County; bd. dirs. Parents Anonymous of Vt., 1988-89, Nat. Alliance Children's Trust Funds, 1990—; chair devel. Vt. Children's Trust Fund, 1989-90. Recipient Social Svcs. Commr.'s award Vt. Agy. Human Svcs., 1987. Mem. Vt. Parent Child Ctr. Network (founding), Family Resource Coalition, Nat. Assn. for Edn. of Young Children, Nat. Alliance of Children's Trust and Prevention Funds (nat. bd. mem.), Children and Family Coun. for Prevention Programs (exec. com., chair devel. com. 1989-90), Nat. Com. for Prevention of Child Abuse (state bd. mem.). Home: 103 Palmer Dr Los Gatos CA 95030 Office: United Way Santa Clara County 2323 Homestead Ave Santa Clara CA 95052

HORKY-MALLOY, LAUREL MEREDITH, educator; b. Chgo., Mar. 4, 1963; d. Raymond Karl and Lillie Mae (Niemann) Horky; m. Robert Anthony Malloy, Dec. 19, 1982; children: Anthony Robert, Eric Andrew. BFA summa cum laude, SW Tex. State U., 1984; student, U. Dallas, Irving, Tex., 1981-82. Cert. provisional tchr. theatre arts and history, Tex. Lead tchr. theatre arts dept. E.M. Pease Mid. Sch., Northside Ind. Sch. Dist., San Antonio, 1985—. Youth dir. Prince of Peace Luth. Ch., San Antonio, 1989—. Mem. Tex. Ednl. Theatre Assn., AAUW, Sierra Club (asst. to newsletter editor Alamo group 1989-90), Kappa Delta Pi. Home: 4419 Avenida Prima San Antonio TX 78233 Office: EM Pease Mid Sch 201 Hunt Ln San Antonio TX 78245

HORN, CAROL ELLEN, fashion designer; b. N.Y.C., June 12, 1936; d. Ely and Luba H. Student, Boston U., 1954-56, Columbia U. Sch. Fine Arts, 1956-58. Head designer Benson & Partners-Outlander Co., N.Y.C., 1968-72, Carol Horn Co., div. Malcolm Starr Inc., N.Y.C., 1972-74; partner, head designer Carol Horn's Habitat, N.Y.C., 1974-83; owner, designer Carol Horn Sportswear, N.Y.C., 1983—; critic Fashion Inst. Tech., N.Y.C.; guest designer Shenkar Coll. Fashion and Textiles, Tel Aviv. Recipient Coty Fashion award, 1975, Wool Knit award Women's Knitwear Assn., 1975. Democrat. Jewish. Office: Carol Horn Sportswear 575 7th Ave New York NY 10018

HORN, DAISY ANDERSON, company executive; b. Newark, Oct. 4, 1929; d. Edward and Impi (Dufua) Anderson; m. John D., Mar. 17, 1951; children: David, Martin, Wade, Craig, Jeffrey, Jennifer, John. BA, Montclair State, 1952. Assr. dir. Somerset O.I.C., Somerville, 1975-78; exec. dir. Young Women Christian Assn., Plainfield, 1978—; Editor, YWCA Mag., Plainfield, 1979. Vice pres., bd. Edn., Bridgewater, 1980-86. Named Woman of Yr., NJ Bus. Women Owners, Frontier Club. Mem. Human Services Commission (pres.), Project Alert/Dudley House, Plainfield Concerns Com., Kiwanis (pres.). Home: 1861 Middlebrooke Rd Bound Brook NJ 08805 Office: YWCA of Plainfield 232 E Front St Plainfield NJ 07060

HORN, GAYE BURKHOLDER, programmer, systems analyst; d. David R. and Carol (Kirtland) Burkholder; 1 child, Zachary. AAS, Wayne Community Coll., 1986; BA, N.C. Wesleyan Coll., 1989. Adminstrv. asst. Community Arts Coun., Goldsboro, N.C., 1986-88; programmer analyst Northern Telecom Inc., Raleigh, N.C., 1988—. Fundraiser, co-chair local PTA, 1988-89; coord. fund drive Arts Coun., 1986; asst. leader Girl Scouts Am., 1987-90. Mem. Data Processing Mgmt. Assn. (pres. student chpt.), Phi Theta Kappa (v.p.). Home: 113 Clairmont Rd Goldsboro NC 27530

HORN, JOAN KELLY, congresswoman; b. St. Louis; M. E. Terrence Jones; 6 children from previous marriage. B in Polit. Sci., U. Mo., St. Louis, 1973, M in Polit. Sci., 1975. Pre-sch., elem. sch. Montessori tchr.; founder pre-schs. St. Louis and St. Joseph, Mo.; adj. faculty dept. polit. sci. U. Mo., St. Louis; with St. Louis County Office Community Devel., 1977-80, St. Louis Housing Authority, 1980-82; prin. Community Cons. Inc.; elected to Congress from Mo. dist. 2, 1990. Author articles on pub. policy issues. Mem. Dem. State Com. Mem. U. Mo. Alumni Alliance, U. Mo.-St. Louis Alumni Assn. (bd. dirs.). Office: US Ho of Representatives Offices of Ho Members Washington DC 20515*

HORN, KAREN NICHOLSON, banker; b. Los Angeles, Sept. 21, 1943; d. Aloys and Novella (Hartley) Nicholson; m. John T. Horn, June 5, 1965; 1 child. B.A., Pomona Coll., 1965; Ph.D., Johns Hopkins U., 1971. Economist bd. govs. FRS, Washington, 1969-71; v.p., economist First Nat. Bank, Boston, 1971-78; treas. Bell of Pa., Phila., 1978-82; pres. Fed. Res. Bank, Cleve., 1982-87; chmn. and chief exec. officer Bank One Cleveland NA, Cleve., 1987—; bd. dirs. TRW, Inc., Eli Lilly Co., Rubbermaid. Vice-chmn., trustee Case Western Res. U., Cleve.; trustee Rockefeller Found., Johns Hopkins U., Balt., Cleve. Clinic Found., Cleve. Orch., Cleve. Tomorrow, Greater Cleve. Roundtable. Office: Bank One Cleve NA 1255 Euclid Ave Cleveland OH 44115

HORN, KIM MARIE, advertising and marketing executive; b. Decatur, Ill., Aug. 7, 1964; d. James LeRoy and Carole Jean (Nelson) M. BS in Mktg., So. Ill. U., 1986. Mgr. The Ltd., Phoenix, 1986-87; account exec. Auto Svcs., Phoenix, 1987; advt. mgr. Virgo Pub., Scottsdale, Ariz., 1987-89; owner, mgr. Network Mktg. & Assocs., Tempe, Ariz., 1989—. Mem. NAFE. Democrat. Methodist.

HORN, LINDA ANNE, remodeling company executive; b. Kansas City, Mo., Nov. 17, 1943. Owner Bus. Svcs., Doraville, Ga.; purchasing agt., credit mgr. Jim Walter Papers, Atlanta; bus. mgr. Sims Remodeling Co., Tucker, Ga.; speaker in field. Contbr. articles to profl. jours. Mem. NAFE, Credit Women's Assn., Profl. Purchasing Agts. Assn. Home: 4200 English Oak Dr Doraville GA 30340

HORN, MARIAN BLANK, judge; b. N.Y.C., 1943; d. Werner P. and Mady R. Blank; m. Robert Jack Horn; children: Juli Marie, Carrie Charlotte, Rebecca Blank. Student, Barnard Coll., Columbia U.; student in law, Fordham U. Bar: N.Y. 1970, D.C. 1973, U.S. Supreme Ct. 1973. Asst. dist. atty. Bronx County, N.Y., 1969-72; assoc. Arent, Fox, Kintner, Plotkin & Kahn, 1972-73; project mgr. Am. U. Law Sch. study on alts. to conventional criminal adjudication U.S. Dept. Justice, 1973-75; litigation atty. Fed. Energy Adminstrn., 1975-76; sr. atty. office gen. counsel strategic petroleum res. br. Dept. Energy, 1976-79, dep. asst. gen. counsel for procurement and fin. incentives, 1979-81; dep. assoc. solicitor div. surface mining Dept. Interior, 1981-83, assoc. solicitor div. gen. law, 1983-85, prin. dep. solicitor, acting solicitor, 1985; judge U.S. Claims Ct., 1986—; adj. prof. law Washington Coll. Law, Am. U., 1973-76. Office: US Claims Ct 717 Madison Pl NW Washington DC 20005

HORN, PAULA LOIS, small business owner, editor, writer; b. N.Y.C., Jan. 20, 1947; d. Herman and Sadie Florence (Spiegelburd) H. BA, Albany State U., 1969; MS, Hofstra U., 1972; MA, NYU, 1974; PhD, U. So. Calif., 1980. Reading cons. and specialist Seaford, N.Y. and Branford, Conn., 1971-74; instructional designer Systems Devel. Corp., Santa Monica, Calif., 1978-79; pvt. cons., 1980—; ednl. tng. cons. U So. Calif., Los Angeles, 1982-85; mktg. tng. cons. Xerox Corp., El Segundo, Calif., 1985-86; software documentation specialist, Ashton-Tate Corp., Torrance, Calif., 1986-88; owner Tng. Ops. Profits, Studio City, Calif., 1988—; ednl. tng. cons. Nat. Tng. Systems, Santa Monica, 1979-80; ednl. tng. cons. Learning Systems, Encino, Calif., 1980-81; media tng. cons. Media Learning Systems, Pasadena, Calif., 1980; researcher and instructional devel. Northridge U., Calif., 1984-85. Author: Economics Analysis for Business, 1982; (with others) RapidFile, 1987; instr., designer, editor: Consultants' Handbook, 1986. Mem. Nat. Soc. Performance and Instrn., Soc. Applied Learning Tech. (bd. dirs.), Assn. Tng. and Devel., Soc. Tech. Communication, Mensa, Phi Delta Kappa, Phi Delta Epsilon. Avocations: writing, reading, concerts, movies, theater. Home: 11023 Fruitland Dr #4 Studio City CA 91604 Office: Tng Ops Profits Studio City CA 91604

HORN, ROBERTA CLAIRE, hospice volunteer organization administrator; b. New Brunswick, N.J.; d. John and Ruth (Holden) Teitscheid. BA cum laude, U. Calif., Berkeley, 1985; postgrad., New Sch. for Social Rsch., N.Y.C. Owner Roberta Horn Photography, Kennebunkport, Maine; cons. History of Print exhbn. Xerox Corp., 1978; reading tutor. One-woman show (photography) Portraits of Serenity. Mem. acquisition bd. for Am. collection Am. Sch. in London Libr., 1976-78; hotline vol. Pacific Ctr. for Human Devel., Berkeley, 1984-85; leader Girl Scouts U.S., China Lake, Calif., 1969-61, Rochester, N.Y., 1972; den mother Cub Scouts Am., Rockville, Md., 1965; mem. condominium bd. City of San Francisco, 1981-84; bd. dirs. Caring Unltd. Family Violence Shelter, Sanford, Maine, 1986-88; program specialist children's summer camp Bishopswood, Camden, Maine, 1990. Recipient awards for photography. Mem. DOVIA, Maine State Hospice Assn., Dirs. of Vol. Orgns., York Art Assn., Art Guild of the Kennebunks (former v.p.), Maine Women in the Arts (former pres.), C.G. Jung Found., Psi Chi. Office: PO Box 3081 Kennebunkport ME 04046

HORN, ROSE MARY, volunteer; b. Lancaster, Pa., Sept. 12, 1921; d. Frank Michael and Josephine Josepha (Kirchner) Abel; m. George Thomas Horn, Sept. 15, 1943; children: George (dec.), Elizabeth, Philip, Rose Mary, Ann. BS, Coll. of New Rochelle, N.Y., 1943; postgrad., Franklin & Marshall Coll., 1943-45, 90, Conn. Coll., 1945, Lanc. Theol. Sem., 1967, Hershey Med. Ctr., 1977, Millersville U., 1989, So. Meth. U., 1990. Cert. tchr., Pa. With advt. dept. Hager Dept. Store, Lancaster, 1943-44; tchr. McCaskey High Sch., Lancaster, 1944-46; substitute tchr. Columbia (Pa.) Sch. Dist., 1965-75; prin. St. Peter Sch., Columbia, 1975-86; ret., 1986; mem. adv. bd. IU's Prin.'s Assn., Lancaster, 1984-86; del. Harrisburg (Pa.) Cath. Diocese Synod, 1986—. Trustee Columbia Library, 1965-75; vol. Literary Coun., Lancaster, 1989—, Meals on Wheels, Columbia, 1986—. Mem. Mountwaybia Club (sec. 1988—), Columbia C. of C. Republican. Roman Catholic. Home: RD #3 Box 197 Columbia PA 17512

HORN, SUSAN ANDREWS, company executive; b. Boston, May 6, 1946; d. Arthur Wood and Marion (Saunders) Chapman; m. Richard Patrick Horn. AA, Colby-Sawyer Coll., 1966; BA, Hiram Coll., 1970. Founder, pres. Gem Island Software, Reading, Mass., 1985-90; dir. Gem Island Software, Carlisle, Mass., 1990—. Class historian Wellesley High Class, 1964; leader, mem. bd. dirs. Camp Fire, Reading, Antiquarian Soc., Reading, 1990—; steering com. officer Reading 350th Celebration, 1989—. Mem. Omicron Beta. Office: Gem Island Software PO Box 804 Carlisle MA 01741

HORN, SUSAN DADAKIS, statistics educator; b. Cleve., Aug. 30, 1943; d. James Sophocles and Demeter (Zessis) Dadakis; m. Roger Alan Horn, July 24, 1965; children: Ceres, Corinne, Howard. BA, Cornell U., 1964; MS, Stanford U., 1966, PhD, 1968. Asst. prof. Johns Hopkins U., Balt., 1968-76, assoc. prof., 1976-86, prof. stats. and health svcs. rsch. methods, 1986—. Fellow Am. Statist. Assn.; mem. Am. Pub. Health Assn., Biometric Soc., Assn. for Health Svcs. Research, Sigma Xi, Phi Beta Kappa, Phi Kappa Phi. Presbyterian. Home: 12101 Falls Rd Hunt Valley MD 21030 Office: Johns Hopkins U 624 N Broadway Baltimore MD 21205

HORNBAKER, ALICE JOY, author; b. Cin., Feb. 3, 1927; BA cum laude and honors in Journalism, San Jose State U., 1949; children: Christopher Albert, Holly Jo, Joseph Bernard III. Asst. woman's editor San Jose Mercury-News, 1949-55; owner, mgr. Frisch Big Boy Restaurant, Cin., 1955-68; dir. pub. relations Children's Home Soc. Calif., Santa Clara, 1968-71; asst. dir. pub. relations United Fund Calif., Santa Clara, 1971—; editor Tristate Sunday Enquirer mag., 1986—, columnist Generations Tristate mag.; editorial dir. Writers Digest Sch., Cin., 1971-75; columnist, critic, mag. writer, reporter, copy editor Tempo sec. Cin. Enquirer, 1975—, also book editor and critic, columnist for Aging, feature writer Tempo sect.; reporter feature segments on aging WKRC-TV; tchr. adult edn. Forest Hills Sch. Dist., Thomas More Coll., 1973—; author: Preventive Care: Easy Exercise Against Aging, 1974; byline in People, Modern Maturity, Sr. Advocate, NATR Jour., and others; contbr. fiction to Enquirer mag.; freelance mag. writer. Recipient Bronze award in Am. health journalism, Am. Chiropractic Assn., 1977, 78, Golden Image award Assn. Ohio Philanthropic Homes, 1989; 1st place for feature writing Cin. Editors Assn., 1983. Mem. Blue Pencil of Ohio State U. (pres. 1981-82), Women in Communications, Ohio Newspaper Women's Assn. (v.p. 1981-83, 1st place human interest story, 1977-85, 2d place columnist award 1979, Tops in Ohio award 1982, M.M. McMullen 2d place award 1982, Recognition award 1985), Soc. Profl. Journalists (treas. 1981-82). Office: The Cin Enquirer 617 Vine St Cincinnati OH 45201

HORNBERGER, DEBORAH ANN, certified registered nurse anesthetist; b. Lackawanna, N.Y., Apr. 4, 1957; d. Robert Henry and Lillian Mae (Muscato) H. AAS in Nursing, Trocaire Coll., 1978; BS in Nursing, B'Youville Coll., 1980; MS in Anesthesia, SUNY, Buffalo, 1983. RN, N.Y. Staff RN in burn unit and intensive care unit Sheehan Emergency Hosp., Buffalo, N.Y., 1978-83; cert. RN anesthetist Buffalo Gen. Hosp., 1983—. Mem. Am. Assn. of Nurse Anesthetists. Republican. Roman Catholic.

HORNBURG, TANYA V., technical consultant; b. Rochester, N.Y., Oct. 25, 1960; d. Donval Paul Louis Hornburg and Catrin-Maria (Haas) Pilkanis. BA in Polit. Sci., Boston U., 1982. Sr. canvassar Mass. Fair Share, Boston, 1983-84, field mgr., 1984, ea. regional sales mgr., 1984-85; head direct sales Matrix, Boston, 1986; adminstrv. supr. PSDI, Cambridge, Mass., 1986-87, tech. cons., 1988—. Mem. NAFI, Project Mgmt. Inst. Episcopalian. Office: PSDI 20 University Rd Cambridge MA 02138

HORN-DALTON, KATHY ELLEN, health facility administrator; b. Latrobe, Pa., Apr. 12, 1952; d. William Irving and Stella Bertha (Denisiuk) Horn; m. Glenn Holbert Dalton, Aug. 4, 1973. BS in Social Work, W.Va. U., 1975, MSW, 1976; PhD in Adminstrn., Columbia Pacific U., 1983. Registered psychotherapist. Counselor Womens Info. Ctr., Morgantown, W.Va., 1973; psychiatric aid Torrance (Pa.) State Hosp., 1974; group home counselor Sommerset Bedford Mental Health Ctr., Rockwood, Pa., 1974; shop foreman Southwest Wyo. Rehab. Ctr., Rock Springs, 1975-76, exec. dir., 1976-81, pres., administr., 1981—; researcher emotionally disturbed/mentally retarded project Div. Vocat. Rehab., Cheyenne, Wyo., 1985; CD grants adminstr. Sweetwater County, Rock Springs, Wyo., 1982-83. Author: Develop and Design an Energy Efficient Sheltered Workshop, 1983, Job Placement Results of a Job Training Partnership Act Program in a Rural Sheltered Workshop, 1985; contbr. articles to profl. jours. Mem. Wyo. Devel. Disabilities Council, 1978, Wyo. Pvt. Indsl. Council, 1983, adv. bd. U. No. Colo., Greeley, 1978; state advisor U.S. Congl. Adv. Bd., Washington, 1984, YWCA. Mem. Wyo. Assn. Rehab. Facilities (legis. chmn. 1981-83), Nat. Assn. Social Workers (cert.), Exec. Females Assn., Bus. Profl. Women's Assn., Pilot Butte Sand Drag Assn., Intermountain Sand Drag Assn., Nat. Sand Co. Assn., Nat. Hot Rod Assn. Office: SW Wyo Rehab Ctr 2632 Foothill Blvd Suite 107 Rock Springs WY 82901

HORNE, CHARLOTTE ANN HOLCOMBE, real estate executive; b. Anniston, Ala., Feb. 5, 1938; d. Charlie Gardy and Ola Bell (Little) Holcombe; m. Robert (Bobby) Edward Horne, Nov. 6, 1954; children—Robbie Sheila Horne Owen, Gary Wayne Horne, Shannon Michelle Horne Lambert. Cert. real estate appraiser, Ala. With credit dept. Hudson's, Anniston, 1971; sec. Super Valu Warehouse, Anniston, 1972; realtor Service Realty, Anniston, 1978-85, Howell Realty, Anniston, 1985—. Voter, dep. registrar, election poll worker, Anniston, 1970—. Mem. Women's Council of Realtors (charter mem., v.p. 1984, pres. 1985, Woman Yr. 1987), Calhoun County Area Bd. Realtors (Million Dollar Sales club 1983-87, life mem., named to Sales Honor club 1980, 81, 82, Realtor of Yr. 1986, bd. dirs. state and local 1985-87), DAR. Baptist. Club: Christian Women's (exec. com.). Lodge: Elks (exec. sec. 1983). Home: 1113 Caswell Dr Anniston AL 36201 Office: 1325 Quintard St Anniston AL 36201

HORNE, JANIS MAYO, investment executive; b. Hampton, Va., June 13, 1955; d. Walter B. and Mattie Harris (Mayo) H. BA with highest honors, Coll. of William and Mary, 1977; postgrad., U. Wis., 1977-79. Investment adminstr., asst. mgr. ops. Bailard, Biehl & Kaiser, Inc., Menlo Park and San Mateo, Calif., 1980-84; assoc. portfolio mgr. Bailard, Biehl & Kaiser, Inc., San Mateo, 1984-87, v.p., 1987—; sec., asst. treas. Bailard Biehl & Kaiser Internat. Fund, San Mateo, 1982, 85—, Bailard Biehl & Kaiser Fund Group, San Mateo, 1986, 89—; rep. Bailard Biehl & Kaiser Fund Svcs., San Mateo, 1987—; dir. shareholders rels. Bailard, Biehl & Kaiser, Inc., San Mateo, 1987-88. Sunday sch. tchr. various Episcopal chs., Williamsburg, Va., 1976-77, Madison, Wis., 1977-79, Palo Alto, Calif., 1982-88. Mem. Security Analysts San Francisco, Investment Counsel Assn. Am., Inst. Chartered Fin. Analysts, History Students Orgn. (sec. Williamsburg chpt. 1975-76, pres. 1976-77), Phi Beta Kappa, Omicron Delta Epsilon, Phi Alpha Theta. Republican.

HORNE, MARCY ANNE, communications educator; b. Pullman, Wash., Jan. 6, 1961; d. Donald Bruce and Mary Lee Tenwick; m. Jack Chandler Horne, Nov. 23, 1985; 1 child, David Chandler. BA in Communications, Wash. State U., 1985, MA, 1988. Bus. mgr. Pullman Herald, 1981-85; asst. prof. Lewis-Clark State Coll., Lewiston, Idaho, 1989—. Editor alumni publ. The Communicator, 1985. Area chmn. Am. Heart Assn., Clarkston, Wash., 1990. Mem. Women in Communications Inc. Home: 2346 Hillview Ct Clarkston WA 99403

HORNER, CONSTANCE J., federal office administrator; b. Summit, N.J., Feb. 24, 1942; d. David Earl and Cecelia (Murphy) McN.; m. Charles Edward Horner, May 7, 1965; children: David Bayer, Jonathan Purcell. BA in English Lit., U. Pa., 1964; MA in English Lit., U. Chgo., 1967. Dep. asst. dir. policy planning and evaluation ACTION Agy., Washington, 1981-82, acting assoc. dir. domestic & anti-poverty ops., 1982-83, dep. assoc. dir. for VISTA & service-learning, 1982-83; assoc. dir. for econs. & govt. Office of Mgmt. and Budget, Washington, 1983-85; dir. Office of Personnel Mgmt., Washington, 1985-89; under sec. HHS, 1989—. Mem. Pres.'s Commn. on White House Fellowships, Pres.'s Commn. on Exec. Exchange. Republican. Office: Dept of HHS Office of the Sec 200 Independence Ave SW Washington DC 20201*

HORNER, MARY KAY HALL, banker; b. Kansas City, Mo., Apr. 27, 1940; d. Joshua Motter and Mary Elizabeth (Phillips) Hall; m. Charles Dallas Horner, Aug. 18, 1962; children: Charles W., Katherine H., Stephen B. BA cum laude, Vassar Coll., 1962; MusM cum laude, U. Mich., 1964. Pvt. music tchr. Kansas City, 1964-74; agt. Voyageur Travel, Fairway, Kans., 1978-81; asst. v.p. United Mo. Bank, Kansas City, 1982-84; sr. v.p. Johnson County Bank, Prairie Village, Kans., 1984—. Active Leadership Kans., 1987; pres. Jr. League, Kansas City, 1974-75, chmn. Jr. League Midwest Coun., 1976-77; chmn. Greater Kansas City ARC, 1987-90; adv. bd. Midwest Red Cross, 1990—; bd. dirs., adv. bd. Shawnee Mission (Kans.) East Sch., 1980-82, Fine Arts Guild William Jewell Coll., Liberty, Mo., 1982-87; bd. dirs., treas. Prairie Village Mchts. Assn., 1984—; v.p., pres. Voluntary Action Bd., 1975-80; pres., sec. Reinhardt Homes Assn., 1976-80; mem. Kansas City Bicentennial Commn., 1976. Mem. Vis. Nurses Assn. (bd. dirs. 1984—), Kansas City C. of C., Pres.'s Club. Republican. Episcopal. Office: Johnson County Bank 6940 Mission Rd Prairie Village KS 66208

HORNER, MATINA SOURETIS, college president emerita, corporate executive; b. Boston, July 28, 1939; d. Demetre John and Christine (Antonopoulos) Souretis; m. Joseph L. Horner, June 25, 1961; children: Tia Andrea, John, Christopher. AB cum laude, Bryn Mawr Coll., 1961; MS, U. Mich., 1963, PhD, 1968; LLD (hon.), Dickinson Coll., 1973; LLD, Mt. Holyoke Coll., 1973; LLD (hon.), U. Pa., 1975, Smith Coll., 1979, Wheaton Coll., 1979, U. Mich., 1989; LHD (hon.), U. Mass., 1973, Tufts U., 1976, U. Hartford, 1980, U. New Eng., 1987, Bentley Coll., 1989, New Eng. Coll., 1989, Pine Manor Coll., 1989, Hellenic Coll., 1990, Am. Coll. Greece, 1990; DLitt (hon.), Claremont U. Ctr. and Grad Sch., 1988. Teaching fellow U. Mich., Ann Arbor, 1962-66, lectr. motivation personality, 1968-69; lectr. social relations Harvard U., Cambridge, Mass., 1969-70, asst. prof. clin. psychology, 1970-72, cons. univ. health svcs., 1971-89, assoc. prof. psychology, 1972-89; pres. Radcliffe Coll., Cambridge, 1972-89, pres. emerita, 1989—; exec. v.p. TIAA-CREF, N.Y.C., 1989—; bd. dirs. Time, Inc., Boston Edison Co. Co-author: The Challenge of Change, 1983; contbr. psychol. articles on motivation to profl. jours. and chpts. to books. Mem. adv. coun. NSF, 1977-87, chair, 1980-86; bd. trustees Twentieth Century Fund, 1973—, Am. Coll. of Greece, 1983-90, Mass. Eye and Ear Infirmary, 1986—, Com. for Econ. Devel., 1988—; bd. trustees Mass. Gen. Hosp., Inst. Health Professions, 1988—; bd. dirs. Coun. for Fin. Aid to Edn., 1985-89, Revson Found., 1986—, Beth Israel Hosp., 1989—; bd. dirs. Women's Rsch. and Edn. Inst., 1979—, chair rsch. com., 1982—; mem. Coun. on Fgn. Rels., 1984—; exec. com. ACE Bus. Higher Edn. Forum, 1984-86; exec. com. New Eng. Colls. Fund, 1980—, 2d v.p., 1984-85, 1st v.p., 1985-88, pres., 1988-89; mem. nat. panel to study declining test scores Coll. Entrance Exam. Bd., 1976-77; exec. com., chair task force Pres.'s Commn. for Nat. Agenda for 1980s, 1979-80; adv. com. Women's Leadership Conf. on Nat. Security, 1982—; exec. com. Coun. on Competitiveness, 1986-89; chair task force on health care Challenge to Leadership Conf., 1987-89. Recipient Roger Baldwin award Mass. Civil Liberties Union Found., 1982, citation of merit Northeast Region NCCJ, 1982, Career Contbn. award Mass. Psychol. Assn., 1987. Mem. NOW (nat. corp. adv. bd. of legal def. and edn. fund 1984—), Assn. Am. Colls. (com. chair), Nat. Inst. Social Scis. (medal for outstanding svc. 1973), Phi Beta Kappa, Phi Delta Kappa, Phi Kappa Phi.

HORNER, MAXINE EDWYNA CISSEL, state legislator; b. Tulsa, Jan. 17, 1933; d. Earl Henry Sr. and Corrine (Burton) Cissel; m. Donald Montell Horner Sr., 1954; children: Shari, Donald Montell Jr. BS in Pers. Mgmt., Langston U. Personnel adminstr. Tulsa Job Corps Ctr., 1971-75; dir. minority women's employment U.S. Dept. Labor, 1975-81; staff asst. U.S Rep. James Jones, Tulsa, 1984-86; mem. Okla. State Senate, 1986—; vice chmn. human resources com. 1987—; mem. bus. and labor, criminal jurisprudence, fin. coms., 1987—; chmn. govt. ops. & agy. oversight com., 1989—; mem. appropriations com., 1989—. Vol. VIP Read Aloud Program; v.p. North Tulsa Heritage Found., 1984—; pres. adv. bd. North Tulsa YMCA, 1985-86; active Corp. Membership Dr. Okla. Sickle Cell Anemia Found., Gov.'s Task Force on Affirmative Action, Simon Estes Scholarship Found., Health and Human Svcs. Com. for Nat. Conf. State Legislators, Children, Families and Social Svcs. Com., Dem. Nat. Platform Com.; chair Okla. Legis. Black Caucus; co-chair 1988 Nat. Black Caucus State Legislators Conf. Tulsa. Recipient spl. recognition Okla. Say No To Hate Crime Coalition, academic scholarship Wiley Coll., Marshall, Tex., 1951, Outstanding Community Svc. awards Tulsa Urban League, North Tulsa Bus. and Profl. Women, Tulsa Job Corps, Sunray DX Oil Co., Omega Psi Phi, grant Harvard U., MPA Program, Mid-Career Profession. Mem. NAACP, LWV, Nat. Assn. Black Social Workers, Dem. Women Action Group, Delta Sigma Theta. Baptist. Home: 3917 N Elgin Tulsa OK 74106 Office: PO Box 351 Tulsa OK 74101

HORNER, SALLY MCKAY MELVIN, academic administrator; b. Fayetteville, N.C., Nov. 17, 1935; d. John Stephen and Lila Williams (Chesnutt) Melvin; m. William W. Horner, June 9, 1953 (div. 1983); children: Stephanie McKay Horner Toney, John Wesley. BS in Chemistry, U. N.C., 1957, PhD in Inorganic Chemistry, 1961. Rsch. assoc., instr. U. N.C., Chapel Hill, 1961-67; prof. chemistry Meredith Coll., Raleigh, N.C., 1967-78, chmn. dept. chemistry and physics, 1972-78, asst. to pres., dir. instnl. rsch., 1975-78; dean arts and scis. U. Charleston, W.Va., 1978-81, provost, 1978-81, v.p. adminstrn. and fin., 1981-83, acting pres., 1984; vice chancellor planning, adminstrn., and fin. U. S.C.-Coastal Carolina Coll., Myrtle Beach, 1984—; physics cons. Research Triangle (N.C.) Inst., 1967; cons. gen. adminstrn. U. N.C., 1977-78, Bd. Regents, Charleston, 1983-87; mem. accreditation team So. Assn. Colls. and Schs., Atlanta, 1983—; speaker in field; nat. forum Am. Coun. on Edn. Women Adminstrs., Phoenix, 1980. Contbr. articles to profl. jours. Exec. com., bd. dirs. YWCA, Charleston, 1983-84; trustee Kanawha Players Theatre, Charleston, 1983-84; treas. Wheelwright Coun. for Arts, Conway, S.C., 1986—. Mem. Am. Chem. Soc., (sec., chmn. elect), S.C. Assn. Women in Higher Edn. (bd. dirs. 1987—), Order of Valkyries, Myrtle Beach C. of C. (fin. com. 1988—), Soc. Sigma Xi, Phi Beta Kappa. Home: 608D N 35th Ave Myrtle Beach SC 29578 Office: U SC Coastal Carolina Coll PO Box 1954 Myrtle Beach SC 29578

HORNER, WINIFRED BRYAN, educator, researcher, consultant; b. St. Louis, Aug. 31, 1922; d. Walter Edwin and Winifred (Kinealy) Bryan; m. David Alan Horner, June 15, 1943; children: Winifred, Richard, Elizabeth, David. AB, Washington U., St. Louis, 1943; MA, U. Mo., 1961; PhD, U. Mich., 1975. Instr. English U. Mo., Columbia, 1966-75, asst. prof. English, 1975-80, chair lower div. studies, dir. composition program, 1974-80, assoc. prof., 1980-83, prof., 1984-85, emeritus prof., 1985; Radford chair rehetoric and composition, prof. English Tex. Christian U., Ft. Worth, 1985—. editor: Historical Rhetoric; An Annotated Bibliography of Selected Sources in English, 1980, The Present State of Scholarship in Historical Rhetoric, 1983, Composition and Literature, Bridging the Gap, 1983; author: Rhetoric in a Classical Mode, 1987. Inst. for the Humanities fellow U. Edinburgh, 1987; NEH grantee, 1976, 87. Mem. Internat. Soc. for History Rhetoric (exec. coun. 1986), Rhetoric Soc. Am. (bd. dirs. 1981, pres. 1987), Nat. Coun. Writing Program Adminstrs. (v.p. 1977-85, pres. 1985-87), Coll. Conf. on Composition and Communication (exec. com.), Modern Lang. Assn. (mem. del. assembly 1981). Office: Tex Chrisitan U English Dept Fort Worth TX 76129

HORNE'Y, CHRISTEL ADELE, small business owner; b. Munich, Nov. 1, 1938; came to U.S., 1959; d. Maxemillian and Marieluise (Stephan) Schmid; m. Richard Arlen Horne'y, Oct. 15, 1961 (div. 1979); children: Michaela Marieluise, Richard Eberhard. Student Dental Asst., U. Dentistry, Munich, 1955-57, student Dental Tech., 1957-59. Cert. dental technician. Founder Studio of Dental Ceramics, Indpls., 1967, owner, 1967—; pub., owner Shaderite Corp., 1988-89; cons., lectr. body chemistry, Indpls., 1975-79; dor. for Ind. Fund for Dental Health Assn., Chgo., 1983-84. Vol. Am. Legion, Lebanon, Ind., 1975—; pres. Med. Mission (div. Ch. Women United), Lebanon, 1976-79. Fellow Dental Lab. Assn. Ind. (bd. dirs. 1980-82). Republican. Roman Catholic. Avocations: Ballroom dancing, crossword puzzles, golf, travel, gin rummy, languages. Home: 9620 Greentree Dr Indianapolis IN 46268 Office: Studio of Dental Ceramics 3906 W 86th St Indianapolis IN 46268

HORNICK, KATHERINE JOYCE KAY, artist; b. Chelan, Wa., Jan. 2, 1940; d. Donald Dale and Dorothy Eleanor (Tilton) Shipton; m. Dan Lewis Hornick, Apr. 6, 1959; children: Tod A. and Daniel D. Student, Kinman Bus. U., Spokane, 1957-58, Shoreline Community Coll., Bothell, 1972-74. Owner The Traveling Gallery, Bothell, Wa., 1969-74; juror NW Pastel Soc., Redmond, Wa., 1978; resident artist Qraz Gallery, Seattle, 1968-70; represented by Bainbridge Arts & Crafts, Bainbridge Island, Wash., 1989—, Oceanlake Studio Gallery, Lincoln City, Oreg., 1989—; condr. Bainbridge Island Studio Tour, 1988-90; lectr. Community Groups & Sch. Puget Sound Area, 1969-89; tchr. Kay Hornick Studios Bothell, 1972-75. Recipient Hon. Mention Charles & Emma Frye Museum Seattle, 1988. Assoc. Mem. NW Watercolor Soc., Chpt. Mem. Nat. Museum Women in Arts, Bainbridge Arts and Crafts (bd. dirs. 1989-90).

HOROWITZ, BEVERLY PHYLLIS, occupational therapist; b. N.Y.C., Jan. 10, 1949; d. Abe Joseph and Blanche (Reich) Postman; m. Stuart Daniel Horowitz, July 15, 1973; children: Elizabeth, Sharon, Amy. BA, SUNY, Stony Brook, 1971; MS, Columbia U., 1975. Lic. occupational therapist, N.Y. Tchr. English, Thomas Alva Edison High Sch., Jamaica, N.Y., 1972-73; occupational therapist St. Charles Hosp., Port Jefferson, N.Y., 1975-79, Vis. Nurse Svc. Huntington, Huntington Station, N.Y., 1980—, Gurwin Jewish Geriatric Ctr., Commack, N.Y., 1988-90; pvt. practice Huntington Station, 1980—; occupational therapist, cons. Hilaire Farm Nursing Home, Huntington Station, 1980—, Muscular Dystrophy Assn., Hauppauge, N.Y., 1980-83, 88-89, Brookhaven Health Care Facility, Patchogue, N.Y., 1988; adj. faculty Touro Coll., Huntington, N.Y, 1989—; book reviewer Am. Jour. Occupational Therapy, Rockville, Md., 1981-86; mem Occupational Therapy Adv. Bd. Touro Coll., 1988—. Workshop presenter Lindenhurst (N.Y.) Pub. Libr., 1987, Northport (N.Y.) Pub. Libr., 1989; mem. exec. bd. Maplewood-South Huntington Schs. PTA, 1989. Recipient cert. appreciation N.Y. State Occupational Therapy Assn., 1980, 82, 83. Mem. Am. Occupational Therapy Assn., Nat. Coun. on Aging. Office: 29 Aldrich St Huntington Station NY 11746

HOROWITZ, ESTHER, speech pathology educator, retired; b. N.Y.C., Dec. 17, 1920; d. Israel and Dora (Altschuler) H. BA, Bklyn. Coll., 1940; MA, U. Wis., 1949; PhD, Columbia U., 1959. Cert. mem. Am. Speech, Hearing, Lang. Assn. Speech clinician Queens (N.Y.) Coll. Speech Clinic, 1944-46; tchr. of speech improvement N.Y.C. Pub. Schs., Bklyn., 1946-50; from instr. to prof. of speech Hofstra U., Hempstead, N.Y., 1950-81, dir. speech clinic, 1953-67. Co-author: Guidelines to Better Speech, 1965; contbr. articles to profl. jours. Recipient cert., The Arts in Britain Today, U. London, 1950. Avocations: music, theatre, arts and crafts. Democrat. Jewish. Home: 147-07 Charter Rd Jamaica NY 11435

HOROWITZ, SYLVIA TEICH, chemistry educator; b. N.Y.C., Dec. 11, 1922; d. Abraham and Gertrude (Green) T.; m. Robert Miller Horowitz, Nov. 29, 1953; children: Jonathan, David, Daniel. BA, Bklyn. Coll., 1943; PhD, Columbia U., 1949. Research assoc. Columbia U. Coll. Physicians and Surgeons, N.Y.C., 1950-53, U. Mich., Ann Arbor, 1953-55; assoc. prof. Calif. State U., L.A., 1969—. Contbr. articles to profl. jours. Mem. Am. Chem. Soc., Sigma Xi. Home: 800 Fairfield Circle Pasadena CA 91106

HORRIDGE, PATRICIA EMILY, education educator; b. Marshall, Tex., Jan. 17, 1937; d. Earl Theodore and Beatrice Mary (Wynne) H. BS, U. Tex., 1958; MS, U. Houston, 1965; PhD, Tex. Woman's U., 1969. Asst. buyer Joske's of Houston, 1959-60; tchr. Deer Park (Tex.) Ind. Sch. Dist., 1960-66; asst. prof. Baylor U., Waco, Tex., 1966-68, Fla. State U., Tallahassee, 1969-72; assoc. prof. U. Southwestern La., Lafayette, 1972-73; chmn., assoc. prof. U. Ky., Lexington, 1973-76; chmn., assoc. prof. Tex. Tech U., Lubbock, 1976-85, chmn., prof., 1985-90, prof., 1990—; reviewer Home Econs. Rsch. jour., 1982—, Clothing and Textiles Rsch. jour., 1983—. Contbr. articles to profl. jours. Recipient Disting. Rockwell Rsch. Professorship, Rockwell Fund, Inc., Dallas, 1990-92. Fellow Assn. Coll. Profs. of Textiles and Clothing (planning coun. 1978-81, cen. region pres. 1981, nat. exec. bd. 1984-86, proceedings editor 1990-91); mem. Am. Home Econs. Assn. (cert. home economist 1987—), Daughters Republic of Tex. (v.p. 1983-85), DAR. Republican. Presbyterian. Office: Texas Tech Univ PO Box 4170/Coll Home Econs Lubbock TX 79409

HORSLEY, PAULA ROSALIE, accountant; b. Smithfield, Nebr., Sept. 7, 1924; d. Karl and Clara Margaret (Busse) Fenske; m. Phillip Carreon (dec.); children—Phillip, James, Robert, David, Richard; m. Norby Lumon, Apr. 5, 1980. Student AIB Bus. Coll., Des Moines, 1942-44, YMCA Coll., Chgo., 1944-47, UCLA Extension, 1974. Acctg. mgr. Montgomery Ward & Co., Denver, 1959-62; acct. Harman & Co., C.P.A.s, Arcadia, Calif., 1962-67; controller, officer G & H Transp., Montebello, Calif., 1967-78; comptroller Frederick Weisman Co., Century City, Calif., 1978-80; chief fin. officer Lutheran Shipping, Madang, Papua, New Guinea, 1980-82; prin. Village Bookkeeper, acctg. cons., Monreno Valley, Calif., 1982-89; chief fin. officer Insight Computer Products and Tech., Inc., San Diego, 1988—. Vol. crises counselor, supr. and instr. Melodyland Hotline, Anaheim, Calif., 1976-79. Mem. Riverside Tax Cons., Nat. Assn. for Female Execs., Internat. Platform

Assn. Republican. Lutheran. Avocations: church activities, reading, cooking, phys. fitness. Home: 4660 N River Rd SP 129 Oceanside CA 92054 Office: Insight Computer Products and Techs Inc 4883 Ronson Ct Ste T San Diego CA 92111

HORST, NANCY CARROLL, county recorder; b. Bloomville, Ohio, Jan. 20, 1933; d. Frank Carl Wyndham and Desee Loree (Smith) Snare; m. Carl Robert Horst, Mar. 26, 1949; children: Catherine Blum, Debra Polgar, Diane Loebig. BA in Communications, Capital U., 1985. Advt. clk. Star Beacon, Ashtabula, Ohio, 1963-65; receptionist Ashtabula, 1965-66; adminstrv. sec. Kent State U., Ashtabula, 1968-70; librarian, sec. Ashtabula Area City Schs., 1971-83; freelance writer Ashtabula, 1974-77; recorder Ashtabula County, Jefferson, Ohio, 1985—; editor Ohio Recorders Assn. Newspaper, 1986—. Contbr. articles to profl. jours. Mem. Ashtabula County Dems., 1974—; v.p. Women Dems., Ashtabula, 1988—. Mem. Women Bus. Owners of Western Res., Ashtabula County Data Processing Bd., Ashtabula County Soc. Handicapped. Home: 3611 Dickenson Rd Ashtabula OH 44004 Office: Ashtabula County Recorder 25 W Jefferson St Jefferson OH 44047

HORST, PAMELA JANE, educational administrator; b. Lancaster, Pa., Nov. 3, 1957; d. Benjamin Henry and Virginia Ann (Suydam) H. BS, Lock Haven U., 1979; MA, Villanova U., 1987. Tchr. Melmark Sch., Berwyn, Pa., 1979-82, asst. dir., 1988—; tchr. Martin Luther Sch., Plymouth Meeting, Pa., 1982-85, asst. dir., 1985-87, dir., 1987-88; exec.-on-duty Silver Springs Residential Treatment Ctr., Plymouth Meeting, 1986-88. Vol. Melmark Home, Berwyn, 1980-82, Silver Springs Residential Treatment Ctr., 1983—, Children's Hosp. Phila., 1987—. Mem. Assn. for Supervision and Curriculum Devel., Kappa Delta Pi. Republican. Home: 20 Bishop Hollow Rd B-5 Newtown Square PA 19073 Office: Melmark Sch Wayland Rd Berwyn PA 19312

HORSTMAN, NANCY JEAN CROCKER, educational administrator; b. Lafayette, Ind., May 18, 1945; d. Robert Bennett and Elsie Jean (Chapin) Crocker; m. Allen Henry Horstman, Aug. 3, 1968; children: Matthew Henry Crocker, Frederick Robert Crocker. BA, Albion Coll., 1967; MS in Edn., Ind. U., 1970; EdS, Mich. State U., 1987. Cert. tchr., in elem. adminstr., Mich. Kindergarten tchr. Cambridge (Mass.) Schs., 1967-68, Indpls. Pub. Schs., 1969-72; tchr. elem. schs. Vallejo (Calif.) Unified Schs., 1972-75, 76-77; Fulbright-Hayes exch. tchr. Inner London Edn. Authority, 1975-76; various temp. ednl. positions Mich., 1979-84; tchr. Chpt. 1 reading Litchfield (Mich.) Schs., 1985-87; elem. sch. prin. Morenci (Mich.) Area Schs., 1987—; cons. NW Schs., Jackson, Mich., 1985. Mem. United Way, Albion, Mich., 1985-86. Janice Marston scholar Mich. State U., 1985. Mem. NAESP, Mich. Elem. and Mid. Sch. Prins. Assn. (curriculum and instrn. commn. 1987—), Lenawee Elem. and Mid. Sch. Prins. Assn., AAUW (pres. Albion 1981-83), Kiwanis, Phi Beta Kappa, Phi Kappa Phi. Democrat. Methodist. Office: Morenci Elem Sch 517 E Locust St Morenci MI 49256

HORSTMAN, SUZANNE RUCKER, certified financial planner; b. Coral Gables, Fla., June 27, 1945; d. Thomas John, Jr. and June Ethel Agusta (Stones) R.; BBA, Fla. Atlantic U., 1971, MBA, 1975. Cert. fin. planner; lic. real estate agt. Assoc. dir. Am. Soc. Cons. Pharmacists, 1971-73; chpt. specialist Epilepsy Found. Am., 1973-74; assoc. dir. devel. Fairfax Hosp. Assn. Found., Springfield, Va., 1974-81; dir. devel. Arlington (Va.) Hosp. Found., 1982-86; prin. Suzanne June Rucker, Cert. Fin. Planner, Falls Church, Va., 1986—; instr. George Washington U.; seminar speaker in field. Bd. dirs. Ronald McDonald House Washington, Salvation Army Aux. Washington, Rep. Working Women's Forum. Fellow Nat. Assn. Hosp. Devel. Republican. Lodge: Optimists.

HORSTMANN, DOROTHY MILLICENT, physician, educator; b. Spokane, Wash., July 2, 1911; d. Henry J. and Anna (Hunold) H. AB, U. Calif., 1936, MD, 1940; DSc (hon.), Smith Coll., 1961; MA (hon.), Yale, 1961; D Med. Scis. (hon.), Women's Med. Coll. of Pa., 1963. Intern San Francisco City and County Hosp., 1939-40, asst. resident medicine, 1940-41; asst. resident medicine Vanderbilt U. Hosp., 1941-42; Commonwealth Fund fellow, sect. preventive medicine Sch. Medicine, Yale U., New Haven, 1942-43; instr. preventive medicine Sch. Medicine, Yale U., 1943-44, 45-47, asst. prof., 1948-52, assoc. prof., 1952-56, assoc. prof. preventive medicine and pediatrics, 1956-61, prof. epidemiology and pediatrics, 1961-69, John Rodman Paul prof. epidemiology, prof. pediatrics, 1969-82; John Rodman Paul prof. epidemiology, prof. pediatrics emeritus, sr. research scientist Sch. Medicine Yale U., 1982—; instr. medicine U. Calif., 1944-45. Recipient Albert Coll. award, 1953, Gt. Heart award Variety Club Phila., 1968, Modern Medicine award, 1974; James D. Bruce award ACP, 1975, Thorvald Madsen award State Serum Inst. (Denmark), 1977, Maxwell Finland award Infectious Disease Soc.-Am., 1978; named Disting. Alumni award U. Calif. Med. Sch., 1979, Master ACP; NIH fellow Nat. Inst. Med. Research, London, 1947-48. Master ACP; fellow Am. Acad. Pediatrics (hon.); mem. NAS, Am. Soc. Clin. Investigation, Am. Epidemiol. Soc. (v.p. 1974-75), Am. Pediatric Soc., Am. Soc. Virology (coun. 1983-84), Assn. Am. Physicians, Infectious Diseases Soc. Am. (pres. 1974-75, coun. 1972-74), Soc. Epidemiologic Rsch., Pan-Am. Med. Assn., Internat. Epidemiol. Assn., Royal Soc. Medicine (hon., epidemiology and preventive medicine sect.), Conn. Acad. Sci. and Engring., European Assn. Against Virus Diseases, Soc. African Soc. Pathologists (hon.), Sigma Delta Epsilon (hon.). Home: 11 Autumn St New Haven CT 06511 Office: Yale U Sch Medicine Epidemiology & Pub Health PO Box 3333 New Haven CT 06510

HORTMAN, CAROLYN L., engineering executive; b. Butler, Ga., Nov. 18, 1957; d. Joe Harold and Bonneal (Joiner) Locke; m. George (Wayne) Hortman, Dec. 12, 1986; children: Ashley, Shae, Brandi, Jennifer. Grad. high sch., Butler. Cert. time study and methods engr. Machine operator Oxford Shirt Co., Reynolds, Ga.; plant mgr. McCrackin Industries, Inc., Conley, Ga. Mem. adv. bd. Upson Tech. Sch. Mem. NAFE. Address: PO Box 423 Hwy 128 Reynolds GA 31076

HORTON, ANN MITCHELL, health organization executive; b. Memphis, Apr. 14, 1949; d. Foy B. and Frances Louise (Mashbern) Mitchell; m. Steven Michael Horton, Dec. 20, 1970; children: Matthew William, Emily Frances. BS, U. Tenn., 1970; MA in Speech Pathology, Memphis State U., 1972. postgrad. No. Ill. U., 1973, 74, Chgo. State U., 1974, Nat. Coll. Edn., 1975, U. Tenn., 1976, 84, U. Cin., 1984, 85. Lic. speech pathologist, Tenn.; cert. speech tchr., Tenn. Grad. asst. Memphis State U., Osceola, Ark., 1971-72, clin. supr., 1972; coord. speech and lang. programs Northwest Suburban Spl. Edn. Coop., Palatine, Ill., 1972-75, coord. reading programs, 1974-75; spl. svcs. coord. for handicapped children East Tenn. Children's Rehab. Ctr., Knoxville, 1975-76; speech pathologist cons. Nat. Health Corp., Athens, Tenn., 1976-83, eastern regional coord. for communication disorders svc., 1983-86, corp. coord. communication disorders svc.s, 1986—, founder Athens Out-Patient Rehab. Program. Contbr. articles to profl. publs. Mem. Nat. Assn. Female Execs., Nat. Health Corp. (co-chmn. quality assurance com. 1982—, co-chmn. supportive personnel com. 1985—, legis. coun. 1990—), Am. Speech, Lang. and Hearing Assn. (supportive personnel com. 1987—), Tenn. Speech and Hearing Assn. (peer rev. com. 1979—, adv. bd. to Blue Cross/Blue Shield 1980-84). Home: 404 Cutlas Rd Englewood TN 37922 Office: Athens Health Care Ctr Box 766 1204 Frye St Athens TN 37303

HORTON, BARBARA ELIZABETH, sales executive; b. Lexington, N.C., Aug. 21, 1953; d. Hazel Knox Horton. BS, Coker Coll., Hartsville, S.C., 1975. Tennis dir. Careel Bay, Cruz Bay, St. John, 1982-88, Beverly Hills (Calif.) Country Club, 1988-89; dir. sales and pub. relations Peter Burwash Internat., Van Nuys, Calif., 1989—; tennis dir. King Ranch Health Spa & Fitness Resort, King City, Ont., Can.; treas.-sec. St. John Racquet Club, 1982-88; Caribbean reg. dir. Peter Burwash Internat., St. John, 1982-88. Contbr. articles to profl. jours. Spokeswoman Am. Lung Assn., 1982-88. Mem. U.S. Profl. Tennis Assn., U.S. Tennis Assn., Century City C. of C., Lioness. Repubican. Methodist. Home and Offie: King Ranch Health Spa, & Fitness Resort, RR 2, King City, ON Canada LOG 1KO

HORTON, BARBARA MARION DEADY, fund developer; b. Oswego, NY, Dec. 14, 1930; d. Harold Eugene and Marion Cecilia (Irwin) Deady; m. Charles Laurence, June 21, 1952; children: Deborah Christine Hovatter, Elizabeth Caroline Michael, Walter Arnold, Patrick Joseph. BS, Northwestern U., Evanston, Ill., 1952. Profl. Reg. Parliamentarian. Resource devel. dir. United Way Atlantic County, N.J., 1986--. Mem. P.E.O. (chpt. pres. 1986-88), Alpha Chi Omega (nat. treas. 1980-85), Holly Shores Girl Scout Coun., Frontier Girl Scout Coun. (Thanks Badge 1973, 87), Atlantic Coun. Women's Chamber, Pub. Rels. Coun. Republican. Roman Catholic. Home: 1930 Mary Jane Ln Linwood NJ 08221

HORTON, JEANETTE, municipal government official; b. Paterson, N.J., Dec. 1, 1938; d. David and Mary (Carpenter) Potash; m. Troy Horton, Oct. 31, 1958. Student, Broward Community Coll., 1970-72, Barry U., 1982, Fla. Atlantic U., 1983-84, Fla. State U., 1985. Cert. mcpl. clk., Fla. Bookkeeper Fla. Housewares, Miami, Fla., 1961-65; asst. to comptroller Gulf Stream Press, Miami, 1965-70; comptroller Chrysler Plymouth, Miami, Fla., 1970-75; municipal clk., fin. dir. Village of Biscayne Park, Fla., 1975—. Commr. Cooper City, Fla., 1971-73. Mem. Fla. Assn. City Clks. (scholarship 1985-87, scholarship chmn. 1988-89), Am. Bus. Women (Woman of Yr. award 1985, pres., v.p. 1985-87), Fla. Assn. City Clks. and Fin. Dirs., Bus. and Profl. Women (pres. 1981), Internat. Mcpl. Clks. Assn., Personnel Mgmt. Assn. Democrat. Roman Catholic. Home: 515 SW 61 Terr Hollywood FL 33023 Office: Village of Biscayne Park 640 NE 114th St Biscayne Park FL 33161

HORTON, MADELINE MARY, financial executive, consultant, financial and estate planner; b. Chgo., Mar. 1, 1939; d. James P. and Priscilla Mary (Caruso) Fiduccia; m. Richard J. Dickman, July 7, 1962 (div. 1981); children: James Earl, Suzanne Dickman Noel; m. Larry B. Horton, June 30, 1984; stepchildren: Michele Rene, Margot Lyn Horton Parsons. BA in Math. cum laude, Rosary Coll., River Forest, Ill., 1960; MS in Math., U. Miami, Coral Gables, Fla., 1962; postgrad., U. Va., 1974-78. Instr. in math. U. Miami, Coral Gables, 1962-63; prin. Dickman Deductions, Charlottesville, Va., 1974-77; instr. devel. math. Piedmont Community Coll., Charlottesville, Va., 1974-78; health affairs planner U. Va. Med. Ctr., Charlottesville, 1978-80; zone mgr. Investors Diversified Svcs., Inc., Charlottesville, 1980-83; fin. cons. Merrill Lynch, Charlottesville, 1983-86; mgr., fin. cons. Prudential-Bache Securities, Inc., Charlottesville, 1986-87; investment broker Wheat First Securities Inc., Charlottesville, 1987; pres., fin. cons., co-founder Horton Fin. Svcs. Inc., Charlottesville, 1987—. Humor columnist Charlottesville Daily Progress, 1971; featured in article Va. Bus. monthly mag., 1988. Mem. Internat. Mgmt. Coun. (sec. Charlottesville chpt. 1986-88, v.p. 1988-89), Internat. Assn. for Fin. Planning, Inst. Cert. Fin. Planners (assoc.), NAFE, Internat. Platform Assn., Kappa Gamma Pi. Republican. Roman Catholic. Home: 3866 Lake Park Rd Earlysville VA 22936 Office: Horton Fin Svcs Inc One Morton Dr Ste 100 Charlottesville VA 22901

HORTON, MILDRED G., state government official; b. Waresboro, Ga., May 18, 1929; d. Willie Fairel and Luscinda Allbritton Keaton; m. Curtis F. Horton, De. 12, 1970; children: Robert L. Gandy Jr., Brenda Horton Poole, Leighann King. Student, St. Johns Community Coll., Am. Inst. Banking. Dir. dept. adminstrn. St. Johns River Water Mgmt. Dist., Palatka, Fla.; asst. cashier Exch. Bank of Palatka; asst. exec. dir. St. Johns River Water Mgmt. Dist., Palatka; owner, sec., treas. Shamrock Greenhouses, Inc. Mem. Fla. Govt. Fin. Officers Assn., NAFE, Putnam Soc., Rotary (charter Palatka Sunrise Club). Home: 10 Thompson Dr East Palatka FL 32131

HORVAT, EDWINA MARIE, city official; b. Youngstown, Ohio, Sept. 9, 1953; d. Edward Joseph and Mary Frances (Yerman) H. BS in Bus. Edn., Kent State U., 1975; MBA, Cleve. State U., 1984. Mktg. sec. ESB Brands, Inc., Cleve., 1975-76; sales mgr. Scene Entertainment Weekly, Cleve., 1976-78; area mgr. Revlon Inc., Grand Rapids, Mich., 1979-83; software trainer Threshold Data Tech., Cleve, 1985-86; dir. adminstrn. Planned Parenthood Greater Cleve., 1986-87; personnel officer City of Shaker Heights (Ohio), 1987—. Bd. dirs. West Side Community Mental Health Ctr., Cleve., 1987—; rec. sec. Berkshire Condominium Assn. Bd. Trustees, Lakewood, Ohio, 1989; mediator Lakewood Law Dept., 1989. Mem. Internat. Personnel Mgmt. Assn. (sec. Greater Cleve. chpt. 1989—), Greater Cleve. Personnel Coun., 13th Street Racquet Club. Democrat. Roman Catholic.

HORWITH, SUSAN KARDOS, banker; b. Allentown, Pa.; m. Brian K. Horwith. BS, Pa. State U., 1979; cert., Am. Inst. Banking, 1987; postgrad., Lubin Grad. Sch. Bus. Internal auditor investment banking and treasury Royal Bank Can., N.Y.C., 1985-87; unit head - personal banking Bank N.Y., N.Y.C., 1987-89, credit trainee, 1988-89, asst. treas., pvt. banker, 1989—. Named one of Outstanding Young Women Am., 1979. Mem. NAFE. Office: Bank NY 706 Madison Ave New York NY 10021

HORWITZ, KATHRYN BLOCH, professor of medicine; b. Sosua, Dominican Republic, Feb. 20, 1941; came to U.S., 1952; d. Werner Meyerstein and Olga (Schlesinger) Bloch; m. Lawrence David Horwitz, June 14, 1964; children: Phillip Andrew, Carolyn Anita. BA, Barnard Coll., 1962; BS, NYU, 1966; PhD, U. Tex., Dallas, 1975; postdoctoral, U. Tex. Sch. Medicine, 1978. Instr. U. Tex. Sch. Medicine, San Antonio, 1978-79; asst. prof. U. Colo. Sch. Medicine, Denver, 1979-84, assoc. prof., 1984-89, prof. of medicine, pathology and molecular biology, 1989—; cellular physiology panel NSF, 1985-88; biochem. endorinology study sect. NIH, 1989—; scientific adv. bd. Molecular Oncology, Inc., Gaithersburg, Md., 1990—. Author numerous research papers. Chair, scientific adv. bd. Cancer League of Colo., 1987—; mem. NOW, ACLU, Common Cause. Recipient Nat. Bd. award Med. Coll. Pa., 1986, Wilson Stone award M.D. Anderson Hosp. and Tumor Inst., 1976, Rsch. Career Devel. award Nat. Cancer Inst., 1981-86; grantee NIH, NSF, Am. Cancer Soc., Nat. Found. Cancer Rsch. Mem. Endocrine Soc. (program com. 1989-91, nominating com. 1989-91, chair 1991), Am. Fedn. Clin. Rsch., Am. Soc. Cell Biology, Am. Assn. Cancer Rsch., Western Soc. Clin. Investiagting, AAAS. Democrat. Jewish. Office: U Colo Dept Medicine Box B-151 4200 E 9th Ave Denver CO 80262

HOSEA, JULIA HILLER, communications executive, paralegal; b. Cin., Oct. 19, 1952; d. Clifford John and Nancy Carol (Elberg) Hiller; m. Jon Michael Ausman, Nov. 3, 1973 (div. 1978); m. Robert Arthur Hosea, Mar. 22, 1987. BA, Allegheny Coll., 1975; cert., Inst. Paralegal Tng., Phila., 1975. Gen. paralegal Pettigrew & Bailey, Miami, Fla., 1975-76, Joseph J. Weisenfeld Law Offices, Miami, 1976-81; corp. paralegal Wood & Lamping, Cin., 1981-85; pension specialist Katz, Teller Brant & Hild, Cin., 1985-89; owner, mgr. Chrysalis Communications, Cin., 1989—; adj. instr. Coll. Mt. St. Joseph, Cin., 1984—. Contbr. articles to profl. publs. Mem. Cin. Paralegal Assn. (pres. 1984-85), Nat. Fedn. Paralegal Assn. (chmn. pension sect. 1986-87, editor Nat. Reporter 1988—). Office: 550 Woodbrook Ln Cincinnati OH 45215

HOSEA, LINDA MARX, psychotherapist; b. Temple, Tex., July 15, 1954; d. Albert and Inez Louise (Helms) Marx; m. Thomas J. Hosea, Mar. 13, 1976 (div. 1990). BS in Psychology, Tex. A&M U., 1976, MS in Psychology, 1984. Counselor Neuropsychiatry Assocs., Bryan, Tex., 1980-83, Brazos Family Inst., Bryan, 1983-85; chem. abuse counselor Hosp. Corp. Am./Greenleaf Hosp., Bryan, 1985-87; pvt. practice Anthony Arden PLD & Assocs., Bryan, 1987-89; program coord. Hosp. Corp. Am./Gulf Pines Hosp., Houston, 1989—. Bd. dirs. Brazos County Rape Crisis Ctr., 1983-89. Recipient Dr. Frist Humanitarian award Hosp. Corp. Am., 1986; named Vol. of Yr. Brazos County Rape Crisis Ctr., Bryan, 1988. Mem. Am. Psychol. Assn., Tex. Assn. Alcoholism and Drug Abuse Counselors, Brazos Valley Psychol. Assn. Lutheran. Home: 14545 Bammel N Houston TX 77014 Office: HCA Gulf Pines Hosp 205 Hollow Tree Ln Houston TX 77090

HOSEK, CHAVIVA MILADA, Canadian provincial official; b. Chomutov, Czechoslovakia, Oct. 6, 1946; d. Emil Hosek and Hedy (Weiss) Pivko. BA with honors, McGill U., Montreal, Que., Can., 1967; AM, Harvard U., 1968, PhD, 1972. Asst. prof. Victoria Coll. U. Toronto, Ont., Can., 1972-78, assoc. prof., 1978—; ptnr. Gordon Capital Corp., Toronto, 1985-87; M.P., cabinet minister Govt. of Ont., Toronto, 1987—; mem. organizing com. Nat. Econ. Summit, Ottawa, 1984-85; mem. Econ. Coun. Can., Ottawa, 1986-87, Canadian Del. to Quadrangular Forum, Tokyo, 1986. Editor: Circle & Labyrinth: Essays in Honour of Northrop Frye, 1983, Lyric Poetry Beyond New Criticism, 1985; contbr. articles to profl. jours. Mem. steering com. Ont. Com. on Status of Women, 1947-81; exec. mem. Nat. Action Com. on Status of Women, Toronto and Ottawa, 1981-86, pres., 1984—. Recipient Woman of Distinction award Toronto YWCA, 1986; named Woman of Yr., B'Nai B'rith Women, 1984. Jewish. Office: Ministry of Housing, 777 Bay St 10th Fl, Toronto, ON Canada M5G 2E5

HOSKIN, SANDRA RUBLE, medical equipment company executive, nurse; b. Chgo., Apr. 21, 1935; d. Robert Adrian and Hallie Jane (Pence) Ruble; m. Ronald Alan Budgett, Dec. 30, 1960 (div. 1973); 1 child, Laura Adrianne; m. James William Hoskin, May 20, 1974. RN, Ill. Masonic Hosp., Chgo., 1957; BSA, Coll. of St. Francis, 1979; MBA, Houston Bapt. U., 1983. RN, Ind., Tex. Staff, head nurse Meml. Hosp., South Bend, Ind., 1960-72; dir. nursing Carlysle Nursing Home, South Bend, 1972-78, Healthwin Hosp., South Bend, 1978-80; surgical supr. The Meth. Hosp., Houston, 1980-82; relief supr. Polly Ryon Hosp., Richmond, Tex., 1982-84; pres. Am. Med. Equipment Co., Houston, 1984—. Bd. mem. Homeowners Assn., Missouri City, Tex., 1986-87. Mem. Nat. Assn. Med. Equipment Dealers, Tex. Assn. Med. Equipment Dealers, Richmond Pk. Homeowners Assn. (treas. 1990), Great Dane Club, Sports Car Club. Republican. Methodist. Home: 3527 Richland Park Dr Richmond TX 77469 Office: Am Med Equipment Co 1841 Old Spanish Trail Houston TX 77054

HOSKINS, DEBORAH LEBO, hospital executive; b. Flemington, N.J., Feb. 6, 1960; d. Stephen and Doris Maude (Faulks) L. BS in Acctg., Elizabethtown Coll., 1982; postgrad., Pa. State U., Middletown, 1990. Sr. auditor Peat Marwick, Harrisburg, Pa., 1982-86; chief fin. officer Rehab. Hosp. of York (Pa.), 1986-88; v.p. for fin. Community Gen. Hosp., Thomasville, N.C., 1988—. Mem. AICPA, Healthcare Fin. Mgmt. Assn. Presbyterian. Office: Community Gen Hosp 207 Old Lexington Rd Thomasville NC 27360

HOSKINS, GERALDINE, hospital nursing administrator; b. Maysville, Ky., Aug. 15, 1940; d. Vernon Garrett Hoskins and Ivetti H. Hoskins Candy. Cert., Christ Hosp. Sch. Nursing, Cin., 1961; AA, U. Cin., 1975. Cert. nursing adminstr. Staff nurse, evening supr. Adams County Hosp., West Union, Ohio, 1961-63; staff nurse, then head nurse, then supr. Christ Hosp., Cin., 1963-69; asst. supr., then supr. med. nursing Bethesda Hosp. Oak, Cin., 1969-70; dir. emergency and intensive care Bethesda Hosp. North, Cin., 1970-71, mgr., 1971-72, asst. v.p., 1972-80; ind. contractor, securities salesperson, Fla., 1980-81; asst. v.p. Jewish Hosp., Cin., 1981, v.p., 1981-89, sr. v.p., 1989—; ind. neighborhood nurse practitioner, Cin., 1972—; career counselor U. Cin.; mem. adv. bd. co-op. edn. dept. Coll. Mt. St. Joseph on the Ohio, 1982, mem. adv. bd. dept. bus., 1982-88; presenter in field. Mem. Am. Hosp. Assn., Ohio Hosp. Assn., Ohio Soc. Nurse Execs., Cin. Soc. Hosp. Nurse Execs., Nat. League Nursing, Ohio League Nursing, Ohio Co-op. Edn. Assn. Republican. Avocations: travel, spectator and participatory sports, swimming, reading, music. Home: 6542 Kentuckyview Dr Cincinnati OH 45230 Office: Jewish Hosp Cin Inc 3200 Burnet Ave Cincinnati OH 45229

HOSKINSON, CAROL ROWE, former teacher; b. Toledo, Mar. 10, 1947; d. Webster Russell and Alice Mae (Miller) Rowe; m. C. Richard Hoskinson, June 8, 1969; 1 child, Leah Nicole. BS in Edn., Ohio State U., 1968; MEd, Ga. State U., 1972. Tchr. Whitehall City Schs., Columbus, Ohio, 1968-69; tchr. DeKalb County Schs., Decatur, Ga., 1969-74, Mt. Olive (N.J.) Twp. Schs., 1974-75, DeKalb County Schs., Decatur, 1975-79; substitute tchr. DeKalb County Schs., Decatur, 1980—, Fulton County Schs., Atlanta, 1989—. Pres. Esther Jackson PTA, Roswell, Ga., 1988-89; treas. Women of the Ch., Roswell, 1983-84; chairperson local sch. adv. Esther Jackson, Roswell, 1989-91; del. Women and Constrn. Conv., Atlanta, 1988; security vol. Dem. Nat. Conv., Atlanta, 1988; com. chair Esther Jackson PTA, Roswell; mem. Supt.'s Adv. Com. Named Vol. of Yr. Fulton County Schs., 1988-89. Mem. AAUW (v.p. Atlanta chpt. 1984-86, edn. scholarship honoree 1984, 86), Atlanta Lawn Tennis Assn., U.S. Tennis Assn., Roswell Hist. Soc., Chattahoochee Nature Ctr., Zoo Atlanta, SciTrek, High Mus. Art, Ga. PTA, Ohio State Alumni Assn., Ga. State Alumni Assn. Democrat. Presbyterian. Home: 1670 Branch Valley Dr Roswell GA 30076

HOSMER, KATHERINE, educator; b. Dillonvale, Ohio, Dec. 6, 1928; d. Adam and Rosina (Silvero) Ciotti; m. Chester H. Hosmer, Aug. 27, 1950 (dec. 1984); children: Carol Hosmer Morgan, David, Rose Marie Hosmer Haws, Diana Hosmer Cowden. BEd, Kent State U., 1971. Substitute tchr. Stark County, 1961-77; tchr. reading Minerva (Ohio) Local Sch. Dist., 1977—; pvt. tutor, Louisville, 1961—. Mem. NEA, Ohio Edn. Assn., Educators Polit. Action Com. Protestant.

HOSS, JANALEE, small business owner; b. Harrison, Ark., Dec. 6, 1939; d. John Wilson and Joye Belle (Moore) Johnson; m. James Luddington Stewart, Nov. 1, 1959 (div. 1973); children: James Luddington, Jeffrey William; m. Joseph Hoss, 1974. Grad. high sch., La Mesa, Calif. Sec. San Diego County, El Cajon, Calif., 1957-60; adminstrv. sec. Stronberg Datagraphix, El Cajon, 1967-70; sec. Anesthological Group, La Mesa, Calif., 1970-72, Allstate Ins. Co., San Diego, 1973-76; cons., dir. Mary Kay Cosmetics, Inc., Spring Valley, Calif., 1975—; owner Exec. Sec. Svc., La Mesa, 1987—. Press chmn. La Mesa Jr. Woman's Club, 1971-72. Home: 10049 Rothgard Rd Spring Valley CA 92078

HOSTETLER, JOYCE DETWILER, gifted/talented education educator; b. Columbiana, Ohio, Oct. 21, 1939; d. Lester William and Mary Edith (Ziegler) D.; m. Donald Hugh Hostetler, June 11, 1960; children: Julie Anne Hostetler Graber, Mark David. BS in Edn., Ohio State U., 1964; M Liberal Studies, U. Toledo, 1988. Cert. tchr., Ohio. Tchr. Doylestown (Ohio) Sch., 1959-60, Columbus (Ohio) Sch., 1960-64, St. Clare Ch., Farmington, Mich., 1969-72; tchrs. abroad program Mennonite Cen. Com., Tanzania, Africa, 1964-67; substitute tchr. Findlay (Ohio) Schs., 1979-84; tchr. gifted/talented McComb (Ohio) Schs., 1984-87; coord. enrichment Fostoria (Ohio)/St. Wendelin Schs., 1987—. Author: Venture Club Handbooks, 1988-90; curriculum writer Summer-Dorney Grant Project, 1984; contbr. articles to profl. jours. Edn. com. Hancock County Humane Soc., Ohio, 1984-85; bd. dirs. Career Info. Bur., Hancock County, 1989-90; county coord. Odyssey of Mind, Findlay, 1985. Mem. AAUW (edn. chair 1990-91), Ohio Acad. Sci. (historic researcher 1988-90), Nat. Assn. Gifted Children, Ohio Assn. Gifted Children. Office: St Wendelin Sch SWAN Prog 400 N Wood St Fostoria OH 44830

HOTCHKISS, SALLY MCMURDO, university administrator; b. Leominster, Mass., Sept. 13, 1929; d. Montagu Henry and Mary Frances (Fisher) McMurdo; m. Sanford Norman Hotchkiss, Feb. 13, 1954; children: Charles Montagu, Douglas Logan. AB, Randolph-Macon Woman's Coll., 1949; MA, U. Minn., 1950, PhD, 1959. Lic. psychologist, Ohio. Instr., chmn. dept. psychology Rockford (Ill.) Coll., 1953-54; study dir. U. Pitts., 1961-66; asst. prof. psychology Youngstown (Ohio) State U., 1968-74, assoc. prof. psychology, 1974-78, prof. psychology, 1978—, assoc. provost, dean grad. studies, 1982—; mem., sec., examiner, pres. Ohio Bd. Psychology, Columbus, 1978-83. Editor: Survey of American Pathologists, 1966; contbr. articles to profl. jours. Bd. dirs., pres. Mahoning County Diagnostic and Evaluation Clinic, 1977-81; bd. dirs. Hospice of Youngstown, 1978-87, Goodwill Industries, Youngstown,1988—. Mem. Am. Psychol. Assn., Midwestern Psychol. Assn., Ohio Psychol. Assn., Phi Beta Kappa, Phi Kappa Phi (chpt. pres.), Delta Kappa Gamma (chpt. pres.). Republican. Episcopalian. Home: 7667 Hitchcock Rd Boardman OH 44512

HOTTENSTEIN, EVELYN JEANETTE KENNY, communications executive; b. Glasgow, Mont., Mar. 4, 1948; d. Daniel Patrick and Miriam (Phelan) Kenny; m. Glenn Hottenstein, 1969 (div.); children: Erin, Kimberly. BA, Carroll Coll., 1970-72. Cert. tchr. English tchr. Mont. State Sch. for Girls, Helena, 1970-72; exec. dir. Camp Fire Council, Helena, 1972-73; mgr. exec. orientation program Camp Fire, Inc., Englewood, Colo., 1974-76; owner, mgr. H&G Devel Co., Cheyenne, Wyo., 1976-78; owner Lifework Assocs., Denver, 1978—; prin. Pub. Speaking for the Profl., Denver, 1979—, pres., 1979—; pres. The Ctr. for Intercultural Communication, Denver, 1987—; pub. speaker, instr. U. Colo., Denver, 1982—. cons. Assn. for Vol. Adminstrn.; mem. Gov.'s Commn. on Status of Women, Mont., 1973-79; bd. dirs. Unitarian Universalist service com. Mem. Am. Soc. Tng. and Devel. (career devel. tng. group), Nat. Assn. Women Bus. Owners, Nat. Speakers Assn. Office: Pub Speaking for the Profl 1776 Lincoln #814 Denver CO 80203

HOUCK, SHARON LU THOMAS, general manager; b. Roaring Spring, Pa., Oct. 6, 1952; d. Guy Emory and Delores Ruby (Blackstone) Thomas; m. Donald DeLuca, June 14, 1981 (div. July, 1988); m. John Anthony Houck, Nov. 11, 1988; 1 child, Paul Adam. Student, Tidewater Community Coll.,

1976, Va. Commonwealth U., 1980, Old Dominion U., 1982, Essex Community Coll., 1989—. Gen. mgr. Greyhound Food Mgmt. Restaura Dining Svc., Phoenix, 1975--. Mem. NAFE, NOW, Nat. Geog. Soc., Nat. Audubon Soc., Balt. Mus. of Art. Republican. Home: 2221 Corsica Rd Baltimore MD 21221

HOUGAN, CAROLYN AILEEN, writer; b. New Iberia, La., Dec. 16, 1943; d. Samuel Arvid and Elisabeth (Case) Johnson; m. James Richard Hougan, Dec. 17, 1966; children: Daisy Case, Matthew Edwards. BA, U. Wis., Madison, 1966. Writer, 1980—. Author: Shooting in the Dark, 1984, The Romeo Flag, 1989. Mem. Wash. Ind. Writers.

HOUGH, JANET GERDA CAMPBELL, research company scientist; b. Glen Ridge, N.J., Dec. 22, 1948; d. Ralph William and Gerda Lydia (Baarck) Campbell; m. John Harrison Hough, Oct. 1, 1966 (div.); 1 child, Laura Leigh. Student Temple U. and Tyler Sch. Art, Phila., 1970-72, Pa. Acad. Fine Arts, 1972, Camden County Coll., Blackwood, N.J., 1973-75; B.S., Thomas Jefferson U., 1977. Lab. animal technician Inst. Med. Rsch., Camden, N.J., 1972-75; rsch. technician dept. biochemistry Thomas Jefferson U., Phila., 1976, phlebotomist, hematology technician, 1976-78, med. technologist spl. hematology, 1978-79, rsch. technician dept. med. genetics, 1979-80; with micromedic systems Rohm & Haas, Horsham, Pa., 1981-83; micromedic Internat. Clin. Nuclear Inc., Costa Mesa, Calif., and Horsham, 1983—. Collaborator, editor textbook Hematology for Medical Technologists, 1984; poet, illustrator Thought Progressions, 1984. Charter mem. Nat. Rep. Presdl. Task Force, 1984—, mem. Nat. Rep. Senatorial Com., 1984—, Rep. Presdl. Citizen's Adv. Commn., 1989—. Mem. N.J. Hos. Assn., Am. Poetry Assn. (pub. anthologies 1986—). Roman Catholic. Avocations: drawing, painting, long-distance walking. Office: ICN Micromedic Systems Inc 102 Witmer Rd Horsham PA 19044

HOUGH-DUNNETTE, LEAETTA MARIE, industrial organizational psychologist; b. Crookston, Minn., Mar. 26, 1947; d. Mervin Byron and Hazel Viola (Hier) Hough; m. Marvin Dale Dunnette, Feb. 2, 1980. BA summa cum laude, U. Minn., 1970, MA, 1973, PhD, 1981. Adminstrv. fellow U. Minn., Mpls., 1969-70; rsch. asst. Personnel Decisions, Inc., Mpls., 1970-73; teaching asst. U. Minn., Mpls., 1973-74; rsch. psychologist Personnel Decisions Rsch. Inst., Mpls., 1975-80, v.p., 1980-88, exec. v.p., 1988—; editorial asst. Marvin Dunnette, Mpls., 1971-75; adj. prof. U. Minn., Mpls., 1982—. Co-editor Handbook of Industrial and Organizational Psychology, 1990. Recipient Eva O. Miller fellowship U. Minn., 1974-75. Mem. Am. Psychol. Assn., Am. Psychol. Soc., Soc. for Indsl. & Organizational Psychology, U.S. Del. for Friendship Among Women, Phi Beta Kappa, Sigma Epsilon Sigma. Home: 370 Summit Ave St Paul MN 55102 Office: Personnel Decisions Rsch 43 Main St S E Ste 405 Minneapolis MN 55414

HOUGH-GOLDSTEIN, JUDITH ANNE, entomology educator; b. Ann Arbor, Mich., Aug. 27, 1950; d. Paul Van Campen Hough and Barbara (Raymond) Evans; m. Carl Goldstein, July 31, 1983; children: Joshua, Kate. BA, Harvard U., 1972; MS, Cornell U., 1977, PhD, 1981. Staff officer NAS, Washington, 1972-74; asst. prof. U. Del., Newark, 1981-88, assoc. prof., 1988—. Co-author books; contbr. articles to profl. jours. Named one of Oustanding Young Women of Am., 1985, runner-up Award for Excellence, Grad. Women in Sci., 1981. Mem. Entomological Soc. Am. (chair com. on pub. info. 1989-90), AAAS, Sigma Xi. Office: U Del Dept Entomolgy & Applied Ecology Newark DE 19717-1303 :

HOUGHTELIN, CHERYL ANN, organization executive; b. Pitts., June 4, 1957; d. Bruce Arnold and Virginia May (Gallagher) H. BS, Ind. U., 1978, cert. in environ. studies, 1978. Naturalist Brown County State Park, Ind. Dept. Natural Resources, Nashville, 1978-79; naturalist, tchr. YMCA Camp Gard Outdoor Ednl. Ctr., Hamilton, Ohio, 1980-82; aquatic coord. YMCA of Palm Beaches, West Palm Beach, Fla., 1983-84, assoc. aquatic dir., 1984-85, aquatic dir., 1985-86, program dir., 1986-88, sr. dir. programs, 1989-90; assoc. br. dir. YMCA of Palm Beaches, 1990—; facilitator Innovative Leisure, Inc., Lake Worth, Fla., 1987—; cluster aquatic coord., tng. chmn. YMCA's South Fla., 1988—. Bd. dirs. Parent and Child Ctr., West Palm Beach, 1986—, chmn. bd., 1987. Recipient award of merit YMCA of U.S.A., 1987, 89. Mem. Assn. Profl. Dirs., Fla. Recreation and Park Assn. (cert.), NAFE. Roman Catholic. Office: YMCA of Palm Beaches 2085 S Congress West Palm Beach FL 33406

HOUGHTON, JUDITH DEAN, choreographer, consultant; b. Rawlins, Wyo., Dec. 4, 1939; d. Irvin C. and Dorothy H. (Ingram) Houghton. Student U. Tex., Austin, 1957-59. Cert. meeting profl. Faculty dance dept., So. Meth., U., Dallas, 1964-65; choreographer numerous themes parks, U.S., 1965-76, Miss Teenage America telecast, Dallas, 1964-80, Miss U.S.A. and Miss Universe Inc., telecasts, 1977—, numerous civic groups, Dallas, 1954—; sr. ptnr. Charles Meeker, Jr. and Assoc., Dallas, 1967-76; cons., dir. corp. meetings, exec. producer Dr Pepper Co., Dallas, 1964—, producer centennial events, 1984-85; dir. corp. meetings, exec. producer Seven-Up Co., 1986—; ptnr., choreographer Charlie's Place, Fort Worth, 1973-76, Incredible Charlie's Dinner Theatre, Dallas, 1976-78. Active Nat. Cheerleaders Assn., Dallas area orgns., 1965—. Mem. Meeting Planners Internat. (pub. relations com. 1982-84, edn. com. 1985-86, bd. dirs. 1986-87, v.p. pub. relations 1987-88). Republican. Author: Miss Teenage America Tells How to Make Good Things Happen, 1976.

HOUK, NANCY (MIA HOUK), research astronomer; b. Potsdam, N.Y., July 18, 1940; d. William George and Justine (White) H. BS, U. Mich., 1962; MS, Case Inst. Tech., 1964; PhD, Case Western Res. U., 1967. Rsch. assoc. Case Western Res. U., Cleve., 1967-70; rsch. assoc. dept. astronomy U. Mich., Ann Arbor, 1970-73, asst. rsch. scientist, 1973-77, assoc. rsch. scientist, 1977-85, rsch. scientist, 1985—; vis. rsch. assoc. Kapteyn Lab. U. Groningen The Netherlands, 1970. Author: Michigan Spectral Catalogue vols. 1-4, 1975, 78, 82, 88; contbr. numerous articles to profl. jours. Recipient grant NSF, 1971—. Fellow Inst. Religion In Age of Sci. (coun.); mem. AAAS (sec. astronomy sect. 1989—, nominating com.), Internat. Astron. Union (sci. organizing commn. 45), Am. Astron. Soc. Democrat. Presbyterian. Office: Univ Mich Dept Astronomy 1041 Dennison Bldg Ann Arbor MI 48109-1090

HOULE, DIANE ELIZABETH, registered nurse, medical coordinator; b. Boston, Feb. 14, 1930; d. Luis Francisco Vargas and Florence H. (Dussault) Rennebaum; (div. 1973); children: Judy, Elizabeth, John. RN, St. Elizabeth's Sch. Nursing, Brighton, Mass., 1952. Cert. ins. rehab. specialist. Surg. asst., office nurse Lahey Clinic, Boston, 1952-54; asst. head nurse pediatric ward St. Elizabeth's Hosp., Brighton, 1952-56; staff obstet. unit Aramco Hosp., Dharan, Saudi Arabia, 1956-58; RN shift supr. rehab. ward Contra Costa County Hosp., Martinez, Calif., 1972-74; vis. nurse Contra Costa County Pub. Health Dept., Concord, Calif., 1974-82; rehab. nurse Intra Corp., Oakland, Calif., 1982-84; med. coord. Royal Ins. Co., Walnut Creek, Calif., 1984—; Bd. mem. Registered Ins. Nurse Group, San Francisco Bay Area, 1985-87, 90—. Mem. Friends of the San Francisco Symphony. Democrat. Home: 595 El Pintado Rd Danville CA 94526 Office: Royal Ins 1600 Riviera Walnut Creek CA 94596

HOULE, FRANCES ANNE, physical chemist; b. Pasadena, Calif., Oct. 22, 1952; m. Willian Dinan Hinsberg, Oct. 7, 1978; children: William, Monique. Student, Whittier (Calif.) Coll., 1970-72; BA in Chemistry, U. Calif., Irvine, 1974; PhD in Chemistry, Calif. Inst. Tech., Pasadena, 1979. Postdoctoral researcher Lawrence Berkeley Lab. U. Calif., 1979-80; mem. rsch. staff IBM Rsch. Div., San Jose, Calif., 1981—; instr. short courses Am. Vacuum Soc., 1984—, Soc. for Photo-Instrumentation Engrs., 1984—. Assoc. editor Jour. of Vacuum Sci. & Tech., 1989—; inventor selective deposition of copper, etching of Si by SF6 gas; contbr. articles to profl. jours. IBM fellow Calif. Inst. Tech., 1977, U. Calif., Berkeley, 1980. Mem. Am. Vacuum Soc. (exec. com. thin film div. 1988-89, scholarship trustees com. 1990—). Office: IBM Rsch Div Almaden Rsch Ctr 650 Harry Rd San Jose CA 95120

HOULE, RITA C., nurse educator; b. Providence, June 14, 1947; d. Andre Raoul and M.B. Irene (Thibodeau) H. BS in Nursing, Salve Regina Coll., 1978; MS in Nursing, U. R.I., 1987; postgrad., Johnson & Wales U., 1989—. RN. Staff nurse R.I. Hosp., Providence, 1968-70, asst. nurse care coord., 1970-75, nursing care coord., 1975-80; clinician R.I. Hosp. Dept. Edn. and Rsch., Providence, 1980-87, clin. specialist, 1987-89, clin. educator, 1989-90; occupational health nurse practitioner Pratt & Whitney, East Hartford, Conn., 1990—; visiting instr. Northeastern U. Coll. Continuing Edn., Boston, 1989—. Co-author: H.E.L.P., 1986. Mem. NAFE, Am. Nurses Assn., Assn. Nursing Profls., R.I. State Nursing Assn., Sigma Theta Tau. Roman Catholic.

HOUSE, CARLEEN FAYE, area marketing representative; b. Sparta, Wis., Dec. 14, 1950; d. Clarence Frederick and Ida Mae (Murdock) Anderson; m. Gregory Allen House, Aug. 25, 1984. BS, U. Wis., 1978, MS, 1982. Cert. engr., Wis. Prin. Customized Rsch. and Design, 1979—; sci. tchr. Wis. Ednl. System, 1981-82; systems analyst Hewlett Packard, 1982-83, software systems engr., 1983-86, MIS dir., 1986-88, area project dir., 1988-90, area mktg. rep., 1990—; chief exec. officer House Research, 1986—; pres. HPII Lt. Partnership, 1987—, Chisago County Office Supply, Chisago City, Minn., 1988—; area project dir. Hewlett Packard, 1988—; dir. devel. House Properties One, 1985—; pres. HPII Ltd. Partnership, 1986—. Mem. Women in Engring., Aircraft Owners and Pilots Assn., Omicron Nu, League of Women Voters. Republican. Lutheran. Home and Office: 10579 Point Pleasant Rd Chisago City MN 55013

HOUSE, KAREN ELLIOTT, financial executive, former editor, reporter; b. Matador, Tex., Dec. 7, 1947; d. Ted and Bailey Elliott; m. Arthur House, Apr. 5, 1975 (div. Sept. 1983); m. Peter Xann, June 4, 1984; children: Petra, Jason. B.J., U. Tex., 1970; postgrad. Inst. Politics, Harvard U., 1982. Edn. reporter Dallas Morning News, 1970-71, with Washington bur., 1971-74; regulatory corr. Wall Street Jour., Washington, 1974-75, energy and agr. corr., 1975-78, diplomatic corr., 1978-84; fgn. editor Wall Street Jour., N.Y.C., 1984-89; v.p. Dow Jones Internat. Group, 1989—; dir. German-Am. Coun., 1988—; bd. dirs. Coun. Fgn. Rels.; trustee Boston U.; mem. dean's adv. coun. U. Tex. Sch. Journalism, Austin, 1985; mem. adv. bd. Ctr. Strategic Internat. Studies; mem. vis. com. Harvard U. Ctr. Internat. Affairs. Recipient Edward Weintal award for Diplomatic Reporting, Georgetown U., 1980-81, Edwin Hood award for Diplomatic Reporting Nat. Press Club, 1982, Disting. Achievement award U. So. Calif., 1984, Pulitzer prize for Internat. Reporting, 1984, Overseas Press Club Bob Considine award, 1984, 88; Harvard fellow, 1982. Fellow Nat. Acad. Arts and Scis. Home: 58 Cleveland Ln Princeton NJ 08540 Office: Dow Jones & Co 200 Liberty St New York NY 10281

HOUSE, MARY ANNE, medical college official; b. Augusta, Ga., Dec. 6, 1950; d. Jack Wilton and Mary Sinclair (Mew) Garrett. Student, Med. U. S.C. Sch. Nursing, 1969-72; BS in Nursing, Med. Coll. Ga., 1974, MS in Nursing, 1979. RN, Ga. Nursing asst. St. Joseph Hosp., Augusta, 1968; nursing asst., ward clk. U. Hosp., Augusta, 1969-74, staff nurse, shift supr., 1974-79; nursing technician Med. U. S.C., Charleston, 1973; sr. surg. transplant coord. Med. Coll. Ga., Augusta, 1979-85, adminstr. organ procurement program, 1985—; clin. instr. dept. adult nursing Med. Coll. Ga. Sch. Nursing, Augusta, 1988—. Author: ABC's of Kidney Transplantation at the Med. Coll. Ga.; editor: South Eastern Organ Procurement Found. Procurement Manual; contbr. numerous articles to profl. publs. Recipient outstanding svc. award Ga. Lions Eye Bank, 1983, Norm Weaver award Nat. Kidney Found. Ga., 1984, cert. of achievement AAUW, Augusta, 1986, merit award South Eastern Organ Procurement Found., 1987. Mem. Am. Registry Transplant Coord. (rep. to bd. dirs., cert. procurement/preservation), N.Am. Transplant Coords. Orgn. (nat. sec. 1981-82, 85-86, editor nat. newsletter 1982-88, chmn. numerous coms.), Am. Coun. on Transplantation, United Network for Organ Sharing, Assn. Nurses Endorsing Transplantation, Assn. Organ Procurement Orgns. (nat. sec. 1989-90). Republican. Episcopalian. Home: 1141 Georgia Ave North Augusta SC 29841 Office: Medical College Georgia 15th St Augusta GA 30912

HOUSE, SUSAN PATRICIA, advertising and public relations executive; b. Denver, Sept. 7, 1959; d. Albert Richard Jr. and June (McPherson) H. BA in Humanities, U. Tex., 1980. Media dir., account exec. Yudell Communications, Inc., Houston, 1980-86; bur. chief S.W. Pub. Rels. Newswire, Houston, 1986-89; mgr. regional sales Businesswire, L.A., 1989; media and pub. rels. cons. House Media Svcs., Houston, 1989—. Mem. Houston-Chiba City Sister City Com. Mem. Cultural Arts Coun. Houston, Mus. Fine Arts, Contemporary Arts Mus., Inst. Internat. Edn., The Asia Soc., Oriental Ceramic Soc., Japan-Am. Soc. Houston, S.W. Mus. L.A. Republican. Presbyterian.

HOUSEMAN, ANN ELIZABETH LORD, educational administrator, state official; b. New Orleans, Mar. 21, 1936; d. Noah Louis and Florence Marguerite (Coyle) Lord; m. Evan Kenny Houseman, June 25, 1960; children: Adrienne Ann, Jeannette Louise, Yvonne Elizabeth. BA, Barnard Coll., 1957; MA, Columbia Univ., 1962; PhD, Univ. Del., 1969. Cert. elem. prin., secondary sch. prin. State supr. reading Dept. Pub. Instrn., Del., 1977-79; prin. M.L. King, Jr. Elem. Sch., Wilmington, Del., 1979-80; adminstr., exec. dir. Del. State Arts Coun., Wilmington, 1980-84; acting dir. Div. Hist. and Cultural Affairs State of Del., Wilmington, 1983-84, prin. P.S. du Pont Intermediate Sch., Wilmington, 1984—; dir. Mid-Atlantic States Arts Consortium, Balt., 1980-84. Mem. adv. bd. Rockwood Mus., Wilmington, 1981—; bd. dirs. Opera Del., Wilmington, 1984—, Del. Theatre Co., Wilmington, 1984—. Contbr. articles to profl. jours. Mem. Diamond State Reading Assn. (pres. 1977-78), Psi Chi, Phi Delta Kappa. Republican. Presbyterian. Office: PS DuPont Intermediate Sch 34th and Van Buren Sts Wilmington DE 19802

HOUSER, LOUISE KELLEY, health care administrator; b. Bowman, S.C., Feb. 22, 1919; d. George Quillie and Byrdie Lucile (Stephens) Kelley; B.S., S.C. State Coll., 1941, M.S., 1959; m. John W. Houser, Jr., Sept. 18, 1943; children—John W., George D. Tchr. public schs., Marion County, S.C., 1941-44; tchr. sci. Ga. Sch. for Deaf, 1959-61; tchr. pub. schs., Rome, Ga., 1961-68; dir. personnel Brentwood Med. Care Home, Ga., 1967-71; adminstr. Brentwood Nursing Home, 1972-77; adminstr. Brentwood Park, Three Rivers Health Care Co., Rome, Ga., 1977—, pres. bd.; adminstrv. cons., 1988—; bd. dirs., v.p. The Nepenthe Group, Inc.; bd. dirs. Murphy-Harpst-Vashti, Inc. Bd. dirs. Rome Girls Club. Mem. Rome Council on Human Relations, Ga. Health Care Assn., Am. Health Care Assn., Ga. Soc. Activity Dirs., Ga. Dental Soc. Aux. (past pres.), Am. Cancer Soc. (past pres. Floyd County div.), Aux. Nat. Dental Assn. (past pres., mem. exec. bd.). Home: 121 Jackson St Rome GA 30161 Office: Moran Lake Rd Rome GA 30161

HOUSTON, CAROLINE MARGARET, editor; b. Harrogate, Eng., May 8, 1964; came to U.S., 1975; d. William H. and Sylvia (Fineron) H. BA in Internat. Studies and Mid East Studies, George Mason U., 1989, postgrad., 1990—. Cert. fluency in Farsi and French. Editor Maxim Techs., Vienna, Va., 1988-89; sec. Am. Near East Refugee Aid, Washington and Israel, 1989-90; asst. sec., treas. World Resources Inst., Washington, 1990—; devel. cons. Legacy Internat., Jerusalem, 1990—. Violinist with semi-profl. orchs., 1972-84. Mem. NOW, Amnesty Internat. Mem. NAFE, Internat. Studies Assn., Mid. East Inst., Mid. East Studies Assn., World Affairs Coun., Inst. Policy Studies, Friends of Kennedy Ctr. Home: 3225 Kenney Dr Falls Church VA 22042

HOUSTON, DORINE SYME, educator; b. Mpls., June 4, 1951; d. George Stevenson and Charlotte Antoinette (Ulrich) Syme; m. Stuart Sidney Houston, Aug. 15, 1976. BA, Temple U., 1973; diploma in translation, U. of Madrid, 1974; MA, Temple U., 1980. Instr. in English Instituto Briam, Madrid, 1973-76; pvt. practice translator, cons. Phila., 1976-85; instr. in English Am. Lang. Acad. Beaver Coll., Glenside, Pa., 1985-87, Jefferson Bus. Coll., Phila., 1987-88; tchr. ESL, coord. Univ. of the Arts, Phila., 1988—. Player Fairmount Park Women's Softball League, Phila., 1984—, Hillers Field Hockey Team, Phila., 1987—; asst. to ward leader 8th Ward Reps., Phila., 1978—; bell ringers guild St. Mark's Episcopal Ch., Phila., 1985—, needlepointers guild, 1986—. Mem. Tchrs. of English to Speakers of Fgn. Langs., Delaware Valley Translators Assn. (pres. 1982-84), Pa. TESOL (2d v.p. Phila. chpt. 1989-90, 1st v.p. 1990—).

HOUSTON, ELIZABETH REECE MANASCO, teacher, consultant; b. Birmingham, Ala., June 19, 1935; d. Reuben Cleveland and Beulah Elizabeth (Reece) Manasco; m. Joseph Brantley Houston; 1 child, Joseph Brantley Houston III. BS, U. Tex., 1956; MEd, Boston Coll., 1969. Cert. elem. tchr., Calif., cert. spl. edn. tchr., Calif., cert. community coll. instr., Calif. Tchr., elem. Ridgefield (Conn.) Schs., 1962-63; staff, spl. edn. Sudbury (Mass.) Schs., 1965-68; staff intern Wayland (Mass.) High Sch., 1972; tchr., home bound Northampton (Mass.) Schs., 1972-73; program dir. Jack Douglas Ctr., San Jose, Calif., 1974-76; tchr. specialist spl. edn., coord. classroom svcs., dir. alternative schs. Santa Clara County Office of Edn., San Jose, Calif., 1976—; instr. San Jose State U., 1980-87, U. Calif., Santa Cruz, 1982-85; cons. Houston Research Assocs., Saratoga, Calif., 1981—. Author: (manual) Behavior Management for School Bus Drivers, 1980, Classroom Management, 1984, Synergistic Learning, 1986. Grantee Santa Clara County Office Edn. Tchr. Advisor Program U.S. Sec. Edn., 1983-84; Recipient President's award Soc. Photo-Optical Instrumentation Engrs., 1979, Classroom Mgmt. Program award School Bds. Assn., 1984, Svc. to Youth award Juvenile Ct. Sch. Adminstrs. of Calif., 1989. Mem. Assn. for Supervision and Curriculum Devel., Assn. Calif. Sch. Adminstrs., Council Exceptional Children, Juvenile Ct. Sch. Adminstrs. of Calif. (bd. dirs.). Home: 12150 Country Squire Ln Saratoga CA 95070 Office: Santa Clara County Office Edn 100 Skyport Dr San Jose CA 95115

HOUSTON, GLORIA, author, education educator; b. Marion, N.C., Nov. 24, 1940; d. James Myron and Ruth (Greene) H.; married, Sept. 3, 1966 (div. 1986); stepchildren: M. Diane Gainforth, Julie Ann McLendon. BS, Appalachian State, 1959-63; MEd., U. S.Fla., 1980-83, PhD, 1989. Cert. Tchr., N.C., La., Tex., Fla. Flight attendant Delta Airlines, Atlanta, 1964-66; music tchr. Irving Ind. Schs., Tex., 1968-71; humanities, music, English tchr. Hillsborough Co. Schs., Tampa, Fla., 1972-82; lit., writing cons. various orgns., 1979—; coord. Suncoast Young Authors Conf. Coll. Edn., U. So. Fla., Tampa, 1985—, adjunct instr., 1982-87, vis. asst. prof., author-in-residence, 1989—; cons. IBM/Goodhousekeeping Tell Me a Story Project, 1989; lectr. in field; presenter workshops Fla. Eng. Tchrs., nationwide. Author: (juvenile and young adult) My Brother Joey Died, 1982, The Year of the Perfect Christmas Tree, 1988 (Pubs. Weekly Best Seller List, other commendations), Littlejim, 1990, others; pub. numerous books; contbr. articles to various publs., mags. Fla. Endowment for the Humanities scholar, Tampa 1988—; grantee Jr. League Tampa, Fla. Nat. Bank, Hazen Found.; recipient Disting. Alumnae award Appalachian State U., 1990. Mem. Authors Guild, Nat. Counc. Tchrs. English, Fla. Coun. Tchrs. English, Internat. Reading Assn., Fla. Reading Assn., Soc. Children's Book Writers, The Authors Guild, Delta Kappa Gamma.

HOUSTON, WHITNEY, vocalist, recording artist; b. East Orange, N.J., Aug. 9, 1963; d. John R. and Cissy H. HHD (hon.), Grambling U. Trained under direction of mother; mem. New Hope Bapt. Jr. Choir, 1974; background vocalist Chaka Khan, 1978, Lou Rawls, 1978, Cissy Houston, 1978, appeared in Cissy Houston night club act; record debut (duet with Teddy Pendergrass) Hold Me, 1984; albums include Whitney Houston, 1985, Whitney, 1986; songs include Greatest Love of All, Saving My Love For You, Didn't We Almost Have It All, You're Still My Man; fashion model Glamour Mag., Seventeen mag., 1981. Recipient Grammy award, 7 Am. Music awards, 4 #1 Single Record awards; named Artist of Yr. Billboard mag., 1986. Grammy award for Best Female Pop Performance, 1985, 87; Winner Am. Music award, 1985 (2), 1986 (5), 1988 (2). Office: care Solters Roskin Friedman Inc 45 W 34th St New York NY 10001*

HOUX, SHIRLEY ANN, personal and business services company executive, consultant, researcher; b. Claremore, Okla., Nov. 1, 1931; d. George Warren and Alta Zena (Starkweather) Pritchard; m. William Dean Munson, June 1, 1951 (div. June 1962); children—Debra Kay, Diana Sue, Donna Lynn; m. Leonard Houx, June 22, 1963; 1 child, David Leonard. Student in bus. Okla. State U., 1949-50. Sec. Jack Gordon, P.A., Claremore, Okla., 1947-48; sec., personnel mgr. Gulf Oil Corp., Tulsa, 1950-51; exec. sec. to wing comdr. U.S. Air Force, Cocoa Beach, Fla., 1951-53; exec. sec. to gen. counsel Houston So., P.A., Stillwater, Okla., 1957-60; exec. sec. to exec. v.p. and sr. v.p. Williams Cos., Tulsa, 1962-64; owner, chief exec. officer Hallmark Exchange, Inc., Tulsa, 1981—; cons. small bus., Tulsa, 1981—; mem. small bus. adv. bd. Tulsa Jr. Coll., 1983—. Author: (drama) Wedding Rehearsal for the Bride of Christ, 1985. Contbg. editor The Chronicle, 1984. Co-creator, producer foot health program, 1967 (Am. Podiatry Assn. Outstanding award 1968); creator, advt. campaign for Cystic Fibrosis Found.: I'm One...Be One, 1978. Pres. women's aux. Okla. Podiatry Assn., Tulsa, 1966-82; sec.-treas. Okla. bd. examiners Okla. Podiatry Assn., 1969-76; nat. audio-visual chmn. women's aux. Am. Podiatry Assn., 1976; pres. Tulsa Cerebral Palsy Assn., 1977, Cystic Fibrosis Found. Aux., Tulsa, 1979. Named Miss Claremore, Claremore Bus. and Profl. Women, Okla., 1949; recipient Two-Star award Pure D'Lite Co., 1982. Mem. Nat. Assn. Female Execs., Tulsa C. of C. Democrat. Avocations: fashion design; the arts; writing.

HOVELL, SUSAN M., mortgage loan administrator, consultant; b. LaCrosse, Wis., Jan. 6, 1961; d. Stanley Allen and Rose Marie (Edhlund) Holter; m. Raymond Allan Hovell, Oct. 15, 1983. BS, Winona (Minn.) State U., 1983; MA, St. Mary's Coll., Winona, 1990. Paralegal Nemes and Hansen, Ltd., Winona, 1982-84; adminstrv. asst. Merchants Nat. Bank, Winona, 1984-86, loan officer, 1986-87, asst. cashier, 1987-89, asst. mgr., 1989—; tech. asst. Winona State U. paralegal program, 1984—; instr. Winona Area Tech. Coll., 1989, Winona State U., 1990, Western Wis. Tech. Coll., LaCrosse, 1989, 90. Pres. YWCA, Winona, 1990; bd. dirs. Women's Resource Ctr., 1985-89. Mem. AAUW, Fin. Women Internat. (Minn. v.p. 1990—), Winona Exchange Club. (pres. 1988, outstanding mem. 1987), Winona Area C. of C. (pres.'s club 1989). Home: RR1 Box 1557 Trempealeau WI 54661 Office: Mchts Nat Bank 102 Plaza E Winona MN 55987

HOVEN, DEBORAH CAMILLE, nurse; b. Salem, Oreg., Oct. 26, 1955; d. Lorin Alfred and Sylvia Beryl (Spillman) H. BS in Nursing, Oreg. Health Scis. U., 1978; cert. in cardiovascular nursing, Stanford U. Hosp., 1986. RN, Oreg., Calif. Staff nurse Salem Hosp., 1979-80, IUC and CCU staff nurse, relief charge nurse, 1980-85; staff nurse Stanford (Calif.) U. Hosp., 1986-87, HomeMed, Menlo Park, Calif., 1987-88, Med. Personnel Pool, San Jose, Calif., 1988-89; home care nurse Western Med. Svcs., San Jose, 1989—; staff nurse YMCArdiac Therapy Program, Salem YMCA, 1985. Mem. World Affairs Coun., Am. Assn. Critical Care Nurses, Am. Heart Assn. (mem. coun.). Home: 847 Roble Ave Apt 4 Menlo Park CA 94025

HOVET, MARY R., assistant school superintendent; b. Brunswick, Md., May 6, 1917; d. Hilleary Cleveland and Nellie (Barger) Rockwell; m. Kenneth Orian Hovet, Sr., Aug. 10, 1952 (dec.); 1 child, Kenneth Orian, Jr. AB with honors, Hood Coll., 1938; MA, NYU, 1951; EdD, George Wash. U., 1971. From tchr. to v. prin. Bd. Edn., Frederick, Md., 1938-48; from supr. high schs. to asst. supt. Bd. Edn., Howard County, Md., 1948-81; mathematician Dept. Commerce, Washington, 1945-48; instr. W. Md. Coll, Westminster, 1953, U. Md., Coll. Pk., 1950-52, Munich, Germany, 1954, U. Minn., Mpls., 1949. Mem. Howard County (Md.) Mental Health Adv. Bd., Com. Awds. Hood Coll., Howard County Extension Homemakers Coun. (pres.), Howard County Gen. Hosp. Aux., Law related Edn. Program for Md. Schs., Florence Bain Sr. Ctr. Adv. Coun. (sec.), Md. Los Income Housing Coalition; elder Presbyn. Ch. Recipient fellowship Physics Case Inst. Tech.; elected First Inst. Sci. Tchrs. Thomas A. Edison Found. Mem. AAUW (pres.), Bus. Profl. Club (state pres., pres. Frederick chpt.), Md. Assn. Supervision Curriculum Devel. (state pres.), Hood Coll. Alumnae Assn.; bd. trustees State Us. and Colls. Democrat. Home: 9901 Evergreen Ave Columbia MO 21046

HOVIS, CHERIE LYNN, business owner, nurse assistant; b. Portland, Oregon, Apr. 12, 1952; d. Richard James Raymond Wayne and Maxine Mildred (Rober) Bolman; m. Dale Anthony Kraft (div. 1971); 1 child, Racquel Lee; m. Donald Ray Hovis, Dec. 21, 1987. Cert., Mtn. Pk. Nursing Home, 1989. Owner Profl. Locators, Tigard, Oregon, 1988—. Home: 11585 S W 98th Tigard OR 97223

HOVIS, LORRAINE BAUGHER, county commissioner; b. York, Pa., Jan. 26, 1942; d. Chester Raymond and Miriam Helen (Lightner) Baugher; m. Raymond L. Hovis; children: Michelle, Steven, Michael. Grad. high sch., York, 1959. Exec. dir. Leadership York, 1977-84; commr. County of York, 1984—, pres. bd. commrs., 1988—; bd. dirs. Pa. State Agrl. Land Preservation Bd., 1989, Pa. Job Tng. Coordination Coun., 1989; adv. bd. Pa. Child and Adolescent Service System Program, Pa. Mental Health/Mental

Retardation, York County Convention and Visitors Bur., Children and Youth Services, Juvenile Detention Home. Campaign chmn. United Way York County, 1989; trustee York Hosp., 1982—; bd. dirs. United Way Pa., Harrisburg, 1987-89; del. Dem. Nat. Convention, Atlanta, 1988; pres. Arts Coun. York County, Atkins House Adv. Bd., Jr. League York, 1976-77, 81-82. Named Elected Official of Yr. York County C. of C., 1989, one of Women Who Have Made a Difference YWCA, 1986, one of Outstanding Young Women Am., 1978; recognized for contbn. to volunteerism YWCA, 1989; recipient Community Service award AFL-CIO, 1980. Mem. Nat. Assn. County Commrs. (health and welfare sterring com. 1985—), Pa. State Assn. County Commrs. (human svcs. com. 1985—). Lutheran. Home: RD #2 Box 260 Wrightsville PA 17368 Office: County of York One W Market Way York PA 17401

HOWARD, AUGHTUM LUCIEL SMITH, retired mathematics educator; b. Almo, Ky., Nov. 10, 1906; d. Leander E. and Anna (Wright) Smith; m. Noel Judson Howard, Jan. 6, 1929; children: Carl Eugene, Robert Alvin. BA, Georgeown Coll., 1926; postgrad., U. Mich., 1927; MS, U. Ky., 1938, PhD, 1942. Lab technician Parke Davis Drug Co., Detroit, 1926-27; tchr. Marshall County High Sch., 1927-29; grad. asst. math. dept. U. Ky., 1936-41, fellow, 1941-42; assoc. prof. math. Ky. Wesleyan Coll., 1942-46, prof., 1946-58; assoc prof. Eastern Ky. State Coll., Richmond, 1958-62, prof., 1962-73; mem. curriculum study com.; commn. on pub. edn., State of Ky., 1961. Tchr. adult Sunday sch. class Richmond 1st Christian Ch., 1971-78, deacon, 1986-87, elder, 1989—. Mem. AAUP, Math Assn. Am. (chmn. Ky. sect. 1944-46, lectr. 1953-55, sec.-treas. 1949-51, 69-71, cert. of meritorious svc. 1988), Richmond Women's Club, Sigma Xi. Home: 206 Pembroke Dr Richmond KY 40475

HOWARD, CHERYL LYNN, human services administrator; b. Compton, Calif., Oct. 2, 1947; d. Robert Eugene and Dolores Elizabeth (Warnke) H.; ptnr. Annette Joy Van Dyke, July 1, 1974. BA, U. Idaho, 1969. Shelter dir. Northwoods Coalition for Battered Women, Bemidji, Minn., 1979-81; tng. & tech. assistance coord. Minn. Coalition for Battered Women, St. Paul, 1981-83; legal advocate Domestic Abuse Project, Mpls., 1982-83, legal advocacy coord., 1983-86, community intervention dir., 1986-88, acting dir., 1987-88; dir. YWCA House of Peace, Cin., 1988—. Bd. dirs. Harriet Tubman Women's Shelter, Mpls., 1985-87; pres. Past-time Bookstore & Women's Ctr., Spokane, Wash., 1978; rep. Subcom. Mpls. Human Rights Commn., 1986-87; co-coord. Wash. NOW, 1974-76.

HOWARD, DEBORAH SUSANNE, graphic designer, illustrator; b. Lakewood, Ohio, Oct. 1, 1956; d. Jay and Rita Charlotte (Schefft) Howard. BFA, Bowling Green State U., 1978. Typographer Lorain (Ohio) Printing Co., 1978-79; artist Morgan Art/Photography, Cleve., 1979-80; art dir. Sonnhalter & Assocs., Cleve., 1980-85, Communications Concepts, Toledo, 1985-87; prin. Howard Design, Toledo, 1985—. Exhibited in group shows Women Alive!, 1987, Toledo Artists Assn., 1988. Recipient merit in graphic excellence Mead Co., 1989. Mem. Advt. Club Toledo (Addy 1990), Women in Communications Inc. (Merit award 1989). Office: Howard Design PO Box 178197 Toledo OH 43617

HOWARD, ELIZABETH, corporate communications and marketing executive; b. Littleton, N.H., Apr. 24, 1950; d. Ellis Woodruff and Elizabeth (Millar) H.; m. Charles A. Schwefel, May 12, 1984. BA, U. N.H., 1972; MS, Pratt Inst., 1985. Dir. corp. pub. rels. Nat. Distillers, N.Y.C., 1978-85, Chem. Corp., N.Y.C., 1980-85; dir. pub. rels. Transway Internat Corp., White Plains, N.Y., 1985; pres. Corp. Communications Group Millennium Inc., N.Y.C., 1986; pres. Elizabeth Howard & Co., N.Y.C., 1987—. Contbr. articles to profl. mags. Bd. dirs. Katharine Gibbs Sch. Scholarship Found., 1987-88; bd. dirs. Hamilton-Madison Settlement House, N.Y.C., 1984-89, pres., 1987-89. Mem. Global Econ. Action Inst., Women Execs. Pub. Rels. (bd. dirs. 1984-87), Fin. Women's Assn. Home: 4 Coachmen's Sq New Canaan CT 06840 Office: 501 Fifth Ave New York NY 10017

HOWARD, IRMGARD KEELER, biochemistry educator; b. Phila., Jan. 21, 1941; d. Clyde Edgar and Johanne Berta-Marie (Abel) Keeler; m. David Allyn Howard, Mar. 21, 1969; children: Deborah Keeler, William Keeler, Eleanor Elizabeth, Stephen James. AB magna cum laude, Duke U., 1962, PhD, 1970. Asst. prof. of chemistry Houghton (N.Y.) Coll., 1970-74, assoc. prof., 1974—; rsch. assoc. in biochemistry Duke U., Durham, N.C., 1980-81; nutrition show host Sta. WJSL Radio, Houghton, 1984-86. Contbr. articles to profl. jours.; contbr. musical compositions to recordings. Rsch. coord. Concerned Citizens of Allegany County, Belmont, N.Y., 1989—. Recipient Hawkhill award, Hawkhill Assocs., 1987. Mem. Am. Chem. Soc. (nat. tour speaker 1989—), Am. Assn. for Clin. Chemistry, N.Y. Acad. Scis., Phi Beta Kappa. Presbyterian. Office: Houghton Coll Chemistry Dept Houghton NY 14744

HOWARD, JACQUELINE SUE, hospital administrator; b. South Bend, Ind., Mar. 26, 1954; d. Thomas Leslie and Marion Jean (Reed) H. RN diploma, DePaul Hosp., St. Louis, 1976; BS, U. Mo., St. Louis, 1985; MBA, Lindenwood Coll., 1988. Staff nurse DePaul Hosp., St. Vincents Div., St. Louis, 1976-80; asst. dir. nursing mgmt. Weldon Springs Hosp., St. Charles, Mo., 1980-83; dir. nursing Weldon Springs Hosp., 1983-86; nursing cons. Hawthorn Children's Psychiat. Hosp., St. Louis, 1986-87; dir. nursing Hawthorn Children's Psychiat. Hosp., 1987-88, asst. adminstr., 1988, exec. dir., 1988—; cons. M.A. Kabir Psychiatry, Inc./Centrec, St. Louis, 1986-89, Healthcare Svcs. Am., Inc., La., Fla., 1986, Compre Treatment unit Lindell Hosp., St. Louis, 1986, Koala Chem. Dependency Ctr., St. Louis, 1986. Mem. Assn. Mental Health Adminstrs. Home: 701 S Skinker Ste 705 Clayton MO 63105 Office: Hawthorn Children's Psychiat Hosp 1901 Pennsylvania Saint Louis MO 63133

HOWARD, JANET ANNE, associations; b. Brownwood, Texas, Aug. 2, 1946; d. S.J. Jr. and Martha (Dublin) Howard. Student, Am. U., 1964-66; BA, U. Texas, 1969. Exec. Asst. U.S. Sen. Ralph Yarborough, Washington, 1969-71; exec. asst. to v.p. E-Systems, Inc., Arlington, Va., 1971-72; co-owner Profiles, Inc., Washington, 1972-73; adminstr. impeachment staff Jud. Com., Washington, 1973-74; exec. asst. Sen. John Glenn, Washington, 1975-77, Sen. Don Riegle, Washington, 1977; nat. dir. Dem. Ho. & Sen. Coun. & Annual Congl. Dinner, Washington, 1978-80, Democrats for the 90s, Washington, 1984—; cons. Democratic Senatorial Campaign Com., Washington; spl. asst. to Mrs. W. Averell Harriman, 1980—. Vol. Fundraising Cancer Soc. Mem. Woman's Nat. Democratic Club (governing bd.), Delta Gamma. Episcopalian. Home: 3032 N St NW Washington DC 20007

HOWARD, JANET SCHLENKER, non-profit organization administrator; b. Jamestown, N.D., Nov. 8, 1950; d. Harold and Alvina (Nitshke) Schlenker; m. James R. Howard, Feb. 21, 1976 (div. July 1980). BA in Social Work, U. N.D., Grand Forks, 1972. Social worker McIntosh County Welfare, Ashley, N.D., 1972-74; social worker med. svcs. div. N.D. Dept. Human Svcs., Bismarck, 1974-76; health edn. coordinator Beltrami Health Ctr., Mpls., 1977-81, adminstrv. dir., 1981-83; resource devel. cons. St. Paul Retired Sr. Vol. Program, 1984-85; exec. dir. Advocating Change Together, Mpls., 1985-88; with Mpls. Pub. Housing Authority, 1988—; vol., trainer Crossroads, Jamestown, N.D., 1974-76; health educator Control Data Corp., Mpls., 1979; cons. on grantwriting Harriet Tubman Women's Shelter, Mpls., 1984; cons. Turtle Island Holistic Health Community, St. Paul, 1984-85, Intermedia Arts Minn., Mpls., 1989, Reflective Leadership Ctr., Hubert H. Humphrey Ctr., U. Minn., Mpls., 1989; bd. mem. Cooperating Fund Drive, St. Paul, 1985-88. Vol. Minn. Aids Project, Walkathon, Mpls., 1988-89, Wildlife Rehab. Ctr., U. Minn., St. Paul, 1989. Recipient awards Minn. Legislature, 1987, Non-Profit Advocacy award Minn. Coun. Non Profits, Duluth, 1988, Community Svc. award Minn. Assn. Rehab. Facilities, St. Paul, 1989. Mem. Nat. Soc. Fund Raising Execs. Mem. Unity Ch. Home: 2203 E 38th St Minneapolis MN 55407

HOWARD, JOAN ALICE, artist; b. N.Y.C., Apr. 28, 1929; d. John Volkman and Mary Alice Devlin; m. Robert Thornton Howard, June 26, 1949; children: Barbara Jo, Robert Thornton Jr., Gregory Lyon, Brian Devlin. Student, Hunter Coll., 1947-48, UCLA, 1967-68, Los Angeles Valley Coll., 1970-71. Dir., choreographer Acad. Dance, Floral Park and Forest Hills, N.Y., 1947-57; dir. dance. Cath. Parochial schs., N.Y.C., Bklyn., and Floral Park, N.Y., 1948-55; chmn. dept. dance Molloy Coll., 1958-67; artist sta. KNBC-TV, Los Angeles, 1967-74, NBC, N.Y.C., 1974-78, sta. WNBC-TV, N.Y.C., 1978-79; artistic dir. Brookville (N.Y.) Sch., 1980-85; dir. dance N.Y.C. YMCA, 1948; founder, dir. Queens-Nassau Regional Dance Theatre, 1950-55; choreographer Molloy Coll. Dance Theatre, 1959-67; cons. prenatal exercise, L.I., N.Y., 1980—; judge art show Westbury (N.Y.) Mural Project, 1979. One-woman show Dime Savings Bank, Manhasset, 1986-87, Nardin Gallery Fine Arts, 1990, Chase Manhattan Bank, 1990—, Ridgefield (Conn.) Guild Gallery, 1989-90; exhibited in group shows at Valley Ctr. Arts Gallery, Los Angeles, 1968-72, Home Savs. and Loan Art Exhibits, Los Angeles, 1969-70, Westwood Art Gallery, Los Angeles, 1972, Onion Gallery, Los Angeles, 1972, North Ridge Women's Ctr. Gallery, Los Angeles, 1972, Great Neck (N.Y.) Ctr. Gallery, 1976, A&S Gallery, Manhasset, 1976, Gloria Vanderbilt Designers Showcase, 1978, Manhasset Library Gallery, 1985-89, Great Neck House Gallery, 1986-87, Hutchins Gallery C.W. Post Coll., L.I., 1986-89 (award 1986, 87, 88, 89, 90), Dime Savs. Bank, Mass., N.Y., European Am. Bank, 1988, Nardin Fine Arts, Cross River, N.Y., 1989, Manhasset Gallery, 1985-89, Hutchins Gallery, C.W. Post Coll., L.I. U., 1990, Plandome Gallery, N.Y.C., 1990; exhibited in juried show Nassau County (N.Y.) Mus. Fine Arts, Roslyn, 1985, Plandome Gallery, N.Y., 1987-88, Greatneck House Gallery, 1986-89 (hon. mention), East Meadow Libr. Gallery, 1988, Freeport Gallery, 1988, Ridgefield (Conn.) Gallery, 1989, Shelter Rock Gallery, 1989, Mardin Gallery Fine Arts, 1989, Ridgefield Gallery Portrait Show, 1989-90, Ridgefield Artists' Guild, 1989, Plandome Gallery, Gt. Neck, 1987-89, Ridgefield (Conn.) Gallery, 1989-90, Shelter Roca Gallery, N.Y., 1989, Nardin Gallery, Cross River, N.Y., 1989 choreographer contemporary ballet Crucifixtion, 1960, Persephone, 1961, Cubes of Truth, 1962, Somewhere, 1965; appeared on radio show Coast to Coast on a Bus, 1939-47; Broadway prodn. Lady in the Dark, 1940-42; performed ballet in TV show Stars of Tomorrow, 1942, Sleeping Beauty, 1942. Dem. committeewoman, Glen Cove, N.Y., 1954-58. Recipient Del Rey Perpetual Race championship trophy, 1974, Little Sabot Perpetual Race trophy, 1972-74, So. Calif. Women's Sailing Conf. sabot championship, 1972-74, 1st Woman trophy Olympic Regatta, 1973. Mem. Dance Educators Am., Manhasset Art Assn., Women's Sailing Com. of U.S. Yacht Racing Union (fund raiser 1980-81), Am. Watercolor Soc. (aux.), Women's C. of C. L.A., Tri-County Artists Ridgefield Art Guild. Clubs: Calif. Yacht (Los Angeles) (Women's Perpetual Race trophy 1972-74), Sports Car of Am. Home and Office: 19 Autumn Ridge Rd South Salem NY 10590

HOWARD, JOERENA YOUNG, principal; b. Bains, La., Feb. 27; d. Preston and Emma (White) Young; m. McErvin Howard, Dec. 25, 1951; children: Francessca, Bridgette, Brian, Charlette, McErvin Jr., Lenette. BA, So. U., Baton Rouge, La., 1954; MEd, Boston U., 1977, postgrad., 1978. Cert. elem. tchr., La. Tchr. East Baton Rouge Sch., Baton Rouge, 1954-55, U.S. Sch. System, France and Germany, 1958, 65-66; tchr. Rapides Parish Sch., Alexandria, La., 1960-63, asst. prin., tchr., 1981—; tchr. Eng. Air Force Base Sch., Alexandria, 1963-65, 66-71, Holland Elem. Sch., Satellite Beach, Fla., 1972-75, U.S. Sch. Pattonville, Fed. Republic Germany, 1975-80. Sunday sch. tchr. Nazarene Bapt. Ch., Alexandria, 1982, youth counsel, 1982—. Mem. La. Edn. Assn., Top Ladies of Distinction (v.p. 1986, teens dir. 1981), Harmony Club (pres. 1984, award 1986). Democrat. Baptist. Home: 3612 11th St Alexandria LA 71302

HOWARD, JUDITH LOIS, artist, business owner; b. Chippewa Falls, Wis., Mar. 31, 1936; d. Roland Martin and Dorothy Lois (McCulloch) Hanson; m. William Lee Howard, Mar. 22, 1959; children: Christian Scott, Craig Matthew. BA, San Jose (Calif.) State U., 1958; MS, So. Oreg. State Coll., 1973. Mem. faculty San Jose State U., 1963; art specialist Medford (Oreg.) Sch. Dist., 1966-78; artist, designer Hanson Howard Gallery, Ashland, Oreg., 1979—; cons. in field. Commr. Oreg. Arts Commn., Salem, 1983—. Mem. Oreg. Advs. for the Arts, Arts Coun. So. Oreg., Schneider Mus. of Art. Republican. Methodist. Office: Hanson Howard Gallery 82 N Main St Ashland OR 97520

HOWARD, KATHLEEN, computer company executive; b. Norman, Okla., Nov. 3, 1947; d. Robert Adrian and Jane Elizabeth (Morgens) Howard; m. Lawrence W. Osgood, Aug. 10, 1968 (div. Sept. 1970); m. Norman Edlo Gibat, Oct. 15, 1971. Student U. Okla., 1966-68. Typesetter, Selenby Press, Norman, 1968-72; owner, pres. Noguska Industries, Fostoria, Ohio, 1973—; co-founder Home Wine Mchts., Chgo., 1976; cons. Bechtel Corp., Ann Arbor, Mich. and Gaithersburg, Md., 1980—; chairperson Am. Software Project, 1985. Co-author, illustrator: Lore of Still Building, 1972; co-author: Making Wine, Beer and Merry, 1973, Computer Comix Mag., 1986; also jours. and bus. mgmt. software. Treas. United Way of Fostoria, 1986-88, 2d v.p. 1988—; bd. dirs. Pvt. Industry Council, 1988—. Recipient Disting. Service award Bechtel Corp., 1983, Founders award Home Wine and Beer Trade Assn. Chgo., 1976. Mem. Better Bus. Bur., Nat. Fedn. Ind. Bus., C. of C. (bd. dirs. 1986—), Employer's Assn. Toledo, Altrusa Internat. Club (sec. Fostoria chpt. 1984-85, pres. 1986-88, editor dist. #5 1988-90). Avocations: painting, printing, travel, reading. Office: Noguska Industries 735-741 N Countyline Fostoria OH 44830

HOWARD, LINDA ANN, banker; b. Huntington, N.Y., June 6, 1953; d. Jack Francis and Catherine Dolores (Moon) Canino. Student Suffolk County Community Coll., Selden, N.Y., 1971-72, L.I. U., 1977-80, SUNY-Westbury, 1986—. Teller, Chase Manhattan Bank, Great Neck, N.Y., 1972-74, gen. clk., teller, Douglaston, N.Y., 1974-78, platform asst., 1978, asst. mgr., Seaford, N.Y., 1978-79, br. mgr., asst. treas., Massapequa and West Islip, N.Y., 1979-85, 2d v.p., Melville, N.Y., 1985-86, 2d v.p., district mgr., Huntington, N.Y., 1987-89, 2d v.p., dist. mgr., Forest Hills, N.Y., 1989—. Treas., West Islip Mus., 1982-85; bd. dirs. West Islip Chamber Orch., 1982-85, Brentwood Family Health Ctr., N.Y., 1982-86; mem. 110/Action Bus. Assn., Melville, 1985—; treas., 1987—; treas. Nassau/Suffolk HealthSystems Agy., 1987—. Recipient Sr. Citizen Appreciation award Southside Hosp., Bayshore, N.Y., 1984, 85. Mem. Nat. Assn. Bank Women (pres. 1988-89). Roman Catholic. Avocations: golf; gardening. Home: 20 Middleville Rd Northport NY 11768 Office: Chase Manhattan Bank NA 70-46 Austin St Forest Hills NY 11375

HOWARD, M. FRANCINE, chemist; b. Catarina, Tex., July 29, 1939; d. Volney Ward and Millicent Beatrice (Zobal) H. BSc in Chemistry, Tex. Woman's U., 1961, MSc in Chemistry, 1966, PhD in Chemistry, 1979. Technician II M.D. Anderson Hosp. and Cancer Inst., Houston, 1959, 62; instr. chem. lab. San Antonio Coll., 1963-64, U. Ky., Lexington, 1965-67; assoc. prof. chemistry Ashland (Ky.) Community Coll., 1967-71; exchange sci. instr. Bendigo (Victoria, Australia) Tchrs. Coll., 1972; instr. chemistry Tarrant County Jr. Coll., Fort Worth, 1976-78, Eastern Ill. U., Charleston, 1978-80; clin. chem. supr. Humana Hosp. Met., San Antonio, 1980—. Mem. AAUW (life, program v.p. 1981, bd. mem. 1982-85), Iota Sigma Pi (life)., Altrusa Internat. (bd. 1981-89, pres. 1985-86).

HOWARD, MARGUERITE EVANGELINE BARKER (MRS. JOSEPH D. HOWARD), travel and investment company executive, civic worker; b. Victoria, B.C., Can., July 30, 1921; d. Reuel Harold and Frances Penelope (Garnham) Barker; brought to U.S., 1924, naturalized, 1945; BA, U. Wash., 1943; m. Joseph D. Howard, June 16, 1952; children: Wendy Doreen Frances, Bradford Reuel. Vice pres., dir. Howard Tours, Inc., Oakland, Calif., 1953—; co-owner, gen. mgr. Howard Travel Service, Oakland, 1956—, mng. dir. Howard Hall, Berkeley, Calif., 1964-75; co-owner, asst. mgr. Howard Investments, Oakland, 1960—; sec., treas. Energy Dynamics Inc. Bd. dirs. Piedmont council Campfire Girls, 1969-79, pres., 1974-79, mem. nat. council, 1972-76, zone chmn., 1974-76, 77-83, zone coordinator, 1976, nat. v.p., 1975, nat. bd. dirs., 1976-83, trustee Camp Augusta, 1988—, bd. dirs. Alameda Contra Costa council, 1984—; bd. dirs. Oakland Symphony Guild, 1969-87, pres., 1972-74; mem. exec. bd. Oakland Symphony Orch. Assn., 1972-74, bd. dirs., 1972-86; 1st pres. Inner Wheel Club of East Oakland, 1983-84; bd. dirs. Piedmont Jr. High Sch. Mothers Club, 1968-69. Recipient Wohelo Order award Campfire, Inc, 1985. Mem. Oakland Mus. Assn., U. Wash. Alumni Assn., East Bay Bot. and Zool. Soc., Young Audiences, Am. Symphony Orch. League, Assn. Calif. Symphony Orchs., Chi Omega Alumni Seattle, Chi Omega East Bay Alumni Berkeley. Republican. Clubs: Womens Univ. (Seattle); Womens Athletic (Oakland) (bd. dirs. 1986—). Home: 146 Bell Ave Piedmont CA 94611 Office: Howard Tours Inc 526 Grand Ave Oakland CA 94610

HOWARD, MARY MERLE PRUNTY, environmental engineering executive; b. Columbus, Miss., Nov. 20, 1942; d. Merle Charles Jr. and Eugenia (Wyatt) Prunty; m. William Leroy Phillips Jr., Sept. 7, 1964 (div.); 1 child, William Leroy III; m. Paul King Howard, Nov. 26, 1976. BA, U. Ga., 1964, MA, 1968; diplomate Edn. Ministry, U. the South, 1981. Editor Harland Bartholomew and Assocs. Inc., Memphis, 1973, planner, 1973-79, assoc., 1979-85, head dept. environ. planning, 1978-85; sr. planner Kimley-Horn and Assoc. Inc., West Palm Beach, Fla., 1985-86; pres., chief exec. officer Resource Engring. and Planning Inc., West Palm Beach, 1986—; bd. dir. Resource Engring. and Planning Inc. Active Jr. League, Memphis, The Palm Beaches, 1979-86, sustainer, 1986—; vol. Boy Scouts Am., Memphis, 1978-79; trustee Grace-St. Luke's Sch., Memphis, 1980-83. Mem. Assn. Am. Geographers (panelist 1982-83), Nat. Assn. Female Execs., Am. Planning Assn., Am. Inst. Certified Planners, Memphis Geographic Soc. (founder, pres. 1983-84), Palm Beach County Planning Congress, Profl. Svcs. Mgmt. Assn. (south Fla. chpt., founding mem., bd. dirs.), Chi Omega (pres. 1963-64). Democrat. Episcopalian. Club: Med. Wives (Memphis) (pres. 1972-73). Home: 31 Cambria Rd Palm Beach Gardens FL 33410 Office: Resource Engring Planning 3920 RCA Blvd Suite 2001 Palm Beach Gardens FL 33410

HOWARD, PATRICIA ANN, artist, mail order graphics company executive; b. Akron, Ohio, July 8, 1950; d. Robert Edwin Dudley and Margaret Eleanor (Johnsen) Sharp; m. Douglas Peter Sherman, Apr. 25, 1970 (div. Dec. 1980); children: Todd, Tyler; m. Alan Waller Howard, June 13, 1981; children: Zachary, Benjamin. Student, Miami U., Oxford, Ohio, 1969-71, Rocky Mountain Sch. Art, Denver, 1981-82, Colo. Inst. Art, 1983-84. Word processing sec. St. Regis Papr Co., Denver, 1976-77, supr. personnel dept., 1978-80; exec. loan sec. Centennial State Bank, Englewood, Colo., 1977-78; personnel recruiter Honeywell Inc., Littleton, Colo., 1980-81; freelance draftswoman Aurora, Colo., 1981-83; freelance wall graphic artist Aurora, 1983-84; owner, mgr., artist Howard Graphics, Loveland, Colo., 1984—. Mem. Ladies Golf Assn. Democrat. Home and Office: 1240 W 6th St Loveland CO 80537

HOWARD, PAULA WALTON OLLICK, marketing professional; b. Cleve., Sept. 22, 1944; d. John Sebastian and Margaret Marie (Hribar) Walton; m. Edward Wilson Ollick; children: Tanya Marie, Teresa Nicole, Andrew John. Licensed practical nurse, W-E Sch. of Practical Nursing, Willoughby, Ohio, 1964; BA in Bus. Adminstrn., Lake Erie Coll., 1985. Licensed practical nurse. Practical nurse Huron Rd. Hosp., Cleve., 1964; vol. Peace Corps U.S. Govt., Bolivia, 1964-65; radio newscaster WHOA, San Juan, P.R., 1971-76; newsanchor CATV Pinpoint Today, San Juan, 1975-76; editor Jour. Nsps., Euclid, Ohio, 1976-79; dir. pub. relations Cuyahoga County Mental Health Bd., Cleve., 1979-81; assoc. dir. event mgmt. Univ. Hosps., Cleve., 1981-85; dir. mktg. Univ. Suburban Health Ctr., South Euclid, Ohio, 1985-86, The Victor S. Voinovich Co., Cleve., 1986-89; pres. Aha! Mktg., Spl. Events, Cleve., 1989—. Chmn. Mentor (Ohio) Cable TV Commn., 1976-77; founder, editor Parish Ch. Newsletter, Mentor, 1979-82; pres. Lake Catholic High Sch. Parents Assn., Mentor, 1986-87; co-founder Ohio Says No to Drugs, Cleve., 1988—; mem. steering com. Cleve. Communicates Coun., 1989—. Recipient Cleve. Communicators award, Women In Communications, Cleve., 1983, Bronze Quill award, Internat. Assn. Bus. Communicators, Cleve., 1984. Mem. Pub. Rels. Soc. Am. (bd. dirs. Cleve. 1980-88, Lighthouse award 1980, pres. 1988), The Press Club of Cleve. (bd. dirs. 1977, Excellence in Journalism award 1988), Cleve. Soc. Communicating Arts, NAFE. Democrat. Roman Catholic. Office: Aha! Mktg Spl Events 530 Euclid Ave #230 Cleveland OH 44115

HOWARD, RUTH COLETTE, marketing professional; b. Holland, Mich., May 23, 1958; d. Benjamin Richard and Marion Hazel (Helder) Van Slooten; m. Mark Allyn Howard. AB, Hope Coll., 1980; MBA, U. Mich., 1982. Asst. product mgr. S.C. Johnson & Son, Inc., Racine, Wis., 1982-84; assoc. product mgr. S.C. Johnson & Son, Inc., Racine, 1984-85, product mgr., 1985-87; product mgr. Steelcase, Inc., Grand Rapids, Mich., 1987—. Bd. dirs. Big Sister of Racine, Wis., 1987. Republican. Office: Steelcase Inc PO Box 1967 Grand Rapids MI 49501

HOWATSON, MARIANNE, publisher; b. Paisley, Ayrshire, Scotland, May 16, 1948; d. Alexander Bremner and Anne Francis (Carrol) H.; m. Richard H. Friedberg. Bachelor Edn., Craigie Coll., 1968; Diploma, Jordan Hill Coll., 1969; postgrad., Harvard Bus. Sch., 1982-83. Advt. dir. Gen. Media, N.Y.C., 1976-79, assoc. pub., 1979-83; sr. v.p. Mag. Pub. Am., N.Y.C., 1983-86; pub., v.p. Am. Express Pub., N.Y.C., 1986-87; pub. Conde Nast Pubs., N.Y.C., 1987—; vice-chmn. Pubs. Council M.P.A., N.Y.C., 1986-88; chmn. Am. Mag. Conf., 1987. Contbr. articles to profl. jours. Mem. Andy Award Com., Fashion Group (bd. dirs.). Office: Self Mag 350 Madison Ave New York NY 10017

HOWATT, HELEN CLARE, library director; b. San Francisco, Apr. 5, 1927; d. Edward Bell and Helen Margaret (Kenney) H. BA, Holy Names Coll., 1949; MS in Libr. Sci., U. So. Calif., 1972; cert. advanced studies Our Lady of Lake U., 1966. Joined Order Sisters of the Holy Names, Roman Cath. Ch., 1945. Life teaching credential, life spl. svcs. credential, prin. St. Monica Sch., Santa Monica, Calif., 1957-60, St. Mary Sch., L.A., 1960-63; tchr. jr. high sch. St. Augustine Sch., Oakland, Calif., 1964-69; tchr. jr. high math St. Monica Sch., San Francisco, 1969-71, St. Cecilia Sch., San Francisco, 1971-77; libr. dir. Holy Names Coll., Oakland, Calif., 1977—. Contbr. math. curriculum San Francisco Unified Sch. Dist., Cum Notis Variorum, publ. Music Libr., U. Calif., Berkeley. Contbr. articles to profl. jours. NSF grantee, 1966, NDEA grantee, 1966. Mem. Cath. Libr. Assn. (chmn. No. Calif. elem. schs. 1971-72), Calif. Libr. Assn., ALA, Assn. Coll. and rsch. Librs. Home and Office: 3500 Mountain Blvd Oakland CA 94619

HOWE, EVELYN FREEMAN, cultural organization administrator; b. Spartanburg, S.C., Jan. 11, 1929; d. D. Odell and Jane Tabitha (Bryson) Freeman; m. Jack Dean Howe, June 10, 1950; children: Andrew Walter, Angela Jane. BA, Limestone Coll., 1948; MA in Edn., Winthrop Coll., 1967. Social studies tchr. Whitmire (S.C.) High Sch., 1948-50; tchr. 2d grade Beaverdam Elem. Sch., Gaffney, S.C., 1950-51; social worker Portsmouth (Va.) Welfare Dept., 1952-54; caseworker Cherokee County Dept. Social Svcs., Gaffney, 1955-58; tchr. 6th grade Draytonville Elem. Sch., Gaffney, 1960-67; prin., librarian Corinth & Alma Elem. Schs., Gaffney, 1967-74; tchr. 6th grade Blacksburg (S.C.) Elem. Sch., 1974-81; tchr. 5th grade J. Paul Beam Elem. Sch., Gaffney, 1981-87; exec. dir. Cherokee County Literacy Assn., Gaffney, 1987—. Pres. Cherokee Hist. and Preservation Soc., Gaffney, 1987-88. Recipient Svc. to Community award Limestone Coll., 1978, Svc. to Coll., 1989. Mem. Cherokee County Social and Health Orgn. Coun. (sec. 1987—), Cherokee County Literacy Assn. (trainer 1986—, pres. Gaffney chpt. 1970-85), Cherokee County Reading Coun. (1st pres. Gaffney chpt. 1985-86), Cherokee County Sch. Dist. Task Force on Reading Improvement (subcom. chair 1988—), S.C. Edn. Assn. (bd. dirs. Columbia chpt. 1983-87), Limestone Coll. Alumni Assn. (sec. bd. Gaffney chpt. 1986—), Delta Kappa Gamma (sec. Gaffney chpt. 1988—), AAUW (pres. Gaffney chpt. 1960-62, 74-76). Democrat. Presbyterian. Home: 219 Crestview Dr Gaffney SC 29340 Office: Cherokee County Literacy 300 E Rutledge Ave Gaffney SC 29340

HOWE, LENORE ANN, furniture company executive; b. Ludlow, Mass., Feb. 16, 1948; d. Emile Arthur and Charlotte Moria (Shearer) Babineau; m. Gerald Wright, Aug. 12, 1967 (div. 1979). BS, U. Mass., 1968; student, Mercy Hosp. Sch. Med. Technol., Springfield, Mass., 1968. Registered Med. Technol., Mass. Med. technologist U. Mass. Health Ctr., Amherst, 1968-71; various positions agrl. and forestry programs Rochester, N.H., 1972-75; staff assoc. New Eng. Mcpl. Ctr., Durham, N.H., 1975-77; owner, exec. Rural Assocs. Cons., Stafford, N.H., 1978—; gen. ptnr. North Woods Chair Shop, Canterbury, N.H., 1981—; cons. R.L. Polk & Co., Detroit, 1978-81. Author: Training Manuals Reports, 1975-80; Editor: Opportunities Newsletter 1976-77. Chmn. Strafford County Land Adv. Com., Dover N.H., 1978-80; mem. adv. bd. Stafford County Forest, Dover N.H. 1975-82, Merrimack County Forest, Concord N.H. 1983-86, Canterbury Conservation Commn., N.H. 1984-90. Recipient Best in U.S. Shaker Chairmaker award Crafts of Am. Harper & Row, 1988. Mem. Alpha Lambda Delta, Alpha Delta Theta. Democratic. Roman Catholic. Home and Office: 237 Old Tilton Rd Canterbury NH 03224

HOWE, MAROLYN LOUISE, chemical engineer; b. Memphis, Jan. 17, 1957; d. William Chew and Lucretia Louise (Alldredge) H.; m. Gerald

Francis Lenski, Feb. 16, 1985. BS in Chemistry, Christian Brothers Coll., Memphis, 1979; BS in Chem. Engring., Christian Brothers Coll., 1981. Registered profl. engr. in tng., Tex. Lectr. Christian Brothers Coll., Memphis, 1980-81; petroleum engr. Texaco, USA, Midland, Tex., 1981-85; chem. engr. Hess Environmental Svcs., Inc., Memphis, 1987—; chem. engr. Crittenden County, emergency response planning com., Marion, Ark., 1988—. Vol. Alzheimer Day Care Ctr., Memphis, 1987—, Crittenden Meml. Hosp., West Memphis, Ark., 1972-73; vol. asst. for waste water permitting City Atty. of West Memphis, 1989—. NSF rsch. fellow, 1974, 78. Mem. AAUW, Soc. Petroleum Engrs., Am. Chem. Soc., Nat. Assn. Corrosion Engrs. (cert. corrosion technologist), Am. Soc. Safety Engrs. Methodist. Office: Hess Environmental Svcs 2565 Horizon Lake Dr Ste 120 Memphis TN 38133

HOWE-ELLISON, PATRICIA MARY, investment banker; b. Chgo., Sept. 14, 1928; d. Harry Michael and Helen Mary (Maloney) Howe; student Barat Coll., Lake Forest, Ill., 1944-47, Goodman Theatre, Chgo., 1947; m. Ernest O. Ellison, Sept. 23, 1977. Instl. sales asst. Blyth & Co., 1954-55; with L.F. Rothschild & Co., 1957-82, mgr. San Francisco br., 1965-82, partner, 1968-82, pres., 1982—; chmn. Corp. Capital Investment Advisors, 1984—; chief exec. officer Capitalcorp, Inc., San Francisco, 1989—, also bd. dirs; mng. dir. Thrift Investment Services, 1984—. Trustee U. San Diego, Women's Forum West. Mem. Securities Industry Assn., San Francisco Bond Club, Equestrian Order Holy Sepulchre, Opera Guild. Republican. Roman Catholic. Clubs: World Trade, Metropolitan, Bankers, Villa Taverna, Bankers (dir.), Bel Air Bay. Office: Capitalcorp Inc 655 Montgomery St San Francisco CA 94111

HOWELL, ALLIE RHEA, medical records director; b. Ropesville, Tex., July 23, 1927; d. Alfred and Allie Olivia (Northam) Martin; m. Raymond Cecil Gordon, Aug. 26, 1945 (dec. Nov. 1955); m. Seale Cecil Edward, Dec. 31, 1959 (dec. Mar. 1967); m. Richard Elea Howell, Nov. 17, 1972; children: Kenneth Ray, Barbara Kay. Accredited med. records technician. Med. sec. Meth. Hosp., Lubbock, Tex., 1954-55; med. records dir. West Tex. Hosp., Lubbock, 1955—. Mem. Am. Med. Records Assn., Tex. Med. Records Assn., Caprock Med. Records Assn. Home: 4605 63rd St Lubbock TX 79414 Office: W Tex Hosp 1401 9th St Lubbock TX 79401

HOWELL, BARBARA FENNEMA, research chemist; b. Chgo., Dec. 18, 1924; d. Nick and Fern Alma (First) Fennema; m. Wilbur Alexander Howell, June 29, 1946; children: Susan Barbara, Gary Wilbur, Michael Owen. BA, U. Minn., 1946; MS, Kans. State U., 1949; PhD, U. Mo., 1964. Asst. prof. Kans. State Coll. of Emporia, 1964-69; postdoctoral fellow U. Mo., Rolla, 1969-71; rsch. chemist Nat. Inst. Standards and Tech., Gaithersburg, Md., 1971-87; materials engr. David Taylor Rsch. Ctr., Annapolis, Md., 1987—. Contbr. articles to profl. jour. Recipient Gordon award Chem. Soc. Washington, 1987. Mem. AAAS, Am. Chem. Soc. (councilor 1983-89). Democrat. Methodist. Office: David Taylor Rsch Ctr Code 2844 Annapolis MD 21402

HOWELL, BONNIE HOWARD, hospital administrator; b. Ithaca, N.Y., Dec. 7, 1947; d. Robert Leon and Helen Elizabeth (Ryerson) Howard; m. James Ward Delaney Howell, Jr., Feb. 17, 1950; children: Carolyn Elizabeth, Kathryn Helene. BS, Cornell U., 1970, MPA, 1972. Planning assoc. Areawide & Local Planning Health Action, Syrauсse, N.YL, 1972-74; adminstr. Community Med. Ctr., Aurora, N.Y., 1974-76; asst. adminstr. Tompkins Community Hosp., Ithaca, 1974-79, adminstr., 1979—; bd. dirs. Tompkins County Trust Co. Contbr. articles to profl. publs. Bd. dirs. United Way Tompkins County, Ithaca, 1986-88. Mem. Am. Coll. Healthcare Execs., Downtown Bus. Women, Rotary. Baptist. Home and Office: Tompkins Community Hosp 101 Dates Dr Ithaca NY 14850

HOWELL, CATHARINE ANN, accountant; b. Tampa, Fla., Mar. 23, 1949; d. William Justin and Faith Catharine (Clark) Nunnally; m. Gary Allen Howell, Aug. 2, 1969; children: Nancy Michelle, Christopher Michael. BS with honors, Atlanta Christian Coll., 1971; postgrad., Okla. City U., 1979, U. Ky., 1979, Cen. State U., Edmond, Okla., 1980-84. CPA, Okla. Auditor, rate analyst State of Okla., Oklahoma City, 1980-83; mcpl. acct. City of Oklahoma City, 1983-85, 85-88, airport acctg. supr., 1985, contr., 1988—. Mem. allocations com., mental health subcom., United Way Oklahoma City, 1987—; vol. tutor, Literacy Vols. of Am., Oklahoma City, 1988—. Fellow Oklahoma City Mgmt. Devel. Acad.; mem. Oklahoma Soc. CPAs (vice-chmn. govtl. acctg. and audit com. 1987), Nat. Govt. Fin. Officers Assn. (spl. rev. com. 1988), Oklahoma Govt. Fin. Officers Assn., AICPA. Office: City of Oklahoma City 100 N Walker St Oklahoma City OK 73102

HOWELL, EMBRY MARTIN, researcher; b. Bethesda, Md., Nov. 18, 1945; d. David Grier and Louise (McMichael) Martin; m. Joseph Toy Howell III, Dec. 28, 1965; children: Andrew Martin, Jessica Ramsey. AB, Barnard Coll., 1968; MSPH, U. N.C., 1972; postgrad., George Washington U. Computer programmer Corp. Trust Co., N.Y.C., 1968; computer programmer dept. city and regional planning U. N.C., Chapel Hill, 1969-70; summer intern State Bd. Health, Raleigh, N.C., 1972; rsch. asst. dept. ob-gyn Georgetown U. Hosp., Washington, 1972-73; health planner, biostatistician Health Systems Agy. No. Va., Falls Church, 1973-75; biostatistician Nat. Capital Med. Found., Washington, 1975-79; dir. SysteMetrics, Inc., Washington, 1979—; speaker in field. Contbr. numerous articles to profl. jours. Vol. Children's Hosp. Hospice; organizer Washington/Balt. Network Assn. Social Scis. in Health. USPHS trainee, 1971-72. Mem. Am. Pub. Health Assn., Assn. for Social Scis. in Health, Assn. for Pub. Policy Analysis and Mgmt., Am. Evaluation Assn., Phi Beta Kappa.

HOWELL, JOYCE ANN, lawyer; b. Haddonfield, N.J., Dec. 15, 1955; d. Harry O. and Mary Ann (Beaudet) H. BS, Shippensburg U., 1977, MLS, 1980; MA, St. John's Coll., Annapolis, Md., 1983; JD, Rutgers U., 1986. Bar: N.J. 1986, Pa. 1986, U.S. Dist. Ct. N.J. 1986, U.S. Ct. Appeals (3d cir.) 1987, U.S. Mil. Ct. Appeals 1987, D.C. 1988. Law clk. to presiding judge equity div. N.J. Chancery Ct., Atlantic City, 1986-87; assoc. Riker, Danzig, Scherer & Hyland, Morristown, N.J., 1987—. Staff mem. Rutgers Law Jour., 1985-86. NEH fellow, 1981, Roothbert Found. fellow, 1982, 83; Rutgers Law Sch. Alumni grantee, 1985. Mem. ABA, N.J. Bar Assn., Morris County Bar Assn., N.J. Women Lawyers Assn. (v.p. 1989-90), Pa. Bar Assn., D.C. Bar Assn. Democrat. Roman Catholic. Office: Riker Danzig Scherer & Hyland 1 Speedwell Ave Morristown NJ 07960-1981

HOWELL, LAURA SUE, real estate executive; b. Mt. Pleasant, Tex., Mar. 30, 1937; d. Robert Ernest and margaret Josephine (Riddle) Mangum. Student, Kilgore Jr. Coll., Longview, Tex., 1974-75. Cert. apt. mgr.; accredited resident mgr. Apt. mgr. Smith, Andrews & Piperato, H.P.I., Longview, Tex., 1979-83, Robert A. McNeil Corp., Longview and Dallas, 1983-87, Southmark, Johnstown Corp., Addison, Tex., 1987—. Mem. Dallas Mus. Art. Mem. Inst. Real Estate Mgmt., Greater Longview Area Apt. Assn. (bd. dirs. 1980-84, sec. 1983-84, product chmn. 1982), Tex. Apt. Assn. (bd. dirs. 1983-84), Addison Athletic Club. Republican. Baptist. Office: Shadowood Apts 14500 Marsh Ln Addison TX 75234

HOWELL, LINDA KAY, electrical contractor; b. Ord, Nebr., Sept. 22, 1946; d. Eugene C. and Mildred F. (Rich) Vanosdall; m. Larry D. Allen, Mar. 15, 1965 (div.); m. Ronald G. Moore, Sept. 26, 1970 (1983); m. Charles E. Howell, Dec. 10, 1983; children: Laurie Lynn Allen Lane Eugene Allen, Leath Mardell Moore. Postgrad., S.W. Community Coll., Creston, 1968, ICS, Scranton, 1987. Waitress Skylark Cafe, Bedford, Iowa, 1959-64; waitress sec. S.W. Community Coll., Creston, 1969-71; sec. to buyer Nat. Fabrics, Pompano Bch., Fla., 1971-73; sec., bookkeeper Personalized A/C, Boca Raton, Fla.; mgr. Biscuit King Restaurant, Ladson, S.C., 1980; bookkekeper Lonzies A/C, S.C., 1980-82; owner of own bus. C & L Fixit Renamed Howell Services, Summerville, 1982--. Mem. Nat. Assn. of Female Exec. Home: 111 Cynthia Ln Summerville SC 29485

HOWELL, MARY ELIZABETH, small business owner; b. Galesburg, Ill., Feb. 19, 1942; d. John A. Shaner and Elizabeth N. (Bowen) Knowles; m. Murrell D. Howell, Dec. 22, 1969; children: Cherie, Thomas, Dean, Murrell. Cert., Alamo Beauty Coll., 1961; student, Jane Grace Sch. Dress Design, 1973; BS in Bus. Adminstrn., U. Redlands, 1985. Owner, operator Howell's Acctg., Minot, N.D., 1972-78; gen. mgr. Gravel Products, Inc., Minot, 1978-80; controller Bluebird Internat., Inc., Denver, 1981-83; owner, pres. Magnetic Power Systems, Huntington Beach, Calif., 1984—; free-lance cons. Huntington Beach, 1984—; acctg. and budget cons. for mfg., health care, real estate, electronics, academia and personal svcs.; owner Cosmetics For Me, Huntington Beach, 1987—; cons., sr. fin. analyst U. Calif., Irvine, 1987—. Copyright Thin Graille of Insanity etching; patentee rail system, pitch control ground effect vehicle; designer needlework, costumes and hair-styles for amateur theater groups; developer cosmetic cream. Leader Girl Scouts USA, Minot, 1973-75, den mother Boy Scouts Am., Minot, 1974, fund raiser Minot AFB Little League and Youth Orgn., 1975; active Hadassah, 1975—, Temple Sharon sisterhood, Costa Mesa, Calif., 1986—. Mem. NAFE, Nat. Assn. Accts. Orange Coast (dir. 1982, 83, v.p. edn. and profl. devel. 1984, 86, sec. 1985, v.p. adminstrn. 1987, pres. 1988, nat. community svc. com. 1989-90), Toastmasters (cert., pres. 1989). Republican. Jewish. Office: Magnetic Power Systems PO Box 1115 Huntington Beach CA 92647

HOWELL, REBECCA ELIZABETH, pilot, driving educator, safety consultant; b. San Antonio, May 23, 1952; d. David Ray and Glenna Ruth (Walters) H.; m. Robert Wayne Sykora, Aug. 22, 1970 (Div. July 1974); m. Donald Homer Kelley, Dec. 23, 1976 (div. Oct. 1977). BS in Pharmacy, U. Houston, 1976; MS, Tex. A&M U., 1983. Clk. Mohrmann Drug Store, Gonzales, Tex., 1968-70, various pharmacies, Houston, 1970-76; staff pharmacist Community Hosp. of Brazosport, Freeport, Tex., 1977-82; owner Safe Cycling Cons., Austin, Tex., 1981—; instr., supr. drivers edn. Austin (Tex.) Driving Sch., 1984-88; cons. Tex. Dept. Pub. Safety, Austin, 1984—; pilot Mandot & Howell Flying Svc., Austin, 1986—, Air South Commuter, Inc., Birmingham, Ala., 1987, Am. Eagle DFW, Tex., 1988—. Contbr. articles to profl. jours. Cons. contract labor Motorcycle Safety Found., Irvine, Calif., 1983—. Mem. Internat. Soc. Women Airline Pilots, Am. Motorcycle Assn., Tex. Motorcycle Riders Assn., Airplane Owners and Pilots Assn., Tex. Automobile Dealers Assn. (pilot 1983—), U.S. Parachute Assn. Home and Office: Safe Cycling Cons PO Box 858 Manor TX 78653

HOWELL, SAUNDRA LEAH, nurse; b. Maryville, Tenn., Feb. 20, 1945; d. Frank Huston and Fern (Morrison) Caldwell; m. Roy Lee Goodman, MAy 28, 1967 (dec. 1985); m. Sherill Eugene Howell, June 14, 1986. Diploma in nursing, U. Tenn., 1966. RN, Tenn. Staff nurse Univ. Tenn. Hosp., Knoxville, 1966-67, Good Samaritan Hosp., Cin., 1967-70, Ft. Sanders Hosp., Knoxville, 1970-72; staff nurse VA Med. Ctr., Bay Pines, Fla., 1972-76, Johnson City, Tenn., 1976—. Trainee Johnson City Emergency Rescue Squad, 1988. Mem. Emergency Nurses Assn. (cert.). Republican. Baptist. Club: Thunderbolt Country. Lodge: Order Eastern Star. Home: Rt 3 Box 131 Kentland Dr Johnson City TN 37604 Office: VA Mountain Home Johnson City TN 37684

HOWERY, SHARON C., marketing executive; b. Newark, Apr. 24, 1962; d. John and Dorothy (Weishaple) H. BA, Boston Coll., 1984; MBA, Fordham U., 1988. Sales rep. Kimberly Clark Corp., Neenah, Wis.; asst. mktg. mgr. Poly Bio Marine, Inc., Orange, N.J.; account exec. Nielsen Mktg. Rsch., Northbrook, Ill. Mem. Am. Mktg. Assn., NAFE, Beta Gamma Sigma, Alpha Mu Alpha. Home: 34 Mayhew Dr South Orange NJ 07079

HOWES, CAROL SUSAN, petroleum engineer; b. Great Bend, Kans., Feb. 27, 1960; d. Thomas Byron and Mary Diane (Staffelbach) Smith; m. Hal Ivan Howes, Nov. 29, 1986. BS in Petroleum Engring., U. Tex., 1982. Engring. trainee Anadarko Prodn. Co., Denver, 1982-83, reservoir engr., 1983-85; sr. reservoir engr. Anadarko Petroleum Corp., Denver, 1985-90, staff reservoir engr., 1990; staff reservoir engr. Anadarko Petroleum Corp., Houston, 1990—. Mem. Soc. Petroleum Engrs., Soc. Petroleum Well Log Analysts, Alliance Francaise, Alpha Xi Delta. Republican. Methodist. Office: Anadarko Petroleum Corp 16801 Greenspoint Park Dr Ste 200 Houston TX 77060

HOWES, WENDY ELIZABETH, small business owner, commercial interior designer, medical design specialist; b. Liberal, Kans., May 6, 1951; d. Wallace Addison and Shirley (Corman) H. BFA, North Tex. State U., 1973. Store planning specialist Sears, Roebuck & Co., 1973-75; corp. interior designer, space planner Rockwell Internat., 1975-77; account exec. Westgate Fabrics, Inc., 1977-79; prin. Inner Spaces Interiors, Dallas, 1979—. Republican. Mem. Ch. of Christ Scientist. Office: Inner Spaces Ste 112 7822 Meadow Park Dr Dallas TX 75230

HOWINGTON, PAMELA KAY, telephone company official; b. Gainesville, Ga., Oct. 16, 1958; d. Leroy Allan and Elosie (Ragsdale) H. BBA, Ga. State U., 1980, MBA, 1984. Analyst So. Bell Co., Atlanta, 1980-84; staff analyst Bell South Svcs., Atlanta, 1984-88; mgr. Bell South Svcs., Birmingham, Ala., 1988—. Baptist. Office: Bell South Svcs 1876 Data Dr N506B Birmingham AL 35244

HOWL, JOANNE HEALEY, veterinarian; b. Mariemont, Ohio, Mar. 16, 1957; d. Joseph Daniel and Claire Helen (Baillargeon) H.; m. Arthur Wesley Howl, May 12, 1990. Grad., U. Tenn., 1987. Groom Salvi Stables, Meadowlands, Pa., 1977-78; weaver Minnewawa Mfg., Knoxville, Tenn., 1979-81; various positions U. Tenn., 1981-83; sr. lab. animal technician Lab Animal Facility, Knoxville, 1983-84; gnotobiology technician U. Tenn., Knoxville, 1984-86; assoc. vet. Mynatt Vet. Clinic, Knoxville, 1987-89; veterinary med. officer U.S. Dept. of Agr. Animal and Plant Health Inspection Svcs., Raleigh, N.C., 1989-90; assoc. veterinarian Rocky Gorge Animal Hosp., Laurel, Md., 1990—. Mem. Am. Vet. Med. Assn., Am. Animal Hosp. Assn., Am. Assn. Feline Practitioners. Roman Catholic. Home: 9222 Canterbury Riding Laurel MD 20723 Office: Rocky Gorge Animal Hosp 7515 Brooklyn Bridge Rd Laurel MD 20723

HOWLETT, PHYLLIS LOU, athletics conference administrator; b. Indianola, Iowa, Oct. 23, 1932; d. James Clarence and Mabel L. (Fisher) Hickman; m. Jerry H. Howlett, Jan. 2, 1955 (dec.); children: Timothy A., Jane A.; m. Ronlin Royer, Dec. 30, 1977. BA, Simpson Coll., 1954. Psychometrist Drake U., Des Moines, 1956-57, asst. to men's athletics dir., 1974-79; asst. dir. athletics U. Kans., Lawrence, 1979-82; asst. commr. Big Ten Conf., Schaumburg, Ill., 1982— ; mem. NCAA Football TV Com., 1980-87, chmn. NCAA com. on women's athletics, 1987—, exec. com., 1990—; exec. com. Nat. Assn. Collegiate Dirs. of Athletics, 1986—; NCAA Women's Golf Com., 1983-89, spl. com. Women's Basketball TV, 1989—. Chmn. Iowa Commn. Status of Women, 1976-79; pres. Vol. Bur. of Greater Des Moines, 1969-70, Arts and Recreation Council of Greater Des Moines, 1975, Iowa Children's and Family Svcs., 1973; nat. pres. Assn. Vol. Burs., Inc., 1972-73, svc. award. Recipient certs. of appreciation Des Moines C. of C., State of Iowa, Drake U. Mem. Nat. Assn. Dirs. of Collegiate Athletics, Council Collegiate Women Athletic Adminstrs. (bd. dirs.), Jr. League, Simpson Coll. Alumni Achievement award, 1988. Inductee Simpson Coll. Hall of Fame. Republican. Office: 1111 Plaza Dr Ste 600 Schaumburg IL 60173-4990

HOWLETT-GONZALEZ, STEPHANIE ANN, home care facilites sales representative, nurse; b. Kansas City, Kans., Dec. 23, 1957; d. Wayne Stewart and Anna Marie (Barancik) H.; m. John B. Gonzalez; children: Vincent, Anthony. AA, Kansas City Community Coll., 1979. RN. Critical care nurse Providence-St. Margarets Health Ctr., Kansas City, Kans., 1979-82; primary pvt. duty nurse Quality Care In, Kansas City, Mo., 1980-81; dir. nursing Profl. Nursing Service, Kansas City, Mo., 1981-86; med. services cons. Crawford Health and Rehab. Services, Kansas City, Mo., 1986; sales rep. HOMEDCO, Lenexa, Kans., 1986—, mem. presidents adv. coun., 1989—; v.p. Progressive Enterprises, Inc.; mem. adv. bd. Olsten Health Care Services, Kansas City, Mo., 1986—, utilization rev. com., 1986—, budget com., 1987. Mem. Mo. Voters Freeze, Kansas City, 1986, Kansas City (Kans.) Jr. League, 1987; active Vols. in Prisons. Named one of Outstanding Young Women Am., 1987. Mem. Nat. Rehab. Assn., Assn. Rehab. Nurses, Support Hospice Oncology Profls., Kansas City Met. Discharge Coordinators, Kansas City Regional Homecare Assn. (edn. com., infusion therapy com.), NAFE. Republican. Home: 10507 College Kansas City MO 64137 Office: HOMEDCO 14653 W 95th St Lenexa KS 66215

HOWORTH, LUCY SOMERVILLE, lawyer; b. Greenville, Miss., July 1, 1895; d. Robert and Nellie (Nugent) Somerville; m. Joseph Marion Howorth, Feb. 16, 1928. A.B., Randolph-Macon Woman's Coll., 1916; postgrad., Columbia U., 1918; J.D. summa cum laude, U. Miss., 1922. Bar: Miss. 1922, U.S. Supreme Ct. 1934. Asst. in psychology Randolph-Macon Woman's Coll., 1916-17; gauge insp. Allied Bur. Air Prodn., N.Y.C., 1918; indsl. research nat. bd. YWCA, 1919-20; gen. practice law Howorth & Howorth, Cleveland, Greenville and Jackson, Miss., 1922-34; U.S. commr. So. Jud. Dist. Miss., 1927-31; assoc. mem. Bd. Vet. Appeals, Washington, 1934-43; legis. atty. VA, 1943-49; v.p., dir. VA Employees Credit Union, 1937-49; assoc. gen. counsel War Claims Commn., 1949-52, dep. gen. counsel, 1952-53, gen. counsel, 1953-54; ptnr. James Somerville & Assocs. (overseas trade and devel.), 1954—; atty. Commn. on Govt. Security, 1956-57; pvt. law practice Cleveland, Miss., 1958—; mem. nat. bd. cons. Women's Archives, Radcliffe Coll.; mem. lay adv. com. study profl. nursing Carnegie Corp. N.Y., 1947-48; chmn. Miss. State Bd. Law Examiners, 1924-28; mem. Miss. State Legislature, 1932-36, chmn. com. pub. lands, 1932-36; treas. Com. for Econ. Survey Miss., 1928-30; mem. Research Commn. Miss., 1930-34. Editor: Fed. Bar Assn. News, 1944; assoc. editor: Fed. Bar Assn. Jour., 1943-44; editor: (with William M. Cash) My Dear Nellie-Civil War Letters (William L. Nugent), 1977; contbr. articles profl. jours. Keynote speaker White House Conf. on Women in Postwar Policy Making, 1944, at conf. on opening 81st Congress. Recipient Alumnae Achievement award Randolph-Macon Woman's Coll., 1981, Lifetime Achievement award Schlesinger Libr. of Radcliffe Coll., 1983; named for her outstanding lifetime achievements by Senate Concurrent Resolution, adopted by Senate and Ho. of Reps., 1984; recipient Excellence medal Miss. U. for Women, 1990. Mem. AAUW (nat. dir., 2d v.p. 1951-55, mem. found. 1960-63), Nat. Fedn. Bus. and Profl. Women's Clubs (nat. dir.; rep. to internat. 1939, chmn. internat. conf. 1946), Nat. Assn. Women Lawyers, Miss. Library Assn. (life), Miss. Hist. Soc. (dir. 1982—, Merit award 1983), DAR, Daus. Am. Colonists, Am. Legion Aux. (past sec. Miss. dept.), Assembly Women's Orgns. for Nat. Security (chmn. 1951-52), Phi Beta Kappa, Pi Gamma Mu, Phi Alpha Delta, Alpha Omicron Pi (Wyman award 1985), Delta Kappa Gamma, Omicron Delta Kappa, Phi Kappa Phi (hon.). Democrat (del. nat. conv., 1932). Methodist. Club: Soroptimist (Washington). Address: 515 S Victoria Ave Cleveland MS 38732

HOWSARE, LEORA ALIC NAGEL, educator; b. Canton, Ohio, June 13, 1908; d. Homer Henry and Myrtle Julia (Wyman) Lautzenheiser; m. Edward John Nagel, Aug. 29, 1937 (dec. Feb. 1945); m. James Shannon Howsare, Dec. 5, 1950 (dec.Aug. 1960). BS in Edn., Kent State U., 1938; student, Ohio State U., 1934-36. Cert. (life) tchr., Ohio. Tchr. Stark County Schs., Ohio, 1927-29, Canton (Ohio) City Schs., 1929-37; missionary, tchr. Kalinea Acad., Philippines, 1939-45; nat. promotional sec. Women's Soc. of World Svc., Evang. United Brethren Ch., Dayton, Ohio, 1945-50; tchr. Manchester (Ohio) Schs., 1952-55, Tallmadge (Ohio) City Schs., 1955-73. Contbr. articles to profl. jours. Jennings scholar Martha Holden Jennings Found., 1966-67; named Woman of Influence, Internat. Toastmistress Clubs, Great Lakes Region, 1969, one of 100 Women in Mission, United Meth. Women East Ohio, 1986. Mem. Bus. and Profl. Women (pres. 1963-64), AAUW (legis. chair 1971-75), Travelers' Club of Kent (pres. 1979-80, 84-85), Delta Kappa Gamma (fellowship chair 1987-89). Republican. Methodist. Home: 4285 Kent Rd 571C Stow OH 44224

HOXIT-SMITH, LINDA CAROLINE, choreographer, educator; b. Bremerton, Wash., Mar. 13, 1953; d. Johnny Ray and Beverly Joyce (Miller) Hoxit; married, June 22, 1990. Student, Olympic Jr. Coll., 1970-71, U.S. Internat. U., San Diego, 1971-73, UCLA, 1976, U. So. Calif., 1977-78. Choreographer, dancer Ray Anthony's Bookends, world tour, 1975, Nikki Whiskey, Tokyo, 1975, Ski Time Revue, Aspen, Colo., 1980, Mr. Blackwell Girl, L.A., 1981, Wrangler Jeans, L.A., 1983; choreographer Monie-Poco Diapers, Tokyo, 1983; choreographer, tchr. dance Roberts Sch. Dance (formerly Ballet Acad. Performing Arts), 1983—; choreographer Wash.-Idaho Dairy Assn., Seattle, 1987—; choreographer episode Northern Exposure CBS Universal Studios, 1990; educator Barbizon Modeling Schs. Internat., 1990. Choreographer Miss Kitsap, Kitsap County, Wash., 1984, Ms. Issaqua (Wash.) Pageant, 1985. Scholar San Francisco Ballet Co., 1967-68, Ford Found., 1967-68, Robert Joffrey Ballet Co., 1969-70, U.S. Internat. Univ. Sch. of Performing and Visual Arts, 1971-73. Mem. Screen Actors Guild, AFTRA, Actors Equity Assn. Democrat.

HOYER, JESSE LEE, ceramic engineer; b. Denver, June 20, 1960; d. Asa Lee and Patricia Louise (Hughes) H. BS, Ga. Inst. Tech., 1983. Ceramic engr. U.S. Bureau Mines, Tuscaloosa, Ala., 1978-83, researcher, 1983—. Contbr. articles to profl. jours. Explorer Advisor Boy Scouts Am. Tuscaloosa, 1986-87; Keyperson Combined Fed. Campaign Tusaloosa, 1988. Recipient spl. achievement award U.S. Bur. Mines, 1988, Engr. of Yr. award, Tuscaloosa, 1989. Mem. Am. Ceramic Soc., Southeastern Sec. Am. Ceramic Soc. Baptist. Office: US Bureau Mines Capstone Dr PO Box L Tuscaloosa AL 35486

HOYER, PHYLLIS SCARBOROUGH, educator; b. Salisbury, Md., Oct. 14, 1938; d. Paul Daniel and Norma (Luettinger) Scarborough; m. Lawrence Cogswell Hoyer, July 8, 1961; children: Brian Lawrence, Andrew Scarborough. BS, Hood Coll., 1960; MEd, Towson State U., 1986; post grad., Hood Coll., U. Md. Cert. early childhood edn., home econs., Md. Tchr. Anne Arundel County Bd. of Edn., Annapolis, Md., 1960-61, Washington County Bd. of Edn., Hagerstown, Md., 1961-64, Frederick County Bd. of Edn., Md., 1972—; chairperson communication com., 1984-85; tchr. adv. com., 1977-80, 87-89; team leader, 1989—; rep. kindergarten class, 1989—. Instr. Frederick County YMCA, 1976-79; participating mem. Earthwatch, Orca Survey, 1989. Mem. NEA, Md. State Tchrs. Assn., Frederick County Tchrs. Assn. (Tchrs. rep. 1980-83), Nat. Orgn. for Women, Fiji Coral Communities. Republican. Home: 8398 Cub Hunt Ct Walkersville MD 21793 Office: Thurmont Elementary Sch 805 E Main St Thurmont MD 21788

HOYLAND, JANET LOUISE, clergyman; b. Kansas City, Mo., July 21, 1940; d. Robert J. and Dora Louise (Worley) H.; B.A., Carleton Coll., 1962; postgrad. in music (Mu Phi Epsilon scholar 1966), U. Mo. at Kansas City, 1964-67; M.L.A., So. Meth. U., 1979; MDiv, St. Paul Sch. Theology, 1986. Policy writer Lynn Ins. Co., Kansas City, 1963-64; music librarian U. Mo. at Kansas City, 1966-68; benefit authorizer Social Security Adminstrn., Kansas City, Mo., 1969-75, tech. specialist, 1976-79, claims authorizer, 1980-83; pastor Mercer United Meth. Ch., 1986-88, Adrian (Mo.) United Meth. Ch., 1988—; piano tchr. Leta Wallace Piano Studio, Kansas City, 1963, 68; piano accompanist Barn Players, Overland Park, Kans., 1972-75, Off Broadway Dinner Playhouse, Inc., Kansas City, 1973. Co-chmn. Project Equality work area, 1971; work area chmn. on ecumenism Council on Ministries, 1969-70; sec. fair housing action com. Council on Religion and Race, Kansas City, 1968; chmn. adminstrv. bd. Kairos United Meth. Ch., 1982; active ward and precinct work Democratic Com. for County Progress, 1968. Mem. Baton Soc. Kansas City Symphony, Friends of Art Kansas City, Fellowship House Assn. Kansas City, Internat. Platform Assn., Kansas City Mus. Club (chmn. composition dept. 1967-68), Lions Club (treas.), Mu Phi Epsilon (v.p. Kansas City 1968, sec. 1971, pres. 1975-76), Pi Kappa Lambda. Mailing Address: Adrian United Meth Ch 802 N Houston Adrian MO 64720

HOYLE, CYNTHIA LYNN, urban planner, consultant; b. Norman, Okla., Mar. 25, 1957; d. Elmer Joe Hoyle and Carol Lavada (Hames) Winton; m. Sheldon Harley Katz, June 15, 1986; 1 child, Sarah Elizabeth. Student, Am. Inst. Fgn. Study, Cambridge, England, 1975, U. Tulsa, 1975-77; BA in Social Work, U. Okla., 1979, M in Regional and City Planning, 1981. Community organizer NOW, Oklahoma City, 1981-82; rsch. asst. Met. Libr. System, Oklahoma City, 1982-85; assoc. planner City of Oklahoma City, 1985, traffic planner, 1985-87; pres. Planning Cons., Stillwater, Okla., 1987—; environ. advisor Planning Commn., Stillwater, 1990. Precinct chmn. Payne County Dem. Party, Stillwater, 1987-89; del. Okla. Dem. Party, 1984. Mem. AAUW (div. officer 1985—, pub. rels. awards 1985, 86, seed grant 1984), Am. Planning Assn. (chpt. pres. 1989—, CPC grant 1989), Am. Inst. Cert. Planners (cert.), Inst. Transp. Engrs., Sierra Club. Unitarian.

HOYT, CHARLEE ILDORA, management executive; b. Bluefield, W.Va., May 21, 1936; d. Charles Ives Van Cleve and Kathryn Margarete (Harden) Perrow; m. Ronald Reiner Hoyt, 1959 (div. 1983); children: Dean Christopher, Jason Allen. BA in Edn., U. Fla., 1959, MEd, 1962, postgrad., 1963-64. Cert. spl. edn. tchr. Tchr. Amherst County Schs., Elon, Va., 1958; tchr. spl. edn. Marion County Schs., Ocala, Fla., 1959-61; counselor Univ.

Counseling Ctr., Gainesville, Fla., 1962-63, Sunland Tng. Ctr., Gainesville, 1963; mem. community faculty Minn. Met. State Coll., Mpls., 1972-83; mem. council City of Mpls., 1975-86; ptnr. Van Cleve Assocs., 1980-87; pres. Van Cleve, Doran & Bruno, Inc. 1987—; corp. officer BAM Leasing Co., Inc., 1987—; dir. human resources Pascua Yagu Tribe; mem. faculty Govt. Tng. Service, St. Paul, 1978-86, Ariz. Govt. Tng. Services; pres. Minn. Women in City Govt., St. Paul, 1978-79; mem. Met. Land Use Adv. Bd., St. Paul, 1978-83; bd. dirs. Transp. Adv. Bd., St. Paul, 1979-81; mem. conf. faculty League of Minn. Cities, St. Paul, 1979-82; bd. dirs. Met. Council Criminal Justice Adv. Bd., St. Paul, 1979-82; pres. Women in Mcpl. Govt., Nat. League of Cities, Washington, 1980-81, founder minority caucus coalition, 1982, dir., 1982-84; curriculum cons. Nat. Women's Edn. Fund, Washington, trainer, 1982—. Presenter numerous workshops; contbr. articles to profl. jours. Mem. Women Helping Women YWCA, 1987—; various offices with Republican Party, Minn., 1970-86 ; pres. Burroughs Elem. Sch. PTA, Mpls., 1973-74; panelist White House Conf., 1981; chmn. Senator Durenburger's Task Force on Women's Issues, Mpls., 1981-84; bd. dirs. Nat. Conf. Rep. Mayors and Council Mems., 1984-85; mem. Senator Durenburger's Intergovtl. Relations Adv. Com., Mpls., 1984-86; bd. dirs. Twin Cities Internat. Program, Mpls., 1983-86; participant Women's Dialogue US/USSR, Moscow, 1985; trustee Council Internat. Programs, Cleve., 1985—; bd. dirs. At the Foot of the Mountain Theater, Mpls., 1985-86, Tucson Ctrs. for Women and Children, 1988—; bd. dirs. GOP Feminists, Hamline U. Ctr. for Women in Govt.; mem. Nat. Women's Polit. Caucus, Hennepin County Women's Polit. Caucus; mem. Tucson Support for Success Team, 1986—, Tuscon YWCA Women Helping Women; bd. dirs. Tucson Ctrs. Women and Children. Mem. Am. Soc. Training and Devel., Minn. Women Elected Ofcls. (pres. 1983-85), Izaak Walton League, Tucson C. of C. Methodist. Club: Remington Investment (pres. 1968-70) (Mpls.). Avocations: lapidary, music, handwork, camping, science fiction. Home: 6932 E Second St Tucson AZ 85710

HOYT, KATHLEEN ELIZABETH, computer analyst; b. Battle Creek, Mich., Sept. 20, 1953; d. John Bill and Patricia Ann (Mack) Howerton; m. Robert Vern Huff, Sept. 30, 1972 (div. 1979); m. James Merlin Hoyt, Dec. 19, 1981; 1 child, Tara Ann. AS in Bus. Data Processing, State Tech. Inst., Memphis, 1981; BBA in Info. Systems summa cum laude, Nat. U., 1987. Computer operator Utrex, Memphis, 1978-79; programmer Coca-Cola Bottling Co., Memphis, 1979-81; computer asst. Dept. of Def.-Civil Svc., Edwards AFB, Calif., 1981-82; technician software documentation Gen. Exectric, Palmdale, Calif., 1982-83; computer specialist Fallbrook (Calif.) Ag-Lab., 1983-84; analyst computer systems Dept. of Navy-Civil Svc., Camp Pendleton, Calif., 1984-90; owner, prin. Computing Made Easy, Fallbrook, 1990—; tech. expert Marine Corps Tactical Systems Support Activity, Camp Pendelton, 1985-88, instr. data link simulation, 1987-88, project officer, 1986-88. With USAF, 1972-77. Faculty scholar Nat. U., 1986. Mem. Armed Forces Communications Electronics Assn., NAFE, Fallbrook Music Soc., Nat. Charity League, Nat. U. Student Alumni Assn. Democrat. Presbyterian. Office: Computing Made Easy 1369 Friends Way Fallbrook CA 92028

HOYT-HOCH, PEGGY JANE, human resources executive; b. St. Louis, Mar. 20, 1954; d. Harold Gavin and Evelyn (Holland) Hoyt; m. Howard Ian Hoch, May 21, 1981; children: Daniel Alexander, James Ian, David Michael, Patricia Anne-Lauren. BS in Polit. Sci., Ariz. State U., 1977; postgrad. in indsl. and labor rels., Cornell U., 1978-79. Flight attendant Am. Airlines, N.Y.C., 1977-78, instr., 1979-81; mgr. personnel devel. N.Y. Airlines, Inc., N.Y.C., 1981-83, dir. human resources, 1983-86; dir. human resources Ogden Allied Svcs., N.Y.C., 1986-88, v.p. benefits dept., 1988—. Vol. Home-Sch. Assn., Forest Hills, N.Y., 1988—. Ariz. State U. scholar, 1977. Mem. Am. Soc. for Pers. Adminstrn., Profit Sharing Coun. of Am. (legis. and legal com. profit sharing 1990—), Employers Coun. on Flexible Compensation. Democrat. Roman Catholic. Office: Ogden Allied Svcs 2 Pennsylvania Pla New York NY 10121

HRADEL, ELIZABETH HARD (ELIZABETH JACKSON HARD), artist; b. Saginaw, Mich., Mar. 27, 1908; d. Herbert Aaron and Kate Jackson (Jackson) Hard; m. Joseph R. Hradel, Jan. 1, 1936; children: Anna Marie, Michael Florian. BA, Mich. State U., East Lansing, 1933; student, U. Wis., 1929-30. Community coord. Chippewa Indian Group, 1963-65; freelance artist. Mem. AAUW, Srt Reach, Sierra. Democrat. Home: 6482 S Mission Mount Pleasant MI 48858

HRIC, PATRICIA ANN, insurance executive; b. Dover, N.J., Mar. 4, 1944; d. George Paul and Agnes Victoria (Gula) H. Student, Vale Sch. of Ins., Springfield, N.J., 1975. Asst. dir. ARC Sch. of Ins., Denville, 1975—; owner, ptnr. Castellini & Hric Ins. Cons. & Ednl. Svcs., Denville, 1978—. Mem. Nat. Assn. Ins. Women (pres. N.W. N.J. chpt. 1974-75, bd. dirs. 1983, chmn. edn. region I 1982-83, numerous coms.), Ins. Brokers Assn. N.J. (co-edn. dir.). Roman Catholic. Home: 18 Highland Trail Denville NJ 07834 Office: CHIS Ins Cons & Edn One Indian Rd Denville NJ 07834

HRISTAKIS, BARBARA, health insurance company professional; b. Athens, Greece, Aug. 23, 1951; came to U.S., 1970; d. Fotios and Anna Anagnostidou H. BA in Biology, Queens Coll., CUNY, 1976; med. asst. cert., N.Y. Sch. Med.-Dental Assts., 1977; M Mgmt. Auditing, New Sch. Social Rsch., 1989; postgrad., NYU, 1989—. Med. asst. Queens Profl. Group, 1976-77; claims analyst Blue Cross-Blue Shield N.Y., N.Y.C., 1978-83, coord. quality assurance, 1983-86, dept. head, 1986-87, unit mgr. customer svc., 1987-88, project leader, 1988-89; project mgmt./orgn.-system analyst Advanced Tech., N.Y.C., 1989—. Dir. youth ministry group St. Demetrius Greek Orthodox Ch., Quens, 1982-85; vol. presdl. elections Nassau County Dem. Com., Port Washington and Lake Success, N.Y., 1989. Mem. Am. Assn. for Info. and Image Mgmt. (profl.). Home: 1 Maple Dr Apt 3B Great Neck NY 11021

HSU, CHING-HSIN, conductor, bassist; b. Keelung, Taiwan, Republic of China, Oct. 7, 1956; came to U.S., 1981; d. Ying-Shyr and Yueh-Shur (Lin) H. BA, Nat. Tiawan Normal U., Taipei, Taiwan, 1980; MusM, Hartt Sch. of Music, 1984, artist diploma, 1985. Bassist Taipei Mcpl. Symphony Orch., 1979-80; piano instr. Kung-Jen Music Sch., Taipei, 1979-81; condr. Young People's Orch., Hartford, Conn., 1983-86; conductor Loomis Chaffee Sch., Windsor, Conn., 1985-86; asst. condr. Hartt Contemporary Players, Hartford, 1985-86; music dir. St. Cloud (Minn.) State U. Orch., 1986—, Heartland Symphony Orch., Little Falls, Minn., 1988—; music dir. Central Minn. Youth Orch., St. Cloud, 1989—; condr. in residence Peter Brith Festivals, Jacksonville, Oreg., 1990—; bassist St. Cloud Symphony Orch., 1987—. Named one of Outstanding Young Women of Am., 1988; Chamber Orch. Series grantee, Central Minn. Arts Coun., St. Cloud, 1989, Faculty Improvement grantee, St. Cloud State U., 1987, 88, 89. Mem. Am. Symphony Orch. League, Cond. Guild, Minn. Music Educator Assn., Am. String Tchrs. Assn., Pi Kappa Lambda. Office: St Cloud State U PA 238 720 4th Ave S Saint Cloud MN 56301-4498

HSU, LAURA HWEI NIEN LING, microbiologist, educator; b. Kwei-Yan, People's Republic of China, Aug. 22, 1939; came to U.S., 1961; d. Shao-Wen and Jeanette (Chiang) Ling; m. Thomas Tseng-Chuang Hsu, July 20, 1963; children: Lynne Ling, Mia Ming. BS with honors, Acadia U., Nova Scotia, Can., 1961; MS, Cornell U., 1964; PhD, U. Miami, 1974. Cert. microbiologist. Supr. lab. Evanston (Ill.) Hosp., 1963-66, instr. med. tech., 1964-66; instr. sci. St. Francis Sch. of Nursing, Evanston, 1966-68; lectr. med. tech. Northwestern U., Chgo., 1967-68; rsch. asst. prof. U. Miami, Coral Gables, Fla., 1974-79; instr. biology Rice U., Houston, 1980-84, dir. programs Continuing Studies, 1984—; vis. assoc. prof. Nat. Taiwan U., Taipei, 1978-79; mem. faculty senate/student com. U. Miami, 1977-78; coord. exptl. biology, Rice U., 1980-84; vis. fellow plant pathology, Cornell U., Ithaca, N.Y., 1982. Contbg. author: Molecular Evolution-Pre and Biological, 1972, Molecular Evolution and Protobiology, 1984, International Review of Cytology, 1987. Judge essay contest, The Houston Post and Friends of Houston Pub. Libr., 1988; chmn. community cultural affairs, Chinese Community Cultural Ctr., Houston, 1989;invited participant Asian Community, Mayor's Citizen's Assistance Group, Houston, 1989; active scholarship com. Chinese Profl. Club, Houston, 1988. Named Clara Marchall Scholar, Acadia U., 1961; recipient grant Rice U., 1981. Mem. Am. Soc. Clin. Pathologists, Internat. Soc. Study of the Origin of Life, Chinese Acupuncture Sci. Rsch. Found., Am. Soc. Microbiologists, Assn. Women in Sci., Sigma Xi, Epsilon Tau Lambda. Office: Office Continuing Studies Rice Univ PO Box 1892 Houston TX 77251

HU, SCARLETT HSICHIA, information systems administrator; b. Chia-I, Republic of China, Dec. 28, 1957; came to U.S., 1979; d. Frank Y.C. and Ging-Sheng (Cheng) H. BBA with honor, Nat. Taiwan U., 1979; MBA, UCLA, 1981; MS in Computer Sci., U. So. Calif., 1988. Lic. real estate salesman, Calif. Applications cons. Sci. Time Sharing Corp. Inc., L.A., 1980-83, account mgr., 1983-84; sr. system analyst Home Savs. Am., L.A., 1984-86; supr. info. ctr., asst. v.p. Irwindale, Calif., 1988-89; dir. MIS, Houlihan, Lokey, Howard & Zukin, L.A., 1989—; founder Hu & Cheng Career Strategists, L.A., 1987—. Columnist China Ladies mag., Taipei, Republic of China, 1983—. Group leader Voice of Los Angeles Choir, 1980—. Mem. Chinese MBA Assn. (co-chairperson 1985—), Info. Ctr. Mgmt. Assn., So. Calif. Profl. Office Systems Users Group, Assn. Female Execs. Office: Houlihan Lokey Howard Zukin 1930 Century Park W Ste 200 Los Angeles CA 90067

HUANG, ALICE SHIH-HOU, microbiology, molecular genetics educator; b. Nanchang, Kiangsi, China; came to U.S., 1949; d. Quentin K.Y. and Grace Betty (Soong) H.; m. David Baltimore, 1968. Student Wellesley Coll., 1957-59; BA, Johns Hopkins U., 1961, MA in Microbiology, 1963, PhD, 1966. Postdoctoral fellow Salk Inst. for Biol. Studies, San Diego, 1967; postdoctoral fellow dept. biology MIT, Cambridge, 1968-69, research assoc., 1969-70; asst. prof. microbiology and molecular genetics Harvard U., Boston, 1971-73, asst. prof. faculty of arts and scis., 1971-73, assoc. prof. microbiology and molecular genetics, 1973-78, prof., 1979—; prof. microbiology in health sci. and tech. Harvard-MIT Program, 1979—; sci. assoc. Channing Lab. and dept. med. microbiology Boston City Hosp., 1971-73; dir. labs. of infectious diseases Children's Hosp., Boston, 1979-89; vis. asst. prof. Academia Sinica, Nat. Taiwan U., Taipei, 1966, lectr., 1970; vis. assoc. prof. virology Rockefeller U., N.Y.C., 1975-76; Wellcome vis. prof. U. Miss., 1980. Assoc. editor Revs. of Infectious Diseases, 1978—. Mem. editorial bd.: Intervirology, 1973—, Archive of Virology, 1975-78, Jour. Virology, 1976—, Microbial Pathogenesis, 1985. Contbr. numerous articles to profl. jours. Recipient Research Career Devel. award USPHS., 1972-77, Eli Lilly award, 1977; Alumni citation Nat. Cathedral Sch., Washington, 1978; John Hay Whitney Found. fellow, 1960-61, Burroughs Wellcome traveling fellow, 1979. Fellow Infectious Diseases Soc. Am.; mem. AAAS, Am. Soc. Microbiology (pres. 1988-89), Am. Soc. Biol. Chemists, Am. Soc. Virology, Am. Acad. Microbiology, Academia Sinica (Taiwan), Sigma Xi. Office: Harvard U Med Sch Dept Microbiology & Molecular Genetics 25 Shattuck St Boston MA 02115

HUANG, THERESA C., librarian; b. Nanking, China; m. Theodore S. Huang, Dec. 25, 1959. B.A., Nat. Taiwan U., 1955; M.S. in L.S., Syracuse U., 1958. Cataloger, Harvard U., Cambridge, Mass., 1958-60; with Bklyn. Pub. Library, 1960-78, regional librarian, 1978—. Joint compiler bibliography: Asia: A Guide to Books for Children, 1966; Nuclear Awareness, 1983; The U.S.A. through Children's Books, 1986, 88. Mem. ALA, Assn. Library Service to Children, Pub. Library Assn., Chinese Am. Librarians Assn., Asia Pacific Am. Librarians Assn. Office: Bklyn Pub Libr 1743 86th St Brooklyn NY 11214

HUBBARD, ELIZABETH LOUISE, lawyer; b. Springfield, Ill., Mar. 10, 1949; d. Glenn Wellington and Elizabeth (Frederick) H.; m. A. Jeffrey Seidman, Oct. 27, 1974 (div. May 1982). Student Millikin U., 1967-69; B.A., U. Ky., 1971; J.D. with honors, Ill. Inst. Tech.-Chgo. Kent Coll. Law, 1974. Bar: Ill. 1974, U.S. Dist. Ct. (no. dist.) Ill. 1974, U.S. Ct. Appeals (7th cir.) 1976, U.S. Supreme Ct. 1984. Atty. Wyatt Co., Chgo., 1974-75, Gertz & Giampietro, Chgo., 1975-76, Baum, Sigman, Gold, Chgo., 1976-81, Elizabeth Hubbard, Ltd., Chgo., 1981—; legal counsel NOW, Chgo., 1978—, sec., 1977. Editor Chgo. Kent Law Rev., 1970. Bd. dirs., mem. The Remains Theatre, 1985—. Mem. Chgo. Bar Assn. (fed. civil procedure com.), Ill. State Bar Assn. Democrat. Home: 441 E Erie St Chicago IL 60611 Office: 55 E Monroe Chicago IL 60603

HUBBARD, JULIA FAYE, accountant; b. Lebanon, Tenn., Apr. 27, 1948; d. Joe Pate Jr. and Rachel (Trice) H.; m. Teddy Clifton Wallin, Sept. 4, 1971 (div. June 1981). BSBA, Tenn. Technol. U., 1970; postgrad. in Acctg., U. Tenn., 1974-77. Sec. Sch. Nursing Vanderbilt U., Nashville, 1970-71; bookkeeper Ingram Corp., Nashville, 1971-72; acct., bookkeeper White & Ensor CPA's, Birmingham, Ala., 1972-74, Internat. Div. Joe M. Rodgers Constrn. Co., Nashville, 1974-79; supr. Ryan, Connelly, Primm & Outhier CPA's, Nashville, 1979-83; prin. Taylor & Assocs. CPA's, Nashville, 1983-86; owner, mgr. Julia F. Hubbard, Acctg. & Cons., Nashville, 1986—; asst. to developer, project coord. R.B. Investments Co., Nashville, 1985; owner, designer Juliana Fashion Accessories, Nashville, 1986—. Mem.-at.-large Hendersonville (Tenn.) Arts Coun., 1985—; bd. dirs., cons. Tenn. Assn. Dance, treas. Fellow Nat. Assn. Accts. (officer, bd. dirs. 1981-85). Republican. Methodist. Office: 25 Music Sq E Nashville TN 37203

HUBBARD, MARGARET ANNA, medical sonographer; b. Erie, Pa., May 4, 1947; d. John and Lucy (Love) Hamilton; m. William John Hubbard, June 12, 1965 (div. 1978); children: William John II, Michelle Renee. Grad., Genesee Hosp. Sch., Rochester, N.Y., 1980. Sonographer Strong Meml. Hosp., Rochester, 1980; radiologic tech. and sonographer Wilson Health Ctr., Rochester, 1981, IDE Radiology, Rochester, 1982-84; sonographer Copland, Hyman and Shackman, Balt., 1984-85, George Washington U., Washington, 1985-87, Washington Ultrasound, 1987-89, South Bay Radiology, San Diego, 1989; prin. Ultrasound Assocs., San Diego, 1989—. Vol. with abused children, San Diego, 1989—. Mem. Am. Registry Radiologic Techs., Soc. Diagnostic Med. Sonographers. Roman Catholic. Home and Office: 11219 Provencal Pl San Diego CA 92128

HUBBARD, SANDRA BEAMER, sales manager; b. Cin., Mar. 9, 1962; d. Allyn Richard and Joyce Ann (Sponsel) Beamer; m. Richard Randall Hubbard, Dec. 30, 1983. PhB, Miami U., Oxford, Ohio, 1983; student, Harvard U., 1986-88. Promotions asst. Newbury Coll., Boston, 1984; adminstrv. asst. Law Offices Ed Hintliam, Boston, 1984-85; mgr. nat. sales Rainbowworld Cards, Boston, 1985-89; mgr. territory sales Krikorian Miller Assoc., Bedford, Mass., 1989—; cons. in field. Mem. U.S. Jr. C. of C. (bd. dirs. 1989—, State of Mass. Speak-Up winner 1990), Kappa Delta. Congregationalist. Home and Office: 32 Eddy St Mansfield MA 02048

HUBBARD, SANDRA SUE, educational administrator; b. Indpls., Dec. 10, 1959; d. Stanley Burton and Maurine A. (Simpson) Beach; m. Earl B. Hubbard, Oct. 4, 1957; 1 child, Lauren Ashley. BS, Ind. U., 1982. Rsch. asst. Ind. U., Indpls., 1981-82; sales intern IBM, Indpls., 1981-82; gov.'s fellow State of Ind., Indpls., 1982-83, svcs. procurement specialist, 1983-85, svcs. procurement supr., 1985-87, dep. dir. purchasing, 1987-89; dir. purchasing Indpls. Pub. Schs., 1989—. Mem. Young Leaders for Mutz, Indpls., 1988. Mem. Ind. Assn. Sch. Bus. Ofcls., Accolade, Ind. U. Woman's Club (nominating chmn. 1986), Beta Gamma Sigma, Sigma Pi Alpha. Republican. Quaker. Home: 9425 Goodway Ct Indianapolis IN 46256 Office: Indpls Pub Schs 120 E Walnut St Rm 117 Indianapolis IN 46204

HUBBARD, VERONICA LYNNE, computer software consulting company executive; b. Adrian, Mich., Jan. 12, 1960; d. Joseph Harris and Aileen (Brown) H. Student, U. Mich., 1978-79, Kalamazoo Coll., 1979-82. Retail mgr. Mac Dee Assocs., Silver Spring, Md., 1982-84; office mgr. Suite 550 Corp., Bethesda, Md., 1984-88; assoc. CACI Inc., Comml., Washington, 1988-90; v.p. Task Force, Inc., N.Y.C., 1990—. Mem. NAFE, N.Y.C. C. of C., NOW, Mensa, Kalamazoo Coll. Alumni Assn. (steering com.), Arlington Players. Office: Task Force Inc 11 Maiden Ln Ste 10E New York NY 10038

HUBER, DEANNA LYNN, sales professional; b. Hammond, Ind., Oct. 20, 1959; d. John Virgil and Joan Marie (Eads) H. BS in Indsl. Mgmt., Purdue U., 1982. Systems engr. Electronic Data Systems, Chgo., 1982-83; with tech. mktg. div. Gen. Electric Co., Indpls., 1983-85; ultrasound sales rep. Cin., 1985-87; nuclear medicine rep. Indpls., 1987-88; ultrasound rep. Acuson Computed Sonography, Kansas City, Kansas, 1988—. Speaker Appalachian Soc. Radiol. Technologists, Prestonsburg, Ky., 1985, Ind. Radiol. Technologists, West Lafayette, 1986. Mem. Sigma Soc. (bd. dirs. 1986), Purdue Alumni Club, Alpha Omicron Pi. Republican. Roman Catholic.

HUBER, SISTER MARGARET ANN, college president; b. Rochester, Pa., July 27, 1949; d. Francis Xavier and Mary Ann (Socash) H. B.S. in Chemistry, Duquesne U., 1972; M.S.A., U. Notre Dame, 1975; Ph.D., U. Mich., 1979. Joined Sisters of Divine Providence of Pittsburgh, Pa.; jr. high tchr. St. Martin Sch., Pitts., 1971-72; asst. to acad. dean LaRoche Coll., Pitts., 1972-75; research assoc. U. Mich., Ann Arbor, 1978; dir. planning LaRoche Coll., 1978-80, exec. v.p., 1980-81, pres., 1981—. Mem. Am. Assn. for Higher Edn. Democrat. Roman Catholic. Office: LaRoche Coll 9000 Babcock Blvd Pittsburgh PA 15237-5828*

HUBER, MARSHA ANNE, teacher; b. Jonesboro, Ark., Mar. 1, 1953; d. Arvil C. and Janna Estelle (Bishop) Kaffka; m. Bryan Leslie Huber, Oct. 3, 1975; children: Laura Day, Lisa Kaye. BS in Edn., Ark. State U., 1973, MS in Edn., 1975, EdS, 1990. Cert. tchr., Ark. Tchr. Nettleton Schs., Jonesboro, 1973-76, Weiner (Ark.) Sch., 1976-78, Jonesboro Schs., 1986—. Leader Crowley's Ridge coun. Girl Scouts U.S.A., 1984-86. Mem. Assn. Supervision and Curriculum Devel., Internat. Reading Assn., NEA, Ark. Edn. Assn., DAR (jr. membership chmn. 1986-88), Jonesboro Classroom Tchrs. Assn. (pres.), Alpha Delta Kappa, Kappa Delta Pi, Phi Delta Kappa. Mem. Christian Ch. (Disciples of Christ). Home: 2302 Rusher Jonesboro LA 72401

HUBER, MIRIAM ELAINE, communications consultant, publishing company executive; b. Chillicothe, Ohio, Jan. 17, 1940; d. William Jacob and Judith Angela (Schumaker) Huber; B.S. in Physics, Heidelberg Coll., Tiffin, Ohio, 1962; M.B.A., Capital U., 1980; m. Thomas Denney Alexander, Jan. 10, 1972. Tchr. physics Am. Acad. for Girls, Uskudar, Turkey, United Ch. Bd. for World Ministries, 1963-67; sci. editor Charles E. Merrill Pub. Co., Columbus, Ohio, 1967-74, prodn. mgr., 1980-89; project mgmt. and tech. communications cons., La Grange, Ohio, 1989—; graphic arts, photo compositor Beaver Press, Columbus, 1975-77; communications specialist Ranco Controls, Columbus, 1977-79. Mem. Heidelberg Fellows. Mem. Columbus Soc. for Communicating Arts, Project Mgmt. Inst. (cert. 1987). Episcopalian. Avocations: aviation, choral music. Home and Office: 159 Loperwood Ln LaGrange OH 44050 Office: 936 Eastwind Dr Westerville OH 43081

HUBER, RITA NORMA, civic worker; b. Cin., July 16, 1931; d. Andrew Elwood and Mary Gertrude (Hille) Stewart; student Cin. Coll. Conservatory Music, 1949-50, Berlitz Sch., Cin., 1951-52; m. Justin G. Huber, July 17, 1954; children: Monica Ann, Sarah Marie, Rachel Miriam. Tchr. Russian lang. for officers' wives Ft. Sill, Okla., 1955-56; bd. dirs. United Community Svcs., Cedar Rapids, Iowa, 1969; founder, chairperson Linn County Consumers League, 1969-70; founder, pub. rels. dir. Cedar Rapids Rape Crisis Svcs., 1974—; owner/operator Hurber Janitorial Svcs., 1982-84; chairperson Linn County Dem. Womens Club, 1966-67, Linn County Com., Eugene McCarthy for Pres., 1967-68; campaign mgr. Delores Cortez for Iowa Legislature, 1968, Jan V. Johnson for Iowa Legislature, 1970, Stanley Ginsberg for county supr. Linn County, 1974, E.L. Colton for Cedar Rapids pub. safety commr., 1977; chairperson Linn County Dem. Cen. Com., 1976-77, 88—; state coord. Jerry Brown for Pres., 1976; chairperson Pat Kane for Linn County Recorder, 1982; chmn. Linn County Bd. Health, 1982-85; instr. parliamentary procedures Cedar Rapids Women's Community Leadership Inst., 1975-77; lectr. local colls. and svc. orgns.; tchr. conversational Russian, Pierce Elementary Sch., Cedar Rapids, 1976; instr. Russian, Community Edn. div. Kirkwood Community Coll.; mem. care rev. com. Pineview Care Ctr., Cedar Rapids, 1987—. Named to Iowa Dem. Party DVP Hall of Fame, 1986. Mem. Am. Inst. Parliamentarians. Roman Catholic (extraordinary minister of Eucharist). Composer: She is Risen, 1973. Home: 2050 Glass Rd NE Cedar Rapids IA 52402

HUBER, VANDRA LEE, businesss educator, consultant; b. Salt Lake City, July 18, 1949; d. Fred L. and Twila Blanche (Jacobs) H.; m. Michael Krolewski, June, 1986. BS cum laude, U. Utah, 1971, MS in Econs., 1978; MBA, Ind. U., 1981, D Bus. Adminstrn. in Human Resources, 1982. Cert. bus. communicator. Reporter, editor Salt Lake City Tribune, 1971-77; dir. communications Utah Social Services, Salt Lake City, 1977-79; instr. Ind. U., Bloomington, 1979-82; asst. prof. Cornell U., Ithaca, N.Y., 1982-85; asst. prof. human resources and mgmt. U. Utah, Salt Lake City, 1985-87; asst. prof. human resources and organizational behavior U. Wash., Seattle, 1987-89, assoc. prof., 1989—; cons. nonprofit orgns. Rochester, Salt Lake City, Seattle; mem. adv. bd. Cornell Inst. Social and Econ. Research, 1983-85. Author: Personnel and Human Resource Management, 1990; contbr. over 25 articles to profl. jours. Treas. Community Crisis Ctr., Salt Lake City, 1978-79. Social Sci. Research Council grantee, 1982; Richard Irwin Dissertation grantee, 1982. Mem. Internat. Assn. Bus. Communicators (Intermountain Outstanding Communicator 1978), Acad. Mgmt. (Dorothy Harlow researcher 1986, ascendent scholar 1987, Fritz Roethlisberger, 1988), Am. Psychol. Assn., Am. Inst. Decision Scis. Democrat. Episcopalian. Home: 18831 NE 140th Pl Woodinville WA 98072 Office: U Wash Sch Bus DJ-10 Seattle WA 98112

HUBERT, GABRIELLE MARY, history instructor; b. Tomah, Wis., Mar. 7, 1922; d. Herman August and Martha Ann (Mistele) H. BA, Mount Mary Coll., 1951; MA, Cath. U., 1957, PhD, 1964. Elem. tchr. St. John's Sch., South Milwaukee, Wis., 1942-50; elem. sch. prin. St. Francis Sch., Ottawa, Ill., 1951-57, St. John Sch., Little Chute, Wis., 1958-59; instr. Dominican Coll., Racine, Wis., 1964-70; assoc. prof. Morehouse Coll., Atlanta, 1970-75; spl. edn. tchr. Ga. Earned Release Ctr., Milledgeville, 1975-77; prof. history Columbia (Tenn.) State Community Coll., 1978—; tchr. Laubach Adult Literacy Program, Columbia, Tenn., 1979—. Producer (audio visual programs); James K. Polk, 1979, The TVA, The Cherokees, 1982, Sites of the Civil War, 1984. Chairperson Voter Registration Campaign, Columbia, 1984; workshop leader Columbia State Women and politics Seminar, Columbia, 1984; speaker Tenn. Speaker's Bur. on the Constn., 1987. Recipient Columbia State Disting. Faculty award 1989; named Woman of Yr. Bus. and Profl. Women, Columbia, 1984; Mellon Found. grantee Vanderbilt U., Nashville, 1986. Mem. AAUW (v.p. Columbia br., state chmn. com. on internat. affairs 1985), Racine Dominicans, Phi Alpha Theta. Roman Catholic. Office: Columbia State Community Coll Hampshire Pike Columbia TN 38401

HUBERT, HELEN BETTY, epidemiologist; b. N.Y.C., Jan. 22, 1950; d. Leo and Ruth (Rosenbaum) H.; m. Carlos Barbaro Arostegui, Sept. 11, 1976 (div. May 1987). BA magna cum laude, Barnard Coll., 1970; MPH, Yale U., 1973, M of Philosophy, 1976, PhD, 1978. Rsch. assoc. Yale U., New Haven, Conn., 1977-78; rsch. epidemiologist Nat. Heart, Lung and Blood Inst., Bethesda, Md., 1978-84; rsch. dir. Gen. Health, Inc., Washington, 1984-87; sr. rsch. assoc. Stanford (Calif.) U., 1988 --. Peer review Am. Jour. Epidemiology, Am. Jour. Pub. Health, Chest, Jour. Am. Med. Assn., Archives Internal Medicine; contbr. articles to profl. jours. and chpts. to books. Vol. Children's Hosp., Stanford, 1988 --. Mem. Am. Heart Assn., Am. Coll. Epidemiology, Soc. Epidemiologic Rsch., Coun. Epidemiology, Arthritis Health Profls. Assn., Sigma Xi (Grant-in-Aid for Rsch. 1978), Phi Beta Kappa. Office: Stanford U Med Ctr 750 Welch Rd Stanford CA 94304

HUBERT-GRENIER, STEPHANIE RAE, executive recruiter, mortgage consultant; b. Tomah, Wis., Apr. 3, 1959; d. Robert Louis and Eleanor Blakeley (Carey Murray) Hubert. BS, U. Wis., LaCrosse, 1985. Intervention specialist Assn. for Retarded Citizens, Vista, Calif., 1985-86; jr. loan processor/shipper Metmor Fin., Inc., San Diego and L.A., 1986-88; asst. processor Century 21 Mortgage Corp., Burlington, Mass., 1988-89; mortgage cons. First Mass. Mortgage, Westford, 1989—; recruiter sales mgmt. A.L. Williams, North Reading, Mass., 1990—. Office: A L Williams 348 Park St W Suite 106 North Reading MA 01864

HUBLITZ, SUE, sales professional; b. N.Y.C., June 6, 1940; d. Lincoln and Katherine (Daly) H. BA in Speech Therapy, Hofstra Coll., 1962; M, Columbia U., 1968. Head occupational therapy dept. St. Agnes Hosp., White Plains, N.Y., 1971-76; program coordinator devel. disabilities North Shore U. Hosp., Manhasset, N.Y., 1976-78; sales rep. Becton-Dickinson, Rutherford, N.J., 1978-81, Argus Surg. Co., Inc., Mt. Vernon, N.Y., 1981—. Mem. Am. Assn. Occupational Therapist (cert.). Home: 765 N Broadway

18B Hastings-on-Hudson NY 10706 Office: Argus Surg Co Inc 6 North St Mount Vernon NY 10550

HUCKABEE, CAROL BROOKS, psychologist; b. Marion, Ohio, Aug. 2, 1945; d. William Richard and Marjorie (Beal) Brooks; m. Roy M. Huckabee, Dec. 22, 1967; 1 child, Lear Elizabeth. BA, U. Colo., 1967; MS, NYU, 1982, PhD, 1985. Lic. psychologist, N.Y., Conn. Psychology intern Downstate Med. Ctr., Bklyn., 1982-84; staff psychologist Blythedale Children's Hosp., Valhalla, N.Y., 1984-86; dir. psychol. svcs. Arms Acres Hosp., Carmel, N.Y., 1986-88, cons., 1988-89; cons. psychologist Putnam Community Hosp., Carmel, 1988—; pvt. practice Brewster, N.Y., 1987—; sch. psychologist N.Y.C. Bd. Edn., 1984—. NIMH clin. tng. grantee, 1980-81, 81-82. Mem. Am. Psychol. Assn., N.Y. State Psychol. Assn., Conn. State Psychol. Assn. Democrat. Office: 155 Main St Brewster NY 10509

HUCKNALL, NANETTE VEDA, finance company executive; b. Elyria, Ohio, Jan. 13, 1933; d. Bert H. and Henrietta C. (Goldsmith) H. BFA, Cooper Union, NY, 1952-56, 1975. Art dir. Lampert Agy., N.Y.C., 1959-61, Pritchard Wood Inc., N.Y.C., 1961-62, Clairol Inc., N.Y.C., 1964-68, United Jewish Appeal Fedn., N.Y.C.; dir. creative services Devel. Corp. Israel, N.Y.C., 1985-; ptnr. Vidax Internat., N.Y., 1988. Design in Graphis Annual, 1972-73. Co-founder, bd. dirs. Ctr. for Peace Through Culture Internat., N.Y., 1978—. Mem. NAFE. Home: 336 C Adolphus Ave Cliffside Park NJ 07010 Office: Devel Corp Israel 730 Broadway New York NY 10003

HUDAK, KRISTEN M., bank executive. BA, U. Fla.; MBA, U. Miami, Fla. Fin. analyst Southeast Banking Corp., Miami, 1975-76, mgr. corp. acctg., 1976-78, asst. contr., 1978-80, v.p., 1980-83, sr. v.p. corp. fin. div., 1983-84, sr. v.p., contr., 1984—. Office: Southeast Banking Corp 1 SE Financial Ctr Miami FL 33131*

HUDDLESTON, DONNA RUTH, engineer; b. Cookeville, Tenn., July 26, 1958; d. Donald Forrest and Norma Ruth (Bumbalough) H. BS in Indsl. Engring., U. Tenn., 1983, postgrad., 1990. Gen. engr. U.S. Dept. Energy, Oak Ridge, Tenn., 1983—; mem. sponsor's com. WATTEC, Oak Ridge, 1988-89, Federally Employed Women, Inc., Oak Ridge, 1987—. Parish contact Episcopal Singles Fellowship, Knoxville, 1988-90. U. Tenn. scholar, 1976. Mem. Inst. Indsl. Engrs., Soc. Mfg. Engrs. (treas. 1989—), Soc. Women Engrs. Office: US Dept Energy PO Box 2001 Oak Ridge TN 37831-8557

HUDDLESTON, KATHY NASH, educational materials sales professional; b. Bozeman, Mont., Apr. 12, 1949; d. John Thomas and Katherine Fay (Metcalf) Nash; m. Gordon J. Huddleston, Aug. 7, 1971; children: Bridget Kaitrin, Ryan Sean. BS in Elem. Edn., Mont. State U., 1971, postgrad., 1989. Cert. tchr., reading specialist, Wyo. Tchr. Jefferson Elem. Sch., Green River, Wyo., 1971-74, Washington Elem. Sch., Green River, 1975-76; dir. Treasure Island Pre-sch., Butte, Mont., 1978-89; dist. sales mgr. World Book-Childcraft, Butte, 1988—; bd. dirs. Community Curriculum Adv. Com., Butte, 1982-85, Home Econs. Adv. Com., Butte, 1982-85; pub. rels. dir. Early Childhood Task Force, Butte, 1985-89. Troop leader Butte area Girl Scouts U.S., 1980-83; bd. dirs. Hillcrest PTA, Butte, 1981-85. Mem. AAUW, Mont. State U. Alumni Assn., Nat. Assn. Edn. Young Children, Hawthorne Community Ctr. Assn. (bd. dirs., pres. 1986-89), Toastmasters (ednl. v.p. 1988-89), Alpha Omicron Pi Alumni (pres. 1985-88). Democrat. Roman Catholic. Home and Office: World Book Childcraft 3430 N Hillcrest St Butte MT 59701

HUDDLESTON, LAUREN B., futurist researcher, oil company executive, human resource developer; b. Nashville, Nov. 19, 1933; d. John and Chattie (Rich) H.; m. Gilbert Taylor, Aug. 25, 1950 (div. July 1972); children: Jeffrey, Charles, Marianne; m. Robert W. Fisher, Apr. 5, 1976. BA, Stephens Coll., 1980; MSW, U. Denver, 1984, PhD, 1988. Clinician, psychotherapy tchr. Halcyon, Inc., Lafayette, Ind., 1972-76; biofeedback specialist New Orleans Ctr. for Psychotherapy, 1976-78; cons. organizational design and human resource devel., orgnl. design The Anchoring System, Denver, 1972—; adminstrv. dir., v.p. Bradden Exploration, Denver, 1981-86; pres., chief exec. officer Fisher Energy Group, Denver, 1986—; developer wellness and peer counseling program Srs. Resource Ctr. Jefferson County, Denver, 1982-84; bd. dirs. Sight Savers Internat. Co-organizer Citizens for Responsible Devel. of Bergen Park, Evergreen, Colo., 1983—; dean search com. Grad. Sch. Social Work, Denver U., 1982—; bd. dirs. Sight Savers Internat., Washington; cons. to bd. Urban Peak for Homeless Youth, Denver. Mem. Nat. Assn. Social Workers, World Future Soc., Internat. Transactional Analysis Assn. (clin. cert.), Ind. Petroleum Assn. Mountain States, Am. Mgmt. Assn. Office: Fisher Energy Group 1020 15th St Ste 4-l Denver CO 80202

HUDDLESTON, MARILYN ANNE, international business financier; b. Fayetteville, N.C., Jan. 28, 1953; d. Allen Paul and Julia Jewel (Hill) Miller; m. Roby Dwayne Huddleston, Sept. 13, 1946; children: Michelle, Christopher, Mathew, Danyel, Michael. MBA in Real Estate and Fin., Central Tex. U., 1974; diploma Acad. of Real Estate, 1977; postgrad. El Paso Community Coll. Owner, fin. cons. Cherokee Fin. Investments, Killeen, Tex., 1983-88; owner, broker All Am. Ins. Agy., Killeen, 1984-88; realtor, assoc. Exec. Fin., Austin, Tex., 1986-88; owner Geodesic Homes of Tex., Killeen, 1984-88; chmn. bd. dirs. Wall St. Internat., 1988—. Author: Miracle Baby at Bracken Ridge Hospital, 1979; Financial Consulting Made Easy, 1983. Pres. Mil. Council of Catholic Women, Stuttgart, Fed. Republic Germany, 1980, Non-Commnd. Officers Wives, Stuttgart, 1980-82, Ciudad del Niño Orphanage Assn., Killeen, 1979—; instr. Christian Religion, Killeen, 1976-88. Recipient Silver Poet award World of poetry Poets, 1989. Mem. Nat. Assn. Female Execs., Internat. Assn. Bus. and Fin. Cons. (hon.), Fort Hood Bd. Realtors, Nat. Assn. Realtors, Tex. Assn. Realtors Soc. Female Execs. (v.p. 1984-86), Internat. Soc. Financiers (cert.). Republican. Roman Catholic. Avocations: singing; writing; tennis; golf; macrame. Home: PO Box 493 Salado TX 76571

HUDDLESTON, VIRGINIA BYRN, critical care nurse consultant, educator; b. Murfreesboro, Tenn., Dec. 7, 1959; d. Robert Alvis Jr. and Virginia Byrn (Sanders) H. BS in Nursing, Baylor U., Dallas, 1983; MS in Nursing, Vanderbilt U., 1988. RN, Tex., Tenn. Staff nurse Parkland Meml. Hosp., Dallas, 1983-85, asst. head nurse, 1985-86; cons., lectr. Barbara C. Mims Assocs., Lewisville, Tex., 1989—; mem. adj. faculty, cons., clin. preceptor Vanderbilt U., Nashville, 1988—. Author: (monograph) Multisystem Organ Failure: A Pathophysiologic Approach, 1990; contbr. chpts. to books. Vol. leader Young Life, Dallas and Lubbock, Tex., 1979-82. Harold Stirling Vanderbilt scholar, 1986-87. Mem. Am. Assn. Critical Care Nurses (cert.), Sigma Theta Tau.

HUDGENS, ALLETTA JERVEY, psychologist, social worker, educator; b. Greenville, S.C., Apr. 13, 1930; d. James Wilkinson and Alletta (Wood) Jervey; m. Richard Watts Hudgens, June 21, 1952 (div. Mar. 1972); children: Peter, Mary, Helen; m. Roy Victor Dorn, May 14, 1988. BA, Mary Baldwin Coll., 1951; MSW, Washington U., St. Louis; 1956; PhD, U. Minn., St. Paul, 1982. Lic. cons. psychologist, Minn. Elem. tchr. Elkton (Md.) Schs., 1951-52, Clayton (Mo.) Schs., 1952-54; social worker U. Va. Hosp., Charlottesville, 1956-58, U. N.C. Hosp., Chapel Hill, 1959-61, U. Minn. Hosp., Mpls., 1973-76; rsch. assoc. CEMREL, St. Louis, 1969-71; family therapist U. Minn., Mpls., 1977-80, Abbott-Northwestern Hosp., Mpls., 1982-84; pvt. practice St. Paul, 1984—; asst. prof. psychology St. Mary's Coll., Mpls., 1987—; workshop leader on women's and family issues various schs. and orgns., Mpls., St. Paul, 1976—. Contbr. articles to profl. jours., chpt. to book. Mem. Am. Psychol. Assn., Am. Assn. Marriage and Family Therapists, Minn. Psychol. Assn., Minn. Assn. Women Psychologists, Minn. Coun. Family Rels. Home: 2800 Lakeside Ct Saint Paul MN 55117 Office: 2233 N Hamline Ste 550 Roseville MN 55113

HUDGINS, CATHERINE HARDING, business executive; b. Raleigh, N.C., June 25, 1913; d. William Thomas and Mary Alice (Timberlake) Harding; m. Robert Scott Hudgins IV, Aug. 20, 1938; children: Catherine Harding, Deborah Ghiselin, Robert Scott V. BS, N.C. State U., 1929-33; grad. tchr. N.C. Sch. for Deaf, 1933-34. Tchr. N.C. Sch. for Deaf, Morganton, 1934-36, N.J. Sch. for Deaf, Trenton, 1937-39; sec. Dr. A.S. Oliver, Raleigh, 1937, Robert S. Hudgins Co., Charlotte, N.C., 1949—, v.p., treas., 1960—, also bd. dirs. Mem. Jr. Svc. League, Easton, Pa., 1939; project chmn. ladies aux. Profl. Engrs. N.C., 1954-55, pres., 1956-57; pres. Christian High Sch. PTA, 1963; program chmn. Charlotte Opera Assn., 1959-61, sec., 1961-63; sec. bd. Hezekiah Alexander House Restoration, 1949-52, Hezekiah Alexander House Aux., 1975—, treas., 1983-84, v.p., 1984-85, pres., 1985-89; sec. Hezekiah Alexander Found., 1986—; past chmn. home missions, annuities and relief Women of Presbyn. Ch., past pres. Sunday Sch. class. Mem. N.C. Hist. Assn., English Speaking Union, Internat. Platform Assn., Mint Mus. Drama Guild (pres. 1967-69), Internat. Biog. Ctr. Eng. (dep. dir. gen.), Daus. Am. Colonists (state chmn. nat. def. 1973-74, corr. sec. Virginia Dare chpt. 1978-79, 84-85, state insignia chmn. 1979-80), DAR (mem. nat. chmn.'s assn., rec. sec. nat. officers club 1990—, chpt. regent 1957-59, chpt. chaplain 1955-57 N.C. program chmn. 1961-63, state chmn. nat. def. 1973-76, state rec. sec. 1977-79, state regent 1979-82, hon. chmn. N.C. Geneal. Register 1982, nat. vice chmn. S.E. region Am. Indians 1989—, rec. sec. Nat. Officers Club 1990—), Children Am. Revolution (N.C. sr. pres. 1963-66, sr. nat. corr. sec., 1966-68, sr. nat. 1st v.p. 1968-70, sr. nat. pres. 1970-72, hon. sr. nat. pres. life 1972—, 2d v.p. Nat. Officers Club, 1st v.p. 1977-79, pres. 1979-81), Huguenot Soc. N.C., Carmel Country Club (Charlotte), Viewpoint 24 Club, (v.p. 1986, pres. 1987). Home: 1514 Wendover Rd Charlotte NC 28211 Office: Robert S Hudgins Co PO Box 17217 Charlotte NC 28211

HUDGINS, PATRICIA MONTAGUE, biology educator; b. Buckhannon, W.Va., Jan. 31, 1938; d. Richard Wells and Clella (Barger) Montague; m. Guy Hugh Bons, June 30, 1975; children: Leslie, Audrey, Monica. BS, W.Va. U., 1959, MS, 1960, PhD, 1966. Instr. pharmacology Med. Coll. Va., Richmond, 1966-68, asst. prof., 1968-72, assoc. prof., 1972-75; assoc. prof. Kirksville (Mo.) Coll. Osteo. Medicine, 1975-80, prof. physiology, 1980-89; prof. functional biology W.Va. Sch. Osteo. Medicine, Lewisburg, 1990—. Bd. dirs. Planned Parenthood N.E. Mo., 1976—, Am. Heart Assn. Mo. affiliate, 1983—, Mo. Dept. Health Cancer Control Program, 1986—; mem. rev. com. Mo. Dept. Health Arthritis Program, 1984—. Mem. Am. Soc. for Pharmacology and Exptl. Therapeutics, Kirksville Optimist Club. Office: WVa Sch Osteo Medicine 400 N Lee St Lewisburg WV 24901

HUDGINS-BONAFIELD, CHRISTINE ANN, editor; b. Chilocothe, Ohio, Dec. 1, 1954; d. Malcolm M. and Ruby Helen (Star) H.; m. Michael J. Bonafield, Apr. 8, 1981; 1 child, Kirsten Blair Bonafield. BS, Auburn U., 1977; postgrad., U. Ala., 1977-79. Reporter Huntsville (Ala.) Times, 1975; asst. press sec. Sen. John Sparkman, Washington, 1976; reporter Wash. Post, 1977, Minn. Star/Tribune, 1979-84, Nuclear Energy McGraw-Hill, Washington, 1984-85; writer internat. corr. McGraw-Hill, Geneva, 1985-86; data editor Communications Week, Washington, 1986—; Author: Auburn Alabama Jokes, 1975. Mem. LWV, AP, Minn. Edn. Assn., Sigma Delta Xi. Club: Nat. Press.

HUDSON, ARLENE, environmental activist; b. Oakland, Calif., Apr. 17, 1936; d. Clyde Edward and Helen Therese (Cerutti) McIrvin; m. James Joseph Coté, Mar. 28, 1958 (div. 1963); 1 child, Steven Michael. BA in Psychology, Calif. State U., Sacramento, 1976, postgrad., 1977-78. Campaign mgr. various state, fed. and local campaigns, Sacramento, 1967-72; exec. field dir. Dem. State Cen. Com., Sacramento, 1967-68; mem. staff Calif. Legis., Sacramento, 1969-72; founder, chmn., editor newsletter The Group for Alternatives to Spreading Poisons, Nevada City, Calif., 1983—; mem. Cascade Holistic Econ. Cons., Eugene, Oreg., 1984—. Founding mem. Toxics Coordinating Project, San Francisco, 1985—; mem. Com. for Sustainable Agriculture, 1986—, mem. mktg.-order subcom., 1986—; bd. dirs. NW Coalition for Alternatives to Pesticides, Eugene, 1987—; mem., chmn. tech. writing com. Nevada County Adv. Com. on Air Pollution, 1988—; mem. Nevada County Greens Alliance, 1988—, Hazardous Waste Transfer Facility Siting Com. for Nevada County, 1989—, North Columbia Schoolhouse Cultural Ctr., 1980—, Nevada County Hazardous Waste Task Force, 1987—, chair tech. sub-com., 1988-90; mem. Cen. Valley Hazardous Waste Minimization Com., 1990—, Rural Def. League; co-founder Calif. Coalition for Alternatives to Pesticides, Arcata and Eureka, 1983—, pres., chmn. bd. dirs., 1989—. Mem. Sierra Club (chmmn. toxic subcom. Sierra Nevada group 1985-88), Amnesty Internat., Better World Soc., Coun. for Livable World, Nat. Peace Inst. Found., People's Med. Soc., Earth First, Nat. Resources Def. Coun., Nevada County C. of C., Greenpeace, Planning and Conservation League, North Columbia Schoolhouse Cultural Ctr., South Yuba River Citizen's League, Siskiyou Mountains Resource Coun. (life). Mem. Universal Life Ch. Home and Office: 10984 Ridge Rd Nevada City CA 95959

HUDSON, BETTY ELIZABETH HAMILTON, elementary educator; b. Bryn Mawr, Pa., Nov. 22, 1945; d. Alexander Moag and Elsie Evelyn (Hamilton) Lyon; m. George Naylor, June 11, 1966 (dec. Jan. 1988); children: Heather, George Naylor; foster children: Mark Rodalunas, Chad Rodalunas. BA, Davis and Elkins Coll., 1967. Cert. gifted and elem. edn. tchr. Mgr. Base Nursery Iraklion Air Sta., Crete, Greece, 1967-69; tchr. Yorktown (Va.) Sch. Dist., 1969-72; tchr., coord. gifted program Smyrna (Del.) Sch. Dist., 1977-87; tchr. gifted children Christina (Del.) Sch. Dist., 1987—; state dir. Odyssey of the Mind, Del., 1984-87; advisor to class of 1987 Smyrna High Sch., 1983-87; v.p.-del. Aerospace Edn. Found., 1989—. Chairperson Old Dover (Del.) Days Crafts Display, 1974; mem. task force statewide Commn. of Gifted Edn., Christina Task Force for Gifted Edn. Semifinalist, Del. Tch. in Space Program, Dover, 1985. Mem. AAUW (chairperson marionette show 1974, chairperson women's book sale 1976-77), NEA, Del. Edn. Assn., Del. Talented and Gifted Orgn. (pres.-elect), Christina Edn. Assn., Macintosh Users Del., Alpha Sigma Phi (Sweetheart 1966), Phi Delta Kappa, Phi Mu. Democrat. Presbyterian. Home: 101 Sonant Dr Newark DE 19713 Office: Brookside Elem Sch Marrows Rd Newark DE 19711

HUDSON, ELIZABETH, communications executive; b. Atlanta, July 16, 1949; d. Willis and Ruth (Thomas) Johnson; m. E. Boyd Matson, 1985; children: Erica Elizabeth, Taylor Douglas. ABJ, U. Ga., 1971; D in Comml. Sci., St. John's U., 1986. Copywriter Sta. WCBD-TV, Charleston, S.C., 1972-73; promotion dir. Sta. WCIV-TV, Charleston, 1973-76, Sta. WAVE-TV, Louisville, 1976-77, Sta. WSB-TV, Atlanta, 1977-78; v.p. corp. projects NBC, N.Y.C., 1979-80, v.p. corp. relations, 1980-82, v.p. corp. rels. and advt., 1982-84, v.p. corp. and media rels., 1984-89, sr. v.p. corp. communications, 1989—; bd. dirs. Kidsnet, Washington. Bd. dirs. N.Y. YWCA, 1985-86. Recipient John Drewry Outstanding Alumni award U. Ga., 1983, Outstanding Young Profl. award S.C. Bus. and Profl. Women, 1975. Mem. Internat. Radio and TV Soc. (pres. 1988-90), Am. Women in Radio and TV (bd. dirs. 1988—). Office: NBC Corp Communications 30 Rockefeller Pla New York NY 10112

HUDSON, ELIZABETH GAULT, retired educator; b. Garrett County, Md., Dec. 5, 1906; d. Clement Wilson and Peachie Eliza (Wolfe) H. BA, U. Richmond, 1927; MA, Coll. William and Mary, 1955. Cert. history, math., English, and Latin tchr., Va. Tchr. King and Queen County Schs., Va., 1927-28, Middlesex County Schs., Va., 1928-42, Chesterfield County Schs., Va., 1942-75; ret., 1975. Named to Hall of Fame, Chesterfield (Va.) Sr. High Sch. Coun., 1989. Mem. Am. Assn. Ret. Persons (instr. transp. dept. 1975-85, asst. coord. 1985—), Psi Chi, Delta Kappa Gamma, Alpha Delta Kappa. Baptist.

HUDSON, JACQUELINE, artist; b. Cambridge, Mass.; d. Eric and Gertrude (Dunton) H.; student Columbia U., Art Students League, Sch. of the Nat. Acad. One-woman shows: Burr Gallery, N.Y.C., Rockport (Mass.) Art Assn., Present Day Club, Princeton, N.J., Maine Art Gallery, Wiscasset, Moulson Union, Bowdoin Coll., 1979; group shows: NAD, Pa. Acad. Fine Arts, Library of Congress, Cin. Mus., Riverside Mus., Portland (Maine) Mus. Art, Dayton Art Inst., Bixler Mus., Colby Coll., Maine Art Gallery, Wiscasset, Bowdoin Coll., Farnsworth Mus., Rockland, Maine, Vallombreuse Gallery, Palm Beach, Fla., Galerie Salammbo, Paris, many others; represented permanent collection Library of Congress; pvt. collections. Recipient Pennell Purchase prize Library of Congress, 1951; Allen Kander Found. award Rockport Art Assn., 1957, Thelma Karr Graphic Prize, 1986; Edith Wengenroth Meml. prize, 1971, 75; Alice Standish Buell Meml. prize Nat. Assn. Women Artists, 1968, Helen Turner Graphic prize, 1974, Donna Miller Meml. prize, 1980; 3d graphic prize Butler Inst. Am. Art, 1983. Mem. Art Students League, Nat. Assn. Women Artists. Rockport Art Assn. (Bronze medal 1989), Lincoln County Cultural and Hist. Assn., Monhegan (Maine) Assos. (chmn. mus. com. 1963-67). Home: Monhegan Island ME 04852 Other: Federal St Wiscasset ME 04578

HUDSON, JOYCE ANN, psychologist; b. Lynchburg, Va., Aug. 26, 1938; d. Walter Patterson Sr. and Doris Addie (Rowles) Drinkard; m. Clarence W. Hudson, Apr. 20, 1958; children: Wilton, Robin, Debbie, Glenn. BS with high honors, Va. Commonwealth U., MS, PhD, 1978. Lic. psychologist, Va.; lic. clin. psychologist, Va.; cert. sex therapist, Va. Instr. in psychiatry Med. Coll. Va., Richmond, 1978—, clin. instr. in psychiatry, 1980—; pvt. practice psychology Richmond, 1980—; clin. instr. psychiatry Med. Coll. Va. Hosp., Richmond, 1978—. Fellow Internat. Coun. Sex Edn. and Parenthood; mem. Am. Assn. Sex Educators, Therapists and Counselors, Am. Psychol. Assn., Va. Psychol. Assn. Office: Assoc Therapists & Counselors 3600 W Broad St Ste 393 Richmond VA 23230

HUDSON, LINDA, health care executive; b. Tuscaloosa, Ala., Feb. 12, 1950; d. Elvin and Clara (Duke) Hudson; m. Charles Garrett Kimbrough, May 26, 1984. BS in Edn., U. Ala., 1971; MS in Psychology, U. So. Miss., 1984. Recreational therapist West Ala. Rehab. Ctr., Tuscaloosa, 1971-72; flight attendant Delta Air Lines, Miami and New Orleans, 1972-80; pvt. practice psychotherapist Hattiesburg (Miss.) and Atlanta, 1984—; program dir. Eating Disorders Adventist Health System/West, Atlanta, 1985-88, regional dir./cons., 1986-87, exec. dir. mental health svcs., 1988-89; nat. cons., 1986; owner Hudson Cons. Assocs., 1989—. Contbr. articles to profl. jours. Mem. Covington Jr. Svc. League, La., 1981-83; co-chmn. St. Tammany Rep. Polit. Action Com., 1980-81; coord. United Way of St. Tammany Parish, 1979-80. Mem. NAFE, Am. Assn. Marriage and Family Therapists, Women Healthcare Execs., Atlanta Women's Network. Democrat. Baptist. Office: 1090 S North Chase Pkwy Ste 222 Marietta GA 30067

HUDSON, MARGARET STOVER, educational administrator; b. Roanoke, Va., Sept. 27, 1947; d. Charles Marvin and Magdalene Virginia (Hobson) Stover; m. John David Hudson, Mar. 1, 1974; 1 stepchild, John David, Jr. B.B.A. cum laude, Roanoke Coll., 1971. Cashier, bookkeeper Roanoke Coll., Salem, Va., 1965-74, controller, 1974-79, dir. fin. and adminstrv. services, 1979-84, bus. mgr., 1984—; customer relations rep. Nat. Cash Register Co., Roanoke, 1974; trustee Diguid-Spencer Trust, Salem, 1976—, Harold Harris Unitrust, Salem, 1983—, James W. Sieg Unitrust, Salem, 1984—, Lois C. Fisher Unitrust, Salem, 1984—, June Cheelsman Unitrust, 1984—, Rural and Thelma Meadors Annuity Trust, Salem, 1985—, Rural E. Meadors Unitrust, 1986—, Jospeph A. Lucado Unitrust, 1989—. Bd. dirs. Va. Choral Soc., Salem, 1974. Mem. Nat. Assn. Coll. and Univ. Bus. Officers, Nat. Assn. Accts., Coll. and Univ. Personnel Assn., So. Assn. Coll. and Univ. Bus. Officers, Va. Dressage Assn., U.S. Dressage Fedn.. Methodist. Club: Roanoke Valley Figure Skating. Lodge: Rotary. Home: 6539 Laban Rd NW Roanoke VA 24019 Office: Roanoke Coll 6530 Fairway Estates Roanoke VA 24018

HUDSON, MOLLY ANN, advertising executive; b. Detroit, Apr. 27, 1941; d. Gabriel Nathanial and Beatrice Meriam (Joshel) Alexander; m. Leonard Atkins, June 18, 1961 (div. 1963); 1 child, Sidney Louis; m. Patrick Hudson, May 4, 1968 (widowed 1974); m. Arnold Leonard Rosen, June 20, 1982. Student, U. Colo., 1958-59, Wayne State U., 1959-61. Supr. creative dept. D'Arcy, MacManus, Benton & Bowles, Detroit, 1965-71, Campbell-Ewald Co., Detroit, 1971-83; sr. v.p. Campbell-Ewald Co., N.Y.C., 1987—, group sr. v.p., 1986-87; sr. v.p. Lintas N.Y., N.Y.C., 1987—. Food editor Met. Detroit, 1983-84; pub. (newsletter) The Food Enthusiast, 1983-85. Recipient Outstanding Achievement award Am. Women in Radio and TV, 1977; named Ad Woman of Yr., Women's Ad Club, 1980; named to Acad. Women Achievers, YWCA, 1986. Mem. Advt. Club N.Y., Advt. Women N.Y. Jewish. Office: Lintas NY One Dag Hammarskjold Pla New York NY 10017

HUDSON, MYRA LINDEN FRANK, consultant; b. Richmond, Va., Oct. 26, 1950; d. J. C. and Myra Teresa (Lanzarone) Frank; m. Timothy Franklin Long (div. Jan. 1981); m. Robert Andrew Hudson. BA, Erskine Coll., 1972; student, Inst. Fin. Edn., 1982-88. Chief activities therapist S.C. Dept. Corrections, Columbia, 1973-75, acting prin., 1975-77, coll. coord., 1977-78; owner, operator Carolina Coast Seafood, Aiken (S.C.) and Beaufort (S.C), 1978-80; from teller to savs. counselor Security Fed. Savs. & Loan, Aiken, 1981-83; customer svc. rep. Bankers 1st Savs. & Loans, Augusta, Ga., 1983-84, mgr. br. adminstrn., 1984-85; coord. automated teller machines, banking officer 1st Fed. Savs. Bank, Brunswick, Ga., 1985-88; ptnr., cons. electronic banking/computer programming RAH Systems, Brunswick, Ga., 1988—; ptnr. specific application software devel., sales, mktg. Details & More, Greenville, S.C., 1989—; lectr. S.C. Edn. Tchrs. Assn., Columbia, 1974, S.C. Assn. Social Workers, Columbia, 1975, Bus. & Profl. Women's Club, Columbia, 1978; small bus. owner, distbr. Nuskin product line, 1987—; ind. mktg. rep. Network 2000/U.S. Sprint; computer specialist Top Svcs., Inc., Duncan, S.C., 1990—, adminstrv./sales mgr. Custom Catering div. Appeared with Aiken Community Theatre, 1981. Mem. hospice com. Am. Cancer Soc., Augusta, 1981; lectr. St. John's United Meth. Ch., 1981-82. Mem. NAFE, Internat. Platform Assn., Brunswick-Golden Isles C. of C. Democrat. Home and Office: Details & More 407 Mauldin Rd Greenville SC 29605

HUDSON, SUNCERRAY ANN, university administrative assistant, research grants manager; b. San Francisco, Jan. 20, 1960; d. Charles Hudson and Nan Katherine (Coleman) Taylor. BA, U. San Francisco, 1982; student, Southeast Community Coll., San Francisco, 1988. Stock transfer clk. The Bank of Calif., San Francisco, 1983-85; prin. clk. U. Calif., San Francisco, 1985-87, adminstrv. asst. II, 1987-88, adminstrv. asst. III, 1988—; ind. dealer Nat. Safety Assocs., Inc., San Francisco, 1990—. Mem. NAFE, Gamma Phi Delta (youth adv. Rho chpt. 1990—). Office: U Calif 521 Parnasus Ave Campus Box 020 PO Box 0440 San Francisco CA 94143

HUDSON, TAJQUAH JAYE, healthcare facility administrator; b. Paris, Tex., Oct. 16, 1959; d. Bob and Ramona (Pollan) Dennison; m. Russell O. Hudson, May 24, 1981. BS, E. Cen. Okla. State U., 1981; MS in Health, Wichita State U., 1987. Program coord. Valley View Hosp., Ada, Okla.; mgr. regional mktg., communications EQUICOR-Equitable HCA Corp., Wichita, Kans.; mgr. product devel. Ptnrs. Nat. Health Plans, Kansas City, Kans.; speaker in field. Mem. NAFE, Am. Coll. Health Care Execs., Kans. Forum for Women Health Care Execs. (student assoc.). Home: 16023 W 83d Terr Lenexa KS 66219

HUDSON-YOUNG, JANE SMITHER, real estate investor; b. Altavista, Va., July 5, 1937; d. Victor Nelson and Elois Reynolds Smither; A.A.S. summa cum laude in Mgmt., Central Va. Community Coll., 1978; m. J. Lee Hudson, May 15, 1954; 1 child, Michael Edward; m. Gordon M. Young, July 9, 1989. Adminstrv. asst. Altavista (Va.) High Sch., 1954-55; with Lane Co., Inc., Altavista, 1956-89, exec. sec. to chmn. bd., 1976-81, exec. sec. to chmn. exec. com., 1981-84, spl. asst. for pub. rels. communications, 1984-86, acct. exec. nat. accts, 1986, asst. sales mgr. contract div., 1986-87, mktg. adminstr., 1988-89; realtor R. B. Carr & Co., Altavista, 1980-87, assoc. broker, 1985-87; mem. adv. bd. Am. Fed. Savs. and Loan, 1985—; pres. Hudson-Young Investments, 1989—. Mem. town coun. Town of Altavista, 1980-86; sec. Altavista Community Improvement Coun., 1981-82; mem. bd. deacons First Bapt. Ch., Altavista, 1980-83. Mem. Va. Assn. Realtors, Corr. Lynchburg (Va.) News., 1966-72. Home and Office: 2200 Beverly Heights Altavista VA 24517

HUESTIS, DOROTHY LOUISE, retired education educator; b. Milw., June 20, 1911; d. Ludwig Henry and Dorothy (Anressohn) Kottnauer; m. David LaDomus Huestis, Sept. 2, 1938; children: Barbara Louise Huestis Jones, Robert D. BA, Ind. U., 1932, MA, 1933. Cert. elem. and secondary tchr., Ohio. Tchr. history, geography, Latin, and biology Mays (Ind.) Consol. Sch., 1934-35; home visitation tchr. of physically handicapped Milw. Pub. Schs., 1935-36; pvt. tchr. kindergarten, Steubenville, Ohio, 1950-58; elem. tchr. Steubenville Schs., 1959-69; instr. edn. dept. Bethany (W.Va.) Coll., 1969-79; cons., editor material for profl. jours. lectr. on European, African, Asian and S.Am. travels, also on metrics, women's careers, flowers; dir. NW ordinance grant Ohio Humanites Coun., 1987; clk. of vestry, lic. lay leader St. Stephen's Episcopal Ch.; mem. exec. com. People's Law Sch., Steubenville, 1989; bd. dirs. ALIVE, shelter program for abused women,

Steubenville, 1980—; vol., profl. worker Girl Scouts U.S.A. RCIE fellow, India, 1973. Mem. AAUW (past pres.), Phi Beta Kappa, Eta Sigma Phi, Delta Kappa Gamma. Home: 121 Bryden Rd Steubenville OH 43952

HUETHER, BARBARA LEE, microbiologist; b. North Adams, Mass., July 18, 1954; d. Clyde William and Elizabeth (Woodbridge) H. BA, U. Tex., 1976; MPH, U. S.C., 1986. Med. lab. specialist Wilford Hall USAF Med. Ctr., San Antonio, 1978-81; dept. head microbiology McLeod Regional Med. Ctr., Florence, S.C., 1981-84; microbiologist 2 S.C. Bur. Labs., Columbia, 1986—; adj. faculty Midlands Tech. Coll., Columbia, 1986-88; grad. asst. U. S.C., 1986. Editor: Guide to Services at the Bureau of Laboratories, 1988. Sgt. USAF, 1976-81. Mem. Am. Soc. Clin. Pathologists (cert. med. technologist, microbiologist). Episcopalian. Home: 6905 Cleaton Rd A102 Columbia SC 29206 Office: SC Bur Labs PO Box 2202 Columbia SC 29202

HUF, CAROL ELINOR, tax service company executive; b. Milw., Apr. 21, 1940; d. William Weiss and Florence H. (Melcher) Weiss Lange; m. Walter Franklin Huf, Sept. 9, 1961; children: Mardell Leslie, Walter Albert III. Student Valparaiso U., 1958-60, Waukesha County Tech. Inst., 1968-69. Tax preparer H & R Block, Milw., 1967-84, instr. tax sch., 1969-83; job service interviewer State of Wis., Waukesha, 1984; pres. Personalized Tax Service, Inc., West Allis, Wis., 1984—, div. mgr. A.L. Williams, 1986. Vol. worker Girl Scouts US, Waukesha, 1970-80, Boy Scouts Am., Waukesha, 1975—; swimming referee Wis. Interscholastic Athletic Assn., Milw., 1972-84. Recipient awards Boy Scouts Am. Mem. Wis. Womens Pub. Links Golf Assn. (sr. v.p. 1986-88—, 2d v.p. 1988—, state tournament chairperson 1987, 90), Nat. Assn. Tax Practitioners (Wisc. bd. dirs. 1989-91), Wis. Assn. Accts., Met. Swimming Ofcls., Edgewood Golf Club (pres. Big Bend, Wis. 1984—). Lutheran. Home: 17825 Westward Dr New Berlin WI 53146 Office: Personalized Tax Service Inc 10533 W National Ave West Allis WI 53227

HUFF, GAYLE COMPTON, advertising agency executive; b. Washington, Nov. 28, 1956; d. Walter Dale and Jeanne (Parker) C.; m. Lanny Ross Huff, May 22, 1982. B in Gen. Studies, U. Mich., 1978. Mgr. br. merchandising CBS Records, Chgo., 1978; local promotion, mktg. mgr. CBS Records, Indpls., Boston, N.Y.C., 1978-81; spl. projects supr. Pickwick Internat. Musicland Group, Mpls., 1981-82; account exec. Campbell-Mithun Advt., Mpls., 1982-85; mktg. mgr., communications Universal Foods Corp., Milw., 1985-86; nat. advt. mgr. Thorobred Advt. Agy. (Jockey Internat., Inc.), Wis., 1986-88; dir. consumer and trade advt. Thorobred Advt. Agy. (Jockey Internat., Inc.), 1988-89, v.p. advt., 1990—. Mem. Traffic Audit Bur. for Media Measurement (bd. dirs. 1988—), Assn. Nat. Advertisers (print advt. com.). Office: Thorobred Advt 2300 60th St Kenosha WI 53140

HUFF, NANCY RUTH, citrus groves administrator, investments executive; b. Cin.; d. Norman Vincent and Marie (Voss) H.; m. William H. Brady, Sept. 9, 1961 (div. Apr. 1971); children—William Huff, Sherry Lynn. B.A., Newton Coll. of the Sacred Heart, Mass., 1961. Asst. to pres. Star Fruit Co., Lake Alfred, Fla., 1961-71; mgr., pres. Huff Groves, Winter Haven, Fla., 1971—; pres Star Investments, Winter Haven, 1980—; v.p. Allapattah Operating Co., Fort Pierce, Fla., 1982—, pres. Alpat Grove care Co., Fort Pierce, 1982—. Mem. Fla. Citrus Mutual, Indian River Citrus League (com. mem.), Women in Citrus, Fla. Citrus Women. Republican. Clubs: Lake Region Yacht and Country, Gardania Garden. (v.p. 1974-78) (Winter Haven); Citrus (Orlando, Fla.). Avocations: photography, pilot, dance, tennis. Office: PO Box 7167 Winter Haven FL 33883

HUFF, SHEILA LEVERNE WILLIAMS, educator; b. Louisville, Oct. 21, 1953; d. Robert Leverne and Inez (Blair) Williams; m. Billy Charles Huff, June 28, 1975; 1 child, Joshua Blake. BA in Art, Morehead (Ky.) State U., 1975; MLS, Spalding U., Louisville, 1986, EdS, 1989. Cert. tchr., Ky. Tchr. art and computer sci. Sacred Heart Acad., Louisville, 1976—; mem. teacher tng. staff Office Cath. Schs., Louisville, 1986, 89, cons. in field. Compiler textbook: Computer Literacy, 1988. Vol. Am. Cancer Soc., Louisville, 1988—; dir. student mural Kusair Children's Charities, 1989-90. Mem. Nat. Art Educators Assn., Ky. Educator Technology Conv., Computer Using Educators, Ky. Art Educators Assn. Democrat. Presbyterian. Home: 10505 Larkhall Ct Louisville KY 40223 Office: Sacred Heart Acad 3175 Lexington Rd Louisville KY 40223

HUFFAKER, CARLA SUE, legal assistant; b. Wilson, Okla., Jan. 24, 1951; d. Carl Leon and Betty Sue (Haliburton) H. BA, Cen. State U., Edmond, Okla., 1974, MA, 1979; AA, Rose State Coll., 1985. Legal asst. Miller, Glover & Hail, Oklahoma City, 1985-86; freelance legal researcher Mitchell, Williams, Selig & Tucker, Little Rock, 1987-90; trial asst. Merritt, Rooney, Collier & Rooney, Oklahoma City, 1989-90, Merritt & Rooney, Oklahoma City, 1990—; legal researcher Bates Engring., Oklahoma City, 1990—. Active press rels. Vice-Pres.'s advance team, Oklahoma City, 1987, Pres.'s advance team, 1989; exec. bd. dirs. Okla. County Rep. Party 1989, precinct chmn., 1989. Mem. Cen. Okla. Assn. Legal Assts., Okla. Trial Lawyers Assn. (assoc. mem.), 14th Air Force Veterans Assn. (assoc. mem.) Tri-City Rep. Women's Club (newsletter editor 1987-89), Okla. Fedn. Rep. Women (state essay chmn. 1989-90). Church of Christ. Home: 4909 N Linn Oklahoma City OK 73112-8358

HUFFMAN, CELIA ANN, librarian; b. Lorain, Ohio, June 2, 1953; d. Russell Edward and Betty Marie (Riggle) Kyger; m. Robert Dale Huffman, Feb. 1980. AA in Gen. Studies, Lorain County Community Coll., Elyria, Ohio, 1975; BA in History, Kent State U., 1977, MLS, 1978; Cert. ednl. media, Bowling Green State U., 1981. Cert. tchr. ednl. media, K-12. Substitute tchr. Lorain City Schs., 1979-82; children's libr. Cuyahoga County Pub. Libr., Parma, Ohio, 1982-85, Brooklyn, Ohio, 1985-86, Brook Park, Ohio, 1986—. Reviewer books, videos for librs. Mem. ALA, Assn. for Libr. Svc. to Children (microcomputer software evaluation com.), Ohio Libr. Assn., NAFE. Republican. Mem. Christian Ch. Home: 1303 W 21st St Lorain OH 44052 Office: Cuyahoga County Pub Libr Brook Park Br 6155 Engle Rd Brook Park OH 44142

HUFFMAN, CLAUDIA SUE, data processing executive; b. Denver, Dec. 3, 1954; d. C. and Patricia Ruth (Wilson) DiMercurio; m. Lawrence Paul Huffman, June 14, 1980 (div. 1987). BA, U. Louisville, 1977; MLS, Ind. U., 1979. Dept. head New Albany (Ind.) Pub. Libr., 1980-81; circulation mgr. Louisville Free Pub. Libr., 1981-83, automation mgr., 1983-87; sys. support Data Rsch. Assocs., St. Louis, 1987-88, software analyst, 1988-90; ref. librarian St. Charles (Mo.) Pub. Library, 1989—. Mem. Data Rsch. Assocs. Users' Group (sec. 1984-86), ALA, Library Adminstrn. and Mgmt. Assn., Digital Equip. Computer Users' Soc., Beta Phi Mu. Democrat. Home: 1771 Russet Valley Dr Saint Louis MO 63146 Office: Data Rsch Assocs 1276 N Warson Rd Saint Louis MO 63132

HUFFMAN, H. ARLENE, bank officer; b. Paxton, Ill., June 18, 1933; d. Edward V. and Mabel R. (Johnson) Bankson; m. Richard M. Huffman, Nov. 25, 1953; children: Melinda Huffman Etter, Mark, David. Student Ind. Bus. Coll. With Community State Bank, Royal Center, Ind., 1969—, asst. cashier, 1975—, asst. trust officer, 1975-87, ins. dept. mgr., 1978—. Helper for elderly Helping Hands, Royal Center; past pres. Progressive Club, Royal Center. Mem. Ind. Agts. Assn. Office: Community State Bank 101 N Chicago St Royal Center IN 46978

HUFFMAN, MARY FRANCES, retired educator; b. Montgomery, Ala., Apr. 30, 1911; d. Mary Huffman; m. Alexander Lee, June 28, 1936 (div. Aug., 1938); 1 child, Patricia Day Smoke. BS, Ala. State U., 1951, MEd, 1961; postgrad., Southern U., Baton Rouge, La., 1960, Beloit Coll., 1963, Talladega Coll., 1963-64. Cert. elem. and secondary tchr., Ala. Tchr. Elem. Schs., Troy, Ala., 1929-30, Prattville, Ala., 1930-32, Lowndes County, Ala., 1932-42, Union Springs, Ala., 1943-45, Montgomery, 1945-73. Sec. Nat. Caucus & Ctr. on Black Aged; sec. Congress of Christian Edn., 1955—; counselor Montgomery-Antioch Dist., Ala. State Women; mem. YMCA program com., 1969; treas. Alonzo Mitchell OES 636, Montgomery, 1980; sunday sch. tchr. Holt Street Bapt. Ch., sec. matrons circle; hostess, crusader, counselor libr./sec. Holt Street Jour.; sec. Montgomery County Multi-Black Caucus. Mem. AAUW, NEA, Assn. Retired Tchrs. Am., Montgomery County Retired Tchrs. Assn., AARP, Twelve Tribes (rec. sec., Montgomery, Ala.). Home: 955 Erskine St Montgomery AL 36108

HUFFMAN, MONA LOU, healthcare executive; b. Washington, Pa., Nov. 3, 1956; d. Robert Holly Sr. and Dolores (Gilmore) Durbin; m. Warren D. Huffman Jr. Diploma in nursing, OVGH Sch. Nursing, 1977; BSN, West Liberty (W.Va.) Coll., 1984; MS in Nursing, Duquesne U., 1990. Cert. in Nursing Adminstrn. Staff nurse ICU and cardiac care unit Washington Hosp., 1977-82, head nurse telemetry unit, 1982-86; mgr. cardiology dept. Suburban Gen. Hosp., Pitts., 1986-90. Mem. Am. Assn. Criticl Care Nurses, Am. Heart Assn., Coun. on Cardiovascular Nursing, Am. Assn. Cardiovascular and Pulmonary Rehab., Bus. and Profl. Women's Assn., Sigma Theta Tau. Home: 236 Clare Dr Canonsburg PA 15317

HUFFMAN, NONA GAY, investment retirement specialist; b. Albuquerque, June 22, 1942; d. William Abraham and Opal Irene (Leaton) Crisp; m. Donald Clyde Williams, Oct. 20, 1961; children—Debra Gaylene, James Donald. Student pub. schs. Lawndale, Calif. Lic. ins., securities dealer, N.Mex. Sec. City of Los Angeles, 1960, Los Angeles City Schs. 1960-62, Aerospace Corp., El Segundo, Calif., 1962-64, Albuquerque Pub. Schs., 1972-73, Pub. Service Co. N.Mex., Albuquerque, 1973; rep., fin. planner Waddell & Reed, Inc., Albuquerque, 1979-84; broker Rauscher Pierce Refsnes, Inc., 1984-85; rep., investment and retirement specialist Fin. Network Investment Corp., 1985-89, John Hancock Fin. Svcs., 1989—; tchr. money mgmt. seminars for sr. citizens ctr.; instr. U. N.Mex. Sr. Citizen Continuing Edn. Mem. Profl. Orgn. Women (co-chmn.), Women in Bus. (Albuquerque chpt.), Internat. Assn. Fin. Planners. Office: John Hancock Fin Svcs 2155 Louisiana NE Ste 4000 Albuquerque NM 87110

HUFFMAN, PAMELA IONE, financial executive; b. Lynwood, Calif., Oct. 1, 1948; d. Donald Leroy and Ione Mae (Arduser) Hogelen; m. Paul Les Huffman, Jan. 3, 1970; 1 child, Darin Paul. BS in Acctg., Calif. State U., Long Beach, 1975; MBA, Chapman Coll., 1990. Acct. St. Francis Hosp., Lynwood, 1975-76, Richard Murray, CPA, Los Alamitos, Calif., 1978, Community Psychiat. Ctrs., Santa Ana, Calif., 1976-78; sr. acct. Community Psychiat. Ctrs., Laguna Hills, Calif., 1978-79, asst. contr., 1979-82, contr., 1982-89, asst. treas., 1989—. 3d v.p. women's aux. Pop Warner Football, Anaheim Hills, Calif., 1982, lst v.p., 1983, pres., 1984. Mem. Nat. Investor Rels. Inst. Republican. Office: Community Psychiat Ctrs 24502 Pacific Park Dr Laguna Hills CA 92656

HUFFMAN, TEELA LOUISE LEWELLEN, medical center administrator; b. Tulsa, May 17, 1948; d. Delmar Huron and Joliet Arlie (Russell) Lewellen; m. Clyde Dean Huffman, Sept. 30, 1980. Student, Okla. State Tech. Inst. Keypunch operator T.G.&Y. Co., Oklahoma City, 1966-68; keypunch supr. Nat. Sharedata Co., Oklahoma City, 1968-71; computer operator Insured Aircraft Title Co., Oklahoma City, 1972-74; prodn. supr. Computer Mgmt. Corp., Oklahoma City, 1974-79; acct. mgr. Automatic Data Processing Co., Tulsa and Chgo., 1979; ops. mgr. Baptist Med. Ctr., Oklahoma City, 1979-86; dir. mgmt systems South Community Hosp., Oklahoma City, Okla., 1986—. Mem. Assn. for Computers Ops. Mgrs., Nat. Assn. Female Execs., Southwest Software Users Group, Am. Health Assn., Electronic Computing Health Oriented, Healthcare Info. and Mgmt. Systems Soc. of Am. Hosp. Assn. Republican. Baptist. Avocations: photography; travel; working with children. Home: 1617 College Ave Oklahoma City OK 73106 Office: South Community Hosp 1001 SW 44th St Oklahoma City OK 73109

HUFFMAN-HINE, RUTH CARSON, adult education administrator, educator; b. Spencer, Ind., Sept. 13, 1925; d. Joseph Charles Carson and Bess Ann Taylor; m. Joe Buren Hine; children: Paulette Walker, Larry K., Annette M. AA in Fine Arts, Ind. Cen. Coll., 1967; BS in Edn., Butler U., 1971; MS in Adult Edn., Ind. U., 1976. Cert. elem. edn. Subs. tchr. Met. Sch. Dist. Wayne Twnshp., Indpls., 1956-60; tchr. of homebound Met. Sch. Dist. Decatur Twnshp., Indpls., 1964-66; adult edn. tchr. Met. Sch. Dist. Wayne Twnshp., Indpls., 1971-75, adminstr. adult edn., 1975—; cons. Ind. Adoption System, Indpls., 1985—; regional rep. Ind. Assn. Adult Adminstrs., 1984—; program rep. Ind. Literacy Coordinators, Indpls., 1985—; speaker, mem. literacy research and evaluation com. Ind. Adult Literacy Coalition, Indpls., 1980-86. Author: Driving Regulations and Courtesies; coauthor Learning for Everyday Living, 1978, Table Approach to Education, 1984, Developing Educational Competencies for Individuals Determined to Excel, 6 vols., 1980 (ERIC System award 1980), (ERIC System award 1985), Collection, Evaluation, Dissemination of Special Research Projects, 1984, Automobile Driving Rules and Regulations, 1988. Vice com. person Rep. Orgn., Indpls., 1968-72; charter mem., sec. Project READ, LITERACY, 1988. Mem. Internat. Reading Assn. (Celebrate Literacy award 1984), Ind. Assn. for Adult Edn. (treas. 1984—, Outstanding Adult Educator 1979), Beta Phi Delta (pres. 1986—), Beta Phi, Delta Kappa Gamma (v.p. 1985-86, fellowship chmn. 1982-84), Phi Delta Kappa. Republican. Mem. Christian Ch. Home: 50 Abner Creek Pkwy Danville IN 46122 Office: Adult Basic Edn Ctr 5248 W Raymond St Indianapolis IN 46241

HUFNAGEL, ELLEN M., management information systems educator; b. Clarion, Pa., Jan. 10, 1948; d. Leon C. and Jeanne C. (Cousins) H. BA in Liberal Arts, Pa. State U., 1969, MS in Mktg., 1976; PhD in Bus. Adminstrn., U. Pitts., 1988. Mgmt. cons. Arthur Andersen, N.Y.C., 1970-71; owner, mgr. Ellen's Fabrics, etc., State College, Pa., 1972-76; systems engr. IBM Corp., Phila., 1976-77; systems analyst Scott Paper Co., Phila., 1977-79, fin. auditor, 1979-80; supervising cons. Coopers and Lybrand, Phila. and Dallas, 1980-83; dir. mgmt. info. systems UCCEL Corp., Dallas, 1983-85; asst. prof. U. South Fla., Tampa, 1988—. Roger Ahlbrandt fellow U. Pitts., 1988; U. Pitts. Rsch. grantee, 1988. Mem. Assn. for Computing Machinery, Acad. of Mgmt. Home: 14160 Fennsbury Dr Tampa FL 33624 Office: U South Fla Coll of Bus Adminstrn Tampa FL 33620

HUFNAGEL, LINDA ANN, biology educator, researcher; b. Teaneck, N.J., Nov. 7, 1939; d. Ernest Albert and Frances Marie (Hrbek) H.; m. Dov Jaron, 1969; children: Shulamit, Tamara; m. Robert Van Zackroff, June 1984. BA, U. Vt., 1961, MS, 1963; PhD, U. Pa., 1967. Lectr. U. Pa., Phila., summer 1967; NSF postdoctoral fellow Yale U., New Haven, 1967-69; rsch. assoc. Columbia U., N.Y.C., 1970; asst. prof. Oakland Community Coll., Farmington, Mich., 1970; rsch. assoc. Wayne State U., Detroit, 1971-73; lectr. biology U. R.I., Kingston, 1973-75, asst. prof., 1975-79, assoc. prof., 1979-86, prof., 1986—, dir. cen. electron microscope facility, 1973—. NSF rsch. grantee U. R.I., 1975, Am. Heart Assn. rsch. grantee, 1979; Steps fellow Marine Biol. Lab., Woods Hole, Mass., 1978, 79. Office: Univ R I Kingston RI 02881

HUFSTEDLER, SHIRLEY MOUNT (MRS. SETH M. HUFSTEDLER), lawyer, former federal judge; b. Denver, Aug. 24, 1925; d. Earl Stanley and Eva (Von Behren) Mount; m. Seth Martin Hufstedler, Aug. 16, 1949; 1 son, Steven Mark. BBA, U. N.Mex., 1945, LLD (hon.), 1972; LLB, Stanford U., 1949; LLD (hon.), U. Wyo., 1970, Gonzaga U., 1970, Occidental Coll., 1971, Tufts U., 1974, U. So. Calif., 1976, Georgetown U., 1976, U. Pa., 1976, Columbia U., 1977, U. Mich., 1979, Yale U., 1981, Rutgers U., 1981, Claremont U. Ctr., 1981, Smith Coll., 1982, Syracuse U., 1983, Mt. Holyoke Coll., 1985; PHH (hon.), Hood Coll., 1981, Hebrew Union Coll., 1986, Tulane U., 1988. Bar: Calif. 1950. Mem. firm Beardsley, Hufstedler & Kemble, L.A., 1951-61; practiced in L.A., 1961; judge Superior Ct., County L.A., 1961-66; justice Ct. Appeals 2d dist., 1966-68; circuit judge U.S. Ct. Appeals 9th cir., 1968-79; sec. U.S. Dept. Edn., 1979-81; ptnr. firm Hufstedler, Kaus & Beardsley, L.A., 1981—; dir. Hewlett Packard Co., US West, Inc., Harman Industries Internat. Mem. staff Stanford Law Rev, 1947-49; articles and book rev. editor, 1948-49. Trustee Calif. Inst. Tech., Occidental Coll, 1972-89, Aspen Inst., Colonial Willamsburg Found., 1976—, Constl. Rights Found., 1978-80, Nat. Resources Def. Coun., 1983-85, Carnegie Endowment for Internat. Peace, 1983—; bd. dirs. John T. and Catherine MacArthur Found., 1983—. Named Woman of Yr. Ladies Home Jour., 1976; recipient UCLA medal, 1981. Fellow Am. Acad. Arts and Scis.; mem. ABA, L.A. Bar Assn., Town Hall, Am. Law Inst. (coun. 1974-84), Am. Bar Found., Women Lawyers Assn. (pres. 1957-58), Am. Judicature Soc., Assn. of Bar of City of N.Y., Coun. on Fgn. Relations, Order of Coif. Office: Hufstedler Kaus & Beardsley 355 S Grand Los Angeles CA 90071

HUGGARD, EILEEN ELISABETH, lawyer; b. N.Y.C., Apr. 12, 1957; d. Raymond Francis and Carol Jean (Kinsella) H. AAS, Agrl. and Tech. Coll. SUNY, Farmingdale, 1977; BA summa cum laude with highest honors in Communication Arts, Hofstra U., 1980; JD, Georgetown U., 1983. Bar: D.C. 1983, N.Y. 1989. Assoc. Pellegrin & Levine, Chartered, Washington, 1983-86; atty. FCC, Washington, 1987-88; atty., telecommunications policy analyst N.Y.C. Energy and Telecommunications Office, 1988—. Mem. ABA, Women's Bar Assn. of D.C., Women in Communications, Fed. Communications Bar Assn., Phi Beta Kappa, Pi Sigma Alpha. Roman Catholic. Office: NYC Energy and Telecommunications Office 49-51 Chambers St New York NY 10007

HUGGINS, MARY LOUISE WHITE, English educator, small business owner; b. Big Wells, Tex., Jan. 7, 1933; d. Edwin Horatio and Cora Edith (English) White; m. Chester Huelon Huggins, Sept. 23, 1961; children: Mary Catherine, Clarice Nell, Lloyd Jefferson, Henry Nuelon, Chester Horatio. BA in English and Spanish, Tarleton State U., Stephenville, Tex., 1979, MA in Teaching, 1981. Cert. secondary tchr., Tex. Sec., bookkeeper Hico (Tex.) Pub. Sch., 1969-76; instr. English, Tarleton State U., 1983—, dir. summer program, 1987—; clk., bookkeeper Blair's Hardware, Hico, 1972-83; owner, operator Mary's Garden, Stephenville, 1987—. Pres. Erath County Women's Polit. Caucus, Stephenville; speaker to garden clubs, 1986—. Named Erath County Woman of Yr., Erath County Com., 1989. Mem. Conf. Coll. Tchrs. English, Assn. Tchrs. Tech. Writing, South Cen. Women's Studies Assn., Tarleton State U. Faculty Women's Club (treas. 1988-89), AAUW (pres. Stephenville br. 1987), Am. Iris Soc., Johnson County Iris and Daylily Soc. (pres. 1987-88, lst v.p. 1989-90). Home: 867 W Elm Stephenville TX 76401

HUGH, LORI EVAN, inventory and cost accounting manager; b. Charleston, W.Va., Feb. 6, 1959; d. Perry W. and Vivien (Perrine) Woofter; m. Jeffrey Ronald Hugh, Nov. 16, 1984. BS in Mining Engring., W.Va. U., 1983, BS in Petroleum Engring., 1984; postgrad., Colo. Sch. Mines, 1985; M.A. in Bus. Adminstrn., Framingham State U., 1991. Mining engr. Consol. Coal Co., Blacksville, W.Va., 1980-84; engring. technician U.S. Bur. Mines, Denver, 1985-86; econ. evaluator Colo. Dept. Health, Denver, 1986; asst. contr. Reynolds Bros. Inc., Canton, Mass., 1987-88; inventory and cost acctg. mgr. L.E. Mason, Boston, 1988—; cons. to various internat. firms, 1987; publicity dir. W.Va. U. chpt. Soc. Mining Engrs., Morgantown, 1983; guest speaker in field. Contbr. articles to profl. jours. Rugby coach W.Va. U. Women's Rugby Team, 1981. Republican. Episcopalian. Home: 12 Inman St Hopedale MA 01747

HUGHES, ANITA HART, hospital services executive; b. Oxford, N.C., Aug. 2, 1960; d. Lynwood Bryan and Mary Leigh (Hart) H. AA, Peace Coll., 1980; BS in Med. Records Adminstrn., East Carolina U., 1982; M in Health Svcs. Adminstrn., U. of S.C., 1989. Registered records adminstr. Asst. dir. med. records N.C. Meml. Hosp., Chapel Hill, 1982-85; dir. med. records Spartanburg (S.C.) Regional Hosp., 1985-86; dir. med. records and utilization mgmt. Greenville (S.C.) Hosp. System, 1986—; clin. site instr. Med. U. of S.C., Charleston, 1986—, East Carolina U., Greenville, 1986—. Project leader March of Dimes, Spartanburg, 1986. Mem. Am. Med. Records Assn. (mem. project team 1989, cert., elector 1990), S.C. Med. Record Assn. (pres. 1988-89), S.C. Hosp. Assn. (speaker 1986—, chmn. utilization rev. com. 1990), Phi Kappa Phi, Phi Theta Kappa. Democrat. Baptist.

HUGHES, ANN, professional association administrator; b. Adrian, Mich., Dec. 11, 1944; d. Harold Rex and Alice (Griewahn) Johnston; m. Philip Ernest Hughes, Aug. 6, 1966; children: Philip, Matthew. BA in Bus. Adminstrn. and Mgmt., Siena Heights Coll., 1982. Asst. mgr. book store Siena Heights Coll., Adrian, 1975-80, sec. to registrar, 1980-82, dir. alumni, 1982-85; v.p. Lewanee County C. of C., Adrian, 1985-90, gen. mgr., 1988-90, exec. v.p., 1990—. Mem. adv. coun. St. Joseph Acad., Adrian, 1987—; mem. bus. coun. Siena Hts. Coll., 1986—; bd. dirs. Jr. Achievement, Adrian, 1989—, Goodwill-Lenawee assn. Retarded Citizens, Adrian, 1988—. Mem. NAFE, Am. Communications Coun., Nat. Assn. Membership Dirs., Am. Chamber Execs., Mich. Chamber Execs. Roman Catholic. Office: Lewanee County C of C 216 N Main St Adrian MI 49221

HUGHES, ANN HIGHTOWER, economist, government official; b. Birmingham, Ala., Nov. 24, 1938; d. Brady Alexander and Juanita (Pope) H. B.A., George Washington U., 1963, M.A., 1969. Asst. U.S. trade rep. Exec. Office of Pres., Washington, 1978-81; dep. asst. sec. trade agreements Dept. Commerce, Washington, 1981-82, dep. asst. sec. Western Hemisphere, 1982—. Recipient Meritorious Exec. award Pres. of U.S., 1982, 88. Office: Dept Commerce 14th & Constitution Ave NW Room 3826 Washington DC 20230

HUGHES, ANN NOLEN, mental health counselor; b. Ft. Meade, Md., Apr. 8, 1933; d. George M. and Georgie T. Nolen; m. Edwin L. Hughes, Oct. 21, 1961; 1 child, Andrew G. BS in Psychology, Rollins Coll., 1985, MA in Counseling, 1986; student in pub. speaking and human rels., Dale Carnegie Inst., 1981; student, Duke U., 1950-52. Lic. mental health counselor. Supr. top secret control, audio/visual small parts supply U.S. Govt., Continental U.S. and Tokyo; adminstrv. sec. System Devel. Corp., Rand Corp., Santa Monica, Calif.; adminstrv. asst., editor, exec. sec., adminstrv. sec. Aerospace Corp., El Segundo, Calif.; staff therapist Circles of Care, Melbourne, Fla. Various leadership positions PTA, Pittsford, N.Y. and Brookfield, Wis., 1968-81. Mem. AAUW, Am. Assn. Counseling and Devel., Assn. for Specialist in Group Work, Am. Mental Health Counselors, Space Coast Ski Club, Space Coast PC User's Group, Kappa Kappa Gamma. Presbyterian. Home: 447 Pauma Valley Way Melbourne FL 32940

HUGHES, ANNE ROSEMARIE, lawyer; b. Elizabeth, N.J., Apr. 17, 1955; d. Vincent Leo and Eileen Beatrice (Menard) Hughes. B in Social Work, Tex. Woman's U., 1977; JD, Lousiana State U., 1985. Attorney Anne R. Hughes, Prof. Law Corp., Baton Rouge, La., 1986--. Dir. Beacon House Adoption Svcs., Inc., Port Allen, La. Mem. ABA, Am. Trial Lawyers Assn., La. State Bar Assn. Democrat. Roman Catholic. Office: 601 Meriam St Piaquemine LA 70764

HUGHES, BARBARA ANN, dietitian, public health administrator; b. McMinn County, Tenn., July 22, 1938; d. Cecil Earl and Hannah Ruth (Moss) Farmer; B.S. cum laude in Home Econs. Carson Newman Coll., Jefferson City, Tenn., 1960; M.S. in Instl. Mgmt., Ohio State U., Columbus, 1963; M.A. (Adonarium Judson scholar), So. Bapt. Theol. Sem., 1968; M.P.H. in Public Health Adminstrn., U. N.C., Chapel Hill, 1972; postgrad. in nutrition U. Iowa, 1974, U. N.C., 1975-85, Case Western Res. U., 1979, Walden U.; PhD 1988 ; m. Carl Clifford Hughes, Oct. 13, 1962. Dietitian, instr. Riverside Meth. Hosp., Riverside Whitecross Sch. Nursing, Columbus, 1963-66; consulting dietitian eastern region N.C. Bd. Health, Raleigh, 1968-73; dir. Nutrition and Dietary Services br., div. Health Services, N.C. Dept. Human Resources, Raleigh, 1973-89, also dir. Women-Infants-Children Program; pres. Hughes and Assocs.; cons. dietitian Mt. Holly Nursing Home, Louisville, 1967-68; adj. instr. Case Western Res. U., Cleve., 1988-89; adj. asst. prof. dept. nutrition Sch. Public Health, U. N.C., Chapel Hill; mem. adv. bd. Hospitality Edn. program N.C. Dept. Community Colls., 1974-80, adv. com. Ret. Senior Vol. Program, Raleigh and Wake County, N.C., 1975-79, N.C. Network Coordinating Council for End-Stage Renal Disease, 1975, Nat. Adv. Council on Maternal, Infant, and Fetal Nutrition, Spl. Supplemental Food Program for Women, Infants, and Children, Dept. Agr., 1976-79, adv. com. Nutrition Edn. and Tng. program N.C. Dept. Public Instruction, 1978-80; coord. undergrad. program in gen. dietetics East Carolina U.; adv. council N.C. Gov.'s Office Citizen Affairs; lectr., cons.; cons. dietitian Augusta Victoria Hosp. and Jerusalem (Israel) Crippled Childrens Center, 1968; witness U.S. congressional and Senate hearings in field. Active edn. programs Pullen Memorial Bapt. Church, Raleigh, deacon, 1976-80, area ministry capt., 1977-78, personnel com., 1978-80; bd. dirs. Community Outreach, 1989—; dietitian/dir. food service archeol. expedition to Israel, 1968; bd. dirs. N.C. Literacy Assn. 1978-83, pres., 1981-83; v.p. Wake County Literacy Council, 1986-87; trustee Gardner-Webb Coll., Boiling Springs, N.C., 1979-82, chmn. curriculum com., 1981-82; chmn. Coalition Pub. Health Nutrition, 1983-85; del. various Democratic Convs., 1981-84, precinct sec.-treas., 1981-83, 1st vice chmn., 1983-85, chair, 1985-87; chmn. adv. bd. dept. home econs. Carson-Newman Coll. Named Woman of Yr., Wake County, 1975, N.C. Outstanding Dietitian of Yr., 1976, N.C. Outstanding Dietitian, Southeastern Hosp. Conf. for Dietitians, 1978; recipient Disting. Alumna award Carson-Newman Coll., 1983. Mem. AAUW (life, pres. Raleigh br. 1971-75, pres. N.C. div. 1978-80, nat. bd. dirs. 1980-82, area rep. 1980-82, nat. edn. found. bd. dirs. 1987-91), Am. Dietetic

Assn. (del. 1971-74, 87-89, pres. N.C. state assn. 1976-77, N.C. network legis. coordinator 1978-81, nat. nominating com. 1979-80, nat. chmn. council on practice 1982-83, chair legislation and pub. policy com. 1985-87, area coord. Ho. of Dels. 1989-92), Am. Public Health Assn. (exec. com. So. br. 1977-87, sec.-treas. 1979-80, 1st v.p. 1980-81), So. Health Assn. (pres. 1982-83, chair nominating com. 1985-86, Spl. Meritorious award 1989), Assn. State and Territorial Pub. Health Nutrition Dirs. (pres. 1977-79, dir. 1981-89, liaison to Assn. Faculties Grad. Program in Pub. Health Nutrition, chair legis. and pub. policy com. 1984-89, Commendation award 1989), N.C. Council Foods and Nutrition (dir. 1976-78, chmn. membership 1975, nominating com. 1979). N.C. Council Women's Orgns. (mem. at large, bd. dirs. 1989-92), Am. Acad. Health Adminstrn., Soc. Nutrition Edn., Nutrition Today Soc., N.C. Acad. Public Health, Ohio State U. Alumni Assn. (life), U. N.C. Gen. Alumni Assn. (life), U. N.C. Public Health Alumni Assn. (life), Altrusa Internat. (pres. Raleigh club 1973-74, dir. 1976-78, 1st vice gov. 1978-79, chmn. nomination com. 1980-82, gov. dist. Three, 1979-80, internat. vocat. servics chmn. 1977-79, 1st v.p. 1985-87, pres.-elect 1987-89, pres. 1989-91), Altrusa Internat. Found. (1st v.p., pres. 1989-91), Women's Forum N.C. Co-author: Diet and Kidney Disease, Assn. for N.C. Regional Med. Program, 1969; contbr. numerous papers, articles to symposia, periodicals in field, vol. areas. Home: 4208 Galax Dr Raleigh NC 27612

HUGHES, BARBARA BRADFORD, nurse; b. Bragg City, Mo., Jan. 21, 1941; d. Lawrence Hurl Bradford and Opa Jewel (Prater) Puttin; m. Robert Howard Hughes, Dec. 9, 1961; children: Kimberly Ann Hayden, Robert Howard II. ASN, St. Louis Community Coll., 1978; student, Webster U., 1980. RN, Mo. Med. surg. nurse Alexian Bros. Hosp., St. Louis, 1979-80; staff nurse Midwest Allergy Cons., St. Louis, 1980; nurse high altitude Aviation Nurse, Ltd., St. Louis, 1980-81; med. surg. staff charge nurse Bethesda Gen. Hosp., St. Louis, 1987-89; pvt. practice real estate mgmt., 1962—. Vol. Luth. Hosp., St. Louis, 1967-70; mem. Mo. Botanical Garden, St. Louis, 1976—, St. Louis Aviation Mus., 1984—, St. Louis Zoo Friends Assn., 1986-87, Sta. Channel 9-Ednl. TV, St. Louis, 1986—; vol. blood drive ARC, St. Louis, 1980; vol. health tchr. Spartan Aluminum Products, Sparta, Ill., 1984. U. Mo. scholar, 1959. Mem. Am. Nurses Assn., Mo. Nurses Assn., Internat. Flying Nurses Assn., Mo. Pilots Assn., U.S. Pilots Assn. Republican. Club: Tyospaye. Home: 736 Windsor Harbor Rd Imperial MO 63052

HUGHES, BARBARA SUZANNE, lawyer; b. Chgo., Feb. 9, 1943; d. William Owen and Catherine Alice (Janssen) H.; m. Burr S. Eichelman Jr., June 27, 1964 (div. June 1982); children: Kathryn Elise, Andrew Burr. BA, U. Chgo., 1964, MA, 1968; JD, U. Wis., 1986. Bar: Wis. 1986. Elem. tchr. Homewood (Ill.) Pub. Schs., 1964-67; cancer edn. program coord. Wis. Clin. Cancer Ctr. and U. Wis. Hosp., Madison, 1980-84; assoc. atty. Stolper, Koritzinsky, Brewster & Neider, S.C., Madison, 1986—; lectr. U. Wis. Law Sch., Madison, 1988; regular speaker I Can Cope cancer program St. Mary's Hosp., 1988-89. Co-author: Clinical Health Maintenance Vol. 6: Cancer of the Breast Guidebook, 1985; author and co-author of numerous cancer prevention videotapes. Mem. Luther Meml. Ch. choir, Worship and Music com.; correspondent, bd. dirs. Cambrian Heritage Soc. Madison, 1988—. Mem. ABA, Legal Assn. for Women, Wis. State Bar Assn., Dane County Bar Assn., Madison Estate Coun., Nat. Acad. Elder Law Attys., Pi Lamda Theta. Office: Stolper Koritzinsky et al 7617 Mineral Point Rd Madison WI 53717

HUGHES, CAROLYN, artist; b. Penasco, N.Mex., Jan. 19, 1921; d. Jose Ildefonso and Lenore (Martinez) Sandoval; m. Gale Winfield Hughes, June 6, 1946; 1 child, Gale Winfield Hughes Jr. Creator, soft sculpture dolls; copy-right for name Peg People, 1972. Home: 516 Amherst Dr SE Albuquerque NM 87106

HUGHES, CAROLYN JEANNE, financial services professional; b. Bklyn., Jan. 17, 1957; d. Anthony Arthur and Carmela Marie (Ranieri) Stanganelli. BBA in Fin. magna cum laude, Adelphi U., 1979, MBA in Fin. and Investments, 1982. Asst. domestic cash mgr. Sterling Drug, Inc., N.Y.C., 1979-80; cash mgr. Quality Care, Inc., Rockville Centre, N.Y., 1980-82; asst. v.p. Bank of Am., N.Y.C., 1982-83; mgr. Merrill Lynch & Co., N.Y.C., 1983-84; cash mgr. to v.p. Prudential-Bache Securities, Inc., N.Y.C., 1984-88; mktg. officer Associated Capital Investors, San Francisco, 1988—. exec. asst. to chmn. Prudential-Bache Securities, Inc./Dem. Bus. Council, Washington, 1985. Mem. Delta Mu Delta (series 7 registered rep.).

HUGHES, CHRISTINE GEORGETTE, infosystems specialist; b. San Francisco, Nov. 1, 1946; d. George F. Hughes and Patricia M. (Connolly) Anderson; m. Abraham E. Ostrovsky, July 17, 1980. BA, San Francisco Coll. for Women, 1968. Pub. relations asst. Macy's, San Francisco, 1969-71; sales mgr. Lanier Products, San Francisco, 1976-77; systems analyst Xerox Corp., Stamford, Conn., 1976; product mgr. Savin Corp., Stamford, 1972-75, 77-80; dir. ops. Quantum Sci., N.Y.C., 1981-83; v.p., dir. Gartner Group, Stamford, 1983-89; pres. Myriad Group, Coral Gables, Fla., 1989—. Pub. Media Letter. Precinct chmn. Reps., Coral Gables, Fla., 1980. Mem. Office Systems Research Assn., Inst. Info. Research, Soc. Computing and Info. Processing. Republican. Roman Catholic. Office: Myriad Group PO Box 142 075 Coral Gables FL 33114

HUGHES, DELIA ANN, executive vice president; b. Houston, Tex., Apr. 5, 1947; d. Glenn Wyman and Myrtle Prudence (Coward) W.; children: Mary Catherine, Cynthia Ann. C. of C. Exec. Cert. Mgr. Sonora C. of C., Sonora, Tex., 1985-87; engring. sec. Appleton Electric Co., Stephenville, Tex., 1987-88; exec. v.p. Azle C. of C., Azle, Tex., 1988—; adv. dir. Projects with Industry, Weatherford, Tex., 1988-89, W. Tex. C. of C., Abilene, Tex., 1986-88. Pres. 4H Leaders Assn., Sonora, 1986; V.P. Women of the Ch. S. John's Episcopal Ch., Sonora, 1985; Mem. Sonora Woman's Club, Sonora, 1976-87, Beta Sigma Phi, Ft. Worth, 1988—. Named Woman of the Year Sutton Co. 4H Club, Sonora, 1984; recipient TCCE scholarship, 1989, CCEAWT scholarship SMU Inst., 1990. Mem. C. of C. Exec. Assn. W. Tex. (bd. dirs., newsletter editor 1989-91), Tex. C. of C. Exec. Assn., Alpha Chi Omega Alpha Phi. Republican. Episcopal. Office: PO Box 1528 Azle TX 76020

HUGHES, DOROTHY TODD, retired music educator; b. Bedford, Ind., Sept. 5, 1898; d. John Richard and Addie May (Todd) H. Diploma, U. Cin., 1922; BS in Music Edn., NYU, 1928, MA in Music, 1932; postgrad., Stanford U., 1931, Ind. U., 1956-57. Life cert. music educator, Pa., Ohio. Supr. of music Johnson City (Tenn.) Pub. Schs., 1921-24, Ashtabula (Ohio) Pub. Schs., 1924-26; asst. prof. music Ohio U., Athens, 1928-29; supr. of music Ohio Pub. Schs., Lakewood, 1929-30; assoc. prof. music Millersville (Pa.) U., 1931-63. Author: Piano Fun with Family and Friends, 1936, Creative Rhythms, 1941, Rhythmic Games and Dances, 1942. Mem. AAUW, Pa. Assn. Sch. Retirees, Women's Welsh Clubs Am., Cambrian Soc. Delaware Valley, Sigma Alpha Iota (chaplain 1974-75, chpt. photographer 1977-79, Rose of Honor award 1977). Republican. Home: 12 Harp Rd Levittown PA 19056

HUGHES, ETHEL LENA, nursing home administrator; b. Spindale, N.C., Mar. 16, 1933; d. William Angus and Ruth Jane (Early) Laughter; m. Claude Fitzpatrick Hughes, Feb. 28, 1954 (div. Jan. 1986); children: Steven Patrick, Alan Lee. RN diploma, Spartanburg Gen. Hosp., Spartanburg, S.C., 1953. Night supr. Abbeville County Meml. Hosp., Abbeville, S.C., 1961-62; nurses aide instr. Manpower Devel.-Tng. Act, Abbeville, 1963-64; dir. nursing Abbeville Nursing Home, Inc., 1968-78, adminstr., 1978—; founder, owner Carolina Springs Laundromat, Inc., 1986—; cons. to adminstrn. Fountain Inn (S.C.)Convalescent Home, 1979-88, J. Health Care, Simpsonville, S.C., 1979-80, Nat. Health Enterprises, Greenville, S.C., 1980-81, Granville Club, Hilton Head, S.C., 1982-83, Sandstrom Home, Myrtle Beach, S.C., 1989; founder, owner, pres. The Guest House, Inc., Abbeville, 1971-81; founder, owner, v.p., sec. Abbeville Nursing Home, Inc., 1968—; mem. med. rev. bd. Blue Cross/Blue Shield S.C., 1974-76, Medicaid Rev. Bd., S.C., 1979-84. Co-Author: (revised & updated manual) How to be a Nurses Aide, 1975. Charter pres. Jay-C-Ettes, Spartanburg, S.C., 1956-57; state rep. McCalls' Congress on Better Living, S.C., 1960; den mother Cub Scouts, Abbeville, 1963-66; pres. Abbeville County Tuberculosis Assn., 1962-66, Women's Soc. Christian Svc., Main St. United Meth. Ch., Abbeville, 1971-72, High Meadows Country Club, Abbeville, 1980-82, Abbeville County Rep. Women's Club, 1988—; bd. dirs. Abbeville County Dept. Health, 1963-65; mem. coun. on aging City of Abbeville, 1964-66 and others. Mem. Am. Coll. Health Care Adminstrs., S.C. Health Care Assn. (dept. health and environ. control liaison com., utilization rev. com., payment for svc. com., peer rev. com., Blue Cross/Blue Shield liaison com., skilled conf. chmn.), President's award 1978), Abbeville County Republican Women's Club (pres. 1988—), Greenwood Country Club, High Meadows Country Club (pres. 1980-82, v.p. 1982-84). Methodist. Office: Abbeville Nursing Home Inc Thomson Circle Abbeville SC 29620

HUGHES, FAYE ADELE, educator; b. New London, Conn., Oct. 11, 1946; d. Irvin Albert and Hazel Adele (Trahan) H. B.S., Central Conn. State Coll., 1969; M.Ed., U. Hartford, 1971; Cert. Advanced Study, Trinity Coll., 1978, M.A., 1981; postgrad. Yale U., 1983-86, U. Conn., 1985-87, Century U., 1987—. Pre-primary tchr. Vine St. Sch., Hartford, Conn., 1969; 2d grade tchr. Barbour Sch., Hartford, 1969-70; mem. curriculum writing team Hartford Bd. Edn., 1970-71; English and reading tchr. Batcheldor Sch., Hartford, 1971, Burns Sch., Hartford, 1971-72; English, reading and social studies tchr. T.J. Quirk Middle Sch., Hartford, 1972—, head tchr. social studies dept., 1988-89; lectr., cons. in field; bd. dirs. Conn. Consortium for Law Related Edn., 1979—; instr. Hartford Tchr. Ctr., Hartford Tchrs. Acad., 1988—; bd. dirs. Conn. Council Social Studies, 1978-81, chmn. Hartford Regional chpt., 1980-81. Democratic campaign worker Town of Newington and Conn. State Fedn. Tchrs., 1979—; Sunday sch. tchr. St. Mark's Ch., Mystic, Conn., 1961-64, St. Mark's Ch., New Britain, Conn., 1964-69; bd. dirs. Central State Coll. Alumni, 1971-76, sec. to bd., 1974-76; adv. com. social studies curriculum devel. team Conn. Dept. Edn.; bd. dirs. Newington Homeowners and Taxpayers, 1984-86. Presdl. Award scholar, 1966; recipient Honorable Mention award Conn. State Celebration of Excellence in Teaching, 1989. Mem. Assn. for Study of Conn. History, Conn. Ctr. for Ind. Historians, Conn. Assn. for Advancement of Russian and East European Studies, Hartford Fedn. Tchrs., Conn. Fedn. Tchrs., Winterthur Guild, Smithsonian Instn., Am. Mus. Natural History, Am. Fedn. Tchrs., Nat. Council for Social Studies, Conn. Council for Tchrs. of English, New Eng. Council for Tchrs. of English, Assn. Supervision and Curriculum Devel., Conn. Council Social Studies, Conn. Assn. Supervision and Curriculum Devel. (contbr. to jour.), Phi Delta Kappa (U. Conn. chpt. v.p. program, 1989-90, v.p. membership 1990—), Beta Sigma Phi, Pi Lamda Theta. Democrat. Episcopalian. Home: 39 Hunters Ln Newington CT 06111 Office: Thomas J Quirk Middle Sch 85 Edwards St Hartford CT 06120

HUGHES, J. DEBORAH, health care administrator; b. Pitts., Mar. 24, 1948; d. James Francis and Margaret Veronica (Wiullmier) H. Diploma in nursing, Columbia Sch. Nursing, Pitts., 1969; BSN, La Roche Coll., 1987; M of Pub. Mgmt., Carnegie-Mellon U., 1988. Cert. nursing adminstr., med. staff coord. Staff nurse Forbes Health System, Pitts., 1969-78, head nurse recovery, 1978-79, supr. nursing, 1979-84, clin. asst. to med. dir., 1984-88, dir. med. staff svcs., 1988-90; quality tracking mgr. Humana, Inc., Lousiville, 1990—. Mem. Am. Assn. Critical Care Nurses, Am. Assn. Operating Room Nurses, League Intravenous Therapy, Am. Hosp. Assn., Nat. Assn. Med. Staff Svcs., Pa. Assn. med. Staff Svcs., NAFE. Office: Humana Inc 500 W Main Bldg The Humana Bldg Louisville KY 40201-1438

HUGHES, JANE WOLFORD, educational administrator, speaker, writer; b. Detroit, June 8, 1920; d. Frank Ralph and Corinne Marie (Ouellette) Gerbig; m. Eugene Wolford, Sept. 23, 1944 (dec. Nov. 11, 1969); children—Diane, Maureen, Michael, John, James, Joseph, Marie Therese; m. 2d, John P. Hughes, June 1, 1972; 8 stepchildren. Student St. Mary Coll. and St. Cyril and Methodius Sem., Orchard Lake, Mich., 1972-73, St. Joseph's Coll., Cin., 1966-67, U. Detroit, 1965-68, Wayne State U., 1943-44; Ph.B., Marygrove Coll., 1942. Fashion copywriter J.L. Hudson Dept. Store, Detroit, 1942-44; dir. pub. relations Archdiocese of Detroit, 1959-62; chmn. pub. relations Nat. Council Cath. Women, Washington, 1960-64; dir. adult edn. Archdiocese of Detroit, 1966-85; mem. Nat. Think Tank, U.S. govt., Washington, 1972; chairperson leadership conf. Mich. Cath. Conf., 1977; mem. com. on edn. U.S. Cath. Conf., 1982-85; mem. nat. adv. com. Adult Catechesis Exec. Com., 1974—; mem. faculty St. Mary Coll., Orchard Lake, 1977, 81, St. John Sem., Plymouth, Mich., 1981—; workshop and keynote speaker in field. Authors manuals; contbr. articles, chpts. to profl. publs.; writer, producer ednl. and tng. TV programs, 1968-72; editor: Working with Adult Learners, 1981. Mem. Round Table Christians and Jews, Detroit, 1962-68; mem. City of Detroit United Community Services, 1965-67; mem. Detroit Commn. on Human Relations, 1967-69; mem. Detroit Get Out and Vote Commn., 1968. Recipient Mother Domittala award Marygrove Coll., 1967, Key to City award City of Detroit, 1968; 1st place creativity award Adult Edn. Assn. Mich., 1968-69, creativity award hon. mention, 1970. Mem. Nat. Cath. Edn. Assn. (bd. dirs. 1967-76, Pres.'s award 1976), Religious Edn. Assn. U.S.A. and Can. (dir. 1976-80), Adult Edn. Assn. U.S.A. (chmn. religious sect. 1976-82). Clubs: Women's Economic, Press (Detroit). Office: 34053 Brittany Dr Farmington Hills MI 48331

HUGHES, JUDITH LEE, dance studio owner; b. St. Petersburg, Fla., Nov. 23, 1940; d. Douglas Prescott and Elsie Lee (Shippey) Johnson; m. Frank C. Hughes III, Dec. 27, 1966; children: Halyn Lee, Frank Collins IV. Student, Adelphi Coll., 1958-60. Tchr. ballet Eckerd Coll., St. Petersburg, 1965-68; owner, tchr. Judith Lee Johnson Studio of Dance, St. Petersburg, 1962—; ptnr. Dance Inc. of Pinellas, St. Petersburg, 1987—; artistic advisor St. Petersburg Civic Ballet, Inc., 1965-74; mem. artistic adv. bd. Fla. West Ballet Co., 1987-91; co-dir. City Ctr. Ballet Co. Tampa/St. Petersburg, 1962-64; competition judge Dance Masters of Am., Fla. chpt. 1988. Choreographer numerous local organizations. Vol. coord. Tarpon Springs (Fla.) Mid. Sch., 1982-83, mem. Student Activities Com., 1981-87. Recipient Woman in the Arts award St. Petersburg Symphony Guild. Mem. State Dance Assn. Fla., Pinellas County Dance Tchrs. Assn. (bd. dirs. 1986—). Club: St. Petersburg Jr. Womens. Home: 2160 Diane Ct Clearwater FL 34623 Office: Judith Lee Johnson Studios 2033-54 Ave N Saint Petersburg FL 34689

HUGHES, JUDY LYNNE, organization executive; b. San Antonio, Mar. 23, 1939; d. Timothy Endemond Gristy and Clovis Ruth (Mooring) Linville; m. Donald E. LaMora, Nov. 12, 1960 (div. Aug. 1980); children: Grant, Leigh, Eric.; m. William J. Hughes, May 11, 1984. Student, Tex. Tech. U., 1956-60. News reporter Colorado Springs (Colo.) Gazette Telegraph, 1960; vice chair pub. rels. Nat. Fedn. Rep. Women, Washington, 1974-76; 2d v.p. Nat. Fedn. Rep. Women, Denver, 1978-82, 1st v.p., 1982-86, pres., 1986-90, immediate past pres., 1990—; ofcl. del. U.S. State Dept., El Salvador, 1989. Co-chmn. Workforce 2000 Bush/Quayle Campaign, Washington, 1989; western rep. to sec. U.S. Dept of Interior, Washington, 1989; mem. RNC Com. Minority Participation, Washington, 1989. Named Rep. Women of Yr. Shelby County Rep. Woman's Club, 1988. Mem. Am. News Woman's Club (assoc.), Pikes Peak Rep. Woman's Club (Colorado Springs). Home: 1743 Sand Lily Dr Golden CO 80401 Office: Dept Interior 1743 Sand Lily Dr Golden CO 80401 also: Denver West Office Pk Bldg 3 Golden CO 80401

HUGHES, JUDY SANDERS, entrepreneur; b. Thomaston, Ga., Jan. 25, 1957; d. Charles William and Lonelle (Evans) Sanders. AB, Wesleyan Coll., Macon, Ga, 1979. Assoc. in Risk Mgmt. Asst. mgr. So. Bell Tel. & Tel., Albany, Ga., 1979-80; asst. staff mgr. So. Bell Tel. & Tel., Atlanta, 1981-85; risk mgr. BellSouth Corp., Atlanta, 1985—; a. Recipient Acad. Excellence award Ins. Inst. Am., 1987. Mem. Atlanta Risk Ins. Mgmt. Soc. (Cristy award 1987). Republican. Presbyterian. Office: BellSouth Corp 13G05-1155 Peachtree St Atlanta GA 30367

HUGHES, JULIANA GENINE, accountant; b. Sioux City, Iowa, Sept. 27, 1962; d. Jay Lewis and Constance Jean (Brown) McDole; m. Randall James Hughes, Jan. 19, 1962. Student, Western Iowa Tech. Community Coll., Sioux City, 1981-82, Briar Cliff Coll., Sioux City, 1982-83. Office asst. Roush Service Co., Dakota City, 1983-85; pension adminstrv. asst. Nat. Med. Enterprises, L.A., 1985-88; acct. Bel-Air Savings and Loan, L.A., 1988-89; sr. acctg. asst. Mpls. Inst. Arts, 1989—. Republican. Office: 2400 3d Ave S Minneapolis MN 55404

HUGHES, KAREN LU, lawyer; b. Ottawa, Ill., Nov. 12, 1947; d. Mervin L. and Doris A. (Stangeland) Osmond; m. John Hughes, July 24, 1971 (div. 1985); children: Douglas, Thomas, Jane. BA, Luther Coll., 1969; JD, Valparaiso U., 1972. Bar: Ind. 1972, U.S. Dist. Ct. (no. dist.) Ind. 1974, U.S. Ct. Appeals (7th cir.) 1975, U.S. Supreme Ct. 1978. Assoc. Hoeppner, Houran, Wagner & Evans, Valparaiso, Ind., 1972-75, Hoover Law Firm, Valparaiso, 1976, Hoeppner, Wagner & Evans, Valparaiso, 1977-85; pvt. practice Valparaiso, 1985-87, Knox, Ind., 1987-88; assoc. Lucas, Holcomb & Medrea, Merrillville, Ind., 1988—; adj. prof. law Valparaiso U., 1985. Mem. Porter County Police Merit Bd., Valparaiso, 1983-85, Porter County Coun., 1985—, pres., 1989—; bd. dirs. Porter County Emergency Med. Svc., 1985-88, Northwest Ind. Forum, 1986—; commr. Northwest Ind. Regional Planning Commn. for Lake, Porter and LaPorte Counties, 1988—, sec., 1990. Mem. ABA, Ind. State Bar Assn., Porter County Bar Assn., Fed. Bar Assn., Lake County Bar Assn., Ind. C. of C. , Tri Kappa. Republican. Lutheran. Home: 708 Hastings Terr Valparaiso IN 46383 Office: Lucas Holcomb & Medrea 300 E 90th Dr Merrillville IN 46410

HUGHES, KAREN WOODBURY, botany educator, academic administrator; b. Madison, Wis., Aug. 15, 1940; d. Lowell Angus and Dorothy (Naylor) Woodbury. BS with honors in Genetics and Stats., U. Utah, 1962, MS in Genetics and Stats., 1964, PhD in Genetics, 1972; postgrad., U. Hawaii, 1966, Oreg. State U., 1968-69. Instr. Galludet Coll. for Deaf, Washington, 1965-66, Bangkok Internat. Sch., 1966-69; dir. Rock Mountain States Cancer Registry U. Utah, 1971-72, rsch. assoc., 1972-73; asst. prof. U. Tenn., Knoxville, 1973-79, mem. genetics com., 1973—, assoc. prof., 1979-84, leadership rev. com., 1980-81, botany devel. com., 1982-83, assoc. head dept. botany, faculty adv. com. to Biology Bus. Office, 1984-85, prof., 1984—, vice-provost for rsch., 1985-86, search com., 1985-87, head dept. biology, mem. biology consortium, natural scis. divisional com., 1985—, dir. info. and devel. svc. Office of Rsch., 1986, devel. com., 1986-88, liberal arts budget com., 1988-89; assoc. dir. genetic biology NSF, 1980-81, panel mem. small bus. innovations program and devel. biology, 1984; mem. adv. bd. Selby Bot. Gardens, E. Young Micropropagation Ctr., 1982-84; sec. USDA Regional Project Cellular and Molecular Genetics for Crop Improvement, 1983, pres.-elect 1983-84, pres. 1984-85; panel mem. for plant growth and devel. USDA Competitive Grants, 1985, 86, 87; mem. plant physiology/pathology rev. team Clemson U., 1985; chair Tenn. Symposia on Plant Cell and Tissue Culture, 1978, 80, 84; co-chair symposium and workshop on plant cell and tissue culture, Peshawar, Pakistan, 1988; speaker various profl. and ednl. orgns. Editor tobacco issue: Plant Molecular Biology Newsletter; reviewing editor: In Vitro, 1983-86, Plant Growth Regulator Soc., 1985-88; cons. editor Plant Cell Tissue and Organ Culture; contbr. numerous articles to profl. and scholarly jours.; presenter numerous sci. papers to symposia and other groups. Competitive grantee USDA, 1979-82, 82-83, 84-86; grantee NSF, 1980-81, 84, 84-85, 86, U.S. Dept. of Energy, 1984-85, U.S. Forest Svc., 1984-85, Martin Marietta, 1984-87, Rockefeller Found. Biotech., 1989-90, Glockner Found., 1990—. Mem. AAAS, Tissue Culture Assn. (sec. plant div. 1978-80, exec. bd. 1980-82, v.p. plant div. 1980-82, coun. mem. 1980-84, pres. plant div. 1982-84, chair and speaker workshop on transformation of higher plants), Internat. Plant Tissue Culture Assn. Office: U Tenn Dept of Botany Knoxville TN 37996-1100

HUGHES, L. JANE, insurance company official; b. Oklahoma City, Aug. 14, 1950; d. George William and E. Doral (Stone) Hopper; divorced; 1 child, Cyndee Jayne. BS, U. Okla., 1972. CPCU; AIC. Tchr. Moore (Okla.) Pub. Schs., 1972-77; substitute tchr. various sch. dists., Denver, 1977-79; field rep. Equifax Svcs., Denver, 1980-82; claims adjuster SAFECO Ins. Co., Denver, 1982-86, claims supr., 1986-88, claims analyst, 1988—. Mem. Nat. Assn. Ins. Women, Soc. CPCU. Democrat. Methodist. Office: SAFECO Ins Co 12499 W Colfax St Lakewood CO 80219

HUGHES, LINDA J., newspaper editor; b. Princeton, B.C., Can., Sept. 27, 1950; d. Edward Rees and Madge Preston (Bryan) H.; m. George Ward, Dec. 16, 1978; children: Sean Edward, Katherine Ruth. BA, U. Victoria, 1972. Reporter, legis. bur. chief Victoria (B.C.) Times, 1972-76; with Edmonton (Alta., Can.) Jour., 1976—, from reporter to asst. mng. editor, 1987—. Southam fellow U. Toronto, Ont., Can., 1977-78. Office: Edmonton Jour, 10006 101st St Box 2421, Edmonton, AB Canada T5J 2S6*

HUGHES, MARCIA ANNE, communications specialist; b. Omaha, Mar. 1, 1962; d. Thomas Charles and Janet Lee (Steuerwald) Matt; m. Scot Andrew Hughes, Oct. 22, 1988; 1 child, Katharine LeeAnne. AA in Journalism, Des Moines Area Community Coll, 1982; BS in English/Journalism, Northwest Mo. State U., 1984. Reporter, editor Boone (Iowa) News-Republican Newspaper, 1980-84; youth employment counselor Community Svcs. Inc., Maryville, Mo., 1984; editor Materials Performance Jour. Nat. Assn. Corrosion Engrs., Houston, 1985-86; dir. pub. info. Indian Hills Community Coll., Ottumwa, Iowa, 1986-88; communications specialist SMMPA, Rochester, 1988—. Editor Sigma Alpha Iota internat. music fraternity, 1982-84. Dir. women's housing Indian Hills Community Coll., 1987-88, exec. coun., mgmt. coun., affirmative action adv. com., fund raising coordination com., fringe benefits com., 1986-88; sec. bd. dirs. Ottumwa (Iowa) Community Players, Inc., 1987-88; pub. rels. advisor bd. dirs. Iowa Jr. Miss. Assn., Ottumwa, 1987-88; youth advisor St. Elizabeth Ann Seton Cath. Ch., Houston, 1985; talent div. coord., promotions chmn. Boone County Jr. Miss Pageant, Boone, Iowa, 1981-83. Named one of Outstanding Young Women Am., 1987; recipient Nat. Stephen Bufton Meml. Edn. award Am. Bus. Women's Assn., 1982-83, 83-84, E. Sherrille Brown award Des Moines Area Community Coll., 1982; Dawson scholar Northwest Mo. State U., 1983-84, Gilbert Whitney Madralier scholar Northwest Mo. State U., 1983-84. Mem. Northwest Mo. State U. Alumni Assn., Des Moines Area Community Coll. Alumni Assn., Phi Theta Kappa. Roman Catholic. Office: SMMPA 500 1st Ave SW Rochester MN 55902

HUGHES, MARIE SHARON, marketing professional; b. Balt., May 20, 1955; d. Edward Conlan and Mary Genevieve (Deinlein) H. BA, Towson State U., 1977; MBA, George Washington U., 1978. Mktg. mgr. Tower Fed. Credit Union, Ft. Meade, Md., 1979—; mem., dir. Balt. Credit Union Mktg. Co-op., 1987—, Capitol Mktg. Group, Washington, 1986—. Recipient Golden Mirror award Credit Union Execs. Soc., 1979-88, Trailblazer award Md. Credit Union League, 1986-90. Mem. Am. Mktg. Assn. (v.p. communications 1986-87, bd. dirs. 1987-88, v.p., sec. 1988-89, pres. elect 1989-90, pres. 1990-91), Fin. Mktg. Assn. (charter), Women in Advt. and Mktg., Beta Gamma Sigma. Democrat. Roman Catholic. Home: 8420 Each Leaf Ct Columbia MD 21045 Office: Tower Fed Credit Union Box 123 Annapolis Junction MD 20701

HUGHES, MARY ELIZABETH, interior designer; b. Charleston, W.Va., Sept. 7, 1940; d. Denver Lewis and Ida Frances (Fink) Morgan; m. George Charles Hughes, June 27, 1964; children: George Charles IV, Justin Morgan, Mary Frederick. Student, Randolph-Macon Woman's Coll., 1958-60; BS, W.Va. U., 1963; AAS, Art Inst. Pitts., 1981. Cert. secondary edn., interior design. French tchr. Kanawha County Schs., Charleston, W.Va., 1963-64, Marshall County Schs., Moundsville, W.Va., 1964-70; sr. designer Boury, Inc. Contract Design, Wheeling, W.Va., 1985-87; head designer Stone and Thomas Design Studio, Wheeling, 1987-88; dir. archtl. design Boury, Inc. Contract Design, Wheeling, 1988—; owner Hughes/Design, Glen Dale, W.Va., 1981—; guest lectr. history of furniture Art Inst. Pitts., 1990. Designer Jonathan's Seafood Restaurant, Rochester, N.Y., 1986-87, Sheraton Inn South, Pitts., 1986-87, Elby's Restaurants, Ohio, Pa., W.Va., 1985-88, Shoney's Restaurants, Columbus, Ohio, 1989—. Mem. Hist. Landmarks Commn., Marshall County, W.Va., 1986—; interior furnishings com. W.Va. Gov.'s Mansion, Charleston, 1986-89; bd. dirs. W.Va. Mansion Preservation Found., Charleston, 1989—; bd. dirs., past pres. No. Panhandle Behavioral Health Ctr., W.Va., 1981—; bd. dirs. ARC, Ohio Valley chpt., 1987—; stewardship commn. Episcopal Diocese of W.Va., Charleston, 1988—; mem. Jr. League Wheeling, pres. 1976-78; treas. Episcoopal Churchwomen W.Va., 1976-78. Named Interior Design Alumni of Yr. Art Inst. Pitts., 1990. Mem. Am. Soc. Interior Designers (profl.), Inst. Bus. Designers, Chi Omega, Kappa Delta Pi, Alpha Delta Kappa. Republican. Home: 509 Wheeling Ave Glen Dale WV 26038 Office: Hughes Design 509 A Wheeling Ave Glen Dale WV 26038

HUGHES, PAULA GUILFOYLE, academic administrator; b. Houston, Feb. 14, 1955; d. Guy Millard and Gloria (Rast) Guilfoyle; m. Dennis Craig Hughes, May 7, 1977; children: Eric, Andy and Alissa (twins), Samuel. B in Bus. Adminstrn., Tex. A&M U., 1976. Pers. coord. Diagnostic Ctr. Hosp., Houston, 1976-77; asst. dir. pers. svcs. Beaver County Hosp. Dist., San Antonio, Tex., 1978-80; prin. Paula Hughes and Assocs., Houston, 1984-86; placement dir. Tex. Sch. Bus., Houston, 1986-87; adminstrv. dir. Bish Mathis

INst., Tyler (Tex.) Comml. Coll., 1987. Mem. Tex. Assn. Pvt. Schs., East Tex. Pers. Assn., Assn. of Former Students Tex. A&M, Tyler C. of C. (edn. com.), Tyler Toastmasters Internat. Republican. Mem. Ch. of God. Internat. Office: Bish Mathis Institute 3111 WNW Loop 323 Tyler TX 75702

HUGHES, SUE MARGARET, librarian; b. Cleburne, Tex., Apr. ; d. Chastain Wesley and Sue Willis (Payne) H. BBA, U. Tex., Austin, 1949; MLS, Tex. Woman's U., 1960, PhD, 1987. Sec.-treas. pvt. corps. Waco, Tex., 1949-59; asst. in public services Baylor U. Library, Waco, 1960-64; acquisitions librarian Baylor U. Library, 1964-79, acting univ. librarian, summer 1979, 87—, dir. Moody Library, 1980—, and acting univ. librarian, 1989—. Mem. AAUP, ALA, Southwestern Library Assn., Tex. Library Assn., AAUW, Delta Kappa Gamma, Beta Phi Mu, Beta Gamma Sigma. Methodist. Club: Altrusa. Office: Baylor U Box 7148 Waco TX 76798

HUGHES, WAUNELL MCDONALD (MRS. DELBERT E. HUGHES), retired psychiatrist; b. Tyler, Tex., Feb. 6, 1928; d. Conrad Claiborne and Bernice Oletha (Smith) McDonald; B.A., U. Tex. at Austin, 1946; M.D., Baylor U., 1951; m. Delbert Eugene Hughes, Aug. 14, 1948; children—Lark, Mark, Lynn, Michael. Intern VA Hosp., Houston, 1951-52; resident Parkland Hosp., Dallas, 1964-67; practiced gen. medicine in Tyler, Tex., 1952-64; acting chief psychiatry service VA Hosp., Dallas, 1967-68, asst. chief, 1968-73, chief Mental Hygiene Clinic and Day Treatment Center, 1973-82, unit chief acute inpatient psychiatry Med. Center, 1982-88; clin. instr. psychiatry Southwestern Med. Sch., U. Tex. Health Sci. Center, Dallas, 1968-88 . Chmn. pre-sch. vision and hearing program Pilot Club, Tyler, 1960-64. Mem. Am. Med. Women's Assn. (pres. Dallas 1980-81), Am. Psychiat. Assn., Am. Group Psychotherapy Assn., (pres. Dallas chpt. 1984-86), North Tex. Soc. Psychiat. Physicians (co-chair MHMR pro bono clinic com. Dallas chpt. 1989—), Dallas Area Women Psychiatrists (archivist 1985—), Alpha Epsilon Iota (pres. 1950-51). Home: 3428 University Blvd Dallas TX 75205

HUGHES, YVONNE LEE, career planning administrator; b. St. Louis, Mar. 10, 1940; D. Sidney Monroe and Bessie Beatrice (Addington) B; 1child, Stephen G. Lee. BA, Harris Stowe Coll., St. Louis, 1962; postgrad., U. Mo., 1976. Elem. tchr. St. Louis Pub. Schs., 1962-75; elem. counseling Riverview Gardens Sch. Dist., St. Louis, 1975--. Mem. Panhellenic Greek Orgn., Mo. State Counselor Assn., Zeta Phi Beta Sorority. Roman Catholic. Home: 1550 Northwinds Estate Apt Saint Louis MO 63136 Office: Riverview Gardens Sch Dist 1550 Northwinds Est Apt 409 Saint Louis MO 63136

HUGHS, MARY GERALDINE, accountant, social service specialist; b. Marshalltown, Iowa, Nov. 28, 1929; d. Don Harold, Sr., and Alice Dorothy (Keister) Shaw; A.A., Highline Community Coll., 1970; B.A., U. Wash., 1972; m. Charles G. Hughs, Jan. 31, 1949; children: Mark George, Deborah Kay, Juli Ann, Grant Wesley. Asst. controller Moduline Internat., Inc., Chehalis, Wash., 1972-73; controller Data Recall Corp., El Segundo, Calif., 1973-74; fin. adminstr., acct. Saturn Mfg. Corp., Torrance, Calif., 1974-77; sr. acct., adminstrv. asst. Van Camp Ins., San Pedro, Calif., 1977-78; asst. adminstr. Harbor Regional Ctr., Torrance, Calif., 1979-87; active bookkeeping svc., 1978—; instr. math. and acctg. South Bay Bus. Coll., 1976-77. Sec. Pacific N.W. Mycol. Soc., 1966-67; treas., bd. dirs. Harbor Employees Fed. Credit Union; bd. dirs. chair svcs. for developmentally disabled of Long Beach, Inc.; mem. YMCA Club. Recipient award Am. Mgmt. Assn., 1979. Mem. Beta Alpha. Republican. Methodist. Author: Iowa Auto Dealers Assn. Title System, 1955; Harbor Regional Center Affirmative Action Plan, 1980; Harbor Regional Center - Financial Format, 1978—; Provider Audit System, 1979; Handling Client Funds, 1983. Home and Office: 18405 Haas Ave Torrance CA 90504

HUKILL, BETH ANN, systems analyst; b. Lansing, Mich., June 6, 1962; d. James Ronald and Joan Mary (Premo) Ackley; m. Brook Robert Hukill, June 15, 1985. BBA in Mgmt., Iowa State U., 1985. Staff cons. Price Waterhouse, Washington, 1985-86; systems analyst JTEK Mgmt. Cons. Inc., Ft. Wayne, Ind., 1986—. Mem. Assn. Systems Mgmt. (prs. Ft. Wayne chpt. 1989-90, outstanding chpt. svc. award 1989). Republican. Roman Catholic. Office: JTEK Mgmt Cons Inc 10427 Leo Rd Ste 103 Fort Wayne IN 46845

HULBERT, MARY FRANCES, radiology technologist; b. Moultrie, Ga., May 18, 1942; d. John David and Lena Mae (Lanier) Herndon; m. Robert Alan Hubert, May 9, 1940. Cert., Sch. Radiologic Tech., Atlanta, 1962, Broome Community Coll., Binghamton, N.Y., 1970; student, SUNY, Binghamton, 1975; cert., Cath. Hosp. Assn., St. Louis, 1977. Registered radiol. technologist, Fla. Staff technologist Laurens County Hosp., Dublin, Ga., 1962; staff technologist Ideal Hosp., Endicott, N.Y., 1963-65, asst. chief technologist, 1965-74; radiology adminstr. Lourdes Hosp., Binghamton, 1974-80; chief technologist Tallahassee (Fla.) Meml. Regional Med. Ctr., 1980, dir. radiology, 1980—; instr. Broome Community Coll., Binghamton, 1965-68, adv. mem. radiology program, 1974-80; instr. CPR Am. Heart Assn., Binghamton, 1976-77; adv. mem. Tallahassee Community Coll., 1980-86; advisor Thomas Tech. Vocat., 1988—. Mem. Am. Soc. Radiologic Technologists, Fla. Soc. Radiologic Technologists, Big Bend Radiol. Soc., Triple Cities Radiologic Soc. (life), Toastmasters Internat. Democrat. Baptist. Office: Tallahassee Meml Regional 1300 Miccosukee Rd Tallahassee FL 32308

HULING, KENDALL FAYE, media consultant; b. Lynwood, Calif., Nov. 6, 1965; d. Gary Paul and Dulcilee (Danielson) H. AA, Columbia Basin Coll., Pasco, Wash., 1985; BA in History, Whitman Coll., 1987. Sales rep. KONA Radio, Pasco, 1989; media cons. KORD Radio, Pasco, 1989—. Coach youth basketball program Bethlehem Luth. Sch., Kennewick, Wash., 1983-90; active Columbia Basin Coll. Alumni Found., 1990—. Mem. Women in Communications, Products Indsl. Expn. Home: 1606 S Quincy Pl Kennewick WA 99337 Office: KORD Radio 2621 W A St Pasco WA 99301

HULIN-SALKIN, BELINDA, writer; b. Lafayette, La., July 3, 1954; d. Adam Joseph and Audrey Mae (Breaux) Hulin; m. Richard Alan Salkin, Nov. 24, 1979. BA in Communications, Loyola U., New Orleans, 1975; MS in Urban Studies, U. New Orleans, 1983. Reporter, producer Sta. WYLD Radio News, New Orleans, 1975; entertainment editor Monroe (La.) Morning World, 1975-77; pub. info. dir. Mental Health Assn., New Orleans, 1978-79; asst. editor Focus mag., Phila., 1980-82; freelance writer Collingswood, N.J., 1982—; contbr. Money mag., N.Y.C., 1982—, Advt. Ag., Chgo., 1983—, Jewish Exponent, Phila., 1986—, Incentive Mktg. mag., N.Y.C., 1986—, Mtgs. and Convs. mag., Secaucus, N.J., 1986—; contbg. editor N.J. Mo., Morristown, 1987—, Continental mag., Austin, Tex., 1987—, Cosmopolitan mag., N.Y.C., 1988—, Applause mag., Phila., 1988—. Editor: Home Improvement Workbook, 1979, Springhouse Report newsletter, 1985; contbg. editor Phila. mag., 1986—. Counselor Crisis Line, New Orleans, 1979. Mem. Phila. Writers Orgn., Am. Soc. Journalists and Authors, Women's Equity Action League. Democrat. Home: 100 Woodlawn Ave Collingswood NJ 08108

HULKA, BARBARA SORENSON, epidemiology educator; b. Mpls., Mar. 1, 1931; d. Herbert Fritchof and Mable (Alquist) Sorenson; m. Jaroslav Fabian Hulka, Nov. 13, 1954; children: Carol Ann, Gregory Fabian, Bryan Herbert. BS, Radcliffe Coll., 1952; MS, Juilliard Sch. Music, 1954; MD, Columbia U., 1959, MPH, 1961. Diplomate: Am. Bd. Preventive Medicine; Lic. physician, Pa., N.C. Research asst. prof. U. Pitts., 1966-67; asst. prof. U. N.C., Chapel Hill, 1967-71, assoc. prof., 1972-76, prof., 1977—, chmn. dept. epidemiology, 1983—, Kenan prof., 1987—; adj. prof. medicine Duke U. Med. Ctr., Durham, N.C., 1982—; chmn. epidemiology and disease study sect. NIH, 1979-83; bd. sci. counselors Nat. Cancer Inst., 1980—; mem. Inst. of Medicine com. toxic shock syndrome Nat. Acad. Sci., 1981-82; mem. Sci. Rev. and Evaluation Bd. subcom. VA, 1983—; mem. subcom. on long-term effects of short-term exposure to chem. agts. Nat. Acad. Scis., 1985—; mem. preventive medicine and pub. health test com. Nat. Bd. Med. Examiners, 1985—; mem. consensus conf. on smokeless tobacco Nat. Cancer Inst. Panel, 1986. Mem. editorial bd. Postgrad. Medicine, 1985—; contbr. articles to profl. jours., chpts. to books. Health Resources Administrn. grantee, 1975-77; tng. grantee in cancer epidemiology Nat. Cancer Inst., 1980—; prostate cancer grantee Nat. Cancer Inst., 1983-85; travel study fellow WHO, 1978. Mem. Soc. Epidemiol. Research (pres. 1975-76, exec. com. 1973-77), Am. Pub. Health Assn. (governing council 1976-78, chmn. epidemiol. sect. 1976-77), Am. Epidemiol. Soc., N.C. Pub. Health Assn. (award for excellence, stats. and epidemiology sect. 1975), Am. Coll. Preventive Medicine (bd. regents 1986), Nat. Acad. Scis. (com. on passive smoking 1985—), Inst. of Medicine, Delta Omega. Home: 2317 Honeysuckle Dr Chapel Hill NC 27514 Office: U NC Sch Pub Health Rosenau Hall CB#7400 Chapel Hill NC 27599

HULL, ELAINE MANGELSDORF, psychology educator; b. Houston, Aug. 15, 1940; d. Paul August and Mary Eleanor (Stephens) Mangelsdorf; m. Richard Thompson Hull, May 30, 1962; 1 child, Geoffrey Alaric (dec.). BA, Austin Coll., Sherman, Tex., 1963; PhD, Ind. U., 1967. Asst. prof. psychology SUNY, Buffalo, 1967-73, assoc. prof., 1973-86, prof., 1986—, dir. biopsychology grad. program, 1986—. Author: Study Guide to Accompany Kalat's Biological Psychology, 1988; contbr. articles to sci. jours. Recipient Chancellor's award for excellence in teaching SUNY, Buffalo, 1975, award for teaching SUNY Students Assn., 1986. Mem. Soc. for Neurosci., Internat. Soc. for Psychoneuroendocrinology, AAAS, Ea. Psychol. Assn., N.Y. Acad. Scis. Democrat. Home: 51 Pryor Ave Tonawanda NY 14150 Office: SUNY Park Hall Buffalo NY 14260

HULL, ELIZABETH ANNE, English professor; b. Upper Darby, Pa., Jan. 10, 1937; d. Frederick Bossart and Elizabeth (Schmick) H.; m. Dean Carlyle Beery, Feb. 5, 1955 (div. 1962); children: Catherine Doria Beery Pizarro, Barbara Phyllis Beery Wintczak; m. Frederik Pohl, July 1984. Student, Ill. State U., 1954-55; AA, Wilbur Wright Jr. Coll., Chgo., 1965; B in Philosophy, Northwestern U., 1968; MA, Loyola U., Chgo., 1970, PhD, 1975. Teaching asst. Loyola U., Chgo., 1968-71; prof. English, coord. honors program William Rainey Harper Coll., Palatine, Ill., 1971—; judge nat. writing competition Nat. Coun. Tchrs. of English, 1975—. Co-editor: (with F. Pohl) Tales from the Planet Earth; contbr. articles to profl. jours. Pres. Lexington Green Condominium Assn., Schaumburg, Ill., 1982-84; bd. dirs. Hunting Ridge Homeowner's Assn., Palatine, 1984-86. Mem. MLA, Midwest MLA, Popular Culture Assn., Sci. Fiction Rsch. Assn. (editor 1981-84, sec. 1987-88, pres. 1989—), Ill. Coll. English Assn. (pres. Chgo. chpt. 1975-77), World Sci. Fiction Assn. (N.Am. sec. 1978—). Democrat. Home: 855 S Harvard Dr Palatine IL 60067 Office: William Rainey Harper Coll 1200 Algonquin Rd Palatine IL 60067

HULL, JANE LAUREL LEEK, nurse, administrator; b. Ontario, Calif., July 4, 1923; d. William Abram and Susan Bianca (Pethick) Leek; R.N., Columbia Presbyn. Sch. Nursing, 1944; B.A., Redlands U., 1977; ; m. James B. Hull, Oct. 10, 1944 (dec.); children—James W., William P., Kenneth D. Supr. obstetrics Sch. Nursing, Mid-Valley Hosp., Peckville, Pa., 1945-46; surg. nurse acute nursing Scranton (Pa.) State Hosp., 1947-52; nurse San Antonio Community Hosp., Upland, Calif., 1953-55; office nurse H.L. Archibald, Upland, 1965; vis. nurse Pomona West End Inc., continuity of care coordinator, Montclair, Calif., 1968-73, exec. dir., 1973—; tchr. ARC nursing course to high sch. students. Recipient Woman Achiever award, Pomona Valley, 1983, Excellence in Edn. award Nat. Assn. Home Care, 1988. Treas. PTA, Pomona, Calif.; vol. exec. dir. Inland Hospice Assn., 1979-80, accreditation commn., 1988-89. Nat. Found. for Hospice/Home Care, 1988. Mem. Calif. Nurses Assn. (pres. dist. 53 1958), Calif. Assn. for Health Services at Home (dir.), Calif. League Nursing, Nat. Homecaring Council (dir.). Republican. Club: Zonta (Ontario, Upland, pres., 1976). Organizer Homemaker Dept. in Vis. Nurse Assn., 1972; developer (with Don Baxter Corp.) plugs for in-dwelling Foley catheters, 1963. Home: 543 W F St Ontario CA 91762 Office: 170 W San Jose Claremont CA 91711

HULL, KATHRYN BLOMQUIST, music teacher, arts consultant; b. Sanders, Idaho, June 14, 1928; d. Willett S. and Ruby V. (Simons) Blomquist; m. Robert M., Apr. 28, 1957 (div. 1990); children: Laurice, Craig, Eric. BA, Pasadena Coll., 1949. Piano Tchr. Ind. music tchr., composer Glendale, Calif., 1949—; supr. of office svcs. Stanford Rsch. Inst., Palo Alto & L.A., 1951-57; statis. analyst Pacific Fin., L.A., 1957-59; music tchr. Mt. Olive Christian Elem. Sch., La Crescenta, Calif., 1971-73; mng. dir. Guild Opera Co., Hollywood, Calif., 1985-87; exec. dir. Glendale Regional Arts Council, Calif., 1982-90; pub. Delos Publs., Verdugo City, Calif., 1984—; cons. For the Arts, Glendale, Calif., 1986—; chief devel. officer ArtScope, Palm Desert, Calif., 1987—; tchr. music theory Coll. of Desert, Palm Desert, 1990—; bd. dirs. Glendale Chamber Orch., 1983-89, Glendale Youth Orch., 1989-90. Contbr. articles to profl. jours. Fine Arts Task Force Glendale Unified Sch. Dist., 1983; bd. dirs. Pasadena Boys Choir, 1982—. Recipient Hon. Svc. award Calif. Congress of Parents & Tchrs., 1977, Svc. to the Arts award Glendale Reg. Arts Coun., 1979; Dedication of Symphony No. 1 Brooke Halpin, Pasadena, 1982. Mem. AAUW, Assocs. of Brand Library and Art Ctr., Music Tchrs. Nat. Assn. (bd. dirs. Cin. 1983), Glendales C. of C. (amb. 1978-90), Calif. Assn. Profl. Music Tchrs. (bd. dirs. 1968—), Bus. and Profl. Women's Club. Republican. Presbyterian. Home and Office: PO Box 947 La Quinta CA 92253

HULL, LOUISE KNOX, retired elementary educator, administrator; b. Springfield, Mo., May 24, 1912; d. William E. and Ruby Joe (Bradshaw) K.; m. Berrien J. Hull, Jan. 1, 1953. B.S. in Edn., Southwest Mo. State U., 1933; postgrad. Colo. U., 1939, Northwestern U., 1945; M.A., NYU, 1952. Cert. elem. and secondary tchr., Mo. Elem. tchr. R12 Sch. Dist., Springfield, 1936-70, supr. tchr., 1956-70, mem. adv. com. to supt., 1955-57. Chmn. Christian edn. com. Westminster Presbyn. Ch., 1953-66, trustee, 1983-86, chmn. bd. trustees, 1986, circle chair, 1986-89, mem. women's adv. bd., 1987-89; pres. Women of Ch., 1970-73, pres. bd. trustees, 1983—; life mem. Wilson Creek Found., Springfield, 1954-67; sec. Greene County Hist. Soc., Springfield, 1960—; mem. Springfield Little Theater Guild, 1970—, Hist. Preservation Soc., Springfield, 1980—; docent Mus. Ozarks, Springfield, 1976-85; chmn. dist. III, John Calvin Presbterial, 1974-76, sec., 1977-80. Mem. Springfield Retired Tchrs. Assn. (life), Ozarks Genealogy Soc (sec. 1985-87, pub. info. rep. 1987-89), DAR (Rachel Donelson chpt.), Mo. Fedn. Women's Clubs (chmn. home life com. 1986-89), Alpha Delta Pi (treas. house corp. 1932-60), Alpha Delta Kappa (sec. 1965-67). Club: Sorosis (Springfield) (pres. 1980-82, chmn. hobby dept. 1986-88, chmn. fine arts dept. 1988-90).

HULL, MARGARET RUTH, artist, educator, consultant; b. Dallas, Mar. 27, 1921; d. William Haynes and Ora Carroll (Adams) Leatherwood; m. LeRos Ennis Hull, Mar. 29, 1941; children: LeRos Ennis, Jr., James Daniel. BA, So. Meth. U., Dallas, 1952, postgrad., 1960-61; MA, North Tex. State U., 1957, postgrad. R.I. Sch. Design, 1982. Art instr. W.W. Bushman Sch., Dallas Ind. Sch. Dist., 1952-57, Benjamin Franklin Jr. High Sch., Dallas, 1957-58; art instr. Hillcrest High Sch., Dallas, 1958-61, dean, pupil personnel counselor, 1961-70; tchr. children's painting Dallas Mus. Fine Art, 1956-70; designer, coordinator visual art careers cluster Skyline High Sch., Dallas, 1970-71, Skyline Career Devel. Ctr., Dallas, 1971-76, Booker T. Washington Arts Magnet High Sch., Dallas, 1976-82; developer curriculum devel./writing art, 1971-82; artist, ednl. cons., 1982—; mus. reprodns. asst. Dallas Mus. Art, 1984—. Group shows include Dallas Mus. Fine Arts, 1958, Arts Magnet Faculty Shows, 1978-82, Arts Magnet High Sch., Dallas Art Edn. Assn. Show, 1981, D'Art Membership Show, Dallas, 1982-83; represented in pvt. collections. Trustee Dallas Mus. Art, 1978-84. Mem. Tex. Designer/Craftsmen, Craft Guild Dallas, Fiber Artists Dallas, Dallas Art Edn. Assn., Tex. Art Edn. Assn., Nat. Art Edn. Assn., Dallas Counselors Assn. (pres. 1968), Delta Delta Delta.

HULL, NICOLE KAROL, marketing professional; b. Hampton, Va., Feb. 7, 1964; d. Philip Henry and Karol (Willis) H. BA in English, Va. Polytechnic Inst., 1988. Profl. clotheir John Norman, Inc., Blacksburg, Va., 1985-86, 87-88; asst. sr. product mgr. Entre Computer Ctrs., Inc., Vienna, Va., 1986, contracts negotiator/software buyer, 1986-87; product mktg. mgr. Govt. Tech. Svcs., Inc., Chantilly, Va., 1988—. Author product guide bulletins, pamphlets, 1986. Mem. Disaster Team Am. Red Cross, Fairfax, Va., 1986—; instr. CPR, first aid, Fairfax, 1986—; mem. First Aid Corps, 1986—, Easter Seals, Blacksburg, 1984, 86. Mem. NAFE, Nat. Parks and Conservation Assn., World Wildlife Assn. Jewish. Home: 12939C Grays Pointe Rd Fairfax VA 22033-2136 Office: Govt Tech Svcs Inc 4100 Lafayette Center Dr Chantilly VA 22021

HULL, RITA PRIZLER, accounting educator; b. Lone Tree, Iowa, Mar. 29, 1936; d. Ernest Ralph and Mildred Lennis (Huskins) Prizler; m. J.W. Hull, May 29, 1954 (div. 1963); children: Mark, Marshall; m. John O. Everett, Sept. 1, 1976. BA in Acctg., Augustana Coll., Rock Island, Ill., 1967; MA in Acctg., Western Ill. U., 1973; PhD in Bus. Adminstrn., Okla. State U., 1978. CPA, Ill.; cert. internal auditor, Ill. Auditor Price Waterhouse & Co., Chgo., 1967-70; asst. prof. acctg. Bowling Green (Ohio) State U., 1976-78; assoc. prof. No. Ill. U., DeKalb, 1978-82; prof. Va. Commonwealth U., Richmond, 1982—. Contbr. articles, papers to profl. publs. Mem. Am. Soc. Women Accts. (treas. Richmond chpt. 1986-87, sec. 1987-88, pres. 1988-90), Am. Acctg. Assn. (acctg. educator award com. 1988-90, Trueblood Seminars com. 1987-88), AICPA, Inst. Internal Auditors, Acad. Acctg. Historians, NOW (treas. Richmond chpt. 1987-89). Democrat. Home: 810 Keats Rd Richmond VA 23229 Office: Va Commonwealth U Box 4000 1015 Floyd Ave Richmond VA 23284

HULL, SUZANNE WHITE, retired cultural institution administrator, writer; b. Orange, N.J., Aug. 24, 1921; d. Gordon Stowe and Lillian (Siegling) White; m. George I. Hull, Feb. 20, 1943 (dec. Mar. 1990); children: George Gordon, James Rutledge, Anne Elizabeth. B.A. with honors, Swarthmore Coll., 1943; M.S. in L.S., U. So. Calif., 1967. Mem. staff Huntington Libr., Art Gallery and Bot. Gardens, San Marino, Calif., 1969-86, dir. adminstrn. and pub. svcs., 1972-86, also prin. officer. Author: Chaste, Silent and Obedient, English Books for Women, 1475-1640, 1982, 88; editor: State of the Art in Women's Studies, 1986. Charter pres. Portola Jr. High Sch. PTA, L.A., 1960-62; pres. Children's Service League, 1963-64, YWCA L.A., 1967-69; mem. alumni council Swarthmore Coll., 1959-62, 83-86, mem.-at-large, 1986-89; mem. adv. bd. Hagley Mus. and Libr., Wilmington, Del., 1983-86, Betty Friedan Think Tank, U. So. Calif., 1985—; hon. life mem. Calif. Congress Parents and Tchrs.; bd. dirs. Pasadena Planned Parenthood Assn., 1978-83, mem. adv. com., 1983—; founder-chmn. Swarthmore-L.A. Connection, 1984-85, bd. dirs., 1985—; founder Huntington Women's Studies Seminar, 1984, mem. steering com. 1984—; bd. dirs. Pasadena Girls Club, 1988—,. Mem. Monumental Brass Soc. (U.K.), Renaissance Soc., Brit. Studies, Conf., Western Assn. Women Historians, Beta Phi Mu (chpt. dir. 1981-84). Home: 1465 El Mirador Dr Pasadena CA 91103 Office: 1151 Oxford Rd San Marino CA 91108

HULME, DARLYS MAE, banker; b. Buckingham, Iowa, Apr. 2, 1937; d. Leland James and Dorothy Mae (Nation) Philp; m. Harlan Dale Hulme, Dec. 4, 1955 (div. Nov. 1971); children: Debra Jean Hulme Hanneman, Richard Dale. Student Iowa Sch. Banking, 1974, Sch. Bank Adminstrn. U. Wis.-Madison, 1982. Bookkeeper, Farmers Savs. Bank, Traer, Iowa, 1953-55, asst. cashier, 1962-72, v.p., 1973-83, sr. v.p., 1983—, also sec. bd. dirs.; acct. North Tama Housing, Inc., Traer, 1974—; sec. to bd. Talen, Inc., Talen Aviation, Ltd., Traer, Farmers Savs. Bank Trust, Vinton, Iowa, 1988—, also sec. to bd.; dir., sec. to bd. Sunrise Hill Care Ctr., Traer; mem. Iowa State Banking Bd., 1985—. Mem. Nat. Assn. Bank Women (group treas. 1980-81, group v.p. 1981-82, group pres. 1982-83, state membership chair 1983-84, regional membership chair 1984-85), Iowa Bankers Assn. (mem. edn. com. 1985-86). Republican. Methodist. Club: PEO (Traer) (corr. sec. 1988). Avocations: gardening, traveling. Home: 701 S Main St Traer IA 50675 Office: Farmers Savs Bank 611 2d St Traer IA 50675

HULNICK, MARY R., university official, psychologist; b. July 1, 1944; m. Herbert Ronald Hulnick. AA, Kendall Coll., Evanston, Ill.; BA, Morningside Coll., 1966; MS, Iowa State U., 1968, PhD, 1971. Lic. psychologist, marriage, family and child counselor, Calif. Counselor Ballard Jr. High Sch., Huxley, Iowa, 1968-69; asst. prof. dept. counseling, counseling psychologist U. Idaho, Moscow, 1971-74; assoc. prof. N.Mex. State U., Las Cruces, 1974-79; co-dir. Effective Living Seminars, Las Cruces, 1979-81; pvt. practice, Los Cruces, Santa Monica, 1975—; acad. v.p. U. Santa Monica, 1981—; dir. psychol. svcs. Baraka Holistic Ctr., Santa Monica, 1982-84. Co-author: Fiscal Fitness: Financial Freedom in 8 Minutes a Day.; contbr. articles to profl. jours. Recipient award Am. Pers. Guidance Assn.; rsch. fellow Iowa State U., 1969-71; grantee N.Mex. State U., 1977. Mem. Am. Psychol. Assn., Assn. Counseling and Devel., Am. Assn. Marriage and Family Therapists (clin.), Assn. Transpersonal Psychology, Assn. Humanistic Psychology, Psi Chi, Sigma Tau Delta. Home: 1680 Michael Ln Pacific Palisades CA 90272 Office: U Santa Monica 2107 Wilshire Blvd Santa Monica CA 90403

HULSEY, TAMMY KAYE, accountant; b. Gainesville, Ga., Apr. 18, 1961; d. Robert Richard and Patricia Anne (Burnett) Hulsey. AS, Gainesville (Ga.) Jr. Coll., 1981; BBA, North Ga. Coll., 1983. Cashier A & P Grocery, Gainesville, Ga., 1977-83; med. transcriber N.E. Ga. Med. Ctr., Gainesville, 1983-86; jr. acct. Mitsubishi Cons. Elec. Am., Braselton, Ga., 1986—. Mem. Phi Theta Kappa, Phi Kappa Phi. Home: 7 H Ave (Chicopee) Gainesville GA 30504 Office: Mitsubishi Consumer Elec Am PO Box 299 Braselton GA 30517

HULT, KAREN MARIE, political science educator; b. Gary, Ind., Apr. 26, 1956; d. Robert Julius and Rita Ann (Mayer) H. BA, Creighton U., 1978; postgrad., Harvard U., 1979; PhD, U. Minn., 1984. Asst. prof. govt. Pomona Coll., Claremont, Calif., 1984-89, assoc. prof., 1990, dir. program in pub. policy analysis, 1988-90; assoc. prof. polit. sci. Va. Poly. Inst. and State U., Blacksburg, 1990—; analyst HHS, Washington, 1982; cons. Orange County Grand Jury. Author: Agency Merger and Bureaucratic Redesign, 1987, Governing Public Organizations, 1990. Mem. Am. Polit. Sci. Assn., Midwest Polit. Sci. Assn., Western Polit. Sci. Assn., Am. Soc. for Pub. Adminstrn., LWV, AAUW (Palmer fellow 1987-88). Democrat. Roman Catholic. Office: Va Poly Inst and State U Polit Sci Dept Blacksburg VA 24061

HUMBERT, PAMELA, small business owner; b. N.Y.C., Oct. 28, 1941; d. Bernhard and Helen (Jobin) Zuckermann. BS in Psychology, Columbia U., 1965; MEd in Devel. Psychology, Tchrs. Coll., 1967, MS in Rehab. Counseling, 1969; MS in Bus. Policy, Columbia U., 1979. Lic. psychologist N.Y. Vocational counselor Greenwich House Counseling Ctr., N.Y.C., 1968-70; counselor N.Y. State Substance Abuse, N.Y.C., 1970-72; dir. Irene Byron Drug Rehab. Ctr., Ft. Wayne, Ind., 1972-73; cons. various cos., 1972-80; owner Pompeian Studios, Bronxville, N.Y., 1980—. Mem. Am. Psychol. Assn. (assoc.). Republican. Episcopalian. Club: City Island (N.Y.) Yacht. Home and Office: 90 Rockledge Rd Bronxville NY 10708

HUMFLEET, HAROLYN J., accountant; b. St. Paul, Jan. 13, 1946; d. Harold R. and F. Jean (Baird) Erickson; m. Orville D. Humfleet, July 25, 1986; children: Kayle, Kory. BS, U. N. Fla., 1985, MBA, 1986; AS, Tidewater Community Coll., 1983. CPA. Police officer City of Virginia Beach (Va.); staff act. Newman Constrn. Co., Virginia Beach; owner H&K Bookkeeping Svc., Virginia Beach; comptroller Queens Constrn. Co., Virginia Beach; sr. acct. Dayton, Piercey and Knapp CPAs, Simsbury, Conn. Mem. Nat. Assn. Accts., NAFE, Beta Gamma Sigma. Home: 15 Crestview Rd Tariffville CT 06081 Office: 53 Quarry Rd Simsbury CT 06070

HUMLICEK, EVELYN CLARICE, volunteer, retired nursing educator; b. Tamora, Nebr., Apr. 10, 1923; d. George Edward and Anna Marie (Polacek) H. BS in Nursing, Creighton U., Omaha, 1947; MS in Edn., U. Omaha, 1953; M Nursing Adminstrn., U. Minn., 1958. RN. Staff nurse St. Joseph's Hosp., Omaha, 1945-47; instr. St. Joseph's Hosp. Sch. of Nursing, Omaha, 1947-50; assoc. chief nursing edn. VA Med. Ctr., Omaha, 1950-85; mem. Nebr. Medicare Beneficiary Adv. Com., 1989—. Counselor Vol. Intervening for Equity, Omaha, 1985—, Am. Assn. Ret. Persons, Omaha, 1986—. Recipient Outstanding Career award chief med. dir. VA, Washington, 1985. Mem. Nebr. Nurses' Assn. (Profl. Achievement award dist. II 1976). Home: 4220 Spring Omaha NE 68105

HUMMEL, DANA D. MALLETT, librarian. B.A. in Art History, Smith Coll., 1957; M.A. in Library and Info. Sci., Denver U., 1968; postgrad. Def. Lang. Inst., 1961, Instituto Mexicano-Norteamericano de Relationes Culturales, 1962, John F. Kennedy Ctr. for Spl. Warfare, 1974, Nat. War Coll., 1976, No. Va. Bus. Sch., 1978, Cath. U. Am., 1981. Head librarian, adminstrn., Howard AFB Library, C.Z., 1969-70; asst. librarian Holmes Intermediate Sch., 1970-71; tchr. Spanish and substitute tchr. J.E.B. Stuart High Sch., 1972-77; sec. Office of exec. dir.-Africa The World Bank, 1978-79; personal sec. to rector Falls Ch. (Va.), 1979-81; mgr. Info. Services Ctr., BDM Internat. subs. Ford Aerospace Co., McLean, Va., 1981-88. Mem. vestry Falls Ch. Episcopal Ch., 1982; del. Republican State Conv., 1981, 86; pres. Ravenwood Civic Assn., 1979-80, 80-81, 81-82; rep. Mason Dist., Fedn. Civic Assns.; mem. ann. plan rev. task force Mason Dist., 1981-82; gov. trustee Fairfax County Pub. Libr. Bd., 1982-88; chmn. bd. trustees Fairfax County. Named Outstanding Woman of Yr., Fairfax County Bd. Suprs. &

Com. of Women, 1982. Mem. AAUP, ALA, Am. Soc. for Info. Sci., Spl. Libraries Assn., Va. Library Assn., D.C. Library Assn., Women in Def., Jr. League Sarasota, Fla. Home: 7355 Villa D'Este Dr Sarasota FL 34238

HUMMEL, MARILYN MAE, educator; b. Cleve., June 20, 1931; d. John Winfield and Meta E. (Timm) H. BS, Ohio U., 1953. Cert. elem. educator. Elem. tchr. Lakewood (Ohio) Bd. of Edn., 1953-83. Mem. Centennial Planning Com., Lakewood, Ohio 1989. Jennings scholar, 1969-70; named Tchr. of the Yr., Franklin Sch., 1983. Mem. Coll. Club West, Delta Kappa Gamma. Republican. Presbyterian.

HUMPHREY, CARLETTA SUE, fiber optics executive; b. Longmont, Colo., Dec. 4, 1954; d. Robert Edward and Shirley (Ann) H. Materials mgr. Ball Corp., Boulder, Colo., 1978-82; document control mgr. Raycom Systems, Boulder, 1983-85, purchasing agt., 1985-89; inventory mgr. Raycom Systems, 1989—; cons. City of Greeley (Colo.), 1986. Mem. Nat. Assn. Purchasing Mgmt. (Achievement award 1986). Office: Raycom Systems Inc R-6395 Gunpark Dr Boulder CO 80301

HUMPHREY, DONNA CLAIRE, teacher; b. N.Y., Dec. 25, 1962; d. Donald Julis and Emma Jean (Jackson) H. BA, Binghamton U., N.Y., 1984; MFA, Columbia U., N.Y., 1988. Cert. tchr. Asst. to dir. Alvin State Sch., N.Y., 1985--; asst. to producer Lefrak Prodn., N.Y., 1987; asst. supr. Shubert Orgn., N.Y., 1987--; tchr. Berkeley Sch., N.Y., Katherine Gibbs Sch., N.Y., 1988--. Home: 547 Riverside Dr Apt 6 D New York NY 10027

HUMPHREY, JAYNE HULBERT, government official; b. Oakland, Calif., Apr. 1, 1947; d. Jack W. and Clare Roberta (Hittle) Hulbert; m. Donald James Humphrey, Nov. 11, 1983. Student Northwestern U., 1964-66, San Francisco State U., 1969-70. With various fed. govt. agencies, Washington, 1964-67; program asst. U.S. Dept. HUD, Washington, 1968, elderly housing program technician, San Francisco, 1969-70, housing rep., coordinator, 1970-75, dir. housing devel. div., 1975-83, dep. regional housing dir., 1983-87 , mgr. Honolulu office, 1986-87, dir. housing devel. div., 1987—; pres. Hulbert Humphrey, Inc., Fairfax, Calif., 1985—; instr. Calif. Mortgage Bankers Assn., Calif. Dept. Real Estate, Sacramento, 1985—; chief negotiator, mem. mgmt. contract with union HUD, San Francisco, 1983-84; mem. rev. bd. performance standards HUD, 1986-87. Named Woman of Yr., U.S. HUD, 1985, recipient 7 outstanding performance awards, 1976-87, superior accomplishment award, 1988, Disting. Service nominee, 1979, spl. achievement award, 1972, 73, 75, Commendation 19th Guam Legislature; named hon. citizen City of Alameda, Calif., 1971. Mem. Fed. Mgrs. Assn., Nat. Soc. Female Execs., Am. Soc. Pub. Adminstrn. Democrat. Presbyterian. Club: Commonwealth. Avocations: music; computers. Office: Dept Housing and Urban Devel 450 Golden Gate Ave Box 36003 San Francisco CA 94102-3448

HUMPHREY, KAREN, mayor, media consultant; b. Cin., Sept. 27, 1945; m. Ken Clarke, Sept. 1973; 4 stepchildren. BA in Humanities, U. So. Calif., 1966. TV news field reporter, anchor, producer, 1967-79; with Sta. KFSN-TV, Fresno, Calif., 1970-79; free-lance media cons. and advisor, 1979-81; mem. planning commn. City of Fresno, 1979-81, mem. city coun., 1981-89, mayor, 1989—; mayor Calif. Commn. on Crime Control and Violence Prevention, 1981-83; mem. Fresno-Clovis Met. Solid Waste Commn., chmn., 1985—; bd. dirs. Fresno Conv. and Visitors Bur., Fresno County Econ. Devel. Corp. Mem. AFTRA, LWV, NOW, Nat. League Cities (bd. dirs. 1986-88), League Calif. Cities (numerous coms., bd. dirs. 1985-88), Women in Mcpl. Govt., Nat. Women's Polit. Caucus, Phi Beta Kappa, Phi Kappa Phi, Alpha Epsilon Rho. Office: Office of Mayor 2326 Fresno St Fresno CA 93721*

HUMPHREY, KAY LYNN, business educator; b. Russellville, Ark., May 30, 1960; d. Louie Adam and Ruth Geraldine (Waid) H. BS, Ark. Tech. U., 1981; MEd, U. Ark., 1986; EdS, U. So. Miss., 1988. Cert. tchr., Ark. Bus. instr. Rich Mountain Community Coll., Mena, Ark., 1982—. Chmn. North Cen. Accreditation Com., Mena, 1987-88, 89-90, Student Affairs Com. Rich Mountain Community Coll., 1988-90. Mem. AAUW (v.p. 1985-87, scholarship 1987), Ark. Bus. Edn. Assn. (v.p. 1985-86, Award of Merit 1981), Ark. Two-Yr. Coll. Assn. (sec. 1988-89), Extension Club (v.p. 1986-87), Delta Kappa Gamma, Delta Phi Epsilon. Democrat. Baptist. Home: 422 Mena #4 Mena AR 71953 Office: Rich Mountain Community Coll 601 Bush St Mena AR 71953

HUMPHREY, LOUISE IRELAND, civic worker, horsewoman; b. Morehead City, N.C., Nov. 1, 1918; d. R. Livingston and Margaret (Allen) Ireland; m. Gilbert W. Humphrey, Dec. 27, 1939; children:Margaret (Mrs. K. Bindhart), George M. II, Gilbert Watts; ed. pvt. schs. Mem. corp., adv. bd. Tall Timbers Rsch. Inc. Nurse's aide ARC, 1944-64; past. dir. Nat. City Bank, Cleve., Nat. City Corp., Cleve., 1981-86; trustee Mus. Arts Assn.; hon. trustee, past pres. Vis. Nurse Assn.; hon. trustee Lake Erie Coll., life trustee United Way Cleve., trustee Archbold Hosp., Thomasville, Ga.; hon. trustee Case Western Res. U.; bd. dirs. Monticello (Fla.) Opera House; mem., past trustee, 2d v.p. Jr. League Cleve.; pres. bd. dirs. Met. Opera Assn., N.Y.; bd. mem. Lincoln Ctr., N.Y.; bd. dirs. Thomas County Entertainment Found.; past pres. No. Ohio Opera Assn.; mem. adv. bd. Coll. of Veterinary Medicine Bd. U. Fla., gainseville; past mem. Ohio Arts Council, 1975-85; treas., trustee Wildlife Conservation Fund Am.; former master foxhounds Chagrin Valley Hunt, Gates Mills, Ohio; past dir., zone v.p. U.S. Equestrian Team, Inc., now hon. life dir.; mem. Garden Club Cleve.; bd. dirs., past pres. Nat. Homecaring Council; treas., bd. mem. Wildlife Legis. Fund Am.; bd. dir. Thomasville Cultural Ctr.; mem., vice chmn., commr. Fla. Game and Fresh Water Fish Commn.; mem. Jr. League, Tallahasse, Fla. Home: Woodfield Springs Plantation Miccosukee FL 32309

HUMPHREY, SHIRLEY JOY, state representative, education consultant; b. Cheyenne, Wyo., May 26, 1937; d. Verlan E. and Inez M. (Tanner) R.; m. John E. Humphrey, Aug. 9, 1959; children: Michael Scott, Marci Lynne. BS in HOme Econs., Wyo. U., 1960. High sch. tchr. dist. #2 Laramie Sch. Dist., Albin, Wyo., 1964-75; high sch. tchr. dist. #1 Laramie Sch. Dist., Cheyenne, 1975-80; coll. instr. Laramie County Community Coll., Cheyenne, 1980-85; civil rights coord. Wyo. State Dept. Edn., Cheyenne, 1987—; mem. Wyo. State Legislature, Cheyenne, 1983—; pres. Wyo. Home Econs. Tchrs., 1964-70. Bd. dirs. Laramie County Fair, Cheyenne, 1975-85; mem. Women's Civic League, Cheyenne, 1970—, Sr. Citizens Adv. Coun., Cheyenne, 1985—. Recipient Disting. Svc. award Future Homemakers Am., 1988; named Hon. State Farmer Future Farmers Am., 1982. Mem. Kappa Kappa Gamma Alumna (pres. 1974-75). Democrat. Presbyterian.

HUMPHREYS, ROBERTA MARIE, astronomer, educator; b. Indpls., May 20, 1944; d. Robert T. and Mary C. (Furnas) H.; m. Kris D. Davidson, June 10, 1976; 1 child, Rowan M.H. BA, Ind. U., 1965; MS, U. Mich., 1967, PhD, 1969. Rsch. assoc. Steward Obs. U. Ariz., Tucson, 1970-72; asst. prof. U. Minn., Mpls., 1972-76, assoc. prof., 1976-83, prof., 1986—; adv. com. NSF Astronomy Commn., Washington, 1981-84; astronomy and astrophysics survey, Nat. Acad. Scis., Washington, 1989-90. Recipient Taylor award for disting. rsch. U. Minn., 1985; named Sloan Found. Fellow, Alfred P. Sloan Found., 1976, Humboldt Disting. Sr. Scientist, Alex. Von Humboldt Found., Fed. Republic Germany, 1988. Mem. Am. Astron. Soc., Internat. Astron. Union, Astron. Soc. Pacific, AAAS, Assn. Univ. Rsch. Astronomy (bd. dirs. 1981-84), Phi Beta Kappa. Office: Dept Astronomy/Univ Mich 116 Church St SE Minneapolis MN 55455

HUMPHRIES, DEBORAH ANN, corporate executive; b. Hope, Ark., Jan. 27, 1955; d. Wayburn Dean and Joretta Ann (Sims) H. BBA, U. Tex., 1976. Adminstrv. asst. Here's Life New York, N.Y.C., 1976-77; pres. D.A. Humphries and Assocs., N.Y.C., 1977-78, Express Computer Supplies, San Francisco, 1984-87; v.p. Clean Image, Inc., San Francisco, 1985—; pres. Win/Win Co., San Francisco, 1987—, Newbold Enterprises, San Francisco, 1989—; flight attendant Am. Airlines, San Francisco, 1978, 87-88; cons., San Francisco, 1983—. Author: Passenger Power, 1987; contbg. editor: Passengers' Best Friend, 1987; patentee in field. Mem. Friends of the Libr., San Francisco. Mem. Nat. Recycling Coalition, Bay Area Career Women, Tex Ex Club (Austin). Democrat. Office: Clean Image Inc 6 Bridge Ave San Anselmo CA 94960

HUMPHRIES, ELLEN THOM, banker; b. Oskaloosa, Iowa, Aug. 4, 1947; d. Theodore A. Thom and Catherine A. (Wilkes) Betts; m. Quinn F. Humphries, Jr., Dec. 4, 1965 (div. Feb. 1979); 1 child, Laura Amanda Kelly Humphries. Diploma, Killeen Comml. Coll., Tex., 1966. Banking officer, asst. mgr. First Nat. Bank, Metairie, La., 1967-78; banking officer Jefferson Bank & Trust, Metairie, 1978-80; banking officer, mgr. First Nat. Bank, Metairie, 1980-84; v.p. Gulf Fed. Savs. Bank, Metairie, 1984-85; account exec. First Fin. Bank, New Orleans, 1985-87; asst. v.p., mgr. Sussex Trust Co., 1987—. Bd. dirs. New Orleans YWCA, 1982-85; cons. Jr. Achievement. Mem. Metairie Cen. Bus. Dist. Assn. (sec. 1982-83, pres. 1983-84), Greater Georgetown C. of C. (bd. dirs., treas.), Georgetown Bus. Assn. (chairperson fin. women internat. awards & scholarship com., cons., tchr. jr. achievement), Nat. Assn. Bank Women (exec. com. diamond state chpt.). Lutheran. Avocations: drama, dance, swimming, reading, youth counseling.

HUMPHRIES, JOAN ROPES, psychologist, educator; b. Bklyn., Oct. 17, 1928; d. Lawrence Gardner and Adele Lydia (Zimmermann) Ropes; m. Charles C. Humphries, Apr. 4, 1957; children: Peggy Ann, Charlene Adele. BA, U. Miami, 1950; MS, Fla. State U., 1955; PhD, La. State U., 1963. Part-time instr. U. Miami, Coral Gables, Fla., 1964-66; prof. dept. psychology Miami-Dade Community Coll., 1966—. Pres. Inst. Evaluation, Diagnosis and Treatment, Miami, 1987—, bd. dirs. 1975—, v.p. 1975-87. Recipient Cert. of Achievement Phi Lambda, 1987. Mem. AAUP (pres. Miami-Dade Community Coll. chpt. 1988—, v.p., sec., mem. exec. bd., v.p. Fla. conf. 1986-88), Biofeedback Soc. Am. (pres. 1989—), Biofeedback Assn. Fla. (pres. 1990—), Internat. Platform Assn. (gov.), Am. Psychol. Assn., AAUW, Dade County Psychol. Assn. (Fla. chpt.), Colonial Dames 17th Century, N.Y. Acad. Scis. (life), Regines in Miami, Soc. Mayflower Descs. (elder William Brewster colony). Democrat. Clubs: Country of Coral Gables, Jockey (life). Editorial staff, maj. author: The Application of Scientific Behaviorism to Humanistic Phenomena, 1975; researcher in biofeedback and human consciousness. Home: 1311 Alhambra Circle Coral Gables FL 33134 Office: Miami Dade Community Coll North Campus 11380 NW 27th Ave Miami FL 33167

HUNDLEY, MARITHA RENEE, purchasing director; b. Covington, Ky., Aug. 23, 1961; d. Bert and Dorothy Pearl (Lainhart) H.; m. Anthony Wayne McKnight, Aug. 22, 1981 (div. 1986). Student, So. Ohio Coll., 1979-80, Ky. Coll. Bus., 1980-81. With Saalfeld Paper, Cin., 1982—, dir. purchasing, 1988—. Mem. NAFE, Order Eastern Star. Republican. Home: 2686 La Feuille Circle #1 Cincinnati OH 45211 Office: Saalfeld Paper Co 2701 Spring Grove Ave Cincinnati OH 45225

HUNEYCUTT, ALICE RUTH, lawyer; b. New Haven, Jan. 10, 1951; d. C. Jerome and Alberta (Piner) H.; m. Howard Mark Bernstein, Nov. 28, 1981; children: Ashley Laughton, Laura Whitney. BA in History, Duke U., 1972; JD, U. Miami (Fla.), 1979. Bar: Fla. 1980, U.S. Dist. Ct. (so. dist.) Fla. 1980, U.S. Ct. Appeals (5th cir.) 1980, U.S. Dist. Ct. (mid. dist.) Fla. 1982, U.S. Ct. Appeals (11th cir.) 1982. Corp. counsel Burger King Corp., Miami, 1980-82; assoc. Stearns Weaver Miller Weissler Alhadeff & Sitterson, P.A., Tampa, Fla., 1982-84; ptnr. Stearns Weaver Miller Weissler Alhadeff & Sitterson, P.A., Tampa, 1984—. Bd. dirs. Am. Heart Assn., Tampa, 1986—, chmn. elect, 1988-89, 89—, chmn., 1990—. Mem. ABA (subcom. franchising, small bus. com., corp., banking and bus. law sect.), Fla. Bar Assn. (Pres.'s Pro Bono Service award 1987), Fla. Assn. Women Lawyers, Kiwanis. Democrat. Methodist. Home: 526 21st Ave NE Saint Petersburg FL 33704 Office: Stearns Weaver Miller Weissler Alhadeff & Sitterson PA One Tampa City Ctr Ste 3300 Tampa FL 33602

HUNGATE, SUE CAROL, financal analyst, sales executive; b. San Antonio, Nov. 4, 1957; d. Joseph Irvin and Betty Lou (Hatzenbuehler) Hungate. BA, U. S.C., Columbia, 1978. Student asst. U. S.C., Columbia, 1975-78, research asst. Affiliated Computer, Dallas, 1978-79; media planner/buyer Bloom Advt., Dallas, 1979-81; customer service EDS/Cunadata, Dallas, 1981-82, regional rep., Charlotte, N.C., 1982-86; account mgr. Broadway & Seymour, Charlotte, 1986-87; sr. sales exec. Citicorp Info. Resources, Charlotte, 1989—. Mem. AAUW, NAFE, Am. Mgmt. Assn., Am. Bus. Women's Assn., Carolina Ambassadors, Fin. Women Internat., Pi Beta Phi. Methodist. Avocations: piano, reading, outdoor sports, sailing, water skiing. Home: 2709 New Hamlin Way Charlotte NC 28210-5800 Office: 2709 New Hamlin Way Charlotte NC 28210

HUNING, DEBORAH GRAY, actress, dancer, audiologist; b. Evanston, Ill., Aug. 23, 1950; d. Hans Karl Otto and Angenette Dudley (Willard) H.; divorced; 1 child, Bree Alyeska. BS, No. Ill. U., 1981, MA, 1983. Actress, soloist, dancer, dir. various univ. and community theater depts., Bklyn., Chgo. and Cranbrook, B.C., Can., 1967—; ski instr. Winter Park (Colo.) Recreation Assn., 1975-79; owner The Good Earth Sprout Farm, Winter Park, 1978-79; audiologist, ednl. programming cons. East Kootenay Ministry of Health, Cranbrook, 1985—; house photographer C Lazy U Ranch, Granby, Colo., 1979; master of ceremonies East Kootenay Talent Showcase, EXPO '86, Vancouver B.C., Can., 1986; creator, workshop leader A Hearing Impaired Child in the Classroom, 1986. Contbr. articles to newspapers, 1986. Sec., treas. Women for Wildlife, Cranbrook, 1985-86; assoc. mem. adv. bd. Grand County Community Coll., Winter Park, Colo., 1975-77; assoc. mem. bd. dirs. Boys and Girls Club of Can., Cranbrook, 1985. Mem. Nat. Assn. Gifted Children, Internat. Marine Animal Trainers Assn. Home: 3716 146th Ave SE Bellevue WA 98006

HUNKIN, MARY LOUISE, educator, behavior specialist; b. Willimantic, Conn., Sept. 27, 1950; d. Alfred James and Erdis Leara (Hopkins) H. BS, Ga. State U., 1972, MEd, 1976; postgrad., Nova U. Cert. in mental retardation, behavior disorders, Ga. Staff worker Ga. Retardation Ctr., Atlanta, 1970-72; tchr. Fulton County Schs., Atlanta, 1972-73, Ga. Retardation Ctr., Atlanta, 19.73-78; instrnl. supr. North Fulton County Tng. Ctr., Atlanta, 1973-78; tchr. Gwinnett County Pub. Schs., Lawrenceville, Ga., 1981—; regional cons. Gospel Light Publs., Ventura, Ga., 1981-86; pvt. tutor, cons., pres. Specialized Teaching, Atlanta, 1981—; profl. advisor Parent-to-Parent, Atlanta, 1985-87; mem. adv. bd. Sheltering Arms Child Care Ctr., Duluth, Ga., 1986-88. Author 24 insvc. tng. guides, 1973—. Mem. Ga. Trust for Hist. Preservation, 1975—; project chmn. Jr. League Atlanta, 1986—; bd. dirs. T.A.S.K., agy. employed handicapped, Atlanta, 1987—. Named Tchr. of Yr., Oaklandn Ctr. for Severely Handicapped, 194, Gwinnett Vocat. Ctr., 1988, Outstanding Vol., Jr. League Atlanta, 1987, 88. Mem. Assn. for Retarded Citizens, Autism Soc. Am. (Outstanding Tchr.-Adv. award 1984), Am. Vocat. Assn., Assn. for Supervision and Curriculum Devel., Nat. Coun. for Exceptional Children, Ga. Assn. for Exceptional Children (Direct Svc. award 1985), Atlanta Coun. for Exceptional Children, Joel Chandler Harris Assn. (bd. dirs. 1988—). Republican. Office: Gwinnett Vocat Ctr 990 McElvaney Ln Lawrenceville GA 30245

HUNLEY, W. HELEN, Canadian provincial government official; b. Acme, Alta., Can., Sept. 6, 1920. Student pub. schs., Rocky Mountain House, Alta.; LL.D., U. Alta., 1985. Telephone operator Carstairs, Acme and Calgary, Alta.; with implement and truck dealership, ins. agy. Rocky Mountain House, 1948-57, owner, 1957-68; owner, mgr. Helen Hunley Agys. Ltd., ins. agy., Rocky Mountain House, 1968-71; town councillor Rocky Mountain House, 1960-66, mayor, 1966-71; elected mem. Legis. Assembly Province of Alta., Edmonton, 1971-79, minister without portfolio, 1971-73, solicitor-gen., 1973-75, minister social services and community Health, 1975-79, lt. gov., 1985—. Formerly active numerous community affairs and vol. agys., including Can. Red Cross, Can. Boy Scouts, Recreation Bd., Alta. Girls Parliament, Provincial Mental Health Adv. Council; hon. patron numerous assns. Served to lt. Can. Women's Army Corps, 1941-45. Office: Province of Alta, Legislature Bldg, Edmonton, AB Canada T5K 2B6*

HUNNEWELL, RUTHANN BAFFO, marketing professional; b. Wilmington, Del., Nov. 28, 1954; d. Charles Matthew and Joanne (Goodwin) Baffo; (div. Dec. 1984). Practical cert., U. Dijon (France), 1975; BA in French, Ohio Wesleyan U., 1976; MBA in Mktg., U. Conn., 1985. Assoc. field dir. Aulino Baen Market Rsch., Wilton, Conn., 1976-77, Guideline Rsch., N.Y.C., 1977-79; sr. project dir. De Kadt Market Rsch., Greenwich, Conn., 1979-83; sr. market rsch. analyst Richardson-Vicks, Inc., Wilton, 1983-85; mgr. market rsch. Frito-Lay, Inc., Dallas, 1985-88; assoc. dir. market rsch. Motts, Div. Cadbury Schweppes, Stamford, Conn., 1988-89; dir. global mktg. coord. and rsch. Cadbury Schweppes, Inc., Stamford, 1989—; cons. Ind. Jewelers Orgn., Westport, Conn., 1983; guest speaker U. Conn., Stamford, 1982. Active Jr. League of Greenwich, 1988; health and fitness instr. Turtle Creek Manor, Dallas, 1987-88; ICU vol. Norwalk (Conn.) Hosp., 1982; lectr. Career Motivation Program, N.E. Utilities, Norwalk, 1983-84. Recipient Outstanding Student Achievement award, The Wall Street Jour., N.Y.C., 1985. Mem. European Soc. Market Rsch., Beta Gamma Sigma, Alpha Mu Alpha, Kappa Kappa Gamma. Episcopalian. Home: 1465 E Putnam Ave 625 Old Greenwich CT 06870 Office: Cadbury Schweppes High Ridge Pk Stamford CT 06905

HUNT, BRENDA LEIGH, telecommunications specialist; b. Washington, Dec. 26, 1960; d. Allen Wayne and Mary Virginia (Oliver) Atkins; m. Kevin David Hunt, Aug. 12, 1990. Sr. communications tech. analyst Sovran Bank Md., Hyattsville, now communications officer. Mem. NAFE.

HUNT, JEAN, archeopsychologist; b. Gainesville, Ga., Dec. 11, 1932; d. Thomas Cleland and Eunice Dean (Lord) H.;m. Fletcher Earle Gaulden, Jr., July 25, 1952 (div. 1967); children: Frances Dean Gaulden Beebe, Craig Hunt Gaulden, Margaret Stanford Gaulden. BA, Winthrop Coll., 1953; MA, Furman U., 1957. Instr. Furman U., Greenville, 1960-64; pers. asst. Celanese Plastics Co., Greer, S.C., 1964-66; pers. dir. Cryovac, Duncan, 1966-70; asst. pers. dir. U. N.C., Chapel Hill, 1970-73; psychol. assoc. I La. State Penitentiary, Angola, 1981-82; sch. psychologist E. Baton Rouge Pub. Schs., Baton Rouge, 1982-83; psychol. assoc. III N.W. La. State Sch., Bossier City, 1983—; chief exec. officer Hunt Assocs., Inc., Pubs., 1990—. Author: Tracking the Flood Survivors; producer (TV documentaries) The Megalith Builders, 1988, Atlantis Emerging, 1989; identified modern survival of megalith builder lang. Grantee Richard Lounsbery Found., 1985. La. Mounds Soc. (pres., editor 1986—), Inst. for Study Am. Cultures (speaker), Am. Psychol. Assn. (assoc.), Am. Mensa. Home: 3330 Eastwood Dr Shreveport LA 71105

HUNT, JUDITH ANN, dean faculty affairs; b. Providence, R.I., Dec. 1, 1939; d. Joseph McVicker and Esther Mathilde (Dahms) H. AB, Brown U., 1960; MS and PhD, Northwestern U., Evanston, Ill., 1964. Postdoctoral fellow NSF, Cambridge U., Eng., 1964-65; asst. prof. to prof. Calif. State U., Hayward, 1965-87, assoc. v.p., faculty affairs and rsch., 1976-87, dean, faculty affairs, Office of the Chancellor, 1987—. Am. Psychol. Assn. Democrat. Unitarian. Office: Calif State Univ/Chancellor 400 Golden Shore Long Beach CA 90802

HUNT, LINDA, actress; b. Morristown, N.J., Apr. 2, 1945. Student, Interlochen Arts Acad., Mich., Goodman Theatre and Sch. of Drama, Chgo. Off-Broadway theater debut in Down by the River, 1975; A Metamorphosis in Miniature, 1982 (Obie award), Little Victories, 1983; Top Girls, 1983 (Obie award); films include Dune, 1984, The Year of Living Dangerously, 1983 (Academy award for best supporting actress), The Bostonians, 1984, Eleni, 1985, Silverado, 1985, Popeye, 1980, Waiting for the Moon, 1987; Broadway appearance in Ah, Wilderness!, 1975, End of the World, 1984 (Tony nomination); in N.Y. Shakespeare Festival prodn. Aunt Dan and Lemon, 1985, Peter Brook's prodn. Cherry Orchard, 1988. Office: care Triad Artists Inc 10100 Santa Monica Blvd 16th Fl Los Angeles CA 90067

HUNT, LINDA MARIE, hospital official; b. Chgo., Sept. 13, 1947; d. Allen A. and Marie (Romano) Gregory; m. Bernard H. Hunt, Jr. (div.); children: Jason Alan, Lisa Marie. BS, U. Phoenix, 1987. Adminstrv. asst. Old Tucson/Old Vegas, 1975-78; asst. mgr. W & W Mktg. Corp., Houston, 1978-83; adminstr. profl. rels. Tucson Gen. Hosp., 1983-84; mgr. Romero Road Med. Clinic, Tucson, 1984-89; mgr. physician svcs. El Dorado Hosp. and Med. Ctr., Tucson, 1989—. Bd. dirs. Flowing Wells Community Effort Coun., 1988; mem. Concerned Women for Am., 1986—. Mem. NAFE, Am. Guild Patient Account Mgmt. Baptist. Office: El Dorado Hosp and Med Ctr 1400 N Wilmot Rd Tucson AZ 85712

HUNT, LYNDA JOYCE, registered nurse; b. Houston, Aug. 17, 1951; d. Lonnie and Ruth (Franklin) H.; 1 child, Kania Ruth. BSN, U. Tex., 1974; cert. in women's health care, U. Tex., Dallas, 1982. Cert. Ob-gyn. Nurse John Sealy Hosp., Galveston, 1978-82; pub. health nurse State of Tex., Houston, 1978-82; family planning nurse practitioner Planned Parenthood, Houston, 1982-87; nurse Harris County Hosp. Dist., Houston, 1987-89; practitioner Homeless Health Clinic Project, Houston, 1988—; ob-gyn. nurse practitioner City of Houston Health Dept., 1989—; part-time obstertic nurse Jefferson Davis Hosp. 1978--. Counselor Task Force for Helping Place Unsheltered Homeless in Shelters; active Coalition for Homeless of Houston and Harris County, Girl Scouts U.S. Mem. NAFE. Democratic. Baptist. Home: 2514 Milwaukee Houston TX 77026

HUNT, MARTHA, sales executive, researcher; b. N.Y.C., May 17, 1924; d. Paul Andrew and Monika (Dobberstein) Pankau; children: Philip Brian Hunt, Susan Monica Hunt. Student, Syracuse U., 1943-47. Asst. controller Commonwealth Fund, N.Y.C., 1947-50; sales tech. Caldwell & Bloor, Mansfield, Ohio, 1958-61; sales promotion mgr. Vita Craft Corp., Shawnee, Kans., 1964-90, cons., 1990—; mem. Meeting Planners Internat., Kans. City, 1982—. Author and editor: cookbooks, 1965—. Pres. League Women Voters, Akron, Ohio, 1951-53; gov. Soroptimist Internat. of Am., Kans. City, 1978-80 (bd. dirs., Phila. 1978-80); pres. Soroptimist Internat. Kans. City, 1973-74. Recipient Meritorious Svc. award, Kans. City Police Dept., 1975, Disting. Govs. award, Soroptimist Internat. Am., Phila., 1978-79, 79-80. Mem. Shepherds's Ctr. (bd. dirs. Kans. City, Mo. chpt., 1972—; Outstanding Mem., nat. bd. dirs. 1990), Rose Brooks Ctr. (Vol. Svc. award 1985; v.p. 1984-85), Safehome, Inc (bd. dirs. 1979—, Outstanding Contbn. award 1988), Metro Citizens Crusade Against Crime Kans. City (pres. 1983), Kappa Kappa Gamma (pres. 1948-49), Alumnae Assn. (N.Y.C.). Republican. Presbyterian. Office: Vita Craft Corp 11100 W 58th St Shawnee KS 66203

HUNT, MARY LOU, counselor, small business owner; b. Bell, Calif., Apr. 23, 1932; d. David Allen and Ruth Irene (Bolton) Smith; m. Earl Busby Hunt, Dec. 20, 1954; children: Robert David, Susan Mary, Alan James, Steven Thomas. BA in Psychology, Stanford U., 1954, MA in Psychology, 1954. Tchr., counselor Women's Guidance Ctr. U. Wash., Seattle, 1972; from sec. to pres., cons. counselor Individual Devel. Ctr. Inc., Seattle, 1972-86, pres., dir., 1986—, also bd. dirs. Contbr. chpt. to book Management Preparation for Women, 1978. Bd. dirs. Seattle Day Nursery Assn., 1974-76, Focus on Part-Time Employment, Seattle, 1976, Together in Employment, Seattle, 1982-85, Classical Music Supporters, 1987—. Mem. Am. Assn. Counseling and Devel., Wash. State Assn. Counseling and Devel., Am. Soc. for Tng. and Devel. (bd. dirs. Seattle 1979-82, membership dir. 1980-82), Soc. Human Resources Mgmt., Nat. Career Devel. Assn., Puget Sound Career Devel. Assn (pres. 1988-89), Washington Career Devel. Assn. (co-pres. 1989-90, pres. 1990—). Office: Individual Devel Ctr 1020 E John St Seattle WA 98102

HUNT, MARY REILLY, organization executive; b. N.Y., Apr. 17, 1921; d. Philip R. and Mary C. (Harten) Reilly; m. Robert R. Hunt, Apr. 10, 1943,; children: Marianne Schram, Philip R., Robert R., Elise Paul. Student, CCNY, 1939. Tax investigator Ind. Dept. Revenue, 1970-80; pres. Ind. Right to Life, 1973-77; dir. devel. Nat. Right to Life Com., Washington, 1979—, hon. bd. mem., 1983—; pres. Mary Reilly Hunt & Assoc., Inc., South Bend, Ind., 1985—. Bd. dirs., v.p. YWCA, 1968-73; bd. dirs. Mental Health Assn. St. Joseph Co., 1972-78; candidate for state legislature, 1988; mem. St. Joseph County Rep. precinct com., South Bend, 1964-79, alt. del. to Nat. Rep. Conv., 1978, 84, 88. Mem. NAFE, Women Bus. Owners, South Bend Symphony Women's Assn. Republican. Roman Catholic. Home and Office: Nat Right to Life Com 1102 N Lafayette Blvd South Bend IN 46617

HUNT, SUE WHITTINGTON, accountant; b. Greenville, Miss., Nov. 23, 1952; d. Robert Bryan Sr. and Dale (Montgomery) W.; m. Ronnie Charles Hunt, Dec. 28, 1974; children: Andrew W., Emily P. AA in Bus., Holmes Jr. Coll., 1972; BBA, Delta State U., 1974; MBA, Miss. Coll., 1985. Acct. J. Milton Newton, Inc., Jackson, Miss., 1975-76; acct., auditor Dept. of Pub. Welfare, Jackson, Miss., 1976-81; chief fiscal officer Miss. Worker's Compensation Commn., Jackson, Miss., 1982-85; budget analyst IV Dept. Fin. and Adminstrn., Jackson, Miss., 1985—. Mem. PTA, Clinton Pub. Schs.,

1986—. Mem. Assn. Govt. Accts. (sec. Jackson chpt. 1986-87, pres.-elect Jackson chpt. 1987-88, pres. Jackson chpt. 1988-89, bd. dirs. 1989—, named Outstanding Chpt. Pres. for Southcentral Region 1988-89), Am. Soc. Women Accts. (treas. Jackson chpt. 1984-85, 1st v.p. 1985-86, pres.-elect 1986-87, pres. 1987-88, bd. dirs. 1988-89), Career Forum, MBA Assn. of Miss. (sec. 1989-90), Internat. Platform Assn. Methodist. Home: 1707 Melrose Pl Clinton MS 39056 Office: Dept Fin and Adminstrn 901 Walter Sillers Bldg Jackson MS 39201

HUNT, WANDA HOLDER, state legislator; b. Bakersville, N.C., Mar. 22, 1944; d. Farrell Robert and Jane (Ledford) Winterhalter Holder; m. Robert Frank Hunt, Mar. 24, 1962; 1 dau., Donna Lynn. Student Appalachian State U. Asst. purchasing Appalachian State U., Boone, N.C., 1965-70; with purchasing/personnel Ceralon Mfg., Aberdeen, N.C., 1972-77; with purchasing office N.C. Dept. Transp., Raleigh, 1977-82; account exec. Pinehurst, Inc. (N.C.), 1984—; mem. N.C. Senate, 1983—, vice-chair edn. com., 1983-84, chmn. sr. citizens com., 1985-86. Mem. bd. edn., Carthage, N.C., 1976-82; precinct chair Democratic party, Pinehurst, N.C., 1974-75; sec. Democratic party, Carthage, N.C., 1975. Recipient award Heart Fund; Disting. Service awards Moore County, 1983, Social Services Bd., Moore County, 1983; Vol. Service award Nat. Cystic Fibrosis, Pinehurst, N.C.; named Disting. Woman, State of N.C., Raleigh, 1984. Mem. Women in State Govt., N.C. State Govt. Employees Assn., N.C. Status of Women, N.C. Heart Fund Assn., Nat. Conf. State Legislatures (pensions com. 1985-86), State Legislators' Network (So. legis. conf. 1985-86), Travel Council N.C. (legis. com.), N.C. Council Hearing Impaired. Democrat. Presbyterian. Home: PO Box 1335 Pinehurst NC 28374*

HUNT, WANDA SUE, marketing executive; b. Weiser, Idaho, July 28, 1950; d. Donald M. and Ruth Ann (Jones) H. Postgrad., N.W. Coll. Bus., 1969. With trust dept. First Interstate Bank of Wash., Seattle, 1969-78, with investment dept., 1978-82, investment officer, 1982-84, asst. v.p., 1984-86, mgr. investments, 1986-88, v.p. and mgr. sales, 1988—. Active Big Sisters; vol. fireman King County, Seattle, 1986—; pres. Lewis & Clark Condo's, Seattle, 1985-88; active various charitable orgns.; bd. dirs. U. Child Devel. Sch., 1985-88, Epilepsy Ctr., 1989-90, Boys and Girls Club, 1989-90. Recipient Banker of Yr. award First Interstate, 1987, Emerald Gerung award for outstanding community svc., 1989. Mem. Women's Bus. Exch., Rotary (bd. dirs. Emerald City club 1988-89). Home: 15625 42d Ave S #7 Seattle WA 98188 Office: First Interstate Bank PO Box 160 Seattle WA 98111

HUNTE, BERYL ELEANOR, mathematics educator, consultant; b. N.Y.C.. BA, Hunter Coll., 1947; MA, Columbia U., 1948; PhD, NYU, 1965. Tchr. maths. Friends Sem., N.Y.C., 1957-62; asst. prof. maths. Rockland Community Coll., Suffern, N.Y., 1962-63; instr. in maths., supr. tchr. trainees NYU, N.Y.C., 1964; with Borough of Manhattan Community Coll., N.Y.C., 1964-67, 70-73; prof. maths Borough of Manhattan Community Coll., 1970—; acting dean acad. affairs Borough of Manhattan Community Coll., N.Y.C., 1987-88; dean for spl. projects CUNY, N.Y.C., 1988-89; assoc. U. Seminar on Higher Edn., Columbia U., N.Y.C., 1989—. Author: (with others) (textbook) Mathematics Through Statistics, 1973. Mem. YWCA of Greater N.Y., N.Y.C.; bd. dirs., sec. UN Assn. of N.Y., N.Y.C., 1980-86. NSF fellow, summer 1960, 1963-64, Chancellor's Faculty fellow CUNY, 1980. Mem. N.Y. Acad. Scis., Am. Math. Soc., Acad. for Humanities and Scis., Am. Assn. Community and Jr. Colls., UN Assn. N.Y.C. Office: Borough Manhattan Coll 199 Chambers St New York NY 10007

HUNTER, CAROLE A., municipal government official; b. Derby, Conn., Apr. 13, 1941; d. James Edward and Matilda Ann (Byrd) Brown; m. James R. Hunter, Jr., June 2, 1939; children: James Russell III, Kimberly Ann, David Harding, Nichole Lynette. Student, Stone Bus. Coll., 1958-60; student, El Paso Communit Coll., 1981-85. Sec. New Haven Redevel. Agy., 1960-64; sec. fin. & acctg. office Ft. Richardson, Anchorage, 1965-67; sec., maintenance dir. Ft. Bliss, El Paso, 1968-70; sec., adminstrv. asst. various offices City of El Paso, 1973—, city clk., 1985—. Mem. Foster Grandparent Adv. Coun., El Paso; chair supervisory com. El Paso Employees Fed. Credit Union. Democrat. Baptist. Office: City of El Paso 2 Civic Center Pla El Paso TX 79935

HUNTER, CHARLOTTE RAE, international personnel officer, educator; b. Denver, Nov. 7, 1942; d. Ralph Emil and Edmae Marie (Landry) H.; m. Michael Eugene Waters, July 28, 1962 (div. 1977); children—Paige D., Michelle R.; m. Brent M. Knight, June 21, 1986. B.A., DePaul U., 1971; M.Ed., U. Ill., 1974, Ph.D., 1979. Cert. profl. in human resources. Publs. editor Ill. Office Edn., Springfield, 1972-73; dir. rsch. Triton Coll., River Grove, Ill., 1976-78; personnel dir. G.D. Searle & Co., Dallas, 1978-81, Saxon, Chgo., 1981-84; personnel officer, chief internat. recruitment div. World Bank, Washington, 1984-85, internat. recruitment chief, 1985—; adj. faculty Elmhurst Coll. (Ill.), 1983-84; mem. State Adv. Coun. on Adult, Vocat. Edn., Ill., 1977-79. Editor: Ill. Career Ednl. Jour., 1972; contbr. writings to publs. Commr. Ill. Commn. on Status of Women, 1975-79; bd. dirs. Nat. Assn. Commns. for Women, 1976-77; coordinating com. Internat. Women's Yr., Ill., 1977. EPDA fellow, 1973-75; recipient cert. of leadership YWCA Chgo., 1977. Mem. Am. Soc. Personnel Adminstrs., Employment Mgmt. Assn., Nat. Assn. Corp. and Profl. Recruiters, Phi Delta Kappa. Office: World Bank 1818 H St NW Washington DC 20433

HUNTER, DEBBIE ANN, customer service specialist; b. Doylestown, Pa., Aug. 21, 1952; d. Franklin David and Jacqueline Rosilie (Humes) Bishop; m. William Franklin Hunter, June 24, 1978; children: William Franklin Jr., Jason David. BS in Edn., West Chester (Pa.) Coll., 1974. Customer svc. rep. H.A. Thompson, Inc., Paoli, Pa., 1974-77, B.G. Balmer, Inc., Devon, Pa., 1977-80, Goins & Hewitt Agy., Paoli, 1980-84; office mgr. Francis A. Hall, Inc., West Chester, 1984—. SEc. Chester County SPCA, West Chester, 1986-87, Caln Elem. Sch. PTA, Thorndale, Pa., 1988-89, pres., 1990—. Mem. Ind. Agts. Assn., Ins. Women of the Main Line (sec. Bryn Mawr, Pa. chpt. 1977-80). Office: Francis A Hall Inc PO Box 491 West Chester PA 19381

HUNTER, DONNA VENÉ, nurse; b. Birmingham, Ala., Aug. 20, 1958; d. Charles Lee Black and Betty Jean (Hunter) Lipscomb. BSN, U. Ala., Birmingham, 1980; MS, Tex. Women's U., Dallas, 1990. Staff nurse Univ. Hosp., Birmingham, 1980-85; staff nurse, charge nurse Meth. Med. Ctr., Dallas, 1985-86; staff nurse VA Med. Ctr., Dallas, 1986—, ICU in-svc. tng. coord., 1989—. Lt. USNR, 1988—. Mem. NAFE, NAACP, AACCN, Minority Adoption Coun., Mt. Olive Bapt. Ch. Nursing Guild, Nat. Naval Officers Assn., Naval Res. Assn. Home: 2610 Nikos Pl Apt 143 Arlington TX 76006 Office: VA Med Ctr 4500 S Lancaster St Dallas TX 75216

HUNTER, ELIZABETH IVES-VALSAM, fashion consultant; b. Boston, Sept. 26, 1945; d. Theodore William James and Dorothy (Sachs) Valsam; m. Robert Douglas Hunter, Oct. 12, 1968; children: Catherine Bowen, Nathaniel Vose, Dorothy Sachs. BA with honors in Econs. and Polit. Sci., McGill U., Montreal, Que., Can., 1967. Asst. to libr. dir. Emerson Coll., Boston, 1971-73; asst. examiner Fed. Res. Bank, Boston, 1974-76, sr. analyst, 1976-79; asst. treas. State St. Bank, Boston, 1979-82; fashion cons. Needham, Mass., 1989—; Summer rsch. fellow McGill U., Montreal, 1968. Editor: Boston Painters 1900-1930, 1986 (New Eng. Booksellers award 1986), Sargent's Murals at the Boston Public Library, 1988, The Twilight of Painting, 1990. Advisor Gammell Studio Trust, Boston, 1981—; overseer Boston Opera Assn., 1985—; incorporator Beaver Country Day Sch., Chestnut Hill, 1988—; trustee Chestnut Hill Sch., 1989—. Mem. Fashion Group Internat. (Boston chpt.). Episcopalian. Home and Office: 178 South St Needham MA 02192

HUNTER, HOLLY, actress; b. Atlanta, Mar. 20, 1958; d. Charles Edwin and Opal Marguerite (Catledge) H. BFA, Carnegie-Mellon U., 1980. Appeared in feature films Broadcast News (Best Actress award N.Y. Film Critics Circle 1988, Best Actress award Berlin Film Festival 1988), Raising Arizona, Always, Miss Firecracker; TV prodns. Roe vs. Wade (Best Actress Emmy award 1989) A Gathering of Old Men; Broadway stage prodns. Crimes of the Heart, The Wake of Jamey Foster; regional stage prodns. Buried Child, A Doll's House, Artichoke; other stage prodns. include A Lie of the Mind, L.A., Battery, N.Y.C., The Person I Once Was, N.Y.C. Bd. dirs. Calif. Abortion Rights Action League. *

HUNTER, JILL B., marketing professional; b. Taylor, Pa., July 27, 1962; m. Robert H. Sperling. Student in Bus., Villanova U., 1984—. Mktg. coord. Gilbreth Internat., Phila., 1984-87; mktg. dir. Gitano, N.Y.C., 1987—. Office: Gitano 20 W 33rd St 12th Fl New York NY 10001

HUNTER, JOAN ELIZABETH, metal products executive; b. Camden, N.J.; m. John H. Hunter; 1 child, Kelly L. Student, Monroe County Area Vocat. Sch., Pa. State U., 1984-87. Mgr. sales office, sales adminstr. Bustin Indsl. Products, Inc., East Stroudsburg, Pa., 1988-89, mktg. mgr., 1990—. Mem. AMA, NAFE, Am. Mktg. Assn., Women in Bus., C. of C. (vice chair). Office: Bustin Indsl Products Inc 401 Oak St East Stroudsburg PA 18301

HUNTER, KAREN ANN, publishing executive; b. Phila., Aug. 16, 1945; d. Bernard Sarkis and Ann A. (Engdahl) Kalayjian. BA, Coll. Wooster, 1966; MA, Cornell U., 1967; MS in Library Sci., Syracuse U., 1971; MS in Bus. Adminstn., Columbia U., 1976. Asst. to pres. Elsevier-North Holland Pub. Co., N.Y.C., 1976-78, clin. pub., 1978-80; planning dir. Elsevier Sci. Pubs., Amsterdam and N.Y.C., 1980-85, v.p., asst. to chmn., 1985—. Contbr. articles on pub. and strategic planning to profl. jours. Named Book Woman, Women's Nat. Book Assn., 1987. Mem. Soc. Scholarly Pub., Internat. Group Sci. Technical and Med. Pubs., Internat. Group Profl. and Scholarly Pub., Assn. Am. Pubs. (exec. coun. PSP div. 1989—), Phi Beta Kappa, Phi Alpha Theta. Home: 139 Grovers Ave Bridgeport CT 06605 Office: Elsevier Sci Pubs 655 Ave of the Americas New York NY 10010

HUNTER, KAY FRANCES TURNER, education administrator; b. Grambling, La., Sept. 7, 1934; d. Grady and Wilhelmina (Thomas) Turner; m. Roger Lee Hunter, Aug. 27, 1968. BS magna cum laude, Grambling State U., 1955; MS, U.Wis., Madison, 1960. Cert. tchr., supr., adminstr., La., Tex. Tchr. Washington Sch., Lake Charles, La., 1955-63, Burkburnett (Tex.) Elem. Sch., 1969-71; asst. prof. Grambling Lab. Sch., 1963-69, Fed. City Coll., Washington, 1971-78; coord. Dallas Ind. Sch. Dist., 1978-82, instructional specialist, 1982-84, dean of instruction, 1984-89, dir., 1989—; cons. Institutional Svcs. for Edn., Washington, 1973-74; reviewer Addison Wesley Pub. Co., Menlo Park, Calif., 1984-85; cons., reviewer Riverside Pub. Co., Chgo., 1984-85. Author articles, curriculum materials. Co-chair March of Dimes drive, Lake Charles, 1962; troop leader Grambling area Girl Scouts U.S., 1964-69. So. Edn. Found. fellow to Hampton Inst., Va., 1964. Mem. Nat. Alliance Black Sch. Educators, Tex. Alliance Black Sch. Educators (state bd. 1989—), Assn. Supervision and Curriculum Devel., Internat. Reading Assn., Alpha Kappa Alpha, Alpha Kappa Mu, Phi Delta Kappa. Baptist. Home: 1341 Mill Stream Dr Dallas TX 75232

HUNTER, KIM (JANET COLE), actress; b. Detroit, Nov. 12, 1922; d. Donald and Grace Mabel (Lind) Cole; m. William A. Baldwin, Feb. 11, 1944 (div. 1946); 1 dau., Kathryn Emmett; m. Robert Emmett, Dec. 20, 1951; 1 son, Sean Emmett. Ed. pub. schs.; student acting with, Charmine Lantaff Camine, 1938-40, Actors Studio. First stage appearance, 1939; played in stock, 1940-42; Broadway debut in A Streetcar Named Desire, 1947; appeared in: tour Two Blind Mice, 1950, Darkness at Noon, N.Y.C., 1951, The Chase, 1952, N.Y.C., tour They Knew What They Wanted, 1952, The Children's Hour; revival, N.Y.C., 1952, The Tender Trap, N.Y.C., 1954, Write Me a Murder, N.Y.C., 1961, Weekend, N.Y.C., 1968, The Penny Wars, N.Y.C., 1969; And, Miss Reardon Drinks a Little; tour, 1971-72, The Glass Menagerie, Atlanta, The Women, N.Y.C., 1973, In Praise of Love, 1975, The Lion in Winter, N.J., 1975, The Cherry Orchard, N.Y.C., 1976, The Chalk Garden, Pa., 1976, Elizabeth The Queen, Buffalo, 1977, Semmelweiss, Buffalo, 1977, The Belle of Amherst, N.J., 1978, The Little Foxes, Mass., 1980, To Grandmother's House We Go, N.Y.C., 1981, Another Part of the Forest, Seattle, 1981, Ghosts, 1982, Territorial Rites, 1983, Death of a Salesman, 1983, Cat on a Hot Tin Roof, 1984, Life with Father, 1984, Sabrina Fair, 1984, Faulkner's Bicycle, 1985, Antique Pink, 1985, The Belle of Amherst, 1986, A Delicate Balance, 1986, Painting Churches, 1986, Jokers, 1986, Remembrance, 1987, Man and Superman, 1987-88, The Gin Game, 1988, A Murder of Crows, 1988, Watch on the Rhine, 89; frequent appearances summer stock and repertory theater, 1940—; appeared, Am. Shakespeare Festival, Stratford, Conn., 1961; film debut in: The Seventh Victim, 1943; other motion pictures include Tender Comrade, 1943, When Strangers Marry (re-released as Betrayed), 1944, You Came Along, 1945, A Canterbury Tale, 1949, Stairway to Heaven, 1946, A Streetcar Named Desire, 1951 (acad. award for best supporting actress), Anything Can Happen, 1952, Deadline U.S.A., 1952, Storm Center, 1956, Bermuda Affair, 1957, The Young Stranger, 1957, Money, Women, and Guns, 1958, Lilith, 1964, Planet of the Apes, 1968, The Swimmer, 1968, Beneath the Planet of the Apes, 1970, Escape from the Planet of the Apes, 1971, Dark August, 1975, The Kindred, 1987, Two Evil Eyes, 1990; made TV debut on, Actors' Studio program, 1948; numerous TV appearances include Requeim for a Heavyweight, 1956, The Comedian, 1957, both on Playhouse 90, Give Us Barabbas on, Hallmark Hall of Fame, 1961, 63, 68, 69, Love, American Style, Colombo, Cannon, Night Gallery, Mission Impossible, The Magician, 1972-73, Marcus Welby, Hec Ramsey, Griff, Police Story, Ironside, Med. Center, Bad Ronald, Born Innocent, 1974, Ellery Queen, 1975, Lucas Tanner, This Side of Innocence, Once an Eagle, Baretta, Gibbsville, Hunter, 1976, The Oregon Trail, 1977, Project: U.F.O., Stubby Pringle's Christmas, 1978, Backstairs at the White House, 1979, Specter on the Bridge, 1979, Edge of Night, 1979-80, F.D.R.'s Last Year, 1980, Skokie, 1981, Scene of the Crime, 1984, Three Sovereigns for Sarah, 1985, Hot Pursuit, 1985, Private Sessions, 1985, Martin Luther King, Jr.: The Dream and the Drum 1986, (CBS TV film) Drop Out Mother, 1987, (NBC-TV miniseries) Cross of Fire, 1989, Murder, She Wrote, 1990; rec. From Morning 'Til Night (and a Bag Full of Poems), RCA Victor, 1961, Come, Woo Me, Unified Audio Classics, 1964, The Velveteen Rabbit cassette Simon & Schuster, 1989. Author: Kim Hunter-Loose in the Kitchen, 1975. Recipient Donaldson award for best supporting actress in A Streetcar Named Desire 1948, also on Variety N.Y. Critics Poll 1948, for film version 1952, winner Look award, Hollywood Fgn. Corrs. Golden Globe award, Emmy nominations for Baretta 1977, Edge of Night 1980, Fla. Carbonell (for Big Mama in Cat on a Hot Tin Roof) award 1984. Mem. Acad. Motion Picture Arts and Scis., ANTA, Actors Equity Assn. (council 1953-59), Screen Actors Guild, AFTRA.

HUNTER, MARY ANDERSON, health care administrator; b. Caldercruix, Scotland, Aug. 18, 1949; came to U.S., 1968; d. Alexander and Kate (Colquhoun) H. BS in Acctg., Westfield State U., 1984; MBA in Healthcare Mgmt., Western New Eng. Coll., 1988. Accts. receivable mgr. Vis. Nurse Assn., Springfield, Mass., 1968-83; fin. officer Rehab. Assocs., Inc., West Springfield, Mass., 1983-87; adminstr. Challenge Phys. Therapy & Rehab., P.C., West Springfield, 1987—. Mem. Agawam (Mass.) Bd. Registrars, 1987—; sec., vice chmn. Rep. Town Com., Agawam; chmn. adv. bd. Order of Rainbow for Girls, East Longmeadow, Mass., 1974-82. Mem. Order of Eastern Star. Republican. Lutheran. Office: Challenge Phys Therapy 71 Park Ave West Springfield MA 01089

HUNTER, NADENE DENISON, physician; b. Quincy, Ill., June 2, 1918; d. Walcott and Blanch Nadene (Babb) Denison; m. Harold Wallace Hunter, Oct. 19, 1944; children: Wallace Jr., Josiah W., Nadene B., Melville W., Sara E., James W., Helen C., Martha L., Walcott W. BS, Wash. State U., Pullman, 1939; MS, Tulane U., New Orleans, 1940, MD, 1944. Med. intern Charity Hosp., New Orleans, 1944-45; psychiatrist N.Y. State Dept. Mental Health, West Brentwood, 1946-48; pvt. practice psychiatry Central Islip, N.Y., 1949-59, Sonyea, N.Y., 1963-67; sr. supervising psychiatrist N.Y. State Dept. Mental Health, Sonyea, 1947-48, 65-68; supervising psychiatrist, 1968-71; asst. dir. Craig Colony, Sch., 1971-76; dir. Hosp. Craig Devel. Ctr., 1976-82; med. dir. Livingston County Health Dept., Mt. Morris, N.Y., 1986—; adv. bd. Univ. Affiliated Prog. DD, Rochester, 1984—; exec. bd. Genesee Coun. BSA, Batavia, N.Y., 1986—. Author; Parasite Diagnosis, 1942, Chagas Disease Preliminary Studies, 1942-43. Chmn., Mem. Mental Health Bd. Livingston County, N.Y., 1968-78, Mem. Community Svcs. Bd., Livingston County, 1987—; Vestry, Warden St. Johns Ch., Mt Morris, 1977—; Diocesan Coun. Episcopal Diocese Rochester, 1985—. Recipient Silver Faun Boy Scouts Am. Genesee Coun., 1973. Mem. Livingston County Med. Soc. (pres. 1972), N.Y. State Med. Soc. (sec./treas. 1978—), AMA, Am. Psychiatric Assn., Am. Acad. Family Physicians, Eastern Star (dist. dep. matron 1977, 84, dist. dep. grand matron 1986), Amaranth (royal matron 1987-89), Neuron Club (Rochester, N.Y., sec.). Republican. Anglican. Home: 9930 S Dansville Rd Dansville NY 14437

HUNTER, NAOMI ELIZABETH, music therapist; b. East Palestine, Ohio, Oct. 21, 1916; d. Frederick M. and Martha May (Green) Bott; m. Clayton Lynn Hunter, Jan. 13, 1940 (dec. Jan. 1969); 1 child, Phillip Lowell (dec.); 1 adopted child, Marsha Lynn. BA in Music, Youngstown State U., 1974; postgrad., Duquesne U., 1975. With David Anderson High Sch. Libr., Lisbon, Ohio, 1938-40, Lepper Libr., Lisbon, 1955-56; intern in music therapy Norristown State Hosp.; Pvt. music tchr. Lisbon, Ohio, 1945—; proprietor Hunter's News & Book Store, Lisbon, 1963-70; music therapist Montessori Sch., Lisbon, 1976-88; social worker Col. County Welfare Dept., Lisbon, 1977; creative writing tchr. Kent State U.-Salem, Salem, Ohio, 1979-82; music therapist Northside Hosp., Youngstown, Ohio, 1986; speaker on music therapy, radical life changes, writing/creativity; dir. Hunter's ARt Show. Contbr. poetry to profl. jours. Dir. Daily Vacation Bible Sch., Lisbon; dir. music programs, Wellsville, Ohio; mem. adv. bd. RSVP, Lisbon; former troop leader Girl Scouts U.S.A. Mem. AAUW, Nat. Assn. Music Therapy (registered, cert.), Lisbon Federated Music Club (scholarship com. 1980-89), Friends Am. Art, Order Ea. Star, White Shrine Jerusalem, Epsilon Sigma Alpha. Republican. Presbyterian. Home and office: 426 N Jefferson St Lisbon OH 44432

HUNTER, SALLY I., interior designer; b. East Liverpool, Ohio, Oct. 8, 1936; Charles E. and Thelma E. (Rice) H. BA, Kalamazoo Coll., 1958. Certified Am. Soc. Interior Designers. Interior designer The Higbee Co., Cleve., 1958-70; interior designer, v.p. Collectors Gallery & Interiors, Lakewood, Ohio, 1970—. Mem. Nat. Trust for Hist. Preservation, Cleve. Mus. Natural History. Mem. Am. Soc. Interior Designers (profl.), Cleve. Mus. Art. Home: 22535 Detroit Rd Rocky River OH 44116 Office: Collectors Gallery & Interiors 14518 Detroit Ave Lakewood OH 44107

HUNTER, SONIA L., retail executive; b. Ayshire, Iowa, Jan. 21, 1933; d. Roland Frank and Evelyn (Anderson) Nohlgren; 1 child, Greta Lynn. BEd, BS, Oreg. State U., 1955. Tchr. Salem (Oreg.) pub. schs., 1955-62; various sectl. positions various cos., 1962-76; property mgr. Reeve/Maillet Group, Bellevue, Wash., 1976-79; ptnr. Beaumont-Hunter Food Brokerage, Bellevue, 1979-81; real estate salesperson Eastlake Realty, Kirkland, Wash., 1981-86; owner Bellevue Florist, 1987—; bd. dirs. Career Floral Design Inst., Bellevue, 1989. Pres. Bayview Homeowners Assn., Kirkland, 1984, bd. dirs., 1983-86. Mem. Soc. Am. Florists, Florist Transworld Delivery, Teleflora, Coast Guard Aux. (sec. 1978-79). Republican. Home: 9715 NE Juanita Dr Kirkland WA 98034 Office: Bellevue Florist 832 102nd St NE Bellevue WA 98004

HUNTER, STACY H., administrative assistant; b. Copiague, N.Y., Sept. 29, 1963; d. Thomas B. and Joan D. (Gomes) Barnett; m. Thomas Charles Hunter, May 5, 1984; 1 child, Brittany Kathleen. Grad. high sch., West Babylon, N.Y. Adminstrv. asst. North Shore Elec. Contractors, East Farmingdale, N.Y., 1981-84; accounts receivable adminstrv. asst. N.J. Ednl. Computer Network, Edison, 1984-85; computer assoc. Villa Banfi, Farmingdale, N.Y., 1985-86; adminstrv. asst. to pres. RKO Warner, N.Y.C., 1986; v.p. Olds Securities Corp., N.Y.C., 1986—; v.p. Graphic Consultants Corp., Highlands, N.J., 1986—. Republican. Roman Catholic. Home: 1 Scenic Dr Apt 1410 Highlands NJ 07732 Office: Olds Securities Corp 150 E 58th St Ste 2406 New York NY 10155

HUNTER, SUE PERSONS, former state official; b. Hico, Tex., Aug. 21, 1921; d. David Henry and Beulah (Boatwright) Persons m. Charles Force Hunter; children: Shelley Hunter Richardson, Kathy Hunter McCullough, Margaret Hunter Brown. BA, U. Tex., 1942. Air traffic controller CAA (now FAA), San Antonio and Houston, 1942-52; writer Bissonet Plaza News, 1969-72; coordinator Goals for La., 1971-74; adminstrv. dir. Jeff Publs. Inc., 1974; press sec. Jefferson Parish Dist. Atty., 1972-75, communications cons., 1975-78; adminstr. Child Support Enforcement Div., 1979-85; contbg. editor The Jeffersonian, 1975-76. Pres. United Ch. Women East Jefferson (La.), 1958-59, LWV Jefferson Parish, La., 1961-64; pres. LWV La., 1967-71, also bd. dirs., 1962-67; mem. probation services com. Community Services Council, Jefferson, 1966-73, v.p., 1970-72; mem. Library Devel. Com. La., 1967-71, Nat. Com. for Support of Pub. Schs., 1967-72; mem. Goals Found. Council Met. New Orleans, 1969-75, sec. 1970, 72; mem. Goals La. Task Force State and Local Govt., 1969-70; pres. MMM Investment Club, 1969-72; bd. dirs. New Orleans Area Health Planning Council, 1969-75, Friends of Westminster Tower, 1986, Coun. for Internat. Visitors, 1990—; mem. adv. council La. State Health Planning, 1971-76; title I adv. council La. State Dept. Edn., 1970-72; vice chmn. Jefferson Women's Polit. Caucus, 1977-78, chmn., 1979, treas., 1980; bd. dirs. New Orleans Area/Bayou-River Health Systems Agy., 1978-82, pres., 1980, 81; mem. Task force for La. Talent Bank of Women, 1980; exec. bd. La. Child Support Enforcement Assn., 1980-86, pres., 1982-84; bd. dirs., legis. chmn. Nat. Child Support Enforcement Assn., 1983-86; mem. Gov.'s Commn. on Child Support Enforcement, 1984-88; mem. La. Statewide Health Coordinating Council, 1980-83, mgmt. com. edn. fund League of Women Voters La., 1988-89. Recipient Outstanding Citizens award Rotary Club, Metairie, La., 1962, River Ridge award, 1976. Mem. Am. Assn. Individual Investors (pres. New Orleans chpt. 1986-88), New Orleans Panhellenic (pres. 1956-57), Les Pelicaneers (pres. 1988-90), Alpha Xi Delta. Presbyterian (elder). Home: 210 Stewart Ave River Ridge LA 70123

HUNTER, SUSAN GAIL, publishing executive; b. Akron, Ohio, Aug. 3, 1950; d. Robert A. and Genevieve G. (Reneker) H. BA, Wittenberg U., 1972. Prodn. editor Charles E. Merrill Pub., Columbus, Ohio, 1972-75; copy editor W.B. Saunders Co., Phila., 1975-77, assoc. med. editor, 1977-79, mktg. dir., 1979-83; dir. mktg. Am. Chem. Soc., Washington, 1983-85; v.p., dir. mktg. Butterworth Pubs., Stoneham, Mass., 1985—. Mem. STM Internat. Pubs., Am. Med. Pub. Assn. (bd. dirs. 1990—), Soc. Scholarly Pub., Boston Bookbuilders, Literacy Vols. of Am., Mensa, Sigma Kappa (sec. 1987—). Home: 15 Terrace Park Reading MA 01867 Office: Butterworth Pubs 80 Montvale Ave Stoneham MA 02180

HUNTER, VALERIE JEAN DEXTER, real estate broker; b. Hackensack, N.J., Sept. 27, 1943; d. Perry and Vera May (Bates) D.; married, Sept. 5, 1965 (div. Mar. 1986); children: Kevin David, Keith Perry; m. William G. Hunter, Aug. 22, 1987. Grad. high sch., Lyndon Center, Ver. Dept. sec. U.S. C. of C., Washington, 1961-63; sec. The Cosmodyne Corp., Hawthorne, Calif., 1963; receptionist, pvt. sec. Sta. WTWN radio, St. Johnsbury, Ver., 1964-65; adminstrv. sec. Sanders Assocs., Inc., Nashua, N.H., 1967-72; co-owner, sec., bookkeeper Gallup Adjustment Service, Skowhegan, Maine, 1975-82; realtor Century 21 Whittemore's Real Estate, Skowhegan, 1981-87; realtor-broker Century 21 Nason Realty, Winslow, Maine, 1987—. Mem. Maine Assn. Realtors, No. Kennebec Valley Bd. Realtors, No. Kennebec Valley Multiple Listing Service, Lakewood Ladies Golf Assn. Home: Augusta Rd Neck Rd Winslow ME 04901 Office: Century 21 Nason Realty 11 Bay St Winslow ME 04901 Mailing Address: PO Box 598 Waterville ME 04901

HUNTER-BONE, MAUREEN CLAIRE, magazine editor; b. Teaneck, N.J., Aug. 18, 1946; d. Eugene Francis and Audrey Dolores (Connellan) Hunter; m. Stanley Bone, Nov. 2, 1974; children: John Hunter Bone, Caroline Vandervoort Bone. BA in English lit., St. Mary's Coll., Notre Dame, Ind., 1968. Writer Scholastic Mags., N.Y.C., 1968-69, asst. editor, 1969-71, assoc. editor, 1971-76, editor, 1976-79; freelance writer N.Y.C., 1979-87; sr. editor 3-2-1 Contact Mag., N.Y.C., 1987; editor Kid City Mag., N.Y.C., 1988-90, editor-in-chief, 1990—. Author: First Follow Nature, 1970, Adventures with a 3-Spined Stickleback, 1972. Mem. nat. ednl. adv. com. U.S. Bicentennial Com., Washington, 1988—; bd. advisors Epiphany Community Nursery Sch., N.Y.C., 1987—. Mem. Am. Soc. Mag. Editors, Ednl. Press Assn. (Disting. Achievement award 1988, 89). Office: Childrens TV Workshop One Lincoln Plaza New York NY 10023

HUNTLEY, ALICE MAE, manufacturing executive; b. Atoka, Okla., May 9, 1917; d. Joseph LaHay and Lula May (Stapp) Howe; BA U. Okla., 1939; m. Loren Clifford Huntley, Nov. 7, 1942; children—Loren Lee, Marcia Lynn. Reporter, McAlester (Okla.) News Capital, 1939-41; sec., asst. to pres. and chmn. bd. N.Am. Aviation, L.A., 1941-63; v.p., co-owner Tubular Specialties Mfg., Inc., L.A., 1966—. Former sec. 1st Baptist Ch. of Westchester; sec. Westchester-Del Rey Republican Women, 1959-60; assoc. mem. Rep. State Cen. Com., 1973. Cert. profl. sec.; named Outstanding Sec. in So. Calif., So. Calif. chpt., 1954, Internat. Sec. of Yr., 1955 (both Nat. Secs.

Assn.). Home: 1645 San Pablo Dr Lake San Marcos CA 92069 Office: 13011 S Spring St Los Angeles CA 90061

HUNTTING, CYNTHIA COX, artist; b. San Francisco, Sept. 2, 1936; d. E. Morris and Margaret (Storke) Cox; m. Edward Tyler Huntting Jr., Mar. 8, 1969 (div. 1974). BA, Smith Coll., 1958; San Francisco Art Inst., 1959. Artist Emporium White House, San Francisco, 1958-61; artist, staff Pace Program Stanford U., 1962-64; artist World Affairs Council No. Calif., San Francisco, 1964-67; artist pvt. practice San Francisco, 1968—; mem. Modern Art Council Bd. San Francisco Mus. Modern Art, 1970-78. Active Jr. League San Francisco, Inc. Republican. Episcopalian. Clubs: Town and Country, Metropolitan, Calif. Tennis. Home and Office: 2720 Lyon St San Francisco CA 94123

HUOT, RACHEL IRENE, biologist, researcher; b. Manchester, N.H., Oct. 16, 1950; d. Omer Joseph and Irene Alice (Girard) H. BA in Biology cum laude, Rivier Coll., 1972; MS in Biology, Cath. U. Am., 1976, PhD in Biology, 1980. Sr. technician Microbiol. Assocs., Bethesda, Md., 1974-77; chemist Uniformed Svcs. Univ. of Health Scis., Bethesda, 1977-79; biologist Nat. Cancer Inst., Bethesda, 1979-82; postdoctoral fellow S.W. Found. for Biomed. Rsch., San Antonio, 1982-85, asst. scientist, 1985-87, staff scientist, 1987-88; instr. U. Tex. Health Sci. Ctr., San Antonio, 1988-89; asst. prof. La. State U., New Orleans, 1990—; judge sr. div. Alamo Regional Sci. Fair, San Antonio, 1989—. Vol. ARC; active Stephen Ministry. NSF grantee, 1972-74; NIH Rsch. Svc. award, 1983-86. Mem. AAAS, LWV, N.Y. Acad. Sci., Tissue Culture Assn., Am. Soc. for Microbiology, Fedn. Am. Scientists, Sci. Club (pres. 1971-72), St. Vincent De Paul Soc., Sierra, Sigma Xi, Iota Sigma Pi, Delta Epsilon Sigma. Democrat. Roman Catholic. Home: 3440 Edenborn Ave #5 Metaire LA 70002 Office: U New Orleans Sch Medicine Dept Urology 1542 Tulane Ave New Orleans LA 70112

HUPALO, MEREDITH TOPLIFF, artist, illustrator; b. Tarpon Springs, Fla., Apr. 28, 1917; d. Walter and Maurine (Martin) Topliff; cert. in design Pratt Inst., 1938; m. Nicholas Hupalo, July 13, 1940 (dec. Sept. 1977); children: Walter Topliff, John Nicholas. One-woman shows: Tarpon Springs Public Libr., 1945, Valley Stream (N.Y.) Mus., 1962, Contemporary Arts, Inc., N.Y.C., 1966, Jet Clubs Internat., N.Y.C., Henry Waldinger Libr., Valley Stream, N.Y., 1977, East River Savs. Bank, Valley Stream, 1978; two-person show: Art League of Daytona Beach, 1986; represented in permanent collection Valley Stream Pub. Libr., Tarpon Springs (Fla.) Pub. Libr., Eastern Airlines Exec. Offices, N.Y.C.; tchr. printmaking Nassau County (N.Y.) Home Extension Svc.; art adviser Valley Stream Mus., 1962-64; illustrator Eastern Airlines, 1964-68; artist Shell Oil Co., 1968-70; designer Continental Can Co., N.Y.C., 1970-73; art tchr. Astor (Fla.) Community Ctr., 1980-82. Recipient spl. award oil painting 34th Nat. Spring Exhbn. Nat. Art League L.I., 1964, gold medal in oil painting 35th Membership Show, 1965; 1st pl. fine art Fla. Silver Springs Arts & Crafts Festival, 1980; 1st place award Umatilla Fall Festival (Fla.), 1983 merit award, 1985; merit award Tampa Realistic Artists, 1984; Best in Show award Nat. League Am. Pen Women, 1984; 1st pl. Fla. Extension Homemakers Cultural Arts; Award of Distinction, Pioneer Art Settlement, 1987, 3d pl., 1989. Mem. Fla. Watercolor Soc. (assoc., participating artist II), Nat. Art League L.I. (treas. 1959-60), Art League of Daytona Beach (Lillian Gittner Meml. award 1988), Fla. Watercolor Soc. (assoc.), Nat. League Am. Pen Women (2d. pl. Daytona Beach, Fla. br. 1987), Mus. Arts and Scis., DeLand Mus. (3d pl. 1988), Astor Area C. of C. (dir. 1981-82). Methodist. Works include Paintings With Markers, 1972. Home: 55809 Dale Cir Astor FL 32102

HUPP, PATRICIA E., executive assistant, freelance writer, consultant; b. St. Louis, June 22, 1950; d. Joseph Francis and Marguerite Betty (Langendorf) Walsh; divorced; 1 child, Joe L. BA cum laude, Maryville Coll., St. Louis, 1988. Exec. asst. Dr. Pepper/Seven-Up Cos., St. Louis, 1979—; freelance corr. West County Publs., St. Louis, 1988—; pub. rels. cons. Polish Am. Cultural Soc., St. Louis, 1988—; pub. rels. coordinator Alexandra Ballet Co., St. Louis, 1988—, bd. dirs. Event co-chairperson Hands Across Am., St. Louis; mem. publicity com. Jr. League St. Louis; fund-raiser Troup 808 Boy Scouts Am., St. Louis; vol. Big Bros./Big Sisters, Step Up! St. Louis; symphony benefit com. St. Louis Civic Singles Adv. Com.; pub. rels. chairperson Festival of Trees Gala, St. Louis; bd. dirs. St. Louis Easter Seal Soc., regional sec., 1898-90; bd. dirs. St. Louis Squires and Ladies Charitable Found., v.p.; bd. dirs. A Single Response. Mem. Internat. Assn. Bus. Communicators, Women's Commerce Assn. (mem. community svc., dinner program coms.), Chandon Club, Delta Epsilon Sigma. Republican. Roman Catholic. Office: Dr Pepper/Seven-Up Cos 8900 Page Ave Saint Louis MO 63114

HURAJT, ANDREA RUTH, controller; b. Cleve., Feb. 29, 1948; d. Andrew Steve and Ruth (Gamary) H.; m. Larry Edward Buehner, May 12, 1988. Student, Dyke Coll., Cleve., 1971-72, Cuyahoga Community Coll., Parma, Ohio, 1984-88. Acct. C.E. Basic, Inc., Cleve., 1973-83; office mgr., acct. Bassichus Co., Cleve., 1983-85; office mgr. Ross Equipment, Cleve., 1985-89; sec.-treas. Associated Equipment Corp., Cleve., 1985-90; contr. Ross Equipment, Cleve., 1988-89; owner, sec.-treas. G.A.L. Family Corp., 1988—; sec.-treas. Associated Equipment Corp., Cleve., 1985—, Bean's Pl., 1988—. Mem. Profl. Women's Assn., Cleve. Women Working (past v.p.). Democrat. Lutheran. Home: 4790 Andrea Ln Cleveland OH 44109 Office: GAL Family Corp 4790 Andrea Ln Cleveland OH 44109

HURBANIS, BRENDA LOUISE, educator; b. Chgo., Nov. 3, 1949; d. Paul Hurbanis and Mary Jane (Adams) Della Toffalo. BS, Frostburg State Coll., 1972; MEd, Western Md. Coll., 1976; EdD, U. Md., 1986. Elem. tchr. Washington County Pub. Schs., Hagerstown, Md., 1972-74, Anne Arundel County Pub. Schs., Annapolis, Md., 1974-75; tchr. language, arts Anne Arundel County Pub. Schs., Annapolis, 1975-77, guidance counselor, 1977-79, guidance dept. chairperson, 1979-81, guidance resource counselor, 1981-83, coordinator instructional leadership program, 1983—; coop. tchr. Anne Arundel County Pub. Schs., 1976-77, counselor trainer 1981-82; cons. Queen Anne's County Pub. Schs., Centerville, Md., 1983-85. Author (handbooks): Guidance Curriculum Handbook, 1982, Discipline, 1982, School Climate Survey, 1986, Strategic Planning Handbook, 1989. Bd. dirs. Ocean Time Homeowners Assn., Ocean City, Md., 1986—, pres., 1989—. Recipient Community Service award United Way Cen. Md., 1978, Counselor of Yr. award Md. Sch. Counselors Assn., 1981, Counseling Contbns. award Md. Personnel and Guidance Assn., 1981, Disting. Service award Anne Arundel County Tchrs. Assn., 1981, Pres.' Service award, 1981. Mem. Assn. for Supervision and Curriculum, Md. Assn. Counseling and Devel. (bd. dirs. 1980), Md. Edn. Assn. (rep. 1975-81), Md. Mid. Sch. Assn., Nat. Orgn. Devel. Network, Anne Arundel County Counselor's Assn. (pres. 1980, Pres.'s Service award 1981). Democrat. Lutheran. Home: 8403 High Ridge Rd Ellicott City MD 21043 Office: Anne Arundel County Pub Schs Freetown Elem Sch Glen Burnie MD 21061

HURCHALLA, MAGGY RENO, county commissioner; b. Miami, Fla., Dec. 11, 1940; d. Henry Olaf and Jane (Wood) Reno; m. James Hurchalla, Nov. 26, 1960; children: James, Robert, Jane, George. BA, Swarthmore Coll., 1962. Mem. water bd. County of Martin, Stuart, Fla., 1972-74, commr., 1974—; mem. Regional Planning Coun., Stuart, 1974, 80-84. Author: (booklet) Woods and Bushes of Martin County, 1974. Named Conservationist of Yr. Fla. Audubon Soc., 1984; recipient Land and Water award Fla. Wildlife Fedn., 1984. Democrat. Home: 5775 SE Nassau Ter Stuart FL 34997 Office: Martin County 2401 Monterey Rd Stuart FL 34997

HURD, SHIRLEY DYER, health care administrator; b. Atlanta, Jan. 8, 1940; d. Martin and Geneva (Thomas) Dyer; m. Albert Hurd Jr., June 10, 1957; children: Reginald, Zachery. BS in Nursing, Cath. U. Am., 1972; MA, Cen. Mich. U., 1978; DS, Pacific Western U., 1980; MA, U. Colo., 1973. RN. Emergency room coord. Penrose Hosp., Colorado Springs, Colo.; bldg. coord. St. Elizabeth Hosp., Washington; clin. dir. Capitol Hill Hosp., Washington; clin. coord. Commn. Human and Health Svcs., Washington; cons. in field. Active Nat. Women's Polit. Caucas, Inner Circle Rep. Party. Recipient Speech award, 1989. Mem. NAFE, Internat. Tng. Communication Network. Presbyterian. Home: 14541 Carona Dr Silver Spring MD 20904 Office: 2700 Martin L King Ave Washington DC 20032

HUREWITZ, SHARON JOY, communications company executive; b. Phila., July 18, 1959; d. Herbert Benedict Hurewitz and Arlene Renee (Bilker) Finston. BA in Polit. Sci., Temple U., 1981; postgrad., Villanova U., 1982-89. Programmer/analyst JACA Corp., Ft. Washington, Pa., 1981-83; sr. analyst/programmer Smith Kline Bio-Sci. Labs., King of Prussia, Pa., 1983-86; software engr. GTE Data Svcs., Tampa, Fla., 1986-88; tech. staff Telenet Communications Corp., Reston, Va., 1988-89; internat. program mgr. Sprint Internat. (formerly Telenet Communications Corp.), Reston, 1989—. Assoc. editor Tandem Users Jour., 1988-90, mng. editor 1986-87; editor NRTUG Newsletter, 1983; contbr. articles to profl. jours. Treas. Summerridge Condominium Assn., Reston, 1989; legis. aide State Rep. Joseph A. Lashinger, Norristown, Pa., 1979, 80; coord. Super Sunday Com., Norristown, 1980. Future Leaders scholarship Temple U., 1979. Mem. NOW, Internat. Tandem Users Group (bd. dirs. 1986-87). Republican. Office: Sprint Internat Comm 12490 Sunrise Valley Dr VARESB322J Reston VA 22096

HURLEY, ALLYSON KINGSLEY, dentist; b. Buffalo, June 15, 1949; d. Norman and Marion (Legler) Kingsley; m. Lawrence Joseph Hurley, May 28, 1977, 1 child, Michael William. Student, Barat Coll., 1967-68; degree in dental hygiene, Marquette U., 1970, BS, 1971; DDS, Howard U., 1977. Pvt. practice dental hygiene, Washington, 1971-77; resident VA Hosp., Lyons, N.J., 1977-78; gen. practice dentistry, Chatham, N.J., 1978—; attending dentist Overlook Hosp., Summit, N.J., 1979—, dir. resident adminstrn., 1980—, mem. edn. com., 1981—; clin. instr. dental hygiene Union County Tech. Inst., Scotch Plains, N.J., 1979-81, mem. selection com. for dental dept., 1987; coord. kindergarten-4th grades dental health program Chatham Boro Sch. System, 1978—; active oral cancer screening program Chatham Boro Jr. Women's Club, 1980-82. Editor, contbg. author newsletter Word of Mouth, 1981—; author: (booklet) Your Child's Teeth, 1984. Alumni recruiter Marquette U., Morris County, N.J., 1977—; bd. dirs. Am. Cancer Soc., Morris County, 1981-83; chair Scholarship Found. of the Chathams, Inc., 1985—. Fellow Acad. Gen. Destistry; mem. ADA, Tri-County Dental Soc. (bd. dirs. 1982-83), Internat. Platform Assn., N.Y. Acad. Scis., Columbia U. Dental Study Club (treas. 1980—), No. N.J. Women's Study Club (pres. 1980-82, 86-89, sec. 1983—), Newcomer's Club Chatham Township. Republican. Roman Catholic. Office: Allyson Kingsley Hurley DDS 585 Main St Chatham Township NJ 07928

HURLEY, CHERYL JOYCE, publishing company executive; b. Pitts., Oct. 30, 1947; d. John and Violet Dernorsek; m. Kevin Hurley, July 27, 1974. Lang. and lit. cert., Université de Lyon, France, 1968; A.B., Ohio U., 1969; M.A., U. Mich., 1971. Research assoc. MLA, N.Y.C., 1972-74, dir. spl. programs, 1974-79; pub. The Library of America, N.Y.C., 1979—, pres., 1988—; cons. in field. Contbr. articles to profl. jours. Rackham fellow, 1969-70. Mem. Am. Studies Assn. (com. on publs. 1983—), Mecox Yacht Club (Bridgehampton, L.I.), Grolier Club, Bridgehampton Club, Phi Beta Kappa, Alpha Lambda elta, Phi Sigma Iota, Phi Kappa Phi. Home: 4 E 88th St New York NY 10128 Office: Libr of Am 14 E 60th St New York NY 10022

HURLEY, ELAINE MARGARET, information systems specialist; b. Lowell, Mass., July 30, 1958; d. John Thomas and Rita (Coffey) H. BS magna cum laude, U. Lowell, 1984. Office mgr. Town of Dracut (Mass.) Sewer Dept. Mem. NAFE. Office: 1196 Lakeview Ave Dracut MA 01826

HURLEY, GIOVANNA MARIA, psychologist; b. Biddleford, Maine, Jan. 20, 1952; d. Daniel Edward and Maria (Phillips) H.; m. James Edward Fortin, Aug. 29, 1981; 1 child, Kate. BA in Psychology, Wheaton Coll., Norton, Mass., 1974; MEd in Counseling Psychology, Boston Coll., 1978, postgrad., 1979—. Lic. psychol. examiner, Maine. Asst. staff psychologist Wientham (Mass.) State Sch., 1974-78, staff psychologist, 1978, prin. psychologist, 1978-79; trainee in psychology Children's Hosp., Boston, 1979-80; grad. asst., lectr. Boston Coll., Chestnut Hill, Mass., 1980-81; clin. fellow, teaching fellow MGH Bunker Hill Health Ctr./Boston Coll., 1981-83; psychologist Region West Family Counseling Svc., Newton, Mass., 1982-83, Maine Bur. Mental Retardation, Portland, 1983-85; pvt. practice Casco, Maine, 1985—; cons. YWCA Teen Pregnancy Program, Portland, 1989, Portland-Lewiston Bur. Mental Retardation, 1985—, ARC Respite Program, Portland, 1989—, Farmington (Maine) Child Devel. Svcs., 1989—. Mem. Am. Psychol. Assn., Maine Psychol. Assn. Democrat. Roman Catholic.

HURLEY, LINDA KAY, psychologist; b. Kansas City, Mo., June 4, 1951; d. James O. and Phyllis L. (Steil) H.; m. Gregory S. Burgin, Nov. 28, 1987. BS, U. Mo., 1973; BA, Am. U., 1978, MA, 1983, PhD, 1986. Lic. psychologist, Tex. Assoc. psychologist Tarrant County Mental Health/Mental Retardation, Ft. Worth, 1983-84; intern in med. psychology Oreg. Health Scis. U., Portland, 1984-85; instr. in pediatrics and psychology U. Tex. Southwestern Med. Ctr., Dallas, 1985-88, asst. prof., 1988-90; psychologist, dir. tng. Child Study Ctr., Ft. Worth, 1990—; bd. trustees Ronald McDonald House (Friends of Ft. Worth Children, Inc.), 1986-89. With USAF, 1974-77. Mem. Am. Psychol. Assn. (clin. psychology div., clin. child psychology sect.), Soc. Pediatric Psychology, Assn. Advancement of Behavior Therapy, Soc. Rsch. in Child Devel., Tex. Psychol. Assn., Dallas Psychol. Assn., Phi Kappa Phi. Office: Child Study Ctr 1300 W Lancaster Fort Worth TX 76102

HURLEY, MARJORIE BRYAN, bank executive; b. Ft. Worth, Feb. 13, 1941; d. Everett and Ollie Rhea (McKinney) Bryan; m. Doyle Andrew Hurley, Mar. 15, 1958; children: Gregory Dean, Jeffrey Alan. Cert. in bank mktg., U. Colo., 1978; cert. in bank mktg. mgmt., U. Ga., 1984. Asst. mktg. Bank of the S.W. (now BancOne-Houston), Houston, 1965-75; asst. v.p., dir. mktg. Union First Nat. Bank (now First Am. Bank), Washington, 1975; v.p., dir. mktg. United Mo. Bancshares, Inc., Kansas City, 1979-88, sr. v.p., 1988—. Advisor: (textbook) Marketing for Bankers, 1982. Mem. Advt. Club of Kansas City (treas. 1985-86, sec. 1986-87, 88-89, bd. dirs. 1984—, v.p. membership 1990—, Ad Woman of Yr. award 1983), Bank Mktg. Assn. (pres. Heart of Am. chpt. 1988-89). Republican. Baptist. Office: United Mo Bancshares Inc 928 Grand Kansas City MO 64106

HURLEY, MARLENE EMOGENE, oil company executive; b. Chamois, Mo., July 23, 1938; d. Eugene Arthur Harrison and Mary Elizabeth (Turner) Meredith; m. Aaron Downs Hurley, Nov. 25, 1956; children: Mitchell Kelly, Aaron Downs Jr. Cert. oil and gas acctg., frontline mgr. Acct. McGrath Constrn. Co., Tulsa, 1964-66, G&T, Inc., G&T Constrn. and Valley Supply Co., Tulsa, 1965-67; acctg. supr. Automation Industries, Inc., Boulder, Colo., 1968-73; office mgr., chief acct. Automotive Svcs., White Rock Investments, JWD Corp., 3 Constrn. Div., Boulder, 1973; freelance acct. various cos., Boulder, 1974-76; treas., contr. Quicksilver, Inc., Colo. X-Ray, Colo. Processor Svc., Broomfield, 1974-79; contr. Hartford House, Ltd., Boulder, 1979-80; adminstrv. asst., mgr. Joint Acct. Payables Freeport McMoran, Inc., McMoran Oil & Gas, Midlands Oil, Lakewood, Colo., 1980-86; chief fin. officer Transp. Engring. Systems, Inc., Broomfield, 1987-88; asst. treas., contr. Altex Industries Inc., Altex Oil, Parrish Oil Tools, Denver, 1989—; cons. Spruce Realty, Boulder, 1974-76, Aaron Associated Affiliates, Lafayette, Colo., 1987-88. Mem. Rebekah lodge (past madam pres. 1966-67). Democrat. Home: Rte 7 Box 405 Golden CO 80403 Office: Altex Industries Inc 1430 Larimer St Denver CO 80202

HURLEY, PRISCILLA R., advertising executive; b. Cleve., May 29, 1940; d. Charles Wesley and Martha (Cretors) Ruddick; m. Edward D. Hurley. BA, Ohio Wesleyan U., 1962; MBA, Pace U., 1983. Sales asst. Ashland Chem., Dublin, Ohio, 1977-78; asst. to v.p. Nestle Co., White Plains, N.Y., 1978-79; advt. mgr. Edn. Mgmt. Corp., N.Y.C., 1979-86; dir. advt. Manhattan East Ste. Hotels, N.Y.C., 1986—; bd. dirs. Egis Corp., Mount Vernon, N.Y. Founder Marysville Community Theater, Ohio 1974. Recipient Mktg. award Pace U. N.Y.C. 1983. Mem. Advt. Women N.Y., Ft. Hill Players White Plains, Greenwich Choral Soc. Office: Manhattan East Ste Hotels 505 E 75th St New York NY 10021

HURST, CAROLYN JEAN, editor, writer; b. Rapid City, S.D., Jan. 21, 1958; d. Gene R. and Alice Louise (Oshner) H.; m. Steven L. Perry, Aug. 8, 1980; children: Natalie Hurst Perry, Evan Hurst Perry. Student, U. Idaho, 1976-77, 78-79; BS in Broadcast Journalism, S.D. State U., 1980. Asst. producer Sta. KUID-TV, Moscow, Idaho, 1978-79; asst. editor Volga (S.D.) Tribune, 1979-81; editor Crow Publs., Denver, 1981-82; news editor Kitsap County Herald, Poulsbo, Wash., 1983; editor Oudoor Empire Pub., Seattle, 1982-83, asst. to pres., 1983-85, cover editor, 1983—; cons. Windemere Real Estate, Silverdale, Wash., 1987—. Editor Fishing and Hunting News Freshwater Fish Maps, 1985. Mem. Phi Kappa Phi, Pi Gamma Mu, Kappa Tau Alpha. Home: 375 NW Sigurd Hanson Rd Poulsbo WA 98370 Office: Windermere Real Estate/H&M 3100 NW Bucklin Hill Rd Silverdale WA 98383

HURST, CATHERINE BEYER, computer company official, writer, editor; b. Ithaca, N.Y., Dec. 23, 1944; d. Robert Thomas and Margaret Ellen (Fletcher) Beyer; children: Brian David, Timothy Beyer. BA in Philosophy cum laude, Newton Coll. Sacred Heart, 1966; postgrad., Cath. U. Am., 1966-67; MBA with honors, Northeastern U., 1988. Sec., bookkeeper Techbuilt, Inc., Cambridge, Mass., 1967-70; editor alumnae publs. Newton (Mass.) Coll., 1970-75; freelance writer, 1975-77; tech. writer Epsilon, Inc., Burlington, Mass., 1977-82; mgr. tech. info. Epsilon, Inc., Burlington, 1982-83, mgr. online svcs., 1983-85, mgr. applications dev., 1985-86, mgr. new product documentation and tng., 1986-88, dir. program mgmt. in rsch. and devel., 1988-90, account dir., 1990—; seminar speaker women's resource com. Boston Coll., Chestnut Hill, Mass., 1977, 86. Contbr. numerous articles to various publs. Chmn., co-chmn. 5th, 10th, 15th, and 20th reunions Newton Coll., 1971-86, class sec., 1966—; founding mem., treas. Acton (Mass.) Jr. Women's Club, 1972-76; treas. McCarthy-Towne Parent Tchr. Student Orgn., 1980-81; publicity chmn. Acton Boxborough Boys' Swim Team Boosters, 1986-90; chmn. Project Graduation 1990, Acton. Named One of Top 10 Alumni Publs. Editor, Am. Coll. Pub. Rels. Assn., 1974. Mem. Beta Gamma Sigma. Roman Catholic. Home: 146 Willow St Acton MA 01720 Office: Epsilon Inc 50 Cambridge St Burlington MA 01803

HURST, CHRISTINA MARIE, respiratory therapist; b. San Diego, Jan. 29, 1955; d. Harvey Joseph Breighner and Doris Romaine (March) March-Breighner; m. Harry Richard Hurst IV, Dec. 19, 1982; children: Heather Erin, Ian Richard. AAS, Del. Tech. Coll., 1989. Cert. respiratory therapist Med. Ctr. Del., Christiana, 1989—; registered respiratory therapist Med. Ctr. Del., Christina, 1990—; instr. basic. cardiopulmonary rescusitation, Wilmington, Del., 1989-90; speaker Senate Labor Rels. Com., 1987. Vol. preschool asthma program Am. Lung Assn. Del., Wilmington, 1989, Del. Epilepsy Found. Wilmington, 1988-90; exec. coun. State Adv. Coun. for Svcs. to Handicapped, Dover, Del., 1989-90; charter mem. parent support group Children with Epilepsy, Wilmington, 1988-90. Mem. Am. Assn. for Respiratory Care, Epilepsy Found. Am., Phi Theta Kappa. Home: 518 Pheasant Run Bear DE Office: Med Ctr Del Stanton Ogletown Rd Newark DE 19713

HURST, FLORA MIA MOLEY, paralegal, office manager; b. New Orleans, Aug. 23, 1953; d. Victor Frank and Laura Elizabeth (Diggs) Moley; m. Matthew Grant Hurst, Jan. 23, 1976. BA, Southea. La. U., 1974. Cert. speech tchr., La. Tchr. Immaculata High Sch., Marrero, La., 1976-77; legal sec. Hammett, Leake, Hammett, P.L.C., New Orleans, 1978-79, Beard, Blue, Schmidt, P.L.C., New Orleans, 1979; legal sec., office mgr. Babovich, McDowell & Bukaty, New Orleans, 1979-84; paralegal, office mgr. Edward F. Bukaty, III, P.L.C., Metairie, La., 1984—. Coach Carrollton Playground, New Orleans, 1978; vol. Jefferson (La.) Nursing Home, 1983, Wayne M. Babovich for Coun. campaign, New Orleans, 1984, St. Dominic Summer Softball, New Orleans, 1985, Peta Silver Spring Monkey Rescue, New Orleans, 1988, Rep. Nat. Conv., 1988. Mem. Internat. Primate Protection League, Jefferson SPCA, Bucks and Does Carnival Club, Krewe of Aquila Carnival Club, People for the Ethical Treatment of Animals, Physician's Com. for Responsible Medicine, Adopt an Animal for the New Orleans Zool. Gardens. Democrat. Roman Catholic. Office: One Galleria Blvd Ste 900 Metairie LA 70001

HURST, FRANCES ETHEL WEEKLEY, retired librarian; b. Birmingham, Ala., Feb. 27, 1919; d. Harold Hudson and Nota Leigh (Windham) Weekley; m. Henry Odessa Hurst, Sept. 8, 1947 (dec. 1962); children: Rosalind Frances Hurst Minderhout, Walter Henry; m. Kenneth Dean, 1983 (div. 1987). BA in Edn., U. Ala., 1941; BA in LS, Emory U., 1945. Tchr. pub. schs. of Ala., 1941-44, 50-52, 1957-62; librarian TVA, Wilson Dam, Ala., 1945-46, U. Ala., Tuscaloosa, 1946-50, 62-69; case worker Talladega County Dept. Pub. Welfare, Talladega, Ala., 1952-53; librarian Jefferson State Community Coll., Birmingham, 1969-87. Mem. AAUW, Ala. Edn. Assn., NEA, Ala. Ret. Tchrs. Assn., Capstone Coll. Edn. Soc., Nat. Alumni Asn. of U. Ala., Am. Assn. Ret. Persons, Kappa Delta Pi, Pi Tau Chi, Triangle. Methodist. Home: 1641 5th St NW Birmingham AL 35215

HURST, SUSAN DIANE, adolescent counselor; b. Kansas City, Mo., May 9, 1957; d. Harold Norman and Phyllis Dee (Shaw) H.; m. Daniel Sneh, Apr. 20, 1986; 1 child, Jonathan Caleb. Student, Hebrew U. Jerusalem, 1977-78; BA with honors, U. Tex., 1979; MA in Psychology, U. Mo., Kansas City, 1981. Crisis counselor Middle Earth Crisis Ctr., Austin, Tex., 1976-77; recreational therapist Austin State Hosp., 1978-79; teaching asst. U. Mo., 1980-81; tchr. Jewish Edn. Coun., Overland Park, Kans., 1980—; teen specialist, project dir. Jewish Family and Children's Svcs., Overland Park, 1986—; tour leader Ramah Seminars in Israel, Jerusalem, summers 1980-85. Mem. teen com. Stop Violence Coalition, Shawnee Mission, Kans., 1986-87; mem. edn. and tng. com. Planned Parenthood, Kansas City, 1988—; mem. adolescent activities com. Kansas City Mayor's Coun. on Youth Devel., 1986—; tchr. Project STAR: Students Taught Awareness and Resistance, Kansas City, 1986. Recipient award Nat. Assn. Jewish Family, Children's and Health Profls., 1989. Mem. Assn. Jewish Family and Children's Agy. Profls., Adolescent Resource Network. Office: Jewish Family-Childrens Svc 5801 W 115th St Ste 103 Overland Park KS 66211

HURT, KATHA CONNOR, state legislator, elementary school teacher; b. Hays, Kans., May 29, 1947; d. Jess Alan and Verna Grace 9Razak) C. BS in Elem. Edn., Fort Hays U., 1969; MS in Elem. Edn., Kans. State U., 1975. Tchr. Colby (Kans.) Pub. Schs., 1969-71, Manhattan-Ogden (Kans.) Schs., 1972—; state legislator State of Kans., Topeka; mem. Edn. com., Local Gov. com., Pensions, Investments and Benefits com., 1989 Interim com. Energy and Natural Resources. mem. Friendship Tutoring Adv. bd., 1980-88, chair. 1983-88; mem. long rang planning com. First United Meth. Ch., 1984-86, ch. and soc. com. 1987—; mem. Flint Hills Econ. Lifelines com. Mem. Assn. for Supervision and Curriculum Devel., Internat. Reading Assn., Tchrs. Applying Whole Lang., PTA, NEA, KNEA, NEA Manhattan (pres. 1981-83, negotiations team mem. 1980-84, polit. action com. chair 1984-85, tchr. rights com. chair 1985-86, Kans. NEA bd. dirs. 1983-89, bd. dirs. liaison to reading circle 1983-89, bd. dirs. liaison to instructional advocacy commn. 1985-89), Accreditation Adv. Com. State Bd. Edn. Home: 1921 Anderson Ave Manhattan KS 66502 Office: State Capitol Rm 281-W Topeka KS 66612

HURT, PAMELA DENISE, chemist, spectroscopist; b. Highland, Ill., Apr. 2, 1964; d. David Densil and Judy Ella (Wilke) H. BS in Chemistry, So. Ill. U., 1987. Chemist Environ. Analysis, Florissant, Mo., 1986-88, Chemir Labs., St. Louis, 1988—. Mem. Am. Chem. Soc. Home: 43 Camrose Green Collinsville IL 62234 Office: Chemir Labs 2806 S Brentwood Blvd Saint Louis MO 63144

HURVITZ, CAROLE HUGHES, pediatrian, hematologist; b. London, Dec. 10, 1942; came to U.S., 1968; d. Richard and Rosemary Helen (Knight) Hughes; m. Richard J. Hurvitz, Jan. 31, 1969; children: Graham, Mark, Keith, Andrew. MB BChir, U. Sheffield, Eng., 1967. House officer King Edward VII Hosp., Windsor, Eng., 1967-68; fellow pathology Health Scis. Ctr., UCLA, 1968-69; resident in pediatrics Cedars of Lebanon Hosp., L.A., 1969-71; fellow hematology and oncology Children's Hosp., L.A., 1971-72; pvt. practice L.A., 1972-75; pediatric hematologist Cedars-Sinai Med. Ctr., L.A., 1972-79, dir. pediatric hematology-oncology, 1979—, acting dir. pediatrics, 1984-86, assoc. dir. pediatrics clin. affairs, 1986—; assoc. clin. prof. pediatrics UCLA Sch. Medicine. Fellow Am. Acad. Pediatrics; mem. L.A. Pediatric Soc. (v.p. 1989-90, pres.-elect 1990—), Am. Soc. Hematology, Am. Soc. Clin. Oncology. Office: Cedars-Sinai Med Ctr 8700 Beverly Blvd Box 48750 Los Angeles CA 90004

HURWITZ, MICHELE LESLIE WEBER, communications specialist; b. Chgo., Oct. 26, 1959; d. Edward and Barbara (Taradash) W.; m. Benjamin Alan Hurwitz, Nov. 12, 1989. BS in Journalism, U. Ill., Urbana, 1981. Writer Benefit Trust Life Ins. Co., Chgo., 1981-82; acct. exec. USI Communications PR Firm, Chgo., 1982-83; copywriter Assocs. Printing Svc.,

Glenview, Ill., 1983-84; media rels. mgr. Am. Acad. of Pediatrics, Elk Grove Village, Ill., 1984-89, dir. pub. rels., 1989—; communications cons. Master Brew Beverages, Inc., Northbrook, 1981—; tchr. READ NOW, Wheeling, Ill., 1988. Contbr. articles to profl. jours. Recipient Honorable Mention Spectra '88 Internat. Assn. of Bus. Communicators, Silver Trumpet award Publicity Club of Chgo. Mem. Publicity Club of Chgo. Home: 2452 Towne Blvd Arlington Heights IL 60004 Office: Am Acad of Pediatrics 141 Northwest Point Blvd Elk Grove Village IL 60009

HUSAK, SUSAN M. V. (CHELSEA MANN), media and communications executive, writer, musician; b. Havertown, Pa., Aug. 30, 1961; d. John Joseph and Dorothy Phyllis (Dispensiere) Erdlen; m. Steven Husak, May, 1986 (div. 1990). BA in Communications, Glassboro (N.J.) State Coll., 1983; postgrad., U. of Arts, Phila. Asst. editor Jersey Woman Mag., Marlton, 1983-85; v.p. Interstate Ins., Somerdale, N.J., 1985-87; advt. and editorial asst. Regal Communications, Moorestown, N.J., 1987-88; adminstrv. asst. Adams and Braverman Advt. Inc., Phila., 1989-90, Rosanio, Bailets & Talamo Inc., Cherry Hill, N.J., 1990—; pub. rels. writer Val Vasil Health Entertainment, Blackwood, N.J., 1986-87; advt. and editorial rep. Phantom Press Publs., New Haven, Conn., 1989—; freelance writer, musician and performing artist., 1978—. Author: The Christmas Carousel, 1990; composer numerous songs; editor: Avant Mag., 1981. Fundraiser N.J. Humane Soc. for Animals, Newark, 1989; active various animal rights and environ. activities. Recipient 1st place award for graphic short story Marvel Comics, 1985, 1st place award for poetry World of Poetry, 1988. Mem. Phila. Writers Orgn. Home: 128-6 Kirkbride Rd Voorhees NJ 08043

HUSSAR, SUSAN RAE, electrical engineer; b. Detroit, Dec. 6, 1951; d. Louis Edward and Thelma Pauline (Dickerson) Fritz; m. Gary Michael, Sept. 9, 1972 (div. Dec. 1988). BSEE, U. Mich., Ann Arbor, 1980. Engr. The Budd Co., Detroit, 1980-81, mfg. engr., 1981-83, product engr., 1983-85; applications engr. Robert Bosch Corp., Farmington Hills, Mich., sr. applications engr., 1985-86; engring. supr. Robert Bosch Corp., Mich., 1986-89; ABS design engr. Ford Motor Co., Dearborn, Mich., 1989—; P.A.C. com. mem. The Budd Co., Troy, 1982-85, Soc. Automotive Engrs., Detroit, 1980—; Tire & Rim Assn., Dayton, 1983-85; EI facilitator The Budd Co., Troy, 1983-85. Com. Mem. Am. Lung Assn., Ann Arbor, 1988-89. Mem. IEEE, Soc. Automotive Engrs., Travis Pointe Country Club. Republican. Home: 5790 Cherrywood Dr 1704 West Bloomfield MI 48322

HUSSAR, SUSAN VICKERY, insurance brokerage executive; b. Des Moines, Oct. 24, 1958; d. James Alexander and Dorothy Estelle (Gross) Vickery; m. Ted William Hussar, Feb. 15, 1986. BS in Psychology, U. Iowa, 1981. V.p. Kirke-Van Orsdel Inc., Washington and Des Moines, 1982—. Mem. D.C. Profl. Ins. Women (newsletter editor 1984-85), Potomac Bus. and Profl. Women (treas. 1990-91), Jr. League Washington. Republican. Episcopalian. Office: Kirke-Van Orsdel Inc 2000 Pennsylvania Ave 7100 Washington DC 20006

HUSSAR, SYBIL ANNE, town committee woman, volunteer; b. N.Y.C., May 29, 1929; d. August M. and Nelle (Moore) H.; divorced; 1 child, Damian Michael. BA, Marymount Coll.; postgrad., Columbia U. Mgr. Log Cabin Farms, Armonk, N.Y.; asst. pers. dir. Sonotone Corp., Elmsford, N.Y.; pers. interviewer Pan Am, N.Y.C.; dir. of student rels. Hilton Hotels; social svc. worker West County Social Svc. Dept., White Plains, N.Y.; dog breeder, Armonk, N.Y., 1950—. Active vol. A.C.S.; vice chmn. Repub. Town Com., North Castle, N.Y., 1955—. Home: 2625 Muirfield Ct West Palm Beach FL 23414

HUSSEIN, PATTIE YU, public relations executive; b. Washington, Nov. 15, 1956; d. Michael Yung-An and Marie (Chang) Y.; d. Sharif Raouf Hussein, June 21, 1980. BS in Journalism, U. Md., 1977; cert. Journalism, NYU, 1977; cert. Arabic Lang., Middle East Inst., Wash., 1981; MA in Communications, U. Md., 1982. Editorial asst. The Washington Star Newspaper, 1977, daily dealine "Today's News" writer, 1977-79; asst. dir. univ. relations U. Md., College Park, 1979-82; communications cons., fed. systems div. IBM, Bethesda, Md.; v.p. Porter/Novelli, Washington, 1987—; bd. mgrs. pub. relations agy. Omnicom, 1987—; account exec. Needham Porter Noville, Washington, 1983-84; sr. account exec. Doremus Porter Novelli, Washington, 1984-86; cons. Mount Vernon Coll., Washington, 1982. Recipient Bronze award, Film/Video, Addy award, Cert. of Excellence, "Treat It for Life" PSA Campaign, Washington Advt. Club, Mercury award, 1989, ATME award, 1990. Mem. Pub. Relations Soc. Am. (Recipient Thoth award, Nat. Capital chpt.), Nat. Assn. Gov. Communications (Recipient Gold Screen award), Communicators Excellence to Black Audiences (Recipient Excellence award), World Inst. Black Communicators, Washington Women in Pub. Relations, Redbook Assn. Edn. in Journalism, Silver Spring Bus. Profl. Women, Publicators Com. Alumni (recording sec.). Democrat. Roman Catholic. Office: Porter/Novelli 1001 30th St NW Washington DC 20007

HUSSELMAN, GRACE, innkeeper, educator; b. Paterson, N.J., July 24, 1923; d. Edward and Lydia (Kliphouse) Van Allen; B.A., William Paterson Coll.; m. Samuel Husselman, June 3, 1944; children—Samuel Glenn, Howard Lloyd. With personnel office Wright Aero. Corp., Fairlawn, Pub. 1942-45; library asst. Wyckoff (N.J.) Pub. Library, 1964-66; library dir. Allendale (N.J.) Pub. Library, 1967-81; elem. sch. tchr., assoc. ednl. media specialist, 1981-84; owner Ye Olde Buckmaster Inn, 1984—. Reading Merit Badge counselor Boy Scouts Am.; pioneer guide Pioneer Girls, nat. youth v.p., sec. friendship circle; sec. bookstore com. Christian Growth Ministries; sec. Ladies Aid Soc., Shrewsbury Community Ch.; bd. deacons Shrewsbury Community Ch.; bd. dirs. Shrewsbury Library, Vt. Mem. N.J., Bergen-Passaic library assns., Hist. Soc. of Shrewsbury (pres./sec.), Kappa Delta Pi. Club: Captains and Mates Yacht. Home: Lincoln Hill Rd Shrewsbury VT 05783

HUSSEY, CAROL ANN, university official; b. Plainview, Tex., Jan. 11, 1955; d. Roland Fountain and Acine (Webb) H. BA with high honors, U. Tex., 1977, postgrad., 1978-79. Dir. devel. rsch. and records St. Edward's U., Austin, Tex., 1980-85, registrar, 1985—. Mem. Austin Civic Orch., 1986—. Recipient Leadership award YWCA, Austin, 1986. Mem. Am. Assn. Collegiate Registrars and Admissions Officers, So. Assn. Collegiate Registrars and Admissions Officers, Tex. Assn. Collegiate Registrars and Admissions Officers, Nat. Assn. Intercollegiate Athletics, AAUW, Phi Beta Kappa, Psi Chi, Alpha Lambda Delta. Home: 602-B Texas Ave Austin TX 78705 Office: St Edward's U 3001 S Congress Ave Austin TX 78705

HUSSEY, JOLEE CHILDS, media specialist; b. Tupelo, Miss., June 2, 1948; d. Thomas Everett and Arey Lee (Stephens) Childs; m. Charles Logan Hussey. BA, U. Miss., 1970, MSS, 1972, MLS, 1984. Chemistry librarian U. Miss., Oxford, 1972-74, 1984-88; media specialist, 1988--, Oxford City Schs., 1988--. Commr. State Hosp. Commn., Jackson, Miss., 1984-86; bd. dirs. Oxford Endowment for Pub. Edn., Oxford-Lafayette County Pub. Libr. Recipient Spirit of Svc. award Oxford City Schs., 1987, Community Disting. Svc. award, 1989. Mem. AAUW, Am. Libr. Assn., Miss. Libr. Assn., Jr. Aux., Phi Kappa Phi, Kappa Delta Pi. Democrat. Home: 54 David St Oxford MS 38655 Office: Oxford City Schs Bramlett Blvd Oxford MS 38655

HUSSEY, NAN MARIE, store executive; b. Wenatchee, Wash., Aug. 14, 1957; d. Charles William and Sarah Alice (Fulkerson) Hussey. Student, Whitworth Coll., 1977; BA in Bus., German Lit., Hope Coll., 1981. Asst. mgr. Arvey Paper & Office Products, Austin, Tex., 1982-83; store mgr. Arvey Paper & Office Products, Elk Grove, Ill., 1983-84, Bellevue, Wash., 1984--. mem. Common Cause, 1976, Amnesty Internat., 1985, Nat. Orgn. Women, 1987. Mem. Summa Cum Laude, Phi Beta Kappa. Democrat. Office: Arvey Paper & Office Products 1910 132d Ave NE Bellevue WA 98005

HUSTON, ANJELICA, actress; b. Los Angeles; d. John and Enrica Huston. Student, Loft Studio. Actress appearing in Hamlet, Roundhouse Theatre, London, Tamara, Il Vittorale Theatre, L.A.; appeared in films including A Walk with Love and Death, 1969, Hamlet, 1969, The Last Tycoon, 1976, The Postman Always Rings Twice, 1981, This is Spinal Tap, 1984, The Ice Pirates, 1984, Prizzi's Honor, 1985 (Academy award for best supporting actress, N.Y. and L.A. Film Critics award), Captain Eo, 1986, Gardens of Stone, 1987, The Dead, 1987 (Best Actress award Ind. Filmakers 1987), Mr. North, 1988, Witches, 1989, A Handful of Dust, Crimers and Misdemeanors, 1989, Enemies, A Love Story, 1989; TV films The Cowboy and the Ballerina, 1984, Faerie Tale Theatre, A Rose for Miss Emily, Lonesome Dove, 1989, The Grifters, 1989. Office: care William Morris Agy Inc 151 El Camino Beverly Hills CA 90212

HUSTON, ANNETTE LYNN, retail chain executive; b. Roanoke, Va., Jan. 1, 1963; d. George William and Avis L. (Brown) H. AS, Va. Western Community Coll., Roanoke, 1984; BA summa cum laude, Roanoke Coll., 1987; postgrad. in History, Va. Poly. Inst. and State U., 1987-90; postgrad. in Bus. Adminstrn., Averett Coll., 1990—. Sales assoc. Sidney's Inc., Rocky Mount, Va., 1980-82; night mgr. Sidney's Inc., Roanoke, 1982-83, asst. store mgr., 1983-84, buyer, 1984-85, supr., 1985-87, v.p. field ops., 1987—; lectr. mktg. high schs., Va., N.C., S.C., Tenn., Md., Pa., 1987—. Tchr. Rocky Mount Recreation Dept., 1980. Franklin County High Sch. scholar, 1981; Va. Poly. Inst. and State U. scholar, 1987-89, rsch. grantee, 1988. Mem. Nat. Hist. Assn., Roanoke Bus. Mchts. Assn., Phi Theta Kappa, Phi Soc., Phi Alpha Theta, Phi Gamma Mu. Democrat. Baptist. Home: Rte 1 Box 34 Redwood VA 24146 Office: Sidney's Inc PO Box 2740 Roanoke VA 24001

HUSTON, MARGO, journalist; b. Waukesha, Wis., Feb. 12, 1943; d. James and Cecile (Timlin) Bremner; student U. Wis., 1961-63; A.B. in Journalism, Marquette U., 1965; m. James Huston, Dec. 9, 1967 (div.); 1 son, Sean Patrick. Editorial asst. Marquette U., Milw., 1965-66; feature editor, reporter Waukesha Freeman, 1966-67; feature reporter Milw. Jour., 1967-70; reporter Spectrum, women's and food sections, 1972-79, editorial writer, 1979-84, polit reporter, 1984—, asst. picture editor, 1985—; instr. mass communications U. Wis., Milw. Recipient Penney-Mo. award for consumer abortion series, 1975, Pulitzer Prize for investigation into plight of elderly, 1977, Clarion award, 1977, Knight of Golden Quill award, Milw. Press Club, 1977, Wis. AP writing award, 1977, special award Milw. Soc. Profl. Journalists, 1977, Penney-Mo. Paul Myhie award for excellence, 1978; By-Line award Marquette U. Coll. of Journalism, 1980; Wis. UPI best editorial award, 1982; Wis. Women's Network award for journalist achievement for women's issues, 1983 Mem. Nat. News Council (dir.), Investigative Reporters and Editors, Nat. Conf. Editorial Writers, Sigma Delta Chi. Club: Milw. Press. Office: Milwaukee Journal 333 W State St Milwaukee WI 53201

HUTCHERSON, CAROLYN ANN, state regulatory agency executive; b. Jackson, Miss., Jan. 4, 1944; d. Bertrand K. and Frances A. (Keith) Melton; m. Robert W. Hutcherson, Sept. 5, 1965; children: Kimberly, Kristin. Diploma, Gilfoy Sch. Nursing, Jackson, 1965; BSN, Miss. Coll., 1977; MS, U. So. Miss., 1978. Staff nurse cardiovascular recovery Miss. Bapt. Med. Ctr., Jackson, 1980-81; asst. prof. Miss. Coll., Clinton, 1978-81; instr. Ga. Bapt. Med. Ctr., Atlanta, 1981-82, Kennesaw Coll., Marietta, 1982-83; exec. dir. Ga. Bd. Nursing, Atlanta, 1983—. Bd. dirs. Nat. Coun. State Bd. Nursing, 1987—, pres. 1990—. NIMH trainee 1978; named Alumna of Year, Miss. Coll. 1984. Mem. Am. Nurses Assn., Am. Orthopsychiat. Assn., Nat. League for Nursing, Ga. Exec. Women's Network, Ga. Women's Health Adminstrn. Network, Sigma Theta Tau. Home: 4131 Gregory Manor Cir Smyrna GA 30082 Office: Ga Bd Nursing 166 Pryor St SW Atlanta GA 30303

HUTCHERSON, KAREN F., nursing administrator; b. Winston-Salem, N.C., Oct. 1, 1951; d. John Fulghum and Viola Sprinkle Shaw; m. Victor J. Hutcherson, Dec. 18, 1970; children: Shannon Renae, Ashley Michelle. Diploma, N.C. Bapt. Hosp. Sch. Nursing, 1972; BSN, N.C. A&T State U., 1981; MBA, Wake Forest U., 1990. RN. Staff nurse N.C. Bapt. Hosp., Winston-Salem, 1972; oncology nurse clinician Bowman Gray Sch. of Med., Wake Forest U., Winston-Salem, 1972-81, oncology nurse educator, 1981-87, dir. nursing cancer ctr., 1982-87; clin. coord. nursing svcs. Bowman Gray Sch. Medicine, Wake Forest U., Winston-Salem, 1987—; curriculum coord., primary instr. Cancer Ctr., Bowman Gray Sch. of Med., Wake Forest U., 1980-87, numerous coms.; speakers bur. A-H Robins Pharms. Co., 1983-88; cons. S.E. Cancer Control Consortium, Winston-Salem, 1987—; presenter in field. Author: Patient Education in Understanding Cancer: An Introductory Handbook, 1986; co-author: Understanding Cancer Treatment: A Guide for You and Your Family, 1988, Cancer Chemotherapy Guidelines, 5th edit., 1985. chmn. western div. nursing com. N.C. Am. Cancer Soc., 1981-82, speakers bur., 1982—, bd. dirs., 1988—; mem. spl. rev. com. clin. community oncology program Nat. Cancer Inst., Bethesda, Md., 1987;. Mem. Am. Nurses Assn., Am. Acad. Ambulatory Nursing Adminstrn., Med. Ctr. Nursing Assn., Piedmont Oncology Assn. (numerous coms.), Oncology Nursing Soc. (mem. com.), SE Cancer Control Consortium, N.C. Nurses Assn. (legis. com. 1989, vice chmn. community health coun., del. convention 1987, 88, 89), Sigma Theta Tau. Home: 754 Lacock Ave Rural Hall NC 27045 Office: Bowman Gray Sch of Med 300 S Hawthorne Rd Winston-Salem NC 27103

HUTCHESON, JANET REID, radiologist; b. N.Y.C., Feb. 21, 1934; d. John George and Ida Kauderer; m. Robert H. Hutcheson, Dec. 29, 1956; 1 child, Jonathan Edward; m. Eugene Streicher, Aug. 9, 1979. BA, Barnard Coll., N.Y.C., 1955; MD, U. Tenn., 1959. Intern St. Thomas Hosp., Nashville, 1961-62; resident in radiology Vanderbilt U., Nashville, 1962-65; instr. radiology Vanderbilt U., 1965-67, asst. prof. radiology, 1967-75; staff radiologist Group Health Assn., Washington, 1979-80, Drs. Prominski et al, Arlington, Va., 1980-85; pvt. practice specializing in radiology Washington, 1985-88; staff radiologist Laurel Beltsville Hosp., Laurel, Md., 1988—. Capt. USN, 1975-79. Democrat. Episcopalian. Home: 6521 Greentree Rd Bethesda MD 20817 Office: 14201 Laurel Park Dr #106 Laurel MD 20707

HUTCHINGS, LEANNE VON NEUMEYER, communications executive, research consultant, writer; b. L.A.; d. F. Louis and Greta Catherine (Clifford) von Neumeyer; children: Marc Lane, Kristin LeAnne, Michael Lane, Jamie Laird, Jeremy Leif, Bret Louis. Student Brigham Young U., 1962. V.p. Steenhoek Neeley von Neumeyer Assocs., Cons.; researcher, writer, owner Heritage Tree, Arcadia, Calif., 1970—; internat. bd. advisors, dir. protocol Neeley Scholarship Found., 1988-89; dir. pub. communications Ch. of Jesus Christ of Latter-day Saints, So. Calif., 1975—, dir. community relations, 1984—, asst. dir. area coun., 1984—; seminar coord. R.E.D.I., Inc., L.A., 1982—, corp. rels. dir., 1984—; design cons. H.M.J. Jewelers, L.A., 1985—; mem. nat. adv. coun. motion picture studio Brigham Young U., Provo, Utah, 1986-89; adminstrv. dir. Pasadena Geneal. Libr., Calif., 1977-82; writer, coproducer KBIG, Sideband Div. Radio, L.A., 1979-80; exec. assoc adminstr. Calif. Bicentennial Found. for the U.S. Constitution, 1987; regional cons. Latter-Day Sentinel Newspaper, L.A., 1985-89; mem. internat. bd. advisors, bd. dir. protocol Neeley Internat. Scholarship Found., L.A., 1985-89, exec. dir., 1988-89; mem. com. on child pornography legis. L.A. County Commn. on Obscenity & Pornography, 1988, chmn. pub. info. portfolio com., 1988—; artist. Author: Honored Heritage, 1975, Woman's Place of Honor, 1976, Prologue and Tapestry, 1976, Moments with the Prophets, 1977, You're Elected Charlie Brown, 1977, Reaching for the Stars, 1975, Up, Up and Away, 1978, Traditions, 1979, All About You, 1980, Southern California: The Earthquake Threat, 1981, Quake!: Preparing Home, Family and Community, 1982, The Peregrine Papers, 1986; columnist: Heritage Tree Foothill Intercity News, 1977-79, Women's Exponent Southern Calif. edit.; Sentinel; journalism series, 1978-80; also articles, collected works, stage trilogy; art exhibits include Wilshire Alma Exhibit, 1985, The Grand Artists Hall, 1986-88. Pres. Daus. Utah Pioneers-Los Angeles County, 1983-85; instr. Arcadia chpt. ARC, L.A., 1983-85; mem. Community Coordinating Coun., Arcadia, 1983-86; mem. exec. bd. Calif. Utah Women, L.A., 1977-79, 85-86, chmn. L.A. County Commn. Pub. Rels. Portfolio, 1988; exec. dir. Neeley Scholarship Found., 1989—. Recipient Mother of Yr. award Ch. of Jesus Christ of Latter-day Saints, Arcadia, 1979. Best of Exhibit award Sculptor's West Workshop, 1982. Mem. NAFE, Assn. Latter-Day Media Artists (assoc. editor Voice of ALMA 1978-83, exec. bd. 1977-81, chmn. spl. events, 1985—, internat. bd. govs. fellow 1981-83), Bus. Industry Conf. Earthquake Preparedness Project, Am. Film Inst., LDS Bookseller's Assn., Deseret Bus. and Profl. Assn., Nat. Mus. Women in the Arts (charter), Arcadia Tournament of Roses Assn., Arcadia C. of C. (chmn. industry commn. of women's div. 1983-85, mem. exec. bd. 1985-86), Am. Family Soc. Washington (coord. So. Calif. chpt. 1988). Republican. Mem. Ch. of Jesus Christ of Latter-Day Saints. Avocations: sculpting, oil painting, violin. Office: REDI Inc 112 W 9th St Ste 922 Los Angeles CA 90015

HUTCHINS, CYNTHIA ANN, optician; b. Beverly, Mass., Aug. 1, 1962; d. Warren Bertram and Carole Marie (Poor) H. AS, Salem State Coll., 1982. Registered dispensing optician, Mass.; cert. Am. Bd. Opticianry. Optometric technician Cambridge Eye Assocs., Danvers, Mass., 1984-85; ops. mgr. Precision Optics, Danvers, 1985—; exec. mgr. Parrelli Optical, Danvers, 1985—; asst. dir. edn. Essex Optical Corp., Hamilton, Mass.; cons. Cape Ann Optical, Danvers. Foster parent Christian Children's Fund, Va., sponsor Covenant House, N.Y., mem. Ctr. for Environmental Edn., Washington, mem. Audubon Soc., Mass. Mem. Mass. Assn. Registered Dispensing Opticians, Bus. Women's Tng. Inst., NAFE. Roman Catholic. Home: 26 Burley St Wenham MA 01984 Office: Parrelli Optical 40 Enon St Beverly MA 01915

HUTCHINS, DIANNE, computer analyst; b. Spartanburg, S.C., Apr. 22, 1953; d. James Charles and Frances (Lawter) H. BA in Mgmt., U. S.C., 1989. Cert. prodn. and inventory mgr. Personnel asst. White Bag Co., Spartanburg, 1977-78; realtor Peachtree Realty, Spartanburg, 1978-81; prodn. planner Andrews Bearing Co. (div. of Ina Bearing), Spartanburg, 1981-87; programmer Ina Bearing, Spartanburg, 1987-89; master scheduler, computer analyst Hartness Internat., Greenville, S.C., 1989—; computer cons. Ina Bearing Co., 1989-90; notary pub., S.C., 1990. Mem. Am. Prodn. and Inventory Control Soc., NAFE. Republican. Baptist. Home: 200 Heywood Ave Apt 301 Spartanburg SC 29302 Office: Hartness Internat PO Box 26509 Greenville SC 29616

HUTCHINS, MARYGAIL KINZER, research analytical chemist, materials analyst; b. L.A., Jan. 17, 1940; d. James Nicklus and Amelie Melina (Lacoste) Kinzer; m. Robert Owen Hutchins, Sr., June 16, 1962; children: Robert Owen Jr., Richard James. BA in Chemistry, Mt. St. Mary's Coll., 1961; MS in Organic Chemistry, St. Joseph's U., 1977; PhD in Organic Chemistry, Temple U., 1981. Tchr., technician various schs., Ind., Pa., 1964-76; grad. rsch. asst. Temple U. and Fels Rsch. Found., 1976-81; advanced product devel. chemist LNP Corp., Malvern, Pa., 1981-86; analytical chemist ICI Advanced Materials, Exton, Pa., 1986—. Contbr. numerous articles to profl. jours. Mem. Am. Inst. Chemists, Soc. Adv. Materials & Process Engring., The Fiber Soc., SPE, Am. Chem. Soc., Phila. Organic Chemists Club, Soc. of Plastics Engrs., Soc. for Creative Anachronisms. Office: ICI Advanced Materials 475 Creamery Way Exton PA 19341

HUTCHINS, PAMELA ELIZABETH, janitorial service executive; b. Torrance, Calif., May 23, 1947; d. Clyde Campbell and Adele (Gilbert) Beaver; m. Phillip Cogan, Mar. 22, 1970, (div. Jan., 1979); m. Charles Roy, Aug. 12, 1979; stepchildren: Karlen, Jennifer. AA, El Camino City Coll., Torrance, 1967; BA, UCLA, 1969; postgrad., Calif. U., Northridge, 1970. Office mgr. Planned Parenthood, Bellevue, Wash., 1974-76; owner Janitorial Svcs. and Supplies, Bellevue, Wash., 1978—. Past pres. People for Abandoned Pets, Bellevue, 1983-89. Mem. Issaquah C. of C., Humane Soc., Greenpeace, Animal Protection Inst., Am. Sunbathing Assn. Democrat. Jewish. Home: 230 165 Ave SE Bellevue WA 98008 Office: H&N Janitorial Svcs 230 165 Ave SE Bellevue WA 98008

HUTCHINSON, MARGARET BLAKESLEE, library director; b. Trenton, N.J., Dec. 27, 1942; d. E. Harold and Ann M. Blakeslee; m. Travis George Hutchinson, Dec. 26, 1942; children: David Travis, Peter Blake. BA, Douglass Coll., 1964; MLS, Rutgers U., 1990. Libr. asst. Essex Fells (N.J.) Sch., 1975-78, Livingston (N.J.) Pub. Libr., 1988, Ocean County Libr., Surf City, N.J., 1989; libr. dir. Holland Soc. N.Y., N.Y.C., 1989—. Bd. dirs. Essex Fells PTA, 1976-78; chmn. Essex Fells Community Field Day, 1977; founder Internat. Book Discussion Group, The Hague, The Netherlands, 1979. Mem. ALA, N.J. Libr. Assn., AAUW (br. pres. Caldwell, N.J. 1972-74), Conn. Hist. Soc., Morris Area Genealogy Assn., Gt. Books Orgn. Home: 161 Devon Rd Essex Fells NJ 07021 Office: Holland Soc NY 122 E 58th St New York NY 10022

HUTCHINSON, VIRGINIA NETTLES, librarian; b. Richmond, Va., Feb. 7, 1936; d. Joseph and Virginia (Davies) Nettles; m. John Michael Robin H., Oct. 3, 1959; children: Catherine Pierce, Peter Anthony. BA in English Lit., Mary Washington Coll., 1958. Librarian D.C. Pub. Library, Washington, 1958-59, 66-67; asst. to communications cons. Govt. Employees Ins. Co., Washington, 1973-78, librarian, 1978—. Mem. ALA, Am. Soc. Personnel Adminstrn., Special Libraries Assn. Democrat. Club: Book Discussion Group (Chevy Chase, Md.). Home: 113 Hesketh St Chevy Chase MD 20815 Office: Goodwin Learning Ctr GEICO Pla Washington DC 20076

HUTCHISON, ELIZABETH MAY, nurse; b. Broomfield, Colo., Apr. 14, 1924; d. Percy William and Frances May (Cram) Marion; m. James Donald Hutchison, Dec. 9, 1945; children: John William, Daniel James, Janet May Morrell, Ronald Raymond. RN, U. Denver, 1945. Polio staff nurse Children's Hosp., Denver, 1945-53; home care staff nurse Weld County Health Dept., Greeley, Colo., 1970-73; community health coord. for adult health Boulder (Colo.) County Health Dept., 1973-87. Author: Adult Health Conference Protocol, 1985; editorial staff: Lafayette History Book, 1989. Mem., historian, docent, Lafayette Hist. Soc., 1978-89. Recipient Recognition award Boulder County, 1981, Appreciation award Boulder City-County Health Dept., 1976. Mem. Non-Practicing and Part-time Nurses Assn., DAR. Democrat. Methodist. Home: 778 Applewood Dr Lafayette CO 80026 Office: Lafayette Miners' Mus 108 E Simpson PO Box 186 Lafayette CO 80026

HUTCHISON, JEANNE SLANINGER, mathematics educator; b. Newburgh, N.Y., Nov. 13, 1942; d. Paul Vincent and Loveda Laura (Peterson) Slaninger; m. Gerald Andrew Hutchison, Feb. 4, 1967 (dec. 1977); 1 child, Michael; m. Joseph M. Fontana, Aug. 27, 1988. BS, Creighton U., 1964; MA, UCLA, 1967, PhD, 1970. Asst. prof. math. U. Ala. at Birmingham, 1970—. Contbr. articles to profl. jours. Mem. AAUP, Am. Math. Soc., Math. Assn. Am. Office: U Ala Birmingham Dept Math University Station Birmingham AL 35294

HUTCHISON, KARON ELAINE, customer service manager; b. Brawley, Calif., May 3, 1951; d. Clifton Eugene and Loretta Marie (Denton) Coates; m. Ronald Adams, June, 1968 (div. Aug. 1971); m. John Wendell Hutchison, Dec. 3, 1971; children: Melanie Lynn, John Bradley. Cert., H&R Block, 1982. Dental asst. Drs. Williams & Moss, Brawley, 1969-71; pvt. practice piano tchr. Calif., 1971-75; cons. Mary Kay Cosmetics, Calif., 1971-75, Family Health Program, Long Beach, Calif., 1975-77; model SuzYum Originals, Honolulu, 1981-82; supr. word processing ctr. Nat. Systems Mgmt., Arlington, Va., 1982-85; customer svc. mgr. McCaw Telepage, Honolulu, 1986—. Vice pres. Awa La Wahine, Honolulu, 1981. Mem. Pageant Profls. (candidate hostess Honolulu chpt. 1988—), Network Systems (rep. Honolulu chpt. 1989—). Republican. Home: 1202 Kaeleku St Honolulu HI 96825 Office: McCaw Telepage 1020 Auahi St Honolulu HI 96814

HUTCHISON, KAY BAILEY, state treasurer; b. Galveston, Tex., July 22, 1943; d. Allan and Kathryn Bailey; m. Ray Hutchison. Student, U. Tex., 1961-64, LLB, 1967. Bar: Tex. 1967. TV news reporter Houston, 1969-71, pvt. practice law, 1969-74; press sec. to Anne Armstrong, 1971; vice chmn. Nat. Transp. Safety Bd., 1976-78; asst. prof. U. Tex., Dallas, 1978-79; sr. v.p., gen. counsel Republic of Tex. Corp., Dallas, 1979—; of counsel Hutchison Boyle Brooks & Fisher, Dallas; mem. Tex. Ho. of Reps., 1972-76; elected treas. of Tex., 1990. Fellow Am. Bar Found., Tex. Bar Found.; mem. ABA, State Bar of Tex., Dallas Bar Assn., U. Tex. Law Alumni Assn. (pres. 1985-86). Republican. *

HUTCHISON, LINDA TAYLOR, state official; b. Danville, Va., May 15, 1952; d. Frederick Lyttleton and Shirley (Peters) H. BFA, Va. Commonwealth U., 1975; postgrad., Anthropology Film Ctr., Santa Fe, 1978. Tchr. fine arts Warren County Pub. Schs., Front Royal, Va., 1975-78; media resource coord. N.Mex. Dept. Edn., Santa Fe, 1979; media specialist Anthropology Film Ctr., 1979-80; freelance documentary producer and dir. Santa Fe, 1980-82; audio-visual specialist N.Mex. State Libr., Santa Fe, 1982-83; state coord. N.Mex. Film Commn., Santa Fe, 1983-85, asst. dir., 1985-87, dir., 1987—. Project dir. Through Other Eyes, 1981; co-producer The High Road, 1983; producer Songs of the Wilderness, 1984. Mem. Assn. Film

Commrs. Internat. Office: NMex Film Commn 1050 Old Pecos Trail Santa Fe NM 87501

HUTCHISON, PAT, nurse, administrator; b. Omaha, Mar. 4, 1943; d. Earl Edward and Sylvia Lorraine (Kronen) Moore; m. James M. Hutchison, June 23, 1963; children—Michael, Danny. Diploma in nursing, St. Joseph's Sch. Nursing, 1968; student Central Ariz. Coll., 1976-82; BS in Health Service Adminstrn., U. Phoenix, 1983; BS in Nursing, U. Phoenix, 1988. R.N.; cert. in advanced cardiac life support, Ariz. Nurse Armish Maag Hosp., Teheran, Iran, 1969-71; supr. Hoemako Hosp., Casa Grande, Ariz., 1973-84; asst. dir. nursing Casa Grande Regional Med. Ctr., 1984-86, nursing supr., 1986—. Nursing chmn. ARC, Casa Grande, 1986—, also bd. dirs., instr. disaster tng., 1982—; instr. cardiopulmonary resuscitation Am. Heart Assn., Casa Grande, 1978—. Recipient Care award Ariz. Hosp. Assn., 1984, Service and Appreciation award Bus. and Profl. Women's Assn., 1984. Mem. Ariz. Nurses in Mgmt., Emergency Nurses Assn. Democrat. Roman Catholic. Avocations: traveling; camping; boating; reading. Home: 1308 N Center St Casa Grande AZ 85222 Office: Casa Grande Regional Med Ctr 1800 E Florence Blvd Casa Grande AZ 85222

HUYER, ADRIANA, oceanographer, educator; b. Giessendam, The Netherlands, May 19, 1945; arrived in Can., 1950; came to U.S., 1975; d. Jacob Catharinus and Sophia (Van Loon) H.; m. Robert Lloyd Smith. BS, U. Toronto, 1967; MS, Oreg. State U., 1971, PhD, 1974. Scientific officer Marine Scis. Branch, Ottawa, Can., 1967-73; rsch. scientist Marine Environ. Data Svc., Ottawa, Can., 1974-75; rsch. assoc. Oreg. State U., Corvallis, 1975-76, rsch. asst. prof., 1976-79, asst. prof., 1979-80, assoc. prof., 1980-85, prof., 1985—; vis. scientist Csiro Marine Labs, Hobart, Australia, 1988. Contbr. articles to profl. jours. Mem. AAAS, Am. Meterol. Soc., Am. Geophys. Union, Can. Meterol. and Oceanographic Soc., Am. Soc. Limnology and Oceanography. Office: Coll Oceanography Oreg State Univ Corvallis OR 97331-5503

HUYLER, MARTHA JUANITA, systems consultant; b. Jersey City, Dec. 3, 1941; d. George and Margaret (Mattey) Faulk; m. Richard Huyler, Sept. 5, 1964; children: Mark, Eric. BA, Hope Coll., 1963; MS, Rutgers U., 1965. Programmer, analyst Ednl. Testing Svc., Princeton, N.J., 1964-66, Arlington (Va.) County Sch. Bd., 1966, Bur. Comml. Fisheries, Beaufort, N.C., 1966-68; systems analyst, cons. Ednl. Testing Svc., Princeton, 1968-81; software cons. Ortho Pharm. Corp., Raritan, N.J., 1981-86; systems cons. N.J. Ednl. Computer Network, Edison, N.J., 1986-89, Montclair State Coll., Upper Montclair, N.J., 1989—. Author: The Bergen County Huylers, 1983. Treas. North Branch (N.J.) Reformed Ch., 1984—. Mem. Somerville Area AAUW (pres. 1981-83, v.p. 1979-81). Office: Sea-Land Svc Inc PO Box 1050 Elizabeth NJ 07207

HUYSMAN, ARLENE WEISS, psychologist; b. Phila.; d. Max and Anna (Pearlene) Weiss; B.A., Shaw U., 1973; M.A., Goddard Coll., 1974; Ph.D., Union Grad. Sch., 1980; m. Pedro Camacho; children—Pamela Claire, James David. Actress, dir. Dramatic Workshop, N.Y.C., 1956-68; music and drama critic and columnist Orlando (Fla.) Sentinel Star, 1966-68; psychodramatist Volusia County Guidance Center, Daytona Beach, Fla., 1966-68; free-lance journalist, 1968-70; psychodramatist Psychiat. Inst., Jackson Meml. Hosp., Miami, 1972-77, dir. Adult Day Treatment Center, 1974-77, dir. Lithium Clinic, 1976-77; psychodramatist South Fla. State Hosp., Hollywood, 1971-72; psychotherapy supr., neurosci. program coordinator St. Francis Hosp., 1984—, clin. dir. Family Workshop, 1985—, dir. Adult Day Treatment Ctr., 1987—; asst. prof. Med. Sch., U. Miami, 1976—; Mem. adv. panel Fine Arts Council Fla., 1976-77; mem. Fla. Gov.'s Task Force on Marriage and the Family Unit, 1976, 89-90; vol. Rec. for Blind, 1974—. Recipient Best Dirs. award and Best Actress award Fla. Theatre Festival, 1967. Mem. Am. Psychol. Assn., Fla. Psychol. Assn., Mental Health Assn. Dade County, Internat. Assn. Group Psychotherapy, Am. Soc. Aging, Am. Assn. Group Psychotherapy and Psychodrama, Moreno Acad., Fedn. Partial Hospitalization Study Groups, Fla. Assn. Practicing Psychologists (bd. dirs., pres. 1987—). Office: Ctr Psychol Growth 3050 Biscayne Blvd Miami FL 33137

HWA, MILLIE HUI, automation mechanical engineer; b. Beijing, China, Nov. 23; came to U.S., 1984; d. Shen Liang and Lily (Wan) H. BSME, Li-Ming U., Shen Yang, China, 1984; MSME, Ariz. State U., 1988. registered profl. engr., Ariz., Calif. Researcher Mech. Engr. in Aerospace, Tempe, Ariz., 1985-86; instr. machine control systems Ariz. State U., Tempe, 1986-88; researcher Garrett Turbine Engine Co., Phoenix, 1987-88; product mech. engr. Advanced Diagnostic Med. Systems, Inc., Dublin, Calif., 1988; mech. engr. Ford Labs., Dublin, 1988; automation design engr. Adaptive Intelligence Corp., Milpitas, Calif., 1989; mech. engr. MEICOR, Fremont, Calif., 1989—; mfg. engr. Fluorocarbon Corp Flo-Med div., Fremont, Calif., 1989. Rsch. asst.: Flow Instability in Thermally Stratified Flows, 1986. Mem. Robotic Internat., Soc. Mfg. Engring. Methodist. Office: Flo-Med Div 326 Warren Ave Fremont CA 94539

HYATT, ELAINE MILLER, business owner, educator; b. Atlanta, June 22, 1951; d. Lowell Leaman and Eloise (West) Miller; m. Andrew Lewis Hunter Hyatt, Feb. 20, 1971; 1 child, Dempsey. BA, U. N.C., 1989. Cert. secondary English tchr., N.C. Bookkeeper Drs. Lusk, Townsend & Karb, Greensboro, N.C., 1976-81; adminstrv. asst. Kelly Temp. Svcs., Greensboro, 1982-86; owner Quarrywoods Qtr. Horses, Staley, N.C., 1986—. Mem. Am. Qtr. Horse Assn., N.C. Tchrs. of English, N.C. Qtr. Horse Assn. Home: Rt 1 Box 52A-5 Staley NC 27355

HYATT, MARGARET ELIZABETH, nurse; b. Warren, Pa., Apr. 4, 1959; d. Emerson Singen and Anne Louise (Krantz) H. BS in Nursing, Villa Maria Coll., Erie, Pa., 1981. RN, Mass. Staff nurse St. Vincent Health Ctr., Erie, Pa., 1982-86, Traveling Nurse Corps, 1986-88; primary nurse Beth Israel Hosp., Boston, 1988—. Mem. Sigma Theta Tau. Democrat. Roman Catholic. Home: 195 Park Dr 44 Boston MA 02215 Office: Beth Israel Hosp 6 S 330 Brookline Ave Boston MA 02215

HYDE, DAWN STAUFFER, human resources consulting firm executive; b. Balt., May 27, 1954; d. Donald Ross Stauffer and Dorothy Jane (Borcher) Portera; m. Jonathan Hynson Hyde, Nov. 11, 1989. BA, Goucher Coll., 1976; MAS, Johns Hopkins U., 1983. Sr. profl. in human resources; accredited exec. in personnel. Personnel asst. Am. Nat. Bldg. & Loan, Balt., 1976-77; dir. personnel Fallston (Md.) Gen. Hosp., 1977-79; personnel officer Mercantile Safe Deposit & Trust, Balt., 1979-84; pres. Berkshire Assocs., Inc., Balt., 1983—. Bd. dirs. Balt. Urban League, 1989— (Disting. Svc. award 1985, 87), chmn. adv. bd. info. processing tng. ctr., 1985. Mem. Md. Assn. Affirmative Action Officers (v.p. 1989—), Md. Career Devel. Assn., Goucher Alumni Assn. (sec. 1986-89), The Johns Hopkins Club. Democrat. Lutheran. Office: Berkshire Assocs Inc 1205 York Rd Ste 34 Lutherville MD 21093

HYDE, ELIZABETH HOWE, cattle rancher; b. Princeton, N.J., Mar. 8, 1920; d. Paul Edward and Harriet (Rinaker) Howe; m. Frederick W. Hyde, July 28, 1943 (dec. 1987); children: Mary, Susan, Frederick W., Rhoda. Student, U. Ariz., 1937-39, McGill U., Montreal, 1939-40, U. Vt., summer 1940; BS in Home Econs., Cornell U., 1941. Comparison shopper Sears Roebuck & Co., Chgo., 1941; jr. statistician, cost of living dir. Bur. Labor Statistics, U.S. Dept. Labor, Washington, 1941-44; ptnr. Yamsay Land & Cattle Co., Bly, Oreg., 1945-80; statis. asst. Blymill, Weyerhaeuser Co., Bly, 1974-76, 1976-79; newspaper columnist CowBelle Corner, 1963-75, 72-75. Mem. Am. Nat. Cattle Women (sec. 1976), Oreg. Cattle Women (pres. 1975-76), Klamath County Cattle Women, AAUW (pres. 1964-65), Am. Assn. Individual Investors, Klamath Hospice, Merle West Med. Ctr. Guild (v.p. 1967). Republican. Home: 1200 Lynnewood Klamath Falls OR 97601

HYDE, GERALDINE VEOLA, secondary education educator, retired; b. Berkeley, Calif., Nov. 26, 1926; d. William Benjamin and Veola (Walker) H.; m. Paul Hyde Graves, Jr., Nov. 12, 1949 (div. Dec. 1960); children: Christine M. Graves Klykken, Catherine A. Graves Hackney, Geraldine J. Graves Hansen. BA in English, U. Wash., 1948; BA in Edn., Ea. Wash. U., 1960, MA in Edn., 1962. Cert. tchr. K-16, Wash.; life cert. specialist in secondary edn., Calif. English educator Sprague (Wash.) Consol. Schs., 1960-62, Bremerton (Wash.) Sch. Dist., 1962-63, Federal Way (Wash.) Sch. Dist., 1963-66; English, journalism and Polynesian humanities educator Hayward (Calif.) Unified Sch. Dist., 1966-86. Charter mem. Hist. Hawai'i Found., Honolulu, 1977—; founding mem. The Cousteau Soc., Inc., Norfolk, Va., 1975—; life mem. Hawai'ian Hist. Soc., Honolulu, 1978—; mem. Moloka'i Mus. and Cultural Ctr., Kaunakaka'i, 1986—, Bishop Mus. Assn., Honolulu, 1973—. Mem. Jr. League of Spokane (life), U. Wash. Alumni Assn. (life), Ea. Wash. Alumni Assn. (life), Nat. Conservancy of Hawaii. Republican. Episcopalian.

HYDE-JACKSON, M. DEBORAH, neurosurgeon; b. Laurel, Miss., Jan. 18, 1949; d. Sellus Hyde and Ann (Huff) McDonald; m. James Joseph Jackson, June 28, 1986. BS in Biology, Tougaloo Coll, Miss., 1970; MS in Biology, Cleve. State U., 1973; MD, Case Western Reserve U., Cleve., 1977. Diplomate Am. Bd. Neurol. Surgery. Resident Univ. Hosps., Cleve., 1978-82; neurosurgeon Guthrie Med. Ctr., Sayre, Pa., 1982-87; pvt. practice Canoga Pk., Calif., 1987—. Contbg. author: The Courage of Conviction, 1985. Mem. AMA, Congress Neurol. Surgeons, Nat. Med. Assn., Alpha Omega Alpha. Democrat. Office: Deborah Hyde-Jackson MD 7230 Med Ctr Dr #600 Canoga Park CA 91307

HYDEN, DOROTHY LOUISE, marketing executive; b. Fort Collins, Colo., July 19, 1948; d. Douglas Stewart and Elizabeth Lenore (Stewart) Neilson; m. Michael J. Daley, Dec. 27, 1969 (div.); 1 child, Shannon; m. Howard E. Hyden, July 17, 1976; children: Kent Stewart, Tiffany Nicole. BA, U. Calif., Santa Barbara, 1970; MBA, Pepperdine U., 1980. Head tchr. Sawyer Bus. Coll., Anaheim, Calif., 1974-75, admissions rep., 1975-76; mktg. specialist Anthony Schs., Orinda, Calif., 1976-77; adminstrv. dir. Escrow Tng. Ctr., Orinda, Calif., 1977-78; pvt. practice consulting Mpls., 1979-88; exec. v.p. Hyden, Hyden and Assocs., Mpls., 1988—. Mem. ASTD, NAFE, PEN, Bus. and Profl. Advt. Assn., Pepperdine U. Alumni Assn., U. Calif. at Santa Barbara Alumni Assn., Internat. Platform Assn., Am. Soc. for Tng. and Devel. Republican. Episcopalian. Home and Office: 7415 Hyde Park Dr Minneapolis MN 55439

HYDEN, ELAINE, auditor; b. Herrin, Ill., Jan. 10, 1949; d. Luther H. and Dorothy (Roberts) H.; m. Thomas J. Ziglinski; 1 child, Elizabeth. BS in Journalism, So. Ill. U., Carbondale, 1971; BS in Acctg., So. Ill. U., 1980. CPA, Ill.; cert. internal auditor, fraud examiner. Cost acct. So. Ill. U., 1972-78, internal auditor, 1980-84, internal audit mgr., 1984-85; exec. dir. audits So. Ill. U., Carbondale, Springfield and Edwardsville, 1985—; bd. dirs. So. Ill. U. Credit Union, 1984-87. Bd. dirs. Carbondale Women's Ctr., 1982-83. Named one of Outstanding Young Women of Am., 1984. Mem. AICPA, Inst. Internal Auditors (cert. of excellence 1983, mem. internat. govt. rels. com. 1989—), Nat. Assn. Cert. Fraud Examiners. Home: 2103 Lerin Ln Marion IL 62959 Office: So Ill U Internal Audit Office 111 Greek Row Carbondale IL 62901

HYDER, JEANNE MCEACHERN, lawyer; b. Bremen, Ga., Sept. 1, 1962; d. James Sterling Jr. and Nancy Morrow (Hughes) McEachern; m. James Davis Hyder, Jr., Feb. 20, 1988. BA, Brenau Coll., 1984; JD, Mercer U., 1987. Bar: Ga. 1987. Assoc. Fulcher, Hagler, Reed, Obenshain, Hanks & Harper, Augusta, Ga., 1987—. Vol. March of Dimes, Augusta, 1989. Mem. ABA, Ga. Bar Assn., Augusta Bar Assn., Def. Rsch. Inst., Network Augusta, Richmond County Mus., Phi Alpha Theta. Republican. Methodist. Office: Fulcher Hagler Reed et al 520 Greene St Augusta GA 30901

HYERS, JUDITH GEGENHEIMER, marketing communications executive; b. Greenport, N.Y., July 8, 1945; d. Harold Walter and Helen Payne (Ramsdell) Gegenheimer; m. Ralph Rushton Browning III, Dec. 16, 1967 (div. June 1974); 1 child, William Ireland Browning; m. L. Cameron Hyers, Feb. 1, 1975 (div. Mar. 1989). BA in English, Wheaton Coll., 1967. Rsch. analyst, sales exec. Xerox Edn. Group, Stamford, Conn., 1971-75; v.p., pres. Hyers/Smith Inc., East Norwalk, Conn., 1975—; chmn., chief exec. officer The Gegenheimer Group Ltd., N.Y.C., 1989—; sec., mem. exec., audit, and compensation coms. Baldwin Tech. Co., Inc., Rowayton, Conn., 1984—. Mem. SeaSide Place Residence Assn. (sec.), WPA Mural Restoration Com. (former pres.). Home: 12 SeaSide Place East Norwalk CT 06855 Office: The Gegenheimer Group Ltd 99 Madison Ave New York NY 10016

HYMAN, BETTY HARPOLE, technical equipment consultant; b. Jasper, Tex., Nov. 20, 1938; d. Russell Charles and John Francis (Hilton) Harpole; m. Arthur Siegmar Hyman (dec.); children: Norma Sullivan, Eric, Jonathan, Lee Ann. BA in Psychology, U. Tex., San Antonio, 1979. Spl. project coord. Tex. Stores, San Antonio, 1975-79; communications cons. Southwestern Bell Tel., Midland, Tex. and San Antonio, 1980-82; tech. cons. AT&T, San Antonio, 1983-85, 88—, Intelliserve Corp., Dallas, 1987-88; cons. IMS Group, San Antonio, 1985-87. Mem. devel. com. San Antonio Spl. Olympics; mem. San Antonio Conservation Soc., 1975—, San Antonio World Affairs Coun., 1985—; bd. dirs. South Tex. Childrens' Habilitation Ctr., San Antonio, 1985-87. Mem. Am. Bus. Women's Assn. (program com. 1987-88), Tex. Tennis Assn. (ranked player 1976-90), Prime Time Tennis Club (v.p. 1985-86). Republican. Presbyterian. Home: 18 Westwood Rd Asheville NC 28803 Office: 901 W Trade 4th Fl Charlotte NC 28202

HYMAN, MARY BLOOM, science education programs coordinator; m. Sigmund M. Hyman, 1947; children: Carol Ann Hyman Williams, Nancy Louise. BS, Goucher Coll., 1971; MS, Johns Hopkins U., 1977. Asst. dir. Edn. Md. Sci. Ctr., Balt., 1976-81, dir. edn., 1981—; trustee Goucher Coll. Mem. quantitative literacy com. Md. State Dept. Edn., edn. outreach adv. panel Smithsonian Inst.; mem. Nat. Urban League Preschool Sci. Collaborative. Recipient Disting. Women award Gov.'s Office, Annapolis, Md., 1981; Meritorious Svc. award Johns Hopkins U., 1983; Outstanding Svc. to Sci. Edn. award. Assn. Sci. Dept. Chairmen of Balt. County Pub. Schs., 1989. Mem. Fund for Ednl. Excellence (bd. dirs.), Md. Assn. Sci. Tchrs. (bd. dirs.), Women in Math/Sci. Task Force Md. State Dept Edn., Phi Beta Kappa, Phi Delta Kappa. Home: 10815 Longacre Ln Stevenson MD 21153

HYMAN, TRINA SCHART, illustrator; b. Phila., Apr. 8, 1939; d. Albert Henry and Margaret Doris (Bruck) Schart; m. Harris Joel Hyman, May 29, 1959 (div. 1968); 1 child, Katrin. Student, Phila. Mus. Sch. Art, 1956-59, Boston Mus. Sch. Fine Arts, 1959-60, Konstfackskolan, Stockholm, 1960-61. Free-lance illustrator, 1961—; art dir. Cricket mag., LaSalle, Ill., 1971-79, staff artist, 1979-88; greeting card artist, designer Pawprints Inc., Jaffrey, N.H., 1980—; free-lance figurine designer The Franklin Mint, Franklin Ctr., Pa., 1982—. Author: How Six Found Christmas, 1969, Self-Portrait, 1979; reteller: Sleeping Beauty, 1975, Little Red Riding Hood, 1983; illustrator 132 books. Recipient Horn Book award for illustration Boston Globe, 1973, Caldecott Honor Book award ALA, 1989, Caldecott medal ALA, 1985. Mem. Graphic Artists Guild, Soc. Children's Book Writers (Golden Kite award 1984).

HYMES, NORMA, internist; b. N.Y.C., July 29, 1949; d. Richard and Ellen (Posner) H.; m. Vincent M. Esposito, Nov. 1978 (div.); 1 child, Richard Hymes-Esposito. BS, Oberlin Coll., 1971; MD, Mt. Sinai, 1975. Diplomate Bd. of Internal Medicine. Intern, resident Maimonides Med. Ctr., Bklyn., 19175-78; internist Manhattan Health Plan, N.Y.C., 1978-81, Manhattan Med Group, P.C., N.Y.C., 1981—. Mgr. The Colonnade Condominium, N.Y.C., 1982-85; trustee N.Y. Soc. For Ethical Culture, N.Y.C., 1989—. Mem. Am. Coll. of Physicians, Am. Med. Women's Assn. Office: Manhattan Med Group 172 Amsterdam Ave New York NY 10023

HYNES, MARY ANN, publishing executive, lawyer; b. Chgo., Oct. 26, 1947; d. Ernest Mario and Emma Louise (Noto) Iantorno; m. James Thomas Hynes, Jan. 25, 1969; children: Christina, Nicholas. Student, Loyola U., 1967; JD, John Marshall Law Sch., 1971, LLM in Taxation, 1975. Bar: Ill. 1971, U.S. Dist. Ct. (no. dist.) Ill. 1971. Exec. editor, law editor Commerce Clearing House, Inc., 1971-79, asst. sec, counsel, 1979-80, v.p., gen. counsel, 1980—. Chief crusader United Way/Crusade of Mercy; v.p., bd. dirs., legis. and policy chmn., chmn. membership Chgo. Crime Commn.; mem. nat. strategy forum Midwest Council Nat. Security; adv. council Chgo. Symphony Orch. Chorus; deanery del. Chgo. Archdiocesan Pastoral Council; pres. local sch. bd., 1984-87; bd. dirs. local YWCA.; corp. council inst. planning com. Northwestern U. Sch. Law; mem. pres.' coun. Mus. Sci. and Industry, Chgo. Mem. ABA (chmn. publs. com., corp. law depts. com., sect. corp., banking and bus. law sect., 1987—, computer law com., litigation sect.), Ill. State Bar Assn. (corp. law dept. sect. coun.), Chgo. Bar Assn., Internat. Bar Assn., Women's Bar Assn. Ill. (former bd. dir., found. adv. bd.), Internat. Fedn. Women Lawyers, Nat. Assn. Women Lawyers, Am. Corp. Counsel Assn., Am. Soc. Corp. Secs., Computer Law Assn., Justinian Soc. Lawyers, Law Club of the City of Chgo., Legal Club of Chgo. (exec. com. 1987), Execs. Club of Chgo., Chgo. Club. Roman Catholic. Office: Commerce Clearing House Inc 2700 Lake Cook Rd Riverwoods IL 60015

IACHETTI, ROSE MARIA ANNE, teacher; b. Watervliet, N.Y., Sept. 22, 1931; d. Augustus and Rose Elizabeth Archer (Orciuolo) Iachetti; BS, Coll. St. Rose, 1961; MEd, U. Ariz., 1969. Joined Sisters of Mercy, Albany, N.Y., 1949-66; tchr. various parochial schs. Albany (N.Y.) Diocese, 1952-66; tchr. Headstart Program, Troy, N.Y., 1966; tchr. fine arts Watervliet Jr. and Sr. High Sch., 1966-67; tchr. W.J. Meyer Sch., Tombstone, Ariz., 1968-71, Colonel Johnston Sch., Ft. Huachuca, Ariz., 1971-78; tchr. Myer Sch., Ft. Huachuca, 1978—, coord. program for gifted and talented, 1981-85. Ann. chmn. Ariz. Children's Home Assn., Tombstone, 1973-74; trustee Tombstone Sch. Dist. #1, 1972-80; active Dem. Club; mem. Bicentennial Commn. for Ariz., 1972-76, Tombstone Centennial Commn., 1979-80, chmn. Centennial Ball, 1980; pres. Tombstone Community Health Svcs., 1978-80; mem. Tombstone City Coun., 1982-84, Inner Senatorial Cir., 1989—; governing bd. Southeast Ariz. Area Health Edn. Coun., 1985—; pres. S.E. Health Edn. Coun., 1990—; patron Our Lady of Santa Rita Abbey, Met. Opera Guild. Mem. Ariz. Edn. Assn. (so. regional dir. 1971-73), Ft. Huachuca Edn. Assn., Tombstone Dist. 1 Edn. Assn. (pres. 1969-71), Ariz. Sch. Bd. Assn., NEA (del. 1971-73), Ariz. Classroom Tchrs. Assn. (del. 1969-71), Internat. Platform Assn., Tombstone Bus. and Profl. Women's Club, Am. Legion Aux., Tombstone Assn. Arts, Inner Senatorial Circle, Pi Lambda Theta, Delta Kappa Gamma, (pres. 1982-84), Phi Delta Kappa (historian 1979-82, 2d v.p. 1982-83). Home: Round Up Trailer Ranch Box 725 Tombstone AZ 85638 Office: Myer Sch Fort Huachuca AZ 85613

IACONE, MARGE, small business owner; b. Bklyn., Feb. 13, 1943; d. Thomas and Margaret Lucy Fiore; children: Donna Avanti, Debra Iacone. Student, Adelphia Sch. Bus., 1958, Morris County Vocat. Sch., 1977, Caldwell Coll., 1989. Gen. mgr. Guaranteed Premium Loan Co., Bklyn., 1963-65; claims inspector Universal Car Loading & Distbn., N.Y.C., 1965-68; quality motor control insp. Nash Controls, Fairfield, N.J., 1968-69; gen. mgr. Roman's Mobile Elec. Co., Caldwell, N.J., 1969-72; gen. mgr. Exptl. Plastic Molds Corp., Fairfield, 1972-86, owner, pres., 1986—. Contbr. articles to profl. jours. Indsl. commr. Fairfield Indsl. Commn., 1986-87; vice chmn. Mayor's Adv. Com., Fairfield, 1987-88; mem. The Steeple Fund Com., 1986-88. Fellow Soc. Plastics Industry, West Essex C. of C.; mem. Fairfield Bus. Industrialists (pres. 1986-89), Rotary (treas. 1987—, v.p. 1989—). Office: Exptl Plastic Molds Corp 3 Spielman Rd Fairfield NJ 07006

IADAVAIA, ELIZABETH ANN, real estate developer; b. N.Y.C., June 28, 1960; d. Vincent Anthony and Sally (D'Angelo) I. BA in Econs., Georgetown U., 1982. With Montifiore Hosp. Neurophysiology Labs., N.Y.C., 1979-80; with Sch. of Bus. Adminstrn. Georgetown U., Washington, 1981-82; with Kolter Devel. Corp., N.Y.C., 1983-85, Merrill Lynch Realty, Stamford, Conn., 1985-88, Crown Group Real Estate Devel. & Fin., White Plains, N.Y., 1988—. Pres. VIP Young Adult Club, 1985-87. Mem. N.Y. State MBA Assn., Sch. of the Holy Child Alumni Assn. (bd. dirs., chmn. Rye, N.Y. chpt. 1983—), Georgetown U. Alumni Assn. (class chmn. 1986—), Women in Sales Assn., Nat. Second Mortgage Assn., VIP Young Adult Club (pres. 1985-87). Home: 17 Archer Dr Bronxville NY 10708

IADEROSA, GINA MARIE, public relations executive; b. Cleveland, May 24, 1960; d. Gregory Benjamin and Jo-Ann Marie (Stangato) I. Student, John Carroll Univ., Cleve., 1982. Mktg. asst. IBM, Cleve., 1981-83; publs. editor Robert A. Sherman & Assocs., Warren, Ohio, 1983-84; communications editor Macmillan Pub. Co., N.Y.C., 1984-86; asst. dir. pub. relations Cartier, N.Y.C.; dir. pub. relations, advt. Carlos Falchi, N.Y.C., 1987--; pub. relations Christine Jaguin, Inc., cons. Debora Kuchme, Inc., Finesse Fashion Buying, N.Y.C., 1987--. Editor in chief Macmillan newsletter, 1985. Vol. 1980 Presidential Campaign, 1980, mem. Maison de Francais, Cleve., 1981. Mem. Female Exec. Roman Catholic.

IANTOSCA, MARYANN, communications executive; b. Newark, Mar. 11, 1958; d. Ralph Anthony and Janet Sarah (Monnetti) I. BA, U. S.C., 1981; AS, Taylor Bus. Inst., Bridgewater, N.J., 1985. Nurses aide Lambertville (N.J.) Nursing Home, 1975-76; waitress Mauros Pizza, Columbia, S.C., 1978-80; pantry chef Colligans Stockton (N.J.) Inn, 1979; cert. tng. tech. Hunterdon Devel. Ctr., Clinton, N.J., 1981-83; asst. treas. 1st Fidelity Bank, Flemington, N.J., 1983-85; assembly operator Burroughs Corp., Flemington, 1983-85; computer operator AT&T Communications, Piscataway, N.J., 1984-87; course developer, network adminstr., mgr. AT&T Communications, Morristown, N.J., 1987-88; trainer, network adminstr. AT&T Communications, Murray Hill, N.J., 1988—; network cons.-sales AT&T Network Svcs., Chesapeake, Va., 1989-90. Counselor Spl. Olympics, Clinton, 1981-82. Mem. Nat. Soc. for Performance and Instrn. (tng. mgr. 1988—), Nat. Female Execs. Assn., Toastmasters, Sigma Chi (sec. 1978-80). Home: 821 Creekside Crescent Chesapeake VA 23320

IAROSSI, NANCY SEMLER, reading specialist; b. Camden, N.J., Oct. 6, 1949; d. George Carlton and Sally (Kappel) Semler; m. Frank Edmund Jr. Iarossi, May 15, 1971; children: Brian George, Kimberly Ann. AS, York Coll., 1970; BA magna cum laude, Montclair State Coll., 1976; MEd, George Mason U., 1986. Tchr. social studies Pope Paul High Sch., Clifton, N.J., 1976-79; reading specialist G.C. Round Elem. Sch., Manassas, Va., 1986—. Author: (with other) (handbook) Race Against Drugs, 1989; contbr. handbook Rmedial Program Plan, 1988. Mem. City of Manassas Remedial Program, 1988-89, City of Manassas Substance Abuse Com., 1989-90. Mem. Internat. Reading Assn., Va. Reading Assn., Greater Washington REading Coun., Gen. Fed. Woman's Club (past pres.), Kappa Delta Pi, Pi Gamma Mu. Republican. Episcopalian. Home: 15343 Maywood Dr Dumfries VA 22026 Office: G C Round Elem Sch 10100 Hastings Dr Manassas VA 22110

IAVARONE, GRACE, associate for university business services; b. Albany, N.Y., Feb. 9, 1961. BBA in Acctg., Siena Coll., 1983. CPA, N.Y. Sr. acct. Ernst & Whinney Albany, N.Y., 1983-85; controller Credit Union Ctr., Albany, 1985-90; assoc. for univ. bus. svcs. SUNY, Albany, 1990—. Mem. AICPA, N.Y. Soc. CPA's, Nat. Assn. Accts., Assn. Credit Union League Execs. Democrat. Roman Catholic. Home: 25B 7 Pine Ln Albany NY 12203 Office: SUNY State University Pla Rm 5426-A Albany NY 12246

IBA, BARBARA JEAN YOUNG, government agency administrator; b. Ellwood City, Pa., Oct. 18, 1937; d. Robert Harold and Ellen Lucille (Newton) Young; R.N., Presbyn.-Univ. Hosp., Pitts., 1958; student Bethany (W.Va.) Coll., 1958-59; B.S. in Nursing, U. Pitts., 1961; postgrad. Am. U., 1980; m. Edward Toshikatsu Iba, Oct. 23, 1965; children—Jennifer Emi, Robert Yoshio. Staff nurse Presbyn.-Univ. Hosp., 1958-59, Bethany Coll., 1958-59; nursing instr. Presbyn.-Univ. Hosp., 1959-64; nurse, population genetic researcher Nat. Inst. Dental Research, NIH, Bethesda, Md., 1964-74, equal opportunity coordinator, 1974-80, acting fed. women's program mgr., 1980-84, fed. women's program mgr., 1984-88; mgr. handicap program Pub. Health Svc., Rockville, Md., 1988—; chief of staff Equal Opportunity Evaluation Task Force, 1979-80; mem. Woodside Child Care Program Task Force, Silver Spring, Md., 1973-79; vice chmn. NIH Child Care Program Adv. Coms., 1973-74. Chmn., Parents of Preschoolers, Inc., 1974-75; mental retardation adv., Washington. Fed. nurse trainee, 1960. Recipient Equal Opportunity Achievement award Nat. Inst. Dental Research, 1978; Dir.'s award NIH, 1980. Mem. Women's Equity Action League, Federally Employed Women, Kensington Bus. and Profl. Women (1st v.p. 1985-86). Home: 8716 Milford Ave Silver Spring MD 20910 Office: Pub Health Svcs Parklawn Bldg Rockville MD 20857

IBBS, PATRICIA JOHNSON, employee benefits consultant, business owner; b. Chgo., Nov. 7, 1938; d. Gustave Carl and Helen Irene (Hackett) Johnson; m. William C. Ibbs, Sept. 5, 1959 (div. 1981); children: Scott Michael, Alison Jean. BA, Northwestern U., 1970; postgrad., Seabury-Western Theol. Sem., 1975. Pub.'s rep. Midwest Media Sales, Wilmette, Ill., 1968-72; assoc. editor Charles D. Spencer & Assoc., Chgo., 1972-86; prin.

PJI Benefits, Atlanta, 1986—, Employee Benefits Edn. Assn., Atlanta, 1986—; mem. editorial adv. bd. Employee Benefit News, McLean, Va., 1986—. Author: Dental Benefit Programs: Design and Operations, HMO Marketing: Benefit Manager's Perspective, Flexible Benefits; contbr. articles to profl. jours. Citizen liaison Chgo. Police Dept., 1965; mem. bd. edn. City of Evanston, Ill., 1968; jr. warden St. Luke's Episcopal Ch., Evanston, 1984-85, sr. warden, 1985-86; poll watcher Dem. Party, Chgo. and Evanston, 1965-74. Recipient Community Svc. award Atlanta City Coun., 1988. Mem. Chgo. chpt. Women in Employee Benefits (co-founder). Home: 24313 Plantation Dr Atlanta GA 30324 Office: PJI Benefits 3390 Peachtree Rd NE #1000 Atlanta GA 30326

ICE, BILLIE OBERTA, retail executive; b. Grantsville, W.Va., July 17, 1962; d. Clovis Drexel and Sherron Lea (Fowler) I. BA, Glenville (W.Va.) State Coll., 1984. Asst. mgr. Hecks Discount Dept. Stores, Nitro, W.Va., 1985-87; softlines mgr. Hills Dept. Stores, Canton, Mass., 1987-89, ops. mgr., 1989—. With U.S. Army, 1981-82. Mem. Nat. Assn. Female Execs., VFW Ladies Aux., Am. Legion. Democrat. Baptist. Home: PO Box 45 Wellsburg NY 14894 Office: Hills Dept Stores Lake Hills Pla Horseheads NY 14845

ICHINO, YOKO, ballet dancer; b. L.A.. Studies with Mia Salvenska, L.A. Mem. Joffrey II, N.Y.C., Joffrey Ballet, N.Y.C., Stuttgart Ballet, Fed. Republic Germany; tchr. ballet, 1976; soloist Am. Ballet Theatre, 1977-81; guest appearances, 1981-82; prin. Nat. Ballet Can., Toronto, Ont., 1982—; various guest appearances including World Ballet Festival, Tokyo, 1979, 82, with Alexander Godunov and Stars, summer 1982, Sydney Ballet, Australia, N.Z. Ballet, summer 1984, Ballet de Marseille, 1985-87, Deutsche Opera Ballet Berlin, Fed. Republic Germany, 1985—, Munich Opera Ballet, 1987-89, Australian Ballet, 1987, 89; tchr. numerous ballet workshops and summer sessions. Recipient medal Third Internat. Ballet Competition, Moscow, 1977. Offices: Nat Ballet Can, 157 King St E, Toronto, ON Canada M5C 1G9

IDA, VERA, lawyer; b. Romania, Jan. 8, 1952; came to U.S., 1979; d. Eugene and Anna (Low) Gerendas; m. Nathan Ida, May 12, 1971; children: Michelle, Jonathan. BA in Tech. Journalism with distinction, Colo. State U., 1983; JD cum laude, U. Akron, 1988. Bar: Ohio 1988. Law clk. Akron (Ohio) City Law Dept., 1987-88; law clk. to judge U.S. Dist. Ct. (no. dist.) Ohio, Akron, 1989—. Mem. citizens' rev. panel, Akron United Way, 1988-89. Mem. ABA, Ohio State Bar Assn., Akron Bar Assn., Phi Kappa Phi. Home: 666 San Moritz Dr Akron OH 44313

IENGO, VALERIE, small business owner; b. Queens, N.Y., Dec. 2, 1955; d. Anthony and Genevieve (DePhillips) I. Student, Pasco Hernando Coll., 1987-90. Press mechanic John's Press Svc., East Meadow, N.Y., 1968-72; specialist Val's Heidelberg Svc., Port Richey, 1972—; free lance photographer (Heidelberg specialist). Author repair manuals in field. Mem. Phi Theta Kappa. Home and Office: 9130 Prosperity Ln Port Richey FL 34668

IGLEHEART, ELIZABETH ROBBIN, employee benefits consultant; b. Bronxville, N.Y., Oct. 6, 1957; d. Jerome and Madelyn Narcissus (Yeskolski) Rakov; m. William Stewart Igleheart, Oct. 23, 1982; 1 child, Alexandra Houghton. BS in Indsl. and Labor Rels., Cornell U., 1979; MBA in Mktg., U. Conn., 1986. Mgmt. trainee Aetna Life & Casualty, Hartford, Conn., 1979-82, sr. mktg. cons., devel. adminstr., 1983-85; dir. mktg., dir. product devel. Ptnrs. Nat. Health Plan, Las Colinas, Tex., 1985-88; v.p., managed care Vol. Hosp. Am., Las Colinas, 1988-89; cons. Towers Perrin, Dallas, 1989—; speaker Dallas Human Resources Mgmt. Assn., 1990, Am. Electronics Assn., Dallas, 1990—; keynote speaker EPIC Healthcare System Quar. Dirs. Meeting, 1990; break-out session leader Tex. Soc. Human Resources, 1990. Co-author: (textbook case study) Marketing Strategy and Planning, 1985. Industry recruiter March of Dimes, Dallas, 1990; speaker Conn. Nat. Abortion Rights Action League, Hartford, 1980-82; supporter Friends of Child Care Dallas; chairperson Cornell Phonathon, 1983-85; sponsor 500, Inc., 1985—. Mem. Southwest Pension Conf., Cornell Alumni Class (officer 1979—), Univ. Club Dallas (profl. women's com.). Republican. Presbyterian. Home: 4811 Mill Creek Pl Dallas TX 75244 Office: Towers Perrin 12377 Merit Dr Ste 1200 Dallas TX 75251-3234

IGLESIAS, MARIA ADELA, education specialist; b. Sancti Spiritus, Las Villas, Cuba, Oct. 3, 1950; came to U.S., Nov. 1960; d. Jorge Antonio and Adela (Orizondo) I. BA, Fla. State U., 1972; MEd, Fla. Atlantic U., 1976; postgrad. U. Mass., 1985—. Spl. edn. dept. head, tchr. Palm Beach County Schs., Boynton Beach, Fla., 1976-80, Dade County Pub. Schs., Coral Gables, Fla., 1980-84; bilingual spl. edn. tchr. Boston Pub. Schs., Jamaica Plain, Mass., 1984-85; ednl. specialist III, Mass. State Dept. Edn., Arlington, 1985-87; program advisor/compliance dept. spl. edn. Boston Pub. Schs., 1987—; cons. Fla. Career Coll., Miami, 1982-83; adj. prof. dept. spl. edn. U. Mass., Boston, 1987—; tutor SW Miami Boys Clubs, 1983-84. Mem. Council Exceptional Children, Am. Fedn. Tchrs., Boston Tchrs. Union, Boston Assn. Sch. Adminstrs. and Suprs. Democrat. Roman Catholic. Avocations: tennis, biking, jogging.

IGLEWICZ, RAJA, state agency administrator, researcher, industrial hygienist; b. Farenwald, Germany, Nov. 27, 1945; naturalized citizen, 1964; d. Max and Ethel (Dworeska) Brody; m. Boris Iglewicz, May 24, 1973; children: David, Alana. BSN cum laude, Temple U., 1975, MS in Occupational and Environ. Health, 1980; postgrad., Harvard U., 1984-85. naturalized citizen, 1963; RN, N.J.; cert. indsl. hygienist. RN Garden State Hosp., Marlton, N.J., 1975-79; indsl. hygienist Allied Chem. Corp., Marcus Hooks, Pa., 1980; program specialist N.J. Dept. Health, Trenton, 1980-84, rsch. scientist, 1985-89, program mgr., 1990—; pres. ANSTAD Corp., statewide, 1984-85; cons. ANSTAD, Cherry Hill, N.J., 1984-89. Recipient Cert. Appreciation, County of Cumberland, 1970; Albert Einstein honor scholar, 1971. Mem. Am. Indsl. Hygiene Assn., Am. Pub. Health Assn. Home: 1912 Rolling Ln Cherry Hill NJ 08003

IKEDA, DONNA RIKA, state legislator; b. Honolulu, Aug. 31, 1939; d. William G. and Lillian (Kim) Yoshida; div.; children: Rika, Aaron, Julie. BA in Speech, U. Hawaii. Substitute tchr., 1969-71; legis. researcher Hawaii Rep. Research Office, 1971-74; asst. v.p. Grand Pacific Life Ins. Ltd., Honolulu, 1989—; former mem. Hawaii Ho. of Reps.; mem. Hawaii State Senate. Office: State Senate State Capitol Rm 202 Honolulu HI 96813

IKLE, DORIS MARGRET, energy conservation company executive; b. Frankfort, Germany, May 28, 1928; came to U.S., 1937, naturalized, 1945; d. Richard and Sonia (Pappenheimer) Eisemann; m. Fred Charles Ikle, Dec. 23, 1959; children—Judith, Miriam. B.A., NYU, 1949, M.A., 1953; postgrad. Columbia U., 1957. Economist, Nat. Bur. Econ. Research, N.Y.C., 1949-56, Rand Corp., Santa Monica, Calif., 1957-60, Inst. Energy Analysis, Washington, 1976-77; cons. U.S. Dept. Commerce, Washington, 1975-76; pres. Conservation Mgmt. Corp., Bethesda, Md., 1977—; adv. council Am. for Energy Independence, 1985—; cons. in field. Author: The Complete Energy Audit Book, 1980, (software) RCS and CACS Audit Systems, 1984. Contbr. articles to profl. jours. Home: 7010 Glenbrook Rd Bethesda MD 20814 Office: Conservation Mgmt Corp 2204 Morris Ave Bordentown NJ 08505-9998

IKUTA, LINDA MACKENNA, nurse; b. Winchester, Mass., July 7, 1952; d. Gilbert James III and Shirley M. (Washburn) MacK.; m. Dale Tadashi Ikuta, Sept. 25, 1983; children: Emily Aiko, David Joseph Hiroyuki. Diploma in nursing, Fall River (Mass.) Sch. Nursing, 1974; AA in Sci., SUNY, Albany, 1978; BSN, U. Phoenix, 1987. RN, Mass. Nurse women's ward Boston City Hosp., 1974; cardiac and hematology nurse Baystate Med. Ctr., Springfield, Mass., 1974-76; neonatal nurse ICU UCLA Hosp. & Clinics, West L.A., 1976-79; sr. nurse intensive care nursing Stanford Univ. Hosp., Palo Alto, Calif., 1979—; lectr. perinatal outreach Stanford U., 1980-88. Mem. Moneray Bay (Calif.) Aquarium, 1984—; nursing mother, mem. Milk Bank of San Jose Aux., 1984, 88. Mem. Southwestern Assn. on Indian Affairs. Democrat. Buddhist. Home: 822 N 6th St San Jose CA 95112 Office: Stanford U Hosp 300 Pasteur Dr Palo Alto CA 94305

ILCHMAN, ALICE STONE, college president, former government official; b. Cin., Apr. 18, 1935; d. Donald Crawford and Alice Kathryn (Biermann) Stone; m. Warren Frederick Ilchman, June 11, 1960; children: Frederick Andrew Crawford, Alice Sarah. BA, Mt. Holyoke Coll., 1957; MPA, Maxwell Sch. Citizenship, Syracuse U., 1958; PhD, London Sch. Econs., 1965; LHD, Mt. Holyoke Coll., 1982, Franklin and Marshall Coll., 1983. Asst. to pres., mem. faculty Berkshire Community Coll., 1961-64; lectr., asst. prof. Ctr. for South and Southeast Asia Studies U. Calif.-Berkeley, 1965-73; prof. econs. and edn., dean Wellesley (Mass.) Coll., 1973-78; asst. sec. ednl. and cultural affairs Dept. State, 1978; asso. dir. ednl. and cultural affairs Internat. Communication Agy., 1978-81; advisor to sec. Smithsonian Instn., 1981; pres. Sarah Lawrence Coll., Bronxville, N.Y., 1981—; intern, asst. to Sen. John F. Kennedy, 1957; dir. Peace Corps Tng. Program for India, 1965-66; chmn. com. on women's employment NAS. Author: The New Men of Knowledge and the New States, 1968, (with W.F. Ilchman) Education and Employment in India, The Policy Nexus, 1976. Trustee Mt. Holyoke Coll., 1970-80, Mass. Found. for Humanities and Pub. Policy, 1974-77, East-West Center, Honolulu., 1978-81 Expt. in Internat. Living, The Markle Found., The Rockefeller Found., The U. of Cape Town, South Africa, Corp. Adv. Bd.; mem. Smithsonian Council, Yonkers Emergency Fin. Control Bd., Am. Ditchley Found. Program Com., Internat. Research and Exchange Bd., Com. for Econ. Devel.; bd. dirs. N.Y. Telephone Co. Mem. Nat. Acad. Pub. Adminstrn., NOW Legal Def. Edn. Fund, Coun. Fgn. Rels., Cosmpolitan Club (N.Y.C.), Century Assn. (N.Y.C.), Bronxville Field Club. Home: 935 Kimball Ave Bronxville NY 10708 Office: Sarah Lawrence Coll Bronxville NY 10708

ILDERTON, JANE WALLACE, small business owner; b. Gainesville, Ga., Mar. 10, 1936; d. William Lewis and Fay E. (Montgomery) Wallace; m. James Wilson Ilderton, June 12, 1954; children: James Wilson Jr., Mark Joseph, Andrew William. Grad. high sch., Gainesville. Owner, operator Designs by Jane, Charleston, S.C.; mfr., designer SGM Baby Bags Co., 1988—. Mem. Market Mchts. Assn., Charleston Trident C. of C., Smocking Arts Guild of Am. Episcopalian. Office: Designs by Jane 188 Meeting St Charleston SC 29401

ILEY, JANET MATHIS, controller; b. Sonora, Tex., June 7, 1959; d. Ray Seth and Mary Oma (Hanson) Mathis; 1 child, Matthew Clinton Iley. BBA, Tarleton State U., 1981, postgrad., 1987—. Acct. Columbian Peanut Co., Deleon, Tex., 1981-83; cost acct. Dr. Pepper, Dallas, 1983-84; controller DeLeon (Tex.) Hosp. Dist., 1984—. Mem. Tex. Hosp. Assn. of Fin. Officers. Democrat. Methodist. Office: DeLeon Hosp Dist 407 S Texas DeLeon TX 76444

IMBODEN, PATRICA ALTOM, advertising company executive; b. Indpls., May 24, 1961; d. Howard Lowell and Sharon Lee (Roney) Imboden. BA, DePauw U., 1983; postgrad., U. Dayton, 1988. Communication asst. L.M. Berry & Co., Dayton, Ohio, 1984-85; sales promotion coord. L. M. Berry & Co., Dayton, 1985-87; account exec. L. M. Berry & Co., Carlisle, Pa., 1987--. Mem. Dayton Art Inst., 1987—, Dayton Performing Arts, 1988; fundraiser. Mem. Internat. Assn. of Bus. Communicators, Nat. Assn Exec. Females. Republican. Methodist. Home: 1420 Green St Harrisburg PA 17025

IMBRIGATO-FESSON, PAULINE-MARIA, clinical psychologist; b. Mineola, N.Y., Aug. 7, 1946; d. Paul and Audrey (Yancey) Imbrigato; m. William Cleveland Fesson, Nov. 18, 1989. BS, Hampton (Va.) U., 1968; MSW, NYU, 1973; M Psychology, Pa. State U., 1980, PhD in Clin. Psychology, 1984. Case worker N.Y.C. Dept. Social Svcs., 1968-74; psychiat. social worker Cen. City Community Mental Health Ctr., L.A., 1974-77, Charles Drew Med. Sch., L.A., 1977—, Thalians Mental Health Ctr., Cedars Sinai Hosp., L.A., 1977-78; clin. psychologist Nat. Children's Ctr., Washington, 1984-85; clin. psychologist for spl. edn. D.C. Pub. Schs., Washington, 1985—; cons. Comprehensive Care Group Homes, Washington, 1986—. Mem. Am. Assn. Psychologists, Assn. Black Psychologists, Assn. Black Social Workers, Delta Sigma Theta. Democrat. Baptist. Office: DC Pub Schs Spl Edn Moten Assessment Ctr Elvans and Morris Rd SE Washington DC 20020

IMEL, PRISCILLA BROWN, accountant; b. Wichita, Kans., Jan. 6, 1954; d. Jack Leon and Charlotte (Kagey) Brown; m. Norman Leon Imel, Nov. 27, 1976; children: David Neil, Sherri Kagey, Colleen Hannah. BA in Sec. Edn./Bus. Adm., William Woods Coll., Fulton, Mo., 1976. Sec. edn. tchr. Wichita Pub. Schs., Kans., 1976-77; accts. payable mgr. Sunflower Beef Co., Wichita, 1978-79; real estate agt. Century 21, Grove & Co., Wichita, 1978-79; acctg. mgr. Eidson Metal Products Inc., Albuquerque, 1979-81; contr. Eidson Metal Products Inc., 1981-84, 86-87, Constrn. Rental & Supply, Albuquerque, 1984-86; acctg. mgr. Leedshill-Herkenhoff, Inc., Albuquerque, 1987-90; exec. v.p. Nat. Assn. Credit Mgrs. N.Mex. Inc., Albuquerque, 1990—. Leader Girl Scouts U.S., Rio Rancho, N.Mex., 1985—. Mem. Nat. Assn. Credit Mgrs. (credit and fin. devel. div. pres. 1988-89). Republican. Methodist. Home: 3409 20th Ave SE Rio Rancho NM 87124 Office: Nat Assn Credit Mgrs NMex PO Box 30108 Albuquerque NM 87190

IMGRUND, BERNADINE WOJTANOWSKI, nurse educator; b. Connellsville, Pa., Mar. 13, 1936; d. Joseph S. and Wanda V. (Zielinski) Wojtanowski; m. David J. Imgrund, Oct. 8, 1960; children: David K., Kristi-Anne. Nursing degree, Mercy Sch. of Nursing, Pitts., 1956; BS, Boston Coll., 1960; EdM, Columbia U. Tchrs. Coll., 1969. RN, N.J., Ill., Pa. Coord. West Jersey Sch. Nursing, Camden, N.J., 1960-61; instr. St. Joseph's Hosp. Sch. Nursing, Paterson, N.J., 1962-64, Hackensack (N.J.) Hosp. Sch. Nursing, 1964-69; asst. prof. nursing Widener U., Chester, Pa., 1978-79; health coord. Coll. DuPage, Glen Ellyn, Ill., 1984-85; pub. health nurse DuPage County Health Dept., Wheaton, Ill., 1989—. Leader Camp Fire, Naperville, Ill., 1980-85, bd. dirs., 1983; pres. svc. ministry St. Raphael Ch., Naperville, 1980-82; mem. Chgo. Coun. Fgn. Ministry, 1983-89, Naperville Art Assn., 1988—, election judge con. 1983-86, precinct com. capt., 1988—. Mem. AAUW (reader peace and nat. security group 1982-84, state com. woman's equity 1984), Great Decisions Group (facilitator, leader 1982-89, pub. libr. liaison), Disting. Ill. Nurses (bd. dirs. 1986-88), Ill. State Nurses, Pi Lambda Theta. Democrat. Roman Catholic. Home: 1239 Elizabeth Ave Naperville IL 60540

IMMEL, CYNTHIA LUANNE, flight attendant; b. Spokane, Wash., Oct. 21, 1958; d. Robert Leon and Barbara Ann (Milholland) I. Student, U. Minn., 1981. Asst. profl. photographer U. Minn., 1977, sr. pub. events attendant, 1978; flight attendant Pan Am., N.Y.C., 1979—; swim coach and instr. Carleton Coll., Northfield, Minn.; judge, attendant Spl. Olympics, Baton Rouge, 1982; pub. event rels. Pan Am. N.Y., 1981-85. Artist: Mural, 1973. Named Outstanding Athlete Coaches award, Northfield, 1977, Am. Legion Outstanding Citizen award, Northfield, 1977. Mem. Ind. Union Flight Attendants, Pi Beta Phi. Republican. Methodist. Home: 1220 S Washington St Northfield MN 55057

INDART, MONICA JEANNE-MARIE, psychologist; b. Buffalo, Wyo., June 9, 1958; d. Jean and Louise (Sagarzazu) I.; m. Thomas J. Morgan, May 19, 1979 (div. 1990). BS, U. Wyo., 1981; MA, U. Tulsa, 1983; postgrad., Rutgers U., 1985—. Rsch. asst. psychology dept. U. Tulsa, 1981-83; substance abuse therapist Bright Sky, Tulsa, 1983-84; psychol. asst. Child Guidance Ctr. Okla. Dept. of Health, Okmulgee, 1984-85; staff psychologist N.J. Dept. Human Svcs./Marlboro Psychiat. Hosp., 1985-89; admissions coord. Marlboro Psychiat. Hosp., 1989—; appointed mem. Div. Mental Health and Hosps. AIDS Task Force, 1989, Div. Mental Health and Hosps. Clin. Experts Panel for the Chronically Mentally Ill., 1989—. Contbr. articles to profl. jours. Vol. Hyacinth Found., New Brunswick, N.J., 1988—; mem. N.J. Women & AIDS Network, 1989—. Mem. Am. Psychol. Assn. (assoc.), N.J. Psychol. Assn., N.J. Acad. Psychology, Mental Health Emergency Svcs. Assn., Nat. Abortion Rights Action League, NOW, Greenpeace, Wilderness Soc., Earthwatch, Phi Beta Kappa, Phi Kappa Phi. Democrat. Home: 305 Nassau St Princeton NJ 08540 Office: Marlboro Psychiat Hosp Sta A Rt 520 Marlboro NJ 07746

INDICK, JANET, sculptor, educational administrator; b. Bklyn., Mar. 3, 1932; d. Charles and Sarah (Goldsmith) Suslak; m. Benjamin Philip Indick, Aug. 23, 1953; children: Michael Cory, Karen Leigh Indick Maizel. B.S. in Art, Hunter Coll., 1953, postgrad., 1953; postgrad. New Sch., 1961-62. Tchr. kindergarten pub. schs., Elizabeth, N.J., 1953-54; dir. nursery sch. Teaneck Jewish Ctr., N.J., 1964—. Executed commd. sculpture Netzach Yisroel, Teaneck Jewish Ctr., 1974, Etz Chaim 1981, Sanctuary Wall Menorah 1983, Temple Beth Rishon, Wyckoff, N.J., 1981, 83, Menorah, Franklin Lakes Pub. Sch., 1983; one-woman shows include Maurice M. Pine Gallery, Fairlawn (N.J.) Pub. Libr., 1990; exhbns. include Morris (N.J.) Mus., 1979, 84, Bergen (N.J.) Mus., 1981, Newark Mus., 1982, Jersey City Mus., 1983, Hebrew Tabernacle, N.Y.C., 1984, Parsons Gallery, N.Y.C., 1984, Lillian Heidenberg Gallery, N.Y.C., 1984—, Chubb Corp., N.J. solo, 1985, N.J. Art Ctr., Summit, 1985, Galleria Maray, N.J., 1986, Vineyard Gallery, N.Y.C., 1986, Edward Williams Gallery Fairleigh Dickinson U., solo 1986, Artforms Gallery, Red Bank, N.J., 1987, Lillian Kornbluth Gallery, Fairlawn, N.J., 1988. Nat. Assn. Women Artists Traveling Exhbns., 1989-90, Fgn. Traveling Exhbns., India, 1989-90, Columbus (Ohio) Mus. Fine Art, 1989-90, Balt. Mus. Art, 1989-90. Advisor Teaneck Arts Adv. Bd., 1982—. Recipient sculpture prize Nat. Assn. Painters and Sculptors, 1970-80, Merit award IFFRA/AIA Forum on Religion, Art and Architecture, 1984; N.J. State Council Arts fellow, 1981. Mem. Sculptors Assn. N.J. (v.p. 1988—), Sculptors League Internat., Nat. Assn. Women Artists (juror, sculpture prize 1974), N.Y. Soc. Women Artists (juror), Women's Caucus Art (juror). Democrat. Jewish. Home: 428 Sagamore Ave Teaneck NJ 07666 also: care Lillian Heidenberg Gallery 50 W 57th St New York NY

INFANTE, DAISY INOCENTES, sales and real estate executive; b. Marbel, The Philippines, Aug. 3, 1946; came to U.S., 1968; d. Jesus and Josefina (Inocentes) I.; m. Enerico Malong Sampang, Sept. 20, 1968 (div. 1981); children: Desiree Josephine, Dante Fernancio, Darrell Enerico; m. Rosben Reyes Ogbac, Jan. 30, 1987; children: Peter Ross, Analisa Frances. AA with highest honors, Notre Dame of Marbel, Philippines, 1963; AB in English magna cum laude, U. Santo Tomas, Manila, 1965, BS in Psychology, 1966; MA in Communications, Fairfield U., 1971. Columnist, writer Pinoy News mag., Chgo., 1975-76, Philippine News, Chgo., 1977-80; cons. EDP Cemco Systems, Inc., Oak Brook, Ill., 1980-81; pres. Daisener, Inc., Downers Grove, Ill., 1980-82; cons. EDP Robert J. Irmen Assocs., Hinsdale, Ill., 1981-82; pres. Data Info. Systems Corp., Downers Grove, Ill., 1982-84; broker, co. mgr. Gen. Devel. Corp., Chgo., 1984-86; columnist, writer Via Times, Chgo., 1984-86; owner, pres. Marbel Realty, Chgo., 1984-88; exec. v.p. Dior Enterprises, Inc., Chgo., 1986-88; real estate sales mgr. M.J. Cumber Co., Grand Cayman, Cayman Islands, 1988-89, Vet. Real Estate, Orlando, Fla., 1989-90, All Star Real Estate, Inc., Orlando, 1990—. Author: Poems of My Youth, 1982; (lyrics and music) My First Twenty Songs, 1981; featured contbr. poems: American Poetry Anthology, Vol. VII, no. 4; inventor fryer-steamer. Sec. Movement for a Free Philippines, 1984. Mem. NAFE, Am. Soc. Profl. Exec. Women, Philippine C. of C. (sec. Chgo. chpt. 1985), Bayanivan Internat. Ladies Assn., Lions (twister Fil-Am. club 1978-79). Roman Catholic. Office: All Star Real Estate Inc 710 E Colonial Dr Ste 200 Orlando FL 32803

INFERRERA, MARIE ANTOINETTE, advertising executive; b. Camden, N.J., Feb. 11, 1958; d. Carmen J. and Antoinette E. (Monzo) I. BA, Rider Coll., 1980. Advt. copywriter Provident Mutual Life, Phila., 1980-82; copywriter Inst. for Sci. Info., Phila., 1982-83, media buyer, 1983-84; advt. specialist Rohm & Haas, Phila., 1984-85, advt. mgr., 1985—. Bd. dirs. Daisy Ln. Condominium, Mt. Laurel, N.J., 1986-88; judge State Edn. Editors Competition, Trenton, N.J., 1989. Recipient Bell Ringer award Bus. Profl. Advertisers Assn., 1988. Mem. Bus. Profl. Advertisers Assn. Republican. Roman Catholic. Office: Rohm & Haas Co Independence Mall W Philadelphia PA 19105

INFIELD, MARTHEA MAE, mental health service executive; b. Cleve., Dec. 31, 1929; d. Neil Edward and Freda Margaret (Schray) Bowler; m. Dwight Hosak Infield, Nov. 14, 1953; children: Susan, Dwight David, Donald, Elisabeth. B.B.A., Fenn Coll., 1952; M.S., Case Western Res. U., 1970. Asst. to overseas div. mgr. Goodyear Tire & Rubber, Akron, Ohio, 1953-54; social worker Lucas County Welfare Dept., Toledo, 1964-65; social worker protective services Cuyahoga County Welfare Dept., Cleve., 1967-68; crisis counselor Crisis Intervention Team, Cleve., 1970-72, coordinator, 1972-74, exec. dir., founder CIT Mental Health Services, 1974—. Republican. Presbyterian. Home: 8381 Celianna Strongsville OH 44136 Office: CIT Mental Health Services 2177 S Taylor Rd University Heights OH 44118

INGALLS, ANNA MAY, English instructor, real estate investor; b. Wayne, Mich., Sept. 18, 1941; d. Louis A. and Margaret A. (Faling) Diedrich; m. Melvyn V. Ingalls, Oct. 19, 1963 (div. June 1982); children: Joy Anita, Todd Louis. BA, Mich. State U., 1962; MA, U. Mich., 1963. Cert. English tchr., Calif., Mich. Textbook writer Fidler Co., Grand Rapids, Mich., 1963-64; tchr. English Godfrey Lee Schs., Grand Rapids, 1964-66; English instr. Southwestern Coll., Chula Vista, Calif., 1966—. Author in field; contbr. articles to profl. jours. Woodrow Wilson fellow U. Mich., 1962-63. Mem. Calif. Tchr.'s Assn., Nat. Coun. Tchrs. of English. Office: Southwestern Coll 900 Otay Lakes Rd Chula Vista CA 92010

INGALLS, JEREMY, poet, educator; b. Gloucester, Mass., Apr. 2, 1911; d. Charles A. and May E. (Dodge) Ingalls. AB, Tufts Coll., 1932, AM, 1933; student, U. Chgo., 1938-39; LHD, Rockford Coll., 1960; LittD, Tufts U., 1965. Asst. prof. English Lit. Western Coll., Oxford, Ohio, 1941-43; resident poet, asst. prof. English lit. Rockford (Ill.) Coll., 1948-50, successively assoc. prof. English and Asian studies, prof., chmn. div. arts, chmn. English dept., 1950-60; Fulbright prof. Am. lit., Japan, 1957; Rockefeller Found. lectr. Kyoto Am. Studies seminar, 1958. Author: A Book of Legends, 1941, The Metaphysical Sword, 1941, Tahl, 1945, The Galilean Way, 1953, The Woman from the Island, 1958, These Islands Also, 1959, This Stubborn Quantum, 1983, Summer Liturgy, 1985, The Epic Tradition and Related Essays, 1989; translator (from Chinese): A Political History of China, 1840-1928 (Li Chien-Nung), 1956, The Malice of Empire (Yao Hsin-Nung) (in Japanese), 1970, Tenno Yugao (Nakagawa), 1975. Recipient Yale Series of Younger Poets prize, 1941, Shelley Meml. award, 1950, and other awards for poetry; appointed hon. epic poet laureate United Poets Laureate Internat., 1965; Guggenheim fellow, 1943, Chinese classics rsch. fellow Republic of China, 1945, 46, Am. Acad. Arts and Letters grantee, 1944, Ford Found fellow Asian studies, 1952, 55. Fellow Internat. Inst. Arts and Letters; mem. Assn. Asian Studies (life), The Authors Guild, Modern Lang. Assn. (chmn. Oriental-We. lit. relations conf.), Poetry Soc. Am., New Eng. Poetry Soc., Dante Soc. Am. (life), Phi Beta Kappa, Chi Omega. Episcopalian. Home: 6269 E Rosewood St Tucson AZ 85711

INGALLS, MARIE CECELIE, state legislator, retail executive; b. Faith, S.D., Mar. 31, 1936; d. Jens P. and Ida B. (Hegre) Jensen; m. Dale D. Ingalls, June 20, 1955; children: Duane, Delane. BS, Black Hills State Coll., 1973, MS, 1978. Elem. tchr. Meade County Schs., Sturgis, S.D., 1957-72, Faith Sch. Dist. 46-2, 1973-76; elem. prin. Meade Sch. Dist. 46-1, Sturgis, 1976-81; owner, operator Ingalls of Faith, Sturgis, 1978-83; mem. S.D. House Reps., Pierre, 1986—. Recipient Woman of Achievement award City of Sturgis, 1986. Mem. S.D. Cattlewomen, Faith C. of C. (pres. 1988), Sturgis C. of C., Optimists, Zonta (hon.). Republican. Lutheran. Home: HCR PO Box 31 Mud Butte SD 57758 Office: Ingalls 1032 Main St Sturgis SD 57785

INGEBRIGTSEN, CATHERINE WILLIAMS, rehabilitation consultant, health education specialist; b. Lake Charles, La., May 28, 1955; d. Thomas Humphrey and Jane Catherine (Caldwell) Williams; 1 child, Jennifer Catherine Bittle. BS, Old Dominion U., 1978, MS summa cum laude, 1983; diploma profl. nursing, Norfolk Gen. Hosp., 1978. Intensive care unit nurse DePaul Hosp., Norfolk, Va., 1979-80; cons. Internat. Rehab. Assn., Virginia Beach, Va., 1980-82; ptnr., pres., cons. OccuSystems, Norfolk, 1982-85; prin., pres. Cathy Bittle & Assocs., Norfolk, 1985—; health edn. cons. Peninsula Health Dept., Newport News, Va., 1985—, dir. grant writing program, 1985-86; educator Diabetes Inst., Virginia Beach, 1984-88; speaker in field. Com. mem. Tidewater Health Fair Task Force, Norfolk, 1983. Lt. Nurse Corps Res. Program USN, 1988—. Mem. Am. Assn. Counseling and Devel., Am. Assn. Phys. Health, Edn., Recreation and Dance, Old Dominion U. Grad. Student Assn. (pres. 1982-83), Phi Kappa Phi. Republican. Roman Catholic. Avocations: sailing, biking, skiing, running, rollerskating. Home: 122 Cathedral Dr North Wales PA 19454 Office: Cathy Bittle & Assocs PO Box 271 Montgomeryville PA 18936

INGEMI, MARTHA CATHERINE, pharmacist; b. Ware, Mass., May 19, 1963; d. John Joseph and Theresa Mary (Foley) I. BS in Pharmacy, U. Conn., 1986. Registered pharmacist, Mass. Profl. sales rep. Syntex Labs., Inc., Palo Alto, Calif., 1986-87; pharmacist CVS Pharmacy, Worcester, Mass., 1987—. Democrat. Roman Catholic.

INGISH, KAREN S., library manager, librarian; b. Chgo., Apr. 24, 1947; d. Anthony John and Annette (Stakenas) Vesely; m. Stephen J. Ingish, Apr. 22, 1972; children: Holly J., Anthony E. BA, U. Ill., 1970; MLS, Rosary Coll., 1987. Reference librarian Poplar Creek Pub. Library, Streamwood, Ill., 1985-86; info. specialist Gorman Pub., Chgo., 1986-88; mgr. library and info. svcs. Ameritech Svcs., Schaumburg, Ill., 1988—. Trustee Poplar Creek Library, Streamwood, 1988—. Mem. ALA, Spl. Library Assn., Streamwood Women's Club (bd. dirs. 1979-80). Office: Ameritech Svcs Inc 1900 E Golf Rd Schaumburg IL 60173

INGLEHART, MARITA ROSCH, education researcher and educator; b. Ludwigshafen, Fed. Republic Germany, Aug. 23, 1951; came to U.S., 1984; d. Karl Julius and Rita (Schreck) Rohr; m. Ekkehard Rosch, Aug. 13, 1973 (div. May 1978); m. Ronald Franklin Inglehart, Apr. 5, 1986; 1 child, Ronald Charles; stepchildren: Elizabeth, Rachel. Diploma in psychology, U. Mannheim, Mannheim, Fed. Republic Germany, 1975, PhD, 1981, Habilitation, 1983. Asst. prof. U. Mannheim, 1975-78; rsch. scientist Ctr. for Decision Making, U. Mannheim, 1978-83; lectr. U. Mannheim, 1983-90; rsch. assoc. Ctr. for Rsch. on Learning and Teaching, U. Mich., Ann Arbor, 1986—; vis. prof. U. Mich., Ann Arbor, 1984-86, adj. asst. prof., 1986—. Author: Kritischelebens-Ereignisse, 1988; editor: Integration von Immigranten, 1979. Mem. Am. Psychol. Assn., Am. Psychol. Soc., German Soc. Psychology, European Assn. of Exptl. Social Psychology. Roman Catholic. Home: 2626 Geddes Ave Ann Arbor MI 48104 Office: U Mich Dept Psychology 580 Union Dr Ann Arbor MI 48109

INGLESBY, BEVERLY FISHER, sales executive; b. Portland, Oreg., July 8, 1954; d. Meredith Lowell and Betty Jean (Adam) Fisher; m. Thomas William Inglesby, Nov. 14, 1980; 1 child, Shannon. BS, U. Oreg., 1977. Ad mgr. Daisy Kingdom, Portland, 1976-78; media buyer, dir. McDonald, Babb & Clarkson, Portland, 1978-80; with sales dept. Blair Radio Sales, Portland, 1980-82; sales mgr. N.W., Portland, 1982—; founder, chmn. bd. Advt. Industry Emergency Fund of Portland, 1987—. Advisor Kappa Kappa Gamma House, Eugene, Oreg., 1989—. Mem. Portland Ad2 (1st v.p. 1977-80), Portland Advt. Fedn. (chmn., treas., 1st v.p. 1986—, pres. 1990—). Republican. Prebyterian. Home: 2025 SW Mt Hood Ln Portland OR 97201 Office: Northwest TV Sales 1501 SW Jefferson St Portland OR 97201

INGLETT, BETTY LEE, media services administrator; b. Augusta, Ga., Oct. 6, 1930; d. Wilfred Lee and Elizabeth Arelia (Crouch) I. BS in Edn., Ga. State Coll. for Women, 1953; MA in Library, Media and Edn. Adminstrn., Ga. So. U., 1980; EdD in Edn. Adminstrn., Nova U., 1988. Tchr. James L. Fleming Elem. Sch., Augusta, Ga., 1953-63, Murphey Jr. High Sch., Augusta, 1963-64, Sego Jr. High Sch., Augusta, 1964-68, Glenn Hills High Sch., Augusta, 1968-75; media specialist Nat. Hills Elem. Sch., Augusta, 1975-80; prin. Lake Forest Elem. Sch., Augusta, 1980-84, Joseph R. Lamar Elem. Sch., Augusta, 1984-86; dir. ednl. media services Richmond County Bd. Edn., Augusta, 1986—; owner, operator Betty Inglett Enterprises, Augusta. Contbr. articles to profl. jours. Bd. dirs. Am. Heart Fund, 1975-80, Am. Cancer Fund, 1986—; del. Dem. State Conv., 1982; council mem. PTA. (life), 1985. Named Adminstr. of Yr., 1988-89. Mem. Richmond County Edn. Assn. (sec. v.p. 1961-63, Adminstr. of Yr. 1989-90), AAUW (v.p. 1957-59), NEA, Ga. Assn. Edn., Ga. Assn. Ednl. Leaders, Ga. Library Media Dept., Ga. Library Assn., Ga. Assn. Instructional Tech., Ga. Assn. Curriculum Instructional Supr., Profl. Leadership Assn., Cen. Savannah River Area Library Assn., Alpha Delta Kappa, Phi Delta Pi, Phi Delta Kappa. Baptist. Office: Ednl Media Services 3148 Lake Forest Dr Augusta GA 30909

INGRAM, DOROTHY STAMPS, librarian; b. Nashville, Aug. 1, 1946; d. Robert Franklin and Sue Perkins (Craig) Stamps; m. Elwood L. White, June 13, 1973 (div. Aug. 1978); m. George Emory Ingram, May 17, 1985. BA, Vanderbilt U., Nashville, 1968; MLS, Peabody Coll., Nashville, 1971. Advtg. writer Dawson, Daniels, sullivan & Dillon, Nashville, 1968-69; librarian U. Ga., Marietta, 1971-74, Southern Tech. Institute, Marietta, 1974-75, Joslyn Art Museum, Omaha, Nebr., Southern Coll. of Technology, Marietta, Ga., 1979--. v. chrmn. edn Young Careers of the High Museum of Art, Atlanta, Ga., 1985-86. Recipient Outstanding Faculty award So. Tech. Found., Marietta, 1988, 90. Mem. ASTD, Ga. Libr. Assn., Southeastern Libr. Assn., Atlanta Area Bibliographic Instrn. Group (chmn. profl. devel. 1985-86, vice pres., pres. elect 1989-90, pres. 1990—), Nat. Soc. Performance and Instrn, Ga. Appalachian Trail Club, Lake Lanier Sailing Club. Democrat. Home: 1682 N Pelham Rd NE Atlanta GA 30324 Office: Southern Coll of Technology 1100 S Marietta Pkwy Marietta GA 30060

INGRAM, JOYCE ELAINE, nurse; b. Greenville, Pa., Jan. 12, 1947; d. George William Ingram and Rachel Marie (Sarver) Green. Diploma, Presbyn. U. Hosp. Sch. Nursing, Pitts., 1967. RN, Ariz., Pa., Tenn. Staff nurse Am. Hosp., South Miami, Fla., 1972-73; staff nurse Jackson Meml. Hosp., Miami, Fla., 1968-72, nursing supr., dir. pediatric nursing, 1973-77; staff nurse Children's Hosp. of Pitts., 1968, head nurse, nursing supr., staffing coordinator, 1977-85; staffing coordinator Scottsdale (Ariz.) Meml. Hosp.-North, 1985-89; staff nurse Vanderbilt Med. Ctr., Nashville, 1989—. Home: 556 Michele Dr Antioch TN 37013

INGRAO, DEBORAH ANN, puzzle creator; b. Jamestown, N.Y., Dec. 15, 1950; d. Phillip Maynard and Dorothy Ruth (Scheffler) York; m. Alleyn Angelo Ingrao, Sept 16, 1972 (div. 1988); children: Alyssa, Renee, Christopher. Grad., Maple Grove Jr.-Sr. High Sch., Bemus Point, N.Y., 1962-68. Dietary aide Fenton Park Nursing Home, Jamestown, N.Y., 1968-69; floating dock assembler Metallic Ladder Mfg. Co., Randolph, N.Y., 1969-72; asst. chef Matador Restaurant, Jamestown, N.Y., 1974-75, Gov. Fenton Restaurant, Jamestown, N.Y.; freelance writer, 1983; puzzle creator Dell Puzzle Magazine, 1984—. Chmn. PTO Bush Sch., Jamestown, N.Y. 1985. Mem. Falconer Rod and Gun Club N.Y. (pres. 1986-87), Skyline Archery Club Jamestownh N.Y., Nature Conservancy, World Wildlife Fund, NOW. Home: Rd #1 Dutch Hollow Rd Jamestown NY 14701

INGULFSEN, CHARLENE, hospital communications executive; b. Toronto, Ont., Can., Mar. 29, 1964; came to U.S., 1964; d. Gordon and Virginia (Quinnell) Burton; m. Tore Ingulfsen, Aug. 16, 1987. BS magna cum laude, Southwestern Adventist Coll., Keene, Tex., 1987. Pub. rels. asst. Southwestern Adventist Coll., 1983-85, 86-87; asst. mgr. Radio Syv, Troms, Norway, 1985-86; program dir. Sta. KJCR, Keene, 1986-87; dir. communication Ardmore (Okla.) Adventist Hosp., 1987—. Mem. Ardmore C. of C. (President's Club). Adventist. Office: Ardmore Adventist Hosp 1012 14th Ave NW Ardmore OK 73401

INMAN, CHRISTAL D., engineering technician; b. Mt. Airy, N.C., May 5, 1964; d. Arnold R. Sr. and Glenda Fay Inman. AAS, Guildford Tech. Community Coll, 1984; postgrad., Forsyth Tech. Community Coll. Technician Diversified Control Systems, Greensboro, N.C.; engring. technician City of Winston-Salem (N.C.). Mem. Inst. Transp. Engrs. (bd. dirs., affiliate dir.), N.C. Soc. Engrs., Winston-Salem Engring. Club (sec.). Home: 4570 Paula Dr Winston-Salem NC 27127 Office: PO Box 2511 Winston-Salem NC 27102

INNES, GEORGETTE MEYER, real estate and insurance broker; b. Wilmington, Del., Mar. 20, 1918; d. George and Flora Sue (Saunders) Meyer; m. Andrew T. Innes, Jr., Nov. 26, 1947 (dec.). Grad. high sch.; cert. appraiser Villanova Coll, 1974. Lic. Realtor, Pa.; ins. broker. Realtor, Phila., 1945—; ins. broker, Phila., 1946—, also appraiser. Mem., speaker Juniata Park Civic Assn., Phila., 1984. Recipient Knights Legion award Italian-Am. Press, 1971. Mem. Phila. Women's Realty Assn. (pres. 1949-51; Woman of Yr. 1972-73; pres. bd. govs. 1949-85), Am. Bus. Women's Assn. (chpt. v.p. 1971, Businesswoman of Yr. 1971), North Phila. Realty Bd. (v.p. 1975, 76, pres. 1977, Gustav A. Wick award 1979), Delaware Council Realty Bds. (sec. 1974), Real Estate Multiple Listing Burs. (treas. 1972-76), Nat. Assn. Realtors (sec.-treas. and v.p. chpt. 1975-80), Phila. Bd. Realtors (v.p. residential div. 1975), Sigma Lambda Soc. (chpt. pres. 1948). Avocations: golf; dancing; gardening; cooking; embroidery. Home: 2012 Roma Way Boynton Beach FL 33435-6506

INNES, P. KIM STURGESS, management consultant; b. Ottawa, Ont., Can., Mar. 29, 1955; d. Roy and Sydney Claire (Chamberlain) S.; m. W. Campbell Innes, May 12, 1984. BSc in Engring. Physics, Queen's U., Kingston, 1977; MBA with distinction, U. W. Ont., 1984. Registered profl. engr., Alta. Gas pipelines engr. Nat. Energy Bd., Ottawa, 1977-78; reservoir engr. Esso Resources Can. Ltd., Calgary, Alta., Can., 1978-80, corp. planning analyst, 1980-82; cons. McKinsey and Co., Toronto, Ont., 1984-88; v.p., asst. to pres. Greyhound Lines of Canada, Calgary, 1988-89; v.p. devel. Relax Hotels and Resorts, Calgary, Can., 1989—; mgmt. cons. in pvt. practice Calgary, 1990—; trustee Queen's U. 1987—, bd. dirs. bookstore 1975-77, mem. univ. council, 1979—; bd. dirs. Alberta Sci. Ctr., 1989—. Mem. Assn. Profl. Engrs., Geologists and Geophysicists Alta, Queen's U. Alumni Assn. (pres. 1980-82). Home: Box 1 Site 32, RR 12, Calgary, AB Canada T3E6W3

INNIS, PAULINE, author, newspaper company executive; b. Devon, Eng.; came to U.S., 1954; m. Walter Deane Innis, Aug. 1, 1959. Attended U. Manchester, U. London. Author: Hurricane Fighters, 1962; Ernestine or the Pig in the Potting Shed, 1963; The Wild Swans Fly, 1964; The Ice Bird, 1965; Wind of the Pampas, 1967; Fire from the Fountains, 1968; Astronumerology, 1971; Gold in the Blue Ridge, 1973, 2d edit., 1980; My Trails (transl. from French), 1975; (with Mary Jane McCaffery) Protocol, 1977; Prayer and Power in the Capital, 1982, The Secret Gardens of Watergate, 1987, Attention: A Quick Guide to the Armed Services, 1988. Bd. dirs. Washington Goodwill Industries Guild, 1962-66; membership chmn. Welcome to Washington Club, 1961-64; co-chmn. Internat. Workshop Capital Speakers' Club, 1961-64; pres. Children's Book Guild, 1967-68; dir. Ednl. Communications; bd. dirs. Internat. Conf. Women Writers and Journalists; mem. criminal justice com. D.C. Commn. on Status of Women; founder vol. program D.C. Women's Detention Center; chmn. women's com. Washington Opera, 1977-79; mem. Liaison Com. for Med. Edn., 1979—; nat. trustee Med. Coll., Pa., 1980—; bd. dirs. Khalil Gibran Found., 1983—; mem. Edn. Commn. for Fgn. Med. Grads., 1986—. Named Hoosier Woman of Yr., 1966. Mem. Soc. Woman Geographers, Authors League, Smithsonian Assocs. (women's bd.), English-Speaking Union (dir.), Spanish-Portuguese Group D.C. (pres. 1965-66), Brit. Inst. U.S., Am. Newspaper Women's Club (pres. 1971-73), Nat. Press. Club, Sulgrave Club. Home: 2700 Virginia Ave NW Washington DC 20037 also: Skipper's Row Gibson Island MD 21056

INNIS-JURKO, ANGELA RENEE, accountant; b. Alva, Okla., Jan. 25, 1961; d. Roy Dean and Bertha June (Bower) Innis. BS in Acctg., Oklahoma City U., 1983. CPA. Mem. corp. acctg. staff Okla. Pub. Co., Oklahoma City, 1983-86, Dallas, 1986-88; fin. analyst BTI Systems Inc., Oklahoma City, 1988-89; controller Whitetail, Inc., Oklahoma City, 1989—. Mem. Am. Inst. CPAs, Okla. Soc. CPAs, Amnesty Internat., Alpha Phi. Methodist. Office: Coburn Optical Industries 1701 S Cherokee PO Box 627 Muskogee OK 74402-0627

INSCOE, JENNIFER LYNN, loan company executive; b. Washington Island, Wis., Sept. 13, 1947; d. Clifford Charles and Betty Delores (Greenfeldt) Young; m. Robert Daniel Inscoe, Dec. 31, 1966 (div. 1981); children: Stephanie Lynn, Robyn Elizabeth. Student, Trinity Coll., Deerfield, Ill., 1965-67, Community Coll., 1979, 80, 87. Real estate agt. Merrill Lynch, Manassas, Va., 1980-82, ReMax Olympic, Manassas, 1982—; loan officer Mfrs. Hanover Mortgage, N.Y.C., 1981-83, Epic Mortgage Co., Woodbridge, Va., 1983-84, Sovran Mortgage, Manassas, 1984-86, Am. Home Funding, Manassas, 1987—. Mem. Fauquier Bd. Realtors (Warrenton, Va.), Prince William Bd. Realtors (Manassas, Va.), Mortgage Bankers Assn., No. Va. Builders Assn. Republican. Baptist. Home: 7581 Margate Ct 203 Manassas VA 22110 Office: Am Home Funding 7794 Donegan Dr Manassas VA 22110

INSELMAN, LAURA SUE, pediatrician; b. Bklyn., Nov. 2, 1944; d. Alexander M. and Rae (Bloom) Inselman. BA, Barnard Coll., 1966; MD, Med. Coll. Pa., 1970. Diplomate Am. Bd. Pediatrics, Am. Bd. Pediatric Pulmonology. Intern and resident St. Lukes Hosp. Ctr., N.Y.C., 1970-73; fellow in pediatric pulmonary disease Babies Hosp., N.Y.C., 1973-76; chief pediatric pulmonary div. Interfaith Med. Ctr., Bklyn., 1976-81; chief pediatric pulmonary div. North Shore Univ. Hosp., Manhasset, N.Y., 1981-86; clin. dir. pediatric pulmonary div. Newington Con. Children's Hosp., 1987—; asst. prof. pediatrics Cornell U. Med. Coll., N.Y.C., 1981-86; asst. clin. prof. pediatrics, Yale U. Sch. Medicine, New Haven, 1987—; asst. prof. pediatrics, U. Conn. Health Ctr., Farmington, 1987—; mem. staff Good Samaritan Hosp., West Islip, N.Y., 1982-87. Bd. dirs. Am. Lung Assn. Nassau-Suffolk, East Meadow, N.Y., 1983-86. Fellow Am. Acad. Pediatrics, Am. Coll. Chest Physicians; mem. Am. Thoracic Soc., Am. Fedn. Clin. Research, N.Y. Acad. Medicine, Harvey Soc., Soc. Pediatric Research. Office: Newington Children's Hosp 181 E Cedar St Newington CT 06111

INTILLI, SHARON MARIE, television associate director; b. Amsterdam, N.Y., Aug. 11, 1950; d. Francisco Joseph Intilli and Virginia Eleanor (Tallman) Monaco. Cert., Paralegal Inst., 1973; student, Fordham U., 1975-79. Group assoc. editor Matthew Bender & Co., N.Y.C., 1974-77; prodn. sec. 20/20 program, ABC, N.Y.C., 1977-78, prodn. assoc., 1979-80, program prodn. asst., 1980-82; legal contract adminstr. ABC Sports, N.Y.C., 1978-79; assoc. dir. Capital Cities/ABC, N.Y.C., 1982—; dir., assoc. dir. freelance projects. Contbg. editor Bender's Forms of Discovery, Vols. 15 & 16, 1975. Mem. Bd. Health and Econ. Redevel. Com., Hillsdale, N.J., 1989—. Recipient Ouststanding Individual Achievement cert. Nat. Acad. TV Arts & Scis., 1980-81. Mem. Dirs. Guild of Am.

INTVELD, MARJORIE LEE, public relations executive; b. Hebron, N.D., Oct. 6, 1936; d. Carl Dubs and Elma (Reich) Iblings, m. Delmar IntVeld, Aug. 31, 1957; children: Steven Albert, Richard William. BA, Bethel Coll., 1960; postgrad., Lang. Sch. Costa Rica, Goshen, Ind., 1974; LNHA, U. Minn., 1978. Clk. typist Bur. of Indian Affairs, Billings, Mont., 1955-56; cashier Miller Hosp., St. Paul, 1957-60; social worker Ramsey County Welfare Dept., St. Paul, 1960-62; missionary Bapt. Gen. Conf., Evanston, Ill., 1963-74; sales rep. Apache Jewelers, St. Anthony, Minn., 1974-75; credit mgr. Buttreys, St. Anthony, 1975; pub. relations coord. Presbyn. Homes of Minn., St. Paul, 1975-84, dir. of corp. pub. relations, 1984—; cons. Assn. of Prebyn. Homes, Mpls., 1988—. Vice chair pub. relations com. Minn. Assn. of Homes for Aging, Mpls., 1988-89; chair Christian Women, St. Paul, 1984-86. Recipient Athena nomination C. of C., 1987. Mem. Pub. Relations Soc. of Am., Internat. Assn. of Bus. Communicators. Home: 7412 Knollwood Dr Mounds View MN 55112 Office: Presbyn Home of Minn 3220 Lake Johanna Blvd Saint Paul MN 55101

IODICE, ELAINE, software engineer; b. Cambridge, Mass., Oct. 16, 1947; d. Arthur Peter and Mary Elizabeth (Stefanelli) I.; m. Ian Gordon Prittie, July 27, 1980. BFA, Boston Conservatory Music, 1969; BSC, U. Victoria (B.C., Can.), 1982. Programmer Software Products Internat., San Diego, 1982-83; mem. tech. staff Hughes Aircraft Co., San Diego, 1983-85, 86-87; cons. Reading, Eng., 1985; sr. software engr. Automated Systems Inc., San Diego, 1987—. Contbr. articles to profl. publs. Mem. Assn. for Computing Machinery, Am. Assn. Artificial Intelligence. Office: Automated Systems Inc 4105 Soriento Valley Blvd San Diego CA 92121

IODICE, JODY DIMENO, psychotherapist; b. Jan. 21, 1953; d. Peter Ronald and Josephine Margaret (DiMeno) I. BA, Mercer U., Atlanta, 1981; MSW, U. Ga., 1983. Clin. social work intern Nat. Inst. Mental Health, Highlands Mental Health Ctr., Canton, Ga., 1982; researcher U. Ga. Sch. of Social Work, Athens, 1983; from post-masters fellow to treatment coordinator Ga. Mental Health Inst., Atlanta, 1983-85; pub. relations cons. Atlanta Depression Holiday Hot Line; psychotherapist West Paces Ferry Psychiatric Ctr., Atlanta, 1985-87; pvt. practice psychotherapist Alcohol and Drug Aftercare Therapeutic Svcs., 1987--; allied profl. staff Laurel Heights Hosp., 1985--, clin. social work cons. West Paces Ferry Psychiatric Ctr., Atlanta, 1987--, adv. bd. mem., cons. family therapist, Schizophizenic Treatment and Rehabilitation Inc., Decatur, 1987--. Mem. Atlanta Historical Soc., 1970, Arts Festival of Atlanta, 1980, High Museum of Art, 1989, Alpha Delta Pi Sorority, Athens, 1973/. Mem. Nat. Assn. Social Workers (Ga. chpt.), Nat. Assn. of Alcoholism and Drug Abuse Counselors, Ga. Addiction Counselors' Assn., U. Ga. Alumni Assn. (pres. 1986-88). Democrat. Roman Catholic. Office: Monteith Commons Ste 205 1708 Peachtree St NW Ste 205 Atlanta GA 30309

IORFIDA, DIANE MARY, health care executive; b. Chgo., Sept. 21, 1954; d. Boleslaus and Genevieve Marie (Sumara) Laskowski; m. Samuel Joseph Iorfida, Sept. 13, 1975. BA in English, DePaul U., 1975, postgrad. 1975-76; MS, U. Notre Dame, 1984; MMOB, Ill. Benedictine Coll., 1987. Lic. tchr., Ill. Tng. coordinator Saxon Home Care Ctrs., Chgo., 1971-75; reading specialist Dept. Spl. Edn., LaGrange, Ill., 1975-76; tng. coordinator LaGrange State Bank, 1976-78; dir. tng. and personnel Garatoni & Assocs., South Bend, Ind., 1978; asst. dir. personnel Elkhart (Ind.) Gen. Hosp., 1978-80, dir. personnel, 1980-84; corp. asst. v.p., dir. human resources Ravenswood Health Care Corp., Chgo., 1984-88; sr. v.p. human resources Univ. Hosps. of Cleve., 1988—. Editorial bd. Jour. Am. Soc. Personnel Adminstrn. Mem. Ind. Soc. Hosp. Personnel Adminstrn. (bd. dirs. 1980-84, pres. 1983-84), Am. Compensation Assn., Am. Soc. Personnel Adminstrn., Ohio Soc. Healthcare Human Resources Adminstrn., Human Resources Mgmt. Assn. Chgo., Am. Soc. Healthcare Human Resources Adminstrn. (bd. dirs. 1987—). Office: Univ Hosps of Cleve 2074 Abington Rd Cleveland OH 44106

IPACH, CYNTHIA ANN, pharmaceutical executive; b. Covington, Ky., June 2, 1963; d. Edward Richard and Nancy Jo (Werbich) Salzer; m. Ronald Paul Ipach, May 6, 1989. BS, Coll. of Mount St. Joseph, 1985. Regulatory affairs mgr. Duramed Pharms., Inc., Cin., 1985—; v.p., sec. Great Escapes Travel, Inc., Cin., 1990—. Mem. Am. Assn. Pharm. Scientists, Regulatory Affairs Profls. Roman Catholic.

IRELAND, CAROL E., draftsman; b. Deluth, Ga., June 25, 1956; d. Raymond Hugh Wilson and Grace Eudora Goss; m. Eogene Darren Ireland (dec. Nov. 1983); children: Jay John, Lisa Grace. Student, Ft. Worth Sch. Bus., 1982-84. Notary pub., Ga. Design draftsman Phoenix Investments Ltd., Ft. Worth, 1982-83; asst. to engring. mgr. Besteel Industries Inc., Ft. Worth, 1983-88; draftsman, CAD operator Cob County Sch. Bus., Marietta, Ga., 1988—; freelance design drafter, Marietta, 1988—. Vol. Kent Nursing Home, Ft. Worth, 1983-88. Democrat. Roman Catholic. Office: Cobb County Sch Dist 440 Glover St Marietta GA 30060

IRELAND, CINDY JEAN, business owner; b. Witchita, Kans., Jan. 28, 1959; d. Webster Edwin and Pauline Grace (Bass) I.; m. Larry Harlin Rand, Aug. 27, 1975 (div. 1978); children: Travis Lee, Troy Jason. BFA, U. No. Iowa, 1987. Owner Ireland Design & Pub., Cedar Falls, Iowa, 1988—. Mem. MacUser Group. Home: 810 W 25th Cedar Falls IA 50613 Office: Ireland Design & Pub 2016 College St Cedar Falls IA 50613

IRELAND, PAMELA WOODHULL, retail executive; b. Englewood, N.J., May 14, 1957; d. Lloyd Owen and Frances Woodhull (Valentine) I. BA magna cum laude, Hobart and William Smith Coll., 1979. Asst. buyer B. Altman & Co., N.Y.C., 1979-80, sr. asst. buyer, 1980-82, buyer children's accessories and sleepwear, 1982-83, buyer infants and toddler apparel, 1983—, buyer children's sleepwear, 1987—. Mem. St. Bartholomews Community Club,, Sandbar Beach and Tennis Club, Phi Beta Kappa. Avocations: tennis, travel. Office: Frederick Atkins Inc 1515 Broadway New York NY 10036

IRLAND, LORRAINE, telecommunications analyst; b. Newark, Dec. 21, 1946; d. Allen Robert and Evelyn (Lusardi) Zensen; m. Michael Joseph Berger, Feb. 13, 1966 (div. 1971); 1 child, Michael Louis Berger; m. James Frederick Irland, Dec. 28, 1983; 1 child, Kevin Frederick. AA in Bus. Mgmt., Diablo Valley Coll., 1979; BA in Bus. Adminstrn., Upper Iowa U., 1983; MS in Corp. Planning, U. Pa., 1986. Communications cons. Pacific Telephone & Telegraph Co., San Francisco, 1969-80; industry cons. AT&T, Basking Ridge, N.J., 1981-84; systems cons. Pitney Bowes, Inc., San Antonio, 1985-86, Nurses Finders, San Antonio, 1986-87; telecommunications analyst United Svcs. Automobile Assn., San Antonio, 1987—. Mem. AAUW, NAFE, Am. Cancer Soc. (pub. info com.), Am. Mktg. Assn. Republican. Clubs: Goebel Collector's (N.Y.); Model A Ford Am. (recording sec., San Antonio chpt.). Avocations: antiques, needlepoint, fashion design, antique Model A cars, floral arranging. Home: 5801 Spring Village San Antonio TX 78247 Office: United Services Automobile Assn 9800 Fredericksburg Rd San Antonio TX 78288

IRVIN, KATHRYN JEANETTE, educator; b. Tallahassee. BA, Fla. A&M U.; MEd, Fla. Atlantic U. Tchr., Palm Beach County Schs., West Palm Beach, Fla., 1969—, head tchr. adult spl. edn., 1985—, media rep. adult edn., 1985-86, chair self-study, exceptional student edn., philosophy and objectives coms., 1986-87; owner Kathryn Irvin's Creative Assembly. Author: Black, Brown and Amber, 1979, Comes a Riderless Horse, 1983, reading home tutoring system Tutor Your Child, 1983; compiler, editor Where to Find Thrift Treasures, 1988, Where to Buy Antiques in Palm Beach County, 1989. Dir. Kambi Youth Theatre, West Palm Beach, 1979-82; tech. dir. Performing Arts Summer Sch., Palm Beach Gardens, Fla., 1983-84, 85; mem. Palm Beach Coun. Arts, Lake Worth Art League. Recipient 1st place award Cleveland Creative Arts, Tenn., 1981, Walter Bogle award Creative Arts Guild, 1983; grantee Palm Beach County Edn. Found., 1987. Mem. NEA, South Fla. Poetry Assn., Nat. Writers Club (hon. mention 1983), Fla. Freelance Writers Assn. (1st pl. awards 1984, 85, 3rd pl. 1990), Classroom Tchrs. Assn., North Palm Beaches Arts Soc., Lake Worth Art League, Palm Beach Vocat. Assn. Avocations: drawing, painting, collecting art objects. Home: 312 Baker Dr West Palm Beach FL 33409

IRVIN, LYNDA ELARE, educational administrator; b. Portsmouth, Ohio, Feb. 3, 1950; d. George Arthur and Wilma Ursula (Lynd) I. BS, Ohio State U., 1972, MA, 1984. Tchr. Worthington (Ohio) City Schs., 1972-84, adminstrv. specialist personnel, 1984-85; prin. Bexley (Ohio) City Schs., 1985-87, Dublin (Ohio) City Schs., 1987—. Hist. docent Worthington Hist. Soc., 1980—; v.p. Worthington Community Chorus, 1984-86; Twig mem. Children's Hosp. Guild, Columbus, 1984—; mem. First Community Ch., usher, mission coun., parish life coun., adult edn. small group instr. Fellow Nat. Assn. Elem. Prins.; mem. Ohio Assn. Elem. Prins., Assn. Curriculum and Devel., Buckeye Assn. Sch. Adminstrs. (legis. com.), Franklin County Prins. Assn. (pres. 1989—), Phi Delta Kappa, Delta Zeta Sorority. Presbyterian. Home: 5853 Harvest Oak Dublin OH 43017 Office: Indian Run Sch 80 W Bridge St Dublin OH 43017

IRVINE, FRANCES GERALDENE, educator; b. Paris, Tex., Mar. 27, 1940; d. Barham W. and Lucy Elizabeth (Matthews) Simmons; m. James Richard Irvine, Nov. 8, 1959. BS, Stephen F. Austin U., 1962. Cert. elem. and secondary tchr., Colo., Tex. 1st grade tchr. Sabine Pass (Tex.) Sch. Dist., 1962-63; 2d grade tchr. Baytown (Tex.) Ind. Sch. Dist., 1963-64; 1st, 2d, 3d grade tchr. Poudre R-1 Sch. Dist., Ft. Collins, Colo., 1965-69; 4th grade tchr. Poudre R-1 Sch. Dist., Ft. Collins, 1970—; 2d grade tchr. Iowa City (Iowa) Sch. Dist., 1969-70; research sabbatical Scottish State Schs., 1977-78. Named Outstanding Young Educator Jaycees, Ft. Collins, 1972; grantee NDEA, 1967. Mem. Nat. Council of Tchrs. of English, Internat. Reading Assn. (local sec. 1974-75, sch. rep. 1985—), Alpha Delta Kappa (Zeta chpt., corr. sec. 1984-86), Alpha Chi. Democrat. Episcopalian. Home: 1555 Miramont Dr Fort Collins CO 80524 Office: Poudre R-1 Sch Dist 312 Princeton Rd Fort Collins CO 80525

IRVINE, PHYLLIS ELEANOR KUHNLE, university administrator; b. Germantown, Ohio, July 14, 1940; d. Carl Franklin and Mildred Viola (Erisman) Kuhnle; m. Richard James Irvine, Feb. 15, 1964; children: Mark, Rick. BSN, Ohio State U., 1962, MSN, 1979, PhD, 1981; MS, Miami U., Oxford, Ohio, 1966. Staff nurse VA Ctr., Dayton, Ohio, 1962-66; mem. nursing faculty Miami Valley Hosp. Sch. Nursing, Dayton, 1968-78; teaching asst., lectr. Ohio State U., Columbus, 1979-82; assoc. prof. Ohio U., Athens, 1982-83; prof., dir. NE La. U., Monroe, 1984-89; dir., prof. sch. nursing Ball State U., Muncie, Ind., 1989—; cons. Drexel U., Phila., 1986; reviewer Addison-Wesley Pub. Co., Phila., 1984—, Health Edn. jour., Phila., 1987, Jour. Profl. Nursing, Phila., 1986. Contbr. articles to profl. jours. Mem. Mayor's Commn. on Needs of Women, La., 1984—; 1st v.p., bd. dirs. United Way of Ouachita, La., 1986—. Tandy Corp. grantee, 1986. Mem. Am. Nurses Assn., La. Nurses Assn., Monroe Dist. Nurses Assn. (bd. dirs.

1985—), Internat. Council Women's Health Issues (bd. dirs. 1986—), Assn. for the Advancement Health Edn., Sigma Theta Tau. Office: NE La U 700 University Ave Monroe LA 71209-0460

IRVING, AMY, actress; b. Palo Alto, Calif., Sept. 10, 1953; m. Steven Spielberg, Nov. 27, 1985 (div.); 1 child, Max Samuel; 1 son with Bruno Barreto. Student, Am. Conservatory Theatre, London Acad. Dramatic Art. Films include Carrie, The Fury, Voices, Honeysuckle Rose, The Competition, Yentl, Mickey and Maude, Rumplestiltskin, Crossing Delancey, A Show of Force, 1990; TV appearances include: The Rookies, Policewoman, Happy Days, Panache, I'm A Fool, Dynasty, Voices, Once An Eagle, Showtime, 1985, (miniseries) Anastasia: The Mystery of Anna Anderson, 1986; appeared as Juliet in Romeo and Juliet, Seattle Repertory Theatre, 1982-83; appeared on Broadway in Amadeus, 1981-82, Heartbreak House, 1983-84, off Broadway The Road to Mecca, 1988. •

IRVING, GITTE NIELSEN, educator; b. Copenhagen, Nov. 5, 1954; came to U.S., 1976; d. Sven Aage and Aase (Espersen) Nielsen; m. Richard Frederick Irving, June 5, 1976; children: Erik Christian, Emilie Jessica. BA, U. Iceland, Reykjavik, 1976; MEd, Lesley Coll., 1977. Cert. elem. tchr., spl. edn. tchr., Mass.; cert. by Mass. Gen. Hosp. in use of Orton-Gillingham strategies for remediation of dyslexia, 1989. Spl. edn. aide Brookline (Mass.) Pub. Schs., 1977-78; spl. edn. tchr. Ashland (Mass.) Pub. Schs., 1978-81, Greater Lawrence Ednl. Collaborative, Andover, Mass., 1981-82; owner, dir. Comprehensive Academics, Inc., Winchester, Mass., 1983—; guest columnist Winchester Star, 1986; mem. com. early edn. planning Winchester Pub. Schs., 1986, com. missions and social concerns United Meth. Ch., Winchester, 1987, co-chair 1988-90, adv. council Spl. Edn. Parents, Winchester, 1985—. Editor spl. edn. presch. newsletter, 1985-86; guest columnist Winchester STar, 1986. Vice pres. Neighborhood Cooperative Nursery Sch., Winchester, 1989, 1988-90. Home: 12 Stone Ave Winchester MA 01890 Office: Comprehensive Academics 573 Main St Winchester MA 01890

IRVING, JOYCE ARLENE, social worker, consultant; b. LaGrange, Tex., Aug. 8, 1945; d. Major Lee and Cora (Williams) Brown; m. Daniel Lamar Irving, Dec. 4, 1966; children: Dana Lorraine, Jerren Alan. AA, Sacramento City Coll., 1971; BA, Calif. State U., Sacramento, 1975, MSW, 1978. Program and tng. asst. Social Scis. Tng. Div., Sacramento, 1965-73; investigator, interviewer Social Svcs. Fraud Unit, Sacramento, 1973-76; social worker Sacramento County Social Svcs., 1976-80; casework specialist Calif. State Dept. Youth Authority, 1980-86, background investigator, 1986-88, casework specialist, 1988—; historian, editor Jack & Jill of Am., Sacramento, 1986-89, program dir., 1990—; cons. Group Home Inc., Sacramento, 1989-90. Mem. Assn. Black Correctional Workers (treas., exec. bd. 1988-90, Pres.'s award 1985, 89), Black Child Inst., Calif. Correctional Peace Officers Assn. (exec. bd. Sacramento chpt. 1990—), Nat. Assn. Univ. Women, Delta Sigma Theta. Home: 9845 Florin Rd Sacramento CA 95829 Office: Calif Dept Youth Authority 3001 Ramona Ave Sacramento CA 95826

IRVING, WANDA ELAINE, communications executive; b. Selma, Ala., Sept. 19, 1953; d. Clifford Actavius and Lettye Idell (Sellers) Cox; m. Samuel Monroe Irving Jr., Dec. 21, 1974; children: Samuel Monroe III, Shalon Mau Rene, Simone Marcus (dec.). Student, Middlebury (Vt.) Coll., 1971-73; cert. of excellence, Casa de Cultura, San Luis Potoshi, Mex., 1974; AB, Dartmouth Coll., 1975. Radio news reporter Sta. WBEC, Pittsfield, Mass., 1969-71; br. mgr. Meier & Frank div. May Co., Portland, Oreg., 1975-77; exec. dir. mktg. Spiral Works, Inc., Portland, 1977-80; coord. spl. events Willamette U., Salem, Oreg., 1980-83; program coord. Oreg. Pub. Broadcasting, Portland, 1983-84; advocacy specialist County of Multnomah, Portland, 1985-86; chief exec. officer On Target Promotions, Inc., Portland, 1986-87; dir. communications svcs. Environ. Svcs., Portland, 1987—; pub. rels. cons.; pub. rels. mgr. for A.C. Green, L.A. Laker, 1985; dir. devel. Ctr. for Urban Edn., 1986-87. Author: 1989: A Clean Water Odyssey, 1989; editor Minority Business Directory of Oregon, 1985; inventor Koupon Kollector, 1985, (game) Along Freedom's Trail, 1986. Legis. rep. small bus. Gov. of Goldschmidt, Portland, 1986; bd. dirs. Social Character Renewal Program, Portland, 1975-85; commr. Portland Cable Commn., 1987-89, Juvenile Svcs. Rev. Bd., Portland, 1988. Named Businesswoman of Yr. Evangelistic Ctr., Portland, 1980. Mem. Internat. Assn. Bus. Communicators (cert.), Am. Mgmt. Assn., NAFE, Women in Communications, Inc., Blacks in Govt., City Club Portland. Office: Environ Svcs 1120 SW 5th Ave Rm 400 Portland OR 97204

IRWIN, G. STORMY, retired paper manufacturing professional; b. Melrose Park, Ill., Sept. 4, 1929; d. Charles W. and Mary E. (Worthley) I. With Zellerbach Paper Co. (div. Mead Co.), Sacramento, 1952-85, ret., 1985. Mng. editor, pub., owner Women in Softball mag. (Women in Sports 1957-72), 1957-78. Coach, mgr., participant Sacramento City Leagues. Recipient 1st place awards for continuous coverage of softball for non-daily publ. under 50,000 circulation Nat. Softball Broadcasters and Writers Assn., 1965, 66, 67, 69, 71, 72, 73; won 30 titles in volleyball, basketball, flag football, and softball Sacramento City Leagues, 1950-90; named to Sacramento Softball Assn. Hall of Honor, 1980. Home: 1945 Piner Rd #85 Santa Rosa CA 95403

IRWIN, LINDA BELMORE, consultant; b. Portland, Oreg., Apr. 29, 1950; d. Calvin C. and Dorothy B. (Belmore) Harper; m. David Gordon Carpenter, May 28, 1978 (div. Feb. 1986); m. Michael Hugh Irwin, June 24, 1989. Student Portland State U., 1968-72. With Hyatt Regency-New Orleans, 1975-78, catering Hyatt-Regency-Capitol Hill, Washington, 1978-80, dir. catering Hyatt-Anaheim, Calif., 1978-80; mgr. Dockside Yacht Sales, Annapolis, Md., 1981-85; dir. sales and mktg. Loew's Hotel, 1985-86; dir. mktg. Annapolis Marriot, 1986-88; ind. mktg. cons., Washington and Dallas, 1988-90; div. dir., CSS, Inc., Dallas, 1990—; ambassador State of Md., Annapolis, 1986-88; mktg. chair Tourism Council Annapolis and Anne Arundel County; curricula advisor Anne Arundel Community Coll.; mem. fund raising com. Ch. Circle Beautification Trust. Mem. Nat. Banquet Mgrs. Guild (founder Los Angeles chpt.), Nat. Assn. Female Execs. (area dir. 1985—), Annapolis C. of C. (ambassador 1985-88), Greater Washington Soc. of Assn. Execs., Anne Arundel Trade Council, Md. Tourism Council (adv. bd.), Internat. Platform Assn. Republican. Episcopalian. Avocations: sailing, travel, literature, calligraphy, ballet. Office: CSS Inc 2929 LBJ Frwy Ste 101 Dallas TX 75234

IRWIN, MARY FRANCES, language professional; b. Portland, Oreg., Oct. 18, 1925; d. Curtiss Henry Sabisch and Gladys Frances (Giles) Strand; m. Harry Elmer Hartman, Sept. 6, 1946 (div. June 1970); children: Evelyn Frances, Laura Elyce, Andrea Candace; m. Thomas Floyd Irwin, Apr. 11, 1971. BA, U. Wash., 1964-68; postgrad., Seattle Pacific, 1977-79, Antioch U., Seattle, Wash., 1987, Heritage Inst., Seattle, Wash., 1987. Educator language Kennewick (Wash.) Dist. #17, 1970-88; guide Summer Study Tours of Europe, 1971-88. Sec. Bahai Faith, 1971-88, librarian, Pasco, Wash., 1985-88. Mem. Nat. Fgn. Lang. Assn., Wash. Assn. Fgn. Lang. Teaching, Nat. Edn. Assn., Wash. Edn. Assn., Kennewick Edn. Assn. Home: 1119 W Margaret Pasco WA 99301 Office: Kamiakin High Sch 600 N Arthur Kennewick WA 99336

IRWIN, MIRIAM DIANNE OWEN, miniature book publisher, writer; b. Columbus, Ohio, June 14, 1930; d. John Milton and Miriam Faith (Studebaker) Owen; m. Kenneth John Irwin, June 5, 1960; 1 child, Christopher Owen Irwin. BS in Home Econs., Ohio State U., 1952, postgrad. in bus. adminstrn., 1961-62. Editorial asst. Am. Home Mag., N.Y.C., 1953-56; salesman Owen Realty, Dayton, Ohio, 1957-58, Clevenger Realty, Phoenix, 1958-59; home economist Columbus and So. Ohio Electric Co., 1959-60; pub. Mosaic Press, Cin., 1977—; owner Bibelot Bindery, 1987—. Author: Lute and Lyre, 1977, Forty is Fine, 1977, Miriam Mouse's Survival Manual, 1977, Miriam Mouse's Costume Collection, 1977, Miriam Mouse's Marriage Contract, 1977, Miriam Mouse, Rock Hound, 1977, Silver Bindings, 1983; editor: Tribute to the Arts, 1984; contbg. author Publisher's Favorite, 1988; illustrator: Corals of Pennekamp, 1979. Daytime crew chief Wyoming Life Squad, Ohio, 1966-71. Mem. Internat. Guild Miniature Artisans, Miniature Book Soc. (past bd. dirs., chairperson 1987-89), Am. Philol. Assn., DAR, Soc. for Promotion of Byzantine Studies, Wyo. Women's Club. Republican. Presbyterian. Avocation: book collecting. Home and Office: 358 Oliver Rd Cincinnati OH 45215

ISAAC, BINA SUSAN, data processing executive; b. Nainital, India, Jan. 9, 1958; came to U.S. 1980; d. Rajan Kurian and Susan (Thomas) George; m. Mathew Isaac, July 14, 1980; children: Sonya Susan, Shawn George. BA, Sarah Tucker Coll., Tirunelveli, India, 1978; MA, Madurai U., India, 1980; MEd, U. Toledo, 1981, MBA, 1984. Coord. computer svcs. and computer ctr. Lourdes Coll., Sylvania, Ohio, 1984-85; dir. computer svcs. and computer ctr. Lourdes Coll., Sylvania, 1985—, part-time instr., 1985—; instr. Lifelong Learning Ctr., Sylvania, 1985—. Mem. Assn. Systems Mgmt., SIG 3X Inc. (spl. interest group). Home: 3851 Barleyton Circle Sylvania OH 43560 Office: Lourdes Coll 6832 Convent Blvd Sylvania OH 43560

ISAAC, YVONNE RENEE, healthcare executive, director; b. Cleve., Apr. 13, 1948; d. Leon Warren and Vernice Leona (Hallom) I.; m. Harold E. Rhynie, Dec. 30, 1984. BA, Sarah Lawrence Coll., 1970; MS, Rensselaer Poly. Inst., 1973, Bklyn. Poly. Inst., 1976. Market researcher GE Co., Phila., 1971-72; cons., planner SPA/Redco (subs. Perkins & Will), Chgo., 1972-75; sr. assoc. Perkins & Will, N.Y.C., 1975-76, project mgr., 1978-81; supply assoc. Mobil Oil Corp., N.Y.C., 1976-78; project mgr. Ehrenkrantz Group, D.C., N.Y.C., 1981-84; asst. dir. Met. Transp. Authority, N.Y.C., 1984-86; group dir. N.Y.C. Health & Hosps. Corp., N.Y.C., 1986—; vis. assoc. prof. Pratt Inst., Bklyn., 1977; asst. prof. Columbia U. Grad. Sch. Architecture and Planning, N.Y.C., 1977-78. Democrat. Home: 649 St Marks Ave Brooklyn NY 11216 Office: NYC Health & Hosps Corp Harlem Ambulatory Care Bldg Project Harlem Hosp Ctr-Old Nurses Residence 506 Lenox Ave New York NY 10037

ISAAC NASH, EVA MAE, educator; b. Natchitoches Parish, La., July 24, 1936; d. Earfus Will Nash and Dollie Mae (Edward) Johnson; m. Will Isaac Jr., July 1, 1961 (dec. May 1970). BA, San Francisco State U., 1974, MS in Edn., 1979, MS in Counseling, 1979; PhD, Walden U., 1985; diploma (hon.), St. Labre Indian Sch., 1990. Nurse's aide Protestant Episcopal Home, San Francisco, 1957-61; desk clk. Fort Ord (Calif.) Post Exchange, 1961-63; practical nurse Monterey (Calif.) Hosp., 1963-64; tchr. San Francisco Unified Schs., 1974; counselor, instr. City Coll. San Francisco, 1978-79; tchr. Oakland (Calif.) Unified Sch. Dist., 1974—; pres. Sch. Adv. Council, Oakland, 1977-78; advt. writer City Coll., San Francisco, 1978; instr. vocat. skill tng., Garfield Sch., Oakland, 1980-81; pub. speaker various ednl. insts. and chs., Oakland, San Francisco, 1982—. Recipient Community Svc. award Black Caucus of Calif. Assn. Counseling and Devel., 1988, Cert. of Recognition, 1990; named Citizen of the Day, Sta. KABL, 1988. Mem. Internat. Reading Assn., Nat. Assn. Female Execs., Am. Personnel and Guidance Assn., Assn. Supervision and Curriculum Devel., Calif. Personnel and Guidance Assn., Phi Delta Kappa. Democrat. Office: Oakland Unified Sch Dist 1025 Second Ave Oakland CA 94606

ISAACOFF, DANA MARGOLIA, military officer; b. Bklyn., Nov. 9, 1960; d. Isadore and Helen Ruth (Lamhut) I. BS, Cornell U., 1982; MA, New Sch. for Soc. Rsch., N.Y.C., 1984; student, MIT, present. Commd. 2d lt. U.S. Army, 1982; platoon leader and asst. ops. officer U.S. Army, Hoechst, West Germany, 1984-86; adjutant U.S. Army, Hoechst, 1986-87; comdr. U.S. Army, Frankfurt, 1987-88; student U.S. Army, Cambridge, Mass., 1989—. Filmmaker: Respect, 1982. Mem. Armed Forces Communications Electronic Assn. Home and office: 38 Madison Ave #1 Cambridge MA 02140

ISAACS, HELEN COOLIDGE ADAMS (MRS. KENNETH L. ISAACS), artist; b. N.Y.C., Jan. 17, 1917; d. Thomas Safford and Martha (Montgomery) Adams; student Miss Hewett's classes, N.Y.C., Miss Porter's Sch., Farmington, Conn., Fontainbleau (France) Sch. Art and Music, 1935, Art Students League, 1936; m. Kenneth L. Isaacs, Mar. 10, 1949; children: Kenneth Coolidge, Anne Isaacs Merwin. Agt., Child's Gallery, Boston; one-woman shows at Child's Gallery, 3 times exhibited in group shows Allied Artists, N.Y., Boston Arts Festival; portraits of various prominent persons; murals in various pub. bldgs., Boston, Rochester, N.Y., Pittsfield, Mass., Daytona, Fla.; represented in painting and drawing collections Fogg Mus., Cambridge, Mass., Nat. Mus. Women in the Arts, Washington. Mem. Colonial Dames Am. Clubs: Colony (N.Y.C.); Chilton (Boston). Home: 68 Beacon St Boston MA 02108

ISAACSON, ARLINE LEVINE, food and beverage/hotel executive; b. Bklyn., Jan. 28, 1946; d. Harry and Sally (Fogelman) Levine; m. Leslie Robert Isaacson, Oct. 31, 1964 (div. July 1970); 1 child, Eric Michael. A.A.S. in Hotel and Restaurant Mgmt., N.Y.C. Tech. Coll., 1983. Restaurant and lounge mgr. Holiday Inn, N.Y.C., 1982-83; mgr. Astors, St. Regis Hotel, N.Y.C., 1983-84; banquet and conf. mgr. Mariner 15 Conf. Ctr., N.Y.C., 1984-85; dir. banquets, confs. and sales Sardi's Restaurant Corp., N.Y.C., 1985-87; dir. catering sales Days Inn Hotel, N.Y.C., 1987—. Dem. vol. Koch Relection Campaign, N.Y.C., 1985. Mem. Food and Beverage Mgrs. Assn. (sec. 1984-88), Roundtable for Women in Food Service (treas. 1986-87), Meeting Planners Internat., Soc. Incentive Travel, Hotel Sales and Mktg. Assn., Internat. Food Service Execs., N.Y.C. Tech. Coll. Alumni Assn. (bd. dirs. 1986—, v.p. 1986-87). Jewish. Avocations: dancing; travel; theatre; gourmet cooking. Home: 1836 E 18th St Brooklyn NY 11229 Office: Days Inn Hotel 440 W 57th St New York NY 10019

ISAACSON, EDITH LIPSIG, civic leader; b. N.Y.C., Jan. 18, 1920; d. I.A. and Bertha (Evans) Lipsig; m. Selian Hebald; children: Anne Mandelbaum, Selian Jr.; m. William J. Isaacson. Student, Radcliffe Coll., 1936-39, 41; LLB, St. Lawrence U., 1943. Pres. Forest Knolls Corp., N.Y.C., 1960—, Norman Homes Corp., N.Y.C., 1968—; cataloguer Nat. Collection Fine Arts, Smithsonian Instn., 1969-72. Author biographies Am. artists; writer club handbooks. Fellow Pierpont Morgan Library, N.Y.C.; mem. Carnegie Council Ethics Internat. Affairs, founders com. Am. Symphony Orch., N.Y., 1962; nat. sec. Women's Am. Orgn. Rehab. through Tng., 1950; trustee Allergy Found. Am. Mem. Radcliffe Coll. Alumni Assn. (chmn. clubs 1966). Clubs: Harvard (N.Y.C.), Cosmopolitan (N.Y.C.) (bd. govs. 1987—); Radcliffe (pres. Washington chpt. 1969) (pres. N.Y. chpt. 1959, 63, bd. sponsors 1974).

ISBELL, VIRGINIA, state legislator; b. Chinook, Mont., May 8, 1932; d. Domenico Renda and Bessie M. (Newton) Renda; cert. med. sec. No. Mont. Coll., 1953; m. Donald D. Isbell, Oct. 11, 1953; children—David, Daniel, Mahealani, Iwalani, Richard. Tchr., Kona (Hawaii) Schs., 1962-72; mgr. Wilmot Boone, M.D., Allan Hubacker, M.D., Kona Coast Med. Group, Inc., Kailua, Kona, Hawaii, 1972-78; mem. Hawaii Ho. of Reps., 1980—. Bd. dirs. Kona Family YMCA; active ARC. Named Woman of Yr., Mayor's award, 1980. Democrat. Mem. Ch. of Jesus Christ of Latter-day Saints. Club: Soroptimist (past pres.).

ISELIN, SALLY CARY, writer; b. Nahant, Mass., June 16, 1915; d. Charles Pelham and Edith Goddard (Roelker) Curtis; m. Lewis Iselin, June 14, 1935; children: Edith Byron, Sarah Morrison. Student, Harvard U., 1933. Editorial asst. sports and fgn. news depts. Newsweek mag., N.Y.C., 1942-45; soc. and non-fiction editor Town & Country Mag., N.Y.C., 1945-48; reporter, researcher Life Mag., N.Y.C., 1948-50; writer-contact CBS, N.Y.C., 1951; fashion editor Women's Home Companion, N.Y.C., 1956; freelance writer. Fund raiser Planned Parenthood, 1935—, Robert Kennedy for Senate, 1964. Democrat. Episcopalian. Club: Colony. Home: Belfast Rd Camden ME 04843

ISENNOCK, MARY ROSE, company executive; b. Rocks, Md., July 24, 1925; d. Bower Colvard and Floreta Eudora (Turner) Reeves; m. Francis Raymond Isennock, June 27, 1946; children: David, Judy. BS in Elem. Edn., Towson State Tchrs. Coll., 1946; MEd, U. Md., 1952. Cert. tchr. elem. edn. Elem. tchr. Harford County (Md.) Pub. Schs., Bel Air, 1945-47, Prince George's County (Md.) Pub. Schs., Upper Marlboro, Md., 1947-51, Balt. County Pub. Schs., Towson, Md., 1951-53, Prince George's County (Md.) Pub. Schs., Upper Marlboro, Md., 1953-76; rsch. interviewer Booz Allen, Phila., 1983—; tax counselor elderly Am. Assn. Ret. Persons, Washington, 1978—, overall coord.; area health seminar Hartford County Ret. Tchrs., Aberdeen, Md., 1983; sec., treas. Family Firm of Forest Hill Realty, Inc., 1975—. Pres. Md. Geneal. Soc., Balt., 1985-87; historian Centre United Meth. Ch., 1985—. Mem. Am. Assn. Ret. Persons (asst. state dir. 1985-88), Md. Ret. Tchrs. Assn. (ann. meeting chmn. 1984—), Hartford County Ret. Tchrs. Assn. (pres. 1982, 83), Hartford County and State Grange (state chmn. scholarship com. 1984-87), Educators Travel Club (bd. dirs. 1978—). Democrat. Home: 2520 Rocks Rd Forest Hill MD 21050

ISENOR, LINDA DARLENE, grocery retailer, marketing professional; b. Calgary, Alta., Can., Oct. 3, 1955; d. Frank Carl and Mavis Ella (Jarnett) Kachmarski; m. Larry Douglas Isenor, Oct. 13, 1973. So. Alta. Inst. Tech.; Diploma in Mktg., SAIT, Calgary, 1988. Cashier to asst. mgr. G&S Restaurants Balmoral Ltd., Calgary, 1972-74; cashier, supr. Calgary Coop. Assn. Ltd., 1974-75, supr., 1975-78, head cashier, 1978-80, asst. grocery merchandiser, 1980-81, grocery merchandising specialist, 1981-82, grocery procurement specialist, 1982-83, supr. pricing and costing, 1983—. Office: Calgary Coop Assn Ltd, 200 S 8500 MacLeod Trail SE, Calgary, AB Canada T2H 2N1

ISHAM, CAROLYNN CLOUGH, advertising executive; b. Waverly, Iowa, Feb. 6, 1947; d. Richard Clough and Wilma Marie (Gerberding) I.; m. Paul E. Pitman, June 29, 1985. BA, U. Iowa, 1969. Tech. editor Honeywell, Newton, Ma., 1969-71; ptnr. Insight (Graphic Design), 1971-74; exec. v.p. Berenson, Isham & Ptnrs., Inc., Boston, Ma., 1974—. Mem. Assn. of Advt. Adminstr. (pres. 1987-89), Advt. Club of Boston, New England Broadcasting Assn., New England Direct Mktg. Assn., Annisquam Yacht Club, Manchester Harbor Boat Club. Home: 89 Pine St Manchester MA 01944 Office: Berenson Isham & Ptnrs Inc 31 Milk St Boston MA 02109

ISHAM, KATHRYN LANE, medical psychologist, pain specialist; b. New Haven, Feb. 15, 1955; d. Robert Lind and Marion (Clements) Isham; m. William Carl Nolte II, Oct. 8, 1988 (div.). BA cum laude, Tulane U., 1977; MEd, S.W. Tex. State U., 1980; EdD, Baylor U., 1986. Diplomate Am. Acad. Pain Mgmt. Dir. residence hall S.W. Tex. State U., San Marcos, 1978-79; rsch. asst. Powell and Assocs., Austin, Tex., 1979-80; ednl. diagnostician Brown Schs., Austin, 1980-81; rsch. asst. U. Tex. Health Sci. Ctr., Dallas, 1983-84, instr. in psychiatry, 1984-87; program dir. Pain Therapy Ctrs., Greenville, S.C., 1987-89; psychologist PMS program Greenville Hosp. System, 1988—, clin. specialist, 1989—. Mem. Jr. League of Dallas, 1983-87, Jr. League of Greenville 1987—, The Met. Arts Coun., Greenville, 1989—. Victor T. Null scholar Baylor U., 1982-83. Mem. Am. Psychol. Assn., Assn. for the Advancement of Behavioral Therapy, Alpha Lambda Delta, Kappa Delta Pi, Psi Chi. Republican. Home: 1102 Summit Dr Greenville SC 29609 Office: Pain Therapy Ctrs 100 Mallard St Greenville SC 29601

ISLER, VICKI JAN, lawyer; b. Elizabeth, N.J., July 29, 1955; d. Sidney and Dorothy (Millberger) I.; m. J. Mitchell Grossman, June 12, 1977; children: Lisa Isler, Drew Isler and Jenna Isler (twins). BA, Colgate U., 1977; JD, Yeshiva U., 1980. Bar: N.J. 1980, U.S. Dist. Ct. N.J. 1980, U.S. Dist. Ct. (so. and ea. dists.) N.Y. 1985, U.S. Supreme Ct. 1986. Dep. atty. gen. div. Law and Pub. Safety N.J. Atty. Gen.'s Office, Trenton, 1980-84; assoc. Brenner Wallack & Hill, Princeton, N.J., 1984, Budd, Larner, Kent, Gross, Rosenbaum, Picillo, Greenberg & Sade, Short Hills, N.J., 1985-87, Earer Siegal Fersko, P.A., Westfield, N.J., 1987-89; ptnr. Giordano, Halleran & Ciesla, Middletown, N.J., 1989—; adj. prof. environ. law Seton Hall U. Law Sch., Newark, 1987; lectr. and seminar panelist, 1986-89. Violist Plainfield (N.J.) Symphony Orch., 1980-86; mem. adv. bd. Environ. Expo, 1986—; mem. adv. bd. Bur. Indsl. Sites, Trenton, 1987—. George Cobb fellow, 1974; named Belkin scholar, 1979. Mem. ABA, N.J. Bar Assn. (chmn. Environ. Law Sect. 1988-89, del. bd. govs. 1987—), LWV. Office: Giordano Halleran & Ciesla 270 State Hwy 35 Middletown NJ 07748

ISOM, HARRIET WINSAR, ambassador; b. Heppner, Oreg., Oreg., Nov. 4, 1936; d. Blaine Eugene and Evelyn (Struve) I. BA, Mills Coll., 1958; MA in Law and Diplomacy, Tufts U., 1960. Fgn. affairs analyst USAF, 1960-61; joined Fgn. Svc., U.S. Dept. State, Washington, 1961; various positions in Africa and Asia; dep. chief mission Am. Embassy, Bujumbura, Burundi, 1974-77; consul Am. Consulate, Medan, Sumatra, Indonesia, 1977-78; polit. counselor Am. Consulate, Jakarta, Indonesia, 1978-81; chargé d'affaires Am. Embassy, Vientiane, Laos, 1986-89; sr. assignments officer Bur. Pers. Dept. State, Washington, 1982-84, dir. Korean affairs Bur. East Asian and Pacific Affairs, 1984-86; amb. to People's Republic Benin, Cotonou, 1989—. Address: Am Embassy Cotonou People's Republic of Benin Dept State Washington DC 20521-2120

ISRAEL, MARGIE OLANOFF, psychotherapist; b. Atlantic City, Apr. 30, 1927; d. Herman and Mary (Salter) Olanoff. Student U. Miami, 1945-46, 50, Am. Acad. Dramatic Arts, 1946-47; B.A. in Psychology cum laude, Hunter Coll., 1970; M.S.W. with honors in fieldwork, Hunter Sch. Social Work, 1972; psychoanalytic tng. N.Y. Soc. Freudian Psychologists, 1965-70, Manhattan Ctr. for Advanced Psychoanalytic Studies, 1972-74, 76; m. Allan Edward Israel, Sept. 20, 1953; 1 child, Janet. Bd. cert. diplomate in clin. social work Am. Bd. Examiners of Clin. Social Workers. Celebrity interviewer Lunchin' with Marge radio show Sta. WFPG, Atlantic City, 1947-48; co-host Steel Pier Midnight radio show, 1949; publicity writer Hy Gardner Astor Hotel, N.Y.C., 1948; writer theatrical interviews Miami (Fla.) Daily News, 1950-51; sec. to exec. dir. Hebrew Old Age Ctr., Atlantic City, 1951-55; sec. to dir. TV-films and radio Nat. Office, Am. Cancer Soc., N.Y.C., 1959-66, asst. to dir. TV-films and radio, 1966-70; social worker Bellevue Hosp., N.Y.C., 1972-76; field instr. social work N.Y. U., 1975-76; pvt. practice psychotherapy, N.Y.C., 1973—. Fellow N.Y. State Soc. Clin. Social Work Psychotherapists, Am. Orthopsychiat. Assn.; mem. Nat. Assn. Social Workers, Acad. Cert. Social Workers, N.Y. Acad. Scis., Psi Chi. Office: 201 E 28th St Ste 1F New York NY 10016

ISRAEL, VIVIANNE WINTERS, publishing executive; b. Inglewood, Calif., Mar. 29, 1954; d. Robert Reynolds and Annie Laura (Ripley) Winters; m. Richard Clyde Israel, May 30, 1976 (div. 1985); 1 child, Tiffany Carissa. RN, El Camino Coll., Torrance, Calif. Fashion model Los Angeles, 1957-70; critical care nurse Northridge Med. Ctr., Reseda, Calif., 1977-80, St. Joseph Med. Ctr., Burbank, Calif., 1980-81; exotic animal handler, trainer Gentle Jungle, Corona, Calif., 1980-81; coronary care nurse Mercy Med. Ctr., Reading, Calif., 1981-85; critical care nurse Norrell/CCSI, Los Angeles, 1985-87; pres. Pacific Coast Publs., Rolling Hills Estates, Calif., 1986—. Vol., co-dir. edn. Wildlife Way Sta., Little Tajunga, Calif., 1987—. Mem. Pubs. Mktg. Assn., Book Publicists of So. Calif., Book Publicists San Diego, Execs. of South Bay, NAFE, Am. Booksellers Assn., Women's Nat. Book Assn., Pubs. Group West, Women's Internat. Network, Walters Internat. Speakers Bur., Internat. Assn. of Ind. Pubs., Am. Businesswomens Assn., Internat. Platformers Assn. Baptist. Home: 1180 W Locust Ave Anaheim CA 92802 Office: Pacific Coast Pubs 710 Silver Spur Rd Ste 126 Rolling Hills Estates CA 90274-3695

ISRAELSKY, ROBERTA SCHWARTZ, speech pathologist, audiologist; b. N.Y.C., July 19, 1954; d. Julian H. and Sylvia (Fenster) Schwartz; m. Brad Richard Israelsky, June 24, 1984; children: Erica, Evan. BA, Temple U., 1976; MA, Hahnemann Med. Coll., 1977, Trenton State, 1978. Lic. by Am. Speech, Lang., Hearing Assn. N.J. Speech/language pathologist W Deptford Twp Sch., W. Deptford, N.J., 1978-81, Sunny Day Autistic Sch., Cherry Hill, N.J., 1981-83; adj. prof. sign lang., voice and articulation Glassboro St. Coll., Glassboro, N.J., 1982-89; speech, sign lang. pathologist and diagnostician Camden Co. Educ. Serv. Comm., Stratford, N.J.; pvt. practice Voorhees, N.J., 1983—; prof. speech Camden County Coll., Blackwood, N.J.; adult supr. B'nai B'rith Girls, Cherry Hill, N.J., 1975-77; cons. Sign Lang. Assn. N.J., 1983—. Author, Hearing and Publication, Consumer Guide to Hearing Aids, 1978. v.p. ORT, Cherry Hill, 1986-89, Women Tech. Soc., 1988-89, Hadassah, 1985-89. Mem. Tri County Speech/Hearing, ASHA, NJSHA. Democrat. Jewish. Home and Office: 20 Jacamar Dr Voorhees NJ 08043

ISSERMAN, JOAN LOUISE, lawyer; b. St. Louis, Apr. 25, 1952; d. Philip and Elizabeth (Cohen) I. Student, Fleming Coll., Lugano, Switzerland, 1969-70, U. Colo., 1970-71; BA in Polit. Sci., U. Mo., 1974; RN, BS in Nursing, St. Louis U., 1976, JD cum laude, 1980. Bar: Mo. 1981, U.S. Dist. Ct. (ea. dist.) Mo. 1981, U.S. Ct. Appeals 1981, Ill. 1981, Colo. 1984, U.S. Dist. Ct. Colo. 1984. RN St. Louis Children's Hosp., 1976-77; assoc. Shepherd, Sandberg & Phoenix, St. Louis, 1980-82; risk mgr. Luth. Med. Ctr., Wheat Ridge, Colo., 1983—. Named Outstanding Young Woman Am., 1984. Mem. ABA, Mo. Bar Assn., Colo. Bar Assn., Denver Bar Assn., Am. Acad. Hosp. Attys., Am. Soc. Healthcare Risk Mgmt., Colo. Health

Lawyers Assn. (bd. dirs. 1984-85), Colo. Hosp. Assn. Risk Mgrs. (founder, pres. 1985). Jewish. Office: Luth Med Ctr 8300 W 38th Ave Wheat Ridge CO 80033

ISSOKSON-SILVER, KAREN LEE, marketing/advertising executive; b. Hyannis, Mass., Apr. 3, 1965; d. Stanley Edward and Louise Ellen (Spritz) I. BS in Communication summa cum laude, Boston U., 1987. Asst. account exec. Backer Spielvogel Bates Worldwide, N.Y.C., 1987-88; account exec. Partnership for a Drug Free Am., N.Y.C., 1988-89, assoc. dir., 1989, v.p., assoc. dir., 1989—. Vol. Planned Parenthood of N.Y., 1989—. Two/Ten scholarship Stride Rite Corp., 1985. Mem. Women in Communications, Inc., Boston U. Alumni Assn. Office: Partnership Drug Free Am 666 Third Ave New York NY 10017

ISTOMIN, MARTA CASALS, performing arts administrator; b. P.R., Nov. 2, 1936; d. Aguiles and Angelica M. (Martinez) Montanez; m. Pablo Casals, Aug. 3, 1957 (dec. 1973); m. Eugene Istomin, Feb. 15, 1975. Student, Mannes Coll. Music, N.Y.C., 1950-54; Mus.D. (hon.), World U., P.R., 1972; L.H.D. (hon.), Marymount Coll., 1975; Doctorate (hon.), U. P.R., 1984, Dickinson Coll., Carlisle, Pa., 1986; D (hon.), Shenandoah Coll., 1986, Interam. U., P.R., 1989. Prof. cello Conservatory Music, San Juan, P.R., 1961-64; vis. prof. cello Curtis Inst., Phila., 1974-75; co-chmn. bd., music dir. Casals Festival, 1974-77; artistic dir. John F. Kennedy Center for Performing Arts, Washington, 1980-90; dir. Harcourt Brace Jovanovich, Inc., N.Y.C., cons. Latin Am. ednl. projects. Trustee Marlboro Sch. Music and Festival; trustee Marymount Sch., N.Y.C., World U. Recipient Puerto Rican Fedn. Women's Clubs award, 1967; award for cultural achievements City of San Juan, 1975; Nat. Conf. Puerto Rican Women award, 1975; Casita Maria medal for outstanding contbns. to culture N.Y.C., 1978; Outstanding Contbns. Performing Arts in Nation's Capitol award, 1983; Family Place Outstanding Community Service award, 1986; Mayor's Excellence in Service Arts award, Washington, 1986; Nat. Fedn. Music Clubs citation, 1987; named Outstanding Woman of Yr. P.R., 1975; Woman of Achievement Sta. WETA-TV, Washington, 1981; Order of Isabella the Cath. govt. Spain, 1986; Officer, Order Arts and Letters govt. France, 1986; Officer's Cross Order Merit govt. Fed. Republic Germany, 1987. Roman Catholic.

ITJEN, PHYLLIS D., retail executive; b. Passaic, N.J., Oct. 13, 1951; d. August and Joanne (Aquilina) D'Alessandro; m. Brian A. Itjen, Apr. 1, 1979; 1 child, Shannon Alys. Owner, gen. mgr. Sweet Shoppe, Etc., Lyndhurst, N.J.; adminstrv. pers. coord. Watson Machine Co., Paterson, N.J.; office mgr. Servometer Corp., Cedar Grove, N.J.; owner Gen. SAI Pers. Svcs., West Paterson, N.J.; pres. SAI Expressions Unltd., Inc., West Paterson. Mem. NAFE, Nat. Fedn. Ind. Bus., Indsl. Mgmt. Assn., Mail Order Assocs. Home: 220 A Overmount Ave West Paterson NJ 07424

ITSON, SONJA PATRICA, information systems executive; b. Denver, Dec. 22, 1943; d. Raymond G. and Gladys F. (Mills) Green; m. Joe A. Itson, Sept. 17, 1966; 1 child, Erica Rae. BA in Geology, Occidental Coll., 1966; MS in Geology, San Diego State U., 1971. Technician Dept. Water Resources State of Wash., Olympia, 1966-68; researcher Scripps Instn. of Oceanography, La Jolla, Calif., 1971-74; instr. geology dept. San Diego State U., 1974; with County of San Diego, 1974—, environ. planner, planning chief, zoning adminstr., 1986-88, regional urban info. system chief, 1989—. Bd. dirs., v.p., fin. officer Homeowners Assn., San Diego, 1986—. Mem. Assn. Environ. Profls. (charter), Urban and Regional Info. Systems Assn. (charter, chair com. 1990—), Am. Planning Assn., NAFE, Internat. Assn. Runners and Walkers (vol.), Calif. Elected Women's Assn., Toastmasters (pres., dist. historial San Diego chpt. 1979, 80), Sigma Delta Epsilon (treas. 1973-74). Home: 3633 Seahorn Circle San Diego CA 92130 Office: County of San Diego 8525 Gibbs Dr Ste 100 San Diego CA 92123

ITTS, ELIZABETH ANN DUNHAM, psychotherapist, consultant, designer; b. Columbus, Ohio, May 11, 1928; d. Dalton Dee and Elizabeth Farrell (Beck) Dunham; m. Frank Joseph Itts, June 23, 1951; children: Cynthia Ann Robbins, Mark Dunham, Deirdre Elizabeth Jones, Andrea Lee Schoenfeld. Student, St. Mary of the Springs, Columbus, Ohio, 1946-47; BFA in Archtl. Design, Ohio State U., 1950; MS in Edn. Guidance, Youngstown (Ohio) State U., 1979. Lic., cert. counselor Nat. Bd. Cert. Counselors. Dir. activity ctr. pilot program Mahoning County Health Dept., Youngstown, 1974-76; dir. Career Devel. Ctr. for Women, Youngstown, 1978-79; asst. to dir. Youngstown State U. Alumni Assn., 1979-81; pvt. practice psychotherapist, cons., 1981-85, 87—; dir. career planning, placement and spl. programs Kent State U., Salem, Ohio, 1985-87; archtl. designer, co-owner Renaissance Design Group, Columbus, 1988—; writer grants funding for workshops, 1980-81; established career planning and placement office Kent State U., Salem, 1985, initiated and developed human svcs. tech. degree, 1986-87; writer acad. challenge grants. Mem. Planning and Zoning Commn., Canfield, Ohio, 1980—, Ohio Speakers Forum, 1990, Friends of Art (Butler Art Gallery), Youngstown, 1965—, Ohio Hist. Soc., Columbus, 1984—; chmn. nominating com. United Way Scholarship Commn., Youngstown, 1978-82. Mem. Am. Assn. Counseling and Devel., Ea. Ohio Counselor's Assn., Jr. Women's League (v.p. Canfield chpt. 1970-71). Roman Catholic. Home and Office: 820 Blueberry Hill Canfield OH 44406

ITZCOWITZ, EDEN BETH, manufacturing company executive; b. Bklyn., Aug. 10, 1962; d. Emanuel and Helene Bonnie (Warshaw) Amrani; m. Nathan B. Itzcowitz,. BA, BSS, Oswego State U., 1984. Office mgr. Man Am. Creations, Tappan, N.Y., 1984--. Mem. So. Jewelry Travelers Assn. Jewish.

IVAN, MARIAN O'LOANE, risk manager; b. Rochester, N.Y., July 31, 1956; d. J. Kenneth and Barbara (Gearhart) O'Loane; m. J. Pierre Ivan, June 16, 1979 (div. Sept. 1983); 1 child, Damien James. BA, U. Toronto, Can., 1977. Lic. ins. broker, Calif. Broker's asst. Fred S. James (now Sedgwick James), San Francisco, 1979-81; surplus lines broker Stewart Smith West, San Francisco, 1982-84; account exec. Dalton & McGrath, San Francisco, 1984-85, Sedgwick James Group, Paris, San Francisco, 1985-88; risk mgr. The RREEF Funds, San Francisco, 1989—. Fund raiser French Am. Internat. Sch., San Francisco, 1986—. Mem. Nat. Coun. Real Estate Investment Fiduciaries, Risk and Ins. Mgmt. Soc. Democrat.

IVENS, MARY SUE, microbiologist, mycologist; b. Maryville, Tenn., Aug. 23, 1929; d. McPherson Joseph and Sarah Lillie (Hensley) I.; B.S., E. Tenn. State U., 1949; M.S. (NIH research trainee), Tulane U. Sch. Medicine, 1963; Ph.D., La. State U. Sch. Medicine, 1966; postgrad. Oak Ridge Inst. Nuclear Studies, Emory U. Sch. Medicine. Dir. microbiol. and mycol. labs. Lewis-Gale Hosp., Roanoke, Va., 1953-56; rsch. mycologist Ctrs. Disease Control, Atlanta, 1957-60; rsch. assoc. La. State U. Sch. Med., 1963-66, instr. medicine, 1966-72, instr. Microbiology, 1966-72, clin. prof., 1972—; dir. mycology lab, La. State U. Sch. Med., 1963-72; lectr. Sch. Dentistry, La. State U. Med. Ctr., 1968-70; assoc. prof. natural scis. Dillard U., New Orleans, 1972—; assoc. Marine Biol. Lab., Woods Hole, 1978— ; cons. in field. Commr. WHO conf. on ctr. for Mycotic sera 1969; chmn. Gold Medal Award Com. Sigma Xi, 1978; mem. La. assn. def. counsel expert witness bank, 1985—; Bd. dirs. Girl Scouts Coun. La., Community Relationships Greater New Orleans, Zoning Bd. River Ridge (La.); mem. exec. bd. River Ridge Civic Assn., 1982—, sec., 1982-84; chmn. pers.l bd. Riverside Bapt. Ch., River Ridge. Recipient Rosicrucian Humanitarian award, 1981; Macy fellow, MBL, Woods Hole, 1978-79; grantee NSF, NIH; diplomate Am. Bd. Microbiology. Mem. Internat. Soc. Human and Animal Mycology, Med. Mycological Soc. Am., Am. Soc. Microbiology (nat. com. on membership 1983-87), AAAS, Nat. Inst. Sci., Sigma Xi. Author articles in field. Home: 408 Berclair Ave New Orleans LA 70123 Office: Dillard U Div Natural Sci New Orleans LA 70122

IVERSEN, NANCY M., human resource consultant; b. Racine, Wis., Dec. 31, 1928; d. Arthur and Anna (Jensen) I. BS in Indsl./Orgnl. Psychology, U. Wis., Parkside, 1987; MS in Mgmt., U. Wis., Racine, 1989. Supr. Wis. Bell Telephone, Racine, 1945-83; human resource cons. Iversen Mgmt. Cons., Racine, 1989—. Mem. Am. Psychol. Soc., Am. Mgmt. Assn., NAFE.

IVERSON, ANN CUMMINGS, advertising agency executive; b. N.Y.C., May 23, 1941; m. Clifton Iverson Jr. Assoc. in Bus. Adminstrn., Briarcliff Coll., 1961; student, London Sch. Econs., 1962-64. Mktg. asst. Garland-Compton Ltd., 1961-64; with BBDO, 1965-70, account exec., 1969-70; account exec. Ogilvy & Mather, Inc., 1970-77; v.p., account supr., then sr. v.p. Ogilvy & Mather, Inc., Houston; sr. v.p. Ogilvy & Mather Advt., N.Y.C., 1987—. Office: Ogilvy & Mather Advt 309 W 49th St Worldwide Pla New York NY 10019*

IVERSON, GENIE, author, writer; b. Newport News, Va.; d. Elmer Victor and Willa (Okker) I.; m. Theodore W. Clymer. Student, N.Y. U., 1964-65; BA, U. Calif., Berkeley, 1966. Freelance writer United Press Internat., San Francisco, 1967-68; staff reporter, youth editor Contra Costa Times, Walnut Creek, Calif., 1968-71; reporter Lesher New Bur, Martinez, Calif., 1971-72; freelance author, writer. Author: Jacques Cousteau, 1976, Louis Armstrong, 1976, Margaret Bouke-White, 1980, I Want To Be Big, 1979, (play) The Goose That Laid Gold Eggs, 1982, The Robbers and The Fig Tree, 1982, The Boy Who Called Wolf, 1989. Mem. Soc. of Children's Book Writers. Home: PO Box 222138 Carmel CA 93923

IVES, ADRIENE DIANE, real estate executive; b. Washington, Oct. 6, 1951; d. Edwin Forrest and Carolyn Elizabeth (Wray) Warner; m. Perry Nelson Ives, May 12, 1972; children: Jesse Warner, James Robert. BS, U. Md., 1973. Tchr. Charles County (Md.) Bd. Edn., 1973-83, Broad Creek Day Sch., Ft. Washington, Md., 1983-85; sales counselor L.K. Farrall, Ltd., Camp Springs, Md., 1985—; tchr. real estate Farrall Inst., Waldorf, Md., 1990—; tchr. Christian Children's Ministry, Washington, 1982-83; v.p. The Warner Corp., Washington, 1982-83; bd. dirs. Nat. Plumbing Supply, Inc., Washington; devel. agt. Burgundy Farm Country Day Sch., Alexandria, Va., 1986-88; instr. real estate edn. Farrall Inst., 1990. Author: Nat. City Christ Church, 1988, 89; contbr. articles to jours. Bd. dirs. Broad Creek Country Day Sch., 1982-83; bd. deaconesses Nat. City Christian Ch., Washington, 1989—. Recipient Citizenship award Prince Georges County Police, Forestville, Md., 1986. Mem. Nat. Assn. Realtors (Cert. Residential Specialist award 1988), Md. Assn. Realtors (Grad. Realtors Inst. award 1987), Prince Georges Assn. Realtors, Women's Coun. Realtors, Realtors Nat. Mktg. Inst. (mem. residential sales coun. 1988), Realtors Polit. Action Com. Republican. Mem. Christian Ch. (Disciples of Christ). Office: LK Farrall Ltd Realtors 6339 Allentown Rd Camp Springs MD 20748

IVES, COLTA FELLER, museum curator, educator; b. San Diego, Apr. 5, 1943; m. E. Garrison Ives, June 14, 1966; 1 child, Lucy Barrett. BA, Mills Coll., 1964; MA, Columbia U., 1966. Staff Met. Mus. Art, N.Y.C., 1966-75, curator charge prints and photographs, 1975—; adj. prof. Columbia U., 1970—. Author: The Great Wave 1974, Art Libraries Assn. award, 1975, The Flight Into Egypt, 1972, (with others) The Painterly Print, 1980, R. Rauschenberg. Photos In & Out City Limits: New York, 1981, French Prints in the Era of Impressionism and Symbolism, 1988, Pierre Bonnard: The Graphic Art, 1989. Chmn. grants com. Met. Mus. Art, 1986-87. Mem. Print Council Am. (exec. bd. 1975-77, 84-87, v.p. 1989—). Club: Grolier (N.Y.C.). Office: Met Mus Art Fifth Ave at 82nd St New York NY 10028

IVES, ELINOR RANDOLPH, retired physician; b. Tucson, Ariz., Nov. 29, 1906; d. Eugene Semmes and Anna (Waggaman) I. MD, Cornell Med. Sch., N.Y.C., 1933. Diplomate Am. Bd. Neurology and Psychiatry. Substitute psychiatrist Merced County Mental Health Dept., L.A. Mem. L.A. Soc. Neurology and Psychiatry, Nat. Fedn. Catholic Physicians Guilds, L.A. County Med. Women's Assn., Nat. Guild Catholic Psychiatrists, World Fedn. Mental Health, Word Med. Assn., L.A. Physicians Art Assn. Republican. Roman Catholic. Home: 5636 Berkshire Dr Los Angeles CA 90032

IVEY, HELENE GORES, realtor; b. Entwistle, Alta., Can.; d. Stephen and Anna (Roemer) Gores; m. Alfred Guy Pete Ivey, May 10, 1945; children: Sarah Lane, Helene Roemer. AB, U. N.C., 1932, postgrad., 1933-34, 40; postgrad., Cath. U. Am., 1941-45, Harvard U., 1950-51. Instr. advanced German Mercer U., 1933-34; social worker Bibb County Welfare Dept., Macon, Ga., 1934-36, Works Progress Adminstrn., western N.C., 1940-41; supr. ARC, Washington, 1940-45; writer Chapel Hill (N.C.) Weekly, 1955-58; mgr. Ivey Realty Co., Chapel Hill, 1958—. Publicity chmn., dir. N.C. State Congress PTA, 1955-57. Mem. Nat. Assn. Realtors, N.C. Assn. Realtors, Chapel Hill Bd. Realtors, LWV (dir. 1951-54).

IVEY, JUDITH, actress; b. El Paso, Tex., Sept. 4, 1951; d. Nathan Aldean and Dorothy Lee (Lewis) I. B.S., Ill. State U., 1973. Actress plays in Chgo., N.Y.C.: The Sea, 1974, The Goodbye People, The Moundbuilders, Oh, Coward, 1977-78, Bedroom Farce, 1979, Dusa, Fish, Stas and VI, 1980, Piaf, 1980-81, The Dumping Ground, 1981, The Rimers of Eldritch, 1981, Pastorale, 1982, Two Small Bodies, 1982, Second Lady, 1983, Hurlyburly, 1984; Broadway plays: Steaming, 1982-83, Blithe Spirit, 1987; films include: Harry and Son, 1984, The Lonely Guy, 1984, The Woman in Red, 1984, Brighton Beach Memoirs, 1986, Hello Again, Sister Sister, Miles from Home, 1988, Everybody Wins, 1990; TV films include: The Shady Hill Kidnapping, Dixie Changing Habits, We Are The Children; TV series: Down Home, 1990. Winner Tony award 1983 (for Steaming), 85 (for Hurlyburly). Office: care ICM 8899 Beverly Blvd Los Angeles CA 90048*

IVEY, KAY ELLEN, state educational agency administrator; b. Repton, Ala., Oct. 15, 1944; d. Boardman Nettles and Barbara Elizabeth Ivey. BS, Auburn U., 1967; cert. in mktg., U. Colo., 1975; cert. in banking, U. South Ala.; cert. in Strategic Leadership for State Execs., Duke U., 1989. Tchr., coach forensics Rio Linda (Calif.) High Sch., 1968-69; asst. v.p. Mchts. Nat. Bank, Mobile, Ala., 1970-79; cabinet officer Office of the Gov., State of Ala., Montgomery, 1979-81; reading clk. Ala. Ho. Reps., Montgomery, 1981-82; exec. v.p. St. Margaret's Hosp. Found., Montgomery, 1982-85; asst. to exec. dir., nat. chmn. for govt. relations and communications Ala. Commn. Higher Edn., Montgomery, 1985—; owner, cons. Ivey Enterprises, Montgomery, 1982—; speaker in field. Editor (audio-visual presentation) What Price Freedom (award of Excellence), 1976, St. Margaret's Hosp. Heart tabloid, 1983. Mem. adv. bd. Sch. Bus. Auburn U., 1980-83; candidate Ala. State Auditor, 1982; sec. Ala. div. Am. Cancer Soc., 1985—; bd. dirs. Ala. Girl's State Sch., 1983-85, Stetson Hoedown Rodeo Queen's Pageant, Montgomery, 1986—; bd. trustees Sheriff's Boys and Girls Ranches. Mem. Indsl. Developers Ala., Young Men's Bus. Orgn., Pub. Relations Council Ala. (bd. dirs. 1976-82), DAR (state chmn. 1985-86), Alpha Gamma Delta (disting. citizen award 1986). Republican. Presbyterian. Home: 609 Thorm Pl Montgomery AL 36106

IVEY, REANEÉ NANETTE, educational administrator; b. Greenville, N.C., July 17, 1957; d. Joseph Thomas Ivey and Marion (Gorham) Wilkes. BS, Hampton Inst., 1979; MEd, Ga. State U., 1986, postgrad., 1989—. Cert. speech pathologist, N.C., Ga. Speech pathologist Pitt County Schs., Greenville, 1979-81; speech pathologist Atlanta Pub. Schs., 1981-90, liaison specialist, 1990—. Active Ben Hill United Meth. Ch., Atlanta. Mem. NEA, Women in Communication, Internat. Network Schs. (steering com. 1985—), Ga. Assn. Speech and Hearing, Pub. Rels. Student Soc. Am., Alpha Kappa Mu, Kappa Delta Pi, Delta Sigma Theta.

IVINS, MARSHA S., aerospace engineer, astronaut; b. Balt., Apr. 15, 1951; d. Joseph L. Ivins. BS in Aerospace Engring., U. Colo., 1973. Lic. pilot. Engr. NASA-Lyndon B. Johnson Space Ctr., 1974—, with crew sta. design br., 1974-80, engr. flight simulation, 1980—, astronaut, 1985—, mission specialist shuttle flight STS-32, 1990. Mem. Exptl. Aircraft Assn., 99's, Internat. Aerobatic Club. Address: NASA Johnson Space Ctr Astronaut Office Houston TX 77058*

IVORY, MING MARIE, political scientist; b. Tokyo, Aug. 28, 1949; d. T. Austin and E. Virginia (Christine) I. BS, Tufts U., 1971; MA, U. Pa., 1973; PhD, MIT, 1986. Rsch. asst. Smithsonian Inst., Washington, summer 1970, 71; faculty assoc. Hampshire Coll., Amherst, Mass., 1973-75; profl. asst. NSF, Washington, 1975; sci. reporter Sta. WVHY-FM, Phila., 1976; profl. asst. Office of Sci. Advisor World Bank, Washington, 1977; cons. Internat. Sci. & Tech. Inst., Washington, 1978-79; sci. policy specialist U.S. Agy. for Internat. Devel., Washington, 1979-80, environ. protection specialist, 1980-85; asst. prof. Creighton U., Omaha, 1986—. Del. Mass. Govs. Conf. on Librs. and Info. Svcs., 1978; elected del. White House Conf. on Librs. and Info. Svcs., 1979. Mem. Am. Polit. Sci. Assn., Soc. for Internat. Devel., Soc. for Social Studies of Sci. Democrat. Unitarian. Home: 13746 Military Rd Omaha NE 68142 Office: Creighton U Polit Sci Dept Omaha NE 68178

IWANSKI, MARIE IDA, healthcare administrator; b. Wisconsin Rapids, Wis., Oct. 13, 1948; d. Adam John and Mary Elizabeth (McNamee) I. BS in Psychology, U. Wis., Stevens Point, 1974, M Rehab. Psychology, 1978. Record clk., pers. clk. Consol. Papers, Inc., Wisconsin Rapids, 1966-71; child care worker, dorm head Norris for Boys, Inc., Mukwonago, Wis., 1974-76; adminstrv. sec. State of Wis., Madison, 1978-79; health planning analyst Wis. Dept. Health and Social Svcs., Madison, 1979-89. Bd. dirs. Nat. Spinal Cord Injury Assn., 1981-87; mem. adminstrv. com. State Employees Combined Campaign, 1983-89, chmn., 1988. Mem. AACD, Internat. Platform Assn., Nat. Rehab. Assn., Am. Biog. Inst. Rsch. Assn., Am. Rehab. Counseling Assn., Nat. Spinal Cord Injury Assn. (bd. mem. emeritus Madison Area chpt.). Home: 302 Kent Ln Apt 202 Madison WI 53713

IZENOUR, CHRISTINE, lighting designer; b. San Antonio, Jan. 22, 1949; d. Charles Stevens and Elizabeth Christine (Lien) I. AA in Fine Arts, Pensacola (Fla.) Jr. Coll., 1970; BA in Metaphysics, Am. Nat. Inst., Calabasas, Calif., 1986; B in Indep. Studies, U. South Fla., 1983. Sr. stage operator Walt Disney World, Orlando, Fla., 1971-74; lighting designer Ch. St. Sta., Orlando, 1974-76; prodn. asst. Quinn Martin Prodns., Hollywood, Calif., 1977-79; lighting designer Walt Disney Prodns., Epcot, Fla., 1979-83; design engr. Hubert Wilke, Inc., North Hollywood, Calif., 1984-86; researcher, writer Am. Nat. Inst., 1986-87; freelance designer, writer Glendale, Calif., 1986-88, Santa Monica Mountains Conservancy, Malibu, Calif., 1988-89; sr. designer Francis Krahe & Assocs., Newport Beach, Calif., 1989—. Columnist Westar Courier newspaper, 1986. Water safety instr. ARC, Ft. Walton Beach, Fla., 1966-76; vol. Cerebral Palsy Telethons, Orlando, 1974-75; co-founder Cathedral Players, Orlando, 1975; marshal Olympic Torch Run, Los Angeles, 1984. Fellow Nat. Thespian Soc., 1967. Mem. Nat. Assn. Female Execs., Phi Kappa Phi. Republican. Home: 6720 Franklin Pl #303 Hollywood CA 90028 Office: 4701 Von Karmon Ave Ste 100 Newport Beach CA 92660

IZZO, LUCILLE ANNE, sales representative; b. Rochester, N.Y., Apr. 1, 1954; d. Peter George and Dorothy June (Cusimano) I. Grad. high sch., Rochester. Regional sales mgr. T.R. Miller Co., Inc., New Milford, Conn., 1986-87; program mgr. Jr. Achievement SW Conn., Stamford, 1987-88, adviser, cons., 1986—; sec. Eastman Kodak Co., Rochester, 1972-84; consumer products sales rep. Eastman Kodak Co., Oklahoma City, 1984-86; copy products sales rep. Eastman Kodak Co., Stamford, 1988—. Bus. cons. Region One Jr. Achievement Conf., 1988, 90; guest speaker West Conn. Jr. Achievement Conf., 1990. Mem. NAFE. Home: 166 Old Brookfield Rd Apt 1-5 Danbury CT 06811 Office: Eastman Kodak Co 1266 Main St Stamford CT 06902

JABLECKI, DONNA MAE, biology educator; b. Muskogee, Okla., Jan. 13, 1943; d. James William and Beulah Mae (Murray) Blankenship; m. Lawrence Thomas Jablecki, Aug. 24, 1963; children: Nathaniel Thomas, Sarah Elizabeth. BS in Biology, Bethany Nazarene Coll., 1965; MST, Middle Tenn. State U., 1973. Cert. tchr., Tenn., Tex. Biology tchr. Madison High Sch., Nashville, 1965-68; tchr. U.S. Forces Dependent Schs., Eng., 1968-76; sci. tchr. Brazoswood High Sch., Clute, Tex., 1976-78, chmn. dept., biology tchr., 1978—; adj. lectr. U. Houston, Clear Lake, 1988; prin. investigator grant NSF, Clute, 1985-87. Sec. bd. dirs. Brazosport Symphony Orch., 1986—, soloist, 1985-88; mem. Brazosport Symphony Chorale, 1985—; bd. dirs. Brazosport Music Theater, 1981; mem. Women's Ctr. of Brazoria County, Angleton, Tex. Recipient Excellence award Pres. Reagan, 1985, Commendation award Gov. of Tex., 1986. Mem. Assn. Presdl. Awardees in Sci. (sec. 1986-88), Sci. Tchrs. Assn. Tex. (com. mem.), Nat. Sci. Tchrs. Assn., Nat. Assn. Biology Tchrs. Democrat. Episcopalian. Home: 910 S Walker Angleton TX 77515 Office: Brazoswood High Sch 302 W Brazoswood Dr Clute TX 77531

JABLIN, LAURIE CLARK, real estate company executive; b. Hall County, Ga., May 9, 1921; d. Joseph Thomas and Josephine (Jones) Clark; m. Frederick Jablin, Feb. 4, 1944 (div. 1973); children: Jo Anne, Juliana. Student, Catawba Coll., 1940, Realtors Inst., Chgo., 1973. Cert. accredited land counselor Realtors Land Inst.; broker N.J. Real Estate Commn., Ga. Real Estate Commn. With various radio stas., 1947-57; owner, prin. broker Radium Realty, Albany, Ga., 1965-79, Century 21-Radium Realty, Albany, 1979-80; broker Doane Western, Inc., St. Louis and Albany, 1980-81; ind. broker, appraiser, Albany, 1981-85; sr. counselor mktg. rsch. Yankelovitch, Skelly & White, N.Y.C., 1985-87; broker VTY Realty, Atlantic City, 1986-87; broker, land specialist Price Real Estate, Ventnor City, N.J., 1987—; broker Mercado Realty, Pleasantville, N.J., 1988—. Pres. Radium Springs Civic Assn., 1977; reader for blind Libr. of Congress, 1976. Mem. Nat. Assn. Realtors (real estate fin. com. 1988—), Ga. Realtors Inst. (gov. 1971-73), Ga. Assn. Realtors (bd. dirs. 1971-73), Woman's Coun. Realtors (pres. 1971), Albany Bd. Realtors (ednl. dir. 1975-76), Realtors Land Inst. (accredited cons.), Nat. Audubon Soc. (life, bd. dirs. 1983-85, Albany), Nat. Hist. Trust, Internat. Toastmistress Club (pres. Albany chpt. 1962-63). Democrat. Presbyterian. Home: 27 Hege Dr Apt 8 Lexington NC 27292

JACANGELO, PIA MARIA, social worker; b. Glen Ridge, N.J., Aug. 10, 1954; d. Joseph Gerard and Thelma (Bisignano) J. BA, Montclair State U., 1976; MSW, Ohio State U., 1980. Diplomate in Clin. Social Work. Mental health clinician N.J. med. sch. Community Mental Health Ctr., Newark, 1981—; pvt. practitioner Fairfield, N.J., 1986—; cons. Ctr. for Eating Disorders, Livingston, N.J., 1988—; specialist in eating disorders, 1986—. Mem. Passaic County Mental Health Assn., Am. Anorexia & Bulimia Assn. (group leader 1988—), Nat. Assn. Social Workers, Acad. Cert. Social Workers. Home: 31A Richland Ct Clifton NJ 07012 Office: 124 Little Falls Rd Fairfield NJ 07006

JACK, NANCY RAYFORD, supplemental resource company executive, consultant; b. Hughes Springs, Tex., June 23, 1939; d. Vernon Lacy and Virginia Ernestine (Turner) Rayford; m. Kermit E. Hundley, Dec. 19, 1979; 1 child by previous marriage: James Bradford Jack, III. C.B.A., Keller Grad. Sch. Mgmt., 1980; cert. in acctg, Harper Coll., 1972, cert. in corp. law and tax law, paralegal, 1973. Sr. sec. Gould, Inc., Rolling Meadows, Ill., 1971-73; staff asst. Gould, Inc., 1973-74, asst. sec., 1974-77, corp. sec., 1977-89, v.p., 1985-89; pres. The Corp. Ofcl. Sec., Wheaton, Ill., 1989—. Recipient cert. of leadership YWCA Met. Chgo., 1975. Mem. Am. Soc. Corp. Secs., Meadow Club, St. Charles Country Club, Beta Sigma Phi. Republican. Home: 1040 Creekside Dr Wheaton IL 60187

JACK, PHYLLIS HARRIS, corporate family strategist, educational consultant; b. Charlotte, N.C., Aug. 23, 1934; d. William Thomas and Connie LaVerne (Childers) Harris; children: Michael Harris, Julie Dawn Jack Rodgers. BA, U. N.C., 1965, MEd, 1969; postgrad., North Tex. State U., 1982-83. Cert. tchr., N.C., Tex. Elem. tchr. Chapel Hill (N.C.) Pub. Schs., 1965-68; staff devel. coordinator Learning Inst. N.C., Durham, 1969-72; child devel. specialist Tex. Dept. Human Resources, Ft. Worth, 1975-77; child care tng. coordinator North Tex. State Univ., Denton, 1978-81; dir., owner Resources for Children, Inc., Ft. Worth, 1984-88; pvt. practice Ft. Worth, 1988—; instr. Tarrant County Jr. Coll., Ft. Worth, North Tex. State U., 1982—; frequent guest speaker; appearances on TV; coordinator for tng. in establishment of pub. sch. kindergarten program in State of N.C., 1972-73. Editorial rev. bd. Child Care Quarterly, Austin, 1984—. Trustee Tarrant County Youth Collaboration, 1982-86; bd. dirs. Tarrant County Med. Aux., 1983-84; adv. bd. Ft. Worth's A Better Childhood Com.; coord. Tex. State Parent Action. Recipient Brous Outstanding Advocate award, 1984. Mem. Nat. Assn. for the Edn. of Young Children (governing bd. nominee 1988—, nat. field rep. 1983—), Tex. Assn. for the Edn. of Young Children (state pres. 1982-83), Fort Worth Assn. for the Edn. of Young Children (pres. 1976-78), Southern Assn. for Children Under Six (com. chair 1978-80, conf. co-chair 1987), Rotary, Phi Beta Kappa, Phi Delta Kappa. Methodist. Club: Ft. Worth Woman's (v.p. and auditor 1983-86). Lodge: Rotary.

JACKLE, KAREN DEE, real estate executive; b. Santa Ana, Calif., June 26, 1945; d. Franklin Suits and Dorothy (Miller) Todd; m. Paul Herman Jackle, Oct. 12, 1968; children: Lara Irene, Julie Maureen. Student, Calif. State U., Long Beach, 1967. Elem. tchr. L.A. City Schs., 1967-68; social worker Los Angeles Dept. Pub. Social Svcs., 1968-70; with Seablue Pools, Salisbury, Rhodesia, 1970; co-owner Paul Jackle & Assocs., Huntington Beach, Calif., 1971—, property mgr., appraiser, 1973-86; property developer, mgr. Paul

Jackle & Assocs., Huntington Beach, 1986—. Mem. Sister City Club, Huntington Beach, 1986—. Mem. AAUW. Office: 18652 Florida St Ste 360 Huntington Beach CA 92648

JACKOBS, MIRIAM ANN, dietitian; b. Sioux City, Iowa, Apr. 8, 1940; d. Abraham and Mary (Wadedo) Kaled; m. John Joseph Jackobs, Aug. 28, 1965; children: Mark James, Daniel Michael, Thomas Vincent. Student, St. Louis U., 1962; BS, Briar Cliff Coll., 1963; MS, Iowa State U., 1965. Lic. in dietetics, Ohio. Instr. nutrition Ariz. State U., Tempe, 1965-67, Willoughby (Ohio) Eastlake Sch., 1967-69; clinical dietitian Migrant Clinic of Seneca County, Tiffin, Ohio, 1969-75; nutrition instr. Heidelberg Coll., Tiffin, 1969-75; founder, cons. dietitian Nutrition Cons. Svcs., 1974—; oncology dietitian Hall Radiation Ctr., Cedar Rapids, 1983-87; nutrition instr. Mt. Mercy & Coe Colls., Cedar Rapids, 1976-87; clinical dietitian The Brethren's Home, Greenville, Ohio, 1987-89; dir. dietary dept. Washington Manor Retirement Ctr., Centerville, Ohio, 1989-90; instr. Kettering (Ohio) Adult Sch., 1988-90, Mount St. Joseph Coll., 1989—. Author: (book) Food Prep Manual, 1968, Diet Manual, 1988; contbr. articles on nutrition to prof. jours. Com. chmn. LWV, Ohio and Iowa, 1970-82; fund raising chmn. PTA, Cedar Rapids, 1984-86; unit leader dist. coun. Boy Scouts Am., 1973-88; organizer Greenville Summer Symphony, Ohio, 1988. Recipient Silver Beaver award Boy Scouts Am., St. George award Archdiocese Dubuque, 1985; Gen. Foods Found. fellow Iowa State U., 1965. Mem. Am. Dietetic Assn., Ohio Dietetic Assn., Ohio Cons. Dietitions (newsletter editor 1988—), Greater Cin. Dietetic Assn., Dayton Dietetic Assn. (chmn. 1987—), Greater Cin. Cons. Dietitians, Gerontology Practice Group, Cedar Rapids Youth Orch., Coe Woman (pres. 1977-78). Roman Catholic. Home and Office: Nutrition Cons Svcs 7733 Westwind Ln Cincinnati OH 45242

JACKOWIAK, PATRICIA, lawyer; b. Chgo., Feb. 3, 1959; d. Leonard John and Margaret Mary (Iozzi) J. BA, Loyola U., Chgo., 1981; JD, John Marshall Law Sch., 1984. Bar: Ill. 1985. Asst. state's atty. Cook County, Chgo., 1987-89, supr. trial atty. bur. child support enforcement, legal advisor law student's spl. and perjury projects, chmn. employee rels. com., 1988-89, com. mem. domestic rels. div. Pro-se task force, 1989; dep. commr. Consumer Protection div. Dept. Consumer Svcs. City of Chgo., 1989—; summer atty. Ct. Claims and Antitrust div. Office of Ill. Atty. Gen., 1985, 86; com. mem. domestic rels. div. Cook County The Pro-Se Task Force Com.; mem. Chgo. div. Ford Consumer Appeals Bd., 1989—. Pres. Santa Lucia Sch. Bd., Chgo., 1987—; chairperson Santa Lucia Parish Carnival Com., 1987—; chairperson employee rels. com. Child Support div., 1988-89; dir. religious edn. Santa Lucia Parish, 1985—; mem. freshman recruiting and fundraising coms. Parents Assocs. Loyola U., Chgo., 1987—; mem. elder care task force Dept. Health, Aging and Disability and Dept. Consumer Svcs., City of Chgo., 1989—. Mem. ABA, Chgo. Bar Assn., Blue Key, Pi Sigma Alpha. Democratic. Roman Catholic. Office: Dept of Consumer Svcs 121 N LaSalle Chicago IL 60602

JACKSON, ANDREA CARROLL, public relations executive, lobbyist, writer, photographer; b. Lockesburg, Ark., Jan. 8, 1945; d. Jake Charles and Lola Evelyn (Hale) Carroll; m. Ronald William Jackson, Dec. 23, 1967 (div. Jan. 1978). B.S. in Edn., Henderson State U., 1967; postgrad. in journalism La. State U., 1981-82. Phys. edn. tchr. Lamar Consol. Schs., Ark., 1967-68; field advisor Ark. Post coun. Girl Scouts U.S., Pine Bluff, 1969-74, pub. rels. dir. Ouachita coun., Little Rock, 1974-79; program and pub. rels. dir. Baton Rouge Area YWCA, 1979-81; editor Bayou Country Publs., Plaquemine, La., 1981-83; communications dir. Am. Lung Assn. of Ark., Little Rock, 1984—; owner, operator TLC Pet Care Svc.; freelance writer, photographer; editor: (tng. manual) Safe Homes Project for Battered Women, 1981; Ark. Women's Rights OURS newspaper, 1985-86. Recipient Excellence in color slide photography awards Ouachita Girl Scout Coun. and Girl Scouts U.S., 1978; Outstanding Svc. award Baton Rouge Area YWCA, 1980. Mem. Ark. Press Women (feature writing awards, 2 in 1982, 3 in 1983, 2 interview awards 1984, 2 broadcast awards 1984, 87, writing editing and interviewing, 1985, 86), Congress of Lung Assn. Staff, Sierra Club (chpt. newsletter editor, exec. com. mem., lobbyist). Avocations: movies, hiking, whitewater rafting. Home: 3507 W 4th Little Rock AR 72205 Office: 211 Natural Resources Dr Little Rock AR 72205

JACKSON, ANGELA RAMONA, case manager; b. Toledo, June 19, 1952; d. Issac and Mona Lois (Talmadge) J. EdB, U. Toledo, 1983; postgrad., Bowling Green State U., Ohio. Youth counselor East Toledo Helping Hand, 1983-85; probation officer Lucas County Dept. Court Svcs., Toledo, 1985-87; case mgr. Lucas County Bd. Mental Health, Toledo, 1987—. Publisher playwriting, Baby Bro, 1989. Bd. dirs. Intensive Bus. Edn. Adv. Com., Toledo, 1987—, United Way Allocations Com., Toledo, 1989—; vol. Fair Housing, Toledo, 1988—; Dem. Committeeman Toledo, 1986-88, ward chmn. Toledo, 1988. Recipient 3d proze poetry contest, 1982, honor roll, 1981, U. Toledo. Mem. NAACP, U. Dem. Club. Office: Lucas County Bd Mental Retardation 2001 Lollingwood Blvd Toledo OH 43624

JACKSON, ANNE (ANNE JACKSON WALLACH), actress; b. Pitts.; d. John Ivan and Stella Germaine (Murray) J.; m. Eli Wallach, Mar. 5, 1948; children: Peter, Roberta, Katherine. Studied with Sanford Meisner and Herbert Berghof at Neighborhood Playhouse, with Lee Strassberg at Actor's Studio. Profl. debut: Cherry Orchard; mem. Am. Repertory Co.; Broadway plays include: Summer and Smoke, Oh, Men! Oh, Women!, Middle of the Night, Major Barbara, Rhinoceros, Luv, Waltz of the Toreadors, Diary of Anne Frank, 1978, Twice Around the Park, 1982-83, Nest of the Woodgrouse, 1984, Café Crown, 1989, off-Broadway plays: The Typists, The Tigers; film appearances include: So Young, So Bad, 1950, Secret Life of an American Wife, 1968, Dirty Dingus McGee, 1970, Lovers and Other Strangers, 1970, The Shining, 1980, Sam's Son, 1985; TV appearances include: 84 Charing Cross Road, Private Battle, Everything's Relative, 1987—; TV films: Family Man, Golda I and II, Out on a Limb, Baby M, 1988; author: (autobiography) Early Stages, 1979. Recipient Obie award. Office: care Internat Creative Mgmt 8899 Beverly Blvd Los Angeles CA 90048

JACKSON, ANNE, publishing executive; b. Stavanger, Norway, Mar. 17; d. Palmer and Gudren (Herlofsen) Nerbo; children: Daniel, John. AA, Greenville Tech. Sch., 1983. Sec. to advt. mgr. Square D. Co., Park Ridge, Ill.; CSI specialist 1st Fed. Savs. and Loan Assn., Greenville, S.C.; circulation mgr. Chem. Sources Internat., Inc., Clemson, S.C.; interviewer ProGen Rsch. Mem. NAFE. Republican. Baptist. Office: Chem Sources Internat Inc PO Box 1824 Clemson SC 29633

JACKSON, BENITA MARIE, physician; b. Englewood, N.J., Aug. 14, 1956; d. Benjamin A. and Gloria L. (Smith) J. AB in Biochemistry, Mount Holyoke Coll., 1978; MD, Howard U. Coll. of Med., 1982; MPH, Emory U. Med. Sch., 1989. Resident internal med. Georgetown Med. Svc. DC. Gen. Hosp., Wash., 1982-83; resident pathology George Wash. U., Wash., 1983-84; resident internal med. Howard U. Hosp., Wash., 1984-86; staff physician internal med. Group Health Assn., Wash.; resident pub. health/ preventive med. Morehouse Sch. Medicine Ga. div. Pub. Health, Atlanta, 1987-89. Mem. Am. Pub. Health Assn., Nat. Med. Assn. Office: Morehouse Sch of Medicine D 720 Westview Dr SW Atlanta GA 30010

JACKSON, BETTY EILEEN, music and elementary school educator; b. Denver, Oct. 9, 1925; d. James Bowen and Fannie (Shelton) J. MusB, U. Colo., 1948, MusM, 1949, MusB. Edn., 1963; postgrad. Ind. U., 1952-55, Hochschule fur Musik, Munich, 1955-56. Cert. educator Colo., Calif. Tchr., accompanist, tchr. H.L. Davis Vocal Studios, Denver, 1949-52; teaching assoc. U. Colo., Boulder, 1961-63, vis. lectr., summers 1963-69; tchr. Fontana Unified Sch. Dist., Calif., 1963—, pvt. studio, 1966—; lectr. in music Calif. State U., San Bernardino, 1967-76; performer, accompanist, music dir. numerous musical cos. including performer, music dir. Fontana Mummers, 1980—, Riverside Community Players, Calif., 1984—; performer Rialto Community Theatre, Calif., 1983—. Performances include numerous operas, musical comedies and oratorios, Cen. City Opera, Denver Grand Opera, Univ. Colo., Ind. Univ. Opera Theater (leading mezzo); oratorio soloist in Ind., Ky., Colo., and Calif., West End Opera (lead roles), Riverside Opera (lead roles); Judge, Inland Theatre League, Riverside, 1983—; mem. San Bernardino Cultural Task Force, 1981-83. Fulbright grantee, Munich, 1955-56; named Outstanding Performer Inland Theatre League, 1982-84; nominee Tchr. of Yr. Fontant Unified Sch. Dist., 1990-91; recipient Outstanding Reading Tchr. award, 1990. Mem. AAUW (bd. dirs., cultural chair 1983-86), NEA, Nat. Assn. Tchrs. Singing (exec. bd. 1985—), Internat. Reading Assn., Music Educators Nat. Conf., Calif. Tchrs. Assn., Calif. Elem. Educators Assn., Fontana Tchrs. Assn., Music Tchrs. Assn., Arrowhead Reading Coun., San Bernardino Valley Concert Assn. (bd. dirs. 1977-83), Internat. Platform Assn., Order Eastern Star, Kappa Kappa Iota (v.p. 1982-83). Avocations: community theater and opera, travel, collecting Hummels and plates. Home: PO Box 885 Rialto CA 92377

JACKSON, BETTY LOU, real estate developer; b. Wichita, Kans., Mar. 31, 1927; d. Orville John and Ida Mabel (Wolfe) Deason; m. James L. Jackson, July 2, 1966 (dec. Feb. 1983); children: Rebecca Lou, Jennifer Mae. AA, SW Baptist U., Bolivar, Mo., 1946; BA, Cen. Mo. State U., 1963; MA, U. Mo., 1964. Salesperson Sears, Kansas City, Mo., 1943-44; bookkeeping clk. Hallmark Cards, Kansas City, Mo., 1945-46; civil service Camp Pendleton, Oceanside, Calif., 1947; sec. Ford Motor Co., Kansas City, Mo., Jim Taylor Olds Co., Independence, Mo., 1952-54; tchr. Consol. Sch. Dist. #2, Mo., 1954-55; tchr. adminstr. Consol. Sch. Dist. #2, Raytown, Mo., 1963-78; owner mgr. B.J.'s Florist Car Wash Laundramat, Stockton, Mo., 1979-82; owner, ptnr. J and S Realty, Stockton, Mo., 1983—; officer J-S Corp., Stockton 1986-90. Mem. Nat. Assn. Realtors, 5-County Bd. Realtors, Mo. Bd. Realtors, Mo. C. of C., AARP. Democrat. Baptist. Home: Lakeview Cir Owl Haven Estates Stockton MO 65785 Office: J-S Realty Stockton Lake Pla PO Box 159 S Hwy 39 Ste 106 Stockton MO 65785

JACKSON, CAROL FRANCES, moving company executive; b. Falmouth, Ky., Sept. 15, 1938; d. Roy Wilson and Alma C. (Field) Johnting; m. Forrest Edward Jackson, Aug. 23, 1957; children: Mary Ann Jackson Pennington, David A., Marsha, Douglas, Roy Andrew. Student, Transylvania Coll., 1956-57; grad., Miller Bus. Coll., Cin., 1957. Sec. Cin. Gas and Electric Co., 1958-59; bookkeeper moving co. Cin., 1968-71; now owner, sec.-treas. Apollo Moving Specialist, Inc., Daytona, Fla., 1985—. Vol., Cannon Falls (Minn.) Elem. Sch., 1980-83, Boy Scouts Am., Brownies. Democrat. Office: Apollo Moving Specialists Inc 771 Fentress Blvd Daytona Beach FL 32114

JACKSON, CAROLYN WITTORFF, professional organization executive, political campaign manager; b. Inman, Kans., Sept. 24, 1953; d. Arnold and Marcelyn (Peterson) W. BS, Kans. State U., 1975, MS, 1981. Extension home economist Harvey County, Newton, Kans., 1975-86; dir. membership Am. Home Econs. Assoc., Washington, 1986-89, Fairfax County C. of C., Vienna, Va., 1989-90; campaign mgr. Dick Nichols for Congress, McPherson, Kans., 1990. Recipient Woman of Yr. Newton Kans. Civic and Community Svc., 1983; nominated Bus and Profl. Women' Young Careerist, 1983. Mem. NAFE, Am. Home Econs. Assn., Am. Soc. Assn. Execs. (membership promotion sect.), Kans State U. Alumni Assn. (nat. capital area chpt.), Epsilon Sigma Phi, Alpha Rio (Horizon award, 1982). Republican. Methodist. Home: 201 Oak Park Dr Apt D McPherson KS 67460 Office: PO Box 411 McPherson KS 67460

JACKSON, CLAUDINE EDITH, radiologist; b. Denver, Aug. 14, 1934; d. Claude Eugene and Edith Alice (Taylor) Bailey; m. Carl Eugene Holloman, June 5, 1950 (dec. 1967); children: Carol Gene, Judy Ann, Claudia Mae; m. William Charles Jackson, Aug. 14, 1969; children: William Charles II, Tammy Lynne. Student, Surety Real Estate, Virginia Beach, Va., 1979; AS, Tidewater Community Coll., Virginia Beach, 1981. Cert. radiologist. Mem. real estate sales Mary Spady Realty, Norfolk, Va., 1979-80; owner Custom Cakes, Virginia Beach, 1975—; x-ray tech. Cutler Army Hosp., Ft. Devens, Mass., 1986-87; x-ray tech. EKG, phlebotomist Henry Haywood Hosp., Gardner, Mass., 1987; X-ray tech. Emerson Hosp., Concord, Mass., 1988-89, Winchendon (Mass.) Health Ctr. sub. Henry Heywood Hosp., 1989—. V.p. LWV, Moore, Okla., 1968. Democrat. Lutheran.

JACKSON, CONSTANCE CORDICE, reading consultant; b. Winchester, Mass.; d. Conrad and Florence (Smith) Cordice; m. Eugene B. Jackson. BS in Elem. Edn., Boston U., 1963, MEd in Reading, Lang., Elem. Edn., 1966, EdD in Reading, Elem. Edn., 1974. Tchr. Scituate (Mass.) Pub. Schs., 1963-64; tchr. Marshfield (Mass.) Pub. Schs., 1964-68, reading cons., 1968-89; teaching fellow Boston U., 1972. Bd. dir. Marshfield Right to Read Effort, 1973-76. Com. Mem. NEA, Internat. Reading Assn., Mass., Marshfield tchrs. assns., Mass. Reading Assn., Delta Kappa Gamma, Pi Lambda Theta. Home: PO Box 126 N Marshfield MA 02059 Office: Box 126-195 Oak St North Marshfield MA 02059

JACKSON, DELLA ROSETTA HAYDEN, civic worker, educator, author; b. Mill Spring, N.C., Mar. 2, 1905; d. Robert Twitty and Amanda (Petty) Hayden; B.A., Johnson C. Smith U., 1948; M.A., N.C. Coll., 1956; m. G. Franklin Davenport, Sept. 28, 1930 (dec. Jan. 1936); children—Evelyn Frances Davenport Petty, Amanda Elizabeth Davenport Gray, Robert Franklin; m. 2d, Clarence Eugene Jackson, Oct. 30, 1943 (dec. Mar. 1951); children—Mae Carolyn Jackson Williams, Clarence Stinson. Tchr., Stony Knoll Sch., Polk County, N.C., 1927-30, Tryon Sch., 1930-31, Pea Ridge Sch., 1932-39, Union Grove Sch., 1939-48, Edmund Embury Sch., 1949-51, Cobb Elementary Sch., Tryon, N.C., 1951-65; tchr. adult edn. Isothermal Community Coll., Mill Spring, N.C., 1971-77; organizer, librarian Stony Knoll Community Library, 1937—, pres., 1972—, also chmn. bd. trustees; spl. edn. tchr. Polk Central High Sch., Mill Spring, 1966-69; resource person Polk County Community Schs., 1982—. Mem. Central Highlands Health Council, 1968-70; 2d v.p. Polk County Homemakers Council; pres. Polk County Extension Homemakers, 1974-75; sec.-treas. Polk County Community Devel. Council; mem. Polk County Family Life Study Com., 1978-79; mem. Ancillary Manpower Planning Bd., Region C, 1972-82, mem. exec. com., 1976-83; leader 4-H clubs, 1965-85; v.p. Polk County Child Devel. Council, 1971-75, Eastern Appalachian Children's Council, 1971-73; chmn. Polk County Child Care Com., 1971-73; mem. Polk County Emergency Med. Service Adv. Com., 1973-75, Polk County Commn. on Aging, 1974—, N.C. Child Care, N.C. Children's 100; bd. dirs. Isothermal Health Council, sec., 1972-76; bd. dirs. Polk County Mental Health Council, 1972-73, St. Luke Hosp. Aux., 1970-77, 85—, Regional Health Council Eastern Appalachia, 1970-77, Polk County unit Am. Cancer Soc., 1979-82; bd. govs., mem. exec. com. Western N.C. Health System Agy., 1977-81, mem. resource devel. com., 1978-81; steering com. Gov.'s Regional Conf. on Leadership Devel. for Women, 1978-79; mem. Region C Employment and Tng. Adv. Com., 1978-83, Polk County Interagy. Council, 1978-81, Polk County Family Life Council, 1978; club rep. Polk County Community Resource Council, 1986—; parliamentarian Grand Ct. Order Calanthe, N.C., 1985; v.p., bd. dirs. Polk County Lit. Coun., 1988—. Named Mother of Year, Afro, 1948, Mother of Year, Homemakers Council Polk County and Western Dist. N.C., 1971; recipient cert. service N.C. Recreation Soc., 1962; cert. leadership for service Western N.C. Community Devel. Program Asheville Agrl. Devel. Council, 1962; award for outstanding leadership and service Western N.C. Devel. Assn., 1979, Woman of Year, 1979; cert. of appreciation Western N.C. Health System Agy., 1981; cert. of award Polk County Hist. Assn., 1980; Sunday Sch. Tchr. of Yr., Stony Knoll C.M.E. Ch., 1980; inducted into Second Wind Hall of Fame, 1990. Mem. LWV (dir. 1970—), Stony Knoll Recreation Soc., Polk County Hist. Assn. Clubs: Order of Calanthe (worthy counselor), Stony Knoll Community (pres. 1959-62). Author: Special Approaches for Sunday School in Small Churches, 1981; Poems of Experience and Emotion, 1981; Twenty Little Prayers, 1981; Let My People Go, 1982; If (Meditations on Christ's Promises), 1989. Home: 433 Haque Rd Mill Spring NC 28756 Office: Box 95 Spring NC 28756

JACKSON, DOLLY JOYCE, educator; b. Orangeburg, S.C., Jan. 6, 1932; d. Hammie Murray and Dolly Conley (Robinson) J. BS, Winthrop Coll., 1953; MS, U. Tenn., 1965, EdD, 1969. Tchr. phys. edn. Jr. high L.A. Pub. Schs., 1959-60; tchr. phys. edn. San Jacinto High Sch., Houston, 1960-62; from tchr. to prin. Rome (Ga.) City Schs., 1962-69; prof. Berry Coll., Mt. Berry, Ga., 1969—. Contbr. articles to profl. jours. Mem. AAUW (bd. dirs. Rome chpt. 1968—, pres. 1968-70), LWV (pres. Rome chpt. 1987-89, bd. dirs. 1990—), Delta Kappa Gamma (pres. 1970-72, parliamentarian 1984—), Kappa Delta Pi (sponsor 1988—). Democrat. Baptist. Office: Berry Coll Box 5019 Mount Berry GA 30149

JACKSON, ELAINE FRANCIS, children's librarian; b. Attleboro, Mass., Jan. 30, 1945; d. Robert Wheaton and Thelma Arlene (Bullock) Francis; m. Jeffrey Jon Jackson, Aug 21, 1965; children: Timothy Mark, Rebecca Lyn. BS in Edn., Bridgewater State Coll., 1966, MEd in Sch. Librarianship, 1990. Cert. elem. tchr., sch. libr., unified media specialist. Tchr. Elizabeth Pole Sch., Taunton, Mass., 1966-67, Braddock Elem. Sch., Annandale, Va., 1967-68, Apalachin-Owego Elem., Apalachin, N.Y., 1968-69, Brick House Sch., Taunton, 1977-83; head libr. Berkley Pub. Libr., Berkley, Mass., 1986-88; children's libr. Norton (Mass.) Pub. Libr., 1989—. Sec. Raynham (Mass.) Youth Soccer, 1978-86. Mem. AAUW, New Eng. Libr. Assn., Mass. Libr. Assn. (exec. bd. children's issues sect.), Order of Eastern Star (worthy matron Rose Croix chpt. 1976-77, sec. 1978-87, dep. grand matron Grand Chpt. Mass. 1978-79). Office: Norton Pub Libr PO Box U Norton MA 02766

JACKSON, FREDA LUCILLE, clergywoman, church administrator, editor; b. Sikeston, Mo., Sept. 15, 1928; d. Jesse Freda and Ruby Lucille (Carter) Andres; student Three Rivers Jr. Coll., 1969, Central Bible Coll., Springfield, Mo., 1973; B.S., Drury Coll., 1980; M.A. in Bibl. Lit., Assemblies of God Theol. Sem., 1986; m. Thomas Lowell Jackson, Oct. 2, 1947; children—Stephen Andres, Elizabeth Ann, Thomas Dean. Bookkeeper, Aduddel Wholesale Auto Parks, Sikeston, 1947-48; pvt. sec. to v.p. So. Ice & Coal Co., Memphis, 1948-49; sec. firm Bailey & Craig, Sikeston, 1950-56, firm Blanton & Blanton, 1956-57; ordained to ministry Assemblies of God Ch., 1983; promotions coordinator, editor deferred giving and trusts dept., gen. council Assemblies of God, Springfield, Mo., 1974—; tchr. English, Central Bibl. Coll., 1986—. Mem. Alpha Sigma Lambda, Womens Ministries, Maranatha Aux. Editor: New Dimensions, 1979—, Maranatha newsletter, 1977; contbr. articles to denominational publs. Home: 2407 W Atlantic St Springfield MO 65803 Office: 1445 Boonville Ave Springfield MO 65802

JACKSON, GERALDINE, small business owner; b. Barnesville, Ga., Oct. 30, 1934; d. Charles Brown and Christine (Maddox) J.; 1 child, Prentiss Andrew. Nurses aide Grady Hosp., Atlanta; mail handler U.S. Post Office, Cicero, Ill.; sec., tour guide Walgreens Lab., Chgo.; credit clk. Sterling Jewelers, Atlanta; owner, broker Gerris Automobile Leasing Svc., Atlanta. Mem. Nat. Law Enforcement Officer Meml. Fund; active Sacred Heart League. Mem. AARP, DAV, Internat. Assn. Chiefs Police, Ga. Sheriff's Assn., Nat. Right To Life. Democrat. Home: 1890 Myrtle Dr SW #422 Atlanta GA 30311

JACKSON, HAZEL, educator; b. Valdosta, Ga., Jan. 18, 1963; d. Arthur Franlin and Betty Jean (Adkins) J. AA, Brewton-Parker Coll., Mt. Vernon, Ga., 1983; BS, N. Ga. Coll., 1986; MS, Valdosta State Coll., 1990. Cert. tchr., Ga. Tchr. severe and profound mental handicaps Colquitt County Bd. Edn., Moultrie, Ga., 1986-89; tchr. learning disabled and behavior disordered Garrison-Pilcher Elem. Sch., Thomasville, Ga., 1989-90; tchr. severe and profound mental handicaps Magnolia-Chappelle Sch., 1990—. Mem. NAFE, Assn. for Supervision and Curriculum Devel., Coun. for Exceptional Children. Baptist. Office: Magnolia-Chappelle Sch Magnolia Rd Thomasville GA 31792-9801

JACKSON, HELEN CASSANDRA, educator; b. Washington, Feb. 10, 1951; d. Robert Alfonso and William Mae (McCrary) Murray; m. John Dubois Conway, Apr. 19, 1969 (div. Mar. 1976); children: Bagiyyah, Malik, Isa; m. John Wanel Jackson Jr., Aug. 25, 1983; children: Zakiya, John. BS in Physics and Math., U. D.C., 1977; postgrad., Johns Hopkins U., 1978-80. Aerospace mathematician NASA/Goddard, Greenbelt, Md., 1978-80; physicist, engr. Western Union, Fairfax, Va., 1980-81; test engr. Telesystems Comsat, Fairfax, 1981-82; sr. elec. engr. NASA/Bendix, Greenbelt, Md., 1982-83; home educator Yirah Youch Acad., Tex., Pa., 1983—; pres., prin. investigator Electro genesis, Petersburg, Tenn., 1987—; computer instr. City Temple Jr. Acad., Dallas, 1984-85; electronics instr. Ala. A&M U., Huntsville, 1987-89; cons. rsch. scientist Tenn. Applied Phys. Scis., Fayetteville, 1989-90; mentor, engr. NASA/Summer Inst. in Tech., Greenbelt, 1978-80; radio speaker Sta. WHUR Radio, Washington, 1972-73; panel guest pub. TV, 1989. Author numerous books, 1978-83, (with others) Home School Burnout, 1988, Great Poems of the Western World, 1979. Lobbyist Eagle Forum, Nashville, 1988—, Home Sch. Assn., Dallas, Harrisburg, Pa., 1984-88; GED tutor for disadvantaged, Petersburg, 1985—. Named Outstanding Nat. Homemaker, Eagle Forum, 1988; participant Torch Run Winter Olympic Relays, 1980. Mem. NAFE, Tenn. Homesch. Assn. Home: Rt 2 Box 131 K Petersburg TN 37144

JACKSON, HERMOINE PRESTINE, psychologist; b. Wilmington, Del., Mar. 11, 1945; d. Herman Preston and Ella Brooks (Roane) Jackson. BA, Elizabethtown (Pa.) Coll., 1967; MA, Ohio State U., 1979, PhD, 1990. Tchr. Wilmington (Del.) pub. sch. sys., 1967-68, Phila. Pub. Sch. Sys., 1968-74; psychologist Midland (Mich.) Hosp., 1979-81, Cen. Mich. U., Mt. Pleasant, 1979-81, West Seneca (N.Y.) Devel. Ctr., 1981—; mem. admissions/discharge com. St. Augustine Ctr., Buffalo, 1983—. Co-author test manual: Manual of Assessment Instruments for the MR/DD Population, 1978. Task force mem. Youth Task Force, Buffalo, 1989. Named Outstanding Instr., Cen. Mich. U., 1981. Mem. Am. Psychol. Assn., Am. Assn. on Mental Retardation, Coalition of 100 Blk. Women (corres. sec. 1988—). Home: 1 Norwalk Ave Buffalo NY 14216 Office: West Seneca Devel Ctr 1200 East and West Rd West Seneca NY 14224

JACKSON, JANE W., interior designer; b. Asheville, N.C., Aug. 5, 1944; d. James and Willie Mae (Stoner) Harris; m. Bruce G. Jackson; children: Yvette, Scott. Student, Boston U., 1964; BA, Leslie Coll., 1967; postgrad., Artisan Sch. Interior Design, 1980-82. Tchr. Montessori, Brookline, Mass., 1969-72; interior designer, owner Nettle Creek Shop, Honolulu, 1980-88; owner Wellesley Interiors, Honolulu, 1988—. Active Mayor's Com. for Small Bus., Honolulu, 1984. Mem. Am. Soc. Interior Design Industry Found., Honolulu Club. Democrat. Office: Wellesley Interiors PO Box 1365 Kaneohe HI 96744

JACKSON, JANICE THERESA, pharmacist; b. Jasper, Fla., Nov. 3, 1960; d. Wilmer and Henrietta Deloris (Udell) J. BS, Fla. A&M U., 1982; postgrad. in pharmacy, U. Ill., Chgo. Lic. pharmacist, Ala., Fla. Grad. pharmacy intern U. Pharmacy, Tampa, Fla., 1982-83, Tampa Gen. Hosp., 1983-84; relief retail pharmacist Jack Eckerd, Inc., Gainesville, Fla., 1984-90; staff pharmacist Marion Community Hosp., Ocala, Fla., 1984-89, Putnam Community Hosp., 1989-90; researcher in med. microbiology. Mem. NAACP (sec. local chpt.), Am. Soc. Hosp. Pharmacists, Fla. Pharmacy Assn., Alachua County Assn. Pharmacists, Kappa Psi (v.p. Psiettes 1981). Mem. A.M.E. Ch. Home: 4421 NW 20th Terr Gainesville FL 32605 Office: Putnam Community Hosp Hwy 20 W Palatka FL 32078-0778

JACKSON, JENNIFER CLAY, broadcast executive; b. Lexington, Ky., Apr. 25, 1960; d. Julian Jr. and Betty Jean (Fields) J. BA in Communications, U. Ky., 1982. Activities dir. Meadowbrook Care Home, Lexington, 1983; receptionist Lexington Computer Store, 1983-85; traffic mgr. Learning Channel, Lexington, 1985-90. Sunday sch. tchr. local Bapt. Ch.; cheerleader coach Little League, Lexington. Mem. NAFE. Home: 1155 Oakwood Dr Lexington KY 40511 Office: 1045 Georgetown Rd Lexington KY 40511

JACKSON, JEWEL, state youth authority official; b. Shreveport, La., June 3, 1942; d. Willie Burghardt and Bernice Jewel (Mayberry) Norton; children: Steven, June Kelly, Michael, Anthony. With Calif. Youth Authority, 1965—, group supr., San Andreas and Santa Rosa, 1965-67, youth counselor, Ventura, 1967-78, sr. youth counselor, Stockton, 1978-81, parole agt., 1986, treatment team supr., program mgr., Whittier and Ione, 1981—; speaker U. Pacific Youth Motivational Project, Stockton, 1985-89. Mem. Women in Criminal Justice-North (co-chair 1974-76), Assn. Black Correctional Workers (chpt. v.p. 1979, editor newsletter 1978-80). Avocations: reading, horseback riding, writing poetry and short stories, designing clothing. Home: PO Box 898 Ione CA 95640

JACKSON, JOY JUANITA, educator; b. New Orleans, Oct. 8, 1928; d. Oliver Daniel and Oneida Christina (Drouant) Jackson; student La. State U., 1946-49; B.A., Tulane U., 1951, M.A., 1958, Ph.D., 1961. Feature writer New Orleans Times-Picayune, 1951-56; instr. Nicholls State Coll., Thibodaux, La., 1961-62, asst. prof., 1962-66; asst. prof. Southeastern La. U., Hammond, 1966-68, asso. prof., 1968-73, prof. history, 1973—, dir. Center for Regional Studies and univ. archives, 1982—. AAUW Irma E. Voight fellow, 1960-61. Mem. Am., La. (dir. 1966-68, pres. 1977-78), So. Hist. Assn., S.E. La. Hist. Assn. (pres. Hammond 1978), Oral History Assn.

Author: New Orleans in the Gilded Age, 1969. Home: 1411 University Dr Hammond LA 70401

JACKSON, KARLA LYNN, management information services account representative; b. West Point, N.Y., Nov. 3, 1956; d. Fred D. and Margaret Erika (Buckmann) Spinks; m. David Jefferson Ashmore, Feb. 19, 1977 (div. Dec. 17, 1979); 1 child, Erika Margaret Augusta; m. Randy Robert Jackson, Aug. 25, 1990. BA, Ind. U.-Purdue U. at Indpls., 1982; MS, Ind. U., 1986. Mgr. Eastside Chiropractic Clinic, Indpls., 1978-80; English tutor univ. div. Ind. U.-Purdue U. at Indpls., 1980-82, composition instr. English dept., 1982-83, tech. writer computing services, 1983-84; tech. writer Ind. U. Adminstrv. Computing, 1984-87; computer tng. coordinator Melvin Simon and Assocs., Inc., Indpls., 1987-88, customer support administrator, 1988-90, MIS account rep., 1990—. Author 4 articles, 5 book revs. and 20 pub. poems; editor: Literary Jour., Genesis, All-Am. Mag., Am. Collegiate Press Assn., 1983. Mem. Indpls. Nuclear Weapons Freeze, Inc. Mem. Soc. Tech. Communication (Cert. of Achievement 1985), Info. Ctr. Mgmt. Assn. (treas.), Sigma Delta Chi, Pi Lambda Theta. Democrat. Roman Catholic. Office: Melvin Simon & Assocs Inc 2 West Washington Indianapolis IN 46207

JACKSON, KATE, actress; b. Birmingham, Ala., Oct. 29, 1949; d. Hogan and Ruth Jackson; m. Andrew Stevens, Aug. 23, 1978 (div. 1981); m. David Greenwald, 1982 (div. 1984). Student, U. Miss.; student, Birmingham U.; grad., Am. Acad. Dramatic Arts, 1971. Worked as model. Appeared in TV series Dark Shadows, 1966-71, The Rookies, 1972-76, Charlie's Angels, 1976-79, The Scarecrow and Mrs. King, 1983-87; TV appearances include Movin' On, The Jimmy Stewart Show; TV movies include: Satan's School for Girls, 1973, Death Cruise, 1974, Killer Bees, 1974, Death Scream, 1975, Charlie's Angels, 1976, Death at Love House, 1976, James at 15, 1977, Topper, 1979, Inmates: A Love Story, 1981, Thin Ice, 1981, Listen to Your Heart, 1983, Baby Boom, 1988; motion picture appearances include: Dirty Tricks, 1981, Making Love, 1982; dir. numerous episodes The Scarecrow and Mrs. King. Recipient 3 Emmy award nominations Nat. Acad. TV Arts and Scis. Mem. AFTRA, Screen Actors Guild, Actors Equity Assn., Dirs. Guild Am. Office: care Triad Artists Inc 10100 Santa Monica Blvd 16th Fl Los Angeles CA 90067*

JACKSON, KAY LYN, telecommunications executive; b. Ft. Worth, Sept. 11, 1962; d. Elbert Sam and Mildred Ann (Streeter) J. AA, Tarrant County Jr. Coll., 1983; postgrad., U. Tex. With telecommunications dept. R-N Communications, Arlington, Tex., 1982-85, Communications Corp. Am., Dallas, 1985, Expertel, Inc., Dallas, 1985-86; with ins. dept. Farmers Ins. Co., Dallas, 1986-87; with Southwestern Bell Telecom, 1987-88; with telecommunications dept. Bozell, Inc., Dallas, 1988-89; with Octel Communications, Dallas, 1989—; telecommunications cons., Dallas, 1985—. Octel Communications scholar, 1989, Southwestern Bell Telecom-Tech scholar, 1987-88. Women in Communications scholar, 1980; recognized for support 20001 Lrng. Ctrs., 1989. Mem. NAFE, Internat. SLI Users Assn. (chmn. conf. com. 1989—). Democrat. Methodist. Home: 300 Bluegrass Ln Euless TX 76039

JACKSON, LELA EVELYNE, corporate executive; b. Mesilla Park, N.Mex. Feb. 11, 1941; d. Willie L. and Ruth (Boggess) Ashworth; m. Robert C. Jackson, Apr. 21, 1969; children—Cynthia Sams, Edward Taber, Elizabeth Taber Brown; adopted children—Shiela Prokuski, Robert Jackson, Regina Jackson. B.A. in Acctg., Bakersfield Coll., 1970; cert. fed. taxation Tex. A&M U., 1983. Ptnr. Personalized Bookkeeping, Bakersfield, 1969-71, Jackson & Jackson, Vivian, La., 1977-79; pres. Le Jac Inc., Vivian, 1979—. Subsect. mem. Nat. Republican Com., Washington, 1982—. Mem. North Caddo C. of C. (co-founder, sec. 1980-81), Profl. Cons. Baptist. Avocations: fishing; gardening; reading. Home: PO Box 747 Vivian LA 71082 Office: Le Jac Inc 219 W Kentucky Vivian LA 71082

JACKSON, LOIS KATHRYN, educational institution executive; b. Flint, Mich., July 31, 1927; d. Milo N. and Edith (Kelly) Wood; m. Warren G. Jackson, Oct. 27, 1945; children—Connie L., Edith A., Christine K. B.A. cum laude, Asbury Coll., 1956; student U. Coimbra, Lisbon, Portugal, 1957-59, Scarritt Coll., Vanderbilt U., 1956-57. Treas., cost acct. Mobil Home Co., 1948-52; missionary educator Bd. Global Ministries, United Meth. Ch., Angola, Zaire, 1959-77; administrv. asst. to supt. Navajo United Meth. Mission Sch., Farmington, N.Mex., 1978-81; bus. mgr. Navajo Mission Acad., Farmington, 1981-87, compt., 1988-89; bus. ops. analyst Presbyn. Med. Svcs., 1990—; office mgr. Tech, Inc., 1989-90, Mass/Mutual Ins. Co, 1990—. Past chmn. program Council on Ministries United Meth. Ch. Mem. Nat. Assn. Female Execs., Am. Mgmt. Assn., Am. Inst. Profl. Bookkeepers.

JACKSON, LOLA HIRDLER, art instructor; b. Faribault, Minn., Mar. 2, 1942; d. Earl Arthur and Marian Barbara (Pavek) Hirdler; children: Carilyn, Cherilyn, Marc. BS in Art Edn., Mankato State U., 1972, MA, 1975. Cert. tchr. Art instr. YWCA, Mankato, Minn., 1968-70, Mankato (Minn.) Area Vocat. Tech. Inst., 1971-72; pres., tchr., art dir. Jackson Studios, Mankato, Minn., 1969-78; art tchr. New Richland (Minn.) High Sch., Mankato (Minn.) State U., 1973-74; pres. Lola Ltd. Lt'ee Art Distbn., N.C., 1976—; tchr., art Lincoln Sch. Math. and Sci. Tech., Greensboro, N.C., 1988-90, chmn. dept., 1988, 89—; tchr., chmn. art dept. Shallotte Mid. Sch., 1990—; pres., bd. mem. Fine Arts Inc., Gallery 500, Mankato, 1972-75. Staff artist The Reporter, 1970-73. Bd. mem. Mankato Area Found., 1976-83. Recipient award Busch Found. Minn. Arts Coun., Nat. Endowment Arts, 1974. Mem. Profl. Pictures Framers Assn., N.C. Assn. of Edn. Republican. Roman Catholic.

JACKSON, LORA RUTHE THOMPSON, parliamentarian, corporate executive; b. Ft. Worth, Oct. 29, 1920; d. John Lyle and Florence (Ector) Thompson; m. Vernon Jackson, Sept. 10, 1944; children: Xanna Yvonne Jackson Young, Jorja Annette Jackson Clemson. Student, Ft. Worth Christian Coll., 1960, Christian Coll. of S.W., 1969. Registered profl. parliamentarian. Clk. mail and advt. Mut. Benefit Ins. Co., 1940-42; clk. to exec. sec. N.Am. Aviation, 1942-45; exec. sec. TEMCO Mfg., 1945-47, Luscombe Aircraft, 1947-50; sec., gen. office supr. SA-SO Sign Mfg. Co., 1950-53; co-owner All-Quality Sign Co., 1953-59; co-owner, v.p., office supr., dir. pub. relations Jackson Vending Supply, Inc., Grand Prairie, Tex., 1959—; tchr., judge parliamentary law; bd. dirs. 1st Nat. Bank Red Oak. Host, dir.: (cable TV show) It's Happening in Grand Prairie, 1981—, History of Grand Prairie, 1981—; producer, dir. city council's agenda preview weekly on govt. cable TV channel; contbr. articles on parliamentary law, beautification and community improvement, and cultural arts to mags. Mem. Dallas County Sch. Bd., 1974—, Dallas County Hist. Commn., 1974-82, Grand Prairie Civil Def. Commn., 1959—; chmn. Grand Prairie Arts and Hist. Preservation Commn., 1976-85, Grand Prairie Bi-Centennial, 1974-76; mem., past chmn. Grand Prairie Community and Home Improvements Commn., 1964-85; mem. spl. funds com. Grand Prairie Ind. Sch. Dist.; state treas. Keep Tex. Beautiful, Inc., 1987; active local, council and dist. PTA's; regional v.p. Tex. PTA; hon. life mem. Nat. Congress Parents and Tchrs., Tex. Congress Parents and Tchrs.; Grand Prairie Hosp. Aux.; mem. council City of Grand Prairie, 1985—, mayor pro-tem, 1986-88. Recipient Mrs. Lyndon B. Johnson Environ. Keep Am. Beautiful award, 1977, award in conservation Tex. Forest Service, 1976; named Woman of Yr., Grand Prairie Daily News, 1979. Mem. Grand Prairie Friends of the Library (pres. 1978-80), Grand Prairie C. of C. (pres. 1982, Women of Yr. 1967, Citizen of Yr., 1969), Nat. Assn. Parliamentarians (nat. pub. relations chair 1987-89), Tex. Assn. Parliamentarians (state pres. 1974-75), North Tex. Assn. Parliamentarians (pres. 1988—), Beautify Tex. Council (state pres. 1976-78, Tex. Bluebonnet State award 1978), Grand Prairie Hist. Orgn., (life, sec., founding pres.). Democrat. Mem. Ch. of Christ. Clubs: Grand Prairie Bus. and Profl. Women's (treas., pres. 1983-84, Woman of Yr. 1976, 82), Grand Prairie Garden (pres., Woman of Yr. 1975). Lodge: Soroptimists (corr. sec. Grand Prairie chpt., regional parliamentarian nat. chpt.). Home and Office: 200 Meyers Rd Grand Prairie TX 75050

JACKSON, LORETTA YOUNG, real estate broker, consultant; b. Chickasha, Okla., Feb. 6, 1935; d. Clarence and Lillie Bell (Curry) Blunt; m. Harold Wayne Jackson; children: Cynthia Wyvonne Jackson Anderson, Limon Jackson. Diploma in real estate, Blackwood Bus. Coll., 1978; BS in Bus. Adminstrn. and Sociology, U. Sci. and Arts of Okla., 1984; postgrad., U. Okla., 1985. Gen. ledger bookkeeper Pool Mortgage Co., Chickasha, 1967-69, asst. mgr., loan supr., 1971-84; asst. loan supr. Am. Express Internat. Bank, Heilbronn, Fed. Republic of Germany, 1969-71; chief teller, bookkeeper Okla. Nat. Bank & Trust, Chickasha, 1971; campaign coord., cons. Youth Svcs. of Grady County, Chickasha, 1985-86; instr. real estate Can. Valley Area Vocat.-Tech, Chickasha, 1988—; owner, broker, cons. Jackson Real Estate, Chickasha, 1988—. Mem. Pres.'s Carter Conf. on Black Community Concerns, Washington, 1979; chmn., co-chmn., sec., treas. Grady County Dem. Cen. Com., Chickasha, 1975-83; sec.-treas. Dem. Party Okla., 1983-87; mem. U. Sci. and Arts of Okla. Found., 1984—, sec., 1989; chmn. Chickasha City Planning Commn., 1985—; bd. dirs. Okla. State Banking Bd., Oklahoma City, 1980—. Named Woman of Yr., Bus. and Profl. Women, 1979, 80. Mem. Nat. Assn. Realtors, Grady County Bd. Realtors, Bus. and Profl. Women, LWV (treas. Okla. chpt. 1989—), AAUW (chmn. 1989—, Outstanding Woman of South Plains award 1982), Ambassadors (pres. Chickasha chpt. 1985), Order Eastern Star, Heriones of Jeroines (most ancient matron), Pi Gamma Mu (life). Home: 322 E Dakota Ave Chickasha OK 73018

JACKSON, LADY LOYD APPLEBY, personnel executive; b. Toccoa, Ga., July 8, 1946; d. Samuel Cecil and Lillian Loyd (Collins) Appleby; m. Joseph Howard Torrence, July 27, 1968 (div. 1973); 1 dau., Katherine Loyd; m. Thomas Houston Jackson, May 3, 1974; children: Thomas Houston, Jr., John Andrew. B.A., Mary Baldwin Coll., 1968. Cert. profl. in human resources. Exec. trainee Sears, Roebuck & Co., Phila., 1968-69; tng. adminstr. Genesco, Inc., Nashville, 1969-72; adminstrv. asst. State Tenn. Dept. Human Svcs., Nashville, 1972-73, dir. office svcs., 1973-77, dir. personnel, 1977-80; dir. personnel ARC, Nashville, 1980-81; asst. dir. personnel Nashville Electric Svc., 1981—; sec.-treas. The Guide Co., Inc., 1984—. Vice chmn. bd. Mcpl. Auditorium Bd., Nashville, 1976-77; sec., treas. Tenn. Personnel Adv. Council, Nashville, 1978-79; mem. Outlook Nashville Personnel Com., Leadership Nashville, 1986-87; bd. dirs. United Methodist Neighborhood Ctrs., Nashville, 1984—, chmn. personnel com., 1985; bd. dirs. ARC Nashville chpt., 1988—, Am. Lung Assn. Tenn., 1988—; cons. Jr. Achievement, 1986. Recipient Laurel Soc. award Mary Baldwin Coll., 1968, Bess Maddox award, 1987; named Woman of Yr. Bus. and Profl. Women's Club, 1987. Indsl. Personnel Assn. (chmn. operating com. 1982-83), Indsl. Personnel Assn. (sec. treas. v.p. 1984, pres. 1985), Am. Soc. Personnel Adminstrs. (program com. chmn. 1984, sec. 1986, v.p. 1987, pres. Nashville chpt. 1988), Internat. Assn. Quality Circles (co-founder, dir. Central Tenn. chpt. 1982-83, James House Williamson award 1989). Democrat. Mem. Woodmont Christian Ch. Office: Nashville Electric Svc 1214 Chruch St Nashville TN 37203

JACKSON, LYNDA KAY, leasing company executive; b. Ottumwa, Iowa, Sept. 26, 1949; d. James Leon and Evelyn Melosina (Hartwig) J. Student, Iowa State U., 1967-70. From sec. to state comptroller Iowa State Dept. Transp., Ames, 1967-70; cash analyst McCall Pattern Co., Manhattan, Kans., 1970-71; credit analyst Beneficial Fin., Manhattan, 1971-72; mgmt. trainee CIT Fin. Services, Des Moines, 1973-75; loan mgr. CIT Fin. Services, Ft. Dodge, Iowa, 1975-76; dist. sales mgr. CIT Fin. Services, St. Louis, 1976-80; v.p. sales TriContinental Leasing Corp., Paramus, N.J., 1980-86; v.p. Copelco Credit Corp., Upper Saddle River, N.J., 1986—. Republican. Baptist. Home: 24 Peach Hill N Ramsey NJ 07446 Office: Copelco Credit Corp 10 Mountainview Rd Upper Saddle River NJ 07458

JACKSON, MARY L., health services executive; b. Phila., June 25, 1938; d. John Francis and Helen Catherine (Peranteau) Martin; m. Howard Clark Jackson III, Dec. 17, 1954; children: Michael, Mark, Brian. Student Bucks County Community Coll., 1977-83. Asst. mgr. retail div. Sears Roebuck & Co., Bensalem, Pa., 1972-77; educator, adminstr., dir. Trevose Behavior Modification Program, Pa., 1975—, leadership tng. workshops, 1979—; salesman Makefield Real Estate, Morrisville, Pa., 1977-78; mortgage fin. cons. Tom Dunphy Real Estate, Feasterville, Pa., 1978-81; weight loss cons., Hulmeville, Pa., 1984—. Writer monthly column The Modifier, 1977—. Mem. Bucks County Bd. Realtors, Hulmeville Hist. Soc. (a founder, charter mem.). Democrat. Presbyterian. Avocations: reading; classical music; speed walking; knitting; fishing. Home: 218 Main St Hulmeville PA 19047

JACKSON, MONA BETHEL, educational administrator, assistant prinicipal; b. Miami, Fla., Mar. 7, 1947; d. Charles E. Bethel and Olga Isabel (Goodman) Bethel Williams; m. Herman Jackson, Dec. 31, 1968; children: Keane Sean, Herman. BS, Fla. A&M U., 1969; MEd, Fla. Atlantic U., 1973. Cert. tchr., Fla. Sci. tchr. Dade County pub. schs., Miami, 1970-74, sci. tchr./counselor, 1974-75, counselor, 1975-82, ednl. specialist, 1982-84, project mgr., 1984-86, asst. prin., 1986—; cons.; curriculum coordinator Perrine Crime Prevention Program, Miami, 1979-82. Author: (manual) Dollars and Cents: A Guide for Scholarship Applicants, 1980, Focus on Careers, 1984. Pres., Dade County Sickle Cell Found., 1983-86; sec. bd. dirs. Haitian Refugee Ctr., Miami, 1983-85; vestry Christ Episcopal Ch., 1984-86. Named Tchr. of Yr., Drew Jr. High Sch., 1972; recipient plaque Dade County Sickle Cell Found., 1981. Mem. Dade County Personnel and Guidance Assn. (pres. 1983-84, plaque 1984), Fla. Assn. Counseling and Devel. (pres.-elect 1985-86, pres. 1986-87, conv. exec. 1986-87, plaque 1985, 87), Fla. Assn. Sci. Tchrs., Women Involved Now, Phi Delta Kappa, Delta Sigma Theta (pres. Beta Alpha chpt. 1967-68, pres. Miami chpt. 1976-80). Democrat. Sec. vestry Christ Episcopal Ch., 1984-86.—. Home: 8970 SW 126th Terr Miami FL 33176

JACKSON, MONA MARIA, accountant, educator; b. Stockholm, Apr. 30, 1944; came to U.S., 1964; d. John Sigvard and Elsa Maria (Evert) Alshammar; m. Julius Leon Jackson, Dec. 31, 1976; children: Timothy John, Mercedes Maria, Julius Deon. BA in Bus. cum laude, U. Guam, 1985; postgrad. in edn., Calif. State U., 1986. Mgr. Security Pacific Nat. Bank, Davis, Calif., 1967-73; acct. R.J. Reynolds Co., Davis, 1973-78; supr. Bank Am., North Highlands, Calif., 1978-80; office mgr. U. Guam, Mangilao, 1983-85; instr. acct. banking and fin. Barclay Coll., San Bernardino, Calif., 1985-87; sr. acct. City of Moreno Valley, Calif., 1987-88; instr. acctg. Nat. Bus. Inst., Riverside, Calif., 1988—; tchr. adult edn. Colton (Calif.) Joint Unified Sch. Dist., 1986—; computer cons., Moreno Valley, 1988—; real estate agt. Tarbell, Realtors. Com. mem. Shared Housing, Riverside, 1988—. Mem. Am. Soc. Pub. Adminstrs., Am. Soc. Women Accts. Democrat. Lutheran. Club: Exchange (Moreno Valley). Home: 24673 Ormista Dr Moreno Valley CA 92388 Office: Nat Bus Inst 4300 Central Ave Riverside CA 92506

JACKSON, MURIEL GRACE, university official; b. Wood-Ridge, N.J., Apr. 21, 1929; d. John David and Lillian Grace (Rogers) Kappeler; B.A., Keuka Coll., 1950; M.S., Columbia U. Sch. Journalism, 1952; grad. U. Mich. Inst. Acad. Adminstrv. Advancement, 1973, Oreg. Mgmt. Devel. Program, 1974; m. Rudolph Lorenz, Mar. 27, 1955 (dec. Nov. 1965); children—John Martin, Tracy Ann, Andrea Grace; m. 2d, Ross E. Jackson, June 10, 1967. Pub. relations asst. St. Lawrence U., 1950-51; editorial asst. Ridgewood (N.J.) News, 1952-53; reporter Binghamton (N.Y.) Press, 1953-56; adminstrv. asst. to pres. San Jose State Coll., 1966-69; asst. to pres. U. Oreg., 1969-75, dir. univ. relations, 1974-79, asst. for adminstrn., 1979-85, asst. v.p. for adminstrn., 1985—, dir. univ. bookstore, 1977-84. Troop leader Western Rivers Council Girl Scouts U.S.A., 1973-74; troop treas. Oreg. Trails Council Boy Scouts Am., 1973-74; sr. warden Episcopal Ch. of the Resurrection, Eugene, Oreg., 1973-74; chmn. Central Convocation Episcopal Diocese of Oreg., 1974-76; spl. events chmn. Lane County (Oreg.) United Way, 1976, 77; bd. dirs. Lane County Cancer Soc., 1978-80; bd. dirs. Lane Meml. Blood Bank, 1979-86, pres., 1984-85. Recipient Disting. Alumna award Keuka Coll., 1975. Mem. Council Advancement and Support of Edn., Eugene C. of C. (chmn. univ. affairs com. 1978, 81, 82), State Bar Assn. Oreg. (mem. bd. state profl. responsibility 1987, 88, 89), Lane County Rubicon Soc. Republican. Home: 2149 Lake Isle Ct Eugene OR 97401 Office: U Oreg 202 Johnson Hall Eugene OR 97403

JACKSON, PATRICIA LEE (MRS. CLIFFORD L. JACKSON), psychologist; b. N.Y.C.; d. Albert George and Lisbeth P. (Lee) Scharf; B.A., Barnard Coll.; M.A., Ph.D., Tchrs. Coll. Columbia U.; m. Clifford L. Jackson. Dir. psychol. testing R. H. Macy & Co., Inc., 1941-49; employment dir. Alexander's Dept. Stores, Inc., Bronx, N.Y., 1949-52; asst. prof. psychology Hunter Coll., N.Y.C., 1951-66, asso. prof., 1966-77, coordinator of counseling services, 1959-71; research dir. Klein Inst. for Aptitude Testing, Inc., N.Y.C., 1953-59, asst. v.p., 1957-59; pvt. practice in psychotherapy, 1964—. Trustee Alfred Adler Inst.; v.p. bd. trustees Ch. of Healing Christ (Emmet Fox Ch.), N.Y.C. Mem. AAAS, Am. Assn. Counseling & Devel., Am. Psychol. Assn., Am. Statis. Assn., Am. Group Psychotherapy Assn., N.Y. Soc. Clin. Psychologists. Author articles in field. Home: 129 E 35th St New York NY 10016-3884

JACKSON, PATRICIA PIKE, director major leadership and gifts, volunteer; b. Pasadena, Calif., May 25, 1960; d. William Byrd and Noelle Irene (Schmutz) J. BA in Psychology, Scripps Coll., 1982; MBA, Claremont (Calif.) Grad. Sch., 1990. Asst. mgr. Pacific Bell, San Jose, Calif., 1982-83; asst. dir. ann. giving Scripps Coll., Claremont, 1983-84; dir. campaign activities Claremont McKenna Coll., 1984-86, dir. corp. rels., 1986-88; dir. major and leadership gifts Mt. Holyoke Coll., S. Hadley, Mass., 1988—; mem. Townhall of L.A., 1985—; sec. Coun. for Advancement and Support of Edn., Calif., 1987-88; co-chair Parents Fundraising Conf., N.E. states, 1989-90; v.p. for programs AAUW, Amherst, Mass., 1990—. Mem. wider rels. Oneonta Congl. Ch., S. Pasadena, Calif., 1983-85, stewardship chair, 1985-88; deacon First Congl. Ch., S. Hadley, 1988—. Mem. AAUW (v.p. programs 1990—), NAFE, Bus. and Profl. Women (Young Careerist award 1987), NOW. Democrat. Office: Mt Holyoke Coll Mary Woolley Hall South Hadley MA 01075

JACKSON, PAULETTE WHITE, nursing administrator, agency executive; b. New Orleans, Jan. 19, 1949; d. Lawrence III and Velma (Jones) White; m. Robert Wardell Tate, June 30, 1964 (div. 1969); children—Robert Jr., Detra Jeanene; m. Tommy Lee Jackson, July 20, 1974; 1 child, Byron. B.S. in Nursing, Southeastern La. U., 1980. Staff nurse Capitol Home Health, Baton Rouge, 1980-81; dir. nursing svc. Hill Haven Nursing Home, Baton Rouge, 1981; nephrology nurse BMA Baton Rouge, 1981-82; staff nurse Ammon's Home Health, Baton Rouge, 1981-83; supr. Greenwell Springs Hosp., La., 1983; owner, adminstr. Faith Home Health Svcs., Baton Rouge, 1983—; pres., owner Abundant Life Nursing Svc., Inc., Baton Rouge, 1989—. Recipient Outstanding Bus. Achievement award Wybirk & Assocs. Inc., 1984. Mem. Beta Beta Beta. Democrat. Avocations: reading; skating; swimming. Home: 5589 Monarch Ave Baton Rouge LA 70811 Office: Faith Home Health Svcs 2034 Wooddale Blvd Ste A Baton Rouge LA 70806 also: Abundant Life Nursing Svc Inc 2055 Wooddale Blvd Baton Rouge LA 70806

JACKSON, REBECCA ANN, controller; b. Harrisburg, Pa., Apr. 2, 1955; d. Edward Richard and Lois Clare (Kuhn) Lewis; m. Keith William Jackson, Oct. 11, 1980; children: Neil Christopher, Eric Daniel. BS, Ind. U. of Pa., 1977. Staff acct. Peat, Marwick, Mitchell & Co., Pitts., 1977-78, sr. acct., 1979, mgr., 1980-81; controller Friendship Fed. Savs. and Loan Assn., Pitts., 1982; asst. v.p. Landmark Savs. Assn., Pitts., 1982-85, v.p. fin. div., 1985—. Mem. AICPA, Pa. Inst. CPAs. Republican. Roman Catholic. Office: Landmark Savs Assn 335 Fifth Ave Pittsburgh PA 15222

JACKSON, ROBERTA PLANT, systems analyst; b. Sharptown, Md.; d. Robert Sidney and Hazel Marie (Adkins) Willing; m. Larry Jackson, Aug. 5, 1988; children: Ryan Plant, Scott, Virginia. BS, U. Md., 1970; cert. project mgmt., IBM Info. Systems Mgmt. Inst. Lead analyst deposits Nat. Bank Ga., Atlanta; programmer analyst Seaboard RR, Jacksonville, Fla.; sci. programmer Univac-Fed. Systems Goddard Space Ctr., NASA, Greenbelt, Md.; systems analyst Credit Bur. Inc. Ga., Atlanta. Mem. NAFE, Am. Mgmt. Assn., Atlanta Jaycees. Home: 5033 Charlemagne Way Lilburn GA 30247

JACKSON, RUTH ROBERTSON, insurance company executive; b. Grady County, Okla., Apr. 17, 1939; d. Gordon James and Rose Viola (Ritter) Robertson; m. Mahlon Bruce Slocum, Dec. 30, 1957 (div. 1972); children: Laura Wynn Robertson, Jill Michele Hawkins; m. Gilbert Shepard Jackson, May 31, 1987. Student, Okla. Coll. for Women, 1957-58, Midwestern U., 1961, El Centro Community Coll., 1980. Legal sec. Wichita County Judge, Wichita Falls, Tex., 1960-62, Douglas E. Bergman Law Firm, Dallas, 1962-64; sec. claims Excalibur Ins. Co., Dallas, 1971-75; sr. sec. claims Excalibur Ins. Co., Carrollton, Tex., 1975-79, asst. sec., treas., 1979-84, pres., 1984—; supr. compliance Excalibur Holdings, Inc., Carrollton, 1979-82, dir. compliance and analysis, 1982-84, dir. underwriting, 1984. Mem. NAFE. Republican. Mem. Metrocrest Bible Ch. Home: 2663 Via Los Altos Carrollton TX 75006 Office: Excalibur Ins Co PO Box 115003 Ste 319 1929 Beltline Carrollton TX 75011-5003

JACKSON, SARAH CURRY, real estate executive; b. Gadsden, Ala., Feb. 18, 1934; d. John Wesley and Lula Nancy (Williams) Curry; m. L.A. Underwood (div. 1972); children: Jeffrey Keith, Sharon Elaine Javis; m. W. Earl Jackson, Aug. 4, 1973; children: Gary Earl, Rodney Lamar. Student, U. Ala., Gadsden, 1952-53. Collection supr. Sears, Roebuck & Co., Gadsden, 1952-76; realtor C21 Dave Anderson Realty, Inc., Sebring, Fla., 1976-81, Scholfield Realtor, Bradenton, Fla., 1981-84, Neal & Neal Realty, Inc., Bradenton, 1984-89, AF&G Realty, Inc., Bradenton, 1989, Neal & Neal Realtors, Bradenton, 1990—; bd. dirs. Manatee County Bd. Realtors, Bradenton, 1982-87, sec., 1987-89, pres.-elect, 1989, pres. 1990—; mem. svc. com. Fla. Assn. Realtors, Orlando, 1989—. Sec. Rep. Women's Forum Fed., Manatee County, 1986, pres.-elect, 1987, pres., 1988, bd. dirs., 1989; precinct committee woman, 1989—. Republican. United Methodist. Office: Neal & Neal Realtors Inc 6220 Manatee Ave W Bradenton FL 34209

JACKSON, SHARON PATRICE, research analyst; b. Washington, Feb. 4, 1958; d. Archibald and Frances (Armwood) J. B.A., Catholic U., 1980; M.A., Johns Hopkins U., 1982. Pub. info. specialist White House Council on Environ. Quality, Washington, 1980-81; research analyst NAACP, Washington, 1981-82; intelligence analyst U.S. Dept. Def., Washington, 1982—. Vol. D.C. Youth Orch. Mem. NAFE, Women in Internat. Security (bd. dirs.), Network of Women in Slavic Studies (bd. dirs.), Johns Hopkins U. Alumni Assn., Cath. U. Alumni Assn. Avocation: cooking, reading.

JACKSON, SHIRLEY CRITE, government agency executive; b. Memphis, June 4, 1940; d. Golden and Lucinda (Berry) Crite; B.A. in Elem. Edn., Northeastern U., 1961, M.A. in Applied Linguistics and English Lang., 1966; postgrad. U. Chgo., George Washington U., 1967-77; Ed.D. in Curriculum and Instrn., Cath. U. Am., 1982; m. Allen D. Jackson, July 5, 1969; 1 son, Dewyane Anthony. Tchr., Chgo. Public Schs., 1961-66, high sch. English cons., 1966-68, coordinator reading, lang. arts, high sch. English programs, 1968-72; communication skills and math. cons., program coordinator D.C. Health Pub. Co., Lexington, Mass., 1972-75; prof. U. Maine, Portland/Gorham, 1975-77; tech. asst. to state depts. edn. Right to Read Program, U.S. Office Edn., Washington, 1975, program devel. br. chief Right to Read Program, 1975-77, dep. dir. program, 1977, dir. program, 1977-78, dir. Nat. Basic Skills Improvement Program, 1978-81, dir. basic edn. programs, 1979-81, acting dep. asst. sec. ednl. support programs, 1981-82, dir. state and local ednl. programs, 1982; asso. dir. Teaching and Learning Research Programs Nat. Inst. Edn., 1982—; dir. edn. Young Astronaut Council; conf. speaker; dir. analysis and data collection service Office Civil Rights, Washington; mem. Nat. Brain Trust on Edn. of Congressional Black Caucus; mem. adv. council Nat. Center for the Book, Library of Congress; mem. nat. adv. council ERIC Reading/Communication Skills; mem. exec. devel. council Horace Mann Learning Center, also mem. exec. resources bd.; mem. task panel Pres.'s Commn. on Mental Health; mem. literacy task panel White House Conf. on Libraries; speaker. Sr. Usher, missionary Allen Chapel A.M.E. Ch., Washington, 1975—; developer, chairperson Operation Coll. Bound: Hosts, 1980-82; active Boy Scouts Am.; v.p. Shugart Jr. High Sch. PTA, 1976; mem. Prince George's County Parents Integration Task Force, 1975-76. Recipient Outstanding Alumni award Northeastern U., 1987. Cert. tchr., Ill.; recipient profl. certs. U.S. Dept. Edn., 1976, 78, 80, 81; Recognition cert. U.S. Office of Edn., 1981; others. Mem. Internat. Reading Assn., Assn. Supervision and Curriculum Devel., Am. Ednl. Research Assn., Nat. Council Negro Women, NAACP, Nat. Urban League, Alpha Kappa Alpha, Phi Delta Kappa. Author Manuals and articles in field. Home: 2120 Keating St Temple Hills MD 20748 Office: 1211 Connecticut Ave Washington DC 20036

JACKSON, SHIRLEY STROTHER, federal agency programs and grants analyst; b. Washington, Mar. 21, 1940; d. Thomas and Lillian (Washington) Strother. AS in Bus. Adminstrn., Southeastern U., 1987, BS summa cum laude in Mktg., 1988. Payroll clk., then supr. Naval Fin. Office U.S. Naval

Sta., Washington, 1958-63; sec. Office of Gen Counsel Fed. Power Commn., Washington, 1963-64; sec. to asst. sec. community devel. and dep. under sec. HEW, Washington, 1964-71; adminstrv. asst. ACTION Agy. div. Office of Dep. Assoc. Dir. of VISTA, Washington, 1971-73; staff asst. to commr. Consumer Product Safety Commn., Washington, 1973-76; staff asst. to asst. sec. consumer and regulatory functions HUD, Washington, 1976-77; office mgr., sec. Newman & Hermanson Co., Washington, 1977; sec., then bus. devel. specialist, regional coord. dept. commerce Minority Bus. Devel. Agy., Washington, 1978—; assoc. real estate agt. Colonial Homes, Inc., Ft. Washington, Md., 1978-81, J. Rob Robinson, Inc., Silver Hills., Md., 1981-85. Tutor Operation Rescue, Washington, 1983; vol. Providence Hosp. Ctr. for Life, Washington, 1983; vol. tutor adult basic edn. program Md. schs., Montgomery County, 1988; vol. Lincoln Theater Project, Washington, 1989—. Recipient Group Incentive award Minority Bus. Devel. Agy., 1984, Performance award, 1980, 83, Cert. of Recognition, 1986, Outstanding Performance award, 1987, 88, 89; Southeastern U. scholar, 1988. Mem. NAFE, NAACP, Am. Mgmt. Assn., Am. Mktg. Assn., Nat. Assn. MBA Women, Nat. Mus. Women in Arts, Pinochle Club (sec. 1982-83). Democrat. Baptist.

JACKSON, SUSAN ROBERTA, geologist; b. Erie, Pa., May 30, 1949; d. Casimir Charles and Josephine Stephany (Olszewski) J.; m. Alan Mitchell, June 8, 1985. BS in Anthropology, U. Pitts., 1971; MS in Geology, Vanderbilt U., 1983; postgrad., Tulsa U., 1987, Okla. State U., 1989. Devel. geologist Western Res. Oil Co., Nashville, 1978-82; geologic rsch. asst. Vanderbilt U., Nashville, 1982-84; postgrad. rsch. fellow Morgantown (W.Va.) Energy and Tech. Ctr., 1984-85; assoc. geologist, project leader Nat. Inst. Petroleum and Energy Rsch., Bartlesville, Okla., 1985-87, rsch. geoscientist, 1987—; project leader Nat. Inst. Petroleum and Energy Rsch., Bartlesville. Contbr. articles to profl. publs. Mem. NAFE, Am. Assn. Petroleum Geologists, Soc. Petroleum Engrs., Soc. for Econ. Paleontologists and Mineralogists, Tulsa Geol. Soc. Office: PO Box 2128 Bartlesville OK 74005

JACKSON, SYLVIA, insurance claims professional; b. N.Y.C.; d. Anath E. and Bianca (Creque) J. Student, Boston U. Lic. ins. broker, Calif. Claims mgr. Corkin Ins. Agy., Newton, Mass., 1988-89; asst. claims mgr. Phoenix Fire & Marine Ins. Co., Charlotte Amalie, V.I., 1985-87; claims mgr. Phoenix Fire & Marine Ins. Co., Newport Beach, Calif., 1989—; also dir. Phoenix Fire & Marine Ins. Co.; bd. dirs. Phoenix Brokerage, Jackson's Ins. Agy., Inc. Mem. NAFE, FundAm., New Decision (bd. dirs.). Office: Phoenix Fire & Marine Ins 2901 W Coast Hwy Ste 150 Newport Beach CA 92663

JACKSON, TARRA, association executive; b. Las Vegas, Nev., Sept. 11, 1964; d. Elijah and Doretha (Harvey) Green; m. Tracy Jackson, Apr. 23, 1988; 1 child, Tarisha. Student, U. Nev., Las Vegas, 1983-86. Asst. mgr. New Town Tavern & Casino, Las Vegas, 1986-89; reg. dir. Miss Black Sophisticate Internat., Carson City, Nev., 1989—; skin care cons. Mary Kay Cosmetics, Dallas, 1990—. Treas., The Family Youth Orgn., Inc., Las Vegas, 1983—; exec. dir. Little & Jr. Miss Black Sophisticate Internat. pageants; v.p. Miss. Black Sophisticate Internat.; active Family Youth Orgn. Mem. NAFE. Democrat. Baptist. Office: New Town Tavern & Casino 600 W Jackson Las Vegas NV 89106

JACKSON, THERESA ANN, engineer; b. Liberal, Kans., Apr. 22, 1959; d. Robert Filmore and Theresa (Wiesle) Jackson. BS in Edn., W. Tex. State U., Canyon, Tex., 1981; A in Applied Electronics, DeVry Inst. Tech., 1986. Phlebotomist Luth. Gen. Hosp., Pk. Ridge, Ill., 1982-84; dir. intramurals DeVry Inst. Tech., Chgo., 1985-86; electonic bench tech. Northrop Def. Systems, Rolling Meadows, Ill., 1986-87; field service engr. Telemotive Indsl. Controls, Chgo., 1987-. Judge, Valentine Boys, Girls Club, Chgo., 1988. Roman Catholic. Home: 3344 S Wallace Chicago IL 60616 Office: Telemotive Div Maxtec Inter 6470 W Cortland Chicago IL 60635

JACKSON, TONYA ELISHE, accountant; b. Meridan, Miss., Sept. 15, 1965; d. Raymond S. and Barbara J. (Williams) J. BS in Mgmt., R.I. Coll., 1987. Sweetener acct. Pepsi-Cola Corp., Chestnut Hill, Mass., 1987-89; property acct. Winn Mgmt. Co., Boston, 1989—. Mem. NAFE, Am. Mktg. Assn. Home: 3 James St Norton MA 02766-2413

JACKSON, VELMA LOUISE, lawyer; b. Sewickley, Pa., Aug. 2, 1945; d. Matthew Edward and Sarah Frances (Carter) J. BS, Duquesne U., 1968; MEd, U. Pitts., 1977; JD, U. Cin., 1982. Bar: W.Va. 1985, Pa. 1986. Chemist Calgon Corp., Pitts., 1969-70; mgr. lab. svcs. Polytech Inc., Cleve., 1970-76; engr. Procter & Gamble Co., Cin., 1976-79; v.p. F.U.T.U.R.E. Assocs., Sewickley, 1982—; law clk., jud. asst. Orphans Ct. div. Ct. Common Pleas, Pitts., 1985-89; pvt. practice Pitts., 1989—; environ. cons. Creative Mgmt. Systems, Detroit, 1979-81; tech. writer O.H. Materials Inc., Findlay, Ohio, 1980-81; instr. bus. law Carlow Coll., Pitts., 1986—; bd. dirs. Sentinel Fin. Svcs. Inc. Author: (poems) Four Drummers, 1989, Echoes of the Heart, (legal) A Light in the Darkness, 1987; contbr. articles to profl. jours.; developed cut plant preservative, 1975. Bd. dirs. Sewickley Community Ctr., 1983-89, Group Against Smog and Pollution, Pitts., 1987—; treas. Quaker Valley Dist. Dems., 1984—, commr. Police Civil Svcs. Commn., Sewickley, 1986—; invitee Citizen Amb. Project to India, Republic of China and USSR Internat. Amb. Programs Inc., Spokane, Wash., 1987, 88. Mem. ABA, AAUW, Nat. Assn. Colored Women's Club (local pres. 1985-87, state 1st v.p. 1988—), Nat. Assn. Negro Bus. and Profl. Women, Pa. Bar. Assn., W.Va. Bar Assn., Delta Sigma Theta. Baptist. Home: 339 Little St Sewickley PA 15143

JACKSON, VERNICE PREWITT, educator; b. Corona, Ala., Aug. 20, 1929; d. Jonas Oliver and Lena (Sanders) Prewitt; m. George Washington Jackson, July 28, 1949; children: Geoffrey, Georgette, Gerome, Geonice, Georita, Geonita. BA, Stillman Coll., 1954; MA in Elem. Edn., U. Ala., Tuscaloosa, 1977. Elem. tchr. Hale County Bd. Edn., Greensboro, Ala., 1957-69; elem. tchr. Tuscaloosa City Bd. Edn., 1970-88, adult basic edn. tchr., 1989—; faculty rep. East End Sch. Profl. Educators, Tuscaloosa, 1978-79; rep. Pegasus Continuous Progress Reading Program of Tuscaloosa, 1981-82; mem. Tuscaloosa City Bd. Textbook Com., 1983-84; mem. adv. bd. com. Emergency Sch. Asst. Act, Tuscaloosa, 1976-77. Editor (3d grade social studies unit) Map Skills, 1976, (3d grade skill lesson plans) Pegasus Reading Program, 1975. Vol. Leukemia Soc., Tuscaloosa, 1987, Tuscaloosa Preservation Soc., 1990; mem. polit. action com. Profl. Educators Of Tuscaloosa City, 1988; mem. NAAAP (Mother of Yr. plaque 1988, Crown 1988-89). Mem. AAUW (chairperson telephone com. 1989-90), Tuscaloos Retired Tchrs. Assn., Am. Assn. Retired Persons. Democrat. Baptist. Home: 2925 16th St Tuscaloosa AL 35401

JACKSON, WILMA (DARCY DEMILLE), columnist, public relations consultant; b. Chgo., Dec. 17; d. R.L. and Sophia O. Littlejohn; B.S. in Urban Studies/Sociology, U. Mich., 1977; cert. in urban studies Mich. State U., 1977; m. Gordon Chester Jackson, July 1, 1959; children: Carole Harris, Linda Luten, Jill, Shelley Bethay. Feature writer and columnist Sepia mag., Ft. Worth, 1961-81; columnist Hip mag., 1963-81, Soul-Teen mag., 1973-81, Bronze Thrills mag., 1957—, also feature writer, 1956—, Chgo. Daily Defender, 1959-61; feature writer Flint (Mich.) Jour., 1981—, columnist Dear Wilma, 1982-90; pub. rels. cons. A. Gail Mazaraki, cons., 1982—; syndicated columnist Associated Negro Press, 1959-64, women's editor, 1959-61; reporter and feature writer Negro Press Internat., 1964-65; market rsch. interviewer Barlow Survey Svc., Chgo., 1958-59; owner, mgr. Medi-Rary Lit. Agy., 1963—; assoc. editor Vines mag., 1980—; instr. Jordan Coll., 1982—, Mott Community Coll., 1984—; travel cons. Monarch Travel, 1989—; guest lectr. creative writing U. Mich., Flint, 1977-78, 1989—; adv. Black Fashion Mus., N.Y.C., 1979-80; pub. rels. dir. The Links, Inc., 1979—, also chmn. internat. trends and svcs.; eval. specialist and instr. The Kennedy Ctr., Flint, 1979-83; bus. liaison rep., tchr. Flint Community Schs.; cons. Manulife Ins., Timeshares, Inc. Mem. pub. affairs com. YWCA; bd. dirs., mem. adv. coun. Mich. League for Human Svcs. Recipient 3 Woman of Yr. awards , 1983, Media Women Humanitarian award, 1983, numerous writing awards. Mem. Am. Bus. Women's Assn. (Nu-Lite chpt.), Nat. Assn. Media Women (Woman of Yr. award 1978, pres. 1978-80, Newsmaker award 1988), Flint Writers Club (v.p. 1973-74), Greater Flint Art Guild, U. Mich. Alumni Assn., Paint and Palette Art Group, Grand Blanc Arts Guild, Flint Inst. Arts, Phi Delta Kappa. Democrat. Office: 615 Lippincott Blvd Flint MI 48503

JACKSON-GILLISON, HELEN LUCILLE, lawyer; b. Colliers, W.Va., July 9, 1944; d. George William and Helen Loretta (Wells) Jackson; m. Edward Lee Gillison Sr.; 1 child, Edward Lee II. BS cum laude, West Liberty State Coll., 1977; JD, W.Va. U., 1981. Bar: W.Va. 1981, U.S. Dist. Ct. (so. and no. dists.) W.Va. 1981. Sole practice Weirton, W.Va., 1981—. Bd. dirs. Blot Out Litter Today, Inc. Clean Community System, Weirton, W.Va. Civil Liberties Union, ARC, Weirton, Sheltered Workshop of W.Va., Hancock County, Housing Authority, Weirton, Ft. Steuben council Boy Scouts Am.; with office of sec. W.Va. Northern Community Coll., 1983—, adv. council friends of coll., 1983—, bd. dirs. 1983—, chmn. bd. advisors, 1988; civil service commr. City of Weirton Police Dept., 1987; mem. People to People Internat. Citizen Ambassador Program. Recipient Black Atty. Yr. award BALSA W.Va. Coll. Law, 1986. Mem. ABA, Assn. Trial Lawyers Am., Mountain State Bar Assn. (bd. dirs.), Nat. Bar Assn., Hancock Bar Assn., W.Va. Trial Lawyers Assn. (bd. govs. 1986—, pub. relations com.), W.Va. Bar Assn. (bd. govs. 1986—, various coms.), Weirton Bus. and Profl. Women's Club (chmn. polit. action com. 1982-83), Assn. Community Coll. Trustees (assoc.), NAACP (bd. dirs. Steubenville chpt. 1982-84), Million Dollar Club, Internat. Platform Assn., Phi Alpha Delta. Democrat. Baptist. Home: 264 Lakeview Dr Weirton WV 26062 Office: 3139 West St Weirton WV 26062

JACKY, DORIS VICTORIA, business owner; b. Walla Walla, July 21, 1928; d. Oscar Melvin and Bessie Juliana (Bruce) Anderson; m. Carl Frederick Jacky Jr., Sept. 4, 1948; children: Linda, Karen, Diane, Janet, Ellen, Lance. BA, Wash. State U., 1950. Sec. Libby's Cannery, Walla Walla, Wash., 1946, 47, 48, Birdseye Snider Quick Freeze, Walla Walla, 1950; sec.-treas. Jacky's Flowers, Walla Walla, 1970—, co-owner, mgr., 1980—. Mem. Credit Women Internat., Florists Transworld Delivery Assn., Am. Floral Soc., N.W. Florists Assn., Soc. Am. Florists, Altrusa (v.p. Walla Walla chpt. 1988-90, pres. 1990—). Home: 616 S Palouse Walla Walla WA 99362 Office: Jackys Flowers & Greenhouse 1127 S 2d PO Drawer C Walla Walla WA 99362

JACOB, LOUISE HELEN, educator; b. Cameron, Wis., May 19, 1924; d. Howard Walter and Agnes Augusta Elizabeth (Berger) Melbye; m. Wayne Thompson Jacob, July 21, 1956; children: Robert Douglas, Steven Allan. BS, Wis. State Coll., River Falls, 1946; MS, U. Wis., 1952; postgrad., Columbia U., N.Y.C., summer 1955. Cert. tchr., Minn., Wis. English tchr. Barron (Wis.) Pub. Schs., 1946-48, Watertown (Wis.) Pub. Schs., 1948-52; dormitory counselor U. Wis., Madison, 1951-52; English tchr. Madison Pub. Schs., 1952-56, Robbinsdale (Minn.) Area Schs., 1956-59, 66—; chmn. English dept. Sandburg Jr. High Sch., Robbinsdale, 1976-87; condr. seminars on gifted edn. Minn. Dept. Edn., 1969-75, on women's rights, 1970-80. Del., precinct chairwoman, state edn. platform com. Rep. Party, Robbinsdale, 1964-74; mem. Robbinsdale Human Rights Commn., 1967. Mem. Robbinsdale Fedn. Tchrs. (legis. chmn. 1970-73, chmn. women's rights 1974-76), LWV (bd. dirs., chmn. pub. rels., v.p. Robbinsdale chpt. 1957-59), AAUW. Lutheran. Home: 4436 Beard Ave N Robbinsdale MN 55422 Office: Cooper High Sch 8230 47th Ave N New Hope MN 55428

JACOB, M. TERESA C., psychology educator; b. Belo Horizonte, Brazil, Oct. 18, 1948; came to U.S., 1977; d. Romeu and Maria (Castilho) J.; 1 child, Rachel. MS, U. Brasilia, 1977; PhD, U. Calif., San Diego, 1985. Asst. prof. Fed. U. Minas Gerais, Brazil, 1973-75; teaching asst. U. Calif., San Diego, 1978-85, rsch. assoc., 1985—; lectr. San Diego State U., San Marcos, Calif., 1988; asst. prof. Palomar Coll., San Marcos, 1989—. Contbr. articles to profl. jours.; contbr. poetry to lit. mags. Bd. dirs. Ctr. for Women Studies and Svcs., San Diego, 1987-89. CAPES grantee, 1978-82, Nat. Rsch. Coun. grantee, 1973-77, Nat. Cancer Inst. grantee, 1988-89. Mem. Am. Psychol. Assn., Western Psychol. Assn., Latina Leadership Network.

JACOB, MARY JANE, curator; b. N.Y.C., Jan. 5, 1952; d. Elmer J. and Catherine (Marino) J.; m. Russell L. Lewis. BFA, U. Fla., 1973; MA in Art History, U. Mich., 1976. Assoc. curator modern art Detroit Inst. of Arts, Mich., 1976-80; curator Mus. of Contemporary Art, Chgo., 1980-83, chief curator, 1983-86; chief curator Mus. Contemporary Art, L.A., 1986-89, ind. curator, 1989—. Author: Forest of Signs: Art in the Crisis of Representation, 1989 Mario Merz, 1989, also numerous exhbn. catalogues; contbg. author: Christian Boltanski: Lessons of Darkness, A Quite Revolution: British Sculpture Since 1965, 1987, Jannis Kounellis, 1986, Gordon Matta-Clark, A Retrospective, 1985, The Woven and Graphic Art of Anni Albers, 1985, In the Mind's Eye: Dada and Surrealism, 1984, The Amazing Decade: Women and Performance Art 1970-1980, 1983; Magdalena Abakanowicz, 1982, The Rouge: The Image of Industry in Art of Charles Sheeler and Diego Rivera, 1978; contbr. articles and essays to profl. jours. Home and Office: 707 W Jr Terr Chicago IL 60613

JACOB, NANCY LOUISE, finance educator; b. Berkeley, Calif., Jan. 15, 1943; d. Irvin Carl and Ruby (Roberts) Feustel; m. George B. Fotheringham, Dec. 22, 1972; 1 child, Randy. BA magna cum laude, U. Wash., 1967; PhD in Econs. magna cum laude, U. Calif., Irvine, 1970. Econ. analyst, summer research staff Ctr. for Naval Analysis, Arlington, Va., 1969, chmn. dept. fin., bus. econs. and quantitative methods, 1978-81; with Weyerhaeuser Co., Tacoma, 1963-65; mem. faculty U. Wash., Seattle, 1970—, dean Sch. Bus. Adminstrn., 1981-88, prof. fin., 1981—; trustee Coll. Retirement Equities Fund., N.Y., 1980—; bd. dirs. Puget Sound Power and Light Co., Bellevue, Wash., Rainier Bancorp., Seattle. Co-author: Basic: An Intro to Computer Programming Using Basic Language, 1979, Investments, 1984, 88; contbr. articles to profl. jours. Bd. dirs. Pacific Coast Banking Sch., Seattle, 1981-88, Jr. Achievement, Seattle, 1982-84, Wash. Council on Internat. Trade, Seattle, 1981—. Recipient Wall St Jour. Achievement award U. Wash., 1967; NDEA Title IV fellow, 1968-70. Mem. Am. Econ. Assn., Am. Fin. Assn. (bd. dirs. 1975-77), Western Fin. Assn. (bd. dirs. 1976-78), Seattle Soc. Fin. Analysts, Fin. Mgmt. Assn. (program com. 1977), Phi Beta Kappa, Alpha Kappa Psi. Club: Rainier, Washington Athletic, Columbia Tower (Seattle). Office: U Wash Grad Sch Bus Adminstrn Seattle WA 98195*

JACOB, RUTH ANN, sales executive; b. Flint, Mich., Nov. 14, 1945; d. Theodore Sargis and Charlotte (Isaac) J. A.A., Flint Jr. Coll., 1968; B.F.A., San Francisco Art Inst., 1971; M.F.A., U. Mich., 1974. Asst. buyer, clk. Saks Fifth Ave, Evanston, Ill., 1974-75; receptionist Gazebo Salon, Park Ridge, Ill., 1975-76; receptionist, asst. mgr. Marc Salon, Chgo., 1976-77; mgr. salon Drake Hotel Salon, Chgo., 1977-78; br. coordinator Glemby Internat., Chgo., 1979-81; owner, bookeeper Mark/James Inc., Chgo., 1981-89, cons., 1989—; sales-distributor R. Lang Enterprise, Chgo., 1989—; instr. fine arts North Shore Arts, Winnetka, Ill., 1975-76, Goddard Coll., Plainfield, Vt., 1974-75; co-owner Creations & Things, Flint, Mich., 1975-76; teaching asst. U. Mich., Ann Arbor, 1973-74. Mem. Old Town Art League, Chgo., 1983. Recipient award Craft Commitment Exhbn., Rochester, Minn., 1974, Assyrian scholar Am. Nat. Exhbn., Chgo., 1974, Plaque, Metro-Help, Chgo., 1981; grantee San Francisco Art Inst., 1971, Kiwanis, Flint, 1971. Mem. U. Mich. Alumni Assn. Republican. Presbyterian. Club: Women's Workout (Chgo.). Avocations: painting; sewing.

JACOBOZZI, VIVIAN MARIE, retail store executive; b. Montenero, Italy, Apr. 24, 1933 (parents Am. citizens); d. Andrea and Adelia Z. (Tornincasa) Iacobozzi; student public schs., Lorain, Ohio. Acct., Caravan Inn, Phoenix, 1963-67; office mgr. AME Food Service, Scottsdale, Ariz., 1967-70, v.p., 1970-78, pres., 1978-81, also dir.; pres., owner Remembrance Inc., 1983—; treas. Arcos Dress Shop, Sun City, Ariz., 1973—. Recipient plaque March of Dimes, 1978. Mem. Nat. Assn. Meat Purveyors (hon.), Livestock Mktg. Assn. (trustee). Republican. Roman Catholic. Home: 2836 N 76th Pl Scottsdale AZ 85251 Office: 7129 6th Ave Scottsdale AZ 85251

JACOBS, ABIGAIL CONWAY, biochemist; b. St. Louis, Nov. 11, 1942; d. Hertsell and Anne (Sinai) Conway; m. Verne L. jacobs, Juen 26, 1969; children: Naomi, Aviva. BS in Chemistry, U. Mich., 1964; PhD in Biochemistry, U. Calif., Berkeley, 1968. Rsch. assoc. Weitzmann Inst. of Sci., Rehovot, Israel, 1968-71, Queens U. of Belfast, No. Ireland, 1971-72; biosci. writer Tracor Jitco, Inc., Rockville, Md., 1979-82; sr. toxicologist Carl Tech Assoc. Inc., Rockville, 1982-89; sr. biochemist Tech. Resources, Inc., Rockville, 1989—. Mem. AAAS, Am. Chem. Soc., N.Y. Acad. Sci., Sigma Xi.

JACOBS, ANNA C., retail executive; b. Washington, Mar. 21, 1939; d. Samuel and Thelma Lee (Harris) Egelnick; m. Hudgins Franklin Wheeler, June 20, 1957 (div. 1981); children: Terry J., Donald F., Deborah J.; m. Morton Edward Jacobs, Feb. 21, 1982. Grad. high sch. Bill collector Miles Glass Co., Washington, 1955; with Smith Transfer & Storage, Washington, 1955-57; statis. typist Dept. HEW, Washington, 1957-58, Dept. Agr., Washington, 1958-60; sec.-treas. Modern Age, Inc., Rockville, Md., 1975-79; tchr. June Andrus Aerobic Dancing, Silver Spring, Md., 1978-80; sales rep. Bassett Table Co., Martinsville, Va., 1975-79; chief exec. officer Jakanna Woodworks, Inc., Rockville, 1980—; cons. in field. Republican. Episcopalian. Office: Jakanna Woodworks Inc 12174 Nebel St Rockville MD 20852

JACOBS, AUDREY ARDYS, teacher; b. Loup City, Nebr., Oct. 27, 1927; d. Merle Webster and Alice Marie (McBeth) Jarmin; m. Alan Ebon Jacobs, June 3, 1951 (div.); children: Patrick Alan, Roger Lee. BS, Oreg. State U., 1950. Cert. tchr., Oreg., Idaho. Tchr. Oakland (Oreg.) High Sch., 1950-51, Vale (Oreg.) Union High Sch., 1952-58, Fruitland (Idaho) High Sch., 1962-64, Ontario (Oreg.) Jr. High Sch., 1969—; sec. Eastern Oreg. Uniserv., Baker, 1986-88. Precinct person Dem. Central Com., Ontario, 1983, 89; pres. Malheur County Cancer Soc., 1975-80; mem. Treasure Valley Chorale, Ontario, 1950—, pres., 1989—; chmn. Community Corrections, Ontario, 1984-86; chmn. Malheur County Health Svcs., Ontario, 1982-84; mem. Dove, Ontario, 1981; del. Dem. Nat. Convention, Atlanta, 1988. Mem. Oreg. Edn. Assn. (pres. Ontario Assn. 1984-86, chmn. legis. coun. 1987—), NEA, AAUW (chmn. Ontario Assn. 1979-81). Presbyterian. Home: 125 SW 13th St Ontario OR 97914 Office: 8-C Sch Dist Ontario OR 97914

JACOBS, AUGUSTA ADELLE, recycling company executive, retired educator; b. Portsmouth, Ohio, Nov. 25, 1925; d. Jacob Harry and Rose (Levine) J. BS, U. Cin., 1947; postgrad. Ohio U., Ohio State U.; grad. Kathleen Bushe and Dody Howard Sch. Modeling, 1954. Tchr. bus. East High Sch., Portsmouth, 1947-51, Green High Sch., Franklin Furnace, Ohio, 1951-87; office sec. Eagle Iron Co., Portsmouth, 1957-75, purchasing agt., 1975-77, asst. mgr., ptnr., 1977—, v.p., sec., 1985—. Bd dirs. Am. Cancer Soc. Scioto County; mem. recycling taskforce City of Portsmouth, 1989—; tchr. Sunday Sch., Temple Beneh Abraham, also bull. editor; pres. Jewish Temple Sisterhood; capt. fund drives United Way; vol. drive Am. Heart Assn., 1989—, March of Dimes, 1989—. Mem. NEA, Southeastern Ohio Tchrs. Assn., Ohio Bus. Tchrs. Assn., Green Local Tchrs. Assn., Portsmouth C. of C., AAUW (past pres. Portsmouth, rec. sec. Ohio div. 1956-58, bd. dirs. Ohio div. 1956-60, bulletin editor, program com. 1987-88, co-chair Women's Work-Women's Worth seminar, chairwoman Choices for Tomorrow's Women Portsmouth br. 1989-90, bd. dirs. 1986-88), Portsmouth Bus. and Profl. Women's Club (pres., chair legis. com. and recycling drive), Portsmouth Women's Networking Orgn. (charter mem.), Delta Kappa Gamma (pres. Alpha Beta Chpt. 1959-61, asst. auditor 1987-88, mem. scholarship and auditing coms., 1988—), Phi Delta Kappa (mem. initiation com. 1989—, mem. auditing, scholarship and social coms. 1990). Republican. Home: 2840 N Hill Rd Portsmouth OH 45662 Office: Eagle Coal & Iron Co 1015 Washington St Portsmouth OH 45662

JACOBS, BELLA HERTZBERG, gerontologist; b. Bklyn., Mar. 22, 1919; d. Rubin and Pauline (Klaif) Hertzberg; m. Lewis Jacobs; children: Ronald, Paula, Barbara. BA, U. Richmond (Va.), 1940; MA, George Washington U., 1970; EdD, U. So. Calif., 1981. Program asst. Health and Welfare Council, Washington, 1967-68; profl. asst. B'nai B'rith Career and Counseling Service, Washington, 1970-72; sr. program mgr Nat. Council on the Aging, Washington, 1972-88; cons. in field Washington, 1988—; mem. nat. adv. com. later years Am. Found. for Blind, N.Y.C., 1981-83; mem. info consortium Adminstrv. on Aging, Washington, 1983-85. Author: Senior Centers and the At-Risk Older Person, 1980 (with other) A Guidebook for the Educational Goals Inventory, 1984, Organizing a Literacy Program for Older Adults, 1986. Mem. Mont. Co. Commn. on Aging; bd. dirs. Lit. Vols. of Am. Mem. Gerontol. Soc., Assn. Adult and Continuing Edn., Assn. Counseling and Devel. Democrat. Jewish. Clubs: Woodmont, Press. Home and Office: 2925 Greenvale Rd Chevy Chase MD 20815

JACOBS, CHRISTIE JEAN, lawyer; b. Damariscotta, Maine, Aug. 27, 1961; d. Winton O'Brien and JoAnn (Waltz) J. AB, Vassar Coll., 1983; JD, Cath. U. of Am., 1990. Paralegal specialist Nationwide Info. Svcs., Albany, N.Y., 1984-86; customer svc. rep. Blue Cross & Blue Shield, Albany, 1986-87; legal intern U.S. Dept. Labor, Washington, 1988-89; legal intern IRS, Washington, summer 1989, atty. adviser, 1990—; arbitrator Autoline Dispute Resolution Better Bus. Bur., Buffalo, 1986-87; student rep. faculty com. Appointments and Promotions, Washington, 1988-89. Tax preparer Vol. Income Tax Assistance, Washington, 1987—. Recipient Spl. Merit award U.S. Dept. Labor, 1988. Mem. ABA (student liaison sect. on taxation 1989-90, appointee to com. on sales, exchs. and basis 1990—), Moot Ct. Assn., Nat. Panel Consumer Arbitrators, Phi Alpha Delta. Democrat. Home: 1616 Q St NW #C Washington DC 20009

JACOBS, DEBRA MCQUAIA, banker; b. Rochester, N.Y., Nov. 11, 1950; d. Francis Milton and Virginia (Conover) McQuaig; m. Paul Howard Jacobs, Sept. 5, 1970 (div. 1978); m. William Joseph Buttaggi, May 27, 1983; children: Alana, William. BS summa cum laude, Syracuse U., 1971; MBA, U. Rochester, N.Y., 1981; grad., Stonier's Grad. Sch. Banking, 1986. From mgmt. trainee to sr. v.p. Cen. Trust Co., Rochester, 1971-85; from sr. v.p. to exec. v.p. and chief adminstrv. officer SunBank, Sarasota (Fla.) County, N.Am., 1985—; dean br. mgmt. acad. SunBanks of Fla., Orlando, 1990—; mem. faculty Stonier's Grad. Sch. Banking, Washington, 1990—; instr. Am. Inst. Banking, 1982-85. Chmn. Com. of 100, Sarasota, 1989-90; mem. steering com. Citizens for Responsible Solutions, Sarasota, 1990—; campaign auditor Park Ridge Hosp. Found., 1977; mem. adv. bd. Monroe County Lilac Festival, 1980-81, mem. teen pageant adv. com., 1980-84; mem. corp. membership com. United Way Greater Rochester, 1984-85; mem. fin. com., bd. of mgrs. Strong Meml. Hosp., 1985; chmn. fin. com., bd. dirs. Western Monroe Mental Health Ctr., 1979-82; chmn. revolving loan fund Monroe County Indsl. Devel. Corp., 1982-85. Mem. Nat. Soc. to Prevent Blindness (chmn. Sarasota/ Manatee, Fla. chpt. 1988-90), N.Y. State Bankers Assn. (consumer legis. com. 1984-85), Rochester Area C. of C. (women's coun. 1977-84, bd. trustees 1980-85), Nat. Assn. Banking Women (sec. 1978), Sarasota C. of C. (ambassador 1986, grad. 1987, bd. dirs., exec. com. 1989-90), Zonta (v.p. 1980). Republican. Lutheran. Office: SunBank/Sarasota County NA PO Box 2138 Sarasota FL 34230

JACOBS, ELEANOR ALICE, retired clinical psychologist, educator; b. Royal Oak, Mich., Dec. 25, 1923; d. Roy Dana and Alice Ann (Keaton) J. B.A., U. Buffalo, 1949, M.A., 1952, Ph.D., 1955. Clin. psychologist VA Hosp., Buffalo, 1954-83; EEO counelor VA Hosp., 1962-79, chief psychology service, 1979-83; clin. prof. SUNY, Buffalo, 1950-83; speaker on psychology to community orgns. and clubs, 1952—; Mem. adult devel. and aging com. NICHD, HEW, 1971-75. Researcher for publs. on hyperbaric medicine, hyperoxygenation effect on cognitive functions in aged. Recipient Outstanding Superior Performance award Buffalo VA Hosp., 1958, Spl. Recognition award SUNY, Buffalo, Spl. Recognition award SUNY, 1971; W.L. McKnight award Miami Heart Inst., 1972; Adminstrs. commendation VA, 1974; Dirs. commendation VA Med. Center, Buffalo, 1978; Disting. Alumni award SUNY, Buffalo, 1983; named Woman of Yr. Bus. and Profl. Women's Clubs, Buffalo, 1973. Mem. Am. Psychol. Assn., Eastern Psychol. Assn., N.Y. State Psychol. Assn., Am. Group Psychotherapy Assn., Am. Soc. Group Psychotherapy and Psychodrama, Psychol. Assn. Western N.Y. (Disting. Achievement award 1976), Group Psychotherapy Assn. Western N.Y., Undersea Med. Soc., Sigma Xi. Home: 221 Pleasant Ave N, Ridgeway, ON Canada L0S 1N0

JACOBS, ILENE B., electrical equipment company executive, treasurer; b. Boston, May 12, 1947; d. William and Sylvia (Mintz) Brenner; m. Richard B. Jacobs, June 15, 1969; children: Aaron, Wendy. BA, U. Mass., 1969; cert. in adv. mgmt. prog., Harvard U., 1982. Cash mgmt. officer Shawmut Bank of Boston, 1969-74; mgr. money and banking Digital Equipment Corp., Maynard, Mass., 1974-80, asst. treas., 1981-84, v.p., treas., 1984—. Treas.

Congregation Beth El, Sudbury, Mass., 1985—. Mem. Nat. Assn. Corp. Treas. (bd. dirs.), Soc. Internat. Treas. Republican. Jewish.

JACOBS, JANE, author; b. Scranton, Pa., May 4, 1916; d. John Decker and Bess Mary (Robison) Butzner; m. Robert Hyde Jacobs, Jr., May 27, 1944; children—James Kedzie, Edward Decker, Mary Hyde. Author: Downtown Is For People in The Exploding Metropolis, 1959, The Death and Life of Great American Cities, 1961, The Economy of Cities, 1969, The Question of Separatism, 1980, Cities and the Wealth of Nations, 1984, (juvenile) The Girl on the Hat, 1989. Address: care Random House 201 E 50th St New York NY 10022

JACOBS, KAREN LOUISE, medical technologist; b. Kingston, N.Y., May 7, 1943; d. William Charles and Vera Elizabeth (Kelly) Jacobs; BS in Applied Tech., Empire State Coll., 1976; MS in Pub. Service Adminstrn., Russell Sage Coll., 1982. Sr. lab. technician, hosp. lab. supr. City of Kingston (N.Y.) Labs., 1962-68; sr. rsch. asst. Dudley Obs., Albany, N.Y., 1972-75; lab. adminstr. Albany Med. Coll., 1976—, mem. faculty, 1982—; mem. infection control com. and subcoms. on AIDS mgmt. and human immunodeficiency virus universal precautions Albany Med. Ctr. Infection Control, 1987—. Bd. dirs. chpt. Leukemia Soc. Am., 1983-87; judge sci. and tech. summer issue on excellence in Am. U.S. News and World Report. Mem. Clin. Lab. Mgmt. Assn. (del. citizen amb. program to China 1989), Am. Soc. Clin. Pathologists, Sierra Club, Earthwatch, Nat. Speleological Soc., Helderburg-Hudson Grotto. Home: 37B Picotte Dr Albany NY 12208 Office: Albany Med Coll Div Hematology and Oncolgy 47 New Scotland Ave Albany NY 12208

JACOBS, KATHLEEN CALDWELL, business educator; b. High Point, N.C., Apr. 8, 1940; d. Thomas and Alene (Ridley) Caldwell; m. Arthur Thomas Jacobs, Apr. 11, 1960; children: Sharon, Arthur Jr., Debra. BA, Wright State U., Dayton, Ohio, 1977; MA, Central Mich. U., 1980; MBA, So. Ill. U., 1985; EdD, Temple U., 1987. Tng. instr. U.S. Dept. Def., Kleber Kaserne, Fed. Republic Germany, 1970-74, Wright Patterson AFB, Ohio, 1974-78, Dover AFB, Del., 1978-80; grad. MBA program dir. So. Ill. U., Edwardsville, 1980-85; assoc. prof. bus. adminstrn. Wilmington Coll., Dover, Del., 1985-87; adj. prof. internat. bus. mgmt. Webster U., St. Louis, 1987-88; assoc. prof. bus. adminstrn. Wesley Coll., Dover, 1988—; chief exec. officer, pres. Career Devel. and Edn. Cons., Dover, 1987—; speaker, presenter conf. in field. Contbr. articles to profl. publs. Mem. AAUP, Am. Ednl. Rsch. Assn., Assn. on Study of Higher Edn., NAFE, Nat. Assn. Minorities with Doctorate Degrees, AAUW (bd. dirs. Dover chpt. 1988), Nat. Urban League, Del. State C. of C. (rep. for Wesley Coll. 1989—), Cen. C. of C. (rep. for Wesley Coll. 1989—), Beta Gamma Sigma, Omicron Tau Theta, Sigma Iota Epsilon. Republican. Office: Wesley Coll 120 N State St Dover DE 19901

JACOBS, LIBBY (MARY ELIZABETH MILLER), theater director; b. Omaha, Mar. 31, 1947; d. George Erwin and Hilda Frances (Nevin) Miller; m. John Francis Jacobs Jr., Aug. 16, 1969; children: Michele Nevin, John Francis III. BA, Hood Coll., 1969; MEd, Va. Commonwealth U., 1973; MA, U. Mich., 1976. Tchr. Henrico County Sch. System, Richmond, Va., 1969-70, Richmond City Sch. System, 1970-71; cons. loan dept. Security Fed. Savs. & Loan, Richmond, 1971-73; instr. Concordia Luth. Coll., Ann Arbor, Mich., 1977-78; dir. Coach House Theatre, Akron, Ohio, 1980-85, 87—; founder, dir. Actors' & Playwrights' Theatre, Akron, Ohio, 1985—. Author: (plays) Sparks, 1984, The Gospel According To Omaha, 1985, Harsh Criticism, 1986. Named Woman of Yr. in Creative Arts, Women's History Project, 1987. Mem. NOW, Ohio Theatre Alliance. Episcopalian. Home and Office: 618 N Portage Path Akron OH 44303

JACOBS, LINDA LEE, advertising executive; b. Freeport, Ill., Apr. 4, 1961; d. Howard Donald and Marjorie Lucille (Metz) J. Diploma, Freeport High Sch., Ill., 1979; AA, Highland Community Coll., Freeport, Ill., 1981; BA in Journalism, No. Ill. U., Dekalb, 1984. Copywriter Gander Mountain Inc., Wilmont, Wis., 1984-85, asst. merchandising mgr., advt. mgr., 1986-89; mktg. mgr. Johnson Smith Co., Bradenton, Fla., 1989—. Recipient Wis. Direct Mktg. Assn., Milw. 1985. Nat. Assn. Female Execs. Office: Johnson Smith Co 4514 19th St Ct E Bradenton FL 34206

JACOBS, MARIAN BECKMANN, corporate professional; b. Teaneck, N.J., Dec. 20, 1935; d. Frederick J. and Marguerite J. (Thoma) Beckmann; BA cum laude (Grace Potter Rice fellow), Barnard Coll., 1957; MA (Columbia scholar, Qunicy Ward Boese fellow, James Furman Kemp fellow), Columbia, 1959, PhD, 1963; m. Warren R. Jacobs Jr., Sept. 5, 1959 (dec.); children: Laura Diane, Anita Michelle; m. 2d, Donald H. Norman, Jan. 9, 1975 (dec.). Research asst. mineralogy dept. Columbia, N.Y.C., 1960-63; research asso. Lamont-Doherty Geol. Obs. of Columbia, Palisades, N.Y., 1963—; asst. prof. oceanography Ramapo Coll. of N.J., Mahwah, 1974-76; sr. analyst market and industry research for polymers and spl. chems. ARCO Chem. Co., Inc. subs. Atlantic Richfield Co., 1976-89; mgr. bus. and devel. Environ. and Engring Cons. Svcs. Dunn Geosci. Corp., Parsippany, N.J., 1989—. NSF grantee, 1965-66, 66-67, 69-71, 71-72, 72-73. Mem. Soc. Plastic Engrs., AAAS, Mineral Soc. Am., Geol. Soc. Am., Phi Beta Kappa, Sigma Xi. Contbr. articles to profl. jours. Research X-ray diffractions and fluorescence studies deep-sea sediments and particulate matter in sea water. Home: 7 Robin Rd PO Box 572 Mahwah NJ 07430 Office: Dunn Geosci Corp Environ & Engring Cons Svcs 299 Cherry Hill Rd Parsippany NJ 07054

JACOBS, MARILYN SUSAN, psychologist, author; b. Bklyn., Mar. 23, 1952; d. Robert Paul and Ena (Selby) J. BS, SUNY, Stony Brook, 1974, George Washington U., 1977; MA, Calif. Sch. Profl. Psychology, L.A., 1984, PhD, 1986. Lic. psychologist, Calif. Postdoctoral assoc. psychoanalytic psychotherapy Wright Inst., L.A., 1986-87; clin. psychologist Forensic Svcs. Bur. L.A. County Dept. Mental Health, 1987-89; clin. psychologist CIGNA Healthplans, L.A., 1989—; pvt. practice L.A., 1986—; adj. asst. prof. Calif. Sch. Profl. Psychology, 1989—. Author: American Psychology in the Quest for Nuclear Peace, 1989. Mem. Am. Psychol. Assn. (bd. dirs. div. 39 women and psychoanalysis), Calif. Psychol. Assn. L.A. County Psychol. Assn., Health Psychology Com. Office: 1314 Westwood Blvd Ste 206 Los Angeles CA 90024

JACOBS, MARION KRAMER, psychologist; b. Brooklyn, N.Y., Jan. 11, 1938; b. Bklyn. Jan. 11, 1938; d. Milton Julius and Edith (Rosenel) Kramer. BA, Brooklyn Coll., 1959; PhD, U. South Calif., 1969. Assoc. prof. of bio med. and psychology W.Va. U., 1969-73; dir., counseling ctr. U. Calif., Irvine, 1973-77; adj. prof. and coordinator psychology clinic UCLA, 1977—, co-dir., co-founder Calif. Self-Help Ctr., 1984—. Contbr. rsch. articles to profl. jours. Mem. Am. Psychological Assn., Western Psychological Assn., Calif. State Psychological Assn. Democratic. Jewish. Office: UCLA Psychology Dept 405 Hilgard Ave Los Angeles CA 90077

JACOBS, MARY KATHRYN, nurse; b. Sioux City, Iowa, Oct. 20, 1947; d. Jack and Georgia I. (Hungerford) J.; m. John F. Finkleman, Sept. 20, 1980 (div. Apr. 1983); 1 child, Jack. Diploma in nursing, Meth. Hosp. Sch. of Nursing, 1968; student, Morningside Coll., 1972-73, U. Tex., 1976. Med. staff nurse St. Luke's Med. Ctr., Sioux City, 1968, staff nurse ICU and critical care unit, 1968-70, clin. instr., freshman theory instr., 1970-72; pediatric office nurse Dr.'s Labowskie, Thomson & Genrich, Colorado Springs, Colo., 1972-76; critical care float nurse Med. Pers. Pool., Colorado Springs, 1972-75; med. and surg. staff nurse Dr.'s Hosp., El Paso, Tex., 1976; critical care staff nurse and unit tchr., head nurse, supr. St. Luke's Episcopal Hosp., Houston, 1977-80; coronary care unit staff nurse, assoc. unit dir. McKennan Hosp., Sioux Falls, 1982-87; nurse educator, 1987-89; unit dir. critical care stepdown unit McKennan Hosp., Sioux Falls, 1989—; critical care book reviewer Brady Communications, Englewood Cliffs, N.J., 1987—. Mem. Smithsonian Inst., Washington, 1985—; assoc. mem. Nat. Trust for Hist. Preservation, Washington, 1985—; charter mem. Nat. Mus. Women in the Arts, Washington, 1985—. mem. NAFE, Nat. League for Nursing, Am. Heart Assn., Am. Assn. Critical Care Nurses, Siouxland chpt. of Am. Assn. Critical Care Nurses, Soc. Critical Care Medicine, Tiger Cubs. Eastern Orthodox. Office: McKennan Hosp 800 E 21st St Sioux Falls SD 57101

JACOBS, RACHEL ISABELLE, communications specialist; b. Chgo., Jan. 1, 1945; d. Samson Martin and Bertha Evelyn (Stites) J.; m. Michael Roy Baumert, Sept. 7, 1966 (div. Feb. 1970); 1 child, Eric Samson. AS, Murray Coll., Tishomingo, Okla., 1965; BA in Edn., East Cen. U., Ada, Okla., 1969; postgrad., U. Okla., 1972; student, Okla. Bapt. U., 1970-71. Cert. art edn. tchr., Okla.; lic. social worker, real estate agt., Okla. Caseworker Okla. Dept. Human Svcs., Shawnee, 1968-69; tchr. kindergarten Shawnee Pub. Schs., 1969-72; coord. pub. rels. Ralph Graves for Senator, Shawnee, 1972; sales mgr. pub. rels. Young Hotel Corp., San Diego, 1972-73; food svc. day mgr. Hillcrest Country Club, Oklahoma City, 1973-74; freelance artist, Oklahoma City, 1974-75; interior decorator Frisch's of Cin., Oklahoma City, 1975-76; mgr. wearables T.G.& Y Stores, Bethany, Okla., 1976; dispatch clk. Southwestern Bell Telephone, Oklahoma City, 1976—; cons. on career images, resumes, Oklahoma City, 1989—. Contbr. poetry to Westlake Ripples. Catalyst Citizens for Smoke-Free Am., Oklahoma City, 1976—; vol. Okla. Ho. of Reps., 1988, Salvation Army, 1989, Sooner Olympics, 1989; mem. bd. Westlake Presbyn. Ch., Oklahoma City, 1990—. Recipient award for dedication and svc. teaching Jefferson Sch. PTA, Shawnee, 1972. Mem. Communications Workers Am. (steward 1978-89), Alumni Assn. Murray Coll., Alumni Assn. Okla. Bapt. U. Democrat. Office: Southwestern Bell Telephone 2301 N Olie Oklahoma City OK 73106

JACOBS, RANDI S., financial planning firm executive; b. N.Y.C., Dec. 22, 1955; d. Selwyn and Marjorie (Slater) J. BSBA, Bucknell U., 1977; MBA, Case Western Res. U., 1978. CPA, N.Y. Supr. Ernst and Whinney, Boston; v.p. Morgan Guaranty Trust Co., N.Y.C., Creative Fin. Programs, Teaneck, N.J. Mem. AICPA. Home: 1077 River Rd #606 Edgewater NJ 07020

JACOBS, RITA GOLDMAN, anesthesiologist, health facility administrator; b. N.Y.C., Jan. 15, 1927; d. Joseph and Miriam (Feinstein) Goldman; m. Daivd Jack Jacobs, Nov. 28, 1952; children: Etta Miriam, Meme Jacobs Rasmussen. BA, NYU, 1947; MD, Women's Med. Coll. Pa., 1951. Diplomate Am. Bd. Anesthesiology. Intern Queens (N.Y.) Gen. Hosp., 1951-52; resident in anesthesia Columbia Presbyn. Med. Ctr., N.Y.C., 1952-54, attending anesthesiologist, 1954-58; attending anesthesiologist Meml. Sloan Kettering Cancer Ctr., N.Y.C., 1958-71; assoc. prof. anesthesiology Cornell Med. Sch., N.Y.C., 1968-71; anesthesiologist Berkshire Med. Ctr., Pittsfield, Mass., 1971—; chmn. dept. anesthesiology Berkshire Med. Ctr., Pittsfield, 1975-84, med. dir. pain clinic, 1986—; med. dir. Crane Ctr. for Day Surgery, Berkshire Med. Ctr., Pittsfield, 1984—; pres. Berkshire Anesthesiologist, PC, Pittsfield, 1975-84, sec., 1984-90. Author, researcher: (scientific exhibit) Use of Microhematocrits in Monitoring Changes in Blood Volume During and After Surgery, 1960 (1st Prize Postgrad. Assembly of N.Y. State Soc. of Anesthesiologists); contbr. articles to med. jours. Fellow Am. Coll. Anesthesiologists; mem. AMA, Mass. Med. Soc., Mass. Anesthia Assn., Berkshire Dist. Med. Soc. (v.p. 1986-88, sec. 1988—), LWV. Democrat. Jewish. Office: Berkshire Med Ctr 725 North St Pittsfield MA 01201

JACOBS, ROSETTA See LAURIE, PIPER

JACOBS, SHEILA GAIL MCNEIL, health educator; b. Akron, Ohio, May 24, 1953; d. Kenneth Lee McNeil and Lois Lenora (Turpin) Jones; m. Paul Alan Jacobs, Aug. 23, 1987. BS, Bowling Green (Ohio) State U., 1975, MEd, 1976. Instr. health edn. Northeastern U., Boston, 1976-80; coord. health promotion program U. Mass., Boston, 1980-82, asst. to exec. dir. Health Svc., 1982-88; dir. health promotion Beder Health Assocs., Braintree, Mass., 1988-89; health edn. behaviorist Med-Plan Weight Mgmt. Program Faulkner Hosp., Boston, 1989—. Rep. speaker's bur. Mass. Passenger Safety program, Boston, 1985—; reviewer citizen's rev. com. on community and youth devel. United Way of Massachusetts Bay, Boston, 1981-84; leader, vol. Patriot's Trail coun. Girl Scouts of U.S., Dorchester, Mass., 1984-86. Mem. Am. Coll. Health Assn., Soc. Pub. Health Educators, Am. Lung Assn. (chairperson smoking or health guidance com. 1984—, bd. dirs. 1985—, exec. com. 1987—), Mass. Choice and Religious Coalition for Abortion Rights, NOW. Democrat. Unitarian Universalist. Office: Faulkner Hosp Med-Plan Weight Mgmt Program Boston MA 02130

JACOBSEN, PAMELA, special education coordinator, consultant, counselor; b. Cleve., June 25, 1947; d. Michael Antony and Mary (Pappas) Hoty; m. William Henry Jacobsen, Aug. 21, 1971 (div. 1982). B.S. in Elem. Edn., Baldwin-Wallace Coll., 1969; postgrad. in learning disabilities, Akron U., 1971-72; M.Ed. in Educating Handicapped, Adams State Coll., 1976. Tchr. Strongsville Schs., Ohio, 1969-71, lang. disabilities tchr., 1971-73; educationally handicapped itinerant tchr. Dist. 60, Pueblo, Colo., 1973-74, educationally handicapped lab. educator, 1974-77, educationally handicapped resource tchr., 1977-79, emotional/behavior disorder educator, 1979-86; child study team specialist, 1986—; educator Summer Champ Camp for Asthmatics, Woodland Park, Colo., 1983-86. Author: Correct and Effective Use of Placement and Procedures for Emotionally Disordered Students, 1985. Active Pueblo Nature Ctr., 1981—; area chmn. Channel 8 Pub. TV Auction, 1982-87; bd. dirs. Altrusa Club of Pueblo, 1986; nominating com. Columbine Girl Scout Council, 1984-86. Recipient Hon. Mention award Gov. Colo., 1985; Service award Champ Camp Program, 1984, 85. Mem. Nat. Assn. Female Execs., Bus. and Profl. Women, Phi Delta Kappa (v.p. 1985-87, pres. 1987-89), Delta Kappa Gamma. Greek Orthodox. Club: Pueblo Athletic. Avocations: golf; hiking; reading. Home: 1100 W 26th St Pueblo CO 81003 Office: Keating Staff Devel Ctr Cen Child Study Office 215 E Orman Ave Pueblo CO 81004

JACOBSEN, REBECCA HANSON, psychologist; b. Dallas, Oreg., Mar. 1, 1949; d. Earl Willard and Virginia (Van Mourik) H.; m. Michael Anthony Jacobsen, Sept. 25, 1970; 1 child, Leif Peter. BA, CCNY, 1972, MS, 1974; MS, U. Ga., 1980, PhD, 1982. Lic. psychologist, Ga., Calif. Asst. rsch. scientist N.Y. State Psychiat. Inst., 1974-77; grad. teaching asst. U. Oreg., Eugene, 1978-79; psychology intern. VA Med. Ctr., Durham, N.C., 1980-81; asst. prof. Med. Coll. Ga., Augusta, 1983-86; clin. psychologist VA Med. Ctr., Augusta, 1982-86, V.A. Med. Ctr., Sepulveda, Calif., 1986—; clin. asst. prof. Fuller Theol. Sem., Pasadena, Calif., 1987—; tng. fellow Ind. Consultation Ctr., Bronx, 1974-77. Contbr. articles to profl. jours. U. Ga. fellow, 1981-82. Mem. Am. Psychol. Assn., Nat. Orgn. VA. Psychologists, Western Psychol. Assn., Psychologists in Pub. Svc. Democrat. Avocations: tennis, gourmet food, bird-watching, needlework.

JACOBSEN, SUSAN MARIE, art museum educator and program director; b. Tyler, Minn., June 25, 1949; d. Henry M. and Wilburta (Sanderson) J.; m. Jerome A. Downes, Apr. 26, 1980. Student, U. Minn., 1967-68; BA, S.W. State U., Marshall, Minn., 1982. Intern edn. div. Mpls. Inst. Arts, 1972-73, coord. art program for tchrs. and students, 1973-74, coord. young people's program, 1974-88, supr. young people's program, 1988-89, supr. pub. programs, 1989—; instr. Compas, St. Paul, 1974-75; mem. adv. bd. edn. dept. Minn. Mus. Art, St. Paul, 1978-79; mem. adv. bd. Children's Mus., St. Paul, 1979-82. Author exhbn. and children's gallery guides Mpls. Inst. Mem. operating support rev. panel community group II, Minn. Arts Bd., 1986-88. Mem. Nat. Art Edn. Assn., Minn. Art Edn. Assn., Minn. Assn. Mus., Minn. Alliance for Arts in Edn., Am. Assn. Mus. Home: 515 5th Ave SE Minneapolis MN 55414 Office: The Mpls Inst Arts 2400 3d Ave S Minneapolis MN 55404

JACOBSON, ANN REISNER, organizational consultant and mediator; b. Berlin, Apr. 25, 1926; d. Fred and Eugenia (Goldman) Reisner; m. Elliot Jacobson, Sept. 1, 1946; children: Mark, Steven, Susan. BA, U. Mo., Kansas City, 1946; MSW with high distinction, U. Kans., 1967. Caseworker Kans. Child Welfare Service, Kansas City, 1965-66; group worker Mattie Rhodes Community Ctr., Kansas City, Mo., 1966-67; project dir. Carver Neighborhood Ctr., Kansas City, 1967-71; exec. dir. Vol. Action and Info. Ctr., Kansas City, 1971-85; v.p. vol. and community resources Heart of Am. United Way, Kansas City, 1986-89; pres. Ann Jacobson & Assocs., Kansas City, 1989—; instr. vol. mgmt. Pioneer Community Coll., Kansas City, 1978—, U. Kans. Sch. Social Welfare, 1989—. Author: Volunteer Management Handbook: For Effective Development of Volunteer Programs, 1985, Self Study Manual for Information and Referral Services, 1987; editor Standards and Guidelines for Field Volunteerism, 1979. Chair, founder Vol. Bur. of Kansas City, Mo., 1966-71; chair Vols. in Edn., 1969; mem. nat. com. Goodwill Industries of Am., 1969-73; bd. dirs. Nat. Ctr. for Vol. Action, 1969-76; v.p. Regional Health and Welfare Council, 1971-72; mem. Mayor's Human Rights Commn., 1972, Mayor's Fair Housing Commn., 1972; del. World Assembly of Jewish Agys. in Israel, 1971—; mem. adv. com. U. Mo. Sch. Social Work, 1975; charter mem., mem. steering com. U. Mos. Kansas City Disting. Fellows Program, 1986—; v.p. Congregation B'nai Jehudah, 1986-89; pres. Jewish Fedn., 1989—, mem. Council of Jewish Fedns. Bd., 1989—; bd. dirs. NCCJ, 1983—; mem. Nat. Jewish Fedn. and Council, Kansas City, Mo., pres. women's div. 1968-71; mem. Nat. Fedn. Temple Sisterhoods, com., 1967-69; mem. Union Am. Hebrew Congregations, commn. 1966-72. Recipient Community Service award Regional Health and Welfare Council, 1969, Matrix Table award Theta Sigma Phi, 1972, Germaine Monteil award, 1975; cited for Outstanding Corp. Achievement Kansas City Times, 1986. Mem. Acad. Cert. Social Workers, Am. Soc. Pub. Adminstrn., AAUP, Mo. Assn. Social Welfare, Nat. Assn. Social Workers (chmn. Mo. coun. 19174-75, pres. 1975-77), Mid-Am. Family Mediation Assn. (v.p. 1986-89), Allinace Info. and Referral Svcs. (nat. bd. dirs. 1982—), Nat. Assn. Vol. Burs. (chmn. 1978-80, editor newsletter 1971-77, pres. 1970-72). Home: 615 W Meyer Blvd Kansas City MO 64113 Office: 615 W Meyer Blvd Kansas City MO 64113

JACOBSON, ANNA SUE, finance company executive; b. Ft. Smith, Ark., Aug. 13, 1940; d. Ray Bradley and Joy Anna (Person) McAlister, (stepfather) Cleve J. McDonald, Sr.; m. Lyle Norman Jacobson, Nov. 23, 1958; children: Lyle Michael, Daniel Ray, Julie Anne, Eric Joseph. Cert. in Fin. Planning, Coll. for Fin. Planning, 1984. Certified fin. paraplanner. Office mgr. Twin Cities Lithographic Inst., St. Paul, 1963-66; sec., St. Paul, Mpls., 1971-78; asst. to pres., office mgr. Planners Fin. Svcs., Mpls., 1978-85, asst. corp. treas., 1987-88; fin. paraplanner McAlmont Investment Co., Mpls., 1985-88, office mgr., 1988—; registered rep. McAlmont Investment Co., 1989—; ind. fin. cons.; bd. dir. Planners Fin. Svcs.; mem. bd. advisors Coll. for Fin. Planning, Denver, 1982—; speaker various orgns. Co-creator Paraplanning Profession Advisor; asst. sales cons. Skie & Assocs., St. Louis Park, Minn., 1987—. Del. Dem. Farmer Labor Com., St. Paul, 1980; campaign chmn. mayoral election, Roseville, Minn., 1983, county commr., city coun. election, Roseville, 1980, 84; local chmn. for passage of ERA, Minn.; mem. Am. Lung Assn., St. Paul; past. pres. PTA, Minn.; mem. exec. coun. Boy Scouts Am., 1977-81; mem. adv. bd. Sch. Dist. 623, Roseville, Minn., 1978-81; fund raising com. mem. Twin Cities Pub. TV Sta., 1975—. Recipient Volunteerism award State of Minn., 1981, Cert. of Appreciation Minn. Bicentennial Com., 1976. Mem. Internat. Assn. Fin. Planning, Twin Cities Assn. Fin. Planners, Internat. Assn. Bus. and Profl. Women (bd. dirs. 1977-86, pres. 1980-82, Woman of Yr. 1982), Concordia Acad. Booster Club, Beta Sigma Phi Nu Phi Mu Chpt. Democrat. Lutheran. Avocations: tennis, riding, reading, piano, playing the harp. Home: 2171 Dellwood Ave N Roseville MN 55113

JACOBSON, BONNIE BROWN, energy consulting company executive, statistician; b. Annapolis, Md., Feb. 15, 1952; d. Albert Robert and Ruth Marie (Pauk) Brown; m. Peter Roy Jacobson, Apr. 28, 1979. BS cum laude, LaRoche Coll., Pitts., 1974; MS, U. Pitts., 1976. Rsch. assoc. Squibb Inst. Med. Rsch., Princeton, N.J., 1976-78; assoc. statistician N.E. Utilities Svc. Co., Hartford, Conn., 1978-80, statistician, 1980-82, sr. statistician, 1982-83, mgr. consumer rsch., 1983-87, corp. statistician, 1987-89; project mgr. energy div. ICF Resources Inc., Fairfax, Va., 1989—; chmn. Space Access, Inc., 1989-90; cons. stats., Hartford, 1976-89; adviser Electric Power Rsch. Inst., Palo Alto, Calif., 1978-89; evaluation prin. investigator Conn. Low Income Weatherization Conservation Program, 1988—; rsch. plan developer Conn. Energy Assistance Study Project, Hartford, 1983-84. Rsch scholar U. Pitts., 1974-76. Mem. NAFE, Am. Statis. Assn., Am. Mktg. Assn., Electric Utility Market Rsch. Coun. Home: 12302 Sleepy Lake Ct Fairfax VA 22033 Office: ICF Resources Inc 9300 Lee Hwy Fairfax VA 22031

JACOBSON, ELAINE ZEPORAH, clinical psychologist; b. Bklyn., Feb. 10, 1942; d. Julius Y. and Eleanor (Lebowitz) Finkelstein; m. Howard Jacobson, June 10, 1965; children: Michael, Daniel, Joel, David. AB summa cum laude, Bklyn. Coll., 1963; PhD, Adelphi U., 1968. Lic. psychologist, Ill. Staff psychologist Staten Island (N.Y.) Mental Health Soc., 1967-68; staff psychologist Adler Zone Ctr., Champaign, Ill., 1968-71, chief psychologist MI children's program, 1981-82; rsch. cons. Eric Clearinghouse, Urbana, Ill., 1976-77, Mediax, Urbana, 1977-78; assoc. psychotherapist Family Svc. Champaign County, Champaign, 1977-81, 84-85; staff psychologist Wizo Found., Jerusalem, 1979-80; clin. supr. dept. psychology and psychol. clinic U. Ill., Champaign, 1986-88; pvt. practice Champaign, 1977-81, 84—; founding chair Patient Adv. Bd. dept. ob-gyn., Carle Hosp., Urbana, 1972-74. Active Hillel Found., U. Ill., 1975—; Zionist affairs chair Hadassah, Champaign, 1980-83. USPHS fellow Adelphi U., 1963-67. Mem. Am. Psychol. Assn., Ill. Psychol. Assn., Champaign Area Psychol. Soc., Phi Beta Kappa. Democrat. Jewish. Office: 1 Greencroft Dr Champaign IL 61821

JACOBSON, EVE MAXINE, editor; b. N.Y.C., July 22, 1961; d. Murray Norman and Rosalind Deborah (Prost) J. BA cum laude, Barnard Coll., 1982; M Internat. Affairs, cert., Columbia U., 1989. Reporter Rockland County Times, Haverstraw, N.Y., 1983; rsch. asst. Am. Jewish Com., N.Y.C., 1987-89; editor Women's Am. Orgn. for Rehab. through Tng., N.Y.C., 1989—. Dean's fellow Columbia U., 1988-89. Mem. Am. Soc. Mag. Editors, Assn. for Israel Studies, Am. Friends Peace Now, Women's Am. Orgn. for Rehab. Through Tng. Office: Women's Am ORT 315 Park Ave S New York NY 10010

JACOBSON, HELEN GUGENHEIM (MRS. DAVID JACOBSON), civic worker; b. San Antonio; d. Jac Elton and Rosetta (Dreyfus) Gugenheim; m. David Jacobson, Nov. 6, 1938; children: Elizabeth, Dorothy Miller. BA, Hollins Coll. With news and spl. events staff NBC, N.Y.C., 1933-38. 1st v.p. San Antonio, Bexar County coun. Girl Scouts U.S.A., 1957-63; Tex. State rep. UNICEF, 1964-69; bd. dirs. U.S. com. UNICEF, 1970-80, hon. bd. dirs., 1980—; bd. dirs. Nat. Fedn. Temple Sisterhoods, 1973-77, Temple Beth-El Sisterhood, Youth Alternatives, Inc.; bd. dirs. Community Guidance Ctr., chmn. bd., 1960-63; bd. dirs. Sunshine Cottage Sch. for Deaf Children, chmn. bd., 1952-54; pres. Community Welfare Coun., 1968-70; pres. bd. trustees San Antonio Pub. Libr., 1957-61; trustee Nat. Coun. Crime and Delinquency, 1964-70, San Antonio Mus. Assn., 1964-73; bd. dirs. Cancer Therapy and Rsch. Found. South Tex., 1977—, sec., 1977-83; pres. S.W. region Tex. Coalition for Juvenile Justice, 1977-79; chmn. Mayor's Commn. on Status of Women, 1972-74; del. White House Conf. on Children, 1970; mem. Commn. on Social Action of Reform Judaism, 1973-77; chmn. Foster Grandparent project Bexar County Hosp. Dist., 1968-69; sec. Nat. Assembly for Social Policy and Devel., 1969-74; pres. women's com. Ecumenical Ctr. for Religion and Health, 1975-77; mem. criminal justice planning com. Alamo Area Coun. of Govts., chmn., 1975-77, 1987-88; mem. Tex. Internat. Women's Yr. Coordinating Com., 1977; co-chmn. San Antonio chpt. NCCJ, 1980-84; chmn. United Negro Coll. Fund Campaign, 1983, 84; sec. Avance; trustee Target 90/Goals for San Antonio, 1986-90. Recipient Headliner award for civic work San Antonio chpt. Women in Communications, 1958, Nat. Humanitarian award B'nai B'rith, 1975; named Vol. Woman of Yr. Express-News, 1959; honoree San Antonio chpt. NCCJ, 1970, Nat. Jewish Hosp., 1978; inductee San Antonio Women's Hall of Fame, 1986, others. Mem. Nat. Coun. Jewish Women (Hannah G. Solomon award 1979), Symphony Soc. (women's com.), Argyle Club. Home: 207 Beechwood Ln San Antonio TX 78216

JACOBSON, JOAN, speech pathologist, audiologist, educator; b. Hull, Iowa, Apr. 26, 1924; d. Fred and Mary (Hoogschagen) Elsinga; m. John Jacobson, June 1, 1945 (div. 1952). BA, Morningside Coll., 1944; MA, Syracuse U., 1948, PhD, 1958. Cert. of clin. competence in speech pathology and audiology. Speech clinician Brookline Pub. Schs., Mass. Gen. Hosp., 1951-57; rsch. assoc. Syracuse (N.Y.) U., 1957-58; asst. prof. speech pathology and audiology Eastern Ill. U., Charleston, 1958-62; faculty St. Cloud State U., Minn., 1962—, now prof. Mem. Am. Acad. Rehabilitive Audiology, Am. Cleft Palate Assn., Minn. Speech Lang. and Hearing Assn. (recipient honors 1984), Am. Auditory Soc. Presbyterian. Avocation: tournament bridge. Home: 412 1/2 7th Ave S Saint Cloud MN 56301 Office: St Cloud State U Speech Clinic Saint Cloud MN 56301

JACOBSON, JUDITH HELEN, state senator; b. South Bend, Ind., Feb. 26, 1939; d. Robert Marcene and Leah (Alexander) Haxton; m. John Raymond Jacobson, 1963; children—JoDee, Eric, Wendy. Student U. Wis.-

Milw. and Madison, 1957-60. Mem. Mont. Senate, 1980—. Mem. Nat. Conf. State Legislators (human resources com. 1981—, del. Mont. Med. Aux. (legis. chmn. 1981—). Democrat. Lutheran.*

JACOBSON, LOUISE GROVES, nutritionist, educator; b. Kittanning, Pa., Oct. 10, 1938. BS in Home Econs., Ind. U. of Pa., 1960; MS in Food and Nutrition, Ind. State U., 1974; postgrad., Memphis State U. Lic. nutritionist and dietitian, Tenn. Dietitian Stouffers Restaurant, Pitts., 1960-61; home econs. tchr. North Hills Sch. System, Pitts., 1961-64; clin. dietitian Bellevue Suburban Hosp., Pitts., 1964-67; nutrition instr. Youngstown (Ohio) State U., 1967-72; food service dir. Saga Food Services, St. Mary's of the Woods, Ind., 1972-73; home econs. tchr. Normandy Sch. System, St. Louis, 1973-74; assoc. prof. Shelby State Community Coll., Memphis, 1974-81; nutritionist and health edn. coordinator Health First Med. Group, Memphis, 1981—; nutritionist nat. health edn. com. Prudential Ins. Co., Roseland, N.J., 1987-88; nutrition cons. for several privately owned orgns.; reviewer Soc. for Nutrition Edn., Oakland, Calif., 1987-88. Author numerous booklets and videos. Active Brooks Art Mus., Memphis, 1983-87; vol. Memphis in May, 1982-88, Ctr. for So. Folklore, Memphis, 1982-88, Friends of the Orpheum, Memphis, 1982-88, Metal Mus., Memphis, 1984-88, Theatre Memphis, 1982-86. Mem. Am. Dietetic Assn. (edn. chmn. 1977-78, chmn. scholarship 1981-83), Tenn. Dietetic Assn. (state seat 1978-80), Memphis Dist. Dietetic Assn. (pub. relations 1980, long range planning chmn. 1986, outstanding dietitian 1980), Memphis Area Nutrition Coun. (treas. 1986), Bridge Club, Ind. U. of Pa. Mid-South Alumni Assn. (chmn.). Republican. Presbyterian. Home: 6567 Poplar Woods Cir S #1 Germantown TN 38138 Office: Health First Med Group 6445 Poplar Ave Memphis TN 38138

JACOBSON, MINDY SUE, art psychotherapist, educator; b. N.Y.C., July 25, 1954; d. Murray and Joan Lois (Rubenstein) Leiner; m. Christopher Harold Jacobson, Mar. 9, 1980 (div. 1984); 1 child, Stephanie Beth; m. Michael Morris Elovitch, Aug. 28, 1988. Student, Union Coll., Schenectady, 1972-74; BA, SUNY, Stony Brook, 1975; MS in Creative Arts Therapy, Hahnemann U., 1978; cert. in adminstrn. social svcs., Temple U., 1985. Sr. art psychotherapist Friends Hosp., Phila., 1978—; pvt. practice Phila., 1982—, 1987—; clin. instr. Hahnemann U., Phila., 1979—, instr. continuing edn. grad. sch., 1990-91; clin. instr., supr. Trenton (N.J.) State Coll., 1989; cons. U.S. Naval Regional Med. Ctr., Phila., 1978; article reviewer Dissociation, 1989; presenter in field; pres. Windowtalk, Inc., Phila. Contbr. articles to profl. jours. Speaker on preventive child abuse Jewish Fedn. Phila., 1988, 89; asst. Brownie leader Girl Scouts U.S.A., Melrose Park, Pa., 1988-91. Mem. Am. Art Therapy Assn. (profl., registered), Internat. Soc. for Study Multiple Personality Disorders/Dissociative States (profl.), Delaware Valley Art Therapy Assn. (profl., treas. 1979-82, newsletter com.). Democrat. Jewish. Office: Friends Hosp 4641 Roosevelt Blvd Philadelphia PA 19124-2399

JACOBSON, MIRIAM NACHAMAH, lawyer; b. Westfield, Mass., Feb. 25, 1941; d. Bernard and Rose (Heller) J.; m. S. David Scher, Apr. 23, 1978. BA summa cum laude, CUNY, 1975; JD, Yale U., 1978. Bar: Pa. 1978, U.S. Dist. Ct. (ea. dist.) Pa. 1978. Assoc. Mesirov, Gelman, Jaffe, et al, Phila., 1978-82, Cohen, Shapiro, Polisher, et al, Phila., 1983; v.p., assoc. counsel Fidelity Bank, N.A., Phila., 1984-87; prin. Law Offices of Miriam N. Jacobson, Phila., 1987—. Co-founder, treas. Lawyers Com. Reproductive Rights, Phila., 1981-85; bd. dir. Yale Law Sch. Fund, New Haven, Conn.; active Nat. Abortion Rights Action League, Planned Parenthood. Mem. ABA, Pa. Bar Assn. (real property and banking sects.), Phila. Bar Assn. (real property and banking sect.), Women Real Estate Attys. (organizer, coordinator 1979—), ACLU, Nat. Orgn. for Women; Nat. Assn. of Women Lawyers, Bus. Women's Network, Nat. Women's Polit. Caucus, Nat. Assn. Women Bus. Owners. Office: Law Offices Miriam N Jacobson 1528 Walnut St Philadelphia PA 19102

JACOBSON, NANCY HELEN, nurse, consultant, educator; b. Lansdowne, Pa., Nov. 16, 1947; d. Homer Pierce and Helen Irwin (Duffy) Tillotson; m. Philip William Jacobson, Dec. 11, 1976; children—Jeneane Renee, Abbe Nicole. Diploma Chester County Hosp., 1968; B.S.N., U. Pa., 1973, M.S.N., 1978. Lic. R.N.; cert. med. surg. nurse, Pa.; cert. nutrition support nurse, Pa. Staff nurse Hosp. of U. Pa., Phila., 1968-79, head nurse, 1970-73, staff devel. instr., 1973-79; instr. Holy Family Coll., Phila., 1979-83; cons. nursing, Phila., 1983—; curriculum specialist Med. Coll. Pa., Phila., 1985-87; assoc. dir. continuing nursing edn., The Med. Coll. Pa., 1987—, cons. 1982-85; cons. United Home Health Services, Phila., 1984-86, Springhouse Corp., Phila., 1984-87, W.B. Saunders Co., Phila., 1986—, Vis. Nursing Assn. Eastern Montgomery County, 1986—; guest lectr. continuing edn. various agys., 1977—. Co-editor RN Bds. Rev. for NCLEX-RN 1987, 88, 89; contbr. articles to profl. jours. Instr. ARC, Phila., 1985, cons. needs assessment, 1985, coordinator student project, 1985. Recipient Profl. Nurse Traineeship award Dept. HEW, 1977. Mem. Am. Nurses Assn. (cert. med., surgical nurse 1987), Pa. Nurses Assn. (continuing edn. approval rev. panel 1987-88), League of I.V. Therapy Edn. (guest lectr. at 1985, 87 convs.), Pa. Assn. for Gifted Edn., Sigma Theta Tau (chair nominating com.). Home: 617 Elkins Ave Elkins Park PA 19117 Office: Med Coll Pa 3200 Henry Ave PO Box 12608 Philadelphia PA 19129

JACOBSON, PATRICIA ANNE FITTS, lawyer; b. Buffalo, N.Y., Dec. 1, 1946; d. Francis Michael Fitts and Ruth Marie (Condon) Fitts Hawkins; m. Carl Whitney Jacobson, June 7, 1969; children—Berit Elissa Jacobson; Matthew Michael Fitts Jacobson. B.A. in Polit. Sci. and Econs., Rosary Coll., River Forest, Ill., 1968; M.A. in Polit. Sci., Boston U., 1973; J.D., Case Western Res. U., Cleve., 1980. Bar: Ohio 1980. Seminar dir. UN Assn./U.S.A., N.Y.C., 1968-69; tchr. English, Chinese Middle Sch. and Chinese U. Hong Kong, 1971-73; continuing edn. planner cons. U. Mich., Ann Arbor, 1973-77; research assoc. Case Western Res. U., 1978-79; assoc. Hahn, Loeser and Parks, Cleve., 1980-82; ptnr. Wickens, Herzer & Panza Co., L.P.A., Lorain, Ohio, 1982—; chairperson Com. on Goals of Mich. Edn. State Dept. Edn., Lansing, 1976-77. Editor: Volume 30 Case Western Res. Law Rev., 1979-80. Consulting lawyer, mem. devel. adv. com. Nord Ctr. for Mental Health, Elyria/Lorain, Ohio, 1982—; mem. lawyers adv. com. ACLU, Cleve., 1981—, bd. dirs., Oberlin, Ohio, 1982-86 . mem. Com. of Concerned Asian Scholars (mem. editorial bd. 1969-71), ABA, Lorain County Bar Assn., Nat. Health Lawyers Assn. Home: 336 Reamer Pl Oberlin OH 44074 Office: Wickens Herzer & Panza Co LPA 1144 W Erie Ave Lorain OH 44052

JACOBSON, SHARYN RENEE, interior designer; b. St. Petersburg, Fla., Sept. 14, 1946; d. Ted Philip and Sylvia (Heller) Wittner; m. Richard Elliot Jacobson, Apr. 20, 1967; children: Todd Aron, Marc Steven, Caron Eve. Student, U. Fla., 1964-65; student, Tampa U., 1965-67. Pres. Interiors, Inc., St. Petersburg, Fla., 1979—. Bd. dirs. Hillel Day Sch., Tampa, 1986. Mem. Am. Soc. Interior Designers, Internat. Furnishing and Design Assn., Nat. Hist. Preservation. Republican.

JACOBSON, SUSAN DENE, librarian; b. St. Paul, Sept. 13, 1949; d. Payson Bernard and Shirley Thelma (Goldman) J. Student, Conn. Coll., 1967-69; BA, Bowdoin Coll., Brunswick, Maine, 1971; MS, Simmons Coll., Boston, 1972. Acquisitions libr. Yale U., New Haven, Conn., 1972-74; head acquisitions libr. Youngstown (Ohio) State U., 1974—; insight leader, game leader English Festival Youngstown State U. Bd. dirs. alumni coun. Bowdoin Coll., 1976-80. Mem. ALA (co-chmn. libr.-vendor rels. discussion group 1982-83, chmn. computer applications in librs. subcom. 1984-85), Phi Kappa Phi. Office: WF Maag Libr Youngstown State U 410 Wick Ave Youngstown OH 44555

JACOBVITZ, ROBIN SMITH, psychology educator, consultant; b. Sharon, Pa., Sept. 8, 1953; d. Jack Edward and Patricia Ann (Reardon) Smith; m. Robert H. Jacobvitz, June 13, 1987. BA, Lake Erie Coll., Painesville, Ohio, 1975; MA, NYU, 1977; PhD, U. Mass., 1983. Postdoctoral fellow U. Minn., Mpls., 1983-85; asst. prof. psychology U. N.Mex., Albuquerque, 1985—; sci. cons. Gen. Mills Corp., Mpls., 1985, Md. Pub. TV, Owings Mills, 1988—. Contbr. articles to profl. jours. Recipient Nat. Rsch. Svc. award NIMH, 1983-85. Mem. Am. Psychol. Assn., Soc. for Rsch. in Child Devel., Psychonomic Soc., Sigma Xi (treas. U. N.Mex. chpt. 1988—). Democrat. Jewish. Home: 8831 Henriette Wyeth NE Albuquerque NM 87122 Office: U NMex Dept Psychology Albuquerque NM 87131

JACOBY, MARY JEAN, human resources professional; b. Westfield, Mass., Apr. 10, 1955; d. Benjamin M. Jacoby and Barbara Ann (Quigley) Smith. BS, Miami U., Oxford, Ohio, 1977; MA, U. Va., 1983; Cert. Communications, Communications Sch., Rep. Nat. Com. Polit. Edn., 1984; Cert. Inst. for Bus. and Community Devel., U. Richmond, 1985. Hospitality hostess Walt Disney World Co., Inc., Lake Buena Vista, Fla., 1977-78; community affairs sec. Sta. KBTV TV, div. Gannett Corp., Denver, 1979-81; instr. U. Va., Charlottesville, 1981-83; mid-atlantic admissions rep. Edn. Mgmt. Corp., Pitts., 1983-84; dir. communications, research Va. Reps., Richmond, 1984-86; ind. pub. relations mktg. cons. Richmond, 1986-87; regional sales mgr. McKendree and Co., Inc., Richmond, Va., 1987-89; mgr. corp. tng. and devel. Blue Cross and Blue Shield Va., Roanoke, 1989—; chairperson pub. relations and recruitment, com. chairperson Met. Richmond, Inc. Chairperson pub. rels. and recruitment coms., bd. dirs. Big Bros.-Big Sisters Met. Richmond, 1984—, regional rep., 1989; co-chairperson pub. rels. Va. Spl. Olympics, Richmond, 1986—; chmn. svc. planning com. St. Paul's Episc. Ch., 1989. Recipient Pub. Svc. award for Outstanding Svc., United Way, Denver, 1980, Commendation for Professionalism, FBI, 1981, Commendation for Humanitarian Svc., DAV, 1981; named one of Outstanding Women in Am., 1986; named Outstanding Vol. of Yr., United Way, Richmond, 1989, Big Sister of Yr., Big Bros. Big Sisters Met. Richmond, 1988. Episcopalian. Home: 3155 #16 Berry Ln SW Roanoke VA 24018 Office: Blue Cross and Blue Shield 602 S Jefferson St Roanoke VA 24011

JACOBY, TERESA MICHELLE, animal behaviorist; b. El Dorado, Ark., Feb. 12, 1956; d. Ray Ralph and Billie Jean (Burns) Phillips; m. Robert Gregory Oshel Jr., June 23, 1973 (div. Sept. 1975); m. Max Mason Jacoby, Aug. 30, 1976; children: Misty Marie, Melany Michelle. BS in Animal Psychology, Pa. State U., 1980. Nat. spokesperson, show judge Am. Dog Breeders Assn., Salt Lake City, 1984—; owner Rocking J Ranch, Emory, Tex. Mem. S.W. Pit Bull Assn. (charter, founding, past pres.), Lone Star State Pit Bull Club (past sec.), Endangered Breed Assn. (nat. rep.), Responsible Dog Owners of Tex. (founding), North Tex. Pit Bull Club, Am. Quarter Horse Assn., World Wildlife Fedn., Greenpeace. Baptist. Home: 110 E Small Hill Dr Grand Prairie TX 75050 Office: Animal Med & Surg Hosp 600 Airport Frwy W Irving TX 75062

JACOVEC, JOANNE MELLOW, financial executive; b. N.Y.C., June 19, 1946; d. Joseph Anthony and Muriel Louise (Tricarick) Mellow; m. Albert Charles Jacovec, Oct. 2, 1971; children Suzanne Elizabeth, Laura Marie. BA, Trinity Coll., Washington, 1968; MS, Fordham U., 1975; postgrad., U. N.C. Asst. prin. Winston-Salem (N.C.) Forsyth County Schs.; project mgr. comptrollers, tng. coord. pers. dept. R.J. Reynolds Tobacco Co., Winston-Salem, mgr. customer svcs. and ops. support; speaker, cons. in field. Chmn. steering com. United Way, 1989-90; vol. Habitat for Humanity, 1990. Mem. Nat. Assn. Accts. (bd. dirs., Outstanding Mem.), NAFE, Internat. Customer Svc. Assn. Roman Catholic. Home: 340 Westoak Trail Winston-Salem NC 27104 Office: RJ Reynolds Tobacco Co PO Box 3000 401 N Main St Winston-Salem NC 27102

JACOX, ADA KATHRYN, nurse, educator; b. Centreville, Mich.; d. Leo H. and Lilian (Gilbert) J. B.S., Columbia U., 1959; M.S., Wayne State U., 1965; Ph.D., Case Western Res. U., 1969. R.N. Dir. nursing Children's Hosp.-Northville State Hosp., Mich., 1961-63; assoc. prof., then prof. Coll. Nursing Univ. Iowa, Iowa City, 1969-76; prof., assoc. dean Sch. Nursing U. Colo., Denver, 1976-80; prof., dir. research ctr. sch. nursing U. Md., Balt., 1980-90, dir. ctr. for health policy rsch., 1988; prof. sch. nursing Johns Hopkins U., Balt., 1990—; dir. Ctr. for Health Policy Rsch. U. Md. Grad. Sch., Balt., 1988-90. Co-author: Organizing for Independent Nursing Practice, 1977 (named Book of Yr., Am. Jour. Nursing); A Process Measure for Primary Care: The Nurse Practitioner Rating Form, 1981 (named Book of Yr., Am. Jour. Nursing). Editor: Pain: A Sourcebook for Nurses, 1977 (named Book of Yr., Am. Jour. Nursing). Chair AIDS study sect. NIH, 1990—; co-chair pain mgmt. guidelines panel AHCPR, 1990. Carver fellow, U. Iowa, 1972; cert. Disting. Achievement in Nursing Research and Scholarship, Alumni Assn. Columbia U. Tchrs. Coll., 1975. Fellow Am. Acad. Nursing; mem. Am. Nurses Assn. (dir. 1978-82, 1st v.p. 1982-84), Am. Nurses Found. (pres. 1982-85), Am. Acad. Nursing, Nat. Acad. Scis. (com. on nat. needs for biomed. and research personnel 1984-87), Inst. of Medicine, AMA (mem. health policy agenda work group 1983-86). Office: Johns Hopkins U Sch Nursing 600 N Wolfe St Baltimore MD 21205

JACQUES, CAROLE, Canadian legislator; b. June 12, 1960; m. Jean-Claude Dubé, 1988; 1 child, Mila. Grad., U. Sherbrooke. Lawyer; mem. Ho. of Commons, 1984—. Mem. Can. Bar Assn., Que. Bar Assn. Progressive Conservative. Office: House of Commons, Parliament Bldgs, Ottawa, ON Canada K1A 0A6*

JADERBORG, JEAN ANN, librarian; b. Washington, D.C., Feb. 22, 1955; d. Harold Arvid and Lois May (Neaderhiser) J. BS in English, Eastern Ill. U., 1976; MLS, U.Ill., 1981. Libr. asst. Lincoln Libr., Springfield, Ill., 1977-80, children's libr., 1980-83, br. head, 1983—; '. Mem. choir Laurel United Meth. Ch., Springfield, 1980—, chairperson edn. com., 1989. Mem. ALA, Ill. Libr. Assn., (I READ Ill. Reading Enrichment & Devel. 1987-90, 1992 chairperson I READ 1990-93). Office: Lincoln Libr West Branch 1251 W Washington Springfield IL 62702

JAE, sculptress, jewelry designer, educator; b. Bklyn., Jan. 9, 1947; d. Benjamin and Shirley (Salles) Shareff. BA, Pace U. art tchr., lectr. Brandeis U., N.Y.C., 1989-. Exhibited in shows at Am. Hellenic Soc., Athens, Greece, 1973, Met. Mus. Art, N.Y.C., Bklyn. Mus. Art, Arts Club N.Y.C., and others in Italy, Spain, Mex., Can., Republic of South Africa, Argentina, Equador. Tchr. ESL Internat. Ctr., N.Y.C., 1987—. Mem. Internat. Women Assn. Arts, Nat. Mus. Women in the Arts. Home and Office: 48 W 73d St New York NY 10023

JAEGER, JUDY DURRANCE, advertising consultant; b. Atlanta, Oct. 26, 1950; d. Sim James and Maggie Elizabeth (Dunn) Durrance; m. Richard Robert Jaeger III, May 18, 1974; children: Richard Robert IV, Kathryn Elizabeth, Laura Suzanne. ABJ, U. Ga., 1972, MA, 1975. Supr. spl. svcs. Miami U., Oxford, Ohio, 1975; advt. asst. Info Works, New Orleans, 1976-77; advt. mgr. Carolina Enterprises, Asheville, N.C., 1978; copy writer Sta. WAAA, Winston-Salem, N.C., 1979-80; prin. Atlanta, 1982—. Docent Audubon Zoo, New Orleans, 1977; vol. Am. Lung Assn. Ga., Atlanta, 1983-88. Mem. Alpha Xi Delta (pres. Atlanta-Clayton County alumnae chpt. 1984-85). Home: 361 Summerwood Dr Stockbridge GA 30281

JAFFE, CAROLINE RUTH, association communications executive; b. N.Y.C., Feb. 26, 1961; d. Israeli A. and Judith (Snyder) J. BA, Oberlin Coll., 1983. Editorial asst. Ea. Paralyzed Vets. Assn., N.Y.C., 1984-85, assoc. editor, 1985-87, asst. dir. communications, 1987-88, dir., 1988-89; dir. communications Nat. Student Nurses Assn., N.Y.C., 1990—. Contbr. articles, poetry, fiction to various publs. Alumni admissions rep. Oberlin Coll., 1984-89. Mem. N.J. Soc. Assn. Execs., Internat. Assn Bus. Communicators, N.Y. Road Runners Club. Office: Nat Student Nurses Assn 555 W 57th St New York NY 10019

JAFFE, JOANNE WILSON, editor; b. N.Y.C., Aug. 11, 1942; d. Ben and Evelyn Olga (Perlman) Wilson; m. Ira Jaffe, June 28, 1967 (div. 1972). BA, Bryn Mawr (Pa.) Coll., 1964; MFA, Columbia U., 1968; MA, UCLA, 1971. Mng. editor Artist's Proof/Pratt Graphic Art Ctr., N.Y.C., 1966-67; editorial assoc. L.A. County Mus. Art, 1971-74; editor Architectural Digest, L.A., 1977-86; editor-in-chief (founding) Angeles Mag., L.A., 1988—; cons. Modern Maternity Mag., Lakewood, Calif., 1987-88, Calif. Mag., 1990—. Designer wearable art, costume elements for film; works exhibited Arco Gallery, L.A., San Francisco Mus. Modern Art, Oakland Mus., others. Democrat. Jewish. Office: Angeles Mag 11601 Wilshire Blvd Los Angeles CA 90025

JAFFE, LOUISE, English language educator, creative writer; b. Bronx, N.Y., May 17, 1936; d. Joseph and Anna (Movitz) Neuwirth; m. Steven Jaffe, Aug. 26, 1962 (div. 1975); 1 child, Aaron Lawrence. BA, Queens Coll., 1956; MA, Hunter Coll., 1959; PhD, U. Nebr., 1965. Instr. Kingsborough Community Coll., Bklyn, 1965-67, asst. prof., 1967-70, assoc. prof. English, 1970-88, prof., 1989—. Author: Hyacinths and Biscuits, 1985, Wisdom Revisited, 1987, also numerous poetry and fiction stories. Mem. editorial bd. Community Review CUNY, 1984—; faculty adv. student lit. mag., 1983—. Recipient First prize N.Y. Poetry Forum, 1980, First prize, First honorable mention Shelley Soc. N.Y., 1983, 84, and others. Mem. Mensa, Poets and Writers Inc., Shelley Soc. of N.Y., Writers Union, Feminist Writers Guild, Democrat. Jewish. Avocations: creative writing, scrabble, crossword puzzles, people-watching, attending and giving poetry readings. Home: 2411 E 3rd St Brooklyn NY 11223 Office: Kingsborough Community Coll Oriental Blvd Manhattan Beach Brooklyn NY 11223

JAFFE, PHYLLIS SHELLEY, lawyer; b. N.Y.C., Feb. 13, 1925; d. Robert and Jessie (Sinick) Shelley; m. Frederick Stanley Jaffe, Aug. 7, 1947 (dec. Aug. 1978); children: Paul, David, Richard. BA, Queens Coll., 1944; JD, Columbia U., 1949. Bar: N.Y. 1949, U.S. Dist. Ct. (so. dist.) N.Y. 1981, U.S. Ct. Appeals (2d cir.) 1984, U.S. Dist. Ct. (no. dist.), N.Y., 1986. Pvt. practice, Ossining, N.Y., 1953-69; editor Prentice-Hall, Englewood Cliffs, N.J., 1969-71; specialist labor relations N.Y.C. Bd. Edn., 1971-72; staff atty. Bd. Coop. Ednl. Services, Yorktown Heights, N.Y., 1972-75; ptnr. Plunkett & Jaffe, P.C., White Plains, N.Y., 1975—. Mem., pres. Ossining Bd. Edn., 1964-69. Served as sgt. WAC, U.S. Army, 1944-46. Mem. Westchester County Bar Assn., Women's Bar Assn. N.Y. State. Jewish. Avocations: tennis, gardening. Office: Plunkett & Jaffe PC 1 N Broadway White Plains NY 10601

JAFFE, RONA, author; b. N.Y.C., June 12, 1932; d. Samuel and Diana (Ginsberg) J. BA, Radcliffe Coll., 1951. Sec. N.Y.C., 1952; assoc. editor Fawcett Publs., N.Y.C., 1952-56. Author: The Best of Everything, 1958, Away From Home, 1960, The Last of the Wizards, 1961, Mr. Right Is Dead, 1965, The Cherry in the Martini, 1966, The Fame Game, 1969, The Other Woman, 1972, Family Secrets, 1974, The Last Chance, 1976, Class Reunion, 1979, Mazes and Monsters, 1981, After the Reunion, 1985, An American Love Story, 1990. Office: care Morton Janklow 666 5th Ave New York NY 10103

JAFFE, SUSAN, ballerina; b. Washington; m. Paul Connelly. Student, Md. Sch. Ballet; student, Sch. Am. Ballet, Am. Ballet Theatre Sch. With Am. Ballet Theatre II, 1978-80; with Am. Ballet Theatre, 1980—, soloist, 1981-83, prin., 1983—. Repertoire includes: Le Corsaire, Apollo, La Bayadere, Bouree Fantastique, Carmen, Cinderella, Concerto, Duets, Giselle, The Guards of Amager, Push Comes to Shove, Symphonie Concertante, others; created role Lynne Taylor-Corbett's Great Galloping Gottschalk; appeared Spoleto in An Evening of Jerome Robbins Ballets, 1982; appeared with Kirov Ballet, 1988. Office: Am Ballet Theatre 890 Broadway New York NY 10003*

JAFFE, SUSAN LYNN, manufacturing company executive; b. N.Y.C.; d. Irving and Beatrice (Albert) J.; children by previous marriage: Robert Wayne, Stephen Mark. BS, Boston U., 1964; postgrad., Hofstra U., C.W. Post U. Elem. sch. tchr. Long Beach, N.Y., 1964-67; pres. Fashions by Appointment, Glen Cove, N.Y., 1967-71; adminstrv. asst. Peerless Sales Corp., Elmont, N.Y., 1967-71; sales mgr., then mktg. dir. United Utensils Co., Inc., Port Washington, N.Y., 1973-78; v.p. ops. and control United Molded Products div. United Utensils Co., Inc., Port Washington, 1978—. Past fund raiser Glen Cove Community Hosp., Geln Cove Library. Home: 249 12th Ave Sea Cliff NY 11579 Office: United Utensils Co Inc Yennicock Ave Port Washington NY 11050

JAFFE, SUZANNE DENBO, investment banker, entrepreneur; b. Washington, Apr. 17, 1943; d. Milton Carl and Beatrice (Altman) Denbo; m. Howard M. Jaffe, Sept. 10, 1967 (div. 1973). BA, U. Pa., 1965; postgrad., NYU, 1965-67. Picture researcher Time, Inc., N.Y.C., 1967-68; analyst L.M. Rosenthal & Co., N.Y.C., 1968-69, Standard & Poor's Intercapital, Inc., N.Y.C., 1969-70; portfolio mgr., ptnr. Century Capital Assocs., N.Y.C., 1971-81; v.p. Highland Capital Corp., N.Y.C., 1982; exec. v.p. Lehman Mgmt. Co., Inc., N.Y.C., 1982-83; dep. compt. N.Y. State, N.Y.C., 1983-85; pres. S.D.J. Assocs., N.Y.C., 1985-89; mng. dir. Angelo, Gordon & Co., N.Y.C., 1990—; bd. dirs. Crossroads Capital LP, Hartford, Conn. Trustee U.S. Social Security-Medicare, Washington, 1984—, Fordham U., 1984—; assoc. trustee U. Pa., 1987—; bd. dirs. Planned Parenthood, N.Y.C., 1976-83, Employees Retirement Income Security Act adv. coun. Dept. of Labor, Washington, 1985-88, Investor Responsibility Rsch. Ctr., 1984-85, Coun. Governing Bds. State Colls. and Univs.; Overseas Edn. Fund Internat., N.Y. women in bus. com.; mem. adv. com. Children's Aid Soc. Mem. Internat. Women's Forum (bd. dirs.), Women's Forum (bd. dirs., treas. 1987-89), Fin. Women's Assn. (treas. 1985-87), Columbia U. Grad. Sch. Bus. Adv. Bd., Harmonie Club (N.Y.C.), Economic Club (N.Y.C.). Democrat. Jewish. Home: 401 E 88th St #5D New York NY 10128 Office: Angelo Gordon & Co 245 Park Ave 26th Fl New York NY 10167

JAFFE, SYLVIA SARAH, art collector, former medical technologist; b. Detroit, May 16, 1917; d. Sam and Rose (Rosmarin) Turner; BS in Med. Tech., U. Wis., 1940; m. David Jaffe, Nov. 8, 1942. Med. technologist Watts Hosp. Lab., Durham, N.C., 1940-45; rsch. hematology technologist in leukemia Sloan Kettering Meml. Hosp. Lab., N.Y.C., 1946-47; chief med. technologist in hematology Arlington (Va.) Hosp. Lab., 1948-55; chief technologist in diagnostic hematology Georgetown U. Hosp., Washington, 1959-70; collector 19th century and 20th century art, 1970—. Art collections include spl. collection of Winslow Homer Wood, block engravings and collection by 19th Century French graphic artist. Mem. Col. Williamsburg (Va.) Found., hon. citizen. Mem. Am. Soc. Med. Technologists, Am. Soc. Clin. Pathologists (assoc.), Am. Women in Sci., Corcoran Gallery Art, Pa. Acad. Fine Arts, Sierra Club, Nat. Wildlife Fed., World Wildlife Fund., Nat. Audubon Soc., Nat. Trust Hist. Preservation, The Washington Print Club, U. Wis. Alumni Assn., Boston Mus. Arts, Nat. Mus. Women in Arts (charter), Sierra Club, Greenpeace, Soc., Wilderness Soc. Democrat. Jewish. Club: Pioneer Women. Contbr. articles to profl. socs. Address: 1913 S Quincy St Arlington VA 22204

JAFFE-BARZACH, AMY EILEEN, marketing executive, consultant; b. Schenectady, N.Y., May 3, 1961; d. Samuel Ellis and Laurie Ellen (Rothstein) J. BS in Econs., SUNY, Albany, 1982; postgrad. in bus. Rennsalear Poly. Inst. Account exec. Retail Mktg. Cons., Albany, 1981-83; regional mktg. mgr. The Pyramid Cos., Glens Falls, N.Y., 1983-84; mktg. mgr., then dir., The Rouse Co., Springfield, Mass., 1984-88; dir. mktg. Bronson & Hutensky, Hartford, Conn., 1988-89, v.p., mktg., 1989—; cons. Childsplay Mag., Springfield, 1984—; bd. dirs. Creative Edge, N.Y.C. Mem. steering com. Young patrons of the Quadrangle Mus., Springfield, Mass., 1984—; bd. dirs. Leukemia Soc. Am., Springfield, 1984—. Mem. Bus. and Profl. Women's Club (Young Careerist award 1984), New Eng. Mktg. Dirs. Council, Advt. Club Western Mass., Pub. Rels. Soc., Women in Communications, Internat. Coun. Shopping Ctr. Democrat. Jewish. Club: Appalachian Mt. (Hartford, Conn.). Home: 26 Forest Hills Ln West Hartford CT 06117 Office: Bronson & Hurtensky City Place 34th Fl Hartford CT 06103

JAFFEE, EILEEN KAREN, biochemist; b. N.Y.C., May 7, 1954; d. Ira and Shirley (Kantor) J.; m. George Douglas Markham IV, July 14, 1983; 1 child, Elizabeth. BS in Chemistry, SUNY, Cortland, 1975; PhD in Biochemistry, U. Pa., 1979. Postdoctoral fellow Harvard U., Cambridge, 1979-81; asst. prof. Havorford (Pa.) Coll., 1981-83; rsch. asst. prof. Thomas Jefferson U., Phila., 1983-84, U. Pa., Phila., 1984—. Contbr. articles to profl. jours. Recipient grad. fellowship NSF, NIH grants, 1981—. Mem. Am. Chem. Soc., Am. Soc. Biochemistry and Molecular Biology, AAAS, Sigma Xi. Office: Univ Pa 4001 Spruce St Philadelphia PA 19104-6002

JAFFER, NAVIN, marketing professional; b. Kisumu, Kenya, Aug. 25, 1958; came to U.S. 1970; d. Amirali and ShahSultan (Nazrali) Jaffer; m. Gregory John Ramage, Dec. 13, 1985. SB in Mechanical Engring., MIT, 1979; MBA, U. Chgo., 1984; postgrad. elec. engring.-computer sci., U. N.C. and N.C. State U., 1989—. Process engr. Polaroid Corp., Waltham, Mass., 1979-80; design engr. Zenith Electronics, Northbrook, Ill., 1980-83; mktg. specialist Gen. Electric-Med. Systems, Milw., 1984-85; bank officer/analyst NCBC Corp., Charlotte, N.C., 1985-87; tech. mktg. analyst Sun Microsystems, Inc., Research Triangle Park, N.C., 1987-89; cons. IMC Corp., Chapel Hill, N.C., 1989—. Vol. Orange County Rape Crisis Ctr., Chapel Hill, 1988-89. Recipient AFL-CIO scholarship, N.Y., 1975. Mem. Assn. Computer

Mfg. and Engring., Tau Beta Pi, Eta Kappa Nu. Democrat. Moslem. Home and Office: 500 Quinn Ct Chapel Hill NC 27516

JAGIELSKI, KAREN IRENE, organization executive; b. Hartford, Conn., Aug. 10, 1962; d. Edward Joseph and Irene Leocadia (Mazurkiewicz) J. BA, Bates Coll., 1986. Constitent caseworker Conn. Senate, Hartford, 1986; vol. VISTA, Hartford, 1987-88; researcher, writer Conn. Coalition for Homeless, Wethersfield, Conn., 1988; lobbyist Conn. NOW, Hartford, 1989—. Author: Connecticut Resource Guide to Sheltering, 1988. State of Conn. scholar, 1980-84, Bates Coll. scholar, 1980-85, Geoffrey law scholar, 1983; Watson Found. fellow, 1986-87. Mem. Conn. Coalition for Choice. Office: Conn NOW 32 Grand St Hartford CT 06106

JAHAN, MARINE, dancer, actress, singer; b. Le Plessis-Aux-Bois, France, Sept. 17, 1958; came to U.S., 1976; d. Raoul Henry and Anne (LaPeyre) J. Uncredited dance double for J. Beals in Flashdance; featured dancer in Streets of Fire; dancer, co-author (fitness video) Freedanse. Office: Move 'N GrowInc 1025 Ocean Ave Ste 101 Santa Monica CA 90403

JAHDE, JUDY A., community health nurse, consultant; b. Beatrice, Nebr., July 23, 1949; d. Harry L. and JoAnn R. (Heble) Scott; m. Marv J. Jahde, Apr. 17, 1972; children: Jennifer D., Sarah A., Matthew J. Diploma, Bryan Meml. Sch. Nursing, Lincoln, Nebr., 1970; student, U. Nebr., 1970-72, Coll. St. Francis, Joliet, Ill., 1981—. Insvc. instr., staff devel./patient teaching coord. Family Hosp., Milw., 1973-80; insvc. edn. coord. in ob-gyn., pediatrics, geriatrics Iowa Luth. Hosp., Des Moines, 1982-86; home health care nurse Norrell Home Health Care Svcs., West Des Moines, Iowa, 1986; nurse, case mgr. Related Health Svcs., West Des Moines, 1986-87; home care nurse St. Francis Hosp. and Med. Ctr., Topeka, 1987-88; med. case mgr. Quality Managed Care, Inc., Overland Park, Kans., 1988—. Mem. Home Health Care Adminstrs. Group. Home: 14114 Woodward Overland Park KS 66223

JAHN, BILLIE JANE, nurse; b. Byers, Tex., Dec. 12, 1921; d. Thomas Oscar and Molly Verona (Kennemer) Downing; student Scott and White Sch. Nursing, 1941-42, U. Mich., 1973-75; B.S. in Nursing, Wayne State U., 1971; M.S., East Tex. State U., 1976, Ph.D., 1982; m. Edward L. Jahn, Dec. 6, 1942; children—Antoinette R., James T., Thomas L., Edward L., Janette E. Staff nurse Warren Meml. Hosp., Centerline, Mich., 1957-61; supr. nursing service Mich. Dept. Mental Health, Northville, 1962-71, Franklin County (Tex.) Hosp., 1972-74; instr. nursing Paris (Tex.) Jr. Coll., 1975-80; nurse educator VA, Waco, Tex., 1981-82; exec. v.p., dir., sr. nursing cons. Dos Cabezas, Inc., Mt. Vernon, Waco and Temple, Tex., 1981—; adj. faculty U. Tex.-Arlington, 1985—; mem. dept. phys. medicine and rehab. Scott and White Hosp., Temple, Tex., 1985—; head nurse dept. physc. med. and rehab.; cons. East Tex. State U., Texarkana, 1978—. adj. faculty U. Tex.-Arlington. Vol., ARC, 1971—; den mother Boy Scouts Am., 1960-62; sec. PTA, Warren, Mich., 1960-62; v.p., Temple, Tex., 1957-58. Mem. AAAS, Nat. League Nursing, Nat. Assn. Rehab. Nurses (rev. bd. Rehab. Nursing Inst. 1986—, Rehab. Nursing Found., 1989—), Tex. League Nursing, AAUP, Nat. Assn. Female Execs., Am. Assn. Curriculum and Supervision, Phi Delta Kappa, Kappa Delta Pi.

JAHN, NORMA JEAN, finance administrator, actress, singer musician; b. Galveston, Tex., Sept. 17, 1926; d. Oran Henry and Helen Angela (Seale) J.; m. Lester A. Balaski, Oct. 22, 1944 (div. 1957); children: Beverly Sue, Belinda Lou; 1 stepchild, Bonnie Jean; m. Charles F. Brass, Dec. 12, 1957 (div. 1959). Student high sch. Dancer, singer Florence Coleman Dance Sch., Port Arthur, Tex., 1929-33; dance instr. Ella Lu Pau Dance Sch., Houston, 1934-40; singer Bg Band Era, various locations, 1941-44; with Model-Billboards Orange Crush, Chgo., 1942; model-print John Robert Powers, N.Y.C., 1943-44; star Norma King Show WWL Radio, Roosevelt Hotel, New Orleans, 1968-69; musicians payroll acct. Warner Bros. Records Inc., Burbank, Calif., 1973—. Bd. dirs. Toluca Lake (Calif.) Commerce Assn., 1988. Named Hon. Citizen, Mayor Victor H. Schiro, City of New Orleans, 1967, Key to the City of New Orleans, 1967; recipient Outstanding Svc. award, USNR, 1968; named Outstanding Vol., New Orleans Recreation Dept., 1968. Mem. Screen Actors Guild, Am. Fedn. Musicians, Am. Fedn. TV and Radio Artists, Associated Latter-Day Media Artists (bd. dirs. membership 1979-84, Donna King Conklin award 1986, Bravo award 1986), Am. Film Inst., The Actor's Ctr., Lincoln Continental Owner's Club. Democrat. Morman. Office: Warner Bros Records Inc 3300 Warner Blvd Burbank CA 91510

JAIN, PUSHPA RANI, radiation oncologist, educator; b. Jabalpur, India, July 5, 1935; came to U.S., 1973; d. Behari Lal and Rama (Narad) J.; adopted children, Vivek, Anand, Poonum. BSc, U. Sagar, India, 1955; MB BS, U. Nagpur, India, 1960; MD in Ob.-Gyn., U. Bombay, 1973. Diplomate, Am. Bd. Radiology. Intern Med. Coll. Nagpur, 1960-61, house surgeon ob-gyn., 1961-62; asst. surgeon Kasturba Hosp., BHEL(I) Ltd., Bhopal, India, 1962-73; fellow in solid tumors Univ. Hosps., Madison, Wis., 1974-75; resident in radiation oncology SUNY, Syracuse, 1975-77, Roswell Pk. Meml. Inst., Buffalo, 1977-78; fellow in radiation oncology Meml. Sloan Kettering Cancer Ctr., N.Y.C., 1978-80; asst. prof. W.Va. U. Health Sci. Ctr., Morgantown, 1980-84; assoc. prof. W.Va. U. Health Sci. Ctr., 1984—; cons., Louis A. Johnson VA Hosp., Clarksburg, W.Va., 1982—. Mem. Am. Soc. Therapeutic Radiation and Oncology, Radiol. Soc. N.Am., Am. Coll. Radiology, Am. Endocurie Therapy Soc., W.Va. State Med. Soc. Office: WVa U Health Sci Ctr Morgantown WV 26506

JAIN, SUNITA DULI, education educator; b. Bamora, India, Feb. 11, 1938; came to the U.S., 1965; d. Kundan Lal and Phoola Bai (Saraf) Katharaya; m. Duli C. Jain, Dec. 25, 1951; children: Avanindra, Ahamindra. BS in Edn., Queens Coll., 1982, MS in Edn., 1986. Tchr. N.Y.C. Bd. Edn., N.Y., 1971-86; edn. assoc. asst. N.Y.C. Bd. Edn., 1986—. Treas. Jain Study Circle, N.Y., 1987—. Mem. United Fed. Tchrs. Home: 99-11 60 Ave Flushing NY 11368 Office: 1930 Andrews Ave Bronx NY 10453

JAINI, YOLANDA MARIE JIMENEZ, principal, educator; b. San Antonio, Feb. 12, 1950; d. Jose and Juanita (Paez) J.; m. Ashok Kumar Atmaram, Dec. 31, 1971; children: Rajendra, Lachmi, Radhika, Amar Lachman, Subhash, Durga. BA, St. Mary U., San Antonio, 1976; MA, Tex. A&I U., 1977, EdD, 1986. Cert. elem., ESL and bilingual tchr., Tex., supr., mid mgr., supt. Tchr. trainee title VII Harlandale Ind. Sch. Dist., San Antonio, 1970-72; tchr. bilingual Edgewood Ind. Sch. Dist., San Antonio, 1972-76, Crystal City (Tex.) Ind. Sch. Dist., 1976-77, San Antonio Ind. Sch. Dist., 1977-78; instr. edn. dept. Tex. A&I U., Kingsville, 1978-79; asst. supt. for curriculum and instruction Asherton (Tex.) Ind. Sch. Dist., 1979-82; asst. prof. reading Tex. A&I U., Kingsville, 1982—; tchr., developer prek Harlandale Ind. Sch. Dist., San Antonio, 1985-87, acad. coord., 1987-90; pres. RIM, Inc., San Antonio, 1988—. U.S. Office of Edn. grantee, 1970-71, 76-77; HEW fellow, 1977-80. Mem. Assn. for Supervision and Curriculum Devel., Tex. Assn. Sch. Adminstrs., NAFE, Indo-Am. Entrepreneur Assn. Democrat. Baptist. Home: 109 S Gardenview San Antonio TX 78213

JAKAB, IRENE, psychiatrist; b. Oradea, Rumania; came to U.S., 1961, naturalized, 1966; d. Odon and Rosa A. (Riedl) J. MD, Ferencz József U., Kolozsvar, Hungary, 1944; lic. in psychology, pedagogy, philosophy cum laude, Hungarian U., Cluj, Rumania, 1947; PhD summa cum laude, Pazmany Peter U., Budapest, 1948; Dr honoris causa, U. Besançon, France, 1982. Diplomate Am. Bd. Psychiatry. Rotating intern Ferencz József U., 1943-44; resident in psychiatry Univ. Hosp., Kolozsvar, 1944-47, resident in neurology, 1947-50; resident internal medicine Univ. Hosp. for Internal Medicine, Pécs, Hungary, 1950-51; chief physician Univ. Hosp. for Neurology and Psychiatry, Pécs, 1951-59; staff neuropathol. rsch. lab. Neurol. Univ. Clinic, Zurich, 1959-61; sect. chief Kans. Neurol. Inst., Topeka, 1961-63; dir. rsch. and edn., 1966; resident psychiatry Topeka State Hosp., 1963-66; asst. psychiatrist McLean Hosp., Belmont, Mass., 1966-67; assoc. psychiatrist McLean Hosp., 1967-74; prof. psychiatry U. Pitts. Med. Sch., 1974-89, prof. emerita, 1989—, co-dir. med. student edn. in psychiatry, 1981-89; dir. John Merck Program, 1974-81; mem. faculty dept. psychiatry Med. Sch., Pecs, 1951-59; asst. Univ. Hosp. Neurology, Zurich, 1959-61; assoc. psychiatry Harvard U., Boston, 1966-69, asst. prof. psychiatry, 1969-74, program dir. grad course mental retardation, 1970-87; lectr. psychiatry, 1974—. Author: Dessins et Peintures des Aliénés, 1956, Zeichnungen und Gemälde der Geisteskranken, 1956; editor: Psychiatry and Art, 1968, Art Interpretation and Art Therapy, 1969, Conscious and Unconscious Expressive Art, 1971, Transcultural Aspects of Psychiatric Art, 1975; co-editor: Dynamische Psychiatrie, 1974; editorial bd.: Confinia Psychiatrica, 1975-81; contbr. articles to profl. jours. Recipient 1st prize Benjamin Rush Gold medal award for sci. exhibit, 1980, Bronze Chris plaque Columbus Film Festival, 1980, Leadership award Am. Assn. on Mental Deficiency, 1980; Menninger Sch. Psychiatry fellow, Topeka, 1963-66. Mem. AMA, Am. Psychol. Assn., Am. Psychiat. Assn., Société Medico Psychologique de Paris, Internat. Rorschach Soc., N.Y. Acad. Scis., Internat. Soc. Psychopathology of Expression (v.p. 1959—), Am. Soc. Psychopathology of Expression (chmn. 1965—, Ernst Kris Gold Medal award 1988), Royal Soc. of Medicine (affiliate), Internat. Soc. Child Psychiatry and Allied Professions, Internat. Assn. Knowledge Engrs. (v.p. for medicine), Deutschsprachige Gesellschaft für Psychopathologie des Ausdruckes (hon.), Deutschsprachige Gesellschaft fur Psychopathologie des Ausdrucks (Prinzhorn prize 1967). Home and Office: 74 Lawton St Brookline MA 02146

JAKES, KAREN SORKIN, biologist; b. Washington, June 18, 1947; d. George Y. and Goldie (Friedman) Sorkin; m. Peter Herbert Jakes, Aug. 23, 1970; children: Susan Johanna, Aaron George. BS in Chemistry, Brown U., 1969; PhD, Yale U., 1974. Asst. for rsch. Rockefeller U., N.Y.C., 1971-75, rsch. assoc., 1976-90. Contbr. articles to profl. jours. Vice pres. Trinity Sch. Parents Assn., N.Y.C., 1983-85, treas., 1988—. Mem. AAAS, ASM. Office: Albert Einstein Coll Medicine Dept Physiology 1300 Morris Park Ave Bronx NY 10461

JAMES, AMABEL BOYCE, freelance writer; b. Balt., Oct. 13, 1952; d. John Cowman George and Barbara Allen (Cobb) Boyce; m. Hamilton Evans James, Aug. 25, 1973; children: Meredith Evans, Rebecca Lee, Hamilton Boyce. AB, Wellesley Coll., 1974. Chartered fin. analyst, 1981. Systems analyst John Hancock Mut. Life Ins. Co., Boston, 1974-75; asst. buyer Lord & Taylor, N.Y.C., 1975; economist Lionel D. Edie, N.Y.C., 1977, E.F. Hutton & Co., N.Y.C., 1978-79, Schroder Capital Mgmt., N.Y.C., 1979-82; freelance writer N.Y.C., 1984—; cons. Keck & Co., N.Y.C., 1984. Editor, contbr. author numerous articles to popular mags., newsletters. Vol. Jr. League City of N.Y., 1975—; docent Nat. Acad. Design, 1986—; bd. dirs. Friends Henry St. Settlement House, 1977-80, Vacations and Sr. Ctrs. Assn., 1984—. Named Margaret Brand Smih lectr. So. Meth. U. Sch. Continuing Edn., 1980. Mem. N.Y. Soc. Security Analysts/ Fin. Analyst Fedn., River Club of N.Y.C., Colony Club, Tokeneke Club. Republican. Episcopalian. Home and Office: 1001 Park Ave New York NY 10028

JAMES, ANNE See WIENS, DEBORAH

JAMES, BARBARA WOODWARD, small business owner, business consultant; b. Owensboro, Ky., Feb. 14, 1936; d. J.T. and Thelma (Newman) Woodward; m. William E. James, Feb. 19, 1951 (div. June 1953); 1 child, Keith Douglas. Vice pres., Fla. Containers Inc., Sebring, 1978-81; v.p. Barda Services Inc., Tampa, Fla., 1981-87; v.p., gen. mgr. BJ's Lounge of Tampa, Inc., 1982—; founder, owner Flamingo Bar and Grill, Clearwater, Fla., 1987—, BJ's Lounge, Tampa, 1989—. Democrat. Roman Catholic. Office: 900 N Dale Mabry Tampa FL 33609

JAMES, CYNTHIA ANN, transportation company official; b. Canton, Ohio, Sept. 2, 1956; d. Richard Eugene and Rose Marie (Steed) J. BA, Miami U., Oxford, 1978. Pers. mgr. Avanti Mgmt. Co., Canton, 1979-80; mgmt. trainee Roadway Express, Inc., Toledo, 1981-81; city dispatcher Roadway Express Inc., Muskegon, Mich., 1981-82; sales rep. Roadway Express, Inc., Warren, Mich.; terminal mgr. Roadway Express, Inc., Port Huron, Mich., 1987-90; nat. account exec. Roadway Express, Inc., Taylor, Mich., 1990—. Mem. Candlelight Youth Coun., Canton, 1971-75, co-chmn., 1973-74. Recipient Outstanding Youth in Community Svc. award Gov. State of Ohio, 1973. Republican. Methodist. Home: 5590 Lapeer Rd #2A Port Huron MI 48060 Office: Roadway Express Inc 22701 Van Born Rd Taylor MI 48180

JAMES, DIANA MARIE, hospital food service director; b. Barksdale AFB, La., Sept. 4, 1955; d. Edward Edward and Florence Agnes (Mals) J.; m. Brian Andrew Braden, Dec. 18, 1981 (div. Mar. 1988). BS in Bus. Mgmt., U. Md., 1985; MS in Human Resource Mgmt., Golden Gate U., 1988. With USAF, 1973, advanced through grades to staff sgt., resigned, 1981; adminstrv. specialist VA/Kellogg Community Coll., Battle Creek, Mich., 1981; food svc. supr. Mich. Air Nat. Guard, Battle Creek, 1981-82, N.D. Res., Minot, 1982; diet technician Williamsburg (Va.) Landing, 1985-86, food prodn. mgr., 1986-89; dir. of dietary Charter Hosp., Charlottesville, Va., 1989—; svcs. supr. Va. Air Nat. Guard, Sandston, 1987—; adj. instr. food svc. Va. Air Nat. Guard. 1989—. Facilitator Young Adult Community Cath., Charlottesville, 1990—. Mem. Golden Gate U. Alumni Assn., U. Md. Alumni Assn., Phi Kappa Phi. Home: 292 Four Seasons Dr Charlottesville VA 22901

JAMES, DOT (DOROTHY ANN), researcher, writer, fund-raiser, editor; b. San Antonio, Sept. 14, 1938; d. Royal Percy and Eloise (Ohlen) J. BA in History, So. Meth. U., 1960; MA in Edn., Stanford U., 1962; postgrad., U. San Francisco, 1984-85, U. Santa Cruz, 1987-88. Cert. in secondary edn., Calif., human svcs. counseling. Mgmt. analyst Dept. of Navy, Treasure Island, Calif., 1963-65; tchr. pub. high sch. Gilroy, Calif., 1965-69, Caldwell, Idaho, 1969-71; editor in chief Venus mag., Palo Alto, Calif., 1973-75; ptnr., chief exec. officer F.S. Button Mfg. Co., San Jose, Calif., 1975-83; exec. dir. AIDS Found. of Santa Clara County, San Jose, Calif., 1983-84; free-lance mgmt. cons. and writer San Jose, 1984—; office mgr. Adult Independence Devel. Ctr., Santa Clara, Calif., 1987; dir. vols. Emergency Housing Consortium, San Jose, 1987-88; coord. community devel. Shelter Against Violent Environments (S.A.V.E.), Fremont, Calif., 1988; with devel. office Santa Clara U., 1988-90; chief exec. officer Paladin Editorial Svcs., San Jose, 1990—. Designer/mfr. feminist slogan buttons housed in Women's Collection, Smithsonian Inst., Washington; contbr. monographs and articles to profl. pubs. Active various women's rights, environ., animal welfare, orgns. for developmentally and physically disabled, gay rights, pub. health groups, 1962—; bd. dirs. Aris Project, Campbell, Calif., 1987-88; crisis intervention counselor Suicide Crisis Svc. of Santa Clara County, San Jose; commr. City of San Jose Human Rights Commn. Grantee Nat. Def. Edn. Act, 1967, Coe Found., 1969; Nonprofit Orgn. Mgmt. Inst. scholar, 1984. Mem. Stanford Bay Area Profl. Women, Nat. Soc. of Fundraising Execs., Santa Clara County Hist. and Geneal. Soc. Democrat. Home and Office: 4260 Camden Ave San Jose CA 95124

JAMES, EDITH JOYCE, steel company executive; b. Chgo., May 22, 1926; d. John and Rebecca Miriam (Fischer) Shaiova; m. W. Ivan James, Dec. 29, 1958 (div. 1970). Student, Hunter Coll., 1944-45, Northwestern U., 1945-47, Ill. State U., 1963-66, Washington U., 1966-70. Acctg. supr. Panelit, Inc., Skokie, Ill., 1958-62; compt. Johnstone Constrn., Bloomington, Ill., 1962-66; asst. dir. housing Washington U., St. Louis, 1966-70; v.p., gen. mgr. William A. Miller Machine and Elevator, St. Louis, 1970-76; founder, pres. James Elecvator Co. and E.J. Elevator Co., St. Louis, 1977-85; pres. J & J Installers, Inc., St. Louis, 1976—; pres. Erector and Riggers St. Louis, 1986—. Mem. Am. Sub-contractors Assn. (v.p., bd. dirs. St. Louis chpt.), St. Louis Cou. Constrn. Employers (sec., bd. dirs. St. Louis Goaltenders), Nat. Assn. Miscellaneous Ornamental Archtl. Porducts Contractors (bd. dirs.). Democrat. Jewish. Office: J & J Installers Inc 4301 Arco Ave Saint Louis MO 63110

JAMES, GENEVA BEHRENS, educator; b. Marietta, Minn., Mar. 23, 1942; d. Siegfried and Dora (Schoenrock) Behrens; BS, Mankato State U., 1963; m. Howard James, Aug. 2, 1963; children: Scott, Dawn. Tchr. English high schs., Minn., 1964-65; instr. acctg., Adult Continuing Edn., Bellevue, Nebr., 1971-75, dir. Adult Basic Edn. Ctr., 1974—, vol. coordinator, 1983—, instr. secondary schs., 1980—, instr. computer literacy, 1984—; Pilot Computer Program, 1987-88, seminar presenter Nebr. State Advt. Edn. Assn., 1986, Commn. on Adult Basic Edn., 1987. Mem. exec. com. Boy Scouts Am., 1974-80; mem. metro community task force, 1986-88. Mem. AAUW, Nat. Assn. Public and Continuing Adult Edn., Adult and Continuing Edn. Assn. Nebr., NEA, Nat. Council Tchrs. English (dist. curriculum com. 1985—), Alpha Delta Kappa. Republican. Lutheran. Home: 1314 Hansen Ave Bellevue NE 68005 Office: 2221 Main St Bellevue NE 68005

JAMES, GLEDA JO, mineral water company executive; b. Atlanta; d. Oscar Lee and Jewell Odessa (Hancock) Brown; m. William Edward James, Jan. 6, 1951 (dec. Oct. 1982); children—Jennifer James Camp, Gregory, Susan. Art student, Naples, Italy, 1962-65; student, Wilmington Coll., 1966-67. Owner, James House Restaurant, Lithia Springs, Ga., 1971-84; real estate sales agt. Finch Realty, Lithia Springs, 1984-85; owner, pres., chmn. bd. Lithia Springs Mineral Water Co., Inc., 1983—, also Cave Spring Pure Water Co. Inc., also Deer Lick Springs Inc. Pres., Lithia Springs Civic Club, 1978; curator Family Dr. Mus., 1984—; mem. Ga. Trust for Hist. Preservation, 1985—; chmn. Tourist Hist. Commn. Recipient Best Painting in Show award Jacksonville Artists Club, N.C., 1966, Homemaker of Yr. award Congl. Dist. Ga. Homemakers, 1970. Mem. Internat. Bottled Water Assn. (pub. relations com. 1984, Pub. Relations award 1984, 85), Sweetwater Hist. Soc. (pres. 1979-85), Atlanta Hist. Soc. Methodist. Avocations: collecting medical memorabilia; historical preservation.

JAMES, HELEN SPENCER, president ceo, technology company; b. New Bedford, Mass., Dec. 29, 1936; d. Edward Kendall and Anne (Lima) Spencer; m. David Thomas James, Nov. 6, 1957; children: Stacey A., Susan L., Sheryl M. BA, U. Tenn., Knoxville, 1981; Student, Ut. Coll. Law, Knoxville, 1981-82. Legal sec. McGuire & McGuire, New London, Conn., 1956-57; adm. asst. Clinch River Home Health, Inc., Clinton, Tenn., 1986-88; pres. ceo Bethel Valley Resources, Inc., Oak Ridge, Tenn., 1988--. Vice Chmn. Anderson Cty Repub. Party Clinton, 1983--; Dir. Recording for the Blind Oak Ridge Tenn., 1983-89, Home Aide Svc. Anderson Cty Clinton, 1986-88. Recipient Phi Beta Kappa Phi Beta Kappa Soc. Epsilon Tenn., 1981, Phi Kappa Phi Phi Kappa Soc. Tenn., 1980, Golden Key Nat. Honor Soc. Tenn., 1980, Beta Gamma Phi Beta Gamma Phi Soc. Tenn., 1978. Mem. Am. Assn. Radon Scientists and Technologists, N.Am. Radon Assn. Republican. Christian. Home: 805 Heritage Hill Dr Clinton TN 37716 Office: Bethel Valley Resources Inc PO Box 3022 Oak Ridge TN 37831

JAMES, JEANNIE HENRIETTA, educator; b. Greenville, S.C., Dec. 5, 1921; d. Portice J. and Essie Virginia (Ross) J.; B.S., Berea (Ky.) Coll., 1945; M.S., U. N.C., 1949; postgrad. Iowa State U., 1955-56; Ed.D., Pa. State U., 1965. Tchr. home econs. Stowe (Vt.) High Sch., 1945-48; asst. prof., asso. prof. home econs. Lincoln Meml. U., Harrogate, Tenn., 1949-59; asst. prof., asso. prof. Ill. State U., Normal, 1959-75; asso. prof. early childhood edn. U. S.C., Columbia, 1975-79, Spartanburg Meth. Coll., 1980; mem. Ill. White House Conf. on Children and Youth, 1969-70. Mem. Nat., S.C. assns. for edn. young children, Soc. for Research and Child Devel., AAUP, World Orgn. for Edn. Children, S.C. Home Econs. Assn., So. Highlands Handicraft Guild, Am. Home Econs. Assn. (program chmn. sect. 1977-79), AAUW, Phi Kappa Delta, Zeta Tau Alpha. Contbr. articles to profl. jours. Home: Belmont Estates #205 Fountain Inn SC 29644

JAMES, JENNIFER AUSTIN, information service company executive; b. N.Y.C., Aug. 26, 1943; d. Francis Wadsworth and Dorothy (Muller) James; m. Jeffrey Pritchard Parker, Mar. 25, 1966 (div. July 1975); children: Lisa Lynn and Lora Paige (twins). BA, Marietta Coll., 1965. Founder, pres. GLOBALDATA Services, Inc., New Canaan, Conn., 1985—. Mem. NAFE, Am. Chem. Soc. (nat. affiliate), Info. Industry Assn., Internat. Platform Assn. Republican. Episcopalian. Office: GLOBALDATA Svcs Inc Valley Ln New Canaan CT 06840

JAMES, KATHRYN KANAREK, electrical engineer; b. N.Y.C., July 16, 1949; d. Jesse Jay and Dora Dorothy (Sader) Kanarek; m. Hugh R. James, Aug. 1982 (div.). BS, MIT, 1969, MSEE, EE, 1971. Computer analyst Computer Systems Engring., North Billerica, Mass., 1971-72; staff mem. MIT Lincoln Lab., Lexington, Mass., 1972-73, MITRE Corp., Bedford, Mass., 1973-76, Analytical Systems Engring. Corp., Burlington, Mass., 1976-77; elec. engr. Combined Arms Combat Devel. Activity U.S. Army, Ft. Leavenworth, Kans., 1978-86; rsch. staff Inst. Def. Analyses, Alexandria, Va., 1986—. Mem. Jr. Women's Symphony Alliance, Kansas City, 1980-86. Grad. fellow Nat. Sci. Found., 1969-71. Mem. IEEE, NAFE, Armed Forces Communications and Electronics Assn., Nat. Coun. Jewish Women (life), Tau Beta Pi, Eta Kappa Nu, Sigma Xi. Jewish. Club: Toastmasters (pres. local chpt. 1976). Home: 3726 King Arthur Rd Annandale VA 22003 Office: Inst for Def Analyses 1801 N Beauregard Alexandria VA 22311

JAMES, KAY, federal agency administrator; b. Portsmouth, Va., June 1, 1949; d. Susie Armistead Coles; m. Charles Everett James; children: Charles Jr., Elizabeth, Robert III. BS, Hampton (Va.) Inst., 1971. Traffic svc. advisor C&P Telephone, Roanoke, Va., 1971-72; group supr. C&P Telephone, Roanoke, 1973, force mgr., 1974; conf. coord. devel. disabilities project State of Va., Richmond, 1978-79; asst. to housing coord. Housing Opportunities Made Equal, Richmond, 1980-81, dir. community edn. and devel., 1981-83; personnel dir. Cir. City Stores, Beltsville, Md., 1983-85; dir. pub. affairs Nat. Right to Life Com., Washington, 1985-88; now asst. sec. pub. affairs Dept. Health and Human Svcs., Washington; pres. Black Ams. for Life, Washington, D.C., 1985-88; asst. sec. pub. affairs HHS Office of the Sec., Washington, D.C., 1989—; mem. White House Com. on Children, Washington, D.C., 1988, White House Task Force on Blacks, Washington, D.C., 1988, Nat. Coalition on Pro-Family Issues, Washington, D.C., 1988; co-founder Nat. Family Inst., Washington, D.C., 1987. Contbr. numerous articles to jours. and newspapers. Republican. Presbyn. Office: Dept Health and Human Svcs Pub Affairs 200 Independence Ave SW Washington DC 20201

JAMES, MARGARET NEAL, home remodeling company executive; b. Caruthersville, Mo., Apr. 6, 1942; d. Hardy Neal and Margaret Irene (Medlin) Privett; m. Charles Rayburn James, Apr. 14, 1962; children: Edward Neal, Lori Ann. Student, Tidewater Community Coll., Virginia Beach, Va., 1977-78. Nurse's aide Pemiscot Meml. Hosp., Hayti, Mo., 1958-61, ward clk., 1961-62; sales clk. J.C. Penney Co., Memphis, 1974-75; tchr.'s aide Virginia Beach Schs., 1977-81; owner, mgr. Prestige Remodeling, Dyersburg, Tenn., 1982—. Pres. Am. Field Svc., Dyersburg, 1987-89. Mem. Am. Bus. Women's Assn. (pres. 1988-89), Homebuilders Assn. Dyer County (exec. officer 1988-89). Republican. Baptist. Home: 2109 Starlight Dyersburg TN 38024 Office: Prestige Remodeling 1775 Pioneer Rd Dyersburg TN 38024

JAMES, MARGE ELIZABETH, company finance executive; b. Akron, Ohio, June 6, 1925; d. Richard Thomas and Georgia Elizabeth (Wilson) Brett; m. John Clyde James, Sept. 5, 1948; children: Nancy Evelyn James Lamb, Elaine Susan James Simmons. BS in Biology with distinction, U. Akron, 1947; postgrad., Brookhaven Community Coll., Dallas, 1980, 81. Supr. chem. lab. City Hosp., Akron, 1948-52; med. technologist Stouder Meml. Hosp., Troy, Ohio, 1952-54, supr. chem. lab., 1957-72; treas. Women's S.W. Fed. Credit Union, Dallas, 1981—; also bd. dirs. Women's S.W. Fed. Credit Union; fin. v.p. Apli-Tech, Inc., Dallas, 1984—, also bd. dirs. Pres. Newcomers, Farmers Branch, Tex., 1975; mem. Friends of the Libr., Farmers Branch, 1980—, City Charter Rev. Com., Farmers Branch, 1982. Mem. NOW, AAUW (pres. 1978-80, interbr. coun. 1980-82, vol. designer credit union software), LWV. Democrat. Home: 14416 Tanglewood Dr Farmers Branch TX 75234 Office: Womens SW Fed Credit Union PO Box 35471 Dallas TX 75235

JAMES, MARIE MOODY, clergywoman, musician, vocal music educator; b. Chgo., Jan. 23, 1928; d. Frank and Mary (Portis) Moody; m. Johnnie James, May 25, 1968. B Music Edn., Chgo. Music Coll., 1949; MusM, Roosevelt U., 1969, MA, 1976; DD, Internat. Bible Inst. and Sem., Plymouth, Fla., 1985. Ordained to ministry Pentecostal Ch., 1976; cert. vocal music tchr., Ill. Key punch operator Dept. Treasury, Chgo., 1950-52; tchr. Posen-Robbins Bd. Edn., Robbins, Ill., 1952-59; tchr. vocal music Englewood High Sch., Chgo., 1964-84; music counselor Head Start, Chgo., 1965-66; exec. dir. House of Love DayCare, 1983, 88, Mary P. Moody Christian Acad., 1989, supt., 1989. Composer, arranger choral music: Hide Me, 1963, Christmas Time, 1980, Come With Us, Our God Will Do Thee Good, 1986, The Indiana House, 1987, Behold, I Will Do a New Thing, 1989. Organist Allen Temple A.M.E. Ch., 1941-45; asst. organist Choppin A.M.E. Ch., 1945-49; organist-dir. Progressive Ch. of God in Christ, Maywood, Ill., 1950-60; missionary Child Evangelism Fellowship, Chgo., 1955-63; unit leader YWCA, New Buffalo, Mich., 1956-58; min. of music God's House of All Nations, Chgo., 1960-80; pastor God's House of Love, Prayer and Deliverance, Robbins, 1982—; chmn. Frank and Mary Moody Scholarship Com., 1984—; dir. music Christian Women's Outreach

Ministry, 1984—; mem. Robbins Community Coun., 1987—; camp counselor Abraham Lincoln Ctr., 1951-53. Coppin A.M.E. Ch. scholar, 1946. Mem. Music Educators Nat. Conf., AFT. Democrat. Club: Good News (tchr. 1987— Robbins, Ill.). Home: 8154 S Indiana Chicago IL 60619

JAMES, MARIE RUPPERT, financial consultant; b. N.Y.C., Sept. 13, 1942; d. John Arthur and Nellie (Huber) Ruppert; m. Michael Joseph James, Jr., June 5, 1976. B.B.A., Baruch Coll., CCNY, 1979; A.A., Alfonsus Coll., 1963. C.L.U.; chartered fin. cons. Tchr., St. John's Villa, Santiago, Chile, 1963-67; dir. head start Archdiocese of N.Y., Bronx, 1967-68; officer mgr. Frederick B. Ayer & Assocs., Inc., N.Y.C., 1968-77; fin. cons. N.Y. Life, Westchester, N.Y., 1979—; mem. estate planning council Westchester, 1986—. Lector, leader of song St. Barnabas Ch.; mem. com. bequests and planned gifts Archdiocese of N.Y. Mem. Nat. Assn. Life Underwriters (pres. elelct), Am. Soc. CLUs (bd. dirs. Westchester chpt.), Life Underwriter Tng. Coun. (chmn.), Beta Gamma Sigma Alumni. Republican. Roman Catholic. Club: Westchester Chorale. Avocations: choral singing; trapshooting. Office: Marie R James & Assocs 37 Saw Mill River Rd Hawthorne NY 10532-1500

JAMES, MARYELLEN, executive search company administrator; b. Rockville Centre, N.Y., Nov. 27, 1960; d. Gerard Joseph and Mary Agnes (Mullany) Smith; m. Thomas J. James, June 21, 1985; 1 child, Robert Thomas. BS in Psychology, So. Conn. State U., 1982. Sr. assoc. Richards Cons. Ltd., Westport, Conn., 1982-85; personnel specialist Gen. Datacom Industries, Inc., Middlebury, Conn., 1985-86; research mgr. J. Redmond & Assocs., Inc., Danbury, Conn., 1986-87; research dir. Employment Opportunities, Danbury, Conn., 1987; ind. cons. New Fairfield, Conn., 1987—. Mem. Nat. Assn. Female Execs.

JAMES, MONA HINKLE, educator; b. Stout's Mills, W.Va., July 21, 1935; d. Harley Robert and Jean (Powell) Hinkle; m. James Lee James, Mar. 19, 1956; children: Jeffrey James, Judith James Sloyer, Jon James. BS in Early Childhood, Ga. State U., Atlanta, 1970, ME in Reading Instruction, 1974; AA in Secretarial Svcs., Glenville (W.Va.) State Coll., 1955. Cert. tchr., Ga. Sec. NASA, Cleve., 1957-60; tchr. North Ridgeville (Ohio) Sch. System, 1965, Elyria (Ohio) City Sch. System, 1966-67, Cobb County Sch. System, Marietta, Ga., 1970-71, 72-80; reading specialist Federally Funded Inner-City Program, Grand Rapids, Mich., 1972; ret., 1980. Elected to Gilmer County Bd. Edn., Glenville, 1990; vol. YES, W.Va., Glenville, 1989—; mem. Gilmer County Indsl. Devel. Assn., Glenville, 1989—, Friends of Gilmer Pub. Libr., 1985—; sec. bd. dirs. Wesley Found., 1989—; treas. Gilmer County Hist. Soc., 1987—. Mem. W.Va./Gilmer County Assn. Ret. Sch. Employees, Literacy Vols. Gilmer County (pres., tutor 1984—), AAUW (v.p., sec. 1983—), W.Va. Fedn. Women's Clubs. Democrat. Methodist. Home: Rt 1 Box 64 Glenville WV 26351

JAMES, SHEILA ANN, advertising executive; b. St. Paul, Feb. 3, 1937; d. Festus Patrick and Mae Agnes Tierney; m. Stuart James; children: Morgan, Owain. BA, U. Minn., 1959. Media analyst J. Walter Thompson, N.Y.C., 1959-61; media rsch. dir. L.C. Gumbinner Advt. Agy., N.Y.C., 1961-63; sr. v.p. Longines Wittnauer, New Rochelle, N.Y., 1964-76; pvt. practice, 1976-79; pres. Harbor Assocs., Greenwich, N.Y., 1979—; v.p. Electronic Mktg. Assn., N.Y.C., 1984—; v.p., dir. N.Y. Showroom, Lynchburg, Va., 1988—. Contbr. articles to mags.; producer, dir. numerous TV commls. Mem. Direct Mktg. Assn. (ECHO award 1985), Brit. Direct Mktg., CTAM. Office: Harbor Assocs 280 Railroad Pla Greenwich CT 06830

JAMES, SHEILA FEAGLEY, museum docent; b. Passaic, N.J., Dec. 22, 1925; d. John Pontz and Elizabeth (O'Neil) Feagley; m. James Malcolm Becker, Apr. 5, 1947 (dec. 1950); children: Pamela, James, Jr.; m. Paul Lenihan, Mar. 18, 1955; (div. June, 1961); children: Winifred, Paul Jr.; m. David Lee James, May 26, 1962; children: Brian David, Adam Wells. BA magna cum laude, Fairleigh Dickinson U., 1975; postgrad., U. Hawaii-Manoa, 1978-82. Counselor and libr. Morris County Jail, Morristown, N.J., 1970-75; interpreter Mission Houses Mus., Honolulu, Hawaii, 1980-85, 90—; storyteller The Storyhour-Manoa, Honolulu, 1983-85, San Francisco Pub. Libr., 1986-87; docent Mus. of Fine Arts, San Francisco, 1986-87, Field Mus. Nat. History, Chgo., 1987-90, Mus. Contemporary Art, Chgo., 1987-90, Art Inst. Chgo., 1987-90, Honolulu Acad. of Arts, 1990—; interviewer Radio Station KNDI, Honolulu, 1984. Author: (Hawaiiana poetry) Color Me Hawaiian, 1979; (Hawaiiana Children's Book) Halani and the Big Bed, 1986 (Yes Conf. award 1986). Bd. dirs. League of Women Voters, Honolulu, 1981-82. Recipient Grant AAUW, Honolulu, 1984. Mem. AAUW (bd. dirs. Hawaii Pacific div. 1978-84, Honolulu Br. 1978-84, San Francisco Br. 1986-87), Art Inst. Chgo., Mus. Contemporary Art, Chgo., Field Mus. Natural History, Chgo. Home: 823 Koko Isle Circle Honolulu HI 96825

JAMES, SUELLEN HOLLIMAN, public information officer; b. Albany, Ga., May 30, 1931; d. John Herbert and Gervaise (Maddox) Holliman; m. Jerry Fuller James, Nov. 25, 1953 (div. 1972); children: Mark Wane, Kenneth Kirk. BSBA, Ga. Coll., 1952. Rsch. asst. Fed. Res. Bank, Atlanta, 1952; exec. sec. Regents of Univ. System, Atlanta, 1952-53; tchr. bus. dept. George Washington High Sch., Agana, Guam, 1953-54; pub. info. officer Albany C. of C., 1977-78, community promotions dir., newsletter editor, 1978-82, dir. conv. and vis. bur., 1982—. Mem. Ga. Hospitality and Travel Assn. (bd. dirs. 1984—, treas. Greater Albany chpt. 1985-91), Ga. Assn. Conv. and Vis. Bur. (bd. dirs. 1989-90), Southwest Ga. Tourism Assn. (pres. 1990), Nat. Tour Assn., Ga. Soc. Assn. Execs., Soc. Govt. Meeting Planners, Women in Network. Home: 3609 Shannon Rd Albany GA 31707 Office: Albany Conv and Vis Bur 225 W Broad Ave Albany GA 31701

JAMES MAYER, SUSAN SMYTH, lawyer, freelance writer; b. Florence, S.C., Jan. 25, 1955; d. John Jay and Caroline Moore (Orr) J. BFA, Stephens Coll., 1976; JD, Syracuse (N.Y.) U., 1983. Bar: Md. 1984; cert. secondary edn. tchr., Mo. Tchr. English Thomas Hayward Acad., Ridgeland, S.C., 1977-78, Middleton Mid. Sch., Goose Creek, S.C., 1979; assoc. Law Offices of James L. Mayer, Elliott City, Md., 1984—. Recipient Cert. of Honor Mo. Writer's Guild, 1976, 2d place award Baltimore Sun Short Fiction Contest, 1989. Mem. ABA, Md. Bar Assn., Howard County Bar Assn., Md. Trial Lawyers Assn. Republican. Presbyterian. Office: Law Office James L Mayer 10801 Hickory Ridge Rd Columbia MD 21044

JAMESON, DOROTHEA, sensory psychologist; b. Newton, Mass., Nov. 16, 1920; d. Robert and Josephine (Murray) Jameson; B.A., Wellesley Coll., 1942; M.A. (hon.), U. Pa., 1973, DSc (hon.) SUNY, 1989; m. Leo M. Hurvich, Oct. 23, 1948. Research asst. Harvard, 1941-47; research psychologist Eastman Kodak Co., Rochester, N.Y., 1947-57; research scientist N.Y.U., 1957-62; vis. scientist Venezuelan Inst. Sci. Research, 1965; research asso. to prof. Psychol. and Inst. Neurol. Scis., U. Pa., 1962-74, Univ. prof. U. Pa., 1975—; vis. prof. Center Visual Sci., U. Rochester, 1974, Columbia U., 1974-76, fall 1986; vis. com. of Bd. of Overseers Harvard U., 1989—; cons. in field. Mem. Nat. Adv. Eye Council, NIH, 1985-89; corp. bd. Woods Hole Oceanographic Inst., 1978-84, 85—; U.S. Nat. Com. Internat. U. Psychol. Scis., 1985—; Nat. Acad. Sci.-NCR Commn. on Human Resources, 1977-80, chmn. com. on vision, 1980-81. Recipient I.H. Godlove award Inter-Soc. Color Council, 1973; Alumnae Achievement award Wellesley Coll., 1974; Deane B. Judd award Assn. Internationale 'de Couleur, 1985; Hermann von Helmholtz award Cognitive Neurosci. Inst., 1987; fellow Center for Advanced Study in the Behavioral Scis., 1981-82. Mem. Soc. Exptl. Psychologists (Howard Crosby Warren medal 1971), Am. Psychol. Assn. (Distinguished Sci. Contbn. award 1972), Am. Psychol. Soc. (William James fellow 1989), NAS, Am. Acad. Arts and Scis., AAAS, Assn. Research in Vision and Ophthalmology, Biophys. Soc., Internat. Brain Research Orgn., Internat. Research Group Color Vision Deficiencies, Optical Soc. Am. (Tillyer medal 1982), Psychonomic Soc., Soc. Neurosci., Sigma Xi. Co-author: The Perception of Brightness and Darkness, 1966; co-author introduction and English translation: Outlines of a Theory of the Light Sense, 1964 (E. Hering); co-editor, author chpt.; Visual Psychophysics: Handbook of Sensory Physiology, Vol. VII/4, 1972; contbr. articles to profl. jours. Office: U Pa 3815 Walnut St Philadelphia PA 19104-6196

JAMESON, PATRICIA MARIAN, government agency administrator; b. Pitts., Mar. 17, 1945; d. Vernon L. and Dorothy Leam (Wilson) J.; B.A., Northwestern U., 1967; M.A., Ohio State U., 1969, with HUD, 1970—, project mgr., Detroit, 1976-77, acting dir. housing mgmt., 1978, dep. area mgr. Milw. Area Office, 1978-85, acting area mgr., 1979-80, 82, regional dir. adminstrn. Chgo. Regional Office, 1985—. Mem. Chgo. Council on Fgn. Relations. Recipient Quality Performance award HUD, 1973, 75, 80, Outstanding Performance award, 1980, 85, 87, 88; NDEA fellow, 1967-69. Mem. Am. Mgmt. Assn., Nat. Assn. Female Execs., NOW, ACLU, Fed. Execs. Inst. Alumni Assn., Phi Beta Kappa, Pi Sigma Alpha. Office: 626 W Jackson Blvd Rm 602 Chicago IL 60606

JAMESON, PAULA ANN, lawyer; b. New Orleans, Feb. 19, 1945; d. Paul Henry and Virginia Lee (Powell) Bailey; children: Paul Andrew, Peter Carver. B.A., La. State U., 1966; J.D., U. Tex., 1969. Bar: Tex. 1969, D.C. 1970, Va., 1973, N.Y. 1978, U.S. Dist. Ct. D.C. 1970, U.S. Dist. Ct. (ea. dist.) Va. 1976, U.S. Ct. Appeals (D.C. cir.) 1972, U.S. Ct. Appeals (4th cir.) 1976, U.S. Ct. Appeals (5th cir.) 1978, U.S. Supreme Ct. 1973, U.S. Ct. Appeals (2d cir.) 1985. Asst. corp. counsel D.C. Corp. Counsel's Office, 1970-73; sr. asst. county atty. Fairfax County Atty.'s Office, Fairfax, Va., 1973-77; atty. Dow Jones & Co., Inc., Princeton, N.J., 1977-79, house counsel, 1979-81, asst. to chmn. bd., 1981-83, house counsel, dir. legal dept., 1983-86; sr. v.p., gen. counsel, corp. sec., PBS, Alexandria, Va., 1986—; bd. dirs. Advanced TV Test Ctr. Inc.; trustee Copyright Soc. USA. Mem. ABA (co-chair electronic media div.), Fed. Communications Bar Assn., D.C. Bar Assn., N.Y. State Bar Assn., Assn. of Bar of City of N.Y. Democrat. Roman Catholic. Office: PBS 1320 Braddock Pl Alexandria VA 22314-1698

JAMES-ROBERTS, BRENDA, lawyer, nurse; b. Trinidad, W.I., Oct. 27, 1957; came to U.S., 1973; d. Paul and Cynthia Bernadine (Augustus) James; m. Lynn Ernest Roberts, Aug. 17, 1985; children: Lynn Ernest III, Brendan P.. BS, Adelphi U., 1980; JD, Hofstra U., 1985. Bar: N.Y. 1986, Del. 1986; R.N., N.Y., Del. Staff nurse ICU Riverside Hosp., Wilmington, Del., 1980-86; staff nurse Lydia E. Hall Hosp., Freeport, N.Y., 1986—; asst. city solicitor City of Wilmington, 1987—; of counsel, Wilmington Youth Devel. Corp., 1987—. Mem. ABA, N.Y. State Bar Assn., Del. State Bar Assn. Office: City of Wilmington 800 French St Wilmington DE 19801

JAMISON, SHEILA ANN ENGLISH, finance company executive; b. Hattiesburg, Miss., July 19, 1950; d. Stanley Gear and Vivian (Gillis) English; m. Troy James Creel, Dec. 21, 1968 (div. 1980); m. Richard Allen Jamison, Oct. 24, 1981. BS in Mgmt. magna cum laude, Fairleigh Dickinson U., 1986. Purchasing asst. Dept. Hosps. State La., Independence, 1973-77; sales rep. Fisher Sci., Houston, 1977-79; account v.p. Paine Webber, Clifton, N.J., 1981-87; asst. br. mgr., assoc. v.p. Dean Witter Reynolds, Inc., N.Y.C., 1987—; speaker The Cons. Firm, Saddle Brook, N.J., 1987. Dir. Gene Michael Scholarship Fund, Bergenfield, N.J., 1986; mem. fund raising com. Tomorrow's Children Fund, Hackensack, N.J., 1987; mem. Group Against Smoking Pollution, 1987—. Mem. Direct Investment Adv. Bd., Barron's High Tech Round Table, Internat. Platform Assn., Phi Zeta Kappa, Delta Mu Delta, Phi Omega Epsilon. Baptist. Office: Dean Witter Two World Trade Ctr 73rd Fl New York NY 10048

JAMISON, SUSAN CLAPP, librarian; b. Pitts., Mar. 21, 1929; d. Harlan Luther and Irene Julia (Krause) Clapp; m. Robert Beatty Jamison, Dec. 19, 1947; children: Linda Jamison Larkin, Stephen Robert. BA in History and English, Coll. Staten Island, CUNY, 1971; M.A. in Am. Studies, U. Del., 1972, Am. History, 1974; MLS U. Md., 1979. Bus. asst. Dr. Robert L. Jacobson, 1960-71; real estate sales Walter Reno Watson Agy., Staten Island, N.Y., 1960-63; tchr. Dover High Sch. (Del.), 1973-75; adj. prof. Wilmington Coll., New Castle, Del., 1975—; asst. dir. Dover Pub. Library, 1980-85; dir. Corbit-Calloway Meml. Library, Odessa, Del., 1975—; grant writer Del. Humanities Forum, Wilmington, 1979-81; mem. speakers bur., 1982-83, evaluator, 1978—; pres. Central Del. Library Consortium, 1982-85. Author: The Face of a Town: the Corbit-Calloway Meml. Library, 1979; author 8 books and programs Yesterday & Today, series 1979-81; contbr. articles to profl. jours; editor and project dir., Six Tricentennial Views of Kent County, 1983-85; author, advisor A Legacy from Del. Women, 1987. Active in Odessa Women's Club, Del., 1975—; host of open house Christmas In Odessa, 1976—; founder, chmn. Septemberfest, 1982; art chmn. Del. Fed. Women's Clubs, 1980-82; publicity chmn. Kent County Tricentennial Commn., Dover, 1983. Recipient Facts on File award for reference pub. ideas, 1985. Mem. ALA (Del. councilor 1989—), Kent Library Network (v.p. 1982-84, pres. 1984-85), Del. Library Assn. (pres. pub. library div. 1979-81, pres. 1985-86, councilor to ALA 1989—), Del. Folklife Assn. (treas. 1987—). Home: Starr-Lore House Main St Odessa DE 19730 Office: Corbit-Calloway Meml Libr 2d and High Sts Odessa DE 19730

JAMISON, VIRGINIA PATTERSON, civic worker; b. Rochester, N.Y., Dec. 24, 1918; d. Walter Richard and Ida May (Lewis) Patterson; m. King Arcy Jamison, Sept. 20, 1943; children: Michael Ray, Gary Wayne, Gregory Martin, Walter Richard, Karen May. BA, Keuka Coll., Keuka Park, N.Y., 1940; MA, Syracuse (N.Y.) U., 1942; postgrad., U. Va., 1942-43. Libr. attendant Rochester Pub. Libr., summers 1939,40; sec. to pres. and dean of women Keuka Coll., summer 1941; clk./sec. Ritter Co., Inc., Rochester, summer 1942; sec. (fellow) Sch. Romance Langs., U. Va., 1942-43; file clk./sec. Hazel-Atlas Glass Co., Wheeling, W.Va., 1944; clk./sec. Med. Sch. Office, U. Rochester, 1948; with Kelly Girl Co., various locations, 1971-72; substitute sec. Bristol Steel & Iron Wks., Inc., Bristol, Va., 1972-74; sec., bookkeeper, adminstrv. asst. YWCA, Bristol, 1975-84; ret.; bd. dirs. YWCA, 1961-70, 71-74, 85—, pres., 1986. Mem. AAUW (pres. 1959-63, treas. 1982-86), Bristol Music Club, YW Women's Club. Pres. Welcome Wagon, 1956; active various charitable orgns. Mem. AAUW (treas. 1982-86, pres. 1959-63), Bristol Music Club, YW Women's Club. Republican. Presbyterian.

JAMPOLE, DIANA PATRICIA, editor; b. Santiago, Chile, May 8, 1958; came to the U.S., 1981; naturalized, 1989; d. Leon and Louisa (Drapkin) Zeldis; m. Stanley Jampole, Oct. 16, 1981 (div. July, 1985). BA, Tel Aviv U., Israel, 1983; MA, Ariz. State U., 1984, MBA, 1989. Cert. instr. Bus. supr. DentaHealth of Ariz., Scottsdale, 1984; bus. mgr. Dr. Goldman and Bohlin, N.Y., 1985; investment unit mgr. Mfs. Assn. of Israel, Tel Aviv, 1985-86; asst. editor Pacitic Sociological Assn., Tempe, Ariz., 1987-89; bus. mgr. Cecil C. Barton DDS, 1989—; bus. cons., Tempe, 1985—. Mem. NAFE, World Trade Ctr. of Israel, Grad. Alliance of Soc. Students, Beta Gamma Sigma, Alpha Kappa Delta. Jewish. Home: 5200 S Lakeshore Dr #136 Tempe AZ 85283

JAMSHIDI, SIMIN, satellite communications executive; b. Tehran, Iran, June 1, 1956; came to U.S., 1974; d. Hamid Jamshidi and Nofar Golestan. BSEE, George Washington U., 1978, MS in Communications Engring., 1980. Program analyst COMSAT, Washington, 1979; mem. tech. staff INTELSAT, Washington, 1980-84, sys. devel. officer, 1984-86, digital svcs. mgr., 1986-88; product mgr. satellite data svcs. GTE Spacenet, McLean, Va., 1988—. Mem. Eta Kappa Nu, Tau Beta Pi. Office: GTE Spacenet 1700 Old Meadow Rd McLean VA 22102

JANAZZO, DONNA LYNN, sales executive; b. New Britain, Conn., Dec. 8, 1948; d. Maurice Janazzo and Dorothy Joan (Ingerson) Reid; divorced. Student, Quinnipiac Coll., Hamden, Conn., 1966-67. Sales and svc. rep. L'Eggs Hosiery, West Hartford, Conn., 1974-76; fleet sales mgr. Stephen World Wheels, Bristol, Conn., 1977—. Mem. Nat. Assn. Fleet Adminstrs. (assoc.), Nissan Century Club, Automotive Fleet and Leasing Assn., Pontiac Sales Masters Club, Cadillac Crest Club, Toyota Sales Soc., Sunshine Club (sec. 1985-90). Underlined information (hone address) will not appear in final publication. Office: Stephen World Wheels 1097 Farmington Ave Bristol CT 06010

JANCUK, WILMA ANN, chemical engineer; b. Cleve., Nov. 15, 1944; d. Andrew L. and Josephine (Yushkiewicz) Diskant; m. Richard J. Jancuk, Oct. 28, 1967 (div. 1979); 1 child, David. B.Chem.Engring., Ohio State U., 1967; MS in Chem. Engring., IIT, Chgo., 1973; MS in Environ. Engring., IIT, 1975. Registered profl. engr., Ill., N.J.; cert. indsl. hygienist, safety profl., hazardous materials mgr. Student engr. Allied Chem. Co., Syracuse, N.Y., 1966; engr. Goodyear Tire & Rubber Co., Akron, Ohio, 1967-69; devel. engr. Western Elec. Co., Chgo., 1969-75; sr. engr. AT&T, Princeton, N.J., 1975-88, sr. staff engr., 1988—; cons. in field; chmn. conf.symposium HazMat, Atlantic City, 1984-85. Contbr. articles to profl. jours. Del. People to People Citizen Ambassador Prog., 1989. Recipient Tech. Achievement award, AT&T, 1972, 87, Tribute to Women in Industry award, YWCA, 1987. Mem. Am. Soc. Safety Engrs., Am. Indsl. Hygiene Assn., ACS, Inst. Hazardous Matls., PrinCen Bridge Club. Republican. Roman Catholic. Home: 11 Hart Ave Hopewell NJ 08525 Office: AT&T PO Box 900 Princeton NJ 08540

JANDURA, PAULA, high technology development company executive; b. Cleveland, Tenn., Nov. 26, 1952; d. Paul Conley Davis and Louise (Clem) Davis-Bowers; m. Albert Jandura, May 28, 1977. AA in Journalism, Thornton Coll., 1973. Adminstrv. mgr. CNA Ins., Chgo., 1973-78; v.p. adminstrn. Interphase Corp., Dallas, 1979—. Mem. Addison Ctr. Theatre, Addison, Tex., 1987—. Mem. Nat. Assn. for Female Execs., Am. Soc. Notaries, Am. Mgmt. Assn. Republican. Baptist. Office: Interphase Corp 13800 Senlac St Dallas TX 75234

JANECEK, LENORE ELAINE, insurance specialist, consultant; b. Chgo., May 2, 1944; d. Morris and Florence (Bear) Picker; M.A.J. in Speech Communications (talent scholar), Northeastern Ill. U., 1972; postgrad. (Ill. Assn. C. of C. Execs. scholar) Inst. for Organizational Mgmt., U. Notre Dame, 1979-80; M.B.A., Columbia Pacific U., 1982; cert. in C. of C. mgmt. U. Colo., 1982; m. John Janecek, Sept. 12, 1964; children—Frank, Michael. Adminstrv. asst., exec. dir. Ill. Mcpl. Retirement Fund, Chgo., 1963-65; personnel mgr. Profile Personnel, Chgo., 1965-68; personnel rep. Marsh Instrument Co., Skokie, Ill., 1971-73; restaurant mgt. Gold Mine Restaurant and What's Cooking Restaurant, Chgo., 1974-76; pres., owner Secretarial Office Services, Chgo., 1976-78; founder, pres. Lincolnwood (Ill.) C. of C. and Industry, 1978-87; pres. Lenore E. Janecek & Assocs., Lincolnwood, 1987—; rep. 10th dist. U.S. C. of C., 1978—. Mem. mktg. bd. Niles Twp. Sheltered Workshop; pres. Lincolnwood Sch. Dist. 74 Sch. Bd. Caucus; bd. mem., officer, founder Ill. Fraternal Order Police Ladies Aux.; bd. dirs., officer Lincolnwood Girl's Softball League, PTA; bd. dirs. United Way, 1982-83; mem. sch. curriculum com. Lincolnwood Bd. Edn.; appointed by Pres. Reagan to the Selective Svc. Bd., 1983; pres. United Way, Skokie Valley, Ill., 1989. Recipient Disting. Grad. of Yr. Nat. Honor Soc., 1985; chosen one of Top 100 Women Leaders in Am., 1988. Mem. Am. C. of C. Execs., Ill. Assn. C. of C. Execs., Women in Mgmt. (local officer), NAFE, Am. Notary Soc., Ill. LWV, Nat. Council Jewish Women, Hadassah. Jewish. Home: 6707 N Monticello St Lincolnwood IL 60645 Office: 4433 W Touhy Suite 550 Lincolnwood IL 60646

JANES, MARONEE FLEMING, vision consultant; b. Fairmont, W.Va., Jan. 22, 1929; d. David Phillips and Evalena (Ford) Fleming; m. Robert Glenn Janes, June 5, 1948 (div. June 1981); children: Pamela Snyder, David, Rovert G. Jr., Anne, Thomas F. AB in Elem. Edn., Fairmont (Va.) State Coll., 1963; MA in Speech Communications, W.VA. U., 19832; cert. in visual handicap, Vanderbilt U., 1985. Spl. edn. tchr. Marion County Sch., W.Va., 1981-85; vision cons. Georgetown County Schs., S.C., 1985—. Bd. dir. All Sts. Episcopal Ch. Women, Pawleys Island, S.C., 1988—, Sunday sch. tchr., 1989—; neighborhood chmn. Vandalia Coun. Girl Scouts U.S., 1964-66, pres., 1973-74; v.p. Black Diamond Coun., 1974—; mem. Marion County Humanities Coun., 1972-74, Gov.'s Commn. on Drug Abuse, 1971—, Gov.'s Critical Issues com., 1971; mem. adv. bd. Town and Gown Theater, 1967—. Mem. Assn. Rehab. of Blind and Visually Handicapped, Jr. League of Fairmont (pres. 1968-70, sustaining), Assn. Rehab. and Edn. for the Blind, Women's Aux. W.Va. Med. Assn. (pres. 1972-73), Women's Aux. Marion County Med. Aux. (pres. 1956-66), Green Hills Garden Club (bd. dirs. gardeners 1972-74, Fairmont). Republican. Gamma Chi Chi. Episcopalian. Home: 193 Belle Isle Villas Georgetown SC 29440

JANESCH, MARY JEAN, legal assistant; b. Pitts., Nov. 26, 1928; d. Eugene Michael and Rosella Irene (Brubaker) Diethrich; m. Eugene Clair Afflerbach, Nov. 26, 1948 (dec. Dec. 1954); children: Vicki L. Disabato, Steven E., Amy J. Lozano, Jody A. Flores; m. Aloysius Carl Janesch, June 26, 1959. Grad. high sch., Cheyenne, Wyomimg, 1946. Cert. legal asst., Ariz., legal sec. Legal sec. William R. Malsh Atty, Tucson, 1958-59, Harris and Brown Attys., Tucson, 1959-61; per sec. TransAmerica Bldg., Tucson, 1961-62; legal sec. Merchant Parkman, Miller and Pitt, Attys., Tucson; legal asst. Superior Ct. Commr. James M. Howsare, Tucson, 1965-71; legal sec., asst. Kenneth L. Allen, Atty, 1975-86; legal asst. Bilby and Shoenhair, P.C., Tucson, 1986-89, Chandler, Tullar, Udall & Redhair, Tucson, 1989—, Mesch, Clark & Rothschild, P.C., Tucson; instr. Pima Community Coll., Tucson, 1974-88. Co-author Ariz. Assn. of Legal Secretaries Manual, 1983. Named Legal Sec. of the Year Tucson Legal Secretaries Assn., 1969-82, Ariz. Assn. of Legal Secretaries, 1982. Mem. ABA, Ariz. Bar Assn., Pima County Bar Assn., Nat. Assn. Legal Assts., Tucson Assn. Legal Assts., Ariz. Women's Lawyers' Assn. Democrat. Roman Catholic. Office: Mesch Clark & Rothschild PC 259 N Meyer Ave Tucson AZ 85701

JANEWAY, ELIZABETH HALL, author; b. Bklyn., Oct. 7, 1913; d. Charles H. and Jeannette F. (Searle) Hall; m. Eliot Janeway; children: Michael, William. Student, Swarthmore Coll.; A.B., Barnard Coll., 1935; Ph.D. in Lit. (hon.), Simpson Coll., Cedarcrest Coll., Villa Maria Coll.; D.H.L. (hon.), Russell Sage Coll., 1981, Florida Internat. U., 1988, Simmons Coll., 1989. Asso. fellow Yale. Author: The Walsh Girls, 1943, Daisy Kenyon, 1945, The Question of Gregory, 1949, The Vikings, 1951, Leaving Home, 1953, Early Days of the Automobile, 1956, The Third Choice, 1959, Angry Kate, 1963, Accident, 1964, Ivanov Seven, 1967, Man's World, Woman's Place, 1971, Between Myth and Morning: Women Awakening, 1974, Powers of the Weak, 1980, Cross Sections: From a Decade of Change, 1982, Improper Behavior, 1987; contbr. to: Comprehensive Textbook of Psychiatry, 2d edit, 1980, Harvard Guide to Contemporary American Writing, 1979, also short stories and critical writing in periodicals and newspapers. Past chmn. N.Y. State Coun. Humanities; bd. dirs. NOW Legal Def. and Edn. Fund, Fedn. State Humanities Coun. Recipient educator's award Delta Kappa Gamma, 1972; named Disting. Alumna Barnard Coll., 1979; recipient Medal of Distinction, 1981. Mem. Authors Guild (council), Authors League Am. (council), PEN, Phi Beta Kappa (hon.). Home: 15 E 80th St New York NY 10021

JANIAK, JANE MARIE, librarian; b. Bklyn., Jan. 10, 1947; d. Charles Joseph and Jane Rosalie (Michalski) J. BA, Fordham U., 1968; MLS, Columbia U., N.Y.C., 1970. Sr. info. technologist Shell Oil Co., N.Y.C. and Houston, 1968-71; libr. Caltex Petroleum, N.Y.C., 1971-72; chief libr. Port Authority of N.Y. & N.J., N.Y.C., 1972—. Mem. ALA, Spl. Librs. Assn., Associated Info. Mgrs. Office: Port Authority NY & NJ One World Trade Ctr New York NY 10048

JANICKI, SUZANNE LYNN, chemist; b. Flushing, Mich., Apr. 17, 1961; d. John David and Sharon Jean (Smith) Kruger; m. Paul David Janicki, Nov. 16, 1985. BS in Chemistry, Mich. State U., East Lansing, 1983. Intern Synchro Start Products, Skokie, Ill., 1981, Nat. Fertilizer Devel. Plant, Muscle Shoals, Ala., 1982; sr. devel. chemist Dow Chem. Co., Midland, Mich., 1983—; mem. industry adv. com. for polymeric materials Underwriters Labs., 1989—. Bd. dirs. Midland Concert Band, 1988. Mem. Soc. Plastic Engrs., ASTM. Republican. Home: 2310 Old Pine Trail Midland MI 48640 Office: Dow Chem Co 433 Bldg Midland MI 48667

JANLE, ELSA MARIE, project manager sensor technology; b. Phila., Pa., Dec. 23, 1941; d. Otto Ludwig Janle and Elsa Karolyn Gratz.; m. Philip H. Swain, Aug. 24, 1963; (div. 88); children: Sheryl Swain, Briana Swain. BS, Ursinus Coll., Collegeville, 1963; MS, Purdue U., W. Lafayette, 1966, PhD, 1979. Rsch. assoc. Purdue U., West Lafayette, Ind., 1979-80; rsch. scientist Purdue U., West Lafayette, 1980-81, instr., 1987—; rsch. assoc. Ind. U. Sch. of Medicine, Indpls., 1981-83; cons. Ash Med. Systems, West Lafayette, 1984-86, sr. rsch. assoc., 1986-88; project mgr. Ash Med. Systems, W. Lafayette, 1988--. Contbr. articles to profl. jours.; patentee in field. Recipient Sbir Phase II Nat. Inst. Health, 1987-89, Sbir Phase I Nih, 1986, Sbir Phase I Nih, 1988. Mem. Am. Diabetes Assoc., Am. Chem. Soc., Am. Soc. for Artificial Internal Organs. Office: Ash Med Systems 2701B Kent Ave West Lafayette IN 47906

JANOCK, MARCIA LINDA, real estate company executive; b. June 17, 1960; d. Irving W. and Baila (Issokson) J. BS, U. Bridgeport (Conn.), 1982. Acct. exec. Hynson Westcott & Dunning, Balt., 1984-85; v.p. Progressive Acquisitions Inc., Miami, Fla., 1987-89; pres. Janock Internat. Enterprises, Malden, Mass., 1989-90, Harvard Cons. Group-Marcia Janock & Assocs. Joint Venture, 1990—. Fundraiser Am. Heart Assn., Mass., 1987-88; asst. chmn. fundraising local polit. campaign, 1988; mem. Nat. Rep. Congl. Com., 1988, 89, Rep. Presdl. Task Force, 1990. Mem. Am. Assn. Self-Emploiyed,

Am. Assn. Individual Investors, Assn. Profl. and Exec. Women, Assn. MBA Execs., Am. Soc. Microbiology, Mass. Chief Police Assn. Republican. Jewish. Home and Office: 47 Essex St Malden MA 02148

JANOSIK, EVELYN JOYCE, real estate company officer; b. Chgo., Sept. 3, 1933; d. John and Anna Lucille (Palesh) Jakab; m. Jerry Richard Janosik, Aug. 6, 1955; children: Michael Charles, Cynthia Elaine, Sandra Anne. BA in Edn., Miami U., Oxford, Ohio, 1955. Cert. tchr., real estate broker. Salesperson Skowronek Corp., Cicero, Ill., 1946-53; typist Cory Corp., Chgo., 1953-55; tchr. Merrilville (Ind.) Sch. Bd., 1955-56; ref. libr. Bendix Aerospace Corp., Mishawaka, Ind., 1956-57; tchr. South Bend (Ind.) Sch. Corp., 1957-59, Mishawaka (Ind.) Sch. Bd., 1967-70; real estate broker Coldwell Banker Anchor R.E., South Bend, 1974-85; v.p. J&E Realty, Mishawaka, 1978-90; pres. Great Lakes Safety Assocs., Mishawaka, 1986-90; cons. in field. Mem. MADD (South Bend chpt.), Sierra Club, Greenpeace, Nat. Coun. State Garden Clubs, Inc. (sec. 1962-63, v.p. 1963-64, pres. 1964-65, historian 1975-76, Artistic Creativity award 1971, Artistic Distinction 1973, Artistic Tri-Color 1973, Horticulture Award of Merit 1975), French Lick Springs Golf & Tennis Resort Club, 10 K Club. Republican. Meth. Home: 16191 Chandler Blvd Mishawaka IN 46544 Office: Great Lakes Safety Assoc 16191 Chandler Blvd Mishawaka IN 46544

JANOUSEK, JUDITH ANN, finacial industry consultant; b. Chgo., July 25, 1940; d. Anton C. and Emily R. (Bajza) J. AA in Bus. Morton Coll., 1960; BS in Bus. Mgmt., Elmhurst Coll., 1981; postgrad. U. Ill., 1981-82, U. Ga., 1984-85; AA in Paralegal Studies, MacCormac Coll., 1984. Lic. real estate broker, Ill. Supr. Olympic Fed. Savs. and Loan Assn., Berwyn, Ill., 1960-65; corp. asst. sec. Clyde Fed. Savs. and Loan Assn., North Riverside, Ill., 1965-75, Proviso Fed. Savs. and Loan Assn., 1975-79; mgr. acctg. dept. Fidelity Fedn. Savs. and Loan Assn., Berwyn, 1979-80; asst. v.p. lending collections Security Fed. Savs. and Loan Assn., Chgo., 1980-86; cons. CEO Assistance, Inc., Oakbrook Terr., Ill., 1986-89; unit mgr. purchase approval and funding dept. Sears Mgmt. Corp., Schaumburg, Ill., 1989—. Mem. AAUW, NAFE, Nat. Assn. Bank Women, Soc. Loan Underwriters, Women in Networking, Cath. Alumni Club, Dialogue for Blind, Bus. and Profl. Women's Club (local and dist. sec. 1968-70). Roman Catholic. Office: Sears Mgmt Corp 1375 E Woodfield Rd Schaumburg IL 60173

JANOVEC, MADELINE MEZA, art educator; b. L.A., Feb. 14, 1935; d. Joachim Joseph and Martha (Meza) J.; m. Morton Kaplan, 1964 (div. 1973); 1 child, Pietra Anna. BS, Portland (Oreg.) State U., 1971. Instr. art Clark Community Coll., Vancouver, Wash., 1978—, Mt. Hood Community Coll., Gresham, Oreg., 1989—; vis. art faculty exploration of visual lang. Evergreen State Coll., Vancouver, 1987-88; co-leader contemporary art tours to western Europe, 1986—. Eighteen one-woman shows; exhibited in 22 group shows. Neighborhood assoc. Brooklyn Action Core, Portland, 1990. Mem. Women's Caucus for Art (founding pres. Portland 1987-90, Oreg. chpt.). Home: 902 SE Franklin Ave Portland OR 97202 Studio: 4460 SE Franklin Portland OR 97202

JANOWIAK, SANDRA LOGAN, funeral service company executive; b. Lansing, Mich., Apr. 25, 1955; d. Carol Edward and Ardis M. (West) Rogers; m. James A. Logan, Jr., Oct. 24, 1981 (dec. Sept. 1983); m. Christopher S. Janowiak, Mar. 7, 1987. Student in social work, Eastern Mich. U., 1978—. Office supr. Bur. Vocational Rehab., Ann Arbor, Mich., 1978-79; adminstrv. asst. reception ctr. Jackson State Prison, Mich., 1979-81; co-owner Janowiak Funeral Home, formerly Geer-Logan Funeral Home, Ypsilanti, Mich., 1981-83, pres., owner, 1983-89. Exec. bd. Women Bus. Owners Com., Ypsilanti, 1983—; adv. bd. Salvation Army, 1983-86; mem. exec. com. Pvt. Industry Council, Washtenaw County Mich., 1987-88. Mem. Ypsilanti C. of C., Nat. Funeral Dirs. Assn., Mich. Funeral Dirs. Assn., Women in Funeral Service Assn., Zonta Internat, Ypsilanti Club (pres. 1989-90). Democrat. Baptist. Home and Office: 320 N Washington St Ypsilanti MI 48197

JANSA, KARLENE RAE, retail executive; b. Anthon, Iowa, Jan. 28, 1946; d. Carl Hans and Dorothea Mary (Hansen) Bumann; m. Edward Otto Jansa, May 14, 1969 (div. 1985); children: Mary, Edward, Al, Karlene. Grad. high sch., Correctinville, Iowa, 1964. Mgr. Shay's Boutique, Hoquim, Wash., 1970-80, Candle Cut, Sergeant Bluff, Iowa, 1981—. Author: My Heart Speaks to Thee, Vol. II, 1983, P.S. God Loves You, 1984, Hearts On Fire, Vol. II, 1985, Our World's Best Loved Poems, 1986. Mem. Ch. Club Ladies (sec. 1985-87, Club award 1987), Sioux Land Singers (Vocal award 1988), Cosmopolitan Club (pres. 1988-90, Esquire award 1989). Democrat. Home: Rt 1 Box 25 Salix IA 51052

JANSEN, BARBARA, dental laboratory owner, technician; b. Lodz, Poland, Dec. 18, 1954; came to U.S., 1961; d. Henryk and Zofia (Zielinski) Jaszczak. Student, Northeast Met. Regional Vocat., Wakefield, Mass., 1975. Dental asst. Chelsea (Mass.) Dental Assocs., 1974-75; dental technician Mass. Dental Prosthetics, Boston, 1975-78, Excell Porcelain Dental Lab., Everett, Mass., 1978-79, New Eng. Dental Prosthetics, Chelsea, 1979-80, Woburn (Mass.) Dental Ceramics, 1980-82, Hirshberg Dental Assocs., Wellesley, Mass., 1982-84; dental ceramicist Profl. Lab. Svc., Watertown, Mass., 1984-90; dental lab. owner Laminates Plus, Framingham, Mass., 1990—; presenter seminars Forum Transformational Seminars; con. in field. Mem. Nat. Bur. Certifiction, Study Group for Dental Labs., Eastern Inter Club Ski League. Office: Laminates Plus 81 Clinton St Framingham MA 01701

JANSEN, GWENDOLYN BETH, office manager; b. Le Mars, Iowa, Feb. 4, 1955; d. James Henry and Elizabeth Jeanette (Byker) J. Med. sec. degree, Western Iowa Tech., 1974. Cert. med. asst.-adminstrv. Med. sec. Sheldon Meml. Hosp., Sheldon, Iowa, 1974-77; office mgr. Michael F.E. Jones, M.D., Sioux City, Iowa, 1977—. Mem. Am. Assn. Med. Assts. (treas. 1980-82, v.p. 1982-83, pres.-elect. 1983-84, pres. 1984-85 Iowa chpt., Profl. Achievement award 1989), Siouxland Med. Office Mgrs. (pres. 1988-89). Home: 1711 25th St Sioux City IA 51104

JANSON, BARBARA JEAN, publisher; b. Mason City, Iowa, Mar. 7, 1942; d. Harley Arnold and Helen Victoria (Henrickson) J.; m. W. John Shallenberger, Feb. 24, 1963 (div. Sept. 1980); children: Mona, Ann; m. John Batty Henderson, Sept. 8, 1984 (div. 1990). BS in Math., Iowa State U., 1965; MS in Math., Trinity Coll., 1970; MBA, U. R.I., 1982. Cert. math. tchr., Iowa, N.Y., Conn. Math. tchr. Pub. High Schs., Avon, Farmington, Bloomfield, Conn., 1966-68, Ulster Acad., Kingston, N.Y., 1971-73; math. instr. Ulster County Community Coll., Kingston, 1973; math. editor Houghton Mifflin Co., Boston, 1974-77; math. instr. Bristol County Community Coll., Fall River, Mass., 1977-78; asst. dir. editorial Am. Math. Soc., Providence, 1978-81, dir. of publ., 1982-85; pres. Janson Publs., Inc., Providence, 1985—; rep. sci. publ. com. Am. Heart Assn., 1986-90; mem. R.I. State Adv. Commn. on Libraries. Editor: Scholarly Publishing: Managing Today, Planning for Tomorrow, 1986. Bd. dirs. Planned Parenthood of R.I., Providence, 1986-87, First Parish Unitarian Ch., Beverly, Mass., 1975-76; mem. steering com. Am. Math. Project, Berkeley, Calif., 1986—; mem. oversight com. Resources Math. Reform Ednl. Devel. Ctr., Newton, Mass.; adv. mem. R.I. State Coun. on Librs. Recipient Mortar Bd. award Iowa State U., 1965. Mem. Soc. for Scholarly Publishing (bd. dirs. 1986-90, chair annual meeting 1985), N.Y. Acad. Sci., AAAS, Am. Math. Soc., Math. Assn. Am., Nat. Council Tchrs. Math., Assn. Am. Publishers (jours. com. 1983-85), Nat. Assn. Women Bus. Owners, LWV. Unitarian. Home: 45 Olney St Providence RI 02906 Office: Janson Publs Inc 222 Richmond St Ste 105 Providence RI 02903

JANTZ, CYNTHIA M., librarian; b. McKenzie, Tenn., Nov. 8, 1957; d. Willfred and Mary (Cantrell) J. AS, Vol. State Community Coll., 1977; BS, Bethel Coll., 1979; MLS, Vanderbilt U., 1988. Cert. tchr., Tenn. Tchr. Union Elem. Sch. Sumner County Bd. Edn., Gallatin, Tenn., 1979-82; English and reading tchr. T.W. Hunter Mid. Sch. Sumner County Bd. Edn., Hendersonville, Tenn., 1982-90, libr. T.W. Hunter Middle Sch., 1990—; cheerleading sponsor T.W. Hunter Mid. Sch., Hendersonville, 1983-90. Mem. choir St. Luke Cumberland Presbyn. Ch.; sect. leader Hendersonville Community Singers, 1987—. Bob Hope Honor scholar, 1977-78, Hutchins scholar, 1978-79. Mem. NEA, Internat. Reading Assn. (local chpt.), Tenn. Edn. Assn., Sumner County Edn. Assn., Tenn. Assn. Middle Schs., Gamma Beta Phi. Home: PO Box 156 Hendersonville TN 37077 Office: TW Hunter Mid Sch 3140 Long Hollow Pike Hendersonville TN 37075

JANUTOLO, SARAH CATHERINE, finance company executive; b. Bluefield, Va., May 29, 1935; d. Milton L. Farmer and Ruth (Woodyard) Dey; m. Benny Ray Janutolo, Aug. 24, 1953; children: Dan, Sheila, Devona. Grad. high sch., Bluefield, W.Va. With Elliott Brokerage Co., Bluefield, 1953-55, F.W. Woolworth, Bluefield, 1954-55, Black Diamond Collection, Bluefield, 1956-58; from clk. to corp. treas. Citizens Budget Co., Youngstown, Ohio, 1962-83; asst. mgr., officer, mgr. Bell Fin. Co., Youngstown, 1983—. Mem. Ohio Consumer Fin. Assn. (bd. dirs. Columbus, Ohio 1988—), Am. Bus. Women's Assn. (pres. Tri County chpt. 1981, pres. 1984, 87-88, 89—, Woman of the Yr. 1982, Boss of Yr. award 1989), Altrusa Club of Youngstown (pres. 1971, Altrusan of the Yr. 1971). Home: 31 Sycamore Dr New Middletown OH 44442 Office: Bell Fin Co 4800 Market St Youngstown OH 44512

JANZEN, NORINE MADELYN QUINLAN, medical technologist; b. Fond du Lac, Wis., Feb. 9, 1943; d. Joseph Wesley and Norma Edith (Gustin) Quinlan. BS, Marian Coll., 1965; med. technologist St. Agnes Sch. Med. Tech., Fond du Lac, 1966; MA, Cen. Mich. U., 1980; m. Douglas Mac Arthur Janzen, July 18, 1970; 1 son, Justin James. Med. technologist Mayfair Med. Lab., Wauwatosa, Wis., 1966-69; supr. med. technologist Dr.'s Mason, Chamberlain, Franke, Klink & Kamper, Milw., 1969-76, Hartford-Parkview Clinic, Ltd., 1976—. Substitute poll worker Fond du Lac Dem. Com., 1964-65; mem. Dem. Nat. Com., 1973—. Mem. Am. Soc. Med. Tech. (people to people clin. lab. scientist del. to People's Republic of China 1989), Nat. Soc. Med. Technologists (awards com. 1984-87, 88—, chmn. 1986-88, nominations com. 1989—), Wis. Assn. Med. Technologists (chmn. awards com. 1976-77, 84-85, 86-87, treas. 1977-81, pres.-elect 1981-82, pres. 1982-83, dir. 1977-84, 85-87, Mem. of Yr. 1982, numerous svc. awards, chair ann. meeting 1987-88), Milw. Soc. Med. Technologists (pres. 1971-72, bd. dir. 1972-73), Communications of Wis. (originator, chmn. 1977-79), Southeastern Suprs. Group (co-chmn. 1976-77), LWV, Alpha Delta Theta (nat. dist. chmn. 1967-69, nat. alumnae dir. 1969-71), Alpha Mu Tau. Methodist. Home: N 98 W 17298 Dotty Way Germantown WI 53022 Office: Hartford-Parkview Clinic 1004 E Sumner St Hartford WI 53027

JAPAR, SUSAN ELIZABETH, obstetrical nurse practitioner; b. Bronx, N.Y., Jan. 8, 1949; d. Romeo and Susan (Kuklish) J.; m. William R. Coffman. BS in Nursing, Hunter Coll., 1970; ob/gyn nurse practitioner cert. U. Kans. Med. Ctr., 1975; MS, U. Calif., San Francisco, 1977. Med.-surg. staff nurse Albert Einstein Hosp., Bronx, 1970-72; staff nurse USAF Hosp., 1972-74; nurse practitioner, Grand Forks AFB, N.D., 1974-75; USAF Hosp., Clark AFB, Philippines, 1977-78; course supr. USAF, 1978-83; gynecol. nurse practitioner USAF Hosp., Myrtle Beach AFB, S.C., 1983-88; gynecol. nurse practitioner USAF Clinic, Hickom AFB, Hawaii, 1988—; ob-gyn nurse practitioner cons. to surg. gen. USAF, 1982—; ob-gyn nurse practitioner cons. tactical air command USAF, 1986-88; vis. lectr. U. Okla. Health Scis. Ctr. Mem. Uniformed Nurse Practitioner Assn., Nurses Assn. of Am. Coll. Ob-Gyn (chmn. Armed Forces Dist. 1983-85). Lutheran. Author: Diagnosis and Treatment of Vulvovaginitis, 1982, 4-part series on contraception, 1983.

JAQUITH, MARTHA ANN, radar engineer; b. Winchester, Mass., May 31, 1962; d. Robert Adford and Shirley Kathleen (White) J. BS in Computer Sci., Merrimack Coll., 1984. Engr. Mitre Corp., Bedford, Mass., 1982-85, Raytheon, Bedford and Sudbury, Mass., 1985—. Republican. Office: Raytheon EDL 528 Boston Post Rd Sudbury MA 01776

JARET, KATHE A., psychologist; b. N.Y.C., May 8, 1952; d. Irving L. and Elaine (Karelitz) J. BA, Bklyn. Coll., 1973, MS, 1975; PhD, U. Conn., 1988. Lic. psychologist, R.I. Psychologist North Kingstown (R.I.) Sch. Dept., 1977—, South County Child & Family Cons., Peacedale, R.I., 1988—; psychologist intern Washington County Med. Health Ctr., Charlestown, R.I., 1988; instr. R.I. Coll., Providence, 1989. Mem. Am. Psychol. Assn., Nat. Assn. Sch. Psychologists, Am. Edn. Rsch. Assn., Internat. Assn. Sch. Psychologists (conf. program com. 1990). Office: South County Child & Family Cons 1058 Kingstown Rd PO Box 301 Peacedale RI 02883

JAROSKI, JILL ANN, dental hygienist, researcher, educator; b. Rhinelander, Wis., Apr. 23, 1956; d. Raymond John Jaroski and Anna Mae (Venne) Juday. BS in Dental Hygiene, Marquette U., 1987; MS, U. Wis., Stout, 1990. Dep. coroner Forest County Sheriff's Dept., Crandon, Wis., 1982-83; dental hygienist Dr. Damian Fennig, Peridontics and Orthodontics, West Allis, Wis., 1983-87; rsch. dental hygienist, regulatory affairs specialist Vipont Pharm., Inc., Ft. Collins, Colo., 1987-88; clin. studies coord., clin. rsch. programs Med. Coll. of Wis., Milw., 1989—; adj. prof. in microbiology, human anatomy, physiology Mount Senario Coll. Author: (with others) chpt. Comprehensive Dental Hygiene Care, 1988. Mem. Sigma Alpha Phi. Home: 927 N 2nd St Bruce WI 54819

JARRELL, IRIS BONDS, educator, business executive; b. Winston-Salem, N.C., May 25, 1942; d. Ira and Annie Gertrude (Vandiver) Bonds; m. Tommy Dorsey Martin, Feb. 13, 1965; 1 child, Carlos Miguel; m. 2d, Clyde Rickey Jarrell, June 25, 1983; stepchildren—Tamara, Cris, Kimberly. Student U. N.C.-Greensboro, 1960-61, 68-69, 74-75, Salem Coll., 1976; B.S. in Edn., Winston-Salem State U., 1981; postgrad. Appalachian State U., 1983, Gardner-Webb Coll., 1989. Cert. tchr., N.C. Resource person Winston-Salem Dental Health Plan; substitute tchr. Winston-Salem/Forsyth County Schs., 1967—; tchr. Rutledge Coll., Winston-Salem, 1982-84; owner, mgr. Rainbow's End Consignment Shop, Winston-Salem, 1983-85; tchr. elem. edn. Winston-Salem/Forsyth County Sch. System, 1985—. Contbr. poetry to mags. Mem. Assn. of Couples for Marriage Enrichment, Winston-Salem, 1984-86, Forsyth-Stokes Mental Health Assn., 1985-86. Mem. Internat. Reading Assn., N.C. Assn. Adult Edn., Forsyth Assn. Classroom Tchrs., Nat. Assn. Female Execs., NOW. Democrat. Baptist. Avocations: singing; writing; sewing; crewel embroidery; gardening; reading. Home: 1008 Gales Ave SW Winston-Salem NC 27103

JARRELL, SHEREE GIPSON, occupational therapist; b. Dallas, Sept. 3, 1955; d. William Lloyd and Gladys Laverne (Herndon) Gipson; m. James Franklin Jarrell, II, Feb. 14, 1986. BS, Tex. Woman's U., Denton, 1977; postgrad., Tex. Woman's U. Registered occupational therapist, Tex. Staff therapist Baylor U. Med. Ctr., Dallas, 1977-79; sr. therapist Baylor U. Med. Ctr., 1979-86, asst. dir., 1986-89, dir., 1989—. Mem. Am. Occupational Therapy Assn., Tex. Occupational Therapy Assn. (recognitions chair 1988—, state conf. prog. chair 1988-89), Trinity North Occupational Therapy Assn. (dist. chair 1989—), Occupational Therapy Assn. Dallas (chair mental health 1980-83). Home: 6458 Westlake Dallas TX 75214 Office: Baylor Univ Med Center 3500 Gaston Ave Dallas TX 75246

JARRELL, VALERIE CANTRELLE, secretary, bookkeeper; b. Houma, La., Oct. 6, 1962; d. Armojen John and Earline Mary (Poche) Cantrelle; m. Thomas Jacob Jarrell, Apr. 27, 1985; 1 child, Brittany Paulette. Grad. high sch., Galliano, La.; cert., H&R Block Tax Sch., New Orleans, 1986. Notary public, La. Bank teller, bookkeeper South Lafourche Bank & Trust, Larose, La., 1980-81; sec. Murphy Cheramie Crewboats, Inc., Galliano, 1981-82; sec., bookkeeper Picciola & Assocs., Inc., Galliano, 1982—; pres. Community Bookkeeping and Tax Svcs., Cut Off, La., 1986—. Mem. exec. coun., Our Lady of Rosary Ch., Larose, 1977-85; mem. Cajun Festival Assn., Galliano, 1982—. Mem. NAFE, La. Assn. Notary Publics. Democrat. Roman Catholic.

JARRETT, ALEXIS, insurance professional; b. Independence, Kans., July 2, 1948; d. Robert Patterson and Betty June (Johnson) J.; m. Victor K. O'Yek, Apr. 12, 1987. BS, U. Minn., Duluth, 1970; postgrad., U. Mo. Lic. in Property and Casualty Ins., Ind., Life and Health Ins., Ind.; cert. coach, Minn. Tchr. Esko (Minn.) Pub. Schs.; pvt. practice Schererville, Ind.; asst. dir. athletics, head coach U. Mo., Columbia. Contbr. articles on sports to newspapers. Sponsor Lake County (Ind.) High Sch. Girls Basketball Banquet; mem. indsl. rsch. liason program Ind. U., Bloomington; bd. dirs. Samaritan Counseling Ctr., N.W. Ind. Mem. Nat. Assn. Life Underwriters, Ind. Assn. Life Underwriters, Lake County Med. Soc. Aux. (pres.), Am. Bus. Women's Assn. (pres. New Image chpt. 1983, named Woman of Yr.). Address: 2330 Wicker Ave Schererville IN 46375

JARRETT, DIANA LOUISE, television producer; b. Flint, Mich.; d. Bennie James and Gwendolyn (Taylor) J. Student, Flint Jr. Coll., Penland (N.C.) Sch. of Crafts, 1967, Herbert Berghof Studios, N.Y.C., 1972. Producer The Word Shop, L.A.; co-producer LAP Art Ltd., N.Y.C.; film cons. County of Hawaii Dept. Rsch. and Devel., Hilo. Producer numerous archaeological documentary films. Mem. AFTRA, SAG.

JARRETT, TERESA YVONNE, medical data specialist; b. Newton, N.C., Aug. 10, 1953; d. Henry and Shirley Edwina (Scronce) J. AAS in Secretarial Scis., Catawba Valley Tech. Coll., Hickory, N.C., 1973; B of Bus., Appalachian State U., 1978. Utilization rev. coord. Catawba Meml. Hosp., Hickory, 1973-82, planning coord., 1982-84, utilization mgmt. coord., 1984-87; diagnosis related groups coord. Frye Regional Med. Ctr., Hickory, 1987-89, oncology data mgr., 1989—; pres. bd. dirs. Catawba County Employees Credit Union, 1977; cons. utilization rev. area hosps., 1980-87; owner Just Bear-ly Crafts, Newton, 1980—, Teresa Y. Jarrett Lettering Svc., Newton, 1980-90. Active Catawba unit Am. Cancer Soc., 1982—, sec. bd. dirs., 1985, pres. bd. dirs., 1987, pub. edn. chairperson, 1990; advisor Teen Dems. Catawba County, 1990. Mem. N.C. Tumor Registrar's Assn., Southeastern Craft and Hobby Assn. Methodist. Home: Rte 1 Box 378 Newton NC 28658 Office: Frye Regional Med Ctr 420 N Center St Hickory NC 28601

JARUZELSKI, JANINA ANNE, lawyer; b. Pitts., Apr. 23, 1958; d. John Jan and Katharine Spencer (Heywood) J. Cert., Leningrad State U., USSR, 1979; AB in History magna cum laude, Princeton U., 1980; JD, U. Pa., 1984. Bar: N.Y. 1986, D.C. 1988, U.S. Ct. Appeals (D.C., 6th and 9th cirs.) 1987, U.S. Dist. Ct. (D.C. cir.) 1989, U.S. Supreme Ct. 1989. Intern Trenton, N.J. bur. N.Y. Times, 1979-80; asst. editor Macmillan Pub. Co., N.Y.C., 1980-81; law clk. Atty. Gen. State of N.J., Trenton, 1982, Paul, Weiss, Rifkind, Wharton & Garrison, N.Y.C., 1983, Cir. Judge U.S. Ct. Appeals, Washington, 1984-85; asst. counsel to clk. U.S. Ho. of Reps., Washington, 1985—. Exec. editor for rsch. and writing U. Pa. Law Rev., 1983-84; contbr. articles to newspapers. Nat. Merit scholar, 1976; Teagle scholar, 1983. Mem. Princeton (N.Y.C.) Club, Nat. Dem. (D.C.) Club. Democrat. Episcopalian. Office: US Ho of Reps H-112 The Capitol Washington DC 20515

JARUZELSKI, KATHARINE HEYWOOD, administrative secretary; b. Tulsa, Okla., Nov. 17, 1929; d. Harold Elston and Eva (Spencer) Heywood; m. John J. Jaruzelski, July 7, 1956; children: Janina Anne, Barratt Heywood. BA, Bowling Green State U., 1950. Adminstrv. sect. Town of Westfield, N.J.; sec. Westfield Recreation Commn., 1974-79; adminstrv. sec. McCune Estate Office, Pitts., 1953-56. Editor Episcopal Monthly mag., 1985-90; author: The Heywood Family, 1975. Mem. Coll. Woman's Club of Westfield (pres. 1975-76, editor newsletter 1984-90), Westfield Hist. Soc., DAR, Soc. Mayflower Descendants N.J. (state sec. 1965-70), League of Women Voters (bd. dirs. 1962-69), Am. Geneal. Soc., Alpha Gamma Delta. Episcopalian. Home: 475 Channing Ave Westfield NJ 07090 Office: Westfield Mcpl Bldg 425 E Broad St Westfield NJ 07090

JARVILL-MCCORD, JUDI LYNNE, health care administrator; b. Yakima, Wash., Aug. 11, 1944; d. Floyd Milton Guthrie and Freeda (Lorraine) Davie; m. Robert Alan Jarvill, Aug. 8, 1964 (div.); children: Traci Lyn, Jon Robert; m. Lance O. McCord, Dec. 3, 1989. AS in Nursing, Chemeketa Community Coll., Salem, Oreg., 1976. RN, Oreg. Head nurse ICU Salem Hosp., 1976-86; dir. nursing Serenity Ln., Eugene, Oreg., 1986-88; adminstr. Rogue Valley Serenity Ln., Cen. Point, Oreg., 1988—. Task force mem. So. Oreg. Drug Awareness, Medford, Oreg., 1988-89; bd. dirs. Valley Health Credit Union, Salem, 1984-86, So. Oreg. State Coll., Ashland, 1988—, Women Entrepreneurs of Oreg., Medford, 1989—, ARC, 1989—; mem. Drug and Pregnancy Task Force, Medford, 1989—, Student Retention Initiative, Medford, 1989—. Mem. Kiwanis, Medford C. of C. (bd. dirs. 1988—), Cen. Point C. of C. Republican. Office: Rogue Valley Serenity Ln 600 S 2d St Central Point OR 97502

JARVIS, BARBARA ANN, transportation executive; b. San Francisco, May 5, 1946; d. Steve and Irma Vivien (Ford) Jarvis; m. Andre Pardow Mitchell (div. Jan. 1973); children: Kristin Dion, Damien Pardow Mitchell; m. Michal Kamionko, Nov. 15, 1987. Student, Skyline City Coll., 1975. Entertainment booking agt. Joe Tex, singer, San Francisco, 1979-82; entertainment booking agt., pres., owner MJM Prodns., San Francisco, Sacramento, 1982-84; dir. transp. Kaiser Permanente Med. Ctr., San Francisco, 1982—. Bd. dirs. HIV Continuum, San Francisco, 1989; transp. dir. San Francisco Kaiser Neighborhood & Health Plan Mem. Free Svc., 1984-89. Mem. Joint Institutional Transp. Brokers' Assn. (pres.), Institutional Mcpl. Parking Assn. (speaker, Award Transp. Excellence IMPC Conv. 1989), Rides for Bay Area Commuters (advisor to new TSM mgrs. 1984—, Achievement Award in Transp. 1989, Best Transp. Program of 1989-90 Yr. award, 1990), San Francisco Tennis Club. Democrat. Roman Catholic. Office: Kaiser Permanente Med Ctr 2425 Geary Blvd San Francisco CA 94115

JARVIS, BARBARA ANNE, lawyer; b. Kansas City, Mo., Apr. 14, 1934; d. Herman Edward and Marjorie Maude (Graber) Spitzenfeil; A.A., Kansas City Jr. Coll., 1953; B.S. in Polit. Sci. magna cum laude, Ariz. State U., 1976, J.D., 1979; m. Thomas B. Jarvis, Sept. 9, 1965; 1 son, Kenneth Mark. Technologist Menorah Med. Center, Kansas City, Mo., 1955-56, Ariz. State U. Student Health Service, 1960-62, Scottsdale (Ariz.) Bapt. Hosp., 1962-65; chief technologist Skyline Lab., Globe, Ariz., 1967-72; practice law, Phoenix, 1979—. Sec. Globe Planning and Zoning Commn., 1970-75; assoc. coordinator Women's Polit. Caucus Ariz.; 1st vice chmn. Ariz. Democratic Com.; mem. Dem. Nat. Com. from Ariz.; chmn. neighborhood rehab. com. Phoenix Urban Form, 1976-77, mem. steering com., 1976-79; mem. Phoenix Bd. Adjustment, 1977-82, chmn., 1980-81; chmn. Village 4 Planning Com., City of Phoenix; chmn. citizens adv. com. Ariz. Dept. Corrections, 1983-85, Paradise Corridor, 1986-88; planning commn. City of Ashland, Oreg., 1989—; bd. dirs. Salvation Army, Globe, Gila Pueblo campus Eastern Ariz. Coll., Gila County Guidance Clinic. Mem. Am. Bar Assn., State Bar Ariz., State Bar Orge., Maricopa County Bar Assn. (co-chmn. alternatives to sentencing com. 1980-81), Ariz. Assn. Criminal Justice, Nat. Orgn. Criminal Def. Lawyers, Oreg. Criminal Def. Lawyers Assn., Ariz. Women Lawyers, Women in Law (chmn.), Ariz. State U. Law Sch. Alumni Assn., Charter 100, Pi Sigma Alpha, Phi Kappa Phi. Office: 1159 Emma Ashland OR 97520

JARVIS, SHIRLEY KAYE, real estate executive; b. Huntington, W.Va., Feb. 11, 1942; d. Thurman Albert and Naomi Elizabeth (Simpson) Chapman; m. James Edward Jarvis, Jan. 3, 1964; children: Donald Christopher, James Courtney. Student, Alderson-Broaddus Coll., 1960-61; Grad. Realtors Inst., Parkersburg Community Coll., 1980. Cert. lab. technician Cabell Huntington (W.Va.) Hosp., 1962-72; realtor Toney Gallery of Homes, Huntington, 1972-79, Era Galaxie, Huntington, 1979-83, H.E. Pilcher and Co., Huntington, 1983; pres., owner The Property Shoppe, Inc. Realty, Barboursville, W.Va., 1983—. Dir. Huntington Womens Bowling Assn., 1981-90; photographer Calvin Evans Evangelistic Crusade, Montego Bay, Jamaica, 1986-89, Moscow, 1990. Recipient Winners Circle award ERA, 1982, Presdl. award Local and State Realtors Assns., 1989. Mem. Nat. Assn. Realtors (multiple listing svc. policy com. 1987-88, community svcs. com. 1989-90), W.Va. Assn. Realtors, Womens Coun. Realtors (state sec. 1987—, state pres. 1990, 3d v.p. 1987), Huntington Bd. Realtors (bd. dirs. 1982—, pres. 1990, multiple listing svcs. and computer affiliates com. 1987—, Realtor of Yr. 1987-88, 89-90), Life Time Million Dollar award 1978-88), Kiwanis (1st v.p.), W.Va. Womens 600 Club (Parkersburg, bd. dirs. 1981-86), Huntington Womens 600 (pres. 1982-87). Republican. Baptist. Home: PO Box 231 Ona WV 25545 Office: The Property Shoppe Inc Realty 6468 Farmdale Rd Barboursville WV 25504

JARY, MARY CANALES, business owner; b. Premont, Tex., Nov. 22, 1936; d. Gus and Ruth (Shively) Canales; m. Lloyd Walker Jary, Apr. 18, 1958; children: Lloyd Walker III, Elisa Jary Long, Bettina Canales, Pamela Ann. Student, Rollins Coll., 1955-56, U. Tex., 1956-58, Incarnate Word Coll., 1959-60, Trinity U., 1966—. Prin., owner Restoration Assocs., San Antonio, 1985—. Pres. San Antonio PTA, 1971; vice chmn. Night in Old San Antonio, 1989—; bd. dirs. San Antonio Conservation Soc., 1972-90. Mem. Am. Inst. Conservation (assoc.), AIA (aux. pres. San Antonio chpt. 1970). Republican. Roman Catholic.

JASICA, ANDREA LYNN, mortgage banking executive; b. Orlando, Fla., Aug. 21, 1945; d. Walter S. and Florence E. (Pasek) J. AA in Pre Bus.

Adminstrn. cum laude, Orlando Jr. Coll., 1965; BS with honors, Rollins Coll., 1976. Sec. Am. Mortgage Co. Fla. Inc., Orlando, 1965-68; closing specialist Charter Mortgage Co., Orlando, 1968-70, Gen. Guaranty Mortgage Co. Inc., Winter Park, Fla., 1971; sr. loan processor C.E. Brooks Mortgage Co. Inc., Orlando, 1971-79; v.p. mktg. Twin Homes Ltd., Orlando, 1980-83; asst. v.p., mgr. region Atlantic Mortgage and Investment Corp. subs. Atlantic Nat. Bank, Orlando, 1984-86; v.p. Commerce Nat. Mortgage Co., Winter Park, 1987-88; supr. Bur. of Census, U.S. Dept. Commerce, Orlando, Fla., 1990—; real estate assoc. Atlantic-to-Gulf Realty Inc., 1972-73, Medel Inc., Maitland, Fla., 1973-74; instr. Mortgage Personnel Svcs. Inc. Contbr. articles to profl. jours. Mem. Valencia Community Coll. Alumni (bd. dirs. 1983-85), Home Builders Assn. Mid-Fla. (assoc., mem. mortgage fin. com., pubs. chmn. 1985, 88, mem. aux. 1985, mem. sales and mktg. council 1984, 85), Orlando Area Bd. Realtors (affiliate, mem. edn. com. 1988), Greater Orlando Assn. Profl. Mortgage Women (chartered, chmn. scholarship com. 1986-87), Mortgage Bankers Assn. Cen. Fla., Fla. Assn. Mortgage Brokers, Nat. Secs. Assn. (asst. treas. Orlando chpt. 1965-71, chmn. future secs. com. 1971).

JASINSKI-CAIDWELL, MARY L., pharmacy technician; b. Chester, Pa., May 8, 1959; d. A. Robert and Helen M. Jasinski; m. William A. Caldwell. Student, Loyola Coll., Balt., 1980; BS, Goldey Beacom Coll., Wilmington, Del., 1982. Registered orthotic fitter; cert. sr. pharmacy technician. Gen. mgr. City Pharmacy Inc., Elkton, Md.; recruiter Golden Beacon Coll., Wilmington, Del.; counselor mastectomy patients City Pharmacy, Elkton, Md.; disc jockey, promoter, Garfield's Restaurant, Elkton; counsellor, advisor Cecil County Birthrite, Elkton. Recipient J.W. Miller award; Alpha Chi scholar, Lindback scholar. Mem. NAFE, Am. Mgmt. Assn., Cecil County C. of C., Alpha Chi. Republican. Roman Catholic. Office: City Pharmacy Inc 723 Bridge St Elkton MD 21921

JASKO, LILLIAN EVELYN, bank executive; b. Union, N.J., Jan. 24, 1933; d. John Paul and Amelia (Durian) J. BA, Vassar Coll., 1955. Asst. v.p., asst. sec. Allied Bank Internat., N.Y.C., 1969-73, v.p., corp. sec., 1973-79; sr. v.p., corp. sec. Allied Bank Internat., N.Y., 1981-88, sr. v.p., corp. sec., country mgr., account officer for Japan, 1983-88, sr. v.p., chief adminstrv. officer, 1981-88; sr. v.p., corp. sec. Allied Internat. Bancorp, Inc., 1981-88; sr. v.p., dir. planning and bus. strategies Banco Portugues do Atlantico, N.Y., 1988—. Contbr. articles on trade, investment and banking to profl. jours. Vol. community orgns., related orgns. and coms. Vassar Coll.; v.p., bd. dirs. Friends of Glen Ridge (N.J.) Libr., 1986—; trustee Freeman Gardens Assn., 1988—. Mem. Nat. Coun. Women U.S., Inc. (bd. dirs.), Pan Pacific and Southeast Asia Women's Assn. U.S., Inc. (bd. dirs., v.p.), Fin. Women's Assn., Global Econ. Action Inst., Alumnae Vassar Coll. (past bd. dirs., treas.), Vassar Club (Essex County, N.J., pres.). Office: Banco Portugues do Atlantico 2 Wall St New York NY 10005

JASPER, DORIS JEAN BERRY, nurse; b. Banner, Miss., Sept. 12, 1933; d. William Richard and Lena Martha (Gambill) Berry; m. Lyman W. Jasper, Jan. 8, 1949; children: Richard L., Lynn William. Student, Blytheville (Ark.) Sch. Nursing, 1949, Purdue U., Westville, Ind., 1979-80, Lake Mich. Coll., Benton Harbor, 1977-80. Staff nurse St. Anthony's Hosp., Michigan City, Ind., 1951-66; pvt. duty nurse Michigan City, 1962-68; emergency rm. nurse St. Anthony's Hosp., 1968-74; charge nurse, emergency rm. nurse Meml. Hosp., Michigan City, 1974-75; pvt. duty nurse Three Oaks, Mich., 1972-84, Michigan City, 1981-88; staff nurse Alpha Christiansan Registry, New Buffalo, Mich., 1988—; pvt. practice Three Oaks, 1989—; pvt. practice No. Ind., So. Mich.; co-owner, mgr. grain farm. Mem. Bus. and Profl. Women's Orgn. (legis. chair dist. 2 1987-88, rec. sec. dist. 2, exec. bd. mem.). Republican. Baptist. Home and Office: 101 Jasper Dr Three Oaks MI 49128

JAUQUET-KALINOSKI, BARBARA, library system administrator; b. Crystal Falls, Mich., Mar. 12, 1948; d. Herbert Francis and Lenore Mary (Roell) Jauquet; m. Gregory Clem Kalinoski, Nov. 12, 1983; children: Stacia Amee, Sara Amee, Michael Thomas and Thomas Michael (twins.). BS, No. Mich. U., 1970; MLS, Western Mich. U., 1974. Adminstrv. asst. Mid-Peninsula Libr. System, Iron Mountain, Mich., 1970-74, asst. dir., 1975-79; periodical libr. U. Wis., Superior, 1980; dir. N.W. Regional Libr., Thief River Falls, Minn., 1981—. Bd. dirs. Discovery Place Child Care Ctr., Thief River Falls, 1990. Named Woman of Honor, AAUW, 1990. Mem. ALA, Minn. Library Assn., Thief River Falls C. of C. (mem. com.), Rotary Club (pres.-elect). Roman Catholic. Office: NW Regional Library 101 E 1st ST Thief River Falls MN 56701

JAVARAS, BARBARA KARIOTIS, educator; b. Chgo., Oct. 3, 1946; d. Theodore and Bessie (Janopoulos) Kariotis; m. James J. Cutrone, July 13, 1965 (div. Mar. 1971); children: John Nicholas, Christine Nicole; m. Paul Basil Javaras, June 24, 1983. Assoc. in Liberal Arts, Wright Jr. Coll., Chgo., 1972; BS, Chgo. State U., 1974; MA, Northern Ill. U., 1979. Cert. tchr., prin., spl. edn. tchr., pre-vocat. coord., Ill. Educator New Horizon Ctr. for Handicapped, Chgo., 1975; rehab. supr. Leyden Devel. Ctr., Franklin, Ill., 1977-78; ednl. facilitator Chgo. Regional Project Chpt. 1, 1978--; ednl. specialist DuPage Supplemental Project Chpt. 1, Chgo.; treas. Learning Games Libr. Assn., Oak Park, Ill., 1985—, coord., 1983-86, assisted with catalog, 1986; presenter programs in field. Dem. election judge, Elmwood Park, Ill., 1976; troop leader Elmwood Park area Boy Scouts Am., 1975-77; bd. dirs. Plato Sch., Chgo., 1986-89; adv. bd. West Suburban Spl. Recreation Assn., Elmwood Park, 1986-87. Mem. Coun. Exceptional Children, Greek Womens Univ. Club, Hellenic Profl. Soc., Phi Delta Kappa. Home: 7223 Oak St River Forest IL 60305

JAVOREK, JUDETH NEWHAM, nursing administrator; b. Sydney, Australia, Nov. 6, 1950; d. Ken and Joan (Nicholson) Newham; m. Jan. Javorek, 1972; 1 child, Jolly. Diploma in nursing, Canberra (Australia) Hosp., 1972; BS, Seattle City Coll., 1980; MA, Webster U., St. Louis, 1983. RN, Oreg., S.C., Wash., Mich. Asst. dir. nursing Providence Med. Ctr., Portland, Oreg., Med. U. S.C., Charleston; dir. nursing Group Health Corp., Seattle; v.p. patient care Holland (Mich.) Community Hosp. Mem. Mich. Orgn. Nurse Execs. (chmn. issues com.), Nightengale Soc. (bd. govs.), Sigma Theta Tau. Home: Pier Love 2324 Lakeshore Fennville MI 49408

JAWORSKI, KAREN ARNOLD, real estate broker; b. Niagara Falls, N.Y., Nov. 12, 1941; d. Stuart Frary and Mary Ellen (Miner) Arnold; m. Edwin J. Jaworski, July 27, 1963; children: John Stuart, Jennifer Ann, Scott Edwin. BA in Edn., SUNY, Oswego, 1963. Grad. Realtors Inst.; cert. residential specialist; notary public. Tchr. Edmeston (N.Y.) Sch., 1963-64, Ridgefield (N.J.) Sch., 1964-67, Harwich (Mass.) Jr.-Sr. High Sch., 1975-80; real estate broker Katherine Cove Real Estate, Harwich Port, Mass., 1979-80, Florence Crockett Real Estate, West Dennis, Mass., 1982-86, Karen Jaworski Real Estate, West Dennis, 1986-89; real estate broker Peter McDowell Assocs., Dennisport, 1989—, mgr. Chmn. Harwich Town Govt. Study Com., 1976-78; bd. dirs. Am. Cancer Soc., 1990, chmn. jail 'n bail, 1990. Mem. Cape Cod and Islands Bd. Realtors (RPAC chmn. 1983-84, program chmn. 1984-85, edn. com. 1987-90, chmn. grievance com. 1990—). Republican. Home: 113 Bank St Harwich Port MA 02646 Office: Peter McDowell Assocs 11 Route 28 Dennisport MA 02639

JAY, NORMA JOYCE, artist; b. Wichita, Kans., Nov. 11, 1925; d. Albert Hugh and Thelma Ree (Boyd) Braly; m. Laurence Eugene Jay, Sept. 2, 1949; children—Dana Denise, Allison Eden. Student Wichita State U., 1946-49, Art Inst. Chgo., 1955-56, Calif. State Coll., 1963. Illustrator Boeing Aircraft, Wichita, Kans., 1949-51; co-owner Back Door Gallery, Laguna Beach, Calif., 1973-88. One-woman shows Milcir Gallery, Tiburon, Calif., 1978, Newport Beach City Gallery, 1981; group shows include Am. Soc. Marine Artists ann. exhbns., N.Y.C., 1978-86, Peabody Mus., Salem, Mass., 1981, Mystic Seaport Mus. Gallery, Conn., 1982-85, Grand Cen. Galleries, N.Y., 1979-84, The Back Door Gallery, Laguna Beach, Calif., 1973-88, Mariners' Mus., Newport News, Va., 1985-86, Nat. Heritage Gallery of Fine Art, Beverly Hills, Calif., 1988—, Md. Hist. Mus., 1989; represented in permanent collections including James Irvine Found., Newport Beach, Niguel Art Assn., Laguna Niguel, Calif., Deloitte, Haskins & Sells, Costa Mesa, Calif., M.J. Brock & Sons Inc., North Hollywood, Calif., others. Recipient Best of Show award Ford Nat. Competition, 1961, First Pl. award Traditional Artists Exhbn., San Bernadino County Mus., 1976, Artist award Chriswood Gallery Invitational Exhbn., Rancho California, Calif., 1973. Fellow Am. Soc. Marine Artists (charter); mem. Niguel Art Assn. (first pres. 1968, hon. life mem. 1978), Artists Equity, Am. Artists Profl. League, Laguna Beach C. of C. Republican.

JAYNE, CYNTHIA ELIZABETH, psychologist; b. Pensacola, Fla., June 5, 1953; d. Gordon Howland and Joan (Rockwood) J. AB, Vassar Coll., 1974; MA, SUNY, Buffalo, 1978, PhD, 1983. Lic. psychologist, Pa. Instr. dept. psychiatry Temple U. Sch. Medicine, Phila., 1982-84, asst. prof., 1984-85, asst. dir. outpatient services, asst. dir. residency tng., 1982-85, clin. asst. prof., 1985—; pvt. practice psychology Phila., 1985—. Contbr. articles to profl. jours. Soc. for Sci. Study Sex scholar, 1981; Sigma Xi grantee, 1981, Kinsey Inst. Dissertation award, 1983. Mem. Am. Psychol. Assn., Ea. Psychol. Assn., Soc. for Sci. Study Sex (bd. dirs. 1984-86). Office: 1213 Locust St Philadelphia PA 19107

JAYNE, ROBYN CHRISTINA, financial administrative secretary; b. Chestertown, Md., June 14, 1969; d. Ronald Edward and Roselma Catherine (Jones) J. Grad. high sch., Worton, Md.; student, Washington Coll., 1987-91. Sec. Kent County Roads Dept., Chestertown, Md., 1987; waitress, caterer Washington Coll. Dining Svc., Chestertown, 1987-89; sec. Randall Cooper CPA, Chestertown, 1988—; waitress Fin, Fur and Feather Inn, Rock Hall, Md., 1983—; tutor, Chestertown, Md., 1988—. Democrat. Roman Catholic. Home: S Main St PO Box 164 Rock Hall MD 21661 Office: Randall L Cooper CPA Washington & Greenwood Ave Chestertown MD 21620

JECKLIN, LOIS U., art corporation executive, consultant; b. Manning, Iowa, Oct. 5, 1934; d. J.R. and Ruth O. (Austin) Underwood; m. Dirk C. Jecklin, June 24, 1955; children: Jennifer Anne, Ivan Peter. Student, State U. Iowa, 1953-55, 60-61, 74-75. Residency coord. Quad City Arts Coun., Rock Island, Ill., 1973-78; field rep. Affiliate Artists, Inc., N.Y.C., 1975-77; mgr., artist in residence Deere & Co., Moline, Ill., 1977-80; dir. Vis. Artist Series, Davenport, Iowa, 1978-81; pres. Vis. Artists, Inc., Davenport, 1981-88; pres., owner Jecklin Assocs., 1988—; cons. writer's program St. Ambrose Coll., Davenport, 1981, 83, 85; mem. com. Iowa Arts Coun., Des Moines, 1983-84; panelist Chamber Music Am., N.Y.C., 1984, Pub. Art Coun., Cedar Rapids, Iowa, 1984; panelist, mem. com. Lt. Gov.'s Conf. on Iowa's Future, Des Moines, 1984. Trustee Davenport Mus. Art, Nature Conservancy Iowa; mem. steering com. Iowa Citizens for Arts, Des Moines, 1970-71; bd. dirs. Tri-City Symphony Orchestra Assn., Davenport, 1968-83; founding mem. Urban Design Council, HOME, City of Davenport Beautification Com., all Davenport, 1970-72. Recipient numerous awards Izaak Walton League, Davenport Art Gallery, Assn. for Retarded Citizens, Am. Heart Assn., Ill. Bur. Corrections, many others; LaVernes Noyes scholar, 1953-55. Mem. Am. Coun. for Arts, Assn. Performing Arts Presenters, Ann. Coll. Univ. Community Arts Adminstrs., Nat. Assembly Local Arts Agys., Crow Valley Golf Club, Outing Club, Rotary. Republican. Episcopalian. Home and Office: 2717 Nichols Ln Davenport IA 52803

JEDWILL, JUDITH MARY, health system professional; b. Detroit, Feb. 28, 1941; d. Donald William and Ruth Elaine (Morrissette) Hansen; m. Richard Allen Jedwill, Nov. 15, 1986; 1 stepchild, Hugh Park. AA in Mktg., Schoolcraft Coll., Livonia, Mich., 1987; student, Detroit Coll. Bus., 1988—. Med. sec. Health Alliance Plan-Metro Med. Group, Detroit, 1979-84, sr. exec. sec., 1984-88; med. sec. Henry Ford Health System, Detroit, 1988-89, governance technician, 1989—. Canvasser Southfield, Mich. area Am. Cancer Soc., 1988—; vol. Henry Ford Health System Hospice Care Program, Detroit, 1990—. Mem. Zonta Internat. Office: Henry Ford Health System 600 Fisher Bldg Detroit MI 48202

JEFFERDS, MARY LEE, environmental education executive; b. Seattle, July 16, 1921; d. Amos Osgood and Vera Margaret (Percival) J.; AB, U. Calif. at Berkeley, 1943, gen. secondary teaching cert., 1951; MA, Columbia U., 1947; cert. Washington and Lee U., 1945. Sec. Fair Play Com. Am. Citizens Japanese Ancestry, 1943-44; adminstrv. asst. U.C. Alumni Assn. book Students at Berkeley, 1949; dir. Student Union Monterey Jr. Coll., 1949-50; mgr. Nat. Audubon Soc. Conservation Resource Ctr., Berkeley, 1951-66; dir. Nat. Audubon Soc. Bay Area Ednl. Svcs., 1966-71; curriculum cons. Project WEY, U. Calif. Demonstration Lab. Sch., Berkeley, 1972-83. Cons. Berkeley Sch. Dist., Alameda County Schs. Mem. land- use com. Environ. Edn. com. East Bay Mcpl. Utility Dist., 1968-87; mem. steering com. Nat. Sci. Guild, Oakland Mus., 1970-76; community adviser Jr. League of Oakland, 1972-76. Mem. Berkeley Women's Town Coun., 1970—; mem. NAACP.; bd. dirs. East Bay Regional Park Dist., 1972—, pres., 1978-80, 88-90; bd. dirs. Save San Francisco Bay Assn., 1969—, People for Open Space, 1977-86, Calif. Natural Areas Coordinating Coun., 1968-90, Living History Ctr., 1982-85; mem. steering com. Bay Area Environ. Edn. Alliance, 1982-85, regional planning com. Assn. of Bay Area Govts., 1988—, exec. com. Citizens for Eastshore State Park, 1985—; v.p. Friends of Bot. Garden, U. Calif., Berkeley, 1976-80, trustee, 1986—. With USAAF, 1944-46. Recipient Merit award Calif. Conservation Coun., 1953; Woman of Achievement award Camp Fire Girls, 1976; Merit award Am. Soc. Landscape Architects, 1979, Conservation award Golden Gate Audubon Soc., 1985. Mem. AAUW (Calif. com. 1970-73), Prytanean Alumnae, Inc. (pres. 1969-71, chmn. adv. coun. 1971-73, adv. com. Urban Creeks Coun. 1986—), Nature Conservancy (chmn. no. Calif. chpt. 1970-71), LWV, Regional Parks Assn., Nat. Women's Polit. Caucus, Golden Gate Audubon Soc., Sierra Club (environ. edn. com. No. Calif. chpt. 1973-77), U. Calif. Alumni Assn., Inst. Calif. Man in Nature, Calif. Assn. Recreation and Park Dists. (v.p. 1978-81, 1988-90, Outstanding Bd. Mem. award 1989), Calif. Elected Women for Edn. and Rsch., Preserve Area Ridgelands Calif. Native Plant Soc., Planning and Conservation League, Urban Ecology, Cousteau Soc., Soroptomists, Pi Lambda Theta, Mortar Board, Gavel (pres.). Democrat. Mem. adv. com. Natural History Guide Series U. Calif. Press, 1972—. Home: 2932 Pine Ave Berkeley CA 94705

JEFFERS, IDA PEARLE, management consultant, volunteer; b. Houston, Tex., Sept. 5, 1935; d. Stanford Wilbur and Ida Pearle (Kinkead) Oberg; m. Samuel Lee Jeffers, Aug. 29, 1956; children: John Laurence (dec.), Julie Elizabeth, Melinda Leigh. Student, U. Colo., 1953-56; BA in History, U. N.Mex., 1957. Asst. to mayor City of Albuquerque, 1978, dir. capital improvements, 1979-81; pres. Orgn. Plus, 1988—; guest lectr. U. N.Mex. Albuquerque Pub. Sch., 1968-71. Chmn. Comprehensive Plan Rev., Bond Issue, various coms., Albuquerque, 1968—; mem. Middle Rio Grand Coun. Govts., Albuquerque, 1972-74; mem. Environ. Planning Commn., Albuquerque, 1972-77, chmn. 1975-76; chmn. Citizen Adv. Group, Community Devel., Albuquerque, 1974-75; mem. Jr. League, Albuquerque, 1966—, bd. dirs. 1970-76; mem. N. Mex. Architect, Engrs. Joint Practice Bd. 1978-85, chmn. 1983-85; treas. St. Mark's Episcopal Ch., 1983-86; pres. Eldorado High Sch. Parents, Albuquerque, 1985-86; pres. Regional Conservation Land Trust, Albuquerque, 1987—; trustee Found., Study and Care of Organic Brain Damage, Houston, 1972-82, pres. 1982—; mem. Urban Transp. Planning Policy Bd., 1972-74; chmn. community advisors Albuquerque Youth Symphony, 1985—; founder, chair Friends of Sandia (N.Mex.) Sch., 1965-68, chmn. devel. pre-sch. bd., 1974; mentor Leadership Albuquerque, 1987—; bd. dirs. Good Govt. Group, Albuquerque, 1988—, treas. 1988—; mem., treas. Albuquerque Arts Alliance, 1988—; mem. Albuquerque All Faiths, All Faith's Receiving Home Aux., 1964-68, sec. 1966, Jr. Women Club, 1963-66, Chaparral Coun. Girl Scouts leaders, 1971-73, selections chmn., 1973-74, Albuquerque Tutorial Coun., 1967-69. Recipient Disting. Pub. Svc. award, State of N. Mex., 1975, Disting. Woman of N. Mex. award, N.Mex. Women's Polit. Caucus, 1976, Golden Talon award Eldorado High Sch., Albuquerque, 1985, Panhellenic Coun. Disting. Alumnae award 1979. Mem. Rotary, Delta Gamma (pres. 1963-67, chmn. collegiate adv. bd. 1968-71, Cable and Shield awards 1970, 77). Republican. Episcopalian.

JEFFERS, SUZANNE, actress; d. Roy Althouse and Rita Middleton; B.S., Calif. State Poly. U.; M.A., U. Calif., Berkeley, 1976; m. Michael B. Jeffers, Aug. 14, 1977; 2 children. Flight attendant TWA, 1970-75; instr. Marymount Manhattan Coll., N.Y.C., 1976; also ind. bus. cons., 1974-75; TV journalist, TV co-host, spokesperson, also cons. to corps. in tng. and devel., 1976-79; pres. Corp. & Media Cons., Inc., N.Y.C., 1979-83; actress, TV journalist, 1983—; lectr. in field. Chmn. bd. Children's Oncology Soc. N.Y., 1977-83. Named an outstanding working woman of U.S., 1981. Mem. Nat. Acad. TV Arts and Scis., Nat. Acad. TV Program Execs., U. Calif. Alumni Assn., Jr. League Orange County, Actors Equity Assn., AFTRA. Episcopalian. Clubs: Carousel, Pacific, River (N.Y.C.). Address: 813 Emerald Bay Laguna Beach CA 92651

JEFFERSON, ANNE MORGAN, handcraft magazine editor; b. Worcester, Mass., Apr. 16, 1935; d. Myles and Janet (McChesney) Morgan; m. David Rowe Jefferson, June 22, 1957; children: David Rowe Jr., Peter Hamilton. BA, Sarah Lawrence Coll., 1957. Editor Knitting World, Cross-Stitch Plus, other mags. House of White Birches, Berne, Ind., 1978—. Mem. Profl. Knitwear Designers Guild (bd. dirs. 1989—), Knitting Guild Am. Office: House of White Birches 4 Oak Dr PO Box 158 Hampton Falls NH 03844

JEFFERSON, CHERYL MAY, producer, screenwriter; b. Chgo., Sept. 28, 1954; d. Norman William and Dolores May (June) J. BS in TV Arts and Scis., U. Ill., 1976. Prodn. asst. Sta. WTTW-TV, Chgo., 1976; researcher, prodn. asst., news writer Sta. WLS-TV, Chgo., 1976-78; account exec. J. Walter Thompson, Chgo., 1978-79; film producer Ency. Britannica Ednl. Corp., Chgo., 1979-83; sr. scriptwriter, exec. producer U.S. Gypsum Co. (name now USG Corp.), Chgo., 1983—. Author: Lyons Den, 1987, Love Shroud, 1988, Hellfire, 1989; contbr. childrens film reviews to mags. Recipient Golden Eagle award Am. Indsl. Film Assn., 1983; Silver Plaque award Chgo. Internat. Film Festival, 1982-83; Italian Med. Assn. Gold Cup award Salerno, Italy Film Festival, 1980; Golden Eagle award Cine Internat. Film Festival. Mem. Romance Writers Am. (pres. Chgo. North chpt. 1989), Chgo. Women's Fiction (founder), U. Ill. Alumni Assn., Sigma Delta Chi. Lutheran. Office: USG Corp 101 S Wacker Dr Chicago IL 60606

JEFFERSON, KRISTIN MARIE, museum director; b. Tacoma, Jan. 15, 1947; d. Edward Harold and Helen Marie (Chandler) J. BA, Bard Coll., 1968; MFA, Hunter Coll., 1974. Facilities adminstr. Sterling Inst., Washington, 1969-71; prof. art CUNY, 1971-79; art dealer N.Y.C., 1979—; founding pres., exec. dir. Mus. of World Art, 1989—. Author: She-Images of Woman in Art, 1983, Magic in the Mind's Eye-Alchemy of Collecting, 1987; curator mus. quality art exhibits, 1982—; film maker documentaries and art pieces, 1971—. Mem. pub. rels. staff Sotheby's benefit for Cath. Relief Svcs. to Benefit the Famine Victims of Ethiopia, 1985. Episcopalian. Home: 330 W 56th St New York NY 10019

JEFFERSON, LILA RAE, librarian; b. Monroe, La., Sept. 23, 1953. BA, NE La. U., 1974; MLS, La. State U., 1975. Interlibr. loan libr. Big Country Libr. System, Abilene, Tex., 1976-83, asst. coord., 1983—; mem. state and regional publicity com. Tex. Conf. Libr. and Info. Svcs., 1990-91. Recipient 1st Pl. award Operation Lifesaver Tex. Jaycees, 1988, 1st Pl. award for newsletter, 1990. Mem. Tex. Libr. Assn. (membership com. 1978-80, dist. rep. 1979, alt. councilor jr. mem. round table 1980, chmn. round table 1982), AAUW (program v.p. 1984-85, del. internat. conf. 1984, former legis. chmn., rec. and corr. sec.), Abilene Jaycees (sec. 1989-90, New Jaycee of Month award 1988, Key Jaycee award 1988, 89, Exec. Office of Yr. 1989-90, Exec. Office of Quarter 1989-90). Office: Big Country Libr System Abilene TX 79601

JEFFERSON, SANDRA TRAYLOR, choreographer, ballet coach; b. Tarboro, N.C., Feb. 28, 1942; d. Charles Labon and Doris Vivian (Parker) Traylor; m. Milton Franklin Jefferson, July 2, 1960; children: Mark Franklin, Todd Christopher. Student, Parks Sch. Dance, Petersburg, Va., 1947-58, Sch. of the Richmond (Va.) Ballet, 1958-60; diploma, Julia Mildred Harper Sch. Dance, Richmond, 1960; studied with Robert David Brown, Sterling, Va., 1978-80. Soloist Ballet Impromptu, Richmond, 1958-60; freelance dance instr. Chantilly, Va., 1968-70; ballet coach Artistic Skating Club of Sterling, 1980; founder, dir. Ballet for Skaters, Manassas, Va., 1980-89; artistic dir. No. Va. Artistic Skating Club, Manassas, 1986-89; cons. in choreography No. Va. Artistic Skating Club, Manassas, 1986-89; artistic dir. Artistic Skating Club Manassas, 1989; founder, dir. Ballet for Skaters, Seabrook, Md., 1989—; choreographer, ballet coach Nat. Capitol Dance and Figure Club, Seabrook, Md. and Washington, 1989—. Developer: Brosano Technique Vocabulary of Movement, 1986; co-developer (artistic skating technique) Brosano Technique, 1981. Social dir. Jaycee-ettes, Winchester, Va., 1963-67; mem. Can. World Team and the U.S. Olympic Sports Festival Team. Recipient Achievement award Jaycee-ettes, Winchester, 1963, 64, 65, 66, 67, U.S. S.E. Soc. of Roller Skating Tchrs. Am. award, 1988, nat. skating medals in U.S. and Can. Mem. Profl. Dance Tchrs. Assn., Inc., Soc. Roller Skating Tchrs. Am. (World Decoration of Excellence award 1989), U.S. Amateur Confederation Roller Skating, Nat. Dance Assn., Am. Alliance for Health, Phys. Edn., Recreation and Dance, Nat. Assn. for Sport and Phys. Edn., Va. Alliance for Arts Edn., Assn. for Supervision and Curriculum Devel., Internat. Platform Assn. Methodist. Home: 507 S Maple Ct Sterling VA 22170

JEFFORDS, LYNN REDDING, lighting designer, architect; b. Glen Ridge, N.J., Sept. 5, 1957; d. Harold Thompson and Alice Louise (Green) Redding; m. John Dobson Jeffords, Sept. 20, 1986. BArch, Pratt Inst., 1980. Registered architect, N.J. Mech. engring. draftsman Kunstadt Assocs., N.Y.C., 1978; structural engring. draftsman Le Messurier Assocs., N.Y.C., 1979; archtl. designer draftsman Hardy Holzman Pfeifer Assoc., N.Y.C., 1980-81; lighting designer project mgr. Jules Fisher & Paul Marantz, Inc., N.Y.C., 1981-90; lighting designer, architect prin. Jeffords Architecture & Lighting Design, Denver, 1990—. Contbr. articles to profl. jours. Tour guide Mus. Modern Art, N.Y.C., 1980, Lighting Designers Forum, N.Y.C., 1990. Mem. AIA, Internat. Assn. Lighting Designers, Illuminating Engring. Soc. Roman Catholic. Office: 2830 E 13th Ave Denver CO 80206

JEFFREY, NOELA MARY, publishing executive; b. Reading, Pa., Dec. 11, 1941; d. John Theodore and Mary M. (Linkowski) Slapikas; m. Alexander MacLean Jeffrey, June 22, 1968; children: Alexander Maclean Jr., Douglas Duart. BA, Seton Hill Coll., 1963. Corr. Harcourt, Barce, Javanovich, N.Y.C., 1963-65; editor Publs. of Most. Reverend Fulton J. Sheen, N.Y.C., 1965-68; editor, assoc. pub. Wells Pubs., Pasedena, Calif., 1985—. Editor Printing Jour., 1988. Bd. dirs. Graphic Arts Alliance, Pitts., 1990—; mem. adv. com. graphics communications dept. Pasadena City Coll., 1988—; mem. various bd. positions Pasadena Jr. Phil. Com., 1982-86, assoc., 1986—; community svc. positions Little League, PTA, 1972—. Named Pioneer of Yr. Printing Industries So. Calif., 1990. Mem. Graphic Arts Suppliers Assn., Indsl. Graphics Assn., In Plant Mgmt. Assn., L.A. Phil. Affiliates. Democrat. Roman Catholic. Home: 330 Rosita Ln Pasadena CA 91105

JEFFREY, SHARON LEE, teacher; b. Abilene, Kans., Mar. 18, 1944; d. Robert L. and Dorothy D. (Schaaf) Gresham; m. GErald Wallace Jeffrey, . BS summa cum laude, Fort Hays State U., Hays, Kansas, 1989. Clerk typist Farm Bur. Ins., Manhattan, Kansas, 1962-63; sec. Kansas State U., Manhattan, Kansas, 1963-65; bookkeeper Steele Oil Co., Leoti, Kansas, 1973-77, Unruh Electric Co., Leoti, Kansas, 197476; tax acct. Leoti, Kansas, 1977-85; adminstr. Gingerbread House Preschool, Leoti, Kansas, 1975—; contracting preschool adminstrv. High Plains Spl. Edn. Cooperative, Garden City Kansas 1979-82, Russell Child Devel. Assn., Garden City Kansas. Sec. Wichita County Med. Care Bd., Leoti, Kansas, 1980-82; bd. dirs Kanza FM Pub. Radio, Pierceville, 1987—; Kansas Pub. TV com.; vice chair KOOD/KSWK Pub. TV bd. dirs., Bunker Hill. Recipient Leadership award Kans. Class, 1989. Mem. Kansas Early Childhood Adminstrs., Nat. Assn. Edn. Young Children,. Lutheran. Office: Gingerbread House Presch 811 W M St Leoti KS 67861

JEFFREY, SUSAN WINDER, finance company executive; b. Richmond, Va., Mar. 15, 1951; d. Richard Peris and Jeanne Winston (Pitts) J.; m. Gary Steven Jacobson, Mar. 3, 1973 (div. Jan. 31, 1984). AB, U. Va., 1973; MBA in Internat. Finance, NYU, 1986. Sculptor Charlottesville, Va., 1973-76; assoc. editor Doubleday & Co., Inc., N.Y.C., 1977-83; co-founder Five Fox Enterprises, N.Y.C., 1983-86, Drummond's Pub. Co., Hong Kong, 1986, Innosearch Corp., N.Y.C., 1986-87; producer, writer Today Show/Nat. Broadcasting Co., N.Y.C., 1987; mgr., fin. strategist Am. Internat. Group, N.Y.C., 1988—. Author: Drummond's Guide to Hong Kong Art & Antique Dealers, 1986. Treas., dir. 227 Tenants Corp., N.Y.C., 1982—. Mem. Phi Beta Kappa. Democrat. Home: 31-33 Mercer St New York NY 10013

JEFFREYS, MARGARET VILLAR (PEGGI JEFFREYS), oil company executive; b. Pensacola, Fla., Mar. 1, 1953; d. William Edward and Betty Sue

(Cimiotti) Villar; m. E. Geoffrey Jeffreys, Feb. 28, 1975. Student, Pensacola Jr. Coll., 1971-72; numerous seminars. Sec., treas. Major Oil Co., Jackson, Miss., and Mobile, Ala., 1973-75, v.p., 1975-77; v.p. The Jeffreys Co., Inc., Mobile, 1977—. Mem. Fine Arts Mus. of the South, Mobile, English Speaking Union, Mobile, Sociedad Mobile Malaga; pres. Art Patrons League, Mobile, 1982-83, 1st v.p. 1981-82, treas., 1979-81, allied arts coun. rep. 1982-83; pres. Freedoms Found at Valley Forge, Mobile, 1983-84, v.p. for awards, 1982-83, v.p. for edn. 1980-82; pres. midtown Mobile Assn., 1980—; treas. Women of Trinity Episcopal Ch., Mobile, 1982-84, pres. 1989-90; dir. Wilmer Hall Children's Home, Mobile, 1990—. Mem. Ind. Petroleum Assn. Am. (bd. dir. 1985—), Ala. Petroleum Landmen's Assn. (sec. 1983-84, bd. dir. 1986-89), Am. Assn. Petroleum Landmen. Episcopalian. Home: 1810 Old Government St Mobile AL 36606 Office: The Jeffreys Co Inc 1509 Government St Ste 100 PO Box 66227 Mobile AL 36660-1227

JEFFRIES, BETTY SARAH, writer; b. Chgo., Ill., Sept. 19, 1925; d. Herman and Anna (Ceplow) J.; m. Emanuel H. Demby, June 07, 1965. BA, U. Chgo., 1945; LLD, Chang U., Seoul, 1968. Writer CBS, Chgo., 1942-43, Arthur Meyerhoff Co., Chgo., 1943-46, ABC, N.Y.C., 1955-56. Author: Half the World is a Bride (Miles Anderson award for Best Prose Play on Contemporary Am. Life), Psychoneurosis of a Sound Effect, ABC World Security Workshop series (World Security Workshop award); film festival editor: Filmakers Newsletter; sr. film critic: The Common Good; freelance writer newspaper articles. Mem. Am. Assn. of Pub. Opinion Rsch. Office: Demby & Assocs 141 E 44 St New York NY 10017

JEFFRIES, MARSHA DENELL, hospital purchasing and contract administrator; b. Chgo., Oct. 2, 1954; d. Rudolph Donald and Lucille (Grant) Brumfield; m. Clinton Wayne Jeffries, May 10, 1980. AA, Loop Jr. Coll., Chgo., 1979. Sec. various fed. agencies and U. Chgo., Chgo., 1972-77; purchasing agt. VA West Side Med. Ctr., Chgo., 1977-82; contract specialist VA West Side Med. Ctr., 1982-85, VA Mktg. Ctr., Hines, Ill., 1985-87; chief purchase & contract VA Lakeside Med. Ctr., Chgo., 1987—. Democrat. Pentecostal.

JEGEN, SISTER CAROL FRANCES, religion educator; b. Chgo., Oct. 11, 1925; d. Julian Aloysius and Evelyn W. (Bostelmann) J. BS in History, St. Louis U., 1951; MA in Theology, Marquette U., 1958, PhD in Religious Studies, 1968; hon. degree, St. Mary of the Woods, Terra Haute, Ind., 1977. Elem. tchr. St. Francis Xavier Sch., St. Louis, 1947-51; secondary tchr. Holy Angels Sch., Milw., 1951-57; coll. tchr. Mundelein Coll., Chgo., 1957—; adv. coun. U.S. Cath. Bishops, Washington, 1969-74; trustees Cath. Theol. Union, Chgo., 1974-84. Author: Jesus the Peace Maker, 1986, Restoring Our Friendship with God, 1989; editor: Mary According to Women, 1985. Participant Nat. Farm Worker Ministry, Fresno, Calif., 1977—; mem. Pax Christi, U.S.A., 1979—, Jane Addams Conf., Chgo., 1989. Recipient Loyola Civic award Loyola U., Chgo., 1981; named one of 100 Women to Watch Today's Chgo. Woman, 1989. Mem. Cath. Theol. Soc. Am., Coll. Theology Soc., Cath.-Jewish Scholars Dialog, Liturgical Conf. Democrat. Roman Catholic. Home and Office: Mundelein Coll Dept Religious Studies 6363 N Sheridan Rd Chicago IL 60660

JEGLINSKI, PATRICIA ANN, banker; b. Fort Fairfield, Maine, Apr. 5, 1938; d. Sherman Leander Todd and Leigh Mae (McLaughlin) Sutton; m. Charles Robert Jeglinski, Nov. 19, 1960; children: Stephanie Frances, David Gregory, John Andrew. Student, U. Maine, 1956-57; AA, Sawyers Bus. Coll., Pasadena, 1959; student, Boston U., 1959, Am. Banking Inst., 1977-79. Exec. sec. credit dept. William Filene & Sons, Inc., Boston, 1959-66; sr. credit analyst Uni-Serv Corp., Cambridge, Mass., 1966-70; stock balancing clk. Am. Optical-Cool Ray, Chelsea, Mass., 1972-73; customer svc. supr. Met. Credit Union, Chelsea, 1973-79; with Suffolk County Sheriff, Boston, 1979; Boston Herald, Chelsea, 1979-80; teller Boston Edison Credit Union, 1980—. Home: 95 Bellingham #3 Chelsea MA 02150

JELLISON, GRETCHEN GAYHART, art educator; b. Reynoldsville, Pa., Jan. 15, 1908; d. Henry Adam and Mary Ann (Beer) Gayhart; m. William Livingston Jellison, Aug. 13, 1932; 1 child, William Henry. BA, U. Mont., 1930. Tchr. Kalispell, Mont., 1930-32; illustrator Rocky Mountain Lab., Hamilton, Mont., 1932-36. Troop leader Girl Scouts U.S., Kalispell and Hamilton, 1931-32; founder, pres. Bitteroot Arts Guild, Hamilton, 1970. Mem. AAUW (past pres. Hamilton chpt.). Home: 504 S 3d St Hamilton MT 59840

JELSTROM, EVELYN MAJA, nurse; b. Ft. Lauderdale, Fla., Dec. 28, 1955; d. Harry Carl and Margaret Cecilia (Van Duzer) Jelstrom; m. Louis Vincent Gabaldoni, Feb. 28, 1981 (div. Dec. 1985). Cert. Nurse Anesthetist Practitioner. Staff/charge nurse Tufts-New England Med. Ctr. Hosp., Boston, 1977-79; staff nurse Intensive Care Unit Sinai Hosp., Balt., 1979-80; cert. nurse anesthetist practitioner Arlington (Va.) Hosp., 1982-84; adminstr. Dr. Louis V. Gabaldoni, Hagerstown, Md., 1984; cert. nurse anesthetist practitioner and quality assurance coordinator Dr. Rosy T. Javate/Commonwealth and Fair Oaks Hosps., Fairfax, Va., 1984-88. Sec., bd. dirs. Nat. Retinitis Pigmentosa Found. Mass. chpt., 1975-77; sec., treas. Simmons Coll. Class of 1977. Mem. Am. Assn. Nurse Anesthetists, Va. Assn. Nurse Anesthetists (mem. govt. relations com. 1987-88), Md. Assn. Nurse Anesthetists, Nat. Assn. Female Executives, Alexandria Singers, Westminster Singers, Washington D.C. Alumnae Club of Simmons Coll. (bd. dirs.), Simmons Coll. Honor Soc. Republican. Presbyterian.

JEMISON, CHERYL LYNNE, small business owner, artist; b. Tulsa, Sept. 16, 1959; d. Fred J. Payton and Rose Mary (Featherston) Payton-Taber; m. Daron Douglas Jemison, Mar. 16, 1961. Student, Jenks High Sch., 1977, Tulsa Co. Vo-Tech., 1977. Lic. Cosmetologist, Okla. Fashion model Cherrie Siegfried Agy., Tulsa, 1979-81; communications officer Broken Arrow (Okla.) Police Dept., 1981-86; owner Cheryl's Craft Cottage, Rex, Georgia, 1987--. Bd. dirs. Rainbow House. Mem. Nat. Soc. Tole and Decorative Painters, Inc., Valley Hill Homemakers (pres. 1988-89). Democrat. Office: Cheryl's Craft Cottage 6459 Highway 42 Ste #12 PO Box 524 Rex GA 30273

JEN, JOANNE PAULINE, sales force/marketing management consultant; b. Oakland, Calif., June 1, 1967; d. Joseph Jwu-Shan and Salina (Fond) J. BA, Northwestern U., 1988, postgrad. Intern Campbell Soup Co., Camden, N.J., 1986; intern Citicorp Savs. Ill., Chgo., 1987-88; bus. analyst ZS Assocs., Evanston, Ill., 1988-89, sr. bus. analyst, 1989—. Author poetry Am. Poetry Assn., 1985. Chmn. Young Chicagoans fo Prevention of Child Abuse, Chgo., 1989—; bd. dirs. Greater Chgo. Coun. for Prevention Child Abuse, 1989—; judge Ill. Jr. Miss Scholarship Program, Bolingbrook, Ill., 1987-88. Mem. Kappa Delta. Home: 1507 Oak Ave 1W Evanston IL 60201 Office: ZS Assocs 1800 Sherman Ave Evanston IL 60201

JEN, KAI-LIN CATHERINE, nutritionist; b. Taipei, Taiwan, Republic of China, July 18, 1949; came to U.S., 1972; d. Chih-Chung and Yu-Lan (Wong) J.; m. Paul Kuang-Hsien Lin, Aug. 5, 1978; children: Elizabeth, John. BS, Nat. Taiwan U., Taipei, Taiwan, Republic of China, 1971; MA, Wayne State U., 1975, PhD, 1977. Asst. rsch. scientist U. Mich., Ann Arbor, Mich., 1979-83; asst. prof. S. Ill. U., Carbondale, Ill., 1983-84; from asst. prof. to assoc. prof. Wayne State U., Detroit, Mich., 1984—. Contbr. articles to profl. jours. Mem. AAAS, Am. Inst. Nutrition, Am. Diabetes Assn., Am. Physiol. Soc., N. Am. Assn. Study Obesity, Sigma Xi. Office: Wayne State U Dept Nutrition Detroit MI 48202

JENKINS, ADRIENNE BETH, market research analyst, marketing consultant; b. West Chester, Pa., Mar. 27, 1963; d. Norman Rodney and Kathleen Louise (Erb) J.; m. Gerard Stephen Batkowski, Oct. 11, 1986 (div. 1990). BS in Mktg., Pa. State U., 1985; postgrad., Temple U., 1988-90. Market rsch. analyst Southeastern Mktg., Stuart, Fla., 1985; sales specialist GE, Pittsfield, Mass., 1986; rsch. assoc. Nat. Aanalysts-Booz Allen, Phila., 1987; market rsch. analyst Rorer Internat. Pharms., Ft. Washington, Pa., 1988-90; sr. market rsch. analyst Rorer Pharm. Corp. (USA), Ft. Washington, 1990—. Cons., vol. Abington (Pa.) Art Ctr., 1990, Greater Phila. Cultural Alliance, 1990. Scholar Campbell Soup Co., 1981. Mem. Am. Mktg. Assn., Internat. Pharm. Market Rsch. Group, NAFE. Office: Rorer Pharm Corp 500 Virginia Dr Fort Washington PA 19034

JENKINS, ANNE ELIZABETH GREEN, pediatric therapist; b. Richmond, Va., May 18, 1944; d. John P. and Dorothy Mae (Williams) Green; B.S., (Rehab. Service Adminstrn. scholar), N.Y.U., 1972; M.A. (Minority Student grad. fellow), Columbia Tchrs. Coll., 1975, Ed.M., 1976; Ph.D. candidate, U. N.C.-Greensboro; m. Earnest Jenkins, June 1, 1964; children—Frederick Anthony, April Kaché, August Kali. Occupational therapist Harlem Hosp., N.Y.C., 1972-74, Blythedale Children's Hosp., Valhalla, N.Y., 1974-77; developmental disabilities specialist Amos Cottage Bowman Gray Sch. Medicine, Winston-Salem, N.C., 1977; dir. Early Intervention Program, Forsyth/Stokes counties, Winston-Salem, 1977-80, learning disabilities specialist, 1980—; pvt. practice; 1984—; mem. faculty N.Y.U. Sch. Edn., N.Y.U. Med. Sch., U. N.C.-Chapel Hill, Winston-Salem State U., 1984—; founder, dir. Visions of the Children, Lexington, N.C., 1986, Piedmont Achievement Ctr. Winston-Salem, N.C.; cons. pre-schools and developmental day-care ctrs., U.S. Dept. Edn., 1987—. Mem. Am. Occupational Therapy Assn., Smithsonian Instrn., Center Study Sensory Integrations, Am. Burn Assn. Roman Catholic. Designer hand orthotics, adaptive equipment for the handicapped. Home: 2931 Springhaven Dr Winston-Salem NC 27103

JENKINS, BILLIE BEASLEY, film company executive; b. Topeka, June 27, 1943; d. Arthur and Etta Mae (Price) Capelton; m. Rudolph Alan Jenkins, Nov. 1, 1935; 1 child, Tina Caprice. Student, Santa Monica City Coll., 1965-69. Exec. sec. to v.p. prodn. Screen Gems, L.A., 1969-72; exec. asst. Spelling/Goldberg Prodns., 1972-82; dir. adminstrn. The Leonard Co./Mandy Films, 1982-85, v.p., 1985-86; exec. asst. to pres. and chief oper. officer 20th Century Fox Film Corp., L.A., 1986-90, dir. prodn. svcs.and resources Fox Motion Pictures div., 1990—; dir. adminstrn. 20th Century Fox Film Corp. Asst. to exec. producer: (films) War Games, 1984, Spacecamp, 1986; (movies for TV) Something about Amelia, 1984, Alex, The Life of a Child, 1985; (series) Paper Dolls, 1985, Cavanaughs, 1987, Charlie's Angels, Rookies, others. Mem. Women in Film Assn. (bd. dirs. 1989-91), NAFE, Black Women's Network, Am. Film Inst., Independent Feature Prodns./West, Motivating Our Students Through Experience, The Alliance of Motion Picture and TV Producers (studio planning council div.). Office: 20th Century Fox Inc 10202 W Pico Blvd Los Angeles CA 90034

JENKINS, BRENDA GWENETTA, early childhood education specialist; b. Durham, N.C., Aug. 11, 1949; d. Brinton Alfred and Ophelia Arden (Eaton) Jenkins. BS, Howard U., 1971, MEd, 1972, Cert. Spl. Edn., 1973-75; postgrad. Trinity Coll., Am. U., U. D.C., 1976—. Cert. aerobics instr. Nat. Dance-Exercise Instr.'s Tng. Assn. Cheerleader coach Howard U., Washington, 1971-86 ; aerobics instr. D.C. Pub. Schs., 1982—, tchr., 1972—; v.p. Nerdlihc Corp., Washington, 1985—; ptnr. Jenkins, Trapp-Dukes and Yates Partnership; aerobic instr. for handicapped Council for Exceptional Children, Washington, 1982, recreation services City of Rockville, Md., 1986—; isnstr. Washington Tchrs.; instr. aerobics Langdon Park Recreation Ctr. Washington Dept. Recreation, 1988—; rep. Union Bldg, 1987—. Recipient Conscientious Service award D.C. Pub. Schs., 1985; Outstanding Recognition award Howard U. Alumni Cheerleaders Assn., 1984 (award renamed The Brenda G. Jenkins Outstanding Cheerleader Award, 1987); Outstanding Service awards Kappa Delta Pi, 1978, 79, 81, 82, 84; citation Washington Tchrs. Union, 1985; Appreciation cert. D.C. Dept. Recreation, 1985, others; nominee Agnes Meyer Outstanding Tchr. award, 1988, Theodore R. Hogans Jr. Pub. Service award, 1988. Mem. Am. Fedn. Tchrs., Theta Alpha chpt. Kappa Delta Pi (exec. com.), Howard U. Alumni Cheerleaders Assn. (cofounder 1977) Democrat. Avocations: alumni cheerleading, fashion design, cooking, dancing, poetry writing.

JENKINS, CAROL ANN, government official; b. Mt. Vernon, Ohio, July 7, 1948; d. Paul Nathaniel and Mary Beatrice (Staunton) J.; m. Michael William Comeau, June 7, 1975 (div. May 1982); children: Christopher Paul, Shawn Michael. BA in Social Work, U. Ky., 1971. Personal staffing specialist USAF, Washington, 1973-80; personnel staff specialist EPA, Washington, 1980-84, Def. Logistics Agy., Def. Constrn. Supply Ctr., Office of Civilian Personnel Staffing Br., Columbus, Ohio, 1984—. Commr. Gahanna (Ohio) Soccer Assn., 1986-. Recipient Sustained Superior Performance award EPA, 1983. Mem. Phi Beta Kappa. Republican. Roman Catholic. Home: 290 Rocky Fork Dr N Gahanna OH 43230 Office: DLA/DCSC-KSSC 3990 E Broad St Columbus OH 43215

JENKINS, CAROL ANNE, educator; b. Kearny, N.J., Mar. 1, 1945; d. Lawrence Augustine and Sara (Ball) J. BA, Malone Coll., 1968; MA in Religious Edn., Chgo. Grad.Sch. Theology, 1969; MA in Sociology, Western Mich. U., 1972; PhD in Sociology, Kans. State U., 1986. Asst. prof., program dir. various orgns., Grand Rapids and Livonia, Mich., 1970-73; asst. prof. Judson Coll., Elgin, Ill., 1973-74, No. State Coll., Aberdeen, S.D., 1974-75, Henry Ford Community Coll., Dearborn, Mich., 1975-76, Wheeling (W.Va.) Coll., 1976-78, Tabor Coll., Hillsboro, Kans., 1978-82; instr. Kans. State U., Manhattan, 1982-85; assoc. prof. Biola U., La Mirada, Calif., 1985—; bd. dirs., chairwoman bd. Faculty Student Union, La Mirada, Christian Conciliation Svcs. of Orange County, Calif.; cons. in field. Author: Thanatology: Discussions On Death & Dying, 1986, Social Problems: Issues and Their Opposing Viewpoints, 1987, Toward An Understanding of Social Thought, 1987, Toward an Understanding of Sociological Theory, 1989; contbr. chpts. to books and articles to profl. jours. Vol. umpire Hillsboro Recreation Dept., 1980-82; speaker Kiwanis, Hillsboro, 1981, Marquette High Sch., 1982; vol. Cedar Hill Mobile Country Club, Fullerton, Calif., 1986—. Instnl. Rsch. grantee, 1990. Mem. Am. Sociol. Assn., Pacific Sociol. Assn. (program chmn. 1988), Midwest Sociol. Assn. (undergrad. edn. com. mem. 1982-85), Rural Sociol. Soc. (mem. com. 1988-90), Assn. Christians Teaching Sociology (nat. program chmn. 1981, 82, 90), Religious Edn. Assn., AAUW, William Lock Singers Players, Alpha Kappa Delta. Mennonite. Home: 2851-19 Rolling Hills Dr Fullerton CA 92635

JENKINS, CLARA BARNES, educator; b. Franklinton, N.C.; d. Walter and Stella (Griffin) Barnes; BS, Winston-Salem State U., 1939; MA, N.C. Ctl. U., 1947; EdD, U. Pitts., 1964; postgrad., N.Y.U., 1947-48, U. N.C.-Chapel Hill, 1963, N.C. Agrl. and Tech. State U., 1971; m. Hugh Jenkins, Dec. 24, 1949 (div. Feb. 1955). Tchr. pub. schs., Wendell, N.C., 1939-43, Wise, N.C., 1943-45; mem. faculty Fayetteville State U., 1945-53, Rust Coll., Holly Spring, Miss., 1953-58; asst. prof. Shaw U., 1958-64; prof. edn. and psychology St. Paul's Coll., Lawrenceville, Va., 1964—; vis. prof. edn. Friendship Jr. Coll., Rock Hill, S.C., summer 1947, N.C. Agrl. and Tech. State U., 1966-83. Former mem. bd. dirs. Winston-Salem State U. Notary pub., N.C.; United Negro Coll. Fund Faculty fellow, 1963-64; Am. Bapt. Conv. grantee, 1963-64. Mem. AAUP, Nat. Soc. for Study Edn., NEA, AAUW, Am. Hist. Assn., Va. Edn. Assn., Am. Acad. Polit. and Social Sci., AAAS, Internat. Platform Assn., Assn. Tchr. Educators, History Edn. Soc., Doctoral Assn. Educators, Am. Assn. Higher Edn., Am. Soc. Notaries, Acad. Polit. Sci., Am. Psychol. Assn., Soc. Research in Child Devel., Am. Soc. Notaries, Marquis Biog. Library Soc., Jean Piaget Soc., Philosophy of Edn. Soc., Soc. Profs. Edn., Am. Soc. Notaries, Phi Eta Kappa, Zeta Phi Beta, Phi Delta Kappa, Kappa Delta Pi. Episcopalian. Home: 920 Bridges St Henderson NC 27536 Office: St Paul's Coll Lawrenceville VA 23868

JENKINS, DAMITA JO, sales professional, industrial engineer; b. Indpls., Aug. 24, 1963; d. Lois Jean Zollicaffer. BS in Indsl. Engring., Purdue U., 1986. Indsl. engring. intern EG&G Idaho, Idaho Falls, summer 1984; indsl. engr. Square D Co., Cedar Rapids, Iowa, 1986-88; asst. mgr. Volume Shoe Corp., Indpls., 1988—; mgr. prodn. control Standard Locknut & Lock Washer Inc., Carmel, Ind., 1989—; part-time computer operator Ctr. for Leadership Devel., Indpls., 1989-90; mktg. cons. J&H Inc., Indpls., 1988—. Home: 3004 N Gale St Indianapolis IN 46218

JENKINS, FRANCES OWENS, retail owner; b. Leonard, Tex., Nov. 12, 1924; d. R. Melrose and Maureen (Durrett) Owens; m. William O. Jenkins (div. 1961); children: Steven O., Tamara. Student theatre arts East Tex. State U., 1939-42, Ind. U., 1945-48, U. Tenn., 1954-56. Fashion model Rogers Modeling Agy., Boston, 1950-52, Rich's, Knoxville, Tenn., 1955-60; owner, instr. Arts Sch. of Self-Improvement and Modeling, Knoxville, 1959-69; owner, pres. Fran Jenkins Boutique, Knoxville, 1964—; cons. Miss Am. Pageant, Knoxville, 1958-66. Actress Carousel Theatre, Knoxville, 1955-58. Home: 8833 Ccve Point Ln Concord TN 37922

JENKINS, GLORIA DELORES, former airline official; d. David and Johnnie Sue (Smith) Barnes; extension student City U. N.Y.; cert. fund raising N.Y. U., 1982; m. John Elmo Jenkins, 1960 (dec.); children—Gloria Susan, Melanie Yvette Treadwell, Carol Lynn, Jonathan Edward. With Pan Am. World Airways, 1955-82, mgmt. prodn. planning aircraft service control maintenance and engring. JFK Airport, N.Y.C., 1979-82, mgmt. powerplant planning A/C engine maintenance and engring., 1982; mem. FAA Speakers Cadre. Exec. bd. Hansel & Gretel Inc., 1977-79; pres. Addisleigh Park Civic Orgn., 1960; mem. John E. Jenkins Meml. Scholarship Fund, 1980; mem. exec. bd. Queens council Boy Scouts Am., chair ethnic outreach com.; chairperson United Negro Coll. Fund Pre-Telethon, 1987-88. Recipient various service awards. Mem. Nat. Assn. Female Execs. (network dir.), NAACP (br. exec. bd.). Mem. A.M.E. Ch. Clubs: Hansel and Gretel (past nat. pres.), Toastmistresses.

JENKINS, HELEN HEATH, educator, communications professional; b. N.Y.C., Nov. 20, 1952; d. Clarence MacDonald and Nonna Schön (Sandes) Heath; m. Reginald Lorenzo Jenkins, Apr. 6, 1974; children: Halima, Omar. BA, Macalester Coll., 1974; MBA, Howard U., 1982; postgrad., U. Md. Cert. advanced profl. Md. State Dept. Edn. Assoc. account exec. Chesapeake and Potomac Telephone Co., Washington, 1982; account executive AT&T, Oakton, Va., 1983; tchr. Montgomery County Pub. Schs., Rockville, Md., 1985. Mem. NAACP, MCABSE, NEA, Beta Gamma Sigma. Home: 13108 Wilton Oaks Dr Silver Spring MD 20906

JENKINS, IRENE, lecturer, writer on religion, nurse; b. McKeesport, Pa., May 23; d. Robert and Fannie (Mason) Watts; m. Leamond Penn, Nov. 7, 1960 (div.); children: Kevin Lee, Monique Lorae; m. Theodore R. Jenkins, Nov. 9, 1980. Student, Louise Sudoga McClintic Sch. of Nursing, Pitts., 1960; student, UCLA, 1971. RN, N.J. Various RN positions, 1960—; charge RN Community Clinic for Jersey Shore Med. Ctr., Neptune, N.J., 1982-83, Cen. Jersey Blood Bank, Shrewsburg, N.J., 1984—; mission worker in The Domincan Republic, 1989—. Contbr. articles to Re Souners Gospel Tidings; semiweekly radio min., Pasadena, Calif., 1977-78; weekly cable TV min., Wilmington, Del., 1985. Evangelist Ch. of God in Christ, 1968—. Recipient Good Ambassadorship award for outstanding mission work, U.S. Pres. Jimmy Carter, 1979. Mem. Creative Writers Assn., Aglow Christian Women's Fellowship. Democrat. Home: 22 Country Club Dr Neptune NJ 07753

JENKINS, KATHY, health facility administrator; b. Fayetteville, N.C., Apr. 1, 1955; d. Leo J. Eisenback Jr. abd Geraldine Humpich; m. Alan Jenkins, Mar. 20, 1982; children: Brian Alan, Scott Alan. BS, U. Louisville, 1977. Asst. lab. dir. Humana Hosp. Audubon, Louisville, Ky.; supr. immunology lab. NKC Inc., Louisville, med. technologist immunology lab., blood bank. Mem. Am. Soc. Clin. Pathologists (cert. med. technologist), Louisville Soc. Med. Technologists (Technologist of Yr., 1989). Address: 5901 Orville Dr Louisville KY 40213

JENKINS, LOUISE SHERMAN, nurse researcher; b. Normal, Ill., Jan. 19, 1943; d. Fred and Zylpha Louise (Garrett) Sherman; m. Gary L. Jenkins, Oct. 30, 1965 (div. July 1976). BS, No. Ill. U., 1979; MS, U. Md., Balt., 1982, PhD, 1985. Asst. head nurse intensive care Community Meml. Hosp., LaGrange, Ill., 1963-65; head nurse coronary care Lutheran Gen. Hosp., Park Ridge, Ill., 1965-69; nurse clinician hemodialysis unit Evanston Hosp., Evanston, Ill., 1969-74; head nurse Skokie Valley Community Hosp., Skokie, Ill., 1974-75; faculty dept. continuing edn. Northwest Community Hosp., Arlington Heights, Ill., 1975-80; Walter Schoeder chair in nursing research U. Wis. Milw. Sch. Nursing and St. Luke's Med. Ctr., Milw., 1987—. Mem.-at-large Coun. Cardiovascular Nursing, Dallas, 1989—; chairperson membership com. Am. Heart Assn.; bd. govs., chairperson nursing research com. Am. Heart Assn. Milw., 1988—. Fellow, clin. nurse scholar Robert Wood Johnson Found., U. Calif., San Francisco, 1985-87. Mem. Wis. Nurses Assn. (bd. dirs. 1988—), Midwest Nursing Research Soc. (research sect. chair 1988—), Coun. Nurse Researchers, Am. Assn. Cardiovascular & Pulmonary Rehab., Soc. for Behavioral Medicine. Office: U Wis Milw School of Nursing 1909 E Hartford Ave Milwaukee WI 53201

JENKINS, MADGE MARIE, management educator, consultant; b. Dearborn, Mich., Oct. 19, 1938; d. Lem and Margaret Mary (Tulloch) VicKroy; m. Robert Eugene Brennan, Dec. 28, 1958 (div. 1965); 1 child, Richard; m. George Henry Jenkins, Aug. 15, 1967. Student Systems Inst., Detroit, 1965, Henry Ford Community Coll., 1965-67; B.A. cum laude, U. Mich., 1976; M.P.A., Wayne State U., 1978. Ops. mgr. Custom Lab., Dearborn, Mich., 1967-68; mgr. Jenkins Wedding Studies, Dearborn, 1968-74; unit dir. dept. recreation City of Dearborn, 1976-78; enumerator Dept. Agr., Seattle, 1978-79; coordinator Stillaguamish Ctr., Arlington, Wash., 1979-80; asst. prof. mgmt., coordinator mgmt. dept. Lima Tech. Coll., Ohio, 1980—; mem. Adv. Bd. Continuing Edn., Bellingham, Wash., 1978-80, Marysville, Wash., 1979-80; mgmt. cons. Jenkins & Jenkins, Cario, Ohio, 1984—; cons. Ctr. for Bus. and Econ. Research, Western Wash. U. 1979-80. Elder, Columbus Grove Presbyterian Ch., Ohio, 1982-83. Mem. Acad. Mgmt., Am. Mgmt. Assn., Am. Assn. Pub. Adminstrn., Am. Soc. Tng. and Devel., Am. Assn. Personnel Adminstrn. Republican. Club: 8-16 Cine (Detroit). Lodge: Toastmasters (v.p. local chpt. 1981-82). Office: Ohio State U Lima Tech Coll Campus Lima OH 45804

JENKINS, MARGARET AIKENS, educational administrator; b. Lexington, Miss., May 14, 1925; d. Joel Bryant and Marie C. (Threadgill) Melton; m. Daniel Armstrong, May 21, 1944 (div. 1950); children—Marie Cynthia, Marsha Rochelle; m. Gabe Aikens, June 29, 1954 (div. 1962); m. Herbert Jenkins, May 21, 1966. Student, Chgo. Conservatory of Music, 1959, Moody Bible Inst., Chgo., 1959, Calif. State U.-Northridge, 1984; HHD (hon.), Payne Acad., 1984, Pentecostal Bible Coll., 1988, So. Calif. Sch. Ministry, 1990. Clk., U.S. Signal Corps, Chgo., 1944, Cuneo Press, Chgo., 1948-52, Ford Aircraft, Chgo., 1952-58, Corps of Engrs., Chgo., 1958-64; progress control clk. Def. Contract Adminstrn. Service Region, Los Angeles, 1966-73; founder, adminstr. Celeste Scott Christian Sch., Inglewood, Calif., 1976—; founder, pres. Mary Celeste Scott Meml. Found., Inc., Inglewood, 1973—; pub., writer, founder Magoll Records, Chgo., 1958-64, M&M Aikens Music, 1957—; mem. Inglewood Coalition Against Drugs, 1987—; radio broadcast Look and Live Sta. KTYM, Inglewood, Calif., 1986—; Mayor of Inglewood Ann. Prayer Breakfast Com., 1988. Recipient Cert. Appreciation, Mayor of Inglewood, 1984, Mayor of Los Angeles, 1980, State Senator, 1975, State Rep., 1976; named Woman of Yr., Los Angeles Sentinel, 1982, Inglewood C. of C., 1982. Mem. Broadcast Music Inc., Am. Fedn. TV and Radio Artists, Nat. Assn. Pentecostal Women and Men Inc. Avocations: religion, writing and recording music, education. Home: 11602 Cimarron Ave Los Angeles CA 90047 Office: Celeste Scott Christian Sch 930 S Osage Ave Inglewood CA 90301

JENKINS, MELODY STINSON, library director; b. Cin., Mar. 3, 1951; d. George Herbert Jr. and Vera Verne (Jones) Stinson; m. Stephen Jack Jenkins, May 20, 1978; children: Margaret Ruth, George Watt. BS in Edn., Western Carolina U., 1973; MLS, U. Ky., 1975. Tchr. language arts Oak Hills Local Sch. Dist., Cin., 1974-75; children's libr. Moultrie (Ga.)-Colquitt County Libr., 1975-76, dir., 1976—. Mem. Ga. Libr. Assn., Moultrie Rotary. Presbyterian. Office: Moultrie-Colquitt Cty Libr 204 5th St SE Moultrie GA 31768

JENKINS, MILDRED N., coomputer company executive; b. Meringo, Ind., June 1, 1928; d. John Herman and Georgia Nell (Summerland) Jungers; m. Robert E. Jenkins, Jan. 14, 1960 (dec. 1978); children: James Edward, George Alan, Deborah Marion, Robert Edison. Engraver Tampa, Fla., 1968-70; tchr.'s aide East Elem. Sch., Ocean Springs, Miss., 1970-72; engraver CalWest Trophies, Chula Vista, Calf., 1972-75, Oceanside, Calif., 1976-77; engraver Trophies and Awards, San Diego, 1975-76; sales mgr. Calco Computers, Oceanside, 1980-87, owner, 1987—; pres. Commodore Users Group, Oceanside, 1980-85; pres. Palomer Ham Radio, Vista, Calif., 1978-79. Author 2 poems. Mem. Nat. Assn. for Female Execs., Am. Assn. Ret. Persons, Rancho Santa Margarita Gem Soc. (sec., editor), DAV Aux. Home: 4815 Stephanie Pl Oceanside CA 92056 Office: Calco Computers 1723 Oceanside Blvd Oceanside CA 92054

JENKINS, MYRA ELLEN, historian, archivist; b. Elizabeth, Colo., Sept. 26, 1916; d. Lewis Harlan and Minnie (Ackroyd) Jenkins; B.A. cum laude,

U. Colo., 1937, M.A., 1938; Ph.D., U. N.Mex., 1953. Instr. pub. schs., Climax, Colo., 1939-41, Granada, Colo., 1941-43, Pueblo, Colo., 1943-50; fellow U. N.Mex., 1950-52, asst., 1952-53; free-lance historian and hist. cons., Albuquerque, 1953-59; archivist Hist. Soc. N.Mex., Santa Fe, 1959-60; sr. archivist N.Mex. Records Center and Archives, 1960-69, dep. for archives, 1968-70; N.Mex. state historian, 1967-80; ret., 1980; instr. St. Michael's Coll., 1962-63, Coll. of Santa Fe, 1966-74, 81-82; assoc. prof. N.Mex. State U., 1983; assoc. adj. prof. U.N. Mex., summer 1982, 84, 86; rsch. cons., 1980—. Mem. Western History Assn., Hist. Soc. N.Mex., Phi Beta Kappa, Phi Kappa Phi, Phi Alpha Theta, Kappa Delta Pi. Democrat. Episcopalian. Author: (with Albert H. Schroeder) A Brief History of New Mexico, 1974; Guides and Calendars to the Spanish, Mexican and Territorial Archives of New Mexico; contbr. articles to profl. jours. and book revs. Home: 1022 Don Cubero St Santa Fe NM 87501

JENKINSON, JUDITH APSEY, librarian; b. Monroe, Mich., Apr. 9, 1943; d. Robert Henry Williams and Caroline (Pardee) Stephenson; m. Arnold Apsey, July 1, 1962 (div. 1977); 1 child, Amy Lou; m. Leif Jenkinson, May 21, 1977, 1 stepchild, Karl J. A.A., Alpena Community Coll., 1964; B.A., Mich. State U., 1966; Arts M.L.S., U. Mich., 1969. Elem. tchr., Lincoln, Mich., 1966-68, high sch. librarian, 1969-72; elem. librarian, Ketchikan, Alaska, 1972-75, 90—, high sch. librarian, 1975-90. Mem. Ketchiken Community Coll. Council, 1980-84, pres., 1984-85; del. Alaska Democratic Conv., 1982, 88; dir., producer, actress, mem. stage crew First City Players, 1972—; commr. Ketchikan Gateway Borough Planning Commn., 1989—. Mem. ALA, NEA, AAUW, NOW, LWV, Ketchikan Edn. Assn., NEA-Alaska, Women's Internat. League for Peace and Freedom, Alaska Library Assn. VFW Aux., Swinging Kings Square Dancers (pres. 1985-86), Eagles, Women of the Moose, Delta Kappa Gama. Home: Box 5342 Ketchikan AK 99901 Office: 2610 4th Ave Ketchikan AK 99901

JENKINS-TURNER, JUDY, informations systems specialist; b. Stephenville, Tex., Mar. 28, 1948; d. Harold Smith and Gaberella A. Butler; 1 child, Stefani LuAnn. Student, Temple U. Cert. CPIM. Bus. systems coord. FMC, Stephenville, Tex.; also materials analyst. Mem. Cross Timbers Bus. and Profl. Women's Club, Greater Fort Worth APICS Chpt. Home: 2800 NE 2d St #100 Mineral Wells TX 76067 Office: 2825 W Washington St PO Box 1377 Stephenville TX 76401

JENKS, SARAH ISABEL, retired nursing administrator; b. Springfield, Mo., May 5, 1913; d. George S. and Mary (Laing) Cuckie; diploma St. Joseph Mercy Hosp., 1934; student U. Calif. Extension, 1959-70, West Coast U., 1974, 78; m. Dean F. Thompson, June 16, 1936 (dec. 1949); 1 son, Dean F.; m. 2d, Kermit Jenks, June 17, 1951. Staff nurse Calif. Hosp., Los Angeles, 1936-37, head nurse, 1937-38, supr., 1938-40; indsl. nurse May Co., Los Angeles, 1940-43; office nurse, Burbank, Calif., 1944-45, Fort Dodge, Iowa, 1946-57; office mgr. Inglewood Med. Clinic ret., 1985; 1957-58; occupational health nurse, Hawthorne, Calif., 1958-72; supervising nurse Occupational Health Service, Los Angeles County, 1972-75; chief occupational health nurse Naval Regional Med. Center, Long Beach, Calif., 1975-81; adminstrv. nurse Occupational Health Center, U. Calif.-Irvine, 1981-85, ret., 1985; nursing chmn. ARC, 1964-70. Recipient Schering Occupational Health Nurse award, 1979; named Nurse of Yr., Harbor Area Assn. Occupational Health Nurses, 1985; Sarah I. Jenks scholarship established in her honor U. Calif.-Irvine, 1985. Mem. Am. Nurses Assn. (chmn. occupational health nurse forum 1968-72), Calif. State Nurses Assn. (pres. Centinela Valley 1963-65), Calif. State Occupational Health Nurses Assn., Am. Assn. Occupational Health Nurses, United Scottish Soc. Democrat. Presbyterian. Home: 1000-6 Williams Dr Fort Dodge IA 50501

JENKS, VINA JANE, claims representative; b. Toppenish, Wash., Mar. 18, 1931; d. Dow Lefield and Ruth Gladys (Jenks) Ashford; m. Melbourne Eugene Jenks, Dec. 25, 1952 (dec. Nov. 1987); 1 child, William Randall. Student, Chemeketa Community Coll., 1978—. With ID bur. Oreg. State Police Dept., Salem, 1949-55, supr. clerical dept., 1953-55, clk. typist patrol office, 1956-59; sec. pers. dept. Boeing Airplane Co., Seattle, 1952-53; lithographer Moore Bus. Forms, Salem, 1959-65; clk. Marion County Dist. Ct., Salem, 1965; with Social Security Adminstrn., 1965—; telephone svc. rep. Social Security Adminstrn., San Diego, 1976-77; claims rep. Social Security Adminstrn., Salem and Albany, Oreg., 1978—. With USNR, 1950-54. Mem. Am. Fedn. Govt. Employees (union rep.). Democrat. Methodist. Home: 2015 Nomad Ct SE Salem OR 97306 Office: Social Security Adminstrn 633 Waverly Ave SE Albany OR 97321

JENKS-DAVIES, KATHRYN RYBURN, retired educator, civic worker; b. Lynchburg, Va., Oct. 9, 1916; d. Charles Arthur and Jessie Katherine (Moorman) Ryburn; m. Thomas Edgar Jenks Jr., Sept. 9, 1941 (dec. June 1975); children: Thomas Edgar III, Jessika, Timothy; m. Robert E. Davies, Dec. 27, 1986. BS, State Tchr. Coll., 1938; postgrad., Mary Washington Coll., 1947-48, U. Va., 1957-58, William and Mary Coll., 1967-68, Va. Commonwealth U., 1969-70. Tchr. various schs., Grundy, Va., 1939-41; phys. therapist U.S. Army, Ft. Bragg, N.C., 1942; operator motor pool U.S. Army, Ft. Still, Okla., 1943-44; occupational therapist U.S. Army, Augusta, Ga., 1944-45; instr. phys. edn. King George (Va.) High Sch., 1947-48; instr. phys. edn. Stratford (Va.) High Sch., 1949-50, substitute tchr., 1950-53; owner, dir. Kay's Kindergarten, Fredericksburg, Va., 1959-82. Featured in Fredericksburg Times mag., The Free Lance-Star and Richmond Newspapers. Counselor Girl Scouts U.S., Grundy, Va., 1939-41; life mem. Kenmore Assn., 1949—; mem. Hist. Fredericksburg Found., Inc., 1953—, Mental Health Bd., 1978-84; founder Ford Franklin Found., 1968-78; commr. Fredericksburg Clean Community Commn., 1976—; rep. United Way, Fredericksburg; art ceramics instr. Community Ctr. of Fredericksburg, 1950-80; bd. dirs. Miss Fredericksburg Fair Pageant, 1965-85; participant community parades; coord. Fredericksburg Fair, 1988-90. Recipient Virginia Ellison Vol. Svc. award Fredericksburg Clean Community Commn., 1976-87, Recognition of Svc. award, 1983-84, 1st, 2nd. and 3rd pl. trophies community parades, awards radio Stas. WFLS and WFVA, 1949-89. Mem. AAUW (advt. chmn. travelogue 1971-89, Donor Honoree award 1983, bd. dirs. 1971-79), Lioness Club (bd. dir. 1968-87, Lioness Tamer 1984, Tongue Wagger 1985), Soroptimist Internat. Fredericksburg (life mem., sec. 1971-73, pres. 1973-75, bd. dirs. 1971-78, First Class Pub. Recognition Trophy 1986, Women Helping Women award 1982), Order of Eastern Star, Nat. League of Fredericksburg (bd. dir., Svc. Recognition Trophies 1963, 69, 80), Izaac Walton League (bd. dir. Dog Mart parade 1965-71). Republican. Episcopalian. Home: #8 Blair Rd Fredericksburg VA 22405-3025

JENNETT, SHIRLEY MARIE SHIMMICK, hospice executive, nurse; b. Jennings, Kans., May 1, 1937; d. William and Mabel C. (Mowry) Shimmick; m. Nelson K. Jennett, Aug. 20, 1960 (div. 1972); children: Jon W., Cheryl L.; m. Albert J. Kukral, Apr. 16, 1977 (div. 1990). Diploma, Rsch. Hosp. Sch. Nursing, Kansas City, Mo., 1958. RN, Mo., Colo., Tex., Ill. Staff nurse, head nurse Rsch. Hosp., 1958-60; head nurse Penrose Hosp., Colorado Springs, Colo., 1960-62, Hotel Dieu Hosp., El Paso, Tex., 1962-63; staff nurse Oak Park (Ill.) Hosp., 1963-64; staff nurse, head nurse, nurse recruiter Luth. Hosp., Wheat Ridge, Colo., 1969-79; owner, mgr. Med. Placement Svcs., Lakewood, Colo., 1980-84; vol. primary care nurse, admissions coord., team mgr. Hospice Metro Denver, 1984-88, dir. patient and family svcs., 1988, exec. dir., 1988—; mem. adv. com. Linkages Assn. for Older Adults, Denver, 1989—. Community liaison person U. Phoenix, 1988—. Mem. Am. Nurses Assn., Colo. Nurses Assn., Nat. Hospice Orgn. (standing rev. com.), Colo. Hospice Orgn. (bd. dirs., v.p. 1990—). Republican. Mem. Ch. of Religious Sci. Office: Hospice of Metro Denver 3955 E Exposition Ave Denver CO 80209

JENNEY-WEST, ROXANNE ELIZABETH, accountant, financial consultant; b. Balt., Jan. 12, 1960; d. Clarence LeRoy and Dorothy Ella (Berger) Jenney; m. Daniel Eugene West, Oct. 27, 1984; children: Colleen Jenney, Daniel Eugene Jr. BS in Acctg., U. Md., 1983. CPA, Md. Staff acct., asst. contr. B.F. Saul Co., Chevy Chase, Md., 1981-84; contr., chief fin. officer FWB Bancorp., Rockville, Md., 1984-86, Mercy Med. Svcs. Inc., Las Vegas, Nev., 1986-89; owner, pres. Jenneywest Fin. Svcs., Inc., Las Vegas, Nev., 1989—. Mem. AICPA, NAFE, U.S. C. of C., Md. Assn. CPAs. Home: 4317 Mott Circle Las Vegas NV 89102

JENNINGS, B. JOELLE, educator; b. Phila., Nov. 8, 1944; d. John Joseph and Foresta (Cianfrogna) Rodgers.; m. James T. Jennings, Sept. 25, 1971 (div. 1981). BA, Holy Family Coll., Phila., 1966; postgrad. in edn. Immaculate Heart Coll., L.A., 1977. Cert. tchr., Calif. Intake worker Mental Health Devel. Ctr., L.A., 1966-69; adminstrv. asst. L.A. Mut. Ins. Co., 1969-70; sec. med. staff Queen of Angels Hosp., L.A., 1970-76; tchr. sci. L.A. Unified Sch. Dist, 1977-79; sci. chmn. New Jewish High Sch., L.A., 1980-83; rsch. mgr. Heidrick & Struggles, L.A., 1983-87, 89—; search support coord., Heidrick & Struggles, 1988—; cons. ednl. pvt. psychotherapist, Woodland Hills, Calif., 1979—. Hospice vol. St. Joseph Med. Ctr., Burbank, Calif. Office: 300 S Grand Ave Ste 2400 Los Angeles CA 90071

JENNINGS, JEANNE ELIZABETH, hotel sales and marketing professional; b. N.Y.C., Oct. 13, 1961; d. John Joseph and Mary Jean (Buckner) J. BSBA, Boston U., 1983. Banquet mgr. East River Restaurant Assn., N.Y.C., 1983-85; account exec., then sales mgr. The Drake Swissotel, N.Y.C., 1985-87, dir. of sales, 1987-89, dir. sales and mktg., 1989—. Mem. Nat. Bus. Traffic Assn., N.Y. Visitors and Conv. Bur., Assn. Corp. Travel Execs., Hotel Sales and Mktg. Assn. Republican. Roman Catholic. Home: 315 E 72d St New York NY 10021 Office: The Drake Swissotel 440 Park Ave New York NY 10021

JENNINGS, MADELYN PULVER, communications company human resources executive; b. Saratoga Springs, N.Y., Nov. 23, 1934; d. George Joseph and Martha (Walsh) Pulver. BA in Bus. and Econs., Tex. Woman's U., 1956. Asst. dir. pub. rels. Slick Airways, Dallas, 1956-58, VIP Svcs., Inc., N.Y.C., 1958; asst. to pres. Smith, Dorian & Burman, Hartford, Conn., 1959; bus. mktg. planning GE, Bridgeport, Conn., 1960-68, mgr. manpower planning, 1968-71, mgr. environ. support operation, 1971-73, mgr. employee rels., 1973-76; v.p. human resources Standard Brands, Inc., N.Y.C., 1976-80; sr. v.p. pers. Gannett Co., Arlington, Va., 1980—; corp. adv. bd. NOW legal def. and edn. fund; adv. com. U. Ill. Inst. Labor and Indsl. Rels.; mem. sec's. commn. on achieving necessary skills U.S. Dept. of Labor, adv. com. Fed. Workforce Quality Assesment. Bd. sponsor trustees U. Va. Colgate Darden Sch. of Bus. Adminstrn.; trustee Russell Sage Coll.; bd. dirs. Am. Press Inst., Tex. Woman's Univ. Found., Corp. YADDO; mem. conf. bd./former chair, exec. com./adv. coun. Human Resources Mgmt., The Internat. Alliance; bd. visitors John S. Knight Fellowship. Mem. Human Resources Roundtable, Sr. Personnel Execs. Forum, Human Resources Planning Soc., Newspaper Personnel Rels. Assn., Sr. Personnel Execs. Roundtable, Am. Newspaper Pubs. Assn. (former chair human resources com.), Bus. Roundtable (employee rels. com.), Soc. Human Resource Mgmt. (strategies and issues coun.), Labor Policy Assn. (bd. dirs.). Home: 3520 Duff Dr Falls Church VA 22041 Office: Gannett Co Inc 1100 Wilson Blvd Arlington VA 22234

JENNINGS, MARCELLA GRADY, rancher, investor; b. Springfield, Ill., Mar. 4, 1920; d. William Francis and Magdalene Mary (Spies) Grady; student pub. schs.; m. Leo J. Jennings, Dec. 16, 1950 (dec.). Pub. relations Econolite Corp., Los Angeles, 1958-61; v.p., asst. mgr. LJ Quarter Circle Ranch, Inc., Polson, Mont., 1961-73, pres., gen. mgr., owner, 1973—; dir. Giselle's Travel Inc., Sacramento; fin. advisor to Allentown, Inc., Charlo, Mont.; sales cons. to Amie's Jumpin' Jacks and Jills, Garland, Tex. investor. Mem. Internat. Charolais Assn., Los Angeles County Apt. Assn. Republican. Roman Catholic. Home and Office: 509 Mt Holyoke Ave Pacific Palisades CA 90272

JENNINGS, NANCY ANN, retired educator; b. Bristow, Okla., July 11, 1932; d. John Linard and Charlie Estelle (Hooper) Stucker; m. Jerald Leon Jennings, June 4, 1951; children: Jan, Catherine Jennings Hackman, Elizabeth. BS, U. Okla., 1956; MS, Washburn U., Topeka, Kans., 1974. Cert. elem. tchr., Kans. Tchr. Whitson Grade Sch. Dist. 501, Topeka, 1970-75, Delia Grade Sch Dist. 321, St. Marys, Kans., 1978-79, Silver Lake (Kans.) Grade Sch. Dist. 372, 1979-85, ret., 1985. Mem. NEA (life), Internat. Reading Assn. (sec. 1983-84), Mulvane Art Ctr., Kans. Wildflower Soc., Kans. Hist. Soc., Topeka Aux. of Kans. Engring. Soc. (pres. 1987-88), DAR (regent Topeka chpt.), AAUW (bd. dirs.), Woman's Club (2d v.p. 1989-91), Alpha Delta Kappa (pres. 1989-91), Kappa Delta Pi, Alpha Phi (2d v.p. 1988-90). Presbyterian. Home: 11340 NW 13th Rd Topeka KS 66615-9614

JENNINGS, TONI, state senator, construction company executive; b. Orlando, Fla., May 17, 1949; d. Jack C. and Margaret (Murphy) J. BA, Wesleyan Coll., Macon, Ga., 1971; postgrad., Rollins Coll., 1972-73. Pres. Jack Jennings and Sons, Inc., Gen. Contractors, Orlando, 1973—; mem. Fla. Ho. of Reps., 1976-80; mem. Fla. Senate, 1980—, Republican leader pro tempore, 1982-83, 85, 86, Rep. leader, 1984, 86-88. legis. del. Orange County, 1980-82, 86-88; chmn. econ. profl. and utility regulation; mem. appropriations, Sub A, Ins., Regulated Industries, Rules and Calendar, Transp. coms. Active Sr. Citizens Adv. Council, Rep. Women's Federated Club of Winter Park, Orlando Women's Rep. Club Federated. Recipient Spl. Commendation award Fla. Restaurant Assn., 1979, Meritorious Service award Fla. Fedn. Humane Socs., 1979, Disting. Alumni award Wesleyan Coll., 1981, Freedom award Women for Responsible Legislation, 1982, Support of Law Enforcement award Fla. Sheriffs Assn., Outstanding Efforts award Tampa Missing Children Help Ctr., 1983, Outstanding Svc. award Grocers' Assn. Fla., 1983, Legis. award Fla. , 1983, Legis. award Fla. Chiropractic Assn., 1983, 86, Appreciation award Fla. Med. Assn. and Physicians of Fla., 1983, Second Ann. Frank J. Fahrenkopf, Jr. Outstanding State Minority Leader award, 1988, Annual Legis. award for Leadership in Econ. Devel. Legislation award Fla. C. of C., 1987; Legislator of Yr. Orange County Young Rep. Club, 1980-81. Mem. Orlando Area Bd. Realtors (Friend of Realtors award 1989), Builders and Contractors, Cen. Fla. Builders Exch., Delta Kappa Gamma, Phi Kappa Phi, Kappa Delta Epsilon. Office: Fla Senate Dist #15 1032 Wilfred Dr Orlando FL 32803

JENNINGS, SISTER VIVIEN ANN, academic administrator; b. Jersey City, May 18, 1934; d. Eugene O. and Alice (Smith) J. BA, Caldwell Coll., 1960; MA in English, Cath. U. Am., 1966; MS in Telecommunications, Syracuse U., 1980; PhD in English, Fordham U., 1972; EdD (hon.), Providence Coll.; LittD (hon.), Caldwell Coll. Assoc. prof. English Caldwell Coll., 1960-69; instr. broadcasting writing Syracuse U., 1979-80; with community affairs dept. Sta. WIXT TV, Syracuse, N.Y., 1980; dir. telecommunications Barry U., 1982-83; dir. pub. affairs Cath. Telecommunications Network Am., 1983-84; pres. Caldwell Coll., 1984—; originator, designer campus TV studios Caldwell Coll., Barry U.; curriculum planner, coord. new grad.-level curriculum in telecommunications Barry U.; lectr. on ednl. and media issues. Producer: Centenary Journey, 1981, Advent Vesper Chorale, 1981, American Immigrant Church, 1982; co-producer The Boat People, 1980. Founder, dir. Children"s TV Experience; founder Project Link Ednl. Ctr., Newark; bd. trustees Las Casas Fund for Cheyenne and Arapaho Indians. Mem. Assn. Cath. Colls. (coord. nat. teleconf.), Assn. Ind. Colls. (pres.'s group), Cath. Telecommunications Network Am. (bd. trustees), Providence Coll. (bd. trustees). Office: Caldwell Coll 9 Ryerson Ave Caldwell NJ 07006

JENNINGS, WANDA BETH, special educator; b. Amherst, Tex., July 30, 1947; d. James Powell and Doris Elenor (Kauffman) Wedel; m. William Bryan Jennings III, Dec. 28, 1967. BS in Edn., Tex. Tech. U., Lubbock 1969; MS in Edn., East Tex. State U., Commerce, 1978. Cert. elem. tchr., Tex. Spl. edn. tchr. Ysleta Schs., El Paso, Tex., 1974-75, Bracket Schs., Brackettville, Tex., 1975-76; tchr. Culberson County, Guadalupe, Van Horn, Tex., 1976-78; spl. edn. tchr. Lower Yukon Schs., Mountain Village, Alaska, 1978-79; curriculum writer Western Regional Resource Ctr., Anchorage, 1979-81; gifted tchr. Kodiak Island (Alaska) Schs., 1981-82; tchr, handicapped Dept. of Defense Dependents Sch., Kaiserslautern, Germany, 1982-87; spl. edn. tchr. Yupiit Schs., Tuluksak, Alaska, 1987-89; tchr. mentally retarded children Boise (Idaho) Schs., 1989—. Author: (poetry) I Am a River, 1981 (Alaska Coun. on the Arts award). Recipient Merit award Alaska Dept. Edn., 1989. Mem. NEA, Beta Sigma Phi (Woman Yr. award 1984, 87). Home: 2504 Anderson Boise ID 83702

JENRETTE, RITA CARPENTER, actress, writer; b. San Antonio, Nov. 25, 1949; d. Carney Hunt and Reba (Garlington) Carpenter; m. John Wilson Jenrette, Sept. 10, 1976 (div. July 1981). BA in History cum laude, U. Tex., 1971. Dir. research Rep. Party Tex., Austin, 1972-74; lectr. Taft Polit. Inst. Trinity U., San Antonio, 1974; dir. research, writer Rep. Nat. Com., Washington, 1974-75; research assoc. Office Tech. Assessment, Washington, 1975-77; dir. mktg. Bridgewater U.S.A., N.Y.C., 1986—; reporter This Evening, interviews include Imelda Marcos, Lech Walesa. Author: My Capitol Secrets, 1981, Conglomerate, 1986; appeared in Fantasy Island, Edge of Night, Kate & Allie, The Equalizer; stage debuts include The Philadelphia Story, A Girl's Guide to Chaos; feature film End of the Line; reporter-at-large PM mag., interviews include Imelda Marcos, Lech Walesa, Raisa Gorbachev, Muammar Qaddafi. Vol. Partnership for Homeless, N.Y.C., 1985-87, Spl. Olympics, N.Y.C., 1980-87; fund-raiser AMFAR, N.Y.C. and Washington, 1986-87. Recipient Critics award Drama-Logue, 1982. Mem. Dutch Reform Ch.

JENSEN, ANNE TURNER, automobile service company executive; b. Upper Providence Twp., Pa., Sept. 15, 1926; d. Ellwood Jackson and Elizabeth Addis (Downing) Turner; student Hood Coll., 1944-45, Phila. Coll. Pharmacy and Sci., 1945-46, 47-48; m. Harry Frederick Jensen, Jr., Apr. 13, 1946; children—Frederick Howard, Richard Jordan, Peter Hielm. Legal sec. Robertson & Turner, Media, Pa., 1950-51; sec. Luncheon-is-Served, Media, 1951-53; asst. sec., treas. Delvale Realty Corp., Media, 1955-59; bookkeeper Turner Realty Co., 1960-64, William H. Turner, Atty., 1960-64, Media Auto Service, 1957-74; sec. Media Auto Service, Inc., 1957—. Capt. Heard Fund Dr., 1958-60. Republican. Presbyterian. Clubs: DAR (chpt. regent 1971-74, state corr. sec. 1977-80, nat. chmn. 1974-77), Daughters of Am. Colonists, Daughters of Colonial Wars (state treas. 1974-77, 80-83), Magna Carta Soc., Daus. of 1812, Navy League U.S. (N.Y. Council).

JENSEN, DELORES (DEE JENSEN), physical education educator; b. Harvey, N.D., Apr. 20, 1944; m. Owen Jensen, Dec. 28, 1968. BS, Valley City State U., 1966; MA, No. Ariz. U., 1973. Master cert. official track and field, level 1 coaching cert. Bus., phys. edn. instr. Hatton (N.D.) Pub. Schs., 1966-72; phys. edn. instr. Midway Sch. Dist., Inkster, N.D., 1972-74; student svcs. asst., women's track coach N.D. State Coll. Sci., Wahpeton, 1974-77, bus. instr., women's track coach, 1974—; exec. com. U.S. Women's Track and Field, 1989—, U.S. Olympic Sports Festival, 1987—; mem. Xth Pan Am. Games Officials Selection Com., 1985-86, Olympic Trials Offcls. Selection Com., 1988. Head mgr. Goodwill Games, 1990. Named Coach of Yr. Nat. Jr. Coll. Coaches Assn., 1986, Olympic Offcl., Track and Field,1984, Nat. Athletics Officials Com., 1984—, co-mgr., U.S. Olympic Sports Festival, Baton Rouge, 1985, mgr., U.S. Olympic Sports Festival, Norman, Okla., 1989, Nat. Sports Festival, Baton Rouge. Mem. AAUW (treas. 1982-85), U.S. Women's Track and Field Coaches Assn. (exec. com. 1986-1988), Alpha Delta Kappa (pres. Eta chpt. 1976-78, treas., exec. com. N.D. chpt. 1982-84), Kiwanis (bd. dirs. 1989—). Home: 1621 N 5th St Wahpeton ND 58075 Office: ND State Coll Sci Old Main Wahpeton ND 58076

JENSEN, DORIS J., educational administrator; b. Sterling, Colo., Aug. 10, 1939; d. Clarence J. and Lillian Lucille (Lawrie) Buckley; m. R. Blair Jensen, Aug. 28, 1960; children—Steven J., Cheryl B. A.A., Graceland Coll., 1959; B.S., Central Mo. State U., 1961, M.A. in English, 1964; PhD in Higher Edn. Adminstrn., U. Mo.-Kansas City, 1988. English instr. Central Mo. State U., Independence, 1969-74, U. Mo., Kansas City, 1974-80; registrar Cleveland Chiropractic Coll., Kansas City, 1980-81, dean student affairs and admissions, 1981-88. Mem. Am. Assn. Coll. Registrars and Admissions Officers, Mo. Assn. Coll. Registrars and Admissions Officers, Nat. Assn. Student Personnel Adminstrs, Phi Lambda Theta.

JENSEN, ETHEL ROXANNE, hotelier; b. Minot, N.D., Oct. 5, 1938; d. Lyle James Thompson and Hazella Marion (Jones) Blake; m. J. Walter Richard Peters, Nov. 14, 1959 (div. 1975); 1 son, J. Chandler; m. Ivan Raymond Jensen, June 1, 1978. Cert. secondary tchr., N.D. Adminstrv. officer U. N.D. Grad. Sch., Grand Forks, 1974-78; owner, mgr. Ambassador Motel, Grand Forks, 1978—; mem. N.D. Ho. of Reps., 1989—. Author weekly newspaper column Valley View, 1980-82. Bd. dirs. Greater Grand Forks Symphony, 1979-80; founding mem., treas. Greater Grand Forks Arts and Humanities Coun., 1980-81; charter v.p. Greater Grand Forks Conv. Bur., 1981-82, pres., 1982-83, 83-84; chmn. Affordable Housing Coun. Home Loan Bank of Des Moines, 1990—. Mem. Am. Hotel/Motel Assn., Greater Grand Forks Hotel/Motel Assn. (pres. 1979-81), Phi Beta Kappa. Unitarian. Club: Quota (treas. 1982-83). Lodge: Rotary, Lioness (charter pres. 1982-83). Avocations: art, music, lit. Home: 3707 Belmont Rd Grand Forks ND 58201 Office: Ambassador Motel 2021 S Washington St Grand Forks ND 58201

JENSEN, HANNE MARGRETE, pathology educator; b. Copenhagen, Dec. 9, 1935; came to U.S., 1957; d. Niels Peter Evald and Else Signe Agnete (Rasmussen) Damgaard; m. July 21, 1957 (div. Apr. 1987); children: Peter Albert, Dorte Marie, Gordon Kristian, Sabrina Elisabeth. Student, U. Copenhagen, 1954-57; MD, U. Wash., 1961. Resident and fellow in pathology U. Wash., Seattle, 1963-68; asst. prof. dept. pathology U. Calif. Sch. Medicine, Davis, 1969-79, assoc. prof., 1979—, dir. transfusion svc., 1973—; McFarlane prof. exptl. medicine U. Glasgow, Scotland, 1983. Office: U Calif Sch Medicine Dept Pathology Davis CA 95616

JENSEN, HELEN, musical artists management company executive; b. Seattle, June 30, 1919; d. Frank and Sophia (Kantosky) Leponis; student pub. schs., Seattle; m. Ernest Jensen, Dec. 2, 1939; children: Ernest, Ronald Lee. Co-chmn., Seattle Community Concert Assn., 1957-62; sec. family concerts Seattle Symphony Orch., 1959-61; hostess radio program Timely Topics, 1959-60; gen. mgr. Western Opera Co., Seattle, 1962-64, pres. 1963-64; v.p., dir., mgr. pub. rels. Seattle Opera Assn., 1964—, preview artists coord., 1981-84; bus. mgr. Portland (Oreg.) Opera Co., 1968, cons., 1967-69; owner, mgr. Helen Jensen Artists Mgmt., Seattle, 1970—. First v.p. Music and Art Found., 1981-84, pres. 1984-85. Recipient Cert., Women in Bus in the Field of Art, 1973; award Seattle Opera Assn., 1974; Outstanding Svc. award Music and Art Found., 1984. Mem. Am. Guild Mus. Artists, Music and Art Found. (life), Seattle Opera Guild (life, pres., award of distinction 1983, parliamentarian 1987-89), Ballard Symphony League (sec.), Portland Opera Assn., Portland Opera Guild, Seattle Civic Opera Assn. (pres. 1981-89), 200 Plus One, Aria Preview, Lyric Preview Group (chmn. 1988—), Past Pres. Assembly (pres. 1977-79, parliamentarian 1987-88), Pres.'s Forum (1st v.p. 1990—, program vice chmn. 1987-88), North Shore Performing Arts Assn. (pres. 1981), Women of Achievement (past pres's. assembly, chmn.), Helen Jensen Hiking Club. Home: 19029 56th Ln NE Seattle WA 98155 Office: 716 Joseph Vance Bldg Seattle WA 98101

JENSEN, JAKKI RENEE, retail company executive; b. Eugene, Oreg., Mar. 1, 1959; d. Philip William Jensen and Mary Katherine (Sommers) Henderson; m. Johnny Claiborne Hawthorne, May 7, 1983. Student, Oreg. State U., 1977-78; student (hon.), Portland State U., 1978-81. With Nordstrom Co., Beaverton, Oreg., 1981—; mgr. cosmetics Nordstrom Co., Beaverton, 1984; mgr. cosmetics Nordstrom Co., Walnut Creek, Calif., 1984-86, buyer cosmetics, 1986-88; buyer cosmetics Nordstrom Co., San Francisco, 1988—. Affiliate, vol. San Francisco Soc. for Prevention of Cruelty to Animals, 1990—. Republican. Home: 213 Elderwood Dr Pleasant Hill CA 94523 Office: 865 Market St San Francisco CA 94103

JENSEN, JANE THIELKE, counseling center administrator; b. Lakewood, Wis., May 13, 1933; d. Gilbert William and Laura (Huss) Thielke; children: Colene Jensen Acker, Greg, Grant, Garrett. BS in Psychology, U. Wis., 1978; MS in Profl. Devel., U. Wis., Stout, 1981. Cert. mental health counselor, Wis., divorce mediator, Wis. Community services specialist Dane County Mental Health Ctr., Madison, Wis., 1973-76; pvt. practice divorce counseling Madison, 1976-78; instr. Madison Area Tech. Coll., Madison, 1973-78; dir., owner, counselor, divorce mediator Divorce Counseling and Mediation Ctr., Madison, 1978—; divorce cons. clergy cts., attys., sch., colls., employee assts. program to bus., Madison, 1973—; creator, presentor Crisis of the Holidays, Single Parent Burnout workshops, divorce groups and women groups, single parents without custody, 1973—. Mem. Gov.'s Women's Adv. Bd., Madison, 1978-82, Single Women/Single Parent Taskforce, Madison, 1978-82; bd. dirs. Fathers for Equal Justice, 1990; co-chair Gender Bias Data Com., 1990. Recipient Nat. Recognition award Cable TV, Madison, 1974. Mem. Wis. Outpatient Clinics, Investment Club (pres.). Home and Office: 7402 Friendship Ln Middleton WI 53562

JENSEN, JENNIFER JO, corporate trainer; b. Audubon, Iowa, May 27, 1960; d. Leo Christian Theodore and Audrey Byrd (Jones) J. BA in English-Theatre, Dana Coll., 1982. Dir. sales and mktg. Scope Cable TV Gt. Plains Communications, Blair, Nebr., 1982-85; asst. dir. admissions Dana

Coll., Blair, 1985-87; dir. human resources Intellisell Inc., Omaha, 1987-89; telemktg. sales mgr. Jones Oil Co., Lincoln, Nebr., 1989; corp. trainer Seller's Choice, Inc., St. Paul, 1989-90; software trainer Edina (Minn.) Realty, 1990—; cons. in telemktg. and human resources, 1990—; judge Iowa High Sch. Speech Assn., 1979—. Com. mem. Nebr. Jr. Miss Com., Blair, 1984-89; bd. dirs. Blair Community Theatre, 1985-87, pres. 1987; charter mem. Blair World of Entertainment Series, 1985, chmn., 1988. Recipient best cameo award Blair Community Theatre, 1982. Mem NAFE, Mid-Am. Direct Mktg. Assn., Danish Brotherhood Am. Republican. Lutheran. Office: Edina Realty 6800 France Ave Edina MN 55431

JENSEN, JODEEN MARIE, corporate trainer; b. Lusk, Wyo., Jan. 24, 1964; d. Gary Dean and Evelyn Louise (Stoddard) Jensen. BA magna cum laude, William Jewell Coll., 1986; MA in English, N.E. Mo. State U., 1988. Dir. communications Profl. Resource Ctr., Leawood, Kans., 1986-87; instr. English, N.E. Mo. State U., Kirksville, 1987-88; placement liaison Project Refocus, U. Mo., Kansas City, 1988-89; corp. trainer Gov. Employees Hosp. Assn., Kansas City, 1989—; freelance writer for profl. jours. and popular mags. Contbr. poetry to various publs. Mem. Am. Soc. for Tng. and Devel. (Kansas City chpt.). Methodist. Home: 15430 E 45th Ter Independence MO 64055 Office: Gov Employees Hosp Assn PO Box 10304 Kansas City MO 64110

JENSEN, KATHERINE KEMP, insurance company executive; b. Canandaigua, N.Y., July 22, 1955; d. Harry Frederick and Charlotte Ruth (Doebereiner) Kemp; m. Fred E. Jensen, Mar. 7, 1987; stepchildren: Brett, Stacey, Marceil. BA, Siena Coll., 1976. Cert. property and casualty ins. instr. Dir. local programs N.Y. State Assembly, Albany, 1976-77; assoc. realtor Grad. Realtor Inst. LaLonde Realty, Inc., Fairport, N.Y., 1978-81; ops. unit mgr. Allstate Ins. Co., Rochester, N.Y., 1981-84; adminstrv. svcs. mgr. Allstate Ins. Co., Rochester, 1984-88; market sales mgr. Allstate Ins. Co., Jamestown, 1988 --. Chmn. N.Y. State Teen Age Reps., 1973-74; mem. N.Y. State Rep. Platform Com., 1974; mem. Perinton Rep. Com., 1978-88, chmn., 1985-88; mem. Zoning Bd. Appeals, Perinton, N.Y., 1981-88, chmn., 1985-88. Recipient Mary Ann award N.Y. State Reps., 1974. Mem. Jamestown Area C. of C., Jamestown Sch. and Bus. Alliance, Empire State Paint Horse Club (pres. 1986-87). Home: RD 1 Lottsville Rd Columbus PA 16405 Office: Allstate Insurance Co 560 W 3d St Jamestown NY 14701

JENSEN, KATHRYN PATRICIA, public broadcaster; b. Fairbanks, AK, June 20, 1950; d. Edward Leroy and Doris Patricia (Fee) Bigelow; m. Timothy Lyle Jensen, May 19, 1973; 1 child, Alexander Morgan. BA, U. Alaska, 1974. Sta. mgr., program dir. Sta. KUAC-FM U. Alaska, Fairbanks, 1976-82; acting gen. mgr. Sta. KUAC-FM-TV U. Alaska, Fairbanks, 1981-82, gen. mgr., 1982-87; gen. mgr. Sta. WCPN-FM, Cleve., 1987—; mem. vis. com. Coll. Edn. Cleve. State U., 1990. Trustee Mid-Town Corridor, Cleve., 1988-89, Libr. Found., Fairbanks, 1985-88. Recipient Elaine B. Mitchell award Alaska Pub. Radio Network, 1988. Episcopalian. Office: WCPN (FM) The Cleve Centre 3100 Chester Ave Cleveland OH 44114

JENSEN, LOREN ANN, human resources specialist; b. Grand Island, Nebr., Jan. 10, 1953; d. Lorentz and Leona (Barden) Semon. BA, U. Nebr., 1974, MBA, 1984, postgrad. in Health Edn., 1986—. Exec. dir. Healthy Lifestyle Concepts, Lincoln, Nebr., 1982-86; corp. cons. Dale Carnegie Systems, Tucson, Ariz., 1986-87; br. mgr. Pac-Tel Paging, Tucson, 1987-89; exec. dir., founder AJL Enterprises, Tucson, 1988—; featured in Cosmopolitan mag., 1989. Bd. dirs. 3HO Superhealth, Tucson, 1986—; adminstrv. bd. mem. St. Francis in Foothills, Tucson, 1987—, mem. chair., 1988—; mem. svcs. coord. Wellness Coun. Tucson, 1990—; coord. Earth Day, 1990; mem. People Ethical Treatment Animals. Named Mgr. of Yr. Mem. NAFE. Methodist. Home: 2713 N Essel Dr Tucson AZ 85715 Office: 6627 E Carondelet Dr Tucson AZ 85710

JENSEN, MARLENE F., magazine publisher; b. Aurora, Ill., Apr. 16, 1947; d. Benjamin Waldo Fann and Sylvia Ida (Brott) Burch; m. Raymond Neils Jensen, Jan. 11, 1970 (div. Sept. 1975). BA in Psychology, Calif. State U., Los Angeles, 1972; MBA, Fordham U., 1981. Editor, pub., owner Sportswoman Mag., Los Angeles, 1972-76; bus. mgr. ABC Leisure Mags., N.Y.C., 1977-79; dir. acquisitions CBS Mags., N.Y.C., 1979-81, pub. audio mag., 1982-83; v.p., pub. Home Mechanix Mag., N.Y.C., 1983-86; v.p. mags. Springhouse Corp., Pa., 1986-89; pres. Jensen Group, High Bridge, N.J., 1989; cons. Bus. Supporting the Arts, Phila., 1987. Author: Women's Sports, 1975, Women Who Want to Be Boss, 1987. Named to Woman Achievers Hall of Fame YWCA, N.Y.C., 1984. Mem. Assn. Bus. Pubs. (chmn, pubs. com., 1987), Mensa.

JENSEN, REGINA BRUNHILD, psychotherapist; b. Bredstedt, Germany, Oct. 26, 1951; came to U.S., 1973; d. Karl Adolf and Hildegard (Weiss) Schlosser; m. Benny Hvitfelt Jensen, July 31, 1976; stepchildren: Anita, Lisa. BS in Physiotherapy, Krankengymnastik Schule, Tuebingen, 1971; MA in Counseling Psychology, Vt. Coll., 1983; PhD Human Behavior, Ryokan Coll., 1984; PhD Clin. Psychology, Sierra U., 1987. Physiotherapist Urban Krankenhaus, Berlin, 1971-73; staff physiotherapist Werner & Beck Physical Therapy, Santa Maria, Calif., 1976-83; pvt. practice health cons. Santa Ynez, 1982—; cons. Jensen Enterprises, Solvang, 1975—, Alexander & Jensen Assocs., L.A., 1983-85; adolescent crisis counselor Santa Ynez Valley High Sch., 1984-86; tutor, program coordinator Sierra U., Santa Monica, 1985—; dir. Inst. for Human Systems Integration, Santa Ynez, 1985—; founder, clin. dir., The Learning Ctr., 1987—. Author: Education for the Medical Consumer, 1983, To Liberate or to Enslave, 1985, How To Buy Back Your Soul, 1987; publisher Fully Alive Publs., 1988—; pub., founder Healing Art Expressions, 1987—; contbr. articles to profl. papers and jours. Mem. Am. Psychol. Assn. (divs. for media and health psychology), Calif. Assn. For Marriage and Family Therapists, Am. Assn. for Counseling and Devel., Orgnl. Devel. Network. Home and Office: 2880 Baseline Ave #B Santa Ynez CA 93460

JENSEN, SHERYL RUFENACHT, health claims processing executive; b. Urbana, Ill., Sept. 14, 1956; d. James William and Alice Marie (Cullison) Rufenacht; children: Chad Eric Baxter, Graham David, Collin James. Student, Columbia Coll., 1990. Recipient eligibility supr. Nat. Heritage Ins. Co., Austin, Tex., 1982-85; fin., cash, adjustments supr. Electronic Data Systems, Little Rock, 1985-88; support svcs. supr. GTE Data Svcs., Jefferson City, Mo., 1988, support svcs. mgr., 1988—. Mem. Jefferson City C. of C., Capital City Jaycees (sec.). Office: GTE Data Svcs 313 Ellis Blvd Jefferson City MO 65101

JEPPESEN, SUSAN QUANDT, marketing executive; b. Milw., Sept. 8, 1954; d. Raymond W. and Ruth M. (Sievers) Quandt; m. Edward Kersten (div.); 1 child, Jennifer Elizabeth; m. Eric Jeppesen; 1 child, Katherine Joan. BS in Acctg., Valparaiso U., 1976; MBA, U. Wis., 1978. Acct. E.C. Hicks & Assocs., Merrillville, Ind., 1976-77; market rsch. analyst Wis. Telephone Co., Milw., 1979, S.C. Johnson & Son Inc., Racine, Wis., 1980; sales fin. cons. Wis. Telephone Co., Milw., 1981-82; mgr. sales support AT&T Info. Systems, Chgo., 1983; comptroller Ameritech Communications Inc., Chgo., 1984, dir. product mgmt., 1984-86, dir. New Bus. Devel. and Systems Integration, 1987; sr. dir. mktg. communications, Ill. Bell, 1988; div. mgr. customer and community rels., 1989—; prof. mktg. Alverno Coll., Milw., 1982; instr. mktg. Milw. Area Tech. Coll., 1982; chmn. membership Infant Welfare Ctr. Clarendon, 1988—; mem. Grace Ch.; mem. parish life com. com. St. Helen's Guild. Mem. Am. Mktg. Assn (pres. Milw. chpt. 1982-83, pres. 1981-82, v.p. communications 1980-81), Chgo. Zool. Soc. (Leadership Greater Chgo. fellow). Home: 6009 N SHore Dr Whitefish Bay WI 53217 Office: 411 E Wisconsin Ave Ste 519 Milwaukee WI 53202

JEPSON, HELEN ANNA, nurse administrator; b. Moline, Ill., June 24, 1947; d. Andrew and Myrtle (Bastable) Jepson. Diploma, Moline Pub. Hosp. Sch. Nursing, 1971; BSN, Marycrest Coll., 1975; MSN, No. Ill. U., 1978, EdD, 1984. RN; cert. in biofeedback. Staff nurse Moline Pub. Hosp., 1971-75, maternal-child educator, 1975-79; staff nurse Kishwaukee Community Hosp., DeKalb, Ill., 1980-86; maternal-child educator No. Ill. U., DeKalb, 1979-86; dir. nursing adminstrn. Sycamore (Ill.) Mcpl. Hosp., 1986-87; dir. nursing dept. MacMurray Coll., Jacksonville, Ill., 1987—. Contbr. articles to profl. jours. Vol., Am. Red Cross, Ill., 1979—; bd. dirs. Ednl. Day Care, Jacksonville, 1987—. Mem. Am. Nurses Assn. (coms.), Childbirth Edn. Assn. (advisor), Sigma Theta Tau (pres. 1981-83). Home: 500 W State St Jacksonville IL 62650

JERGE, MARIE CHARLOTTE, minister; b. Mineola, N.Y., Dec. 26, 1952; d. Charles Louis and Helen Marie (Scheld) Scharfe; m. James Nelson Jerge, Aug. 27, 1977. AB, Smith Coll., 1974; MDiv, Luth. Theol. Sem. of Phila., 1978. Pastor St. Mark Evang. Luth. Ch., Mayville, N.Y., 1978-88; co-pastor Zion Evang. Luth. Ch., Silver Creek, N.Y., 1983-88; asst. to the bishop Upstate N.Y. Synod, Buffalo, 1988—; bd. dirs. Acad. Preachers, Phila., 1982—. Chairperson Chautauqua County Commn. of Family Violence and Neglect, Mayville, 1981-82, bd. dirs., 1978-88. Named one of outstanding Young Women in Am., 1980. Home: 370 Borden Rd West Seneca NY 14224 Office: Upstate NY Synod 49 Linwood Ave Buffalo NY 14209

JERKINS, GRACE MAE, retired educator; b. Rockville, Ind., Sept. 1, 1904; d. Claude Franklin and Jessie Beatrice (McKee) Gossett; m. Frank Edward Jerkins, Dec. 29, 1943 (dec. July 1970). BS in Edn., Ind. State U., Terre Haute, 1937; postgrad., Colo. State U., 1938. Tchr. Vigo County Pub. Schs., New Goshen, Ind., 1923-25, Elkhart (Ind.) Pub. Schs., 1927-43; jr. high social studies and lang. arts tchr. Gary (Ind.) Pub. Schs., 1944-58. Author: Chronicles of the Gossett Family, 1985. Del. UNESCO, Boston, 1961; former conductor fund drive for channel 11, City of Gary; former vol. with handicapped children. Mem. Nat. Retired Tchrs., AAUW (fellow 1969-70, membership award 1987), Ind. Hist. Assn., N.W. Ind. Women's Club (chmn. civic gourp, legis. advisor), Bus. and Profl. Women's Club, Pi Gamma Mu, Phi Alpha Theta. Republican. Presbyterian. Home: 520 S Vermillion Pl Gary IN 46403

JERKOFSKY, MARYANN, virologist, educator; b. Alameda, Calif., Feb. 18, 1943; d. Gus Joseph and Helen Louise (Babel) J. BA, U. Tex., 1965; PhD, Baylor Coll. Medicine, 1969. Postdoctoral fellow Pa. State Med. Ctr., Hershey, 1969-72, rsch. assoc., 1972-73, instr. microbiology, 1973-74; rsch. asst. prof. Med. Sch. U. Miami (Fla.), 1974-76; asst. prof. U. Maine, Orono, 1976-81, assoc. prof., 1981—; vis. researcher U. Amsterdam, The Netherlands, 1983; vis. prof. Am. U. Les Cayes, Haiti, 1988, 1990. Contbr. articles to profl. jours. Recipient pre-doctoral fellowship NIH, 1966-69. Mem. AAAS, Am. Soc. Microbiology, Am. Soc. Virology, Phi Beta Kappa, Sigma Xi (dissertation award 1969), Phi Kappa Phi. Democrat. Roman Catholic. Office: U Maine Dept Microbiology 281 Hitchner Hall Orono ME 04469

JERNIGAN, GAIL FIVEASH, financial executive; b. Del., May 31, 1951; d. Charles O. and Dorothy (Deaver) Fiveash; m. R.V. Deats III, May 19, 1973 (div. 1984); m. J. Jerrel Jernigan, Jan. 1, 1988; children: Jeffery, Clay. BS, N.C. State U., 1973. Substitute tchr. Kinston (N.C.) City Schs., 1973-75; cost and property control clk. Lenoir County Bd. Edn., Kinston, 1975-78; life ins. agt. N.Y. Life Ins. Co., Kinston, 1979-85; stock broker Wheat First Securities, Kinston, 1985-88; budget analyst DuPont, Savannah River Co., Aiken, S.C., 1988-89; sr. environ. analyst Westinghouse, Savannah River Co., Aiken, 1989—. Overall chmn. United Way, Kinston, 1987, mem budget com., Barnwell, 1988-89, bd. dirs., 1988—. Named to Outstanding Young Women Am., 1981. Mem. Jaycees (pres. local chpt. 1983, Disting. Citizen award 1986, Outstanding N. Carolinian award 1986).

JERNIGAN, MARIAN SUE, fashion merchandising professional; b. Chattanooga, Dec. 18, 1940; d. John Marion and Coye M. (Cunningham) Hayes; m. G. William Jernigan, Dec. 22, 1969. BS, Purdue U., 1962, MS, 1964, PhD, 1968. Exec. trainee Hutzler Bros. Co., Balt., 1963-64; dept. mgr. L.S. Ayres & Co., Lafayette, Ind., 1964-65; instr. Purdue U., W. Lafayette, Ind., 1965-66; asst. prof. La. State U., Baton Rouge, 1968-73; assoc. prof. Fla. State U., Tallahassee, 1973-76, N. Tex. State U., Denton, 1976-83; acting dir. N. Tex. State U., 1980-83; prof. fashion merchandising Tex. Woman's U., Denton, 1983—. Co-author: Merchandising Mathematics for Retailing, 1984, Fashion Merchandising and Marketing, 1990. pres. Internat. Toastmistress, Lewisville, Tex., 1983. Mem. Fashion Group Internat., Assn. Coll. Profs. Textiles and Clothing, Am. Home Econs. Assn., Am. Collegiate Retailing Assn., Costume Soc. Am. Tex. Home Econs. Assn. (div. sec.), Zeta Tau Alpha (advisor to student chpts.), Delta Kappa Gamma, Alpha Lambda Delta, Omicron Nu, Phi Upsilon Omicron. Methodist. Office: Tex Womens U PO Box 22509 Denton TX 76204

JERNOW, JANE LIU, pharmaceutical chemist, pharmaceutical manager; b. Shangai, Peoples Republic China, July 1, 1938; d. Henry Liu and Shan Yao; m. Stanley Kenneth Jernow, Dec. 12, 1965; 1 child, Allison. BS, U. Ill., 1958, MS, 1961; PhD, Pa. State U., State College, 1963. Scientist Sterling Winthrop Rsch. Inst., Rensselaer, N.Y., 1968-69; program dir. NAS, Washington, 1986-89; mgr. Hoffmann-LaRoche Inc., Nutley, N.J., 1971—. NIH postdoctoral fellow Cornell U., Ithaca, N.Y., 1963-65; recipient Tribute to Women in Industry award, N.J., 1982, Transfer of Know How Tech. award UN, N.Y.C., 1985. Mem. AAAS, Am. Chem. Soc., Assn. Women in Sci., Sigma Xi, Phi Tau Phi. Democrat. Home: 6671 32d St NW Washington DC 20015 Office: Hoffmann-LaRoche Nutley NJ 07110

JERSEY, DEIRDRE IRENE, public relations executive; b. Bronx, N.Y., Aug. 7, 1946; d. George Vincent and Edith Marion (Bruder) Ketchum; m. Ira FredericK Jersey, May 8, 1965; children: Ira Jr., Richard George. AA, Suffolk Community Coll., Selden, N.Y., 1981; BA, St. Joseph's Coll., Patchoque, N.Y., 1984. Journalist Record Newspapers, Port Jefferson, N.Y., 1981-84; pres. Pub. Images Inc., Hauppauge, N.Y., 1984—, Pub. Image Printing, Hauppauge, 1989—. Vice chmn. Brookhaven Small Bus. Adv. Coun., 1987—; bd. dirs. Boy Scouts Am., Suffolk County Coun., 1989-90, YMCA, Brookhaven, N.Y., 1988-89. Named Women in Bus. Advocate of Yr. Small Bus. Adminstrn., 1990. Mem. Nat. Assn. Women Bus. Owners (pres. L.I. 1989-91), L.I. Communicators Assn., Nat. Sch. Pub. Rels. Assn. (Golden Achievement award 1987), N.Y. Sch. Pub. Rels. Assn. (fin. chmn. 1987-89). Republican. Lutheran. Office: Public Images Inc 1328 Motor Parkway Hauppauge NY 11788

JERSON, CAROL ANNE, industrial engineer, quality facilitator; b. Worcester, Mass., Feb. 17, 1957; d. Samuel Albert and Anne Rose (Shablin) Alukas; m. Jack Ted Jerson, Sept. 16, 1983. BS magna cum laude, Emerson Coll., 1979, MS, 1982. Loss prevention rep. Liberty Mut. Ins. Co., Boston and Miami, 1980-81, Am. Gen. Fire and Casualty, Houston, 1982-83; ednl. cons. Boeing Mil. Airplane Co., Wichita, Kans., 1983-85; cons. Liberty Mut. Ins. Co., Boston, John Hancock Ins. Co., Boston, Am. Inst. Banking, Boston, 1979-80, Mitre Corp., Bedford, Mass., Patricia Stevens Career Coll., Wichita, Kans.; adj. instr. Patricia Stevens Career Coll., 1989, Widener U., 1989 Host cable TV Carol Alukas Show, 1974-75; co-host radio show That's Life, 1974-75; vol. Wichita Radio Reading Service. Recipient Gold Key award Emerson Coll., 1977. Active Jr. Achievement of Delaware Valley. Mem. Assn. Safety Engrs., Soc. Advancement Mgmt. (sec. 1980), North Dade C. of C., Houston C. of C., Am. Helicopter Soc., Inst. Indsl. Engrs., Assn. Quality and Participation, Gamma Sigma Sigma. Lodge: Lionesses (3d v.p., co-founder Auburn).

JERVIS, SALLY ANN, director; b. Scranton, Pa., Mar. 15, 1937; d. William and Edith (Beebe) Jervis. BS in Recreational Edn., Pa. State U., 1959. Supt. playgrounds Wyo. Valley Playground Assn., Wilkes-Barre, Pa., 1959-62; dir. recreation City of Wilkes-Barre, 1962-65; dir. pk., recreation Luzerne County, Wilkes-Barre, 1965-69; exec. dir. Pa. Woods Girl Scout Coun., Wilkes-Barre, 1969—; bd. Adult Svcs. Unlimited, Plains, Pa., 1985-89. Pres. Pa. Recreation and Parks Soc., 1967-68; chairperson Macy Utilization Girl Scouts of U.S., 1976-81; mem. Oakwood Park Townhouse Assn., 1977-81; mem. Boro Coun., 1982-86; pres. Greater Pittston Sanitary Authority, 1986—. Mem. PTA Coun., Wilkes-Barre Area Sch. Bd., Women's Club. Democrat. Baptist. Home: 135 Haverford Dr Laflin PA 18702 Office: Penn's Woods Girl Scouts Pa Woods Coun 10 S Sherman St Wilkes-Barre PA 18702

JESESEKE, ELLEN FRANCES, computer programmer, corporate computer graphic artist; b. Saddle Brook, N.J., Sept. 3, 1954; d. Frank Alexander and Helen (Kandravy) J. BA in Fine Arts, certs. in art edn. and computer sci., magna cum laude, William Paterson Coll., 1976; cert. in comml. art, Sch. Advt. Art, Bloomfield, N.J., 1977; certs. in microcomputers, CES Tng. Sch., River Edge, N.J., 1985; certs. in computer graphics, Pratt Inst., The New Sch., N.Y.C., 1985-86; VAX cert., Digital Equipment Corp., N.Y.C., 1987; cert. in computer documentation, Am. Mgmt. Assn., 1988. Tchr. art N.J. Sch. Systems, 1976-79; visual merchandising artist Hahne's & Co., Montclair, N.J., 1979-80; health aide, art therapy asst. John F. Kennedy Rehab. Ctr., Edison, N.J., 1980-81; interior designer Carriage House, River Edge, N.J., 1981-82; mainframe programmer PDP 11/70, data processing tech. writer and documentation coord., corp. comml. artist, graphic project coord. Christian Salvesen, Secaucus, N.J., 1982—, co. rep. computer and graphic seminars, confs. and tradeshows, 1984—, corp. computer graphics artist, 1987—, personal computer and computer graphics rsch. coord., writer and artist employee newsletter, mainframe programmer VAX cluster 8250, 1988—, company art library coord., company art photographer, 1989—. Mem. Nat. Computer Graphics Assn., Digital Equipment Computers Users Soc., Nat. Assn. Desktop Pubs., Am. Mgmt. Assn., Nat. Assn. Female Execs., Assn. for Women in Computing, Nat. Tng. and Computer Network, Pi Lambda Theta. Russian Orthodox. Home: 260 Fourth St Saddle Brook NJ 07662 Office: Christian Salvesen 1 Enterprise Ave Secaucus NJ 07094

JESKE, DEBORA RAE, research scientist; b. Connellsville, Pa., Nov. 14, 1952; d. Harold John and Gladys Laroux (Bryner) Rutter; m. Theodore Francis, Oct. 30. 1981; child;ren: Sarah Jane, Rachel Anne, Ursula Diane. BS in Chemistry cum laude, Waynesburg Coll., 1974; PhD in Chemistry, U. Pitts., 1978. Rsch. chemist Westvaco Corp. R&D Lab, Laurel, Md., 1978-83; rsch. scientist Union Camp Corp., Princeton, NJ, 1983—. Contbr. articles to Jour. Applied Physics. Mem. Trinity United Meth. Ch. Mem. Am. Chem. Soc., Tech. Assn. Pulp and Paper, Tech. Assn. Graphic Arts. Democratic. United Methodist. Home: 14 Carolina Ave Trenton NJ 08618

JESKE, LUCILLE, advertising executive; b. Milw., Feb. 6, 1931; d. Carl Reinhold and Adele (Bergmann) J. BS, Marquette U., 1954. Ordained Stephen minister Luth. Ch. Copy, editorial and direct advt. mgr. JC Penney Catalogs, N.Y.C.; ind. mktg. cons. Westport, Conn. Neighborhood canvasser Cancer Assn., Heart Fund, Westport, Conn., 1990. Mem. Women in Communications, N.Y. Women in Bus., Direct Mail Mktg. Assn. (cert.), Theta Sigma Phi (treas., Milw. chpt.). Home: 1 Redcoat Rd Westport CT 06880

JESSUP, RACHEL LUTZ, banker; b. Stamford, N.Y., Nov. 30, 1962; d. Sayers Albert and Joan (Marquit) Lutz; m. Joel Mark Jessup, Oct. 22, 1988. BA in Psychology, Alfred U., 1984. Traffic mgr. WZOZ Radio, Oneonta, N.Y., 1984-85; acct. exec. WZOZ Radio, Oneonta, 1985, announcer, 1985-86, 1989—; customer svc. rep. Key Bank of Eastern N.Y., NA, Oneonta, 1986; mgmt. trainee Key Bank of Eastern N.Y., NA, Albany, 1986-87; fin. svc. rep. Key Bank of Eastern N.Y., NA, Oneonta, 1987-88, fin. svcs. officer, 1988-89, regional sales officer, 1989-90, fin. svcs. officer, 1990—; mem. Mohawk Valley Econ. Devel. Dist. Inc., Mohawk, N.Y., 1989—. Bd. dirs. Oneonta YMCA, 1988—; vol. United Way of Delaware and Otsego Counties, 1989 (Vol. of Year 1989). Mem. AAUW, Leatherstocking Candlelighters, Oneonta Rotary Club. Democrat. Home: 27 Luther St Oneonta NY 13820

JETER, KATHERINE LESLIE BRASH, lawyer; b. Gulfport, Miss., July 24, 1921; d. Ralph Edward and Rosa Meta (Jacobs) Brash; m. Robert McLean Jeter, Jr., May 11, 1946. BA, Newcomb Coll. of Tulane U., 1943; JD, Tulane U., 1945. Bar: La. 1945, U.S. Dist. Ct. (we. dist.) La. 1948, U.S. Tax Ct. 1965, U.S. Supreme Ct. 1971, U.S. Dist. Ct. (ea. dist.) La. 1975, U.S. Ct. Appeals (5th cir.) 1981, U.S. Dist. Ct. (mid. dist.) La. 1982. Assoc. Montgomery, Fenner & Brown, New Orleans, 1945-46, Tucker, Martin, Holder, Jeter & Jackson, Shreveport, 1947-49; ptnr. Tucker, Jeter, Jackson and Hickman and predecessors, Shreveport, 1980—; judge pro tem 1st Jud. Dist. Ct., Caddo Parish, La., 1982-83; mem. adv. com. to joint legis. subcom. on mgmt. of the community; pres. YWCA of Shreveport, 1963; hon. consul of France; Shreveport; pres. Little Theatre of Shreveport, 1966-67; pres. Shreveport Art Guild, 1974-75; mem. task force crim justice La. Priorities for the Future, 1978; pres. LWV of Shreveport, 1950-51. Recipient Disting. Grad. award Tulane U., 1983. Mem. La. State Law Inst. (mem. coun. 1980—, adv. com. La. Civil Code 1973-77, temp. ad hoc com. 1976-77), Pub. Affairs Rsch. Coun. (bd. trustees 1976-81, exec. com. 1981—, area exec. committeeman Shreveport area 1982), ABA, La. Bar Assn., Shreveport Bar Assn. (pres. 1986), Nat. Assn. Women Lawyers, Shreveport Assn. for Women Attys., C. of C. Shreveport (bd. dirs. 1975-77), Order of Coif, Phi Beta Kappa. Baptist. Contbr. articles on law to profl. jours. Home: 3959 Maryland Ave Shreveport LA 71106 Office: 401 Edwards St Ste 905 Shreveport LA 71101-3146

JEWETT, SALLY JEAN, independent video producer; b. Phila., May 9, 1953; d. William Orrington and Sarah Elizabeth (Kluttz) J.; m. Julian Whitaker, May 16, 1983 (div. 1986); m. Tom J. Brocato, Aug. 20, 1989. BA in English and Polit. Sci., Bowling Green State U., 1974. Prodn. asst. Sta. KYW-TV, Phila., 1974-75, assoc. producer, 1975-76, field producer, 1976-79; nat. segment producer PM Mag., San Francisco, 1979-81; producer Group W Entertainment, L.A., 1981; field producer Entertainment Tonight, L.A., 1981-84; owner On The Scene Prodns., L.A., 1984—. Producer: (videotapes) Tahiti, 1987 (Pacific Area Travel Assn. Grand Prize), Abortion for Survival, 1989 (Golden Cinema award). Mem. NAFE, NOW, Publicist's Guild Am., Dir.'s Guild Am. Office: On The Scene Prodns Inc 5900 Wilshire Blvd #1400 Los Angeles CA 90036

JIALANELLA, GLORIA JEAN, realtor; b. Staten Island, N.Y., July 7, 1942; d. Theodore and Cornelia (Castelletti) Wetz; children: Robert Lloyd, Crystal Keefer, Thomas. Grad. high sch., Akron, Ohio, 1960. Field tng. supr. Kroger Co., Solon, Ohio, 1962-82, Orlando, 1982-88; realtor Hightower & Assocs., 1989—. Mem. Am. Soc. Tng. and Devel., Nat. Orgn. Women. Home: 4549 Point Lookout Rd Orlando FL 32808

JIA-YUAN, CHARLOTTE, physical process engineer; b. Shanghai, People's Republic China, Aug. 10, 1958; came to U.S., 1983; d. Jian-Chang Jia and Wei Zhang; m. Zhongjian Yuan, May 13, 1989. BS in Physics, Shanghai Tchrs. U., 1982; MS in Physics, U. Mo., Rolla, 1985, MSEE, 1987. Instr. Shanghai Tech. Sch., 1982-83; teaching asst. U. Mo., Rolla, 1984-88, rsch. asst., 1987-88; sr. process engr. B. Philips Display Components Co., Ann Arbor, Mich., 1988-89; process engr. I Motorola, Inc., Schaumburg, Ill., 1989—. Mem. IEEE, Am. Phys. Soc., Smithsonian Assocs. Home: 94 Mulberry Ln Streamwood IL 60107 Office: Motorola Inc F-12 1301 E Algonquin Rd Schaumburg IL 60196

JIBBEN, LAURA ANN, state agency administrator; b. Peoria, Ill., Oct. 1, 1949; d. Charles Otto and Dorothy Lee (Skaggs) Becker; m. Michael Eugene Hagan, July 7, 1967 (div. Apr. 1972); m. Louis C. Jibben, July 14, 1972. BA in Criminal Justice, Sangamon State U., 1984; MBA, Northwestern U., 1989. Asst. to chief of adminstrn. Ill. Dept. Corrections, Springfield, 1974-77, exec. asst. to dir., 1977-80, dep. dir., 1980-81; mgr. toll services Ill. Tollway Dept., Oak Brook, 1981-86; chief adminstrv. officer Regional Transp. Authority, Chgo., 1986—, fund mgr. loss financing plan, 1987—, also, chmn. pension trust; cons. labor studies Sangamon State U., Springfield, 1981. Apptd. mem. Transp. Adv. Bd. City of Naperville, 1988—. Recipient Appreciation award VFW, Chgo., 1983, award Ill. State Toll Hwy. Authority, 1986. Mem. Nat. Assn. Female Execs., Women's Transp. Seminar, Am. Mgmt. Assn., Human Resource Mgrs. Assn. Chgo., The Planning Forum, Beta Sigma Phi (treas., v.p., corr. sec. Naperville and Easton, Ill. chpts.).

JIMENEZ, ARLENE MARIE, energy industry executive; b. Salinas, Calif., June 20, 1959; d. Melvyn Howard and Gertrude Lorraine (McKernan) Krause; m. Waldo Rafael Jimenez, June 1, 1985. AA in Merchandising, Fashion Inst. Design, L.A., 1981; BA, U. La Verne, Calif., 1981; MBA in Mgmt., U. Bridgeport, 1986. Salesperson Bullocks, West Covina, Calif., 1976-81; asst. buyer Bullocks Wilshire, L.A., 1981-82; mgr. ops. Pacific Sunwear of Calif., Newport Beach, 1982-85; research asst. U. Bridgeport, Conn., 1985-86; commodity broker Chilmark Commodities Corp., Stamford, Conn., 1986-87; br. mgr. Sovereign Commodities Corp., Stamford, 1987; corp. auditor Louis Dreyfus Corp., Wilton, Conn., 1987—; pipeline scheduler ops. Louis Dreyfus Energy Corp., Wilton, 1989-90. Mem. Nat. Rep. Com., Washington, 1987. Mem. NAFE. Roman Catholic. Home: 1169 Hope St C-5 Stamford CT 06907 Office: Louis Dreyfus Energy Corp 10 Westport Rd Wilton CT 06897-0810

JIMENEZ, BETTIE EILEEN, small business owner; b. LaCygne, Kans., June 8, 1932; d. William Albert and Ruby Faye (Cline) Montee; m. William R. Bradley, Aug. 21, 1947 (div. Sept. 1950); 1 child, Shirley; m. J.P. Jimenez, Feb. 20, 1951 (div. Nov. 1978); children: Pamela, Joe Jr., Robin Michelle. Student, Ft. Scott Jr. Coll., Paola, Kans., 1979-81. Reporter LaCygne Jour., 1943-45; union recorder I.L.G.W.U., Paola, 1956-57; mgr. Estes Metalcraft, Osawatomie, Kans., 1977-82; owner El Rey Tavern, Osawatomie, 1980-89. Home: 516 Walnut Osawatomie KS 66064

JINKS, SHARON JEAN, electronics executive, consultant; b. Bklyn., Nov. 1, 1947; d. Robert James and Mary Elizabeth (Beckler) Nelson; m. Daryl Allen Jinks, May 18, 1969; children: Robert Nelson, Heidi Jean. AAS in Early Childhood, Jr. Coll. of Albany, N.Y., 1967. Tchr. Gloversville (N.Y.) Day Nursery, 1965-67; with Jones and Naudin Leather, Gloversville, 1976-87; v.p. D.A.J. Electronics, Gloversville, 1984—; resource specialist Schenectady (N.Y.) Community Action, 1988—; v.p. Kingsborough Sch. of N.Y., Gloversville, 1976-78, pres., 1979-81; supt. St. James Luth. Ch. Sch., Gloversville, 1980-87, choir dir., 1978-85. Leader Girl Scouts Fulton County, Gloversville, 1980-84, Boy Scouts Am., Gloversville, 1978-84; chairperson Christian Edn. of St. James Luth. Ch., Gloversville, 1982-87, advisor youth group, 1984-87. Mem. Displaced Homemakers Club (sec. Johnstown, N.Y. chpt. 1989—). Republican. Lutheran. Home: 356 Bleecker St Gloversville NY 12078

JOACHIM, BRIGITTA GOLDEN, writer, advertising agency executive, media consultant; b. Berlin; d. Carl and Gisele (Zeisel) Golden; children: Nancy, Lynne Joachim-Flanders, James Golden. Student, Manhattan Sch. Mus., 1947-49; cert. TV workshop, Hofstra U., 1972, BA cum laude, 1973, MA with honors, 1976; postgrad., Columbia U., 1973-74. Cert. speech pathologist, N.Y. Election interviewer CBS News, N.Y.C., 1970; communications specialist South Nassau Communities Hosp., Nassau County, N.Y., 1970-74, Assn. for Help Retarded Children, Brookville, N.Y., 1970-74, Beth Israel Hosp., N.Y.C., 1970-74; talent and rsch. coord. Am. Alive NBC-TV, N.Y.C., 1978-79; creative dir./writer Jim Sant Andrea Shows Producers, N.Y.C., 1979-82; pres., creative dir. Media for 80's, N.Y.C., 1982—; nursery sch. tchr. Hendrix St. Day Nursery, 1950-52; prof. media and communications Touro Coll., N.Y.C., 1987—; media cons. Researcher Investigative News Group, N.Y.C., 1987—; judge radio and TV Internat. Clio awards, 1981—; media writer Writers Conf. to China, 1984; finalists judge Am. Film Festival, 1986-87; judge Internat. Film and Video Awards, 1987—; mem. blue ribbon panel Emmy awards, 1987—. Editor ednl. film Mother and Child, 1976; scriptwriter The Chase is On, A Breed Apart, Women of Louisiana, Model of Tommorrow, Sexually Speaking, Stress, 1981-88, The New You (Physicians Med. Pub.) 1988. Past pres. Westbury PTA, Old Westbury, N.Y.; active Lincoln Ctr. Theatre, Mus. Modern Art; host, sponsor fgn. students AFS; dir. Children's Video Project, 1990-91. Mem. Nat. Acad. TV Arts and Scis. (forum producer N.Y. chpt. 1978, mem. nominating com. bd. govs.), N.Y. Alumni Assn. (mem. Hofstra U. exec. bd.), N.Y. Women in Film, Cinema Club, Sigma Pi. Jewish. Office: Media for 80's 60 W 66th St Ste 20E New York NY 10023

JOB, ANNE MARIE, newspaper business editor, writer; b. Jackson, Mich., Mar. 7, 1956; d. Louis J. and Lottie (Safidlo) J. BS, Mich. State U., 1978; postgrad., U. Va. Automotive writer AP, Detroit; automotive editor Detroit Free Press; exec. bus. editor Detroit News. Recipient Batten fellowship, Davenport fellowship. Mem. NAFE, Women's Econ. Club, Soc. of Am. Bus. Editors and Writers, Darden Sch. of Bus. Forum (pres.). Office: 9373 W Sample Rd Coral Springs FL 33065

JOBE, ALICE, transportation executive; b. Little Rock, Nov. 24, 1935; student Long Beach City Coll., 1960-61; m. K.L. Jobe, Mar. 12, 1957; 1 dau., Cathy. With Nat. Equity Life Ins. Co., Little Rock, 1954-55, Cash Wholesale Co., Little Rock, 1956-57; with Bekins Internat., subs. Bekins Co., Wilmington, Calif., 1959-77, v.p., 1971-77; v.p. Imperial Internat., Inc., Torrance, Calif., 1977-78, exec. v.p., 1978-80, dir., 1977-81; pres. Imperial Van Lines Internat., Inc., 1980-81; industry cons., 1981-82; founder, pres. Caddo Internat., freight forwarding, Los Alamitos, Calif., 1982—. Mem. Household Goods Forwarders Assn. (exec. com. 1977-78), Nat. Def. Transp. Assn. (life), Am. Soc. Profl. Women. Republican. Office: Caddo Internat 3662 Katella Ave Ste 209 PO Box 739 Los Alamitos CA 90720

JOBE, SHIRLEY A., librarian; b. San Bernadino, Calif., Oct. 10, 1946; d. Fines and Luejeannia (Armstrong) J.; m. Lonnie Parker, March 1969; (div.) 1974; 1 child, Robyn Nicole. BA, E. Tex. State U., Commerce, 1968; MSLS, Simmons Coll., Boston, 1971. Cataloger Fla. Meml. Coll., 1968-70; head librarian John F. Kennedy Library, Boston, 1971-84, Boston Globe, 1984. Author catalogs, bibliographies, book reviews. Recipient Boston Black Achievers award 1987; EDPA fellow U.S. Dept. Edn., Boston, 1970. Mem. Mass. Black Librarians Network Boston, Spl. Librarians Assn. Wash. Home: 54 Mt. Pleasant Cambridge MA 02140

JOBSON, MAREDA BELL, semiconductor company executive; b. Wilkes Barre, Pa., May 17, 1946; d. William Andrew and Kathleen Mary (Kinsey) Bell; m. Charles Thompson Jobson, Aug. 14, 1970; children: Paul Thompson, Adam Robert. BA, Fontbonne Coll., 1968. Actuarial asst. Travelers Ins. Co., Hartford, Conn., 1968-69, Gen. Am. Life Ins. Co., St. Louis, 1969-73; programmer/analyst Allied Supermarkets, Oklahoma City, 1973-78; programmer McGraw-Hill, Hightstown, N.J., 1979-80; data analyst McGraw-Hill, Hightstown, 1980-81; data specialist NSA/ARMS, Cherry Hill, N.J., 1981-82; adminstr. data base RCA Solid State, Somerville, N.J., 1982-84; mgr. data base adminstrn. Gen. Electric Solid State, Somerville, 1984-89; cons. Fairfax, Va., 1989—. Bd. dirs. Pickwick Pebble Hill Sch., Doylestown, Pa., 1983-84, sec.-treas., 1984-85. Mem. Delaware Valley Cullinet Software Users Group (pres. 1984-88), Integrated Database Mgmt. Systems Users Assn. (bd. dirs. 1985-88, sec.-treas. 1986-88). Home: 9810 Perrott Ct Fairfax VA 22031

JOERGER, ERICA ANN, account executive; b. Houston, Jan. 22, 1965; d. Arthur Peter and Susan Helen (Patton) J. BBA, U. Tex., 1987. Sales rep. Pillsbury Co., Austin, Tex., 1988-89; account exec. Pillsbury Co., Tyler, Tex., 1989—. Mem. NAFE, NOW. Democrat. Roman Catholic. Home: 5100 Sweetbriar Ln #536 Tyler TX 75703 Office: Pillsbury Co Inc 4965 Preston Park Blvd #190 Plano TX 75093

JOFFE, WENDY A., psychologist; b. Medville, Pa., Sept. 4, 1947; d. Jerome S. and Shirley (Newman) Siebert; m. Seymour Joffe, Oct. 17, 1971 (dec. Feb. 1973); 1 stepchild, David Joffe; m. James Michael Fendelman, Mar. 1, 1981; children: Joel, Andrew, Max. MA in Spl. Edn., Boston U., 1970; BA in Psychology, Case Western Res. U., 1982; PhD in Psychology, U. Miami, Fla., 1979. Vocat. counselor James E. Scott Family Health Ctr., Miami, 1970-71, mental health coord., 1971-72, trainer, clinician, 1972-75; asst. prof. psychology St. Thomas U., Miami, 1975-80; clin. dir. Family Life Ctr. of Fla., Miami, 1977—; adj. prof. psychology U. Miami, 1976-85; tng. cons. Health & Rehabilitative Svcs., Miami, 1974-75, 81, State of Fla., Miami, 1979-80, Fla. Dept. Youth & Family Devel., Miami, 1979-82. Author: Stages of Recovery, 1990. Named one of Outstanding Therapists, Town & Country mag., 1988. Mem. Am. Assn. Marriage and Family Therapists (supr.), Am. Family Therapy Assn. (clin.), Am. Psychol. Assn. (clin.), Dade County Psychol. Assn. (clin.), NOW. Democrat. Jewish. Office: Family Life Ctr of Fla 1550 Madruga Ave #516 Miami FL 33146

JOHANKNECHT, LORI JO, infosystems specialist; b. Pk. Ridge, Ill., Sept. 14, 1961; d. Arland Kent and Sonja Lou (Gross) J. BS in Bus., Valparaiso U., 1983; MBA, Lewis U., 1990. Computer systems user rep. Reynolds & Reynolds Co., Elk Grove Village, Ill., 1983-87; sr. systems acctg. coord. Waste Mgmt., Inc., Oak Brook, Ill., 1987—. Mem. Fin. Mgmt. Assn., Alpha Xi (bd. reps. 1984-86, sec. 1987-89). Democrat. Mem. Christ Ch. Office: Waste Mgmt Inc 3003 Butterfield Rd Oak Brook IL 60148

JOHANNSSON, VICTORIA ANN, advertising professional; b. Fayetteville, N.C., July 28, 1964; d. Thorgrimar and Truus (Lauffer) J. BA in Communications, N.C. State U., 1987. Researcher 82d Airborne Mus., Ft. Bragg, N.C., 1984-85; prodn. asst. Ctr. for Pub. Broadcasting, Raleigh, N.C., 1985-87; media planner, traffic mgr. Rizzo Cohn & Ptnrs., Boston, 1987-90; media planner, buyer KK & M Advt., Boston, 1990—. Pub. rels. vol. Make a Wish Found., Boston, 1988. Mem. Ad Club Boston, N.C. State U. Alumni Assn. (co-chmn. New Eng. chpt. 1987—). Office: KK & M Advt 1616 Soldiers Field Rd Boston MA 02135

JOHANSEN, KATHLEEN MARIE, public relations executive; b. Albany, N.Y., Sept. 26, 1961; d. John Christian and Barbara (Busse) J. BA, St. Mary's Notre Dame (Ind.), 1984; postgrad., Columbia U., 1984. Rsch. assoc. Conn. Rsch. Assocs., Greenwich, 1985; sales dir. Book of Books, Stamford, Conn., 1986; grants technician Grants Office - City of Stamford, 1987; asst. dir. devel. The Floating Hosp., Inc., N.Y.C., 1988; dir. pub. rels. William Pitt Real Estate Corp., Stamford, 1989-90; publicity cons. pub. rels., spl. events New Canaan, Conn., 1990—. Co-author: Another Look at the Rainbow, 1984, Care-Giving in the Community Hospital, 1985. Coord. vols. Christopher Shays for Congress, Fairfield County, Conn., 1987; campaign coord. Chris Burnham for State Rep., Stamford, 1987, 88; dir. Tony Fenton Bike Tour for Cystic Fibrosis, Fairfield County, 1989, 90; publicity chairperson New Canaan Tenn Ctr. Adult Bd., 1989, 90; flutist New Canaan Town Band, 1977-90. Recipient Recognition award Cystic Fibrosis Found., 1989. Mem. Women in Communications, Jr. League, Fairfield County Pub. Rels. Assn. Republican. Roman Catholic. Home: 23 Green Meadow Ln New Canaan CT 06840

JOHN, DOREEN ANN, psychologist; b. Wilkes-Barre, Pa., Aug. 29, 1949; d. Gerard John and Dora Margaret (Maffei) Serafini; m. Anthony Paul John, Sept. 1, 1975. BA in Psychology, Wilkes Coll., 1972; MA in Psychology, Marywood Coll., 1979. Lic. clin. psychologist, Pa.; cert. reahab. counselor, nat. counselor. Caseworker Project Outreach, Nanticoke, Pa., 1972-75; project coor. Hazleton/Nanticoke Mental Health, 1975-79; adolescent family therapist Children and Youth Svcs., Luzerne County, Pa., 1979-80; rehab. specialist Internat. Rehab. Svcs., Kingston, Pa., 1980-84; psychologist John Heinz Inst. for Rehab. Medicine, Wilkes-Barre, 1984-88; psychologist behavioral medicine dept. Mercy Hosp., Scranton, Pa., 1988—. Mem. Little Theater of Wilkes-Barre, 1980—, Bob Niznik Dance Co., Kingston, 1981—; vol. Valley Santa, Wilkes-Barre, 1984—. Mem. Am. Psychol. Assn., Am. Assn. Counseling and Devel. Home: 98 E Vaughn St Kingston PA 18704

JOHN, YVONNE MAREE, interior designer; b. Leeton, New South Wales, Australia, Sept. 8, 1944; came to U.S., 1966; d. Percy Edward and Gladys May (Markham) Thomas; m. Michael Peter John, Aug. 20, 1966; children: Michael Christian, Stephen Edwin Dennis. Student, Buenaventura Coll., 1969, U. Calif., Santa Barbara, 1975; cert., United Design Guild, 1975; AA, Interior Design Guild, 1976; Diploma, Internat. Correspondence Sch., 1976. Designer Percy Thomas Real Estate, Leeton, 1960-66; cosmetologist, artist Bernard's Hair Stylists, Ventura, Calif., 1966-67, 74-73; cosmetologist Banks Beauty Salon, Chgo., 1968-69; owner, mgr. Yvonne Maree Designs, Ventura and Olympia, Wash., 1978—; owner, cosmetologist Mayfair Salon, Leeton, 1962-66; owner, mgr. Y.M. Boutique, Griffith, Australia, 1965-66. Contbr. numerous short stories and poems to newspapers; artist numerous pen and ink drawings; one man show Royal Mus. Sydney, Australia, 1954. Artist Ventura County Gen. Hosp., 1970's. Recipient Cash and Cert. awards Sydney Newspapers, 1950's, Ribbon awards Sydney County Fairs, 1950's. Mem. Am. Platform Assn. Office: Yvonne Maree Designs PO Box 2143 Olympia WA 98507

JOHNIGAN, SANDRA KAY, bank executive; b. Estherville, Iowa, Sept. 11, 1947; d. Glenn and Betty Jean (Williams) Thomas; m. William D. Johnigan (div. Aug. 1981); m. Donald C. Ellwood. BSBA in Acctg., U. Tulsa, 1969. CPA, N.Y., Tex., Okla. Mgr. Arthur Young, Okla., 1974-78; prin. Arthur Young, Dallas, 1978-81, ptnr., nat. dir. real estate and savs. and loans, 1981-88; pres. Coast-to-Coast Fin. Corp., N.Y.C., 1988—, also bd. dirs.; pres. Superior Fed. Savs. Bank, Hinsdale, Ill., 1988—, also bd. dirs.; mem. adv. coun. Fed. Home Loan Bank. Contbr. articles to profl. jours. Vol., cons. Arts and Bus. Coun.; contbr. acquisitions Met. Mus. Art; vol. City Meals on Wheels; contbr. Cen. Park Conservancy. Mem. AICPA (chair), N.Y. State Soc. CPAs, Conf. de la Chaine des Rotisseurs. Office: Superior Fed Savs Bank 911 N Elm St Hinsdale IL 60521

JOHNS, AVIS SHETTER, computer professional; b. Mt. Joy, Pa., Feb. 6, 1935; d. Park S. and Mildred C. (Auker) Shetter; m. William W. Johns, Mar. 28, 1953; children: Michael Lee, Sandra Kay Johns Wolfe. Student, Millersville (Pa.) State Coll., 1967-68; AA, Cochise Coll., Sierra Vista, Ariz., 1975; MA, U. No. Colo., 1981. Acctg. technician Donegal Sch. Dist., Mt. Joy, 1964-67; sec. to prin. Donegal High Sch., Mt. Joy, 1967-70; clk.-typist U.S. Army Intelligence Ctr. and Sch., Ft. Huachuca, Ariz., 1972-73; clk. stenographer U.S. Army Communications System Agy., Ft. Huachuca, Ariz., 1973-75; sec., stenographer U.S. Army Communications Command, Ft. Huachuca, Ariz., 1975-79; computer systems programmer Joint Test Element, TRI-TAC, Ft. Huachuca, Ariz., 1979-83; computer specialist U.S. Army Communications Command, Ft. Huachuca, Ariz., 1983-87; infosystems mgmt. specialist U.S. Army Info. Systems Command, Ft. Huachuca, Ariz., 1987-89, inspection program analyst, asst. inspector gen., 1989—; sec. Fed. Women's Program, Ft. Huachuca, 1976-77; treas., Federally Employed Women, Ft. Huachuca, 1976-78. Mem., sec. Sierra Vista Commn. on Human Rels., 1985-86; dep. registrar for voters Cochise County, Sierra Vista, 1986-88; tutor Huachuca Area Alliance for Literacy; active Sierra Vista United Meth. Ch. Mem. AAUW (v.p.), Am. Bus. Women's Assn. (publicity chair 1988-89; Ariz. Winning Women in Govt. award 1987, Woman of Yr. 1990), Huachuca Art Assn. (treas. 1983-85), Internat. Tng. in Communications (past officer, coun. pres. 1989-90), Armed Forces Communications-Electronics Assn. (membership v.p. 1988—). Republican. Home: 4920 Laguna Ave Sierra Vista AZ 85635 Office: US Army InfoSystems Command ATTN ASIG-P Fort Huachuca AZ 85613-5000

JOHNS, BEVERLEY ANNE HOLDEN, special education administrator; b. New Albany, Ind., Nov. 6, 1946; d. James Edward and Martha Edna (Scharf) Holden; m. Lonnie J. Johns, July 28, 1973. BS, Catherine Spalding Coll., Ky., 1968; MS, So. Ill. U., 1970; postgrad., Western Ill. U., 1973-74, 79-80, 82, U. Ill., 1984-85. Cert. adminstr., tchr. Ill. Demonstration tchr. So. Ill. U., Carbondale, 1970-72; instr. MacMurray Coll., Jacksonville, Ill., 1977-79; intern Ill. State Bd. Edn., Springfield, 1981; program supr. Four Rivers Spl. Edn. Dist., Jacksonville, Ill., 1972—; chmn. Ill. Edn. of the Handicapped Coalition, 1982-89; conf. coord. Ill. Alliance, Champaign, 1982—; bd. dirs. Jacksonville Area Assn. Retarded Citizens; lectr. to profl. confs.; cons. in field. Author: Report on Behavior Analysis in Edn., 1972; editor: Position Papers of Ill. Council for Exceptional Children, 1981; contbr. articles to profl. jours. Govt. rels. chmn. Internat. Council Exceptional Children, 1984-87; fed. liason Ill. Adminstrs. Spl. Edn., 1985-86. So. Ill. U. fellow, 1968; resolution honoring Beverly H. Johns 60th Ann. Internat. Council for Exceptional Children Conv., 1982; cert. of recognition Ill. Atty. Gen., 1985. Recipient Lifetime Achievement award Ill. Coun. for Exceptional Children, 1989; named Jacksonville Woman of the Yr. Bus. and Profl. Women, 1988. Mem. Assn. Retarded Citizens (com. 1982—), Assn. Supervision and Curriculum Devel., Ill. Council for Children With Behavioral Disorders (founder, past pres., presdl. award 1985, meritorious mem. award), Ill. Alliance for Exceptional Children (v.p 1982—), Ill. Council Exceptional Children (past pres., chmn. govt. relations com. 1982—, governing bd. 1984—, Presdl. award 1983), West Cen. Assn. for Citizens with Learning Disabilities (founder, com. chair 197—), Delta Kappa Gamma (chpt. pres. 1988-90). Roman Catholic. Avocation: world travel. Home: PO Box 340 Jacksonville IL 62651 Office: Four Rivers Spl Edn Dist 936 W Michigan Jacksonville IL 62650

JOHNS, CAROL JOHNSON, physician, educator; b. Balt., June 18, 1923; d. Ashmore Clark and Elsie Greacen (Carstens) Johnson; BA, Wellesley Coll., 1944; MD, Johns Hopkins U., 1950; DHL (hon.), Coll. Notre Dame of Md., 1981; m. Richard James Johns, June 27, 1953; children: James Ashmore, Richard Clark, Robert Shanard. Intern, Johns Hopkins Hosp., 1950-51, asst. resident in medicine, 1951-53, fellow, 1953-54, physician outpatient dept., 1953-64, dir. Sarcoid Clinic, 1962—, active staff, 1964—, dir. med. clinic, 1967-76, dir. hosp. quality assurance, 1974-79, mem. hosp. med. bd., 1971-79; asst. in medicine Johns Hopkins U., 1951-58, instr., 1958-67, asst. prof., 1967-71, assoc. prof., 1971—, adv. bd. Applied Physics Lab., 1974-78; acting pres. Wellesley Coll., 1979-81, asst. dean, dir. continuing edn., 1981—; chmn. bd. Balt. City PSRO, 1975-79; pres. Internat. Sarcoid Conf., 1984; mem. pulmonary allergy adv. com. FDA, 1973-75; faculty adv. editorial bd. Johns Hopkins U. Press, 1981-84. Contbr. articles to med. jours., chpts. in textbooks. Mem. vestry Ch. of Redeemer, 1967-70, sr. warden, 1976-79, layreader; bd. trustees Calvert Sch., 1968-72; bd. trustees Wellesley Coll., 1971-90, exec. com., 1971-80, 84-90, chmn. nat. devel. fund, 1975-80, trustee fin. com., 1979—, chmn. trustee faculty relations com., 1984-90; trustee St. Paul's Sch. for Girls, 1973-75; bd. dirs. Stetler Rsch. Fund for Women, 1971-79, 84—; mem. Armed Forces Epidemiol. Bd., 1985—; bd. regents Univ. Health Scis., 1985—. Named Med. Woman of Yr. Med. Coll. Pa., 1984. Mem. Am. Clin. Climatol. Assn. (v.p. 1987), Am. Thoracic Soc., Balt. City Med. Soc., Johns Hopkins Med. Surg. Assn. (sec.-treas. 1981-87, pres. 1987-89), Johns Hopkins Women's Med. Alumni Assn. (pres. 1957-59, dir.), Md. Med. Chirurg. Faculty (coun. 1978-79), Soc. Med. Coll. Dirs. Continuing Edn., Alliance for Continuing Med. Edn. (coun. 1987—), Phi Beta Kappa, Sigma Xi, Alpha Omega Alpha (bd. dirs. 1978-87, v.p. 1985-86, pres. 1986-87), Johns Hopkins Club, Wellesley Coll. Club, Mt. Vernon Club, Cosmos Club. Episcopalian. Home: 203 E Highfield Rd Baltimore MD 21218 Office: 17 Turner 720 Rutland Ave Baltimore MD 21205

JOHNS, DIANNA ROSE, fundraiser; b. Akron, Ohio, Oct. 1, 1951; d. William Louis and Jennie Rose (Palmeiri) J. BA in Econs., Ohio State U., 1977. Rsch. mgr. ophthalmology Ohio State U., Columbus, 1973-77; rsch. mgr. cardiology VA Hosps. U. Iowa, Iowa City, 1977-82; mgr. Makiannika, Atlanta, 1982-84; dir. spl. events Met. Atlanta March of Dimes, 1984-87; nat. dir. spl. events Nat. Offices Arthritis Found., Atlanta, 1987—; cons. on spl. events Atlanta C. of C., 1988—, cons. on galas and spl. events Nexus Contemporary Art Ctr., Atlanta, 1988—. Contbr. articles to profl. jours. Mem. exec. com. Bus. Vols. for Arts, Atlanta; bd. dirs. Nexus Contemporary Art Ctr., Atlanta, YWCA, Atlanta, 1983; chmn. planning com. Midtown YWCA, Atlanta, 1982-83. Mem. Nat. Soc. Fund Raising Execs., Bus. and Profl. Women's Club Atlanta (treas. 1982-83), Atlanta Women's C. of C. Democrat. Office: Athritis Found Nat Offices 1314 Spring St Atlanta GA 30309

JOHNS, ELIZABETH JANE HOBBS, educational administrator; b. Roanoke Rapids, N.C., July 18, 1941; d. Florence Eugene and Elizabeth Holt (Massey) Hobbs; m. Lewis Clarence Johns, Apr. 7, 1961; children: Karen Anne Johns Cuccaro. AA with honors, Valencia Community Coll., 1984; BSBA with honors, Fla. So. Coll., 1988; postgrad. in mgmt., Fla. Inst. Tech., 1989—. Med. receptionist Dr. Harold Knowles, Orlando, Fla., 1959-61; sec. Martin Marietta Aerospace%, Orlando, 1961-77; edn. adminstr. Martin Marietta Aerospace, Orlando, 1977—; chair bd. credit union Martin Marietta Orlando (Fla.) Aerospace, 1987—; bd. dirs. Martin Marietta Fed. Credit Union, 1978—. Mem. community adv. bd. sch. continuing edn. Hamilton Holt Sch., continuing edn. council for women Valencia Community Coll., 1984—. Named one of Outstanding Women in Bus., 1985, one of Top Ten Employees, Martin Marietta Aerospace, Orlando, 1983, one of Top 100, 1978. Mem. Am. Bus. Women's Assn., Valencia Community Coll. Alumni Assn. (bd. dirs. 1984—), Orlando C. of C. (post secondary edn. task force), Phi Theta Kappa. Republican. Methodist. Home: 3201 Holliday Ave Apopka FL 32703 Office: Martin Marietta Electronics & Missiles Group Orlando Ops Box 5837 MP 147 Orlando FL 32855

JOHNS, LEE RHEA, nurse; b. Birmingham, Ala., Aug. 7, 1956; d. Llewellyn William Jr. and Jane Elizabeth (Green) Johns. BS in Sociology, Jacksonville (Ala.) State U., 1978; BS in Nursing, U. Ala., Birmingham, 1983; grad., Sch. Aerospace Medicine, Brooks AFB, Tex., 1989. RN, Ala., S.C. Staff oncology nurse U. Ala. Med. Ctr., 1983-84; staff hospice nurse AMI Brookwood Med. Ctr., Birmingham, 1984-86; patient care coord. oncology unit Bapt. Med. Ctr. Montclair, Birmingham, 1986-87, staff nurse one day surgery dept., 1987-88; hospice nurse clinician Greenville (S.C.) Hosp. System, 1988—; flight nurse aeromed. evacuation USAFR, Charleston AFB, S.C., 1989—. With USNG, 1986-88; 1st lt. USAFR, 1988—. Mem. Oncology Nursing Soc. (v.p. Birmingham chpt. 1986-88), Nat. Hospice Orgn., Aerospace Med. Assn., Res. Officers Assn., Jacksonville State U. Alumni Assn. (pres. Jefferson/Shelby County chpt. 1988), Palmetto Ski and Outing Club, Greenville Singles Club (v.p. 1989-90). Republican. Roman Catholic. Office: Greenville Hosp System 701 Grove Rd Greenville SC 29605

JOHNS, MARGY GOVER, director extended programs, educator; b. Somerset, Ky., Sept. 7, 1931; d. Milton E. and Margaret Ellen (Beattie) Gover; m. Jerry Johns, Dec. 15, 1951; 1 child, Joni Lynn Johns Gibson. BS, Ea. Ky. U., 1955, MA, 1965. Tchr. Harlan County Sch. Bd., Somerset, 1955-59, Somerset Schs., 1959-65; with counseling and admissions dept. Somerset Community Coll., 1965-66, assoc. prof. polit. sci., community svcs. coord., 1979-84, chief educator, community svc. coord., 1979-84, dir., 1986—; bicentennial coord. State of Ky., Frankfort, 1975-76; mem. State of Ky. Gov.'s Com. on Literacy; planner Ky. energy conservation program Murray State U. Sec., v.p. Ky. Dem. Women., 1972-82, 5th dist. dir., 1978-80; del. Nat. Dem. Conv., 1976, 80; vice chmn. County Dem. Exec. Com., Somerset, 1980-83. mem. Somerset and Pulaski C. of C. (chmn. cert. cities 1988). Home: 409 Clements Somerset KY 42501 Office: Somerset Community Coll 808 Monticello Rd Somerset KY 42501

JOHNS, TRACI LORRAINE, administrative assistant, writer; b. Whittier, Calif., Dec. 26, 1964; d. Ray Linn and Eleanor Lorraine (Guidas) J. BA in Journalism, Duquesne U., 1986. Freelance writer Pitts. Post Gazette, 1985-86; intern-dir. Pitts. Cable TV, 1986-87; corr. Union Leader Corp., Manchester, N.H., 1987-89; adminstrv. asst. Corp. Exec. Svcs., Londonderry, N.H., 1989—; freelance writer Pitts. Bus. Times-Jour., 1983-86; writer fed. courthouse AP, Pitts., 1984-87; dir. pub. rels. advt. Pitts. Cable TV, 1986; contbg. writer for Comics Scene and Starlog Mags. Dir. community TV show Tea and Testimony, 1987; plays include The Collector, 1986; video grapher: Special Agent: Hudson Marr. Mem. Soc. Profl. Journalists (student sec. 1985), Women in Communications (profl. chpt. treas. 1990-91), Red Masquers. Home: 590 Beech St Apt 4 Manchester NH 03104 Office: Corp Exec Svcs 75 Gilcreast Rd Londonderry NH 03053

JOHNSEN, DEBRA LEE, teacher; b. Harlan, Iowa, Feb. 12, 1257; d. Robert Dean Heistand and Kathryn (Adamson) Walpus; m. Gale Lynn, Aug. 12, 1978; children: Jason, Sara, Brandon. Postgrad., Iowa State U., 1979; student, Buena Vista Coll. Cert. teacher. Bus. tchr. Dunlap Community Sch., Iowa; asst. head bookkeeper 1st Nat. Bank, Woodbine, Iowa, 1981-83; summer youth coordinator JTPA, Shelby County. Chairperson Phase III Steering Com., Dunlap, 1987—, Dunlap Tchrs. Orgn., 1987—; pres. United Meth. Women's Circle, Woodbine, 1988. Mem. Iowa Bus. Edn. Assn., Nat. Bus. Edn. Assn. Democrat. Office: Dunlap Community Sch 1102 Iowa Ave Dunlap IA 51529

JOHNSON, ADDIE COLLINS, educator, former dietitian; b. Evansville, Ind., Feb. 28; d. Stewart and Willa (Shamell) Collins; m. John Q. Johnson, Sept. 6, 1958; 1 child, Parker. BS, Howard U., 1956; MEd, Framingham State Coll., Mass., 1967. Registered dietitian, Mass. Dietitian Boston Lying-In Hosp., 1957-61; dietitian Diet Heart Study, Harvard U. Sch. Pub. Health, Boston, 1962-63; tchr. Foxboro (Mass.) Pub. Sch., 1967—; dietitian Sch. Medicine Boston U., 1975-77, Westinghouse Health Systems, Boston; faculty Dept. Nursing Boston State Coll., 1979-82; nutrition cons. Head Start program Westinghouse Sch., Boston, 1979-82; instr. Dept. Nursing U. Mass., 1981—, Bridgewater State Coll., Mass., 1982—; mem. state adv. council Dept. Edn. Bur. Nutrition Edn., 1981-83. Bd. dirs. Norfolk-Bristol County Home Health Assn., Walpole, Mass., 1975-78; presenter Nat. Social Studies Assn., Boston, 1984-85; instr./trainer health services edn. ARC, 1987—. Mem. AAUW, Am. Dietetic Assn., Am. Home Econs. Assn., Eastern Mass. Home Econs. Assn. (dir. 1978), Mass. Tchrs. Assn. (higher edn. com. 1984-87), Soc. Nutrition Edn., NAACP (life), Delta Kappa Gamma (journalist Iota chpt. 1986—), Delta Sigma Theta. Home: 92 Morse St Sharon MA 02067 Office: Foxboro Mechanic St Foxboro MA 02035

JOHNSON, AMY LEIGH, pediatrician; b. Chippewa Falls, Wis., July 2, 1955; d. Elmer Eugene Jr. and Caroline Jesse (Lanzer) Nelson; m. David Michael Johnson, June 12, 1982; children: Owen David, Melodie Rachel. BS in Med. Tech., U. Wis., Oshkosh, 1977; MD, Med. Coll. Wis., 1982. Diplomate Am. Bd. Pediatrics. Intern and resident in pediatrics U. Tenn., Memphis, 1982-85; staff physician Children's Hosp. Wis., Milw., 1985-88; pvt. practice Monroe, Wis., 1988—. Fellow Am. Acad. Pediatrics (jr.); mem. Order Eastern Star. Office: Monroe Clinic 1515 10th St Monroe WI 53566

JOHNSON, ANITA LOCY, marketing executive; b. Cleve., Sept. 25, 1955; d. John Judd and Ann Elizabeth (Hefner) Locy; m. Brian Kelly Johnson, Jan. 5, 1985. Student, MIT, 1977-78, Institut D'Etudes Politiques, Paris, 1975-76; BA, Rice U., 1977; MBA, U. Tex., 1984. Economist Tex. Dept. Water Resources, Austin, 1979-80; product mgr. Intel Corp., Austin, 1982-84; product mgr. Intel Corp., Portland, Oreg., 1984-85, mktg. mgr., 1985-88; corp. devel. mgr. Intel Corp., Houston, 1988—. Jack G. Taylor Presdl. scholar, 1981, NSF scholar, 1977, Schlumberger scholar, 1975. Mem. Phi Beta Kappa. Office: Intel 7322 Southwest Frwy Houston TX 77074

JOHNSON, ANNE BRADSTREET, research physician, educator; b. Boston, Mar. 5, 1927; d. Stafford F. Johnson and Catherine (Tyler) Stadie; m. Jack Minkoff, June 19, 1948; children: Ellen Louise, Paul Andrew. BA, Cornell U., 1948, MD, 1951. Diplomate Am. Bd. Internal Medicine, Am. Bd. Anat. Pathology and Neuropathology. Pvt. practice internal medicine Cleve., 1955-57; from instr. to asssoc. prof. Albert Einstein Coll. Medicine, Bronx, N.Y., 1962—, now assoc. prof. depts. pathology and neurosci. Contbr. articles to profl. jours. Grantee NIH, Nat. Multiple Sclerosis Soc., United Leukogystrophy Found. Mem. AAAS, Am. Assn. Neuropathologists, Histochem. Soc., Am. Soc. Cell Biology, Internat. Acad. Pathology, Soc. for Neurosci., N.Y. Acad. Scis. Office: Albert Einstein Coll Med Dept Pathology K 604 1300 Morris Park Ave Bronx NY 10461

JOHNSON, ANNE MARCOVECCHIO, book publishing executive; b. Staten Island, N.Y., May 22, 1931; d. Martin and Wilhelmina (Baldaccheri) MarcoV.; m. Hugh Johnson, Sept. 25, 1965 (dec. Feb. 1987). BA, Hunter Coll., 1953. Exec. sec. Doubleday & Co., Inc., N.Y.C., 1953-57; exec. sec. Random House, Inc., N.Y.C., 1957-67, asst. to pres., 1967-69, div. v.p., 1969-89, also bd. dirs. Bd. dirs. Fund for Free Expression, N.Y.C., 1975, Helsinki Watch, N.Y.C., 1979, Ams. Watch, N.Y.C., 1981. Mem. Assn. Am. Pubs. Internat. Freedom to Publish, Essex County Country Club (West Orange, N.J.). Home: 140 Hepburn Rd Clifton NJ 07012

JOHNSON, BADRI NAHVI, sociology educator, real estate business owner; b. Tehran, Iran, Dec. 1, 1934; came to U.S., 1957; d. Ali Akbar and Monir (Khazraii) Nahvi; m. Floyd Milton Johnson, July 2, 1960; children: Robert, Rebecca, Nancy, Shahla. BS, U. Minn., 1967, MA, 1969. Stenographer Curtis 1000, Inc., St. Paul, 1958-62; lab. instr. U. Minn., Mpls., 1966-69, teaching asst., 1969-72; chief exec. officer Real Estate Investment and Mgmt. Enterprise, St. Paul, 1969—; instr. sociology Anoka-Ramsey Community Coll., Coon Rapids, Minn., 1973—; commentator, bd. dirs., sponsor pub. radio KFAI, Mpls., 1989—; producer, commentator, sponsor Iranian program pub. TV, Mpls., 1990—. Interpreter Immigration and Naturalization Svcs., St. Paul, 1970—; organizer Iranian earthquake disaster relief, 1990. Recipient earthquake relief orgn. citation Iranian Royal Household, 1968. Mem. NEA, Minn. Edn. Assn., Sociologists of Minn., U. Minn. Alumni Assn. Home: 1276 E Iowa Ave Saint Paul MN 55106 Office: Anoka-Ramsey Community Coll 11200 Mississippi Blvd NW Coon Rapids MN 55433

JOHNSON, BARBARA CONVERSE, infosystems specialist, freelance writer; b. Bronxville, N.Y., July 6, 1955; d. Stephen Hardy and Mary L. (Booth) J. BA in Hispanic Studies, Cornell U., 1977; MBA, U. Chgo., 1981. Lic. massage therapist, N.Y. Coordinator outreach program Westchester Hispanic Coalition, White Plains, N.Y., 1977-78; purchasing agt. J.S. Svc. Ctr. Corp., Mamaroneck, N.Y., 1978-79; coordinator internat. program UNICEF/1st Earth Run, N.Y.C., 1986; asst. controller Chem. Bank, N.Y.C., 1981-84, info. systems cons., 1984-86, mgr. human resource info. systems, 1987-88, systems devel. cons., 1988—. Vol. tutor The Internat. Ctr., N.Y.C., 1984-85. Mem. Boston Computer Soc., Am. Massage Therapy Assn., Manhattan Yacht Club, Skating Club of N.Y. Presbyterian. Home: 45 Walker Ave Rye NY 10580

JOHNSON, BARBARA JANE, sales representative; b. Chgo., Aug. 19, 1946; d. Sidney and Norma Mona Shaffer; B.A. in Sociology and Psychology, U. Ill., 1968; postgrad. M.B.A. program, Roosevelt U., 1971-72; m. Gary Johnson, Aug. 25, 1968; 1 child, Eric Michael. Asst. personnel dir. Associated Mills, Chgo., 1967-69, Scholl Mfg. Co. Inc., Chgo., 1969-71; nurse recruiter Cook County Hosp. Governing Com., Chgo., 1971-73; recruiter Mt. Sinai Hosp., Chgo., 1973-76; sales rep. Stryker Corp., Kalamazoo, 1976-81, area trainer; sales rep. Physio Control, Schaumberg, Ill., 1981-88, regional sales dir. Hosp. Satellite Network, L.A., 1988-89, midwest regional sales dir., 1989—; with Sensormedics Corp., Anaheim, Calif.; founder Chgo. Area Nurse Recruiters; cons. positions as nurse recruiter. Vice pres. Budlong Community Action Group, 1979—; advisor Jr. Achievement, 1969-72; auction com. Ednl. TV; trustee Mt. Sinai/Schwab Rehab. Ctr., 1983—. Recipient Lee Stryker sales award, 1979. Mem. Assn. of Operating Room Nurses (sponsor). Recipient first place Recruitment Brochure for Chgo. Area Bus. Communicators, 1975; salesman of year, 1979; first woman to achieve nat. award, 1979.

JOHNSON, BARBARA JEAN, business owner; b. Bay City, Mich., Apr. 18, 1952; d. John Joseph and Irene Mildred (Heller) Galbraith; m. Robert Joseph Johnson, Sept. 2, 1972; children: Keith, Tamara, Jeffrey. Student, Delta Coll., 1970-71, Lake Superior State Coll., 1971; cert. mcpl. treas., Mich. State U., 1986. Treas. Pinconning (Mich.) Twp., 1978-89; sec. Bay County (Mich.) 911 Bd. Dirs., 1984-88; trustee No. Bay Ambulance Bd., Pinconning, 1986-88, Bay County Twp. Officers Assn., 1978-89; owner B&K Appraisal, Pinconning, 1988—; treas. No. Bay Ambulance, Pinconning, 1988. Mem. League Dem. Women, Bay County, 1986—, Mich. Dem. Cen. Com., Bay County, 1984—, St. Michael's Home & Sch. Orgn., Pinconning, 1981—, treas., 1985-89. Mem. Mich. Mcpl. Treas. Assn., Mcpl. Treas. Asn. U.S. and Can. (cert.), Mich. Mcpl. Fin. Officers Assn., Mich. Assessors Assn. Roman Catholic. Home: 5135 N Mackinaw Rd Pinconning MI 48650 Office: B&K Appraisal 5315 N Mackinaw Rd Pinconning MI 48650

JOHNSON, BARBARA SUE, nurse; b. Dallas, Feb. 4, 1952; d. DeVon N. and Mary Jo (McHam) Bills; m. Thomas Allen Johnson, Feb. 14, 1986; 1 child, Samantha Nicole. Grad., All Saints Hosp. Sch. Nursing, Ft. Worth, 1984; nurse degree, Collin County Coll., Plano, Tex., 1989. Lic. vocat. nurse, R.N., Tex. Nurse mgr. Dallas County Health Dept., Dallas, 1984-88, Oak Lawn Community Svcs., Dallas, 1988-89; utilization rev. nurse Prudential Healthcare Systems North Tex., Dallas, 1989—. Vol. Am. Cancer Soc., 1988; instr. ARC. Recipient Golden Rule award J.C. Penney Co., Dallas, 1988. Mem. Assn. Nurses in AIDS Care, Lic. Vocat. Nurses Assn. Tex. Baptist. Home: 3104 Comanche Trail Plano TX 75074-2719 Office: Prudential Healtcare System 6060 N Central Expwy 750 Dallas TX 75206

JOHNSON, BEATRICE BROOKSHIRE, nurse; b. Meridian, Miss., Apr. 30, 1957; d. Warren Lee and Cora Mae (Roberts) Brookshire; m. Andrew Lee Johnson, Jan. 4, 1980; children: Reuben, Amber. Assoc. Gen. Edn., Meridian Jr. Coll., Miss., 1980; Assoc. Nursing, Meridian Jr. Coll., 1981; B. Nursing, U. So. Miss., 1988. RN, Miss. Grad. nurse F.G. Riley Meml. Hosp., Meridian, Miss., 1981; staff nurse Forrest Gen. Hosp., Hattiesburg, Miss., 1981-82; charge nurse Forrest Gen. Hosp., 1982-85; pub. health nurse Miss. State Dept. Health, Hattiesburg, 1985-88; supervising nurse Miss. State Dept. Health, 1988—. Bd. Trustees Instn. Higher Learning scholar, 1987-88. Mem. State Employees Assn. Miss. (sec. 1989—), Gamma Beta Phi. Methodist. Home: 905 N 30th Ave Hattiesburg MS 39401 Office: Miss State Dept Health 2801 Hwy 11 Bypass Hattiesburg MS 39401

JOHNSON, BETH EXUM, lawyer; b. Beaumont, Tex., July 4, 1952; d. James Powers Jr. and Betty Jean (Clement) Exum.; m. Walter William Johnson, Apr. 25, 1981. BA in Psychology, Tulane U., 1974; JD, Loyola U., New Orleans, 1985; LLM in Energy and Environ., Tulane U., 1989. Bar: La. 1985, U.S. Dist. Ct. (ea. dist.) La. 1985, U.S. Dist. Ct. (we. and mid. dists.) 1989. Paralegal McCloskey, Dennery, Page & Hennesy, New Orleans, 1975-80; oil and gas abstractor of title Frawley, Wogan, Miller & Co., New Orleans, 1980-82; lawyer, trust officer Hibernia Nat. Bank, New Orleans, 1985—; mem. faculty La. succession practice Tulane Univ., New Orleans, 1990—; faculty La. succession practice Tulane U., New Orleans, 1990—. Mem. New Orleans Estate Planning Coun. Mem. ABA, La. Bar Assn., New Orleans Bar Assn., Fed. Bar Assn. , Am. Assn. Petroleum Landmen, Petroleum Landmen's Assn. New Orleans, Friends of City Pk., City Club, Premier Athletic Club, Phi Alpha Delta, Kappa Alpha Theta. Home: 959 Harrison Ave New Orleans LA 70124 Office: Hibernia Nat Bank 313 Carondelet St Rm 301 New Orleans LA 70130

JOHNSON, BETSEY LEE, fashion designer; b. Hartford, Conn., Aug. 10, 1942; d. John Herman and Lena Virginia J.; m. John Cale, Apr. 4, 1966; 1 dau., Lulu; m. Jeffrey Olivier, Feb. 7, 1981. Student, Pratt Inst., N.Y.C., 1960-61; B.A., U. Syracuse, 1964. Editorial asst. Mademoiselle mag., 1964-65; ptnr., co-owner Betsey, Bunky & Nini, N.Y.C., from 1969; owner retail stores N.Y.C, L.A., San Francisco, Coconut Grove, Fla., Venice, Calif., Boston, Chgo. Prin. designer: Paraphernalia (owned by Puritan Fashions, Inc.), 1965-69; designer, Alvin Duskin Co., San Francisco, 1970; head designer: Alley Cat by Betsey Johnson, div. LeDamor, Inc., 1970-74; free-lance designer for, Jr. Womens div. Butterick Pattern Co., 1971, Betsey Johnson's Kids Children Wear for new div, Shutterbug, Inc., 1974-77, Betsey Johnson for, Jeanette Maternities, Inc., 1974-75; designer first line womens clothing for, Gant Shirtmakers, Inc., 1974-75; Tric-Trac by Betsey Johnson, Womens Knitwear, 1974-76; children's wear for Butterick's Home Sewing catalog, from 1975; head designer jr. sportswear co.: childrens wear for Star Ferry by Betsey Johnson and Michael Milea, 1975-77; owner, head designer, B.J., Inc., designer wholesale co., N.Y.C., 1978, pres., treas., B.J. Vines, N.Y.C., owner, Betsey Johnson store, N.Y.C., from 1979 (Recipient Mademoiselle mag. Merit award 1970, Coty award 1971, 2 Tommy Print awards 1971); owner 3 retail stores in N.Y.C., 2 in Los Angeles, 1 San Francisco, 1 in Miami. Mem. Coun. Fashion Designers Am., Women's Forum. Office: Betsey Johnson Co 209 W 38th St New York NY 10018 also: 110 E 9th St Ste A889 Los Angeles CA 90079

JOHNSON, BETTY ANNE, nurse; b. Centerville, Iowa, Sept. 14, 1924; d. Delazon Marion and Lucy Glen (Guernsey) Wilson; m. Vern William Johnson (dec. Oct. 1966); children: Richard Hugh, Russell William, John Allen. Grad., St. Joseph Sch. Nursing, Ottumwa, Iowa, 1946; BS in Health Arts, Coll. of St. Francis, Joliet, Ill., 1982. RN, Iowa. Tchr. Albany Sch., Bloomfield, Iowa, 1942-43; nurse Ottumwa Hosp., 1946-49, 78-83, Balboa Hosp., San Diego, 1949-50, Davis County Hosp., Bloomfield, Iowa, 1955-66, 74-78; nurse, pediatrics dept. St. Joseph Hosp., Ottumwa, 1967-73; nurse Glenwood (Iowa) State Hosp. for Retarded, 1973-74; substitute house parent Rainbow Acres, Ranch for Handicapped Adults, Camp Verde, Ariz., 1984-87; supr. Foothills Cave Ctr., Cottonwoord, Ariz, 1985-87; with Kachine Point Health Ctr., Sedona, Ariz, 1987-89. Home: 425 S Willard St Ottumwa IA 52501

JOHNSON, BETTY JEAN, physical therapist; b. Caribou, Maine, Apr. 25, 1958; d. Wyllard Pierce and Norma Louise (Rackliffe) J. BS, U. Maine, Presque Isle, 1980; BS in Phys. Therapy, U. New Eng., 1990. Tchr. Limestone (Maine) High Sch., 1980-82, Caribou High Sch., 1982-83, Caribou Intermediate Sch., 1983-84, Stockholm (Maine) Elem. Sch., 1984-85; preloader United Parcel Svcs., Ft. Fairfield, Maine, 1984-85; phys. therapy aide Swedish Med. Ctr., Englewood, Colo., 1985-86; coach volleyball U. Maine, Presque Isle, 1986; tutor computer lab. U. New Eng., Biddeford, Maine, 1987-90; phys. therapist Cary Med. Ctr., Caribou, 1990—. Faculty scholar U. New Eng., 1989-90. Mem. Am. Phys. Therapy Assn. Liberal. Lutheran. Home: PO Box 1193 Caribou ME 04736

JOHNSON, BETTY ZSCHIEGNER, treasurer-secretary; b. Portage, Wis., June 20, 1933; d. Roy Lamar and Emma Minnie (Stoeckman) Zschiegner; m. Sidney Darrell. Student, Cen. Bible Coll., 1951-54. Organist First Assembly of God Ch., Memphis, 1954—, sec., bookkeeper, 1954-64; sec., treas. Delta Services, Inc., Memphis, 1968—; bookkeeper First Assembly of God Ch., Memphis, 1974-77; sec., treas. Quality Built Homes, Inc., Memphis, 1976—. Named Central Bible Coll. scholar, 1954. Mem. Home Builders Assn. Republican. Office: Delta Services Inc PO Box 38926 Memphis TN 38183

JOHNSON, BEVERLY KAY, marketing executive; b. Ponca City, Okla., May 15, 1939; d. Maynard F. and Flossy N (Lowe) Sallee; children: Debi, Paul; m. Leif Johnson, June 1, 1987. BA, Pt. Loma Coll., 1961; MA, Calif. State U., 1967. Choral conductor Cen. Oregon Community Coll., Bend, 1970-80, Azusa (Calif.) Pacific U., 1980-81; owner Davis & Assoc., Brea, Calif., 1981—. Producer 5 videos, 20 audio tapes, 1986—; speaker in field. Fund raiser Easter Seals. Mem. Nat. Assn. Female Execs., So. Calif. Vocat. Edn. Orgn. (bd. dirs. 1964-69), Nat. Assn. Single Adult Leaders. Republican.

JOHNSON, BEVERLY PHILLIPS, bank officer; b. Richmond, Va., May 14, 1963; d. Harold Thomas and Betty Lucille (Trammell) Phillips; m. Robert Mark Johnson, Nov. 29, 1985. BS, Lee Coll., Cleveland, Tenn., 1985. Comptroller Frank White Co., Cleveland, 1983-86; credit analyst 1st Am. Nat. Bank, Chattanooga, 1986-88; mortgage banker 1st Am. Nat. Bank, Cleveland, 1988-89; comml. real estate banker 1st Am. Nat. Bank, Chattanooga, 1989—. Div. campaign chairperson United Way Bradley County, Cleveland, 1987—; treas. Cleveland Community Concert Assn., 1989—. Mem. Cleveland/Bradley Home Builders Assn. (assoc.), Cleveland Bd. Realtors (assoc.), Cleveland Country Club (assoc.), Jaycees, Civitan (bd. dirs. Cleveland chpt. 1984—, pres.-elect 1990), Pillars Club, Lee Coll. Pres. Circle. Republican. United Methodist. Home: 1220 Bramblewood Tr Cleveland TN 37311 Office: 1st Am Nat Bank 725 Broad St Chattanooga TN 37402

JOHNSON, BRENDA JEAN, trucking company executive; b. River Falls, Wis., July 30, 1965; d. Theodore Edmund and Lorraine Theresa (Sieben) J. BS, St. Cloud State U., 1987. Tax temporary Dakota County Treas., Hastings, Minn., 1988; performance mgr. D. Biscoe Trucking, Inc., Cottage Grove, Minn., 1988—. Bd. dirs. Womens Volleyball League, Hastings, Minn., 1989. Mem. NAFE, Hastings C. of C. (tournament dir. 1988, 89). Roman Catholic. Home: 3440 Cannon St Hastings MN 55033 Office: D Biscoe Trucking Inc 10473 80th St S Cottage Grove MN 55016

JOHNSON, BRENDA LEE, laboratory director; b. Corfu, N.Y., Feb. 13, 1960; d. Daniel David and Carroll Lee (Timms) Stanley; m. Glenn Alan Johnson, Apr. 1, 1978; children: Jessica Lee, Danielle Marie. Student, Cumberland Sch. Med. Tech., Cookeville, Tenn., 1979-8l. Lic. lab. technologist, Tenn. Lab. technician Rhea County Med. Ctr., Dayton, Tenn., 1980-81; lab. technologist, lab. dir. Acadia St. Landry Hosp., Church Point, La., 1982-88, lab. dir., 1988—. Mem. Am. Soc. Med. Technologists, Am. Med. Technologists. Presbyterian. Home: 206 N Eastern Ave Crowley LA 70526 Office: Acadia St Landry Hosp 8l0 S Broadway Church Point LA 70525

JOHNSON, BRENDA LEE, reading teacher; b. Jamestown, N.Y., Oct. 5, 1950; d. Herbert Edwin and Betty Lou (Steck) J.; m. Donald Alfred Vining, Dec. 23, 1976 (div. Nov. 1982). Student, U. Buffalo, 1971; BA in Edn., SUNY, Fredonia, 1971, MEd in Reading, 1975, postgrad., 1989—. Cert. elem. and reading tchr. Tchr. remedial reading Jamestown Pub. Schs., 1980-81; tchr. Panama (N.Y.) Cen. Sch., 1972-80, reading educator, 1981—; reading educator and developer Program for At Risk Students, Jamestown Boys and Girls Club/Pvt. Industry Coun., 1987-90. Creator various reading and writing curriculum series, 1987-90. Mem. NEA (del. local region 1987-89), Internat. Reading Assn. (pres., bd. dirs. Chautauqua Coun. 1984-89, Pres.'s award 1988), Assn. for Supervision and Curriculum Devel., Nat. Coun. Tchrs. Eng., N.Y. State ACE, Chautauqua County Reading Task Force (chmn. 1984-86), SED (congruence steering com. 1988—, adminstrv. intern Panama Cen. div. 1990-91), Women of the Moose, Eastern Star. Home: 240 Valley View Ave Jamestown NY 14701 Office: Panama Cen Sch Panama NY 14767

JOHNSON, CAROLYN ANNE, advertising agency executive; b. Detroit, July 3, 1948; d. Raymond John and Margaret Louise (Middlemiss) Cully; m. Phillip Alan Johnson, Mar. 24, 1973. BA in Advt., Mich. State U., 1970. Copywriter Cochrane Chase & Co., Inc. (now AC&R Advt., Inc.), Irvine, Calif., 1971-73, copy dir., from 1973, v.p., from 1978, sr. v.p.; now sr. v.p. and creative dir. AC&R Advt., Inc., Irvine. Recipient numerous awards Art Dirs. N.Y., Advt. Club N.Y., others. Office: AC&R Advt Inc PO Box 19792 Irvine CA 92713*

JOHNSON, CAROLYN ELIZABETH, librarian; b. Oakland, Calif., May 29, 1921; d. Ferdinand Orin and Clara Wells (Humphrey) Hassler; m. Benjamin Alfred Johnson, Feb. 12, 1943; children—Robin Rebecca, Anne Elizabeth, Delia Mary. B.A., U. Calif.-Berkeley, 1946; cert. librarian Calif. State U., Fullerton, 1960; M.L.S., Immaculate Heart Coll., 1968. Asst. children's librarian Fullerton Pub. Library, Calif., 1951-59, coord. children's svcs., 1959-81, city librarian, 1981—; instr. Rio Hondo City Coll., Whittier, Calif., part time 1970-72, Calif. State U.-Fullerton, 1972-77; ; vice chmn. 3d Pacific Rim Conf. Council, 1983-86; mem. Korczak award com. U.S. Bd. Books for Young People, 1988. Author: The Art of Walter Crane, 1988. Mem. Library Tech. Tng. Adv. Com., Fullerton Coll., 1970; founding bd. dirs. Youth Sci. Ctr., Fullerton, 1958. Named Profl. Woman of Yr., N. Orange County YWCA, 1986. Mem. ALA, Calif. Library Assn. (chmn. children's service div.), Orange County Library Assn. (v.p.), So. Calif. Coun. on Lit. for Children and Young People (pres. 1979-81, Dorothy C. McKenzie award 1987), PTA (life), AAUW, LWV, Phi Beta Kappa, Theta Sigma Phi. Methodist. Home: 644 Princeton Circle E Fullerton CA 92631

JOHNSON, CATHERINE AUGUSTA LEWIS, youth service worker; b. Mobile, Ala., Dec. 31, 1937; d. Claude H. and Mabel L. (Miller) Lewis; m. Charlie Johnson, Jr., Apr. 22, 1967; children—Roderick Earl, Cyrus Aleric, Traci Elizabeth. Student Bishop State Coll., 1958, U. Colo., 1971, 72, Westminster Community Coll., 1985. With Ridge Regional Ctr. for Mental Retardation, Wheat Ridge, Colo., 1964-81; youth service worker A, Adams County Detention Ctr., Brighton, Colo., 1981-85, youth service worker B, 1985—; exec. producer Songwriters Choice in Christian Music, (program series) Denver Community TV; owner Kathy A.L.'s Music Pub. Co.; music min. Mem. Denver chpt. ARC, Denver Pub. Libr. Recipient profl. awards Mem. ASCAP, Internat. Platform Assn., Colo. Songwriters and Musicians Assn., Nashville Songwriters Assn., Rocky Mountain Writers Guild, Am. Cablevision Littleton-Community Producers' Network. Seventh-day Adventist. Avocations: songwriting, singing, producing and directing, tennis, swimming. Home: 12243 E 53d Ave Denver CO 80239

JOHNSON, CATHERINE COMMON, newspaper executive; b. Watertown, N.Y., Feb. 12, 1914; d. James Allison and Minna (Anthony) Common; B.A., St. Lawrence U., 1935; M.S. in Journalism, Columbia U., 1937; m. John Brayton Johnson, June 21, 1941; children: John Brayton, Ann Catherine, Deborah Jane, Harold Bowtell. Reporter, editor Watertown (N.Y.) Daily Times, 1937-41, editorial and spl. features writer, 1950—; v.p., sec. Johnson Newspaper Corp., owners Watertown Daily Times, Batavia Daily News, Malone Evening Telegram, Catskill Daily Mail; dir. Creg Systems Corp., Watertown. Vice chmn. Thousand Islands State Park Commn. Recipient Alumni citation St. Lawrence U., 1972, Athletic Hall of Fame inductee, 1987. Mem. Nat. League Am. Pen Women, North Country Artists Guild, AAUW (pres. Jefferson br. 1981-82). Republican. Presbyterian. Club: Coll. Women of Jefferson County (pres. 1954-56). Home: 221 Flower Ave W Watertown NY 13601 Office: 260 Washington St Watertown NY 13601

JOHNSON, CATHERINE GRYMES, real estate salesperson; b. Oklahoma City, Feb. 19, 1952; d. Herman Jr. and Mary (Visant) Grymes; m. Robert Dale Johnson; children: Justin Robert, Mary Elizabeth. Student, U. Tenn., 1970-71, Memphis State U., 1971-74. Rental agt. Avis Rent-A-Car, Memphis, 1974; clk. The Galbreath Co., Memphis, 1974-75; sales rep. Cook-Treadwell & Harry, Inc., Memphis, 1975-76; dept. mgr. Internat. Harvester Credit Corp., Memphis, 1976-81; customer service mgr. Am. Wallcoverings (div. The Arton Group), Memphis, 1981-82, retail store mgr., 1985-86; sales rep. The Arton Group, Memphis, 1985-87; real estate salesperson, 1989—. Mem. Olive Branch (Miss.) New Beginnings Civic Orgn., 1985—. Mem. Am. Soc. Internal Designers, Constrn. Specifications Inst., Nat. Safety Assn., Pi Beta Phi. Club: King's Daughters (Memphis) (pres. 1970). Home and Office: 7188 Larkfield Cove Olive Branch MS 38654

JOHNSON, CATHLEEN, public relations executive. BS, No. Ill. U., 1973. Former account exec. Richardson & McElveen; with Evelman Pub. Rels., Chgo., 1979—, v.p., 1984-85, sr. v.p., 1985—. Office: Edelman Pub Rels 211 E Ontario St Chicago IL 60611*

JOHNSON, CECILIA ANN, educator, researcher; b. Panama City, Fla., Nov. 22, 1940; d. Lott Warren and Cecilia Ann (Kuhlman) Middlemas; m. Joseph Asberry Johnson, Mar. 21, 1970 (dec.). B.A., Agnes Scott Coll., 1962; M.A., Emory U., 1964, Ph.D., 1976. Golf profl. 1963; instr. Ga. State Coll., Atlanta, 1964-66; instr. world history Northwestern State U., Natchitoches, La., 1970-74, 85—; adj. prof. Gulf Coast Community Coll. Pres. Natchitoches Humane Soc., 1972—; bd. dirs. La. Humane Soc., 1983—. Mem. Inst. Hist. Research (London), South Central Renaissance Conf., Met. Opera Guild, Audubon Soc. Democrat. Roman Catholic. Fla. State Women's Golf Assn. champion, 1956, 59. Avocations: reading; humane work; music. Home: 305 Poete St Natchitoches LA 71457

JOHNSON, CHARLOTTE VERNE, sales account executive; b. Tampa, Fla., Mar. 26, 1944; d. Calvin Phylemon and Theda Karleen J. B, Kans. State U., 1966. Acct. mgr., office mgr. Rainbow Photo, Kansas City, Kans., 1966-70, plant mgr., sales rep., 1970-74; regional mgr. GAF Corp., Wayne, N.J., 1974-78; sales rep. Olympus Corp., Woodbury, N.Y., 1978-80, regional mgr., 1980-81, dir. nat. accts., 1981-83, v.p. sales, 1983-85, v.p. nat. accts., 1985—; supplier rep. Catalog Showroom Merchandiser, 1982-83, Discount Store News, 1984. Photographer Kansas City Zool. Gardens, 1976-78, Breed mag., 1977-78, Am. Kennel Club, 1976-78. Mem. Nat. Premium Sales Execs., Nat. Assn. Female Execs., Photo Mktg. Assn., Nat. Arbor Soc., Nat. Wildlife Soc., Leavenworth (Kans.) Kennel Club. Office: Olympus Corp Crossways Park Woodbury NY 11791

JOHNSON, CHERI JEAN, real estate company executive; b. Chico, Calif., Oct. 14, 1959; d. Eugene Albert Johnson and Helene Frances (Treckeme) Meyer. BA, Calif. State U., Sacramento, 1983; M Adminstrn., U. Calif., Davis, 1989. Shipping and invoice clk. Jalmar Press, Sacramento, 1976-81; order desk clk., driver Sacramento Blood Ctr., 1982-84; analyst Calif. Dept. Health Svcs., Sacramento, 1985-87, Commn. on State Fin., Sacramento, 1988-89; dir. rsch. Stover Co., Sacramento, 1990—. Contbr. articles to profl. publs. Bd. dirs. Sacramento Coun. for Internat. Students, 1984-85, pres., 1985-86; mem. Sacramento Old City Assn., 1989—. Mem. AAUW (chmn. internat. rels. Sacramento br. 1984-86), Nat. Assn. Bus. Economists, Am. Assn. Individual Investors, Am. Inst. Real Estate Appraisers, Psi Chi (life). Home: 1321 33d St Sacramento CA 95816 Office: Stover Co 1721 2d St Sacramento CA 95814

JOHNSON, CHLOE RENE, community economic developer; b. Dallas, Oct. 18, 1939; d. William Porter and Vera Lee (Skinner) Riggs; m. Doyle K. Chaddick, Dec. 1, 1956 (div. July 1976); 1 child, Susan Kay; m. Walter Lee Johnson Jr., Apr. 30, 1983. Cert. indsl. developer; registered chamber executive. Exec. v.p. Quitman (Tex.) C. of C., 1973-76, Waxahachie (Tex.) C. of C., 1976-78, Grand Prairie (Tex.) C. of C., 1978-80; mgr. community devel. Tex. Econ. Devel. Commn., Austin, 1980-86; prin. Johnson & Assocs., Austin, 1986—. Recipient Community Svc. award Plano C. of C., 1971, Community Svc. award County of Wood, 1975. Mem. Tex. Indsl. Devel. Council (dir., com. chmn. 1975—), So. Indsl. Devel. Council (com. chmn. 1981—), Am. Indsl. Devel. Council (com. chmn. 1983—). Democrat. Baptist. Home and Office: 8308 Tecumseh Dr Austin TX 78753

JOHNSON, CHRISTINE M., transportation executive; b. Laramie, Wyo., Sept. 1, 1948; d. Albert Lenard and Dorothy (Hulet) MicKelson; m. Michael Johnson, July 15, 1968 (div. 1978); m. Milton Pikarsky, Oct. 25, 1979 (dec. 1989). BA, U. Ill., Chgo., 1970, M Urban Planning and Policy, 1976, PhD, 1978. Lectr. rsch. assoc. U. Ill., 1975-78, asst. prof., 1979; dir. mktg. Checker Taxi Co., Chgo., 1981-82; dir. rsch. Am. Pub. Works Assn., Chgo., 1982-84; asst. dir. planning and devel. Port Auth. N.Y., N.Y.C., 1984-88, dir. office transp. planning, 1988-90; asst. commr. policy and planning N.J. Dept. Transp., Trenton, 1990—; Chair person nat. Ride Sharing Rsch. Conf., Washington, 1981; cons. in field. Contbr. articles to profl. jours. Mem. transp. task force Chgo. Cen. area Com., mem. steering com. Met. Planning and Housing coun.; mem. N.J. Gov.'s Waterfront Devel. Com., N.J. Monorail Legisl. Commn., N.J. Clean Air Steering Com. Named to Acad. Women Achievers, N.Y. YWCA, 1989. Mem. Nat. Assn. Vanpool Oprs. (past bd. dirs.), Inst. Traffic Engrs., Am. Pub. Works Assn., Womens Equity, Women's Transp. Seminar. Reorganized Ch. of Jesus Christ of Later-day Saints. Home: 7 Ashford Dr Plainsboro NJ 08536 Office: N J Dept Transp CN600 Trenton NJ 08625

JOHNSON, CHRISTINE MARIE, leather apparel designer, consultant; b. Mason City, Iowa, Dec. 4, 1952; d. Elizabeth Ann (Swarner) Johnson; m. Michael Robert Salier, Aug. 5, 1978 (div. Mar. 1983). AS in Fine Arts, No. Iowa Community Coll., 1973; student, U. Wis., 1971; BFA in Interior and Illustration Design, Am. Inst. Fine Arts, 1975, MFA in Interior and Illustration Design, 1975. Pvt. practice tailor, clothing designer Mason City, 1966-84; freelance interior designer N.Y.C. and Des Moines, 1974-82; leather garment designer, mgr. Under My Skins, Mason City, 1984—; instr. apprentices Under My Skins, 1987—. Mem. PETA, Calif., 1986—, Friends of the Earth, London, 1989—. Mem. am. Leatherworkers Assn., Internat. Tanners Assn. Republican. Methodist. Office: Under My Skins 1022 N Adams Mason City IA 50401

JOHNSON, CHRYSTA LEA, registered nurse; b. Paris, Tex., Mar. 19, 1949; d. Herschel Albert and Shirley Louise (Linthicum) Lynch; m. Robert Micheal Johnson, Aug. 30, 1969 (div.); children: Judy Lea, Robert Thomas. Student, Tex. Womans U., 1967-69; Assoc. in Nursing, Cook County Coll., 1974. RN, Tex. Head nurse of surg. fl. Flow Meml. Hosp., Denton, Tex., 1974-79; nursing dir. First Tex. Med. Clinic, Denton, 1979-81; head nurse surg. fl. Denton (Tex.) Regional Med. Ctr., 1981-90; office nurse and surg. nurse F. Jeffery Charney, M.D., Denton, 1990—; Charter mem. Am. Acad. Ambulatory Nurses Assn., 1981. Mem. Am. Heart Assn. (bd. dirs. 1988—, CPR instr. 1977—, CPR instr. trainer 1989—), Confederate Air Force (col. 1987—). Republican. Episcopalian. Home: 1800 Westminster #11 Denton TX 76205

JOHNSON, CONSTANCE ANN TRILLICH, small business owner, lawyer, writer, researcher, lecturer; b. Chgo., Apr. 16, 1949; d. Lee and Ruth (Goodhue) Trillich; m. Robert Dale Neal, Dec. 25, 1972 (div. 1988); 1 child, Adam Danforth; m. Lewis W. Johnson Jr., Feb. 14, 1990. BA in French, U. Tenn., 1971, cert. Sorbonne, 1970; MLn, Emory U., 1979; JD, Mercer Law Sch., 1982. Bar: Ga. 1982; cert. Reiki therapist level III. Reservationist AAA, Tampa, Fla., 1971-72; libr. tech. asst. I, Mercer U., Macon, Ga., 1973-74, libr. tech. asst. III, 1974-78; teaching asst. Mercer Law Sch., Macon, 1981; asst. prof. Mercer Med. Sch., Macon, 1980-82; pvt. practice, Macon, 1982-86; min. Ch. Tzaddi, 1986-89; writer/researcher ADC Project, 1988-89; min. Alliance of Divine Love, 1988—; of counsel Read Found., Evansville, Ind., 1989—; mgr. Lifestream Assocs., 1989; freelance editor Page Design Co., 1989; assoc. AA Computer Care, Longwood, Fla., 1989; owner Christian Computer Care, 1990—; founder House of the Lord, 1989—; rsch. asst. Ctr. Constl. Studies, Macon, 1983; researcher ADC Project, 1988-89; instr. bus. Wesleyan Coll., Macon, 1982; owner Christian Computer Care, Longwood, 1990—. Editor (periodical) Ray of Sunshine, 1989. Bd. dirs. Unity Ch., Middle, Ga., 1987, Sec., 1987. Bd. dirs. Macon Council World Affairs, 1981-82, Light of Creative Awareness, Northville, Mich., 1989; mem. Friends Emory Libraries, Atlanta, 1980-87; mem. Friends Eckerd Coll. Library, St. Petersburg, Fla., 1980-87. Mem. ABA, Am. Soc. Law and Medicine, Am. Judicature Soc., DAR (Kaskaskia chpt.), Mercer U. Women's Club (treas. 1974, pres. 1986, bd. dirs. 1987), Am. Assn. U. Women, Friends of the Library, Mid. Ga. Gem and Mineral Soc., Macon Mus. Arts and Scis., La Leche League (sec. 1985), Phi Alpha Delta. Republican. Office: Christian Computer Care 370 North Hwy 17-92 Longwood FL 32750

JOHNSON, CRYSTAL DUANE, psychologist; b. Houston, Mar. 2, 1954; d. Alton Floyd and Duane (Mullican) J.; m. Donald Beecher Hart, Mar. 21, 1989. BA, U. Tex., 1983, MS, 1985. Lic. profl. counselor, psychol. assoc. Student devel. specialist U. Tex., Tyler, 1985-86, intake counselor, 1986-88; staff psychologist Sabine Valley Ctr., Longview, Tex., 1988-89, Mental Health/Mental Retardation Ctr. of East Tex., Tyler, 1988-89; pvt. practice psychologist Tyler, 1989—; counselor Plan A Coop., Henderson, Tex., 1990—. Mem. Smith County Humane Soc., Tyler, 1985—, Humane Soc. of the U.S., Washington, 1987—. Mem. Am. Psychol. Assn., Tex. Psychol. Assn., East Tex. Psychol. Assn.

JOHNSON, DANA LISA, apparel designer; b. N.Y.C., June 16, 1958; d. Johnny and Freda (Clark) J. AAS in Art, Fashion Inst. of Tech., N.Y.C., 1979. Designer's asst. I.Appel, N.Y.C., 1979-81, Lady Ester, N.Y.C., 1981-83; asst. designer Bestform, L.I., 1983-86; designer, patternmaker Durelle Lingerie, N.Y.C., 1986—. Mem. NAFE. Home: 880 St Nicholas Ave New York NY 10032

JOHNSON, DEBORAH JEAN, real estate company executive; b. Phoenix, Apr. 24, 1953; d. Forrest Willard and Pauline Laverne (Childress) Long; m. Barry Williams Eisenach, Feb. 16, 1974 (div. 1980); m. Albert Austin Johnson, Jan. 24, 1981 (div. 1984); children: Justin Edward, Lisa Marie. Student, Mesa Jr. Coll., 1971-72, Westminster Community Coll, 1977; cert., Jones Real Estate Sch., 1983, Legal Awareness Tng. Program, 1987. Receptionist, sec. Telecommunications Inc., Denver, 1972-73; office mgr. United Drywall & Painting Inc., Denver, 1973-80; bookkeeper, asst. acct. Gam & Co., Portland, Oreg., 1981; contr. Realities Inc., Denver, 1983-84; real estate assoc. ERA Award REalty, Arvada, Colo., 1985-86; real estate assoc. Re/Max West Inc., Arvada, 1986-89, Lakewood, Colo., 1989—; acct. Smith, Brooks, Bolshoun & Co., Denver, 1980. Coach, Arvada Soccer Assn., 1985-86. Mem. Colo. Assn. Realtors, Realtor Corpac 99 Club, RE/MAX Pres.'s Club, Exec. Club, 100 Percent Club. Home: 6773 Welch Ct Arvada CO 80004 Office: Re/Max West Inc 3000 Youngfield St Ste 350 Lakewood CO 80215

JOHNSON, DEBORAH SUE, archaeology, forensic civil research and close range photogammetry consultant; b. Rochester, N.Y., May 18, 1948; d. Hobart Warren and Jean Phyllis (Bassage) Hondorf; m. Michael Chee Johnson, Aug. 14, 1976; children: Kristi Anne, Ryan Michael. BA in Anthropology, SUNY, Binghamton, 1970; MA in Anthropology, U. Ariz., Tucson, 1972; postgrad., Ariz. State U., Phoenix, 1974—. Cert. community coll. tchr., Ariz. Instr. anthropology Mesa Community Coll., Phoenix, 1976-79; civil designer WBC (Griner Engineering), Phoenix, 1979, Collar, Williams and White Engring., Phoenix, 1979-81, Henningson, Durham and Richardson Engring., Phoenix, 1982-84; photogrammetrist, civil designer, archaeologist, dir. mktg. Andrews Atherton, Inc., Phoenix, 1984-87; prin. Rsch. Assocs., Phoenix, 1987—; instr. anthropology South Mt. Community Coll., Phoenix, 1990—. Contbr. numerous articles to profl. jours. Leader Brownie Troup, Phoenix, 1988—, Girl Scout Troop, 1988—. NSF grantee, 1970; recipient Student Paper award Anthrop. Soc., 1969. Mem. Am. Soc. for Photogrammetry and Remote Sensing, Soc. for Am. Archaeology, Ariz. Archeol. Coun., Profl. Assn. Diving Instrs. (cert. advanced diver with night specialty), Archaeol. Conservancy, Smithsonian Inst. Methodist. Club: Al Houris Middle Eastern and North African Dance Co. (dir. 1976—). Home and Office: 10211 S 43rd Pl Phoenix AZ 85044

JOHNSON, D'ELAINE ANN HERARD, artist; b. Puyallup, Wash., Mar. 19, 1932; d. Thomas Napoleon and Rosella Edna (Berry) Herard; m. John Laffette Johnson, Dec. 22, 1956. B.F.A., Central Wash. U., 1954; M.F.A., U. Wash., 1958, postgrad. U. London, 1975—. Instr. art Seattle Pub. Schs., 1954-78, Mus. History and Industry, Seattle, 1954-56; dir. Mt. Olympus Estate, Edmonds, Wash., 1971; cons. art groups, Wash. State, 1954—. lectr. Cen. Wash. State U., Seattle PTA, Creative Arts Assn., Everett, Everett Community Coll., Women's Caucus for Art, Seattle, numerous others; served as art juror for numerous shows. Founder Mt. Olympus Preserve for Arts, Edmonds, Wash., 1971, sponsor art events, 1971—; active Wash. Coalition Citizens with Disabilities. Exhibited in group shows: Fry Art Mus., Seattle, 1964, Seattle Art Mus., 1959, Henry Art Gallery, Seattle, Vancouver Maritime Mus., B.C., Can., 1981, N.S. Art Mus., Can., 1971, Whatcom Mus., Bellingham, Wash., 1975, State Capitol Mus., Olympia, Wash., 1975, Corvallis State U., Oreg., 1982, Newport Mus., Oreg., Nat. Artist Equity, 1972, Belluvue Art Mus., Seattle, 1989, Rosicrusian Egyption Mus., San Jose, Calif., 1990; over 300 exhibits 1950—, over 1200 paintings through 1970. Elected to Wash. State Art Commn. Registry, Olympia, 1982; recipient numerous awards. Mem. Nat. Artist Equity, Internat. Soc. Artists, The Cousteau Soc., Am. Council for Arts, Nat. Women's Studies Assn., Assn. Am. Culture, Internat. Platform Assn., Nat. Pen Women Assn., Kappa Delta Pi, Kappa Pi. Avocations: scuba diving, camping, travel, violin, writing. Home and Office: 16122 72d St Ave W Edmonds WA 98020

JOHNSON, DIANA LYNN, law clerk; b. Pearisburg, Va., Dec. 23, 1954; d. Ted James Sr. and Thelma Ilene (Kirk) J. BS, Radford U., 1977. Law clk. Warren, Gibb and Scheid, P.C., Narrows, Va., 1977—; cons. Anderson and Assocs., Inc., Blacksburg, Va., 1983-84; abstractor Record Data Va., Richmond, 1985—. Author poetry book. Campaign mgr. Dem. Ted Johnson Jr. for Congress, 9th Dist. Va., 1974. Mem. Relief Soc., DAR (invitee). Mem. LDS Ch. Home: 1501 Wenonah Ave Pearisburg VA 24134 Office: Warren Gibb and Scheid PC 225 Main St Narrows VA 24124

JOHNSON, DIANE WEINBERG, software analyst; b. Phila., Oct. 20, 1951; d. Fred Schwartz and Esther (Merion) Weinberg; m. Terry Alan Johnson, June 10, 1951; children: Kimberly, Ashley. BA, Am. U., 1973; MBA, U. Ga., 1980. Project leader YMCA, Arlington, Va., 1973-74; ctr. dir. Pr. Wm. Co. Parks and Recreation, Dale City, Va., 1974-78; account exec. Automatic Data Processing, Dallas, 1980-81; programming support analyst Cable Data, Sacramento, 1982—; mem. Women in Cable, Sacramento, 1982—. V.p. Coll. Green East Homeowner's Assn., 1987—; precinct leader Dem. Women's Club, 1988, com. chair, 1989, v.p. 1990—. Mem. Smithsonian Inst. Jewish.

JOHNSON, DIANNE BALL, accountant; b. Bristow, Okla., Feb. 2, 1959; d. Robert Russell Ball and Marlene (Moss) Watts; m. Douglas Ogden Johnson, July 1, 1981; children: Kristen Marie, Charles Ogden. Student, Trinity U., 1977-78; BBA in Engring. Mgmt., U. Tex., 1982. Accounts mgr. Capital City Contractors, Inc., Austin, Tex., 1984-88; acctg. mgr. Video Telecom Corp., Austin, 1988—. Pres. and Banowsky scholar Trinity U., 1977-78. Presbyterian. Office: Video Telecom Corp 1908 A Kramer Austin TX 78758

JOHNSON, DONNAMAE ELAINE, technologist; b. Grand Rapid, Minn., Feb. 21, 1951; d. Howard Severt and Donnabelle Francine (Henry) Landey. Cert., U. Salzburg, 1972; BA in German, Anderson U., 1975; AA in Nuclear Medicine, Prince George's Community Coll, 1980. Russian linguist U.S. Army Security Agy., Augsburg, Germany, 1973-77; staff technologist Sinai Hosp., Balt., 1980; supr. nuclear cardiology Wash. Hosp. Ctr., 1980-87; instr. Prince George's Community Coll., Largo, Md., 1981-88; supr. nuclear cardiology Nat. Insts. Health, Bethesda, Md., 1987; chief technologist Veterans Adminstrn. Med. Ctr., Wash., 1987—; advisor Prince George's Community Coll., Largo, 1982--. Contbr. articles to profl. jours. Mem. Soc. Nuclear Medicine (treas. 1985-86, chmn. 1986-87, pres. 1986-87, del. 1988-), Verification of Involvement in Continuing Edn., Nat. Assn. for Female Execs., Aircraft Owners and Pilots Assn. Home: 9225L Brandy Ln Laurel MD 20707 Office: VA Med Ctr 50 Irving St NW Washington DC 20422

JOHNSON, DORA MYRTLE KNUDTSON, principal; b. Bryant, S.D., Sept. 4, 1900; d. Knudt Guttorm and Margit Knudtson; m. Arthur Johnson, Jan. 31, 1949 (dec. Aug. 1949); 1 stepdaughter, Doris Miller. BA, St. Olaf Coll., 1923; MA, U. Wash., Seattle, 1941. Sr. high sch. tchr. math. Gaylord (Minn.) Sch. Dist., 1923-26, Madison (S.D.) Sch. Dist., 1926-43; dean of girls Madison (Wis.) Sch. Dist., 1932-41, prin., 1941-43; high sch.tchr. math. Kansas City (Mo.) Sch. Dist., 1943-49; dean of women Mo. Christian Coll., Columbia, 1950-57; ret. Mo. Christian Coll., 1958; cons. AAUW, Kansas City, 1969-71. Editor: A History of the Mo. Div. of AAUW, 1946-76. Mem. AAUW (br. pres. Madison, S.D., state chmn., fellowship found. Kansas City 1963-67, state pres. Kansas City 1967-69, nat. com. for ednl. found. D.C. chpt. 1971-75, honorary life mem. 1989, Significant Svc. award 1989), Internat. Assn. of Univ. Women, Internat. Relations Coun., Friends of Art. Democrat. Lutheran. Home: 10000 Wornall Rd Apt 1402 Kansas City MO 64114

JOHNSON, DOROTHY, mayor; m. Rue C. Johnson; 5 children. BS, U. Utah; postgrad., Ind. U. Mem. bdn. edn. City of Appleton, Wis., 1977-80, mayor, 1980—. Mem. Wis. Retirement Rsch. Com., Fox River Mgmt. Commn.; bd. dirs. Fox Valley Water Quality Agy. Named Woman of Yr., State of Wis. Bus. and Profl. Women, 1982; Paul Harris fellow Rotary. Mem. Wis. Alliance of Cities. Office: City Hall PO Box 1857 Appleton WI 54913*

JOHNSON, DOROTHY PHYLLIS, counselor, art therapist; b. Kansas City, Mo., Sept. 13, 1925; d. Chris C. and Mabel T. (Gillum) Green; B.A. in Art, Ft. Hays. State U., 1975, M.S. in Guidance and Counseling, 1976, M.A. in Art, 1979; m. Herbert E. Johnson, May 11, 1945; children—Michael E., Gregory K. Art therapist High Plains Comprehensive Mental Health Assn., Hays, Kans., 1975-76; art therapist, mental health counselor Sunflower Mental Health Assn., Concordia, Kans., 1976—, co-dir. Project Togetherness, 1976-77, coordinator partial hospitalization, 1978—, out-patient therapist, 1982—; dir. Swedish Am. State Bank, Courtland, Kans., 1960—, sec., 1973-77. Mem. Kans., Am. art therapy assns., Am. Mental Health Counselors Assn., Am. Assn. for Counseling and Devel., Kans. Assn. for Counseling and Devel., Assn. for Humanistic Psychologists, Assn. Transpersonal Psychologists, Assn. Specialists in Group Work, Phi Delta Kappa, Phi Kappa Phi. Contbr. articles to profl. jours. Home: Box 200 Courtland KS 66939 Office: 520 B Washington St Concordia KS 66901

JOHNSON, EDDIE BERNICE, state senator, educator; b. Waco, Tex., Dec. 3, 1935; d. Lee Edward and Lillie Mae (White) J.; m. Lacy Kirk Johnson, July 5, 1956 (div. Oct. 1970); 1 child, Dawrence Kirk. Diploma in Nursing, St. Mary's Coll. of South Bend, 1955; BS in Nursing, Tex. Christian U., 1967; MPH in Pub. Adminstrn., So. Meth. U., 1976; LLD (hon.), Bishop Coll., 1979, Jarvis Coll., 1979, Tex. Coll., 1989. Chief psychiat. nurse psychotherapist Vets. Hosp., Dallas, 1956-72; state rep. Tex. Ho. Reps. Dist. 33-0, Dallas, 1972-77; regional dir. HEW, Dallas, 1977-79; exec. asst. to adminstr. for primary health care policy HEW, Washington, 1979-81; v.p. Vis. Nurse Assn. of Tex., Dallas, 1981-87; mem. Tex. Ho. of Reps., dist. 23, 1986—; cons. div. urban affairs Zales Corp., Dallas, 1976-77; exec. asst. personnel div. Neiman-Marcus, Dallas, 1972-75; pres. Eddie Bernice Johnson & Assocs., Inc., Metroplex News, Dallas-Ft. Worth Airport. Bd. dirs. ARC. Recipient Citizenship award Nat. Conf. Christians and Jews, 1985; named an Outstanding Alumnus St. Mary's Coll. of Nursing, 1986. Mem. Alpha Kappa Alpha. Office: Tex State Senate PO Box 12068 Austin TX 78711

JOHNSON, EDNA HAFNER, court administrator; b. Canton, Ohio, Apr. 1, 1942; d. Harold Ralph and Edna Mary (Pope) Hafner; m. Charles Cleason Johnson, May 4, 1963 (div. Feb. 1970); 1 child, Elizabeth Anne. BS in Journalism, U. Fla., 1983, BS in Pub. Rels., 1984. Cert. family mediator, Fla. Sec. Pratt & Whitney Aircraft Co., West Palm Beach, Fla., 1963-66; exec. sec. Charles R. Dorsey Ins. Co., West Palm Beach, 1966-67, Butler Aviation Co., West Palm Beach, 1967-68, RCA Computer Systems, Palm Beach Gardens, Fla., 1968-74; asst. ct. adminstr. State of Iowa, Le Mars, 1984-87; jud. asst. State of Fla., West Palm Beach, 1974-80; dep. ct. adminstr., dir. family mediation State of Fla., Titusville, 1987—. Author: How To Use System 36 in Iowa, 1986; editor: Watch Dog in Tallahassee, 1983. Mem. Nat. Assn. Ct. Mgmt., Acad. Family Mediators, Assn. Family and Conciliation Cts., AAUW, Beta Sigma Phi. Home: PO Box 348 Sanford FL 32772 Office: Ct Adminstrn 301 N Park Ave Sanford FL 32771

JOHNSON, ELIZABETH DIANE LONG, lawyer; b. Pasadena, Calif., Nov. 16, 1945; d. Volney Earl and Sylvia Irene (Drury) Long; m. Lynn Douglas Johnson, Oct. 22, 1966; 1 child, Barbara Annette. BA, U. of Houston, 1967; JD, Rutgers U., 1980. Bar: N.J. 1980, U.S. Dist. Ct. N.J. 1980, Pa. 1984, U.S. Supreme Ct. 1986. Pvt. practice Riverside, N.J., 1980—; Pub. defender, Riverside Twp., 1988—; speaker Bur. Comprehensive Justice Ctr. Burlington County, 1987—. Del. Women in Law to Peoples Republic of China Citizen Amb. Program of People to People Internat., 1989; mem. Tenby Chase Civic Assn., Delran, N.J., 1972-87, treas. 1976, v.p. 1974; trustee Drenk Mental Health Ctr., 1988—. Mem. ABA, N.J. Bar Assn., N.J. Women Lawyers Assn., Burlington County Bar Assn. (chair, bench and bar com. 1989—), Burlington County Bar Found. (trustee 1988-89, treas. 1988-89), Assn. Trial Lawyers Am. (N.J. chpt.), Internat. Platform Assn., Soc. for the Right to Die, Nat. Trust for Hist. Preservation, Mensa, Rotary Internat., Phi Alpha Delta, Delta Gamma. Methodist. Office: 23 Scott St Ste C PO Box 274 Riverside NJ 08075

JOHNSON, ELIZABETH HILL, foundation administrator; b. Ft. Wayne, Ind., Aug. 21, 1913; d. Harry W. and Lydia (Buechner) Hill; m. Samuel Spencer Johnson, Oct. 7, 1944 (dec. 1984); children: Elizabeth Katharine, Patricia Caroline. BS summa cum laude, Miami U., Oxford, Ohio, 1935; MA in English Lit., Wellesley Coll., 1937; postgrad., U. Chgo., 1936. Cert. tchr., Ohio. Pres., co-founder S.S. Johnson Found., a Calif. Corp., San Francisco, 1947—. Mem. Oreg. State Bd. Higher Edn., Salem, 1962-75, Oreg. State Edn. Coordinating Com., Salem, 1975-82, Oreg. State Tchr. Standards and Practices Commn., Salem, 1982-89; bd. dirs. Lewis and Clark Coll., Portland, Oreg., 1985—, Pacific U., Forest Grove, Oreg., 1982—, Sunriver Prep. Sch., 1983—, Oreg. Hist. Soc., Portland, 1985—, Cen. Oreg. Dist. Hosp., Redmond, 1982—, Oreg. High Desert Mus., Bend, Oreg. Health Decisions, 1986—. Lt. USNR, 1943-46. Named Honoree March Dimes White Rose Luncheon, 1984; recipient Aubrey Watzek award Lewis and Clark Coll., 1984, Cen. Oreg. 1st Citizen award, Abrams award Emanual Hosp., 1982. Mem. Am. Assn. Higher Edn., Am. Assn. Jr. Colls., Assn. Supervision and Curriculum Devel., Soroptimists (hon.), Phi Beta Kappa, Phi Delta Kappa, Delta Gamma, Beta Sigma Phi. Republican. Lutheran. Club: Francisca (San Francisco); Town, University, Waverly (Portland). Home: 415 S Canyon Dr Redmond OR 97756 Office: SS Johnson Found 441 S Canyon Dr Redmond OR 97756

JOHNSON, ELIZABETH JACKSON, town councilwoman; b. Birmingham, Ala., Jan. 16, 1925; d. Leicester LeMont and Hazel Ione (Elliott) Jackson; m. Hugo C. Johnson; children. AB in Am. Govt., Harvard, Cambridge, Mass., 1947. Stenographer Hercules Powder Co., Birmingham, Ala., 1943-44; sec. Prof. Charles T. Copeland, Cambridge, Mass., 1945-46, Harvard U. Hist., Govt., Econ. Tutorial Office, Cambridge, Mass., 1947-50; sec. to dean Wichita State U., Wichita, Kans., 1961-64; adm. officer U. Pitts., Grad. Sch. Pub. Internat. Affairs, 1964-66; commr. elected Civil Service Commn., Ohara Township, Pa., 1974-76; hist. tour guide Low Country Adventures, Ltd., Hilton Head Island, 1985—; council-at-large Town of Hilton Head Island, S.C., 1987-89. Pres. Squaw Run Area Watershed Assn., Ohara Twp., Pa., 1977-81. Recipient Conservation award Keystone Chap. Soil Conservation Soc. Am. Mem. Am. Assn. U. Women Fox Chapel Br. Pa. (V.P. 1972-74). Republican. Episcopalian. Home: 21 Donax Rd Hilton Head Island SC 29928

JOHNSON, ELLEN CHRISTINE, marketing executive; b. St. Paul, Mar. 10, 1948; d. Arnold Elwood and Betty Jane (Bruening) Damsgaard; m. Neal Frank Johnson, June 21, 1969; 1 child, April Holly. BA in Advt., U. Minn., 1971; MBA, Coll. St. Thomas, 1985. Dir. pub. rels. Children's Home Soc. Minn., St. Paul, 1971-73, asst. dir. devel., 1973-78; coord. pub. rels. Minn. Hosp. Assn., Mpls., 1978-80; dir. mktg., pub. rel. Unity Med. Ctr., Mpls., 1980-83; exec. dir. Unity Health Found., Mpls., 1983-85; mgr. mktg. product Health One Corp., Mpls., 1985-87; pres., chief exec. officer Ellstar Mktg. Corp., Mpls., 1987—. Contbg. author: Fifty Effective Print Ads for Hospitals, 1986, Profiles in Hospital Marketing, 1984; editor (newsletter) Women in Sr. Mgmt., 1987. Recipient Mpls. YWCA Leadership award, 1985, MacEachern citation Acad. Hosp. Pub. Rels., 1979. Fellow Am. Soc. for Hosp. Mktg. and Pub. Rels. (pres. 1985); mem. Pub. Rels. Soc. Am. (accredited, pres. Minn. chpt. 1982, Silver Anvil award 1983), Minn. chpt. Am. Mktg. Assn. Presbyterian. Office: Ellstar Mktg Corp Ct Internat #210N 2550 University Ave W Saint Paul MN 55114

JOHNSON, ELLEN RANDEL, real estate broker; b. Canton, Miss., May 9, 1916; d. Robert Colquhoun and Laura Arabella (Taylor) Randel; m. Floyd Everett Johnson Sr.; children: Dolly Mae Johnson Day, Floyd Everett Johnson Jr. Student, Blue Mountain Coll., 1934-35; course in real estate, Miss. Realtors Inst., 1976-77. Bookkeeper E. Constantin, Jr., Yazoo City, Miss., 1951-54, 56-59; draftsman Miss. State Hwy. Dept., Yazoo City, 1955; office mgr. Miss. Chem. Corp. Fed. Credit Union, Yazoo City, 1963-66; freelance journalist Yazoo Herald, 1970-74; broker, owner Ellen Johnson Realty, Yazoo, 1977; broker, assoc. Phyllis Waltman Realtors and Century 21 Beard & McMahan Realtors, Hattiesburg, Miss., 1978-79; broker, owner Ellen Johnson, Realtor, Hattiesburg, 1980-90. Author: The Dining Table for Candida Patients, 1988; contbr. articles to profl. jours. Charter dir. Yazoo Arts Council, 1973-75; chmn. civic quiz Am. Bus. Women's Assn., Hattiesburg, 1987. Mem. Nat. Assn. Realtors (Omega Tau Rho medal 1984), Nat. Women's Council Realtors, Miss. Women's Council Realtors (gov. 1984, v.p. 1983-84, by-laws chmn. 1984, Realtor of Yr. 1984), Hattiesburg Women's Council Realtors (v.p. 1982-83, Realtor of Yr. 1984), Miss. Assn. Realtors (by-laws com.), Hattiesburg Bd. Realtors (bd. dirs., com. chmn. 1979, 81, 84, v.p. multiple listing service 1982-83, pres. 1983-84, treas. 1987, Realtor of Yr. 1984). Republican. Baptist. Clubs: Mozart (Yazoo City) (pres. 1969); Miss. Music (Jackson) (jr. festival chmn. 1973-75). Home and Office: 1302 Estelle Hattiesburg MS 39402

JOHNSON, EVELYN BRYAN, flying service executive; b. Corbin, Ky., Nov. 4, 1909; d. Edward William and Mayme Estelle (Fox) Stone; grad. Tenn. Wesleyan Jr. Coll., 1929; student U. Tenn., 1930-32; m. Wyatt J. Bryan, Mar. 21, 1931 (dec. 1963); m. 2d, Morgan N. Johnson, Feb. 25, 1965 (dec. 1977). With Morristown (Tenn.) Flying Service, Inc., 1947—, chief flight instr., 1949—, sec.-treas., 1949-62, pres., 1962-82; mgr. Moore Murrell Airport, 1962—. Gov.'s appointee Tenn. Aero. Commn., 1983-86, v. chmn., 1987-89, chmn., 1989—. Recipient Carnegie Hero medal, 1958, Service to Mankind award Morristown Sertoma Club, 1981; named Flight Instr. of Yr., Nashville dist., 1973, 79, So. region, 1979, Nat., 1979 (all FAA); Outstanding Alumnus, Tenn. Wesleyan Coll., 1981. Mem. Morristown Area C. of C., Nat. Assn. Flight Instrs. (dir., treas. 1987-89), Ninety-Nines, Whirly Girls, Aircraft Owners and Pilots Assn., CAP, Silver Wings (Woman of Yr. 1981, bd. dirs. 1987—). Republican. Baptist. Home: Rural Rt 1 Osage Hills Jefferson City TN 37760 Office: PO Box 1013 Morristown TN 37816

JOHNSON, FATIMA NUNES, chemist; b. Makati, Rizal, The Philippines, Jan. 1, 1939; came to U.S., 1959; d. Carlos L. and Pureza (d'Eca) Nunes; m. Edgar M. Johnson, Sept. 9, 1967; children: Victoria C., David M. BS in Chemistry, Adamson U., Manila, 1959; MS, Boston Coll., 1961, PhD in Organic Chemistry, 1964. Sr. staff chemist Arthur D. Little, Cambridge, Mass., 1964-69; rsch. chemist Edgewood (Md.) Arsenal, 1969-70; scientist U.S. Pharmacopeia, Rockville, Md., 1971-90; sr. staff officer food chems. codex NAS, Washington (D.C.), 1990—. Contbr. articles to profl. jours.; patentee cen. nervous system depressants. Mem. Am. Chem. Soc., Am. Assn. Pharm. Scientists (charter). Roman Catholic. Home: 5315 Renaissance Ct Burke VA 22015 Office: Nat Acad Scis Food and Nutrition Bd 2101 Constitution Ave NW Washington DC 20418

JOHNSON, FRANCES E., public relations executive; b. Nama Kogen, Wis., May 12, 1936; d. Lloyd E. and Ada E. (Estep) Denman; m. Albert A. Johnson, Oct. 6, 1953; children: Netty, Douglas, Grant. Buyer Real Mdse. Lit Bros., Phila.; bank card rep. Meridian Bank Corp., Reading, Pa.; pvt. practice real estate mgmt. Panama City Beach, Fla.; pvt. practice pub. relations Ranch House Inn, Panama City Beach, Fla. Inst. of Diving award for contbn. to Internat. Mus. Home: 601 E Gulf Blvd Panama City Beach FL 32413 Office: 651 Clara Ave Panama City Beach FL 32407

JOHNSON, FRANCES FLAHERTY, career development specialist, retired educator; b. Hamlet, N.C., Feb. 23, 1916; d. John Lawrence and Mary Elizabeth (Shortridge) Flaherty; m. Clifton Jerome Johnson, Nov. 27, 1940 (dec. 1953); 1 child, Carolyn Johnson Koch. BS, State Tchrs. Coll., Fredricksburg, Va., 1936; MEd, U. N.C., 1958; postgrad. U. Oslo, 1963, U. Vienna, Austria, 1967; student Shetland Islands tradition and crafts, Lerwick, Scotland, 1979. Tchr. Cumberland County Schs., Godwin, N.C., 1936-37; tchr. Aberdeen Schs., N.C., 1937-39, prin., 1939-41; counselor Fayetteville Schs., N.C., 1958-64, Winston-Salem Forsyth Schs., N.C., 1964-65; cons. Dept. Pub. Instrn., Raleigh, N.C., 1965-71; project dir. Dare-Hyde-Tyrrell Schs., Manteo, N.C., 1971-73; vocat. counselor Wake Schs., Raleigh, 1973-74; now ret. contbg. mem. Smithsonian Inst., Washington, 1988—; active SITES and outreach programs. Mem. Am. Assn. for Adult and Continuing Edn. (del. for people-to-people visit to Soviet Union and to People's Republic China 1983), Am. Assn. for Counseling Devel., Asia Soc. Avocation: traveling.

JOHNSON, GAIL DELORIES, forensic chemist, toxicologist; b. Chgo., Sept. 30, 1957; d. Roger George and Delories B. (Reppert) J. BS in Chemistry, No. Ill. U., 1980. Quality control chemist Standard Pharmacal Corp., Elgin, Ill., 1980; forensic chemist Ill. Racing Bd. Lab., Elgin, 1980-82, Analytical Techs., Inc., Tempe, Ariz., 1982-84; analytical chemist Nichols Inst., San Juan Capistrano, Calif., 1985-87; forensic chemist, toxicologist, GC/MS group leader Damon Reference Labs., Rancho Cucamonga, Calif.,

1987—. Mem. Am. Chem. Soc., Am. Inst. Chemists. Office: Damon Reference Labs 10532 Acacia St Ste B-1 Rancho Cucamonga CA 91730

JOHNSON, GERALDINE ESCH, language specialist; b. Steger, Ill., Jan. 5, 1921; d. William John Rutkowski and Estella Anna (Mannel) Pietz; m. Richard William Esch, Oct. 12, 1940 (dec. 1971); children: Janet L. Sohngen, Daryl R., Gary Michael; m. Henry Bernard Johnson, Aug. 23, 1978 (dec. 1988). BSBA, U. Denver, 1955, MA in Edn., 1958, MA in Speech Pathology, 1963; vocat. credential, U. No. Colo., 1978; postgrad., Metropolitan State Coll. Cert. speech therapist, Colo.; cert. tchr., Colo. Tchr. music Judith St. John Sch. Music, Denver, 1946-52; tchr. West High Sch., Denver, 1955-61, chmn. bus. edn. dept., 1958-61, reading specialist, 1977-78; speech therapist, founder South Denver Speech Clinic, 1965-71; tchr. Educationally Handicapped Resource Rm., Denver, 1971-74, Diagnostic Ctr., The Belmont Sch., Denver, 1974-77; speech-lang. specialist elem. and jr. high schs., Denver, 1978-86; itinerant speech-lang. specialist various elem. and jr. high schs., Denver, 1978—; ret. Denver Pub. Sch. System, 1986; home lang tchr. Early Childhood Edn., Denver, 1975; mem. Ednl. TV Adv. com., Colo.; sec. Cen. Bus. Edn. Com., Colo; tchr. letter writing clinics, local bus., Denver, 1960—. Former judge Colo. State Speech Festivals; demonstrator, lectr. Speech-Lang. and Learning Disabilities area Colo. Edn. Assn., 1971-73. Recipient Spl. Edn. award Denver Pub. Schs., 1986. Mem. Speech-Lang.-Hearing Assn. (cert.), U. Denver Sch. Bus. Alumni Bd., Beta Gamma Sigma, Kappa Delta Pi, Delta Pi Epsilon. Home: 2780 S Vance Way Denver CO 80227

JOHNSON, GWENAVERE ANELISA, artist; b. Newark, S.D., Oct. 16, 1909; d. Arthur E. and Susie Ellen (King) Nelson; m. John Wendell Johnson, Dec. 17, 1937; 1 child, John Forrest. Student, Mpsl. Sch. Art, 1930; BA, U. Minn., 1937; MA, San Jose State U., 1957. Cert. gen. elem., secondary, art tchr., Calif. Art tchr., supr. Austin (Minn.) Schs., 1937-38; art tchr. Hillbrook Sch., Los Gatos, Calif., 1947-52; art tchr., supr. Santa Clara (Calif.) Pub. Schs., 1952-55; art tchr., dept. chmn. San Jose (Calif.) Unified Schs., 1955-75; owner Tree Tops studio, San Jose, 1975— Juried shows: Los Gatos Art Assn., 1976-79, 85-88, Artist of Yr., 1988 (1st and 2d awards), 83, 84 (Best of Show awards), Treeside gallery, Los Gatos, 1980, 81 (1st awards); Livermore Art Assn., 1977 (2d award), Los Gatos Art Mus., 1981 (1st award), 82 (2d award), Rosicrucean Mus., 1983, Centre d'Art Contemporian, Paris, 1983; creator Overfelt portrait Alexian Bros. Hosp., San Jose, Calif., 1977; exhibited in group shows Triton Art Mus., 1983—. Recipient Golden Centaur award Acad. Italia, 1982, Golden Album of prize winning Artists, 1984, Golden Flame award Academia Italia, 1986, others. Mem. San Jose Art League, Los Gatos Art Assn. (Artist of Yr. 1988), Santa Clara Art Assn. (Artist of Yr. 1983, 3 First awards 1989), Soc. Western Artists, Artists Equity, Nat. League Am. Penwomen (corr. sec., Merit Achiever award), Academia Italia. Home and Office: 2054 Booksin Ave San Jose CA 95125

JOHNSON, JAMIE, lawyer; b. N.Y.C., Nov. 16, 1947; d. Roy Sigvard Johnson and Ruth (Gouldon) Kaufman. Student, Briarcliff Coll., 1965-67; AB cum laude, Middlebury Coll., 1969; JD, U. Chgo., 1972. Assoc. Gardner Carton & Douglas, Chgo., 1972-76; atty. Montgomery Ward & Co., Chgo., 1976-77, Playboy Enterprises Inc., Chgo., 1977-78; assoc. Rogers Hoge & Hills, N.Y.C., 1979-83, Jones Hirsch & Bull, N.Y.C., 1983-84, Fish & Neave, N.Y.C., 1984-87, Kramer, Brufsky & Cifelli, Southport, Conn., 1987—. Contbg. author: Trademark Law Practice Forms, Vols. I and II, 1989. Recipient Prix de Paris, Condé Nast, 1969. Mem. U.S. Cycling Fedn., Phi Beta Kappa. Office: Kramer Brufsky & Cifelli 181 Old Post Rd Southport CT 06490

JOHNSON, JANET HELEN, Egyptology educator; b. Everett, Wash., Dec. 24, 1944; d. Robert A. and Jane N. (Osborn) J.; m. Donald S. Whitcomb, Sept. 2, 1978; children: J.J., Felicia. BA, U. Chgo., 1967, PhD, 1972. Instr. Egyptology U. Chgo., 1971-72, asst. prof., 1972-79, assoc. prof., 1979-81, prof., 1981—; dir. Oriental Inst., 1983-89; research assoc. dept. anthropology Field Mus. of Natural History, 1980-84. Author: Demotic Verbal System, 1977, Thus Wrote 'Onchsheshonqy, 1986, (with Donald Whitcomb) Quseir al-Qadim, 1978, 80; editor: (with E.F. Wente) Studies in Honor of G.R. Hughes, 1977. Smithsonian Instn. grantee, 1977-83; NEH grantee, 1978-81, 81-85; Nat. Geog. Soc. grantee, 1978, 80, 82. Mem. Am. Rsch. Ctr. in Egypt (bd. govs. 1979—, exec. com. 1984-87, 90—, v.p. 1990—). Office: U Chgo Oriental Inst 1155 E 58th St Chicago IL 60637

JOHNSON, JANET LOU, real estate executive; b. Boston, Aug. 22, 1939; d. Donald Murdoch and Helen Margaret (Slauenwhite) Campbell; m. Walter R. Johnson, Mar. 31, 1962; children—Meryl Ann, Leah Kathryn, Christa Helen. Student Boston U., 1959, Gordon Coll., Hamilton, Mass., 1962-64. Adminstr., account exec. Fuller/Smith & Ross, Boston, 1958-63; adminstr. Walter R. Johnson, P.E., Gloucester, 1970-76; broker Realty World, Gloucester, 1976-77, Hunneman & Co., Gloucester, 1977-79; pres., owner Janet L. Johnson Real Estate, Gloucester, 1979—. Mem. Mass. Assn. Realtors (bd. dirs. 1985-87), Nat. Assn. Realtors, Cape Ann C. of C., Cape Ann Bd. Realtors (pres. 1984-85, state dir. 1985-86), Greater Salem Bd. Realtors. Home: 35 Norseman Ave Gloucester MA 01930 Office: Janet L Johnson Real Estate 79 Rocky Neck Ave Gloucester MA 01930

JOHNSON, JANICE C., financial manager; b. Quantico, Va., Apr. 4, 1956; d. Weldon W. and Agnes (Klasko) J. BA, Frostburg State U., 1978; MBA, George Washington U., 1984. Bus., fin. mgr. Advanced Marine Enterprises, Inc., Arlington, Va.; contract adminstr. VSE Corp., Alexandria, Va. Mem. NAFE. Home: 4737 Colonel Ashton Pl Upper Marlboro MD 20772

JOHNSON, JANICE DENICE, trade school executive; b. Torrance, Calif., May 20, 1955; d. Motlow and Beanice (Barnett) Woods; m. Luis Ernesto Johnson, June 26, 1987; 1 child, Jeannee Lunice. Student vocat. edn., UCLA, 1982. Mgr. Jasiano's Beauty Supply and Salon, Compton, Calif., 1976-80; mgr., instr. U. Cosmetology, Compton, 1980-85; instr. Wilfred Beauty Acad., L.A., 1985-86; owner, mgr. Beauty and Me, L.A., 1986-87; career-placement coord. Wilfred Ednl. Corp., Hollywood, Calif., 1987—; cons. Nat. Assn. Black Svcs., Inglewood, Calif., 1989—. Recipient award YWCA, Compton, 1984. Home: 20526 Fuero Dr Walnut CA 90016 Office: 5042 Ferndale St Los Angeles CA 90016

JOHNSON, JANICE KAY, school system administrator; b. Burke, S.D., Apr. 12, 1946; d. Ladik and Mae (Weinrich) Janousek; m. Terry Max Johnson, June 11, 1968. BS in Elem. Edn., Dakota State Coll., 1968; MS in Elem. Edn., So. Ill. U., 1969; PhD in Sci. Edn., Syracuse (N.Y.) U., 1976. Cert. tchr., Ill., N.Y., Ariz.; cert. sch. adminstr., Ariz. Tchr. East St. Louis (Ill.) Schs., 1968-69, East Syracuse-Minoa (N.Y.) Schs., 1969-74; faculty assoc. Ariz. State U., Tempe, 1976-77, sr. mgmt. analyst, 1979-82; program developer Mesa (Ariz.) Community Coll., 1977-79; curriculum coord. Glendale (Ariz.) Union High Sch. Dist., 1982—; grant proposal reviewer NSF, Washington, 1978-81, Fund. for Improvement in Postsecondary Edn., Washington, 1980-82; cons. Tolleson (Ariz.) High Sch. Dist., 1988—, Cartwright Sch. Dist., Phoenix, 1989—. Contbr. numerous articles to profl. jours. Mem. Washington Elem. Sch. Dist., Phoenix, 1985—, pres., 1987-88, North Phoenix Rep. Women. Mem. Ariz. Sch. Bd.'s Assn., Nat. Sch. Bd.'s Assn., Nat. Sci. Tchr.'s Assn., NAFE. Lutheran. Home and Office: 901 W Las Palmaritas Phoenix AZ 85021

JOHNSON, JANICE MARIE, lawyer, accountant; b. Atlanta, June 25, 1954; d. Wendell Berdette and Annie Martha (Pounds) Johnson. BA, Millsaps Coll., 1975; JD, George Washington U., 1978. Law clk. Joseph P. Bornstein, Washington, 1976; sr. tax specialist Peat, Marwick, Mitchell & Co., Washington, 1977-79; dir. nat. tax practice Oppenheim, Appel, Dixon & Co., N.Y.C., 1981-85; tax ptnr. BDO Seidman, N.Y.C., 1985—; guest on radio and TV talk shows. Contbr. articles to profl. jours. Mem. D.C. Mayor's Revenue Policy Adv. Com., 1980-81; chmn. Arthur S. Fleming Awards Luncheon, 1981; v.p., dir. Bonwit Plaza Unit Owners Assn., 1980-81; chmn., bd. dirs. Am. Ballet Comedy Dance Troupe; mem. Congressman Charles Rangel's Task Force on Taxes, 1988—; bd. dirs. YWCA of N.Y.C.; pres. Accts. for Pub. Interest, 1989—; trustee Fifth Ave. Presbyn. Ch., 1988—. Mem. AICPA (tax forms subcom. of fed. tax div.), D.C. Soc. CPAs (bd. govs. 1981), ABA, D.C. Bar Assn., N.Y. Soc. CPAs (mem. tax exec. com.), Assn. of Bar of City of N.Y., Downtown D.C. Jr. C. of C. (bd. dirs., Exceptional Service award 1980), Miss. Soc. CPAs, Miss. Soc. of Washington, Accts. Club Am. (bd. govs. 1990). Democrat. Home: 30 W 63d St Apt 19J New York NY 10023 Office: BDO Seidman 15 Columbus Circle New York NY 10023

JOHNSON, JEAN ELAINE, nurse, psychologist; b. Wilsey, Kans., Mar. 11, 1925; d. William H. and Rosa L. (Welty) Irwin. B.S., Kans. State U., 1948; M.S. in Nursing, Yale U., 1965; M.S., U. Wis., 1969, Ph.D., 1971. Instr. nursing Iowa, Kans. and Colo., 1948-58; staff nurse Swedish Hosp., Englewood, Colo., 1958-60; in-service edn. coordinator Gen. Rose Hosp., Denver, 1960-63; research asst. Yale U., New Haven, 1965-67; assoc. prof. nursing Wayne State U., Detroit, 1971-74; prof. Wayne State U., 1974-79; dir. Center for Health Research, 1974-79; prof. nursing, assoc. dir. oncology nursing Cancer Center, U. Rochester, 1979—; Rosenstadt prof. health research Faculty Nursing, U. Toronto, fall 1985. Contbg. author: Handbook of Psychology and Health, vol. 4, 1975; contbr. articles to profl. jours. Recipient Bd. Govs. Faculty Recognition award Wayne State U., 1975; award for disting. contbn. to nursing sci. Am. Nurses Found. and Am. Nurses Assn. Council for Nurse Researchers, 1983; grantee NIH, 1972—. Fellow AAAS; mem. Inst. Medicine, Nat. Acad. Sci. (com. on patient injury compensation 1976-77, membership com. 1981-86, governing council 1987-89), Am. Nurses Assn. (chmn. council for nurse researchers 1976-78, mem. commn. for research 1978-82), Acad. for Behavioral Medicine Research, Sigma Xi, Am. Psychol. Assn., Omicron Nu, Phi Kappa Phi. Home: 1412 East Ave Rochester NY 14610 Office: U Rochester Cancer Ctr 601 Elmwood Ave Rochester NY 14642

JOHNSON, JENNIFER RHAE, graphic designer, computer graphics consultant; b. Washington, Mar. 10, 1964; d. James Richard and JoAnn Nira (Diehl) Johnson. BA, Pa. State U., 1986. Designer, computer graphics cons. Grafik Communications, Ltd., Alexandria, Va., 1986—. Artwork pub. in Print Mag. Annual, 1988, 89. Mem. Washington Apple Pi, Am. Morgan Horse Assn., Am. Quarter Horse Assn., U.S. Dressage Fedn. Democrat. Methodist. Home: 7007 S Osborne Rd Upper Marlboro MD 20772 Office: Grafik Communications Ltd 300 Montgomery St Alexandria VA 22314

JOHNSON, JETSIE LOUISE, family nurse practitioner, consultant; b. Newport News, Va., Apr. 7, 1944; d. Breavoid Milton and Jetsie (Johnson) White; m. Henry Johnson Jr., Feb. 24, 1963; children: Cheryl Johnson Holmes, Henry Breavoid, Daryl Jay, Shamala Michelle. AAS magna cum laude, Thomas Nelson Community Coll., Hampton, Va., 1974; BS, Hampton U., 1985, MSN, 1987. RN, Va.; cert. family nurse practitioner. Staff nurse Hampton Gen. Hosp., 1974-77; nurse practitioner Alvin Bryant, M.D., Hampton, 1978-80, VA Med. Ctr., Hampton, 1980-81; staff nurse VA Med. Ctr., Richmond, Va., 1983-84; nurse practitioner Naval Regional Med. Ctr., Norfolk, Va., 1981-82; nurse supr. Commonwealth Health Care, Hampton, 1982—; staff nurse Med. Coll. of Va., Richmond, 1988; nurse practitioner Ea. State Hosp., Williamsburg, Va., 1984—; preceptor Old Dominion U., Norfolk, 1981-82, Hampton U., 1988-89; hon. instr. nurse practitioner program Med. Coll. of Va., 1979-80; cons. Alvin Bryant, M.D., 1981—; mem. adv. coun. Hampton U. Nursing Ctr., 1989-90; pres. Minority Cancer Task Force, Hampton, 1989—; corr. sec. Dept. Mental Health/Mental Retardation and Substance Abuse Svcs. Nurse Practitioner Practice Group, 1989—. Co-leader Girl Scouts U.S., Hampton, 1985-86; v.p. La Progressive Ten, Hampton, 1982; pres. Young Profls. of Tidewater, Hampton, 1980-81. Recipient Cert. of Appreciation, Minority Cancer Task Force, 1985; NIMH Tng. grantee Dept. HHS, 1985, 86. Mem. Va. Coun. Nurse Practitioners, Phi Theta Kappa, Sigma Theta Tau. Democrat. Home: 66 Santa Barbara Dr Hampton VA 23666 Office: Ea State Hosp Drawer A Williamsburg VA 23187

JOHNSON, JO ANN, nursing educator; b. Orlando, Fla., May 31, 1938; d. Joe Wynne and Posy (Edwards) Prichard; m. David L. Johnson, Aug. 3, 1963; children: Leslie Ann, David Wynne. BSN, Vanderbilt U., 1960; MA, Columbia U., 1962; MPA, U. So. Calif., 1972, D of Pub. Adminstrn., 1973. Pub. health nurse County of Orange, Fla., 1960-61; instr. nursing U. Va., 1962-64; asst. prof. nursing Calif. State U., L.A., 1965-75, assoc. prof. nursing, from 1975, now chmn. dept. nursing. HEW spl. fellow U. So. Calif., 1972. Office: Calif State U-LA Dept Nursing 5151 State University Dr Los Angeles CA 90032*

JOHNSON, JOAN B., cosmetics company executive; b. 1929. With Johnson Products Co., 1954—, v.p., from 1965, treas., 1975—, also chmn. bd. Office: Johnson Products Co 8522 S LafayetteAve Chicago IL 60620*

JOHNSON, JOAN BERNICE, nurse; b. Kilkenny, Minn., Dec. 30, 1939; d. Joseph and Albina (Budin) Viskocil; m. Thomas Williams, Aug. 1971 (div. 1975); m. Dennis D. Johnson, June 8, 1979; 1 child, Jeffrey; stepchildren: Brenda, Erik. Diploma in nursing, St. Cloud Hosp., 1960; BS in Nursing, St. Catherine's Coll., St. Paul, 1987. RN, Minn. Staff nurse St. Cloud (Minn.) Hosp., 1960-62; team leader St. Luke's Hosp., St. Paul, 1962-65; recovery room nurse Coney Island Hosp., Bklyn., 1965-66; sch. nurse NYU Health Svc., N.Y.C., 1966-68; nurse USAF Regional Hosp., Va., 1968-70, Brookdale Hosp. Employee Health Ctr., N.Y.C., 1970; pediatric nurse U. Minn., Mpls., 9708; charge nurse Queen of Peace Hosp., New Prague, Minn., 1971-85, bay supr., 1985-90, asst. dir. nursing, 1990—. Capt. USAF, 1968-70. Roman Catholic. Home: 24545 Cedar Point Rd New Prague MN 56071 Office: Queen of Peace Hosp 301 2d St NE New Prague MN 56071

JOHNSON, JOAN BRAY, insurance company adminstrator; b. Kennett, Mo., Nov. 19, 1926; d. Ples Green and Mary Scott (Williams) Bray; m. Frank Johnson Jr., Nov. 6, 1955; 1 child, Victor Kent. Student, Drury Coll., 1949-51, Cen. Bible Inst. and Coll., 1946-49. Staff writer Gospel Pub. Co., Springfield, Mo., 1949-51; sec. Kennett Sch. Dist. Bd. Edn., 1951-58; spl. features corr. Memphis Press-Scimitar, 1959-60; sec. to v.p. Cotton Exchange Bank, Kennett, 1959-60; proposal analyst Aetna Life Ins. Co., El Paso, Tex., 1960-64, pension adminstr., 1964-71; office mgr. Brokerage div. Aetna Life Ins. Co., Denver, 1971-78; office adminstr. Life Consol. div. Aetna Life Ins. Co., Oakland, Calif., 1979-82; office adminstr. PFSD div. Aetna Life Ins. Co., Walnut Creek, Calif., 1983-86; office adminstr. PFSD-Health Mktg. div. Aetna Life Ins. Co., Sacramento, 1986-89; regional adminstr. Aetna Life Ins. Co., Hartford, Conn., 1989—. Officer local PTA, 1964-71; pres. Wesley Service Guild, 1968-71; den mother Boy Scouts Am. Recipient Life Service award PTA, 1970. Fellow Life Office Mgmt. Assn. (instr. classes); mem. Assn. Bus. and Profl. Women, Life Underwriters Assn., DAR, Last Monday Club, Opti-Mrs., Allied Arts Club. Democrat. Methodist. Home: 2415 La Estrella Dr Henderson NJ 89014 Office: 151 Farmington Ave Hartford CT 06156

JOHNSON, JOANNE MARY, marketing and real estate executive, real estate broker; b. Bklyn., Mar. 28, 1947; d. John Peter and Anne Marie (Alesi)) Da Prato; m. John Daryl Johnson, Feb. 15, 1969; children: Jodi Lynn, Shaun Bryan. Student, Bkly. Coll., 1969; AA, Coll. of Staten Island, 1986; student, Univ. No. Tex., 1987—. Profl. asst. Price Waterhouse, N.Y.C., 1982-86, real estate mktg. mgr., 1990—; mktg. supr. real estate services group Price Waterhouse, Dallas, 1986-90; Editor: (newsletter) Real Estate Update, Real Estate Securities & Capital Markets. Editor (newsletter): Real Estate Update, 20/20 Vision. Bd. dirs. Tex. Soc. to Prevent Blindness. Mem. Nat. Assn. Female Execs., Nat. Assn. Real Estate Editors, The Kamen Found., North Tex. Assn. Real Estate Profls., Assn. Acctg. Mktg. Execs., Inc. Republican. Roman Catholic. Club: Brookhaven Country (Dallas). Home: 1312 Royal Palm Ln Carrollton TX 75007 Office: Price Waterhouse 1700 Pacific Ave Ste 1400 Dallas TX 75201-4698

JOHNSON, JOSEPHINE POWELL, power and light company manager; b. Goldsboro, N.C., Apr. 23, 1941; d. William Howard and Vennie Ann (Johnson) Powell; m. William Gene Stephenson, Dec. 24, 1959 (dec. Feb. 1979); 1 child, Teresa Lynn; m. 2d, Amos James Johnson Jr., Aug. 15, 1981; stepchildren—Amos James III, Edward Spencer, Brian Keith. Student Fayetteville Tech. Inst., 1975-79, Mt. Olive Coll., N.C., 1980-83. With Carolina Power & Light Co., 1961—, adminstrv. asst. to dist. mgr., Goldsboro, N.C., 1979-80, area mgr., Mt. Olive, 1980-86, area bus. mgr., Goldsboro, 1986-87; pres. Mt. Olive Bus. Devel. Corp., 1987—; pres. Bus. Industry Assn. for Duplin, Samson and Wayne County, 1987—. Bd. dirs. United Way, Wayne County, N.C., 1983—, Am. Heart Assn. Wayne County, 1987, Goldsboro Edn. Found., 1987 ; bd. dirs., pres. Mt. Olive Indsl. Com. of 100, 1984; bd. dirs. Com. of 100 Wayne County, 1987; precinct vice chmn. Cumberland County, Manchester Twp., N.C., Mem. Am. Bus. Womens Assn. (v.p. 1983), N.C. Bus. and Profl. Women U.S.A. (v.p. 1982), C. of C. (v.p., bd. dirs. 1980—). Democrat. Home: 117 Club Knolls Mount Olive NC 28365 Office: S Center St Goldsboro NC 27530

JOHNSON, JOY DUVALL, psychotherapist, educator; b. Syracuse, Jan. 10, 1932; d. Sylvanus Milne and Evelyn Ruth (Millis) Duvall; m. Ray M. Johnson Jr., Sept. 9, 1951; children: Kenneth Steven, Linda Ouellette. AB, U. Chgo., 1951, BA, 1963, MA in Social Work, 1965. Program dir. Henry Hart Jewish Community Ctr., 1965-66; group supr. Inpatient, Outpatient, 1966-67; chief social worker Ill. Dept. of Mental Health, Chgo., 1966-69; therapist in pvt. practice Chgo., 1969-90, trainer, cons.; assoc. prof. Jane Addams Coll. of Social Work, 1969-90, prof. emerita, 1990—. Author: Use of Groups in Schools, 1977, The Art of Dating, 1969; contbr. articles to profl. jours. Mem. Acad. of Cert. Social Workers, Assn. of Family Mediators, Am. Soc. of Sex Edn., soc. of Clinical & Experimental Hyposis, Council on Social Work Edn., Nat. Assn. of Social Workers, Council on Social Work Edn. Home and Office: Joy Johnson & Assocs 526 St Andrews Ct Lady Lake FL 32159

JOHNSON, JOYCE ANN, educator; b. Phila., Dec. 7, 1950; d. Walter Scott and Marie Therese (Uhlman) J. BA in Elem. Edn., Bethany (W.Va.) Coll., 1973. Elem. tchr. Avalon (N.J.) Bd. Edn., 1973—. Mem. NEA, N.J. Edn. Assn., Cape May County Edn. Assn. (chmn. fund raising 1987-90), Avalon Edn. Assn. (pres. 1985-90), Embroiders Guild Am., Country Shore Woman's Club (trustee 1989-90, treas. 1990—). Democrat. Episcopalian. Home: 46 Jill Ave Box 986 Marmora NJ 08223

JOHNSON, JUDITH ANN, educational administrator; b. Bklyn.; d. Charles Washington and Gwendolyn (Allen) Lockley; divorced; children: Pamela, Paul. BA, Bklyn. Coll., 1961; MA, NYU, 1966; cert. advanced study, SUNY, New Paltz; postgrad., Columbia U., 1984—. Tchr. N.Y.C. Pub. Schs., 1960-62, guidance counselor, 1964-66, coordinator of guidance, 1967-73; career resource specialist N.Y.C. Labor Dept., 1962-64; asst. prin. Mamoroneck (N.Y.), 1974-79; dir. instnl. svcs. So. Westchester Boces, Port Chester, N.Y., 1979-85; dir. curriculum elem. edn. Nyack (N.Y.) Pub. Schs., 1985—. Co-author ednl. materials. Mem. Rockland Ctr. for Arts, West Nyack, N.Y.; bd. dirs. YMCA, Nyack. Recipient Founders award Westchester Prins. Ctr., 1988. Mem. Assn. for Supervision and Curriculum Devel. (sec. N.Y. chpt. 1986-88, nat. bd. dirs. 1986-88), Am. Ednl. Rsch. Assn., Nat. Assn. Black Sch. Educators, Phi Delta Kappa. Democrat. Baptist. Home: 48 Fessler Dr Spring Valley NY 10977 Office: Nyack Pub Schs S Highland Ave Nyack NY 10960

JOHNSON, JUDITH KAY, lawyer; b. Indpls., Apr. 15, 1939; d. Winfield D. and Bessie M. (Townsend) Wood; m. Edward R. Johnson, June 22, 1963 (div. 1974); m. Adrian E. Flatt, Aug. 11, 1990. BA, Butler U., 1961; MA, So. Meth. U., 1969, JD, 1975. Bar: Tex. 1975. Tchr. pub. schs., various locations, Ind., Ill., Ariz. and Tex., 1961-70; instr. Sch. Law So. Meth. U., Dallas, 1975; assoc. Worsham, Forsythe, Sampels & Wooldridge, Dallas, 1975-81, ptnr., 1981—; speaker at tax and retirement confs.; discussion leader So. Meth. U. Symposium for Women, 1975—. Ann. fund chair Sch. Law, So. Meth. U., 1987-89, pres. alumni coun., 1989—, bd. visitors, 1988—; trustee Butler U. Mem. Dallas Bar Assn. (mem. employees benefits exec. compensation sect.), ABA (mem. employees benefits and exec. compensation com.), State Bar Tex. (mem. compensation and employee benefits com., sect. taxation), Dallas Art Mus., Phi Alpha Delta. Presbyterian. Office: Worsham Forsythe Sampels & Wooldridge 2001 Bryan St Ste 3200 Dallas TX 75201

JOHNSON, JUDY SHERRILL, business educator, educational consultant; b. McComb, Miss., Aug. 27, 1944; d. Samuel Benton and Eunice (Ikard) Sherrill; m. Bill Johnson, Dec. 27, 1985; stepchildren: Christie, Karen, Laurie, Leslie. BSC, U. Miss., 1966; postgrad. U. Fla., 1967, Fla. Atlantic U., 1971, 73, 76, U. Cen. Fla., 1984, Ark. State U., 1981. Lic. tchr. N.C., Tenn., Ala., Fla., Miss. Mem. faculty Santa Fe Jr. Coll., Gainesville, Fla., 1966-68, Broward County Bd. Pub. Instrn., Ft. Lauderdale, Fla., 1968-76; tchr. Huntsville City Sch., Ala., 1976-81; ednl. cons., sales rep. McGraw-Hill Book Co., N.Y.C., 1981-85; cons. Hillsborough County Bus. Edn. Tchrs., Tampa, Fla., 1982; mem. adv. bd. Pinellas County Indsl. Arts Dept., Clearwater, Fla., 1982-84; mem. adv. bd. bus. edn. Pinellas County, Clearwater, 1984-85, Hillsborough High Sch., Tampa, 1982-85, Gaither High Sch., Tampa, 1984-85, chmn. adv. bd. adult night sch., 1985; judge state contests Miss., 1977, Fla., 1982-85. Active Rep. Party of Fla., 1982-85; mem. Symphony Guild, Ft. Lauderdale; project advisor Huntsville Christian Women's Club, 1987-88; sec. United Meth. Women's Club First United Meth. Ch., 1988; v.p. Heritage Quilters Huntsville, 1987-88, pres., 1988-89; chair mini-retreat First United Meth. Ch., Huntsville, 1988-89; retreat com. worker, mem. planning com. Tenn. Valley Women's Retreat, 1988; tchr., leader Precept Bible Study, Precept Ministeries, 1988, Community Bible Study, 1989; vol. Huntsville Land Trust, 1988-89. Named Runner-up Advisor of Yr. Fla. Future Bus. Leaders Am., 1974. Mem. Delta Pi Epsilon, Alpha Delta Kappa (treas. 1980-81, various coms.), Phi Mu Alumnae (pres. 1969-71, collegiate dir. State of Fla. 1968-69, state day coord. 1970), Beta Sigma Phi, Phi Beta Lambda Alumnae, du Midi Gen. Federated Women's Club (publicity chmn. 1989-90). Avocations: cross stitch, sewing, fishing, gardening. Home: 1409 Governors Dr Huntsville AL 35801

JOHNSON, JULIE ELIZABETH, accountant; b. Salisbury, Md., Nov. 30, 1962; d. Clyde George and Edith Margaret (Crowther) J.; m. Francis Lafferty, Nov. 24, 1984. BS, Towson St. U., 1984. Internal auditor Cheasapeake Rim & Wheel, Balt., 1984-85; mgr. Princess Anne (Md.) Pharmacy, 1985-88; tax acct. Ellin & Tucker Chartered, Balt., 1985-88; tax acct. Noxell Corp., Hunt Valley, Md., 1988-89, sr. acct., 1989—. Republican. Methodist. Office: 11050 York Rd Hunt Valley MD 21030

JOHNSON, KAREN ANNE, communications executive; b. Huntington, N.Y., June 24, 1962; d. Edward Frederick and Carol Mary (Anderson) J. BS in Communications, Appalachian State U., Boone, N.C., 1984. Staff asst. U.S. Congressman Duncan Hunter, Washington, 1985-87; dir. communications working ptnrs. program Rep. Nat. Com., Washington, 1987; editor liability alert Capitol Group, Washington, 1987-88; dir. communications and polit. affairs Nat. Fedn. Rep. Women, Washington, 1988—; dir. gubernatorial debate communications Va. Fedn. Rep. Women, Washington, 1988—, Tex. Fedn. Rep. Women, McAllen, Tex., 1989; staff mem. Presdl. Transition Term, Washington, 1988-89. Editor The Rep. Women mag., 1988—. Dir. Va. coalition Dole for Pres., Arlington, 1987-88; mem. women's coalition George Bush for Pres., Washington, 1988; staff mem. Presdl. Transition Term, Washington, 1988-89. Mem. Women in Communications, Inc., Rep. Communications Assn., Jr. League Washington, Fed. City Rep. Women's Club (pres. 1989—). Roman Catholic. Republican. Home: 529 E Nelson Ave Alexandria VA 22301 Office: Nat Fedn Rep Women 310 1st St SE Washington DC 20003

JOHNSON, KAREN B., mayor; b. Buffalo, May 12, 1942; m. Lyman Johnson; children: Kent, Eric. AB, Radcliffe Coll., 1964. Coun. mem. City of Schenectady, N.Y., 1976-83, pres. city coun., 1980-83, mayor, 1983—. Chmn. bd. Schenectady United Way. Recipient Saul King award Schenectady United Way, 1987; named Woman of Yr., Mohawk Pathways Girl Scout Coun. Mem. AAUW, LWV (Susan B. Anthony award Schenectady chpt. 1980), Jr. League Schenectady. Office: City Hall Jay St Schenectady NY 12305*

JOHNSON, KAREN JANE, electrical engineer; b. Lake Charles, La., Sept. 6, 1953; d. Edward Lee and Betty Jane (Pylate) J. BSEE, La. State U., 1978. Registered profl. engr., Tex., assoc.; cert. mgr. Quality engr. Boeing Aerospace, Houston, 1978-81; space shuttle mission contr. Rockwell Space Ops., Houston, 1981-86, tech. asst., 1986—, sr. engr., 1990—; speaker on profl. engr. registration. Author tng. manual, 1987. Vol. Big Sisters Houston, 1987-88; mem., rep. to bd. Pasadena (Tex.) Philharm. Soc., 1986-88; mem. Contraband Swing Band, 1981-86, pres. 1986; mem. Cultural Arts Coun. Houston, 1984—; chmn., performer Challenger benefit dance A Family Affair, 1986; chmn. publicity com. Rockwell United Way, 1987. Named Rockwell Woman of Yr. Women's Adv. Bd. Bay Area Bank and Trust, Women in New Growth Svcs., 1987. Mem. AIAA (sr. mem., sec. 1987-88, chmn. publicity 1987, councillor 1988—, Woman of Mo. 1988, teller's com. 1989), Nat. Mgmt. Assn. (Rockwell chpt., profl. devel. com. 1987—, chmn.

mgmt. week com. 1988, mem. relations booster 1988-90), Inst. Cert. Profl. Mgrs. (cert. assoc. mgr.). Democrat. Presbyterian. Home: 1620 Bay Area Blvd #504 Houston TX 77058 Office: Rockwell Space Ops 600 Gemini Houston TX 77058

JOHNSON, KAREN KAY, continuing education director; b. Pittsfield, Ill., Jan. 22, 1949; d. Garl Edward and Dorothy Mae (Coultas) Hileman; m. Robert Curtis Johnson, Jan. 22, 1967; children: David Curtis, Daniel Brent. AA, Odessa Coll., 1973; BA, U. Tex., Odessa, 1975, MA, 1985; doctoral studies, Tex. Tech. U., 1989—. Art dir. The Odessan Mag., Odessa, Tex., 1970-75; news bur. chief San Angelo Standard Times, Odessa, 1975-77; v.p. mktg. Odessa C. of C., 1977-83; dir. bus. & profl. programs Odessa Coll., 1985-87, continuing edn. dir., 1987—. Recipient Ada Carter Johnson award Bus. & Profl. Women's Club, 1983, Woman of the Year Tex. Press Women, 1984. Mem. Tex. Adminstrs. of Continuing Edn., Tex. Assn. Continuing Edn., Bus. & Profl. Women (pub. relations chmn. 1984-85), Women's Info. Network. Democrat. Presbyterian. Home: PO Box 482 Odessa TX 79760 Office: Odessa Coll 201 W University Odessa TX 79764

JOHNSON, KAREN L., food products executive; b. 1940. BS, U. Wis., 1961, MS, 1962. Home economist, supr. Pillsbury Co., Mpls., 1962-72, dir. consumer svcs. refrigerated products div., 1972-76; dir. consumer affairs foods div. Borden, Inc., Columbus, Ohio, 1976-77, v.p. consumer affairs consumer products div., 1977-83, v.p. consumer affairs, 1983—. Office: Borden Inc 180 E Broad St Columbus OH 43215*

JOHNSON, KATHARYN PRICE (MRS. EDWARD F. JOHNSON), civic worker; b. Smyrna, Del., Mar. 24, 1897; d. Lewis M. and Jennie Cairl (Smithers) Price; grad. Centenary Coll., 1915; student Goucher Coll., 1915-18; m. Edward F. Johnson, Nov. 16, 1920; children—Edward A., Jane Cairl Johnson Kent. With Liberty Loan Com. for Md. and Liberty Loan Assn. of Balt., 1918-20; pres. Women's Guild Hitchcock Meml. Ch., 1930-32; dir. Scarsdale Woman's Club, 1933-36; dir. White Plains Thrift Shop, 1930-43, pres, 1936-43; mem. exec. com. Scarsdale Community Fund, 1934-38; active Scarsdale council Girl Scouts, 1937-53, commr., 1939-41, now hon. mem. Scarsdale-Hartsdale council, 1953-69; mem. region 2 com. Girl Scouts U.S.A., 1942-56, mem. nat. bd., exec. com., 1947-55, chmn. orgn. and mgmt. dept., 1952-55, mem. nat. field com., 1943-55, mem. equipment service com. 1956-69, mem. internat. com., 1956-60, mem. meml. gifts com., 1974-81; mem. Bd. Edn., Scarsdale, N.Y., 1943-46; disaster chmn. Scarsdale chpt. ARC, 1942-45; mem. Commn. Human Rights, 1958-69, Commn. Status of Women, 1957-69; rep. World Assn. Girl Guides and Girl Scouts to UN, 1957-71, mem. NGO com. on UNICEF, 1965-72, sec., 1968-70; participant World Confs., World Assn. Girl Guides and Girl Scouts, Greece, 1960, Denmark, 1963, Japan, 1966, Finland, 1969, Can., 1972, Eng., 1975, Iran, 1978, World Conf., U.S., 1984. Recipient Juliette Low World Friendship medal Girl Scouts USA, 1984. Mem. Nat. Council Women U.S., Scarsdale Hist. Soc., Olave-Baden-Powell Soc. (founder), Pi Beta Phi. Republican. Presbyterian. Clubs: Scarsdale Woman's (life), Scarsdale Golf, Nat. Women's Republican; Shenorock Shore. Home: 165 Brewster Rd Scarsdale NY 10583

JOHNSON, KATHERINE HOLTHAUS, health care marketing professional; b. Denver, Mar. 19, 1961; d. William Philip and Barbara Kristine (Nielsen) Holthaus; m. Robert Scott Johnson. B in Applied Math. Engring., U. Colo., 1983; postgrad., U. Denver, 1984-85, 87—. Acctg. intern Cooper, Haugen & Co., CPAs, Englewood, Colo., 1982-84; market analyst mktg. dept. Porter Meml. Hosp., Denver, 1985-88; account exec. Tallant LaPoint & Ptnrs., Inc., Englewood, 1988—. Judge, vol. 4-H Clubs, Met. Denver, 1979—; supt. Sunday sch. Ascension Luth. Ch., Littleton, Colo., 1985-87. Recipient 2 Advantage awards Adventist Health System, 1987. Mem. Soc. for Healthcare Planning and Mktg., Am. Hosp. Assn., Acad. for Health Svcs. Mktg., Am. Mktg. Assn., Alpha Chi Omega. Republican. Office: Tallant LaPointe & Ptnrs Inc 5200 DTC Pkwy #400 Englewood CO 80111

JOHNSON, KATHRYN BARRETT, controller, writer; b. Washington, May 6, 1941; d. O'Connor Barrett and Grace Wilson (Schultz) Woodward; m. Gary James Rowley, Mar. 1961 (div. Jan. 1969); children: Mark Christopher, Tammi Lynn and Terri Noelle (twins); m. Harold Robert Johnson, June 5, 1970. Student, U. Tex., Arlington, 1959-61. Traffic mgr. KNOK Radio, Ft. Worth, 1960-64, WBAP Radio, Ft. Worth, 1968-69; media dir. Aylin Advt. Agy., Dallas, 1969-72; mktg. dir. The Hill Cos., Dallas, 1972; media dir., contr. Crume & Assocs., Dallas, 1972-80; reporter, editor Charlevoix Country Press-Walloon Lake Sun, Boyne City, Mich., 1980-82; dir. adminstrn. Energy Mktg. Group, Petoskey, Mich., 1982-85; bookkeeper U.S.-U.S. English, Petoskey, 1985—; contr. Town & Country Cedar Homes, Petoskey, 1987—. Author murder dinners, 1988—; editor (newspaper) Experience Summer, 1987—. Treas. Recycle North, Petoskey, 1986—. With M.I. Corps, USAR, 1974-80. Mem. Am. Women in Radio & TV (pres. and v.p. Ft. Worth chpt. 1968-70, pres. and treas. Dallas chpt. 1971-73), Zonta (treas. Petoskey chpt. 1989, 90). Democrat. Methodist. Home: 08076 Ferry Rd East Jordan MI 49727 Office: Town & Country Cedar Homes US 131 S Petoskey MI 49770

JOHNSON, KATHY ANN, insurance agent; b. Portland, Oreg., Sept. 30, 1956; d. Edgar Scott and Bettymae (King) H.; m. Douglas Michael Johnson, Nov. 7, 1981; 1 child, Robert Douglas. BS, Oreg. Coll. Edn., 1978; MS, We. Oreg. State Coll., 1981. Cert. elem. tchr., Oreg. Tchr. Glendale (Oreg.) Pub. Schs., 1978-79, Salem (Oreg.) Pub. Schs., 1979-82; owner, agent State Farm Ins., Issaquah, Washington, 1983—. Mem. Toy and Gift Bank of Issaquah, 1984; active Salmon Days, Rotary Run, 1987-90. Named to Half Millionaire Club State Farm Ins., 1984, Outstanding Young Women of Am. award, 1984; recipient Legion of Honor award State Farm Ins., 1987-88; named an Honor Agt. Fire and Auto Ins., 1989. Mem. NAFE, Issaquah Women Profls. (chmn. 1984), Bus. Womens Inst., Issaquah C. of C. (Rotary (dir. club svc. 1989-90). Republican. Presbyterian. Office: State Farm Ins 240 NW Gilman Blvd Suite C Issaquah WA 98027

JOHNSON, LADY BIRD (MRS. LYNDON BAINES JOHNSON), wife of former President of U.S.; b. Karnack, Tex., Dec. 22, 1912; d. Thomas Jefferson Taylor; B.A., U. Tex., 1933, B.Journalism, 1934, D.Letters, 1964; L.L.D., Tex. Woman's U., 1964; D.Letters, Middlebury Coll., 1967; L.H.D., Williams Coll., 1967, U. Ala., 1975; H.H.D., Southwestern U., 1967; m. Lyndon Baines Johnson (36th Pres. U.S.), Nov. 17, 1934 (did Jan. 22, 1973); children: Lynda Bird Johnson Robb, Luci Baines. Mgr. husband's congl. office, Washington, 1941-42; owner, operator radio-TV sta. KTBC, Austin, Tex., 1942-63, cattle ranches, Tex., 1943—. Hon. chmn. Nat. Headstart Program, 1963-68, Town Lake Beautification Project. also cotton and timberlands, Ala. Mem. Advisory council Nat. Parks, Historic Sites, Bldgs. and Monuments; bd. regents U. Tex., 1971-77, mem. internat. conf. steering com., 1969; trustee Jackson Hole Preserve, Am. Conservation Assn., Nat. Geog. Soc.; founder Nat. Wild flower Research Ctr., Austin, 1982. Recipient Togetherness award Marge Champion, 1958; Humanitarian award B'nai B'rith, 1961; Businesswoman's award Bus. and Profl. Women's Club, 1961; Theta Sigma Phi citation, 1962; Disting. Achievement award Washington Heart Assn., 1962; Industry citation Am. Women in Radio and Television, 1963; Humanitarian citation Vols. of Am., 1963; Peabody award for White House TV visit, 1966; Eleanor Roosevelt Golden Candlestick award Women's Nat. Press Club; Damon Woods Meml. award Indsl. Designers Soc. Am., 1972; Conservation Service award Dept. Interior, 1974; Disting. award Am. Legion, 1975; Woman of Year award Ladies Home Jour., 1975; Medal of Freedom, 1977; Nat. Achievement award Am. Hort. Soc., 1984. Life mem. U. Tex. Ex-Students Assn. Episcopalian. Author: A White House Diary, 1970. Address: LBJ Libr 2313 Red River Austin TX 78705*

JOHNSON, LAURA ANN, computer/infosystems engineer; b. Shreveport, La., June 9, 1959; d. Willie and Willie Delores (Griffin) J. BS, La. Tech. U., 1980; MBA, SUNY, Buffalo, 1984. Eligibility worker II Caddo Office of Family Security, Shreveport, 1981-82; systems engr. Electronic Data Systems, Dallas, 1984—. County conv. del. Dem. Party of Collin County, Plano, Tex., 1988. Baptist. Home: 18790 Lloyd Dr Apt 1027 Dallas TX 75252

JOHNSON, LAVERNE ST. CLAIR, elementary teacher; b. Danville, Va., Dec. 27, 1929; d. Emanuel Linwood and Lula St. Clair (Yarbrough) White; m. Cornell A. Johnson, Apr. 10, 1955 (div. Apr. 1982); children: Cassandra St. Clair, LeBrahne Cornell. Student, Howard U., 1950-55, Allen U., 1955; BA, Queens Coll., 1977, MA, 1986. Cert. in reading edn., common br., N.Y. Asst. tchr. 1st Hebrew Day Nursery, Bklyn., 1967-75; tchr. United Youth Action Day Care, Bklyn., 1977-80, Charles R. Drew Day Care Ctr., Queens Village, N.Y., 1980-83, N.Y.C. Bd. Edn., Bklyn., 1983—. Composer childrens' music; author: (childrens' poems) Fall Time Fall Time, 1974. Mem. Com. to Eliminate Media Offensive to African People, St. Albans, N.Y., 1988—, Dem. Club, St. Albans, Bklyn. Philharmonic Chorus, St. Albans Congl. Ch. choir, Howard U. Choir, other choral groups. Mem. United Fedn. Tchrs. Howard U. Alumni Club (sec. L.I. chpt. 1970-79(, Lioness (v.p. Cambria Heights, N.Y. 1980-82, cert. of appreciation 1980-89).

JOHNSON, LESLIE JONES, electrical engineer; b. High Point, N.C., Jan. 1, 1958; d. Charles Jackson and Virginia (Hudson) Jones; m. Thomas Graves Johnson, Feb. 4, 1984; 1 child, Christopher James. BS in Philosophy, N.C. State U., Raleigh, 1979, BS in Math, 1980; MS in Elec. Engring., U. Calif., Irvine, 1984. Tech. Staff Rockwell Internat., Anaheim, Calif., 1980—. Author: Contbr. articles to profl. jours. Mem. Applied Dynamics Internat. Users Soc., Soc. of Computer Simulation, Digital Equipment Corp. Users Soc., Rockwell Softball Orgn. (treas. 1984—). Republican. Methodist.

JOHNSON, LILLIAN BEATRICE, sociologist, educator, counselor; b. Wilmington, N.C., Nov. 8, 1922; d. James Archie and Mary Gaston (Atkins) J. A.A., Peace Coll., 1940; B.R.E., Presbyterian Sch. Christian Edn., 1942; M.S., N.C. State U., 1965, Ph.D., 1972. Dir. Christian edn. First Presbyn. Ch., Pensacola, Fla., 1945-47, Greenwood, S.C., 1947-48, Durham, N.C., 1948-51; club dir. Army Spl. Services, No. Command, Japan, 1951-53; teenage dir. YWCA, Washington, 1953-56, assoc. exec. Honolulu, 1956-59, exec. dir. Tulsa, 1959-62; instr. N.C. State U., 1962-72; asst. prof. Greensboro Coll., 1972-75; mem. faculty sociology dept. Livingston U., 1975-89; pvt. practice family counselor, Fayetteville, N.C., 1989—. Ct. counselor, mediator Cumberland County Dispute Resolution Ctr. Mem. Am. Sociol. Assn., So. Sociol. Soc., Nat. Council Family Relations, N.C. Council on Family Relations. Home: 405-A Trade Wind Dr Fayetteville NC 28314 Office: 310 Green St Fayetteville NC 28301

JOHNSON, LINDA, librarian. BA in English, U. Ariz., 1971, MLS, 1974; MA in Edn. Adminstrn., Santa Clara U., 1988. Head govt. pub. dept. Santa Clara (Calif.) U., 1974-88, bibliographer psychology and edn. Orradre Libr., 1986-88; chief govt. documents Unit-Reference and User Edn. Div. Clark Libr. San Jose (Calif.) State U., 1984-88, chief Govt. Publs. Dept., 1988—; Reviewer govt. documents Govt. Publ. Rev. Reviewer govt. documents Govt. Publ. Rev. Co-chmn. Adv. Bd. South Bay Coop. Libr. Systems, 1988-89. Mem. ALA, Assn. Coll. and Research Libr. (sec. edn. and behavioral scis.), Libr. Adminstrn. and Mgmt. Assn., Calif. Acad. and Research Librs., Calif. Libr. Assn. (chmn. 1983, nominating com. 1988—), Am. Assn. Higher Edn., No. Calif. Assn. Law Librs., No. Calif. Bus. Librs., Govt. Documents Roundtable, Map and Geography Roundtable, We. Assn. Schs. and Colls. (accreditation team 1983, 84), Phi Beta Kappa (v.p. membership No. Calif. chpt. 1986-88), Phi Kappa Phi, Beta Phi Mu, Pi Lambda Theta. Home: 466 Boynton Ave #16C San Jose CA 95117

JOHNSON, LINDA ARLENE, oil distributor; b. Sparta, Wis., Mar. 6, 1946; d. Clarence Julius and Arlene Mae (Yahnke) Jessie; children: Darrick, Larissa. With Union Nat. Bank & Trust Co., Sparta, 1964-69, Hill, Christensen & Co., CPA's, Tomah, Wis., 1969-75; owner Johnson of Wis. Oil Co., Inc., Tomah, 1969—; with Larry's Express, Inc., Tomah, 1975-78; owner Johnson Rentals, 1979—, Johnson of Wis. Transport Co., Inc., Tomah, 1982—. Mem. St. Paul's Luth. Ch., Tomah. Mem. Petroleum Marketers Assn. Am., Nat. Assn. Convenience Stores, Nat. Fedn. Ind. Bus., Am. Trucking Assn., Wis. Assn. Convenience Stores, Petroleum Marketers Assn. Wis., Wis. Ind. Businessmen, Inc., Tomah Area C. of C. Home and Office: 612 Kilbourn Ave Tomah WI 54660

JOHNSON, LINDA DIANE, nurse, administrator; b. Forest Grove, Oreg., Feb. 11, 1947; d. Harold D. and Anna Alice (Wolf) J. BS in Nursing, U. Oreg., Portland, 1969; MS in Nursing, U. Tex., San Antonio, 1978; PhD, U. Pa., 1989. RN, Pa., Oreg., Del. Staff nurse in psychiatry VA Hosp., San Antonio, 1973-75, mental health nurse coord., 1975-78, instr. in nursing svc., 1978-79; assoc. chief nursing svc. for edn. trainee VA Med. Ctr., Little Rock, 1980; assoc. chief nursing svc. for edn. VA Med. Ctr., Coatesville, Pa., 1980-88, assoc. chief nursing svc. for ops., 1988-90; healthcare edn. specialist Dept. Vet. Affairs Office Acad. Affairs, Washington, 1990—; asst. dir. instrn. Practical Nursing (91C) Program U.S. Army Res. Forces Sch., Wilmington, Del., 1984-89, dep. dir. for adminstrn., 1989—; adv. com. Practical Nursing Program Ctr. for Arts and Tech., Coatesville, 1986-90. Capt. Nurse Corps, U.S. Army, 1969-73, maj. Res. Mem. Assn. Mil. Surgeons U.S., Nurses Orgn. VA, Res. Officers Assn., Del. and Am. Nurses Assn. Home: 332 Barclay St Coatesville PA 19320 also: 6820 Ericka Ave Alexandria VA 22310 Office: Dept Vet Affairs Office Acad Affairs Associated Nurses Professions Edn Program Svcs 810 Vermont Ave NW (143C3) Washington DC 20420

JOHNSON, LINDA JOYCE, sales executive; b. Lowell, Mass., Nov. 6, 1956; d. Emil and Esther Muriel (Ayer) Zabierek; m. James M. Johnson, Sept. 5, 1975 (div. Nov. 1979). Mfg. adminstr., M/A-Com., Inc., 1979, sales administr., 1979-81, sales specialist, 1981-84; regional sales mgr. Hyletronics, Inc., Littleton, Mass., 1984; regional sales mgr. Frequency Sources, Chelmsford, Mass., 1984-86; regional sales mgr. Sanders Assocs., Manchester, N.H., 1986-88; v.p., co-owner Computer Decisions, Inc., Derry, N.H., 1988—. Mem. Nat. Contract Mgmt. Assn., Nat. Assn. Female Execs., Women in Electronics, Women In Def., Computer Decisions, Inc. (bd. dirs.), Assn. Old Crows. Avocations: golf, piano, reading. Home: 5 Walnut Hill Rd Derry NH 03038 Office: Computer Decisions Inc PO Box 368 E Derry NH 03041

JOHNSON, LINDA LIGON, management executive; b. Charleston, S.C., Mar. 22, 1949; d. Elisha James and Lonie Opal (Steele) Ligon; m. William Sharpe Johnson, Oct. 1969 (div. Sept. 1973); children: Darby, Kelly. Student, U. S.C., 1971-77, Richland Tech., Columbia, S.C., 1978-79. Bldg. mgr. Richland Med. Pk., Columbia, S.C., 1973-76; adminstr. S.C. State Housing Authority, Columbia, 1980-83; property mgr. Westminster Co., Columbia, 1983—; dist. mgr. Westminster Co., Raleigh, N.C., 1984-90; v.p. property mgmt. Darby Devel. Co., Charleston, S.C., 1990—. Mem. Raleigh Bd. Realtors, 1988; bd. dirs. Wake County Family Homes. Mem. Nat. Inst. Real Estate Mgmt., Raleigh Inst. Real Estate Mgmt., Raleigh Area Office Bus. Assn. Republican. Methodist.

JOHNSON, LINDA MARIE, federal government manager; b. Garden City, Mich., Mar. 25, 1940; d. Earl Marion and Elizabeth Johanna (Anderson) J. BA, Dickinson Coll., 1961. Claims rep. Social Security Adminstrn., Dearborn, Mich., 1961-66; field rep. Social Security Adminstrn., Defiance, Ohio, 1966-69; ops. supr. Social Security Adminstrn., Lima, Ohio, 1969-71; sr. staff asst. Social Security Adminstrn., Cleve., 1971-72; staff devel. assoc. Social Security Adminstrn., Dallas, Balt., 1972-73; planning specialist Social Security Adminstrn., Dallas, 1973-76, ombudsman, 1976-77; dist. mgr. Social Security Adminstrn., Pasadena, Tex., 1977—. Chmn. Combined Fed. Campaign, Houston, 1982-83, United Way of Tex. Gulf Coast, Houston, 1983-84. Named Woman of Yr. Tex. Fedn. Bus. and Profl. Women, 1987; recipient Community Svc. award Social Security Mgmt. Assn., 1987, Chairman's award Houston Fed. Exec. Bd., 1985. Mem. Bus. and Profl. Women (pres. 1975-76, dist. dir. 1977, nat. found. chmn. 1987-89, state found. chmn. 1978-80, 85-86), Social Security Mgmt. Assn. (exec. officer 1988-89, v.p. 1982-84), Social Security Regional Pub. Info. Com (chmn. 1985-89), Houston Fed. Exec. Bd. (chmn. 1985-86). Democrat. Lutheran. Office: Social Security Adminstrn 1800 Dabney Dr Pasadena TX 77502

JOHNSON, LIZABETH LETTIE, insurance agent; b. Dallas, Aug. 24, 1957; d. Winfred Herschel Johnson and Mary Francis (Flowers) Goff; children: Brandi, Elissa. Student, Georgetown (Ky.) Coll., 1975-76, U. Ky., 1976-78. Staff analyst Met. Ins. Co., Lexington, 1979-81, ins. agt., 1981-82; sr. account agt. Allstate Ins. Co., Lexington, 1982—. Vol. Big Bros./Big Sisters, 1979-84, Life Adventure Camp, 1989—; hotline counselor Lexington Rape Crisis Ctr., 1984—, bd. dirs., 1988—; vol. Christians in Community Service, 1986—; mem. Ky. Spl. Needs Adoption Support Group, 1985—. Fellow Life Underwriting Tng. Council; mem. NAACP, Nat. Assn. Life Underwriters. Democrat. Baptist. Office: Allstate Ins Co 694 New Circle Rd NE Room 3 Lexington KY 40505

JOHNSON, LORI ANNE, banker; b. Garden City Park, N.Y., Oct. 10, 1963; d. Robert Frederick and Kathleen Helen (Smith) J. BS, St. Johns U., Jamaica, N.Y., 1986; MBA, St. Johns U., 1988. Grad. asst. St. John's U., Jamaica, N.Y.; systems analyst Chase Manhattan Bank, N.Y.C. Mem. NAFE, St. John's U. Alumni Assn., St. John's U. Alumnae Assn. Home: 128 Atlantic Ave Garden City Park NY 11040

JOHNSON, LUAN, educational program developer, trainer, researcher; b. Provo, Utah, Apr. 27, 1956; d. Jack R. and Colleen (Kesler) J. BA, Brigham Young U., 1981, MA, 1984. Dir. Teaching Resource Ctr., Provo, 1980-84; teaching asst. communications dept. Brigham Young U., Provo, 1982-83; counselor Master Acad., Salt Lake City, 1985; ednl. designer, program mgr. City of Sunnyvale, 1986—; free-lance editor, 1984-85; tutor, 1984-85. Pres. Youth Assn. Retarded Children, Brigham City, 1976-77. Mem. Phi Kappa Phi. Republican. Mormon. Avocation: collecting and flying kites. Home: 205 B Red Oak Dr W Sunnyvale CA 94086 Office: Dept Pub Safety 700 All American Way Sunnyvale CA 94086

JOHNSON, LYNNE ARDELL, lawyer; b. Spokane, Wash., Oct. 25, 1951; d. Gaylar Winton and Donna Lucille (Tolford) J. AB in Econs. with departmental honors and distinction, Vassar Coll., 1973; JD, Yale U., 1976. Bar: Ga. 1977, N.Y. 1981. Asst. to gen. counsel Systems and Technics, S.A., Gland, Switzerland, 1976-77; assoc. Powell, Goldstein, Frazer & Murphy, Atlanta, 1977-79, Fried, Frank, Harris, Shriver & Jacobson, N.Y.C., 1979—; v.p., bd. dirs. 155 W. 15th St. Corp., N.Y.C., 1984—. Contbg. author: Exit Age: Reconsidering Compulsory Education for Adolescents: Studies in Law, Education and Social Science, 1981. Hon. grad. fellow for legal studies, 1973-74. Mem. ABA, Am. Soc. Internat. Law, Internat. Bar Assn., Inter-Am. Bar Assn., Assn. Immigration and Nationality Lawyers, N.Y. County Lawyers' Assn., State Bar Ga., Soc. Univ. Patent Adminstrs., Lotus Club. Office: One New York Pla New York NY 10004

JOHNSON, MARCELITE ELAINE, computer management executive, consultant; b. Savannah, Ga., Mar. 19, 1949; d. Leon and Jane (Mohr) Dingle; m. Melvin Norman Johnson, Dec. 22, 1968; children—De Andra Chanet, Monet Nichelle, Melvin Roschaun. B.A. in Math., U. Colo.-Boulder, 1972; M.S. in Edn., Ind. U.-Bloomington, 1979; postgrad. U. So. Calif., Stuttgart, Fed. Republic Germany, 1984-85. Programmer analyst Hewlitt-Packard, Colorado Springs, 1979-81; sr. systems analyst Penrose Hosp., Colorado Springs, 1982-83; systems mgr. Penrose Cancer Hosp., Colorado Springs, 1981-82; systems mgr. Civilian Personnel Office U.S. Army, Stuttgart, 1983-85; br. support mgr. Wang Deutschland GmbH Fed. Systems Dist., Stuttgart, 1985-87; tng. mgr. European bus. svcs. Wang EAME Hdqrs., Brussels, 1987—; lectr. U. Colo., 1980, City Colls. Chgo., Stuttgart, 1983-85. Mem. Nat. Assn. Female Execs., Alpha Kappa Alpha. Episcopalian. Avocations: tennis; bridge. Office: Wang EAME, Rue Col Bourgstraat III, B-1140 Brussels Belgium

JOHNSON, MARGARET HELEN, welding executive; b. Chgo., June 3, 1933; d. Harold W. and Clara J. (Pape) Glavin; m. Odean Jack Johnson, Nov. 18, 1950; children: Karen Ann, Dean Harold. Student Moody Bible Inst., 1976-78. V.p., sec. Sunshine Welding, Inc., Chgo., 1956—, also dir.; trustee SWCEPS, Chgo., 1963—. Author: Living Faith, 1973, 80, Lord's Ladder of Love, 1976, God's Rainbow, 1982; contbr. articles to religion mags. Life mem. Rep. Presdl. Task Force, 1982—, trustee, 1986-88; charter founder Ronald Reagan Rep. Ctr., 1987; mem. Lake View Neighborhood Group, Chgo., Small Group Ch. Community; active Mary, Seat of Wisdom Cath. Women's Club, 1970—, renew facilitator 1986-88, co-chairperson 1986-88; Sunday sch. tchr., 1985. Mem. ASCAP, Fedn. Ind. Small Bus., Internat. Platform Assn., Women's Aglow Fellowship Internat. Home: 20 Hawley Ct Grayslake IL 60030

JOHNSON, MARGARET HILL, educational administrator; b. Dundee, Scotland, June 26, 1923; d. John Barnet and Isabella Rae (Watson) Hill; came to U.S., 1946, naturalized, 1957; student Inverness (Scotland) Royal Acad., 1940, Edinburgh (Scotland) Royal Coll. Art, 1940-43; doctoral candidate U. Mass., Amherst, 1980—; children—Ann Hill Doughty, James Appleton Doughty (dec.), Joanna Elizabeth Johnson. Latin and remedial English tutor Harvey Sch., N.Y.C., 1947-52; tchr. athletics Pingree Sch. for Girls, Hamilton, Mass., 1959-61; tchr. Shore Country Day Sch., Beverly, Mass., 1952-59; asso. dir. Theodore S. Jones & Co., design mgmt. cons., Milton, Mass., 1961-72; dir. career planning and placement Mass. Coll. Art, 1972—, coordinator human services; design cons. Theodore S. Jones & Co.; speaker Lesley Coll., 1977, Cambridge (Mass.) Community Schs., 1977—, MIT, Harvard U., R.I. Sch. Design, Hofstra U. Served with Brit. Women's Royal Naval Service, 1943-46. Mem. Coll. Placement Council, Mass. Assn. Women Deans and Counselors, Nat. Assn. Women Deans, Adminstrs. and Counselors, Am. Assn. Higher Edn., Coll. Art Assn. Am., Eastern Coll. Placement Officers, Arts Dirs. Club Boston, Graphic Artists Guild. Author: (with others) Your Future in Art and Design, 1977. Home: Box 75 Off Summer St Marshfield MA 02051 Office: 621 Huntington Ave Boston MA 02115

JOHNSON, MARGARET KATHLEEN, educator; b. Baylor County, Tex., Oct. 30, 1920; d. George W. and Julia Rivers (Turner) Higgins; m. Herman Clyde Johnson, Jr., July 27, 1949 (dec.); 1 child, Carolyn Kay. B.S., Hardin-Simmons U., 1940; M.Bus. Edn., North Tex. State U., 1957, Ed.D., 1962. Clk. Farmers Nat. Bank, Seymour, Tex., 1940-41; adminstrv. sec. U.S. Navy, Corpus Christi, Tex., 1941-46; adminstrv. asst. Hdqrs. 8th Army, Yokohama, Japan, 1946-49; instr. Coll. Bus. Adminstrn., U. Ark., 1957-60; teaching fellow Sch. Bus. Adminstrn., North Tex. State U., 1960-62, instr., 1962-63; asst. prof. bus., tchr. edn. and secondary edn. Tchrs. Coll., U. Nebr., Lincoln, 1963-65; asso. prof. Tchrs. Coll., U. Nebr., 1966-70, prof., 1970—; guest lectr. U. N.Mex., 1967, Curriculum Devel. in Bus. Edn., N.S. Dept. Edn., 1969, North Tex. State U., 1970, East Tex. State U., 1972; in Policies Commn. for Bus. and Econ. Edn., 1979-83. Author: Standardized Production Typewriting Tests series, 1964-65, National Structure for Research in Vocational Education, 1966; co-author: Introduction to Word Processing, 1980, 2d edit., 1985, Introduction to Business Communication, 1981, 2d edit., 1988; editor: Nat. Bus. Edn. Assn. Yearbook, 1980. Recipient United Bus. Edn. Assn. award as outstanding grad. student in bus. edn. North Tex. State U., 1957, award for outstanding service Nebr. Future Bus. Leaders Am., 1968; Mountain-Plains Bus. Edn. Leadership award, 1977; merit award Nebr. Bus. Assn., 1979. Mem. Nat. Bus. Edn. Assn. (exec. bd. 1975, 76-78), Mountain-Plains Bus. Edn. Assn. (exec. sec. 1970-73, pres. 1975), Nebr. Bus. Edn. Assn. (pres. 1966-67), Nebr. Council on Occupational Tchr. Edn., Delta Pi Epsilon. Office: U Nebr 529 Nebraska Hall Lincoln NE 68588

JOHNSON, MARIE LOUISE, college dean; b. Chgo., June 28, 1933; d. Frederick Douglas and Pearl Louise (Bailey) J. BA, U. Ill., 1954, MS, 1958; PhD, Ill. Inst. Tech., 1971. Chief psychometrist student counseling service U. Ill. Navy Pier, Chgo., 1956-61, U. Ill. Chgo. Circle Campus, 1965-71; assoc. dean of students U. Ill., Chgo., 1971—; with Chgo. Bd. Edn., 1971-89; exec. dir. student acad. svcs. The Fielding Inst., Santa Barbara, Calif., 1989—; mem. adv. com. long-term care study sect. Nat. Ctr. Health Services Research HEW, Washington, 1976-77, cons., 1977-81; cons. women's identities study Chgo. State U., 1980-81; mem. health services devel. grants Dept. Health and Human Resources, Washington, 1977-81; charter mem. adv. bd. Bur. Child Study Chgo. Bd. Edn., 1981—. Mem. adv. bd. model cities Altgeld Quality of Life Project, Chgo., 1976-77. Mem. Am. Assn. Counseling and Devel., Am. Coll. Personnel Assn., Nat. Assn. Black Psychologists, Nat. Assn. Women Deans, Adminstrs. and Counselors, U. Ill. Black Alumni Assn. (pres. 1985—), Alpha Lambda Delta, Psi Chi, Alpha Kappa Alpha, Alpha Gamma Pi. Mem. United Ch. of Christ. Home: 409 Rosario Dr Santa Barbara CA 93110 Office: The Fielding Inst 2112 Santa Barbara St Santa Barbara CA 93103

JOHNSON, MARILYN ANN, real estate appraiser; b. Lansing, Sept. 20, 1946; d. Ralph Eugene and Helen Beatrice (Boor) Moulton; m. Mark Glenn, Sept. 26, 1945; children: Randy, Paul. BA magna cum laude, Vanderbilt U., 1970. Salesperson Webster Realty, Mentor, Ohio, 1976-79; comml. appraiser Ostendorf Morris Co., Cleve., 1979-86; ptnr. No. Ohio Appraisals, Willoughby, 1986-90; pres. Johnson & Sherman, Inc., Willoughby, 1990—; adj. instr. Lakeland Community Coll., Mentor, 1980; co-instr. Bldg. Owners and Mgrs. Assn., Cleve., 1985. Mem. admin. coun. Hope Ridge United Meth. Ch., Mentor, 1990—. Mem. Am. Inst. Real Estate Appraisers (Cert. MAI), Soc. Real Estate Appraisers (Cert. SRPA, Young Adv. Coun. 1984-85, discussion leader 1986), Nat. Assn. Realtors, Willoughby C. of C., Comml. Real Estate Women Cleve. Inc., Phi Beta Kappa. Office: Johnson & Sherman Inc 38120 W Spaulding St Willoughby OH 44094

JOHNSON, MARILYN JUNE, stockbroker, financial planner; b. Milw., July 17, 1934; d. Bjarne Leonard and Stella Virginia (Gronert) J.; children: James Marc Withers, Chris Withers, Laura Lyn Withers. BS magna cum laude, U. Md., 1975; MA, George Washington U., 1978. Teaching fellow George Washington U., Washington, 1975-77; adminstrv. asst. Harris, Kerr, Foster, Irvine, Calif., 1978-79; pension cons. Prudential Ins. Co., L.A., 1979-85; stockbroker, cert. fin. planner Prudential-Bache Securities, Thousand Oaks, Calif., 1985—. Mem. AAUW, Omicron Delta Epsilon, Alpha Sigma Lambda, Phi Kappa Phi. Office: Prudential Bache Securities 125 Auburn Ct Thousand Oaks CA 91362

JOHNSON, MARILYN RAE, writer, producer; b. La Crosse, Wis., June 27, 1958; d. Melvin Leonard and Dorothy (Rieder) J. BA in English magna cum laude, Viterbo Coll., 1979; MS in Ednl. Media, U. Wis., LaCrosse, 1988. News coord. Viterbo Coll., La Crosse, 1979-80; freelance writer La Crosse, 1980-81, 82-83; scriptwriter Trane Co., La Crosse, 1981-82, 84-88; communications specialist Mayo Clinic, Rochester, Wis., 1983; writer, producer AVS, Inc., La Crosse, 1989—. Elder First Presbyn. Ch., La Crosse, 1986—. Mem. Women in Communications, Inc. (LaCrosse chpt. membership com. 1988-90, pres. 1990-91), Internat. TV Assn., Urbandale Pk. Condominium Assn. (pres. 1986—, reas.). Office: AVS Inc 2109 Ward Ave La Crosse WI 54601

JOHNSON, MARION JOYCE FRYE, educator; b. Traverse City, Mich., Aug. 18, 1932; d. Howard Clarence and Ferne Marion (Wilson) Frye; m. Harold Cumings Johnson; children: Robin Ann, Gary Cumings, Gregory Harold. BA, Alma Coll., 1954. Cert. tchr., Ohio. Tchr. high sch. Chelsea Area Schs., Chelsea, Mich., 1954-56, Wayne Meml. High Sch., Wayne, Mich., 1956-57, Anacostia High Sch., Washington, 1957-58; substitute tchr. USDESEA Schs., Sembach, Fed. Republic of Germany, 1973-75; high sch. tchr. Fairborn High Sch., Fairborn, Ohio, 1975—; regional judge (writing) Nat. Coun. Tchrs. of English, Fairborn, 1987—; clinician creative writing Ohio Coun. Tchrs. of English and Lang. Arts, Columbus, Ohio, 1987; organizer elem. sch. libr., Wiesbaden Air Base, Fed. Republic of Germany, 1972. Editor Chapel Newsletter, McGuire Air Force Base, 1968, OWC Newsletter, Sembach Air Force Base, 1974. Mem. 1st Presbyn. Ch., Fairborn, 1985—, mem. choir, 1985—. Mem. AAUW (bd. dirs. 1989-90), Rotary-Anns (pres. Fairborn chpt. 1986-87). Republican. Home: 328 Bowman Dr Fairborn OH 45324 Office: Fairborn High Sch 900 E Dayton Yell Springs Fairborn OH 45324

JOHNSON, MARLENE, lieutenant governor; b. Braham, Minn., Jan. 11, 1946; d. Beauford and Helen (Nelson) J.; m. Peter Frankel. BA, Macalester Coll., 1968. Founder, pres. Split Infinitive, Inc., St. Paul, 1970-82; pres., bd. dirs. Face to Face Health and Counseling Clinic, 1977-78; with Working Opportunities for Women, 1977-82; lt. gov. State of Minn., St. Paul, 1983—; founder, past chmn. Nat. Leadership Conf. Women Execs. in State Govt.; mem. exec. com., midwestern chair Nat. Conf. Lt. Govs. Chmn. Minn. Women's Polit. Caucus, 1973-76, Dem.-Farmer-Labor Small Bus. Task Force, 1978, Child Care Task Force, 1987, Nat. Conf. of Lt. Govs., 1987; dir. membership sect. Nat. Women's Polit. Caucus, 1975-77; vice chmn. Minn. Del. to White House Conf. on Small Bus., 1980; co-founder Minn. Women's Campaign Fund, 1982; founder, past chmn., Nat. Leadership Conf. Women Execs. in State Govt.; bd. dirs. Nat. Child Care Action Campaign; chair Children's 2000 Commn. Recipient Outstanding Achievement award, St. Paul YWCA, 1980, Disting. Svc. award St. Paul Jaycees, 1980, Disting. Citizen citation, Macalester Coll., 1982, Disting. Contributions to Families award Minn. Council on Family Relations, 1986, Minn. Sportfishing Congress award, 1986, Children's Champion award Children's Def. Fund, 1989, Jane Preston award Minn. State Coun. on Vocat. Tec. Edn., 1989; named dir. World Press Inst., Ten Putstanding Young Minnesotans Minn. Jaycees, 1980; Swedish Bicentennial Commn. grantee, 1987. Mem. Nat. Assn. Women Bus. Owners (past pres.). Office: Office of Lt Gov Room 121 State Capitol Aurora Ave Saint Paul MN 55155

JOHNSON, MARTHA JO (MARTY JOHNSON), public relations professional, publisher; b. Salisbury, N.C., June 3, 1947; d. Joseph Wayne and Martha (Deibert) J.; m. Philip Duke Stukey, Dec. 20, 1969 (div. 1976); 1 child, Peter Duke; m. John F. McGinn, July 4, 1980 (div. 1986). AA, St. Petersburg Jr. Coll., 1968; BS in Journalism, U. Fla., 1970. Dir. advt. agy., 1980-84; dir. corp. communications Nat. Mall Monitor, Clearwater, Fla., 1984-86; pub. rels. agy. dir. Indian Rocks Beach, Fla.; pres. M. Johnson & Assocs., Advt. and Pub. Rels., 1986—; founder, pub. Celebrate Life! mag., 1988—; chief exec. officer Unimedia Corp., 1989—. Dir. communications Internat. New Thought Alliance, Fla. West Coast Dist., 1987—; bd. dirs. Pinellas Habitat for Humanity, St. Petersburg, 1984-85. Recipient Addy award Advt. Fedn., 1986. Mem. Bay Area Profl. Writers Guild. Office: PO Box 247 Indian Rocks Beach FL 34635

JOHNSON, MARY ALICE, magazine editor; b. Rochester, Ind., Apr. 16, 1942; d. Nolan Lee and Alice Lavida (Ruede) Lewis; m. Manford Warren Johnson, May 28, 1960; children: Nola (dec.), John Jay, June Jeannette Johnson Sorber. Grad. high sch., Hillsboro, Oreg., 1960. Owner, baker, decorator Mary's Custom Cakes and Cake Parts, St. Helens, Oreg., 1980-87; founder, mng. editor Sugar Art Sharing Confectionary Ideas mag., 1986—; chmn. Sugar Art Ltd. Partnership, McMinnville, Oreg., 1986—, Sugar Art Party Plan, McMinnville, 1987—; creator products for hobbyist and handicapped decorators, 1969—; tchr. cake decorating, candy and gingerbread houses, 1981—; cons., presenter cake decorating and sugar art demonstrations, various youth clubs and area high schs. Leader, Country Kids and Friends 4-H, St. Helens, 1979-85; organizer rural fire dept., Rainier, Oreg.; Sunday sch. tchr. Luth. Ch., 1956-74, officer women's groups, 1960-77; sec. Tualitan Vallye Rabbit Breeders Assn., 1964-67, fair dinner booth chmn., 1965-66; ballot clk. Columbia County Election Bd., 1972-80; decorated cake supt. Columbia County Fair, 1983-85; decorations chmn. Christian Women's Club, McMinnville, 1989—; founder youth hobby club Pettis Fours Club, 1989. Winner awards for entries in numerous county and state fairs, cake shows. Mem. NAFE, Women Entrepreneurs Oreg., Internat. Cake Exploration Soc. Republican. Lutheran. Office: Sugar Art Ltd Partnership 300 E 3d St McMinnville OR 97128

JOHNSON, MARY ANN, pension fund consultant; b. Butte, Mont., Mar. 6, 1945; d. Kenneth Allen and Hazel Mary Ann (Walker) Lehner; m. Robert E. Johnson, Apr. 19, 1969. Student, NYU, 1968-69; BA, U. Redlands, 1967. Rsch. analyst Laird Inc., N.Y.C., 1968-70; adminstrv. asst. TeleSession Co., N.Y.C., 1970; assoc. Loeb, Rhoades and Co., N.Y.C., 1971-76; adminstrv. asst. Mgmt. Asset Corp., Westport, Conn., 1977-79; prin. Rogers, Casey and Barksdale, Inc., Stamford, Conn., 1979-87, Berg Fiduciary Cons., Port Chester, N.Y., 1988; pres. Tremont Ptnrs., Inc., New Canaan, Conn., 1989—; speaker in field. Office: Tremont Ptnrs Inc 39 Pine St New Canaan CT 06840

JOHNSON, MARY ANN, human resources professional; b. Elizabethtown, N.C., June 24, 1950; d. Donnie and Adell (Hair) J.; married, 1979 (div. 1985). Student, Bladen Tech. Coll.; cert. in computer tng., N.C. Dept. Human Resources, 1987; student, Nat. Edn. Corp., Scranton, Pa. Notary pub., N.C. Clk. teller Carolina Power & Light Co., Elizabethtown, 1971-72; ctr. dir. Four County Community Svcs., Inc., Elizabethtown, 1972-87; program cons. N.C. Dept. Human Resources, Raleigh, 1987—, lead trainer, 1989—; trainer N.C. Dept. Social Svcs. staff on pub. assistance certification. Recruiter Rep. Minority Coun. Eligibility Info. Svcs. State Dept. DHR, manual devel. coord., Raleigh and Elizabethtown., 1989—. Mem. NAFE, Nat. Bus. Women Assn. Home: 2801 Fenham Ct Raleigh NC 27604 Office: NC Dept Human Resources Anderson Hall 695 Palmer Dr Raleigh NC 27603

JOHNSON, MARY ELIZABETH, retired college educator; b. Powhatan Pt., Ohio, Mar. 10, 1905; d. John McFadden and Nancy Ramsay (Shannon) J. BA, Muskingum Coll., New Concord, Ohio, 1926; MA, U. Mich., 1933; postgrad., Northwestern U., 1956, 60, Ohio State U., 1946, 68. Cert. in edn., speech correction, Ohio, 1960. Tchr. Moundsville (W.Va.) High Sch., 1926-37, dean of girls, 1935-37; chmn. English dept. Martins Ferry (Ohio) High Sch., 1937-44, instr. speech, 1944-48; asst. prof. Muskingum Coll., 1948-52, assoc. prof. speech, 1952-72, emeritus assoc. prof., 1972—; chmn. drama and poetry reading conf. Muskingum Coll., 1946-68, communications area, 1950-53, acting chmn. dept. speech, 1965-66, adviser Nat. Collegiate Players, 1957-65; author Ohio dist. state scholarship tests in English for secondary schs., 1941, 43, 46. V.p. Women's Forum, New Concord, 1966-67; mem. First Community Village Coun., Columbus, Ohio, 1984, 85; chmn. Children's Hosp. Twig #15, Columbus, 1987, 88. Mem. AAUW, Am. Assn. Ret. Persons, Am. Speech and Hearing Assn., Ohio Speech and Hearing Assn., Comparative Edn. Soc. (seminar and field study in Europe 1967), Ohio Ret. Tchrs. Assn., Heritage Club, Parchment Club (pres. New Concord chpt. 1968, 78), Delta Kappa Gamma Internat. (pres. Psi, Alpha Delta State 1941-43, pres. Alpha Psi chpt. 1951, state recording sec. 1965-67). Democrat. Presbyterian.

JOHNSON, MARY LYNN, chemistry educator, consultant; b. Pampa, Tex., Mar. 12, 1938; d. E. Ray and L. Hortense (Allison) Miller; m. James Jefferson Johnson, Jr., Aug. 17, 1957; children: Melinda Ann, James Jefferson III. Student, West Tex. State U., 1955-57; BS in Scis., U. Tex.-El Paso, 1958; MS, N.Mex. State U., 1961; PhD, Pa. State U., 1970. Air pollution chemist El Paso City-County Health Dept., Tex., 1959-60, 61-63, Tex. State Health Dept., El Paso, 1963-64; air pollution spl. fellow USPHS, HEW, University Park, N.Mex., 1960-61, University Park, Pa., 1964-68; asst. prof. chemistry U. Tex.-Arlington, 1968-75; chemistry instr. Hockaday Sch., Dallas, 1975-86, Brookhaven Coll., Dallas, 1979-87, Highland Park Ind. Sch. Dist., 1986—; indsl. cons. combustion and air pollution problems, 1965-75. Contbr. articles to profl. jours. Fellow Am. Inst. Chemists, mem. People to People Citizen Ambassadors. Mem. Am. Chem. Soc., Internat. Union Pure and Applied Chemistry, Combustion Inst. Democrat. Congregationalist. Avocations: reading; antiques; piano. Home: 3004 Croydon Denton TX 76201 Office: Highland Park High Sch 4220 Emerson Dallas TX 75205

JOHNSON, MARY MURPHY, social services director; b. N.Y.C., Mar. 5, 1940; d. Richard and Nora (Greene) Murphy; m. Noel James Johnson, Oct. 8, 1961; children: Valerie Johnson Brogan, Donna Homan, Noreen Marie, Richard. BA in English, History and Sociology magna cum laude, Jacksonville State U., 1983, MA in History, 1984, B in Social Work magna cum laude, 1987. Cert. gerontology specialist. Asst. acticities dir. Jacksonville (Ala.) Nursing Home, 1985-86; social services dir. Beckwood Manor, Anniston, Ala., 1987—; Cons. in field. Editor: Vladivostak Diary, 1987. Mem. Ala. Archaeol. Soc., Coosa Valley Archaeol. Soc. (sec. 1982-87), Soc. Ala. Archivists, Human Services Council, Phi Eta Sigma, Phi Alpha Theta, Sigma Tau Delta, Omicron Delta Kappa. Russian Orthodox. Clubs: Non Commd. Officers Ladies Aux. (pres. 1970-71), Non Commd. Officers Wives (Germany) (pres. 1965-66).

JOHNSON, MARY SUSAN, transportation company professional; b. Bloomingdale, Ind., Nov. 19, 1937; d. William Blaine Shade and Goldina VandaVeer (Newlin) Brown; children: Roger, Tisa, Julia, Angela, Robert, William. Grad. high sch., Rockville, Ind. Road driver Roadway Express, Chgo. Heights, Ill., 1977—. Mem. Am. Motorcycle Assn., Am. Bikers Aim Toward Edn., Am. Radio Relay League, Am. Radio Emergency Svc. (Lake County), Porter County Amateur Radio Club, Internat. Platform Assn. Home and Office: PO Box 316 Griffith IN 46319

JOHNSON, MARY TEEL, pianist, educator; b. Warsaw, Ind., Sept. 28, 1921; d. William Rollin and Leona Gladys (Haines) Teel; m. Delman Howard Johnson, June 1, 1946; 1 child, Spencer Teel. BA in Piano and Music Edn., Wash. State U., 1943; M in Piano, L.A. Conservatory, 1951-52; studies with Madame Rosina Lhevinne, L.A., 1951-52. Jr. high music and Am. history tchr. Tacoma (Wash.) Pub. Sch. System, 1943-44; pvt. piano tchr. Tacoma, 1944-50, San Gabriel, Arcadia, Calif., 1950-63, Mpls., 1963-84; musician, writer Monterey, Calif., 1984—; Am. history vol. Monterey Peninsula Unified Sch. Dist., 1985-88; speaker Minn. Music Tchrs. Assn., Mpls, 1986, Steinway & Sons, N.Y.C., 1987, Calif. Music Tchrs. Assn., Monterey, 1987, 88, AZ Music Tchrs. Assn., Phoenix, 1990. Author: Keys to Successful Piano Lessons, 1986. Solicitor, presenter commemorative prints of Statue of Liberty and Signing of Constitution to all pvt. and pub. schs. on Monterey Peninsula, 1987. Recipient State and Nat. Am. Heritage award DAR, 1986, Best Chpt. Program award, DAR, 1987, Resolution of Appreciation Bd. Edn. Monterey Peninsula Unified Sch. Dist., 1986. Mem. DAR, Monterey County Symphony Guild (officer 1984—). Republican. Home: 13 Deer Forest Dr Monterey CA 93940

JOHNSON, MARY VERONICA, nurse, private investigator; b. Syracuse, N.Y., Dec. 27, 1945; d. Zachariah Irving and Beulah Therese (Hill) Hotaling; m. Anthony Alan Fugo, July 4, 1964 (div. 1971); m. Wayne Raymond Johnson, July 11, 1974 (div. 1987); children: William John, David Jeffrey. Lic. Practical Nurse, Sheridan Vocat. Coll., Hollywood, Fla., 1972. Staff nurse Hollywood Meml. Hosp., 1972-74; office nursing supr. Drs. Johnson and Cofran, Hollywood, 1974-86; nursing supr. Hollywood Diagnostics Ctr., 1986-89; prin. Guardian Detective Agy., Hollywood, 1987-88; svc. coord. hosp. linen div. Am. Svc. Corp. Am.; staff nurse Hospice House, Hollywood, 1988—. Pub. Luther Meml. Luth. Ch. newsletter, Hollywood, 1983-87. Chmn. adv. bd. McArthur High Sch., Hollywood, 1981, 82, 85, supr. vols., 1984-86, v.p. band boosters, 1982; local capt. Pembroke Pines (Fla.) Citizen's Crime Watch, 1984-88; mem. crew "Day Tripper" Cruises Inc., Pompano Beach, Fla., 1987-88; dir. youth group Luther Meml. Luth. Ch., 1976-79, dir. activities, 1980-82; bd. dirs. Greater Hollywood YMCA, 1987—. Recipient Outstanding Service award McArthur High Sch., 1985, 86. Mem. NAFE, Older Women's League, Am. Cancer Soc., United Singles of Am. Office: Hollywood Diagnostics Ctr 4224 Hollywood Blvd Hollywood FL 33021

JOHNSON, MARYANN ELAINE, educational administrator; b. Franklin Twp., Pa., Nov. 1, 1943; d. Mary I. Sollick; B.S. in Elementary Edn., Mansfield State Coll., Pa., 1964; M.S. in Elementary Edn., U. Alaska, College 1973; Ed.D., Wash. State U., Pullman, 1981; married. Tchr. Nayatt Sch., Barrington, R.I., 1964-66, North Sch., North Chicago, Ill., 1966-67, Kodiak (Alaska) On-Base Sch., 1967-71; reading coordinator Eastmont Sch. Dist., East Wenatchee, Wash., 1974-77, now asst. supt. Sec. Parent Advisory Com., 1974-76. Mem. Assn. Supervision and Curriculum Devel., Wash. State Assn. Supervision and Curriculum Devel. (bd. dirs. 1986-89, pres. elect 1989-90, Educator of Yr. 1981), NEA, Wash. Assn. Sch. Adminstrs. (bd. dirs., chmn. curriculum and instrn. Job-Alike, profl. devel. com., Project Leadership, pres. elect 1986-87, pres. 1987-88, leadership award, 1986, Exec. Educator 100 1988, pres. 1987-88, chmn. WASA 21st century scholarship com. 1988-89), Am. Assn. Sch. Adminstrs. (resolutions com. 1988-89, com. for advancement of sch. adminstrs. 1989-92), Delta Kappa Gamma (pres. 1982-84), Phi Delta Kappa, Phi Kappa Phi. Named Eastmont Tchr. of the Yr., 1973-74. Office: 460 N E 9th St East Wenatchee WA 98802

JOHNSON, MARYANNA MORSE, small business owner; b. Oxford, Miss., Dec. 21, 1936; d. Hugh McDonald and Anna Sullivan (Virden) Morse; children: Julianna, John, Cymthia, Mary. Student, Miss. U. for Women, 1957; BS in Nursing (cum laude), Tex. Woman's U., 1986. RN, Tex. Health promotion facilitator Addison, Tex.; co-founder, owner Large Internat. Bus., Carrollton, Tex. Mem. Sigma Theta Tau. Home: Box 707 Addison TX 75001

JOHNSON, MAXINE FRAHM, bank executive; b. Mason City, Iowa, Dec. 18, 1939; d. Peter Jr. and Emily Marian (Bistline) Frahm; m. Robert W. Johnson, June 3, 1962; children: Brenda Lynn, Janine Suzanne. BA, Grinnell Coll., 1961; MBA, U. Pitts., 1976. Contract writer Bankers Life Co., Des Moines, 1961-62; music tchr. Haworth (N.J.) Pub. Sch., 1962-63; pvt. practice Setauket, N.Y., 1963-65, Joliet, Ill., 1965-70, Glenshaw, Pa., 1970-76; trust officer Pitts. Nat. Bank, 1976-82; sr. trust officer Bank of New England, N.A., Boston, 1982-84, v.p., 1984-90, head personal trust adminstrn., 1990—; adj. faculty Northeastern U., Dedham, Mass., 1989—, New Eng. Banking Inst., 1984—. Author: Implications of the Generation Skipping Transfer Tax for Trust Administrators, 1980. Trustee Boston Conservatory. Mem. Inst. Cert. Fin. Planners, Boston Estate Planning Coun., Pi Kappa Lambda, Delta Gamma Sigma, Rotary. Office: Bank of New England N A 28 State St MA BOS13TRU Boston MA 02106

JOHNSON, MELISSA BRUCE, accountant, business owner; b. Durant, Okla., Oct. 5, 1952; d. Kenneth Sawyer and Mary Norma (Henderson) Bruce; m. David Lee Curry, Nov. 15, 1971 (div. May 1977); 1 child, Christine Michelle; m. Ronald Lynn Johnson, July 9, 1977; children: Cody Lynn, Ronald Kenneth. AS in Bus. Adminstrn., Grayson County Coll., 1986; student, U. N. Tex., 1988—. Bookkeeper, pharmacy clk. Burtis Drug, Inc., Denison, Tex., 1970-77; office mgr. Lankford Roofing Co., Inc., Denison, 1977-78, 81-85; acct. Robert S. Black, Denison, 1978-81; pvt. practice Denison, 1981—; acct. The Learning Tree, Denison, 1986-88; office adminstr. Michael W. Wiginton, CPA, Denison, 1988—. Campaign worker to elect Ben F. Bruce to U.S. Congress, Arlington, Tex., 1978; rm. chairperson Mayes PTA, Denison, 1984—; mem. Hughes PTA, Denison, 1985-87; den leader Texama Valley coun. Boy Scouts Am., Denison, 1986-88. Mem. St. Luke's Parish Sch. Parents Club (v.p. Denison chpt. 198-485, ann. bazaar chairperson 1985), Phi Theta Kappa. Republican. Baptist. Home: 131 S Hickory St Denison TX 75020

JOHNSON, MELISSA RAMIREZ, psychologist; b. N.Y.C., July 18, 1953; d. Fausto Arturo and Joan Phyllis (Schwartz) Ramirez; m. Robert Bruce Johnson, June 15, 1974; children: Laura Rebecca, David Colin. BA, Duke U., 1974; PhD, U. N.C., 1980. Psychologist Franklin (Pa.) Regional Med. Ctr., 1982-85; rsch. assoc., clin. asst. prof. U. N.C. Sch. Medicine, Chapel Hill, 1980-82; psychologist, clin. asst. prof. pediatrics Wake Area Health Edn. Ctr., U. N.C. Sch. Medicine, 1986—. Contbr. articles to profl. jours. Bd. dirs. Exch. Club Child Abuse Prevention Program, Raleigh, N.C., 1988-90, Specialized Svcs. for Children, Raleigh, 1988-90. Fellow Am. Orthopsychiat. Assn.; mem. Am. Psychol. Assn., N.C. Psychol. Assn., Soc. for Pediatric Psychology, Am. Profl. Soc. on the Abuse of Children, Internat. assn. for Infant Mental Health. Democrat. Office: Wake Med Ctr Peds AHEC 3000 New Bern Ave Raleigh NC 27610

JOHNSON, MILDRED IRENE, business educator; b. Oakland, Iowa, Feb. 27, 1924; d. Roy McKinley and Erna Emma (Klopping) F.; m. Robert Douglas Johnson, July 14, 1945; children: Douglas Wells, Lynn Anne. BSBA, Colo. State U., 1965, MS in Bus. Adminstr., 1968. Instr. Colo. State U., Fort Collins, 1967-78, asst. prof., 1979-82, lectr., 1983-85, asst. prof. emeritus, 1986—; cons. numerous firms and organizations including Bell Tel. Labs., Murray Hill , N.J., 1983-85, Houghton Mifflin Co., Boston, 1985, Western Temporary Svcs., Fort Collins, 1982, Colo. Pub. Health Assn., Denver, 1983, Poudre R-1 Schs., Fort Collins, 1983-84, Colo. Vocat. Edu. Assn., Denver, 1977. Contbr. articles to profl. jours.; co-producer: (video tape) Computer Tex Analysis, 1983, (film) Administrative Office Mng. and Bus. Tch. Edu., 1980; co-author: (computer manual) Business Report Computer Manual, 1983. Vol. Salvation Army, Fort Collins, 1981-86, Girl Scouts U.S., Arvada, Colo., 1961, 4-H Clubs, Fort Collins, 1965, March Dimes, Denver, Boy Scouts Am., Denver, 1957-60, ARC, Denver, 1951, Am. Cancer Soc., Fort Collins; bd. dirs. First Presbyn. Ch. Found., Fort Collins, 1990—, com. chmn. Fort Collins Audubon Soc., 1982-85; com. mem. United Way, Fort Collins, 1977-84; sec., bd. dirs., Fort Collins Symphony Guild, 1989—; patron Fort Collins Symphony and Lincoln Ctr. for Performing Arts, 1979-80. Mem. Assn. for Bus. Communications, Colo. State U. Alumni Assn., Faculty Club (bd. dirs. 1979-83), Quota Internat. (sec. 1981, bd. dirs. 1981-86, cons. 1983-84, dist. 9 sec., treas. 1982), Rotary (communications com. 1990—), Phi Omega Pi, Beta Epsilon, Delta Pi Epsilon (sec. 1983-85, bd. dirs. 1983-85), Beta Gamma Sigma, Phi Kappa Phi (historian 1974, treas. 1975, sec. 1976, 77, v.p. 1978, pres. elect 1979, pres. 1980, bd. dirs. 1974-80, regional v.p. 1983-89, nat. regent 1989—, nat. trustee 1983—, nat. dir. 1983—, nat. v.p. Phi Kappa Phi Found. 1986-89). Republican. Presbyterian. Home: 1330 Calabasas Ct Fort Collins CO 80525 Office: Colo State U Mgmt Dept Fort Collins CO 80523

JOHNSON, MILLICENT VIVIAN, mental health nurse consultant; b. Carrington, N.D., Mar. 16, 1910; d. Peter and Katherine (Pepple) J. BS, U. Minn., 1940; MS, Columbia U., 1956. Clinic nurse Scott County Med. Clinic for Poor, Davenport, Iowa, 1932-38; pub. health nurse Washington County Health Dept., Washington, Iowa, 1940-41; sch. nurse Mendota (Ill.) Bd. Edn., 1941-43; nurse cons. ARC, St. Louis, 1943-45, 47-54; sch. nurse Clinton (Iowa) Bd. Edn., 1945-47; mental health nurse cons. Wagner Luth. Coll., Staten Island, N.Y., 1956-62; mental health pub. health nurse cons. Balt. Health Dept., 1962-66, Vis. Nurse Assn., Omaha, 1966-74; ret., 1974. Vol. Rep. party, various civic orgns., Omaha, 1966—. Presbyterian. Home: 5828 Lafayette Ave Omaha NE 68132

JOHNSON, NANCY ANN, accounting manager; b. Chgo., Dec. 31, 1955; d. Louis E. and Verlaine (Heusler) J. BS in Acctg., Clemson U., 1977; MBA, U.N.C., Charlotte, 1981. CPA, N.C. Fin.-acctg. acct. Duke Power Co., Charlotte, 1977-79, supr. customer billing and acctg., 1979-81, acct., 1981-82, supr. acctg. systems, 1982-85, mgr. materials and fuel acctg., 1985-88, acctg. systems devel. mgr., 1988-89, mgr. acctg. controls and systems devel., 1988-90, project coord., 1990—. Bd. dirs. Safe Drive Found., Charlotte, 1986-87, 89—; bd. dirs. Queen City Jaycees, Charlotte, 1984, sec., 1985, v.p. membership, 1986; mem. Metrolina Jaycees, Charlotte, 1987, Charlotte Jaycees, 1988—. Mem. Nat. Assn. Accts. Office: Duke Power Co 422 S Church St Charlotte NC 28242-0001

JOHNSON, NANCY C. PICKLES, academic director; b. Jamaica, N.J., Apr. 8, 1950; d. Thomas Francis and Mary Grace (crinnion) Pickles. BS, U. Md., 1972, postgrad., 1988; M in Edn., Boston U., 1975. Sec., registrar Boston U., Nato Base, Italy, 1973-74; med. tech. Onslow Meml. Hosp., Jacksonville, N.C., 1974-75; program dir. Coastal Carolina Community Coll., Jacksonville, 1975-80; instr. sci. Dept. Def. Schs., Camp Zama, Japan, 1980-81; chmn. Biology dept. St. Maur Internat. Sch., Yokohama, Japan, 1981-82; med. technologist USN Hosp., Bethesda, Md., 1982-83, Malcolm Grow Med. Ctr., Andrews AFB, Md., 1983-86; head corr. Naval Sch. Health Scis., Bethesda, 1986-87; acad. coord. U. Md., Balt., 1987-90; dir., clin. lab. officer Walter Reed Army Med. Ctr., Washington, 1990—. Vol. Boy Scouts Am., Accokeek, Md., 1989—, treas. local troop, 1990—. Mem. NAFE, Md. Assn. for Higher Edn., Am. Soc. Clin. Pathologists. Roman Catholic. Office: Walter Reed Army Med Ctr Clin Officer Lab Course Washington DC 20307-5001

JOHNSON, NANCY ELIZABETH, bookseller; b. Des Moines, July 21, 1953; d. Walter Eugene and Frances Goodman (Eaton) J. BS, Drake U., 1975. Page Legislature State of Iowa, Des Moines, 1967-69, asst. bill clk., 1970-71; pub. rels. Conv. and Visitors Bur., Des Moines, 1975-76; antique show promoter Collector's Extravaganza, Denver, 1976-77; bookseller The Library, Des Moines, 1977—; book reviewer Collectors Jour., 1985—, Mtn. States Collector, Evergreen, Colo., 1986—; cons. Antiques Am., Davenport, Iowa, 1989—. Mem. Am. Booksellers Assn., Internat. Booksellers Fedn., Upper Midwest Booksellers Assn., Nat. Assn. Dealers in Antiques (book reviewer newsletter 1987—), Nat. Assn. Women Bus. Owners, Bohemian Club, Alpha Kappa Delta, Kappa Delta Pi, Psi Chi. Republican. Protestant. Home: 2737 E Euclid Ave Des Moines IA 50317 Office: The Library Collectors Extr 1301 E Euclid Ave # 6 Des Moines IA 50316

JOHNSON, NANCY FAYE, nurse; b. Crookston, Minn., Apr. 30, 1951; d. Kermit E. and G. Elaine (Schroeder) Nordlum; m. David Joseph Johnson, Sept. 4, 1976; children: Jason Joseph, Matthew Eric. Student, Pacific Luth. U., 1969-70, Bemidji State U., 1970-71; cert. in nursing, Agassiz Valley Sch., 1972, St. Luke's Sch. Nursing, 1976. With Riverview Hosp., Crookston, 1972—, head nurse, 1979-84, staff nurse, 1985—; instr. prenatal and Lamaze classes, Crookston, 1976-83; bd. dirs. adv. coun. Practical Nursing, East Grand Forks, Minn. Mem. Cub Scout coun., Crookston, 1987—; del. Ind. Rep. County Conv., Crookston, 1988—; chairperson Ann. Nurse's Fund Raiser, Crookston, 1977-86, Nurse's Scholarship Com., Crookston, 1976-86; bd. dirs. ARC Bd., Polk County, 1970. Mem. Minn. Nurse's Assn. (bd. dirs. 1985-87, pres. Dist. 1 chpt. 1986-88), NAFE, Minn. Head Nurse Orgn. (chairperson 1982-84), Am. Nurse Nat. Conv. (state del. 1985-87, 90—), Jaycee's. Lutheran. Office: Riverview Hosp Minnesota St Crookston MN 56716

JOHNSON, NANCY LEE, congresswoman; b. Chgo., Jan. 5, 1935; d. Noble Wishard and Gertrude Reid (Smith) Lee; m. Theodore H. Johnson, July 16, 1958; children—Lindsey Lee, Althea Anne, Caroline Reid. B.A., Radcliffe Coll., 1957; postgrad., U. London, 1957-58. Vice chmn. Charter Commn. New Britain, Conn., 1976-77; mem. Conn. Senate from 6th dist., 1977-82, 98th-102nd Congresses from 6th Dist. Conn., Washington, 1983—. Lectr. Am. art New Britain Mus. Am. Art, 1968-71; pres. Friends of Library, New Britain Pub. Library, 1973-76; pres. Radcliffe Club No. Conn., 1973-75; bd. dirs., pres. Sheldon Community Guidance Clinic, 1974-75; dir. religious edn. Unitarian Universalist Soc. New Britain, 1967-72, pres., 1973-75; bd. dirs. New Britain Symphony Soc., 1975-77, Plainville Group Home, 1975-76, United Way New Britain, 1976-79. Recipient Outstanding Vol. award United Way, 1976; English Speaking Union grantee, 1958-59. Republican. Home: 141 S Mountain Dr New Britain CT 06052*

JOHNSON, NAOMI MARIE, retired home economist; b. Oskaloosa, Kans., Jan. 30, 1910; d. Henry Lewis and Bessie (Buck) J. BS in Home Econs., Kans. State U., 1932, MS in Clothing and Textiles, 1949; postgrad., Columbia U., 1951, Tex. Women's Coll., 1962. Tchr. home econs. Smith Hughes High Sch., Scottsville, Kans., 1937-38; extension home economist Kans. State U., Manhattan, 1944-76; home economist Neosho County Extension Svc., Erie, 1938-44; ret., 1976. Mem. Riley County Mus., Manhattan, Arkins Mus. Friends Art, Kansas City, Mo., Kans. State Mus., Topeka. Fellow Am. Home Econs. Assn. (50 Yr. Mem. award 1985); mem. Kans. Home Econs. Assn. (treas. 1940, 54 Yr. Mem. award 1989), AAUW (publicity com.), AARP (membership com.), Nat. Assn. Ret. Fed. Employees (v.p. 1986-87), DAR, Riley Co. Geneal. Soc. (past pres.), Fashion Group, Costume Soc. Am., Delta Kappa Gamma, Epsilon Sigma Phi (40 Yr. Mem. award Alpho Rho chpt. 1960). Republican. Presbyterian. Home: 2307 Chris Dr Manhattan KS 66502

JOHNSON, NORA ANN TONER, investments and property management executive; b. Juneau, Alaska, Mar. 1, 1952; d. Felix and Mary Fredericka V. Toner; m. Paul Evert Johnson, Dec. 29, 1981. BBA, U. Portland, 1978. Village acct. Sealaska, Juneau, 1978-79; jr. acct. Alaska Div. Legis. Audit, Juneau, 1979-81; propr. Chicagof Charters, Elfin Cove, Alaska, 1981—, Elfin Gen. Supply, Elf Inn, J. & M. Fish Co., 1983—. Treas. Community of Elfin Cove Non-Profit Corp., 1984—; mem. Elfin Cove Adv. Sch. Bd., 1985-88. Mem. Nat. Fedn. Ind. Businesses, Elfin Cove Hist. Soc. (sec./treas. 1986—), Elfin Cove Library Assn. (pres. 1986—). Democrat. Roman Catholic. Office: J&M Fish Co 2222 Elf Inn Way Elfin Cove AK 99825

JOHNSON, NORINE GOODE, psychologist; b. Indpls., Dec. 3, 1935; d. Frank and Marie (Collins) Goode; B.A., DePauw U., 1957; Ph.D., Wayne State U., 1972; postgrad. Harvard Med. Sch., 1975-77; m. Charles W. Johnson, Aug. 23, 1958; children: Cammarie, Kathryn Carroll, Margaret Ellen. Psychology cons. to pediatrics Univ. Hosps. Cleve., 1968-69; asst. clin. prof. dept. neurology Boston U. Med. Sch., 1976—; adj. prof. psychology Boston Coll., 1978-84; dir. psychology Kennedy Meml. Hosp., Brighton, Mass., 1970-88; pres. ABCS Psychology Resources, 1988—. Pres. area bd. Mental Health and Retardation, 1973, regional bd., 1974; mem. Gov.'s Adv. Council Mental Health and Mental Retardation, 1974-76, chairperson children's subcom., 1976. NIMH scholar, trainee. Fellow Mass. Psychol. Assn. (pres. elect 1980, pres. 1981-83, dir., bd. profl. affairs 1977-79, chairperson 1977-78, liaison to Mass. Psychiat. Soc. 1978); mem. Am. Psychol. Assn. (co-chair fin. com. 1987-89, exec. com. assn. psychology internship ctrs. 1985-88, council of reps. 1985-88, div. 35 chair fin. com. 1987—), Assembly Scientist Practitioner Psychologists (treas. 1988—), Div. Women Psychologists (chair fin. com. 1987—), Psi Chi. Club: Boston Athletic. Home: 13 Ashfield St Roslindale MA 02131 Office: 111 Willard St Suite 2B Quincy MA 02169

JOHNSON, NORMA HOLLOWAY, federal judge; b. Lake Charles, La.. B.S., D.C. Tchrs. Coll., 1955; J.D., Georgetown U., 1962. Bar: D.C. bar 1962, U.S. Supreme Ct. bar 1967. Pvt. practice law Washington, 1963; atty. Dept. Justice, Washington, 1963-67; asst. corp. counsel D.C., 1967-70; judge D.C. Superior Ct., 1970-80, U.S. Dist. Ct. (D.C. dist.), Washington, 1980—; Bd. dirs. Nat. Children's Center, Washington, National Street Law Inst. Mem. Am. Bar Assn., Nat. Bar Assn., D.C. Bar, Nat. Council Juvenile Ct. Judges, Am. Judicature Soc. (dir.), Nat. Assn. Women Judges (dir.). Office: US Dist Ct US Courthouse 3d & Constitution Ave NW Washington DC 20001*

JOHNSON, NORMA J., specialty wool grower; b. Dover, Ohio, Aug. 30, 1925; d. Jasper Crile and Mildred Catherine (Russell) J.; student Heidelberg Coll., 1943; cert. drafting techniques Case Sch. Applied Sci., 1944; student Western Res. U., 1945-47, Ohio State U., 1951, Muskingum Coll., 1965; AA, Kent State U., 1979, Buckeye Joint Vocat. Sch., 1979-84; m. Robert Blake Covey, Oct. 7, 1951 (div. 1960); 1 child, Susan Kay. Instr. arts and crafts Univ. Settlement House, Cleve., 1944; mech. draftswoman Nat. Assn. Civil Aeros., Cleve., 1944-46; mfrs. rep. Nat. Spice House, 1947-49; tchr. econs., home econs., English, math, history, high sch., Tuscarawas County Sch. System, New Philadelphia, Ohio, 1962-69; owner, mgr., operator Sunny Slopes Farm, producer of specialty wools and grains, Dover, Ohio, 1969—. Tchr., Meth. Sunday Sch., 1956-61; chaplain Winfield PTA, 1960; program dir. Brandywine Grange, 1960-62; troop leader Girl Scouts, U.S.A., 1961-70. Recipient cert. of merit Tuscarawas County Schs., 1965, Ohio Wildlife Conservation award Tuscarawas County, 1972, 1st and 3d premiums for handspinning fleece, Ohio State Fair, 1984, 8th and 10th premiums, Mich. Stat Fair, 1985, proclamation Bd. Commrs. Tuscarawas County. Mem. Mid States Wool Growers, Am. Angus Assn., Am. Tree Farm System, Nat. Arbor Day Found., Nat. Wildlife Fedn., Ohio Nut Growers Assn., Midwest Weavers Assn., Canton Weavers and Spinners, Ohio Arts and Crafts Guild, Tuscarawas County Geneal. Soc., Inc., Tuscarawas County Hist. Soc. Bldg. designed and constructed interior facilities for the Scheuer-Haus. Home and Office: Rt 1 Box 398 Dover OH 44622

JOHNSON, OPAL BURTON, educator; b. Mercer County, W.Va., May 30, 1929; d. Martin Luther and Annie Elizabeth (Gentry) Burton; m. Eugene Hunter Johnson, Mar. 13, 1948; children: Eugene Hunter Jr., Nancy Gayle Johnson Canady. BA, King Coll., Bristol, Tenn., 1966; MA in Teaching, East Tenn. State U., 1977. Cert. elem. tchr., Va. Tchr. Bristol (Va.) Sch. System, 1966—. Named Tchr. of Yr., Bristol (Tenn.-Va.) Rotary Club, 1989. Mem. NEA, Va. Edn. Assn., Bristol Edn. Assn., Phi Kappa Phi, Phi Delta Kappa. Presbyterian. Home: 1106 Holston Ave Bristol TN 37620

JOHNSON, PAM MCALLISTER, newspaper publisher, consultant; b. McAlester, Okla., Apr. 14, 1945; d. Elmer Reuben and Esther Queen (Crump) McAllister; m. Donald Nathanial Johnson, June 8, 1968; children—Jason, Dawn. B.S., U. Wis., 1967, M.S., 1971, Ph.D., 1977. Assoc. prof. journalism U. Wis. Madison, 1971-78; assoc. prof. Norfolk State U. (Va.), 1979-81; gen. exec. Gannett Co., Inc., Bridgewater, N.J., 1981—; asst. to pub. The Ithaca Jour., N.Y., 1981, pres., pub., 1981—; dir. First Bank Ithaca. Bd. dirs. St. Bonaventure U., Olean, N.Y., Sta. WCNY-TV, Syracuse, N.Y.; mem. adv. bd. Nat. Youth Communication, Syracuse, 1983. Mem. Nat. Assn. Black Journalists, Nat. Assn. Edn. in Journalism, N.Y. State Pubs. Assn., Am. Newspaper Pubs. Assn., N.Y. Assn. Black Journalists, Ithaca Bus. and Profl. Women. Club: Zonta. Office: Ithaca Jour 123 W State St Ithaca NY 14850*

JOHNSON, PATRICIA ANITA, arts association administrator; b. Chgo., Mar. 17, 1944; d. Theodore and Johnie (West) Richardson; m. James A.; children: David, Todd. BA, Oberlin Coll., 1965; postgrad., U.S. Internat. U., San Diego, 1985. Curator Brockman Gallery, Los Angeles, 1976-78; cultural affairs coordinator San Diego Community Coll., San Diego, 1982-85; dir. S. Dallas Cultural Ctr., Dallas, 1985-88; exec. dir. Jamaica Arts Ctr., Jamaica, N.Y. Bd. dir. San Diego State U. Art Council, 1983-85, San Diego Pub. Art Adv. Bd., 1985-; Chmn. San Deigo Mus. of Art-African Arts Com., 1983-84. Am. Assn. of Mus., Inroads. Democrat. Protestant. Office: Jamaica Arts Ctr 16104 Jamaica Ave Jamaica NY 11432

JOHNSON, PATRICIA BURKE, educator; b. Butte, Mont., Mar. 30, 1941; d. Clifford William and Ada (Givogre) Burke. BS, Mont. State U., 1963, postgrad., 1985—; MA, Ind. U., 1969; postgrad., various univs., 1970-89. Cert. physics, math., earth sci. tchr., Mont. Tchr. math. Opheim (Mont.) Schs., 1963-64, Manhattan (Mont.) Schs., 1964-65; instr. math. Mont. State U., Bozeman, 1965; tchr. earth, life and phys. sci. C.R. Anderson Sch., Helena, Mont., 1966-72; tchr. physics and earth sci. Capital High Sch., Helena, 1972-89; securities broker Edward D. Jones and Co., Eugene, Oreg., 1989-90, Adams, Hess, Moore & Co., Eugene, 1990—; dir. Aerospace Workshop, Carroll Coll., Helena, 1980-85; asst. Canyon Ferry Limnological Inst., Helena, summers 1982-89; judge aerospace exhibits county fair, Helena, 1983-85; regional rep. Smithsonian Air and Space Mus., Washington, 1982; speaker to elem. schs. and community orgns., 1976—. Mem. Helena Citizens' Coun., 1985-89, chmn., 1988; vice chmn. Helena City Planning Bd., 1986-87; mem. Lewis and Clark-Helena Consol. Planning Bd., 1987-88; participant, class sec. Leadership Helena, 1986-87, mem., program co-coord. steering com., 1987-89, also others; mem. Congress on Aerospace Edn., San Diego, 1988. Mamed Nat. Aerospace Tchr. of Yr., Nat. Congress on Aerospace Edn., 1988, Woman of Distinction Soroptimists, 1988; recipient Mont. Outstanding Sci. Tchr. award Mont. Power Co., 1978, silver achievement award YWCA, Helena, 1988, Crown Circle award Nat. Congress on Aerospace Edn., San Diego, 1988., cert. of merit Helena Airport Bd., 1988; Mont. Tchr. in Space candidate NASA, 1985; GM scholar, 1959-63, U. Dayton scholar, 1977, U. Calif.-Davis scholar, 1977; NSF grantee, 1968-69. Mem. Nat. Sci. Tchrs. Assn., Mont. Sci. Tchrs. Assn., Mont. Earth Sci. Tchrs. Assn. (charter), NEA, Mont. Edn. Assn., Helena Edn. Assn. (exec. bd., com. mem.), Mont. Acad. Scis., Aircraft Owners and Pilots Assn., Mont. Assn. Female Execs. (charter, membership com. 1986-88), Mont. Pilots Assn. (state western v.p. 1988, pres. Helena Hanger 1981), Mont. Antique Airplane Assn. (charter, sec. 1978-81), Delta Kappa Gamma, Alpha Delta Kappa. Office: PO Box 1377 Eugene OR 97440

JOHNSON, PATRICIA DUREN, health insurance company executive; b. Columbus, Ohio, Oct. 22, 1943; d. James and Rosetta J. Duren; m. Harold H. Johnson, Jr., Dec. 25, 1965; 1 child, Jill. BS in Edn., Ohio State U., 1965. Tchr. various locations, 1966-72; sales rep. ITT Hartford, Portland, Oreg., 1972-73; sr. v.p. Blue Cross of Calif., 1975—. Bd. dirs. Am. Cancer Soc., 1988—. Mem. Am. Hosp. Assn., Women in Health Adminstrn., Delta Sigma Theta. Office: Blue Cross of Calif 21555 Oxnard St Woodland Hills CA 91367*

JOHNSON, PATRICIA GAYLE, corporate communication executive, writer; b. Conway, Ark., Oct. 23, 1947; d. Rudolph and Frances Modene (Hayes) J. Student U. Calif., Irvine, 1965-68. Advance rep. Disney on Parade, Los Angeles, 1971-75; mktg. dir., dir. field ops. Am. Freedom Train, 1975-77; publ. rels. mgr. Six Flags, Inc., Los Angeles, 1977-81; mgr. corp. communications Playboy Enterprises, Inc., Los Angeles, 1981-82; external rels. mgr. Kal Kan Foods, Inc., Los Angeles, 1982-86; v.p. Daniel J. Edelman, Inc., 1986-88; sr. v.p. Amies Advt. and Pub. Rels., Irvine, 1988-89; dir. pub. rels. World Vision, Monrovia, Calif., 1989—; lectr. U. So. Calif., UCLA, Calif. State U., Northridge, Calif. State U., Dominguez Hills. Mem. Pub. Rels. Soc. Am. (past officer), Pub. Affairs Council, Delta Soc. (advisor). Mem. Foursquare Gospel Ch. Collaborator TV scripts; contbr. articles to various consumer and profl. mags. Office: World Vision 919 W Huntington Dr Monrovia CA 91016

JOHNSON, PATRICIA HARDY, early childhood specialist pre-school provider; b. Washington, Sept. 14, 1933; d. Dennis and Ira Bell (McGarrah) Hardy. BS, Miners Tchrs. Coll., Washington, D.C., 1955; MA, NYU, 1962; EdD, U.S. Internat. U., San Diego, 1989. Cert. tchr. elem. physically handicapped, mentally handicapped, learning handicapped, supervision, sch. psychologist, adminstrn. Resource specialist L.A. Unified Sch. Dist.; prin., asst. prin. L.A. Child Guidance Clin.; owner, pres. Raintree Inn, Inc., L.A. Author: Raintree Inn Incorporated's Complete Child Care Center's Curriculum Guide, 0-27 Months; contbr. articles to profl. jours. Mem. usher bd. and hospitality com. Eternal Promise Bapt. Ch., L.A. Spl. Edn. grantee State of Calif.; numerous fellowships received from Univs. Mem. NAFE, Am. Assn. Ret. Persons, NYU Alumni, UCLA Alumni, Beta Pi Sigma, Gamma Theta Upsilon. Democrat. Home: 5007 Rainbow's End Culver City CA 90230 Office: 6611 Rugby Ave Ste A Huntington Park CA 90255

JOHNSON, PATRICIA MARY, publisher; b. Evanston, Ill., Mar. 14, 1937; d. Harold W. and Florence M. (Miller) J.; children: William, Nancy, Richard. Degree in Interior Design LaSalle U., Chgo., 1972; student Art Inst., Chgo., 1970-73. Owner Decor Interior Design, Chgo., 1972-76; interior design communicator, producer/host weekly syndicated cable TV program on interior design, 1980-86; owner Design Communications, Rosenhayn, N.J., 1976-85; exec. dir., founder Corp. for Disabled/Handicapped, 1985—, A Positive Approach, Inc. Recipient award N.J. Gov., 1985, Practitioner of Yr. award N.J. Rehab. Assn., 1987, Humanitarian Service award United Cerebral Palsy, 1987, Jefferson award NBC, 1988, Healing Community United Nations Pub. award, 1989. Author: Eliminating Barriers from Your Lifestyle, 1988; contbr. articles to profl. jours. and consumer mags.; also radio broadcaster.

JOHNSON, PAULA BARNES, psychology educator; b. Boston; d. Robert Bostwick and Elizabeth (Paterson) B. BA, UCLA, 1967, MA, 1969, PhD, 1974. Acting asst. prof. psychology U. Calif., Santa Cruz, 1972-74, asst. prof., 1974-77; assoc. rsch. psychologist UCLA, 1977-80; prof. Calif. Sch. Profl. Psychology, L.A., 1980—; cons. UCLA-Neuro-Psychiat. Inst., Media Studies, 1976-79, Rand Corp., Santa Monica, Calif., 1976-79, prenatal alcohol abuse prevention and recovery L.A. County Office Alcohol Programs, 1989. Co-author: Women and Sex Roles, 1978; contbr. articles to profl. jours., 1971—. Mem. Flying Drs. of Mercy, 1981-88. Rsch. grantee UCLA, 1977. Mem. Internat. Soc. Polit. Psychology, Peace Psychology Rsch. Group, Soc. for Psychol. Study of Social Issues (rsch. grantee 1989), Psychologists for Social Responsibility. Democrat. Office: CSPP 2235 Beverly Blvd Los Angeles CA 90057

JOHNSON, PAULINE, immunologist, scientist; b. Batley, Yorks, Eng., May 29, 1959; came to U.S., 1986; d. Keith and Clarice Annie (Spedding) J. Student, Liverpool (Eng.) U., 1980; PhD in Biochemistry, Dundee (Scotland) U., 1983. Postdoctoral scientist Cellular Immunology Unit Med. Rsch. Coun., Oxford, Eng., 1983-86; postdoctoral scientist cellular immunology unit The Salk Inst., La Jolla, Calif., 1986—. George Hirst Meml. fellow, 1979, Beit Meml. rsch. fellow, 1983-86, Cancer Rsch. Inst. fellow, 1986-89. Mem. British Biochem. Soc. (editorial advisor 1989—), British Soc. Immunology. Office: The Salk Inst PO Box 85800 La Jolla CA 92016

JOHNSON, PHYLLIS KAY, sales executive; b. Vernon, Tex., Dec. 15, 1955; d. Wilbert Arnold and Mildred Ruth (Forster) Kieschnick; m. Evertte Neal Johnson, Feb. 23, 1980 (div. 1987). BBA, Tex. Tech. U., 1978. Sales rep. R.J. Reynolds Tobacco, Wichita Falls, Tex., 1978-79, area sales rep., 1979-84; asst. div. mgr. R.J. Reynolds Tobacco, Ft. Worth, 1984-85, tng. and devel. mgr., 1985-86, spl. accounts mgr., 1986-87; div. sales mgr. R.J. R. Nabisco, Memphis, 1987—. Republican. Home: 251 Summerfield Ln Cordova TN 38018

JOHNSON, RAYMONDA THEODORA GREENE, humanities educator; b. Chgo., Jan. 12, 1939; d. Theodore T. and Eileen (Atherley) Greene; m. Hulon Johnson, June 27, 1964; children: David, Theodore, Alexander. BA in English, DePaul U., 1960; MA in English, Loyola U., Chgo., 1965. Cert. high sch. English tchr., Ill. Tchr. high sch. English, Chgo. Pub. Schs., 1960-65; instr. English, Harold Washington Coll., City Coll. Chgo. (formerly Loop Coll.), Chgo., 1965-66, asst. prof., 1966—, faculty advisor coll. newspaper, 1989. Grade rep. parents coun., v.p. parents coun. mid. sch. Latin Sch., Chgo., 1974—, trustee, 1987—; cubmaster, leader cub scouts Boy Scouts Am., Chgo., 1974-81; active black creativity adv. com. Mus. Sci. and Industry, Chgo., 1985—. Recipient svc. award religious edn. program St. Thomas the Apostle Ch., Chgo., 1984. Mem. Twigs Mothers Club (pres. 1982-84), Alpha Kappa Alpha. Democrat. Roman Catholic. Home: 6747 S Bennett Ave Chicago IL 60649

JOHNSON, REBECCA MCGEORGE, sales representative, textile consultant; b. Roanoke, Va., Aug. 10, 1948; d. Gilbert Wesley and Lydia Pauline (Brooks) McGeorge; m. James Edin Johnson. AA, Lees McRae Coll., Banner Elk, N.C., 1968; BS, Mars Hill Coll., 1971. Cert. home economist, Va. Extension agt., writer monthly newsletter Va. Poly. Inst. and State U., Hanover and Appomattox, 1971-83; tchr., Campbell County Sch. System, Lynchburg, Va., 1973-74; sales rep. Baldwin, Md., 1987—. Mem. Am. Home Econs. Assn., Md. Home Econs. Assn., Woman's Club Denton (Md., sec. 1986-87), Gun Powder Garden Club (Balt., v.p. 1989-91). Office: Box 334 Phoenix MD 21131

JOHNSON, ROSEMARY WRUCKE, personnel management specialist; b. Leith, N.D., Sept. 21, 1924; d. Rudolph Aaron and Metta Tomina (Andersen) Wrucke; m. Robert Johnson Jr., Sept. 28, 1945 (div. 1964). Student, GW U., Wash. D.C., 1944-45, 47, Nat. Art Sch., Wash. D.C., 1943-45. Supr. FBI, Wash. D.C., 1952-65, Displaced Persons Commn., Franfurt, Germany, 1965-81; mng. orgn. design cons. Arlington, Va., 1981--. Mem. Classification and Compensation Soc., Nat. Soc. of Former, FBI Women (membership chmn. 1985--). Lutheran. Home and Office: 2525 N 10th St #820 Arlington VA 22201

JOHNSON, RUTH ANN, sales executive; b. Chgo., Feb. 4, 1947; d. Raymond Fred and Ann Laura (Olson) J. BSBA, Northwestern U., 1968. With sales and mktg. dept. Xerox Corp., Houston, 1977-80, Bell & Howell, Houston, 1980-85; v.p. sales Bowe Systems, Hicksville, N.Y., 1985-89; nat. dir. sales C.O.P.E., Inc., Tucson, 1989—. Governing mem. N.Y. chpt. Women's Polit. Caucus, 1984—. Mem. Am. Mgmt. Assn., NAFE, U.S. Golf Assn., U.S. Tennis Assn. Home: 200-32 Shearwater Ct W Port Liberte NJ 07305

JOHNSON, SANDRA JEAN, teacher, civic leader; b. Oregon City, Oreg., Oct. 15, 1945; d. Vernon Davis and Ruth Alice (Plummer) Gill; m. Ronald C. Johnson; children: Steve, Scott. BS in Elem. Edn., Dana Coll., 1982; MS in Elem. Edn., Wayne State Coll., 1988. Cert. elem. tchr., tchr. mentally handicapped. Preschool dir., tchr. Anita, Iowa, 1974-76. Exec. sec. 1st Luth. Ch. Women, Blair, Nebr., 1987-89; mem. hosp. aux. Meml. Community Hosp., Blair, 1988—. Mem. NEA, AAUW, Ft. Calhoun Edn. Edn. (pres. 1987-88), Met. Reading Club. Home: 2560 Northgate Blair NE 68008

JOHNSON, SANDRA JOYCE, personnel management specialist; b. Oakland, Calif., Feb. 28, 1949; d. Alex Little and Dorothy Mae (Sims) Grate; m. Gus Lewis, Jr., Aug. 22, 1966 (div. 1969); children: Maurice, Cherie Lewis; m. Eugene Johnson, June 9, 1979. Student, Laney Jr. Coll., 1969-71. Payroll supr. Dept. of Treasury, San Francisco, 1974-79; payroll supr. Naval Supply Ctr. Dept. of Navy, Oakland, 1979-81; employee rels. specialist Dept. of Navy, Mil. Sealift Command Pacific, Oakland, 1981-84; pers. staffing specialist Dept. of Navy, Oakland, 1984-86, employee devel. specialist, 1986-87, supervisory employee devel. specialist, 1987-88, pers. mgmt. specialist, 1988-90, staffing and classification specialist, 1990—. Mem. NAACP, Employee Activity Assn. (pres. 1987-90), Oakland Assn. Recreation and Employee Svcs. (pres. 1989—), Nat. Coun. Negro Women (pres. 1990), Esoteric Social and Civic Club (pres. 1986—), Bay Area Media Coalition (sec. 1985-89), Elks (daughter ruler 1990), Kappa Alpha Psi Silhouettes (v.p. 1988-90). Democrat. African Methodist Episcopal. Home: 6363 Conlon Ave El Cerrito CA 94530-1668

JOHNSON, SARILYN JOAN, real estate broker; b. Kokomo, Ind., June 25, 1932; d. Cleon Frederick Meister and Iris Marie (Detamore) Clark; m. Richard D. Johnson, Dec. 24, 1948 (div. 1963); children: Douglas Kent, Kimberly Mae; m. Glenn E. Johnson, May 3, 1965. Cert. real estate, Edison Coll., Ft. Myers, Fla., 1978. Cert. real estate broker. Office clk. Kimm Paint Co., Muncie, Ind., 1952-56; office mgr. Muncie Reclamation and Supply, 1956-61; office mgr., bookkeeper C.E. Geckler, MD, Muncie, 1961-65; office mgr. C. Bibler Supply Co., Inc., Muncie, 1966-72; real estate broker Raso & Mascarello Realty, Inc., Cape Coral, Fla., 1978-88; realtor, mgr. property management dept. Century 21 Birchwood Realty, Cape Coral, 1988—. Contbr. articles to profl. jours. Mem. Rep. Nat. Com., Washington, 1987. Mem. Nat. Assn. Female Execs., Am. Bus. Women Assn., Bus. and Profl. Women, Women's Council Realtors (pres. 1981-82, Woman of Yr. 1983), Cape Coral Bd. Realtors (bd. dirs. 1986—, Realtor Assoc. of Yr. 1981), Cape Coral C. of C. Lodge: Order Eastern Star. Home: 4508 Santa Barbara Blvd Apt 101 Cape Coral FL 33914 Office: Century 21 Birchwood Realty Inc Cape Coral FL 33904 also: 5510 SW 4th Pl #508 Cape Coral FL 33914

JOHNSON, SHARON JEAN, public relations professional; b. Augsburg, Fed. Republic of Germany, Aug. 15, 1962; d. Arthur Jackson and Jean Francis (Rickett) B.; m. Kevin Lenard Johnson. BS in Pub. Relations, N. Tex. State U., 1984. Reporter North Tex. Daily Newspaper, Denton, 1982-83, editor, 1983; media asst. Vance-Mathews Advt., Inc., Beaumont, Tex., 1985; traffic asst., news writer Pyle Communications Media Group, Beaumont, 1985; film dir., dir. pub. service Sta. KFDM-TV, Beaumont, 1985-87; coordinator pub. edn. Del. Council on Crime and Justice, Wilmington, 1987-88; program coordinator United Way of Del., Wilmington, 1988-89; corp. rels. specialist Allstate Ins. Co., Northbrook, Ill., 1989—. Contbr. articles to profl. pubs. Memm. Internat. Assn. Bus. Communicators, NAFE. Democrat. Baptist. Home: 1397 Huntington Dr Mundelein IL 60060

JOHNSON, SHARON KAY HANEROFF, speech and language pathologist; b. Peoria, Ill.; d. Arthur August and Cecilia M. (Lamanski) H.; separated; children: Kent T., Blake D., Lance C., Eric S. BA, So. Ill. U., Edwardsville, 1969, MS, 1980; postgrad., St. Louis U., 1989—. Cert. high sch. tchr., Ill.; cert. elem. and secondary speech and language impaired tchr., Ill.; Lic. speech pathologist, Mo., Ill. Instr. adult edn. U.S. Dependent Schs. European Area, Karlsruhe and Kaiserslautern, Fed. Republic Germany, 1971-75; tchr., chairperson mid. sch. exploration program Tehran (Iran) Am. Mid. Sch., 1975-77; speech and language pathologist Miss. Valley Rehab. Inc., Alton, Ill., 1980-82; chief speech pathologist St. Joseph's Hosp., Alton, 1982-85; pres., speech pathologist Practical Communication Speech and Language Svcs., Alton, Ill., 1985—; dir. adaptive skills program for head injured Impact, Inc., Alton, 1986—; cons. Alton Meml. Hosp., St. Joseph's Hosp., Alton, The Vis. Nurse Assn. Greater St. Louis, Beverly Farm Found. Inc., Vaughn Home Health Care & Svcs. Inc.; grant writer, dir. Adaptive Skills Program for Head Injured Persons. Contbg. author Whole Aphasia Catalog, 1986. Bd. dirs. Ill. Gov.'s Planning Coun. on Devel. Disabilities, 1988, Ill. Gov.'s Adv. Coun. for Ind. Living, 1987; mem. strategic planning com. Nat. Head Injury Found., Washington, 1990. Ill. Cancer Soc. scholar U. Ill., Urbana, 1984. Mem. Am. Speech and Hearing Assn., Ill. Head Injury Assn. (pres. 1988—, spl. friend award 1988), Southwestern Ill. Speech and Hearing Assn., Phi Kappa Phi, Pi Lambda Theta. Office: Practical Communication Inc Rehab Svcs Ste 406 200 W Third St Alton IL 62002

JOHNSON, SHARON MARIE BLOM, public relations executive; b. Blue Earth, Minn., Aug. 19, 1937; d. Frithjof and Mildred Pearl (Mundale) Blom; m. Dale Hughes Johnson, May 31, 1958 (div. July 1982); children: Eric Arthur, Karan Marie, Peter Frederick. Student, Mankato State U., 1955, Waldorf Coll., 1956, Rice U., 1984. Asst. dir. placement Iowa State Univ., Ames, 1956-58; owner various bus. Houston, 1972-76; mgr. fin. Mitsui & Co. (U.S.A.) Inc., Houston, 1977-86; guest lect. Univ. Houston, 1983-85; mgr., devel. dept. Mitsui & Co. (U.S.A.) Inc., Houston, 1986-88; dir. pub. rels., editor co., newsletter Mitsui & Co. (U.S.A.), Inc., Houston, 1988--. editor, Mitsui Sunshine News. Fund raiser, Children's Museum, Jacksonville, 1965-71, Various Pol. Mem. Women's Club, Plaza Club. Republican. Home: 1822 Barker-Cypress #2202 Houston TX 77084 Office: Mitsui & Co (USA) Inc 1000 Louisiana Ste 5700 Houston TX 77002

JOHNSON, SHAWANA P., sales executive; b. Cleve., Apr. 4, 1957; d. Raymond and Lois (Wilson) J. AS, Miami U., Oxford, Ohio, 1977; BS, West Liberty State Coll., W.Va.; MBA, Cleve. State U., 1983. From mgr. mktg. to mgr. nat. mktg. Gen. Elec. Consulting Svcs. Corp., Rockville, Md., 1983-87; dir. N.Am. sales Earth Observ. Satellite Co. (subs. Gen. Elec. & Hughes Aircraft Co.), Lanham, Md., 1988—. Mem. Am. Mktg. Assn., Exec. Mgmt. Program. Home: 6569 Cross Creek Trail Backsville OH 44141

JOHNSON, SHERRI DALE, educational consultant; b. Drumright, Okla., May 15, 1948; d. William Dale and Leota Mae (Mann) Roberts; m. James Earl Johnson, Aug. 5, 1972; children: Tara Nicole, Taylor Nichele. BS, Okla. State U., 1970; MS, North Tex. State U., 1980. Cert. secondary tchr., Tex., Okla. Tchr. English and speech Nathan Hale High Sch., Tulsa, 1970-76, Dallas Community Coll.-El Centro, 1976-77; tchr. speech and journalism Haggard Mid. Sch., Plano, Tex., 1976-78, Carpenter Mid. Sch., Plano, 1978-79, Clark High Sch., Plano, 1979-81; tng. cons. Dallas County Mental

Health Assn., Dallas, 1984-87; dir. PhoneFriend, Plano, 1987—; ednl. cons. Plano Sch. Dist., 1987—. Author: Latchkey Survival Course: Handbook for Parents and Children, 1987. Tchr. suicide prevention Crisis Ctr. Collin County, Plano, 1989—; coord. S.T.O.P. prog. Vines High Sch. PTO, Plano, 1988-89, pres., 1989—; cons. W.H.O. prog. Mental Health Assn., Dallas, 1987—; mem. speakers bur., chmn. childrens' youth com. Collin County Mental Health Assn., Plano, 1989—; mem. counselors' adv. com. Plano I.S.D., 1987—; com. mem. Keep Plano Beautiful Task Force, 1989—; chmn., founder Focus on Children, Child Abuse Prevention Coalition, 1989—. Named Plano Vol. of Yr. Edn. Category, 1989. Mem. NEA, AAUW, Tex. Educators Assn. Democrat. Home: 3420 Regent Dr Plano TX 75075 Office: PhoneFriend PO Box 260225 Plano TX 75026

JOHNSON, SHIRLEY ANN, health care executive; b. Detroit, Apr. 12, 1944; d. Edward James and Verdia (Kegler) Joseph; children: Cynthia Elaine, Gerald Essex, Natalie Ann. AS, Highland Park Coll., Mich., 1975; BS, Mercy Coll., Detroit, 1982; MS, U. Detroit, 1984. Lab. technician Children's Hosp. of Mich., Detroit, 1964-69, med. lab. technician, 1973-84; mgr. implementations Comprehensive Health Svcs., Detroit, 1985-86, adminstr., 1987-89; exec. cons. Blue Care Network S.E. Mich., Southfield, 1989—. Mem. Am. Acad. Med. Adminstrs., Nat. Assn. Female Execs., Greater Detroit Area Health Council, Soc. Healthcare Planning & Mktg. Democrat. Methodist. Home: 15390 Hubbell Detroit MI 48227 Office: Blue Care Network Mich 27000 W 11 Mile Rd Southfield MI 48086

JOHNSON, SHIRLEY ELAINE, management consultant; b. Terre Haute, Ind., Sept. 15, 1946; d. Mervil Ray and Sarah Kathryn (Tucker) W.; m. Richard E. Johnson Jr., Sept. 23, 1964 (div. 1974); children: Richard Alan, Gary Michael Sr. AA, Coll. Dupage, 1980; student, DePaul U., 1988—. Sec. to v.p. fin. Cenco Inc., Oak Brook, Ill., 1972-74, exec. asst. to group pres., 1974-75, asst. to chmn., 1975-77, corp. personnel/office mgr., 1977-80; corp. sec. Acadia Petroleum Corp., Denver, 1980-82; mgr. office Chapman, Klein & Weinberg, PC, Denver, 1982-84; asst. to chmn. The Heidrick Ptnrs., Inc., Chgo., 1984—. Mem. Am. Mgmt. Assn., Am. Soc. Personnel Adminstrs., DuPage Personnel Assn. (sec. 1979), Exec. Women Internat., Nat. Assn. Female Execs. Home: 7309 Hartford Downers Grove IL 60516 Office: The Heidrick Ptnrs Inc 20 N Wacker Dr Ste 2850 Chicago IL 60606

JOHNSON, SONDRA LEA, accountant; b. Kansas City, Mo., May 11, 1952; d. Albert John Oscar and Dorothy Mae (Hudgens) J. AA, Longview Coll., 1972; BSBA cum laude in Acctg., Cen. Mo. State U., 1974, MBA, 1980. CPA, Mo. Acct. Farmland Industries, Kansas City, 1974-76; acct., auditor Ernst & Whinney, Kansas City, 1976-79, Laventhol & Horwath, Kansas City, 1980-81; corp. acct., mgr. Butler Mfg. Co., Kansas City, 1981-84; audit supr. Grant Thornton Internat., Kansas City, 1984-89; internat. internal auditor Marion Merrell Dow, Kansas City, 1989—; specialized instr. nat. continuing edn. tng. program, Grant Thornton Internat., various locations U.S.A.; acctg. instr. Cen. Mo. State U., Warrensburg, 1979-80, Rockhurst Coll., Kansas City, 1981-82, Avila Coll., Kansas City, 1989-90. Mem. AICPAs, Nat. Assn. Accts., Mo. Soc. CPA's, Women's C. of C. of Kansas City, Phi Kappa Phi. Democrat. Lutheran. Office: Marion Merrell Dow 9300 Ward Pkwy Kansas City MO 64114

JOHNSON, STEPHANIE LYNN, quality assurance professional; b. Chgo., Apr. 10, 1962; d. Clarence Johnson and Pearline (Pope) Haywood. Student, Tenn. State U., Nashville, 1986. VCC weight engr. Bell Helicopter Textron, Hurst, Tex., 1986-88; quality assurance engineer Andrew Corp., Denton, Tex., 1988—; mem. adv. coun. occupaitonal tech. edn. Denton Sch. Dist., 1989—; mem. textbook selection com. sci. dept. Ft. Worth Sch. Dist., 1987-88. Big Sister, Big Bros. and Sisters Tarrant County, Ft. Worth, 1987-88; youth and edn. adv. com. Martin Luther King Jr. Ctr., Denton, 1988-89; industry rep., steering com. Denton Adopt-A-Sch. Program, Denton, 1988—; sr. choir mem., coll. coord., announcement clk. Mt. Olive Bapt. Ch., Arlington, Tex., 1988—. Recipient Spl. Project Recognition, Ft. Worth Adopt-A-Sch. Program, 1988—. Mem. Nat. Soc. Black Engrs. (campus advisor 1989—), NAACP, Tex. Alliance for Minorities in Engring. (industry rep. 1986—), Tenn. State U. Nat. Alumni Assn., 100,000 Club Southside YMCA of Chgo. Baptist. Office: Andrew Corp Tex 2701 Mayhill Rd Denton TX 76205

JOHNSON, SUSAN BURGESS, county administrator; b. Ridley Park, Pa., June 26, 1948; d. Vincent Byard and Lucy May (Wilkerson) Burgess; m. Stewart Alden Johnson, Aug. 8, 1970; 1 child, Lauren. BA, Coll. William & Mary, 1970; MSA, George Washington U., Washington, 1979. Pers. mgr. SBA, Washington, 1977-80, NASA, Washington, 1976-77, 80-84; pers. mgr. and orgn. dir. NOAA, Washington, 1984-88; county adminstr. King George County, King George, Va., 1988-89. Mem. IPMA (bd. dirs. fed. sector 1985-88). NAFE, ICMA, VACO, King George C. of C., Optimist Internat., Kappa Delta, Kappa Delta Pi, Beta Sigma Phi. Republican. Home: Box 1918 Dahlgren VA 22448 Office: NASA Hdqrs Code DE Washington DC 20546

JOHNSON, VALERIE SHARON, ombudsman; b. Wyandotte, Mich., Aug. 25, 1950; d. Glenn Clare Hedrick I and Patricia Arlene (Waldron) Wiggins; m. James Johnson (dec. Oct. 1984); children: D.J., Ronald, David, Kyle, Jimmy, Nicole. BA, Spring Arbor Coll., 1976. Mgr. regulatory hotline State of Mich., Lansing, 1979, dir. women bus. owners program, 1980, indsl. agt., 1981-83; bus. ombudsman, pub. speaker Mich. Commerce Dept. and Gov. Blanchard, Lansing, 1984—; instr. bus. courses Mich. Dept. Commerce. Bd. dirs. Concerns Police Survivors, Mich., Mich. Victims Alliance, Mich. Tech. Coun.; mem. leadership Cen. Meth. Ch. Traverse City, Mich.; bd. dirs. Mich. Tech. Coun.; mem. Grand Traverse LWV. Mem. Mich. Indsl. Developers Assn., Mich. Assn. for Academically Talented, Lansing Assn. for Academically Talented, LWV, Foster Parents Assn., Traverse City Econ. Club (bd. dirs.), Optimists. Republican. Office: care Traverse City C of C PO Box 387 Traverse City MI 49685-0387

JOHNSON, VICKI LYNN, legal secretary; b. Mpls., Nov. 20, 1961; d. Arnold Eino and Marian Gail (Hanson) J.; 1 child, Erin Nichole Leary. Student, N.D. State U., 1980-84, Va. Western U., 1990—. Adminstrv. asst. Ebenezer Soc., Mpls., 1987-88; law office sec. Law Office of Tonita M. Foster, Roanoke, Va., 1988-89; sec. Woods, Rogers & Hazlegrove, Roanoke, 1989—; judge N.D. State Sci. Fair, 1983. Big sister Big Brothers, Sisters, Fargo, N.D., 1982, Salvation Army Shelter for Battered Women, Roanoke, 1989. Mem. Nat. Assn. Legal Secs. Democrat. Baptist. Home: 215 Oak Dr Blue Ridge VA 24064 Office: Woods Rogers & Hazlegrove 105 Franklin Rd SW Roanoke VA 24064

JOHNSON, VICKI R., insurance company executive; b. Glens Falls, N.Y., June 19, 1952; d. Leonard H. and Rose (Petrosky) J. A.B., Franklin and Marshall Coll., 1974; postgrad. U. Portland, 1979-80; M.B.A., UCLA, 1986. Group mgr. The Prudential, San Diego, 1974—; mem. Oreg. Accident and Health Claim Assn., 1976-81. Pres., Ridgeview Condominium Assn., 1978-81; mem. Los Angeles Olympic Organizing Com., 1984. Fellow Life Mgmt. Inst.; mem. Los Angeles Accident and Health Claim Assn., The Woods Homeowners Assn., UCLA Alumni Bd. (dir. at large, exec. MBA). Home: 1691 Neptune Ave Leucadia CA 92024 Office: 9171 Towne Center Dr #380 San Diego CA 92122

JOHNSON, VICKY LYNN, lawyer; b. Crete, Nebr., July 18, 1955; d. Robert E. Jr. and Verna Mae (Henning) J. BA, U. Nebr., 1977; JD, U. Tex., 1980. Bar: Nebr. 1981. Investigator City of Sioux Falls, S.D., 1982-86; ptnr. Buhrmann Johnson & Wilson, Crete, 1986-88, Johnson & Wilson, Crete, 1989—. Active Saline County Child Abuse/Neglect Network, Crete, 1988-89; bd. dirs. YWCA, Sioux Falls, 1986, sec. bd. dirs., Lincoln, Nebr., 1988—. NSF scholar U. Nebr., 1976; Alt. Regent's scholar U. Nebr., 1973. Mem. Nebr. State Bar Assn., 7th Jud. Bar Assn. (treas. 1987-89), Rotary (v.p. Crete club 1988—), Phi Beta Kappa. Democrat. Office: Johnson & Wilson 334 E 13th St NE Crete NE 68333

JOHNSON, VICTORIA KAPRIELIAN, medical educator; b. The Bronx, N.Y., June 30, 1959; d. Walter V. and Julia (Hachigian) K.; m. Lemmuel Owen Johnson, Sept. 29, 1990. BA, Brown U., 1981; MD, UCLA, 1985. Diplomate Am. Bd. Family Practice. Resident Duke-Watts Family Practice, Durham, N.C., 1985-88; fellow UCLA Family Medicine, L.A., 1988-89; asst. clin. prof. Duke U. Med. Ctr., Durham, N.C., 1989—; dir. inpatient svc. Div. Community Medicine Duke U., 1989-90, dir. sports medicine, 1989—, dir. arts medicine, 1989—, dir. predoctoral edn. in family medicine, 1990—. Mem. Am. Acad. Family Physicians (pub. com. 1985, mental health com. 1986-88), N.C. Acad. Family Physicians (edn. com. 1989—, med. sch. affairs 1990—), Soc. Tchrs. Family Medicine.

JOHNSON, VILIA JOCELYN, perfume company executive; b. Bamberg, S.C., Dec. 21, 1953; d. John Franklin and Mary Elizabeth (Covington) J. BA in Lang. and Lit., BA in Social and Behavioral Scis., U. S. Fla., 1974. Sales clk. Sandcastle Swimwear, N.Y.C., 1975-76; market rep. Allied Stores Mktg., N.Y.C., 1976; retail buyer Mabley and Carew, Cin., 1977-78, Richman Gordman, Omaha, 1978-84; account exec. Cosmair Inc., Kansas City, Kans., 1984-85, Dallas, 1985; regional sales mgr. Cosmair Inc., St. Louis, 1986-87; asst. v.p., mgr. field sales Cosmair Inc., Dallas, 1987-89, L.A., 1990—. Office: Cosmair Designer Fragrances 575 Fifth Ave New York NY 10017

JOHNSON, ZOE ANN, accounting executive; b. Madison, Wis., Oct. 26, 1960; d. Gordon Heldt and Betty Ann (Rynders) J.; m. John Paul Seabolt, May 18, 1985. BBA with distinction, U. Wis., 1982. CPA, Wis., Tex. Sr. auditor Arthur Andersen & Co., Dallas, 1982-85; contr. Lyn Zanville, Inc., Dallas, 1985-86; mgr. gen. acctg. Meth. Hosps. of Dallas, 1986-89, mgr. planning, 1989—; bd. dirs. Meth. Hosp. Employee Fed. Credit Union. Mem. Healthcare Fin. Mgmt. Assn. Republican. Presbyterian. Office: Meth Hosps of Dallas 301 W Colorado Dallas TX 75208

JOHNSON BLANKENSHIP, ELIZABETH ANN, nurse; b. Pueblo, Colo., Jan. 10, 1952; d. James Jewell and Evalyn Marie (Hutchison) Carter; married; children: Gretchen, Ashley. Student, Sacred Heart Coll., Wichita, Kans., 1973-74; AS in Nursing, U. Cen. Ark., 1975; BS in Nursing, U. Tex., Arlington, 1988. R.N., Ark., Okla., Tex. Staff nurse Conway (Ark.) Meml. Hosp., 1975-76; dir. nursing Russellville (Ark.) Nursing Ctr., 1976-78; nursing cons. Ark. Office Long-Term Care, Little Rock, 1978-80; dir. nursing Stella Manor Nursing Ctr., Russellville, 1980-81; agy. dir. Vis. Nurses Assn., Fayetteville, Ark., 1981-82; dir. profl. svcs. Sooner Home Health Agy., Stilwell, Okla., 1982-84; exec. dir. Regional Health Systems, Inc., Muskogee, Okla., 1984-90; dir. nursing Cleburne Meml. Hosp., Heber Springs, Ark., 1990—; cons. home healthcare, Muskogee. Co-author: Patient Education in Home Care, 1988; contbr. articles to profl. jours. Muskogee regional coord., United Way, 1988. Mem. Nat. Home Care Assn., Okla. Home Health Care Assn., Am. Soc. Parenteral and Enteral Soc., Tex. Nurses Assn., Muskogee C. of C., Sigma Theta Tau. Democrat. Home: PO Box 753 Heber Springs AR 72543

JOHNSON-CHAMP, DEBRA SUE, lawyer, educator; b. Emporia, Kans., Nov. 8, 1955; d. Bert John and S. Christine (Brigman) Johnson; m. Michael W. Champ, Nov. 23, 1979; children: Natalie, John. BA, U. Denver, 1977; JD, Pepperdine U., 1980; postgrad. in library sci. U. So. Calif., 1983—. Bar: Calif. 1981. Sole practice, Long Beach, Calif., 1981-82, Los Angeles, 1981-87; legal reference librarian, instr. Southwestern U. Sch. Law, Los Angeles, 1982-88; adj. prof. law, 1987-88; atty. Contos & Bunch, Woodland Hills, Calif., 1988—. Editor-in-chief: Southern Calif. Assn. Law Libraries Newsletter, 1984-85. Contbr. articles to profl. journs. Mem. law rev. Pepperdine U., 1978-80. West Pub. Co. scholar, 1983; trustee United Meth. Ch., Tujunga, Calif., 1986—. Recipient H. Wayne Gillis Moot Ct. award, 1980, Vincent S. Dalsimer Best Brief award, 1979. Mem. ABA, So. Calif. Assn. Law Libraries, Am. Assn. Law Libraries, Calif. Bar Assn., Southwestern Affiliates, Friends of the Library Los Angeles. Democrat. Home: 5740 Valerie Ave Woodland Hills CA 91367 Office: Contos & Bunch 5855 Topanga Canyon Blvd Suite 400 Woodland Hills CA 91367

JOHNSON-GRAYUM, JANE ROBIN, dentist; b. San Antonio, Jan. 14, 1957; d. James Robert and Jacquelyn E. (Oualline) Johnson; m. Harry Wesley Grayum, Dec. 29, 1983. AA, San Antonio (Tex.) Jr. Coll., 1977; BA in Biology, U. Tex., 1980; DDS, U. Tex. Dental Br., Houston, 1984. Dentist McAleese & Grayum Family Dentistry, Houston. Home: 4315 Celestite Houston TX 77072 Office: McAleese & Grayum Dentistry 14179 Highway 290 Houston TX 77040

JOHNSON-LESSON, CHARLEEN ANN, teacher, insurance executive; b. Battle Creek, Mich., June 10, 1949; d. Kenneth Andrews Leeson and Ila Mae (Weed/Lesson) McCutcheon; m. Lynn Boyd Johnson, Aug. 8, 1970; children: Eric Andrew, Andrea Marie. BA, Spring Arbor Coll., 1971; MS in Reading, Western Ill. U., 1990. Cert. elem. and secondary tchr., Mich., elem. tchr., Ill., reading K-9, Ill. Tchr. Hanover (Mich.) Horton Schs., 1972-73, Virden (Ill.) Elem. Sch., 1984-90; ins. agt. State Farm, 1990—. Music dir., pianist Zion Luth. Ch., Farmersville, Ill., 1979-88, organist, pianist Olvie St. Friends, Battle Creek, 1961-67; cheerleading advisor, 1969-70; collegiate varsity cheerleader, 1967-69. Recipient Honor the Educator award World Book, 1988. Mem. AUA, Internat. Reading Assn., Virden Edn. Assn., Ill. Edn. Assn., Nat. Edn. Assn., Alpha Upsilon Alpha. Home: RR 1 Box C-77 Virden IL 62690 Office: State Farm Ins 2410 N Springfield Virden IL 62690

JOHNSTON, ARDENA CROWSON, public secretary, bookkeeper; b. Ackerman, Miss., June 25, 1929; d. Earl Oakley and Bernice Ora (Moss) Crowson; m. Everette C. Johnston, Aug. 20, 1946 (div. Aug. 1985); children: Billy Earl, Beverly (dec.), Allen Lee. Student, King Coll., Bristol, Tenn., 1947-48, U. Miss., 1949. Cert. of licence for ministry. Sales clk. Walker's 5 & 10 Cent Store, Louisville, Miss., 1943-46; full charge bookkeeper Dill & Norris Sheet Metal & Heating, Columbus, Miss., 1963-66; final analysis clk. Miss. Bapt. Med. Ctr., Jackson, 1981-85; owner Reliable Bookkeeping & Typing Svc., Richland, Miss., 1986—; tax preparer income taxes and state sales taxes. Author: Successful Living, 1984. Vol. counselor on personal and tax matters. Mem. Miss. Businesswomen (corr. sec.), Nat. Assn. Female Execs. Methodist. Home: 105 Pearl Ave Richland MS 39218-9568

JOHNSTON, CHRISTINA JANE, real estate executive, mortgage broker, educator; b. Toronto, Ont., Can., June 3, 1952; d. George Elmer and Mary Selina (Northey) J. BA with honors, U. Western Ont., London, 1975. Researcher, writer House of Commons, Ottawa, Ont., 1975-77; adminstrv. mgr. sales Marco Beach Realty, Marco Island, Fla., 1977-79; pres., owner Marco Summit Realty, Marco Island, 1979-82; v.p., mortgage broker Windjammer of Marco, Marco Island, 1979—; instr. Realty World Acad., St. Petersburg, Fla., 1979-81; pres., mgr. Fla. Sun Realty Co., Sarasota, 1982-86; v.p., mgr. Fla. Home Properties & Comml. Realty, Inc., 1986-87; mgr. 1st So. Trust Realty Corp., 1987—; bd. dirs., chmn. edn. com. Sarasota Bd. Realtors, 1985-86, also mem. realtors polit. action com. 1985—; pres. So. Gulf Council Realty World, 1980-82; bd. dirs. First Fla. region Broker's Council, Realty World, 1982-84; pres. Women's Council of Realtors, Marco Island, 1988; dir. Marco Island Bd. Realtors, 1987-89; pres. Marco Multi-List, 1989. Contbr. articles to profl. jours. Pres. Young Progressive Conservatives, Cambridge, Ont., 1968-70. Recipient Office of Yr. award Realty World, 1980, Top Listing Office award, 1981, Spl. award for Prodn., 1981, Million Dollar Sales Awards Marco Beach and Realty World, 1979-81; named Realtor of Yr. Marco Island Bd. Realtors, 1988. Mem. Sarasota C. of C., Marco Island C. of C. (chmn. Expo '82). Home: 1215 Edington Pl Apt L-4 Marco Island FL 33937

JOHNSTON, DOLORES MAE MASCIK (MRS. ROBERT EDGAR JOHNSTON), cultural organization administrator; b. Conneaut, Ohio, May 26, 1927; d. Michael Morris and Roberta Mary (Jacobs) Mascik; m. Robert Edgar Johnston, Mar. 19, 1950; children: Kirk, Christine, Mark. BS, Ohio State U., 1949. Lic. med. technologist; registered profl. parliamentarian. Researcher hematology dept. Ohio State U., Columbus, 1949-54; med. technologist Youngstown (Ohio) Hosp. Assn., 1954-55; med. technologist Eli Lilly Clin. Research Labs., Indpls., 1955-57, Green Bay, Wis., 1958-60. Mem. Green Bay Community Chorus, 1966-70, Bach Choir of Green Bay, 1970-80, St. Norbert Coll. Collegiate Chorale, 1980—; pack officer Boy Scouts of Am., 1970-71; co-chmn. ARC Blood Bank, 1970-72, mem. Lakeland chpt. steering com., 1974-76, 78-79, vol. chmn. blood bank vols., 1976-80; bd. dirs. Lakeland chpt. ARC, 1980-87, chmn. 1983-85, rep. to Badger Region blood services com., 1979-81, 82-83, rep. to Pere/Marquette div. council, 1980-82; vol. worker Mobile Meals, 1971—; pres. Brown County Med. Soc. Aux., 1969-70, dir., 1973-78, parl., 1989—; mem. Brown County Rep. Women's Club, 1969—; bd. dirs. Wis. Polit. Action Com., 1972-73; bd. dirs. Curative Workshop Rehab. Ctr., 1975-85, sec., 1976-78, pres., 1980-82; chmn. Ind. Living Program Council, 1982-85; sec. bd. dirs. Brown County United Way Council of Agys., 1975-76. Recipient Outstanding Mem. award Brown County Med. Aux., 1973-74, Vol. of Yr. award Lakeland chpt. ARC, 1981, Med. Services award Brown County Med. Soc., 1982, 31st Ann. Brotherhood award B'nai B'rith, 1984; named YWCA Women of Yr., 1977. Mem. Women's Aux. State Med. Soc. Wis. (pres. 1973-74, parliamentarian 1981-87, hon. membership conf. 1987), AMA Aux. (N.C. regional family health chmn. 1974-75, N.C. regional area counselor Project Bank, 1975-76, 76-77, nat. project bank coordinator 1977-78, nat. rec. sec. 1979-80, chmn. nat. health projects 1978-79, nat. historian, 1980-81), Wis. Assn. Parliamentarians (pres. 1987-89), Aesculapian Soc. (charter), Land O'Lakes Region Parliamentarian, Brown County Med. Soc. Aux. (pres. 1969-70), P.E.O. (chpt. treas. 1970-72, state conv. treas. 1976, chpt. pres. 1985-87), Internat. Tng. in Communication (parliamentarian 1989-90), Alpha Lambda Delta, Alpha Chi Omega. Lutheran. Clubs: Federated Women's, Jr. Women's., Fox Valley (treas. 1989-90). Lodge: Order Eastern Star, Shriners. Home: 3285 Waubenoor Dr Green Bay WI 54301

JOHNSTON, DONNA FAYE, color consultant, production art director; b. Stromburg, Nebr., Oct. 16, 1941; d. Verlin James and Roberta Carola (Larsen) Fellows; m. Robert Carl Johnston, May 2, 1964 (div. 1965); 1 child, Karla Kathliene. BFA, Kansas City Art Inst., 1963; journeyman cert., Graphic Communications Union, 1980; cert. color correction, Vocat. Tech. Edn., 1980. Prodn. mgr. H.H. Harney Advt., Lincoln, Nebr., 1966-68; lead mech. art and trainer Bozell & Jacobs Advt., Omaha, 1968-70; mech. art spl. account Dudycha Studio, Omaha, 1970-72; prodn. mgr. Oliver Advt., Kansas City, 1972-73; prodn. and color correction artist Vile/Goller Fine Arts, Kansas City, 1973-79; color correction artist K&A Lithographing, Kansas City, 1979-80, Chroma-Graphics, Kansas City, 1980-81; color correction artist and quality control Orent Graphic Arts, Omaha, 1981-86; color correction supr. Epsen-Hillmer Graphics Co., Omaha, 1986—; printing cons. Margo Kries-Entrepreneur, Stromsburg, 1987—, Willie Plith-Photographer, Omaha, 1987—. Author monthly newsletter Am. Singles, 1986. Mem. Landmarks, Omaha, 1986-87, Westport Art Assn., Kansas City, 1979-80, Earthwatch, Watertown, Mass., 1985-87, Nat. Geographic Soc., 1984-85. Mem. Omaha Club Printing House Craftsmen (bd. dirs.), Nat. Assn. Female Execs., Am. Singles of Omaha (pub. relations dir. 1986-87, author monthly newsletter 1986), Parents Without Ptnrs. (Outstanding Service award 1986). Methodist. Office: Epsen-Hillmer Graphics Co 2000 California Omaha NE 68102

JOHNSTON, ERIN ELAM, paralegal; b. Greensboro, N.C., Feb. 18, 1958; d. Harper J. and Mary (Glendinning) Elam; m. Clark Presley Johnston, Nov. 15, 1980; 1 child, Houston Tyler. BA, Appalachian State U., 1980; paralegal studies, Meredith Coll., 1985. Cert. legal asst. 1987. Legal sec. Griffin, Deaton, Horsley & Bailey, Reidsville, N.C., 1981-83; paralegal William F. Horsley, P.A., Reidsville, 1983-88, Donaldson & Horsley, P.A., Greensboro, N.C., 1988-89, Michael Lewis Attys., Winston-Salem, N.C., 1989—. Contbr. articles to various jours. Mem. Reidsville City Schs. Drug Task Force, 1987—. Named Legal Sec. of the Year Rockingham County Legal Secs., 1987. Mem. N.C. Acad. Trial Lawyers (chmn. legal assts. com.), N.C. Assn. Legal Secs. (credentials chmn. 1989). Democrat. Presbyterian. Home: PO Box 25132 Winston-Salem NC 27114-5132 Office: White And Crumpler 11 W Fourth St Winston-Salem NC 27101

JOHNSTON, GRACE ELIETTE, newspaper advertising executive; b. Middleboro, Mass., Feb. 5, 1957; d. Edward George and Eliette Helene (Racine) J. BA in Sociology, Gordon Coll., Wenham, Mass., 1978. Activity dir. Heritage Hall Nursing Home, Agawam, Mass., 1978-79; advt. account exec. Transcript-Telegram, Holyoke, Mass., 1979-82, mgr. retail advt., 1982-85; mgr. retail advt. Burlington (Vt.) Free Press, 1985-88; advt. dir. Rutland (Vt.) Herald, 1988—. Bd. dirs. United Way Rutland County, 1990. Recipient New Kid on Block award United Way Rutland County, 1989. Mem. New Eng. Newspaper Advt. Execs. Assn. (Bright Idea award 1989), New Eng. Newspaper Assn. (speaker 1982—), Internat. Newspaper and Mktg. Execs., Rotary (sec., bd. dirs. Rutland 1989-91). Republican. Office: Rutland Herald 27 Wales St Rutland VT 05701

JOHNSTON, GWINAVERE ADAMS, public relations consultant; b. Casper, Wyo., Jan. 6, 1943; d. Donald Milton Adams and Gwinavere Marie (Newell) Quillen; m. H.R. Johnston, Sept. 26, 1963 (div. 1973); children: Gwinavere G., Gabrielle Suzanne; m. Donald Charles Cannalte, Apr. 4, 1981. BS in Journalism, U. Wyo., 1966; postgrad., Denver U., 1968-69. Editor, reporter Laramie (Wyo.) Daily Boomerang, 1965-66; account exec. William Kostka Assocs., Denver, 1966-71, v.p., 1969-71; exec. v.p. Slottow, McKinlay & Johnston, Denver, 1971-74; pres. The Johnston Group, Denver, 1974—; adj. faculty U. Colo. Sch. Journalism, 1988—. Bd. dirs. Leadership Denver Assn., 1975-77, 83-86, Mile High United Way, 1989—. Mem. Pub. Rels. Soc. Am. (pres. Colo. chpt. 1978-79, bd. dirs. 1975-80, 83-86, nat. exec. com. Counselor's Acad. 1988-90, profl. award), Colo. Women's Forum, Rocky Mountain Pub. Rels. Group (founder), Com. of 200, Denver Athletic Club, Denver Press Club. Republican. Home: 717 Monaco Pkwy Denver CO 80220 Office: The Johnston Group 1512 Larimer St #720 Denver CO 80202

JOHNSTON, JANIS CLARK, psychologist, consultant; b. South Bend, Ind., Jan. 5, 1947; d. Robert Dale and Lois Treasure (Whitacre) Clark; m. Mark Emmett Johnston, June 14, 1969; children: Ryan Clark, Megan Gale. BA with distinction, Manchester Coll., 1969; MEd, Boston U., 1970, EdD, 1974. Lic. psychologist; cert. sch. psychologist. Psychol. examiner Harvard Pre-Sch. Project, Cambridge, Mass., 1973-74; sch. psychologist Lexington (Mass.) Pub. Schs., 1972-78; therapist and trainer Acorn Employee Assistance Program, Phila., 1979-81; sch. psychologist Oak Park-River Forest (Ill.) High Sch., 1981-89; pvt. practice family therapy and systems consultation Oak Park, Ill., 1984—; instr. Boston U., 1974-75; clin. asst. prof. and supr. psychologist Hahnemann Med. Coll. and Hosp., Phila., 1978-81; cons. Acorn, Chgo., 1984-88. NDEA Title IV fellow, 1969-72. Mem. Am. Psychol. Assn., Nat. Assn. Sch. Psychologists, Ill. Sch. Psychologists Assn. (region 1 Sch. Psychology Practitioner of Yr. 1984), Psychologists for Social Responsibility, LWV, NOW.

JOHNSTON, JONI ELIZABETH, clinical psychologist; b. Sarasota, Fla., Oct. 29, 1960; d. Manley Thurston and Sara Elizabeth (Bruner) J.; m. Stuart A. Thomson, Aug. 11, 1984 (div. Jan. 1989). BS in Psychology, Auburn U., 1981; MS in Clin. Psychology, Fla. Inst. Tech., 1984, D Clin. Psychology, 1985. Lic. clin. psychologist, Tex. Staff psychologist Dallas Child Guidance Clinic, 1985-87; cons. Neurobehavioral Inst. Dallas, 1987-88; pvt. practice Psychiatry & Psychology Assocs., Dallas, 1988—. Bd. dirs. Arts For People, Dallas, 1988-89; mem. Dallas Women's Found., 1989—, North Dallas C. of C., 1988-89. Mem. Am. Psychol. Assn., Dallas Psychol. Assn. (com. chair 1988—), Mental Health Assn. (chmn. May is Mental Health Month com. 1989, bd. dirs. Dallas chpt. 1989—, speaker's bur. 1987—). Office: 7515 Greenville Ave 806 Dallas TX 75231

JOHNSTON, JOSEPHINE ROSE, chemist; b. Cranston, R.I., Aug. 9, 1926; d. Robert and Rose (Varca) Forte; m. Howard Robert Johnson, Mar. 7, 1949; 1 child, Kevin Howard. Student, Carnegie Inst., 1945-47; BS, Mich. State U., 1972, MA, 1973; postgrad., MIT, 1973—. Med. technologist South Nassau Community Hosp., Rockville Centre, N.Y., 1947-50; med. technologist Mich. State U., East Lansing, 1950-53, faculty specialist, 1966-76; dept. pathology Albany (N.Y.) Med. Ctr., 1953-54; med. lab. supr. Bulova Watch Co., Jackson Heights, N.Y., 1954-57; sr. chemistry technologist Mid Island Hosp., Bethpage, N.Y., 1958-66; sr. rsch. assoc. Uniformed Svcs. Univ., Bethesda, Md., 1976-78; asst. to chmn. dept. physiology Uniformed Svcs. Univ., Bethesda, 1978-82, assoc. to chmn., 1982—. Contbr. articles in field to profl. jours. Mem. Analytical Chem. Soc., Data and Electronic Soc., Internat. Platform Assn. Lutheran. Office: 6813 Woodville Rd Mount Airy MD 21771

JOHNSTON, KAREN QUEALLY, rehabilitation director; b. Yonkers, N.Y., Mar. 3, 1952; d. Terence Dennis and Ann S. Queally. BS in Phys. Therapy, NYU, 1974; MS Health Care Adminstrn., Iona Coll., 1983. Phys. therapist Burks Rehab. Ctr., White Plains, N.Y., 1974-79; phys. therapy dir. St. Patrick's Home, Bronx, N.Y., 1979-80; rehab. dir. Cabrini Nursing

Home, Dobbs Ferry, N.Y., 1980-84; asst. adminstr. Met. Jewish Geriatric Ctr., Bklyn., 1984-85; rehab. dir. E. Bay Hillhaven, Alameda, Calif., 1985-86; regional rehab. dir. No. Calif. Hillhaven, Richmond, Calif., 1986-88; East Bay Area dir. No. Calif. Hillhaven, Richmond, 1988-89; dir. rehab. Kaiser Oakland, Calif., 1989—; cons. in field; instr. at various univs. Recipient Robert B. Power Award for Excellence in Health Care Systems Mgmt., 1984. Mem. Am. Phys. Therapy Assn. (treas. 1988—, rep. at Assy. of Reps. 1987—). Home: 519 Santa Teresa Millbrae CA 94030 Office: Kaiser Oakland Med Ctr 280 W MacArthur Blvd Oakland CA 94611

JOHNSTON, LYNNE S. C., property manager; b. Washington, Aug. 28, 1947; d. Louis P. and Thelma (Posey) Carstensen; children: Julie Catherine Johnston-Fuentes, Joseph Jonathan. Student, Portland Community Coll., Oreg., Portland State U.; DD (hon.). Asst. to v.p., dean sch. medicine U. Oreg., Eugene; asst. to v.p. mid Atlantic region Western Devel. Corp., Georgetown, Washington; corp. systems analyst, mktg. rep. Indsl. Tech. Internat., Falls Church, Va.; sector govt. property adminstr. Sci. Applications Internat. Corp., McLean, Va. Contbr. articles to profl. jours. Mem. NAFE, Nat. Property Mgmt. Assn. (cert. personal property specialist, co-founder northern Va. chpt.), Am. Soc. Profl. and Exec. Women, Oreg. State Mgmt. Assn.

JOHNSTON, MARY ELLEN, nursing educator; b. Roswell, N.Mex., June 4, 1951; d. E. Bernard and Jane (Shugart) J. BSN, Baylor U., 1973; MSN, Oral Roberts U., 1982. Staff nurse crit. care dept. Tucson Med. Ctr., 1973-74; charge nurse med. unit St. Mary's Hosp., Roswell, 1975; instr. nursing Ea. N.Mex. U., Roswell, 1975—; faculty advisor for Phi Theta Kappa. Mem. ANA (cert. med./surgical nursing), DAR, P.E.O., N.Mex. Nurses Assn. (pres. dist. V), Baylor U. Nurses Alumni Assn., Philanthropic and Ednl. Orgn., Daus. of Am. Colonists, Altrusa Club Roswell, Sigma Theta Tau.. Republican. Methodist. Home: 2715 N Kentucky Ave #16 Roswell NM 88201 Office: Ea NMex U PO Box 6000 Roswell NM 88202-6000

JOHNSTON, NANCY DAHL, data processing specialist; b. Waco, Tex., Sept. 18, 1954; d. Howard Edward and Gladys Marie (Haynes) Dahl; children: Russell Edward, Dennis Aaron. Student, Tex. Woman's U., Denton, Victor Valley Coll., Victorville, Calif. Accounts mgr. Pacific Physicians' Svcs., Loma Linda, Calif., 1978-81; data processing coord. Denton County, Denton, 1986-89; exec. asst. Jet-Line Svc., Inc., Portland, Maine, 1989—. Mem. NAFE, Mcpl. Software Users Group (sec. 1988-89), Greenpeace. Home: 42-B Blueberry Ln Gray ME 04039

JOHNSTON, PATRICIA CARYL, social worker; b. Neuilly-Sur-Seine, France, Apr. 12, 1954; d. Bruce Foster and Harriet Lou (Pollins) J. BA in Psychology, Stanford U., 1976; MSW, U. Denver, 1978. Lic. clin. social worker, Colo. Social worker Jefferson County Pub. Schs., Golden, Colo., 1978—; pvt. practice psychotherapy Lakewood, Colo., 1989—; faculty cons. Inst. for Child Abuse and Neglect, Lakewood, 1985-86. Bd. dirs. Met. Child Protection Coun., Denver, 1980-83, v.p.; vol. Sexual Assault Program Luth. Hosp., Wheat Ridge, Colo., 1983-87, chairperson, 1984-86; bd. dirs. Denver Women's Chorus, 1987-89, pres. 1988-89, v.p. 1987-88). Named Vol. of Yr., Vol. Connection, 1986. Mem. nat. Assn. Social Workers (cert., presenter sch. social work conf. Feb. 1985, profl. symposium Nov. 1985), Colo. Child Protection Coun., Jefferson County Edn. Assn., Colo. Assn. for Children of Alcoholics and Other Addictions. Democrat. Home: 3484 W 36th Ave Denver CO 80211

JOHNSTON, RUBY CHARLOTTE, nurse; b. Freedom, Nebr., Oct. 6, 1918; d. William Murray and Delia Isabel (Morgan) Phillips; student Nebr. Sch. Agr., Curtis, 1932-36, U. Colo., Boulder, summer 1938; R.N., Denver Gen. Hosp., 1945; m. Gerald William Johnston, Sept. 19, 1943; 1 son, Leo F. Rural sch. tchr., 1936-41; sec. supt.'s office Nebr. Sch. Agr., 1941-42; staff nurse Denver Gen. Hosp., 1945-46; office nurse, Cambridge, Nebr., 1946-47; staff nurse St. Catherine's Hosp., McCook, Nebr., 1947-56, LaGrange County Hosp., LaGrange, Ind., 1956-58; obstet. supr. LaGrange County Hosp., 1958-68, dir. nurses, 1968-70; dir. nurses Miller's Merry Manor, LaGrange, 1970-76; county health nurse LaGrange County Health Dept., LaGrange, 1976-80, part-time staff nurse, 1980—; chmn. exec. com. Ind. Nurses Assn. Geriatric Conf., 1975-77; deacon Presbyt. Ch. Bd. dirs. N.E. Ind. chpt. Am. Lung Assn., 1981-89; Co-coordinator Focus on Health, LaGrange, 1982-85. Registered Mem. Ind. Nurses Assn., Nurses Assn. Am. Coll. Obstetricians and Gynecologists, Am. Legion Aux. Republican. Clubs: Bus. and Profl. Women's, Eastern Star, River Oaks Extension. Home: Rural Route 2 Box 298 Howe IN 46746 Office: Cour House Annex LaGrange IN 46761

JOHNSTON, VIRGINIA EVELYN, editor; b. Spokane, Wash., Apr. 26, 1933; d. Edwin and Emma Lucile (Munroe) Rowe; student Portland Community Coll., 1964, Portland State U., 1966, 78-79; m. Alan Paul Beckley, Dec. 26, 1974; children—Chris, Denise, Rex. Proofreader, The Oregonian, Portland, 1960-62, teletypesetter operator, 1962-66, operator Photon 200, 1966-68, copy editor, asst. women's editor, 1968-80; spl. sects. editor (UPDATE), 1981-83, 88—; editor FOODday, 1982—; pres. Matrix Assos., Inc., Portland, 1975—, chmn. bd., 1979—; cons. Democratic party Oreg., 1969, Portland Sch. Dist. No. 1, 1978. Mem. Women in Communications, Inc., Inst. Profl. and Managerial Women, Nat. Assn. Female Execs., Eating and Drinking Soc. Oreg. (pres.), We. Culinary Inst. (mem. adv. bd.), Portland Culinary Alliance (mem. adv. bd.). Democrat. Editor Principles of Computer Systems for Newspaper Mgmt., 1975-76. Home: 4140 NE 137th Ave Portland OR 97230 Office: 1320 SW Broadway Portland OR 97201

JOHNSTONE, PAULA SUE, medical technologist; b. Springfield, Mo., July 5, 1947; d. Nathan Paul and Ima Louise (Glenn) Johnstone. BS, S.W. Mo. State U., 1969. Cert. med. technologist Am. Soc. Clin. Pathologists. Vol., Cox Med. Ctr., Springfield, 1964-68; lab., office aide Springfield Med. Lab., 1964-68; chief technologist Springfield Gen. Osteo. Hosp., 1969-73; staff technologist St. John's Regional Health Ctr., Springfield, 1973-75, evening supr., 1975-76, asst. adminstrv. dir., 1976-86; clin. lab. coordinator, 1986-89; lab. computer coord., 1989—. Dir., Glidewell Baptist Ch. Tng., Springfield, 1984-85, chmn. budget and fin. com. 1986-87. Mem. Am. Soc. Med. Technologists, Nat. Cert. Agy. Med. Lab. Personnel, Mo. Soc. Med. Technologists (pres. 1976-77, columnist newsletter 1976-77), Nat. Assn. Female Execs., S.W. Mo. State U. Alumni Assn. Baptist. Clubs: Nat. Travel, Frommer's Dollarwise Travel Club. Avocations: European travel; reading; knitting; house plants. Home: Route 5 Box 495C Springfield MO 65803 Office: St John's Regional Health Ctr 1235 E Cherokee Springfield MO 65804

JOHNSTONE, SALLY MAC, educational association administrator, psychology educator; b. Macon, Ga., Dec. 8, 1949; d. Ralph E. and Maxine A. Johnstone; m. Stephen R. Tilson, 1977. BS, Va. Poly. Inst., 1974, MS, 1976; PhD, U. N.C., 1982. Lectr. European div. U. Md., Heidelberg, Fed. Republic of Germany, 1982-84; instr. psychology U. Md., College Park, 1984-89, asst. dean, 1984-86, dir. Ctr. for Instructional Telecommunications, 1986-89; dir. Western Coop. for Ednl. Telecommunications, Boulder, Colo., 1989—; cons. Grand Valley State U., Grand Rapids, Mich., 1989, Can. Distance Learning Devel. Centre, Edmonton, Alta., Can., 1989, Program for Educating Nurses via Satellite Links, Charleston, W.VA., 1988-89, Fairleigh Dickinson U., Teaneck, N.J., 1990; invited panelist U.S. Dept. Edn., Washington, 1990—; vice chair distance learning com. Md. Higher Edn. Com., Annapolis, Md., 1988-89. Mem. Ednl. Access Com., Prince George's County, Md., 1986-89; sci. fair judge U. Hills. Elem. Sch., Md., 1986-89. Annenberg/CPB Project grantee, 1988; recipient Disting. Rsch. award Nat. U. Continuing Edn. Assn., 1989. Mem. Am. Psychology Assn., Internat. Teleconferencing Assn., Pub. Svc. Satellite Consortium. Office: Western Coop Ednl 1540 30th St Boulder CO 80301-9752

JOINVILLE, PATRICIA KAY, distributorship branch manager; b. Woonsocket, R.I., Apr. 4, 1955; d. Henry David and Katherine (Horbaychuk) J. Tng. supr., asst. mgr. Assoc. Fin. Svcs., R.I., Pa., 1977-81, Tex., 1977-81; inside sales rep. Bearings, Inc., Dover, N.H., 1982-85; branch mgr. outside sales Eastern Bearings, Inc., Portsmouth, N.H., 1985—. Vol. Portsmouth Regional Hosp., 1989. Named Outstanding Airman of 1988 N.H. Air Nat. Guard. Mem. Bus. & Profl. Women (2nd v.p. 1986-87). Roman Catholic. Home: 2 Maplewood Ave Dover NH 03820 Office: Eastern Bearings Inc 270 West Rd Portsmouth NH 03801

JOKERST, CAROL ANN, religious group leadership team member; b. St. Louis, Mar. 28, 1939; d. Oliver W. and Mary Virginia (Prendergast) J. BA, Incarnate Word Coll., 1964; MA, St. Louis U., 1971, Duquesne U., 1974. Cert. jr./sr. high sch. tchr. Tchr. St. Dismas Sch., Florissant, Mo., 1962-63; tchr. Incarnate Word Acad., St. Louis, 1964-71; dir. formation Sisters of Charity of Incarnate Word, San Antonio, 1974-80, gen. adminstrv. team, 1984—; exec. dir. Religious Formation Conf., Washington, 1980-83; dir. mission effectiveness Incarnate Word Health System, San Antonio, 1983-84; chmn. bd. Spohn Health Care System, Corpus Christi, Tex., 1985—; bd. dirs. Santa Rosa Health Care System, San Antonio, Incarnate Word Health System, San Antonio, Incarnate Word Coll., San Antonio. Tchr. G.E.D. Program, St. Louis, 1967-69; vol. chaplain Med. Ctr. Hosp. (County), San Antonio, 1977-80. Mem. Religious Formation Conf. (bd. dirs. 1976-78), World Future Soc., Nat. Vocation Conf., Tex. Conf. Catholic Health Care Facilities. Democrat. Roman Catholic.

JOLIN, PEGGY, state legislature; b. London Springs, Oreg., Mar. 21, 1952; d. Paul and Loraine Wopschall; m. Dennis Jolin; 1 child, Sean. Student, Antelope Valley Coll., Lane Community Coll., U. Oreg. Rep. Oreg. Ho. of Reps., 1980-87; senator Oreg. State Senate, 1989—; majority whip, 1983; chair Sunset Rev. Com., 1985, mem. 1987; chair Consumer and Bus. Affairs Com., 1987, Ins. Task Force Com., 1987, Telecommunicaitons and Consumer Affairs Com., 1989—; vice chair Bus. Econs. and Fin. Com., 1989—; mem. Lane County Budget Com., 1977-78, House Leadership Policy Com., 1987, Transp. Com., 1987, Trade and Econ. Devel. Com., 1989—, Tourism Com., 1989—; speaker's alternate Legis. Trade and Economy Com., 1987; appointed to Western Coun. of State Govs. Com. on Econ. Devel. and Internat. Trade. Named Outstanding Young Woman Am., 1985. Home: 31251 Joe Geer Rd Cottage Grove OR 97424 Office: Senate Chamber Salem OR 97310

JOLINSKI, JENNY RAMIREZ, information management specialist; b. Pueblo, Colo., June 20, 1947; d. Paul Sr. and Frances (Hernandez) Ramirez; m. Edwin Clinton Bailey, Nov. 1, 1969 (div. 1982); 1 child, Jean Ramirez Bailey; m. John Henry Jolinski, Apr. 28, 1984. BA, So. Colo. State Coll., Pueblo, 1969; MSLS, U. N.C., 1972. Rsch. assoc. Sch. Medicine U. N.C., Chapel Hill, 1972-73; libr., instr. Atkins Libr. U. N.C., Charlotte, 1973-75; cons. Am. Heart Assn., Dallas, 1975-76; realtor Merrill Lynch Realty, Orlando, Fla., 1980-83; mktg. mgr. Landstar Homes, Kissimmee, Fla., 1983-85; asst. dir. Harcourt Brace Jovanovich, Orlando, 1985—. Mem. Assn. for Info. and Image Mgmt., Spl. Librs. Assn., ARMA Internat., NAFE. Democrat. Roman Catholic. Home: 112 Cinnamon Dr Orlando FL 32825 Office: Harcourt Brace Jovanovich 6277 Sea Harbor Dr Orlando FL 32887

JONDAHL, TERRI ELISE, sales and marketing professional; b. Ukiah, Calif., May 6, 1959; d. Thomas William and Rebecca (Stewart) J. AA in Bus. Adminstrn., Mendocino Coll., 1981; postgrad., Columbia Pacific U., 1989—. Sec. to planning commn. County of Mendocino, Ukiah, Calif., 1977-80; office systems analyst County of Mendocino, Ukiah, 1980-83; micro systems analyst Computerland of Annapolis, Md., 1983-84; controller Continental Mfg. Inc., Nacogdoches, Tex., 1984-87; mktg. mgr. Continental Mfg. Inc., Nacogdoches, 1987-89, dir. sales and mktg., 1989—, sec., treas., 1985—; bd. dirs. Doubledave's Pizzaworks, Inc., College Station, Tex., 1988—; cons. acct. Drosia Trading Inc., Nacogdoches, 1988-89. Co-author: National Federation of Business & Professional Women Local Organization Revitalization Plan, 1989. Mem. Mktg. Edn. Adv. Council Nacogdoches Ind. Sch. Dist., 1989. Mem. Tex. Fedn. Bus. & Profl. Women (dist. dir. 1989-90), Nacogdoches Bus. & Profl. Women (pres. 1987-88), Ukiah Bus. & Profl. Women (pres. 1981-82), Nat. Assn. Female Execs., Nacogdoches County C. of C. Home: 5303 Scenic Dr Nacogdoches TX 75961 Office: Continental Mfg Inc 2306 Rayburn Dr Nacogdoches TX 75961

JONES, ANGELA, media relations specialist; b. Vicksburg, Miss., Mar. 2, 1959; d. Horatio Erwin and Bessie Ree (Crump) J. BS, U. So. Miss., 1980. Announcer Sta. WJDX-AM/WZZQ-FM, Jackson, Miss., 1980-81; news dir. Sta. WVMI-AM/WQID-FM, Biloxi, Miss., 1981-86; news reporter WWL News Radio, New Orleans, 1986-87; news producer, editor Mut. Broadcasting/NBC Radio, Washington, 1988-89; pub. rels. counsel Nat. Fedn. Ind. Bus., Washington, 1989—. Mem. Women in Communications, Am. Women in Radio and TV, Radio-TV News Dirs. Assn. Democrat. Methodist. Office: Nat Fedn of Ind Bus 600 Maryland Ave SW #700 Washington DC 20024

JONES, ANNABEL MARIE, lawyer; b. Oklahoma City, Nov. 18, 1953; d. William Lloyd and Betty Mae (Conner) J. BA with distinction, U. Okla., 1976; JD, 1979. Bar: Okla. 1979, U.S. Dist. (we. dist.) Okla. 1981, U.S. Dist. (ea. dist.) Okla. 1989. Law clk. to judge U.S. Dist. Ct. Okla., Oklahoma City, 1979-80; assoc. gen. counsel Okla. Securities Commn., Oklahoma City, 1980-82; sr. atty. Samson Prodn. Svcs. Co., Tulsa, 1982—. Mem. Tulsa Phil. Vol. Coun., 1986-90, Tulsa Ballet Theatre Guild, 1986-90, Leadership Tulsa, 1988—, Okla. Bar Assn. Select Com. on Securities Law, Oklahoma City, 1986—; bd. dirs. Big Bros. and Sisters Green County, Tulsa, 1989—. Mem. ABA (state regulation sec. oil and gas subcom. Chgo. chpt. 1986—, fed. regulation sec. Chgo. chpt. 1986—, state regulation securities com. Chgo. 1986—, fed. regulation securities com. Chgo. 1986—), Gamma Phi Beta, Phi Beta Kappa, Phi Delta Phi. Democrat. Office: Samson Prodn Svcs Samson Pla 2W 2d Tulsa OK 74103

JONES, ANNE ELIZABETH, motor license agent, insurance executive; b. Chgo., Nov. 26, 1945; d. George Edward and Betty Jane (Wise) Sybrant; m. Brenton Elvis Jones, Aug. 15, 1965 (div. June 1980); children: James Devon, Douglas Edward, Robert Derrick. Student, Ark. City Jr. Coll., Kans., 1962-64, Okla. State U., 1964-65. Credit mgr. Koppel's, Bartlesville, Okla., 1966-67; collector Am. Collection Agy., Bartlesville, 1967-72; office mgr. Paul Stumpff & Assocs., Bartlesville, 1972-82; owner A.J. Leasing, Inc., Tulsa, 1982—, Sooner Assocs., Inc., Tulsa, 1982—; motor lic. agt. Cen. Tag Agy., Tulsa, 1982—. Mem. Motor Lic. Agts. Assn. (exec. v.p. 1984-85, polit. liaison 1984, tchr. ins. and lic. law 1984, legis. chmn. 1986-87, exec. v.p., 1987—, liaison commn. sec. 1988-89, state sec. 1989-90), Ins. Women Tulsa (legis. chmn. 1984, pub. relations chmn. 1985, tchr. ins. classes 1979-85, cert. profl. ins. woman, bylaws chmn., 1987, chmn. pubs. 1989-90), Nat. Odometer Enforcement Assn., Midwest Taskforce on Odometer Enforcement, Soc. Cert. Ins. Counselors (apprentice faculty), Soc. of Cert. Ins. Svc. Reps. (seminar instr. 1989, 90), Nat. Assn. Ins. Women (state orgn. chmn. 1985, Rookie of Yr. 1981, regional winner Lace Speak-Off 1985, 1st Runner-up Nat. Speak-Off 1985, Region vi chmn. pub. relations, 1986-87), Tulsa C. of C., Okla. Soc. Chartered Ins. Counselors (charter), Profl. Ins. Agts. Okla. (seminar instr. 1979-90), Ind. Ins. Agts. Okla. (seminar instr. 1979-83), Toastmasters (Tulsa) (various offices, Area 1 Gov., 1987-88). Avocations: pub. speaking, motivational seminars, antique dealing, oil painting, photography. Office: Cen Tag Agy 2702 E 15th St Tulsa OK 74104

JONES, ANNE MARKEY, health science facility administrator, consultant; b. Winston-Salem, N.C., Jan. 16, 1953; d. Andrew Joseph and Mary I. (Ayers) Markey; m. Larry Joseph Imes, Oct. 8, 1977 (separate). BSN, U. N.C., 1974. RN. Staff nurse N.C. Bapt. Hosp., Winston-Salem, 1974-78; staff nurse II pediatrics dept. Charlotte (N.C.) Meml. Hosp., 1978-79; neurology nurse specialist neurology dept. Bowman Gray Sch. of Medicine, Winston-Salem, 1979-81, lectr. in neurology, 1982-89; dir. vascular lab. Montefiore Med. Ctr. Albert Einstein Coll. of Medicine, Bronx, 1989—; ednl. coord. Bowman Gray Sch. of Medicine, 1981-89. Mem. Young Dems., Winston-Salem, 1972-76. Mem. Soc. Vascular Tech. (pres. 1985-86), Am. Registry Diagnostic MEd. Sonographers (bd. dirs. 1987—), Am. Heart Assn. (stroke coun.). Roman Catholic. Office: Montefiore Med Ctr Vascular Lab 111 E 210th St Bronx NY 10046

JONES, ANNIE WALTON, educator; b. Marshall, Tex., Nov. 3, 1952; d. Ollie and Obelia (Brown) Walton; m. Roger Lee Jones, Aug. 21, 1987; children: Ardis Delano Walton, Kristie Elease Walton Jones. BA, Wiley Coll., 1976; cert. in teaching, 1981; MEd Guidance, Counseling, Prairie View Med. Coll., 1984. Respiratory technician Meml. Hosp., Marshall, 1974-76; rural housing asst. E-TEX.HUDCO, Marshall, 1977-78; housing adminstr. City of Marshall Housing Authority, 1978-79; from payroll clk. to adminstrv. asst. for devel. Wiley Coll., Marshall, 1979-81; tchr. Marshall Ind. Sch. Dist., 1982—. Mem. Tex. State Tchrs., NEA, Tex. Vocat. Guidance Assn. (auction com. 1988-89), Nat. Assn. Curriculum Devel., Nat. Assn. Female Execs., Women's Softball Club, Delta Sigma Theta (life). Democrat. Baptist. Home: 408 S Callum St Marshall TX 75670 Office: Marshall Ind Sch Dist 700 W Houston St Marshall TX 75670

JONES, ARDITH BROCKA, health occupations educator; b. Aplington, Iowa, July 26, 1940; d. Herman Henry and Kathryn (Bengen) Brocka; m. Lester Tyler Jones, Apr. 9, 1962; children: Trent Tyler, Lance David, Kevin Neal. BA, U. Iowa, 1962; postgrad., U. Minn., 1981—. Cert. vocat. edn. tchr., Minn.; cert. med. technologist, Am. Soc. Clin. Pathologists. Chief med. technolgist Meml. Hosp., Pullman, Wash., 1962-64; med. technologist Dist. Meml. Hosp., Forest Lake, Minn., 1977-78, Bethesda Luth. Hosp., St. Paul, 1979-82; exec. dir. Health Occupations Students of Am., Dept. of Edn. State of Minn., St. Paul, 1982-84, health occupations specialist, 1984-89, Health Occupations Students of Am. adv., 1982-89; bd. dirs. Nat. Health Occupations Students of Am., Dallas, 1987-88. Mem. charter commn. City of White Bear Lake (Minn.), 1979-83; election judge City of White Bear Lake, 1976-83, pres. Willow Elem. Sch. PTA, White Bear Lake, 1977-81; parent advisory chair Mariner High Sch., White Bear Lake, 1982-84. Mem. Nat. Assn. of State Adminstrs. of Health Occupations Edn., Am. Vocat. Assn., Minn. Vocat. Assn., AAUW (v.p. White Bear Lake chpt. 1988--), LWV, Antique Club. Republican. Home: 2215 South Shore Blvd White Bear Lake MN 55110

JONES, AUDREY HOWARD, management consultant; b. Bklyn., May 13, 1928; d. Edward Richard and Venie Ednora (Jacobs) Howard; BA, Hunter Coll., 1949; MS in Marine Sci., L.I. U., 1969; m. Farrell Jones, June 16, 1951; children: Joanne Kathryn and Jacqueline Elinor (twins). Rsch. biochemist Manhattan Eye, Ear and Throat Hosp., 1949-51, Downstate Med. Coll., SUNY, Bklyn., 1952-58; instr. biology Nassau Community Coll., Garden City, N.Y., also cons. Environ. Assocs. and Urban Edn., Inc., 1970-73; environ. scientist, then EEO mgr. L.I. Lighting Co., Hicksville, N.Y., 1972-79, personnel policies and svcs. mgr., 1979-86, mgr. tng. and devel., 1986-90, mgmt. cons., 1990—; adj. asst. prof. N.Y. Inst. Tech., 1979-80; field faculty adv. Goddard grad. program Norwich U., 1981-83; lectr. SUNY, Farmingdale; mem. career svcs. adv. bd. Adelphi U., 1981—. Mem. citizens adv. com. N.Y. State Coastal Zone Mgmt. Program; mem. L.I. regional adv. com. N.Y. State External High Sch. Diploma Program; assoc. trustee L.I. Jewish Med. Ctr. Recipient various svc. awards, certs. appreciation. Mem. Am. Gas Assn. (various coms. 1975-84), Edison Electric Inst. (various coms. 1975-84), L.I. Assn. (chmn. personnel dirs. council 1980-81), LWV, NAACP, L.I. Center for Bus. and Profl. Women (pres. 1982-84), Delta Sigma Theta. Democrat. Unitarian-Universalist. Clubs: Zonta, 100 Black Women of L.I. Home: 22 Driftwood Dr Port Washington NY 11050 Office: LI Lighting Co 175 E Old Country Rd Hicksville NY 11801

JONES, BARBARA CHRISTINE, educator, linguist, creative arts designer; b. Augsburg, Swabia, Bavaria, Fed. Republic Germany, Nov. 14, 1942; came to U.S., 1964, naturalized, 1971; d. Martin Walter and Margarete Katharina (Roth-Rommel) Schulz von Hammer-Parstein; m. Robert Edward Dickey, 1967 (div. 1980); m. Raymond Lee Jones, 1981. Student U. Munich, 1961, Philomatique de Bordeaux, France, 1962; BA in German, French, Speech, Calif. State U., Chico, 1969, MA in Comparative Internat. Edn., 1974. Cert. secondary tchr., community coll. instr., Calif. Fgn. lang. tchr. Gridley Union High Sch., Calif., 1970-80, home econs., decorative arts instr., cons., 1970-80, English study skills instr., 1974-80, ESL coordinator, instr. Punjabi, Mex. Ams., 1970-72, curriculum com. chmn., 1970-80; program devel. adviser Program Devel. Ctr. Supt. Schs. Butte County, Oroville, Calif., 1975-77; opportunity tchr. Esperanza High Sch., Gridley, 1980-81, Liberty High Sch., Lodi, Calif., 1981-82, resource specialist coordinator, 1981-82; Title I coordinator Bear Creek Ranch Sch., Lodi, 1981-82, instr., counselor, 1981-82; substitute tchr. Elk Grove (Calif.) Unified, 1982-84; freelance decorative arts and textiles designer, 1982—; internat. heritage and foods advisor AAUW, Chico, Calif., 1973-75; workshop dir. Creative Arts Ctr., Chico, 1972-73; workshop dir., advisor Bus. Profl. Women's Club of Gridley, 1972-74; v.p. Golden State Mobile Home League, Sacramento, 1980-82. Designer weavings-wallhangings (1st place 10 categories, Silver Dollar Fair, Chico, 1970). Mem. United European Am. Club, Am. Assn. German Tchrs., U.S. Army Res. Non-Commd. Officer's Assn. (ednl. adv. 1984-86), Kappa Delta Pi. Avocations: weaving, fiber designs, swimming, skiing, internat. travel and culture. Home: 2485 Viejo Dr Lake Havasu City AZ 86403

JONES, BEATRICE, television executive; b. Nashville, Jan. 24, 1953; d. Thomas Jefferson and Pearlie Bee (Saunders) J. Student, Bentley Coll., 1974; BS in Commerce, N.C. Cen. U., 1975; MA in Pub. Affairs & Human Svcs. Adminstrn., Rider Coll., 1989; cert. mgmt. and adminstrv. analysis program, Trenton State Coll.; postgrad., MIS Tng. Inst., Boston, USDA Grad. Sch. Auditor N.J. Dept. Trans., Trenton, 1976-78; mgmt. compliance officer N.J. Dept. Higher Edn., Trenton, 1978-86; mgr. finance and acctg. N.J. Pub. Broadcasting Authority, Trenton, 1986—; chair community adv. bd. for ednl. opportunity fund program Mercer County Community Coll. Chair recruitment Big Bros./Big Sisters Assn., Trenton; mem. minority arts com. Friends of N.J., Trenton; 2d v.p. N.J. Black Adminstrs. Network; chair tickets N.J. Black Am. Heritage Festival, 1988; mem. Dropout Prevention Planning Collaborative; corr. sec. Nat. Polit. Congress Black Women; youth advisor N.J. Black Issues Conv. Youth Leadership Devel. Inst.; mem. adv. coun. Rider Coll. Ednl. Opportunity Program. Named Mercer County Big Sister of Yr., 1980, 84, one of Outstanding Young Women of Am., 1984; recipient N.J. Black Admisntrs. Network Pres.' award, 1986. Mem. Nat. Assn. Govt. Accts. (social dir. Trenton br.), Nat. Assn. Female Execs., Nat. Assn. Univ. Women, Pub. Telecommunications Fin. Mgmt. Assn., Trenton chpt. NAACP. Home: 1018-B Prospect St Trenton NJ 08638 Office: NJ Pub Broadcasting Authority 1573 Parkside Ave #CN777 Trenton NJ 08625

JONES, BERNICE, psychotherapist; b. Birmingham, Ala., June 10, 1941; d. Freeman and Lee Emma (Kemp) Carter; children: Aleta LaVern Gibson, Duvelle Jones, Raeshay Jones. BSN, Wayne State U., Detroit, 1978; MS, Wayne State U., 1981; PhD, Internat. Bible Inst. & Sem., Orlando, Fla., 1982. Counselor/cons. Macomb Med. Commons, Mt. Clemens, Mich., 1981-84; psychotherapist Jones Counseling Svc., Mt. Clemens, 1984—; psychology intern Wayne County Clinic for Child Study, Detroit, 1988-89. Author: Sex and Morality, 1981, Hot Flashes, 1983; contbr. articles to profl. jours. Commr. Civil Svc. Commn. of Mt. Clemens, 1986; v.p. Community Relations Bd. Mt. Clemens, 1983-85. U. Detroit grad. scholar, 1987-89. Mem. Network for Chirstian Women, Am. Assn. Sex Educators, Therapists and Counselors, Am. Assn. Marriage and Family Therapy, Soroptomist. Democrat. Ch. of Christ. Home: 45 Mulligan Dr Mount Clemens MI 48043 Office: Jones Counseling Service 45 Mulligan Dr Mount Clemens MI 48043

JONES, BETTY KATE, accountant, director; b. Union City, Tenn., Aug. 26, 1952; d. Cloyce Eugene and Katie P. (Reeves) J. BSBA, U. Tenn., 1974. CPA, Tenn. Tax mgr. Price Waterhouse, Memphis, 1974-81; mgr. taxes Nucor Corp., Charlotte, N.C., 1981-84; tax dir. Hosp. Corp. Am., Nashville, 1984—. Mem. AICPAs, Tenn. Soc. CPAs, Tax Execs. Inst., Young Leaders Assn. Home: 508 Lynwood Blvd Nashville TN 37205 Office: Hosp Corp Am One Park Pla Nashville TN 37203

JONES, BEVERLY ANN MILLER, nursing executive, patient services executive; b. Bklyn., July 14, 1927; d. Hayman Edward and Eleanor Virginia (Doyle) Miller. BSN, Adelphi U., 1949; m. Kenneth Lonzo Jones, Sept. 5, 1953; children—Steven Kenneth, Lonnie Cord. Chief nurse regional blood program ARC, N.Y.C., 1951-54; asst. dir., acting dir. nursing M.D. Anderson Hosp. and Tumor Inst., Houston, 1954-55; asst. dir. nursing Sibley Meml. Hosp., Washington, 1959-61; assoc. dir. nursing svc. Anne Arundel Gen. Hosp., Annapolis, Md., 1966-70; asst. adminstr. nursing Alexandria (Va.) Hosp., 1972-73; v.p. patient care svcs., Longmont (Colo.) United Hosp., 1977—; instr. ARC, 1953-57; mem. adv. bd. Boulder Valley Vo.-Tech Health Occupations Program, 1977-80; chmn. nurse enrollment com. D.C. chpt. ARC, 1959-61; del. nursing adminstrs. good will trip to Poland, Hungary, Sweden and Eng., 1980. Contbr. articles to profl. jours. Bd. dirs. Meals on Wheels, Longmont, Colo., 1978-80, Longmont Coalition for Women in Crisis, Applewood Living Ctr., Longmont; mem. Colo. Hosp. Assn. Task Force on Nat. Commn. on Nursing, 1982; mem. utilization com. Boulder (Colo.) Hospice, 1979-83; mem. council labor rels. Colo. Hosp. Assn., 1982-87; mem.-at-large exec. com. nursing svc. adminstrs. Sect. Md. Nurses' Assn., 1966-69. Mem. Am. Orgn. Nurse Execs. (chmn. com. membership svcs. and promotions, nominee recognition of excellence in nursing adminstrn.), Colo. Soc. Nurse Execs. (dir. 1978-80, 84-86, pres. 1980-81, mem. com. on nominations 1985-86). Home: 853 Wade Rd Longmont CO 80503 Office: PO Box 1659 Longmont CO 80503

JONES, BILLIE MCCLEARY, retired music educator; b. Seattle, July 10, 1913; d. William Smith and Eva Emaline (Anderson) McCleary; m. Willis Marion Jones, Sept. 17, 1938 (div.); 1 child, Robert William. BA, U. Wash., 1935. Music supr. Waterville (Wash.) Pub. Schs., 1936-38; piano instr. Olympic Jr. Coll., Bremerton, Wash., 1945-48; music specialist Seattle Pub. Schs., 1959-70; ret., 1970. Mem. AAUW (pres. Casas Adobes br., Tucson, 1988-89, recipient Svc. award 1989, rec. sec. Ariz. area 1990—), PEO Club (treas. Tucson chpt. 1984-85), Tucson Musical Arts Soc. (sec. 1987-88), Questors Club (sec. Tucson chpt. 1989-90), Ladies Mus. Club (treas. Seattle chpt. 1965-67), Pi Lambda Theta, Mu Phi Epsilon (named Alumnus of Yr. 1979).

JONES, CAROL M. E., controller; b. Paterson, N.J., May 7, 1949; d. William Gregory and Jane Marie (Tamboer) Angiono. Student, Elon Coll., 1967-69. Model miscellaneous agencies N.Y., N.J., 1966—; Paralegal Jack B. Ehrich, Esquire, Hackensack, N.J., 1973-77; contr. J & K Constrn., Towaco, N.J., 1986-89, Mktg. Mobility Cons. & Contracting, Co., Inc., Morristown, N.J., 1989—. Mem., bd. dirs. Barn Theatre, Montville, N.J., 1974—, Peckanack Players, Wayne, N.J., 1979—; asst. treas. Republicans Abroad, Paris, 1982-84. Roman Catholic. Office: Office-Mobility Cons & Contracting Co Inc 176 Morris St Morristown NJ 07960

JONES, CAROLINE ROBINSON, advertising executive; b. Benton Harbor, Mich.; d. Ernest and Mattie Robinson; 1 child, Anthony R. B.A., U. Mich., 1963. Copywriter J. Walter Thompson, N.Y., 1963-68, v.p., co-creative dir. Zebra Assocs., Inc., N.Y., 1968-71; copywriter Kenyon & Eckhardt, N.Y., 1971-74; ptnr., creative dir. Black Creative Group, N.Y., 1974-77; v.p., creative group head Batten, Barton, Durstine & Osborn, Inc., N.Y., 1977; exec. v.p., creative dir. Mingo-Jones Advt., N.Y., 1978-86; pres. Caroline Jones Advt. Inc., N.Y.C., 1986—. Bd. dirs. N.Y. Advt. Council, L.I.U., Nat. Urban League, NOW Legal Def. Fund. Recipient creative advt. awards Clio, One Show, ANNY, NYMRAD, Art Dirs., CEBA, and others; Matrix award Women in Communications. Mem. Nat. Acad. TV Arts and Scis., Delta Sigma Theta (Lillian award 1985), Internat. Radio TV Soc. Home: 200 E 65th St Apt 26C New York NY 10021 Office: Caroline Jones Advt Inc 1290 Ave of the Americas New York NY 10104*

JONES, CAROLYN ELIZABETH, small business owner; b. Middleboro, Mass., Sept. 5, 1931; d. King Israel and Kleo Estelle (Hodges) Evans; m. John Homer Jones, Sept. 9, 1966 (dec. July 1986); 1 child, David Everett. BA in English, Tift Coll., 1952; M of Religious Edn., Carver Sch. Missions and Social Work (now So. Bapt. Theol. Sem.), 1958; BA in Art, Mercer U., 1982. Cert. secondary tchr., Ga. Tchr. McDuffie County Bd. Edn., Thomson, Ga., 1952-53, Colquitt County Bd. Edn., Norman Park, Ga., 1953-55; missionary Home Mission Bd. SBC, New Orleans and Macon, 1958-66; spl. edn. tchr. Bibb County Bd. Edn., Macon, 1968-70, 75-79; owner, operator Laney Splty. Advertising Co., Macon, 1986—. Contbr. numerous articles and poems to profl. jours.; copyright Converts game, 1979. Bible tchr. YWCA, Macon, 1980-85, clk.-trustee, deacon 1st Bapt. Ch., Macon. Mem. Macon-Bibb County C. of C., Alumnae Assn. Tift College, Greater Macon Women Bus. Owners Club. Democrat. Club: Ad of Cen. Ga. Office: Laney Splty Advt Co 2451 Kingsley Dr Macon GA 31204

JONES, CAROLYN ELLIS, publisher, retired employment agency and business service company executive; b. Marigold, Miss., Feb. 21, 1928; d. Joseph Lawrence and Willie Decelle (Forrest) Peeples; m. David Wright Ellis, May 30, 1945 (div. 1966); children—David, Lyn, Debbie, Dawn; m. Frank Willis Jones, Jan. 1, 1980. Student La. State U., 1949. Owner, mgr. Personnel and Bus. Service, Inc., Greenwood, Miss., 1962-88, now v.p.; owner Honor Pub. Co., Greenwood, 1988—. Author: The Lottie Moon Storybook, 1985; Editor: An Old Soldier's Career, 1974. Contbr. articles to religious and gen. interest publs. Mem. adv. bd. career edn. Greenwood Pub. Schs., 1975-76, mem. adv. bd. vocat.-tech. dept., 1975-88; conf. leader Miss. Bapt. Convention Singles Retreat, 1980; Mission Service Corps del. Home Mission Bd., So. Bapt. Conv., Hawaii, 1979. Mem. Greenwood C. of C. (edn. com. 1980—, guest speaker career day program local high sch.), Mothers Against Drunk Drivers, Altrusa Internat., Nat. Fedn. Ind. Bus., Miss Delta Rose Soc., Miss. Native Plant Soc., Gideon Aux. (pres. 1986-88). Avocations: writing, rose exhibitions. Office: Honor Pub 802 W President Greenwood MS 38930

JONES, CHRISTINE ELIZABETH, healthcare marketing executive; b. Alexandria, La., Jan. 20, 1959; d. Thomas Nelson Jr. and Beverly Stuart (Koch) J. BS in Home Econs. Edn., Miss. U. for Women, 1981; MS in Pub. Rels., U. So. Miss., 1984. Admissions rep. Miss. U. for Women, Columbus, 1981-83; dir. pub. rels. Healthcare Svcs. Am./Hillcrest Hosp., Birmingham, Ala., 1984-85; regional mktg. coord. Healthcare Svcs. Am., Birmingham, 1985-87; dir. mktg. Bapt. Med. Ctr.-Princeton, Birmingham, 1987-88; asst. adminstr. mktg. Mid-South Hosp., Memphis, 1988-89; pres. Impact Healthcare Mktg. Consultants, Memphis, 1988-90; dir. mktg. devel. The Willough at Naples, Fla., 1990—. Bd. dirs. Touch-A-Life Group Home, Memphis, 1988-89; mem. Miss. U. for Women Alumni Bd., 1985-90; jr. high sch. adviser Woodland Presbyn. Ch., Memphis, 1988-89. Mem. NAFE, Am. Mktg. Assn., Sales and Mktg. Execs. of Memphis, Polo Club Naples, Miss. U. for Women Young Alum Assn. (chmn. 1988-90, pres. Birmingham chpt. 1985-87), Am. Hosp. Assn., Phi Kappa Phi. Republican. Office: The Willough at Naples 9001 E Tamiami Trail Naples FL 33962

JONES, CLARICE CARMODY, teacher; b. Watervliet, Mich., Oct. 5, 1906; d. Joseph Edward and Sophia (Barth Weber) Carmody; m. Clair Francis Platt, Aug. 2, 1926 (dec. 1972); m. Edward E. Jones, Aug. 5, 1977 (dec. 1986). BA, Western Mich. U., Kalamazoo, 1937; MSW, U. Mich., 1943; D in Pub. Svc. (hon.), Western Mich. U., 1986. Tchr. Detroit Pub. Schs., Detroit, 1925-26; substitute tchr. Kalamazoo Pub. Schs., Mich., 1926-35; bookkeeper Classified Advt. Sales Gazette, Kalamazoo, Mich., 1935-37; social worker Emergency Relief Adminstra., Kalamazoo, Mich.; child welfare worker State of Mich., Battle Creek, Mich., 1943-45; exec. sec. Mich. Children's Aid Soc., Mich., 1945-47; chief psychiatric social worker Kalamazoo Child Guidance Clinic, Mich., 1947-56, adminstrv. asst., 1956-67; field instr. U. Mich., Kalamazoo, Mich., 1943-67; lectr. Intermittently U. Mich. Sch. of Social Work, 1947-67; assoc. prof. Western Mich. U., Kalamazoo, 1967-74. Contbr. articles to profl. jours. Del. White House Conf. on Children and Youth, Washington, 1950-60; chmn. bd. dirs. AARP, Washington, 1984-86, bd. dirs. Fed. Credit Union, 1987—; mem. statewide coord. coun. Task Force on Alzheimers. Recipient Am. Heritage award Sr. Power Day, Lansing, 1984, Harry J. Kelly award Mich. Soc. of Gerontology, Flint., Mich., 1984, Numerous Certs. of Appreciation and awards, 1985. Mem. Am. Assn. of U. Profs., Edison Neighborhood Bd. of Dirs., YWCA Program Com., Common Cause, Mich. Welfare League, Sr. Power Day Task Force, Mich., Sr. Advocates Coun. and Liaison for AARP Joint State Legis. Com., Mich. Soc. of Gerontology, Med. Care Adv. Coun., State Health Planning Counc., Western Mich. U. Found. (bd. dirs.). Home: 4040 Greenleaf Circle #308 Kalamazoo MI 49008

JONES, CLAUDELLA ARCHAMBEAULT, medical institute executive, educator; b. Holgate, Ohio, Sept. 25, 1938; d. Claude Edmund and Marjorie Elizabeth (Warren) Archambeault; children: Christopher Mark, Daniel Sullivan, Anne Elizabeth. Diploma Mercy Sch. Nursing, Toledo, 1959, U. Mich., 1972. R.N., Ohio, Mich. Mem. surg. staff St. Charles Hosp., Toledo, 1959; asst. to staff physician Casa Marina Hotel and USCG, Key West, Fla., 1959-60; charge nurse labor and delivery Monroe County Gen. Hosp., Key West, 1959-60; charge nurse emergency room Jackson Meml. Hosp., Miami, Fla., 1960; mem. oper. rm. staff Good Samaritan Hosp., Los Angeles, 1961; charge nurse, medicine, surgery, pediatrics Defiance (Ohio) Hosp., 1961-62; staff nurse, rehab. Tampa Gen. Hosp., 1961-62; float and pvt. duty nurse U. Mich., 1962-64, mem. staff neurosurgery, otology, ophthalmology U. Mich. Med. Ctr., Ann Arbor, 1964-66, head nurse burn unit, 1966-68; mem. project staff Evaluation and Demonstration of a Model Burn Unit, Ann Arbor, 1968-71; dir. burn care technician program U. Mich. Burn Ctr., St. Joseph Mercy Hosp., 1969-71; editor publs. dept. Nat. Inst. for Burn Medicine, Ann Arbor, 1971—, ednl. coord., 1971-75, dir. edn., 1975—, adminstr. inst., 1982—; project mgr. Nat. Burn Info. Exchange, 1972—, W.K. Kellogg Found. Gt. Lakes Regional Burn Care Demonstration Project, 1975-77; mgr. Burn Info. Triage System, 1976-78; co-chmn. Rehab. of Burned Patient Seminars, 1975—. Mem. Am. Burn Assn. (Disting. Service award 1978), Assn. Critical Care Nurses, Mich. Nurses Assn., Am. Nurses Assn., Internat. Soc. Burn Injuries. Author: Nursing the Burned Patient, 1973, Procedures for Nursing the Burned Patient, 1975, Teaching Basic Burn Care, 1975; Emergent Care of the Burn Victim, 1977; editor, author: A Decade of Progress in Burn Medicine: Nat. Inst. for Burn Medicine, 1980; Reconstruction and Rehabilitation of the Burned Patient (I. Feller, W.C. Grabb), 1980; editor Am. Burn Assn. newsletter, 1970, NBIE Newsletter, 1980; editor: Frederick A. Coller: A Remembrance, 1987, Fire Safety Burn Prevention and Immediate Care for Older Adults Training the Trainer, 1990; mem. editorial bd. Dimensions of Critical Care Jour., 1981-82, Burns, Jour. of Burn Care and Rehab., 1982. Office: 909 E Ann St Ann Arbor MI 48004

JONES, DARLENE FRANCES, state correctional officer; b. Chgo., Dec. 31, 1959; d. James and Susie (Williams) Estes; children: Cassie, Victor II. AA, Bakersfield (Calif.) Coll., 1989. Cert. peace officer. Drug counselor Pomona (Calif.) Crisis Ctr., 1984-89; correctional sgt. Calif. Dept. of Corrections, Bakersfield, 1989-90, correctional counselor, 1990—; investor real estate. Active in Young Black Reps. Recipient Pomona Unified Sch. Dist. award.

JONES, DIANNE POWELL, health services administrator; b. Mooresville, N.C., Jan. 30, 1963; d. Andrew Jefferson Jr. and Elizabeth Ann (Gentry) Powell; m. Rodney John Jones, May 14, 1988. BA, BS, Meredith Coll., Raleigh, N.C., 1984. Dir. pub. rels. and human resource devel. Piedmont chpt. ARC, Spartanburg, S.C., 1984-87; programs mgr. United Way of Piedmont, Spartanburg, 1988; mgr. mobile mammography svcs. Spartanburg Regional Med. Ctr., 1988—; first aid instr., ARC, 1987—; educator, AIDS Network Spartanburg, 1987—; mem. Spartanburg Breast Cancer Task Force, 1989. Mem. Am. Cancer Soc., Bus. Profl. Women of Spartanburg (named Young Career Woman of the Yr. for Spartanburg County 1989), Pilot Club Spartanburg. Republican. Baptist. Home: 405 Grassland Rd Campobello SC 29322

JONES, DONNA MARILYN, real estate broker, legislator; b. Brush, Colo., Jan. 14, 1939; d. Virgil Dale and Margaret Elizabeth (McDaniel) Wolfe; m. Donald Eugene Jones, June 9, 1956; children: Dawn Richter, Lisa Shira Stuart. Student, Treasure Valley Community Coll., 1981-82; grad., Realtors Inst. Cert. residential specialist. Co-owner Parts, Inc., Payette, Idaho, 1967-79; dept. mgr., buyer Lloyd's Dept. Store, Payette, Idaho, 1979-80; sales assoc. Idaho-Oreg. Realty, Payette, Idaho, 1981-82; mem. dist. 13 Idaho Ho. of Reps., Boise, 1987-90, mem. dist. 10, 1990—; assoc. broker Classic Properties Inc., Payette, 1983—. Co-chmn. Apple Blossom Parade, 1982; mem. Payette Civic League, 1968-84, pres. 1972; mem. Payette County Planning and Zoning Commn., 1985-88, vice-chmn. 1987; field coordinator Idaho Rep. Party Second Cngl. Dist., 1986; mem. Payette County Rep. Cen. Com. 1978—; precinct II com. person, 1978-79, state committeewoman, 1980-84, chmn. 1984-87. Recipient White Rose award Idaho March of Dimes, 1988; named Payette/Washington County Realtor of Yr., 1987. Mem. Idaho Assn. Realtors (legis. com. 1984-87, chmn. 1986, realtors active in politics com. 1982—, polit. action com. 1986, polit. affairs com. 1986-88, chmn. 1987, bd. dirs. 1984-88), Payette/Washington County Bd. Realtors (v.p. 1981—, state dir. 1984-88, bd. dirs 1983—, sec. 1983), Bus. and Profl. Women (Woman of Progress award 1988, 90, treas. 1988), Payette C. of C. Republican. Home: 1911 First Ave S Payette ID 83661 Office: Classic Properties 333 S 9th St Payette ID 83661

JONES, DORIS ELAINE, veterinarian; b. Cleburne, Tex., Apr. 18, 1955; d. Charles Allen and Helen Doris (Riley) J. BS in Vet. Medicine, Tex. A&M U., 1979, DVM, 1980. Vet. asst. Burleson (Tex.) Animal Hosp., 1973-75; mem. staff surg. dept. Small Animal Clinic, Tex. A&M U., College Station, 1974-80; veterinarian Lake County Vet. Clinic, Graham, Tex., 1980-82; prin. Dry Creek Vet. Clinic, Graham, 1982—; vet. adviser Humane Soc. Young County, Inc., Graham, 1983—. Mem. Am. Vet. Med. Assn., Tex. Vet. Med. Assn., Am. Heartworm Soc., Cornell Feline Health Ctr., Humane Soc. Young County (bd. dirs. 1983—), Graham C. of C.

JONES, DORIS MAE, court reporting company executive; b. Allentown, Pa., Nov. 24, 1938; d. Michael C. and Ann (Fedor) Hardony; m. Lewis M. Horwitz, Mar. 14, 1964 (div. 1984); children: Monica B., Pamela L. BS, Mich. State U., 1960; postgrad. Cleve. Marshall Law Sch., 1962; cert. Emery Sch., 1975. Ct. reporter Doris O. Wong Assocs., Boston, 1975-79; ofcl. reporter U.S. Dist. Cts., Boston, 1979-81; pres. Doris M. Jones & Assocs., Boston, 1980—, bd. dirs., sec. Lawrence Extended Day Program, Brookline, Mass., 1977-81; steering com. hospitality program, Episcopal Diocese, Boston, 1984—, co-chair, 1987. Mem. Nat. Shorthand Reporters Assn., Mass. Shorthand Reporters Assn. (sec. 1977-79, bd. dirs. 1977-80), Greater Boston C. fo C. (mem. Execs. Club), Phi Gamma Nu, Delta Zeta. Avocations: reading, traveling, cooking, public speaking. Address: Doris M Jones & Assocs Inc 59 Temple Pl Boston MA 02111

JONES, EDITH HOLLAN, judge; b. Phila., Apr. 7, 1949; d. O. Roger and Edith (Lingle) Hollan; m. Sherwood O. Jones, Dec. 27, 1973; children: Andrew and David. BA, Cornell U., 1971; JD with honors, U. Tex., 1974. Bar: Tex. 1974, U.S. Supreme Ct. 1979, U.S. Ct. Appeals (5th and 11th cirs.), U.S. Dist. Ct. (so. and no. dists.) Tex. Assoc. Andrews & Kurth, Houston, 1974-82, ptnr., 1982-85; judge U.S. Ct. Appeals (5th cir.), 1985—. Gen. counsel Rep. Party of Tex., 1981-83. Mem. ABA, State Bar Tex. Presbyterian. Office: US Ct Appeals 8631 US Courthouse 515 Rusk Ave Houston TX 77002*

JONES, EDITH IRBY, physician; b. Conway, Ark., Dec. 23, 1927; d. Robert and Mattie (Buice) Irby; m. James Beauregard Jones, Apr. 16, 1950; children: Gary, Myra, Keith. BS, Knoxville Coll., 1948; MD, U. Ark., 1952. Intern Univ. Hosp., Little Rock, Ark., 1952-53; gen. practice medicine Hot Springs, Ark., 1953-59; resident in internal medicine Baylor Coll. Medicine, Houston, 1959-62; practice medicine specializing in internal medicine Houston, 1962—; mem. staff Meth. Hosp., Houston, Hermann Hosp., Houston, Riverside Gen. Hosp., Houston, St. Elizabeth Hosp., Houston, St. Anthony Ctr., Houston, St. Joseph Hosp., Houston, Thomas Care Ctr., Houston; mem. staff Town Park, Houston, chief of staff; clin. asst. prof. medicine Baylor Coll. Medicine, U. Tex. Sch. Medicine, Houston; dir. Prospect Med. Lab.; bd. dirs., sec. Mercy Hosp. Comprehensive Health Care Group; ptnr. Jones, Coleman and Whitfield; grand med. examiner Ct. Calanthe Jurisdiction, Tex.; cons. Social Security Agy., Tex. Pub. Welfare Dept., Vocat. Rehab. Assn., Tex. Rehab. Commn.; bd. dirs. Standard Savs. Assn., Houston; numerous others. Contbr. articles to profl. jours. Bd. dirs. Houston Internat. U., Drug Addiction Rehab. Enterprise, March of Dimes, Houston, Odessey House, Houston; mem. adv. bd. Houston Council on Alcoholism; mem. com. for revising justice code, Harris County, Tex.; chmn. bd. trustees Knoxville Coll.; impartial hearing officer Houston Ind. Sch. Dist.; trustee Mut. Assn. for Profl. Service; mem. Community Welfare Planning Assn., Friends of Youth, Human Services Adv. Council, Houston; mem. bd. visitors U. Houston; numerous others. First black to receive BS and MD degrees from U. Ark; Dr. Edith Irby Jones Day proclaimed by State of Ark., 1985, City of Little Rock, 1985, City of N.Y.C., 1986; named One of 30 Most Influential Black Women Houston, 1984; inducted into Tex. Black Women's Hall of Fame, 1986; commended by Calif. Senate, 1969; proclamation by city council, Houston, 1985, Mayor of Houston, 1986; recipient cert. of citation Ho. of Reps. State of Tex., 1986; portrait placed in entrance hall U. Ark. for Med. Scis., 1985; numerous others. Mem. AMA, Am. Med. Women's Assn. (v.p. Houston chpt.), Nat. Med. Assn. (past pres.), Lone Star Med. Assn., Harris County Med. Assn., Houston Med. Forum, Tex. Assn. Disability Examiners, Bus. and Profl. Women, Nat. Council of Negro Women, Inc. (v.p. Dorothy Height chpt.), NAACP, PTA, YMCA, Alpha Kappa Mu, Delta Sigma Theta, Eta Phi Beta. Democrat. Clubs: Links, Inc., Top Ladies of Distinction, Girl Friends, Inc., Women of Achievement, Inc. (Hall of Fame 1985). Lodge: Order Eastern Star. Home: 3402 S Parkwood Dr Houston TX 77021 Office: 2601 Prospect St Houston TX 77004

JONES, ELEANOR ILLSTON, foundation executive; b. Ithaca, N.Y., Nov. 6, 1924; d. Cady Pangburn and Laura H. (Buck) Illston; m. Don L. Jones, Dec. 24, 1942 (div. 1980); children: David M., Amy L., Evan W., Anne L., Matthew D., Peter W. Diploma, Practical Bus. Coll. Freelance writer for newspapers, religious periodicals, trade papers, 1949-68; dir. pub. relations Harding Hosp., Worthington, Ohio, 1968-85; dir. Harding Evans Found., Worthington, 1985—; cons. Bd. Devel. Network:; founder, 1st pres. Tele-Mom Inc. Trustee Directions for Youth, Zonta Service Found.; trustee, v.p. adminstr. Columbus Area Internat. Program, 1980-86; chmn. adv. com. on mental health and retardation tech. Columbus Tech. Inst., 1970-78. Recipient first award Excellence in Column Writing, Kans. Press Assn., 1956, 58; Outstanding Service award Columbus Tech. Inst., N. Area Mental Health Services, Harding Hosp. Mem. Nat. Assn. Hosp. Devel. (fellow, dir. Region VI, v.p. edn. found.), Ohio Assn. Hosp. Devel., Worthington Area C. of C. (chmn. bd. 1989). Democrat. Methodist. Club: Columbus Metro, Zonta. Lodges: Order Eastern Star. Home: 823 Franklin Ct Worthington OH 43085 Office: 445 E Granville Rd Worthington OH 43085

JONES, ELIZABETH M., program director secondary school district; m. Robert Fresley Jones; children: Mark, Suzanne, Wendy. BA, Carrol Coll.; MS, U. Wis., Milw., 1976, PhD, 1984. Cert. tchr., prin., curriculum dir., Wis. Edn. cons., adj. prof. Nat.-Louis U., Evanston, Ill., 1985—; program project coord. Sch. Dist. of Kettle Moraine, Wales, Wis., 1987—; speaker, staff devel. leader. Contbr. articles to profl. jours. Recipient Leadership award Sch. Dist. Kettle Moraine, grant Nat. Endowment for the Humanities; named Tchr. of Yr. Mem. AAUW, NEA, Milw. Women's Symphony League, Wis. Assn. of Educators of Gifted and Talented, Wis. Coun. for Gifted and Talented, Assn. for Supervision and Curriculum Devel., State Task Force on Restructuring Schs., Wis. Edn. Assn., Edn.-For-Employment Coun., Peaks of Excellence, Inc., (bd. pres., editor), Phi Delta Kappa. Republican.

JONES, ELIZABETH WINIFRED, biology educator; b. Seattle, Mar. 8, 1939; d. Kenneth Clifford Harris and Dorothea (Dowty) J. BS, U. Wash., 1960, PhD, 1964. Postdoctoral fellow MIT, Cambridge, 1964-67, instr. in biology, 1967-69; asst. prof. Case Western Res. U., Cleve., 1969-74; assoc. prof. Carnegie Mellon U., Pitts., 1974-82, prof., 1982—; vis. scientist Sch. Medicine Wash. U., 1981-82; adj. prof. in psychiatry U. Pitts., 1985—; mem. genetics tng. com. NIH, Bethesda, Md., 1972-73, mem. genetics study sect., 1976-80, 84-86, chair, 1990—. Editor: (book) Molecular Biology of the Yeast Saccharomyces, (2 vols.), 1981, 82; (jours.) Genetics, 1980—, Yeast, 1984—; assoc. editor Ann. Rev. of Genetics, 1990—. Recipient Rsch. Career Devel. award NIH, 1971-74, 75-77. Fellow AAAS; mem. Am. Soc. Microbiology, Am. Soc. Cell Biology, Genetics Soc. Am. (pres. 1987). Office: Carnegie Mellon U 4400 5th Ave Pittsburgh PA 15213

JONES, ERIKA ZIEBARTH, lawyer; b. Washington, June 10, 1955; d. Thomas Arthur and Ruth (Helm) Ziebarth; m. Gregory Monroe Jones, June 2, 1978; 1 child, Katherine Anne. AB, Georgetown U., 1976, JD, 1980. Bar: D.C. 1980, U.S. Ct. Appeals (D.C. cir.) 1987, U.S. Supreme Ct. 1987. Atty., regulatory analyst U.S. Office Mgmt. and Budget, Washington, 1980-81; spl. counsel Nat. Hwy. Traffic Safety Adminstrn., Washington, 1981-85, chief counsel, 1985-89; of counsel Mayer, Brown and Platt, Washington, 1989—. Bd. dirs. Immaculata Coll. High Sch., 1985-88. Mem. ABA (com. vice-chmn. 1989—), Fed. Bar Assn. (com. chmn. 1988—), Women's Bar Assn. D.C., D.C. Bar Assn., Phi Beta Kappa. Republican. Roman Catholic. Home: 6612 31st Pl NW Washington DC 20015 Office: 2000 Pennsylvania Ave NW Washington DC 20006

JONES, EVELYN CLEMENTINE, college administrator; b. Harvey, W.Va., Mar. 10, 1921; d. Robert Lee and Emma Tuschan (Calloway) Robinson. Student, Wheeling Coll.; student in theology, sociology & govt., U. So. Calif.; DD (hon.), U. Ea. Fla. Founder, dir. various assns., 1970-79, W.Va. chpt. Nat. Polit. Women, 1981—, Martin Luther King Jr. Community Coll., Mt. Hope, W.Va., 1981—; tchr. literacy, Fayette County. Co-chairperson W.Va. Rainbow Coalition, Mt. Hope, 1984—; active St. Anthony's Guild, Oak Hill, W.Va. Mem. Nat. Congress Black Women, Cath. Daus. Am., Delta Sigma Theta (award). Address: Box 429 Mount Hope WV 25880

JONES, GAIL, teacher; b. Birmingham, Ala.; d. Johnnie and Edith B. (Baker) J. BA, Ala. A. & M. U., Huntsville, 1972; MA, U. Ky., 1974. Cert. elem. tchr., Ky. Tchr. Jefferson County Bd. Edn., Louisville, Ky. Editor: Anthology of Writing by participants in Louisville Writing Project. Mem. NEA, Ky. Edn. Assn., Jefferson County Tchrs. Assn., Greater Louiville Eng. Coun., The Nat. Writing Project, Nat. Coun. Tchrs. of Eng. (presenter Ky. Coun. 1984), Assn. for Supervision and Curriculum Devel., Nat. Sci. Tchrs. Assn., City-wide Boeling Tchrs.' League. Office: Roosevelt-Perry Elem Sch 1606 Magazine St Louisville KY 40203

JONES, GENIA K., critical care and emergency supervising nurse; b. Dallas, Dec. 21, 1954; d. Joe and Juanita Sue (White) Self; m. Paul L. Jones, June 1, 1986. ADN, Cedar Valley Coll., 1976, mgmt. cert., 1980; sci. update, Mountain View Coll., Dallas, 1984. RN; cert. basic life support, advanced cardiac life support, emergency nurse. Asst. dir. nursing svcs. Four Season's Conv. Ctr., Dallas, 1977-78; with surgery dept. Dallas/Ft. Worth Med. Ctr., 1978-80; dir. nursing Med. Staffing Svcs., Dallas, 1980, Reproductive Svcs., Inc., Dallas, 1981; adminstrv. supr. Dallas Family Hosp., 1982-85; patient care coord. emergency dept. Dallas S.W. Med. Ctr., 1985-90; internat. flight nurse Air Ambulance Network, Inc., Dallas, 1987—; instr. I.V. therapy, 1980—; cons., advisor, 1980—. Recipient Citizens award, Certs. Apprecition, HOSA Nat. Leadership Conf.; Internat. Biog. Assn. fellow, 1990. HOE-HOSA ptnr., Am. Heart Assn., Nurse's Svc. Orgn., Tex. Nurse's Assn., Emergency Nurse's Assn. Home: 106 Burkett Ln Red Oak TX 75154

JONES, GLORIA ELLEN, corporate design firm executive; b. Beaver Dam, Wis., Aug. 30, 1948; s. Henry P. and Theresa Sylvia (Alsum) Westra; m. Jerald W. Kuiper, June 21, 1965 (div. Jan. 1975); children—Bill, Bob, Heather; m. Robert W. Jones, Jr., July 16, 1977. Student U. Wis.-Oshkosh, 1970-73, Harvard Sch. Design, 1985, Northwestern U., 1985-86. Sales dir. The Star, Oshkosh, 1975-76; account exec. The Post Corp., Appleton, Wis., 1976-78; prin. Rehab. Specialists, Appleton, 1978-82, Jones Appraisal Service, Appleton, 1978-82, Interior Design Firm, Appleton, 1980-82; v.p. Bischoff/Lincoln, Chgo., 1982-85; pres. Jones Design Group, 1985—. Bd. sec. A Better Chance, Oshkosh, 1974. Named Mrs. Wisconsin, 1980. Mem. Internat. Assn. Bus. Communicators, Young Execs. (v.p. communications 1984-85), Women in Mgmt. (v.p. mktg. 1984, 2d v.p. 1985), Am. Soc. Interior Designers. Democrat. Presbyterian. Avocations: writing, reading, golf. Home: 1927 Sherman Ave Apt 1S Evanston IL 60201 Office: Jones Design Group 10-102 Merchandise Mart Chicago IL 60654

JONES, IRENE MARGARET, commercial banker; b. Staten Island, N.Y., June 11, 1965; d. Stuart G. and Jacqueline H. (Byrnes) J. BA in Econs., Furman U., 1987. Mgmt. trainee First Union Nat. Bank, Jacksonville, Fla., 1987-88; credit mgr. First Union Nat. Bank, Miami, Fla., 1988-90, comml. banker, 1990—. Fundraiser United Way of Dade County, Miami, 1989. Mem. AAUW, NAFE, Phi Beta Kappa. Roman Catholic.

JONES, J. DULIN, writer, film producer; b. Hollywood, Calif., Sept. 6, 1957; d. John Dulin and Helen Mae (Weaver) J. BA, Calif. State U., Long Beach, 1980. Developer mini-series and TV series Embassy Communications, Los Angeles, 1981-84; assoc. to producer Hotel Aaron Spelling Prodns., Los Angeles, 1984-85; writing intern Sundance Film Inst., Los Angeles, 1985; feature film story analyst Carson Prodns., Los Angeles, 1985-86; freelance screenplay and play writer Los Angeles and N.Y.C., 1986—. Author: (screenplays) Fade Away, 1986, No Other Love, 1987, Story of the Century, 1988, Jack and Mike, 1989, (play) Cousin Judy, 1989. Bd. dirs. Sterling Circle of Aviva Ctr. for Girls, 1990. Mem. ACLU, ECO (TV and film coms.), Writers Guild Am., Ind. Feature Project, Am. Film Inst., Sundance Film Inst. (pre-selection com. 1985-87), People for Am. Way, Habitat for Humanity, Amnesty Internat., Delta Gamma.

JONES, JAMIE DENISE See WATFORD, JAMIE DENISE

JONES, JANICE JOANNE, hospital administration executive; b. Yakima, Wash., Dec. 8, 1953; d. Clifford Milton and Joanne (Fisher) J.; m. Richard A. Sparks, June 23, 1979 (div. June 1986); m. Jerry D. Kracht, Nov. 26,

1987. Student, NYU, 1974-75; BA, U. Washington, 1976, M in Hosp. Adminstrn., 1980. Day treatment counselor Group Health Coop., Mental Health, Seattle, 1976-77; rsch. asst. Child Devel. Mental Retardation Ctr., Seattle, 1978-80; ambulatory care mgr. U. Health Svcs., U. Mass., Amherst, 1980-83; spl. projects coord. Good Samaritan Community Healthcare, Puyallup, Wash., asst. v.p., 1984-86, v.p., 1986—; provider rep. Puget Sound Health Systems Agy., Seattle, 1987—. V.p. bd. Second City Chamber Music Series,. Mem. Tacoma-Pierce County C. of C. (provider rep., 1987—), Am. Coll. Healthcare Execs. Office: Good Samaritan Community Healthcare 407 14th Ave SE Puyallup WA 98371

JONES, JANICE LOUISE, researcher, writer; b. Selma, Calif., Dec. 17, 1956; d. Howard Edward Jones and Betty Irene (Fulbright) Thornbury. BA in Journalism, Calif. State U., Fresno, 1980; postgrad., Claremont Grad. Sch., 1988-89. Researcher, freelance contbr. L.A. Times, 1980—. Mem. AAUW (co-dir. L.A. chpt. 1988-89, fellowship 1988-89). Home: 16551 Mariana Circle Huntington Harbour CA 92649 Office: LA Times Times Mirror Sq Los Angeles CA 90053

JONES, JEAN MELODY, grants administrator, consultant; b. Bridgeton, N.J., Sept. 11, 1949; d. Eldon Hall Wesley and Jean (Rodriquez) Adams; m. Winston F. Nash; children: Jayme Marie, Eldon Vance. AA in Bus. Adminstrn., Golden Gate U., 1976, BA in Adminstrn. Justice, 1977, M in Pub. Adminstrn., 1979. With display advt. Vineland (N.J.) Times jour., 1971-74; vets. coordinator. Stockton State Coll., Pomona, N.J., 1980-82; asst. dir. ednl. opportunity fund program Stockston State Coll., Pomona, N.J., 1982-85, dir. opportunity fund program, 1985-87; grants adminstr. Jacksonville (Fla.) Transp. Authority, 1987—; recruiter Minority Officer Recruitment N.J. Air Nat. Guard, 1983—; mediator Community Justice Inst. Atlantic County, Atlantic City, N.J., 1986-87. With USN, 1975-80, cpt. N.J. Air Guard, 1981—. U. North Fla. Govt. fellow, 1989. Mem. Cert. Pub. Mgrs. Soc. of N.J. (com. mem. 1984-87), Nat. Assn. Black Women in Higher Edn., N.J. Assn. Vets. Program Asminstrs., Non-Commn. Officer Assn. of N.J. Democrat. Roman Catholic. Office: Jacksonville Transp Authority 100 N Myrtle St Jacksonville FL 32203

JONES, JEANNE ELISE DUMAS, educational administrator; b. Ft. Worth, July 21, 1949; d. Armand and Margaret Dean (Woleben) Dumas; m. Kenneth Ronald Jones, 1970; 1 child, Jennifer. BA, North Tex. State U., 1972, MEd, 1984; MA, U. Tex., Arlington, 1981. Cert. provisional secondary edn. history, Eng., midmgmt. cert., Tex., secondary supr. cert., Tex. Eng. tchr. Southwest High Sch., Ft. Worth, 1973-85; summer sch. administrator Ft. Worth Ind. Sch. Dist., 1985-86; vice prin. Dunbar Mid. Sch., 1985-88; dean of students Y.O.U. U. North Tex., Denton, 1987-89; asst. prin. Dunbar Sixth Grade Sch., Ft. Worth, 1988—. Mem. Vice Prin's. Task Force, 1987-88. Named Outstanding Greek Woman, 1970; recipient Circle T Girl Scout Coun. Adult Ten Yr. award, 1983. Mem. Vice Prins. Leadership Acad. Task Force (chmn.), Tex. Elem. Prins. and Suprs. Assn., Assn. for Supervision and Curriculum Devel., Phi Delta Kappa, Delta Kappa Gamma (sec. and rsch. com. 1987-89), Alpha Xi Delta (treas. 1987-89). Presbyterian. Office: Dunbar Sixth Grade Sch 5100 Willie Fort Worth TX 76105

JONES, JEANNIE CROMEANS, publishing executive; b. Helena, Ark., Jan. 19, 1949; d. Ardie Leaton and Ruth Beatrice (Rowan) Cromeans; m. Douglas Wendell Jones, May 7, 1971 (div. Sept. 1989); m. Douglas Wendell Jones; children: Jennifer Dana (dec.), Steven Douglas. Student, San Diego State Coll., 1968, Phillips County (Ark.) Community Coll., 1969-70, Memphis State U., 1980. Comml. artist Bradford Printing Co., Helena, 1969-70, Branch-Smith Pub. Co., Inc., Ft. Worth, 1970-71; owner, publisher DeSoto County Tribune and Pub. Co., Inc. & Home Market Mags., Olive Branch, Miss., 1972—. Supporter Disabled Am. Vets Assn., Humane Soc. Am., Miss. Humane Soc., Memphis Humane Soc. Mem. Greenpeace, Miss. Press. Assn. Republican. Home: 8141 Hunters Hill Cove Olive Branch MS 38654 Office: DeSoto County Tribune Pub Co Inc Home Market Mags Olive Branch MS 38654

JONES, JOAN MEGAN, anthropologist; b. Laramie, Wyo., Sept. 7, 1933; d. Thomas Owen and Lucille Lenoir (Magill) J; m. James Caldwell Merritt, June 20, 1980. BA, U. Wash., 1956, MA, 1968, PhD, 1976. Mus. educator Burke Mus. U. Wash., Seattle, 1969-72; anthropologist Quinault Indian Nation, Taholah, Wash., 1976-77; researcher, corp. officer Profl. Anthropology Consulting Team/Social Analysts, Seattle, 1977-79; research assoc. dept. anthropology U. Wash., Seattle, 1982—; research investigator Dept. Social and Health Services State of Wash., Seattle, 1977; vis. lectr. Dept. Anthropology U. B.C., Vancouver, 1978; research specialist Artsplan Arts Alliance Wash. State, Seattle, 1978; vis. instr. Dept. Anthropology Western Wash. U., Bellingham, 1981; cons. in field. Author: Northwest Coast Basketry and Culture Change, 1968, Basketry of Quinault, 1977, Native Basketry of Western North America, 1978, Art and Style of Western Indian Basketry, 1982, Northwest Coast Indian Basketry Styles. Wenner-Gren Found. Anthrop. Research fellow, 1967-68; Ford Found. fellow, 1972-73; Nat. Mus.'s. Can. grantee, 1973-74. Fellow Am. Anthrop. Assn., Soc. Applied Anthropology; mem. Nat. Assn. Practicing Anthropologists, Assn. Women in Sci., Skagit Valley Weavers Guild (v.p. Skagit County chpt. 1985-86, 89-90, corr. sec. 1988-89), Whidbey Weavers. Office: U Washington Dept Anthropology Seattle WA 98195

JONES, JULIA FAYE GRIGGS, educator; b. Peterstown, West Va., July 9, 1945; d. Joseph Lee and Vivian Pearl (Ferguson) Griggs; m. Giles Monroe Jones,. BS in Edn., Concord Coll., 1970; MS in Edn., Radford U., 1975. Interpreter, translator Celanses Fibers Corp., Pearisburg, Va., 1987, Fairchild Corp., Glen Lyn, Va., 1988; tchr., librarian Peterstown High Sch., 1970-89. Campaign worker W.Va. House Del., Union, 1988; organizer St. Jude's; European travel leader, 1977, 80, 89; active Monroe County Reading Coun. Finalist Tchr. of Yr. Monroe County, 1988. Mem. W.Va. Edn. Assn., Monroe County Edn. Assn., W.Va. Tchrs., W.Va. Libr. Assn., Concord Coll. Alumni Assn. Democrat. Baptist.

JONES, KAREN ANNETTE, civic volunteer; b. Grand Prairie, Tex., Feb. 16, 1941; d. Ballard Dorsie and Iris Alvern (Hampton) Hutchison; m. Jerry Raymond Jones, Mar. 16, 1963; children: Lisa Rene Jones Burleson, Karen DeAnn Jones. BS, McMurry Coll., Abilene, Tex., 1963. Sec. McMurry Coll., Abilene, 1959-63, Continental Oil Co., Abilene, 1963; substitute tchr. Abilene Pub. Schs., 1967-68; tchr. continuing edn. Mountainview Community Coll., Dallas, 1974; floral designer/sec. Christopher Design, Dallas, 1978-80. Bd. dirs., sec. Wesley Rankin Community Ctr., Dallas, 1989—; adminstrv. bd. Inglewood United Meth. Ch., Grand Prairie, Tex., 1986—. Mem. AAUW (sec. 1988—), Grand Prairie Women's Club (bd. dirs. 1986-88). Democrat. Methodist. Address: 2118 Wellington Dr Grand Prairie TX 75051

JONES, KATHLEEN ANN, nuclear medicine technologist; b. Allentown, Pa., July 15, 1964; d. Edward Thomas and Catherine Marie (Steve) Jones. BS in Nuclear Med. Tech. magna cum laude, Cedar Crest Coll., Allentown, Pa., 1986. Cert. in nuclear med. tech. Staff nuclear med. technologist The Allentown (Pa.) Hosp.-Lehigh Valley Hosp. Ctr., 1986—, clin. coordinator, 1988—; Editor ednl. progs. Jour. Nuclear Med. Tech., 1990—. Mem. Soc. Nuclear Medicine (treas. 1988-90), Lehigh Valley Soc. Nuclear Medicine Technologists (pres. 1989-90), Del. Valley Soc. Nuclear Medicine Technologists. Democrat. Roman Catholic. Home: 1214 Washington St #8 Whitehall PA 18052 Office: Lehigh Valley Hosp Ctr 1200 S Cedar Crest Blvd Allentown PA 18103

JONES, KATHLEEN NAEFELI, mental health services professional; b. Easton, Pa., June 28, 1947; d. Gerard Andrew and Marguerite Hope (Johnson) Haefeli; m. John Richard Jones, June 18, 1966; children: Evan Richard, Victoria Haefeli. BA, James Madison U., Harrisonburg, Va., 1971; MEd, Kutztown (Pa.) U., 1980; PhD, Lehigh U., Bethlehem, Pa., 1990. Cert. counselor. Counselor Pa. State U., Schuylkill Campus, Schuylkill Haven, Pa., 1981-83; grad. asst. Counseling Svc., Lehigh U., Bethlehem, 1984-86; staff therapist Wholistic Health Care Svcs./Good Shepherd, Allentown, Pa., 1987-89, interim dir., 1979-90; asst. dir. Wholistic Health Care Svcs./Good Shepherd, Allentown, 1990—; cons. counselor Family Life Svcs., Topton, Pa., 1980-81; adj. instr. Albright Coll., Reading, Pa., 1982, Moravian Coll., Bethlehem, 1986; cons. counselor Profl. Assn. Network, Pottsville, Pa., 1986-89, Pa. State Schuylkill Campus, 1988-89; co-dir. equal opportunity grant Pa. State U., Schuylkill campus, 1989. Co-chair Organizing Project for Schuylkill County Commn. for Women, 1989, Schuylkill County Commn. for Women, 1990, Schuylkill County Women's Conf., 1988. Lehigh U. alumni fellow, Bethlehem, 1983-84. Mem. AAUW, Am. Assn. Counseling and Devel., Pa. Psychol. Assn., Pa. Counseling Assn. (sec. 1982-88, Grad. Student of Yr. 1987), Chi Sigma Iota. Office: Wholistic Health Care Svcs 1006 S 6th St Allentown PA 18103

JONES, KATHRYN CHERIE, pastor; b. Breckenridge, Tex., Nov. 26, 1955; d. Austin Thomas and Margaret May (Mohr) J. BA, U. Calif., San Diego, 1977; MDiv, Fuller Theol. Sem., 1982. Assoc. pastor La Jolla (Calif.) United Meth. Ch., 1982-84; pastor in charge Dominguez United Meth. Ch., Long Beach, Calif., 1984-88, San Marcos (Calif.) United Meth. Ch., 1988—; coord. chaplains Pacific Hosp., Long Beach, 1986-88. Bd. dirs. So. Calif. Walk to Emmau Community, L.A., 1987-88, San Diego chpt., 1988—. Mem. Christian Assn. Psychol. Studies, Evangs. for Social Action. Democrat. Office: San Marcos United Meth Ch PO Box 126 San Marcos CA 92069

JONES, KATHRYN KRISTY, data processing executive; b. Princeton, Ind., Oct. 4, 1958; d. Billy Gene and Julia (Stiles) Kolb; m. Thomas Eugene Jones, Jan. 12, 1980; children: Amber Nichole, Joshua Thomas. AS, Vincennes U., Ind., 1978; BBA, U. Evansville, Ind. Asst. mgr. Long John Silvers, Princeton/Evansville, Ind., 1975-78; keypunch operator Potter & Brumfield, Princeton, 1978; computer programmer Potter & Brumfield, 1978-83, mkt. research analyst, 1983-86, mktg. sys. analyst, 1986—; personal computer cons.; instr. personal computers Ivy Tech., Evansville, 1989—. Active Princeton Area Betterment, 1985—. Recipient Quality Quest award, Potter & Brumfield, 1985; named one of Outstanding Young Women of Am., 1987. Mem. Princeton Bus. and Profl. Women's Orgn., Am. Prodn. and Inventory Control Soc. Home: RR 2 Box 209A Princeton IN 47670 Office: Potter & Brumfield 200 S Richland Creek Dr Princeton IN 47671

JONES, KATHY ELAINE, broadcasting professional; b. Bartow, Fla., July 26, 1958; d. Payton Lester and Carrie Mae (Hall) J. BS, Fla. State U., 1980. Cert. broadcast engr. Paralegal Getty Oil Co., L.A., 1981-82; comml. coord. Sta. KTLA Channel 5, L.A., 1982-84; programming asst. Sta. KMPC Radio, L.A., 1984—. Spl. event coord. South Cen. Foster Parents Assn., L.A., 1986—; pub. rels. dir. United Women Prayer Power Fellowship, Ontario, Calif., 1989—; bus. mgr. Prayer and Faith Gospel Community Choir, L.A., 1981—; asst. playground dir. Sugar Ray Youth Found., L.A., 1986-90; vol. choir dir. Fred C. Nelles Youth Authority, Whittier, Calif., 1987-89. Mem. Pub. Interest Radio & TV Ednl. Soc., Women in Communications Inc. Office: Golden West Broadcasters 5858 Sunset Blvd Los Angeles CA 90028

JONES, LAURA ANN, marketing professional; b. Melrose Park, Ill., July 16, 1963; d. Edward Vincent and Marilyn Ann (Panoch) J. BA in Journalism, No. Ill. U., 1985. Sales rep. Metrovision Inc., Palos Hills, Ill., 1980-83; telemarketer Amoco Oil Co., DeKalb, Ill., 1984-85; adminstrv. asst. Pappageorge Haymes Ltd., Chgo., 1985-87; mktg. rep. Textile Craft Co., Chgo., 1987-88, mktg. dir., 1988—. Mem. Delta Nu (treas. Delta Gamma chpt. 1987, pres. 1988-90). Office: Textile Craft Co 3446 N Southport Ave Chicago IL 60657

JONES, LAURA ANN, radio announcer, production assistant; b. Mishawaka, Ind., Oct. 22, 1968; d. Michael David Jones and Susan Lynn (Gebel) Moore. BS in Telecommunications, Ball State U., 1990. Announcer, news anchor WCRD Radio, Muncie, Ind., 1989; producer, dir. Ball State U. Journalism Workshop, Muncie, 1989; announcer, recording engr., producer, news anchor WBST Radio, Ball State U., Muncie, 1988—; voice over announcer Rutter Communications, Muncie, 1990. Recipient David Letterman Intern award, 1990. Mem. Women in Communications (sec. 1988-90), Alpha Epsilon Rho (rec. sec. 1989-90). Democrat. Home: 802 W Ashland Muncie IN 47303

JONES, LAURETTA MARIE, artist, computer artist, graphic designer, educator; b. Cleve., Mar. 13, 1953; d. Richard Llewellyn and Loretta (Jares) J. BFA, Cleve. Inst. Art, 1975; postgrad., N.Y. Inst. Tech., 1981, 87. Instr. Sch. Visual Arts, N.Y.C., 1984—, dir. undergraduate computer studies, 1988-90; adj. prof. art Manhattanville Coll., Purchase, N.Y., 1985-86; cons. Trintex, White Plains, N.Y., 1986-87, IBM Gallery Sci. and Art, N.Y.C., 1987-88; cons. graphic design IBM T.J. Watson Rsch. Ctr., Yorktown Heights, N.Y., 1988-90, adv. graphic designer, 1990—. Exhibited collages, drawings in shows worldwide, 1983—; represented in permanent collection Franklin Inst., Phila. Mem. Nature Conservancy, 1978—, People Am. Way, 1985—. Mem. Nat. Computer Graphics Assn. (speaker 1987), Small Computers Arts Network (speaker 1984-89), Computer Arts Discipline Graphic Artists Guild (founding, steering com. 1984-88), N.Y.C. chpt. Assn. Computing Machinery's Spl. Interest Group Graphics (editor newsletter, bd. dirs. 1986—), Am. Inst. Graphic Arts, Amnesty Internat., Greenpeace, NOW. Office: IBM TJ Watson Rsch Ctr PO Box 704 J2-A31 Yorktown Heights NY 10598

JONES, LAWASSA B., legal assistant; b. Ringgold, Ga., Mar. 27, 1938; d. Charles Benjamin and Martha Elizabeth (Gaddis) Brackett; m. Richard R. Jones, June 13, 1956; children Cherie Haggard, Gemma Jenkins, Richard Jr. AAS, Cleveland (Tenn.) State Community Coll., 1978, student contracts law, computer literacy, 1986; BS, Covenant Coll., Lookout Mountain, Ga., 1990. Cert. legal asst. corp. and bus. specialist, Tenn. Asst. to office mgr. Arlen Shopping Ctrs. Co., Chattanooga, 1976-78; corp. paralegal Stophel, Caldwell and Heggie PC, Chattanooga, 1978-86, Stophel and Stophel PC, Chatanooga, 1986-87; bus. mgr. Master Plan Jewelry, Cleve., Tenn., 1987—. Mem. viewers adv. com. WTCI, Chattanooga, 1984-90; tutor Opportunity for Adult Reading, Cleveland, 1986—. Mem. Nat. Assn. Legal Assts., Tenn. Paralegal Assn. (founder, past pres., editor newsletter, bd. dirs. east region 1986-90). Democrat. Home: 3370 Jackson Circle SE Cleveland TN 37323 Office: PO Box 3723 Cleveland TN 37320-3723

JONES, LEWANNA, nurse consultant, small business owner; b. Nofolk, Va., Nov. 22, 1955; d. Eldon Dock and Johnnie Doris (Tarver) J. ADN, Lamar U., 1978. RN, Tex. Change nurse, asst. Park Place Hosp., Port Arthur, Tex., 1978-84; assoc. coord. critical care dept. Park Place Hosp., Houston, 1984-85; chief exec. officer Utimate Home Health Care, Inc., Nederland, Tex., 1986—; cons. Concepts of Care, Inc., R. Jones & Assocs., Orange, Tex.; cons. supr. Meml. Home Health Care, Houston; bd. dirs. Tex. Ctr. for Home Care Develop., Inc. Mem. Adv. Com. to State Bd. of Nurse Examiners, Tex. Mem. NAFE, ANA, Tex. Orgn. Nurse Execs., Nat. Assn. Health Care, Tex. Nurses Assn., Tex. Assn. Home Health Agys. (clin. practice com., polit. action coun.), Intravenous Nurse Soc. Office: Ultimate Home Health Care Inc PO Box 1714 Nederland TX 77627

JONES, LILLIE AGNES, retired educator; b. Leroy, Iowa, Nov. 25, 1910; d. Orace Wesley and Lorena Floy (Buffum) Davis; m. John Hammond Jones, May 27, 1938; children: John Harry, Mary Agnes Jones Edwards. BA, Colo. State Coll., 1937. Cert. elem. tchr., Colo. Elem. tchr. Weld County Sch. Dist. 8l, Kersey, Colo., 1930-34, Weld County Sch. Dist. 12l, Erie, 1934-38, Longmont (Colo.) Pub. Schs., 1955-59, Adams County Sch. Dist. 12, Thornton, Colo., 1959-67, Littleton (Colo.) Pub. Schs., 1967-69; Farmington (N.Mex.) Pub. Schs., 1969-76, ret., 1976; cataloger Longmont Pub. Libr., 1953-55. Kersey High Sch. scholar, 1928. Mem. Nat. Ret. Tchrs. Assn., N.Mex. Ret. Tchrs. Assn. (life), Pub. Employees Retirement Assn., Colo. Ret. Sch. Employees Assn., AAUW (life, past treas. Longmont), Alpha Delta Kappa (rec. sec., historian Sun City, Ariz. 1980, 82). Democrat.

JONES, LILLIE MADISON, school system administrator; b. Brevard, NC, Dec. 8, 1942; d. James Arthur Sr. and Lillie Reesie (Norman) Madison; m. Frederick Nathaniel Jones, Sept. 3, 1965; children: Adelina Giselle, Frederick Nathaniel II. BA, Bennett Coll., Greensboro, N.C., 1965; MS, A & T State U., 1977; EdS, Va. Polytechnic Inst., Blacksburg, Va., 1984, EdD, 1986. Cert. Edn. Adminstrn. High Sch. Eng. Tchr. William Penn High Sch., High Point, N.C., 1965-66; French tchr. William Penn High Sch., High Point, 1968; Eng. tchr. T. Wingate Andrews High Sch., High Point, 1968-73, High Point Cen. High Sch., 1974-76; adminstrv. asst. Northeast Jr. High Sch., High Point, 1976-78; prin. Leonard St. Alternative Sch., High Point, 1978-81; prin. for instr. Northeast Mid. Sch., High Point, 1981-83; asst. and assoc. supr. High Point Pub. Schs., 1983—; reality therapist cons. for various orgns. on various topics. Author: book, 1986; editor: parent-tchrs. conf. 1989; speaker on various topics. Pres. High Point Affiliate-Nat. Black Child Devel., 1988, High Point Alumnae Delta Sigma Theta Sorority, 1981-83; dir. United Methodist Ch. Dist., High Point, 1986-88; chmn. Personnel, Children's Home, Winston-Salem, N.C., 1989—; loaned exec. United Way, 1986. Recipient Meritous Svc. award, Bennett Coll., Greensboro, N.C., 1987, Scholarship Nat. Training Lab., UNCF, Crystal City, Va., 1988-89. Mem. Assn. for Supr. & Curriculum Devel., Nat. Assn. of Ach. Adminstrn. (Supr. Acad., Colo. Springs, Colo. 1986), Nat. Assn. of Pupil Personnel Adminstrs., Am. Personnel & Guidance Assn., Phi Delta Kappa, Delta Kappa Gamma, Top Ladies Club of Guilford County. Democrat. Home: 1105 Cedrow Dr High Point NC 27260 Office: High Point Pub Schs 900 Eng Road High Point NC 27260

JONES, LINDA LOUISE, library director; b. Jefferson, Iowa, Sept. 7, 1946; d. Ralph M. and Helen E. (Wind) J. BA, Evangel Coll., 1968; MLS, U. No. Iowa, 1972, U. South Fla., 1989. Tchr. Benton Community High Sch., Van Horne, Iowa, 1968-71; librarian Melcher (Iowa) Dallas Schs., 1972-76; dir. library Open Bible Coll., Des Moines, 1976-84, Southeastern Coll., Lakeland, Fla., 1984—. Mem. ALA, Southeastern Library Assn., Fla. Library Assn., Assn. Christian Libraries, Fellowship Christian Librarians and Info. Scientists, Phi Kappa Phi. Office: Southeastern Coll 1000 Long Fellow Blvd Lakeland FL 33801

JONES, LINDA R. WOLF, organization executive; b. Jersey City, Sept. 4, 1943; d. Eugene Leon and Lottie (Pinkowitz) Rubin; m. Frank Paul Jones, Oct. 21, 1973 (div. Nov. 1987); 1 child, Elisabeth Noel. AB, Bryn Mawr Coll., 1964; MA, Yale U., 1968; DSW, Yeshiva U., N.Y.C., 1985. Dir. planning and tng. N.Y.C. Dept. Employment, 1971-77; dir. legislation N.Y.C. Community Devel. Agy., 1977-78; supervisory legis. analyst N.Y.C. Human Resources Adminstrn., 1978; sr. policy analyst Community Svc. Soc. N.Y., 1978-85; dir. pub. policy YMCA Greater N.Y., 1985-89; dir. spl. projects Phoenix House, N.Y.C., 1990—; mem. adj. extension faculty Cornell U./N.Y. State Sch. Indsl. and Labor Rels., N.Y.C., 1975-80; dir. Nonprofit Coordinating Com. N.Y., N.Y.C., 1986—, Govt. Affairs Profls., N.Y.C., 1989—. Mem. editorial bd. New Eng. Jour. Human Svcs., 1981—; contbr. articles to profl. jours. Mem. Civic Affairs Forum, N.Y.C., 1985—; mem. legis. task force N.Y. State Gov.'s Office Vol. Svc., N.Y.C., 1987—. Mem. Women in Govt. Rels., Am. Pub. Welfare Assn. (dir. 1982), Bryn Mawr Club Westchester (bd. mem., past pres. 1974—), Princeton Club. Home: 377 Westchester Ave Apt 2L Port Chester NY 10573 Office: Phoenix House 164 W 74 St New York NY 10023

JONES, LISA ELLEN, newscaster; b. Longview, Tex., May 15, 1959; d. Claude Felton and Jewell Loyce (Burns) Fitts; m. Michael Ray Jones, June 20, 1980 (div. Jan. 1986). BS in Elem. Edn., Okla. State U., 1982, BS in Radio, TV and Film/News and Pub. Affairs, 1987. Tchr. various elem. schs. Okla., 1983-86; anchor, reporter Sta. KTMC, McAlester, Okla., 1985-86; reporter, news intern Sta. KTUL-TV, Tulsa, 1986, Sta. KJRH-TV, Tulsa, 1986; anchor, reporter, producer Sta. KTEN-TV (affiliate ABC), Denison, Tex., 1987-89; anchor, reporter Sta. KSNF-TV (affiliate NBC), Joplin, Mo., 1989—; instr. journalism East Cen. U., Ada, Okla., fall 1987. Recipient Best Documentary award Okla. Assn. Broadcasters, 1986; Okla. Gridiron Found. scholar, 1986-87. Mem. Women in Communications, Alpha Epsilon Rho. Office: Sta KSNF-TV Tri-State Broadcasting 1502 Cleveland Ave Joplin MO 68402

JONES, LISA GAIL, personnel manager; b. Chester, Pa., June 1, 1960; d. Dudley and Pauline H. Jones. BS in Design and Merchandising, Drexel U., 1982. Asst. store mgr. Lookin Good, Phila., 1980; head of stock, buying office intern Strawbridges & Clothier, Phila., 1980-81; group mgr. sportswear Hecht's Dept. Store, Hyattsville, Md., 1982-84; asst. buyer Hecht's Dept. Store, Arlington, Va., 1984-86; personnel dir. Hecht's Dept. Store, 1986-87; personnel mgr. Marshalls Dept. Store, Rockville, Md., 1988—. Mem. NAFE, Human Resources Network, Retail Action Group (sec. 1985-86). Democrat. Office: Marshalls 12051 Rockville Pike Rockville MD 20852

JONES, LORA LEE, construction executive; b. Indpls., Aug. 8, 1962; d. Jack W. and Dorothy L. (Gerking) McGuire; divorced. Student, Mooresville High Sch., 1981. Office mgr. ABC Erecting, Inc., Mooresville, Ind., 1989—. Mem. Hoosier Girls State, Terre Haute, Ind., 1980. Republican. Home: Rte 1 Box 394A Coatesville IN 46121

JONES, LORELLA MARGARET, physics educator; b. Toronto, Ont., Can., Feb. 22, 1943; came to U.S., 1948; d. Donald Cecil and F. Shirley (Patterson) J. BA, Harvard U., 1964; MSc, Calif. Inst. Tech., 1966, PhD, 1968. From postdoctoral fellow to instr. Calif. Inst. Tech., Pasadena, 1967-68; asst. prof. physics U. Ill., Urbana, 1968-70, assoc. prof. physics, 1970-78, prof. physics, 1978—. Fellow Am. Phys. Soc. (div. particles and fields); mem. AAUP (chpt. pres. 1989-90). Office: U. Ill Dept Physics 1110 W Green St Urbana IL 61801

JONES, M. COLLEEN, educational consultant; b. Kansas City, Mo., Nov. 20, 1950; d. Richard Jewel and Willie Mae (Clark) Thompson; m. Melvin Wallase Jones, Oct. 27, 1973. BBA, U. Iowa, 1972; MBA, U. So. Calif., 1973. Asst. to pres., rsch. analyst, assoc. Office Instnl. Rsch., Tenn. State U., Nashville, 1973-74; asst. to dean grad. studies, instr. office adminstrn. U. Tenn. Coll. Bus. Adminstrn., Knoxville, 1974-75; dir. spl. support svcs. U. Iowa, Iowa City, 1975-8l; internal auditor Office Insp. Gen., U.S. Dept. Edn., Washington, 198l-82; cons. M.A.E. Enterprises, Washington, 1982—; grad. teaching fellow George Washington U., Washington, 1984-87. Mem. editorial bd. Mid-Am. Assn. Ednl. Opportunity Program Personnel Jour., 1986—. Mem. adv. bd. Project Enrich, D.C. Pub. Schs., 1982-88; mem. planning com. ward IV, Georgia Avenue Day, Washington, 1983; mem. Coalition 100 Black Women, Washington, 1983—. Recipient Trio Achiever award Nat. Coun. Ednl. Opportunity Assns., 1983; WoodWilson fellow, 1973, Inst. Ednl. Leadership fellow, 198l-82, AAUW fellow, 1987-88. Mem. Orgnl. Behavior Teaching Soc., Orgnl. Devel. Network, Nat. Soc. for Performance and Instrn. Networking (chmn. 1985-86), Assn. Black Women in Higher Edn. (bd. dirs. 1985-87), Alpha Kappa Alpha. Baptist. Home: l4l9 Underwood St NW Washington DC 20012-2827

JONES, MADONNA MARY, corporate professional; b. Indpls., June 12, 1940; d. Cecil Thomas and Margaret Mary (Kroeger) Seal; m. Samuel E. Jones; children: Jeffrey K., Gregory A., Joelyn K., J. Douglas, Dorinda K.; m. 2d, Samuel E. Jones, Mar. 24, 1979. Student, I.B.M., Indpls., 1959. Key punch operator auditors dept. State House, Indpls., 1959; key punch operator Crane (Ind.) Naval Depot, 1960-61; bookkeeper Tom Daily Furniture, Washington, Ind., 1961-71, mgr., 1973-78; bookkeeper Plainville (Ind.) Mill and Elevator, 1972; corp. sec. Jones Engring. Inc., Ind., 1979—. Bd. dirs. Community Concert Assn. Recipient Vol. Svc. award, Nat. Extension Homemakers Coun., 1987, Commemorative Medal of Honor, 1988. Mem. NAFE, Internat. Bus. and Profl. Women (Woman of Yr. 1985), Harned Home C. of C. (bd. dirs.), West Boggs Kasting Assn. Republican. Roman Catholic.

JONES, MALINDA THIESSEN, telecommunications company executive; b. Perryton, Tex., Jan. 23, 1947; d. Chester Francis Thiessen and Bobbye Pearson (Wallis) Schwalm; m. Hollis Bass Jones, Mar. 21, 1969 (div. 1972); 1 child, Reshad. B.A. in Psychology, U. Mo.-Kansas City, 1975. Rsch. asst. U. Kans. Med. Ctr., Kansas City, 1975-77; owner, mgr. Metro Shampoo Co., Kansas City, Mo., 1977-79; regional mgr. U.S. Telecom, Dallas, 1981-82, staff asst. to pres., Dallas, 1983-84, sr. planner, 1984-85; dir. mktg. Telinq Systems Inc., Richardson, Tex., 1985-86, dir. bus. devel. and corp. communications, 1986—; v.p. mktg. Dakota Group, Inc., 1989—; cons. in field. Editor conf. presentations, bus. plans. Vol. tchr. Sch. for Learning Disability, Operation Discovery, Kansas City, 1973-75; corp. liaison exec. assistance program Dallas C. of C./Dallas Ind. Sch. Dist., 1984; chmn. com. Therapeutic Riding Tex., Dallas, 1985. Recipient Outstanding Contbr. award Dallas Ind. Sch. Dist., 1984. Mem. NAFE, Nat. Mus. Assn. for Women in Arts, Assn. Women Entrepreneurs Dallas. Home: 1122 Overlake Dr Richardson TX 75080 Office: Dakota Group Inc 1217 Digital Dr Richardson TX 75081

JONES, MARGARET DORIS, small business owner; b. Mechanicsville, Md., June 15, 1942; d. George Henry and Cora Madeline (Goldsmith) Murphy; m. Joseph Paul Jones, Jr., Sept. 3, 1960; children—Joseph Paul Jones III, Margaret Dedie. Student, U. Md., 1972-74, George Washington U., 1969, Mgmt. Devel. Ctr. Md., 1978. Telephone operator C&P Telephone Co., Md., Leonardtown, 1960-62; tchr., tchr's aid Leonardtown Bd. Edn., 1967-70; with trial magistrate's system, 1970-71; dist. ct. clk. St. Mary County Dist. Ct., Leonardtown, 1971-86, mem. grievance com., 1976-77; assoc. L. K. Farrell Realtors, Ltd.; owner Jones Countryside Antiques, Crafts and Collectibles. Sec., v.p. Hollywood Ladies Aux. Fire Dept., Md., 1965-70; sec. Oakville Elem. Sch. PTA, Mechanicsville, 1968; ; mem., chmn. Father Andrew White PTA, Leonardtown, 1972-80; worker St. Mary Ryken PTA, Leonardtown, 1976-84; coordinator Dist. Ct. United Way campaign, 1984; past mem. Fraternal Order of Police Sec. for Domestic Abuse/Sexually Assaulted Task Force, St. Mary's County. Mem. So. Md. Bd. Realtors (Disting. Sales Assoc. of Yr. 1989). Democrat. Roman Catholic. Avocations: sewing; art; family history. also: L K Farrell Realtors Ltd PO Box 716 Lexington Park MD 20653

JONES, MARGARET MARY, insurance company consultant; b. Worcester, Mass., June 26, 1963; d. George Victor and Jenny Mary (Acquaro) J. AA in Euro-studies, Franklin Coll., Lugano, Switzerland, 1983; BS in Econs., St. Michael's Coll., Winooski, Vt., 1985; MBA, Anna Maria Coll., Paxton, Mass., 1990. Internat. investor World Bank, Washington, 1986-87; claims adjuster Liberty Mut. Ins. Co., Worcester, 1987-89; planning cons. Liberty Mut. Ins. Co., Boston, 1989—. Staff asst. Worcester city coun. campaign, 1987-88, Mondale Ferraro presdl. campaign, Vt., 1984-85; vol., area rep. Edn. Found., Les Exchange Culturelle. Mem. French Libr., Am. Albanian Nat. Orgn. Republican. Roman Catholic. Home: 115 Walnut St Unit 2 Stoughton MA 02072 Office: Liberty Mut Ins Co 175 Berkeley St Boston MA 02074

JONES, MARGIE IRENE, credit manager; b. Lebanon, Tenn., Apr. 14, 1951; d. Claude Clarence and Ethel Dee (Barnes) Head; m. Billy Gene Jones, May 4, 1968; 1 child, Heather Ann. Student, Vol. State Community Coll., Lebanon, 1983-85. With Maremont Corp., Nashville, 1979-82, sr. sales analyst, 1982-84, sr. credit mgr., 1988—. Mem. Nat. Assn. Credit Mgmt. (pres., founder credit women's ednl. group 1985-87), Nat. Assn. Credit Mgmt. (chairperson S.E. chpt. 1986-87). Home: 3053 Boulder Park Dr Nashville TN 37214

JONES, MARGUERITE JACKSON, educator; b. Greenwood, Miss., Aug. 12, 1949; d. James and Mary G. (Reedy) Jackson; m. Algee Jones, Apr. 4, 1971; 1 child, Stephanie Nerissa. BS, Miss. Valley State U., 1969; MEd, Miss. State U., 1974; Specialist in Community Coll. Teaching, Ark. State U., 1983; postgrad. U. Ark., 1982. Tchr. English Henderson High Sch., Starkville, Miss., 1969-70, creative writing Miami (Fla.) Coral Park, 1970-71, English, head dept. Marion (Ark.) Sr. High Sch., 1971-78, East Ark. Community Coll., Forrest City, 1978-79; migrant edn. supr. Marion (Ark.) Sch. Dist., 1979-83; mem. faculty Draughons Coll., Memphis, 1978-83; asst. prof. State Tech. Inst., 1984—; cons. writing projects; condr. workshops for ednl. bus., civic groups; bd. dir. Tng. Inst., The Cathedral of Bountiful Blessings Ch. Mem. Nat. Coun. Tchrs. English, Ark. Assn. Profl. Educators, Assn. Supervision and Curriculum Devel. Home: 1239 Meadowlark Ln Memphis TN 38116 Office: State Tech Inst 5983 Macon Grove Memphis TN 38134

JONES, MARIAN ILENE, educator; b. Hawarden, Iowa, Oct. 3, 1929; d. Henry Richard and Wilhelmina Anna (Schmidt) Stoltenberg; m. Paul Irving Jones, June 14, 1958 (dec. Feb. 1985). BA, U. La Verne, 1959; MA, Claremont Grad. Sch., 1962; PhD, Ariz. State U., 1971. Cert. tchr., Iowa, Calif. Elem. tchr. Cherokee (Iowa) Sch. Dist., 1949-52, Sioux City (Iowa) Sch. Dist., 1952-56, Ontario (Calif.) Pub. Schs., 1956-61, Reed Union Sch. Dist., Belvedere-Tiburon, Calif., 1962-65, Columbia (Calif.) Union Sch. Dist., 1965-68; prof. edn. Calif. State U., Chico, 1972—. Contbr. articles to profl. jours. Mem. Internat. Reading Assn., AAUW, Phi Delta Kappa, Delta Kappa Gamma. Home: 1675 Manzanita Ave Apt 14 Chico CA 95926 Office: Calif State U Dept Edn Chico CA 95929

JONES, MARY ALICE, investment banking professional; b. Balt., May 2, 1965; d. Richard Anthony and Mary Dorothy (Macatee) J. BBA summa cum laude, Loyola Coll., Balt., 1987, MBA, 1989. Corp. fin. assoc. Ferris, Baker, Watts, Inc., Balt., 1987-89; rsch. assoc., bank stock analyst Alex Brown and Sons, Inc., Balt., 1989—. Mem. Balt. Bond Club, Balt. Security Analysts Soc., Fin. Mgmt. Assn. Balt. (pres. 1986-87), Loyola Sailing Club, Nat. Assn. Security Dealers, Alpha Sigma Nu. Republican. Roman Catholic. Home: 9109 Lyons Mill Rd Owings Mills MD 21117 Office: Alex Brown & Sons Inc 135 E Baltimore St 16th Fl Baltimore MD 21202

JONES, MARY ELLEN, biochemist; b. La Grange, Ill., Dec. 25, 1922; d. Elmer E. and Laura A. (Klein) J.; BS, U. Chgo., 1944; PhD, Yale U., 1951; children: Ethan Vincent Munson, Catherine Laura Munson. AEC fellow, Am. Cancer Soc. fellow, assoc. biochemist Mass. Gen. Hosp., Boston, 1951-57; asst. prof. grad. dept. biochemistry Brandeis U., Waltham, Mass., 1957-60, assoc. prof., 1960-66; assoc. prof. dept. biochemistry Sch. Medicine, U. N.C., Chapel Hill, 1966-68, prof. depts. biochemistry and zoology, 1968-71; prof. dept. biochemistry Sch. Medicine, U. So. Calif., 1971-78; prof., chmn. dept. biochemistry Sch. Medicine, U. N.C., Chapel Hill, 1978-89, Kenan prof. biochemistry, 1980—; mem. study sect. Am. Cancer Soc., 1971-73, NIH, 1971-75; mem. sci. adv. bd. Nat. Heart, Lung and Blood Inst., 1980-84; mem. metabolic biology study sect. NSF, 1978-81; mem. Merit rev. bd. VA, 1975-78; mem. life sci. com. NASA, 1976-78; pres. Chairs of Assn. Med. Sch. Depts. Biochemistry, 1985; mem. Nat. Adv. Gen. Med. Scis. Council, 1988—. Am. Cancer Soc. scholar, 1957-62; NIH grantee, 1957—; NSF grantee, 1957-90. Mem. Am. Chem. Soc. (councilor 1975-79, nominating com. 1971-72, chair 1973-74), Am. Soc. Biol. Chemists (councilor 1975-78, 81-84, pres. 1986), Nat. Acad. Scis., Inst. Medicine of Nat. Acad. Scis. (councilor 1984-87), Assn. Women in Sci., AAAS, N.Y. Acad. Sci., Sierra Club, Sigma Xi. Democrat. Unitarian. Club: Appalachian Mountain. Contbr. numerous articles on biochem. research to sci. publs.; editorial bd. Jour. Biol. Chemistry, 1975-80, 82-87, Cancer Research, 1982-86; assoc. editor Can. Jour. Biochemistry, 1969-74. Office: U NC Dept Biochemistry & Nutrition Chapel Hill NC 27599-7260

JONES, MARY LOUISE HELFRICH, pediatrics, obstetrics-gynecology nurse; b. Dover, Del., Sept. 7, 1944; d. Anthony G. and Mary Jane (Brown) Helfrich; m. William Frank Jones, June 6, 1965; children: Michelle Lynn, Matthew Sean. BSN cum laude, Southern Coll., Collegedale, Tenn., 1980; MSN, U. Fla., 1985, postgrad., 1986—; RN, Washington Hosp Ctr., 1965. RN, D.C., Fla. Clin. coord. Ob-gyn, head nurse pediatrics, pediatric ICU Orlando (Fla.) Regional Med. Ctr.; coord. perinatal ctr., head nurse OB Fla. Hosp. Med. Ctr., Orlando, dir. perinatal-pediatrics; Cons. for programmed/space planning, family centered perinatal svcs. Contbr. articles to profl. pubs. Area leader, walking mother March of Dimes, 1981-88. Mem. Assn. Ob-Gyn and Neonatal Nurses (Fla. congress on nursing orgns.), ANA (bioethics coun., cert. nurse adminstr., cert child birth educator), Nat. Perinatal Assn., So. Regional Nursing Soc., Fla. Healthy Mothers/Healthy Babies Coalition, Coun. of Nurse Researchers, Commn. on Future of Nursing in Fla., Sigma Theta Tau (Alpha and Theta Epsilon chpts.). Roman Catholic.

JONES, MONIKA, data processing executive; b. Burlington, Vt., May 7, 1949; d. Paul and Frieda (Windisch) Desforges; m. Dennis E. Jones (div. 1974); children: Dennis E. Jr., Anthony B. Data processing mgr., mktg. services officer, customer support rep. Exchange Bank & Trust, Tampa, Fla., 1974-82; asst. v.p., v.p. data processing First Fla. Bank. N.A., Tampa, 1982-90; dir. profl. svcs. Systems Mgmt. Engring., Inc., Tampa, 1990—. Mem. Am. Inst. Banking (edn. adminstr. Tampa chpt. 1979-83, Banker of Yr. Tampa chpt. 1981-82), Nat. Assn. Female Execs. Home: 17923 Holly Brook Dr Tampa FL 33647 Office: Systems Mgmt Engring Inc 10012 N Dale Mabry Ste 219 Tampa FL 33618

JONES, NANCY C., construction executive; b. Cody, Wyo., Mar. 16, 1942; d. John Carl and Catherine (Schaff) Buckingham; m. William D. Norman, Feb. 5, 1965 (div. 1972); 1 child, Kelly Blue; m. Raymond M. Jones, May 31, 1974; children: Dan, Stephen, Renee, Kelly, Susie. Student, Colo. State U., 1963-65. Owner J.B. Blue Restaurant, Gillette, Wyo., 1968-74; pres. WoodBuck, Inc., Sheridan, Wyo., 1973—; bd. dirs. Shayne and Shortco, Inc., Belen, N.Mex., 1983—. Republican. Roman Catholic. Home: 1415 Easy St Sheridan WY 82801 Office: Shayne & Shortco Inc 385 Rio Communities Belen NM 87002

JONES, NANCY LANGDON, financial planner; b. Chgo., Mar. 24, 1939; d. Lewis Valentine and Margaret (Seese) Russell; m. Lawrence Elmer Langdon, June 30, 1962 (div. 1970); children: Laura Kimberley, Elizabeth Ann; m. Claude Earl Jones, Jan. 1, 1973. BA, U. Redlands, Calif., 1962. Cert. fin. planner; registered investment advisor. Bookkeeper Russell Sales Co., Santa Fe Springs, Calif., 1962-70; office mgr. Reardon, McCallum & Co., Upland, Calif., 1970-77; broker, assoc. ERA Property Ctr., Upland, 1977-84; registered rep. Fin. Network Investment Corp., Pasadena, Calif., 1984—; pvt. practice fin. planning Upland, 1984—; adj. faculty Coll. Fin. Planning, Denver, 1986—. Leader Spanish trails coun. Girl Scouts Am., 1974-81; Asst. League of Upland. Recipient Hon. Svc. award Valencia Elem. Sch., 1978. Mem. Internat. Assn. Fin. Planners (pres. San Gabriel Valley chpt. 1987-88), Am. Bus. Women's Assn. (sec. Upland chpt. 1984-85, Woman of Yr. award 1988, pres. Upland chpt. 1989-90), Inst. Cert. Fin. Planners (bd. 1990—), Nat. Coun. Exchangers (sec. 1986-87), Women's Bus. Network (pres. 1987-88), Registry of Fin. Planning Practitioners, Inland Valley Profls. (charter), Upland C. of C., Screen Actors Guild. Home and Office: 2485 Mesa Ter Upland CA 91786

JONES, NANCY LYNNE, secretarial service executive; b. Larned, Kans., Nov. 27, 1938; d. Jack Edward and Grace May (Linder) Doerr; m. Alva Ray Jones Jr., Dec. 28, 1957; children: Jeffrey Ray, Michael Alan (dec.), Elizabeth Kay, Douglas Edward. BA, San Jose State U., 1975. Tchr., pianist Nancy L. Jones Piano Studio, Eugene, Oreg., Calif., Wash., 1954—. Composer seven 20th Century piano compositions, 1990, (choral work) Perfect Peace, 1976. Rec. sec. Music Tchrs. Assn. of Calif., Santa Clara, 1974-75. Mem. Oreg. Music Tchrs. Assn. (corr. sec. Eugene chpt. 197-88). Home and office: Bits & Bytes Secretarial Svc 1508 W 26th Ave Eugene OR 97405

JONES, OLIVET BENBOW, management consultant; b. Winston-Salem, N.C., July 10, 1954; d. Alexander Oliver and Pauline (Lyons) Benbow; m. William Neal Jones. AB, Smith Coll., 1976; postgrad., Northwestern U., 1978-79. Mgmt. trainee Leo Burnett USA, Chgo., 1976-78; with First Nat. Bank Chgo., 1978-80; account exec. Essence Communications, Chgo., 1980-82; v.p. human resources James H. Lowry & Assocs., Chgo., 1982-83; dir. pub. rels. James H. Lowry & Assocs., 1983, dir. exec. search, 1984-85, v.p., 1985—. Contbr. articles on mgmt. to various publs. Bd. dirs., Joseph Holmes Dancers, Chgo., 1989—; nat. trustee, Boys and Girls Clubs of Am.

JONES, PATRICIA PEARCE, biologist, educator; b. N.Y.C., Jan. 27, 1947; d. Charles Albert and Lucy Joy (Kapilow) Pearce. BA, Oberlin Coll., 1969; PhD in Biology with distinction, Johns Hopkins U., 1974. Postdoctoral fellow Med. Ctr. U. Calif., San Francisco, 1974-76, Sch. Med. Stanford (Calif.) U., 1976-78; asst. prof. dept. biological scis. Stanford U., 1983—, prof., 1990—, chair PhD program in immunology, 1988—; Mem. Immunology Study sect. NIH, 1983-87. Mem editorial bd., assoc. editor Jour. Immunology, 1983-86; transmitting editor Internat. Immunology, 1989—; contbr. articles to profl. jours. Recipient fellowship Arthritis Found., 1974-77, NSF, 1977-78, Founders Prize Tex. Instruments Found., 1984. Mem. Am. Assn. Immunologists (chmn. publs. com. 1986-90), Sigma Xi. Home: 639 Arastradero Rd Palo Alto CA 94306 Office: Stanford U Dept Biological Scis Stanford CA 94305-5020

JONES, PATSY D., educator; b. Simsboro, La., Mar. 6, 1926; d. Talmage and Dora Melissa (Ward) Durrette; m. W.R. Rowland, Oct. 6, 1946 (dec. Sept. 1982); children: Malissa Rickman, W. Roger, Shelby A.; m. Claude S. Jones, June 21, 1985; children: Linda Kelley, Karen Evans. BS, East Tenn. State U., Johnson City, 1947; MS, East Tenn. State U., 1976, postgrad, 1980—; MA, U. Tenn., 1978. Cert. elem. tchr., Tenn., tchr. spl. edn. Tchr. Unicoi County Sch. System, Erwin, Tenn., 1947-49; tchr. Kingsport (Tenn.) City Sch. System, 1949-54, 60-78, tchr. spl. edn., 1978-85; ret.; dir. mus. Andrew Jackson Sch., Kingsport, 1969-79. Editor Sr. Newsletter Chit Chat, 1987-89. Newsletter editor sr. group First Baptist Ch.; bd. dirs. Netherland Inn Assn., steering com. chairperson. Mem. Kingsport Ret. Tchrs. Assn. (pres. 1987-89), Kingsport Hon. Tchrs. Sorority (chartered, treas. 1965, silver sister 1989), Am. Assn. Ret. People (sec. 1989). Democrat. Baptist. Home: 853 Mimosa Dr Kingsport TN 37660

JONES, RACHEL M., former educator, real estate agent; b. Ahoskie, N.C., July 1, 1929; d. George Washington and Lollie Eldo (Gatling) Manly; m. Edward Thomas Jones, Aug. 22, 1970; children: Antonio, Julie, Mark, Kimberely. BS, Agrl. and Tech. Coll., 1953; MA, Bklyn. Coll., 1976, M in Adminstrn. and Supervision, 1980. Tchr. home econs. Jr. High Sch. 265, Bklyn., 1962-64; dean girls med. program Jr. High Sch. 117, Bklyn., 1968-79, tchr. reading, sci., 1980-81, asst. prin., 1980-86; realtor Bklyn., 1987—; owner variety store, 1985-87. Pres. East 56th St Block Assn., 1975—. Recipient Cert. Community Planning Bd., 1985. Mem. Bklyn. Coll. Alumni, Am. Home Econs. Assn., Bklyn. Assn. Supervision and Curriculum Devel., N.Y. Nat. Assn. Black Educators. Lodge: Order Eastern Star. Home: 47 E 56th St Brooklyn NY 11203

JONES, REBECCA ANN, medical records professional; b. Muncie, Ind., June 22, 1946; d. John Everett and Moscelyn A. (Turner) Whitesell; m. Charlie Paul Jones, Aug. 1, 1965; children: Julie Ann, John Paul, Jay Alan. BS, Ind. U. Sch. Medicine, Indpls., 1974. Asst. dir. dept. med. records Community Hosp. Indpls., 1974-75; dir. med. records, quality assurance, utilization rev. Ball Meml. Hosp., Inc., Muncie, 1975—; med. record cons. local long-term care facilities, 1975—. Participant Acad. Community Leadership, Muncie Delaware C. of C., 1986. Mem. Am. Med. Record Assn., Ind. Med. Record Assn. (chmn. pub. rels. com. 1978, continuing edn. com. 1981). Republican. Mem. Soc. of Friends. Home: RD 1 Box 108E Daleville IN 47334 Office: Ball Meml Hosp Inc 2401 University Ave Muncie IN 47303

JONES, REGINA NICKERSON, public relations executive; b. Los Angeles, Sept. 23, 1942; d. Leslie Augustus and Luedelia (Triggs) Nickerson; children: Kenneth Leon, Kevin Christopher, Keith Fitzgerald, Kory Reginald, Karen Regina. Bookkeeper, sec. Carson Realty, Los Angeles, 1958; radio telephone operator Los Angeles Police Dept., 1962-66; owner, publisher Soul Publs., Los Angeles, 1966-83; v.p. pub. relations Solar Records-Dick Griffey Prodns., Los Angeles, 1983-86; pres., owner Regina Jones & Assocs, Los Angeles, 1985—. Recipient Outstanding Women in Bus. Image award NAACP, 1980. Mem. Nat. Assn. Media Women, Black Music Assn. (exec. council), NAACP, Urban League.

JONES, RENAE SPENCER, marketing professional; b. Dickson, Tenn., Dec. 15, 1960; d. William Roger and Genny L. Spencer. BA, David Lipscomb Coll., 1983. Mgr. Gen. Distbg. Co., Burns, Tenn., 1975-83; bill clk. Tenn. Ho. of Reps., Nashville, 1982; dir. human resources Universal Plastics, Inc., Cookeville, Tenn., 1983—. Contbg. editor: Women Organizing Women, 1989—. Mem. exec. bd., water safety chmn. Putnam County ARC, Cookesville, 1986-90; bd. dirs. Putnam County United Way, 1988; prizes and donations chair Putnam County Cystic Fibrosis Bike-a-Thon; pub. rels. chair, bd. mem. Upper Cumberland Alliance Against Domestic Violence; pres. Cookeville-Putnam County Clean Air Commn., 1989-90; active Tenn. Coun. for Future Women in the Workplace; vol. WCTE-TV. Mem. Tenn. Bus. and Profl. Women (young careerist chair 1989-90, bd. dirs.), Cookeville Bus. and Profl. Women (1st v.p. 1987-88, v.p. 1988-90), AAUW (bd. dirs. 1987—). Club: Toastmasters (Cookeville) (pres. 1988, area gov. 1989-90). Home: 191 E 15th Apt 4 Cookeville TN 38501

JONES, RENEE KAUERAUF, health care administrator; b. Duncan, Okla., Nov. 3, 1949; d. Delbert Owen and Betty Jean (Marsh) Kauerauf; m. Dan Elkins Jones, Aug. 3, 1972. BS, Okla. State U., 1972, MS, 1975; PhD, Okla. U., 1989. Statis. analyst Okla. State Dept. Mental Health, Okla. City, 1978-80, divisional chief, 1980-83, adminstr., 1983-84; assoc. dir. HCA Presbyn. Hosp., Okla. City, 1984—; adj. instr. Okla. U. Health Sci. Ctr., 1979—; assoc. staff scientist Okla. Ctr. for Alcohol and Drug-Related Studies, Okla. City, 1979—; cons. in field. Assoc. editor Alcohol Tech. Reports jour., 1979-84; contbr. articles to profl. jours. Capt. USNR, 1985. Mem. Am. Pub. Health Assn., Assn. Health Svcs. Rsch., Alcohol and Drug Problems Assn. N.Am., N.Y. Acad. Scis., So. Sleep Soc. (sec.-treas. 1989—), Phi Kappa Phi. Democrat. Methodist. Home: 215 NW 20th Oklahoma City OK 73103 Office: HCA Presbyn Hosp NE 13th at Lincoln Blvd Oklahoma City OK 73104

JONES, ROBIN ARBUCKLE, academic program coordinator, consultant; b. San Francisco, Sept. 29, 1962; d. Thomas Leroy and Donna (Ellis) Arbuckle; m. Lt. Grey Charles Jones, July 31, 1988. Student, Diablo Valley Coll., 1981-83, Richmond Coll., London, 1983; BA, U. Calif., Santa Barbara, 1985; postgrad., U. Kans., 1989—. Instr. U. Kans., Lawrence, 1985-87; employment cons. Haskell Indian Jr. Coll., Lawrence, 1986-87; employment svcs. specialist Mont. State Employment Svc., Great Falls, 1987-90; program coord. master's adminstrv. scis. program U. Mont., Malmstrom AFB, 1990—; cons. 1st Interstate Bank, Great Falls, 1988, Malmstrom AFB Youth Ctr., Great Falls, 1988. Mem. YWCA, Great Falls, 1988—. Mem. Internat. Assn. Personnel in Employment Security (pres. 1989—), Officer Wives Club (scholarship 1989-90), Gamma Pi Beta (pres. Great Falls chpt. 1987—). Home: 2 Birch St Great Falls MT 59405 Office: U Mont 840 MSSQ/MSE Malmstrom AFB MT 59402-5000

JONES, ROXANNE HARPER, state legislator; b. N.C., May 3, 1928; d. Gilford and Mary (Bruton) Harper; m. James H. Jones, 1957 (dec.); children: Patricia Hill, Wanda Crews. Student pub. schs. Bd. dirs. Pa. Minority Bus. Devel. Authority, Pa. Legis. Black Caucus, 1985—, Pa. Intra-Govtl. Long Term Care Coun.; minority chmn. urban affairs and housing com., mem. pub. health and welfare com., community and econ. devel. com., Democratic policy coms., aging and youth com. Pa. State Senate, 1985—. Recipient Nat. Welfare Rights Orgn. Leadership award Nat. Welfare Rights Orgn., 1972, Woman of Yr. award Zeta Phi Beta, 1985, Achievement cert. Nat. Coun. Negro Women, 1985. Bd. dirs. Ams. for Democratic Action; co-chmn. Coalition Concerned Citizens; exec. dir. Phila. Citizens in Action; mem. Allegheny West Found. Mem. Apolstolic Ch. Home: 2330 W Allegheny Ave Philadelphia PA 19132 Office: Pa State Senate Harrisburg PA 17120

JONES, SALLY DAVIESS PICKRELL, writer; b. St. Louis, June 4, 1923; d. Claude Dildine and Marie Daviess (Pittman) Pickrell; m. Charles William Jones, Sept. 2, 1943; 1 son, Matthew Charles. Student, Mills Coll., Oakland, Calif., 1941-43, U. Calif.-Berkeley, 1944, Columbia, 1955-58. Author: (novel) The Lights Burn Blue, 1947. Mem. UN Women's Guild, Fgn. Policy Assn., Nat. Coun. Women, Asia Soc., English-Speaking Union, Met. Mus. Art, Internat. Platform Assn., Internat. Women's Forum. Episcopalian. Address: 311 E 58th St New York NY 10022

JONES, SHARON LESTER, psychotherapist; b. Stuart, Fla., Mar. 26, 1944; d. Andrew Morrison and Dorothy Virginia (Atkinson) Lester; b. James Baker Jones, June 12, 1965; children—James Timothy, Jennifer Lynn. A.B. cum laude, U. Miami, 1966; M.A., U. Tulsa, 1980; postgrad. in family therapy, Houston Family Inst., 1980-82. Psychotherapist Interface Counseling Ctr., Houston, 1980—; Mem. Am. Assn. Marriage and Family Therapists, Houston Marriage and Family Therapist Assn. (bd. dirs. 1983—, pres.), Nat. Council Family Relations, Am. Assn. Profl. Hypnotherapists, Assn. Neuro Linguistic Programming (master programmer 1983-85), Pi Beta Phi (bd. dirs. Houston 1988—). Republican. Methodist. Avocations: jogging; raquetball; reading; camping. Office: Interface Counseling Ctr 5015 Westheimer Suite 3260 Houston TX 77056

JONES, SHERYL CASSANDRA, marketing professional; b. Utica, N.Y., Jan. 1, 1947; d. Ronald Gray and Marjory Helen (Holiday) J.; children: Eric Alonso, Lilia Carolyn. BS, Rochester (N.Y.) Inst. Tech., 1969; postgrad. in Bus. Adminstrn., Our Lady of the Lake U., San Antonio, 1990—. Lic. Comml., Instrument Airplane and Rotorcraft. Regional mktg. mgr. Narco Avionics, San Jose, Calif.; exec. dir. The Whirly Girls, San Antonio, 1978-81; regional mktg. mgr. Bell Helicopter Textron, Ft. Worth, 1981-89; v.p. Sidlinger Computer Corp., San Antonio, 1989-90; dir. mktg. ALCOR, San Antonio, 1990—. Named Most Proficient Pilot of Yr., Bell Salesman of Yr., 1987. Mem. Ninety Nines, The Whirly-Girls, Aircraft Owners and Pilots Assn. Lutheran. Office: 10130 Jones-Maltsberger Rd San Antonio TX 78216

JONES, SUSAN ANN, economic development consultant; b. Gloversville, N.Y., May 5, 1959; d. William Francis and Mary Elizabeth (Cocker) J. AB in Econs., Cornell U., 1981; M in Planning, U. Calif., Berkeley, 1984. Legal aide dept. law State of N.Y., Binghamton, 1981-82; preservation planner Cambridge (Mass.) Hist. Commn., 1984; econ. devel. specialist Cambridge Systematics, 1984-87, assoc., 1987-88; sr. assoc. Cambridge Systematics, Berkeley, 1988-90, acting dir., 1990—; speaker Calif. Transp. and Pub. Works Conf., Garden Grove, 1989—, Workforce 2,000 Conf., U. Wis. and U.S. Dept. Labor, Milw., 1988, Nat. Coun. Urban Econ. Devel., Transp. and Devel. Conf., 1990, mem. exec. bd. for conf. devel. Editor: newsletter Architects, Designers, and Planners for Social Responsibility, 1984-85. Mem. exec. com. Human Race Roadrace, Boston, 1986-88; mem. Berkeley County-Rec. Softball League. Mem. Calif. Assn. Local Econ. Devel., Am. Coun. for Urban Econ. Devel., Nat. Coun. for Urban Econ. Devel. Waterfront Ctr. Democrat. Office: Cambridge Systematics 2855 Telegraph Ave Ste 305 Berkeley CA 94705

JONES, SUSAN DORFMAN, writer; b. N.Y.C., Oct. 4, 1939; d. Joseph and Sarah (Sorrin) Dorfman; m. William Harry Jones, Sept. 18, 1960; children: Jeffrey Scott, Eric David, Timothy Mark. BA, Syracuse U., 1961. Pres., owner Antiques Corp. Am., 1972-77; communications officer Riggs Bank, Washington, 1978-81; mgr. publs. Potomac Electric Power Co., Washington, 1981-82; sr. mgr. corp. communications MCI Corp., Washington, 1982-83; dir. corp. communications Sears World Trade, Washington, 1983-85; dir. corp. communications and govt. rels. Oxford Devel. Corp., Bethesda, Md., 1985-87; communications expert pub. health svc./health and human svcs. U.S. Alchohol, Drug Abuse, Mental Health Adminstrn., Rockville, Md., 1989—; free-lance writer, cons., Washington, 1975—; radio personality Sta. 4KQ, Brisbane, Australia, 1962; adj. prof. communications Am. U., Washington, 1978-82. Author, editor, project mgr. corp. ann. reports; writer sch. bd. candidates and home rule campaign speeches, Washington, 1970-76. Treas. D.C. Recreation Dept., 1973-79; bd. dirs. Murch Elem. Sch., Washington, 1969, 73. Recipient 1st pl. award for columns N.Y. Press Assn., 1961, Gold Quill award Internat. Assn. Bus. Communicators, 1980. Mem. Internat. Assn. Bus. Communicators (treas. 1981), Nat. Assn. Bank Women, Women in Telecommunications, Nat. Press Club, Pub. Rels. Soc. Am. Democrat. Jewish. Home and Office: 7300 Burdette Ct Bethesda MD 20817

JONES, TONYA GALE, construction executive; b. Sullivan, Ind., Sept. 11, 1948; d. Harlan Carther and Nina Marie (Summers) Thomas; m. Murray Bonham Jones, May 23, 1973 (div. Apr. 2, 1985); children: Jessica Anne, Mercedes Elizabeth. BA, Ill. State U., 1971; grad., Realtors Inst., Ill., 1977. Lic. broker, Ill., Tenn. Bus. devel. coord. Realty World Midwest Regional Hdqrs., Oakbrook, Ill., 1978-80; project coord. Hewelett & Norton, Inc., Nashville, 1980-82; v.p. R & D Schultz & Assocs., Inc., Nashville, 1982-85; pres. Mark IV Enterprises, Inc., Nashville, 1985—; 4 yr. mayoral appointment Met. Govt. of Davidson County, Nashville. Bd. dirs. YWCA, Bloomington, Ill., 1974-78. Mem. Nashville Mid. Tenn. Homebuilders (bd. dirs. 1985—), State of Tenn. Homebuilders Assn. (bd. dirs. 1987—), Maury County Homebuilders Assn. (liason 1988—), Nashville Homebuilders Assn., Nashville C. of C., Comml. Builders Coun., DAR, Colonial Dames, Ill. Soc. of Mayflower Descendants, Ea. Star. Office: Mark IV Enterprises Inc 104 Woodmont Blvd Ste 203 Nashville TN 37205

JONES, VALERIE KAYE, insurance company executive; b. Cleve., Oct. 26, 1956; d. Daniel Edward and Katherine (Donaldson) J. BS with high honors, Ohio U., 1978; postgrad., Cleve. State U. Lic. ins. agt. Asst. personnel dir. The Higbee Co., Cleve., 1977-78; tchr. learning disabilities and behavior disorders Cleve. Heights-Univ. Heights (Ohio) Sch., 1978-83; mem. ins. specialist CUNA Mut. Ins. Group, Madison, Wis., 1983-84, rep. group coverages, 1984-87, field communications adminstr. cen. dist., 1987-88, sr. field communications adminstr., 1988—; bd. sec. Liberty Hill Credit Union, Cleve., 1978-83. Asst. to dir. directory project Cuyahoga Spl. Edn. Service Ctr., 1974; mem. 21st Dist. Congl. Caucus, Cleve., 1984. Mem. Nat. Assn.

Female Execs., Delta Sigma Theta. Democrat. Home: 37456 Spring Ln Farmington Hills MI 48018 Office: CUNA Mut Ins Group 20800 Civic Ctr Dr Southfield MI 48076

JONES, VICTORIA LYNN, marketing executive; b. Cin., June 26, 1955; d. Thomas Anson and Patricia Mary (McCarthy) J. BA, Northwestern U., 1977, M.Mgmt., 1983. Tchr. English Hamilton County Pub. Schs., Cin., 1977-79; sales rep. Telephone Mktg. Svcs., Cin., 1979-80, Alpha Audio Visual, Cin., 1980-81; mktg. asst. Baxter. Fenwal div., Deerfield, Ill., summer 1982; mktg. asst. Aunt Jemima Quaker Oats, Chgo., 1983-84; mktg. mgr. new products Mayfair Games, Niles, Ill., 1984-86; assoc. product mgr. Old Spice Am. Cyanamid Shulton USA Div., Clifton, N.J., 1986-88; product mgr. new products Pope & Talbot, Eau Claire, Wis., 1988-89; dir. advt. Wis. Milk Mktg. Bd., Madison, 1989—; Admissions cons. J.L. Kellogg Grad. SCh., Evanston, Ill., 1986—. Mem. NAFE, Am. Mktg. Assn., Am. Soc. Advt. and Promotion, Kellogg Alumni Assn., Am. Soc. Advt. Profls., Game Mfrs. Assn. Am. (cons. 1984-86, commendation award 1986). Office: Wis Milk Mktg Bd 8418 Excelsior Dr Madison WI 53717

JONES, WANDA FAYE, library media specialist; b. Little Rock, May 7, 1949; d. Hoyt and Marcella (Durnie) Williams; m. Robert David Jones, Nov. 22, 1978; 1 child, Robert David. BS in Edn., Ouachita Bapt. U., Arkadelphia, Ark., 1971, MS in Edn., 1975; MLS, Tex. Woman's U., 1980. Cert. English tchr., in libr. media, Ark. Libr. media specialist Carthage (Ark.) Pub. Sch., 1971-74, Harris Elem. Sch., North Little Rock, Ark., 1974-77, Jacksonville (Ark.) Elem. Sch., 1977-83, North Pulaski High Sch., Jacksonville, 1983—; conf. and workshop presenter, 1982—. Co-author curriculum guides; contbr. articles and revs. to Ark. News and Views. Mem. standards com. for media program Ark. State Libr., 1983; mem. Cen. Ark. Friends of Libr., Friends of Zoo. Recipient award for exemplary libr. program U.S. Dept. Edn., 1986. Mem. Ark. Assn. Instrnl. Media (com. mem. 1977—, chmn. student media festival 1987-88), Ark. Edn. Assn. (conf. chmn. libr. media div. 1982-84), Ark. Libr. Assn. (chmn. poster session 1989), Ark. Assn. Sch. Librs. (v.p. 1983, pres. 1984). Baptist. Office: North Pulaski High Sch 718 Harris Rd Jacksonville AR 72076

JONES, WINONA NIGELS, library media specialist; b. St. Petersburg, Fla., Feb. 24, 1928; d. Eugene Arthur and Bertha Lillian (Dixon) Nigels; m. Charles Albert Jones, Nov. 26, 1944; children: Charles Eugene, Sharon Ann Jones Allworth, Caroline Winona Jones Pandorf. AA, St. Petersburg Jr. Coll., 1965; BS, U. South Fla., 1967, MS, 1968; Advanced MS, Fla. State U., 1980. Libr. media specialist Dunedin (Fla.) Comprehensive High Sch., 1967-76; libr. media specialist, chmn. dept. Fitzgerald Middle Sch., Largo, Fla., 1976-87; dir. Media Svcs. East Lake High Sch., 1987—. Active Palm Harbor and Pinellas County Hist. Soc. Named Educator of Yr. Pinellas County Sch. Bd. and Suncoast C. of C., 1983, 88, Palm Harbor Woman of Yr. Palm Harbor Jr. Women's Club, 1989. Mem. ALA (coun. 1988-92), NEA, AAUW, Fla. Assn. Media in Edn. (pres.), U. So. Fla. Alumni Assn., Assn. Ednl. Communication and Tech. (div. sch. media specialist, coms.), Am. Assn. Sch. Librs. (com., pres.-elect 1989, pres. 1990—), Southeastern Libr. Assn., Fla. Libr. Assn., Assn. Supervision and Curriculum Devel., Fla. State Libr. Sci. Alumni, U. South Fla. Libr. Sci. Alumni Assn. (bd. dir.), Phi Theta Kappa, Phi Rho Pi, Beta Phi Mu, Kappa Delta Pi, Delta Kappa Gamma (parliamentarian 1989-90, legis. chmn. 1990), Inner Wheel Club, Pilot Club, Civic Club, Order of Eastern Star (Palm Harbor, past worthy matron). Democrat. Home: 911 Manning Rd Palm Harbor FL 34683 Office: 1300 Silver Eagle Dr Tarpon Springs FL 34689

JONES-SMITH, JAYNE E., therapist; b. Kansas City, Mo., Jan. 10, 1952; d. Melvin and Imalda Mae Bess Jones; m. Darryle C. Smith, Aug. 30, 1980; 1 child, Jason. BS in Psychology, Southeast Mo. State U., Cape Giradeau, 1974, MA in Psychiatric Counseling, 1980. Lic. profl. clin. counselor. Adult basic edn. tchr. Cape Giradeau (Mo.) Vocat. Tech.; mental health therapist St. Francis Community Mental Health, Cape Giradeau; team leader Good Samaritan Hosp., Dayton, Ohio. Mem. adv. bd. MHT program Sinclair Community Coll. Mem. NAFE, Order of Eastern Star (past worthy matron), Giradeau Bus. and Profl. Women's Club (past pres.). Democrat. African Methodist Episcopalian. Home: 468 Fountain Ave Dayton OH 45405 Office: 2831 Salem Ave Dayton OH 45406

JONG, ERICA MANN, author, poet; b. N.Y.C., Mar. 26, 1942; d. Seymour and Eda (Mirsky) Mann; m. Michael Weitman, 1963 (div. 1965), m. Allan Jong (div. Sept. 1975); m. Jonathan Fast, Dec. 1977 (div. Jan. 1983); 1 dau., Molly; m. Kenneth David Burrows, Aug. 5, 1989. B.A., Barnard Coll., 1963; M.A., Columbia U., 1965. Faculty, English dept. CUNY, 1964-65, 69-70, overseas div. U. Md., 1967-69; mem. lit. panel N.Y. State Council on Arts, 1972-74; faculty Bradford Writers Conf. Middlebury, Vt., 1982. Author: (poems) Fruits & Vegetables, 1971, Half Lives, 1973, Loveroot, 1975, At the Edge of the Body, 1979, Ordinary Miracles, 1983; (novels) Fear of Flying, 1973, How to Save Your Own Life, 1977, Fanny: Being the True History of the Adventures of Fanny Hackabout Jones, 1980, Parachutes & Kisses, 1984, Serenissima, 1987; (poetry and non-fiction) Witches, 1981; (juvenile) Megan's Book of Divorce, 1984, (novel) Any Woman's Blues, 1990. Recipient Bess Hokin prize Poetry mag., 1971, Alice Faye di Castagnola award Poetry Soc. Am., 1972; named Mother of Yr., 1982; Nat. Endowment Arts grantee, 1973. Mem. Authors Guild (coun. 1975—), Poets and Writers Bd., Writers Guild Am.-West, P.E.N., Author's Guild Coun., Phi Beta Kappa. Office: care Ed Victor Inc 9255 Sunset Blvd Los Angeles CA 90069

JONKOUSKI, JILL ELLEN, materials scientist, ceramic engineer, educator; b. Chgo.; d. Joseph Louis and Ruth (Reichhardt) J. BS in Ceramic Engring., U. Ill., MS in Ceramic Engring. Former researcher Battelle Meml. Inst., Columbus, Ohio; former ceramic engr. Austenal Dental, Inc., Chgo.; rsch. scientist BIRL Indsl. Rsch. Lab., Northwestern U., Evanston, Ill.; former mem. adj. faculty Triton Coll., River Grove, Ill. Mem. Am. Ceramic Soc. (speaker tech. presenter 1983, 84), Nat. Inst. Ceramic Engrs., Am. Soc. Metals Internat., U. Ill. Alumni Assn. Office: Northwestern U BIRL 1801 Maple Evanston IL 60201-3135

JONTZ, PAULINE, museum director, college administrator; b. Akron, Ohio, Oct. 26, 1928; d. Clinton Charner and Lora Elizabeth (Hunter) Prather; m. Leland D. Jontz, June 25, 1950; children: James Prather, Mary Lee Jontz Turk. AB, Ind. U., 1949. Accredited Pub. Relation Soc. Am., Nat. Soc. Fund Raising Execs. Dir. devel. and pub. relations Children's Mus. Indpls., 1963-82; exec. dir. Conner Prairie, Noblesville, Ind., 1982—; v.p. Earlham Coll., Noblesville, 1982—. Bd. dirs. Morris Butler Hist. Home, 1988—. Recipient Disting. Alumni award Ind. U., 1985, Matrix award Women in Communications, 1988, Sagamore of Wabash award Gov. of Ind., 1988; named Woman of Achievement, Ind. Women's Press Club, 1976. Mem. Am. Assn. for State and Local History (bd. dirs. 1989—), Indpls. Conv. and Visitors Assn. (bd. dirs. 1988—), Consortium of Arts Adminstrs. (v.p. 1989—), Ind. U. Journalism Alumni Assn. (treas. 1988—), Indpls. Rotary Club (bd. dirs. 1990—). Methodist. Office: Conner Prairie 13400 Allisonville Rd Noblesville IN 46060

JOOSTEMA, BRENDA ANN, nursing administrator; b. Morristown, N.J., May 8, 1958; d. Wiley Allen and Beverly Ann (Riebel) Arnold. BS in Nursing, W.Va. Wesleyan Coll., 1981. RN, N.J. Staff nurse Morristown Meml. Hosp., 1981-82; clinician A in psychiatry Med. Coll. Va. Hosp., Richmond, 1984-85; charge nurse King James Care Ctr., Chatham Twp., N.J., 1985-86; charge nurse Cheshire Home, Florham Park, N.J., 1982-83, asst. dir. nursing, 1986-87; asst. dir. nursing N.J. Ea. Star Home, Bridgewater, 1987—. Mem. Assn. Nursing Adminstrs. (assoc. LTC facilities N.J. area), Alpha Gamma Delta. Home: 11 Garfield Ave Madison NJ 07940 Office: NJ Ea Star Home 111 Finderne Ave Bridgewater NJ 08807

JORANKO, SARA R., language professional, English, educator; b. Hamilton, Ohio, Oct. 31, 1936; d. Robert Michael and Garnet Rosalie (Thomas) O'Friel; m. Ronald James Joranko, June 13, 1959; children: David Brian, Mary Gillian. Diploma, Jewish Hosp. Sch. Nursing, Cin., 1957; BA in English, John Carroll U., Cleve., 1980, MA, 1985. RN, Ohio. Staff nurse to head nurse Ohio State U. Hosp., Columbus, 1957-60; part-time instr. John Carroll U., Cleve., 1982-88, instr., 1988—; part-time instr. Ursuline Coll., Pepper Pike, Ohio, 1987. Mem. MLA, Nat. Coun. Tchrs. of English. Roman Catholic. Office: John Carroll U Cleveland OH 44118

JORDAN, BARBARA C., lawyer, educator, former congresswoman; b. Houston, Feb. 21, 1936; d. and Arlyne J. B.A. in Polit. Sci. and History magna cum laude, Tex. So. U.; J.D., Boston U., 1959. Bar: Mass. 1959, Tex. 1959. Adminstrv. asst. to county judge County of Harris, Tex.; mem. Tex. Senate, 1966-72; pres. pro tem, chmn. Labor and Mgmt. Relations Com. and Urban Affairs Study Com.; mem. 93d-95th congresses from 18th Dist. Tex.; mem. com. judiciary, com. govt. ops.; mem. spl. task force 94th Congress; mem. steering and policy com. House Democratic Caucus; Lyndon B. Johnson pub. svc. prof. U. Tex., Austin, 1979-82, Lyndon B. Johnson Centennial chair in nat. policy, 1982—; mem. UN panel on multinat. corps. in South Africa and Namibia; dir. numerous cos. Author: Barbara Jordan—Self Portrait, 1979. Named One of 10 Most Influential Women in Tex., One of 100 Women in Touch With Our Time, Harpers Bazaar mag.; headed Redbook mag. poll Women Who Could Be Pres.; Dem. Woman of Year Women's Nat. Dem. Club; Woman of Year in Politics, Ladies Home Jour.; recipient Eleanor Roosevelt humanities award, 1984, Charles Evans Hughes Gold medal Nat. Conf. Christians and Jews; Barbara Jordan Fund established in her honor Lyndon B. Johnson Sch. Pub. Affairs. Mem. ABA, Tex. Bar Assn., Mass. Bar Assn., Houston Bar Assn., NAACP, Delta Sigma Theta. Baptist. Office: U Tex Lyndon B Johnson Sch Pub Affairs Austin TX 78713*

JORDAN, BARBARA SCHWINN, painter; b. Glen Ridge, N.J.; d. Carl Wilhelm Ludwig and Helen Louise (Jordan) Schwinn; m. Frank Bertram Jordan, Jr.; children: Janine Jordan Newlin, Frank Bertram III. Grad. N.Y. Sch. Fine and Applied Art (Parsons), N.Y. and Paris; student Grand Cen. Art Sch., Art Students League, Grand Chaumiere, Academie Julien-Paris, Columbia U., NAD. Illustrator mags. including Vogue, 1930's, Ladies Home Jour., Saturday Evening Post, Colliers, Good Housekeeping, Cosmopolitan, McCall's, American, Town and Country, 1940's-50's. Women's Jour., Eng., Hors Zu, Fed. Republic Germany, Marie Claire, France, other fgn. publs., 1950's-60's. Portrait painter, including Queen Sirikit, Princess Margaret, Princess Grace; freelance painter, 1970—; one-man shows include Soc. of Illustrators, 1940, 50, Barry Stephens Gallery, 1950, Bodley Gallery, N.Y.C., 1971, 80, Community Coll., West Mifflin, Pa., 1973, Duquesne U., 1973; exhibited in group shows including NAD, 1955, Royal Acad., London, Guild Hall, N.Y., 1981, Summit N.J. Art Ctr., 1981, Meredith Long Gallery, Houston, 1983, Mus. Soc. Illustrators, N.Y., 1985, The Marcus Gallery, Sante Fe, 1985, 86, The Gerald Peters Gallery, Santa Fe, 1985, 86, Brandywine Mus., Pa., 1986, New Britain (Conn.) Mus. Am. Art, 1986, works represented Holbrook Collection, Ga. Mus. Art, Eureka Coll., Ill., New Britain Mus. Am. Art, Mus. of the Soc. of Illustrators, N.Y.C., Brandywine Mus., Pa., Sanford Low Meml. Collection, Del. Art Mus., Wilmington, Mus. Am. Illustration, N.Y.C., Glenbow Mus., Calgary, Alberta, Can., various pvt. and gallery collections; lectr., instr. illustration Parsons Sch., 1952-54; founder adv. coun. Art Instrn. Sch., 1956-70. Chmn. art com. UNICEF greeting cards, 1950-61 mem. com. Spence Chapin Sch., Philharm. Soc., 1950's-60's. Winner prizes Art Dirs. Club, 1950, Guild Hall, 1969. Assoc. mem. Guggenheim Mus. Mem. Cosmopolitan Club N.Y. Author: Technique of Barbara Schwinn, 1956; World of Fashion Art, 1968. Home and Studio: Mecox Rd RR 1 Box 882 Water Mill NY 11976

JORDAN, BETTY SUE, retired educator; b. Lafayette, Tenn., Sept. 4, 1920; d. Aubrey Lee and Geneva (Freeman) West; m. Bill Jordan, Oct. 22, 1950; 1 child, L. Nicha. Student, David Lipscomb Coll., 1939-41; BS, U. Tenn., 1943; registered dietitian Duke U. Hosp., 1945; MEd, Clemson U., 1973. Dietitian U. Ala., Tuscaloosa, 1945-46, Duke U., Durham, N.C., 1946-48, Stetson U., DeLand, Fla., 1948-50, Furman U., Greenville, S.C., 1950-52; elem. tchr. Greenville County Schs., S.C., 1952-66, tchr. orthopedically handicapped, 1966-85. Mem. NEA, Assn. Childhood Edn. (treas. 1980-85), United Daus. Confederacy (pres. Greenville chpt. 1978—), Greenville Woman's Club, Lake Forest Garden Club (pres. 1970-71, 77-79, 80-81, historian 1981-87), Greater Greenville Rose Soc. (pres. 1983-84), Am. Rose Soc. (accredited rose judge 1986, rose arrangement judge, cons.), Clarice Wilson Garden Club (pres. 1987-89), Delta Kappa Gamma (pres. Tau chpt. 1976-78, state chmn. communications 1979-81, state chmn. rsch. 1983-85, leadership/mgmt. seminar 1989), Kappa Kappa Iota (state pres. 1972-73, conclave pres. 1983-85), Democrat. Methodist. Avocations: collecting antiques, growing roses, flower arranging. Home: 21 Lisa Dr Greenville SC 29615

JORDAN, CAROL LYNN, editor; b. Cleve., July 1, 1956; d. Harold Vedell and Vunice Irene (Nash) J. BS, Ohio U., 1979. Reporter Lake County Telegraph, Painesville, Ohio, 1979-84, Fairchild Publs., N.Y.C., 1984-86; asst. news editor Fairchild Publs., 1987-88; news editor Fairchild Publs., 1988-89; mng. editor Capital Cities/ABC Inc., 1990—. Mem. New Hope Scholarship Com., Jersey City, 1989, New Hope Flower Guild, Jersey City, 1986-89. Mem. Nat. Assn. Black Journalists, Black Women in Publishing. Democrat. Baptist. Office: Fairchild Publs 7 E 12th St New York NY 10003

JORDAN, GRACE ELLEN, retired educator; b. Somerville, N.J., Apr. 30, 1928; d. George William and Grace Alma (Beams) Hedge; m. John Russell Jordan, July 14, 1946; children: John R., Ellen B., Patricia A. BA, Calif. State U., Long Beach, 1967, MEd, 1975. Cert. sec. edn. tchr., Calif. Sec. Douglas Aircraft, El Sequndo, Calif., 1955-63; tchr. L.A. Unified Sch. Dist., 1967—; reading specialist Brevard County Schs., Merritt Island, Fla., 1970-71. Chmn. United Way, Carson, Calif., 1986-87. L.A. Ednl. Partnership grantee. Mem. Nat. Coun. Tchrs. English, Phi Delta Kappa, Delta Kappa Gamma (v.p. 1987—, Educator of Yr. award 1990). Roman Catholic. Home: 11222 Kensington Rd Los Alamitos CA 90720

JORDAN, HARRIET MARIE, sales executive; b. Gloucester Pt., Va., Dec. 15, 1959; d. Harry Randolph and Esther Marie (Hall) J.; m. Dana K. Bohannon, Dec. 17, 1977 (div. Aug. 1980). BSBA, Christopher Newport Coll., 1985. Teller United Va. Bank, Newport News, 1978-79; br. office coord. Legg Mason Wood Walker, Newport News, 1979-81; office mgr. Pilot Life Ins. Co., Newport News, 1981-82; office asst. U.S. Govt., Ft. Eustis, Va., 1982-86; assoc. acct. Newport News Shipbuilding, 1986; 1st mate, navigator ARKADAS Charters, Bahamas, 1986-87; capt., 1st mate, navigator ARKADAS Charters, Christiansted, St. Croix, 1987-88; group mdse. and sales mgr. Burdines, Ft. Lauderdale, Fla., 1988—. Republican. Home: 1460 SE 15th St Apt B Fort Lauderdale FL 33316 Office: 2314 E Sunrise Blvd Fort Lauderdale FL 33304

JORDAN, JOAN KOWALSKI, financial executive; b. N.Y.C., Dec. 5, 1941; d. John J. and Adella (Brenner) Kowalski; m. John P. Jordan, Oct. 26, 1968 (dec. Sept. 1979). BA, Western Coll. for Women, 1963; postgrad., NYU, 1964-66, SUNY, Binghamton, 1971, William Patterson Coll., 1973-74. Sr. mcpl. bond analyst Dun & Bradstreet, Inc., N.Y.C., 1963-68; analyst Fed. Res. Bank of N.Y., 1968-69; tchr. Windsor (N.Y.) Cen. Sch. Dist., 1970-72; asst. treas. Chase Manhattan Bank, N.Y.C., 1972-80; sr. mcpl. bond analyst L.F. Rothschild, Unterberg, Towbin, N.Y.C., 1980; sr. underwriter AMBAC Idemnity, N.Y.C., 1980, v.p., mgr., 1981-86, first v.p., 1987—. Mem. Nat. Fedn. of Mcpl. Analysts, Mcpl. Bond Women's Club, Women's Bond Club of N.Y., Mcpl. Analysts Group of N.Y., Western Coll. Alumnae Assn. (first v.p. 1986—). Office: AMBAC Idemnity 1 State Street Pla New York NY 10004

JORDAN, JUDITH VICTORIA, clinical psychologist, educator; b. Milw., July 28, 1943; d. Claus and Charlotte (Backus) J.; m. William M. Redpath, Aug. 11, 1973. AB, Brown U., 1965; MA, Harvard U., 1968, PhD, 1973. Diplomate Am. Bd. Profl. Psychology. Psychologist Human Relations Service, Wellesley, Mass., 1971-73; assoc. psychologist McLean Hosp., Belmont, Mass., 1978—; dir. women's studies program McLean Hosp., Belmont; asst. dir. tng. psychology dept. McLean Hosp., 1982—; vis. scholar Stone Ctr. Wellesley Coll., 1985—; instr. in psychology Harvard U., 1988—; cons. in field. Author: Empathy and Self Boundaries, 1984, (with others) The Self in Relation, 1986; editor, author: Relational Self in Women. Mem. Am. Psychol. Assn., Mass. Psychol. Assn. (bd. dirs. 1983-85), Phi Beta Kappa. Office: McLean Hosp 115 Mill St Belmont MA 02178

JORDAN, KAREN GAIL, controller; b. Memphis, Dec. 8, 1950; d. Lawrence Fletcher and Joy Tyler (Ward) Lambert; m. Marvin Lee Jordan, Aug. 2, 1946; children: Stephen Eric, Cheryl Lynn, Jennifer Leigh. BA in Acctg. Cum Laude, Memphis State U., 1981. CPA. Staff acct. Fouts and Morgan, CPA's, Memphis, 1981-82; controller Montesi Groceries, Memphis, 1982-84; contr. Alverno Memphis Corp., 1984-86, Guy's Formalwear, Inc., Memphis, 1986-90, Joseph DeFranco, MD, Germantown, Tenn., 1990—. Mem. Nat. Assn. Pub. Accts., Tenn. Soc. of CPA's. Republican. Home: 1774-B 6th Crompton Sq Memphis TN 38134 Office: Joseph DeFranco MD 7655 Poplar Ave Ste 385 Germantown TN 38138

JORDAN, LORNA, news director; b. Washington, D.C., Nov. 3, 1958; d. Edwin C. and Mary (Kahle) J.; m. John A. Romano, Aug. 30, 1986. PhB, Miami U., 1981. News reporter WING-AM, Dayton, Ohio, 1981-84, WHIO-AM, Dayton, Ohio, 1984-85, WKRC-AM, Cin., 1985-87; from news reporter to news dir. WVXU-FM, Cin., news dir., 1988--; stringer Nat. Pub. Radio, Washington, D.C., 1987--, CBS News, N.Y., 1987-88. Bd. dirs YWCA, Kettering, Ohio, 1985-87. Mem. Soc. for Profl. Journalists, Kappa Delta. Office: WVXU FM Radio Station 3800 Victory Pkwy Cincinnati OH 45207

JORDAN, LUCILLE GALLOWAY, retired educational administrator; b. Transylvania County, N.C.; d. Thomas Pleasant and Mary Sue (Fisher) Galloway; m. Frederick L. S. Jordan, Dec. 24, 1945; 1 child, Noelle Thomasina. BS, U. Tenn., Knoxville, 1948; MEd, U. Ga., 1964, EdD, 1966; postdoctoral study U Calif.-Santa Barbara, 1970, U. Colo., 1973, U. Keele, Staffordshire, Eng., 1974. Cert. tchr., adminstr., supr., Ga. Tchr. pub. schs. N.C., Tenn., Ga.; clin. prof. edn. U. Ga., 1966-78; assoc. state supt. schs. State of Ga. Dept. Edn., Atlanta, 1978-88. Author: The Five Senses, 1967; Learning Opportunities Surround Us, 1968; Does Individualization Make a Difference?, 1973. Co-author: Humanities Programs Today, 1970; Collaboration for Teacher Education, 1978; Educational Manpower, 1969. Bd. trustees, mem. exec. com. Ga. Econs. Council, 1980-88, emeritus trustee, 1989—. Recipient Global Apple award Am. Forum for Global Edn., 1989. NSF fellow, 1974. Mem. AAUW (trustee edn. info. and referral system 1983—), Assn. Supervision and Curriculum Devel. (nat. pres. 1981-82; leadership award 1984), Phi Delta Kappa. Baptist. Clubs: Atlanta Athletic, Nat. Assistance League. Avocations: travel, sewing, collecting historical plates. Home: 2310 N Peachtree Way Dunwoody GA 30338

JORDAN, MARY ANN, research biologist; b. Mpls., July 31, 1940; d. Richard Charles and Freda (Laudon) J.; m. Paul Warren Lommen, Sept. 25, 1965 (div. 1982); children: Andrea, Kate; m. David Scott Johnson, Jan 14, 1984. Student, Carleton Coll., 1958-60; BA magna cum laude, U. Minn., 1962; MS, PhD, U. Rochester, 1968; postgrad., Stanford U., 1963. Postdoctoral fellow in biology Washington U., St. Louis, 1969; research assoc. biology U. Mich., Ann Arbor, 1971-72; research assoc., lectr. Utah State U., Logan, 1974-77; research biologist U. Calif., Santa Barbara, 1978-82, asst. research biologist, lectr., 1982—. Contbr. articles to profl. jours. Treas. Goleta (Calif.) Civic Ballet, 1984-85. Fellow NSF, USPHS, NIH. Mem. AAAS, Am. Soc. Cell Biology, LWV. Unitarian. Club: Tennis (Santa Barbara). Office: U Calif Dept Biol Scis Santa Barbara CA 93106

JORDANA, ANN M., health facility administrator; b. North Tonowanda, N.Y., Dec. 23, 1935; d. W. Kenneth and Ann Marie (Pfarr) Poland. Diploma, Sch. Radiologic Technologists, Trenton, N.J., 1985. Cert. clin. med. asst.; cert. adminstrv. med. asst.; registered radiologic-technologist. Office mgr. Drs. Ans and Flax P.A., Hollywood, Fla.; adminstr. Doctor's Diagnostic Ctr., Hollywood; lectr. in field. Mem. adv. bd. Broward Community Coll. Med. Assisting Program. Named Broward County Med. Asst. of Yr., 1971. Mem. Am. Assn. Med. Assts. (pres. 1988-89, recipient Outstanding Svc. award 1980, v.p. 1987-85, sec.-treas. 1985-87), Fla. Assn. Med. Assts. (pres. 1972), Broward County Med. Assts. Assn. (pres. 1970-75), Hollywood C. of C. Republican. Roman Catholic. Home: 3500 Mystic Pointe Dr Tower 400 #1106 Aventura FL 33180 Office: Doctors Diagnostic Ctr 210 S Federal Hwy Hollywood FL 33020

JORDON, DEBORAH ELIZABETH, lawyer; b. Pitts., June 24, 1951; d. Joseph Mitchell and Marjorie Odessa (Glaude) J. BA, Brown U., 1972; JD, Yale U., 1975. Bar: Pa. 1975, N.Y. 1978, U.S. Dist. Ct. (ea. and so. dists.) N.Y., 1978. Law clk. to presiding justice U.S. Dist. Ct. (ea. dist.) Pa., Phila., 1975-77; assoc. Paul, Weiss, Rifkind, Wharton & Garrison, N.Y.C., 1977-79; asst. to mayor City of N.Y., 1979-82; counsel to pres. CCNY, 1982-84; sr. atty. NBC, N.Y.C., 1984-87, asst. gen. atty., 1987-88, gen. atty., 1988-89, sr. gen. atty., 1989—; v.p. NBC Internat. Ltd.; bd. dirs. NBC Europe, Inc.; chmn. bd. dirs. Harlem Legal Svcs., Inc., N.Y.C.; bd. dirs. Met. Assistance Corp., N.Y.C. Bd. dirs. N.Y.C. Sports Commn., Bennett Coll., Greensboro, N.C., 1985—, Lifelong Learning Program, N.Y. 1981-82, Marymount Manhattan Coll., N.Y.C., 1984-87. Named Achiever in Industry Harlem YMCA, N.Y.C., 1988. Mem. Phi Beta Kappa. Roman Catholic. Home: 200 W 79th St New York NY 10024 Office: NBC Inc 30 Rockefeller Pla New York NY 10112

JORGENSEN, JUDITH ANN, psychiatrist; b. Parris Island, S.C.; d. George Emil and Margaret Georgia Jorgensen; B.A., Stanford U., 1963; M.D., U. Calif., 1968; m. Ronald Francis Crown, July 11, 1970. Intern, Meml. Hosp., Long Beach, 1969-70; resident County Mental Health Services, San Diego, 1970-73; staff psychiatrist Children and Adolescent Services, San Diego, 1973-78; practice medicine specializing in psychiatry, La Jolla, Calif., 1973—; staff psychiatrist County Mental Health Services of San Diego, 1973-78, San Diego State U. Health Services, 1985-87; psychiat. cons. San Diego City Coll., 1973-78, 85-86; asst. prof. dept. psychiatry U. Calif., 1978—; chmn. med. quality rev. com. Dist. XIV, State of Calif., 1982-83. Mem. Am. Psychiat. Assn., San Diego Soc. Psychiat. Physicians (chmn. membership com. 1976-78, v.p. 1978-80, fed. legis. rep. 1985-87), Am. Soc. Adolescent Psychiatry, San Diego Soc. Adolescent Psychiatry (pres. 1981-82), Calif. Med. Assn. (alternate del.), Soc. Sci. Study of Sex, San Diego Soc. Sex Therapy and Edn., San Diego County Med. Soc. (credentials com. 1982-84). Club: Rowing. Office: 470 Nautilus St Suite 211 La Jolla CA 92037

JORGENSEN, NORA JUNE, civic volunteer; b. Salina, Kans., May 31, 1927; d. Leon Paul and Edith Ethel (Giersch) S.; m. Alfred Vincent, Feb. 25, 1961; (div. May 16, 1988); children: Ann Wallace, Kathy Christiansen, Mary Grace Crosby, David Geoffroy. Student, Marymount Academy, Salinas, Saint Mary Coll., Xavier, Calif. bd. dirs. Cover Girls, OCPAC, Big Canyon Philharmonic, Newport Beach, 1987-88. Bd. dirs. Children's Home Soc. (pres.), Hoag Heart Inst., Hoag Hosp. Donor Recognition Com., Ctr. Dance Alliance, OCPAC, Newport Beach, 1962-86; liaison Hoag Hosp. Cancer Ctr.; deacon St. Andrew's Presbyn. Ch., Newport Beach, 1978; founding mem. DC Performing Arts Ctr., Newport Beach, 1980, Opera Pacific, 1984, Ctr. 1000, Cancer Ctr., Newport Beach, 1987; pres. Camelot Guild, Newport Beach, Chariot Champions, Newport Beach, 1984; v.p. Orange County Master Chorale, Newport Beach, 1987—. Recipient Outstanding Support award, Chariot of Champions, Spirit of Life Award, City of Hope; Named Woman of Yr., Orange County Mag. Mem. Incoming Chair. Asst. League, Hoag Hosp., Sherman Gardens, Founders Plus. Republican. Presbyterian. Home: 1533 Antigua Way Newport Beach CA 92660

JORY, MARCIA LYNN, trust officer, lawyer; b. Portland, Oreg., Mar. 29, 1955; d. Fred Merle and Laura Jean (Watson) J.; m. Ray C. Kennedy, Aug. 23, 1980; children: Adam Barrett, Bryce Taylor. BA, U. Puget Sound, 1977; JD, U. Oreg., 1980. Assoc. Maletis & James, P.C., Portland, 1980-82, Furrer & Scott, Tigard, Oreg., 1983-88; trust officer 1st Interstate Bank of Oreg., Portland, 1988—. Elder Westminster Presbyn. Ch., Portland, 1989—; bd. dirs. YMCA of Portland, 1982-89, 1st v.p., 1985, pres. bd. dirs. 1986-88, bd. dirs. Samaritan Counseling Ctr., 1983-85; assoc. Emanuel Hosp. Assoc.'s Coun., Portland, 1985—. Mem. ABA, Oreg. Bar Assn., Multnomah County Bar Assn., Washington County Bar Assn., City Club of Portland. Office: 1st Interstate Bank of Oreg 1300 SW 5th PO Box 2971 Portland OR 97208

JOSELL, JESSICA (JESSICA WECHSLER), public relations executive; b. Balt., June 17, 1943; d. Maury J. and Rose E. (Lodin) Snyder; m. Neil B. Josell, Apr. 30, 1965 (dec. Nov. 1967); m. Steven James Wechsler, Jan. 12, 1980. BA, U. Fla., 1965. V.p., gen. mgr. Morton Dennis Wax & Assocs., N.Y.C., 1976-81; v.p. The Raleigh Group, Ltd., N.Y.C., 1981-87; pres. Josell Communications, Inc., N.Y.C., 1981—; exec. officer, bd. dirs. The Bridge, Inc., N.Y.C. Office: Josell Communications Inc 185 West End Ave #22-C New York NY 10023-5539

JOSEPH, ELEANOR ANN, director medical records, consultant; b. Cleve., Mar. 6, 1944; d. Emil and Eleanor (Leelais) Dienes; m. Abraham Albert Joseph, Oct. 28, 1984. BS in Math. cum laude, Cleve. State U., 1978. Accredited record technician. Asst. dir. med. records Suburban Hosp., Warrensville Heights, Ohio, 1963-77; coder Shaker Med. Ctr., Shaker Heights, Ohio, 1965, Huron Rd. Hosp., Cleve., 1965; instr. Cuyahoga Community Coll., Cleve., 1970-72; dir. med. records Hillcrest Hosp., Mayfield Heights, Ohio, 1977-84; med. records technician Vis. Nurse Assn., Cleve., 1985; coord. med. record svcs. Ctr. for Health Affairs/Greater Cleve. Hosp. Assn., 1985-88, dir. coding svcs., 1988-89, dir. health record svcs., 1989—; cons. in field, Cleve., 1976—; mem. speakers' bur. Hillcrest Hosp., Mayfield Heights, Ohio, 1978-84; adv. com. Cuyahoga Community Coll., Cleve., 1973-80, instr. 1970-72; cons. Suburban Pavilion, Manor Care Nursing Homes, Luth. Home, Cleve., 1976-88. Co-author: (manual) Quality Assurance Program for Medical Records Department, 1981, Dollars and Sense: A Reference Guide to Coding and Prospective System Reimbursement Issues, 1988; co-editor: Care and Management of Health Care Records, 1988. Active Holden Arboretum, Kirtland, Ohio, 1975—, Ohio Hist. Soc., Columbus, 1975—. Mem. Am. Med. Record Assn. (mem. long term care sect., membership com. 1989, charter mem. assembly on edn. 1989), N.E. Ohio Med. Record Assn. (pres. 1982-83, counselor 1983, edn. com. 1984, 87, chmn. nominating com. 1986, treas. 1979, v.p. 1980, mem. cons. com. 1987—, del. for state assn. mems. at nat. annual meeting Am. Med. Record Assn. 1989, 90), Pres.'s award 1983), Am. Coll. Healthcare Execs., Ohio Med. Record Assn. (legis. com. 1989—). Democrat. Lutheran. Office: Ctr for Health Affairs Greater Cleve Hosp Assn 1226 Huron Rd Cleveland OH 44115

JOSEPH, HARRIET, English literature educator; b. Montreal, Que., Can., Mar. 14, 1919; came to U.S., 1944; d. Samuel and Hanna Mai (Brown) Bloomfield; m. Edward D. Joseph, Aug. 16, 1942; children: Leila Muriel, Alan Pinto, Brian Daniel. BA, McGill U., Montreal, Que., 1941; MA, Bryn Mawr Coll., 1942. Instr. to assoc. prof. English lit. Pace U., Pleasantville, N.Y., 1966-81; prof. Pace U., Pleasantville, 1981—. Author: Shakespeare's Son-in-Law: Man & Physician, 1964; contbr. articles on Eng. litr. to jours. Active LWV, Scarsdale, N.Y. Mem. AAUW, MLA, Sheakespeare Assn. Am., Am. Jewish Congress, Am. Women's Orgn. for Rehab. Through Tng., Author's League. Home: 9 Putnam Rd Scarsdale NY 10583 Office: Pace U Bedford Rd Pleasantville NY 10570

JOSEPH, HOLLY J., insurance company executive; b. St. Paul, Dec. 10, 1956; d. Earl W. and Virginia Ann (Jones) Smith; m. Earl C. Joseph II, Dec. 24, 1974. BA cum laude, Coll. of St. Catherine, St. Paul, 1979; MA in Internat. Mgmt., Coll. of St. Thomas, St. Paul; student, Longman Security Schs. Lic. life, accident and disability, 1986. Credit authorization supr. J.C. Penney Co., Mpls., 1978-82; credit supr. J.B. Hudson Jewelers, Mpls., 1982-85; dist. sales dir. Purple Cross Plan, Mpls., 1986—; guest lectr. U. Minn., 1987-89. Bd. dirs. Merri-Grove Co-op, pres. Mem. Mpls. Postal Customer Coun., Mpls. Consumer Credit Assn., Japan-Am. Soc. Minn., Alliance Française, Toastmasters. Home: 365 Summit Saint Paul MN 55102

JOSEPH, JOYCE MARIE See AMIN, JAMILLAH MAARIJ

JOSEPH, JUDITH R., publishing executive; b. Newark, Sept. 18, 1948; d. Siegmund and Yolanda (Klein) J.; B.A. with honors, N.Y.U., 1970; M.A., U. Va., 1973; m. Alan M. de Vries, June 1982; 1 child, Elizabeth Martha. Sales rep. Prentice-Hall Pub., Inc., 1973-75; pub. social sci. and humanities texts D. Van Nostrand Co., Inc., N.Y.C., 1975-79, v.p., publs. dir., 1979-81; sr. editor vocat. and tech. texts John Wiley & Sons, Inc., N.Y.C., 1981-87, exec. editor Architecture, Design and Hospitality Mgmt., Van Nostrand Reinhold Co., N.Y.C., 1987—, v.p. editorial dir., 1989—. Mem. Am. Assn. Pub., Soc. Scholarly Pub., NOW.

JOSEPH, MARY THOMAS, insurance professional; b. Bradenton, Fla., July 16, 1958; d. Jimmie Frank and Maggie Bea (Hill) Thomas; m. Jean Claude Joseph, Dec. 22, 1984. BS in Criminal Justice, U. So. Fla., 1980, BS in Speech Communication, 1980. Lic. life ins. sales rep., Fla. Mgmt. trainee State Farm Life Ins. Co., Winter Haven, Fla., 1982-84, svc. supr., 1984—. Mem. NAFE, Toastmasters Internat., Delta Sigma Theta, Sigma Iota Epsilon. Democrat. Mem. Church of Christ. Home: 1113 Hillcrest Dr NE Winter Haven FL 33880 Office: State Farm Life Ins Co 3425 Lake Alfred Rd Winter Haven FL 33880

JOSEPH, ROSALINE R., hematologist/oncologist; b. N.Y.C., Aug. 21, 1929; d. Joseph and Malca (Rosenberg) Resnick; m. Robert J. Joseph, Jan. 2, 1954; children: Joy S., Nina B. AB, Cornell U., 1949; MD, Women's Med. Coll. Pa., Phila., 1953; MS, Temple U., 1958. Instr. dept. medicine Temple U. Med. Ctr., Phila., 1957-60; assoc. in medicine Temple U. Med. Ctr., 1960-63, asst. prof. medicine, 1963-69, assoc. prof. medicine, 1969-77; course co-coordinator Sys. Oncology Interdisciplinary Course, 1968-73; prof. medicine, dir. Med. Coll. Pa., Phila., 1977; course coordinator Med. Coll. Pa., 1978, dir. hematology/oncology, to date; pres. med. staff Med. Coll. Pa., 1990—. Contbr. articles to profl. jours. Del. dir. Am. Cancer Soc., 1989—. Recipient Lindback award for disting. teaching, Christian & Mary Lindback Found., 1982, Am. Cancer Soc. Div. Disting. Svc. award, 1987. Fellow ACP; mem. Am. Soc. Hematology, Am. Soc. Clin. Oncology, Alumni Assn. Med. Coll. Pa. (pres. 1988-90). Office: Med Coll of Pa 3300 Henry Ave Philadelphia PA 19129

JOSEPH, SUSAN B., lawyer; b. N.Y.C., June 1, 1958. BS in Econ. and Bus. Mgmt., Ramapo Coll. of N.J., 1981; JD cum laude, Seton Hall U., 1985. Bar: N.J. 1985, U.S. Dist. Ct. N.J. 1985, N.Y. 1988. Legal asst. Prudential Ins. Co. Am., Newark, 1982-85; assoc. Fox & Fox, Newark, 1985-86, Elkes, Maybruch & Weiss, P.A., Freehold, N.J., 1986-87; asst. counsel N.Am. Reins. Corp., N.Y.C., 1987—. Vol. campaign Bill Bradley for Senate, Union, N.J., 1984, 90; vol. Starlight Found., N.Y.C., 1988—, Victims for Victims, 1989—. Mem. ABA, N.J. Bar Assn. (spl. com. on entertainment law 1988—), Assn. Bar City N.Y., Am. Philatelic Soc., The Strollers (provisional). Home: 747 Valley St Apt 3K Maplewood NJ 07040

JOSEPHS, BABETTE, legislator; b. N.Y.C., Aug. 4, 1940; d. Eugene and Myra A. J.; m. Herbert B. Newberg, Jan. 28, 1962; children: Lee Aaron Newberg, Elizabeth Newberg. BA, Queens Coll., 1962; JD, Rutgers U., 1976. Sole practice Phila., 1976-78; exec. dir. Nat. Abortion Rights Action League of Pa., Phila., 1978-80, Citizens Coalition for Energy Efficiency, Phila., 1980-81; pvt. practice cons., fundraiser Phila., 1981-84; mem. Pa. Ho. of Reps., Phila., 1984—. Bd. dirs. ACLU. Mem. Phila. Bar Assn. Democrat. Jewish. Office: 1229 Chestnut St Box B Philadelphia PA 19107

JOSEPHS, BONNIE PRISCILLA, lawyer; b. Verona, N.J., Oct. 11, 1938; d. Paul and Helen (Joelson) J.; children: Melodie Winawer, Paul. BA, Smith Coll., 1960; JD, NYU, 1966. Bar: N.Y., 1966. Editor MacFadden Publs., N.Y.C., 1960, Hearst Mags., N.Y.C., 1961-62, Del Publs., N.Y.C., 1962, Grosset & Dunlap, N.Y.C., 1962-63; assoc. Cravath, Swaine & Moore, N.Y.C., 1966-69, London, Buttenwieser & Chalif, N.Y.C., 1969-74; ptnr. London, Buttenwieser, Bonem & Valente, N.Y.C., 1975, Buttenwieser & Josephs, N.Y.C., 1976-77; prin. Bonnie P. Josephs, N.Y.C., 1978—. Author: (with others) Political and Civil Rights, 1966, Child's Play, 1965; contbr. articles to profl. jours. Mem. Assn. of Bar of City of N.Y. (arbitration and alternate dispute resolution com. 1986-89, sci. and law com. 1989), Assn. Trial Lawyers Am. Democrat. Jewish. Home: 173 Riverside Dr New York NY 10024 Office: 1414 Sixth Ave New York NY 10024

JOSEPHS, CAROLYN BRENDA, typesetter, commercial and graphic artist; b. Bklyn., Feb. 19, 1964; d. Leonard and Kay Lois (Natowitz) J. AA in Graphic Design and Photography, Nassau Community Coll., Garden City, N.Y., 1983; BS in Graphic Design, Buffalo State Coll., 1985. Paste-up and mech. artist Penton Learning Systems, N.Y.C., 1986; typesetter Nassau Pennysaver, Freeport, N.Y., 1986-87; typesetter, layout and mechs. RMP Pub. Svcs., Freeport, 1987; newspaper ad layout artist Bklyn. Marketeer, 1987-88; mag. layout artist Starlog Press, N.Y.C., 1988; typesetter Volt Info. Scis., N.Y.C., 1988—. Contbr. articles to profl. jours. Vol. artistic skills Buffalo Psychiat. Ctr. Mem. Graphic Artists Guild, NAFE, Greenpeace, N.Y. Road Runners Club. Democrat. Jewish. Home and Office: 1045 E 59th St Brooklyn NY 11234-2505

JOSEY, DEBORAH K., civilian military employee; b. Cin., Sept. 10, 1949; d. J. Sidney and Blanche (A.) Smith; m. Ben E. Josey, Nov. 29, 1983. Student, Western Mich. U., Army Correspondence Course, Newport News, Va. Personnel asst. RAF, Bentwaters, U.K.; tng. technician USAF, Elgin AFB, Fla. Mem. NAFE, Federally Employed Women (treas.). Home: PSC 2 Box 939 APO New York NY 09405

JOSLYN, BETSY ANN, actress; b. Staten Island, N.Y., Apr. 19, 1954; d. Frederic Marshall and Marie Louise (Sidnam) J. BA, Wagner Coll., 1975. Recording artist Book-of-the-Month Club Records. Broadway performances include Into the Woods, 1988, Sunday in the Park With George, 1985-86, A Doll's Life, 1982, Sweeney Todd, 1980-81; also performed in off-Broadway and regional theater including The Fatasticks Light up the Sky; performer West Side Story, Opernhaus Zurich, Switzerland; TV appearances include Sweeney Todd, The Merv Griffin Show, As the World Turns, THe Guiding Light; soloist at Kennedy Ctr. prodn. Of Thee I Sing/Let 'Em Eat Cake; recording Sondheim. Mem. AFTRA, SAG, AEA.

JOSSELYN, SHARON HOLLADAY, educator; b. Vernon, Tex., Dec. 30, 1950; d. Otis Orran and Glenna Jean (Rogers) Holladay; children: Dianna Lorrainne Gruber, Kenneth Richard Cook, step-children: Gerald James Cook Jr., Carl Fred Cook, Rodney Allan Josselyn. Cert. computer sci., Can. Coll., Redwood City, 1986; AA in Liberal Arts and Child Devel., Am. River Coll., Sacramento, 1990. Dir., owner Sharon's Family Day Care, Redwood City, 1974-80; instr., coach Am. Youth Soccer Orgn., Redwood City, 1980-84; supr., tutor F.C. Joyce Elem. Sch., Northhighlands, Calif., 1987-88; caseworker, tutor Woodacre Group Home (for abused children), Carmichael, Calif., 1988; tchr., asst. Am. River Coll. Child Care Ctr., Sacramento, 1988-90; coord., head tchr. Inverness Pvt. Sch., Carmichael, Calif. Author: Sing with Your Child, 1988, The ABC's Language, 1988, Art at My Level, 1989, Family Information Booklet, 1989. Mem. NAFE, NOW, Nat. Assn. for Edn. of Young Children. Baptist.

JOST, BARBARA DINGER, retail executive, graphic designer; b. Kittanning, Pa., Sept. 3, 1947; d. Raymond and Elizabeth Annzonetta (King) Dinger. AA, Wheeler Sch. Mdsing. & Retail, Pitts., 1967; student, U. Pitts. Gen. mgr. Hardman Eastman Studios, Inc., Pitts., 1973—; cons. in field. Democrat. Lutheran. Mem. NAFE, Mercedes Benz Club of Am. Home: 2916 Harcum Way Pittsburgh PA 15203

JOU, JEANETTE BIKLING, business owner; b. Toysun, Republic of China, Sept. 29, 1945; came to U.S., 1982; d. Man Ho Moy and Cheung Ngor (Cho) Chan; m. Shin Shan Jou, July 11, 1970; children: Penny Susan, Jason Peter. Mgr., owner Jeanette's Food Market, N.J., 1982-85; gen. mgr. Coliseum Motel, Greensboro, N.C., 1985-87; mgr. Burger King, N.J., 1982-85, Taco Bell Pepsico Inc., Greensboro, 1987-88; owner Restaurant Las Lumpias, Venezuela, 1974-82, Golden Chopsticks, Greensboro, 1987—. Home: 2815 Gwaltney Rd Greensboro NC 27407 Office: Golden Chopsticks 201-C Century Blvd Kernersville NC 27284

JOVANOVITCH, MILENA, editor, journalist; b. London, July 26, 1951; came to U.S., 1958; d. Stevan and Mirjiana (Tupanjanin) J. BA, Smith Coll., 1973. Adminstr. asst. Coun. Fgn. Rels., N.Y.C., 1974-76; reporter N.J. Herald, Newton, 1976-79, Westchester-Rockland Newspapers, White Plains, N.Y., 1979-84; contbg. reporter N.Y. Times, 1984—; gen. editor Prodigy Svcs. Co., White Plains, 1987—. Mem. Soc. Profl. Journalists, Women in Communications, Deadline Club, Smith Coll. Club of Westchester.

JOYCE, ANNE RAINE, editor, director; b. South Bend, Ind., Oct. 2, 1942; d. James Agee and Marjorie Elizabeth (Gilstrap) Raine; m. Glenn Russell Joyce, Aug. 19, 1962; 1 child, Adam Russell. AB, Cen. Meth. Coll., 1962; MA in French, U. Mo., 1966; MA in Linguistics, U. Iowa, 1979. Cert. tchr., Mo. Tchr. Centralia (Mo.) High Sch., 1962-64; instr. Coe Coll., Cedar Rapids, Iowa, 1978-79, Georgetown U., Washington, 1980-83; asst. editor Am.-Arab Affairs, Washington, 1983-84, editor, dir. publs., 1984—. Mem. edn. com. Fairfax County (Va.) PTA Bd., 1986-88. U.S. Dept. Def. fellow, 1964-66; recipient Recognition award Am.-Arab Affairs Coun., 1988, Disting. Alumni award. Cen. Meth. Coll., 1990. Mem. Middle East Studies Assn., LWV (fin. chair Fairfax county chpt. 1981—). Home: 6916 Tulsa Ct Alexandria VA 22307 Office: Am-Arab Affairs Coun 1730 M St NW #512 Washington DC 20036

JOYCE, BERNITA ANNE, federal government agency administrator; d. Albert A. and Margaret C. Joyce. BA, Duchesne Coll.; MBA, U. Santa Clara, 1968, PhD, 1974; m. Kenneth B. Lucas, Aug. 2, 1975. Adminstr., Soc. of Sacred Heart, Menlo Park, Calif. and Seattle, regional adminstr., San Francisco, 1969-71; with Wolfe & Co., CPA's, Washington, 1971-72; fin. dir. Nat. Forest Products Assn., Washington, 1972-74; budget and fiscal officer ICC, Washington, 1974-77, Office Mgmt. and Budget, 1977-80; asst. dir. mgmt. svcs. Bur. Mines, Dept. Interior, 1980-85, asst. dir. Office Program Analysis Dept. Interior, 1985—. Author: Financial Viability of Private Elementary Schools. Mem. AICPA, NAFE, Sr. Execs. Assn., Exec. Women in Govt., Assn. Govt. Accts., Assn. for Pub. Policy Analysis and Mgmt., Beta Gamma Sigma. Home: 6001 Bradley Blvd Bethesda MD 20817

JOYCE, BEVERLY JOAN, nurse; b. Springfield, Ohio, Aug. 19, 1945; d. William Andrew and Mary Catherine (Kramer) Palmer; m. Jesse Carey Stiggins, June 23, 1961 (div. 1966); children: Jesse Carey Jr., Carl Brian, Catherine Dunnell. AS in Nursing, Fla. Jr. Coll., 1977. RN, Fla.; cert. human immunodeficiency virus counselor. Staff nurse Univ. Hosp., Jacksonvillle, Fla., 1978-81, Quality Care, Jacksonville, 1979-80; staff nurse Meml. Med. Ctr., Jacksonville, 1981-82, charge nurse, 1982-87, asst. head nurse, 1988, nurse mgr., 1988—; nurse house supr. St. Catherine's Labour Manor, Jacksonville, 1979-80; resolve through sharing counselor La Crosse (Wis.) Luth. Hosp., 1986—; family counselor Through The Tears, 1990. Mem. Am. Assn. Critical Care Nurses (treas. 1990—), Nat. Orgn. Nurse Execs. (middle mgmt. coun. 1988—), Nat. Assn. Female Execs., Amnesty Internat. U.S.A. Democrat. Lutheran. Office: Meml Med Ctr 3625 University Blvd S Jacksonville FL 32216

JOYCE, FLORENCE V. MIENERT (MRS. GEORGE T. JOYCE), civic worker; b. Fosston, Minn., Feb. 13, 1923; d. William P. A. and Clara (Lindfors) Mienert; R.N., Ancker Hosp. Sch. Nursing, St. Paul, 1944; student U. Minn., 1944-45; m. George T. Joyce, Aug. 8, 1946; children—Roberta Eileen, Elizabeth Anne. Bd. dirs. N. Central Iowa chpt. ARC, 1960-66, 67-73, nursing services chmn., 1967-75; pres. Vols. Service League, St. Joseph Mercy Hosp., Mason City, Iowa, 1959-61; leader Girl Scouts U.S.A., 1948-66; bd. dirs. YWCA, 1963-66, Community Achievement award, 1979; pres. Charles MacNider Art Guild, Mason City, 1972-73, membership council 1973-80; mem. River City Hist. Preservation Bd., 1986-88; precinct chmn. Cerro Gordo County Republican Central Com., 1974-82, co-chmn., 1984-86; mem. fund raising com. Hospice of Cerro Gordo, Mason City, Iowa, 1982-85. Mem. Am. Nurses Assn., Iowa Nurses Assn., Iowa Dist. 10 Nurses Assn. (dir. 1981-84), Nat. Trust for Historic Preservation, Cerro Gordo County Med. Aux., Ancker (Hosp.) Nursing Alumni Assn. Club: Mason City Womans (dir. 1965-75, pres. 1969-70). Roman Catholic. Home: 259 N Crescent Dr Mason City IA 50401

JOYCE, MARILYN SCHMIDT, training company executive; b. Covington, Ky., Sept. 3, 1942; d. Robert Andrew and Rita Marie (Stadtmiller) S.; m. Clayton Robert Joyce, Nov. 29, 1975; stepchildren—David Joyce, Kathryn Joyce Keehn, Robert Joyce. B.A., Thomas More Coll., 1964; M.Ed., Xavier U., 1968. Tchr., Colerain High Sch., Cin., 1964-68; tchr. N.E. High Sch., Ft. Lauderdale, Fla., 1968-69; chmn. dept. curriculum devel. Henderson High Sch., Atlanta, 1969-75; trainer, mgr. URS Corp., Seattle, 1977-80; founder, pres. Joyce Inst., Seattle, 1981—; ergonomics tng. cons. GTE, 1983—, Boeing Co., Seattle, 1981—; speaker Internat. Sci. Conf., 1986, Nat. Safety Coun. Conf., 1986. Editor tng. courses: Dataspan, 1981, Datahealth, 1985. Author: Ergonomics: Humanizing the Automated Office, 1989; co-author tng. manual: Managing Office Ergonomics, 1986, Pro-Read, 1972. Mem. Human Factors Soc., Am. Soc. Tng. and Devel., Am. Mgmt. Assn., Seattle C. of C. (trustee 1988), Columbia Tower Club, Ranier Club, Rotary. Republican. Roman Catholic. Home: 2220 40th Ave E Seattle WA 98112

JOYCE, PAMELA-ANN LEONG, marketing consultant; b. Honolulu, Feb. 16, 1948; d. Kwai Wood and Sara (Lau) Chun; 1 child, Ryan Courtney. BA, U. Calif., Berkeley, 1970. Customer svc. rep. Pacific Telephone Co., Berkeley, 1970-74; communications cons. Pacific Telephone Co., Fremont, Calif., 1974-78; bus. devel. specialist Pacific Telephone Co., San Francisco, 1978-81, account exec., 1981-82; chief exec. officer, pres. Claremont Rockridge Home Video, Oakland, Calif., 1982-86; pres. Pamela-Ann Joyce, Cons., Alameda, Calif., 1982—. Sec., editor Boy Scouts Am., Alameda, 1983—. Werner Scott scholar U. Calif., Berkeley, 1969-70; Bd. Regents scholar U. Hawaii, Honolulu, 1966-68. Mem. AAUW (newsletter editor 1987), U. Calif. Alumni Assn. (China chpt., pres. 1988), Sigma Omicron Pi. Office: 150 Basinside Way Alameda CA 94501

JOYE, AFRIE SONGCO, minister; b. Guagua, Pampanga, Philippines, Aug. 8, 1942; came to U.S. 1968; d. Emilio Lelay and Elmerita (Atienza) Laus Songco; m. Charles James Joye, Aug. 28, 1971. BA in Christian Edn., Harris Meml. Coll., Manila, 1963; MA in Christian Edn., Scarritt Grad. Sch., Nashville, 1970; PhD in Theology and Religious Edn., Claremont Sch. Theology, Calif., 1980. Dir. Christian edn. First United Meth. Ch., Naga, Philippines, 1963-66; dist. Christian Edn. coordintor Bicol-Palawan Region of United Meth. Ch., 1963-66; dir. Christian Edn. Cen. United Meth. Ch., Manila, 1966-68; dir. youth ministry and student ctr. Cen. United Meth. Ch., 1970-71; instr. psychology and Christian edn. Philippin Christian Coll./ Harris Meml. Coll., Manila, 1970-71; nat. dir. Christian edn. in Asian and Native Am. chs. Gen. Bd. Discipleship, Nashville, 1976-79; dir Christian Edn. Aldersgate United Meth. Ch./John Wesley United Meth. Ch., Charleston, S.C., 1971-74; minister Christian edn. Community United Meth. Ch., Huntington Beach, Calif., 1987-90; assoc. minister Laguna Hills (Calif.) United Meth. Ch., 1990—; cons./trainer in Christian edn. Editor: Program Ideas and Training Designs for Pacific and Asian American Church Schools, 1981; contbr. articles to profl. jours. Nat. mem. Bread for the World, Fellowship of Reconciliation, Amnesty Internat. Coolidge Colloquium fellow, Assn. for Religion and Intellectual Life, 1989. Mem. AAUW, Nat. Christian Educators Fellowship, Am. Acad. Religion, Assn. of Profs. and Researchers of Religious Education, Nat. Fedn. Asian Am. United Meth. Office: 24442 Moulton Pkwy Laguna Hills CA 92653

JOYNER, SUZANNE DIMASCIO, marketing executive; b. Phila., Dec. 2, 1942; d. Placido L. and Lillian G. (Smith) Mosca; m. Richard DiMascio, Dec. 26, 1963 (div. Nov. 1976); children: Christopher, Jeffrey; m. James H. Joyner III, Jan. 1, 1980; children: James IV, Gordon, Christopher, Richard, Jeffrey. RN; cert. nurse specialist in gerontology. Dir. nursing North Pa. Convalescent Home, Lansdale, 1976-78; clin. research assoc. Pharmacia, Piscataway, N.J., 1978-80, product mgr., 1980-85, sr. product mgr., 1985-86, group product dir., 1986-88; mktg. exec. Wyeth Ayers Internat. Co., Phila., 1988—, sr. product mgr., 1988—. cons. nursing, 1977-79; cons. Thane Assocs., 1983-86. Author: (manual) Debrisan for Wound Care, 1977. Republican. Roman Catholic. Avocations: walking, swimming, aerobics. Home: 26 Solebury Mountain Rd New Hope PA 18938 Office: Wyeth Internat Co 150 Rodor Chester Rd Radnor PA 19101

JOYNER-KERSEE, JACQUELINE, track and field athlete; b. East St. Louis, Ill., Mar. 3, 1962; d. Alfred Sr. and Mary Joyner; m. Bob Kersee, Jan. 11, 1986. BA in History, UCLA, 1985. Winner 4 consecutive Nat. Jr. Pentathlon Championships; silver medalist, heptathlon Olympics, 1984; winner heptathlon Goodwill Games, Moscow, 1986; winner heptathlon, world record of 7161 points U.S. Olympic Festival, 1986; winner USA/ Mobil Outdoor Track and Field Championship, 1987; winner, long jump and heptathlon World Track and Field Championships, 1987; gold medalist, long jump 24'3'12 and decathlon, world record 7291 Olympics, 1988; Grand Prix Indoor Champion, winner indoor world record 55m hurdlers 7:37, 1989. Recipient Sullivan award, 1987, Jesse Owens award, Am. Black Achievement award Ebony Mag., 1987; named Athlete of Yr. Track & Field News, 1986, Female Athlete of Yr. AP, 1987, 1st Female Athlete of Yr. award Sporting News, 1988. Office: Athletics Congress/USA PO Box 120 Indianapolis IN 46206 also: US Olympic Commn care Media Info 1750 E Boulder St Colorado Springs CO 80909*

JOZEF, SALLY SCHLEY, law firm marketing director; b. Milw., Feb. 26, 1962; d. Edward George and Imogene (Powrie) Schley; m. Paul Alan Jozef, May 13, 1989. BS, Northwestern U., 1984; postgrad., U. Wis., 1985-86; Student, Ealing Coll., London, 1982. Pub. rels. and fund devel. asst. St. Francis Children's Ctr., Milw., 1983; project asst. Kirkland & Ellis law firm, Chgo., 1984-85; law clk. Mulcahy & Wherry, S.C., Milw., 1986; regional mktg. coord. Am. Arbitration Assn., Phoenix, 1987-89; dir. client rels. Burch & Cracchiolo, P.A. law firm, Phoenix, 1989—. Mem. Nat. Assn. Law Firm Mktg., Women in Communications Inc. (recognitions chair 1990—), Northwestern Alumni Assn., Svc. Club Milw., Kappa Alpha Theta, Alpha Lambda Delta. Home: 1147 E Rovey Ave Phoenix AZ 85014 Office: Burch & Cracchiolo PA 702 E Osborn Rd Phoenix AZ 85014

JU, TERESA LIN, insurance company director; b. Taipei, Republic of China, Feb. 25, 1950; Came to U.S., 1971; d. Yun and Huei (Chun) Lin; m. Shy-Ming Ju, Feb. 23, 1943; children: Nancy, Patricia. MS, Fairleigh Dickinson U., 1985. System analyst SwissRe, N.Y.C., 1980-83; mktg. mgr. System Automation Consultants, Inc., Colts Neck, N.J., 1983-84; dir. strategic systems Continental Ins., N.Y.C., 1984—; dep. project mgr. SHARE, Chgo., 1986—. Chinese Folk Dance 1st Place Winner, Taipei, 1966. Mem. Assn. for Computing Machinery, Holmdel Republican Club, Chinese Computing Club (chairperson 1986—). Home: 59 Takolusa Dr Holmdel NJ 07733 Office: Continental Ins Corp 180 Maiden Ln New York NY 10038

JUBEARK, SANDRAA MELVIN, real estate appraiser; b. Tampa, Fla., Oct. 18, 1948; d. Albert and Martha (Anderson) Melvin; children: Ronnie, Kevin, Julian. Degree in nursing, Adult Tech. Coll., Tampa, Fla., 1967. Practical nurse various locations, 1967-88; pres., owner Heavenly Rest Ltd., Augusta, Ga., 1988—; mortgage banker, fin. cons. New Beginnings, Ltd., Augusta, 1982—, tax. cons., 1985—. Author weekly column Finances and You, 1982-83. Counselor, Debtors Anonymous, Augusta, 1987—; vol. reading instr., 1984—, United Way, Augusta, 1984-88; mem. Burn Found. Augusta, 1987-88. Mem. LPN Assn., Am. Bus. Women Assn., Network Augusta. Republican. Home: 307 Greene St Augusta GA 30901

JUCKETT, MARGARET GREGORY, management educator; d. Roy Burlington and Vada (Exline) Gregory; m. John LeRoy Juckett, June 26, 1954; children: Roy Gregory, Jay Lowell. BS, W.Va. Wesleyan Coll., 1943; MA, U. Ky., 1946; MBA, Monmouth Coll., West Long Branch, N.J., 1975. Bus. instr. W.Va. Pub. Sch. System, Buckhannon and Lost Creek, Meredith Coll., Raleigh, N.C., 1949-52; chair dept. bus. Wesley Coll., Dover, Del., 1952-54; assoc. prof. mgmt. Monmouth Coll., 1956—, chair dept. mgmt. and mktg., 1981-86, chair dept. mgmt., 1986-87; vis. prof. Kean Coll, Madison, N.J., summer, 1985, 87; instr. Garden State chpt. Am. Savs. and Loan Assn.; prof. continuing edn. Am. Mgmt. Assn., West Long Branch, N.J. Mem. AAUW, Acad. Mgmt., Zonta Internat. (past sec., pres., bd. dirs., current chair status of women com.), Kappa Delta Pi, Delta Pi Epsilon, Delta Mu Delta. Office: Monmouth Coll Dept Mgmt West Long Branch NJ 07764

JUDAH, JANEEN SUE, petroleum engineer; b. Houston, Sept. 29, 1959; d. Russell Jr. and Jacqueline Marie (Williams) J. BS, Texas A&M U., 1980, MS, 1983; MBA, U. Tex., 1987. Registered profl. engr., Tex., Okla., N. Mex. Instr. Tex. A&M U., College Station, 1982-83; engr. Bass Enterprises Prodn. Co., Midland, Tex., 1981-82; engr. Arco Oil & Gas Co., Midland, 1983-90, Houston, 1990—. Bd. dirs. March of Dimes, Midland, 1987-90, Midland Arts Assembly, 1989-90, Am. Heart Assn., Midland, 1989-90—; chmn. allocations, campaign sect. United Way, Midland, 1986-90; mem. Houston Symphony League, 1990—, Houston Opera Guild, 1990—. Mem. Soc. Petroleum Engrs. (chmn. 1989), Leadership Midland, Phi Mu (nat. collegiate fin dir. 1988—, nat. fin. dir. 1990—). Republican. Baptist. Office: Arco Oil & Gas Co PO Box 1346 Houston TX 77251

JUDD, JACQUELINE VOGEL, educator; b. Edgerton, Wis., May 9, 1939; d. Ira Charles and Mabel Helen (Pratt) Vogel; m. Stanley Samual Judd, Jr., June 2, 1962; children: Gretchen Judd Cottrell, Stanley Samual III. BE, U. Wis., Whitewater, 1963, MS in Teaching, 1975. Cert. elem. tchr., Wis. Tchr. North Milton Rural Sch., Milton, Wis., 1959-61, Harmony Sch., Milton, 1961-

64, Footville (Wis.) Elem. Schs., 1964-67; tchr., unit leader Madison Elem. Sch., Janesville, Wis., 1967-74; tchr., team leader Harrison Elem. Sch., Janesville, 1974-88, Marshall Mid. Sch., Janesville, 1988—; presenter, speaker in field. Bd. dirs., pres. Friends Janesville Libr., 1982-88; chmn. centennial com. Janesville Libr., 1986, trustee, 1987—; bd. dirs., chmn. youth svcs. com. YWCA, Janesville, 1987—. Named Woman of Distinction, YWCA, 1989. Mem. Assn. for Individually Guided Edn., Wis. Assn. Mid. Level Educators, AAUW, Rock Valley Astronomers Club, Elk Ladies (chmn. scholarship com. Janesville 1989—). Home: 2125 E Rugby Rd Janesville WI 53545 Office: Marshall Mid Sch 408 S Main St Janesville WI 53545

JUDD, MARY JO, public relations executive; b. Clinton, Iowa, May 29, 1949; d. John David and Ruth Harriette (Capion) Hart; m. James J. Snyder, June 27, 1971 (div. 1975); 1 child, Alys Anne; m. Robert Allen Judd, May 26, 1976; 1 child, Timothy Hart. BA in Pub. Rels., Mary Crest Coll., Davenport, Iowa, 1990, postgrad., 1990—. Tchr. baton twirling park dists. and YMCA's, Clinton, 1967-71, No. Chgo. suburbs, 1971-72; Davenport, Iowa, 1985-86; tchr.'s aide, cheerleading coach Malta (Ill.) Jr. and Sr. High Schs., 1980-81. Originator, chmn. POW-MIA Christmas Tree Vigil and Candlelight Svc., Miss. Valley chpt. Vietnow, chair pub. rels., 1987-88; co-chair substance abuse awareness Wilson Grade Sch. PTA, Davenport, 1988-89; developer Kids are Super alcohol and drug prevention program, Ill. Racing Industry Assistance Program, 1989; pub. rels. chair Miss LeClaire Valley Pageant, 1989-90. Mem. Internat. Acad. Accredited Twirling Tchrs. (life). Episcopalian. Home: 4105 Greenway Dr Davenport IA 52804

JUDD, NAOMI, country musician; m. Larry Strickland; children: Wynonna, Ashley. Mem. country mus. duo The Judds; songs include Had a Dream for the Heart, 1983, Mama He's Crazy, (Grammy award), 1984, Why Not Me, (Single of Yr. Country Music Assn.), 1984, Girls Night Out, 1985, Rockin' with the Rhythmn of the Rain, 1986; albums include Why Not Me?, The Judds, Rockin' with the Rhythm, River of Time, 1989. Recipient Grammy award, 1989, duet award (with Wynonna Judd), Acad. Country Music, 1984, 85, 86, 89, Vocal Duo award (with Wynonna Judd), Country Music Assn., 1988, 89.

JUDD, WYNONNA, country western musician; b. 1964; d. Naomi Judd. Mem. country western mus. duo The Judds; songs include Had A Dream, 1983, Mama He's Crazy, 1984, Why Not Me, 1984, Love Is Alive, 1985, Have Mercy, 1985, Grandpa, 1986; albums include The Judds, Why Not Me?, Rockin' with The Rhythm, River of Time, 1989. Recipient: Grammy, 1989, duet award (with Naomi Judd), Acad. Country Music, 1984, 85, 86, 89, Vocal Duo award (with Naomi Judd), Country Music Assn., 1988, 89.

JUDELL, CYNTHIA N., craft company executive; b. N.Y.C., Mar. 23, 1924; d. Luma L. and Stella E. (Robins) Kolburne; m. Samuel Judell, Oct. 30, 1949; children—Joy C., Neil H.K. B.S.E.E., Antioch Coll., Yellow Springs, Ohio, 1945; M.A., Columbia U., 1948. Cert. secondary tchr. Engr., Jet Propulsion Lab., Pasadena, Calif., 1946-47; tchr. math., sci. Leonard Sch. for Girls, N.Y.C., 1948-49; substitute tchr. Bd. Edn., Ridgefield, Conn., 1964-67; part-time tchr. Bd. Edn., Brookfield, Conn., 1967-73; ptnr. T W M Enterprises, Wilton, Conn., 1976—. Dep. registrar of voters Town of Wilton, 1977—; elected mem. Bd. of Tax Rev., Wilton, 1980-87; treas. Town Assn., Inc., Wilton, 1980-84. Recipient Intergroup scholar Columbia U., 1948. Mem. LWV (budget chair, treas. Conn. chpt. 1978-86, treas. Wilton chpt. 1986-88), Conn. Soc. Women Engrs. (treas. 1971-72). Office: T W M Enterprises PO Box 266 Wilton CT 06897

JUDGE, JOANNE MARY, health care facility executive; b. Kingston, Pa., July 10, 1952; d. Michael Joseph and Mary (Koval) J. BS in Acctg., St. Joseph U., Phila., 1974. CPA, Pa. Mem. audit staff Touche Ross & Co., Phila., 1974-76; contr. Community Hosp. of Lancaster, Pa., 1976-78, dir. fiscal affairs, 1978-83, v.p. fin., 1983-86, acting adminstr., 1986-87, pres., 1987—; chmn. hosp. adv. coun. Capital Blue Cross, 1989—; mem. Pa. Health Care Cost Containment Coun., 1989-92. Contbr. to profl. publs. Bd. dirs., treas. YMCA, 1986-89, v.p., 1989-90, pres., 1990—; bd. dirs. Vis. Nurse Home Care Assn., 1983-90, chmn. planning com., 1986; bd. dirs. Emergency Health Svcs. Fedn. Southcentral Pa., 1984-90, treas., 1985-90; treas. Lancaster County Emergency Med. Svcs. Coun., 1978-90; mem. conceptual team, faculty Leadership Lancaster, 1984-90; com. mem. United Way, 1982-90, asst. chair, 1990; mem. task force, profl. adv. com. Lancaster Easter Seal Soc., 1986-90; bd. dirs. Lancaster Cleft Palate Clinic, 1990—. Mem. AICPA, Healthcare Fin. Mgmt. Assn. (nat. bd. dirs. 1986-90, nat. bd. examiners 1983-86, Appalachian chpt. pres. 1983-84, chmn. elect 1990—), Nat. Assn. Accts. (pres. Lancaster chpt. 1984-85), Accts. 52 Club, Pa. Inst. CPAs, Am. Coll. Healthcare Execs., Am. Osteo. Hosp. Assn. (affairs coun. 1988, 89, chmn. 1990), Am. Hosp. Assn. (ho. of dels. 1990—), Coll. Osteo. Healthcare Execs., Hosp. Assn. Pa. (policy rev. group Southcentral regional coun. 1988-90), Pa. Osteo. Hosp. Assn. (treas. 1988-90), C. of C. Found. (bd. dirs 1987—). Democrat. Roman Catholic. Home: 67 Deer Ford Dr Lancaster PA 17601 Office: Community Hosp Lancaster 1100 E Orange St PO Box 3002 Lancaster PA 17604-3002

JUE, SUSAN LYNNE, interior designer; b. Berkeley, Calif., July 7, 1956; d. Howard Lynn and Rosie (Fong) J. AA with honors, Cabrillo Coll., 1977; BA, Calif. Coll. Arts and Crafts, 1979. Interior designer Lucasfilm Ltd., San Anselmo, Calif., 1980-81, Whisler-Patri Architects and Planners, San Francisco, 1982, Barry Reischmann Design Studio, San Francisco, 1983, Kaplan, McLaughlin, Diaz Architects and Planners, San Francisco, 1984-85; Gensler & Assocs., Architects San Francisco, 1985, Hirano Assocs., San Francisco, 1987-88, Clocktower Design, San Ramon, Calif., 1988-89, Reel/Grobman & Assocs., San Francisco, 1989—. Chmn. Salvation Army Gateway Project, 1990. Mem. Inst. Bus. Designers (newsletter editor No. Calif. chpt. 1987-88, resource index com. 1987-88, chmn. graphic com. 1987-89, mem. Ronald McDonald House com. 1988-89, Cert. of Appreciation 1989), Designers Lighting Forum. Home: 1810 Bonita Ave Apt C Berkeley CA 94709

JUEL, TWILA EILEEN, teacher; b. Audubon, Iowa, Feb. 8, 1948; d. Niels Christian and Norma Eileen (Wahlert) J. BS in Edn., Dana Coll., Blair, Nebr., 1970; MS in Edn., U. Nebr. Omaha, 1975. Cert. Tchr., Nebr. Tchr. Millard Pub. Schs., Omaha, Nebr., 1970-. Mem. NEA, Nebr. Edn. Assn., Millard Edn. Assn., Phi Delta Kappa. Democratic. Lutheran. Home: 16146 Arbor Ct Omaha NE 68130

JUENEMANN, SISTER JEAN, hospital administrator, nun; b. St. Cloud, Minn., Nov. 19, 1936; d. Leo A. and Teresa M. (Oster) Juenemann. Diploma St. Cloud (Minn.) Sch. Nursing, 1957; student Coll. St. Benedict, 1957-59; BS cum laude in Nursing, Seattle U., 1967; MHA, U. Minn., 1977. Joined Order of St. Benedict, Roman Catholic Ch., 1959; dir. nursing svc. Queen of Peace Hosp., New Prague, Minn., 1963-65, 67-77, asst. adminstr., 1967-77, chief exec. officer, 1977—; speaker at confs. Chmn. Community Com. for Prevention Chem. Abuse, New Prague, 1975-80; bd. dirs. St. Cloud (Minn.) Hosp., St. Benedict's Coll., St. Joseph, Minn. Named participant Itasca Seminar on Leadership, Mpls. Found., 1979; Bush Found. summer fellow Cornell U., U. Calif., Berkeley, 1982. Fellow Am. Coll. Healthcare Execs.; mem. Am. Hosp. Assn. (Chief Exec. Officer Yr. 1989), Soc. Health care Planning & Mktg., Cath. Hosp. Assn., AAUW (past pres. New Prague chpt.), Women's Health Leadership Trust, New Prague Opportunities, Sigma Theta Tau. Avocations: Hardanger, walking, cooking.

JULANDER, PAULA FOIL, state agency administrator; b. Charlotte, N.C., Jan. 21, 1939; d. Paul Baxter and Esther Irene (Earnhardt) Foil; m. Roydon Odell Julander, Dec. 21, 1985; 1 child, Julie McMahan Shipman. Diploma, Presbyn. Hosp. Sch. Nursing, Charlotte, N.C., 1960; BS magna cum laude, U. Utah, 1984; postgrad., Brigham Young U. RN, Utah. Nurse various positions Fla. and S.C., 1960-66; co-founder, office mgr. Am. Laser Corp., 1970-79; gen. staff nurseoper. rm. Salt Lake Surg. Ctr., Salt Lake City, 1976-79; self employed Salt Lake City; teaching asst. U. Utah, Salt Lake City; rep. Utah State Legislature Coms.; adj. faculty mem. Brigham Young U. coll. Nursing, 1987—. Pres. Utah Nurses Found., 1986-88; mem. Statewide Task Force on Child Sexual Abuse, 1989-90, Utah Nursing Resource Study, 1985-90, State Feasibility Task Force for Nurses, 1985—, LWV, Women's Polit. Caucus, Statewide Abortion Task Force, 1990, Junior League Svc. Orgn., Salt Lake City, adv. bd. Interwest Quality Improvement Resource Ctr., 1989-90, adv. com. for health svcs. adminstrn. Interdept'l. Masters Program, 1990, Task force on Strengthening Hosp. Nursing, 1989-90, Progressive Elective Ofcls. Project of the Western States Ctr., 1989-90. Mem. ANA (del. conv. 1986-90), Utah Nurses Assn. (legis. rep. 1987-88, pres.), Nat. Orgn. Orgn. Women Legislators, Sigma Theta Tau, Phi Kappa Phi. Home: 1467 Penrose Dr Salt Lake City UT 84103 Office: Utah Nurses Assn 1058 E 900 S Salt Lake City UT 84105

JULIAN, ELLEN RUTH, psychometrician; b. Pasadena, Tex., June 12, 1957; d. Frank Miles and Martha Ellen (Parse) J.; m. Gerald Wayne Ellege, Apr. 27, 1985. BS, So. Meth. U., 1978; MS, Fla. State U., 1982, PhD, 1985. Asst. evaluator Dallas Ind. Sch. Dist., 1978-81; rsch. asst. Fla. State U., Tallahassee, 1981-85; psychometrician Nat. Bd. Med. Examiners, Phila., 1985—; tutor and cons. in field. Contbr. articles to profl. jours. Mem. Am. Ednl. Rsch. Assn., Fla. Ednl. Rsch. Assn. (Disting. Paper award 1985), AAUW, Nat. Coun. Measurement in Edn. Office: Nat Bd Med Examiners 3930 Chestnut St Philadelphia PA 19104

JULIAN, MICHELE DENISE, research company executive; b. Wilmington, Del., Jan. 23, 1954; d. Stanford and Ida Margaret (Lea) Simpson; m. Raymond Charles Julian, May 27, 1979. B.A., Boston Coll., 1976; M.S. in Mgmt., Lesley Coll., 1984. Personnel asst. Star Market, Cambridge, Mass., 1976-78; personnel adminstr. Charles T. Main Co., Boston, 1978-80; sr. personnel rep. Orion Research Co., Cambridge, 1980-86; personnel mgr., Prime Computer, 1987—. Contact person for student alumni relations Boston Coll., Chestnut Hill, Mass., 1983-84. Mem. Internat. Assn. Personnel Women, Am. Soc. Personnel Mgmt.Democrat. Episcopalian. Office: Orion Research Inc 529 Main St Schraffts Ctr Boston MA 02129

JULIE, ORA MCBRIDE, electronics executive; b. Texarkana, Tex., Mar. 8, 1939; d. Octave Otis and Cleo (Unger) McBride; m. Joebe Julie. Student, So. Meth. U., 1957-58, Arlington State Coll., 1958-59, Marymount Coll., N.Y.C., 1977. Asst. gen. mgr. Sanday, Inc., N.Y.C., 1965—; v.p. Julie Rsch. Labs., Inc., N.Y.C., 1971—. Mem. DAR, Nat. Contract Mgmt. Assn. Office: Julie Rsch Labs Inc 508 W 26th St New York NY 10001-5504

JULIFS, SANDRA JEAN, community action agency executive; b. Jersey City, July 12, 1939; d. Roy Howard and Irma Margrete (Barkhausen) Walters; m. Harold William Julifs, July 22, 1961; children: David Howard, Steven William. BA, U. Va., 1961; postgrad., U. Minn., 1962-63, Mankato State Coll., 1963. Tchr. St. James (Minn.) Pub. Schs., 1961-62; substitute tchr. Sleepy Eye (Minn.) Pub. Schs., 1963-67, home bound tutor, 1967; lay reader, rater U. Wis., Stevens Point, 1968; co-founder Family Planning Service Portage County, Stevens Point, 1970-72; family planning dir. Tri-County Opportunities Coun., Rock Falls, Ill., 1971-77; energy programs coord. Tri-County Opportunities Coun., Rock Falls, 1977-78, planner, EEO officer, 1978-83, pres., chief exec. officer, 1983—; bd. dirs., sec. Ill. Ventures for Community Action, Springfield, 1983—. Mem. Nat. Community Action Found., Washington, 1987—. Recipient Appreciation award Western Ill. Agy. on Aging, 1980, 81, Spl. Recognition award Ill. Head Start and Day Care Assn., Recognition award Ill. Community Action Fund, 1984. Mem. AAUW, NAFE, Am. Soc. Pub. Adminstrn., Whiteside County Welfare Assn. (chair 1986-87), Lee County Welfare Assn. (sec.-treas. 1983-84), Nat. Community Action Assn., Ill. Community Action Assn. (com. chair 1985-88, dir. exec. com. 1986—, treas. 1988, 89, sec. 1989, 90, Recognition award 1985-89). Lutheran. Office: Tri-County Opportunities Coun 405 Emmons Ave PO Box 610 Rock Falls IL 61071

JULIUSSON, MARGUERITE, film production executive, sales representative; b. Bklyn., Nov. 2, 1956; d. John Joseph and Margaret (Murphy) Lobiak; m. Steven Victor, Apr. 25, 1981 (div. Mar. 1990). BA in English, Le Moyne Coll., Syracuse, N.Y., 1978. Art producer Nat. Lampoon Mag., N.Y.C., 1979-81; assoc. producer Wyse Advt., N.Y.C., 1981-82; sales rep. Glenn Films, Chgo., 1983-84; sr. sales rep. The Artists Co., Chgo., 1984—. Mem. Grant-A-Wish. Home: 1658 N Orchard St Chicago IL 60614 Office: The Artists Co 1658 N Orchard St Chicago IL 60614

JUMPER, CINDY ANN, import-export company executive; b. Dallas, Feb. 4, 1954; d. Troy Robert and Mary Jean (Pierce) Mitchell; 1 child, Bobby Joe. Mgr. EZ Mart Stores, Inc., Texarkana, Tex., 1984-86; pres. Kilgore's Finest Imports, Kilgore, Tex., 1989—. Mem. NAFE, NOW, Internat. Traders, Alice Allen Rebekah Lodge #216. Home and Office: PO Box 2381 Kilgore TX 75663

JUNCKER, KAREN POST, early childhood educator, administrator; b. Houston, Apr. 12, 1944; d. Ben Gibson and Mary Lou (Giddings) Post; children: Grant, Meredith. BS, Purdue U., 1966; MEd, Bowling Green (Ohio) U., 1970; Degree in Nursery Sch. Adminstrn., Calif. State U., Fullerton, 1983; cert., Pacific Oaks Coll., Pasadena, Calif., 1986. Home svc. rep. Ind., Mich. Electric Co., Benton Harbor, Mich., Ohio Power Co., Fremont; early childhood edn. instr. Village Pre-Sch., Yorba Linda, Calif.; dir. early childhood edn. Temple Beth Emet, Anaheim, Calif. Mem. Nat. AEYC, Calif. AEYC (grantee), State Bd. Orange County AEYC (pres.), Assn. for Early Jewish Edn. (sec.), Nat. Jewish Early Childhood Network (bd. dirs., v.p.), Omicron Nu, Phi Delta Kappa. Jewish. Home: 19631 Monteano Ln Yorba Linda CA 92686 Office: 1770 W Cerritos Anaheim CA 92804

JUNG, DORIS, dramatic soprano; b. Centralia, Ill., Jan. 5, 1924; d. John Jay and May (Middleton) Crittenden; m. Felix Popper, Nov. 3, 1951; 1 son, Richard Dorian. Ed., U. Ill., Mannes Coll. Music, Vienna Acad. Performing Arts; student of, Julius Cohen, Emma Zador, Luise Helletsgruber, Winifred Cecil. Debut as Vitellia in: Clemenza di Tito, Zurich (Switzerland) Opera, 1955, other appearances with, Hamburg State Opera, Munich State Opera, Vienna State Opera, Royal Opera Copenhagen, Royal Opera Stockholm, Marseille and Strasbourg, France, Naples (Italy) Opera Co., Catania (Italy) Opera Co., N.Y.C. Opera, Met. Opera, also in Mpls., Portland, Oreg., Washington and Aspen, Colo.; soloist: Wagner concert conducted by Leopold Stokowski, 1971; with, Syracuse (N.Y.) Symphony, 1981, voice tchr., N.Y.C., 1970—. Home: 40 W 84th St New York NY 10024

JUNG, HILDA ZIIFLE, physicist; b. Gretna, La.; d. William Christian and Leonora Margaret (Giboney) Ziifle; m. Julius Robert Jung Jr., Nov. 2, 1968. BS, Tulane U., 1943. Engring. release clk. Higgins Aircraft Co., Michoud, La., 1943-44; rsch. physicist So. Regional Rsch. Ctr., USDA, New Orleans, 1944-79; retired, 1979. Contbr. articles to profl. jours.; patentee chem. process. Named Woman of Yr. New Orleans Fed. Exec. Bd., 1978. Mem. AAAS, Am. Chem. Soc. (sec. La. sect. 1977), Orgn. Profl. Employees Dept. Agr. (life, pres. 1978, Profl. of Yr. 1979), Nat. Assn. Retired Fed. Employees (1st v.p., legis. chmn., 1980, pres. 1981, pub. rels. officer 1984, 89-90), Am. Assn. Retired Persons (chmn. social com. 1989), Sigma Xi. Lutheran.

JUNG, LADONNA, radiologist; b. N.Y.C., Oct. 30, 1960; d. George S. and Kay (Han) Chung. BA magna cum laude, Columbia U., N.Y.C., 1982; MD, NYU, 1987. Rsch. asst. dept. neurology UCLA, 1980-81, Harvard U., Boston, 1982; tchr. chemistry St. Ann's Sch., Brooklyn Heights, N.Y., 1982-83; resident in internal medicine Lenox Hill Hosp., N.Y.C., 1987-88; resident in radiation oncology Hosp. of U. Pa., Phila., 1988—. Mem. Jr. com. Boys' Club N.Y.; sponsor Mus. of City of N.Y. Marine Biol. Lab. scholar, 1981. Mem. AMA, Assn. Therapeutic Radiology and Oncology, Med. Soc. State N.Y. Presbyterian. Home: 712B Country Club Pkwy Mount Laurel NJ 08054 also: care Convertine 500 E 77th St New York NY 10021 Office: U Pa Hosp 2 Donner Dept Radiation Oncology 3400 Spruce St Philadelphia PA 19104-4283

JUNG, LARAMIE JANE, educational fundraiser, administrator; b. Dayton, Ohio, Oct. 8, 1951; d. William Earl and Betty Jane (Weidner) Althoff; m. Stephen Vincze, Apr. 30, 1971 (div. Aug. 1987); children: Stephanie J., Alexander C., Andrew M.; m. Mark Alan Jung, Nov. 5, 1988. BA in English, U. Dayton, 1979, MBA, 1984, postgrad., 1984-87. Acctg. asst. Totenko Co., Ltd., Dayton, 1974-75; admissions sec. U. Dayton, 1976-78, admissions counselor, 1978-79, asst. to dir. fin. aid and adminstrn., 1979-81, asst. dir. fin. aid and adminstrn., 1981-84, dir. alumni rels. and ann. support programs, 1984-87; dir. instl. advancement Black Hills State U., Spearfish, S.D., 1987-90; assoc. v.p. devel. U. Evansville (Ind.), 1990—. Bd. dirs. Tales & Scales, Am. Cancer Soc. Mem. Nat. Soc. Fundraising Execs., Tri-state Assn. Fundraising Execs. (sec.), Coun. for Advancement and Support of Edn. (com. vice chair, pres. S.D. chpt., Outstanding Young Women Am. 1987), Spearfish C. of C., Optimists (bd. dirs.). Lutheran. Home: 1726 Glenmoor Rd Evansville IN 47715

JUNGBAUER, MARY ANN, chemistry educator; b. Phoenix, Oct. 8, 1934; d. Max and Irene (Kirchner) J.; 1 child, Richard Lincoln Richards. BA, Immaculate Heart Coll., 1957; MS, U. Notre Dame, 1961, PhD, 1964. Sci. tchr. L.A. Archdiocese, Long Beach, Calif., 1956-59; rsch. asst. U. Notre Dame (Ind.), 1959-63; asst. prof. chemistry Immaculate Heart Coll., L.A., 1963-67; assoc. prof. chemistry Drew U., Madison, N.J., 1967-69; assoc. prof. chemistry Barry U., Miami, Fla., 1969—, chair dept. chemistry, 1980—; vis. prf. Mt. St. Mary's Coll., L.A., 1965-67, Biscayne Coll., Miami, 1972-74. Rsch. grantee Rsch. Corp., 1964-68, tech. grantee Coun. of Independent Colls., 1987-90. Home: 704 Jeronimo Dr Coral Gables FL 33146 Office: Barry U 11300 NE 2d Ave Miami FL 33161

JUNGBLUTH, CONNIE CARLSON, investment banker; b. Cheyenne, Wyo., June 20, 1955; d. Charles Marion and Janice Yvonne (Keldsen) Carlson; m. Kirk E. Jungbluth, Feb. 5, 1977; children: Tyler, Ryan. BS, Colo. State U., 1976. CPA, Colo. Sr. acct. Rhode Scripter & Assoc., Boulder, Colo., 1977-81; mng. acct. Arthur Young, Denver, 1981-85; asst. v.p. Dain Bosworth, Denver, 1985-87; v.p. George K. Baum & Co., Denver, 1987—; bd. dirs. Security Diamond Exchange, Denver. Active Denver Estate Planning Coun., 1981-85; organizer Little People Am., Rocky Mountain Med. Clinic and Symposium, Denver, 1986; adv. bd. Children's Home Health, Denver, 1986-89; fin. adv. bd. Gail Shoettler for State Treas., Denver, 1986; bd. advisors U. Denver Sch. Accountancy, 1986-89; campaign chmn. Kathi Williams for Colo. State Legis., 1986. Named one of 50 to watch, Denver mag., 1988. Mem. AICPA, Colo. Soc. CPAs (strategic planning com. 1987-89, isntr. bank 1983, trustee 1984-87, pres. bd. trustees 1986-87, bd. dirs. 1987-89, Pub. Svc. award 1985-87, chmn. career edn. com. 1982-83), Colo. Mcpl. Bond Dealers, Metro North C. of C. (bd. dirs. 1987-90), Denver City Club (bd. dirs. 1987-88), Pi Beta Phi.

JUNKER, CHRISTINE ROSETTA, swine production executive; b. Burlington, Iowa, June 10, 1953; d. Roland Lee and Janet Elaine (Kapotas) Wiemann; m. Theodore Henry Junker, Mar. 10, 1977; 1 child, Nolan Robert. Assocs. of Animal Sci., Hawkeye Inst. Tech., 1977; student, U. No. Iowa, 1984-85. Drafstman Confinement Specialists, Mediapolis, Iowa, 1973-75; herdsman X-L Pork, Cedar Falls, Iowa, 1976-77; livestock specialist Tasco, Inc., Shell Rock, Iowa, 1977-81; problem accounts specialist I.F.G. Leasing, Parkersburg, Iowa, 1981-86; pres. Pork Purveyors, Ltd., Parkersburg, 1986-88, 89—; gen. mgr. div. Pork Purveyors Doane Farm Mgmt. Co., Parkersburg, 1988-89; founder div. Pork Purveyors, Ltd. Craft Store, Parkersburg, 1990—; mem. adv. com. animal sci. dept. Hawkeye Inst. Tech., Waterloo, Iowa, 1988-90; coord. Parkersburg Econ. Devel., 1990—. Producer children's album with 5 original songs, 1989; contbr. articles to profl. jours. Mediator Iowa Farmer/Creditor Mediation Svc., 1987—. Named Outstanding Alumni All Agrl. Club, Hawkeye Inst. Tech, 1979. Mem. Iowa Pork Producers, Parkersburg C. of C. Home: RR 2 Box 100 Parkersburg IA 50665 Office: Pork Purveyors Ltd PO Box 596 222 3d St Parkersburg IA 50665

JUNKER, SANDRA JEAN, military officer; b. Binghamton, N.Y., Dec. 18, 1947; d. Frank Cameron Wayman Sr. and Louise Lucille (DeLarco) Wayman; m. Melvin Rudolph Junker, April 11, 1970. Student, U. Alaska, 1973-76, Liberty U., 1989—. Enlisted U.S. Army, 1969, advanced through grades to sgt. 1st class, 1983; radiol. technician USA MEDDAC Sandia Base, Albuquerque, 1969-71, Kimbrough Army Hosp., Ft. Meade, Md., 1971-73, Ft. Richardson, Anchorage, 1973-77, Walter Reed Army Med. Ctr., Washington, 1977-79; field recruiter Richmond RBN, Petersburg, Va., 1979-83, nurse recruiter, 1983-85; sta. comdr. Charlotte RBN, Lenoir, N.C., 1985-87, Hickory, N.C., 1987-88; recruiter trainer Charlotte RBN, Asheville, N.C., 1988-89; with quality control non-commissioned officer mil. processing and entrance sta. Charlotte (N.C.) RBN, 1989; sta. comdr. Houston RBN, Beaumont, Tex., 1989—, Orange, Tex., 1990—. Leader Girl Scouts U.S. Mem. Nat. Assn. Female Execs., Altrusa, NOW. Avocations: cross stitching, crochet, reading, sewing. Home: 6360 Mayhaw Dr Beaumont TX 77708 Office: 109 McArthur Circle Orange TX 77630

JURASKA, JANICE MARIE, psychology educator; b. Berwyn, Ill., Feb. 9, 1949. BA, Lawrence U., 1971; MA, U. Ill., 1975; PhD, U. Colo., 1977. NIMH postdoctoral fellow psychology dept. U. Ill., Champaign, 1978-80; from asst. prof. to assoc. prof. psychology dept. Ind. U., Bloomington, 1980-85; assoc. prof. psychology dept. U. Ill., Champaign, 1986—. Co-editor: Developmental Neuropsychobiology, 1986. Grantee NIH, NIMH, NSF, John D. and Catherine T. MacArthur Found. Mem. Soc. for Neuroscience, Internat. Soc. for Devel. Psychobiology, Internat. Acad. Sex Rsch., Am. Psychol. Soc., Phi Beta Kappa. Office: U Ill 603 E Daniel Champaign IL 61820

JURCZAK, PATRICIA JEAN, public affairs manager; b. Pitts., Apr. 20, 1962; d. Joseph Anthony and Barbara (Christian) Raffaele; m. Christopher Michael Jurczak, Sept. 19, 1987. BA in Journalism (cum laude), Duquesne U., 1984. Pulliam fellow The Phoenix Gazette, Phoenix, 1984; art, lifestyle reporter Lawton (Okla.) Pub. Co., 1984; regional correspondent Fairchild Pub., Pitts. Bur., 1986-87; pub. relations writer Ind. (Pa.) Hosp., 1987-89; mgr., pub. affiars The Hosp. Coun. Western Pa., Warrendale, 1990—. Recipient Pulliam Fellow award Pulliam Found., 1984; named Outstanding Young Woman Am., 1984. Mem. Women In Communications, Inc. (v.p. 1986-88, v.p. fin. 1990—), Pub. Soc. Health Care Orgn. (asst. v.p. 1990-92, job placement). Roman Catholic. Home: 819 Churchill Ct Mars PA 16046

JUREK, EILEEN JEAN, material analyst, small business owner; b. Whiting, Ind., Oct. 25, 1947; d. Joseph Valentine and Olga Catherine (Aranowski) Gallas; m. Mark Stephan Jurek, Oct. 9, 1973; children: Jennifer, Stacey. Student, Purdue U., Hammond, Ind. Exec. sec. Sears, Roebuck, Chgo., 1971-76; sec. Inland Steel Co., Chgo., 1976-78; analyst Union Tank Car, East Chicago, Ind., 1978—; owner, mgr. Networks, temp. svc., Whiting, 1981—; model No. Ind. Art Assn., Munster, 1981—. Liturgist St. John Bapt. Ch., Whiting, 1989-90. Mem. NAFE, Whiting C. of C. Home: 2018 Stanton Ave Whiting IN 46394

JURICH, JULIE ANN, family and child therapist; b. Toledo, June 18, 1946; d. Anthony and Lillian Agnes (Tomes) Vavrik; m. Anthony P. Jurich, June 18, 1971 (div. Dec. 1979); m. Donald S. Holand, Dec. 31, 1988. BS, Ohio State U., 1968; MEd, MS, Penn. State U., 1970; PhD, Kans. State U., 1978. Cert. marriage family therapist, Kans.; cert. sex therapist, Kans. Elem., secondary guidance counselor Tyrone (Pa.) Area Sch Dist., 1970-72; homebound instr. Manhattan (Kans.) Area Sch. Dist., 1973-74; family and child therapist Community Mental Health Svcs., Ft. Riley, Kans., 1974-87; marriage and family therapist Op. Bridge, Omaha, 1987-88; instr. Met. Community Coll., Omaha, 1988-89; marriage and family therapist The Hudson Ctr., Omaha, 1989—; adj. prof. U. Nebr., Omaha, 1989—. Contbr. articles to profl. jours. Mem. Am. Assn. Marriage and Family Therapists, Soc. Pediatric Psychology, Am. Assn. Sex Educators and Counselors, Am. Psychol. Assn., Am. Assn. for Counseling and Devel. Home: 2125 N 125 Circle Omaha NE 68164 Office: The Hudson Ctr 12111 Pacific St Omaha NE 68154

JURMAN, CLAUDIA LYNNE, travel agent; b. Huntington, N.Y., Sept. 3, 1956; d. Harry Richard Jurman and Rea Fiske; m. Robert Jay Shulman, Dec. 16, 1978 (div. Nov. 1989); 1 child, Jeremy Edward. Student, Ithaca Coll., Ithaca, 1974-76, Pace U., 1980-81, 89—, Katharine Gibbs, Melville, 1977-78. Sec. Pace U., White Plains, N.Y., 1978-81; receptionist First Boston/Shelternet, Tarrytown, N.Y., 1983; office mgr. Tenex Communications, White Plains, 1983-85; bus. mgr. Bano Buick/Chrysler, Mt. Kisco, N.Y., 1985-86; customer svc. mgr. Tannon Devel., White Plains, 1986-87; billing mgr., customer svc. mgr. Mercedes Airport Svc., N.Y., 1987-89; travel agt. Hollowbrook Travel, Garrison, N.Y., 1989—. Den Leader Boy Scouts Am. Beacon, 1988—. Recipient Westchester C. of C. Secreterial Success award, C. of C. Pace U. White Plains, 1980, WPRPGA, 1981. Mem. NAFE. Republican. Presbyterian. Office: Hollowbrook Travel Allsport Rte 9 Fishkill NY 12524

JUST, GEMMA RIVOLI, advertising executive; b. N.Y.C., Nov. 29, 1921; d. Philip and Brigida (Consolo) Rivoli; B.A., Hunter Coll., N.Y.C., 1943; m. Victor Just, Jan. 29, 1955. Copy group head McCann Erickson, N.Y.C., 1958-62; copy. supr. Morse Internat., N.Y.C., 1962-67; v.p., dir. creative svcs. Deltakos div. J. Walter Thompson, N.Y.C., 1967-75; v.p., copy dir. Sudler & Hennessey, div. Young & Rubicam, N.Y.C., 1980-87; sr. v.p., assoc. creative dir. copy, 1987-88, ret., 1989. Mem. Episcopal Women's Club of Ch. of Incarnation, N.Y.C., also ch. altar guild. Named Best Writer, Art Dirs. Club N.Y., 1979, Best Writer Young & Rubicam, 1981; recipient Aesulapius awards Modern Medicine mag., 1980-88. Mem. Coun. Communications Socs., Pharm. Advt. Coun., Am. Med. Writers Assn. (exec. com. 1973). Home: 155 E 38th St Apt 5D New York NY 10016

JUSTICE, DOROTHY DOBBS, food equipment manufacturing company executive; b. Woodstock, Ga., Apr. 13, 1932; d. Eugene Tiller and Bertha (Roe) Dobbs; m. Lester Joseph Justice, June 10, 1950. Student Marsh Bus. Coll., Atlanta, 1948-49. Office mgr. Norris Candy Co., Atlanta, 1964-68; exec. asst. Cornelius Co., Atlanta, 1968-70; v.p. adminstrn. Remarco, Atlanta, 1970-73; v.p. Refresco Internat., Atlanta, 1973-82, pres., chief exec. officer, 1982—; pres., chief exec. officer, Modular Engring. Corp., Atlanta, 1984-89; pres., chief exec. officer Decorative Accents, Inc., 1990—. Pres. Mountain Park Homeowners Assn., Stone Mountain, Ga., 1984—. Mem. Nat. Assn. Food Equipment Mfrs. Democrat. Baptist. Clubs: Big Canoe Golf and Tennis (Ga.); Stone Mountain Garden, Stone Mountain Women's. Avocations: interior decorating; flower arranging. Home: 1524 Carlton Ave Stone Mountain GA 30087 Office: Modular Engring Corp PO Box 1748 Stone Mountain GA 30086

JUSTICE, INGRID COOPER, marketing executive; b. Detroit, Mar. 23, 1958; d. William Allen and Auguste Ingrid (Schneider) C.; m. Christopher Scott Justine, Mar. 17, 1990. BA in German, Ind. U., 1980; M in Internat. Bus., U. S.C., 1985. Sales asst. W. Bill Ltd., London, 1980-81; export clk. Pass Confirming Ltd., London, 1981-82; adminstrv. asst. Union-Transport Gmbh, Duesseldorf, West Germany, 1984-85; planning analyst Robert Bosch Corp., Farmington Hills, Mich., 1985-88, mktg. adminstr., 1988-89; mkt. analyst TRW Steering and Suspension, Sterling Heights, Mich., 1989—. Recipient cert. Goethe Inst., Atlanta, 1984. Mem. Automotive Market Rsch. Coun. (mem. light vehicle O.E. com. 1988—). Democrat. Unitarian-Universalist. Office: TRW Steering and Suspension 34201 Van Dyke Ave Sterling Heights MI 48077-6512

JUSTICE, KATHLEEN MURPHY, corporation executive; b. Los Angeles; d. Patrick Joseph and Marie Margaret (Cremins) Murphy; m. John A. Justice (dec.); children: Kevin Patrick Muno, Therese Marie Hernandez, Maureen Ann Hensley, Michael Lawrence Muno, Lawrence Matthew Muno. BS in Nursing, Mount St. Mary's Coll., 1956; pub. health cert., health and devel. credential, nursing edn. teaching credential, UCLA, 1970; MSC in Health Svcs. RN. Dir. health svcs. Wiseburn Sch. Dist., Los Angeles; instr. physical edn., health edn. St. Bernard's High Sch.; instr. Am. Red Cross, Beverly Hills, Calif., 1966-67; dir. health svcs. El Camino Coll., El Camino, Calif.; prof. nursing edn. Glendale (Calif.) Coll.; dir. health svcs. Covina Valley (Calif.) Unified Sch. Dist.; dir. health svcs., spl. edn. Los Angeles (Calif.) County Supt. of Schs.; pres. Cal-Brite Inc., Manhattan Beach, Calif., 1985—. Republican. Roman Catholic. Home: 125 Seventh St Manhattan Beach CA 90266 Office: Cal Brite Inc PO Box3391 Manhattan Beach CA 90266

JUSTICE, SUSANNE DOROTHY, medical administrator; b. Flushing, N.Y., Aug. 28, 1942; d. Edward H. and Dorothy E. (Scholl) Lane; m. M.M.T. Justice (dec. Apr. 1980); children: Edward P., Jennifer L.; m. Frank J. Moran, May 18, 1984. Diploma Jackson Meml. Hosp. Sch. Nursing, 1963. R.N., Fla. Group nurse Mt. Sinai Hosp., Miami Beach, Fla., 1963-66; part-time group nurse, 1967-72; head nurse Jackson Meml. Hosp., Miami, 1966-67; hosp. coord., head coord. Fla. Home Health Svcs., Miami, 1972-73; hosp. coord., assoc. dir. nursing Unicare, Inc., Miami, 1973-75; pres., adminstr. Medi-Health of Fla., Inc., 1975—; chief exec. officer Francoa, Inc., 1988—; cons. in field; chmn. adv. com. Medicare Home Health Claims, 1988-89. Author: Problem Oriented Records for Home Health Agencies; mem. editorial adv. bd. Caring mag., 1983-84; contbg. author: Quality Assurance Workbook, 1978, 83. Mem. Nat. Assn. Women Bus. Owners, Fla. Assn. Home Health Agys. (v.p. 1981-83, pres. 1983-85, chmn. liasion com. 1985-88, bd. dirs. 1978-86, 87-88, M.T. Terry Justice Meml. award 1980), So. Fla. In Home Services Consortium (pres. 1981-83), Am. Acad. Med. Adminstrs. (sec.-treas. Fla. chpt. 1983-84, pres. 1985-86, Hardie Lord award 1986, Nat. Disting. Svc. award 1986), Nat. Assn. Home Care (dir. 1980-82, quality assurance com. 1981, ann. meeting com. 1989), Fla. Hosp. Assn. Home Care Coun. (pres.-elect 1989-90, pres. 1990—), Associated Home Health Industries of Fla. (chmn. nominating com. 1989, chmn. liaison com. 1989-90). Lutheran. Home: 2027 NE 121 Rd North Miami FL 33181 Office: Medi-Health of Fla Inc 1550 NE Miami Gardens Dr #304 North Miami Beach FL 33179-4884

JUSTINGER, MARYANN ELIZABETH, mathematics educator; b. Buffalo, Oct. 22, 1951; d. William James and Geraldine Katheryn (Weber) Schwab; m. Paul George Justinger Apr. 1, 1978; 1 child, Rebecca Rose. BA, Daemen Coll., Buffalo, 1973; EdD, SUNY, Buffalo, 1986. Cert. math. tchr., N.Y. Tchr. Holy Family Sch., Buffalo, 1973-74, Buffalo Acad. Sacred Heart, 1974-77; part-time instr. math. Canisius Coll., Buffalo, 1975-78; coll. reporting officer Erie Community Coll., Buffalo, 1977-78, instr. math., 1979-85, asst. prof., 1985-89, assoc. prof., 1989—, indsl. outreach instr., 1983-85; textbook reviewer W.C. Brown, Wadsworth, 1989. Vol. fund raiser PBS, Buffalo, 1977—. Mem. N.Y. State Maths. Assn. Two-Yr. Colls. (legis. chmn. 1989—), AAUW. Republican. Roman Catholic. Office: Erie Community Coll South 4140 Southwestern Blvd Orchard Park NY 14127-2199

JUSTIS, NANCY ANN, director sports information; b. Cedar Rapids, Iowa, Dec. 1, 1950; d. Carroll David and Thelma Mae (Sheffield) Ross; m. Robert Louis Justis, Apr. 23, 1977; 1 child, Nicole Renee. BA, U. Iowa, 1973. Reporter The Coloradoan, Ft. Collins, Colo., 1973-74; asst. editor U. No. Iowa, Cedar Falls, 1974-76, asst. sports info. dir., 1976-79, dir. sports info., 1979—; asst. press chief 1984 Summer Olympics, L.A., 1984, 1987 Pan-Am. Games, Indpls., 1987. Mem. Coll. Sports Info. Dirs. of Am. (Citation for Excellence 1982, 84, 88, 89, 90), Basketball Writers Am., Women in Communications, Inc. (charter, Merit award 1990). Home: 122 Maryhill Dr Cedar Falls IA 50613 Office: U No Iowa 27th & College Cedar Falls IA 50614

JUSTUS, BETTY I., consumer credit counseling manager; b. Arenzville, Ill., June 1, 1930; d. William Allen Davis and Lottie Grace (Shirkey) Faulkner; m. Leon A. Justus, Apr. 12, 1958 (div. 1988); children: Reed C., James Leon. AA, Skagit Valley Coll., Oak Harbor, Wash., 1981. Lic. cosmetologist, Calif. Salesperson trainer Sears Roebuck & Co., Charleston, S.C., 1959-61; mgr. Beauty Shop, San Diego, 1963-64; hairdresser Navy Base Beauty Shop, Guantanimo Bay, Cuba, 1971-72; instr. phys. fitness Spl. Svcs., Agana, Guam, 1976-78; area rep. Consumer Credit Counseling Svc. of Seattle, 1981-90, area mgr., 1990—. Bd. dirs. Help House, Oak Harbor, 1982—; sec., cons. New Leaf, Oak Harbor, 1985-88; chair Car Resources/Coop. Edn. Svc., Mt. Vernon, Wash., 1985—; project coord. Heritage Way hwy. beautification, Oak Harbor, 1988—. Mem. Nat. Found. Consumer Credit, Soroptimist Internat., Bus. and Profl. Women (pres. 1983-84, 86-87), Greater Oak Harbor C. of C. (pres. 1990—), Navy League. Methodist. Home: 2608 W La Mesa St Coupeville WA 98239 Office: Consumer Credit Counseling Svc 4086 400th Ave W Oak Harbor WA 98277

JUVELIS, PRISCILLA CATHERINE, antiquarian bookseller; b. Newark, Sept. 2, 1945; d. Steven and Odelite (Canning) J. B.A., Boston U., 1967. Dir. internat. dept. Harcourt Brace Jovanovich Internat. Corp., N.Y.C., 1971-76; rights dir. The Franklin Library, N.Y.C., 1976-78; owner, pres. Priscilla Juvelis, Inc., Boston, 1980—. Mem. exec. com. Save Venice, Inc. , Boston. Editor, pub.: The Book Beautiful and The Binding as Art, 1983, vols. 1 and 2; author: (with Duncan and de Bartha) Art Noveau and Art Deco Bookbinding, 1989. Mem. Antiquarian Bookseller's Assn. Am. (bd. govs. 1990-92), Mass. and R.I. Bookseller's Assn. (sec. 1983-84, v.p. 1984-86, pres. 1986-88), The Manuscript Soc. (trustee 1987-88, bd. dirs. 1988-90, 90—), Assn. Internat. des Bibliophiles, The Grolier Club. Office: 150 Huntington Ave Boston MA 02115

KAATZ, MARGO JEANNE, registered nurse; b. Bay City, Mich., Mar. 20, 1960; d. Raymond Arthur and Rosemary Helen (Witzke) K. AA/AS, Ventura Coll., 1981; BA, Whittier Coll., 1983; MA, Azusa Pacific U., 1986; postgrad., Whittier Coll. Sch. Law, 1990—. RN, Calif.; cert. chem. dependency nurse, Calif. RN Ventura (Calif.) County Med. Ctr., 1981-83; RN I Presbyn. Intercommunity Hosp., Whittier, Calif., 1983-85; RN II Presbyn. Intercommunity Hosp., Whittier, 1985-87, RN III clin. specialist, 1988-89, nursing supr., 1989—; chem. dependency perinatal expert L.A. County Sheriff's Dept. Substance Abuse Narcotic Edn. Div., L.A., 1990—. Tchr. Grace Luth. Ch., Ventura, 1979-81. Recipient Whittier Coll. Acad. award Alpha Gamma Sigma, Whittier, 1981, W. Roy Newsom scholarship Whittier Coll. Law Sch., L.A., 1990. Mem. Am. Red Cross, Nat. Assn. Perinatal Addiction and Rsch. Edn., Calif. Assn. Nurses in Substance Abuse (L.A. chpt. pres. 1988-89), Nat. Assn. Chem. Dependency Nurses, Calif. Assn. Marriage Family Therapists, NAFE. Republican. Lutheran. Office: Presbyn Intercommunity Hosp 12401 E Washington Blvd Whittier CA 90602

KABACK, ELAINE, career counselor, consultant; b. Phila., Feb. 22, 1939; d. Sol and Evelyn Zitman; student Pa. State U., 1956-58; B.A., Temple U., 1960; M.S., Calif. State U., 1977; children—Douglas, Stephen, Michelle. Tchr. English, Sayre Jr. High Sch., Phila. Public Schs., 1960-62; tchr. English and history Beth Tfiloh Pvt. Day Sch., Balt., 1968-72; mgmt. cons., trainer Sandra Winston Assos., Palos Verdes, Calif., 1975—; counselor Career Planning Ctr. and Mid-Life Ctr., Long Beach City Coll., 1977-78; dir. program devel. Univance Career Ctrs., Inc., Los Angeles, 1978-80; pvt. practice career counseling, 1980—, v.p., cons. Exec. Horizons, Inc., Irvine, Calif., 1989—; coordinator career transition program, trainer/presenter UCLA Extension; cons. in career systems and outplacement. Pres. Palos Verdes chpt. NOW, 1974-76; treas. S.W. chpt. Nat. Women's Polit. Caucus, 1973, 78; bd. dirs. STEP Adult Edn. Programs, Palos Verdes, 1974—, cert. community coll. life counselor, Calif.; cert. tchr., Pa. Mem. Calif. Counseling and Devel., Am. Soc. Tng. and Devel., Am. Assn. Counseling and Devel., Orgn. Devel. Network, Phi Kappa Phi. Office: 24222 Hawthorne Blvd Suite B Torrance CA 90505 also: 11340 W Olympic Blvd Ste 255 Los Angeles CA 90064

KABALA, KAREN LYNN, small business owner; b. Wilmington, Del., Oct. 12, 1963; d. Leonard John and Iria Fatima (Branco) K. AA in Bus., Castle Jr. Coll., Windham, N.H., 1983. Lic. real estate salesperson, N.H. With sales and mktg. dept. Advantage/Trend West, Haverhill, Mass., 1983-86; with sales and mktg. dept. Scopus Corp., Lowell, Mass., 1986-87, sales mgr., 1987-88; owner, operator Affinity Data Products, Salem, N.H., 1988—; with sales dept. Bllinn Realty/Gallery of Homes, Salem, 1985-87. Vol. Salvation Army, Lowell, 1988. Fellow Small Bus. Orgns. (cert. 1989). Roman Catholic. Office: Affinity Data Products PO Box 1550 Salem NH 03079

KABATECK, GLADYS IRENE, counselor; b. Chgo., Sept. 13, 1930; d. Nerses and Arousiag (Mugalian) Odian; m. John Joseph Kabateck, Nov. 27, 1958; children: Brian Stephen, John Richard. BA in Music, Fresno State U., 1952; BA, Calif. State U., L.A., 1981, MS in Counselor Edn., 1986. Cert. life community coll. counselor, student personnel worker and instr., Calif. Learning disabity asst. instrnl. assistance program Glendale (Calif.) Community Coll., 1979-81, counselor coord., 1982—; participant Crisis in Counseling. Mem. Glendale Assistance League; mem. women's com. Glendale Symphony Orch. Assn.; coord. Self-Esteem Workshop; vocat. edn. participant, speaker Thai Embassy; mem. task force com. Child Ctr.; founder bd. dirs. Friends of Coll. Library; mem. adv. bd. Glendale YWCA; com. mem., presenter Women's Hist. Conf.; bd. dirs. Natural Mus. Sci. and Industry. Mem. Calif. Assn. for Counseling and Devel., Calif. Community Coll. Counselors Assn., Profl. Orgn. for Women in Edn. and Re-Entry, Calif. Career Edn. Assn., Bus. and Profl. Women), AAUW, Glendale Community Coll. Patrons Club (bd. dirs.), Music Tchrs. Assn., Town and Gown (U. So. Calif.), P.E.O., Oakmont Country Club, also others. Republican. Home: 1383 Opechee Way Glendale CA 91208 Office: Glendale Community Coll 1500 N Verdugo Rd Glendale CA 91208

KABEL, JOANNE LISA, interior decorating executive; b. Balacynwood, Pa., Sept. 15, 1963; d. Sander Elliot and Ilene Phyllis (Rosner) K. AA, Rider Coll., Lawrenceville, N.J., 1983; student, Decorating Den, Bethesda, Md., 1989. Adminstrv. asst. Brockway Industries, Haddenfield, N.J., 1983-84; adminstrv. legal aide, cons. N.J. State Dept. of Health, Trenton, N.J., 1984-86; adminstrv. aide Corestates Bank, Pennington, N.J., 1986; office mgr., asst. regional dir. Decorating Den Systems, Inc., Marlton, N.J., 1988—. Co-author: (book on poetry) Creative Works, 1970. Campaign mgr. sch. bd. pres. campaign, Delran, N.J., 1978; campaign vol. Re-elect Gov. Kean, N.J.; state rep. Local 1038, CWA, Trenton. Recipient 2nd place award Future Bus. Leaders Am. stenography competition, 1978. Mem. NAFE, NOW, Cherry Hill (N.J.) C. of C., Cherry Hill Young Reps. (vol. sec.), Delta Zeta. Home: 16 Tenby Ln Marlton NJ 08053 Office: Decorating Den Systems Inc 3 Eves Dr Ste 301 Marlton NJ 08053

KABRIEL, MARCIA GAIL, psychotherapist; b. El Reno, Okla., Jan. 8, 1938; d. Gail Frederick and Katherine (Marsh) Slaughter; m. J. Ronald Kabriel, May 25, 1957 (div. Sept. 1985); children—Joseph Charles, Jeffrey Gail, Jae B. BA, U. Okla., 1965, MSW, 1968; postgrad. Am. U. Psychiat. social worker Dept. Mental Hygiene, N.Y.C., 1968-69; psychiat. social worker Washington Hosp. Ctr., 1970-72, assoc. mem. dept. psychiatry, 1972-75, sr. psychotherapist Counseling Ctr., 1972-75; psychotherapist Md. Inst. Pastoral Counseling, Annapolis, Md., 1972—; chief dept. social services Washington Hosp. Ctr., 1979-82, cons. spl. projects, 1974-82; supr. continuing protective services State Md., 1983—; exec. v.p. Kent Island Transport, Inc., 1985—; field instr. Cath. U., Washington, 1973-75, U. Md., 1976-90. Mem. Nat. Assn. Social Workers, Acad. Cert. Social Workers (bd. cert. diplomate). Democrat. Presbyterian. Home: 1416 Regent St Annapolis MD 21403 Office: 104 Forbes St Suite F Annapolis MD 21404

KACEWICZ, LAURA ANN, securities broker, educator; b. Medford, Mass., June 27, 1945; d. Ignatius James and Rita Florence (O'Brien) Bottaro. BA in Polit. Sci., Calif. State U., Long Beach, 1967, MA in Polit. Sci., 1973. Adminstrv. intern City of Signal Hill, Calif., 1973; coll. instr. Long Beach City Coll., 1973-78; securities broker Merrill Lynch, Long Beach, 1978-81, 83-86, Paine Webber, Long Beach, 1981-83, Fin. Network Investment Corp., Long Beach, 1986—; mem. Internat. Assn. Fin. Planners, 1984-88. Contbr. articles Women's Forum, 1988-89. Bd. dirs. Long Beach Symphony, 1985-88; mem. Nat. Women's Polit. Caucus Greater Long Beach, 1983—, Long Beach Symphony Guild, 1984—, L.A. County Art Mus., L.A., 1985—, Long Beach Mus. Art., 1985—. Named Outstanding Student Tchr. Delta Kappa Gamma, 1987. Mem. NAFE, Long Beach C. of C, Pi Lambda Theta. Office: Fin Network Investment Corp 3447 Atlantic Ave Long Beach CA 90807

KACIR, BARBARA BRATTIN, lawyer; b. Buffalo, Ohio, July 19, 1941; d. William James and Jean (Harrington) Brattin; m. Charles Stephen Kacir, June 3, 1973 (div. Aug. 1977). BA, Wellesley Coll., 1963; JD, U. Mich., 1967. Bar: Ohio 1967, D.C. 1980. Assoc. Arter & Hadden, Cleve., 1967-74, ptnr., 1974-79; ptnr. Jones, Day, Reavis & Pogue, Washington, 1980-83, Cleve., 1983—; instr. trial tactics Case-Western Res. U., Cleve., 1976-79; legal rep. for Warner Bros., Twentieth-Century Fox, MGM/UA, Universal, Orion, Columbia, Buena Vista, Paramount, Tri-Star in Ohio litigation. Mem. nat. com. visitors, nat. fund raising com. U. Mich. Mem. ABA, Ohio Bar Assn., D.C. Bar Assn., Cleve. Bar Assn. (trustee 1973-76, treas. 1978-79), Assn. Trial Lawyers Am., Am. Law Inst., Def. Rsch. Inst. Republican. Office: Jones Day Reavis & Pogue 901 Lakeside Ave North Point Cleveland OH 44114

KACLIK, DEBI LOUISE, construction executive; b. Pitts., May 15, 1953; d. John G. and Dolores J. (Grekalskis) K. BA, West Liberty State Coll., 1975; Cert. in Computer Aided Drafting and Design, Pitts. Tech. Inst., 1982; postgrad., Horry-Georgetown Tech. Sch., 1987-88, Columbia Pacific U., 1988—. Program dir. YMCA, Pitts., 1975-78; regional supr. United Rep. Life Ins. Co., Harrisburg, Pa., 1977-80; phys. therapy asst. The Verland Found., Pitts., 1980-81; estimator, mgr. PPS Enterprises, Inc., Pitts., 1981-83; mgr. Wild Sisters Restaurant, Inc., Pitts., 1983-84; v.p., project mgr. Kreisle Bros. Masonry, Ltd., Georgetown, S.C., 1984-85; owner, ptnr., constrn. mgr. Mastco Masonry/Steel, Georgetown, 1986-87; owner, pres. The Brick People, Inc., Surfside Beach, S.C., 1988-89, Charlotte, N.C., 1989—; owner, pres. Kaclik & Assocs., Murrells Inlet, S.C.; presenter news spl. Sta. KDKA-TV, Pitts., 1977; guest speaker Sta. WTAE-TV, Pitts., 1978, Sta. WBTW-TV, Myrtle Beach, S.C., 1987. Instr. water safety, first aid and disaster shelters ARC, Myrtle Beach and Pitts., 1969-85; coord. regional and internat. Cerebral Palsy Games, Pitts., 1981; bd. dirs. N.Am. Riding for the Handicapped, Pitts., 1982; team coordinating asst. nat. telethon teamwalk Am. March of Dimes, Myrtle Beach, 1986-88. Mem. Am. Assn. Subcontractors, U.S. Sidewinder Assn. Democrat. Roman Catholic. Home: 425 Bay Dr Salters Cove Murrells Inlet SC 29576 Office: Kaclik & Assocs 425 Bay Dr Salters Cove Murrells Inlet SC 29576

KACOR, LAURA MARY, mental health center administrator; b. Chgo., Oct. 25, 1958; d. Raymond Frank and Josephine Marie (Mercurio) K. BPh in Psychology, Northwestern U., 1988. Asst. dir. spl. promotions Dominick's Finer Foods, Northlake, Ill., 1976-85; dir. ops. H. Shapiro & Asssocs., Chgo., 1985-87; adminstr. Maine Ctr. for Mental Health, Park Ridge, Ill., 1988—, resource devel. specialist, 1988-89; cons. Zindor Spltys., Niles, Ill., 1989—. Mem. Women in Mgmt. (v.p. mktg. North shore chpt. 1989—), NAFE, Northwestern U. Alumni Assn. (bd. dirs. 1989—), Alpha Sigma Lambda. Republican. Christian Scientist. Office: Maine Ctr for Mental Health 832 Busse Hwy Park Ridge IL 60068

KADABA, PANKAJA KOOVELI, medicinal chemist; b. Perumbavoor, Kerala, India, May 15, 1928; came to U.S., 1953; d. Ananthasubramani Kooveli and Mangala Kooveli (Mangala) Subramanya Iyer; m. Prasad Krishna Kadaba, June 30, 1954; 1 child, Lini S. Kadaba. BS, U. Coll., Trivandrum, India, 1947, MS, 1949; PhD, U. Delhi, India, 1954; postgrad., U. Wis., 1953-54. Lectr. in biochemistry Am. Mission Med. Coll., Vellore, India, 1949-50; lectr. in chemistry U. Delhi, 1950-53; rsch. assoc. Brown U., Providence, 1957-60; instr. in biochemistry Coll. Pharmacy, U. Ky., Lexington, 1965; assoc. prof. chemistry Morehead (Ky.) State U., 1965-66; asst. prof. chemistry Christian Bros. Coll., Memphis, 1966-68; rsch. assoc. Coll. Pharmacy U. Ky., Memphis, 1968-80; asst. rsch. prof. U. Ky., Memphis, 1980-83, assoc. rsch. prof. medicinal chemistry and pharmacognosy, 1983—; vis. assoc. prof. of chemistry U. Ljubljana, Yugoslavia, 1973-74; grad. dissertation advisor U. Ky., 1989—; researcher Antiepileptic Drug Devel. Program NIH, Bethesda, 1976—, Lederle Labs., Pearl River, N.Y., 1983—, CNS Rsch. Inc., Cambridge, Mass., 1989—; rsch. bd. advisors Am. Biog. Inst., 1986—. Author: (with others) Advances in Heterocyclic Chemistry, 1989; patentee in field; contbr. numerous articles to profl. jours. Active Lexington Art League, 1976-82, bd. dirs. 1980-81; chmn. Lexington Art League Critic Club, 1980-81. Rsch. grant NIH, 1982-91. Mem. Am. Chem. Soc., Internat. Soc. Heterocyclic Chemistry, India Chemists and Chem. Engrs. Club (del. 1982). Office: U Ky Coll Pharmacy Rose St Lexington KY 40536-0082

KAEL, PAULINE, film critic, author; b. Petaluma, Calif., June 19, 1919; d. Isaac Paul and Judith (Friedman) K.; 1 child, Gina James. Student, U. Calif., Berkeley, 1936-40; LLD (hon.), Georgetown U., 1972; D. Arts and Letters (hon.), Columbia Coll., Chgo., 1972; LittD (hon.), Smith Coll., 1973, Allegheny Coll., 1979; LHD (hon.), Kalamazoo Coll., 1973, Reed Coll., 1975, Haverford Coll., 1975; DFA (hon.), Sch. Visual Arts, N.Y.C., 1980. Movie critic New Yorker mag., 1968—. Author: I Lost it at the Movies, 1965, Kiss Kiss Bang Bang, 1968, Going Steady, 1970, Deeper into Movies, 1973 (Nat. Book award 1974), Reeling, 1976, When the Lights Go Down, 1980, 5001 Nights at the Movies, 1982, Taking It All In, 1984, State of the Art, 1985, Hooked, 1989; contbg. author: The Citizen Kane Book, 1971; contbr. to numerous other mags. Recipient George Polk Meml. award, 1970, Front Page award Newswomen's Club N.Y., 1974, 83; Guggenheim fellow, 1964. Mem. Phi Beta Kappa (hon.). Office: New Yorker 25 W 43rd St New York NY 10036

KAFKA, ANNE G., lawyer; b. Chgo., Oct. 25, 1920; d. Rudolf D. and Gertrude (Thomas) K. B.A., Oberlin Coll., 1941; LL.D., St. John's U., 1949. Bar: N.Y. 1949, U.S. Dist. Ct. (so. dist.) N.Y. 1950, U.S. Dist. Ct. (ea. dist.) N.Y. 1951, U.S. Ct. Appeals (2d cir.) 1953. Assoc. J.D. Edwards, N.Y.C., 1950-60, C.J. Jones, N.Y.C., 1960-65; ptnr. Jones & Kafka, Mineola, N.Y., 1965-73; sole practice, Patchogue, N.Y., 1973—. Active Suffolk County Democratic Women's Caucus, Hauppauge, N.Y., 1978-80. Recipient award for Excellence, Cleve. Bd. Edn., 1936. Mem. N.Y. State Trial Lawyers Assn., N.Y. County Lawyers Assn., Suffolk County Bar Assn., N.Y. Workers Compensation Bar Assn. (pres. 1976-78, bd. dirs. 1960-82). Democrat. Club: Young Dems., World Federalists.

KAGAN, HENYA, psychologist, educator, counselor; b. Schtetin, Poland, June 19, 1946; came to U.S., 1981; d. Itzhak Schtunzeiger and Adela Vax Friedman; m. Dan Klein, May 18, 1976 (div. 1988); children: Shai Ben-Zvi, Gili Klein (dec.); m. Norman I. Kagan, Aug. 26, 1988. BA in Psychology, Bar-Ilan U., Ramat-Gan Israel, 1975; MA in Counseling Psychology, U. Ill., 1984, PhD in Counseling Psychology, 1986. Psychologist Probation Svcs., Tel Aviv, 1974-75, Shiba Hosp., Ramat Gan, 1975-76; dir. Rehab. Ctr. for Handicapped, AshKelon, Israel, 1978-81; psychologist Psychol. Ednl. Svcs., Ash Kelon, 1978-81; intern counseling ctr. So. Ill. U., Carbondale, 1985-86; asst. prof. U. Ga., Athens, 1986-88, U. Houston, Clear Lake, Tex., 1988—; rsch. cons. emergency med. svc. of fire dept. City of Houston, 1988—. Contbr. articles to numerous publs. Mem. Compassionate Friends, Houston, 1990; vol. various community activities and svcs., 1988—. Grantee rsch. and tng. City of Houston, 1988—. Mem. Am. Psychol. Assn., Am. Psychol. Soc., Am. Ednl. Rsch. Assn., Tex. Psychol. Assn., Houston Psychol. Assn. Jewish.

KAGAWA, KATHLEEN HATSUYO, entrepreneur; b. Honolulu, June 9, 1952; d. Shinso and Jane Fumiko (Murata) K.; m. Masamichi Irimajiri (div. 1977). Student, U. Hawaii, Honolulu, 1970-73, Sophia U., Tokyo, 1973; BSBA, U. Beverly Hills, 1977, MBA, 1979, PhD in Internat. Bus., 1982. Mgr. Flipside Record Shop, Honolulu, 1969-70; producer, singer Victor Records, Tokyo, 1973-76; actress Hawaii Five-O, Honolulu, 1976; co-owner Images Internat. of Hawaii, Honolulu, 1976-79; v.p., sec., hostess East-West Connection TV Show, L.A., 1980-81; dir. pub. rels. Fendi, Beverly Hills, 1981-82; pres. Sky Prodns., Inc., Honolulu, 1982-86; v.p., treas. Born Internat., Inc., Honolulu, 1986-89; pres., dir. Mitsumine (USA) Co. Ltd. aka Chapman's Men's Wear aka Alfred Shaheen Stores, 1989—, Hawaii 5-O Properties, Inc., Honolulu, 1990—; adminstrv. exec., corp. sec. new Tokyo-Hawaii Restaurant Co., Ltd., 1981-89; cons. Schlossberg-Cassidy and Assoc., Washington, 1983-86; sponsor State of Hawaii Nat. Aquaculture Assn., Washington, 1983-86; admissions counselor U. Beverly Hills, Honolulu, 1984-86; pres. K & H Devel. Co., Ltd.; realtor Diamond Head Group subs. New Tokyo Restaurant, 1986, bd. dirs; sec.-treas. Azabu Enterprises Ltd., 1989-90, bd. dirs. Named Best in Backstroke, State of Hawaii Swim Competition, 1968. Mem. Gemological Inst. Am. Alumni Assn., Japan-Am. Soc. of Honolulu, Honolulu Bd. Realtors, Mortgage Broker Assn., Pacific and Asian Affairs Coun., Punahou Alumni Assn., Oahu Country Club. Baptist. Club: Oahu Country (Hawaii). Home: 3215 Kaohinani Dr Honolulu HI 96817

KAGEY, F(LORENCE) EILEEN, retired educator; b. Lima, Ohio, July 29, 1925; d. Joseph Leonard and Florence Elizabeth (Niles) K.; B.S. in Edn., Ball State U., 1952; M.S. in Edn., Ind. U., 1955. Sec., Gen. Electric Co., Ft. Wayne, Ind., 1943-45, 48-49, Farnsworth Telephone and Radio Corp., Ft. Wayne, 1945-48; H.A. Jeep prof. Ball State U., 1949-52; elem. tchr. Harmar Sch., Ft. Wayne, 1952-54, Emerson Sch., Gary, Ind., 1954-58, Sch. 52, Indpls., 1959-61, George Kuny Sch., Gary, 1961-90, ret.; sec. to v.p. Research and Rev. Service of Am., Indpls., 1958-59. Chmn. public relations Calumet Corner chpt. Sweet Adelines, Inc., Munster, Ind., 1980-82, mem., 1977—, bd. dirs., 1981-82. Mem. NEA (life), Am. Fedn. Tchrs. (bldg. rep. Local 4 1979-89), Ind. State Tchrs. Assn., Assn. Supervision and Curriculum Devel., Ind. Assn. Supervision and Curriculum Devel., AAUW (v.p. in-charge program), Kappa Delta Pi. Democrat. Roman Catholic. Author: (juvenile) Jeremy: the People-Dog, 1974. Home: 3040 W 39th Pl Gary IN 46408

KAGIWADA, HARRIET HATSUNE, engineering educator; b. Honolulu, Sept. 2, 1937; d. Kenjiro and Yakue Natsuyama; m. Reynold S. Kagiwada, Aug. 19, 1961; children: Julia, Conan. PhD, Kyoto U., 1963. Math. Rand Corp., Santa Monica, Calif., 1961-68, cons.; adj. assoc. prof. U. So. Calif.,

L.A., 1974-79; sr. scientist Hughes Aircraft Co., El Segundo, 1979-87; chief engr. Infotec Devel. Inc., Camarillo, 1987-89; prof. systems engring. Calif. State U., Fullerton, 1990—. Author: Invariant Imbedding and Time-Dependent Transport Processes, 1963, System Idenification: Methods and Applications, 1974, Integral Equations via Imbedding Equations, 1974, Multiple Scattering Processes: Inverse and Direst, 1975, Numerical Derivatives and Nonlinear Analysis, 1986. Mem. IEEE, Inst. Adv. Engring., Sigma Delta Epsilon (pres. 1990—). Office: Calif State U Fullerton CA 92634

KAHLOW, BARBARA FENVESSY, statistician; b. Chgo., June 26, 1946; d. Stanley John and Doris (Goodman) Fenvessy; m. Lloyd Fitch Reese, Dec. 6, 1969 (div. 1977); m. Allan Howard Young, Mar. 31, 1979 (div. 1982); m. Ronald Arthur Kahlow, Sept. 28, 1985 (sep.). BA, Vassar Coll., 1968. Statistician U.S. Govt./Dept. HEW, Nat. Ctr. Health Statistics, Rockville, Md., 1968-70, Nat. Ctr. for Ednl. Statistics, Washington, 1970-72, Exec. Office of Pres./Office of Mgmt. and Budget, Washington, 1972—. Author: Motor Vehicle Accident Deaths in the U.S.: 1950-69, 1970; contbr. articles to profl. jours. Recipient Quality Svc. award HEW, 1971, Spl. Performance award Office Mgmt. and Budget, 1982, 89; N.Y. State Regents scholar, 1964-68. Mem. Am. Statis. Assn., Foggy Bottom Assn., League of Rep. Women of D.C., Friends of the Kennedy Ctr., Smithsonian Assocs., Washington Vassar Club, Univ. Club Washington. Republican. Episcopalian. Home: 2555 Pennsylvania Ave NW Apt 404 Washington DC 20037 Office: Office Mgmt. & Budget 10235 NEOB Washington DC 20503

KAHN, BLOSSOM, motion picture executive; b. N.Y.C., Aug. 16, 1936; d. Jules Franklin and Anita Beatrice (Arkin) K.; B.A. in English, Hofstra Coll., Hempstead, N.Y., 1958; postgrad. Columbia U. Sch. Journalism, N.Y.C. Exec., story dept. Universal Pictures Corp., N.Y.C., 1963-64; head motion picture, TV and play depts. Curtis Brown Lit. Agy., N.Y.C., 1964-68; pres. Kahn-Penney Lit. Agy., Los Angeles, 1968-77; dir. creative affairs First Artists Prodns., Los Angeles, 1977-78; exec. in charge creative projects Avco-Embassy Pictures, Los Angeles, 1978-82; v.p. prodn. Zupnick Curtis Enterprises, Inc., Los Angeles, 1982-83; v.p. West Coast Packaging & Devel., Polymuse, Inc., 1983—; lectr. Sherwood Oaks Coll., Marymount Coll., Los Angeles. Mem. Women in Film, Women in Communication, Inc. Office: 208 S Beverly Dr Beverly Hills CA 90212

KAHN, FAITH-HOPE, nurse, adminstrator, writer; b. N.Y.C., Apr. 25, 1921; d. Leon and Hazel (Cook) Green; RN, Beth Israel Med. Center, N.Y.C., 1942; student N.Y. U., 1943; m. Edward Kahn, May 29, 1942; children: Ellen Leora, Faith Hope II, Paula Amy. First scrub operating room Beth Israel Hosp., N.Y.C., 1942; supr., operating room Hunts Point Gen. Hosp., 1942; gynecol. reconstrn. procedures researcher Phoenixville (Pa.) Gen. Hosp., 1943, Sydenham Hosp., N.Y.C., 1945; supr. ARC Disaster Field Hosp., Queens, N.Y., 1950-51; adminstr., mgr. team coordinator Dr. Edward Kahn, FACOG, Queens Village, N.Y., 1945—. Inventor, publicity chmn. Girl Scouts U.S.A., 1953; exec. dir. publicity Woodhull Schs., 1956-60, pres., 1961-62; exec. dir. publicity N.Y. Dept. Parks Figure Skating, 1956-70; exec. dir. publicity and applied arts St. John's Hosp., Smithtown, N.Y., 1965-66; state advisor N.Y., U.S. Congressional Adv. Bd., Washington, 1981—; nat. adv. bd. Am. Security Council, 1978—; founder Am. Security Found.; bd. trustees, Am. Police Hall of Fame and Mus., 1983—; mem. Republican Presdl. Task Force, 1986, Statue of Liberty and Ellis Island Centennial Commn., N.Y., 1986—. Recipient citation ARC, 1951, Am. Law Enforcement Officers Assn., Bronze medal Am. Security Council Ednl. Found., 1978, spl. recognition award Center Internat. Security Studies, 1979, Meml. Plate, Patriots of Am. Bicentennial, 1976, Great Seal of U.S.A. Plate, cert. Am. Sons Liberty, 1987, Good Smaritan award, 1987, Justice award Cross of Knights, 1987 Knights of Justice award, 1987; named Knight Chevalier Venerable Order of Michael the Archangel, 1987. Fellow, World Lit. Acad. (life), Acad. Nat. Law Enforcement (hon.); mem. Am. Acad. Ambulatory Nursing Adminstrn., Nurses Assn., Nat. League Nursing, Am. Coll. Obstetricians and Gynecologists, Nat. Assn. Physicians' Nurses, Nat. Critical Care Inst., Assn. Operating Room Nurses, AAAS, Nat. Assn. Female Execs., N.Y. Acad. Scis., Am. Police Acad. (cert. appreciation 1979, 83), Am. Fedn. Police, The Retired Officers Assn., Internat. Platform Assn., Security and Intelligence Found. (cert. appreciation 1986), Internat. Intelligence and Orgnd. Crime Investigators Assn., Smithtown Hist. Soc., Nat. Audubon Soc., NRA. Clubs: Tiyospaye, Paul Revere, Sterlingshire Woman's. Author, editor: The Easy Driving Way for Automatic and the Standard Shift, 1954; (with Edward Kahn) The Pelvic Examination, Outline and Guide for Residents, Internes and Students, 1954; (with Edward Kahn) Traction Hysterosalpingography for Uterine Lesions, 1949; contbr. articles profl. and lay jours. Home: 213 16 85th Ave Hollis Hills NY 11427-1324 Office: 213 16 85th Ave Queens Village NY 11427

KAHN, KATHY, writer, photographer; b. Seattle, Apr. 2, 1945; d. Robert Arthur Moody and Donna (Green) Kelly; children: Simon Peter, Jesse MacDougall. Author: Hillbilly Women, 1973 ; Fruits of Our Labor, 1982. Playwright: The Contest, 1983. Contbr. articles and photographs to internat. mags.; photographic exhbns. Seattle, N.Y.C., Moscow, Leningrad. RecipientMademoiselle Woman of the Yr., 1974; NEH grantee, 1981. Mem. PEN. Home: 151 1st Ave #4R New York NY 10003 Studio: 974 Paseo la Cresta Chula Vista CA 92010-6727

KAHN, LESLIE RUTH, service executive; b. N.Y.C., Jan. 15, 1947; d. Murrey and Florence (Marine) Kahn; child from previous marriage: Steven Craig Ringelheim; m. John Schwartz. AAS, N.Y. Tech. Coll., N.Y.C., 1972; BA, CUNY, 1981. Adminstr. coll. dentistry NYU, N.Y.C., 1967-71; dental hygienist Dr. Steven S. Baron, DDS, Rego Park, N.Y., 1974-79; office mgr. Dr. Jerome Levine, DDS, N.Y.C., 1973-74; dental hygienist Dr. Steven S. Baron, DDS, Rego Park, N.Y., 1974-78; pres. Craig Med. and Dental Pers. Agy., Inc., N.Y.C., 1980—; adj. lectr. CUNY Med. Assts. Sch., 1981, Greater N.Y. Dental Meeting, 1980-86; cons. in field. Contbr. articles to profl. jours. Recipient Academic Excellence award Health Edn. Mem. N.Y. State Dental Hygiene Soc. (hons.), Fla. State Dental Hygienist Soc., Fla. Dental Soc. Office: Craig Pers Agy Inc 25 W 43d St Ste 405 New York NY 10036

KAHN, LINDA ANNE, small business owner; b. Johannesburg, Republic of South Africa, June 21, 1949; came to U.S., 1980; d. Julius and Gita Freda (Katz) Sasto; m. David Kahn, Mar. 22, 1970; children: Robyn, Paul. Student, U. Witwatersrand, Johannesburg, 1967-68; BS in Beauty Therapy, Clinique Valerie, Johannesburg, 1977. Beauty therapist Linda Beauty, Johannesburg, 1977-80; owner, beauty therapist Beauty Kliniek, San Diego, 1983—. Home: 5928 Eton Ct San Diego CA 92122 Office: Beauty Kliniek 3268 Governor Dr San Diego CA 92122

KAHN, LINDA MCCLURE, maritime industry executive; b. Jacksonville, Fla.; d. George Calvin and Myrtice Louise (Boggs) McClure; m. Paul Markham Kahn, May 20, 1968. B.S. with high honors, U. Fla.; M.S., U. Mich., 1964. Actuarial trainee N.Y. Life Ins. Co., N.Y.C., 1964-66, actuarial asst., 1966-69, asst. actuary, 1969-71; v.p., actuary US Life Ins., Pasadena, Calif., 1972-74; mgr. Coopers & Lybrand, Los Angeles, 1974-76, sr. cons., San Francisco, 1976-82; dir. program mgmt. Pacific Maritime Assn., San Francisco, 1982—. Bd. dirs. Pacific Heights Residents Assn., sec.-treas., 1981; trustee ILWU-PMA Welfare Plan, SIU-PD-PMA Pension and Supplemental Benefits Plans, 1982-90, Seafarers Med. Ctr., 1982-90, others. Fellow Soc. Actuaries, Conf. Actuaries in Pub. Practice; mem. Internat. Actuarial Assn. (chmn. subcom. on minority recruiting 1988—), Internat. Assn. Cons. Actuaries, Actuarial Studies Non-Life Ins., Am. Acad. Actuaries, Western Pension Conf. (newsletter editor 1983-85, sec. 1985-88, treas. 1989—), Actuarial Club Pacific States, San Francisco Actuarial Club (pres. 1981), Met. Club, Commonwealth Club, Soroptimists Club (v.p. 1973-74). Home: 2430 Pacific Ave San Francisco CA 94115 Office: Pacific Maritime Assn 635 Sacramento St San Francisco CA 94111

KAHN, MELISSA JAN, lawyer; b. N.Y.C., Dec. 31, 1956; d. Phillip and Ruthe (Rosenzweig) K.; m. Michael Feinstein, June 16, 1985; 1 child, Meryl Jordan Feinstein. BA, Cornell U., 1979; JD, Georgetown U., 1982. Staff atty. Pension Benefit Guaranty Corp., Washington, 1982-84; assoc. Skadden, Arps, Slate, Meagher & Flom, N.Y.C., 1984-85; v.p. Equitable Life Assurance Soc. U.S., N.Y.C., 1986—. Bd. dirs. Martin Feinstein Meml. Cancer Rsch. Found., Deer Park, N.Y., 1986-90. Mem. Fed. Bar Assn., N.Y. State Bar Assn., D.C. Bar Assn., Assn. Pvt. Pension and Welfare Plans (bd. dirs. 1988—), NAM (vice chmn. pension com. 1989—), Employee Retirement Income Security Act Industry Com. (retirement savs. com. 1986—), NOW, Sierra Club. Democrat. Jewish. Office: Equitable Life Assurance 200 Plaza Dr Secaucus NJ 07096

KAHN, NANCY VALERIE, publishing company executive, consultant; b. N.Y.C., Dec. 15, 1952; d. Alfred Joseph and Miriam (Kadin) K. BA magna cum laude, Princeton U., 1974. Dir. prodn. and devel. Bus. Rsch. Publs., Inc.-MacRAE's Directories, N.Y.C., 1984-86; assoc. pub., exec. editor Monitor Pub. Co., N.Y.C., 1987-88; dir. new product devel. Gale Rsch. Inc., N.Y.C., 1988-89; editorial dir. directories and info. devel. A/S/M Communications/Adweek, N.Y.C., 1989—. Univ. scholar Princeton U., 1974. Mem. Info. Industry Assn., N.Y. Directory Pubs. Assn., Washington Directory Assn., Princeton Club. Democrat. Office: A/S/M Communications/Adweek 49 E 21 St New York NY 10010

KAHN, SUSAN BETH, artist; b. N.Y.C., Aug. 26, 1924; d. Jesse B. and Jenny Carol (Peshkin) Cohen; m. Joseph Kahn, Sept. 15, 1946 (dec.); m. Richard Rosenkranz, Feb. 1, 1981. Grad., Parsons Sch. Design, 1945; pupil, Moses Soyer, 1950-57. Subject of: book Susan Kahn, with an essay by Lincoln Rothschild, 1980; One-man shows Sagittarius Gallery, 1960, A.C.A., Galleries, 1964, 68, 71, 76, 80, Charles B. Goddard Art Center, Ardmore, Okla., 1973, Albrecht Gallery Mus. Art, St. Joseph, Mo., 1974, N.Y. Cultural Center, N.Y.C., 1974, St. Peter's Coll., Jersey City, 1978, Heidi Neuhoff Gallery, N.Y.C., 1989; exhibited in group shows Audubon Artists, N.Y.C., Nat. Acad., N.Y.C., Springfield (Mass.) Mus., City Center, N.Y.C., A.C.A., Galleries, N.Y.C., Nat. Arts Club, N.Y.C., Butler Inst., Youngstown, Ohio, Islip Art Mus., East Islip. N.Y., 1989, Fine Arts Mus. of S., Mobile, Ala., 1989, Chatanooga Regional History Mus, 1989, Longview (Tex.) Mus. Art, 1989, ; represented in permanent collections, Tyler (Tex.) Mus., St. Lawrence U. Mus., Canton, N.Y., Fairleigh Dickinson U. Mus., Rutherford, N.J., Syracuse U. Mus., Sheldon Swope Gallery, Terre Haute, Ind., Montclair (N.J.) Mus. Fine Arts, Butler Inst. Am. Art, Youngstown, Ohio, Reading (Pa.) Mus., Albrecht Gallery Mus. Art, St. Joseph(Mo.), Cedar Rapids (Iowa) Art Center, N.Y. Cultural Center, N.Y.C., Edwin A. Ulrich Mus., Wichita, Kans., Wichita State U., Johns Hopkins Sch. Advanced Internat. Studies, Washington, Joslyn Mus., Omaha, U. Wyo., Laramie. Recipient Knickerbocker prize for best religious painting, 1956; Edith Lehman award Nat. Assn. Women Artists, 1958; Simmons award, 1961; Knickerbocker Artists award, 1961; Nat. Arts Club award, 1967; Knickerbocker Medal of Honor, 1964; Famous Artists Sch. award, 1967. Mem. Nat. Assn. Women Artists (Anne Barnett Meml. prize 1981, Solveig Stromsoe Palmer Meml. award 1987, Dorothy Schweitzer award 1990), Artists Equity, Met. Mus., Mus. Modern Art, Nat. Assn. Women Artists (meml. award 1987).

KAHN, TRACY LYNN, botanist; b. Ann Arbor, Mich., May 13, 1955; d. Raymond Henry and Judith Annette (Braden) K.; m. Norman C. Ellstrand, July 2, 1983; 1 child, Nathan. BS in Botany, U. Mich., 1977; PhD in Botany, U. Calif., Riverside, 1987. Lab. dir. Hickerson Flowers Inc., Apopka, Fla., 1977-81; rsch. asst. botany dept. U. Calif., Riverside, 1981-87; NIH postdoctoral fellow genetics dept. U. Calif., Berkeley, 1987-88; postdoctoral fellow U. Calif., Riverside, 1988—; mem. faculty U. Redlands, Calif., 1990—. Mem. Bot. Soc. Am., Toastmasters. Home: 1402 Everton Pl Riverside CA 92507 Office: U Calif Dept Botany Riverside CA 92521

KAHRS, CYNTHIA ANNE, special education teacher; b. Sterling, Colo., Jan. 1, 1948; d. Walter Henry and Bernice Beatta (Klein) K. AA, Northeastern Jr. Coll., Sterling, 1969; BA, U. No. Colo., 1971, MA in Spl. Edn., 1977; Learning Disabled endorsement, Western State Coll., Gunnison, Colo., 1975. Cert. tchr., Colo., Wyo. Spl. edn. tchr. Anna Pettis Sch., Sterling, 1970-71; resource tchr. Buchanan Jr. High Sch., Wray, Colo., 1972-73; spl. edn. tchr. Casper (Wyo.) Elem. Sch., Lone Star Sch., Otis, Colo., 1975-77, Wheatland (Wyo.) Jr. High Sch., 1978-90. Mem. Wyo. Edn. Assn., Platte County Edn. Assn., Coun. Exceptional Children, Assn. Univ. Women (sec. 1988-89). Home: 909 14th St Wheatland WY 82201

KAHRS, SUSAN KIMBERLEY, process development scientist; b. Montclair, N.J., July 16, 1963; d. Jack and June Elizabeth (Stieve) K. BS in Molecular Biology, Lehigh U., 1985; MS in Microbiology, Rutgers U., 1987, postgrad., 1990—. Rsch. scientist Hoffmann-LaRoche Inc., Nutley, N.J., 1987-88; scientist Hoffmann-LaRoche Inc., Belleville, N.J., 1988—. Contbr. articles to profl. jours. Mem. AAAS, Am. Soc. for Microbiology, Theobald Smith Soc. of N.J. Home: 24 Kitchell Rd Denville NJ 07834 Office: Hoffman-LaRoche 111 Franklin Ave Belleville NJ 07011

KAIA, MARILYN JOLOYCE, flower grower; b. Magnolia, Minn., Aug. 9, 1933; d. Loran Byron and Jessie Luella (Remme) Hunter; m. Newton Kekahio, 1955 (div. 1969); adopted children: Shawn Kekahio Labrador, Newton K., Tanya Kekahio Rennoe, Hunter Kea; m. John Francis Kenolio Kaia, July 4, 1974. Student, Grays Harbor Jr. Coll., 1951-52, U. Hawaii, 1958-60, U. Humanistic Studies, 1980-82. Office mgr. Robert Yee Constrn., Honolulu, 1970-75, Kaua Kea Kottages, Hana, Hawaii, 1977-78; mem. office staff Hana Maui Hotel, 1976-77, Helani Gardens, Hana, 1978-87; co-owner, mgr. Kaia Ranch & Co., Hana, 1976—; owner, bed and breakfast hostess Volcano (Hawaii) Heart Chalet, 1970—; part-time tchr., Waianae (Hawaii) High Sch., 1960-63. Bd. dirs., sec. Hana Soil and Water Conservation Dist., 1978-89. Mem. Heleconia Soc. Internat., Hana Flower Growers Assn., Univ. Extension Svc., Am. Bed and Breakfast Assn., Inn Rev. Republican. Home: PO Box 404 Hana HI 96713 Office: Kaia Ranch & Co Ulaino Rd Hana HI 96713

KAIDO, BONNELL DOLORES, medical education administrator; b. Cooperstown, N.Y., Dec. 5, 1951; d. Samuel Wellington and Bernadette Elizabeth (Rafferty) K. AAS in Bus., SUNY, 1972; BS in Bus., Coll. of St. Rose, 1974; MS in Edn., U. Albany, 1978. Bus. educator Sharon Springs Cen. Sch., 1975-80; supr. The Mary Imogene Bassett Hosp., Cooperstown, 1980-82, coord. med. edn., 1982-86, asst. dir. med. edn., 1986—; mem. occupation edn. adv. com. Mohawk Valley Community Coll., Utica, 1986—, svcs. com. Assn. for Hosp. Med. Edn., 1989—; office tech. adv. com. SUNY-Cobleskill, 1988—; dir. Med. Alumni Assn. MIBH, Cooperstown, 1988—; speaker Assn. Hosp. Med. Edn. Spring Inst., 1988-90, N.J. Assn. Med. Edn. New Directions in Med. Edn., 1988, N.J. Med. Soc., Coun. Adminstrn. Direct in Med. Edn. Workshop, 1986, 89, chmn.-elect, 1988—; EMS officer, EMT lab instr. Otsego County Emergency Svcs.; instr. N.Y. CTC. Mem. program com. Am. Lung Assn. Mid. N.Y., Utica, 1987—, Otsego EMS Coun.; CPR inst. ARC. Mem. Delta Kappa Gamma, Delta Pi Epsilon. Democrat. Roman Catholic. Office: The Mary Imogene Bassett Hosp One Atwell Rd Cooperstown NY 13326

KAIGE, ALICE TUBB, retired librarian; b. Obion, Tenn., Jan. 27, 1922; d. George Easley and Lucile (Merryman) Tubb; m. Richard H. Kaige, Aug., 1952; children: Robert H., Richard C., John S. BA, Vanderbilt U., 1944; BS in Libr. Sci., Geo. Peabody Coll., 1947. Libr. Martin (Tenn.) High Sch., 1946-47, Demonstration Sch. Geo. Peabody Coll. Joint U. Librs., Nashville, Tenn., 1947-52; acquisitions libr. Lincoln Libr., Springfield, Ill., 1967-70; office coord. Springfield (Ill.) Chpt. ACLU, 1974; staff rep. Am. Fed. State, County & Mcpl. Employees, Springfield, 1975; libr. Ill. Dept. of Commerce and Community Affairs, Springfield, 1976-89. Vice chmn. Women's Internat. League for Peace and Freedom, 1969-70, various coms., 1970—; treas. Cen. Ill. Women's Lobby, 1971-72; com. on local govt. League of Women Voters, 1973-76; career day com. Urban League Guild, 1970-71; mem. NAACP,steering com. Springfield chpt. ACLU, 1974-75; co-founder West Side Neighborhood Assn., Springfield, 1977. Recipient Elizabeth Cady Stanton award, Springfield Women's Political Caucus, 1982. Mem. Sangamon County Hist. Soc., NOW, Women's Internat. League for Peace and Freedom, War Resisters League, LWV, Springfield Women's Polit. Caucus. Home: 701 S State St Springfield IL 62704

KAIREY, MINDY SUE, gerontological health care specialist; b. L.I., N.Y., Jan. 12, 1963; d. Jules and Selma Jone (Raisler) K.; m. David Robert Manion, June 21, 1987. BS, Pa. State U., State College, 1985; MPA Health Svcs. Adminstrn., U. So. Calif., 1987, MS in Gerontology, 1987. Project dir. Andrus Gerontology Ctr. U. So. Calif., L.A., 1985-87; fellow Blue Cross & Blue Shield Assn., Chgo., 1987-88; mgr. older adult program devel. MacNeal Hosp., Berwyn, Ill., 1988-89; cons. Mercer Meidinger Hansen, Chgo., 1989—. Vol. Ill. Dept. Children and Family Svcs., Chgo., 1988—; mem. adv. coun. Ill. Dept. of Aging, Chgo., 1988-89, Coun. on Aging Long Term Care Task Force, Cicero, Ill., 1988-89. Recipient rsch. assistantship NIH, 1985, 86. Mem. Am. Pub. Health Assn., Am. Coll. Health Execs., Gerontol. Soc. Am. Home: 850 N State St #23C Chicago IL 60610 Office: William M Mercer Inc 10 S Wacker Dr Chicago IL 60606

KAISER, ANN PHILOMENA, special education professor; b. Ellinwood, Kans., Mar. 1, 1948; d. John Fredrick and Loretta Marie (Achatz) K. BS, Kans. State U., 1970; MA, U. Kans., 1973, PhD, 1974. NIH post-doctoral fellow U. Kans., Lawrence, Kans., 1974-75; rsch. assoc. U. Kans., Lawrence, 1975-82; assoc. prof. Vanderbilt U., Nashville, 1982-88, prof., 1988—; rsch. scientist Vanderbilt U. Kennedy Ctr., Nashville, 1982—; chair Dept. Spl. Edn. Vanderbilt U., Nashville, 1984-86; cons. Office of Spl. Edn. Projects-U.S. Dept. Edn., 1988—. Editor: Ecological Perspectives, 1978, Teaching Functional Language, 1983, Preparing Personnel to Work With Persons With Severe Disabilities, 1990, Journal of Assn. for Persons With Severe Handicaps; contbr. articles to profl. jours. Named Educator of Yr., Assn. for Retarded Citizens, 1989; recipient of over 15 grants from state and fed. agys. Fellow Am. Psychol. Assn.; mem. Coun. on Exceptional Children, Assn. for Persons With Severe Handicaps. Office: Dept Spl Edn Vanderbilt U 303 MRL Peabody Nashville TN 37203

KAISER, ANTOINETTE PERRONE, communications executive; b. Pittston, Pa., Feb. 22, 1935; d. Rosario Peter and Annunziata Clementina (Franco) Perrone; m. Robert G. Kaiser, June 22, 1969 (dec. Feb. 1979); 1 child, Kyle Kaiser Swiat. BS in Bus., Empire State Coll., Buffalo, 1984. Asst. mgr. Marine Midland Bank, N.A., Tonawanda, N.Y., 1969-72; dist. ops. officer Marine Midland Bank, N.A., Buffalo, 1972-73, br. ops. officer, 1973-76; gen. mgr. STI-CO Industries, Inc., Buffalo, 1976-79, pres., chief exec. officer, 1979—. Apptd. to def. adv. panel Gov. Mario Cuomo, 1990. Fellow Radio Club of Am.; mem. Am. Prodn. and Inventory Control Soc., Assn. PUb. Safety Communications Officers (comml. adv. com.). Office: STI-CO Industries Inc 11 Cobham Dr PO Box 656 Orchard Park NY 14127

KAISER, JOYCE ANN, government official; b. Jersey City, Aug. 30, 1939; d. Frederick and Louise (Feary) Neebling; m. Gordon Allen Biddle, Sept. 21, 1963 (div. 1974); 1 dau., Adrienne Louise; m. Dennis Lee Kaiser, June 5, 1975 (div. Dec. 1983); m. Burt S. Barnow, July 18, 1987. A.A., Coll. San Mateo, 1959; B.A., Calif. State U.-San Francisco, 1961. With Employment Devel. Dept., Sacramento, Calif., 1965-80; owner Adrienne's Furniture, Davis, Calif., 1975-80; personnel dir. Reagan Transition Team, Washington, 1980-81; exec. asst. to asst. sec. Employment and Tng., Washington, 1981-82, adminstr. policy and research, 1981-82; assoc. asst. sec. of labor Employment and Tng. Adminstrn., Washington, 1982-85; asst. dir. Office Internat. Tng., AID, Washington, 1985—; rep. Nat. Commn. on Employment Policy, Washington, 1981-83. Republican. Presbyterian. Office: AID SA-16 Suite 201 Washington DC 20523

KAISER, KAREN ELIZABETH, advertising agency executive; b. Scottsbluff, Nebr., Feb. 20, 1957; d. William Gerhard and Sally Ann (Porter) K. BA in Communication, U. Minn., 1981. Pres., owner Toucan Unltd., St. Paul, 1983-88; coord. new bus. Clarity Coverdale Rueff Advt., Mpls., 1988-89, mgr. mktg. resources, 1989—; pub. speaker Am. Soc. Interior Decorators, also various ednl. groups, 1988—. Vol. spl. event Children's Home Soc., St. Paul, 1990. Mem. Minn. Advt. Fedn. Office: Clarity Coverdale Rueff 415 1st Ave N Minneapolis MN 55401

KAISER, MARY AGNES, chemist, chemical company executive; b. Pittston, Pa., June 11, 1948; d. Fredolin Anthony and Agnes Regina (Searfoss) K.; m. Cecil Dybowski, May 11, 1979; 1 child, Marta. BS, Wilkes Coll., 1970; MS, St. Joseph's U., Phila., 1972; PhD in Chemistry, Villanova (Pa.) U., 1976. Postdoctorate U. Ga., Athens, 1976-77; research chemist E.I Du Pont De Nemours & Co., Wilmington, Del., 1977-79, supr. research, 1979-86, sr. supr., 1986—. Co-Author: Environmental Problem Solving Using Gas and Liquid Chromatography, 1982; contbr. articles to profl. jours. Mem. Am. Chem. Soc. (chmn. div. analytical chemistry), Fedn. Analytical Chemistry and Spectros Copy Soc. (chmn. governing bd.), Chromatography Forum (chmn.), Sigma Xi (research recognition award 1970), Phi Kappa Phi. Office: DuPont Co Engring Test Ctr PO Box 6094 Newark DE 19714-6094

KAISER, MARY KISTER, research psychologist; b. St. Charles, Mo., Oct. 25, 1956; d. Robert Paul and Mary Virginia (Jost) Kister; m. Franz Nicholas Kaiser, June 21, 1980; 1 child, Alexander Dierich. BA, U. Va., 1977, MA, 1980, PhD, 1982. NIMH postdoctoral fellow U. Mich., Ann Arbor, 1982-84; rsch. psychologist Ames Rsch. Ctr. NASA, Moffett Field, Calif., 1985-89, prin. scientist Ames Rsch. Ctr., 1989—. Cons. editor Jour. of Exptl. Psychology: Human Perception and Performance; contbr. articles to profl. jours. Fellow NSF, 1979-82. Mem. Assn. for Rsch. in Vision and Ophthalmology, Psychonomic Soc., Western Psychol. Assn., Internat. Soc. Ecol. Psychology, N.Y. Acad. Scis. Office: NASA Ames Rsch Ctr Mail Stop 262-3 Moffett Field CA 94035

KAISH, OLGA M., guidance counselor; b. Pitts., Dec. 26, 1927; m. J. Edward Kaish, Aug. 4, 1956; children: Mark Alan, Terri, Todd Alexander, Tanya. BA, Chatham Coll., 1949; MA, Syracuse U., 1956. Cert. secondary tchr., guidance counselor, N.Y. English tchr. Longville (Minn.) Cen. High Sch., 1950-51, Bemidji (Minn.) High Sch., 1951-52; resident dir. Syracuse (N.Y.) U., 1954-56, vocat. counselor women, 1967-70; jr. high sch. counselor Syracuse City Schs., 1956-58; 060 elem. sch. counselor, Solvay (N.Y.) Schs., 1970-76; job placement counselor BOCES Adult Edn. Program, Liverpool, N.Y., 1976-79; high sch. counselor Phoenix (N.Y.) Cen. High Sch., 1979—; cons. Regional Learning Svc., Syracuse. Organizer Camillus (N.Y.) Teen Outreach Program, 1970. Capt. USMC, 1952-56. Mem. AAUW (pres. 1972-74), ASTD, Internat. Tng. Communications (pres. 1982-83), Cen. N.Y. Assn. Children with Learning Disabilities (pres.), N.Y. State Counselors Assn., Oswego County Tchr. Ctr. (v.p., 1987—), Inst. Tng. in Communications (v.p. program, 1989—), Women Marines Assn. (pres. 1986-87). Episcopalian. Home: 102 Southwest Way Camillus NY 13031-1209 Office: John C Bridlebough High Sch 470 Main St Phoenix NY 13135

KAJI, HIDEKO KATAYAMA, pharmacologist; b. Tokyo, Jan. 1, 1932; came to U.S., 1954; d. Sakae and Tsuneko (Matsuda) Katayama; m. Akira Kaji, Aug. 23, 1958; children: Kenneth, Eugene, Naomi, Amy. BS, Tokyo Coll. Pharmacy, 1954; MS, U. Nebr., 1956; PhD, Purdue U., 1958. Vis. scientist Oak Ridge (Tenn.) Nat. Lab., 1962-63; assoc. U. Pa., Phila., 1963-64; rsch. assoc. The Inst. Cancer Rsch., Phila., 1965-66, asst. mem., 1966-76; vis. mem. Max Planck Inst. Molek. Gen., Berlin, 1972-73, Nat. Inst. Med. Rsch., London, 1973; assoc. prof. Jefferson Med. Coll., Phila., 1976-82; vis. prof. Wistar Inst., Phila., 1984-85; prof. pharmacology, molecular and devel. biology, oncogenesis Jefferson Med. Coll., Phila., 1983—; cons. Nippon Paint Co., Ltd., Tokyo, 1990—, Coatesville (Pa.) VA Hosp., 1982-84. Contbr. articles to profl. jours. Fellow NIH (bd. dirs. 1986-89); mem. Am. Soc. Biochemistry and Molecular Biology, Am. Soc. Pharmacol. and Exptl. Therapeutics, Am. Soc. Microbiology, Sigma Xi. Home: 334 Fillmore St Philadelphia PA 19111 Office: Jefferson Med Coll 1020 Locust St Philadelphia PA 19107-6799

KAKAC, KIM ANNETTE, nurse; b. Kirksville, Mo., Dec. 19, 1962; d. Carroll Conrad and Karen Joyce (Corbin) K. BSN, SIUE, Edwardsville, Ill., 1982-88. Life guard, cashier Fairfield Park Dist., Ill., 1981-84, asst. pool mgr., 1985; nurses aide Way Fair Restorium, Fairfield, Ill., 1984-86; student nurse intern Jefferson Barracks Vet. Hosp., St. Louis, Mo.; registered nurse Barnes Hosp., St. Louis, 1988--. Mem. Nat. Student Nurses Assn. Republican. Home: 4205 Ellenwood Apt 202 Saint Louis MO 63116 Office: Barnes Hosp Barnes Hosp Pla Saint Louis MO 63109

KAKASCIK, JOAN, psychologist; b. Passaic, N.J., Jan. 14, 1941; d. John Stephen and Mary (Chowka) K. BA, Paterson State Coll., 1962; MA, Syracuse U., 1964; EdD, Boston U., 1975; postgrad. coll., U.S. Army Command & Gen. Staff, 1981-84. Lic. psychologist, N.J.; cert. sch. psychologist, N.J. Asst. to dean of women Ohio State U., Columbus, 1964-66; dir. internat. student project Greater Boston YMCA, 1967-68; dean of women Curry Coll., Milton, Mass., 1968-72; psychologist Cen. Bergen Community Mental Health Ctr., Paramus, Mass., 1975-77; prin. clin.

psychologist N.J. Dept. Devel. Disabilities, South Orange, N.J., 1978—; chair N.J. Psychology Adv. Com., Trenton, 1986-88. Author: Picture Cookbook, 1980, I.E.P. Resource Package-Social/Emotional Development, 1981, Boston: International Visitors' Guide, 1968. Commr Bergen County Commn. on Status of Women, Hackensack, N.J., 1989—; appointee Gov.'s Commn. Sci. Advisors, Trenton. Lt. col. USNG, 1974—. Recipient N.J. State Senate Resolution, 1977, Twin award Trenton YWCA, 1984. Mem. N.J. Psychol. Assn. (com. chair 1989-90), East Bergen Bus. & Profl. Women (v.p. 1989-91), Am. Psychol. Assn., Assn. Mil. Surgeons-US, N.J. Fedn. Bus. & Profl. Women (planning com. 1990-91), Nat. Guard Assn. NJ (pres. 1989-91), Lt. Daniel W. Lee Armor Assn. (charter). Home: 18 Weller Terr Saddle Brook NJ 07662 Office: NJ Dept Devel Disabilities 76 S Orange Ave South Orange NJ 07079

KALAHAR, PATRICIA ANN, real estate executive; b. Algona, Iowa, Sept. 13, 1956; d. Donald Morris and Shirley LaVonne (Olson) K. AA, Black Hawk Jr. Coll., Moline, Ill., 1975; BS, Iowa State U., 1977; MA, Drake U., 1986. Field dir. Iowa Rep. Central Com., Des Moines, 1978-79; assoc. dir. devel. Graceland Coll., Lamoni, Iowa, 1979-81; dir. devel. Marion High Sch., Omaha, 1981-82; lobbyist, dir. pub. relations Iowa Credit Union League, Des Moines, 1982-84; exec. dir. U.S. Nat. Hot Air Balloon Championship, Indianola, Iowa, 1984-85; exec. v.p. Iowa Homebuilders Assn., Des Moines, 1985-86; mktg. dir. Gen. Growth Co., Des Moines, 1986-87; pub. affairs specialist U.S. Dept. Agr., Des Moines, 1987-89; realtor Baird & Warner Real Estate, Hinsdale, Ill., 1989—; cons. Des Moines Area Community Coll., Ankeny, Iowa, 1985—. Editor: Grandma Olson's Country Cooking, 1988; contbr. articles to profl. publs. Mem. Nat. Assn. Realtors, Ill. Assn. Realtors, DuPage County Assn. Realtors. Republican. Methodist. Home: 2821 Windsor #109 Lisle IL 60532 Office: Baird & Warner Real Estate 108 S Washington Hinsdale IL 60521

KALAYJIAN, ANIE SANENTZ, educator, consultant, psychotherapist; b. Aleppo, Syria; came to U.S., 1971; d. Kevork and Zabelle (Mardikian) K.; m. Shahé Navasart Sanentz, Dec. 16, 1984. BS L.I. U., 1979; MEd, Columbia U., 1981, EdD, 1985, profl. nurses tng. course, 1984; cert. photography, Pratt Inst., 1979. R.N., N.Y. Psychiat. nurse Met. Hosp., N.Y.C., 1979-84; staff psychiat. mental health nurse Manhattan Bowery Project, N.Y.C., 1978-86; instr. Hunter Coll., N.Y.C., 1980-82; prof. Bloomfield Coll., N.J., 1984-85; lectr. Jersey City Coll., 1985; prof. Seton Hall U., South Orange, N.J., 1985-87, grad. program St. Joseph Coll., 1987—. Active com. for presdl. task force on nursing curriculum Soc. for Traumatic Stress Studies; East coast coord. Mental Health Outreach to Earthquake Survivors in Armenia. Recipient Clark Found. scholarship award, 1985; Endowed Nursing Edn., Columbia U., scholar, 1984; Armenian Relief Soc. scholar, 1976-77, Armenian Students Assn. Am. scholar, 1976-78. Fellow Coun. on Continuing Edn., Am. Orthopsychiat. Assn., N.Y. State Nursing Assn. (planning com. nursing edn.); mem. Psychiat. and Mental Health Nursing (coun.), Inst. for Psychodynamics and Origins of Mind, Armenian Students Assn. (treas. 1980-81, pres. 1981-83, scholarship chairperson 1983-85, v.p. Cen. Exec. Com. 1987-88, pres. 1988-89, elected nat. pres. 1988—), Armenian-Am. Soc. for Studies (founder, pres. 1988—), N.Y. Registered Nurses' Assn. (chairperson edn. com.), Kappa Delta Pi (advisor 1989-90), Sigma Theta Tau. Avocations: aerobics; photography; acting. Office: 130 W 79th St New York NY 10024

KALB, MARY ANN, real estate broker; b. Mpls., Apr. 5, 1926; d. Merrill and Annabel (Foss) Hutchinson; m. George L. Kalb, Jan. 4, 1947; children: Merrill Kalb Watrous, Lewis P. BS, U. Nebr., Omaha, 1967. Mem. sales staff Chesley & Alloway Realtors, Medford, N.J., 1970-72, mng. broker, 1972-87; mng. broker Hoopes Better Homes and Gardens Realtor, Medford, 1987-89, B. Gary Scott, Realtors, Medford, 1989—. Pres. Medford Bus. Assn., 1978. Mem. Cert. Residential Brokers, Burlington Bd. Realtors (bd. dirs. 1984-90, pres. 1990), LWV (pres. Medford chpt. 1972-74, chmn. Burlington County coun. 1978), AAUW. Episcopalian. Office: B Gary Scott Realtors 510 Stokes Rd Medford NJ 08055

KALCHBRENNER, THELSEN MARJORIE, small business owner; b. Chgo., Dec. 4, 1936; d. James Russell and Thelsen Clara (Hauk) Hoffheimer; divorced; children: Lori Thelsen, Russell John. Grad. high sch., Chgo. Sec. Continental Bank of Ill., Chgo., 1953-55, Raynor Lithographing, Chgo., 1956-58; adminstrv. and exec. sec. Delta Advt., Chgo., 1974-82; owner, pres., mgr. T.J. Investments and Thelsen Enterprises doing bus. as Fair Muffler Shops, Loves Park, Ill., 1984—. Mem. Loves Park/Machesney Park C. of C. (bd. dirs.). Roman Catholic. Club: YWCA. Lodge: KC. Home: 4555 Trevor Circle Rockford IL 61109 Office: Fair Muffler Shops 130 E Riverside Blvd Loves Park IL 61111

KALE, BARBARA ALICE, social services administrator; d. Leon Ray Lewis and Frances Charlotte (Rohrback) Shearin; m. Corridon Stuart Kale, June 17, 1961 (div. 1987); children: Mark Douglas, Richard Stuart, James Edward, Robin Nadine. BA, U. Wash., Seattle, 1961; MBA, Coll. St. Thomas, St. Paul, 1988. Dir. Speech & Hearing Svcs., Jamestown, N.D., 1972-84; acting dir. Metro Work Ctr., Mpls., 1987-89; exec. dir. Midway Tng. Svcs., St. Paul, 1989—. Bd. Dir. Alpha Opportunities Jamestown, 1983-84; Administrv. Bd. Rosemount United Methodist Ch. Rosemount Minn., 1989. Mem. Nat. Assn. Female Exec. Rep. Protestant. Home: 4549 Lake Park Dr Eagan MN 55122

KALEDO, GRACE LUCILLE, public relations executive; b. Adrian, Mich., Dec. 17, 1928; d. Everett Ray and Ethel (Moore) Deken; student Adrian schs.; m. Charles Gordon Kaledo, June 22, 1946; children: Mary Lou Kaledo Mitchell, Kathryn Sue Kaledo DeMeritt, Larry Michael. Editor, publisher Lenawee Tribune, Adrian, 1968-74; pub. rels. with community svcs. dept. City of Adrian, 1975-79; adminstrv. dir. Croswell Opera House, Adrian, 1983-86, devel. cons.; ptnr. Catalyst Promotions. Past mem. continuing edn. com. Adrian Coll.; bd. dirs. Southeast Travel & Tourism Commn.; co-chmn. Lenawee Heritage Festival; Croswell Players; past pres. Greater Adrian Inter Club Coun.; mem. operational support and outreach com. Mich. Coun. Arts; active Trenton Hills United Brethren Ch. Recipient Outstanding Community Svc. award Adrian Kiwanis, 1971, Svc. to Youth award, 1973. Mem. NAFE, Nat. Fedn. Press Women, League Historic Am. Theatres, Nat. Writers Club, Lenawee C. of C. (travel and tourism com., Maple Leaf award 1986), Mich. Press Women, Civitan (Lenawee), Zonta. Home and Office: 4555 S Mission Rd #525 Tucson AZ 85714

KALICKI, PATRICIA ANN, educator; b. Boston, Mar. 31, 1954; d. Felix C. and Josephine (Vitellaro) Moschella; m. Anthony Michael Kalicki, Oct. 4, 1981; 1 child, Stephen Andrew. BS in Edn., Bridgewater State Coll., 1976; MEd in Spl. Edn., Suffolk U., 1982. Cert. tchr., Mass. Tchr. Our Lady of Lourdes Sch., Jamaica Plain, Mass., 1980-81, Cen. Elem. Sch., South Berwick, Maine, 1981-82; tchr. spl. needs Norton (Mass.) Mid. Sch., 1982—, coord. fundraising spl. needs dept., 1982—; bd. dirs. Bridgewater State Coll. Mem. NEA, Norton Tchrs. Assn. (v.p. 1986-87, 88-89, 89-90), Mass. Tchrs. Assn., Coun. for Exceptional Children, Bridgewater State Coll. Alumni Assn. (bd. dirs. 1983—), Oak Tree Women's League, Women's Club. Roman Catholic. Home: 4 Thayer Rd Medway MA 02053

KALIK, BARBARA FAITH, state legislator; b. Bronx, N.Y., Nov. 8, 1936; d. Albert and Lydia (Cohen) Benowitz; children: Darcie Lynn, Andrew Jay, Lance Jon. Student, CCNY, 1953-56. Owner, operator Jolie Travel Ctr., Inc., Willingboro, N.J., 1968—; mem. N.J. Gen. Assembly, 1978—, assoc. assembly leader, dep. minority leader, 1986, chair task force equitable mgmt. revenue and expenditures, 1990, chmn. revenue, fin. and appropriations com. 1984-85, vice chmn. joint appropriations com., 1986-87, mem. judiciary com., mem. higher edn. and regulated professions com., mem. council, 1971-75; Mayor City of Willingboro, 1974, 77; pres. Willingboro Dem. Club, 1967; Dem. committeewoman Willingboro 16th Dist., 1965-85; vice chmn. Burlington County Dem. Com., 1970-77; mem. Nat. Dem. Policy Commn.; bd. dirs. Spl. Services Sch.; mem. N.J. Job Tng. Coordinating Council, 1984, Mt. Laurel Ballet Co., Burlington County Girl Scout Council. Recipient Area Health Edn. Ctr. award, N.J. State Fedn. Women's Clubs award, Motor Vehicle Employees Appreciation award, Legis. Award for Advocacy for People with Disabilities, 1989, Ann Klein Advocate Honoree State Svc. award, 1989; named Bus. Person of Yr., Rotary Internat., Outstanding Citizen, VFW. Mem. Burlington County C. of C. (pres. 1984). Jewish. Office: Country Club Pla Beverly-Rancocas Rd Willingboro NJ 08046 also: Park Plaza Mall Rte 130 S Edgewater Park NJ 08010

KALIN, KARIN BEA, educator, consultant; b. N.Y.C., June 22, 1943; d. Lawrence Leon and Celia (Siskind) Elkind; children: Laura, Howard. BS, SUNY, Oswego, 1965; MS, CUNY, 1967. Cert. social studies tchr., N.Y. Tchr. Benjamin Franklin High Sch., N.Y.C., 1965-66, Grover Cleveland High Sch., Ridgewood, N.Y., 1967-73; tchr. Aviation High Sch., Long Island City, N.Y., 1979—, sex equity coord., also local equal opportunity coord.; curriculum developer OEO, N.Y.C. Bd. Edn., fall 1985; panelist Aerospace Edn. Workshop for Elem. Tchrs., Career Exploration Seminar, Aerospace Edn. Conf., 1990, East Meadow (N.Y.) Sch. Dist., 1989—; cons. Coll. Aeros., N.Y., 1986; cons. Profl. and Clerical Employees of Internat. Ladies Garment Workers Union, N.Y.C., 1989; with L.I. Coun. for Equal Edn. and Employment, 1990. Mem. Women on Job, Port Washington, N.Y., 1986—; mem. com. Nassau Dem. Com., Westbury, N.Y., 1988—. Grantee Columbia U., 1967, 69, N.Y.C. Bd. Edn., 1983, Nat. Coun. for Humanities, 1985, Project Voice/Move, 1984-85. Mem. N.Y. State Tchr.'s Union, NOW (chairperson women and employment com. Hempstead, N.Y. 1987—, chair consciousness raising com. 1982). Jewish. Home: 700 Barkley Ave East Meadow NY 11554 Office: Aviation High Sch 36th St & Queens Blvd Long Island City NY 11101

KALIN, NANCY JAGGER, interior designer; b. Akron, Ohio, July 7, 1935; d. Paul Warren and Evelyn Marie (Conrad) Jagger; 1 child, Mark. BS in Edn., U. Akron, 1957. Interior designer, owner Kalin Antique Interiors, Middlebranch, Ohio, 1972—. Home and office: PO Box One Middlebranch OH 44652

KALINAUSKAS, NANCY MCRAE, social worker, consultant; b. Boston, Apr. 10, 1948; d. Colin William and Helen Louise (Pence) McRae; m. Romualdas J. Kalinauskas, June 10, 1970 (div. 1989); children: Andrew, Lindsey, Lara. BA, Goucher Coll., 1970; MSW, U. Md., 1972. Lic. social worker. Social worker VA Outpatient Clinic, Balt., 1972-75, Bedford (Pa.) Somerset Mental Health/Mental Rehab., 1975-78; pvt. practice Bedford, 1978—; dir. Bedford Outpatient Office, Twin Lakes Ctr., 1985—; cons. Pennknoll Village Nursing Home, 1978—, Head Start, 1980-89, Donahoe Manor Nursing Home, 1983—. Mem. Bedford County Drug and Alcohol Bd., 1983-84; v.p. Bedford County Human Svcs. Council, 1990—, pres., 1988-89; mem. adv. council Pennknoll Village Home, 1990—. John F. Kennedy Inst. scholar, 1970-72/. Mem. Nat. Assn. Social Workers, AAUW (v.p. br. 1987-89). Democrat. Presbyterian. Home: 220 E Penn St Bedford PA 15522 Office: Twin Lakes Ctr 130 W Penn St Bedford PA 15522

KALINIAK, CATHERINE MARY, federal government offical; b. Grand Rapids, Mich., Mar. 5, 1958; d. Donald Robert and Catherine Ann (Anderson) K. BS, Cen. Mich. U., 1980. News reporter WTWN-AM, Grand Rapids, 1980-81, WKZO-TV, Grand Rapids, 1981-82; press sec. U.S. Congressman Harold S. Sawyer, Washington, 1982-85, Ray Shamie for U.S. Senate, Boston, 1984, U.S. Sen. Dan Quayle, Washington, 1985-88; chief of staff Fed. Railroad Adminstrn., Washington, 1988-89; pub. affairs specialist U.S. Dept. Energy, Washington, 1989—; Tutor Higher Achievement Program, Washington, 1987—. Commr. Capitol Hill Football League, Washington, 1989—. Mem. Rep. Communications Assn. (pres., social program dir. 1982-85), Bush/Quayle Schedule C Assn. Roman Catholic. Home: 123 4th St NE Washington DC 20002 Office: US Dept Energy 1000 Independence SE Rm 8G-087 Washington DC 20585

KALINS, DOROTHY, magazine editor; b. Westport, Conn., Oct. 9, 1942; d. Joseph M. and Gil G. Kalins. Student, Skidmore Coll., 1960-62, Sorbonne, Paris, 1962-63; B.A., Columbia U., 1965. Design writer Home Furnishings Daily, N.Y.C., 1965-68; freelance writer, various publs. including N.Y. Mag., 1969-74; exec. editor Apartment Life Mag., N.Y.C., 1974-78; editor-in-chief Apartment Life Mag., 1978-81, Met. Home Mag., 1978—; bd. dirs. Design Industries Found for AIDS; core faculty Stanford Profl. Pub. course. Author: Researching Design in New York, 1968, Cutting Loose, 1972, The Apartment Book, 1979, The New American Cuisine, 1981; editor: Renovation Style, 1986. Mem. Am. Soc. Mag. Editors (past exec. bd.), Edni. Found. Fashion Inst. of Tech. Office: Met Home 750 3rd Ave New York NY 10017

KALIPOLITES, JUNE TURNER, rehabilitation services professional; b. Grasmere, N.H., Aug. 10, 1932; d. Louis O. and Edith Mae (Allen) Turner; m. Nicholas G. Kalipolites, Feb. 12, 1955; children: George, Stephanie, Athena. AA, Hesser Coll., Manchester, N.H., 1977; BS, U. N.H., 1980; Degree in Rehab. Adminstrn. and Svcs., So. Ill. U., Carbondale, 1982. Cert. rehab. counselor. Office mgr. Harris Upham and Co., Inc., Manchester; rehab. counselor Div. Vocat. Rehab., Nashua, N.H.; rsch. asst. So. Ill. U.; rehab. cons. N.H. Div. Vocat. Rehab., Concord. Author: Projects with Industry: A Unique Concept for Providing Rehabilitation Services to Persons with Severe Disabilities, 1982. LaVerne Noyes scholar. Mem. NAFE, Am. Assn. Counseling and Devel., Nat. Rehab. Assn. (bd. dirs. 1986-87), Nat. Rehab. Adminstr. Assn. (nat. bd. dirs. 1983-87), N.E. Rehab. Counseling Assn. (pres. 1987, bd. dirs. 1977—), N.H. Rehab. Assn. (bd. dirs. 1977—, treas. 1978, 90), Rho Sigma Chi, Chi Sigma Iota. Democrat. Greek Orthodox. Home: 668 Lake Ave Manchester NH 03103 Office: NH Div Vocat Rehab 78 Regional Dr Concord NH 03301

KALISCH, BEATRICE JEAN, nursing educator, consultant; b. Tellahoma, Tenn., Oct. 15, 1943; d. Peter and Margaret Ruth Petersen; m. Philip A. Kalisch, Apr. 17, 1965; children—Philip P., Melanie J. B.S., U. Nebr., 1965; M.S. (USPHS fellow), U. Md., 1967, Ph.D. (USPHS fellow), 1970. Pediatric staff nurse Centre County Hosp., Bellefonte, Pa., 1965-66; instr. nursing Philipsburg (Pa.) Gen. Hosp. Sch. Nursing, 1966; pediatric staff nurse Greater Balt. Med. Center, Towson, Md., 1967; asst. prof. maternal-child nursing Am. U., 1967-68; clin. nurse specialist N.W. Tex. Hosp., Amarillo, 1970; assoc. prof. maternal-child nursing, curriculum coordinator nursing Amarillo Coll., 1970-71; chmn. baccalaureate nursing program, asso. prof. nursing U. So. Miss., 1971-74; prof. nursing, chmn. dept. parent-child nursing U. Mich. Sch. Nursing, Ann Arbor, 1974-86; Shirley C. Titus Disting. prof. U. Mich. Sch. Nursing, 1977—, Titus Disting. prof. nursing mgmt., 1989—; prin., dir. nursing consultation svcs. Ernst & Young, Detroit, 1986-89; prin. researcher USPHS grant to investigate impact of Cadet Nurse Corps on Am. nurses, U. So. Miss., 1971-74; prin. investigator USPH grant to study image of nurses in mass media and the informational quality nursing news, U. Mich., 1977-86; vis. Disting. prof. U. Ala., 1979, U. Tex., 1981, Tex. Christian U., 1983. Author: Child Abuse and Neglect: An Annotated Bibliography, 1978; co-author: Nursing Involvement in Health Planning, 1978, Politics of Nursing, 1982, Images of Nurses on Television, 1983 The Advance of American Nursing, 1986, The Changing Image of the Nurse, 1987; co-editor: Studies in Nursing Mgmt.; contbr. articles to profl. jours. Recipient Joseph L. Andrews Bibliog. award Am. Assn. Law Libraries, 1979; Book of Yr. award Am. Jour. Nursing, 1978, 83, 86, 87, Outstanding Achievement award U. Md., 1987, Distinguished Alumni award U. Nebr., 1985, Shaw medal Boston Coll., 1986. Fellow Am. Acad. Nursing; mem. AAAS, MINOA, Am. Nurses Assn., Nat. League Nursing, Am. Public Health Assn., Am. Mktg. Assn., Am. Hosp. Assn., Mich. Nursing Diagnosis Assn., Sigma Theta Tau, Phi Kappa Phi. Presbyterian. Home: 27675 Chatsworth Rd Farmington Hills MI 48334 Office: U Mich Sch Nursing 400 N Ingalls Bldg Ann Arbor MI 48109

KALISHER, SHEILA LYNN, invention company executive; b. Detroit, July 12, 1944; d. Jack Allyn and Beatrice Sybil (Rosenfeld) Cohen; m. Lester Kalisher, May 8, 1966; children: Aaron James, Lisa Jineen. Student, U. Mich, 1962-63; BA, Wayne State U., 1967. Cert. secondary tchr. Tchr. English Virginia Beach (Va.) Sch. System, 1968-69; pres., chief exec. officer A.L.L.'S. WELL & CO., Livingston, N.J., 1986—. Mem. Women's Am. Orgn. Rehab. Through Tng. (v.p. 1981-82), Nat. Soc. Inventors (sec. pub. rels. 1987—), Welcome Wagon Club (pres. Livingston chpt. 1980-81). Home and Office: 94 N Rockledge Dr Livingston NJ 07039

KALISHMAN, REESA JOAN, accountant; b. Bronx, N.Y., Nov. 4, 1959; d. Samuel and Julia (Fluger) Deutch; m. Stuart Jay Kalishman, Sept. 5, 1981. AA with honors, Miami-Dade Community Coll., 1977; BBA, Fla. Internat. U., 1979. CPA, Fla. Staff acct. Holtz & Co., CPA's, Miami, Fla., 1979-80; semi sr. acct. Holtz & Co., CPAs, Ft. Lauderdale, Fla., 1980-81; staff acct. Oppenheim, Appel, Dixon CPAs, Miami, 1981; agt. IRS, Miami, 1981—; vol. income tax assistance provider IRS, Dade County, Fla., 1983, acting group mgr., tax laws instr., Miami, 1986-87, group mgr. planning and spl. programs div., Ft. Lauderdale, 1987—, group mgr. field exam., Ft. Lauderdale, 1989—; task force witness, participant Dept. Justice, Roanoke, Va., 1986, Miami, 1987. Campaign worker mayoral election North Miami Beach, Fla., 1978. Mem. Am. Inst. CPA's, Fla. Inst. CPA's, Phi Theta Kappa. Republican. Jewish.

KALL, JANICE ELENA, public relations executive; b. San Rafael, Calif., Oct. 14, 1960; d. Dale I. and Fern H. (Phillipsen) Parker; m. Joseph F. Kall, June 25, 1982 (div. Nov. 1989); 1 child, Jasmine L. BA in Journalism, Calif. State U., Long Beach, Calif., 1982; postgrad., San Diego State U., 1988. Cons. Computhink, Redondo Beach, Calif., 1982-84; staff writer Hi-Tech Pub. Relations, San Francisco, 1984-85; writer Talaris Systems, San Diego, 1985-89; pub. relations mgr. Computer Accessories Corp., San Diego, 1989—. Contbr. numerous articles to various computer jours. Mem. Computer & Electronics Mktg. Assn. Home: 595 Montview Dr Escondido CA 92025 Office: Computer Accessories/Proxima 6610 Nancy Ridge Dr San Diego CA 92121

KALLGREN-MILLER, JANINE ANN, radio station production manager; b. Palo Alto, Calif, Jan. 20, 1962; d. James Allen Kallgren and Helen Susan Baranowski; m. Bernard G. Miller, Sept. 24, 1983. BA, U. Mo., Columbia, 1983. Announcer Sta. KBIA, Columbia, Mo., 1981; comml. producer Sta. KFMZ, Columbia, 1983; announcer Radio Glen, Southampton, Eng., 1983-84; info. desk asst. Manchester (Eng.) Internat. Airport; announcer Sta. WITF, Harrisburg, Pa., 1986-87; program dir. Sta. WSCL, Salisbury, Md., 1987-88; prodn. mgr. Sta. WWFM, Trenton, N.J., 1988—. Vol. Special Olympics Princeton, N.J., 1988; Oboeist Trenton Symphony Trenton, N.J., 1988--. Republican.

KALLMAN, KATHLEEN BARBARA, marketing professional; b. Aurora, Ill., Mar. 23, 1952; d. Kenneth Wesley and Germaine Barbara (May) Eby; m. John Kenneth Kallman, Sept. 27, 1975; 1 child, Erin Marie. Legal sec. Sidley & Austin, Chgo., 1973-76, Winston & Strawn, Chgo., 1976-78; exec. sec. Beatrice Cos., Inc., Chgo., 1978-81, adminstrv. asst., 1981-83, asst. to chmn. bd. dirs., 1983-84, asst. v.p., 1984-85; pres., mng. dir. Stratxx Ltd., Chgo., 1985—. Mem. Chgo. Council on Fgn. Relations, 1986—. Mem. Am. Soc. Profl. and Exec. Women. Roman Catholic. Club: Internat. (Chgo.). Office: Stratxx Ltd Chicago IL 60611

KALLMAN, MARY JEANNE, biopsychology educator, researcher; b. Alexandria, Va., May 27, 1948; d. Ira Semon and Carol Louise (Gardinier) Davis; m. William Michael Kallman, Dec. 20, 1969. BS in Psychology, Lynchburg Coll., 1970; MS in Biopsychology, U. Ga., 1974, PhD, 1976. Post-doctoral fellow dept. pharmacology Med. Coll. Va., Richmond, 1976-79, rsch. assoc. dept. pharmacology, 1979, asst. prof., 1980-83; asst. prof. dept. psychology U. Miss., University, 1983-86; dir. grad. exptl. program dept. psychology and pharmacology dept. psychology and pharmacology U. Miss., University, 1986—; rsch. asst. dept. psychology U. Ga., 1970-73, 74-75, dept. psychiatry U. Miss. Med. Ctr., 1973-74; adj. asst. prof. dept. psychology Va. Commonwealth U., 1976-77; grant reviewer EPA, March of Dimes, document reviewer EPA. Contbr. chpts. to 5 books, numerous articles to profl. jours. Recipient Outstanding Rsch. Program award Miss. Psychol. Assn., 1986. Mem. AAAS, APA, Am. Soc. Pharmacology and Exptl. Therapeutics, Neuroscis., Behavioral Pharm. Soc., Behavioral Teratology Soc., Behavioral Toxicology Soc., SouthEastern Psychol. Assn., South Cen. Soc. Toxicology, Southeastern Pharm. Soc., Sigma Xi. Methodist. Office: Dept Psychology Univ of Miss University MS 38677

KALLNER, NINA CORY, educator; b. Colfax, ind., Sept. 19, 1921; d. Herschel Floyd and Lena Jeanette (Hutchinson) Cory; m. Robert Clayton Kallner, Nov. 28, 1921; children: Beverly Kay, Linda Carol. BS, Ball State U., 1961, MA, 1966. Cert. elem. edn. tchr., libr. sci. Tchr. Anderson Community Schs., Anderson, Ind., 1961-64, 65—. Mem. AAUW (pres. local chpt. 1982, 85-86). Democrat. Mem. Disciples of Christ Ch. Home: 2527 Albert St Anderson IN 46012

KALLSEN, PAMELA KAY, health facility administrator; b. Fresno, Calif., June 19, 1951; d. Richard Lewis and Delynn (Eaken) Seyller; m. Ronald E. Bragg, Feb. 2, 1974 (div. Mar. 1983); children: Leslie, Laura; m. Gene W. Kallsen, Feb. 25, 1989. BA in Home Econs., Calif. State U., Fresno, 1974; BS in Edn., Memphis State U., 1978. Mgr. Fashion Fabrics, Kennewick, Wash., 1974-75; univ. teaching asst., secondary tchr. Memphis City Schs., 1977-79; co-owner Spraywest, Fresno, 1980-82; dir. wellness St. Agnes Med. Ctr., Fresno, 1982-83, asst. dir. pub. relations, 1983-84; adminstr. dir. Calif. Eye Inst., St. Agnes Med. Ctr., Fresno, 1984—; coordinator med. skills courses, Calif., 1985—, Calif. Heart Symposium, Yosemite, Calif., 1985. Fund raiser St. Agnes Assocs., Fresno; mem. adv. coun. Blind Babies Foun. Mem. Am. Acad. Ophthalmic Adminstrs., Am. Acad. Ophthalmology, Womens Health Care Execs., Fresno Womens Network, Blind Babies Found. (adv. coun.), Lions. Republican. Presbyterian. Home: 887 E Catalina Circle Fresno CA 93720 Office: 5771 N Fresno Ste 110 Fresno CA 93710

KALRA, BERALDINE LELI, police officer; b. N.Y.C.; d. Pasquale Augustus and Rosaria Carmella (Caputo) Leli; m. Arjun Dev Kalra, Nov. 15, 1981; 1 child, Steffen Anthony Kaplan. BS cum laude, N.Y. Inst. Tech., Old Westbury, 1976; MA in Forensic Psychology, CCNY, 1979. Spl. investigator N.Y. Atty. Gen., N.Y.C., 1976-77; police officer N.Y.C. Police Dept., 1973-84; counselor N.Y. Assn. for New Ams., N.Y.C., 1989—. Sec. Policewoman's Endowment Assn., N.Y.C. With USAR, 1975-79.

KALSTAD, KRISTEN ANDREA, transportation executive; b. Annapolis, Md., Mar. 6, 1948; d. Henry Morris and Elizabeth (McKnight) K.; divorced; 1 child, Heidi Kalstad Rork. Student, Bergen Community Coll., 1969-70, Paterson State Tchrs. Coll., 1970; A summa cum laude, Anne Arundel Community Coll., 1979; B, U. N.Mex., 1982, postgrad., 1983; student, Embry Riddle Aero. U., 1981. Flight instr. Sunport Aviation, Albuquerque, 1980-81; co-pilot SW Med. Air Transport, Albuquerque, 1981; flight instr. Crestview Aviation, Albuquerque, 1981-83; flight attendant TWA, N.Y.C., 1970-83; regional airline pilot Big Sky Airlines, Billings, Mont., 1983-85; airline pilot, flight engr. Ea. Airlines, Washington, 1985-88; 1st officer Ea. Airlines, Boston, 1988-89; flight officer Pan Am. World Airways, 1989—. Mem. Internat. Social Affiliation of Women Airline Pilots, Airline Pilots Assn. Democrat. Home: 111 Round Bay Rd Severna Park MD 21146

KALTENBACH, SHIRLEY JEAN, educational consultant; b. Torrance, Calif., Sept. 19, 1948; d. Hubert Leonard and Theodore Shirley (Hunt) K. BA in History, Westmont Coll., Santa Barbara, Calif., 1971; postgrad., U. S.C., 1975-76; MS in Computer Sci., River Coll., Nashua, N.H., 1986. Cert. tchr., Calif., N.H. Asst. mgr. stationery, books, camera Broadway Dept. Store, Torrance, 1968-69; mgmt. trainee Bullock's Dept. Store, Torrance, 1971-72; substitute tchr. Palos Verdes (Calif.) Sch. Dist., 1972-74; spl. edn. tchr. Redondo (Calif.) Union High Sch. Dist., learning disability tchr., 1974-75; spl. edn. tester So. Pasadena (Calif.) Sch. Dist., 1975-76; learning disabilities specialist Hudson (N.H.) Meml. Sch., 1976-85; lectr. River Coll., Nashua, N.H., 1985—; course developer Digital Equipment Corp., Nashua, N.H., 1987—; sec. Staff Devel. Com., Hudson N.H. 1981-82; chairperson Staff Devel. Com., Hudson N.H. 1982-84. Recipient Fellowship award U. S.C. 1975. Mem. Nashua Choral Soc. Republican. Office: Digital Equipment Corp 110 Spit Brook Rd Nashua NH 03062

KALUZNIACKI, SOPHIA BARBARA, veterinarian; b. Warsaw, Poland, May 11, 1942; came to U.S., 1952; d. Roman Julius and Stena (Zubrzycki) Kaluzniacki; m. George G. Kulesza, Dec. 27, 1971; 1 child, Christina. Student, U. Ariz., 1960-63, Ariz. State U., 1963-64; D.V.M., Wash. State U., 1968. Asst. prof. U. Ariz., Tucson, 1968-70; staff veterinarian Humane Soc. Ariz., Phoenix, 1970-71; pvt. practice vet. medicine, Green Valley, Ariz., 1971—. Contbr. articles to profl. jours. Adv. bd., sec. Pima County Animal Control, Tucson, 1978-89, chair, 1989—; mem., sec. Ariz. State Bd. Vet. Examiners, Phoenix, 1980-87; bd. dirs. Soc. Prevention Cruelty to Animals of Ariz., Inc., Tucson, 1972—. Mem. AVMA, Ariz. Vet. Med. Assn., So. Ariz. Vet. Med. Assn. Address: Green Valley Animal Hosp 220 E Duval Rd PO Box D Green Valley AZ 85622

KAMALI, NORMA, designer; b. N.Y.C., June 27, 1945; d. Sam and Estelle (Grub) Mariategui; grad. Fashion Inst., 1965. With Kamali Ltd., 1967-78; owner, designer O.M.O. Norma Kamali, N.Y.C., 1978—. Recipient Coty Winnie award, 1981, Return award, 1982, Hall of Fame award, 1983; Women's Fashion Designer of Yr. award Council Fashion Designers Am., 1983; Award for Innovative Use of Video Council of Fashion Designers Am., 1986; Fashion Group honoree, 1986, CEDA award, 1986, Community Service award, 1985. Office: 11 W 56th St New York NY 10019*

KAMATOY, LOURDES AGUAS, artist; b. San Fernando, Pampanga, Philippines, June 29, 1945; came to U.S., 1966; d. Juan Gutierrez and Segunda Mercado (De La Cruz) Aguas; m. Ernesto Gabriel Kamatoy, Apr. 28, 1973; 1 child, Lisette Marie. BA in English, U. Santo Tomas, Manila, Philippines, 1964; MA in Ednl. Theatre, NYU, 1972; overseas cert. theatre, Rose Bruford Coll. Speech, Kent, Eng., 1966. Supr. Arthur Andersen & Co., N.Y.C., 1966-73; instr. theatre U. So. Ind., Evansville, 1973-75; pres. Bodega, Evansville, 1975-79; artist rep. Lulu Represents, Chgo., 1986-89; ptnr. MK Videostar, Chgo., 1989—. Pres. Evansville Arts and Edn. Coun., 1983; v.p. U. Evansville Theatre Soc., 1984; panelist Ind. Arts Commn., Indpls., 1985; bd. dirs. Arts Insight, Indpls., 1985, USI Soc. Arts & Humanities, Evansville, 1988. Mem. Petroleum Club (Evansville), Columbia Club (Indpls.). Democrat. Roman Catholic. Office: 70 W Huron St #1702 Chicago IL 60610

KAMERMAN, SHEILA BRODY, educator, social worker; b. U.S., Jan. 7, 1928; d. S. Lawrence and Helen (Golding) Brody; m. Morton Kamerman, Sept. 11, 1947; children: Nathan Brody, Elliot Herbert, Laura Kamerman-Katz. B.A., NYU, 1946; M.S.W., Hunter Coll., 1966; D. Social Welfare, Columbia U., 1973. Social worker N.Y.C. Dept. Social Services, 1966-68; social work supr. Bellevue Psychiat. Hosp., 1968-69; research assoc., sr. research assoc. Columbia U. Sch. Social Work, 1971-79, assoc. prof. social policy and planning, 1979-81, prof., 1981—; assoc. prof. Hunter Coll. Social Work, 1977-79; chmn. NAS-NRC panel on work, family and community, 1980-82; mem Com. Child Devel. Research and Pub. Policy, 1983-88 ; mem. com. on prenatal care, Inst. Medicine , 1986-88; cons. in field, mem. numerous social welfare coms. and adv. bds.; mem. Gov. Cuomo's Task Force on Poverty and Welfare Reform, 1986-87, adv. com . on Work and Family, 1987-88, UN Expert group on Family Policies. Author: (with Alfred J. Kahn) Not for the Poor Alone, 1975, Social Services in the United States, 1976, Social Services in International Perspective, 1977, Family Policy: Government and Families in Fourteen Countries, 1978, Child Care, Family Benefits and Working Parents, 1981, Parenting in an Unresponsive Society, 1980, Maternity and Parental Benefits and Leaves, 1980, Helping America's Families, 1982, Maternity Policies and Working Women, 1983, Income Transfers for Families with Children, 1983, Child Care: Facing the Hard Choices, 1987, The Responsive Work Place, 1987, Child Support: From Debt Collection to Social Polciy, 1988, Mothers Alone: Strategies For a Time of Change, 1988, Privatization and the Welfare State, 1989, Social Services for Children, Youth and Families in the United States, 1990; contbr. numerous articles to profl.jours. Recipient Hexter award Hunter Coll. Sch. Social Work, 1977, Nat. Leadership award in Social Policy, Heller Sch. Brandeis U.; named to Hunt Coll. Hall of Fame, 1981; fellow Ctr. Advanced Study in Behavioral Scis., 1983-84. Mem. Nat. Assn. Social Workers, Am. Pub. Welfare Assn., Am. Soc. Pub. Adminstrn., Assn. Policy Analysis and Mgmt., Phi Beta Kappa. Home: 1125 Park Ave New York NY 10128

KAMINKOWITZ, GRACE, writer, consultant, public official; b. N.Y.C., May 23, 1935; d. Louis and Gertrude (Noachs) K. BA, U. Iowa, 1955; postgrad., Northwestern U., 1956-58. Copywriter, retail advt. mgr. Montgomery Ward & Co., Chgo., 1955-61; advt. copy chief, v.p. mktg. Helene Curtis Industries, Inc., Chgo., 1961-75; v.p., pres. New Dimensions Mktg., Inc., Chgo., 1975-84; pub. affairs cons. Grace Kaminkowitz Enterprises, Chgo., 1984—; polit. columnist Today's Chgo. Woman, 1986—; aging columnist Pioneer Press, Wilmette, Ill., 1988—; polit. columnist Crain's Chgo. Bus., 1989—; commr. Ill. Human Rights Commn., Chgo., 1988—; bd. dirs., v.p., sec. ASN Pub. Co., San Marcos, Calif., 1977—. Contbr. articles to profl. jours. and mags. Nat. steering com. Nat. Women's Polit. Caucus, Washington, 1985—; exec. bd. Ill. Women's Polit. Caucus, Springfield, 1983—; chair Chgo. Women's Polit. Caucus, 1983-90; v.p. ERA Ill., Chgo., 1980-82; adv. com. Ill. Gov.'s Coun. on Health and Phys. Fitness, Springfield, 1980—. Recipient Golden Trumpet award Publicity Club Chgo., 1967, 1968, Superior Communications award Am. Assn. Port Authorities, 1977. Mem. AAUW (exec. bd. Chgo. br.), Bus. and Profl. Women, Chgo. Area Pub. Affairs Group, Chgo. Women in Govt. Rels., Women in Communications, Inc. (pres. Chgo. chpt., 1966-67, Disting. Svc. award 1968, 70, Headliner 1980). Democrat. Jewish. Home: 1143S Plymouth Ct #501 Chicago IL 60605 Office: Ill Human Rights Commn 100 W Randolph St Chicago IL 60605

KAMINSKI, JANELLE KAY, sales executive; b. Hinsdale, Ill., Nov. 18, 1962; d. Roy Partain Davis and Virginia Lea (Tolley) Duke; m. Ronald Paul Kaminski, July 5, 1980. Student, Elmhurst Coll., 1980-81. Customer svc. clk. Aromat Corp., Elk Grove Village, Ill., 1982-84, sales coord., 1984-85, exec. sec., 1985-86, supr. customer svc., 1986-88, sr. supr. sales adminstrn., 1988-90, asst. mgr., distbr. sales, 1990—. Sect. leader Christ Ch. Choir, Oakbrook, Ill., 1984-86. Mem. NAFE. Republican. Office: Aromat Corp 921 Lively Blvd Elk Grove Village IL 60007

KAMINSKI, KAREN SUE, occupational therapist; b. Ft. Hood, Tex., Dec. 7, 1955; d. Emiljan and Irene Louise (Heck) K.; m. Jeff Ian Macleod, Sept. 12, 1952. BS in Occupational Therapy, U. Tex., 1981; MA in Behavioral Scis., U. Houston, Clear Lake, 1989. Therapist UTMB Moody State Sch., Galveston, Tex., 1981-83, Shriners Burn Inst., Galveston, 1983-88, UTMB Pediatrics, Galveston, 1988—. Author, presentor: Activities of Daily Assessment of Severely Burned Children, 1985, Use of a Modified Swedish Knee Cage With Burned Children Ambulation, 1985, Pediatric Burn Rehabilitation, 1986, Problems in Scarring and Contracture Management, 1987. Mem. Silk Stocking Hist. Assn., Galveston, 1984--, Galveston Hist. Found., 1984--. Mem. Am. Occupational Therapy Assn., Am. Burn Assn., Internat. Soc. for Burn Injures. Office: U Tex Med Branch OT Galveston TX 77550

KAMINSKI, MADOLYN ANDREA DESILVA, registered nurse, educator; b. St. Louis, Apr. 20, 1952; d. Anthony George and Sherry (Simmer) DeSilva; m. Mark Stefan Kaminski, May 30, 1981; 1 child, Andrea Thayne. RN, Barnes Hosp. Sch. Nursing, St. Louis, 1975. Lic. RN, Mo., Calif., Mass., Mich. Staff nurse Barnes Hosp., St. Louis, 1975-81, asst. head nurse, 1975-81; ednl. coordinator life support tng. ctr. Stanford (Calif.) Med. Ctr., 1981-86; staff nurse intermediate intensive care Catherine MacCauley Health Ctr., Ann Arbor, Mich., 1986-87; instr. postgrad. edn. U. Mich. Med. Ctr., Ann Arbor, 1986—; affiliate faculty Am. Heart Assn., Santa Clara County, Calif., 1981-86, Mich., 1986-87. Tech. advisor, site coordinator various community CPR tng. projects. Mem. Am. Heart Assn. (Service awards), Am. Assn. Critical Care Nurses (chmn. mktg. com. 1988-90, Service award 1987), U. Mich. Women's Faculty Club (welcoming com. 1988-90). Roman Catholic.

KAMINSKY, JUDITH GERSON, marketing executive; b. Columbus, Ga., Oct. 4, 1942; d. Harry and Inez (Witt) Gerson; m. Sidney Fine Kaminsky, June 30, 1963; children: Jana Leigh, Beth Ann. Student, Ind. U., 1960-61, U. Ga., 1961-64. V.p., treas. Bi-State Broadcast, Inc., Columbus, 1972-85; dir., mktg. Peach State Pub. Radio, Atlanta, 1985—; co-owner, co-mgr. Sta. WPNX Radio, Columbus, 1971-85; mktg. dir. Peach State Pub. Radio Network, Atlanta, 1985—. Bd. dirs. Springer Opera House, Columbus, 1970-72, Southeastern Music Ctr., 1988—; charter mem. Columbus Mus.; mem. Springer Guild, Columbus, 1970-75, Columbus Symphony Women's Assn., 1970-75, 88—; chmn. nominating com. Concharty Coun. of Girl Scouts, Inc., 1988—, bd. dirs., 1989-92. Fellow Internat. Biog. Assn.; mem. NAFE, Am. Mktg. Assn. (v.p. 1986-87, bd.. dirs. 1987-88), Prof. Bus. communications (v.p. 1986-88), Columbus Area Network for Profl. and Exec. Women. Avocations: reading, gourmet cooking and baking, writing. Office: Peach State Pub Radio 1540 Stewart Ave SW Atlanta GA 30310

KAMINSKY, LAURA, composer, arts presenter; b. N.Y.C., Sept. 28, 1956; d. Leonard and Eva Deborah (Sarna) Kaminsky. BA, Oberlin Coll., 1978; MA, CUNY, 1980. Adj. faculty New Sch., N.Y.C., 1980-82, CCNY, 1980-82; dir. Network for Learning, N.Y.C. and Houston, 1980-83; founder, artistic dir. Musicians' Accord, N.Y.C., 1980—; assoc. dir. edn. 92d St. Y, N.Y.C., 1984-88; artistic dir. The Town Hall, N.Y.C., 1988—; recording artist Mode Recordings; cons. Mary Flagler Cary Charitable Trust, N.Y.C., 1990; cons., panelist Colo. Council on Arts and Humanities, Denver, 1990; panelist Am. Composers Alliance, N.Y.C., 1988—. Composer solo, chamber and orchestral works. Bd. govs. N.Y. Found. for Arts, 1987—. Millay Colony for Arts fellow, 1984, 86; Va. Ctr. for Creative Arts fellow, 1985, 89, 90; recipient ASCAP-Chamber Music Am. award, 1989, citation for creative svc. to arts Community Pres. Borough of Manhattan, 1989; N.Y. State Coun. on Arts rec. grantee, 1987, N.Y. State Coun. on Arts commn., 1988-89, Infusion Chamber Ensemble commn., 1990. Jewish. Office: Town Hall 123 W 43d St New York NY 10036

KAMISAR, SANDRA LEE, federal agency administrator, publishing consultant; b. Washington, Apr. 15, 1937; d. Harry and Betty (Bass) K. AA, George Washington U., 1956; cert. med. sec., Strayer Bus. Coll., Washington, 1957. With Office of Prevention, Edn. and Control Nat. Heart, Lung and Blood Inst., Bethesda, Md., 1957—, chief pubs. mgmt. sect., supr. writing and editing Office of Prevention, Edn. and Control, 1977—; cons. printing and pub. NIH, Bethesda, 1979—. Editor: Dietary Management of Hyperlipoproteinemia. Bd. trustees Temple Shalom, Chevy Chase, Md., 1982—; sec. Mid-Atlantic Council Union of Am. Hebrew Congregations, Washington, 1990. Mem. Nat. Assn. Govt. Communications, Assn. Reform Zionists of Am. (v.p. membership Washington chpt.). Democrat. Home: 6140 Utah Ave Washington DC 20015

KAMMERDEINER, NANCY ALYCE, city official; b. Natrona Heights, Pa., Jan. 25, 1946; d. Ivan M. and Sylvia E. (Klingensmith) K.; m. F. Gerald Callan, Oct. 17, 1987. BA in Polit. Sci., Allegheny Coll., 1967; MPA, Syracuse U., 1969. Program asst. informational devel. br. AID, New Delhi, 1968; adminstrv. analyst Office of Mng. Dir., City of Phila., 1969-72, mgmt. analyst Office of Mayor, 1972-80, fin. svcs. adminstr. Office Dir. of Fin., 1980-86, mgr. human resources info. ctr., 1986-88, asst. to dir. fin., 1988—; treas. Southeastern Regional Coun. for Intergovtl. Personnel Act, Phila., 1972-80. Mem., chmn. rev. com. United Way Southeastern Pa., Phila., 1982-89; bd. dirs. Big Sisters Phila., 1989; mem. self evaluation com. Greater Phila. coun. Girl Scouts U.S.A., 1989. Mem. Am. Soc. for Pub. Adminstrn. (council 1971-89, pres. 1973-74), Leadership Inc. Office: City of Phila 1400 Mcpl Svcs Bldg Philadelphia PA 19102

KAMMEYER, SONIA MARGARETHA, real estate agent; b. Stockholm, June 21, 1942; came to U.S., 1964; d. Bengt Henrik and Margot Elsa M. (Hodin) Sjoberg; m. Whitman Ridgway, June 13, 1964 (div. 1978); children: Sean, Siobhan; m. Kenneth C.W. Kammeyer, Dec. 28, 1982. Student, Fleisher's Art Meml. Sch., Phila., 1966-69. With Ben Bell Real Estate, Lanham, Md., 1972-73, Robert L. Gruen Real Estate, Silver Spring, Md., 1973-81, Panarama Real Estate, Silver Spring, 1981-82, Long & Foster Real Estate, Inc., Silver Spring, 1982—. Mem. Montgomery County Bd. Realtors, Howard County Bd. Realtors, Washington D.C. Bd. Realtors, Swedish Profl. Women. Home: 14600 Triadelphia Mill Rd Dayton MD 21036 Office: Long & Foster Real Estate 11307 Georgia Ave Wheaton MD 20902

KAMON, PAULINE MCDOUGAL, real estate developer; b. Fairmont, W.Va., June 29, 1925; d. Paul Erwin and Lena Pearl (Curry) Hartley; m. George Earl McDougal, May 17, 1941 (dec. 1973); children: Sue Ann, Paula Jean, Chris Douglas, Jonathan Kelly, Stacy Lynn. Student, U. Pitts., Poly. Inst., Bethel Park, 1986, GRI Inst., Valley Forge, Pa., 1988. Cert. real estate agt. Office mgr. Ace Exterminators & Water Proofing Co., Bethel Park, Pa., 1962-74; bookkeeper, clk. Pa. Assn. Notaries, Pitts., 1975-79; exec. sec. W. Pa. Conf. Ctr. United Meth. Ch., Pitts., 1979-86; real estate agt. Coldwell Banker Real Estate, Bethel Park, 1986--; co-chmn. Spl. Olympics, 1987; mem., task force Coldwell Banker Real Estate, Pitts., 1988; mem. exec. com. Coldwell Banker Real Estate, 1989. Author: God I Didn't Want To Be A Widow; contbr. articles to profl. jours. Lay leader United Meth. Ch., Bethel Park, Pa., 1976—; chmn. staff parish pers. United Meth. Ch., 1988—, mem. met. correlating com. W. Pa. Conf., 1975-78; vol. Teen Hotline, 1972-74. Mem. Dravo Srs. (conf. bd. trustees). Republican. Office: Coldwell Banker Real Estate 1815 Washington Rd Pittsburgh PA 15241

KAMPF, CINDY ALISE, public relations executive; b. Honolulu, Aug. 14, 1961; d. Joel and Isobel Linda (Cohen) K. BA, Muhlenberg Coll., Allentown, Pa., 1983; grad., Syracuse U., 1983-85. Project mgr. Hemming and Gilman, Inc., N.Y.C., 1985-86; asst. account exec. Dorf & Stanton Communications, Inc., N.Y.C., 1986-87; spl. events coord. Dorf & Stanton Communications, Inc., 1987-88; account exec. Keyes Martin Pub. Rels., Springfield, N.J., 1988—. Area chmn. Hands Across Am., N.J., 1986; mem. young profls. com. Cancer Care of N.J.; fundraiser spl. events Am. Indian Coll. Fund. Mem. Pub. Relations Soc. Am., Pro Bono, Muhlenberg Metro. Alumni Asn. (v.p.), Newhouse Alumni Assn. Home: 99 Westminster Rd Chatham NJ 07928 Office: Keyes Martin Pub Rels 841 Mountain Ave Springfield NJ 07081

KAMPH, PATRICIA ANN, comptroller; b. Detroit, Jan. 6, 1956; d. Carl John Sr. and Helen (Rydzewski) Krawczyk; m. John George Kamph III, Oct. 1, 1977 (div. Nov. 1987); children: John IV, Carl, Dennis. Student, Schoolcraft Coll., 1986-87. Data processing mgr. Cox Instrument Div., Detroit, 1973-78; compt., adminstrv. asst. Reider Racing Ent., Inc., Taylor, Mich., 1985—. Mem. NAFE, Am. Soc. for Woman Accts., Am. Mgmt. Assn. Republican. Roman Catholic. Office: Reider Racing Ent Inc 12351 Universal Dr Taylor MI 48180

KAMSLER, VICTORIA ALEXANDRA ASHCROFT, political philosopher; b. Passaic, N.J., Apr. 18, 1960; d. George Gabriel and Elizabeth Ashcroft (Allison) K. Student, Centro de Estudios Hispanicos, Madrid, 1979, The Sorbonne, Paris, 1980, London Sch. Econs., 1981; AB in Internat. Studies, Bryn Mawr Coll., 1982; D Phil cand. in politics, Oxford (Eng.) U., 1987. Intern 99th Congress, Congresswoman Patricia Schroeder, Washington, 1985, 100th Congress, Sen. Edward M. Kennedy, Washington, 1986; pub. policy cons. ICF Inc., Washington, 1986; lobbyist Mass. Citizen Action, Boston, 1987; teaching fellow Harvard U., Cambridge, Mass., 1987—, tutor in govt. Currier House, founder Feminist Polit. Theory Group, 1988—. Danforth award for excellence in teaching, Harvard U., 1989. Mem. Am. Philos. Assn., Am. Polit. Sci. Assn., Boston Athenaeum Club. Democrat. Home: 235D Highland Ave Somerville MA 02143 Office: Harvard U Currier House Linnaean St Cambridge MA 02138

KANE, AGNES BREZAK, pathologist, educator; b. Danbury, Conn., Nov. 3, 1946; d. John Edward and Mary Elizabeth (Hatfield) Brezak; m. David E. Kane, June 22, 1970. BA, Swarthmore Coll., 1968; MD, Temple U., 1974, PhD, 1976. Diplomate Am. Bd. Pathology. Resident Temple U. Hosp., Phila., 1975-76, 77-78; postdoctoral fellow Karolinska Inst., Stockholm, 1976-77; asst. prof. Temple U. Sch. Medicine, Phila., 1977-82; asst. prof. Brown U., Providence, 1982-87, assoc. prof. pathology, 1987—; mem. merit rev. bd. for basic scis. VA, Washington, 1984-86; cons. R.I. Commn. for Safety and Occupational Health, Providence, 1986—; commr. Commn. to Identify Occupational Diseases, Providence, 1987-88; mem. rev. com. Nat. Inst. Environ. Health Scis., Research Triangle Park, N.C., 1988—. Contbr. articles on exptl. pathology to sci. publs. Lucretia Mott fellow Swarthmore Coll., 1969-71; recipient Rsch. Career Devel. award NIH, 1981-86. Mem. Am. Assn. Pathologists (women's com. 1987—, program com. 1990—), Assn. Women Med. Faculty Brown U. (founder, coord.), Women in Medicine (faculty advisor Brown U. chpt.; Mary Putnam Jacobi award 1986), Phi Kappa, Sigma Xi. Office: Brown Univ Box G Providence RI 02912

KANE, CAROL, actress; b. Cleve., June 18, 1952. Stage debut in The Prime of Miss Jean Brodie, Pub. Theatre, N.Y.C., 1966, also appeared at Charles St. Playhouse, Boston ; other N.Y.C. theatre appearances include Ring 'round the Bath Tub, 1972, The Tempest, 1974; film appearances include Carnal Knowledge, 1971, The Last Detail, 1974, Dog Day Afternoon, 1975, Hester Street, 1975 (Acad. award nomination for Best Actress), Harry and Walter Go to New York, 1976, Annie Hall, 1977, Valentino, 1977, The World's Greatest Lover, 1977, The Mafu Cage, 1977, When a Stranger Calls, 1979, The Muppet Movie, 1979, La Sabina, 1979, Les Jeux, 1980, Norman Loves Rose, 1982, Racing With the Moon, 1984, All is Forgiven, 1985-86, Jumpin' Jack Flash, 1986, Ishtar, 1987, License to Drive, 1988, Scrooged, 1988, The Princess Bride, 1989, Joe Versus the Volcano, 1990, The Lemon Sisters, 1990; stage appearances include The Effect of Gamma Rays on Man in the Moon Marigolds, 1978, Tales from the Vienna Woods, 1979, Benefit of a Doubt, 1979, The Tempest and Macbeth at Lincoln Center, 1980, Sunday Runners in the Rain, 1980, The Debutante Ball, 1988, Frankie and Johnny in the Clair de Lune, 1988; appeared in TV film Many Mansions, in TV series Taxi, 1981-83, American Dreamer; films An Invasion of Privacy, 1983, Burning Rage, 1984, All is Forgiven, 1986, Drop Out Mother, 1988. Recipient Emmy award for outstanding supporting actress in a comedy series, 1981. Office: care ICM 8899 Beverly Blvd Los Angeles CA 90048*

KANE, KATHLEEN ELIZABETH, insurance service executive; b. Hartford, Conn., Dec. 17, 1961. BBA, U. Montevallo (Ala.), 1982. Lic. disability, property and casualty ins. agt. Quality control analyst Collateral Mortgage, Ltd., Birmingham, Ala., 1983-85; sr. svc. specialist Cuna Mutual Ins. Group, Birmingham, 1985—. Mem. NAFE, LWV. Home And Office: 150 Snowbird Dr Apt 123 Birmingham AL 35209

KANE, MARGARET BRASSLER, sculptor; b. East Orange, N.J., May 25, 1909; d. Hans and Mathilde (Trumpler) Brassler; m. Arthur Ferris Kane, June 11, 1930; children: Jay Brassler, Gregory Ferris. Student, Packer Collegiate Inst., 1920-26, Syracuse U., 1927, Art Students League, 1927-29, N.Y. Coll. Music, 1928-29, John Hovannes Studio, 1932-34; PhD (hon.), Colo. State Christian Coll., 1973. head craftsman for sculpture, arts and skills unit ARC, Halloran Gen. Hosp., N.Y., 1942-43; 2d v.p. Nat. Assn. Woman Artists, Inc., 1943-45; sec. to exec. bd. Sculptors Guild, Inc., 1942-45, chmn. exhbn. com., 1942, 44; Jury mem. Bklyn. Mus., 1948, Am. Machine & Foundry Co., 1957; com. mem. An American Group, Inc. Work exhibited at Jacques Seligmann Gallery, N.Y., Whitney Ann. Exhbns., all Sculptors Guild Mus. and Outdoor Shows, Nat. Sculpture Soc. Ann. Bas-Relief Exhbn., 1938, Whitney Mus. Sculpture Festival, 1940, Bklyn. Mus. Sculptors Guild, 1938, Bklyn. Soc. Artists, 1942, Lawrence (Mass.) Art Mus., 1938, N.Y. World's Fair, 1939, Sculptors Guild World's Fair Exhbn., 1940, Robinson Gallery, N.Y., 1939, Traveling Mus. and Instns., 1938, Lyman Allyn Mus., 1939, Met. Mus., Internat. Exhbns., 1940, 1949, Roosevelt Field Art Ctr., N.Y.C., 1957, Phila. Mus., N.Y. Archtl. League, Nat. Acad., Penn. Acad., Chgo. Art Inst., Am. Fedn. Arts, Riverside Mus., Montclair Mus., Grand Cen. Art Galleries, Lever House, N.Y.C., 1959-81, Rye (N.Y.) Library, 1962, Lever House Sculptors Guild Ann. Exhbn., 1973-81, N.Y. Bot. Garden, 1981, Sculptors Guild 50th Anniversary Exhbn., Lever House, 1987, 88, 89, 1st Bi-Coastal exhibits San Francisco, Collection Donald Trump, 1988, Shidoni Galleries, Santa Fe, N.Mex., 1989, Am. Sculpture, Hofstra Mus., 1990; also exhbns. of nat. scope, 1938—; solo sculpture exhbn., Friends Greenwich (Conn.) Library, 1962; executed plaque for Burro Monument, Fairplay, Colo.; exhibited N.Y. Bank for Savs., 1968, Mattatuck Mus., Con., 1967, Lamont Gallery, N.H., 1967, Phila. Art Alliance Exhibition Sculpture of the American Scene, 1987, Am. References (Artists) Chicago, 1989—; executed: 18 foot carving in limewood depicting History of Man; reprodns. in Contemporary Stone Sculpture, 1970, Contemporary American Sculptures, Am. References, Chgo., 1989—; contbr. articles to mags.; feature article in Greenwich (Conn.) Time, 1990. Recipient Anna Hyatt Huntington award, 1942, Am. Artists Profl. League and Montclair Art Assn. Awards, 1943; 1st Henry O. Avery Prize, 1944; Sculpture Prize Bklyn. Soc. Artists, Bklyn. Mus., 1946; John Rogers Award, 1951; Lawrence Hyder Prize, 1952, 54; David H. Zell Meml. Award, 1954, 63; hon. mention U.S. Maritime Commn., 1941 and; A.C.A. Gallery Competition, 1944; Med. of honor for sculpture Nat. Assn. Women Artists, 1951; Med. of honor for sculpture Nat. Acad. Galleries, N.Y.; prize for carved sculpture, 1955; animal sculpture, 1956; 1st award for sculpture Greenwich Art Soc., 1958, 60; 1st award for sculpture Annual New Eng. Exhbns., Silvermine, Conn. Fellow Internat. Inst. Arts and Letters (life); mem. Sculptors Guild (charter), Nat. Assn. Women Artists (2d v.p. 1943-44), Artists Council, U.S.A., Bklyn. Soc. Artists, Greenwich Soc. Artists (council), Pen and Brush, Internat. Sculpture Center, Silvermine Guild Artists, Nat. Trust for Historic Preservation.; Mem. Internat. Soc. Artists (charter). Home and Studio: 30 Strickland Rd Cos Cob CT 06807

KANE, MARILYN ELIZABETH, small business owner; b. Butler, Pa., May 7, 1941; d. James and Anna (Supko) Holot; m. Paul D. Kane Sr., May 6, 1961; children: Kristina Marie, Paul D. Jr., Marilyn E. Grad. high sch., Butler, Earl Wheeler Modeling, Pitts., 1960; student, Palmer Talent Agy., N.Y.C., 1983—, UCLA, 1988. Cert. to teach modeling through World Modeling Assn. Exec. dir. Kane Finishing and Modeling Sch., Butler, 1970—; former instr. personal devel. Butler County Community Coll.; exec. dir. Kane Model and Talent Mgmt., Butler, 1970—. Fashion photographer Kane Sch. and Mgmt., 1980—; pageant dir. Miss Butler County USA, Cameo Model USA, Butler, 1977—; pageant judge various local, state, nat. levels competitions, 1970—. Mem. World Modeling Assn. (named Dir of Yr. 1978, 79, 85, Jr. Internat. Fashion Model 1979, 80, 81, 83, life). Democrat. Byzantine Catholic. Home: 203 Reiber Ave Butler PA 16001 Office: Kane Finishing & Modeling Sch 1022 N Main St Butler PA 16001

KANEB, ELIZABETH M., nursing home administrator; b. Massena, N.Y., Jan. 16, 1958; d. Edward John and Catherine Margaret (Meinhold) K. BA, St. Lawrence U., 1979; MBA, Clarkson U., Potsdam, N.Y., 1988. Lic. nursing home adminstr. Asst. adminstr. Highland Nursing Home, Inc., Massena, 1983—; sec. Kaneb Realty Corp.

KANE-VANNI, PATRICIA RUTH, lawyer, consultant; b. Phila., Jan. 12, 1954; d. Joseph James and Ruth Marina (Rameriz) Kane; m. Francis William Vanni; Feb. 14, 1980; 1 child, Christian Michael. AB, Chestnut Hill Coll., 1975; JD, Temple U., 1985. Bar: Pa. 1985, U.S. Ct. Appeals (3d cir.) 1988. Freelance art illustrator Phila., 1972-80; secondary edn. instr. Archdiocese of Phila., 1980-83; contract analyst CIGNA Corp., Phila., 1983-84; jud. aide Phila. Ct. of Common Pleas, 1984; assoc. atty. Anderson and Dougherty, Wayne, Pa., 1985-86; atty. cons. Bell Telephone Co. of Pa., 1986-87; assoc. corp. counsel Independence Blue Cross, Phila., 1987—; cons. Coll. Consortium on Drug and Alcohol Abuse, Chester, Pa., 1986-89. Contbr. articles and illustrations to profl. mags. Committeewoman Dem. Party, Lower Merion, Pa., 1983-87; judge Delaware Valley Sci. Fairs, Phila., 1986, 87. Recipient Legion of Honor award Chapel of the Four Chaplins, 1983. Mem. ABA, Pa. Bar Assn., Phila. Bar Assn. (Theatre Wing), Brehon Law Soc., Phila. Assn. Def. Counsel, Nat. Health Lawyers Assn., Phila. Hispanic Bar Assn., Phi Alpha Delta. Democrat. Roman Catholic. Home: 32 E Levering Mill Rd Bala Cynwyd PA 19004 Office: Independence Blue Cross Legal Dept 42d Fl 1901 Market St Philadelphia PA 19103

KANFER, RUTH, psychologist; b. St. Louis, Feb. 1, 1955; d. Frederick H. and Ruby Kanfer. BA, Miami U., Oxford, Ohio, 1976; MA, PhD, Ariz. State U., 1981. Med. psychology intern health scis. ctr. U. Oreg., Portland, 1980-81; NIMH postdoctoral fellow U. Ill., Champaign, 1981-83, vis. asst. prof. psychology, 1983-84; asst. prof. psychology U. Minn., Mpls., 1984-89; office naval rsch. summer faculty rsch. fellow USN Personnel Rsch. and Devel., San Diego, 1987; vis. scholar Stanford U., Palo Alto, Calif., 1988; assoc. prof. psychology U. Minn., Mpls., 1989—. Editorial bd. Jour. Applied Psychology, 1990—, Organizational Behavior and Human Decision Processes, 1989—; co-editor: Abilities Motivation and Methodology: The Minnesota Symposium on Learning and Individual Differences, 1989; contbr. articles to profl. jours. Fellow NIMH, 1976. Mem. Am. Psychol. Assn. (Disting. Sci. award for an early career contribution to psychology 1989), Am. Psychol. Soc., Acad. Mgmt. Assn., Internat. Assn. Applied Psychology, The Psychonomic Soc., Midwestern Psychol. Assn., Sigma Xi. Office: U Minn Dept Psychology Elliott Hall 75 E River Rd Minneapolis MN 55455

KANG, BANN C., immunologist; b. Kyungnam, Korea, Mar. 4, 1939; d. Daeryong and Buni (Chung) K.; came to U.S., 1964, naturalized, 1976; A.B., Kyungpook Nat. U., 1959, M.D., 1963; m. U. Yun Ryo, Mar. 30, 1963. Intern, L.I. Jewish Hosp.-Queens Hosp. Center, Jamaica, N.Y., 1964-65, resident in medicine, 1965-67; teaching asso. Kyungpook U. Hosp., Taegu, Korea, 1967-70; fellow in allergy and chest Creighton U., Omaha, 1970-71; fellow in allergy Henry Ford Hosp., Detroit, 1971-72; clin. instr. medicine U. Mich. Hosp., Ann Arbor, 1972-73; asst. prof. Chgo. Med. Sch., 1973-74; chief allergy-immunology Mt. Sinai Hosp., Chgo., 1975—; asst. prof. Rush Med. Sch., Chgo. 1975-84, assoc. prof., 1984-86; assoc. prof. U. Ky. Coll.

Medicine, 1987—; cons. allergy-immunology Edgewater Hosp., Chgo., 1976—, St. Anthony's Hosp., Chgo., 1976—, NHLBI, 1989—; mem. Experimental Transplantation Adv. Bd., Ill., 1985-86, Diagnostic and Therapeutic Tech. Assessment (AMA), 1987—, Gen. Clin. Rsch. Com. (NIH), 1989—; counselor Chgo. Med. Soc., 1984-86, mem. policy com., adv. com. to health dept. Chgo. and Cook County, 1984-86. Recipient NIH award U. Mich., 1972-73. Diplomate Am. Bd. Internal Medicine, Am. Bd. Allergy-Immunology. Fellow ACP, Am. Acad. Allergy; mem. Am. Fedn. Clin. Research, AMA, Inter-Asthma Assn. Contbr. over 40 articles to profl. jours. Home: 2716 Martinique Ln Lexington KY 40509 Office: U Ky Coll Medicine 629 Albert B Chandler Med Ctr 800 Rose St Lexington KY 40536

KANG, KYOUNG SOOK, teacher; b. Seoul, May 29, 1942; came to U.S., 1972; m. Young woo Kang, Feb. 26, 1972; children: Paul, Christopher. BA in Edn., Sookmyung Woman's U., Seoul, 1972; MS in Edn., Purdue U., 1987. Cert. elem. tchr., Ind. Clk., youth dept. Red Cross of Korea, Seoul, 1962-64; clk. Samho Trading Co., Seoul, 1965-67; field trainee Pa. State Office for the Blind, Harrisburg, 1967-68; assoc. exec. dir. Rehab. Ctr. for the Blind of Korea, Seoul, 1970-72; orientation and mobility tchr. for the blind Gary (Ind.) Community Sch. Corp., 1977—; Sunday sch. tchr. Chunho-dong Meth. Ch., Seoul, 1958-59, Namsan Meth. Ch., Seoul, 1960-62, Westminster Presbyn. Ch., Munster, Ind., 1981-82. Author: Two Candles Shining in the Darkness of the World, 1990. Leader Seoul Girl Scout coun., 1961-62. Recipient Cert. Appreciation, Korean Assn. Spl. Educators, 1978, Paul Harris award Rotary Internat., Evanston, Ill., 1987, Cert. Appreciation Gary Dept. Spl. Edn., 1988. Mem. AAUW (life), Coun. for Exceptional Children. Home: 8116 Meadow Ln Munster IN 46321 Office: Lincoln Achievement Ctr 1988 Polk St Gary IN 46407

K'ANG, VERSA CLARICE, museum director; b. Victoria, Va., May 28, 1939; d. Ralph Jennings Holder and Clara Hayworth (Weir) Holder Fischer; m. Jay Stephen Anderson, Aug. 11, 1961 (div. 1973); children: Max Kuika'hi, Mark Kuikawa'; m. Lyle Kekahi K'ang, Dec. 19, 1974; 1 child, Micah Ka'aona. BA in Edn., U. Wash., 1961; MA in Am. Studies, U. Hawaii, 1973; postgrad., Cen. Wash. U., 1980. Cert. tchr., Hawaii. Tchr. South Cen. Sch. Dist., Seattle, 1961-63, Kamehameha Schs., Honolulu, 1963-68; tchr., ctr. supr. lang. arts multi-cultural ctr. Hawaii County Econ. Opportunity Coun., Honokaa, 1976-78; counselor, supr. People for People, Yakima, Wash., 1978-83; exec. dir. Yakima Valley Mus. and Hist. Assn., 1983—; cons. dept. interdisciplinary studies Heritage Coll., Toppenish, Wash., 1982-83. Contbr. articles on Yakima Valley heritage to various publs. Co-chmn. Gov.'s Commn. on Youth and Leisure Time Activities, Honolulu, 1972-73, sub-com. Wash. State Centennial Commn., Olympia, 1985—; mem. Yakima County Tourism Coun., 1988, Yakima Conventer Ctr. Commn., 1989—; mem. bd. adv. Yakima Nation Cultural Mus. Mem. Am. Assn. State and Local History, Am. Assn. Mus., Wash. Mus. Assn., Wash. State Folklife Coun. (founding bd. dirs. 1983), Yakima C. of C., U. Wash. Alumni Assn., Assn. Washtinton Gens. (hon. gen.), Kiwanis (bd. dirs.), Phi Kappa Phi. Mormon. Lodge: Kiwanis (bd. dirs.). Home: 910 S 25th Ave Yakima WA 98902 Office: Yakima Valley Mus and Hist Assn 2105 Tieton Dr Yakima WA 98902

KANGAS, JULIE ELIZABETH, dentist; b. Massena, N.Y., Mar. 1, 1956; d. Richard Tauno and Fannie Evelyn (Nikkola) K.; m. William Randolph Jungman, May 9, 1981; children: Robert William Kangas Jungman, brian Christopher Kangas Jungman. BS, Boise State U., 1977; DDS, U. So. Calif., 1981. Dentist Dr. Richard Katnik DDS, Inc., San Diego, 1981-82, San Diego Dental Health Ctr., La Mesa, Calif., 1982-83, Dr. Philip Menna DDS Inc./Personal Dental Plan, El Cajon, Calif., 1983-85; owner, dentist Citracado Dental Group, Escondido, Calif., 1982—. Editor, contbr. (newsletter) Word of Mouth, 1985—. Vol. dentist Children's Dental Health North, San Diego, 1988; vol. screening dentist Boys & Girls Club, Escondido, 1989—; mem., treas. Escondido Dental Health Acad., 1984-85; vol. speaker local preschs. La Petite Acad., Lion & Lamb Presch., Escondido, 1988—. Western Interstate Com. Higher Edn. scholar, 1977-81, Pres.'s scholar Boise State U., 1974. Mem. NAFE (coord. 1989-90), San Diego County Dental Soc., Calif. Dental Assn., ADA, Pacific Acad. Esthetic Dentistry (charter), San Diego Women Dentists (charter, exec. com. 1986-87), Am. Assn. Women Dentists, Escondido C. of C., Psi Omega. Office: Citracado Dental Group 306 W El Norte #E Escondido CA 92026

KANICK, VIRGINIA, radiologist; b. Coaldale, Pa., Nov. 10, 1925; d. Martin and Anna (Pisklak) K. BA, Barnard Coll., 1947; MD, Columbia U., 1951. Diplomate Am. Bd. Radiology. Intern Western Reserve U. Hosps., Cleve., 1951-52; resident in radiology St. Luke's Hosp., N.Y.C., 1952-55, attending radiologist, 1955-74; acting dir. radiology St. Luke's Roosevelt Hosp., N.Y.C., 1981-84, dep. dir. of radiology, 1984-89; ptnr. West Side Radiology, N.Y.C., 1989—; clin. prof. radiology Coll. Physicians and Surgeons Columbia U., N.Y.C., 1975—; pres. Med. Bd. St. Luke's Roosevelt Hosp., 1980-82. Contbr. articles to profl. jours. Bd. dirs. Health System Agy. of N.Y.C., 1978-81. Fellow Am. Cancer Soc., 1955. Fellow Am. Coll. Radiology; mem. Am. Roentgen Ray Soc., Radiol. Soc. N.Am., N.Y. County Med. Soc. (sec., dir. 1978—), N.Y. State Radiol. Soc. (bd. dirs. 1975—). Republican. Roman Catholic. Home: 560 Riverside Dr Apt 17B New York NY 10027 Office: West Side Radiology 1090 Amsterdam Ave New York NY 10025

KANNARD, JANICE ALISA, pharmaceutical plant manager; b. Glendale, Calif., Aug. 13, 1952; d. Vernon William Jones and Betty Lou (Davis) Alsberg; m. Don A. Kennard Aug. 18, 1990. BS in Biochemistry, Calif. Polytech. State U., 1976. Asst. chemist McGaw Lab., Irvine, Calif., 1976-78, asst. research scientist, 1978-80, quality control supr., 1980-82; quality assurance mgr. Allergan Pharms., Irvine, Calif., 1982-83, production mgr., 1983-86, plant mgr., 1986—. Mem. C. of C. Women Bus. Republican. Office: Allergan Pharm 2525 Pullman Ave Santa Ana CA 92705

KANNER, ELLEN, writer; b. Miami, Fla., Jan. 3, 1961; d. Lewis Mitchell and Marcia Miriam (Jervis) K.; m. Benjamin David Bohlmann. BA, Bennington (Vt.) Coll., 1983. Freelance writer The Miami News, 1983-85; mgr. Bookworks, Inc., Miami, 1983-85; freelance writer Tokyo, 1985-87; claims rep. SAG, Miami, 1988—. Author: (novel) Geographic Cure, 1988, (video) Mom Was Wrong, 1988, (diet video) Mouthtraps, Inc., 1988; contbr. to mags. Vol. alumni com. Bennington Coll., 1988—; mem. Orion com. South Fla. chpt. ARC, Miami, 1989—. Mem. S. Fla. Zool. Assn., Hist. Assn. So. Fla., Coconut Grove Writers Workshop, Nat. Soc. Arts and Letters. Democrat. Jewish.

KANNER, ELLEN BARBARA, clinical psychologist; b. Newark, Apr. 22, 1950; d. S. Lee and Elsie (Frumkin) K.; m. Brian R. Donovan, June 10, 1973; children: Gregory Kanner, Rebecca Kanner. BA in Psychology, Smith Coll., 1972; MA in Clin. Psychology, Fordham U., 1974, PhD in Clin. Psychology, 1980. Lic. psychologist N.Y. Psychology aide Behavior Modification Program Northampton (Mass.) State Hosp., 1972-73; psychology intern Kings County Hosp., Bklyn., 1975-76; part time psychology work various clinics, N.Y., 1976-77; psychologist Kings Park (N.Y.) Psychiat. Ctr., 1980-83; pvt. practice Huntington, N.Y., 1983—. Unitarian. Office: 205 East Main St Huntington NY 11743

KANNRY, SYBIL, psychotherapist, consultant, b. Tulsa, Okla., Oct. 1, 1931; d. Julius and Celia Bertha (Triger) Zeligson; m. Daniel Kannry, June 12, 1977; children by previous marriage: Jeffrey Alan Shames, Erica Leslie Shames, Jonathan Adam Shames. Student U. Colo., 1949-51; BA, U. Okla., 1953; MSW, NYU, 1974. Diplomate in Clin. Social Work; cert. clin. social worker, N.Y.; credentialled alcoholism counselor; cert. employee assistance profl. Tchr. piano, Tulsa, 1956-61; psychiatric social worker Essex County Hosp., Cedar Grove, N.J., 1974-75, Rockland Psychiat. Ctr., Spring Valley, N.Y., 1975, adult team supr., 1975-78, adult team supr., Haverstraw, N.Y., 1978, clinic supr., Orangeburg, N.Y., 1978-83, clinic dir., Yonkers, N.Y., 1983-84; founder, dir. Indsl. Counseling Assocs., South Nyack, N.Y., 1982-84, Ctr. for Corp. and Community Counseling, South Nyack, 1984—; founder, pres. Tulsa Assn. for Childbirth Edn., 1957-59. Fellow Soc. Clin. Social Work Psychotherapists; mem. Am. Assn. Marriage and Family Therapy (clin. mem.), N.Y. Milton H. Erickson Soc. for Psychotherapy and Hypnosis, Nat. Assn. Social Workers, Am. Orthopsychiat. Assn., Acad. Cert. Social Workers, Employee Assistance Profl. Assn., Soc. Clin. and Exptl. Hypnosis. Home and Office: 2 Clinton Ave South Nyack NY 10960

KANTER, ROSABETH MOSS, management educator, consultant, writer; b. Cleve., Mar. 15, 1943; d. Nelson Nathan and Helen (Smolen) Moss; m. Stuart Alan Kanter, June 20, 1963 (dec. Mar. 1969); m. Barry Alan Stein, July 2, 1972; 1 child, Matthew Moss Kanter Stein. BA in Sociology magna cum laude, Bryn Mawr Coll., 1964; MA, U. Mich., 1965, PhD, 1967; postgrad., Harvard U. Law Sh., 1975-76; MA (hon.), Yale U., 1978, Harvard U., 1986; DSc (hon.), Bucknell U., 1980, Babson Coll., 1984, Bryant Coll., 1986, Bentley Coll., 1990; LHD (hon.), Antioch U., Westminster Coll., 1984, Suffolk U., N. Adams State Coll., 1987, Colby-Sawyer Coll., 1988, U. New Haven, 1989; DCL (hon.), Union Coll., 1987; LLD (hon.), Regis Coll., 1987; DSS (hon.), Fla. Internat. U., 1990. Vis. prof. mgmt. MIT, 1973-74, Harvard U., 1979-80; from assoc. to asst. prof. Brandeis U., 1967-77; prof. Yale U., 1977-86; Class of 1960 prof. mgmt. Harvard U. Bus. Sch., 1986—; cons. BellSouth, Apple Computer, Procter & Gamble, IBM, Internat. Harvester Co., Honeywell Corp. and numerous others; trustee Coll. Retirement Equities Fund, N.Y., 1985—; dir. Ctr. for New Democracy, Washington, 1985-87; trustee Am. Leadership Forum, Houston, 1982-86; mem. work group on entrepreneurship Pres.'s Commn. Indsl. Competitiveness, 1984; Govs.'s innovation adv. com. Commonwealth of Mass, chair subcom., 1986; mem. Spl. Commn. on Employee Involvement and Ownership, Mass., 1986-87; mem. Gov.'s Commn. Rev. Anti-Takeover Laws, Mass. 1988; Katz-Newcomb lectr. in social psychology U. Mich., 1986; Disting. speaker Orgn., Theory, Careers and Women in Mgmt. divs. Nat. Acad. Mgmt., 1987; Lilly Found. Disting. lectr. Nat. Assn. Community Leadership Orgns., 1985; Leavey Disting. lectr. U. Santa Clara, 1984; vis. scholar Newberry Libr. Program in Humanities, Chgo., 1973, Norwegian Rsch. Coun. on Sci., and Humanities, Oslo, 1980; Kellogg Found. 50th Anniv. lectr. Am. Assn. Higher Edn., 1979, Blazer lectr. U. Ky., 1974, Davidson lectr. U. N.H., 1975; Sigma Chi scholar-in-residence Miami U., Oxford, Ohio, 1978; bd. dirs. Goodmeasure Software Corp., Cambridge, Mass., Am. Productivity and Quailty Ctr., Houston, Ames Dept. Stores, Nichols Inst. Author: Work and Family in the U.S., 1977, Men and Women of the Corporation, 1977 (C. Wright Mills award 1977), The Change Masters, 1983, (with M.S. Dukakis) Creating The Future: The Massachusetts Comeback and Its Promise for America, 1988, When Grants Learn to Dance, 1989 (Johnson Smith Knicely Exec. Leadership award 1990), plus 5 other books, also monographs; mem. editorial bd. Human Resource Mgmt. jour., 1982-89, Orgn. Dynamics jour., 1983-85, 89, Jour. Bus. Venturing, 1985-89, Jour. Contemporary Bus., 2987-89, others; adv. bd. Society jour., 1987-89; editor Harvard Bus. Rev., 1989—; contbr. over 100 articles to profl. jours., books, mags. (2 articles Harvard Bus. Review McKinsey award). Incorporator Babson Coll., 1984—, Boston Children's Mus., 1984—; bd. dirs. Nat. Orgn. Women Legal Def. and Edn. Fund, N.Y., 1979-86, Ctr. New Democracy, Washington, 1985—. Named Woman of the Yr. New Eng. Women's Bus. Owners, 1981, Internat. Assn. Personnel Women, 1981, MS mag., 1985; named to Cleve. Heights High Sch. Hall of Fame, 1986, Working Woman Hall of Fame AT&T/Working Women mag., 1986, Ohio Women's Hall of Fame, 1990; recipient Athena award Intercollegiate Assn. Women Students, 1980, Gold medal award Big Sister Assn. Greater Boston, 1985, Women Who Make a Difference award Internat. Women's Forum, 1988, Richard M. Cyert award Profl. Excellence Carnegie-Mellon U. Grad. Sch. Indsl. Adminstrn., 1989, Project Equality award, 1990; Guggenheim fellow; numerous research grants. Fellow Acad. Mgmt. (Disting. speaker mgmt. cons. div. 1985), Am. Soc. Quality & Participation; mem. Am. Sociol. Assn. (exec. council 1982-5), Eastern Sociol. Soc. (exec. com. 1975-78, Gellman award, 1978), Com. of 200 (founder), Internat. Women's Forum. Office: Harvard U Bus Sch Teele 218 Boston MA 02163

KANTOREK, SANDRA SCHWAHL, optometrist; b. Newark, Sept. 18, 1952; d. Charles Richard and Mary (Costabile) Schwahl; m. John Vito Kantorek, Aug. 17, 1974; children: Christopher, Heather. Student, Douglass Coll., 1970-72; OD, Mass. Coll. of Optometry, 1976. Clinical instr. New England Coll. of Optometry, Boston, 1976-78; pvt. practice Union, N.J., 1978--; low vision specialist St. Barnabas Med. Ctr., Livingston, N.J., 1986--. Adv. Bd. Head Start Program, 1985--. Mem. Am. Optometric Assn. (contact lens, low vision sect. mem.), Mid Jersey Opt ometric Soc., Tri-County Optometric Soc., Beta Sigma Kappa (Silver Medal Award). Office: 1485 Morris Ave Union NJ 07083

KANY, JUDY C(ASPERSON), state senator; b. June 29, 1937; d. Helmer C. and Florence P. Casperson; m. Robert Kany, Aug. 16, 1958; children: Kristin, Geoffrey, Daniel. BBA, U. Mich., 1959; MPA, U. Maine-Orono, 1976. Mem. Maine Ho. Reps., 1975-82, Maine Senate, 1982—, chmn. Maine's Adv. Commn. on Radioactive Waste, 1981-87, Joint Standing Com. Legal Affairs, Joint Standing Com. on State Govt., 1982-86, Joint Standing Com. Energy and Natural Resources, 1983-84, 89—, mem. Commn. on Maine's Future, 1976, 87-89; mayor Waterville, Maine, 1987-89. Democrat. Home: 18 West St Waterville ME 04901 Office: Maine State Senate Augusta ME 04333

KAO, KAREN PATRICIA, advertising executive; b. Rochester, N.Y.; d. Peter Te-Sung and Patricia (Chang) K. BS, Cornell U., 1988. Media planner Young & Rubicam, N.Y.C., 1988-89; account exec. Grey Advt., N.Y.C., 1989—. Instr. YMCA, N.Y.C., 1989, Cornell Club, N.Y.C., 1988-89. Mem. Ad Club. Home: 488 E 74th St New York NY 10017 Office: Grey Advt 777 3d Ave New York NY 10017

KAPLAN, AMY LOUISE, educator; b. N.Y.C., June 14, 1950; d. Max and Anne Esther (Langsam) K. BA, U. Conn., 1972, MA, 1978; postgrad., Fairfield U., 1979-82, N.Y. Med. Coll., 1982-83. Cert. tchr., Conn. Tchr. Columbia (Conn.) Bd. Edn., 1972-73, Manchester (Conn.) Bd. Edn., 1973-74, Trumbull (Conn.) Bd. Edn., 1974-79; project dir. Weston Group, Westport, Conn., 1981; tchr. Easton (Conn.) Bd. Edn., 1983-84; dir. Learning Ctr., Westport, 1983—; tchr. Westport Bd. Edn., 1984-89; agt. Mass. Mutual, Fairfield, Conn., 1990; tchr. Collier County (Fla.) Pub. Schs., 1990—. Mem. Dem. Town Com., Fairfield, 1987; fundraiser Hole-in-the-Wall Gang Day Camp, Westport, 1987-88. Mem. NEA, Conn. Edn. Assn. (assembly rep. 1975), Flying Eagles Club (bd. dirs. Stratford, Conn. 1986).

KAPLAN, ANN RUTH, small business owner; b. N.Y.C., Jan. 14, 1938; d. Abraham H. and Bertha (Goodman) Maslow; m. Jerome I. Kaplan, Dec. 18, 1965; 1 child, Jeanne. Student, Bennington Coll., 1956-58, Brandeis U., Waltham, 1962-64. Rsch. asst. Wellesley Human Rels. Svc., 1960-63, New Design Project Boston Floating Hosp., Boston, 1963, Joint Admissions Project Mass. Mental Health Ctr., Boston, 1964-65; owner/dir. Artifacts Gallery, Indpls.; juror Lafayesta Craft Fair, Ind., 1985, Watertower Art Fair, Louisville, 1988. Bd. dirs. Columbus Assn. for Childbirth Edn., Abortion Edn. Soc. of Ohio, Arts Ind. (Newspaper), Ind. Pro-choice Action League, Ind. Film Soc. Mem. Am. Craft Council. Democrat. Jewish. Office: Artifacts Gallery 6327 Guilford Avenue Indianapolis IN 46220

KAPLAN, CAREY, English literature educator; b. Boston, Dec. 16, 1943; d. Bertram David and Rose Marie (Doolan) Halperson. BA, Barnard, 1965; MA, U. Chgo., 1968; PhD, U. Mass., 1972. Prof. English lit. St. Michael's Coll., Colchester, Vt., 1972—. Editor (with Ellen Rose, essays) Alchemy of Survival, 1986 (NEMLA Best citation 1986), Approaches to Teaching; co-author: (with Ellen Rose) Doris Lessings Golden Notebook, 1987, The Canon and the Common Reader, 1990. Mem. Gov.'s Commn. Mental Health, Vt., 1983-86; pres. Doris Lessing Soc., 1984-86. Mem. MLA. Home: 284 Colchester Ave Burlington VT 05401 Office: St Michaels Coll Colchester VT 05439

KAPLAN, CAROL BLAKELY, communications executive; b. Oak Ridge, Tenn., Sept. 17, 1945; d. John Paul and Tinque June (Spann) Blakely; m. Jonathan Wall Kaplan, July 29, 1967 (div. 1976). BA, Swarthmore (Pa.) Coll., 1967; MS, U. Pa., 1971. Tchr. Sch. Dist. of Phila., 1967-68, 69-70, Monona (Wis.) pub. schs., 1968-69, Prince Georges Co. pub. schs., Upper Marlboro, Md., 1971-74; assoc. rsch. scientist Am. Inst. Rsch., Palo Alto, Calif., 1974-82; dir. corp. communications Boole & Babbage, Sunnyvale, Calif., 1982--. Editor BooleanWorld, 1986-88, Info. Exec., 1983, Jour. of Capacity Mgmt., 1982-83, Inside Software Engring., 1982-84. Coordinator United Way campaign, Sunnyvale, 1984-87. Mem. AAUW, Mt. View Tennis Club (pres. 1987). Democrat. Office: Boole & Babbage 510 Oakmead Pkwy Sunnyvale CA 94086

KAPLAN, DIANE SUSAN, radio broadcasting executive; b. Bklyn., Feb. 26, 1957; d. Theodore Sharon and Eleanor J. (Wasserman) K.; m. Melvin H. Sather, Sept. 12, 1987; stepchildren: Jay, Jerry, Charles. BA in Communications and Women's Studies summa cum laude, U. Pa., 1977. Dir. pub. affairs Sta. WXPN-FM, U. Pa., Phila., 1975-76, program dir., 1976-77, dir. pub. info., 1977-79; gen. mgr. Sta. KALX-FM, U. Calif., Berkeley, 1979-81; program mgr. Calif. Pub. Broadcasting Commn., Sacramento, 1981-83; exec. dir. Alaska Pub. Radio Network, Anchorage, 1983-90, pres., chief exec. officer, 1990—. Commr. Anchorage Telephone Commn., 1985; active Anchorage Women's Commn., 1986-88, People for the Am. Way; bd. dirs. United Way, Anchorage, 1988-89. Mem. Alaska Press Club (treas., bd. dirs. 1986-89), Chugach Conf. Planning Com., Anchorage C. of C., Rotary Club, Phi Beta Kappa. Home: Box 726 Eagle River AK 99577 Office: Alaska Pub Radio Network 4640 Old Seward Hwy Ste 202 Anchorage AK 99503

KAPLAN, ERICA LYNN, typing and word processing service company executive, pianist; b. Jamaica, N.Y., Aug. 6, 1955; d. George William and Raylia (Eagle) Kaplan; m. James Laurence Kellermann, Feb. 26, 1982. B in Mus., Manhattan Sch. Music, N.Y.C., 1976, M in Mus., 1979. Clk. dept. edn. 92d St. Y, N.Y.C., 1972-76, assoc. dept. pub. rels., 1977-78, catalogue coord., sec. to exec. dir., 1978, assoc. dept. performing arts, 1978-79, assoc. dir. dept. publs., 1979-80; pres. Erica Kaplan Typing/Word Processing/Music Svcs., N.Y.C., 1980—; piano soloist Huntington (N.Y.) Philharmonia, 1975; rehearsal pianist, performance accompanist The Mikado, Playwrights Horizons, N.Y.C., 1975, Fiona in Swan Song, N.Y.C., 1986; mus. dir., accompanist A Salute to Vaudeville/A Tribute to Fred Astaire, N.Y.C., 1980—; mus. dir., pianist Portrait of a Man, Hyde Pk. (N.Y.) Festival Theatre, 1981, Am. Renaissance Theater, N.Y.C., 1982, 86, The Fantasticks, Dalton Sch., N.Y.C., 1983; performance accompanist Okla., Theatreworks, Bklyn., 1984; resident pianist Am. Renaissance Theater, N.Y.C., 1981—; audition accompanist Interboro Repertory Theater, N.Y.C., 1986—; accompanist, vocal lessons class Stuyvesant Adult Ctr., N.Y.C., 1988—. Translator and annotator with additional mus. examples: L'Anacrouse dans la Musique Moderne, 1978; composer (songs) Four by Feiffer, 1978, Hey Boys, 1984, Unborn Child, 1988. Mem. New Eng. Anti-Vivisection Soc., Boston, 1982—, Nat. Anti-Vivisection Soc., 1988—, Common Cause, Washington, 1983—, SANE/FREEZE, 1988. Mem. Am. Fedn. Musicians, NAFE, Union Concerned Scientists. Democrat. Jewish. Avocations: theater, travel.

KAPLAN, HELENE LOIS, lawyer; b. N.Y.C., June 19, 1933; d. Jack and Shirley (Jacobs) Finkelstein; m. Mark N. Kaplan, Sept. 7, 1952; children: Marjorie Ellen, Sue Anne. AB cum laude, Barnard Coll., 1953; JD, NYU, 1967; LLD (hon.), Columbia U., 1990. Bar: N.Y. 1967. Pvt. practice law N.Y.C., 1967-78; ptnr. Webster & Sheffield, N.Y.C., 1978-86, counsel, 1986—; bd. dirs. The May Dept. Stores Co., Met. Life Ins. Co., Chem. Banking Corp., Chem. Bank, Mobil Corp., Verde Exploration Ltd. Trustee N.Y. Council for the Humanities, 1976-82, chmn., 1978-82; trustee Barnard Coll., 1973-83, chmn., 1983—, trustee Columbia U. Press, 1977-80, MITRE Corp., 1978—, N.Y. Found., 1976-86, Mt. Sinai Hosp. Med. Ctr. and Med. Sch., 1977—, John Simon Guggenheim Meml. Found., 1981—, NYU Law Ctr. Found., 1985-87, Carnegie Corp. N.Y., 1979—, vice chmn., 1981-84, chmn., 1984-91; trustee Inst. for Advanced Study, 1986—, Neuroscis. Research Found., 1986—, Am. Mus. of Natural History, 1989—; mem. adv. com. of U.S. Sec. of State on South Africa, 1986-88; mem. N.Y. State Gov.'s Task Force on Life and the Law, 1985—; trustee N.Y.C. Pub. Devel. Corp., 1978-83, vice chmn., 1979-82; trustee Olive Free Library; bd. dirs. Am. Arbitration Assn., 1978-82, Catskill Ctr. for Conservation and Devel., 1981—; mem. Women's Forum, Inc., 1982—; mem. council Rockefeller U., 1984—; mem. Bretton Woods Com., 1985—; mem. Carnegie Council on Adolescent Devel., 1986—, Carnegie Commn. on Sci., Tech., and Govt., 1988—; ptnr. N.Y.C. Partnership, 1987—. Mem. ABA, N.Y.C. Bar Assn. (com. on philanthropic orgn. 1975-81, recruitment of lawyers 1978-82, com. on profl. responsibility 1980-83), N.Y. State Bar Assn., Coun. Fgn. Rels., Am. Acad. Arts & Scis., Am. Philos. Soc., Cosmopolitan Club, Coffee House Club, Century Assn. Home: 146 Central Pk W New York NY 10023 Office: 237 Park Ave 20th Fl New York NY 10017

KAPLAN, HUETTE MYRA, business educator, training consultant; b. Chgo., July 11, 1933; d. Max and Jeannette (Smith) Lazan; m. Jerrold M. Kaplan, Feb. 14, 1954; children: Lawrence, Jeffrey. BS in Bus. Edn., DePaul U., 1971. Instr. Pub. Svc. Careers Program State of Ill., Chgo., 1971-72; instr., dir. Patricia Stevens Bus. Sch., Chgo., 1972; relocation mgr., tng. specialist, dir. tng. and devel. Zurich-Am. Ins. Cos., Chgo. and Schaumburg, Ill., 1972-80; pres., tng. cons. H.K. & Assocs., Lansing, Ill., 1980—; tng. dir. Calumet Area Literacy Coun., Hammond, Ind., 1985—; trainer Chgo. Literacy Coordinating Ctr., 1988—; instr. Purdue U.-Calumet, Hammond, 1976—. Bd. dirs. Temple Beth El, Hammond, 1986-88, Calumet Area Literacy Coun., 1990; mem. task force Chgo. Coalition for Edn. and Tng. for Employment, 1984-86. Mem. Nat. Bus. Edn. Assn., Am. Soc. for Tng. and Devel., Human Resources Mgmt. Assn. Jewish. Home and Office: HK & Assocs 2843 192d St Lansing IL 60438

KAPLAN, JANET GORDON, music educator; b. Boston, Nov. 30, 1938; d. Morris and A. Ruby (Perlman) G.; children: Beth, Deborah, Paul. AA, Los Angeles Valley Coll., 1968; BA, Calif. State U., 1984, MA in Ednl. Psychology, 1987. Intern social work Los Angeles Children's Bur., 1982, Valley Hosp. Med. Ctr., Van Nuys, Calif., 1983; tchr., coach, judge string music Los Angeles County Schs., 1983—; cons. San Fernando Valley Community Concerts, Van Nuys. Pres. Los Angeles Philharmonic Docents, 1977-80. Mem. Music Tchrs. Assn. (pres. east valley br. 1989—), Am. String Tchrs. Assn., Mu Phi Epsilon (pres. 1980-82, 88-89, Outstanding Musician 1958, Music Therapy award 1981-84, Edn. award 1986).

KAPLAN, (NORMA) JEAN GAITHER, teacher; b. Cumberland, Md., Dec. 14, 1927; d. Frank Preston and Elizabeth (Mcneil) Gaither; m. Robert Lewis Kaplan, Dec. 4, 1959; 1 child, Benjamin Leigh. AB in Edn., Madison Coll., Harrisonburg, Va., 1950; MA in Edn., U. Va., 1956, postgrad., 1957-61, 76. Tchr. Frederick County Sch. System, Winchester, Va., 1950-51, Washington County Sch. System, Hagerstown, Md., 1951-55, Charlottesville (Va.) Sch. System, 1955-60, York County (Va.) Sch. System, 1962, Newport News Sch. System, Denbigh, Va., 1963, Internat. Sch. Bangkok, 1965-67; tutor Reston Reading Ctr., Fair Fax County, Va., 1972-74; tutor (homebound) Fairfax County (Va.) Sch. Systems, 1974-78; pvt. practice pvt. tutor Middleburg, Va., 1978—; pres. Tutorial Services, Inc., McLean, Va., 1985-87, sec. The Rumson Corp., Middleburg, Va., 1981—. Mem. No. Va. Conservation Coun., Fairfax County, Va., 1976-81; bd. dirs. Nat. Environ. Leadership Coun., 1990—. Mem. AAUW, LWV, Bangkok Am. Wives Assn., Tuesday Afternoon Club (pres. 1974-75), Ayr Hill Garden Club, Kappa Delta Pi, Slpha Sigma Tau. Home and Office: Atoka Chase PO Box 1943 Middleburg VA 22117

KAPLAN, JOCELYN RAE, financial planning firm executive; b. Lynbrook, N.Y., Apr. 23, 1952; d. Eugene S. and Adeline (Dembo) K. B.S., Northwestern U., 1975. Cert. fin. planner. Ins. agt. Fidelity Union Life Ins. Co., College Park, Md., 1976-77, Bankers Life Ins. Co., Rockville, Md., 1977-80; fin. planner Reutemann & Wagner, McLean, Va., 1980-82; fin. planning casewriter McLean Fin. Group, 1982-83; dir. fin. planning DeSanto Naftal Co., Vienna, Va., 1983-85; pres. Advisors Fin., Inc., Vienna, 1985—. Founding mem., treas. Congregation Bet Mishpachah, Washington, 1981, v.p., 1982, pres., 1983. Recipient Nat. Quality award Nat. Assn. Life Underwriters, 1978; Agt. of Yr. award Gen. Agt. and Mgrs. Assn., 1978. Mem. Internat. Assn. Fin. Planners, Inst. Cert. Fin. Planners, Registry of Fin. Planning Practitioners. Home: 5000 N 17th St Arlington VA 22207 Office: Advisors Fin Inc 2200 Clarendon Blvd Ste 1110 Arlington VA 22201

KAPLAN, JUDITH HELENE, corporate professional; b. N.Y.C., July 20, 1938; d. Abraham and Ruth (Kiffel) Letich; m. Warren Kaplan, Dec. 31, 1958; children: Ronald Scott, Elissa Aynn. BA, Hunter Coll., 1955; postgrad., New Sch. for Social Rsch., 1955-56. Registered rep. Herzfeld & Stern, N.Y.C., 1963; agt. New York Life Ins. Co., N.Y.C., 1964-69; registered rep. Scheinman, Hochstin & Trotta, 1969-70; v.p. Alpha Capital Corp., N.Y.C., 1970-74; pres. Tipex, Inc., N.Y.C., 1966-84; v.p. Alpha Pub. Relations, N.Y.C., 1970-73; pres. Utopia Recreations Corp., 1971-73, Howard Beach Recreation Corp., 1972-73; chmn. bd. Alpha Exec. Planning Corp., 1970-72; field underwriter N.Y. Life Ins. Co., 1974-75; pres. Action Products Internat. Inc., 1978-87, chairperson, 1980—, Ronel Industries, Inc., 1982-84; participant White House Conf. on Small Bus., 1979. Author: Woman Suffrage, 1977; co-author: Space Patches-from Mercury to the Space Shuttle, 1986; contbg. editor: Stamp Show News, M & H Philatelic Report; creator, producer Women's History series of First Day Covers, 1976-81; contbr. articles to profl. jours. Active Wyo. adv. on woman suffrage; trustee Found. for Innovative Lifelong Edn. Inc., 1986-88. Named Outstanding Young Citizen Manhattan Jaycees, Small Bus. Person of Yr. State of Fla, 1986. Mem. NOW (ins. coord. nat. task force on taxes, v.p. N.Y. chpt., co-founder Ocala/Marion County chpt. 1982, bd. women's adv. coun. Ocala and Marian Counties 1986-88), Nat. Women's Polit. Caucus, Women Leaders Round Table, Nat. Assn. Life Underwriters, Assn. Stamp Dealers Am., Am. First Day Cover Soc. (life), Am. Philatelic Soc. (life), Bus. and Profl. Women, AAUW. Home: 577 Silver Course Circle Ocala FL 32672 Office: 344 Cypress Rd Ocala FL 32672

KAPLAN, LAURA GARCIA, utilities executive; b. Hollywood, Fla., Mar. 11, 1957; d. Thomas Tubens and Felicia (Acebal) Garcia; m. Steven Kaplan; 1 child, Kristin. BSEE, U. Miami, 1979. Various positions Fla. Power and Light Co., Miami, 1980-88, constrn. services mgr., 1988—. Counselor Soc. Abused Children, Kendall, Fla., 1985-86; instr. Jr. Achievement, Miami, 1986-87, Adult Illiteracy Program, 1987. Early admission scholar U. Miami, 1975. Mem. Leadership Miami Assn., Greater Miami C. of C. Republican. Roman Catholic. Club: Hurricane. Home: 1270 NW 133 Ave Sunrise FL 33323 Office: Fla Power & Light Co 701 Lincoln Rd Miami Beach FL 33139

KAPLAN, LINDA F., advertising executive; b. N.Y.C., Jan. 15, 1951; d. Marvin and Bertha (Cohen) K.; m. Fred Thaler, May 30, 1987. BA, CCNY, 1972, MA in Music, 1975. Music lectr. CCNY, 1972-74; performer, musical dir., writer N.Y.C., 1974-75; freelance writer Brain Res., N.Y.C., 1975-77; copywriter J. Walter Thompson Agy., N.Y.C., 1978-80, sr. v.p., 1982—; lectr. Mercy Coll., Dobbs Ferry, N.Y., 1986. Composer popular songs. Com. mem. United Jewish Appeal, N.Y.C., 1986. Recipient nine Clio awards, 1981-86, Silver Lion award Cannes Film Festival, 1986; named One of the Top 100 People in Advt. Under 40, Ad Ages, 1984, Top 100 Women in Advt., 1988. Mem. Phi Beta Kappa. Democrat. Jewish. Office: J Walter Thompson Agy 466 Lexington Ave New York NY 10017

KAPLAN, LOIS JAY, writer, composer, sculptor, consultant; b. Chgo., Feb. 6, 1932; d. Banjamin Eli and Birdie (Goodman) K. MusB, DePaul U., 1958; MS in Recreation Adminstrn., U. Wis., Madison, 1963; MA in Art, Lit., Music, Jacksonville (Ala.) State U., 1978; postgrad. in music and humanities, Fla. State U. Music dir. U. Chgo. Settlement House, 1953-56; dir. Chgo. Stadium Band, 1956-58; stage mgr., music dir. Univ. Theatre, U. Chgo., 1957-59; producer, dir. entertainment shows U.S. Army Svc. Clubs, Europe, 1959-61; summer camp dir. various youth camps, 1961-63, 74; tchr. music, art, lit, band dir. Chgo. Pub. Schs., 1956-59, 61-63; recreation cons., lectr. on arts Anniston, Ala., 1980—; commd. 2d lt. U.S. Army, 1963, advanced through grades to lt. col., ret., 1986; tchr. English Pusan U., Korea, 1965-66. Contbr. articles to profl. jours., critiques and revs., poems and short stories to Chgo. Daily News, Chgo. Sun-Times, Chgo. Today, New Yorker, N.Y. Mag., DePaulia, Cardinal Mag., others; music compositions include: La Salle Street Sketches, Pallas Athena, Song and March, This Indeed We'll Defend, Salute to the Citizen Soldier, Phantasies #1-3 (electronic music), and Serving the Cause of Democracy; sculpture series includes: I. Complexity; II. Implosion; III. Kaleidoscope. Decorated Army Commendation medal; recipient Diploma di Benemerenza, Centro Studi e' Scambi Internazionali (CSSI), 1980, Diploma D'Onore, 1982, Diploma di Medaglia d'oro, 1985, others. Fellow Internat. Acad. Poets (Cambridge, Eng.), Centro Studi e' Scambi Internat. Acad. Leonardo Da Vinci (Rome), World Lit. Acad. (Cambridge, Eng.); mem. Nat. Recreation and Parks Assn., Am. Fedn. Musicians U.S. and Can., Internat. Soc. Contemporary Music, Nat. Music Educators Assn., Ala. Coun. Arts and Humanities (com. chmn., prog. executor), Assoc. Photographers Internat. Photographic Soc. Am., Audubon Soc., Nat. Arbor Day Found., Nat. Wildlife Fedn., Nat. Wilderness Soc., others. Home: 616 Lenwood Dr Anniston AL 36206

KAPLAN, MADELINE, law firm administrator; b. N.Y.C., June 20, 1944; d. Leo and Ethel (Finkelstein) Kahn; m. Theodore Norman Kaplan, Nov. 14, 1982. AS, Fashion Inst. Tech., N.Y.C., 1964; BA in English Lit. summa cum laude, CUNY, 1982; MBA, Baruch Coll., 1990. Free-lance fashion illustrator N.Y.C., 1965-73; legal asst. Krause Hirsch & Gross, Esquires, N.Y.C., 1973-80; mgr. communications Stroock & Stroock & Lavan Esquires, N.Y.C., 1980-86; dir. adminstrn. Cooper Cohen Singer & Ecker Esquires, N.Y.C., 1986-87, Donovan Leisure Newton & Irvine Esquires, N.Y.C., 1987—. Contbr. articles to profl. jours. Founder, pres. Knolls chpt. of Women's Am. Orgn. Rehab. Through Tng., Riverdale, N.Y., 1979-82, v.p. edn., Manhattan region, 1982-83. Mem. Assn. Legal Adminstrs., Am. Soc. Tng. and Devel., Adminstrv. Mgmt. Soc.

KAPLAN, PATRICIA ANN, advertising executive; b. Hinsdale, Ill., Oct. 19, 1952; d. Arthur and Dorothy Ileane (Smith) Pielet; m. Peter John Kaplan; 1 child, Chase. BS in Spl. Edn., U. Miami, 1974. Spl. edn. tchr. Dade County Pub. Schs., Naranja, Fla., 1974-75; steel broker Metalon Inc., Northbrook, Ill., 1975—; advt. exec. Norcom Inc., Northbrook, 1983—. Office: Norcom Inc 35 Burning Tree Ln Deerfield IL 60015

KAPLAN, SANDRA LEE, physical therapist, educator; b. Lakewood, N.J., Jan. 2, 1956; d. Edward S. and Adele (Lee) K. BS, U. Conn., 1978; MS, Ohio State U., 1984; postgrad., NYU, 1985—. Lic. phys. therapist, Ohio, Conn., W.Va., N.Y. Phys. therapist Maumee Valley Phys. Therapy Svcs., Toledo, 1978-80, Hamilton County Bd. of MRDD, Cin., 1982-82; pvt. practice Columbus, Ohio, 1982-84; instr. Nisonger Ctr., Columbus, 1983-84; acad. coord. clin. edn. W.Va. U., Morgantown, 1984-85; pvt. practice phys. therapy Blyn., 1985—; asst. prof. phys. therapy program L.I. U., Blyn., 1987—, interim co-dir. phys. therapy program, 1988-89. Trustee Park Slope Jewish Ctr., Bklyn., 1988—. Mem. Am. Phys. Therapy Assn., N.Y. Road Runners Club, Phi Kappa Phi. Office: LI U University Pla M1008 Brooklyn NY 11201

KAPLAN, SHARI ANN, health care services executive; b. Boston; d. Alan Foster and Rae Charlotte (Gladstone) Friedenn; m. Stanley Kaplan, Mar. 15, 1962; children: Wayne D., Lisa D., Dean M. AB, U. Miami, 1962; MS, U. Wis., Milw., 1976. Instr. U. Miami, Coral Gables, Fla., 1964-66; exec. dir. Arthritis Found. Wis., Milw., 1976-82; corp. fin. officer First Wis. Nat. Bank, Milw., 1982-84; exec. v.p. Milw. Ins., 1984-88; pres. MCM Corp., Milw., 1986-88, Milw. Equity Svcs., 1986-88; v.p. devel. Universal Med. Bldgs., Milw., 1988; v.p. ops., v.p. health svcs. United Health, Inc., Milw., 1988—; exec. v.p. United Profl. Cos., Milw., 1989—; clin. instr. dept. medicine Med. Coll. Wis., Milw., 1978—. Gov. appointee State of Wis. UN Commn., 1989—; bd. dirs. Devel. Corp. for Israel, 1988—; mem. steering com. Gov.'s Trade Commn. to Israel, 1988; bd. dirs. NCCJ, 1986—; chmn. corp. campaign Benedict Ctr. for Criminal Justice, Wis., 1987-88. U.S. Dept. HHS fellow, 1973-76. Mem. Hadassah (v.p. 1988—), Golda Maier Club (chmn. 1989—). Democrat. Jewish. Home: 11541 N Laguna Dr Mequon WI 53092 Office: United Health 105 W Michigan St Milwaukee WI 53203

KAPLAN, SHEILA, university official; b. Bklyn.. BA in European History, CUNY, PhD in Modern European History; MA, Johns Hopkins U. Instr. history CUNY System; dir. Spl. Baccalaureate Program CUNY; v.p. acad. affairs Winona (Minn.) State U.; vice chancellor for acad. affairs Minn. State U. System; chancellor U. Wis.-Parkside, Kenosha, 1986—. Bd. dirs. Kenosha Area Devel. Corp., Racine County Econ. Devel. Corp.; chmn. bd. Council for Adult and Experiential Learning. Office: U Wis-Parkside Office of Chancellor PO Box 2000 Kenosha WI 53141-2000*

KAPLAN, SLYVIA ALLISON, retired elementary school educator, civic worker; b. Rochester, N.Y., Aug. 26, 1917; d. Morris and Esther (Hoffenberg) Garelick; m. Ralph Allison, Dec. 25, 1940 (dec. 1956); children: James, Stephen; m. Burton Kaplan, Dec. 20, 1957 (dec. 1983). Degree in teaching, SUNY, Brockport, 1938, BS summa cum laude, 1958. Tchr. pub. schs. Rochester, N.Y., 1938-40; case worker Dept. Pub. Welfare, Rochester, 1940-41; tchr. pub. schs. Rochester. Dist. dir. Genesee Valley PTA, 1958-60, also N.Y. state chmn. for exceptional child, for cultural arts, chmn. conv. mgmt., chmn. various PTA orgns., 1955-58; v.p. Women's Human Rels. Coun.; chmn. Rochester-Monroe County Youth Bur., 1974-76, Brighton (N.Y.) Youth Bur., 1962-73; del. Gov.'s Conf. on Children and Youth, 1969; mem. White House Conf. on Children and Youth, 1970, Gov. Rockefeller's Adv. Coun. on Children and Work, 1976; N.Y. state del. White Ho. Conf. on Children and Youth, 1970; bd. dirs., chmn. drug com. Monroe County Citizens Planning Coun., 1967-68; chmn. town mgmt. study com. Town of Brighton, 1976; exec. com. United Way Greater Rochester, 1976-79; bd. govs. Rossmoor Scholarship Found., 1989—. Recipient ann. award N.Y. State Div. Youth, 1969, Woman of Yr. award Brighton Rotary, 1969, Spl. Citation,Town of Brighton, 1972, Nat. Vol. Activist award, 1977, United Way award, 1979, 12th Ann. Civic award Rochester C. of C., 1976. Mem. AAUW (adv. com. endl. fund, co-chair scholarship com. Walnut Creek br. 1988-89), LWV, PTA (hon. life), Planned Parenthood. Home: 4332 Terra Granada Dr Walnut Creek CA 94595

KAPLAN, SYLVIA YALOWITZ KAPLAN (MRS. MILTON I. KAPLAN), librarian, educator; b. Chgo., May 23, 1921; d. Max and Gertrude (Yalowitz) K.; Ph.B., Northwestern U., 1956; M.A. in L.S., Rosary Coll., 1961, postgrad., 1962; postgrad. U. Ill., 1965-69, HEA Inst. on Reclassification, Rosary Coll., 1969, DePaul U., 1970; doctoral candidate (scholar, grad. asst.) U. Pitts., 1980-86; m. Milton I. Kaplan, Apr. 5, 1959. Asst. librarian Argonne Nat. Lab., U. Chgo., 1943-50; chief med. librarian Mcpl. Tb Sanitarium, Chgo., 1953-57; sch. librarian, Gary, Ind., 1957-59; librarian Inst. Applied Research, U. Chgo., 1961-62; chief librarian, instr. med. bibliography Chgo. Med. Sch., 1960-64; librarian Michael Reese Hosp. Sch. Nursing, Chgo., 1964-66; chief librarian Ill. Dept. Mental Health, 1967-70; instr. library sci. Northeastern Ill. State Coll., 1970—; asst. prof. library sci. Eastern Ill. U., Charleston, 1970—. Mem. AAUW, AAUP (officer), Med. Library Assn. (cert.), Am. Assn. Library Schs., Spl. Libraries Assn., Assn. Acad. Librarians, Internat. Assn. Semantics, Hadassah, Internat. Platform Assn. (hon.), Delta Kappa Gamma (hon.; scholar 1979). Democrat. Jewish. Contbr. revs. to profl. jours. Office: Eastern Ill U Dept Library Sci Charleston IL 61920

KAPNEK, WENDY N., public relations executive; b. Trenton, N.J., Sept. 13, 1960; d. Walter Joseph and Dolores Jean (Miller) O'Brien; m. Theodore H. Kapnek III. BA, Syracuse U., 1982. Account exec. Ardrey Inc. Pub. Rels., Edison, N.J., 1982-84; account supr. Lewis, Gilman & Kynett Inc. Pub. Rels., Phila., 1984-86; v.p., account supr. Ketchum Pub. Rels., Phila., 1986—; bd. dirs. Phila. Urban Fin. Corp. Recipient Bellringer award Community Rels. Report, 1989, Mercury award Larami Comm/Media Com, N.Y.C., 1989. Mem. Pub. Rels. Soc. Am. (Pepperpot award 1987, 88), PHila. Club Advt. Women, PPRA, Women In Communication (chmn. career day). Democrat. Jewish. Home: 631 Moreno Rd Penn Valley PA 19072 Office: Ketchum Pub Rels One Independence Philadelphia PA 19106

KAPP, NANCY GLADYS, savings and loan executive; b. Oak Park, Ill., Jan. 23, 1945; d. Andrew John and Gladys Abigail (Johnson) McClintock; m. Ted Martin Kapp, Sept. 28, 1973; children—Adam, Natalie, Pamela. B.S.Ed., No. Ill. U., DeKalb, 1968; postgrad. Nat. Coll. Edn., Evanston, Ill., 1969-70. Tchr. elementary/jr. high sch. Dist. 96, Riverside, Ill., 1968-71, high sch. substitute tchr., 1971-72; personnel dept. sec. St. Paul Fed. Bank For Savs., Chgo., 1971-73, sr. exec. sec. to pres., 1973-80, adminstv. asst. legal dept., 1980—. Dir., chmn. Community Sch. of Galewood, Chgo., 1983-84; mem. Republican Nat. Com., 1979—; sponsor GOP Victory Fund, Rep. Party, Washington, 1982—; mem. Rep. Presdl. Task force, 1984—. Mem. Nat. Assn. Female Execs., AAUW, Nat. Assn. Exec. Secs., Nat. Paralegal Assn. Republican. Episcopalian. Office: St Paul Fed Bank For Savs 6700 W North Ave Chicago IL 60635

KAPPA, MARGARET MCCAFFREY, resort hotel consultant; b. Wabasha, Minn., May 14, 1921; d. Joseph Hugh and Verna Mae (Anderson) McCaffrey; B.S. in Hotel Mgmt., Cornell U., 1944; grad. Dale Carnegie course, 1978; cert. hospitality housekeeping exec.; m. Nicholas Francis Kappa, Sept. 15, 1956; children—Nicholas Joseph, Christopher Francis. Asst. exec. housekeeper Kahler Hotel, Rochester, Minn., 1944; exec. housekeeper St. Paul Hotel, 1944-47, Plaza Hotel, N.Y.C., 1947-51; exec. housekeeper, personnel dir. Athearn Hotel, Oshkosh, Wis., 1952-58; dir. housekeeping The Greenbrier, White Sulphur Springs, W.Va., 1958-84; cons., 1984—; tchr. housekeeping U.S. and fgn. countries; cons.; vis. lectr. Cornell U. Author: (with others) Managing Housekeeping Operations, 1989. Pres. St. Charles Borromeo Parish Assn., White Sulphur Springs, 1962, v.p., 1980, 82; tech. adv., host 2 ednl. videos Am. Hotel and Motel Assn., 1986. Recipient diploma of honor Société Culinaire Philanthropique, 1961. Mem. Cornell Soc. Hotelmen (pres. 1980-81, exec. com. 1981-82), Nat. Exec. Housekeepers Assn. (pres. N.Y. chpt. 1950), N.Y.U. Hotel and Restaurant Soc. (hon. life). Republican. Roman Catholic. Clubs: Nat. Woman's; Quota (charter mem. Greenbrier County). Home and Office: 323 W Main St Wabasha MN 55981

KAPPLER, LYDIA PATRICIA, electronics executive; b. Trenton, N.J., Apr. 15, 1958; d. Harry Patrick and Lydia Jane (Arnold) Kappler. Various mgmt. positions Lionel Leisure Inc., Phila., 1976-83; product merchandiser IMAGIC Co., Los Gatos, Calif., 1983; sales rep. CAL-ABCO Inc., Woodland Hills, Calif., 1983-84, area mgr., 1984, dist. mgr., 1984-85, mgr. regional sales east coast, 1985-87, mgr. nat. accounts, 1989—. Mem. NAFE. Democrat. Roman Catholic. Home: 21500 Burbank #305 Woodland Hills CA 91367 Office: CAL-ABCO Inc 6041 Variel Ave Woodland Hills CA 91367

KAPTSAN, HELEN, telephone company executive; b. Moscow, Russia, July 10, 1960; d. Abram and Galena (Metropolsky) Kaptsan; m. John Joseph Leyden, Oct. 9, 1982 (div. 1988). BA in Econs., Fordham U., 1981; Dipl. in Sys. Analysis, NYU, 1986; postgrad., Fordham U., 1983. Staff mgr. corp. planning N.Y. Telephone, 1979, staff mgr. residence mkts., 1980, staff mgr. bus. mkts., 1980-81, assoc. staff dir. forecasting, 1981-87; staff dir. spl. svcs. N.Y. Telephone, N.Y.C., 1987—. Participant NYNEX Choices Prog. to jr. high sch. students. Mem. NAFE, Assn. of Mgmt. Women. Home: 105 Garth Rd #6D Scarsdale NY 10583 Office: New York Telephone 140 West St #1502 New York NY 10007

KAPTUR, MARCIA CAROLYN, congresswoman; b. Toledo, June 17, 1946. B.A., U. Wis., 1968; M. Urban Planning, U. Mich., 1974; postgrad., U. Manchester, (Eng.), 1974. Urban planner; asst. dir. urban affairs domestic policy staff White House, 1977-79; mem. 98th-102nd Congresses from 9th Dist. Ohio, 1983—. Bd. dirs. Nat. Ctr. Urban Ethnic Affairs; adv. com. Gund Found.; exec. com. Lucas County Democratic Com.; mem. Dem. Women's Campaign Assn. Mem. Am. Planning Assn., Am. Inst. Cert. Planners, NAACP, Urban League, Polish Mus., U. Mich. Urban Planning Alumni Assn. (bd. dirs.), Polish Am. Hist. Assn. Roman Catholic. Clubs: Lucas County Dem. Bus. and Profl. Women's, Fulton County Dem. Women's. Office: US House of Reps 1228 Longworth House Bldg Washington DC 20515*

KARABATSOS, ELIZABETH ANN, aerospace industry executive; b. Geneva, Nebr., Oct. 25, 1932; d. Karl Christian and Margaret Maurine (Emrich) Brinkman; m. Kimon Tom Karabatsos, Apr. 21, 1957 (div. Feb. 1981); children: Tom Kimon, Maurine Elizabeth, Karl Kimon. BS, U. Nebr., 1954; postgrad., Ariz. State U., 1980; Cert. contemporary exec. devel., George Washington U., 1985. Instr. bus. Fairbury (Nebr.) High Sch., 1954-55; staff asst. U.S. Congress, Washington, 1955-60; with Karabatsos & Co. Pub. Relations, Washington, 1960-73; conf. asst. to asst. adminstr. and dep. adminstr. Gen. Services Adminstrn., Washington, 1973-76; dir. corr. Office Pres.-Elect, Washington, 1980; assoc. dir. adminstrv. services Pres. Personnel-White House, Washington, 1981; dept. asst. to Sec. and Dep. Sec. Def., Washington, 1981-86, asst. to, 1987-89; dir. govt. and civic affairs McDonnell Douglas Helicopter Co., Mesa, Ariz., 1989-90, gen. mgr. gen. svcs., 1990—. Mem. Nat. Mus. Women in Art, Washington, Rep. Women's Fed. Forum, Washington. Mem. AAUW, Office of Sec. Def. Sr. Profl. Women, Women in Def. (sec. 1987), Pi Omega Pi, Pi Beta Phi. Episcopalian. Lodge: Order Eastern Star. Home: 7818 E Montebello Ave Scottsdale AZ 85250

KARAN, DONNA (DONNA FASKE), fashion designer; b. Forest Hills, N.Y., Oct. 2, 1948; m. Mark Karan; 1 child, Gabrielle. BFA, Parsons Sch. Design, 1987. With Addenda Co., to 1968; with Anne Klein & Co., N.Y.C., 1968-84; co-designer Anne Klein & Co., 1971-74, designer, 1974-84; owner, designer Donna Karan New York, N.Y.C., 1984—. Showed first complete collection for Anne Klein & Co. in 1974; collaborator on Anne Klein collections with Louis dell'Olion. Recipient Coty award, 1977, awards Coun. of Fashion Designers of Am., 1985, 86; co-recipient (with Louis dell'Olio) Coty Hall of Fame citation, 1982, Coty award, 1984. Office: Donna Karan Co 550 Seventh Ave New York NY 10018*

KARASICK, CAROL, advertising agency executive; b. N.Y.C., 1941. BS in Mktg., Boston U., 1962. With Compton Advt., 1962-65, Ted Bates, 1966-75, Lever Bros., 1977-78, Saatchi & Saatchi DFS, Inc., N.Y.C., 1979—. Mem. election com. Pres G. Ford, 1976. Office: Saatchi & Saatchi DFS Inc 375 Hudson St New York NY 10014

KARASIK, BRENDA-LEE, employee development specialist; b. Worcester, Mass., Mar. 11, 1947; d. Earl Randolph and Jessie Leone (Waite) Pratt. BA, Worcester State Coll., 1968; MS, Troy (Ala.) State U., 1978; postgrad., Nova U., 1985—. Guidance counselor Army Edn. Ctr., Wiesbaden, Fed. Republic of Germany, 1968-72; tchr. Ft. Riley, Junction City, Kans., 1972-75; edn. specialist Air Force Edn. Ctr., Zweibrucken, Fed. Republic of Germany, 1975-77; guidance counselor Air Force Edn. Ctr., Washington, 1977-80; edn. specialist hdqrs. U.S. Dept. of Army, Alexandria, Va., 1980-81, 1981-88, edn. program adminstr. hdqrs., 1988-89; tng. and devel. specialist Naval Ocean Systems Ctr., San Diego, 1989—. Contbr. articles to profl. jours. Mem. Assn. for the Devel. of Computer Based Instructional Systems, Am. Mgmt. Assn., Am. Soc. for Tng. and Devel., Fed. Ednl. Tech. Assn., Human Factors Soc., NAFE, Nat. Soc. for Performance and Instruction, Pentagon PC Users Group, Soc. for Applied Learning, Spl. Interest Group for Optical Media in Edn., Phi Delta Kappa. Office: Naval Ocean Systems Ctr 271 Catalina Blvd San Diego CA 92152

KARDON, JANET, museum director, curator; b. Phila.; d. Robert and Shirley (Drasin) Stolker; m. Robert Kardon, Nov. 19, 1955; children: Ross, Nina, Roy. BS in Edn., Temple U.; MA in Art History, U. Pa. Lectr. Phila. Coll. Art, 1968-75, dir. exhbns., 1975-78; dir. Inst. Contemporary Art, Phila., 1978-89, Am. Craft Mus., N.Y.C., 1989—; cons., panel mem. Nat. Endowment for Arts, 1975—; mus. panel mem. Pa. Coun. on Arts, Phila., 1988—; U.S. commr. Venice Biennale, Venice, 1980. Curated and created essays for 30 exhbns., including Laurie Anderson, Robert Mapplethorpe, David Salle. Grantee Nat. Endowment for Arts, 1978. Mem. Assn. Art Mus. Dirs. Club: Cosmopolitan. Home: Rittenhouse Pla 1901 Walnut St Apt 21-A Philadelphia PA 19103 Office: Am Craft Mus 40 W 53d St New York NY 10019

KAREGA, DEBORAH ANNETTE, nurse manager; b. Detroit, Apr. 16, 1953; d. LeRoy and Dorothy Marie (Browning) Mitchell; m. Che Ali Karega; 1 child, Lisa. ADN, Wayne County Community Coll., 1981; AAS, BAS, Siena Heights Coll., 1984; MS, Cen. Mich. U., 1988. RN, Mich. Staff nurse Mt. Carmel Mercy Hosp., Detroit, 1982-85; charge nurse Sacred Heart Rehab. Ctr., Detroit, 1985-88; unit nurse mgr. N.W. Gen. Hosp., Detroit, 1988; staff nurse Olsten Health Care Svcs., Southfield, Mich., 1988—; emergency rm. nurse trauma team Mt. Carmel Mercy Hosp., Detroit, 1989—; unit nurse mgr. Mich. Health Care Corp., Detroit, 1989—. Bd. dirs. Grateful Home for Women, Detroit, 1988. Nurse corp USNR, 1987—. Mem. NAFE, Siena Heights Coll. Alumni Assn., U.S. Naval Inst., Wayne County Community Coll. Alumni Assn., Naval Reserve Assn., Cen. Mich. U. Alumni Assn. Democrat. Lutheran. Home: 16215 Roanoke Dr Apt 102 Southfield MI 48075

KARELITZ-LESHAY, MAXINE HOFFMAN, nursing service agency executive; b. Bklyn., May 29, 1942; d. Jacob and Jean Lorraine (Fierstein) Hoffman; m. Julian Robert Karelitz, Oct. 2, 1960 (div. Dec. 1963); 1 child, Gavin Alexander Karelitz; m. Steven Vedder LeShay, Apr. 17, 1982. B.A., Bklyn. Coll., 1976; M.S.W., Barry Coll. Sch. Social Work, Miami Shores, Fla., 1978. Cert. social worker, N.Y. Social worker Seminole Indian Reservation, Hollywood, Fla., 1976-78, Children's Home Soc., Fort Lauderdale, Fla., 1977-78, United Cerebral Palsy, N.Y.C., 1978-80; instr. sociology and social work Glassboro State Coll., N.J., 1980-88; dir. and cons. social services N.J. Meml. Home, Vineland, N.J., 1980-86; exec. dir., founder Women On Their Own, Inc., Malaga, N.J., 1982—. Mem. Guideposts Women's Consortium, Glassboro State Coll., 1984-88, mem. adv. bd. career direction for single parents and homemakers, 1985-87; adv. citizen advocacy Assn. Retarded Citizens, Gloucester County, N.J., 1985-87; mem. Reach planning sub-com., Gloucester County, N.J., 1987-88; active People Against Spouse Abuse, Woodbury, N.J., 1986-87. Named hon. capt. U.S. Naval Res., 1980; child welfare trainee Barry Coll. Sch. Social Work, 1977-78. Mem. Christian Science Ch. Office: Women On Their Own Inc PO Box O Malaga NJ 08328

KARELL, PATRICIA PAYNE, lawyer; b. Yankton, S.D., Oct. 3, 1955; d. Richard Clifford and Marina Elizabeth (Schmidt) Payne; m. Stephen Dolan Bell, Dec. 21, 1979 (div. Jan. 1988); children: Jordan Elaine, Lauren Meredith; m. Allan Karell, June 23, 1990. Student, Creighton U., 1973-74; BA, U. S.D., 1976, JD, 1979. Bar: S.D. 1979, Minn. 1980, Mont. 1987. Dep. state's atty. Minnehaha County State's Atty.'s Office, Sioux Falls, S.D., 1979-80; house counsel Gt. Am. Ins. Co., St. Paul, 1980-82, Wausau Ins. Co., Edina, Minn., 1988-84; assoc. Cousineau, McGuire, Shaughnessy & Anderson, Mpls., 1982-83, Crowley, Haughey, Hanson, Toole and Dietrich, Billings, Mont., 1987—; spl. asst. atty. Gen. State of Mont. Bd. dirs. Family Svc., Inc., Billings, 1988—. Mem. ABA, Mont. State Bar, Minn. State Bar, S.D. State Bar, Mont. Def. Trial Lawyers Assn., Mortar Bd., Phi Beta Kappa. Republican. Evangelical. Home: 2323 Ash St Billings MT 59101 Office: Crowley Haughey et al 490 N 31st St Billings MT 59101

KARI, SHELLEY LYNN, personnel director; b. Blue Earth, Minn., May 2, 1957; d. Leo Verner and Blanche Lillian (Johanek) K.; m. Kenneth Edwin Lay, Nov. 1, 1980. BA in Chemistry, U. Minn., 1979. Exec. sec. nat. hdqrs. Coast to Coast Stores, Mpls., 1979-80; sales rep. Proctor and Gamble, Milw., 1980; sales assoc. Thimbles, Mpls., 1981; mdse. mgr. Target Stores, Mpls., 1981-86; v.p. Replacements Ltd., Greensboro, N.C., 1986-88; exec. dir. exec. placement network Shelley Group Ltd., Portland, Me., 1989—; sec. Postal Customers Coun., Greensboro, 1987-88. Mem. NAFE, Va. Assn. Female Execs., Sigma Sigma Sigma. Lutheran. Office: Shelley Group Ltd 89 Auburn St Ste 1079 Portland ME 04103

KARK, JOANNE BARBARA, health physicist, educator; b. Newark, Sept. 18, 1953; d. Jon Joseph and Anna Rose (Peters) K.; m. Robert Norton McVey, Mar. 24, 1979 (div. Apr. 1980). BS, Villanova U., 1975; postgrad., Colo. State U., 1984-85. Cert. nuclear medicine technologist. Analytical chemistry technician SpectroChem Labs., Inc., Franklin Lakes, N.J., 1976-77; nuclear medicine technologist Albert Einstein Med. Ctr., Phila., 1977-79; biol. technician Oak Ridge (Tenn.) Nat. Lab., 1979-81, radiol. technician, 1981-84; nuclear safety health physicist I, Ill. Dept. Nuclear Safety, Glen Ellyn, 1986—; instr. radiation safety Oakton Community Coll., Des Plaines, Ill., 1989—. Contbr. articles to profl. jours. Recipient program cert. of appreciation Suburban Bldg. Ofcls. Conf., 1988. Mem. Soc. Nuclear Medicine (assoc.), Health Physics Soc. (plenary, treas. Midwest chpt. 1989—, pub. info. com. 1989—). Roman Catholic. Office: Ill Dept Nuclear Safety Bldg C Ste 200 800 Roosevelt Rd Glen Ellyn IL 60137

KARKUT, BONNIE LEE, dental office manager; b. Muskegon, Mich., Feb. 7, 1934; d. Fay Henry Hohenstein and Doris Catherine (Nelson) Collins; m. Joseph Paul Karkut, Dec. 29, 1956; children: Deborah, Joseph, Bradley, Elizabeth. BA in Speech Pathology, Mich. State U., 1955; postgrad. studies, U. Hawaii, 1956, U. Mich., Saginaw, 1959. Cert. speech pathologist. Speech pathologist Pub. Schs., Muskegon, Mich., 1955-56, Saginaw, Mich., 1956-59; office mgr. Dental Office, Naples, Fla., 1984—. Pres. Saginaw (Mich.) County Dental Aux., 1978-79. Mem. AAUW, Fla. Dental Assn. (dental asst. and aux. sect.), Delta Zeta (program chmn. 1988-89), Panhellenic Soc. Republican. Roman Catholic. Home: 2570 Crayton Rd. Naples FL 33940 Office: Dental Office 850 Central Ave Bldg #103 Naples FL 33940

KARL, HELEN WEIST, pediatric anesthesia educator, researcher; b. N.Y.C., Oct. 28, 1948; d. Edward C. and Louise (Stursberg) Weist; m. Stephen R. Karl, June 1, 1974 (div. 1990); children: Katherine L., Thomas R., John W. BA in Philosophy, Smith Coll., 1970; MD, U. Va., 1976. Diplomate Am. Bd. Anesthesiology, Nat. Bd. Med. Examiners. Intern in surgery Hartford (Conn.) Hosp., 1976-77, resident in anesthesia, 1977-79;

fellow in pediatric anesthesiology Children's Hosp. of Phila., 1979-81; staff anesthesiologist St. Christopher's Hosp. for Children, Phila., 1981; asst. prof. anesthesiology and pediatrics Pa. State U., Hershey, 1981-90; asst. prof. anesthesiology U. Washington, 1990—; Parker B. Francis fellow in pulmonary rsch. Pa. State U., Hershey, 1986-88. Contbr. articles to profl. jours. Grantee Am. Lung Assn. of Pa., 1986-88. Fellow Am. Acad. Pediatrics (sec. on anesthesiology com. on drugs 1989—); mem. Am. Soc. Anesthesiologists (task force for preparation self-evaluation exam. 1982-83), Am. Med. Women's Assn., Am. Thoracic Soc., Internat. Anesthesia Rsch. Soc., Wash. Soc. Anesthesiologists, Soc. Cardiovascular Anesthesiologists, Anesthesia Patient Safety Found. Office: Children's Hosp & Med Ctr 4800 Sand Point Way NE Seattle WA 98105

KARLAN, LUANN FLORIO, medical management and research consultant; b. Bklyn., Oct. 20, 1954; d. F. Anthony and Barbara Ann (Fehlker) Florio. Student, CUNY, Bklyn., 1972-77; student, Columbia U., 1974, 75, Pace U., 1977. Cert. tchr. pvt. vocat. schs., N.Y. Rsch. assoc. animal studies dept. urology Meml. Sloan-Kettering Cancer Ctr., N.Y.C., 1977-79; dir. fin. Med. Practice Adminstrn., N.Y.C., 1979-85; clin. trials coord. pharm. industry N.Y.C., 1985-87; regional dir. Dorex, Inc., Orange, Calif., 1988—; pres., owner Venturemedicus, Inc., N.Y.C., 1987—; cons. Sci. Advisory, Bar Ilan U., Ramat Gan, Israel, N.Y.C., 1987-90. Instr. Handicapped Riders (children), New Eng., 1987—. Social Sci. scholar Bklyn. Coll. Sch. Social Scis., CUNY, 1975-77. Mem. U.S. Dressage Fedn. (del., asst. editor newsletter 1990), New Eng. Dressage Assn. (bd. dirs.), Sch. Am. Ballet (assn. mem.), Art Student's League N.Y. Home: 27 W 72th St New York NY 10023 Office: Venturemedicus Inc 27 W 72th St Ste 212 New York NY 10023

KARLE, ISABELLA, chemist; b. Detroit, Dec. 2, 1921; d. Zygmunt Apolonaris and Elizabeth (Graczyk) Lugoski; m. Jerome Karle, June 4, 1942; children: Louise Hanson, Jean Marianne, Madeleine Tawney. BS in Chemistry, U. Mich., 1941, MS in Chemistry, 1942, PhD, 1944; DSc (hon.), U. Mich., 1976, Wayne State U., 1979, U. Md., 1986; LHD (hon.), Georgetown U., 1984. Assoc. chemist U. Chgo., 1944; instr. chemistry U. Mich., Ann Arbor, 1944-46; physicist Naval Rsch. Lab., Washington, 1946—; mem. exec. com. Am. Peptide Symposium, 1975-81, adv. bd. Chem. and Engring. News, 1986-89. Mem. editorial bd. Biopolymers Jour., 1975—, Internat. Jour. Peptide Protein Rsch., 1981—; contbr. articles to profl. jours. Recipient Superior Civilian Service award USN, 1965, Fed. Women's award U.S. Govt., 1973, Annual Achievement award Soc. Women Engrs., 1968, Annual Achievement award U. Mich., 1987, Dexter Conrad award Office Naval Rsch., 1980, WISE Lifetime Achievement award Women in Sci. and Engring., 1986, award for disting. achievement in sci. Sec. of Navy, 1987, Gregori Aminoff prize Swedish Royal Acad. Scis., 1988, Adm. Parsons award Navy League U.S., 1988, Ann. Achievement award CCNY, 1989; named to Michigan Women's Hall of Fame, 1989. Fellow Am. Inst. Chemists. (Chem. Pioneer award 1984); mem. NAS, Am. Crystallographic Assn. (pres. 1976), Am. Chem. Soc. (Garvan award 1976, Hillebrand award 1970), Am. Phys. Soc., Biophys. Soc. Home: 6304 Lakeview Dr Falls Church VA 22041 Office: Naval Rsch Lab Code 6030 Washington DC 20375

KARLEN, JANICE MARIE, economist, educator, consultant; b. Elizabeth, N.J., Oct. 29, 1953; d. Victor Joseph and Leona Mary (Metz) K. BS, Kean Coll., 1974; MBA, Rutgers U., 1975; EdS, Seton Hall U., 1980, EdD, 1984. Auditor Exxon Corp., Florham Park, N.J., 1975-76; asst. registrar Essex County Coll., Newark, 1977-79, instl. researcher, 1979-80; asst. to v.p. N.J. Inst. Tech., 1980-83; dean bus. div. Antelope Valley Coll., Lancaster, Calif., 1984-86; v.p. Erie Community Coll., Williamsville, N.Y., 1986-88; pvt. practice cons. Elizabeth, N.J., 1988—; prof. CUNY/LaGuardia Community Coll., 1988—. Contbr. articles to profl. jours. Mem. AAUW (edn. chairperson 1986), Lancaster C. of C. (bd. dirs. 1985), Amherst C. of C., Soroptomists (internat. leadership chairperson 1985), Phi Delta Kappa, Kappa Delta Pi. Democrat. Home: 635 Magie Ave Elizabeth NJ 07208

KARLIN, ELYSE ZORN, marketing professional, writer; b. N.Y.C., July 21, 1950; d. Edgar Seymour Zorn and Ruthellen (Schlanger) Strain; m. Alan Cohen, May 28, 1972 (div. 1975); m. Andrew Karlin, Sept. 12, 1982; one child, Harris Karlin. BJ, U. Mo., 1972. Reporter McGraw-Hill Pub. Co., Boston, 1972-76; asst. to pres. Silton/Turner Advt., Boston, 1976-78; freelance writer Boston, 1978-80; assoc. mktg. mgr. MLI Industries, Watertown, Mass., 1980-81; assoc. mgr. dir. mail sales H.E. Harris & Co., Boston, 1981-83; sr. acct. exec. Ayer Direct, N.Y.C., 1983-85; acct. supr. Kobs & Brady Advt., N.Y.C., 1985-86; sr. v.p. mgmt. supr., mem. exec. com. DFS Direct Saatchi & Saatchi, N.Y.C., 1983-86; pres. EK Assocs. Direct Mktg. Cons., New Rochelle, N.Y., 1986—; chmn. Direct Mktg. Cooperative. Author: Massachusetts No-Fault Divorce Kit, 1980, Massachusetts Will Kit, 1980, The Best Baby Gift, 1988, Collectible Bisque and China Children Figurines 1850-1950, 1990; contbg. editor Collectors, Clocks & Jewelery Mag., Heritage, others. Mem. Direct Mktg. Club of N.Y.C. (judge student ECHO awards 1986), Am. Soc. Jewelry Appraisers, Victorian Soc., Jewelry Historians Soc., Soc. for Women in Edn. Home and Office: 10 Elk Ave New Rochelle NY 10804

KARLIN, MURIEL SCHLOSBERG, information systems analyst, consultant; b. Mt. Vernon, N.Y., Dec. 19, 1940; d. Nat and Lee (Karlin) Schlosberg; children: Leeza Beth Watstein, David Michael Watstein. BA in Psychology, Clark U., 1962; MS in Computer Sci., NYU, 1986. Programming cons. N.Y.C. Bd. Edn., Bklyn., 1983; systems engr. Electronic Data Systems, Woodbury, N.Y., 1983-84; documentation mgr., systems adminstrn. mgr. Instinet Corp., N.Y.C., 1987—; instr. Info. Techs. Inst., NYU, N.Y.C., 1987. Enrichment coordinator, v.p. Ridge Rd. Elem. Sch. PTA, North Haven, Conn.; mem. North Haven Ednl. Council. Mem. NAFE, Assn. Computing Machinery. Home: 77 Bleecker St New York NY 10012

KARLSON, DIXIE D., educator; b. White Owl, S.D., Apr. 7, 1941; d. Elmer Cliford and Gertrude Berniece (Fluhrer) Weyer; m. Alfred Leroy Karlson, May 29, 1964; children: Leroy, Karl, Twyla, Lyla, Clayton. BS in Edn., Black Hills State U., Spearfish, S.D., 1972, MEd, 1981. Tchr. Stetter Sch., Butte County, Belle Fourche, S.D., 1964-65, Horse Creek Sch., Newell, S.D., 1965-73, Nisland (S.D.) Sch., 1974-76, 1976-90; tchr. San Bernardino (Calif.) Unified Sch. Dist., 1990—; guest instr. Black Hills State Coll., summer, 1982-84. Sun. sch. tchr. Vacation Bible Sch., 1970-73; ch. bd. sec., audit com. Nisland Ind. Community Ch., 1971-74; treas. Nisland PTO, 1979-81; pres. Newell PTO, 1976-77; active 4-H, No. Hills Reading Coun., Kindergarten Workshop Black Hill State , 199o, others. Mem. NAFE, Delta Kappa Gamma (pres. 1988—), Sunshine Gals Extension (treas. 1979-85). Republican.

KARLSON, KAREN LOUISE, radiologist; b. N.Y.C., May 6, 1950; d. Lloyd Alfred and Antoinette Sofia (Petersen) Bolling; B.A., CCNY, 1971; M.D., Columbia U., 1975; m. Thomas J. Karlson, May 19, 1971; children—Aurora, Alexandra. Intern, St. Vincent's Hosp., N.Y.C., 1975-76; resident Columbia Presbyn. Med. Center, 1976-79; fellow, 1979-80, asst. prof., 1980-81; attending radiologist, St. Barnabas Med. Ctr., Livingston, N.J.; chairperson dept. radiology, 1987—; asst. clin. prof. radiology UMDNJ, 1987;, asst. prof. Cornell U. Med. Center-N.Y. Hosp. Mem. Columbia U. Coll. Physicians and Surgeons, Black and Latin Students Orgn., Am. Coll. Radiology, Radiol. Soc. N.Am. Lutheran. Contbr. articles to profl. jours. Home: 6 Orchard Ln Livingston NJ 07039 Office: St Barnabas Med Ctr Dept Radiology Livingston NJ 07039

KARMAZIN, NELLY, pathology educator; b. Odessa, USSR, May 25, 1930; came to U.S., 1978; d. Jacob Yankelevich and Riva Krimershmoys; m. Valentin Karmazin, Feb. 24, 1952 (div. 1973); 1 child, Ilya. MD, Kishinev State Med. Inst., Kishinev, USSR, 1952. Pediatrician City Hosp., Soroki, USSR, 1952-53; gen. practitioner Grushevo Med. Ctr., Moldavia, USSR, 1953-54; resident pediatrics Kishinev State Med. Inst., 1954-56; pediatrician Republican Pediatric Hosp., Kishinev, 1956-69; chief dept. med. statistics Oncology Inst., Kishinev, 1969-77; resident pathology Thomas Jefferson Med. Sch., Phila., 1980-84; pediatric pathology fellow St. Christopher's Hosp. for Children, Phila., 1984-85; pathologist St. Christopher's Hosp. for Children, 1985-89; asst. prof. pathology sch. medicine Temple U., Phila., 1989—. Contbr. articles to profl. jours.; author abstracts in field. Fellow Coll. Am. Pathologists. Republican. Jewish. Office: St Christophers Hosp for Children Erie Ave at Front St Philadelphia PA 19134-1095

KARNATH, JOAN EDNA, editor; b. St. Paul, July 14, 1947; d. Charles Omar and Marie Edna (Gorg) League; m. Richard John, July 24, 1971 (div. Mar. 1981). BS in Elem. Edn., Winona State U., 1970, MS in Elem. Edn., 1978. Tchr. Ind. Sch. Dist. 234, Rushford, Minn., 1971-82; beauty cons. Mary Kay Cosmetics, Dallas, 1982-84; hostess Ramada Hotel, Inc., St. Paul, 1983-84; coord., computer ctr. 3M Co., St. Paul; lead editor Unisys Corp., St. Paul, 1984—; mem, sec. Rushford Edn. Assn., 1971-82. Precinct Chairwoman Ind. Reps., Winona, 1980-81; Sec. Eden Home Assn., Eagan, 1987—. Mem. AAUW, Nat. Edn. Assn., Minn. Edn. Assn., U. Minn. Global Edn. Com., Profl. Editors Network, Toastmasters Internat. Republican. Roman Catholic. Home: 4423B Clover Ln Eagan MN 55122 Office: Unisys Corp 2276 Highcrest Rd Roseville MN 55113

KARNES, BETTEJANE, civic volunteer; b. Bridgeport, Conn., May 7, 1926; d. Karl Harry and Charlotte (Blake) Larson; m. Victor Veikko Lehtinen, Aug. 2, 1947 (dec. June 1960); children: Victor, Eric, Gregory, Christopher; m. John Wesley Karnes, Mar. 7, 1964; 1 child, Nathan Bryant. BS, U. Conn., 1946, MA, 1961. High sch. tchr. Glastonbury (Conn.) Bd. Edn., 1946-47, Killingly (Conn.) Bd. Edn., 1947-48, Plainfield (Conn.) Bd. Edn., 1959-64. Chair Recycling Com., Storrs, Conn., 1980-85; mem. Earth Day Planning Com., Storrs, 1980-85; 1st v.p. Women's Club of Storrs, 1986-88; coord. hospitality Vols. of Nat. History Mus. of Conn., Storrs, 1986-88; chair, originator Lic. Practical Nurse Scholarship Program, Willimantic, Conn., 1988—; mem. coun. Storrs Congl. Ch., founder after kindergarten care program, 1988; area chair Ch. Women United in Conn., Meriden, 1986-88, state pres., 1988—; trustee Christian Conf. Conn., 1988—. Mem. AAUW (sec. Storrs chpt. 1986-88), LWV (chair state energy commn. 1965—). Democrat. Mem. United Ch. of Christ. Home: 353 N Eagleville Rd Storrs CT 06268

KARNES, LUCIA ROONEY, psychologist; b. Moncton, N.B., Can., Mar. 9, 1921; d. Charles William and Jean Waring (Robson) Rooney; m. Thomas Campbell Karnes, June 7, 1946; children: Eleanor, Campbell, Timothy, Charles. BS, Ga. State Coll., 1942; MA, Emory U., 1946; PhD, U. N.C., 1967. Tchr. Decatur Girls High, Decatur, Ga., 1942-46; tchr. Summit Sch., Winston-Salem, N.C., 1947; prof. Salem Coll., Winston-Salem, 1949-54, 60-77; lang. therapist Bowman Grey Sch. Medicine, Winston-Salem, 1950-57, Orton Reading Ctr., Winston-Salem, 1957-72; dir. Ctr. for Spl. Edn., Salem Coll., Winston-Salem, 1972-77; pvt. practice psychology Winston-Salem, 1977—; dyslexic cons. Patterson Sch., Lenoir, N.C., 1977—, Jefferson Acad., Winston-Salem, N.C., 1980—, Greenfield Sch., Wilson, 1986—, Wingate Coll., Wingate, N.C., 1988—. Creator Using Computers in Psychology courses, 1972; author (video) Teaching Dyslexics, 1975. Founder, pres. state bd. LWV, Winston-Salem, 1953; pres. state bd. AAUW, Winston-Salem, 1950-54; bd. dirs. YWCA, Winston-Salem, 1950-54; v.p. bd. dirs. Arts Coun., Winston-Salem, 1954-60. Named Outstanding Reading Tchr., Reading Assn., Winston-Salem, 1982. Mem. Orton Dyslexia Soc. (v.p. bd. dirs. 1960-77), Am. Psychol. Assn., N.C. Psychol. Assn., Assn. for Children with Learning Disabilities (v.p. bd. dirs. 1972—), Sorosis Club, Delta Kappa Gamma. Democrat. Presbyterian. Home: 200 Lamplighter Circle Winston-Salem NC 27104

KARNEY, DEA ILENE, sales and marketing professional; b. Ft. Lauderdale, Fla., Mar. 2, 1965; d. Donald Ray Sr. and Ilene (Brauchler) K. BS, Fla. State U., 1987. Sr. account exec. Data Access Corp., Miami, Fla., account exec.; sales instr. Dale Carnegie. Mem. Pompano Beach Ch. of God. Mem. NAFE, Am. Mktg. Assn., Fla. State U. Alumni Assn., Am. Bus. Women's Assn. Office: 14000 SW 119th Ave Miami FL 33186

KARNIOL, HILDA HUTTERER, artist, educator; b. Vienna, Austria, Apr. 28, 1910; d. Simon and Josephine (Weisman) Hutterer; student Acad. for Women, Vienna, 1926-30, Mrs. Olga Konetzny-Maly and A. F. Seligman, Vienna, 1925-28; m. Frank Karniol, June 25, 1933; 1 son, William George. Over 100 one-man shows, including Susquehanna U., 1952-73, Pa. State Mus., Harrisburg, 1954, Neville Mus., Green Bay, Wis., 1958, Addha Artzt Gallery, N.Y.C., 1960, Cornell Library Gallery, Ithaca, N.Y., 1960, Drexel Inst. Tech., Phila., 1960, Farnsworth Mus., Rockland, Maine, 1960, Mary Buie Mus., Oxford, Miss., 1960, Columbus (Ga.) Mus., 1962, Rutgers U., 1965-66, Laurel (Miss.) Rogers Mus., 1962; La Salle Coll., Phila., 1964; Hallmark Art Gallery, Kansas City, Mo., 1967, U. Ill., Urbana, 1968, U. Minn., St. Paul, 1969, U. Mich., 1969, U. Ky., Elizabethtown, 1970, La. State U., New Orleans, 1971, Kans. State Coll., Pittsburg, 1972, Purdue U., 1973, Invitational Art Exhbn., Painters of Central Pa., State Coll., 1982, 83; represented in permanent collections at St. Vincent Arch Abbey, Latrobe, Pa., Susquehanna U., Selinsgrove, Pa., Lincoln Sch., Honesdale, Pa., Del. Art Center, Wilmington, HEW, Lycoming Coll., Williamsport, Pa., Bloomsburg (Pa.) State Coll., Lewisburg (Pa.) Art Council; instr. fine arts Susquehanna U., 1959-75; lectr., artist-in-residence Fed. Govt. Cultural Enrichment Program for Clearfield, Clinton, Centre and Lycoming counties, Pa., 1967; art adviser Sunbury Bicentennial Com., 1972; demonstrator, exhibitor Laurel State Festival, Wellsboro, Pa., 1975. Recipient 1st prize in portraiture Berwick (Pa.) Arts Center, 1965; purchase prize Lewisburg Arts Festival, 1975, 1st prize, 1978, Distinguished Citizen award, Susquehanna U., Selinsgrove, Pa, 1988. Mem. Susquehanna Art Soc., Société d'Honneur Française, Pi Delta Phi, Sigma Alpha Iota. Home: 960 Race St Sunbury PA 17801

KARNOWSKY, DEBORAH, advertising agency executive. V.p., sr. v.p. W.B. Doner & Co., Southfield, Mich., until 1989; exec. v.p. Lintas Campbell-Ewald, Warren, Mich., 1989—. Recipient numerous creative awards. Office: Lintas Campbell-Ewald 30400 Van Dyke Ave Warren MI 48093*

KAROL, MERYL H., immunotoxicology educator; b. N.Y.C., Aug. 10, 1940; m. Paul Jason; children: Darcie, Deverin, Meredith. BS, Cornell U., 1961; PhD, Columbia U., 1967. NIH fellow SUNY-Stony Brook, 1967-68; research assoc. U. Pitts., 1974-76, research asst. prof., 1976-79, assoc. prof., 1979-85, prof. immunotoxicology, 1985—; advisor numerous govt. health adv. bds., agys.; lectr. in field. Editorial bd. Methods in Toxicology; contbr. articles to profl. jours. Recipient Women in Sci. award U. Mich., 1986. Mem. AAAS, Am. Chem. Soc., Am. Thoracic Soc., Am. Conf. Govt. Indsl. Hygienists, Soc. Toxicology (Frank R. Blood award), N.Y. Acad. Scis., Am. Assn. Immunologists. Avocations: sports, decorating, design, travel. Office: U Pitts Dept Environ Occ Health 130 De Soto St Pittsburgh PA 15261

KAROL, PAMALA MARIE, author; b. Hollywood, Calif., Mar. 29, 1950; d. Joseph Karol and Rene Franc (Jackson) Innocent. Diploma, U. Paris, 1973; BA in Communication Arts, Columbia Coll., L.A., 1974; postgrad., Loyola-Marymount U., L.A., 1974-76. With U. Calif., Berkeley, 1967-70. Author: The Mayan, 1988, Adventures on the Isle of Adolescence, 1989; author (film) Adventures on the Isle of Adolescence, 1989. U.S. rep. Winter Olympics Writers Festival, Calgary, Can., 1988. Calif. Arts Coun. Artists' fellow in lit., 1989; recipient Acad. Am. Poets prize, 1986; Am. Motion Picture Arts and Scis. grantee, 1974, 75. Mem. Poetry Soc. Am., Acad. Am. Poets. Office: Bone Scan Records 6520 Selma Ave Ste 562 Hollywood CA 90028

KARP, JUDITH ESTHER, oncologist; b. San Diego, July 15, 1946; d. Louis Moses and Bella Sarah (Perlman) K.; B.A. in Chemistry, Mills Coll., Oakland, Calif., 1966; M.D., Stanford U., 1971; m. Stanley Howard Freedman, Sept. 21, 1975. Intern medicine, jr. resident in medicine Stanford Hosps., 1971-72; asst. resident in medicine Johns Hopkins Hosp., 1972-73; clin. and research fellow oncology Johns Hopkins Med. Sch., 1973-75, instr. oncology and medicine, 1975-78, asst. prof., 1978-85, assoc. prof., 1985—; speaker Internat. Congress Chemotherapy, Vienna, Austria, 1983; mem. consensus com. Immuno-compromised Host Soc., 1987-88. Recipient Aurelia Henry Reinhardt prize Mills Coll., 1966, Cancer Research award Washington chpt. Awards for Research Coll. Scientists, 1975; San Diego Heart Assn. grantee, 1965-67; Am. Cancer Soc. Jr. clin. faculty fellow, 1976-79. Diplomate Am. Bd. Internal Medicine; recipient Resolution of Commendation, State of Md., 1982; Recognition award City of Balt., 1984. Mem. Am. Soc. Hematology, Am. Soc. Clin. Oncology, Cell Kinetics Soc. (clin. counsellor governing council 1985-87), Am. Soc. Microbiology, Immunocompromised Host Soc., Internat. Soc. Exptl. Hematology, Nat. Bd. Med. Examiners, Phi Beta Kappa. Democrat. Jewish. Home: 3422 Manor Hill Rd Baltimore MD 21208 Office: Johns Hopkins Hosp Oncology Ctr 600 N Wolfe Baltimore MD 21205

KARPAN, KATHLEEN MARIE, state official, lawyer, journalist; b. Rock Springs, Wyo., Sept. 1, 1942; d. Thomas Michael and Pauline Ann (Taucher) K. B.S. in Journalism, U. Wyo., 1964, M.A. in Am. Studies, 1975; J.D., U. Oreg., 1978. Bar: D.C. 1979, Wyo. 1983, U.S. Dist. Ct. Wyo., U.S. Ct. Appeals (D.C. and 10th cirs.). Asst. news editor Cody Enterprise, Wyo., 1964; press asst. to U.S. Congressman Teno Roncalio U.S. Ho. of Reps., Washington, 1965-67, 71-72, adminstrv. asst., 1973-74; asst. news editor Wyo. Eagle, Cheyenne, 1967; free-lance writer, 1968; teaching asst. dept. history U. Wyo., 1969-70; desk editor Canberra Times, Australia, 1970; dep. dir. Office Congl. Relations, Econ. Devel. Adminstrn. U.S. Dept. Commerce, Washington, 1979-80, atty. advisor Office of Chief Counsel, Econ. Devel. Adminstrn., 1980-81; campaign mgr. Rodger McDaniel for U.S. Senator, Wyo., 1981-82; asst. atty. gen. State of Wyo., Cheyenne, 1983-84, dir. Dept. Health and Social Services, 1984-86, sec. of state, 1987—. Del. Democratic Nat. Conv., San Francisco, 1984, Atlanta, 1988; del., chmn. platform com. Dem. State Conv., Douglas, Wyo., 1984. W.R. Coe fellow, 1969. Mem. D.C. Bar Assn., Wyo. Bar Assn., Nat. Assn. Secs. State, Bus. and Profl. Women, Am. Pub. Welfare Assn., Nat. Assn. Lt. Govs., Nat. Assn. Secs. of State, Rotary. Roman Catholic. Lodge: Zonta. Home: 410 W 2d Ave Cheyenne WY 82001 Office: Wyo Sec of State State Capitol Cheyenne WY 82002

KARPEN, MARIAN JOAN, financial services executive; b. Detroit, June 16, 1944; d. Cass John and Mary (Jagiello) K.; A.B., Vassar Coll., 1966; postgrad. Sorbonne, Paris, N.Y. U. Grad. Sch. Bus., 1974-77. New Eng. corr. Women's Wear Daily, Fairchild Publs.-Capital Cities Communications, 1966-68, Paris fashion editor, TV and radio commentator Capital Cities Network, 1968-69; fashion editor Boston Herald Traveler, 1969-71; nat. syndicated newspaper columnist and photojournalist Queen Features Syndicate, N.Y.C., 1971-73; account exec. Blyth Eastman Dillon, N.Y.C., 1973-75, Oppenheimer, N.Y.C., 1975-76; v.p., mcpl. bond coordinator Faulkner Dawkins & Sullivan (merged Shearson Hayden Stone), N.Y.C., 1976-77; mgr. retail mcpl. bond dept. Warburg Paribas Becker-A.G. Becker (merger Becker Paribas into Merrill Lynch), N.Y.C., 1977-79, sr. v.p. and prin., 1977-84; sr. v.p., ltd. ptnr. Bear Stearns & Co., 1984-87, assoc. dir., 1987-90; pres., prin. The EuroEast Cons. Group, Inc., N.Y.C., 1990—; lectr. fin. seminars, 1978—; mem. bus. adv. council U.S. Rep. Senate. Mem. benefit com. March of Dimes, 1983; mem. Torchlight Ball com. Internat. Games for Disabled, 1984, other benefit coms.; friend vol. Whitney Mus. Am. Art. Recipient Superior Prodn. award Becker Paribas, 1983. Mem. Nat. Assn. Securities Dealers (registered rep.), N.Y. Stock Exchange (registered rep.), N.Y.C. Women's Econ. Roundtable, Am. Soc. Profl. and Exec. Women, AAUW, U.S. Figure Skating Assn., Fishing Club of Am. (angler's honor roll), English Speaking Union, Vassar Club N.Y. (bd. dirs., mem. exec. com.), Skating Club (N.Y.C. and Boston). Past editorial bd. Retirement Planning Strategist; contbr. articles and photographs to newspapers and mags. Home: 233 E 69th St New York NY 10021 Office: The EuroEast Cons Group Inc 230 Park Ave Ste 924 New York NY 10169

KARPF, JUANITA, music educator; b. Rochester, N.Y., Oct. 31, 1951; d. John Andrew and Carol Jean (Boyce) K. BM, State U. Coll., Potsdam, N.Y., 1973; MM, U. Ga., 1986, doctoral student, 1986. Music tchr. Auburn (N.Y.) City Schs., 1973-75; music tchr. Fayetteville-Manlius Schs., Manlius, N.Y., 1976-77, Altamont Sch., Birmingham, Ala., 1977-79, Bibb County Schs., Macon, Ga., 1979-84; instr. music Mercer U., Macon, 1981-84, U. Ga., Athens, 1984—; music dir. Macon Symphony Youth Orch., 1982-84. Contbr. articles to Notable Black Am. Women, 1990. Performer recital Weill Recital Hall, N.Y.C., 1989. Mem. Am. Musicological Soc., Am. String Tchrs. Assn., Coll. Music Soc., Am. Fedn. Musicians, Atlanta Fedn. Musicians, Ga. Cello Soc., Lanier Symphony Orch., AAUW (Athenian scholar 1988), Nat. Women's Studies Assn., Sonneck Soc. Office: U Ga School of Music Athens GA 30602

KARPIEL, DORIS CATHERINE, state legislator; b. Chgo., Sept. 21, 1935; d. Nicholas and Mary (McStravick) Feinen; m. Harvey Karpiel, 1955 (div.); children—Sharon, Lynn, Laura, Barry. A.A., Morton Jr. Coll., 1955; B.A., No. Ill. U., 1976. Real estate sales assoc. Bundy-Morgan BHG; coordinator Bloomingdale Twp. Republican Presdl. Hdqrs., Ill., 1960, 64, 68; former pres. Bloomingdale Twp. Rep. Orgn.; mem. Twp. Ofcls. of Ill.; trustee Bloomingdale Twp., 1974-75, supr., 1975-80; precinct committeewoman Bloomingdale Twp. Rep. Central Com., 1972, chmn., 1978-80; mem. Ill. Ho. of Reps., 1979-82, Ill. State Senate from 25th Dist., 1984—. Mem. Am. Legislators Exchange Council, Rep. Orgn. Schaumberg Twp.; former sec. Dupage County Suprs. Assn.; former sec. Dupage County Twp. Ofcls.; mem. Dupage County Women's Rep. Orgn., Meml. Hosp. Guild, Am. Cancer Soc. Mem. LWV, DuPage Bd. Realtors, Pi Sigma Alpha. Clubs: Bloomingdale Roselle and Streamwood Country, University Women's, St. Walters Women's. Office: Ill State Capitol Bldg Springfield IL 62706 Other: 400 Lake St #220 Roselle IL 60172-3572*

KARPINSKI, PATRICIA ANNE, psychologist; b. Blue Island, Ill., Apr. 25, 1948; d. Edmund James and Elsie Gertrude (Hlavatovich) K. BA, Roosevelt U., Chgo., 1971, MA, 1977; postgrad., Spalding U., Louisville, 1989—. Cert. psychologist. Tchrs. aide Ill. Inst. Visually Handicapped, Chgo., 1975; intern psychology Rehab. Inst. Chgo., 1976-77; therapist River Region Mental Health/Mental Retardation Bd., Louisville, 1977-78; therapist, psychologist Seven Counties Svcs., Louisville, 1978—. Roosevelt U. grantee, Chgo., 1974-75. Mem. Am. Psychol. Assn. (assoc.), Am. Psychol. Soc., Midwestern Psychol. Assn., Ky. Psychol. Assn. (assoc.). Democrat. Unitarian. Home: 1412 Willow Ave Apt 31 Louisville KY 40204 Office: Seven Counties Svcs 1512 Crums Ln Louisville KY 40216

KARPOFF-MANDELL, GINA D., sales executive; b. Northridge, Calif., July 26, 1964; d. Morris Isadore and Ruda Harriet (Zuckerman) Karpoff; m. Dale Alan Mandell, Sept. 10, 1988. AA, L.A. Pierce Coll., Woodland Hills, Calif., 1982; student, Calif. State U., Northridge, 1986—. Telemktg. supr. ITT-C.O.P.A., Canoga Park, Calif., 1980-82; exec. sec. Hanover Consumer Fin. Co., Encino, Calif., 1982-84; indsl. saleswoman Zero Corp.-Zero Halliburton, Pacoima, Calif., 1984-87; aerospace account mgr. engring. and archtl. sales Bruning div. AM Internat., Santa Fe Springs, Calif., 1987—; real estate saleswoman James R. Gary, Ltd., Woodland Hills, 1989—. Mem. San Fernando Valley Bd. Realtors. Office: Bruning Div AM Internat 10349 Heritage Park Dr Ste 3 Santa Fe Springs CA 90670

KARR, ELIZABETH MCRAE, hospital executive; b. Birmingham, Ala., July 9, 1953; d. James Neal and Donna Mae (Paige) McRae; divorced; children: Kristopher Ryan, Brian Heath. A in Nursing, Jefferson State Jr. Coll., 1974; cert. in Health Services Adminstrv. Devel., U. Ala., Birmingham, 1985, BS in Hosp. Adminstrn., 1987. RN, Ala. Staff nurse Cooper Green Hosp., Birmingham, 1974-83, operating room supr., 1981-83; clin. dir. Druid City Hosp., Tuscalousa, Ala., 1983-88; dir. surg. services Brookwood Hosp., Birmingham, 1983-88, Huntsville (Ala.) Hosp., 1988—; cons. Tuscalousa Surg. Ctr. Vol. local March of Dimes, 1980, ARC, 1981. Grantee March of Dimes, 1971, Davis & Geck, 1982. Mem. Assn. Operating Room Nurses (bd. dirs. 1982-84), Surg. Soc. Huntsville Ala. Republican. Methodist. Avocations: camping, canoeing, reading. Home: 10033 Willow Cove Rd Huntsville AL 35803 Office: Huntsville Hosp 101 Sivley Rd Huntsville AL 35801

KARR, KARI BETHANY WARD, psychologist; b. Abilene, Tex., Apr. 3, 1951; d. Harry Harrison and Kathleen Margaret (Thostenson) Ward; m. Chesley Warren Karr, Oct. 31, 1980. BA summa cum laude, U. N.Mex., 1973, MA, 1978; PhD, Ariz. State U., 1983. Lic. psychologist, Tex. Ariz., N.Mex. Therapist N.Mex. Penitentiary, Santa Fe, 1979-80; counseling intern Ariz. State U., Tempe, 1980-82; psychol. intern Good Samaritan Med. Ctr., Phoenix, 1982-83; counseling psychologist U. Tex., El Paso, 1984-87; dir. counseling, assistance and referral service U. N.Mex., Albuquerque, 1988—; detoxification counselor Recovery of Alcholics, Santa Fe, 1978-79; program coord. Casa Porvenir Halfway House, Santa Fe, 1978; group therapist Youth, Etc., Phoenix, 1980; chair ethics El Paso Psychol. Assn., 1987; chair, insurance subcommittee, New Mex. Psychol. Assn., 1989; v.p. League of Acad. Women. 2d v.p. NAACP, Santa Fe, 1980; del. El Paso County Democratic Conv., 1984; bd. dirs. Casa Blanca Halfway House, El Paso, 1984-87; mem. Theatre Arts Corp. Named one of Outstanding Young Women of Am., 1979, 83. Mem. Am. Psychol. Assn. (elected N.Mex. member-at-large 1990, chair ins. subcom. 1989—), El Paso Psychol. Assn.

(parliamentarian 1984-87, chair ethics com. 1987), Rocky Mountain Ednl. Research Assn., Phi Beta Kappa, Phi Kappa Phi. Jewish.

KARSEN, SONJA PETRA, Spanish educator emeritus; b. Berlin, Apr. 11, 1919; came to U.S., 1938, naturalized, 1945; d. Fritz and Erna (Heidermann) K. Titulo de Bachiller, 1937; B.A., Carleton Coll., 1939; M.A. (scholar in French), Bryn Mawr Coll., 1941; Ph.D., Columbia U., 1950. Instr. Spanish Lake Erie Coll., Painesville, Ohio, 1943-45; instr. modern langs. U. P.R., 1945-46; instr. Spanish Syracuse U., 1947-50, Bklyn. Coll., 1950-51; asst. to dep. dir. gen. UNESCO, 1951-52, Latin Am. Desk, tech. assistance dept., 1952-53, mem. tech. assistance mission Costa Rica, 1954; asst. prof. Spanish Sweet Briar Coll., Va., 1955-57; assoc. prof., chmn. dept. Romance langs. Skidmore Coll., Saratoga Springs, N.Y., 1957-61, chmn. dept. modern langs. and lits., 1961-79, prof. Spanish, 1961-87, prof. emerita, 1987; Fulbright lectr. Free U., Berlin, 1968; mem. adv. and nominating com. Books Abroad, 1965-67. Author: Guillermo Valencia, Colombian Poet, 1951, Educational Development in Costa Rica with UNESCO's Technical Assistance, 1951-54, 1954, Jaime Torres Bodet: A Poet in a Changing World, 1963, Selected Poems of Jaime Torres Bodet, 1964, Versos y prosas de Jaime Torres Bodet, 1966, Jamie Torres Bodet, 1971, Ensayos de Literatura E Historia Iberoamericana/Essays on Iberoamerican Literature and History, 1988, Papers on Foreign Languages, Literature and Culture, 1982-87, 88; editor: Lang. Assn. Bull., 1980-83; mem. editorial adv. bd.: MOdern Lang. Studies; contbr. articles to profl. jours. Decorated chevalier dans l'Ordre des Palmes Academiques, 1964; recipient Leadership award N.Y. State Assn. Fgn. Lang. Tchrs., 1973, 76, 78, Nat. Disting. Leadership award, 1979, Disting. Service award, 1983, 86, Capital Dist. Fgn. Language Disting. Service award, 1987; recipient Spanish Heritage award, 1981, Alumni Achievement award Carleton Coll., 1982; exchange student auspices Inst. Internat. Ednl. at Carleton Coll., 1938-39; Buenos Aires Conv. grantee for research in Colombia, 1946-47; faculty research grantee Skidmore Coll., summer 1959, 61, 63-64, 67, 69-70, 73, ad hoc faculty grantee, 71, 78, 85. Mem. Am. Assn. Tchrs. Spanish and Portuguese, Nat. Assn. Self-Instrnl. Lang. Programs (v.p. 1981-82,pres. 1982-83), AAUW, AAUP, MLA (del. assembly 1976-78, Mildenberger medal selection com 1984-86), El Ateneo Doctor Jaime Torres Bodet (founding mem.), Nat. Geog. Soc., Instituto Internacional de Literatura Iberoamericana, Asociacion Internacional de Hispanistas, UN Assn. U.S.A., Am. Soc. French Acad. Palms, Fulbright Alumni, Phi Sigma Iota, Sigma Delta Pi. Home: PO Box 441 Saratoga Springs NY 12866

KARST, JUDY WARD-STEINMAN, broadcasting executive; b. Monroe, La., Feb. 15, 1941; d. Irving and Daisy Leila (Ward) Steinman; m. Charles Edward Karst, Dec. 27, 1965 (div. 1980); children: Alexander, Alicia, Jacqueline. BA cum laude, La. Coll., 1960; double MA with honors, U. Hawaii, 1962; PhD with honors, Tulane U., 1971. Prof. Chulalongkorn U., Bangkok, Thailand, 1963-64; adj. prof. La. State U., Baton Rouge, 1976-78; news dir. KDBS, Inc., Alexandria, La., 1977-80, asst. to gen. mgr., 1980-83, sta. mgr., 1983-85, gen. mgr., 1985—. Author news documentary, 1988 (award). Bd. dirs. Easter Seals La., New Orleans, 1987—; pres. Alexandria-Pineville Women's Commn., 1979-80, Work Against Rape and Helpline, Alexandria, 1975-78; mem. Rapides Parish Dem. Exec. Com., 1986—. Recipient Investigative Reporting award AP, 1987, 88, 89, Continuing Coverage award AP, 1989; named Woman of Yr., Bus. and Profl. Women Alexandria, 1987, Woman Who Can, Rapides Library, 1987. Mem. La. Emergency Preparedness Assn. (sec. 1987, bd. dirs., Merit award 1988), Nat. Assn. Broadcasters (chmn. TV and radio polit. action com. 1989—), La. Assn. Broadcasters (bd. dirs. 1988—, chmn. TV and radio polit. action com. 1988—, Promotion of Yr. award 1988), Central La. Media Assn. (pres. 1987—), Daus. of King. Episcopalian. Office: KDBS Inc 1515 Jackson St Alexandria LA 71301

KARSTIEN, DIANA C., small business owner; b. Phila., Dec. 28, 1946; d. Adrian and Bernice (Mooney) Clark; m. Robert E. Karstien, Dec. 29, 1984; 1 child, Theresa Jolstad. Cert. in floral design. Adminstrv. asst. Mylcorp., Phila., The Clark Group, Inc., Trenton, N.J., Golden Cradle, Cherry Hill, N.J.; owner Diana's Floral Specialties, Lindenwold, N.J. Mem. Sons of Italy (recipient Sons of Italy award), Sq. Cir. Sportsmen Club, English Setter Club, Silver Wings Adult Cyclists, Psi Alpha Xi. Roman Catholic. Home: 321 3d Ave Lindenwold NJ 08021 Office: Diana's Flora Specialties 250 Gibbsboro Rd Lindenwold NJ 08021

KARTHAUSER, PATRICIA FARLEY, computer services executive; b. Neptune, N.J., Nov. 12, 1952; d. William Henry and Elizabeth Entwisle (Hughes) Farley; m. Clifford Paul Karthauser, Aug. 2, 1975; children: Kristin, Laura, Garrett. BS, Nebr. Wesleyan U., 1975. Programmer FBI, Washington, 1976-78; programmer, analyst, database analyst State of Nebr., Lincoln, 1978-80; sr. programmer, analyst Control Data Corp., Lincoln, 1980-85; sr. systems analyst Lincoln Tel.& Tel., 1985-86; dir. computer svcs. SRI Gallup, Lincoln, 1986—. Bd. dirs. Children's Zoo, Lincoln, 1987-89. Mem. Assn. for Systems Mgmt., HP Users Group. Office: Gallup Orgn Inc 300 S 68th Street Pl Lincoln NE 68510

KARU, GILDA M., lawyer, government official; b. Oceanport, N.J., Dec. 1, 1951; d. Harold and Ilvy (Meriloo) K.; m. Frederick F. Foy, May 23, 1981. AB, Vassar Coll., 1974; JD, Ill. Inst. Tech., 1987. Bar: Ill. 1987, U.S. Dist. Ct. (no. dist.) Ill. 1987. Quality control reviewer Food and Nutrition Svc. USDA, Robbinsville, N.J., 1974-77, team leader, 1977-78, supr., 1978-81; sect. chief Food and Nutrition Svc. USDA, Chgo., 1981—; employer advisor Ctr. for Rehab. and Tng. Disabled Persons, Chgo., 1986—. North-central dir. Estonian Am. Nat. Coun., N.Y.C.; v.p. 1st Estonian Evang. Luth. Ch., Chgo. Recipient Letters of Commendation USDA, 1975, 77, 79, 80, Cert. of Merit, 1985, Cert. of Appreciation Ctr. for Tng. and Rehab. Disabled, 1986, Cert. of Recognition William A. Jump Meml. Found., 1987, Arthur S. Flemming award Washington Downtown Jaycees, 1987, Ill. Dem. Ethnic Heritage award, 1989. Mem. ABA, Ill. Bar Assn., Chgo. Bar Assn., Am. Pub. Welfare Assn., Nat. Assn. Female Execs., Mensa, Vassar Club (treas. Chgo. chpt. 1988—, v.p. 1990—). Office: USDA Food and Nutrition Svc 50 E Washington St Chicago IL 60602

KARUKSTIS, KERRY KATHLEEN, chemistry educator; b. Buffalo, June 16, 1955. BS in Chemistry, Duke U., 1977, PhD in Phys. Chemistry, 1981. Postdoctoral researcher U. Calif., Berkeley, 1981-84; prof. chemistry Harvey Mudd Coll., Claremont, Calif., 1984—. Contbr. articles to profl. jours. NIH Nat. Rsch. award, 1981-84; James B. Duke fellow Duke U., 1980-81, Nat. Merit scholar Duke U., 1973-77. Mem. Am. Chem. Soc., Biophys. Soc., Am. Soc. for Photobiology, Sigma Xi, Phi Beta Kappa. Office: Harvey Mudd Coll Dept Chemistry Claremont CA 91711

KASA, PAMELA D., lawyer; b. 1943. BSChemE, Rensselaer Poly. Inst., 1965; JD, Georgetown U., 1968; LLM, NYU, 1980. Sr. patent atty. Bristol-Myers Co., N.Y.C., from 1976, sec., 1982—, v.p., 1985—, also assoc. gen. counsel; assoc. counsel Clairol, Inc., 1978-80, v.p., counsel, 1980-82. Office: Bristol-Myers Co 345 Park Ave New York NY 10154*

KASAKOVE, SUSAN, interior designer; b. Newark, N.J., Nov. 11, 1938. BFA, U. Buffalo, 1958, Hunter Coll., 196; postgrad., N.Y. Sch. of Interior Design, 1960-64, New Sch. for Social Rsch., 1967-68, Pratt Inst., 1968-69. Asst. interior designer Rodgers Assocs., N.Y.C., 1964-66; interior designer Walter Dorwin Teague Assocs., N.Y.C., 1966-70; sr. interior designer N.Y. State Facilities Devel. Corp., N.Y.C., 1970—. Interior designs include projects for Eli Lilly & Co., Bank of Bermuda, Quaker Oats Corp., N.Y. State Office of Mental Health, N.Y. State Office of Mental Retardation, Cattaraugus County, Warren County. Reading tutor Vols. for Children's Svcs., N.Y.C., 1976-82; chair Friends of White Plains (N.Y.) Symphony, 1981-83; vol. dept. Asian Studies Met. Mus. Art, N.Y.C., 1988—, vol. guide edn. dept., 1978—; Rep. treas. 11th Ward, Yonkers, N.Y., 1979-81. Recipient Outstanding Svc. to Sch. award Rockland County (N.Y.) Lions Club, 1955. Home: 793 Palmer Rd Apt 3-F Bronxville NY 10708 Office: NY State Facilities Devel Corp 909 3d Ave New York NY 10022

KASE-POLISINI, JUDITH BAKER, educator; b. Wilmington, Del., Dec. 13, 1932; d. Charles Robert and Elizabeth Edna (Baker) Kase; B.A., U. Del., 1955; M.A., Case Western Res. U., 1956; m. James F. Polisini; stepchildren—James, Elizabeth, John, Katherine, Ann. Tchr., dir. children's theatre Agnes Scott Coll., 1956, U. Tenn., 1957, U. Md., Germany, 1958-60, Denver Civic Theatre, Denver U., Kent Sch. for Girls, 1960-61; dir. children's theatre U. N.H., Durham, 1962-69; dir. theatre resources for youth, Somersworth, N.H., 1966-69; assoc. prof. theatre U. South Fla., Tampa, 1969-74, assoc. prof. edn., 1975-83, prof., 1984—, artistic dir. ednl. theatre, 1976—; project dir. Hillsborough County Artists-in-Schs. Evaluation and Inservice Project, 1980-82. Bd. dirs. Fla. Alliance for Arts Edn., sec., 1976-77, vice-chmn., 1979-82, chmn. 1982-84; chmn. Wingspread Conf. on Theatre Edn., 1977; drama adjudicator Nat. Arts Festival, Ministry of Edn., Bahamas, 1975, 76, 79, 80; regional chmn. Alliance for Arts Edn., chmn. nat. adv. council, mem. edn. adv. com., 1986-88; J.F. Kennedy Center for Performing Arts, 1983—; cons. theatre edn. and prodn. Recipient Disting. Book of Yr. award, 1989; Am. Theatre of the John F. Kennedy Ctr. for Performing Arts, fellow, 1989. Mem. Children's Theatre Assn. Am. (pres.-elect 1975-77, pres. 1977-79, chmn. symposia 1981-85, spl. recognition citation 1984), Am. Theatre Assn. (chief div. pres.'s coordinating council 1977-78 commn. on theatre edn. 1982—), Speech Communication Assn. (elected), Southeastern, Fla. Theatre Confs., Nat. Theatre Conf. (Sara Spencer award 1980), Internat. Assn. Theatres for Children and Youth, Fla. Assn. for Theater Edn. (theatre edn. of yr. award 1986), Fla. Conf. Tchrs. English, United Faculty Fla., Tampa Mus. Democrat. Episcopalian. Club: Carrollwood Village. Author: The Creative Drama Book: Three Approaches, other books; editor: Creative Drama in a Developmental Context; Children's Theatre, Creative Drama and Learning, Drama as a Meaning Maker; contbr. articles to profl. jours.; pub. playwright; dir. plays. Home: 5321 Taylor Rd Lutz FL 33549 Office: U South Fla Dept Secondary Edn Tampa FL 33620

KASH, FRANCYS KAYGEY, civic worker, service organization executive; b. Sioux City, Iowa, Feb. 25, 1921; d. Jacob David and Ida (Schwab) Maron; student pub. schs., Sioux City; m. Louis Kash, Dec. 17, 1939; 1 dau., Leslie Jo Kash Brodie. Dir., Columbia Savs. and Loan Assn., Beverly Hills, Calif., 1976-81; v.p. 1st Pacific Bank, 1981-83; public affairs/cultural cons. Los Angeles County, 1983—. Vice pres. B'nai B'rith Women, Washington, 1965-76, mem. exec. bd., 1958, treas., 1963-65, internat. pres., 1976-78, chmn. constitution-policy com., 1982-86, former chmn. Anti-Defamation League planning com., life mem. exec. com., hon. life mem. Commn.; former commr. Hillel, B'nai B'rith Youth Orgn.; guest lectr. U. Calif. Extension, Los Angeles, 1977; mem. exec. com. western region, U.S. Com. for UNICEF, 1966; mem. Los Angeles City Human Relations Commn. Adv. Com., 1963—; chair JFC Greater Los Angeles Bd. Govs., 1987—; del. to U.N. End Decade Cof., Nairobi, 1985; mem. Calif. Atty. Gen. Constl. Rights Adv. Com., 1962-64; bd. govs. Jewish Fedn. Council Greater Los Angeles, 1984—. Named Woman of Achievement, N.Y. Women's Div. of Anti-defamation League, 1976; recipient Recognition for Outstanding Efforts award L.A. County Com. for Women, 1988, Outstanding Service award State of Israel, 1973, Los Angeles Mayor award, 1976-77. Mem. Jewish Fedn. Council (bd. dirs. 1958-76, pres. women's conf. 1960-61, bd.dirs. exec. com. 1987—), Sisterhood Congregation Mogen David (life), JFC, GLA (bd. dirs, exec. com. B'nai B'rith Internat. (bd. govs., adm. com., Dove of Peace award 1987). Home: 9311 Alcott St Los Angeles CA 90035

KASHDIN, GLADYS SHAFRAN, painter, educator; b. Pitts., Dec. 15, 1921; d. Edward M. and Miriam P. Shafran; m. Manville E. Kashdin, Oct. 11, 1942 (dec.). BA magna cum laude, U. Miami, 1960; MA, Fla. State U., 1962, PhD, 1965. Photographer, N.Y.C. and Fla., 1938-60; tchr. art, Fla. and Ga., 1956-63; asst. prof. humanities U. South Fla., Tampa, 1965-70, assoc. prof., 1970-74, prof., 1974-87, prof. emerita, 1987—; works exhibited in 58 one-woman shows, 38 group exhbns.; maj. touring exhibits include: The Everglades, 1972-75; Aspects of the River, 1975-80; Processes of Time, 1981-89; represented in permanent collections: Taiwan, Peoples Republic of China, Columbus Mus. Arts, LeMoyne Art Found., Tampa Internat. Airport, Tampa Mus. Art, Kresge Art Mus.; lectr.; adv. bd. Hillsborough County Mus., 1975-83. Mem. U. S. Fla. Status of Women Com., 1971-76, chmn., 1975-76. Recipient Women Helping Women in Art award Soroptimist Internat., 1979, Citizens Hon. award Hillsborough Bd. County Commrs., 1984, Mortar Bd. award for teaching excellence, 1986. Mem. NOW, AAUW (1st v.p. Tampa br. 1971-72), Phi Kappa Phi (chpt.-pres. 1981-83, artist/scholar award 1987). Home: 441 Biltmore Ave Temple Terrace FL 33617 Office: U South Fla CPR 361 Tampa FL 33620

KASHKA, MAISIE SCHMIDT, nursing educator; b. Abilene, Kans., Jan. 2, 1938; d. Oliver H. and Ruby (Alexander) Schmidt; m. Leroy E. Kashka, July 14, 1962 (div. Nov. 1979); children: John, James, Sarah. BSN, U. Kans., 1960, M Nursing, 1977; PhD, Tex. Woman's U., 1987. Staff nurse U. Kans. Med. Ctr., Kansas City, 1960-61, 66-69; instr. Florence Cook Sch. Practical Nursing, Kansas City, 1961-62, 65-66; staff nurse U. Kans. Med. Ctr., Kansas City, 74-75, Wyandot County Mental Health Ctr., Kansas City, 1975-76; instr. Johnson County Community Coll., Overland Park, Kans., 1977-79; instr., asst. prof. nursing U. Kans., Kansas City, 1979-83; asst. prof. nursing Tex. Christian U., Ft. Worth, 1983-88, Tex. Woman's U., Denton, 1988—. Contbr. articles to profl. jours., chpts. to books. Bd. dirs. LVW, Shawnee Mission, Kans., 1965. Mem. Am. Nurses Assn., U. Kans. Nurses Alumni Assn., Sigma Theta Tau, Phi Kappa Phi. Democrat. Roman Catholic. Home: 2705 N Bell Denton TX 76201 Office: Tex Woman's U Coll Nursing Denton TX 76204

KASHOU, JEAN LEE, hardware and software manufacturing company executive; b. Milw., May 4, 1945; d. Laverne John and Evelyn Mary (Dickinson) Williams; m. George C. Kashou, Sept. 9, 1967 (div. May 1980). G-rad. high sch., Milw.; student, Bus. Sch., Ft. Lauderdale, Fla. Exec. sec. Will Ross Inc., Milw., 1969-71, Indsl. Fuel Oil, Milw., 1977-82; office mgr. Kashou Carpet Co., Milw., 1971-77, Logan Prodns., Milw., 1983-84, 85-88, I.A.H.B., Portola Valley, Calif., 1984-85; adminstr. 3Computer Co., Santa Clara, Calif., 1988-89; adminstr. office chmn. 3Com Corp., Santa Clara, Calif., 1989—. Former campaign mgr. Stephen Leopold for State Rep., Milw. Office: 3Com Corp 3165 Kifer Rd Santa Clara CA 95052

KASI, LEELA PESHKAR, pharmaceutical chemist; b. Bombay, July 15, 1939; came to U.S., 1971; d. Subbaraman and Lakshmi (Shastri) Peshkar; m. Kalli R. Kasi, June l0, 197l. BS, U. Bombay, India, 1958; PhD, U. Marburg, W. Germany, 1968. Jr. chemist Khandelwal Labs., Bombay, India, 1958-59; trainee Farbwerke Hoechst, Frankfurt, W. Germany, 1960; teaching asst. U. of Marburg, W. Germany, 1967-68; sr. chemist Boehringer-Knoll Ltd., Bombay, India, 1969-7l; mgr. quality control Health Care Industries, Michigan City, Ind., 1972-77; asst. chemist U. Tex. MD Anderson Cancer Ctr., Houston, 1979-90, assoc. chemist, 1990—; asst. prof. chemistry U. of Tex. MD Anderson Cancer Ctr., Houston, 1982—; mem. graduate faculty U. Tex. 1984-. Contbr. articles to profl. jours. Co-investigator/investigator rsch. grant Tex. Higher Edn. Bd., 1990—; also two rsch. contracts from pvt. industries, 1989—. Grantee Sub-Contract Rsch. NIH, 1988-89; co-investigator several rsch., Nat. Cancer Inst., 1989—; co-investigator/investigator rsch. grant Tex. Higher Edn. Bd., 1990-92; two rsch. contracts from pvt. industries, 1989-91. Mem. AAAS, Soc. of Nuclear Medicine, N.Y. Acad. of Sci., Sigma Xi. Home: 4710 McDermed Houston TX 77035 Office: U Tex MD Anderson Cancer Ct 1515 Holcombe Blvd Houston TX 77030

KASINDORF, BLANCHE ROBINS, educational administrator; b. N.Y.C., May 18, 1925; d. Samuel David and Anna (Block) Robins; B.A., Hunter Coll., 1944; M.A., N.Y.U., 1948; postgrad. Cornell U., 1946-50; m. David Kasindorf, July 1, 1960. Tchr. pub. schs., Bklyn., 1945-56; instr. Bklyn. Coll., 1956-57; asst. in research for Puerto Rican study Ford Found. and N.Y.C. Bd. Edn., 1956-57; asst. prin. N.Y.C. Pub. Schs., 1957-59; research asso. ednl. programming and stats. N.Y.C. Bd. Edn., 1959-63, coordinator spl. edn. liaison div. child welfare for Bur. Curriculum Research, 1963-64; jr. prin., integration coordinator Bklyn. Sch. Dist. 44, 1964-65; prin. Pub. Sch. 8, Bklyn., 1965-87; cons. to numerous social agys. Mem. NEA, Council Exceptional Children, N.Y.C. Elementary Sch. Prins., Council Supervisory Assns. Contbr. to profl. publs.; also editor instructional materials. Home: 1655 Flatbush Ave Brooklyn NY 11210

KASKE, CAROL MARGARET VONCKX, educator; b. Elgin, Ill., Feb. 5, 1933; d. J. Newell and Frances M. (Fitchie) Vonckx; m. Robert E. Kaske, June 4, 1958 (dec. Aug. 1989); 1 child, Richard J. BA, Washington U., St. Louis, 1954; MA, Smith Coll., 1956; PhD, Johns Hopkins U., 1964. Lectr. Peabody Conservatory, Balt., 1957-58, Duke U., Durham, N.C., 1959-60; lectr. women's campus U. N.C., Greensboro, 1961; lectr. U. Ill., Champaign-Urbana, 1961-64; lectr., asst. prof. Cornell U., Ithaca, N.Y., 1963-85, assoc. prof., 1985—; cons. in field. Co-author, editor: Marsilio Ficino, 3 Books on Life, 1989; mem. editorial bd. Spenser Ency. and Spenser Soc., 1977—, mem. exec. coun., 1979-81; contbr. articles to profl. jours. Mem. Internat. Assn. for Neo-Latin Studies, Modern Lang. Assn., Renaissance Soc. Am., AAUP. Democrat. Episcopalian. Home: 121 N Quarry St Ithaca NY 14850 Office: Cornell U GS 252 Ithaca NY 14853

KASKINEN RIESBERG, BARBARA KAY, author, composer, musician, music educator; b. Manistee, Mich., June 26, 1952; d. Norman Ferdinand and Martha Agnes (Harju) Kaskinen; m. David H. Riesberg, Feb. 14, 1985. AA, Broward Community Coll., Coconut Creek, Fla., 1978; BA with honors, Fla. Atlantic U., 1981; postgrad., Nova U., 1989—. Instr. adult piano Atlantic High Sch., Delray Beach, Fla., 1981-82; organist, combo dir. Affirmation Luth. Ch., Boca Raton, Fla., 1981-86; studio musician, composer/arranger Electric Rize Prodns., Margate, Fla., 1982—; ind. instr. piano, electronic keyboard and guitar. Margate, 1979—; bass and keyboard player Electric Rize Band, Margate, 1982—; in-house composer and arranger Hansen House, Miami Beach, Fla., 1987-88; co-founder Oasis Coffee House, Boca Raton, Fla., 1990—. Author: Barbara Riesberg's Adult Electronic Keyboard Course Book I, 1988, Books II and III, 1989. Reporter Coalition to Stop Food Irradiation, Broward, Fla., 1989. Mem. NOW, ASCAP, Fla. Atlantic U. Alumni Assn. Home: 6601 NW 22nd St Margate FL 33063

KASKIW, PAMELA IRENE See HANLON, PAMELA IRENE

KASLE, ANITA L., fashion consultant; b. New Bedford, Mass., Oct. 30, 1929; d. Myer and Ethel (Margolis) Goldberg; m. Herbert David Kasle, Apr. 3, 1927; children: Marlene, Wendy, Nancy. Student, Keuka Coll., Keuka Park, N.Y., 1947-48, U. Mo., 1948-49, Butler U., Indpls., 1950. Owner Nito-Joi Present, Inc., Zionsville, Ind., 1972-73; fashion dir. L. Strauss/Regency Rm., Indpls., 1974-78; fashion cons./speaker Fashion Your Image, Carmel, Ind., 1978—; fashion show coord. and commentator Alliance Indpls. Mus. Art, 1985. Bd. dirs. North Group Symphony, Indpls, 1984-89, Dance Kaleidoscope, Indpls., 1986-88; mem. Indpls. Opera Guild, 1982—, Beethoven Found., Indpls., 1986—. Recipient Outstanding Civic Leader award Girls Inc., 1990; named No. 1 Fashion Cons., Indpls. mag., 1985. Mem. Fashion Group Inc., Nat. Speakers Assn., Nat. Profl. Saleswomen, Internat. Platform Assn.

KASMIR, GAIL ALICE, insurance company official, accountant; b. N.Y.C., Aug. 19, 1958; d. Fred and Evelyn Silvie (Mailman) K. BSBA summa cum laude, U. Cen. Fla., 1979. CPA, Fla. Acct. Ernst and Young, Orlando, Fla., 1979-83; fin. mgr. Harcourt Brace Jovanovich (Harvest Life Ins. Co.), Orlando, Fla., 1983-85; sr. v.p., treas., sec., cons. to bd. dirs., mem. investment com. LifeCo Investment Group, Inc. and subs. Nat. Heritage Life Ins. Co., Maitland, Fla., 1985-89, exec. v.p., 1990—; bd. dirs., sec. LifeCo Mktg. Svcs., Inc., 1990—. Vol. Am. Cancer Soc., 1987—, Am. Soc. for Cancer Research, 1987—. Fellow Life Office Mgmt. Assn.; mem. Am. Inst. CPAs, Fla. Inst. CPAs, Ins. Acctg. and Systems Assn., Beta Alpha Psi, Beta Gamma Sigma. Republican. Jewish. Home: 1160 Woodland Terr Trail Altamonte Springs FL 32714 Office: 1101 N Lake Destiny Dr #200 Maitland FL 32751

KASPER, SUSAN KATHRYN, psychologist; b. Irvington, N.J., Sept. 3, 1944; d. Albert Frank and Frances Marie (Coleman) DeFrancisco; m. Ronald S. Kasper, July 16, 1966 (div. May 1982); 1 child, Andrew S. Kasper; m. Joseph Pucilowski, May 5, 1990. BA magna cum laude, Kean Coll., 1966, MA with distinction, 1971; MA, Fairleigh Dickinson U., 1977; PhD, Hofstra U., 1982. Lic. psychologist, N.Y., N.J. Fifth grade tchr. Parsippany (N.J.) Sch. System, 1966-67; adj. asst. prof. gen. and child psychology County Coll. of Morris, Randolph, N.J., 1972-79; mental health profl. crisis intervention Pequannock Mental Health Ctr., Pompton Plains, N.J., 1979-81; sr. clin. psychologist Essex County Hosp. Ctr., Cedar Grove, N.J., 1982-87; cons. Hagedorn Ctr. for Geriatrics, Glen Gardner, N.J., 1987-88, Psychol. Consultants Group, Randolph, 1986—; pvt. practice psychologist Randolph, 1983—; trainer parent group Pequannock Mental Health Ctr., Pompton Plains, N.J. 1979; adj. faculty child abnormal psychology Fairleigh Dickinson U., Madison, N.J., 1988. Author (rsch.) Psychological Abuse, 1982. Trainer Morris County Hotline, Denville, N.J., 1975, 76; co-founder Morris County Assn., Denville, 1970; vol. occupational therapy Greystone Park (N.J.) Psychiat. Hosp., 1972-73. N.J. Jr. fellow in psychology, 1976-77; recipient Cert. of Appreciation, Vol. Action Coun., Morris County, N.J., 1974, Outstanding Svc. award Nat. Assn. for Mental Health, 1974. Mem. Am. Psychol. Assn., Ea. Psychol. Assn. N.J. Acad. Psychology, Gerontol. Soc. N.J., N.J. Psychol. Assn. (com. on aging 1986-89, pub. info. com. 1990), Morris County Psychologists, Morris County Assn. for Mental Health (bd. dirs. 1973-77, v.p. 1976-77, co-chair vol. tng. com. 1974, Vol. of Yr. 1974), Kappa Delta Pi. Home and office: 151 Dover Chester Rd Randolph NJ 07869

KASPRZAK, JOYCE ANN, weight loss company executive; b. Greensburg, Pa., Sept. 28, 1946; d. Benjamin Steven and Palma Christine (Policastro) De Rosa; m. Richard E. Reid, Nov. 1, 1966 (div. Nov. 1977); 1 child, Brian Scott; m. 2d, Alan Lee Kasprzak, June 25, 1978. B.A. in Communication Arts, U. Dayton, 1967, postgrad., 1969-70; A.M.A., Wright State U., 1985; cert. chief exec. officer devel. program, 1987. Social worker Welfare Dept., Dayton, Ohio, 1967-68; tchr. St. James Elem. Sch., Dayton, 1968-71, St. Helen Elem. Sch., Dayton, 1972-73; pres., dir. The Diet Workshop, Dayton, 1973—, mem. nat. adv. bd., 1980—; chmn. creative cuisine Am. Heart Assn., 1979-80. Contbr. Diet Corner column several newspapers, 1974-79. Founder U. Dayton Scholarship Fund, 1981, U. Dayton Endowment, 1986. Recipient numerous awards for outstanding performance Nat. Diet Workshop, 1974-90; awards for fund-raising activities Nat. CARE Assn., 1976, St. Jude's Hosp., Memphis, 1977, 78, ARC, Dayton, 1979, 80; award Salute to Women Entrepreneurs, Lazarus of Dayton, 1986. Mem. Women in Communications, Pres.'s Roundtable, Dayton C. of C., Dayton Area Heart Assn. (bd. dirs.), U. Dayton Pres.'s Club. Roman Catholic. Office: The Diet Workshop PO Box 5817 3220 N Main St Dayton OH 45405-0817

KASSEBAUM, NANCY LANDON, senator; b. Topeka, July 29, 1932; d. Alfred M. and Theo Landon; children: John Philip, Linda Josephine, Richard Landon, William Alfred. BA in Polit. Sci, U. Kans., 1954; MA in Diplomatic History, U. Mich., 1956. Mem. Maize (Kans.) Sch. Bd., 1972-75; mem. Washington staff Sen. James B. Pearson of Kans., 1975-76; mem. U.S. Senate from Kans., 1979—, mem. fgn. relations com., labor and human resources com., banking, housing and urban affairs com., spl. com. on aging. Republican. Episcopalian. Office: US Senate 302 Russell Senate Bldg Washington DC 20510*

KASSEWITZ, RUTH EILEEN BLOWER, retired hospital executive; b. Columbus, Ohio, May 15, 1928; d. E. Wallett and Helen (Daub) Blower; BS in Journalism-Mgmt., Ohio State U., Columbus, 1951; m. Jack Kassewitz, July 28, 1962 (dec.); 1 step child, Jack. Copywriter, Ohio Fuel Gas Co., Columbus, 1951-55, Merritt Owens Advt. Agy., Kansas City, Kans., 1955-56; account exec. Grant Advt., Inc., Miami, Fla., 1956-59; account supr. Venn/Cole & Assocs., Miami, 1959-67; dir. communications Ferendino/Grafton/Candela/Spillis Architects & Engrs., Miami, 1967-69; dir. communications Dade County Dept. Housing and Urban Devel., Miami, 1969-72; dir. communications Met. Dade County Govt., 1972-78; adminstr. pub. rels. U. Miami/Jackson Meml. Med. Ctr., 1978-90, ret., 1990. Pres., U. Miami Women's Guild, 1973-74; bd. dirs. Girls Scouts Tropical Fla., 1974-76, 81-83, Lung Assn. Dade-Monroe Counties, 1976-87; mem. exec. com. Miami-Dade Community Coll. Found.; pres. Mental Health Assn. Dade County, 1982; mem. Miami Ecol. and Beautification Com., 1978—, also bd. dirs.; bd. govs. Barry U., Miami, 1981-83; trustee Nat. Humanities Faculty, 1981-83; trustee United Protestant Appeal, 1984—; mem. Greater Miami Urban Coalition; treas., past chmn. Health, Edn., Promotion Council, Inc.; adv. bd. Miami's for Me, 1987-88; mem. Coral Gables Cable TV Bd., 1983-86; ch. moderator Plymouth Congl. Ch., 1986-88; community adv. bd. Jr. League Greater Miami, Inc., 1989—. Recipient Disting. Service award Plymouth Congl. Ch., Miami, 1979; Ann Stover award, 1983, Golden Image award, Fla. Pub. Relations Assn., 1987. Mem. Public Relations Soc. Am. (pres. South Fla. chpt. 1969-70, nat. chmn. govt. sect. 1973-74, nat. dir. 1974-78; continuing edn. council 1981-83; Silver Anvil award 1973, Assembly del. 1970-73, 86-89), Internat. Platform Assn., Women in Communications (pres. Greater Miami chpt. 1962-63; Clarion award 1973, 75, Community Headliner 1985), Fla. Hosp. Assn., South Fla. Hosp. Public Relations Assn., Miami Internat. Press Club (bd. dirs. 1986-87), Miami Forum, Greater Miami C. of C. (gov. 1983-86), Fla. Women's Alliance, Rotary (bd. dirs. Miami club 1989—, pub. rels. chmn.). Home: 1136 Aduana Ave Coral Gables FL 33146

KASTEN, DIANE LYNN, typesetting company executive; b. St. Louis, Mar. 9, 1947; d. Edmund Louis and Elsie Joan (Schaffernegger) K. Typist Ralston Purina Co., St. Louis, 1965-69; typesetter, supr. ITT Hamilton Ins. Co., St. Louis, 1969-71; typesetter Old Olive Printing Svcs., St. Louis, 1971-73; owner, operator The Hyper Typer, St. Louis, 1973—. Chairwoman, bd. dirs. St. Louis Effort for AIDS. Democrat. Mem. Unity Ch. Home: 5252 Bancroft Ave Saint Louis MO 63109 Office: Hyper Typer 760 Office Pkwy Ste 38 Saint Louis MO 63141

KASTL, DIAN EVANS, lawyer; b. Oklahoma City, Jan. 5, 1953; d. Jim and Hazel Corrine (Hill) Evans; m. David G. Kastl, May 18, 1970, Feb. 6, 1987; children: Shea P., R. Patricia. BS in Nursing, U. Okla., 1975, MA in Journalism, 1979; BS in Journalism, U. Md., 1976; JD, Loyola U., 1984; LLM in Trade Regulation, NYU, 1985. Bar: N.J. 1985, N.Y. 1985, Fla. 1985, U.S. Dist. Ct. N.J. 1985, La. 1987, D.C. 1987, U.S. Dist. Ct. (ea., mid. and we. dists.) La. 1987, U.S. Ct. Appeals (5th cir.) 1987. Rsch. asst. NYU Sch. Law, N.Y.C., 1984-85; assoc. Trenam, Simmons, Kemker, Scharf, Barkin, Frye O'Neil, Tampa, Fla., 1985-87, Chaffe, McCall, Phillips, Toler & Sarpy, New Orleans, 1987—. Mem. editorial bd., comments editor Loyola Law Rev., 1983-84. Bernard and Pauline Lasker scholar, 1984-85. Mem. ABA (chmn. computer programs subcom. patent trademark and copyright sect. 1988-89), N.Y. Bar Assn., La. Bar Assn., New Orleans Bar Assn., Sigma Delta Chi, Kappa Tau Alpha. Democrat. Home: 23 Spinnaker Ln New Orleans LA 70124 Office: Chaffee McCall Phillips Toler & Sarpy 1100 Poydras St New Orleans LA 70163

KASTLER, BONNIE LOU, account representative; b. Oswego, N.Y., Nov. 10, 1956; d. Franklin Roosevelt Kastler and Nancy Ann (Garrison) Polacek; m. Richard D. Mace, Nov. 16, 1974; (div. 1984); children; Jason R. and Rebecca L. Regents Diploma, Mexico Acad. & Cen. Sch., Mexico, 1970-74. Clerical (work study) Howell Ins., Mexico, N.Y., 1974--; cna sr. policy service clk. CNA Ins. Group, Liverpool, N.Y., 1977-81; underwriting tech. Unigrd Ins., Liverpool, N.Y., 1981-86; asst. commercial lines mgr. Eastern Shore Assn., Fulton, N.Y., 1986-88; metropolitan acct. rep. Fulton, N.Y., 1988--. Founder & Dir., Palermo Twirlettes, Mexico, N.Y., 1974-87; Bd. of Parks & Recreation - Palermo, Palmermo Town Park, N.Y., 1985. Named Miss N.Y. State Future Bus. Leaders of Am., 1974, Met. 1989 Fast Start award winner for Syracuse Region, Met. Leaders Club. Mem. Am. Bus. Women's Assn., Syracuse Assn. Life Underwriters (season ticket chmn. 1989, Key Person 1989). Republican Methodist.

KASTLER, NANCY JANE MEADE, clinical research biomedical engineer; b. Webster City, Iowa, Aug. 24, 1959; d. John Richard abd Mary Virginia (Steil) Meade; m. William J. Kastler, Sept. 13, 1978; (div. 1982); children: William Jason and Jamie Lee. AA, Iowa Cen. Community Coll., Ft. Dodge, 1980; BS, Iowa State U, Ames, 1982; MS, U. Minn., Mpls., 1988, postgrad., 1989. Cert. engr.-in-tng. Process devel. engr. The Pillsbury Co, Mpls., 1982-86; research scientist Medtronic Inc., Mpls., 1987-88; sr. engr. Baxter Healthcare, Inc., Mpls., 1988-89; mgr. vascular graft R & D, Angeion Corp., Plymouth, 1989-90; mgr. cell barrier devices Hana Biologics, Alameda, Calif., 1990—; lectr., organizer Artificial Organs Course, U. Minn., Mpls., 1988-89, 89-90. Co-author: Work in Hydrogels in Medicine, 1988. Mem. Minn. Women's Consortium St. Paul, 1989. Recipient Grad. Sch. Fellowship U. Minn. Mpls., 1986, Forstrom Fellowship U. Minn. Mpls., 1986. Mem. Am. Inst. Chem. Engr., Tau Beta Pi Engring., Am. Soc. Profl. Exec. Women. Independent. Home: 3924 Hanly Rd Oakland CA 94602 Office: Hana Biologics 850 Marina Village Pkwy Alameda CA 94501

KASTNER, SHAY DAVIDSON, sales and marketing professional, consultant; b. El Paso, Tex., Oct. 2, 1944; d. Clyde William and Mae Vivian (Thurman) Davidson; (div. 1975); 1 child, Tiffney Thurman Kastner. Student, Tex. Women's U., 1962-63, U. Tex., 1963-64, San Jose (Calif.) State U., 1965-67; BA, U. Ark., 1975; MA, San Jose (Calif.) State U., 1982. Ind. jewelry mfr. Little Rock and San Jose, 1971-80; N.E. account mgr., mgr. sales and exec. tng. Corvus Systems, Inc., San Jose, 1980-84; pvt. practice San Jose, 1984—. Author: Token-Ring Component & Configuration Guide, 1990. Coord. 1st Soviet/U.S. High-Tech. Trade Summit and Conf., Santa Clara, 1990. Mem. NAFe. Office: PO Box 1504 Los Gatos CA 95031

KASZA, ELIZABETH A., accounting professional; b. Morristown, N.J., Sept. 28, 1958; d. Joseph F. and Mary (O'Sullivan) Gray; div.; 1 child, Kenneth W. Kosza. AA in Bus. with highest honors, Middlesex Coll., Edison, N.J., 1988; student, Rutgers U., 1988—. Acctg. mgr. Astro Molding Inc., Old Bridge, N.J., 1976—. Mem. Nat. Assn. Accts. (honor award 1988), Middlesex Alumni Assn. (honor award 1988). Roman Catholic. Office: Astro Molding Inc Rte 1 Old Bridge NJ 08857

KATCHUR, MARLENE MARTHA, nurse administrator; b. Belleville, Ill., Dec. 20, 1946; d. Elmer E. and Hilda B. (Gutherz) Wilde; m. Raymond J. Katchur, Feb. 22, 1969; 1 child, Nickolas Phillip. BSN, So. Ill. U., 1968; MS in Health Care Adminstrn., Calif. State U., L.A., 1982. RN; cert. critical care nurse. Staff nurse Los Angeles County-U. So. Calif. Med. Ctr., 1968-69, critical care nurse, 1969-73, asst. head nurse med. intensive care unit, 1974, head nurse intensive coronary care unit, 1975-78, nursing supr. internal medicine nursing, 1978-81, assoc. nursing dir. internal medicine nursing, 1981-83, fiscal analysts and info. systems coord., 1983-89, patient-centered info. systems cons., 1989—. Mem. Sheriff's Relief Assn. Mem. Am. Assn. Critical Care Nurses, Nat. Critical Care Inst. Edn., Am. Heart Assn., So. Ill. U. Alumni Assn. (life), Health Svcs. Mgmt. Forum, Orgn. Nurse Execs. Calif. (membership com.), Am. Soc. Profl and Exec. Women, Nat. Assn. Female Execs., Soc. for Clin. Data Mgmt. Systems (bd. dirs. 1990—), AAUW, Soc. Med. Computer Observers (charter), Am. Legion Aux., Nat. Hist. Soc., Jobs Daus. (past honor queen). Office: LA County-U So Calif Med Ctr 1200 N State St Rm 1118 Los Angeles CA 90033

KATER, KATHRYN, nursing educator, consultant; married; 1 child. BSN, St. Louis U., BS, MSN, 1984. RN. Staff nurse Barnes Hosp., instr.; instr. advanced EKG and cardiac assesment Courses Barnes Hosp., Manchester; nurse specialist cardiovascular surgery Washington U. at Barnes Hosp., St. Louis; translator; nursing computer programer; researcher. Contbr. numerous articles to nursing jours. Mem. Critical Care Nurses Assn., Nat. Nurses Adv. Bd. for Myasthenia Gravis Found., Midwest Nursing Rsch. Soc. (recipient blue ribbon), Sigma Theta Tau, Delta Lambda. Episcopalian. Home: 577 Princeway Ct Manchester MO 63011

KATKE, MARY LOU, nurse; b. Big Rapids, Mich., Mar. 16, 1959; d. Richard Peter and Janet Louis (Bell) K. Assoc., Ferris State U., Big Rapids, 1979. Staff nurse med./surg. Mecosta County Gen. Hosp., Big Rapids, 1979, staff nurse emergency rm., 1980-83; critical care float nurse E.W. Sparrow Hosp., Lansing, Mich., 1983-84; nursing supr. Mecosta County Gen. Hosp., Lansing, 1984-88, head nurse emergency rm., 1988-90, mgr. emergency rm., 1990—. Home: 13640 120th Ave Rodney MI 49342 Office: Mecosta County Gen Hosp 405 Winter Big Rapids MI 49307

KATSAKIORES, PHYLLIS, small business owner, city councilor; b. Saugus, Mass., Sept. 22, 1934; d. Robert D. and Eva M. (Clemonts) Harrie; m. Charles Hemeon, Sept. 11, 1954 (div.); children: Debbie, Charles, Laurie; m. George N. Katsakiores, Oct. 9, 1983. Grad. high sch., Saugus. City councilor Town of Derre, N.H., 1985; rep. State of N.H., 1985; rep., chair Rockingham County, Derry, 1986-88; owner Retail Grocery Super-Store, Derry. Chmn. Rockingham Rep. Party, 1978-86. Mem. Am. Legis. Exch. Coun., Orgn. Women Legislators. Home: 1 Bradford St Derry NH 03038

KATSON, ROBERTA MARINA, entrepreneur; b. Albuquerque, Oct. 5, 1947; d. Robert V. and Penelope (Papafrangos) Katson; student Emory U., 1966-67, Ga. State U., 1967-69; m. Cyrus Butner, 1980; children: Justin Cyrus, Renee Alexis. BA, U. N.Mex., 1974, MA, 1977. Gen. mgr. Window Rock (Ariz.) Motor Inn, Navajo Reservation, 1972-73; research asst. dept. econs. U. N.Mex., Albuquerque, 1974-75, research asso. Resource Econ. Group, 1975-77; economist program analysis Econ. Devel. Adminstrn., Dept. Commerce, Washington, 1977-79; economist Dept. Energy, Washington, 1979-84; cons. Calligraphic Design, Fairfax, Va., 1986-88, owner, 1989—. Mem. Phi Kappa Phi, Omicron Delta Epsilon. Democrat. Contbr. articles to profl. jours. Home: 11901 St Johnsbury Ct Reston VA 22091 Office: Calligraphic Design 8802 Glade Hill Rd Fairfax VA 22031

KATT, BONITA KAY, small business owner; b. Columbus, Ohio, July 20, 1941; d. Robert W. and Pauline M. (Lawrence) Egnew; m. Douglas E. Katt, Aug. 16, 1980; children: Michael, Mitchell. BEd, Ohio State U., 1964. Mgr. Steak & Ale Restaurants, Toledo; dir. prepared foods Churchill Supermarkets, Inc., Sylvania, Ohio; owner, mgr. The Wallpaper Co., Toledo; arbitrator Better Bus. Bur., 1987—; cons. Nat. Decorating Products Assn., 1989. Mem. Zonta Internat. (pres. Toledo chpt. 1990), Nat. Assn. Women in Constrn., Women Bus. Owners Assn. (past pres.), Sylvania C. of C. Republican. Methodist. Office: 2955 N Reynolds Rd Toledo OH 43615

KATZ, ELAINE MARCIA, nuclear engineering educator; b. Chgo., Oct. 31, 1942; d. Hymen and Esther (Schnidman) K. BSME, Purdue U., 1963; MS, U. Tenn., 1971, PhD, 1975. Registered profl. engr., Tenn. Mech. engr. Met. Sanitary Dist, Chgo., 1963-64, J.F. Pritchard & Co., Kansas City, Mo., 1964-66, Rust Engring. Co., Birmingham, Ala., 1966-68; sr. nuclear engr. Combustion Engring. Inc., Windsor, Conn., 1973-76; fgn. research assoc. French AEC, 1976-77; from asst. to assoc. prof. nuclear engring. U. Tenn., Knoxville, 1977—; summer faculty participant Oak Ridge Associated Univs., 1981. Summer faculty fellow NASA-ASEE Johnson Space Ctr., Houston, 1988, ASME congl. fellow as sci. advisor for Sen. Jim Sasser, Tenn., 1985, Lilly Found. fellow, 1978-79. Mem. ASME, Am. Soc. Engring. Edn., Am. Nuclear Soc., Soc. Women Engrs. (student sect. faculty advisor). Home: 1431 Cherokee Trail Apt 106 Knoxville TN 37920 Office: U Tenn Dept Nuclear Engring Knoxville TN 37996-2300

KATZ, GLORY WEISBERGER, advocate for the disabled; b. N.Y.C., Aug. 11, 1928; d. Abraham Harry and Rose (Polstein) W.; m. Harvey L., June 12, 1949; children: Susan Katz Miller, Arne H. BA, Syracuse U., N.Y., 1949; MA, Columbia U., 1966. Tchr. Bd. Coop. Ednl Svcs., Port Chester, 1966-85; tchr., head Bd. Coop. Ednl Svcs., Rye Brook, N.Y., retired; V.p. Yonkers League for Retarded, 1985--. pres. Parents Adv. Com. Spl. Yonkers Citizens 1984--; chmn. Yonkers Women's Div. United Jewish Appeal Fedn. White Plains 1988-89;. Recipient Mental Health award Westchester County Dept. Community Mental Health, 1990. Mem. Bd. Visitors Rockland Psychia. Ctr., Orangeburg, N.Y. (pres.1986-87), Yonkers Council Dept. Comn. Mental Health, Mental Health Assn. Westchester, Assn. for NY State Educators of Emotionally Disturbed, Assn. for Children with Learning Disabilities (Cert. Appreciation award 1976). Democratic. Jewish. Home: 89 Oval Court Yonkers NY 10710

KATZ, HILDA, artist; b. June 2, 1909; d. Max and Lina (Schwartz) K. Student, Nat. Acad. Design; student (3 awards; New Sch. Social Research scholarship), 1940-41. Author: (under pen name Hulda Weber) poems including numerous anthologies, spl. ltd. edit., 1987-88; anthologies include The Bloom, 1984-85, 87, Perfume and Fragrance, 1988, 89, Lightning & Rainbows, 1989, 90; contbr.: numerous poems, short stories to books and mags. including Humpty Dumpty's Mag. (publ. for children); contbr. commemorative poetry to mus. and govt. including Pres. Ronald W. Reagan, 1985, series of poems in N.Y. State Mus. of Albany, 1987, Yad Vashem Meml. Archives, Jerusalem, 1987, Mus. of Jewish Heritage, 1988, Jewish Theol. Sem. of Am., 1989; one-woman exhbns. include: Bowdoin Coll. Art Mus., 1951, Calif. State Library, 1953, Print Club Albany, N.Y., 1955, U. Maine, 1955, 58, Jewish Mus., 1956, Pa. State Tchrs. Coll., 1956, Massillon Mus., 1957, Ball State Tchrs. Coll., 1957, Springfield (Mass.) Art Mus., 1957, Miami Beach (Fla.) Art Ctr., Richmond (Ind.) Art Assn., 1959, Old State Capitol Mus. La., other exhbns. include: Corcoran Bienniale Library of Congress, Am. in the War Exhbn, N.Y. State Mus. of Albany, 1989, Jewish Theol. Sem. of Am., 1989, 26 mus., Am. Drawing anns. at: Albany Inst., Nat. Acad. Design, Conn. Acad. Fine Arts, Bklyn. Mus., Delgado Mus., Art-U.S.A., 1959, Congress for Jewish Culture, Met. Mus. Art., Springfield (Mo.) Art Mus., Children's Mus. Hartford, Conn., Miniature Printers, Peoria (Ill.) Art Ctr., Pa. Acad. Fine Arts, Originale Contemporate Graphic Internat., France, Bezalel Nat. Mus., Israel, Venice (Italy) Bienniale, Royal Etchers and Painters Exchange Exhibit, Eng., Bat Yam Mus., Israel, Paris, France, 1958, 59, Am.-Italian Print Exchange, numerous libraries, artists socs., invitational exhbns. include, Rome, Turin, Venice, Florence, Naples (all Italy), Nat. Academe Muse, France, Israel, USIA exhbns. in, Europe, S. Am., Asia, Africa; represented spl. collections, U.S. Nat. Mus., 1965, U. Maine, 1965, Library of Congress, 1965-71, Met. Mus. Art, 1965-66, 80, Nat. Gallery Art, 1966, Nat. Collection Fine Arts, 1966-71, 78, Nat. Air and Space Mus., 1970, N.Y. Pub. Library, 1971, 78, U.S. Mus. History and Tech., 1972, Naval Mus., 1972, Ft. Lewis Coll., Durango, Colo., 1980-81, Boston Pub. Library, 1980-81, Israel Nat. Mus., Jerusalem, 1980-81, State Mus. Albany, N.Y., 1980, N.Y. State Mus. Archives, Albany, 1979-89; also represented in permanent collections Balt. Mus. Art, Franklin D. Roosevelt, Fogg Mus., Harvard, Santa Barbara (Calif.) Art Mus., Syracuse U., Colorado Springs Fine Arts Ctr., Pennell Collection, Am. Artists Group Prize at Samuel Golden Coll., U. Minn., Calif. State Library, Pa. State Library, Bezalel Nat. Mus., Archives Am. Art Smithsonian Instn. (art and poetry), Washington, Archives and State Mus. Albany, N.Y. (120 works), Newark Pub. Library, Addison Gallery Am. Art, Bat Yam Municipal Mus., Safed Mus., Israel, Pa. State Tchrs. Coll., Richmond Art Assn., Peoria (Ill.) Art Ctr., Boston Pub. Library, St. Margaret Mary Sch. Art, Musee Nat. d'Art Modern, Yad Vashem Meml. Archives, Jerusalem (poetry), 1987, N.Y. State Mus. and Archives, 1989; spl. collections paintings, drawings and prints acquired by 19 nat. and internat. mus./archives including U.S. Nat. Mus., Washington, 1965, Univ. Maine Art, 1965, Libr. Congress, Washington, 1965, 71, Met. Mus. N.Y., 1965, 80, Nat. Coll. Fine Arts, 1966, 71, 78, Nat. Gallery Art, 1966, Nat. Air & Space Mus., 1966, N.Y. Pub. Libr., 1971, 78, Nat. Mus. History/Tech., 1971, Mus. City N.Y., 1978, Jewish Mus. N.Y., 1979, N.Y. State Mus. Albany, N.Y., 1979-90, Israel Mus., 1980, Ft. Lewis Coll. Mus., 1980, Smithsonian, 1979, Yad Vashem Meml. Mus./Archives, 1987, Mus. Jewish Heritage, N.Y., 1989, Jewish Theological Seminary Am., 1989, Jewish Nat. & Univ. Libr., Israel, 1990. Represented as artist and poet: Miss. Art Assn. Internat. Water Color Club award 1947, 51, New Haven Paint and Clay Club, purchase award Peoria Art Ctr. 1950, Print Club Albany 1962, also Library of Congress, U. Minn., Calif. State Library, Met. Mus. Art, Pa. State Tchrs. Coll., Art Assn. Richmond, Ind., N.Y. Pub. Library, Newark Pub. Library, St. Margaret Mary Sch. Art Coll., landscape award Soc. Miniature Painters, Gravers and Sculpture, James Joyce award Poetry Soc. Am. 1975; presented spl. commemoration to Yad Vashem Meml. Hist. Site, Jerusalem, 1987; named Dau. of Mark Twain 1970; life fellow Met. Mus. Art; named to Exec. and Profl. Hall of Fame (plaque of honor 1966). Recipient World Order of Narrative Poets; named Membro Honoris Causa dell'Accademia di Scienze, Letteri, Arti Classe Accademica "Nobel", Milan, 1974, 75, Classe Storia Letter-Atura Americana, Milan, 1978, Exec. and Profl. Hall of Fame-Life, 1966; named A Daughter of Mark Twain, 1970; Met. Mus. fellow, 1966. Fellow Internat. Acad. Poets (founder 1977); mem. Soc. Am. Graphic Artists (group prize 1950), Print Club Albany (N.Y.), Boston Printmakers (award 1955), Washington Printmakers (exhbns.), Conn. Acad. Fine Arts, Am. Color Print Soc., Audubon Artists (group exhbns., award 1944), Phila. Water Color Club (group exhbns.), Nat. Assn. Women Artists (award 1945, 47), Print Council Am., Hunterdon Art Center, Internat. Platform Assn., Poetry Soc. Am., Artists Equity N.Y., Authors Guild, Inc., Accademia Di Scienze, Lettere, Arti-Milano, Italy (Consigliere, named hon. mem. as artist 1974, author/poet 1975, Nobel designate 1978); Academia Di Scienze. Lettere, Arti, Classe. Office: 915 W End Ave Apt 5D New York NY 10025

KATZ, JANE, educator; b. Sharon, Pa., Apr. 16, 1943; d. Leon and Dorothea (Oberkewitz) Katz; B.S. in Edn., CCNY, 1963; M.A., NYU, 1966; M.Ed., Columbia Tchrs. Coll., 1972, Ed.D., 1978. Mem. faculty Bronx Community Coll., CUNY, 1964—, prof. phys. edn., 1972—; mem. U.S. Round-the-World Synchronized Swim Team, 1964; synchronized swimming solo tour of Eng., 1969; founding co-organizer, coach 1st Internat. Israeli Youth Festival Games, 1970; mem. winning U.S. Maccabiah Swim Team, 1957; vice chmn. Metro Master AAU Swim Team, 1974—; mem. AAU Nat. Masters All-Am. Swimming Team, 1974—, synchronized swimming solo champion, 1975; speaker, judge in field. Trainee Fed. Adminstrn. Aging, 1971-72; mem. Internat. Hall. of Fame, Ft. Lauderdale, Fla. Named Healthy Am. Fitness Leader U.S. Jaycees and the Pres's. Coun. on Phys. Fitness, 1987, Outstanding Masters Synchroured Swimming, 1987; winner CCNY Towsend Harris Acad. medal, 1989. Mem. AAHPER, U.S. Com. Sports for Israel (dir., co-chmn. women's swimming com. 1970—), Nat. Jewish Welfare Bd., Internat. Aquatics. Author: Swimming for Total Fitness, A Progressive Aerobic Program, 1981; Swimming Through Your Pregnancy, 1983; W.E.T. Workouts: Water Exercises and Techniques to Help You and Tone Up Aerobically, 1985; Fitness Works: Blueprint for Lifelong Fitness, 1988; papers in field. Address: 400 2d Ave Apt 23B New York NY 10010

KATZ, KATHY SILVER, psychologist, educator; b. N.Y.C., May 9, 1947; d. Albert M. and Lola (Galvin) Silver; m. Richard J. Katz, June 21, 1970; children; Marisa S., Eliza J. BA, U. Pa., 1968; PhD, Rutgers U., 1974. Lic. Psychologist, Md., D.C. Psychology intern Judge Baker Guidance Ctr., Boston, 1972-73; postdoctoral fellow Children's Hosp. Med. Ctr., Boston, 1974-75; asst. prof. pediatrics Georgetown U. Med. Ctr., Washington, 1975-83, staff psychologist, 1975-83, assoc. prof. of pediatrics, 1983—; dir., infant follow-up Georgetown U. Child Devel. Ctr., Washington, 1978-88, dir. psychology, 1983—; adj. assoc. prof. psychology Cath. U., Washington, 1983—; cons. in field. Author: Chronically Ill and At Risk Infants, 1989; contbr. articles to profl. jours. panel mem. Dist. Govt. Task Force on Personnel Preparation for Pub. Law 99-457, Washington, 1989—. Grantee U.S. Dept. Edn., 1985-88, 86-89, 88-91, 89—, March of Dimes, 1988-89. Mem. Am. Psychol. Assn. (exec. bd. div. on children, youth and families 1988—), Soc. Pediatric Psychology, Am. Assn. Mental Retardation. Office: Georgetown U Med Ctr 3800 Reservoir Rd NW CG-52 Bles Bldg Washington DC 20007

KATZ, LYNN FRANCES, psychology educator, consultant; b. Pitts.; d. Cecil and Miriam (Friedman) Schwartz; m. David N. Katz, Jan. 27, 1959. BS, U. Pitts., 1959, MS, 1962, PhD, 1965. Lic. psychologist, Pa. Asst. prof. psychology dept. U. Pitts., 1965-68, asst. prof. ednl. psycholgy dept., 1968-72, assoc. prof. psychology in edn. dept., 1972—; cons. psychologist Allegheny County Juvenile Ct., Pitts., 1964—. Contbr. articles to profl. jours. Mem. Am. Psychol. Assn., Western Pa. Sch. Psychologists Assn., Assn. for Moral Edn.

KATZ, MARILYN FAYE, communications consultant; b. Chgo., Aug. 28, 1945; d. Phillip and Lucile (Berman) K.; m. Robert Scott Chambers, Nov. 15, 1985; children: Halley, Grady. Student, Northwestern U., 1964-68. Rsch. activist Join Community Union, Chgo., 1965-69; freelance writer L.A., 1969-71; researcher, writer Urban Policy Rsch. Inst., Beverly Hills, Calif., 1972-73; writer, producer, dir. Profl. Rsch., Inc., L.A., 1974-77; nat. sec. New Am. Movement, Chgo., 1977-79; writer, producer, dir. Goldsholl Films/Television Theatre, Chgo. and N.Y.C., 1979-83; media dir. Harold Washington for Mayor campaign, Chgo., 1982-83; pres. MK Communications, Chgo., 1983—; adviser to mayor of Chgo, 1983-87; polit. cons., 1990; cons. Nat. Equity Fund, Chgo., 1987—, Local Initiatives Support Corp., N.Y.C., 1986—, City Colls. of Chgo., 1987—. Author: The Glass House Tapes, 1973; writer, producer films. Founder Chgo. Women's Union, 1970, L.A. Women's Union, 1972; founder, pres. Reproductive Rights Nat. Network, 1978. Grantee Russell Sage Found., N.Y.C., 1972, Ping & Carol Feary orgn., N.Y.C., 1973. Fellow Leadership Greater Chgo.; mem. Cook County Dem. Women (founder, bd. dirs.), Lakewood Balmoral Resident's Coun. (bd. dirs.). Home: 5418 Magnolia St Chicago IL 60640 Office: MK Communications 359 W Chicago Ave Chicago IL 60610

KATZ, MARTHA LESSMAN, lawyer; b. Chgo., Oct. 28, 1952; d. Julius Abraham and Ida (Oiring) Lessman; m. Richard M. Katz, June 27, 1976; 1 child, Julia Erin. AB, Washington U., St. Louis, 1974; JD, Loyola U., Chgo., 1977. Bar: Ill. 1977, U.S. Dist. Ct. (no. dist.) Ill. 1977, Calif. 1981, U.S. Dist. Ct. (so. dist.) Calif. 1981, U.S. Dist. Ct. (no. dist.) Calif. 1982. Assoc. Fein & Hanfling, Chgo., 1977-80, Rudick, Platt & Victor, San Diego, 1981-82, 84—; asst. sec., counsel Itel Corp., San Francisco, 1982-84. Active Friends of Mayor's Adv. Bd. on Women. Mem ABA (corp. banking and bus. law, taxation sects.), Ill. Bar Assn., San Diego County Bar Assn., Lawyers Club San Diego (work options com.), Career Women's Network (steering, com. and co-chmn. 1990 conf.), Anti Defamation League (civil rights com.), Phi Beta Kappa. Jewish. Office: Rudick Platt & Victor 1770 4th Ave San Diego CA 92101

KATZ, MICHELE WYNNE, marketing professional; b. Buena Park, Calif., Dec. 21, 1962; d. Milton and Piri (Gross) K. BA, UCLA, 1984, MBA, 1989. Account coord. Needham Harper Worldwide/Rubin Postaer & Assocs., L.A., 1985-87; assoc. mktg. mgr. Taco Bell Corp., Irvine, Calif., 1989—. Mem. Ctr. 500, Orange County, 1990. Mem. Anderson Mgmt. Alumni Assn., Kappa Kappa Gamma. Democrat. Jewish. Office: Taco Bell Corp 17901 Von Karman Irvine CA 92714

KATZ, MIRIAM LESSER, psychotherapist, educator; b. Petah-Tikva, Israel, Aug. 29, 1942; came to U.S., 1965; d. Kurt and Ilse (Fliess) Lesser; m. Adrian Izhack Katz, Mar. 31, 1965; 1 child, Iris Ellen. Diploma in nursing, Beilinson U. Tel-Aviv, 1962; B Gen. Studies, Roosevelt U., Chgo., 1976; MA, U. Chgo., 1977. RN Ill.; lic. psychotherapist Am. bd. Med. Psychotherapist. Head nurse Beilinson Med. Ctr. Tel-Aviv U., Petah-Tikva, 1962-65; operating room nurse Yale U. Med. Ctr., New Haven, 1965-67; surg. nurse U. Chgo. Med. Ctr., 1968-75; rsch. asst. dept. child psychiatry U. Chgo., 1976-80, child and adolescent psychotherapist, 1980—, lectr. in psychiatry, 1988—; psychiat. cons. Head Start, Chgo., 1980-84. Contbr. articles to profl. jours. Mem. Am. Psychol. Assn., Am. Assn. Counseling Psychologists, World Fedn. Mental Health. Home: 1125 E 53d St Chicago IL 60615 Office: U Chgo Dept Psychiatry 5841 S Maryland St Chicago IL 60637

KATZ, NANCY SUE, lawyer; b. Indpls., July 26, 1954; d. Irwin and Ann (Baker) K. AB, Oberlin Coll., 1976; JD, U. Mich., 1980. Bar: Mich. 1980, U.S. Dist. Ct. (ea. dist.) Mich. 1980, U.S. Dist. Ct. (we. dist.) Mich. 1981, U.S. Ct. Appeals (6th cir.) 1981. Staff atty. U.S. Dist. Ct. (ea. dist.) Mich., Detroit, 1980-81; assoc. Pepper, Hamilton & Scheetz, Detroit, 1981-88; assoc. gen. counsel ANR Pipeline Co., Detroit, 1988—. Mem. ABA, State Bar Mich., Detroit Bar Assn., Fed. Bar Assn. Home: 523 McKinley St Plymouth MI 48170 Office: 500 Renaissance Ctr Detroit MI 48243

KATZ, PHYLLIS ALBERTS, developmental research psychologist; married; 2 children. AB in Psychology summa cum laude, Syracuse U., 1957; PhD in Devel. Clin. Psychology, Yale U., 1961. Assoc. prof. psychology CUNY, 1969-72, chairperson devel. psychology sect. PhD program in edn., 1969-75, acting exec. officer PhD program in edn., 1974-75, prof., 1973-76; dir. Inst. Rsch. on Social Problems, Boulder, 1975—; adj. prof. U. Colo., Boulder, 1980—. Editor: Sex Roles: A Jour. of Research, 1976—, Towards the Elimination of Racism, 1976; co-editor: Eliminating Racism: Profiles in Controversy, 1988; contbr. book chpts. on racism, gender-role rsch. and only-child rsch.; mem. editorial bd. Archives of Sexual Behavior, 1975—; contbr. numerous articles to profl. jours. Trustee Colo. Music Festival, 1982-84, pres. bd. trustees, 1984-85; mem. City of Boulder planning com. Cultural Arts Ctr.; bd. dirs. Women's Found. Colo., 1986—. USPHS trainee Yale U., 1956-59; grantee NYU Arts and Sci. Research, 1963-66, CUNY Faculty Research, 1973, Nat. Inst. Child Health Human Devel., 1966-68, 68-72, 79-81, 81-83, 87-91, Office of Child Devel., 1972-75, Nat. Inst. Mental Health, 1977-79, 84-86, NSF, 1984-86. Mem. Am. Psychol. Assn. (jour. editor 1974-77, chairperson child advocacy com. 1973, exec. com. 1980—, head affirmative action com. 1981—, council rep. 1983-86, div. pres. 1986-87, fellow divs. 7, 9, 35 and 45), Women's Found. of Colo., Southeastern Psychol. Assn., Soc. Research in Child Devel., Assn. Women in Sci., Sigma Xi. Home: 1035 Pearl St 5th Fl Boulder CO 80302

KATZ, ROBIN NANCY, commercial real estate management executive; b. Bklyn., Aug. 15, 1963; d. Joel Katz and Gail Florence (Wander) Holzman. BA, UCLA, 1984; MBA, Calif. State U., Northridge, 1989. Cert. prin. broker dealer. Bookkeeper CPR Investment Corp., L.A., 1983-84; asst. property mgr. Realty Ctr. Mgmt., L.A., 1984-86; property mgr. CPR Properties, L.A., 1987; property mgr., ptnr. Graymont Group, L.A., 1988-89; pres. Graymont Mgmt. Co., L.A., 1989—; pres. Graymont Securities, Inc., L.A., 1987-89. Mem. Internat. Coun. Shopping Ctrs., Women in Retail Real Estate, Nat. Assn. Security Dealers. Office: Graymont Mgmt Co Inc 233 Wilshire Blvd Ste 295 Santa Monica CA 90401

KATZ, SUSAN AUDREY, producer, director, writer; b. Bklyn., May 14, 1956; d. Nathan and Pearl (Kron) K.; m. Stephen Anthony Sheehan, Aug. 31, 1986. BA in TV-Radio with honors, Bklyn. Coll., 1978; cert. in film, NYU, 1987. Assoc. producer BC Presents Sta. WNYC-TV, N.Y.C., 1977-78; traffic producer Sta. WNEW-TV, N.Y.C., 1978-79, syndicated tape mgr., 1979-80; promotion mgr. Sta. WWYZ-FM, Waterbury, Conn., 1980-82; dir. promotions Sta. WATR-TV, Waterbury, 1980-82; dir. creative services Sta. WTXX-TV, Waterbury, 1980-85; editor in chief Bandshell Publs., Bklyn., 1985—; co-owner Katz Sheehan Media, Bklyn. and Bridgeport, Conn., 1985—. Newsletter editor N.Y. State Senator Marty Markowitz, 1978—; dir. advt. Bucci for Bridgeport mayor, 1985, Moran for Bridgeport mayor, 1989; exec. producer Taste of Bridgeport, 1988; active numerous corp., comml. and polit. prodns. Recipient Telly award, 1985, Echo award Direct Mktg. Assn., 1986. Democrat. Jewish. Office: Katz Sheehan Media 140 Summit St Bridgeport CT 06606 also: Katz Sheehan Media 243 McDonald Ave Brooklyn NY 11218

KATZEL, JEANINE ALMA, journalist; b. Chgo., Feb. 20, 1948, d. LeRoy Paul and Lia Mary (Arcuri) Katzel; B.A. in Journalism, U. Wis., 1970; M.S. in Journalism, Northwestern U., 1974. Publs. editor U. Wis. Sea Grant Program, Madison, 1969-72; editor research div. agrl. sch. U. Wis., Madison, 1972; research editor Prism mag. AMA, Chgo., 1972-73; free lance writer, 1974-75; lit. editor Plant Engring. mag. Tech. Pub. Co., Barrington, Ill., 1975-76, news editor, 1976-77, asso. editor, 1977-79, sr. editor, 1979—; sr. editor Plant Engring mag Cahners Pub., Des Plaines, Ill., 1987—. Judge assoc. ann. competition Engring. Coll. Mag., 1978-83, 85—. Recipient Elsie Bullard Morrison prize in Journalism, U. Wis., 1969; Peter Lisagor award in bus. journalism, 1983. Mem. Women in Communications, Am. Soc. Bus. Press Editors (pres. Chgo. chpt. 1977-78), Soc. Profl. Journalists, Soc. Fire Protection Engrs., Am. Inst. Plant Engrs., Am. Inst. Chem. Engrs., Am. Chem. Soc., Nat. Audubon Soc., Nat. Fire Protection Assn. (tech. com. on fire pumps), Am. Soc. Safety Engrs., Internat. Soc. Fire Service Instrs., No. Ill. Computer Soc., Phi Kappa Phi. Home: 708 Cimarron Dr Cary IL 60013 Office: 1350 E Touhy Ave PO Box 5080 Des Plaines IL 60018

KATZEN, SALLY, lawyer; b. Pitts., Nov. 22, 1942; d. Nathan and Hilda (Schwartz) K.; m. Timothy B. Dyk, Oct. 31, 1981; 1 child, Abraham Benjamin. BA magna cum laude, Smith Coll., 1964; JD magna cum laude, U. Mich., 1967. Bar: D.C. 1968, U.S. Supreme Ct. 1971. Congl. intern Sente Subcom. on Constl. Rights, Washington, 1963; legal rsch. asst. civil rights div. Dept. Justice, Washington, 1965; law clk. to Judge J. Skelly Wright U.S. Ct. Appeals (D.C. cir.), 1967-68; assoc. Wilmer, Cutler & Pickering, Washington, 1968-74, ptnr., 1975-79, 81—; gen. counsel Coun. on Wage and Price Stability, 1979-80, dep. dir., 1980-81; pub. mem. Adminstrv. Conf. U.S., 1988—; mem. exec. com. Prettyman-Leventhal Inn of Court, 1988-90, counselor, 1990—; mem. Jud. Conf. for D.C. Cir., 1972-81, 83-90. Editor-in-chief U. Mich. Law Rev., 1966-67. Mem. com. visitors U. Mich. Law Sch., 1972-90. Fellow ABA (ho. of dels. 1978-80, 89—, coun. adminstrv. law sect. 1979-82; chmn. adminstrv. law and regulatory practice sect. 1988-89, governing com. forum com. communications law 1979-82, chmn. standing com. Nat. Conf. Groups 1989—), D.C. Cir. Com. on Bicentenial; mem. D.C. Bar Assn., Women's Bar Assn., FCC Bar Assn. (exec. com. 1984-87, pres. 1990—), Women's Legal Def. Fund (pres. 1977, v.p. 1978), Order of Coif. Home: 4638 30th St NW Washington DC 20008 Office: Wilmer Cutler & Pickering 2445 M St NW Washington DC 20037-1420

KATZENSTEIN, THEA, retailer; b. N.Y.C., Mar. 30, 1927; d. Carl E. and Lillian (Rosenblatt) Schustak; m. William Katzenstein, Sept. 10, 1950; children: Leo, Ranee. Student, Sarah Lawrence Coll., 1948-50; BS, Columbia U., 1962, MA, 1967. Pres. Gallery A., N.Y.C., 1967-71, Melita, N.Y.C., 1972-77, TK Studio, Coral Gables, Fla., 1977—; adj. prof. of jewelry Fla. Internat. U., 1989-90. Author: Early Chinese Art and The Pacific Basin, 1967; painting, graphics and jewelry represented in numerous pvt. collections. Mem. Soc. North Am. Goldsmiths, Enamel Guild South, Nat. Enamelist Guild, Fla. Soc. Goldsmiths, Fla. Craftsmen, Zonta (sec. Coral Gables chpt. 1989—). Democrat. Jewish. Home: 625 Biltmore Way Coral Gables FL 33134

KATZFEY, PATRICIA ANN, marketing professional; b. Springfield, Mo., Nov. 23, 1956; d. Harry Lee and Virginia Lucille (Nelson) Self; m. Michael Anthony Katzfey, Sept. 5, 1981. BS in Mktg., S.W. Mo. State U., 1978, BS in Data Processing, 1980; postgrad., Lake Forest (Ill.) Grad. Sch., 1988—. Cost acct. Lily Tulip, Inc., Springfield, Mo., 1980-82; mktg. mgr. Sajac Co., Beaver Dam, Wis., 1983-84; support cons. Bank of Ill., Champaign, 1984-85; mktg. analyst Air Products & Chems., Allentown, Pa., 1985-86; distbn. mktg. mgr. Oneac Corp., Libertyville, Ill., 1987-88; product mgr. Videojet Systems, Internat., Elk Grove, Ill., 1988—. Mem. Am. Mktg. Assn. Office: Videojet Systems Internat 2200 Arthur Ave Elk Grove IL 60007

KATZIR, PAMELA, educator; b. N.Y.C., Mar. 13, 1938; d. Isador H. and Anne E. Goldberg; 1 child, Dan. BA cum laude, Adelphi U., 1959; MS in Edn., CCNY, 1965; postgrad., Hebrew U., U. Miami, Fla. Cert. lang. arts and social studies tchr., Fla. Tchr. Dade County Pub. Schs., Miami; instr. Miami-Dade Community Coll.; tchr. Ministry of Edn., Jerusalem, East Meadow (N.Y.) Pub. Schs. Numerous leadership offices in community. Mem. Law Related Edn. Assn., Nat. Coun. for the Social Studies (com. on religion), Nat. Coun. Tchrs. of English (com. on alternative edn.), Coun. for Exceptional Edn., Internat. Reading Assn., Fla. Reading Assn., Phi Delta Kappa Found. Home: 16950 W Dixie Hwy Miami FL 33160

KATZMAN, ANITA, author; b. N.Y.C., Feb. 6, 1920; d. Louis and Sylvia (Fox) Butensky; m. Nathan Katzman, Mar. 29, 1942 (dec. 1965); children: Mark, Drew, Bruce, Mindi. BA, N.Y. U., 1940. Author: My Name is Mary 1975. Founders Bd. Asolo Performing Arts Ctr., Sarasota Fla.; Bd. Dirs. Asolo Theater Festival Assn.; Devel. Bd. USF Gerontology Ctr., Tampa Fla., Sarasota-Manatee Jewish Found., Sarota Fla., Fla. Council Libraries. Recipient GTE Community Adv. Panel 1973, Community Acheivement award Women's Resource Ctr. Sarasota 1988, West Coast Woman Newspaper Sarasota 1989. Mem. The Author's Guild, The Author's League Am., Pan Pacific & Southeast Women's Assn., Lotus Club. Democratic. Office: PO Box 56 Sarasota FL 34230-0056

KATZMAN, DONNA JEANNE, marketing executive; b. Ft. Worth, Apr. 8, 1945; d. John Carter Wilson and Milded Lucille (Beaver) Lindhout; m. Kenneth Douglas Katzman, Nov.9, 1965 (div. June 1983); children: Brett Eric, Jeffrey Pratt, Scott Bradley, Rebecca Kathleen. Student, Rice U., 1967. Profit improvement officer Monumental Life Ins. Co., Balt., 1977-80; sales rep. Contel Advt., Kansas City, Mo., 1981-85; mktg. mgr. Armour Cape & Pond, Inc., Atlanta, 1985-88; mktg. dir. Jones, Nall & Davis, Inc., Atlanta, 1989—. Bd. dirs. Women Together, Balt., 1975-78. Named Outstanding Sales Rep. Am. Advt. Dist., Atlanta, 1985, fellow with distinction Life Office Mgmt. Assn., 1980. Mem. LWV (com. chmn. 1972-80), Soc. Mktg. Profl. Svcs., Nat. Assn. Female Execs., Ga. Indsl. Developers Assn., Ga. Assn. Phys. Plant Adminstrn., Dunwoody North Driving Club (coach 1986). Republican. Episcopalian. Office: Jones Nall & Davis Inc 57 Forsyth St Ste 800 Atlanta GA 30303

KATZMAN, PATRICIA DIANE, mechanical engineer; b. Detroit, Sept. 28, 1964; d. Sidney Herbert and Mary Floy (Schulz) K. BSME, Bradley U., 1987. Staff mech. engr. Argonne (Ill.) Nat. Lab., 1983-84, Sundstrand Corp., Rockford, Ill., 1985-86, GE, Lynn, Mass., 1988—. Mem. ASME, Tau Beta Pi. Home: 66 Lee St Apt 1 Marblehead MA 01945 Office: GE 1000 Western Ave Lynn MA 01910

KATZOWITZ, LAUREN, public affairs consultant. BS in Comparative Lit. with honors, Brandeis U., 1970; MS with honors, Columbia U., 1971. With, Newsweek mag., then Phila. Bull.; free-lance writer, editor, cons., until 1975; cons. Ford Found., 1972-75; mgr. PBS programs Exxon Corp., 1978-81, Great Performances, Live From Lincoln Ctr., Dance in America, NOVA, The MacNeil/Lehrer Report; communications mgr. Exxon Rsch. and Engring. Co., 1981-84; regional liaison Europe and Africa, Exxon Corp., 1984-86; exec. dir. Found. Svc., UJA/Fedn. of Jewish Philanthropies, 1986—; pres. LK Consulting, 1986—. Pres. Bronx Ednl. Svcs.; trustee Women's Action Alliance, Am. Friends of Inst. Internat. d'Etudes Musicales, St. Maximin, France, B'nai B'rith Hillel/Jewish Assn. for College Youth. Named one of 12 Women to Watch in the Eighties, Ladies' Home Jour., 1979. Regional Finalist Pres.'s Commn. on White House fellow, 1984. Office: LK Consulting 505 E 79th St New York NY 10021

KAUFFMAN, LAURA TAVEL, advertising professional; b. Boston, Sept. 19, 1956; d. Kenneth Mark and Pepita Lorraine (Urbina) K.; m. John Timothy Henson. BA cum laude, Windham Coll., 1977; MA, George Mason U., 1988; postgrad., U. Mass., 1977. Coord. consumer communications Am. Gas Assn., Arlington, Va., 1979-86, mgr. advt. svcs., 1986-90; mgr. advt. Am. Gas Assn., Arlington, 1990—. Contbr. articles to profl. jours. Mem. Utility Communicators Internat., Bus./Profl. Advertisers Assn., Advt. Club of Washington, Inc. Office: Am Gas Assn 1515 Wilson Blvd Arlington VA 22209

KAUFFMAN, M. JANE, guidance counselor; b. Batavia, N.Y., Sept. 2, 1935; d. Edward Joseph and Loretta Viola (Garraghan) K. BS, SUNY, Buffalo, 1957; MS, Canisius Coll., 1964. English tchr. Kenmore (N.Y.) Sch. System, 1957-62; guidance counselor Williamsville (N.Y.) Sch. Dist., 1962—; polit. action com. N.Y. State United Tchrs., 1983—, state chmn., 1985, western N.Y. polit. action coordinator, state dir. E.D. #2, 1989—. Labor studies adv. bd. Erie Community Coll., Buffalo, 1986—; govt. relations com. Erie County United Way, 1987—; mem. Erie County Dem. Com., Buffalo, 1986—, nominating com. Amherst (N.Y.) Dem. Com., 1987—. Mem. Am. Fedn. Tchrs., Williamsville Tchrs. Assn. (exec. bd.), Buffalo AFL-CIO Council (polit. del. 1983—), N.Y. State United Tchrs. (Western N.Y. Leadership award 1989, dir. election dist. #2), Western N.Y. Consortium Guidance Counselors, Phi Delta Kappa. Roman Catholic. Office: NY State United Tchrs 5350 Main St Williamsville NY 14221

KAUFFMAN, MARGARET ANNE, public relations executive; b. St. Louis, Sept. 9, 1945; d. Tom Harry and Margaret Ruth (Siebert) Goddard; m. William Francis Kauffman, June 29, 1968; children: Kathryn Ruth, Juliet Lynn. BJ, U. Mo., 1968, postgrad., 1983-84, 89; postgrad. Jefferson Coll., 1984-85, 88. Writer Am. Nat. Stores, St. Louis, 1968-69, J.C. Penny Co., St. Louis, 1969; dir. pub. info. St. Louis Dept. Health and Hosps., 1969-71, Jefferson Coll., Hillsboro, Mo., 1979—. Editor, Jefferson Coll. News, 1979—. Founding mem., sec.-treas. Friends Jefferson Coll., 1980-87; opinion leader contact program com. Missourians for Higher Edn.; mem. am. coun. on edn. nat. identification program Women in Higher Edn. Adminstrn.; mem. adminstrv. bd., Union United Methodist Ch., St. Louis, 1976—; chmn. blood dr. ARC, St. Louis, 1976-77. Recipient MacEachern award Am. Hosp. Assn., 1970. Mem. Mo. Assn. Community Jr. Colls., United Methodist Women, Phi Delta Kappa. Home: 6601 Bancroft Saint Louis MO 63109 Office: Jefferson Coll PO Box 1000 Hillsboro MO 63050

KAUFFMAN, PEG, advertising executive, marketing consultant; b. Erie, Pa., Apr. 19, 1944; d. Eric Alfred and Agnes Mary (Logue) Jonsson; m. Walter L. Kauffman, July 15, 1966; children: Walter L., Eric Barton, Leslie Ann, Andrew John. Student parochial schs., Erie. Advt. account rep. The Greensheet, Erie, 1983-85, Lake Shore Visitor, Erie, 1985-86; cons. Geary & Hill Mktg., Erie, 1986-88; pres. Kauffman Assocs. Mktg. and Advt., Erie, 1988—. Editor Erie Philharm. Newsletter, 1977-78. Bd. dirs. YWCA, Erie, 1979-80; corr. sec. Hamot Aid Soc., Erie, 1980-81; v.p. Erie Philharm. Women's Assn., 1980-81; active Erie Civic Ballet, Erie Art Mus. Mem. Am. Bus. Women's Assn. (pres., 1989 Woman of Yr.), NAFE, Nat. Assn. Women Bus. Owners (mem.-at-large). Democrat. Roman Catholic. Clubs: Woman's of Erie, Erie Advt. Avocations: needlepoint, hot air ballooning, walking. Home: 1135 W 10th St Erie PA 16502

KAUFFMAN, SANDRA D., state legislator; b. Osceola, Nebr., Jan. 26, 1933; d. James Richard and Erma Grace (Heald) Daley; m. Larry Allen Kauffman, Sept. 4, 1955; children: Claudia Kauffman Boosman, Matthew Allen. BA, U. Nebr., 1954; postgrad., U. Kansas City, summer 1957. Tchr. Falls City (Nebr.) High Sch., 1954-55, Westport High Sch., Kansas City, Mo., 1955-59; sales rep. Manson Industries, Topeka, Kans., 1974-75; dir. pub. affairs Bishop Hogan High Sch., Kansas City, 1985-86; mem. Mo. Ho. of Reps., Jefferson City, 1987—. Mem. Kansas City Citizens Assn., 1981—, 1983—, Kansas City Consensus, 1985—, Kansas City Selective Svc. Bd., 1982—; mem. women's coun. U. Mo., Kansas City, 1986; mem. adv. coun. St. Joseph Health Ctr., Kansas City, 1988. Recipient Friend of Edn. award Ctr. Edn. Assn., 1986; named Mem. of Yr., Mo. Congress Parents and Tchrs., 1979. Mem. Nat. Order Women Legislators, Am. Legis. Exch. Coun., Nat. Coun. State Legislatures, Nat. Congress Parents and Tchrs. (hon., life), South Kansas City C. of C., Grandview C. of C., Mo. Women's Coun. on Econ. Devel. and Tng. Republican. Methodist. Home: 620 E 90th Terr Kansas City MO 64131 Office: Mo Ho of Reps House Post Office Jefferson City MO 65101

KAUFMAN, ANN, architect, educator; b. St. Louis, Sept. 7, 1954; d. Rudolf Ernst-Felix and Edith Mary (Greiderer) K. B.A., Wesleyan U., 1976; M. Arch., Columbia U., 1981. Designer, James, Stewart Polshek & Ptnrs., Architects, N.Y.C., 1981-82; exec. dir. Am. Architecture: Innovation and Tradition, Columbia U., N.Y.C., 1982-83; designer, architect Arata Isozaki and Assocs., Tokyo, 1983-85, Bond, Ryder, James Architects, N.Y.C., 1985-87, Robert E. Meadows Architect, N.Y.C., 1987—; curator of exhibitions Columbia U., 1982—, adj. asst. prof. architecture, 1984—; lectr. architecture Princeton U., 1989—. Editorial cons. The Japan Architect, Tokyo, 1983-84. Contbr. articles to profl. jours. William Kinne scholar Columbia U., 1980; Henry Luce Found. scholar, 1983. Mem. Architects for Social Responsibility, Japan Soc. Democrat. Office: Robert E Meadows Architect 40 Dover St New York NY 10038

KAUFMAN, CHARLOTTE KING, artist, educational administrator; b. Balt., Dec. 5, 1920; d. Ben and Belle (Turow) King; A.B., Goucher Coll., 1969; M.P.H., Johns Hopkins U., 1972, M.Ed., 1976; m. Albert Kaufman, July 22, 1945; children—Matthew King, Ezra King. Dir. public relations Balt. Jewish Community Center, 1962-67; research and editor Johns Hopkins U. Sch. Hygiene and Public Health, Balt., 1969-72, admissions officer, 1972-74, dir. admissions and registrar, 1974-86, dir. study cons. program undergraduates, 1986-89, pub. health adviser, 1989—. Mem. Am. Pub. Health Assn., Am. Assn. for Higher Edn., Am. Assn. Collegiate Registrars and Admissions Officers, Artists Equity Assn. (v.p. Md. chpt. 1988—), Delta Omega. Democrat. Jewish. Home: 1 E University Pkwy #1501 Baltimore MD 21218 Office: Mergenthaler Hall JH Homewood Campus Charles and 33d Sts Baltimore MD 21218 Studio: 3000 Chestnut Ave Mill Centre 223 Baltimore MD 21211

KAUFMAN, ELAINE SUE SOMMERS, educator; b. Bklyn., Dec. 25, 1933; d. Samuel and Lily Vivian (Schiller) Sommers; m. Harold Alexander Kaufman, June 24, 1956; children: Michele Beth, Roy Sommers. BA, Bklyn. Coll., 1955; MEd, U. Pitts., 1959. Cert. elem., spl. edn., reading tchr., reading specialist, N.Y., Pa., N.J. Elem. tchr. East Meadow (N.Y.) Pub. Schs., 1955-56, Pitts. Pub. Schs., 1956-61; elem. tchr. Piscataway (N.J.) Bd. Edn., 1961-63, supplemental tchr., 1972-80, learning strategist, 1980-82, tchr. handicapped, 1982—; cons. Piscataway Adult Edn. Adv. Coun., 1975-79. Counselor Piscataway Helpline, 1971-73; pres. Women's Am. ORT, Piscataway, 1970-73, North Cen. N.J. regional v.p., 1973-75; v.p. Pitt Dames, U. Pitts., 1957-58; trustee Anshe Emeth, 1977-78, v.p., pres. Couples Club, 1977-79; active Planned Parenthood. Frick Commn. scholar, 1958. Mem. NEA, N.J. Edn. Assn., Piscataway Tchrs. Assn., Middlesex Reading Coun. (membership chmn. 1987-88, parliamentarian 1988-89, Outstanding Contbr. award 1987), NOW, AAUW, Brandeis Women's Assn. (life Middlesex chpt.), Phi Kappa Delta. Home: 142 Fountain Ave Piscataway NJ 08854 Office: Schor Mid Sch N Randolphville Rd Piscataway NJ 08854

KAUFMAN, JANE, information company executive; b. Appleton, Minn., Nov. 11, 1947; d. William Carl and Patricia Anne (Hurley) K.; m. Andrew Joseph Pennella, May 12, 1979. BA, Bennington Coll., 1969; MSOR, NYU, 1973, MA, 1975, PhD, 1978. Mem. tech. staff Bell Labs., Holmdel, NJ, 1969-73; rsch. assoc. Warner Lambert Co., Milford, Conn., 1977-78; mgr. mktg. svcs. GE, Bridgeport, Conn., 1978-84; mgr. bus. devel. GE, Fairfield, Conn., 1984-85; v.p. market strategy U.S. West, Denver, 1985-88; v.p. mktg. McGraw-Hill, N.Y.C., 1988-90; pres. venture co., corp. dir. bus. devel. NYNEX, White Plains, N.Y., 1990—. Home: 180 Blackwood Ln Stamford CT 06903 Office: NYNEX 1113 Westchester Ave White Plains NY 10604

KAUFMAN, JANICE HORNER, foreign language educator; b. Mattoon, Ill., Apr. 30, 1949; d. Daniel Ogden and Julia Betty (McDermid) Horner; m. Richard Boucher Kaufman, June 24, 1972; children: Julia Ogden, Richard Pearse. AB, Duke U., 1971; MA in Liberal Studies, Hollins Coll., 1979; postgrad., NYU, 1986. Tchr. Roanoke (Va.) City Pub. Schs., 1971-72, North Cross Sch., Roanoke, Va., 1974-82; instr. in French Va. Poly. Inst. and State U., Blacksburg, 1984-86, 88, 90—, asst. dir fgn. lang. camps, 1984-85, administrv. dir., 1986; French, English interpretor translator Coll. Architecture and Urban Studies, Blacksburg, 1988; instr. in French Hollins Coll., Roanoke, 1989-90, Radford (Va.) U., 1989, 90—; student counselor Am. Inst. Fgn. Study, Greenwich, Conn., 1977; session leader Russell County Pub. Schs., Lebanon, Va., 1985, Va. Assn. Ind. Schs., Richmond, 1986. Sustaining mem. Jr. League of Roanoke Valley, Inc., 1989—; treas. Women of Christ Ch., 1984-86, Sunday sch. tchr. Christ Episcopal Ch., Blacksburg, Va., 1987-89. Mem. Am. Assn. of Tchrs. of French, Am. Coun. on the Teaching of Fgn. Lang., N.E. MLA. Home: 1406 Highland Circle Blacksburg VA 24060

KAUFMAN, JUDITH LASKER, health association administrator; b. N.Y.C., May 27, 1942; d. Lewis and Miriam (Greenspan) Lasker; m. Jerome B. Kaufman, June 29, 1967; children: Jonathan Lasker, Jeffrey Paul. BA, Alfred U., 1963, MS, 1965. Dir. N.Y.C. campaign Planned Parenthood, 1965-66; mktg. rep. IBM Corp., N.Y.C., 1966-70; chief exec. officer Champaign-Urbana (Ill.) Conv. and Vis. Bur., 1984-86; dir. pub. relations Penta, Champaign, 1986; dir. Leukemia Soc. Am. Inc., Urbana, 1986—. Pres. Champaign Children's Home and Aid Soc. Ill., 1972—; past v.p. Jr. League Champaign-Urbana; founder, mem. regional adv. com. Dept. Family and Children's Services, Champaign, 1978—; chair Urbana Juvenile Justice Rev. Com., 1983—. Mem. Exec. Club Champaign-Urbana, Twin Cities Bus. and Profl. Women's Club, Women's Bus. Council, Champaign-Urbana C. of C., Rotary. Jewish. Home: 2104 Zuppke Dr Urbana IL 61801 Office: Leukemia Soc Am Inc 123 W Main St #220 Urbana IL 61801

KAUFMAN, PHYLLIS CYNTHIA, lawyer, author, theatrical producer; b. Phila., Nov. 4, 1945; d. Harry and Gertrude (Friend) K. BA cum laude, Brandeis U., 1967; JD, Temple U., 1974. Bar: Pa. 1974, U.S. Dist. Ct. (ea. dist.) Pa. 1974. Pvt. practice entertainment law, Phila., 1977—; exec. producer Playhouse in the Park, Phila., 1979; dir. entertainment Caesar's Hotel-Casino, Atlantic City, N.J., 1980-81; v.p. entertainment Sands Hotel-Casino, Atlantic City, 1981-83; v.p. Kanadus Entertainment Inc., Toronto, 1982—; v.p., chief fin. officer Bright Techs., Inc., N.Y.C. and Phila., 1989—. Co-author: No-Nonsense Financial, Real Estate, Career and Legal Guides, 1985—; assoc. editor Temple Law Quarterly. Bd. dirs. Phila. Coll. Performing Arts, 1977-85, Creative Artists Network, 1986-88, Phila chpt. ALS Assn., 1986—, Phila. Civic Ballet, 1989—; bd. advocates Fox Chase Cancer Ctr., 1989—. Ford Found. grantee, 1965-67. Mem. Phila. Bar Assn. Democrat. Office: Bright Techs 1500 Locust St #3805 Philadelphia PA 19102

KAUFMAN, SHELLEY S., psychologist; b. Syracuse, N.Y., July 16, 1953; d. Elliott Alexander and Arlene Phyllis (Wolfe) K.; m. Timothy James Burke, Nov. 27, 1977; children: Marin, David. BA, Ariz. State U., 1975, MA, 1977, M Counseling, 1978, PhD, 1984. Lic. psychologist, Ariz. Tchr. Aliet Ind. Sch. Dist., Houston, 1975-76; elem. sch. counselor Chandler Unified Sch. Dist., Chandler, Ariz., 1978-80,1985-86; from child therapist to psychologist Jane Wayland Ctr., Phoenix, 1086-88; psychologist Inst. Neurodevelopmental Tng., Phoenix, 1988; outpatient clin. dir. Wayland Family Ctrs., Phoenix, 1988—; cons. NOVA, Phoenix, 1989—, Terros, Phoenix, 1989—; faculty assoc. Ariz. State U., Tempe, 1987-89; assoc. med. staff St. Luke Hosp., Phoenix, 1989—, Charter Hosp. East Valley, Chandler, Ariz., 1989—. Mem. Am. Psychol. Assn., N.Y. Acad. Scis., Phi Delta Kappa. Democrat. Jewish. Home: 1966 E Kentucky Ln Tempe AZ 85284

KAUFMAN, SUSAN JANE, banker; b. Denver, Nov. 13, 1942; d. William Douglas and Catherine Sue (Orrison) Morrison; m. Jerry Allen Kaufman, Mar. 10, 1962; children: Eric Douglas, Carrie Annette. BA, U. Colo., 1968; MA, U. Denver, 1972; MBA, John F. Kennedy U., Orinda, Calif., 1981. Cert. fin. planner. Br. mgr., asst. v.p. Citicorp Savs., Orinda, 1981-87, area staff officer, L.A., 1987—; mgr. Wells Fargo Bank, L.A., 1987-89, asst. v.p. br. mgr., Arcadia, Calif., 1989—. Mem. Internat. Coun. Fin. Planners, Inst. Cert. Fin. Planners, Jr. League, Arcadia C. of C., Rotary Internat., Delta Gamma. Republican. Home: 1528 Sheridan Rd Glendale CA 91206 Office: 747 W Duarte Rd Arcadia CA 91007

KAUFMAN-LEVY, BARBARA, psychologist; b. Bklyn., Apr. 8, 1954; d. Martin Charles and Toby (Shapiro) Kaufman; m. David Theodore Levy, Sept. 7, 1987; 1 child, Jeffrey Kaufman-Levy. BA magna cum laude, Queens (N.Y.) Coll., 1975; MA, U. Buffalo, 1977; EdD, U. Rutgers, 1985. Lic. psycholgist, Md., Washington, D.C. Couselor, psychologist, adj. instr. dept. psychology Seton Hall U., South Orange, N.J., 1977-82; psychologist Wayne (N.J.) Counseling Ctr., 1982-85, Rutgers Community Health Ctr., New Brunswick, N.J., 1985-87; counselor, psychologist Cath. U., Washington, 1988; pvt. practice Silver Spring, Md., 1988—. Mem. Am. Psychol. Assn., Md. Psychol. Assn., Phi Beta Kappa. Home and Office: 414 Ellsworth Dr Sliver Spring MD 20910

KAUFMANN, SYLVIA NADEAU, office equipment sales company executive; b. Eagle Lake, Maine, Dec. 1, 1940; d. Edwin Joseph Nadeau and Emily (Beaulieu) Gadbois; m. Max Daniel Kaufmann, Sept. 21, 1958 (div. 1985); children: Mark A., Laura A., Max D. Jr. Grad. high sch., East Hartford, Conn., 1958. Bookkeeper United Bank and Trust, Hartford, Conn., 1959-66; real estate agt. Barcombe Agy., South Windsor, Conn., 1967-74; sales rep. Duplicating Methods Co., East Windsor, Conn., 1974-80; gen. mgr., officer Duplicating Methods Co., East Windsor, 1980—. Commr. ethics commn. Town of Enfield, Conn. Mem. Nat. Office Machine Dealers Assn., North Cen. Conn. C. of C., Bus. Profl. Women Greater Hartford, Exec. Females Inc. Democrat. Roman Catholic. Home: 6 Hoover Ln Enfield CT 06082 Office: Duplicating Methods Co 170 North Rd East Windsor CT 06088

KAUGER, YVONNE, state supreme court justice; b. Cordell, Okla., Aug. 3, 1937; d. John and Alice (Bottom) K.; m. Ned Bastow, May 8, 1982; 1 child, Jonna Sinclair. BS magna cum laude, Southwestern State U., Weatherford, Okla., 1958; cert. med. technologist, St. Anthony's Hosp., 1959; J.D., Oklahoma City U., 1969. Med. technologist Med. Arts Lab., 1959-68; assoc. Rogers, Travis & Jordan, 1970-72; jud. asst. Okla. Supreme Ct., Oklahoma City, 1972-84, justice, 1984—; mem. appellate div. Ct. on Judiciary; mem. State Capitol Preservation Commn., 1983-84; mem. dean's adv. com. Oklahoma City U. Sch. Law. Founder Gallery of Plains Indian, Colony, Okla., Red Earth, 1987; active Jud. Day, Girl's State, 1976-80; keynote speaker Girl's State Hall of Fame Banquet, 1984; bd. dirs. Lyric Theatre, Inc., 1966—, pres. bd. dirs., 1981; past mem. bd. dirs. Civic Music Soc., Okla. Theatre Ctr., Canterbury Choral Soc.; mem. First Lady of Okla.'s Artisans' Alliance Com. Named one of Outstanding Young Women Am., U.S. Jaycees, 1967, Byliner Honoree, Women in Communications, 1984, Woman of Yr., Oklahoma City chpt. Bus. and Profl. Women's Club, 1984, Woman of Yr., High Noon, 1985, Judge of Yr., Okla. Trial Lawyer's Appellate, 1987; adopted by Cheyenne-Arapaho tribes, 1984; honored by Okla. Hospitality Club, Ladies in the News, 1985; recipient Disting. Alumni award Southwestern Okla. State U., 1986, Oklahoma City U., 1986, Pioneer award Downtown Now, 1989; named Outstanding Appellate Judge Okla. Trial Lawyers Assn., 1987. Mem. ABA (law sch. accreditation com.), Okla. Bar Assn. (law schs. com. 1977—), Washita County Bar Assn., Washita County Hist. Soc. (life), St. Paul's Music Soc., Iota Tau Tau, Delta Zeta (Disting. Alumna award 1988, State Delta Zeta of Yr. 1987, Nat. Woman of Yr. 1988). Episcopalian.

KAVADAS-PAPPAS, IPHIGENIA KATHERINE, teacher, consultant; b. Manchester, N.H., Oct. 24, 1958; d. Demetrios Stefanos and Rodothea (Palaiologou) K.; m. Constantine George Pappas, July 29, 1979; children: George Demetrios, Rodothea Constance. BA, U. Detroit, 1980; MAT summa cum laude, Oakland U., 1985. Cert. tchr., Mich. Pre-sch. tchr. Assumption Nursery Sch., St. Clair Shores, Mich., 1977-80, bd. dirs., interim dir., 1984; Sunday sch. tchr. Assumption Greek Orthodox Ch., St. Clair Shores, 1985—; chairperson persch. curriculum com. Greek Orthodox Archdiocese Dept. Religious Edn., Brookline, Mass., 1987—; cons. Assumption Nursery Sch., 1985—. Co-author: Pre-school Curriculum Manual for

Greek Orthodox Archdiocese, 1990. Mem. Assumption Greek Orthodox Ch. Philoptochos Soc., 1978-87; trustee Assumption Nursery Sch., 1979—. Recipient Vol. Svc. award Angus Elem. Sch., 1989. Mem. Nat. Assn. for the Edn. Young Children. Office: Assumption Greek Orthodox 21800 Marter Rd Saint Clair Shores MI 48080

KAVALER, SUSAN ADLER, clinical psychologist; b. N.Y.C., Jan. 31, 1950; d. Solomon and Alice (Zelikow) Weiss; m. Thomas Kavaler, July 12, 1970 (div. 1975); m. Saul Michael Adler, Aug. 14, 1983. PhD in Clin. Psychology, Adelphi U., 1974. Psychologist Beth Israel Hosp., N.Y.C., 1974-76, Manhattan Psychiat. Children's Ctr., N.Y.C., 1977-80; pvt. practice psychotherapy-psychoanalysis, N.Y.C., 1976—; sr. supr., tng. analyst Internat. Sch. Mental Health Practitioners; mem. faculty Postgrad. Ctr. Mental Health, N.Y.C., 1984-86; mem. faculty, supr. Nat. Inst. Pychotherapies, N.Y.C., 1985—; sr. supr., tng. analyst Internat. Sch. Mental Health Practitioners, 1985—; bd. dirs., supr. Bklyn. Inst. Psychotherapy, 1985—, mem. psychoanalytic inst. faculty; adj. prof. Union of Experimenting; tng. analyst Internat. Sch. Mental Health Practitioners. Contbr. chpts. to books, articles to profl. jours. Recipient Post-grad. Ctr. Hon. award, 1984, 85. Mem. NAFE, Am. Psychol. Assn. (bd. dirs., chairperson pub. info. com. for psychoanalysis div.), Nat. Inst. for Psychotherapies Profl. Assn. (chair writing group 1984-90, cert. psychoanalyst, psychotherapist), Postgraduate Psychoanalytic Soc. (speaker), Women's Psychotherapy Referral Svc. Jewish. Office: 115 E 9th St New York NY 10003

KAVIN, REBECCA JEAN, health science executive; b. Dodge, Nebr., June 29, 1946; d. William Wilber Walsh and Dorothy Eleanor (Watson) Williams; m. Paul Babcock, May 15, 1965 (div. Sept. 1976); m. E. Iraj Kavin, Apr. 23, 1977; children: Mark Bijan, Seana Shereen. Cert., Ohio U., 1963. Claims adjuster San Found. for Med. Care, San Diego, 1968-70; adminstrv. asst. Friendly Hills Med. Group, La Habra, Calif., 1971-77; office mgr. Robert M. Peck and Sergio Blesa, M.D., Pasadena, Calif., 1978-81; pres. Provider Mgmt. Assocs., La Canada, Calif., 1981—; speaker Continuing Edn. Dept. UCLA, 1985, Hosp. Coun. of So. Calif., L.A., 1986, Am. Acad. Med. Preventics, L.A., 1986. Contbr. articles to profl. jours. Mem. Am. Guild Patient Account Mgrs. (speaker L.A. chpt. 1986), U.S. C. of C. Republican. Presbyterian. Office: Provider Mgmt Assocs 2441 Honolulu Ave Montrose CA 91020

KAVOUNAS, ANITA MARIE, credit collections manager; b. Glendale, Calif., Dec. 13, 1956; d. Marton and Ruth (Raadlund) Ellefsen; m. Gregory Theodosios Kavounas, May 21, 1986; 1 child, Reed Dennis Copsey Jr. Student, Calif. State U., L.A.; cert., U. So. Calif., L.A., 1986. Regional contacts and collections mgr. Lerch, Bates and Assocs., Inc., La Crescenta, Calif.; dist. coord. Otis Elevator Co./United Techs., Glendale, Calif.; facilities mgr. Poly Imports, L.A.; mng. ptnr. World Wide Parrot Imports, Montebello, Calif.; guest lectr. in field. Mem. NOW, NAFE, Nat. Assn. Credit Mgrs., Nat. Assn. Women in Constrn. Republican. Lutheran. Office: Lerch Bates & Assocs 2953 Honolulu Ave La Crescenta CA 91214-3912

KAWA, MARCIA LYNNE, business owner, contractor; b. Trinidad, W.I., July 7, 1957; came to U.S., 1958; d. Willard George and Wanda Rose (Chamberlain) Bastron; m. Yokawa, Feb. 26, 1987; children: Randy, Tracy, Sherri, Michah. With Golden West Coll. Police Acad., Huntington Beach, Calif., 1975-76; office mgr. Allen Mobileasing, Garden Grove, Calif., 1977-78, Kawa Co., Anaheim, Calif., 1978-86; owner Marlee Constrn. Parts & Svcs., Ontario, Calif., 1985—; v.p. Kawaco, INc., Ontario, 1986—. Mem. Future Farmers of Am. Boosters (pres. Don Lugo chpt. 1990—). Office: Kawaco Inc 1355 S Parkside Ontario CA 91761

KAWAGUCHI, MEREDITH FERGUSON, lawyer; b. Dallas, Feb. 5, 1940; d. Hugh William Ferguson and Ruth Virginia (Perdue) Drewery; m. Harry H. Kawaguchi, Apr. 22, 1977. BA, U. Tex., 1962, MA, 1968; JD, So. Meth. U., 1977. Bar: Tex. 1977. Legal examiner gas utilities div. Tex. Railroad Commn., Austin, 1977-84, legal examiner oil and gas div., 1984-89, asst. dir. gas utilities and liquified petroleum gas sect. of legal div., 1989-90; cons. in law, lectr. to profl. confs. Author position paper Tex. Energy Natural Resources Adv. Council. Mem., Sorority Adv. Coun., Austin, 1980-88, Japanese-Am. Citizens League, Houston, 1981—, Exec. Women in Tex. Govt., Austin, 1984. Recipient Cert. of Recognition Tex. Railroad Commn., 1982, Outstanding Svc. award, 1987. Mem. ABA, Tex. Bar Assn., Travis County Bar Assn. (oil gas and mineral law sect.), Travis County Women Lawyers Assn., Exec. Women in Tex., Internat. Platform Assn. Home: 5009 Westview Dr Austin TX 78731 Office: Tex Railroad Commn 1701 N Congress Austin TX 78711-2967

KAWMY, SUSAN YOST, educator; b. Bklyn., Feb. 14, 1950; d. John Gantt and June Ardith (Goodman) Yost; m. Karim Fred Kawmy, Aug. 17, 1974; children: Jumana Maria, Rashad Fouad, Marya Melissa. BS, Colo. State U., 1972; MEd, U. Ariz., 1973. Resource tchr. Edn. Svc. Unit, Hastings, Nebr., 1973-74, 85-87, Scottsdale (Ariz.) Pub. Schs., 1974-76; resource tchr., cons. Universal Am. Sch., Kuwait, 1977-78, Am. Sch. Kuwait, 1979, Al Bayan Sch., Kuwait, 1979-82; pvt. practice Susan Kawmy Lang. and Learning Specialist, Kuwait, 1976-84; resource tchr., diagnostician Hastings Pub. Schs., 1986-87; spl. edn. cons. Kawmy and Assocs., Kuwait, 1987-89; outreach project dir. Kuwait Spl. Edn. Soc., 1989—; cons. Al Bayan Sch., Ctr. for Evaluation and Teaching; founder, mem. sch. bd. Khalifeh Sch.; designer mainstream support team Kuwait Pvt. Schs. Mem. Mental Health Specialists Support Group. Mem. Kuwait Spl. Edn. Soc., YWCA Internat. Club. Republican. Episcopalian. Home: c/o Pepsi Co Internat, PO Box 9351, Dubai United Arab Emirates Office: Kawmy and Assocs, 7351 Trade Ctr Level 23, Dubai 13122, Kuwait Permanent: c/o Dr J G Yost Rte 4 Box 4 Hastings NE 68901

KAY, ELIZABETH ALISON, zoology educator; b. Kauai, Hawaii, Sept. 27, 1928; d. Robert Buttercase and Jessie Dowie (McConnachie) K. BA, Mills Coll., 1950, Cambridge U., Eng., 1952; MA, Cambridge U., Eng., 1956; PhD, U. Hawaii, 1957. From asst. prof. to prof. zoology U. Hawaii, Honolulu, 1957-62, assoc. prof., 1962-67, prof., 1967—; research assoc. Bishop Mus., Honolulu, 1968—. Author: Hawaiian Marine Mollusks, 1979; editor: A Natural History of The Hawaiian Islands, 1972. Chmn. Animal Species Adv. Commn., Honolulu, 1983-87; v.p. Save Diamond Head Assn., Honolulu, 1968-87, pres., 1987—; trustee B.P. Bishop Mus., Honolulu, 1983-88. Fellow Linnean Soc., AAAS; mem. Marine Biol. Assn. (Eng.), Australian Malacol. Soc. Episcopalian. Office: U Hawaii Manoa Dept Zoology 2538 The Mall Honolulu HI 96822

KAY, ELIZABETH ANN, media consultant; b. Providence, Dec. 20, 1956; d. Milton Charles and Anna (Levy) Kay. BS in Elem. Edn., Northeastern U., Boston, 1980. Pub. rels. assoc. New Eng. Aquarium, Boston, 1980-84; freelance producer, series producer, researcher Evening Mag., WBZ-TV, Boston, 1984-88; cons. H.A. Perry Fond. Media Rels., 1st Ann. Internat. Submarine Races, Boston, 1989; media cons. on environ. issues, 1989—; ptnr. Seafarers Expeditions, Inc., Bangor, Maine, 1984—; bd. dirs. Boston Harborfest, 1987—; chmn. mktg. com., trustee Sea Edn. Assn., Woods Hole, Mass., 1985—. Contbr. articles to profl. jours. Explorer Advisor of the Yr., Boy Scouts Am., 1978. Jewish. Home: 5 Forest St Wakefield MA 01880

KAY, HELEN (MRS. HERBERT J. GOLDFRANK), writer; b. N.Y.C., Oct. 27, 1912; d. Hyman and Terese (Herman) Colodny; student public schs. Washington, writer workshops N.Y.U., Bank State Coll.; m. Herbert John Goldfrank, Dec. 25, 1933; children—Lewis Robert, Deborah, Joan. Editorial research Time mag., N.Y.C., 1936, Fortune mag., 1937, Labor Press, SMCWA News, 1943-44, CIO News, 1945. Bd. dirs. Learning to Read Through the Arts at the Guggenheim, 1980. Mem. Authors League, PEN, Soc. Children's Book Writers. Author: Snow Birthday, 1955; One Mitten Lewis, 1955; City Springtime, 1957; A Pony for the Winter, 1959; Lincoln, A Big Man, 1958; Abe Lincoln's Hobby, 1961; How Smart Are Animals, 1963; The Secrets of the Dolphin, 1964; A Stocking for a Kitten, 1965; Picasso's World of Children, 1965, reprinted, 1977; An Egg is for Wishing, 1966; Man and Mastiff, 1967; Apes, 1970; The First Teddy Bear, 1985; The Staff of the Shepherd, 1983; many others. Address: 375 Nannyhagen Rd Thornwood NY 10594

KAY, M. JANE, utility executive; b. Detroit, Aug. 31, 1925; d. Albert A. and Celia (Betzing) Kay. BS, U. Detroit, 1948; MA, Wayne State U., 1952; MBA, U. Mich., 1963. Sr. personnel interviewer employment Detroit Edison Co., 1948-60, personnel coord. for women, 1960-65, office employment adminstr., 1965-70, gen. employment adminstr., 1970-71, dir. personnel svcs., 1971-72, mgr. employee rels., 1972-77, asst. v.p. employee rels., 1977-78, v.p. employee rels., 1978-82, v.p. adminstrn., 1982—; bd. dir. First Am. Bank-SE Mich., Bon Secours of Mich. Healthcare System, Inc.; tchr. U. Detroit Evening Coll. Bus. and Adminstrn., 1963-75; seminar leader div. mgmt. edn. U. Mich., 1968-74, Waterloo Mgmt. Edn. Centre, 1972-77. Mem. Mich. Employment Security Adv. Coun., 1967-81; chmn. bd. dirs. Detroit Inst. Commerce, 1976-79; exec. bd. NCCJ, 1980—, nat. trustee, 1984-88. Recipient Alumni Tower award U. Detroit, 1967, Headliner award Women Wayne State U., 1970, Wayne State U. Alumni Achievement award, 1974, Career Achievement award Profl. Panhellenic Assn., 1973; named one of Top Ten Working Women of Detroit, 1970, Alumnus of Yr., U. Detroit, 1981; cert. Adminstrv. Mgmt. Soc. Am. Soc. Personnel Adminstrn; inducted in Mich. Women's Hall of Fame, 1988. Mem. Internat. Assn. Personnel Women (pres. 1969-70), Women's Econ. Club (v.p. 1971-72, pres. 1972-73), Personnel Women Detroit (pres. 1960-61), U. Detroit Alumni Assn. (pres. 1964-66), Phi Gamma Nu (nat. v.p. 1955-57). Office: 2000 2nd Ave Detroit MI 48226

KAY, MARGARET J., psychologist; b. Washington, Apr. 16, 1951; d. Joseph Allen and Joan (Auchter) Brown; m. Jeffrey Edward Kay, Nov. 24, 1984; children: Meghan Joan, Jennifer Elizabeth. BA, Ind. (Pa.) U., 1973; MS, U. Waterloo, Ontario, Canada, 1977. Licensed Psychologist. Cert. Sch. Psychologist. Diplomate Am. Bd. Med. Psychotherapists. Research asst. Dept. Air Force, Washington, 1973; mgmt. trainee Hamilton Bank, Lancaster, Pa., 1973-74; psychologist Reality Home Svcs. for Children, Waterloo, Ontario, Canada, 1976-77; chief psychologist, v.p. Pan Am Corp., Hershey, Pa., 1977-81; psychologist, owner Lancaster (Pa.) Psychol. Svcs., 1981—; cons. in field. Author: Parent Power: Understanding Right To Education Laws, 1980. Sec. Lancaster LD Pvt. Sch. Project, 1988—. Recipient Cert. of Appreciation Lancaster Assn. for Children & Adults with Learning Disabilities, 1985. Mem. Am. Psychol. Assn., Orton Dyslexia Soc., Pa. Psychol. Assn. Republican. Roman Catholic. Home: 600 Randolph Dr Lititz PA 17543 Office: 2818 Lititz Pike Lancaster PA 17543

KAY, MARY ELLEN, financial adviser; b. Sewickley, Pa., June 21, 1947; d. Edmond and Virginia (Stueber) Kay; student Point Park Jr. Coll., 1964-65, Carnegie-Mellon U., 1965-69, N.Y. Inst. Fin., 1970-73; m. Randolph Rudisill Croxton, Apr. 19, 1969 (div. 1985); m. Lance R. Rembar, Sept. 15, 1990. Stockbroker, Dupont-Walston, N.Y.C., 1971-73, Shearson-Am. Express, N.Y.C., 1973-75; sr. v.p. A.G. Becker, N.Y.C., 1975-84, Bear Stearns & Co., N.Y.C., 1984-87, Oppenheimer & Co., N.Y.C., 1987—; sr. v.p., portfolio mgr. Cowen Trilogy Mgmt., 1990—; pres. K & W Music, N.Y.C., 1980—, Easy St. Music Prodns., N.Y.C., 1979—; mus. performer, writer 1978-81; cons. in field. Adv. bd. First Women's Bank, N.Y.C., 1974-75; chmn.'s adviser U.S. Congl. Adv. Bd., 1983—; mem. Senatorial Inner Coun. Recipient Lyric Competition award Internat. Am. Song Festival, 1981. Mem. Am. Soc. Composers Authors and Publs. Author: A Time to Remember, 1980. Home: 16 E 84th St Apt 3-B New York NY 10028

KAY, MARY PATRICIA, laboratory manager; b. Gary, Ind., Feb. 20, 1947; d. Ernest P. and Madeline M. (Holland) Brandt; m. Michael L. Kay, Sept. 13, 1969; children: Matthew A., Marcus A. BS in Biology, Marian Coll., 1968; student, South Bend Med. Found., 1968. Dir. blood bank Dukes Meml. Hosp., Peru, Ind., 1968-83; asst. lab. mgr. Dukes Meml. Hosp., Peru, 1980-83, lab. mgr., 1983--; dir. guest relations Dukes Meml. Hosp., Peru, 1986--; chemistry cons. Du Pont, Wilmington, Del., 1988--; prof. adv. panel Med. Lab. Observer, Oradell, N.J., 1988--. Mem. Psi Iota Xi (sec., 1987-88, pres., 1988--), Clin. Lab. Mgmt. (program chair, 1987-89), ASCP (sec. 1986-87). Roman Catholic. Home: 313 N Walnut St Peru IN 46970 Office: Dukes Meml Hosp Grant & Boulevard Peru IN 46970

KAY, SUSAN BARCUS, plastic surgeon; b. Stockton, Calif., Sept. 28, 1948; d. Robert Kirkpatrick and Betty Jane (Sullivan) B.; m. Gregory Louis Kay, Sept. 26, 1981; children—Brittany Paige, Morgan Allison. AB with distinction, Cornell U., 1970; MD, U. Rochester, 1975. Diplomate Am. Bd. Plastic Surgery. Intern Johns Hopkins Hosp., Balt., 1975-76, resident, 1976-77; resident U. Louisville, 1977-78, Barnes Hosp.-Washington U., St. Louis, 1978-81; instr. plastic surgery Washington U. Sch. Medicine, St. Louis, 1981-83; asst. prof. plastic surgery Baylor Coll. Medicine, Houston, 1983-85; asst. prof. plastic surgery UCLA, 1985—. Chmn. ad hoc com. on black studies Cornell U., Ithaca, N.Y., 1969; coordinator voter registration drive, Rochester, N.Y., 1972. NSF research grantee Cornell U., 1969; Teaching asst. grantee Cornell U., 1969-70; recipient Faculty Letters of Commendation, U. Rochester Sch. Medicine and Dentistry, 1972, 73. Mem. Am. Soc. Plastic and Reconstructive Surgeons, Am. Med. Women's Assn., Phi Beta Kappa. Office: UCLA Med Ctr Dept Plastic Surgery Los Angeles CA 90024

KAY, SUZANNE MAHLBURG, geochemist, educator; b. Rockford, Ill., May 30, 1947; d. Milton William and Norine Elizabeth (Zortman) Mahlburg; m. Robert Woodbury Kay, June 4, 1975; children: Jennifer Elizabeth, Alexander Marshall. BS, U. Ill., 1969, MS, 1971; PhD, Brown U., 1975. Postdoctoral fellow UCLA, 1975-76; postdoctoral fellow Cornell U., Ithaca, N.Y., 1976-78, rsch. assoc., 1978-82, sr. rsch. assoc., 1983-90, acting assoc. prof., 1990—; vis. assoc. Calif. Inst. Tech., Pasadena, 1982. Editor: Plutonism from Antarctica to Alaska, 1990. Fulbright scholar, 1989. Fellow Geol. Soc. Am., Mineralog. Soc. Am.; mem. Am. Geophys. Union, Sigma Xi. Home: 102 Genung Cir Ithaca NY 14850 Office: Cornell U Dept Geol Sci Ithaca NY 14853

KAYE, ELIZABETH ANN, educational administrator; b. Chillicothe, Mo., Aug. 18, 1951; d. John William and Mildred Louise (Tompkins) K.; m. John Tryneski, May 26, 1984; 1 child, John Michael Tryneski. BA, Northwestern U., 1973. Editorial asst. Northwestern U. Press, Evanston, Ill., 1973-74; asst. to pres. D.B. Sutherland Group, Chgo., 1974-75; asst. promotion mgr. U. Chgo. Press, 1975-78; publicist Loop Ctr. YWCA, Chgo., 1978-80; dir. spl. svcs. Loop Ctr. YWCA, 1980-81; project mgr. seminars Phoenix-Hecht Inc., Chgo., 1981-83; dir. alumni relations IIT, Chgo., 1984-87; dir.. centennial IIT, 1987—. Bonbright scholar, 1973. Mem. Nat. Soc. Fund Raising Execs., Phi Beta Kappa. Office: IIT Centennial Office 10 W 33rd St Chicago IL 60616

KAYE, JUDITH SMITH, state judge; b. Monticello, N.Y., Aug. 4, 1938; d. Benjamin and Lena (Cohen) Smith; m. Stephen Rackow Kaye, Feb. 11, 1964; children: Luisa Marian, Jonathan Mackey, Gordon Bernard. BA, Barnard Coll., 1958; LLB cum laude, NYU, 1962; LLD (hon.), St. Lawrence U., 1985, Union U., 1985, Pace U., 1985, Syracuse U., 1988, L.I. U., 1989. Assoc. Sullivan & Cromwell, N.Y.C., 1962-64; staff atty. IBM, Armonk, N.Y., 1964-65; asst. to dean Sch. Law NYU, 1965-68; ptnr. Olwine Connelly Chase O'Donnell & Weyher, N.Y.C., 1969-83; judge N.Y. State Ct. Appeals, N.Y.C., 1983—; bd. dir. Sterling Nat. Bank. Contbr. articles to profl. jours. Former bd. dirs. Legal Aid Soc. Recipient Vanderbilt medal NYU Sch. of Law, 1983, Medal of Distinction, Barnard Coll, 1987. Fellow Am. Bar Found.; mem. Am. Law Inst., Am. Coll. Trial Lawyers, Am. Judicature Soc. (bd. dirs. 1980-83). Democrat. Home: 101 Central Pk W New York NY 10023 Office: Ct Appeals 20 Eagle St Albany NY 12207

KAYE, JUDY, actress; b. Dec. 11, 1948; d. Jerome Joseph and Shirley Edith (Silverman) K. Student, UCLA. Appeared in plays Fiddler on the Roof, Godspell, You're a Good Man Charlie Brown, 1968, Jesus Christ Superstar, 1972, (N.Y. debut) Grease, 1977, On the Twentieth Century, 1978, Moony Shapiro Songbook, 1980, Oh Brother!, 1981, Four to Make Two, 1982, Love, 1984, Side by Side by Sondheim, Paper Mill Playhouse, Millburn, N.J., 1984-85, Windy City, Paper Mill Playhouse, 1985, The Phantom of the Opera (Tony award for featured actress in a mus.), 1988—. Jewish. Office: care William Morris Agy 1350 Ave of the Americas New York NY 10019*

KAYE, MELANIE FERN, obstetrician, gynecologist; b. Albany, N.Y., Feb. 4, 1960; d. Jesse and Shirley (Poskanzer) K. BS, Georgetown U., 1981; MD, Albany Med. Coll., 1985. Diplomate Nat. Bd. Med. Examiners. Rsch. assoc. Higher Edn. Rsch. Inst., Washington, 1979-80, Am. Soc. Allied Health Professions, Washington, 1980; rsch. asst., translator Kennan Inst. for Advanced Russian Studies, Washington, 1980-81; sci. investigator Los Alamos (N.Mex.) Nat. Labs., 1982, 83; researcher depts. oncology and thoracic surgery Albany Med. Ctr., 1984-85; intern, then resident George Washington U. Hosp., Washington, 1985-89; obstetrician-gynecologist Ob-Gyn. Affiliates, Greenbelt, Md., 1989—, Holy Cross Hosp., Silver Spring, Md., 1989—; supr. residents Holy Cross Hosp., Silver Spring, 1989—. Contbr. articles to profl. jours. Jr. fellow Am. Coll. Obstetrics and Gynecology; mem. Phi Beta Kappa, Alpha Omega Alpha. Jewish. Home: 9803 Bristol Sq Ln 204 Bethesda MD 20814

KAYLOR, BARBARA BROTMAN, advertising executive, pilot; b. Balt., Dec. 15, 1959; d. Don N. and Phyllis Eve (Block) Brotman; m. Marc Lawrence Kaylor; m. Aug. 18, 1984; 1 child, Paige Leigh. BA, Lynchburg Coll., 1981. Media dir. Image Dynamics Inc., Balt., 1981-84, treas., 1983—, v.p., 1984-86, exec. v.p., 1986—; pres. Air Inc., Balt., 1984—; pub. svcs. com. Am. Advt. Fedn., Washington, 1987-89. Bd. govs. Goodwill Industries,, Balt., 1988—, AMC Cancer Rsch., Balt., 1986-87, Levindale Geriatric Hosp., Balt., 1987-89; vice chmn. Assoc. Jewish Charities, Balt., 1987; chmn. Young Execs. Forum, Loyola Coll., 1989-91. Mem. Advt. Assn. of Balt. (pres. 1989-90, v.p. 1986-89, treas. 1984-86, sec. 1983-84). Democrat. Office: Image Dynamics 1101 N Calvert St Baltimore MD 21202

KAZAN, KATHRYN LUKINS, clinical social worker; b. Louisville, Sept. 23, 1957; d. Milton Elliott and Nancy Jean (Sellars) Lukins; m. Timothy Jay Kazan, July 28, 1979 (div. Jan. 1986); 1 child, Luellen Sara. BA, Ariz. State U., 1979; MSSW, U. Tex., Austin, 1985. Cert. social worker, advanced clin. practitioner. VISTA worker Flagstaff (Ariz.) Women's Resource Ctr., 1980-82; staff therapist, eating disorders unit Hays Meml. Hosp., San Marcos, Tex., 1985-86; psychotherapist Austin, 1986-87, Austin Psychotherapy Assocs., 1987—; workshop facilitator William Whisenant, PhD, Austin, 1987—; presenter, cons. Flagstaff Polce Dept., 1980-82, No. Ariz. U., 1980-82. Mem. Nat. Assn. Social Workers, Am. Assn. Counseling and Devel., Assn. for Humanistic Psychology, Assn. for Exptl. Edn. Office: Austin Psychotherapy Assocs 7719 Woodhollow Dr #152 Austin TX 78703

KAZANIWSKYJ, LUBOMYRA MARIA, physician; b. Chgo., May 13, 1957; d. Julian and Marie (Chotyneckyj) Maleckyj; m. Andrew L. Kazaniwskyj, June 2, 1979; children: Mark Andrij, Vera Christina, Andrea, Diana. BS, U. Ill., Chgo., 1979; DO, Chgo. Coll. Osteopathic Med., 1983. Diplomate Am. Bd. Family Practice. Rotating internship Chgo. Osteopathic Hosp., 1983-84; residency Rush Presbyn. St. Luke's Med. Ctr. and Christ Hosp., Chgo. and Oak Lawn, Ill., 1984-86; office practice Christ Hosp. Affiliation, Oak Lawn, 1986—; preceptor, instr. Rush Med. Coll., Oak Lawn, 1986—. Mem. AMA, Am. Acad. Family Practice, Ill. State Med. Soc., Ill. Acad. Family Physicians, Chgo. Med. Soc. Office: 4700 W 95th St Oak Lawn IL 60453

KAZIMIR, GINA ANN, public relations, marketing executive; b. Perth Amboy, N.J., Oct. 9, 1964; d. Andrew Steven and Nancy Carol (Neapolitan) K.; m. Philip Matthew Caruso Jr., July 25, 1986. Student, Georgetown U., 1982-84; BA, Rutgers U., 1986. Art cons. Circle Fine Art, Woodbridge, N.J., 1984-85; asst. creative dir. J.B. Ross-Linea Inc., New Brunswick, N.J., 1985-86; owner, chief exec. officer G.A. Kazimir & Co., Balt., 1986-89; dir. arts mgmt. U. Md., 1988-89; dir. pub. affairs and mktg. Corcoran Gallery of Art, Washington, 1989—; cons. D.B. Prodns., Washington, 1982-85, Jeuesses Musicales-USA, N.Y.C., 1986-89. Cons. Nomadic Theatre, Washington, 1986; vol. Balt. Choral Arts Soc., 1987-89. Nat. Merit, Rutgers and Leopold Schepp scholar, 1982. Mem. NAFE, Pub. Rels. Soc. Am., Am. Arts Alliance, Mensa. Office: Corcoran Gallery of Art Arts Mgmt Washington DC 20006

KAZLE, ELYNMARIE, production stage manager, producer; b. St. Paul, June 22, 1958; d. Victor Anton and Marylu (Gardner) K. BFA, U. Minn., Duluth, 1982; MFA, Ohio U., 1984. Prodn. mgr. Great Lakes Shakespeare, Cleve., 1983; prodn. stage mgr. San Diego (Calif.) Opera, 1984, PCPA Theaterfest, Santa Maria, Calif., 1986-87; stage mgr. Bklyn. Acad. Music, 1987; assoc. producer Am. Theater Actors, N.Y.C., 1988—; prodn. stage mgr. Time Flies When You're Alive, West Hollywood, Calif., 1988—; assoc. producer Paulmark Prodns., L.A., 1988-90; asst. advt. display Wall St. Jour., L.A., 1988-89. Editor, pub.: (newsletter) The Ohio Network, 1984—; producer Santa Monica Playhouse, 1989—. Mem. Stage Mgrs. Assn., Stage Mgrs. Assn. L.A. (assoc. dir.), U.S. Inst. Theatre Tech. (bd. dirs.), Actors Equity Assn., Phi Kappa Phi, Delta Chi Omega (past pres. 1978). Office: Santa Monica Playhouse 1211 4th St Santa Monica CA 90401

KEANE, LAURA MEACHAM, marketing professional; b. St. Petersburg, Fla., Feb. 11, 1962; d. Robert Colegrove and Katharine (Miller) Meacham; m. Martin Patterson Keane, June 17, 1989. BA in Lit., Eckerd Coll., 1983. Dir. market rsch. Am. Diversified Captial, West Palm Beach, Fla., 1983-85; market analyst Landauer Assocs., West Palm Beach, 1985; v.p. market rsch. Southeastern Mktg., Stuart, Fla., 1986-89; mgr. mktg. and advt. Nicklaus/Sierra Devel. Corp., Tampa, Fla., 1989—; cons. in field, 1983—. Office: Nicklaus/Sierra Devel Corp 15436 N Florida Ave Tampa FL 33613

KEARNEY, ELIZABETH IRENE, consulting firm executive, writer; b. New Burnside, Ill., Dec. 7, 1934; d. E. William Edmondson and Verna P. (Greer) Eppley; m. M.L. Kearney, Feb. 7, 1953 (div.); children: Michael, Kim. BA, UCLA, 1954; MA, U. Pa., 1959, PhD in Bus. Tchr., program dir. Pasadena Unified Sch. Dist., Calif., 1959-84; v.p. Managex, Inc., Houston, 1984, Cole/Kearney Co., South Pasadena, 1984; pres. Kearney Enterprises, L.A., 1979-85; chief exec. officer Kearney/Bandley Enterprise, Inc., 1985—. Author: How to Increase Your Vocabulary, 1964; How To Write A Term Paper, 1965; The American Novel: A Study Guide to 36 Great Books, 1966; The Continental Novel: A Bibliography of Criticism, Vol. I, 1967, Vol. II, 1982; Everyone's A Customer, 1986, People Power, 1987, MLM Is Big Business, 1988, Customers run Your Company, 1989. Contbr. articles to profl. jours. Past editor CAG Communicator, Pipelines Newsletter, Previews newspaper. Pres. Terr. Park Assn., 1984—; bd. dirs. Pasadena Edn. Found.; vol. Nat. Trust Hist. Preservation, 1980—; adv. gifted children Calif. Advs. Gifted Edn., 1967—. Recipient Best Reference Book award ALA, 1967; fellow NDEA, 1968, Johns Hopkins U., 1971. Mem. Golden Voice, Nat. Speakers Assn., Leads Club, Women's Referral Services, Pasadena C. of C. (chmn. com. 1983-85). Republican. Episcopalian. Avocations: travel, writing, reading, historical preservation.

KEARNEY, GRETCHEN WARNER, college official; b. Hammond, Ind., Dec. 14, 1955; d. R. Douglas and Mary Lee (Kennard) Warner; m. Terrence John Kearney, Aug. 28, 1982. BA, DePauw U., 1978; MA, Ind. U., 1981; postgrad., Loyola U., Chgo., 1984—. Exec. dir. Terre Haute (Ind.) Symphony Assn., 1981-82; asst. to pres. Chgo. Sch. Profl. Psychology, 1983-85; dir. acad. advising and retention Sch. Art Inst. Chgo., 1985-88; v.p. for acad. planning Montay Coll., Chgo., 1988-90; asst. dean for acad. affairs Barat Coll., Lake Forest, Ill., 1990—; presenter ann. conf. Nat. Acad. Advising Assn., 1987; mem. Bridges Interdisciplinary Conf. Loyola U., 1990. Fellow NEA, 1981. Mem. Nat. Assn. for Student Personnel Adminstrs., Assn. for Study Higher Edn., Am. Assn. for Higher Edn., Ill. Coll. Personnel Assn. (sec.), Phi Beta Kappa, Alpha Lambda Delta, Delta Zeta. Roman Catholic. Office: Montay Coll 3750 W Peterson Ave Chicago IL 60659

KEARNEY, JUDY MILLER, marketing executive; b. Danville, Pa., July 6, 1940; d. Paul Victor and Mary Alice (Becker) Frye; m. Thomas W. Kearney; children: Deborah, Ross. BA, Juniata Coll., 1962. Dir. mktg. Tampa (Fla.) Hilton of Riverside, dir. sales and mktg.; acting dir. sales Sheraton Valley Forge Hotel and Conv. Ctr., King of Prussia, Pa.; sales mgr. Host Farm, Lancaster, Pa.; dir. sales Radisson Pla. Hotel, Orlando, Fla. Mem. NAFE, SMART, ASAE, HSMA, OOCVB. Home: 256 Harbor Dr Winter Garden FL 34787

KEARNEY, PATRICIA ANN, university administrator; b. Wilkes-Barre, Pa., May 15, 1943; d. William F. and Helen L. (Hartz) K. BA, Mich. State U., 1965; MSEd, Ind. U., 1966. Head resident advisor Western Ill. U., Macomb, 1966-68; asst. v.p. SUNY, Buffalo, 1968-70; asst. dean student life Lock Haven (Pa.) State Coll., 1970-72; dir. residential life U. Calif., Davis, 1974-83, bus. mgr., 1983-85, dir. housing and food services, 1985-90, asst.

vice chancellor student affairs, 1990—; speaker nat. and state convs. Contbr. articles to profl. jours. Mem. Am. Coll. Personnel Assn. (pres.), Am. Mgmt. Assn., Am. Soc. Tng. and Devel., Assn. Coll. and U. Housing Officers Internat., Sierra Club. Home: 714 Borchard Ct Woodland CA 95695 Office: U Calif 127 Student Housing Davis CA 95616

KEARNEY, ROSE THERESA, nursing educator; b. Glen Falls, N.Y., July 8, 1951; d. James J. and Helen F. (Oprandy) K. BS with honors, Keuka Coll., 1973; MN, U. Fla., 1976, PhD, 1987. Assoc. prof. U. of South Fla., Tampa; asst. prof. La. State U. Med. Ctr., New Orleans; project coord. indigent health care U. Fla., Gainesville; dir. nursing SUNY Coll. at New Paltz, 1988—. Mem. Ulster County unit nursing edn. com. Am. Cancer Soc., 1990—, mem. rep. assembly, 1990—; bd. dirs. Mid-Hudson Consortium for Avancement of Edn. for Health Profls., 1988—, mem. scholarship com., 1989-90, com. chair, 1990, mem. nursing edn. com., 1988-90; mem. profl. devel. program SUNY, Albany, 1989—; mem. adv. coun. Ulster County Community Coll., 1989—; mem. adv. regional planning group for early intervention svcs. United Cerebral Palsy Ulster County, Inc and Children's Rehab. Ctr., 1989—. Mem. Am. Nurses Assn., SRNEF, N.Y. State Coun. of Deans, Nat. League for Nursing, Profl. Nursing Network, Sigma Theta Tau. Roman Catholic. Home: 34 Prospect St New Paltz NY 12561 Office: SUNY Coll at New Paltz Dept Nursing VLC 205 New Paltz NY 12561

KEARNEY, SHEILA PATRICIA, educator; b. Lynn, Mass., Mar. 16, 1933; d. Michael Bernard and Julia Therese (O'Brien) K. BS in Edn., Salem State Coll., 1954, MS in Edn., 1967; Cert. of Advanced Grad. Study, Boston U., 1981. Cert. elem. tchr. Tchr. Town of Saugus, Mass., 1954-56; tchr. remedial reading Stanley Sch., Swampscott, Mass., 1956-57; tchr., 1957—; head tchr. Stanley Sch., Swampscott, 1982-89; instr. Mass. Migrant Edn. Program, Gloucestersite, 1984—; mem. computer com., fine arts coun., curriculum com., reading and writing com. Swampscott Sch. System. Mem. Swampscott Town Meeting, Swampscott Democratic Com. Named Tchr. of Yr. Swampscott Edn. Assn., 1988-89; Horace Mann grantee Town of Swampscott, 1988-89. Mem. Mass. Tchrs. Assn. (profl. ethics com.), North Shore Reading Assn., Swampscott Edn. Assn. (bldg. rep., bargaining com.) Northeast Coalition of Ednl. Leaders, Whole Lang. Assn., Delta Kappa Gamma (2d v.p. 1984-86, 1st v.p. 1986-88, pres. 1988— Omega chpt.). Roman Catholic. Home: 14 Shackle Way Swampscott MA 01907

KEARNS, PATRICIA LOUISE, marine surveyor; b. Ohio, Apr. 7, 1944; d. John Henry and Willamina (Krull) Byrne; m. Robert M. Kearns, Aug. 3, 1963 (div. 1971) children: Michael, Jennifer. Cert., Stuart Sch. of Bus. Adminstrn., Asbury Park, N.J., 1963. Marina mgr. Herring Bay Marina, Deale, Md., 1974-76; yacht broker Cruising Ctr., Inc., Annapolis, Md., 1976-80, Fitzsimmons-Huckins Yacht Brokers, Annapolis, 1980, Interyacht, Inc., Annapolis, 1980-85; sailing instr. Womanship, Inc., Annapolis, 1985—; with yacht sales dept. Hans Christian Yachts, Inc., Annapolis, 1985-88; marine surveyor, propr. Marine Assocs., Ltd., Annapolis, 1988—; yacht delivery capt., USCG lic. operator Passenger Carrying Vessels, Annapolis, 1985—; speaker Boat Owners Assn. of the U.S., Alexandria, Va., 1989—; sr. sailing coach U.S. Naval Acad. Mem. Am. Boat & Yacht Coun. (bd. dirs. 1988—), Society of Naval Architects and Marine Engrs. (assoc.), Nat. Assn. Profl. Women Mariners (founder 1987), Nat. Assn. Marine Surveyors. Roman Catholic. Home and Office: 982-101 Spa Rd Annapolis MD 21403

KEARSE, AMALYA LYLE, federal judge; b. Vauxhall, N.J., June 11, 1937; d. Robert Freeman and Myra Lyle (Smith) K. B.A., Wellesley Coll., 1959; J.D. cum laude, U. Mich., 1962. Bar: N.Y. 1963, U.S. Supreme Ct. 1967. Assoc. Hughes Hubbard & Reed, N.Y.C., 1962-69; ptnr. Hughes Hubbard & Reed, 1969-79; judge U.S. Ct. Appeals (2d cir.), 1979—; lectr. evidence N.Y. U. Law Sch., 1968-69. Author: Bridge Conventions Complete, 1975, 3d edit., 1990, Bridge at Your Fingertips, 1980; translator, editor: Bridge Analysis, 1979; editor: Ofcl. Ency. of Bridge, 3d edit, 1976; mem. editorial bd. Charles Goren, 1974—. Bd. dirs. NAACP Legal Def. and Endl. Fund, 1977-79; bd. dirs. Nat. Urban League, 1978-79; trustee N.Y.C. YWCA, 1976-79, Am. Contract Bridge League Nat. Laws Commn., 1975—; mem. Pres.'s Com. on Selection of Fed. Jud. Officers, 1977-78. Named Women's Pairs Bridge Champion Nat. div., 1971, 72, World div., 1986, Nat. Women's Teams Bridge Champion, 1987. Mem. ABA, Assn. of Bar of City of N.Y., Am. Law Inst., Lawyers Com. for Civil Rights Under Law (mem. exec. com. 1970-79). Office: US Ct Appeals US Courthouse Foley Sq New York NY 10007

KEATING, ANNE FRASER, recruiting executive; b. Rockville Center, N.Y., Apr. 27, 1955; d. Pierson Keating and Elizabeth Nelson. BA in Philosophy, Yale U., 1977; MBA in Mktg., U. Pa., 1982. Asst. dir. undergrad. admissions, dir. transfer admissions Yale U., New Haven, 1977-80; adminstrv. officer Brown Bros. Harriman, N.Y.C., 1982-85; exec. recruiter Bentley & Evans, N.Y.C., 1986-87, Stricker, Sur & Assocs., N.Y.C., 1987—. Team mem. U.S. Field Hockey Assn., Colorado Springs, Colo., 1977-80, v.p. fin. and adminstrn., 1982-84; team mem. U.S. Lacrosse, 1977-78. Mem. Yale U. Alumni Assn. (co-chmn. schs. com. 1982—), Yale Alumnae Lacrosse Assn. (pres. 1978-88). Office: Stricker Sur & Assocs 717 Fifth Ave New York NY 10022

KEATING, LAUREL, humanities educator, theatrical director; b. Los Angeles, Dec. 29, 1924; d. Charles and June Elaine (Smith) K. BS, UCLA, 1945; MA, Syracuse U., 1952, PhD, 1973; EdD, Arts Complex, Rochester, N.Y., 1988. Instr. Moravian Coll., Bethlehem, Pa., 1952-54; dir. women's program Sta. WSBA-TV, York, Pa., 1954-56; lectr. Hunter Coll., N.Y.C., 1958-60; asst. prof. SUNY, Cortland, 1960-62; assoc. prof. humanities Yeshiva U., N.Y.C., 1962-87; moderator numerous TV series; theatre dir. numerous prodns.; author: Notes on Speech, 1973; contbr. articles to profl. jours. Served with USN Waves, 1945-46. Mem. Popular Culture Assn., Ednl. Film Library Assn., Assn. Ednl. Communication and Tech. Club: New Community Cinema (N.Y.). Home: 1112 Washington Dr Centerport NY 11721

KEATON, FRANCES MARLENE, sales representative; b. Redfield, Ark., July 1, 1944; d. John Thomas and Pauline (Hilliard) Wells; m. Larry Ronald Keaton, Sept. 17, 1946. Cert. in acctg., Draughon's Sch. Bus., 1972. Lic. ins. agt. Acctg. supr. Home Ins. Co., Little Rock, 1962-70; auditor St. Paul Ins. Co., Little Rock, 1970-74; spl. agt. Continental Ins. Co., Little Rock, 1974—. Vol. Ark. Sch. for the Blind, Little Rock, 1968. Mem. Little Rock Field Club, Casualty Roundtable, Auditor's Assn., Ins. Women, Underwriters Roundtable, The Executive Female, Ind. Ins. Agts. Assn., Profl. Ins. Assn. Democrat. Baptist. Home and Office: 111 Red River Dr Sherwood AR 72116

KEATS, SHEILA, musician, educator; b. Bayonne, N.J., Dec. 7, 1929; d. Irving and Helen (Saskin) K. Student, Radcliffe Coll., 1947-48, Syracuse U., 1948-50; BS, Juilliard Sch., 1954. Adminstrv. asst. Juilliard Sch. Music, N.Y.C., 1953-56, mng. editor Juilliard Rev., dir. alumni activities, 1956-60, staff accompanist, 1972—; mgr., press rep. Goldman Band, N.Y.C., 1960-68; staff writer student program Lincoln Ctr., N.Y.C., 1968-73; assoc. dir., head piano dept. Sch. for Strings, N.Y.C., 1971—, sec.-treas., 1977—; program annotator Am. Symphony Orch., N.Y.C., 1968-72, also program notes for various performances in Carnegie Hall, Avery Fischer Hall, Town Hall, N.Y.C.; ofcl. accompanist Suzuki Inst. and Internat. Confs., Stevens Point, Wis., San Diego, Amherst, Mass., 1973-83; vis. prof. Universidad Internacional Menendez Pelayo, Santander, Spain, summer 1990. Editor, author: Manhattan School of Music Catalog, 1969; contbr. articles to profl. publs. Mem. Suzuki Assn. Ams. (registered tchr., cert. tchr. trainer), Am. Fedn. Musicians. Home: 155 W 68th St Apt 704 New York NY 10023 Office: Sch for Strings 419 W 54th St New York NY 10019

KECK, BARBARA ANNE, management consulting company executive; b. Goshen, Ind., Aug. 10, 1946; d. Howard and Mary Elizabeth (Taylor) Brumbaugh; m. Gerald Nadel, June, 1966 (div. 1972); Chad Whitney Keck, May 16, 1976; children: Martin Whitney, Matthew James Howard. BA cum laude, Rutgers U., 1968; MBA, Harvard U., 1976. Communications specialist U.S. Dept. Agrl., New Brunswick, N.J., 1968-71; asst. dir. pub. rels. dept. Hill & Holliday, Boston, 1971-73; dir. advt. and pub. rels. Paperback Booksmith, Boston, 1973-74; mktg. mgr. food packaging Continental Can Co. Hdqrs., Stamford, Conn., 1976-79; chmn., chief exec. officer Keck & Co. Bus. Cons. Inc., N.Y.C., 1979-85; pres. Keck & Co. Bus. Cons., Atherton, Calif., 1985—. Sec. N.J. Tenants Assn., 1969-70; bd. dirs. Puppetry Guild Greater N.Y., N.Y.C., 1981-84. Mem. Inst. Mgmt. Cons., Women in Mgmt. (founder 1978, pres. 1979-80), Harvard Bus. Sch. Club (San Francisco). Episcopalian. Home and Office: 410 Walsh Rd Atherton CA 94025

KECK, JUDITH MARIE BURKE, government agency administrator; b. Springfield, Ohio, Feb. 24, 1938; d. John T. and Mary Elizabeth (Kaliher) Burke; m. Henry J. Reinhardt, Feb. 22, 1958 (div.); 1 child, Lucy L.; m. James E. Keck, Feb. 18, 1978. BS in Mgmt., Park Coll., 1983; MA in Mgmt., Cen. Mich. U., 1985; postgrad., Def. Systems Mgmt. Coll., 1986, Air War Coll., 1989; PhD, Pacific Western U., 1990. Cert. govt. contracting officer, govt. program mgr. Billeting officer USAF, Zweibrucken AFB, Fed. Republic Germany, 1969-72; commissary officer Edwards AFB, Calif., 1972-74; procurement agt. George AFB, Calif., 1974-76; chief contract adminstrn. Nellis AFB, Nev., 1976-78; chief services contracting Grand Forks AFB, N.D., 1978-81; contracting officer aero. systems div./air launched cruise missile div. Wright Patterson AFB, Ohio, 1981-85, program mgr. aero. systems div./B-1 Bomber, 1985-87, program mgr. aero. systems div. project Tomorrow, 1987—, chief acquisition mgmt. HQ, aero. systems div., 1990—; instr. systems mgmt. Air Force Inst. Tech., Wright Patterson AFB, 1985, quality assurance, 1981; dir. fed. women's program George AFB, 1976. Mem. aero. systems div. Exec. Combined Fed. Campaign, 1989—. Mem. Am. Assn. for Artificial Intelligence, Nat. Contract Mgmt. Assn., Air Force Assn., Nat. Assn. Mil. Comptrollers, NAFE, Sigma Iota Epsilon. Democrat. Roman Catholic. Home: 8022 Philadelphia Dr Fairborn OH 45324

KEDDERIS, PAMELA JEAN, insurance company executive; b. Waterbury, Conn., May 15, 1956; d. Leo George and Evelyn Helen (Fenske) K. Student, U. Nice, 1976-77; B.A., Assumption Coll., 1978; M.B.A., U. New Haven, 1981. Credit analyst, Citytrust Bank, Bridgeport, Conn., 1980-81, sr. credit analyst, 1981-82, fin. analyst, 1982-83, seminar leader, 1981-83; planning analyst Continental Ins. Co., N.Y.C., 1983-84, sr. planning analyst, 1984-85, dir. planning, 1985-87, asst. v.p. 1987—. Active YMCA, Union, N.J., 1985—; mem. Planning Forum. Mem. NAFE, North Shore Animal League. Democrat. Lutheran. Avocations: music, traveling. Home: 1166 Schmidt Ln North Brunswick NJ 08902

KEDING, ANN CLYRENE, freelance copywriter; b. Ft. Benning, Ga., Aug. 31, 1944; d. Porter Bill and Clyrene (Stull) Maxwell; children from previous marriage: Robert, Jeff. BA in Psychology, Calif. State U., Fullerton, 1973, MA in Psychology, 1975; postgrad., U. So. Calif., 1980-83. Instr. psychology Calif. State U., Fullerton, 1974-76, Golden West Coll., Huntington Beach, Calif., 1976-78; mktg. sch. project dir. Foote, Cone & Belding, L.A., 1978-80; copywriter Yuguchi & Krogstad, L.A., 1980-82, Hamilton Advt., L.A., 1982-84, Grey Advt., L.A., 1984-85; freelance copywriter L.A., Eugene, Calif. and Oreg., 1985—; asst. prof. U. Oreg., Eugene, 1986—. Author: How to Produce Creative Advertising, 1990; writer TV commls., advt. campaigns, brochures. Mem. adv. coun. L.A. Commn. on Assaults Against Women, 1985—. Recipient Pub. Citation Govt. Calif., 1985, Humanitarian award L.A. Commn. Assaults Against Women, 1986; Gannett fellow, 1987, 88. Mem. Am. Acad. Advt., Calif. State U. Fullerton Alumni Assn., Phi Kappa Phi (bd. dirs. 1974-75). Office: U Oreg Sch Journalism Eugene OR 97403

KEEBLER, LOIS MARIE, educator; b. Jasper, Ala., Nov. 24, 1955; d. Roosevelt T. and Marie (Smiley) K. Student, Cen. State U., Wilberforce, Ohio; cert., Ala. Regional Hosp. Cert. tchr., Ala. Democrat. Baptist.

KEEFE, JANET CATHRYN, employment services executive; b. Lindsay, Calif., Aug. 18, 1947; d. Earl Loren and Ina Mae (Redmond) Shryer; children: Stephanie, Kate; m. James F. Keefe, Dec. 24, 1985. AA, Mt. San Antonio Coll., 1967; student, Calif. State U., L.A., 1969-72. Sales mgr. Griswolds Hotel & Restraunt, Claremont, Calif., 1976-78; sales rep. Ocean Pacific Sunwear, Tustin, Calif., 1978-81; owner The Wardrobe Co., Laguna Beach, Calif., 1981-83; mgmt. cons. Julian Ryder & Assocs., Manhattan Beach, Calif., 1985-88; exec. dir. tng. and devel. Apple One Employment Svcs., Glendale, Calif., 1988—. Mem. Calif. Assn. Placement Counselors, Am. Soc. Tng. and Devel. Office: Apple One Employment Svcs 327 W Broadway Ste B Glendale CA 91204

KEEFER, RHONDA JEAN, data processing executive; b. Elmira, N.Y., May 20, 1959; d. Ronald Burger; m. Steven L. Keefer; 1 child, Robert Atlee. BS, Pa. State U., 1981. Sr. sales rep. Datapoint Corp., Bala Cynwyd, Pa., 1981-82; dist. sales mgr. Commodore Bus. Machines, West Chester, Pa., 1982-83; sales exec. Digital Equipment Corp., Blue Bell, Pa., 1983—. Mem. Jaycees (bd. dirs. Lansdale br. 1986-87, v.p. 1987—). Home: 100 Hunter Ln North Wales PA 19454 Office: Digital Equipment Corp 1740 Walton Rd Blue Bell PA 19422

KEEFER, YVONNE JUNE KELSOE, religious organization administrator; b. Gotebo, Okla., Oct. 2, 1935; d. Carl Clifford and Zelma Phoebe (Bond) Kelsoe; m. James Albert Keefer, June 8, 1956; children: Steven Dale, Brian Lee. BS in Home Econs., Okla. State U., 1966. Ednl. dir. 1st So. Bapt. Ch., Lawrence, Kans., 1969-70; dir. campus ministries U. Kans., Lawrence, 1969-82; exec. dir. Woman's Missionary Union, Family Ministry, Partnership Missions Kans. Nebr. Conv. So. Bapts., Topeka, Kans., 1983—; chmn. 1990-91 dated plan Woman's Missionary Union So. Bapt. Conv., Birmingham, Ala., 1987-88. Assoc. editor The Campus Minister, 1980-82. Chaplain Lawrence Police Dept., 1976-83; mem. Friends of Art, Lawrence; exec. bd. Kaw Valley Assn., Topeka, 1970-82; bd. dirs. Wellspring Found., Prairie Village, Kans., 1984—, Douglas County Mental Health Assn., Lawrence, 1979-82. Mem. Assn. So. Bapt. Campus Ministers (nat. v.p. 1982-83), Exec. Dirs. Woman's Missionary Union, Phi Kappa Phi, Omnicron Nu, Phi Upsilon Omnicorn, Pi Zeta Kappa (Outstanding Mem. award, nat. v.p.). Republican. Club: PEO (Lawrence) (pres. 1981-82). Home: 4011 W 13th Lawrence KS 66044 Office: Kans Nebr Conv So Bapts 5410 W 7th Topeka KS 66606

KEEGAN, BRIDGET ANN, chemist, environmental engineer; b. New Haven, Conn., Jan. 13, 1951; d. Michael J. Keegan and Maryanne Smithkowski. BS, BA, MS, U. New Haven, 1988; postgrad., Rensselaer Poly. Inst., 1989—. Engr. Dept. of Def., New London, Conn., 1977—. Contbr. several articles to prof. jours. Mem. Air Pollution Control Assn., Audubon Soc., Nature's Conservancy, 700 Club. Home: Naval Underwater Systems Ctr Smith St New London CT 06320

KEEGAN, JANE ANN, insurance executive, consultant; b. Watertown, N.Y., Sept. 1, 1950; d. Richard Isidor and Kathleen (McKinley) K. BA cum laude, SUNY-Potsdam, 1972; MBA in Risk Mgmt., Golden Gate U., 1986. CPCU. Comml. lines mgr. Lithgow & Rayhill, San Francisco, 1977-80; risk mgmt. account coordinator Dinner Levison Co., San Francisco, 1980-83; ins. cons., San Francisco, 1983-84; account mgr. Rollins Burdick Hunter, San Francisco, 1984-85; account exec. Jardine Ins. Brokers, San Francisco, 1985-86; ins. cons., San Francisco, 1986-87, ins. adminstr. Port of Oakland, 1987—, risk mgr., 1989—. Vol. San Francisco Ballet vol. orgn., 1981—, Bay Area Bus., Govt. ARC disaster conf. steering com., 1987-88, 89; mem. Nob Hill Neighbors Assn., 1982—. Mem. Nat. Safety Mgmt. Soc., CPCU Soc. (spl. events chairperson 1982-84, continuing profl. devel. program award 1985, 88), Risk and Ins. Mgt. Soc. (dep.). Democrat. Roman Catholic. Home: 1635 Clay St Apt 1 San Francisco CA 94109

KEEL, CHERYL ANN, labor specialist, nurse; b. N.Y.C., Sept. 11, 1946; d. Cleveland Milton Jenkins and Gwendolyn Lucille (Bland) Trice; m. Joe Davis Keel, Apr. 2, 1965; 1 child, Derrick Vonn. Student, NYU, 1967, Liberty (Va.) U. Staff nurse Bklyn. Hosp., 1965-67, Meml. Hosp., Chapel Hill, S.C., 1967-68, Loris (S.C.) Community Hosp., 1968-69; sch. nurse Horry County Dept. of Edn., Conway, 1969-78; indsl. nurse AVX Corp., Myrtle Beach, 1978-84, facilitator, 1984—; cons. AVX, Myrtle Beach and Juarez, Mex., 1988—. Mem. com. Am. Heart Assn., Myrtle Beach, 1985-87; mem. Bus. Ethics Forum, Conway, 1989; bd. dirs. CASA, Myrtle Beach, 1984-87, Am. Cancer Soc., Myrtle Beach, 1988-89; sec., mem. Citizens Against Spouse Abuse. Recipient Cert., Fed. Women's Program, 1988. Mem. Assn. for Quality and Participation (exec. bd. 1989), Am. Bus. Women's Assn. (chair com. 1984—, Woman of Yr. 1986-87), Toastmasters (v.p. 1988, dist. lt. gov. Myrtle Beach 1989—), NAFE. Democrat. Baptist. Office: AVX Corp 17th Ave South Myrtle Beach SC 29578

KEELAND, DELPHA FLORINE, librarian; b. Glendive, Mont., June 3, 1925; d. Fred Peter and Anna (Buller) Deckert; m. Charles William Keeland, July 25, 1943; children—Charles, Richard James, Norma Lynn, Princess Ann, Ramona Joy, Dixie Lee, Dana Scott. Student pub. schs., Richey, Mont. Nurses aide McCone County Hosp., Circle, Mont., 1962-66, 74-76; owner Trail's End Cafe, Olympia, Wash., 1967-71; librarian Richey Pub. Library, Mont., 1980—. Mem. V.F.W. Aux., Am. Legion Aux. Methodist. Office: Richey Pub Library Richey MT 59259

KEELER, JANET BRADFORD, advertising executive; b. Northampton, Mass., Mar. 14, 1947; d. Howard Newton and Nancy Strobridge (Alger) S.; m. Lawrence Pierson Keeler III, Aug. 30, 1970 (div.). BA, U. Vt., 1969; MLS, Ind. U., 1972; M in Internat. Mgmt., Am. Grad. Sch. Internat. Mgmt., 1974. With N W Ayer, N.Y.C., 1975-89, sr. v.p., exec. acct. dir., 1988—. Mem. Beverly Yacht Club (Marion, Mass.). Republican. Congregationalist. Home: 1140 5th Ave #9C New York NY 10128 Office: NW Ayer Inc Worldwide Plaza 825 Eighth Ave New York NY 10019

KEELER, KATHLEEN MARIE, food service executive; b. Liberty, N.Y., Apr. 16, 1957; d. Kenneth Lynn and Betty Theresa (Pammer) K. AAS in Office Mgmt., Sullivan County Community Coll, 1977, AS in Bus. Adminstrn., 1979. Mgr., bookkeeper Kapito Bros.'s Tires, Monticello, N.Y., 1975-84; ophthalmological asst., med. bookkeeper Dr. Theodore N. Isseks, Liberty, 1981-86; gen. supr., mgr. Mercury Pizzeria & Restaurant, Monticello, 1986-87; v.p., gen. mgr. Dodge Inn Restaurant, Inc., Rock Hill, N.Y., 1987—. Instr. water safety advanced lifesaving courses ARC, Monticello, 1980—; volleyball referee for area high schs., 1979-80. Mem. NAFE, Phi Theta Kappa. Methodist. Home: Box 110 Rock Hill NY 12775 Office: Dodge Inn Restaurant Inc 18 Lake Louise Marie Rd Rock Hill NY 12775

KEELER, MARIAN RITA, credit union executive; b. Cambridge, Mass., Apr. 26, 1930; d. Everett O. and Margaret E. (MacLean) Misaner; children: Joan R. Hoysradt, Fred R. Hoysradt, Jean R. Hoysradt. Student, Bentley Sch. Acctg. and Fin., Boston, 1949. Mgr., treas. Manchester (Mass.) Town Employees Fed. Credit Union, 1969-84; mgr. Beverly (Mass.) Mcpl. Employees Fed. Credit Union, 1984-87; pres., chief exec. officer Stoneham (Mass.) Mcpl. Employeess Fed. Credit Union, 1987—. Mem. Mass. Credit Union Assn. (sec. Roy F. Bergengren chpt. 1979—, bd. dirs. 1989—), Lions (treas. 1990). Roman Catholic. Home: PO Box 59 Manchester MA 01944 Office: Stoneham Mcpl Employees Fed Credit Union 40 Pine St Stoneham MA 02180

KEELEY, PAMELA ANN, artist; b. Springfield, Ill., July 18, 1950; d. Richard Eugene and Mary Ann (Puckett) K.; 1 child, Celeste Erin Cole. Grad. in nursing, St. John's Hosp., Springfield, 1972; BFA, Cornish Coll. Arts, Seattle, 1988; MA in Fine Art with distinction, U. N.Mex., 1990. RN, Ill. Staff nurse St. John's Hosp., 1972-73, Meml. Med. Ctr., Springfield, 1973-76, St. Joseph's Hosp.-U. Colo. Med. Ctr., Denver, 1976-77, Swedish Hosp., Seattle, 1977-78; pvt. office nurse, tchr. Seattle, 1978-79; staff nurse, rsch. coord. U. Wash. Hosp. and Sch. Medicine, Seattle, 1980-88; tchr. art Albuquerque Pub. Schs. Community Edn., 1989; teaching asst. sculpture dept. U. N.Mex., Albuquerque, 1989—. Author: The Rest of Your Life, 1988 (Gallery award ASA 1988). Nurse vol. Cath. Relief Svcs., Kamput Refugee Camp, Thailand, 1980; co-founder Springfield Gay Liberation, 1972-75, Colo. 1st Feminist Credit Union, Denver, 1976; mem. Ill. Gays for Legis. Action, 1974; co-dir. Lesbian Mothers Nat. Def. Fund, Seattle, 1977. Emily Morse scholar Cornish Coll., Seattle, 1986-87, Carl Jung scholar, 1987. Democrat. Home: 113 B Princeton SE Albuquerque NM 87106

KEEN, BRENDA DENNISTON, lawyer; b. Ft. Smith, Ark., Dec. 5, 1949; d. James Pritchard and Era Erline (Jones) D.; m. Dean Edward Keen, June 23, 1973 (dec. June 1990); 1 child, Duncan Denniston. BA, U. Houston, 1972, JD magna cum laude, 1975. Bar: Tex. 1975, U.S. Dist. Ct. (so. dist.) Tex. 1975. Assoc. Haynes & Fullenweider, P.L.C., Houston, 1975-79, v.p., ptnr., 1979-87; ptnr., officer Wallis & Keen, P.C., Houston, 1988—. Contbr. articles to legal publs. Fellow Am. Acad. Matrimonial Lawyers (treas. Tex. chpt. 1989—), Tex. Bar Found., Houston Bar Found.; mem. State Bar Tex. (family law coun. 1989—). Roman Catholic. Office: Wallis and Keen PC One Riverway Ste 2525 Houston TX 77056

KEEN, CHARLOTTE ELIZABETH, marine geophysicist, researcher; b. Halifax, N.S., Can., June 22, 1943; d. Murray Alexander and Elizabeth Randell (Cobb) Davidson; m. Michael J. Keen, May 11, 1963 (div.). B.Sc. with 1st class honors, Dalhousie U., Halifax, 1964, M.Sc. with 1st class honors, 1966; Ph.D., Cambridge U., (Eng.), 1970. Research scientist Atlantic Oceanographic Lab., Energy, Mines, Resources, Dartmouth, N.S., 1970-74, Geol. Survey of Can., Atlantic Geosci. Centre, Dartmouth, 1972—; chmn. Can. Nat. Com. Lithosphere; mem. Can. Nat. Com. Internat. Union Geol. Scis., Geodesy and Geophysics, Iternat. Commn. Marine Geology. Contbr. articles to sci. jours. Recipient Young Scientist medal Atlantic Provinces Inter-Univ. Commn. Sci., 1977. Fellow Royal Soc. Can., Geol. Assn. Can. (past pres.'s medal 1979), Am. Geophys. Union; mem. Can. Geophys. Union. Anglican. Home: 9 Wenlock Grove, Halifax, NS Canada B3P 1P6 Office: Atlantic Geosci Ctr, Bedford Inst Oceanography, Dartmouth, NS Canada B2Y 4A2

KEEN, MARIA ELIZABETH, academic administrator; b. Chgo., Aug. 19, 1918; d. Harold Fremont and Mary Eileen Honore (Dillon) K. AB, U. Chgo., 1941; postgrad., U. Wyo., summer 1943; MA, U. Ill., 1949; postgrad., U. Mich., 1957. Tchr. high sch. Wyo., 1942-43, Mich., 1943-44; tchr. Am. Coll. for Women, Istanbul, Turkey, 1944-47; mem. faculty U. Ill., Urbana, 1967-88, prof. emerita, 1988—. Mem. Champaign Community Devel. Com.; com. mem. YWCA, YMCA. Mem. AAUP (treas.), Animal Protection Inst., Defenders of Wildlife, LWV, Nat. Assn. Fgn. Student Advisors, Am. Inst. Biol. Scis., Nat. Council Tchr. Educators, U. Ill. Athletic Assn. (sec., dir.), Ont. Geneal. Soc., AAAS, Orton Dyslexia Soc., Phi Kappa Epsilon. Baptist. Home: 608 S Edwin St Champaign IL 61821

KEENAN, BEVERLY OWEN, customer service professional; b. Medicine Lodge, Kans., July 29, 1948; d. Neil Harrington and Bertie Geneva (Nurse) Owen; m. Donald Joseph Livingston, Jan. 29, 1963 (div. Mar. 1975); children: Virginia, Rebecca, Wesley, Carrie, Lee; m. Theodore Wayne Keenan, Apr. 23, 1975; 1 child, James. Student, Okla. State U., 1978-79. Field rsch. person Nat. Analysts, Phila., 1977-79; agt. Daily Oklahoman, Stillwater, Okla., 1979-80; distbr. Rocky Mountain News, Denver, 1980-82, dist. mgr., 1982-88; nat. sales dir. Frame Enterprises, Oklahoma City, 1988; customer svc. rep. MCI Telecommunications Corp., 1989—; leader seminars, 1986—. Supporting mem. Women's Crisis Ctr., Castle Rock, Colo., 1986-87; speaker Women in Transition Groups, Littleton, Colo., 1987-89. Mem. Nat. Assn. Female Execs., Mensa. Club: Appaloosa Horse (Moscow, Idaho).

KEENAN, JOAN MARIE, clinical laboratory manager; b. Lorain, Ohio, Jan. 31, 1949; d. Stanley Joseph Sobieski and Mary Elizabeth Sklarek; m. Thomas Howard Keenan, Feb. 5, 1972; children: Mary Catherine, Carolyn Alice. BS, Notre Dame Coll., South Euclid, 1970; MS, Cleve. State U., 1972. Clin. chemist Lorain Community Hosp., 1970-71; chemistry supr. St. John's Hosp., Cleve., 1971-77; clin. chemist All Children's Hosp., St. Petersburg, 1977-78; chemistry supr. HCA Largo (Fla.) Med. Ctr. Hosp., 1978-79, asst. lab. mgr., 1979-83, lab. mgr., 1983—; advisory St. Petersburg Jr. Coll. Med. Lab. Tech. Prog. St. Petersburg, Fla., 1984--, HCA Distributed Info. Systems Nashville, 1987--. Supr. Licensure State Fla. Mem. Am. Soc. Clin. Pathologists, Clin. Lab. Mgr. Assn. Roman Catholic. Home: 3269 Hyde Park Dr Clearwater FL 34621 Office: HCA Largo Med Ctr Hosp 201 14th St SW Largo FL 34640

KEENAN, KATHLEEN MARGARET, biostatistician, educator; b. St. Paul, May 24, 1934; d. Robert James and Margaret (Spoden) K. BA, St. Catherine Coll., St. Paul, 1956; MS, U. Minn., 1958, PhD, 1964. Asst. prof. U. Minn., St. Paul, 1964-68; asst. prof. U. Minn., Mpls., 1968-69, assoc. prof. Sch. Dentistry, 1969—. Contbr. sci. articles to profl. jours. Am. Pub.

Health Assn. fellow, 1971. Mem. AAAS, Am. Genetic Assn., Am. Soc. Human Genetics, Am. Statis. Assn., Biometric Soc., N.Y. Acad. Scis., Minn. Acad. Sci. (pres. 1977-78), Sigma Xi. Office: Sch Dentistry U Minn 515 Delaware St SE Minneapolis MN 55455

KEENAN, RETHA ELLEN VORNHOLT, nurse, educator; b. Solon, Iowa, Aug. 15, 1934; d. Charles Elias and Helen Maurine (Konicek) Vornholt; BSN, State U. Iowa, 1955; MSN, Calif. State U., Long Beach, 1978; m. David James Iverson, June 17, 1956; children: Scott, Craig ; m. Roy Vincent Keenan, Jan. 5, 1980. Publ. health nurse City of Long Beach, 1970-73, Hosp. Home Care, Torrance, Calif., 1973-75; patient care coord. Hillhaven, L.A., 1975-76; mental health cons. InterCity Home Health, L.A., 1978-79; instr. Community Coll. Dist., L.A., 1979-87; instr. nursing El Camino Coll., Torrance, 1981-86; instr. nursing Chapman Coll., Orange, Calif., 1982, Mt. Saint Mary's Coll., 1986-87; cons., pvt. practice, Rancho Palos Verdes, Calif., 1987-89, L.A., 1989—. Contbg. author: American Journal of Nursing Question and Answer Book for Nursing Boards Review, 1984, Nursing Care Planning Guides for Psychiatric and Mental Health Care, 1987-88, Nursing Care Planning Guides for Children, 1987, Nursing Care Planning Guides for Adults, 1988, Nursing Care Planning Guides for Critically Ill Adults, 1988. Cert. nurse practitioner adult and mental health, 1979; mem. Assistance League of San Pedro, Palos Verdes, Calif. Bd. dirs. Luth. Ch. NIMH grantee, 1977-78. Mem. AAUW, Nurses Assn., Calif. Nurses Assn., Am. Nurses Assn. Coun. on Psychiatric and Mental Health Nursing, Phi Delta Gamma, Sigma Theta Tau, Phi Kappa Phi, Delta Zeta (bd. dirs.). Republican. Avocations: travel, writing, reading. Home: 27849 Longhill Dr Rancho Palos Verdes CA 90274

KEENAN-ABILAY, GEORGIA ANN, service representative; b. Denver, Oct. 3, 1936; d. Lawrence Edward and Helen Kathleen (Gray) K.; m. Charles Henry Dupree, May 31, 1958 (div. Nov. 1977); children: Phoenix, Therese, Mark, John; m. Joseph D. Abilay, Nov. 26, 1988. BA, Regis Coll., 1968; MA, St. Thomas U., 1978. With reservations United Airlines, Denver, 1956-57; stewardess Trans World Airlines, Chgo., 1957-58; in elem. edn. Notre Dame Sch., Denver, 1969-72; dir. religious edn. Notre Dame Parish, Denver, 1972-77, Archdiocese Denver, 1977-80; v.p., treas. Kilfinane and Cook, Denver, 1980-82; dir. human resources Cosmopolitan Hotel, Denver, 1982-83, Kaanapali Beach Hotel, Lahaina, Hawaii, 1983-85, Royal Lahaina Resort, Hawaii, 1985—; corp. dir. human resources Hawaiian Hotels and Resorts, Lahaina, 1988; trainer Amfac Hotels and Resorts, Hawaii, 1984-86; vice chmn. Maui Hotel Assn., 1987; bd. dirs. Project 714, Lahaina, 1987. Bd. dirs. Archdiocesan Women's Bd., Denver, 1981-83, Passages, Denver, 1980-83, Maui Econ. Devel. Bd., Kahalui, 1984; chairperson Charity Walk, 1984-86. Named Handicapped Employer of Yr., State of Hawaii, 1987. Mem. Council Hawaii Hotels, Am. Soc. Personnel Assn. Club: Distributive Edn. of Am. (Hawaii) (bd. dirs. 1984—). Home: 4002 Mahinahina Lahaina HI 96761 Office: Royal Lahaina Resort 2780 Kekaa Dr Lahaina HI 96761

KEENE, EVELYN, advertising executive; b. Chelsea, Mass., Oct. 18, 1922; d. Abraham and Ida (Winer) Brown; m. Alfred M. Keene (dec.); children: Judith Keene Greenspan, Leila, Michael A. BS in Journalism cum laude, Boston U., 1945. Gen. assignment reporter UPI, Boston, 1945-55, Boston Globe, Boston, 1968-75; exec. Keene Advt. Specialities Inc., Boston, 1980—. Mem. Hadassah, Boston; vol. Combined Jewish Philanthropies of Boston. Mem. Charles River Watershed Assn. Democrat. Home: 33 Pond Ave #B203 Brookline MA 02146 Office: Keene Advt 137 South St Boston MA 02111

KEENE, MARGARET GIRTHEL, retired educator; b. Haysi, Va., Nov. 8, 1915; d. Perry Evans Gilbert and Fannie Lillian Pucket; m. Cecil Edward Keene, Sept. 2, 1936 (dec. July 1989); children: Jama K. Lori, Andrea K. Wynegar, John Gilbert. BS, East Tenn. State U., 1964. Elem. tchr. Bristol (Tenn.) City System, 1964-83. Mem. AAUW (chair legis. program 1988-90), Bristol Tenn. Retired Tchr.'s Assn. (informative and protective svcs. com. chmn. 1985-89), Republican Women's Orgn. Baptist. Home: 616 Greenfield Pl Bristol TN 37620

KEENE-BURGESS, RUTH FRANCES, army official; b. South Bend, Ind., Oct. 7, 1948; d. Seymour and Sally (Morris) K.; m. Leslie U. Burgess, Jr., Oct. 1, 1983; children: Michael Leslie, David William, Elizabeth Sue, Rachael Lee. BS, Ariz. State U., 1970; MS, Fairleigh Dickinson U., 1978; grad., U.S. Army Command and Gen. Staff Coll., 1986. Inventory mgmt. specialist U.S. Army Electronics Command, Phila., 1970-74, U.S. Army Communications-Electronics Material Readiness Command, Fort Monmouth, N.J., 1974-79; chief inventory mgmt. div. Crane (Ind.) Army Ammunition Activity, 1979-80; supply systems analyst Hdqrs. 60th Ordnance Group, Zweibruecken, Fed. Republic Germany, 1980-83; chief inventory mgmt. div. Crane (Ind.) Army Ammunition Activity, 1983-85, chief control div., 1985; inventory mgmt. specialist 200th Theater Army Material Mgmt. Ctr., Zweibruecken, 1985-88; analyst supply systems U.S. Armament, Munitions and Chem. Command, Rock Island, Ill., 1988-89; specialist logistics mgt. U.S. Army Info. Systems Command, Ft. Huachuca, Ariz., 1989—. Mem. Federally Employed Women (chpt. pres. 1979-80), NAFE, Soc. Logistics Engrs., Assn. Computing Machinery, Am. Soc. Public Adminstrn., Soc. Profl. and Exec. Women, Assn. Info. Systems Profls., AAAS, NOW. Democrat. Jewish. Home: 4916 W Pinchot Ave Phoenix AZ 85031

KEENER, LARKELYN, programmer/analyst consultant; b. Hollywood, Calif., May 29, 1945; d. Larkin Vernon and Evelyn June (Meyers) Mulkey; m. Ted Anthony Keener, Aug. 18, 1968. BA in Anthropology, U. Calif., Berkeley, 1968. Jr. programmer The Svc. Bur. Corp., San Jose, 1969-70; assoc. programmer IBM Sys. Devel. Div., San Jose, 1970-71; programmer/analyst IBM DP Div., Portland, 1971-77; owner Swallow Ridge Computer Svc., Bend, Oreg., 1981—. Mem. Cen. Oreg. Llama Assn. (sec. 1990—), Tech. oriented Businesses of Cen. Oreg., AAUW (v.p. 1983-88). Democrat. Office: Swallow Ridge Computer Svc PO Box 7111 Bend OR 97708

KEENER, LINDA MARIE, computer company executive; b. Rapid City, S.D., Jan. 28, 1953; d. Kenneth Read and Ann Elaine (Backer) Hankins; m. Douglas Rex Keener, June 29, 1974; children: Kathryn Diane and Brian Douglas (twins). Cert. in bus. adminstrn., Midwest Bus. Coll., Ft. Collins, Colo., 1973; BSBA, U. Colo., Colorado Springs, 1979. Various adminstrv. positions Hewlett-Packard Co., Colorado Springs, 1974-79, mktg. assoc., 1979-80, buyer, 1980-82, supr., 1982-83, mgr. prodn. sect., 1983-86, mgr. prodn., 1986-88; mgr. prodn. control Cray Rsch. Inc., Colorado Springs, 1988-89; mgr. prodn. sect. Hewlett Packard Co., Loveland, Colo., 1989—. Loaned exec. United Way, 1983; vol. Colorado Springs Jr. League, 1986—.

KEENEY, DEBRA ANN, marketing executive, director; b. N.Y.C., July 8, 1954; d. Thomas William and Mariacivita (Vellucci) K.; m. Richard Lee Narburgh, Feb. 28, 1981; 1 child, Christopher Narburgh. BA, Rider Coll., 1976; MA, New Sch. of Social Rsch., 1980. Rsch. assoc. Opinion Rsch. Corp., Princeton, N.J., 1979-82; account exec. McGraw-Hill Rsch., N.Y.C., 1982-85; prin. DAK Rsch., Ewindsor, N.J., 1985-87; dir. telephone interviewing ctr. McGraw-Hill, Hightstown, N.J., 1987-89; dir. market rsch. Datapro/McGraw-Hill, Delran, N.J., 1989—; cons. SBA, Trenton, N.J., 1986-87; instr. SBA, Mercer County Coll., Trenton, 1986-87. Moderator Youth Speaks Up, Princeton, 1980-88. Mem. Am. Mktg. Assn., Mktg. Rsch. Assn., Rider Coll. Alumni Assn. (bd. dirs. Lawrenceville, N.J. chpt. 1986—). Roman Catholic. Office: Datapro 600 Delran Pkwy Delran NJ 08075

KEENON, UNA H. R., municipal court judge; b. Nashville, Dec. 30, 1933; d. Charles and Mary (Gowins) Harris; m. Harold K. Miller, Dec. 18, 1976; 1 child, Gregory M. Rhodes. BA, Tenn. State U., 1953; JD cum laude, Cleve.-Marshall Law Sch., 1975. Bar: Ohio 1975, U.S. Dist. Ct. (no. dist.) Ohio 1977. Social worker Davidson County Welfare Dept., Nashville, 1953-57, Cuyahoga County Welfare Dept., Cleve., 1957-60; tchr. Cleve. Bd. Edn., 1960-74; lawyer Legal Aid Soc., Cleve., 1975-78; atty.-in-charge juvenile div. Pub. Defender, Cleve., 1978-80; ptnr. Johnson, Keenon & Blackmon, Cleve., 1980-83; mng. atty. UAW Legal Svcs., Cleve., 1983-86; judge East Cleveland (Ohio) Mcpl. Ct., 1986—; coord. juvenile project Criminal Justice Coord. Com., Cleve., 1976-78. Founding pres. Black Women Polit. Action Com., Cleve., 1982-86; trustee Cleve. Treatment Ctr., 1984—, Cuyahoga County Pub. Libr., Cleve., 1985—, Phyllis Wheatley Assn., Cleve., 1987—, YWCA, East Cleveland, 1990. Recipient Leodis Harris Advocacy award Criminal Justice Coun., Cleve., 1981, Gov.'s Spl. Recognition award, Ohio Gov., 1987, 89, Meritorious Svc. award East Cleveland Black Police Officers Assn., 1988-89, Exemplary Svc. award Phyllis Wheatley Assn., 1990. Mem. Assn. Mcpl./County Judges (trustee), Mcpl. Judges Assn., Kiwanis Club East Cleveland (svc. award 1989), Alpha Kappa Alpha. Democrat. Baptist. Home: 16101 Cleviden Rd East Cleveland OH 44112 Office: East Cleveland Mcpl Ct 14340 Euclid Ave East Cleveland OH 44112

KEEP, JUDITH N., federal judge; b. 1944. B.A., Scripps Coll., 1966; J.D., U. San Diego, 1970. With Defenders Inc., 1971-73; pvt. practice law, 1973-76; asst. U.S. atty. Calif., 1976; judge Mcpl. Ct., San Diego, 1976-80, U.S. Dist. Ct. (so. dist.) Calif., San Diego, 1980—. Office: US Dist Ct 940 Front St San Diego CA 92189*

KEEPING, SHARON MARIE, programmer, analyst; b. Yonkers, N.Y., Nov. 1, 1954; d. Henry Charles and Marietta (Galgano) K.;m. Ron M. Davenport, June 15, 1974 (div. Aug. 1977); 1 child, Christopher Ron Davenport. AAS, Pitt Community Coll., 1988. Programmer Hamilton Beach, Inc., Washington, N.C., 1988-90; programmer/analyst AS/400 City of Greenville, N.C., 1990—.

KEESHEN, KATHLEEN KEARNEY, public relations executive; b. N.Y.C., Dec. 4, 1937; d. James William and Hannah "Pauline" (Mansfield) Kearney; 1 child (by previous marriage), John Christopher Day; m. Walt Keeshen Jr.; stepchildren: Michael Patrick Keeshen, Walt John Keeshen III, Kathleen Marie Keeshen, William Thomas Keeshen, Ralph Timothy Keeshen. BA in English, U. Md., 1959, MA in Journalism, 1973, PhD in Am. Studies, 1983; postgrad., Stanford U., Belmont, Calif., 1988—. Cert. profl. sec. Congl., legal, med., acad., corp. sec. various, East and Midwest, 1954-63; sec. Washington Systems Ctr. IBM, Bethesda, Gaithersburg, Md., 1963-64; pers. adminstr. IBM, Bethesda, 1964-66, mgr. suggestion dept., 1966-70, communications specialist, 1970-73; lab. communications mgr. Systems Communications Div. IBM, Manassas, Va., 1974-76; communications staff corp. hdqrs. IBM, Armonk, N.Y., 1977-83; communications and community rels. mgr. Almaden Rsch. Ctr. IBM, San Jose, Calif., 1983—. Contbr. articles to profl. jours.; lectr. in field. Adv. bd. San Jose Pub. Libr. Found., 1988, Friends of San Jose Pub. Libr., 1987—, Silicon Valley Info. Ctr., 1986—; mem. exec. com. Friends of San Jose Pub. Libr. 1989 Spring Gala Benefit. Mem. Am. Journalism Historians Assn., Assn. for Edn. in Journalism and Mass Communications, Women in Communications, Am. Studies Assn., Dean's First Edition Club, Coll. of Journalism, U. Md., Sigma Delta Chi, Calif. Writers Club, Alpha Xi Delta, San Jose Profl. Womens Literary Assn. Office: IBM Almaden Rsch Ctr 650 Harry Rd San Jose CA 95037

KEESLING, KAREN RUTH, lawyer; b. Wichita, Kans., July 9, 1946; d. Paul W. and Ruth (Sharp) K. BA, Ariz. State U., 1968, MA, 1970; JD, Georgetown U., 1981. Bar: Va. 1981, Fla. 1981. Asst. dean of women U. Kans., Lawrence, 1970-72; exec. sec., sec.'s adv. com. on rights and responsibilities of women HEW, Washington, 1972-74; dir. White House Office of Women's Programs, Washington, 1974-77; head civil rights and equal opportunity sect., Gov. Div., Congl. Rsch. Svc. Libr. Congress, Washington, 1977-80; legis. aide Sen. Nancy Kassebaum, Washington, 1979-81; mem. pers. office staff Office of Pres.-elect, Washington, Jan. 1981; pvt. practice Falls Church, Va., 1981-88; dep. for Equal Opportunity Dept. AF, Washington, 1981-82, dep. asst. sec. Manpower Res. Affairs and Installations, 1982-83; prin. dep. asst. sec. Manpower Res. Affairs, 1983-87; prin. dep. asst. sec. Readiness Support Dept. AF, Washington, 1987-88, prin. dep. asst. sec. Manpower and Res. Affairs, 1988, asst. sec. Manpower and Res. Affairs, 1988-89; pvt. practice Falls Church, Va., 1990—. Mem. Nat. Fedn. Republican Women's Club, Washington, 1975, Nat. Women's Polit. Caucus, Washington, 1980. Named one of Ten Outstanding Young Women of Am., 1975; recipient Ariz. State U. Alumni Achievement award, 1976, Elizabeth Boyer award Women's Equity Action League, 1986, Meritorious Civilian award USAF, 1987, Woman of Distinction award Nat. Conf. Coll. Women, Student Leaders and Women of Distinction, 1988, Exeptional Civilian Svc. award USAF, 1988. Mem. Va. Bar Assn., Fla. Bar Assn., Va. Fedn. Bus. and Profl. Women's Clubs (2d v.p. 1987-88, 1st v.p. 1988-89, pres.-elect 1989-90, pres. 1990—), No. Va. Women Atty.'s Assn. (steering com. 1990—), Va. Bus. and Profl. Women's Found. (bd. trustees 1985—), The Women's Inst. Inc. (adv. coun. 1985—), Outstanding Young Women of Am. (bd. advisors 1983—), US Com. for the UNIFEM (gen. counsel 1983—), P.E.O. (Wichita), Pi Beta Phi. Home: 3504 Stoneybrae Dr Falls Church VA 22044 Office: 252 N Washington St Falls Church VA 22046

KEETON, KATHY MERLE, publisher; b. Republic of South Africa, Feb. 17, 1939; d. Keith and Queenie K.; m. Jan. 17, 1988. Student, Royal Ballet Sch., London. Vice chmn. Gen. Media Internat., N.Y.C., 1969—; Pres. Omni mag., N.Y.C., 1978—, Longevity Mag. Author: (with Yvonne Baskin) Woman of Tomorrow, 1985; exec. producer TV program Omni: Visions of Tomorrow, The New Frontier. Active Fund for the Aging (City Meals on Wheels), Corp. Blood Drive, Nat. Coalition Against Censorship. Mem. AIAA, Amateur Astronomers Assn., Am. Space Found., Robotics Internat. SME, Space Generation Found., L-5 Soc. Office: Omni Mag 1965 Broadway New York NY 10023

KEGLER, BRENDA JEAN, speech/language pathologist; b. Columbia, S.C., Feb. 24, 1949; d. William Arledge and Mary (Shelton) Arledge Murray; m. Clarence Cornell Kegler, May 8, 1971; children: Kimbrelly Nicole, Clarence Cornell II. BS, S.C. State U., Orangeburg, 1971; MS, Winthrop Coll., 1981. Speech/language pathologist Richland County Dist. I, Columbia, S.C., 1971-72, Chester County (S.C.) Schs., 1972-74, Rock Hill (S.C.) Sch. Dist. III, 1980-89, New Hanover County Schs., Wilmington, N.C., 1989—. Mem. AAUW (chmn. edn. found. program 1983), N.C. Assn. Augmentative Communication, Speech/Language and Hearing Area Resource Exchange, Newcomer's Club (sec. 1981), Delta Sigma (corresponding sec. Rock Hill chpt. 1984). Democrat. Methodist. Home: 2215 Sterling Pl Wilmington NC 28403

KEGLEY, JACQUELYN ANN, philosophy educator; b. Conneaut, Ohio, July 18, 1938; d. Steven Paul and Gertrude Evelyn (Frank) Kovacevic; m. Charles William Kegley, June 12, 1964; children: Jacquelyn Ann, Stephen Lincoln Luther. BA cum laude, Allegheny Coll., 1960; MA summa cum laude, Rice U., 1964; PhD, Columbia U., 1971. Asst. prof. philosophy Calif. State U., Bakersfield, 1973-77, assoc. prof., 1977-81, prof., 1981—; vis. prof. U. Philippines, Quezon City, 1966-68; grant project dir. Calif. Council Humanities, 1977, project dir. 1980, 82; mem. work group on ethics Am. Colls. of Nursing, Washington, 1984-86. Author: Introduction to Logic, 1978; editor: Humanistic Delivery of Services to Families, 1982, Education for the Handicapped, 1982; mem. editorial bd. Jour. Philosophy in Lit., 1979-84; contbr. articles to profl. jours. Bd. dirs. Bakersfield Mental Health Assn., 1982-84. Mem. N.Y. Acad. Scis., Philosophy of Sci. Assn., Soc. Advancement Am. Phil. soc. (chmn. Pacific div. 1979-83, nat. exec. com. 1974-79), Philosophy Soc., Soc. Interdisciplinary Study of Mind, Am. Philosophical Assn., Dorian Soc., Phi Beta Kappa. Democrat. Lutheran. Home: 7312 Kroll Way Bakersfield CA 93309 Office: Calif State U Dept Philosophy & Religious Studies Bakersfield CA 93309

KEHLE, MARY JANE, psychologist; b. Gary, Ind., Jan. 13, 1937; d. John Richard and Hattie Irene (Cleckner) Wicoff; m. A. Paul Kehle, Dec. 20, 1958; children: Elizabeth Kay, Deborah Diane, Anna Maria. Diploma in nursing, Presbyn.-St. Luke's Hosp., Chgo., 1958; BA, Stephens Coll., Columbia, Mo., 1976; MA, U. No. Colo., 1978; PhD, Ariz. State U., 1985. RN, Ill.; lic. psychologist, Ariz. Staff nurse Ravenswood Hosp., Chgo., 1958-59, office of pvt. practice physician, Chgo., 1959-60; sch. nurse Perry Sch., Phoenix, 1962-64; counselor Phoenix Meml. Hosp., 1979-80; instr. Glendale (Ariz.) Community Coll., 1978-80; pvt. practice Phoenix, 1978—; presenter seminars on human sexuality. Author: You're Nearly There, 1973, In the Middle, 1987. Mem. Am. Psychol. Assn., Am. Bd. Med. Psychotherapists, Am. Bd. Sexology (diplomate), Am. Assn. Sex Educators, Therapists and Counselors (cert.). Presbyterian. Office: 1901 E Thomas Rd Ste 208 Phoenix AZ 85016

KEHLEY, DEBORAH ANNE, merchandiser; b. Queens, N.Y., May 11, 1966; d. Clifford Ray and Helen Josephine (Narbut) K. AS, Burlington County Coll., 1986; BS, Monmouth Coll., 1988. Office asst. Rapid Lift Svc. Co., Inc., Delair, N.J., 1985-89; mdse. mgr. J.C. Penney Co., Trenton, N.J., 1989—. Mem. NAFE, Delta Phi Epsilon Alumni. Republican. Roman Catholic. Home: 17 E Woodcrest Ave Maple Shade NJ 08052 Office: JC Penney Co Rte 1 at Quakerbridge Rd Trenton NJ 08052

KEHOE, SUSAN, automotive training specialist; b. Cleve., Dec. 5, 1947; d. John William and Mary Margaret (Swicia) Kehoe; m. Gerald Nicholas, May 15, 1970 (div.); children: Patricia, Mark. BA, U. Detroit, 1970; MA, Oakland U., 1980, PhD, 1983. Cert. secondary tchr., Mich. Trainer ESL Utica Community Schs., Mich., 1974-78; coord. program Oakland Univ., Rochester, Mich., 1980-83; adj. prof. mktg. Wayne State Univ., Detroit, 1983-85, U. Mich., Ann Arbor, 1984-85; pres., owner The Kehoe Group, Birmingham, Mich., 1983-89; trainer, program designer Gen. Motors, Detroit, 1984-89; trainer, cons. Nat. Steel, Ecorse, Mich., 1984-89; tng. specialist electronics div. Ford Motor Co., Ypsilanti, Mich., 1989—. Presenter Nat. Reading Conf., 1981, 83, Internat. Reading Assn., 1982, Am. Edn. Rsch. Assn., 1982, Conf. on Coll. Composition, 1984; mktg. com. Detroit Symphony Orch. Mem. Am. Soc. For Tng. and Devel., Detroit Soc. Clubs. Club: Econ. of Detroit. Avocations: art, travel, music. Home: 3858 Lincoln Dr Birmingham MI 48010 Office: Ford Motor Co Electronics div PO Box 412 Ypsilanti MI 48197

KEHOE, VERONICA MCAULEY, producer, actress; d. Martin J. and Veronica M. (McCarthy) Lally; m. John P. Kehoe, Dec. 1, 1984, 1 child, Allise S. McAuley; stepchildren: Maura, John, Kevin, Brendan. Student, Marymount Manhattan Coll., 1978, 83-84. Exec. dir., founder The Gypsy Road Company, Inc., N.Y.C., 1987—; founder, exec. dir. The Twenty-First Century Playwrights Festival, 1989—; co-founder, mem., bd. dirs. Kehoe, White, Savage & Co., Inc., 1969; founding mem., bd. dirs. Theatre XII Repertory, ESP Repertory; mem. Raft Theatre, N.Y.C.; founding mem. Eastside/Westside Repertory, L.A. Founding mem. N.Y. Women's Found. Mem. SAG, AFTRA, AEA, Am. Acad. Dramatic Arts (alumna 1976).

KEIFER, MARY CARTER, law educator; b. Charlottsville, Va., Sept. 21, 1946; d. Carter Lewis and Anne Harrison (Crathorne) Loth; m. John Louis Keifer, Aug. 29, 1970; children—Marcy, Lisa, Kate, Kristin. AB in Math., Converse Coll., 1968; JD, U. Va., 1971. Bar: Ohio 1971, U.S. Dist. Ct. 1974. Staff atty. Toledo Legal Aid Soc., 1971-74; assoc. prof. bus. law, mem. faculty senate Ohio U., Athens, 1974—. Contbr. papers to legal procs. Mem. Athens City Recreation Bd., 1978-83, pres., 1980; mem. Athens City Bd. Edn., 1978—, pres., 1984; sec. bd. govs. J. Warren McClure Athens Edn. Found.; officer Athens Coop. Nursery Bd., 1975-77; bd. dirs. Athens Swim Club. Recipient Faculty-Staff Contbn. award Coll. Bus. Adminstrn. Ohio U, 1988. Mem. Ohio State Legal Services Assn. (trustee), Tri-State Bus. Law Assn. (pres.), Ohio State Bar Assn., Athens City Bar Assn. Presbyterian. Club: Athens Jr. Women's. Avocations: reading, lap swimming. Home: 201 Longview Heights Athens OH 45701 Office: Ohio U 216 Copeland Hall Athens OH 45701

KEIL, BEVERLY, human resources specialist; b. 1946. BS, Rochester Inst. Tech., 1968; MBA, SUNY, 1975. With Carborundum, Niagara Falls, N.Y., 1971-75; pers. mgr. Northwest Industries, Inc., Chgo., 1975-77, Olin Corp., Stanford, Conn., 1977-79; v.p., dir. human rels. Post-Newsweek Stas., Inc., 1979; dir. human resources Washington Post Co., 1979-86, v.p. human resources, 1986—. Office: Washington Post Co 1150 15th St NW Washington DC 20071*

KEINLEN, HELEN HORSLEY, educator; b. Lovell, Wyo., Mar. 11, 1927; d. William Watts and Glen (Croft) Horsley; m. Joseph Stanley Kienlen, Dec. 20, 1948; children: Jerome, Shelley, Kyle, Kent. AA, U. Utah, 1946; BS in Elem. Edn., U. Wyo., 1948; MS in special edn. reading, Fort Hays State U., 1965. Tchr. Lincoln Elem. Sch., Casper, Wyo., 1948-49, Stanton Sch., Laramie, Wyo., 1949-50, Worland Sch. System, 1951-85; dir. Reading Workshop, Hays, Kans., 1965; pres. Title III State Com., Cheyenne, Wyo., 1969-74; chmn. Wyo. State Gifted and Talented Edn. Com., Cheyenne, ž1972-76; presenter to Wyo. Elementary Tchrs., Worland, 1985-89. Den mother Boy Scouts of Am., Worland, Wyo., 1958, 1965; rep. women's club Fed. of Womens' Clubs, Worland, 1952-75; cancer edn. chmn. Am. Cancer Soc., Worland, 1970-74. Named Wyoming State Tchr. of Year, Wyo. Edn. Assn., Cheyenne, 1968; Outstanding Elem. Tchr of Am., 1974; Outstanding Woman of the Community, Bus. and Profl. Women's Assn., Worland, Wyo., 1989. Mem. AAUW (officer 1956-65), Internat. Educators Assn. (award com. 1984-85), Delta Kappa Gamma, (pres. 1980-82). Republican. Mormon. Home: 911 S 8th St Worland WY 82401

KEIRNAN, ELLEN LOUISE, paralegal specialist; b. Waukegan, Ill., Sept. 8, 1949; d. Thomas Sebastian and Rita Geraldine (Kelly) K.; m. William P. Sams, Aug. 4, 1972 (div. Dec. 1986). BA in English, Quincy Coll., 1971; MBA, Lake Forest Grad. Sch. Mgmt., Ill., 1984. Legal sec. Legal Referral Bur. of Lake County, Waukegan, 1971-73, paralegal, 1973-76; legal sec. Outboard Marine Corp., Waukegan, 1976-78, paralegal, 1978-82, paralegal specialist, 1982—. Mem. Waukegan Symphony Chorus, 1990; participant Explorer Scouts Career Devel., 1990. Mem. Ill. Paralegal Assn., Nat. Paralegal Assn., Women's Exec. Creative Alliance Network, Nat. Fedn. Paralegal Assocs., U.S. Golf Assn., Bonnie Brook Women's Golf Assn. Home: 928 N County St Waukegan IL 60085 Office: Outboard Marine Corp 100 Sea-Horse Dr Waukegan IL 60085

KEISER, KAREN LYNNE, health facility executive; b. Dayton, June 29, 1960; d. Charles William and Doris Eloise (Preston) Keiser. B.A., Oglethorpe U., Atlanta, 1983. Program coord. Muscular Dystrophy Assn., Atlanta, 1983-85, dist. dir., Palm Beach, Fla., 1985-86; dir. women's health ctr. Ga. Bapt. Med. Ctr., Atlanta, 1986-88; dir. mktg. Psychiat. Inst. Atlanta, 1988-89; dir. mktg. Brawner Hosp., Atlanta, 1989—. Author, editor: MDA Monthly News, 1985-86. Recipient Oglethorpe award Student Govt. Assn., 1982. Mem. planning com. Atlanta Dogwood Festival. Mem. Am. Mktg. Assn., Nat. Bus. Assn. Female Execs., Am. Soc. for Hosp. Mktg. and Pub. Rels., Jr. C. of C., Women's C. of C. (chmn. community devel. com. 1988-89, bd. dirs. 1989—), Toastmasters, Atlanta Track Club. Roman Catholic. Avocations: running, outdoor sports, horseback riding. Home: 8372-R Roswell Rd Atlanta GA 30350

KEISER, NANCY EYMAN, management consultant; b. Dallas, May 11, 1947; d. Leland Virgil and Alma Nadine (Handley) Ingram; m. Terry David Eyman, July 18, 1966 (div. 1976); children: Laura Kathleen, Michael David; m. Larry Harold Keiser, June 24, 1978; 1 child, Kimberly Beth. BA magna cum laude, Harding U., 1970; MS, U. North Tex., 1980. Edn. and tng. coord. Cen. Tex. Coun. of Govts., Belton, Tex., 1973-78; community edn. coord. Tex. Dept. Human Resources, Belton, 1978-79; communications coord. Human Resource Ctr., U. Tex., Arlington, 1980-81; asst. area dir. Tex. Commn. on Alcoholism, Arlington, 1981-83; dir. Corp. Dymanmics, Ft. Worth, Tex., 1984; mgmt. trainer Tex. Instruments, Dallas, 1984-85; communication coord. CPC Arlington-Gen. Motors, Arlington, 1985-87; sr. cons. Baker & Co., Dallas, 1987-89; ind. tng. and process cons. Arlington, 1989—; cons. long range steering com., St. Andrew Christian Ch., Arlington, 1989. Contbr. articles to Esprit mag. Charter mem. St. Andrew Christian Ch., 1989; bd. dirs. Theatre Arlington, 1980-81; mem. Arlington Social Svc. Task Force, 1986. Mem. USO Tour Group, Harding U., Searcy, Ark. 1966. Mem. Am. Soc. Tng. and Devel., Alpha Chi. Disciples of Christ. Home and Office: 2321 Briarwood Blvd Arlington TX 76013

KEISTLER, BETTY LOU, accountant, tax consultant; b. St. Louis, Jan. 2, 1935; d. John William and Gertrude Marie (Lewis) Chancellor; m. George E. Keistler, Aug. 3, 1957 (div. Mar. 1981); children: Kathryn M. Morrissey, Deborah J. Birsinger. AS, St. Louis U., 1956; BBA, U. Mo., 1986. Asst. treas. A. G. Edwards & Sons, St. Louis, 1956-57; owner, mgr. B. L. Keistler & Assoc., St. Louis, 1969-82; contr. Family Resource Ctr., Inc., St. Louis, 1982-87; registered rep. Equitable Fin. Svcs., Mo., 1987; bus. mgr. Mo. Bapt. Coll., St. Louis, 1987-88, Barnes Hosp. Sch. of Nursing, St. Louis, 1989; cons. in field, St. Louis, 1982—; registered rep. Equitable Fin. Services, 1987—. Treas. Pkwy. Townhouses At Village Green, Chesterfield, Mo., 1985-87; exec. core United Way Greater St. Louis, 1984—; mem. U. Mo. Alumni Assn., 1987—; rep. to the bd. alumni assn. U. Mo., St. Louis., 1988—. Scholar Phillip Morris Corp., St. Louis, 1982-84. Mem. Am. Bus. Women Assn. (v.p. 1978-79, pres. 1979-80, treas. nat. conv. 1981, Woman of

Yr. 1979-80), Am. Soc. Women Accts., Ind. Accts. of Mo. (sec. 1978-79, v.p. 1980-81, state sec. 1978-79), St. Louis Women's Commerce Assn., 1904 World's Fair Soc., Internat. Platform Assn., Am. Biog. Inst. (hon. advisor, rsch. bd. advisors nat. div. 1989), Alpha Sigma Lambda (life, treas. 1985-87), NAFE. Republican. Baptist. Home: 14524 Bantry Ln Chesterfield MO 63017

KEITH, JUANITA ORTON, health education writer, consultant; b. St. Cloud, Minn., Dec. 2, 1917; d. Herbert Oliver and Myrtice Ellen (Cooley) Orton; m. Donald Johnson Keith, June 20, 1942; children: Carol Jean, Ned Orton. AA, Des Moines Area Community, 1974; BFA, Drake U., 1976, MS, 1986. Sec. Rex Granite Co., St. Cloud, 1936-37; acct. Northwestern Bell Telephone Co., Mpls., 1937-44; mgr. Telco Credit Union, Mpls., 1945-46; mgr. news desk Devel. Office, Drake U., Des Moines, 1966-68; dir. pub. rels. Bob Allen Cos., Des Moines, 1969-71; freelance writer, 1953—; holistic health cons., workshop facilitator, 1977—; counselor, tester Broadlawns Hosp., Des Moines, 1973-75. Author: Your Radiant Body, 1980; contbr. numerous articles to various publs.; former weekly columnist Urbandale News. Pub. rels. vol. Des Moines Mayor's Task Force, 1968-69, YWCA, Des Moines, 1970-72; formerly active PTA, Meth. Ch. Clairol scholar, 1975. Mem. AAUW (dir. communications Des Moines 1987-89), LWV. Office: Archer Creative Press PO Box 7087 Grand Sta Des Moines IA 50309

KEITH, MARY ELLEN, lawyer, writer; b. San Angelo, Tex., Dec. 5, 1938; d. William Earnest and Nettie May (Ketchum) Davenport; m. Francis Edwin Harvick, Jr., June 14, 1960 (dec. 1966); 1 child, Jeanette Neal Harvick Keith; m. Donald M. Keith, Jan. 19, 1968. Student, San Angelo Jr. Coll., 1957-58; BA, U. Tex., 1968; JD, U. Houston, 1970. Bar: Tex. 1970. Reporter Austin (Tex.) Am. Statesman, 1961-64; women's editor Galveston (Tex.) Daily News, 1964-67; asst. atty. gen. State of Tex., Austin, 1970-72, grant coord., supr. pub. info. Office of Gov., 1976-80; pvt. practice, Houston, Corpus Christi, Tex., 1972-76, Marshall, Tex., 1980-81; instr. journalism and communications Wiley Coll., Marshall, 1981-84; staff atty., investigator Tex. Commn. on Jud. Conduct, Austin, 1984-87; ptnr. Keith & Keith, Livingston, Tex., 1987—. Author: The Scarlet Cord, 1985, Das Haus an der Mauer, 1989; columnist Believer's Guide mag., 1985. Organizer, chmn. Com. for Juvenile Ctr., Galveston, 1967; lectr. to religious and civic groups, 1967—; legis. chmn. War Against Drugs, Marshall, 1983; sec. Am. Cancer Soc., Livingston, 1988-89. Recipient various awards Headliner's Club, 1960's, 2d place award AP Mng. Editors, 1967, Criminal Def. Lawyers Project award Office of Gov., State of Tex., 1979, Disting. Svc. award Tex. Commn. on Jud. Conduct, 1987. Mem. State Bar Tex. (editor newsletter adminstrv. law sect. 1988—), Order of Barons, Advocates. Office: 400 N Washington Ave Livingston TX 77351

KEITH, PAULINE MARY, artist, illustrator, writer; b. Fairfield, Nebr., July 21, 1924; d. Siebelt Ralph and Pauline Alethia (Garrison) Goldenstein; m. Everett B. Keith, Feb. 14, 1957; 1 child, Nathan Ralph. Student, George Fox Coll., 1947-48, Oreg. State U., 1955. Illustrator Merlin Press, San Jose, Calif., 1980-81; artist, illustrator, watercolorist Corvallis, Oreg., 1980—. Author 5 chapbooks, 1980-85; editor: Four Generations of Verse, 1979; illustrator Sagebrush Girl, 1981; contbr. poetry to anthologies and mags.; one-woman show Roger's Meml. Library, Forest Grove, Oreg., 1959, Corvallis Art Ctr., 1960, Human Resources Bldg., Corvallis, 1976; exhibited in group shows Nolan's Dept. Store, Corvallis, 1959-61, Hewlett-Packard Co., Corvallis, 1984, 85. Co-elder First Christian Ch. (Disciples of Christ), Corvallis, 1988-89, co-deacon, 1980-83; sec. Hostess Club of Chintimmini Sr. Ctr., Corvallis, 1987, pres., 1988-89. Recipient 1st prize Benton County Fair, 1982, 83, , 88, 89, 2nd prize, 1987, 3d prize, 1984, 90. Mem. Oreg. Assn. Christian Writers, Internat. Assn. Women Mins., Linn-Benton Diabetes Assn., Am. Legion Aux. (elected post post II Corvallis chpt. 1989-90), Corvallis Art Guild, Chintimmini Artists, Chintimmini Writers. Republican. Office: PO Box 825 Corvallis OR 97339

KEITH, PENNY SUE, mayor, educator; b. Louisville, Sept. 15, 1949; d. John G. Jr. and Edna Lee (Butler) K. AS, U. Ky., 1974; BS, U. Louisville, 1978, MEd in Spl. Edn., 1982, MEd in Curriculum Studies, 1984. Cert. tchr., Ky. Adv. tchr. St. Stephan Martyr Sch., Louisville, 1978-80; tchr. learning disabled students South Oldham Mid. Sch., Crestwood, Ky., 1980—; pub. rels. liason South Oldham Mid. Sch., 1987—; mayor City of Parkway Village, Ky., 1990—. Editor: Through the Eyes of 6th Graders, 1978, Interview with Famous People in the Louisville Times, 1987. Commr. City of Parkway Village, Louisville, 1982-85, 88-89, treas. 1986. Mem. NEA, Ky. Mcpl. League, Ky. Cols., Oldham County Edn. Assn., Atwood Sr. Citizens (pres. 1985—). Democrat. Methodist. Home: 850 Melford Ave Louisville KY 40217 Office: South Oldham Mid Sch 6403 W Hwy 146 Crestwood KY 40014

KEITH, SUSAN BETH KNOBBS, information systems, operations executive; b. La Harpe, Ill., Aug. 18, 1951; d. William Franklin and Alberta Ruth (Shoemate) K. Personnel coord. Sheaffer Pen Co., Ft. Madison, Iowa, 1973-76, computer operator, 1976-81; computer operator Better-Bilt Aluminum Products, Smyrna, Tenn., 1981-85, lead operator, supr., 1985-89, mgmt. info. systems ops. mgr., 1989—. Mem. NAFE, Assn. Computer Ops. Mgmt., Data Processing Mgmt. Assn., Altai Software S.E. User Group (chairperson 1987, chairperson steering com. 1988), Aircraft Owners and Pilots Assn., Mid-Tenn. Assn. Contingency Planners. Democrat. Office: Better-Bilt Aluminum Products Co Inc 704 12th Ave Smyrna TN 37167

KEITH, THERESA DAY, personnel executive; b. Chattanooga, July 18, 1962; d. James W. Day and M. Rebecca (Godsey) Geren; m. Gregory M. Keith, Feb. 14, 1987. BS cum laude, U. Tenn., 1984, MS magna cum laude, 1987. Lab technician Ashland Ter. Animal Hosp., Chattanooga, 1984-87; personnel mgr. Gold Bond, Inc., Hixson, Tenn., 1987—; corp. mem. Healthcare Coalition/Worksite Wellness Coun., Chattanooga, 1987—. Bd. dirs. Ulster Project East Tenn., Chattanooga, 1989; mem. Vol. Choices, Chattanooga, 1987. Mem. Soc. for Human Resource Mgmt., Psi Chi. Office: Gold Bond Inc 5485 Hixson Pike Hixson TN 37343

KEITH-MUSELIN, BRENDA KAY, health care facility administrator; b. Middletown, Ohio, Nov. 13, 1947; d. James Edward and Eva May (Alexander) Keith; m. Walter Ellery Muselin, Aug. 30, 1968 (div. Sept. 1978); children: Ellery Linn Muselin, Thomas James Muselin. Nursing diploma, St. Elizabeth Med. Ctr., 1968; cert. in cardiology, Ohio State U., 1968; student, Miami U., Ohio, 1969-70, 80; BS in Health Edn., Cen. State U., Wilberforce, Ohio, 1976; M in Hosp. and Health Adminstrn., Xavier U., 1976. Dist. health nurse Clearcreek Local Schs., Springboro, Ohio, 1969-81; asst. charge nurse emergency dept. Southview Hosp., Dayton, Ohio, 1980-84; relief charge nurse emergency dept. Stubbs Meml. Health Ctr., Waynesville, Ohio, 1983-85; charge nurse emergency dept. Bethesda Care Warren County, Lebanon, Ohio, 1984-86; instr. staff devel. Clinton Meml. Hosp., Wilmington, Ohio, 1985-86; dir. Quaker Heights Health Care Ctr, Waynesville, Ohio, 1986-87; pres. Keilin, Inc., Dayton, 1987—; instr. State of Ohio, Wayne Twp., 1979, asst. instr. Ohio Regents Clinton Meml. Hosp., 1984—. Active Southwestern Ohio Am. Heart Assn., Warren County br. ARC, Wayne Local PTO, Waynesville Soccer Assn., Waynesville Little League, Athletic Assn., Tri-State Health Adminstrs. Forum, Warren County Health Planning Bd., Miami U. Health Edn., Outdoor Edn. Workshop. Mem. Am. Hosp. Assn., NAFE, South Metro Dayton C. of C. (amb. 1988—). Methodist. Home: PO Box 482 Waynesville OH 45068 Office: Keilin Inc 2912 Springboro W Dayton OH 45439

KELCHNER, DIANE LYNN, orchestra administrator; b. Camden, N.J., Dec. 14, 1956; d. Donald Ambrose and Dorothy Edna (Brown) K. BS in Bible, MusB in Performance, Phila. Coll. Bible, 1980; cert. mgmt. seminar, Am. Symphony Orch. League, 1987. Free-lance musician and tchr., 1980—; assoc. editor Auerbach Pubs., Inc., Pennsauken, N.J., 1981-83; founder, dir. Seacoast Ensembles, Pennsauken, 1984—; dir. audience devel. Concerto Soloists Chamber Orch., Phila., 1983—; ptnr. Marilyn Jewelers, Phila., 1989—; pres. vol. com. Christian Symphony Orch., Langhorne, Pa., 1984-86; asst. dir. music Fellowship Evangelical Free Ch., Mt. Laurel, N.J., 1983—; co-dir. Christian Musicians Svc., Pennsauken, 1983-87. Alumni rep. Phila. Coll. Bible, Langhorne, 1982-86, sec. exec. com., 1984-85; vol. March of Dimes, Haddon Heights, N.J., 1980—, Pennsauken Twp. Town Watch, 1981—, With USNR, 1989—. Mem. Internat. Horn Soc., Am. Symphony Orch. League, Am. Fedn. Musicians, Nat. Wildlife Fedn., Nat. Fedn. for Decency.

KELEHEAR, CAROLE MARCHBANKS SPANN, legal administrative assistant; b. Morehead City, N.C., Oct. 2, 1945; d. William Blythe and Gladys Ophelia (Wilson) Marchbanks; m. Henry M. Spann, June 5, 1966 (div. 1978); children: Lisa Carole, Elaine Mabry; m. Zachariah Lockwood Kelehear, Sept. 15, 1985. Student Winthrop Coll., 1963-64; grad. Draughon's Bus. Coll., 1965; cert. in med. terminology Greenville Tech. Edn. Coll., 1972; grad. Millie Lewis Modeling Sch. Cert. med. asst. Office mgr. S.C. Appalachian Adv. Commn., Greenville, 1964-68, Wood-Bergheer & Co., Newport Beach and Palm Springs, Calif., 1970-72; asst. to Dr. J. Ernest Lathem, Lathem & McCoy, P.A., Greenville, 1972-75, Robert E. McNair, McNair, Konduros, Corley, Singletary and Dibble Law Firm, Columbia, S.C., 1975-77; office mgr. Dr. James B. Knowles, Greenville, 1977-78, Constangy, Brooks & Smith, Columbia, 1978-83; legal asst. to sr. ptnr. William L. Bethea Jr., Bethea, Jordan & Griffin, P.A., Hilton Head Island, S.C., 1983-88; adminstrv. asst. to Dr. Rajko D. Medenica, Hilton Head Island, 1988—; notary pub.; vol. Ladies aux. Greenville Gen. Hosp., 1966-72, South Coast Hosp., Laguna Beach, Calif., 1973, St. Francis Hosp, Greenville, 1974-76, Hilton Head Island Hosp., 1983—. Mem. Hilton Head Hosp. Aux., Profl. Women's Assn. Hilton Head Island, Am. Bus. Women's Assn., Nat. Assn. Female Execs., Am. Soc. Notaries, Beta Sigma Phi. Home: PO Box 21174 Hilton Head Island SC 29925

KELL, CARLA SUE, federal agency administrator; b. Highland Park, Mich., Sept. 15, 1952; d. Carl William and Margie May (Cannon) Bodner; m. Joseph Mark Kell, Oct. 10, 1971 (div. Dec. 1980). Student, Anderson Coll., 1970-71, Glendale Coll., 1976-77, Ariz. State U., 1978-79, Mesa Coll., 1979-80. Private tutor English, Federal Republic of Germany, 1971-74; office mgr. Bell & Schore, Rochester, Mich., 1974-75, COL Press, Phoenix, 1978-80; publicity mgr. O'Sullivan Woodside & Col, Phoenix, 1980-81, gen. mgr., 1982-84; pub. relations/promotion cons. GPI Publs., Cupertino, Calif., 1985; pub. cons., 1985-88; project adminstr. FAA, 1988—; account coordinator Bernard Hodes Advt., Tempe, Ariz., 1981; cons. freelance mktg., Phoenix, 1983. Vol., Fiesta Bowl Parade Com., Phoenix, 1983, FAA Airport Improvement Program Project.

KELLAIGH, KATHLEEN, producer; b. N.Y.C., June 28, 1955; d. Joseph Anderson and Alice Rendell (French) Kelly; m. Joel Wayne Robertson, Oct. 1, 1988; 1 child. BFA summa cum laude, U. Ill., 1976. Performer United Stage, Mich., 1977-78, Hartman Stage, Conn., 1978-79, Guiding Light-CBS TV, N.Y.C., 1979-81; dir. Center Stage Bravo, 1981-82; performer Nassau Rep., N.Y., 1983-84, Sail-Away Prodns., World Cruises, 1983-86; producer Adonai Arts Found.-Narnia, N.Y.C., 1986; performer All My Children, N.Y.C., 1987, America's Most Wanted, Fox TV, N.Y.C., 1988; producer, assoc. producer Adonai Arts Found., N.Y.C., 1988—; make-up artist Sarah Caldwell's Bicentennial Prodn., Pa., 1976; make-up artist/;instr. Nat. Acad. Dance, 1974-77; playwright in residence Little Theatre/Genesius Guild, Ill., N.Y., 1971-72, 81—. Author play: The Separate World, 1971, Chapter 33, 1981; poetry pub. in Am. Poetry Anthology, 1989. Chmn. Episcopal Peace Fellowship, N.Y.C., 1982-86; mem. Diocesan Task Force on World Peace, N.Y., 1982-88. Phi Kappa Phi Acad. scholar, 1975-76. Mem. Am. Fedn. TV and Radio Artists, Screen Actors Guild, Actors Equity Assn., Actors Fund, Episcopal Actors Guild, Genesius Guild (sec. 1987-88), Phi Kappa Phi.

KELLAM, DIANE CELINE FIDI, insurance executive; b. New Britain, Conn., July 6, 1950; d. Victor C. Sr. and Filomena (Lombardo) Fidi; m. David Corbin Kellam III, Feb. 11, 1977. Student, Cath. U. Am., 1967. Personal ins. mgr. Charles H. McDonough Sons, Inc., Bloomfield, Conn., 1978-82; ins. account exec. H.D. Segur, Inc., Waterbury, Conn., 1982-85; v.p. ISU Internat., San Francisco, 1985-89; pres., chief exec. officer ISU East, Inc., Farmington, Conn., 1989—. Mem. Jr. League of Greater New Britain, New Britain Gen. Hosp. Aux., Catholic Family Svcs. (adv. bd., bd. trustees), Hospice of Greater New Britain. Mem. Hartford Assn. of Ins. Women, Nat. Assn. Ins. Women, Mary Immaculate Acad. Alumni Assn. (treas.), New London County Mut. Ins. Adv. Coun., VFW Post 511 Women's Aux. Roman Catholic. Home: 80 Adams St New Britain CT 06052 Office: 270 Farmington Ave Ste216 Farmington CT 06032

KELLEHER, DEBRA LEE, health organization administrator; b. Indpls., May 10, 1958; d. Donnis Leon nand Marilyn Lee (Smith) Winegar; m. T. William Kelleher, Sept. 13, 1986; 1 child, Ryan William. BA, Miami U., Oxford, Ohio, 1980. From field rep. to branch dir. Arthritis Found., Ohio, 1981-83, exec. dir., 1984—; mem. Human Health Services for Health Dept., Cin., 1986-88. Dir. policy com. United Way, Cin., 1988—, campaign chmn., 1989-90; mem. edn. com. Nat. Arthritis Found., Atlanta, 1987—, mem. ho. of dels., 1989, mem. corp. policies com., 1989-90. Mem. Nat. Soc. Fund Raising Execs., Cin. Small Bus. Assn., Cin. C. of C., Madeira Bus. Assn., Miami U. Alumni Assn., Delta Delta Delta. Republican. Presbyterian. Home: 5848 Charter Oak Dr Cincinnati OH 45236 Office: Arthritis Found 7811 Laurel Ave Cincinnati OH 45243

KELLEHER, JUDITH CHARLENE (JUDITH CHARLENE GIVENS), retired nurse; b. Dean, Tex., Aug. 5, 1923; d. Charles C. and Jessie I. (Griffin) Givens; m. Daniel R. Kelleher, June 29, 1947 (dec.); children: Patricia Kelleher Sullivan, Pamela Kelleher Millonida, Daniel C., Dennis A. Degree in Nursing, San Joaquin Gen. Hosp. Sch., Stockton, Calif., 1948; AA, Am. River Coll., Sacramento, 1976; BSN, PHN, Calif. State U., Sacramento, 1976; MSN, NP, Calif. State U., Long Beach, 1986. RN. Staff nurse VA Hosp., Oakland, Calif., 1948; office nurse Oakland, 1948-50; pub. health nurse Calif. Youth Authority, Santa Rosa, Calif., 1950-52; staff nurse, office nurse Concord (Calif.) Community Hosp., 1953-66; house supr. Marlina Hosp., Lynwood, Calif., 1966; head nurse emergency dept. Downey (Calif.) Community Hosp., 1966-71; adminstrv. head nurse emergency dept. Brookside Hosp., Richmond, Calif., 1971-73; supr. emergency, operating, PAR, CCU and ICU depts. Brookdale Hosp., Oakland, 1973; dir. emergency dept. nursing San Leandro (Calif.) Meml. Hosp., 1973-75; staff nurse Kaiser Hosp., Sacramento, Calif., 1975-79; charge nurse Kaiser Hosp., Bellflower, Calif., 1979-81; triage nurse Kaiser Hosp., Anaheim, Calif., 1981-86; served various coms. State Health Dept.; faculty Coll. Surgeons Am. Acad. Orthopaedic Surgeons U. Calif. at San Francisco, Davis and Long Beach, 1971-89. Editorial bd. Jour. Emergency Nursing, 1974; editorial cons. R.N. mag., 1972-74; contbr. articles to numerous nursing publs. Mem. ARC, Downey PTA, Downey, Calif. Recipient Life Svc. award Downey PTA, 1971. Mem. AAUW, Emergency Nurses Assn. (co-founder 1970, bd. dirs. 1970-77, nat. pres. 1973-74), Univ. Assn. Emergency Physicians (liaison nurse 1974), Am. Nurses Assn., Calif. Nurses Assn., Nat. League Nursing, Fedn. Specialty Nurses (charter mem.), Sigma Theta Tau. Democrat. Roman Catholic.

KELLEHER, LISA ANN, insurance company executive; b. Plainfield, N.J., Oct. 15, 1960; d. Henry George Clauer and Georgiana Rose (Wannag) Sweetman. BA in Journalism, Pace U., 1978—. Documentation and closing specialist Mcpl. Issues Servic Corp., 1982-84, mgr. documentation and closing dept., 1984—; v.p., asst. sec. Mcpl. Bond Investors Assurance Corp., White Plains, 1987—. Mem. Nat. Assn. Female Execs. Republican. Presbyterian. Office: Mcpl Bond Investors Assurance Corp 113 King St Armonk NY 10504

KELLER, DARLA LYNN, trust manager, organization consultant; b. Lemon, S.D., Jan. 7, 1956; d. Donald Dwight and Bonna Claire (Gilbert) K.; m. Jerry Jerome Eskridge, Aug. 27, 1984 (div. Dec. 1988); children: Lisha Saree, Aram Josias. Diploma, Minn. Sch. Bus., 1975. Sec. Hirschfield's Inc., Mpls., 1974-75, Lionel D. Eide & Co., Mpls., 1975-76; client adminstr. Resource Trust Co., Mpls., 1976—; trust mgr. Archer Trust, Mpls., 1981—; cons. Larry Wilson Enterprises, Mpls., 1987—. Treas. Como Park Elem. Sch. PTA, St. Paul, 1989—, St. Croix-East Central cou.Girl Scouts U.S., 1986—. Home: 1315 N Dale St Saint Paul MN 55117 Office: Archer Trust 105 S Fifth St #712 Ste 466 Minneapolis MN 55402-1251

KELLER, JOYCE GARVER, association executive, writer; b. Cleve. Sept. 28, 1947; d. John H. and Zelda (Gershowitz) Garver; m. Steven Ray Keller, 1967; 1 child, Stuart Alan. Assoc. dir. ACLU of Ohio, 1972-78; polit. campaign cons., Columbus, Ohio, 1978-80; ops. supr. U.S. Census Bur., Columbus, 1980; exec. dir. Ohio Women, Inc., Columbus, 1980-82, People for the Am. Way, Columbus, 1982-85; gen. mgr. Health Power of Columbus, Inc., 1986-87 ; QA/UR and compliance mgr. Health Power Mgmt. Co., Columbus, 1987-88, v.p. HMO ops., 1988—; cons. various univs. Contbr. articles to profl. jours. and mags.; creative cons. TV documentary "Focus: Censorship", 1983 (Ohio State Bar Assn. Media award 1985). Bd. dirs. Alliance for Coop. Justice, Columbus, 1977-80, Ohio Hunger Task Force, Columbus, 1981-84, Columbus Area Women's Polit. Caucus, 1978-82 (Dem. Task Force chmn., 1987); selection com. Ohio Women's Hall of Fame, Columbus, 1983; adv. Ohio Tchr. Edn. and Cert., Ohio Dept. Edn., 1984. Recipient Community Service award Ohio Ho. of Reps., 1982, City of Columbus and Franklin County, 1978, Civil Liberties award ACLU of Ohio Found., 1983, Friend of Edn. award Ohio Edn. Assn., 1986. Mem. Nat. Assn. Female Execs., Nat. Women's Polit. Caucus (nat. site selection com.), Columbus Bus. and Profl. Women's Club, Nat. Council Jewish Women, Columbus Area C. of C. (mem. pres.'s Roundtable, 1986). Democrat. Office: Health Power Mgmt Corp 560 E Town St Columbus OH 43215

KELLER, LORETTA SCHERTZ, artist, art therapist, freelance journalist; b. N.Y.C., Aug. 19, 1928; d. Isidore Schertz and Rose Flichtenfeld; m. Herbert Bishop Keller, Feb. 1, 1953 (separated 1986); children: Debra S., Steven S. BA, Hunter Coll., 1957; MA in Human Devel., Pacific Oaks Coll., Pasadena, Calif., 1989. Art therapist Altadena, Calif., 1973—; reporter Star News, Pasadena, Calif., 1978-79; freelance writer Altadena, 1979—. One-woman shows include Jack Carr Gallery, Pasadena, Riverside (Calif.) Art Mus.; represented in permanent pvt. collections; contbr. articles to newspapers and other publs. including L.A. Times. Vol. Pasadena Heritage, 1978—, Pasadena Foothills Dem. Club, 1978; mem. adv. coun. Altadena Libr., 1990—. Recipient 1st prize 12th Ann. Fiesta de Artes, La Mirada, Calif., 1973. Home and Studio: 1526 Gaywood Dr Altadena CA 91001

KELLER, MARGARET GILMER, English educator; b. Harrisburg, Pa., July 11, 1922; d. Charles Greenawalt and Mary Ellen (Sullivan) Gilmer; m. George Henry Keller III, July 13, 1940; children: Mary Ellen, Margaret Marie, George Henry. AB, Trinity Coll., 1933, AM, Columbia U., 1934; cert. 1942, cert. State Tchrs. Coll., Bloomsburg, Pa., 1934; Acting chmn. history dept., Trinity Coll., Washington, 1935-36, chmn. classical dept., Convent Sacred Heart, 1936-37, Steelton (Pa.) High Sch., 1937-41; adj. prof. English dept. Rutgers U., 1946—, mem. dean's adv. com. U. Coll., 1968, also advisor to women's clubs U. Coll.; chmn. classical dept., Glen Rock (N.J.) High Sch., 1956-59, chmn. fgn. lang. dept, 1959—. Active Am. Cancer Soc., Community Chest ARC, Girl Scouts U.S.A.; mem. nominating bd. Ridgewood (N.J.) Nursing Service, 1959-60; Republican county committeeman; trustee Trinity Coll. (life), 1963-67, 1974—, chmn. 75th Anniversary Fund, 1974-75. Honored by Rutgers U., 1953, 61, 65, 71, 82, 87, Newman Province of N.J., 1963, Nat. Jaycees, 1973, Middle States Assn. Comm. on Secondary Schs., 1970, 74; recipient Robert Ax citation Glen Rock High Sch., 1971, Case Inst., 1976, Alumnae Service award Trinity Coll., 1977, 87, Pres.'s medal, 1982; named Outstanding Tchr. of Yr., Rutgers U., Newark, 1982, Disting. Prof. of Yr., 1988-89. Mem. NEA, N.J. Edn. Assn., Am. Classical Soc., AAUW (former dir.), Archeol. Inst. Am., MLA, Suprs. Assn. N.J. (sec. 1973-76), Am., N.J., Mid-Atlantic States classical socs., AAUP, Chaplain's Aid Assn., Trinity Coll. Alumnae Assn. (nat. pres. 1963-67, recipient Nat. Achievement award, 1987), Rutgers Alumni Assn. (hon., advisor), Phi Chi Theta (hon.), Alpha Sigma Lambda (hon., advisor). Clubs: Newman (adviser Rutgers U.), Univ. Coll. Women (hon. Rutgers U.), Coll. Home: 200 Phelps Rd Ridgewood NJ 07450 Office: Rutgers U New Brunswick NJ 08901

KELLER, MARGARET MARIE, lawyer, educator; b. N.Y.C., Oct. 1, 1944; d. George H. and Margaret (Gilmer) K.; m. James T. Holmes, Dec. 27, 1969 (div. Aug. 1985); 1 child, James T. III; m. Donald A. Sperling, Jan. 2, 1988. AB cum laude, Trinity Coll., Washington, 1965; JD, Columbia U., 1968, MS in Adminstrv. Medicine, 1972. Bar: N.Y. 1968, N.J. 1972. Assoc. DeForest & Duer, N.Y.C., 1969-71, 76-78, ptnr., 1979—; atty. HEW, N.Y.C., 1971-77, Moreland Act Commn., N.Y.C., 1976; grad. instr. Sarah Lawrence Coll., Bronxville, N.Y., 1981—. Bd. dirs. Camphill Found., Kimberton, Pa., 1986—. Recipient Disting. Svc. award HEW, 1977. Mem. Assn. Bar City N.Y. (chmn. com. on medicine and law 1979-82). Office: DeForest & Duer 90 Broad St New York NY 10004

KELLER, MARY LYNN, television account executive; b. Houston, May 29, 1958; d. John Rankin and Margaret Patricia (Boothe) K. BS in Advt., U. Tex., 1980. Account exec. Houston Chronicle, 1982-84, Marschalk Advt. Agy., Houston, 1984-85; asst. account exec. Penny & Pengra Advt. Agy., Houston, 1985; account exec. Sta. KHOU-TV, CBS, Houston, 1985—. Recipient 10th dist. award for excellence in advt. Am. Assn. Advt. Agys., 1980, Membership Dir. of Yr. award Am. Advt. Fedn., 1985. Mem. Ad 2 (membership dir. 1982-84). Republican. Roman Catholic. Home: 2701 Revere Apt 219 Houston TX 77098 Office: Sta KHOU-TV 1945 Allen Pkwy Houston TX 77011

KELLER, PAMELA DIANE, communications executive; b. Abilene, Tex., June 5, 1958; d. Bill Merl and Mary Margaret (Ridgley) K. BA in Journalism and Advt., Central State U., 1981; student, U. Okla., 1976-80. Copywriter Tupper Advt., Oklahoma City, 1980-81; account mgr. New Res. Group, Inc., Oklahoma City, 1981-89, sec./treas., 1985-89, v.p., 1988—, also bd. dirs.; communications specialist Romo Corp., Denver, 1990—. Copywriter TV commls. (Addy award 1981). Named one of Outstanding Young Women of Am., 1989. Mem. Am. Soc. Female Execs. Republican. Presbyterian. Home: 1374 S Fulton Way G-206 Denver CO 80231 Office: Romo Corp 10455 W 6th St Denver CO 80215

KELLER, RENÉE SUSAN, editor periodical; b. N.Y.C., Aug. 14, 1960; d. Harold Robert and Mabel Madeline (Rickard) K. BA in English Literature, Herbert H. Lehman Coll., 1983. Editorial intern FIND/SVP, N.Y.C., 1982; libr. clk. Herbert H. Lehman Coll., N.Y.C., 1981-83; legal libr. asst. Kronish, Lieb, Shainswit, Weiner and Hellman, N.Y.C., 1983-85; reader svc. corr. Parade Publs., Inc., N.Y.C., 1985-89, asst. articles editor, 1989—. Mem. Women in Communications (program com. 1989). Office: Parade Publs Inc 750 Third Ave New York NY 10017

KELLER, SUSAN AGNES, insurance officer; b. Moline, Ill., July 12, 1952; d. Kenneth Francis and Ethel Louise (Odendahl) Hulsbrink; m. Kevin Eugene Keller, June 20, 1981; 1 child, Dawn Marie. Grad. in Pub. Relations, Patricia Stevens Career Coll., 1971; grad. in Gen. Ins., Ins. Inst. Am., 1986. CPCU; lic. ins. agt., real estate agt. Comml. lines rater Bitiminous Casualty Corp., Rock Island, Ill., 1973-78; with Roadway Express, Inc., Rock Island, 1978-81; front line supr. Yellow Freight System, Inc., Denver, 1982-83; supr. plumbing and sheet metal prodn. Bell Plumbing and Heating, Denver, 1983-84; v.p. underwriting Golden Eagle Ins. Co., San Diego, 1985—; cons. real estate foreclosure County Records Service, San Diego, 1986-89. Vol. DAV, San Diego, 1985—; notary pub. Mem. Soc. Chartered Property and Casualty Underwriters, Profl. Women in Ins., Nat. Assn. Female Execs. Roman Catholic. Home: 449 Jamul Ct Chula Vista CA 92001 Office: Golden Eagle Ins Co 7175 Navajo Rd San Diego CA 92119

KELLER, TERESA GALE, education educator; b. Columbia City, Ind., July 14, 1958; d. John Walter and Frances Betheleen (North) Blain; m. Michael Gene Keller, Apr. 10, 1982; 1 child, Blain Michael. BSc. in Mktg., Ball State U., 1980, Postgrad., 1989. Instr. Muncie (Ind.) Opportunities Industrialization, 1980-83; sec. Indsl. Trust & Savings Bank, Muncie, 1986; instr. secretarial sciences Ind. Vocat. Tech. Coll. Anderson Campus, 1986–. Fund raiser Muscular Dystrophy Assn., Anderson, 1986, Am. Cancer Soc., Anderson, 1987-88; Christmas drive coord. Women's Alternatives, Anderson, 1988—. Mem. Profl. Secs. Internat., Nat. Bus. Edn. Assn., Ind. Assn. Adult and Continuing Edn. Office: Ind Vocat Tech Coll 325 West 38th St Anderson IN 46013

KELLER, WANDA KATE, health industry specialist; b. Nome, Alaska, Sept. 9, 1961; d. Lester Robert Sr. and Martha (Avessuk) K. Diploma, Alaska Bus. Coll., Anchorage, 1979-80; student, Anchorage Community Coll., 1985-87. Sr. clk. typist Alyeska Pipeline Svc. Co., Anchorage, 1982-84; administr. asst. Artic Slope Tel. Co., Prudhoe Bay, 1984; sr. sec. Alaska Native Review Commn., Anchorage, 1984-85; health info. specialist Southcentral Found., Anchorage, 1987-88, community health rep. supr.,

1988-89; with Alaska Native Health Bd., Anchorage, 1989—; health fair coord. McLaughlin Youth Ctr., Anchorage, 1987-89.; chairperson Community Health Rep. bd. dirs., 1989—; vice chairperson Community Health Rep. tng. com., 1989—; ct. adv. for battered Native women with Alaska Women's Resource Ctr. Medal winner at World Eskimo-Indian Olympics, Native Youth Olympics, Artic Winter Games; named Overall Female Athlete, Spirit Days Traditional Games, 1988. Home: PO Box 101265 Anchorage AK 99510

KELLERMAN, JOAN M., psychologist; b. N.Y.C., July 3, 1953; d. Arthur J. and Meriam (Gorfine) K.; m. Jack Demick, Aug. 30, 1981; 1 child, Lisbet Kate. BA, York Coll., 1975; MA, Clark U., 1977, PhD, 1980; student, Boston U. Sch. Medicine, 1981. Intern Boston Vets. Adminstrn. Hosp., 1978-79; postdoctoral fellow Boston U. Sch. Medicine, 1980-81; clin. fellow McLean Hosp., Belmont, Mass., 1980-81; staff psychologist South Shore Counseling Ctr., Hanover, Mass., 1986—; pvt. practice Agoraphobia Treatment and Research Ctr. New Eng., Boston, 1981—; staff psychologist South Norfolk Community Services, Inc., Mass., 1981-82; clin. coordinator South Norfolk Community Services, Inc., Foxboro, Mass., 1982-83; clin. dir. South Norfolk Community Services, Inc., Norwood, 1983-86; assoc. psychologist Bay State Psychol. Assocs., Inc., Boston, 1984-86; dir. psychology Arbour Hosp., Jamaica Plain, Mass., 1986--; dir. research Agoraphobia Treatment & Research Ctr., Boston, 1981—; cons. psychologist Quincy City Hosp., 1985-88; dir. psychology Arbour Hosp., Jamaica Plain, 1986--. dir. research Agoraphobia Treatment & Research Ctr., Boston, Sharon, 1981—; cons. psychologist Quincy City Hosp., 1985-88. Mem. Am. Psychol. Assn., Ea. Psychol. Assn., New Eng. Psychol. Assn., N.Y. Acad. of Sciences. Jewish. Home: 5 Owl Dr Sharon MA 02067 Office: Arbour Hosp 279 Robinwood Ave Jamaica Plain MA 02192

KELLERMAN, SALLY CLAIRE, actress; b. Long Beach, Calif., June 2, 1937; d. John Helm and Edith Baine (Vaughn) K.; m. Richard Edelstein, Dec. 19, 1970; 4 step-daughters; m. Jonathan Krane, 1980. Student, Los Angeles City Coll., Actor's Studio, N.Y.C. Stage appearances include Singular Man, N.Y.C., Breakfast at Tiffany's; films include A Little Romance, MASH, Brewster McCloud, Last of the Red-Hot Lovers, Foxes, Reflection of Fear, Slither, Lost Horizon, The Big Bus, Head On, Rafferty and the Gold Dust Twins, The Boston Strangler, Loving Couples, The April Fools, Welcome to L.A., Serial, For Lovers Only, 1982, Dempsey, 1983, September, Gun, 1983, Back to School, 1986, That's Life, 1986, Meatballs III, 1987, Three for the Road, 1987, You Can't Hurry Love, 1988, Someone to Love, 1988; also TV roles Chrysler Theatre, Mannix, It Takes a Thief; TV film Verna: USO Girl, 1978, Elena, 1985; miniseries Centennial, 1978-79. Recipient nominations Acad. and Golden Globe awards for MASH. Mem. Actor's Equity, AFTRA. Office: care Agy Performing Arts 9000 Sunset Blvd #1200 Los Angeles CA 90069*

KELLERS, KATHLEEN MARIE, federal government postal administrator; b. Jersey City, Jan. 19, 1956; d. Edward Vincent and Maria Joyce (Mehok) Keegan; m. Timothy Robert Kellers, Sr., Oct. 3, 1981; children: Timothy Robert Jr., Jaye Joyce. B.A., Rutgers Coll., 1978. Letter carrier U.S. Postal Service, Toms River, N.J., 1978-83; supt. postal ops., Brielle, N.J., 1987; postmaster, Sea Girt, N.J., 1987—; distr. safety instr., Cherry Hill, N.J., 1985. Recipient cert. appreciation Del. Valley Distr. U.S. Postal Service, 1985, cert. appreciation New Brunswick Div. Career Awareness Conf., 1987, 88. Mem. Nat. Assn. Letter Carriers, Nat. Assn. Postal Suprs., Nat. Assn. Postmasters of U.S. Roman Catholic. Avocations: reading; needlework; gardening. Home: PO Box 391 Brielle NJ 08730 Office: US Postal Service 800 The Plaza Sea Girt NJ 08750-9998

KELLEY, ALICE MARY, educator; b. Ludington, Mich., Aug. 5, 1920; d. Thomas Phillips and Martha Elthina (Olmstead) McMaster; m. Robert E. Reynolds Sr., May 3, 1941 (div. 1970); children: Robert E., Thomas R., Barbara Ann Reynolds Christmann; m. Irving McLeod Kelley, Dec. 23, 1973. AB, San Diego State U., 1958, MA, 1963. Cert. secondary tchr., Calif. Tchr. English Cajon Valley Sch. Dist., El Cajon, Calif., 1958-63; tchr. English San Diego Unified Sch. Dist., 1963-70, resource tchr., curriculum writer, 1963-70, tchr. English and Journalism, 1970-76; dept. chmn. San Diego City Schs., 1968-70, adminstv. coun., 1967-70. Sec., San Diego Mus. of Art-East County chpt., 1987-88, treas. 1988-89. Recipient Prin. Sch. award, Freedom Found., San Diego, 1968. Mem. AAUW, DAR, Soc. for Women in Ed., Alpha Delta Kappa.

KELLEY, BETTY MARIE, restaurant owner, cook; b. Oil City, Pa., Feb. 23, 1955; d. Robert Charles Miles and Ethel Eleanor (Kelley) Miles. Grad. high sch., high sch., Titusville, Pa. lectr. Cambridge Grange, 1990—. Owner Betty's Restaurant, Cambridge Springs, Pa., 1980—. Mem. U.S.C. of C., Cambridge Grange (chaplain 1987-90, lectr. 1990—). Republican. Baptist. Office: Betty's Restaurant 164 Venango Ave Cambridge Springs PA 16403

KELLEY, BRENDA CAROLE, product designer; b. Rumford, Maine, July 27, 1945; d. Norman Adam and Anne Marie (Bernard) Young; m. Robert L. Kelley, Jan. 27, 1964 (div. 1975); children: Bryan Courtney, Bruce Christopher, Barry Craig; m. Steven Edward Meredith, Feb. 24, 1989. Student, Butera Sch. Art, Boston, 1963-64, So. Maine Vocat. Tech. Inst., Portland, 1978-81, 82-83, Pacific Northwest Coll. Art, Portland, Oreg., 1987—, U. Oreg., 1988, Ctr. for Creative Studies, 1975-77. Illustrator, keyline artist Fed.'s Dept. Store, Detroit, 1976; computer coord. R.L. Polk & Co., Detroit, 1975, 77; advt. account exec. Jour. Tribune Newspapers, Biddeford, Maine, 1977-79; drafter, pipe designer E.C. Jordan Engring., Portland, Maine, 1979-82; design product mgr. Nike Athletic Co., Oreg., N.H, 1983-85; dir. design cons. Kelley Design Svcs., Portland, Oreg., 1989—. Holder 65 patents in athletic footwear. Vol., Brick Store Hist. Mus., Kennebunk, Maine, 1978-79; ofcl., Kennebunk Hist. Commn., 1981-85. Recipient numerous advt. and art awards from profl. orgns. Methodist. Home: 8009 NW Reed Dr Portland OR 97229 Office: Kelley Design Svcs 8009 NW Reed Dr Portland OR 97229

KELLEY, CHRISTINE RUTH, business owner, consultant; b. St. Louis, Oct. 14, 1951; d. John Weatherhead and Mary Christine (Echkout) K.; 1 child, Jennifer Christine. AS in Nursing, St. Louis Community Coll., 1975; BA in Bus. Mgmt., Webster U., 1988, postgrad, 1988—. Charge relief and staff nurse St. Luke's W., Cardinal Glennon, St. Louis, 1975-77; pub. health nurse Vis. Nurse Assn., St. Louis, 1977-78; chief flight nurse Tri-Star Aviation, St. Louis, 1978-80; agy. nurse Med. Staffng, Med.-Staff, Dallas, 1980-83; charge relief and psychiatric staff nurse/counselor St. John's Mercy Med. Ctr., St. Louis, 1983-85, adolescent psychotherapist/counselor, 1985; dir. air ambulance div. Jet Svcs., Inc., Chesterfield, Mo., 1985-87; pres., chief exec. officer Air-Med. Internat., Inc., St. Louis, 1987—; bus. cons. Genesis Learning Sytems, Creve Coeur, Mo., 1989—; assisted Dept. Health State of Mo. in writing air ambulance regulations for fixed wing aircraft, 1988. Mem. Regional Commerce & Growth Assn., St. Louis, 1986—, 89—; State Adv. Coun. for Emergency Med. Svcs., Jefferson City, Mo., 1988—. Mem. Profl. Aeromed. Transport Assn. (bd. dirs. 1988—), Assn. Air Med. Svcs., Nat. Assn. Women Bus. Owners, Mo. Emergency Med. Svcs. Alliance, Nat. Flight Nurse Assn., Regional Commerce and Growth Assn's. Pres.'s Club, Mothers Club. Republican. Office: Air-Med Internat Inc 62 St Charles Pl Saint Louis MO 63119

KELLEY, GEORGIA, real estate development, consultant; b. San Francisco, Jan. 15, 1947; d. George Francis and Irene Jane (Malavazos) K.; m. Daniel Schimenti, June 19, 1967 (div. 1973); m. Joseph Michael Daniels, Aug. 5, 1989. BSBA, U. San Francisco, 1976; M in City Planning, U. Calif., Berkeley, 1981. Asst. to planning dir., City of Hercules KCA Engrs. Surveyors & Planners, San Francisco, 1978-81; asst. proj. mgr. Inland Steel Devel. Corp., San Rafael, Calif., 1982-83; cons. urban planning & devel. mgmt. Georgia Kelley Urban Planning, Design & Devel., Mill Valley, Calif., 1983-84; ptnr., urban planner, landscape designer Kelley-Hook, Mill Valley, Calif., 1984-87; constrn. coord. The Innisfree Cos., Tiburon, Calif., 1986-88; real estate devel. cons. Fairfax, Calif., 1988—; Hercules Project mgr. Gelsar, Daly City, Calif., 1989—. Mem. Econ. Devel. Task Force, City of Hercules, Calif., 1989—; Devel. Strategy Planning Task Force, 1989-90, West County 2000 Steering Com., 1990—. Office: 273 Cypress Dr Fairfax CA 94930

KELLEY, JACQUIE, state legislator; m. Mark Kelley. Ed., S.D. State U., U. Colo., U. Minn. PNP; state senator from dist. 24 S.D. Senate. Democrat. Roman Catholic. Home: HCR 37-28 Camelot Pierre SD 57501*

KELLEY, LINDA EILEEN, marketing specialist, sales consultant; b. Osceola, Iowa, June 10, 1950; d. Marion Gale and Frances (Steele) McKinnie; m. Dennis Dean Kelley, Aug. 3, 1969 (div. 1980); 1 child, Jennifer Lynne. Student, U. No. Iowa, 1969. Classified advt. mgr. Creston (Iowa) News-Advertiser, 1971-79, advt./promotion mgr., 1981-82; classified advt. promotion specialist Des Moines Register & Tribune, 1979-81; assoc. cons. K. Bordner Cons., Inc., Bloomington, Minn., 1982-84; sales devel. rep. Mpls. Star & Tribune, 1983—; pres. Cities Best Values Direct Mail; instr. advt. Hennepin Jr. Coll., Mpls.; cons. small bus. Author: Retail Advertising for the Small Business, 1986—. Methodist.

KELLEY, MARIAN HERBST, public relations executive; b. Austin, Tex., Feb. 27, 1959; d. Harvey Raymond and Lila Dean (Finley) Herbst; m. Mark J. Kelley, Dec. 13, 1986. BA in Journalism, Tex. Tech. U., 1981. Pub. rels. asst. Tracor, Inc., Austin, Tex., 1981-86; mgr. pub. rels. Tracor, Inc., 1986—. Bd. dirs. Capital Area Easter Seal Rehab. Ctr., Austin, 1988—; vol. Laguna Gloria Art Mus., Austin, 1982—; communications com. United Way/Capital Area, Austin, 1989—. Named Competent Toastmaster, 1984. Mem. Pub. Rels. Soc. Am. (1986-87), Tex. Pub. Rels. Assn. (bd. dirs. 1988—). Office: Tracor Inc 6500 Tracor Ln Austin TX 78725

KELLEY, MARSHA CHRISTINE, state official; b. Pittsfield, Ill., Aug. 11, 1965; d. Vernon Aaron and Carolyn Muriel (Ervin) K. BA in Econs., Western Ill. U., 1987. Bookkeeper V.H. Callender Constrn. Co., Pittsfield, 1986; acct. Nature House Inc., Griggsville, Ill., 1987-88; exec. I, budget analyst Ill. Dept. Pub. Aid, Springfield, 1988—. Mem. NAFE, Phi Beta Lambda. Home: 1819 Seven Pines Rd Apt 3 Springfield IL 62704 Office: Ill Dept Pub Aid 100 S Grand Springfield IL 62762

KELLEY, PATRICIA HAGELIN, geology educator; b. Cleve., Dec. 8, 1953; d. Daniel Warn and Virginia Louise (Morgan) Hagelin; m. Jonathan Robert Kelley, June 18, 1977; children: Timothy Daniel, Katherine Louise. BA, Coll. of Wooster, 1975; AM, Harvard U., 1977, PhD, 1979. Instr. New Eng. Coll., Henniker, N.H., 1979; asst. prof. U. Miss., University, 1979-85, assoc. prof., 1985-89, acting assoc. vice chancellor acad. affairs, 1988, prof., 1989—, assoc. dean, 1989—; program dir. NSF, Washington, 1990—. Contbr. articles to profl. jours. Deacon Bethel Presbyn. Ch., Olive Branch, Miss., 1985—. Predoctoral fellow NSF, 1976-79; rsch. grantee NSF, 1986-89, 90-92. Mem. Paleontol. Soc. (coun. 1984-85, chair SE sect. 1984-85) Geol. Soc. Am., AAAS, Miss. Acad. Scis., Paleontol. Rsch. Inst., Sigma Xi, Phi Beta Kappa. Presbyterian. Office: U Miss Dept Geology & Geol Engring University MS 38677

KELLEY, SANDRA DEE, manufacturing company executive; b. Hot Springs, S.D., Aug. 9, 1937; d. Edwin Donald and Lucile Olga (Wickstrom) Kachelhoffer; m. Arvid S. Lundy, June 14, 1959 (div. 1974); children: Jayne Elaine Gerlach, Bill S. Lundy, Alice Ann Hill; m. Gregory Michael Kelley, Aug. 16, 1975; 1 stepchild, Michael R.B. BS, S.D. State U., 1959; student, Coll. of Santa Fe, 1970-71, 78; MA, N.Mex. Highlands U., 1972; EdD, N.Mex. State U., 1984. Pres. bd. dirs. Creative Living Assocs., Los Alamos, 1973-76; adminstrv. aide Los Alamos (N.Mex.) Unitarian Ch., 1974-75; asst. drama dir. Los Alamos High Sch., 1976-80; grad. teaching asst. N.Mex. State U., Las Cruces, 1980-84; rsch. asst. Ysleta Ind. Sch. Dist., El Paso, Tex., 1983; asst. dir. FIPSE Project N.Mex. State U. Las Cruces, 1983-84; editor Diversified Tech. Svc., Inc., El Paso, 1985, ednl. technologist, 1985, project mgr., 1985-87; tech. mgr. Diversified Tech. Svc., Inc., Oklahoma City, 1987—; mem. accreditation team North Cen. Assn., 1983; recorder Quality Edn. Conf., Las Cruces, 1982-83; pres. N.Mex. State U. Grad. Sch. Council, Las Cruces, 1982-83. Leader, camp dir. Girl Scouts of Am., Los Alamos, 1967-69; counselor Santa Fe Crisis Ctr., 1970-78. S.D. Home Econs. Assn. scholar, 1955. Mem. ASTD, NAFE, Am. Ednl. Rsch. Assn., Assn. Supervision and Curriculum Devel., Assn. for Ednl. Communications and Tech., Fed. Ednl. Tech. Assn., Soc. Applied Learning Tech., N.Mex. State Writing Inst. Assoc., Phi Delta Kappa, Phi Kappa Phi. Democrat. Mem. Unitarian Ch. Home: 6630 S May Ave Apt F Oklahoma City OK 73159 Office: Diversified Tech Svc Inc 1233 Sovereign Row Ste B3 Oklahoma City OK 73108

KELLEY, SHEILA SEYMOUR, public relations executive, political consultant; b. Bronxville, N.Y.; d. William Joseph and Jane (Seymour) K.; m. Robert Max Kaufman, 1959. BA magna cum laude, Syracuse U., 1949. Reporter Yonkers Herald Statesman, N.Y.C., 1950; reporter, editor Close Up column Herald Tribune, N.Y.C., 1950-53; writer, producer Sta. WNBC-TV, N.Y.C., 1953-54; media cons. to Senator Jacobs K. Javits, N.Y.C., 1956-74; press sec. Senator Jacobs K. Javits, Washington, 1958-61; account supr., v.p. Harshe Rotman Druck, N.Y.C., 1961-76; founder, pres. VOTES, Inc., N.Y.C., 1973-75; v.p. Doremus Pub. Rels., N.Y.C., 1976-86; v.p., exec. v.p., 1987-90, mng. dir., exec. v.p., 1990—. Mem. Pub. Rels. Soc. Am. (accredited), Women Execs. Pub. Rels. (pres. 1987-88), Phi Beta Kappa. Republican. Office: Gavin Anderson Doremus & Co 11 W 42th St New York NY 10036

KELLISON, DONNA LOUISE GEORGE, accountant, educator; b. Hugoton, Kans., Oct. 16, 1950; d. Donald Richard and Zepha Louise (Lowry) George. BA in Elem. Edn. with honors, Anderson (Ind.) U., 1972; MS in Elem. Edn., Ind. U., 1981. CPA; Ind.; lic. tchr., Ind. Tchr. elem. Maconaquah Sch. Corp., Bunker Hill, Ind., 1972-73; office mgr. Eskew & Gresham, CPA's, Louisville, Ky., 1973-78; para-profl. Blue & Co., Indpls., 1979-83, tax compliance specialist, 1983-84, tax sr., 1984-86, tax supr., 1986-87, tax mgr., 1987-90, tax prin., 1990—. Vol. Children's Clinic, Indpls., 1985—. Mem. Network Women in Bus., Am. Inst. CPA's, Ind. CPA Soc., Tax Inst. Presbyterian. Club: Toastmasters (Indpls.) (sec. 1986). Home: 9318 Embers Way Indianapolis IN 46250 Office: Blue & Co PO Box 80069 Indianapolis IN 46280-0069

KELLMAN, CHERYL ANNE, computer consultant; b. Port of Spain, Trinidad and Tobago, Aug. 17, 1962; came to U.S., 1967; d. Clyde and Merle (Patrick) K. Student, Bernard H. Baruch Coll., 1980. Lic. real estate agt., appraiser, N.Y. Acct. Harbor Mgmt. Corp., N.Y.C., 1983-84; mgmt. supr. Zeal Mgmt. Corp., N.Y.C., 1984-85; real estate saleswoman Buchbinder & Warren, N.Y.C., 1985-86, Dowling & Peltz Ltd., Bklyn., 1987-88; bookkeeper Kalmon Dolgin Affiliates, Inc., Bklyn., 1986-88, computer cons., 1988—; computer cons. Centra Software, N.Y.C., 1988—, Migdol Realty Mgmt., Inc., N.Y.C., 1988-89. Pres. 305-307 Prospect Owners Corp., Bklyn., 1988-89; vol. Bklyn. Mus., 1988. Mem. NAFE. Democrat. Roman Catholic. Office: CK Computerized Solutions 305 Prospect Pl #2C Brooklyn NY 11238

KELLNER, EILEEN WYNNE, hospital administrator; b. Passaic, N.J., Oct. 29, 1929; d. Michael Edward and Rita Beatrice (Smith) Wynne; m. William Gilbert Kellner, Sept. 20, 1953; children: Patricia J., Peter G. BA, Wellesley Coll., 1951; MBA, CUNY, 1971. Exec. tng. squad Macy's, N.Y.C., 1951-53; mgr. Smith Youth Ctr., Passaic, 1953-56; adminstrv. resident Westchester Med. Ctr., Valhalla, N.Y., 1971; sr. clinic adminstr. Mt. Sinai Hosp., N.Y.C., 1972-78; asst. adminstr. N.Y. Hosp., White Plains, N.Y., 1978-80; bus. mgr.- dept. neurology Columbia U., N.Y.C., 1981-86; adminstrv. mgr. Columbia Presbyn. Eastside, N.Y.C., 1986—. Pres. PTA, Greenburgh Cen. 7 Sch. Dist., Hartsdale, N.Y., 1968-69; chmn., bd. trustees Community Unitarian Ch., White Plains, N.Y., 1983-84; bd. trustees Search for Change, White Plains, 1989—. Mem. Am. Coll. Health Care Execs., Am. Coll. Med. Group Adminstrs. Democrat. Unitarian-Universalist. Home: 60 Birchwood Ln Hartsdale NY 10530 Office: Columbia Presbyn Eastside 38 E 61 St New York NY 10021

KELLOGG, DOROTHY M., state legislator; b. Mpls., July 26, 1920; d. Carl Howard and Marie (Mundhenke) Sorteberg; m. Lawrence Strong Kellogg, 1940; children: Lawrence Edmund, Ralph Curtis, Jean Marie Jostad. Grad. high sch., Watertown, S.D. Former mem. S.D. Ho. of Reps.; mem. S.D. State Senate. Mem. LWV, Bus. and Profl. Women, Watertown C. of C. Democrat. Methodist. Home: Rte 2 Box 123 Watertown SD 57201*

KELLOGG, NANCY JEAN, project director; b. Malden, Mass., Apr. 16, 1957; d. William Everett and Arlene Frances (Hurton) K. BS, Boston U., 1979; MPA, Suffolk U., 1990. Registered occupational therapist. Sr. occupational therapist Lynn (Mass.) Pub. Schs., 1980-85; program coord. Mass. Kennedy Meml. Hosp. for Children, Boston, 1986-88; project dir. Mass. Easter Seal Soc., Worcester, 1989—; pvt. practice Boston, 1988-89. Mem. Am. Occupational Therapy Assn. (rsch. symposium for devel. disabilities 1987), Boston Computer Soc., Rehab. Engrs. Soc. N.Am. Office: Mass Easter Seal Soc 484 Main St Worcester MA 01608

KELLS, PHYLLIS ELAINE, artist, teacher, writer; b. Peoria, Ill., Dec. 9, 1932; m. Louis Robert Kells, Aug. 23, 1958; children: Robert Phillip, Eric Louis. BFA, Bradley U., 1956, MFA, 1958. Cert. elem. high sch., spl. art tchr., Ill. Freelance portrait painter, landscape, still life painter Washington, Ill., 1951—; editorial artist Peoria Jour., 1953-56; tech. illustrator Caterpillar Tractor Co., East Peoria, Ill., 1956-57; elem. tchr. art Peoria Pub. Schs., 1958-67; dir. after sch. art program Ist Federated Ch., Peoria, 1972-73; grad. asst. instr. art Bradley U., Peoria, 1956-57; instr. art history, lectr. Ill. Cen. Coll., East Peoria, 1973-80; freelance writer, Washington, 1987—; art demonstrator, judge art shows. One women shows includes Lincoln Meml. Courthouse, Metamora, Ill, 1977, U. Unitarian Ch., Peoria, Ill., 1977, YWCA Tea Room Gallery, Peoria, 1978, Universalist Unitarian Ch., Peoria, 1980; exhibited in group shows at Peoria Savs. Art Festivals, 1976, 77, Ill. Cen. Coll. Faculty Show, 1977, Ill. Cen. Coll. Fine Art Exhibits, 1975-87, Jubilee Coll. Autumn Fest, 1983-89, Brimfield, Ill., Peoria's One Senseational Weekend, 1987, Ill. Art League Exhibit at Lakeview Mus., Peoria, 1988. Bd. dirs. Universalist Unitarian Ch., Peoria, 1976. Bradley U. Fedn. scholar, 1955-56. Mem. Chimes, Delta Phi Delta. Republican.

KELLUM, CARMEN KAYE, apparel company executive; b. Greensburg, Pa., Oct. 15, 1952; d. Bruce Lowell and Mildred Louise (Montgomery) Taylor; m. John Douglas Kellum, Aug. 2, 1975 (div. May 1987). Student, MacMurray Coll., 1971-72, Elgin Community Coll.; AA, Coll. DuPage, 1975; BA with honors, Nat. Coll. Edn., 1978. Cert. tchr. Aide occupational therapy Mercy Ctr., Aurora, Ill., 1972-76; tchr. behavior disorders Lake Park High Sch., Roselle, Ill., 1978-80, Salk Pioneer Sch., Roselle, 1980-81; mgr. So-Fro Fabrics Stores, Chgo., Lombard and Joliet, Ill., 1981-84; offshore coord. Florsheim Shoe Co., Chgo., 1984-90; mgr. in tng. Linens N Things, Deerfield, Ill., 1990—. Mem. Orton Dyslexia Soc., Nat. Assn. Female Exec., Kappa Delta Pi. Lutheran. Home: 30 W 156 Wood Ct and Hwy 59 Bartlett IL 60103 Office: Linens N Things Cadwell Corners 19 Waukegan Rd Deerfield IL 60015

KELLY, ALISON MARY, registered nurse anesthetist; b. Yonkers, N.Y., Feb. 13, 1955; d. Vincent Paul and Dorothy (Egan) Kelly. AS in Nursing, U. Bridgeport, 1974; BA in Biology, U. Colo., 1983; MS in Anesthesia, Mt. Marty Coll., 1986. Staff RN Saratoga Springs (N.Y.) Hosp., 1974-76, Boulder (Colo.) Community Hosp., 1977-80; RN St. Anthony's Hosp., Denver, 1982-84; staff RN, high risk labor U. Colo. Health Sci. Ctr., Denver, 1980-84; staff cert. registered nurse anesthetist Southeast Anesthesia and Assocs., Charlotte, N.C., 1986-87, Albemarle Anesthesia and Assocs., Elizabeth City, N.C., 1987—; instr. Boulder Community Hosp. Childbirth Inst., Boulder, Colo., 1977-80. Mem. Am. Assn. Nurse Anesthetists. Home: 2410 Dan & Mary St Elizabeth City NC 27909 Office: Albemarle Anesthesia Assocs Eringhaus St Elizabeth City NC 27909

KELLY, ANASTASIA DONOVAN, lawyer; b. Boston, Oct. 9, 1949; d. Charles A. and Louise V. Donovan; m. Thomas C. Kelly, Aug. 23, 1980; children: Michael, Brian. BA, Trinity Coll., 1971; JD magna cum laude, George Washington U., 1981. Bar: D.C. 1982, Tex. 1982. Analyst Air Line Pilots Assn., 1971-74; dir. employee benefits Martin Marietta Corp., Bethesda, Md., 1974-81; assoc. Carrington, Coleman, Sloman & Blumenthal, Dallas, 1981-85, Wilmer, Cutler & Pickering, Washington, 1985-90; ptnr. Wilmer, Cutler & Pickering, 1990—; gen. counsel Coupe St. Thomas Ltd., 1981-85; advisor William Kissinger Fin. Planners, Timonium. Md., 1985—. Named one of Outstanding Young Women of Am., 1980. Mem. ABA, Dallas Bar Assn., Order of Coif. Republican. Roman Catholic. Home: 5727 Moreland St NW Washington DC 20015 Office: Wilmer Cutler Pickering 2445 M St NW Washington DC 20037

KELLY, ANNE C., retired city official; b. Buffalo, Mar. 6, 1916; d. John Patrick and Elizabeth Marie (Edwards) Donohue; m. Thomas Edward Kelly, Apr. 19, 1941; children: Maureen Anne, Michael Thomas, Edward John, Kevin Joseph, Theresa Elizabeth Callahan. Student SUNY-Buffalo. Tchr., St. Teresa Sch., Yonkers, 1956-64; clk. City of Buffalo, 1964, sec. to comptroller, 1967-70, coun. clk., 1970-76, sr. coun. clk., 1976-81. Com. woman N.Y. Democratic Com., 1970-87, mem. exec. bd., 1970—; vice chmn. Erie County Dem. Com., 1985—; past pres. Mercy League of Buffalo Mercy Hosp., Nash Ladies Guild, South Side Dem. Club; mem. Women for Downtown Buffalo. Roman Catholic. Clubs: Daus. of Erin, Nash Ladies. Lodge: KC (past pres. Nash guild). Home: 9 Haig Place #603 Dunedin FL 33528

KELLY, BARBARA REYNOLDS, real estate developer; b. Phila., June 29, 1953; d. James Paul Reynolds and Emma T. (Vassallo) Scott; m. Russell A. Kelly, Aug. 18, 1973. BA, Rutger State U., 1978; MBA, LaSalle U., 1985. Staff acct. Strouse Greenberg and Co., Phila., 1978-79, mgr. acctg., 1979-86; asst. v.p. Helmsley-Greenfield, Phila., 1986-89; prin. Real Estate Info. Svc. Corp., Cherry Hill, N.J., 1990—. Corp. chmn. United Way, Phila, 1986. Mem. Comml. Real Estate Women (chmn. membership 1986-88, v.p. 1988-89, pres. 1989—), LaSalle Alumni Assn. (steering com. 1988—), Internat. Coun. Shopping Ctrs. Republican. Roman Catholic. Home: 12 Orchard Way Mount Laurel NJ 08054 Office: Real Estate Info Svc Corp 1040 Kings Hwy N Cherry Hill NJ 08034

KELLY, BRENDA JOYCE, management consultant; b. Baytown, Tex., Sept. 13, 1950; d. James Richard and Ruby Lee (Battle) K. BA, Sam Houston State U., 1971; MA, U. Houston, 1979. Assoc. editor Kentron Hawaii Ltd., Houston, 1973-74; tech. writer Lockheed Corp., Houston, 1974-80, quality of worklife and productivity project engr., 1980-86; community health care specialist Peace Corp, Port-au-Prince, Haiti, 1986-87; pvt. practice process cons. Port-au-Prince, 1987-88, Houston, 1988-90, Europe, Australia, Africa, South Am., Asia, U.S., 1990—. Community asst. Students for Preservation Afro-Am. Dignity and Equality, Huntsville, Tex., 1971; instr., cons. Communities and Cities in Schs., Galveston, Tex., 1986; facilitator Tex. Risk Communication Project Com., Houston, 1989. Mem. Orgn. Devel. Network, Mus. Heritage Soc., Heroin of Jericho, Mosley. Democrat. Baptist. Home and Office: 372 DeKalb Ave #5-I New York NY 11205 Office: PO Box 96266 Houston TX 77213-6266

KELLY, CAROL WHITE, company executive; b. Shreveport, La., Dec. 23, 1946; d. Verlin Ralph and Mary Louise (Humphries) White; m. James Patrick Kelly, June 6, 1968; children: Mary Louise, Christopher John. BA, Centenary Coll. La., Shreveport, 1968. Corp. sec., treas. Kelly & Assocs., Atlanta, 1986—. Mem. Atlanta Hist. Soc., Atlanta Ballet Guild (life), High Mus. Art, Episcopal Ch. Women (sec.-treas. 1976-80), Chi Omega Alumnae Assn. (pres. 1979-80). Office: Kelly & Assocs PC 200 Galleria Pkwy Ste 1510 Atlanta GA 30339

KELLY, CATHERINE MAKEM, educator; b. Phila., June 3, 1948; d. Albert Bernard and Michelina Theresa (Burzichelli) Makem; m. William Francis Kelly, Apr. 4, 1981. BS, West Chester (Pa.) State U., 1970; MEd, Temple U., 1977, MA, La Salle U., Phila., 1990. Cert. French and Spanish tchr., Pa. Part-time and substitute tchr. Rantoul (Ill.) Schs., 1982-83; security mgr. Carson, Pirie, Scott, Urbana, Ill., 1983-84; merchandiser Amb. Card Co., Mechanicsburg, Pa., 1985-86; tchr. French, Archdiocese of Phila., Lansdale, Pa., 1970-77; tchr. French and Spanish Archdiocese of Phila., 1986—. Vol. Assoc. Svc. for Blind, Phila. and Harrisburg, Pa., 1985; active

St. John's Hospice, Phila., 1987—. Capt. U.S. Army, 1977-81. Recipient ribbons for cooking and crafts Balt. Art Mus., 1980, Champaign County, Ill., 1981, 82, 83. Mem. Am. Assn. Tchrs. French, AAUW (br. pres. 1982-84), Sigma Delta Pi. Democrat. Roman Catholic.

KELLY, CHRISTINE ANN, small business owner, educator; b. Bklyn., May 11, 1952; d. William John and Joan Ellen (Sullivan) K. AAS in Acctg., Kingsborough Community Coll., 1973; BS in Phys. Edn., Bklyn. Coll., 1976. Cert. physical edn. tchr., N.Y. Head softball coach C.W. Post Coll., Greenvale, N.Y., 1979-84; sales mgr. Karnival Sports Ctr., Bklyn., 1984-88; owner, founder Shortstop Silkscreening, S.I., N.Y., 1988—; tchr. St. Edmund High Sch., Bklyn., 1979-81; adj. lectr. Kingsborough Community Coll., Bklyn., 1984—; head coach softball Empire State Games, N.Y., 1987—. Bd. dir. holiday basketball tournament Tournament of Champions, N.Y., 1986—. Mem. Sporting Goods Mfg. Assn., N.Y. Bd. Ofcls. for Women Sports. Democrat. Roman Catholic. Office: Shortstop Silkscreening 1235 Bay St Staten Island NY 10305

KELLY, DOROTHY ANN, college president; b. Bronx, N.Y., July 26, 1929; d. Walter David and Sarah (McCauley) K. B.A., Coll. New Rochelle, 1951; M.A., Catholic U., Washington, 1958; Ph.D., U. Notre Dame, 1970; Litt.D. (hon.), Mercy Coll., Dobbs Ferry, N.Y., 1976; LL.D. (hon.), Nazareth Coll. of Rochester, N.Y., 1979; D.H.L. (hon.), Coll. St. Rose, 1981, Manhattan Coll., 1979. Mem. faculty Coll. New Rochelle, N.Y., 1957—, chmn. dept. history, 1965-67, acad. dean, 1967-72, acting pres., 1970-71, pres., 1972—; trustee, vice chmn. Commn. Ind. Colls. and Univs. State of N.Y., 1977-78, chmn. bd. trustees, 1978-80, mem. govt. relations com., 1980—; chmn. Com. Higher Edn. Opportunity, 1977; mem. commr. edn. Adv. Council on Higher Edn. for N.Y. State, 1975-77, subcom. on postsecondary occupational ed., 1975-77; exec. com. Empire State Found. Ind. Liberal Arts Colls., 1975—, vice chmn., 1977-81, chmn., 1981—; trustee, mem. exec. com. Assn. Colls. and Univs. State of N.Y., 1976-80; mem. exec. com. Assn. Colls. Mid-Hudson Area, 1976—, pres., 1979-81; mem. com. on purpose and identity Assn. Cath. Colls. and Univs., 1975-80; mem. Neylan Coll. steering com., 1978—, mem. bishops and pres. com., 1979—; mem. adv. council on fin. aid to students Office Edn., HEW, 1978—; chmn. Women's Coll. Coalition, 1981-83; trustee United Student Aid Funds, 1980—; chmn. govt. relations adv. com. Nat. Assn. Ind. Colls. and Univs., 1981-82, chair, 1982-88; mem. Westchester County Assn., 1980—, bd. dirs. 1985-87; bd. dirs. Assn. Am. Colls., 1983-86; bd. trustees Tchrs. Ins. and Annuity Assn. Am., 1987—, Cath. U. Am., 1988—; bd. dirs. Ursuline Sch., New Rochelle, 1988—, Ann. Coun. on Edn., 1990—. Bd. dirs. New Rochelle Hosp. Med. Ctr., 1988—, NCCJ, 1989—. Mem. AAUP, Am. Hist. Assn., AAUW, Nat. Fedn. Bus. and Profl. Women, Am. Assn. Higher Edn., Nat. Assembly Women Religious. Address: Coll New Rochelle New Rochelle NY 10801*

KELLY, DOROTHY HELEN, pediatrician, educator; b. Fitchburg, Mass., July 29, 1944. BS in Nursing magna cum laude, Fitchburg State Co., 1966; BS with distinction, Wayne State U., 1968, MD with distinction, 1972. Diplomate Am. Bd. Pediatrics. Intern dept. pediatrics Mass. Gen. Hosp., 1972-73, resident in pediatrics, 1973-75, fellow in pediatrics pulmonary medicine, 1976-79; teaching fellow Harvard Med. Sch., Boston, 1973-75, clin. fellow, 1972-75, instr. in pediatrics, 1975-81, asst. prof. pediatrics, 1981-89, assoc. prof. pediatrics, 1989—; assoc. dir. pediatric pulmonary unit, Mass. Gen. Hosp., 1988—; cons. HEW/Bur. Community Health Svcs. 1979-80, FDA 1985, 88, ECRI 1987-88, others; active task force on prolonged apnea, Am. Acad. Pediatrics, 1978; chmn. apnea adv. com. Nat. Sudden Infant Death Syndrome Found., 1979-81, sci. rev. com. 1981; com. mem. anesthesiology and respiratory therapy devices panel-FDA, Ctr. for Devices and Radiol. Health, 1990—; chmn. physicians' coun., Nat. Assn. Apnea Profls., 1990—, others. Reviewer several jours. in field; contbr. numerous articles to profl. jours. Recipient Woman of Vision award Nat. Soc. for Prevention of Blindness, Mass. Affiliate, 1981, First Disting. Alumni award Fitchburg State Coll., 1984, grants in field. Mem. Am. Med. Woman's Assn., Am. Bd. Pediatrics, Am. Acad. Pediatrics, Am. Thoracic Soc., Internat. Pediatric Soc., Assn. for Psychophysiol. Study of Sleep, Soc. for Pediatric Rsch., Mass. Thoracic Soc., Eas. Soc. for Pediatric Rsch. Home: 39 Drummer Rd Acton MA 01720

KELLY, EILEEN PATRICIA, management educator; b. Steubenville, Ohio, Oct. 24, 1955; d. Edward Joseph and Mary Bernice (Cassidy) K. BS, Coll. Steubenville, 1978; MA, U. Cin., 1979, PhD, 1982. LPA, Ohio; sr. profl. in human resources. Lectr. U. Cin., 1981-82; asst. prof. bus. Creighton U., Omaha, 1982-87; chmn. mgmt., mktg. and systems dept., 1986-88, assoc. prof., 1987-88, coordinator project Minerva, 1987-88; assoc. prof. La. State U., Shreveport, 1988—, chmn. dept. mgmt. and mktg., 1988—; comml. arbitrator, 1988—. Contbr. articles to profl. jours. and acad. presentations. Mem. Acad. Mgmt, Am. Bus. Law Assn., Soc. Human Resource Mgmt., Internat. Platform Assn., Beta Gamma Sigma (faculty advisor 1985-88). Roman Catholic. Office: La State U Coll Bus 8515 Youree Dr Shreveport LA 71115

KELLY, EULA MAE CURRIE, retired journalist; b. Olsburg, Kans., Aug. 6, 1906; d. Charles and Nancy Almira (Fleming) Currie; m. Henry Jervey Kelly, May 23, 1936 (div. 1946); 1 child, Thomas Jervey. BS in Journalism, Kans. State U., 1928, MS in English Lit., 1929, BS in Home Econs. and Journalism, 1951. Asst. editor woman's page Kansas City (Mo.) Star, 1929-31, reporter, feature writer, 1931-36; asst.editor coop. extension svc. Kans. State U., Manhattan, 1943-52; field editor home dept. Capper's Farmer mag., Topeka, 1952-60; public writer USDA, Washington, 1960-71; ret., 1971; freelance mag. writer, 1943-52. Mem. Women in Communications (profl., pres. 1976, Kans. Disting. Journalist award 1958, Nat. Disting. Journalist award 1984, cert. of appreciation 1989), Am. Assn. Coll. Editors, Home Economists in Bus., AAUW (group chmn. 1975, 84, 89-90), Am. Assn. Ret. Persons (publicity chmn. 1973-74), Nat. Assn. Ret. Fed. Employees, Quill Club, Mortar Bd., Phi Kappa Phi, Omicron Nu. Democrat. Episcopalian. Home: 2121 Meadowlark Rd Apt 40 Manhattan KS 66502

KELLY, JEAN MCCORMICK, advertising agency executive; b. Norwalk, Conn., June 13, 1938; d. John M. and Dorothy (Bennett) McCormick; m. Kevin E. Kelly, Sept. 18, 1982; children—Gregory, Geoffrey, Stefanie. B.S., U. R.I., 1960. Copywriter Montgomery Ward, N.Y.C., 1960-62; asst. advt. dir. Advertiser Democrat newspaper, Norway, Maine, 1963-65; copy chief/women's editor Sta.-WMTW-TV, Poland Spring, Maine, 1965-67; continuity dir. Sta.-WEAT-TV-AM-FM, West Palm Beach, Fla., 1967-70; s. creative dir. William F. Haselmire Advt., West Palm Beach, 1970-85; ptnr. The Kodi Group, West Palm Beach, 1985-90, The Intercom Mktg. Group, West Palm Beach, 1987-90; v.p. Manis, Monda, Allen, Inc., West Palm Beach, 1990—. Republican. Catholic. Av. (pres. 1976-77) (Palm Beach, Fla.). Home: 356 Golfview Rd #309 North Palm Beach FL 33408 Office: Manis Monda Allen Inc 929 Clint Moore Rd Boca Raton FL 33487

KELLY, JOSEPHINE KAYE, social worker; b. Grand Rapids, Mich., May 30, 1944; d. Clark Everet Peterson and Dorothy Jane (Mudd) Schaefer; m. Raymond Luke Kelly, July 19, 1969; children: William Lawrence, Kenneth James. BA with honors, Grand Valley State Coll., 1967; postgrad., Western Mich. U., 1984—. Registered social worker. Exec. dir. Voluntary Action Ctr., Grand Rapids, 1977-79; project coord. Area Agy. on Aging, Grand Rapids, 1977-79; program coord. Aquinas Coll., Grand Rapids, 1979-80; psychiat. social worker Kent Oaks Psychiat. Unit, Grand Rapids, 1987-88; continued care social worker St. Mary's Hosp., Grand Rapids, 1987-88; co-owner Hidden Lake Farm, Conklin, 1969—; med. social worker Alpine Manor Inc., Grand Rapids, 1988—. Trustee Chester Twp., 1984—, mem. canteen svcs. unit, 1984—; mem. planning bd. St. Mary's Hosp., Grand Rapids, 1981-82; mem. lay adv. bd. Cath. Info. Ctr., Grand Rapids, 1983-85, pres., 1984-85; pres. Coun. on Aging of Kent County, Grand Rapids, 1979-80, mem. 1977—; mem. transp. adv. commn. Coopersville (Mich.) Area Pub. Schs., 1977-81; sec. Conklin Food Coop, 1977-80; bd. dirs. Women's Resource Ctr., Grand Rapids, 1977-79, steering com., 1972-73. Mem. Am. Soc. Pub. Administrn., Am. Legion (aux.), Mich. Beefalo Breeders Assn. (sec./treas. 1982-84), Am. Beefalo World Registry, Vol. Mgmt. Assn. Western Mich. (founder, 1st pres. 1975-76), Conklin Brotherhood Assn. Republican. Roman Catholic. Home: 3616 Coolidge St Conklin MI 49403 Office: Alpine Manor Inc Social Svcs Dept 1050 Four Mile Rd NW Grand Rapids MI 49504

KELLY, KATHLEEN SUE, academic dean; b. Duluth, Minn., Aug. 6, 1943; d. Russell J. and Idun N. Mehrman; m. George F. Kelly, Apr. 29, 1961; children: Jodie A., Jennifer L. AA, Moorpark (Calif.) Coll., 1971; BS in Journalism, U. Md., College Park, 1973, MA in Pub. Rels., 1979, PhD in Pub. Communication, 1989. Accreditated pub. rels. Dir. pub. info. Bowie (Md.) State Coll., 1974-77; asst. to dean, instr. Coll. Journalism U. Md., College Park, 1977-79, assoc. dir. devel., 1979-82; v.p. Mt. Vernon Coll., Washington, 1982-83; dir. devel. U. Md., College Park, 1983-85, assoc. dean, lectr. Coll. Journalism, 1985-88, asst. dean Coll. Bus. and Mgmt., 1988—; cons. NASA, NIH, Mt. St. Marys Coll., 1986—; lectr. CASE, Pub. Rels. Soc. Am., 1987—. Dir. Anne Arundel County Student Trade Found., Annapolis, Md., 1986-89. Named Outstanding Faculty Mem., Panhellenic Assn., U. Md., 1986. Mem. Pub. Rels. Soc. Am. (chmn. ednl. and cultural orgn. sect. 1989, pres. Md. chpt. 1986-87, President's Cup 1981), Nat. Soc. Fund Raising Execs., Coun. Support and Advancement Edn. (N.H. Women's Forum 1983), Women in Higher Edn., Md. C. of C. (pub. rels. com. 1989—), Phi Kappa Phi. Democrat. Home: 317 Thomas Rd Severna Park MD 21146 Office: U Md Coll Bus and Mgmt College Park MD 20742

KELLY, LEONTINE T. C., clergywoman; b. Washington; d. David D. and Ila M. Turpeau; m. Gloster Current (div.); children: Angella, Gloster Jr., John David; m. James David Kelly (dec.); 1 child, Pamela (adopted). Student W.Va. State Coll.; grad. Va. Union U., 1960; M.Div., Union Theol. Sem., Richmond, Va., 1969. Formerly sch. tchr.; former pastor Galilee United Meth. Ch., Edwardsville, Va.; later mem. staff Va. Conf. Council on Ministries; pastor Asbury United Meth. Ch., Richmond, 1976-83; mem. nat. staff United Meth. Ch., Nashville, 1983-84; bishop Calif.-Nev. Conf., San Francisco, 1984-88. Vis. prof. evangelism and witness Pacific Sch. Religion, Berkeley, Calif., 1988—. Office: 316 N El Camino Real #112 San Mateo CA 94401

KELLY, MARGUERITE STEHLI, fashion executive, consultant; b. N.Y.C., June 9, 1931; d. Henry E. and Grace (Hays) Stehli; m. Charles J. Kelly, Jr., Dec. 23, 1962; children: Marguerite Grace, Lisa Stehli. BA, Bryn Mawr Coll., 1953. Exec. trainee Macy's, N.Y.C., 1953-54, asst. buyer, 1954-57; buyer Bloomingdale's, N.Y.C., 1957-63; pres. Maggie, Inc., Wayzata, Minn., 1964-86; also brs. Maggie, Inc., Georgetown, D.C., 1964-70, Locust Valley, N.Y., 1970-75; ret., 1986. Mem. com. for spl. fund Foxcroft Sch., Middleburg, Va., 1974-76, trustee, 1978-87; mem. alumnae coun. Brearley Sch., N.Y.C., 1973-75; trustee Abbott Northwestern Hosp., Mpls., 1984-86. Mem. Woodhill Club, Piping Rock Club (Locust Valley). Episcopalian.

KELLY, MARILYN VERONICA, management consultant; b. Jersey City, Jan. 29, 1947; d. William Henry and Agnes (Greener) K. BA, Rutgers U., 1968; MA, Goddard Coll., 1980. Acting project leader RCA Corp. Staff, N.Y.C., 1968-70; systems analyst programmer Litton Zabel, N.Y.C., 1970-72; dept. mktg. stats. Melnor Industries, Moonachie, N.J., 1972-75; prin. Body Psychedynamics, Plainfield, N.J., 1980—; pvt. practice Plainfield, 1981—. Contbr. articles to profl. jours. Mem. N.Y. Acad. Scis., Internat. Transactional Assn., Orgn. Devel. Network.

KELLY, MARY LOUISE, computer science educator; b. Jacksonville, Fla., Mar. 6, 1952; d. Walter B. and Katherine (Pace) K. AA, Fla. Jr. Coll., 1975; BA, U. North Fla., 1977, MEd, 1982; MAT, Jacksonville (Fla.) U., 1986. Cert. tchr., Fla. Mid-mgmt. adminstrv. asst. Voyager Life Ins. Co., Jacksonville, 1981-84; instr. Fla. Jr. Coll., Jacksonville, 1984-84, 87; tchr. computer sci. Duval County Sch. Bd., Jacksonville, 1984-89; asst. prof., data processing Palm Beach Community Coll., Lake Worth, Fla., 1987—. Advisor Data Processing Mgmt. Assn. Palm Beach Community Coll. Mem. DPMA, Fla. Assn. Computer Educators, Kappa Delta Pi. Democrat. Office: 4200 Congress Ave Sta 29 Lake Worth FL 33461

KELLY, MATTIE CAROLINE MAY, business executive; b. Vernon, Fla., Mar. 12, 1912; d. William W. and Mary Alice (Russ) May; m. Coleman Lee Kelly, Mar. 26, 1932 (div. June 1971); children: Carnera Lee, Lila Bernarr, Imogene Kelly, Carol Kelly, Cecelia Kelly Sims; m. Paul Sims, July 13, 1973 (div. May 1979). Tchr. pub. schs., Fla., 1928-33, 37; pres. Kelly Boat Svc., Inc., 1980—, Kelly Homes, Inc., Destin, Fla., to 1978; co-owner, trustee Coleman L. Kelly Trust; co-organizer, owner, pres. Radio Sta. WMMK-FM, Destin. Author: (poetry) Songs and Sonnets From the Sea, 1964. Mem. Okalosa County Dem. Com., 1958—, exec. adv. bd., 1956-72; mem. State Dem. Exec. Com., mem. adv. bd., 1966-70, del. nat. conv., 1968, 72. Bd. dirs. Destin Libr., 1956—, Fla. League Arts, 1980-81; bd. dirs. Okaloosa County chpt. ARC, 1954-60, chmn., 1957-58; adv. bd. diversified coop. tng. Choctawhatchee High Sch., 1960—; camp counsellor Senior Hi, Camp Weed, 1964; patron Stagecrafters, Okaloosa Community Concert Assn.; Benefactor Ft. Walton Beach Ballet Assn., Symphony Assn.; sponsor Playground Mut. Concert Assn.; founder, promoter, supporter Mattie M. Kelly Fine Arts Ctr., Destin, donor land and funds; mem. coordinating coun. for arts Okaloosa-Walton Jr. Coll., 1965—, rep. to Fla. Arts Coun., 1966—; patron Okaloosa County Symphony, Ft. Walton Beach Ballet Assn.; adv. bd. Okaloosa County Mental Health Assn., 1978—, Women's Theatre Workshop Okaloosa-Walton Jr. Coll., 1978—; chmn. Historic Sites Commn., Okaloosa-Walton; mem. Protestant Episcopal Ch., adminstr., supt. ch. sch., 1953-60, dist. chmn. christian edn., 1958-61, asst. organist, tchr., del. adult conf. 1957, 59, del. religious TV programming workshop, 19555-56, dist. v.p., 1961-64, pres. ch.-women diocese Fla., 1965-68. Recipient award ARC, 1960, award for arts for N.W. Fla., Gov. Fla., 1982, Gov.'s citation, 1983, Harmony award Soc. Preservation Encouragement Barber Shop Quartet Singing in Am., 1983, Neptune award, 1989. Mem. AAUW (charter, legis. com. 1971—), Am. Camellia Soc., Nat. Writers Club, General Soc. Okaloosa County, N.Y. Bot. Gardens Club, Okaloosa County Concert Assn., Nat. Hist. Soc., Playground Poets Assn. (coord. 1977—), Ft. Walton Beach C. of C. (edn. com., mem. host com., Ross and Nell Marler Citizenship award 1982), Fla. Boatsmen's Assn. (sec. 1972—), Hist. Soc. Okaloosa and Walton Counties, Ft. Walton Beach Woman's Club (chmn. fine arts com. 1957-58), Woman's Club (v.p. 1958-59), Gulf Coast Dem. Women's Club, Assoc. Coun. Arts, Choctaw Bay Music Club. Address: PO Box 425 Indian Bayou Destin FL 32541

KELLY, MAUREEN ANN, systems accountant; b. N.Y.C., July 13, 1965; d. William J. and Frances C. (Scanlon) K. BS, U. Ariz., 1987. Acct. U.S. Govt. Dept. of the Army, Ft. Huachuca, Ariz. Mem. Am. Soc. Mil. Comptrollers (treas. Cochise chpt. 1990—), Golden Key Nat. Honor Soc., Beta Gamma Sigma. Office: US Army Intelligence Ctr and Ft Huachuca Attn ATZS-RMF Fort Huachuca AZ 85613-6000

KELLY, MAXINE ANN, property developer; b. Ft. Wayne, Ind., Aug. 14, 1931; d. Victor J. and Marguerite E. (Biebesheimer) Cramer; m. James Herbert Kelly, Oct. 4, 1968 (dec. Apr. 74). B.A., Northwestern U., 1956. Sec., Parry & Barns Law Offices, Ft. Wayne, 1951-52; trust sec. Lincoln Nat. Bank & Trust Co., 1956-58; sr. clerk stenographer div. Mental Health, Alaska Dept. Health, Anchorage, 1958-60; office mgr. Langdon Psychiat. Clinic, 1960-70; propr. A-1 Bookkeeping Service, 1974-75; ptnr. Gonder-Kelly Enterprises & A-is-A Constrn., Wasilla, Ark., 19756; sales assoc. Yukon Realty/Gallery of Homes, Wasilla, 1989; sec. Rogers Realty, Inc., Wasilla, 1989, dir., 1989—. Dir. Alaska Mental Health Assn., Anchorage, 1960-61; pres., treas. Libertarian Party Anchorage, 1968-69, Alaska Libertarian Party, 1969-70. Mem. AAUW (life), Anchorage C. of C., Whittier Boat Owners Assn. (treas. 1980-84). Home: 4000 Steven Dr Wasilla AK 99687 Office: Rogers Realty Inc 2061 Palmer-Wasilla Hwy Wasilla AK 99687

KELLY, PAMELA SUE, purchasing manager; b. Jersey City, Nov. 26, 1953; d. Alfred and Mary Jane (Miller) Klansky. BS, Katherine Gibbs Coll., 1971. Ops. project mgr. Am. Svc. Control, Ft. Lauderdale, Fla.; dir. purchasing; v.p. Svc. Control Corp., Phoenix. Mem. NAFE. Republican. Roman Catholic.

KELLY, PATRICIA MARGUERITE MARY, administrative services executive, photographer; b. New City, N.Y., May 25, 1930; d. Joseph Francis and Ann Hackett K.; m. Edward Nathan Jaffe, Apr. 27, 1960; 1 child, Ann Linda; m. Wayne Cook, Apr. 18, 1977 (div. 1978). Student, Acad. St. Joseph, Brentwood, U. Conn., Stanford, 1950, Hunter Coll., N.Y.C., 1960, Wash. Sch. Bus., N.Y.C., 1950. Cert. Photography. Exec. dir. Diners/Fagazy Travel Sch., 1969-70; pres. Kelly's Exec. Adminstrv. Personal Svcs.,

1977-89; exec. asst. Monterey (Calif.) Peninsula Found., 1980-82; pres. Squeukie B. King Kelly Co., 1984—; owner Piecefull Collections, Bandon-by-the-Sea, Oreg. Editor, author: Marine News mag., 1950; author: Civil Service Leader, 1950. V.P. Ridgefield Young Rep., Conn., 1952; Treas, Sec. Sr. Class, Southampton, N.Y., 1948; Exec. Asst. Mayor, City Adminstrn., Carmel-by-the-sea, Calif., 1983-84. Recipient Good Conduct Medal Immaculate Comception, Tuckahoe, N.Y., 1940; Named Miss Ideal Girl U.S. Army-Keesler Field, Biloxi Miss., 1940. Mem. Nat. Trust for Hist. Preservation, Screen Actors Guild (aka Kelly Jaffe), AFTRA (aka Kelly Jaffe), Am. Film Inst., Nat. Wildlife Fedn and Wilderness Soc., Actors Equity Assn. Independent Republican. Roman Catholic. also: Piecefull Collections 155 Baltimore Ave Bandon-by-the-Sea OR 97411

KELLY, ROCHELLE-LOUISE, marketing professional, clothing designer; b. Pueblo, Colo., July 29, 1961; d. John Russell and Georgina Frances (Woodward) K. BS, U. So. Colo., 1984. Assoc. brand mgr. Better Brands Atlanta, 1984-86; mktg. cons. Peachtree Mktg., Atlanta, 1986; young adult mktg. specialist Coffee Devel. Group, Denver, 1986—; designer, ptnr. Kelyco Western Wear, 1987—; mem. pub. rels. position, mktg. Nat. High Sch. Rodeo Assn., Denver, 1987—. Mem. Jr. League Denver. Office: 7777 E Yale Ste A-307 Denver CO 80201

KELLY, SALLY M(ARIE), pathologist; b. Bridgeport, Conn.; d. James F. and Elizabeth R. (Burke) K. AB, Conn. Coll., 1943; MA, U. Wis., Madison, 1944, PhD, 1946; MD, NYU, 1963. Diplomate Am. Bd. Pathology (Clin.). Rsch. fellow Bklyn. Botanic Garden, 1945-47; instr. Simmons Coll., Boston, 1947-48; asst. prof. Vassar Coll., Poughkeepsie, N.Y., 1948-51; sr. rsch. scientist N.Y. Dept. Health, Albany, 1951-64, assoc. rsch. scientist, 1964-67, rsch. physician, 1967—; teaching asst. U. Wis., Madison, 1946, Columbia U., N.Y.C., 1946-47; rsch. fellow Harvard U., Cambridge, Mass., 1947-48; resident in clin. pathology, Albany Med. Ctr. Hosp., 1968-70; rsch. assoc. prof. Albany Med. Coll., 1974—. Author: Biochemical Methods in Medical Genetics, 1977; editor: Birth Defects: Risks and Consequences, 1976, Clinical Genetics: Problems in Diagnosis and Counseling (with others), 1982; contbr. articles to profl. jours. Lalor Found. fellow, Wilmington, Del., 1950-51; Brown-Hazen Fund fellow in med. edn., Rsch. Corp., N.Y.C., 1958, 60-63. Fellow AAAS, Coll. Am. Pathologists; mem. Phi Beta Kappa. Office: NY State Dept Health Wadsworth Ctr Labs & Rsch Albany NY 12201

KELLY, SHANNON LYNN, stockbroker; b. Monterey, Calif., Sept. 10, 1956; d. Leonard Howard and Joni Dorothy (Twitchell) Higginbotham; m. Brian Andrew Kelly, Sept. 12, 1982. A.A., U. South Fla., 1974-76; B.A., U. Hawaii, 1979. Outer islands mgr. Gatliff Corp., Honolulu, 1979-81; stockbroker Paine Webber Jackson & Curtis, Honolulu, 1981-89; fin. advisor, analyst State of Hawaii, 1989—; freelance poetry writer. Recipient Golden Poet award Am. Poetry Assn., 1987. Mem. Investment Soc. Hawaii (bd. dirs.). Republican, Honolulu Bd. Realtors.

KELLY, SHARON LEE, writer, editor; b. Phila., Oct. 10, 1965; d. George Francis and Beverly Ann (Taylor) K. BA in English, Villanova (Pa.) U., 1987; postgrad., Beaver Coll., 1988—. Sales promotion editor Prudential Ins., Ft. Washington, Pa., 1987—. Committeewoman Rep. Party, Doylestown, Pa., 1988—; literacy tutor Vols. in Teaching Alternatives, Doylestown, 1990—; pub. rels. chair Bucks County Conservancy, Doylestown, 1989—; chairperson Bucks County Young Reps., Doylestown, 1989—. Mem. Women in Communications, Inc. Home: 777 Wallace Dr Warminster PA 18974

KELLY, SUSAN CROCE, corporate affairs professional; b. Berkeley, Calif., Feb. 6, 1947; d. D. Fred and Helen June (Morris) Croce; m. James Michael Kelly, Jan. 30, 1970 (div. 1977); 1 child, Brendan Croce Kelly. BS, Purdue U., 1969; MA, St. Louis U., 1973. Reporter St. Louis Globe Democrat, 1969-72; reporter, photographer Springfield (Mo.) Newspapers Inc., 1973-76; pub. rels. specialist Monsanto St. Louis, 1976-78; pub. rels. mgr. Monsanto Europe SA Monsanto Co., Brussels and London, 1978; mgr. editorial svcs., then mgr. sci. communications Monsanto Co., St. Louis, 1979-83, pub. rels. dir., then dir. corp. communications, 1984-85; freelance writer St. Louis, 1986; dir. corp. affairs Sandoz Crop Protection Corp., Des Plaines, Ill., 1987—; mem. pub. affairs oversight coun. Nat. Agr. Chem. Assn., Washington, 1989—; pub. rels. com. Western Agr. Chem. Assn. Author: Route 66, 1988; contbr. articles and features to various mags. and newspapers. Bd. dirs. Theatre Project Co., St. Louis, 1983-86; pub. rels. com. Churchill Meml., Fulton, Mo., 1983—; v.p. Hadley Twp. Dem. Club, Clayton, Mo., 1984; mem. Circle of Friends, Chgo. YMCA, 1989-90. Mem. Pub. Rels. Soc. Am. (chpt. officer 1976—), Soc. Midwest Authors, Exec. Club Chgo. Roman Catholic. Office: Sandoz Crop Protection Corp 1300 E Touhy Ave Des Plaines IL 60018

KELLY, SUZANNE WOODWARD, management consultant, trainer; b. Wichita, Kans., Sept. 10, 1946; d. Wallace Wayne and Julianne (Seitz) Woodward; m. Glenn Lochten Kelly, Jan. 27, 1967 (div. 1989); children: Scott Lochten, Brian Woodward, Matthew MacFerren. BS in Nursing, U. Colo., Denver, 1969; MS in Bus. Administn., U. Denver, Denver, 1985. Reg. nurse. Vis. nurse Denver Vis. Nurses Assn., 1969; founder, childbirth educator Childbirth and Parenting Assn. and Co., Denver, 1969-80; mgmt. cons. Susan Kelly Assoc., Englewood, Colo., 1980—; adj. prof. Met. State Coll. Denver, 1980, 85; cons., trainer, bd. dirs. Tech. Assistance Ctr., 1980-88. Pres. Cherry Hills Rancho Water and Sewer Dist., Englewood 1986—; bd. dirs., pres. Arapahoe County Med. Aux., Englewood pres. 1970-84, bd. dirs. Porter Meml. Hosp. Found., 1979-85; v.p. Jr. League Denver, 1975-87; mem. Leadership Denver, 1982—, 50 for Colo., 1988. Mem. Am. Soc. Training & Devel., Inst. Mgmt. Cons. Presbyterian. Office: 17 Martin Ln Englewood CO 80110

KELLY, TERESA SPARKS, systems application engineer; b. Bluefield, W.Va., Jan. 18, 1963; d. Edward Eugene and Edith Mae (Weiss) Sparks; m. John Westley Kelly, Jr., Oct. 3, 1987. Student, Bluefield State Coll., 1980-84. Equipment application engr. No. Telecom, Inc., Research Triangle Park, N.C., 1985-87, system application engr., 1987—. Mem. NAFE. Home: 6817 Tavernier Ct Apex NC 27502 Office: No Telecom Inc 200 Perimeter Park Dr Morrisville NC 27560

KELLY, VIANA EILEEN, marketing and public relations professional; b. Pueblo, Colo., Feb. 10, 1953; d. Duane Albert and Mary Vinta (Ames) Rockel; m. Douglas Ray Heeren, July 22, 1972 (dec.); children: Douglas Ray, Valissitie Christina; m. Eric Damian Kelly, May 31, 1980; children: Damian Charles, Eliza Jane. Grad., Iowa State U. V.p. bd. dirs. Color Radio, Ltd., Leadville, Colo., 1980-83; mktg. cons. U. Park Mchts. Assn., Pueblo, 1985; mktg. specialist Pueblo Community Coll., 1980-85; grad. asst. Dept. Profl. Studies Iowa State U.; advt. cons. Seal Pharmacy, Pueblo, 1984-85. Bd. dirs. Pueblo Girls Club, 1986-89; active Jr. League of Pueblo, 1982-85; vol. tng. Channel 8 Auction, Pueblo 1988, Leadership Pueblo, 1986; dir. So. Colo. Sci. Olympiad, 1989-90. Mem. AAUW (bd. dirs. 1987), State Bd. Community Colls. (rep., mem. mktg. com. 1985-90), Kiwanis, Colo. Press Club, So. Press Club, Alpha Chi. Home: 1506 13th St Ames IA 50010

KELSEY, FRANCES OLDHAM (MRS. FREMONT ELLIS KELSEY), government official; b. Cobble Hill, Vancouver Island, Can., July 24, 1914; came to U.S., 1936, naturalized, 1956; d. Frank Trevor and Katherine (Stuart) Oldham; m. Fremont Ellis Kelsey, Dec. 6, 1943; children—Susan Elizabeth, Christine Ann. B.Sc., McGill U., 1934; M.Sc., 1935; Ph.D., U. Chgo., 1938, M.D., 1950. Instr., asst. prof. pharmacology U. Chgo., 1938-50; editorial assoc. AMA, Chgo., 1950-52; assoc. prof. pharmacology U. S.D., 1954-57; med. officer FDA, Washington, 1960—; dir. div. sci. investigations FDA, 1967—. Author: (with F.E. Kelsey, E.M.K. Geiling) Essentials of Pharmacology, 1960. Recipient Pres.'s award for Distinguished Fed. Civilian Service (refusal to approve contl. distbn. thalidomide in U.S.), 1962. Mem. Am. Soc. Pharmacology and Exptl. Therapeutics, Soc. Exptl. Biology and Medicine, Am. Med. Writers Assn., International Assn. Teratology Soc., Sigma Xi, Sigma Delta Epsilon. Home: 5811 Brookside Dr Chevy Chase MD 20015 Office: FDA Office of Compliance 7520 Standish Pl Rockville MD 20855

KELSEY, JULIE ANN, automotive executive; b. Chgo., Sept. 1, 1961; d. Ralph Charles and Jean Catherine (Zicarelli) Smejkal; m. Thomas Drake

Kelsey, Oct. 17, 1987. BS in Advt., U. Ill., 1984. Sales trainee Nat. Bus. Lists, Chgo., 1984-85; distbn. analyst Ford Motor Co., Detroit, 1985-86; dist. analyst Ford Motor Co., Indpls., 1986, zone mgr., 1986-88, metro mgr., 1988, dist. merchandising specialist, 1989—. Home: 11651 Capistrano Dr Indianapolis IN 46236 Office: Ford Motor Co PO Box 1992 Indianapolis IN 46206

KELSH, KAREN TERESA, sales executive; b. White Plains, N.Y., Oct. 10, 1963. AA, Gulf Coast Community Coll., 1984; BS in Fashion Mdse., Fla. State U., 1985. Store mgr. Dairy Queen, Panama City Beach, Fla., 1979-83; asst. mgr. Ice Cream Circus, Panama City Beach, 1983; night mgr. Surf Line Shirts, Panama City Beach, 1984; intern Jordan Marsh, Boca Raton, Fla., 1985; exec. trainee Jordan Marsh, Orlando, Fla., 1986; area sales mgr. Jordan Marsh, Altamonte Springs, Fla., 1986-89; group sales mgr. Maison Blanche, Altamonte Springs, 1989-90; cosmetic mgr. Maison Blanche, Tampa, Fla., 1990—. Alt. chmn. Jordan Marsh United Way. Mem. NAFE, Fla. State U. Alumni Assn., Fla. State U. Trustee Club. Office: Maison Blanche 2200 E Fowler Ave Tampa FL 33619

KELSO, GWENDOLYN LEE, silver appraiser, consultant; b. Washington, Jan. 5, 1935; d. Leon Hugh and Katherine Estelle (Henderson) K. Mgr. Shaw & Brown Co., Washington, 1967-71, Chas. Schwartz & Son, Washington, 1972-76; silver appraiser, Washington, 1976—; ptnr. The Silver Lion, Washington, 1983-85; owner, mgr. The Rampant Lion, Washington, 1985—; cons. to FBI and law enforcement agys. and cts., 1982—; appraiser presentation silver aboard U.S. naval vessels and at installations, 1986-88; cataloguer, conservator silver Forbes Mag. Collection, N.Y.C., 1989; mem. USS Alexandria Commning Com. Mem. Internat. Soc. Appraisers (scholar 1989), Am. Soc. Appraisers (candidate for membership), Appraisers Assn. Am., Silver Soc. (London), NAFE, U.S. Naval Inst., Newcomen Soc. U.S. Republican. Episcopalian. Home: 3731 39th St NW Washington DC 20016 Office: The Rampant Lion PO Box 5887 Washington DC 20016

KELTS, SUSAN MARGARET, registered nurse; b. Herington, Kans., Oct. 25, 1949; d. George Cummins and Jeanette Wilhelmina (Frese) Sims; m. K. Alan Kelts, May 1, 1977; children: Eric, Amanda, Gregory, Andrew. Diploma, Stormont Vail Sch. Nursing, Topeka, 1970; BSN, Met. State Coll., Denver, 1977. RN; cert. child/adolescent nursing. Staff nurse pediatrics Stormont Vail Hosp., Topeka, 1970-71; staff nurse Sullivan County Community Gen. Hosp., Liberty, N.Y., 1971-72; staff nurse, team leader U. Colo. Med. Ctr., Denver, 1972-76; pediatric office nurse Menlo Med. Clinic, Menlo Park, Calif., 1976-78; school nurse Menlo Sch. and Coll., Menlo Park, 1978-79; staff devel. instr. McKennan Hosp., Sioux Falls, S.D., 1979-81; staff devel. coord. Rapid City (S.D.) Rahab. Hosp., 1981-84; instr. pediatric nursing sch. of nursing Rapid City Regional Hosp., 1984-86, staff devel. coord. pediatric intensive care, 1986—. Mem. Rapid City Area Child Protection Coun., 1989—, Black Hills Symphony Chorus, Rapid City, 1987—; mem., sec. Wilson Sch. PTA, Rapid City, 1989—; bd. dirs., parent advisor Rapid City Children's Ctr., 1985-90; founder, co-coord. hosp. tour program for children, Rapid City, 1987-90. Mem. Am. Nurses Assn., S.D. Nurses' Assn. (bd. dirs. 1983-87), Assn. for Care Children's Health, AAUW, Sigma Theta Tau. Democrat. Congregationalist. Office: Rapid City Regional Hosp 353 Fairmont Blvd Rapid City SD 57701

KEMBLE-HEISINGER, ANNE, nursing manager, nurse; b. Argentina, Can., Aug. 10, 1956; d. Stanley G. and Mary Frances (Fewer) Heisinger; m. Lee Kemble, June 2, 1984; 1 child, Ilia Bride. BSN, Calif. State U., Fresno, 1979, MSN, 1983, postgrad. Sr. care case mgmt. Calif. Med. Ctr., L.A.; lectr. nursing Calif. State U., Long Beach; lectr. nursing, staff nurse critical care Valley Medicine Ctr., Fresno; presenter in field. Am. Assn. Critical Care Nurses, Greater Long Beach Critical Care Nurses, Orange County Critical Care Nurses (publs. chair). Home: 1821 Delta St Rosemead CA 91770

KEMMERER, SHARON JEAN, computer specialist; b. Sellersville, Pa., Apr. 11, 1956; d. John Musselman and Esther Jone (Landis) K. BS, Shippensburg U., 1978; MBA, Marymount Coll., 1982. Mgmt. analyst Navy Internat. Logistics, Phila., 1978-81; computer systems analyst Navy Supply Systems Commn., Crystal City, Va., 1981-86, Nat. Inst. Standards and Tech., Gaithersburg, Md., 1986—; mem. com. Fed. Women's Program. Contbr. articles, poetry to newspapers. Deacon Alexandria (Va.) Ch., 1985-86, v.p. coun., 1985; moderator Lung Assn., Fairfax, Va., 1986; vol. Project Heart, Washington, 1986-87, Montgomery County Health Buddy, 1988—, Stepping Stones Shelter for Homeless, 1989—. Mem. IEEE Computer Soc. Lutheran. Office: NIST/NCSL Gaithersburg MD 20899

KEMP, BETTY RUTH, librarian; b. Tishomingo, Okla., May 5, 1930; d. Raymond Herrell and Mamie Melvina (Hughes) K.; B.A.L.S., U. Okla., 1952; M.S., Fla. State U., 1965. Extramural loan libr. U. Tex., Austin, 1952-55; libr. lit. and history dept. Dallas Pub. Libr., 1955-56, head Oaklawn Br., 1956-60, head Walnut Hill Br., 1960-64; dir. Cherokee Regional Libr., LaFayette, Ga., 1965-74; dir. Lee County Libr., hdqrs. Lee-Itawamba Libr. System, Tupelo, Miss., 1975—; bd. libr. owners. State of Miss., 1979-83, chmn., 1979-80. Active LWV, United Meth. Women. Mem. ALA, Southeastern Libr. Assn. (sec. pub. libr. sect. 1987-88, continuing edn. and staff devel. com.), Miss. Libr. Assn. (chmn. reprint com 1989—), Am. Assn. of Univ. Women, Nat. Soc. Daus. of War of 1812, United Daus. of the Confederacy, Nat. Soc. Dames of Ct. of Honor, Beta Phi Mu. Democrat. Home: 2112 President Tupelo MS 38801 Office: 219 Madison Tupelo MS 38801

KEMP, SUZANNE LEPPART, educator, clubwoman; b. N.Y.C., Dec. 28, 1929; d. John Culver and Eleanor (Buxton) Leppart; m. Ralph Clinton Kemp, Apr. 4, 1953; children—Valerie Gale, Sandra Lynn, John Maynard, Renee Alison. Grad. Ogontz Jr. Coll., 1949; B.S., U. Md., 1952. Elem. sch. tchr. Mem. Nat. Soc. Women Descs. of Ancient and Hon. Arty. Co., Nat. Soc. Daus. of Founders and Patriots of Am. (corr. sec.), Nat. Soc. Sons and Daus. of Pilgrims, Nat. Soc. U.S. Daus. of 1812 (chpt. organizing pres. 1977-79, state 2d v.p., chpt. v.p. 1979—), Nat. Soc. New Eng. Women (colony pres. 1978-80, Nat. Soc. Colonial Dames XVII Century (state chmn. heraldry and coats of arms 1977-79), Nat. Soc. D.A.R. (chpt. regent 1970-73, chpt. v.p., Md. soc. chmn. transp. 1976-79), Md. State Officers Club, Md. Hist. Soc., Friends of Animals, Defenders of Animal Rights Inc., U. Md. Alumni, English Speaking Union, Star Spangled Banner Flag House Assn., Potter-Balt. Clayworks, Balt. Mus. Art, Walters Art Gallery, Dames of the Court of Honor, Kappa Delta Alumni. Clubs: Baltimore Country; Lago Mar (Ft. Lauderdale, Fla.); Roland Park Women's. Editor: The Spinning Wheel, 1973-76. Home: 1206 Doves Cove Rd Towson MD 21204

KEMPER, DORLA DEAN (DORLA DEAN EATON), real estate broker; b. Calhoun, Mo., Sept. 10, 1929; d. Paul McVey and Jesse Lee (McCombs) Eaton; student, William Woods Coll., 1947-48; B.S. in Edn., Cen. Mo. State U., 1952; m. Charles K. Kemper, Mar. 1, 1951; children: Kevin Keil, Kara Lee. Tchr. pub. schs., Twin Falls, Idaho, 1950-51, Mission, Kans., 1952-53, Burbank, Calif., 1953-57; real estate saleswoman, Minn., 1967-68, Calif., 1971-73; Deanie Kemper, Realtor (name changed to Deanie Kemper, Inc. Real Estate Brokerage 1976), Loomis, Calif., 1974-76, pres., 1976—, also dir. Pres., Battle Creek Park Elem. Sch. PTA, St. Paul, 1966-67; mem. Placer County (Calif.) Bicentennial Commn., 1976; mem. Sierra Coll. Adv. Com., 1981—. Named to Million Dollar Club (lifetime) Sacramento and Placer County bds. realtors, 1978; designated Grad. Realtors Inst., Cert. Residential Specialist. Mem. Nat. Assn. Realtor, Calif. Assn. Realtors, Nat. Assn. Real Estate Appraisers, Placer County (mem. profl. standards com.) bds. realtors, Bd. Calif. regent 1971-73, organizing chpt. regent 1977-79, chpt. dir. 1978-80, state registrar Calif. 1980-82, state vice regent 1982-84, state regent 1984-86, nat. resolutions com.); nat. recording sec. gen. NSDAR, DAR (nat. chmn. units overseas 1983-86). Republican. Mem. Christian Ch. Clubs: Hidden Valley Women's (pres. Loomis club 1970-71, rec. sec. gen. 1986—), Auburn Travel Study (pres. 1979). Home: 8165 Morningside Dr Loomis CA 95650

KEMPER, KATHI JILL, pediatrics educator; b. St. Louis, Feb. 3, 1957; d. Kenneth Eugene and Merline (Briggs) Kemper. BA, U. Chgo., 1978; postgrad., U. N.C. 1978-82, U. N.C., 1982-83. Resident in preventive medicine U. N.C., Chapel Hill, 1983; intern in pediatrics U. Wis., Madison, 1983-84, resident in pediatrics, 1984-86; Robert Wood Johnson gen. acad. fellow in pediatrics Yale U., New Haven, 1986-88; pediatrician Pedi-Care, Essex,

Conn., 1987-88; physician Yale Health Plan, New Haven, Conn., 1987-88; asst. prof. pediatrics U. Wash., Seattle, 1988—; cons. Haber & Flora Inc., New Haven, 1987-88. Contbr. articles to profl. jours. Fellow Am. Acad. Pediatrics; mem. Ambulatory Pediatric Assn., Am. Pub. Health Assn., Western Soc. Pediatric Rsch. Mem. Soc. of Friends. Office: Harborview Med Ctr 325 Ninth Ave Seattle WA 98104

KEMPER, MARLYN JANOFSKY, information scientist; b. Balt., Mar. 26, 1943; d. Louis and Augusta Louise (Jacobs) Janofsky; m. Bennett I. Kemper, Aug. 1, 1965 (dec. June 1987); children: Alex Randall, Gari Hament, Jason Myles; m. Lewis Littman, Apr. 22, 1990. BA, Finch Coll., 1964; MA in Anthropology, Temple U., Phila., 1970; MA in Library Sci., U. S. Fla., 1983; D in Info. Sci., Nova U., 1986. Dir., Hist. Broward County Preservation Bd., Hollywood, Fla., 1979-87; automated systems librarian Broward County Main Library, Ft. Lauderdale, Fla., 1983-86; assoc. prof., dir. info. sci. doctoral program Nova U., Ft. Lauderdale, 1987—. Pub. info. officer Broward County Hist. Commn., 1975-79. Vice chmn. Broward County Library Adv. Bd., 1987—. Recipient Judge L. Clayton Nance award, 1977; Broward County Hist. Commn. award, 1979. Mem. ALA, IEEE, Am. Soc. for Info. Sci., Spl. Libraries Assn., Assn. Computing Machinery, Info. Industry Assn., Beta Phi Mu, Phi Kappa Phi . Author: A Comprehensive Documented History of the City of Pompano Beach, 1982 A Comprehensive History of Dania 1983, Hallandale, 1984, Deerfield Beach, 1985, Plantation, 1986, Davie, 1987, Networking: Choosing A Lan Path to Interconnection, 1987; author weekly columns Ft. Lauderdale News, 1975-79; contbr. articles to Microcomputer Environment: Management Issues, and articles to profl. jours. Home: 2845 NE 35th St Fort Lauderdale FL 33306 Office: Nova U Info Sci Dept 3301 College Ave Parker Bldg Fort Lauderdale FL 33314

KEMPF, MARTINE, voice control device manufacturing company executive; b. Strasbourg, France, Dec. 9, 1958; came to U.S., 1985; d. Jean-Pierre and Brigitte Marguerite (Klockenbring) K. Student in Astronomy, Friedrich Wilhelm U., Bonn, Fed. Republic of Germany, 1981-83. Owner, mgr. Kempf, Sunnyvale, Calif., 1985—. Inventor Comeldir Multiplex Handicapped Driving Systems (Goldenes Lenkrad Axel Springer Verlag 1981), Katalavox speech recognition control system (Oscar, World Almanac Inventions 1984, Prix Grand Siecle, Comite Couronne Francaise 1985). Recipient Medal for Service to Humanity Spinal Cord Soc., 1986; street named in honor in Dossenheim-Kochersberg, Alsace, France, 1987; named Citizen of Honor City of Dossenheim-Kochersberg, 1985, Outstanding Businessperson of Yr. City of Sunnyvale, 1990. Office: Kempf 1080 E Duane Ave Ste E Sunnyvale CA 94086

KENDA, JUANITA ECHEVERRIA, artist, educator; b. Tarentum, Pa., Nov. 12, 1922; d. Carlos Porfirio and Jane Amelia (Gummert) Echeverria; m. William Kenda, Aug. 18, 1940; children: Linda Jane, Carlos Paul, William Porfirio. Student, Stephens Coll., 1940-41, Art Students' League, N.Y.C., 1941-42; BFA, Temple U. and Tyler Art Sch., 1945; student, U. Hawaii, 1969-72. Instr. Phila. Mus. Art, 1940-43, Sr. Acad., Punanou Sch., Honolulu, 1948-49; dir. art edn. Hawaii Dept. Edn., Honolulu, 1952-60; head, creative art sect. Honolulu Acad. Arts, Honolulu, 1958-63; community relations officer, Eastwest Ctr. U. Hawaii, Honolulu, 1967-70; pres. Nat. Soc. Arts and Letters, Downtown Gallery, Honolulu, 1969-76, Am. Women's Club, Asuncion, Paraguay, 1977-79; trustee Tennant Found., Honolulu, 1984—. One woman exhibitions include: Duncan Gallery, N.Y., Da Vinci Gallery, Phila., Downtown Gallery, Honolulu; represented in collections of pres. of Mex., many others. Bd. dirs. Hawaii Art Coun., Honolulu, 1984—, Honolulu Acad. Arts; hon. consul of Mexico in Honolulu, 1969-77; mem. Allentown Art Mus., Peabody Mus. Mem. Hawaii Artist's League (pres. 1984—), Am. Assn. Museums, Internat. Coun. Museums, PEO, Oahu Country Club, Plaza Club. Republican. Episcopalian. Home: 3708 Lurline Dr Honolulu HI 96816

KENDALL, DOLORES DIANE PISAPIA, artist, author, marketing executive; b. Newark, N.J., June 1, 1946; d. Dominick Pisapia and Ann Fanfone Pisapia Kendall. Grad. Berkeley Bus. Coll., East Orange, N.J., 1965; postgrad. Middlesex County Coll., Edison, N.J., 1966-67, Rutgers U., 1967-69, Todd Butler Art Workshop, Edison, 1964-74, art Inst. Boston, 1976, Graham Art Studio, Boston, 1975-77, Sch. Visual Arts, N.Y.C., 1978, NYU, 1977, Advt. Club N.Y., 1978. Proofreader, supr. N.J. State Diagnostic Ctr., Menlo Park, N.J., 1965-75; apprentice, instr. Graham Art Studio, Boston, 1975-77; dir. direct mktg. Boardroom Reports Inc., N.Y.C., 1977-82; pres., chief operating officer Roman Managed Lists, N.Y.C., 1982; dir. direct mktg. Mal Dunn Assocs., N.Y.C., 1983; dir. lists and card deck mgmt. Warren, Gorham & Lamont Inc., N.Y.C., 1984-86, direct mktg. cons., 1986-87; p. Marketry, Inc., N.Y.C. and Bellevue, Wash., 1987—. Exhibited in group art shows: N.Y.C., Boston, Middlesex County, N.J., Somerset County, N.J., Morris, N.J., 1965-74, Greenwich Village Art Show, N.Y.C., 1972, Graham Art Studio, Boston, 1975-77; represented in numerous pvt. art collections throughout the U.S. Author: My Eyes Are Windows, 1972; Feelings and Thoughts (poetry), 1979. Recipient Desi award Direct Mail Mktg. Promotion Package, 1980, Poetry award One Mag., 1972, Internat. Cert. of Recognition for List Day, 1982. Mem. Direct Mktg. Assn. (Echo awards led judges 1982-85, List Day lectr., N.Y.C.), Internat. Poetry Assn. (Clover Collection of Verse VI 1973, Danae in Clover 1973—), Direct Mktg. Creative Guild, Nat. Mail Order Assn. (adv. bd. 1979-80), Nat. Assn. Female Execs., NOW, Direct Mktg. Club N.Y.C., Internat. Platform Assn., Nat. Bus. Circulation Assn. Home: 530 2d Ave New York NY 10016 Office: Marketry Inc 312 E 30th St Suite 14B New York NY 10016

KENDALL, KATHARINE KERR, genealogist, author, historian, researcher; b. Yanceyville, N.C., Oct. 10, 1921; d. Albert Yancey and Mary Johnston (Oliver) Kerr; m. Henry E. Kendall, June 21, 1947 (dec.). AB, Meredith Coll., 1942. Genealogist Raleigh, N.C., 1960—; Mem. Carolina Charter Corp., Raleigh, 1989—. Author: Caswell County N.C. Wills (3 books), 1979, Caswell County N.C. Deeds, 199, History Yanceyville Presbyterian Church, 1976, Person County N.C. Wills, Marriages (2 books) 1980-85. Mem., sec. bd. dirs. Wake County Red Cross, Raleigh, 1967-73; precinct chmn. Wake County N.C. Dem. Party, 1970. Mem. DAR (Samuel Johnston chpt., former regent, Geneal. award), N.C. Geneal. Soc. (charter, 1st treas. 1973—), Nat. Geneal. Assn., Presbn. Hist. Soc., Hist. Preservation Soc. N.C., Wake County Hist. Soc., Caswell County Hist. Soc., Friends N.C. State Archives (life), Friends Meredith Coll. Libr. (life). Presbyterian. Home and Office: 2814 Exeter Circle Raleigh NC 27608

KENDALL, KAY LYNN, interior designer; b. Cadillac, Mich., Aug. 20, 1950; d. Robert Llewellyn and Betty Louise (Powers) K.; 1 child, Anna Renee Easter. BFA, U. Mich., 1973. Draftsman, interior designer store planning dept. Jacobson Stores, Inc., Jackson, Mich., 1974-79; sr. interior designer store planning dept. Jacobson Stores, Inc., Jackson, 1981—; prin. Kay Kendall Designs, Jackson, 1979—; cons. in field. Mem. Am. Soc. Interior Designers (profl. mem., assoc. Cen. Mich. chpt.). Home: 340 Edward St Jackson MI 49201 Office: Jacobson Stores Inc 3333 Sargent Rd Jackson MI 49201

KENDALL, KIM ELIZABETH, clinical psychologist; b. Oakland, Calif., Feb. 2, 1952; d. Jack Douglas and Ruth Evelyn (Butler) K. BS in Psychology, U. Calif., Davis, 1979; PhD in Clin. Psychology, U. Mass., 1985. Lic. psychologist, Mass., Wis., Wash. Acting chief psychology VA Hosp. and Med. Ctr., White River Junction, Vt., 1985-86; pvt. practice psychology Northampton, Mass., 1986; staff psychologist Amherst Coll. Student Health Ctr., Amherst, Mass., 1986, Monroe Clinic, Monroe, Wis., 1986-89; asst. clin. faculty dept. child psychiatry Adolescent Clinic, U. Wash., Seattle, 1989—; clin. supr. behavioral medicine sect. Dartmouth Med. Sch., Hanover, N.H., 1984-85. Co-author: Partners in Health, 1985; contbr. articles to profl. jours. Grantee Sigma Delta Epsilon, 1982, Sigma Xi, 1982. Mem. Am. Psychol. Assn., Nat. Register Health Svc. Providers in Psychology, Soc. Behavioral Medicine, Wash. State Psychol. Assn. Democrat. Office: Univ Wash Child Devel Ctr WJ 10 Seattle WA 98195 also: 1728 E Madison St Seattle WA 98122

KENDALL, LAUREL ANN, geotechnical engineer; b. Detroit, Dec. 4, 1956; d. James McNair and Dorothy Mildred (Frost) K. BSE in Environ. Sci., U. Mich., 1979, MS in Civil Engring., 1983. Registered profl. engr., Mich. Student engr. Bechtel Assocs. P.C., Ann Arbor, Mich., 1979, geotech. engr., 1980-81; geotech. engr. Bechtel Civic & Mineral Corp., Gaithersburg, Md.,

1981-82, Bechtel Power Corp., Midland, Mich., 1983-84; project engr., mgr. NTH Cons., Ltd., Farmington Hills, Mich., 1984—; instr. Lawrence Inst. Tech., Southfield, Mich., 1985—. Mem. ASCE (chmn. geotech. com. 1985-87, bd. dirs. 1987—), Mich. Soc. Profl. Engrs., Engring. Soc. Detroit. Congregationalist. Office: NTH Cons. Ltd 38955 Hills Tech Dr Farmington Hills MI 48055

KENDALL, SCIPIARUTH, programmer analyst; b. Boston, May 29, 1955; d. Scipio Hoover and Connie Lee (Lester) K. BS in Computer Info Systems, Calif. Polytech. U., Pomona, 1986. Noncommd. lab. tech. USAF-George AFB, Victorville, Calif., 1977-81; lab. asst. Covina (Calif.) Reference Lab., 1981-85; credit processor Informative Rsch., Inc., Anaheim, Calif., 1985; inventory specialist Washington Inventory Inc., Riverside, Calif., 1985; tax asst. Borsch Tax Svc., Fullerton, Calif., 1986; phlebotomist Meth. Hosp., Arcadia, Calif., 1986; eligibility worker County of L.A., El Monte, Calif., 1986-87; programmer analyst L.A. County, Downey, Calif., 1987—; commd. lab. technician USAFR, March AFB, Calif., 1981-89, commd. Med. Svc. Corps, 1990—. Canvasser U.S. Savs. Bond of L.A. County, Downey, 1988; fundraiser Brotherhood Crusade and United Way, Downey, 1988; walker March of Dimes L.A. County, Downey, 1989, 90. With USAF, 1977-81, USAFR, 1981—. Recipient Community Support award L.A. County Data Processing Dept., 1990. Mem. NAFE, Orange County Women Networkers, Data Processing Mgmt. Assn., Toastmasters Internat. Office: LA County Data Processing Dept Law Enforcement Systems 9150 E Imperial Hwy Downey CA 92424

KENDIG, PATRICIA HALE, writer, consultant; b. Salt Lake City, Aug. 19, 1934; d. John Carson and Larene Ellen (Feeney) Hale; children: Colleen Patricia, William Fabian Jr., John James. BA in History, Stanford U., 1956. Tech. writer Evans & Sutherland Computer Corp., 1970-74, Western Bancorp., Salt Lake City, 1974-76; prodn. editor Martin Marietta Corp., Washington, 1985—; freelance writer various locations, 1958—; editor Am. Diabetes Assn. newsletter, 1972-73, Marriage Encounter newsletter, 1974-75; adv. bd. Intermountain Cath. newspaper, Salt Lake City, 1981-85. Contbr. articles to various jours., Utah State Hist. Soc. Mag.; columnist Gitmo Gazette, 1963-64, Beaufort (S.C.) Gazette, 1965, Rocky Mountain Rev., 1966. Pub. rels. mgr. for musical and religious orgns., Salt Lake City, 1974-80; bd. dirs. Stanford Alumni of Utah, 1982-84. Mem. AAUW (state div. chair 1982-83, chpt. officer 1980-81), League Utah Writers (chpt. pres. 1972-73), Soc. tech. Communication (award of merit 1987, award of achievement 1988), Stanford Alumni of Washington, D.C. Roman Catholic. Office: Martin Marietta Corp ATS 475 School St Washington DC 20024

KENDRICK, CHERYL DONOFRIO, hospital administrator; b. Troy, N.Y., Feb. 10, 1948; d. Frank Charles and Norma (Martorelli) Donofrio; m. Carleton R. Ayers (div.); children: Joshua Royse, Benjamin Lawrence; m. Ronald Howard Kendrick, June 10, 1989. Student, St. Lawrence U., 1966-69; première degrée, U. Rouen, France, 1968-69; BA in French and English, U. Conn., 1970; postgrad., San Diego State U., 1975-77. Mgr. pub. rels. J.W. Robinson's, San Diego, 1977-81; dir. pub. rels., asst. store mgr. Neiman Marcus, San Diego, 1981-88; dir. Office Procotol, Office of Mayor, San Diego, 1988-89; dir. hosp. and market communications Grossmont Hosp., La Mesa, Calif., 1989—. Bd. dirs. Charter 100, San Diego, 1970—, L.E.A.D. San Diego, Inc., 1987—, Sr. Community Ctrs., San Diego, 1989—. Mem. Am. Soc. Hosp. Mktg. and Pub. Rels., Pub. Rels. Soc. Am., Nat. Assn. Hosp. Devel., Health Care Communicators, San Diego Women in Health Administra. Republican. Office: Grossmont Hosp 5555 Grossmont Center Dr La Mesa CA 92042

KENDRICK, PAMELA ANN, mathematics educator; b. Joplin, Mo., July 6, 1943; d. Laymon Harl and Margaret Alice (Stiers) Morrison; m. Anthony Eugene Kendrick , June 9, 1963. EdB, Pittsburg (Kans.) State U., 1965, MS, 1969. Cert. tchr., Mo., Kans. Computer programmer RCA Missile Test Project, Cape Canaveral Air Force Sta., Fla., 1969-72; statistician NASA Pub. Health Service, Cape Canaveral Air Force Sta., Fla., 1972-73; engr., computer analyst Jet Propulsion Lab., Cape Canaveral Air Force Sta., Fla., 1973-74; instr. math Fla. Inst. Tech., Melbourne, 1974-81; asst. prof. Brevard Community Coll., Cocoa, Fla., 1982—; cons. to various textbook pubs.; dir. computer calculus project in conjunction with Fla. Programs in Excellence, 1988; developer TV stats. course Brevard Community Coll. Recipient Outstanding Alumni award Pittsburg State U., 1975-76; named Fla. Outstanding Young Woman, 1976-77, One of Top 20 Outstanding Young Women Am., 1976-77. Mem. AAUW (sec. Brevard County 1983-85, v.p. programming Brevard County 1986-88), Math. Assn. Am. Democrat. Office: Brevard Community Coll 1519 Clearlake Rd Cocoa FL 32922

KENDRICK, STEPHANIE BIRD, real estate agent; b. Sheridan, Wyo., Dec. 1, 1953; d. Hugh Theodore and Lois Elaine (Huson) Bird; m. Hugh Cumming Kendrick, Dec. 29, 1950; children: Jacob, Hugh. AA, Sheridan Coll., 1983, BS, U. Wyo., 1983; student, Place Real Estate Sch., 1988. Real estate agt., owner KB Brokerage, Inc., Sheridan; ticket sales mgr. Sheridan Rodeo Assn.; exec. sec. WY-MT Indsl. Assn., Sheridan. Author: Western Energy Development: Biophysical/Sociocultural Impacts, The Sunshine House. Mem. Sheridan County Bus. Women, Sheridan County C. of C., Beta Sigma Phi. Home: 420 W Works St Sheridan WY 82801

KENEALLY, MARYANN PAGLIA, educational consultant; b. Phila., Sept. 13, 1942; d. Basil Joseph and Jennie (Caruso) Paglia; div.; children: Susan, Jennifer, Laura. BA, Glassboro State Coll., 1967, MA, 1984. Cert. learning disabled tchr. cons., N.J. Tchr. Brooklawn (N.J.) Sch. Dist., 1967-68, Bellmawr (N.J.) Sch. Dist., 1968-70; dir., tchr. Bellmawr Community Nursery Sch., 1974-82; tchr. Barrington (N.J.) Sch. Dist., 1983-85, Archway Programs, Atco, N.J., 1985-86; learning cons. Camden (N.J.) Sch. Dist., 1986-88, Glassboro (N.J.) Sch. Dist., 1987-88, Camden County Vocat-Tech. Sch. Dist., Sicklerville, N.J., 1989—; sec. Camden County Nursery Sch. Dirs., Cherry Hill, N.J., 1978-79. Mem. Bellmawr Dem. Club, 1984-86. Recipient cert. of appreciation Camden County Girl Scouts U.S., 1981, 82, ARC, Camden, 1983. Mem. Gloucester County Learning Consultants. Roman Catholic. Home: 224 2d Ave Bellmawr NJ 08031 Office: Camden County Vocat Schs 6008 Browning Rd Pennsauken NJ 08109

KENLEY, ELIZABETH SUE, commerce and transportation executive; b. Kansas City, Mo., Oct. 4, 1945; d. Ralph Raymond and Josephine Allen (Wells) Cummins. BS, Kans. U., 1968, MPA, 1972. Asst. city mgr. Winfield (Kans.), 1968-70; adminstrv. asst. Kansas City (Mo.) Police Dept.; 1970; cons., 1973; with E.I. DuPont Co., Kingwood, Tex., 1974—, regional tech. buyer, 1977-79, cons., plant start up, 1979, regional tech. buyer, 1980-82; internat. project buyer Aramco, Houston, 1982-86, quality assurance liaison, supr. refinery no. area projects unit, 1986-89, owner, pres. Internat. Commerce & Transp., Houston, 1988—. Mem. Houston C. of C., Am. Mgmt. Assn. Home: 9632 Briarforest Houston TX 77063 Office: 2215 Harbor Blvd Houston TX 77020

KENLY, JACQUELINE SUEANN, aerospace transportation administrator; b. Portland, Oreg., Aug. 26, 1945; d. Arthur Martin and Mary Kathrin (Brunkala) Miller; m. Robert Kenly, Mar. 5, 1982 (div. Apr. 1983). Student, Wright Jr. Coll., Chgo., 1963-64, Lewis U., Lockport, Ill., 1968-69. Aircraft mechanic Continental Airlines, L.A., 1964-77; plant electrician Procter and Gamble Co., Chgo., 1977-79, Wester Electric, Chgo., 1979; avionics mechanic Am. Airlines, Chgo., 1979-80, sr. instr. aircraft maintenance, 1980-82; sr. instr., tech. specialist Am. Airlines, Tulsa, 1982-84; supr. Am. Airlines, Chgo., 1984—. Sgt. U.S. Army, 1965-68. Mem. Am. Theatre Organ Soc., Chgo. Area Theatre Organ Enthusiasts, Chgo. Hort. Soc., Coachlite Skate Club. Democrat. Roman Catholic. Home: 1330 E Rand Rd #53 Des Plaines IL 60016 Office: Am Airlines PO Box 66033 Chicago IL 60666

KENNAN, ELIZABETH TOPHAM, college president; b. Phila., Feb. 25, 1938; d. Frank and Henrietta (Jackson) Topham; m. Michael Burns, 1986; 1 child, Frank Alexander Kennan. BA summa cum laude, Mt. Holyoke Coll., 1960; MA, St. Hilda's Coll. Oxford U., Eng. 1962; PhD, U. Wash., 1966; LHD (hon.), Trinity Coll., Washington, 1978, Amherst Coll., 1980, St. Mary's Coll., 1982, Oberlin Coll., 1983; LLD (hon.), Smith Coll., 1984; LittD (hon.), Cath. U. Am., 1985, U. Mass., 1988. Asst. prof. history Cath. U. Am., Washington, 1966-70, assoc. prof., 1970-78, dir. mediaeval and Byzantine studies program, 1970-78, dir. program in early Christian humanism, 1974-78; pres. Mt. Holyoke Coll., South Hadley, Mass., 1978—;

lectr. in field; dir. NYNEX Corp., White Plains, N.Y., N.E. Utilities, Hartford, Conn., Berkshire Life Ins. Co., Pittsfield, Mass., Shawmut Bank, Boston; cons. to various colls.; pres. Five Colls., Inc., 1985-; dir. Coun. on Libr. Resources, 1982-; mem. Indo-U.S. Subcommn. of Am. Secretariat. Translator, author: (with John D. Anderson) On Consideration (St. Bernard of Clairvaux), 1976; contbr. articles to profl. publs. Mem. Dana Found., Higher Edn. Program Commn., 1986—; trustee U. Notre Dame, South Bend, Ind. Named Tchr. of Yr., Cath. U. Am., 1977; Marshall scholar, 1960; Woodrow Wilson fellow, 1962. Mem. Mediaeval Acad. Am. (coun. 1984-86), Coun. on Fgn. Rels., Phi Beta Kappa.a. Home: Pres' House Mt Holyoke Coll South Hadley MA 01075 Office: Mt Holyoke Coll Office of Pres South Hadley MA 01075

KENNARD, JOYCE, state judge. Former judge L.A. Mcpl. Ct.; justice Calif. Supreme Ct., Sacramento, 1989—. Office: Calif Supreme Ct Supreme Ct Bldg Sacramento CA 95814*

KENNEDY, BETH BLUMENREICH, film studio executive; b. Detroit, Mar. 11, 1950; d. Leonard and Bernice Blumenreich; m. Michael F. Kennedy; 1 child, Joshua Hayes. BA, U. Mich., 1971; MA, UCLA, 1974; JD, Southwestern U., 1984. Mgr. sensurround dept. Universal Studios, Universal City, Calif., 1975; asst. to studio mgr. Universal Studios, Universal City, 1977, adminstr. transp. dept., 1978, dir. infor systems TV & UP, 1980; v.p., dir. corp. internal mgmt. cons. MCA Inc., Universal City, 1982-86; v.p. planning and adminstrn. Universal Studios, Universal City, 1987-89, sr. v.p. planning and adminstrn., 1989—; regional v.p., gen. mgr. Jud. Arbitration and Mediation Svcs., Inc., 1990. Contbr. articles to profl. jour. Mem. legal com. The Nurtury, Sherman Oaks, Calif., 1988—; bd. dirs. Mar. of Dimes, Nat. Women's Employment and Edn., Inc. Named one of Outstanding Young Women of Am., Outstanding Young Women of Am. awards program, 1980. Mem. ABA, Women in Bus. (mem. com. 1985-88), Orgn. of Women Execs. (chair membership com. 1989, bd. dirs.), Women in Film, Beverly Hills Bar Assn., L.A. County Bar Assn. Office: Universal City Studios 100 Universal City Pla Universal City CA 91608

KENNEDY, CHARLOTTE IRENE, radio station executive; b. Detroit, May 17, 1947; d. Charles William and Betty (Earns) Cossin; m. John Gordon Outlaw, June 11, 1966 (div. 1977); m. Karl Patrick Kennedy, Aug. 28, 1981; 1 child, Lindsay Kathleen. Diploma, Patricia Stevens Finishing Sch, Detroit, 1973. Office mgr., sales agt. WMUZ-AM, Detroit, 1966-73; account exec. WBFG-AM, Detroit, 1973-80, EWXL-AM, Royal Oak, Mich., 1980-82; v.p. Moore Furnace Co., Livonia, Mich., 1982-87; gen. mgr. WLQV-AM, Livonia, 1987—. Presbyterian. Office: WLQV Radio Ste 650 29200 Vassar Dr Livonia MI 48152

KENNEDY, CHERYL LYNN, museum director; b. Pekin, Ill., Nov. 25, 1946; d. Paul Louis and Ann Marie (Bingham) Wieburg; m. Roger Nicholas Kennedy, Feb. 7, 1966; children: Kurt Alan, Kimberly Ann. Grad. high sch., Pekin, Ill. Prin., and profl. quilter Mahomet, Ill., 1976-81; program coord. Early Am. Mus., Mahomet, 1981-85, dir. mus., 1985-86; dir. mus. and edn., 3 parks Champaign County Forest Preserve, Mahomet, 1986—; chmn. Ill. quilt documentation project Early Am. Mus. and Land of Lincoln Quilt Assn., 1986—. Creator and presenter (slide programs) Our Founding Mothers, 19th Century Life. Historian Meth. Local History Com., Mahomet, 1984-86; co-chair Greater Champaign County Area Attractions Coun. Mem. Midwest Mus. Coun., Am. Assn. Museums, Am. Assn. State and Local History Mus., Cong. Ill. Hist. Socs. and Mus. (v.p.), Ill. Heritage Assn., Ill. State Hist. Soc., Champaign County Hist. Soc., Nat. Quilt Assn. and Am. Quilt Soc., Antique Quilt Study Group and the Quilt Conservancy, Nat. Soc. of Fundraising Executives (chmn. of Philanthropic Affairs Com. Home: RR 3 Box 52 Mahomet IL 61853 Office: Early Am Mus PO Drawer 669 Mahomet IL 61853

KENNEDY, CHRISTIE ANN, oil refining and marketing company official; b. Shelbyville, Tenn., Jan. 30, 1950; d. William Herbert and Hazel Muriel (Banfield) K. BS, U. Tulsa, 1973; MPA, U. Tex., 1976. Rsch. assoc. Bur. Pub. Adminstrn., U. Tenn., Knoxville, 1976-78; editor Redact Corp., Tulsa, 1978-79; engring. specialist Crest Engring., Tulsa, 1980-82; documentation specialist Thunderbird Automation Co., Tulsa, 1982-83; writer Bruning CAD, AM Internat., Tulsa, 1983-84; tchr. Tulsa Pub. Schs., 1984-85; supr. tech. publs. Memorex Telex Co., Tulsa, 1985-88; policy and procedures coord. Sun Refining & Mktg. Co., Tulsa, 1988—; cons. to local non-profit orgns., Knoxville, 1976-78, Tulsa, 1979—. Author tech. manuals of hardware, software and engring. and acctg. systems. Trustee Temple Israel, Tulsa, 1985—; bd. dirs. Heritage Acad., Tulsa, 1988—. U. Tex. fellow, 1974-76. Mem. Women in Communication (bd. dirs. Tulsa chpt., co-editor newsletter 1988-89, membership retention com. 1989-90, newsletter editor 1990—). Republican. Home: 134 E 18th St Tulsa OK 74119 Office: Sun Refining & Mktg Co 1907 S Detroit PO Box 2039 Tulsa OK 74102

KENNEDY, COLLEEN GERALYN, nurse, social worker; b. Staten Island, N.Y., Feb. 2, 1955; d. James Martin and Eleanor S. (Dehliner) K.; m. Edward Francis Humphries, July 21, 1990; 1 child by previous marriage, Michael J. Carlucci. AAS in Nursing, Coll. S.I., 1976; BSW, Adelphi U., 1982, MSW, 1984. RN, N.Y. Staff nurse Staten Island Hosp., 1976-80, social work asst., 1980-84, clin. social worker, 1984-85; asst. dir. social work Eger Health Care Ctr., Staten Island, 1985-87; systems analyst program devel. and evaluation St. Vincent's Med. Ctr., Staten Island, 1987-89; asst. dir. Ctr. Chem. Dependency, Bayley Seton Hosp., Staten Island, 1989—, mktg. dir., 1990—. Mem. Staten Island Com. on Alcoholism and Substance Abuse. Mem. NAFE, Nat. Assn. Social Workers, Acad. Cert. Social Workers, Employee Assistance Profls. Assn., Staten Island Preservation League, Nat. Trust Historic Preservation. Democrat. Roman Catholic. Office: Ctr Chem Dependency Bayley Seton Hosp 75 Vanderbilt Ave Staten Island NY 10304

KENNEDY, CORNELIA GROEFSEMA, federal judge; b. Detroit, Aug. 4, 1923; d. Elmer H. and Mary Blanche (Gibbons) Groefsema; m. Charles S. Kennedy, Jr. (dec.); 1 son, Charles S. III. B.A., U. Mich., 1945, J.D. with distinction, 1947; LL.D. (hon.), No. Mich. U., 1971, Eastern Mich. U., 1971, Western Mich. U., 1973, Detroit Coll. Law, 1980, U. Detroit, 1987. Bar: Mich. bar 1947. Law clk. to Chief Judge Harold M. Stephens, U.S. Ct. of Appeals, Washington, 1947-48; assoc. Elmer H. Groefsema, Detroit, 1948-52; partner Markle & Markle, Detroit, 1952-66; judge 3d Judicial Circuit Mich., 1967-70; dist. judge U.S. Dist. Ct., Eastern Dist. Mich., Detroit, 1970-79; chief judge U.S. Dist. Ct., Eastern Dist. Mich., 1977-79; circuit judge U.S. Ct. Appeals, 6th Circuit, 1979—. Mem. Commn. on the Bicentennial of the U.S. Constitution (presdl. appointment). Recipient Sesquicentennial award U. Mich. Fellow Am. Bar Found.; mem. ABA, Mich. Bar Assn. (past chmn. negligence law sect.), Detroit Bar Assn. (past dir.), Fed. Bar Assn., Am. Judicature Soc., Nat. Assn. Women Lawyers, Am. Trial Lawyers Assn., Nat. Conf. Fed. Trial Judges (past chmn.), Fed. Jud. Fellows Commn. (bd. dirs.), Fed. Jud. Ctr. (bd. dirs.), Phi Beta Kappa. Office: US Ct of Appeals 744 US Courthouse 231 W Lafayette St Detroit MI 48226

KENNEDY, DEBRA JOYCE, marketing professional; b. Covina, Calif., July 9, 1955; d. John Nathan and Drea Hannah (Lancaster) Ward; m. John William Kennedy, Sept. 3, 1977 (div.); children: Drea, Noelle. B.S. in Communications, Calif. State Poly. U., 1977. Pub. relations coordinator Whittier (Calif.) Hosp., 1978-79, pub. relations mgr., 1980; pub. relations dir. San Clemente (Calif.) Hosp., 1979-80; dir. pub. relations Garfield Med. Ctr., Monterey Park, Calif., 1980-82; dir. mktg. and community relations Charter Oak Hosp., Covina, 1983-85; mktg. dir. CPC Horizon Hosp., Pomona, 1985-89; dir. mktg. Sierra Royale Hosp., Azusa, 1989—. Mem. Am. Soc. Hosp. Pub. Relations, Healthcare Mktg. Assn., Healthcare Pub. Relations and Mktg. Assn., Covina and Covina West C. of C., West Covina Jaycees. Republican. Methodist. Club: Soroptimists. Contbr. articles to profl. jours.

KENNEDY, DONNA VIRGINIA, financial planner; b. Russell, Kans., Mar. 28, 1948; d. James Don and Dorothy Louise (Bogue) Holt. BBA, Washburn U., 1973. lic. ins. agt., lic. realtor. Editorial cons. Josten's Am. Yearbook Co., Topeka, Kans., 1974-76, asst. product mgr., 1976-78; realtor assoc. Brosius and Slattery, Inc., Topeka, 1978-80, Valley, Inc., Topeka, 1980-82; ins. agt. State Farm Ins. Co., Topeka, 1982-86; dir. mktg. sales Castlewood Constrn., Inc., 1986-87; pres. Creative Patios of Topeka, 1986-87; profl. recruiter Stormont-Vail Regional Med. Ctr., Topeka, 1988-90; fin. planner N.Y. Life Ins. Co., 1990—. Nat. Conv., Don Dougan, Hall of Fame. Mem. C. of C., Topeka Homebuilders Assn. Home: 3411 SW 33d Topeka KS 66614

KENNEDY, DORA FUNARI, school system administrator; b. Bellaire, Ohio, Mar. 8, 1921; m. Edwin Dallas Kennedy, Nov. 5, 1946; 1 child, Dallas C. Kennedy II. BA, Ohio U., 1942; MEd, U. Md., 1957, PhD, 1979. Tchr. Spanish, Latin, English Warren Consol. High Sch. (named changed to Buckeye South High Sch.), Tiltonville, Ohio, 1942-47; tchr. Latin, English Northridge High Sch., Dayton, Ohio, 1947-49; elem. tchr. Carleplace (N.Y.) Elem. Sch., 1949-51, College Park (Md.) Elem. Sch., 1951-59; supr. fgn. langs. Bd. Edn.-Prince George's County Schs., Upper Marlboro, Md., 1959—; cons. Harcourt, Brace, Jovanovich, Orlando, Fla., 1980—, Prentice Hall, Englewood Cliffs, N.J., 1988—, N.E. Conf. Bd. Dirs., 1990-91. Co-author: Complete Guide to Exploratory Foreign Languages, 1985; co-author numerous curriculum guides; contbr. articles to profl. jours. Bd. dirs. Northeast Conf. on Teaching Fgn. Langs., 1984-88 (Nelson Brooks award 1989). Mem. Prince George's County Educators, Md. State Tchrs., Am. Coun. on Teaching Fgn. Langs. (bd. dirs. 1987-88, recording sec. 1989-90, Florence Steiner award for ednl. leadership 1989), Md. Fgn. Lang. Assn. (pres. 1985-86), AAUW (edn. com.), Delta Kappa Gamma, Phi Beta Kappa, Phi Kappa Phi (hon.). Unitarian. Home: 4806 Harvard Rd College Park MD 20740

KENNEDY, ELAINE THERESE, sales executive; b. Dorchester, Mass., Aug. 10, 1937; d. John J. and Helen (McGuire) Conner; m. Vincent L. Pavone, Sept. 14, 1957 (div. June 1986); children: Vincent L., Stephen D., Mark J., Michelle M., Christine M.; m. Richard D. Kennedy, Sept. 25, 1987. Bus. degree, Katherine Gibbs Sch., Boston, 1956; AA cum laude, Oakland Community Coll., Farmington, Mich., 1983; BA, Wayne State U., 1990. Adminstrv. asst. Schostak Bros. Inc., Southfield, Mich., 1977-79; staff asst. GM, Detroit, 1981-83, office mgr. staff asst., 1983-85; regional sales mgr. Kent-Moore Co., Warren, Mich., 1987—; speaker Oakland Community Coll., 1984, 86, Midwest Conf., Mich., Ohio, Ill., 1987—. Past officer Our Lady of Refuge Edn. Com.; former vol. ARC; bd. mem. bd. dirs. PTA, Bloomfield Hills, Mich.; campaign worker Birmingham (Mich.) Dem. Com., 1980, 84; founding mem. Detroit Art Inst. Mem. Nat. Automobile Dealers Assn. (exhibitor 1986—), Mich. Automobile Dealers Assn. (presenter 1985—). Home: 1610 Graefield Birmingham MI 48009 Office: Kent-Moore Co GMDE 28635 Mound Rd Warren MI 48092-3499

KENNEDY, ELIZABETH MAE, musician; b. Medford, Mass., Oct. 16, 1949; d. Thomas Power and Anne Cecelia (Coyne) Sullivan; m. William David Kennedy, Oct. 12, 1970 (div. 1984); children: Mary Elizabeth, Jonathan Martin. AS, NS Community Coll., 1969. Retail sales mgmt. Jordan Marsh Co., Peabody, Mass., 1966-69; retail mgmt. Sears, Roebuck and Co., Lynn, Mass., 1969-70; asst. bookkeeper Henry Leather Co., Peabody, Mass., 1970-76; office mgr. Bartlett and Steadman Co. Inc., Marblehead, Mass., 1981-90; bandleader, performer New England Area, 1983—; music dir., contract organist St. John The Evangelist Ch., Swampscott, Mass., 1985—. Co-author: music and words Dear Mr. Gorbachev, 1988. Organizer Devereux Neighborhood Assn. Mem. Am. Fedn. Musicians Local 126. Democrat. Roman Catholic. Home: 46 Ocean Ave Marblehead MA 01945

KENNEDY, EVELYN SIEFERT, foundation executive, textile restoration specialist; b. Pitts., Nov. 11, 1927; d. Carmine and Assunta (Iacobucci) Rocci; BS magna cum laude, U. R.I., 1969, MS in Textiles and Clothing, 1970; m. George J. Siefert, May 30, 1953 (div. 1974); children: Paul Kenneth, Carl Joseph, Ann Marie; m. Lyle H. Kennedy, II, Oct. 12, 1974 (div. Feb. 1986). With Pitts. Pub. Schs., 1945-50; with Goodyear Aircraft Corp., Akron, Ohio, 1950-54; clothing instr. Groton (Conn.) Dept. Adult Edn., 1958-68; pres. Sewtique, Groton, 1970, Sewtique II, New London, Conn., 1986; v.p. Kennedy Capital Advisors, Groton, 1973-85, Kennedy Mgmt. Corp., Groton, 1974-85, Kennedy InterVest, Inc., Groton, 1975-85; pres., exec. dir. P.R.I.D.E. Found., Inc., Groton, 1978—; clothing cons. Coop. Extension Service, Dept. Agr.; internat. lectr. on clothing for disabled and elderly; adj. faculty U. Conn., Eastern Conn. State Coll., St. Joseph Coll.; hon. prof. U. R.I., assoc. prof., 1987—; fed. expert witness Care Label Law, FTC, 1976; mem. Major Appliance Consumer Action Panel, 1983-89. Regional adv. coun. SBA active corps Execs., Hartford, 1985—; bd. dirs. Small Bus. Devel. Ctr., 1989—, Easter Seal Rehab. Ctr. Southeastern Conn.; bus. adv. council U. R.I., 1979—, trustee, 1985—; active LWV; mem. Groton Vocat. Edn. Adv. Council. Recipient award of distinction U. R.I., 1969, Small Bus. Adminstrn. Adv. of Year, 1984; named Woman of Yr. Bus. and Profl. Women's Club, 1977, Conn. Home Economist of Yr., 1987. Mem. Internat. Sleep Council (consumer affairs rep.), Internat. Soc. Appraisers (panelist FMHA roster, farmer's credit mediator 1989—), Nat. Assn. Bedding Mfrs., Conn. Home Economists in Bus. (founder 1977, Women of Yr. 1987), Nat. Home Economists in Bus. (chmn. internat. relations, nat. fin. chmn. 1986), Am. Home Econs. Assn., Coll. and Univ. Bus. Instrs. of Conn., Am. Accupational Therapy Assn. (resource cons. 1986—), Fashion Group, Omicron Nu, Phi Kappa Phi. Democrat. Roman Catholic. Clubs: New London Zonta, Bus. and Profl. Women's (Outstanding Women of Year 1977). Author: Dressing With Pride, 1980, Clothing Accessibility: A Lesson Plan to Aid the Disabled and Elderly, 1983. Office: 71 Plaza Ct Groton CT 06340

KENNEDY, JACQUELINE ANN, administrative assistant to governor; b. Westerly, R.I., Feb. 8, 1947; d. Raymond Geoffrey and Josephine Ann (Faulise) Burns; m. Stephen Manning Kennedy, Sept. 11, 1965; children: Geoffrey Joseph, Jocelyn Beth, Ashley Manning. Grad. high sch., Cambridge, Mass. Adminstrv. asst. Appellate div. Dept. Employment Security, Concord, N.H., 1979-83; adminstrv. asst., scheduler Gov. John H. Sununu, Concord, 1983-89; adminstrv. asst. scheduling and appointments Office Chief of Staff to Pres., Washington, 1989—. Chmn. bd. Dunbarton N.H.) Sch. Bd., 1975-85; firefighter Cunbarton Vol. Fire Dept., 1981-85. Mem. Rep. Women's Club (sec. Salem chpt. 1972-76). Home: RR 2 Box 207 Concord NH 03301 Office: Exec Office of the Pres 1600 Pennsylvanie Ave NW Washington DC 20500

KENNEDY, JOAN CANFIELD, volunteer; b. Wash., Mar. 24, 1931; d. Austin Francis and Gertrude Rita (MacBride) Canfield; m. Keith Furnival Kennedy, Feb. 11, 1956; children: Joseph Keith, Austin Robert, Thomas Canfield, Richard Furnival. BA, Coll. New Rochelle, 1953. Dir. Coll. of New Rochelle Alumnae Assn., 1977-81, 89-; chmn. Coun. Human Rels., Scarsdale, N.Y., 1983-85; dir. Scarsdale Chpt. LWV, 1974-85, Charlotte-Mecklenburg, N.C. chpt., 1985-89, pres., 1989-; bd. dirs. New Neighbors League, 1986-87, Shalom Homes, 1987-88; trustee Ctr. Preventive Psychiatry, White Plains, N.Y., 1973-85. Recipient Ursulas Laurus Citation, 1968, Angela Merici award, 1988; named New Neighbor of Yr. New Neighbors League, 1987. Mem. Niantic Bay Yacht Club, Larchmont (N.Y.) Yacht Club. Roman Catholic. Home: 1441 Carmel Rd Charlotte NC 28226

KENNEDY, JOSEPHINE, travel agent; b. Staten Island, N.Y., Mar. 25, 1914; d. Rocco Michael and Angelina (Brunetti) Ricci; m. George William Kennedy (dec. Sept. 1988); children: George William Jr., Dian Catherine Kendrick. Cert., Inst. Cert. Travel Agts., Wellesley, Mass., 1977. Mgr., founder Happy Landings Agy., Westbury, N.Y., 1934-36; owner Jo Kennedy's Travel Agy., Inc., Floral Pk., N.Y., 1936—. Mem. Am. Soc. Travel Agts., Inst. Cert. Travel Agts.

KENNEDY, KATHY IRENE, public health researcher; b. Yonkers, N.Y., May 25, 1956; d. John James Kennedy and Jean Marie (Baldassare) Jarusinsky; m. Walter Benson Vernon, Sept. 6, 1980; children: Margaret Amelia, Gordon Fitzgerald. AB in Psychology, Boston Coll., Chestnut Hill, Mass., 1978; MA in Psychology, Assumption Coll., Worcester, Mass., 1981; postgrad., U. N.C., 1981-82. Rsch. asst. Med. Found., Boston, 1976; tching. asst. Dept. Psyhcology, Boston U., Chestnut Hill, 1978-79; rsch. asst. Mass. Mental Health Ctr., Boston, 1978-79; tching. asst. Dept. Psychology, Assumption Coll., Worcester, 1979-80; project asst. Family Health Internat., Rsch. Triangle Park, N.C., 1980-82, rsch. analyst, 1984-87, sr. rsch. analyst, 1984-87, rsch. assoc., 1987—; bd. dirs. Nat. Coalition Nat. Family Planning, 1987—; tech. adv. Inst. Internat. Studies Family Planning, 1985—; presentor, trainer in field. Contbr. articles to profl. jours. Recipient numerous scholarships and grants in field. Mem. AAUW, Am. Public Health Assn., Internat. Couns. Sex Edn. PArenthood. Home: 1121 Snderson St Durham NC 27705 Office: Family Health Internat 2224 E Chapel Hill Nelson Hwy Triangle Pk Research Triangle Park NC 27709

KENNEDY, KAY J., researcher-writer; b. S.D.; d. Edward James and Marie Amelia (Bowman) K.; B.A. in Geology, U. Wyo., 1931. Reporter, Gt. Falls (Mont.) Leader, 1944-45, Denver Post, 1945, Alaska Daily Empire, Juneau, 1950-51, Fairbanks (Alaska) Daily News-Miner, 1952-56; chief news bur. Alaska Visitors Assn., Seattle, 1957-60; news bur. chief Alaska Travel Promotion Assn., 1961-62; pub. relations Wien Alaska Airlines, Fairbanks and Anchorage, 1966-70; freelance research-writer, 1936—; producer 1st 2 Alaska Travel manuals, 1957-58; 68; author original copy Alaska Sunset Discovery Book, 1963, Wien Brothers Story, 1967. Recipient Lulu award Los Angeles Advt. Women, 1958; named Wash. Woman of Achievement, Wash. Press Women, 1978. Mem. Nat. Fedn. Press Women (Woman of Achievement 1987), Outdoor Writers Assn. Am., Alaska Press Women (founder, pres. 1961; awards 1969, 71, Nat. Woman of Achievment 1987), Wash. Press Women (award 1959), Soc. Am. Travel Writers. Clubs: Alaska Press (award 1959). Address: 330 3d Ave #407 Fairbanks AK 99701

KENNEDY, MARILYN MOATS, management consultant, writer; b. Kansas City, Kans., Apr. 15, 1943; d. Orin Lloyd Sr. and Georgia (Jeffries) Moats; m. Daniel Joseph Kennedy Jr., June 3, 1967; 1 child, Anne Evelyn. BS in Journalism, Northwestern U., 1965, MS, 1966. Asst. prof., assoc. dean DePaul U., Chgo., 1966-77; owner Career Strategies, Wilmette, Ill., 1975—. Author: Office Politics, 1980, Career Knockouts, 1981, Salary Strategies, 1983, Powerbase, 1985, Office Warfare, 1986, Glamous Guide to Office Smarts, 1986. Mem. Women in Communications (pres. Chgo. chpt. 1979-80, Nat. Headliner 1986), Headline Club (pres. Chgo. chpt. 1975-76). Republican. Presbyterian. Office: Career Strategies 1153 Wilmette Ave Wilmette IL 60091

KENNEDY, MELANIE SPROUL, pathologist, educator; b. Lima, Ohio, Oct. 21, 1942; d. James W. and Clellah L. (Stotts) Sproul; m. Bruce H. Kennedy, Feb. 20, 1965 (div. 1990); 1 child, Melita L. BA, Ohio N. U., 1964; MD, Ohio State U., 1968. Diplomate Am. Bd. Pathology. Intern Mt. Carmel Hosp., Columbus, Ohio, 1969-70; resident Mt. Carmel Hosp., Columbus, 1973-75, 76-78; med. dir. Cen. Ohio Red Cross Blood Ctr., Columbus, 1971-76; med. dir., specialist in blood banking program Ohio State U. Hosps., Columbus, 1981—, dir. transfusion svc., 1982-90; assoc. prof. pathology Ohio State U., 1984—, assoc. dean student affairs Coll. Medicine, 1989—; consulting physician Meml. Hosp. Union County, Marysville, Ohio, 1980—. Editor textbooks: Alternative Education Methods for Continuing Education, 1987, Perinatal Transfusion Therapy, 1990; contbr. chpt.: Therapeutic Use of Blood Components, 1991. Recipient Transfusion Med. Acad. award NIH, 1985. Fellow Coll. Am. Pathologists; mem. Ohio Assn. Blood Banks (pres. 1981-84), Am. Assn. Blood Banks, Am. Med. Women's Assn. (br. pres. 1973), Assn. Women in Sci. (pres. Cen. Ohio chpt. 1989-90, Outstanding Scientist award 1986), Ctr. Sci. and Industry, Planned Parenthood. Office: Ohio State U Coll Medicine 370 W 9th St Columbus OH 43210

KENNEDY, TAMYRA MACHELE, community relations information officer; b. Wise, Va., June 11, 1958; d. Paul Wilmot and Celia Estyl (Graham) Kennedy. AAS in Drafting, Mountain Empire Community Coll, Big Stone Gap, Va., 1981; BA in English, Clinch Valley Coll., Wise, 1981. Lic. profl. coll. tchr. Reporter Coalfield Progress, Norton, Va., 1984-85; tchr. English Lee County Sch. System, Jonesville, Va., 1985-87; community relations info. technician Mountain Empire Community Coll., Big Stone Gap, Va., 1987-90, info. officer, 1990—; chmn. Mktg. and Retention Com., Big Stone Gap, 1989—. Mem. AAUW, Assn. Classified Employees (chmn. profl. devel. 1989—), Order Eastern Star (worthy matron 1985-86), Pocohontas Rebekah Lodge (noble grand 1988—). Home: 220 E 1st St N Apt 4 Big Stone Gap VA 24219 Office: Mountain Empire Commun Coll Drawer 700 Big Stone Gap VA 24219

KENNEDY, VARINA (KAY KENNEDY), publishing company executive, writer; b. Newark, Ark., Dec. 4, 1940; d. Estel Charles and Valerie (Murphy) Kuehnert; m. Joseph Kennedy, Nov. 7, 1959. Cert. in interior design Clover Park Tech. Sch., Tacoma, 1972; student Solano Coll., Calif., 1972-73, San Bernardino Valley Coll., Calif., 1980. Designer trainee Breuner's Home Furnishings, Pleasant Hill, Calif., 1972-73; decorator cons. J.C. Penney Co., Concord, Calif. and North Little Rock, Ark., 1973-76; interior designer Walls Galore & More, Inc., North Little Rock, 1976-78, Nickell Flooring, San Bernardino, Calif., 1978-79; freelance designer, San Bernardino, 1980-83; owner Comprehensive Design Services, Tacoma, 1984-87, Creative Concepts, Tacoma, 1987-89; pres. Page One Press, Inc., Tacoma, 1989—; columnist Business People/Profiles, Pierce County Bus. Examiner, 1987-89; pres. Washington Home Bus. Network, 1988—. Contbr. numerous articles on design, color and small bus. to mags. and newspapers. Mem. NAFE, Color Mktg. Group, Nat. Trust for Historic Preservation, Pacific N.W. Writers Conf., Am. Soc. Interior Designers (assoc.). Office: Page One Press Inc 9330-D Bridgeport Way SW #40 Tacoma WA 98499

KENNEDY, YVONNE KENNINGTON, educator, retired; b. Boston, Tex., Nov. 25, 1919; d. Thomas W. and Elva Mae (Clemens) Kennington; m. Harvey W. Kennedy; children: Tom M., Cherry Kennedy Santee. BS in Edn., Henderson State U., 1949, MS, 1956; postgrad., Ariz. State U., 1956-70. Cert. elem. tchr., Ark. Tchr. high sch. LePanta, Ark., 1941-43; acct. Union R.R., Texarkana, Tex., 1943-46, Cotton Belt Mo. Pacific, Tex. Pacific/ Kans. City So.; tchr. elem. Texarkana Pub. Sch., 1946-47, Arkadelphia Pub. Sch., 1949-56; tchr. U.S. Govt. Interior Indian Sch., Phoenix, 1956-58, Scottsdale Sch. Dist., Phoenix, 1958-84; ret., 1984; grade level chmn. Scottsdale Sch. Dist., 1960-62. Bd. dirs. Phoenix Symphony Guild, 1983-85; mem. Phoenix Art Mus., 1960-89, Ariz. Hist. Soc., Phoenix, 1980-89, Mental Health Guild, Phoenix, 1985-89, Phoenix Symphony Aux., 1986-89. Mem. Nat. Soc. Arts and Letters, Patron Art Drama, English Speaking Union (bd. dirs. 1980-86), AAUW, Alpha Kappa Delta (pres. Maricopa County 1964-66, regional pres. 1966-68). Democrat. Baptist. Home: 5037 E Weldon Ave Phoenix AZ 85018

KENNEDY-SHIELDS, KATHLEEN ANN, health care administrator; b. Bklyn., Sept. 9, 1951; d. Vincent B. and Ann M. (Dunlap) Kennedy; m. Paul J. Shields, May 6, 1977; 1 child, Christopher Ryan. BA, U. South Fla., 1973; MS magna cum laude, St. Johns U., 1977. Child care worker Mission of Immaculate Virgin, S.I., 1973-74, caseworker, 1974-76; caseworker S.I. Devel. Ctr., 1976-77, team leader, 1977-78, placement specialist, 1978-80, program planning specialist, 1980-83, community service adminstr., 1983-86; dir. S.I. Planning and Devel., 1986—; dir. planning and devel. N.Y. State Office Mental Retardation and Devel. Disabilities, 1986—; project cons. to numerous orgns. including On Your Mark, Inc., S.I., Assn. for Children with Retarded Mental Devel., N.Y.C., Ind. Living Assocs., Bklyn., Eden II for Autistic Children, S.I., and many others; dir. planning Willowbrook Closure Exec. Task Force, 1986-87. Active Commr.'s Task Force for Redesign of N.Y.C. Service Delivery System, 1989, N.Y. State Task Force of Needs and Assessment and Evaluation, 1988—, Commr.'s Task Force on Strategic Planning in N.Y.C., 1988—; panelist Commr.'s Forum Planning for the Future, 1988—; vice chmn. Critical Community and Capital Projects Taskforce, 1986-89; den mother Boy Scouts Am., S.I., 1988—. Named Woman of Yr. On Your Mark, Inc., 1989; recipient Commendation Mission of Immaculate Virgin, 1989. Mem. N.Y. State Women and Govt., Boro Dispute Panel for Multiply Disabled. Roman Catholic. Home: 650 Victory Blvd Apt 4B Staten Island NY 10301 Office: Staten Island Devel Disabilities Services 1150 Forest Hill Rd Staten Island NY 10312

KENNELLY, BARBARA B., congresswoman; b. Hartford, Conn., July 10, 1936; d. John Moran and Barbara (Leary) Bailey; m. James J. Kennelly, Sept. 26, 1959; children: Eleanor Bride, Barbara Leary, Louise Moran, John Bailey. BA in Econs, Trinity Coll., Washington, 1958; grad., Harvard-Radcliffe Sch. Bus. Adminstrn., 1959; M.A. in Govt, Trinity Coll., Hartford, 1971. Mem. Hartford Ct. of Common Council, 1975-79; sec. of state State of Conn., Hartford, 1979-83; mem. 98th-102nd Congresses from 1st Dist. Conn., Hartford. Trustee Trinity Coll., Hartford, Conn.; previously active in numerous civic, polit., and govt. orgns. in Greater Hartford, Conn. Democrat. Roman Catholic. Office: 204 Cannon House Office Bldg Washington DC 20515

KENNELLY, SISTER KAREN MARGARET, college administrator; b. Graceville, Minn., Aug. 4, 1933; d. Walter John Kennelly and Clara Stella Eastman. BA, Coll. St. Catherine, St. Paul, 1956; MA, Cath. U. Am., 1958; PhD, U. Calif., Berkeley, 1962. Joined Sisters of St. Joseph of Carondelet, Roman Cath. Ch., 1954. Prof. history Coll. St. Catherine, 1962-71, acad. dean, 1971-79; exec. dir. Nat. Fedn. Carondelet Colls., U.S., 1979-82; province dir. Sisters of St. Joseph of Carondelet, St. Paul, 1982-88; pres. Mt. St. Mary's Coll., L.A., 1989—; cons. N. Cen. Accreditation Assn., Chgo., 1974-84, Ohio Bd. Regents, Columbus, 1983-89; trustee colls., hosps., Minn., Wis., Calif., 1972—. Editor, co author: American Catholic Women, 1989; author: (with others) Women of Minnesota, 1977. Fulbright fellow, 1964, Am. Coun. Learned Socs. fellow, 1964-65. Mem. Am. Hist. Soc., Am. Cath. Hist. Soc., Medieval Acad., Am. Assn. Rsch. Historians on Medieval Spain. Roman Catholic. Home and Office: Mt St Mary's Coll 12001 Chalon Rd Los Angeles CA 90049

KENNER, CAROLE ANN, nursing educaor; b. Cin., Sept. 19, 1953; d. Lester O. and Betty A. Waugh. BSN, U. Cin., 1976; MSN, Ind. U., 1983, DNS, 1988. Assoc. prof. nursing U. Cin., asst. prof. nursing; asst. head nurse Children's Hosp. Med. Ctr., Cin., staff nurse. Instr. CPR, ARC. Mem. NAACOG (ednl. coord. Ohio chpt., coord. Greater Cin. chpt.), Sigma Theta Tau. Home: 5678 Pleasant Hill Rd Milford OH 45150

KENNEY, LISA MICHELLE, academic administrator; b. L.A., Nov. 20, 1962; d. Charles Spencer and Romaine (Rauser) K. BA, Point Loma Coll., San Diego, 1986. Instrnl. aide Sacramento (Calif.) Unified Sch. Dist., 1986; substitute tchr. Antioch (Calif.) Unified Sch. Dist., 1987; instr. Active Learning, Inc., Corte Madera, Calif., 1987, supr., mgr., program delivery, 1987-89, v.p., gen. mgr., 1989—. Co-Chairperson Marin County Task Force on Self Esteem and Personal and Social Responsibility, 1988—. Mem. Commonwealth Club (San Francisco). Democrat. Office: Active Learning Inc 21 Tamal Vista Blvd Corte Madera CA 94925

KENNEY, ROSEMARY, data processing specialist; b. Seven Oaks, Kent, Eng., Oct. 7, 1945; came to U.S., 1947; d. Michael and Marjorie (Bennett) Reilly; m. Lawrence James Kenney, Jan. 9, 1971; 1 child, Brian James. AS in Data Processing, Suffolk Community Coll., Selden, N.Y., 1969; BBA in Acctg., Dowling Coll., Oakdale, N.Y., 1975, MBA, 1984. Programmer Citicorp, Melville, N.Y., 1969-73, systems analyst, 1973-75, pvt. label programming mgr., 1975-79, assn. programming mgr., 1979-84, mgr. assn. svcs., 1984-87; process mgr. Citicorp, Hagerstown, Md., 1987-89, tech. planner, 1989—. Mem. AAUW (bd. dirs. Hagerstown br., community chmn. 1989—), Dowling Coll. Alumni Assn. (alumni coun. 1985-87). Home: Rte 10 Box 71 Hagerstown MD 21740 Office: Citicorp 1 Citicorp Dr Hagerstown MD 21740

KENNEY-WALLACE, GERALDINE, chemistry and physics educator; b. London, Mar. 29, 1943. Assoc., Royal Inst. Chemistry, 1965; MS, U. B.C., 1968, PhD in Chemistry, 1970. Research assoc. biophysics Oxford U., 1964-66; chemistry fellow U. B.C., 1970-71; assoc. Radiation Lab. U. Notre Dame, 1971-72; from instr. to asst. prof. Yale U., 1972-74, asst. prof. chemistry, 1974-78, assoc. prof., 1978-80; prof. chemistry, physics U. Toronto, from 1980; chmn. sci. Council of Can., Ottawa, Ont., 1987-90; pres. McMaster U., Ont., 1990—; vis. scientist chemistry Argonne Nat. Lab., 1973—, Poly. Sch. of Paris, 1981; vis. prof. Stanford U., 1985-86. Recipient Corday-Morgan medal, 1979, Noranda award, 1984; Alfred P. Sloan fellow, 1977-79; Killam Research fellow, 1979-81; Guggenheim fellow, 1983; E.W.R. Stealil fellow, 1984. Mem. The Chem. Soc., Am. Chem. Soc., Am. Phys. Soc., Optical Soc. Am., InterAm Photochem Soc. Office: McMaster U, Office of Pres, Hamilton, ON Canada L8S 4L8*

KENNY, JANE A., federal agency administrator; b. Conn., Oct. 5, 1945; d. John K. Grad., Coll. New Rochelle; MPA in Govt. Mgmt., Am. U. Mgmt. analyst Computer Scis. Corp., 1977-79, U.S. Dept. Justice, Washington; staff asst. Nat. Assn. Schs. of Pub. Affairs and Adminstrn., Washington; spl. asst. to V.P. Office of V.P., Washington; dir. Exec. Secretariat GSA, Washington; dir. VISTA, SCSP ACTION Agy., Washington, 1986-88. Office: ACTION Office of Dir 1100 Vermont Ave NW Washington DC 20525

KENNY, SHIRLEY STRUM, college administrator; b. Tyler, Tex., Aug. 28, 1934; d. Marcus Leon and Florence (Golenternek) S.; m. Robert Wayne Kenny July 22, 1956; children: David Jack, Joel Strum, Daniel Clark, Jonathan Matthew, Sarah Elizabeth. BA, BJ, U. Tex., 1955; MA, U. Minn., 1957; PhD, U. Chgo., 1964; LHD (hon.), U. Rochester, 1988. Chair English dept. U. Md., College Park, 1973-79, provost Arts and Humanities, 1979-85; pres. CUNY Queens Coll., Flushing, 1985—. Author: The Conscious Lovers, 1968, The Plays of Richard Steele, 1971, The Performers and Their Plays, 1982, The Works of George Farquhar, 2 vols.,1988; editor: British Theatre and the Other Arts, 1984; contbr. numerous articles to profl. jours. Bd. dirs. Carnegie Found. for the Advancement of Teaching, Goodwill of Greater N.Y. Recipient Disting. Alumnus award U. Chgo. Club Washington, 1980, Svc. and Leadership award N.Y. Urban League, 1988; named Outstanding Woman, U. Md., 1983, Outstanding Alumnus, U. Tex. Coll. Communication, 1989. Mem. Am. Handel Soc. (exec. bd.) MLA, Am. Soc. for Theatre Rsch., Am. Soc. for 18th Century Studies, Bibliog. Soc. Va., Sigma Alpha Iota. Office: City U Queens Coll Kissena Blvd Flushing NY 11367

KENNY-WELCH, SUSAN MARIE, management consultant; b. Boston, Jan. 14, 1955; d. Joseph Francis and Mary Catherine (McCormick) Kenny; m. Neal E. Colman, Apr. 30, 1978 (div. 1982); m. Norman D. Welch, Sept. 16, 1988. BBA, U. Mass., 1976. Asst. mgr. Bay Bank Middlesex, Burlington, Mass., 1976-79; adjuster Liberty Mutual Ins. Co., Boston, 1979-81, Holyoke Mutual Ins. Co., Salem, Mass., 1981-84; pres. Welch Appraisals, Inc., Peabody, Mass.; cons. Glen Sand and Gravel Corp., N.H., 1989-, Welch. Assocs., Inc., Peabody, Mass., 198--. Mem. NOW, Bus. and Profl. Women. Nat. Assn. Female Executives. Office: Welch Appraisals Inc PO Nox 2126 West Peabody MA 01960

KENSICK, HELEN LORRAINE, public relations executive; b. Jersey City, Dec. 4, 1948; d. Stanley Edward and Helen (Karren) K. BA, U. Mass., 1970, PhD, 1984; postgrad., U. Geneva and Oxford U., 1975. Writer, instr. U. Mass, Amherst, 1972-79; media specialist U. Chgo., 1979-81; speech writer Chgo. Mercantile Exchange, 1981-82; cons., writer, editor Edmund Smason, Inc., Chgo.; mgr. BBDM Pub. Relations, Chgo., 1984—; bd. dirs. Nana Solbrig Chgo. Moving Co.; bd. editors Mass. Studies in English, Amherst, 1975-77. Editor Mass. Daily Collegian, Amherst, 1967-70. Media cons. Michael Dukakis Profl. Campaign, Chgo., 1987-88, Lehnhoff Sch. of Music and Dance, Chgo., 1979. Mem. Dickens Reading Group. Democrat. Nat. Catholic. Home: 5521 Blackstone Ave Chicago IL 60637 Office: Bender Browning et al Advt 444 N Michigan Ave Chicago IL 60611

KENSINGER, TINA R., entrepreneur, author; b. Poteau, Okla., Jan. 28, 1961; d. John Franklin and Ruthann (Cannon) Shiflett; m. Darryl E. Kensinger, May 31, 1986. BA, Ouachita Bapt. U., 1983; postgrad., So. Bapt. Theol. Sem. Office mgr., exec. sec. Cintas Corp., Ft. Smith, 1987-88; sales rep. House of Lloyd, Ft. Smith, 1987-89; employment counselor Snelling and Snelling, Ft. Smith, Ark., 1988; freelance author, entrepreneur Greenwood, Ark., 1988—. Active MADD. Mem. NAFE, Bapt. Women's Assn. (bd. dirs.). Democrat. Home and Office: 99 Chippewa Circle Greenwood AR 72936

KENT, JILL ELSPETH, government official; b. Detroit, June 1, 1948; d. Seymour and Grace (Edelman) K.; m. Mark Elliott Solomons, Aug. 20, 1978. BA, U. Mich., 1970; JD, George Washington U., 1975, LLM, 1979. Bar: D.C. 1975. Mgmt. intern U.S. Dept. Transp., Washington, 1971-73; staff analyst Office Mgmt. and Budget, Exec. Office of Pres., Washington, 1974-76; legis. counsel U.S. Treasury Dept., Washington, 1976-78; dir. legis. reference div. Health Care Financing Adminstrn., Washington, 1978-80; sr. budget examiner Office Mgmt. and Budget, Exec. Office Pres., Washington, 1980-84; chief Treasury, Gen. Services, OMB, 1984-85; dep. asst. sec. for departmental fin. and planning U.S. Dept. Treasury, 1985-86; dep. asst. sec. for dept. fin. and mgmt., 1986-88; asst. sec. of the Treasury, 1988-89, chief fin. officer, U.S. Dept. State, 1989—; pres. S&K Properties Investment Partnership, Washington, 1979—; lectr. D.C. Pub. Schs.; participant charter exec. devel. program Office Mgmt. and Budget, 1984; bd. dirs. Mobile Med. Care Inc., 1987—. Trustee Newport Sch., 1988—. Recipient Adminstrs. award Health Care Financing Adminstrn., 1980; named one of Top 40 Performers, Management mag., 1987. Mem. ABA, D.C. Bar Assn., Pres's. Council on Mgmt. Improvement. Republican. Home: 5300 27th St NW Washington DC 20015 Office: Dept of State Washington DC 20520

KENT, JOAN SWAFFORD, real estate broker; b. L.A., Aug. 14, 1927; d. Henry Watson and Lillian (Stanton) Swafford; m. William Kent III, Sept. 3, 1955; children—Lucinda, Nicholas, Augustus. Student Bennington Coll., 1947-48, U. Calif.-Berkeley, 1945-1947; BA, UCLA, 1950. Cert. real estate broker. Sales assoc. Frank Howard Allen, Stinson Beach, Calif., 1970-75, Seadrift Co. Realtors, Stinson Beach, 1975-76, Cushman and Wakefield, San Francisco, 1976-80; broker assoc. Hill and Co., San Francisco, 1981—. Bd. dirs. San Francisco Symphony, 1981-87; active in Modern Art Council, San Francisco, 1957—; Edgewood Aux., San Francisco, 1956—; assoc. dir. San Francisco Opera Guild, 1958—; mem. Childrens Theatre Assn., San Francisco, 1958—; charter mem. art mus. council L.A. County Mus. Art Volunteer Council, San Francisco Symphony. Mem. Marin County Bd. Realtors, San Francisco Bd. Realtors. Republican. Episcopalian. Clubs: Town & Country, San Francisco Golf, Seadrift Beach and Tennis. Avocations: golf, reading, music, swimming, hiking, gardening. Office: Hill & Co 2107 Union St San Francisco CA 94123

KENT, KAREN IRENE, transportation executive; b. Ashtabula, Ohio, July 24, 1944; d. Herman Henry and Winifred Melissa (Havens) Smith; m. Larry Leroy Kent, June 26, 1965; children: Ronald Bruce, Donald Bryan. Student, Kent State U., Ashtabula, 1962-63, Durham Bus. Coll., Phoenix, 1964-65. Bookkeeper Osselaer Constrn. Co., Phoenix, 1978; from moulding clk. to jr. auditor S.W. Forest Industries, Phoenix, 1964-68, 74-76, 79-81; asst. bookkeeper Bookbinder Fin. Corp., Phoenix, 1982; gen. auditing clk. Cen. Ariz. Distbg. Co., Glendale, 1983; acct. Inspiration Consol. Copper Co., Phoenix, 1983, SMP Mech. Contractors Inc., Phoenix, 1984; co-owner, v.p. Canyon States Transp. Inc., Phoenix, 1984—. Cons. Birthright of Phoenix, 1969-75; program chmn. Phoenix Bapt. Hosp. Auxiliary, 1969-74; child find advocate Ariz. Dept. Edn., Phoenix, 1978—; team mother Pop Warner Football, 1980-83, Little League Baseball, Phoenix, 1978-83; treas. PTO, Phoenix, 1978-83, Skyhawk Parent Alliance, Glendale, 1986-88; active After 5 Christian and Profl. Women, 1985-90. Mem. Phoenix C. of C. (pres.'s exchange 1986—). Republican. Baptist. Home: 2913 W Muriel Dr Phoenix AZ 85023 Office: Canyon States Transp Inc 21630 N 19th Ave Suite B-3 Phoenix AZ 85027-2717

KENT, LESLIE ANN, fraternity executive; b. Boston, Nov. 8, 1955; d. William James and Nellie Jean (Smith) K. BA, UCLA, 1978, MBA, 1981, MLS, 1987. Asst. v.p. Bank of Am., Los Angeles, 1981-85; info. specialist Medialink Internat. Corp., Pasadena, Calif., 1985-88; mgr. Advanced Info. Mgmt., Seal Beach, Calif., 1988-89; exec. dir. Pi Lambda Theta, Bloomington, Ind., 1989—; intern Rodleian Libr., Oxford (Eng.) U., 1986. Fellow UCLA, 1986. Mem. ALA, Nat. Assn. Female Execs., UCLA Alumni Assn., Am. Soc. for Info. Sci., Spl. Libraries Assn. (program com. mem. 1987-89), Sierra Club. Libertarian. Home: 2909 Sare Rd Apt 15 Bloomington IN 47401 Office: 4101 E 3d St Bloomington IN 47407

KENT, NANCY LEE, teacher; b. Balt., Aug. 30, 1956; d. Lawrason Lee and Orpha Jeanne (Wolfe) K. BA in Elem. Edn., Coll. of William and Mary, 1978. Cert. tchr., Va. Tchr. York County Schs., Yorktown, Va., 1978-81, 83—; clk. typist, counselor Langley AFB, Hampton, Va., 1984, 86; summer counselor NASA Langley Rsch. Ctr., Hampton, 1978-81, 83, 85, 87, 88. Deacon, Denbigh Presbyn. Ch., 1987—, sec., 1987-88, fin. co-chmn., 1988-89, stewardship chmn. 1989—; bd. dirs. Tabb Elem. Sch. Parent, Tchr., Student Orgn., 1984-90, Va. Peninsula Am. Heart Assn., 1987—; mem. Va. Ind. Polit. Network. Mem. Am. Bus. Women's Assn. (edn. chmn., local chpt.-Woman of Yr. 1988), York Edn. Assn., Va. Edn. Assn., NEA, Jr. League of Hampton Rds., Hampton Rds. Jaycees (pres. 1988-89, chmn. bd. 1989-90, regional dir. Va. 1989-90, state chaplain of Va. 1990—), Va. State Reading Assn., Newport News Reading Coun. Home: 938 Etna Dr Newport News VA 23602

KENT, ROBERTA B., literary agent; b. N.Y.C., Sept. 7, 1945; d. Robert B. and Rose (Linker) K. BA magna cum laude, NYU, 1967, MA, 1969; postgrad., Princeton U., 1967-68. Asst. to head literary dept. Creative Mgmt. Assocs., N.Y.C., 1969-70; asst. to pres. Curtis Brown Ltd., N.Y.C., 1970-72, literary agt., v.p. dept. motion pictures, 1978-79; ptnr., literary agt. W.B. Agy., N.Y.C., 1972-78; literary agt., v.p. dept. motion pictures Kohner-Levy Agy., Los Angeles, 1979-81; literary agt. The Ufland Agy., Beverly Hills, Calif., 1981-83; literary agt., v.p. literary dept. S.T.E. Representation, Ltd., Beverly Hills, 1983—. Mem. Phi Beta Kappa. Democrat. Office: STE Representation Ltd 9301 Wilshire Blvd Beverly Hills CA 90210

KENT, SALLY LITHERLAND, sculptor; b. Port Arthur, Tex., Oct. 2, 1937; d. William Francis and A. Juanita (Dawson) Litherland; m. James Jerry Kent, Sept. 8, 1956; children: Charlotte, William James, Christopher. Student, Hunter Coll., N.Y.C., 1955-56; BFA, Calif. Coll. Arts and Crafts, Oakland, 1985, MFA, 1988. Glaze chemist Calif. Coll. Arts and Crafts, Oakland, 1986-88; San Francisco, 1988—, photographer sculpture, 1986—, sculptor, painter, 1988—. One-woman shows include The Art Store Gallery, Oakland, 1987, Calif. Coll. Arts and Crafts Grad. Gallery, Oakland, 1988, Cochise Coll. Gallery, Sierra Vista, Ariz., 1990. Mem. Internat. Sculpture Ctr. Office: 1001 A O'Reilly Ave San Francisco CA 94129

KENTON SMITH, WANDA GAYLE, marketing professional; b. Atlanta, July 25, 1957; d. Howard Burton and Mary Elizabeth (McElroy) Kenton; m. Kenneth A. Smith, May 26, 1979; 1 child, Chelsea Linnea. BA in Journalism, Auburn U., 1979. Advt. copywriter Levitz Furniture, Miami, Fla., 1979-80; editor World Publs. Inc., Winter Park, Fla., 1980-82; pres. Kenton Smith Communications Inc., Orlando, Fla., 1982-84; dir. mktg. Regal Marine Industries, Inc., Orlando, 1984-90; dir. sales and mktg. svcs. Regal Marine Industries, Inc., 1990—; pub. relations and mktg. cons., Cen. Fla. Editor: The Winning Edge, 1982, Deferring Fraud, 1984; contbr. articles to numerous consumer mags. Coord. atty. gen. campaign State of Ala., Guntersville, 1979; regional and state dir. pub. communications Mormon Ch., Orlando, 1983-87, young women's pres., 1987-90, adviser Single Adult Program. Mem. Sales and Mktg. Execs. (bd. dirs. 1988—, chmn. pub. rels. com. 1988-90, Outstanding Women in Bus. award 1984, named SME Sec. 1990—, elected officer), Boating Writers Internat., Nat. Marine Mfrs. Assn. (sales promotion com.), Fla. Motion Picture and TV Assn. Republican. Office: Regal Marine Industries Inc 2300 Jetport Dr Orlando FL 32809

KENVIN, HELENE ENID, lawyer, organization executive, author; b. N.Y.C., Oct. 25, 1941; d. Melvin C. and Ethel (Wiesenthal) Schwartz; m. Howard Kenvin, Sept. 24, 1981; children: Fred Andrew, Seth Alan. AB magna cum laude, Brown U., 1962; LLB, Columbia U., 1965. Bar: N.Y. 1965, U.S. Dist. Ct. (so. and ea. dists.) N.Y. 1967, U.S. Ct. Appeals (2d cir.) 1967, U.S. Ct. Appeals (7th cir.) 1970, U.S. Supreme Ct. 1970. Pvt. practice N.Y.C., N.Y., 1965—; pres. The Caucasus Network, Esopus, N.Y., 1984—; mem. faculty Rutgers U. Law Sch., Camden, N.J., 1972-83; campus fellow Brown U., Providence, 1973; vis. lectr. Jewish Theol. Sem., N.Y.C., 1976, Columbia U., N.Y.C., 1977. Author: Lawyering, 1976, Justice by the Book: Aspects of Jewish and American Criminal Law, 1976; This Land of Liberty: A History of America's Jews, 1986; contbr. articles to legal jours. Mem. Jewish Geneal. Soc. (exec. coun. 1977-83, editor Dorot 1985-86), Phi Beta Kappa (vis. scholar 1979-81). Office: The Caucasus Network PO Box 218 Esopus NY 12429

KENWORTHY, JEAN MARIE, marketing manager; b. Clarks Summit, Pa., Feb. 12, 1960; d. Paul James and Dorothy Marie (Raub) K. BS in Mktg., Pa. State U., 1983. Svc. mgr. Casa Lupita Restaurants, Inc., Newark, Ohio, 1983, Jacksonville, Fla., 1984, Marlton, N.J., 1985-86; sales rep. MacMillan Publ. Co., Allentown, Pa., 1986-89; mktg. mgr. W.B. Saunders Co., Phila., 1989—. Roman Catholic. Home: 3901 Conshohocken Ave 6403 Philadelphia PA 19131 Office: WB Saunders Co The Curtis Ctr Independence Sq W Philadelphia PA 19106-3399

KENWORTHY, LUCRETIA MINA, controller; b. Winchester, Ind., Sept. 27, 1962; d. David Russel and Hazel Leona (Irvin) K.; 1 child, Kathy Lou. Student, Ind. U. East, 1988—. Acctg. clk. Lajitas Hotels, Terlingua, Tex., 1983; controller Greenville (Ohio) Inn, 1985—. Brownie leader Girl Scouts U.S., Lynn, Ind., 1989-90; coach YMCA, Lynn, 1989. Mem. NAFE.

KENYON, DAPHNE ANNE, economist; b. Augusta, Ga., Aug. 14, 1952; d. Lawrence Austin and Shirley (Knaus) Kenyon; m. Peter George Kachavos, Oct. 22, 1988. BA, Mich. State U., 1974; MA in Econs., U. Mich., 1976, PhD in Econs., 1980. Asst. prof. Dartmouth Coll., Hanover, N.H., 1979-83; sr. analyst U.S. Adv. Commn. on Intergovt. Relations, Washington, 1983-85; fin. economist U.S. Treasury Dept., Washington, 1985-87; sr. research assoc. Urban Inst., Washington, 1987-88; Lincoln fellow Lincoln Int. of Land Policy, Cambridge, Mass., 1988—; cons. U.S. IRS Adv. Panel, Washington, 1987—. Assoc. editor Urban Studies, 1988—; editor: Coping with Mandates, 1987, Intergovernmental Tax and Policy Competition, 1989; contbr. articles to profl. jours. Mem. N.H. Gov. Revenue Adv. Com. Concord, 1982. NSF grad. fellow, 1974. Mem. Am. Econ. Assn., Nat. Tax Assn., Pub. Choice Soc., Nat. Tax Jour. (referee). Roman Catholic.

KENYON, JOSEPHINE, teacher; b. Catskill, N.Y., Jan. 13, 1944; d. Richard Ellis and Katherine Turrell; 1 child, Jacqueline Darquea. AAA, SUNY, Oneonta; BA, Calif. State U.; teaching cert., Toranto Teachers Coll., 1969-70. Elem. tchr. Alex. Muir Sch., Toranto, Canada, 1970-72, Earlville Elem Sch., Earlville, N.Y., 1972-87; gifted talented tchr. Earlville Elem. Sch., 1987-89; gifted and talented coord. Fairport (N.Y.) Cen. Sch., 1989—. Mem. program com. Chenango County Coun. of the Arts, Norwich. Mem. Advocay for Gifted and Talented Educ., Delta Kappa Gamma.

KENYON, JUDITH ELEANOR, nurse, real estate company official; b. Ballston Spa, N.Y., Apr. 22, 1948; d. Horace Henry and Eleanor Rose (Barker) K.; m. Robert Patraw, June 11, 1978 (div. June 1985); 1 child, David Kenyon. AAS magna cum laude, Jr. Coll. Albany (N.Y.), 1975. RN, N.Y. Asst. dir. traffic WMHT-Pub. TV, Schenectady, N.Y., 1967-68; mem. cardiac nursing staff St. Clare's Hosp., Schenectady, 1975-77; pvt. duty nurse Tri-Cities, Latham, N.Y., 1977-81; clinic nurse Planned Parenthood, Schenectady, 1981-85; supr. nurse Bapt. Retirement Ctr., Scotia, N.Y., 1983-87; charge nurse VA Hosp., Albany, 1987—. 2d lt. USAR Nursing Corp, 1987—. Mem. Phi Theta Kappa. Republican. Lutheran. Home: 327 Glen Ave Scotia NY 12302 Office: VA Hosp Albany Holland Ave Albany NY 12000

KENYON, JULIA CAROLINE, retired educator; b. Harvard, Nebr., Jan. 3, 1919; d. Peter J. and Anna Marie (Bartholoma) Pauley; m. Meril T. Kenyon, May 10, 1949. BS, U. Nebr., 1941; MEd, Colo. State U., 1968, postgrad., 1980; postgrad., Oreg. State U., 1965, U. No. Colo., 1970, Utah State U., 1979, others. Tchr. home econs., Philips, Nebr., 1941-43, Grand Island, Nebr., 1943-44; FHA supr. home econs. Loup City (Nebr.) Schs., 1945-46; mgr. home extension program Perkins County, Nebr., 1947-59; tchr. home econs. Holyoke (Colo.) High Sch., 1959-84. Hon. vol. local Heart Assn.; chair Holyoke Heart Assn.; vol. Meals on Wheels. Served with WAVES, USN, 1944-46. Recipient Outstanding Home Econs. Humanitarian award State of Colo., 1977. Mem. NEA, Colo. Edn. Assn. (profl. affairs com.), Holyoke Edn. Assn. (pres. 1975), Am. Vocat. Assn., Colo. Vocat. Assn., Colo. Assn. Vocat. Tchrs., Am. Home Econs. Assn., Colo. Home Econs. Assn., Gen. Fedn. Women's Clubs (dist. treas. Nebr. 1954-55, pres. 1954-55), Sigma Kappa, Delta Kappa Gamma (pres. local chpt.). Methodist. Clubs: Venango Fairy Dell (pres.), Mary Jane Extension. Lodge: Order Eastern Star (past matron). Home: 205 S Belford St Holyoke CO 80734 Office: PO Box 193 Holyoke CO 80734

KEOGH, HEIDI HELEN DAKE, publishing executive; b. Saratoga, N.Y., July 12, 1950; d. Charles Starks and Phyllis Sylvia (Edmunds) Dake; m. Randall Frank Keogh, Nov. 3, 1973; children: Tyler Cameron, Kelly Dake. Student, U. Colo., 1972. Reception, promotions Sta. KLAK, KJAE, Lakewood, Colo., 1972-73; account exec. Mixed Media Advt. Agy., Denver, 1973-75; writer, mktg. Jr. League Cookbook Devel., Denver, 1986-88; chmn., coordinator Colorado Cache & Creme de Colorado Cookbooks, 1988—; speakers bur. Mile High Transplant Bank, Denver, 1983-84, Writer's Inst., U. Denver, 1988; bd. dirs. Stewart's Ice Cream Co., Inc., Jr. League, Denver. Contbr. 6 articles to profl. jours. Fiscal officer, bd. dirs. Mile High Transplant Bank; blockworker Rep. Party, Littleton, Colo., 1980-84, Heart Fund, Cancer, Littleton, 1978—; fundraising vol. Littleton Pub. Schs., 1980—; vol. Arapahoe (Colo.) Advocates for Children, 1988—, Families First, 1989—. Mem. Jr. League Denver (Jr. League pub. rels., bd. v.p. ways and means, 1989—), Columbine Country Club, Gamma Alpha Chi, Pi Beta Phi Alumnae Club (pres. Denver chpt. 1984-85). Episcopalian. Home: 63 Fairway Ln Littleton CO 80123

KEOGH, MONICA LEVERONE, small business owner; b. Mpls., June 22, 1954; d. Joseph Paul and Genevieve Gertrude (Ozark) L.; m. Richard John Keogh, Sept. 10, 1977; children: Robert William, Gregory Laurence. BA, Coll. St. Catherine, 1976; postgrad., Art Ctr. Coll. of Design, Pasadena, Calif., 1983-84. Art dir. Envision Art & Design, Houston, 1979; graphics supr. Baylor Coll. Medicine, Houston, 1979-83; art dir. 3/0 Internat., Houston, 1984; art dir., owner Monica Keogh Design, Houston, 1985—; assoc. art dir. Baxter & Korge, Houston, 1989—. Recipient Typographic Excellence award Type Dirs. Club, 1986. Mem. Women In Communications, Inc., Am. Assn. Graphic Arts, Houston Calligraphy Guild. Roman Catholic. Office: Monica Keogh Design 8323 Westglen Houston TX 77063-6309

KEOHANE, NANNERL OVERHOLSER, college president, political scientist; b. Blytheville, Ark., Sept. 18, 1940; d. James Arthur and Grace (McSpadden) Overholser; m. Patrick Henry III, Sept. 16, 1962 (div. May 1969); 1 child, Stephan; m. Robert Owen Keohane, Dec. 18, 1970; children: Sarah, Jonathan, Nathaniel. BA, Wellesley Coll., 1961, Oxford U., Eng., 1963; PhD, Yale U., 1967. Faculty Swarthmore Coll., Pa., 1967-73, Stanford U., Calif., 1973-81; fellow Ctr.for Advanced Study in the Behavioral Scis. Stanford U., 1978-79, 87-88; pres., prof. polit. sci. Wellesley (Mass.) Coll., 1981—; bd. dirs. State St. Boston Corp., IBM. Author: Philosophy and the State in France: The Renaissance to the Enlightenment, 1980; co-editor: Feminist Theory: A Critique of Ideology, 1982. Trustee WGBH Ednl. TV Found., 1981—, Colonial Williamsburg Found., 1988—; bd. dirs. Carnegie Found. for Advancement of Teaching, 1986—. Marshall scholar, 1961-63; AAUW dissertation fellow. Mem. Council on Fgn. Relations, Phi Beta Kappa, Cosmopolitan Club (N.Y.C.), Saturday Club (Boston), Comml. Club (Boston), Algonquin Club. Democrat. Office: Wellesley Coll Office of Pres Wellesley MA 02181-8201

KEON, LINDA ELIZABETH, veterinarian; b. Boston, Jan. 29, 1950; d. Howard T. and Eleanor M. (Hilberg) Rich; m. Thomas L. Keon, Feb. 10, 1973 (div. Oct. 1985). AS, Mass. Bay Community Coll., Watertown, 1969; BS, Salem State Coll., 1972; MEd, Suffolk U., 1975; DVM, U. Mo., 1986. Lic. veterinarian, Pa., Va. Fla. Tchr. Acton-Boxborough High Sch., 1972-74; instr. bus. North Shore Community Coll., Beverly, Mass., 1974-75, So. Vt. Coll., Bennington, 1975-76, Lansing (Mich.) Community Coll., 1976-78; grad. asst. Mich. State U., 1978-79; instr. organic chemistry U. Notre Dame, Ind., 1979-81; vet. technician U. Mo., Columbia, 1981-83; staff veterinarian Steinbach Vet. Hosp., Blue Bell, Pa., 1986-88, Trevose (Pa.) Vet. Ctr., 1988-90, Best Friends' Animal Clinic, Miramar, Flas., 1990—. Active Honor Code Com. SCAVMA, Columbia, 1983-85. Mem. NEA, Am. Vet. Med. Assn. (rep. student chpt. 1983-85), Am. Animal Hosp. Assn., Mo. Vet. Med. Assn., Ea. Bus. Tchrs. Assn., Cornell Feline Health Ctr., Columbia Kennel Club, Pennypack Watershed Assn., Aircraft Owners and Pilots Assn., 99's Women's Pilot Assn. Home: 967 Wesley Ave Huntington Valley PA 19006 Office: River Run Animal clinic 9981 Miramar Pkwy Miramar FL 33025

KEPHART, LORI MAUREEN DU'MONT, administrative assistant; b. Santa Monica, Calif., Apr. 2, 1968; d. Vernon and Virgina Lee (Vieth) Von Baron; m. Thomas Lynn Kephart, July 22, 1989. Student, Santa Monica Coll. Administrv. asst. Jardine Emett & Chandler, L.A.; receptionist Galaxy Temps, West L.A.; dept. mgr. Millers Outpost, Santa Monica; asst. mgr. Thom Mc Ann, Santa Monica. Mem. Internat. Order of the Rainbow Girls (rep. Mo. chpt. 1988-89, Grand Cross of Color). Home: 3724 Inglewood Blvd #7 Los Angeles CA 90066

KEPLER, ELISE ANNE, marketing consulting company executive; b. Chicago Heights, Ill., July 31, 1964; d. Thomas Furman and Patricia Anne (Boehler) Kepler. BA, Bucknell U., Lewisburg, Pa., 1986; postgrad., LaSalle U., Phila. Asst. dir. mktg. Genesis Data Systems, Harrisburg, Pa., 1986-87; mktg. mgr. SofCor, Inc., Berlin, N.J., 1987-88; maj. sys. team mem. GE/RCA Telephone Sys., Bala Cynwyd, Pa., 1988-89; mktg. mgr. RCA Bus. Telephone Systems, Mt. Laurel, N.J., 1989-90; pres., owner DANE Assocs., Winston-Salem, N.C., 1989—; sec., treas. Steward Homes, Inc., Nashville, 1989—. Patentee on software. Active Big Bros./Big Sisters, Lewisburg, 1982-86. Lt. U.S. Army, 1986, with Res. 1986—. Recipient DAR award, 1982. Mem. NAFE, NOW, Am. Mgmt. Assn., Am. Mktg. Assn., Sales and Mktg. Execs. Internat., Toastmasters Internat. Republican. Office: Dane Assocs 1001 S Marshall St Ste 31 Winston-Salem NC 27101

KEPLER, PATRICIA ANNE, nursing home administrator; b. Rochester, N.Y., Mar. 15, 1942; children: Elise Anne, T. Scott. Student, Elizabethtown (Pa.) Coll., 1983, Pa. State U. Exec. dir. Kanawha Hospice Care, Inc., Charleston, W.Va., 1983-86; adminstr. Care Haven of Pt. Pleasant, W.Va., 1986-88; asst. v.p. alt. funding Rebound, Inc., Hendersonville, Tenn., 1988-89; exec. dir. Steward Homes, Inc., 1988-90, Shepherd's Ctr. of West End, Nashville, 1989—; appointee Gov. of W.Va. Health Planning Task Force; pres. Outreach Pulmonary Rehab. Svcs.; pres. Steward Homes, Inc. Mem. NAFE, Zonta (treas.), Kiwanis, Sigma Phi Omega. Home: 7308 Harding Rd Nashville TN 37221 Office: Shepherds Ctr West End PO Box 50818 Nashville TN 37205

KEPNER, JANET SUMNER, secondary educator; b. Hartford, Conn., May 27, 1936; d. William Saville and Jane Rockwell (Sumner) Grainger; m. Charles David Kepner III, Dec. 28, 1957; children: Kimberly Jean Kepner McCahill, Kristin Ann (dec.). BS in Physical Edn., Boston U., 1958. Cert. health and phys. edn. tchr., Conn. Substitute tchr. Avon (Conn.) Pub. Schs., 1964—. Sec./treas. United Fund, Avon, 1989; chmn. Natural Resources Comm., Avon, 1980-84; vice chmn. Fisher Meadows Devel. Commn., Avon; mem. Rep. Town Com., Avon, 1988—; leader Girl Scouts USA, Avon, 1965-70. Mem. Sargent Coll. Club (pres. Hartford 1969-70), Avon Women's Club, Kappa Kappa Gamma (chmn. ways and means com. Hartford 1969-70). Republican. Episcopalian. Home: 192 Haynes Rd Avon CT 06001

KEPNER, RITA MARIE, sculptor, writer, editor, international military public affairs officer; b. Binghamton, N.Y., Nov. 15, 1944; d. Peter Walter and Helena Theresa (Piotrowski) Kramnicz; m. John C. Mattiesen; 1 child, Stewart. Student, Elmira Coll., 1962-63; BA, Harpur Coll., SUNY, 1966; postgrad., Okla. U., 1988; diplome of merit (hon.), Acad. Bedriacense, Calvsatore, Italy, 1984. One-woman shows include Willoughby Wallace Meml. Gallery, Branford, Conn., 1967, Penryn Gallery, Seattle, 1970, 73, 76, Haines Gallery, Seattle, 1975, Zoliborz Gallery, Warsaw, Poland, 1981, Yorkshire 510, Norman, Okla.; group shows include SUNY, Binghamton, 1966, Manawata Art Gallery, Palmerston North, N.Z., Modern Art Mus., Seattle, 1976, Portland (Oreg.) Art Mus., 1976, Die Roemer Gallery, Wiesbaden, Fed. Republic Germany, 1988; major works include Peace Pipe, Zalaegerszeg, Hungary, Human Forms in Balance, City of Seattle, 1975, Unity, City of Znin, Poland, 1976, Rough to Smooth, Seattle Pub. Library, 1978; instr. sculpture Evergreen Coll., Olympia, Wash., 1974-78; instr. exptl. coll. U. Wash., 1972-74; informal visual arts amb. between U.S. and Poland, 1976-81; pres. fed. women's program coun. Seattle dist., 1985-86; fed. women's project mgr., Schweinfurt, Fed. Republic Germany, 1986-87, Wiesbaden, 1988; artist-in-residence City of Seattle, 1975, 77-78; del. Internat. Sculptors Conf., Toronto, Ont., Can., 1978; writer, editor, pub. affairs specialist Seattle dist. U.S. Army CE; pub. affairs officer Wiesbaden (Fed. Republic Germany) Milcom Hdqrs., 1987-88; editor Schweinfurt, Fed. Republic Germany, 1986-87. Co-founder Bainbridge Island Arts Coun.; VISTA vol., 1982-84; bd. dirs. Aradia Med. Clinic, Seattle, 1972-74, 88-89; founder Chimacum (Wash.) Sch. Dist. Learning Boosters, 1989; loaned exec. to govt. campaigns United Way, 1989; 1st aid trainer Medic I, Seattle, 1989—; trainer for campaign coords. and key workers, 1989; elected co-chair Marrowstone Island Groundwater Com. Dept. of Ecology, Wash. State; mem. adv. com. Seawater Interusion Team. Recipient merit award for superior journalistic achievement U.S. Army CE, 1984, 85, 2d place news category competition award, 1985, 86; suggestion award Dept. Army, 1984, ofcl. commendation, 1985, 86, 87, 90, Cert. achievement Washington Assn. Educators of the Talented and Gifted, 1990; Kosciuszko Found. grantee, 1975, 76, 79, 81. Mem. Internat. Artists Assn. of UNESCO, Paris Artists Equity Assn., Internat. Artists Cooperation (Edewecht, Fed. Republic Germany), N.W. Multihull Assn. (commodore 1974). Holder USCG capt. lic. for passenger carrying aux. sailing vessels up to 50 tons, 1980—. Contbr. articles to N.W. Arts, Seattle Post Intelligencer, Leonardo mag., Polska Panorama, Poland mag. Home: 6681 Flager Rd Nordland WA 98358-9629 Office: Pub Affairs Office Puget Sound Naval Shipyard Bremerton WA 98314-5000

KEPPLER, BILLIE JO, special education educator; b. Hartford, Conn., July 30, 1949; d. William Abraham and Lena (Wernikoff) Levine. BS, U. Conn., 1971; MS, Cen. Conn. State U., New Britain, 1975. Cert. maths. and spl. edn. tchr., Conn. Tchr. spl. edn. McDonough Sch., Hartford, 1971—; tchr. maths. Sphere, Simsbury, Conn., summer 1980-81, Migratory Children's Program, Hartford, summer 1982-83, program leader, summer 1984; chairperson, monitor spl. edn. program McDonough Sch., Hartford, 1981-86; cheerleading advisor Hartford Pub. High Sch., 1984-85; coord. Conn. Celebration of Teaching, Windsor, 1987-90. Author: (handbook) McDonough Discipline Handbook, 1989. Named Tchr. of the Yr., Hartford Bd. Edn., 1983; Dodge Found. grantee, 1989-90. Mem. Hartford Fedn. Tchrs., Phi Delta Kappa. Jewish. Home: 25 Rye Ridge Pkwy West Hartford CT 06117 Office: McDonough Sch 100 Wilson St Hartford CT 06106

KEPURAITIS, PEGGY MARY, electrical engineer; b. Chgo., Feb. 21, 1961; d. Edward D. and Therese D. (Mocny) K. BSEE, U. Ill., 1984; MS in Computer Sci., U. Ill., Chgo., 1989. Elec. engr. II communications sector Motorola, Inc., Schaumburg, Ill., 1984-85, elec. engr. I, 1985-87, sr. software engr., 1987-88, engring. group leader, 1988—. Mem. NAFE, Chgo. Jaycees (treas. 1985, subchmn. jr. citizenship 1986, project chmn. 1987). Home: 4116b W Addison Chicago IL 60641 Office: Motorola Corp 1301 E Algonquin Rd Schaumburg IL 60196

KERES, KAREN LYNNE, English educator; b. Evanston, Ill., Oct. 22, 1945; d. Frank and Bette (Pascoe) K.; BA, St. Mary's Coll., 1967; student U. Notre Dame, 1967-68; MA, U. Iowa, 1969. Assoc. prof. English, humanities, fine art William Rainey Harper Coll., Palatine, Ill., 1969—, Palomer Coll., San Marcos, Calif., 1990—; cons. bus. communications. Mem. MLA, Ill. Assn. Tchrs. English, Am. Fedn. Tchrs., Nature Conservancy, Mensa. Home: 222 Fairfield Dr Island Lake IL 60042 Office: William Rainey Harper Coll Dept Liberal Arts Palatine IL 60067

KERKEL, LYNN, middle school educator; b. Baton Rouge, Nov. 14, 1942; d. Peter Phillip and Rosa Emaline (Dunnam) K.; m. James O. Skidmore, Dec. 23, 1972 (div. Jan. 6, 1978). AA, Mt. San Antonio Jr. Coll., 1962; BE, Kent State U., 1965, MEd in Reading, 1973. Cert. elem. educator, reading specialist, Ariz., Mich. Elem. educator Willoughby (Ohio) Eastlake Bd. Edn., 1965-84, mid. sch. educator, 1984—; inservice instr. Willoughby-Eastlake Bd. Edn. Named to South High Sch. Hall of Fame Willoughby-Eastlake Bd. Edn., 1989. Mem. Willoughby Eastlake Tchr. Assn. (past pres. 1981-86, grievance co-chair, 1965—), Galilee Shrine #41 Order of the White Shrine of Jerusalem, Ohio Edn. Assn. (rep. 1970—), NEA (rep. 1979—), Northeastern Ohio Edn. Assn., Internat. Reading Assn., Delta Kappa Gamma Soc. Internat. Democrat. Methodist. Home: 5457D Millwood Ln Willoughby OH 44094

KERLEY, JANICE JOHNSON, personnel executive; b. Coral Gables, Fla., Nov. 28, 1938; d. Howard Love and Lois Dean (Austin) Johnson; m. Bobby Joe Kerley, May 16, 1959; children: Janice Elisabeth Kerley Vela, Meredith Ann Kerley Tucker. AA, Stephens Coll., 1958; B in Music Edn., U. Miami, Fla., 1960. Tchr. Dade County Pub. Schs., Miami, 1960-69; asst. to v.p. engr. Racal-Milgo, Inc., Miami, 1972-80; dir. sales and mktg. B. Joe Kerley, Realtor, Miami, 1980-83; dir. customer service, ops. mgr. Modern-Age Furniture Co., Miami, 1983-85; chief exec. officer Adia Pers. Svcs., Greensboro, Winston-Salem, N.C., 1985—. Named Small Businessperson of Yr. Greensboro Area C. of C., 1988. Mem. Am. Bus. Women's Assn. (nat. bd. dirs. 1978-79, trustee nat. scholarship fund 1978-79, named one of top ten businesswomen, 1988). Office: Adia Personnel Services 315-B Pomona Dr Greensboro NC 27407 also: 4300 Indiana Ave Ste 35 Winston-Salem NC 27106

KERMEEN, SHARON KAY, social services worker; b. Caledonia, Mich., Dec. 2, 1938; d. Wayne Earl and Crystal Doreen (Johnson) K. Grad. high sch., Middleville, Mich. Typist clk. Barry County Dept. of Social Services, Hastings, Mich., 1957-69, clerical supr., 1970-72, eligibility examiner, 1970-72, assistance payments worker, 1972—. Mem. cast Hastings Civic Players, 1963. Mem. Mich. State Employees Assn. (sec. treas., v.p.), United Auto Workers, Hastings Bus. and Profl. Women's Club (corr. sec., 2d v.p.). Home: 321 S Broadway Middleville MI 49333

KERN, ANGELINE FRAZIER, educational administrator; b. Jackson, Tenn., Apr. 27, 1939; d. William Raymond and Sarah Louise (Harris) Frazier; divorced; children: Tiffany Louise, Kevin James. BA, Lambuth Coll., Jackson, 1961; MA, Memphis State U., 1962; postgrad., U. Tenn., 1963. Tchr. phys. edn. Jackson City Schs., 1960-62; tchr. English, guidance counselor Georgian Hills Jr. High Sch., Memphis, 1962-65; guidance counselor Colonial Jr. High Sch., Memphis, 1965-70; adminstrv. asst. Kingsbury High Sch., Memphis, 1970-72; prin. Avon Elem. Sch., Memphis, 1972-77, Balmoral Elem. Sch., Memphis, 1977—. Mem. adv. bd. East Memphis YMCA, 1984-87; mem. Memphis City Beautiful Commn., 1985-89; pres. St. John's Creek Home and Garden Club, Memphis, 1968-70. Recipient Youth Svc. award YMCA, Memphis, 1983, Vol. Recognition award, 1986, Patron of Youth award, 1987. Mem. NEA, Nat. Assn. Elem. Sch. Prins., Assn. for Sch. Curriculum Devel., Tenn. Assn. Elem. Sch. Prins. (fall conf. planning com. 1985), Memphis Pub. Sch. Prins. Assn. (auditing com. 1983-85), Memphis State U. Rebounders, Educators Bridge Club, Phi Delta Kappa, Delta Kappa Gamma (fin. chmn. Epsilon chpt. 1976-84, corr. sect. 1984-86). Republican. Roman Catholic. Office: Balmoral Elem Sch 5905 Grosvenor Memphis TN 38119

KERN, BARBARA PATRICIA, public health administrator; b. Elizabeth, N.J., Sept. 22, 1935; d. Eugene Louis and Wilma Catherine (Pitula) K. BS, Ithaca Coll., 1957; MA, NYU, 1965. Lic. in phys. therapy, N.J., N.Y. Supr. N.Y. State Hosp. Rehab., West Haverstraw, 1958-67; asst. prof. phys. therapy Temple U., Phila., 1967-71; cons. phys. therapy N.J. State Dept. Health, Trenton, 1971-75, coordinator crippled children program, 1975-80, chief spl. child health services, 1980-86, dir. spl. chief health services, 1987—; with N.J. Sr. Exec. Svc., 1989, Wash. State Program for Children with Spl Health Needs, 1989; adminstrv. cons. Va. Crippled Children Program, 1985, Ala. Crippled Children Program, 1982; mem. planning com. Nat. Conf. Fin. Services for Handicapped Children, 1983; project dir. Pediatric AIDS Demonstration Grant, 1989—; cons. in field. Contbg. author: Competencies in Physical Therapy, 1977; contbr. articles to profl. jours. Chmn. prevention com. N.J. Assn. Retarded Citizens, 1981. Mem. Am. Pub. Health Assn., Assn. Maternal and Child Health Programs. Office: NJ State Dept Health CN 364 Trenton NJ 08626

KERN, CONSTANCE ELIZABETH, real estate broker; b. Cleve., Dec. 18, 1937; d. Walter Anthony and Irene (Davies) Matthews; divorced; children: James, David, Douglas, Kathleen. Student, John Carroll U., 1957, Case Western Res. U., 1958; BA in Speech and English, Marietta (Ohio) Coll., 1959; postgrad., Sul Ross State U., Midland, Tex., 1967-68, Comml. Coll. Real Estate, Ft. Worth, 1984, 86. Cert. tchr., Ohio, Tex.; lic. real estate broker, Tex. Tchr. South Euclid and Lyndhurst (Ohio) Schs., 1959-60; sec. Pan Am. Petroleum, Midland, 1960-61; tchr. St. Ann's Sch., Midland, 1967-69; real estate agt. McAfee & Assocs., Arlington, Tex., 1985-86; real estate broker Constance Kern Real Estate, Arlington, 1986—; property mgr., 1986—; property mgr., 1986—; oil operator, investor, Midland and Arlington, 1975—. Vol. Pink Ladies Midland Meml. Hosp., 1970-73; troop leader Brownies Girl Scouts Am., Midland, 1971; vol. speech therapist Children's Service League Cerebral Palsy Ctr., Midland, 1975-76. Mem. Nat. Bd. Realtors, Tex. Bd. Realtors, Arlington Bd. Realtors, AAUW, Pi Kappa Delta. Republican. Roman Catholic.

KERN, JILL PHELPS, marketing executive; b. Boston, Aug. 12, 1956; d. Walter Phelps and Barbara Ann (Cobban) K. BS, MIT, 1977; MBA, U. Chgo., 1983. Quality engr. Babcock & Wilcox, Augusta, Ga.; fin. analyst Northwest Industries, Chgo.; corp. quality analyst Burroughs Corp., Detroit; cons. Digital Equipment Corp., Stow, Mass., 1984-87; mktg. mgr. Digital Equipment Corp., Marlborough, Mass., 1987—. Co-author, editor: Human Resources Management, 1987; contbr. articles to profl. publs. Reader, Mass. Assn. for Blind, Brookline, 1988—. Mem. Am. Soc. Quality Control (sr., bd. dirs. 1990-92, Disting. Svc. award 1985, various coms.). Office: Digital Equipment Corp 600 Nickerson Rd Marlborough MA 01752

KERN, PATRICIA JOAN, media specialist; b. Ft. Wayne, Ind., Dec. 1, 1933; d. Wesley Emery and Ruth Mae (Adams) Pritchett; m. Kenneth Charles Kern, Mar. 9, 1951; children: Ralph, Theresa, Catherine Holman, Norman. BFA, Ft. Wayne, 1976; BA, Indiana U., Ft. Wayne, 1977; MS Ed., St. Francis, Ft. Wayne, 1981, Indiana U., Ft. Wayne, 1983. Art instr. Ft. Wayne Art Inst., Ft. Wayne, Ind., 1975-77; art tchr. South Side High Sch., Ft. Wayne, 1978-81; art history inst. Indiana U., Ft. Wayne, 1979-83; art tchr. k-6 Shambaugh Elem., Ft. Wayne, 1981-82; media tchr. Jefferson Middle Sch., Ft. Wayne, 1982--; art appreciation Inst. Indiana U., 1988--; Painter and Sculptor: Portrait of Lora, 1973 (best of show), 1973, Figure Study, 1973 (1st-Tri-Kappa), 1973, Mandala, 1975 1st-Tri-Kappa), 1975, Portrait of Monica, 1979 (purchase award), 1979. Mem., Ft. Wayne Women's Bureau- Ft. Wayne, Ind., 1977--. Named Beatty scholar Delta Kappa Gamma, Indpls., 1988, runner-up for Outstanding Tchr. award Ft. Wayne Sch., Ft. Wayne, Ind., 1984-85. Mem., Assn. of Indiana Media Educators, Ft. Wayne Edn. Assn., Indiana Stat Tchr. Assn., Nat'l Edn. Assn., Delta Kappa Gamma (2nd v.p., 1988-90). Office: Jefferson Middle Sch 5303 Wheelock Rd Fort Wayne IN 46835

KERN, REGINA FLORA, broadcast executive; b. N.Y.C., Mar. 16, 1948; d. Joshua and Margot (Skapowker) K. BA, NYU, 1969; MA, Yeshiva U., 1972. Asst. dir. Conn. Renaissance, Inc., Westport, 1973-75; acct. exec., show host, producer WMMM/WDJF-FM, Westport, 1975-77; announcer, producer KWIT-FM, Sioux City, Iowa, 1977-78; devel. dir. WNVT-TV, Annandale, Va., 1978-80; pub. participation coord. The Corp. for Pub. Broadcasting, Washington, 1980-82; devel. dir. The Am. U., Washington, 1982-83; gen. mgr. WAMU-FM, The Am. U., Washington, 1983-86; cable gen. mgr. Interstate Gen. Co., Waldorf, Md., 1986-88; system gen. mgr. Jones Intercable Co., Waldorf, 1988—; bd. dirs. The Devel. Exchange, Washington, 1983-86. Pres. United Way of Charles County, Waldorf, 1990, bd. dirs., 1987—; bd. dirs. The Levine Sch. Music, Washington, 1987; sr. tutor Prince George's Literacy Coun., 1983-87. Mem. Kiwanis (bd. dirs. 1989-90), Charles C. of C. (bd. dirs. 1990-93). Democrat. Jewish. Office: Jones Intercable Co 336 Post Office Rd Waldorf MD 20602

KERNAN, BARBARA DESIND, senior government executive; b. N.Y.C., Jan. 11, 1939; d. Philip and Anne (Feuer) Desind; m. Joseph E. Kernan, Feb. 14, 1973. BA cum laude, Smith Coll., 1960; postgrad. Oxford U., 1963; MA, Harvard U., 1963, postgrad. John F. Kennedy Sch. of Govt. Harvard U., 1983; postgrad. in edn. policy George Washington U., 1980. Editor, Harvard Law Sch., 1960-62; tchr. English, Newton High Sch. (Mass.), 1962-63; editor Allyn & Bacon Pubs., Boston, 1963-64; edn. asso. Upward Bound, Edn. Assos., Inc., Washington, 1965-68; edn. program specialist Title I, Elem. and Secondary Edn. Act, U.S. Office Edn., 1969-73; fellow Am. Polit. Sci. Assn., Senator William Proxmire and Congressman Alphonzo Bell, 1973-74; spl. asst. to dep. commr. for elem. and secondary edn. and dir. dissemination, sch. finance and analysis, U.S. Office Edn., 1975-77, chief program analysis br. div. edn. for disadvantaged, 1977-79, chief grant program coordination staff Office Dep. Commr. for Ednl. Resources, 1979-80; chief priority concerns staff Office Asst. Sec. Mgmt., U.S. Dept. Edn., Washington, 1980-81, dir. div. orgnl. devel. and analysis Office of Dep. Undersec. for Mgmt., 1981-86; sr. exec. svc. candidate on spl. project to improve status of women Sec. Transp., Washington, 1983-84, fed. sr. exec. svc., 1986; inducted sr. exec. svc., 1986; assoc. adminstr. for adminstrn. Nat. Hwy. Traffic Safety Adminstrn., Dept. Transp., 1986—. Recipient awards U.S. Office Edn., 1969, 71, 77, U.S. Dept. Edn., 1981-86; scholarships U. Mich., 1956-58, Smith Coll., 1958-60, Harvard U., 1962-63; Am. Polit. Sci. Assn. fellow, 1973-74; Sr. Exec. fellow John F. Kennedy Sch. Govt. Harvard U., 1983.

KERNAN, MARY CATHERINE, education educator; b. Rochester, N.Y., Aug. 22, 1957; d. John Francis and Mary Margaret (O'Brien) K.; m. Glenn Robert Herbert, Aug. 15, 1987. BA in Psychology, SUNY, Geneseo, 1979; MA in Indsl. Orgn./Psychology, U. Akron, 1983, PhD in Indsl. Orgn./Psychology, 1985. Asst. prof. Kent (Ohio) State U., 1985-89, U. Del., Newark, 1989—. Contbr. articles to profl. jours. Recipient grad. rsch. fellowship U. Akron, 1984, summer rsch. and creativity grant Kent State U., 1987, gen. univ. rsch. grant U. Del., 1990. Mem. Acad. Mgmt., Am. Psychol. Assn., Am. Psychol. Soc., Soc. Indsl. and Orgnl. Psychologists. Office: Dept Business Adminstrn Univ Delaware Newark DE 19716

KERNEY, EVELYN LORETTA, utilities executive; b. Tuscaloosa, Ala., Jan. 28, 1945; d. Robert Lee and Arnetta (Green) Palmer; m. Fulton L. Burns, June 21,1964 (div. Oct., 1971); m. Robert Lee Kerney Jr, May 17, 1985. BA, Canisius Coll., Buffalo, 1983, MS, 1985; doctoral studies, SUNY, Buffalo, 1985—. Lic. realtor. Mailgirl N.Y. Telephone, Buffalo, 1965-85, order typist, 1965-70; supr., acting mgr., trainer N.Y. Telephone, Buffalo, N.Y.C., 1970—; real estate sales rep. Mil-Hil Realty, Buffalo, N.Y.C., 1985—; Exec. advisor N.Y. Telephone Jr. Achievment, 1977. Com. mem. Rep. Club, Buffalo Urban League Guild. Mem. Women in Communications, Nat. Assn. of Female Execs., AAUW, Alpha Sigma Lambda. Home: 233 Brunswick Blvd Buffalo NY 14208 Office: Canisius Coll Nat Honor Soc Continuing Edn Buffalo NY 14208

KERN-FOXWORTH, MARILYN LOUISE, journalism educator; b. Kosciusko, Miss., Mar. 4, 1954; d. Jimmie and Manella (Dickens) Kern; m. Gregory Lamar Foxworth, July 3, 1984; 1 child, Gregory Lamar II. BS, Jackson State U., 1974; MS, Fla. State U., 1976; PhD, U. Wis., 1982. Pub. rels. asst. Sta. WJTV, Jackson, Miss., 1974; communications specialist Fla. State U., Tallahassee, 1974; advt. coordinator City of Tallahassee, 1975-76; coll. rels. rep. GTE Automatic Electric, Northlake, Ill., 1977; AM traffic mgr. Sta. WWQM Radio, Madison, Wis., 1978-79; prodn. mgr. Sta. WHA-AM, Madison, 1979-80; columnist, reporter Mid-West Observer, Madison, 1979-80; asst. prof. U. Tenn., Knoxville, 1980-87; prof. Tex. A&M U., College Station, 1987—. Assoc. editor Nashville Banner, 1983; contbr. chpt. to Dictionary Lit. Biography, 1985; contbr. articles to mags. including Black Collegian (Unity award 1985). Co-chair advisory Phyllis Wheatley YWCA, Knoxville, 1983-85. Amon Carter Evans scholar U. Tenn., 1983; recipient Kizzy award Black Women's Hall of Fame, Chgo., 1980, Pathfinder award Pub. Rels. Inst., 1988, PRSSA Adviser of Yr.; named a Woman of Achievement U. Tenn., 1983; fellow Am. Press Inst., 1988, Poynter Inst., 1988; first black person in U.S. to receive a PhD in advt. and pub. rels. Mem. Pub. Rels. Soc. Am. (Recognition of Excellence 1985), Assn. for Ednl. Journalism (nat. com., Research Award 1980), Nat. Communication Assn. (planning com.), Black Media Assn., Alpha Kappa Alpha. Home: 3417 Parkway Terr Bryan TX 77802 Office: Tex A&M U Dept Journalism 230 Reed McDonald College Station TX 77843-4111

KERNODLE, UNA MAE, teacher; b. Jackson, Tenn., Mar. 4, 1947; d. James G. and Mary E. (McLemore) Sikes. B.S. in Home Econs., U. Tenn., 1969; M.Edn., U. Alaska, 1974. Tchr., head dept. vocat. edn. and electives Chugiak High Sch., Anchorage; edn. cons. State of Alaska, Anchorage Talent Bank; presenter Gov.'s Conf. on Child Abuse, Alaska Vocat. Edn. Assn. Conf., Alaska Home Econs. Inst., 1989; state officer Alaska Home Econs. Recipient Gruening award, 1989. Mem. Am. Home Econs. Assn., Anchorage Assn. Edn. Young Children, NEA, Am. Vocat. Assn. Democrat. Baptist. Office: Chugiak High Sch PO Box 218 Eagle River AK 99577

KERNS, CHRISTIANNE FINCH, lawyer; b. Inglewood, Calif., Aug. 11, 1958; d. Daniel Wiley Finch and Winifred (Hahn) Westberg; m. Charles David Kerns, May 12, 1984. BA, Calif. State U., Fullerton, 1980; JD, U. So. Calif., 1985. Bar: Calif. 1985, U.S. Dist. Ct. (cen. dist.) Calif. 1985, U.S. Ct. Appeals (9th cir.) 1985. Assoc. Sheppard, Mullin, Richter & Hampton, L.A., 1985—. Editor-in-chief: Major Tax Planning Jour., 1985, Computer/Law Jour., 1984-85. Mem. ABA, L.A. County Bar Assn., Orange County Bar Assn., Calif. State Bar Assn., Fin. Lawyers Conf. Republican. Presbyterian. Office: Sheppard Mullin Richter & Hampton 333 S Hope St 48th Fl Los Angeles CA 90071

KERNS, GERTRUDE YVONNE, psychologist; b. Flint, Mich., July 25, 1931; d. Lloyd D. and Mildred C. (Ter Achter) B.; B.A., Olivet Coll., 1953; M.A., Wayne State U., 1958; Ph.D., U. Mich., 1979. Sch. psychologist Roseville (Mich.) Pub. Schs., 1958-68, Grosse Pointe (Mich.) Pub. Schs., 1968-86; pvt. practice psychology, Grosse Pointe, 1980—; instr. psychology Macomb Community Coll., 1959-69. Author: A Second Heartbeat, 1979. Mem. Am. Psychol. Assn., Mich. Psychol. Assn., Lakeshore Psychol. Assn. (pres. 1988-89), Psi Chi. Home: 28820 Grant St Saint Clair Shores MI 48081 Office: 63 Kercheval Ste 205 Grosse Pointe MI 48236

KERNS, KIM ANN, company buyer; b. Elizabeth, N.J., July 13, 1960; d. James Leo Murray and Joan Gail (Loveless) Stone; m. Kelvin Max Kerns, June 6, 1987. BA in Gen Sci., Rutgers Coll., 1982. Expeditor Hahnes & Co., Lawrenceville, N.J., 1982-83; jr. buyer AM Cable Communications, Quakertown, Pa., 1983-84; purchasing mgr. Conolog Corp., Somerville, N.J., 1984-86; sr. buyer Liquid Metronics, inc., Acton, Mass., 1986—; treas. Employees Assn. Liquid Metronics Inc., 1988-89. Mem. Nat. Assn. Purchasing Mgmt. (cert.), Am. Prodn. and Inventory Control Soc. Home: 172 Dale Ave Leominster MA 01453 Office: Liquid Metronics Inc 19 Craig Rd Acton MA 01720

KERPER, MEIKE, family violence, sex abuse and addictions educator, consultant; b. Powell, Wyo., Aug. 13, 1929; d. Wesley George and Hazel (Bowman) K.; m. R.R. Milodragovich, Dec. 25, 1963 (div. 1973); children: Dan, John, Teren, Tina, Stana. B.S., U. Mont., 1973; M.S., U. Ariz., 1975; postgrad. Ariz. State U., 1976-78, Columbia Pacific U. Cert. domestic violence counselor, alcoholism and drug abuse counselor, mental health profl. and investigator. Family therapist Cottonwood Hill, Arvada, Colo., 1981; family program developer Turquoise Lodge, Albuquerque, 1982; co-developer abusers program Albuquerque Shelter Domestic Violence, 1984; family therapist Citizens Council Alcoholism and Drug Abuse, Albuquerque, 1984-86; pvt. practice cons. and trainer family violence and treatment, Albuquerque, 1987—; developer sex offender program Union County, Oreg. Co-author: Court Diversion Program, 1985; author Family Treatment, 1982. Lobbyist CCOPE, Santa Fe, 1983-86; bd. dirs. Union County Task Force on Domestic Violence. Recipient commendation Albuquerque Shelter Domestic Violence, 1984. Mem. Soc. for the Sci. Study of Sex, Nat. Assn. Alcoholism Counselors, N.Mex. Assn. Alcoholism Counselors, Delta Delta Delta. Republican. Episcopalian. Club: PEO. Avocations: Art history; reading; Indian culture; swimming; public speaking. Home: 61002 Love Rd Cove OR 97824

KERR, BONNIE LYNN, academic administrator, Spanish educator; b. Youngstown, Ohio, Oct. 6, 1943; d. Charles Edwin and Mary Gray (John) Jennings; m. John Scott Kerr, Aug. 14, 1965. Student, U. Valencia, Spain, 1964; BA, Lake Erie Coll., 1965; postgrad., Middlebury (Vt.) Coll., 1967, 70—. Tchr. Spanish Westover Sch., Middlebury, Conn., 1965-67, Taft Sch., Watertown, Conn., summer 1966; dean of girls Kent (Conn.) Sch., 1970-84, assoc. dir. admissions, tchr. Spanish, 1984—. Vol. Jr. League of Waterbury, Conn., 1965-70, Friends of Kent Libr., 1975, Hosp. Aux., Sharon, Conn., 1970-85. Mem. Coun. for Women in Ind. Schs. Republican. Episcopalian. Office: Kent Sch Corp Kent CT 06757

KERR, CHARLOTTE HERMAN, retired obstetrician-gynecologist; b. Champaign, Ill., May 25, 1920; d. Charles Everett and Gladys (Chaney) Herman; m. John E. Kerr; children: Patricia, Philip. BS, U. Ill., 1940, MD, 1948; MS, Iowa State U., 1944. Fellow Am. Coll. Surgeons, Am. Coll. Ob-Gyn.; diplomate Am. Bd. Ob-Gyn. Instr. Northwestern U. Sch. Medicine, Chgo., 1954-60; pres. Am. Med. Women's Assn., Chgo., 1964; treas. Am. Med. Women's Assn., N.Y.C., 1967, v.p., 1976, pres.-elect, 1977, pres., 1978; councillor Med. Women's Internat. Assn., various cities in U.S., 1978-; cons. in field. Co-editor: (book) American Medical Association Book of Woman

Care. Recipient Alumni Achievement award U. Ill. Dept. Home Econs., 1981, 88, Alumni Faculty Achievement award Dept. Ob-Gyn. Northwestern U., 1988. Mem. Am. Med. Assn., Pinellas County Med. Assn. (bd. govs. 1978-80), St. Petersburg Women's Club, St. Petersburg Garden Club.

KERR, DEBORAH MACPHAIL, cluster sales manager; b. Gettysburg, Pa., June 14, 1951; d. John Archie and Jeanne Alma (Spangler) MacPhail; m. Robert Stair Kerr, Jr., May 25, 1974. BS in Music Edn., Gettysburg Coll., 1973. Selection/tng. coordinator Commonwealth Nat. Bank, Harrisburg, Pa., 1978-79; safety tng. mgr. Ralston Purina Co., Mechanicsburg, Pa., 1979-81; data processing edn. coordinator Hamilton Bank, Lancaster, Pa., 1981-82, dir. mgmt. devel., 1982-83; asst. v.p., dir. manpower devel. Hamilton Bank, subs. CoreStates, Lancaster, 1982-85; asst. v.p., dir. corp. devel. CoreStates Fin. Corp., Phila., 1985-86; asst. v.p. personnel, tng. coordinator, Consumer Banking Group Phila. Nat. Bank, 1986—, v.p., personnel and tng. coordinator, Consumer Banking Group, Phila. Nat. Bank, 1987, v.p., cluster sales mgr., 1988—; mem. corp. adv. bd. Lebanon Valley Coll., Annville, Pa., 1985—; instr. Am. Inst. Banking, Lebanon, 1983-84; mem. tng. degree adv. com. Pa. State U., Middletown, Pa., 1983-84; mem. state edn. exec. adv. com. Pa. Am. Inst. Banking, Harrisburg, 1982; lectr. in field; bd. dirs. ARI; mem. finance com. Del. County Chpt. Girl Scouts, 1989—. Mem. Am. Soc. Tng. and Devel. (chpt. pres. 1981; Leigh Woehling Meml. award 1985, mem. exec. com. human resource devel. careers 1986-87). Avocations: reading, gardening, hiking, camping.

KERR, ELIZABETH MARGARET, educator, writer; b. Sault Ste Marie, Mich., Jan. 25, 1905; d. John Arthur and Katherine Dorothy (Hirth) K. BA, U. Minn., 1926, MA, 1927, PhD, 1941. Instr. English, Tabor Coll., Hillsboro, Kans., 1929-30, U. Minn., Mpls., 1930-37, 38-43, Coll. of St. Catherine, St. Paul, 1937-38; asst. prof. Rockford (Ill.) Coll., 1943-45; instr. Milw. State Coll., 1945-55; assoc. prof. U. Wis., Milw., 1956-59, prof., 1959-70, prof. emeritus English, 1970—. Author: Bibliography of the Sequence Novel, 1950, Yoknapatawpha: Faulkner's Little Postage Stamp of Native Soil, 1969, William Faulkner's Gothic Domain, 1979, William Faulkner's Yoknapatawpha: "A Kind of Keystone in the Universe", 1984. MLA research grantee, 1942, Summer Salary Support grantee U. Wis., Milw., 1959, 1961. Mem. MLA, Dickens Studies, Soc. for Study So. Lit. Democrat. Congregationalist. Home: Fairhaven 435 Starin Rd Whitewater WI 53190

KERR, JOAN ZIEGLER, clinical psychologist; b. Cin., Mar. 29, 1949; d. Paul Fout and Evelyn Marie (Arthur) Ziegler; m. James Morris Kerr, Dec. 27, 1969; children: Timothy Arthur, Joel Wesley. BA, Auburn U., 1973, MS, 1984, PhD, 1987. Lic. psychologist, Ala. Clin. psychologist The Bridgeway Hosp., North Little Rock, Ark., 1986-88, SouthPark Clinic, Huntsville, Ala., 1988—; cons. Ala. Gov.'s Grants "Looking Up" program, Huntsville, 1989-90, Huntsville Action Resource Team, 1989-90. Bd. dirs. Big Bros./Big Sisters of North Ala., Huntsville, 1989-91. Mem. Am. Psychol. Assn., Ala. Psychol. Assn., Ala. Head Injury Found. Presbyterian. Office: SouthPark Clinic 7501 Memorial Pkwy S Huntsville AL 35802

KERR, LISA BRUENING, sales and marketing executive; b. Washington, Apr. 13, 1962; d. David Crick and Lynn Brown (Petersen) Bruening; m. Patrick Thomas Kerr, Oct. 15, 1988. BS in Elem. Edn., The Pa. State U., 1984. Computer operator U.S. Steel, Pitts., 1985-86, Federated Investors, Pitts., 1986; adminstrv. asst. Devel. Dimensions Internat., Pitts., 1986-87; sales and marketing asst. Interstate Hotels Corp., Pitts., 1987—. Republican. Roman Catholic. Home: 912 Arch Ave Pittsburgh PA 15234 Office: Interstate Hotels Corp Pla X 680 Andersen Dr Pittsburgh PA 15220

KERR, MABEL DOROTHEA, psychiatrist, educator; b. Toronto, Ont., Can. (parents Am. citizens); d. George Houston and Mabel (Wark) Kerr; B.S., Ohio State U., 1944; M.D., Columbia, 1950. Intern dept. medicine St. Luke's Hosp., N.Y.C., 1950-51, resident, 1951-52; psychiat. resident Payne Whitney Clinic, N.Y. Hosp., 1952-57; practice medicine, specializing in psychiatry, N.Y.C., 1954—; assoc. attending psychiatrist N.Y. Hosp., 1979—; clin. asst. prof. psychiatry Cornell U. Med. Coll., 1968-79, clin. assoc. prof., 1979—; asst. med. examiner, officer chief med. examiner City of N.Y., 1957-66. Pres., Elmora Found. Fellow N.Y. Acad. Medicine; mem. AMA, Am. Psychiat. Assn., Women's Med. Soc. N.Y. State, Am. Med. Women's Assn. Address: 20 E 68th St New York NY 10021

KERR, NANCY HELEN, psychology educator; b. L.A., June 27, 1947; d. Edmund James and Sally (Byrd) K.; m. David Foulkes, Apr. 19, 1978. BA, Stanford U., 1969; PhD, Cornell U., 1974. Asst. prof. psychology U. Wyo., Laramie, 1974-78; vis. asst. prof. psychology Emory U., Atlanta, 1978-79, asst. prof., 1979-82; vis. asst. prof. psychology Mercer U., Macon, Ga., 1982-83; asst. prof., assoc. prof., now prof. psychology Oglethorpe U., Atlanta, 1983—. Contbr. articles to profl. jours. Recipient James McKeen Cattell award, 1990. Mem. Am. Psychol. Soc., Psychonomic Soc., Southeastern Psychol. Assn., European Sleep Rsch. Soc. Office: Oglethorpe U 4484 Peachtree Rd NE Atlanta GA 30319

KERR, SYLVIA JOANN, educator; b. Detroit, June 19, 1941; d. Frederic Dilmus and Maud (Dirst) Pfeffer; m. Norman Story Kerr, Aug. 6, 1933; children: David, Kathleen. BA, Carleton Coll., 1963; MS, U. Minn., 1966, PhD, 1968. Asst. prof. Augsburg Coll., Mpls., 1968-71; instr. Anoka Ramsey Community Coll., Coon Rapids, Minn., 1973-74; from asst. prof. to full prof. Hamline U., St. Paul, 1974—. Contbr. numerous articles to profl. jours. NIH fellow U. Minn., 1972, 74-75. Office: Hamline U Dept Biology 1536 Hewitt Saint Paul MN 55104

KERRICK, JILL MAUREEN, pharmacist; b. Colville, Wash., Feb. 19, 1964; d. John Charles and Judy Kay (McLaughlin) K. B of Pharmacy, Wash. State U., 1987; postgrad., U. Utah, 1990—. Registered pharmacist. Pharmacy extern Meml. Hosp., Pullman, Wash., 1985; pharmacy intern Hart and Dilatush Pharmacy, Spokane, Wash., 1984-86; pharmacy extern Valley Gen. Hosp., Spokane, Wash., 1987, Group Health Coop., Spokane, 1987; staff pharmacist Fred Meyer Pharmacy, Renton, Wash., 1987—. Vol. leader Young Life, Bellevue, Wash., 1987—. Scholarship Wilburn N. Joyner Fund, Wash. State U., 1985, Spokane Women's Aux. for Wash. Pharm. Assn., 1986. Mem. Am. Pharm. Assn. (sr. class rep. 1986), Kappa Alpha Theta, Lambda Kappa Sigma, Rho Chi. Republican. Home: 120 S 300 E Apt 206 Salt Lake City UT 84111 Office: VAMC 500 Foothill Blvd Salt Lake City UT 84148

KERSCHNER, JOAN GENTRY, state librarian; b. Spencer County, Ind., Sept. 20, 1945; d. Harold Joseph and Alice Ellen (Jones) Gentry; 1 child, Kelly Kacese. BA, Ky. Wesleyan Coll., 1966; MLS, Ind. U., 1972. Tchr. speech and drama Glasgow (Mont.) High Sch., 1966-67; libr. Tom Williams Elem. Sch., Las Vegas, Nev., 1967-68, F. J. Reitz High Sch., Evansville, Ind., 1968-70; librarian Greene County (Ind.) Consol. Sch. Dist., 1970-72; documents libr. Nev. State Libr., Carson City, 1972-80, dir. pub. and tech. svcs., 1980-82, asst. state libr., 1982-86, dir. state libr. and archives, 1986—. Mem. Depository Library Council to Pub. Printer, 1976-79. Recipient Young Writers award Owensboro Messenger/Inquirer, 1967, Charles McCarthy award Coun. State Govts., 1987. Mem. ALA (various offices in govt. documents roundtable), Nev. Library Assn. (pres. 1979-80, spl. citation 1968, 78), Mountain Plain Library Assn., Calif. Library Assn., Western Council State Library Agys., Chief Officers State Library Agys., Spl. Libraries Assn. Office: Nev State Libr & Archives 401 N Carson St Carson City NV 89710

KERSHAW, CAROL JEAN, psychologist; b. New Orleans, Apr. 11, 1947; d. Neal Howard and Gloria Jackson (Moss) Perkins; m. John William Wade, Aug. 20, 1983; stepchildren: Chris Wade, Stephen Wade, Tiffany Wade. BS in Secondary Edn., U. Tex., 1969; MS in Speech Communication, North Tex. State U., 1971, MEd in Counseling, 1976; EdD in Counseling, East Tex. State U., 1979. Lic. psychologist, Tex. Assoc. prof. DeVry Inst., Dallas, 1971-73; instr., counseling psychologist East Tex. State U., Commerce, 1976-78; counselor, instr. Tarrant County Jr. Coll., Hurst, Tex., 1971-74; dir. spl. svcs. Goodwill Industries, Dallas, 1974-76; marriage and family therapist, cons. mental health clinic Tex. Dept. Mental Health and Retardation, Greenville, 1977-78; asst. prof., dir. grad. program in marriage & family therapy Tex. Woman's U., Denton, 1980-83; coord. child devel. dept. Tex. Woman's U., Houston, 1983-88; pvt. practice Inst. for Family Psychology, Houston, 1986—; co-dir. Milton H. Erickson Inst. Houston, 1986—; bd. dirs. Milton H. Erickson Inst. Tex., Houston, 1986—; presenter in field. Author: Therapeutic Metaphor in the Treatment of Childhood Asthma: A Systemic Approach, Ericksonian Monographs, Vol. 2, 1986; co-author: Psychotherapeutic Techniques in School Psychology, 1984, Learning to Think for and Organ, Bridges of the Bodymind, 1980. Sec. Tex. Assn. for Marriage and Family Therapy, 1978-80. Recipient Meritorious Svc. award Tex. Assn. for Marriage & Family Therapy, 1980. Mem. Am. Psychol. Assn, Am. Assn. for Marriage and Family Therapy (clin., approved supr.), Soc. for Exptl. & Clin. Hypnosis, Am. Soc. for Clin. Hypnosis (assoc.), Internat. Soc. for Clin. & Exptl. Hypnosis, Psi Chi. Democrat. Methodist. Office: Inst for Family Psychology 2012 Bissonet Houston TX 77005

KERSTETTER-HULL, JOANNE RITA, financial counseling executive; b. Washington, Oct. 5, 1952; d. Dale David and Patricia Claire (Chisholm) Kerstetter; m. Albert J. Hull, Jr., Jan. 1, 1983; children: Jessica Lynn, Ashley, Jason. BA, U. Md., 1974, MS, 1979. Exec. dir. Consumter Credit Counseling Svc. Greater Washington, Inc., Washington, 1976—; commr. State of Md., Dept. Licensing & Regulation, Balt., 1978-85; Dir. Nat. Found. Consumer Credit, Silver Spring, Md., 1985—, treas., 1988—; dir. Internat. Credit Assn. Greater Washington, Silver Spring, 1989—. Mem. NAFE, Consumer Edn. & Info. Assn. Va., Assn. Fin. Counseling & Planning Edn., Greater Washington Soc. Assn. Execs.

KESCHL, CONSTANCE FRANCES, home economics educator; b. Elizabeth, N.J., Mar. 31, 1949; d. Michael Peter and Helen Ann (Pazahanich) Lokuta; m. Dennis Lee Keschl, Sept. 5, 1970; children: Dennis Kurt, Thomas Michael. BS in Home Econs., Mansfield State Coll., 1971. Cert. tchr., N.J., Maine. Instr., curriculum developer child care Perth Amboy (N.J.) Adult Sch., 1975-76, educator family life/consumer edn., coord. home econs. dept., 1976, supr. sch. cafeteria, 1976, project dir., 1976-78; home econs. educator Livermore Falls (Maine) High Sch., 1979-87; home econs. educator, dept. chairperson Gardiner (Maine) Area High Sch., 1987—; substitute tchr. Manville (N.J.) Pub. Schs., Middlesex (N.J.) Pub. Schs., Union County Tech. Inst. and Vocat. Ctr., Scotch Plains, N.J., 1978-79; cooperating tchr. U. Maine, Farmington, 1980—; home econs. adv. coun. U. Maine, Farmington. Grantee Carl D. Perkins, 1987. Mem. NEA, Maine Tchrs. Assn., Maine Home Econs. Assn. Roman Catholic. Home: 316 Wings Mills Rd Belgrade ME 04917 Office: Gardiner Area High Sch Cedar St Gardiner ME 04345

KESEGI, PAMELA LYNNE, mental health treatment program coordinator; b. Dayton, Ohio, July 24, 1951; d. Calvin Sterling and Frances Jeannette Tawney; m. William Robert Kesegi, Sept.14, 1974; children: Nathan and Chad. BS, Miami U., Oxford, Ohio, 1973; MS, U. Ill., Urbana, 1975. Coord. walk-a-thon United Cerebral Palsy, Champaign, Ill., 1975—; claims & customer service rep. Blue Cross Wash. & Alaska, Seattle, 1976-77; mental health counselor Lake County Mental Health Dept., Waukegan, Ill., 1978-79; tchr. aide Clearmont Sch., Elk Grove, Ill., 1980-81; summer sch. health tchr. Hoffman Estates High Sch., Hoffman Estates, Ill., 1981--; county literacy coord. Cherokee County Literacy Assn., Gaffney, S.C., 1983-86; esl tutor for Vietnamese students Cherokee County Sch. Dist. #1, Gaffney, 1986--; interim literacy dir. Literacy Vol., Corning, N.Y., 1986--; sexual abuse community educator Family Services of Chemung County, Inc., Elmira, N.Y., 1986-87; continuing treatment program coordinator Family Svcs. of Chemung County, Inc., Elmira, N.Y., 1987-90; exec. dir. Amity House/Glynn Community House Crisis Ctr., Inc., Brunswick, Ga., 1990--; vol. literacy tutor Cherokee County Literacy Assn. Gaffney S. C.,1982-86. Advisory Council Cherokee 70001 (youth employment) Gaffney, 1984-86. Mem. NAFE, NOW, AAUW, Laubach Literacy Action. Democrat. Roman Catholic. Office: Amity House/Glynn Community Crisis Ctr Inc PO Box 278 Brunswick GA 31520

KESHAVARZI, SUSAN ROSS, management consultant; b. Los Angeles, Apr. 16, 1947; d. David Henry and Gretchen (Salsman) Ross; m. Mohammad Reza, Dec. 13, 1978, (div. Oct. 1984). BS, U. San Francisco, 1989. Sec. Hughes Aircraft Co., Los Angeles, 1969-79; project adminstr. Hughes Aircraft Co., Carson, Calif., 1979-80; capital resources adminstr. Hughes Aircraft Co., Long Beach, Calif., 1980-86, bus. mgr., 1986—; instr. John Robert Powers, Redondo Beach, 1972-75; interior designer MDR Constrn. Co., Marina Delrey, Calif., 1975-78. Participant Costa Mesa Action Group, 1981--. Mem. Hughes Mgmt. Club. Republican. Moslem.

KESLING, ANNETTE ELIZABETH, interior designer; b. Indpls., Nov. 10, 1931; d. Orel Vance and Letitia Lorretto (Kelly) Sappenfield; m. Paul Frank Bellis, Aug. 25, 1956 (div. 1974); children: Daryl, Vance K., Douglas R., Paula S., Bellis; m. Devon Edmond Kesling, Apr. 28, 1984; children: Diane, David, Robert. Grad., Marion Bus. Coll., Ind., 1949-50; student, Ind. U. Extension, South Bend, 1951-52, Columbus Coll. Arts & Design, 1972-73. Sec. Edward's Iron Works, South Bend, Ind., 1950-54, St. Joseph County Med. Soc., South Bend, 1954-56, St. Edward's Episcopal Ch., Columbus, Ohio, 1962-64; office mgr. Exec. Caterers, Columbus, 1965-72; design cons. Dean & Barry Paint Co., Columbus, 1973-78; owner Annette's Design Studio, Columbus, 1978—; design cons. Heinzerling Mem. M.R. Facilities Columbus, Ohio 1978-79, Phase I and II Columbus Ohio 1981-82, Americare Corp. - Skilled Care Columbus Ohio 1978-83, design cons. Ohio Pres. Homes - Skilled Care Columbus Ohio 1979-82. Mem. Ctr. Sci. Industry Columbus, Ohio 1988, Opera Columbus 1988. Mem. ASID, Columbus Apartment Assn. (bd. dirs. 1976-77). Republican. Episcopalian. Office: Annette's Design Studio 1585 Bethel Rd Columbus OH 43220

KESSINGER, MARGARET ANNE, internal medicine educator; b. Beckley, W.Va., June 4, 1941; d. Clisby Theodore and Margaret Anne (Ellison) K.; m. Loyd Ernst Wegner, Nov. 27, 1971. MA, W.Va. U., 1963, MD, 1967. Diplomate Am. Bd. Internal Medicine and Med. Oncology. Internal medicine house officer U. Nebr. Med. Ctr., Omaha, 1967-70, fellow med. oncology, 1970-72, asst. prof. internal medicine, 1972-77, assoc. prof., 1977-90, prof., 1990—, assoc. chief oncology/hematology sect., 1988—. Contbr. articles to profl. publs. Fellow ACP; mem. Am. Assn. Cancer Edn. (exec. bd. 1987-90), Am. Soc. Clin. Oncology, Am. Assn. Cancer Rsch., Internat. Soc. Exptl. Hematology, Am. Soc. Hematology, Sigma Xi. Republican. Methodist. Office: U Nebr Med Ctr 400 S 42d St Omaha NE 68198

KESSLER, DORIS HENRIETTA, army officer; b. New Kensington, Pa., Sept. 19, 1935; d. Francis Arthur and Dora Mary (Michael) Molinari; BS, Pa. State U., 1957; postgrad., U. Pitts., 1958-68, Am. U., 1972-73; m. Otto F. Kessler, June 1958 (div.). Tchr., Duquesne (Pa.) High Sch., 1958-68; commd. 1st lt. U.S. Army, 1968, advanced through grades to lt. col. Adj. Gen.'s Corps, 1984; instr. Ft. McClellan, Ala., 1968-69; recruiting officer, N.Y.C., 1970-72; chief tng. mgmt. div. Ft. Belvoir, Va., 1972-73; co. comdr., Ft. Jackson, S.C., 1973-75; bn. exec. officer, Ft. Jackson, 1975; ADP officer Computer Systems Command, Ft. Belvoir, 1975-79; project officer Women in the Army Study, Dept. Army, 1977-78; chief staff support sect., software, command, control and communications, Command in Chief Pacific Staff, Camp Smith, Hawaii, 1980-83, chief adminstrv. team U.S. Army Readiness Group, Ft. Sheridan, Ill., 1983-84; automation mgmt. officer 4th Army Planning Group, Ft. Sheridan, 1983-84; dir. adminstrv. and logistical support U.S. Army Res. Components Personnel and Adminstrv. Ctr., St. Louis, 1984-86, ADP plans officer, project mgr. info. systems ISC, 1986-87, info. mgmt. plans officer command and control support activity, Heidelberg, Fed. Republic Germany, 1987—. Committeewoman, Allgheny County, Pitts., 1963-67. Mem. Nat. Assn. Female Execs., Assn. U.S. Army, Internat. Platform Assn., Met. Opera Guild, Met. Mus. Art, Armed Forces Electronic and Communication Assn., Lafayette Sq. Restoration Com. Club: Mil. Dist. Washington Officers, Media, Carnegie. Office: Dept Army Command and Control Support Activity ATTN: ASE-I-CC-PR APO New York NY 09403-0136

KESSLER, JEAN S., insurance company executive; b. New Brunswick, N.J., Oct. 20, 1954; d. John S. and Henrietta Marguerite (Pasquier de Lumeau) Kessler; m. Michael P. Gutzan, Sept. 16, 1984; AS in Mgmt. with highest honors, Middlesex County Coll., 1990; postgrad. Edison State Coll., 1990—. Cert. profl. ins. woman. Sec. to dir. Carter-Wallace, Inc., Cranbury, N.J., 1977-78, exec. sec. to corp. v.p., 1978-80; exec. sec. to v.p. Continental Ins. Co., Cranbury, N.J., 1981, exec. sec. to sr. v.p., 1981-84, exec. sec. to exec. v.p., 1984-89; career trainee Am. Reliance Ins. Co., 1989—. Recipient Sec. of Yr. award Profl. Secs. Internat., 1981-82. Cert. profl. sec. Mem. NAFE, Profl. Secs. Internat. (chmn. civic com. New Brunswick chpt. 1980-81, sec. of yr. com. 1981-82; mem. nominating com. 1981, audit com. 1982, ways and means com. 1981-82), Nat. Assn. Ins. Women (nominating com. 1990), Mensa, Nu Tau Sigma. Office: 1000 Lenox Dr PO Box 6426 Lawrenceville NJ 08648

KESSLER, LEONA HANOVER, interior designer; b. Phila., Sept. 15, 1925; d. Herman and Ida (Gleaner) Hanover; B.S. in Textile Engring. (Sara Tyler Wister scholar), Phila. Coll. Textiles and Sci., 1948; m. Sydney Kessler, Aug. 28, 1948; children—Andrew Louis, Todd Hanover. Pvt. practice interior design and cons. Lee Kessler Interiors, Phila., 1957—; textile designer, stylist, color cons.; mem. faculty Moore Coll. Art, 1970-72, Art Inst. Phila., 1973-78, Phila. Coll. Textiles and Sci., 1972-81; juror textile design and interior design; works exhibited designer showcases, local house tours, faculty shows. Named Alumnus of Month, Textile Engr., 1971. Mem. Am. Soc. Interior Designers (dir. Pa. East chpt. 1967-78, chpt. recognition awards 1974, 80). Author: That Which Was Once a Warp, 1971; contbr. articles and photographs to mags. and newspapers. Address: 3421 Warden Dr Philadelphia PA 19129

KESSLER, MARGARET MARIE, artist, writer; b. Auburn, Ind., Aug. 15, 1944; d. Kenneth Albert and Edna Marie (Cardinal) Jennings; m. Jere Wayne Kessler, June 10, 1962; children: Wade John, Paul David. Freelance artist, writer Richardson, Tex.; tchr. Cloudcroft (N.Mex.) Summer Workshops, Dillman's Creative Art Workshops, Lac Du Flambeau, Wis., Hindes Studio, Charlotte, Tex., art club demonstrations and workshops nationwide. Author, artist: Painting Better Landscapes, 1987 (3d printing); author, artist articles in The Artist's Mag. (oil painting featured on cover, Feb., 1985), North Light Mag., and Southwest Art Mag. Recipient Best Traditional Painting award Hoosier Salon, Indpls., 1983, Best Shoow awards Artists and Craftsmen Associated, Dallas, 1982, 84, 85, 87, Outstanding Tchr. award 1988, Best of Show award Regional Painting and Sculpture Show, Richardson, 1982, 83, 85, Hon. Mention Am. Artist's Profl. League, Salmagundi Club, N.Y.C., 1984, Gold medal Grumbacher Art awards, 1989, Silver, 1982, Bronze, 1983, Top 100 Arts for the Parks award, Jackson, Wyo., 1989. Mem. Artists and Craftsmen Associated (signature mem. 1983, pres. 1985-86). Home and Studio: 330 Ridgehaven Place Richardson TX 75080

KESSLER, MAXINE, restauranteur; b. N.Y.C., Nov. 14, 1935; d. Julius and Mildred (Elfenbien-Rosenblum) K. Grad. high sch., 1953. Ballet dancer Met. Opera House, N.Y.C., 1948-54; profl. dancer Moulin Rouge, Paris, 1956, Casino Monte Carlo (Monaco), Casino Knokke (Belgium) and Casino Weisbaden (Germany), 1957, 36 Chandelles, Paris, 1957, Casino of Travemunda (Germany), Casino of Baden Baden(Germany), Casino of Campioni, Lido Casino (Italy) and Stork Club of London, 1958, Bataclan of Geneva, 1959, Salone Margharita Theatre, Rome, 1960; actress Murder at the Folies Bergere, Paris, 1963, The Key, Copenhagen, 1964; co-owner Sunset Strip Restaurant, N.Y.C., 1986-88, Bonnies by the Bay Restaurant, New Suffolk, N.Y., 1983—; free lance translator, France, N.Y., 1970—. Office: Bonnies by the Bay 725 First St New Suffolk NY 11956

KESSLER, MINUETTA SHUMIATCHER, composer, pianist; b. Gomel, USSR, Sept. 15, 1914; came to U.S., 1930; d. Abraham Isaac Q.C. and Luba (Lubinskaya) Shumiatcher; m. Myer M. Kessler, Sept. 14, 1952; children: Ronald, Jean Kessler Brenner. Grad., Juilliard Sch. Music, 1934, postgrad. diploma, 1936. Founder, owner, pres. Mus. Resources, Belmont, Mass.; music editor The PEN Woman, Washington, 1982-86 (Disting. Service citation 1986); dir., founder Concerts in the Home, 1965-79. Commd. Clavier mag., 1989. Recipient 1st Master Cert. in Piano and Composition, Mass., Can. ASCAP awards, 1945, 46, Brookline Libr. Composition award, 1972, Am. Chamber Music prize, 1984, thirteen composition awards Nat. League Am. PEN Women, 1982, 84, 85, 86, Keys to City of Calgary, Ala., Can., 1951, 1st prize for left hand piano composition Nat. League PEN Women, 1988; Alberta Concerto placed in Time Capsule, Calgary Arts Ctr., 1985. Licentiate Associated Bd. of Royal Coll. and Royal Acad. of Music, London; mem. New Eng. Pianoforte Tchrs. Assn. (pres. 1965-67), Mass. Music Tchrs. Assn. (pres. 1982-83), Music Tchrs. Nat. Assn. (Master cert. 1984, pres. Boston chpt. 1984-86), New Eng. Jewish Music Forum (founder 1963, bd. dirs., v.p.), Friends of Young Musicians (founder 1966), Am. Women Composers (co-pres. Mass. chpt. 1987), Boston Juilliard Alumni Assn. (organizer, founder, pres.). Home and Office: Mus Resources 30 Hurley St Belmont MA 02178

KESSLER-HODGSON, LEE GWENDOLYN, actress; b. Wellsville, N.Y., Jan. 16, 1947; d. James Hewitt and Reba Gwendolyn (Adsit) Kessler; m. Bruce Gridley, June 22, 1969 (div. Dec. 1979); m. Jeffrey Craig Hodgson, Oct. 31, 1987. BA, Grove City Coll., 1968; MA, U. Wis., 1969. Prof. Sangamon State U., Springfield, Ill., 1969-70; personnel exec. Bullock's, Los Angeles, 1971-74; owner Brunnen Enterprises, Los Angeles, 1982—. Author: A Child of Arthur, 1981; producer, writer play including Anais Nin: The Paris Years, 1986; actress appearing in TV movies, mini-series including Roots, 1978, Backstairs at The White House, 1979, Blind Ambition, 1980, Hill Street Blues, 1984-87, Murder By Reason of Insanity, 1985, Hoover, 1986, Creator, 1987, Our House, 1988, Favorite Son, 1988, Lou Grant 1983, 84, Barney Miller, 1979, L.A. Law, 1989, (screenplay) Settlers Way, 1988; recurring role TV series Matlock, L.A. Law, numerous others. Knapp Prize fellow U. Wis., 1969. Mem. Screen Actors Guild, Actors Equity Assn., AFTRA. Republican. Mem. Ch. Scientology. Home: 1527 Adele Pl Thousand Oaks CA 91366

KESTIN, JOAN B., teacher; b. Trenton, N.J., June 23, 1944; d. Samuel and Ethel (Rathauser) Bard; m. Howard H. Kestin, Aug. 22, 1970; children: Bette, Anita. BS in Music in Eng., Boston U., 1966; MEd., U. Ariz., 1970. Cert. Tchr., N.J. Eng. tchr. Trenton high sch., N.J., 1966-69, Hillel Acad., Passaic, N.J., 1984-87; adjunct tchr. Bloomfield Cottage, N.J., 1986-87; Eng. tchr. Passaic (N.J.) High Sch. V.P. PTO-Kennedy Elem. Sch., Wayne 1978; Editor B'nai B'rith, Wayne 1983-85. Recipient Outstanding First Year Tchr. award Trenton Bd. Educators 1967. Mem. Sister of Wayne Conservative Cong. Wayne (Pres. 1980-81). Democrat. Home: 88 Anderson Dr Wayne NJ 07470

KESTNER, ARLENE KATHERINE, psychologist, researcher, educator; b. Chgo., Oct. 9, 1939; d. Henry and Beatrice Florence (Montgomery) Schweigerdt; m. Neil Richard Kestner, June 10, 1967; 1 child, Lars Neil. AA, Cottey Coll., 1959; BS, U. Ill., 1961; MS, Bradley U., 1962; PhD, La. State U., Baton Rouge, 1969. Rsch. assoc. Galesburg (Ill.) St. Rsch. Hosp., 1961-64, Delta Primate Rsch. Ctr., Covington, La., 1965; prof. psychology dept. So. U. A&M Coll., Baton Rouge, 1967—; Editor: Conference Proceedings, 1988, 1989, 1990, Culinary Herb Cookbook, 1988. Vol. Vols. in Pub. Schs., Baton Rouge, 1986-89. Mem. Am. Psychol. Assn., Southeastern Psychol. Assn., Internat. Herb Growers and Marketers Assn. (bd. dirs. 1988—), Zonta Internat. (bd. dirs. Baton Rouge chpt. 1988-89). Office: Southern Univ A&M Coll Dept Psychology Baton Rouge LA 70813

KESTON, JOAN BALBOUL, public relations executive; b. N.Y.C., Feb. 6, 1937; d. Sol and Adele (Gredinger) Balboul; (div. Mar. 1986); children: Lisa, Vicky, Sol. BA, N.Y.U., 1958; postgrad., Rutgers U., 1959; MPA, U. So. Calif., 1981; 1959; postgrad., U. So. Calif., 1986. Br. mgr. Social Security Administrn., Rockville, Md., 1978-86; exec. dir. Pub. Employees Roundtable, Washington, 1986—. Editor: (book) Hagadah, 1972, (newsletter) Unsung Heroes, 1986; co-author: How to Celebrate Public Service Recognition Week (booklet), 1986, 87, 88, 89, 90. Mem. Federally Employed Women, Internat. Personnel Mgrs. Assn., Am. Fgn. Svc. Assn., Profl. Mgrs. Assn., Drs. Pub. Adminstrn. Assn. of U. So. Calif. (treas.), Am. Soc. Pub. Adminstrs. Am., Consortium of Pub. Adminstrn., Fedn. Gov. Info. Processing Couns., World Affairs Coun. Jewish. Home: 330 Lynn Manor Dr Rockville MD 20850

KETCHAM, JULIA ANN, speech pathologist; b. Richmond, Va., Mar. 14, 1943; d. Charles C. and Helen Irene (Neidhardt) Fraze; m. Robert Louis Ketcham, Aug. 22, 1965 (div. 1977); children: Michael Louis, Cynthia Ann. BA, Ind. U., 1965, MAT, 1966. Lic. speech pathologist, Ind. Speech pathologist Met. Sch. Dist. Perry Twp., Indpls., 1965-68, Met. Sch. Dist.

Wayne Twp., Indpls., 1968-69; pvt. practice speech pathology Fort Wayne, Ind., 1972-73; cons. speech pathologist Profl. Diagnostic & Evaluation Svcs., Fort Wayne, 1980-83; speech pathologist Ft. Wayne State Devel. Ctr., 1974-87, dir. speech/lang./hearing dept., 1987—; assoc. faculty dept. audiology and speech pathology Ind. U./Purdue U., Ft. Wayne, 1988—. Mem. Council for Exceptional Children (pres. 1976-77), Ind. Speech and Hearing Assn., Am. Speech, Lang., Hearing Assn., U.S. Soc. Augmentative Alternative Communication, Alpha Gamma Delta, Cousteau Soc. Democrat. Unitarian Universalist. Home: 8442 Cerco St Fort Wayne IN 46815 Office: Fort Wayne State Devel Ctr 4900 Saint Jo Rd Fort Wayne IN 46835

KETLEY, JEANNE NELSON, health science adminstrator; b. N.Y.C., Apr. 18, 1938; 1 child, Alex D. BS, Queens Coll., 1962; MS, Cornell U., 1967; PhD, Johns Hopkins Med. Sch., 1973. Muscular Dystrophy Assn. fellow NIH, Bethesda, Md., 1973-74; staff fellow NIH, Bethesda, 1974-77; chemist FDA, WAshington, 1977-79; exec. sec. in phys. biochemistry Div. Rsch. Grants, NIH, Bethesda, 1979-85, chief spl. rev. sect., 1985-89, chief physiol. scis. rev. sect., 1989—. Contbr. articles to profl. jours. Mem. AAAS, NOW, Am. Chem. Soc., Biophys. Soc., Protein Soc., N.Y. Acad. Scis. Office: NIH Div Rsch Grants Westwood Bldg 203 A Bethesda MD 20892

KETTENHOFEN, GRETCHEN MARIA, director of development; b. Canaan, Conn., Nov. 4, 1935; d. Leo J. and Alice (Stem) K.; m. Gunther Paul Mittendorf, Apr. 19, 1980. BA cum laude, Barnard Coll., 1957. Ops. mgr. Oxtoby-Smith Inc., N.Y.C., 1957-65; survey field dir. Audits and Surveys, N.Y.C., 1966-70; exec. v.p. Slurzberg Rsch., N.Y.C., 1970-79; pres. GK Assocs., 1980-84; adminstrv. asst. Avrett, Free, Ginsberg, N.Y.C., 1985-88; dir. devel. Coun. on Econ. Priorities, N.Y.C., 1989—. Contbr. articles to profl. jours. Vestry mem., chair stewardship com., editor newsletter Episc. Ch. of Holy Apostles; class fund chair Barnard Coll. Mem. NAFE, Women's City Club of N.Y. Home: 153 Dupont St Brooklyn NY 11222

KETTLE, SALLY ANNE, community relations executive; b. Omaha, Feb. 2, 1938; d. Harry Eugene and Elaine Josephine (Winston) Smiley; m. William Frederick Kettle, July 20, 1968 (div. 1973); children: Christopher, Winston. BEd, U. Nebr., 1960, postgrad. Cert. tchr., S.C., Nebr. Tchr. Omaha Pub. Schs., Omaha, 1966-72; owner, mgr. The Rick Rack, Ltd., Lakewood, Colo., 1974-75; coord. merchandising communications 3M, St. Paul, 1978-80, sr. coord. internat. corp. communications, 1981-84; corp. dir. communications Intran Corp., St. Paul, 1984; pres. Sally Kettle & Co., Bloomington, Minn., 1985—; tchr. TV, U. Omaha, 1968-69; community faculty Met. State U., Mpls., 1983—; adj. faculty mem. Sch. Journalism and Mass Communications U. Minn.; speaker numerous orgns. TV hostess City of Bloomington Cable TV, 1984-86. Co-founder Women's Resource Ctr., bd. dirs., mem. adv. bd., 1978-88; chair 13th Precinct, Bloomington, 1978-83; bd. dirs. 41st Sen. Dist., Bloomington, 1982-83; cable TV commr. Bloomington City Coun., 1984-85; pub. rels. com. U.S. Olympic Festival, 1989-90; bd. dirs. Minn. Prayer Breakfast Bd., 1984—; mem. Better Bus. Bur.; founder Ad Rev. Coun.; mem. state cen. com. and platform commn. DFL, 1988-90; bd. dirs. Fellowship Christian Athletes, 1988-89. Named one of Outstanding Young Women of Am., 1965. Mem. Am. Advt. Fedn. (conf. com. 1985-87, pub. svc. com. 1986—), Advt. Fedn. Minn. (bd. dirs. 1982-86), Women's Econ. Roundtable, Internat. Platform Assn., Nat. Grad. Women's Honor Soc., Minn. Press Club (co-chair newsmaker com., bd. dirs. 1989—), Phi Delta Gamma, Kappa Alpha Theta. Mem. Assemblies of God Ch. Home: 10321 Morris Rd Bloomington MN 55437

KETTLEWOOD, BEA CARD, artist, retired educator; b. Pompton Plains, N.J., June 7, 1929; d. James Whitfield and Florence B. (Payne) Card; m. James Kettlewood, June 28, 1952. BS, Newark State Coll., 1951; MA, NYU, 1955, EdD in Painting, 1972. Cert. tchr., N.J. Tchr. art New Milford (N.J.) Jr.-Sr. High Sch., 1951-84, chmn. art dept., 1960-84, chmn. art, home econs. and lang. depts., 1981-84; part-time instr. in art extension div. William Paterson Coll., Wayne, N.J., 1963-67; freelance painter, 1959—; free lance illustrator; lectr. in field. Designed stained glass windows for Chapel at Chilton Meml. Hosp. From elder to sr. elder First Reformed Ch., Pompton Plains, N.J., 1987-90. Mem. Woman's Caucus for Art, AAUW (sec. N.J. interbr.), Ringwood Manor Art Assn., Delta Kappa Gamma (chpt. pres. 1978-80). Home: 45 Wilrue Pkwy Pompton Plains NJ 07444

KETZ, LOUISE BILEBOF, literary agent, book producer; b. N.Y.C., Jan. 20, 1945; d. Alexander and Helen Joan (Korz) Bilebof; m. Gerard E. Ketz, Sept. 8, 1973 (div. Apr. 1987). BA, Hunter Coll., 1966. Prodn. editor Macmillan Pub. Co., N.Y.C., 1966-70; mng. editor, sr. editor Charles Scribner's Sons, N.Y.C., 1970-83; pres. Ketz Agy., N.Y.C., 1983—; v.p. Prentice Hall Press, N.Y.C., 1985; v.p., pub. J.K. Lasser Tax Guides, 1985. Exec. editor Ency. of Am. Mil., 1990—. Tchr. English, Sch. Vols. N.Y., N.Y.C., 1987; editor 19th Precinct Community Coun., N.Y.C., 1989. Mem. Editorial Freelancers Assn., Am. Hist. Assn., U.S. Commn. for Mil. History. Roman Catholic. Office: 1485 1st Ave New York NY 10021

KEUCHEN, TOISTER ELAINE, employment agency executive; b. Bklyn., Nov. 5, 1930; d. Murray Toister and Elizabeth Stein; m. Herbert Keuchen; 1 child, Susannah. Student, U. Fla., 1952. Occupational therapist Stony Lodge Hosp., Ossining, N.Y., 1966-75; pres. Crickett Employment Agy. and Pers. Svc., Ossining.

KEULEGAN, EMMA PAULINE, special education educator; b. Washington, Jan. 21, 1930; d. Garbis H. and Nellie Virginia (Moore) K. BA, Dumbarton Coll. of Holy Cross, 1954. Cert. tchr. elem. and spl. edn. Tchr. St. Dominic's Elem. Sch., Washington, 1954-56, Sacred Heart Acad., Washington, 1956-59, Our Lady of Victory, Washington, 1959-63, St. Francis Acad., Vicksburg, Miss., 1963-78, Culkin Acad., Vicksburg, 1978—. Treas. PTA, Vicksburg, 1980. Mem. Internat. Reading Assn. (pres. Warren County chpt.), Colonial Dames 17th Century (state v.p. 1987-89, state pres. 1989), Daus. Am. Colonists (chaplain 1985-89, 2d v.p. 1989), DAR (chpt. regent 1967-69). Republican. Roman Catholic. Home: 215 Buena Vista Dr Vicksburg MS 39180 Office: Culkin Elem Sch Rt 11 Box 63 Vicksburg MS 39180

KEUPPER, LILLIAN MARIE, banker; b. Gillespie, Ill., Feb. 25, 1920; d. Hugo William and Ann Marie (Carroll) K. Student, Webster Coll., St. Louis, 1940-41. Cashier Peoples State Bank Gillespie (Ill.), 1970—, sr. v.p., 1982-86, exec. v.p., 1986—. Treas. Sch. Dist. 7, Gillespie, 1980—; sec. Gillespie Pub. Libr., 1982—; sec.-treas. Holy Cross Cemetery Assn., Gillespie, 1985—. Democrat. Roman Catholic. Home: 807 S Macoupin St Gillespie IL 62033 Office: Peoples State Bank 121 S Macoupin St Gillespie IL 62033

KEWLEY, SHARON LYNN, systems analyst; b. Geneseo, Ill., Sept. 23, 1958; d. James Leslie and Geraldine (Myers) K. BBA with honors, U. Miami (Fla.), 1988. Gen. agent Varvaris & Assocs., Cedar Rapids, Iowa, 1981-84; programmer, analyst U. Miami, Coral Gables, Fla., 1984-88; systems analyst Metro Dade County, Miami, 1988—. Mem. NAFE, Kendall Jaycees, Nat. Gold Key Honor Soc. Republican. Lutheran. Office: Metro Dade County 5680 SW 87th Ave Miami FL 33173

KEY, DOROTHY LAUSBERG, financial consultant; b. Arnold, Pa., Oct. 28, 1947; d. Robert Joseph and Alice Mae (Smith) Lausberg; m. Robert Joseph Key, May 10, 1976 (div. 1982). BA in Rehab. Edn., Pa. State U., 1969. CLU; chartered fin. cons., 1986. Social caseworker Harmarville Rehab. Ctr., Pitts., 1969-75; sales rep. Key Bellevilles, Inc., Leechburg, Pa., 1975-82; agt. Prudential Ins. Co., Pitts., 1982-84; assoc. SMA Fin. Svcs., Pitts., 1984-89; dir. adv. mktg. Sun Fin. Group, 1989—. Mem. Life Underwriters Polit. Action Com., Pitts., 1985-89; active Pitts. Press Old Newsboy campaign Children's Hosp. Mem. Am. Soc. CLU and Chartered Fin. Cons., Nat. Assn. Life Underwriters, Pitts. Assn. for Fin. Planning., Pitts. Life Underwriters Assn. (bd. dirs.), No. Allegheny County C. of C. (v.p., bd. dirs.). Democrat. Roman Catholic. Club: Zonta. Lodge: Rotary. Avocations: reading, cultural events, continuing education, public speaking, civic activites. Office: Sun Fin Group One Station Sq The Landmarks Bldg Pittsburgh PA 15219

KEY, MARY RITCHIE (MRS. AUDLEY E. PATTON), linguist, author, educator; b. San Diego, Mar. 19, 1924; d. George Lawrence and Iris (Lyons) Ritchie; children: Mary Helen Key Ellis, Harold Hayden Key (dec.), Thomas George Key. Student, U. Chgo., summer 1954, U. Mich., 1959; M.A., U. Tex., 1960, Ph.D., 1963; postgrad., UCLA, 1966. Asst. prof. linguistics Chapman Coll., Orange, Calif., 1963-66; asst. prof. linguistics U. Calif., Irvine, 1966-71; assoc. prof. U. Calif., 1971-78, prof., 1978—, chmn. program linguistics, 1969-71, 75-77, 87—; cons. Am. Indian langs., Spanish, in Mexico, 1946-55, S.Am., 1955-62, English dialects, 1968-74, Easter Island, 1975, Calif. Dept. Edn., 1966, 70-75, Center Applied Linguistics, Washington, 1967, 69; lectr. in field. Author: numerous books including Comparative Tacanan Phonology, 1968; Male/Female Language, 1975, Paralanguage and Kinesics, 1975, Nonverbal Communication, 1977, The Grouping of South American Indian Languages, 1979, The Relationship of Verbal and Nonverbal Communication, 1980, Catherine the Great's Linguistic Contribution, 1980, Polynesian and American Linguistic Connections, 1984, Comparative Linguistics of South American Indian Languages, 1987, General and Amerindian Ethnolinguistics, 1989; founder, editor: newsletter Nonverbal Components of Communication, 1972-76; mem. editorial bd.: Forum Linguisticum, 1976—, Lang. Scis., 1978—, La Linguistique, 1979—, Multilingua, 1987—; contbr. articles to profl. jours. Recipient Friends of Library Book award, 1976, hon. mention, Rolex awards for lalng. project Computerizing the Langs. of the World, 1990; U. Calif. Regent's grantee, 1974, Fulbright-Hays grantee, 1975; Faculty Rsch. fellow, 1984-85. Mem. Linguistic Soc. Am., Am. Dialect Soc. (exec. council; regional sec. 1974-83), Internat. Reading Assn. (dir. 1968-72), Delta Kappa Gamma (local pres. 1974-76). Office: U Calif-Irvine Program in Linguistics Irvine CA 92717

KEY, RAMONA THORNTON, health facility administrator; b. Little Rock, Ark., Dec. 13, 1939; d. J.P. and H. Belle (Jones) T.; m. Charles E. Winters, Jan. 21, 1961 (dec. Dec. 1965); children: Lesa Trujillo, Kellie Scarpa, Dale Winters; m. George Trujillo, May 24, 1970 (dec. July 1977); 1 child, Melinda Trujillo; m. Dennis Russell Key, May 15, 1982 (div. Feb. 1988). BS in Psychology, Southwestern Coll., 1963; cert. coronary intensive care, U. Tenn., 1973; postgrad., Memphis State U., 1979-81. RN, Tenn. Nurse various hosps., 1961-72; dir. personal adjustment ctr. Mental Health and Retardation Ctr., Oxford, Miss., 1972-75; cons. Interagy. Commn.'s Devel. Disabilities Tng. program State of Miss., 1974-75; coord. for adult acute psychiat. svc., liaison with local mental health ctr. Boulder (Colo.) Psychiat. Inst., 1975-77; head nurse behavior modification VA Hosp., Memphis, 1978-81; hosp. supr. Vista Sandia Psychiat. Hosp., Albuquerque, 1981-85, dir. nursing svcs., 1985-88; dir. nursing svcs. U. N.Mex. Mental Health Ctr., Albuquerque, 1988-90, Charter Hosp., Albuquerque, 1990—; leader health workshops, Miss., 1974; bd. dirs. Nurse Profl. Standards Bd., VA Med. Ctr., Memphis, 1979-81; mem. faculty U. N.Mex. Coll. Nursing, 1986—. Mem. ANA, N.Mex. Nurses Assn. (CEU com. 19866), N.Mex. Orgn. Nurse Execs. (prgoram chairperson 1987-88), N.Mex. Hosp. Assn. (bd. dirs. hosp. svcs. corp. 1988-90). Democrat. Methodist. Home: 3702 Rose Circle SE Rio Rancho NM 87124 Office: Charter Hosp Albuquerque Dir Nursing Svc 5901 Zuni SE Albuquerque NM 87110

KEYES, DARLYNN LADD, real estate executive; b. Denver, Apr. 14, 1948; d. Ernest Victor and Mary Louise (Webb) K. BS, U. Wyo., 1971. Lic. in real estate, Fla.; cert. real estate broker, Colo. Dir. mktg., ski instr., ski patrol Geneva Basin, Grant, Colo., 1972-78; gen. mgr. Tumbling River Guest Ranch, Grant, 1974-76; owner Above Timberline Outfitters, Grant, 1974—, Keyes Real Estate and Investment Co., Vail, Colo., 1979—; comml. and residential real estate salesperson, 1977-79; interval owner in real estate Streamside of Vail, 1979-80; project dir. real estate Brewster Green, Cape Cod, Mass., 1981-82, Vallarta Torrs, Puerta Vallarta, Mex., 1983-84; real estate salesperson Clube Praia de Ora, Algarve, Portugal, 1984; project dir. real estate Sandstone Creek Club, Vail, 1985-87; sales dir. Gold Point Condos, Breckenridge, Colo., 1987-88; sales mgr. Torres Mazatlan, Mexico, 1988-90; project dir. Hideaway Beach Club, Nazatlan, 1990—; sec., treas. Viking Vacation Internat., Brewster, 1982-83. Mem. Nat. Assn. Exec. Women, Colo. Bd. Realtors, Vail Bd. Realtors, Colo. Cattleman's Assn., Nat. Bd. Realtors, Colo. Wool Growers Assn., Nat. Dude Ranch Assn. (bd. dirs. 1975, Washington rep.), Am. Resort and Residential Devel. Assn., Profl. Assn. Diving Instrs. Clubs: Alpine Garden, Beaver Scuba Divers (Vail); London (Eng.) Gliding. Home and Office: La Marina 809, Apdo 7 Sucursal B, Mazatlan Sinaloa 82000, Mexico

KEYES, EMMALOU, social services administrator, nurse; b. Hutchinson, Kans., Nov. 13, 1931; d. Ferguson and Virginia Lucile (Copenhaver) Reynolds; m. Mark B. Cripe, Nov. 13, 1953 (div. 1962); m. William Robert Keyes, Mar. 24, 1967 (dec. Mar. 1989); children: Lee Edward, Jay Scott. BS in Nursing, Pan Am. U., 1984; MS in Nursing, Corpus Christi State U., 1988. Cert. family nurse practitioner. Pub. health nurse Hidalgo County Health Dept., Edinburg, Tex., 1952-77; family nurse practitioner Hidalgo County Health Care Corp., Edinburg, 1977-79; title XIX screener Tex. Dept. Health, Austin, 1979-80; sch. nurse Progreso (Tex.) Ind. Sch. Dist., 1980-82; clinic services dir. Planned Parenthood, McAllen, Tex., 1982—; bd. dirs., disaster nurse ARC, McAllen; instr. Pan Am. nursing dept. BSN program U. Tex. Mem. Am. Nurses Assn., Tex. Nurses Assn. (dist. pres., treas., bd. dirs.), Am. Pub. Health Assn., Nat. Assn. Nurses in Family Planning, Am. Heart Assn. Episcopalian. Home: 21 S 35th McAllen TX 78501 Office: Planned Parenthood 1017 Pecan McAllen TX 78501

KEYES, JOAN ROSS RAFTER, educator, author; b. Bklyn., Aug. 12, 1924; d. Joseph W. and Hermia (Ross) Rafter; m. William Ambrose, Apr. 26, 1947; children: William, Peter, Dion, Alexandrea. BA, Adelphi U., Garden City, N.Y., 1945; MS, Long Island U., Greenvale, N.Y., 1973. Prodn. asst. CBS Radio, N.Y., 1943-44; cub news reporter Bklyn. Daily Eagle, 1945-46; advt. copywriter Gimbel's Dept. Store, N.Y., 1946-47; adj. prof. L.I. U., Greenvale, N.Y., 1984—; tchr. Port Wash. Pub. Schs., N.Y., 1970--; lectr., cons. pub. sch. dists. nationwide, 1978—; workshop leader Tchrs. English to Speakers Other Langs. convs., 1981—. Author: Beats, Conversations in Rhythm, 1983, (video program) Now Your're Talking, 1987; (computer program) Quick Talk, 1990; contbr. articles to ednl. mags. Participant Rep. Tchrs. Com., Long Island, 1984; Lectr. Our Lady of Fatima Ch., Port Wash., 1987; Vol. Earthwatch, Mallorca, 1988. Mem. Tchrs. of English to Speakers of Other Languages, Am. Fedn. of Tchrs., N.Y. State United Tchrs., Port Wash. Tchrs. Assn. Republican. Roman Catholic. Office: Port Washington Pub Schs Campus Dr Port Washington NY 11050

KEYES, JUDITH DROZ, lawyer; b. Pitts., Jan. 16, 1946; d. Blair Guthrie Huddart and Barbara Jane (Tilden) McCoy; m. Donald Glenn Droz, May 25, 1968 (dec. Apr. 1969); 1 child, Tracy Tilden Droz; m. David Phillip Keyes, June 6, 1970. BS, Pa. State U., 1966; MA in Linguistics, U. Mo., 1970; JD, U. Calif., Berkeley, 1975. Bar: Calif. 1975, U.S. Dist. Ct. (no. and ea. dists.) Calif. 1975. Tchr. Chgo. Pub. High Sch. System, 1966-67; field atty. NLRB, San Francisco, 1975-76; ptnr. Corbett & Kane, Oakland, Calif., 1976—; vis. assoc. prof. Suffolk U. Law Sch., Boston, 1986-87; bd. dirs. Calif.-Nev. Meth. Homes, Oakland, Calif. Mem. ABA, Calif. Bar Assn., San Francisco Bar Assn., Alameda County Bar Assn., Order of the Coif. Democrat. United Ch. of Christ. Office: Corbett & Kane 2000 Powell St Ste 1450 Emeryville CA 94608

KEYSER, GLORIA JEAN, human resources director; b. Easton, Pa., July 28, 1939; d. Edgar Richard and Helen Elizabeth (May) Fraunfelter; m. Gerald David Keyser, May 9, 1959; children: Constance, Deborah, David, Karen, Kevin. Student, East Stroudsburg U., 1957-59; BA, Shippensburg U., 1976; postgrad., Pa. State U., 1982-84, Wilson Coll., 1986. Spl. events coord., customer billing Fashion Lane, Inc., Chambersburg, Pa., 1972-74, pub. rels. cons., 1976-77; dir. Cumberland Valley Humane Soc., Chambersburg, Pa., 1977-79; fed. ind. monitor Franklin County CETA, Chambersburg, Pa., 1979-80, mgr. mktg. and placement, 1980-81; exec. dir. Franklin County Pvt. Industry Coun., Chambersburg, Pa., 1981-84; dir. confs., food svc. ops., continuing studies Wilson Coll., Chambersburg, Pa., 1984-88; dir. human resources Veniez Inn, Hagerstown, Mo., 1988—. Author street map/names, Chambersburg, 1975. Mem. Franklin County Area Devel. Corp., Chambersburg, 1984-89, Tri-County Children and Youth Adv. Bd., Chambersburg, 1982-84, Tri-County Econ. Edn. Found. Bd., Cross Keys, Pa., 1981-84, Bd. of Health, Chambersburg, 1988—; cons. polit. campaigns, Chambersburg, 1988. Mem. Women's Network of Franklin County, AAUW, Chambersburg Hosp. Aux., Pa. Soc. Assn. Execs. Democrat. Roman Catholic. Home: 565 East Catherine St Chambersburg PA 17201

KEYSER, NANCY LEOLA, design engineer; b. Seattle, Wash., Nov. 18, 1943; d. Chelmer Glen and Esther May (Dascher) Witherbee; m. James A. DeBoer, Oct. 13, 1962 (div. Feb. 1970); m. Robert E. Keyser, Dec. 6, 1975 (div. Dec. 1989). Engring. diploma, U. Wash. Salesperson Seattle World's Fair, 1962; accountant, payroll Seattle Credit Bur., 1966-67, Simpson Timber, Seattle, 1967-71; accountant Family Care Ctrs., Seattle, 1971-72, Swanson-Dean Builders, Bellevue, Wash., 1972-73; mfg. engr., planner Boeing Co., Renton, Wash., 1974—; owner Village Tavern, Bellevue, Wash. Active various civic orgns. including Heart Fund and Am. Cancer Soc. Recipient Congress Woman's award, Outstanding Regional Dir. award Nat. Jaycee Women, 1980. Home: 2345 138th SE Bellevue WA 98005 Office: Boeing Company PO Box 3707 MS 64-11 Seattle WA 98124

KEYSERLING, HARRIET H., state legislator; b. N.Y.C., Apr. 4, 1922; d. Isadore and Pauline Hirschfeld; m. Ben Herbert Keyserling, June 24, 1944; children—Judy, Billy, Paul, Beth. B.A. in Econs., Barnard Coll., 1943. Mem. S.C. Ho. of Reps., 1977—, mem. joint legis. energy com., chair joint legis. com. cultural affairs, 1984—; bd. dirs. Palmetto Fed. Savs. and Loan Assn. Organizer Beaufort County LWV; mem. nuclear wast consultation com. SE Compact Commn. for Low Level Racioactive Waste Mgmt.; mem. adv. panel on nuclear waste disposal office of Tech. Assessment of U.S. Congress, 1979-82; mem. exec. com. Nat. Conf. State Legislatures, 1979-82, vice chmn. com. on energy, 1982, chmn. women's network, 1981-82; mem. adv. com. to U.S. Commn. on Civil Rights. At-large mem. Beaufort County Council, 1975-77; chair, founder S.C. Women in Govt.; bd. dirs. Spoleto Festival U.S.A., Beaufort County Open Land Trust, Penn Ctr. of Sea Islands; chair Legislative Com. Cultural Affairs. Mem. Nature Conservacny (bd. dirs.). Democrat.

KEYSTON, STEPHANI ANN, small business owner; b. Baytown, Tex., Aug. 6, 1955; d. Herbert Howard and Janice Faye (Stowe) Cruickshank; m. George Keyston III, Oct. 8, 1983; 1 child, Jeremy George. AA with honors, Merced Coll., Merced, Calif., 1975; BA in Journalism with distinction, San Jose State U., 1976. Reporter, Fresno (Calif.) Bee, 1974-75; reporter, photographer Merced (Calif.) Sun-Star, 1974-77; pub. info. officer Fresno City Coll. (Calif.), 1977-80; dir. communications Aerojet Tactical Systems Co., Sacramento, 1980-83; co-owner, v.p. Keyco Landscape Contractor Inc., Auburn, Calif., 1984—. Co.-coordinator Aerojet United Way Campaign, 1981; Aerojet Tactical Systems Co. coordinator West Coast Nat. Derby Rallies, 1981-83. Mem. Internat. Assn. Bus. Communicators (dir. Sacramento chpt. 1983), Citrus Heights C. of C. (v.p. 1983). Republican. Home: 13399 Lakeview Pl Auburn CA 95603 Office: Keyco Landscape Contractor Inc 10594 Combie Rd Ste 6476 Auburn CA 95603

KEZLARIAN, NANCY KAY, communications company executive; b. Royal Oak, Mich., Aug. 26, 1948; d. Barkev A. and Nancy (Israelian) K. Student, U. Vienna, Austria, 1969; BA, Albion Coll., 1970; MA in Theatre and TV, U. Mich., 1971. Cert. secondary tchr., Mich., Calif. Tchr. West Bloomfield Hills (Mich.) High Sch., 1971-76; tchr. ESL, L.A. Pub. Schs., 1976-80; personnel dir. Samuel Goldwyn Co., L.A., 1985-86; dir. adminstrn. and human resources Act III Communications, L.A., 1986—; owner, mgr. KAZ, painted clothing co., L.A., 1980—. Writer, actress My Seventeenth Summer, The Big Blue Marble, 1979 (Emmy award for childen's TV programming). Named Tchr. of Yr., West Bloomfield Hills High Sch., 1976. Mem. SAG, Personnel and Indsl. Rels. Assn. (legis. rep. dist. 5 1989, 90). Office: ACT III Communications 1800 Century Park E Ste 200 Los Angeles CA 90067

KHACHIGIAN, MEREDITH J., retail executive; b. Dec. 13, 1944. Student, Coll. of Sequoias, 1963, U. Calif., 1963; BA in Sociology, U. Calif., Santa Barbara, 1966. Exec. asst. Brokaw, Schaenen & Clancy, 1966-69; sales rep. Cherchez Les Campigions, 1980-83; retail sales A Store for Cooks, 1885-89; bd. regents U. Calif., 1987—, vice chmn., 1989-90; bd. trustees Calif. State Summer Sch. Arts; bd. dirs. U. Calif. Irvine Found. Trustee Cecil H. and Ida M. Green Found. for Earth Scis.; appointed by Gov. George Deukmejian Commn. for Rev. of the Master Plan for Higher Edn., 1985-87; mem. Rep. Women Federated; chmn. Early Childhood Edn. Program, 1975-79; del. AAUC Legis. Conf., 1984, 86. Named Honoree AAUW Ednl. Found. Program. Mem. Calif. at Santa Barbara Alumni Assn. (former pres., bd. dirs., mem. exec. com., former chmn., club com.), Am. Assn. of Univ. Women (pres. 1979-80), Nat. Asst. League (Capistrano Valley chpt. 1978—), Parent Tchr. Fellowship, Guardian Angels.

KHAN, CHAKA, singer; b. Chgo., Mar. 23, 1953; 1 child, Milini. Singer Rufus musical group, 1972-76, Warner Bros. Records, 1978—. Albums include Rags to Rufus, 1974, Rufus Featuring Chaka Khan, 1975, Chaka, 1979, Naughty, 1980, Whatcha' Gonna Do For Me, 1981, Chaka Khan, 1982, I Feel For You, 1984, Destiny, 1986, CK, 1989. Recipient Grammy awards for group vocal and vocal arrangements, 1983, for best rhythm & blues female vocal, 1983, 84. Office: care Geffen Records 9130 Sunset Blvd Los Angeles CA 90069*

KHANSARY, PHYLLIS JUNE, communications executive; b. Elgin, N.D., Feb. 20, 1960; d. William Richard and Eunice June (Ensminger) Bond; m. Mark Khansary, Sept. 16, 1983. BS, Moorhead State U., 1982; MBA, Nat. U., 1989. Purchasing adminstr. CCH Computax Inc., Torrance, Calif., 1983-87; mgr. adminstrn. Pedersen Communications, Gardena, Calif., 1987—; owner Khansary Wholesale Merchandising, Long Beach, Calif., 1989—. Mem. NAFE. Office: Pedersen Communications 13724 Harvard Pl Ste A Gardena CA 90249

KHARASCH, VIRGINIA SISON, pediatric pulmonary physician; b. Manila, Aug. 14, 1956; came to U.S., 1983; d. Gregorio Beljano and Luz (Mendoza) Sison; m. Sigmund Joseph Kharasch, Dec. 29, 1956. BS in Zoology, U. of Philippines, 1977, MD, 1981. Diplomate Am. Bd. Pediatrics. Intern Med. Ctr. Manila, 1981-82; staff physician Presdl. Sect. Command Hosp., Philippines, 1982; resident in pediatrics Phoenix Hosp., 1983-84, Michael Reese Hosp./U. Chgo., 1984-86; mem. pediatric staff Michael Reese Health Plan and Hosp., Chgo., 1986-87; pediatric pulmonology specialist Harvard U./Children's Hosp., Boston, 1987-89; clin. asst. in medicine Children's Hosp., Boston, 1990—; instr. Med. Sch. Harvard U., Boston, 1990—; basic sci. researcher Harvard U. Sch. Pub. Health, 1987-90; cons. Cystic Fibrosis Ctr., Boston, 1987-90. Contbr. articles to med. jours. Rsch. fellow Nat. Rsch. Coun. of The Philippines, 1982. Fellow Am. Acad. Pediatrics; mem. AMA, Am. Coll. Chest Physicians, Pi Gamma Mu, Phi Kappa Phi, Phi Sigma. Office: Childrens Hosp 300 Longwood Ave Boston MA 02115

KHATAMI, MAHIN, molecular biologist; b. Tehran, Iran, May 9, 1943; came to U.S., 1969; d. Kazim and Badri Khatami. BS in Chemistry, Tchr. Tng. Coll., Tehran, 1964; MA in Biochemistry, SUNY, Buffalo, 1977; PhD in Molecular Biology, U. Pa., Phila., 1980. Instr. chemistry and physics sr. high schs., Tehran, 1964-69; instr. biochemistry Phila. Coll. Podiatric Medicine, 1975; rsch. assoc. physiology U. Va., 1980-81; postdoctoral rsch. assoc. Fox Chase Cancer Inst., Phila., 1981-82; asst. prof. ophthalmology U. Pa., Phila., 1985—; symposium dir. U. Pa. Ann. Symposium Diabetic Complications, Phila., 1989—; speaker Japan, Iran, India, U.S.A. Contbr. articles to profl. jours., chpts. to books. Iran Ministry of Sic. grad. student fellow, 1977-80; Juvenile Diabetes Found. Internat. summer student program grantee, N.Y.C., 1988-90; recipient Rsch. Svc. award NIH, Nat. Rsch. Svcs., Bethesda, Md., 1982-85. Mem. Assn. for Rsch. in Vision and Ophthalmology, Soc. Exptl. Biology and Medicine, Am. Diabetes Assn., N.Y. Acad. Scis., Internat. Programs Com. U. Pa. Home: 1019 Radnor House Rosemont PA 19010 Office: Scheie Eye Inst 51 N 39th St Philadelphia PA 19104

KHELIL, NAJAT ARAFAT, physicist; b. Nablus, Palestine, Jordan, July 5, 1942; came to U.S., 1962.; d. Tawfic A. and Shuhra S. Arafat; m. Chakib M. Khelil, Oct. 5, 1964; children: Sina, Khaldoun. BS in Physics and Chemistry, Cairo U., 1960; MS in Nuclear Physics, Ohio State U., 1965; PhD, North Tex. State U., 1974. Assoc. prof. U. Algiers, Algeria, 1974-80, George Washington U., Washington, 1981-84, Shaw U., Raleigh, N.C., 1985; cons. Orgn. Arab Students, Washington, 1984—; researcher Nat. Bur. Standards, Gaithersburg, Md., 1981-82. Vol. Am. Cancer Soc., Heart Fund; bd. dirs. United Holy Land Fund, Chgo., 1986—, Rainbow Coalition, 1987—; pres. Union Palestinian-Am. Women, 1986-89. Fulbright scholar Am. Info. Service, 1962-63. Mem. Am. Phys. Soc., Union Palestinian Engr., Council Pres.'s Arab-Am. Orgn. (chairperson 1987), Arab Women's Council (pres. 1986—), Moslem Women's Assn. (v.p. 1986—), Sigma Pi Sigma. Moslem. Home: 11209 Hunt Club Dr Potomac MD 20854

KHIREIWISH, LAURIE OWEN, English and reading educator; b. Dallas, Mar. 1, 1957; d. Harry Hancock and Patricia Deane (Harman) Owen; m. Subhi A. Khireiwish, June 9, 1984 (div. 1982); 1 child, Kirk Willhoite. BS in Elem. Edn., Tex. Woman's U., 1978, MEd in Lang. Disabilities, 1981. Spl. edn. tchr. English and reading Strickland Jr. High Sch., Denton, Tex., 1979—; core team leader student assistance program, campus liaison Strickland Jr. High Sch., 1986—, mem. drug edn. steering com., dept. chair, spl. edn. liaison, 1987—; co-leader D.I.S.D. strategic planning action team, 1990—. Mem. PTA. Mem. Nat. Coun. Tchrs. of English, Coun. for Exceptional Children, Tex. Assn. Children with Learning Disabilities, Tex. Coun. Tchrs. of English, Delta Kappa Gamma. Presbyterian. Home: 812 Moss Ross Ln Aubrey TX 76227 Office: Strickland Jr High Sch 324 Windsor Denton TX 76201

KIBLER, VIRGINIA ELAINE, psychologist; b. Oakland, Calif., June 25, 1951; d. Gordon Markwood and Eleanor (Fried) K.; m. John Richard Barr, Mar. 17, 1985; children: Jason Sidney Kibler Barr, Rachael Hannah Kibler Barr. BS, Mich. State U., 1973; MS, Ohio U., 1976, PhD, 1978. Lic. psychologist, Mont., Colo. Asst. prof. Eastern Mont. Coll., Billings, 1979-82; asst. prof. Mont. State U., Bozeman, 1983; psychologist Billings Counseling Assocs., 1980-87; postdoctoral fellow Houston Child Guidance Ctr., 1989; pvt. practice counselor Houston, 1990—; adj. prof. Eastern Mont. Coll., Billings, 1982-84, psychologist, cons., 1984-85. Contbr. articles to profl. jours. Mem. exec. com. AAUP, Billings, 1980-81, pres., 1981-82. Dreikurs Tuition scholar Rudolph Dreikurs Inst., Badgastein, Austria, 1982, scholar Ohio U., 1976, Mich. Competitive scholar State of Mich., 1969. Mem. Am. Psychol. Assn., N.Am. Soc. Adlerian Psychology, Am. Assn. for Counseling and Devel., Internat. Assn. Marriage and Family Counselors, Chi Sigma Iota. Home: 15710 Woodcroft Dr Houston TX 77095

KIBRICK, ANNE K., nursing educator, university dean; b. Palmer, Mass., June 1, 1919; d. Martin and Christine (Grigas) Karlon; m. Sidney Kibrick, June 16, 1949; children: Joan, John. R.N., Worcester (Mass.) Hahnemann Hosp., 1941; B.S., Boston U., 1945; M.A., Columbia Tchrs. Coll., 1948; Ed.D., Harvard U., 1958; L.H.D. (hon.), St. Joseph's Coll., Windham, Maine, 1973. Asst. edn. dir. Cushing VA Hosp., Framingham, Mass., 1948-49; asst. prof. nursing Simmons Coll., Boston, 1949-55; dir. grad. div. Boston U. Sch. Nursing, 1958-63, dean, 1963-68, prof., 1968-70; chmn. dept. nursing Boston Grad. Sch. Arts and Sci., 1970-74; chmn. sch. nursing Boston State Coll., 1974-82; dean Sch. Nursing U. Mass., Boston, 1974-88, prof., 1988—; cons. div. nursing USPHS, 1964-68; cons. Nat. Student Nurses Assn., 1985-88; mem. nat. adv. council nurse tng. USPHS, NIH, 1968-73; cons. Hebrew U.-Hadassah Med. Orgn., Jerusalem, 1971—; mem. Inst. Medicine of Nat. Acad. Scis., 1972—, mem. steering com. costs of edn. of health professions, 1972-74; mem. Nat. Med. Audiovisual Tng. Center, 1972-76, Gov.'s Com. and Area Bd. Mental Health and Mental Retardation, Nat. Commn. for Study Nursing and Nursing Edn., 1970-73; mem. faculty com., regent's external degree program in nursing SUNY, 1974-82; mem. hosp. mgmt. bd. U. Hosp., U. Mass., 1976-81; dir. Medic Alert, Am. Jour. Nursing Co.; cons. Cumberland Coll. Health Scis., New South Wales, Australia, 1986, Menoufia U., Shibin El Kom, Egypt, 1987. Mem. editorial bd. Mass. Jour. Community Health. Bd. dirs. Brookline Mental Health Assn., Met. chpt. ARC., Children's Ctr. Brookline and Greater Boston, Inc., 1984—, Boston Health Care for the Homeless, 1988—. Fellow Am. Acad. Nursing; mem. Nat. Mass. Leagues Nursing (pres. 1971-73), Am. Nurses Assn., Mass. Nurses Assn. (dir. 1982-86), AIDS Internat. Info. Found. (founding mem. 1985), Mass. Nurses Found. (v.p. 1983-86), Nat. Acads. of Practice, Mass. Med. Soc. (bd. dirs. postgrad. med. inst. 1983—, exec. com. 1989—), Mass. Blueprint 2000, Sigma Theta Tau, Pi Lambda Theta. Home: 381 Clinton Rd Brookline MA 02146

KIDD, AGNES JUANITA, retired educator; b. Guntown, Miss., Aug. 12, 1918; d. Holbert Thomas and Allie Pearl (Coleman) Hopkins; m. Clyde Earl Kidd, Nov. 24, 1937 (dec. 1981); children: Kenton Earl, Mary Kathryn. BS, E. Cen. State U., Ada, Okla., 1939; MEd., Cen. State U., Edmond, Okla., 1954. Cert. classroom tchr., counselor, pub. relations. Tchr. Putnam City Jr. High Sch., Oklahoma City, 1954-59; counselor, dean of girls Putnam City High Sch., Oklahoma City, 1959-70; dir. high sch. relations Cen. State U., Edmond, 1970-75; dir. info. svcs. Tulsa Vo-Tech Sch., 1975-80; bd. dirs. Okla. Edn1. TV Authority, Oklahoma City, Okla. Educator's Credit Union; mem. Com. 100 Study Educators, Oklahoma City, 1984; sr. intern Sen. David Boren, Washington, 1985; mem. NEA Rev. Bd. for Tchr's Rights, Washington, 1981-86. Pres. MacDowell Club Allied Arts, Oklahoma City, 1985-87; charter mem. Okla. Acad. for State Goals, Oklahoma City, 1986—; mem. Okla. Heritage Assn., Oklahoma City, 1986—; chair com. Okla. Jefferson-Bryan Democratic Women, Oklahoma City, 1970. Named to Educator's Hall of Fame, Phi Delta Kappa, Oklahoma City, 1986; recipient Juanita Kidd Courtyard OETA Channel 13 Bravo award, 1988. Mem. Okla. Edn. Assn. (Juanita Kidd Room, Hdqr. Bldg. named in her honor, life, pres. 1983-84, Kate Frank Meritorious award 1980), World Confeden. Teaching Professin (del. 1972), NEA (life), Kappa Kappa Iota (pres. Oklahoma City chpt. 1985-86), Delta Kappa Gamma (pres. Oklahoma City chpt. 1986-88), Phi Delta Kappa. Mem. Christian Ch. Home: 8023 NW 104th St Oklahoma City OK 73162

KIDD, DEBRA JEAN, communications executive; b. Chgo., May 13, 1956; d. Fred A. and Jean (Pezzopane) Winchar; m. Kim Joseph Kidd, July 22, 1978; children: Jennifer Marie, Michele Jean. AA in Bus. with high honors, Wright Jr. Coll., 1977. Legal sec. Sidley & Austin, Chgo., 1977-80; investment adminstr. Golder, Thoma & Co., Chgo., 1980-81, exec. asst., 1981-84; sales rep. Dataspeed, Inc., Chgo., 1984, midwestern regional mgr. Dataspeed, Inc., Chgo., 1985; communications cons. Chgo. Communications, Inc., Chgo., 1986—; owner, founder Captain Kidd's Video, Niles, 1981-84. Vol. Am. Lung Assn., Chgo., 1979; vol. tchr. CCD Our Lady Mother of Ch., Norridge, Ill., 1981-83; vol. Parents Who Care, 1988—. Mem. NAFE, Nat. Assn. Bus. Women, Nat. Assn. Profl. Saleswomen, Nat. Network of Women in Sales, Bus. and Profl. Women's Club, Phi Theta Kappa. Roman Catholic. Avocations: camping; snow and water skiing; horseback riding; sailing; reading; needlepoint.

KIDD, PATRICIA EILEEN, advertising executive; b. Wilmington, Del., July 21, 1952; d. Stephen and Geraldine (Meyers) K. BS in Psychology, Hood Coll., 1974. V.p. Astro Publs., Princeton, N.J., 1974-78; pub. rels. account exec. James Neal Harvey Advt., N.Y.C., 1978-81; advt. account exec. Warren Muller Dolobowsky, Inc., N.Y.C., 1981-82; sr. account exec. William Esty Advt., N.Y.C., 1982-84; v.p., account supr. Cunningham & Walsh Advt., N.Y.C., 1984-86; chmn. Duracom, Inc. Video Mktg., N.Y.C., 1986-88; account rep. Mapes and Ross Mktg. Rsch., Princeton, 1988—. Chmn. Crosstown-62, Sr. Transp., Princeton, 1976-77. Mem. Jaycees (pres. Princeton chpt. 1977-78), Hood Coll. Alumni Assn. (pres. N.Y.C. chpt. 1982-88). Democrat. Presbyterian.

KIDD, REBECCA MONTGOMERY (LOUISE KIDD), artist; b. Muncie, Ind., Nov. 29, 1942; d. Joe Bucklyn and Mary Marguerite (Mark) Montgomery; corr. student comml. art, Famous Artists Schs.; cert. of completion corr. course U. Sci. and Philosophy, Waynesboro, Va., 1976; m. Ben Roy Kidd, Apr. 10, 1964; children—Daniel Ben, Diana Piper. Painter in oils, pastels; painter in realism, impressionism and abstract styles; character painter, 1966—; portrait painter and drawer, 1962-81, 83—; outdoor scene, still life, floral painter, 1969—; children's story illustrator, 1972-74; restorer old houses, 1972-81; adaptor of master's paintings, 1974-82; miniature painter, 1974-82; film illustrator, 1975; Am. Indian painter, 1975-81; trading pin designer, 1977, 78; lithograph printmaker, 1977; monotype printmaker, 1978-84; one woman show: Roadside Gallery, Melfa, Va., 1982; group shows include: Roadside Gallery, 1977—, The Gallery, Ct. Plaza, Salisbury, Md., 1977-84, Queens Coll., Cambridge U., 1982. Mem. Quality Edn. Accomack County (Va.), Exec. Com., 1979-80. Mem. Eastern Shore Art League (constn. and bylaws chmn. 1979, dir. 1982), Visual Artists and Galleries Assn., Nat. Mus. Women in Arts (charter), Nat. Trust Historic Preservation (assoc.), Internat. Platform Assn. (merit award and popular choice award 1984 conv.). Address: 9 Lake St Onancock VA 23417

KIDDER, MARGOT, actress; b. Yellowknife, Can., Oct. 17, 1948; m. Tom McGuane, 1975 (div.); 1 dau., Maggie; m. John Heard. Student, U. B.C. Began career in Can. theater and TV; film debut in Gaily, Gaily, 1969; other films include Quackser Fortune Has a Cousin in the Bronx, 1970, Sisters, 1972, Gravy Train, 1974, The Great Waldo Pepper, 1975, The Reincarnation of Peter Proud, 1975, 92 in the Shade, 1977, Superman, 1978, The Amityville Horror, 1979, Superman II, 1981, Some Kind of Hero, 1981, Trenchcoat, 1983, Superman III, 1983, Little Treasure, 1985, Superman IV; starred in TV series Nichols, 1972, TV movie Honky Tonk, 1974; other TV appearances include Mod Squad, Vanishing Act, 1986, Hoax, 1986, Louisiana, The Glitter Dome, Body of Evidence, 1988. Office: Marion Rosenberg Office 8428 Melrose Pla Ste C Los Angeles CA 90069*

KIEBALA, SUSAN MARIE, accounting and management educator; b. Bay City, Mich., Aug. 22, 1952; d. Edwin Edward and Ruth May (Jarvela) Bukowski; m. Joseph Kiebala, Oct. 6, 1973; children: James, Adam, Kara. BS, Ferris State Coll., 1973; MBA, Western Mich. U., 1977. Acct. Consumers Power Co., Jackson, Mich., 1973-76, Eaton Corp., Marshall, Mich., 1976-78; instr. acctg. Kellogg Community Coll., Battle Creek, Mich., 1978-89; asst. prof. Olivet (Mich.) Coll., 1990—; adj. instr. Davenport Coll., Kalamazoo, 1989—. Coord. Youth Soccer League, Marshall, 1986—; sec./treas. Marshall Soccer Boosters, 1987-88; chmn. Marshall Citizens for Quality Schs., 1988; treas. Com. for Quality Schs., 1989; co-chmn. Fin. Com. Millage, 1989; neighborhood capt. Am. Cancer Soc., 1987—; treas. St. Joseph's Guild of St. Mary's Ch., Marshall, 1989—. Recipient Gold Apple award Marshall Pub. Schs., 1988. Home: 527 Sherman Dr Marshall MI 49068 Office: Olivet Coll 407F Mott Olivet MI 49076

KIEFER, KIT ANNETTE, editor; b. Wausau, Wis., Dec. 18, 1958; d. Arthur Clarence and Mae Evelyn (Wagner) K.; m. Jon Andrew Brecka, Sept. 26, 1985 (div. Jan. 1990); children: J.J., Jeff, Gwinneth. BA in Journalism and Polit. Sci., U. Wis., River Falls, 1981. Asst. editor 13-30 Corp., Knoxville, Tenn., 1981-85; editor Krause Publs., Iola, Wis., 1986—; writer Search, Amherst, Wis., 1986-90, Trapper & Predator Caller, Iola, 1988-90; cons. Paul M. Green Inc., Madison, Wis., 1987-90. Author: The Post-Nuclear Collegian, 1985, The Top 100, 1990. Vol. League of Pollsters, Amherst, 1988, St. Mary of Mt. Carmel Divorcees Against Drugs, Ahmerst, 1989. Recipient Excellence in Design award Wis. Pottery League, 1988, Roger award Portage County Poetry Soc., 1989, Salesperson of Yr. award Wicker Plus, 1989. Mem. Amherst Range Riders (sec.-treas. 1988-90). Republican. Lutheran. Home: 376-2 Lincoln St Amherst WI 54406 Office: Krause Publs 700 E State St Iola WI 54490

KIEFERT, ALICE STOCKWELL, designer, civic worker; b. Des Moines, June 7, 1929; d. John Fred and Anna Regina (Wiczek) Stockwell; m. D.E. Kiefert, Sept. 10, 1949 (sep.); children: Anna Marie Kiefert Shoemaker, Timothy John. Student, Layton Sch. Art, Milw., 1947-49, Waukesha (Wis.) Tech. Coll., 1972. Saleswoman Gimbel's, Milw., 1945-46, Sarah Coventry, Ocono, Wis., 1969; bookkeeper 1st Wis. Nat. Bank, Milw., 1947-48; asst. bookkeeper Columbia Hosp., Milw., 1948-49; designer, saleswoman Lake Country Interiors, Ocono, 1970; nursing asst. Waukesha County Vis. Nurses, Ocono, 1974-76; asst. mgr., saleswoman Woman's Apparel, Ocono, 1979-81; designer, owner, mgr. Originals by Alice Kiefert, Oconomowoc, Wis., 1980-89. Fund raiser numerous orgns.; past mem. bldg. fund Oconomowoc YMCA; past pres., bd. dirs. Oconomowoc Women's Club, Oconomowoc Libr., Meml. Hosp. Oconomowoc; organizer Festival of Arts, Oconomowoc, 1975-80; former instr. first aid ARC, Milw.; past bd. dirs., leader, camp counselor Girl Scouts U.S.A., Milw.; pres., svc. vol. G.G. Graham Aux. Post, 1983, VFW, Milw., 1947-57, others. Recipient community svc. award Mother's March on Polio, 1954, Oconomowoc Centennial Com., 1974, Waukesha County Vol. Action, also others. Mem. LWV, Music Club. Home: 5879 Mary Ln Oconomowoc WI 53066

KIEFFER, SUSAN FAYE, advertising executive; b. Sheboygan, Wis., July 17, 1962; d. Charles and Gladys Lydia (Lorenz) Hamann; m. James William Kieffer, July 29, 1989. A, U. Wis., Sheboygan, 1983; BA, U. Wis., LaCrosse, 1985. Account exec. Jacobson Rost, Sheboygan, 1986—. Vice pres. Big Bros./Big Sisters, Sheboygan, 1987—. Mem. Nat. Orgn. Female Profls. Lutheran. Home: 1807 N 6th St Sheboygan WI 53081 Office: Jacobson Rost 529 Ontario Ave Sheboygan WI 53081

KIEFFER, SUSAN WERNER, geologist; b. Warren, Pa., Nov. 17, 1942. BS in Physics and Math., Allegheny Coll., 1964; MS in Geol. Scis., Calif. Inst. Tech., 1967, PhD in Planetary Scis., 1971; DSc (hon.), Allegheny Coll., 1987. Postdoctoral research geochemist UCLA, 1971-73, asst. prof. geology, 1973-79; geologist U.S. Geol. Survey, Flagstaff, Ariz., 1979—; rsch. prof. Ariz. State U., Tempe, 1988—; prof. geology Ariz. State U., 1990—. Co-editor: (with A. Navrotsky) Microscopic to Macroscopic: Atomic Environments to Mineral Thermodynamics, 1985. Alfred P. Sloan Found. fellow, 1977-79; W.H. Mendenhall lectr., U.S. Geol. Survey, 1980; recipient Disting. Alumnus award Calif. Inst. Tech., 1982; recipient Meritorious Service award Dept. Interior, 1986, Spendiarov award Soviet Acad. of Scis., 1990. Fellow Am. Geophys. Union, Mineral. Soc. Am. (award 1980), Geol. Soc. Am., Meteoritical Soc.; mem. Nat. Acad. Scis., Am. Acad. Arts Scis. Office: Ariz State U Geology Dept Tempe AZ 85287-1404 also: Ariz State U Geology Dept Tempe AZ 85287-1404

KIEFFER-ANDREWS, MARILYN JOANNE, nurse, midwife; b. Michigan City, Ind., Dec. 3, 1947; d. Edward Charles and Eleanor Mae (Coughlin) Hinkley; m. Lowell Eugene Andrews, Apr. 25, 1987. AA, Immaculate Jr. Coll., 1968; BS in Nursing, Loyola U., 1972; MS, U. Utah, 1977; postgrad., The Union Inst., 1990—. Pub. health nurse Indian Health Service, Phoenix, 1972-73, Newtown, N.D., 1973-74; staff nurse U. Utah Med. Ctr., Salt Lake City, 1974-77; staff nurse midwife Phoenix Meml. Hosp., A.R.E. Clinic, Phoenix, 1980-82; pvt. practice, 1982-88; adminstr., owner Birth & Family Ctr., Phoenix, 1983-85; commissioned officer cons. clinician Phoenix Indian Hosp. USPHS, 1987-89; psychiat. nurse practioner Crisis Clinic and Homeless Program, Phoenix, 1989—; cons. Ariz. Midwife Adv. Bd., Phoenix, 1980--. Contbr. articles to profl. jours. Mem. Toast Master's Internat., Phoenix, 1982-86, Ariz. Coalition for Effective Health Care, Phoenix, 1983-85, Ariz. Bus. Alliance, Phoenix, 1983-85, Ariz. Women's Town Hall, Phoenix, 1986. Mem. Am. Coll. Nurse-Midwives, Chpt. V, IV ACNM (vice chmn. 1980-82, 1983-85, chair 1978-80), Nat. Assn. Obstetric and Gynecol. Nurses, Am. Pub. Health Assn., Sigma Theta Tau, Women Emergin, Musaleim Seis. Democrat. Episcopalian. Home: 7543 N 20th St Phoenix AZ 85020

KIELSMEIER, CATHERINE JANE, school system administrator; b. San Jose, Calif; d. Frank Delos and Catherine Doris (Sellar) MacGowan; M.S., U. So. Calif., 1964, Ph.D., 1971; m. Milton Kielsmeier; children—Catherine Louise, Barry Delos. Tchr. pub. schs. Maricopa, Calif.; sch. psychologist Campbell (Calif.) Union Sch Dist., 1961-66; asst. prof. edn. and psychology Western Oreg. State Coll., Monmouth, 1966-67, 70; asst. research prof. Oreg. System Higher Edn., Monmouth, 1967-70; dir. spl. services Pub. Schs., Santa Rosa, Calif., 1972—. Mem. Sonoma County Council Community Services, 1976—, Sonoma County Orgn. for Retarded/Becoming Independent, 1978—. Mem. Council for Exceptional Children. Club: Commonwealth of Calif. Home: 7495 Poplar Dr Forestville CA 95436 Office: 211 Ridgeway Ave Santa Rosa CA 95402

KIENBAUM, KAREN SMITH, lawyer; b. Flint, Mich., Aug. 10, 1943; d. George Arnold and Ellen Janice (Wills) Smith; 1 child, Ursula. BA in History and Edn., U. Mich., 1965; JD, U. Detroit, 1975. Bar: Mich. 1975. Tchr. Donoero High Sch., Royal Oak, Mich., 1966-72; dep. defender Legal Aid and Defender Assn., Detroit, 1975-77; assoc. Blue Cross Blue Shield, Detroit, 1977-78, asst. gen. counsel, 1981-90; supervising counsel ins. and legis. divs. Ford Motor Co., Dearborn, Mich., 1990—. Mem. Mich. Bar Assn. (appointee prepaid legal svcs. 1978-85), Detroit Bar Assn. (chmn. corp. sect. 1985-88, Chair person of Yr. labor sect. 1983, dir. 1987—, mem. exec. com.), ACCA (bd. dirs. 1985—, dir. minority demonstration program 1988—, 1st v.p. 1989, pres. 1990), DBA Found. (trustee 1987—), Grosse Pointe Hunt Club. Home: 6 Jefferson Ct Grosse Pointe Park MI 48230 Office: Ford Motor Co Parkland Towers W 3 Parklane Blvd Ste 1500 Dearborn MI 48126

KIENER, MARY ELAINE, nursing educator; b. Cleve., June 24, 1950; d. John Anthony and Elaine Cecelia (Kaster) K. BS in Nursing, Marquette U., 1973; MS in Ednl. Adminstrn., U. Wis., Milw., 1979, PhD in Urban Edn., 1983. Clin. nurse Univ. Hosps., Cleve., 1973-74; nursing supr. Whitecliff Manor Extended Care Facility, Cleveland Heights, Ohio, 1974-75; family care nurse Family Hosp., Milw., 1976-77; dir. tng. supportive svcs. Interfaith Program for Elderly, Milw., 1977-78; nursing specialist employment and tng. project U. Wis.-Milw. Sch. Allied Health Professions, 1978-79; teaching asst. U. Wis.-Milw. Sch. Edn., 1979-82; asst. prof. dept. nursing Ball State U., Muncie, Ind., 1982-84; program coord. Sigma Theta Tau, Indpls., 1984-86; asst. prof. Coll. Nursing Mich. State U., East Lansing, 1986—; nurse, mobile examiner Nat. Med. Cons. Inc./Kimberly Nurses, Milw., 1977; nurse counselor Weight Loss Clinic Am., Milw., 1977; gerontol. nurse Dr. and Mrs. Josef Kindwall, Milw., 1978-79; cons. Med. Coll. Wis., Office Continuing Edn., Milw., 1979-80, Interfaith Program for Elderly, Milw., 1978-79, Spotlight Theatre, 1989-90. Editor: (with R.M. Barnard and J. Fawcett) Directory of Nurse Researchers, 2d edit., 1987; contbr. articles to profl. jours.; cast mem. in community theater prodns., 1988-89. Soprano soloist Ind. Renaissance Fair, 1983; recording sec. Unitarian Universalist Ch. of Lansing, 1986-87, bd. mem., 1988, v.p. bd. trustees, 1989; mem. Greater Lansing Quest for Peace Com., 1987; mem. Grand Ledge Spotlight Theatre, Inc. Actor's Workshop, 1988—; grant devel. cons., 1989. Mem. Am. Assn. Adult and Continuing Edn. (mem. speakers bur. 1987-88), Am. Nurses Assn. (coun. continuing edn. 1986—, Mich. Nurses Assn. (coun. on continuing edn. 1986—, continuing edn. adv. com. 1989), Self-Directed Learning Network, Nat. League Nursing, Soc. Rsch. in Edn., Midwest Nursing Rsch. Soc., Phi Delta Kappa, Sigma Theta Tau (chartering officer 1990). Home: 1027 Seymour Lansing MI 48906

KIENKER, KAREN ANN, physical medicine and rehabilitation physician; b. Kansas City, Mo., Apr. 26, 1951; d. Kenneth Louis and Norma Clare (Innes) K. BA, Cen. Meth. Coll., 1973; MD, U. Ill., Rockford, 1977. Diplomate Am. Bd. Phys. Medicine and Rehab. Intern Columbus-Cuneo-Cabrini Med. Ctr., Chgo., 1978; resident in phys. medicine and rehab. Rehab. Inst. Chgo., 1978-81; instr. U. Wis. Hosp. and Clinics, Madison, 1981-82, asst. prof., 1982-84; staff physiatrist Iowa Meth. Med. Ctr., Des Moines, 1984—. Coord. Foster Parents Plan Vol. Support Group 204, Des Moines, 1987—. Fellow Am. Acad. Phys. Medicine and Rehab.; mem. Am. Congress Rehab. Medicine, Am. Pain Soc., Altrusa (rec. sec. Des Moines, 1987-88). Democrat. Unitarian. Home: 8892 Summit Clive IA 50325 Office: Iowa Meth Med Ctr 1200 Pleasant St Y310 Des Moines IA 50309

KIER, ANN B., pathology educator; b. Littlefield, Tex., June 26, 1949; d. Robert Merlin and Martha (Bond) Yarbrough; m. Friedhelm Schroeder, Dec. 9, 1978; 1 child, Hilary. BA, U. Tex., 1971; BS, Tex. A&M U., 1973, DVM, 1974; PhD, U. Mo., 1979. Diplomate, Am. Coll. Lab. Animal Medicine. NIH postdoctoral fellow U. Mo., Columbia, 1976-79; asst. prof. U. Mo., 1979-84, assoc. prof., 1984-87; assoc. prof. dept. pathology U. Cin. Med. Sch., 1978—, dir. histopathology lab., 1988—; cons. NIH, Washington, 1983—, Comparative Pathology, Frann Sci., Cin., 1987—. Contbr. to numerous sci. publs. Grantee NIH, 1980—. Mem. Am. Assn. Pathologists, AAAS, Am. Assn. Lab. Animal Sci. Home: 134 Wrenwood Ln Terrace Park OH 45174 Office: Dept Pathology U Cin 231 Bethesda Ave Cincinnati OH 45267-0529

KIERNAN, M. C. (CASEY KIERNAN), science policy analyst, biologist; b. Albany, N.Y., Mar. 7, 1956; d. Peter Delacy and Mary Agnes (Reilly) K. BS, Georgetown U., 1979, MS, 1981, MPhil, 1982; PhD in Biology, Yale U., 1984. Phys. scientist EPA, Annapolis, Md., 1979; sr. interferon technician Meloy Labs., Springfield, Va., 1980; instr. gen. biology Yale U., New Haven, 1981-82, instr. advanced cell biology and electron microscopy, 1982; instr. plant physiology U. Minn., 1984; program officer Govt.-Univ.-Industry Rsch. Roundtable, Nat. Acad. Scis., Washington, 1984-88; sr. program officer NAS, Washington, 1988—. Grantee NIH, 1980-84, Am. Cancer Soc., 1982. Mem. AAAS, N.Y. Acad., Scis. Home: 6205 N 22d St Arlington VA 22205 Office: NAS 2101 Constitution Ave Washington DC 20418

KIES, CONSTANCE VIRGINIA, nutrition educator, scientist; b. Blue River, Wis., Dec. 13, 1934; d. Guerdon Francis and Gertrude Caroline (Pitts) K. BS, U. Wis., Platteville, 1955, MS, U. Wis., Madison, 1960, PhD, 1963. Lic. dietitian, Tex.; lic. tchr., Wis. English tchr. Rothschild-Schofield area schs., Wis., 1955-56; tchr., librarian Pontage High Sch., Wis., 1956-58; research asst. U. Wis., Madison, 1960-63; dietition instr. Madison Gen. Hosp., Wis., 1960-63; asst. prof. U. Nebr., Lincoln, 1963-65, assoc. prof., 1965-68, prof. human nutrition, 1968—. Editor: Bioavailability of Iron, 1983, Bioavailability of Calcium, 1985, Bioavailability of Manganese, 1987, Bioavailability of Copper, 1990, Plant Foods for Human Nutrition; contbr. articles to profl. jours. Recipient Disting. Alumni award U. Wis., 1974. Grantee Ross-Abbott Labs., 1982. Mem. Am. Chem. Soc. (Dinsting. Svc. award 1987), Inst. Nutrition, Soc. for Clin. Nutrition, Am. Assn. Cereal Chemists, Am. Dietetics Assn. (registered dietitian), Am. Oil Chemists Assn., Soc. Enteral and Parenteral Nutrition, Am. Home Econs. Assn. (Borden award 1973). Congregationalist. Home: 3341 Holdredge Apt 9 Lincoln NE 68503

KIESEL, MARJORIE JEAN, accountant; b. L.I., N.Y., Jan. 14, 1960; d. George and Grace (Mast) Kiesel. BS summa cum laude, SUNY, Plattsburgh, 1982; MBA, Pace U., 1986. Cert. mgmt. acct. Mgr. IBM, Tarrytown, N.Y., mgmt. acct. Mem. NAFE, Nat. Assn. Accts., Am. Mgmt. Assn.. Home: 18 Circle Dr Aqua Vista Danbury CT 06811 Office: 540 White Plains Rd Tarrytown NY 10592

KIESLING, JUANITA HASELOFF, real estate broker; b. Vernon, TX, Jan. 23, 1935; d. Herbert Karl and Ottilie Rose (Obenhaus) H.; m. Ernst Willie Kiesling, Aug. 25, 1956; children: Carol, Chris, Max. BBA, Tex. Tech U., 1957, MBA, 1974. Instr. Tex. Tech U., Lubbock, 1971-76; real estate agt. Land and Assocs., Lubbock, 1977-80; owner, broker Chapman South, Realtors, Lubbock, 1980-82, Nita Kiesling, Realtors, Lubbock, 1982-88; adminstrv. mgr. WestMark, Realtors, Lubbock, 1988—; Bd. dirs. Lubbock Housing Fin. Corp. Bd. dirs. Am. Heart Assn., Lubbock, 1985-86; chmn. adv. council Lutheran Social Service, Lubbock, 1986-87; dir. Caprock Girl Scouts Council, Lubbock, 1984-88; com. chair Citizens Adv. Com. for Capital Improvements, Lubbock, 1985-86; budget div. United Way, Lubbock, 1986-88. Mem. Lubbock Bd. Realtors (Realtor of Yr. award 1986, chmn. bd. 1990), Tex. Assn. Realtors (chmn. fin. procedures com., mgmt. adv. com. 1986, bd. dirs. 1989—), Sales Execs. Assn. (bd. dirs. 1983-84), Lubbock C. of C. (com. mem. 1982—), Toastmasters, Soroptimists (pres. 1987-88). Home: 4912 94th St Lubbock TX 79424 Office: West Mark Realtors 7008 Indiana Lubbock TX 79413

KIESSEL, RUTH ANN, social worker; b. Cleve., Aug. 6, 1945; d. Arthur and Ruth Ann (Engelhart) Kistemaker; m. Richard Joseph Kiessel, Mar. 22, 1968; children: Kristine Marie, Debora Renee. BA, Wittenberg U., Springfield, Ohio, 1967; postgrad., Smith Coll., Northampton, Mass., 1967-68; MSW, U. Md., Balt., 1980; postgrad., Frostburg (Md.) State U., 1988. Group facilitator Alcohol Safety Action Program, Fairfax, Va., 1981-83; residential program coordinator Family Svc. of Montgomery County, Gaithersburg, Md., 1981-83, group facilitator, 1983-87, coordinator svcs. for srs. program, 1983—; guest lectr. Cath. U., Washington, 1982-83; BSW field supr. Hood Coll., Frederick, Md., 1981-82; MSW field supr. Cath. U., Washington, 1985-87, U. Md., Balt., 1988-89; mem. Study Group on Mental Health on Elderly, Montgomery County, 1988; mem. long-term care com., Montgomery County, 1986; mem. Up-county Sr. Svcs., Coordinators Com., 1986—; mem. Coordinating Com. for Housing for Handicapped Individuals, 1983; mem. ind. living com. Montgomery County Commn. on Handicapped Individuals. Convenor, organizer Coalition on Mental Health Srs., Montgomery County, 1989; rep. project home oversight com. Md. Assn. Psycho-Social Svcs., 1983. Recipient Cert. of Appreciation, Widowed Persons Svc., Md., 1988. Mem. Nat. Assn. Social Workers, Alzheimer's Disease and Related Disorders Assn., Older Women's League, Mental Health Assn., Md. Gerontol. Assn., League Women Voters, Psi Chi (sec. 1966-67). Office: Family Svc Montgomery 1 W Deer Park Rd Gaithersburg MD 20877

KIGGINS, MILDRED L., telemarketing firm executive; b. Hempstead, N.Y., Sept. 14, 1927; d. Wolfgang and Hannah Ingeborg (Olsson) Weissmann; m. Andrew Edward Kiggins, Jan. 8, 1962 (div. 1982); children: Daniel

Mark, David Bruce. Diploma, Donovan Bus. Coll., Hackensack, N.J., 1945, Luther Coll. Acad., 1947. Exec. sec. Am. Machine & Foundry Inc., Stamford, Conn., 1954-61; telemktg. rep. Adult Independence Devel. Ctr., 1977—, Harry Schoenfeld Ins. Services & Design, Los Gatos, Calif., 1985—; sec. Salois & Parrott, Cert. Shorthand Reporters, 1985—. Tchr. Sunday sch. St. John's Lutheran Ch., Stamford, 1948-50. Mem. Nat. Assn. Female Execs. Republican. Avocations: gardening, music, sports, church activities. Home: 4644 Pinto River Ct San Jose CA 95136

KIIHR, ELIZABETH MARIE, automotive product/process engineer; b. Dayton, Ohio, Feb. 16, 1963; d. Michael Vito and Sandra Lee (Barsalou) Donisi; m. Thomas John Kiihr Jr., Sept. 17, 1988. BSEE, GM Inst., 1986; postgrad., U. Mich., 1989—. Mfg. and machine controls engr. Delco Products, GM, Dayton, 1986-87, prodn. supr., 1987-88; sr. process engr. Kelsey-Hayes Co., Fenton, Mich., 1988-89; future devel. engr. AC Rochester, GM, Flint, Mich., 1989—. Adviser Jr. Achievement, 1986-88. Recipient Outstanding Young Citizen award, 1981. Mem. NAFE, Soc. Mfg. Engrs., Coll. Alummi (class sec. 1989—), Alpha Sigma Alpha. Office: AC Rochester GM 300 N Chevrolet Ave Flint MI 48555

KILBANE, ADRIENNE F., small business owner; b. Chgo., Jan. 19, 1933; d. Herbert E. and Edna M.(Qualmann) Seyring; m. Robert H. Kilbane, Feb. 24, 1951 (div. 1974); children: Robbyn Kilbane McFadden, Lawrence H., Gregory A., David J. AA, Lake County Jr. Coll., 1981; BA, Barat Coll., 1984. Lic. real estate Ill. Med. asst. Med. Office, Grayslake, Ill., 1960-70; treas. sch. dist., sec. to supt. Spaulding Sch. Dist. 58, Waukegan, Ill., 1970-74; sec. sch. fin. office Highland Park (Ill.) Dist. #108, 1974-83; asst. to dir. Waukegan Pk. Dist., 1983-84; assoc. real estate Corder Realty, Waukegan, 1978—; pres., owner Ice Cream Harbor Inc., Waukegan, 1984—. Pres. PTO, Waukegan, 1963-64; leader Girl Scouts Am., Waukegan, 1958-63; den mother Boy Scouts Am., 1962-71; active Big Bros./Big Sisters, U. Ill. Coop. Extension Svc.; bd. dirs. 4-H. Mem. Art Inst. Chgo., Lincoln Pk. Zool. Soc., Nat. Assn. Realtors, NAFE, Nat. Assn. Prevention Cruety Animals, Am. Cancer Inst., World Wildlife Fund, No. Ill. Tourism Council, Ill. Conv. and Tourism Bur., Waukegan Lake County C. of C. (bd. dirs.), Altrusa Internat., Exchange Club, Duck's Unltd., Phi Theta Kappa. Republican. Lutheran. Home: 605 Frolic Ave Waukegan IL 60085

KILBOURN, JOAN PRISCILLA, microbiologist; b. Portland, Oreg., June 15, 1936; d. Jesse W. and Iris M. (Chenoweth) Payne; m. Lee Ferris Kilbourn, June 11, 1961; children: Laurie Jane, Ellen Mae. BS in Gen. Sci., U. Oreg., 1958, MS in Microbiology, 1960; PhD in Microbiology, Oreg. State U., 1963. Grad. rsch. asst. microbiology dept. Oreg. State U., Corvallis, 1961-63; instr. biology dept. U. Oreg., Eugene, 1963-66; rsch. assoc. pediatrics dept. U. Oreg., 1966-68; tutor sci. and math., GED program Portland Community Coll. Adult Lit. Project, 1968-80; med. technologist and environ. surveillance officer VA Hosp., Portland, 1971-74; assoc. dir. biology svcs. ICN Med. Labs., Inc., 1974-76; instr. div. continuing edn. Portland State U., 1977, Clackamas Community Coll., 1978, Physicians Med. Lab., 1979, 81; dir. vaccine rsch. Willamette Lab., 1980-82; lab. dir. Miracle Med. Lab., 1979-84; lab. dir., owner Cons. Clin. and Microbiol. Lab., Inc., Portland, 1984—; instr. clin. pathology U. Oreg. Med. Sch., 1973-74; rsch. cons., 1976—; adv. Nat. Com. for Clin. Lab. Standards, also observer; cons. CHOICE; microbiology time study vol. Coll. Am. Pathologists; mem. adv. bd. NW Sci. Exposition, 1988—. Reviewer Current Microiology jour., Sci. Software Quarterly jour., other sci. books and films; vol. editorial bd. Dictionary of Microbiology; contbr. numerous articles to profl. jours.; patentee in field. Chmn. Mary Dimond Scholarship Fund, Lewis and Clark Coll. Recipient 3 Recognition awards Am. Soc. Clin. Pathologists for Continuing Med. Lab. Edn.; grantee Portland VA Hosp., Flow Labs., Inc., Wampole Labs. div. Carter-Wallace, Inc., Hoffmann-LaRoche, Inc., Gen. Diagnostics. Mem. AAAS (reviewer sci. books, films), Am. Soc. Microbiology, Nat. Registry Microbiologists, Am. Soc. Clin. Pathologists, Assn. Advancement Med. Instrumentation, N.Y. Acad. Sci., Assn. Women in Sci., Sigma Xi, Iota Sigma Pi (chmn. Dr. Marie Berg Scholarship Fund), Sigma Delta Epsilon. Democrat. Episcopalian. Home: 3178 SW Fairmount Blvd Portland OR 97201 Office: Cons Clin and Microbiol Lab Inc 1033 SW Yamhill St Profl Bldg Ste 101 Portland OR 97205

KILBOURNE, BARBARA JEAN, health and human services executive; b. Milw., Mar. 21, 1941; d. Burton Conwell and Marjorie Janet (Tufts) K.; m. Kenneth Keith Kauffman, Feb. 10, 1962 (div. 1983). BA, U. Minn., 1972; MBA, Coll. St. Thomas, St. Paul, 1980. Adminstr. Ebenezer Soc., Mpls., 1974-85; v.p., dir. housing Walker Residence and Health Svcs., Inc., Mpls., 1985-88; exec. v.p. Oblate Ministries Health and Aging, West St. Paul, Minn., 1988—; bd. dirs. Westminster Resident Svcs. Corp., St. Paul, 1990—, River Region Health Svcs., Red Wing, Minn., 1990—, Sr. Housing, Inc., Mpls., 1986—, Ancilla Health Sys., Chgo., 1990—; pres. Tekakwitha Nursing Home, Sisseton, S.D., Apt. Community Our Lady of the Snows, Belleville, Ill., Madonna Towers, Rochester, Minn.; cons., speaker in field; mem. commn. on aging Cath. Charities USA, Washington, 1989—; presenter workshops, symposia. Author: Family Councils in Nursing Homes, 1981. Chair bd. dirs. Dakota, Inc., Eagan, Minn., 1985—; project chair Dialog 2000, Dakota County, Minn., 1988—. Mem. Minn. Assn. Homes for Aging (treas. 1984-86, bd. dirs. 1977-86, 89—), Gerontol. Soc. Am. Republican. Episcopalian. Home: 416 S 5th St Stillwater MN 55082 Office: Oblate Ministries Health and Aging Ste 212 60 E Marie St West Saint Paul MN 55118

KILCUP, CLARA GRIEGO, desktop publishing business owner; b. Albuquerque, Sept. 2, 1960; d. Henry and Filomena (Sanchez) Griego; m. Glen William Kilcup, Sept. 12, 1986. BA in Psychology and French, Willamette U., 1982. Lic. real estate agt. English asst. Ministère de l'Education, Lycée le Castel, Dijon, France, 1982-83; program dir. La Pasada Halfway House, Albuquerque, 1983-86; owner The Written Image, Albuquerque, 1987—. Mem. Nat. Alliance Homebased Businesswomen, Albuquerque Women in Bus., Mac Women, Phi Sigma Iota, Psi Chi. Democrat. Office: The Written Image 920 Gold Ave SW Albuquerque NM 87102

KILGORE, BERNICE JEWELENE, teacher; b. Troup, Tex., Aug. 1, 1918; d. Bonnie Bess and Fannie Bell (Thompson) Ross; m. Berry Bannon Kilgore, Aug. 16, 1947; children: Judy Lynn, Berry Micheal. BA, Tex. Coll., 1950; MA, Tex. So. U., 1958. Tchr. Olney (Tex.) Pub. Schs., 1941-43; prin. Quanah (Tex.) Pub. Schs., 1943-46; tchr. Monahans (Tex.) Pub. Schs., 1946-47; head tchr. Kermit (Tex.) Pub. Schs., 1947-65, tchr. history and geography, 1965-81, substitute tchr., 1981-83, ret., 1981. Author poems and poetry; writer musical ballards: Shady Lane, You Won's Get Away From Me. Founder Jr. Historians, Kermit, 1971-81; sec. Community Civic Club, Kermit, 1987—; del. Dem. State Conv., Houston, 1988; vol. Nursing Ctr., Kermit, 1986-89. Mem. Tex. Ret. Tchrs. Assn., Am. Assn. Ret. Persons, Nat. Ret. Tchrs. Assn., Friends of Edn., Nat. Council of Social Studies. Democrat. Home: 531 North Ave B Kermit TX 79745

KILGORE, CATHERINE C., economic geologist, researcher; b. Los Angeles, Dec. 25, 1956; d. Donald Evan and Elsie Ellen (Walden) Cook; m. Thomas Jefferson Kilgore, III, Aug. 5, 1978; 1 child, Devin Walden. BS in Geology, Fort Lewis Coll., 1978; postgrad. in mineral econs. Colo. Sch. Mines, 1981-82. Geologist U.S. Geol. Survey, Denver, 1979, Colo. Dept. Health, Denver, 1979-80, U.S. Bur. Mines, Denver, 1980-88, supervisory minerals specialist, 1988—. Author info. circulars, articles. Recipient spl. achievement award U.S. Bur. Mines, 1983, 86. Mem. Soc. Mining Engrs. (session chmn. 1986). Avocations: stained glass art, gourmet cooking. Office: US Bur Mines MAFO Bldg 20 Denver Fed Ctr Denver CO 80225

KILGORE, KATHERINE GAYLE, small business owner; b. Pound, Va., Nov. 26, 1945; d. Woodrow W. and Florence Elizabeth (Sturgill) Adams; m. James D. Kilgore, Oct. 19, 1968 (div. Oct. 1986); children: Christopher D., Sean Patrick. BS, East Tenn. State U., 1968. Tchr. Wise County Schs., Va., 1968-69; prodn. typist Thompson & Litton, Inc., Wise, 1970-76, word processing supr., 1976-78, contract specialist, specifications writer, 1978-88; prin. K. Gayle Kilgore Cons. Svcs., Wise, 1988—. Adminsitr. Adams Scholarship Fund; treas. J.J. Kelly Quarterback Club; active various youth community activities. Mem. Order Eastern Star. Baptist. Avocations: reading, roller skating, walking, embroidery. Home: PO Box 1284 219 Spring Ave Wise VA 24293 Office: K Gayle Kilgore Cons Svcs Box 889 219 Spring Ave Wise VA 24293

KILGROW, JULIE MAYNES, state agency director; b. Huron, S.D., Nov. 9, 1940; d. Charles William and Almira Rose (Summers) Maynes; m. Alan R. Gardner, Jan. 1, 1985; children: Julie Katharine, Jennifer Worth, John Charles. BS in Edn., U. Utah, 1962. Cert. secondary tchr., Utah. Tchr. Evergreen Jr. High Sch., Salt Lake City, 1962-63; with fin. devel. dept. YWCA, Boise, Idaho, 1979-82; v.p. mktg. 1st Security Bank, Boise, 1982-87; dir. Dept. Employment State of Idaho, Boise, 1987—; v.p., cons. bus. Channel Enterprises, Inc., Boise, 1985—. Pres. Boise Jr. league, 1977, Boise Allied Arts, 1978, United Way Ada County, 1980; mem. 2nd century com. United Way Am., Arlington, Va., 1986; chair Mayor's Blue Ribbon Com. Urban Devel., Boise, 1985; bd. trustees Boise Stae U., 1986; bd. dirs. Interconf. of Employment, 1986. Mem. Crane Country Club. Democrat. Episcopalian. Home: 2057 White Pine Ln Boise ID 83706

KILHAM, SUSAN SOLTAU, aquatic ecologist; b. Duluth, Minn., Jan. 22, 1943; d. Edward Henry and Charlotte Mae (Gustafson) Soltau; m. Peter Kilham, Sept. 4 1967 (dec. 1989). BS, Eckerd Coll., St. Petersburg, Fla., 1965; PhD, Duke U., 1971. Teaching asst. Duke U., Durham, N.C., 1965-67; rsch. assoc. Duke U., 1970-71; guest investigator Woods Hole Oceanographic Inst., Woods Hole, Mass., 1972, 79-80; lectr. U. Mich., Ann Arbor, 1973; asst. rsch. scientist U. Mich., 1973-80, vis. assoc. prof., 1989-90, assoc. rsch. scientist, 1980—. Editorial bd Jour. Great Lakes Rsch., 1981-83, Limnology and Oceanography, 1988—; contbr. articles to profl. jours. NSF oceanographic traineeship, 1967-70; recipient McArthur Alumnus award, Eckerd Coll., 1977; Max Planck Soc. scholar, 1988. Mem. Am. Soc. Limnology and Oceanography, Phycol. Soc. Am., Internat. Soc. Theoretical and Applied Limnology, Internat. Assn. for Great Lakes Rsch., AAAS, Ecol. Soc. Am., Internat. Soc. Diatom Rsch., Internat. Phycol. Soc. Home: 812 Duncan St Ann Arbor MI 48103 Office: University of Michigan Dept Biology Ann Arbor MI 48109-1048

KILKEARY, NAN M., communications specialist; b. Evergreen Park, Ill., Sept. 17, 1943; d. Robert M. and Barbara E. (Bailey) Lundberg; m. William P. Kilkeary, Dec. 17, 1966 (div. Aug. 1978); children—Timothy T., Christopher K. B.S., U. Ill., 1965; postgrad. U. Chgo., 1974-75. Editor, UPI Broadcast, Chgo., 1966-67, 69; asst. mgr. press relations CNA, Chgo., 1971-74; account supr. Harshe-Rotman & Druck, Chgo., 1974-76; dir. communications Allstate, Northbrook, Ill., 1976-81; v.p. communications Investors Diversified Services, Mpls., 1981-82; dir. communications Montgomery Ward, Chgo., 1982-85; pres. Kilkeary Communications, 1985—; pres. Quik Read, 1987—; sr. v.p. mktg. communications and strategic planning Wieboldt Stores, Inc., Chgo., 1986-87; owner, mgr. O'Rourke's Pub., Chgo., 1966-75. Author: The Good Communicator, 1987; contbr. articles to profl. jours. Founder, Ill. Housewives for ERA, Evanston, Ill., 1972; bd. dirs. New City YMCA. Recipient Golden Trumpet, Publicity Club Chgo., 1975, 79, 80, Shaunessy award, 1979, 80; Pres. award Internat. Assn. Bus. Communicators, 1979. Mem. Pub. Relations Soc. Am. (silver anvil 1977, 79), Nat. Investor Relations Inst. (chpt. dir. 1975-80), Women in Communications. Democrat. Unitarian. Club: Carleton.

KILKELLY, MARJORIE LEE, state legislator; b. Hartford, Conn., Dec. 1, 1954; d. Bruce Hamilton and Corlys Lucille (Lux) Brewer; children: Jeffrey Jr., Robert, Sarah A.E. BS in Human Services, N.H. Coll., 1986, MS in Community Econ. Devel., 1986. Asst. to dir. Lincoln County Summer Youth Employment Program, Wiscasset, Maine, 1978; coordinator Community Food & Nutrition Program Coastal Enterprises, Inc., Wiscasset, 1978-79, Coastal Econ. Devel. Corp., Wiscasset, 1979-80; dir. Head Start Program Coastal Econ. Devel. Corp., Bath, Maine, 1980-84; asst. instr. N.H. Coll., Manchester, 1985-86; dir. Jr. Tots Wiscasset Recreation Program, 1985-88; dir. food services Boothbay Sch. Dept., Boothbay Harbor, Maine, 1985-88; owner Hurricane Hill Catering Co., Wiscasset, 1989—; elected mem. 114th Legis. State of Maine, 1988—; treas. Coastal Enterprises Inc., Rundlet Block, Wis., 1981—; rep. to Internat. Conf. on Econ. Devel., New Delhi, 1983—. Former mem. Blaine House Conf. on Families Planning Com., 1979-80; active Maine Human Services Council Sta. 23, Augusta, Maine, 1980-88; Sunday sch. tchr., lecter. St. Philips Episcopal Ch., Wiscasset, 1984-85; chair coordinating com. St. Philips Food Bank, 1986-88; chair Wis. Dem. Com., 1986—; nat. chmn. schs. S.O.S. Nat. Hunger Awareness Program, Denver, 1986—; elected mem. 113th Legis. State of Maine, 1986—, 114th Legis., 1988, candidate 115th Legis., 1990. New England Rural fellow, Coun. State Govts. Toll fellow; grantee Maine Welfare Edn. Employment Tng. Program, 1983. Mem. Bus. and Profl. Women (Maine Young Career Woman award 1989), Huntoon Hill Grange Club, Lincoln County Pamona Grange Club, Sportsmans Alliance Club of Maine. Democrat. Episcopalian. Clubs: B.P.W. (Damariscotta, Maine); CONA (Newcastle, Maine). Home: W Alna Rd PO Box 180 Wiscasset ME 04578 Office: Maine Ho Reps Augusta ME 04333

KILLACKEY, DOROTHY HELEN, educator, real estate professional; b. Pitts., Mar. 29, 1927; d. Edward G. and Dorothy Marie (Krauss) Buschow; m. Feb. 5, 1949 (div. Sept. 1985); children: Thomas, Maureen, Nancy, Edward. BA, Columbia U., 1948; MS, Western Conn. State U., Danbury, 1971; 6th Yr. Profl. Deg., Western Conn. State U., 1980. Tchr. Brewster (N.Y.) pub. schs., 1965-89; tchr. title I summer sch. Govt. Title I, Brewster, 1973-80; from real estate salesman to broker Spectra Realty, Brewster, 1983—; ch. parochial bd. dirs. St. Lawrence O'Toole Ch., Brewster, 1974-76; pres. J.F. Kennedy Sch. Union, Brewster, 1975-77. Nancy Barrelle scholar Western Conn. State U., 1979. Mem. Phi Delta Kappa, Delta Kappa Gamma. Home: 401 Stonewall Ln Brewster NY 10509

KILLE, MARY JEAN, realtor; b. Boyd, Wis., Aug. 7, 1937; d. Izola (Gillis) Lorenz; m. Patrick David Kille, June 30, 1956 (div. Jan. 1977); children: Cindy, Steve, Bob, Ben, Jennifer. Salesperson Wiebolts Dept. Store, Waukegan, Ill., 1971-72; owner Florist & Wholesale, Mundelein, Ill., 1972-78; realtor Baird & Warner, Libertyville, Ill., 1979-82, Merrill Lynch, Libertyville, 1982-87, RE-MAX Suburban, Inc., Libertyville, 1987—. Mem. Nat. Assn. Realtors, Ill. Assn. Realtors. Home: 18865 Linden Ave Grayslake IL 60030

KILLEA, LUCY LYTLE, state legislator; b. San Antonio, July 31, 1922; d. Nelson and Zelime (Pettus) Lytle; B.A., Incarnate Word Coll., San Antonio, 1943; M.A. in History, U. San Diego, 1966; Ph.D. in History, U. Calif., San Diego, 1975; m. John F. Killea, May 11, 1946; children: Paul, Jay. Research analyst for Western Europe, Army Intelligence, Spl. Br., Washington, 1944-48; adminstrv. asst. Dept. State, London, 1946; econ. officer Econ. Coop. Adminstrn., The Hague, Netherlands, 1949; research analyst CIA, Washington, 1948-56; part time book reviewer USIS, 1956-60; teaching and research asst. U. Calif., San Diego, 1967-72; exec. dir., exec. v.p. Fronteras de las Californias, San Diego, 1974-78; mem. City Council, San Diego, 1978-82, dep. mayor, 1982, mem. planning commn., 1978; mem. Calif. State Assembly, 1982-89; mem. Calif. State Senate, 1989—; lectr. socioeconomics of Baja, Calif. and Mex., Southwestern Coll., Chula-Vista, 1976; lectr. dept. history San Diego State U., 1976-77; participant, organizer, panelist, moderator confs. in field, U.S., Mex.; mem. Palm City Sanitation Dist., 1978-82, Met. Transit Devel. Bd., 1978-82. Regional Employment and Tng. Consortium Bd., 1978-80, City-County Reinvestment Task Force, 1978-80. Bd. trustees San Diego Zoöl. Soc., 1976-78; mem. San Diego County Cultural Heritage Com., 1971-78, vice chmn., 1973-75; mem. Hist. Site Bd., City San Diego, 1968-75, vice chmn., 1971-75; bd. dirs. San Diego Hist. Soc., 1971-77; chmn. Internat. Com. Conv. and Visitors Bur., 1978, host com., 1976-77; adv. bd. Sharp Hosp.; bd. dirs., com. mem. Friends of Library, U. Calif., San Diego; founding mem. Caridad Internacional; mem. James S. Copley Library Adv. Council, U. San Diego, 1981—; active community orgns. including LWV, Fine Arts Soc. San Diego, YWCA, San Diego Mus. Art, San Diego Chpt. ARC, Dimensions, Aardvarks Ltd., Pacific Beach Hist. Soc., San Diego Symphonic Assn. Research grantee, Justice Found., 1965, U. Calif., San Diego, 1971; recipient awards, Conf. Calif. Hist. Socs., 1966, Inst. for Protection of Children, City of Tijuana and Tijuana Com., 1966, Alice Paul Award, Nat. Women's Polit. Caucus, 1982; named one of 12 Women of Valor, Beth Israel Sisterhood of Temple Beth Israel, San Diego, 1966, Woman of Accomplishment, Bus. and Profl. Clubs. San Diego, 1979, Woman of Yr., San Diego Irish Congress, 1981; honored Leukemia Soc., 1980; named alumna of distinction Incarnate Word Coll., San Antonio, 1981. Mem. Nat. Women's Polit. Caucus, Calif., Women in Bus., Mus. Photog. Arts, San Diego Arts Center, Nat. Trust Historic Preservation, San Diego Hist. Soc. (life), San Diego County Congress of History, Travelers Aid Soc., Navy League, Vietnam Vets. Assn. Mid City C. of C., San Diego C. of C., Nat. Assn. State Legislatures, NCCJ, World Affairs Council, Am. Fgn. Service Assn., Incarnate Word Alumnae Assn., U. San Diego Alumni Assn., U. Calif. San Diego Alumni and Friends, Calif. Elected Women's Assn. for Edn. and Research (bd. 1980-85, sec., treas., 1980-81, v.p. 1982-85). Democrat. Roman Catholic. Clubs: Catfish, Army-Navy (Arlington, Va.). Contbr. writings to publs. in field. Office: State Capitol Rm 4062 Sacramento CA 95814

KILLEBREW, ELLEN JANE (MRS. EDWARD S. GRAVES), cardiologist; b. Tiffin, Ohio, Oct. 8, 1937; d. Joseph Arthur and Stephanie (Berlont) K.; B.S. in Biology, Bucknell U., 1959; M.D., N.J. Coll. Medicine, 1965; m. Edward S. Graves, Sept. 12, 1970. Intern, U. Colo., 1965-66, resident 1966-68; cardiology fellow Pacific Med. Center, San Francisco, 1968-70; dir. coronary care, Permanent Med. Group, Richmond, Calif., 1970-83; asst. prof. U. Calif. Med. Center, San Francisco, 1970-83, assoc. prof., 1983—. Robert C. Kirkwood Meml. scholar in cardiology, 1970; recipient Physician's Recognition award continuing med. edn. Diplomate in cardiovascular disease Am. Bd. Internal Medicine. Fellow ACP, Am. Coll. Cardiology: mem. Fedn. Clin. Research, Am. Heart Assn. (research chmn. Contra Costa chpt. 1975—, v.p. 1980, pres. chpt. 1981-82, chm. CPR com. Alameda chpt. 1984). Home: 30 Redding Ct Tiburon CA 94920 Office: 280 W MacArthur Blvd Oakland CA 94611

KILLEN, MELANIE ANN, assistant professor of psychology; b. Berkeley, Calif., Sept. 11, 1957; d. Duncan Campbell Killen and Marcia Nadine Savin. BA, Clark U., 1978; MA, U. Calif., Berkeley, 1982, PhD, 1985. Asst. prof. psychology Wesleyan U., Middletown, Conn., 1985—; vis. faculty fellow Yale U., New Haven, 1990-91; Mellon faculty fellow Wesleyan U., Middletown, 1987; panel rev. mem. Am. Ednl. Rsch. Assn. Contbr. chpts. to books and articles to profl. jours. Recipient Founder Region fellowship Soroptimist Internat. Am., Berkeley, 1984, Chancellor's Patent fund Chancellor U. Calif., Berkeley, 1984, Spencer grant Spencer Found., Chgo., 1989-90, Pedagogical Devel. grant Pres. Wesleyan U., Middletown, 1990-91. Mem. Soc. Rsch. in Child Devel., Jean Piaget Soc., Am. Psychol. Assn. Office: Wesleyan U Dept Psychology Middletown CT 06457

KILLEN-WOLF, ANNE, marketing professional; b. Carlisle, Eng., July 16, 1959; came to U.S., 1963; d. John Killen and Maureen (Diamond) McRae. BA, Calif. State U., Long Beach, 1982. Asst. br. mgr. Orange Micro, Anaheim, Calif., 1982-83, br. mgr., 1983, internat. sales mgr., 1983-84, mktg. mgr., 1984-85; sales rep. Sperry Corp., Orange, Calif., 1985-86; account mgr. UNISYS (formerly Sperry Corp.), L.A., 1986-88; mgr. strategic programs Hughes Aircraft Corp., L.A., 1988-89; edn. devel. mgr. Apple Computer, Inc., Newport Beach, Calif., 1989—. Vol. Youth Motivation Task Force, L.A., 1988—, Make-A-Wish Found., L.A., 1987—; mem. Commn. on Child Pornography and Obscenity, L.A., 1988. Mem. Gamma Phi Beta (advisor 1984-85). Office: Apple Computer Inc 18301 Von Karmen Ste 1000 Irvine CA 92714

KILLIAN, IRIS LOUISE, human resources executive; b. Hickory, N.C., Aug. 28, 1962; d. James Clinton and Dorothy Louise (Booker) K. BS in Pub. Health, U. N.C., 1984; MBA, Duke U., 1986. Tutor, counselor U. N.C., Chapel Hill, 1981-84; tng. specialist Siecor Corp., Hickory, N.C., 1986-87; prodn. supr. Siecor Corp., Hickory, 1987-89, employee involvement facilitator, supr. telephony cable plant tng. and devel., 1989—; assoc. Am. Med. Internat., Atlanta, 1985. Mem. Community Rels. Coun., Hickory, 1987—, Lead Program Adv. Com., Durham, N.C., 1986—, Mfg. Resources Planning Adv. Com., Morganton, N.C., 1988—; organist Clinton Tabernacle African Meth. Episcopal Ch., Hickory, 1978—. Mem. Nat. Black MBA Assn. Methodist. Home: 656 First Ave SE Hickory NC 28602

KILLIANY, CATHERINE ANN, home entertainment rental executive; b. Cambridge, Ohio, Feb. 9, 1957; d. Anthony Henry and Barbara Jane (VanAman) Kruk; m. David Andrew Killiany, July 14, 1975; children: Jason Andrew, Joseph Anthony, Connie Marie. Owner, mgr. Uncle Dave's Family Entertainment Ctr., Cambridge, 1986—; exec. v.p. Rententertainment Concepts, Inc., Cambridge, 1988-89. Home: 4985 Skyline Dr Cambridge OH 43725 Office: Rententertainment Concepts Inc 500 S 9th St Cambridge OH 43725

KILLINGBECK, LINDA ANN, financial analyst; b. New Haven, Conn., Feb. 7, 1961; d. Rowland R. and Ethel M. (Belfanc) K. BA, Yale U, 1982; MBA, Pace U., 1987. Asst. controller Mech. Plastics Corp., Pleasantville, N.Y., 1982-87; fin. analyst Zierick Mfg. Corp., Mt. Kisco, N.Y., 1987-88; cost analyst Ciba-Geigy Corp., Ardsley, N.Y., 1988—; computer cons. C.W. Brown Inc., White Plains, N.Y., 1988. Mem. NAFE, Yale Women's Lacrosse Assn. (bd. dirs. 1988—), Yale Women's Basketball Assn. (bd. dirs. 1983-85). Avocations: skiing, travling, computers. Home: 802 Williamsburg Dr Mahopac NY 10541 Office: Ciba-Geigy Corp 444 Saw Mill River Rd Ardsley NY 10502

KILLORY, DIANE SILBERSTEIN, lawyer; b. White Plains, N.Y., Apr. 13, 1954; d. Morton Stanley and Estelle (Keller) Silberstein; m. Joseph Edward Killory Jr. BA summa cum laude, U. Rochester, 1976; JD cum laude, Harvard U., 1979. Bar: D.C. 1979. Assoc. Steptoe & Johnson, Washington, 1979-83; spl. counsel for legal policy FCC, Washington, 1983, sr. legal advisor to Commr. Patrick, 1983-86, gen. counsel, 1986-89; ptnr. Morrison & Foerster, Washington, 1989—. Mem. Phi Beta Kappa. Office: FCC 1919 M St NW Washington DC 20554

KILMARTIN, SUZANNE, professional society administrator; b. Manhattan, Kans., Feb. 25, 1945; d. Paul E. and Bonna Jean (Boren) Peterson. BA, San Francisco State U., 1967, MA, 1970. Editor/exec. asst. Brandwein Assocs., San Francisco, 1975-78; communications dir. Retail Furniture Assn. of Calif., San Francisco, 1980-82; exec. dir. Phila./Del. Valley Restaurant Assn., Phila., 1985-86; exec. asst. Nat. Adoption Ctr., Phila., 1986-87; exec. dir. Phila. Assn. Life Underwriters, Phila., 1988—; instr. of English, Cittone Inst., Mt. Laurel, N.J., 1989—. Mem. Del. Valley Soc. of Assn. Execs., NAFE. Democrat. Episcopalian. Office: Phila Assn Life Underwriter 1315 Walnut St Ste 1617 Philadelphia PA 19107

KILMER, SHEILA AGNES, art consultant; b. Green Bay, Wis., June 3, 1942; d. Kenneth Gregory and Mary Josephine (De Wane) Kane; m. Bruce Norbert Kilmer, Sept. 5, 1942 (div. Dec. 1979); children: Bridget, Barrett. BS, U. Wis., Oshkosh, 1965; MS, U. Wis., Green Bay, 1979. Elem. tchr. Cudahy Pub. Schs., Cudahy, Wis., 1962-63; elem. tchr. Columbus Pub. Schs., Columbus, Wis., 1965, Sun Prairie Pub. Schs., Sun Prairie, Wis., 1965-66; elem. tchr. art Sun Prairie Pub. Schs., 1966-67, Salt Lake City Pub. Schs., 1967-68, Ashwaubenon Pub. Schs., Green Bay, 1969-84; art cons. Stevens Fine Art Gallery, Detroit, 1984-85, Heritage Art Cons. Svcs., Troy, Mich., 1985-87, Art Expression, Inc., Troy, 1985—. Mem. beautification awards com. Troy C. of C., 1986-88; speaker, chairperson, psychic, healer, min. Ctr. Enlightenment, Royal Oak, Mich., 1986—. Home: 2844 Charter Blvd 102 Troy MI 48083 Office: Art Expression Inc 1721 Crooks Rd Ste 100 Troy MI 48084

KILPATRICK, ANITA See STAUB, ANITA

KILPATRICK, CAROLYN CHEEKS, state representative, educator; b. Detroit, June 25, 1945; d. Marvell and Willa Mae (Henry) Cheeks; divorced; children: Kwame, Ayanna. AS, Ferris State Coll., Big Rapids, Mich., 1965; BS, Western Mich. U., 1972; MS in Edn., U. Mich., 1977. Tchr. Murray Wright High Sch., Detroit, 1972-78; mem. Ho. of Reps. State of Mich., 1978—; del. Dem. Convs., 1980, 84, 88; majority whip Ho. of Reps.; mem. House Appropriations Com. Rep. Detroit Substance Abuse Advisory Council; participant Mic. African Trade Mission, 1985, UN Internat. Women's Conf., 1986; del., participant Nairobi (Kenya) Internat. Agriculture Show Mich. Dept. of Agriculture; mem. resource com. TV documentary Your Children, Our Children; bd. trustees Henry Ford Hosp. Recipient Anthony Wayne award Wayne State U., Disting. Legislator award Gentlemen of Wall Street, Burton-Abercrombie award 13th Dem. Congl. Dist.

Mem. Nat. Orgn. 100 Black Women, Nat. Black Caucus of State Legislators (chairperson Mich. legis. session 1983-84), Nat. Order Women Legislators, Nat. Orgn. Black Elected Legis. Women (treas.). Mem. Pan African Orthodox Christian Ch. Office: Ho Reps 105 Capitol Bldg Lansing MI 48909

KILPATRICK, RUBY NAPPIER, nursing educator; b. Deweyville, Tex., July 25, 1925; d. Emery Ellis and Annie Ethel (Oxley) Nappier; m. Rufus Underwood Kilpatrick, Mar. 23, 1946; children—Rufus Underwood, Emery Dale, William Gerard, Ruby Dianne, Bradford Lee. Diploma in nursing St. Mary's Sch. Nursing, 1945; B.S.N., Lamar U., 1979, MEd, 1984. Pub. health nurse City of Galveston, Tex., 1945; pvt. duty nurse Ofcl. Nursing Bur., Beaumont, Tex., 1946-47; regular relief nurse Bapt. Hosp., Beaumont, 1949-51; emergency room nurse, head nurse med. floor, charge nurse on coronary care St. Elizabeth Hosp., Beaumont, Tex., 1968-74; clin. instr. Lamar U., Beaumont, 1974-83, instr., 1983-86; sec.-treas. Kilpatrick's Bonded Warehouse, Beaumont, 1960—; mem. State Nursing Adv. Com. to Spl. Com. on Post-secondary Edn. Sec.-treas. Cub Scouts, Boy Scouts Am., Beaumont, 1983; mem. Legis. Wives, Austin, 1957—. Mem. Tex. Congress Parents and Tchrs. (life), Lamar U. Alumni Assn. (life), Dist. Nurses Assn. Dist. 12 (dir. 1982-84, 86-88, legis. chmn. 1982-84, pres. 1984-86, Nurse of Yr. 1989), Mental Health Assn. Beaumont (adv. com.), Tex. Nurses Assn., Tex. Assn. Coll. Tchrs., Sigma Theta Tau Democrat. Mem. Ch. of Christ. Club: Woman's (sec. 1973-74) (Beaumont). Home: 785 Randolph Cir Beaumont TX 77706 Office: Lamar Univ Dept Nursing PO Box 10081 Beaumont TX 77710

KILQUIST, HELEN LEONARD, retired social service worker; b. Farmingdale, N.Y., Oct. 3, 1912; d. George Emil and Mabel Helen (Hall) K. BA, Cornell U., 1933; MA in Religious Edn., Hartford (Conn.) Sem. Found., 1956; MS, U. of Hartford, 1980. Clk. N.Y. State Labor Dept., Albany, 1937-39; sr. clk. N.Y. State Employment Svc., Binghamton, 1939-43; employment interviewer N.Y. Sate Employment Svc., Binghamton, Jamestown, 1943-55; dir. religious edn. Hartford Episcopal Ch., 1956-57, Springfield (Mass.) Episcopal Ch., 1957-58, Manchester (Conn.) Episcopal Ch., 1958-60; social worker Conn. Dept. Income Maintenance, Hartford, 1960-84; ret., 1984. Vol. tutor basic reading Literacy Vols., 1986-87, English as 2d lang., 1988—; vol. Hartford Hosp., 1987-89. Mem. Hartford Sch. of Religious Edn. Alumni Assn. (pres. 1958-60), Larrabee Assn. (v.p. 1985-89), AAUW (internat. rels. chmn. 1986-88), Cornell Club (dir. Hartford chpt. 1986-88), Cornell Womens Club (pres. greater Hartford chpt. 1964-65).

KILTY, LEAOLA ANGELLEANA, small business owner; b. Weatherford, Tex., Apr. 9, 1936; d. Clearance Edward and Angelleana (Miller) Dugan; m. Charles Alexander Kilty, Aug. 9, 1954; 1 child, Deborah Lea. AA in Bus. Adminstrn., Los Angeles Community Coll., 1976; BS in Bus. Adminstrn., Calif. State U., Northridge, 1983; cert. in graphoanalysis, Internat. Graphoanalyst Assn., Chgo., 1986. Office mgr. Vallepac Inc., San Fernando, Calif., 1969-71; bookkeeper Thorn Refrigeration Corp., Pacoima, Calif., 1971-74, exec. asst., 1977—; clk. accounts payable Hope Community Mental Health Ctr., Lakeview Terrace, Calif., 1974-75, fin. counselor, 1975, mgr. acctg. dept., 1975-77; owner Handwriting Revelations, Mission Hills, Calif., 1986—; document examiner, handwriting identifier Mission Hills, 1989—; cons. in field. Mem. Club 100 San Fernando YWCA, 1984—; recording sec. Sylmar (Calif.) Assn., 1986-87. Mem. The Exec. Female, Bus. and Profl. Women San Fernando (recording sec. Tri-Valley dist. 1984-85, v.p., program chair 1985-86, pres. 1986-87, found. chair 1987—, Club Bull. award 1986-87, Coro Track Meml. award 1986-87, North Hollywood Stblzn. award 1986-87, Blood Bank award 1986-87), So. Calif. Graphoanalyst Soc. (life), Calif. State U. Alumni Assn. Republican. Home: 13682 Shablow Ave Sylmar CA 91342 Office: Thorn Refrigeration Corp 13721 Desmond St Pacoima CA 91331

KILWIEN-MECK, SHERRI RAE, educator; b. National City, Calif., Oct. 4, 1960; d. Raymond David Kilwien and Catherine Marie (Sekora) Phillips. BJ, U. Tex., 1981, cert. secondary English, Journalism, 1985; MS, Tex. A&I U., 1990. lic. real estate sales. Co-owner Meck Properties, Austin, 1983-85; owner, operator Travis Bookkeeping Svcs., Missoula, Mont., 1983-85; owner Redi-Temp, Missoula, 1985; co-owner East San Antonio Travel Mgmt., 1985—; tchr. Sam Houston High Sch., San Antonio Independent Sch. Dist., San Antonio, 1985—. Bd. dirs. Bexar County Child Welfare Bd., Bexar County Community Guidance Ctr.; mem. youth com. M.L. King Commn., San Antonio Mus. Assn., San Antonio Performing Arts Assn., Inst. Texan Cultures, Mind Sci. Found.; corp. devel. com. San Antonio Festival, Am. Film Inst., United Way Crisis Intervention Bd.; participant, presenter, coord. San Antonio Youth Literacy; mem. I Have A Dream Found. (gala com.), Project Any Baby Can corp. doll campaign. Mem. NAFE, DAR, Assn. Tex. Profl. Educators, Journalism Edn. Assn., Nat. Coun. Tchrs. English, Women in Communications Inc., River City Bus. & Profl. Women's Club, Colonial Dames Soc. Am., Leadership San Antonio. Republican. Roman Catholic. Office: Sam Houston High Sch 4635 E Houston San Antonio TX 78220

KIM, CHUNG HEE, real estate developer; b. Seoul, Korea, Dec. 27, 1937; came to U.S. 1961; d. Yong Nam and Mi Ock Kim; children: John W., Kristina M. BA, Seoul Nat. U., 1960. Pres. Comstock Investment Co., Mountain View, Calif., 1976—. Office: Comstock Partnership 2290 California St Mountain View CA 94040

KIM, JIN KYUNG, medical scientist; b. Seoul, Korea, Dec. 13, 1939; d. Yong Jo and Chun Ki (Jung) K. BS, Ewha Womans U., 1961; MS, Mich. State U., 1972; PhD, U. Colo., 1975. Teaching asst. Yonsei U., Seoul, 1961-69; rsch. asst. Mich. State U., 1969-72; rsch. assoc. U. Colo., 1972-75; post doctorate fellow Mayo Clinic, Rochester, Minn., 1975-78; asst. prof. U. Colo., 1978-85, assoc. prof., 1985—. Mem. Am. Soc. Nephrology, Internat. Soc. Nephrology, Am. Fedn. Clin. Research, Am. Soc. Renal Biochemistry and Metabolism. Office: U Colo Health Scis Ctr 4200 E 9th St Denver CO 80262

KIM, LAURA KYUNG-HWA, investment banker; b. Seoul, South Korea, July 18, 1961; d. Tony Jai and Lucia Sook-Chul (Shin) K. BA in Music, UCLA, 1984; MBA in Fin., U. Chgo., 1988. Investment acct. Pacific Investment Mgmt. Co., Newport Beach, Calif., 1984-85; mktg. adminstr. Prudential Asset Mgmt. Co., L.A., 1985-86; assoc. Bank of Am. Corp. Fin., N.Y.C., 1988—. Presbyterian. Home: 600 Columbus Ave #9G New York NY 90024 Office: Bank of Am Corp Fin 335 Madison Ave 6th Fl New York NY 90017

KIM, MI JA, academic dean; b. Seoul, Jan. 23, 1940; came to U.S., 1966; d. Si Hyung and Jung Kwon (Ahn) Lee; m. Heung Soo Kim, Jan. 14, 1964; children: Yoon Hi and Joseph. BS in Nursing, Yon Sei U., Seoul, 1962; PhD, U. Ill., Chgo., 1975. Staff nurse Severance Hosp., Seoul, 1962-63; health nurse Am. Embassy, Seoul, 1963-66; asst. prof. Coll. Nursing/Univ. Ill., Chgo., 1975-79, assoc. prof., 1979-84, interim assoc. dean for rsch., 1984-86, assoc. dean rsch., dir. grad. studies, 1986-87, assoc. dean acad. affairs, dir. grad. studies, 1987-88, acting dean, 1988-89, prof., dean, 1989—; cons. Levine Assocs., Kensington, Md., 1989—, Bd. Regents Higher Edn., Boston, 1989, Nat. Ctr. Nursing Rsch., Bethesda, Md., 1987—. Named Univ. Scholar, U. Ill., 1985-88, Outstanding Nurse Educator, Korean Nurses Assn., Seoul, 1983; recipient Book of Yr. award Am. Jour. Nursing, 1984, Golden Apple award, students of Coll. Nursing, U. Ill., 1976, 78. Fellow Am. Acad. Nursing; mem. North Am. Nursing Diagnosis (bd. dirs. 1985—), Am. Thoracic Soc., Chgo. Lung Assn. (bd. dirs. 1977—), Chgo. Heart Assn. (bd. govs. 1980-88), Am. Physiol. Soc., Sigma Theta Tau (Disting. Lectr. 1987). Office: Coll Nursing/Univ Ill 845 S Damen Ave Chicago IL 60612

KIM, SANGDUK, biochemistry educator, researcher; b. Seoul, Korea, June 15, 1930; came to U.S., 1954; d. Tak Won and chungHee (Kil) K.; m. Woon Ki Paik, June 15, 1959; children: Margaret, Dean, David. MD, Korea U., Seoul, 1953; PhD, U. Wis., 1960. Intern Evang. Deaconess Hosp., Milw., 1954-55; rsch. assoc. U. Wis., Madison, 1959-61, U. Ottawa, Ont., Can., 1961-66; rsch. assoc. Fels Inst. Temple U., Phila., 1966-73, sr. investigator Fels Inst., 1973-78, assoc. prof. biochemistry Fels Inst., 1978-90, prof. biochemistry, 1990—. Author: (monograph) Protein Methylation, 1980; editor: Protein Methylation, 1990. NIH Rsch. grantee, 1973-81, NSF Rsch. grantee, 1979-85, Nat. Multiple Sclerosis Rsch. grantee, 1985—. Mem. Am. Soc. Biol. Chemists, Am. Assn. for Cancer Rsch., N.Y. Acad. Sci., Am. Chem. Soc., Am. Soc. for Neurochemistry. Home: 7818 Oak Ln Rd Cheltenham PA 19012 Office: Temple U Fels Inst 3420 N Broad St Philadelphia PA 19140

KIM, SYNJA P., corporate business planner; b. Seoul, Republic of Korea; came to U.S., 1967; d. Byung Jae and Jung-D (Kim) Park; m. Sang Joo Kim, Dec. 4, 1976. BS in Acctg., Va. Commonwealth U., 1971; MBA in Fin. and Multinat. Mgmt., U. Pa., 1986. Jr. analyst Am. Fgn. Ins. Assn., N.Y.C., 1971; internal auditor Ethan Allen, Inc., Danbury, Conn., 1972-74, sr. acct., 1975-77; sr. acct. Carolina Power & Light Co., Raleigh, N.C., 1978-79, fin. analyst, 1980-82, sr. fin. analyst, 1983-87; mgr. budget planning and fin. analysis Internat. Life and Group, CIGNA Worldwide, Phila., 1987-89; mgr. bus. planning CIGNA Internat. Fin. Svcs., Phila., 1989, dir. bus. planning, 1989—; pres. Inst. Korean-Am. Studies, 1986—; instr. Korean-Am. Lang. Sch., Rsch. Triangle Park, N.C., 1979-81; guest speaker Raleigh C. of C., 1982; program coordinator Nat. Coun. for Internat. Visitors Ctr., Rsch. Triangle Park, N.C., 1984-87. Mem. Nat. Assn. Accts. Republican.

KIMBALL, FRANCES ADRIENNE, physiologist; b. Oakland, Calif., May 2, 1939; d. Elmore Norton and Gladys Catherine (Oliver) K. BA, U. Calif., Berkeley, 1961; MA, Calif. State U., Chico, 1970; PhD, Cornell U., 1973. Cert. tchr., Calif. Rsch. asst. Reed Coll., Portland, Oreg., 1961-68; rsch. scientist The Upjohn Co., Kalamazoo, Mich., 1973-85, sr. project mgr., 1985-89; acting dir. project mgmt. The Upjohn Co., Kalamazoo, 1989—. Editor: The Endometrium, 1982, New Approaches to the Study of Benign Prostatic Hypeplasia, 1984. Pres. bd. dirs. Planned Parenthood Southwest Mich., Kalamazoo, 1979-85. NIH grad. fellow Cornell U., 1970-73. Mem. Phi Kappa Phi. Office: Upjohn Co Kalamazoo MI 49001

KIMBALL, JOAN HARWOOD, dentist; b. Dorchester, Mass., May 30, 1956; d. Walter Edward and Frances Joan (Zetes) Harwood; m. Glenn Philip Kimball, June 18, 1982; children: Lauren, Glenn, Kara. BS, U. N.H., 1978; DMD, Boston U., 1982. Resident VA Hosp., Jamaica Plain, Mass., 1982-83; dentist Katsur & Assocs., Pitts., 1983-84, Allegheny Dental Group, McKeesport, Pa., 1984, Allegheny Dental Assocs., Pitts., 1984-86; pvt. practice Bradford, Mass., 1987—. Mem. ADA, Merrimack Valley Dental Assn., Mass. Dental Soc., Phi Beta Kappa. Home: 46 Rutherford Ave Haverhill MA 01830 Office: 10 Doane St Bradford MA 01835

KIMBALL, MARY HOLT, educator; b. Janesville, Wis., Oct. 2, 1934; d. Earle Frank and Mildred (Beahm) Holt; m. Robert Parker Kimball, June 30, 1962; children: Emily Beth, Laura Ann, Peter Markham. BA in French, Beloit (Wis.) Coll. Cert. tchr. in English-as-second-lang. French/history tchr. Piedmont High Sch., Piedmont, Calif., 1958-60; English/social studies tchr. La Vista Jr. High, Hayward, Calif., 1960-62; French tchr. Garfield Jr. High, Madison, Wis., 1962-64, Burlingame Intermediate, Burlingame, Calif., 1964-66; tchr. English-as-second-lang. Klein Forest High Sch., Houston, 1982—. Author: The Heritage of North Harris County, 1977. Mem. AAUW, NEA, Tex. State Tchrs. Assn., Tex. Tchrs. Speakers Other Langs., Phi Beta Kappa. Republican. Presbyterian.

KIMBLE, GLADYS AUGUSTA LEE, nurse, civic worker; b. Niagara Falls, Can., June 28, 1906; d. William and Florence Augusta Baker (Buckton) Lee; naturalized citizen of the U.S.; RN, Christ Hosp., Jersey City, 1929; BS, Columbia U. Tchrs. Coll., 1938, MA, 1948; m. George Edmond Kimble, Jan. 5, 1952. Nurse, Willard Parker Hosp., N.Y.C., 1931; asst. and supervisory relief nurse Margaret Hague Maternity Hosp., Jersey City, 1931-37; staff nurse, relief supr. Manhattan Eye, Ear and Throat Hosp., N.Y.C., 1937-38; sr. staff, asst. nurse supr. Vis. Nurse Svc., N.Y.C., 1938-41; sr. pub. health nurse USPHS, Little Rock, 1941-43; pub. health supr. Providence Dist. Nursing Assn., 1943-46; edn. dir. Jersey City Pub. Health Nursing Svc., 1946-49, also instr. Seton Hall U., South Orange, N.J., 1947-49; pub. health nurse cons. U.S. Inst. Inter-Am. Affairs, Brazil, 1949-51; dir. pub. health dept. Englewood (N.J.) Hosp., 1951-53; nurse coord. exch. visitor nurse program Overlook Hosp., Summit, N.J., 1964-71. Recipient Appreciation award for svc. rendered Providence Hosp., 1944; Woman of Yr. award Essex County Bus. and Profl. Women, 1968. Fellow Am. Pub. Health Assn. (life), mem. Sarasota Geneal. Soc. (charter). Episcopalian. Lodges: Daus. of the Nile, Nyla (Sarasota, Fla.) (charter), Ladies Oriental Shrine of N. Am. (SAR-I Ct. 79), Royal Order of Jesterettes, Eillim Ives #18, Sarasota. Home: 4540 Bee Ridge Rd Villa 12 Sarasota FL 34233

KIMBRELL, ANNA MARGARET, educator; b. Sweet Springs, Mo., Jan. 8, 1927; d. Charles Arthus and Selma Leota (Rohrbach) Scrivner; m. Joseph Mitchell Kimbrell, June 5, 1948; children: Susan Lizbeth Cooke, Drusilla Gaye Kimbrell, Amelia Ann Hull. BM, Cen. Meth. Colll., 1948; postgrad., Cen. Mo. State U., 1953, 64, 85, Ottawa (Kans.) U., 1976, U. Mo., Kansas City, 1965, 83. Music educator Higbee (Mo.) High Sch., 1948-49; music educator Stover (Mo.) High Sch., 1951-54; English tchr. Versailles (Mo.) High Sch., 1954-56; lang. arts instr. Palmer Jr. High Sch., Independence (Mo.) Sch. Dist., 1966-87. Pres. Independence Community Tchrs. Assn./Mo. State Tchrs. Assn., 1980-81, Hawthorne Literary Soc. Federated Women, Versailles, 1954-55; coord., bd. dirs. Shepherd Ctrs., Independence, 1988-89; chair higher edn., mem. adminstrv. bd. First United Meth. Ch., 1989-91. Named Community Tchrs. Assn. Leader of Yr., Mo. State Tchr. Assn., 1983-84. Mem. AAUW (chairperson community com., bd. dirs.), Independence Retired Tchrs. (chair, bd. dirs., historian), Mo. State Retired Tchrs. Assn., Kansas City Swiss Soc., Elswood Meadows Garden Club (bd. dirs., sec.), Phi Beta (life). Democrat. Home: 2705 Berry Ave Independence MO 64057

KIMES, BEVERLY RAE, editor, writer; b. Aurora, Ill., Aug. 17, 1939; d. Raymond Lionel and Grace Florence (Perrin) K.; m. James H. Cox, July 6, 1984. B.S., U. Ill., 1961; M.A. in Journalism, Pa. State U., 1963. Dir. publicity Mateer Playhouse, Neff's Mills, Pa., 1962, Pavillion Theatre, University Park, Pa., 1963; asst. editor Automobile Quar. Pubs., N.Y.C., Princeton, N.J., 1963-64, assoc. editor, 1965-66, mng. editor, 1967-74, editor, 1975-81; editor The Classic Car, 1981—. Bd. dirs. Auburn-Cord-Duesenberg Mus., Milestone Car Soc.; mem. internat. coordination com. Nat. Automotive History Collection, Detroit Pub. Library. Recipient Cugnot award Soc. Automotive Historians, 1978, 79, 83, 85, 86, Thomas McKean trophy, 1983, 85, 86, Moto award Nat. Assn. Automotive Journalists, 1984, 85, 86. Mem. Internat. Motor Press Assn., Milestone Car Soc. (bd. dirs.), Soc. Automotive Historians (pres. 1987-89). Author: The Classic Tradition of the Lincoln Motor Car, 1968; (with R.M. Langworth) Oldsmobile: The First Seventy-Five Years, 1972; The Cars That Henry Ford Built, 1978; (with Rene Dreyfus) My Two Lives, 1983; (with Robert C. Ackerson) Chevrolet: A History from 1911, 1984; The Standard Catalog of American Cars 1805-1942, 1985; The Star and the Laurel: The Centennial History of Daimler, Mercedes and Benz, 1986; editor: Great Cars and Grand Marques, 1976; Packard: History of the Motor Car and the Company, 1979; Automobile Quarterly's Handbook of Automotive Hobbies, 1981.

KIMES, SHERYL ELAINE, business educator; b. St. Louis, Apr. 14, 1954; d. John Alfred and Alpha Louise (Johnson) K. AB, U. Mo., 1975; MA in Pub. Adminstrn., U. Va., 1977; MBA, N.Mex. State U., 1983; PhD, U. Tex., 1987. Energy coord. St. Louis County, St. Louis, 1978-79; energy analyst Londe-Parker-Michels, St. Louis, 1979-82; teaching asst. N.Mex. State U., Las Cruces, 1982-83, 198; project mgr. Technol. Innovation Ctr., Las Cruces, 1983-84; asst. instr. bus. U. Tex., Austin, 1984-85, rsch. asst., 1985-86; asst. prof. bus. N.Mex. State U., Las Cruces, 1986-88, Cornell U., Ithaca, N.Y., 1988—. U. Tex. fellow, 1984-86. Mem. Decision Sci. Inst., Inst. Mgmt. Sci., Ops. Mgmt. Assn. Office: Cornell U 335 Statler Hall Ithaca NY 14853

KIMM, BARBARA CHANDLER, healthcare adminstrator; b. Ogdensburg, N.Y., Nov. 30, 1936; d. Ralph James and Pearl (McFadden) Chandler; m. Richard Clearwater Kimm, Aug. 19, 1978; 1 child, Susan. BS in Health Adminstrn., Colby Sawyer Coll., 1958. Dsir. med. data svcs. Crouse Irving Meml. Hosp., Syracuse, N.Y., 1958-61, 64-67, asst. v.p. adminstrn., 1980—; dir. med. data svcs. Community Gen. Hosp., Syracuse, 1969-80; lectr. health adminstrn. New Sch. for Social Rsch., Syracuse, spring 1989; chmn. porf. med. adv. com. Home Health Providers, Inc., Syracuse, 1989—. Past officer Jr. League of Syracuse; bd. dirs. Home Aides of Cen. N.Y., Syracuse, 1985—, Consol. Industries, Syracuse, 1987—. Mem. Med. Record Assn. N.Y. State (pres. 1975-76, Disting. Mem. award Cen. N.Y. chpt. 1985), N.Y. Assn. Quality Assurance Profls. (treas. 1984-86), Cen. N.Y. Assn. Quality Assurance (pres. 1982-84), Healthcare Fin. Mgmt. Assn., Everson Mus. Mems. Coun., Syracuse Stage Guild, Weighlock Guild. Home: 5069 Pine Valley Dr Fayetteville NY 13066 Office: Crouse Irving Meml Hosp 736 Irving Ave Syracuse NY 13210

KIMMEL, CAROLE ANNE, scientist, developmental toxicologist; b. Lexington, Ky., Apr. 26, 1944; d. Ernest Edward and Sunbeam Blackburn (Moore) Davis; m. Gary Lewis Kimmel, Aug. 22, 1970; 1 child, Rebecca Anne. BS, Georgetown (Ky.) Coll., 1966; PhD, U. Cin., 1970. Postdoctoral fellow U. Cin., 1970-72; teratologist U.S. EPA, Cin., 1972; instr. anatomy Harvard U. Med. Sch., Boston, 1972-73; sr. staff fellow Nat. Inst. Environ. Health Sci., Research Triangle Park, NC, 1973-77; research scientist, br. chief Nat. Ctr. for Toxicological Rsch., Jefferson, Ark., 1977-84; developmental toxicologist U.S. EPA, Washington, 1984—. Chmn. missions com. St. James Episcopal Ch., Potomac, Md., 1989—. Mem. Neurobehavioral Teratology Soc. (pres. 1989-90), Teratology Soc. (pres. 1990—), Soc. Toxicology (chmn. bd. publs. 1989-90), European Teratology Soc. Democrat. Home: 607 Somersworth Way Silver Spring MD 20902 Office: US EPA 401 M St SW (RD-689) Washington DC 20460

KIMMEL, JOYCE FRANCES, training and development officer; b. Lakeport, Calif., Aug. 31, 1948; d. Emmanuel Rinehart and Clare Sophia (Dunnebeck) K.; 1 child, Jason Jeremiah Pageau. BA magna cum laude, Calif. State U., Chico, 1971, MA with distinction, 1973. Cert. community college instr. Instr. Allan Hancock College, Santa Maria, Calif., 1973-78; botanist U.S. Forest Service, Eureka, Calif., 1979-86; employee dev. specialist U.S. Forest Service, San Francisco, Calif., 1986-88, regional training officer, 1988—; dep. forest supr. U.S. Forest Svc., San Francisco, 1990; botanical cons. U.S. Forest Service, Eureka, Calif., 1979-80. Contbr. article to profl. jours. Asst. scout leader South San Francisco, Calif. Boy Scouts Am., 1986—. Recipient Instr. Improvement Grant, Allen Hancock College, 1977. Mem. Natl. Org. Dev. Network, Bay Area chapt. Democrat. Office: U.S. Forest Service 630 Sansome St San Francisco CA 94111

KIMMICH, SARA JANE, bioengineer, researcher; b. Mexico City, Mex., Jan. 26, 1963; came to U.S., 1979; d. Hernando Julio and Sara Ann (Reid) Jimenez; m. Mark Raymond Kimmich, June 9, 1987. ScB in Bioengineering, Tex. A&M U., 1986. Rsch. lab. technician SYNTEX, Palo Alto, Calif., 1987-88; rsch. coord. Alamo Bone and Joint Clinic, San Antonio, Tex., 1988—; rsch. coord. Alamo Rsch. and Devel. Inc., San Antonio, 1988—, S.W. Found. Biomedical Rsch., San Antonio, 1989—, S.W. Rsch. Inst., San Antonio, 1988—, Alamo Rehab., San Antonio, 1988—. Designer (testing machine design) rotational torque, 1988. phlebotomist vol. Veteran's Hosp., San Antonio, 1983; vol. Challenge of the Lumbar Spine, San Antonio, 1988-89; rsch. vol. Bone Bank Found., San Antonio, 1988-90. Mem. IEEE, Bioelectric Repair and Growth Soc., Engring. in Medicine and Biology (fundraising chmn. 1986), Cadeuces Soc. Office: Alamo Bone and Joint Clinic 4330 Medical Dr Ste 200 San Antonio TX 78229

KIMURA, LILLIAN CHIYEKO, human service agency executive; b. Glendale, Calif., Apr. 7, 1929; d. Homer and Hisa (Muraki) Kimura; B.A., U. Ill., 1951, M.S.W., 1954; postgrad. Inst. for Nonprofit Mgmt., Columbia U., 1985. Program dir. Olivet Community Center, Chgo., 1954-68; dir. Olivet Service Area, Chgo. Commons Assn., 1968-71; program cons. Nat. Bd. YWCA of U.S.A., 1971-78; dir. mid-states region, 1978-80, exec. field services, 1980-83, asst. exec. dir., 1984-86, assoc. exec. dir., 1987—. Pres., Japanese Am. Service Com., 1973-79; bd. dirs. Nat. Japanese Am. Citizens League, 1972-79, 88—, chairwoman bd. Pacific Citizens League, 1988—; gov., 1974-79, pres. N.Y. chpt., 1986. Mem. Acad. Cert. Social Workers, Assn. Social Workers, Nonprofit Mgmt. Assn. (bd. dirs.) Office: 726 Broadway New York NY 10003

KINARD, AGNES DODDS, lawyer, historian, author; b. Pitts.; d. Robert James and Agnes Julia Raw; m. Morton Frank, June 4, 1944 (div. 1958); children: Allan Dodds, Michael Robert, Marilyn Morton; m. James Pinckney Kinard, Dec. 27, 1961. BA in History cum laude, U. Pitts., 1936; LLB, U. Pitts, 1939; JD, U. Pitts., 1961; postgrad., Chatham Coll., 1980. Bar: Pa. 1940. Law researcher Reed, Smith, Shaw & McClay, Pitts., 1940-41; Lynne A. Warren, N.Y.C., 1940-41; exec. sec. Allegheny County War Price and Ration Bd., Pitts., 1941-44; British Colonies section chief, asst. to the deputy adminstr. Lend-Lease Adminstrn., Washington, 1944-46; women's editor, columnist Canton (Ohio) Economist, 1946-58; assoc. broker, sales Kelly Wood Real Estate, Pitts., 1959-72; broker, pres., co-owner Mountain Real Estate Co., Inc., Confluence, Pa., 1973-83. Author: Historical Survey of the Landscape Design Society of Wetern Pennsylvania: 1962-83, 1983, Celebration of Carnegie in Pittsburgh, 1981, The Jane Holmes Reidence-A Century of Caring, 1982, Seasons of the Heart, 1988-89, Fanfare for Fifty Year, 1989, History of the Pitttsburgh Symphony Association, 1939-1989, 1989; commd. symphony by Nikolai Lopatnikoff for the Pitts. Symphony Orch., 1972. Bd. dirs. Pitts. Plan for Art, Sch. Vol. Assn., Pitts. Youth Symphony Orch. Assn., Pitts. Symphony Assn.; founder, mem. Rachel Carson Homestead Assn., Pioneer Crafts Council (founder, pres., co-chmn. Long Range Planning com.). Recipient Award of Merit Pitts. History and Landmark Found. Mem. Pitts. Civ. Garden Ctr. (life), Nat. Council State Garden Clubs (life), landscape design critic, Nat. Soc. Arts & Letters (life), Landscape Design Soc. of We. Pa. (founding bd. mem., past pres., recipient Helen S. Hull Plaque for Lit. Horticultural Interest, 1986), Carnegie Mus. of Art Women's Com., Kappa Kappa Gamma.

KINCANNON, FELICE, advertising agency executive. With Hill, Holliday, Connors, Cosmopoulos, Inc., Boston, 1975—, v.p., then sr. v.p., exec. v.p., 1988—. Office: Hill Holliday Connors Cosmopulos Inc 200 Clarendon St Boston MA 02116*

KIND, PHYLLIS DAWN, immunologist; b. Sidney, Mont., July 31, 1933; d. Dan E. and Margaret (Erickson) K. B.A., U. Mont., 1955; M.S., U. Mich., 1956, Ph.D., 1960, postgrad. 1960-63. Instr., U. Colo.-Denver, 1963-65, asst. prof., 1965-71; research microbiologist NCI-NIH, Bethesda, Md., 1971-74; assoc. prof. dept. microbiology George Washington U., Washington, 1974-79, prof., 1979—; mem., chmn. NSF Grad. Fellowship Eval. Panel, Washington, 1979-81; ad hoc mem. of NIH Study sect., 1976—. Contbr. articles to profl. jours. NSF fellow, 1955-59; NIH fellow, 1963-64. Mem. Am. Soc. Microbiology (div. chmn. 1975-76), Am. Assn. Immunologists, Am. Soc. Histocompatibility and Genetics, AAAS, Soc. Exptl. Biology and Medicine, Assn. Women in Sci., NIDA (study sect. 1986-90), Sigma Xi, Phi Kappa Phi. Avocations: sailing, skiing, tennis, swimming, bird-watching. Office: George Washington U Med Ctr 2300 I St NW Washington DC 20037

KINDALL, CHARLOTTE ELOISE, management consultant, trade association administrator; b. Norton, Kans., June 26, 1944; d. Alfred and Alice Elizabeth (Hadley) Kopp; m. David Kindall, Mar. 30, 1962; children: Chris, Kem, Kyle. Student, Colby (Kans.) Community Coll. Mgmt. cons. Norton; mgmt. cons., dir. Norton Area C. of C., 1984—. Active Pioneer County Devel., 1988—. Mem. U.S. Chamber Inst. (bd. dirs. 1989-90, mem. task force commn.), Kans. C. of C. Execs., N.W. Kans. Travel Coun. (pres. 1989-90), Bus. and Profl. Women (Woman of Yr. 1985), Travel Industries Assn. Kans. (bd. dirs. 1989-90). Home: 1014 Truman Dr Norton KS 67654 Office: Chamber of Commerce 112B N State St Norton KS 67654

KINDRED, JOAN HOVER, actress, civic worker, home economist; b. Poughkeepsie, Nov. 28, 1930; d. Ernest William and Florence (Christiansen) Hover; B.S., U. Md., 1953; m. John Joseph Kindred, III, Aug. 25, 1956 (div. Aug. 1980); 1 dau., Drewry Ann. Promotion and speech writer Sta. WTOP, Washington, 1953-54; producer, star daily TV women's culinary arts show Sta. WRC, Washington, 1955-56; home economist Potomac Electric Power Co., 1956; producer, star indsl. and comml. film for TV, 1956-59; pres. Snark, Ltd., repertory group, N.Y.C., 1969-72. Vice pres., bd. dirs. Twilight Park Assn., 1971-75; bd. dirs. Sheltering Arms Children's Service, 1974-87, treas. aux., 1975-77. Republican. Presbyterian.

KING, ANN BEATRICE, art director; b. Washington, Feb. 12, 1957; d. Robert Joseph and Phyllis Mary (McCann) Goodreau; m. Darrell Ray King, July 2, 1983; 1 child, Andrew Darrell. BFA, Corcoran Sch. Art, Washington, 1979. Supervising graphic designer City of Alexandria (Va.) Print

Shop, 1982-84; designer J. Maxine & Martin, McLean, Va., 1984-85; asst. art dir. Irv Kline & Assocs., Alexandria, 1985-87; art dir. Mt. Vernon Realty, Alexandria, 1987—. Mem. Art Dirs. Club Met. Washington. Home: 5390 Cleburne Ln Woodbridge VA 22192 Office: Mt Vernon Realty 1700 Diagonal Rd 6th Fl Alexandria VA 22314

KING, ANN STOCKMAN, librarian, educator; b. N.Y.C., Nov. 6, 1931; d. Frank J. and Natalie A. Stockman; m. Albert M. King; 3 children. BS in Edn., So. Conn. State Coll., New Haven, 1959; MLS, So. Conn. U., 1974; postgrad., St. Joseph's U., Hartford, Conn., 1988. Cert. elem. tchr., media specialist, Conn. Libr. Fairfield (Conn.) Pub. Schs., 1974—. Mem. Mill River Wetlands Com., Fairfield, 1965—; v.p. AAUW, 1975-77, sec., 1982-84. Claire Fulcher Internat. scholar AAUW, 1988. Mem. Conn. Ednl. Media, Fairfield County Sch. Librs., Southwestern Libr. Coun. Office: Fairfield Woods Middle Sch 1115 Fairfield Woods Rd Fairfield CT 06430

KING, BARBARA JEAN, nurse; b. Cape Girardeau, Mo., June 28, 1941; d. Otto Samuel and Goldie Elizabeth (Clover) Fowler; student Weatherford Jr. Coll., 1965; R.N., John Peter Smith Hosp. Sch. Profl. Nursing, 1969. Cert. advanced cardiac life support; m. Charles Basil King, Jr., Sept. 4, 1972; children—Otto Samuel, Christopher Lee. Head nurse pediatrics and isolation County Hosp., also intensive care and coronary care units Small Gen. Hosp., Ft. Worth, 1969-72; dir. nursing service Jarvis Heights Nursing Center, Ft. Worth, 1976-77; dir. nursing services Ft. Worth Rehab. Farm, 1978-80; staff nurse, asst. supr. shift Decatur Community Hosp. (Tex.), 1983-85 ; staff nurse and supr. Burdgeport Hosp., 1986— instr. vocat. nursing Cooke County Coll., Gainesville, Tex., 1981; cons. convalescent centers and hosps. Chmn. child care com. Women of Moose, 1977—; ch. organist Zion Valley Cumberland Presbyterian Ch.; asso. organist St. Matthew Cumberland Presbyn. Ch. Served with M.C., USN, 1962-65. Mem. Dirs. Nursing Homes Assn. Tarrant County (v.p.). Democrat. Home: Route 1 Box 198 Alvord TX 76225

KING, BILLIE JEAN MOFFITT, professional tennis player; b. Long Beach, Calif., Nov. 22, 1943; d. Willard J. Moffitt; m. Larry King, Sept. 17, 1965. Student, Calif. State U. at Los Angeles, 1961-64. Amateur tennis player, 1958-67, profl., 1968—; mem. Tennis Challenge Series, 1977, 78; chief exec. officer U.S. TEAMTENNIS, Chgo., 1985—; Singles champion tournaments Wimbledon, 1966-68, 72, 73, 75, U.S. Open, 1967, 71, 72, 74, U.S. Hardcourt, 1966, Italian Open, 1970, West German Open, 1971, Australian Open, 1968, South African Open, 1966, 67, 69, U.S. Indoor, 1966-68, 71, U.S. Clay Court, 1971, French Open, 1972, Avon, 1980; doubles champion Wimbledon, 1961, 62, 65, 67, 68, 70-73, U.S. Open, 1965, 67, 74, 80, French, 1972, Italian, 1970, South African, 1967-70, Bridgestone, 1976, Virginia Slims, 1974, 76; mixed doubles champion Wimbledon, 1967, 71, 73, U.S. Open, 1967, 71, 73, French, 1967, 70, South African, 1967, Australian, 1968; winner 29 Virginia Slims singles titles, 1970-77, 4 Colgate titles, 1977, Fedn. Cup, 1963-67, 76-79, Wightman Cup, 1961-67, 70, 77, 78; World Tennis Team All-Star, 3 times; host Colgate women's sports TV spl. The Lady is a Champ, 1975; co-founder, dir. Kingdom, Inc., San Mateo, Calif.; sports commentator ABC-TV, 1975-78; co-founder, pub. WomenSports mag., 1974—; founder Women's Tennis Assn., 1973; first woman commr. (TEAMTENNIS League) profl. sports history, 1984; TV commentator HBO-Sports Wimbledon coverage; cons. Virginia Slims World Championship Series; bd. dirs. Callenger Ctr.; amb. Adventures in Movement Charity; nat. spokesperson Literary Vols. Am. Author: Tennis to Win, 1970, (with Kim Chapin) Billie Jean, 1974, (with Cynthia Starr) We Have Come a Long Way, The Story of Women's Tennis, 1988. Named Sportsperson of Yr., Sports Illustrated, 1972; Woman Athlete of Yr., A.P., 1967, 73; Top Woman Athlete of Yr., 1972; Woman of Yr., Time mag., 1976; One of 10 Most Powerful Women in Am., Harper's Bazaar, 1977; One of 25 Most Influential Women in Am., World Almanac, 1977; named to Internat. Tennis Hall of Fame, 1987, Nat. Women's Hall of Fame, 1990. Office: US TeamTennis 445 N Wells Ste 404 Chicago IL 60610

KING, BLONDIE CHERRY, director business college, consultant; b. Shelby, Miss., Mar. 18, 1933; d. Leon and Maudie (Lee) James; m. James Edward King, Dec. 14, 1963 (div. Dec. 1984); 1 child, Beverly Ann Cherry. AA, Diablo Valley Coll., 1979; BVE, San Francisco State U., 1983; MA, Bethune Cookman Coll., 1967, postgrad. Prin. Marion Bus. Coll., Chgo., 1964-74; supr., tchr. Chgo. COIC Orgn., Chgo., 1974-76; counselor, tchr. Peralta Community Coll. Dist., Oakland, Calif., 1978-81; asst. to dir. Spanish Speaking Unity Coun., Oakland, 1983-86; counselor, tchr. S.W. Bus. Coll., San Francisco, 1986-87; counselor, adminstr. Acad. of Stenographic Arts, San Francisco, 1987-89; dir. Dickinson-Warren Bus. Coll., Richmond, Calif., 1990—; internat. demonstrator, model Madame C.J. Walker Betty Coll., Chgo., 1958-76; acad. cons. Brunswick Corp., Chgo., 1968-69; exec. dir. Marion Bus. Coll. Alumni, Chgo., 1974-76. Contbr. articles to profl. jours. Mem. membership com. NAACP, Chgo., 1969-74; mem., sec. Chgo. Urban League, 1972-73; vote registrar community block club, Chgo., 1974-76. Mem. NEA, Calif. Tchrs. Assn., AAUW (Citation 1976, 89), Cen. State Alumni Club (assoc., Plaque 1971), Fantastic Zodiac Ladies (pres. 1972-73, Plaque 1973), Alpha Chi Pi Omega (Citation 1976). Home: 530 Baylor Ct Benicia CA 94510

KING, CANDICE MERIWETHER, psychologist; b. Paducah, Ky., Dec. 21, 1950; d. Corbin and Eleanore (Austin) Meriwether; m. Phillip Crabtree, July 2, 1969 (div. Dec. 1979); 1 child, Bubba; m. Daryl K. Sanderson, Aug. 21, 1982 (dec. Sept. 1987); 1 child, Cassie Lee; m. Gene W. King, Aug. 8, 1988. BA, Murray State U., 1973, MS, 1975, postgrad., 1978. Cert. psychologist, Ky. Child psychologist Paducah (Ky.) Mental Health Cen., 1975-77; dir. psychol. services W.Ky. Easter Seal Cen., Paducah, 1977-78; psychologist McCracken County Sch. System, Paducah, 1978—. Vice chmn. Purchase Area Spouse Abuse Bd., Paducah, 1988. Mem. Ky. Assn. Sch. Adminstrs., W. Ky. Spec. Edn. Coordinators (sec. 1985-87), Women Aware (v.p. 1979-88), Preschool Interagy. Planning Council, Purchase Area Masters' Psychologists (v.p. 1988), Bus. and Profl. Women of Achievement, 1985. Democrat. Baptist. Home: 3735 Jenn Ln Paducah KY 42003 Office: McCracken County Bd Edn 260 Bleich Rd Paducah KY 42003

KING, CAROL LOUISE, city official; b. Detroit, Dec. 10, 1948; d. William Albert and Mary Theresa (Simon) K.; B.A. in English and Speech, Western Mich. U., 1971. Sales rep. Am. Can Co., Detroit, 1973-76; employment counselor, account exec. New Options, In., Detroit, 1976-78; congressional aide, 1978-79; pres. Mich. conf. NOW, 1979-80; placement coordinator Displaced Homemaker Project, Warren, Mich., 1980-82; adminstrv. asst. to Detroit City Councilwoman Maryann Mahaffey, 1982-89; exec. dir. Mich. Abortion Rights Action League, 1989—; legis. liaison, cons. in field. Vice pres. Mich. conf. NOW, 1978-79, pres. Macomb County (Mich.) chpt., 1976-78, nat. chairperson reproductive rights com. 1978-79, nat. bd. dirs., 1980—; bd. dirs. Mich. Welfare Reform Coalition, S.E. Mich. Anti-Rape Network, Sojourner Found.; regional dir. NOW, mem. Mich. Polit. Action Com., nat. bd. dirs. 1980-86; bd. dirs., chairperson pub. affairs Planned Parenthood Detroit, 1980—; founding mem., mem. steering com. Democratic Citizens Caucus, 1980; chmn. Detroit Welfare Reform Coalitions, 1986-89; mem. exec. com. People's Campaign for Choice, 1987-88. Mem. ACLU, Nat. Abortion Rights Action League, Voice of Reason, Older Women's League, Women's Econs. Club Detroit, Detroit Women's Forum. Democrat.

KING, CAROLYN DINEEN, federal judge; b. Syracuse, N.Y., Jan. 30, 1938; d. Robert E. and Carolyn E. (Bareham) Dineen; children: James Randall, Philip Randall, Stephen Randall; m. John L. King, Jan. 1, 1988. A.B. summa cum laude, Smith Coll., 1959; LL.B., Yale U., 1962. Bar: D.C. 1962, Tex. 1963. Practice law Houston, 1962-79; circuit judge U.S. Ct. Appeals 5th Circuit, Houston, 1979—. Trustee, mem. exec. com., treas. Houston Ballet Found., 1967-70; trustee, mem. exec. com. U. St. Thomas, 1988—; mem. Houston dist. adv. council SBA, 1972-76; mem. Dallas regional panel President's Commn. White House Fellowships, 1972-76, mem. commn., 1977; bd. dirs. Houston chpt. Am. Heart Assn., 1978-79; nat. trustee Palmer Drug Abuse Program, 1978-79; trustee, sec., treas., chmn. audit com., fin. com., mem. mgmt. com. United Way Tex. Gulf Coast, 1979-85. Mem. ABA, Fed. Bar Assn., State Bar Tex., Houston Bar Assn., Phi Beta Kappa. Roman Catholic. Office: US Ct Appeals 11020 US Courthouse 515 Rusk Ave Houston TX 77002-2694

KING, CAROLYN MAE, educator; b. Fond du Lac, Wis., Oct. 23, 1946; d. John Francis and Adina Elnora (Bahr) K.; BS, Wis. State U., Oshkosh, 1970; MS, Niagara U., 1974. Tchr. phys. edn. Public Schs. Niagara Falls (N.Y.), 1970-83; women's swim coach Niagara (N.Y.) U., 1975-76; substitute tchr., Niagara Falls, 1983-84, tchr. phys. edn., 1984—, elem. dir., 1987—. Water safety instr. ARC; mem. Nat. Ski Patrol, winter emergency care instr. Recipient award Joseph P. Kennedy Jr. Found., 1972. Mem. Niagara Falls Tchrs., N.Y. State United Tchrs., Am. Fedn. Tchrs., Alpha Kappa Delta. Democrat. Lutheran. Club: College. Home: 459 Chicora Rd Lewiston NY 14092

KING, CHERYL WALLER, writer, conservator of artwork; b. Atlanta, July 17, 1957; d. Robert D. and Belle (Lindler) Waller. BBA, Berry Coll., 1979. Sales major accounts Kerrigan Datamedia Inc.; fin. analyst Dun & Bradstreet, Greenville and Columbia, S.C.; asst. controller Greater Greenville C. of C.; controller Conch Republic Woodworks, Inc., The Headquarters, Inc., Key Largo, Fla.; dir. pub. relations, adminstrv. asst. Mariners Hosp., Plantation Key, Fla. Active ARC, Keys Hosp. Found., Inc. Mem. NAFE, Cousteau Soc., Am. Soc. Profl. And Exec. Women, Amnesty Internat. USA, Greenpeace, Alpha Phi Omega. Home: PO Box 2095 Key Largo FL 33037

KING, CHRISTINE LEDESMA, infosystems specialist; b. N.Y.C., Dec. 15, 1945; d. Ricardo Ledesma and Julia (Benedicto) Ledesma; m. Kenneth K. King Jr., July 29, 1967; children: Michelle Ariadne, Ronald Edward. BA in French, Beaver Coll., Glenside, Pa., 1967; MBA with distinction, Northeastern U., 1985. Pvt. practice translator, interpreter Boston, 1967-74; adminstrv. aide Communication Systems div. GTE Corp., Needham, Mass., 1974-78, mgr. adminstrv. services Bus. Communication Systems div., 1978-81, program mgr. Atlantic Op., 1981-88; bus. area mgr. Govt. Systems div. GTE Corp., 1988—; lectr. telecommunications Northeastern U., Boston, 1981—. Mem. IEEE, Beta Gamma Sigma. Mem. United Ch. Christ.

KING, CHRISTINE PARAN, business analyst, consultant; b. Los Angeles, Aug. 4, 1949; d. Paul Suren and Marjorie Augusta (Jacobs) K. Ed. pub. schs., Fontana, Calif. Sr. engring. technician Atlantic Richfield, Los Angeles, 1973-76; computer coordinator Occidental Petroleum, Irvine, Calif., 1978-79; supr. data processing Stanford Applied Engring., Costa Mesa, Calif., 1979-80; mgr. data processing Chase Manhattan Bank, Heidelberg, Fed. Republic Germany, 1980-81; MIS bus. analyst Apple Computer, Inc., Cupertino, Calif., 1981-85, cons., 1985-87; cons. Keyword Office Tech., San Jose, Calif., 1985; supr. warehouse adminstrn. Nat. Semiconductor, Inc., Sunnyvale, Calif., 1987—; owner jewelry and fine gift shop. Active abused children, homeless causes. Mem. Bus. Women's Assn., Assn. Exec. Saleswomen, Assn. Small Systems Users, No. Calif. PICK Users, Leeds Club. Republican. Home: 1430 Sunshade Ln San Jose CA 95122

KING, CLAUDIA LOUAN, film producer, lecturer; b. Merced, Calif., May 1, 1940; d. Alvin Cecil and Thelma May (Matthew) K.; m. Douglas McLean, July 10, 1965 (div. 1975); children: Kia Gabrielle, Kendra Sue. BA, U. Calif., 1963; MA, Ind. U., 1969. Lectr. U. Fla., Gainesville, 1969-70; asst. prof. U. Nev., Las Vegas, 1973-79; producer Source 17 Prodns., Santa Monica, Calif., 1979-85; freelance producer Chico, Calif., 1985—; freelance producer Chico, Calif., 1985—. Producer Rape is Everybody's Concern, 1978, Los Angeles Personally Yours, 1985; author: (screenplays) The Garden of Eden, 1983, My Sister's Keeper, 1986, Documentary: The Evolution of Women, 1989. Carnegie grantee, 1969; Nev. Endowment for Humanities grantee, 1978. Mem. Women in Film, Coll. Art Assn. Democrat. Home: Rt 1 Box 1476 Orland CA 95926

KING, CORETTA SCOTT (MRS. MARTIN LUTHER KING, JR.), educational association administrator, lecturer, writer, concert singer; b. Marion, Ala., Apr. 27, 1927; d. Obidiah and Bernice (McMurray) Scott; m. Martin Luther King, Jr., June 18, 1953 (dec. Apr. 1968); children: Yolanda Denise, Martin Luther III, Dexter Scott, Bernice Albertine. A.B., Antioch Coll., 1951; Mus.B., New Eng. Conservatory Music, 1954, Mus.D., 1971; L.H.D., Boston U., 1969, Marymount-Manhattan Coll., 1969, Morehouse Coll., 1970; H.H.D., Brandeis U., 1969, Wilberforce U., 1970, Bethune-Cookman Coll., 1970, Princeton U., 1970; LL.D., Bates Coll., 1971. Voice instr. Morris Brown Coll., Atlanta, 1962; commentator Cable News Network, Atlanta, 1980—; lectr., writer; founding pres., chief exec. officer Martin Luther Ling Jr. Ctr. for Nonviolent Social Change Inc. Author: My Life With Martin Luther King, Jr., 1969; contbr. articles to mags.; Concert debut, Springfield, Ohio, 1948, numerous concerts, throughout U.S., concerts, India, 1959, performances, Freedom Concert. Del. to White House Conf. Children and Youth, 1960; sponsor Com. for Sane Nuclear Policy, Com. on Responsibility, Moblzn. to End War in Viet Nam, 1966, 67, Margaret Sanger Meml. Found.; mem. So. Rural Action Project, Inc.; pres. Martin Luther King, Jr. Found.; chmn. Commn. on Econ. Justice for Women; mem. exec. com. Nat. Com. Inquiry; co-chmn. Clergy and Laymen Concerned about Vietnam, Nat. Com. for Full Employment, 1974; pres. Martin Luther King Jr. Center for Nonviolent Social Change; co-chairperson Nat. Com. Full Employment; mem. exec. bd. Nat. Health Ins. Com.; active YWCA; bd. dirs. So. Christian Leadership Conf., Martin Luther King, Jr. Found. Gt. Britain; trustee Robert F. Kennedy Meml. Found., Ebenezer Bapt. Ch. Recipient Outstanding Citizenship award Montgomery (Ala.) Improvement Assn., 1959, Merit award St. Louis Argus, 1960, Distinguished Achievement award Nat. Orgn. Colored Women's Clubs, 1962, Louise Waterman Wise award Am. Jewish Congress Women's Aux., 1963, Myrtle Wreath award Cleve. Hadassah, 1965, award for excellence in field human relations Soc. Family of Man, 1968, Universal Love award Premio San Valentine Com., 1968, Wateler Peace prize, 1968, Dag Hammarskjold award, 1969, Pacem in Terris award Internat. Overseas Service Found., 1969, Leadership for Freedom award Roosevelt U., 1971, Martin Luther King Meml. medal Coll. City N.Y., 1971, Internat. Viareggio award, 1971, numerous others; named Woman of Year Utility Club N.Y.C., 1962, Woman of Year Nat. Assn. Radio and TV Announcers, 1968. Mem. Nat. Council Negro Women (Ann. Brotherhood award 1957), Women Strike for Peace (del. disarmament conf. Geneva, Switzerland 1962, citation for work in peace and freedom 1963), Women's Internat. League for Peace and Freedom, NAACP, United Ch. Women (bd. mgrs.), Alpha Kappa Alpha (hon.). Baptist (mem. choir, guild adviser). Club: Links (Human Dignity and Human Rights award Norfolk chpt. 1964). Address: Martin Luther King Jr Ctr 449 Auburn Ave NE Atlanta GA 30312

KING, DELORES LUVINA, college official; b. Topeka, Apr. 1, 1937; d. Perry Leon Wash and Dorothy Martha (Perkins) Anderson; m. Harry King, Apr. 12, 1959 (div. Apr. 1967). AA, Kennedy-King Coll., Chgo., 1972; BSBA, Roosevelt U., Chgo., 1975. Clk.-typist Montgomery Ward, Chgo., 1956-63, Ill. State Psychiat. Inst., Chgo., 1963-72; records officer, credential specialist Ill. Coll. Optometry, Chgo., 1972—; tng. specialist in gen. ednl. devel. Leader Girl Scouts U.S.A., Chgo., 1967-71; treas. United Meth. Women, Chgo., 1969-72; sec. Nat. Gospel Choirs and Choruses, Chgo., 1984-89, pres. 1989—; mem. Assn. Community Orgns. for Reform Now, Chgo., 1985—. Mem. Am. Collegiate Assn. Registrars and Admissions Officers, Ill. Collegiate Assn. Registrars and Admissions Officers, Roosevelt U. Alumni Assn., Radiant Circle (pres. 1971-86). Democrat. Home: 11114 S Normal Ave Chicago IL 60628

KING, EDWINA L., image consultant; b. Birmingham, Ala., July 2, 1952; d. David and Bertha (Caffee) Lewis; m. David Wesley King III, Nov. 22, 1972. AA in Nursing, San Antonio Coll., 1979. Staff nurse Santa Rosa Med. Ctr., San Antonio, 1980-82; asst. dir. nursing Oakhill Care Ctr., San Antonio, 1982; asst. dir. nursing Four Seasons Nursing Ctr., San Antonio, 1982-83, dir. nursing, 1983-86; staff nurse Profl. Nurses Bur., San Antonio, 1986—; cert. image cons. Beauticontrol, Inc., Dallas, 1989, dir., 1990. Republican. Office: Edwina L King and Assoc 8342 Star Creek San Antonio TX 78251

KING, ELAINE SLATTON, college administrator; b. Greenville, S.C., Apr. 2, 1947; d. Dennis Ralph and Erie Nora (Barnett) Slatton; m. Gary Edward King, Sept. 22, 1946. Grad. high sch., Greer, S.C. Bookkeeper North Greenville Coll., Tigerville, S.C., 1966-73, bus. office mgr., 1973—; auditor North Greenville Assn. Women's Missionary Union, Travelers Rest, S.C., 1985—. Recipient Outstanding Leadership award North Greenville Coll., 1985, Disting. Service award, 1986. Mem. Coll. Univ. Personnel Assn., Foothills Community (Tigerville, S.C.) Club. Republican. Baptist. Home: PO Box 233 Tigerville SC 29688 Office: North Greenville Coll Tigerville SC 29688

KING, ELIZABETH MAUREEN, applications system manager; b. Bellefonte, Pa., Nov. 13, 1957; d. Richard A. and Joanne Sellers King. BA, Pa. State U., University Park, 1979. Mgr. application systems Jack Eckerd Corp., Clearwater, Fla.; systems analyst R.H. Macy, Newark. Betty J. Lockington scholar, Martin Marietta scholar. Mem. NAFE, Gulf Coast Exec. Women, Phi Beta Kappa, Phi Kappa Phi, Pi Sigma Alpha. Home: 12136 73d St N Largo FL 34643

KING, ELIZABETH RAYMOND, geophysicist; b. Halifax, Can., Dec. 5, 1923; d. Harold Skinner and Susan (Raymond) K. AB, Smith Coll., Northampton, Mass., 1947. Geologist U.S. Geol. Survey, Washington, 1948-51, exploration geophysicist, 1951-64; rsch. geophysicist U.S. Geol. Survey, Washington, Reston, Va., 1964—. Contbr. articles to tech. jours. Sec., East Silver Spring (Md.) Citizens Assn., 1983—. Nielson scholar Smith Coll., 1946-47. Fellow Geol. Soc. Am.; mem. Soc. Exploration Geophysicists, Am. Geophys. Union, AAAS, Geol. Soc. Washington, Potomac Geophys. Soc. (founding mem., v.p. 1975-76), Alumnae Assn. Smith Coll. Unitarian. Home: 8403 Hartford Ave Silver Spring MD 20910 Office: US Geol Survey MS927 Nat Ctr Reston VA 22092

KING, GLORIA REED, pharmacist; b. Pine Bluff, Ark., Jan. 13, 1946; d. William Drew and Alvern (O'Steen) Reed; stepdau. Margaret Eastham Reed; m. Eddie Lamar King, June 5, 1965; 1 child, Michael Kay. BS in Pharmacy, U. Ark., 1974, MS in Inst. Pharmacy, 1984. Pharmacy res. U. Ark. Med. Sci. Hosp., Little Rock, Ark., 1974-75; staff pharmacist HCA Doctors Hosp., Little Rock, 1975; pharmacy supr. Drs. Hosp., Little Rock, 1975-76, dir. pharmacy, 1976—. Mem. Ark. Assn. Hosp. Pharmacists (pres. 1985), Ark. Pharmacists Assn. (bd. dirs. 1985), Am. Soc. Hosp. Pharmacists, Rho Chi, Kappa Epsilon (past chpt. sec.). Baptist. Office: 6101 W Capitol Little Rock AR 72205

KING, GWENDOLYN BAIR, public speaker; b. Hartsville, S.C., Oct. 27, 1915; d. William Parlor and Mary Margaret (Scurry) Bair; m. LaBruce Ward King, Dec. 26, 1937; children: John LaBruce King, Margaret Gwendolyn King Farrow. AB, Coker Coll., 1936. With asst. pers. office Libr. Congress, Washington, 1937-39; sec., dir. Libr. Congress, Union Catalog, Washington, 1939-43; asst. to appointments sec. for the President The White House, Washington, 1953-69, dir. correspondence for Pat Nixon, 1969-74; pub. speaker on White House career Calif., 1977—. Contbr. to Presidential Records, The Nat. Archives, Washington, 1988. Dir. Speakers' Bur., Home Hospice, Santa Rosa, Calif., 1985, cert. caregiver, 1982-84; mem. Oakmont Archtl. Com., Santa Rosa Symphony League. Named Paul Harris Fellow, Rotary Internat., 1983, Citizen of the Day, KABL, San Francisco, 1983. Mem. AAUW, Newcomers Club (pres. Santa Rosa chpt. 1977-78), Oakmont Book Club (chmn. 1981-82), Oakmont Golf Club (sec. 1986), Saturday Afternoon Club. Republican. Unitarian Universalist. Home: 451 Pythian Rd Santa Rosa CA 95409

KING, HELEN JELKS, optometrist; b. Balt., July 2, 1958; d. Allen Nathaniel and Mary (Larson) Jelks; m. Christopher Burnette King, June 16, 1983; children: Benjamin, Bryan. BS, Emory U., 1979; Grad., So. Coll. Optometry, Memphis, Tenn., 1983. Lic. optometrist. Optometrist, owner King & King, Englewood, Fla., 1983—. Mem. Fla. Optometric Assn., Profl. and Bus. Women's Orgn., Young Women's Club. Republican. Methodist. Home: 140 S Oxford Dr Englewood FL 34223 Office: King & King ODS PA 1800 Placida Rd Englewood FL 34223

KING, IMOGENE MARTINA, educator, nurse; b. West Point, Iowa, Jan. 30, 1923. Diploma, St. John's Hosp., 1945; B.S. in Nursing, St. Louis U., 1948; M.S. in Nursing, 1957; Ed.D., Columbia U., 1961; Ph.D. (hon.), So. Ill. U., 1980. Instr. med.-surg. nursing St. John's Hosp., St. Louis, 1947-58; asst. prof. nursing, then assoc. prof. Loyola U, Chgo., 1961-66; prof. grad. program in nursing Loyola U, 1972-80; prof. U. South Fla., Tampa, 1980-90, prof. emeritus, 1990—; asst. chief research Grants br. div. nursing HEW, Washington, 1966-68; prof., dean sch. nursing Ohio State U., Columbus, 1968-72; mem. def. adv. com. on women in the services Dept. Def., 1972-75; cons. VA Hosp. Alderman Ward 2, Wood Dale, Ill., 1975-79, chmn. fin. com. Author: Toward a Theory for Nursing, 1971, A Theory for Nursing: Systems, Concepts, Process, 1981, transl. to Japanese, 1983, transl. to Spanish, 1985, Curriculum and Instruction in Nursing, 1986; contbr. articles in nursing to profl. jours., chpts. to books. Recipient Recognition of Contbns. to Nursing Edn. award Columbia U. Tchrs. Coll., 1983, Disting. Scholar award U. So. Fla., 1988-89. Mem. Am. Nurses Assn., Ill. Nurses Assn. (recipient highest recognition award 1975, award 19th dist. 1975), Fla. Nurses Assn. (pres. dist. IV 1983-84, Nurse of Yr. 1984, nursing rsch. award 1985), Fla. Nurses Found. (pres. 1988—), Sigma Theta Tau (counselor 1981-83, pres.-elect 1986-87, pres. 1987-89, Founders award for Excellence in Edn 1989, disting. lectr. 1990, 91), Phi Kappa Phi (scholar award 1986).

KING, JEANNETTE WERTZ, microbiologist, researcher; b. Helena, Mont., July 18, 1937; d. Wesley W. and Virginia (Kelley) Wertz; m. Kenneth L. King, Aug. 17, 1959; children: Virginia, Cynthia, Melanie, Kendall, Kristi. BA, Tex. Christian U., 1959. Rsch. microbiologist Denver Rsch. Inst., 1967-82; dir. energy div. Fairleigh Dickinson Lab., Abilene, Tex., 1982—; asst. rsch. prof. Hardin-Simmons U., Abilene, 1983—. Editor: Bio Recovery Jour., 1987—. Mem. Am. Soc. Microbiology, Soc. Indsl. Microbiology, Ind. Petroleum Assn. Am., Tex. Ind. Producers and Royalty Owners, W. Tex. Oil and Gas Assn., Nat. Stripper Well Assn., Abilene Women's Club, AAUW, PEO (treas. 1986-87), Abilene C. of C. (sci. and tech. com. 1989—). Democrat. Home: 13 Fairway Oaks Blvd Abilene TX 79606 Office: Hardin Simmons U Fairleigh Dickinson Rsch Abilene TX 79606

KING, JENNIFER CAROLYN, marketing and promotions entrepreneur; b. N.Y.C., Oct. 8, 1960; d. Robert Eliot and Dorothy Lucine (Jones) K.; m. Timothy C. Fredel, 1989. Student, U. Colo., Boulder, 1978-81; BA in Bus. Mgmt., Simmons Coll., Boston, 1984. Asst. to exec. dir. SRI Internat., Menlo Park, Calif., 1981-82; dir. mktg. Pacific Ventures, Palo Alto, Calif., 1984-85; pres. JCK Enterprises, Menlo Park, 1985—, Synergistic Designs, San Francisco, 1985—, Rugged Elegance, Kennebunkport, Maine, 1989—. Producer promotional campaign (posters) Medical Alley, 1986, 88, (serigraph and lithograph) Ams. cup campaign Survival of the Fastest, 1987, N. Calif. campaign Biotech Bay, 1989. Recipient Illustration award, Communication Arts, Palo Alto, 1987, Design award, 1987, Graphics Design award, Graphis, Switzerland. Mem. Community Entrepreneurs Orgn., Alumnae Resource Ctr., Simmons Alumnae, Kappa Kappa Gamma. Republican. Presbyterian. Home: 1525 Chestnut St #2 San Francisco CA 94123 Office: JCK Enterprises 927 Hermosa Way Menlo Park CA 94025

KING, JOYCE CALISTRI, columnist; b. Charleroi, Pa., May 26, 1927; d. Jeremiah James and Vera Colette (Hurley) Calistri; m. William Louis King, II, Dec. 22, 1951; children: Mari Joyce, William Louis, III, Donald II. BA, U. Pa. Coll. for Women, 1949. Tchr. Romper Room TV, WTPA-TV, Harrisburg, Pa., 1954-55, WGAL-TV, Lancaster, Pa., 1956-57; hostess, producer Joyce King Show, WHP-TV, Harrisburg, Pa., 1959-60; sta. mgr. WSUB-TV Cable, Shillington, Pa., 1969-70; publicity dir. Bavarian Festival, Barnesville, Pa., 1974-76; wine columnist Reading Eagle, Reading, Pa., 1978—; feature writer Reading Eagle, 1978—; freelance columnist newspapers, mags., 1972—; student activities dir. Reading Hosp. Sch. Nursing, Reading, Pa., 1965-69; newsletter editor Young Republicans, Harrisburg, Pa., 1949-50, AAUW, 1955-56; dir. publicity Green Hills Theatre, Reading, Pa., 1963-67; mem. Pres.'s Art Council. Alvernia Coll. Scholar Am. Legion, U. Pa., 1945. Mem. Am. Women Radio and TV (pres. 1960), AAUW (v.p. 1955). Republican. Roman Catholic. Home: 2624 Whittier Ave Sinking Spring PA 19608 Office: Reading Eagle 345 Penn St PO Box 582 Reading PA 19603

KING, JUDITH ANN, computer operator; b. Little Rock, Sept. 16, 1950; d. Howard and Ida Mae (Stockwell) K. Grad. exec. sec., Draughon Sch. Bus., Little Rock, 1972-73; BA in Sociology, BA in Psychology, U. Ark., 1979, postgrad., 1979-80; postgrad., Rhema Bible Sch., Tulsa, 1991. Vol. Ark. Children's Hosp., Little Rock, 1970-72; salesperson Amway, Little Rock, 1983-85, 89—; telephone computer operator AT&T, Little Rock, 1969—.

Organizer, worker Bush campaign Rep. party, Little Rock, 1988. Office: AT&T 5705 W 65th St Rm 133 Little Rock AR 72209

KING, KATHERINE CHUNGHO, pediatrician; b. Beijing, People's Republic of China, Aug. 27, 1937; came to U.S., 1955; d. Ginpoh Yeh and Wen Ying (Hsu) King; m. Peter A.J. Adam (wid. June 1980); m. Louis H. Li, June 8, 1985. BA, Meredith Coll., 1957; MD, Bowman Gray Sch. Medicine, 1962. Diplomate Nat. Bd. Med. Examiners, Am. Bd. Pediatrics, Am. Bd. Neonatal-Perinatal Medicine. Resident in pediatrics Cleve. Metro Gen. Hosp./Case Western Res. U., 1962-66; instr. of pediatrics Case Western Res. U., Cleve., 1969-71, asst. prof. to assoc. prof. pediatrics, 1971-85, assoc. prof. reproductive biology, 1979-85; assoc. prof. pediatrics Albert Einstein Coll. of Medicine, N.Y.C., 1989—; co-dir. Perinatal Clin. Rsch. Ctr. Cleve. Metro Gen. Hosp., 1969-85, dir. div. hematology, 1981-85; staff hematologist Schneider Children's Hosp., New Hyde Park, N.Y., 1985—. Contbr. articles to profl. jours. Recipient grants for Devel. of Glucose Control, Diabetics Assn. of Greater Cleve., 1968-70, Disordered Fetal Metabolish, NIH, 1983-88, GIP Responses of Newborns, Ross Labs., 1983, Perinatal Outreach, Fan Fox and Leslie R. Samuel Found., N.Y., 1990. Fellow Am. Acad. Pediatrics, Am. Coll. Nutrition; mem. Am. Fedn. Clin. Rsch., Soc. Pediatric Rsch., Ea. Soc. Pediatric Rsch., Am. Diabetes Assn. Home: 19 Gramatan Ct Bronxville NY 10708 Office: Schneider Childrens Hosp New Hyde Park NY 11042

KING, KATHLEEN MURPHY, media center supervisor; b. Danville, Ky., Apr. 3, 1944; d. Dudley C. Sr. and Gladys (Royce) Murphy; children: Robert C. King II, Lydia Marie King. BA, U. Tulsa, 1966; MS, Okla. State U., 1989. Chief exec. officer Data Share, Oklahoma City, 1982-83; exec. adminstr. Whole World Family Pub., Tulsa, 1983-84; supr. media ctr. Coll. of Edn. Okla. State U., Stillwater, 1986—; mgmt. cons. cablecast of Homecoming Parade, Stillwater, 1988—; curriculum design cons. Applied Bus. Telecommunications, San Ramon, Calif., 1990. Writer/producer/dir.: video Tough Love, 1986; producer, co-dir.: radio drama A Turkey's Tale, 1988; writer/producer/dir: radio documentary What Future the Past, 1987; author: manual Cablecasting the Homecoming Parade at Okla. State U., 1989. Mem. Women in Communications, Okla. Broadcast Educators, Internat. TV Assn., Alpha Epsilon Rho. Republican. Episcopalian. Office: Okla State U Media Ctr Coll Edn 203 Gundersen Hall Stillwater OK 74078

KING, LAURA JANE, librarian, genealogist; b. Pemberville, Ohio, Jan. 19, 1947; d. Richard D. and Jessie Florence (Brown) Zepernick; B.A., Bowling Green (Ohio) State U., 1969, M.Ed., 1976; m. Bruce William King, June 17, 1972; 1 child, Christian Andrew. Cert. geneal. lectr.; cert. geneal. record searcher. County extension agt. home econs. Ohio Coop. Extension Svc., Paulding County, 1970-77; local and family historian Pemberville Pub. Libr.; mem. PRIDE com., vocat. home econs. dept. Paulding Exempted Village, 1975—; instr. genealogy Continuing Edn. Bowling Green State U., Eastwood Sch. Dist. Community Edn. Mem. Paulding County Bicentennial Commn., 1975-77; organist 1st Presbyn. Ch., Pemberville, ruling elder, ch. historian. Recipient Tenure award Coop. Extension Svc., 1975; mem. Wood County Citizen's Com. for Bicentennial of U.S. Constn. and NW Ordinance; mem. Pemberville Sch. Adv. Com. Mem. Ohio Geneal. Soc. (pres. Wood County chpt. 1978-80, chmn. pub. rels. chmn. 1982-83, chmn. First Families of Wood County com.), Berks County Geneal. Soc., Palatines to Am., DAR (vice regent chpt. 1975-77, regent chpt. 1979-83, registrar chpt. 1985—, state vice chmn. pages 1978-80, state chmn. lineage rsch. 1980-87, state and div. outstanding jr. mem. 1980, state chmn. membership commn. 1983-87, state recording sec. 1987—, state corr. sec. 1989—, area speaker's staff), U.S. Daus. of 1812 (chmn. state insignia), First Families Ohio, Daus. Union Vets., Nat. Soc. Magna Charta Dames, Colonial Dames 17th Century, Daus. Am. Colonists (chpt. regent 1986—, state chmn. pub. rels., 1987, chmn. mideast region pub. rels.), Bus. and Profl. Women's Club (pres. Paulding 1975-76, v.p. 1974-75), Am. Home Econs. Assn., Ohio Home Econs. Assn. (cert. home economist), Coun. Ohio Genealogists, Colonial Order Crown of Charlemagne, Phi Upsilon Omicron Alumni. Club: Order Eastern Star. Corr. docent DAR Mus., Washington. Home: 14553 N River Rd Pemberville OH 43450

KING, LAUREN JUANITA, chiropractor; b. Baltimore, Wash., Oct. 13, 1951; d. George Rutherford and Edwina J. (Bryant) K.; m. James Jaworski, Aug. 1979 (div. 1981); m. Jeffrey J. Donchez, Mar. 20, 1982; children: Tamar R., Alexander J.R. D of Chiropractic, Palmer Coll., 1973. Diplomate Am. Bd. Chiropractic Orthopedists. Assoc. King Clinic, Mt. Vernon, Wash., 1973-80; ptnr., dir. King Clinics, Inc., Mt. Vernon, 1980-86; dir. King Chiropractic Clinic, Inc., Mt. Vernon, 1986—, Chiropractic Cons., N.W., Inc., Mt. Vernon, 1986—; mem. Wash. State Bd. Examiners, Olympia, 1984—; cons. Wash. Dept. Labor and Industries, Olympia, 1981—. Bd. trustees Western States Chiropractic Coll., Portland, Oreg., 1985-89. Fellow Acad. Chiropractic Orthopedists; mem. Am. Chiropractic Assn., Wash. Chiropractic Assn., Sigma Phi Chi (pres. 1971-72). Home: 17210 68th Ave W Edmonds WA 98026 Office: King Chiropractic Clinic 124 N 18th Mount Vernon WA 98273

KING, LINDA ORR, museum director; b. Washington, June 21, 1948; d. William Baxter and Jayne (Reiser) Orr; m. James McClain King, June 3, 1947; children: David, Adam, Lindsay. BA, La. State U., 1970, MA in Fine Arts, 1971. Fine arts history asst. La. State U., Baton Rouge, 1967-70, grad. asst., 1970-71; assoc. curator La. State Mus., New Orleans, 1971-74; curator Coastal Ga. Hist. Soc./Mus. Coastal History, St. Simons Island, 1984-87; dir. Coastal Ga. Hist. Soc., St. Simons Island, 1987—. Co-editor: (photograph essay) George Francois Mugnier, 1975. Bd. dirs. St. Vincent dePaul Soc., Glynn County, Ga., 1982—, Coastal Area Planning and Devel. Commn.-Adv. Coun. on Historic Preservation, 1987; mem. Glynn County Courthouse Renovation Com., 1989. Recipient Kellogg Career Enhancement award Kellogg Found., 1989. Mem. Ga. Assn. Mus.'s and Galleries (treas. 1987-89), Coastal Mus.'s Assn. (treas. 1987-89). Roman Catholic. Office: Coastal Georgia Hist Soc 101 12th St Saint Simons Island GA 31522

KING, LIS SONDER, public relations executive, writer; b. Roskilde, Denmark; came to U.S., 1956, naturalized, 1961; d. Carl Otto and Gerda Vohnsen (Sonder) Petersen; m. Robert King (div. 1972); 1 dau., Dorte; m. Theodore Allin Pace, 1972; grad. Roskilde Katedralskole, arts degree Sch. Fine Arts, Copenhagen, 1952. Feature writer Berlingske Tidende, Copenhagen, 1956-58; reporter, editor Moreau Pub. Co., Bloomfield, N.J., 1957-59; reporter, editor St. Thomas (V.I.) Daily News, Island Times, San Juan, P.R., 1962-63; editor The Advance, Dover, N.J., 1961-63; pub. relations dir. Fluid Chem. Co., Newark, 1963-64, Keyes, Martin & Co., Springfield, N.J., 1964-69; pres. Lis King Pub. Relations, Mahwah, N.J., 1969—; columnist Harris Pubs., N.Y.C., 1981—, Suburban News, Paramus, N.J., 1986—. Author, editor: St. Thomas Directory, 1962; author: Furniture: Make-Do, Make-Over, Make Your Own, 1977; contbr. articles to various pubs. Mem. Nat. Home Fashions League, Taxpayers Assn. Mahwah. Avocations: travel, gardening, reading, breeding Great Danes. Home and Office: 30 Dundee Ct Box 725 Mahwah NJ 07430

KING, MARCIA, library director; b. Lewiston, Maine, Aug. 4, 1940; d. Daniel Alden and Clarice Evelyn (Curtis) Barrell; m. Howard P. Lowell, Feb. 15, 1969 (div. 1980); m. Richard G. King Jr., Aug., 1980. BS, U. Maine, 1965; MSLS, Simmons Coll., 1967. Reference, field advisory and bookmobile librarian Maine State Library, Augusta, 1965-69; dir. Lithgow Pub. Library, Augusta, 1969-72; exec. sec. Maine Library Adv. Com., Maine State Library, 1972-73; dir. Wayland (Mass.) Free Pub. Library, 1973-76; state librarian State of Oreg., Salem, 1976-82; dir. Tucson Pub. Library, 1982—. Past chmn. bd. dirs. Tucson United Way; chmn. adv. bd. com. Sta. KUAT (PBS-TV and Radio); mem. adv. bd. Resources for Women, Inc., Salvation Army. Mem. ALA, Pub. Library Assn., Ariz. State Library Assn., AAUW, Assn. Specialized and Coop. Library Agys. Unitarian. Office: Tucson Pub Libr 101 N Stone Ave PO Box 27470 Tucson AZ 85726-7470

KING, MARCIA GYGLI, artist; b. Cleve., June 4, 1931; d. Robert Prescott and Ruth (Farr) Gygli; m. Rollin White King, May 10, 1956 (div. 1974); children: Rollin White King Jr., Edward Prescott King. BA, Smith Coll., 1953; MFA, U. Tex., San Antonio, 1981. Docent Nat. Gallery Art, Washington, 1956-60; organizer, dir. docent program McNay Art Mus., San Antonio, 1964-76; art critic Express news, San Antonio, 1976-77; artist N.Y.C., 1979—; lectr. Nat. Gallery Art, Washington, 1956-60, div. continuing edn. U. Tex., 1976, So. Meth. U., Dallas, 1984, McNay Art Mus., San Antonio, 1984, Washington Project for the Arts, 1985, Monserrat Coll. Art, Beverly, Mass., 1987, Whitney Mus., Phillip Morris, N.Y.C., 1988, Lehman Coll. CUNY, 1988; panelist Panel on Women in the Arts, Alexandria, Va., 1978, Washington Project for the Arts, 1985, Corpus Christi (Tex.) State U., 1986. One woman shows include McNenama O'Connor Mus., Victoria, Tex., 1975, Douglas Coll. Rutgers U., New Brunswick, N.J., 1981, McNay Art Mus., San Antonio, 1984, Mattingly Baker Gallery, Dallas, 1984, White Columns, N.Y., 1985, Parker Smalley Gallery, N.Y., Manhattan Marymount, N.Y., 1986, Ferver Gallery, N.Y., 1987, Katzen Brown Gallery, N.Y.C., 1988, 90, Haines Gallery, San Francisco, 1988, Wallace Wentworth Gallery, Washington, 1988, U. N.C., 1989, Valerie Miller Gallery, Palm Desert, Calif., 1989, Cleve. Ctr. for Contemporary Art, 1989-90; represented in collections Bklyn. Mus., Cleve. Mus., Guggenheim Mus., Johnson Mus., Cornell U., Nat. Mus. Women in Arts, Newark Mus., Rogers Coll., Istambul. Recipient James Kirkeby Nat. Meml. award Tex. Watercolor Soc., 1976, Brewer's Digest award Lone Star Brewery Day, 1963, Annual Z.T. Scott award & cir. Tex. Fine Arts Assn., 1970, Ethel T. Drought Meml. award San Antonio Art League Exhbn., 1971, Best of Show award Tex. Watercolor Show, 1971, First Purchase Prize, Tex. Watercolor Show, 1972, First Purchase Prize, 17th Delta Annual, Ark. Art. Ctr., 1974; named Outstanding Woman in San Antonio, Women's Polit. Caucus, 1979. Office: 477 Broome St 63 New York NY 10013

KING, MARCIA JONES, potter, physicist; b. Oak Park, Ill., May 17, 1934; d. Walter Leland Jones and Florence W. (Dull) Anderson; m. James Craig King, Nov., 1953 (div. 1966); 1 child, James Craig King, Jr. BS, Johns Hopkins U., 1960, PhD, 1969. Elec. engr. Electronic Communications, Inc., Timonium, Md., 1959-63; research assoc. theoretical particle physics Syracuse (N.Y.) U., 1969-72; asst. editor The Physical Rev. Brookhaven Nat. Lab., Upton, N.Y., 1972-74; physicist Argonne (Ill.) Nat. Lab., 1974-78; pvt. practice potter and physicist Syracuse, N.Y., 1978—. Contbr. articles to profl. jours.; exhibiter pots throughout cen. N.Y. Mem. AAAS, Am. Physical Soc., Syracuse Ceramic Guild (pres. 1982-84), Phi Beta Kappa, Sigma Xi. Democrat. Home and Office: 228 Buckingham Ave Syracuse NY 13210

KING, MARGARET ANN, communications educator; b. Marion, Ind., Feb. 27, 1936; d. Paul Milton and Janet Mary (Broderick) Burke; m. Charles Claude King, Aug. 25, 1956; children: C. Kevin, Elizabeth Ann, Paul S., Margaret C. Student, Ohio Dominican, 1953-56, U. Kans., 1980-81; BA in Communication, Purdue U., 1986, MA in Pub. Communication, 1990. Regional rep. Indpls. Juv. Justice Task Force, 1984-85; tchr. asst. dept. communication Purdue U., West Lafayette, Ind., 1986—. Charter bd. mem. Tippecanoe Council Drug & Alcohol, Lafayette, Ind., 1985; grad., mem. Leadership Lafayette, 1983. Purdue U. fellow, 1986-87. Mem. Speech Communication Assn. Am., Cen. States Communication Assn. (conv. paper 1989), Golden Key Nat. Hon. Soc., Phi Kappa Phi. Republican. Roman Catholic. Home: 1613 Redwood Ln Lafayette IN 47905 Office: Purdue U Dept Communication West Lafayette IN 47907

KING, MARY JANE, communications and media relations specialist; b. Tuscaloosa, Ala., Nov. 18, 1950; d. John Argyle and Mary Jane (Whitten) K. BA with high hon., Agnes Scott Coll., 1972; MA, Emory U., 1974. Coord. publicity The Omni (Atlanta Coliseum Inc.), 1975-76; sr. pub. rels. specialist Ga. Dept. Industry, Trade and Tourism, Atlanta, 1976-79; freelance writer Atlanta, 1980-81; events editor Emory U., Atlanta, 1981-83, program asst. Emory Ctr. for Internat. Studies, 1984-86; communications coord. Capital City Club, Atlanta, 1986-88; communications and cultural affairs officer Can. Consulate Gen., Atlanta, 1988—. Mem. DeKalb dist. com. Atlanta area coun. Boy Scouts Am., 1983—; mem. governing bd. Atlanta Resource Found., 1983—; docent Friends of Zoo Atlanta, 1986—. Named Ga.'s Jr. Miss, America's Jr. Miss Pageant, 1968; Rotary Found. fellow, 1979-80. Mem. Can.-Am. Soc. Southeastern U.S. (editor newsletter 1989—), Atlanta Press Club, Phi Beta Kappa. Presbyterian. Office: Can Consulate Gen One CNN Ctr South Tower Ste 400 Atlanta GA 30303-2705

KING, MARY SMOTHERS, management; b. Memphis, Oct. 28, 1937; d. Dwight Dewitt and Lillian Helen (Flowers) Smothers; m. Charles Stirling King, Jan. 18, 1963 (div. 1982); children: Lillian Lee, Frances Elizabeth, Mary Nell. Student, McNeese U., Lake Charles, La., 1966-67, MusB, 1965; MA, Corpus Christi State U., Tex., 1985. Flight attendant Am. Air Lines, Buffalo, 1962; paralegal Pvt. Law Practice, Lake Charles, La., 1967-78; gen. mgr. Lake Charles Symphony, La., 1978-81; asst. controller White River Drilling Co., Corpus Christi, Tex.; exec. asst. Zoom, Inc. Prodn. Co., Corpus Christi, Tex., 1982-84; exec. dir. Camp Fire Council of Corpus Christi, Tex., 1984-85, USO of S. Tex., Inc., Corpus Christi, 1985—; bd. mem. Lake Charles Symphony, La. 1975-78, Heart Assn., Lake Charles La. 1974, Bethune Day Care Ctr., Corpus Christi Tex., 1986; hon. tailhooker USN, Corpus Christi Tex. 1987—. Composer, Performer: Work for Organ & Voice, Psalm 97 1965; soloist multiple symphonies Operas Little Theatre, Tenn., La., Ark., Tex., 1956-73. Sec. Jr. League Lake Charles La., 1971-73; campaign mgr. Pol. Race for Dist. Judge Calcasieu & Cameron Parishes, La. 1978-79,La. 1978-79. Recipient Commander's award for Pub. Service, U.S. Army, 1989. Mem. Jr. League Corpus Christi, Nat. Assn. Female Execs., Young Men's Bus. Aux. Club Lake Charles (Pres. 1966-67), Lake Charles Club (Pres. 1970-71), Kiwanis Lions Club, Am. Bus. WOmen's Clubs, Rotary Corpus Christi. Republican. Baptist. Home: 1515 Ennis Joslin #107 Corpus Christi TX 78412 Office: USO of S Tex Building 3 Naval Air Station Corpus Christi TX 78419

KING, MARY-CLAIRE, epidemiologist, educator, geneticist; b. Evanston, Ill., Feb. 27, 1946; 1 child, Emily King Colwell. BA in Math., Carleton Coll., 1966; PhD in Genetics, U. Calif., Berkeley, 1973. Asst. prof. U. Calif., Berkeley, 1976-80, assoc. prof., 1980-84, prof., 1984—; mem. bd. sci. counselors Nat. Cancer Inst.; cons. Com. for Investigation of Disappearance of Persons, Govt. Argentina, Buenos Aires, 1984—. Contbr. more than 80 articles to profl. jours. Recipient Alumni Achievement award Carleton Coll. Mem. AAAS, Am. Soc. Human Genetics, Soc. Epidemiologic Research, Phi Beta Kappa, Sigma Xi. Office: U Calif Sch Pub Health Berkeley CA 94720

KING, MARYLEE HANSEN, academic administrator; b. Seattle, Mar. 19, 1946; d. LeRoy Robert and Wilma (Mackenzie) Hansen; m. Norman Bruce King; children: Arthur N., Elizabeth Anne H. BS in Eng. & Journalism, Oreg. State U., 1968; MS in Coll. Adminstrn., Ind. U., 1970. Asst. dir. of residence living Wash. State U., Pullman, Wash., 1970-73; assoc. dir. of residence living Wash. State U., Pullman, 1973-75; coord. instr. of participating cit. edn. prog. Wash. State U., Mabton; prog. devel. and career devel. instr. Bakersfield Coll., Bakersfield, Calif., 1984-86; dir. interdisciplinary studies Marylhurst (Oreg.) Coll., 1988—; instr. Yakima Valley Coll., Sunnyside, Wash., 1977-78; cons., bilingual edn. compliance, State of Wash., Sunnyside, 1977-78. Author: article (with others), Jour. Coll. Student Personnel Adminstrn. 1973, handbook, Handbook for Renters, 1971, prog. guide, Ind. U. Prog. Manual, 1969. Co-leader Campfire Girls, Calif. and Oreg., 1984—; trustee, clk. Richland Sch. Dist. Bd. of Trustees, Shafter, Calif., 1981-86; founder, pres. Adult Day Care Ctr. Alzheimers, Bakersfield, Calif., 1983-86; mem. bioethics com. Eastmorland Hosp., 1989—. Mem. AAUW (branch pres. 1987-89; Oreg. div. bd. issue chmn. 1989—; Barbara Leask Community and Branch Svc. award, Bakersfield, 1986, Hon. Named Gift to Edn. Found. Prog., 1983), Women in Higher Edn. (steering com. 1989—), Jr. League of Portland (sustainer), Delta Kappa Gamma (rsch. chmn. 1988-89). Office: Marylhurst Coll Marylhurst OR 97036

KING, MONICA KAYLA, art gallery director; b. Crowley, L.A., May 14, 1962; d. Joseph Sherwood and Daisy Edith (Kibodeaux) King; m. Jerry Daigle, Aug. 11, 1979. High Sch. Grad., 1975-79. Gallery dir. Crowley Art Assn. Gallery Inc., L.A., 1983-89. Mem. Crowley Art Assn., Acadia Parish Homemakers. Democrat. Baptist. Office: Crowley Art Assn 111 W 3rd St Crowley LA 70527

KING, PATRICIA MILLER, library administrator, historian; b. Bklyn., July 26, 1937; d. Donald Knox and Amy Beatrice (Heyliger) Miller; m. Samuel W. Stein, Jan. 2, 1978 (dec. May 1988); 1 child by previous marriage, Victoria Elizabeth King. A.B., Radcliffe Coll., 1959, A.M., 1961; Ph.D., Harvard U., 1970. Teaching asst. Harvard U., 1965-70; asst. prof. Wellesley Coll., Mass., 1970-71; dir. research Haney Assocs., Concord, Mass., 1971-73; dir. Schlesinger Library, Radcliffe Coll., 1973—, dir. projects. Contbr. articles to profl. jours. Bd. dirs. Nat. Coun. for Rsch. on Women, N.Y.C., 1983—; bd. dirs. Database Task Force, 1986—, treas., 1988-89, chmn. bd., 1989—; trustee Boston Heart Found., 1988—. Grantee in field. Mem. Mass. Hist. Soc., Am. Antiquarian Soc., Orgn. Am. Historians, Am. Hist. Assn., Berkshire Conf. of Women Historians. Home: 3 Whittier St Cambridge MA 02140 Office: Radcliffe Coll Schlesinger Libr 3 James St Cambridge MA 02138-3766

KING, RACHEL HADLEY, religious studies educator; b. Leavenworth, Kans., Apr. 27, 1904; d. Frank Campbell and Georgianna May (Brackett) King; B.A., Smith Coll., 1926; M.A., U. Chgo., 1927, U. Colo., 1931; Ph.D., Yale, 1937, Bible tchr., then head dept. Northfield (Mass.) Sch. Girls, 1928-31, 35-66; tchr. English, Kobe Coll., Japan, 1937-38; adj. prof. Bibl. studies Barrington (R.I.) Coll., 1972-85; vol. tchr. underprivileged children N.Y.C. Pub. Schs., summers 1969-71. Mem. Kobe Corp., 1960—; alumni council Yale Div. Sch., 1968-75. Recipient citation Council Religion in Ind. Schs., 1967. Mem. Am. Acad. Religion, Nat. Assn. Bible Instrs. (chmn. curriculum com. 1946-64), Am. Sch. Oriental Research, So. Bibl. Lit. Presbyterian. Author: George Fox and The Light Within 1650-1660; 1940; God's Boycott of Sin, 1946; Theology You Can Understand, 1956; The Omission of the Holy Spirit from Reinhold Niebuhr's Theology, 1964; The Creation of Death and Life, 1970. Home: The 60 Broadway Providence RI 02903

KING, ROSALYN MERCITA, social science researcher; b. Jacksonville, Fla., Aug. 16, 1948; d. Morris Charles and Marie (Coleman) K. BS, Howard U., 1970, MA, 1972; EdD, Harvard U., 1979. Dir. police youth project NCCJ, Washington, 1970-73; placement coord. U. North Fla., Jacksonville, 1973-74, instr., student support counselor, 1973-75; career edn. program coord. Roxbury/Harvard Sch. Program, Cambridge, Mass., 1976; rsch. analyst Spl. Commn. on Unequal Ednl. Opportunity Mass. Ho. of Reps., Boston, 1977; program coord. Freedom House, Inc., Roxbury, Mass., 1977-78; sr. program assoc. Expand Assocs., Inc., Silver Spring, Md., 1979; sr. assoc., dir. rsch. Mark Battle Assocs., Inc., Washington, 1980; dir. planning, program devel. and tech. assistance PUSH-Excel Inst. Research and Tng., Washington, 1981; rsch. assoc. So. Ctr. Studies in Pub. Policy Clark Coll., Atlanta, 1981-84; pres. Info. Rsch. Network Svc., Alexandria, Va., 1984—, Bathshua's Greetings, Alexandria, 1988—; chief of racial stats. U.S. Bur. Census, Washington, 1988; vis. prof. psychology Coppin State Coll., Balt., 1989-90. Contbr. articles to profl. jours. Mem. Psi Chi, Phi Delta Kappa. Home: 6526 River Tweed Ln Alexandria VA 22312

KING, RUBY THOMPSON, English educator, civic worker; b. nr. Wrightsville, Ga.; d. Charles D. and Maude (Douglas) Thompson; m. Seabron Larry King. Student, South Ga. Coll.; BA, Scarritt Coll., MA; postgrad. George Peabody Coll. Tchrs., U. Ga., Fla. State U., U. Edinburgh (Scotland). Tchr. English, Brunswick, Ga.; tchr. Lowndes County Ga.; tchr. English, Coffee County (Ga.) high schs., 1966—. Apptd. mem. Rep. Nat. Steering Com.; del. Nat. Rep. Conv., New Orleans; Conf. sec. missionary pers. Woman's Soc. Christian Svc.; active numerous local fund drives; coord. Wesleyan Svcs. Guild; 8th Dist. Sci. Fair committeewoman; sponsor Young Teens; charter mem. Tri-Hi-Y Internat., chmn. convocation; field rep. World Field Rsch., Inc.; editor Ga. Bull. Dir. Thompson-King Found.; trustee Florence Crittendon Home, Savannah, Ga.; mem. Pub. Library Bd.; White House appointment Nat. Traffic Safety Coun., Washington; staff Am. Rsch. Bur., Inc. state news reporter Atlanta Jour.; mem. Macon Music Chorus; mem. Nat. Rep. Party Task Force, selected del. for Nat. Rep. Conv. Named Star Tchr., Ga. C. of C., Douglas Citizen of Yr. for disting. community svc.; Albert Schweitzer fellow. Mem. AAUW, BPWC, Home Demonstration Coun. So. Ga., Conf. Hist. Soc., Ga. Edn. Assn. (county chmn. pub. rels.), NEA, Am. Soc. Psychical Rsch., Ga. Assn. Edn., Nat. Assn. English Tchrs., UDC, Internat. Platform Assn., Internat. Assn. Univ. Women, Am. Assn. Univ. Women, D.A.R., Philharmonic Club, Nat. Heritage Commn. Preservation Hist. Shrines, Nat. Hist. Shrine Soc. (patron), Nat. Council Tchrs. English, Am. Security Coun., Canterbury Cathedral Assn., Canterbury Cathedral Preservation Soc., Nat. Shrine/Hist. Trust Preservation, Thespian Soc., Scarritt Alumni Club, Order Eastern Star, Garden Study Club, Fine Arts Club, Woman's Garden Guild Club. Methodist. Author: History of Historic Ebenézer Methodist Church, 1800-1989; author poetry pub. in Am. Anthology of Verse, Nat. Anthology Poetry, Quaderni di Poesia, Anthology of Internat. Poetry; contbr. to poetry jours. in U.S., Scotland, Eng. and Italy. Address: 111 N Gaskin Ave Douglas GA 31533

KING, RUTH ALLEN, management consultant; b. Providence, Oct. 8, 1910; d. Arthur S. and Wilhelmina H. (Harmon) Allen. Grad. Tefft Bus. Inst., Providence, 1929; 1 child, Phyllis King Dunham. Stenographer N.Y. Urban League, N.Y.C., 1929; sec. adminstrn., adminstrv. asst., placement officer, asst. dir. Nat. Urban League Skills Bank, 1929-75; founder/sec. The EDGES Group, Inc., 1969—; minority rels. cons., Hazeltine Corp., Greenlawn, N.Y., 1976—; cons. to exec. v.p. Sony Corp. Am., Park Ridge, N.J., 1980—; selected speaker New Opportunities at Hofstra U. Ann. Grad. Dinner, 1990. Life mem. NAACP. Named Affirmative Action Pioneer Met. N.Y. Project Equality, 1975; Ruth Allen King Scholarship Fund established, 1970; EDGES Ruth Allen King Ann. Excalibur award established, 1978; recipient Ann Tanneyhill award for commitment to Urban League Movement, 1975, Recognition award NCCJ, 1975, Spl. citation Gov. of R.I. and Providence Plantations, 1981; Ruth Allen King Appreciation Day proclaimed in her honor, Providence, 1981, N.Y.C., 1975; citation R.I. Ho. of Reps., 1981; plaque Urban League R.I., 1981; Woman of Yr. award Suffolk (N.Y.) chpt. Jack and Jill of Am., 1982; named one of Am. Top 100 Black Bus. and Prof. Women Dollars & Sense mag., 1986; recipient medallion Whitney M. Young, Jr., 1987, Profl. award Bklyn. Club of the Nat. Assn. Negro Bus. and Profl. Women's Clubs, 1987, numerous others. Mem. N.Y. Pers. Mgmt. Assn., Council Concerned Black Execs., Julius A. Thomas Soc. (charter). Home and Office: 185 Hall St Apt 1715 Brooklyn NY 11205

KING, SANDRA, advertising agency executive; b. Torrance, Calif. Mar. 6, 1944; d. Walter Raymond and Eleanor Christina (Mehlhoff) King; m. George Brayton, Dec. 31, 1974 (div.); 1 son, Beau King. B.B.A., U. Miami, 1966. Sales rep. Chart Pak, N.Y.C., 1966-67; mem. acctg. staff Air Calif., Newport Beach, 1967-69; mktg. rep. U.S. Fin., Sandiego and Santa Ana, Calif., 1969-70, dir. advt. and pub. relations, 1970-72, regional sales mgr., 1972-73; account exec. Hubbert Advt., Tustin, Calif., 1973-74; pres. King Communications, Newport Beach, Calif., 1974—; lectr. career counseling advt. Vol. worker Orangewood Home of Dependent Children, Arthritis Telethon. Designer logo for America's Cup. Recipient 11 Mame awards. Mem. Bldg. Industry Assn. Orange County Advt. Fedn. (Golden Orange award, 3 awards of excellence), Indsl. League Orange County, Sales and Mktg. Council, Bldg. Industry Assn., Home Builders Council. Republican.

KING, SHARON ANN, banker; b. Keene, N.H., Feb. 26, 1944; d. A. Arthur and Florence A. (Mills) McKew; m. Richard P. King, Apr. 20, 1973; 1 child, Diane A. Ba in Hist., Keene State Coll., 1982; diploma, Maine, N.H., Vt. Sch. Banking, Portland, Maine, 1987. Customer svc. officer Conn. River Bank, Charlestown, N.H., 1966-83; asst. treas., retail banking Claremont (N.H.) Savs. Bank, 1983-89; asst. v.p., mgr., retail N.H. Savs. Bank, Concord, 1989—. Mem. New Eng. Safe Deposit Assn. (exec. bd. 1986—), Am. Inst. Banking (pres. NewMont chpt. 1988-89). Office: NH Savs Bank 27 N State St Concord NH 03301

KING, SHERYL JAYNE, educator, counselor; b. East Grand Rapids, Mich., Oct. 29, 1945; d. Thomas Benton III and Bettyann Louise (Mains) K. BS in Family Living, Sociology, Secondary Edn., Cen. Mich. U., 1968, M in Counseling, 1971. Educator Newaygo (Mich.) Pub. Schs., 1968-72; interior decorator Sue King Interiors, Grand Rapids, Mich., 1972-73; dir. girl's unit Dillon Family and Youth Svcs., Tulsa, 1973-74; mgr. Fellowship Press, Grand Rapids, Minn., 1974-76; educator, counselor Itasca Community Coll., Grand Rapids, 1977-81, dept. head, 1980-81, 85-86, 86-87; educator Dist. 318, Grand Rapids, 1977—; bd. dirs., chairperson program com. Marriage and Family Devel. Ctr., Grand Rapids, 1985—. Mem. issues com. No. Minn. Citizens League, Grand Rapids, 1984—, Blandin Found. Study, 1985-86; chairperson Itasca County Women's Consortium, Grand Rapids, 1983-87; Women's Day Conf., Grand Rapids, 1983-87; bd. dir. audio tech. Fellowship of Believers, Grand Rapids, 1974-87, deaconess, 1974—; bd. dir. audio tech Camp Dominion, Cass Lake, Minn., 1976-80; mem. fitness com., chmn. aquatic com., YMCA, Grand Rapids, 1974-87. Recipient 6 Outstanding Svc. awards Fellowship of Believers, 1974-79. Mem. NAFE, Quadna Club, Alpha Delta Kappa. Republican. Home: PO Box 247 Grand Rapids MN 55744 Office: 902 N Pokegama Ave Dist 318 Grand Rapids MN 55744

KING, SUSAN BENNETT, crystal company executive; b. Sioux City, Iowa, Apr. 29, 1940; d. Francis Moffatt Bennett and Marjorie (Rittenhouse) Sillin; divorced. AB, Duke U., 1962. Legis. asst. U.S. Senate, Washington, 1963-66; dir. Nat. Com. for Effective Congress, Washington, 1967-71, Ctr. Pub. Financing of Election, Washington, 1972-75; exec. asst. to chmn. Fed. Election Commn., Washington, 1975-77; commr. U.S. Consumer Product Safety Commn., Washington, 1978, chmn., 1978-81; dir. consumer affairs Corning (N.Y.) Glass Works, 1982, v.p. corp. communications, 1983-86; pres. Steuben Glass, N.Y.C., 1987—; vice chmn. U.S. Regulatory Council, U.S. Govt., Washington, 1979-80; del. Consumer Affairs Orgn. Econ. Cooperation and Devel., Paris, 1980-81. Chairperson bd. visitors inst. policy and scis. Duke U., Durham, N.C., 1985-87, trustee, 1987—; trustee Keuka Coll., Keuka Park, N.Y., 1983-87. Fellow Inst. Politics Harvard U., 1981. Mem. Nat. Consumers League (pres. 1984-85). Democrat. Office: Steuben Glass 715 Fifth Ave New York NY 10022

KING, SUSAN ELIZABETH, artist, publisher; b. Lexington, Ky., Apr. 15, 1947; d. Wallace Lang and Virginia Pierce (Hughes) K.; m. Michael David Oppenheim, 1978. BA in Art, U. Ky., 1971; MA in Art, N.Mex. State U., 1973. Tchr. art Pratt Art Inst., Bklyn., 1971-72; apprentice Byron Temple Pottery, Lambertville, N.J., 1971-72; teaching asst. N. Mex. State U., Las Cruces, 1972-73; founder, artist Paradise Press, L.A., 1975—; tchr., Otis/Parsons Coll., L.A., Scripps Coll. Press, Claremont, Calif.; cons., Nexus Press, Atlanta, 1987; lectr. at various schs., libraries, profl. orgns. Author: I Spent the Summer in Paris, 1984, Lessonsfrom the South, 1986, Lessonsfrom French, 1988; author, printer portfolio Support Living Artists!, 196-89. Bd. dirs., Woman's Bldg., L.A. Artist-in-residence, Women's Studio Workshop, Rosendale, N.Y., 1983, Visual Studies Workshop, Rochester, N.Y., 1984, Nexus Press, Atlanta; grantee Nat. Endowment for Arts, 1980-81. Mem. Paficic Ctr. Book Arts, Alliance Contemporary Book Arts. Office: Paradise Press PO Box 5306 Santa Monica CA 90405

KING, SYLVIA LYNN, accountant; b. Cross Plains, Texas, Jan. 7, 1938; d. Harlon Howard and Marjorie Lynn (Brown) Lacy; m. Carl Lamont King, Nov. 2, 1935; children: Kibb Harlon, Donna Lynn. Cert. Payroll Profl. Acctg. supr. Frito-Lay, Inc., Dallas, 1964—; instr. Principles of Payroll, North Lake Coll., Dallas, 1988-90; chmn. Tex. Payroll Conf., 1990, So. Users Payroll Pers. Systems. Mem. Am. Payroll Assn. (Dallas chpt.). Democrat. Office: Frito-Lay Inc 600 Frito-Lay Tower Dallas TX 75235

KING, TERESA LYNNE, nurse; b. Ft. Scott, Kans., May 8, 1953; d. John Joseph and Lola Faye (Smith) K. BS, Calif. State U., Bakersfield, 1975. RN, Calif. Nurse San Joaquin Hosp., Bakersfield, 1975-79, Bakersfield (Calif.) Cardiovascular, 1979-89. Mem. Calif. Nurses Assn., Peripheral Vascular Nurses, Am. Assn. Office Nurses. Democrat. Protestant.

KING, TERESITA LIM, gynecologist; b. Quezon City, Luzon, Philippines, Jan. 19, 1952; came to U.S., 1979; d. Fernando Go and Martina (Lim) K.; m. Andrew Steven Nakrin, July 5, 1979; 1 child, Joy Cecille Grace Nakrin. BS, U. of Philippines, 1973, MD, 1977. Diplomate Am. Bd. Ob-Gyn. Intern Manila (Philippines) Med. Ctr., 1977-78; rural physician Republic of Philippines, Quezon City, 1978-79; staff physician Northwest Hosp., Chgo., 1979-80; resident ob-byn. U. Ill., Chgo., 1980-84; staff physician, chief ob-gyn. Heritage Hosp., Tarboro, N.C., 1984-88; staff physician, chief gynecologist Community Hosp. of Rocky Mount, N.C., 1986—; tchr. birth control at pub. and pvt. high schs., Berwyn, Ill., Chgo., 1981-84; pub. health physician Cook County, Chgo., 1981-84. University scholar U. of Philippines, 1969-77. Fellow Am. Bd. Obstetricians-Gynecologists; mem. Pre-Medicine Honor Soc., Phi Kappa phi, Pi Gamma Mu. Roman Catholic. Office: 2807 N Main St Tarboro NC 27886

KING, VINETTA ELLEN, real estate rehabilitator, investor; b. Bethesda, Md., May 24, 1949; d. Arthur Mendez and Frances May (Jenkins) Gottschalk; m. Leonard E. King, June 1978 (dec. Aug. 1978). BS, U. Md., 1971. Owner, pres., chmn. bd. A & E Blueprinters Inc., Md., D.C., Va., 1978-82; investor comml. property Washington, 1982—; rehabilitator hist. homes Montgomery County, Md., 1986—. Fellow Kensington Hist. Soc.; mem. Wash. Astrology Forum, Assn. Rsch. Enlightenment.

KING-ATALLAH, HELEN LOUISE, occupational health nurse; b. Waterville, Maine, Jan. 15, 1958; d. Harold and Florence (Levasseur) King; m. Antoine Atallah, Aug. 1, 1987. AS, U. Maine, 1980; lic. emergency med. technician, Kennebec Vocat. Tech. Inst., Waterville, Maine, 1981. RN, Maine. Charge nurse Mid-Maine Med. Ctr., Waterville, 1980-83; occupational health nurse, safety mgr. Warnaco Men's Apparel, Waterville, 1983—; cons. Kennebec Valley Regional Health, Waterville, 1980—, Maine Bur. Health, Augusta, 1989—; vol. Waterville chpt. ARC, 1986—; exec. bd. Maine Cardiovascular Health Coun., Augusta, 1989-90. Recipient Good Citizen award DAR, 1976, Nat. Schering award for outstanding occupational health nurse, Schering Plough Co., 1988. Mem. New Eng. Occupational Health Nurses (bd. dirs. 1988—), Maine Occupational Health Nurses Assn. (recording sec. 1983-85, v.p. 1985-88, pres. 1988—), Maine Chamber Commerce and Industry (subcom. on health 1985), Waterville C. of C., Eta Sigma Gamma. Home: 51 Oakhill Dr Oakland ME 04963 Office: Warnaco Men's Apparel 10 Water St Waterville ME 04901

KING CALKINS, CAROL COLEMAN, hospital administrator; b. L.A., May 31, 1949; d. Harold S. and Gladys (Blumenthal) Coleman; 1 child, Katrina Elizabeth King; m. Michael Steven Calkins, Oct. 10, 1987. BA in Psychology, U. Colo., 1972; MBA, U. No. Colo., 1982. Dir. group living Nat. Jewish Ctr. Immunology and Respiratory Medicine, Denver, 1980-82; dir. clin. support svcs. Nat. Jewish Ctr. Immunology and Respiratory Medicine, 1982-83, dir. spl. projects, 1983-84, asst. dir. adminstrv. svcs., 1984, dir. adminstrv. svcs., 1984—; speaker in field. Recorder improvement process coun. Jefferson County (Colo.) Schs., 1989. Recipient Big Sisters Colo. award 6th Ann. Salute to Women. Mem. Colo. Hosp. Assn. Risk Mgrs. Office: 1400 Jackson St Denver CO 80206

KING-ETTEMA, ELIZABETH DOROTHY, video and film editor, writer, photographer; b. Morristown, N.J., Sept. 29, 1953; d. James Claude and Martha Helene (Dawson) King; m. Dale Frederic Ettema, Feb. 13, 1982; children—Taylor Braam, Claire Elizabeth. B.A. in Art History, UCLA, 1975; postgrad. U. N.M., 1977-78. Writer, Bettis & Parks Advt., Albuquerque, 1975-76; bus. mgr. N.M. Ballet Co., Albuquerque, 1976-78; asst. editor Dury Assocs., Los Angeles, 1978, Another Editing Pl., Los Angeles, 1978-79, Bullywood Prodn., Los Angeles, 1979, Alan Landsburg Prodn., Los Angeles, 1980-81, Columbia TV, Los Angeles, 1982-83; video editor Am. Film Inst., Los Angeles, 1983-85. Video editor Scenario, 1984, U.S. 49/Calif. 1, 1985. Recipient scholarship UCLA Extension, 1979. Mem. Motion Picture and Videotape Editors Guild, Soc. Children's Book Writers, Internat. Documentary Assn. Democrat. Episcopalian. Club: Embroiderer's Guild of Am. (historian chpt. 1984-85, v.p., program chmn. 1987-88). Avocations: photography, embroidery. Home and Office: 7235 Forbes Ave Van Nuys CA 91406

KING-GRISWOLD, KATHY ANN, controller; b. Danville, Pa., Apr. 25, 1957; d. Kenneth A. and Mattie Jane (Boone) King; m. Keith E. Griswold, July 1, 1978. AA, Ea. Nazarene Coll., 1978; BS, SUNY, Saratoga Springs, 1982, postgrad., 1990—. Controller Sugar Creek Stores, Inc., Rochester, N.Y.; asst. to controller Bathique Internat. Ltd., Rochester, 1984—. Mem. Nat. Assn. Accts. (asst. treas., bd. dirs.), Cash Mgmt. Assn. Monroe County (chair membership). Republican. Methodist. Home: 1442 Crittenden Rd Rochester NY 14623 Office: care of Sugar Creek Stores Inc 760 Brooks Ave Rochester NY 14619

KING-HADEN, KELLY LOUISE, flight attendant; b. N.Y.C., Jan. 16, 1959; d. Leon Bouleware and Gloria Sandra (Gardner) King; m. Laurence Paul Haden, Oct. 29, 1988. BA, Boston Coll., 1982. Adminstrv. asst. information systems Fairchild Publs., N.Y.C., 1983-85; flight attendant Pan Am. World Airways, N.Y.C., 1985—; tchr. N.Y.C. Pub. Sch. System, 1986—. Founder, chairperson Matthew C. Walker Scholarship Fund, DeWitt Clinton High Sch., Bronx, N.Y., 1988—; v.p. N.Y. Progressive Bapt. Conv., 1984-85. Named Miss Congeniality Miss Harlem Beauty Pageant, Inc., N.Y.C., 1983.

KING-JOHNSON, MARCIA, technical analyst; b. Sumter, S.C., Dec. 7, 1958; d. Talmadge Everett and Almetta (Waiters) King; m. Calvin Lee Johnson, Jan. 1, 1983; 1 child, Calicia LaToya. BA, Spelman Coll., 1980; MA, Ea. Mich. U., 1986. Leader Girl Scout Coun., Atlanta, 1980-82; vol. Providence Hosp., Southfield, Mich., 1988-89; dep. voter registrar, Southfield, 1989; tutor Literacy Coun., Oakland County, Mich., 1989. Fellow Am. Psychol. Assn.; mem. NAFE, Mich. Assn. Indsl. Orgn. Psychologists, Women's Sports Fedn., Nat. Assn. Black Psychologists, Mich. Psychol. Assn., Delta Sigma Theta. Methodist. Home: 23750 Twining Dr Southfield MI 48075

KINGSBURY, CAROLYN ANN, software systems engineer; b. Newark, Ohio, Aug. 4, 1938; d. Cecil C. Layman and Orpha Edith (Hisey) Layman Dick; m. L.C. James Kingsbury, Apr. 25, 1959; children: Donald Lynn, Kenneth James. BS in Math., BS in Info. and Computer Scis., U. Calif., Irvine, 1979; postgrad. West Coast U., 1982-84. Systems engr., analyst Rockwell Internat., Downey, Calif., 1979-84, system and software engr. Northrop Corp., Pico Rivera, Calif., 1984-89; systems engr. Hughes Aircraft Co., Long Beach, Calif., 1989-90, Fullerton, Calif., 1990—. Pres. PTA, Manhattan Beach, Calif., 1971-73; Cub Scout den mother Boy Scouts Am., Manhattan Beach, 1972-73. Recipient Service award Calif. Congress Parents and Tchrs., 1973, Leadership Achievement award YWCA, Los Angeles, 1980, 84, NASA Achievement awards, 1983. Mem. NAFE, AAUW, Nat. Mgmt. Assn., Newtowners Club (pres. 1962). Republican. Home: 11392 Stonecress Ave Fountain Valley CA 92708 Office: Hughes Aircraft Co 1901 W Malvern Ave PO Box 3310 Fullerton CA 92634

KINGSTON, MAXINE HONG, author; b. Stockton, Calif., Oct. 27, 1940; d. Tom and Ying Lan (Chew) Hong; m. Earll Kingston, Nov. 23, 1963; 1 child, Joseph Lawrence. B.A., U. Calif., Berkeley, 1962; hon. doctoral degree, Eastern Mich. U., 1988, Colby Coll., 1990, Brandeis U., 1990—. tchr. English, Sunset High Sch., Hayward, Calif., 1965-66, Kahuku (Hawaii) High Sch., 1967, Kahaluu (Hawaii) Drop-In Sch., 1968, Kailua (Hawaii) High Sch., 1969, Honolulu Bus. Coll., 1969, Mid-Pacific Inst., Honolulu, 1970-77; prof. English, vis. writer U. Hawaii, Honolulu, 1977; Thelma McCandless Disting. Prof. Eastern Mich. U., Ypsilanti, 1986, Chancellor's Disting. Prof. U. Calif., Berkeley, 1990. Author: The Woman Warrior: Memoirs of a Girlhood Among Ghosts, 1976 (Nat. Book Critics Circle award for non-fiction; cited by Time mag., N.Y. Times Book Rev. and Asian Mail as one of best books of Yr.), China Men, 1981 (Nat. Book award; runner up for Pulitzer prize and Nat. Book Critics Circle award nominee 1988), Hawaii One Summer, 1987, Tripmaster Monkey-His Fake Book, 1989 (PEN West award in Fiction), Through the Black Curtain, 1988; contbr. short stories, articles and poems to mags. and jours., including Iowa Rev., The New Yorker, Am. Heritage, Redbook, Mother Jones, Caliban, Mich. Quarterly. Recipient Mademoiselle Mag. award, 1977, Anisfield Wolf Book award, 1978, Calif. Arts Commn. award 1981, Hawaii award for Lit., 1982, Gov.'s award for the Arts, 1989; NEA writing fellow, 1980, Guggenheim fellow, 1981; named a Living Treasure of Hawaii, 1980, Asian/Pacific Women's Network Woman of the Yr., 1981, Am. Acad. and Inst. Award in Lit., 1990; recipient Women's Com. Major Book Collection award Brandeis U., 1990.

KINKADE, KATE, publishing executive, magazine editor, insurance executive; b. N.Y.C., Jan. 22, 1951; d. Joel M. and Peeta S. (Sherman) Sandleman; m. Patrick Ramsey, June 27, 1981; children: Jamaa Ramsey, Kikanza Ramsey. BS in Speech, Emerson Coll., Boston, 1972; postgrad., Am. Coll., Bryn Mawr, Pa. CLU. Mgr. sales Equitable Life Ins., L.A., 1973-76; agy. v.p. Lincoln Nat. Life Ins. Co., Encino, Calif., 1976-80; chief exec. officer TIME Fin. Svcs., Reseda, Calif., 1980—; mng. editor Calif. Broker, Burbank, Calif., 1981—; exec. v.p. Life Underwriters Assn., Encino, 1978-81. Contbr. articles to profl. jours. Mem. steering com. nat. office Beyond War, Palo Alto, Calif., also Los Angeles regional fin. support and chairperson local chpt., Burbank, Calif., 1984—. Recipient Asst. Prodn. awards Equitable Life, 1973, 77, Lincoln Nat. Life, 1978, 80, Pacific Mut. Life, 1983. Mem. Assn. CLU's. Democrat. Jewish. also: 18107 Sherman Way #205 Reseda CA 91335-4564

KINKEAD, ELLEN JANE, volunteer; b. Penfield, Pa., Jan. 10, 1915; d. John Calvin and Mary Elizabeth (Flynn) McKissick; m. David Charles Kinkead, Sr., Mar. 17, 1939; children: John Calvin, David Charles Jr., Joan Ellen, Alan Robert. BS in Nursing, Duquesne U., 1959; MEd, Indiana U. Pa., 1964. R.N. Gen. staff supr. Clearfield (Pa.) Hosp., 1936-51; clin. instr. Sch. Nursing, Clearfield, 1952-57; dir. nursing and sch. Clearfield Hosp., 1961-71, asst. adminstr. nursing, 1971-73, v.p. adminstrn., 1973-75; coord. Maple Ave. and Bookville (Pa.) Hosps., DuBois, Pa., 1975-78; asst. v.p. Maple Ave. Hosp., DuBois, 1978, cons. vol., 1978-81. Contact person, vol. Parents Anonymous, Clearfield, 1983—, pres., 1983-88. Named Vol. of Yr., Parents Anonymous of Clearfield County, 1988. Mem. AAUW (Risk Challenge award 1989), Am. Assn. Ret. Persons Clearfield County (v.p. 1985-86, 88-90, sec. 1988—). Democrat. Roman Catholic. Home: 415 Elm Ave Clearfield PA 16830 Office: Parents Anonymous 415 Elm Ave Clearfield PA 16830

KINKEAD, VERDA CHRISTINE, non-profit organization executive, consultant; b. Plant City, Fla., Feb. 12, 1931; d. Ernest Glenn and Mina Lee (Alexander) K. Diploma, Bronson Meth. Hosp. Sch., Kalamazoo, 1952; BA in Humanities, Adrian Coll., 1963; MA Guidance-Counseling, Mich. State U., 1964. RN, Mich. Nurse Bronson Meth. Hosp., 1952-54; 2d sr. surg. nurse West Side Med. Group, Kalamazoo, 1954-60; mentor, resident asst. Adrian (Mich.) Coll., 1962-63, head resident, 1964-65, asst. dean student affairs, dean women, 1965-69; co-founder, co-dir. Handicappers Info. Coun. and Patient Equipment Locker, Inc., Alma, 1981-87, pres., chief exec. officer, co-chmn. bd. dirs., 1987—; ednl. asst. East Main Meth. Ch., Kalamazoo, 1959-60. Former editor Saginaw Valley Dynamo; editor Challenger newsletter, 1986—; contbr. poetry to various publs. Bd. dirs. Saginaw Valley br. Nat. Multiple Sclerosis Soc., past treas; sec. bd. dirs., fair sec. Gratiot Agrl. Soc., Ithaca, Mich., 1977-83; vol. counselor Gratiot County Mental Health Ctr., Alma, 1983—; chmn. Gratiot County Early Intervention Coun., 1989—; organizer, group facilitator Ptnrs. in Renewal, Alma, 1989—; lay speaker United Meth. Ch.; mem. Go Grow Gratiot, 1989— (co-chair awards com., 1989-90, chairperson, 1990—). Recipient outstanding svc. award Mich. Coll. Personnel Assn., 1972, Saginaw Valley br. Multiple Sclerosis Soc., 1986, First Lady award Mich. Women's Commn., 1987, vol. leadership award Greater Mich. Found., 1988, Outstanding Alumni award Adrian Coll., 1988. Mem. AAUW (sec. Alma br. 1965), Order Eastern Star (chaplain 1988—, assoc. conductress 1989—), Alma Woman's Club (v.p. 1990—), Phi Delta Kappa. Republican. Home: 3060 N Union Rd Alma MI 48801 Office: Handicappers Info Coun 1022 Michigan Ave Alma MI 48801-1330

KINLEIN, M(ARY) LUCILLE, nurse; b. Ellicott City, Md., Dec. 17, 1921; d. Julius Augustus and Mary Teresa (Plantholt) K.; B.A., Coll. Notre Dame, Balt., 1943; B.S. in Nursing Edn., Catholic U. Am., 1947, M.S., 1953. Asst. prof. nursing Cath. U. Am., 1947-69, dir. masters program in cardiovascular disease nursing, 1962-69; mem. faculty Georgetown U. Sch. Nursing, 1970-74; pres. D.C. Profl. Nurses Exam. Bd., 1955-61, D.C. Practical Nurses Exam. Bd., 1961-67; cons. HEW, 1964-74; ind. general nurse, 1971-79; ptnr. Détente Manor, McLean, Va., 1978-81; vis. prof. U. So. Miss., Hattiesburg, 1975-78, also coordinator Center Nursing Edn., Practice and Research; vis. lectr. univs. Wis., Va., Alaska Pacific U.; mem. Washington Nursing Devel. Conf. Group; founder Nat. Center of Kinlein, 1979, Inst. of Kinlein, 1983. Recipient Alumni Achievement award Coll. Notre Dame, 1973, Cath. U. Am., 1974; Linda Richards award Nat. League Nursing, 1977. Mem. Am. Nurses Assn., Nat. League Nursing, Am. Heart Assn., Sigma Theta Tau, Kappa Gamma Pi. Roman Catholic. Author: Independent Nursing Practice with Clients, 1977; Moving That Power Within, 1983, expanded edit., 1985; Author-editor: Cordising: A New Understanding of Caring, 1986; co-author: Concept Formalization in Nursing, 1973; founder Jour. of Kinlein, 1981. Home: 6700 Belcrest Rd Apt 615 Hyattsville MD 20782 Office: 6525 Belcrest Rd Hyattsville MD 20782

KINNAIRD, MARGARET MARY, educator; d. Frank Anton and Margaret (Bader) Kinnaird. BA, Coll. of St. Rose, Albany, N.Y., 1971; MS, Russell Sage Coll., 1974; EdD, Boston U., 1982. Tchr. Berne-Knox (N.Y.) Westerlo Cen. Sch. Dist., 1973—; adj. curriculum coord. N.Y. State Bd. Edn., Albany, 1983—; pres. Berne-Knox Westerlo Tchr.'s Assn., Berne, 1987-90, elem. computer coord. Author: Computers, Utilizing Modern Technology in Adult and Continuing Education Programs, Albany, N.Y.: The State Education Department, 1988. Mem. PTA (exec. com.), badge counselor Boy Scouts Am. Mem. Am. Ednl. Rsch. Assn., Assn. for Supervision and Curriculum Devel., New Eng. Ednl. Rsch. Orgn., Pi Lambda Theta. Home: 410 Cole Hill Rd East Berne NY 12059 Office: Berne-Knox-Westerlo CSD Helderberg Trail Berne NY 12023

KINNAIRD, NANCY WEBSTER, systems engineer; b. Washington; d. M.L. and Virginia (Armstrong) Webster; children: Mike, Michelle. BS with honors, Purdue U., 1986, MS, 1988. Systems engr. Electronic Data Systems, Kokomo, Ind.; sr. programmer U.S. Dept. Def., France and West Germany. Purdue U. scholar. Mem. Phi Kappa Phi, Alpha Lambda Delta, Pi Gamma Mu. Home: 921 S Gulford Ave Carmel IN 46032

KINNEL, MARY L., educator; b. Dawson, Ga., Sept. 3, 1945; d. James Kinnel and Flora M. (Bunts) Burdine; m. James Riley Lewis, 1964 (div.); children: Anthony, Reginald, Vickie; m. George Wayne Harris; 1 child, Kevin. Student, Gibbs Jr. Coll., St. Petersburg, Fla., 1963-64; BS, Ft. Valley (Ga.) State Coll., 1980, postgrad., 1987—. Tchr. home econs. Monroe County Middle Sch., Forsyth, Ga., 1980-82, Cen. High Sch., Macon, Ga., 1985-86, Wilkinson County Jr. High Sch., Irwinton, Ga., 1987; recruitment cons. Ft. Valley State Coll., 1986, recruitment specialist, 1987—; tchr. arts and crafts, Camp John Hope, Marshallville, Ga., 1980-82. Mem. Ga. Vocat. Assn., Am. Vocat. Assn., NAFE, Assn. Supervision and Curriculum Devel., DAV Aux., Delta Kappa Rho. Democrat. Baptist.

KINNEY, KATHLEEN O'LEARY, social welfare administrator; b. Canonsburg, Pa., Sept. 18, 1942; d. Daniel William and Laura Ellen (Offutt) O'Leary; divorced; children: Ian Michael, Laura Ellen, Nathan Patrick (dec.). Dep. dir, planning officer Community Action Agy., Ashtabula, Ohio, 1970-74; chief exec. officer Lake Area Recovery Ctr., Ashtabula, 1974—, Donahoe Ctr. Corp., Ashtabula, 1975—. Mem. Civic Devel. Corp., 1979—; v.p., bd. dirs. Ashtabula Arts Ctr., 1987—. Recipient Resource Devel. award Ohio Dept. Health, 1985, Gov.'s Spl. Recognition Ohio Gov. Richard Celeste, 1987. Mem. Alcohol and Drug Problems Assn. N.Am. (bd. dirs., chair Women's Commn. 1988—), Women's Alliance for Recovery Svc. (pres. 1987-89), Nat. Network State Assns. (bd. dirs. 1986—), Ohio Gov.'s Coun. Recovery Svcs., Assn. Ohio Substance Abuse Programs (pres. 1985-87), Leadership Ashtabula (charter class). Democrat. Home: 4200 Caylor Ct Ashtabula OH 44004 Office: Lake Area Recovery Ctr 2801 C Court Ashtabula OH 44004

KINNEY, LISA FRANCES, state senator; b. Laramie, Wyo., Mar. 13, 1951; d. Irvin Wayne and Phyllis (Poe) K.; m. Rodney Philip Lang, Feb. 5, 1971; children: Cambria Helen, Shelby Robert. BA, U. Wyo., 1973, JD, 1986; MLS, U. Oreg., 1975. Reference libr. U. Wyo. Sci. Libr., Laramie, 1975-76; outreach dir. Albany County Libr., Laramie, 1975-76, dir., 1977-83; mem. Wyo. State Senate, Laramie, 1985—. Author: (with Rodney Lang) Civil Rights of the Developmentally Disabled, 1986; (with Rodney Lang and Phyllis Kinney) Manual For Families with Emotionally Disturbed and Mentally Ill Relatives, 1988; contbr. articles to profl. jours; editor, compiler pub. relations directory for ALA, 1982. Bd. dirs. Big Bros./Big Sisters, Laramie, 1980-83. Recipient Beginning Young Profl. award Mt. Plains Libr. Assn., 1980; named Outstanding Wyo. Libr. Wyo. Libr. Assn., 1977, Outstanding Young Woman State of Wyo., 1980. Mem. ABA, Nat. Confs. of State Legislatures (various coms.), Laramie C. of C., Snowy Range Internat. Folk Dance Club (pres. 1980-87), Zonta (v.p. 1989—). Democrat. Avocations: photography, dance, reading, traveling, languages. Home: 603 Spring Creek Laramie WY 82070

KINNEY, MARJORIE SHARON, finance and marketing executive; b. Gary, Ind., Jan. 11, 1940; d. David H. and Florence C. Dunning; student El Camino Coll., 1957, 58; LHD (hon.), West Coast U., 1982, Coll. San Mateo, 1987-88; MBA, Pepperdine U., 1989; m. Daniel D. Kinney, Dec. 31, 1958 (div. 1973); children: Steven Daniel, Michael Alan, Gregory Lincoln, Bradford David; m. Bradley Thomas Jr., Nov. 9, 1985 (div. Apr. 1987). Ptnr., Kinney Advt. Inc., Inglewood, Calif., 1958-68; pres. Greeters of Am., 1967-69; chmn. Person to Person Inc., Cleve., 1969-72; pres. Kinney Mktg. Corp., Encino, Calif., 1972-80; sr. v.p. Beverly Hills (Calif.) Savs. & Loan Assn., 1980-84; chmn., pres. Kinney & Assocs., Laguna Niguel, Calif., 1985—; dir. Safeway Stores, Inc., Chubb/Pacific Indemnity Co.; lectr. Bd. dirs. ARC, 1976-81, United Way, 1979-81; trustee West Coast U.; adv. bd. U.S. Human Resources, Womens Legal Edn. Fund; briefing del. to Pentagon Fed. Res. Dept. and White House, 1986; pres. Santa Fe Rep. Women, 1987; co-chair Childcare Action Day, 1986; participant Women of Faith and Courage, program for homeless girls, 1987—; chair Caps for Calypso, clothing project for homeless, 1988. Presbyterian. Office: 81 Palm Beach Ct Laguna Niguel CA 92677

KINOSHITA, KAY, physics researcher, educator; b. Princeton, N.J., July 17, 1954; d. Toichiro and Masako (Matsuoka) K. AB, AM, Harvard U., 1976; PhD, U. Calif., Berkeley, 1982. Rsch. assoc. Harvard U., Cambridge, Mass., 1982-84, asst. prof., 1984-88, assoc. prof., 1988—; spokesperson Nikko-Maru, Tsukuba, Japan, 1984—. Mary Ingraham Bunting Inst. fellow, 1985-87. Mem. Am. Phys. Soc. Office: Harvard U Physics Lab 42 Oxford St Cambridge MA 02138

KINOSIAN, JANET MARIE, journalist; b. Los Angeles, June 20, 1957; d. Kasper John and Carol Grace (Boghosian) K. BA in Psychology, UCLA, 1980; MA in Psychology, Loyola Marymount, 1987. Intern L.A. Mag., 1980-81; staff writer Orange County Media Group, Costa Mesa, Calif., 1982-84; contbg. editor Orange Coast Mag., Costa Mesa, Calif., 1984—; pres. JMK & Co., Brentwood, Calif. Contbr. numerous articles to regional and nat. mags. and newspapers; internationally syndicated by N.Am. Syndicate, Times of London, N.Y. Times Syndicate Sales Corp. Co-founder Campus Coalition for Peace, 1978, Internat. Women's Coalition, 1979; mem. Alliance for Survival, 1978-81, Amnesty Internat., 1980-89, Child Help USA, 1985-89. Mem. APA, Orange County Press Club, Pacific Coast Press Club, Hollywood Women's Press Club, Calif. Assn. Ind. Writers, Am. Soc. Journalists and Anthropologists, Pi Beta Phi. Democrat. Presbyterian. Home: 11692 Chenault St Apt 103 Los Angeles CA 90049 Office: JMK Co Studio One 11692 Chenault St Apt 103 Brentwood CA 90049

KINSER, CAROLYNN HIPPS, executive secretary; d. Robert S. and Vevel M. (Hensley) Hipps; m. Charles Allen Kinser; children: Christy Annette, Cynthia Allison. Student, Walter's State Community Coll., Morristown, Tenn. Exec. sec. Austin Co., Inc., Greeneville, Tenn.; data processing and accounts receivable supr. Takoma Med. Group, Assocs., Greeneville. Named Woman of the Yr.. Mem. Am. Bus. Women's Assn. (past pres., v.p. Marguerite Brumley chpt. edn. com.), United Meth. Women (local pres.), Pilot Club of Greeneville, Tenn. Recording Secs. Home: Rolling Hills Rd Rte 3 Box 141 Greeneville TN 37743

KINSLOW, MARTA BENAVIDES, educator; b. Laredo, Tex, Oct. 30, 1941; d. Matilde and Maria de los Angeles (Hernandez) B.; m. George William Kinslow, June 22, 1968; children: Robert Joseph, Minnie Marie, George William II. BA, U. Tex., 1964. Cert. tchr., Tex. Tchr. M.B. Lamar Jr. High Sch., Laredo, 1964-70, Kitty Hawk Jr. High Sch., Converse, Tex., 1979-83; tchr. aide Redlands (Calif.) Elem. Sch., 1976-79; tchr. math. and computers J.G. Cigarroa Mid. Sch., Laredo, 1983—, dept. head, 1984-89. Historian J.G. Cigarroa Mid. Sch. PTA, 1984-85; v.p. Cigarroa Mid. Sch. Band Parents, 1983-85; tchr. Confrat. Christian Doctrine Blessed Sacrament, Laredo, 1968-70, 77-79. Mem. AAUW (treas. 1984-86, v.p. 1989-91). Democrat. Home: 119 Ceniso Loop Laredo TX 78043 Office: Cigarroa Mid Sch 2600 Palo Blanco Laredo TX 78043

KINTNER, JUDITH ANN, food company executive; b. Idaho Falls, Ida., July 8, 1938; d. John Israel and Golda (Hanks) Bailey; m. Elwood W. Kintner, June 17, 1960 (div. 1989); children: Randall, Laura. BS, Oreg.

State Coll., 1960, MS, 1964; PhD, U. Nebr., 1973. Food technologist Rogers Bros. Co., Idaho Falls, 1960-69; cons. in food tech. Spokane, Wash., 1973-75; project leader Comml. Creamery Co., Spokane, 1975-78; tech. dir. Comml. Creamery Co., 1978—, v.p., 1990—. Contbr. articles to profl. jours. Active 4-H, 1960—; com. chmn. Band Parents Adv. Group, Spokane, 1984-85; quilting advisor Spokane Gifted Children Prog., 1987. Named Tech. Person of the Year, Assn. for Dressings & Sauces, Atlanta, 1988; Gen. Foods/Inst. Food Technologists grad. fellow, 1970-72; Gerber/Inst. Food Technologists undergrad. scholar, 1959-60. Mem. Inst. Food Technologists (sec., pres. 1968-69), Am. Assn. Cereal Chemists, Am. Chem. Soc., Assn. for Sauces and Dressings (tech. adv. com. 1983—), Snack Food Assn. (tech. adv. com. 1988—), Spokane Falls Jewelers Guild (v.p. 1986-87), Spokane Falls Needlework Guild (group leader 1977-78), Zeta Tau Alpha. Republican. Mormon. Office: Commercial Creamery Co S 159 Cedar St Spokane WA 99204

KINTNER, TREVA CARPENTER, retired educator; b. Topeka, Ind., Apr. 27, 1920; d. Adrian and Elizabeth (Burns) Carpenter; m. Loren D. Kintner, Aug. 23, 1946; children: Susan, David. BS, Manchester Coll., North Manchester, Ind., 1944; MS, U. Mo., 1952. Tchr. pub. schs. Milford, Ind., 1944-45, Wakarusa, Ind., 1945-46, Pickerington, Ohio, 1947-48; instr. U. Mo., Columbia, 1952-54; asst. prof. foods U. Mo., 1968-86; ret.; prof. Prince of Songkaa U. Pattani, Thailand, 1986. Contbr. articles to profl. jours. Mem. Kissimmee Women's Club, Kissimmee Garden Club, Ret. Tchrs. Assn. (pres.), AAUW (pres. 1987-89), Sigma Xi, Gamma Sigma Delta (award of merit 1986), Phi Upsilon Omicron (nat. coun. 1989). Address: 2775 Orchid Ln Kissimmee FL 32743

KINYON, JAMIE MICHELE, social services adminstrator; b. Mason City, Aug. 12, 1954; d. Richard James and Mary Kelley; m. Joy Allan Kinyon, Oct. 12, 1985 (div. May, 1988). BA, Wartburg Coll., Waverly, 1972-76; MSW, U. Kans., 1976-78. Social worker Anoka (Minn.) County Human Services, 1978-80; sch. social worker Southern Minn. Spl. Service Coop, Wells, Minn., 1980-82; social worker Blue Earth County Human Services, Mankato, Minn., 1983; project coordinator Amboy (Minn.) Good Thunder Schs.; therapist Phillip Clinic, Mankato, Minn., 1983, Sinnissippi Mental Health Ctr., Ill., 1983-85; social service dir. Magic Valley Regional Med. Ctr., Twin Falls, Idaho, 1985--; bd. mem. Am. Cancer Soc., 1985--, field supr. Coll Idaho, Nampa 1986, cons. High Risk Infant Task Force, Twin Falls, 1988-89. Research asst. Competencies, skills, functions, unique to sch. social work, 1978, competency based edn., 1978. Bd. mem. Community Orgn. for Rehabilitative Efforts, 1985--, chairperson person Twin Falls County Child Team, 1985--. Mem. Am. Hosp. Assn. Social Work, Am. Bd. Cert. Diplomate Social Work, Acad. Cert. Social Workers, Nat. Assn. Social Workers (Idaho chpt.). Roman Catholic. Office: Magic Valley Regional Med Ctr 650 Addison Ave W Twin Falls ID 83303-0040

KINZEY, OUIDA BLACKERBY, retired mathematics educator, photographer, photojournalist; b. Leeds, Ala., Feb. 6, 1922; d. George W. and Kate (Spruiell) Blackerby; m. William Thomas Kinzey, Feb. 6, 1943. AB, Birmingham So. Coll., 1942, EdM, 1959; advanced profl. diploma, U. Ala., 1964. Tchr. math. Phillips High Sch., Birmingham, Ala., 1942-44, Humes High Sch., Memphis, 1944-45; chmn. math. dept. Woodlawn High Sch., Birmingham, 1945-69; assoc. prof. math. Birmingham So. Coll., 1969-84, prof. emeritus, 1984—, dir. vis. profs. program, 1971-75, also mem. alumni leadership bd.; cons., lectr., speaker and workshop dir. throughout S.E. region, Gala adv. bd. Author: (audio-visual text) Creative Teaching Mathematically, 1973, (video) The World of Mathematics, 1990; author, photographer photographic essays; photographs exhibited one man shows including Birmingham So. Coll., 1984, Samford U., 1984, Med. Ctr. East, 1985, Univ. Hosp., 1989, U. Ala., Birmingham, 1989, Birmingham Mus. of Art, 1989. Grantee NSF, 1959, 61, 64, 71, Kellogg Found., 1978, Mellon Found., 1980, 81, 84, Title III, 1982; recipient Grand Nat. award NEA/Kodak, 1984, Cert. of Achievement Birmingham So. Coll., 1990; named an Outstanding Educator of Am., 1972. Mem. AAUW, Ala. Assn. Coll. Tchrs. Math., Ala. Acad. Sci., United Daus. Confederacy, Nat. Coun. Tchrs. Math., Math. Assn. Am., Am. Math Soc. (joint policy bd. math. pub. info. resources com.), Ala. Edn. Assn., Ala. Poetry Soc. Ala. Writers' Conclave, Nat. League Am. PEN Women, Phi Beta Kappa, Kappa Delta Pi, Delta Kappa Gamma, Kappa Delta Epsilon, Kappa Mu Epsilon, Theta Sigma Lambda, Delta Phi Alpha, Alpha Lambda Delta. Speech Arts Club (pres., v.p., sec., treas.). Democrat. Methodist. Avocations: photography, collecting rocks, Indian artifacts and antiques. Home: 1413 Swallow Ln Birmingham AL 35213

KINZIE, MIRIAM ANNETTE, jewelry store owner; b. Cushing, Okla., Aug. 26, 1953; d. Donovan Homer and Lillie Geraldine (Bollinger) Kincaid; m. Philip Kent, June 20, 1981; 1 child, Mirelle Avery. BS, Okla. State U., Stillwater, 1975; MS, Okla. State U., 1980. Sales display buyer McKeown's Showcase, Stillwater, 1972-75, Leonard Jewelry, Stillwater, 1975-76; asst. mgr. Evert's Jewelers, Dallas, 1976-78; asst. buyer Miss Jackson's, Tulsa, 1978-79; rsch. asst. Okla. State U., Stillwater, 1979-81; assoc. prof. La. State U., Baton Rouge, 1980-81; mgr., owner Leonard Jewelry, Stillwater, 1981—; coordinator Fashion Bd., Stillwater, 1972-75. Mem. Okla. Jewelers Assn. (v.p. 1987—), Rotary Anns, Downtown Stillwater Unltd. (mem. com. 1988—), Okla. Jewelers Assn. (v.p.). Democrat. Baptist. Home: 1000 N Star Dr Apt 4 Stillwater OK 74075

KIRBY, COLLEEN, professional society administrator; b. Spring Valley, Ill., Feb. 15, 1948; d. Francis Paul and Margarette Esther (McDonald) Sever; m. James Harold Kirby (div. 1986); 1 child, Aaron. BA, No. Ill. U., 1969; MA, U. Ill., 1971. Librarian So. Ill. U., Carbondale, 1970-72; instr. YMCA, Carbondale, 1971-74, John A. Logan Coll., Carterville, Ill., 1972-74, Oklahaoma City Community Coll., 1978-82; phys. dir. YMCA, Bethany, Okla., 1974-83; dir. program devel. YMCA, Oklahoma City, 1983-85; v.p. program devel. YMCA, L.A., 1985—; v.p. program devel. and tng. Nat. Coun. of YMCA of Japan, Tokyo, 1990—; trainer of trainer YMCA. Co-author: Putting You in Creative Aerobic Dance, 1975, National YMCA's Day Camp Standards, 1980. Mem. Assn. Profl. Dirs. (bd. dirs. phys. edn. com. 1984), Am. Camping Assn., Sierra. Office: YMCA of Japan, 2-3-18 Nishiwaseda, Shinjuku-ku, Tokyo 169, Japan

KIRBY, DEBORAH MACDONALD, rehabilitation psychologist; b. Washington, May 19, 1948; d. Robert Angus and Margarett Mary (Harrison) MacDonald; m. Stephen Edward Kirby, Sept. 6, 1980; 1 child, Jessica Lynn. B.A., George Washington U., 1970; M.Ed., Am. U., 1972. Psychiat. asst. Chestnut Lodge Psychiat. Hosp., Rockville, Md., 1969-70; rsch. psychologist Dept. Army, 1970; clin. intern Am. U., Counseling Ctr., 1972; clin. psychologist Bay County Guidance Clinic, Panama City, Fla., 1972-73; rehab. counselor State of Fla., Panama City, 1974; rehab. psychologist Woodrow Wilson Rehab. Center, Fisherville, Va., 1975-84; dir. Shenandoah Counseling Assocs., P.C., 1981-88, pres., 1989—; mem. med. staff King's Daus. Hosp., Staunton, Va., 1982—, Waynesboro Community Hosp. Author papers in field. Fellow Am. Bd. Med. Psychotherapists (diplomate); mem. Am. Psychol. Assn., Va. Assn. Clin. Counselors, Va. Psychol. Assn., Va. Counselors Assn., Charlottesville-Albemarle Kennel Club (past bd. dir.), Kappa Alpha Theta. Democrat. Office: Shenandoah Counseling Assocs PC PO Box 696 Stanton VA 24401

KIRBY, JERI PATRICIA HALL, educator; b. Dallas, June 4, 1947; d. Charles Patrick and Elizabeth (Green) Hall; m. Michael Fletcher Kirby, Jan. 15, 1972; 1 child, Aaron Keith. BS in Edn., North Tex. State U., 1969; MEd, Stephen F. Austin U., 1976. Cert. elem. and art tchr., Tex. Tchr. elem. Garland (Tex.) Ind. Sch. Dist., 1970-83, Wills Point (Tex.) Ind. Sch. Dist., 1985—. Baptist. Home: Rt 2 Box 147 Canton TX 75103 Office: Wills Point Intermediate PO Drawer 30 Wills Point TX 75169

KIRBY, KATE PAGE, physicist; b. Washington, Dec. 5, 1945; d. Vance Nathaniel and Harriet (Geary) K.; m. Arch William Horst, May 21, 1977; children: Andrew, Elizabeth, Carolyn, Jonathan. AB, Radcliffe Coll., 1967; MS, U. Chgo., 1968, PhD, 1972. Postdoctoral fellow Harvard U. Observatory, Cambridge, Mass., 1972-73; rsch. physicist Smithsonian Astrophys. Observatory, Cambridge, 1973—; lectr. dept. astronomy Harvard U., Cambridge, 1973-83, 84-86; assoc. dir. Harvard-Smithsonian Ctr. for Astrophysics, Cambridge, 1988—. Contbr. articles to profl. jours. Fellow Am. Phys. Soc. (sec.-treas. div. atomic, molecular and optical physics 1984-87, chmn. membership com. 1989-90). Office: Harvard-Smithsonian Ctr for Astrophysics 60 Garden St Cambridge MA 02138

KIRBY, KRISTIE LYNN, psychologist; b. Flora, Ill., Oct. 12, 1953; d. John Warren and Patricia Ann (Porter) K.; m. Richard Michael Kessler. BA, Eastern Ill. U., 1975, MA, 1977; PhD, U. Mont., 1983. Lic. psychologist, Tenn. Assoc. psychologist Southeastern Ill. Mental Health Ctr., Olney, 1977-79; intern dept. psychology Upstate Med. Ctr., Syracuse, N.Y., 1982-83; staff psychologist St. Joseph's Hosp., Syracuse, 1983-84; sr. clin. psychologist Ridgeview Psychiat. Hosp., Oak Ridge, Tenn., 1984-89; prin. Profl. Psychotherapy Assocs., Kingston, Tenn., 1988—; part-time mem. faculty U. Tenn., Knoxville, 1985-86. Contbr. articles to profl. jours. NIMH grantee, 1979. Mem. Am. Psychol. Assn., Soc. for Clin. and Exptl. Hypnosis, Appalachian Psychoanalytic Soc., Tenn. Psychol. Assn., Phi Alpha Eta, Sigma Xi, Psi Chi. Office: Profl Psychotherapy Assocs 1000 Bradford Way Bldg 2 Kingston TN 37763

KIRBY, MARY WEEKS, educator, reading specialist; b. Cheverly, Md., Nov. 23, 1947; d. Isaac Ralph and Dorothea (Huppert) Weeks; m. William Charlie Kirby, Feb. 14, 1976; children: Joie, Fatimah, Tariq. Bachelor in Music Edn., James Madison U., 1969; MEd, Va. Commonwealth U., 1976; cert. Writers' Digest Sch., 1988. Cert. tchr. of music, reading and elem., Va. Music instr. Charles City County Schs., Providence Forge, Va., 1969-70, Hanover Learning Ctr., Va., 1970-72; sales cons. Boykins's Music Shop, Richmond, Va., 1972-74; elem. tchr. New Kent Pub. Schs., Va., 1974—, writing cons., 1980—; owner/operator Wacky Timepieces; presentor ednl. and reading workshops, 1980-82. Sponsor Young Authors' Workshop, New Kent, 1985—; co-chmn., presentor Parents Anonymous of Va., 1984-88; trustee Islamic Ctr. of Va., 1985-88, sec., 1981-85; active Boy Scouts Am., Girl Scouts U.S. Mem. New Kent Edn. Assn. (officer 1977-81), Va. Edn. Assn., NEA, Richmond Area Reading Council (sec. 1982-83), Sigma Alpha Iota (life). Avocations: needlework, reading, swimming. Home: 1309 Bull Run Dr Richmond VA 23231 Office: New Kent Pub Schs Quinton VA 23141

KIRCHNER, ELIZABETH PARSONS, clinical psychologist; b. Balt., July 20, 1928; d. Wilber Fay and Marguerite Victoria (Lindsay) Parsons; m. Henry Paul Kirchner, Nov. 11, 1950; children: Peter, James, Robert. BS, Cornell U., 1950; MS, Pa. State U., 1952, PhD, 1955. Lic. psychologist, Pa. Pvt. practice State College, Pa., 1958—; mem. faculty dept. psychology Pa. State U., University Park, 1965—; psychologist Buffalo State Hosp., 1959-61, U. Buffalo Med. Sch., 1961-64; cons. Pa. Correctional System, 1972-80, VA Hosp., Altoona, Pa., 1973-76, State Hosp. System, Pa., 1975-78, Office of Juvenile Probation and Parole, Bellefonte, Pa., 1983-85, Centre Community Hosp., State College, 1984—, Multiple Sclerosis Soc., Pa., 1989—. Author: Assertive Training in Prison, 1973, Be Your Own Therapist, 1981, Coping with Chronic Illness, 1988; contbr. articles to profl. jours., newspapers. Bd. dirs. state and local ACLU, 1968-75; co-founder Environ. Forum, State College, 1985. Grantee NIH, 1971-73. Mem. LWV, Am. Psychol. Assn., Coun. Human Svcs., Art Alliance Cen. Pa., Pa. Guild Craftsmen, Sierra Club (officer), Sigma Xi. Office: 111 S Allen St Ste 2D State College PA 16801

KIRCHNER, KATHERINE ANN, registered nurse, alcoholism counselor; b. Bay Shore, N.Y., Apr. 18, 1948; d. Arthur Robert and Katherine (Weber) K. AAS in Nursing, Suffolk County Community Coll., 1968; BS in Nursing, C.W. Post Coll., 1976; MA in Health Care magna cum laude, SUNY, Stony Brook, 1986. Staff nurse Southside Hosp., Bay Shore, 1968-69, staff nurse oper. rm., 1974-76, 81-89; insvc. instr. Boston Hosp. for Women, Brookline, Mass., 1969-70; staff nurse med.-surg. Newton Wellesley Hosp., Newton Lower Falls, Mass., 1970-71; nurse-in-charge Univ. Hosp., Boston, 1971-74; nursing team leader Straub Hosp., Honolulu, 1976-80; alcoholism counselor Lighthouse Counseling Ctr., Riverhead, N.Y., 1989—; nursing care coord. Eastern L.I. Hosp., Greenport, N.Y., 1989—. Assn. Oper. Rm. Nurses scholar, 1974; HEW grantee, 1975. Mem. N.Y. State Nurses Assn., N.Y. Fedn. Alcoholism Counselors. Lutheran. Office: Eastern LI Hosp Manor Place Greenport NY 11944

KIRCHNER, LYNN MARIE, human resources executive; b. Middletown, N.Y., Aug. 30, 1956; d. Christian W. and Mary R. (Barberio) K. AA, SUNY, Delhi, 1976; MA in Internat. Bus., SUNY, Cortland, 1978; MBA in Internat. Bus., Tsukuba Daigaku, Tsuchiura, Sakura Japan, 1979. Mgr. Orange County Cable Co., Middletown, 1979-80; mgr. mktg. Am. TV & Communications, Denver, 1980-81; mgr. Weisner Pub., Denver, 1981; dir. human resources Firstours, Denver, 1981-83; sr. dir. pers. Continental Express, Denver, 1983-88; regional dir. human resources Charter Med., Denver, 1988-90; dir. recruitment St. Joseph Hosp., Denver, 1990—. Contbg. author: (poems) World's Greatest Vol. I, 1984, World's Greatest Vol. II, 1985. Vol. Big Bros.-Big Sisters, Denver, 1980-90, Lunker Hunters, Denver, 1988-90, Denver Jr. Symphony Guild, 1981-90. Mem. Nat. Assn. Human Resources (outstanding human resources award 1988), Am. Hosp. Assn., Colo. Hosp. Human Resources Assn., Am. Soc. Pers. Adminstrs., Colo. Hosp. Assn. Home: 9400 E Iliff Ave #311 Denver CO 80231 Office: St Joseph Hosp 1835 Franklin St Denver CO 80231

KIRCHNER, SUZANNE CORNELIA, labor administrator; b. Sunbury, Pa., Nov. 22, 1955; d. John Michael and Marcelle Antoinette Augusta (Mari) K. BS with distinction, Pa. State U., 1976. Dir. Little Oaks Day Care Ctr., State College, Pa., 1976; tchr. Discovery Sch., Harrisburg, Pa., 1976-77; clk. III Pa. Liquor Control Bd., Harrisburg, 1977-78; investigator Office Labor-Mgmt. Standards U.S. Dept. Labor, Pitts., 1978-87; dist. dir. Office Labor-Mgmt. Standards U.S. Dept. Labor, Seattle, 1987—. Mem. NAFE, Fed. Criminal Investigators Assn., Phi Upsilon Omicron. Roman Catholic. Office: US Dept Labor OL-MS 1111 Third Ave Ste 880 Seattle WA 98101-3212

KIRCHOFF, SHAILA RAE, small business owner; b. Mpls., July 20, 1962; d. Elroy Edward and Shirley Ann (Forsberg) K. Student, U. Minn., 1983-85, Monterey Pen. Coll. Asst. to pres. Art Pub./Art Gallery, Santa Monica, Calif., 1986-88; nat. sales dir. Fine Leather Apparel Mfg., Los Angeles, 1988-. Mem. Trancas Riders and Ropers, Creative Inst., Profl. Women's Network of Monterey Pen., Monterey C. of C. Republican. Presbyterian. Office: John Michael Inc 110 E 9th St Ste A285 Los Angeles CA 90079

KIRK, CONSTANCE IONE, former hospital administrator, consultant; b. Neptune, N.J., Apr. 29, 1951; d. Lawrence Lynwood and Ione Louise (Hegstead) Lyford; m. Bartholomew Francis Kirk, Feb. 21, 1987; 1 child, Bartholomew Francis III. BA, U. Conn., 1973; M Health Adminstrn., George Washington U., 1979. Asst. adminstr. Sharp Meml. Hosp., San Diego, 1979-83, assoc. adminstr., 1983-87; adminstrv. cons. U. Calif. San Diego Med. Ctr., 1987; pvt. practice cons. San Diego, 1987—; bd. dirs. Edgemoor Geriatric Hosp., Santee, Calif., 1985-88. Campaign leader Dem. Party, San Diego, 1988. Recipient Tribute to Women in Industry award San Diego YWCA, 1983. Mem. Am. Coll. Healthcare Execs., Nat. Assn. Rehab. Facilities. Home and Office: 4276 Adams Ave San Diego CA 92116

KIRK, HELENE LISA, computer programmer, systems analyst; b. Bklyn., Apr. 6, 1959; d. Stanley and Marilyn (Segall) K.; m. Paul W. Gromadzki, June 18, 1978; (div. Nov. 1985); m. Steven Kirk, Sept. 7, 1986. BBA magna cum laude, CUNY, 1976-80. Computer programmer, systems analyst AT&T, White Plains, N.Y., 1980-88; computer programmer/systems analyst AT&T, Alpharetta, Ga., 1988—; image cons. Beauti Control Cosmetics, 1990—. Democrat. Jewish. Office: AT&T 300 Eastside Dr Alpharetta GA 30201

KIRK, LYNDA POUNDS, stress therapist; b. Corpus Christi, Tex., Dec. 17, 1946; d. James Arthur and Elizabeth Pauline (Sanders) Pounds; m. Edward C. Randolph Kirk, June 10, 1967; children: Leslie Jennifer, Edward Christopher. BA, U. tex., 1977. Therapist Austin (Tex.) State Hosp., 1977-80; dir. stress mgmt. The Hills Med./Sports Complex, Austin, 1980-82; founder, owner Austin Biofeedback Ctr., 1982—, Health Mastery Concepts, Austin, 1982—; cons. State of Tex., Austin, 1983—, City of Austin, 1985—, Lower Colo. River Authority, Austin, 1984—. Author: (book/cassette series) Regenerative Relaxation, 1981; Urological Applications of Biofeedback, Stress Mastery and Peak Performance, 1986. Bd. dirs. South Austin Polit. Action Coalition, 1986-87, South Austin Civic Club, 1983-88, pres., 1987; bd. dirs., treas. Texans for the Preservation of Hist. Structures, 1990—. Mem. Biofeedback Soc. Am., Biofeedback Soc. Tex. (exec. bd., citation award 1989), Behaviorial Medicine Soc. Am., Am. Holistic Med. Assn., Phi Beta Kappa. Episcopalian. Home: 420 Brady Ln Austin TX 78746 Office: Austin Biofeedback Ctr 4207 James Casey Ste 301 Austin TX 78745

KIRK, MARY POWELL, college administrator; b. Tryon, N.C., Jan. 15, 1954; d. Fred Hugh and Betty Louise (Arledge) Powell; m. Charles Thomas Kirk, July 2, 1988; children: Kathryn Louise, Kristin Anne Kirk. BS, U. N.C., Greensboro, 1975; postgrad., E. Carolina U., 1989—. Exec. sec. Fellowship Hall, Inc., Greensboro, 1976-83; office mgr. Warren J. David, P.A., Beaufort, N.C., 1983-84; asst. to pres. Carteret Community Coll., Morehead City, N.C., 1984—. Officer Project Christmas Cheer, Morehead City, 1987—; mem. edn. com. Morehead City Econ. Devel. Coun., 1988—; mem. Morehead City Liaison Com. for Chronically Mentally Ill., 1988-90; mem. Carteret Literacy Coalition, Morehead City, 1987—. Geoffrey Tennant scholar, 1971. Mem. Women in N.C. Higher Edn., N.C. Pub. Info. Officers Assn., Am. Assn. Women in Community and Jr. Colls. Democrat. Baptist. Office: Carteret Community Coll 3503 Arendell St Morehead City NC 28557

KIRK, SUSAN MURRAY, executive assistant, executive secretary; b. Hartford, Conn., July 31, 1953; d. Leonard A. Sr. and Elizabeth (Anderson) Murray; m. Michael William Kirk, July 24, 1982. Student, Sweet Briar (Va.) Coll.; AS magna cum laude, Cen. Va. Community Coll., 1986. Exec. asst. to pres. Gulf Shores Inst., Lecanto, Fla.; adminstrv. asst. to plant mgr. Sparton Electronics, Crystal River, Fla.; exec. sec. to pres. Barnett Bank of Citrus County, Lecanto. Mem. NAFE, Am. Legion Aux., Am. Bus. Women's Assn., Nat. Mus. Women in the Arts, Fla. Pub. Rels. Assn., Phi Beta Lambda. Home: 3101 Twisting Ln Bowie MD 20715

KIRKEMO, ELIZABETH ELLEN, infosystems specialist; b. Washington, Apr. 6, 1962; d. William Joseph Jr. and Roberta Louise (Creech) Dunn; m. Kevin Eugene Kirkemo, Sept. 15, 1990. BS, Mary Washington Coll., 1984; postgrad., U. Phoenix, 1988—. Logistics analyst Syscon Corp., Washington, 1985-88; data mgr. GTE Corp., Mountain View, Calif., 1988—. Vol. Am. Heart Assn., Washington and No. Va., 1988, Hospice of No. Va., Arlington, 1986-87. Roman Catholic. Home: 1201 Sycamore Terr #45 Sunnyvale CA 94086

KIRKHAM, M. B., plant physiologist, educator; b. Cedar Rapids, Iowa; d. Don and Mary Elizabeth (Erwin) K. BA with honors, Wellesley Coll.; MS, U. Wis., PhD. Cert. profl. agronomist. Plant physiologist U.S. EPA, Cin., 1973-74; asst. prof. U. Mass., Amherst, 1974-76, Okla. State U., Stillwater, 1976-80; from assoc. prof. to prof. Kans. State U., Manhattan, 1980—; guest lectr. Inst. Water and Conservancy and Hydroelectric Power Rsch., Inst. Farm Irrigation Rsch., People's Republic of China, 1985, Inst. Exptl. Agronomy, Italy, 1989; vis. scholar Biol. Labs., Harvard U., Cambridge, Mass., 1990. Cons. editor Plant and Soil jour., 1979—; editorial bd. Field Crops Research jour., 1983—; contbr. over 130 articles and papers to sci. jours. NDEA fellow U. Wis., 1968-70, NSF postdoctoral fellow U. Wis., 1971-73, E.I. du Pont de Nemours and Co. summer faculty fellow, 1976; NSF grantee, Office of Water Research and Tech. grantee, U.S. Dept. Agrl. grantee, U.S. Dept. Energy grantee. Fellow AAAS, Am. Soc. Agronomy (editorial bd. 1985—), Soil Sci. Soc. Am. (travel grantee to internat. congress Japan 1990), Royal Meteorol. Soc.; mem. Am. Soc. Plant Physiology (editorial bd. 1982-87), Am. Soc. Horticultural Sci., Internat. Soil Sci. Soc., Bot. Soc. Am., Am. Meteorol. Soc., Crop Sci. Soc. Am. (editorial bd. 1980-84), N.Y. Acad. Sci., British Plant Growth Regulator Soc., Growth Regulator Soc. Am., Phi Kappa Phi, Gamma Sigma Delta, Sigma Xi. Home: 1420 McCain Ln #244 Manhattan KS 66502 Office: Kans State U Evapotranspiration Lab Manhattan KS 66506

KIRKIEN-RZESZOTARSKI, ALICIA MARIA, academic administrator, researcher, educator; b. Lodz, Poland; came to U.S., 1965; d. Leszek Tadeusz and Francesca Irene (Mortkowicz) Kirkien; m. Zygmunt Roman Rzeszotarski, Dec. 14, 1971. MS in Chem. Engring., Polish U. Coll., London, 1951; PhD, U. London, 1955. Asst. prof. chemistry U. W.I., Jamaica, 1956-59, assoc. prof., 1959-61; assoc. prof. U. W.I., Trinidad, 1961-65; assoc. prof. Trinity Coll., Washington, 1966-68, prof. chemistry, 1968—, chair chemistry dept., 1969—; sr. rsch. assoc. George Washington U. Med. Ctr., Washington, 1984. Contbr. numerous articles to profl. jours. Sec., treas. Polish Vets. ASSC, Washington, 1981-83. Univ. Coll. Sr. Rsch. fellow, 1965-66, 71, UCSB, 1967. Mem. Am. Chem. Soc. (adv. bd. Chem. and Engring. News 1978-81), Chem. Soc. Gt. Britain, Polish Inst. Arts and Scis of N.Y., Phi Beta Kappa. Republican. Roman Catholic. Home: 407 Buckspur Ct Millersville MD 21108 Office: Trinity Coll 125 Michigan Ave NW Washington DC 20017

KIRKLAND, BERTHA THERESA (MRS. THORNTON CROWNS KIRKLAND, JR.), engineer; b. San Francisco, May 16, 1916; d. Lawrence and Theresa (Kanzler) Schmelzer; m. Thornton Crowns Kirkland, Jr., Dec. 27, 1937 (dec. July 1971); children: Kathryn Elizabeth, Francis Charles. Supr. hosp. ops. Am. Potash & Chem. Corp., Trona, Calif., 1953-54; office mgr., T.C. Kirkland, elec. contractor, 1954-56; sec.-treas., bd. dirs. T.C. Kirkland, Inc., San Bernardino, Calif., 1958-74; design-install estimator Add-M Electric, Inc., 1972-82, v.p., 1974-82; estimator, engr. Corona Indsl. Electric, Inc. (Calif.), 1982-83; project engr. Fischbach and Moore, Inc., L.A., 1984—. Episcopalian. Club: Arrowhead Country (San Bernardino). Home: 526 E Sonora St San Bernardino CA 92404 Office: Fischbach & Moore Inc 1223 S Flower St Burbank CA 91502

KIRKLAND, MARY JANE, manufacturing executive; b. N.Y.C., Jan. 7, 1937; d. Nicholas and Florence (Paul) Dalvano; (div.); children: Amy, Elizabeth, James, Jennifer. BA, Queens Coll., 1957, MS, 1967. Cert. elem. tchr., N.Y. Tchr. East Meadow (N.Y.) Pub. Schs., 1957-58, Rochester (N.Y.) Pub. Schs., 1958-60; English tchr. Languages Internat., Brussels, Belgium, 1977-79; English language facilitator Essochem, Brussels, 1977-79; internat. contracts adminstr. Servo Corp. of Am., Hicksville, N.Y., 1980-84; sr. subcontracts adminstr. AIL Systems Inc., Deer Park, N.Y., 1984—. Coord. Women Overseas for Equality, Brussels, 1977. Mem. Women in Electronics (treas. 1985-86). Office: AIL Systems Inc Commack Rd Deer Park NY 11729

KIRKLAND, PEGGY ANN, teacher; b. Detroit, Nov. 16, 1947; d. Roy James Griffin and Ada Louise (Newby) Cain; m. Arthur Kirkland Jr., Feb. 24, 1973 (div. Apr. 1980); 1 child, Julian Arthur. BA, Wayne State U., 1970; MA, NYU, 1976; cert. Edn. Specialist, Wayne State U., 1987. Cert. elem. tchr., Mich. Tchr. Lessenger Jr. High Sch., Detroit, 1970-73, New Hyde Park (N.Y.) Meml. High Sch., 1973-75; adj. lectr. La Guardia Community Coll., L.I. City, N.Y., 1976-77; tchr. Southfield (Mich.) High Sch., 1977-81, St. Theresa-Visitation Sch., Detroit, 1981-82; adj. lectr. Lawrence Tech. U., Southfield, 1982-83; dir. alternative edn. program Ferndale (Mich.) High Sch., 1985-86, tchr., coord., 1984—; speaker Nat. Alliance for Bus., Chgo., 1987, Nat. Coun. of Negro Women, Inc., Detroit, 1987. Author numerous poems. Mem., lay reader Old Mariner's Ch., Detroit, 1981—; vol. United Negro Coll. Fund., 1977-83. Recipient Outstanding Tchr. award, Southfield High Sch., 1981. Mem. NEA, NAACP, Assn. for Supervision Curriculum Devel., Chandon Club (Yountville, Calif.), Delta Kappa Gamma. Anglican Catholic. Office: Ferndale High Sch 881 Pinecrest Ferndale MI 48220

KIRKMAN, KAY, fund raising executive; b. Coffeyville, Kans., Oct. 29, 1935; d. Howard E. and Mildred Joy (Bridenstine) Williams; m. William P. Kirkman, Jr, Apr. 23, 1954; children: Kathleen, Deanna, Phillip, Paul. AA, Johnson County Community Coll., Overland Park, Kans., 1976; BA, Park Coll., 1978; MFA, Wichita State U., 1985. Publs. editor Johnson County Community Coll., 1969-75, Wesley Med. Ctr., Wichita, Kans., 1978-80; instr. English and creative writing Mo. So. State Coll., Joplin, 1976-78, Barton County Community Coll., Gt. Bend, Kans., 1983-84, Wichita State U., 1984; dir. employee communications svcs. Pizza Hut, Inc., Wichita, 1981-83; dir. devel. Wentworth Mil. Acad., Lexington, Mo., 1985-90; pub. rels. cons., freelance writer, 1975—. Author: Joplin: A Pictorial History, 1981, Wichita: A Pictoral History, 1982. Bd. dirs. Lexington Hist. Assn., 1986—. Recipient awards of excellence and merit Adv. Club Wichita, 1981, 82, 83, Coun. for Advancement and Support Edn., 1973-75, poetry and short story award Wichita Eagle-Beacon, 1980, Gt. Bend Herald, 1982, Excelsior Springs

Tribune. Mem. Internat. Assn. Bus. Communicators (accredited, accreditation chmn. dist. 5, 1988—), Joplin Writers Assn. (pres. 1979), Lexington Women's Club, Beta Sigma Phi. Presbyterian. Home: 2106 South St Lexington MO 64067 Office: Reach Out Am Inc 6500 N Cosby Kansas City MO 64151

KIRKPATRICK, ANNE SAUNDERS, systems analyst; b. Birmingham, Mich., July 4, 1938; d. Stanley Rathbun and Esther (Casteel) Saunders; m. Robert Armstrong Kirkpatrick, Oct. 5, 1963; children: Elizabeth, Martha, Robert, Sarah. Student, Wellesley Coll., 1956-57, Laval U., Quebec City, Can., 1958, U. Ariz., 1958-59; BA in Philosophy, U. Mich., 1961. Systems engr. IBM, Chgo., 1962-64; systems analyst Commonwealth Edison Co., Chgo., 1981—. Treas. Taproot Reps., DuPage County, Ill., 1977-80; pres. Hinsdale (Ill.) Women's Rep. Club, 1978-81. Club: Wellesley of Chgo. (bd. dirs. 1972-73). Home: 524 N Lincoln Hinsdale IL 60521 Office: Commonwealth Edison Co 72 W Adams Room 1122 Chicago IL 60603

KIRKPATRICK, ELEANOR BLAKE, civic worker; b. Mangum, Okla., Mar. 10, 1909; d. Mack Barkley and Kathryn (Talbott) Blake; m. John Elson Kirkpatrick, June 20, 1932; 1 child, Joan Elson. B.A. in French, Smith Coll., 1931; D.Humanities (hon.), Oklahoma City U., 1968. Ptnr. Kirkpatrick Oil Co., Oklahoma City, Kirkpatrick Oil & Gas, Oklahoma City. Bd. dirs. Kirkpatrick Ctr., Oklahoma City; treas. Kirkpatrick Found., Oklahoma City. Named to Okla. Hall of Fame, Okla. Heritage Assn., Oklahoma City, 1975; recipient Evergreen Disting. Service award Nat. Assn. Mature People, Okla., 1982, Bd. Trustees award Omniplex Sci. Mus., Oklahoma City, 1984, Wall of Fame award Oklahoma City Pub. Sch. Found., 1990; co-founder, hon. pres. Alliance Française, Oklahoma City; bd. mem. Oklahoma Art Ctr. Mem. Oklahoma City U. Opera (bd. dirs.), Soc. and Library Soc. (hon.), Oklahoma City U. Library Soc. (bd. dirs.). Avocation: backgammon. Office: Kirkpatrick Oil Co 1300 N Broadway Dr Oklahoma City OK 73103

KIRKPATRICK, JEANE DUANE JORDAN, political scientist, government official; b. Duncan, Okla., Nov. 19, 1926; d. Welcher F. and Leona (Kile) Jordan; m. Evron M. Kirkpatrick, Feb. 20, 1955; children: Douglas Jordan, John Evron, Stuart Alan. AA, Stephens Coll., 1946; AB, Barnard Coll., 1948; MA, Columbia U., 1950, PhD, 1968; postgrad. (French govt. fellow), U. Paris Inst. de Sci. Politique, 1952-53; LHD (hon.), Mt. Vernon Coll., 1978, Georgetown U., 1981, U. Pitts., 1981, U. West Fla., 1981, U. Charleston, 1982, St. Anselm's, 1982, Hebrew U., 1982, Betheny Coll., 1983, Colo. Sch. Mines, 1983, St. John's U., 1983; Loyola Coll., 1985, Hebrew Union Coll., 1985, Universidad Francisco Marroquin, Guatemala, 1985, Coll. of William and Mary, 1986, U. Mich., 1988. Rsch. analyst Dept. State, 1951-53; rsch. assoc. George Washington U., 1954-56, Fund for the Rep., 1956-58; asst. prof. polit. sci. Trinity Coll., 1962-67; assoc. prof. polit. sci. Georgetown U., Washington, 1967-73, prof., 1973—; sr. fellow Am. Enterprise Inst. for Pub. Policy Rsch., 1977—; Leavey prof. Founds. Am. Freedom, 1978—; mem. cabinet U.S. permanent rep. to UN, 1981-85; co-chmn. task force presdl. election process 20th Century Fund; cons. Am. Coun. Learned Socs., Dept. State, HEW, Dept. Def., intermittently 1955-72; vice chmn. com. on v.p. selection Democratic Nat. Com., 1972-74, mem. nat. commn. party structure and presdl. nomination, 1975; mem. credentials com. Dem. Nat. Conv., 1976; mem. internat. rsch. coun. Cte. for Strategic and Internat. Studies. Author: Foreign Students in the U.S.: A National Survey, 1966, Mass Behavior in Battle and Captivity, 1968, Leader and Vanguard in Mass Society: The Peronist Movement in Argentina, 1971, Political Woman, 1974, The Presidential Elite, 1976, Dismantling the Parties: Reflections on Party Reform and Party Decomposition, 1978, The Reagan Phenomenon, 1983, Dictatorships and Double Standards, 1982, Legitimacy and Force (2 vols.), 1988; contbr. articles to profl. jours.; editor, contbr. various pubs. Trustee Helen Dwight Reid Ednl. Found., 1972—; trustee Robert A. Taft Inst. Govt., 1978—; mem. bd. curators Stephens Coll. Recipient Disting. Alumna award Stephens Coll., 1978, B'nai B'rith Humanitarian award, 1982, award of the Commonwealth Fund, 1983, Gold medal VFW, 1984, French Prix Politique, 1984, Dept. Defense Disting. Pub. Svc. medal, 1985, Spl. award from the Mayor N.Y.C., 1985, Presdl. medal of Freedom, 1985, others; Earhart fellow, 1956-57. Mem. Internat. Polit. Sci. Assn. (exec. coun.), Am. Polit. Sci. Assn. (Hubert Humphrey award 1988), So. Polit. Sci. Assn. Office: Am Enterprise Inst 1150 17th St NW Washington DC 20036

KIRKPATRICK, JOYCELYN, clinical dietitian; b. Apple Valley, Calif., Apr. 11, 1947; d. Paul Franklin and Eleanor Jean (Wilson) K. BS, Calif. State Polytech. U., San Luis Obispo, 1970. Cert. diabetes educator, 1988. Clin. dietitian Ga. Baptist Hosp., Atlanta, 1971-72; clin. dietitian, asst. food svc. dir. Alvarado Community Hosp., San Diego, 1972-76; diabetes educator Eisenhower Med. Ctr., Rancho Mirage, Calif., 1976-83; clin. dietitian Palm Springs (Calif.) Med. Ctr., 1983-85; clin. dietitian, diabetes educator John F. Kennedy Meml. Hosp., Indio, Calif., 1989—; nutrition instr. Coll. of Desert, Palm Desert, Calif., 1976-84, Optifast Weight Loss Program, Rancho Mirage, 1981—; nutrition cons. Vis. Nurses, Riverside County, Palm Desert, 1980-86; pvt. practice Nutrition Wise, Rancho Mirage, 1976—. Co-author: (cookbook) The Guiltless Gourmet, 1983, The Guiltless Gourmet Goes Ethnic, 1990; contbg. editor: ADA Family Cookbook, 1979, 84; contbr. articles to profl. jours. Mem. Young Proff-Organ, McCallum Theater, Palm Desert, 1989, on-air nutrition KPSI Radio - The Desert Health Show, Palm Springs, 1989—. Mem. Am. Dietetic Assn., Am. Heart Assn (bd. dirs. 1988—, Fund Raising award, 1988-89), Am. Diabetes Assn., Diabetes Care and Edn. Assn. (sec. 1980-82), Inland Dist. Dietetic Assn. (Media Satellite award, 1988-89). Republican. Methodist. Office: Nutrition Wise PO Box 499 Rancho Mirage CA 92270

KIRKPATRICK, MARY BETH, educator; b. Sibley, Iowa, July 13, 1951; d. Delbert Aielt and Mary Louise (Helmers) Kruger; m. Glen Alan Kirkpatrick, Dec. 20, 1975; children: Jason D., Joshua James. BA, S.W. State U., Marshall, Minn., 1973; postgrad., U. No. Iowa, 1980-85, U. Nebr., 1987. Cert. secondary sch. tchr., coach. Tchr., coach Sacred Heart (Minn.) Pub. Schs., 1973-74, Tilford Mid. Sch., Vinton, Iowa, 1974—. Author: Everyone Wins, 1986; contbr. articles to profl. jours. Mem. PTA, Grundy Center, Iowa, 1989—; speaker Parent Groups, Iowa, 1988—; participant Congl. Fitness Assessment Day, Washington, 1986. Recipient Govs. Cup Iowa Govs. Coun., Des Moines, 1985, U.S. West Outstanding Tchr. award Iowa U.S. West, Denver, 1988, Christa McAuliffe fellow U.S. Dept. Edn., Washington, 1988. Mem. AAUW, Iowa Girl's & Women's Sports (pres. 1984-85), AAHPERD (Cen. Dist. Secondary Phys. Edn. Tchr. of Yr. award 1985, Iowa chpt. v.p. 1987-88, Secondary Phys. Edn. Tchr. of Yr. award 1986, Disting. Svc. 1988), Nat. Assn. Sport & Phys. Edn., Vinton Golf Club, Grundy Ctr. Golf Club. Republican. United Methodist. Office: Tilford Mid Sch E 13th St Vinton IA 52349

KIRKPATRICK, TRICIA THOMSON, fashion consultant; b. Ft. Smith, Ark., Oct. 17, 1946; d. John Whittier and Erma Doris Thomson; m. Michael Kegler, Nov. 15, 1968 (div. 1975); m. Robert McCann Kirkpatrick, Oct. 10, 1981. Student, Tex. Women's U., 1964-67. Fashion cons. Nieman Marcus, Dallas, 1967. Pres. Irving (Tex.) Symphony League, 1988-89; past pres. Las Colinas Womens Assn., 1986; bd. dirs. Cultural Affairs Council, Irving, 1986—. Mem. Las Colinas Garden Club (founder), Irving Heritage Soc., Literary Guild, Gourmet Club, Jr. Book Review Irving Hosp. Guild, Texas-fest Steering Com. Republican. Methodist. Address: 601 N Durango Irving TX 75062

KIRKPATRICK, VICKI KAREN, county government official; b. Salem, Oreg., July 31, 1952; d. Raymond Elmer and Mildred Margaret (Laver) Goodwin; children: Jaclyn Victoria, Courtney Laver. BS in Psychology, cert. in teaching, U. Oreg., 1974. Sec. Gordon Brunton Realty, Eugene, Oreg., 1974-76; adminstrv. asst. Oreg. Dept. Gen. Svcs., Salem, 1976-78, Oreg. Dept. Revenue, Bend and Salem, 1978-79; tng. and devel. specialist Oreg. Dept. Revenue, Salem, 1979-81, budget and fin. analyst, 1981-83; adminstrv. asst. to dir. health dept. Tacoma-Pierce County, Tacoma, 1984-85, dir. adminstrv. svcs. health dept., 1985—; chair equal employment adv. com. Oreg. Dept. Revenue, 1981-82; cons. to tax ct. judge Oreg. Tax Ct., Salem, 1982. Contbg. author: Budget Manual for Municipal Corporations, 1982. Mem. Pierce County Day Care Task Force, Pierce County, 1985-86; mem. planning com. Ann. Women's Awareness Week, Tacoma, 1984, program chair planning com., 1985. Mem. Nat. Govt. Fin. Officers Assn., Am. Pub. Health Assn., Wash. Fin. Officers Assn. (cert. and awarede designation of Profl. Fin. Officer 1989), Wash. State Assn. of Local Pub. Health Officials, City Club of Tacoma, Rotary (Internat., Tacoma chpt. program com. 1990—). Democrat. Lutheran. Office: Tacoma Pierce County Health 3629 South D St Tacoma WA 98408

KIRKSEY, TERRIE LYNN, multi-purpose senior center administrator, social work consultant; b. Shaw, Miss., Nov. 18, 1958; d. Clarence Clayton and Mary Juanice (King) K. B of Social Work, Delta State U., 1980; MSW, U. Tenn. Ctr. for Health Scis., 1985. Asst. dir. recreational therapy Rosewood Manor, Memphis, 1980, dir. social services, 1981-83; dir. social services Memphis Health Care Ctr., 1980-81, St. Peter Villa, Memphis, 1983-84; asst. dir. Josephine K. Lewis Ctr. for Sr. Citizens, Memphis, 1984-89, dir., 1989—; social work cons. Bapt. Home Plus Home Health Agy., Memphis, 1986—, Hillhaven Raleigh, Memphis, 1989—. Bd. dirs. Ret. Sr. Vol. Program, 1985-89, sec., 1986-87; bd. dirs. Alzheimer's Day Care Inc., sec., 1987-90, pres.-elect, co-carers, 1990; bd. dirs., sec. Memphis/Shelby County Coun. on Aging, 1989—. Mem. Phi Theta Kappa. Democrat. Home: 4055 Chinaberry Cove Memphis TN 38115 Office: Josephine K Lewis Ctr for Sr Citizens 1188 N Parkway Memphis TN 38105

KIRKWOOD, CATHERINE, artist; b. N.Y.C., July 4, 1949; d. Kenneth Munn Kirkwood and Alexa (Dannenbaum) Hirsh; m. Craig Campbell Anderson; children: Heather Dene, Julia Suzanne. Student, Syracuse U., 1967-69, Calif. Coll. Arts and Crafts, Oakland, 1970-71; BFA, U. N.Mex., 1972, MA, 1974. Grad. instr. U. N.Mex., 1973-74; owner, designer Mei Ming Ware, Santa Fe, 1985-89. Exhibited in group shows at include 1972 S.W. Fine Arts Biennial Mus. N.Mex., Santa Fe, Downey (Calif.) Mus. Art Unltd. Exhibit, 1972, 19th Exhbn. Southwestern Prints and Drawings Dallas Mus., 1972, "Woman In Art" U. M.Mex., 1972, Introduction '73 Hills Gallery, Santa Fe, 1973, Gallery Modern Art, Taos, N.Mex., 1973, "Boulder Plus Two" Henderson Mus., Boulder, Co., 1974, 19th Ann. Invitational Art Exhbn., Union, N.J., 1978, Machler Gallery, Phila., 1978, "Provocations & Regenerations" Albuquerque United Artists, 1979, Faculty Show U. N.Mex., Albuquerque, 1979, Tuthill-Gimprich Gallery, N.Y.C., 1980, AIR Gallery, Austin, Tex., 1984, "Southwest '85: A Fine Arts Competition" Mus. N.Mex., Santa Fe, "Own Your Own" Pueblo (Clolo.) Art Ctr., 1985, AAUW Calendar, 1989, Cydney Payton Gallery, Denver, 1989; represented in permanent collections Downey Mus., Am. Telephone and Telegraph Co., Chgo. Democrat. Home: Rte 14 Box 216Y Santa Fe NM 87505

KIRLEY, MARION RACHEL, psychoanalyst, psychotherapist; b. Winthrop, Mass., Aug. 7, 1934; d. Patrick Francis and Hazel Elizabeth (Cody) K. BS in Nursing, Boston Coll., 1959, MS in Nursing, 1967, EdD, 1980. Diplomate Am. Bd. Med. Psychoterapists; cert. psychotherapist, clin. nurse specialist. Staff nurse Mass. Gen. Hosp., Boston, 1959-61, supr. operating room, 1961-63, psychiat. nurse clinician, 1969-74; instr. Mt. Auburn Hosp., Cambridge, Mass., 1963-65; nursing care coord. Danvers (Mass.) State Hosp., 1967-69; inst. Salem (Mass.) State Coll., 1976; nurse clinician San Francisco Gen. Hosp., 1981; asst. psychoanalyst Karen Horney Clinic, N.Y.C., 1981-86, Soloman Carter Fuller Mental Health Ctr. Crisis Intervention, Boston, 1987-89; pvt. practice psychoanalysis Boston, 1987—, N.Y.C., 1989—; pvt. practice Am. Inst. Psychoanalysis Psychotherapy Program, N.Y.C., 1989—; mem. faculty Am. Inst. Psychoanalysis, 1989. Served to capt. U.S. Air Force 1969-71. Mem. Assn. Advancement Psychoanalysis (sec.), Am. Nursing Assn. (cert.), Am. Nurses Council Psychiat. Mental Health Nursing, Mass. Nurses Assn., Am. Inst. Psychoanalysis (cert.). Roman Catholic. Office: 329 E 62d St New York NY 10021 also: 1 Hawthorne Pl Boston MA 02114

KIRMSE, ANNE-MARIE ROSE, educator, researcher; b. Bklyn., Sept. 23, 1941; d. Frank Joseph Sr. and Anna (Keck) K. BA in English cum laude, St. Francis Coll., 1972; MA in Theology with honors, Providence Coll., 1975; PhD in Theology, Fordham U., 1989. Cert. elem. tchr., N.Y. Tchr. elem. sch. Diocese Bklyn., 1962-73; instr. adult edn. Diocese Rockville Centre, N.Y., 1974—; dir. religious edn. St. Anthony Padua Parish, East Northport, N.Y., 1975-83; dir. spiritual programs Diocese of Rockville Centre, 1979—; demonstration tchr. Paulist Press, N.Y.C., 1968-70; cons. Elem. Sch. Catechetical Assocs., Bklyn., 1971-73; mem. adj. faculty grad. program Sem. Immaculate Conception, Huntington, N.Y., 1979-80; adj. instr. Molloy Coll., Rockville Centre, 1985; asst. to Rev. Avery Dulles, Fordham U., Bronx, N.Y., 1988—, rsch. assoc., Laurence J. McGinley chair in religion and soc., 1989—; adj. lectr. St. Joseph's Coll., Patchogue, N.Y. Recipient Dominican scholarship Providence (R.I.) Coll., 1973, Kerygma award Diocese Rockville Centre, 1980, Presdl. scholarship Fordham U., 1988; McGinley fellow Fordham U., 1988. Mem. Sisters of St. Dominic, 1960—, Long Island Women's Ordination Conf. Democrat. Roman Catholic. Office: Fordham U Keating Hall 322 Laurence J McGinley Chair in Religion and Soc Bronx NY 10458

KIRSCH, CHRISTINE JO, chemist; b. Akron, Ohio, Nov. 17, 1950; d. Joseph Stephen and Dorothy Viola (Samuelson) Frederick; m. Gregory Alan Kirsch, Aug. 19, 1978; 1 child, Jonathan Joseph. BS in Biology, Ohio Dominican Coll., 1972; MBA, Capital U., 1983. Chemist Ross Labs., Columbus, Ohio, 1973—. Mem. AAAS. Democrat. Roman Catholic. Home: 9972 Granden St Pickerington OH 43147 Office: Ross Labs 625 Cleveland Ave Columbus OH 43215

KIRSCHBROWN, LITA BRYNA, presidential center executive; b. Jersey City, Nov. 16, 1952; d. Jerome and Sydell (Obolsky) K.; m. Steven Scott D'Arazien, Apr. 11, 1967. BA, Rutgers U., 1974; MBA, Emory U., 1989. Asst. editor Popular Photography mag., N.Y.C., 1974-76; grants adminstr. Am. Soc. for Microbiology, Washington, 1976-78; press sec. to Congress Jim Lloyd, U.S. Ho. of Reps., Washington, 1978-80; publs. coord. U. N.C., Chapel Hill, 1980-82; real estate saleswoman Mayhew Beer Realty, Chapel Hill, 1982-85, Town & Country, Arlington, Va., 1985-87; assoc. dir. devel. Carter Presdl. Ctr., Atlanta, 1989—; grad. asst. Emory U., Atlanta, 1988-89. Editor Ctr. Focus newsletter, 1981 (merit award 1981). Bd. dirs., chmn. fund raising and publicity coms. Orange County Rape Crisis Ctr., Chapel Hill, 1982-84; pres. Mt. Vernon Townhouse Assn., Alexandria, Va., 1985; chmn. planning and zoning com. Mt. Vernon Coun. Citizens Assns., Fairfax County, Va., 1986. Emory U. merit fellow, 1988-89, 87, 88. Mem. Assn. MBA Execs., NAFE, Emory Bus. Club, Gold Key. Democrat. Jewish. Home: 1253 Lenox Circle NE Atlanta GA 30306 Office: The Carter Ctr One Capenhill Atlanta GA 30307

KIRSCHNER, RUTH BRIN, educator; b. Mpls., Mar. 12, 1924; d. Sigman and Leah (Chazankin) Brin; m. Norman Bernard Kirschner, June 19, 1949; children: Sally Jo Kirschner Minsberg, William Arthur. BS cum laude, U. Minn., 1946. Primary tchr. Robert Fulton Sch., Mpls., 1946-52; elem. tchr. St. Louis Park (Minn.) Schs., 1962—; tchr. religious sch. Adath Jeshurun Synagogue, Mpls., 1946-83, Bnai Emet Synagoguue, St. Louis Park, 1989—; primary tchr. Latch Key, Mpls., 1986-88; nursery sch. tchr. Westwood Luth. Ch., St. Louis Park, 1989—; customer svc. rep. Am. Automobile Assn., St. Louis Park, 1985—. Sec. 4th Dist. Dem. Com., St. Louis Park, 1986-90; state del. St. Louis Park Dem. Com., 1986, 88, 90; mem. Community Rels. Coun. St. Louis Park, 1986-88; pres. Friends St. Louis Park Libr., 1987-88, sec., 1990—. Mem. AAUW (sec.-treas. 1970-72, parliamentarian 1974-76), Lioness (pres. Lyn-Lake 1985-86), Alpha Delta Kappa (state scholarship chmn. 1988-90, sec. Gamma chpt. 1990—). Jewish. Home: 3135 Colorado Ave S Saint Louis Park MN 55416

KIRSCHSTEIN, RUTH LILLIAN, physician; b. Bklyn., Oct. 12, 1926; d. Julius and Elizabeth (Berm) K.; m. Alan S. Rabson, June 11, 1950; 1 child, Arnold. B.A. magna cum laude, L.I. U., 1947; M.D., Tulane U., 1951; D.Sc. (hon.), Mt. Sinai Sch. Medicine, 1984; LL.D. (hon.), Atlanta U., 1985. Intern Kings County Hosp., Bklyn., 1951-52; resident pathology VA Hosp., Atlanta, Providence Hosp., Detroit, Clin. Ctr., NIH, Bethesda, Md., 1952-57; fellow Nat. Heart Inst. Tulane U., 1953-54; mem. staff NIH, Bethesda, 1957-72, 74—; asst. dir. div. biologics standards NIH, 1971-72; dep. dir. Bur. Biologics, FDA, 1972-73, dep. assoc. commr. sci., 1973-74; dir. Nat. Inst. Gen. Med. Scis., 1974—, acting assoc. dir. women's health, 1990; bd. dirs. Found. Advanced Edn. Scis.; chmn. grants peer rev. study team NIH; mem. Inst. Medicine, Nat. Acad. Scis., 1982—. Recipient Superior Service award HEW, 1971, 78, Presdl. Meritorious Exec. award, 1980, Presdl. Disting. Exec. Rank award, 1985, Dr. Nathan Davis award, 1990. Mem. Am. Assn. Immunologists, Am. Assn. Pathologists, Am. Soc. Microbiology. Home: 6 West Dr Bethesda MD 20814 Office: Nat Inst Gen Med Scis Westwood Bldg Rm 926 5333 Westbard Ave Bethesda MD 20892

KIRSCHTEN, BARBARA LOUISE, lawyer; b. Chgo., Apr. 11, 1950; d. Robert and Rhea (Rimes) K.; m. James Vincent Feinerman, Oct. 4, 1986. BA, U. Pa., 1972; MA with honors, BA, Cambridge (Eng.) U., 1974; PhD, Harvard U., 1979; JD, Northwestern U., 1982. Bar: N.Y. 1983, D.C. 1987. Assoc. Milbank, Tweed, Hadley & McCloy, N.Y.C., 1982-86, Steptoe & Johnson, Washington, 1986—. Author: The Nonprofit Corporation Forms Handbook, 1990; co-author: Charitable Contributions, 1990; contbr. articles on tax issues to various publs. Mem. ABA (taxation sect.), D.C. Bar (taxation sect., task force on unrelated bus. income tax proposals to House Ways and Means oversight subcom.). Roman Catholic. Office: Steptoe & Johnson 1330 Connecticut Ave NW Washington DC 20036

KIRSTEIN, NAOMI WAGMAN, service executive; b. Israel, Mar. 23, 1937; came to U.S., 1939; BS in Pub. Relations and Communications, Boston U., 1958. With H.E. Harris and Co., 1958-61; coop. advt. mgr. Polaroid Corp., 1961-63; office mgr., pub. relations exec. N.Y. State Council on Arts, 1963-65; pub. relations dir. Mass. chpt. Heart Fund Assn., 1965-66; freelance pub. relations dir. Edward A. Finch Co., 1967-69; freelance pub. relations dir., pres. Rima Newmar Inc., 1970-71; owner, mgr. Wagman Travel, 1972-77, Custom Travel, Brookline, Mass., 1977—; owner Custom Spas Worldwide, 1986—; spa cons. Author: Sun and Daughter Signs, 1974; contbr. articles to profl. publs. Mem. Am. Friends of Israel Soldiers (dir. N.E. region), Women in Travel, Food and Travel Writers Assn. (press mem.), Tau Mu Epsilon. Jewish. Office: Custom Travel Custom Spas Worldwide 1318 Beacon St Brookline MA 02146

KIRTLEY, MARY ELIZABETH, school administrator, educator; b. Mansfield, Ohio, Aug. 27, 1935; d. George S. and Margaret (Wey) K. BA, U. Chgo., 1956; MA, Smith Coll., 1958; PhD, Case Western Res. U., 1964. Asst. prof. Biochemistry Sch. Med. U. Md., Balt., 1965-71, assoc. prof. Biochemistry, 1971-76, prof. Biochemistry, 1976—; dir. grad. studies Dickinson Coll., Carlisle, Pa., 1983—; program dir. NSF, Washington, 1983-84. Office: Dickinson Coll Carlisle PA 17013

KIRWAN, KATHARYN GRACE (MRS. GERALD BOURKE KIRWAN, JR.), retail executive; b. Monroe, Wash., Dec. 1, 1913; d. Walter Samuel and Bertha Ella (Shrum) Camp; m. Gerald Bourke Kirwan Jr., Jan. 13, 1945. Student, U. Puget Sound, 1933-34; BA, BS, Tex. Woman's U., 1937; postgrad., U. Wash., 1941. Libr. Brady (Tex.) Sr. High Sch., 1937-38, McCamey (Tex.) Sr. High Sch., 1938-43; mgr. Milady's Frock Shop, Monroe, 1946-62, owner, mgr., 1962—. Meml. chmn. Monroe chpt. Am. Cancer Soc., 1961—; mem. Snohomish County Police Svcs. Action Coun., 1971; mem. Monroe Pub. Libr. Bd., 1950-65, pres. bd., 1964-65; mem. Monroe City Coun., 1969-73; mayor City of Monroe, 1974-81; commr. Snohomish County Hosp. dist. 1, 1970-90, chmn. bd. commrs., 1980-90; mem. East Snohomish County Health Planning Com., 1979—; mem. Snohomish County Law and Justice Planning Com., 1974-78, Snohomish County Econ. Devel. Coun., 1975-81, Snohomish County Pub. Utility Dist. Citizens Adv. Task Force, 1983; sr. warden Ch. of Our Saviour, Monroe, 1976-77, 89, sr. warden, 1976-77, 89-90. With USNR, 1943-46. Mem. AAUW, U.S. Naval Inst., Ret. Officers Assn., Naval Res. Assn., Bus. and Profl. Women's Club (2d v.p. 1980-82, pres. 1983-84), Washington Gens. (Washington chpt.), Snohomish County Pharm. Aux., C. of C. (pres. 1972). Episcopalian. Home: 538 S Blakely St Monroe WA 98272 Office: 108 W Main St Monroe WA 98272

KISCADEN, LAURA LINNÉA, psychologist; b. Mpls., Nov. 3, 1950; d. Robert Albert and Eleanor Esther (Hultman) K.; m. Roger Russell Alm, Oct. 14, 1983. BA in Psychology, Moorhead (Minn.) State U., 1972; MS Counseling & Guidance, U. N.D., 1974; postgrad., Minn. Sch. Profl. Psychology. Licensed psychologist, Minn. Counselor Cen. Tech. Community Coll., Hastings, Nebr., 1974-76; counselor, dir. career ctr. Anoka-Ramsey Community Coll., Coon Rapids, Minn., 1976-77; counselor Normandale Community Coll., Bloomington, Minn., 1979; career devel. specialist State Dept. Edn., St. Paul, 1978, 80-83, equal ednl. opportunity specialist, 1984—; cons. in field, 1978—; chmn. Affirmative Action Com., 1988—. Mem. dept. edn. del. Minn. Women's Consortium; counselor, speaker Washington County Family Violence Network, 1986; bd. dirs. Explorer Scouts, St. Paul, 1980-83. N.D. Bd. Higher Edn. scholar, 1973-74; named Outstanding Young Woman of Am., Fuller & Dees, 1976. Mem. Am. Assn. Career Devel. (regional dir. 1982), Nat. Coalition Sex Equity Edn., NOW (pres. Hastings chpt. 1975-76), St. Paul C. of C. (youth and edn. task force 1981-83). Office: Minn State Dept Edn 550 Cedar St Saint Paul MN 55101

KISER, DOROTHY MAE HOUSTON, registrar; b. Ft. Sumner, N.Mex., Apr. 26, 1944; d. Robert David and Emma Eunice (Dunlop) Houston; m. Allen R. Kiser, Aug. 28, 1965; children: Mark Allen, Keith Edward. BS, Hardin-Simmons U., 1965, postgrad., 1985—. With Hardin-Simmons U., Abilene, Tex., 1980—, assoc. registrar, 1987-88, registrar, 1988—. Mem. Tex. Assn. Collegiate Registrars and Admissions Officers (sec. 1990—), West Tex. Assn. Collegiate Registrars and Admissions Officers (sec. 1987-88, v.p. 1988-89, pres. 1989-90), AAUW (rep. 1989-90). Baptist. Office: Hardin-Simmons U 2200 Hickory Abilene TX 79698

KISER, KIMBERLY ANNE, contracting company executive; b. Woodruff, Wis., Sept. 7, 1958; d. William and Geraldine Ann (Patnode) K.; m. Marcel Anthony Van Eerd. BA in Sociology, Boston State Coll., 1980; MEd, Harvard U., 1981. Indian child welfare specialist Ketchikan (Alaska) Indian Corp., 1981-82; adminstrv. asst. Ketchikan Vis. Bur., 1982-83; bus. mgr. Sta. KRBD-FM, Ketchikan, 1983-84; mktg. coord. Pool Engring., Ketchikan, 1984-85; pres. Raymond Restoration, Inc., Raymond, Wis., 1985—. Am. Indian Program scholar, 1980. Mem. Women in Constrn., Harvard Bus. Club. Office: Raymond Restoration inc PO Box 65 12000 W Six Mile Rd Caledonia WI 53108

KISER, NAGIKO SATO, librarian; b. Taipei, Republic of China, Aug. 7, 1923; came to U.S., 1950; d. Takeichi and Kinue (Sooma) Sato; m. Virgil Kiser, Dec. 4, 1979 (dec. Mar. 1981). Secondary teaching credential, Tsuda Coll., Tokyo, 1945; BA in Journalism, Trinity U., 1953; BFA, Ohio State U., 1956, MA in Art History, 1959; MLS, cert. in library media, SUNY, Albany, 1974. Cert. community coll. librarian, Calif., cert. jr. coll. tchr., Calif., cert. secondary edn. tchr., Calif., cert. tchr. library media specialist and art, N.Y. Pub. relations reporter The Mainichi Newspapers, Osaka, Japan, 1945-50; contract interpreter U.S. Dept. State, Washington, 1956-58, 66-67; resource specialist Richmond (Calif.) Unified Sch. Dist., 1968-69; editing supr. CTB/McGraw-Hill, Monterey, Calif., 1969-71; multi-media specialist Monterey Peninsula Unified Sch. Dist., 1975-77; librarian Nishimachi Internat. Sch., Tokyo, 1979-80, Sacramento City Unified Sch. Dist., 1977-79, 81-85; sr. librarian Camarillo State Hosp. and Devel. Ctr., Camarillo, Calif., 1985—. Editor: Short Form Test of Academic Aptitude, 1970, Prescriptive Mathematics Inventory, 1970, Tests of Basic Experience, 1970. Mem. Calif. State Supt.'s Regional Council on Asian Pacific Affairs, Sacramento, 1984—. Library Media Specialist Tng. Program scholar U.S. Office Edn., 1974. Fellow Internat. Biographical Assn. (life); mem. ALA, AAUW, Calif. Library Assn., Calif. Media and Library Educators Assn., Asunaro Shoogai Kyooiku Kondankai (Lifetime Edn. Promoting Assn.) (Japan), The Mus. Soc., Internat. House of Japan, Matsuyama Sacramento Sister City Corp., Japanese Am. Citizens League, UN Assn. U.S., Ikenoboo Ikebana Soc. Am., Los Angeles Hototogisu Haiku Assn., Ventura County Archeol. Soc. Mem. Christian Science Ch. Office: Camarillo State Hosp Profl Libr Box 6022 1878 S Lewis Rd Camarillo CA 93011-6022

KISER, SHARON ANN, health facility professional; b. Dayton, Ohio, Aug. 2, 1945; d. Charles Russell and Louise Matilda (Baer) Warner; m. Peter Joseph D'Onofrio, Oct. 16, 1971 (div. June 1976); m. Ronald Eugene Kiser, June 14, 1986; 1 stepchild, Rebecca Erin. Degree in secretarial sci., Miami Jacobs Jr. Coll., 1971; AS in Bus. Adminstrn., Sinclair Community Coll., 1986; BA in Mgmt., Antioch U., 1990. Cert. dir. volunteer services, Ohio. Exec. sec. NCR Corp., Dayton, 1963-78; dir. vol. services Grandview Hosp. and Med. Ctr., Southview Hosp. and Family Health Ctr., Dayton, 1978—; speaker Nat. Osteo. Guild Assn., Dayton, 1981; nat. speaker Am. Soc. Dirs. Vol. Services Ednl. Conf., Houston, 1983, Cin., 1984, Phila., 1986; mem. tng.

com., human resources com. Voluntary Action Ctr. United Way, Dayton, 1983, 86. Contbr. articles to profl. jours. Mem. Ohio Soc. Dir. Vol. Services (mem. chmn. Southwestern Ohio 1981-85, mem. by-laws com. 1980-81, S.W. Ohio's newspaper rep. 1982-84), Am. Soc. Dir. Vol. Services (Creative Achievement award 1983, 84, 86, mem. innovative programming com. 1987). Methodist. Home: 7201 Claircrest Dr Huber Heights OH 45424 Office: Grandview Hosp and Med Ctr 405 Grand Ave Dayton OH 45405

KISLAK, JEAN HART, art director; b. Mineola, N.Y.; d. Frank Ernest and Isabelle Tayor (Ellis) Hart; m. William I. Herendeen, Aug. 22; remarried Louis G. Johnson, Jan. 31; 1 child, Jennifer Taylor; remarried Jay Kislak, Apr. 7, 1985. Student Peace Jr. Coll., Raleigh, N.C., Queens Coll., Charlotte, N.C. With Storer Broadcasting Co., Miami, Fla.; with S.E. Banks N.A., Miami, Fla., 1974-84, art dir., 1974-84; mem. Gov. Fla. Panel Visual Arts, 1980, Dade County Art in Pub. Places, 1979-81; art cons., 1974—. Bd. dirs. Viscaya Mus., Miami, 1963, Beaux Arts, U. Miami, 1968, Theatre Art Patrons, Miami, 1965; trustee Dade County Zool. Soc., 1988—; mem. Bacardi Imports Art Bd., 1983-89, Kislak Art Found., 1986—, Fla. State Bd. Art Coun., 1987, Dade County Ctr. for the Arts Bd., 1989—. Recipient Gov. Fla. award art, 1976, 79, Miami Dade Pub. Library award, 1978, Bus. Com. for Arts award, 1975-79, WPBT Pub. TV award, 1976, 77, 80, Lowe Gallery, U. Miami cert. recognition, 1980, Dade County Art in Pub. Places cert. recognition, 1981, 82. Address: 2 Palm Bay Ct Apt 21W Miami FL 33138

KISSANE, JEAN CHARLOTTE, lawyer; b. Phila., Feb. 6, 1946; d. William C. and Grace A. (McGlade) K. AB, Lycoming Coll., 1968; JD, Widener U., 1986. Bar: Del. 1986, U.S. Dist. Ct. Dela. 1987. Tchr. history Colonial Sch. Dist., New Castle, Del., 1968-86; assoc. Skadden, Arps, Slate, Meagher & Flom, Wilmington, Del., 1986—. Recipient Am. Jurisprudence awards, 1986. Mem. ABA, Del. Bar Assn., Mensa, Phi Delta Phi, Phi Kappa Phi. Democrat. Office: Skadden Arps Slate Meagher & Flom Box 636 1 Rodney Sq Wilmington DE 19899-0636

KISSANE, LEEDICE MCANELLY, retired college educator; b. Denison, Iowa, May 26, 1905; d. Jefferson R. and Minnie (Bigler) McAnelly; m. Donald P. Kissane (dec. 1968); children: Esther Kissane Hodgkinson, John M., James Donald. BA, Cornell Coll., Mt. Vernon, Iowa, 1926; MA, U. Idaho, 1937; PhD, U. Minn., 1967. Cert. tchr. State of Idaho. English educator Idaho State U., Pocatello, 1941-70, dir. Am. Studies program, 1967-70; newspaper columnist Idaho State Jour., Pocatello, 1978-83; Fulbright lectr. in Am. Lit. and Culture U. Iceland, Reykjavik, 1970-72; bd. dirs. Ruth Suckow Meml. Assn., Earlville, Iowa; adviser Idaho Coun. Tchrs. English, 1960-70. Author: Ruth Suckow: A Critical Analytical Study, 1969; contbr. numerous articles. Vol. gallery attendant Grinnell Arts Coun., Grinnell, Iowa, 1983-; mem. Cen. Celebration Com. City of Pocatello, 1982. Fulbright lectr. 1970-72. Mem. AAUW (PAC Northwest Region scholarship grantee), Ret. Tchrs. Assn., Idaho TRet. Tchrs. Assn. (Hall of Fame 1982), Bannock County Hist. Soc. (life), Phi Beta Kappa, PEO Sisterhood Lodge.

KISSEL, ELIZABETH MCCOMBS, corrections professional, administrator; b. Atlanta, Jan. 6, 1958; d. James Norfleet and Rufe Dorsey (Edwards) McCombs; m. Gerald Duane Kissel, Dec. 13, 1980; children: Adam Shane, Dana Kristin, Jared Blane. BS, Brenau Coll., 1980; MS, Ga. State U., 1988. Cert. peace officer, corrections mgr., Ga. Sgt., exec. asst. to chief dep. Gwinnett County Sheriff's Dept., Lawrenceville, Ga., 1980-86; exec. asst. to warden Gwinnett County Bur. Corrections, Dept. Pub. Safety, Lawrenceville, 1987—. Grantee, Atlanta Regional Commn., 1989. Mem. Am. Jail Assn., Am Correctional Assn., Peace Officers Assn. Ga., Ga. Correctional Assn., NAFE. Office: Gwinnett County Corrections PO Box 47 Lawrenceville GA 30246

KISSINGER, MARILYN RUTH, national account development specialist; b. Reading, Pa., Mar. 22, 1947; d. Robert E. and Ruth I. (Strause) K.; children: Kristine Kintzer, Brett Kintzer. BS, Temple U., 1988. Nat. account devel. specialist Am. Equipment Leasing Co., Inc., Reading; dir. sales and mktg. Kissinger Assocs. Computer Systems, Hamburg, Pa., 1989; vocat. instr. Berks Vocat. Tech. Sch., Leesport, Pa., 1979-89; nat. account devel. specialist Flying Hills Corp. Ctr., Shillington, Pa., 1989—. Chairperson, fundraiser Easter Seals Soc. of Berks County. Nominated Tchr. of the Yr., Easter Seal Soc. Mem. NEA, NAFE. Home: 89 Winchester Ct Reading PA 19606

KISTIAKOWSKY, VERA, physics researcher and educator; b. Princeton, N.J., Sept. 9, 1928; d. George Bogdan and Hildegard (Moebius) K.; m. Gerhard Emil Fischer, June 16, 1951 (div. 1975); children: Marc Laurenz Fischer, Karen Marie Fischer. A.B., Mt. Holyoke Coll., 1948, Sc.D. (hon.), 1978; Ph.D., U. Calif.-Berkeley, 1952. Staff scientist U.S. Naval Rsch. Def. Lab., San Francisco, 1952-53; fellow U. Calif.-Berkeley, 1953-54; rsch. assoc. Columbia U., N.Y.C., 1954-57, instr., 1957-59; asst. prof. Brandeis U., Waltham, Mass., 1959-62, adj. assoc. prof., 1962-63; staff mem. MIT, Cambridge, 1963-69, sr. rsch. scientist, 1969-72; prof. physics, 1972—; Phi Beta Kappa lectr., Washington, 1983-84. Author: Atomic Energy, 1959; One Way Is Down, 1967; contbr. articles on nuclear and elem. particle physics to profl. jours. Dir. Coun. for a Liveable World, Boston, 1983—; co-chmn. United Campuses to Prevent Nuclear War, 1987—. Recipient Centennial award Mt. Holyoke Coll., 1972. Fellow AAAS, Am. Phys. Soc. (councilor 1974-77); mem. Assn. for Women in Sci. (pres. 1982-83), Phi Beta Kappa (senator 1988-92). Office: MIT 24-522 77 Massachusetts Ave Cambridge MA 02139

KISTNER, JENNIFER RUTH, sales executive; b. Cin., Sept. 20, 1957; d. John William and Joan Shirley (Dignan) Mohr; m. Jerry Robert Kistner, July 19, 1955; 1 child, Tyler John. BS in Bus., Miami (Ohio) U., 1980. Sales rep. Pro-Tech Systems, Inc., Cin., 1980-81; regional mgr. The Nat. Underwriter Co., Cin., 1981—. Home: 4885 Dominica Way Apple Valley MN 55124 Office: Nat Underwriter Co 14870 Granada Ave Ste 285 Apple Valley MN 55124

KITAGAWA, AUDREY EMIKO, lawyer; b. Honolulu, Mar. 31, 1951; s. Yonoichi and Yoshiko (Nagaishi) K. B.A. cum laude, U. So. Calif., 1973; J.D., Boston Coll., 1976. Bar: Hawaii, 1977, U.S. Dist. Ct. Hawaii, 1977. Assoc., Rice, Lee & Wong, Honolulu, 1977-80; sole practice, Honolulu, 1980—. Exec. editor Internat. Law Jour., 1976. Mem. Historic Hawaii Found., 1984. Mem. Hawaii Bar Assn., ABA, Assn. Trial Lawyers Am., Japan-Hawaii Lawyers Assn. (v.p. 1982—), Law Office Mgmt. Discussion Group, Hawaii Lawyers Care, Phi Alpha Delta. Republican. Club: Honolulu. Office: 820 Mililani St Suite 615 Honolulu HI 96813

KITAZAKI, JEANNE DURNFORD, circuit board fabricator, executive; b. Milw., June 1, 1940; d. James Henry and Doris Delvin (Ellsworth) Durnford; m. William Kitazaki, Aug. 17, 1963 (div. Sept. 1978); children: Doris Julie, Krystal Jeanne. BS, Carroll Coll., 1962. Cert. electroplater, finisher, specialist in electronics. Analytical chemist State of Wis., Madison, 1962-63, Abbott Labs, North Chgo., Ill., 1963-65; rsch. chemist SCM-Microstatics, Skokie, Ill., 1965-67; tech. dir. Oconomowoc Electroplating Co., Inc., Ashippun, Wis., 1979-81; process chemist Master Lock, Milw., 1981-84; dir. product devel. RBP Chemical Corp., Milw., 1984-90; sr. mgr. Pho-Tronics, Milw., 1990—; mem. task group Interconnections, Packaging and Circuitry, Lincolnwood, Ill., 1986—, asst. chmn., 1987—; apptd. by gov. Citizen's Adv. Com. Researched and contbd. sci. articles to profl. jours. Pres. LWV, Watertown, Wis., 1979-81, election reporting, 1990; dir. Libr. Bd., Watertown, 1978-81; mem. citizen's adv. com. on clean water act Gov. State of Wis., 1978-80; mission bd. dirs. United Ch. Christ, Milw., 1986-90. Recipient Edn. award U.S. Dept. Energy, 1974. Mem. NAFE, Women in Sci. Southeastern Wis. (charter), Am. Electroplaters and Surface Finishing Soc. Home: 4420 N Bartlett Ave Shorewood WI 53211

KITCHEN, ANNA LOUISE, psychologist; b. Lyndon, Kans., Feb. 23, 1930; d. Arthur Sellards and Inez Bell (Sherry) K. BA, Baker U., 1952; MA, U. Kans., 1959; postgrad., Am. Acad. Asian Studies, San Francisco, 1960-62, Old Dominion U., Coll. of William and Mary, U. Va. Cert. sch. psychologist, Va. Aide Topeka State Hosp., 1952-54; clin. psychologist Sonoma (Calif.) State Hosp., 1960-62, Kans. Neurol. Inst., Topeka, 1962-68, Cath. Family and Childrens Svcs., Norfolk, Va., 1968-70; psychologist Portsmouth (Va.) City Schs., 1970-73; sch. psychologist Va. Beach City Schs., 1973-88, Lunenburg County Sch. Bd., Victoria, Va., 1988-90; Vol. People with AIDS Group, Norfolk, 1987-88. Mem. Altrusa Womens Club, Norfolk, 1974-75, Shanti Peace Orgn., Norfolk, 1969, ACLU, Norfolk, 1969-70, Presbyn. Women's Circle, Victoria, 1990. Mem. Am. Psychol. Assn. (assoc.), Nat. Assn. Sch. Psychologists, Va. Psychol. Assn., Transpersonal Psychology Assn., Internat. Assn. of Near Death Studies, Inc., Coun. for Exceptional Children, Raphaclite Inst. Home: Rte 1 Box 23 Victoria VA 23974

KITCHEN, CAROL ANNE, social worker; b. Buffalo, July 4, 1941; d. Denis A. and Norma (Caton) K.; m. Robert L. Magee, Apr. 24, 1965 (div. 1981); 1 child, Bruce. AB, Marietta Coll., 1964; MLS, U. Pitts., 1965; MSW, Ohio State U., 1973; M in Philosophy, Drew U., 1989. Cert. clin. social worker. Supervising social worker Salvation Army Family Svc. Bur., Cin., 1974-78; counselor Ctr. for Mental Health, Anderson, Ind., 1978-81, Genesee Coun. on Alcoholism, Batavia, N.Y., 1982-85; supervising social worker Geneva B. Scruggs ICF, Buffalo, 1985-86; counselor United Labor Agy., Newark, 1988-90. Co-coord. Unitarian Universalists for Lesbian & Gay Concerns, Boston, 1987-89. Scholar Unitarian Universalist Assn., Boston, 1989-90; fellow Congregational History Project U. Chgo., 1990—. Mem. AAUW, Nat. Assn. Social Workers, Am. Acad. Religion. Democrat. Unitarian Universalist.

KITCHIN, KATE PARKS, guidance counselor, educator; b. Scotland Neck, N.C., Apr. 16, 1911; d. John Arrington and Norma (Cloman) K. AB, U. N.C., Chapel Hill, 1931; MA, Columbia U., N.Y., 1943. Tchr. Woodland (N.C.)-Olney High School, 1931-36; tchr. English, counselor Rocky Mt. High School, 1936-79; guidance asst. summer sch. Appalachian State Tchrs. Coll., Boone, N.C., 1955, co-guidance dir., 1956, guidance dir., 1960; chmn. Report of So. States Work Conf. on Guidance in Pub. Schs., Daytona, S.C., 1956. contbr. articles to profl. jours. Pres. N.C. Dean's Assn., 1942-44; exec. sec. N.C. Student Coun. Congress, 1952-56; clk. Vestry Ch. of the Good Shepherd, Rocky Mt., 1979-90. Recipient DAR medal of honor, 1988; named Rocky Mt. Tchr. of the Yr., Social Edn. Assn., 1976, Rocky Mt. Woman of Yr., 1950, 1965. Mem. Am. Assn. Ret. Persons (NRTA div.), N.C. Assn. Educators, Nash-Edgecombe Ret. Sch. Pers., Rocky Mt. Jr. Guild, Delta Kappa Gamma (pres. N.C. chpt. 1950-53). Democrat. Episcopalian.

KITCHIN, ROSEMARIE ATKIN, communications company executive; b. Springfield, Ill., June 6, 1939; d. Bernard and L. Lucille (McCarty) Atkin; m. K. Thomas Kitchin, Jr., Dec. 17, 1960 (div. 1974); children: Kraig Thomas, Kevin Thomas. BS in Journalism, Northwestern U., 1961; postgrad., Webster U., Kansas City, Mo., 1984. Dir. pub. rels. Jewish Welfare Fedn. Detroit, 1972-76; owner, mgr. Rm. Communications, Paoli, Pa., 1974-90, Charlotte, N.C., 1990—; mgr. pub. rels. for svc. and parts Chrysler Corp., Highland Park, Mich., 1976-79; mktg. mgr. recreational vehicle parts Chrysler Corp., Center Line, Mich., 1979; account exec. Martin Fromm & Assocs., Inc., Kansas City, 1979-81, v.p., 1981-84; regional sales mgr. for 3 mags. Chilton Co., Atlanta, 1984-86; editor Automotive Mktg. Chilton Co., Radnor, Pa., 1986-88, editor-in-chief, 1988-89, assoc. pub., editor-in-chief, 1989-90; exec. advt. dept. Radiator Splty. Co., Charlotte, 1990—; cons. The Matrix Group, Charlottem 1990—. Mem. Pub. Rels. Soc. Am. (accredited). Office: 5140 Top Seed Ct Charlotte NC 28226

KITTLITZ, LINDA GALE, small business owner; b. Waco, Tex., Jan. 22, 1949; d. Rudolf Gottlieb and Lena Hulda (Landgraf) K. BA in Art, Tex. Tech. U., 1971. Sales rep. Taylor Pub. Co., San Francisco and Dallas, 1972-73, Internat. Playtex Corp., San Francisco, 1974-76, Faberge Inc., San Francisco, 1976-78, Soflens div. Bausch and Lomb Co., San Francisco, 1978-81, Ben Rickert Inc., San Francisco, 1981-86, Golden West Envelope Co., San Francisco, 1987-89; mfr.'s sales rep. Dearing Sales, San Francisco, 1986-87; owner, mgr. Lip Svc. Communications Co., San Francisco, 1988—; sales assoc. R.G. Creations, Inc., San Francisco, 1989—; sales assoc. RG Creations, 1989—. Mem. NAFE, Profl. Women's Network San Francisco (bay area chpt.), San Francisco C. of C. Democrat. Baptist.

KIVEL, MAXINE NANCY, technical writer, editor; b. Sebewaing, Mich., Aug. 8, 1934; d. Morris Bernard Kessler and Irene Nass; m. Joseph Kivel, June 16, 1956 (div. 1982); children: Karen Sue, Patricia Lynn. BA, U. Mich., 1956. Tech. writer, editor Atlanta Rsch. Corp., Alexandria, Va., 1965-68, Bell Tel. Labs., Whippany, N.J., 1968-69, U.S. FDA, Rockville, Md., 1970—. Editor: (tech. newsletter) Radiological Health Bull., 1975. Represented U.S. in World Bridge Olympiad, 1978, 86, 90. Recipient N.Am. Bridge Championship (Women's Pairs), 1986. Mem. Am. Contract Bridge League (life).

KIVELSON, MARGARET GALLAND, physicist; b. N.Y.C., Oct. 21, 1928; d. Walter Isaac and Madeleine (Wiener) Galland; m. Daniel Kivelson, Aug. 15, 1949; children: Steven Allan, Valerie Ann. AB, Radcliffe Coll., 1950, AM, 1951, PhD, 1957. Cons. Rand Corp., Santa Monica, Calif., 1956-69; asst. to geophysicist UCLA, 1967-83, prof., 1983—, also chmn. dept. earth and space scis., 1984-87; prin. investigator of magnetometer, Galileo Mission, Jet Propulsion Lab., Pasadena, Calif., 1977—; overseer Harvard Coll., 1977-83; mem. adv. coun. NASA, 1987—; chair adv. com. NSF, 1986-89, Com. Solar and Space Physics, 1977-86, com. planetary exploration, 1986-87, com. solar terrestial phys., 1989—. Editor: The Solar System: Observations and Interpretations, 1986; contbr. articles to profl. jours. Named Woman of Yr., L.A. Mus. Sci. and Industry, 1979, Woman of Sci., UCLA, 1984; recipient Grad. Soc. medal Radcliffe Coll., 1983, 350th Anniversary Alumni medal Harvard U. Mem. Am. Geophysics Union, Am. Phys. Soc., Am. Astron. Soc.; fellow AAAS. Office: UCLA Dept Earth & Space Scis 6843 Slichter Los Angeles CA 90024

KIZER, CAROLYN ASHLEY, poet, educator; b. Spokane, Wash., Dec. 10, 1925; d. Benjamin Hamilton and M. (Ashley) K.; m. Stimson Bullitt, Jan., 1948 (div.); children—Ashley Ann, Scott, Jill Hamilton; m. John Marshall Woodbridge, Apr. 11, 1975. BA, Sarah Lawrence Coll., 1945; postgrad. (Chinese govt. fellow in comparative lit.), Columbia U., 1946-47; studied poetry with Theodore Roethke U. Wash., 1953-54; LittD (hon.), Whitman Coll., 1986, St. Andrew's Coll., 1989, Mills Coll., 1990. Specialist in lit. U.S. Dept. State, Pakistan, 1964-65; first dir. lit. programs Nat. Endowment for Arts, 1966-70; poet-in-residence U. N.C. at Chapel Hill, 1970-74; Hurst Prof. Lit. Washington U., St. Louis, 1971; lectr. Spring Lecture Series Barnard Coll., 1972; acting dir. grad. writing program Columbia, 1972; poet-in-residence Ohio U., 1974; vis. poet Iowa Writer's Workshop, 1975; prof. U. Md., 1976-77; poet-in-residence, disting. vis. lectr. Centre Coll., Ky., 1979; disting. vis. poet East Wash. U., 1980; Elliston prof. poetry U. Cin., 1981; Bingham disting. prof. U. Louisville, Ky., 1982; disting. vis. poet Bucknell U., Pa., 1982; vis. poet SUNY, Albany, 1982; prof. Columbia U. Sch. Arts, 1982; prof. poetry Stanford U., 1986; sr. fellow in humanities Princeton U., 1986; prof. writing U. Ariz., 1989—; participant Internat. Poetry Festivals, London, 1960, 70, Yugoslavia, 1969, 70, Pakistan, 1969, Rotterdam, Netherlands, 1970, Knokke-le-Zut, Belgium, 1970; sr. fellow humanities council Princeton U., 1986. Author: The Ungrateful Garden, 1961, Knock Upon Silence, 1965, Midnight Was My Cry, 1971, Mermaids in the Basement: Poems for Women, 1984, Yin: New Poems, 1984 (Pulitzer prize 1985), The Nearness of You, 1987; translator Carrying Over, 1988; founder, editor: Poetry N.W., 1959-65; contbr. poems, articles to Am. and Brit. jours. Recipient award Am. Acad. and Inst. Arts and Letters, 1985, award in lit. San Francisco Arts Commn., 1986, Gov.'s awards State Wash., 1965, 85, Pulitzer Prize for Poetry, 1985, Pres.'s medal Ea. Washington U., Theodore Roethke prize, 1988. Mem. ACLU, Amnesty Internat., PEN, Poetry Soc. Am. (Frost medal 1988), Acad. Am. Poets. Episcopalian. Address: 322 E Drachman Tucson AZ 85705

KIZZEE, MARGARET LEIGH, finance editor, investment representative; b. Huntsville, Tex.; d. Amos Ulishes and Minnie Faye (Watkins) Leigh; m. Matthew Kizzee, June 3, 1978; 1 child, Meryl-Ina Samantha. BS with honors, Sam Houston State U.; MBA, Houston Bapt. U., 1989. Registered investment rep., Tex. Page editor Sam Houston State U., Huntsville, 1975-76, assoc. editor, 1976, editor, 1976-77; copy editing intern Roanoke Times & World-News, Va., 1977; fin. writer Bus. & Energy Internat., Inc., Houston, 1978-79; fin. editor Am. Capital Fin. Svcs., Inc. (name now Am. Capital Mgmt. & Rsch., Inc.), Houston, 1980—, resident mgr., 1985—. Sam Houston State U. Alumni Assn. scholar, 1974, Jesse H. Jones Found. scholar, 1976-78; recipient Bill Hay Meml. award Bill Hay Found., 1977. Baptist. Avocations: restoring antiques, collecting rare books and cookbooks, coins and stamps, horticulture. Office: Advantage Capital Corp 2800 Post Oak Blvd Houston TX 77056

KJERULFF, GEORGIANA LUDLOW GREENE, journalist, historian, county official; b. N.Y.C., Oct. 26, 1917; d. Thomas Travers and Edith Frances Ludlow (LeComte) Greene; m. Lauritz Toft Kjerulff; children: Clarice, Kristen, Karen, Lauritz, Thomas. Student, N.J. Coll. for Women; BA in Journalism, La. State U., 1939; postgrad., U. Calif., Berkeley, 1946-47. Fashion copywriter Meyer-Both, N.Y.C., 1940-45; feature writer Melbourne (Fla.) Daily Times, 1959-68; mem. Brevard County Hist. Commn., Melbourne, 1983-84, 88—. Author: Tales of Old Brevard, 1972, Troubled Paradise, Melbourne Village, 1986; editor: Trees of Palo Alto, 1977, Streets of Palo Alto, 1978. Commr. Town of Melbourne Village (Fla.), 1970-72, 85-89, vice mayor, 1985-89. With USNR, 1942-45. Recipient cert. of recognition VA Hosp., 1979, spl. awards Mus. of Man, San Diego, 1983, Writers award State of Calif. Mem. South Brevard Hist. Soc. (pres. 1986-87), Nat. League Am. Penwomen (bd. dirs. Palo Alto chpt. 1987), LWV (bd. dirs.), AAUW (bd. dirs. Melbourne br. 1960-70), NOW (bd. dirs. Palo Alto 1976-77), Unitarian Fellowship (pres. 1986-87, Leadership award 1988). Democrat. Home: 710 Acacia Ave Melbourne FL 32904

KJOS, VICTORIA ANN, lawyer; b. Fargo, N.D., Sept. 17, 1953; d. Orville I. and Annie J. (Tanberg) K. BA, Minot State U., 1974; JD, U. N.D., 1977. Bar: Ariz. 1978. Assoc. Jack E. Evans, Ltd., Phoenix, 1977-78, pension and ins. cons., 1978-79; dep. state treas. State of N.D., Bismarck, 1979-80; free-lance cons. Phoenix, 1980-81, Anchorage, 1981-82; asst. v.p., v.p., mgr. trust dept. Great Western Bank, Phoenix, 1982-84; assoc. Robert A. Jensen P.C., Phoenix, 1984-86; ptnr. Jensen & Kjos, P.C., Phoenix, 1986-89; assoc. Allen, Kimerer & LaVelle, Phoenix, 1989-90, ptnr., 1990—; lectr. in domestic relations. Contbr. articles to profl. jours. Mem. Ariz. Dem. Coun., Western Pension Conf.; bd. dirs. Arthritis Found., Phoenix, 1986-89, v.p. for chpt. devel., 1988-89. Mem. ABA, Ariz. Bar Assn. (exec. coun. family law sect.), Maricopa Bar Assn. (sec. family law com. 1988-89, pres. 1989-90, judge pro tempore 1989—, study com. 1988—), Assn. Trial Lawyers Am., Ariz. Trial Lawyers Assn., Ariz. Women's Lawyers Assn., NOW, Phi Delta Phi. Office: Allen Kimerer & LaVelle 2715 N 3d St Phoenix AZ 85004

KLAJBOR, DOROTHEA M., lawyer, consultant; b. Dunkirk, N.Y., Dec. 2, 1915; d. Joseph M., Sr., and Susan R. (Schrantz) K.; student George Washington U., 1949-52; J.D., Am. U., Washington, 1956. Admitted to D.C. bar, 1957; successively legal asst., legis. atty., atty., 2d asst. to Chief U.S. Marshal, civil rights compliance officer Dept. of Justice, Washington, 1938-70; supr. Town of Dunkirk, N.Y., 1973-76; mem. N.Y. State Liquor Authority, Buffalo, 1976-82. Bd. dirs. Center for Women Govt., Albany, N.Y., 1978-82, Dunkirk Sr. Citizens Ctr., 1983; mem. Chautauqua County Task Force on Aging, 1972-73, Town of Dunkirk Indsl. Devel. Agy., 1972-76, Chautauqua County Planning Bd., 1973-76, No. Chautauqua County Intermcpl. Planning Bd., 1974-76, Chautauqua County Overall Econ. Devel. Planning Bd., 1974-76, Literacy Vols., 1972-76, West Dunkirk Vol. Fire Dept., 1973—; adv. bd. Dunkirk Sr. Citizens, 1974-76; mem. women's div. N.Y. State Democratic Com. Mem. Am. Bar Assn. (life), Fed. Bar Assn., D.C. Bar, Women's Bar Assn. D.C., AAUW, Nat. Lawyers Club, Cath. Daus. Am., No. Chautauqua Club Assocs. (life), Dunkirk Hist. Soc. (life), Kappa Beta Pi. Democrat. Roman Catholic. Clubs: Chautauqua County Dem. Women's (treas. 1974-76), Zonta Internat. (chmn. com. on status of women; Industry Person of Yr. award 1980, Calista Jones award for advancement rights of women 1984), Town of Dunkirk Dem. Home: 91 Forest Pl Fredonia NY 14063

KLAMERUS, KAREN JEAN, pharmacist, researcher; b. Chgo., Aug. 10, 1957; d. Robert Edward and Jane Mary (Nawoj) K.; m. Frederick P. Zeller. BS in Pharmacy, U. Ill., 1980; PharmD, U. Ky., 1981. Registered pharmacist Ky., Ill., Pa. Staff pharmacist Haggin Meml. Hosp., Harrodsburg, Ky., 1980-81, Regional Med. Ctr., Madisonville, Ky., 1982; critical care liasion Regional Med. Ctr., Madisonville, 1982; clin. pharmacist resident U. Nebr., Omaha, 1983; clin. pharmacist cardiothoracic surgery U. Ill., Chgo., 1983-88, clin asst. prof. dept. pharmacy practice, 1983-86, asst. prof., 1986-88, departmental affiliate dept. pharmaceutics, 1986-88; cons. Dimensional Mktg. Inst., Chgo., 1983-88, Channing, Weinbergs' Co., Inc., N.Y.C., 1983-88; sr. pharmacokineticist Wyeth-Ayerst Rsch., Phila., 1988—. Mem. rev. bd. Drug Intelligence and Clin. Pharmacy. Mem. Am. Soc. Clin. Pharmacol. and Therapeutics, Am. Coll. Clin. Pharmacy, Am. Heart Assn., Rho Chi. Office: Wyeth-Ayerst Rsch PO Box 8299 Philadelphia PA 19101-1245

KLANCHER, FAYE ROMELLE, service executive, consultant; b. Virginia, Minn., Jan. 28, 1941; d. Wayne Edwin and Ella Leona (Ortendahl) Nelmark; m. Edward Anthony Klancher, Nov. 26, 1961 (div. June 1977); children: Anthony Edward, Joseph Wayne. Cert. radiology tech., Hibbing (Minn.) Gen. Hosp., 1959; student, U. Minn., 1980-83; BS, Ottawa U., 1988. Chief technologist Pine County Meml. Hosp., Sandstone, Minn., 1959-60; dept. mgr. West Med. Clinic, St. Paul, 1961-70; supr., technologist Abbott Northwestern Hosp., Mpls., 1968-70; dir. Children's Svc. Cons., Mpls., 1970-77; radiology supr. Columbia Park Clinics, Mpls., 1977-80; ptnr. Radiographer Cons., Mpls., 1980-84; prin. technologist U. Minn., Mpls., 1980-83; head dept. radiology Hennepin County Med. Ctr., Mpls., 1983-86; dir. radiology dept. St. Elizabeth Hosp., Beaumont, Tex., 1986—; speaker in field. Roman Catholic.

KLANN, JULIE ANN, business owner; b. Detroit, Apr. 1, 1945; d. Russell Henry and Frances Margaret (Folsom) K. BS, Mich. State U., 1967. Asst. buyer Abraham & Straus, Bklyn., 1968-69, J.C. Penney Co., N.Y.C., 1969-72; buyer Mervyn's Dept. Store, Hayward, Calif., 1973-77, Emporium Capwell Dept. Store, San Francisco, 1978-79, 82-83; sales rep. Arrowhead Jewelry Co., San Rafael, Calif., 1980-81; merchandiser Items of Calif., L.A., 1984; recruiter Alan J. Blair Personnel Svcs., San Francisco, 1985-86; pres., owner Placement Dynamics Agy., Inc., San Francisco, 1986—. Mem. Nat. Assn. Personnel Cons., San Francisco C. of C., Calif. Assn. Personnel Cons. Home: 116 Harvard Ave Mill Valley CA 94941 Office: Placement Dynamics Agy Inc 595 Market St Ste 2610 San Francisco CA 94105

KLAPES, NANCY ARLENE, microbiologist, educator; b. Springfield, Mass., Aug. 20, 1955; d. Constantine Charles and Bonnie Jean (Harms) K. BA in Microbiology, U. N.H., 1977; MS in Environ. Health, U. Minn., 1980, PhD in Environ. Health, 1987. Teaching and rsch. asst. U. Minn., Mpls., 1978-87; specimen receiving technologist II U. Minn. Hosp. and Clinic, Mpls., 1981-87; chemist Twin Cities Rsch. Ctr., Bur. of Mines, Mpls., 1984; postdoctoral rsch. scientist U. Minn., Mpls., 1987-88; rsch. asst. prof. N.C. State U., Raleigh, 1988—. Contbr. articles to profl. jours. Counselor, activity specialist New Eng. Camp Cherith, Alfred, Maine, 1976-80, 88; swim instr. YMCA, 1973-77, 82-86. J. Stanford Smith fellow, 1983-85; USPHS trainee, 1978-79, 80-81; U. Minn. fellow, 1977-78; Daniel Heath Meml. scholar, 1976-77. Mem. Am. Soc. for Microbiology, Sigma Xi, Delta Omega, Alpha Epsilon Delta. Home: 3201-208 Huddlestone Dr Raleigh NC 27612 Office: NC State U Box 7624 Raleigh NC 27695-7624

KLAPPER, GAIL HEITLER, lawyer; b. Denver, May 26, 1943; d. Emmett H. and Dorothy (Shwayder) Heitler; m. Jack A. Klapper, June 25, 1965; children: Dana, Stacy, Amy, Lisa. BA in Polit. Sci., Wellesley (Mass.) Coll., 1965; JD, U. Colo., 1968. Bar: Colo. 1968, U.S. Dist. Ct. Colo. 1968. Pvt. practice Denver, 1968-76, 1983—; White House fellow U.S. Dept. of Interior, Washington, 1976-77; exec. dir. Colo. Dept. Regulatory Agencies, Denver, 1977-81, Colo. Dept. Pers., Denver, 1981-82; candidate Colo. atty. gen. ptnr. Klapper Zimmermann, Denver, 1983-86; of counsel Moye, Giles, O'Keefe, Vermeire & Gorrell, Denver, 1986-89; bd. dirs. United Bank of Denver, U.S. West Communications, Denver, Gold, Inc., Denver. Trustee Wellesley Coll., 1986—; founder, bd. dirs. Pub. Edn. Coalition, Denver, 1984—; bd. dirs. Nat. Jewish Ctr. for Immunology and Respiratory Medicine, Denver, 1986—, vice-chmn., 1987—; bd. dirs. Denver Civic Ventures, 1978—, chmn. 1989—. Recipient Leadership Denver Assn. award, 1984, Norlin award U. Colo., 1987, Pub. Svc. award U. Colo. Grad. Sch. Pub. Affairs, 1987; White House fellow, 1976-77. Mem. ABA, Colo. Bar Assn., Denver Bar Assn., Colo. Forum (bd. dirs.), Colo. Women's Forum (pres. 1980-81). Democrat.

KLASS, KATHIE, public relations professional; b. L.A., Feb. 26, 1951; d. Edgar F. Klass and Sheila E. (Lisker) Lenik; m. Kenneth P. Mabie, June 11, 1972 (div. 1983); m. Daniel L. Rumelt, Nov. 14, 1986. BA, Calif. State U., San Jose, 1973, MA, 1975. Consumer coord. Santa Cruz County Dist. Atty., Santa Cruz, Calif., 1974-81; project mgr. Direct Selling Edn. Found., Washington, 1981-82; exec. officer Calif. State Consumer Adv. Coun., Sacramento, 1982-86; co-chair Consumers Opposed to Secret Taxes, Washington, 1986-87; dir. state and local govt. affairs Nat. Assn. Home Builders, Washington, 1987-89; exec. dir. Issue Dynamics, Inc., Washington, 1989—. Chair Calif. Collection Agy. Adv. Bd., Sacramento, 1978; bd. dirs. Calif. State Cemetery Bd., Sacramento, 1980-82. Cited for pub. svc. Calif. legislature, 1982, 85. Mem. Soc. Consumer Affairs Profls. (treas. D.C. chpt. 1990—, Outstanding Pub. Svc. award L.A. chpt. 1985), Electronic Industries Consumer/Bus. Roundtable. Office: Issue Dynamics Inc Ste 230 901 15th St NW Washington DC 20005

KLASS, LISA ANN, art design company executive; b. Jackson, Mich., Mar. 22, 1962; d. Joseph Benjamin and Martha Lou (Mericle) K.; m. Gary Lee Kinney, Oct. 5, 1986. Student, Jackson Community Coll., 1980-84, 85-86. Owner, pres. Art Design, Horton, Mich., 1982—. Mem. NAFE, Doll Guild Am., Humane Soc., Aircraft Owners and Pilots Assn. Republican. Baptist. Home: 209 Merkle Dr Horton MI 49246 Office: Art Design 2525 Crispell Rd Horton MI 49246

KLASS, PERRI ELIZABETH, pediatrician, writer; b. Tunapuna, Trinidad, Apr. 29, 1958; d. Morton and Sheila Solomon K.; children: Benjamin Orlando Klass, Josephine Charlotte Paulina Wolff. AB, Harvard U., 1979; postgrad., U. Calif., Berkeley, 1979-81; MD, Harvard U., 1986. Diplomate Am. Bd. Med. Examiners. Researcher Inst. Parasitology, Rome, 1981-82; instr. expository writing Harvard U., Cambridge, Mass., 1982-83; resident in pediatrics Children's Hosp., Boston, 1986-89, staff pediatrician, 1989-90; rsch. fellow Boston City Hosp., 1990—. Author: Recombinations (novel), 1985, I Am Having an Adventure (short stories), 1986, A Not Entirely Benign Procedure (essays), 1987, Other Women's Children (novel), 1990; contbr. articles to various publs. Winner O Henry award, Doubleday, 1983, 84. Fellow Am. Acad. Pediatrics (media spokesperson 1989—); mem. PEN, Am. Med. Women's Assn., Mass. Med. Soc.

KLASS, PHYLLIS CONSTANCE, genetic counselor, psychotherapist; b. Scranton, Pa., Aug. 13, 1927; d. Max Gordon and Lina Rachel (Levine) Rich; m. Felix Klass, Sept. 27, 1952 (dec. Mar. 1988); children: Steven, Janet. BA, Syracuse U., 1947; MA, Columbia U., 1948; MS, Sarah Lawrence Coll., 1972. Diplomate Am. Bd. Med. Genetics. Asst. prof. Cornell Med. Coll., N.Y.C., 1972—; dir. genetic counseling program N.Y. Hosp., 1972—; chair genetic counseling Prenatal Diagnosis Lab of N.Y., 1975-81. Fellow Am. Orthopsychiat. Assn.; mem. Nat. Soc. of Genetic Counselors (chair profl. issues com.), Am. Soc. of Human Genetics. Office: New York Hosp Cornell Med Ctr 525 E 68th Street New York NY 10021

KLASSEN, MARGRETA, psychologist, educator; b. L.A., May 4, 1928; d. David Charles and Jessie Irene (Birch) Klassen; m. Richard Caddell Calhoun, May 31, 1946 (dec. Jan. 1984); children: Cathleen, Melissa, Nancy, Richard; m. Donald Cole Wargin, Feb. 14, 1970 (widowed). AA, Chaffey Coll., 1966; BA, Pitzer Coll., 1968; MS, Calif. State U., L.A., 1972; PhD, Claremont (Calif.) Grad. Sch., 1982. Lic. psychologist, Calif. From instr. to counselor Chaffey Community Coll., Alta Loma, Calif., 1972-74; dir. biofeedback program U. La Verne, Calif., 1974-76; asst. prof. Calif. State Poly. U., Pomona, 1986-88; owner Assocs. for Wellness, Claremont, Calif., 1974—; oral commr. Calif. Dept. Consumer Affairs, Sacramento, 1986—; examiner bio-feedback program Cert. Inst. of Am., Wheatridge, Colo., 1984—; stress mgmt. coord. Claremont Coll., 1988—. Editor: History of the Arabian Horse, 1968. Mem. Claremont Hist. Soc., 1989-90. Mem. Am. Psychol. Assn., Assn. for Applied Psychology and Bio-feedback, Inland Empire Bus. Women's Assn. (pres. Upland, Calif. chpt. 1984), Laguna Poets Soc., Audubon Soc., Sierra. Home: 469 W Seventh St Claremont CA 91711 Office: Monsour Counseling Ctr 735 N Dartmouth Ave Claremont CA 91711

KLATZKIN BOCHNER, ROBIN JANE, banker; b. Trenton, N.J., July 5, 1960; d. Clive and Audrey (Kashden) Klatzkin; m. Alan Bochner, Sept. 22, 1990. BSCE, Duke U., 1982; MBA, U. Pa., 1987. Projectmgr. Procter & Gamble Co., Cin., 1982-83; dept. and staff team mgr. Procter & Gamble Co., 1983-85; assoc. Bankers Trust Co., N.Y.C., 1987-88; project mgr. Bankers Trust Co., 1988-89; asst. v.p. Bankers Trust Co., N.Y.C., 1989—; internal cons. Johnson & Johnson Co., Milford, N.J., 1986-87; computer cons. Wharton Grad. Sch. Bus., Phila., 1986-87. Advisor Jr. Achievement, Cin., 1983-85. Mem. Assn. MBA Execs., Am. Mgmt. Assn., Microcomputer Mgrs. Assn., ASCE, N.Y. PC Orgn., Chi Epsilon, Alpha Phi Omega, Wharton Mgmt. Club (pres. 1985-86). Home: 11-01 162nd St Apt 8C Whitestone NY 11357 Office: Bankers Trust Co 130 Liberty St 12th Fl New York NY 10006

KLATZKY, SHEILA R., finance; 1 child, Antoinette. BA, Reed Coll., Portland, 1963-67; MA, U. Chgo., 1967-68, PhD, 1968-70. Asst. assoc. prof. U. Wis., Madison, 1970-75; assoc. prof. Fordham U., Bronx, N.Y., 1975-83; investment sales rep. Williams R.E., N.Y.C., 1984-85; proj. mgr. Finnco Devel. Corp., Poughkeepsie, N.Y., 1985-86; mort. officer Empire of Am. FSB, White Plains, N.Y., 1986—; cons. Fund for City of N.Y., 1980-81, Donnelley Mktg. Info. Svcs., Stamford, Conn., 1983. Author: research monograph, 1970; several articles for profl. jours., 1970-83. Recipient Post Doctoral Fellowship, Soc. Sci. Research Coun. 1970, Fellowship, Ctr.for Adv. Study, Stanford, 1980. Mem. Bd. of Realtors of Westchester County, U. Chgo. Alumnae Club (pres. 1986-87). Home: 469 Rosedale Ave White Plains NY 10605 Office: Time WIll Tell Unlimited Inc 962 Madison Ave New York NY 10021

KLEBANOW, BARBARA ELAINE, teacher; b. N.Y.C., Dec. 6, 1936; d. Joseph Herman and Helen (Feldstein) Klebanow. BA, U. Conn., 1958; MS, Yeshiva U., 1960; profl. diploma U. Conn., 1965; MS, Lehman Coll., 1977. Cert. sch. dist. adminstr., N.Y.; cert. reading specialist, N.Y.; cert. spl. edn. tchr., N.Y. Elem. classroom tchr. North Rockland Central Sch. Dist., Stony Point, N.Y., 1960-64, reading specialist elem. level, 1964-69, reading specialist secondary level, 1969—, adminstrv., intern, 1977-78; Internat. Reading Assn. state coord. for N.Y., 1985—, chair of cert. in reading adv. group, 1987-88. Recipient Celebrate Literacy award Rockland Reading Council, 1987. Fellow Assn. Women Adminstrs. in Westchester, Rockland Reading Council; mem. N.Y. State Reading Assn. (pres. 1983-84, Reading Tchr. award 1987), Phi Delta Kappa. Avocations: travel, reading, handicrafts. Office: North Rockland Cen Sch 117 Main St Stony Point NY 10980

KLEEMAN, ROSSLYN ANETA SHORE, federal agency administrator; b. Mpls., Apr. 20, 1922; d. S. Louis and Tessa (Woolpy) Shore; m. J. Nathan Eiser, Aug. 2, 1942 (dec. June 1945); 1 child, Nancy; m. Richard Pentlarge Kleeman, Jan. 1, 1950; children: Alice, Katherine, David. BS, U. Minn., 1971. Program mgr. HEW, Washington, 1971-72; project dir. Office of Mgmt. and Budget, Washington, 1972-73; asst. dir. U.S. Gen. Acctg. Office, Washington, 1973-79, assoc. dir., 1980-85, sr. assoc. dir., 1986-88; dir. fed. work force future issues U.S. GAO, 1989—. Editor: (column) Pub. Adminstrn. Rev. Jour. Fellow Nat. Acad. Pub. Adminstrn. (bd. trustees); mem. Am. Soc. Pub. Adminstrn. (nat. coun.), Internat. Personnel Mgmt. Assn., Am. Polit. Sci. Assn., Nat. Assn. Schs. Pub. Affairs and Adminstrn., Pub. Employees Roundtable (vice-chair). Home: 3642 Upton St NW Washington DC 20008 Office: GAO 441 G St NW Washington DC 20548

KLEIN, ANNE SCEIA, public relations executive; b. Phila., Apr. 25, 1942; d. Charles B. and Kathryn L. (Lucas) Sceia; m. Gerhart L. Klein, June 19, 1976. BS in Econs., U. Pa., 1964, MA in Communications, 1965. Promotion asst. S.E. Pa. Transit Authority, Phila., 1965; pub. rels. dir. Pa. Lung Assn., Phila., 1965-68; info. dir. H2L2 Architects, Phila., 1968; pub. rels. officer Girard Bank, Phila., 1968-76; acct. exec. Aitkin-Kynett Co., Inc., Phila., 1977; mgr. media rels. Sun Co., Radnor, Pa., 1978-80; mgr. exec. communications Sun Co., Radnor, 1980-82; pres. Anne Klein & Assocs., Inc., Mt. Laurel, N.J., 1982—. Mem. Ethics Com., Mt. Laurel, 1988—; Citizens Adv. Com., Mt. Laurel, 1988—. Recipient Super Communicator of 80's award Women in Communications, 1987. Mem. Pub. Rels. Soc. Am. (accredited, pres. Phila. chpt. 1979, mid-Atlantic chmn. 1984, assembly del. 1980-82, 88—, exec. com. Counselors Acad. 1990—, Pepperpot awards), Pub. Rels. Profls. So. N.J. (chmn. 1987—, pres. 1985-87), Forum Exec. Women (sec. bd. dirs. 1981-83), Phila. Pub. Rels. Assn., Harbor League Club, Peale Club, U. Pa. Faculty Club, Kappa Delta. Office: 533 Fellowship Rd Ste 250 Mount Laurel NJ 08054

KLEIN, BARBARA PINCUS, food scientist, educator; b. N.Y.C., Dec. 30, 1936; d. Herman and Edith (Lebow) Pincus; m. Miles V. Klein, Sept. 2, 1956; children: Cynthia, Gail. BS, Cornell U., 1957, MS, 1959; PhD, U. Ill., 1974. Asst. prof. U. Ill., Urbana, 1986-90, assoc. prof., 1980-85, prof., 1985—, chmn. div. foods and nutrition, 1986-90. Editor: Methods of Vitamin Assay, 1986. Mem. Inst. Food Technologists, Am. Home Econs. Assn. (Borden award 1988), Am. Chem. Soc., Am. Assn. Cereal Chemists, Am. Dietetic Assn., Am. Inst. Nutrition. Office: Univ Ill 905 S Goodwin Ave Urbana IL 61801

KLEIN, CHARLOTTE CONRAD, public relations executive; b. Detroit, June 20, 1923; d. Joseph and Bessie (Brown) K. BA, UCLA, 1945. Corr. UPI, Los Angeles, 1945-46; staff writer CBS, Los Angeles, 1946-47; publicist David O. Selznick Studios, Culver City, Calif., 1947-49, Foladare and Assocs., Los Angeles, 1949-51; publicist to v.p. Edward Gottlieb & Assocs., N.Y.C., 1951-62; v.p. to sr. v.p. Harshe Rotman & Druck, N.Y.C., 1962-78; dir. press/govt. affairs Sta. WNET-TV, N.Y.C., 1978-79; pres. Charlotte C. Klein Assocs., N.Y.C., 1979-84; sr. v.p., group supr. Porter Novelli, N.Y.C., 1984-89; prin. Charlotte Klein Assocs., N.Y.C., 1989—. Contbr. articles to profl. jours. Bd. dirs. Manhattan chpt. Am. Cancer Soc., 1988—. Recipient Cine Golden Eagle, 1977, Matrix award Women in Communications, 1975. Mem. Pub. Relations Soc. Am. (accredited, pres. N.Y. chpt. 1985-86, Silver Anvil award 1978, John Hill award 1988), Women's Forum (bd. dirs. N.Y. chpt. 1986-87), Women Execs. in Pub. Relations (pres. 1965), Vertical Club. Office: 138 E 36th St New York NY 10016

KLEIN, DEBORAH CHERYL, social worker; b. Bryan, Tex., Jan. 23, 1953; d. Sol and Felice Half (Schapiro) K. BA, U. Tex., 1975; MS, Tex.Woman's U., 1980. Cert. social worker-advanced clin. practitioner. Asst. psychologist Austin (Tex.) State Sch., 1975-78; child therapist Tex. Rsch. Inst. Mental Scis., Houston, 1978-80, child therapy supr., 1980-82; clin. therapist DePelchin Children's Ctr., Houston, 1982-87; program therapist Baywood Hosp., Webster, Tex., 1987-88; dir. clin. svcs. Family Svc. Ctr., Galveston, Tex., 1988-89; adminstr. clin. svcs. Family Svc. Ctr., Houston, 1989—. Mme. Nat. Assn. Social Workers, Am. Assn. Counseling and Devel., Am. Mental Health Counselors Assn., Mental Health Assn. Harris County, Tex. Network Children, Youth and Families, Bay Area Counseling Assn., Singles in Svc. to Temple Emanuel (pres. 1982-83), Women's Am. Orgn. Rehab. and Tng. Democrat. Jewish. Office: Family Svc Ctr 18301-A Egret Bay Houston TX 77058

KLEIN, DONA VELLEK, cellist, teacher; b. Chgo., May 21, 1955; d. Donald G. and Ita (Loe) Vellek; m. Daniel M. Klein, Oct. 2, 1988. MusB, New Sch. Music, Phila., 1978. Cellist Buffalo Philharmonic Orch., 1978-81, Camenae Quartet, Buffalo, 1980-81; asst. prin. Atlanta Symphony Orch., 1981—; teaching affiliate artist Emory U., Atlanta, 1982—; prin. cello Atlanta Opera Co., Atlanta, 1986-88; dir. Sempre Sonare A Chamber Music Orgn., Atlanta, 1987—; co-founder, mem. Atlanta Quartet, 1987—; cellist Robert Shaw Inst., France, summer 1988. Mem. Ga. Cello Club Soc. Home: 1147 Brookhaven Ct Atlanta GA 30319

KLEIN, DORIS ELAINE, educator; b. Crawford County, Iowa, May 13, 1929; d. Arthur Leo Ahrenholtz and Myrtle Fay (Cox) Meyer; m. Clifford John Klein, Aug. 25, 1949; children: Curtiss, Lucinda, Nicolette, Timothy, Mary Beth, Jodine. Normal tng. cert., U. No. Iowa, 1947; student, Drake U., 1955-66; BS, Dana Coll., 1975. Elem. tchr. Crawford County Schs., Denison, Iowa, 1947-49, St. Peter Cath. Sch., Defiance, Iowa, 1965-66; kindergarten tchr. Shelby County Schs., Harlan, Iowa, 1955-65, Harlan (Iowa) Community Schs., 1966—. Recipient Tchr. Appreciation award Harlan C. of C., 1988, Outstanding Svc. to Students and Profession award Coll. of St. Mary's-Omaha, 1989. Mem. NEA, Iowa Edn. Assn., Harlan Edn. Assn., AAUW, Am. Legion Aux. Democrat. Roman Catholic. Home: 1202 Durant Harlan IA 51537 Office: Harlan Community Schs 19th and Victoria Sts Harlan IA 51537

KLEIN, DYANN LESLIE, theater properties company executive; b. Clifton, N.J., June 1, 1951; d. Alfred L. and Florence (Slaff) K.; divorced. BA, Ohio State U., 1973; postgrad., Rutgers U., 1976, Sch. Visual Arts, 1983-86. Art therapist Jackson Meml. Hosp., Miami, Fla., 1973-74; prodn. asst. Dom Albi Assocs., N.Y.C., 1974-75; freelance prodn. asst. N.Y.C., 1975-76, freelance designer and stylist, 1976-80; pres. Props For Today, Inc., N.Y.C, 1980—; guest speaker Fashion Inst. of Tech., N.Y.C., 1987, mem. faculty; bd. dirs. Tipps Directory, N.Y.C. Mem. NAFE, Am. Film Inst., Roundtable for Women in Food Svc., Am. Rental Assn., Internat. Spl. Guests Soc., Nat. Assn. Broadcast Employees and Technicians, Advt. Photographers Am. (sustaining mem.). Jewish. Office: Props For Today Inc 121 W 19th St 3d Fl New York NY 10011

KLEIN, ELAINE, magazine publishing executive; b. Bklyn., Mar. 12, 1929; d. Sidney and Bertha (Smith) Laks; m. Melvin Klein, Dec. 23, 1951; children: Cyd Robin Klein Tomack, Amy Susan. Exec. sec. to pres. Muzak Corp., N.Y.C., 1949-55; expeditor The Van Ard Co., Forest Mills, N.Y., 1968-70; dir. spl. sales Playbill Mag., N.Y.C., 1970—. Mem. The New Dramatists, Friars Club. Democrat. Jewish. Office: Playbill Mag 71 Vanderbilt Ave New York NY 10169

KLEIN, ELIZABETH ARCHER, clergy member; b. Richmond, Calif., Oct. 15, 1963; d. George William and Donna (Garman) Archer; m. Jeffrey Marshal Klein, Feb. 14, 1987. AB, Stanford U., 1985; MDiv, Fuller Theol. Sem., Pasadena, Calif., 1989. Ordained to ministry Presbyterian Ch. as reverend, 1990. Intern Knox Presbyn. Ch., Pasadena, 1988-89; pastor San Martin (Calif.) Presbyn. Ch., 1990—. Mem. San Jose Prebyn. Assn., The Fellowship (assoc.). Office: San Martin Prebyn Ch 13200 Lincoln Ave San Martin CA 95046

KLEIN, ESTHER MOYERMAN (MRS. PHILIP KLEIN), publisher; b. Phila., Nov. 3, 1907; d. Louis and Rebecca (Feldman) Moyerman; BS, Temple U., 1929; student U. London, 1954; m. Philip Klein, Apr. 26, 1930; children: Arthur, Karen Louise Klein Mannes. Reporter, Phila. Jewish Times, 1925, Atlantic City Times, 1927; feature writer Pub. Ledger Syndicate, 1928-29, Pub. Ledger, Evening Bull., Phila. Record, 1929-32; pub. relations counsellor, editor Art Alliance Bull., 1945-49; commentator Sta. WPEN, 1949-53; pub. Phila. Jewish Times, 1953-74; author, hist. researcher, 1974—; lectr. women's clubs, 1951—. Del. Internat. Conf. Residential Adult Edn., Holland, 1957, Germany, 1959; participant in first workshop Residential Adult Edn. for Adult Edn. Assn. U.S., 1954. Mem. Gov.'s Commn. on Charitable Orgns., 1969—; chmn. Rittenhouse Sq. Women's com. for Phila. Orch., 1957; organizer bicentennial women's com. Walnut St. Theatre; adv. com. Friends Nat. Independence Hist. Park; chmn. bicentennial program Beth Zion - Beth Israel Congregation; bd. dirs. Rittenhouse Found., Phila. Jewish Times Inst., also dir. ann. cooking festivals; exec. com. Long Beach Island Found. Arts and Scis., N.J. Named Distinguished Dau. Pa.; recipient Gimbel Phila. award, 1975; awards Alumnae Girls High Sch., Phila. Art Alliance, Temple U., City Council Phila., Colonial Hist. Soc.; Klein Recital Hall at Temple U. named in her honor. Mem. Pa. Newspaper Pubs. Assn., Temple U. Alumni (honored at 80th anniversary, 1964), Phila. High Sch. for Girls Alumnae, Hannah Penn House, Emergency Aid of Pa., Chgo. Art Mus., Mus. Modern Art N.Y., Pan Am. Assn. Club: Print. Author: A Guidebook to Jewish Philadelphia, 1965; International House Celebrity Cookbook, 1965; History and Guidebook of Fairmount Park, 1974. Address: 135 S 18th St Philadelphia PA 19103

KLEIN, FAY MAGID, health administrator; b. Chgo., Jan. 12, 1929; d. Victor and Rose (Begun) Magid; m. Jerome G. Klein, June 27, 1948 (div. 1970); children: Leslie Klein Janik, Debra Lynne Maslov. BA in English, UCLA, 1961; MA in Pub. Adminstrn., U. So. Calif., 1971. Cert. health adminstrn. Supr. social workers L.A. County, 1961-65; program specialist Econ. and Youth Opportunity Agy., L.A., 1965-69; sr. health planner Model Cities, L.A., 1971-72; dir. prepaid health plan Westland Health Svcs., L.A., 1972-74; exec. dir. Coastal Region Health Consortium, L.A., 1974-76; grants and legis. cons. Jewish Fed. Council of L.A., 1976-79; planning council Jewish Fed. Councils of So. Fla., Palm Beach to Miami, 1979-82; adminstrv. dir. program in kidney diseases Dept. Medicine UCLA, 1982-84; exec. dir. west coast Israel Cancer Rsch. Fund, L.A., 1984—; cons. Arthritis Found., Los Angeles, 1984, Bus. Action Ctr., Los Angeles, 1982, Vis. Nurses Assn., Los Angeles, 1982. Charter mem. Los Angeles County Mus. of Art, Mus. of Contemporary Art, Los Angeles; cons. Los Angeles Mcpl. Art Gallery, 1979; mem. Art Council Wight Gallery, UCLA. Fellow U.S. Pub. Health, U. So. Calif., 1970-71. Mem. Am. Pub. Health, UCLA Alumni Assn. (life).

KLEIN, GERDA DORIS, mental health center executive; b. Pitts., Oct. 3, 1934; d. Isaac Morris and Rosalind (Ruderman) Friedman; m. Warren Martin Klein, July 1, 1962; children: Peter, Robert, Randi Ellen, David, Jonathan (dec.). BA in Edn., U. Pitts., 1956; MEd, Cleve. State U., 1980. Tchr. English, drama Jean Hay High Sch., Cleve., 1956-60; tchr. English Lorain (Ohio) High Sch., 1962-63; tchr., chmn. dept. English Lake Rider Acad., N. Ridgeville, Ohio, 1969-72; grad. asst. Cleve. State U., 1978-80; instr. Lorain County Community Coll., Elyria, Ohio, 1980-81; adminstrv. asst. W.G. Nord Community Mental Health Ctr., Lorain, 1982-84; dir. communications/devel. W.G. Nord Community Mental Health Ctr., 1984—. Coord. County mental Health Levy camopaign, 1986; bd. dirs. Agudath B'nai Israel Synagogue, Lorain, 1973—, pres., 1984-86; founding bd. dirs., sec. Community Found. of Lorain County, 1980—, Leadership Lorain County, 1984-89; com. chair United Way., Lorain, 1988—; bd. dirs. Leadership Lorain County Alumni Assn., 1990. Mem. Assn. Mental Health Adminstrs., Nat. Assn. Mental Health Info. Officers, Nat. Soc. Fund Raising Execs., Women in Communications, Pi Lambda Theta. Home: 4606 Compass Rose #28 Vermilion OH 44089

KLEIN, HARRIET FARBER, lawyer; b. Elizabeth, N.J., Apr. 30, 1948; d. Melvin Julius and Frances Mildred (Novit) Farber; m. Paul Martin Klein, Sept. 9, 1973; children: Andrew, Zachary. B.A. with honors, Douglass Coll., New Brunswick, N.J., 1970; J.D., Rutgers U., 1973. Bar: N.J. 1973, U.S. Dist. Ct. N.J. 1973. Jud. clk. chancery div. Superior Ct. N.J., 1973-74; assoc. Budd, Larner, Kent, Gross, Picillo & Rosenbaum, Newark, 1974-78; ptnr. Greenbaum, Rowe, Smith, Ravin, Davis & Bergstein (and predecessor), Woodbridge, N.J., 1979—; mem. N.J. State Bd. Bar Examiners, 1987-90, reader, 1977-87; mem. adv. com. on bar admissions N.J. Supreme Ct., 1987-90; mem. Essex-Newark Legal Svcs. Vol. Project, 1983-84. Pres. Sisterhood of Congregation B'nai Israel, Millburn, N.J., 1985-87. Mem. Essex County Bar Assn. (vice-chmn. com. on status of women in law firms 1988-90, vice-chmn. equity jurisprudence com. 1989-90, co-chmn. com. on women in the profession 1990—), N.J. Bar Assn., ABA, Order of Barristers, Phi Alpha Theta. Home: 45 Ridgewood Terr Maplewood NJ 07040 Office: Greenbaum Rowe Smith Ravin Davis & Bergstein PO Box 5600 Woodbridge NJ 07095

KLEIN, IRMA FRANCES, career development educator, consultant; b. New Orleans, Jan. 5, 1936; d. Harry Joseph and Gesina Frances (Bauer) Molligan; m. John Vincent Chelena (dec. 1963); 1 child, Joseph William; m. Chris George Klein, Aug. 14, 1965; 1 stepchild, Arnold Conrad. BS in Bus. Augustine Coll., postgrad. Mktg. Inst., Chgo., Loyola U., Chgo., Realtors Inst., Baton Rouge. Mgr. Stan Weber & Assocs., Metairie, La., 1971-75; tng. dir., 1975-81; cons. Coldwell Banker Comml. Co., New Orleans, 1981; dir. career devel. Coldwell Banker Residential Co., New Orleans, 1982-85; pres. Irma Klein Career Devel., Inc. Instr. U. New Orleans, Bonnabel High Sch., Realtors Inst., La. Real Estate Commn. Author: Career Development, 1982; Training Manual, 1978, Obtaining Listings, 1986, Participative Marketing, 1986, Marketing & Servicing Listings, 1987, Designing Training Curriculum, 1987. Active Friends of Longue Vue Gardens, La. Hist. Assn. Meml. Hall Found. Mem. La. Realtors Assn. (bd. dirs. 1973-74, grad. Realtors Inst. 1976), Jefferson Bd. Realtors (v.p. 1984), Edn. and Resources (cert., pres. La. chpt.), Research Club of New Orleans (pres. 1984-85), Realtors Nat. Mktg. Inst. (ambassador Tex. and La. 1985—, Outstanding Achievement award 1985, cert. broker 1980, residential specialist 1977), Nat. Assn. Realtors (nat. conv. speaker 1986), CRB (pres. La. chpt. 1982-83, chmn. edn.), CRS (pres. La. chpt. 1988—), Forty Scholars Soc., Am. Dental Assts. Assn., Les Quarante Ecolieres. Republican. Roman Catholic. Clubs: Antique Study Group of New Orleans, Confederate Lit. (New Orleans) (pres.), Research (New Orleans). Avocation: antiques.

KLEIN, JO ANN MARTUCCI, corporate communications specialist; b. Mt. Vernon, N.Y., Mar. 4, 1947; d. Joseph Anthony and Ann Gloria Isabell (Paparatto) Martucci; m. Henry Alexander Klein, Oct. 22, 1972. Student in Math., Columbia U., 1965-67; AA, Fairleigh Dickinson U., 1984, BS, 1986. Cert. tchr., spl. edn., N.Y. Exec. asst. Gordon W. White Inc., N.Y.C., 1965-66; asst. editor Columbia U., N.Y.C., 1966-69, mgr. data processing/classified documentation, 1969-72; asst. security officer Riverside Research Inst., N.Y.C., 1972-75; internal cons. Consolidated Edison, N.Y.C., 1975—, dir.-editor Info. Tech. Express newsletter, 1989-90; cons. and lectr. in field. Contbr. articles to profl. jours. Chair major gifts program Juvenile Diabetes Found., N.J. and N.Y. chpt., 1972-90; chair publicity and fundraising Am. Diabetes Assn., N.J., 1985—. Mem. NAFE, Office Products Exchange Network Inc. (founder 1981, pres. 1984-87, chair 1988-90, dir.-editor OPEN newsletter 1984-90), Am. Mgmt. Assn., Assn. Info. Systems Profls., Assn. Women in Computing, Cons. Interface, Am. Soc. Indsl. Security. Avocations: golf, swimming, interior decorating, photography, handicrafts.

KLEIN, KAREN HELENE, manufacturing executive; b. Reading, Pa., Sept. 23, 1960; d. Ronald Norman and Helena Katharine (Schlosser) Bautsch.; m. Joseph Francis Klein, May 26, 1984. BA in Journalism, Pa. State U., 1982. Customer svc. rep. Berk-Tek, Reading, 1982-84, mktg. asst., 1984-85; mktg. asst. Grosfillex, Inc., Reading, 1985-86, asst. to gen. mgr., 1986-87, adminstrn. mgr. N.Am. leisure furniture div., 1988—; cons. Hearth and Home, Gilford, N.H., 1989. Republican. Roman Catholic. Office: Grosfillex Old West Penn Ave Robesonia PA 19551

KLEIN, KAY JANIS, nurse; b. Detroit, Aug. 22, 1942; d. Alexander Michael Corey and Lillian Emiline (Stanley) Kilborn; divorced; children: Tonya Kay, William James, Jason Ronald. Student, C.S. Mott Community Coll., 1960-62, Mich. State U., 1962-64; AA, AS in Nursing, St. Petersburg Jr. Coll., 1978; student, U. South Fla., 1985—. RN; cert. perioperative nurse; cert. varityspist. Mgr. display Lerner Shops, Flint, Mich., 1960-62; layout artist Abdulla Advt., Flint, 1966-67; varitypist, artist City Hall Print Shop, Flint, 1967-70; nurse Suncoast Hosp., Largo, Fla., 1976-78; nurse, coord. plastic surgery svc., perioperative staff nurse Largo Med. Ctr. Hosp., 1978-81, 84—; assoc. dir. nursing Roberts Home Health Svc., Pinellas Park, Fla., 1982-84; inservice edn. instr., dir. video edn., team leader oncology dept. Largo Med. Ctr. Hosp., 1980-81. Editor, illustrator: (book) Some Questions and Answers About Chemotherapy, 1981, Thoughts for Today, 1981; illustrator: (cookbooks) Spices and Spoons, 1982, Yom Tov Essen n' Fressen, 1983; various brochures and catalogues; art work in permanent collection of C.S Mott Jr. Coll., Flint, 1962. Historian Am. Business-women's Assn., Flint, 1968-73 (scholarship 1976); outreach chmn. Temple B'nai Israel, Clearwater, Fla., 1981-85; regional outreach coord. Union of Am. Hebrew Congregations, N.Y.C., 1983-85. Mem. Assn. of Oper. Rm. Nurses, Phi Theta Kappa. Republican. Jewish. Home: 122 Palmetto Ln Largo FL 34640 Office: Largo Med Ctr Hosp 201 14th St SW Largo FL 33540

KLEIN, LAUREN MARSHA, teacher; b. Reading, Pa., July 3, 1957; d. Walter R. and Janice V. (Moyer) Dunn; m. Gary D. Klein, Aug. 27, 1954. BS in Music Edn., Susquehanna U., Selinsgrove, Pa., 1979; MM, Temple U., Phila., 1982. Vocal tchr. Albright Coll., Reading, Pa., 1983-85, Wyomissing Ins. Fine Arts, Reading, Pa., 1983-85, Swarthmore Music, Pa., 1985-86; choral dir. Widener U., Chester, Pa., 1986-88; elem. music tchr. Shipley Sch., Bryn Mawr, Pa., 1986—. Mem. Little Lyric Opera Co. Mem. Nat. Assn. Orff Tchrs., Nat. Singing Tchrs. Assn. Home: 626 E 19th St Chester PA 19013

KLEIN, MICHELE SCHUTTE, information scientist; b. Pitts.; d. Jack and Bette (Braurman) Schutte; m. Kenneth L. Klein; children: Mitchell, Micah. BA, U. Pitts., 1972; MS, Case Western Res. U., 1973. Cert. med. librarian. Head librarian Children's Hosp. Rsch. Found., Cin., 1973; program policy specialist Nat. Health Ins. Co., Austin, Tex.; reference librarian Tex. Med. Assn., Austin, 1978; dir. library svc. Children's Hosp. Mich., Detroit, 1978—. NIH fellow, Bethesda, Md., 1972. Mem. Med. Libr. Assn. (pres. Midwest chpt. 1985), Spl. Libr. Assn., Met. Detroit Med. Libr. Group (pres. 1981), Beta Phi Mu. Office: Childrens Hosp Mich 3901 Beaubien Blvd Detroit MI 48201

KLEIN, NANCY HOPKINS, anthropologist, educator; b. South Bend, Ind., Aug. 3, 1931; d. Lee Edward and Vera Jane (Murphy) Hopkins; m. Edward Jay McGowen III, Mar. 10, 1950 (div. 1962); children: Brooke Hopkins, Lindsay Ann, Cassandra Lee; m. Lawrence George Klein, Aug. 3, 1965. BA, U. Chgo., 1952, MA, 1965; PhD, Northwestern U., 1980. Asst. prof. sociology DePaul U., Chgo., 1965-78; lectr. anthropology San José (Calif.) State U., 1979-83; adj. prof. Whitehead Ctr. U. Redlands, Calif., 1986-89; dir. communication Josephson Inst. Ethics, Marina Del Rey, Calif., 1990—; chmn. bd. dirs. Edn. Satellite Network, L.A., 1988—. Co-author: Problem Solving in Society, 1974. NSF fellow in sci. applied to societal problems, 1975; grantee Ford Found., 1963. Mem. Sigma Xi. Home: 2930 Neilson Way Santa Monica CA 90405 Office: Josephson Inst Ethics 310 Washington St Marina del Rey CA 90292

KLEIN, RUTH B., civic worker, packaging co. exec., poet, author; b. Cin., Jan. 31, 1908; d. Samuel and Minnie (Schunke) Becker; student U. Calif. at Los Angeles, 1926-28, San Jose State Coll., 1928-29; m. Charles Henle Klein, Sept. 23, 1938; children—Betsy Klein Schwartz, Charles Henle, Carla Klein Fee III. Sec., Novelart Mfg. Co., Cin., 1960—, dir., 1960—. Vol. Aid to Visually Handicapped program Cin. sect. Nat. Council of Jewish Women, 1951-82, sec., 1954-56, 63-64, bd. dirs., 1952-70; bd. dirs. Civic Garden Center of Greater Cin., 1956-63, chmn. spl. services for aid to visually handicapped, 1952-82. Mem. Nat. Braille Assn., Greater Cin. Writers League, Verse Writers' Guild Ohio. Club: Contemporary Literary. Author: Latitude of Love; Longitude of Lust, 1979; contbr. poems to various anthologies. Home: 6754 Fair Oaks Dr Cincinnati OH 45237

KLEIN, SHEILA MARGARET, staff development director; b. Ogdensberg, N.Y., Mar. 11, 1943; d. James Patrick and Margaret Marie (Mulligan) Noon; m. David Barry Jenkins, Sr., Feb. 12, 1966 (div. Apr. 13, 1984); children: David Barry Jr., Colleen; m. Philip Stanley Klein, Nov. 28, 1987. BS in Nursing, D'Youville Coll., 1965. Cert. rehab. nurse, cert. ins. rehab. specialist. Pub. health nurse Monroe County Health Dept., Rochester, N.Y., 1965-67; clin. instr. D'Youville Coll., Buffalo, 1969-70; staff nurse Urban Med. Hosp., Marietta, Ga., 1973-77, Visiting Nurse Assn., Atlanta, 1977-80; med. cons. Crawford & Co., Atlanta, 1980-84, tng. specialist, 1984-88, dir. mgmt. tng. & devel., 1988—. Author: Seminar Brochurse, 1986, 88. Co-leader Parental Support Group, Atlanta, 1981; vol. Parental Activist Group, Atlanta, 1987. Mem. Am. Soc. Tng. & Devel. Republican. Messianic Judaism. Home: 2632 Shadow Bluff Marietta GA 30062 Office: Crawford & Co 5620 Glenridge Dr NE Atlanta GA 30342

KLEIN, SUSAN MARSHA, nurse, coordinator, marketing consultant; b. Washington, May 23, 1953; d. Neil Bernard and Frances (Bass) Kabatchnick; m. Leigh Forrest Klein, June 16, 1974; children: Allison Michele, Scott Joseph. Diploma in nursing, Sinai Hosp. Sch. of Nursing, 1974; cert. legal asst. program, George Washington U., 1984. RN, Md. Educator childbirth Parent & Child, Inc., Bethesda, Md., 1978-85; instr. arthritic aquatic Jewish Community Ctr., Rockville, Md., 1983-84; legal asst. Kabatchnick & Kabatchnick, Washington, 1984; coordinator disabled services Capital Centre, Md., 1984—; mem. accesibility adv. coun. Box Office Mgmt. Inst., 1987—; pres., chmn. bd. Disabled Mktg. Cons., 1989—; v.p. Success Network, Inc., 1989—. Bd. dirs. Montgomery County Heart Assn., 1977-80; vol. chmn. com. for tchr. svcs. Parent & Child, Inc., 1978-81; v.p. Hadassah, 1980-81; recording sec. Glenallan Elem. Sch. PTA, 1986-87, pres., 1987-89, E. Brooke Lee Middle Sch. PTA, 1989—. Recipient Mid-Atlantic Region award B'nai B'rith, 1977, Hon. Mention for CPR, Montgomery County Heart Assn., 1977, Ann. award for Community Service Met. Washington Pub. Health Assn., 1978; named one of Outstanding Young Women in Am., 1980, Five Outstanding Young Marylanders, 1980. Mem. Internat. Platform Assn., POWERS (bd. dirs. 1989—), Montgomery County C. of C., Greater Gaithersburg Jaycee Women (external v.p. 1980-81), Md. Jaycetees (arthritis program mgr. 1980-83). Home and Office: Disabled Mktg Cons 1944 Autumn Ridge Circle Silver Spring MD 20906

KLEIN, VIRGINIA SUE, psychotherapist; b. Liberty, N.Y., Dec. 30, 1936; d. Abe and Lillian (Malin) Levine; m. Andrew Klein, Mar. 29, 1959; children: Earl Saul, Holly Jo. BS, Rutgers U., 1972, MSW, 1974, PhD, 1978. Lic. psychotherapist, N.J. Psychotherapist N.J. Correctional Inst. for Women, Clinton, 1973-75; pvt. practice Somerville, N.J., 1974—; producer, host cable TV series Gorwing Up in the 80s, 1986-88, Through the Looking Glass, 1988—; presenter seminars, tng. programs; lectr. and cons. in field; founder, chmn. 4 internat. confs. on incest and related problems, 1987, 88, 89, 90; co-dir. The Tng. Inst., Switzerland, 1989, 90. Author: How to Get Free!, 1985, Bad Mad Boy, Honey Bear, and the Magic, Waterfall (A Continuing Family Story), 1986, I-am, Pa-pah and Ma-me, 1986. Mem. Acad. Cert. Social Workers, Am. Inst. Counseling and Psychotherapy (diplomate), Nat. Assn. Social Workers. Office: Hage Prodns Inc PO Box 21 Somerville NJ 08876

KLEINER, KATHLEEN ALLEN, psychology educator; b. Phila., Nov. 12, 1958; d. William Anton and Marjorie Anne (Fine) K.; m. Roy Owen Gathercoal, Aug. 9, 1988; 1 child, Glen William Gathercoal. AB, Franklin & Marshall Coll., Lancaster, Pa., 1981; MA, PhD, Case Western Res. U., 1985. Teaching asst. Frankln & Marshall Coll., 1980-81; rsch. asst. Case Western Res. U., Cleve., 1981-85; researcher U. Calif., Berkeley, 1985-87; asst. prof. psychology Ind. U.-Purdue U., Indpls., 1987—; summer faculty fellow Ind. U., Bloomington, 1988. Contbr. articles to profl. jours. Evaluation mem. Campaign for Healthy Babies, Indpls., 1990—. Nat. Inst. Child Health and Human Devel. predoctoral fellow, 1981-85; Case Western Res. U. grad. alumni grantee, 1984, Project Devel. Program Interdisciplinary grantee Ind. U.-Purdue U., 1990. Mem. Am. Psychol. Soc., Midwest Psychol. Assn., Soc. Rsch. in Child Devel., Internat. Soc. Infant Studies, Psi Chi. Mem. Soc. of Friends. Office: Ind U-Purdue U 1125 E 38th St Indianapolis IN 46205-2810

KLEINFELD, STEFANIE LYNN, chiropractor; b. N.Y., Aug. 20, 1962; d. Arnold Jay Kleinfeld and Helena (Dressner) Friedman. BS, U. Vt., 1984; D of Chiropractic, Life Chiropractic Coll., 1987. Assoc. Family Chiropractors, South Burlington, Vt., 1988--; pvt. practice Marko Family Chiropractic, South Burlington, 1988--. Mem. Champlain Valley Chiropractic Coun. (sec. 1988—), Internal Chiropractic Assn. Office: 21 Hedgerow Dr Shelburne VA 05482

KLEINFELTER, MARY ANN, marketing executive; b. Perry, Ga., Oct. 22, 1949; d. Melvin Joseph and Margaret (Williams) K.; m. James Allison (div.). BA, U. N.C., 1971; MA, Columbia U., 1975. Direct mail mgr. N.Y. Mag., N.Y.C., 1975-79; mktg. mgr. Am. Mgmt. Assn., N.Y.C., 1979-81; list mgr. Wheeler Group/Drawing Bd., New Hartford, Conn., 1981-83; v.p. brokerage List Svcs. Corp., Ridgefield, Conn., 1983-87; dir. customer acquisitions Daytimers, East Texas, Pa., 1987—. Mem. Direct Mktg. Club N.Y., Am. Mktg. Assn., Phila. Direct Mktg. Club, Direct Mktg. Assn., Phi Beta Kappa. Office: Daytimers 1 Willow Ln East Texas PA 18046

KLEINHANS-KELLEHER, JOAN MARY, insurance company professional; b. Phila., Aug. 13, 1954; d. John P. and Mary (Coleman) Kleinhans; m. Timothy Kelleher, June 11, 1988. BS in BA, Drexel U., Phila., 1976; MBA, Drexel U., 1983. Statistician Acme Markets, Phila., 1976-77; sys. analyst Consolidated Rail Corp., Phila., 1977-83; fin. analyst Cigna, Phila., 1983-85; product mgr. Cigna, 1985-86, bus. analysis cons., 1986-88, pricing cons., 1988—. Mem. Operations Research Soc. of Am., The Inst. Mgmt. Sci. Office: Cigna 1600 Arch St 2 Home Office Philadelphia PA 19103

KLEINLEIN, KATHY LYNN, training and development executive; b. S.I., N.Y., May 2, 1950; d. Thomas and Helen Mary (O'Reilly) Perricone; m. Kenneth Robert Kleinlein, Oct. 30, 1983. BA, Wagner Coll., 1971, MA, 1974; MBA, Rutgers U., 1984. Cert. secondary tchr., N.Y., N.J., Fla. Tchr. English, N.Y.C. Bd. Edn., S.I., 1971-74, Matawan (N.J.) Bd. Edn., 1974-79; instr. English, Middlesex County Coll., Edison, N.J., 1978-81; med. sales rep. Pfizer/Roerig, Bklyn., 1979-81, mgr. tng. ops., N.Y.C., 1981-87; dir. sales tng. Winthrop Pharms. div. Sterling Drug, N.Y.C., 1987-88; dir. tng. Reuters Info. Systems, N.Y.C., 1988—; pres., dir. tng., Women in Transition, career counseling firm; pers. mgmt. officer U.S. Army Res., N.J., 1981-86; cons. Concepts & Producers, N.Y.C., 1981-85. Trainer United Way, 1982-83, mem. polit. action com., 1982—; mem. Rep. Presdl. Task Force, Washington, 1983—. Capt. U.S. Army, 1974-78. First woman in N.Y. N.G., 1974; first woman instr. Empire State Mil. Acad., Peekskill, N.Y., 1976. Mem. Nat. Soc. Pharm. Sales Trainers, Sales and Mktg. Execs., Am. Soc. Tng. and Devel., N.J. Assn. Women Bus. Owners, LWV, Matawan C. of C., Alpha Omicron Pi. Republican. Roman Catholic. Club: Atlantis Divers (N.Y.C.). Home: 53 Ivy Way Matawan NJ 07747 Office: Reuters Info Systems 1700 Broadway St New York NY 10019

KLEINMAN, HYNDA KAREN, cell biologist; b. Boston, May 20, 1947; d. Ernest and Doris (Riman) Fisher; m. Joel C. Kleinman, Dec. 28, 1968; children: Dana, Ruth. BS, Simmons Coll., 1969; MS, MIT, 1971, PhD, 1974. Postdoctoral fellow Tufts U., Boston, 1974-75; staff fellow Nat. Inst. Dental Rsch. NIH, Bethesda, Md., 1975-79, rsch. chemist, 1980-89, chief cell biology, 1985—; vice chmn. Gordon Conf., N.H., 1990; mem. adv. com. Geisinger Inst., Danville, Pa., 1989; mem. program com. Ea. Coast Connective Tissue Conf., Bethesda, 1990. Patentee in field. Recipient Helen Hay Whitney Found. award, 1975; Doerenkamp-Zbinden award Johns Hopkins U., 1987; NIH grantee, 1985, 87. Mem. AAAS, Am. Assn. Cell Biology (program com. 1989-90), Soc. Complex Carbohydrates, Tissue Culture Assn. Office: Nat Inst Dental Rsch NIH 30/407 Bethesda MD 20892

KLEINSCHMIDT, JULIA J., social worker, educator; b. Brownwood, Tex.; m. William M. Kleinschmidt; children: Ann Karen, John Anthony. BA in Zoology, U. Tex., El Paso, 1961; MSW, U. Utah, 1983. Cert. social worker; lic. clin. social worker. Caseworker Austin (Tex.) State Hosp., 1961-64, 66-67, Spring Grove State Hosp., Balt., 1964-66; social worker, program planner Westminster Coll., Salt Lake City, 1983-88; instr. U. Utah, Salt Lake City, 1988—. Editor: (resource dictionary) To You From Me, 1985, 2d edit., 1987; co-editor (monograph) U. Utah, 1990. Mem. Nat. Assn. Social Workers, Health Edn. Utah, AAUW, League Women Voters, Phi Kappa Phi, Eta Sigma Gamma. Home: 1381 E Millbrook Way Bountiful UT 84010 Office: Univ Utah Health Edn Dept HPRN 215 Salt Lake City UT 84112

KLEINSCHNITZ, BARBARA JOY, oil company executive, consultant; b. Granite Falls, Minn., Aug. 25, 1944; d. Arthur William and Joy Ardys (Roe) Green; m. Charles Lewis Kleinschnitz, Dec. 28, 1963; 1 child, Katheryn JoAnn Kleinschnitz Hartsock. BBA, U. Denver, 1983; student, Colo. Women's Coll. Leadman Schlumberger Well Services, Denver, 1968-76; supr., log processing Scientific Software-Intercomp, Denver, 1976-82; tech. cons. Tech. Log Analysis, Inc., Lakewood, Colo., 1982-83; customer support mgr. Energy Systems Tech., Inc., Englewood, Colo., 1983-86; cons. technical Littleton, Colo., 1986—; documentation specialist Q.C. Data, Inc., 1987—; cons. Tech. Log Analysis, Inc., Denver, 1982-83, Energy Systems Tech., 1986—. Vol. Denver Police Reserve, 1973-75. Mem. Nat. Organ. Women, NAFE, Assn. Women Geoscientists, Soc. Profl. Well Log Analysts (bd. dirs. 1989-90, v.p. 1990—), Denver Well Log Soc. (bd. dirs. 1986-87, v.p. 1987-88, pres. 1988-89). Democrat. Roman Catholic. Home: 8692 W Frost Ave Littleton CO 80123 Office: 777 Grant St Ste 111 Denver CO 80203

KLEIS, MARGARET ANNE, sales executive; b. Watertown, Wis., June 28, 1950; d. Cletus David Hasslinger and Margaret Louise (Bergwall) Bartlett; m. John P. Kleis, Aug. 26, 1972 (div. Apr. 1987); 1 child, Mary Elizabeth. Student, U. Wis., 1968-72, Alverno Coll., Milw., 1987—. Producer Island Playhouse, MacKinac Island, Mich., 1975-76; spokes person Allis Chalmers, Milw., 1976-77; sales rep. Tri Media, Milw., 1977-79, Savig Nac and Assocs., Milw.; pres., owner Almar, Kleico, Hartland, Wis., 1980--. Producer: Star Spangled Girl, 9712, Box Convey and Fill Systems, 1987. Treas. St. Charles Home and Sch. Bd., Hartland, Wis., 1988--. Mem. Wis. Assn. Mfrs. Agts., Profl Dimensions, Am. Defense Prepareness Assn. Roman Catholic. Home: 733 E Capitol Dr Hartland WI 53029 Office: Almar Kleico 151 E Capitol Dr Hartland WI 53029

KLEISTER, TAMI RAE, investment bank manager; b. Elyria, Ohio, Jan. 6, 1963; d. Ronald Herman Kleister and Gloria Rae (Bradley) Gilbo. AS, Lorain County Community Coll., Elyria, Ohio, 1983; student, Oberlin (Ohio) Jr. Vocat. Sch., Lor. Community Coll. Mktg. asst. Elyria (Ohio) Savings & Trust Nat., 1980-84; real estate mgr. Starling Realty, Inc., Sarasota, Fla., 1985-86; paralegal Duffey, Judd, Webb, Wood, P.A., Sarasota, 1986-88; branch mgr. Hampton Securities, Inc., Sarasota, 1988—; Coord. Ohio Office Edn. Assn., Elyria, 1980-84; sec. Am. Banking Assn., Elyria, 1980-84; treas. Am. Inst. of Banking, Elyria, 1980-84. Community activator Elyria C. of C., 1980-84; sec. St. Marks Orthodox Ch., Lorain, Ohio, 1982-84; sponsor Fellowship of Christian Athletes, Sarasota, 1987—; fund raiser John & Mable Ringling Mus., Sarasota, 1986—; sec. Make A Wish Found., 1987—; activist, sec. Young Reps., 1988—. Mem. NAFE, Female Execs. Sarasota, Kiwanis. Republican. Home: 440 South Shore Dr Osprey FL 34239

KLEKODA-BAKER, ANTONIA MARIE, forensic handwriting specialist, consultant; b. Grand Rapids, Mich., June 30, 1939; d. Anthony Joseph and Adele Elizabeth (Fifelski) Zoppa; m. Raymond Syl Klekoda, Aug. 31, 1957 (div. 1977); children: Cecilia (dec.), Vanessa, Rhonda, Darla, Norman, Yvette, Patrice; m. Frederick John Baker, Dec. 31, 1986. Student, Davenport Coll., Grand Rapids, Mich., 1956, Aquinas Coll., Grand Rapids, Mich., 1957-58, 77. Organist, choir dir. Basilica of St. Adalbert, Grand Rapids, Mich., 1957-62; music instr. Mich. Acad. of Music, Northern Mich., 1962-63; owner Handwriting Analysis Service, Grand Rapids, 1963-87; editor Garfield Park Assn., Grand Rapids, Mich., 1974-76; feature columnist Grand Rapids Press., 1966-76; staff Diocesan Pubs., Grand Rapids, 1977-85; musician, Convs., community theater, Western Mich. Contbr. over 4000 articles to profl. jours. and mags.; delivered over 3500 lectrs. Resource authority Grand Rapids Pub. Library, 1976—; organizer City Neighborhood Assn., Garfield Park, Grand Rapids, 1973, mem. Greater Grand Rapids Convention Bur., 1984-85. Recipient Safety Engrs. award W. Mich. Chpt. Soc. Safety Engrs., 1985, Holland Rotarian award, Holland, Mich. Rotary Club, 1985, Sparta Rotary award, Sparta, Mich. Rotary Club, 1986. Mem. Nat. Assn. Pastoral Musicians, Nat. Assn. of Document Examiners, Alliance Women Entreprenurs, Grand Rapids Fedn. Musicians, Mich. Graphological Resources (chairperson, woman of the year 1986-87), Data Personnel Mgmt. Assn. Roman Catholic. Home and Office: 325 Aurora SE Grand Rapids MI 49507

KLEMSTINE, EVELYN RENEE, auditor; b. Hamburg, Fed. Republic of Germany, June 25, 1958; came to U.S., 1959; d. James Aurandt and Edith (Meyer) K. BS in Acctg., Va. Polytech. Inst. & State U., 1979; MSBA, Boston U., Stuttgart, Fed. Republic of Germany, 1987. Auditor Naval Audit Svc., Arlington, Va., 1979-82, Defense Audit Svc., Arlington, 1982-83, Armed Forces Recreation Ctr., Garmisch, Fed. Republic Germany, 1983-84; auditor-in-charge Army Internal Review, Stuttgart, Fed. Republic Germany, 1984-87; lead auditor insp. gen.'s office Dept. of Def., Arlington, Va., 1987-90; project mgr. insp. gen.'s office Dept. of Def., Arlington, 1990—; instr. Acctg., Cen. Tex. Coll., Stuttgart, 1986, City Coll. Chgo., Stuttgart, 1987. Author: Functional Training Package on Budgeting and Appropriation Accounting, 1982. Vol. Animal Shelter, Alexandria, Va., 1989. Catholic.

KLEPPER, LESA KAY, hospital executive; b. Rogersville, Tenn., Aug. 12, 1961; d. Leroy Samuel and Volena May (Burdine) K. BS in Bus. Mgmt., Carson-Newman Coll., 1983. Bus. office mgr. Hawkins County Meml. Hosp., Rogersville, 1983-86; dir. patient acctg. Williamson Med. Ctr., Franklin, Tenn., 1986—. Mem. Healthcare Fin. Mgmt. Assn. (treas. 1988—), Order Ea. Star. Republican. Baptist. Home: 1115 Carnton Ln B-4 Franklin TN 37064 Office: Williamson Med Ctr 2021 Carothers Rd PO Box 1600 Franklin TN 37065-1600

KLEREKOPER, LISE CHAMBLEE, child protection services social worker; b. Quantico, Va., Oct. 23, 1964; d. Francis Lymuel Chamblee and Karen (Trofast) Garthright; m. Ralph Cornelis Klerekoper, Dec. 19, 1987. BS, Shepherd (W.Va.) Coll., 1985; MSW, U. Md., 1987. Lic. social worker, Md. Resident in social work The Washington Hosp. Ctr., 1986; intern in social work Montgomery County Health Dept., Rockville, Md., 1987, interim patient svcs. dir. AIDS program, 1987, social work intern AIDS program, 1987; med. social worker Fairfax Hosp., Falls Church, Va., 1988-90; social worker Fairfax County Child Protection Svcs., Fairfax, Va., 1990—. Mem. AAUW, Nat. Assn. Social Workers. Roman Catholic. Home: 319 Foxridge Dr SW Leesburg VA 22075

KLESPIES, LINDA SUE, company administrative executive; b. Akron, Ohio, May 12, 1952; d. Nicholas Joseph and Willie Ruth (Bryan) K. MusB, Mt. Union Coll., 1974; Mus.M., Wichita State U., 1976; BMus Edn., Ohio State U., 1979; postgrad. in Musicology, Ind. U., 1977. Tchr. music Bd. Edn. Findlay (Ohio), 1979-80; mgr. trainee Friendly Restaurant, Canton, Ohio, 1980; asst. mgr. Ponderosa Inc., Kent, Ohio, 1980-82, dist. tng. instr., Kansas City, Kans., 1982, mgmt. devel. designer and instr., Dayton, 1982-83, (assigned to E.S.I. Meats) orgn. devel. specialist, Dayton, 1983-85; personnel adminstr. Frito-Lay, Inc., 1985-86; human resource systems mgr. Stone Container Corp., 1986—. Dir. children's choir Ch. of Master, Akron, 1972-73; dir. choir Salem United Meth. Ch., Wichita, 1974-76; mem. sanctuary choir spl. music team Olive Bapt. Ch.; mem. bd. advisors hospitality mgmt. program Ohio State U., 1984-85, home study div. Cornell U., 1984-85, adj. instr. 1986—, Pensacola Jr. Coll., 1988—. Mem. Am. Soc. Personnel Adminstrn., Internat. Platform Assn., Am. Soc. Tng. and Devel., NAFE, Pensacola Personnel Group, Pensacola C. of C., Mortar Bd., Mu Phi Epsilon, Pi Lambda Theta, Alpha Lambda Delta. Democrat. Baptist. Club: Rainbow Girls (past worthy advisor, capt. drill). Avocations: music, exercise, football, swimming, blown glass and shells collecting. Office: Stone Container Corp 101 Stone Blvd Cantonment FL 32533

KLICK, JEAN E., military officer; b. Chgo., Jan. 15, 1943. BA, Purdue U., 1964; MBA, Stanford U., 1970; grad., Sq. Officer Sch., 1971, Air Command & Staff Coll., 1975, Nat. War Coll., 1982. Commd. 2d lt. USAF, 1964, advanced through grades to brig. gen., 1989; asst. dir. base adminstrn. USAF, England AFB, La., 1965-66; chief pub. div. Hdqrs. 9th Air Force Directorate Adminstrn., Shaw AFB, S.C., 1966-67; exec. officer 432d Tactical Reconnaissance Wing, Udorn Royal Thai AFB, Thailand, 1967-68; chief career control sect. Consol. Base Pers. Office, Homestead AFB, Fla., 1970-72; chief 2d Weather Wing Pers. Div., Wiesbaden AFB, Fed. Republic Germany, 1972-73; chief assignment control div. Dep. Chief of Staff Pers. Hdqrs. USAF Europe, Ramstein AFB, Fed. Republic Germany, 1973; staff dir. for USAF women, then chief pers. plans div. Hdqrs. Strategic Air Command, Offutt AFB, Nebr., 1975-78; dep. mil. asst. and asst. sec. for manpower, res. affairs and installations Dept. Air Force, Washington, 1978-79, mil. asst. to special asst. to sec., dep. sec. def., 1979; comdr. L.A. Air Force Sta., 1982-84; vice-comdr. Arnold Engring. and Devel. Ctr., Arnold AFB, Tenn., 1984-86; insp. gen. Air Force Systems Command, Andrews AFB, Md., 1986-88; dep. comdr. for communications, ops. support and control systems Hdqrs. Space Systems div. Air Force Systems Command, L.A. AFB, 1988-90, vice-comdr. Hdqrs. Space Systems div., 1990—. Office: Air Force Dept Hdqrs Space Systems Div Los Angeles AFB CA 90009-2260*

KLIEBHAN, SISTER M(ARY) CAMILLE, college president; b. Milw., Apr. 4, 1923; d. Alfred Sebastian and Mae Eileen (McNamara) K. Student, Cardinal Stritch Coll., Milw., 1945-48; B.A., Cath. Sisters Coll., Washington, 1949; M.A., Cath. U. Am., 1951, Ph.D., 1955. Joined Sisters of St. Francis of Assisi, Roman Catholic Ch., 1945; legal sec. Spence and Hanley (attys.), Milw., 1941-45; instr. edn. Cardinal Stritch Coll., 1955-62, asso. prof., 1962-68, prof., 1968—, head dept. edn., 1962-67, dean students, 1962-64, chmn. grad. div., 1964-69, v.p. for acad. and student affairs, 1969-74, pres., 1974—, bd. dirs., 1974—. Bd. dirs. Goals for Milw. 2000, 1980-83, treas. Wis. Found. Ind. Colls., 1974-79, 87-90, v.p., 1979-81, pres., 1981-83; bd. dirs. DePaul Hosp., 1982—, Sacred Heart Sch. Theology, 1983—; mem. adv. bd. St. Camillus Campus, 1989—; bd. dirs. Internat. Inst. of Wis., 1984—, Mental Health Assn. Milwaukee County, 1983-87, Pub. Policy Forum, 1987—, Better Bus. Bur. of Wis. Inc., 1989—; mem. TEMPO, 1982—, bd. dirs., 1986-89; bd. govs. Wis. Policy Rsch. Inst., 1987—. Mem. Am. Psychol. Assn., Wis. Assn. Tchr. Educators, Phi Delta Kappa, Delta Epsilon Sigma, Psi Chi, Delta Kappa Gamma, Kappa Delta Pi. Lodge: Rotary (Milw.).

KLIEGMAN, PAULA GOLDEN, social worker; b. Chgo., Mar. 23, 1937; d. Herman H. and Ethel (Kamfner) Golden. BA, Northwestern U., 1958; AM, U. Chgo., 1960. Lic. clin. social worker. Social worker La Rabida Hosp., Chgo., 1960-66, Child and Family Services, Chgo., 1963-66; social worker, assoc. chief social services Dept. Psychiatry Michael Reese Hosp., Chgo., 1966-89, acting chief social worker social work in psychiatry, acting assoc. dir. dept. social work, 1989; pvt. practice Chgo., 1973—; cons. Cicero (Ill.) Family Services, 1980-82; tchr. Inst. Psychoanalysis, Chgo., 1976-79. Contbr. articles on parenting to profl. jours. Mem. Nat. Assn. Social Workers, Assn. Child Psychotherapists (treas. 1978-79). Home: 1607 E 50th Pl Chicago IL 60615 Office: 111 N Wabash #822 Chicago IL 60602

KLIMA, KAREN ANN, ophthalmic photographer; b. Balt., Nov. 27, 1960; d. John Joseph and Carmella Mary (Taresco) K. BA, Coll. of Notre Dame, Balt., 1982. Cert. retinal angiographer. Ophthalmic photographer Wilmer Eye Inst. Johns Hopkins U., Balt., 1982-89; dir. ophthalmic photography Dept. The Retina Ctr. at St. Joseph Hosp., Balt., 1989—; retinal angiographic technician Retinal Vascular Ctr., Johns Hopkins U., 1987—; mem. faculty, instr. Ophthalmic Photographer's Soc., Atlanta, 1990—. Mem. Ophthalmic Photographer's Soc., NAFE, Md. State Fish and Game Protective Soc. Roman Catholic. Home: 3405 Pinewood Ave Baltimore MD 21206 Office: Retina Ctr St Joseph Hosp 7620 York Rd Towson MD 21204

KLIMA, MARTHA SCANLAN, state legislator; b. Balt., Dec. 3, 1938; d. Thomas Moore and Catherine A. (Stafford) Scanlan; m. James Patrick Klima Jr., Apr. 8, 1961; children: Jennifer, J. Patrick III, Andrew. AA, Villa Julie Coll., 1958. Med. stenographer U. Md. Med. Sch., Balt., 1958-63; mem. appropriations com. Md. Ho. of Dels., Annapolis, 1982—; sec. Cen. Md. Health Systems Agy., 1981-83; commr. State Planning Commn., State of Md., 1983—. Del. Rep. Nat. Conv., Dallas, 1984; bd. dirs. Greater Balt. Med. Ctr., Towson, 1986—, Md. Spl. Olympics, 1987—. Named Freshman of Yr., Ho. of Dels., 1984, Woman of Yr. Towsontowne Bus. and Profl. Women's Club; recipient Gov.'s Citation for Outstanding Svc. to Citizens of Md., 1988. Mem. Am. Legis. Exchange Coun. (state chmn. 1987—), Women Legis. Md., Congress of PTA's (hon. life), Balt. County C. of C. (award of merit 1981), Exchange Club (Balt.). Republican. Roman Catholic. Home: 1403 Newport Pl Lutherville MD 21093 Office: Ho Reps Annapolis MD 21401

KLIMAN, SUSAN SCHAEFER, designer; b. Tucson, Dec. 2, 1963; d. John Paul and Helen (Schwarz) Schaefer; m. Douglas Hartley Kliman, Feb. 18, 1989. BArch, Corell U., 1986. Project mgr. Giuliani Assocs. Architects, Washington, 1986-88; designer Richard Luke Architect, Las Vegas, Nev., 1988-89; project mgr. Harris Sharp Assoc. Architects (named changed to HSA Architects Inc.), Las Vegas, 1989—. Instr. swimming, lifeguard Montgomery County Recreation Dept., Silver Spring, Md., 1986-88; Brownie leader Girl Scouts U.S.A., Las Vegas, 1988-89, 2d v.p. Frontier coun., 1989—. Mem. AIA (assoc.), LWV, AAUW, Alpha Phi.

KLIMKOWSKI, SISTER M. ANN FRANCIS, academic administrator; b. Wyandotte, Mich., Jan. 1, 1931; d. Alexander and Mary (Koncki) K. BSE, Bowling Green (Ohio) State U., 1961, MEd, 1967; PhD, U. Toledo, 1983. Tchr. various schs., 1954-72; prin. elem. sch. Mpls., 1972-76; asst. prin. high sch. Oregon, Ohio, 1976-77; founding dir. Lifelong Learning Ctr. Lourdes Coll., Sylvania, Ohio, 1979-81, acting acad. dean, 1981-83, pres., 1983—; mem. Cen. Cath. High Sch. Adv. Council, Toledo, 1983—; bd. dirs. Mid-Am Bank & Trust Sylvania, Ohio. Bd. dirs. Metro-Toledo Chs. United, 1983—; mem. Com. of 100, Toledo, Sylvania Area Community Improvement Corp. Mem. Am. Assn. Higher Edn., Ohio Assn. Ind. Colls. and Univs., Ohio Coll. Assn. (exec. com. 1986—), Toledo C. of C., Sylvania C. of C. Roman Catholic. Lodge: Zonta (profl. women's group Toledo chpt.). Home: 6855 Convent Blvd Sylvania OH 43560 Office: Lourdes Coll Office of the Pres 6832 Convent Blvd Sylvania OH 43560

KLINCK, PATRICIA EWASCO, state official; b. Albany, N.Y., May 13, 1940; d. Albert C. and Mary Ann (Sopko) Ewasco; m. C. Hoagland Klinck, Jr., Sept. 12, 1970; 1 dau., Natalie Childs. B.A. in History, Smith Coll.,

1961; M.S. in L.S, Simmons Coll., Boston, 1963; postgrad. in edn., SUNY, Albany, 1964-67; student sr. exec. program, Harvard U., 1989. Young adult worker Boston Pub. Libr., 1961-63; libr. dir. Colonie Central High Sch., Albany, 1963-67; libr. Libr./U.S.A., U.S. Pavilion, N.Y. World's Fair, summer 1965; libr. dir. Simon's Rock Coll., Gt. Barrington, Mass., 1967-70; regional dir. N.W. Regional Libr. Vt. Dept. Librs., Montpelier, 1970-72; dir. extension svcs. div. Vt. Dept. Librs., 1972-73, 73-74, acting asst. state libr., 1973, asst. state libr., 1974-77, state libr., 1977—; chmn. New Eng. Library Bd., 1979-81; bd. dirs. Chief Officers State Library Agys., 1978-80, vice chmn., 1978-80, chmn., 1981-82; mem. White House Conf. Preliminary Design Commn., 1985-86. Mem. Vt. Bicentennial Commn., 1986—; bd. dirs. Vt. Hist. Soc., 1977—. Mem. ALA (legislation com. 1966-68), Assn. State Library Agys. (bd. dirs. with ALA 1986-88), Assn. Specialized and Cooperative Library Agys. of ALA (bd. dirs.), New Eng. Library Assn., Vt. Library Assn., Vt. Council on Humanities. Home: 47 Brewer Pkwy South Burlington VT 05401 Office: Vt Dept Of Librs 111 State St State Office Bldg PO Montpelier VT 05602

KLINE, AMY JO, sales company executive; b. Clarion, Pa., July 8, 1960; d. Paul Leroy and Leona Ruby (Black) Kline. Diploma, N. Clarion, Leeper. Exec. sec. Clarion (Pa.) County Commn., 1978-82; receptionist Astro Mfg. Co., Inc., Shippenville, Pa., 1983-86; bartender, bookkeeper Vince's Tavern, Leeper, Pa., 1985-86; sales coord. Astro Mgf. Co., Inc., Shippenville, 1986-87; regional sales mgr. Astro Mfg. Co., Inc., Shippenville, 1987--; owner Performance & Accessories, Strattanville, Pa., 1987--. Republican. Methodist. Office: Astro Mfg Co Inc Box 189 Shippenville PA 16254

KLINE, CLAIRE ELLEN, anesthesiologist; b. San Antonio, Mar. 9, 1955; d. Robert and Shirley (Fisher) K.; m. John H.S. Holshouser; 1 child, John H. Clayton. BA, Wellesley Coll., 1977; MD, U. Tex. Health Sci. Ctr., 1981. Resident in anesthesiology U. Tex. Health Sci. Ctr., San Antonio, 1981-84; fellow in pediatric anesthesiology Hosp. for Sick Children, Toronto, Ont., Can., 1984; staff Southwest Tex. Meth. Hosp., San Antonio, 1985—. Bd. dirs. Friends of the McNay Mus., San Antonio, 1987-89; mem. Jr. League of San Antonio. Mem. Am. Soc. Anesthesiologists, AMA, Tex. Soc. Anesthesiologists (alt. del. 1990-92), Tex. Med. Assn., Bexas County Med. Soc. Office: 1022 North Main Ave San Antonio TX 78212

KLINE, GLORIA JEAN, clinical specialist, nurse, college program director; b. Wooster, Ohio, July 6, 1946; d. John F. and Philomena C. (Tomassetti) Oliver; m. William Kline, Oct. 12, 1968; 1 child, William Oliver. BSN, Ohio State U., Columbus, 1970; MSN, U. Akron, Ohio, 1982; diploma in nursing, Mercy Sch. of Nursing, 1967. RN, Ohio; cert. Critical Care Nursing, Med. Clin. Nurse Specialist. Instr. nursing Timken Mercy Med. Ctr., Canton, Ohio, 1974-84, clin. specialist, 1984-90, Eucharistic minister, 1978—; educator Stark Tech. Coll., Canton, med. and surg. specialist, head nursing dept., dir. nursing ADN program. Bd. dirs., mem. speaker bur. East Cen. Ohio div. Am. Heart Assn., Canton, 1980-90; vol. ann. drive Cancer Soc., 1975—. Mem. Am. Nurses Assn., Ohio Nurses Assn., Stark Carroll Dist. Nurses Assn., AACN, NANDA, Alumni Assn. Mercy Sch. Nursing, Sigma Theta Tau, Delta Omega. Republican. Roman Catholic. Home: 337 Commonwealth Ave NE Massillon OH 44646 Office: Stark Tech Coll 6200 Frank Ave NW Canton OH 44720

KLINE, JOYCE SHERYL, materials engineer; b. Malden, Mass., June 18, 1965; d. Herbert Frank and Phyllis Eileen (David) K. BSME, Worcester Poly. Inst., 1987; postgrad., Boston U., 1989—. Customer svc. asst. Life of Am. Ins. Co., Malden, 1981-83; engring. intern New England Metal Spinning Co., Malden, 1985; summer intern Automated Systems div. RCA, Burlington, Mass., 1986; materials application engr. Aircraft Engine Corp. GE, Lynn, Mass., 1987-90; engr. mfg. mgmt. program GE, Plainville, Conn., 1990—. Mem. ASME, Am. Soc. Metals, Worcester Poly. Inst. Regional Club (chair 1988), Worcester Poly. Inst. Panhellenic Assn. (pres. 1986-87), Worcester Poly. Inst. Student Alumni Assn. (chair 1985-86), Alpha Gamma Delta. Jewish. Home: 31 Hawthorne St Malden MA 02148 Office: GE Elec Disbtn and Control 41 Woodford Ave Plainville CT 06062

KLINE, KAREN L., retail store owner; b. Bemidji, Minn., Feb. 12, 1940; d. Kermit S. and Betty A. (Sallberg)Oksendahl; m. James E. Kline, Dec. 27, 1968; children: Julia Elizabeth, James Edward Jr. BA, St. Olaf Coll., 1961; MA, U. Wis., 1964. Tchr. Richfield (Minn.) High Sch., 1964-66; group leader Experiment in Internat. Living., Brattleboro, Vt., 1964-67; sect. head Rotary Internat., Evanston, Ill., 1967-68; tchr. Haven Jr. High Sch., Evanston, 1968-70; adminstrv. asst. Casket Mfg. Am., Evanston, 1972-78; pres. Accent Chgo., Inc., Chgo., 1978—; mem. nat. adv. coun., Experiment in Internat. Living, 1972—; appointee, Chgo. Tourism Coun., 1988—. Bd. govs., Augustana Ctr., Chgo., 1988—. Mem. Nat. Assn. Women Bus. Owners, AAUW, LWV, Rotary. Democrat. Home: 428 Washington Ave Wilmette IL 60091 Office: Accent Chgo Inc 835 N Michigan Ave Chicago IL 60611

KLINE, KRISTINE JO, utility executive; b. Havre, Mont., Oct. 22, 1957; d. Edwin John and Donna Louise (Purdy) Haugen; m. Donald Ralph Kline, June 24, 1978; children: Cole Edwin, Cortney Dawn. AS in Water, Waste Water Tech., No. Mont. Coll., 1978; BS in Microbiology, Mont. State U., 1980. Supt. waste treatment plant City of Havre, 1980—; part-time instr. No. Mont. Coll., Havre, 1981—; field scout Pollution Technics, 1980. Mem. Water Polution Control Fedn., 1978, dir. 1989—. Mem. Water Pollution Control Assn. (chmn. edn. com. 1983-85, pres. 1986-87, mem. com. 1987-88, W.D. Hatfield award 1987-88), AAUW, Beta Sigma Phi. Methodist. Home: 1129 Cleveland Ave Havre MT 59501 Office: City of Havre Box 231 Havre MT 59501

KLINE, LINDA, employment consultant; b. Boston, Aug. 8, 1940; d. George and Eva (Weiner) Kline; B.A. in Biology, Boston U., 1962. Pers. dir. Block Engring. Inc., Cambridge, Mass., 1964-66; brokerage mgr. Eastern Life Ins. Co. N.Y., Boston, 1966-68; mgr. direct placement Lendman Assos., N.Y.C., 1968-72; dir. women-in-mgmt. div. Roberts-Lund, Ltd., N.Y.C., 1972-77; pres. Kline-McKay, Inc., Exec. Search and Outplacement Cons., Maximus Cons., Inc., N.Y.C., 1978—; exec. dir. Majority Money, women's network, 1976-79; tchr. fin. planning for women Marymount-Manhattan Coll., 1977; lectr. and/or cons. women's programs at several colls. and univs. and corps. Co-author: Career Changing: The Worry-Free Guide, 1982. Bd. dirs. Women Bus. Owners Edn. Fund, 1982-86 , Mom's Amazing, 1985-88; community bd. dirs. Mt. Sinai Med. Ctr., 1984—. Mem. Women Bus. Owners N.Y. (bd. dirs. 1978-84), Nat. Coalition Women's Enterprise (adv. bd. 1988-89). Address: 3 E 48th St #6 New York NY 10017

KLINE, LOUISE LETHA, small business owner; b. Cedar Rapids, Iowa, Mar. 6, 1944; d. Harry August and Letha Doris (Risdal) Wendel; m. Gary Allee, Feb. 9, 1963 (div. Sept. 1977); children: Robert Wendel, Brent Edward; m. Sherman M. Kline, Apr. 1, 1978. Grad. high sch., Atkins, Iowa. Cosmetologist Arlene's Beauty Shop, Atkins, Iowa, 1963-64; with sales dept. Fabs Fabrics, Iowa City, 1972-73, Avon, Iowa City, 1973, Killians Dept. Store, Cedar Rapids, Iowa, 1974; custom drapery cons. Armstrongs Dept. Store, Cedar Rapids, 1974-77; custom drapery cons., owner Window Fashions, Cedar Rapids, 1978-83; owner, mgr. Olde World Lace Shoppe, Amana, Iowa, 1983—. Mem. Amana Arts Guild, Profl. Women's Network, Amana Travel Vistors Coun., Lace Guild, Luth. Women's Missionary. Office: Olde World Lace Shoppe 204 C St Amana IA 52203

KLINE, MABLE CORNELIA PAGE, educator; b. Memphis, Aug. 20, 1928; d. George M. and Lillie (Davidson) Brown; 1 dau., Gail Angela Page. Student LeMoyne Coll.; BSEd, Wayne State U., 1948, postgrad. Tchr., Flint, Mich., 1950-51, Pontiac, Mich., 1953-62; tchr. 12th grade English, Cass Tech High Sch., Detroit, 1962—, coord. Study Skills Program; mem. English Book Selection com., 1986—. Life mem. YWCA, NAACP. Detroit Pub. Edn. Fund grantee, 1989. Mem. NEA (life), Assn. Supervision and Curriculum Devel., Am. Fedn. Tchrs., Nat. Council Tchrs. English, Wayne State U. Alumni Assn., Delta Sigma Theta. Episcopalian. Home: 1101 Lafayette Towers W Detroit MI 48207 Office: 2421 2d Ave Detroit MI 48201

KLINE, MIRIAM MARIE, educational administrator, township official; b. Hamburg, Pa., Sept. 28, 1934; d. Emanuel James and Mabel Elsie (Heimbach) Wagner; m. Richard Daniel Kline, Mar. 31, 1956; children—Eugene Richard, Ann Marie Kline Womack. Student pub. schs., Hamburg; student Pa. State U., 1988. Supr. Am. Casualty, Reading, Pa., 1952-55; sec. Hamburg Area Sch. Dist., 1961-85, sec., dir. dist. support services, 1985—; sec.-treas. Twp. of Perry, Shoemakersville, Pa., 1973—. Author: (booklet) Effective Educational Secretary Handbook, 1983, 89. Mem. Berks County Assn. Ednl. Secs. (v.p. 1985-87), Berks County Assn. Twp. Officials, State Assn. Ednl. Secs., State Assn. Twp. Suprs., State Assn. Mcpl. Secs., Pa. Sch. Bds. Assn., Nat. Assn. Ednl. Office Personnel, Pa. Assn. Notaries. Republican. Lodge: Women of Moose. Avocations: quilting; reading; travel. Home: 681 Ridge Rd Shoemakersville PA 19555 Office: Hamburg Area Sch Dist Windsor St Hamburg PA 19526

KLINE, PATRICIA LEE, dental hygienist; b. Inglewood, Calif., July 29, 1941; d. Lee B. and Martha Louise (Myers) K.; m. Boyd Sanford Lemon, Aug. 31, 1963 (div. Jan. 1970); 1 child, Julie Anne. BS in Dental Hygiene, U. So. Calif., 1963. Registered dental hygienist, Calif. Dental hygienist Dr. George Telford, La Crescenta, Calif., 1964-87, Dr. Charles Lilly, Burbank, Calif., 1981—. Mem. Am. Dental Hygienist Assn., Hundred Peaks Sierra Club (chmn. 1988). Democrat. Jewish. Office: care Dr Charles Lilly DDS 303 S Glenaoks Blvd Ste 12 Burbank CA 91502

KLINEDINST, PAMELA LIANE, real estate broker; b. Washington, Apr. 27, 1948; d. William Henry and Lois Aileene (Waddell) K. BA, High Point (N.C.) Coll., 1970. Asst. buyer Garfinckel's, Washington, 1970-73; mgr. Garfinkel's, Washington, 1973-77; asst. store mgr. Harper's, Washington, 1977-78; realtor Realty World-Koepenick, Rockville, Md., 1978-80; realtor, relocation dir. Realty World-Greater Potomac, Gaithersburg, Md., 1980-82; realtor Long & Foster Real Estate, Inc., Bethesda, Md., 1982—; comml. property mgr. Wilkins Ctr., Bethesda, Md., 1980—. Mem. Nat. Commn. on Future of High Point Coll., 1989-90; lay mem. Balt. Ann. Conf. United Meth. Chs., Balt., 1984—; youth del. Rep. Nat. Conv., Miami, Fla., 1972; trustee Concord St. Andrew's United Meth. Ch., Bethesda, 1984—. Recipient Svc. award Literacy Coun. Montgomery County, 1988. Mem. Washington Calligraphers Guild (treas. 1986—), Community Ministry of Montgomery County (treas. 1980-83), Literacy Coun. Montgomery County, Congl. Country Club, Zeta Tau Alpha (chpt. treas. 1968-70). Home: 5000 Battery Ln Bethesda MD 20814 Office: Long & Foster Real Estate 4520 East West Hwy Bethesda MD 20814

KLINEFELTER, HYLDA CATHARINE, obstetrician, gynecologist; b. Gettysburg, Pa., Sept. 28, 1929; d. Roscoe Emanuel and Sara Catherine (Wagner) K.; m. Edward Ralph Kohnstam, June 18, 1955; children: Charles, Kathryn. Student, Gettysburg Coll., 1947-48; AB, U. Pa., 1951; MD, Med. Coll. Pa., 1955. Diplomate Am. Bd. Ob-Gyn. Rotating intern Phila. Gen. Hosp., 1955-56; resident in ob.-gyn. Presbyn. U. Pa. Med. Ctr., Phila., 1956-59; mem. teaching staff Med. Coll. Pa., Phila., 1959-62; rsch. asst. maternal and child health Pa. Hosp., Phila., 1964-66; co-supr. family planning clinic Presbyn. Hosp./U. Pa. Med. Ctr., 1967-68; ptnr. Media (Pa.) Clinic, 1969-81; pvt. practice, 1981-86; ptnr. Granite Run Ob.-Gyn. Assocs., Media, 1986—; mem. staff, Riddle Meml. Hosp., vice chmn. ob.-gyn., 1989—. Contbr. articles to med. jours. Fellow Am. Coll. Ob.-Gyn.; mem. Am. Med. Womens Assn. (past treas. dist. 25), Am. Fertility Soc., Am. Assn. Gyn. Laparoscopists, AMA, Delaware County Med. Soc., Pa. Med. Soc., Fox Valley Civic Assn., Soroptimist, Alphi Xi Delta Alumni. Republican. Lutheran. Home: 264 S Ivy Ln Glen Mills PA 19342 Office: Granite Run ObGyn Assn 1088 W Baltimore Pike Media PA 19063

KLINEFELTER, SARAH STEPHENS, division dean, radio station manager; b. Des Moines, Jan. 30, 1938; d. Edward John and Mary Ethel (Adams) Stephens; m. Neil Klinefelter. BA, Drake U., 1958; MA, U. Iowa, Iowa City, 1968; postgrad., Harvard U., July, 1984, U. Wis., Sept., 1987. Chmn. humanities dept. High Sch. Dist. 230, Orland Pk., Ill., 1958-68; chmn. communications and humanities div. Kirkwood Community Coll., Cedar Rapids, Iowa, 1986-78; prof. English Sch. of the Ozarks, Point Lookout, Mo., 1978-86; gen. mgr. Sta. KSOZ-FM, Point Lookout, 1986—; dean div. of performing and profl. arts Sch. of the Ozarks, Point Lookout, 1989—. Commr. Skaggs Community Hosp., Branson, Mo., 1986—; chmn. Branson Planning and Zoning Commn., 1983; project dir. Mo. Humanities Bd.; commr., examiner North Cen. Assn. Higher Edn., 1978-85; commr. Iowa Humanities Bd., 1971-78; mem. Taney County Planning and Zoning Commn., 1989—. Democrat. Presbyterian. Home: PO Box 828 Point Lookout MO 65726 Office: Sta KSOZ-FM Sch of Ozarks Point Lookout MO 65726

KLING, PHRADIE (PHRADIE KLING GOLD), contracting company official administrator; b. N.Y.C., July 2, 1933; d. Samuel A. and Mary Leah (Cohen) K.; m. Lee M. Gold, Sept. 5, 1955 (div. 1976); children: Judith Eileen, Laura Susan, Stephen Samuel, James David. BA, Sarah Lawrence Coll., 1955; MA in Human Genetics, Sara Lawrence Coll., 1971. Genetic counselor assoc. Coll. Medicine and Dentistry N.J., Newark, 1970-73; assoc. genetic counselor Sarah Lawrence Coll., Bronxville, N.Y., 1970-73; genetic counselor N.Y. Fertility Rsch. Found., N.Y.C., 1971-73; staff assoc., genetic counselor depts. pediatrics, ob-gyn and neurology Columbia U. Coll. Physicians and Surgeons, N.Y.C., 1973-78; asst. in genetics St. Luke's Hosp. Ctr., N.Y.C., 1977-79; health program assoc. Conn. Dept. Health Svcs., Hartford, 1978-84; edn. cons. Conn. Traumatic Brain Injury Assn., Rocky Hill, 1984-85; office mgr. Anderson Turf Irrigation Inc., Plainville, Conn., 1986—; speaker, instr. on health and health ethics issues, Conn., N.Y., N.J., 1971-85; dir. confs. on genetics and traumatic brain injury, 1980-85; project dir. edn. field testing Biol. Scis. Curriculum Study, 1981-83. Mem. Farmington River Watershed Assn., Simsbury, Conn., 1988—; docent Sci. Mus. Conn., West Hartford, 1989—. Recipient citation for dedicated svc. Conn. Safety Belt Coalition, 1985. Mem. AAAS, Am. Human Genetics, Bus. and Profl. Microcomputer Users Group, Conn. Assn. for Jungian Psychology, Conn. Computer Soc., Hastings Ctr., Am. Mensa (chpt. coord. gifted children 1985—). Home: 33 Hunter Rd Avon CT 06001

KLINGBERG, ALICE LILLIAN, elementary school teacher, retired; b. Apr. 16, 1914; d. Carl William and Anna Kathryn Margaret (Jespersen) K. AS, Miss Wood's Sch., 1938; BEd, Nat. Coll. of Edn., Evanston, Ill., 1951, MEd, 1961. Tchr. elem. and music Portland, N.D., 1938-40; tchr. kindergarten Racine, Wis., 1940-79; ret., 1979; chmn. primary sect. Wis. State Conv., Milw., 1961; lectr. in field; mem. archaeology dig in Israel with Wheaton Coll.; faculty Jerusalem Children's Ctr., 1966, 68, 77-79. Tchr. Sunday sch. and adult classes, Racine, 1932-89; pres. state and local ch. orgn.; chmn. Racine County chpt. Girl Scouts U.S., 1970-75. With Civil Def., 1941—, World War II. Mem. Wis. Ret. Tchrs. Assn., Racine County Ret. Tchrs. Assn. (membership com. 1980-88), Racine Zool. Soc., AAUW. Republican. Home: 3932 Spring St Racine WI 53405

KLINGENSMITH, THELMA HYDE (MRS. DON. J. KLINGENSMITH), retired educational administrator; b. Rauville, S.D., May 23, 1904; d. Eber Watson and Ida (Lebert) Hyde; B.A. magna cum laude, John Fletcher Coll., 1928; M.S. in Ed., U. N.D., 1962; m. Don Joseph Klingensmith, Sept. 11, 1930; children: Merle Joseph, Eunice Victoria Klingensmith Evans. Tchr. rural schs., Almont, N.D., 1922-24; exec. sec. Young People's Gospel League, Chgo., 1928-30; asst. supt. Ponca Meth. Indian Mission, Ponca City, Okla., 1936-43; tchr. English, Almont High Sch., 1951-54; supt. schs. Morton County, Mandan, N.D., 1959-73; mem. Am. Assn. Sch. Adminstrs. seminar to Russia, 1969. Bd. dirs. N.D. div. Am. Cancer Soc., 1958-72, chmn. pub. edn. com., 1958-60, sec., 1960-66; sr. v.p. N.D. Young Citizens League, 1959-63, sr. pres., 1963-65; legis. rep. N.D. Coun. County Supts. Assn., 1963-66; adviser Morton County Libr. Bd., 1960—, trustee, 1977-83, 84-89; sec.-treas. Heart River Gospel Assn., 1950-66, dir., 1950—; dir., treas. N.D. Action Com. for Environ. Edn., 1968-75; bd. dirs. Dickinson Coll. Found. 1969-88; v.p. West Wis. Conf., Women's Soc. Christian Svc., Methodist Ch., 1945-46; legis. rep. N.D. Woman's Christian Temperance Union, 1978-89; Western dist. coord. Christian Social involvement N.D. Conf., United Meth. Women, 1979-83; Western dist. coord. Christian Personhood, 1983-85; Dakota area del. Internat. Conf. Christian Heritage in Govt., United Meth. Ch., London, 1981; co-chmn. nat. Conv. Prohibition Party, 1983; treas. N.D. Coun. on Gambling Problems, 1985-88. Named N.D. Mother of the Yr., 1965; recipient citation for conservation edn. Nat. and N.D. wildlife fedns., 1974, Pres.' citation Vennard Coll., 1984, tribute and statuette N.D. Eagle Forum, 1985. Mem. Mandan Hosp. Aux., Mandan Friends of the Libr., N.D. Assn. Sch. Adminstrs., Am. Bible Soc., N.D. Libr. Assn. (trustee citation award 1980, cert. of appreciation 1982), N.D. Libr. Trustees Assn. (v.p. 1967-68, 74-76, sec. 1971-73, dir. 1976-82, pres. 1979-81), N.D. Wildlife Fedn. (chmn. essay contest 1973-78), Marquis Libr. Soc. (adv. mem.). Clubs: Golden Grad of Vennard Coll. (pres. 1981-84) (University Park, Iowa); Zonta (dist. VII chmn. pub. affairs com. 1968-70; del. internat. convs. 1968, 70, 72). Editor: Almont Jubilee History Book, 1956; Morton County Elementary Tchrs. Bull., 1959-73. Home: 206 Collins Ave PO Box 663 Mandan ND 58554

KLINGER, JUDITH ANN, elementary educator; b. Phila., Apr. 3, 1943; d. Ralph Paul and Margaret Elizabeth (Griffiths) Tarbutton; (div.); 1 child, Gayle Michele. BS in Edn., Shipppensburg (Pa.) State Coll, 1964, MEd, 1966. Cert. elem. tchr., Pa. Elem. educator Red Lion (Pa.) Area Sch. Dist., 1964-66, 70—, elem. libr. sci. educator, 1966-69; mem. lang. arts com. Red Lion Sch. Dist., 1988—, mem. whole lang. com., 1990—. Mem. Friends of Kaltreider Meml. Libr., Red Lion, 1989—; Chmn. edn. com. St. Paul;s United Meth. Ch., 1982-87, Sunday sch. supt., 1984-87, chmn. coun. on ministries, 1988-90. Mem. Order of Eastern Star (worthy matron 1974-75). Republican. Home: 706 S Main St Red Lion PA 17356 Office: Mazre C Gable Elem Sch Cedar St Red Lion PA 17356

KLINGER, LINDA ANNE, telecommunications administrator; b. Wenatchee, Wash., Apr. 4, 1949; d. Robert Gene and Elizabeth (Talley) Gormley; m. Marvin Klinger, Aug. 23, 1980. A in Applied Arts, Wenatchee Valley Coll., 1969; student, Wash. State U., 1969-72; BBA, City U., Portland, Ore., 1987. English dept. program coord. Wenatchee Valley Coll., 1972; student activities coord. Edmonds (Wash.) Community Coll., 1973-76; analytical asst. GTE NW, Everett, Wash., 1976, supply specialist, 1976-78, supply adminstr., 1978-80; supply supr. GTE NW, Beaverton, Oreg., 1980-84; mgr. Phone Mart GTE NW, Gresham, Oreg., 1984-88, supr. bus. control orders and maintenance, 1988-89; area supr. Pub. Communications, Everett, Wash., 1989—. Mem. GTE Vol. Network, Beaverton, 1987-89. Recipient Gov's. Award for Volunteerism, Ore., 1984. Mem. Am. Bus. Women (chair edn. com. 1984—, treas. N.W. region 1988-90, lt. gov. N.W. region 1990—). Democrat. Baptist. Lodge: Soroptimist (treas. NW region 1988—). Home: 12322 42nd SE Everett WA 98204

KLINGHOFFER, JUNE FLORENCE, physician, educator; b. Phila., Feb. 12, 1921; d. Harry and Esther (Uram) K.; m. Sidney U. Wenger, June 24, 1947; 1 child, Robert Klinghoffer Wenger. BA, Woman's Med. Coll. Pa., Phila., 1941; MD, Med. Coll. Pa., Phila., 1945. Diplomate Am. Bd. Internal Medicine, Am. Bd. Rheumatology. Intern , then resident Albert Einstein Med. Ctr., Phila., 1945-47; fellow in pathology Woman's Med. Coll. Pa., 1947-48; prof. medicine Med. Coll. Pa., Phila., 1969—, Ethel Russell Morris prof. medicine, 1987—. Contbr. articles to med. jours. Recipient Lindback award for disting. teaching, 1965, Alumnae Achievement award Med. Coll. Pa., 1978. Fellow ACP, Phila. Coll. Physicians; mem. AMA, AAUP, Am. Med. Women's Assn., Assn. Am. Med. Colls., Am. Coll. Rheumatology, Alpha Omega Alpha. Home: 356 Meadow Ln Merion Station PA 19066 Office: Med Coll Pa 3300 Henry Ave Philadelphia PA 19129

KLINK, PATRICIA DE BLANK, investment management company executive; b. N.Y.C., May 7, 1945; d. John Jaffray and Marianne (Roberts) Wallace; m. John Michael Klink. BA in Econs., U. Mich., 1967; MBA, Harvard U., 1969. Dep. mgr. Brown Bros. Harriman & Co., 1969-78; pres. Discount Corp. N.Y. Advisers, 1978—. Mem. Treasury Securities Lunch Club, Money Marketeers, Harvard Club, N.Y. Yacht Club. Office: Discount Advisers 58 Pine St New York NY 10005

KLOCEK, KATHLEEN ANNE, parent educator, writer; b. Pitts., Nov. 5, 1948; d. Alexander and Frances Florence (Tropeck) Kravec; m. Daniel Leonard Klocek, Dec. 26, 1970; children: Joseph, Timothy, Kara, Matthew. B.S., Duquesne U., 1970. Exec. officer mgr. Kaufmann's, Pitts., 1970-71; nat. parenting trainer Am. Soc. Psychoprophylaxis in Obstets./Lamaze, Washington, 1977-81; exec. dir. Parenting Assocs., Verona, Pa., 1980—; dir. devel. Mom's House, Inc., Pitts., 1986-89, dir. funding, 1989—. Contbr. articles to Childbirth Educator mag., 1982—. Mem. Family Resource Coalition, Am. Soc. Psychoprophylaxis in Obstetrics (bd. dirs. 1975-81), Mothers Are People Too Program. Republican. Byzantine Catholic. Avocations: genealogy; ice skating; swimming; reading; photography. Office: Parenting Assocs 8243 Lincoln Rd Verona PA 15147

KLOCKE, MARY MARGARET, softdrink company official; b. New Haven, Oct. 31, 1961; d. Francis John and Ann Marie (Burger) K. BA, Manhattan Coll., 1983; MBA, U. Notre Dame, 1985. Cost analyst Ford Motor Co., Dearborn, Mich., 1985-87; planner Pepsi-Cola Bottling Group, Somers, N.Y., 1987-88; div. planning mgr. Pepsi-Cola East, Somers, 1988-89; mgr. planning and analysis Pepsi-Cola Co., Twinsburg, Ohio, 1989—. Instr. Jr. Achievement Detroit, 1986-87; coord. vols. St. Luke's Community Svcs., Stamford, Conn., 1988-89. Sullivan scholar, 1983, 84. Mem. Phi Beta Kappa, Epsilon Sigma Pi. Democrat. Roman Catholic. Home: 2350 Charney Rd University Heights OH 44118 Office: Pepsi-Cola Co 1999 Enterprise Pkwy Twinsburg OH 44087

KLODOWSKI, AMY MARTHA AUSLANDER, lawyer; b. N.Y.C., Oct. 13, 1952; d. Oscar and Beatrice (Feinberg) Auslander; m. Harry F. Klodowski, Jr., Nov. 12, 1983; children: Deborah Bea, Daniel Francis. BA, Kent State U., 1974; JD, U. Pitts., 1978. Bar: Pa. 1978. Atty. Equitable Resources, Inc., Pitts., 1978-88, gen. counsel Equitable Gas Co. div., 1988-89, cons., 1989—. Mem. ABA, Fed. Energy Bar Assn., Pa. Bar Assn., Allegheny County Bar Assn., Pitts. Athletic Assn., Rivers Club (Pitts.). Office: Equitable Gas Co 420 Blvd of the Allies Pittsburgh PA 15219

KLODZINSKI, BEATRICE DAVIS, management consultant; b. Berkeley, Calif., Dec. 28, 1950; d. H. Virgil and Margie (Snowden) D. BSBA, U. Denver, 1973, MBA, 1974. Asst. adminstr. Davis Nursing Home, Inc., Denver, 1972-76; prof. Universidad De Santo Tomas, Bogota, Colombia, 1977-78; writer, translater Sintesis Economica, Bogota, 1978-79; prof. Universidad Los Andes, Bogota, 1979-80; mgr. Serviminas Ltd., Medellin and Bogota, 1978-81; prof. Eafit U., Medellin, 1982-84; pres. Performance Plus, Sacramento and Trinidad, Colo., 1986—; trainer Colo. State Dept. Health, Denver, 1975; pres. Negodiagnosticos Ltd., Medellin, 1981-85. Adv. Colo. State Legisl. Register Health/Planning Bd., Denver, 1974-75; alt. del. Denver County Rep. Convention, 1971; del. Leadership Denver, 1975. Mem. Nat. Speaker's Assn. (sec. 1986—), Sacramento Women's Network (chair com. 1986), AAUW (pres. Trinidad chpt. 1989-90), Delta Sigma Pi (pres. 1975). Office: Performance Plus Bus Cons PO Box 754 Trinidad CO 81082

KLOEPFER, MARGUERITE FONNESBECK, writer; b. Logan, Utah, Nov. 13, 1916; d. Leon and Jean (Brown) Fonnesbeck; m. Lynn William Kloepfer, Aug. 6, 1937; children: William Leon, Kenneth Lynn, Kathryn Kloepfer Ellis, Robert Alan. BS, Utah State U., 1937. Legal sec. Lynn W. Kloepfer, Atty., Ontario, Calif., 1958-74; freelance writer, novelist Ontario, Calif., 1974—. Author: Bentley, 1979, Singles Survival, 1979, But Where is Love, 1980, The Heart and the Scarab, 1981, Schatten in der Wuste, 1983; contbr. short stories to Seventeen, Women's Day, numerous others; contbr. articles on travel to profl. jours. Pres. Foothill chpt. Nat. Charity League Inc., Ontario, 1965-67, nat. pres., 1968-70; pres. Interfraternity Mother's Clubs council U. So. Calif., Los Angeles, 1971-72, mem. coordinating council, town and gown; pres. Law Aux. San Bernandio County, Calif., 1957-58, Law Aux. Calif., 1974-75. Mem. Moneytalkers Investment Club (pres. 1989). Club: Friday Afternoon (West San Bernandio County) (pres. 1986-87). Home: 306 E Hawthorne St Ontario CA 91764

KLOESMEYER, ILIANA MARISA, beverage company executive, media director; b. Harrisburg, Pa., Sept. 28, 1958; d. Jan and Sonia (Plynaer) K.; m. Bradley Thomas Kloesmeyer Wagner, Oct. 10, 1987. Student, W.Va. U., Morgantown, 1976-78; cert., Katharine Gibbs, Boston, 1978-79; student, Temple U., Phila., 1981-83. Sr. media buyer Sonder Sevitt Advt., Phila., 1983-85; mktg. dir. Cable AdNet, Malvern, Pa., 1985-86; media dir. Phila. Coca-Cola, 1986—; mem. advt. com. Red Cross, Phila., 1986. Counselor Women Organized Against Rape, Phila., 1981; com. mem. Am. Cancer Soc. Phila. Mem. Cable Advt. Bur., TV Radio Advt. Club (TV com.), Alpha Xi

Delta Alumni. Democrat. Presbyterian. Office: Phila Coca-Cola Erie Ave and G St Philadelphia PA 19134

KLONARIS, MARY, marketing executive; b. Weirton, W.Va., Dec. 22, 1928; d. Steve and Cleoniki (Xanthopoulos) Daniels; m. Sam Klonaris, July 17, 1948; children: Nikki Lynne, William Theodore. Student, Ohio State U., Columbus, 1945-47, Cleve. State U., 1971. With svc. dept. Sears Roebuck & Co., Cleve., 1948-51; sec. acctg. dept. Midland Bag Co., Cleve., 1951-54; field researcher Market Rsch. of Cleve., 1966-76; ter. mgr. Spar-Burgoyne-Mktg., Mpls., 1976-90; retail rep. Proctor & Gamble, Cin., 1976-88; pres. Market Tasks, Cleve., 1976—. Treas. St. Constantine and Helen Philoptochos, Cleve., 1987—. Mem. Am. Mtkg. Assn. Eastern Orthodox. Office: Market Task 5395 Huron Rd Lyndhurst OH 44124

KLOOS, JEANETTE DORIS BURNS, environmentalist, state official; b. La Mesa, Calif., Nov. 1, 1950; d. William Richard and Winifred Marion (Smith) Burns; m. William Carl Kloos, July 2, 1978; children: Carl William, Todd Richard. BA in Environ. Studies, U. Calif., Santa Barbara, 1972; MS, Rensselaer Poly. Inst., 1977; BS in Computer Sci., U. Tex., San Antonio, 1984. Environ. specialist Fed. Hwy. Adminstrn., Albany, N.Y., 1973-77, Boston, 1977-78, Arlington, Va., 1978; environ. specialist Fed. Hwy. Adminstrn., Washington, 1978-80, bicycle coord., 1980-81; computer programmer Check-Stop, San Antonio, 1984; environmentalist Oreg. Hwy. Div., Milwaukie, 1985—; scenic area coord. Oreg. Dept. Transp., Milwaukie, 1988—. Contbr. to profl. publs. Recipient 3E award region 1 Hwy. Div. Oreg. Dept. Transp., 1988. Mem. Nat. Assn. Environ. Profls. (cert.), Assn. for Computing Machinery, Women's Transp. Seminar (Mem. of Yr. award Portland 1988), Toastmasters, Alpha Chi. Democrat. Presbyterian. Office: Oreg Dept Transp 9002 SE McLoughlin Blvd Milwaukie OR 97222

KLOPFENSTEIN, MELINDA LEE, accountant; b. Lansing, Mich., Oct. 18, 1944; d. George Wayne and Cecil Lorena (Wilcox) Brown; m. Lee David Klopfenstein, May 28, 1966 (div. May 26, 1981); children: Mark Wayne, Susan Gail. BS in Math, Mich. State U., 1965; BBA in Acctg., Saginaw Valley State Coll., 1978. Bookkeeper Ernst and Whinney, Saginaw, Mich., 1977-79; franchise acct. Tuffy Service Ctrs., Inc., Saginaw, 1980-85, Tuffy Assocs. Corp., Saginaw, 1986; acct. R&D, Inc. doing bus. as Tuffy Muffler, Saginaw, 1986—. Editor Civic Newcomers, Saginaw, 1969. Mem. housing commn. Carrollton Twp., Mich., 1981-82; co-chair Miss Saginaw County, 1973, Luth. Social Svcs. of Mich. Ambassadors, 1988—; sec. Saginaw County Pres.'s Coun., 1988—; treas. Our Saviour Luth. Ch., Saginaw, 1983-87, fin. sec., 1987—. Mem. Mich. State U. Coll. Nat. Sci. Alumni Assn. (bd. dirs.), Jaycees (Saginaw aux. chpt., bd. dirs. 1972-75, Woman of Yr. 1975). Home: #10 Slatestone Dr Saginaw MI 48603

KLOPFER, JOANNE, optometrist; b. Sept. 7, 1954; d. Leopold E. and Fujie (Matsuo) K. BA, Cornell U., 1975; OD, Pa. Coll. Optometry, 1979; MPH, Yale U. Sch. Medicine, 1985. Lic. optometrist, Pa., N.Y., N.J., Md., Del. Fellowship in primary care, The Eye Inst. Pa. Coll. Optometry, Phila., 1979-80, chief resident, The Eye Inst., 1980-81, instr. optometry, 1981-82, asst. prof. optometry and community health, 1983-86, chmn. dept. community health and behavioral sci., 1985-89, assoc. prof. optometry and community health, 1986—; fellowship in preventive ophthalmology Wilmer Inst. of Johns Hopkins U., Balt., 1990—; faculty advisor Student Optometric Svc. to Humanity, Dominica, W.I., 1987, Lapenita, Mexico, 1990; article reviewer Optometry and Vision Sci., Washington, 1989—. Author: PUblic Health and Community Health, 1990; contbr. articles to profl. jours. Faculty advisor Beta Sigma Kappa, Phila., 1985—, Omega Epsilon Phi, Phila., 1984-88. Nominated Clin. Educator of the Yr., Student Coun., Pa. Coll. Optometry, 1989, 90; recipient rsch. grants Am. Optometric Found., Washington, 1985, 86, Ezell Fellowship grantee, 1982-83, Bro. of Yr. award Omega Epsilon Phi, 1978, Nat. Rsch. Svc. award Nat. Eye Inst. Pub. Health Svc., 1990—. Fellow Am. Acad. Optometry; mem. Assn. Rsch. in Vision and Ophthalmology, Am. Pub. Health Assn., Am. Optometric Assn., Am. Soc. Testing of Materials (F-31 com. 1987-89). Office: Johns Hopkins Hosp Dana Ctr Preventive Ophthalmology Wilmer Inst Rm 120 Baltimore MD 21205

KLOPFLEISCH, STEPHANIE SQUANCE, social services agency administrator; b. Rupert, Idaho, Dec. 21, 1940; d. William Jaynes and Elizabeth (Cunningham) Squance; B.A., Pomona Coll., 1962; M.S.W., UCLA, 1966; m. Randall Klopfleisch, June 27, 1970; children—Elizabeth, Jennifer, Matthew. Social worker, Los Angeles County, 1963-67; program dir. day care, vol. services Los Angeles County, 1968-71; div. chief children's services Dept. Public Social Services, Los Angeles County, 1971-73, dir. bur. of social services, 1973-79; chief dep. dir. Dept. Community Services, Los Angeles County, 1979—; with Area 10 Devel. Disabilities, 1981-82; bd. dirs. Los Angeles Fed. Emergency Mgmt. Act, 1985—, pres., 1987; bd. dirs. Los Angeles Shelter Partnership. Mem. Calif. Commn. on Family Planning, 1976-79; mem. Los Angeles Commn. Children's Instns., 1977-78; bd. dirs. United Way Info., 1978-79; chmn. Los Angeles County Internat. Yr. of Child Commn., 1978-79, Los Angeles Shelter Ptnrship., 1987; bd. govs. Sch. Social Welfare, UCLA, 1981-84. Mem. Nat. Assn. Social Workers, Am. Soc. Pub. Adminstrn.

KLOSE, PATSY MAE ELLEN, nursing educator; b. Sebeka, Minn., Dec. 15, 1941; d. George and Iva Louise (McFarlane) Pendergrast; m. Lemoine Harry Klose, Apr. 20, 1963; children: Stephan Craig, Allen James. Diploma, Sister's of St. Joseph Sch., 1962; BS, Moorhead State U., 1978; MS, U. Minn., 1989. Operating rm. and emergency rm. nurse Trinity Hosp., Jamestown, N.D., 1962-63; clinic nurse Jamestown Clinic, Ltd., 1963; operating rm., emergency rm. and pediatric nurse Trinity Hosp., Jamestown, 1964-65; clin. instr. N.D. State Hosp., Jamestown, 1965-87; behavioral outreach nurse Hennepin County Med. Ctr., Mpls., 1988; instr. Statewide Psychiat. Nursing Edn. Program, Jamestown, 1989—; group therapist N.D. State Hosp., Jamestown, 1989—; pre-admission screener Bock Assocs., St. Paul, 1990. Coord. for Jamestown area Dakota Radio Info. Svc., Bismarck, N.D., 1989—. Mem. Am. Nurses' Assn. (psychiat. mental health coun. 1989—), Am. Psychiat. Nurses' Assn., N.D. Nurses Assn. (com. on continuing edn. 1990-93, mem.-at-large psychiat. mental health cou. 1990-93), Task Force on 3rd Party Reimbursement (chair 1989-92), Sigma Theta Tau. Office: Statewide Psychiat Nursing Edn PO Box 1200 Bus Loop East Jamestown ND 58402-1200

KLOSTERMAN, PATRICIA ANN, sales professional; b. Flint, Mich., Dec. 16, 1959; d. Leonard Carl and Florence Josephine (Nichols) K.; m. Clyde Michael Olmstead, July 1, 1989. Student, Mich. State U.; BBA, U. Mich., 1982. Suggestion investigator Buick Motor Div., Flint, 1981-82; customer rels. specialist Buick Motor Div., 1982-83; dist. sales mgr. Buick Motor Div., Kansas City, Kans., 1984-86; dist. sales mgr. Am. Honda Motor Co., Little Rock, 1986-87, San Francisco, 1987—. Big sister, Brig Bros. & Big Sisters, Topeka, 1986; youth group counselor, St. Dominic's Ch., Benicia, Calif., 1989. Republican. Roman Catholic. Home: 731 West I St Benicia CA 94510 Office: Am Honda Motor Co Bldg 300 700 Van Ness ave Torrance CA 90502

KLOTH, RACHELL DARDEN, herbalist; b. Kinston, N.C., May 7, 1939; d. Johnnie White and Susan Winnifred (Stroud) Spychalla; m. N. Rollie Kloth; children: Jonathan, Janine. D. of Reflexology, Bernadean U., 1982; M. Herbalist, Emerson Coll., Canada, 1984. Cert. Reflexologist; Nutritional Cons. Small bus. owner Appleton, Wis., 1978—; cons. in field. Home: 2210 S 57th St West Allis WI 53219 Office: Kloth's Health House 1295 Appleton Rd Menasha WI 54952

KLOTZ, DOROTHEA GLORIA, steel sales executive; b. Bethlehem, Pa., Jan. 11, 1945; d. Harvey William and Lucy Gloria (Martucci) Klotz. BA, Moravian Coll., 1966; postgrad., Lehigh U., 1975-78. Adminstrv. asst. Lehigh U., Bethlehem, Pa., 1974-76; customer svc. rep. Bethlehem Steel Corp., 1976—. Bd. dirs. S.E. Neighborhood Ctr., Bethlehem, 1990—, Community Action Com., 1982—. Recipient Community Svc. award Pa. State Legislature, 1984. Mem. Am. Bus. Women's Assn. (pres. 1988, Woman of Yr. 1986), Bethlehem Bus. and Profl. Women (v.p. 1989-90), AAUW (pres., Woman of Yr. 1984). Democrat. Roman Catholic. Office: Bethlehem Steel Corp 701 E 3d St Bethlehem PA 18016

KLOTZ, FLORENCE, costume designer; b. N.Y.C.; d. Philip K. and Hannah Kraus. Student, Parsons Sch. Design, 1941. Designer: Broadway shows Take Her She's Mine, 1960, Never Too Late, 1962, Nobody Loves An Albatross, 1963, On An Open Roof, 1963, Owl and the Pussycat, 1964, One by One, 1964, Mating Dance, 1965, The Best Laid Plans, 1966, Superman, 1966, Paris Is Out, 1970, Norman Is That You, 1970, Legends, Follies, 1971 (Drama Desk award, Tony award), A Little Night Music, 1973 (Drama Desk award, Tony award), Side By Side Sondheim, 1975, Pacific Overtures, 1976 (Drama Desk award, Tony award, Los Angeles Critic Circle award), On the 20th Century, 1978 (Drama Desk award), Broadway Broadway, Dancin' In The Streets, 1982, Grind, 1984 (Tony award), Jerry's Girls, 1985; (ballet-jazz opus) Antique Epagraph, N.Y.C.; Broadway musicals Rags, 1986, Roza, 1987; Ctr. prodns. Carousel, 1956, Oklahoma, 1956, Annie Get Your Gun, 1956, 4 Baggatelle; movies Something for Everyone, 1969, A Little Night Music, 1976 (Oscar nomination, Los Angeles Critic Circle award); ice shows John Curry's Ice Dancing, 1979; Broadway musical A Doll's Life; ballet 8 Lines, 1986, I'm Old Fashioned (Jerome Robbins), Ives Songs (Jerome Robbins, City of Angels, 1989 (Outer Critics Circle award), Kiss of the Spider Woman, 1989. Democrat. Home: 1050 Park Ave New York NY 10028

KLUBNIKIN, KHERYN, environmental policy analyst; b. L.A., July 21, 1951; d. John and Irene Klubnikin. BS in Biolog. Scis., U. So. Calif., 1973; MS in Environ. Studies with program honors, Calif. State U., Fullerton, 1979. Writer/intern EPA, Washington, 1977; coastal planner Resources Agy. County Planning, Ventura, Calif., 1979-80; natural resource specialist Santa Monica Mountains Nat. Recreation Area Nat. Pk. Svc., Woodland Hills, Calif., 1981-85; project leader for Patuxent Wildlife Rsch. Ctr., U.S. Fish and Wildlife Svc., Md., 1985-87; coord. western environ. issues Nat. Pk. Svc., Washington, 1987—; liaison to President's Task Force on Outer Continental Shelf Leasing and Devel. Mem. Leadership Am. Mem. Soc. for Conservaton Biology, Women in Govt. Rels., LWV, George Wright Soc. (bd. dirs.). Unitarian. Office: US Nat Pk Svc 18th and C Sts NW Washington DC 20013

KLUK, NADA, insurance company executive; b. Munich, Germany, Oct. 22, 1946; d. Marko and Zorka (Medic) Borkovich; m. Ronald Andrew Kluk, June 1, 1968. Lic. real estate agt., Ill. Asst. supr. Washington Nat. Ins. Co., Evanston, Ill., 1969-72, supr., 1972-74, gen. supr., 1974-75, asst. mgr., 1975-77, mgr., 1977-89, mem. mgmt. adv. coun., 1979-81, chmn. group coverages and procedures com., 1985-89, sec. group underwriting com., 1985-89, mem. 75th anniversary com., 1986; sales assoc., real estate agt. Realty Network, Inc., Chgo., 1989—. Vol. Am. Cancer Soc., Chgo., 1980-85; capt. vols. bus. div. United Way, Evanston, 1981-84. Nominee YWCA Leader Luncheon, 1979. Mem. NAFE. Democrat. Roman Catholic. Avocations: reading, walking. Office: Realty Network Inc 7062 W Higgins Chicago IL 60656

KLUMPNER, INGER OLSON, psychology educator; b. Alafors, Starkarr, Sweden, Apr. 26, 1925; d. Joel Olaf and Elsa Maria (Sand) Olson; m. George Henry Klumpner, June 16, 1946; children: George Harold, James Henry. Student, Northwestern U., 1943-44; PhB, U. Chgo., 1946, MA, 1949, postgrad., 1961-64, 67-68; cert., Inst. for Psychoanalysis, Chgo. Instr. Morton Coll., Cicero, Ill., 1969-73; lectr. Roosevelt U., Chgo., 1973-77, Elmhurst (Ill.) Coll., 1977, Rosary Coll., River Forest, Ill., 1977-79; asst. prof. psychology Rosary Coll., 1979—; counselor Orthogenic Sch., U. Chgo., 1946. Active various charitable orgns. in past. Lutheran. Office: Rosary College 7900 W Division St River Forest IL 60305

KLYCE, DOROTHY JEAN WALLECK, utility executive; b. Pitts., Oct. 8, 1942; d. Albert John and Mae (O'Donnell) Walleck; m. Stephen D. Klyce (div.); children: Alexander, Victoria, Nathaniel. BA, Smith Coll., 1964. With La. Power & Light Co., New Orleans, 1980—, mgr. community rels. dept., 1986-89, dir. pub. rels. dept., 1989-90, v.p. pub. rels., 1990—; mem. La. Literacy Task Force, Baton Rouge. Bd. dirs. Girl Scouts U.S., New Orleans. Mem. Women in Communications (Communicator of the Yr. 1989), Inc., Pub. Rels. Soc. Am., La. Press Assn., La. Assn. Broadcasters, LWV (bd. dirs. New Orleans chpt.), Press Club of New Orleans (Community Svc. award 1988). Home: 3800 Mimosa New Orleans LA 70131 Office: La Power & Light Co 317 Baronne St New Orleans LA 70112

KNAFO, DANIELLE SYLVIA, clinical psychologist; b. Morocco, Mar. 18, 1953; came to U.S., 1953; d. Maurice and Rosine (Cohen) Knafo. BA magna cum laude, Tel Aviv U., Israel, 1977, MA magna cum laude, 1979; PhD, CUNY, 1987; postdoctoral student in psychoanalysis, NYU, 1987—. Clin. psychology intern Bronx (N.Y.) Psychiatric Ctr., 1984-85; dir. psychol. svcs. St. Barnabas Hosp., Bronx, 1986-88; pvt. practice N.Y.C., 1987—; psychodiagnostic con. Holliswood (N.Y.) Hosp., 1988-89; supervising psychologist Bronx-Lebanon Hosp. Ctr., 1988-90; adj. lectr. CCNY, Bklyn. Coll., 1982-83; adj. lectr. New Sch. for Social Rsch., 1983-84, mem. faculty Eugene Lang Coll., 1989—; clin. supr. grad. psychology program Pace U., 1988—; reviewer Hosp. and Community Psychiatry, Washington, 1988—; cons. Telecounsel on Abnormal Psychology, PBS. Author: Egon Schiele: A Self in Creation, 1989. Counselor St. Vincent's Hosp. Rape Crisis Program, 1981-84; dir. Suicide Prevention Program, Bronx, 1986-88. Fellow NIMH, 1981, BRA Found. fellow, 1987. Mem. Am. Psychol. Assn., N.Y. Acad. Scis., World Fed. for Mental Health, Internat. Psychohistory Assn. (rsch. assoc.), Israel Psychol. Assn., Women Psychoanalysts (study group). Office: Private Practice 305 West End Ave #5E New York NY 10023

KNAPP, BARBARA CURTIS, marketing and public relations executive, editor; b. Perryopolis, Pa., Nov. 1, 1933; d. Earle Edwin and Elizabeth Boyd (Knox) Curtis; m. Peter Osborn Knapp, June 11, 1957; children: Curtis Merriam, Elizabeth Evelyn. B.S., Kent State U., 1955. Asst. dir. co. history project McGraw-Hill Pub. Co., N.Y.C., 1955-57; sec., dir. law sch. devel. U. Pa., Phila., 1957-59; docent coordinator Cin. Art Mus., 1974-75; dir. pub. relations and mkgt. Dayton Philharmonic Orch. (Ohio), 1979-90, ret., 1990; dir. Dayton Philharmonic Women's Assn., 1976-89. Editor, writer Rhythm and News, 1980-90; book reviewer Dayton Daily News. Assoc. bd. dirs. Dayton Art Inst., 1983-88; bd. dirs. Jr. League Cin., 1972-74; council mem. Jr. League Phila., 1969-71; bd. dirs. New Neighbors League Dayton, 1976. Mem. Am. Women in Radio and TV (pres. Dayton chpt. 1987-88), Women in Communications, Inc., Cardinal Key, Laurels, Alpha Psi Omega. Episcopalian. Home: 1341 Laurelwood Rd Dayton OH 45409

KNAPP, CONSTANCE ANNE, management consultant, educator; b. N.Y.C., Jan. 25, 1948; d. Harold Thomas and Jacqueline (Devine) C. BA, SUNY, New Paltz, 1969; MBA, Fordham U., 1975. Cert. systems profl. Actuarial trainee Home Ins. Co., N.Y.C., 1969-72; tech. rep. Rapidata, Inc., N.Y.C., 1972-74; internat. mgmt. cons. Equitable Life Assurance Soc., N.Y.C., 1974-79; mgr. fin. info. systems N.Y. Times, N.Y.C., 1979-83; owner C.A. Knapp Enterprises, Bklyn., 1984—; asst. prof. Pace U., 1985—; student liaison Assn. for Systems Mgmt., N.Y.C., 1987-89. Contbr. articles to profl. jours. Mem. Inst. Mgmt. Scis., Assn. for Computing Machinery, Assn. for Systems Mgmt. (Outstanding Svc. award 1988), NAFE. Democrat. Mem. United Ch. of Christ. Office: 591 10th St #3 Brooklyn NY 11215

KNAPP, JEAN CARMEN, home economist; b. Denver, Feb. 15, 1921; d. Harvey Iven and Rosamond Lillian (Wheaton) Myers; m. Walter Edward Knapp, Dec. 4, 1943; children: Vicki Jean, Gregory Allen. BS in Home Econs., Western Mich. U., 1943. Cert. sec. and elem. sch. tchr. Tchr. homemaking and English Lawrence (Mich.) Pub. Schs., 1943-44; tchr. homemaking Benton Harbor (Mich.) Schs., 1955-60; chmn., co-chmn. Homemakers in Home Econs., 1980. Nat. rep. United Meth. Women, 1975, dist. sec.; pres. local PTA, city PTA; coun., del. Mich. Rep. Conv. Mem. AAUW, Econ. Club. Mem. Christian Reformed Ch. Home: 1223 Miami Rd Benton Harbor MI 49022

KNAPP, MARILEE TIBERIO, educator; b. Pitts., May 1, 1942; d. Gilbert F. and Isabel (Altier) Tiberio; children: Lauren, Andrew. BS in Bus. Edn., U. Dayton, 1964; MS in Bus. Edn., U. Pitts., 1968; postgrad., Okla. State U., 1982, Wayne State U., 1987—, U. Wis., Eau Clair, 1989. Instr. Duffs Bus. Inst., Pitts., 1966-67, Keystone Oaks High Sch., Pitts., 1967-69, Valley Point High sch., Dalton, Ga., 1973-74, Bradford Sch., Pitts., 1974-76; sales assoc. Twin Pines Real Estate, Mt. Lebanon, Pa., 1976-78; co-op coord., instr., office occupations coord. Mott (Mich.) Community Coll., 1985—; presenter seminar Citizens Bank, Flint, Mich., 1987; presenter Co-op Trends Conf., 1988; organized profl. image workshop, 1989; chairperson Flint Co-op Consortium, 1988—; co-chmn. drive-in co-op workshop GMI Engring. & Mgmt. Inst., 1989. Designer brochures, 1985—. Adv. Com. Genesee area Skill Ctr., Flint, Mich., 1986—; fundraiser Flint United Way, 1986. Recipient "Talented Tenth" award, "Your Spl." award Mott Community Coll. Mem. Nat. Bus. Edn., Midwest Coop. Edn. Assn., NAFE, Coop Edn. Assn., Mich. Coun. Coop. Edn., Flint Women's Forum (edn. chmn. 1987—), South Hills Coll. Club, Toastmaster's Internat. (edn. v.p.). Republican. Roman Catholic. Office: Mott Community Coll 1401 E Court St Flint MI 48503

KNAPP, MILDRED FLORENCE, social worker; b. Detroit, Apr. 15, 1932; d. Edwin Frederick and Florence Josephine (Antaya) K.; B.B.A., U. Mich., 1954, M.A. in Community and Adult Edn. (Mott Found. fellow 1964), 1964, M.S.W. (HEW grantee 1966), 1967. Dist. dir. Girl Scouts Met. Detroit, 1954-63; planning asst. Council Social Agencies Flint and Genessee County, 1965; sch. social worker Detroit public schs., 1967—; field instr. grad. social workers. Mem. alumnae bd. govs. U. Mich., 1972-75, scholarship chmn., 1969-70, 76-80, chmn. spl. com. women's athletics, 1972-75, class agt. fund raising Sch. Bus. Adminstrn., 1978-79; mem. Founders Soc. Detroit Inst. Art, 1969—, Friends Children's Mus. Detroit, 1978—, Women's Assn., Detroit Symphony Orch., 1982-89; vol. Coun. Detroit Symphony Orch., 1990—; trustee, fin. chmn. Children's Mus. Recipient various certs. appreciation. Mem. Nat. Assn. Social Workers, Acad. Cert. Social Workers, Nat. Community Edn. Assn. (charter), Outdoor Edn. and Camping Council (charter), Mich. Sch. Social Workers Assn. (pres. 1980-81), Detroit Sch. Social Workers Assn. (past pres.), Detroit Assn. U. Mich. Women (pres. 1980-82), Detroit Fedn. Tchrs. Methodist. Home: 702 Lakepointe Grosse Pointe Park MI 48230 Office: 8401 Woodward Ave Rm 211 Detroit MI 48202

KNAPP, NANCY HAY, mental health administrator; b. Cleve., June 2, 1922; d. Henry Homer and Aurore Louise (LaCroix) Hay; m. Richard Dominick Knapp, Sept. 11, 1955; 1 child, Pamela Hay. BA, Hunter Coll., 1957; MS in Edn., U. Pa., 1971, EdD, 1987. Nat. cert. counselor; clin. assoc. Am. Bd. Med. Psychotherapists; cert. prevention specialist. Career and edn. counselor Johnson O'Connor Rsch. Found., N.Y.C., 1950-53; counselor, report writer The Pers. Lab., N.Y.C., 1953-63; cons., Chapel Hill, N.C., 1963-65, Phila., 1965-69; dir. profl. svcs. Crossroads Career Planning Corp., Phila., 1978-80; counseling dir., resources for women U. Pa., Phila., 1972-78; dir. consultation and edn. Crozer-Chester Med. Ctr., Upland, Pa., 1980—, chmn. tng. com., 1985—; mem. faculty Main Line Sch. Night, Ardmore, Pa., 1978-80; trainer Pa. Dept. Health, Harrisburg, 1982-85. Author: (tng. manuals) Prevention: Drug Misuse, 1983, Growing, Together, 1985. Bd. dirs. Resources for Women, U. Pa., Phila., 1976-80; mem. steering com. Coalition for Edn./Placement of Women, Phila., 1976-78, coord., 1978-80; mem. Chester (Pa.) Vocat./Ednl. Outreach, 1980-82, dir., 1982-84. Recipient Community Devel. award Pa. Cons. Edn. Coun., 1981; grantee Pa. Dept. Health, 1981, 83. Mem. APA (assoc.), ASCD, Cons. Assn. Greater Phila., Phi Delta Kappa. Home: 326 Sprague Rd Narberth PA 19072

KNAPP, THERESA DANIEL, finance professional; b. Dansville, N.Y., Feb. 19, 1926; d. Walter Caleb and Theresa Margaret (Bacon) K. BS, Nazareth Coll., 1950; MS, SUNY, Albany, 1956. Joined Sisters of St. Joseph of Rochester, Roman Cath. Ch. Bookkeeper Foster-Wheeler Corp., Dansville, N.Y., 1943-44; tchr. bus. edn. Nazareth Acad. High Sch., Rochester, N.Y., 1950-56; tchr. bus. edn. St. Agnes High Sch., Rochester, 1956-67, student activities coord., 1972-75; assoc. chaplain Rochester Inst. Tech., 1967-72; coord. CETA Manpower Program, Geneseo, N.Y., 1975-76; asst. dir. student activities Nazareth Coll. of Rochester, 1976-83, payroll supr., 1983—; mem. rsch. grant com. Nazareth Coll. of Rochester, 1988—; local treas. Sisters of St. Joseph, Rochester, 1988—; treas., bus. mgr. Stage III Prodns., Inc., Rochester, 1976-84. Mem. choral group White House Christmas Tree League, 1973. Mem. Am. Payroll Assn., Nat. Notary Assn., NAFE. Republican. Home: 4141 East Ave Rochester NY 14618 Office: Nazareth Coll of Rochester 4245 East Ave Rochester NY 14610

KNAPP, VICKY KIMBROUGH, nursing coordinator; b. Anniston, Ala., May 20, 1957; d. William E. and Marguerite (Coleman) Kimbrough; m. Harold Eugene Knapp Jr., Aug. 27, 1988. BSN, Jacksonville (Ala.) State U., 1978; MSN, U. Ala., 1982. RN, Ala. Staff nurse ICU N.E. Ala. Regional Med. Ctr., Anniston, 1978-80; staff nurse critical care unit Bapt. Med. Ctr.-Montclair, Birmingham, Ala., 1981-84, edn. coord., 1984—; instr. basic cardiac life Am. Heart Assn., Birmingham, 1984—, mem. affiliate faculty, 1985—, instr. advanced cardiac life support, 1988—. Mem. Ala. Soc. for Healthcare Edn. and Tng. of Am. Hosp. Assn., Toastmasters (pres. Birmingham chpt. 1986). Office: Bapt Med Ctr Montclair 800 Montclair Rd Birmingham AL 35213

KNAPP, VIRGINIA ESTELLA, retired educator; b. Washington, May 11, 1919; d. Bradford and Stella (White) Knapp; B.A., Tex. Tech. U., 1940; M.A., U. Tex. 1948; postgrad. Sul Ross Coll., 1950, Stephen F. Austin U., 1964-68. Tchr. journalism, high schs., Silverton, Tex., 1940-41, Electra, Tex., 1941-42, Joinerville, Tex., 1942-60, Carthage, Tex., 1961-69; tchr. history and journalism Longview (Tex.) High Sch., 1969-80; instr. Trinity U., San Antonio, summer 1972; fellowship tchr. Wall St. Jour., Tex. A&M U., College Station, summers 1964-67. Chmn., Rusk County (Tex.) Hist. Commn., 1980—. Recipient Wall St. Jour. award Outstanding Journalism Tchrs. of Yr., 1965-66; Trail Blazer award Tex. High Sch. Press Assn., 1980; Woman of Yr. award, 1983. Mem. Tex. State Tchrs. Assn., Classroom Tchrs. Assn., Tex. Assn. Jour. Dirs., Rusk County Heritage Assn., Rusk County Hist. Commn., Women in Communications (pres. Longview chpt. 1972-74, Service award 1975), Tex. Press Women, DAR. Episcopalian. Contbr. hist. writing to Ala. Rev., Progressive Farmer, Rusk County C. of C. Brochure, Rusk County Heritage, numerous others. Home: 321 College Ave Henderson TX 75652 Office: 514 N High Henderson TX 75652

KNAPPENBERGER, DOROTHY LAVINA, retired educational supervisor; b. Knox, Pa., Mar. 31, 1906; d. Charles Ervin and Edith Gertrude (DeLoe) K. AA, Stephens Coll., Columbia, Mo., 1924; BA, U. Mo., 1926; MA, Columbia U., 1930. Cert. tchr. Tchr. English and history High Sch., Kiefer, Okla., 1926-27; tchr. English High Sch., Altus, Okla., 1927-29; tchr. English, dir. activities Roosevelt Jr. High Sch., Tulsa, 1930-43; tchr. English and journalism Daniel Webster High Sch., Tulsa, 1943-56; supr. secondary English Tulsa Pub. Schs., 1956-71. Mem. The Gillies-Svc. Orgn., Gilcrease Mus. History and Art, Tulsa, 1980—. Mem. AAUW (hon. life, historian 1990-92), Nat. Coun. Tchrs. English, NEA, Okla. Coun. Tchrs. English, Pilot Club Tulsa (pres. 1972-73). Presbyterian.

KNAUB, CHARLOTTE JUANITA, public health nurse; b. Laurel, Mont., May 15, 1933; d. Clyde Elihu and Wilhelmina Harriet (Goyer) Decker; divorced, 1975; children: Jeffrey Scott, Jonathan Clyde, Laurie Jan. Diploma in nursing, Mont. State U., 1955, BSN, 1968. Clin. nurse/supr. Deaconess and St. Vincent Hosps., Billings, Mont., 1956-67; pub. health nurse Yellowstone County (Mont.) Health Dept., Billings, 1968-71; migrant health project supr., nursing cons. Mont. Dept. Health/USPHS, Billings, Helena, 1971-79; nurse epidemiologist Internat. Rescue Com., Thailand, 1979-80; public health team leader Nat. Coun. Chs., N.Y.C., Somalia, 1981; public health nurse/educator/adminstr. WHO/W. Pacific Regional Office, W. Pacific countries, 1981-89; mktg. assoc. Richard James Realtors, Kent, Wash., 1990; supr. King County Dept. of Health, Seattle, 1990—; cons. World Concern, Seattle, 1980, UN Health Care, Bangkok, Thailand, 1989, Tom Dooley Found., 1989. Contbr. to books and manuals in field. Co-organizer United Fund, Laurel, Mont., chmn. Mont. Friendship Force, Helena, 1977-78. Mem. Internat. Coun. Nurses, UN Civil Servants Assn., Nat. League Nurses, Am. Pub. Health Assn., Mont. State U. Alumni, Wash. State Bd. Realtors. Home: 10210 239th St SE 28 Kent WA 98032

KNAUER, NANCY J., lawyer; b. Phila., July 27, 1961; d. Wilhelm F. Knauer and Barbara J. (Fields) Flaherty. BA in History cum laude, U. Pa., 1981, JD, 1984. Bar: Pa. 1984. Assoc. Ballard, Spahr, Andrews & Ingersoll, Phila., 1984—; mem. faculty Pa. Bar Inst. Legal Practice Series, Harrisburg, 1987—; lectr. Temple U. Sch. Law Grad. Tax Program, Phila., 1988—. Bd. dirs., Pres. Knauer Found. for Hist. Preservation, Phila., 1987—; bd. dirs., asst. sec. Independence Hall Assn., Phila., 1988—. Mem. ABA, Pa. Bar Assn., Phila. Bar Assn. Office: Ballard, Spahr et al 30 S 17th St Philadelphia PA 19103

KNAUER, VELMA STANFORD, retired savings and loan executive; b. Pottstown, Pa., July 4, 1918; d. Chester Miller and Pearl Fretz (Miller) Stanford. Student pub. schs.; m. Joseph Daniel Knauer, Feb. 17, 1940; children: Joseph Daniel, Susan Velma Knauer Metz. With U.S. Axle Co., Inc., Pottstown, 1936-45; with First Fed. Savs. & Loan Assn., Pottstown, 1953-88, contr., 1953-88, asst. treas., 1953-62, asst. sec., 1962-75, treas., 1976-89, ret., 1989. Mem. Am. Soc. Profl. and Exec. Women. Home: 970 Feist Ave Pottstown PA 19464

KNECHT, JULIA ANN, firefighter, paramedic; b. Bayshore, N.Y., July 3, 1959; d. Thomas Francis and Patricia Adele (Lamberta) K. Student, Suffolk County Community Coll., Selden, N.Y., 1978-79, Daytona (Fla.) Community Coll., 1981-83, Seminole County Community Coll., Sanford, Fla., 1984—. Paramedic Flagler County Ambulance Service, Bunnell, Fla., 1983-84, Herndon Ambulance Service, Orlando, Fla., 1984; firefighter, paramedic Seminole County Fire Dept., Sanford, Fla., 1984—; reserve paramedic Daytona Beach Fire Dept., 1983-85; paramedic part time Rural Metro Ambulance Service, Orlando, 1986—. Firefighter, paramedic Osteen (Fla.) Vol. Fire Dept., 1986—. Republican. Presbyterian. Home: 2499 Tipton Dr Deltona FL 32738

KNEE, RUTH IRELAN (MRS. JUNIOR K. KNEE), social worker, health care consultant; b. Sapulpa, Okla., Mar. 21, 1920; d. Oren M. and Daisy (Daubin) Irelan; m. Junior K. Knee, May 29, 1943 (dec. Oct. 21, 1981). BA, U. Okla., 1941, cert. social work, 1942; MA, U. Chgo., 1945. Psychiat. social worker, asst. supr. Ill. Psychiat. Inst., U. Ill. at Chgo., 1943-44; psychiat. social worker USPHS Employee Health Unit, Washington, 1944-46, chief psychiat. social worker, 1946-49; psychiat. social work assoc. Army Med. Ctr., Walter Reed Army Hosp., Washington, 1949-54; psychiat. social work cons. HEW, Region III, Washington, 1955-56; with NIMH, Chevy Chase, Md., 1956-72; chief mental health care adminstrn. br. USPHS, 1967-72, assoc. dep. adminstr. Health Svcs. and Mental Health Adminstrn., 1972-73, dep. dir. Office of Nursing Home Affairs, 1973-74; long-term mental health care cons.; mem. com. on mental health and illness of elderly HEW, 1976-77; mem. panel on legal and ethical issues Pres.'s Commn. on Mental Health, 1977-78; liaison mem. Nat. Adv. Mental Health Coun., 1977-81. Mem. editorial bd. Health and Social Work, 1979-81. Bd. dirs. Hillhaven Found., 1975-86, Cathedral Coll. of the Laity, 1988—, Washington Nat. Cathedral, 1988—. Fellow Am. Pub. Health Assn. (sec. mental health sect. 1968-70, chmn. 1971-72), Am. Orthopsychiat. Assn. (life), Gerontol. Soc. Am., Am. Assn. Psychiat. Social Workers (pres. 1951-53); mem. Nat. Conf. Social Welfare (nat. bd. 1968-71, 2d v.p. 1973-74), Inst. Medicine/Nat. Acad. Sci. (com. study future of pub. health 1986-87), Coun. on Social Work Edn., Nat. Assn. Social Workers (sec. 1955-56, nat. dir. 1956-57, 84-86, chmn. competence study com., practice and knowledge com. 1963-71), Acad. Cert. Social Workers, Am. Pub. Welfare Assn., DAR, U. Okla. Assocs., Women's Nat. Dem. Club, Phi Beta Kappa (assoc. 1985—), Psi Chi. Address: 8809 Arlington Blvd Fairfax VA 22031

KNERLY, MARY JOHNSON, service company executive, business seminar developer; b. Cleve., Feb. 5, 1925; d. Lawrence Redfield and Margaret (Geltz) Johnson; m. Stephen J. Knerly, Sept. 20, 1944; children: Margit Anne Knerly Daley, Stephen J. Jr., Mary Ellen Knerly Kosicki. Student, Lake Erie Coll., Painesville, Ohio, 1942-44; BA, Case Western Res. U., 1946, postgrad., 1948-49. Nursery sch. tchr. Bingham Day Nursery, Cleve., 1945-46; book reviewer Cleve. Press newspaper, 1946-62; ednl. cons. The Lakewood (Ohio) Found., 1957-65; v.p. The Fairmount Theatre of the Deaf, Cleve., 1978-81, pres., 1981-84; pres. Service Service Inc., Cleve., 1984—; owner Beaconhill Ltd., Cleve., 1984—; part-time counselor Svc. Corps Ret. Execs., Cleve., 1987—; bd. dirs. Lake County History Ctr. Columnist The Business Score, Sun Newspapers, Cleve., 1987. Pres. Cleve. Gallery Group, 1960-70; bd. dirs. Cleve. Music Sch. Settlement, 1961—, Cleve. Ballet, 1977-84; mem. exec. com. The Singing Angels, Cleve., 1967—. Mem. Am. Womens' Econ. Devel. Corps, Nat. Assn. Female Execs., Women Bus. Owners Assn., Western Res. Archtl. Historians (pres. 1981-83). Republican. Clubs: City, Twentieth Century, Mid-Day. Office: Service Service Inc 11428 Cedar Ave Rm C-1 Cleveland OH 44106

KNERLY, VICKY W., sales administrator; b. Syracuse, N.Y., Dec. 11, 1961; d. Garry Richard and Barbara Ann (Ward) Wood; m. Stephen R. Knerly, Feb. 28, 1988. AS with honors, Cen. City Bus. Inst., Syracuse, 1984; student, SUNY, Albany, 1981, Fla. Internat. U. Sales adminstr. Bush Klein Realty, Inc., Miami, Fla.; sr. administrv. aide Tampa (Fla.) Electric Co.; legal sec., systems adminstr. Stagg, Hardy & Yerrid, P.A., Tampa; bd. dirs. Compass Project, Inc. Recipient Young Career Woman award Westshore Midday Bus. and Profl. Women. Mem. NAFE, NOW. Democrat. Office: 150 W Flagler St Ste 1500 Miami FL 33130

KNERR, ELIZABETH LORRAINE, computer company executive, educator; b. Three Hills, Alta., Can., June 23, 1949; came to U.S., 1956; d. Bertram Leonard and Edith Covell (McKee) Brandon; children: Cassandra Jo, Shelly Beth; m. Frederic John Knerr, May 21, 1988. Student, Rockmont Coll., 1967-70, Millersville (Pa.) U., 1981-85, Pa. State U., 1988-89. Office mgr. Farm Credit Assn., Lancaster, Pa., 1977-85; dir. tng. The Office Works, Lancaster, 1985-90; pres. PC Focus, Lancaster, 1990—; pvt. practice piano tchr., Denver, 1971-74; youth chair dir. Ch. of the Brethen, Quarryville, Pa., 1987-88; pres. Wordperfect Users Group, Lancaster, 1990—. Mem. adv. bd. Sch. Dist. Lancaster, 1989—, Productivity Ctr., Cerritos, Calif., 1989-90. Mem. Am. Soc. for Tng. and Devel., NAFE, Lancaster C. of C. Republican. Home: 979 May Post Office Rd Strasburg PA 17579 Office: PC Focus 1935 Fruitville Pike #111 Lancaster PA 17601

KNEZO, GENEVIEVE JOHANNA, science and technology policy researcher; b. Elizabeth, N.J., Aug. 8, 1942; d. John and Genevieve (Sadowski) K.; 1 child, Alexandra M. A.B. in Polit. Sci., Douglass Coll., Rutgers U., 1964; M.A. in Sci., Tech. and Pub. Policy, George Washington U., 1981; grad., Nat. Def. U., 1989. With Congl. Rsch. Svc., Libr. of Congress, Washington, 1967—, specialist in sci. and tech., 1979—, head sci., rsch. and tech. sect., 1986-88. Author profl. publs. Mem. AAAS, NOW, D.C.-Brasilia Ptnrs. of Ams., Sierra Club, Phi Beta Kappa, Pi Sigma Alpha. Avocations: whitewater canoeing; hiking; gymnastics; classical music. Home: 606 Oakley Pl Alexandria VA 22302 Office: Libr of Congress Congl Rsch Svc Sci Policy Rsch Div Washington DC 20540

KNIGHT, ALICE DOROTHY TIRRELL, state legislator; b. Manchester, N.H., July 14, 1903; d. Nathan Arthur and Clara (Stiles) Tirrell; m. Norman Knight, Nov. 15, 1952. B.A., U. N.H., 1925, postgrad., 1933; postgrad. Boston U., 1941-42. Tchr. Newton Falls (N.Y.) High Sch., 1925-26; prin. Oswegatchie (N.Y.) Union Sch., 1926-27, Bartlett Sch., Goffstown, N.H., 1932-35; home lighting specialist Pub. Svc. Co. N.H., Manchester, 1935-39; tchr. merchandising Mt. Ida Jr. Coll., Newton Centre, Mass., 1939-45; home svc. dir. Boyd Corp., Portland, Maine, 1945-47; dist. home economist Frigidaire Sales Corp., Boston, 1948-64; mem. N.H. Ho. of Reps., 1967-74, 76-78, 80—; rep to N.H. Gen. Ct., 1967—; mem. joint legis. com. on elderly affairs, 1983—; pres. Greater Manchester Community Concert Assn., 1985-87; co-chmn. Goffstown Bicentennial Com. of the Constn., 1986—. Mem. budget com. Town of Goffstown, 1966-72; mem. Gov.'s Adv. Com. Alcoholism, 1972-73, 74-78, Statewide Health Coordinating Coun., 1977-78, N.H. Hist. Soc.; past pres. bd. dirs. Hillsborough County North Cancer Soc.; bd. dirs. N.H. Cancer Soc. Recipient award N.H. Program on Alcohol and Drug Abuse, 1971, 75, Gov.'s Recognition award Hillsborough County, 1986, Pub. Svc.award Union Pomona Grange, 1987. Mem. Nat. Home Fashions League (pres. 1957-58), Nat. Order State Legislators, Vis. Nurses Assn. (bd. dirs. Greater Manchester chpt. 1981-87), N.H. Coun. World Affairs, Nat. Grange, DAR (regent 1974-76), Nat. Order Women Legislators (treas. 1968-71), Manchester Bus. and Profl. Women (pres. 1972-74), Nat. Soc. New Eng. Women, Order Eastern Star (life), Soroptomist (life, Boston), Goffstown Unity Club, Goffstown Garden Club (pres. 1976-78), Goffstown Shirley Club (pres. 1977-78). Republican.

KNIGHT, ANNE HASKELL, technology education manager; b. Boston, Apr. 14, 1937; d. Eben Brown and Marion Moore (Raymond) Haskell; m. Lewis Emerson Knight, June 2, 1962; children: Christopher, Catherine, Julie. BA, Mt. Holyoke Coll., 1959; MAT, Yale U., 1962. Programmer electronic data processing div. Honeywell, Newton Highlands, Mass., 1959-62; programmer Computations Inc., Harvard, Mass., 1962-65; sec. Whittemore Sch. Bus. Edn. WSBE, U. N.H., Durham, N.H., 1972-74; game project dir. Univ. N.H., Durham, 1974-76, computer specialist, Computer Svcs., 1976-86; mgr. edn. svcs. Acad. Computing Univ. N.H., Durham, 1978-85, mgr. microcomputer resource ctr., 1985-86; instr. Golden Gate U., Newington, N.H., 1977-82, 84-85; instr. div. continuing edn. U. N.H., 1983-84; dir. adminstrv. svcs. N.H. Tech. Inst., Concord, N.H., 1986-88; mgr. tech. edn., Office for Info. Tech. Harvard U., Cambridge, Mass., 1988—. Pres. LWV, Durham, mem. planning bd., Durham, bd. dirs. Los Altas, Calif., 1966-70. Recipient grant Spaulding Potter, Univ. N.H., 1981. Mem. N.H. Assn. for Computer Edn. Statewide (pres. 1980-85, 87-88), Internat. Coun. for Computers in Edn. (bd. dirs. 1985-88, sec. 1986-87), N.Am. Simulation and Gaming Assn. (pres. 1980-82). Episcopalian. Home: 9 Meserve Rd Durham NH 03824 Office: Office Info Tech Harvard U 50 Church St Cambridge MA 02138

KNIGHT, CATHERINE ANNE, marketing professional; b. Chgo., Sept. 2, 0263; d. Charles Gray and Patricia Anne (McBarron) K. BS, Tex. Christian U., 1985. Sec. Shelton W. Greer Co., Panel Div., Houston, 1980-85; with sales Shelton W. Greer Co., Panel Div., Austin, Tex., 1985-86; sales, office mgr. shelton Greer Co., Panel Div., Austin, Tex., 1986-87; regional sales mgr. Shelton Greer Co., Panel Div., Dallas; v.p., mktg. CKA Enterprises, Inc., Arlington, Tex., 1988--; bd. dirs., v.p. CKA Enterprises, Inc., Arlington, 1988--; ind. beauty cons. Mary Kay Cosmetics, Inc., Dallas. Mem. NAFE, Constrn. Specification Inst., Nat. Journalism Honor Soc., Alpha Delta Pi Alumni. Republican. Roman Catholic. Home: 3001 Ave K East #111-c Grand Prairie TX 75050 Office: CKA Enterprises Inc 611 Ryan Plaza Dr #700 Arlington TX 76011

KNIGHT, GLADYS (GLADYS MARIA KNIGHT), singer; b. Atlanta, May 28, 1944; d. Merald, Sr. and Elizabeth (Woods) K.; m. Barry Hankerson, Oct. 1974 (div. 1979); 1 son, Shanga; children from previous marriage: Kenya, James. Grad. coll. Author: lyrics Way Back Home, others; first pub. recital, Mt. Mariah Bapt. Ch., Atlanta, 1948; toured with Morris Brown Choir, 1950-53, recitals local chs. and schs., 1950-53; winner grand prize Ted Mack's Amateur Hour 1952; jazz vocalist, Lloyd Terry Jazz Ltd., 1959-61, mem., Gladys Knight and the Pips (formerly Pips Quartet), 1953—, concert appearances in Eng., 1967, 72, 73, 76, Australia, Japan, Hong Kong, Manila, 1976; rec. artist, Brunswick, 1957-61, Fury, 1961-62, Everlast, 1963, Maxx and Bell, 1964-66, Motown, 1966-73, Buddah, Capitol, Columbia, MCA, 1988; TV appearance Charlie & Co., 1985; produced, appeared in HBO film Sisters in the Name of Love, 1986. Winner 6 gold Buddah records, 1 gold, 1 platinum Buddah album; 4 Grammy awards; named Top Female Vocalist, Blues and Soul mag. 1972; spl. award Washington City Council for inspiration to youth in city, 1972; other awards include Clio, AGVA, NAACP Image, Ebony Music, Cashbox, Billboard, Record World, Rolling Stone, Ladies Home Jour., Am. Music award (with Pips), 1984, 1988. Address: care Shakeji Inc 1589 Golden Arrow Dr Las Vegas NV 89109

KNIGHT, IDA BROWN, retired educator; b. Macon, Ga., Aug. 8, 1918; d. Morgan Cornelius and Ida (Moore) Brown; m. Dempsey Lewis Knight, Apr. 11, 1942; children: Lavera Knight Hughes, Eugene Charles. BS, Spelman Coll., 1940; MS, SUNY, Fredonia, 1958; postgrad., SUNY, 1974, U. Manchester, Eng., 1974. Cert. tchr. home econs. Clothing tchr. Bibb County Vocat. Sch., Macon, 1940-42; tchr. home econs. Ballard Normal Sch., Macon, 1943-45; elem. tchr. Jamestown (N.Y.) Pub. Schs., 1955-77. Sec. Jamestown Community Schs. Coun.; bd. dirs. Jamestown Girls Club, 1960-78. Mem. AAUW, Chautauqua County Ret. Tchrs. Assn., Delta Kappa Gamma (corr. sec. 1963-64). Home: 140 Federal Pl Jamestown NY 14701

KNIGHT, JUNE J., banking executive; b. Hampton, Va., Oct. 28, 1935; d. Junius Elliott and Maggie Rhotenal (Benton) K. Student, Am. Inst. Banking, Newport News, Va., 1955-68; grad., Sch. Bank Mgmt., Charlottesville, Va., 1970. Clk. First Nat. Bank, Newport News, Va., 1954-62; mgmt. credit dept. First & Merchants Nat. Bank, Newport News, 1962-70, asst. cashier, 1968-70; asst v.p. First & Merchants Nat. Bank, Richmond, Va., 1970-74; v.p. First & Merchants Nat. Bank, Richmond, 1974-77; sr. v.p. F&M Sovran Bank, Richmond, 1977-88; exec. officer Sovran Bank, Richmond, 1988—; v.p., dir. Benton-Knight Ltd., Hampton, Va., 1962—. Mem. Robert Morris Assocs., Nat. Assn. Bank Women.

KNIGHT, KAREN A., utility executive; b. Lincoln Park, Mich., Aug. 4, 1939; d. Frank W. and Dorothy M. (Knack) K.; m. David P. Bold, Aug. 18, 1962 (div. Dec. 1974); children: David, Edward. BS, U. N.Mex., 1974, MBA, 1974. Fin. statistician Pub. Svc. Co. of N.Mex., Albuquerque, 1975-77, sr. bus. analyst, 1977-80, dir. stockholder records, 1980-86, asst. corp. sec., 1986—. Mem. Western Securities Transfer Assn., Securities Transfer Assn., Am. Soc. Corp. Secs., Kiwanis. Office: Pub Svc Co of N Mex Alvarado Sq MS0087 Albuquerque NM 87111

KNIGHT, KATHRYN ROSS, education educator; b. Hanford, Calif., May 8, 1927; d. Hugh O. and Amy M. (Ogle) Ross; m. Thomas Lincoln Knight Jr.; children: Sue Ann Knight Hankins, Thomas Ross. Student, U. Calif., Berkeley, 1944-48; BA, Humboldt State U., 1952. Tchr. McKinleyville (Calif.) Sch. Dist., 1952-55; elem. sch. tchr. Arcata (Calif.) Elem. Sch. Dist., 1955-58; instr. English Coll. of Redwoods, Eureka, Calif., 1974-85; lectr. English Humboldt State U., Arcata, 1985—. Active Friends of the Libr. Humbolt County. Mem. AAUW, Hist. Sites Soc., Humboldt State Faculty Wives Club. Democrat.

KNIGHT, KATHY, small business owner, writer; b. Oakland, Calif., June 22, 1950; d. William Pell Bruns and Doris Diana (Koofman)Burrell; m. Paul C. LoCascio, Apr. 29, 1967 (div. Jan. 1979). Student, Radio Electronic Tech. Sch., 1965-67, Albert Merrill Computer Sch., 1988—. Owner, dispatcher At Your Service Limousine, N.Y.C., 1979-87; v.p., art dir. Golden Sphinx Records, N.Y.C., 1980—; financier Recording Project- UFO, N.Y.C., 1980; pres., owner Knight Mfg., N.Y.C., 1987—; mgmt. asst. Curtis Knight Mgmt. & Prodn. Co., N.Y.C., 1976—; assoc. producer Cosmic Prodns., N.Y.C., 1987-88; adminstrv. credit asst. St. Martin's Press, N.Y.C., 1988—; cons. Documentary Jimi Hendrix. Artist for various album covers and posters. Vol. Am. Heart Assn.; mem. Rep. Nat. Com., 1987. Mem. Am. Mus. Natural History, Nat. Audubon Soc., Nat. Arbor Day Found., Nat. Assn. Female Exec., Am. Film Inst. Mayan Order, Christian Children's Fund. Mem. Worldwide Ch. God. Office: St Martin's Press 175 Fifth Ave New York NY 10010

KNIGHT, LAURIE JEAN, bank official; b. Colorado Springs, Colo., July 31, 1963; d. Billie Edward and Violet Imogene (Sandefer) Tillerson; m. Todd Alan Knight, Apr. 20, 1985; children: Rachel Nicole, Kyle Matthew. Student, Am. Inst. Banking, Valparaiso, Fla., 1987. Asst. collection mgr. Vanguard Bank & Trust, Valparaiso, 1986—. Named Outstanding Banker-Educator, Okaloosa-Walton Community Coll., 1989. Mem. Am. Inst. Banking (v.p. edn. Okaloosa County chpt. 1984-89, pres. 1990—), Niceville-Valparaiso C. of C. Home: 318 Seminole St Fort Walton Beach FL 32548 Office: AIB care 23 S John Sims Pkwy Valparaiso FL 32580

KNIGHT, MARGARETT LEE, lawyer, editor; b. Newtown, Ind., Jan. 3, 1923; d. Charles Oscar and Edna (Pace) Smith; m. Robert Cook Knight, June 20, 1961. LL.B., Ind. U., 1945, J.D., 1965; A.B., Mills Coll., 1953; LL.M., Yale U., 1955. Bar: Ind. 1945. Dep. atty. gen. Ind. Home: 1318 Hoover Ln Indianapolis IN 46260 Office: Atty Gen 219 State House Indianapolis IN 46204

KNIGHT, MARGO HAUCK, university official; b. St. Louis, June 7, 1954; d. Victor B. and Margaret (Case) Hauck; m. David Knight, Oct. 26, 1986. BA, Macalester Coll., 1975. With Mfg. Data Systems, Inc., Ann Arbor, Mich., 1975-80; rsch. asst. Tayloe-Murphy Inst., Colgate Darden Grad. Sch. Bus., U. Va., Charlottesville, 1980-8l, dir. rsch. Devel. Office, 198l-82; dir. rsch. Office Alumni and Univ. Rels., Georgetown U., Washington, 1982—. Mem. Am. Prospect Rsch. Assn.

KNIGHT, MARY ANN, secondary school educator; b. Dubuque, Iowa, Nov. 5, 1944; d. Harold V. and Grace C. (Riley) McMahon; m. George Everett Knight, June 10, 1967; children: Michelle, Suzanne, Thomas. BA in English, Clarke Coll., Dubuque; MA, SUNY, New Paltz. Cert. in English edn., N.Y., N.J. Journalist Advertiser-Photo News, Warwick, N.Y., 1974-80; tchr. English St. Stephen's Sch., Warwick, 1980-82; tutor in composition Warwick, 1982-84; tchr. writing SUNY, New Paltz, 1984-86; tchr. English Goshen (N.Y.) High Sch., 1987—. Trustee Albert Wisner Pub. Library, Warwick, 1974-81. Mem. AAUW (past officer), Sigma Tau Delta. Roman Catholic. Home: 10 Lakeview Dr Warwick NY 10990 Office: Goshen High Sch Scotchtown Ave Goshen NY 10924

KNIGHT, SHIRLEY, actress; b. Goessel, Kans., July 5, 1936; d. Noel Johnson and Virginia (Webster) K.; m. John R. Hopkins; children: Kaitlin, Sophie. D.F.A., Lake Forest Coll., 1978. Actress theatre and films. Theater debut in Look Back in Anger, Pasadena (Calif.) Playhouse, 1958, N.Y.C. debut in Journey to the Day, 1963; other N.Y.C. theater appearances include The Three Sisters, 1964, Rooms, 1966, We Have Always Lived in the Castle, 1966, The Watering Place, 1969, Kennedy's Children, 1975 (Tony award), Happy End, 1977; with Bristol (Eng.) Old Vic Theatre in And People All Around, 1967; other appearances in Eng. include A Touch of the Poet, 1970, Antigone, 1971, Economic Necessity, 1973; other U.S. theater appearances include A Streetcar Named Desire, Princeton, N.J., 1976, Happy End, N.Y.C., 1977, Landscape of the Body, Chgo., then N.Y.C., 1977, A Lovely Sunday for Creve Coeur, Charleston, S.C., then N.Y.C., 1979, Losing Time, N.Y.C., 1979, I Won't Dance, Buffalo, 1980, Come Back Little Sheba, N.Y.C., 1984, Women Heroes, N.Y.C., 1986, The Depot, N.Y.C., 1987; film appearances include Five Gates to Hell, 1959, The Dark at the Top of the Stairs, 1960, Sweet Bird of Youth, 1962, House of Women, 1962, Flight from Ashiya, 1964, The Group, 1966, Petulia, 1966, Dutchman, 1967, The Rain People, 1969, The Counterfeit Killer, 1970, Juggernaut, 1974, Beyond the Poseidon Adventure, 1979, Endless Love, 1981, The Sender, 1982; TV films include The Outsider, 1967, Shadow Over Elveron, 1968, Friendly Persuasion, 1975, Medical Story, 1975, Return to Earth, 1976, The Defection of Simas Kudirka, 1978, Champions: A Love Story, 1979, Playing for Time, 1980, With Intent to Kill, 1984. Active Com. for Handgun Control, nat. civil rights orgns., worker for peace. Recipient various acting honors U.S. and abroad. Office: care Triad Artists Inc 10100 Santa Monica Blvd 16th Fl Los Angeles CA 90067

KNIPPENBURG, TRACY, public relations consultant; b. Columbus, Ohio, June 16, 1962; d. Fredrick Ormond and Beverly Ann (Carlisle) K. BS in Journalism, Ohio U., 1984. Media rels. officer DeMoss/Ryan for County Commrs., Franklin County, Ohio, 1984; cons. The Media Group, Inc., Columbus, Ohio, 1985; pub. info. officer Ohio Disaster Svcs. Agy., Columbus, 1985-86; project mgr., pub. info. svcs. Nutech Engrs., Bethesda, Md., 1986-89; sr. assoc. Corp. Response Group, Washington, 1989—. Contbr. articles to newsletters. Mem. Pub. Rels. Soc. Am. Democrat.

KNIPPLE, WENDY LYN, marketing professional; b. Chgo., Oct. 16, 1958; d. Raymond George and Frances Joyce (Plonka) B. BS in Bus., BSJ, U. Colo., 1982, postgrad.; MS in Computer Sci., U. Denver, 1984. Asst. editor Colo. Med. Soc., Denver, 1981; instr. computer sci. U. Denver, 1982-84; adminstrv. asst. CASCO Internat., Inc., Englewood, Colo., 1984-85; computer programmer On-Lion Inc., Denver, 1985-86; owner ind. computer pub. co., Greeley, Colo., 1986-87; exec. asst. strategic mktg. U.S. West Co., Englewood, 1987-88, asst. mgr. strategic mktg., 1988—. Participant foster parent program, Greeley, 1986-87; vol. Samaritan Ho., Denver, 1987—. Republican. Lutheran. Home: 6655 S Williams Crescent W Littleton CO 80121 Office: US West Co 6200 S Quebec St Ste 370 Englewood CO 80111

KNISELY, ANNE MARIE, public relations executive; b. Akron, Ohio, Dec. 3, 1955; d. Carl Edward and Joanne Carr (Bell) K. AA, Henry Ford Community Coll., Dearborn, Mich., 1976; BA, Wayne State U., Detroit, 1978. Staff writer The Mellus Newspapers, Lincoln Park, Mich., 1978-79; reporter, asst. news editor The Mellus Newspapers, 1979-80; pub. rels. asst. Jervis B. Webb Co., Farmington Hills, Mich., 1980-84; asst. dir. pub. rels. Jervis B. Webb Co., 1984, dir. pub. rels., 1984-90; mgr. communications and devel. engineered systems div. United Technologies Automotive, Detroit, 1990—; chmn. Communications '87 Conf., Detroit, 1986-87. Grand winner Mercury awards, Nat. Media Conf. and Pub. Rels. Forum, 1988, Gold winner, 1988. Mem. Pub. Rels. Soc. Am. (dir. 1988-90, chmn. accreditation com. 1989-90, sec. Detroit chpt. 1990—), Internat. Assn. Bus. Communicators (dir. 1987-88), Women in Communications, Am. Mktg. Assn., Engring. Soc. Detroit, Econ. Club. of Detroit.

KNISELY, SALLY, psychotherapist; b. Baraga, Mich., Mar. 17, 1917; d. Henry Samuel and Flora (Hagerman) Knisely; A.B., U. Mich., 1944; M.A., U. Chgo., 1946; Ed.D., Columbia U., 1964. Day nursery caseworker Bur. Family Service, Orange, N.J., 1946-49; caseworker to mentally ill vets. VA, N.Y.C., 1949-53; child psychotherapist Inter-Agy. Guidance Center, Yonkers, N.Y., 1953-58; child psychotherapist Monsey (N.Y.) Mental Health Clinic, 1957-58; child psychotherapist New Rochelle (N.Y.) Guidance Center, 1958-59; pvt. practice psychotherapy, Stamford, Conn., 1968—; cons. numerous nursery sch. and presch. programs. Fellow Conn. Soc. Clin. Social Workers; mem. Am. Orthopsychiat. Assn., Council Psychoanalytic Psychotherapists, Nat. Assn. Edn. Young Children, Soc. Health and Human Values, Nat. Assn. Social Workers, Nat. Assn. of Deaf, Am. Deafness and Rehab. Assn., AAUW, Nat. Bd. Examiners in Clin. Social Work. Home and office: 69 Jordan Ln Stamford CT 06903

KNIZESKI-HOLLANDER, JUSTINE ESTELLE, insurance company executive; b. Glen Cove, N.Y., June 4, 1954; d. John Martin and Elsie Beatrice (Gozelski) Knizeski. B.A., Conn. Coll., 1976; M. Mgmt., Northwestern U., 1981. Customer service supr. Brunswick Savs., Freeport, Maine, 1977-79; investment analyst Bankers Life and Casualty Co., Chgo., 1980-83, dir. corp. planning and analysis, 1983-87; dir. budgets, cost acctg. Blue Cross/Blue Shield of Ill., 1987—. Chmn. bd. dirs. Alternatives, Inc., Chgo., 1984-87, vice chmn., 1987—, bd. dirs., 1983-84; mem. Chgo. Council Fgn. Relations, 1984-85. Mem. Planning Forum. Avocations: sailing; bicycling; traveling; painting.

KNOBLER, CAROLYN BERK, chemist; b. New Brunswick, N.J., Jan. 6, 1934; d. Abraham Albert and Esther (Schilian) Berk; m. Charles Martin Knobler, Jan. 28, 1957; children: Daniel, Michael. BS, George Wash. U., 1955; PhD, Pa. State U., 1959. NSF resident fellow U. Amsterdam, The Netherlands, 1959-60; resident asst., resident chemist,ZWO fellow U. Leiden, The Netherlands, 1960-61, 70-71; resident asst. Calif. Inst. Tech., Pasadena, Calif., 1962-64; from asst. resident chemist to assoc. resident chemist U. Calif., L.A., 1964—; vis. lectr. U. Calif., L.A., 1975; resident chemist U. Canterbury, Christchurch, New Zealand, 1978-79, U. Pierre et Marie Curie, Paris 6 France, 1987, 1983-84 (CNRS). Recipient Herbert Newby McCoy, U. Calif. Dept. Chemistry, 1989. Mem. Am. Phys. Soc., Am. Crystallographic Assn., Phi Beta Kappa, Sigma Xi. Office: U Calif Dept Chemistry 405 Hilgard Los Angeles CA 90024

KNOBLOCH, HILDA, pediatrician, retired; b. N.Y.C., Dec. 14, 1915; d. Philip J. and Minnie (Jacobson) K.; m. Benjamin Pasamanick, May 1, 1942 (div. July 1982). BA, Barnard Coll., 1936; MD, NYU, 1940; MPH, Johns Hopkins U., 1951, DrPH, 1955. Diplomate Am. Bd. Pediatrics, Am. Bd. Preventive Medicine and Pub. Health. Rsch. assoc. Sch. Hygiene and Pub. Health Johns Hopkins U., Balt., 1951-55, asst. prof., 1955; assoc. prof. dept. pediatrics Ohio State U. Coll. of Medicine, Columbus, 1955-62, prof. dept. pediatrics, 1962-66; prof. dept. pediatrics U. Ill. Coll. Medicine, Chgo., 1966-67, Mount Sinai Sch. Medicine, CUNY, 1967-70, Albany (N.Y.) Med. Coll. of Union U., 1970-82; med. specialist N.Y. State Dept. Mental Hygiene, Albany, 1970-81; cons. Meml. Med. Ctr., Savannah, Ga. Editor: Gesell and Amatruda's Developmental Diagnosis, 1974; author: Manual of Developmental Diagnosis, 1980; producer videotapes on normal and abnormal infant devel., 1982; contbr. articles to profl. jours. Fellow Am. Acad. Pediatrics, Soc. for Rsch. in Child Devel., Am. Pediatric Soc., Am. Acad. for Cerebral Palsy; mem. Phi Beta Kappa, Alpha Omega Alpha. Home: 230 E Oglethorpe Ave Savannah GA 31401

KNODEL, ELINOR LIVINGSTON, immunologist, biomedical researcher, writer; b. N.Y.C.; d. Robert Edwin and Elinor (Findley) K.; m. Peter M. Tuhy; 1 child, Elinor Judith Tuhy. BA in Chemistry, Barnard Coll., 1969; PhD in Biochemistry, U. Conn., 1976. Mfg. process chemist clin. systems div. E.I. Du Pont de Nemours & Co., Inc., Wilmington, Del., 1980-85, devel.

chemist clin. systems div., 1985-87, devel. immunologist clin. systems div., 1987-90, with external affairs dept., 1990—. Tech. writer E.I. Du Pont Co., Wilmington, 1990—; contbr. project reports and sci. articles to profl. jours. Stewardship com. chair St. James Episc. Ch., Wilmington, 1987. Mayo Clinic Found. Postdoctoral fellow in neurochemistry, 1978-80, Rockefeller U. Postdoctoral fellow in neuroendocrinology, 1976-77, U. Conn. Rsch. Found. Grad. fellow in biochemistry, 1975-76; Pa. State scholar Barnard Coll., 1965-69. Mem. AAAS, Am. Chem. Soc., Am. Assn. Clin. Chemistry, Tissue Culture Assn., Wilmington Women in Bus. Office: E I Du Pont de Nemours Concord Pla-Quillen Bldg 3411 Silverside Rd Wilmington DE 19810

KNOERNSCHILD, KATHERINE MARY, sales executive; b. Milw., Nov. 7, 1948; d. Carl William and Lucille Ann (Bell) K. Student, U. Wis., 1977. Asst. v.p. sales JBS Assocs., Denver; sales rep. Windmill Vitamin Co., Lincolnwood, Ill.; food stamp outreach coord. Wis. Dept. Health & Social Svcs., Madison; policy analyst Madison Sch. Bd. Mem. CAHA, CADA, RMAUA, NMAWA, MADA, WADA, NAFE. Home: 1873 S Bellaire St #510 Denver CO 80222

KNOLL, ROSE ANN, health facility administrator; b. Marshfield, Wis., Aug. 28, 1954; d. Edward Edwin Jr. and Mary Ellen (Allen) K. BS, U. Wis., 1976; MSA, Cen. Mich. U., 1985; AAS, Communication Coll. of USAF, 1985. Dir. radiology Divine Savior Hosp. and Nursing Home, Portage, Wis.; radiologic technologist Georgetown U. Hosp., Washington; supr. radiology, mgr. USAF Clinic McGuire AFB, N.J.; mgr. radiology Pentagon USAF Flight Medicine Clinic, Washington; dir. imaging svcs. Douglas Community Hosp., Roseburg, Oreg. Staff sgt. USAF, 1979-85. Decorated Good Conduct medal with oak leaf cluster; U. Wis. grantee. Mem. NAFE, AHRA, ASRT, WSRT, Gamma Sigma Sigma. Roman Catholic. Home: 1307 SE Main St Roseburg OR 97470 Office: Douglas Community Hosp Imaging Svcs Dept 738 W Harvard Blvd Roseburg OR 97470

KNOLLE, MARY ANNE ERICSON, psychotherapist, business communications consultant; b. Kilgore, Tex., Jan. 7, 1941; d. Evert Eric and Frances Leone (Scott) Ericson; children by previous marriage: Clay Claflin, Sunny Claflin; m. John W. Knolle, Mar. 14, 1980; children: Sara Anne, Evelyn. BA, North Tex. U., 1962; MA in Communication, U. Tex., 1968; postgrad., UCLA, 1964-66; MA in Psychology, Houston Bapt. U., 1989. Editor co. publs. Gt. S.W. Life Ins. Co., 1962; prof. U. Balt., 1968, Miami (Fla.) Dade Coll., 1968, Savannah (Ga.) State Coll., 1969, U. Houston, 1972-76; dir. pub. relations Alvin (Tex.) Coll., 1970-72; founder, pres. Panorama Programs, Houston, 1972-76; coordinator mgmt. devel. tng. Brown & Root, Inc., Houston, 1970-79; div. founder, mgr. mgmt. and orgnl. devel. systems Diversified Human Resources Group, Inc., Houston, 1979—; founder, pres. Panorama Mgmt. Inst., Houston, 1979—, Panorama Cons., 1980—; pres., therapist Stepfamily Support Ctr., Inc., Houston; cons. moot ct. U. Tex. Law Sch., 1965—. Judge regional speech contest Houston Jaycees; instr. Houston Community Coll., Alvin Community Coll., U. Balt., Savannah St. Coll. Recipient Blockbuster award United Way, 1979. Mem. Am. Soc. Tng. and Devel., Houston C. of C. (chmn. edn. com.), Houston Indoor Tennis Club, Alpha Delta Pi (past pres. alumnae). Presbyterian. Office: 4126 Twelve Oakes Tower Ste 1515 Houston TX 77027

KNOPF, SUSAN LEWIS, sales executive; b. L.A., Feb. 9, 1956; d. Robert Leon Feldman and Cyra (Wolf) Lewis; m. Jonathan Crasilneck Knopf, Apr. 25, 1981; 1 child, Erin Katherine. BA in Mass Communications, U. So. Fla., Tampa, 1977; MA in Pub. Communication, U. Denver, 1979. Free lance corr. WFCA-TV, Tampa, 1977; grad. teaching asst. dept. mass communications U. Denver, 1978-79; writer KMGH-TV, Denver, 1979-80; TV news reporter KTBS-TV, Shreveport, La., 1980-83; beauty cons. Mary Kay Cosmetics, Dallas, 1981-84; mgr. Hunt & Peck, Div. of Salkin & Linoff, Mpls., 1984-85; territory mgr. Kraft, Dairy Group, Phila., 1985-87, account mgr., 1987-88; sales rep. Profl. Detailing Network, N.Y.C., 1989—; founder, dir. Shreveport Journalism Found., 1985-87. Co-author script video tape: Safe Aerobics, 1987. Leader Girl Scouts Am., Shreveport, 1980-81; mem. Citizens for Personal Freedom, New Orleans, 1989—; go-getter WYES-TV, New Orleans, 1989; nat. del. Women's Am. ORT Conv., New Orleans. Recipient 2d Pl. Spot award La. UPI, 1981; named Outstanding Edn. Writer, La. Assn. Educators, 1982. Mem. Women in Communications, Inc., Soc. Profl. Journalists, Women's Am. Orgn. for Rehab. Through Tng., Nat. Abortion Rights Action League, Nat. Coun. Jewish Women, Hadassah, Sierra Club (newsletter editor, dir. 1983-84), NOW. Democrat. Jewish. Home: 6210 Glen Echo Arlington TX 76017

KNOTH, MARGE JUNE, author; b. Lafayette, Ind., Aug. 23, 1944; d. Francis Lawrence and Susie Marie (Johnson) Brettnacher; m. Richard Daniel Knoth, Dec. 18, 1962; children: Lisa Joyce, Nicholas Daniel, April Lorraine, Tonia Suzanne. Diploma, Writer's Digest Sch. of Mag., 1975. Profl. ind. writer Lafayette, 1974—; activity dir., social svc. designee, newsletter editor Comfort Retirement and Nursing Home, Lafayette, 1979-88. Author: Looking Back, 1989, The Professional Activity Director, 1989, Remembering the Good Old Days, 1989, Activity Planning at Your Fingertips, 1990; contbr. articles to profl. jours. and mags. Mem. Tippecanoe County Hist. Soc., Lafayette, 1988-89; sec. Right to Life, Lafayette, sec. Mem. Nat. Fedn. Press Women, Women's Press Club of Ind., Authors and Friends Writers Club (co-founder, leader, sec. 1988—), Nat. Assn. Activity Profls., Women in Communications. Republican. Home: 1907 Vinton Lafayette IN 47904 Office: Valley Press 1907 Vinton Lafayette IN 47904

KNOTT, ELIZABETH B., clergy; b. Phila., July 29, 1927; d. Harry Gustus and Lillian (Leapson) B. BA, Maryville Coll., 1957; BD, McCormick Sem., 1963; MS, Okla. State U., 1970. Bookkeeper Sun Oil Co., Phila., 1946-53; dir. of Christian Edn. Roosevelt Dr. Presbyn. Ch., Milw., 1958-63; assoc. pastor First Presbyn. Ch., Littleton, Colo., 1963-66; pastor First Presbyn. Ch., Tonkawa, Okla., 1966-73; assoc. synod exec. mission funding Synod of Lincoln Trails, Indpls., 1973-80; organizing pastor New Creation Presbyn. Ch., Altoona, Iowa, 1980-83; interim pastor Grace Presbyn. Ch., Springfield, Va., 1984-85, Lewistown (Pa.) Presbyn. Ch., Va., 1986; interim exec. Presbytery of Detroit, 1986-87; synod exec. Synod of Alaska-Northwest, Seattle, 1987—; Mem.-at-large Consultation on Ch. Union, Princeton, N.J., 1975-76; bd. trustees McCormick Sem., Chgo., 1980-83, Sheldon Jackson Coll., Sitka, Ala., 1987—, Whitworth Coll., Spokane, Wash., 1987—; organizing bd. Creative Futures Ctr., Seattle, 1989; vice-moderator Churchwide Coordinating Cabinet, Louisville, 1989; mem. Wash. Assn. of Chs., Seattle, 1987. Organizer of intergenerational arts and crafts fair, City Council, Tonkawa, 1972, organizer of year-round recreation, City Council, Tonkawa, 1971; chairwoman Ch. Employed Women, 1975-76. Recipient Alumni citation Maryville Coll., 1989. Mem. Alban Inst., Assn. for Creative Change, Witherspoon Soc., Presbyn. Health, Edn. and Welfare, Women Execs. Democrat. Home: 106 SW 299th Pl Federal Way WA 98023

KNOTT, TARA DAVIS, evaluation consultant; b. Alexandria, La., Dec. 5, 1943; d. Raoul Lynwood and Ruby Montez (Luneau) Brister; m. David Howard Knott, Aug. 6, 1978. BA in Psychology, Memphis State U., 1971, MA in Speech Pathology, 1975; BA in Speech and Music, La. State U., 1961; PhD in Evaluation Research, Clayton U., 1978. Evaluator family practice dept. U. Tenn. Center for Health Scis., 1976-78; research cons. Deafness Found., 1978, Nat. Hearing Assn., 1978; evaluation cons. Covington Mental Health Center; head data collection Project WOMAN, 1978-79; evaluation cons. Mid South Hosp., Jackson Splty. Hosp.; United Inns, Memphis Mental Health Inst., U. Tenn. Center Health Scis., Rivendell Corp. Am., Hosp. Corp. Am., Meharry Med. Sch.; pres. Evaluation Resources, Inc., First Tenn. Bank, Ford Motor Co., Memphis Mus. System, United Way Greater Memphis, Allied Arts Coun. Greater Chatanooga; cons., tchr., colls. and univs.; mem. Ill. State Bd. Edn. Grantee in alcoholism and drug abuse. Mem. Am. Evaluation Assn., Soc. Neurosci., Employee Assistance Soc. N.Am., Am. Psychol. Assn., Am. Soc. Tng. and Devel., Am. Edn. Research Assn., Am. Fitness in Industry, Tenn. Evaluation Network. Democrat. Methodist. Contbr. articles to profl. jours. Office: 4646 Poplar Ste 509 Memphis TN 38117

KNOTTS, SARAH APRIL, medical manufacturing company executive, nurse; b. Indpls., May 4, 1952; d. A. Frank and Luella Anne (Wilson) Knotts; m. Christopher Goodwin, June 10, 1978 (div. Nov. 1986); children: Julia Faith, Luke Eugene, Averie Amelia. BA in Psychology, Clark U., 1976; AS, Front Range Coll., Westminster, Colo., 1985. RN, Colo. Staff nurse Longmont (Colo.) United Hosp., 1985-88, Boulder (Colo.) Meml. Hosp., 1988; dir. devel. Boulder Impact Monitors, Inc., 1988—. Inventor orthopedic impact monitor. Mem. NAFE, ACLU, Now, Nat. Assn. Orthopedic Nurses, Sierra Club, Psi Chi. Democrat. Home: 8008 Pepple Rd Longmont CO 80503 Office: Boulder Impact Monitors Inc 2525 Arapahoe Ste E-4 Boulder CO 80302

KNOWLER, FAITH MARION, civic worker; b. Muscatine, Iowa, Jan. 22, 1911; d. Will and Mary M. (Dankert) Stamler; m. Lloyd A. Knowler, June 30, 1935; children: Mary Louise, William Clayton. BA, U. Iowa, 1933; postgrad., Washington U., St. Louis, 1933-34; MA, U. Iowa, 1937. Caseworker Citizens Com. for Relief & Employment, St. Louis, 1934-35, U. Hosp. Social Svc. Dept., Iowa City, 1935, 61-63. Co-founder Youth Homes, Inc., Iowa City, 1972, bd. dirs., 1972—, pres. bd., 1978, mem. personnel com., 1985—; mem. Coun. for Internat. Visitors to Iowa City, 1986—; vp. for planning United Way of Johnson County, Iowa City, 1976, bd. dir.s, 1976-79, 87—. Mem. Alumni Assn. U. Iowa, AAUW (pres. 1943-44, bd. dirs. 1944-45), League Women Voters of Johnson County (pres. 1975-77), League Women Voters of Iowa (com. chmn. 1977-79), U. Iowa Alumni Assn., 19th Century Club, Univ. Club (pres. 1966-67), P.E.O. Democrat. Unitarian Universalist. Home: 207 Golfview Ave Iowa City IA 52246

KNOWLES, CAROLINE HOFFBERG, clinical psychologist, educator; b. N.Y.C., Mar. 1, 1926; d. Israel Isaac and Lilly (Salwen) Hoffberg; m. John Albert Meixner, June 6, 1948 (div. 1959); m. William Henry Knowles, June 7, 1971; children: Gabrielle Anne., Eve Rachel. BA, NYU, 1951; MA, Brown U., 1955; PhD, Yale U., 1959, U. Mich., 1963. Diplomate in Clin. Psychology Am. Bd. Profl. Psychology; lic. psychologist, Calif. Asst.prof. psychology Calif. State U., Riverside, 1959-61; lectr. in psychology U. Mich., Ann Arbor, Mich., 1961-67; clin. psychologist Boston U., 1968-71; assoc. prof. Washington Coll., Chestertown, Md., 1971-73; vis. psychologist Vanuatu Gen. Hosp., Port Villa, Vanuatu, 1980-83; bereavement assistance dir. Hospice Svc. of Lake County, Lakeport, Calif., 1984-85; pvt. practice Lakeport, 1987—; instr. in psychology Yuba Coll., Lower Lake, Calif., 1985—, Mendocino Coll., Lakeport, 1989—; cons. in field. Author numerous poems; contbr. articles to profl. jours. Mem. Mental Health Adv. Bd., Lakeport, 1984-85; bd. dirs. No. Calif. chpt. Planned Parenthood, 1986—, chmn. steering com., 1990—; v.p. Lake County chpt. Big Brothers/Big Sisters, 1987—. Univ. scholar Brown U., 1952; USPHS Rsch. fellow Yale U., 1955-57, 57-59. Mem. Am. Psychol. Assn., Assn. for Women in Psychology, Am. Soc. Clin. Hypnosis, Western Psychol. Assn., Calif. State Psychol. Assn., San Francisco Acad. Hypnosis, Sigma Xi. Presbyterian. Home: 3572 Crestwood Dr Kelseyville CA 95451 Office: 1222 S Main St Lakeport CA 95453

KNOWLES, JOCELYN WAGNER, health writer, women's health specialist; b. N.Y.C., Feb. 22, 1918; d. Frederick and Violet Alice (Swain) W.; m. Clive Dorman Knowles, 1950 (div. 1959); 1 child, Katherine Miranda. Student, London Sch. Econs., 1938; BS, Columbia U., 1939, MA, 1940; MPH, UCLA, 1970. Exec. dir. Nat. Physicians Forum, Inc., N.Y.C., 1945-49; West Coast editor Nat. Foremen's Inst. Prentice-Hall Co., L.A., 1959-68; writer, editor The Female Patient mag., N.Y.C., 1980-81; dir. Planned Parenthood of S.W., Silver City, N.Mex., 1981-83; freelance writer N.Y.C., 1977—; asst. to pres. Writers House, Inc., N.Y.C., 1988—; book critic Kirkus Revs., 1989—. Contbr. articles to med. mags.; staff book-reviewer L.A. Times. First woman organizer Brotherhood of Railway Trainmen, 1945-47; publicist Farmers Union of Iowa, Des Moines, 1951, Golden Gate Arboretum, San Francisco, 1976; bd. dirs. Nat. Womens Health Network, 1981-85. NIH grantee U. Calif., L.A., 1968-70; Va. Ctr. for the Arts fellow, Charlottesville, 1976, Woolrich fellow Columbia U., N.Y.C., 1977, Wurlitzer Found. fellow, Taos, N.Mex., 1981. Jewish.

KNOWLES, PHYLLIS BRADFUTE, title insurance company executive; b. Cin., Oct. 16, 1927; d. Fred Lott and Mary (White) Bradfute; m. Harry V. Knowles, Aug. 24, 1950 (div. 1973); children—Pamela A. Fleizach, Debra A. Zakarin. BA, Barnard Coll., 1950. Exec. sec. Carrie Chapman Catt Meml., N.Y.C., 1950-53; pres. Quinbee & Bradfute Internat. Promotions, Eastchester, N.Y., 1957-75; exec. mgr. Urban Developers, Phila., 1975-79, Gibraltar Title & Escrow Co. of Boca Raton, Fla., 1979—. Author: Records of the Town of Eastchester, 1969. Pres. LWV, Eastchester, 1954-56, Eastchester Hist. Soc., 1965-76; treas. West County Hist. Soc., 1970-76; treas. Univ. Arts League, Phila., 1977-79. Mem. Nat. Assn. Notaries. Republican. Methodist. Club: Boca West. Avocations: Doll house building; historian; lecturer. Home: 1626 Bridgewood Dr Boca Raton FL 33434 Office: Gibraltar Title & Escrow Co 3200 N Military Trail Boca Raton FL 33431

KNOX, AGNES RUTH, retired teacher; b. Urbana, Ill., July 15, 1911; d. Charles Wallace and Marie Louise (Lewis) Graham; m. William Wallace Knox, Sept. 5, 1936 (dec. Aug. 1981); children: Virginia, Wallace, Charles, Katherine. AB, U. Mich., 1932, AM, 1937. Teacher. Pres. Harding Sch. PTA, Erie, Pa., 1957-58; pres. LWV, Erie 1963-65. Mem. AAUW (sec. Pa. chpt. 1948-50, pres. Erie chpt. 1948-50), Nat. Lawyers' Wives (sec. 1971-72), Erie Lawyers' Wives (pres. 1970-71), Erie Club, Kahkwa Club. Republican. Presbyterian. Home: 210 W 6th St #PH79 Erie PA 16507

KNOX, BETTY AGEE, art gallery executive; b. Corpus Christi, Tex., Nov. 25, 1936; d. John Wesley and Shirley Margaret (Fugate) Agee; m. Seymour H. Knox, June 15, 1979. BA, U. Tex., 1958. Art cons. Buffalo Fine Arts Acad., 1959-82; pres. Betty Knox Gallery, N.Y.C., 1984—; hon. chairwoman Marine Midland Bank, Inc. Chmn. Guide Dog Found. for Blind, N.Y.C., 1985; mem. exec. bd. Rep. Congl. Leadership Coun., Washington, 1989. Recipient Golden Horseshoe award Met. Opera Assn., 1989, Wall of Honor award Ellis Island Found., 1989, History Marker award U. Tex. Ex-Students Assn., 1989; Yale Art Gallery Assocs. fellow. Mem. Met. Mus. Art, Mus. Modern Art, Whitney Mus. Art (film and video fellows), Circle Nat. Gallery of Art, Albright-Knox Art Gallery, Nat. Horse Show Found. (life), English Speaking Union, Yale Club, Capitol Hill Club (Washington). Episcopalian. Office: 524 E 72d St New York NY 10021

KNOX, DEBORAH CAROLYN, state agency administrator, accountant; b. Manchester, Tenn., Mar. 31, 1962; d. Eugene Clarke and Myrtle Carolyn (Bell) K. BBA in Acctg., Middle Tenn. State U., 1984. CPA, Tenn. Sr. fin. planner Lincoln Fin. Group, Brentwood, Tenn., 1986; staff CPA Charles Tharp & Assocs., Nashville, 1987; staff acct. Dept. Treasury State of Tenn., Nashville, 1984-85, supr. pension payroll Dept. Treasury, 1987, compliance analyst, policy planner, 1988, dir. program acctg. Dept. Fin., Adminstrn., 1988—. Mem. Assn. Govt. Accts., Nat. Assn. CPAs (John Lewis award 1984).

KNOX, HAVOLYN CROCKER, financial consultant; b. Charlotte, N.C., Oct. 20, 1937; d. Earl Reid and Etta Lorane (Wylie) Crocker; m. Charles Eugene Knox, July 20, 1963 (div. 1981); children: Charles Eugene Jr., Sandra Leigh. Cert. Stenography, U. N.C., Greensboro, 1956. Charted Fin. Cons., CLU. Exec. sec. Stellings-Gossett Theatres, Inc., Charlotte, 1956-57; legal sec. McDougle, Ervin, Horack & Snepp, Charlotte, 1957, Pierce, Wardlow, Knox & Caudle, Charlotte, 1957-63; adminstrv. asst. Charlotte-Mecklenburg Planning Commn., 1980; exec. asst. Conn. Mut. Life Ins. Co., Charlotte, 1981-86; assoc. The Hinrichs Fin. Group, Charlotte, 1986—. Ops. dir. Eddie Knox for Mayor campaign, Charlotte; campaign mgr. Herb Spaugh for City Coun., Charlotte, 1981, 83, 85; registration chmn. Kemper Open Golf Tournament, Charlotte, 1976-79; pres. The Legal Aux., Charlotte, 1972-73; bd. dirs. Oratorio Singers of Charlotte, 1986—. Recipient William Danforth Found. award, 1955. Mem. Am. Soc. CLU and ChFC, Nat. Assn. Life Underwriters, Charlotte Assn. Underwriters, Charlotte Estate Planning Coun. Republican. Presbyterian. Club: The Tower (Charlotte). Lodge: Civitan. Home: 2331 Carmel Rd Charlotte NC 28226 Office: The Hinrichs Fin Group 1600 Charlotte Plaza Charlotte NC 28244

KNOX, JACQUELINE MAE, director records and registration; b. New Bedford, Mass., May 13, 1932; d. Rene Cyril Honore and Lorenza (Brizard) Boutin; m. Joe Bert Knox, Apr. 2, 1955; children: Susanne, Phillip, Peter. AA, Brevard Community Coll., Cocoa, Fla., 1973; BA, U. N. Fla., 1985. Vets. advisor Brevard Community Coll., 1973-74, handicapped specialist, 1974-77; adminstrv. asst. St. John's River Community Coll., Palatka, Fla., 1978-84; supr. records dept. U. N. Fla., Jacksonville, 1985-86, dir., 1986—; chmn. honors com. alumni bd. dirs. U. North Fla., 1988—. Mem. Ladies Aux. Lodge 125, Orange Park, Fla., 1986. With USN, 1952-55. Recipient Disting. Alumni award Brevard Community Coll., 1987. Mem. Fla. Assn. Women Deans, Advisors and Counselors, Fla. Assn. Community Colls. (chmn. region II 1984-85), Am. Bus. Women's Assn. (membership chmn. 1978—), NAFE, Blue Key, Phi Theta Kappa (pres. Melbourne chpt. 1972-73). Home: 2170 Orange Ave Orange Park FL 32073 Office: U North Fla 4567 St Johns Bluff Rd S Jacksonville FL 32216

KNOX, REBECCA HOWLAND, occupational therapy consultant; b. Wilmington, Del., May 5, 1943; d. F. Stratton, Jr. and Elizabeth Hussey (Brown) K.; m. Gerald W. McCollum, June 6, 1964 (div. Apr. 1975). BA, Brown U., 1965; cert. Tufts U., 1968; MA, St. Mary's Coll., Winona, Minn., 1983. Lic. occupational therapist, Mass. Occupational therapist Robert Breck Brigham Hosp., Boston, 1968; research asst. Inst. for Family and Youth, Cambridge, Mass., 1968-73; occupational therapy cons. Wellmet Project, Inc., Cambridge, 1973, Boston Area Nursing Homes, 1973—, Ctr. House, South Boston, Mass., 1976—, Wellsprings, Cambridge, 1985—; cons. Liberty Sch., Cambridge, 1974—, Women's Job Counseling Ctr., Cambridge, 1987—; researcher Tigerlily Research, Cambridge, 1985—. Sponsor 2 children Holy Land Christian Mission Internat. (now Children Internat.), 1983—; mem. Harbor Area Mental Health Human Rights Com., Boston, 1985—. Mem. Am. Occupational Therapy Assn., Mass. Occupational Therapy Assn., Internat. Transactional Analysis Assn., Boston Orthomolecular Soc., Assn. for Psychol. Type, NAFE, Mensa, Friends of Boston Bio Ctr. Democrat. Buddhist. Avocations: observing cats, drawing psychol. maps. Office: Wellsprings PO Box 175 Cambridge MA 02141

KNOX, RHONDA LEE, lawyer; b. Kansas City, Mo., July 6, 1960; d. James Bernard and Lois Ilene (DuVall) K. BA summa cum laude, Olivet Nazarene Coll., 1982; JD, Vanderbilt U., 1985. Bar: Colo. 1985. Assoc. Holland & Hart, Colorado Springs, Colo., 1985—. Mem. ABA, Colo. Bar Assn., El Paso County Bar Assn. , Christian Legal Soc., Kiwanis (bd. dirs. Colorado Springs 1988—). Democrat. Nazarene. Home: 5060 Sunsuite Trail Colorado Springs CO 80917 Office: Holland & Hart 1400 Holly Sugar Bldg Colorado Springs CO 80903

KNOX, WILMA JONES, psychologist; b. St. Louis, Feb. 17, 1930; d. Tom Borth and Helen Margaret (Cahill) Jones; m. William Christie Knox, Oct. 10, 1956 (div. Aug. 1969). BA, U.N.C., 1951, MA, 1954; PhD, Pa. State U., 1958. Lic. psychologist, Miss. Intern in psychology VA Med. Ctr. and Regional Office, Pitts., 1955; intern in psychology VA Med. Ctr. (Gulfport Div.), Biloxi, Miss., 1956, staff psychologist, 1957-59, 62-87; staff psychologist VA Med. Ctr. (Gulfport div. CDU), Biloxi, Miss., 1987—, VA Med. Ctr., Sheridan, Wyo., 1959-62; part-time assoc. prof. U. So. Miss., Hattiesburg, 1975-85; adv. com. Harrison County Family Court, Gulfport, 1975-79; editorial referee Jour. of Studies on Alcohol, Rutgers U., N.J., 1976-82. Contbg. author: Encyclopedia Handbook of Alcoholism, 1982; contbr. articles to profl. jours. Named Biloxi VA Career Woman, Lighthouse B&PW Club, 1985. Mem. Am. Psychol. Assn., Miss. Psychol. Assn., Internat. Coun. Psychologists (area chmn. 1985—), Mental Health Assn. in Harrison County (legis. com. chmn. 1971—, named Outstanding Vol. 1979, Outstanding Chmn. 1980), Mental Health Assn. in Miss. (legis. chmn. 1978-84, named Outstanding Vol. 1982, recipient Legis. award 1978), Altrusa Club of Biloxi (pres. 1979, com. chmn. 1985-90), Broadwater Beach Country Club, PEO, Pi Beta Phi Alumni. Republican. Presbyterian. Office: VA Med Ctr Biloxi MS 39531

KNOX-MALEWICKI, DEBRA SUZANNE, state official; b. Monroe, Wis., July 23, 1954; d. Raymond Lester Miskimon and Dorothy Rose (Youngwith) Sewell; m. Robert Allen Malewicki, May 22, 1987; children: Marissa, John Ryan. BA, East Tex. State U., 1980; MBA, U. Wis., Whitewater, 1984. Program mgr. Wis. Innovation Svc. Ctr., Whitewater, 1985—; instr. Lakeland Coll., Sheboygan, Wis., 1986—. Author (with others) Marketing Ingenuity and Invention, 1989. Advisor Phi Gamma Nu, Whitewater, 1986—; chmn. Wis. Gov.'s Task Force on Innovation and and Rsch. and Devel., Small Bus. Conf., Madison, 1987. Mem. Small Bus. Innovations Rsch. Com. (chairperson 1987—), Wis. Bus. Women's Coalition (chairperson conf. 1987—). Office: Wis Innovation Ctr 402 McCutchan Hall U Wis Whitewater WI 53190

KNUDSON, ANN RANKIN, educator; b. Glens Falls, N.Y., May 11, 1933; d. Charles Stephens and Myrtle (Bennett) Rankin; m. Richard Lewis Knudson, June 4, 1930; children: Leesa M., Erik S. BS, Gorham (Maine) State U., 1954; MS, U. Maine, 1961. Cert. tchr. and adminstr., Maine, N.Y. Tchr. Eliot (Maine) Cen. Sch., 1954-55, Bridge St. Sch., Westbrook, Maine, 1955-57, Katahdin Ave. Sch., Millinocket, Maine, 1957-60, Washburn Sch., Auburn, Maine, 1960-62, Poland (Maine) Elem. Sch., 1963-65; tchr., dir. Oneonta (N.Y.) Nursery Sch., 1975—; dir. New Eng. MGT Register, Oneonta, 1964—. Mem. AAUW (current affairs com. 1974-76), Nat. Assn. Edn. of Young Children, Delta Kappa Gamma. Republican. Episcopalian. Home: 21 Franklin St Oneonta NY 13820

KNUTSON, KATHERINE MELLBY, retired teacher; b. Thief River Falls, Minn., Apr. 25, 1910; d. Oscar Frederick and Louise Terese (Grindeland) Mellby; m. Wallace E. Anderson, Jan. 21, 1939 (dec. 1966); 1 child, Rolf Frederick; m. Oscar R. Knutson, Aug. 1981 (dec.). BA, St. Olaf Coll., 1932. Tchr. Joice (Iowa) Pub. Sch., 1932-34, Maynard (Minn.) Pub. Sch., 1934-36, Brainerd (Minn.) Pub. Sch., 1936-39. Active mem. St. Stephen's Luth. Ch., West St. Paul, Minn. Mem. AAUW, St. Paul (Minn.) Women's Club, Cherokee Heights Garden Club (St. Paul). Home: 751 Upper Colonial Dr Mendota Heights MN 55118

KNUTTI, ELIZABETH BLANCHE, nurse officer; b. Elkins, W.Va., Mar. 5, 1945; d. John Howard and Adelaide Eileen (Fullmer) K.; m. Jonas Neale Swecker, Oct. 12, 1985; stepchildren: Terri L. Swecker, Paul R. Swecker, Jill Swecker Dejak. BSN, W.Va. U., 1971. RN. Charge nurse W.Va. U. Hosp., Morgantown, 1966-70, Monongalia Gen. Hosp., Morgantown, 1970-72; commd. nurse officer USPHS, 1972, advanced through grades to comdr., 1989; occupational health nurse Nat. Inst. Occupational Safety and Health, Morgantown, 1990—; ; spirometry instr. Am. Lung Assn., Charleston, W.Va., 1985-89. Co-author: NIOSH/DRDS Spirometry Procedure Manual, 1988. Mem. Am. Nurses Assn., AAUW (pres. 1988-89), USPHS Commd. Officers Assn. (v.p. 1977-79). Republican. Christian and Missionary Alliance. Home: 309 Elmhurst St Morgantown WV 26505 Office: NIOSH/ALOSH 944 Chestnut Ridge Rd Morgantown WV 26505-2888

KOART, NELLIE HART, real estate investor and executive; b. San Luis Obispo, Calif., Jan. 3, 1930; d. Will Carleton and Nellie Malchen (Cash) Hart; m. William Harold Koart, Jr., June 16, 1951 (dec. 1976); children: Kristen Marie Kittle, Matthew William. Student Whittier Coll., 1947-49; BA, U. Calif.-Santa Barbara, 1952; MA, Los Angeles State Coll., 1957. Life diploma elem. edn., Calif. Farm worker Hart Farms, Montebello, Calif., 1940-48; play leader Los Angeles County Parks and Recreation, East Los Angeles, Rosemead, Calif., 1948-51; elem. tchr. Potrero Heights Sch. Dist., South San Gabriel, Calif., 1951-55, vice prin., 1955-57; real estate salesman William Koart Real Estate, Goleta, Calif., 1963-76, real estate investor KO-ART Enterprises, Goleta, 1976—, pres. Wm. Koart Constrn. Co., Inc., Goleta, 1975—; real estate sales person Joseph McGeever Realty Co., Goleta, 1976—; adv. bd. Bank of Montecito, Santa Barbara, Calif., 1983—. Editor: Reflections, 1972. Charter mem. Calif. Regents program Calif. Fedn. Republican Women, 1989; treas. Santa Barbara County Fedn. Republican Women, Alamar-Hope Ranch, 1981-82, treas. County Bd., 1983-84; treas. Com. to Recall Hone, Maschke and Shewczyk, Goleta, 1984; treas. Santa Barbara County Lincoln Club, 1983-87, bd. dirs., 1983—; assoc. mem. state central com. Calif. Republican Party, 1985-87. Mem. Santa Barbara Apartment Assn., Antique Automobile Club of Am. (sec. treas. Santa Barbara 1980-84). Club: Cardinal and Gold (Los Angeles). Avocations: swimming, numismatics, college and professional football. Office: KO-ART Enterprises Post Office Box 310 Goleta CA 93116

KOBAYASHI, ANN H., state legislator; b. Honolulu, Apr. 10, 1937; m.; 3 children. Student Pembroke Coll., Northwestern U. Officer family corp.; former legis. aide, adminstrv. asst. Hawaii Senate, now mem. Senate from 14th Dist. Republican. Office: State Senate Rm 227 Honolulu HI 96813 Home: 3657 Waaloa Way Honolulu HI 96822*

KOBAYASHI, YUMI, financial analyst; b. Tokyo, Apr. 19, 1951; came to U.S., 1980; d. Jin and Katsuko (Sato) K.; m. Masahiro Murakami, Apr. 4, 1977 (div. 1982); m. James W.G. Sagin, Jan. 23, 1984. BA in Econs., Tokyo U., 1975; MBA, Stanford U., 1982. Chartered fin. analyst. Industry analyst The Long-Term Credit Bank Japan, Tokyo, 1975-80; security analyst Paine Webber Mitchell Hutchins, N.Y.C., 1982-84; ptnr. James Sagin Assocs., San Francisco, 1984—; bd. dirs. Sakura Color Products Corp., Union City, Calif. Author: Economic History of the Showa Era, 1988, Medical Industry in Japan, 1980, Survey of the Future Growth of the Electronics Industry, 1978, The Changing Structure of Japanese Industry, 1978. Mem. Akamonkai, San Francisco, 1984—, Gakushikai, Tokyo, 1975—. Mem. Inst. Chartered Fin. Analysts, N.Y. Soc. Security Analysts. Office: James Sagin Assocs 150 Beach Park Blvd Foster City CA 94404

KOBE, KAREN LOUISE, freelance writer; b. Glendale, Calif., Mar. 14, 1962; d. Jesse Edward and Gunilla Birgitta (Jonsson) Coulson; m. Michael Robert Kobe, June 16, 1984; children: Jonathan, Benjamin. BA in English, Tex. A&M U., 1986. Freelance writer, editor, cons. Austin, Tex., 1985—. Mem. Women in Communication, Inc., Soc. Tech. Communication. Republican. Baptist. Home and Office: 5909 Charles Schreiner Tr Austin TX 78749

KOBE, LAN, medical physicist; b. Semarang, Indonesia; naturalized; d. O.G. and L.N. (The) Kobe. BS in Physics, IKIP U., Bandung, Indonesia, 1964, MS in Physics, 1967; MS in Med. Physics and Biophysics, U. Calif.-Berkeley, 1975. Physics instr. Sch. Engring., Tarumanegara U., Jakarta, Indonesia, 1968-72; research fellow dept. radiation oncology U. Calif.-San Francisco, 1975-77; clin. physicist in residence dept. radiation oncology UCLA, 1977-78, asst. hosp. radiation physicist, 1978-80, hosp. radiation physicist, 1980—; instr. radiation oncology physics to resident physicians and med. physics graduate students. Contbr. sci. papers to profl. publs. Newhouse grantee U. Calif.-Berkeley, 1974-75, grantee dean grad. div. U. Calif.-Berkeley, 1975; recipient Pres. Work Study award U. Calif., Berkeley, 1974-75, Employee of Month award UCLA, 1983, Outstanding Service award UCLA, 1986; devel. Achievement award, UCLA, 1988. Mem. Am. Assn. Physicists in Medicine (nat. and So. Calif. chpts.), Am. Assn. Individual Investors (life). Lodge: Rosicrucian Order. Office: UCLA Hosp and Clinics Dept Radiation Oncology Los Angeles CA 90024

KOBER, ARLETTA REFSHAUGE (MRS. KAY L. KOBER), educational administrator; b. Cedar Falls, Iowa, Oct. 31, 1919; d. Edward and Mary (Jensen) Refshauge; BA, State Coll. Iowa, 1940; MA, U. No. Iowa; m. Kay Leonard Kober, Feb. 14, 1944; children: Kay Mary, Karilyn Eve. Tchr. high schs., Soldier, Iowa, 1940-41, Montezuma, Iowa, 1941-43, Waterloo, Iowa, 1943-50, 65-67, co-ordinator Office Edn. Waterloo Community Schs., Waterloo, Iowa, 1967-84; head dept. co-op. career edn. West High Sch., Waterloo, 1974-84. Mem. Waterloo Sch. Health Council; nominating com. YWCA, Waterloo; Black Hawk County chmn. Tb Christmas Seals; ward chmn. ARC, Waterloo; co-chmn. Citizen's Com. for Sch. Bond Issue; pres. Waterloo PTA Council, Waterloo Vis. Nursing Assn., 1956-62, 82—; pres. Kingsley Sch. PTA, 1959-60; v.p. Waterloo Women's Club, 1962-63, pres., 1963-64, trustee bd. clubhouse dirs., 1957-58; mem. Gen. Fedn. Women's Clubs, Nat. Congress Parents and Tchrs.; Presbyterial world service chmn. Presbyn. Women's Assn.; bd. dirs. Black Hawk County Republican Women, 1952-53, United Services of Black Hawk County, Broadway Theatre League, St. Francis Hosp. Found. Mem. AAUW (v.p. Cedar Falls 1946-47), NEA, Internat. Platform Assn., LWV (dir. Waterloo 1951-52), Black Hawk County Hist. Soc. (charter), Delta Pi Epsilon (v.p. 1966-67), Delta Kappa Gamma. Club: Town (dir.) (Waterloo), P.E.O. Home: 3436 Augusta Circle Waterloo IA 50701 Office: 503 W 4th St Waterloo IA 50701

KOBS, ANN ELIZABETH JANE, nursing administrator, consultant; b. Clinton, Iowa, Feb. 13, 1944; d. Francis Hubert and Leora Elizabeth (Sodeman) Boeker; m. Dennis Raymond Kobs, Oct. 15, 1966 (div. 1989); children: Michael, Peter, Amy. Diploma, Mercy Hosp. Sch. Nursing, 1965; BS in Nursing, Marycrest Coll., 1978; MS in Nursing Adminstrn., No. Ill. U., 1981. Staff charge nurse Mercy Hosp., Davenport, Iowa, 1965-66; clin. instr. Marycrest Coll., Davenport, 1967; health care cons., Chgo., 1973—; pre-reviewer for continuing edn. and career counselor in residence Ill. Nurses Assn., Chgo., 1978-80; career devel. cons. Ill. Hosp. Assn., Oak Brook, 1980-81, staff specialist nursing, 1981-83, dir. nursing, Naperville, 1983-84; dir. nursing surg./maternal-child health Alexian Bros. Med. Ctr., Elk Grove Village, Ill., 1984-87; dir. nursing svcs. Rochelle (Ill.) Community Hosp., 1987-89; cons. Medicus Systems Corp., 1989—; lectr. No. Ill. U., 1981-87, St. Xavier Coll., 1987; mem. faculty Aurora U., 1987—; clin. teaching asst. U. Iowa, 1988—; expert witness for med. malpractice cases, 1987—. Mem. City Beautification Commn. Rock Island, 1972-76, also sec., vice-chmn. Mem. Am. Orgn. Nurse Execs. (cons., legis. and regulation com. 1987-89), Ill. Orgn. Nurse Execs. (mem. exec. com., chmn. Task Force on Sunset Ill. Nursing Act 1984-87, pres. 1988-89), Nat. League Nursing, Ill. League Nursing, Sigma Theta Tau. Roman Catholic. Editor: Ill. Nurses Assn. Directory of Baccalaureate Degree Completion Programs for RNs in Ill., 1979; writer, producer, dir.: Nursing: Opportunities Unlimited, 1980.

KOBUS, MONA WRIGHT, air transportation professional; b. Atwood, Kans., June 13, 1932; d. Lawrence Wallace Berry and Adele Rosina (Gulzow) Wright; m. R.J. Wright, Jan. 1952 (div. 1957); m. J.P. Kobus, Nov. 1968 (separated Nov. 1989). BS, U. Ariz., 1961; postgrad., No. Ariz. U., 1966-67, Ariz. State U., 1967-69, 86-87; MPA, Ariz. State U., 1981. Customer rels. rep. Ariz. Pub. Svc. Co., Casa Grande, Flagstaff, Ariz., 1961-67; owner/operator Mona's Clipping Svc., Phoenix, 1969-74; various positions City of Phoenix, 1974—; contract mgr. Phoenix CETA/PSE/PNP, 1978-81; planning, engring., environ. asst. Phoenix Sky Harbor Internat. Airport, 1986—; staff asst. 1988 Citizens Bond Com. for Aviation, Phoenix, 1987-88. Editor, writer (newsletter) Rapsheet, 1972-75; author columns in field, 1961-67. Pres. state home econ. occupations adv. bd. Ariz. State U., 1983-84; mem. City Mgr.'s Women's Issues com., Phoenix, 1989-91, steering com. Svc. Fund Drive, Phoenix, 1984-86; precinct com., Yuma County, Ariz., 1958. Recipient recognition pub. svc. Ariz. Dept. Econs. Security, 1975; named to Outstanding Young Women of Am., 1966. Mem. ASPA (life; nat. com. 1990-91), Am. Home Econs. Assn. (life), Ariz. Home Econs. Assn. (pres. no. region 1965-67), Sinagua Soc. of Mus. No. Ariz., Satisfied Frog Gold Mountain Club, Flagstaff C. of C. (chmn. Indian princesses, Retail Merchants sect. 1965-67), So. Ariz. Hiking Club, Swinging Stars Square Dance Club, Delta Delta Delta. Republican. Lutheran. Home: 5110 North 31st Way 338 Phoenix AZ 85016 Office: Phoenix Sky Harbor Internat Airport 3400 Sky Harbor Blvd Phoenix AZ 85034-4420

KOCH, CAROL HIGGINS, marketing reseach manager; b. Orange, N.J., Mar. 13, 1953; d. Frank and Jean Marie (Cox) Higgins; m. Bruce Stuart, Sept. 1, 1980. BA, Ohio Wesleyan U., 1975; MA, Ohio State U., 1976; MBA, N.Y. U., 1982. Cert. French and German tchr. Asst. tchr. Ohio State U., Columbus, 1976-77; German, French tchr. Montville High Sch., 1978-80; rsch. asst. NYU, 1981-82; sales rep. Viviane Woodard, N.Y., 1982-83; rsch. supr. Bozell, Jacobs, Kenyon & Eckhardt, Dallas, 1983-87; mktg. rsch. mgr. Tex. Instruments Consumer Products div., Dallas, 1987—. Home: 3508 Woodhaven Dr Farmers Branch TX 75234

KOCH, DIANE RUTH, community relations professional; b. Sidney, Ohio, July 16, 1956; d. Harold Roy and Ruthabelle May (Fosnight) K. BMus, Capital U., 1978. Pub. info. coord. Greater Columbus (Ohio) Arts Coun., 1978-79; vol. coord. Prevent Blindness, Columbus, 1979-80; program supr. Leo Yassenoff Jewish Ctr., Columbus, 1981-84; mgr. indsl. div. Manpower Temporary Svcs., Columbus, 1984-85; asst. coord. music in air dept. recreation and parks City of Columbus, 1985, dir. devel. dept. recreation and parks, 1985-88; mgr. community rels. Warner Cable Communications, 1988-89; pres. The Sponsorship Group, Columbus, 1989—; vocal instr., Columbus, 1978-87; cons. Schiller Park Master Planning Project, Columbus, 1987—. Directed numerous musicals for local community theaters, 1978-88; vocal recitalist, Columbus, 1980-82. Bd. dirs., exec. com. Family Counseling Crittenten Svcs., Columbus, 1988—; bd. dirs. Columbus Boys Choir, 1987; steering com. Gazebo Park, Columbus, 1988—; councilmember Columbus Found. Funders Coun., 1988—. Recognized for outstanding artistic achievement Worthington (Ohio) Community Theatre, 1988. Mem. Nat. Cable TV Pub. Affairs Assn., NAFE, Women's Bus. Bd. Lutheran. Home and Office: 980 Bernard Rd Columbus OH 43221

KOCH, EDNA MAE, lawyer; b. Terre Haute, Ind., Oct. 12, 1951; d. Leo K. and Lucille E. (Smith) K.; m. Mark D. Orton. BS in Nursing, Ind. State U., 1977; JD, Ind. U., 1980. Bar: Ind. 1980, U.S. Dist. Ct. (so. dist.) Ind. 1980. Assoc. Dillon & Cohen, Indpls., 1980-85; ptnr. Tipton, Cohen & Koch, Indpls., 1985—; leader seminars for nurses Ball State U., Muncie, Ind., St. Vincent Hosp., Indpls., Deaconess Hosp., Evansville, Ind., others; lectr. on med. malpractice Cen. Ind. chpt. Am. Assn. Critical Care Nurses, Indpls. "500" Postgrad. Course in Emergency Medicine, Ind. Assn. Osteo. Physicians and Surgeons State Conv., numerous others. Mem. ABA, Ind. State Bar Assn., Indpls. Bar Assn., Ind. Trial Lawyers Assn., Am. Nurses Assn., Ind. State Nurses Assn. Republican. Office: Tipton Cohen & Koch 47 S Meridian St Ste 200 Indianapolis IN 46204

KOCH, HELEN ALICE, organist; b. Wymore, Nebr., May 4, 1916; d. Arthur and Estelle (Holbert) Harms; m. Charles Day Quaife, June 18, 1946 (dec. Aug. 1963); children: Janet Lynn, Ruth Ann; m. Erwin Roland Koch, Jan. 26, 1970 (dec.). BA, Hamline U., 1938; MA, U. Minn., 1940. Instr. piano and organ Stephens Coll., Columbia, Mo., 1943-46; organist Meth. Ch., Hampton, Iowa, 1947-63; organist, choir dir. St. Paul's United Ch. Christ, St. Pauul, 1966-72, St. Peter's Luth. Ch., St. Pauul, 1972-75; organist Peace United Ch. Christ, St. Pauul, 1975—. Home: 1625 W Minnehaha Ave Saint Paul MN 55104

KOCH, JOANNE, film society administrator; b. N.Y.C., Oct. 7, 1929; d. John Albert Obermaier and Blanche (Ashman) Persky; m. Oscar A. Godbout Jr., Dec. 24, 1947 (div. July 1967); 1 child, Andrea Godbout; m. Richard H. Koch, Mar. 17, 1967; stepchildren: Stephen R. Koch, Jeremy B. Koch, Chapin F. Koch. BA, Goddard Coll., 1950. Film researcher film dept. Mus. of Modern Art, N.Y.C., 1950-54, tech. dir. film dept., 1963-67; tech. dir. film dept. Grove Press, N.Y.C., 1967-70; exec. dir. Film Soc. Lincoln Ctr., N.Y.C., 1971—. Named Chevalier of Arts & Letters, French Ministry of Culture, 1984. Mem. Soc. Motion Picture & TV Engrs. (assoc.). Office: Film Soc of Lincoln Ctr 140 W 65th St New York NY 10012

KOCH, JUNE QUINT, international construction liaison executive; b. Bklyn., Jan. 18, 1933; d. Eli and Minnie Quint; m. Noel Clinton Koch, Sept. 10, 1967; children—Justin, Monica, Jennie, Gabriel, Elias. B.A., Bklyn. Coll., 1954; M.A., Temple U., 1957; Ph.D., Columbia U., 1965. Instr. Temple U., 1958-65; asst. prof. Widener Coll., 1965-68, Bryn Mawr Coll., 1968-73; dir. Fed. Liaison Phila. '76 Inc., 1973-75; v.p. Koch Assocs., Inc., 1976-80; dir. intergovtl. relations Reagan-HUD Transition Team, 1980-81; dep. undersec. HUD, Washington, 1981-84, asst. sec. for policy devel. and rsch., 1984-87; co-founder, pres. Constrn. Mgmt. & Trading Inc., Vienna, Va. NEH grantee, 1972-73; numerous govt. awards. Mem. Republican Women's Forum, RNC Women's Network, Internat. Platform Assn., Phi Beta Kappa. Jewish. Office: Constrn Mktg & Trading Inc 8150 Leesburg Pike Ste 600 Vienna VA 22182*

KOCH, KIMBERLY ANN, broadcast executive; b. Chgo., May 5, 1964; d. Kenneth Alfred and Patricia Ann (Kelsey) K. BA magna cum laude, U. Utah, 1986. Camera operator Sta. KUTV (affiliate NBC), Salt Lake City, 1985-87; prodn. asst. Sta. KUED-TV (affiliate PBS), Salt Lake City, 1987-89, assoc. producer, 1989—. Mem. Women in Communications, Inc., Phi Kappa Phi, Kappa Tau Alpha, Phi Eta Sigma. Home: 7445 N Tall Oaks Circle Park City UT 84060 Office: Sta KUED-TV 101 Gardner Hall Salt Lake City UT 84112

KOCH, RITA ELIZABETH, computer specialist; b. Middletown, Conn., Mar. 22, 1948; d. Francis Xavier Joseph and Margaret (Whalen) K.; m. Salvatore Sclafani, Dec. 29, 1984; 1 child, Margaret Anne. BA, U. Conn., 1971; postgrad., Calif. State U., Hayward, 1972, New Sch. for Social Rsch., 1982-83, Baruch Coll., 1983, NYU, 1980. Computer programmer U.S. Dept. HUD, Washington, 1977-79, computer specialist, N.Y.C., 1979-84; computer specialist IRS, Washington, 1984-88, HUD, 1988—; mem. Fed. Women's Program, N.Y.C., 1982. Mem. Concord Village Assn.-Communications, Bklyn., 1982-83, Consumer Coun. Health Ins. Plan, N.Y.C.-Bklyn., 1983-84; mem. Capitol Hill Arts Workshop. Mem. NAFE, Computer Soc. of IEEE, Nat. Trust for Hist. Preservation, Capitol Hill Restoration Soc. Avocations: historic preservation, Victorian era, poetry. Home: 535 Second St SE Washington DC 20003

KOCH, SUSAN ELSA, sales executive; b. Hempstead, N.Y., Jan. 29, 1944; d. Bruce Carlton Koch and Jacqueline Raulet Paidas. Student, Carnegie Mellon U., Pitts., 1962-64; BA, Fairleigh Dickinson U., Teaneck, N.J., 1973; MA, Montclair State Coll., 1981. Customer svc. rep. N.J. Bell Telephone Co., 1965-67; asst. prodn. mgr. Modern Packaging mag./McGraw Hill, Inc., 1969-71; asst. book editor Guidepost Mag., N.Y.C., 1973-76; patient svcs. coordinator Nat. Multiple Sclerosis Soc., 1980-81; home econs. tchr. Leonia (N.J.) High Sch., 1981-82; sales cons. Macy's N.E., Paramus, N.J., 1987-88; rsch. consumer specialist Englewood, N.J., 1987—. Contbr. articles to profl. jours. County com. person Dem. Orgn., Leonia, 1976. Recipient Cert. of Achievement, McGraw-Hill, Inc. in graphic arts, 1970. Mem. Closter Animal Welfare Soc., N.Y.C. Opera Guild (vol.), AAUW, Sigma Kappa. Home: 19 W Hudson Ave Englewood NJ 07631

KOCHAMP, KATHERINE ELLEN, food products executive, researcher; b. Lindsay, Calif., Apr. 14, 1946; d. Jack and Orpha (Livingston) K. Student, Hartwell Coll., 1968. Supr. Phillips Petroleum Corp., Sacramento, 1969-77, Atlantic Richfield Corp., Sacramento, 1978-82; with Wallpaper Co., Roseville, Calif., 1983-88, BAg Ladies Coffee Co., Placerville, Calif., 1985—. Mem. NAFE. Democrat. Roman Catholic.

KOCH LIPMAN, CAREL EVELYNN, designer; b. Lincoln, Nebr., Mar. 23, 1960; d. Robert Carl and Gertrude Evelyn (Kornmuller) Koch; m. Ken Lipman, Dec. 16, 1989. B.S., Drexel U., 1982. Design asst. Sydney Carvin Milliken, N.Y.C., 1981, 82-83, Jones New York, N.Y.C., 1983-84; sales rep., designer Asymmetry, N.Y.C., 1984-85; designer Rayman/Ridless, N.Y.C., 1985-87; designer, producer, sales rep. Carel Koch Indsl. Design, N.Y.C., 1983, designer Echo Design Group, Albert Nipon Belts, 1987-88; designer Philip Sand Belts, 1988; with new product devel. dept. Karl Lagerfeld Bijoux div. Victoria Internat., 1988-89; deisgner The 1928 Jewelry Co., 1989—. Mem. NAFE, Phi Eta Sigma, Phi Kappa Phi, Omicron Nu. Avocations: dance, film, art, travel.

KOCHMAN, ROSALIND AXELROD, lawyer; b. Worcester, Mass., Jan. 12, 1937; d. George and Clara (Castleman) Axelrod; m. Marvin C. Kochman, Dec. 21, 1957; children: David, Stephen, Debra. BA, Harvard U., 1958; JD, NYU, 1974. Bar: N.Y. 1975, U.S. Dist. Ct. (so. and ea. dist.) N.Y. 1975, U.S. Ct. Appeals (2nd cir.) 1975. Pres. Nat. Council Jewish Women, Bklyn., 1969-71; asst. consumer specialist N.Y.C. Dept. Consumer Affairs, 1972-73; legal intern Office of Dist. Atty. County of Kings, Bklyn., summer 1973; legal assoc. Cohen, Weiss & Simon, N.Y.C., 1974; pvt. practice law Bklyn., 1978—; legal assoc. Karp & Sommers, N.Y.C., 1981-84; adminstr., legal counsel Kochman Eye Surg. Facility, Bklyn., 1984—. Trustee Community Hosp. Bklyn.; bd. dirs. Prospect Park South Assn. Mem. Am. Soc. Ophthalmic Adminstrs., Nat. Health Lawyers Assn., ABA, N.Y. State Bar Assn., N.Y. County Lawyers Assn., Bklyn. Women's Bar Assn., Radcliffe Club of N.Y., Knickerbocker Field Club. Jewish. Office: Kochman Eye Surg Facility 1301 Ave J Brooklyn NY 11230

KOCUREK, MARY JANE, librarian; b. Beasley, Tex., Aug. 6, 1939; d. Willie Adolph and Annie Ilene (Knesek) Kubelka; m. William John Kocurek, June 10, 1958. AA, Wharton Jr. Coll., 1964; BS in Edn., U. Houston, 1966; MLS, North Tex. State U., 1970. Bakery owner, mgr. Rosenberg, Tex., 1960-67; tchr. Lamar Consol. Ind. Sch. Dist., Rosenberg, 1967-70, librarian, 1970—. Contbr. numerous articles to Mus. Publicity. Bd. dirs. Am. Cancer Soc., Richmond, Tex., 1980—, Hist. Morton Cemetery Assn.; chmn. bd. dirs. Planned Parenthood Ft. Bend, Rosenberg, 1984-86; pres. Ft. Bend Mus. Docents, Richmond, 1985; mem. Richmond Sesquicentennial Steering Com., 1985—; vice-chmn. Ft. Bend County Republican Party, 1968-72. Recipient outstanding contbn. award Ft. Bend Mus., 1986, Planned Parenthood SE Tex., 1986; ednl. achievement award Am. Cancer Soc., 1986. Mem. Tex. Libr. Assn., Classroom Tchrs. Assn. (v.p. 1975-76, legis. chmn. 1985-86, sec. 1989-90), Young Adults Round Table, Phi Theta Kappa, Kappa Delta Pi, Delta Kappa Gamma. Mem. Brethren Ch. Clubs: New Century Garden (pres. 1981-82), Rose-Rich Rep. (publicity chmn. 1985-86) (Richmond). Home: 100 Hillcrest Dr Richmond TX 77469 Office: Lamar Consol Ind Sch Dist 4814 Mustang Ave Rosenberg TX 77471

KOCUREK, PATRICIA TERRAZAS, educator; b. Brownsville, Tex., Mar. 9, 1935; d. Alberto and Bertha (Cortazar) Terrazas; m. Louis J. Kocurek Jr., Aug. 17, 1957; children: Louis J. III, Alberto T., Kristopher M., John R., Patricia A. Student, St. Mary's Coll., Notre Dame, Ind.; BA, Incarnate Word Coll., San Antonio, 1957; MA, Trinity U., 1976. Cert. bilingual tchr. Tchr. chpt. I Harlandale Ind. Sch. Dist., San Antonio; del. NEA, Lome Togo, Melbourne, Australia and San Jose, Costa Rica. Active San Antonio Symphony League; founding mem. Tranchesi Meml. Service Corp.; chairperson Wolf Trail Kids Kamp, Harry Jersig Speech and Hearing Ctr.; meml. chair Sunshine Cottage; precinct chair Bexar County Dems.; mem. exec. com. Ella Austin Community Ctr., Early Learning Inst., 1st v.p.; group leader Little Rock Scripture Soc.; past Christian Child Devel. dir. Our Lady of Grace Ch. Mem. NEA (bd. dirs. Dist. XX), Tex. State Tchrs. Assn. (exec. com., legis. contact), Harlandale Tchrs. Assn. (past pres., v.p., treas.), World Orgn. of the Teaching Profession, St. Monica's Guild, Alumnae of the Sacred Heart, Equestrian Order of the Holy Sepulchre. Democrat. Roman Catholic. Home: 108 Thelma Dr San Antonio TX 78212

KODIS, MARY CAROLINE, marketing consultant; b. Chgo., Dec. 17, 1927; d. Anthony John and Callis Ferebee (Old) K.; student San Diego State Coll., 1945-47, Latin Am. Inst., 1948. Controller, div. adminstrv. mgr. Fed. Mart Stores, 1957-65; controller, adminstrv. mgr. Gulf Mart Stores, 1965-67; budget dir., adminstrv. mgr. Diana Stores, 1967-68; founder, treas., controller Handy Dan Stores, 1968-72; founder, v.p., treas. Handy City Stores, 1972-76; sr. v.p., treas. Handy City div. W.R. Grace & Co., Atlanta, 1976-79; founder, pres. Hal's Hardware and Lumber Stores, 1982-84; retail and restaurant cons., 1979—. Treas., bd. dirs. YWCA Watsonville,1981-84, 85-87; mem. Santa Cruz County Grand Jury, 1984-85. Recipient 1st Tribute to Women in Internat. Industry, 1978; named Woman of the Yr., 1986. Mem. Ducks Unltd. (treas. Watsonville chpt. 1981-89). Republican. Home and Office: 302 Wheelock Rd Watsonville CA 95076

KOEHL, CAMILLE JOAN, accountant; b. Chgo., Nov. 9, 1943; d. Alfonse James and Genevieve V. (Riche) Daurio; children: David A., Laura L., Robert M., Karen M. BS in Acctg., De Paul U., 1976; postgrad., Roosevelt U., 1987—. CPA, Ill.; cert. fin. planner. Treas. Meritex Corp., Carpentersville, Ill., 1966-68; controller Di Com Corp., Glenview, Ill., 1968-73; v.p., treas. Ridge Road Co., Northbrook, Ill., 1982-87, Decker Gardens, Inc., Northbrook, 1979-87, S&L Engring. Co., Northbrook, 1973-87; ptnr. HJS Constrn. Co., Barrington Hills, Ill., 1979—; pres. Lé Tan Ltd., Palatine, Ill., 1984—, IMC Ltd., Barrington Hills, 1985—; owner Camille J. Koehl & Assoc., Barrington Hills, 1978—; pres. Koehl Constrn. and Devel. Corp., Barrington Hills, 1990—, Pressing Matters Ltd., East Dundee, Ill., 1990—. Mem. Ill. CPAs, IBCFP. Home and Office: RR 2 Bow Ln Barrington Hills IL 60010

KOEHLER, CORINNE ANDERSON, financial planner; b. Eau Claire, Wis., Oct. 5, 1949; d. John and Helen (Hanson) Anderson; m. Dennis Paul Koehler, July 9, 1972. BS, U. Wis., Eau Claire, 1972. Cert. fin. planner, 1987. Asst. v.p./br. mgr. Otero Savs. & Loan, Colorado Springs, 1973-81; fin. planner, stock broker Dain Bosworth, Inc., Pueblo, Colo., 1987—. Bd. dirs. United Way of Pueblo, v.p. 1987—; past pres. El Pueblo Boys Ranch, also bd. dirs; trustee Pueblo Community Coll. Found.; bd. dirs. and past pres. Jr. League of Pueblo Inc.; mem. adv. bd. Packard Found.; bd. dirs. Pueblo Zoological Soc., 1988—. Named Vol. of the Year, El Pueblo Boys Ranch, 1988. Mem. Inst. Cert. Fin. Planners, Leadership Pueblo Alumni Assn. Home: 403 Argyle Pueblo CO 81004 Office: Dain Bosworth Inc 5th & Main Pueblo CO 81004

KOEHLER, JANE ELLEN, librarian; b. Belleville, Ill., Oct. 18, 1944; d. Edward William and Elizabeth Ellen (Sanford) Hindman; m. Robert Philip Koehler, Feb. 18, 1936; children: Clare Anne, Beth Ellen. BS, Eastern Ill. U., 1967; MS, U. Ill., 1970. Cert. edn. educator;. Library asst. Belleville (Ill.) Pub. Library, 1964-65; tchr. librarian Sch. Dist. 72, Woodstock, Ill., 1966-73; dir. library services Sch. Dist. 200, Woodstock, 1969-73; dir. youth services Woodstock Pub. Library, 1980-89, asst. dir., 1989—. Author: (short story) Northwest Herald, 1980. Bd. dir. Auxillary Mem. Hosp.; vol. Turning Point (Crisis Intervention), 1978-88; mem. Ill. Literary Heritage Com., 1984-85; chmn. Mem. Hosp. for. Mem. Library Adminstr. Coun. of Northern Ill. (sec. 1990), Woodstock Fine Arts Assn. Republican. Roman Catholic. Home: 13171 Hickory Ln Woodstock IL 60098 Office: Woodstock Pub Library 414 W Judd Woodstock IL 60098

KOELMEL, LORNA LEE, data processing executive; b. Denver, May 15, 1936; d. George Bannister and Gladys Lee (Henshall) Steuart; m. Herbert Howard Nelson, Sept. 9, 1956 (div. Mar. 1967); children: Karen Dianne, Phillip Dean, Lois Lynn; m. Robert Darrel Koelmel, May 12, 1981; stepchildren: Kim, Cheryl, Dawn, Debbie. BA in English, U. Colo., 1967. Cert. secondary English tchr. Substitute English tchr. Jefferson County Schs., Lakewood, Colo., 1967-68; sec. specialist IBM Corp., Denver, 1968-75, pers. administr., 1975-82, asst. ctr. coord., 1982-85, office systems specialist, 1985-87, backup computer operator, 1987—; computer instr. Barnes Bus. Coll., Denver, 1987—; owner, mgr. Lorna's Precision Word Processing and Desktop Pub., Denver, 1987-89; computer cons. Denver, 1990—. Organist Christian Sci. Soc., Buena Vista, Colo., 1963-66, chm. bd. dirs.,Thornton, Colo., 1979-80. Mem. NAFE, Nat. Secs. Assn. (retirement ctr. chair 1977-78, newsletter chair 1979-80, v.p. 1980-81), U. Colo. Alumni Assn., Alpha Chi Omega (publicity com. 1986-88). Republican. Club: Nat. Writers. Lodge: Job's Daus. (recorder 1953-54).

KOENECKE, CAROL YVONNE, administrator; b. Reedsburg, Wis., Jan. 21, 1959; d. Martin Edward and Marlene Levita (Luetkens) K. BA in Psychology, La. State U., 1981; MA, Rollins Coll., 1986. Cert. addictions profl., Fla., alcohol and drug counselor, Tex. Psychiat. technician Mid-Continent Hosp., Olathe, Kans., 1981-82; asst. dir. Drug Abuse Edn. Ctr., Olathe, 1981-82; probation officer Johnson County, Olathe, 1982-83; probation officer, investigator Fla. Dept. Corrections, Orlando, 1983-85; dir. Neighborhood Watch Program Orlando Crime Commn., 1985-86; program counselor Straight, Inc., Orlando, 1986-87, assoc. dir., 1987-89; administr. Straight, Inc., Dallas, 1989—. Vol. Spouse Abuse, Inc., Orlando, 1985, Greenpeace, Washington, 1986—; bd. dirs. YWCA. Mem. Am. Assn. for Counseling and Devel., Am. Mental Health Counselors Assn., Fla. Alcohol and Drug Abuse Assn., Community Leaders Am., Am. Acad. Med. Administrs., Internat. Leaders in Achievement, Alpha Epsilon Delta, Psi Chi, Mu Sigma Rho, Alpha Xi Delta. Republican. Lutheran. Office: Straight Inc 2900 Gateway Ste 600 Irving TX 75063

KOENIG, ELIZABETH BARBARA, sculptor; b. N.Y.C., Apr. 20, 1937; d. Hayward and Selma E. (Rosen) Ulman; m. Carl Stuart Koenig, Sept. 10, 1961; children: Katherine Lee, Kenneth Douglas. BA, Wellesley Coll., 1958; MD, Yale U., 1962; postgrad., Art Students League N.Y., 1963-64, Corcoran Sch. Art, 1964-67. Exhibited one-woman shows including St. John's Coll., Annapolis, Md., 1974, also solo retrospectives Lyman Allyn Mus., New London, Conn., 1978, Rotunda of Pan-Am. Health Orgn., Washington, 1978; group shows include Internat. Dedication Nat. Bur. Standards, Gaithersburg, Md., 1966, No. Va. Mus., Alexandria, 1975, Textile Mus., Washington, 1974-75, Meridian House Internat., Washington, 1980; commd. works include: Free Spirit marble carving Washington Hebrew Congregation, 1978, Monumental Torso bronze for grounds George Meany Ctr. for Labor Studies, 1982; represented in many pvt. collections, U.S. and Europe, 1965—. Recipient 1st prize sculpture Tri-State Regional Exhbn., Md., 1970, 2d and 3d prize sculpture, 1971. Mem. Artists Equity Assn. (v.p. Washington 1977-83), Art Students League N.Y. (life), Internat. Sculpture Ctr., New Arts Ctr. Avocations: reading, gardening. Home: 9014 Charred Oak Dr Bethesda MD 20817

KOENIG, GAY PENNINGTON, pharmacist; b. Portsmouth, Ohio, Jan. 31, 1956; d. Roy Marcus and Norma Gay (Meade) Pennington; m. Paul Jerome, Sept. 24, 1988. BS, U. Kentucky, 1980. Registered pharmacist. Asst. mgr. Revco DS, Inc., Paintsville, Ky., 1980-82, Ashland, Ky., 1982-89; Marietta, Ga., 1989—. Mem. Am. Pharm. Assn., Ky. Pharm. Assn. Republican.

Methodist. Office: Revco DS Inc #1588 2692 Sandy Plains Rd Marietta GA 30066

KOENIG, KIM DIANE, lawyer, writer; b. Tucson, Sept. 22, 1956; d. Theodore Ronald Koenig and Dorothy May (Hegenbart) Yeoman; m. John Rolfing Muenster, July 11, 1982; 1 child, Kailani Koenig-Muenster. BA, Evergreen State Coll., 1978; JD, U. Puget Sound, 1981. Bar: Wash. 1981, U.S. Dist. Ct. (we. dist.) Wash., 1982. Staff atty. Seattle-King County Pub. Defender Assn., 1981-85; spiritual counselor Voices of Light, Rolling Bay, Wash., 1986-89, co-founder, 1986-90; of counsel Mestel & Muenster, Seattle, 1989—; author, writer Bainbridge Island, Wash., 1986—; model Jockey Internat., 1989—; model Jockey Internat., 1989—. Author: Sojourns of the Soul, 1989. Office: PO Box 4630 Rolling Bay WA 98061-0630

KOENIG, MARIE HARRIET KING, public relations director, fund raising executive; b. New Orleans, Feb. 19, 1919; d. Harold Paul and Sadie Louise (Bole) King; m. Walter William Koenig, June 24, 1956; children: Margaret Marie, Susan Patricia. Major in Voice, La. State U., 1937-39; Pre-law, Loyola U., 1942-43; BS in History, U. LaVerne, 1986. Adminstrv. asst. to atty. gen. State of La., New Orleans, 1940-44; contract writer MGM Studios, Culver City, Calif., 1944-46; asst. sec., treas. Found. for Ind., L.A., 1950-56, Found. for Social Rsch., L.A., 1950-56; dir. communications Incentive Rsch. Corp., L.A., 1969-78; rsch. supr., devel. dept. Calif. Inst. Technology, pasadena, Calif., 1969; staff asst. for devel. Rep. Party of L.A., South Pasadena, 1989—. Author: Does the National Council of Churches Speak for You?, 1978; delivered lecture series on U.S. fgn. policy. Hon. citizen Colonial Williamsburg Found.,1987; active Nat. Soc. for Hist. Preservation, 1986, Gene Autry Western Heritage Mus., 1986, Friends of the Huntington Libr., 1986, Town Hall of L.A., 1986-88, Pasadena City Women's Club, 1982-84, The Masquers Club; contbr. mem. L.A. World Affairs Counc., 1990, L.A. County Mus. Art, 1990; past pres. Pasadena Rep. Women Federated; past mem. Opera Guild of So. Calif., 1976; com. mem. Pacific Clinics, 1985-88; past chmn., v.p. programs Bel Air Rep. Women Federated, 1980-85. Recipient Cert. Recognition Calif. State Assembly, 1989, Recognition of Excellence, Achievement and Commitment U.S. Ho. Reps., 1989, Cert. Merit Rep. Presdl. Task Force, 1986, Cert. Appreciation U.S. Def. Com., 1984, Hon. Freedom Fighter award U.S. Def. Com., 1985, Cert. Appreciation Am. Conservative Union, 1983, Cert. Commendation Rep. Cen. Com. L.A. County, 1972, Cert. Appreciation Eisenhower-Nixon So. Calif. Com., 1952. Mem. The Greater L.A. Press Club, The Publicity Club L.A., Women In Communications, Inc. Republican. Home: 205 Madeline Dr Pasadena CA 91105

KOENIG, SHARON ANN, banker; b. Appleton, Wis., Dec. 2, 1947; d. Joseph A. and Dolores Iva (Bergner) Gregorius; m. Stanley Louis Koenig, Aug. 7, 1971; children: Bryan Louis, Lisa In Hee. Student, Carthage Coll., 1966-68; BA, U. Wis., 1971. Residential mortgage loan processor, underwriter First Wis. Nat. Bank Madison, 1971-80, mgr., officer residential mortgage dept., 1980-83, comml. mortgage loan officer, 1983-86, coordinator, officer mortgage and SBA, 1986—. Officer, rep. Nakoma Neighborhood Assn., Madison, 1984-86; vice chmn. Families by Adoption South Cen. Wis., Madison, 1985-87, chmn. 1987-89. Mem. Madison Bd. Realtors, Wis. Mortgage Bankers Assn., Nat. Mortgage Bankers Assn. Home: 4206 Manitou Way Madison WI 53711 Office: First Wis Nat Bank Madison One S Pinckney St Madison WI 53711

KOENIG, SIERRA SUE, accountant; b. Reno, Sept. 23, 1954; d. Raymond Louis and Pearl Ruth (McCann) K.; m. John W. Galarneau, Aug. 2, 1975 (div. Nov. 1977); 1 child, John William. M in Acctg., U. Calif., Davis, 1976. CPA, Calif. Cert. property mgr., Calif. Property mgr. S&M Capital, Sacramento, 1973-76; acct. Main Hurdman, Sacramento, 1977-84; prin. Sierra Svcs., San Diego, 1977—; acct. Stock/ALPER, San Diego, 1985-87; prin. Contractor's Svc. Ctr., El Cajon, Calif., 1988—; cons. Alpine, Calif., 1986—, Sierra Svcs., El Cajon, 1984-87; acct. Drug Edn. Awareness Program, 1988—. Treas. Mothers Against Drunk Drivers, San Diego, 1984; chairperson membership com. Women Escaping a Violent Environment, San Diego, 1984; vol. March of Dimes, San Diego, 1986; Sacramento Area Economical Opportunity Council; mem. Ch. Luth. of the Good Shepard, Alpine. Mem. NAFE (bd. dirs. 1985—), Adam Computer Soc. (sec./treas. 1985-87), Nat. Assn. for Women Accts. Democrat. Office: Sierra Svcs 868 N 2nd St Ste 301 El Cajon CA 92021

KOENIGS, RITA SCALES, lawyer; b. Milw., May 5, 1952; d. John J. and Gertrude M. (Kendall) S. BA, Am. Internat. Coll., 1974; JD, Western New Eng. Coll., 1977. Bar: Mass. 1977, U.S. Dist. Ct. Mass. 1977. Assoc. Joseph & Manganaro, Springfield, Mass., 1977-79, Oberg, Linial & Scales, Springfield, 1979-80; staff trial atty. Mass. Defenders Com., Pittsfield, 1980—; atty.-in-charge Com. for Pub. Counsel Svcs., Pittsfield, 1987-90, Springfield, 1990—. Mem. planning bd. and capital outlay com. City of Pittsfield, 1988-90. Office: Com for Pub Counsel Svcs 1145 Main St Ste 208 Springfield MA 01103

KOERBER, JANET PEARL, lawyer; b. Milw., Nov. 22, 1933; d. Clarence F. and Isabelle L. (Arndt) K. BA, Marquette U., 1964, JD, 1966. Bar: Wis. 1966, U.S. Dist. Ct. (ea. and we. dists.) Wis. 1966, U.S. Ct. Appeals (7th cir.) 1966, U.S. Supreme Ct. 1972, U.S. Tax Ct. 1979. Pvt. practice, Milw., 1966-82, 84—; trustee U.S. Bankruptcy Cts. (ea. dist.) Wis., 1966-69, estate adminstr., 1982-84. Advisor Am. Saddlebred Horse Breeders of Wis., 1977—, Am. Saddlebred Assn. of Wis., 1977—, Matrix Home Health Care Agy. Mem. ABA, Milw. Bar Assn., Wis. Bar Assn., U.S. Selective Svc. Bd. Home: 10635 N Ivy Ct Mequon WI 53092 Office: 1234 N Prospect Ave Milwaukee WI 53202

KOERBER, JOAN PATRICIA, educator; b. Newark, Mar. 23, 1929; d. George Vincent and Catherine Rose (Donahue) Callanan; m. John Calvin Koerber, June 27, 1953; children: John C., Joanne C. BS in Elem. Edn., Newark State Coll., 1952; MA in Adminstrn., Kean Coll., Union, N.J., 1984. Tchr. 15th Ave Sch., Newark, 1952-71, Lincoln Sch., Newark, 1971-78; tchr. chpt. I Newark Bd. Edn., Newark, 1978-79; chapter I coord. Lincoln Sch., 1979-84, basic skills tchr., 1984—; summer sch. coord./prin. Lincoln Sch., 1979-84. Sec. Essex County PTA. Mem. NEA, N.J. Edn. Assn., Essex County Edn. Assn., Newark Edn. Assn., Newark Tchrs. Union, Assn. for Supervising and Curriculum Devel., N.J. State Columbiettes (supreme bd. dirs., past state pres.), Kappa Delta Phi (past pres.), Phi Delta Kappa (past pres.), Kean Coll. Grad. Sch. Coun. (pres.). Home: 95 Midland Pl Newark NJ 07106

KOERBER, MARILYNN ELEANOR, gerontological educator, consultant, nurse; b. Covington, Ky., Feb. 1, 1942; d. Harold Clyde and Vivian Eleanor (Conrad) Hilge; m. James Paul Koerber, May 29, 1971. Diploma, Christ Hosp. Sch. Nursing, Cin., 1964; BS in Nursing, U. Ky., 1967; MPH, gerontology cert., U. Mich. RN, Ohio, S.C. Staff nurse premature and newborn nursery Cin. Gen. Hosp., 1964-65; staff nurse, hosp. discharge planner Vis. Nurse Assn., Cin., 1967-69; asst. dir. Vis. Nurse Assn., Atlanta, 1976-78; instr. Coll. Nursing, U. Ky., Lexington, 1970-71; supr. Montgomery County Health Dept., Rockville, Md., 1971-74; asst. prof. Coll. Nursing, U. S.C., Columbia, 1979-86; Alzheimer's project coord. S.C. Commn. on Aging, Columbia, 1988—; dir. edn. and tng. Luth. Homes S.C., White Rock, 1988—; instr. Coll. Nursing, U. S.C., 1987-89; mem. utilization rev. bd. West Midlands Health Dist., Lexington, 1984—; text item writer, nurse aide cert. Psychol. Corp., San Antonio, 1989; bd. examiners Nursing Home Adm., Columbia, 1990; presenter gerontol. workshops. Contbg. editor: (handbook) Promoting Caregiver Groups, 1984; reviewer gerontology textbooks, 1988; contbr. tng. video and manuals on Alzheimers, 1988 (hon. mention Retirement Rsch. Found. 1989). Del. S.C. Gov. White House Conf. on Aging, Columbia, 1981; chairperson ann. mtg. S.C. Fedn. for Older Ams., Columbia, 1988, 89; sec., editor newsletter Shadblow Homeowners Assn., Columbia, 1989—. USPHS trainee, 1965-67, Adm. on Aging trainee, 1969-70. Mem. ANA (cert. gerontol. nurse 1988, community health nurse 1989), S.C. Nurses Assn., Am. Pub. Health Assn., Gerontol. Soc. Am., S.C. Gerontol. Soc. (treas. 1989—, Rosamond R. Boyd award 1986), Coun. Gerontol. Nursing, Soc. for Pub. Health Educators, Am. Soc. on Aging, Alzheimers Assn. (bd. dirs. Columbia chpt. 1988—), Nat. Coun. on Aging. Democrat. Unitarian Universalist. Home: 1143 Pine Croft Dr West Columbia SC 29169-3138 Office: Luth Homes SC PO Box 497 White Rock SC 29177

KOERNER, JERRY LYNN, county official; b. Owosso, Mich., Aug. 12, 1950; d. Theodore Jr. and Doris (Ashmun) K. BA in Lit. and Psychology, John Wesley Coll., Owosso, Mich., 1974; BBA, Calif. State U. Stanislaus, Turlock, 1984; MBA, Calif. State U., Turlock, 1985. Supr. mail room dept., dir. women's athletics John Wesley Coll., 1974-75; program coord. Merced County Community Action Agy., Merced, Calif., 1981; work study vet.'s rep. Calif. Employment Devel. Dept., Turlock, 1982; employment and tng. specialist Merced County Pvt. Industry Tng. Dept., 1986—. First aid instr. ARC, Eng., 1980; group leader Teen Pregnancy Symposium, Merced, 1989. Sgt. USAF, 1976-80. Mem. AAUW (co-chmn. scholarship fundraiser com. Merced 1989-90), Merced C. of C. (com. 1988). Office: Merced County Pvt Industry Tng Dept 1020 W Main St Merced CA 95340

KOFMAN, MARY ANITA, newspaper manager; b. Mansfield, Ohio, Aug. 20, 1942; d. Harold and Marion Howman; children: Noah, Toby, Molleen, Shannon. Student, U. Ala., Tuscaloosa, NYU. Asst. pub. rels. dir. Jr. Achievement, Inc., N.Y.C., 1960-64; tchr. Tuscaloosa County Sch. System, Northport, Ala., 1980-85; adminstrv. asst. Ala. Press Assn., Birmingham, 1985-87; mgr. Magnolia Clipping Svc., Tuscaloosa, Ala., 1987—. Bd. dirs. Arthritis Found. Mem. NAFE, LWV (bd. dirs.), Tuscaloosa Area Gerontology Assn. Office: 2600 8th St Tuscaloosa AL 35401

KOFSKY, MARIA P., quality assurance professional; b. Baguio City, Philippines, July 11, 1963; d. Eduardo S. and Hermosa (Paman) Paderon; m. Alan J. Kofsky, Sept. 5, 1987. BS in Biology, SUNY, Stony Brook, 1985. Supr. quality assurance Allergan Optical Inc., Woodbury, N.Y., quality assurance supr.; quality assurance supr. Pharmafair Inc., Hauppauge, N.Y.; quality assurance supr. and insp. Barr Lass, Inc., Northvale, N J.; rsch. asst. SUNY, Stony Brook. Home: 8 Dawson Pl Huntington NY 11746

KOGA, ELAINE, controller; b. San Francisco, Feb. 8, 1942; d. Harry Takeo and Mitsuko Kaneko K.; m. Tad T. Murano, July 19, 1964 (div. 1981); children: Michael M., Kevin G. BS, U. San Francisco, 1980. Tax acct. Robert H. Mann, CPA, San Francisco, 1971-72; chief acct. H. Shenson, Inc., San Francisco, 1972-78; asst. controller, acctg. mgr. Esprit De Corp, San Francisco, 1978-80; v.p., controller Marsquare Internat., Inc., San Francisco, 1980; controller Peat, Marwick, Mitchell, CPA, San Francisco, 1981, Armstrong, Bastow, Potter, CPA, San Jose, Calif., 1982, Sofabed Conspiracy, Inc., Berkeley, Calif., 1983-84; asst. v.p., controller Montgomery Capital Corp., San Francisco, 1984—. Mem. Nat. Assn. Accts. (bd. dirs. 1981-84). Home: 1007 Arlington Ln Daly City CA 94014 Office: Montgomery Capital Corp 244 California St Suite 700 San Francisco CA 94111

KOGEN, LINDA SUE, construction company executive; b. Chgo., Aug. 29, 1961; d. Howard M. and Esther Evelyn (Solotky) K. Student, Drake U., 1979-81. Sec. Kogen Enterprises, Highland Park, Ill., 1981-84; pres. Kogen Constrn. Co., Chgo., 1985—. Mem. Project Skill (cert. appreciation 1989), Young Men's Jewish Coun. (designate bd. dirs. mem. 1989). Office: Kogen Construction 1755 Lake Cook Rd Highland Park IL 60035

KOGI, HIROKO, financial analyst; b. Kiryu, Gumma, Japan, Mar. 8, 1955; d. Ryohei and Fusako K. AA, Obirin Coll., 1975; BS in Political Sci., Lindenwood Coll., St. Charles, Mo., 1981; MBA, U. Mo., 1987, MA in Econ., 1988. Asst. to shipbrokers Dodwell and Co. Ltd., Tokyo, 1975-79; with Mercantile Bank N.A., St. Louis, 1982-83; research asst., teaching asst. U. Mo., 1986-88; fin. analyst Mitsubishi Trust and Banking Corp., N.Y.C., 1988-. Mem. NAFE, Omicron Delta Epsilon, Beta Gamma Sigma. Office: Mitsubishi Trust and Bankin 520 Madison Ave 25th Fl New York NY 10022

KOHANKIE, CAROL LANGDON, health facility administrator; b. New London, Conn., July 15, 1940; d. Wilbur Spencer and Mary (Leather) Langdon; m. Robert Watson Kohankie II, Aug. 26, 1967; 1 child, Robert Watson III. BFA in Textile Design, Moore Coll. of Art, Phila., 1963; MEd, U. Hartford, 1968. Exec. dir. Jr. Achievement, Wooster, Ohio, 1980-81; pres. Kie Creations, Flower Mound, Tex., 1981-86; chmn. Christian Community Action Festival of Trees, Lewisville, Tex., 1986-87; assoc. dir. devel. Dallas Ballet, 1987-88; dir. devel. and communications The Winston Sch., Dallas, 1988; dir. devel. Grace Presbyn. Village, Dallas, 1988-90; exec. dir. Deaf Action Ctr., 1990; cons. Dancer's Unltd., Inc., Dallas, 1987-88, Christian Community Action, Lewisville, 1982-87. Chmn. Zip Code Task Force, Flower Mound, 1982-86; mem. Planning and Zoning Commn., Flower Mound, 1983-84; mem. Dallas Com. Internat. Visitors; bd. dirs. Nat. Soc. Fund Raising Execs., 1988—. Named Guardian Angel Christian Community Action, 1987; English Speaking Union travel grantee, Phila., 1962; bd. dirs. Nat. Soc. Fund Raising Exec., 1988—; dir. devel. Grace Presby. Village. Mem. Nat. Soc. Fund Raising Execs. Dallas and Ft. Worth (bd. dirs. Dallas chpt. 1989—), AAUW. Republican. Methodist. Home: 3930 Willow Run Flower Mound TX 75028

KOHLER, CARRIE ANN, industrial relations executive; b. Chgo., Aug. 25, 1963; d. Edward Carl and Dorothy Therese (Springer) Malinowski. BS in Sociology, Iowa State U., 1985, MS in Indsl. Relations, 1987. Field examiner Nat. Labor Relation Bd., Des Moines, 1987; asst. indsl. relations dir. Packaging Corp. Am., Filer City, Mich., 1988—; Am. Arbitration Assn., San Diego, 1986; pres. Am. Soc. Personnel Adminstrn., Ames, Iowa, 1986-87. Author: Thesis, Pre-Hire Agreements in the Constrn. Industry, Past Present and Future 1987. Mem. Jaycees, Manistee Mich., 1988—. Recipient Scholarship award George Von Tungln Scholarship for excellence. Mem. Indsl. Relations Research Assn., Alpha Kappa Delta Sociology Honor Soc. Home: 3271 Lakeshore Rd Manistee MI 49660 Office: Packaging Corp Am 2246 Udell St Filer City MI 49634

KOHLS-STEHMAN, BETTY, financial consultant, management consultant; b. Glencoe, Minn., Dec. 23, 1952; d. Clarence Otto and Pearl Amelia (Tuman) Kohls; m. Carl Knottwell Stehman Jr., Feb. 12, 1984; 1 child, Sandra. BA in Acctg., Winona (Minn.) State U., 1975. Staff auditor Norwest Bank Minn., N.A., Mpls., 1975-78; acct. Regan Cos., Mpls., 1978-79; lead auditor Bemis Co., Mpls., 1980; internal audit mgr. Hartzell Corp., St. Paul, 1980-82; controller Ragon Electronics, St. Paul, 1982-85, Gustafson Constrn., Inc., St. Louis Park, Minn., 1985-88; ind. sales cons. Discovery Toys, Livermore, Calif., 1988—; owner, cons. An Asst. to the Entrepreneur, Wheaton, Md., 1989—. Asst. treas. Berg for Congress campaign, St. Paul, 1980; vol. acct. children's Miracle Network Telethon, Mpls., 1984, 85. Mem. Kensington Bus. & Profl. Women. Republican. Lutheran.

KOHN, JULIEANNE, travel agent; b. Detroit, Apr. 15, 1946; d. Ralph Merwin and Jane Tacke (Meyers) K.; B.A., Heidelberg Coll., Tiffin, Ohio, 1968; postgrad. Eastern Mich. U., 1969-70; diploma Inst. Cert. Travel Agts., 1979. Travel agt. Am. Express Co., Detroit, 1970-73, Thomas Cook Inc., Detroit, 1973-75; mgr. Island Traveller, Grosse Ile, Mich., 1975-76; pres., owner Flying Suitcase, Inc., Grosse Ile, 1976—; ptnr. Tri-Kohn Investments, Grosse Ile, Mich., 1983—. Mem. Am. Soc. Travel Agts., Inst. Cert. Travel Agts. (life). Episcopalian. Club: Grosse Ile Golf and Country. Home: 9781 Hawthorn Glen Dr Grosse Ile MI 48138 Office: 8117 Macomb St Grosse Ile MI 48138

KOHN, KAREN JOSEPHINE, graphic and exhibition designer; b. Muskegon, Mich., Jan. 8, 1951; d. Herbert George and Catherine Elizabeth (Johnson) K.; m. Robert Joseph Duffy Jr. , July 10, 1982; children: Megan Kathleen, Sarah Evelyn. BFA, cum laude, U. Mich., 1973; MFA, Sch. Art Inst. Chgo., 1975. Free-lance designer, Chgo., 1976-77; designer Stevens Exhibits, Chgo., 1977-78; artist-in-residence Chgo. Council on Fine Arts, 1978-79; designer Chgo. Hist. Soc., 1979-81, dir. design, 81-84; prin. Karen Kohn & Assocs., Chgo., 1985—. Work appeared in Mus. News, Kraft Gen. Foods hdqrs. Recipient Superior Achievement award for temporary exhbn. Congress of Ill. Hist. Socs. and Mus., 1985, Superior Achievement award for permanent exhbn., 1989. Mem. Am. Assn. Mus. (Distinctive Merit awards 1982, 84, 85, Highest Honor awards 1982, 83, 84), Nat. Assn. Mus. Exhibitors (Midwest regional rep. 1983-84), Soc. Typog. Arts, Am. Inst. Graphic Artists.

KOHN, LISA, entertainment advertising executive; b. Summit, N.J., Sept. 16, 1963; d. Daniel Joseph Kohn and Mary Anne (Freiman) Miller. BA in Psychology, Cornell U., 1985. Mem. sales and market rsch. staff Demographic Systems, Inc., N.Y.C., 1985-86; account mgmt. asst. NW Ayer, Inc., N.Y.C., 1986; account supr. Grey Entertainment and Media, N.Y.C., 1986—. Home: 533 E 5th St Apt 1 New York NY 10009 Office: Grey Entertainment & Media 875 3d Ave 4th Fl New York NY 10022

KOHN, MARY LOUISE BEATRICE, nurse; b. Yellow Springs, Ohio, Jan. 13, 1920; d. Theophilus John and Mary Katharine (Schmitkons) Gaehr; A.B., Coll. Wooster, 1940; M.Nursing, Case Western Res. U., 1943; m. Howard D. Kohn, 1944; children: Marcia R., Marcia K. Epstein. Nurse, 1943-44, Atlantic City Hosp., 1944, Thomas M. England Gen. Hosp., U.S. Army, Atlantic City, 1945-46, Peter Bent Brigham Hosp., Boston, 1947, Univ. Hosps., Cleve., 1946-48; mem. faculty Frances Payne Bolton Sch. Nursing Case Western Res. U., 1948-52; vol. nurse Blood Service, ARC, 1952-55; office nurse, Cleve., part time 1955—; free-lance writer. Bd. dirs. Aux. Acad. Medicine Cleve., 1970-72, officer, 1976—; mem. Cleve. Health Mus. Aux., Am. Cancer Soc. vol.; mem. women's com. Cleve. Orch., 1970; women's council WVIZ-TV. Mem. Am., Ohio nurses assns., alumni assns. Wooster Coll., Frances P. Bolton Sch. Nursing (pres. 1974-75), Assn. Operating Rm. Nurses, Antique Automobile Assn. Am., Western Res. Hist. Soc., Am. Heart Assn., Cleve. Playhouse Aux., Internat. Fund for Animal Welfare, Cleve. Animal Protective League, U.S. Humane Soc., Friends of Cleve. Ballet, Smithsonian Instn., Council World Affairs, Orange Community Arts Council. Clubs: Cleve. Racquet, Women's City, Women's of Case-Western Res. U. Sch. Medicine. Author: (with Atkinson) Berry and Kohn's Introduction to Operating Room Technique, 5th edit., 1978, 6th edit., 1986, 7th edit. Asst. editor Cleve. Physician, Acad. Medicine Cleve., 1966-71. Home: 28099 Belcourt Rd Cleveland OH 44124

KOITHAN, MARY SUSAN, nursing educator; b. Cin., Feb. 25, 1956; d. Norman J. and Dorothy B. (Harrell) Zemites; m. Ronald Koithan, Sept. 17, 1980; children: Andrea, Matthew. BSN, U. Cin., 1978; MSN, U. Nev., 1986; postgrad., U. Colo. Instr. in nursing U. Nev., Las Vegas; pvt. practice cons., home healthcare educator Las Vegas; instr. Clark County Community Coll., Las Vegas; charge nurse, supr. Desert Springs Hosp., Las Vegas. Bd. dirs., co-chair nursing com., nurse educator, mem. disaster team ARC. Barrick fellow; U.S. Dept. HEW grantee. Mem. AACCN, ANA, Nev. Nurses Assn. (pres. 1990—), Western Inst. Nursing, Western Soc. for Nursing Rsch., Am. Nurses Found., Phi Kappa Phi, Sigma Theta Tau. Home: 658 Valemont Ct Las Vegas NV 89124

KOKOLAKIS-KASTRENAKES, MARIA, advertising executive, consultant, business owner; b. Bklyn., Nov. 10, 1963; d. John and Pagona (Frangos) Kokolakis; m. Michael Kastrenakes, Feb. 17, 1990. BA in English, Dowling Coll., 1984; MS in Mass Communication, Boston U., 1987. Asst. advt. exec. Grey Advt., Inc., N.Y.C., 1986; advt. exec. Garvan Advt., Inc., Hicksville, N.Y., 1987-88; account supr. Kaprielian O'Leary, N.Y.C., 1988-89; pres., owner CommuniK Advt., Inc., Tarpon Springs, Fla., 1989—; market rsch. and new bus. cons. Benito Advt., Tampa, Fla., 1989; program dir. dept. marine sci. internat. workshop on large Eddy simulations U. So. Fla., St. Petersburg, 1990—. Mem. Bus. Profl. Advt. Assn. N.Y . Republican. Greek Orthodox. Office: CommuniK Advt & Mktg Inc 201 E Center St Tarpon Springs FL 34689

KOLASA, KATHRYN KELLY, food and nutrition educator, consultant; b. Detroit, July 26, 1949; d. Marion J. and Blanche Ann (Gasiorowski) K.; m. Patrick Noud Kelly, Jan. 3, 1983. BS, Mich. State U., 1970; PhD, U. Tenn., 1974. Test kitchen home economist Kellogg Co., 1971; instr. dept. food sci. and food systems adminstrn. U. Tenn.-Knoxville, 1973-74; asst. prof. dept. food sci. and human nutrition Mich. State U., East Lansing, 1974-76, assoc. prof., 1976-82; prof., chmn. food, nutrition and instn. mgmt. Sch. Home Econs., East Carolina U., Greenville, N.C., 1982-86, prof., head nutrition edn. and svcs. sect. Dept. Family Medicine, Sch. Medicine, 1986—; mem. subcom. food and nutrition bd. NAS on Uses of the RDA, 1981-83; cons. food and nutrition. Recipient grants in nutrition and food service, 1974—; Kellogg nat. fellow, 1985-88. Mem. Soc. Nutrition Edn. (pres. 1984), Am. Instn. Nutrition, Inst. Food Technologists, Com. on Nutritional Anthropology, Am. Dietetic Assn. Roman Catholic. Author: (with Ann Bass and Lou Wakefield) Community Nutrition and Individual Food Behavior, 1978. Home: 3080 Dartmouth Dr Greenville NC 27858

KOLASKI, CYNTHIA BERTHA, writer; b. Ridgewood, N.J., Nov. 17, 1959; d. Nicholas John and Susan Marian (Gibbs) Bertha; m. Kenneth M. Kolaski, Oct. 14, 1989. BA, Bennington Coll., 1983; JD, Temple U., 1989. Bar: Pa. 1989, N.J. 1989. Asst. editor A.M. Best Co., Oldwick, N.J., 1985-86; free-lance writer Phila., 1989—. Contbg. editor: Most Eligible Women in Philadelphia, 1982. Mem. NOW, ABA, Pa. Bar Assn., Phila. Bar Assn., N.J. Bar Assn. Mem. Soc. of Friends.

KOLATA, GINA, journalist; b. Balt., Feb. 25, 1948; d. Arthur and Ruth Lillian (Aaronson) Bari; m. William George Kolata; children: Therese Bari, Stefan Matthew. BS, U. Md., 1969, MA, 1973; postgrad., MIT, 1969-70. Copy editor Sci. Mag., Washington, 1973-74, writer, 1974-87; reporter N.Y. Times, N.Y.C., 1987—. Co-author: Combatting the Number One Killer: The Scientific Report on Heart Disease, 1978, The High Blood Pressure Book, 1979 (Blakeslee award 1980); columnist Bild der Wissenschaft, 1984-87, Jour. Investigative Dermatology, 1985-87; contbr. articles to mags., newspapers. Coordinator charity dinners So Others Might Eat program, Washington, 1983-87. Recipient William Harvey award E.R. Squibb and Son, 1982. Mem. Nat. Assn. Sci. Writers. Democrat. Roman Catholic. Office: NY Times Sci Times Sect 229 W 43rd St New York NY 10036*

KOLB, BERTHA MAE (BERTHA MAE RAGSDALE), travel agency administrator; b. Dumas, Ark., Nov. 3, 1925; d. Harold Dewey and Hallie Eugenia (Muskelley) Ragsdale; m. Charles Rudolph Kolb, Oct. 9, 1951 (dec. 1982); 1 child, Charles Harold. Student, La. State U., 1959-61. Sec. Le Tourneau Co., Vicksburg, U.S. Govt. Waterways Experiment Sta.; travel agt. Am. Internat. Travel, Inc., 1983-. Pres. Vicksburg Coun. of Garden Clubs, 1972; bd. dirs. Garden Clubs of Miss., 1977-89; active numerous Vicksburg civic svc. clubs, 1953-. Mem. Vicksburg Country Club (pres. ladies orgn. 1969-70), Town and Country Garden Club (pres. Vicksburg chpt. 1973-75). Episcopalian.

KOLB, DORIS, chemistry educator; b. Louisville, Aug. 4, 1927; d. James W. and Mary Agnes (McCracken) Kasey; m. Kenneth E. Kolb, Sept. 18, 1948; children: Kenneth E. Jr., Ronald F., Jerome W. BS, U. Louisville, 1948; MS, Ohio State U., 1950, PhD, 1953. Chemist Standard Oil Ind., Whiting, 1953-57; ass. prof. Corning (N.Y.) Community Coll., 1962-65; prof. Ill. Cen. Coll., East Peoria, Ill., 1967-86; vis. prof. Bradley U., Peoria, Ill., 1986—. Co-author: Glass: Its Many Facets, 1988; contbr. book chpts. in field, articles to profl. jours. bd. dirs. Corning-Painted Post Sch. Dist., Corning, N.Y.; mem. Planned Parenthood (exec. dir. 1966-67, pres. 1976-78). Recipient Gallion Teaching awd. Ill. Cen. Coll., East Peoria, Ill, 1968, Catalyst awd. Chem. Mfrs. Assn., 1981, Vis. Scientist awd. Am. Chem. Soc., W. Conn. sect., 1985. Mem. Am. Chem. Soc. (chmn. elect Chem. Edn. Div. 1990), Ill. Assn. Chemistry Tchrs. (chmn. 1982), Delta Kappa Gamma (fin. chmn. 1988-90). Home: 7309 N Edgewild Dr Peoria IL 61614

KOLB, MARY LORRAINE, real estate company executive; b. La Crosse, Wis., Jan. 26, 1947; d. Thomas and Lorraine M. (Schaffer) Sagear; m. Jerry R. Kolb, May 29, 1971; children: James Thomas, Kelly Robert. Grad. high sch., Holmen, Wis. Loan officer Bank of Holmen, 1968-84; broker, owner Century 21 Gold Banner Realty, Onalaska, Wis., 1986—. Active disaster svcs. human resource system La Crosse County chpt. ARC, 1984—, disaster chmn. Wisconsin River Valley ter., Madison, 1986—. Home: N7138 CTH V Holmen WI 54636 Office: Century 21 Gold Banner Realty 200 Main St Onalaska WI 54650

KOLB, VERA M., chemistry educator; b. Belgrade, Yugoslavia, Feb. 5, 1948; came to U.S., 1973; d. Martin A. and Dobrila (Lopicic) K.; m. Cal Y. Meyers, 1976 (div. 1986). BS, Belgrade U., 1971, MS, 1973; PhD, So. Ill. U., 1976. Postdoctoral fellow So. Ill. U., Carbondale, 1977-78, mem. faculty, 1978-85; assoc. prof. chemistry U. Wis., Parkside, 1985-90, prof. chemistry, 1990—. Editor: Teratogens, Chemicals Which Cause Birth Defects, 1988; contbre. articles to sci. publs.; patentee in field. Violinist Racine (Wis.) Symphony Orch., Civic Orch. Milw. Fulbright grantee, 1973-76; grantee

NIH, 1984-87, Am. Soc. Biochemistry and Molecular Biology, 1988. Mem. Am. Chem. Soc. (task force on occupational safety and health 1980—). Office: Dept Chemistry Univ Wis Parkside PO Box 2000 Kenosha WI 53141

KOLBE, MARGARET ANN, data processing training consultant; b. Chgo., Sept. 19, 1948; d. Walter A. and Catherine M. (Herda) Lisowski; m. Michael Joseph Kolbe, Dec. 8, 1973. B.S. in Psychology magna cum laude, Loyola U., Chgo., 1970; cert. Honeywell Inst. Info. Sci., 1970. Data processing cons. COMSI, Inc., Oak Brook, Ill., 1970-75; v.p. product devel. Deltak, Inc., Naperville, Ill., 1975-84; v.p., ptnr. The Info. Engrs., St. Charles, Ill., 1984—. Author tng. series, also poetry. Ill. Acad. Sci. scholar, 1966. Mem. Ind. Writers Chgo., Soc. Tech. Communication, Assn. Devel. of Computer-based Instructional Systems, Ind. Computer Cons. Assn., Nat. Soc. Performance and Instrn., Nat. Writers Club. Roman Catholic. Avocation: creative writing. Office: Info Engrs 36W290 Crane Rd Saint Charles IL 60175

KOLBESON, MARILYN HOPF, advertising executive, organization and management consultant; b. Cin., June 9, 1930; d. Henry Dilg and Carolyn Josephine (Brown) Hopf; children: Michael Llen, Kenneth Ray, Patrick James, Pamela Sue Kolbeson Lang, James Allan. Student U. Cin., 1947, 48, 50. Sales and mktg. mgr. Cox Patrick United Van Lines, 1977-80; sales mktg. mgr. Creative Incentives, Houston, 1980-81; pres. Ad Sense, Inc., Houston, 1981-87, M.H. Kolbeson & Assocs., Houston, 1987, Seattle, 1987—, The Phoenix Books, Seattle, 1987—; cons. N.L.P. Communications; lectr., cons. in field. Mem. adv. bd. Alief Ind. Sch. Dist., 1981-87, pres., 1983-84; bd. dirs. Santa Maria Hostel, 1983-86, v.p., 1983-84; founder, pres. Mind Force, Houston, 1978-87 and Seattle, 1987—. Mem. Greater Houston Conv. and Visitors Coun., loaned exec., 1986-87; mem. adv. bd. Am. Inst. Achievement, 1986-87; charter mem. Rep. Task Force. Mem. Houston Advt. Splty. Assn. (bd. dirs. 1984-87, treas. 1985, v.p. 1986-87), Inst. Noetic Scis. (charter), Galleria Area C. of C. (bd. dirs. 1986-87), Toastmasters (area gov. 1978), Grand Club (v.p. 1986), Seward Park Community Orgn. Republican. Christian Scientist. Office: 5247 S Brandon Seattle WA 98118

KOLE, JANET STEPHANIE, lawyer, writer, photographer; b. Washington, Dec. 20, 1946; d. Martin J. and Ruth G. (Goldberg) K. A.B., Bryn Mawr Coll., 1968; M.A., NYU, 1970; J.D., Temple U., 1980. Bar: Pa. 1980. Assoc. editor trade books Simon & Schuster, N.Y.C., 1968-70; publicity dir. Am. Arbitration Assn., N.Y.C., 1970-73; freelance photojournalist, N.Y.C., 1973-76; law clk. Morgan Lewis & Bockius, Phila., 1977-80; assoc. Schnader, Harrison, Segal & Lewis, Phila., 1980-85; ptnr. Cohen, Shapiro, Polisher, Shiekman & Cohen, Phila., 1985—; author books including: Post Mortem, 1974; contbr. numerous articles to gen. interest publs., profl. jours.; bd. editors New Am. Rev. Mem. Mayor's Task Force on Rape, N.Y.C., 1972-77; adv. Support Ctr. Child Advs., Phila., 1980—; mem. Phila. Vol. Lawyers for the Arts; steering com. Lawyers for Reproductive Rights. Fellow Acad. Advocacy; mem. Assn. Trial Lawyers Am., ABA (co-div. dir. substantive areas of litigation, chmn. com. on monographs and unpublished papers, com. spl. pubs.). Democrat. Office: Cohen Shapiro Polisher Shiekman & Cohen 12 S 12th St 22d Fl Philadelphia PA 19107

KOLE-HARF, PATRICIA JEAN, journalist, educational consultant, reading specialist; b. Berea, Ohio, Oct. 14, 1937; d. Paul Frederic and Mena (Labordes) Kole; m. Fredric Henry Harf, June 21, 1969. BS in Edn., Baldwin-Wallace Coll., Berea, Ohio, 1959; MS in Edn., Akron U., 1966; Dr. in Edn., Ariz. State U., 1972. Rsch. Ednl. Rsch. Coun. Am., 1967-69; tchr. Berea City Schs., Cleve. and Parma, Ohio, 1969-73; asst. prof. Cleve. State U., 1975—; corr., columnist, freelance writer Chronicle-Telegram, Elyria, Ohio, 1986—; ednl. cons. State of Ohio; syndicated columnist Univerisal Press; diagnotician of reading difficulties. Author teaching materials and tchr. and children's textbooks; contbr. articles to profl. jours.; also advisor to book pubs. Pres. Berea Hist. Soc.; mem. Cleve. Orch. Women's Com.; mem. Rep. Precinct Com., Berea; advisor Cleve. Radio and TV Coun.; tutor of adults and youths unable to read. Named Outstanding Citizen, Berea C. of C., 1965, Ohio State Outstanding Educator Accoc. Prof. C.C.C, 1968. Mem. NOW, Soc. Profl. Journalists (Excellence in Journalism award 1990), Berea C. of C. (Outstanding Citizen 1965), Berea Hist. Soc., Berea Bus. and Profl. Women, Nat. Edn. Assn., Internat. Reading Assn. (cons. and writer for reading tchrs.), Ohio Edn. Assn., Berea Garden Club, Baldwin-Wallace Women's Club, Kiwanis (sec., v.p.), Berea Rep. Club (Mayoral Volunterism award 1987), Press Club of Cleve. Republican. Methodist. Home: 323 Westbridge Berea OH 44017

KOLENC, KOLEEN M., psychologist, instructor; b. Leadville, Colo., July 20, 1951. BA, U. No. Colo., 1973; MA, U. Mo., 1979, PhD, 1984. Instr. math. St. Pius X High Sch., Kansas City, Mo., 1973-74; newspaper staffer Key to the News, Kansas City, 1974-79; counselor, psychologist N.W. Mo. State U., Maryville, 1984-87; instr., psychologist Conception (Mo.) Sem. Coll., 1987—. Mem. Am. Psychol. Assn., Am. Assn. Counseling and Devel., Am. Assn. Marriage and Family Therapists, Mo. Psychol. Assn., Pi Lambda Theta. Office: Conception Sem Coll Conception MO 64432

KOLENUT, ELISA S., sales executive; b. Paterson, N.J., Sept. 20, 1958; d. Martin Edward and Angela (Avolio) Kolenut Finamore. BA in Mktg. and Distributive Edn., Montclair State Coll., 198l. Cert. high sch. tchr., N.J. Tchr. distributive edn. Jefferson Twp. High Sch., Oakridge, N.J., 1981-85; premise sales rep. Nat. Telephone Directory-N.J. Bell Yellow Pages, Paramus, 1985-86, mgmt. trainee, 1985-86, premise sales mgr., 1986-88, account exec. sales mgr., 1988—; sec. Nat. Telephone Directory-Pen-Del Directory Corp. Found., Somerset, N.J., 1988—. Fellow NAFE. Home: 776 Ewing Ave Franklin Lakes NJ 07417 Office: NJ Bell Yellow Pages Nat Telephone Directory 115 W Century Rd Paramus NJ 07652

KOLKER, SONDRA G., fund raising/special events executive; b. N.Y.C., Nov. 30, 1938; d. Morris Henry and Alice (Cohen) Budow; m. Justin William Kolker, Aug. 23, 1958; children: Lawrence Paul, David Brett. Student, Hofstra U. Dir. N.Y.C. Office N.Y. State Dem. Com., 1977-79; v.p., exec. dir. Fund for Higher Edn., N.Y.C., 1980-88; pres. Sondra Kolker & Assocs., Halesite, N.Y., 1988—; spl. cons. Internat. Devel. Svcs. subs. of NMP of Am., Inc., 1989—. Speechwriter for numerous speakers at corp. banquets, 1980-88. Bd. dirs. Huntington (N.Y.) Townwide Fund, 1978—; active in Huntington Hosp. Aux., 1965—, Great Gatsby Soc. for Multiple Sclerosis, 1988—, Marble Hills Civic Assn., Halesite, 1958—; committeewoman Huntington Dem. Com., 1974-82. Recipient Meritorious Svc. award Huntington Twp. C. of C., 1974, 76, 77, 78, Bicentennial Citation Town of Huntington, 1977. Mem. NAFE, LWV, Nat. Soc. Fund Raising Execs., Women in Fin. Devel., L.I. Crafts Guild, Huntington Twp. C. of C., Women's Econ. Round Table, Huntington Bus. and Profl. Women. Jewish. Home and Office: Sondra Kolker & Assocs 4 Everett Pl Halesite NY 11743

KOLKHORST, KATHRYN MACKAY, lawyer; b. Richmond, N.Y., Sept. 21, 1949; d. Bernard Edwin and Jane Mackay (Shaw) K.; m. Mark Finks, 1968 (div. 1972); m. William George Ruddy, Mar. 31, 1979; children: Anna Caroll, Elena Jane. Student, Wellsley Coll., 1966-68; BA, So. Conn. State Coll., 1969; postgrad., Yale U., 1975-77; JD, U. Conn., West Hartford, 1977. Bar: Alaska 1979, U.S. Dist. Ct. Alaska 1982. Reporter New Haven Jour. Courier, 1970-75; law clk. to presiding justice Alaska Supreme Ct., Juneau, 1977-78; asst. atty. gen. State of Alaska, Juneau, 1979-85; ptnr. Ruddy, Bradley & Kolkhorst, Juneau, 1986—. Active Juneau Arts Coun., 1979-82, Juneau Symphony, 1980-84; chairperson Juneau Jazz & Classics, 1987—. Mem. Alaska Bar Assn. Democrat. Presbyterian. Office: Ruddy Bradley & Kolkhorst PO Box 34338 Juneau AK 99803

KOLLER, MARITA A., accountant; b. Chgo., June 6, 1955; d. Frank J. and Jean J. Koller. BA, Western Ill. U., 1976; MPA, Am. U., 1980; AAS, Oakton Coll., 1989. Acct. UOP, Des Plaines, Ill.; computer specialist Baxter Labs., Deerfield, Ill.; actuarial asst. Towers, Perrin, Foster and Crosby, Chgo. U. Ill. scholar. Mem. Am. Mgmt. Assn., Am. Soc. Profl. and Women Execs. Home: 934 Forest Des Plaines IL 60018

KOLLIAS, GEORGIA NICOLETTA, lobbyist; b. Wilmington, Del., Feb. 20, 1961; d. Anthony V. and Polly (Papadopoulos) K. BA in Indsl. Psychology, Boston U., 1981; BA in Internat. Relations, U. Del., 1986, MA in Pub. Adminstrn. with honors, 1988. Money market rep. Del. Trust co., Wilmington, 1981-83; asst. to v.p. corp. planning Big Bros./Big Sisters Am. Nat. Hdqrs., Phila., 1984-86; researcher, cons. Embassy of Greece, Washington, 1987; rsch. assoc. Office Internat. Programs, Newark, Del., 1987-88; exec. asst. to lt. gov. State of Del., Dover, 1988; cons. Kollias Cons., N.Y.C., 1989—; mgr. Inst. Internat. Bankers, N.Y.C., 1988-89; cons. in field. Author: Office of International Programs, 1987, International Resources, 1988, High Tech Task Force Essay, 1988. Greek instr. YMCA, Wilmington, 1987; exec. staff U.S. Senate Campaign, Del., 1988. Named Legis. Fellow Pub. Adminstrn. Inst., 1987. Mem. Am. Soc. Pub. Adminstrn., Internat. Devel. Soc., AAUW, People to People, Phi Kappa Phi Honor Soc. Democrat. Greek Orthodox. Home: 115 Ponds Ln Greenville DE 19807 Office: Kollias Consulting PO Box 2844 New York NY 10185

KOLLINER-KELLY, NONNIE KRIS, administration company executive; b. Placerville, Calif., Sept. 19, 1946; d. Nonnie Eugenia Blomquist; 1 child, N. Kristine Naylor Baker. Mgr. employee benefits Border Steel Rolling Mills, Inc., El Paso, Tex.; owner, pres. Koll-Med, El Paso. Mem. S.W. Pension Conf., NAFE. Office: 1021 Arizona El Paso TX 79902 Office: PO Box 3158 El Paso TX 79923

KOLLOFF, MARGARET PENELOPE BRITTON, associate professor; b. Wayne, Mich., Oct. 2, 1942; d. Erwin Adelbert and Carolyn Ann (Herron) Britton. BA, Kalamazoo Coll., 1964; MA, Ea. Kentucky U., 1971; EdS, Ea. Ky. U., 1974; PhD, Purdue U., 1983. Elem. tchr. Lansing (Mich.) Pub. Sch., 1966-69, Model Lab. Sch., Richmond, Ky., 1969-72; instr. elem. edn. Ea. Ky. U., Richmond, 1972-74, asst. prof. elem. edn.; dir. gifted and talented programs Ball State U., Muncie, Ind., 1981-90, asst. prof. gifted edn., 1984-86, assoc. prof. gifted edn., 1986-90; dir. curriculum Cranbrook Schs., Bloomfield Hills., Mich., 1990—; dir. Ind. Midwest Talent Search, 1983-90, Ind. Gifted Edn. Cadre Program, 1983-90; cons. numerous schs. in Ind. and other states, 1975—. Contbr. articles and book chapters to gifted edn. Recipient Edn. and Rsch. award, Mensa Found, 1988. Mem. Nat. Assn. for Gifted Children (bd. dirs. 1990—, early leader award 1987), Coun. for Exceptional Children, Assn. for Gifted, Phi Delta Kappa. Congregationalist. Office: Ball State U Burris Lab Sch Muncie IN 47306

KOLODNY, NANCY JOAN, psychiatric social worker, writer; b. N.Y.C., Mar. 18, 1946; d. Lawrence Milton and Estelle Vivian (Srebnik) Shapiro; m. Robert Charles Kolodny, June 16, 1966; children: Linda Hillary, Lora Elizabeth, Lisa Michelle. BA, Barnard Coll., 1967; MA, Washington U., St. Louis, 1969, MSW, 1980. Cert. tchr., Mass., Mo. Tchr. University City (Mo.) High Sch., 1967-69, South Boston High Sch., 1970-71, Clayton (Mo.) High Sch., 1971-72; social worker Bulimia Anorexia Self Help, St. Louis, 1981-83; exec. dir. Behavioral Med. Inst., New Canaan, Conn., 1983—. Author: When Food's A Foe: How to Confront and Conquer Eating Disorders, 1987 (Editor's Choice by Booklist 1987, Books for the Teen Age by N.Y. Pub. Lib. 1988-89); co-author: (with others) Smart Choices, 1986 (Young Adult's Choice by Internat. Reading Assn. 1988, Books for the Teen Age by N.Y. Pub. Lib. 1987-88), How to Survive Your Adolescent's Adolescence, 1984. Mem. AAUW (bd. dirs. 1988-89, chmn. comm. on women 1987-88), NASW, Am. Anorexia Bulimia Assn., Kappa Delta Pi. Democrat. Office: Behavioral Med Inst 885 Oenoke Ridge Rd New Canaan CT 06840

KOLSRUD, GRETCHEN SCHABTACH, federal agency administrator; b. Schenectady, N.Y., Jan. 9, 1939; d. Carl and Elizabeth (Paine) Schabtach; m. James Ernest Kolsrud, Sept. 30, 1967 (div. Mar. 1980). BS, McGill U., 1960; MA, Johns Hopkins U., 1963, PhD, 1966. Prin. rsch. scientist Honeywell, Inc., New Brighton, Minn., 1966-67; sr. system scientist Serendipity, Inc., Crystal City, Va., 1967-71; staff scientist BioTech., Inc., Falls Church, Va., 1971-73; program mgr. NASA, Washington, 1973-74; mgr. transp. program Office Tech. Assessment U.S. Congress, Washington, 1974-76, asst. to dir. new, emerging techs., 1976-78, mgr. biol. applications program, 1978-89; sr. assoc. Office Tech. Assessment U.S. Congress, 1989—; cons. Instrument Flight Tng., Inc., Mpls., 1967, U.S. Dept. Transp., Washington, 1971. Gilman fellow Johns Hopkins U., Balt., 1960-61, 63-66; recipient fellowship NSF, Washington, 1961-62, Carnegie Inst. Washington, 1962-63. Fellow AAAS (chair-elect sect. X 1990—), Human Factors Soc. (sec.-treas. 1974-75); mem. U.S. Assn. for Club Rome, Sigma Xi (grantee research 1964-65). Office: Office Tech Assessment US Congress Washington DC 20510

KOLSTE, DEBRA ANN, medical technologist; b. O'Neill, Nebr., June 20, 1953; d. Gerard Joseph and Ardis Loree (Newman) Babl; m. Rex J. Kolste, July 16, 1977; children: Andrew, Alison, Tori. BS in Med. Tech., U. Nebr., Omaha, 1975; postgrad., Wichita State U., 1978-79. Cert. med. tech. Med. tech. U. Nebr. Med. Ctr., 1975-79; med. technician Wesley Med. Ctr., Wichita, Kans., 1979-82, Citizens Med. Ctr., Colby, Kans., 1985—; chmn. wellness fair Colby Wellness Com., 1987—. Bd. dirs. Svc., Awareness, Family Edn. Child Abuse Prevention Commn., Colby, 1982—, Colby Med. Ctr. Aux., 1982—, Drug and Alcohol Coun., Colby, 1988—, Hi-Plains Hospice, Colby, 1986—. Mem. AAUW (pres. Colby 1985-87). Home: 3 Austin Ct Colby KS 67701

KOLTENUK, ADRIENNE RUTH, organization official, civic worker; b. Newark, Aug. 25, 1947; d. David and Eileen (Block) Chinsky; m. Jeffrey Seymour Koltenuk, Mar. 22, 1969; children: Douglas Michael, Danielle Sarene. BA, Rutgers U., 1969. Team leader Del. region NCCJ, Wilmington, Del., 1982, asst. Youth Program, 1983, Youth Program specialist, 1984—, secondary coord., 1988—; facilitator Nat. Office NCCJ., N.Y.C. summer conf., 1989. Vol. Green Circle, NCCJ, 1981—; bd. dirs. Eagle Glen Civic Assn., New Castle, Del., 1973-76, 88—, Millcreek br. AAUW, 1977-80; bd. dirs. Temple Beth El, Newark, Del., 1987-89, Hadassah, 1980-82, 87-89. Recipient Svc. award NCCJ, 1989, Women of Yr. award Temple Beth El, 1989. Office: Del Region NCCJ PO Box 747 Wilmington DE 19899

KOLTON, MARILYN SYLVIA, social services administrator; b. Chgo., Mar. 26, 1944; d. Valentine and Virginia K.; m. Louis Dwarshuis, May 28, 1983. BS in Psychology summa cum laude, Loyola U., Chgo., 1966, MA in Clin. Psychology, 1967, PhD, 1969; post-doctoral fellowship, NIMH, 1969. Lic. psychologist, Ill. Adj. prof. Loyola Univ., Chgo., 1967-68; lectr. dept. psychology U. Mich., 1969-73; project dir. Ctr. for Rsch. on Utilization Sci. Knowledge Inst. Social Rsch. U. Mich., 1969-72; tng. dir. Orgn. Applied Sci. in Soc., 1972-80, pres., 1976-80; field instr. Sch. of Social Work U. Mich., 1977-80; sr. psychologist Consultation and Learning Ctr., 1980; mental health program specialist NIMH, HHS, 1980-81; pediatric clin. psychologist Assocs. in Adolescent Psychiatry, Riveredge Hosp., 1981-83; clin. dir. outpatient clinic Ctr. for Children's Svcs., 1983-86, exec. dir., 1986—; adj. prof. Grad. Sch. of Leadership and Human Behavior U.S. Internat. U., San Diego, 1969, San Diego State U., 1969; lectr. Sch. of Social Work U. Mich., 1980. Author: Cooperative Housing: A Handbook for Effective Operations, 1977, (with others) Innovative Approaches to Youth Services, 1973, The Quality of Medical Care: Evaluation and Improvement, 1975; contbr. numerous articles to profl. jours. Active Mayor's Citizen's Com. on Drug Abuse, Ann Arbor, Mich., 1973; vice-chair Washtenaw County Com. on Status of Women, 1975-76, chair, 1976-78; mem. Washtenaw County Citizen's Com. for Selection of County Adminstr., 1978; bd. dirs. Exec. Club, 1985-86, Private Industry Coun., 1987—. Mem. Nat. Coun. Health Svc. Providers in Psychology, Am. Psychol. Assn. Office: Ctr for Children's Svcs 702 N Logan Danville IL 61832

KOLTOV, NADINE H., financial analyst; b. Boston, Mass., Sept. 9, 1962; d. Frank and Sylvia K. BA, U. Mass., Amherst, 1984; postgrad., Babson Coll., Wellesley, Mass., 1987—. CPA. Sr. auditor Laventhol & Horwath, CPA's, Boston, Mass., 1984-88; sr. fin. analyst Reebok Internat. Ltd., Stoughton, Mass., 1988--. Mem. AICPA, Mass. Soc. CPAs. Office: Reebok Internat Ltd 100 Technology Center Dr Stoughton MA 02072

KOMANDO, KIMBERLY ANN, computer company executive; b. Union, N.J., July 1, 1964. BS in Computer Info. Systems, Ariz. State U., 1985. Mktg. rep. IBM, Phoenix, 1984-85; major account rep. AT&T, Phoenix, 1985-87; exec. v.p. Nationwide Auto Care Ctrs., Phoenix, 1987-88; pres. Komando & Assocs. Inc., Phoenix, 1988—; dist. mgr. UNISYS, Phoenix, 1988—; mktg. cons. and speaker in field. Author: How To Cash In On Auto Malls, 1988; talkshow host; internationally syndicated columnist; contbr. articles to profl. jours. V.p. fundraising Young Reps. Party, Phoenix, 1989—. Office: Komando & Assocs Inc PO Box 44158 Phoenix AZ 85064

KOMISARCZYK, SHIRLEY THERESA, educator; b. Cascade, Md., Nov. 6, 1930; d. Raymond Thomas and Mary Nina (Coyle) Swinscoe; m. Robert Patrick Clonan, May 3, 1952 (div. 1972); children: Richard Clonan, Eileen Clonan Monesson, Brian Clonan, Shirlene Clonan Soos, Christopher Clonan; m. Michael Komisarczyk (div. Oct. 1978). BS in Elem. Edn. cum laude, Fordham U., 1961; MA in Ednl. Adminstrn. and Supervision summa cum laude, Seton Hall U., 1972. Lic. tchr., prin., N.J. Pvt. sec. North Am. Reassurance Co., N.Y.C, 1949-52, 7755 Dependants Sch. Detachment, Karlsruhe, Fed. Rep. Germany, 1952-53, Bank of China, N.Y.C., 1954-57; tchr. Clark (N.J.) Bd. Edn., 1961, Woodbridge Bd. Edn., Colonia, N.J., 1965-68; remedial reading specialist Old Bridge (N.J.) Bd. Edn., 1972—. Mem. Rep. Nat. Com. Mem. N.J. Edn. Assn., Middlesex County Edn. Assn., Women In Edn. Com., Old Bridge Edn. Assn., Am. Assn. Retired Persons (life). Roman Catholic. Home: 71 Carriage Ln Englishtown NJ 07726 Office: Old Bridge Bd Edn Rte 516 Adminstrn Bldg Old Bridge NJ 08857

KOMOROWSKI, CHERYL ANN, librarian; b. Buffalo, Nov. 11, 1956; d. Donald and Carol (Brown) Hoffman; m. Frank Komorowski, Oct. 1, 1976; 1 child, Justine. BS, Buffalo State Coll., 1976. Lic. real estate profl., 1986. Libr. Boylan, Brown, Code, Fowler, Randall and Wilson, Rochester, 1986-88, Arthur Andersen and Co., Rochester, N.Y., 1988—; asst. libr. Harter Secrest and Emery, Rochester. vol. Rochester Philharm. Orch., 1982—.

KOMP, BARBARA ANN, technical publications executive; b. La Porte, Ind., Nov. 3, 1954; d. Gerald Lee and Betty Mae (Schelin) K. BA in Elem. Edn., Ball State U., 1977; student Purdue U., 1984—, Ind. Vocat. Tech. Coll., 1986—; cert. in lang. arts & reading competencies, 1977. Quality control insp. Foreman Mfg. Co., Rolling Prairie, Ind., 1978-80; quality control insp. Weil-McLain Co., Michigan City, Ind., 1980-81, jr. quality control engr., 1981-84, tech. writer, 1984-88. Advisor Jr. Achievement, Michigan City, 1982-84. Mem. NAFE (women mgmt.), Am. Soc. Quality Control (cert., membership chmn. 1981-83, treas. 1984-85), Soc. for Tech. Communication (Tech. Manual Achievement award 1986), Women in Mgmt., N.W. Ind. Desktop Pubs. Avocations: writing childrens' stories, jazz aerobics, photography, volleyball. Office: Weil-McLain A Marley Co Blaine St Michigan City IN 46360

KONCHANIN, LYNN MARIE, pediatrician; b. Oceanside, N.Y., Nov. 30, 1957; d. Peter and Mary (Kowha) K.; m. Richard Steven Mannella, July 14, 1984. BS magna cum laude, Pensselaer Poly. Inst., 1981; D of Medicine magna cum laude, Albany Med. Coll., 1981. Licensed physician, Pa.; diplomate Am. Bd. Pediatrics. Resident in pediatric medicine St. Christopher's Hosp. for Children, Phila., 1981-84; staff pediatrician Pediatric Specialties, Ltd., Langhorne, Pa., 1984—; mem. pediatric staff The Lower Bucks Hosp., Bristol, Pa., 1984—, St. Mary Hosp., Langhorne, 1987—; assoc. mem. pediatric staff St. Christopher's Hosp. for Children, 1984—; pediatric clin. instr. Med. Sch. Temple U., Phila., 1985—; sch. physician Pennsbury Sch. Dist., Bucks County, Pa., 1988-89. Pediatric advisor Focus on Motherhood program Child Home and Community, Bristol, 1986—; mem. adv. bd. Bucks County Dept. Mental Health/Mental Retardation, Doylestown, Pa., 1986—; mem. med. adv. bd. Bucks County Planned Parenthood, Doylestown 1986—; lectr. on nutrition various community groups, Bucks County, 1986—. Fellow Am. Acad. Pediatrics; mem. Pa. Med. Soc., Bucks County Med. Soc. Lutheran. Office: Pediatric Specialties Ltd Oxford Sq Ste 502 370 Middletown Blvd Langhorne PA 19047

KONDY, STEPHANIE MARY, psychologist; b. Miami, Fla., May 26, 1949; d. Matthew Frank and Alice (Jarosz) K. BA, U. Fla., 1972; MA, U. Ala., 1975; EdD, U. Fla., 1987. Psychologist HRS Dist. 8, Ft. Myers, Fla., 1975-77; psychology dir. Landmark Learning Ctr., Miami, 1977-79, dir. programs and svcs., 1979-84; quality assurance dir. United Cerebral Palsy, Miami, 1984-89, residential svcs. dir., 1989—; cons. Star Cons., Fla., 1980—. Author: Leadership Styles, 1987. Chmn. Ladies Guild, Miami Springs, 1989. Mem. Am. Psychol. Assn., Nat. Assn. DD Mgrs., Am. Assn. Mental. Office: UCP Group Home 3 16521 NW 1 Ave Miami FL 33166

KONEZNY, LORETTE M. SOBOL, publishing executive; b. N.Y.C., Sept. 5, 1948; d. Jack and Florence (Silver) Sobol; m. Gerald Walter Konezny, June 4, 1972 (div. 1988); 1 child, Scott David. BS, U. Bridgeport, 1971; postgrad. Adelphi U., 1972-73, Parsons Sch. Design, 1977. Instr., Middle Sch., Malverne, N.Y., 1971-72; pvt. instr. art, L.I., 1972-76; instr. art, adult art end. programs, Rockville Centre, Oceanside and Lawrence, N.Y., 1976-79; pres. Pen Notes, Inc., Freeport, N.Y., 1979—; art cons. Rockville Centre High Sch., 1976-77; exhibited in group shows Adelphi U., 1973, Hewlett East Rockway Temple, 1976, Moscow Internat. Book Fair, 1987; represented in permanent collection Yeshiva U., L.A.; bus. cons. Baldwin C. of C., 1986. Author, pub.: Learning to To Tell Time, 1982, Learning to Print, 1984, Learn Handwriting, 1986, Learn to Write Numbers, 1987; patentee in field; pub. Aprendiendo A Escrbir Las Letras, 1989 exhibited at Moscow Internat. Book Fair, 1987. Mem. L.I. Networking Entrepreneurs (founding pres. 1984-85), Soc. Scribes. Office: 134 Westside Ave Freeport NY 11520

KONIECZNY, SHARON LOUISE, insurance company executive; b. Madison, Minn., July 2, 1952; d. Frank H. and Elenore A. (Mikkelson) K. Student, Dakota Wesleyan U., 1970-71, U. Minn., 1971-72. Sales rep. Advance Schs., Bloomington, Minn., 1972; sales agt. ITT Life Ins., Mpls., 1973-75, mktg. auditor, 1975-76, supr. new bus., 1976-79, mgr. UND Issue, 1979-81, asst. v.p. new bus., 1981-83, asst. v.p.sales support, 1983-87, v.p., sales mktg., 1987—. Mem. United Way, Mpls. (vice chmn. 1984-85, chmn. 1985). Mem. Nat. Assn. Life Underwriters (gen. agy. mgmt. conf.), Am. Mktg. Assn., Nat. Assn. Ins. Women, Soc. Ins. Trainers and Educatores, Internat Assn. Fin. Planners. Democrat. Lutheran. Home: 12610 50th Ave Plymouth MN 55442

KONIOR, LYNNE BARTLETT, marketing communications executive; b. Paoli, Pa., Feb. 21, 1953; d. John B. and Dorothy F. (Lemon) Willey. BS cum laude, U. Mass., Amherst, 1979. Coord. devel. and spl. projects Nat. Recreation and Parks Assn., Arlington, Va., 1979-81; dir. pub. rels. Weight Watchers Eastern Mass. and R.I., Boston, 1981-82; dir. devel. and pub. rels. Nat. Kidney Found. Mass., Boston, 1982-84; v.p. pub. rels. Arnold & Co., Boston, 1984-85; chmn., chief exec. officer King Konior Inc., Boston, 1985-90; dir. communications and pub. rels. WHDH-TV, Boston, 1990—; adv. bd. Hub Express Airlines, 1987—; mem. exec. com., bd. dirs. Nat. Kidney Found. Mass., 1989—. Mem. adv. com. Boston for the World, 1985—; devel. com. U.S. Olympic Com.; devel. cons. Summer Solstice Art Festival, 1984; bd. dirs. Campfire Assn. Mem. Publicity Club New Eng. (Bell Ringer awards 1985, 86, 87, 88, 89, Spl. Merit award 1985), NAFE, Advt. Club Greater Boston. Avocations: ceramics, racquetball, golf. Office: King Konior Inc 87 Summer St Boston MA 02110

KONNICK, DIANNE CHERYL, financial executive; b. New Brunswick, N.J., Feb. 11, 1961; d. Richard Edward and Cathleen Gladys (Bickler) Readdy; m. Christopher Matthew Konnick, Aug. 14, 1982; children: Matthew Roy, Allison Marie. BBA in Finance, Shippensburg State, 1982; postgrad., George Mason U., 1987—. Cert. mgmt. acct. Comml. loan examiner Am. Bank & Trust, Reading, Pa., 1982-83; analyst, asst. fin. officer Meridian Bancorp, Reading, 1983-86; fin. analyst Am. Chem. Soc., Washington, 1986-88, sr. budget analyst, 1988-89; fin. adminstr. Dietrich's Milk Products, Reading, Pa., 1989—. Mem. Inst. Cert. Mgmt. Accts., NAFE, Nat. Assn. Accts. Republican. Roman Catholic. Home: 29 Chestnut St Shillington PA 19607 Office: Dietrich's Milk Products 100 McKinley Ave Reading PA 19605

KONON, NEENA NICHOLAI, interior designer; b. Chgo., Dec. 4, 1951; d. Nicholas Alexander and Marie G. (Korotkoff) K. BFA cum laude, Ohio U., 1973. Interior designer Architectonics, Inc., Chgo., 1973-75, sr. interior designer, 1978-82; interior designer Space Mgmt. Assoc., Inc., Chgo., 1975-78; design prin. Borkon & Konon Assoc., Inc., Chgo., 1982-84; assoc. Perkins & Will, Inc., Chgo., 1984—. Liasion restoration Holy Trinity Russian Orthodox Cathedral, Chgo., 1987, millenium com., 1988. Mem. Chgo.

Real Estate Exec. Women, Internat. Facilities Mgrs. Assn., Chgo. Real Estate Exec. Women. Republican.

KONVALINKA, MARIANNE, beverage company executive; b. Berwyn, Ill., Apr. 2, 1959; d. Edward and Nancy Diana (Hodges) K. BS in Mktg., Colorado State U., 1981. Mgmt. trainee, asst. mgr., then gen. mgr. GRand Am. Fare, Colo., 1981-84; merchandising mgr. Brown-Forman Beverage Co., Denver, 1984-85; sales rep. Brown-Forman Beverage Co., Dallas, 1985-86; market mgr. Brown-Forman Beverage Co., Seattle, 1986—. Contbr. articles to trade publs. Vol., Big Sisters Seattle, 1988—. Mem. Golden Rams Club (v.p. 1979-80, pres. 1980-81). Democrat. Lutheran. Home: 3610 SW Cloverdale St Seattle WA 98136 Office: Brown Forman Beverage Co 14711 NE 29th Pl Bellevue WA 98007

KONZ, HELEN KATHERINE, retired teacher; b. LaPlata, Mo., Mar. 25, 1910; d. Christian C. Kyhl and Dorothea Marie (Holm) Kyhl; m. Frank A. Konz, Apr. 8, 1944 (dec.). BA, U. No. Iowa, 1932; MA, Ohio State U., 1951. Life teaching cert., Ohio. Jr. high tchr. Bode (Iowa) Pub. Schs., 1937-41, Kingsport (Tenn.) Pub. Schs., 1941-45; secondary tchr. of english and drama Columbus (Ohio) Pub. Schs., 1945-75; dir. theatre Columbus (Ohio) Pub. Schs., 1955-73. Pres. Upper Arlington Sr. Ctr., Columbus, 1988; pres., editor Scandinavian Club , Columbus, 1960-64; mem. altar guild Holy Luth. Ch. Recipient Intergenerational Activities award Tremont Elem. Sch., Upper Arlington, 1986, 87-88, 89-90, Appreciation award for leadership and involvement in the community Upper Arlington Coun., 1989. Mem. AAUW (v.p. 1989-91, travel slide presenter), Phi Delta Gamma (treas. 1978-84, nat. fin. com. 1982-83). Home: 3039 Sudbury Rd Columbus OH 43221

KOON, VIVIAN JENKINS, nurse; b. Kershaw, S.C., July 10, 1947; d. John Lee and Mamie (Ramsey) Jenkins; m. Joe R. Koon Jr., Feb. 14, 1976; stepchildren: Robin, Roxie. BSN, U. S.C., 1988; ADN, N.W. Ala. State Jr. Coll., Phil Campbell, Ala., 1973. Staff nurse Anderson (S.C.) Meml. Hosp., 1968-72, Bailey Meml. Hosp., Clinton, 1973-74; head nurse Piedmont regional office S.C. Dept. Mental Retardation, Clinton, 1974—. Vol. ARC. Mem. Am. Nurses Assn., Laurens County Law Enforcement Wives Assn. (pres. 1990—). Home: Rte 2 Box 283 Country Ln Clinton SC 29325 Office: Piedmont Regional Office PO Drawer 239 Clinton SC 29325

KOONTZ, EVA ISABELLE, medical technologist; b. Jetmore, Kans., Feb. 3, 1935; d. Vernon Ward and Lillian Mae (Bell) K. BS in Natural Scis., Sterling (Kans.) Coll., 1957; cert. in med. tech., U. Kans. Med. Ctr., 1958. Office technologist Group Practice, Mission, Kans., 1958-60; chemistry supr. Bethany Hosp., Kansas City, Kans., 1960-64; rsch. asst. pediatric hematology and metabolic rsch. U. Kans. Med. Ctr., Kansas City, Kans., 1964-72, R&D Tech., Providence-St. Margaret's Health Care Ctr., Kansas City, Kans., 1972-74; staff technologist St. Lukes Hosp., Kansas City, Mo., 1974-79; clin. lab. mgr. and supr. Quincy Rsch. Ctr., Kansas City, Mo., 1979-80; staff technologist Lakeside Hosp., Kansas City, Mo., 1980-82; med. technologist supr. Midwest Rsch. Inst., Kansas City, Mo., 1982-88; toxicology supr. Clin. Reference Labs., Inc., Lenexa, Kans., 1988—. Mem. Am. Soc. for Med. Tech., Am. Assn. for Clin. Chemistry, Mo. Soc. Med. Technologists. Republican. Presbyterian. Home: 10251 Cedarbrooke Ln Kansas City MO 64131 Office: Clin Reference Labs Inc 11844 W 85th St Lenexa KS 66214

KOONTZ, NORMA CAROLYN, employee benefits manager; b. Houston, Sept. 6, 1938; d. Austin Wesley and Virgie Beatrice (Brown) Edwards; m. William E. McQueen, Oct. 12, 1957 (div.); children: William E. Jr., Angela; m. Ben Turner, May 27, 1966 (div.); 1 child, Christina; m. Otis Eugene Koontz, Dec. 28, 1978. BA, Tex. So. U., 1985. Writer, editor Community Newspapers, Houston; ins. analyst Cooper Industries, Inc., Houston, 1970-76, mgr. pensions, 1976-81; office mgr. U. Houston, 1981-85; retirement plan adminstr. CRS Sirrine, Inc., Houston, 1985-86, supr. employee benefits, 1986-87, mgr. employee benefits, 1987—; panelist Fidelity Investments Conf., Dallas, 1989—. Columnist Houston Informer, 1983-85; author poetry. Vol., bd. dirs. Women's Christian Home, Houston, 19189—. Recipient Pub. Svc. award Houston Police Dept., 1985, Outstanding Community Svc. award Tex. So. U., 1986. Mem. SW Pension Conf., Houston Benefit Mgrs. Roundtable, Internat. Fedn. Employee Benefit Plans, Soc. Profl. Journalists, Friends Houston Pub. Libr., Houston Black Reps., Tex. Jazz Heritage Soc., Wheatley Alumni Assn. Baptist.

KOONTZ, NORMA JEAN, educator; b. Lafayette, Ind., Nov. 10, 1930; d. Joseph Edward and Margaret (Thompson) Maxwell; m. Willis F. Koontz, Aug. 15, 1953 (dec. 1982); children: Lynn and Tony (twins), Patricia Beth. BS, Ball State U., 1953; MA, Western Mich. U., 1978. Tchr. New Buffalo (Mich.) Schs., 1953-55, South Lyon (Mich.) Schs., 1955-56; tchr. English, Berrien Springs (Mich.) Pub. Schs., 1975—. Contbr. poetry to various anthologies. Chmn. spring project for civic benefit, St. Joseph, Mich., 1980; chmn. coun. on ministries United Meth. Ch., 1986—. Mem. AAUW (nat. scholarship named in her honor 1984). Republican. Home: 1885 Acorn Dr Saint Joseph MI 49085 Office: Berrien Springs Mid Sch One Sylvester Dr Berrien Springs MI 49103

KOONZ, CLAUDIA, historian. Formerly mem. history faculty Coll. of the Holy Cross, Worcester, Mass.; assoc. prof. Duke U., 1988—. Author: Mothers in the Fatherland: Women, the Family, and Nazi Politics, 1987; co-ed. Becoming Visible: Women in European History, 1977. Office: Duke U Dept of History Durham NC 27706*

KOOPMAN, CHERYL, social psychologist; b. Red Bluff, Calif., June 14, 1950; d. William Warren and Norma Jean (Long) K.; m. Thomas K. Dawes, Aug. 22, 1982 (div. Oct. 1986). BA in Psychology, U. California, Berkeley, 1972; MA in Ednl. Psychology, UCLA, 1974; PhD in Ednl. Psychology, U. Va., 1979. Intern U.S. Office of Edn., Washington, 1977; lectr. U. Wis., Milw., 1978-79; post-doctoral fellow Harvard U., Boston, 1979-82, Columbia U., N.Y.C., 1982-87; sr. rsch. fellow Pub. Agenda Found., N.Y.C., 1987-88; rsch. scientist N.Y. State Psychiat. Inst., N.Y.C., 1988—; asst. prof. clin. psychology Columbia U., N.Y.C., 1989—; cons. NSF Grant on Fair Market Value, Columbia U., N.Y.C., 1986-87, Asian-Am. Med. Clinic, Walnut Creek, Calif., 1985, Elmhurst (N.Y.) Hosp. Dept. Emergency Med., 1983-84, Harvard Med. Sch., Boston, 1980-82. Author 6 chpts. of books; contbr. articles to profl. jours. Mem. N.Y. Psychologists for Social Responsibility, N.Y.C., 1982—; co-founder Mass. Psychologists for Social Responsibility, Boston, 1981-82; mem. staff Pub. Citizen Health Rsch. Group, Washington, 1976; vol. Mo Udall's Nat. Campaign for Prea., Washington, 1975. Recipient Viola Bernard award Columbia U. Dept. Psychiatry, N.Y.C., 1988-89; NIMH grantee Columbia Tchrs. Coll., N.Y.C., 1982-84, Harvard Med. Sch., Boston, 1979-81; Ford Found. fellow Columbia U. Sch. Internat. Affairs, 1984-86. Mem. Am. Psychol. Assn., Internat. Soc. Polit. Psychology, Soc. for Psychol. Study of Social Issues, Soc. for Personality and Social Psychology. Democrat. Home: 255 W 84 St #11E New York NY 10024 Office: Columbia Univ, 722 W 168 St Box 29, Dept Psychiatry New York NY 10032

KOOPMANN PARRISH, RETA COLLENE, retail executive; b. Oklahoma City, Feb. 27, 1944; d. Henry William and Hazel (Rollins) Singleton; m. Fred F. Koopmann, June 1, 1963 (div. 1974); 1 child, Rebecca Dawn; m. Walter J. Parrish, Jan 3, 1987. BS, Calif. Coast U., 1987, postgrad. in bus. adminstrn., 1987—. Front end mgr. Kroger Co., Cleve., 1969-72; with acctg. dept. Johns Manville, Denison, Tex., 1972-74; bakery/deli merchandiser Kroger Co., Columbia, S.C., 1974-83; v.p. bakery, deli ops. Kash n' Karry div. Lucky's Inc., Tampa, Fla., 1983-88, Kash n' Karry Food Stores Inc., Tampa, 1988-90; LBO, corp. dir. bakery/deli/sea food ops. United Supermarkets, Inc., Lubbock, Tex., 1990—. Author tng. manuals, 1984, 86, 87. Bd. trustees Jim Borck Ednl. Found., Inc., 1988—; vol. Spl. Olympics, Tampa, 1986, 87, 88; bd. govs. Am. Biog. Inst. Rsch. Assn., 1989—. Mem. NAFE, Internat. Deli/Bakery Assn. (exec. bd. 1986-89), Internat. Platform Assn., Retail Bakers Assn. (bd. dirs. 1980—), Eagles. Republican. Lutheran. Home: 5204 Kenosha Ave Lubbock TX 79413 Office: United Supermarkets Inc 501 66th St Lubbock TX 79413

KOOPMANS, CHERYL BETTE, business educator; b. Rochester, N.Y., July 4, 1950; d. John Leonard and Lois Dinah (Chambery) K. BA in English, U. Rochester, 1974; paralegal cert., Adelphi U., 1974; MBA Fin., Applied Econs., U. Rochester, 1979. Spl. investigator N.Y. State Atty. Gen.'s Office, Rochester, 1975-77; internat. fin. analyst treasury staff Harris Corp., Melbourne, Fla., 1978-80; market research analyst analog div. Harris Corp., 1980-81, communications product mktg. engr. analog div., 1981-82, communications product mktg. mgr. analog div., 1982-84; mgr. market research Harris Semiconductor sect. Harris Corp., 1984-85, dir. market research, 1985-87; asst. prof. bus. St. Mary's Coll. Md., St. Mary's City, 1987—; dir. market research Michael Dowling & Co., Melbourne, 1987—; pres. Research Unlimited, Palm Bay, Fla., 1987—. Asst. treas. Condominiums of Indian Harbour Assn., Indian Harbour Beach, Fla., 1979, treas., 1980. N.Y. State Regents scholar, 1968, U. Rochester Undergrad. scholar, 1968, U. Rochester Grad. scholar, 1977, Purdue U. fellow, 1990. Mem. Am. Mktg. Assn. Democrat. Home: 3235 Hanover Dr Lafayette IN 47905

KOOS, PATRICIA KAY, educator; b. Sidney, Nebr., Sept. 25, 1940; d. Leo J. and Wilma (Snyder) Thomas; m. David E. Koos, June 10, 1961; children: Thomas, Todd. BA, U. No. Colo., 1961. Profl. teaching cert., Iowa. Elem. tchr. Albia (Iowa) Community Schs., 1961-62, Bridgewater (Iowa)-Fontanelle Schs., 1962-63; instr. reading Simpson Coll., Indianola, Iowa, 1971-75; instr. child care Iowa Western Community Coll., Council Bluff, 1977-78; elem. tchr. remedial reading Harlan (Iowa) Community Schs., 1979-89, 1st grade tchr., 1989—. Mem. Harlan Edn. Assn. (sec. 1988-89, del. 1990—), AAUW (1st v.p. 1979-81, pres.1982-83, 2d v.p. 1988-90), Federated Womens Club (v.p. 1984-86, pres. 1986-88, treas. 1990—). Republican. Lutheran. Home: 1406 Southridge Dr Harlan IA 51537

KOOT, SHEILA CASSILY, teacher; b. Bangor, Maine, May 4, 1944; d. Charles F. and Anne F. (Chamberlain) Cassily; m. Gerard M. Koot, June 17, 1967; children: Michael Gerard, Christian Johan. AB in Math, Anna Maria Coll., Paxton, Mass., 1966; MA, SUNY, Stony Brook, 1972. Tchr. math. John Bapst High Sch., Bangor, 1966-67, Dawnwood Jr. High Sch., Centereach, N.Y., 1967-72, Mulcahey Mid. Sch., Taunton, Mass., 1972-77, Taunton High Sch., 1978-83, Dartmouth (Mass.) High Sch., 1983—; Sch. rep. Dartmouth Educators Assn., Southeastern Mass. U., North Dartmouth, Dartmouth Math. Curriculum Group 1984-88. Recipient Rsch. in Math. Edn. award Shell Ctr. for Math. Edn., Nottingham, Eng., 1988. Mem. Nat. Coun. Tchrs. Math., Coll. Club New Bedford (bd. dirs. 1987—). Home: 417 Gulf Rd W South Dartmouth MA 02748

KOPACK, PAMELA LEE (PAMELA LEE MACMINN), business services executive; b. Portland, Maine, July 25, 1951; d. Everett John Foye and Lois Florence (Loveland) MacMinn; student Sears, Roebuck Extension Inst., 1969-73, Newspaper Inst. Am., 1979-85; m. Charles Thomas Kopack, Apr. 2, 1971. Sales staff Sears Roebuck & Co., Cleve., 1966-69, credit collector, 1972-75; exec. sec., asst., Cole Nat. Corp., Cleve., 1976-79; pres. Kopack Svc. Bur., Cleve., 1979—; various positions as employment counselor, travel cons., bridal cons., model, photographer, advt. aide, sales person. Author poetry pub. in Poetry-People, 1975, other publs., 1974—, lyrics for songs recorded on single records and albums, 1974-79; author greeting cards, articles, short stories. Mem. Career Guild (New Feature award 1982), Secs. Workshop, P.S. for Profl. Secs. (Bur. Bus. Practice, article award 1979), Internat. Platform Assn., Nat. Assn. Female Execs. Clubs: Women's Opportunity Workshop, Nat. Assn. Notaries. Recipient poetry award for Facets of a Housewife, pub. in Beyond Verse, 1977. Compiler Royal Doulton Manual for Collectors. Address: 16493 Prospect Rd Strongsville OH 44136-5543 Office: PO Box 81573 Cleveland OH 44181-0573

KOPECKY, PILAR ROSARIO, nurse; b. Quito, Pichincha, Ecuador, Oct. 5; came to U.S., 1967; d. Carlos and Consuelo (Ribas) C.; m. John W. Foster, Nov. 28, 1970 (div. Dec. 1982); m. Jack Kopecky, Oct. 14, 1989. AA in Gen. Edn., Santa Monica Coll., 1974, AA in Nursing, 1975; BS in Nursing, Calif. State U., L.A., 1978. Cert. intensive care and pub. health nurse. Nurse Harbor-UCLA Hosp., Torrance, Calif., 1975-76, O'Connor Hosp., San Jose, Calif., 1979—; mem. clin. practice com. O'Connor Hosp., San Jose, 1982—; mem. Staff III Com., San Jose, 1985-87; me. Standard of Care Com., San Jose, 1987—; coordinator Pacu Quality Assurance Program, San Jose, 1988—. Vol. Health Fair, San Jose, 1985, Run for the Kids, Stanford U., Palo Alto, Calif., 1983—, Juvenile Ctr. Aux., San Jose, 1988—; nurse Interplast, Palo Alto, 1985—. Mem. Am. Soc. Post Anesthesia Nurses, Sierra Club, Beta Sigma Phi (svc. officer 1988—). Home: 7562 Newcastle Dr Cupertino CA 95014 Office: O'Connor Hosp 2105 Forest Ave San Jose CA 95128

KOPENHAVER, JOSEPHINE YOUNG, painter, educator; b. Seattle, June 9, 1908; d. George Samuel and Blanche Cecilia (Castle) Young; m. Ralph Witmer Kopenhaver, Apr. 11, 1931. AB, U. Calif., 1928; MFA (scholar 1936-37), U. So. Calif., 1937; postgrad. Claremont Grad. Sch., 1951, 67, Chouinard Art Inst., 1946-47, Otis Art Inst., 1954-55. Prof. art Chaffee Jr. Coll., Ontario, Calif., 1946-47, L.A. City Coll., 1948-73, Woodbury U., L.A., 1973-76, summer sessions Calif. State U., L.A., 1950, Pasadena City Coll., 1949, Otis Art Inst., L.A., 1959, Pasadena Art Inst., 1948; profl. painter, exhibiting artist, 1933—; cons. Art Historians, Carmel, Calif. Work included in exhibits mus. and pvt. galleries U.S. and Mex., 1933—, including Hatfield Galleries, L.A.; art juror; represented Archives of Am. Art Oakland (Calif.) Art Mus.; reprodns. of paintings in N.Y. Art Rev., 1988, Calif. Art Rev., 1989. Winner first award in oil L.A. Art Festival, 1936, various art awards. Mem. L.A. Art Assn., Nat. Watercolor Soc., Audubon Artists, Artists for Econ. Action, Calif. Tchrs. Assn., L.A. Athletic Club, Zeta Tau Alpha. Office: PO Box 10666 Glendale CA 91209

KOPENHAVER, PATRICIA ELLSWORTH, podiatrist. Student, Columbia U., 1950-53; BA, George Washington U., 1954; MA, Columbia U., 1956; Dr. Podiatric Medicine, N.Y. Coll. of Podiatric Medicine, 1963; postgrad., N.Y. Coll. Podiatric Medicine, 1980. Diplomate Nat. Bd. Podiatry Examiners. Pvt. practice podiatry Greenwich, Conn., 1964—; mem. staff Laurelton Convalescent Hosp., Greenwich. Friends of Greenwich Libr.; publicity dir. Neighbors Club, YWCA, 1968—; bd. dirs. Monmouth Opera Guild, 1965; trustee Monmouth Opera Festival, 1966, v.p., 1964; mem. Greenwich Arts Council; program chmn. Greenwich Women's Republican Club, 1983-84, 4th dist. rep., 1984-85, 1987—; mem. Greenwich Exchange for Women's Work, 1984; chmn. bd. Greenwich Woman's Club Gardeners, 1986—. Recipient Hosp. Fund award for med. research translations ARC. Mem. AAUW, NOW, Am. Podiatry Assn. (career guidance com.), Conn. Podiatry Assn., Fairfield Podiatry Assn., Am. Woman's Podiatry Assn. (sec.), Am. Assn. Women Podiatrists (charter pres. 1969-78), Acad. Podiatry, Am. Podiatry Council, UN Assn. U.S.A., Acad. Podiatric Medicine, (chmn. nominating com. 1981, 1st v.p. 1983-84, chmn. fund raising 1984-85, chmn. women's issues 1985, chmn. community edn. 1989), Am. Podiatric Circulatory Soc., Am. Acad. Sports Medicine, Am. Acad. of Podiatric Sports Medicine (assoc. 1989), George Washington U. Alumni Assn., Columbia Alumni Assn., Fairfield County Alumni Assn. Columbia U., Nat. Fedn. Rep. Women, Bruce Mus., Nature Conservancy, Federated Garden Clubs Conn., Croquet Found. Am., St. Mary Ladies Guild, Greenwich Gardeners, Womans' Club (ways and means com. 1989), English Speak Union, Pi Epsilon Chi. Clubs: Soroptimist Internat. of the Ams., Inc. (vice chmn. program com. 1985—, regional med. scholarship chmn. 1987, med. scholarship chmn. Northeastern region 1988, program dir. 1988—, pres. Greenwich br. 1990—), Toastmasters, Travel (program com. 1984—, Indian com.), Greenwich Women's (chmn. civic and public affairs com. 1970, program chmn. 1983—, pres. 1985-88, scholarship chmn. 1985—, ways and means com. 1989). Home: 2 Sutton Pl S New York NY 10022 Office: 8 Dearfield Dr Greenwich CT 06831

KOPLOVITZ, KAY, communication network executive; b. Milw., Apr. 11, 1945; d. William E. and Jane T. Smith; m. William C. Koplovitz Jr., Apr. 17, 1971. BS, U. Wis., 1967; MA in Communications, Mich. State U., 1968. Radio and TV producer, dir. Sta. WTMJ-TV, Milw., 1967; editor Communications Satellite Corp., Washington, 1968-72; dir. community services UA Columbia Cablevision, Oakland, N.J., 1973-75; v.p., exec. dir. UA Columbia Satellite Services Inc., Oakland, 1977-80; pres., chief exec. officer USA Network, N.Y.C., 1980—. Mem. bd. overseers NYU Grad. Sch. Bus., 1984-87; bd. dirs. Nat. Jr. Achievement, 1986—. Recipient Action for Childrens TV award, 1979, Twin award Ridgewood YWCA, 1980, Matrix award Women in Communications, 1983, Outstanding Alumnus award Mich. State U. Grad. Sch. Bus., 1985, Outstanding Corp. Social Responsibility CUNY, 1986, Women Who Run the World award Sara Lee Corp., 1987; Cable Merit scholar, 1968. Mem. Nat. Cable TV Assn. (advt. com. 1979-82, Idell Kaitz award 1979), Women in Cable (founding bd. mem., membership chmn. 1979-80, v.p. 1981-82, pres. 1982-83), Cable Advt. Bur. (bd. dirs., exec. com., treas. 1981-87, Chmn.'s award for Leadership 1987), Nat. Acad. Cable Programming (bd. dirs. 1984-87), Advt. Council Inc. (bd. dirs. 1985-87), Com. of 200, Womens Forum, N.Y.C. Partnership (bd. dirs. 1987—), Mus. Broadcasting (bd. dirs. 1988—). Office: USA Network 1230 Ave of the Americas 18th Fl New York NY 10020*

KOPMAN, ELIZABETH SUZANNE, health services regional controller; b. Phila., Aug. 27, 1950; d. Frederick and Beatrice (Gans) Perlitch; m. Arthur Kopman, June 21, 1970 (div. June 1986); children: Brad, Jaime. Diploma in Nursing, Temple U., 1971; AA, LaSalle Extension U., 1974; student in Health Care Asministrn., St. Joseph's Coll., 1989. Head nurse Phila. Geriatric Ctr., 1971-73; supr. St. Mary's Hosp., Phila., 1974-75; nursing supr. Ashton Hall Rehab. Ctr., Phila., 1975-78; dir. nursing Northwood Nursing Home, Phila., 1978-80, adminstr., 1980-82; asst. dir. Mayo Nursing Ctr., Phila., 1982-84, adminstr., 1986-88; owner Popcorn Video, Phila., 1984-86; instr. first aid Loesche Sch., Phila., 1982; buyer movies Popcorn Video, Phila., 1984—; mem. products com. GERI-Med, Phila., 1987—, regional contr., 1988-89, regional adminstr., 1989—. Contbr. articles to profl. jours. Coach Max Meyers Athletic Club, Phila., 1985—. Mem. Nat. Assn. of Female Execs., Long Term Nursing Adminstrs. Republican. Jewish. Home: 409 Audubon Terr Philadelphia PA 19116 Office: Geriatric and Med Ctrs 5601 Chestnut St Philadelphia PA 19139

KOPP, JENNIFER LEE, technical illustrator; b. Phoenix, May 30, 1949; d. Leonard Owen and Gloria Belle (Shaffer) Kelly; student Los Angeles Pierce Coll., 1976-78, Moorpark Coll., 1981-83; m. Glenn Robert Kopp, Sept. 7, 1969; children—M. Scott, G. Douglas (dec.). Supr., Volt Tech. Corp., Van Nuys, Calif., 1977-78, project coordinator, El Segundo, Calif., 1978-80; checker in drafting Mainstream Engring., Sherman Oaks, Calif., 1978-79; sr. tech. illustrator Dynaction Resources, Chatsworth, Calif., 1979; sr. tech. illustrator Litton Data Command Systems, Agoura Hills, Calif., 1980-86. Dir. North Shore chpt. Gt. Salton Sea Experience, 1986; dir. Salton Sea Legal Def. Group Systems, Agoura Hills, Calif., 1986-87; firefighter, sec.-treas. North Shore Vol. Fire Co., 1985-86; docent Living Desert, 1986-88. Recipient Presdl. Sports award Pres.'s Council on Phys. Fitness, 1973, 4 awards of Merit for sports L.A. Pierce Coll., 1977, Sportsmanship award Women's Internat. Motorcycle Assn., 1976, Citizenship award, 1978. Mem. North Shore C. of C. (founder 1987, pres., exec. dir. 1987-88), North Shore Litton Data Command Systems Rod and Gun Club (pres. 1982-83, v.p. 1984-85). Home: 101760 Sea Breeze Dr North Shore CA 92254 Office: PO Box 3197 North Shore CA 92254

KOPP, KRISTIN JEAN SVANOE, small business owner, therapist, consultant. BA, U. Wis., 1974; postgrad., Am. Inst. Hypnotherapy, 1990—. Registered hypnotherapist; lic. Avatar master. Pres. Ptnrs. in Progress, Milw., 1986—; dir. Pathways Learning Ctr., 1988—; speaker in field. Author: Creating Tomorrow; host weekly TV talk show Helping Hands, 1990—. Mem. Nat. Speaker's Assn., Wis. Profl. Speakers, Assn. for Humanistic Psychology. Home and Office: 3030 N 80th Milwaukee WI 53222

KOPP, LAURIE, marketing professional; b. Edison, N.J., Jan. 28, 1964; d. Melvin and Augusta Desie (Zimmerman) K. BS in Edn., U. Pa. Product mgr. James River Corp./Dixie Products, Norwalk, Conn.; brand asst. Procter & Gamble, Cin. Mem. Am. Mktg. Assn. (past pres.). Home: 2 Soldiers Field Park #815 Boston MA 02163

KOPP, MELISANDE, lawyer; b. Tulsa, Jan. 14, 1943; d. Hermann George and Mildred Ann (Humphrey) K.; m. Frank Aquila Rogers, June 5, 1986. BA, U. Ark., 1964; postgrad., Ind. U., 1965; JD, NYU, 1976. Attorney United Ch. Christ, N.Y., 1976-78, Estate Lyricist, Dorothy Fields, N.Y., 1978; editor Harcourt Brace Jovanovich, N.Y., 1978-81, Clark Boardman Co., Ltd., N.Y., 1981-82; assoc. Halperin & Marcus, N.Y., 1983-84; law clerk N.Y. Supreme Ct., Bklyn., 1984-85; sr. attorney The State Ins. Fund., N.Y., 1985--. Mem. Greenwich Village Singers, N.Y., 1977—. Mem. Magna Charta Dames. Democrat. Home: 73 W 11th St New York NY 10011 Office: The State Ins Fund 199 Church St New York NY 10007

KOPP, NANCY KORNBLITH, state legislator; b. Coral Gables, Fla., Dec. 7, 1943; d. Lester and Barbara M. (Levy) Kornblith; m. Robert E. Kopp, May 3, 1969; children: Emily, Robert E. III. BA with honors, Wellesley Coll., 1965; MA, U. Chgo., 1968; LittD (hon.) Hood Coll., 1988. Instr. polit. sci. U. Ill., 1968-69; staff spl. subcom. on edn. U.S. Ho. of Reps., Washington, 1970-71; legis. staff Md. Gen. Assembly, Annapolis, 1971-74; mem. Md. Ho. of Dels., 1974—, chmn. appropriations subcom. on edn. and human resources, 1981—; mem. exec. com. Nat. Conf. State Legislators, asst. majority leader, 1987—, chmn. assembly on legislature; exec. com. So. Reg. Edn. Bd. Mem. Am. Polit. Sci. Assn., LWV, AAUW, Common Cause. Democrat. Jewish. Office: Maryland Gen Assembly Lowe House Office Bldg Annapolis MD 21401

KOPP, VIRGINIA ANN, soil conservationist; b. Elmhurst, Ill., June 24, 1959; d. Edward J. and Arlene H. (Krempels) K. BS, U. Ill., 1984; MS, Va. Tech., 1988. Soil conservationist USDA, Halifax, Va., 1988—. Vol. Literacy Program. Mem. NAFE, Soil Sci. Soc. Am., Master Gardeners of Va., Nat. Bridge Appalachian Trail Club, Phi Kappa Phi. Roman Catholic. Office: Soil Conservation Svc PO Box 247 Halifax VA 24558

KOPPEL, AUDREY FEILER, electrologist, educator; b. N.Y.C., Sept. 25, 1944; d. Jules Eugene and Lee (Gibel) Feiler; m. Mark Alyn Koppel, May 28, 1967; children: Jason, Seth. B.A., Bklyn. Coll., 1972; diploma in electrolysis Hoffman Inst., 1975; postgrad. George Washington U., 1984, Essex Community Coll., 1984, Kree Inst., 1980. Electrologist, Bklyn., 1976, Glemby Internat., N.Y.C., 1976-78, Island Electrolysis, Manhasset, N.Y., 1982-84; registrar, supervising instr. Kree Inst., N.Y.C., 1978-82; pres. North Shore Electrolysis, Manhasset, 1982-84; dir., electrologist Bklyn. Studio, 1982—; pres. Ray Internat., 1986—. Editor, author pamphlet Glossary for Electrolysis, 1985; contbr. articles to profl. jours. Active Greater N.Y. coun. Boy Scouts Am., 1977-84; flag lt. Bklyn. Power Squadron. Mem. Am. Electrology Assn. (v.p. 1984—, edn. chmn. 1984—, continuing edn. coord. 1985, chmn. pub. rels. com. 1989—), N.Y. Electrolysis Assn. (corr. sec. 1983-85, pres. 1985-90, bd. trustee 1990—, advisor 1990—), Internat. Guild of Electrologists (merit award 1978). Democrat. Jewish. Clubs: U.S. Power Squadron (flag lt.), Bklyn. Yacht. (v.p. ladies aux. 1989—). Avocations: boating, swimming, music. Office: Bklyn Studio of Electrolysis 2376 E 16th St Suite 1 Brooklyn NY 11229

KOPPES, SARAH CATHERINE, management consultant; b. Kansas City, Mo., Oct. 10, 1962; d. Robert John and Carolyn Jane (Russell) K. BBA, Hope Coll., 1983. Mgr. strategic planning Gen. Dynamics Corp., St. Louis, 1984-87; mgr. Midwest region Data Resources, Inc., Chgo., 1987-88; pres. SCK, Inc., St. Louis, 1988—. Vol. St. Louis Children's Hosp., 1989—.

KOPPULA, MOREEN, physician; b. Kurnool, India; came to U.S. 1977; d. James and Kamala (Kandukuri) R; m. Sampurnarao Koppula, Dec. 29, 1973; children: Patrick, Anthony. MBBS, Guntur Med. Coll., India, 1973. Diplomate Am. Bd. of Anesthesiology. Intership Govt. Gen. Hosp., Guntur, 1973-75; sr. house officer in anesthesia East Birmingham (U.K.) Hosp., 1976-77, Worthing (U.K.) Hosp., 1977; resident Hahnemann Med. Coll. and Hosp., Phlia., 1978-79, Children's Hosp. of Phila., 1979; resident in pediatrics Cooper Med. Ctr., Camden, N.J., 1979-80; chief resident in anesthesia Hahnemann Med. Coll. and Hosp., Phila., 1980-81; fellow in anesthesia Childrens Hosp. of Phila., 1981; mem. staff anesthesiologist Our Lady Of Lourdes Hosp., Camden, 1981-82; mem. staff in anesthesiologist Maricopa Med. Ctr., Phoenix, 1982—, Good Samaritan Med. Ctr., Phoenix, 1983—, St. Joseph's Hosp., Phoenix, 1983—, Phoenix Meml. Hosp., 1983—, Thuderbird Samaritan Hosp., Glendale, Ariz., 1983—, St. Luke's Hosp., Phoenix, 1983—, Tempe (Ariz.) St. Luke's Hosp., 1983—; dir. of obstetrical anesthesia Desert Samaritan Hosp., Mesa, Ariz., 1988—. Mem. Am. Soc. of Anesthesiologist, Ariz. Soc. of Anesthesiologist, Maricopa County Soc. of Anesthesiologist. Republican. Lutheran. Home: 6997 E Paradise Ranch

Rd Paradise Valley AZ 85253 Office: Spring Group PO Box 60070 Phoenix AZ 85082

KOPROWSKA, IRENA, pathologist, cytologist; b. Warsaw, Poland, May 12, 1917; came to U.S., 1944; d. Henryk and Eugenia (Cwi) Grasberg; m. Hilary Koprowski, July 14, 1938; children: Claude, Christopher. BA, Popielewska/Roszkowska, Warsaw, 1934; MD, Warsaw U., 1939. Cert. Am. Bd. Pathology, Internat. Bd. Cytopathology. Intern in medicine Villejuif Lunatic Asylum, Seine, France, 1940; various pathology and rsch. positions, 1942-47; asst. pathologist N.Y. Infirmary for Women and Children, N.Y.C., 1947-49; rsch. fellow dept. of anatomy Cornell U. Med. Coll., N.Y.C., 1950-54; asst. prof. dept. pathology SUNY Downstate Med. Ctr., N.Y.C., 1954-57; assoc. prof. dept. pathology, dir. sch. cytotechnology Hahnemann Med. Coll., Phila., 1957-64, prof. pathology dir. sch. cytotechnology, 1964-70; prof. pathology, dir. cytology lab. Temple U. Med. Sch., Phila., 1970-87, prof. emerita, 1987—; rsch. asst. dept. pharmacology Cornell U. Med. Coll., N.Y.C., 1949-50, rsch. fellow dept. anatomy, 1950-54; cons. WHO, Southeast Asia, India, 1960-85, A.F.I.P. Air Force Cytology Rescreen Project, 1979-80. Contbr. articles to profl. jours. Named one of Women Physicians of the Yr., Polish Am. Med. Assn., 1977; grantee USPHS-Nat. Cancer Insts., 1954-75, rsch. grantee Bender Co., Vienna, Austria, 1983-89. Fellow Am. Soc. Clin. Pathologists (emeritus), Coll. Am. Pathologists (emeritus), Coll. Physicians of Phila., Internat. Acad. Cytology (hon.), Internat. Acad. Pathology (emeritus); mem. Am. Assn. for Cancer Rsch. Inc. (emeritus), Am. Assn. Pathologists Inc. (emeritus), Am. Med. Women's Assn., Am. Soc. Cytology (life med.), Am. Soc. Exptl. Pathology, Argentinian Soc. Cytology (hon.), Path. Soc. Phila. Home: 334 Fairhill Rd Wynnewood PA 19096

KORBEL, ELAINE ELIZABETH, office administrator; b. Farley, Iowa, Aug. 31, 1941; d. Alphonse Mathias and Leonetta Elizabeth (Freking) Link; m. Adrian Charles Korbel, June 4, 1966; children: Douglas Paul, Kari Elizabeth. Student, Loras Coll., Dubuque, Iowa, 1988-89. Sec. John Deere, Dubuque, 1961-67; advisor Telegraph-Herald, Dubuque, 1978-79; office adminstr. Loras Coll., Dubuque, 1983—. Mem. Profl. Women's Network, League Women Voters, Friendship Force. Republican. Roman Catholic. Home: 1750 Horizon Ct Dubuque IA 52001 Office: Loras College 1450 Alta Vista Dubuque IA 52001

KORDA, REVA, advertising executive; b. N.Y.C., Dec. 24, 1926; d. Louis and Yetta (Sussman) Fine; m. William Korda, Sept. 7, 1957; children: Joshua, Natasha. BA magna cum laude, Hunter Coll., 1947. Copywriter Gimbel's, N.Y.C., 1949-50, Macy's, N.Y.C., 1951-53; with Ogilvy & Mather, Inc., N.Y.C., 1953-80; writer Ogilvy & Mather, Inc., 1953-62, sr. v.p., 1962-74, exec. v.p., 1974-80, creative head, 1974-80; dir. Ogilvy & Mather Internat., 1975-80; chmn. Korda Rand Levine Inc., N.Y.C., 1980-83, Reva Korda Cons., Inc., 1983-89. Mem. Phi Beta Kappa. Office: Rte 2 Box 870 Sag Harbor NY 11963

KORDEN, MARY ETHEL, early childhood educator, administrator; b. Camden, N.J., Jan. 13, 1950; d. William Henry Turner and Leola (Pratt) Williams; m. Dolo Lee Korden, Sept. 5, 1987; children: Dana, Iris, Susannah, Chaz, Rita, Jennifer, Paula. AS, Camden County Coll., Blackwood, N.J., 1976; BA, Glassboro (N.J.) State Coll., 1978. Cert. nursery sch. tchr., elem. tchr. Floating tchr. Broadway Family Ctr., Camden, N.J., 1974-75, head tchr., 1975-76; Title I reading and math. tchr. Richland Sch. Dist. I, Columbia, S.C., 1978-80; remedial reading tchr. J.J. Roberts United Meth. Sch., Liberia, 1981-82, kindergarten tchr., 1982-83; head tchr. Delaware County Head Start, Chester, Pa., 1985-87; dir. Glassboro State Coll. Child Care Ctr., Camden, 1987—. Chmn. fundraisers Gorton Town (Liberia) Pub. Sch., 1982-83. Mem. NAFE, NAACP, Nat. Assn. Edn. Young Children, Glassboro State Coll. Parents Club, Liberian Women's Assn. (pres. 1989—). Democrat. Roman Catholic. Home: 212A Garfield Ave Collingswood NJ 08108

KORDUCKI, BARBARA JOAN, former orchestra executive, educator, real estate agent, consultant; b. Milw., May 2, 1956; d. Edward and Rita Korducki. BA in Mass Communication, U. Wis., Milw., 1980; MPA, Seattle U., 1986. News reporter, pub. affairs producer Sta. WUWM, Milw., 1979-81; cons. Adams & Assocs., Seattle, 1981-82; pub. rels. and projects coord. Nat. Multiple Sclerosis Soc., Seattle, 1982-85; pub. rels. and mktg. specialist Planned Parenthood of Seattle-King County, Seattle, 1985-87; mng. dir. N.W. Chamber Orch., Seattle, 1987-90; cons., real estate agent Seattle, 1990—; adj. lectr. journalism Seattle U., 1989—; mem. mktg. task force Bus. Vols. for Arts, 1989-90. Exec. producer (ednl. musical) Henry's Tune, 1990—. Pub. rels. cons. Seattle Urban League/King County Coalition on Teen Pregnancy, 1985-87; bd. dirs. Wash. Literacy, 1982-85; spl. events com. Nat. Multiple Sclerosis Soc., Seattle, 1987-88; panelist Puget Power Blue Ribbon Commn., 1986-87; project advisor Leadership Tomorrow, Seattle, 1986. Mem. N.W. Devel. Officers Assn., Pub. Rels. Soc. Am. (cert., chair Wash. awards 1987—, co-chair Totem awards 1984-86), Seattle Sailing Club (bd. dirs. 1986-87), Seattle Women's Sailing Assn. Democrat. Office: NW Chamber Orch 1305 4th Ave Ste 522 Seattle WA 98101

KOREK, JOAN SUSAN, pharmacist; b. Mpls., Sept. 8, 1957; m. Thomas Gerard Cantu, Jan. 27, 1989. BS in Pharmacy, U. Minn., 1981; PharmD, U. Tex., Austin, San Antonio, 1983. Resident in psychiat. pharmacy U. Tex. and Austin State Hosp., 1984; grad. teaching asst. Coll. Pharmacy U. Tex., Austin, 1982-83; clin. instr. Coll. Pharmacy U. Tex., 1983-84; staff pharmacist Shoal Creek Hosp. Pharmacy, Austin, 1983-84; clin. psychiat. pharmacist U. Utah Hosp. & VA Med. Ctr., Salt Lake City, 1984-88; instr. clin. pharmacy U. Utah, Salt Lake City, 1984-86; asst. prof. clin. pharmacy U. Utah, 1986-88; clin. pharmacist Rosewood Ctr., Owings Mills, Md., 1988-89; dir. pharmacy, clin. pharmacist Walter P. Carter Ctr., Balt., 1989—; clin. asst. prof. sch. medicine U. Md., Balt., 1990—; adj. asst. prof. Coll. Nursing U. Utah, 1987-88; adj. asst. prof. clin. pharmacy U. Md., Balt., 1988-89; cons. psychiat. drug therapy Unita County Counseling Svcs., Evanston, Wyo., 1987-88; asst. prof. clin. pharmacy U. Md., Balt., 1989—. Contbr. articles to profl. jours. Mem. Am. Assn. of Colls. Pharmacy, Am. Coll. Clin. Pharmacy, Am. Pharm. Assn., Am. Soc. Hosp. Pharmacists, Md. Soc. Hosp. Pharmacists. Office: Walter P Carter Ctr 630 W Fayette St Baltimore MD 21201

KOREN, MARY ELAINE, nurse; b. Youngstown, Ohio, Feb. 28, 1950; d. William Emil and Helen Cecilia (Keyser) Sovik; m. Alan G. Koren, Oct. 13, 1979; children: Katie, Michael, Megan. BSN, St. Xavier Coll., 1972; MSN, Loyola U., Chgo., 1975; postgrad., Rush U., 1983-90. Staff nurse Evanston (Ill.) Hosp., 1972-74; staff nurse, practitioner Rush Med. Ctr., Chgo., 1974-75, profl. nurse trainee, 1986-87, 89-90; instr. New Eng. Bapt. Sch. of Nursing, Boston, 1975-76; nurse adminstr. Newton-Wellesley Hosp. (Mass.), 1976-77; asst. prof. U. Ill. Coll., Chgo., 1977-82, George Williams Coll., Downers Grove, Ill., 1983. Contbr. articles to profl. jours. Mem. pub. edn. com. Am. Cancer Soc., Chgo., 1977-83. Mem. AAUW, Am. Nurses Assn., Sigma Theta Tau.

KORETZ, JANE FAITH, biophysicist; b. N.Y.C., Aug. 12, 1947; d. Norman Joseph and Natalie (Cromer) K. BA with high honors, Swarthmore Coll., 1969; PhD in Biophysics, U. Chgo., 1974. Postdoctoral fellow MRC Cell Biophysics Unit King's Coll., London, 1974-76; rsch. assoc. Coll. Med. and Dentistry of N.J., Newark, 1976-77; asst. prof. Dept. Biology Rensselaer Poly. Inst., Troy, N.Y., 1977-83; assoc. prof. Dept. Biology Rensselaer Poly. Inst., Troy, 1983-90, prof., 1990—, assoc. dir. ctr. for biophysics, 1989—; cons. in field; reviewer NIH, 1989—, NSF, 1977—. Contbr. articles to profl. jours. Reader, program producer RISE, Schenectady, N.Y., 1984—. Fellowship Muscular Dystrophy Assn., 1974-76; grantee Nat. Eye Inst.; Fulbright scholarship Ctr. for Internat. Exchange of Scholars, 1991; recipient Henry Fukui Travel award Nat. Found for Eye Rsch., 1989. Mem. Assn. for Women in Sci., Internat. Soc. for Eye Rsch., Optical Soc. Am., Am. Soc. Biochemistry and Molecular Biology, Biophys. Soc. (coun. mem. 1988—), Assn. for Rsch. Vision and Ophthalmology, Sigma Xi. Office: Ctr for Biophysics/Biology Rensselaer Poly Inst Troy NY 12180-3590

KORFHAGE, JOYCE, pharmacist; b. Cleve., Nov. 23, 1948; d. Clinton Jay and Margaret Ethel (Rains) K.; m. Larry J. Leach, July 27, 1969 (div.); 1 child, Shannon Kay Leach. B of Pharmacy, U. Ky., Lexington, 1971. Registered Pharmacist; cert. tissue therapist. Asst. mgr. Taylor Drugs #19, Louisville, 1971-73; pharmacist in charge Norton Drugs, Manhattan, Kans., 1973-75; owner, pharmacist All Care Pharmacy and Home Convalescent Ctr., Louisville, 1976—; cert. positive mental attitude instr. Napeoliom Hill Found. Entertainment chmn. Ky. Pharm. Assn. State Conv., Louisville, 1980; regional chmn. Medic Alert, Louisville, 1981-84; vice chmn. Nard Task Force for Women, Washington, 1981-83; v.p. Derby City Chpt. Spinal Cord Group, Louisville, Ky., 1988-89. Mem. Ky. Med. Equip. Supplier Assn., Jefferson County Pharmacy Assn. (sec. 1976-77, bd. govs. 1990—), Ky. Pharm. Assn., Am. Soc. Parenteral and Enteral Nutrition, Louisville C. of C., Better Bus. Bur., Inst. of Self-Actualization (enrollment com. 1988-89). Methodist. Office: All Care Pharmacy and Home Convalescent Ctr 4434 Cane Run Rd Louisville KY 40216

KORGEN, JUDITH KAY, budget analyst; b. Alma, Mich., Apr. 2, 1939; d. Richard Louis and Doris Eleanor (Odle) Waggoner; m. Ben J. Korgen, Aug. 15, 1959; children: Susan, Jeffry, James. AA, Stephens Coll., 1959; BS, Oreg. State U., Corvallis, 1966. Acct. Oreg. State U., 1966-69; programs analyst Woods Hole (Mass.) Oceanographic Inst., 1974-78; specialist engring. adminstrn. Martin Marietta Manned Space Systems, New Orleans, 1978-82, sr. specialist engring. adminstrn., 1982—. Recipient Silver Snoopy award NASA, 1990. Mem. AAUW (treas. Slidell, La. chpt. 1982-86, pres. 1986-88). Home: 219 Loop Dr Slidell LA 70458 Office: Martin Marietta Systems PO Box 29304 New Orleans LA 70189

KORMOS, KATHLEEN MISICHKO, editorial supervisor; b. Cleve., Oct. 15, 1952; d. William and Verna (Kuruc) Misichko; m. Michael Peter Kormos, Nov. 9, 1985; stepchildren: Michael Peter Jr., Elizabeth Marie. BA in Journalism, Kent State U., 1974. Reporter Chronicle-Telegram, Elyria, Ohio, 1974-80; pub. info. officer City of Cleve., 1981-84; asst. editor PR Newswire, Cleve., 1985-87, sr. editor, 1988, editorial supr., 1988—. Republican. Russian Orthodox. Home: 1379 E Ridgewood Dr Seven Hills OH 44131 Office: PR Newswire 815 Superior Ave #1120 Cleveland OH 44114

KORN, JUDITH ANN, human relations consultant; b. N.Y.C., Mar. 23, 1947; d. Eugene and Bertha (Magaram) Kron; B.A. cum laude, SUNY, Buffalo, 1968; M.A., Columbia Univ. Tchrs. Coll., 1969; m. Barry Paul Korn, Aug. 2, 1969; children—Lisa Michele, Suzanne Leslie, Amy Beth. Speech, hearing pathologist Long Island Jewish Hillside Med. Center, New Hyde Park, N.Y., 1969-71; dir. Human Relations Inst., White Plains, N.Y., 1979—; program coord. Effective Parenting Info. for Children, Briarcliff, N.Y., 1989—; adj. prof. Coll. New Rochelle, 1981-86. Mem. Am. Soc. Tng. and Devel., Am. Assn. for Counseling and Devel., Assn. Humanistic Edn. and Devel., Phi Beta Kappa. Office: 7 Pine Brook Dr White Plains NY 10605

KORNASIEWICZ, PAMELA LOUISE, classification analyst; b. Kittanning, Pa., Sept. 13, 1959; d. Edward Joseph and Helen Louise (Rodgers) K. BS, U. Pitts., 1981; postgrad., U. Calif., Santa Barbara, 1981-83; MBA, U. Pitts., 1986. Bookkeeper Polish Falcons of Am., Ford City, Pa., 1975-77; teaching asst. U. Calif., 1981-83; house mgr., EEO officer Evergreen Homes, Inc., Ford City, Pa., 1984-85; classification analyst Penn State U. Mem. choir Ch. St. Francis of Paola, 1971-74, Spl. Olympics, Evergreen Homes, 1984-85, Hand-in-Hand Festival, U. Pitts., 1980-81. Mem. Coll. and U. Personnel Assn., Fin. Club, Phi Eta Sigma. Office: Pa State U 120 S Burrowes St University Park PA 16801

KORNBLEET, LYNDA MAE, fireproofing and acoustical insulation contractor; b. Kansas City, Kans., June 15, 1951; d. Seymore Gerald Kornbleet and Jacqueline F. (Hurst) Kornbleet Malka. BA, U. St. Thomas, Houston, 1979. Lic. real estate salesperson. Temporary counselor Lyman's Personnel, Houston, 1974-75; real estate salesperson Coldwell Banker, Houston, 1975-77; sales, office mgr. Acme Insulation, Dallas, also Houston, 1977-79; owner, pres. Payless Insulation, Houston, 1979—. Named Contractor of the Yr., Sears Home Improvement, 1988. Mem. Nat. Assn. Remodeling Industry (bd. dirs. Houston 1982-84), Houston Air Conditioning Council (bd. dirs. 1982-83), Cellulose Insulation Contractors (chmn. Houston 1981-82), Houston Bus. Council, 1987-88. Democrat. Jewish. Avocations: bridge, golf, baseball, basketball. Office: Payless Insulation 207 Reinerman St Houston TX 77007

KORNBLUTH, SANDRA JOAN, transportation company administrator; b. N.Y.C., Oct. 27, 1951; d. Louis and Rose (Rosansky) K. BA magna cum laude, Queens Coll., 1973; MA in Romance Langs., Princeton U., 1975. Instr. French lang. Princeton (N.J.) U., 1973-77; mgr. cargo tariffs Air France, N.Y.C., 1977-82; mgr. internat. pricing Emery Worldwide, Wilton, Conn., 1982-86, dir. pricing, 1986-89; pres. Riverview Traffic Group, Trumbull, Conn., 1989—; mem. adv. bd. Cargo Rate Services, Miami, Fla., 1984—. Bd. dirs. Literacy Vols. Greater Norwalk, 1987. Fullbright-Hayes scholar, 1973. Office: PO Box 575 Trumbull CT 06611

KORNEGAY, MERRY LYNN, automotive executive; b. Warrenton, Va., Aug. 5, 1951; d. Edmond Bruce Sr. and Barbara Mary Elizabeth (Herbster) Noland; m. Reid Goff Kornegay Jr.; children: Steven Michael, Michelle Lynn, Barbara Ellen. AS, Cape Fear Community Coll., Wilmington, N.C., 1987. Mgr. Cavalier Motel, Warrenton, 1969-73, Old Town Art and Antique Gallery, Warrenton, 1973-76, Hosp. Automotive, Inc., Wilmington, 1979—. Author poems. Roman Catholic. Home: PO Box 7291 Wilmington NC 28406 Office: Hosp Automotive Inc 46 Covil Ave Wilmington NC 28403

KORNER, CAROL ANN, nurse; b. Bucyrus, Ohio, July 26, 1960; d. James Clayton and Donna May (Eickel) K. AS in Nursing Tech., Marion Tech. Coll., 1982. RN, Ohio. Nursing asst. Marion (Ohio) Gen. Hosp., 1980-82, nurse, 1982—. Scholar Shunk Mfg. Co., 1978-80. Mem. Am. Nurses' Assn. (cert. mental health and psychiat. nursing). Republican. Mem. United Ch. of Christ. Home: 812 S Sandusky Ave Bucyrus OH 44820

KORNER, HILDA, personnel executive; b. N.Y.C., June 2, 1931; d. Manuel and Sadie (Brookman) Troob; m. Herbert Korner, Aug. 1, 1953 (div. Feb. 1971); children—David, Peter. B.S. in Personnel Adminstrn, SUNY-Rochester, 1974. Owner, operator Gallery III, Marin County, Calif., 1964-69; supr. personnel services SUNY-Buffalo, 1970-72, dir. recruitment and promotion of women, 1972-75, coordinator human research devel., 1975-77; mgr. employment Stanford Linear Accelerator Ctr., Calif., 1977-83, asst. personnel dir., 1983-88, mgr. tng. and staff devel., 1988—; instr. D'Youville Coll., Buffalo, 1973-74, Ohlone Coll., Fremont, Calif., 1982-83; co-owner, ptnr. Korn Kompany, Palo Alto, Calif., 1985—. Workshop leader Resource Ctr. for Women, Palo Alto, 1981-83. Avocations: theater; symphony; chamber music; travel; reading. Home: PO Box 7414 Menlo Park CA 94026 Office: Stanford Linear Accelerator Ctr PO Box 4349 Stanford CA 94309

KORNFELD, ROSALIND HAUK, research biochemist; b. Dallas, Aug. 2, 1935; d. Walter L. and Margaret (Wallace) Hauk; m. Stuart A. Kornfeld, June 11, 1959; children: Katherine, Stephen Kerry, Carolyn. BS, George Washington U., 1957; PhD, Washington U., 1961. Post-doctoral rsch. fellow dept. biol. chemistry Washington U., St. Louis, 1961-63; staff fellow NIH, Bethesda, Md., 1963-65; rsch. instr. dept. medicine Washington U., St. Louis, 1965-69, rsch. asst. prof., 1969-71, rsch. assoc. prof., 1971-78, assoc. prof. biochemistry and medicine, 1978-81, prof. medicine and biol. chemistry, 1981—; Mem. com. on cancer immunobiology Nat. Cancer Inst., Bethesda, 1975-78, physiol. chemistry study sect. NIH, Bethesda, 1980-83. Editorial bd. Jour. of Biol. Chemistry, 1981-86; contbr. articles to profl. jours. Named scholar of the Leukemia Soc. Am., Washington U. Sch. Medicine, 1971-76. Mem. Am. Soc. Biochemistry and Molecular Biology, Am. Soc. Hematology, The Soc. for Complex Carbohydrates, Clayton Twp. (Mo.) Dem. Club (pres. 1971-73), Phi Beta Kappa. Democrat. Office: Washington U Sch Medicine Box 8125 660 s Euclid Saint Louis MO 63110

KOROTKIN, AUDREY RHONA, communications executive; b. Phila., Aug. 8, 1957; d. Arthur Lewis and Carol Ruth (Ruffner) K.; m. Don C. Clippinger, Oct. 21, 1989. BA in Russian Area Studies magna cum laude, U. Md., 1979. Prodn. asst. NBC Nightly News, Washington, 1978-79; news anchorwoman Sta. WCBM Radio, Balt., 1978-79; news, sports, anchor reporter Sta. WBAL Radio, Balt., 1979-86; exec. dir. Triple Crown Prodns., Inc., Louisville, 1986-89; pres. Korotkin Assocs. Inc., Louisville, 1989—. Contbg. writer Md. Horse mag., 1985, Racing Action newspaper, 1989—. Mem. Nat. Abortion Rights Action League, Balt., 1980—. Mem. AFTRA, NOW, Turf Publicists Am., Nat. Turf Writers Assn., Md. Racing Writers Assn., Thoroughbred Club Am., Phi Kappa Phi. Democrat. Jewish. Home and Office: 2221 Strathmoor Blvd Louisville KY 40205

KORP, PATRICIA ANNE, management analyst; b. Lincoln, Nebr., Nov. 15, 1942; d. Theodore R. and Elizabeth Anne (Olson) Munn; m. Vince L. Korp, Jan. 15, 1965 (div. 1986); children—Kathleen Anne, Karen Lee Korp Martinez. BS in Journalism, U. Wyo., 1967, MA, 1974. Women's editor Sheridan (Wyo.) Press, 1964-66; pub. info. and research asst. Wyo. Dept. Edn., 1967-69; dir. pub. relations and communications Wyo. Edn. Assn., 1969-71; coordinator info. services Mountain Plains Program, Glasgow, Mont., 1972-73; freelance pub. relations, Laramie, Wyo., 1973-74; pub. info. specialist Bur. Land Mgmt., Rawlins, Wyo., 1975-76, Cheyenne, Wyo., 1976-81, chief Office Pub. Affairs, 1981-85, Washington hdqrs. office, 1985—; communications specialist Wyo. Spl. Olympics, 1978-79. Editor: Wyo. Edn. News, 1969-71; asst. editor Wyo. Horizons, 1976-80, editor, 1980-85. Mem. Wyo. Council Children and Youth, 1976-77. Recipient All-Am. award Ednl. Press Assn. Am., 1st place award Nat. Fedn. Press Women, 1980. Mem. Nat. Fedn. Press Women, Capital Press Women (v.p.), Seton Cath. High Sch. Athletic Assn. (sec. 1981-83, pres. 1984), Sigma Delta Chi. Democrat. Roman Catholic. Office: 18th and C Sts NW Room 5622 Washington DC 20240

KORSHAK, YVONNE, art historian; b. Chgo., May 30, 1936; d. Donald Korshak and Irma B. Jaffe; m. Robert J. Ruben; 1 child, Karin. BA cum laude, Radcliffe Coll., Cambridge, Mass., 1958; MA, U. Calif. Berkeley, 1966; PhD, U. Calif., 1973. Asst. prof. U. Md., College Park, 1972-74, Fordham U., N.Y.C., 1974-75; from asst. prof. to prof. Adelphi U., Garden City, N.Y., 1975—, chairperson Dept. Art and Art History, 1978-81, dir. mus. studies, 1979—. Author: Frontal Faces in Attic Vase Painting, 1987, co-editor: Selections from Permanent Collection, 1983. Recipient Pres.'s award for excellence in teaching, 1990. Mem. Coll. Art Assn. Am., Archaeological Inst. Am., Long Island Art Historians Assn., American Soc. for Eighteenth Century Studies, American Philological Assn. Office: Adelphi U Dept Art and Art History Garden City NY 11530

KORTH, CHARLOTTE WILLIAMS, furniture and interior design firm executive; b. Milw.; d. Lewis C. and Marguerite Peil Brooks; m. Robert Lee Williams, Jr., Oct. 25, 1944 (dec.); children: Patricia, Melissa Williams O'Rourke, R. Brooks; m. Fred Korth, Aug. 23, 1980. Student, U. Wis., 1941. V.p., co-owner Charlotte's Inc., El Paso, Tex., 1951-76; pres. Paso del Norte Design, Inc., El Paso, 1978—; chmn. bd., chief exec. officer Charlotte's, Inc., El Paso, 1979—; mem. adv. bd. Mountain Bell Tel. Co., 1976-79; First City Nat. Bank, El Paso, 1981-86. Mem. women's com. El Paso Symphony Orch.; charter mem. Com. of 200, 1982—, Mus. of Women in the Arts, 1985—; mem. Architectural Adv. Bd.; active U. Tex., Austin. Recipient Silver plaque Gifts and Decorative Accessories mag., 1978; named Woman of Yr., Women's Polit. Caucus, 1979, Outstanding Woman Entreprenuer El Paso, Am. Bus. Women's Assn., 1979. Mem. Am. Soc. Interior Designers (bd. dir. Tex. 1977—), Inst. Bus. Designers, El Paso C. of C. (bd. dir. 1976—), El Paso Women's C. of C., Delta Gamma, Coronado Country Club, El Paso Club, Internat. Club (El Paso), Santa Teresa (N.Mex.) Country Club. Home: 1054 Torrey Pines El Paso TX 79912 also: 4200 Massachusetts Ave Washington DC 20016 Office: Charlotte's Fine Furniture Pepper Tree Square 5411 N Mesa St El Paso TX 79912

KORTH, PENNE PERCY, ambassador; b. Hattiesburg, Miss., Nov. 3, 1942; married; 3 children. Grad., U. Tex., 1964. Sr. Washington assoc., client liaison and rep. trust and estate div. Sotheby's, 1986-89; amb. to Mauritius, Port Louis, 1989—. Co-chmn. Am. Bicentennial Presdl. Inauguration, 1988-89. Office: Am Embassy, Rogers Bldg 4th Fl, John Kennedy St, Port Louis Mauritius*

KORTLANDER, MYRNA, psychotherapist; b. N.Y.C., July 12, 1934; d. Irving and Jean (Feldman) Beckenstein; children: Marc Allen, Don Richard. BA, Hunter Coll., 1975; MSW, Fordham U., 1981. Diplomate Nat. Assn. Social Workers. Staff Alfred Adler Mental Health Clinic, N.Y.C., 1981-83; psychotherapist Lower East Side Svc. Ctr., N.Y.C., 1983-86, L.I. Cons. Ctr., Forest Hills, N.Y., 1986-87; pvt. practice Forest Hills, 1981—. Mem. Nat. Assn. Social Workers, ALMACA. Home: 114-20 Queens Blvd Forest Hills NY 11375

KORTMAN, JOYCE ELAINE, graphic arts company executive, civic worker; b. Holland, Mich., Dec. 24, 1935; d. Henry John and Jeanette (Van Kampen) De Ridder; m. Harris Jay Kortman, May 15, 1956; children: David, Calvin, Lafon, Renee, Mark. Ed., Davenport Coll.; Hope Coll., Western Theol. Sem. Mem. adv. coun. Nat. Inst. Arthritis, Metabolism and Digestive Disease, NIH, 1973-75; mem. West unit Health Systems' Agy. Bd., HEW, 1972-83; active Mich. affiliate Am. Diabetes Assn., 1970—, vice chair nat. coordinating com. for pub. activities, mem. com. on pub. affairs and Mich. del. co-chmn. work group on nat. resources Nat. Commn. on Diabetes, 1975; cons., speaker, and consumer adv. in health; propr. DaCal Printing Co., Heritage Printing Service, Holland; pres. Galien Travel Inc. Mem. adv. bd. Mich. Dept. Pub. Health, 1974—; mem. Commn. on Handicapped Concerns, Mich. Dept. Labor, Holland Christian Schs. PTA; exec. dir. Holland Area Ecumenical, non-profit housing corp. Recipient cert. of appreciation Am. Diabetes Assn., 1970, citation for outstanding contbn., 1973, Vol. of Yr. award, 1976, Meritorious Svc. award, 1976. Mem. Holland C. of C. (1st vice chair bd.), Calvinette Internat. (counselor, co-chair com. on curriculum revision). Office: 16935 Riley St Holland MI 49423

KORTRIGHT, SUZANNE ALAINE, administrative assistant; b. Syracuse, N.Y., Apr. 28, 1954; d. Richard M. and Irene J. (Korycinski) Lawless; children: John Jr., Kevin M. AA, Cen. City Bus. Inst., 1984; student, BOCES, 1986. Adminstrv. asst. Fay's Inc., Liverpool, N.Y.; exec. sec. Syracuse Supply Co. Vol. Vera House, Rape Crisis Ctr., Am. Cancer Soc. Mem. NAFE, NOW, Profl. Secs. Internat., Nat. Audubon Soc., Smithsonian Inst., Cousteau Soc., Greenpeace. Home: 1013 Avery Ave Syracuse NY 13204

KOSACOFF-KARP, PHYLLIS JOYCE, construction company executive; b. N.Y.C., Apr. 1, 1944; d. Louis and Claire (Rubin) Kosacoff; m. Sheldon I. Karp, May 30, 1964 (div. 1974); children: Andrew, Allyson, Michele, Jamie Greg. Student, SUNY, N.Y.C., 1961-63, 72-77. Constrn. mgr., owner Phyllis Joyce Interiors Inc., Plainview, N.Y., 1969-81; constrn. project mgr. HRH Constrn. Corp., N.Y.C., 1981—. Prin. projects include Manufacturer Hanover Trust World Hdqrs., AT&T World Hdqrs., AT&T Infoquest, Thomson McKinnon Securities Fin. Sq., Hartz Assoc., Loews, Corp, The Mediators, E.J. Minskoff Equities, Inc., Orion Pictures Corp., Integrity Life Ins. Mem. Internat. Platform Assn., Internat. Platform Soc. Office: HRH Constrn Corp 1325 Ave of Americas New York NY 10021

KOSAKOWSKI, CYNTHIA MALLETT, marketing professional; b. Patuxent River, Md., Mar. 7, 1957; d. William Ernest and Helen Patricia (Splain) Mallett; m. Bruce S. Kosakowski, Oct. 22, 1983. BA magna cum laude, Mt. Holyoke Coll., 1979; student, Conn. Coll., 1977-78. CLU. With Met. Life Ins. Co., 1979—; mtkg. dir. Met. Life Ins. Co., N.Y.C., 1985-89; asst. v.p. Met. Life Ins. Co., Boston, 1989—; coll. recruiter Mt. Holyoke Coll., 1988—. Mem. Mt. Holyoke Club of Boston. Home: 24 Circle St Marblehead MA 01945 Office: Met Life Ins Co 99 High St 21st Fl Boston MA 02110

KOSCIUCZYK, LISA ANNE, civil engineer; b. Worcester, Mass., Apr. 1, 1959; d. Theodore Emil and Mary Elizabeth (Skudlark) K. BS, Worcester Poly. Inst., 1981. Lic. gen. engr. contractor A, Calif. Sr. civil engr. asst. Los Angeles County Pub. Works Dept., Calif., 1981-85; assoc. project engr. Irving Co., Newport Beach, Calif., 1985-86; project engr. Advanco Constructors, Upland, Calif., 1986—; pres. Lisak Constrn. Co. Inc., Long Beach, 1987—. Coordinator, St. Bartholomew's Young Adults, 1989. Mem. Worcester Poly. Inst. Alumni Assn., Phi Sigma. Democrat. Roman Catholic. Home: 230 Termino Ave #19 Long Beach CA 90803 Office: Advanco Constructors 1500 W 9th St Upland CA 91786

KOSCIUK, LISA MARIE, software engineer; b. Scotch Plains, N.J., July 2, 1965; d. Stanley E. and Carole A. (Dubas) K. BA, Mass. Wellesley Coll., 1988. Systems integrater Cambride (Mass.) Tech. Group, 1988; cons. applications design Cabot Corp., Waltham, Mass., 1988; cons. Phoenix Techs. Ltd., Norwood, Mass., 1988-89; cons. software engr. Lotus Devel. Corp., Cambridge, 1989—; cons. MIS, Mountainside, N.J., 1989-90. Assoc. New Eng. Wildlife Ctr., Mass., 1990—; mem. Sta. WGBH Pub. TV, 1989-90. Mem. Boston Computer Soc., NAFE. Office: Lotus Devel Corp 161 First St Cambridge MA 02142

KOSHLAND, MARIAN ELLIOTT, immunologist, educator; b. New Haven, Oct. 25, 1921; d. Waller Watkins and Margaret Ann (Smith) Elliott; m. Daniel Edward Koshland, Jr., May 25, 1945; children—Ellen R., Phyllis A., James M., Gail F., Douglas E. B.A., Vassar Coll., 1942, M.S., 1943; Ph.D., U. Chgo., 1949. Research asst. Manhattan Dist. Atomic Bomb Project, 1945-46; fellow dept. bacteriology Harvard Med. Sch., 1949-51; asso. bacteriologist biology dept. Brookhaven Nat. Lab., 1952-62, bacteriologist, 1963-65; assoc. research immunologist virus lab. U. Calif., Berkeley, 1965-69, lectr. dept. molecular biology, 1966-70, prof. dept. microbiology and immunology, 1970-89, chmn. dept., 1982-89, prof. dept. molecular and cell biology, 1989—; mem. Nat. Sci. Bd., 1976-82; mem. adv. com. to dir. NIH, 1972-75. Contbr. articles to profl. jours. Mem. Nat. Acad. Scis., Am. Acad. Microbiology, Am. Assn. Immunologists (pres. 1982-1983), Am. Soc. Biol. Chemists, Phi Beta Kappa, Sigma Xi. Home: 3991 Happy Valley Rd Lafayette CA 94549 Office: U Calif Dept Molecular & Cell Biology 439 LSA Berkeley CA 94720

KOSIER, CHRISTINE MARIE, company executive; b. Jacksonville, Fla., Dec. 27, 1956; d. Anthony Francis and Nancy Joann (Vann) Romano; m. Mark Edward Kosier, June 7, 1980 (div. Mar. 1987). BA in Psychology, U. Fla., Gainesville, 1978. Cert. profl. human resources. Clerical and field rep. Equifax Svcs., Jacksonville, Gainesville, Fla., 1969-79; adminstrv. mgr. Carnett div. JM Family Enterprises, Jacksonville, 1979-86; mgr. human resources JM Family Enteprises, Jacksonville, 1986-89; mgr. human resourcesJoyserv Co. Ltd. div. JM Family Enterprises, Jacksonville, 1989—. Mem. Am. Soc. Personnel Adminstrs., Am. Soc. Tng. and Devel., Am. Mgmt. Assn., Human Resource Systems Profls. (chmn. S.E. region 1987), Jacksonville Compensation Assn. Home: 7675 Las Palmas Way Jacksonville FL 32256 Office: Joyserv Co Ltd 1751 Tallyrand Ave Jacksonville FL 32206

KOSINSKY, BARBARA TIMM, librarian; b. St. Louis, July 4, 1942; d. Paul E. and Virginia L. (Borcherding) T.; m. John P. Kosinsky, July 25, 1964; children: James Alan, Bethany Anne. BS in Edn., Concordia Coll., River Forest, Ill., 1964; BA in Computer Sci., North Cen. Coll., Naperville, Ill., 1986; MLS, SUNY, Buffalo, 1972. Cert. tchr., Ill., N.Y. Tchr. St. Paul Luth. Sch., North Tonawanda, N.Y., 1964-67; libr. Trinity Luth. Sch., West Seneca, N.Y., 1971-80, North Cen. Coll., Naperville, 1981-89; regional mktg. rep. Online Computer Libr. Ctr., Dublin, Ohio, 1990—; free-lance writer West Seneca and Naperville, 1978—. Contbr. articles to religious mags. and general interest publs. Mem. ALA, Am. Soc. Info. Sci., Nat. Writers Club., Ill. Libr. Assn. Home: 2721 Rolling Meadows Dr Naperville IL 60564 Office: 1807 S Washington St Ste 380 Naperville IL 60565

KOSKI-PONTON, ELLEN IRENE, sales executive, management consultant; b. Louisville, June 10, 1947; d. Edward Zacharias and Doris Jean (Speer) Koski; m. George Evan Ponton, Oct. 12, 1985; children by previous marriage—Monica Linette Arnold, Matthew David Arnold, Marcus Aaron Arnold; stepchildren—Yvonne Larae Ponton, Colleen Ruth Ponton. AS in Bus. Adminstrn., Tidewater Community Coll., 1983; BA in Interdisciplinary Studies, U. S.C., Lancaster, 1985, EdM, 1988. Adminstrv. asst. Northwestern Mut. Life, Norfolk, Va., 1981-83, asst. dir. mktg., Charlotte, N.C., 1983-84; ind. distbr. Herbalife, Monroe, N.C., 1983—; eligibility specialist Union County Dept. Social Services, 1985-86; mgmt. cons. Dorey Electric, Norfolk, Va., Advanced Marine Enterprises, Virginia Beach, Va., 1982-83; bus. mgr. EOR Monroe Urgent Care and Marshville Med. Ctr., 1986-87; adminstr., South Point Family Practice, P.A., 1987—, state, local, nat. Med. Group Mgrs. Assn., 1988—. Foster parent Ohio Youth Commn., Del, 1976-79, Cath. Family Services, Virginia Beach, 1980-81; pres. Tidewater Assn. Talented and Gifted, Virginia Beach, 1982; vol. Rape Crisis Companion, Monroe, N.C., 1985—. Club: Amateur Trapshooting Assn. (Vandalia, Ohio). Avocations: trapshooting; reading; swimming. Home: 4610 Nesbit Rd Monroe NC 28110

KOSMES, KARA MARIE, accountant; b. Haverhill, Mass., Dec. 29, 1958; d. Theophilos and Mary Josephine (Azzarito) K. BSBA summa cum laude, Merrimack Coll., 1980. Acctg. supr. Haverhill Mcpl. Hosp., 1980-81; acct. John A. Rosatone, P.A., Haverhill, 1981-84; office mgr. Stephanotis Flower Shop, Haverhill, 1986—; sr. acct. William J.F. Murphy, CPA, Haverhill, 1984—; cons. in field. Mem. Winnekenni Found. Lodge: Soroptimist (treas. 1986—) (Haverhill). Home: 35 Westland Ter Haverhill MA 01830 Office: William JF Murphy CPA 396 Main St Haverhill MA 01830

KOSS, ROSABEL STEINHAUER, educator retired; b. Phila., Sept. 3, 1913; d. Arthur H. and Agnes (Temple) Steinhauer; m. Franklyn C. Koss, July 6, 1947 (dec. 1987); children: C. Lynn Knauff, Susan Kreiner, Carolyn Ruef, Rosalind Diehl. BS, Trenton State Coll., 1935; MA, Teachers Coll., N.Y.C., 1942; DEd, Columbia U., 1964. Cert. health edn. specialist, N.J. Supr. health and phys. edn. Flemington (N.J.) Pub. Schs., 1935-37; tchr. health and phys. edn. Ridgewood (N.J.) High Sch., 1937-40, Passaic Valley Regional High Sch., Little Falls, N.J., 1940-48; asst. prof. Montclair State Coll., Upper Montclair, N.J., 1958-61, Upsala Coll., East Ornge, N.J., 1964-71; assoc. to full prof. Ramapo Coll of N.J., Mahwah, N.J., 1971-84; dir. tchr. edn. Ramapo Coll of N.J., Mahwah, 1974-79, prof. emeritus, 1985; adj. prof. Stockton State Coll., Pomona, N.J., 1985—; asst. sport attachee Royal Swedish Embassy, N.Y.C., 1964-74. Author: (with others) Dance for Older Adults, 1988, Mature Stuff. Physical Activity for Older Adults, 1989; contbr. articles profl. jours. Mem. Bd. Edn. Little Falls, N.J., 1954-63; bd. trustees, treas. Bergen County, N.J. Retired Sr. Vol. Program, 1979-84; trustee Realty Owners Assn., Stone Harbor, N.J., 1985-88; commmr. Cape May County Freeholders Adv. Commn. on Women, 1986—; mem. Human Svcs. Adv. Coun., Cape May County, 1989—; vestry St. Mary's Episcopal Ch., Stone Harbor, N.J. Recipient Work Study Grants to Sweden, The Royal Swedish Consulate, N.Y.C., 1968, 70, 72, Athletic Alumni Women's award, Trenton State Coll., 1976; named to Trenton State Coll. Alumni Athletic Hall of Fame, 1987; Rosabel Koss annual award in her honor Am. Alliance Health, Physical Edn., Recreation and Dance. Mem. AAUW, LWV, Am. Alliance Health, Physical Edn., Recreation, Dance (life mem., profl. achievment award, N.J. 1973, honor award fellow, 1979, merit award Eastern Dist., 1980, coun. on aging and adult devel.), Gerontol. Soc. N.J. (parlimentarian 1988-89), Nat. Coun. on the Aging, Internat. Soc. of Comparative Physical Edn. and Sport, Garden Club (docent for Wetlands Inst.). Home: 150 91st St Stone Harbor NJ 08247

KOSSANYI, MARIA, broadcasting company executive; b. Budapest, Hungary, Feb. 19, 1926; came to U.S., 1951; d. Oszkar and Stephanie (Hovany) Monostory; m. Anthony Krasznai, Sept. 20, 1944 (div. 1971); children: Maria-Athonia, Csilla, Patricia; m. Miklos Kossànyi, Jan. 9, 1973; 1 child, Attila. Diploma, U. Budapest. Mgr. Slenderella Internat., Cleve., 1954-58; hungarian program dir. Sta. WZAK, Cleve., 1963-77; gen. mgr. Nationality Broadcasting Network, Cleve., 1977—; cons. Deutsche Welle, Köln, Fed. Republic Germany, 1977—, RAI Italian Broadcasting, 1979—, Swiss Radio Internat., Bern, Switzerland, 1982—, Hungarian Radio-TV, 1963. Exec. producer (video) Slovenia, 1964, Hello Cleveland, 1988, Hungary, 1984, Budapest, 1989. Bd. dirs. Heritage Club, Washington, 1967, All Nation Found., Cleve., 1984; hon. co-chmn. Ohio Celebrates Liberty, Columbus, 1986. Recipient Gov.'s award, 1973, U.S. Congress award, 1982, U.S. Marin award, 1986, various internat. awards. Home: 30006 Lake Rd Bay Village OH 44140 Office: Nationality Broadcasting 11906 Madison Ave Cleveland OH 44107

KOSTER, NOREEN CATHERINE, speech therapist; b. Port Jefferson, N.Y., Oct. 31, 1953; d. Charles Michael and Marjorie Johanna (Saccente) Bubnis; m. Robert John Koster, Mar. 22, 1975; children: Jessica Dawn, Kyle Robert. BS, Worcester State Coll., 1975; MS, Adelphi Coll., 1983. Tchr. Cleary Sch. for Deaf, Ronkonkoma, N.Y., 1976-77; freelance tchr. Dance and Movement, Bohemia, N.Y., 1976-79; tchr. hearing and speech impaired Bd. Coop. Ednl. Svcs. -2, Patchogue, N.Y., 1979-80; speech/lang. therapist presch. handicapped program Bd. Coop. Ednl. Svcs. -2, ISLIP, N.Y., 1980-82, speech/lang. therapist, program facilitator, infant program, 1981-82; speech/lang. therapist pres. handicapped program Bd. Coop. Ednl. Svcs. -2, Terryville, N.Y., 1982-84, speech/lang. therapist dist. based presch. handicapped, 1984-85; speech/lang. therapist dist. based elem., jr. and sr. high sch. program Bd. Coop. Ednl. Svcs. -2, Patchogue, N.Y., 1984—; lectr. Am. Soc. Psychoprophylaxis in Obstretrics 1977-79, Mothers ofTwins Club, Suffolk County, N.Y., 1978, Bd. Coop. Ednl. Svcs. 2, Lang. Workshops for Parents, 1980-85. Vol. Cleary Sch. for Deaf, Ronkonkoma, N.Y., 1974-76; La Leche League, Bohemia libr. 1975, Islip, N.Y. (publicity chmn. 1978, publ. chmn. 1978-80, 1988-90, ways and means chmn.1980-83, co-treas. 1989-90); catechist Roman Cath. Ch. Mem. AAUW (topic chmn. 1977-78, events chmn. 1977-79, child study chmn. 1978-80, 1988-89, pub. rels. chmn. 1979-80), Bd. Coop. Ednl. Svcs. 2 (union rep. 1984-86, racquetball corp. head 1982—). Roman Catholic. Home: 37 Arthur Ave Blue Point NY 11715

KOSTICH, SHIRLEY ANN, health services administrator; b. Milw., June 3, 1944; d. Ferdinand and Vetial (Burbey) Homan; m. Nikola Peter Kostich, May 28, 1969; children: Natasha and Aleksandar. BS, U. Wis., 1967. Case worker social svcs. Unicare, Milw., 1967-69; cons. residential care Unicare, Madison, Wis., 1969-70; with after care team Med. Coll. Wis./Milw. County, 1979-80; administrv. coord. med. svcs. Milw. County Mental Health Complex, 1981—; coordinator Am. Bd. Psychiat. and Neurology Oral Exams, Milw. 1986; cons. seminar Alliance Mentally Ill, Milw. 1985-86. Editor: Newsletter Mental Health Complex, 1986-87. Chmn. Shorewood (Wis.) High Sch. Post Prom Com. 1986; pres. adv. coun. sexual assault treatment ctr. Good Samaritan Med. Ctr. 1987—; coord. Milw. County Mental Health Complex campaign United Way, 1986-89, Silver award, Chmn.'s award. Mem. Editor's Forum (Nat. Competition award), Nat. Assn. Med. Staff Svcs., NAFE. Serbian Orthodox. Home: 3715 N Lake Dr Shorewood WI 53211 Office: Milw County Mental Health Complex 9455 Watertown Plank Rd Milwaukee WI 53226

KOSTIELNEY, JANET LEAH, public relations executive; b. LaPorte, Ind., Apr. 18, 1951; d. Walter Raymond and Betty Jane (Salyer) Wood; m. Alan Arthur Unger, Apr. 24, 1971 (div. 1983); children: Jennifer, Todd, Aaron; m. James Gerald Kostielney, May 10, 1985; stepchildren: Richard, Christina, Tricia. Student, Ball State U., 1969-70; RN, Purdue North Cen. U., Westville, Ind., 1971, degree in mktg., 1990. Sec., office mgr. Haldeman Farm Mgmt. Co., LaPorte, 1967-69; med.-surg., ob-gyn. nurse St. Anthony Hosp., Michigan City, Ind., 1969-72; craft and sewing instr. Tex., N.C., 1972-79; typesetter, graphic artist Merchants Nat. Bank, Indpls., 1979-81; costumer, designer Dunes Theatre, Michigan City, 1981-83; indsl. oil sales rep. Schmock Oil Corp., Michigan City, 1983-84, Berreth Oil Co., Mishawaka, Ind., 1984-85; consumer and pub. rels. rep. Weil-McLain, Michigan City, 1985—; prin. Kostielney Kommunications, Michigan City, 1990—. Columnist: Purdue Rapport, 1989—; editor polit. action newsletter, Michigan City, 1989—; contbr. articles to popular newspapers. Assoc., bldg. dir. Habitat for Humanity, Michigan City, 1987—; co-creator Cath. Youth Group, Michigan City, 1990; pres. PTA, Michigan City, 1984-86. Mem. NAFE, Am. Mgmt. Assn. Republican. Roman Catholic. Home: 226 Loran Rd Michigan City IN 46360 Office: Weil-McLain Blaine St Michigan City IN 46360

KOSTREVA, ADRIENNE LEE GAAL, retail executive, consultant, director; b. Dearborn, Mich., Nov. 7, 1945; d. Michael Andrew and Beatrice Bennett (Herrman) Gaal; m. Daniel J. Kostreva (div.); m. Franklyn Lumsden, 1989. MBA with honors, Roosevelt U., 1980. From asst. buyer to buyer Filene's Basement, Boston, 1967-71; store mgr. Design Research, Boston, 1972-73; store supr. Bargains Unltd., Boston, 1974; dist. mgr. Commonwealth Trading, Inc., Boston, 1975-77; regional mgr. Marshall's Inc., Boston, 1977-78; staff cons. Deloitte Haskins & Sells, Chgo., 1980; dir. mdse. planning The Doody Co., Columbus, Ohio, 1981; pvt. practice cons. Columbus, 1982-83; v.p., dir. stores Charles A. Stevens, Chgo., 1983-85; pres. Adrienne Kostreva/The Retail Leadership Source, Chgo., 1985—; instr. Franklin U., Columbus, 1982-83, Capital U., Columbus, 1982-83, Roosevelt U., Chgo., 1984—; project dir. Chgo. City Wide Coll., Chgo., 1986-87, mem. retail adv. bd., 1987—. Mem. Friends of Chgo. City Ballet, 1983-86; cons. Bd. Devel. Network, Columbus, 1982-83; participant tutoring program 4th Presbyn. Ch., Chgo., 1983-89. Mem. Nat. Retail Fedn., Ill. Retail Mchts. Assn., Chgo. Retail Execs. Assn., Fashion Group, Inc. (treas. Boston chpt. 1971-73), Women's Exec. Network Chgo., Black Retail Action Group, Roosevelt U. Alumni Assn. (bd. dirs., chmn. program com. bd. govs. 1984-88). Office: 230 N Michigan Ave Chicago IL 60601

KOTCHER, SHIRLEY J. W., lawyer; b. Bklyn.; d. Irving and Violet (Miller) Weinberg; m. Harry A. Kotcher; children: Leslie Susan, Dana Anne. BA, NYU; JD, Columbia U. Bar: N.Y. In-house counsel Booth Meml. Med. Ctr., Flushing, N.Y., 1975-83, gen. counsel, 1983—; advisor health care Borough Pres. Queens, N.Y., 1978. Author: Hidden Gold and Pitfalls in New Tax Law, 1970. Mem. ABA (health law forum com.), Nat. Health Lawyers Assn., Am. Acad. Hosp. Attys., Nassau County Bar Assn., Am. Soc. Law and Medicine, Am. Soc. Health Care Risk Mgmt., Assn. for Hosp. Risk Mgmt. N.Y., Greater N.Y. Hosp. Assn. (legal adv. com. 1976—), N.Y. Bus. Group on Health, Self-Ins. Roundtable. Office: Booth Meml Med Ctr Main St Flushing NY 11355

KOTHERA, LYNNE M., clinical psychologist; b. Cleve., Dec. 18, 1938; d. Leonard Frank and Lillian (Shackleton) Kothera; m. Richard Litwin, Oct. 24, 1965. BA with hons., Denison U., Granville, Ohio, 1960; MA, NYU, 1983; PhD, L.I. U., Bklyn., 1989. Dancer Martha Graham Dance Co., N.Y.C., 1961-62, Carmen DeLavallade Dance Co., N.Y.C., 1965-68, Glen Tetley Dance Co., N.Y.C., 1965-69; prin. dancer John Butler's, N.Y.C., 1971; artist-in-residence Boston High Schs. - Title III, 1969-71, Hobart-Smith Coll./Denison U., 1973; auditor N.Y. State Council of the Arts, N.Y.C., 1974-78; predoctoral fellow clin. psychology Yale-New Haven Hosp., 1987-88; postdoctoral fellow neuropsychology Inst. of Living, Hartford, Conn., 1989—. Mem. Am. Psychol. Assn. Democrat. Home: 23 E 11th St New York NY 10003 Office: The Institute of Living Dept Psychology 400 Washingotn St Hartford CT 06106

KOTLER, LOUISE LICHTMAN, volunteer, educator; b. N.Y.C., Apr. 13, 1921; d. Louis and Florence (DeWaltoff) Lichtman; m. Arnold C. Kotler, Sept. 8; children: John David, Nancy. BA, Mount Holyoke, 1941; MFA, Yale U., 1943. Counsellor Tampa (Fla.) Museum Art, 1988—; adj. prof. U. of So. Fla., 1976-83. Bd. trustees Tampa Museum of Art, 1950-90; mem. Art in Pub. Places, Hillsborough County, 1989—; Fla. State Arts Coun., 1983-87. Recipient Mount Holyoke Coll. Genevieve Townsand award, 1941, First Dean's award for Outstanding Svc. to the Arts U. So. Fla., 1985, Award for the Arts Cultural Com. C. of C. 1986. Mem. Yale Club, Yale Drama Sch. Assoc., Mount Holyoke Club, Friends of Art Mount Holyoke. Home: 64 Bahama Circle Tampa FL 33606

KOTOWSKI, CHRISTINE ANNE, nurse; b. Buffalo, Feb. 8, 1947; d. Leonard Michael and Irene (Jedrzejewski) Zmozynski; m. David M. Kotowski, Oct. 26, 1968; children—Jeffrey, Jennifer, Kenneth, Gregory. B.S. in Nursing cum laude, Daemen Coll., N.Y., 1983. RN, N.Y. Nurse's asst. St. Joseph Inter-Community Hosp., Cheektowaga, N.Y., 1978-80; camp nurse Jewish Ctr., Greater Buffalo, Amherst, 1981; charge nurse Williamsville Suburban Nursing Home, N.Y., 1981, day supr., 1982, asst. dir. nursing, 1982-84; nurse cons. Brown and Kelly Law Offices, Buffalo, 1984—; cons. and lectr. in field. Pre-Cana sponsor Our Lady of Blessed Sacrament Ch., Depew, N.Y., 1985-88; supporter Bowmansville Vol. Fire Dept; sec. alumni bd. dirs. Daemen Coll. Nursing, 1988—. Mem. NAFE, Profl. Nurses Assn. Western N.Y., Western N.Y. Paralegal Assn., Delta Epsilon Sigma. Republican. Roman Catholic. Avocations: choir, church projects, tennis, reading. Office: Brown and Kelly 1500 Liberty Bldg Buffalo NY 14202

KOTTLER, SYLVIA BRAVMAN, retired special education educator; b. Wilkes-Barre, Pa., July 11, 1922; d. Philip and Bertha (Friedman) Bravman; m. Barnet Kottler, Mar. 24, 1944; children: Malcolm Jay, Ann Kottler Schindler. BA, U. Md., 1944; MS, Purdue U., 1963; Montessori diploma, St. Nicholas Coll., London, 1971. Cert. speech pathologist, ednl. psychologist. Speech pathologist Wabash Ctr. for Retarded, West Lafayette, Ind., 1963-64; ednl. therapist Achievement Ctr., Purdue U., West Lafayette, 1963-73, prof. spl. edn., 1973-87, prof. emeritus, 1987—; founder, dir. Achievement Ctr. for Children with Spl. Needs, Greenwich, Conn., 1988—; cons. Del. Dept. Pub. Instrn., 1971-80, Gatehouse Sch. Learning Ctr., London, 1973-88, Hyper-Active Children's Support Group, Bognor Regis, Eng., 1980—; cons. div. spl. edn. Ind. Dept. Pub. Instrn., Indpls., 1975-85; lectr. nat. and internat. meetings. Co-author: Developmental Guide to Early Childhood Training, 1976; author: (videotapes and manual) Mainstreaming the Exceptional Learner, 1986, Mainstreaming Exceptional Preschoolers, 1980; contbr. articles to profl. jours. Bd. dirs. United Cerebral Palsy Assn., Tippecanoe County, Ind., 1963-72, Assn. Retarded Citizens, Lafayette, Ind., 1970-87. Recipient Miriam Bender award U. Indpls., 1983. Mem. Assn. for Children with Learning Disabilities, Coun. for Exceptional Children, Nat. Assn. for Edn. Young Children, U.S.A. Toy Libr. Assn. (a founder, bd. dirs. 1981-85), Orton Dyslexia Soc., AAUP. Democrat. Jewish. Office: Achievement Ctr 200 Railroad Ave Greenwich CT 06830

KOTUK, ANDREA MIKOTAJUK, public relations executive, writer; b. New Brunswick, N.J., Oct. 19, 1948; d. Michael and Julia Dorothy (Muka) Mikotajuk. BA, Douglass Coll., Rutgers U., 1970. Pub. relations asst. Wall St. Jour. Newspaper Fund, Princeton, N.J., 1970; editorial asst. Redbook mag., N.Y.C., 1970-71; asst. pub. relations dir. Children's Aid Soc., N.Y.C., 1971-75; assoc. pub. relations dir. Planned Parenthood, N.Y.C., 1975-80; pres. Andrea & Assocs., N.Y.C., 1980—. Writer publicist ads for newsmags., healthcare corps., for non-profit agys.; contbg. editor Arts Mag., 1970-75. Mem. NAFE, Healthcare Businesswomen's Assn., Am. Med. Writers Assn. Office: Andrea & Assocs 36 E 23rd St New York NY 10010

KOTULA, JEANNE, psychologist; b. Orange, N.J., May 18, 1957; d. Edward George and Rita Margaret (Baker) K. BA, Boston U., 1980; MS, Fla. Inst. Tech., 1984, D of Psychology, 1986. Lic. psychologist, Fla. Dir. outreach Women in Distress, Ft. Lauderdale, Fla., 1987-88; psychologist Care Unit, Coral Springs, Fla., 1987-88; dir. pscyhol. svcs. Residential Treatment Ctr., Lake Worth, Fla., 1988-89; pvt. practice Ft. Lauderdale, 1986-89, Stuart, Fla., 1989—. Mem. Am. Psychol. Assn., Fla. Psychol. Assn., Psi Chi. Democrat. Home: 6056 Riverboat Dr Stuart FL 34997 Office: 815 E Osceola St Stuart FL 34995

KOUPAL, JOYCE ANN, marketing executive, consultant; b. Sacramento, Mar. 7, 1932; d. Cecil Wallace and Elizabeth Louise (DeRee) Nash; m. Edwin Augustus Koupal (dec. Mar. 1976); children: Cecil Edwin, Christine Ann, Diane Marie. Exec. dir. People's Lobby, Inc., Los Angeles, 1976—, The Printing Press, Los Angeles, 1977-81; ind. polit. cons. San Rafael, Calif., 1980-82; gen. mgr. Assn. for Advanced Tng. in Behavioral Scis., Los Angeles, 1982-83; owner Koupal Enterprises, Sacramento, 1987—. Author: (with Faith Keating) Success Is Failure Analyzed, 1976. Mem., bd. dirs. Women's Clinic, 1975-87; mem. Los Angeles County Energy Commn., 1975-76. Recipient Sylvia Leventhal Ann. award Assn. for Study of Community Orgns., 1974. Mem. Women's Network. Home and Office: 64 Margarita Terr Novato CA 94947

KOURY, JOANNE MARIE, exercise physiologist; b. Allentown, Pa., Aug. 21, 1957; d. Charles Abraham and Jammely (Hadeed) K.; m. Glenn Guanowsky, May 7, 1989. BA magna cum laude, Cedar Crest Coll., 1979; postgrad., East Stroudsburg U., 1982—. Asst. buyer Wanamaker's Dept. Store, Phila., 1979-80; freelance Rodale Press, Emmaus, Pa., 1980-81; showroom designer Furniture Unltd., Quakertown, Pa., 1981-83; fitness dir. Lehigh Valley Racquet and Fitness Ctrs., Allentown, 1983-89; cons. Health East Inc., Allentown, 1989—. Mem. Am. Coll. Sports Medicine, Internat. Dance Edn. Assn., Am. Alliance for Physical Edn., Recreation and Dance, Pa. Alliance for Physical Edn., Recreation and Dance, Nat. Coun. for Cooperation in Aquatics. Eastern Orthodox.

KOVACH, BARBARA ELLEN, management and psychology educator; b. Ann Arbor, Mich., Dec. 28, 1941; d. Harry Arnold and Margaret Mayne (Buell) Lusk; m. Craig Randall Duncan, Dec. 28, 1963 (div. 1973); children: Deborah Louise, Mark Randall; m. Randall Louis Kovach, May 2, 1981; 1 child, Jennifer Elizabeth. BA magna cum laude, Stanford U., 1963, MA, 1964; PhD, U. Md., 1973. Asst. prof. psychology U. Mich., Dearborn, 1973-77, assoc. prof., 1977-82, prof., 1982-84, chair Dept. Behavioral Scis., 1980-83; dean Univ. Coll. Rutgers U., New Brunswick, N.J., 1984-88, prof. mgmt. and psychology, 1984—, dir. leadership devel. com., 1988—; pres. Leadership Devel. Inst., Princeton, N.J., 1990—; cons. Rochester (N.Y.) Products-Gen. Motors, Grand Rapids, Mich., 1982-87, Ford Motor Co., Dearborn, 1981-82, Mich. Bell Telephone, 1980-81. Author: Sex Roles and Personal Awareness, 1978, 1990, Power and Love, 1982, Organizational Synch, 1983, Adolescent Experience, 1983, The Flexible Organization, 1984, Survival on the Fast Track, 1988, Organization Gameboard, 1989; contbr. articles to profl. jours. Daniel E. Prescott fellow U. Md., 1972; recipient Susan B. Anthony and Faculty Recognition awards U. Mich., 1980. Mem. Am. Psychol. Assn., Acad. Mgmt., Organizational Devel. Network, Phi Beta Kappa. Republican. Episcopalian. Home: 95 Cuyler Rd Princeton NJ 08540 Office: Rutgers U Sch of Bus New Brunswick NJ 08903

KOVACH, MARY JO, marketing professional; b. Chgo. Hgts., Feb. 16, 1959; d. Joseph John and Shirley Ann (Odey); m. Gerald Desmond Bolton, Sept. 11, 1988. BA, Eastern Ill. U., Charleston, 1981. Sales rep. R.D. Irwin, Inc., Homewood, Ill., 1981-83; sales coordinator U.S. Lines, Inc., Oak Brook, Ill., 1983-84; mktg. mgr. Scott, Foresman & Co., Glenview, Ill., 1984-89; sr. sales specialist MacMillan Pub. Co., N.Y.C., 1989—; speaker Chgo. Women in Pub., Chgo., 1986. Chmn. Heart Assn. Blood Drive, Flossmoor, 1977. Recipient Rich Township Outstanding Service, Ill., 1977. Mem. N.O.W., Alpha Phi Fraternity for Women.

KOVACHEVICH, ELIZABETH ANNE, federal judge; b. Canton, Ill., Dec. 14, 1936; d. Dan and Emilie (Kuchan) Kovachevich. BBA in Fin. magna cum laude, U. Miami; JD, Stetson U. Bar: Fla. 1961, U.S. Dist. Ct. (mid. and so. dists.) Fla. 1961, U.S. Ct. Appeals (5th cir.) 1961, U.S. Supreme Ct. 1968. Research and adminstrv. aide Pinellas County Legis. Del., Fla., 1961; assoc. DiVito & Speer, St. Petersburg, Fla., 1961-62; house counsel Rieck & Fleece Guilders Supplies, Inc., St. Petersburg, 1962—; pvt. practice law St. Petersburg, 1962-73; judge 6th Jud. Cir., Pinellas and Pasco Counties, Fla., 1973-82, U.S. Dist. Ct. (mid. dist.) Fla., St. Petersburg, 1982—; chmn. St. Petersburg Profl. Legal Project-Days in Court, 1967. Bd. regents State of Fla., 1970-72; legal advisor, bd. dirs. Young Women's Residence Inc., 1968; mem. Fla. Gov.'s Commn. on Status of Women, 1968-71; mem. Pres.'s Commn. on White House Fellowships, 1973-77; mem. def. adv. com. on Women in Service, Dept. Def., 1973-76; Fla. conf. publicity chmn. 18th Nat. Republican Women's Conf., Atlanta, 1971; lifetime mem. Children's Hosp. Guild, YWCA of St. Petersburg; charter mem. Golden Notes, St. Petersburg Symphony; hon. mem. bd. of overseers Stetson U. Coll. of Law, 1986. Recipient Disting. Alumni award Stetson U., 1970, Woman of Yr. award Fla. Fedn. Bus. and Profl. Women, 1981, ann. Ben C. Willard Meml. award, Stetson Lawyers Assn., 1983, numerous others. Mem. ABA, Fla. Bar Assn., Pinellas County Trial Lawyers, Assn. Trial Lawyers Am., Am. Judicature Soc., St. Petersburg Bar Assn. (chmn. bench and bar com., sec. 1969). Office: US Dist Ct 611 N Florida Ave Rm 310 Tampa FL 33602

KOVELESKI, KATHRYN DELANE, retired educator; b. Detroit, Aug. 12, 1925; d. Edward Albert Vogt and Delane (Bender) Vogt; BA, Olivet (Mich.) Coll., 1947; MA, Wayne State U., Detroit, 1955; m. Casper Koveleski, July 18, 1952; children: Martha, Ann. Tchr. schs. in Mich., 1947-88; tchr. Garden City Schs., 1955-56, 59-88, resource and learning disabilities tchr., 1970-88, ret. 1988. Chmn. bd. christian edn. Congl. Ch. Mem. Bus. and Profl. Women (pres. Garden City 1982-83, Woman of Yr. 1983-84), Mich. Assn. Retired Sch. Personnal, Wayne Lit. Club (past pres., treas. 1988-89), Sch. Masters Bowling League (v.p. 1984-88), Odd Couples Bowling League (pres. 82-83).

KOVITZ, NANCY R., sales promotion agency executive; b. Chgo.; d. Samuel Harold Freed and Julia (Silverman) Stone; m. Alan David Kovitz, Apr. 16, 1961; children: Samuel Howard, Kathryn Ann. BA, U. Chgo., 1960; MLS, Rosary Coll., 1983. Rsch. asst. Newberry Libr., Chgo., 1979-82; info. specialist Peat Marwick Main, Chgo., 1982-84; mgr. info. ctr. Frankel and Co., Chgo., 1984—; lectr. Columbia Coll., Chgo. Contbr. articles to profl. jours.; editor abstracting newsletter. Bd. mem. Internat. Comm. for Women Mus., Chgo., 1983-85. Mem. Spl. Libr. Assns., Am. Libr. Assn.,

AMA, Chgo. Calligraphy Collective. Office: Frankel & Co 111 E Wacker Dr Chicago IL 60601

KOWALCZEWSKI, DOREEN MARY THURLOW, communications company executive; b. London, May 5, 1926; came to U.S., 1957, naturalized, 1974; d. George Henry and Jessie Alice (Gray) Thurlow; BA, Clarke Coll., 1947; postgrad. Wayne State U., 1959-62, Roosevelt U., 1968; m. Witold Dionizy Kowalczewski, July 26, 1946; children: Christina Julianna, Janet Alice, Stephen Robin. Agy. supr. MONY, N.Y.C., 1963-67; office mgr. J.B. Carroll Co., Chgo., 1967-68; mng. editor Sawyer Coll. Bus., Evanston, Ill., 1968-71; mgr. policyholder svc. CNA, Chgo., 1971-73; EDP coord. Canteen Corp., Chgo., 1973-75; mgr. documentation and standards LRSP, Chgo., 1975-77; data network mgr. Computerized Agy. Mgmt. Info. Svcs., Chgo., 1977-86; founder, chmn. Tekman Assocs., 1982—; chpt. sec. Soc. Tech. Communications, 1988—. Pres., Univ. Park Assn., 1980-84. Mem. NAFE, Women in Info. Processing, Chgo. Women in Mgmt., Soc. Tech. Communications, Mensa. Home: 8923 Southview Brookfield IL 60513

KOWALCZYK, DEBORAH A., marketing executive; b. Southington, Conn., July 3, 1951; d. Francis Joseph and Mary G. (Casale) Santy; m. Wayne Henry Kowalczyk, Sept. 13, 1974; children: Lynn, Jill. BA, Elmira (N.Y.) Coll., 1973; MBA, U. Hartford, 1982. Mgr. underwriting adminstrn. CIGNA Corp., Hartford, Conn., 1973-78, strategic planner, 1978-82, product mgr., 1982-85, asst. v.p., 1985-87, v.p., 1987-90; ptnr. Communications PLUS, Windsor Locks, Conn., 1990—; cons. Cambridge (Mass.) Technology Group, 1987—, Challenger Ctr., Alexandria, Va., 1990. Mem. NAFE, Assn. Investment Mktg. and Sales Execs., Nat. Coun. Real Estate Investment Fiduciaries. Home: 37 Strawberry Hill Windsor CT 06095

KOWALCZYK, JEANNE STUART, biology educator; b. Atlanta, Dec. 22, 1942; d. A. Sidney and Martha Ross (Hart) Jones; m. Alex W. Stuart, Sept. 9, 1961 (dec. 1981); m. Bruno Kowalczyk, Jan. 15, 1983. BS, Jacksonville State U., 1966, MS, 1968; PhD, Auburn U., 1972. Head biology dept. Belmont (N.C.) Abbey Coll., 1972-78; prof. biology U. S.C., Spartauburg, S.C., 1978—. Contbr. articles to profl. jours. NSF fellow, 1968-72. Mem. Appalachian Region Electron Microscopist Soc., South East Parasitologist Soc., Sigma Xi, Gamma Sigma Delta, Gamma Beta Phi. Democrat. Roman Catholic. Home: Paradox Farm Gaffney SC 29340

KOWALCZYK, MARYANN MERCEDES, professional association administrator; b. Hazleton, Pa., May 25, 1947; d. Frank Bernard and Mary Josephine (Voytko) K. Student, U. Pa., U. D.C. Staff specialist Nat. Commn. on Rsch., Washington, 1982-83, NAS, Washington, 1983-85; exec. asst. Computer Soc. of IEEE, Washington, 1987-89; corp. dir. IEEE, Inc., N.Y.C., 1989—. Recipient several Svc. awards. Mem. IEEE, NAFE, Nat. Commn. on Rsch., Coun. Engring. Sci. Soc. Execs. Office: IEEE Inc 345 E 47th St New York NY 10017

KOWALSKI, JANE MAE, government contract specialist; b. Lebanon, Oreg., June 18, 1951; d. Stephan Peter and Ardine Inez (Donaldson) K.; m. Romaine F. Douglas (div. 1974); 1 child, Shelly Lee Kowalski. AS in Bus. and Mgmt., Clark County Community Coll., 1989, postgrad., 1989—. Clerk, stenographer Nat. Park Svc., Mammoth, Wyo., 1971-74; clk.-stenographer Bur. Land Mgmt., Dillon, Mont., 1974-75; records mgmt. specialist Bur. Land Mgmt., Dillion, Mont., 1975-76; sec. Bur. Land Mgmt., Las Vegas, Nev., 1976-78, resource clk., 1978-79; mail and file clk. western area power adminstrn. Dept. Energy, Boulder City, Nev., 1979-85, support svc. specialist, 1985-86, purchasing agt., 1986-89, contract specialist, 1989-90; contract specialist Dept. Energy, Phoenix, 1990—. Mem. Purchasing Mgmt. Assn. Southern Nev., Geneal. Soc. Methodist. Home: 1713 E Broadway Rd Tempe AZ 85282 Office: Dept Energy Western Area Power Adminstrn PO Box 200 Boulder City NV 89005

KOZA, JOAN LORRAINE, fabric manufacturing company executive; b. Berwyn, Ill., Apr. 28, 1941; d. Frank Louis and Lorraine Frances (Thomas) K.; BS in Communications, U. Ill., 1963. Office mgr. Dwan Med. Ctr., Summit, Ill., 1959-64; law office mgr. firm Gordon, Reicin & West, Chgo., 1964-73; sales mgr. Ambassador Hotels, Chgo., 1973-76; v.p. sales and mktg. MPC Industries, Inc. & subs., indsl. and recreational fabrics, Chgo., 1976—; owner, mgr. JK Advt., 1977—; pres. Chgo. Legal Secs. Assn., 1970-72; v.p. Ill. Assn. Legal Secs., 1970-73. Pres., chmn. bd. Children's Research Found., 1963-66. Contbg. author: New American Poetry Anthology (Golden Poet award 1988, 89). Named Chgo. Legal Sec. of Yr., 1972, Ill. Legal Sec. of Yr., 1972. Mem. Alpha Lambda Delta, Theta Sigma Pi. Roman Catholic. Home: 546 Banyon Ln LaGrange IL 60525 Office: 4834 S Oakley Pl Chicago IL 60609

KOZAK, MARILYN S., biochemist, educator; b. Akron, Ohio, July 8, 1943; d. John and Agatha (Monsour) K. BS, Marygrove Coll., 1965; MA, Johns Hopkins U., 1967, PhD, 1972. Asst. prof. cell biology Sch. Medicine NYU, N.Y.C., 1978-79; prof. biol. sci. U. Pitts., 1979-89; prof. biochemistry Robert W. Johnson Med. Sch. U. Medicine, Dentistry N.J., Piscataway, 1990—; mem. Molecular Biology Study sect. NIH, Bethesda, Md., 1989—. Office: U Medicine Dentistry NJ 675 Hoes Ln Piscataway NJ 08854

KOZAK, MARLENE GALANTE, engineering company executive; b. Oak Park, Ill., Mar. 31, 1952; d. Joseph Angelo and Josephine (Malatia) Galante; m. Lawrence Edward Kozak, Apr. 16, 1977. BA in Chemistry, BS in Biology, U. Ill., Chgo., 1974, MS in Molecular Genetics, 1976; cert. in mgmt., Am. Mgmt. Assn., Chgo., 1984. Research/teaching asst. U. Ill., Chgo., 1974-76; info. scientist G.D. Searle & Co., Skokie, Ill., 1977-78; info. analyst Arnar Stone Labs. div. Am. Hosp. Supply Corp., 1978-79, sr. info. analyst, 1979-81; mgr. info. services Am. Critical Care div. Baxter-Travenol, 1981-85; dir. info. resources and planning DuPont Pharms. subs. EI DuPont De Nemours, Wilmington, Del., 1986-87, dir. info. svcs. internat., 1987-90; chief adminstrv. officer Clean Air Engring., Palatine, Ill., 1990—; speaker in field. Contbr. articles to profl. jours. Mem. Soc. Info. Mgmt., Assn. Info. Mgrs. Office: Clean Air Engring 207 Woodwork Ln Palatine IL 60067

KOZAROVICH, DONNA LEE, bookkeeper; b. East Liverpool, Ohio, Oct. 15, 1961; d. Samuel L. and Norma J. (Rice) Black; m. Daniel C. Kozarovich, Jan. 5, 1990; 1 child, Daniel C. Jr. AS in Acctg. and Bus. Mgmt., Community Coll. Beaver County, Monaca, Pa., 1988. Billing clk. Silver Star Meats, Inc., McKees Rocks, Pa., 1987-88; acctg. clk. Massey Buick, Pitts., 1988; accounts payable-accounts receiving clk., billing clk. Samson Buick Co., Pitts., 1988-89, accounts receivable clk., 1989, billing clk., 1989; account clk. Mallet's Gateway Terminal, Inc., Pitts., 1989-90; billing clk. Girl Friday Agency, Steubenville Pike, Pa., 1990. Fellow NAFE. Home: 355 Rte 30 Lot 1 RD 2 Clinton PA 15026 Office: 355 Rte 30 Lot #1 RD#2 Clinton PA 15026

KOZBERG, DONNA WALTERS, rehabilitation administration executive; b. Milford, Del., Jan. 1, 1952; d. Robert Glyndwr and Gailey Ruth (Bedorf) Walters; m. Ronald Paul Kozberg, June 8, 1974. BA, U. Fla., 1973, M in Rehab. Counseling, 1974; MFA, CUNY, 1979; MBA, Rutgers U., 1986. Cert. rehab. counselor. Rehab. counselor Office Vocat. Rehab., N.Y.C., 1975-81; area dir. Lift, Inc., Staten Island, N.Y., 1981-83; ea. region dir. pub. relations, advt. Lift, Inc., Mountainside, N.J., 1983-85, v.p., 1985—, v.p., chief fin. officer, 1988; self-employed writer, editor, 1975—. Contbr. articles to profl. jours.; assoc. editor Parachute mag., 1978; editor-in-chief (newsletter) Counselor Adv, 1980. Pres. Com. on Employment of People with Disabilities; trustee Ctr. for Creative Living; bd. dirs. N.J. Adv. Coun. for Independent Living, adv. panel NYU. Mem. Nat. Rehab. Assn. (Spl. citation 1974, grantee 1973), Nat. Rehab. Adminstrs. Assn., Nat. Rehab. Counselors Assn., Poets and Writers, Nat. Assn. Female Execs. Home: 714 Woodland Ave Westfield NJ 07090 Office: Lift Inc PO Box 1072 Mountainside NJ 07092

KOZDEMBA, DOROTHY ANN, marketing professional; b. Newark, N.J., Jan. 13, 1949; d. Anthony L. and Margaret M. (Devecka) K. BS in Med. Tech., U. Bridgeport, 1971; postgrad., Fairleigh Dickinson U., 1979. Registered med. technologist. Staff med. tech. United Hosps. Med. Ctr., Newark, 1971-73, Clara Maass Hosp., Belleville, N.J., 1973-75; tech. svc. rep. Clay Adams, Div. Becton Dickinson, Franklin Lakes, N.J., 1975-76, sales rep., 1976-80, tng. mgr., 1980-81; asst. product mgr. Electro-Nucleonics, Inc., Fairfield, N.J., 1981-82, product mgr., 1982-85, mktg. mgr., 1985-86; mktg. product dir. Johnson & Johnson Profl. Diagnostics, Raritan, N.J., 1986-89; v.p. sales and mktg. Photest Diagnostics, Mahwah, N.J., 1989-90; acct. supr. M.E.D. Communications, Woodbridge, N.J., 1990—; com. mem. Nat. Com. Clin. Lab. Standards, Physician Office, Villanova, Pa., 1986-87; chmn. savs. bond drive, J&J Profl. Diagnostics, Raritan, 1989. Mem. NAFE, Am. Soc. Med. Tech., Biomed. Mktg. Assn., Am. Assn. Clin. Chemistry. Republican. Roman Catholic. Home: 75 Wick Dr Fords NJ 08863 Office: MED Communications 1460 Rte 9 N Woodbridge NJ 07095

KOZDEMBA, KATHLEEN MARY, communications executive; b. Elmira, N.Y., Jan. 24, 1954; d. Thomas Edward and Helen Bernadette (Janeski) K. BA in Journalism, St. Bonaventure U., Olean, N.Y., 1975; MBA, Syracuse U., 1984. Reporter Star-Gazette, Elmira, 1975-77, family news editor, 1977-80, Sunday editor, 1980-81, regional news editor, 1981-82, asst. mng. editor, 1982-83, mng. editor/news, 1983-85; mng. editor The Ithaca (N.Y.) Jour., 1985-87, The Springfield (Mo.) News-Leader, 1987-89; news exec. Gannett Co., Inc., Arlington, Va., 1989—. Mem. AP Mng. Editors (bd. dirs. 1988—), N.Y. AP Assn. (bd. dirs. 1986-87), N.Y. State Soc. Newspaper Editors (treas. 1986-87), Am. Soc. Newspaper Editors, Soc. Profl. Journalists, Women in Communications (com. chmn. 1988). Roman Catholic. Home: 4541 Pinecrest Heights Dr Annandale VA 22003 Office: Gannett Co Inc 1100 Wilson Blvd Arlington VA 22234

KOZELUH, ROBIN IRENE, retail sales executive; b. La Mesa, Calif., Apr. 12, 1962; d. Charles Hampton and Pansy Eleanora (Parkhill) Ratcliffe; m. Jack Elbert Nix, July 5, 1979 (div. Sept. 1983); m. Michael Randall Kozeluh, Oct. 28, 1983. Office mgr. Vern's Svc. Inc., San Diego, 1979-81; circulation mgr. Pubs. Devel. Corp., San Diego, 1981; sales and advt. mgr. Olan Mills Studio, Valdosta, Ga., 1984; vet. technician Goldsboro (N.C.) Vet. Hosp., 1986-87; computer entry specialist Mega Force Temporaries, Goldsboro, 1987; administrv. asst. Beverage Enterprises, Goldsboro, 1987; bus. mgr. Sta. KSUA-FM, Fairbanks, Alaska, 1988; asst. mgr. Far North Atari, Fairbanks, 1989—. Republican. Office: Far North Computers 59 College Rd #217 Fairbanks AK 99701

KOZIK, MARGARET MARY, management consultant; b. N.Y.C., Nov. 7, 1966; d. Andrew Fabian and Joanna Mary (Hartford) K.; m. Lance Richard Brooks, July 25, 1987. BS in Animal Sci. and Agrl. Bus. Mgmt., N.C. State U., 1988. Coord. spl. events Ivey's, Charlotte, N.C., 1983-84; make-up artist Germaine Monteil Cosmetics, Cary, N.C., 1986-87; model scout Baribizon Internat., Raleigh, N.C., 1988; pres., chief exec. officer Personal Image Cons.'s Inc., Raleigh, 1988—; cons. Advanced Micro Devices, Golden Corral Hardee's, Am. Airlines. Author: Building A Better Working Image-Female, 1987, Building A Better Working Image-Male, 1988, Image-The First Impressions, 1989, Effective Organization, 1989, Effective Communication, 1989. Active in Children's Orphanage, Charlotte, 1984-85, Agrl. Ext. Svc., Charlotte, 1984-88. Mem. Assn. Fashion and Image Cons.'s (pres. Carolina's chpt.), 4-H Club (Master Vol. award Wake County chpt. 1989, scholar vet. sci. to N.C. State U.)), The Leads Club. Home: 1717B Collegeview Ave Raleigh NC 27606 Office: Personal Image Cons Inc 3261 Atlantic Ave #200 Raleigh NC 27604

KRA, PAULINE SKORNICKI, French educator; b. Lodz, Poland, July 30, 1934; came to U.S., 1950, naturalized, 1955; d. Edward and Nathalie Skornicki; m. Leo Dietrich Kra, Mar. 10, 1955; children: David Theodore, Andrew Jason. Student Radcliff Coll., 1951-53; BA, Barnard Coll., 1955; MA, Columbia U., 1963, PhD, 1968; Ma, Queens Coll., 1990. Lectr., Queens Coll., City U. N.Y., 1964-65; asst. prof. French, Yeshiva U., N.Y.C., 1968-74, assoc. prof. French, 1974-82, prof., 1982—. Mem. MLA, Am. Assn. Tchrs. French, Am. Soc. 18th Century Studies, Société française d'étude du XVIII siècle, Assn. for Computers and Humanities, Assn. for Literary and Linguistic Computing, Phi Beta Kappa. Author: Religion in Montesquieu's Lettres persanes, 1970; contbr. articles to profl. jours. Home: 109-14 Ascan Ave Forest Hills NY 11375 Office: 500 W 185 St New York NY 10033

KRAETZER, MARY C., sociologist, educator, consultant; b. N.Y.C., Sept. 12, 1943; d. Kenneth G. and Adele L. Kraetzer; m. Kestas E. Silunas. AB, Coll. New Rochelle, 1965; MA, Fordham U., 1967, PhD, 1975. Instr. Mercy Coll., Dobbs Ferry, N.Y., 1969-70, asst. prof., 1970-75, assoc. prof., 1975-79, prof., 1979—; research asst. Fordham U., Bronx, N.Y., 1965-67, teaching asst., 1967-68, teaching fellow, 1968-69, adj. instr., 1971-75, adj. asst. prof., 1975-76; adj. assoc. prof. L.I. U. Grad. Br. Campus Mercy Coll., 1976-79, adj. prof., 1979-81, coordinator M.S. in Community Health Program, 1976-81, adj. prof. Westchester campus, 1988—; rsch. cons. elem. schoolbooks Nat. Council of Chs./Church Women United Task Force on Global Consciousness, N.Y.C., 1971; mem. adv. com. edn. and society div. Nat. Council Chs., 1975-78; mem. evaluation team Middle States Assn. Colls. and Secondary Schs. Commn. on Higher Edn., Monmouth, N.J., 1976. Contbr. chpts. to books, articles to profl. jours. Recipient citation Am. Men and Women of Sci., 1978; Bd. Regents scholar, 1961-65, Fordham U. scholar, 1965-68; Fordham U. fellow, 1968-69; grantee Mercy Coll., 1984, 85, 86, 88; NSF summer intern, 1967. Mem. Am. Sociol. Assn., Am. Pub. Health Assn. Office: Mercy Coll 555 Broadway Dobbs Ferry NY 10522

KRAFFT, MARIE ELIZABETH, chemistry educator; b. Alexandria, Va., Aug. 15, 1956. BS, Va. Polytech. Inst., 1979; MS, Va. Poly. Inst., 1980, PhD, 1983. Postdoctoral Columbia U., N.Y.C., 1983-85; asst. prof. Fla. State U., Tallahassee, 1985-90, assoc. prof. chemistry, 1990—. Recipient Sloan award, N.Y., 1989, Dreyfus Found. scholar, 1989.

KRAFT, ELAINE JOY, community relations and communications official; b. Seattle, Sept. 1, 1951; d. Harry J. and Leatrice M. (Hanan) K.; m. Lee Somerstein, Aug. 2, 1980; children: Paul Kraft, Leslie Jo. BA, U. Wash., 1973; MPA, U. Puget Sound, 1979. Reporter Jour. Am. Newspaper, Bellevue, Wash., 1972-76; editor Jour./Enterprise Newspapers, Wash. State, 1976; mem. staff Wash. State Senate, 1976-78, Wash. Ho. of Reps., 1978-82, pub. info. officer, 1976-78, mem. leadership staff, asst. to caucus chmn., 1980—; ptnr., pres. Media Kraft Communications; mgr. corp. info., advt. and mktg. communications Weyerhaeuser Co., 1982-85; dir. communications Weyerhaeuser Paper Co., 1985-87; dir. community rels. N.W. region Coors Brewing Co. 1987—. Recipient state and nat. journalism design and advt. awards. Mem. Nat. Fedn. Press Women, Women in Communications, Wash. Press Assn. Home: 14329 SE 63d Bellevue WA 98006 Office: 301 116th Ave #550 Bellevue WA 98004

KRAFT, ELISABETH ALLEN, wordprocessor; b. Hagerstown, Md., Nov. 8, 1937; d. William Fuller Lines and Catherine (Wheeler) Burns; m. James Albert Hagy, June 14, 1958 (div. 1966); 1 child, Jennifer Lynn; m. Kenneth James Kraft, July 27, 1968; 1 child, Karen Louise. BS in Edn., U. Md., 1960. Cert. elem. tchr., Md. Tchr. 1st grade Montgomery County Bd. Edn., Kensington, Md., 1960-62; tchr. kindergarten Prince George's County Bd. Edn., College Park, Md., 1965-68; story hour dir. Copper County Community Schs., Houghton, Mich., 1973-74; wordprocessor Harold A. Wheeler, Chassell, Mich., 1988—. Editor, compiler: Wheeler-Alden Family Part I, 1962, Alden-Shedd Families, 1965. Leader, cons., organizer and day care dir. Girl Scouts U.S., Houghton, 1970-85; project planner South Houghton County Community for Action Agy., 1968-78; program chair Keweenaw Unitarian Universalist Fellowship, Houghton, 1987—; mem. Friends of the Land of Keweenaw. Recipient Cert. of Appreciation, Community Action Agy., 1978; named to Upper Peninsula Girl Scouts Hall of Fame, 1987. Mem. Copper County Peace Alliance, Internat. Neighbors (program chair), LWV, AAUW (treas. Copper County chpt. 1987-89), Coaliton for First Amendment Rights. Democrat. Home: Rt 2 Box 72 Chassell MI 49916

KRAFT, LINDA CAROL, marketing executive; b. Ellensburg, Wash., Dec. 30, 1954; d. Albert Patrick and Marjorie Blanche (Hanks) Bruley; m. David Marvin Kraft, Jr., Nov. 23, 1982. Grad., Ellensburg (Wash.) High Sch., 1973. Mktg. asst. GTE, Wenatchee, Wash., 1974-77; svc. advisor GTE, 1977-80, communication cons., 1980-83; sales mgr. Wenatchee Broadcasting Co., 1983-84; pres., chief exec. officer Wheedle Pub., Wenatchee, 1984-87; mktg. dir. Cen. Wash. Bank, Wenatchee, 1987—; cons. Wash. Mus. Assn., Olympia, Wash., 1984-87. Editor: Wheedle (children's series books), 1986. Pub. rels. chmn. Am. Cancer Soc., Chelen/Douglas counties, 1988—. Altrust grantee, 1974. Mem. Career Women's Network (pres. 1985). Republican. Home: 255 N Iowa East Wenatchee WA 98802 Office: Central Wash Bank 301 N Chelan Wenatchee WA 98801

KRAFT-HODGES, JUDITH ANN, postal service worker; b. Highland Pk., Mich., Mar. 4, 1954; d. Robert Joseph and Dorothy Marion (Herman) Kraft; m. Robert E. Wirth, Dec. 18, 1981 (div. Jan. 1984); m. Hugh David Hodges, July 15, 1988; children: Matthew Robert Kraft, Jeremy David Hodges. Student, Macomb County Coll., 1973-75, Mich. Tech. U., 1977-78, U. Md., European br., 1979-83, Columbia Pacific U., 1990—. Cert. substance abuse counselor, Mich. Substance abuse counselor U.S. Army, Wiesbaden, West Germany, 1978-82; mental health counselor U.S. Army, Washington, 1980-82; substance abuse counselor U.S. Govt. Svc., Nurnberg, West Germany, 1983-84; supr. U.S. Postal Svc., Roseville, Mich., 1987-88, Mt. Clemens, Mich., 1988—. Sgt. U.S. Army, 1978-82. Republican. Home: 20569 Piedmont Mount Clemens MI 48043

KRAG, OLGA, interior designer; b. St. Louis, Nov. 27, 1937; d. Jovica Todor and Milka (Slijepcevich) Golubovich. AA, U. Mo., 1958; cert. interior design UCLA, 1979. Interior designer William L. Pereira Assocs., L.A., 1977-80; assoc. Reel/Grobman Assocs., L.A., 1980-81; project mgr. Kaneko/Laff Assocs., L.A., 1982; project mgr. Stuart Laff Assocs., L.A., 1983-85; restaurateur The Edge, St. Louis, 1983-84; pvt. practice comml. interior design, L.A., 1981; pres. Mem. invitation and ticket com. Calif. Chamber Symphony Soc., 1980-81; vol. Westside Rep. Coun., Proposition 1, 1971; asst. inaugural presentation Mus. of Childhood, L.A., 1985. Recipient Carole Eichen design award U. Calif., 1979. Mem. Am. Soc. Interior Designers, Inst. Bus. Designers, Phi Chi Theta, Beta Sigma Phi. Republican. Serbian Orthodox. Home and Office: 700 Levering #10 Los Angeles CA 90024

KRAGE, PATRICIA ANN SHERIDAN, personnel officer; b. Truckee, Calif., Sept. 18, 1852; d. Lawrence P. and Audrie Bernice (Nelson) Sheridan; m. John S., Dec. 29, 1973 (div. Feb., 1987); children: April A., Allison A. BS, U. Wyoming, 1974. Ofice mgr. Deck Law Office, Sioux City, Iowa., 1974-75; sec. Security Nat. Bank, Sioux City, Iowa, 1975, word processing spvr, 1976, personnel asst.; personnel officer Security National Bank, Sioux City, Iowa, 1980--; dir. Minority Outreach Bd., Gordon Chemical Dependency Ctr., Sioux City, 1987--, Family Services, Inc., Sioux City, 1988--. Sec. bd. dirs. Am. Heart Assn., Sioux City, 1988—. Mem. Soc. for Human Resource Mgmt., ALĄACA, Siouxland Pers. Assn. (1st v.p. 1986, pres. 1987, 89-90), Kappa Delta. Democrat. Roman Catholic. Home: 3239 Nebraska St Sioux City IA 51104 Office: Security National Bank 6th and Pierce Sts Sioux City IA 51101

KRAIG, ELLEN, immunology educator; b. Ft. Worth, Feb. 9, 1953; d. Howard I. Kraig and Ida (Abrams) Humphrey; m. David J. Kolodrubetz, June 18, 1978; children: Michael, Daniel. BS, U. Denver, 1975; PhD, Brandeis U., 1980. Postdoctoral fellow Calif. Inst. Tech., Pasadena, 1980-83; asst. prof. U. Tex. Health Sci. Ctr., San Antonio, 1983—; cons. Syntex, Palo Alto; mem. transp. biology and immunology subcom. NIH, 1989—. Contbr. articles to profl. jours. Mem. Recombinant DNA Com, SW Found., San Antonio, 1985—; speaker Bus. of Sci. Meetings, San Antonio, 1987, judge Sci. Fair, San Antonio, 1987—; chair Tex. Immunology Meetings, San Antonio, 1990. Named Disting. Alumna, U. Denver Biology, 1982; Postdoctoral fellow NIH and Cancer Rsch. Inst., 1980-83; rsch. grantee NIH, Welch Found., Morrison Trust, 1983—. Mem. Am. Assn. Immunologists, Am. Soc. Microbiologists, Phi Beta Kappa. Office: UTHSCSA Cell Biology 7703 Floyd Curl Dr San Antonio TX 78284

KRAINIK, ARDIS, opera company executive; b. Manitowoc, Wis., Mar. 8, 1929; d. Arthur Stephen and Clara (Bracken) K. BS cum laude, Northwestern U., 1951, postgrad., 1953-54, DFA (hon.), 1984; LHD (hon.), DePaul U., 1985, Loyola U., 1986, U. Wis., 1986; DFA (hon.), St. Xavier Coll., 1986, Knox Coll., 1987, Columbia Coll., Chgo., 1988, Lake Forest Coll., 1989, Roosevelt U., 1989; LLD (hon.), Albion Coll., 1990; D Mus. Arts (hon.), U. Ill. at Chgo., 1990. Tchr. drama, pub. speaking Horlick High Sch., Racine, Wis., 1951-53; exec. sec., office mgr. Lyric Opera, Chgo., 1954-59; asst. mgr. Lyric Opera, 1960-75, artistic adminstr., 1975-80, gen. mgr., 1981—, gen. dir., 1987—; bd. dirs. No. Trust Co. Mezzo soprano appearing with Chgo. Lyric Opera, 1955-59. Bd. trustees Northwestern U. Recipient Commendatore Italian Order Merit, 1983, Ill. Order Lincoln, 1985, Alumni Merit award Northwestern U., 1986, Award of Achievement Girl Scouts U.S.A., 1987, Dushkin Svc. award Music Ctr. of North Shore, 1987, Thomas De Gaetani award U.S. Inst. Theatre Tech., 1990; named Tribute to Chgo.Women Honoree Midwest Women's Ctr., 1986, one of Chicagoans of Yr. Boys and Girls Club, 1987, Exec. of Yr. Crain's Chgo. Bus., 1990. Mem. Nat. Coun. on the Arts, Ill. Arts Alliance (gov. bd.), Internat. Assn. Opera Dirs., Opera Am. (bd. dirs., pres.), Chgo. Hist. Soc. Guild, Northwestern U. Women's Bd., Northwestern U. Assocs., Northwestern U. Kellog Sch. Mgmt. (adv. coun.), Mortar Bd., Economic Club (bd. dirs.), Commercial Club (Chgo.), Lake Geneva Country Club, Saddle and Cycle Club, Pi Kappa Lambda. Christian Scientist. Office: Lyric Opera of Chgo 20 N Wacker Dr Chicago IL 60606

KRAJCIK, JACKIE LYNN, guidance counselor; b. Wooster, Ohio, Nov. 4, 1959; d. Jack Willard and Faye (Butterbaugh) Harter; m. Anthony Shelby Krajcik, Sept. 4, 1982; 1 child, Daniel Anthony. BS in Edn., Ohio State U., 1982; MS in Edn., U. Akron, 1986. Cert. secondary English tchr., Ohio. English tchr. Northwestern Local Schs., West Salem, Ohio, 1982-88; high sch. guidance counselor Northwestern Local Schs., West Salem, 1988—; varsity basketball coach Northwestern High Sch., West Salem, 1982; varsity volleyball coach, 1983-88. Mem. Ohio Sch. Counselors Assn., Wayne County Counselors Assn., Wayne County Saddle Club. Office: Northwestern High Sch 7569 N Elyria Rd West Salem OH 44287

KRAJOVIC, PATRICIA LOUISE, management executive; b. Altoona, Pa., May 2, 1949; d. Robert H. and Bernadette E. (Sullivan) Slee; m. William A. Rowan Jr., Nov. 19, 1967 (div. 1980); children: William R., Bryan S., Julie R.; m. David W. Krajovic, June 6, 1985; children: Christopher D., Jennifer L. BS, Pa. State U., 1980, MPA, 1981, MBA, 1985. Technician Altoona Hosp., 1967-72; rsch. asst. Pa. State U., University Park, 1972-78; intern Strategic Analysis, Inc., Reading, Pa., 1984; coordinator WIC, Family Health Svcs., Bellefonte, Pa., 1981-83; exec. dir. Shelter Against Violent Environments, Fremont, Calif., 1985-89; dir. adminstrn. Spengler, Nathanson, Heyman, McCarthy & Durfee Law Office, Toledo, 1989—. Task force, adv. bd. Women and Their Children's Housing, San Jose, 1986-88. Mem. Emergency Svcs. Network (vice-chmn. bd. dirs. 1987-88), Nat. Assn. Female Execs. Republican. Roman Catholic. Home: 6847 Morningdew Blvd Maumee OH 43537

KRAKORA-LOOBY, JANICE MARIE, pediatrician; b. Chgo., Jan. 14, 1951; d. Joseph George and Marie Adele (Doleshek) Krakora; m. John Augustus Looby III, July 21, 1979; children: Eileen Loretta, John Augustus IV, James Patrick. BS with honors, Mich. State U., 1972, DVM with honors, 1973; MD with honors, Rush Med. Coll., Chgo., 1987. Assoc. vet. Kohn Animal Hosp., Highland Park, Ill., 1973-75; assoc. vet. Libertyville (Ill.) Animal Hosp., 1976-77, hosp. dir., 1977-82; assoc. vet. Mundelein (Ill.) Animal Hosp., 1982-85; intern and resident in pediatrics Rush-Presbyn.-St. Luke's Med. Ctr., Chgo., 1987-90; pediatrician Vernon Hills (Ill.) Pediatric Assoc. Ltd., 1990—; bd. dirs. Sun Room, Inc., Lake Forest, Ill. Active Lake Forest/Lake Bluff Women's Rep. Club, Sch. St. Mary Parents Club. Paul Harris fellow Rotary, 1988. Fellow Am. Acad. Ppediatrics; mem. Am. Vet. Med. Assn., Am. Med. Women's Assn., AMA, Chgo. Med. Soc., Ill. Med. Assn., Chgo. Pediatric Soc., Lake County Pediatric Soc., Aerospace Medicine Assn. Home: 1764 Bowling Green Dr Lake Forest IL 60045 Office: Vernon Hills Pediatric Assocs Ltd 10 Phillip Rd Vernon Hills IL 60061

KRAKOVER, BRAMBY ANN, college official; b. Denver, Feb. 24, 1962; d. Allen Stanton and Elaine (Golden) K. Lewis and Clark Coll.; BA in Psychology, Lewis & Clark, 1984. Cert. purchasing mgr., materials mgr. Loan clk. Lewis and Clark Coll., Portland, Oreg., 1984, accounts payable clk., 1984-85, buyer, 1985-87, purchasing mgr., 1987—. Mem. Nat. Assn. Ednl. Buyers (2d v.p. 1989—, lst v.p. 1990-91, nat. small schs. com. 1987-90, nat. membership com. 1988-90), Purchasing Mgrs. Assn. Oreg. (bd. dirs. 1989—). Office: Lewis & Clark 0615 SW Palatine Hill Rd Portland OR 97219

KRAKOW, AMY GINZIG, advertising creative executive; b. Bklyn., Feb. 25, 1950; d. Nathan and Iris (Minkowitz) Ginzig; m. Gary Scott Krakow, Nov. 7, 1976. BA in Speech and Theatre, Bklyn. Coll., 1971, postgrad. in TV prodn., 1971. Promotion mgr. Popular Mechanics, N.Y.C., 1976-77; copy mgr. U.S. News & World Report, N.Y.C., 1977-80; promotion mgr. Sta. WINS-Radio, N.Y.C., 1980-82; promotion dir. CBS Mags., N.Y.C., 1982-84, The Village Voice, N.Y.C., 1984-85, N.Y. Woman (Am. Express Pub.), N.Y.C., 1987-89; cons. Silverman Collection, Santa Fe, 1985—; sem. leader Radcliffe Pub. Workshop, 1987—; mem. Mag. Pubs. Congress, 1989. Producer Festival of Street Entertainers, N.Y.C., 1984—, Albuquerque, 1986; contbr. articles to consumer and trade mags. including New York, Family Circle, Working Woman, others; creator, producer, artistic director Ann. Coney Island Tattoo Festival, 1986—, The Psychedelic Festival, 1988. Bd. dirs. Sideshows by the Seashore, Coney Island, U.S.A., Bklyn., 1985—, Bond Street Theater Coalition, 1985—, City Lore, N.Y.C., 1987—. Recipient Addy award, 1985, BPA award, 1981. Mem. Advt. Women N.Y., Delta Phi Epsilon (exec. bd. 1984-85). Home and Office: 57 Warren St New York NY 10007

KRAL, ELIN, healthcare company executive; b. Halden, Norway, Jan. 12, 1940; came to U.S., 1966; d. Ingeman G. and Ebba N. (Johnsen) Jorgensen; m. Frank Kral, Jan. 23, 1967; children: Astrid M., Brian G. BA, Halden Oha, Norway, 1962. Application chemist Princeton Applied Research EG&G, N.J., 1973-78; mkt. research mgr. Vickers Am. Med. Co., Whitehouse Station, N.J., 1978-81; dir. new bus. devel. FCS Comml. Svcs., Flemington, N.J., 1981-84; pres. Iatric Bioproducts for Medicine, Tempe, Ariz., 1984—; bd. dirs. Western Labs., Tempe, Ariz. Innovation Network, Scottsdale. Mem. NAFE, Regulatory Affairs Profl. Soc., Sons of Norway.

KRALL, CATHY ANN, computer systems analyst; b. Lancaster, Pa., Dec. 17, 1954; d. Dale E. and Kathryn Rae (Ney) K. BA in Philosophy, New Coll., Sarasota, Fla., 1975; MA in Philosophy, U. Pitts., 1977, postgrad., 1982—. Computer systems analyst Pa. Dept. Environ. Resources, Harrisburg, 1982-86; chief end-user support Pa. Dept. Environ. Resources, 1986-88, chief distributed systems, 1988—; adj. instr., Harrisburg Area Community Coll., 1985—. Lutheran. Home: 312 N Mount Joy St Elizabethtown PA 17022 Office: Pa Dept Environ Resources 3600 Vartan Way Harrisburg PA 17110

KRALL, VITA, psychologist; b. New Haven, July 9, 1923; d. Moses Adam and Jennie (Alper) K. BA, Antioch Coll., Yellow Springs, Ohio, 1944; MA, U. Iowa, 1945; PhD, U. Rochester (N.Y.), 1951. Lic. psychologist, Conn. Instr. U. Rochester, 1948-51, Mich. State U., East Lansing, 1951-53; sr. clin. psychologist Topeka, 1953-58, Kans. Neurol. Inst., Topeka, 1959-60; staff psychologist Child Guidance Clinic of Greater Bridgeport (Conn.), Inc., 1961-62; psychologist, dir. tng. Michael Reese Hosp., Chgo., 1963-88; rsch. psychologist Hartford (Conn.) Hosp., 1989-90. Author: Developmental Psychodiagnostic Assessment of Children and Adolescents, 1989, Play Therapy Primer, 1989. Recipient Saft award for outstanding instr. Michael Reese Hosp., Chgo., 1983, 87, Disting. Svc. award, Am. Bd. Profl. Psychologists, 1987, Disting. Psychologist, Ill. Psychol. Assn., 1983. Fellow Am. Orthopsychiatric Assn.; mem. Am. Psychol. Assn., Soc. for Rsch. in Child Devel., Soc. for Personality Assessment, Soc. for Pediatric Psychology. Home and Office: 18 Atwater St Milford CT 06460

KRAM, SHIRLEY WOHL, federal judge; b. N.Y.C., 1922. Student, Hunter Coll., 1940-41, CUNY, 1940-47; LLB, Bklyn. Law Sch., 1950. Atty. Legal Aid Soc. N.Y., 1951-53, 1962-71; assoc. Simons & Hardy, 1954-55; pvt. practice law, 1955-60; judge Family Ct., N.Y.C., 1971-83, U.S. Dist. Ct. (so. dist.) N.Y., N.Y.C., 1983—. Author: (with Neil A. Frank) The Law of Child Custody, Development of the Substantive Law. Office: US Dist Ct US Courthouse 40 Foley Sq New York NY 10007*

KRAMER, ALEX-ANN, actress, broadcasting personality; b. Bridgeport, Conn., Mar. 30, 1957; d. Frank William and Angelina Francis (Fortuna) Liptak; m. Anthony Fialko, June 17, 1978 (div. 1981); children: Meaghan Ann Fialko, Sandy Alexis Fialko; m. Mark William Kramer, May 21, 1988. Cert., Conn. Sch. Broadcasting, Stratford, Conn., 1987; cert., Soap Set Acting Studio, Milford, Conn., 1989; student, Mgmt. Broadcasting Coll. Edn. Unit. Chief canine control officer State Dept. of Agr., Hartford, Conn., 1981-83; mgr. Perkin Elmer Corp., Wilton, Conn., 1983-86; on-air personality Sta. WEBE 108 FM, M.L. Media Ptnrs. Ltd., Norwalk, Conn., 1986-88; self-employed actress Kramer Prodns. Inc., Milford, Conn., 1989—; voice-over, actress, T.V./radio Bill Rock Prodns., Stratford, Conn., 1989—; traffic on-air personality Sta. WEZN New City Communications, 1990—; advanced soap opera acting with Walt Wiley (All My Children-ABC-TV), 1989. Producer: radio program, Kaleidoscope, 1987; fund raiser, Muscular Dystrophy, Conceptual Jailhouse, 1989, award 1989. Literacy vol., Bridgeport, Conn., 1988; bd. dirs. Juvenile Diabetes Triathlon, New Haven County, 1987-90; mem. and officer Conn. Seat Belt Coalition, So. Conn., 1988; contbr. personality, Am. Cancer Soc., Paul Newman's Hole in the Wall, 1988; vol. Gang Camp, March of Dimes, MADD, Conn. Burn Care Found. Named Best Credibility on-air, Arbitron/George Burns Reports/Radio, Mr. Report, 1988-89, Consecutive #1 Ratings, Arbitron, Southeastern Conn., 1988-89; recipient, Hon. Muscular Dystrophy, Greater New Haven, Conn., 1988-89. Mem. NAFE, NOW, Nat. Assn. for Women in Broadcasting.

KRAMER, ALICE POULSEN, psychologist; b. N.Y., Jan. 10, 1937; d. Carl M. and Ellen Margarite (Juliusson) Poulsen; m. Milton Dan Kramer, Jan. 9, 1960 (div. Nov. 1971); 1 child, Karen. BA, Queens Coll., 1958; MS cum laude, Long Island U., 1961; PhD, St. John's U., 1973. Lic. Psychologist, N.Y. Lectr. Long Island U., Bklyn., 1961-64; clin. psychologist Logan Meml. Hosp., N.Y., 1974-75; asst. clin. psychologist St. Vincent's Hosp., N.Y., 1970-75; psychologist pvt. practice, N.Y., 1975—; cons. Drug Prevention Program, Bklyn. Cath. Schs., 1975—. Lutheran. Office: 25 W 13th St New York NY 10011

KRAMER, ANNE PEARCE, writer, communications and film executive, educator, psychotherapist, psychoanalyst; m. Stanley Kramer (div.); children: Larry David, Casey Lise. BA magna cum laude, U. So. Calif., MA, 1965, PhD, 1972. Gen. exec. asst. to producer/dir. Stanley Kramer Prodns., prodn. exec., assoc. producer, story editor, casting dir., dialogue dir.; sr. lectr. cinema and comparative lit. U. So. Calif., Los Angeles; acting asst. prof. comparative lit. and film Calif. State U., Long Beach; pres. Cathexis 3, Los Angeles; story editor, v.p. creative affairs Castle Hill Prodns., Inc., Los Angeles, 1978-80; story editor Columbia Pictures, 1981-83, exec. story editor, 1985-88, exec. creative dir., 1983-86, creative cons. to the chmn., 1987—; free-lance cons. film prodn. and editorial pub., 1986—; creative collaborator Clifton Fadiman, Ency. Brit. Films; judge Focus Award for Screenwriting; cons. communications Sta. KPFK-Radio, govt., others. Author: (with others) Directors at Work, 1970, Neo-Metamorphoses-A Cyclical Study, Comparative Transformations in Ovidian Myth and Modern Literature, 1972, Interview with Elia Kazan, 1974, Focus on Film and Theatre. Bd. dirs. Model UN; expert witness on censorship for Los Angeles Dist. Atty.; nurses aide ARC, Children's Hosp.; former pres. Recovery Found. for Disturbed Children; ednl. cons., instr. Camarillo State Mental Hosp.; mem. Psychoanalytic Ctr. Calif. (affiliate). Mem. MLA, AAUP, Women in Film, Delta Kappa Alpha, Phi Kappa Phi, Pi Beta Phi.

KRAMER, CAROL GERTRUDE, marriage and family counselor; b. Grand Rapids, Mich., Jan. 14, 1939; d. Wilson John and Katherine Joanne (Wasdyke) Rottschafer; m. Peter William Kramer, July 1, 1960; children: Connie R. Kramer Sattler, Paul Wilson. AB, Calvin Coll., 1960; MA, U. Mich., 1969; PhD, Holy Cross Coll., 1973; MSW, Grand Valley State U., 1985. Diplomate Internat. Acad. Profl. Counseling and Psychotherapy. Elem. tchr. Jenison (Mich.) Pub. Sch., 1960-64; sch. social worker Grand Rapids Pub. Sch., 1964-73; pvt. practice marriage and family counselor Grand Rapids, 1973—; v.p. Human Resource Assocs., Grand Rapids, 1983-88; guest lectr. Calvin Coll., Mich. State U., Grand Valley State U., 1975-85. Ruling elder First Presbyn. Ch., Grand Rapids, 1975-78; mem. Gerald R. Ford Rep. Women, Grand Rapids, 1973—; bd. dirs. March of Dimes, Grand Rapids, 1980-87; mem. Mich. Bd. of Licensing Marriage Counselors, 1985-88, co-chair pastoral rels. com. Gun Lake Community Ch., 1989—. Named one of Outstanding Young Women in Am., 1974. Fellow Am. Assn. Marriage and Family Therapists; mem. Mich. Assn. Marriage Counselors (awards com. 1988), Nat. Assn. Social Worker., Kent County Family Life Coun. (pres. 1975). Home: 12622 Park Dr Wayland MI 49348 Office: Psychology Ctr 2059 Lake Michigan Dr NW Grand Rapids MI 49504

KRAMER, DEIRDRE ANNE, psychology educator, researcher; b. Jersey City, Dec. 17, 1954; d. John Michael and Katherine Anne (Stanton) K. BA magna cum laude, Syracuse U., 1976; MA, Temple U., 1979, PhD, 1983. Postdoctoral fellow Max Planck Inst., Berlin, 1982-84; asst. prof. psychology Rutgers U., New Brunswick, N.J., 1984-90, assoc. prof., 1990—, faculty resident, gen. edn. programmer, 1989—; presenter at profl. confs., U.S. and fgn. countries; co-organizer, chmn. conf. symposia; ad hoc textbook reviewer McGraw-Hill, Prentice-Hall, Random House; speaker in field; ad hoc jour. reviewer. Joint editor: Transformation in Clinical and Developmental Psychology, 1989; contbr. articles to profl. jours., chpts. to books. Rsch. grantee Temple U., 1978, 81, Rutgers U., 1984-85, 86-87, 88-90, Nat. Inst. on Aging, 1985-86. Mem. Am. Psychol. Assn. (chmn. network com. div. 20, 1989—, mem. program com. 1989-90), Jean Piaget Soc. (program com. 1985—), Gerontol. Soc. Am. Democrat. Office: Rutgers U Dept Psychology Kilmer Campus New Brunswick NJ 08903

KRAMER, DIANA, advertising agency executive; b. N.Y.C., May 18, 1928; d. Anthony Alfred and Dorothy Vernon (Wilkins) Flandina; m. John H. Kramer, Apr. 3, 1948; children: Anthony, Laura. BA, Barnard Coll., 1949. Jr. copywriter, then v.p. and copy chief Mutch, Haberman, Joyce, N.Y.C., 1967-69; sr. copywriter Gaynor & Ducas, N.Y.C., 1969-76; v.p., assoc. creative dir., then sr. v.p. Warwick Advt., N.Y.C., from 1976; with Saatchi & Saatchi Advt., N.Y.C., 1986—, sr. v.p., now exec. v.p. and creative dir. Author song lyrics. Recipient Andy awards, Clio awards, CEBA awards, U.S. Film Festival award. Mem. Advt. Club N.Y. Republican. Roman Catholic. Office: Saatchi & Saatchi Advt 375 Hudson St New York NY 10014

KRAMER, DIANA R., human resources executive; b. N.Y.C., Mar. 10, 1949; d. Joseph and Gloria S.; m. Steven Kramer, May 7, 1975. BA, Glassboro (N.J.) State Coll., 1972; MA, New Sch. Social Research, N.Y.C., 1975; PhD, Fordham U., 1979. Tchr. N.Y.C. Bd. Edn., 1972-80; mgr. human resources and tng. AT&T, Basking Ridge, N.J., 1980-87; mgr. human resources, planning and devel. BASF Corp., Parsippany, N.J., 1987-90; dir. tng. and devel. Agfa Corp., Ridgefield Park, N.J., 1990—. Mem. Am. Psychol. Assn., Human Resources Planning Soc., Am. Soc. Personnel Adminstrs. Adminstrn., Am. Soc. Tng. and Devel., Met. N.Y. Assn. Applied Psychology. Club: Toastmasters. Home: 1 Colonial Way Chatham NJ 07928

KRAMER, ELEANOR, real estate broker, tax practitioner, financial consultant; b. N.Y.C., Feb. 18, 1939; d. Herman I. Kramer and Fay (Berger) Kramer-Levy; m. Richard H. Fitz-Gerald III, Dec. 24, 1959 (div.); m. Gregory F. Navarro, Oct. 1, 1975; children: Brad, Cindy. BA in Speech and Theater, Bkylyn Coll., 1975; MS in Urban Affairs, CUNY, Hunter Coll., 1976. Tchr. cultural arts Bronx (N.Y.) Bd. Edn., 1966-70; real estate broker, pres. Tritown Realty Corp., Mamaroneck, N.Y., 1978-83; pvt. practice tax cons. Mamaroneck, 1983—; adj. prof. sociology Rockland Community Coll., Suffern, N.Y., 1979-85, Westchester Community Coll., Valhalla, N.Y., 1979-85; founder dance therapy St. Vincent's Hosp., N.Y.C.; lectr., demonstrator N.Y.C. Pub. Schs., author, producer, performer, co-creator child edn. programs, 1967-77. Mem. pub. relations com. Bicentennial commn. Village of Mamaroneck, 1976; bd. dirs. Community Action Program, Mamaroneck, 1977-79. Mem. NOW (ad hoc chmn. 1970, co-author women's ednl. seminar Libr. of Congress), LWV (bd. dirs. 1977-80), Nat. Soc. Tax Preparers. Office: PO Box 77 Mamaroneck NY 10543

KRAMER, JANICE KAY, real estate marketing executive; b. Boonville, Mo., Jan. 16, 1944; d. Stanley Monroe and Jewel Mary (Enderlin) K. Student, U. Mo., U. Ill-Chgo. Urban planner Environetic Rsch. Corp., Chgo., 1969-72; sr. analyst Real Estate Rsch. Corp., Chgo., 1972-76; mkt. feasibility cons. J. K. Kramer Real Estate, Chgo., 1976-78; real estate mktg. supr. to mgr. McDonald's Corp., Oak Brook, Ill., 1978-81, staff dir., 1981-84, dir. mkt. devel., 1984—; educator, mkt. evaluation Internat. Mkts. McDonald's Corp. 1981—, Women's Career Devel., 1983—; bus. advisor INROADS, Chgo., 1984—. Recipient Leadership awards YWCA, 1986, 88. Mem. Chgo. Coun. on Fgn. Rels., Columbia Yacht Club. Home: 1400 N State Pkwy Chicago IL 60610 Office: McDonald's Corp Kroc Dr Oak Brook IL 60521

KRAMER, KAREN SUE, psychologist; b. L.A., Sept. 6, 1942; d. Frank Pacheco Kramer and Velma Eileen (Devlin) Moore; m. Stewart A. Sterling, Dec. 30, 1965 (div. 1974); 1 child, Scott Kramer Sterling. BA, U. Calif., Berkeley, 1966; MA, U.S. Internat. U., 1976; PhD, Profl. Sch. Psychology, 1980. Psychometrist U. Calif. Counseling Ctr., Berkeley, 1966-67; social worker Alameda County Welfare Dept., Oakland, Calif., 1967-69; vol. coord. San. Diego County Probation Dept., 1971-73; officer San Diego County Probation Dept., 1973-76; coord. and counselor clin. and outreach programs Western Inst., San Diego, 1976-77; program coord. and counselor Women's Resource Ctr., Oceanside, Calif., 1977-78; pvt. practice psychology San Diego, 1978-81; planner analyst San Diego County Dept. Health Svcs., 1979-81; cons. Calif. Dept. Social Svcs., Emeryville, 1981-83; affirmative action officer State Compensation Ins. Fund, San Francisco, 1983-87; cons., psychologist Office of Prevention Calif. Dept. Mental Health, 1987-89; pvt. practice psychology Berkeley, 1990—; prof. Nat. U., San Diego, 1979-81;; pres. North County Coun. Social Concerns, Vista, Calif., 1977-78; mem. adv. bd. Chinatown Resource Devel. Ctr., San Francisco, 1984-87, San Francisco Rehab. Ctr., 1984-87; bd. dirs. Network Cons. Svcs., Napa, Calif. Mem. Personnel Mgmt. Assn. of Aztlan, Calif. Peer Counselors Assn. (adv. bd. 1987-90, Calif. Prevention Network (bd. dirs. 1989-90).

KRAMER, LYNNE ADAIR, lawyer; b. Oceanside, N.Y., June 25, 1952; d. Paul and Ruth (Kleiner) K.; m. Frederick Eisenbud, Aug. 29, 1976; children: Joshua Kramer-Eisenbud, Benjamin Kramer-Eisenbud. BA, Smith Coll., 1973; JD, Hofstra U., 1976. Bar: D.C. 1976, N.Y. 1977, Va. 1977; assoc. firm Thomas Stanton, Alexandria, Va., 1976-77, firm Dominic A. Barbara, Carle Place, N.Y., 1977-78; sole practice, Commack, N.Y., 1979—; lectr. Suffolk Acad. Law (N.Y.), 1981—; guest lectr. Hofstra U. Law, 1983-84, NITA program, 1985—, Toro Sch. Law, 1982-83. Trustee, Temple Beth David, 1981; legal adviser Human Rights Commn. and Women's Equal Rights Congress Com., 1982-84. Mem. Nassau/Suffolk Women's Bar Assn. (bd. dirs., chmn. judiciary 1982-83, sec. 1983-84, pres. 1984-85), Matrimonial Bar Assn. Suffolk (bd. dirs., treas. 1983-84), Assn. Trial Lawyers Am., ABA (matrimonial and family law com.), N.Y. State Bar Assn. (matrimonial and family law sect.), Suffolk County Bar Assn. (lawyers referral com. 1982-84, cts. com. 1983-84, fee disputes com. and judiciary com. 1985—, bd. dirs. 1986-89, Individual Assignment System Task Force 1988—), Suffolk County Womens Bar Assn. (chair matrimonial and family law com. 1988—), N.Y. State Trial Lawyers, Nassau County Bar Assn., Womens's Bar Assn. State of N.Y. (bd. dirs. 1984-85, judiciary appeals panel 1984-85), Smith Coll. Club Suffolk County (pres. 1982-83). Republican. Jewish. Home: 7 Bradshaw Ln Fort Salonga NY 11768 Office: Lynne Adair Kramer 6165 Jericho Turnpike Commack NY 11725

KRAMER, MARY VINCENT, information specialist; b. Rochester, N.Y., Sept. 30, 1957; d. Leonard Patterson and Ruth Helen (Farrell) V.; m. Dusty Kramer, Nov. 4, 1989. AS in Bus. Adminstrn., Monroe Community Coll., Rochester, 1981; BS in Mgmt., St. John Fisher Coll., 1989. Tech. info. asst. Xerox Corp., Rochester, N.Y., 1979-89; tech. info specialist Xerox Corp., Rochester, 1989—; steering com. Treas. Employee Involvement, 1987—. Recipient William H. Riley award St. John Fisher Coll., 1989, Outstanding Adult Student award Rochester Area Colls., 1989; cert. Appreciation Assn. Info. and Image Mgmt., 1985, Xerox Achievement award, 1984, 89. Mem. NAFE, N.Am. Serials Group, Alpha Sigma Lambda. Republican. Roman Catholic. Home: 54 Winfield Ln Webster NY 14580

KRAMER, MELANY BETH, lawyer; b. Pueblo, Colo., Apr. 30, 1954; d. George David and Grace Rita (Sherwood) K. BA in Lit. and Humanities, Pepperdine U., 1975; JD, U. of the Pacific, 1978. Assoc. Ramsey, Morrison & Keddy, Sacramento, 1980-83, Cooper & Schafer, Sacramento, 1983-85, Barrett, Penney & Byrd, Sacramento, 1985-87, Dummit, Faber & Brown, Sacramento and L.A., 1987—. Vol. Sta. KVIE, Channel 6, Sacramento, 1980—, Sta. KXPR-FM, Sacramento, 1986—. Mem. State Bar Calif., L.A. County Bar Assn., Sacramento County Bar Assn. (community rels. com. 1988). Democrat. Baptist. Office: Dummit Faber & Brown 428 J St Ste 550 Sacramento CA 95814

KRAMER, RUTH, accountant; b. N.Y.C., June 20, 1925; d. Isidore and Sarah (Heller) Kleiner; m. Paul Kramer, Oct. 27, 1946; children: Stephen David, Lynne Adair. BA, Bklyn. Coll., 1946. Registered pub. acct., N.Y. Tchr. elem. sch. N.Y.C. Bd. Edn., 1946-50; acct. Lichtenstein & Kramer, N.Y.C., Lynbrook, N.Y., 1954; jr. ptnr. Paul Kramer & Co., Lynbrook, 1954-56, ptnr., 1956-65, mng. ptnr., 1965—; cons. Nassau County (N.Y.) Dist. Attys. Office, 1956-65; expert witness acctg. matters Nassau County Grand Juries, 1956-65; mem. IRS liaison com. Bklyn. Dist., 1965-76; mem. N.Y. State Bd. for Pub. Accountancy, 1982-89. Troop leader Girl Scouts U.S., 1947-48; chmn. Tri-Town sect. Anti Defamation League, 1952-53; active Heart Fund; pres. Lynbrook Women's Rep. Club, 1956-58; treas. Assembly Candidates Campaign Com., 1964; mem. Nassau County Fedn. Rep. Women, Syosset Woodbury Rep. Club. Named Woman in Acctg., local TV channel, 1974. Mem. Nat. Soc. Pub. Accts. (del.), Empire State Assn. Pub. Accts. (Meritorious Service award, 2d v.p., 1975-76, 1st v.p. 1977-78, pres. 1978-79, Pres.'s award, 2d past pres. exec. bd. 1979-80, 1st past pres. exec. bd. 1981-82, pres. Nassau County chpt. 1962-63, 75-76, state bd. dirs. 1980—, Woman of Yr. award 1982), Tax Inst. C.W. Post Coll., Acctg. Inst. C.W. Post Coll. Clubs: Sisterhood North Shore Synagogue; Am. Jewish Congress, Lynbrook Pythian Sisters (past chief). Home and Office: 23 Hilltop Dr Syosset NY 11791

KRAMER, SANDRA, broadcast communications executive; b. Chgo., Nov. 10, 1943; d. Mortimer Stanton and Ida (Dewoskin) Gold; divorced; children: Kimberly, Kelly, Scott. Acct. exec. Coordinators, Chgo., 1975-77; gen. mgr. Sta. WEEF, Highland Park, Ill., 1977-80; v.p., exec. producer Pub. Interest Affiliates, Chgo., 1980—; v.p., bd. dirs. Chgo. Antique Radio Corp., Inc., 1987—; v.p., sec. Petro Products, Inc., Chgo., 1978—. Exec. producer: (radio div.) Northwestern Reviewing Stand, 1985—, Campbell Playhouse with Helen Hayes, 1986-88, Campbell Souper Stars with Kathy O'Malley, 1988—, Eddie Albert's Medscan, 1985-86, Crain's Bus. Report, 1987—, (radio spl.) Pete Townshend-My Generation, 1985, The JFK Conflict with Edwin Newman, 1988, (audio books) James Burke, 1989; nat. syndicated host (radio series and inflight audio programing) Am. Airlines, Pan Am., Trans World, United Airlines, TWA. Mem. Star Light Found., Broadcast Promotion and Mktg. Execs., Nat. Assn. Broadcasters, New Chgo. Coalition, Jewish United Fund, Anti-Cruelty Soc. Club: East Bank (Chgo.). Office: Pub Interest Affiliates 666 N Lake Shore Dr Ste 800 Chicago IL 60611

KRAMER, SHERRI MARCELLE, association executive; b. Phila., Apr. 14, 1954; d. Irvin and Rhoda Pearl (Levin) K. Student, Montgomery Community Coll., 1971-73; BA, Rutgers U., 1975; paralegal asst. cert., U. Md., 1977. Asst. to counsel U.S. Senator Jacob K. Javits, Washington, 1974-77; legis. asst. U.S. Senator Orrin G. Hatch, Washington, 1977-78; asst. project dir. Coun. Exceptional Children, Reston, Va., 1978-79; sr. legis. analyst Alliance Am. Insurers, Chgo., 1979-83; dir. legis. monitoring Ins. Svcs. Offices, N.Y.C., 1983-86; pres. Kramer Consulting, Ltd., Tampa, Fla., 1986—; asst. exec. dir. Tampa Jewish Fedn., 1987-89; assoc. exec. dir. Jacksonville (Fla.) Jewish Fedn., 1989—; legis. and technical cons., Voc-Ed Handbook for Disabled, U. Wis., 1980. Co-author: Retraining Special Educators in Career Education, 1979. Del., Hillsborough County Human Rights Commn., Tampa, 1987-89; trustee Hillel Found. U. South Fla., Tampa, 1988-89. Mem. Nat. Conf. Christians and Jews, Assn. Jewish Communal Orgns. Profls., Orgn. for Rehab. and Tng., NAFE, Anti-Defamation League, Montgomery County Community Coll. Alumni Assn. (bd. dirs. 1973-81). Office: Jacksonville Jewish Fedn 8505 San Jose Blvd Jacksonville FL 32217

KRAMER, VICKI LEE, elementary education educator; b. Anaconda, Mont., June 7, 1949; d. George Michael and Maybelle (Tolon) Donich; m. Darryl James Henning, July 7, 1972 (div.); 1 child, Anthony Jon; m. Joe Emil Kramer, Dec. 6, 1987. Student, Mont. Tech., 1967-69; BS in Elem. Edn., Western Mont. Coll., 1972; MA in Elem. Adminstrn., U. Mont., 1989. Cert. elem. tchr., adminstr., Mont. Tchr. Sch. Dist. #27, Elliston, Mont., 1972-73; fourth grade tchr. Sch. Dist. #1, Deer Lodge, Mont., 1973-79, first grade tchr., 1979-84, kindergarten tchr., 1984—; charter mem. Home Start, Deer Lodge, 1983, 84. Tour guide Mont. State Prison, Deer Lodge, 1984-87; parish coun. pres. Immaculate Conception Ch., Deer Lodge, 1984-86; vice-chmn. Powell County Meml. Hosp. Found. Drive, Deer Lodge, 1985-86. Mem. Deer Lodge Edn. Assn., Delta Kappa Gamma. Home: 722 Greenhouse Rd Deer Lodge MT 59722 Office: Sch Dist #1 444 Montana Ave Deer Lodge MT 59722

KRAMER, WINIFRED ANITA, marketing professional; b. Opole, Minn., Aug. 29, 1946; d. Joseph Anthony and Katherine Mary (Klimek) Czech; m. Adam Joseph Kramer, Aug. 2, 1985; children: Todd G., Tedd J. Louis; stepchildren: Kenneth J., Keith J., Kevin J. Rental mgr. St. Therese Residence of New Hope, Minn., editor residence newsletter, staff writer nat. publ.; asst. property mgr. Edina (Minn.) Realty Corp. Svcs.; realtor assoc. Century 21 F.R. Lein and Sons, Mpls.; freelance writer and editor. Cub scout leader local chpt. Boy Scouts Am. Mem. NAFE, Ch. Affiliated Women's Group (pres., v.p.), Jr. High Girl's Basketball Athletic Assn. (asst. coach, coach, sec., chmn. fundraiser). Home: 7200 Orchid Ln N Maple Grove MN 55369 Office: 8008 Bass Lake Rd New Hope MN 55428

KRAMM, DEBORAH LUCILLE, lawyer; b. Milw.; d. Hartzell McDonald and Alice Lucille (Johnson) K.; m. Gary Baiz, June 19, 1988. Student, Trinity Coll., Deerfield, Ill., 1971-73; BS, Bradley U., 1974; JD, New Eng. Sch. of Law, 1977; postgrad., Georgetown U., 1978. Bar: N.Y. 1982, Ill. 1980, Mass. 1978. Trademark atty. U.S. Trademark Office, Washington, 1977-78; assoc. Hume, Clement, Willian, Brinks & Olds, Chgo., 1978-81; atty. Avon Products, Inc., N.Y.C., 1981-84; atty. Tiffany & Co., N.Y.C., 1981-84, v.p., sec., 1984-85; counsel Am. Brands, Inc., Old Greenwich, Conn., 1986—. Bd. dirs. Nat. Found. for Advancement for Arts, 1987—; vice chmn., Martha Graham Guild, 1988—; trustee Martha Graham Ctr. for Contemporary Dance, Inc., N.Y.C., trustee, 1989—. Curt Tiege scholar, 1973. Mem. U.S. Trademark Assn. (bd. dirs. 1984-87), Cosmetic, Toiletry and Fragrance Assn. (chmn. trademark com. 1984). Office: Am Brands Inc 1700 E Putnam Ave Old Greenwich CT 06870

KRANITZKY, MARY LISA, construction company executive; b. Schenectady, N.Y., July 20, 1955; d. Charles William Kranitzky, and Shirley Ann (Thomas) Ballou. B.S. in Fin., U. Ala., 1982. Fin. specialist Gen. Electric Co., Birmingham, Ala., 1981-83, supv. acctg. adminstrn., Atlanta, 1984-85, corp. auditor, Schenectady, 1985-87; mgr. fin. analysis and auditing Gen. Electric Constrn. Services, Burkville, Ala., 1988—. Bd. dirs. Birmingham Opera Theater, 1980—. Recipient Acad. Excellence medal Fin. Execs. Inst., 1982. Mem. Beta Gamma Sigma, Phi Kappa Phi, Omicron Delta Epsilon. Episcopalian. Avocations: music; water skiing; reading. Home: 2136 N Sutherland Dr Montgomery AL 36116 Office: Gen Electric Constrn Services One Plastics Dr Burkville AL 36752

KRANKING, MARGARET GRAHAM, artist; b. Florence, S.C., Dec. 21, 1930; d. Stephen Wayne and Madge Williams (Dawes) Graham; BA summa cum laude (Clendenin fellow), Am. U., 1952; m. James David Kranking, Aug. 23, 1952; children: James Andrew, Ann Marie Kranking Eggleton, David Wayne. Asst. to head publs. Nat. Gallery Art, Washington, 1952-53; profl. artist, 1966—; tchr. art Woman's Club Chevy Chase (Md.), 1976-88; guest instr. Amherst Coll.; 1985; one-woman shows: Spectrum Gallery, Washington, 1974, 76, 78, 79, 83, 85, 87, 90, Gallery Kormendy, Alexandria, Va., 1979, Philip Morris U.S.A., Richmond, Va., 1982, 83, 86; group shows include: Balt. Mus., 1974, 76, Corcoran Gallery Art, Washington, 1952, 72, USIA Traveling Exhibit, C. Am., 1978-79, AARP Traveling Exhibition, 1986; represented in permanent collection U. Va., 1979, Philip Morris U.S.A., 1982, 83, U.S. Coast Guard, 1986, 87, 88, AT&T, 1986, 88, Freddie Mac, 1987, 88; traveling exhbn. Nat. Watercolor Soc., 1985-86, Watercolor Color U.S.A., 1987, Am. Watercolor Soc., 1988, Am. Artist mag., 1988, Adirondacks Nat. Exhbn. of Am. Watercolor, 1988, 89, Artitude 7th Internat. Art Competition, N.Y., 1989; ofcl. artist USCG. Mem. Spectrum Gallery Washington, So. Watercolor Soc., Artists Equity, Washington Watercolor Assn., M.W. Watercolor Soc., Acad. Artists, Potomac Valley

Watercolorists (pres. 1981-83), Am. Watercolor Soc. (assoc.), Nat. Watercolor Soc. Roman Catholic. Home: 3504 Taylor St Chevy Chase MD 20815

KRANYIK, ELIZABETH ANN, educator; b. Bridgeport, Conn., Nov. 15, 1957; d. Andrew Ladislaus and Marion Irene (Slater) K. BS summa cum laude, Western Conn. State U., 1979; MA, Fairfield U., 1989. Cert. elem. tchr., Conn. Tchr., program coordinator Fairfield (Conn.) Elem. Summer Sch., 1973-85; tchr. St. Maurice Sch., Stamford, Conn., 1980-82, Our Lady of Lourdes Sch., Melbourne, Fla., 1982-85, St. Pius X Sch., Fairfield, 1985-87, Bridgeport Pub. Schs., 1988—; freelance tutor, Stamford; cons., tchr. Mill River Wetlands Program, Fairfield, 1985-87, Ocean Classroom, Bridgeport, Conn., 1989—. Vol., tour guide H.M.S. Rose Found., Bridgeport, Conn., 1985—. Mem. Alliance Francais (Merit award 1979), Nat. Cath. Educators Assn. Roman Catholic. Home: 1155 Huntington Turnpike Bridgeport CT 06610 Office: Capt's Cove Seaport 1 Bostwick Ave Bridgeport CT 06606

KRANZ, JANET LEE, marketing professional; b. Kalamazoo, Mich., Nov. 19, 1947; d. Herbert Taft and Elnora Louise (Reeder) K.; m. Jose Luis Narezo, Jan. 21, 1972 (div. 1982); m. Richard Lee Clem, Aug. 12, 1985; children: Sara Elizabeth, Kelli Sue. BA, Mich. State U., 1969; cert. in mgmt., Harvard U., 1987; cert. in mktg., Northwestern U., 1989. Account exec. Lansing (Mich.) State Jour., 1970-74; mktg. writer Amway Corp., Ada, Mich., 1974-76; ind. cons. Lansing, Grand Rapids, Mich., 1976-82; dir. mktg. United Way of Capital Area, Lansing, 1982-84, assoc. exec. dir., 1984-87; sr. v.p. United Way of Kent County, Grand Rapids, 1988-89; ind. cons. Grand Rapids, Mich., 1990—; speaker in field; cons. on furniture history, Interior Design mag., 1980, Ball State U., Muncie, Ind., 1980. Mem. com., Gerald R. Ford Presdl. Mus., Grand Rapids, 1980; bd. dirs., United Way of Mason, Mich., 1984-86, Boarshead Regional Theatre, Lansing, 1985-87. Mem. Pub. Rels. Assn. Mich. (bd. dirs. Lansing chpt. 1983-85), Econs. Club Grand Rapids, Grand Rapids Art Mus. Home: 6610 Sunfish Lake Ave Rockford MI 49341

KRASKER, ELAINE S., state legislator; b. Portsmouth, N.H., Apr. 18, 1927; m. Shel Krasker; 3 children. BA, U. N.H., 1949. Mem. N.H. Ho. of Reps., 1975-85; now senator N.H. State Senate. Democrat. Jewish. Home: Little Harbor Rd Portsmouth NH 03801 Office: NH State Senate State Capitol Concord NH 03301*

KRASNY, CHARLOTTE ALTHEA, volunteer; b. Detroit, Nov. 28, 1935; d. Harold Oliver and Charlotte Ruth (Lundberg) Jones; m. Mike S. Krasny, Dec. 21, 1958; children: Mitchell, Robin, Scott, Glenn, Keith. BEd, U. Miami, Coral Gables, Fla., 1958. Cert. secondary sch. tchr. (math). Tchr. Kinloch Park Jr. High, Miami, Fla., 1958-60; tchr. Rickards Jr. High, Tallahassee, Fla., 1960-62, Cen. Jr. High Sch., Melbourne, Fla., 1962-63; vol. Jr. League, Melbourne, Fla., 1964—; musician Melbourne Mcpl. Band, 1965—; tchr. Hoover Jr. High, Indialantic, Fla., 1983-84. Pres., chmn. bd. Melbourne Mcpl. Band, 1975-85; vice-chmn. Melbourne Commn. on Bicentennial of U.S., 1986—; mem. Com. on Centennial of Melbourne, 1987-88. Mem. AAUW, S. Brevard Panhellenic, Jr. League S. Brevard. Republican. Home: 787 Malibu Ln Indialantic FL 32903

KRATOCHVIL, SUSAN MARIE, savings and loan executive; b. Omaha, June 9, 1958; d. Bernard Lee and Kathleen Ann (Watsabaugh) K. Student, Rockhurst Coll., Kansas City, Mo., 1976-77; BS in Elem. Edn., Creighton U., 1980; postgrad., Marquette U., 1982; MEd in Curriculum, U. So. Calif., 1985. Cert. tchr., Nebr.; cert. profl. in human resources. Elem. tchr. St. Columbkille Sch., Papillion, Nebr., 1980-81, Mary Our Queen Sch., Omaha, 1981-84; substitute tchr. Westside Community Schs., Omaha, 1985-86, Omaha Pub. Schs., 1985-86; dir. tng. 1st Fed. Savs. & Loan Assn. Council Bluffs (Iowa), 1986-90; tng. specialist in equasion systems First Data Resources, Omaha, 1990—; owner, prin. Iscript, videoscripting computer cons., Omaha, 1988—. Scriptwriter audio-visual materials. Site coord. student search program Duke U., Omaha, 1981-84; community rep. Midwest Drug Edn. Conf., Omaha, 1983; employee campaign mgr. United Way Midlands, Omaha-Council Bluffs, 1987, 88, 89; computer cons. Chris Abboud for Congress, Omaha, 1990; vice coord community tng. Jr. League Omaha, 1989; program tng. coord. United WayBoardwalk; mentor Girl's Club of Omaha, 1990; edn. chairperson Inst. Fin. Edn chpt. 10, 1990. Recipient Exceptional Vol. award Jr. League Omaha, 1988; Creighton U. scholar, 1980. Mem. Am. Soc. Tng. and Devel., Inst. Fin. Edn. (edn. com. chpt. 10, 1987-89), Nat. Assn. Desktop Pubs., Personnel Assn. Midlands, NAFE, Theta Phi Alpha. Republican. Roman Catholic. Home: 2402 S 13th St Omaha NE 68108 Office: First Data Resources 11128 John Galt Blvd Omaha NE 68179

KRAUCH, VELMA ANN, teacher; b. L.A., Sept. 21, 1916; d. Frank Earl and Susie Velma (Stephens) M.; m. William H. Krauch; (dec.). BA, Immaculate Heart Coll., Los Angeles, 1975; credential in Adult Teaching, UCLA, 1976. Freelance writer Calif., 1967; tchr. Napa Valley (Calif.) Coll., 1982; regional rep. edn. program Nat. Council on Aging, Washington, 1978-81; author-pubs. Calif., 1982; pub. speaker, various orgn. and groups, Calif., 1987--. Author: This is Your Life Story, How to Write It, How to Teach It, 1988 (award Religion in Media 1988). Commn. Vacaville (Calif.) Libr. Commn., 1987—. Mem., Hist. Soc., Geneal. Soc.

KRAUCHICK, DALE ZOBAL, information executive; b. Elizabeth, N.J., Aug. 9, 1955; d. George Frank and Doris May (Beran) Zobal; m. Stephen Francis Krauchick Jr., Apr. 16, 1988. MA in History, West Chester U., 1979, BS, 1977. Employment counselor Snelling and Snelling, Exton, Pa., 1979-80, Workforce, West Chester, Pa., 1980-81; customer svc. rep. Deluxe Check Printers, Paoli, Pa., 1981-85, reg. acct. svc. rep., 1985-87, dept. mgr., 1987—. Mem. West Chester Community Band, Chester County Christian Chorale,. Republican. Home: 122 N Locust Ln Exton PA 19341 Office: Deluxe Check Printers 2 Industrial Blvd Paoli PA 19301

KRAUK, ELSIE ALEXANDRIA, educator; b. N.Y.C., Oct. 28, 1919; d. Harry and Katherine Huczko Harasym; B.A., Hunter Coll., 1941; M.A., Tchrs. Coll., Columbia U., 1942; postgrad. Johns Hopkins U., 1949-56, Towson State U., 1949-50, U. Md., 1956-59; m. Pembroke Mitchell Krauk, July 18, 1943; 1 son, James Mitchell. Tchr. phys. edn. Thomas Johnson Elem. Sch., Balt., 1942-43; social caseworker Dept. Public Welfare, Balt., 1948-49; tchr. grade 4 and 5 Guilford Ave. Elem. Sch., Balt., 1949-52, Glenmount Elem. Sch., 1952-77, ret., 1977; tutor, vol. work, 1977—. Tchr. rep. exec. bd. PTA, 1956-58, 63-65, area tchr. representing Balt., 1961-63. Mem. Ret. Public Sch. Tchrs. Assn., Md. Ret. Tchrs. Assn., NEA. Home: 6216 Walther Ave Baltimore MD 21206

KRAUS, EILEEN S., bank executive. BA, Mt. Holyoke Coll., 1960; MA, Trinity Coll., 1965. Owner, pres. Career Search Resource, 1975-79; v.p. Conn. Nat. Bank, Hartford, 1979-80, sr. v.p., 1980-87, exec. v.p., 1987—. Office: Conn Nat Bank 777 Main St Hartford CT 06115*

KRAUS, JOAN DAVIDA, educational therapist; b. Chgo., Apr. 27, 1933; d. Leo and Ann (Travis) Bramson; m. Samuel Kraus, Nov. 21, 1954; children: Barbara, Edward, Russell. AB, Stanford U., 1954. Life elem. teaching credential, life learning disability specialist credential, Calif. Substitute tchr. Switzer Ctr., Torrance, Calif., 1974-75; learning disabilities specialist Palos Verdes Peninsula Unified Sch. Dist., Rancho Palos Verdes, Calif., 1976-90, mem. supts.'s adv. com., 1984-87; pvt. ednl. therapist, Rancho Palos Verdes, 1990—. Contbr. articles to profl. jours. Vice pres. sisterhood Congregation Ner Tamid, Rancho Palos Verdes, 1969-70; chmn. spl. edn. Palos Verdes Veninsula PTA Coun., 1971-72. Grantee Calif. Dept. Edn., 1985-87. Mem. Assn. Ednl. Therapists (profl., chmn. study group 1986-88), Computer-Using Educators (sec., treas. 1988-90), Ridgecrest Sch. PTA (hon. svc.). Democrat. Home and Office: 6108 Monero Dr Rancho Palos Verdes CA 90274

KRAUS, MOZELLE DEWITTE BIGELOW (MRS. RUSSELL WARREN KRAUS), psychologist, educator; b. Vicksburg, Miss., Sept. 29, 1929; d. Raymond Demar and Henrietta (DeWitte) Bigelow; m. Russell Warren Kraus, Sept. 30, 1961. BS, D.C. Tchr's. Coll., 1952; MA, George Washington U., 1954; EdD., Am. U., 1965.Instr., Dept. Def., Washington, 1952-54; tchr. Wheaton (Md.) High Sch., 1954-55; grad. asst. Am. U., 1955-56; research asst., then assoc. to the late Dr. Leonard Carmichael, former sec. Smithsonian Instn., Washington, v.p. Nat. Geog. Mag., 1956-72; pvt. practice, Washington, 1972—; asso. prof. psychology George Washington U., 1965—; instr. psychology USDA Grad. Sch., 1964—; vis. prof. U.S. Naval Sch. Hosp. Adminstrn., 1968-69; group therapy Salvation Army, Washington, 1980—. Fellow Am. Orthopsychiat. Assn.; mem. AAAS, Am. Psychol. Assn., Va. Psychol. Assn., Nat. Register Health Providers, Internat. Council Psychologists, D.C. Psychol. Assn., DAR, Salvation Army Aux., Phi Delta Gamma, Sigma Xi, Psi Chi, Sigma Kappa, Kappa Delta Epsilon. Episcopalian. Contbr. articles to profl. jours.; author newspaper column Person to Person. Home: 5500 Friendship Blvd 925 N Chevy Chase MD 20815

KRAUS, NANCY PENNE, publishing company executive; b. Norfolk, Va., Jan. 19, 1962; d. James Herman and Betty Jacqueline (Greene) K. BS, U. N.C., Chapel Hill, 1985. Asst. buyer Lord & Taylor, N.Y.C., 1985; sals asst. Jones N.Y., N.Y.C., 1985; auditor Bus. Publs. Audit Circulation, N.Y.C., 1987-88; circulation promotions mgr. Twice & Previews mag. Viare Pub., N.Y.C., 1988-89; mktg. mgr. Video Rev. mag. Viare Pub., 1989—. Mem. Video Software Dealers Assn. Presbyterian. Home: 206 Sullivan St New York NY 10012 Office: Viare Pub 902 Broadway New York NY 10010

KRAUS, NORMA JEAN, industrial relations executive; b. Pitts., Feb. 11, 1931; d. Edward Karl and Alli Alexandra (Hermanson) K. BA, U. Pitts., 1954; postgrad. NYU , 1959-61, Cornell U., 1969-70. Pers. mgr. for several cos., 1957-70; corp. dir. personnel TelePrompter Corp., N.Y.C., 1970-73; exec. asst., speech writer to lt. gov. N.Y. State, Office Lt. Gov., Albany, 1974-79; v.p. human resources, labor relations and stockholder relations Volt Info. Scis., Inc., N.Y.C., 1979—. Co-founder, Manhattan Women's Polit. Caucus, 1971, N.Y. State Women's Polit. Caucus, 1972, vice chair N.Y. State Women's Polit. Caucus, 1978; bd. dirs. Ctr. for Women in Govt., 1977-79. Lt. (s.g.) USNR, 1954-57. Pa. State Senatorial scholar, 1950-54. Mem. Women's Econ. Roundtable, Indsl. Relations Research Assn., Employment Mgmt. Assn., Am. Compensation Assn. Democrat. Avocations: politics, women's rights, breeding Persian cats. Office: Volt Info Scis Inc 101 Park Ave New York NY 10178

KRAUS, PANSY DAEGLING, gemology consultant, editor, writer; b. Santa Paula, Calif., Sept. 21, 1916; d. Arthur David and Elsie (Pardee) Daegling; m. Charles Frederick Kraus, Mar. 1, 1941 (div. Nov. 1961). AA, San Bernardino Valley Jr. Coll., 1938; student Longmeyer's Bus. Coll., 1940; grad. gemologist diploma Gemological Assn. Gt. Britain, 1960, Gemological Inst. Am., 1966. Clk. Convair, San Diego, 1943-48; clk. San Diego County Schs. Publs., 1948-57; mgr. Rogers and Boblet Art-Craft, San Diego, 1958-64; part-time editorial asst. Lapidary Jour., San Diego, 1963-64, assoc. editor, 1964-69, editor, 1970—, sr. editor, 1984-85; pvt. practice cons., San Diego, 1985—; lectr. gems, gemology local gem, mineral groups; gem & mineral club bull. editor groups. Mem. San Diego Mineral & Gem Soc., Gemol. Soc. San Diego, Gemol. Assn. Great Britain, Mineral. Soc. Am., Epsilon Sigma Alpha. Author: Introduction to Lapidary, 1987; editor, layout dir.: Gem Cutting Shop Helps, 1964, The Fundamentals of Gemstone Carving, 1967, Appalachian Mineral and Gem Trails, 1968, Practical Gem Knowledge for the Amateur, 1969, Southwest Mineral and Gem Trails, 1972, revision editor Gemcraft (Quick and Leiper), 1977; contbr. articles to Lapidary jour., Keystone Mktg. catalog. Home and Office: PO Box 600908 San Diego CA 92160

KRAUSE, DAPHNE HYLDA, health and social service agency executive; b. Gloucestershire, Eng., Jan. 14, 1927; came to U.S., 1953; d. Harvey Daniel and Marjorie Evelyn (Penglaze) Paton; children: Deidre, Kenneth, Euan. Ed. pvt. schs., Eng. Founder, pres. Mpls. Age & Opportunity Ctr., Inc., 1967—; adviser govt. leaders and expert on aging throughout U.S., Africa, Can., Egypt, Eng., Fed. Republic Germany, Japan, Norway, also others; testified U.S. Senate and coms. U.S. Ho. of Reps.; guest lectr. numerous univs. including Yale U., U. Minn., U. Tex.; participant Anglo-Am. Conf. on Aging, 1976; speaker, cons. numerous hosps., univs., profl. orgns., govtl. agys.; numerous TV and radio appearances. Contbr. chpt. to books and profl. articles. Bd. dirs. Girl Scouts U.S.A., Mpls., 1950-60, Moblzn. Econ. Resources, Mpls., 1967-75, Abbott-Northwestern Hosp., Mpls., 1975—; past pres. Madison Sch. PTA; past chmn. Loring Nicollet Neighborhood Assn.; past mem. Southside Citizens Adv. Bd.; past vice chmn. Concentrated Employment Program; past mem. Human Rels. Task Force; mem. Mpls. Mayor's-Coun. Adv. Com. on Congregate Care; del. Minn. White House Conf. on Aging; trustee Found. for Hopice and Home Care, 1977—; chmn. Inner City Coun. Girl Scouts U.S., Mpls. Recipient resolution Mayor and City Coun Mpls., 1975, plaque Greater Twin City Area Black Community, 1976, Americanism medal DAR, 1982. Mem. Nat. Assn. for Home Care (not-for-profit rep. 1988—, bd. dirs., spl. recognition award 1987). Office: Mpls Age & Opportunity Ctr 1801 Nicollet Ave S Minneapolis MN 55403

KRAUSE, HEATHER DAWN, data processing executive; b. Kansas City, Kans., May 6, 1956; d. Jack E. Firth and Bonnie Jo (Reeves) Cupps; m. Kerry Murray Krause, May 23, 1981. Cert., Kansas City Skill Ctr., 1980. Cert. drafting tchr., Mo. Assoc. drafter Black & Veatch, Kansas City, Mo., 1980; technician mech. design Wilcox Electric, Kansas City, 1980; coord. CAD design systems Smith & Loveless, Inc., Lenexa, Kans., 1980—; owner Digital Design Technologies, Kansas City, Mo., 1989—; instr. Longview Community Coll., Lee's Summit, Mo., 1987—. Mem. Nat. Computer Graphics Assn., Kansas City Area AutoCAD User's Group, Kansas City CAD User's Group, NAFE. Democrat. Home: PO Box 11314 Kansas City MO 64112

KRAUSE, JOAN MERRY, production manager; b. Milw., Dec. 25, 1935; d. Edward C. Kaczmarek and Lorraine Elsie (Heidemann) Gruman; m. Russell H. Krause, Sept. 11, 1957; children: Katherine Ann, Steven Russell. Continuity dir. Klau-Van Pietersom-Dunlap, Milw., 1969-71; mgr. media svcs. etc. Klau-Van Pieterson-Dunlap, Milw., 1971-72, traffic mgr., 1972-73; traffic mgr. Hoffman-York, Milw., 1973-76; mgr. word processing ctr. YMCA-Main Office, Milw., 1976-77; prodn. mgr. Bozell & Jacobs, Milw., 1977-83, Blair, Inc., Rockford, Ill., 1983-89, McKee & Assocs., Brookfield, Wis., 1989—. Home: 4550 Raven Ln New Berlin WI 53151 Office: McKee & Assocs 12690 W North Ave Brookfield WI 53005

KRAUS-FRIEDMANN, NAOMI, biochemistry educator; b. Budapest, Hungary, July 4, 1933; came to U.S., 1965; d. Jacob and Vilma Krausz; divorced; 1 child, Daphna Friedmann. MS, Hebrew U., Jerusalem, 1960; PhD, Hebrew U., 1965. Instr. sch. medicine U. Pa., Phila., 1968-74; asst. prof. sch. medicine U. Tex., 1974-76, assoc. prof. sch. medicine, 1976-86; prof. sch. medicine U. Tex., Houston, 1986—. Editor: Hormonal Regulation of Guconeogenesis, 1980; contbr. over 100 sci. papers to profl. jours. Mem. Assn. Women in Sci. (pres. Houston Gulf chpt. 1975-77, v.p. Houston Gulf chpt. 1989-90). Office: U Tex Sch Medicine Dept Physiol & Cell Biology Houston TX 77225

KRAUSS, BEATRICE J., psychology educator; b. Portland, Oreg., Dec. 26, 1943; d. Edwin Eugene and Mable Maru (Wilhelm) Osgood; m. Herbert Harris Krauss; children: Michael Conal, Daniel Avram. MusB, Northwestern U., 1965; MA, U. Kans., 1967; PhD, CUNY, 1979. Dir. rsch. Community Sch. Dist. 18, Bklyn., 1978-79; asst. prof. Coll. of New Rochelle, N.Y., 1979-87, assoc. prof., 1987-90, dir. coll. ctr., dir. women's studies, 1989-90; mgr. rsch. group Eric Marder Assocs., N.Y.C., 1986-89; sr. rsch. assoc. Meml. Sloan Kettering Cancer Ctr., N.Y.C., 1990—; treas. Internat. Orgn. for Study Group Tensions, N.Y.C., 1987—. Author: (with others) Living with Anxiety & Depression, 1974; contbr. articles to profl. jours. Cons. Com. on Alcohol and Drug Abuse, Irvington, N.Y., 1983-84; pres. Sleepy Hollow Concert Assn., Tarrytown, N.Y., 1983-85. Coll. of New Rochelle grantee, 1985. Mem. Am. Psychol. Assn. (task force on teaching psychology of women 1982-84), Assn. for Women in Psychology (assoc. editor newsletter 1988), N.Y. Acad. Scis., Ardsley Curling Club, Psi Chi. Home: 6 Downing Ct Irvington NY 10533

KRAUSS, JAMIE GAIL, psychologist; b. N.Y.C., Feb. 19, 1952; d. Robert and Mildred (Rothenberg) K.; m. William Scott Burgey, Oct. 18, 1987; 1child, Shirah Krauss Burgey. BA in Psychology cum laude, U. Colo., 1974; MA, U. Hartford, 1977; PhD, Boston Coll., 1986. Lic. psychologist, Mass. Staff psychologist Framingham (Mass.) Ct. Clinic, 1977-79, Worcester (Mass.) State Hosp., 1979-80; psychologist cons. Dekalb Emergency Mental Health Svc., Decatur, Ga., 1980-81; emergency svcs. clinician The Ctr. for Mental Health, Watertown, Mass., 1981-82; clin. fellow in psychology Mass. Gen. Hosp., Boston, 1983-84; mental health counselor Newton-Wellesley Hosp., Newton, Mass., 1984-85; prin. psychologist, team leader Met. State Hosp., Waltham, Mass., 1985-88; staff psychologist, team leader Quincy (Mass.) Mental Health Ctr., 1988—; supr. Am. Psychol. Assn. internship program Quincy Mental Health Ctr., 1989—; supr. psychology trainees Met. State Hosp., Waltham, 1985-88; clin. fellow in psychology Harvard Med. Sch., Boston, 1983-84; supr. Worcester Family Therapy Tng. Program, 1979-80. Mem. NOW, 1989-90. Grad. Teaching fellow Boston Coll., 1982, Grad. Rsch. fellow Boston Coll., 1985. Mem. Am. Psychol. Assn., Mass. Psychol. Assn. Democrat. Jewish. Office: Quincy Mental Health Ctr 460 Quincy Ave Quincy MA 02169

KRAUSS, MARLENE, surgeon, health and medical products executive; b. Jan. 17, 1945; M. Zachary Berk. BA, Cornell U., 1965; MBA, Harvard U., 1967, MD, 1979. Surgeon, attending physician N.Y. Hosp.; with D. H. Blair & Co., N.Y.C., 1967-75, 86—, mng. dir., from 1967, 1986—; mng. dir. Med-Tech Svcs., N.Y.C., 1989—. Vice chmn. bus. com. Met. Mus. Art, N.Y.C.; mem. Pres.'s Coun. Cornell Women. Office: D H Blair & Co Inc Med-Tech Svcs Div 44 Wall St New York NY 10005*

KRAUSS, SUE ELIZABETH, medical manager; b. Poplar Bluff, Mo., Oct. 29, 1951; d. Raymond Harry and Wanda Elizabeth (Randol) Gibson; 1 child, Emily Sue. AS in Radiol. Tech., Santa Fe Jr. Coll., 1971; student, St. Joseph's Coll., Maine. Radiol. technologist U. Fla., Gainesville, 1971-73; sect. chief Mt. Sinai Hosp., Miami Beach, Fla., 1973-76; asst. chief Miami Heart Inst., 1976-80; radiol. technologist Heights Hosp., Houston, 1981-82; radiol. technician Casa Grande (Ariz.) Regional Med. Ctr., 1983—; adminstrv. mgr. AMMAN, Inc., Casa Grande, 1986—. Mem. Am. Soc. Radiol. Technologists, Am. Registry Radiol. Technologists, Radiology Bus. Mgrs. Assn., Casa Grande Regional Med. Aux., Am. Cancer Soc. Republican. Baptist. Office: AMMAN Inc 900 E Florence Blvd Ste D Casa Grande AZ 85222

KRAUT, BEVERLY RUTH, specialty food broker; b. Long Branch, N.J., Apr. 9, 1952; d. Arthur and Evelyn (Schlossman) K. BA, Colby Coll., 1974. Mgr., buyer Curds & Whey, Oakland, Calif., 1976-83; account rep. Monterey Cheese Co./Otto Roth, South San Francisco, 1983-84, Calif. Sunshine Fine Foods, Co., San Francisco, 1984-86; no. Calif. broker LaTempesta, South San Francisco, 1986—, DeChoix Specialty Foods, Co., South San Francisco, 1986—. Vol. Food Runners, San Francisco, 1988—, Daily Bread, Berkeley, Calif., 1988—. Mem. San Francisco Profl. Food Soc., Am. Inst. Wine and Food. Democrat. Jewish. Home: 5366 Bryant Ave Oakland CA 94618

KRAUT, EVELYN SCHLOSSMAN, retired educator; b. N.Y.C., June 6, 1921; d. Louis and Celia (Singer) S.; m. Arthur Kraut, June 24, 1945 (dec. Oct. 1973); children: Harriette G. Weingast, Alan, Beverly Ruth. BA in Stats., Hunter Coll., N.Y.C., 1941; MA in Gen. Elem. Edn., Kean Coll., Elizabeth, N.J., 1960; EdS in Tchr. Edn., Rutgers U., 1964; PhD in Edn. Theory, Columbia-Pacific U., 1988. Statistician Columbia U., N.Y.C., 1941; engring. asst. Dept. of Army, Ft. Monmouth, N.J., 1942-45; substitute tchr. North Monmouth (N.J.) County Schs., 1957-61; elem. sch. tchr. Eatontown (N.J.) Pub. Schs., 1961-86; math. cons., instr. Austin P. Hepburn Human Resource Ctr., Hallandale, Fla., 1986-88; edn. cons. Contbr. articles to profl. jours. Com. chairperson Hadassah, Rumson, N.J., 1946-70; active Hills Dem. Club, Hollywood, Fla., 1988—, Arts and Culture Ctr., Hollywood, 1986—. Mem. NEA, AAUW (v.p. membership 1986-88), N.J. Edn. Assn., Nat. and World Wildlife Fedn., Hunter Coll. Alumni Assn. (So. Fla. chpt. v.p. programs 1988—), Rutgers U. Alumni Assn. (grad. sch. edn. 1980—), Kean Coll. Alumni Assn. Home: 1201 S Ocean Dr #501 S Hollywood FL 33019

KRAUT, JOANNE LENORA, computer programmer, analyst; b. Watertown, Wis., Oct. 29, 1949; d. Gilbert Arthur and Dorothy Ann (Gebel) K.; BA in Russian, U. Wis., Madison, 1971, MS in Computer Sci., 1973. Computer programmer U. Wis. Sch. Bus., Madison, 1969-72, Milw. Ins. Co., 1973-74; tech. coord. Wis. Dept. Justice, Madison, 1974-83; tech. svcs. supr. CRC Telecommunications (formerly Benchmark Criminal Justice Systems), New Berlin, Wis., 1983-89; sr. programmer/analyst Info. Communications Systems, Pub. Safety Software, Inc., 1989—. Mem. Lakewood Gardens Assn. (dir. 1981-83), Dundee Terrs. Condominium Assn. (officer 1983—). Mem. Phi Beta Kappa. Home: 609 Dundee Ln Hartland WI 53029 Office: N34 W24041 Capitol Dr Pewaukee WI 53072

KRAVETZ, BETH, lawyer, educator; b. Miami, Fla., May 9, 1949; d. Lester and Paula (Davidson) K. Student, So. Ill. U., 1966-68; BA, Fla. Atlantic U., 1970; postgrad., U. Wis., 1970-71; JD, Georgetown U., 1974. Bar: D.C. 1975, Fla. 1976. Legis. asst. Congressman Jerry Patterson, Washington, 1974; pvt. practice Washington, 1974-75, 1987—; govt. relations asst. Nat. Recreation and Park Assn., Rosslyn, Va., 1975-77; dir. govt. relations Smith Bucklin & Assocs., Washington, 1977-79; gen. counsel Nat. Assn. Ins. Brokers, Washington, 1979-81; ptnr. Kravetz & Hearity, Washington, 1981-83; assoc. gen. counsel/govt. relations counsel Home Warranty Corp., Home Owners Warranty and HOW Ins. Co., Washington, 1983-86; adj. prof. law Georgetown U. Law Ctr., Washington, 1983—, Washington Coll. Law, Am. U., Washington, 1987—. Author: Insiders Guide to the Risk Retention Act, 1986; contbr. articles to profl. jours. Named Presidential scholar So. Ill. U., 1968, Panhellenic scholar Fla. Atlantic U., 1970. Mem. ABA. Republican.

KRAVETZ, CAROLYN F., television producer; b. Boston, Feb. 26, 1966; d. Norman M. and Lenore (Leehman) K. BA, Boston U. Coll. of Communicati, 1988. Prodn. asst. WGBH-TV, Boston, 1986, rsch. assoc., 1987-88; assoc. producer WCVB-TV, Boston, 1988—. Mem. Nat. Acad. TV Artist Services.

KRAVITCH, PHYLLIS A., federal judge; b. Savannah, Ga., Aug. 23, 1920; d. Aaron and Ella (Wiseman) K. B.A., Goucher Coll., 1941; LL.B., U. Pa., 1943; LL.D. (hon.), Goucher Coll., 1981. Bar: Ga. 1943, U.S. Dist. Ct. 1944, U.S. Supreme Ct. 1948, U.S. Circuit Ct. Appeals 1962. Practice law Savannah, 1944-76; judge Superior Ct., Eastern Jud. Circuit of Ga., 1977-79, U.S. Ct. Appeals (5th cir.), Atlanta, 1979-81, U.S. Ct. Appeals (11th cir.), 1981—. Trustee Inst. Continuing Legal Edn. in Ga., 1979-82; mem. Bd. of Edn., Chatham County, Ga., 1949-55, Law Sch. Council Emory U. Sch. Law, Atlanta, 1986—; mem. vis. com. U. Chgo. Law Sch., 1990—. Recipient Hannah G. Solomon award Nat. Council of Jewish Women, 1978. Fellow Am. Bar Found.; mem. Am. Bar Assn., Savannah Bar Assn. (pres. 1976), State Bar of Ga., Am. Judicature Soc., Am. Law Inst. Office: US Ct Appeals PO Box 8085 Savannah GA 31412

KRAVITZ, LINDA DELANNE, marketing executive; b. Chgo., May 14, 1947; d. George W. and Jean A. (Lynch) Steinman; m. David J. Kravitz, Nov. 5, 1983; 1 child, Jessica W. BA, Western Mich., 1968; MA, U. Mich., 1970. Prodn. asst. Martin J. Simmons, Chgo., 1974-75; account exec. Frankel & Co., Chgo., 1975-79; mgr. mktg. McDonald's Corp., Oak Brook, Ill., 1979-83, staff dir. adult mktg., 1983-85, head dept. youth mktg., 1985-87, dept. dir. youth mktg., 1987-88, v.p. mktg., 1988—; bd. dirs. Young Astronaut Coun., Washington, 1989—. Office: McDonald's Corp 1 Kroc Dr Oak Brook IL 60521

KREAGER, EILEEN DAVIS, bursar; b. Caldwell, Ohio, Mar. 2, 1924; d. Fred Raymond and Esther (Farson) Davis. B.B.A., Ohio State U., 1945. With accounts receivable dept. M & R Dietetic, Columbus, Ohio, 1945-50; complete charge bookkeeper Magic Seal Paper Products, Columbus, 1950-53, A. Walt Runglin Co., Los Angeles, 1953-54; office mgr. Roy C. Haddox and Son, Columbus, 1954-60; bursar Meth. Theol. Sch. Ohio, Delaware, 1961-86; adminstrv. cons. Fin. Ltd., 1986—; ptnr. Coll. Administrv. Sci., Ohio State U., 1975-80; seminar participant Paperwork Systems and Computer Sci., 1965, Computer Systems, 1964, Griffith Found. Seminar Working Women, 1975; pres. Altrusa Club of Delaware, Ohio, 1972-73. Del. Altrusa Internat., Montreal, 1972, Altrusa Regional, Greenbrier, 1973. Mem. AAUW Assoc. Am. Inst. Mgmt. (exec. council of Inst., 1979); Am. Soc. Profl. Cons., Internat. Platform Assn., Ohio State U. Alumna Assn., Columbus Computer

Soc., Kappa Delta. Methodist. Clubs: Ohio State U. Faculty, Delaware Country. Home: PO Box 214 Worthington OH 43085

KREAMER, BARBARA OSBORN, state legislator. BA, Washington Coll., 1970; M of Liberal Arts, Johns Hopkins U., 1975; JD, U. Md., Balt., 1989. Tchr. Bel Air (Md.) Sr. High Sch., 1971-76; producer, interviewer Sta. WAMD, Aberdeen, Md., 1977-78; commr. Md. Commn. for Women, 1977-85; mem. Harford County (Md.) Coun., 1979-83; del. Md. Gen. Assembly, Annapolis, 1983—; del. Dem. Nat. Conv. 1st Congl. Dist., 1988; Dem. candidate for Congress 1st dist. Md., 1990; pres. Md. Assn. Elected Women, 1985; speaker various Md. confs. Editor Harford County Edn. Assn. newsletter; past editor Washington Elm; contbr. articles to profl. jours. and brochures. Mem. Washington Coll. Vis. Com. Mem. AAUW, NOW (speaker), LWV (speaker), NAACP (speaker nat. conv. workshops on legal issues 1987, 88), County Dem. Clubs. Home: 701 Beards Hill Rd Aberdeen MD 21001 Office: 118 W Bel Air Ave Aberdeen MD 21001

KREBS, JULIA ELIZABETH, biology educator; b. Baton Rouge, Mar. 29, 1943; d. Robert William and Juanita (File) Krebs; m. Roger Kent Hux, Oct. 4, 1980. AB, Oberlin (Ohio) Coll., 1965; MEd, Boston Coll., 1969; MSc, U. Ga., 1972, PhD, 1977. Vol. Peace Corps, Patu Gajah, Perak, Malaysia, 1966-67; tchr. Boston City Schs., 1968-69; teaching/rsch. asst. U. Ga., Athens, 1969-77; prof. biology Francis Marion Coll., Florence, S.C., 1977—. Contbr. articles to profl. jours. Mem. Ecol. Soc. Am., Environ. Edn. Assn. S.C. (sec. 1989—). Office: Francis Marion College Dept of Biology Florence SC 29501

KREBS, MARGARET ELOISE, publishing company executive; b. Clearfield, Pa., Apr. 20, 1927; d. Henry Louis and Delia Louise (Beahan) K.; grad. high sch. With Progressive Pub. Co., Inc., Clearfield, 1945—, bus. office mgr., 1956-60, bus. mgr., 1960-63, asst. to pub., 1963-69, asso. pub., 1981—, dir., exec. v.p., 1969-77, pres., 1977—; v.p./sec. Clearfield Broadcasters, Inc., Stas. WCPA-AM and WQYX-FM, 1965—, dir., 1971—. Mem. Pa. Newspaper Women's Assn., Clearfield Bus. and Profl. Women's Club (pres. 1952-53, dist. membership chmn. 1952-53), Sigma Delta Chi. Democrat. Roman Catholic. Club: Lake Glendale Sailing (sec. 1966—). Home: 526 Ogden Ave Clearfield PA 16830 Office: 206 E Locust St Clearfield PA 16830

KREBSBACH, KAREN K., state legislator; m. Paul Krebsbach; 2 children. BS, Minot State U. Corp. sec. Krebsbach's, Inc.; state senator from dists. 40 and 50 N.D. Senate; mem. adv. bd. SBA. Bd. dirs. Trinity Med. Ctr. Mem. Minot (N.D.) C. of C. Republican. Home: 1715 6th St NW Minot ND 58701*

KREDI, OLGA AMARY, apparel company executive; b. Havana, Cuba, Sept. 22, 1960; d. Nisin and Maria (Giral) Kredi. BA in Bus. Adminstrn., Fla. Internat. U., Miami, 1984. Adminstrv. asst. McDonald, Miami, 1978-81; asst. coord. Miami Dade Community Coll., Kendall, Fla., 1979-84; fiscal asst. II Fla. Internat. U., Miami, 1980-82; asst. office mgr. Gus Nachado, Haileah, Fla., 1982-83; sales and mktg. mgr. Century, Haileah, 1983-86; asst. dir. admissions St. Thomas U., Opa Locka, Fla., 1986-89; asst. pres. Sol Sportswear Inc., Hialeah, 1984—. Mem. Fla. INternat. ZU. Career Senate Assn. (officer 1980), Hialeah C. of C. (vol. 1989). Office: Sol Sportswear Inc 4593 E 10th Ave Hialeah FL 33013

KREEGER, JEAN ANN, insurance company executive; b. York, Pa., July 16, 1950; d. Frank G. and Ardene (Livingstone) Kopp; 1 child, Michelle L. BS, York Coll. of Pa., 1972; MEd, Millersville U., 1973. Lic. ins. agt., Pa. Juvenile probation officer County of York, Pa., 1974-79; agt. State Farm Ins. Co., Dallastown, Pa., 1979-83, agy. mgr., York, 1983—. Mem. Nat. Assn. Life Underwriters (bd. dirs.). Methodist. Lodge: Sertoma (charter). Home: 3708 Cayuga Ln York PA 17402 Office: State Farm Ins 2709 S Queen St York PA 17403

KREER, IRENE OVERMAN, meeting management executive; b. McGrawsville, Ind., Nov. 11, 1926; d. Ralph and Laura Edith (Sharp) Overman; m. Henry Blackstone Kreer, Dec. 22, 1946; children: Laurene (dec.), Linda Kreer Witt. BS in Speech Pathology, Northwestern U., 1948. Speech pathologist pub. schs. Chgo., 1947-49; staff asst., lectr. Art Inst. Chgo., 1962—; pres. Irene Overman Kreer & Assocs., Inc., Chgo., 1962—; bd. dirs., officer SKK Inc., Chgo., 1962—; frequent lectr. on art, architecture Chgo. area; TV appearances representing Art Inst. edn. programs. Formerly bd. dirs. Glenview (Ill.) Pub. Library; mem. Glenview Community Ch. Mem. Field Mus., Chgo. Architecture Found., Smithsonian Assocs., Nat. Trust for Hist. Preservation, Assoc. Alumnae Northwestern U. (bd. dirs. 1975—), Delta Delta Delta. Republican.

KREFTING, CAROL LEE, banker; b. Portland, Oreg., July 26, 1948; d. Richard L. and Irene (Vincent) Noland; m. Charles C. Krefting, Sept. 27, 1968; children: Richard C., Michael J. Student, U. Wash., 1967-68, Stonier Grad. Sch. Rutgers U., 1982-83. Non-profl. Security 1st Nat. Bank, L.A., 1966-67, Seattle 1st Nat. Bank, 1968-72; non-profl. Riggs Nat. Bank, Washington, 1975, from asst. cashier to v.p., 1976-83; v.p. 1st Am. Bank of Va., McLean, 1983-87, 1st Am. Metro Corp, Silver Spring, Md., 1987; sr. v.p. 1st Am. Metro Corp, McLean, 1987—. Contbg. author: Bank Investments, 1982. Mem. Fin. Forum of Wash., NAFE. Office: 1st Am Metro Corp 1970 Chain Bridge Rd McLean VA 22102

KREHEL, ROBERTA MAE, business owner; b. Cleve., Mar. 14, 1927; d. Joseph Myron Keller and Mary Ann (Laskowski) Kulakowski; m. Joseph Yaro Krehel, June 14, 1947; children: Suzanne Matlack, Roberta Graff, Joan Semanisin, Joseph Michael. Student, Cuyahoga Community Coll., 1973, 75. Jr. bookkeeper Victoreen Instrument Co., Cleve., 1946-49; sec. to psychiatrists Parma, Ohio, 1959-62; founder, pres., gen. mgr. S.W. Med. Call Ctr., Inc. Dba Acad. S.W. Answering Svc., Parma, 1961—; sec. Telephone Answering Svcs. of Ohio, 1962-67; pres. T.A.S.O., Ohio, 1969-70, METAS, Ohio, 1988-89. Mem. Parma C. of C., Great Lakes Telemessaging Assn., S.W. Women Bus. Owners, Mid-Eastern Telephone Answering Svcs., Assn. Telemessaging Svcs., Nat. Fedn. Ind. Bus., Internat. Fedn. Ind. Bus. Republican. Home: 1397 W Sprague Rd Broadview Heights OH 44147 Office: Acad SW Answering Svc 1520 W Pleasant Valley Rd Parma OH 44134

KREIDER, CAROLE COMPTON, professional counselor, consultant; b. Boston, Mar. 3, 1939; d. Lemuel Cliff and Dorothy Bell (Leister) Compton; m. Kenneth Gruber Kreider, Dec. 2, 1961; children: Cynthia Louise, Kenneth Brett, Christopher Lee. BS, Simmons Coll., 1960; MA, cert. in family counseling, Bowie U., 1985. Cert. profl. counselor, Md. Mental health counselor Affiliated Community Counselors, Inc., Rockville, Md., 1985—, intake coord., 1990—; seminar leader Adlerian Parenting Workshops, Md., 1984-86. Vol. election precinct, Rockville, 1984, Stepping Stones Shelter, Rockville, Community Block Grants, Rockville, 1989—; group piano coord. Cold Spring Elem. Sch., Rockville. Mem. Am. Assn. for Counseling and Devel., Md. Assn. Counseling and Devel. Democrat. Home: 9232 Copenhaver Dr Potomac MD 20854 Office: Affiliated Community Inc 51 Monroe St Ste 1505 Rockville MD 20850

KREIDER, CYNTHIA LOUISE, company official; b. Boston, Feb. 8, 1963; d. Kenneth Gruber and Carole (Compton) K. Student, Richmond Coll., London, 1983; BS in Polymer Sci., Pa. State U., 1985. Tech. intern Nuclear Regulatory Commn., Washington, 1981-83; rsch. asst. Dept. of Materials, Sci. and Engring. Pa. State U., University Park, 1981-83; devel. chemist Wacker Silicones Corp., Adrian, Mich., 1985-86, sales rep., 1986-87; market devel. specialist Hüls Am. Petrarch Systems Silanes & Silicones Inc., Bristol, Pa., 1987-89; materials specialist Polymerland Inc., subs. Gen. Electric Plastics, Parkersburg, W.Va., 1989—. Contbr. to profl. handbooks. Page Md. Gen. Assembly, Annapolis, 1981. Mem. Am. Soc. Metals. Home: 4400 Grand Central Ave Ste 28 Ashby Glenn Vienna WV 26105 Office: Polymerland Inc Subs GE Plastics 5th and Avery St Parkersburg WV 26102

KREISMAN, JANE SCHEXNAYDER, children's entertainment company executive; b. New Orleans, Jan. 20, 1948; d. Leonard J. and Evelyn (Hebert) Schexnayder; m. Norman R. Kreisman, May 18, 1975; 1 child, Anne. BA, U. New Orleans, 1975; MEd, Tulane U., 1976. Cert. elem. tchr., La. Ednl. therapist Primary Reading Clinic, Metairie, La.; ednl. mgr. Remedial Specialists, Inc., New Orleans; founder, developer, chief exec. officer Good Fairies of Hullen Ridge, Inc., Kenner, La.; entertainment coord. La. Expn., New Orleans, 1984. Author: The Literate Home, 1977, The Good Fairies Training Manual. Mem. NAFE, NAPPS, New Orleans C. of C. (exec. com.), Rivertown USA Assn. (sec.). Address: 509 Williams Blvd Kenner LA 70062

KREITZER, LOIS HELEN, personal investor; b. Pitts., Feb. 2, 1933; d. Franklin and Helen Katherine (Leyda) Maroney; m. William Emil Kreitzer, Nov. 14, 1962. BS, Pa. State U., 1955. Stockbroker Parker Hunter (formerly McKelvy & Co.), Pitts., 1955-62; cons. Pitts., 1962-68, executrix of estates, 1968-82, personal investor, 1975—, shareholder activist, 1970—. Mem. AAUW (life, jrs. sec., v.p., pres. 1960-62), Pa. State U. Alumni Assn. (life), Penn State Club Allegheny County (pres. 1963), Coll. Club Pitts. (life, jrs. v.p., pres. 1959-60), Soroptimist Internat. Pitt. (v.p. 1961), DAR (jrs. treas.-sec., v.p., pres. 1957-60), Colonial Dames of the XVII Century (charter treas.). Republican. Presbyterian.

KREJCSI, CYNTHIA ANN, textbook editor; b. Chgo., Dec. 28, 1948; d. Charles and Dorothea Bertha (Hahn) K.; m. Daniel Neil Ehlebracht, May 16, 1986 (div. Nov. 1988). BA, North Park Coll., 1970; postgrad. Nat. Coll. Edn., 1989—. Prodn. editor Ency. Brit., Chgo., 1970-71, style editor, 1971-72; asst. editor Scott, Foresman & Co., Glenview, Ill., 1972-77, assoc. editor, 1977, editor, 1978-84, sr. editor, 1984—; sr. editor Benefic Press, Westchester, Ill., 1977-78. Mem. NAFE, Chgo. Coun. Fgn. Rels., Smithsonian Instn., Chgo. Women in Pub., Internat. Reading Assn., Nat. Reading Conf. Home: 1425 Partridge Ln Arlington Heights IL 60004 Office: Scott Foresman & Co 1900 E Lake Ave Glenview IL 60025

KREKER, JEANNINE H., media specialist, director; b. Kansas City, Mo., Dec. 10, 1940; d. Jon A. and Jacqueline (Davis) K. Student, U. Kans., 1987—. Psychology asst. Dr. Richard Garland, Lees Summit, Mo., 1986-87; researcher MJM Rsch., Overland Park, Kans., 1988; rsch. dir. Oread Advt., Lawrence, Kans., 1989; rsch. asst. Lees Summit Hosp., 1989-90, rsch. and media dir., 1990—. Mem. P.E.O. Republican. Home: 951 Arkansas J-5 Lawrence KS 66044

KREMENITZER, JANET PICKARD, educator, child development researcher, consultant; b. Bklyn., Sept. 12, 1949; d. Leonard and Francine (Saltzman) Pickard; BA, Queens Coll., City U. N.Y., 1971; MA, Tchrs. Coll. Columbia U., 1972, EdM, 1974, EdD, 1977; m. Martin William Kremenitzer, Dec. 21, 1974; children: Rebecca Jolie, David Aaron. Instr., Barnard Coll. Columbia U., N.Y.C., 1971-73; tchr. Dalton Sch., N.Y.C., 1972-73; lectr. CCNY, 1973-75; asst. prof. Western Conn. State Coll., Danbury, 1977-79; mem. adj. faculty, 1982; ednl. cons., Newtown, Conn., 1979—, coord. Ctr. for Devel. Studies Western Conn. U., 1989—; research cons. Associated Neurologists Danbury, 1982—; research asst. Rose F. Kennedy Center for Research in Mental Retardation and Human Devel., Albert Einstein Coll. Medicine, 1973-74; v.p., founding dir. edn. Maimonides Acad. Western Conn., Inc., 1978-80, bd. dirs., 1978—, coord. early childhood program, 1983—; dir. aerobic fitness program Maimonides Acad., 1987—. Mem. Am. Psychol. Assn., Soc. Research in Child Devel., Internat. Soc. Devel. Psychobiology, AAPHER, Pi Lambda Theta. Club: Hadassah. Address: 39 Brookwood Dr Newtown CT 06470

KREMENTZ, JILL, photographer, author; b. N.Y.C., Feb. 19, 1940; d. Walter and Virginia (Hyde) K.; m. Kurt Vonnegut, Jr., Nov. 1979; 1 child, Lily. Student, Drew U., 1958-59; attended Art Students League, Columbia U. With Harper's Bazaar mag., 1959-60, Glamour mag., 1960-61; pub. relations staff Indian Industries Fair, New Delhi, 1961; reporter Show mag., 1962-64; staff photographer N.Y. Herald Tribune, 1964-65, staff photographer Vietnam, 1965-66; assoc. editor Status-Diplomat mag., 1966-67; contbg. editor N.Y. mag., 1967-68; corr. Time-Life Inc., 1969-70; contbg. photographer People mag., 1974—. Contbr. photography numerous U.S. and fgn. periodicals.; one-woman photography shows Madison (Wis.) Art Center, 1973, U. Mass., Boston, 1974, Nikon Gallery, N.Y.C., 1974, Del. Art Mus., Wilmington, 1975; represented in permanent collections Mus. Modern Art, Library of Congress; photographer: The Face of South Vietnam (text by Dean Brelis), 1968, Words and Their Masters (text by Israel Shenker), 1974; photographer, author: Sweet Pea: A Black Girl Growing Up in the Rural South (foreword by Margaret Mead), 1969, A Very Young Dancer, 1976, A Very Young Rider, 1977, A Very Young Gymnast, 1978, A Very Young Circus Flyer, 1979, A Very Young Skater, 1979, The Writer's Image, 1980, How It Feels When a Parent Dies, 1981, How It Feels to be Adopted, 1982, How It Feels When Parents Divorce, 1984, The Fun of Cooking, 1985, Lily Goes to the Playground, 1986, Jack Goes to the Beach, 1986, Katherine Goes to Nursery School, 1986, Jamie Goes on an Airplane, 1986, Tanya Goes to the Dentist, 1986, Benjy Goes to a Restaurant, 1986, Holly's Farm Animals, 1986, Zachary Goes to the Zoo, 1986, A Visit to Washington, D.C., 1987, How It Feels to Fight For Your Life, 1989, A Very Young Skier, 1990, A Very Young Musician, 1990, A Very Young Gardener, 1990. Recipient Nonfiction award Washington Post/Children's Book Guild, 1984, ACCH Joan Fassler Meml. Book award, 1990. Mem. PEN. Address: care Alfred A Knopf Inc 201 E 50 St New York NY 10022*

KREMER, HONOR FRANCES (NOREEN), advertising executive; b. Ireland, Aug. 9, 1939; came to U.S., 1961; m. Manny Kremer, May 17, 1963; 1 child, Patrick David. BS, CUNY; MS, Baruch Coll. Group sec. Bentalls, Ltd., Kingston-On-Thames, Surrey, Eng., 1954-58, Cen. Secondary Sch., Hamilton, Ont., Can., 1959-61; office mgr. Aschner Assocs., N.Y.C., 1961-63; pub. rels. asst. McMaster U., Hamilton, 1963-64; office mgr. Packaging Components, N.Y.C., 1965-67; head acctg. Shaller Rubin Assocs., N.Y.C., 1967-72, v.p. fin. and adminstrn., 1972-79, sr. v.p., 1979-82, sr. v.p., mem. exec. com., 1982—, sec.-treas. multi-media div., 1972-75; pvt. practice bus. cons., 1986-89; sr. v.p., chief exec. officer, exec. v.p., fin. officer Lewis & Gace Med. Advt., N.Y.C., 1989—, exec. v.p., 1989. Mem. Nat. Fedn. Bus. and Profl. Women (bd. dirs., v.p.), Advt. Fin. Mgmt. Group. Roman Catholic. Office: 1 Bridge Pla Fort Lee NJ 07024

KREMS, SUSAN ALEXANDER, telecommunications specialist; b. Chgo., May 25, 1940; d. Joseph B. and Florence Jean (Cassel) Alexander; children: Steven Michael, Stacy Lynn. Student, U. Ill. Gen. ptnr. Tel-Us Ltd., Beverly Hills, Calif.; pres. 1 800 Telemktg. Inc., Beverly Hills. Mem. TASC (bd. dis., sec.), SNUG (pres. 1990—), ATSI, NAFE, Beverly Hills C. of C. Office: 400 S Beverly Dr #214 Beverly Hills CA 90212

KRENKE, KRISTINE RENEE, correctional institute official; b. Milw., June 1, 1948; d. William John and Genevieve (Meyer) Burke. BS, U. Wis., Oshkosh, 1970; MSW, U. Iowa, 1972. Parole and probation agt. Div. Corrections, Milw., 1972-79, supt. women's ctr., 1979-80; asst. supt. div. corrections Taycheedah (Wis.) Correctional Inst., 1980-89, Kettle Moraine Correctional Inst., Plymouth, Wis., 1989—; speaker feminist approach to addictions Nat. Female Offender conf., Raleigh, N.C., 1987, Am. Correctional Assn., Balt., 1988-89. Creator, developer Together Today For Tomorrow parenting program for incarcerated mothers, 1982, Women and Chems. feminist drug therapy program, 1986. Office: Kettle Moraine Correctional Inst PO Box 31 Plymouth WI 53073

KRENZER, GAIL CLAIRE (GAIL CLAIRE OVERHOLT), pediatric psychologist; b. Omaha, July 27, 1944; d. Donald McLean and Claire Luella (Abbott) Overholt; m. Vernon William Krenzer, June 18, 1966; children: Douglas William, Jeffrey Donald, Andrew Richard. BS with distinction, U. Nebr., 1966, MEd, 1969, cert. in sch. psychology, 1978, PhD, 1980. Cert. tchr., counselor, sch. psychologist, Nebr.; lic. psychologist, Nebr. Tchr. English Tecumseh (Nebr.) Jr. Sr. High Sch., 1966-67; tchr., guidance counselor Cen. High Sch., Omaha, 1967-71; sub. tchr., tchr. adult edn. Omaha Pub. Schs., 1973-76; sch. psychologist Millard Pub. Schs., Omaha, 1979-85; pvt. practice in pediatric psychology Omaha, 1981—; psychologist Omaha Pub. Schs., 1989—; psychologist Svcs. for Crippled Children, Omaha, 1979-83; instr. U. Nebr., Omaha, 1977-79, 82-83, adj. prof., 1985—. Den mother, com. chmn. Boy Scouts Am.; mem. parent adv. com. Talented and Gifted Edn.; unit orgn. chmn. LWV; mem. First Cen. Congl. Ch.; bd. dirs. Meyer Children's Rehab. Inst., 1980—, Creche Child Care Ctr., 1984-86, Hattie B. Monroe Home, U. Nebr. Med. Ctr.; trustee Goodwill Industries Nebr., 1984-90; former cons. Girl's Club of Omaha; mem. Omaha Community Com. on Sch. Desegregation, 1973-74. U. Nebr. career scholar, 1965-66. Mem. Westside High Sch. Booster Club, Westside Middle Sch. Parents Orgn. (leader jr. great books com.), Pi Beta Phi, Phi Delta Kappa. Democrat. Home and Office: 8305 Hickory St Omaha NE 68124

KREPS, JUANITA MORRIS, former secretary of commerce; b. Lynch, Ky., Jan. 11, 1921; d. Elmer M. and Cenia (Blair) Morris; m. Clifton H. Kreps, Jr., Aug. 11, 1944; children: Sarah, Laura, Clifton. AB, Berea Coll., 1942; MA, Duke U., 1944; PhD, 1948; hon. degrees, Bryant Coll., 1972, U. N.C. at Chapel Hill, Denison U., Cornell Coll., 1973, U. Ky., Queens Coll., St. Lawrence U., 1975, Wheaton Coll., 1976, Claremont Grad. Sch., Berea Coll., 1979, Tulane U., Colgate U., 1980, Trinity Coll., 1981, U. Rochester, Grove City Coll., 1984, Davidson Coll., 1990. Instr. econs. Denison U., 1945-46, asst. prof., 1948-50; mem. faculty Duke U., 1955-77, assoc. prof., 1962-68, prof. econs., 1968-77; James B. Duke prof. Duke, 1972-77; asst. provost Duke U., 1969-72, v.p., 1973-77; U.S. sec. commerce, 1977-79; bd. dirs. N.Y. Stock Exchange, 1972-77; bd. dirs. Eastman Kodak Co., ARMCO, UAL Corp., J.C. Penney, AT&T, Deere & Co., Zurn Industries, Inc., Chrysler Corp., Am. Coun. on Germany, Rsch. Triangle Found.; trustee Berea Coll., Duke Endowment, Nat. Humanities Center, 1983-86, HumRRO, 1980-83, Council on Fgn. Relations, 1983-89; mem. bds. overseers Tchrs. Ins. and Annuity Assn. and Coll. Retirement Equities Fund, 1985—; bd. dirs. Nat. Merit Scholarship Corp., 1972-77, Ednl. Testing Service, 1971-77; mem. Nat. Manpower Policy Task Force. Author: (with C.E. Ferguson) Principles of Economics, 2d rev. edit, 1965, Lifetime Allocation of Work and Income, 1971, Sex in the Marketplace: American Women at Work, 1971, Women and the American Economy, 1976; co-author: (with Richard Perlman and Gerald Somers) Contemporary Labor Economics, 1973; Editor: Employment, Income and Retirement Problems of the Aged, 1963, Technology, Manpower and Retirement Policy, 1966, Sex, Age and Work, 1975. named to Presdl. Commn. on Nat. Agenda for the 80's, 1979; recipient N.C. Pub. Service award, 1976; Stephen Wise award, 1978, Woman of Yr. award Ladies Home Jour., 1978, Duke U. Alumni award, 1983, Haskins award Coll. Bus. and Pub. Adminstrn., NYU, 1984, first Corp. Governance award Nat. Assn. Corp. Dirs., 1987, Dir.'s Choice Leadership award Nat. Women's Econ. Alliance Found., 1987, Disitng. Meritorious Service medal Duke U. Alumni, 1987. Fellow AAAS, Gerontol. Soc. (v.p. 1971-72), Am. Acad. Arts and Scis.; mem. Am. Econ. Assn. (v.p. 1983-84), So. Econ. Assn. (pres. 1975-76), AAUP, AAUW (Achievement award 1981), Indsl. Relations Research Assn. (exec. com.). Office: Duke U 115 E Duke Bldg Durham NC 27708

KRESSIN, LORI LEE, university administrator; b. Eau Claire, Wis., July 12, 1959; d. Vernon David and Geraldine Ann (Laatch) Kressin. BS, U. Wis., River Falls, 1981; MSEd, James Madison U., Harrisonburg, Va., 1985. Porter TWA Svcs./Yellowstone Nat. Park, Gardnier, Mont., 1982; ranger Shenandoah Nat. Park, Luray, Va., 1983-88; asst. athletic dir. Yale U., New Haven, 1985-86; facility mgr. U. Va., Charlottesville, 1986-89, asst. athletic bus. dir., 1989—; svc. tech. Bally Lifefitness, Irvine, Calif., 1986—; coach JMU Women's Softball Team, Harisonburg, Va., 1983-85. Mem. AAHPER, Collegiate Coun. of Women Athletic Adminstrs., Women's Sports Found., Nat. Intramural Recreational Sports Assn. Democrat. Christian Ch. Home: 747-D Mountainwood Rd Charlottesville VA 22901 Office: U Va PO Box 3785 University Hall Charlottesville VA 22903

KRESSLER, AMELIA JULIA BRAUN, marketing professional; b. Jacksonville, Fla., Feb. 2, 1944; d. Joseph Francis and Lydia J. (Ruckes) Braun; m. Peter Rockwell Kressler, Sept. 5, 1970; children: Brooke Snowdon, Gwendoline Tory. BA, Stetson U., 1966. Economist Fed. Power Commn., Washington, 1966-67; economist/internat. trade specialist U.S. Dept. of Commerce, Washington, 1967-70; mktg. rsch. mgr. First Pa. Bank, Phila., 1973-76; mktg. cons. PAK Assocs., Wenonah, N.J., 1977-. Bd. dirs. Holly Shores Girl Scouts Coun., Newfield, N.J. (past pres.), 1977-83; sec. United Way of Gloucester County, 1986—; bd. dirs. (N.J.) LWV, 1988—; bd. dirs. (N.J.) AAUW, 1985-89; 4th v.p. Women's Agenda of N.J., 1988, pres. Named 1 of 25 Best and Brightest, Gloucester County Times, 1989; named outstanding vol., Gloucester Dist. Youth & Family Svcs, 1989. Mem. Am. Mktg. Assn. (pres. Phila. chpt. 1977-79). Home and Office: 7 N Jackson Ave Wenonah NJ 08090

KRETSCHMER, DIANE ELISE, marketing executive; b. Chgo., Sept. 28, 1946; d. John and Ruthe (Banes) Majestic; m. Peter J. Kretschmer, Jan. 19, 1978; 1 child, Jonathan David. BA with honors, U. Ill., Chgo., 1971; MBA in Mktg., U. Md., 1981. Assoc. dir. Ctr. for Mgmt. Devel., U. Md., College Park, 1978-82; dir. mktg. Garden State Brickface & Stucco Co., Roselle, N.J., 1982-90; cons., 1990—. Mem. Women's Direct Response Group, Direct Mktg. Club N.Y.

KREUTER, GRETCHEN V., college president; b. Mpls., May 7, 1934; d. Sigmund and Marvyl (Larson) von Loewe; children: David Karl, Betsy Ruth. BA, Rockford Coll., 1955; MA, U. Wis., PhD. Lectr. in Am. Studies Colgate U., Hamilton, N.Y., 1962-67; lectr. in history Coll. St. Catherine, St. Paul, 1969-71, Hamline U., St. Paul, 1971-72; prof. of history Macalester Coll., St. Paul, 1972-73, St. Olaf Coll., Northfield, Minn., 1975-80; asst. to pres. Coll. St. Catherine, St. Paul, 1980-84; asst. to v.p. acad. affairs U. Minn., Mpls., 1984-87; pres. Rockford Coll., Ill., 1987—; mem. chmn. Minn. Humanities Council, St. Paul, 1974-83; bd. dirs. Nat. Assn. State Humanities Commns., Washington, 1984-86. Author: An American Dissenter (McKnight prize 1968), 1969, Running the Twin Cities; editor: Women of Minnesota, 1977, Two Career Family, 1978. Bd. dirs. Kobe Coll. Corp., Regents Coll. (London) Coun. AMCORE Fin. N.A., Rockford Mus. Ctr., Keith Country Day Sch., St. Anthony Hosp., Rockford. Home: 4725 White Oak Ave Rockford IL 61111 Office: Rockford Coll 5050 E State St Rockford IL 61108-2393

KREUTLER, PATRICIA ANN, food products executive; b. Whippany, N.J., Dec. 6, 1945; d. Joseph Philip and Jule Ann (Barber) K.; m. George E. White, Oct. 21, 1972 (div. Aug. 1977). AB in Biology, Merrimack Coll., 1967; PhD, MIT, 1973. Research assoc. MIT, Cambridge, Mass., 1973-75; asst. prof. Simmons Coll., Boston, 1975-81, assoc. prof., 1981-82; mgr. of nutrition The Coca-Cola Co., Atlanta, 1982-87; sect. mgr. nutrition Kraft Gen. Foods, Glenview, Ill., 1987-90; assoc. dir. Kraft Gen. Foods, 1990—; dept. chair of nutrition Simmons Coll., Boston, 1975-82; vis. faculty Fairleigh Dickinson U. Dental Sch., Hackensack, N.J., 1981-82. Author: Nutrition in Perspective, 1980, co-author (2nd edit. 1988). Mem. AAAS, Inst. of Food Technologists, Sigma Xi. Home: 3901 Radcliffe Dr Northbrook IL 60062 Office: Kraft Gen Foods 801 Waukegan Rd Glenview IL 60025

KREUTZKAMPF, JUNE ELIZABETH, social studies and home economics educator; b. Estherville, Iowa, June 13, 1940; d. Albert Olaf Theodore and Pearl Pauline (Wede) K. BS, Iowa State U., 1962, MS, 1970; PhD, U. Minn., 1978. Tchr. pub. schs. Hawarden, Maquoketa and Jefferson, Iowa, 1962-69; asst. prof. SUNY-Buffalo, 1971-74; vis. asst. prof. Brigham Young U., Provo, Utah, 1975-76; asst. prof. Peru State Coll., Nebr., 1979-80; asst. prof., chmn. dept. home econs. U. Minn., Duluth, 1980-84, coord. social studies program, 1984-86, assoc. prof. Dept. Instructional Sci., 1986-90, head Dept. of Instructional Sci., 1990—, pres. univ. edn. assn., 1990—. Bd. dirs. Spirit Mountain Recreational Area Authority, Duluth, 1983-87; pres. univ. edn. assn. U. Minn., 1990—. Mem. NEA, AAUW, Am. Edn. Research Assn., Nat. Council Social Studies, Minn. Edn. Assn. (bd. dirs. 1989—), Assn. Tchr. Educators, Assn. for Supervision and Curriculum Devel., Phi Delta Kappa, Omicron Nu, Kappa Omicron Phi, Beta Sigma Phi. Democrat. Methodist. Advocations: traveling, reading, sewing, photography. Home: 312 Hawkins St Duluth MN 55811 Office: U Minn 231 Bohannon Hall Duluth MN 55812

KREYKES, KATHLEEN KAY, media services executive; b. Iowa City, June 28, 1952; d. Howard Baker and Katharine Eloise (Jennison) Waddell; m. Rodney Dale Kreykes, July 18, 1981. BA, U. Iowa, 1974, MA, 1975. Dir. media svcs. Marshalltown (Iowa) Community Coll., 1975—, pres. faculty senate, 1981-82, 85-86, acting dean instrn., 1986, dir. student orientation, 1986—, adminstrv. intern, 1989. Mem. subcom. Iowa Legis. Task Force on Higher Edn., 1988-89, Iowa Dept. Edn. Task Force, 1989; bd. dirs. Marshall County chpt. ARC, 1990-92. Mem. Iowa Higher Edn. Instructional Resources Consortium (exec. dir. 1985-90), Iowa Ednl. Media Assn. (chmn. pub. rels. com. 1986-88, bd. dirs. 1988-91), NEA, Assn. Edn. Communication Tech., Iowa Edn. Assn., Iowa Assn. Communication Tech. (pres. 1987-89), Iowa Valley Community Coll. Edn. Assn. (pres. 1988-89), Pi Lambda Theta. Home: 2510 S 6th St Apt E36 Marshalltown IA 50158 Office: Marshalltown Community Coll 3700 S Center St Marshalltown IA 50158

KRICK, MARILYN A., internal auditor, accountant; b. New Castle, Pa., Mar. 23, 1952; d. James N. and Twila M. (Wagner) Armstrong; m. Alphonsus D. Krick, Sept. 9, 1983. BS, Clarion (Pa.) State U., 1973. CPA, Pa. Internal auditor Carlisle (Pa.) Hosp. and Health Svcs., F.E. Mgmt. Co., Carlisle; audit specialist comptroller ops. Office of the Budget Commonwealth of Pa., Harrisburg; chief acct. State Pub. Sch. Bldg. Authority, Harrisburg; fin. mgr. West Chester (Pa.) State U. Mem. AICPAs, Assn. Govtl. Accts., NAFE, Am. Women's Soc. CPAs, Inst. Internal Auditors, Healthcare Fin. Mgrs. Assn., Pa. Inst. CPAs. Home: 5600 Stradford Dr Harrisburg PA 17112

KRIEG, DOROTHY LINDEN, soprano, performing artist, educator; b. Moline, Ill., June 19, 1919; d. Carl Victor Lundin and Maybelle Eugenia (Bohman) Linden; m. Eugene D. Krieg, Nov. 24, 1949. Studied piano, voice, pvt. instrs., from 1932; student, Am. Conservatory, 1938-44; studied, opera and oratorio with numerous Maestri. Tchr. Midwestern Conservatory, Chgo., 1947-49; pvt. practice teaching singing Chgo., 1952—; past treas. Nat. Assn. Tchrs. Singing Chgo. Began singing career in vaudeville at age 4; later appeared with Midwest Opera Co.; artist Moments of Opera show, Colosimo's and on TV; appearances in Chgo. area include supper clubs Singer's Rendevous, Caruso's, Singing Sorinis, Pucci's, The Black Forest, Northernaire Showboat in Three Lakes, Wis., ballrooms Drake Hotel, Conrad Hilton Hotel, Blackstone Hotel, others, polit. convs., USO shows; concert artist Chgo. Symphony Orch., from 1950's appearing at Orch. Hall, on tour and on TV with condrs. Fritz Reiner, Rafael Kubelic, George Schick, others; soprano soloist ann. performances Messiah, Marshall Field Choral Soc., 27 yrs., Bryn Mawr Community Ch., Chgo., 17 yrs., Chgo. Temple, 10 yrs., other chs. and temples throughout Chgo.; soloist major oratorio socs. including Swedish Choral Club, Apollo Club, Rockefeller Chapel Choir, Collegium Musicum, St. Louis Bach Soc., Cornell Coll., Calvin Coll., Testor Chorus, Rockford, Ill.; soloist U.S. premieres Vivaldi's Gloria and Handel's Psalm 112, Orch. Hall with Chgo. Symphony; female soloist Chgo. Swedish Glee Club, Chgo. Swedish Male Chorus, Schwaebisher Saengerbund, Chgo. Master Bakers Chorus, Combined German Male Choruses at Civic Opera Ho., others; tchr. voice prodn., phrasing, stage deportment, coach opera, oratorio, English, French and Italian lit., German lieder. Mem. Seal Watch, Can. Magdalen Islands, 1989, 90. 1st pl. winner West Side div. Chicagoland Music Festival Contest, 1939; named Western Springs Music Club scholar. Mem. Greenpeace, Internat. Fund Animal Welfare, Internat. Soc. Animal Rights, People for Ethical Treatment of Animals, Whale Adoption Project. Home: 6700 S Oglesby #1506 Chicago IL 60649 also: 17701 Park #104 Lansing IL 60438

KRIEG, PHYLLIS CHEEK, nurse educator; b. Siler City, N.C., Aug. 7, 1960; d. Charles Joseph and Ida Maye (Willett) Cheek; m. William Ralph Krieg, Feb. 16, 1985. BS in Nursing, U. N.C., Greensboro, 1982, MS in Nursing, 1989. Staff nurse Cone Hosp., Greensboro, 1982-84, primary nurse, 1984-87; clin. nurse specialist, operating rm. Wesley Long Hosp., Greensboro, 1990—. Mem. N.C. Nurses Assn., Assn. Operating Rm. Nurses, Sigma Theta Tau. Republican. Home: 2607 David Caldwell Dr Greensboro NC 27408 Office: Wesley Long Hosp 501 N Elam Ave Greensboro NC 27402

KRIEG, REBECCA JANE, editor; b. Bloomington, Ill., Oct. 7, 1953; d. Russell Edward and Betty Ilena (Clesson) Krieg. BA summa cum laude in Christian Edn., Lincoln Christian Coll., 1977; student U. Ky. Trainer self-help skills for retarded Lincoln Devel Ctr. (Ill.) 1975-76; women's editor Lincoln Courier, 1977-84; campus ministry intern Christian Student Fellowship, U. Ky., Lexington, 1984; copy editor Lexington Herald-Leader, Ky., 1985—. Vol. rep. Cen. Ill. chpt. Cystic Fibrosis Found., 1982-84; a founder Logan County Com. Against Domestic Violence and Sexual Assault, 1983, v.p., bd. dirs., 1983-84; vol. Rape Info. and Counseling Service, Springfield, Ill., 1982-83. Mem. Golden Key, Delta Epsilon Chi. Mem. Christian Ch. Avocations: piano, singing, crocheting, cooking, hiking. Office: Lexington Herald-Leader Main at Midland Lexington KY 40507

KRIEGEL, BETH ANN, accountant; b. Albuquerque, Oct. 16, 1961; d. Arlyn Alvin and Betty Ann (Kallsen) K. B in Acctg., N.Mex. State U., 1983. CPA, Calif., Tex. Sr. auditor Peat Marwick Main, Midland, 1983-85; audit supr. Coopers & Lybrand, Dallas, 1985-88; audit mgr. Pannell Kerr Forster, San Diego, 1988--. Mem. AICPA, Tex. Soc. CPAs (Dallas chpt.), Beta Alpha Psi, Phi Kappa Phi, Beta Gamma Sigma, Chi Omega. Republican. Presbyterian. Home: 3012 Serbian Pl San Diego CA 92117 Office: Pannell Kerr Forster 701 B St Ste 655 San Diego CA 92101

KRIEGER, JANE HELEN, real estate company officer; b. N.Y.C., Dec. 5, 1946. BA, Bklyn. Coll., 1967; MA, George Washington U., 1969; MBA, NYU, 1982. Project mgr. N.Y.C. Housing and Devel. Adminstrn., 1968-74; spl. asst. Legal Aid Soc., N.Y.C., 1974-85; asst. v.p. Morgan Guaranty Trust, N.Y.C., 1985-86; exec. v.p. Grenadier Realty Corp., Bklyn., 1986—; cons. grad. sch. bus. decision lab. NYU, 1985-88. Mem. Women in Housing and Fin. Office: Grenadier Realty Corp 1230 Pennsylvania Ave Brooklyn NY 11239

KRIENKE, CAROL BELLE MANIKOWSKE (MRS. OLIVER KENNETH KRIENKE), realtor, appraiser; b. Oakland, Calif., June 19, 1917; d. George and Ethel (Purdon) Manikowske; student U. Mo., 1937; BS, U. Minn., 1940; postgrad. UCLA, 1949; m. Oliver Kenneth Krienke, June 4, 1941 (dec. Dec. 1988); children: Diane (Mrs. Robert Denny), Judith (Mrs. Kenneth A. Giss), Debra Louise (Mrs. Ed Paul Davalos). Demonstrator, Gen. Foods Corp., Mpls., 1940; youth leadership State of Minn. Congl. Conf., U. Minn., Mpls. 1940-41; war prodn. worker Airesearch Mfg. Co., Los Angeles, 1944; tchr. L.A. City Schs., 1945-49; realtor DBA Ethel Purdon, Manhattan Beach, Calif., 1949; buyer Purdon Furniture & Appliances, Manhattan Beach, 1950-58; realtor O.K. Krienke Realty, Manhattan Beach, 1958—. Manhattan Beach bd. rep. Community Chest for Girl Scouts U.S., 1957; bd. dirs. South Bay council Girl Scouts U.S.A., 1957-62, mem. Manhattan Beach Coordinating Coun., 1956-68, South Coast Botanic Garden Found., 1989—, Long Beach Area Childrens Home Soc. (v.p., 1967-68, pres. 1979; charter mem. Beach Pixies, 1957—, pres. 1967; chmn. United Way, 1967); sponsor Beach Cities Symphony, 1953—. Mem. DAR (life, citizenship chmn. 1972-73, v.p. 1979, 83—), Calif. Retired Tchrs. Assn. (life), Colonial Dames XVII Century (charter mem. Jared Eliot chpt. 1977, v.p., pres. 1979-81, 83-84), Friends of Library, Torrance Lomita Bd. of Realtors, South Bay Bd. Realtors, Nat. Soc. New England Women (life, Calif. Poppy Colony), Internat. Platform Assn., Soc. Descs. of Founders of Hartford (life), Friends of Banning Mus., Hist. Soc. of Centinela Valley, Manhattan Beach Hist. Soc., Manhattan Beach C. of C. (Rose and Scroll award 1985), U. Minn. Alumni (life). Republican. Mem. Community Ch. (pres. Women's Fellowship 1970-71). Home: 924 Highview St Manhattan Beach CA 90266 Office: OK Krienke Realty 1716 Manhattan Beach Blvd Manhattan Beach CA 90266

KRIEPS, MARTHA J., clothing chain marketing official; b. Milw., Dec. 25, 1963; d. Kenneth Karol and Mary Therese (Schatzman) K. BA in Advt., U. Wis., 1986; MS in Direct Mktg., Northwestern U., 1987. Mktg. analyst Eddie Bauer, Inc., Redmond, Wash., 1988—; guest speaker Oreg. Direct Mktg. Assn., 1989. Mem. Puget Consumers Coop., Seattle, 1988. Mem. Woodland Park Zool. Soc., Golden Key, Phi Kappa Phi, Phi Eta Sigma. Office: Eddie Bauer Inc 14850 NE 36th St Redmond WA 98052

KRIER, CYNTHIA TAYLOR, state legislator, lawyer; b. Beeville, Tex., July 12, 1950; m. Joseph Krier, 1982. B.J., U. Tex., 1971, J.D., 1975. Bar: Tex. 1975. Of Counsel Matthews & Branscomb, San Antonio; mem. Tex. State Senate from 26th dist., 1985—. Mem. ABA, Tex. Bar Assn., San Antonio Bar Assn., Omicron Delta Kappa, Phi Kappa Phi, Phi Delta Phi. Republican. Office: Tex State Senate State Capitol Austin TX 78711 also: 301 S Frio San Antonio TX 78207

KRINER, SALLY GLADYS PEARL, artist; b. Bradford, Ohio, Jan. 29, 1911; d. Henry Walter and Pearl Rebecca (Brubaker) Brant; m. Leo Louis Kriner, Feb. 28, 1933; children—Patricia Staab, Jane Palombo. Grad. Arsenal Tech. sch. Indpls.; student Ind. U.-Indpls., 1954, Herron Sch. Art, Indpls., 1958. Exhibited in one woman shows Hoosier Salon, Indpls., 1960, Village Art Gallery, Southport, Ind., 1967, 70, 73, Brown County Art Guild, Nashville, Ind., 1970, 74, 77, 80, 83, 87; group shows include South Side Art League, Indpls., 1959-74, Indpls. Art League, 1959-64, Brown County Art Guild, 1974—; represented in permanent collections Riley Hosp., Indpls., others. Founder Southside Women's Symphony Com., Indpls., 1958; treas. Perry Twp. Republican Club, Ind., 1960-65; pres. State Assembly Women's Club, 1965-67; bd. dirs. ARC, Indpls., 1942-45, Southside Civic Orgn., Indpls., 1954, Clowes Hall Women's Com., Indpls., 1963. Recipient citation ARC, 1946; citation Marion County Meritorious Service Award, 1959; citation Greater Southside Civic Orgn., 1961; Art award Kappa Kappa Kappa, 1967, 68, 70, 71. Fellow Indpls. Art League Found. (numerous awards 1960-66); mem. Southside Art League, Inc. (pres. 1964-65, numerous awards 1964-75, founder), Ind. Artists Club, Inc. (Purchases award 1978), Ind. Heritage Arts, Inc., Rutland Art Assn., Brown County Art Guild (pres. 1980-83, v.p. 1983—), Ind. fedn. Arts Clubs (bd. dirs. 1963-73), Ind. Artist (chmn. prize fund 1974-75), Consignment and appraisal of fine arts, Hoosier Salon, Indpls. Mus. Arts, Nat. Soc. Arts and Letters, Nat. Mus. Women in Arts, Hoosier Group Women in Arts. Presbyterian. Avocation: growing flowers. Home and Studio: Rural Route 3 Box 208 Nashville IN 47448

KRINSKY, CAROL HERSELLE, art history educator; b. N.Y.C., June 2, 1937; d. David and Jane (Gartman) Herselle; m. Robert Daniel Krinsky, Jan. 25, 1959; 2 children. BA, Smith Coll., 1957; MA, NYU, 1960, PhD, 1965. Mem. faculty NYU, 1965—, assoc. prof. art history, 1973-78, prof., 1978—. Author: Vitruvius de Architectura 1521, 1970; Rockefeller Center, 1978; Synagogues of Europe, 1985; Gordon Bunshaft of Skidmore, Owings & Merrill, 1988; Europas Synagogen, 1988; contbr. articles to profl. jours. Bd. dirs. Internat. Survey Jewish Monuments, Urbana, Ill., 1981—, Soc. Archtl. Historians, 1978-80, 1986-89, The Mac Dowell Colony, Inc., 1989—. Am. Coun. Learned Socs. grantee, 1981. Mem. Soc. Archtl. Historians (pres. 1984-86, pres. N.Y.C. chpt. 1977-79), Coll. Art Assn., Planning History Group, Am. Urban History Assn, Women's City Club, Phi Beta Kappa. Office: NYU Dept Fine Arts 100 Washington Sq E New York NY 10003

KRINTZMAN, B. J., real estate broker, television show host; b. Worcester, Mass., Dec. 30, 1946; d. Sumner B. and Shirley R. (Sigel) Cotzin; m. Steven Krintzman, Aug. 9, 1969 (div. Jan. 1978); children: Douglas Andrew, Joshua Barrett. AB, Vassar Coll., 1968; MBA, Harvard U., 1970; postgrad., Boston Coll. Law Sch., 1989—. Lic. real estate broker, Mass. Mng. dir. Boston Shakespeare Co., 1979-82; dir. planning Boston Symphony Orch., 1982-84; talk/game show hostess Newton Continental Cablevision, Mass., 1984-85; real estate broker Hughes Assocs., Newton, 1984—. Mem. adv. bd. WBZ-TV Fund for the Arts, 1982-85; mem. adv. bd. Boston Shakespeare Co., 1982-84, bd. dirs., 1979-82; bd. govs. Harvard Bus. Sch. Alumni Assn., 1983-86; trustee Mass. Cultural Alliance, 1980-84; mem. scholarship com. Worcester County Vassar Club, 1976-82, chairperson, 1982; commr. Human Rights Adv. Bd., Worcester, 1977-78. Named 1 of 10 Outstanding Young Leaders of Greater Boston, Boston Jaycees, 1980. Mem. Greater Boston Real Estate Bd., Harvard Bus. Sch. Assn. (bd. govs. 1983-86). Jewish. Club: New Eng. Backgammon (Boston). Avocations: crossword puzzles, antiques, theater, tennis. Home: 30 Avalon Rd Waban MA 02168 Office: Hughes Assocs 1631 Beacon St Waban MA 02168

KRISCH, JEAN PECK, physics educator; b. Washington, May 23, 1939; d. Robert Eben and Dorothy (Wiley) Peck; m. Alan David Krisch, Aug. 27, 1961; 1 child, Kathleen Susan. BS, U. Md., 1960; MS, Cornell U., 1962, PhD, 1965. Lectr. dept. physics U. Mich., Ann Arbor, 1973-89, assoc. prof. dept. physics, 1989—; assoc. chair for undergrad. programs dept. physics U. Mich., Ann Arbor, 1987—. Contbr. articles to profl. jours. Mem. Am. Phys. Soc., Am. Assn. Physics Tchrs.

KRISE, PATRICIA LOVE, automotive industry executive; b. Indpls., July 28, 1959; d. John Bernard and Ann (Emmons) Love; m. Thomas Warren Krise, Sept. 5, 1987. BA magna cum laude, Hanover Coll., Ind., 1981; MBA with hons., Miami U., Oxford, Ohio, 1982. Substitute tchr. Henry County Sch. Dist., Knightstown, Ind., 1982-83; project mgr. Servaas Labs., Inc., Indpls., 1983-84; sales analyst Ford Motor Co., Mpls., 1984, outstate field mgr., 1984-86, met. field mgr., 1986-87, truck merchandising mgr., 1987-88, merchandising mgr., 1988-89; met. field dir. Denver dist. Ford Motor Co., 1989, market representation specialist Denver dist., 1990—; advisor/presenter Ford Dealer Advt. Fund, Mpls., 1987-88. Recipient Outstanding Mktg. Award, Cen. Region Ford Motor Co., 1987, Wall St. Jour. award, 1981. Mem. Twin Cities Sales Mgrs. Club, Hanover Coll. Alumni Assn., Women's Athletic Assn. (treas. 1979-80), Pre-Law Club (pres. 1980-81), Alpha Delta Pi. Republican. Roman Catholic.

KRITZER, MARGARET ROSE, magnetic resonance imaging scientist; b. Pottstown, Pa., Apr. 6, 1959; d. William Herman and Alice May (Crandall) K. BS in Physics, Case Western Res. U., 1981, MS in Applied Math., 1986. Physicist Technicare Corp., Solon, Ohio, 1981-86; software mathematician Imatron, Inc., South San Francisco, Calif., 1986-89; magnetic resonance imaging scientist Toshiba Am. Magnetic Resonance Imaging, South San Francisco, 1989—; presenter in field. Contbr. articles to profl. jours. Participant San Francisco AIDS Walk, 1989; mem. Soc. Photographic Scientists and Engrs., 1982-85. Home: 2185 Hayes St 7 San Francisco CA 94117 Office: Toshiba Am MRI Inc 280 Utah Ave South San Francisco CA 94080

KRIVOY, KATHY LYNN, marketing and finance specialist; b. Euclid, Ohio, Jan. 6, 1956; d. Douglas D. and Dawna (Allen) K.; m. David Eric Rogers, May 29, 1982. BA in Econs, U. Rochester, 1978, MBA in Mktg. and Fin., 1984. Lic. real estate agt., Pa. Internat. market sales forecaster Eastman Kodak, Rochester, N.Y., 1978-79, domestic film market sales forecaster, 1979-81, analyst Mgmt. Svcs. div., 1981-83, specialist Consumer Products div., 1983-85; account executive U.S. Sales div. Eastman Kodak, Allentown, Pa., 1985-87; ptnr. Gemroi Co., Fredericksburg, Va., 1987-88; asst. to v.p. corp. planning Benjamin Moore & Co., Montvale, N.J., 1988—. Vol. Voluntary Action Ctr., Allentown, 1987; mem. adv. bd. to County Commrs., steering com. Community Svcs. for Children, 1986-88; mem. Jr. League of Bergen County, 1988—, chmn. tng. com. Mem. NAFE, Nat. Paint and Coating Assn. (consumer rsch. com. 1988—), Jr. League Bergen County. Republican. Office: Benjamin Moore & Co 51 Chestnut Ridge Rd Montvale NJ 07645

KRIZ, MARJORIE MINSK, writer; b. Evanston, Ill., May 2, 1920; d. Louis David and Helen (Tavenner) Minsk; m. Jack Jerome Kriz, children: Helen Marshall, John Jerome III. BS, Northwestern U., 1942, MA, 1943; postgrad., Oxford Christ Ch. Coll., 1985, U. Wis., 1986. Prodn. asst. Northwestern U. Theatre, Evanston, 1940-41, pub. rels. dir., 1941-43; writer Am. Theatre Wing, N.Y.C., 1943; reporter, editor City News Bur., Chgo., 1944-54, aviation editor, 1967-71; asst. pub. affairs officer Great Lakes region FAA, 1971-88. Contbr. articles to profl. jours. Bd. dirs. Milw.'s Mitchell Gallery Flight Mus. Mem. Aviation Space Writers Assn., Chgo. Newspaper Reporters Assn. (treas., bd. dir.), Chgo. Press VA Assn., Zeta Phi Eta. Home: 3306 Hayes St Evanston IL 60201-1832

KRIZANOSKY, MARY SUZANNA, water treatment plant operator; b. Evanston, Ill., July 18, 1958; d. Andrew Michael and Margaret Ellen (Kennedy) K. BA, Calif. State U., Sacramento, 1982. Cert. water treatment operator, Calif. Dept. Health Services. Mgr. Sierra Coll. Recycling Ctr., Rocklin, Calif., 1982-83; conservation aide Nat. Park Service, Moab, Utah, 1983; plant operator 1 City of Sacramento, 1984-86, plant operator 2, 1986—. Mem. Internat. Union Operating Engrs., Audubon Soc., Phi Kappa Phi. Home: 4580 Chapparal Dr Placerville CA 95667 Office: City of Sacramento 101 Bercut Dr Sacramento CA 95814

KROEHL, SUSAN ANN, nurse; b. Jersey City, June 26, 1945; d. Edward G. and Mildred Marie (Huff) K. AD in Nursing, Fairleigh Dickison U., 1967; BS in Nursing, Northeastern U., Boston, 1981; MS, Boston Coll., Chestnut Hill, Mass., 1983. Staff nurse Mass. Gen. Hosp., Boston, 1967-69, unit tchr., 1969-71; continuing care coord. Mass. Rehab. Hosp., Boston, 1972-73; surg. rehab. clin. nurse Peter Bent Brigham/Brigham & Women's Hosp., Boston, 1973-82; enterostomal therapy coord. Cath. Med. Ctr., Manchester, N.H., 1984-87, nursing practice coord., 1987-88, nursing practice adminstrv. liaison, 1988—; enterostomal therapy cons. Dana Farber Cancer Ctr., Boston, 1975-81. Mem. div. svc. and rehab. com. Am. Cancer Soc., Manchester, 1984-89, chmn., 1989—, div. bd. dirs. Hillsborough County North unit, 1987-89, mem. nursing edn. subcom., 1984-87. Mem. Internat. Assn. Enterostomal Therapy, Oncology Nursing Soc. Roman Catholic. Office: Cath Med Ctr 100 McGregor St Manchester NH 03102

KROEPLIN, KARLA JOAN, communications specialist; b. Marshfield, Wis., Nov. 18, 1961; d. Karl Frederick and Jean Marlene (Helsten) K. BS in Journalism, U. Wis., 1987. Pres. Wis. Union, Madison, Wis., 1986-87; communications specialist Wis. Dept. Devel., Madison, 1986-89; pro bono coord. Will County Legal Assistance Program, Joilet, Ill., 1990—; freelance writer, designer Bolingbrook, Ill., 1989—. Author, editor: (mag.) Wis. Internat. Trade, 1986-89, (mag.) Finl. Mgrs. Statement, 1990; designer (mag.) Chicagoland Apt. Assn., 1990. Pub. rels. coord. Bolingbrook (Ill.) Silver Anniversary Com., 1990. Mem. Women in Communications, Inc. (treas. student chpt. 1987, scholarship 1987). Home: 325 Musial Circle Bolingbrook IL 60440

KROGH, SARAH ELIZABETH, client access and wire systems manager, accountant; b. Eugene, Oreg., Nov. 9, 1956; d. Arnold Walter and Shirley Elizabeth (Schrock) K. BA, Oreg. State U., 1979. CPA, Oreg. Cons. mgr. Andersen Cons., Portland, Oreg., 1979-90; system mgr. Norwest Tech. Svcs., Mpls., 1990—; past pres.-elect Am. Women's Soc. CPA's Portland, 1987-90. Bd. dirs. Alcohol Safety Action Program, Portland, 1988-90. Office: Norwest Tech Svcs 255 2d Ave S Minneapolis MN 55479

KROKENBERGER, LINDA ROSE, chemist, environmental analyst; b. Ridley Park, Pa., July 17, 1954; d. Roy Frank and Rose Marie (Kraffert) K. BS in Chemistry, Syracuse U., 1976. Radiopharm. chemist Upstate Med. Ctr., SUNY, Syracuse, 1976-78; chemist IT Corp. (formerly West Coast Tech. Services), Cerritos, Calif., 1978-80, analytical chemist, 1980-81, sr. chemist, 1981-84, asst. mgr. lab., 1984-85, project mgr. environ. protection agency, 1985-86; mgr. data control Enseco-Cal Lab., West Sacramento, Calif., 1987; asst. mgr. lab. Sci. Applications Internat. Corp., San Diego, 1987-89; ind. cons. in environ. analytical chemistry and quality assurance, Poway, Calif., 1989—. Recipient Citizenship award DAR, 1972. Mem. Am. Chem. Soc., ASTM, Assn. Official Analytical Chemists, Soc. Environ. Toxicology and Chemistry. Republican. Methodist. Home and Office: 12974 Cree Dr Poway CA 92064

KROLL, CAROLYN K., public administrator; b. Wallingford, Pa., Feb. 2, 1945; d. Charles Carter and Gheretein (Yeatman) Kline; m. James Oliver Kroll, Jan. 5, 1968; children: Erin K., Timothy Albert. BS in Journalism, Northwestern U., 1967; MA in Creative Writing, U. Dallas, 1975; postgrad., Boston U., 1990—. Dist. coord. Mass. Bay Dist. of Unitarian-Universalist Chs., Inc., Boston, 1982-84; head exec. asst. County of Middlesex, Cambridge, Mass., 1984-86; founder, dir. Kids-in-Common Extended Day Program, Watertown, Mass., 1987-89; chief of staff Mass. State Senate, Boston, 1984-86; statewide coord. Mass. Orgn. of Sch. Improvement Couns., Boston, 1986; dir. ops. County of Essex, Salem, Mass., 1987-89. Mem. Watertown (Mass.) Sch. com., 1980-85; del. Dem. State Conv., Boston, 1990; bd. dirs. Mass. Women's Polit. Caucus (treas. 1987-89). Mem. Mass. Mcpl. Assn., Am. Assn. Pub. Adminstrn. Democrat. Home: 90 Russell Ave Watertown MA 02172

KRONE, DEBRA JEAN, marketing professional; b. Knoxville, Tenn., May 3, 1955; d. James William and Ruby A. (Holmes) Floyd; m. Patrick Trainor, Sept. 22, 1973 (div. 1978); 1 child, Amy Michelle; m. Stephen W. Krone, Dec. 23, 1983. BS in Acctg., U. Cin., 1977. Acct. GECC, Cin., 1978-79; sales recruiter Sales Consultants, Cin., 1979-81; area sales mgr. Gorham Textron, Cin., 1981-83; sales rep. Applause, Denver, 1983-84; dist. sales mgr. Waterford Crystal Inc., Denver, 1984-87; freelance sales trainer various cos., Denver, 1987—; healthcare rep. Schering Corp., Morrison, Colo., 1989—. Republican. Baptist. Home: 21 Almond Dr Johnston RI 02919

KRONE, JULIE, jockey; b. Benton Harbor, Mich., July 24, 1963; d. Don and Judy Krone. Began as profl. jockey Tampa Bay (Fla.) Downs, 1980; leading woman jockey in U.S., 1986-88. Races won include Cornhusker Handicap, AK-Star-Ben racetrack, Omaha, 1988, Flower Bowl Handicap, Belmont Park, 1988, Modesty Stakes, Arlington Park, Ill., 1989, Budweiser Md. Classic, Pimlico, 1989. Office: care Jockeys' Guild 20 E 46th St New York NY 10017*

KRONENBERG, INEZ V., academic administrator, small business owner, genealogist, consultant; b. St. Cloud, Minn., Mar. 10, 1937; d. Barney V. and Crescentia M. (Hurrle) K. AA, St. Cloud State U., 1974, B in Elective Studies, 1979. Sec. to v.p. for acad. affairs St. Cloud (Minn.) State U., 1955-77, adminstrv. asst. to v.p. for acad. affairs, 1977-81, cataloging sect., learning resources, 1981-86, office mgr., ctr. for internat. studies, 1986-87, coord. employment opportunities, career libr., Ctr. Career Planning and Placement, 1988—; cons. Creative Memories, 1989—. Co-editor: (newsletter) Minn. Ednl. Sec., 1965-67; editor: (newsletter) Local 753, Am. Fedn. State, County and Mcpl. Employees, St. Cloud State U., 1980-83. Bd. dirs. Stearns County Hist. Soc., St. Cloud, 1988—; mem. Minn. Hist. Soc., St. Paul. Mem. AAUW, Nat. Assn. Ednl. Secs., Minn. Assn. Ednl. Office Personnel, St. Cloud Area Genealogists (pres. 1987—). Home: 1002 South 16 Ave Saint Cloud MN 56301-5236

KRONHOLM, LOUISE BAILEY, public relations executive; b. Boston, Dec. 16, 1934; d. John Moran and Barbara (Leary) Bailey; m. Conrad J. Kronholm, Nov. 7, 1959 (div. 1978); children: Eric, Justin, John, Bailey; m. John A. Carrozzella, 1990. BA, Marymount Coll., Tarrytown, N.Y., 1956; postgrad., Boston U. Sch. of Law, 1956-57, Conn. State U., New Britian, 1957-58. Lic. ins. broker. Agt. John Hancock Ins. Co., Rocky Hill, Conn., 1985--; special events coord. Hartford Arts Council, Conn., 1984--. Staff mem. Dukakis Campaign, Hartford, Conn., 1988; sec. Conn. Law Enforcement Found., 1980—; trustee U. of Conn. Bd. of Trustees, 1978—; pres Hartford Ballet, 1974; lobbyist Masonic Home and Hosp., 1989. Mem. World Affairs Ctr., University Club, Hartford Club, March of Dimes. Democrat. Roman Catholic. Home: 178 Longhill Rd Wallingford CT 06942

KRONNER, JOAN MARIE, sales professional; b. Balt., Nov. 29, 1960; d. Robert J. Sr. and Helen M. (Dee) K. BS, Towson (Md.) State U., 1983. Mem. coord. Electrolux Corp., Balt.; instr. in creative arts Balt. City Dept. Pks. and Recreation; owner Joan Marie Studio, Balt. Mem. Art Guild of Md. (recording sec.). Home: 2607 Evergreen Ave Baltimore MD 21214 Office: 6820 Eastern Ave Baltimore MD 21224

KRONSTAD-JUDGE, ELIZABETH, English educator; b. Ft. Benning, Ga., Nov. 11, 1948; d. Gudmund Havaard and Bettye Jean (Saylor) Kronstad; m. Lou Reed, Jan. 26, 1972 (div. 1972); m. Tim Judge, Nov. 22, 1975; children: Krista Gudrun, Samantha Anne. BPS, SUNY, SAratoga Springs, 1981; MS in Edn., Iona Coll., New Rochelle, 1986; student, Columbia U., 1967-69, No. Va. Community Coll., Alexandria, 1975-77. Stage/lighting dir./dir. The Lou Reed/U.S. and European Tours, 1972-74; ind. theatrical dir. Westchester, N.Y., 1978-84; profl. stage actress, 1974-84; edn. reporter The Chappaqua (N.Y.) Jour., 1983-84; theatre critic The Patent Trader Newspaper, Mt. Kisco, N.Y., 1983-85; film dir., editor Videography, New Rochelle, N.Y., 1983-85; tchr. English, speech Cardinal Spellman High Sch., Bronx, 1985-88; instr. English, theatre, communications Hunter Coll. High Sch., N.Y.C., 1988—; asst. prof. English Iona Coll., New Rochelle, 1987—; head English instr. Bronx Sci. Entrance Exams, Riverdale Jr. High Sch., 1987—; instr. N.Y. Bot. Gardens, The Children's Garden, Bronx, 1988—. Dir., editor film: The Last Mrs. Blakely, 1983; author poetry. Vol. The N.Y. Bot. Gardens, 1987-88; pres. Irvington Gardens Coop. Tenants Orgn., Irvington-on-Hudson, 1980-82. Mem. N.Y. State Alliance for Arts Edn., Nat. Council Tchrs. English, Stuyvesant Yacht Club. Democrat. Presbyterian. Home: 2320 Bronx Park E Bronx NY 10467

KROPAS, CLAUDIA VICTORIA, electronic engineer; b. Boston, Nov. 11, 1957; d. George C. and Virginia M. (Tuinila) K. BS in Applied Math., Fla. Inst. Technology, 1979; BEE, U. Dayton, 1984; MEE, Calif. State U.,

Sacramento, 1988. Cert. engr.-in-tng. Equipment design engr. So. Bell Telephone & Telegraph Co., Ft. Lauderdale, Fla., 1979-83; electronic engr. McClellan AFB, Sacramento, Calif., 1984-85; sr. engr. Aerojet Solid Propulsion Co., Sacramento, 1985-88; rsch. and devel. engr. Wright Rsch. and Devel. Ctr., Wright-Patterson AFB, Ohio, 1989—. Mem. IEEE, Soc. Women Engrs.

KROTH, JEANNIE MAE, nurse; b. Waverly, Ohio, May 3, 1944; d. Reginald Henry and Marjorie Ellen (Stephens) K. LPN, Shawnee State Community Coll., Portsmouth, Ohio, 1980, ADN, 1984. RN, Ohio. Supr., charge nurse Pike Community Hosp., Waverly; from nurse to staff nurse Am. Nursing Care, Columbus, Ohio; staff nurse Ross County Med. Ctr., Chillicothe, Ohio, Mercy Hosp., Portsmouth. Mem. Am. Legion, Phi Theta Kappa. Democrat. Baptist. Home: 98 Fish & Game Rd Waverly OH 45690

KROUSE, ANN WOLK, publishing executive; b. Chgo., Feb. 4, 1945; d. Barnett David and Shirley (Schwartz) Wolk; m. Paul Carl Krouse, Aug. 8, 1964; children: Amy Renee, Beth Diane, Joseph David, Katie Sue. Student, U. Miami, Fla., 1962. Ops. mgr. Playboy Club, Chgo., 1963-64; v.p. Ednl. Communications, Inc., Lake Forest, Ill., 1967—; bd. dirs. URT Industries, Inc., Hialeah Gardens, Fla., Peaches Entertainment Corp., Hialeah Gardens. Pub., co-editor (book) Who's Who Among Black Americans, 1976-88 (Outstanding Reference Book, 1976). Bd. dirs. scholarship found. Ednl. Communications, Inc., 1970—; mem. Jewish United Fund, 1970—, Mothers Against Drunk Driving, 1985—. Mem. Nat. Sch. Pub. Relations Assn., Ednl. Press Assn., Direct Mail Mktg. Assn., Lake Forest Open Lands Assn., Beaver Creek Country Club. Office: Ednl Communications Inc 721 N McKinley Rd Lake Forest IL 60045

KROUSE, DIANE MURRAY, advertising company executive; b. Far Rockaway, N.Y., May 24, 1954; d. Jan and Kathleen (Mann) Murray; m. David Allan Krouse, Oct. 10, 1982; children: Sarah Elizabeth, Michael Dean. BA, Stanford U., 1977. Promotion coord. Beetleboards Internat., L.A., 1977-78; account exec. RAP Communications, L.A., 1978-79; v.p., account supr. D'Arcy, Masius, Benton and Bowles, N.Y.C., 1979-85; sr. v.p., account group dir. D'Arcy, Masius, Benton and Bowles, Los Angeles, 1985—. Mem. Phi Beta Kappa. Home: 2256 Linnington Ave Los Angeles CA 90064 Office: D'Arcy Masius Benton & Bowles Inc 6500 Wilshire Blvd Ste 1000 Los Angeles CA 90048

KROUSKOP, JANICE LOUISE, registered dietitian; b. Pitts., Aug. 31, 1953; d. John William and Martha Sophie (Schmelz) Uncapher; m. Andrew C. Krouskop, June 28, 1975; children: Adam C., Ryan W. BS, Mansfield State Coll., 1974; MPH, U. Tex., Houston, 1979. Home econs. tchr. West View Jr. High Sch., Pitts., 1975; foods and nutrition tchr. Lincoln Sch., Camden, N.J., 1975-76; dietary supr. The Oaks Nursing Home, Wyncote, Pa., 1976-77; nutrition cons. Dairy Coun., Inc., Houston, 1979-81; nutrition instr. Carlow Coll., Pitts., 1981-83; nutrition instr. O'Hara Elem. Sch., Pitts., 1988-90. Classroom vol. O'Hara Elem. PTA, Pitts., 1988-90; activist Peace Links, Pitts., 1985—; deacon, moderator Fox Chapel Presbyn. Ch., 1988, elder, Christian edn. chair, 1990. Coll. scholar Order of Ea. Star, Pa., 1971. Mem. Am. Dietitic Assn. (registered dietitian), Pitts. Dietitic Assn., AAUW (pres. Fox Chapel Area br. 1989-91). Republican. Home: 218 Timber Ridge Rd Pittsburgh PA 15238

KROWN, SUSAN ELLEN, physician, researcher; b. Bronx, N.Y., Sept. 8, 1946; d. Frederick B. and Paula (Hauser) K.; m. Roger E. Pitt, May 18, 1980 (div. 1988); 1 child, Catherine Krown Pitt. AB, Barnard Coll., 1967; MD, SUNY, Bklyn., 1971. Diplomate Am. Bd. Internal Medicine. Intern, then jr. and sr. resident in internal medicine Mt. Sinai Hosp., N.Y.C., 1971-74; with Meml. Sloan-Kettering Cancer Ctr., N.Y.C., 1974—, assoc. mem., 1984—; clin. asst. Meml. Hosp., N.Y.C., 1977-78, asst. attending physician, 1978-82, assoc. attending physician, 1982—; asst. prof. Med. Coll. Cornell U., N.Y.C., 1977-83; assoc. prof. Med. Coll. Cornell U., N.Y.C., 1983—; mem. oncologic drugs adv. com. FDA, Rockville, Md., 1986—; chair oncology com. AIDS Clin. Trials Group, Bethesda, Md., 1990—. Mem. editorial bd. Jour. Interferon Rsch., 1985—, Jour. AIDS, 1988—; contbr. numerous articles to profl. jours. NIH Rsch. grantee; Am. Cancer Soc. Jr. Faculty fellow, 1978-81. Mem. Internat. Soc. for Inteferon Rsch. (coun. 1986—), Soc. for Biol. Therapy (bd. dirs. 1987-89), AIDS Task Force (chair Meml. Sloan Kettering Cancer Ctr. 1989—). Office: Meml Sloan Kettering Ctr 1275 York Ave New York NY 10021

KRPATA, ANNE MARIE, legal administrator; b. Jamaica, N.Y., July 7, 1933; d. Edmund August and Anna (Green) Merwede; m. Raymond John Krpata, Sept. 9, 1951; children: Elizabeth Ann, Douglas. BA, SUNY, Farmingdale, N.Y., 1961. Office mgr. Bros. Coach Corp., Hewlett, N.Y., 1959-70; controller Karey Products, Plainview, N.Y., 1970-77; adminstr., controller Jerry Schultz Co., Bayshore, N.Y., 1977-81; adminstr. dir. McLaughlin & Stern Ballen & Ballen, N.Y.C., 1981-86; fin. and adminnstrn. dir. Gallagher & Gosseen, Mineola, N.Y., 1986—. Mem. ABA, Nat. Assn. Legal Adminstrs. (founder, pres. L.I. chpt. 1987-89). Office: Gallagher & Gosseen 190 Willis Ave Mineola NY 11501

KRUEGER, BETTY JANE, telecommunication company executive; b. Indpls., Oct. 4, 1923; d. Forrest Glen and Hazel Luellen (Taylor) Burns; student Butler U., 1948-49; m. Alan Douglas Krueger, Apr. 4, 1975; 1 son by previous marriage—Michael J. Vornehm. Supr., instr. Ind. Bell Telephone Co., Indpls., 1941-54; supr. communications Jones & Laughlin Steel Co., Indpls., 1954-56, Ford Motor Co., Indpls., 1956-64, U.S. Govt., Camp Atterbury, Ind., 1964-66; dir. communications Meth. Hosp. of Ind., Indpls., 1966-79; pres. owner Rent-A-Radio, Inc. of Ind., Indpls., after 1979; sec.-treas. Communications Unltd., Inc. Former pres. Am. Legion Aux.; chmn. for Ind., Girls State U.S.A., 1972-77; probation officer vol., 1973-74; suicide prevention counselor, 1972-73. Recipient award for outstanding community service Ford Motor Co., 1961. Mem. Am. Soc. Hosp. Engring., Am. Hosp. Assn., Nat. Assn. Bus. and Ednl. Radio, Inc., Internat. Teletypewriters for the Deaf, Asso. Public Safety Communications Officers, Inc., Am. Bus. Women. Methodist. Home: RR 2 Box 119 Franklin IN 46131 Office: 4032 Southeastern Ave Indianapolis IN 46203

KRUEGER, BONNIE LEE, editor, writer; b. Chgo., Feb. 3, 1950; d. Harry Bernard and Lillian (Soyak) Krueger; m. James Lawrence Spurlock, Mar. 8, 1972. Student Morraine Valley Coll., 1970. Adminstrv. asst. Carson Pirie Scott & Co., Chgo., 1969-72; traffic coordinator Tatham Laird & Kudner, Chgo., 1973-74; traffic coordinator J. Walter Thompson, Chgo., 1974-76; prodn. coordinator, 1976-78; editor-in-chief Assoc. Pubs., Chgo., 1978—; editor-in-chief Sophisticate's Hairstyle Guide, 1978—, Sophisticates Beauty Guide, 1978—, Complete Woman, 1981—; pub., editorial services dir. Sophisticate's Black Hair Guide, 1983—. Mem. Statue of Liberty Restoration Com., N.Y.C., 1983; campaign worker Cook County State's Atty., Chgo., 1982; poll watcher Cook County Dem. Orgn., 1983. Mem. Soc. Profl. Journalists, Nat. Assn. Female Execs., Am. Health and Beauty Aids Inst. (assoc. mem.), Sigma Delta Chi. Lutheran. Clubs: Sierra, Cousteau Soc. Office: Complete Woman 1165 N Clark St Chicago IL 60610

KRUEGER, CARYL WALLER, author, lecturer; b. Chgo., Apr. 1, 1929; d. Thomas Floyd and Astrid Alvina (Johnson) W.; m. Cliff W. Krueger, Aug. 11, 1951; children: Chris, Carrie, Cameron. BS, Northwestern U., 1950; postgrad., U. Chgo., 1951, U. Calif., 1971-73. Account exec. Advt. Div., Inc., Chgo., 1952-60, W. S. Meyers Co., Honolulu, 1961-70, Caryl Krueger Assocs., Honolulu, 1963-68; ind lectr. on parent-child relationships, time mgmt., 1969—. Author: Six Weeks to Better Parenting, 1981, 2d edit., 1985, 1001 Things To Do With Your Kids, 1988; contbr. articles to Parade, Sunset, Parents, L.A. Times, C.S. Monitor, other publs. Pres. Oahu League Republican Women, Honolulu, 1968-69, Community Concert Assn., Rancho Santa Fe, Calif., 1983. Named Writer of Yr., Chgo. Advt. Club, 1959, Woman of Yr., Panhellenic Hawaii, 1968; recipient service award Camp Fire Girl Council, Honolulu. Mem. Women in Communications (pres. Honolulu chpt. 1968), Pen Women, AAUW, Phi Beta, Alpha Omicron Pi (pres. Honolulu chpt. 1963). Christian Scientist. Home and Office: 28455 Meadow Mesa Ln Escondido CA 92026

KRUEGER, CATHERINE ANNE, food scientist; b. Michigan City, Ind., June 10, 1961; d. Joseph Thomas and Rose Marie (Linde) K. BA in Microbiology, Miami U., Oxford, Ohio, 1983; postgrad., Purdue U., 1984-86. Assoc. food scientist T.J. Lipton, Inc., Englewood Cliffs, N.J., 1986—. Mem. Inst. Food Technologists. Democrat. Roman Catholic.

KRUEGER, KATHERINE KAMP, lawyer; b. Chgo., Apr. 7, 1944; d. Rudolph Pollay and Josephine Yvette (Marland) Kamp. Student U. Paris, Sorbonne, 1963-64; B.S. magna cum laude, Tulane U., 1965, M.S., 1968; J.D., Northwestern U., 1980. Bar: Tex. 1980, Ill. 1988. Micropaleontologist, Gulf Oil Corp., New Orleans, 1967-68; custodian collections geology Field Mus., Chgo., 1968-76, lectr., 1975-76; lectr. earth sci. Northeastern Ill. U., Chgo., 1977; atty. oil and gas Gulf Oil Corp., Houston, 1980-81, Amoco Prodn. Co., Houston, 1981-87, atty. environ. law Amoco Corp., Chgo., 1987—; atty. litigation Amoco Prodn. Co., Houston, 1989—; bd. dirs. The Eureka Soc., Escondido, Calif., 1974—; vol. lectr. Desk and Derrick, Houston, 1983. Contbr. articles to profl. jours. Campaign vol., poll watcher Ind. Democratic candidate for Ill. Constl. Conv., Chgo., 1968; poll watcher Ind. Democratic candidate for Ill. Rep., Chgo., 1978; del. Dem. Senatorial Dist. 7 Conv., Tex., 1984. NSF Student grantee microbiol. dept. U. Miami Marine Lab., 1960-64; grantee La. Heart Found., Sophie Newcomb Coll. Botany Dept., 1962-63, Grad. Sch. Tulane U. Scholars and Fellows Orgn., 1965-66; named Steinmayer Best Geol. Student, Tulane U., 1965; Houston Bar Found. fellow, 1982—. Mem. ABA, State Bar Tex., Houston Bar Assn., Chgo. Bar Assn., Ill. State Bar Assn., Phi Beta Kappa, Sigma Gamma Epsilon, Eta Sigma Phi. Home: 14027 Memorial Dr #255 Houston TX 77079

KRUEGER, MICHELLE MARY, copywriter; b. Hammond, Ind., June 18, 1963; d. Donald Michael Linos and Judith Ann (Gantenbein) Daniels; m. David Mark Krueger, Aug. 23, 1985; 1 child, Megan Norma. BA, Purdue U., 1985. Office asst. Chicago mag. Sta. WFMT Inc., 1985-86; assoc. Communications for Mgmt., Chgo., 1986-87; copywriter Bus. One Irwin, formerly Dow Jones-Irwin, Homewood, Ill., 1987-88, sr. copywriter, 1988—. Mem. Direct Mktg. Assn., Chgo. Assn. Direct Mktg., Nat. Wildlife Fedn. Home: 2055 W 183d St Homewood IL 60430 Office: Business One Irwin 1818 Ridge Rd Homewood IL 60430

KRUEGER, NANCY ASTA, physical therapist; b. Manhattan Beach, Calif., Jan. 8, 1947; d. Henry Adolph and Asta Ida (Harrison) Graef; m. Gary Patrick Krueger, June 14, 1969. Student, Lewis & Clark Coll., 1964-66; BS, U. So. Calif., L.A., 1969; postgrad., U. So. Calif., Downey, 1980-81. Staff phys. therapist Los Angeles County-U. So. Calif. Med. Ctr., L.A., 1969-71, Stockton (Calif.) State Hosp., 1971; pediatric phys. therapist Calif. Childrens Svcs.-San Joaquin County, Stockton, 1972-73; sr. phys. therapist Calif. Childrens Svcs.-San Diego County, San Diego, 1974-80; mng. dir. therapy svcs. Sharp-Cabrillo Hosp., San Diego, 1981-83; sr. phys. therapist El Cajon (Calif.) Valley Hosp., 1983-84; prin. El Cajon Therapy Assocs., 1984—; cons. Teledyne Ryan Aero., San Diego County, 1984—; speaker in field. Singer Old Globe Madrigal Singers, 1983; vice chair adv. com. Maternal, Child and Adolescent Health, San Diego County, 1987-89; active local polit. campaigns. Fellow Am. Acad. Sports Medicine, Orthopedic Soc.; mem. Juniors of Social Svc., Soroptimist Internat. (sec. El Cajon chpt. 1982), Am. Phys. Therapy Assn. (chmn. Dan Diego dist. 1977-78, bd. dirs. Calif. chpt. 1983-84, mem. nominating com. 1989—), Aux. Am. Optometric Assn. Democrat. Episcopalian. Home: 4657 Rancho Park Ave San Diego CA 92120 Office: El Cajon Therapy Assocs 416 S Magnolia Ave El Cajon CA 92020

KRUEGLER, NANCY ALICE, association executive; b. Troy, N.Y., Dec. 27, 1946; d. Theodore M. and Marjorie M. (James) Pszeniczny; m. Dennis Michael Kruegler, May 11, 1947; children: Laura Margaret, Julie Jean. AA, Albany (N.Y.) Bus. Coll., 1966. Mgr. accounts payable Standard-Rosenbaum, Inc., Latham, N.Y., 1966-75; comptroller Sign-Pro Corp., Watervliet, N.Y., 1975-85; exec. dir. Latham Area C. of C., Latham, N.Y., 1985—. Mem. North Colonie Sch. Dist. substance com., Latham, 1985-88; bd. dirs. Cohoes Commerce & Ind., Cohoes, N.Y., 1983-85; chmn. Consumer Protection Bd., Colonie, 1986—. Mem. Latham Bus. and Profl. Assn. Office: Latham Area C of C 849 New London Rd Latham NY 12110

KRUG, JUDITH FINGERET, association administrator; b. Pitts., Mar. 15, 1940; d. David and Florence (Leiber) Fingeret; m. E. Herbert Krug, Oct. 12, 1963; children: Steven, Michelle. BA in Polit. Theory, U. Pitts., 1961; MA, U. Chgo., 1964. Reference librarian John Crerar Library, Chgo., 1962-63; cataloguer dental sch. libr. Northwestern U., Chgo., 1963-65; rsch. analyst ALA, Chgo., 1965-67, dir. Office Intellectual Freedom, 1967—; exec. dir. Freedom to Read Found., Chgo., 1969—; mem. com. on pub. understanding about the law ABA, Chgo. 1985—. Editor Newsletter on Intellectual Freedom, 1970—, Freedom to Read Found. News, 1972—; exec. producer (film) The Speaker, 1977 (Silver Cindy award 1978, Silver Screen award 1979). Recipient Irita Van Doren Book award Am. Booksellers Assn., 1976, Robert B. Downs award U. Ill., Champaign-Urbana, 1978, Carl Sandburg Freedom to Read award Friends Chgo. Pub. Libr., 1983. Mem. ALA, Phi Beta Kappa (assoc., exec. commn. Chgo. area 1980—). Office: ALA Office for Intellectual Freedom 50 E Huron St Chicago IL 60611

KRUG, KAREN-ANN, healthcare financial executive, accountant; b. Riverdale, N.D., Apr. 22, 1951; d. C. and Elsie (Eide) K.; m. C. Scott James, Aug. 19, 1978. BS, N.D. State U., 1980. CPA, Calif. Mgr. proof transit 1st Nat. Bank Grand Forks (N.D.); sr. acct. Leo E. Bell & Assocs., Grand Forks, 1978-80; dir. project rev. Agassiz Health Systems Agy., Grand Forks, 1980-82; sr. adminstrv. asst. St. Mary's Hosp., Reno; dir. planning and devel. St. Mary's Health Care Corp., Reno, 1982-87; contr. Pacific Presbyn. Med. Ctr., San Francisco, 1987-89; corp. contr. Daughters of Charity Nat. Healthcare System Seton Med. Ctr., Daly City, Calif., 1989-. Vol. Jr. Achievement, Reno, 1984-87, Project Literacy U.S., San Francisco, 1987-88. Mem. AICPA, Calif. Soc. CPA's (healthcare com. 1989—), Healthcare Fin. Mgmt. Assn., Am. Mgmt. Assn. Office: Seton Med Ctr 1900 Sullivan Ave Daly City CA 94015

KRUGER, JOANN, construction executive; b. N.Y.C., Mar. 18, 1930; d. Joseph and Madeline (Masiello) Suozzo; m. Nicholas Kruger, Dec. 7, 1952; children: Gerard, Laura Kruger. Pvt. practice interior design N.Y.C., 1965-71; interior designer, constrn. exec. N. Kruger Inc., Nassau, N.Y., 1971-84; constrn. exec. Janco Constrn. Inc., Nassau, 1984—. Mem. Rep. Senatorial Inner Circle, James Beard Found. Mem. Women in Constrn. Roman Catholic. Home: 445 Centre Island Rd Oyster Bay NY 11771

KRULWICH, TERRY ANN, biochemistry researcher; b. N.Y.C., Apr. 7, 1943; d. Lester S. and Beatrice (Cohen) K.; m. S. Paul Posner, June 10, 1973; children: Jeremy Michael, Adam Jared, Amos Allen. BA, Goucher Coll., 1964; MS, U. Wis., 1966, PhD, 1968; DSc (hon.), Goucher Coll., 1987. Postdoctoral fellow in molecular biology Albert Einstein Coll. Medicine, Bronx, 1968-70; asst. prof. biochemistry Mount Sinai Sch. Medicine of CUNY, N.Y.C., 1970-74, assoc. prof., 1974-81, prof. biochemistry, 1981—, dean, grad. sch. biol. sci., 1981—; mem. cellular and molecular com., basis of disease review com NIH, 1978-81, mem. microbiology, physiololgy and genetics study sect., 1983-87. Editor: The Bacteria, Vol. XII, 1990; editorial bd. Jour. Bacteriology, 1985-90, Microbiol. Reviews, 1983-88. Trustee Ramaz Sch., N.Y.C., 1981—. Predoctoral fellowship NSF, 1964-70; recipient Rsch. Career Devel. award NIH, 1975-80. Mem. Am. Soc. Microbiology (div. chmn. physiol. 1990-91), Am. Soc. for Biochemistry and Molecular Biology, Biophys. Soc., N.Y. Acad. Scis., Harvey Soc. Office: Dept Biochem Mt Sinai Sch 1 Gustave L Levy Pl Box 1020 New York NY 10029

KRUMHOLTZ, CHERYL LYNN, computer operations administrator; b. Dayton, Ohio, Mar. 13, 1966; d. Charles Frances Krumholtz and Mary Patricia (Bruggeman) Reece. Student, U. Dayton, 1984, Wright State U., Dayton, 1985; BS, U. S.C., 1988. With customer svc. Lofino's Inc., Beavercreek, Ohio, 1983-86; acctg. asst. Danis Industries Corp., Dayton, Ohio, 1986, State Printing Co., Columbia, S.C., 1986-87; adminstr. computer ops. Bobbin Blenheim Inc., Columbia, 1987—. Mem. NAFE. Roman Catholic. Home: 646 Holland Circle West Columbia SC 29169 Office: Bobbin Blenheim Inc 1110 Shop Rd Columbia SC 29201

KRUPKA, TINA MARIE, account executive; b. Syracuse, N.Y., Sept. 23, 1961; d. Ronald Walter and Joan Eileen (Staerker) K. Student, U. Coll., Syracuse, N.Y., 1987. With Syracuse Newspaper, 1978—, sales rep., acct. exec., 1986—. Fellow NOW; mem. Alpha Sigma Lambda. Democrat. Roman Catholic. Office: Syracuse Newspapers 1 Clinton Sq Syracuse NY 13202

KRUPNICK, WENDY SUSAN, labor union representative; b. Phila., Apr. 28, 1965; d. Harry and Diane G. (Gottfried) K. BA, Temple U., 1988. Rep., photo editor United Food and Comml. Workers Local 1776, Norristown, Pa., 1988—. Active in Variety Club annual charity drive. Mem. NAFE, Internat. Labor Commmunication Assn., Pa. Labor Communication Assn., AFL-CIO Bucks County Labor Coun. Democrat. Jewish. Home: 1371 Abbey Way Bensalem PA 19020 Office: UFCW Local 1776 3031 Walton Rd Ste 210 Norristown PA 19401

KRUPNIK, VEE M., business executive; b. Chgo.; d. Phillip and Jane (Glickman) K.; m. Melvin Drury, Sept. 24, 1978. B.S., Northwestern U., C.P.A., cert. fin. planner, real estate broker, ins. broker, Ill. Assoc. dir. corp. fin. Weis, Voisin, Cannon, Chgo., 1967-68; pres. PEC Industries Inc., Ft. Lauderdale, Fla., 1969-71; acct., real estate and ins. broker Vee M. Krupnik & Co., Chgo., 1971-73; sales cons. Baird & Warner Inc., Chgo., 1973-81, asst. v.p. comml.-investment div., 1981-85, v.p. corp. group, 1985-89; comml./investment specialist, 1990—. Mem. Internat. Assn. Fin. Planning (bd. dirs. 1985-87), Internat. Council Shopping Ctrs., Nat. Assn. Corp. Real Estate Execs., Nat. Assn. Securities Dealers, Women's Exec. Network, Nat. Assn. Realtors (bd. dirs. 1983-84, comml. investment council), Cert. Comml. Investment Mems. (pres. Ill. chpt. 1983-84), Ill. Assn. Realtors (bd. dirs. 1983-84), Chgo. Bd. Realtors (bd. dirs. 1982-85, 88—), Chgo. Assn. Commerce and Industry, Comml. Investment Multiple Listing Service (pres. 1982-84), Comml. Real Estate Orgn., Network of Women Entrepreneurs, Chgo. Real Estate Exec. Women. Home: 5757 N Sheridan Rd #7A Chicago IL 60660 Office: Baird & Warner Inc 4040 N Lincoln Ave Chicago IL 60618

KRUPP, IRIS MARIE, dermatologist, educator; b. New Orleans, May 1, 1928; d. Philip J. and Ione M. (White) K.; m. Robert E. Post, Sept. 14, 1978. BS, La. State U., 1948; MS, Tulane U., 1955, PhD, 1958, MD, 1971. Resident in dermatology Tulane Med. Ctr., 1973-76; from rsch. asst. to asst. prof. parasitology Tulane U., New Orleans, 1949-65, assoc. prof. psychiatry, neurology and tropical medicine, 1966-76; clin. assoc. prof. dermatology Tulane Med. Ctr., New Orleans, 1977—; pvt. practice dermatology, 1976; pvt. practice dermatology, 1976—; prin. investigator amebiasis rsch. project Cali, Colombia and Durban, South Africa, 1959-67; rsch., edn. assoc. VA Hosp., New Orleans, 1972-73; mem. ad hoc study group on parasitic diseases U.S. Army Med. Rsch. and Devel. Command Walter Reed Army Inst. Rsch., 1973-75, cons. parasitic diseases, 1975-76; cons. tropical diseases Surgeon Gen. U.S., 1973-76; instr. parasitology U. Mich., summer 1954, 55; investigator outbreak amebic dysentery, Barquisimeto, Venezuela. Contbr. articles to profl. jours. Mem. Internat. Soc. for Dermatologic Surgery, Internat. Soc. for Study Vulvar Disease, Am. Acad. Dermatology, Am. Soc. for Dermatologic Surgery, So. Med. Assn., La. State Med. Soc. (del. 1984), Jefferson Parish Med. Soc. Republican. Roman Catholic. Office: Krupp Derm Clinic 3601 Houma Blvd Metairie LA 70006

KRUPP, MARGARET ANN, marketing executive; b. Racine, Wis., May 30, 1956; d. Leslie John and Ruth Margaret (Graham) Kroupa; m. Daniel Robert Krupp, June 18, 1977; 1 child, Andrew Robert. BS in Chem. Process Engring. with honors, U. Wis, 1978; MBA in Mktg. and Fin. with honors, Northwestern U., 1983. Registered profl. engr. Chem. engr., R&D div. S.C. Johnson & Son, Inc., Racine, Wis., 1978-79, safety coord., R&D div, 1979-80, quality assurance shift mgr., R&D div., 1980-83, sr. engr., mfg. div., 1983-84, asst./assoc. product mgr., home care div., 1984-87, staff engr., mfg. div., 1987-89; mgr. pricing and programing J.I. Case Co., Racine, Wis., 1989-90; sr. process engr. Abbott Labs., Inc., North Chicago, Ill., 1990—. Mem. Am. Inst. of Chem. Engrs., Tau Beta Pi. Home: 34235 Russet St Burlington WI 53105 Office: J I Case Co 700 State St Racine WI 53403

KRUSE, ANN GRAY, computer programmer; b. Oklahoma City, Jan. 4, 1941; d. Floyd and Bernice Florence (Follansbee) Gray; A.B., Randolph Macon Woman's Coll., 1963; M.B.A., U. Chgo., 1973; m. Roy Edwin Kruse, Mar. 20, 1971 (dec.). Programming mgr. Ind. Info. Controls, Valparaiso, Ind., 1966-67; systems programmer Nat. Bus. Lists, Inc., Chgo., 1968-69, Am. Steel Foundries, Hammond, Ind., 1970-73; engr. applications programming Bell Helicopter Textron, Fort Worth, 1974-76; lead systems programmer Harris Data Communications, Dallas, 1976-81; sr. systems programmer Lone Star Gas Co., Dallas, 1981-82; sr. software specialist E-Systems, Dallas, 1982—. Republican. Episcopalian. Home: 6128 Blackberry Ln Dallas TX 75248 Office: PO Box 660023 Dallas TX 75266

KRUSE, DONNA HYNES, engineer consultant; b. Phila., Dec. 4, 1956; d. John Francis, Jr. and Aldonna Theresa Ulbinsky Hynes; m. Steven Matthew Kruse, June 25, 1983; children: Christina Marie, Adam Elliott. BS in Mech. Engring., Drexel U., 1979. Registered mech. engr., Tex. Mech. engr. Naval Ship Systems Engring. Station, Phila., 1979-81; instrumentation engr. Day & Zimmermann, Inc., Engring. & Construction Div., Phila., 1981-83; sr. mech. engr. Day & Zimmerman, Inc., Lone Star Div., Texarkana, Tex., 1983-90; prin. Kruse, Taylor & Van Horn, 1990—; instr. Drexel U., Phila., 1982. Unit sec. Sacred Heart Ch. Women's Soc., Texarkana, Tex., 1988—. Recipient Distinguished Svc. award ASME, Phila., 1979. Mem. ASHRAE, MENSA, Tex. Soc. Profl. engrs., Cath. Daughters of Am. Home: 19 Lanshire Dr Texarkana TX 75503 Office: Kruse Taylor & Van Horn 2222 Hampton Rd Texarkana TX 75503

KRUSE, JAN CECILE, nurse; b. Ft. Madison, Iowa, May 31, 1959; d. Herman Joseph and Cecilia Elizabeth (Mehmert) K. BSN, Marycrest Coll., 1981; postgrad. studies in nursing, Tex. Womens U., 1989—. RN. Staff nurse Franciscan Med. Ctr., Rock Island, Ill., 1981-83; staff rn St. Paul Med. Ctr., Dallas, 1983—; orthopedic nurse clinician St Paul Med. Ctr., Dallas, 1989—. Mem. Nat. Assn. Orthopaedic Nurses (rsch. com. 1989—), Dallas Orthopaedic Nurses Assn., Tex. Soc. Health Care Edn. Republican. Roman Catholic. Home: 2240 E Trinity Mills Rd 421 Carrollton TX 75006

KRUSE, PAMELA JEAN, lawyer; b. Miami, Fla., June 3, 1950; d. Robert Emil and Irma G. Kruse. BS, Mich. State U., 1973, MA, 1975, PhD, 1979; JD, U. Mich., 1985. Bar: Mich. 1986. Grad. asst. Mich. State U., East Lansing, 1976-77, asst. intramural dir., 1977-79, labor rels. rep., 1979-81, asst. dir. labor rels., 1981-82; resident mgr. 719 Oakland, Ann Arbor, Mich., 1982-83; rsch. asst. Law Sch. U. Mich., Ann Arbor, 1982-85; jud. clk. U.S. Dist. Ct. (we. dist.) Mich., 1985-86; assoc. Clary, Nantz, Wood, Hoffius, Rankin & Cooper, Grand Rapids, Mich., 1986—. Bd. dirs. Babe Zaharias Golf Tournament, Am. Cancer Soc., 1987—. Recipient Gold and Silver medals U.S. Pan Am. Team, Winnipeg, Man., Can., 1967, Silver medal U.S. Olympic Team, Mexico City, 1968; holder world records swimming 400 meters freestyle, 1967, 200 meters freestyle, 1967, 440-yard freestyle, 1966; inducted to Greater Fort Lauderdale Sports Hall of Fame, 1979. Mem. ABA, State Bar Mich. (exec. coun. young lawyers sect. 1987—), Grand Rapids Bar Assn. (chairperson, exec. bd. dirs. young lawyers sect. 1987—), Mich. Pub. Employer Labor Rels. Assn. (bd. dirs. 1981-82, chmn. manual revision com. 1982), Mich. State U. Alumni Assn. (2d v.p., bd. dirs. 1988—), U.S. Olympians, Phi Delta Kappa, Kappa Alpha Theta. Office: Clary Nantz Wood et al 500 Calder Plaza Bldg Grand Rapids MI 49503

KRUSE, STEPHANIE SHERYL, hospital administrator; b. George, Iowa, July 28, 1956; d. Harold J. and Dena Laura (Kanengieter) K.; m. Craig N. Schriber, Sept. 16, 1989. Grad., St. Luke's Hosp. Nursing Sch., Sioux City, Iowa, 1977; BA in Journalism, Augustana Coll., Sioux Falls, S.D., 1980; postgrad. in bus., U. Nev., 1985—. RN, S.D. Charge nurse Good Samaritan Ctr., Sioux Falls, 1977-79; pub. rels. intern McKennan Hosp., Sioux Falls, 1979-80; dir. pub. rels. St. Luke's Hosp., Aberdeen, S.D., 1980-82; head pub. rels. dept. St. Mary's Hosp., Reno, 1983-85; dir. community rels. and market-sales St. Mary's Health Care Corp., Reno, 1985—; mem. pub. rels. adv. com. U. Nev., Reno, 1988—. Com. chmn. Am. Cancer Soc., Reno, 1986—; bd. dirs. Reno Little Theater, 1988—, also past pres. Recipient gold award for advt. Healthcare Mktg. Report, 1986, 88. Mem. Internat. Assn. Bus. Communicators (pres. local chpt. 1987, Silver award dist. 6, 1985), Am. Mktg. Assn. (bd. dirs. local chpt. 1989—), Am. Soc. for Hosp. Mktg. and Pub.

Rels. (coun. dist. 9, 1984—), Nev. Hosp. Assn. (chmn. pub. rels. com. 1989—), Reno C. of C. (speaker's bur. 1988—), Rotary (bd. dirs.). Office: St Mary's Support Svcs 1155 W 4th St Ste 222 Reno NV 89503

KRUSE, VIRGINIA GILDA, financial officer; b. N.Y.C., Aug. 20, 1921; d. Domenick and Katherine (Rauch) Capuozzo; m. Robert J. Kruse, Oct. 11, 1953. BS, NYU, 1946. Fin. officer Gen. Trade Mark, Labelcraft Inc., Staten Island, N.Y.; tchr. Washington Sch. for Secs., N.Y.C. Bd. dirs. Jaques Marchais Tibetan Mus., Alice Austen House, Inc. Mem. S.I. Bus. and Profl. Women's Assn., AAUW. Home: 710 Oakland Ave Staten Island NY 10310

KRUSHENICK, FRANCES HARRIET, preschool educator; b. N.Y.C., May 21, 1930; d. Herman and Goldie (Epstein) Greenberg; m. John Krushenick, June 1, 1957; children: Andra, Joshua, Jevon. MA, Bank St. Coll. Edn., N.Y.C., 1953. Cert. early childhood edn. tchr., N.Y., N.J. Dir. Little Village Nursery Sch., N.Y.C., 1964-68, Bklyn. Heights (N.Y.) Community Nursery Sch., 1968-72, Lakeshore Presch., Milw., 1973-75; tchr. Cresent Ave. Ch., Fort Wayne, Ind., 1977-79, Temple Emanual Nursery Sch., N.Y.C., 1980-83; dir. Univ. Plaza Nursery Sch., N.Y.C., 1983—. Mem. Nat. Assn. for Edn. Young Children. Office: Univ Plaza Nursery Sch 110 Bleecker St New York NY 10012

KRUSIE, KATHLEEN ROSE, hospital administrator; b. Monticello, Iowa, Mar. 2, 1960; d. John Jerome and Ruth Ann (Muller) Welter; m. Steven Robert Krusie, Aug. 13, 1983; children: Megan Elise, Jason Robert. BA in Zoology, U. Iowa, 1982, MA in Hosp. and Health Adminstrn., 1984. Rsch. asst. Ctr. for Health Svcs. Rsch., Iowa City, 1983; mgmt. assoc. Blue Cross/Blue Shield Iowa, Des Moines, 1983-84, coord., 1985, adminstr., 1985-88; human resources coord. Mercy Hosp., Iowa City, 1988-89; asst. adminstr. Mercy Med. Ctr., Cedar Rapids, Iowa, 1989—. Pres. Sunday sch. class for married couples St. Paul's United Meth. Ch., Cedar Rapids, 1989—, mem. parish rels. com., 1990—. Mem. Nat. Mgmt. Assn. (bd. dirs. Cedar Rapids Met. chpt. 1989-90), Am. Coll. Healthcare Execs., Profl. Womens Network. Home: 3940 Falbrook Dr NE Cedar Rapids IA 52402 Office: Mercy Med Ctr 701 10th St SE Cedar Rapids IA 52402

KRY, REBECCA RIDLEY, foundation administrator; b. Nashville, Dec. 10, 1939; d. Edward Clarke and E. Carlene (Tanner) R.; m. Stig A. Kry, June 10, 1984; children from previous marriage: Carlton C. Rochell Jr., Anne Leslie Rochell. BA, U. So. Miss., 1963. Officer for spl. resources N.Y. Pub. Libr., N.Y.C., 1977-80; v.p. devel. Phoenix House Found., N.Y.C., 1980-85; exec. dir. Damon Runyon-Walter Winchell Cancer Fund, N.Y.C., 1985—. Mem. Women in Fin. Devel. Democrat. Episcopalian. Home: 333 E 68th St New York NY 10021 Office: Damon Runyon Walter Winchell Cancer Fund 131 E 36th St New York NY 10016

KRYGEL, BARBARA A., Small business owner; b. Detroit, Mich., Apr. 30, 1947; d. Joseph Stanley and Clara (Kolodziejczak) Kleczkowski; m. Kenneth Edward, May 03, 1968; children: Carolyn, Kevin. BS, Wayne State, Detroit, 1965, U. Cen. Mich., 1985; Masters in Edn., George Wash. U., 1986. Destination Specialist Inst. of Cert. Tvl. Wellesley Mass, 1988. Tchr. Our Lady Queen of Apostles, Hamtramck, Mich., 1966-67; supr. N Cen. Airlines, Detroit, 1967-71; regional training coordinator Republic Airlines, N. Cen. region, 1971-79; ops. mgr. NW Airlines, Livonia; Inst. Travel Edn. Inst., Southfield, 1979--; owner, pres. Travel Text Assocs., 1979--, Travel Industry Placement Serv., Southfield, 1986--, Travel Edn. Inst., southfield, 1986--; Regional Coordinator Inst. Certified Tvl Agents Southfield Mich., 1986. Author: Textbooks, Ticketing Series 1981, Quick Ticketing Guide, 1982, Co-Author: 15 books in Tvl Agent Series, 1988; Editor: 15 additional Books. ACE Score-Small Bus. Assn. Mem. Soc. Travel and Tourism Educators (sec., treas. 1986-89), Am. Soc. Travel Agts., Detroit Women's Travel Orgn. (Woman of Yr. 1984).

KRYNICKI, MARGARET, personnel director; b. Long Beach, Calif., Nov. 8, 1953; d. Thaddeus S. and Winifred (Kirwan) Krynicki. BA, Calif. State U.-Long Beach, 1976, MA, 1982; postgrad. U. So. Calif. Human resources asst. TRW ISD, Long Beach, 1976-78; personnel adminstr. Mattel, Inc., Hawthorne, Calif., 1978-79, TRW Elec. & Def., Redondo Beach, Calif., 1979-82; employee rels. specialist, employee rels. mgr., dir. indsl. rels. Rockwell Internat./NAA, El Segundo, Calif., 1982-89; dir. pers. Blue Shield Calif., 1989—. Mem. Nat. Mgmt. Assn., Mensa. Office: Blue Shield Calif 6701 Center Dr W Los Angeles CA 90045

KRYSINSKI, LINDA ANN, editorial office supervisor; b. Pitts., Feb. 24, 1957; d. Arthur Anthony and Patricia Ann (Balzer) K. BFA, Carnegie Mellon U., 1979. Systems adminstr. Duncan, Lagnese & Assocs. (now known as Killam Assocs.), Pitts., 1979-86; editorial office supr. Materials Rsch. Soc., Pitts., 1986—; part-time corr. Pitts. Post-Gazette, 1990—; freelance corr. Pitts. Post-Gazette, 1990—. Mem. North Hills Jaycees (Jaycee of Month 1989, Jaycee of Quarter 1990; chmn. project of the year 1989), Nat. Wildlife Fedn., Greenpeace. Republican. Roman Catholic. Home: 121 Hillcrest Dr Pittsburgh PA 15237 Office: Materials Rsch Soc 9800 McKnight Rd Pittsburgh PA 15237

KRZYZAN, JUDY LYNN, automotive executive; b. Buffalo, Sept. 1, 1951; d. James Lambert and Janet Lucille (Grabau) McKellar; m. Ronald Edward Krzyzan, Dec. 21, 1974 (div. Jan. 1989); 1 child, Brian Edward. Student, Erie Community Coll., 1969-70. With counter and delivery M & H Auto Supply, Orchard Park, N.Y., 1973-75; parts counter person Crest Dodge Inc., Orchard Park, 1975-81; parts mgr. Case Chrysler Plymouth, Hamburg, N.Y., 1981-87, Mancuso Chrysler Plymouth, Hamburg, 1987—; supr. Profl. Inventory Assn., N.H., 1976-85. Mem. Chrysler Parts and Svc. Mgrs. Guild (v.p., sec. 1986-87, 89—), The Greater Buffalo Auto Body Guild. Home: 2801 Southcreek Rd Hamburg NY 14075 Office: Mancuso Chrysler Plymouth 5160 Camp Rd Hamburg NY 14075

KSOLL, CHRISTINA MARIA, bank executive; b. Englewood, N.J., Oct. 25, 1964; d. Dieter S. and Katharina (Zielke) K. AB in Biology, Harvard U., 1986. Asst. buyer Bloomingdale's, N.Y.C., 1986-87; assoc. buyer J.C. Penney Co., Dallas, 1987-89; pvt. banking rep. Harris Trust and Savs. Bank, Chgo., 1989—. Vol. Vols. of Ill., 1990. Mem. NAFE, Harvard Club. Home: 2930 Pine Grove St Apt 211 Chicago IL 60657 Office: Harris Trust & Savs Bank 111 W Monroe St Chicago IL 60603

K-TURKEL, JUDI (JUDITH LEAH), writer; b. N.Y.C., Jan. 3, 1934; d. Samuel S. and Pauline (Turkel) Rosenthal; divorced; children: Joseph, Jeffrey Kesselman, David, Kevin Peterson. BA, Bklyn. Coll., 1955. Story and mng. editor Dell Publs., N.Y.C., 1955-58, 62-65; editor-in-chief Sterling, Stearn & KMR Publs., N.Y.C., 1959-62; sr. editor Macfadden-Bartell Publs., N.Y.C., 1966-68; freelance writer N.Y.C. and Wis., 1968-89; pres. P/K Assocs., Inc., Madison, Wis., 1977—; instr. adult edn. Gt. Neck (N.Y.) Pub. Schs., 1973-76, U. Wis., Madison, 1977-82, journalism Madison Area Tech. Coll., 1984-87; lectr. nonfiction writing CW Post Ctr., L.I. U., Manhasset, N.Y., 1976-77; tchr.-in-residence Rhinelander (Wis.) Sch. Arts, 1984-86. Author: (writing as Judi Kesselman) Stopping Out, 1976, (writing as Judi Kesselman-Turkel with Franklynn Peterson) The Do-It-Yourself Custom VanBook, 1977, Vans, 1979, (with others) Eat Anything Exercise Diet, 1979, Snowmobile Maintenance and Repair, 1979, I Can Use Tools, 1981, (textbook) Good Writing, 1980, Test Taking Strategies, 1981, Study Smarts, 1981, Homeowner's Book of Lists, 1981, How to Improve Damn Near Everything Around Your Home, 1981, The Author's Handbook, 1982, rev., 1986, The Grammar Crammer, 1982, Research Shortcuts, 1982, Note-Taking Made Easy, 1982, The Vocabulary Builder, 1982, Getting it Down: How to Get Your Ideas on Paper, 1983, Spelling Simplified, 1983, The Magazine Writer's Handbook, 1983; syndicated computer newspaper columnist, 1979—; contbr. articles to profl. jours. Chmn. non-partisan Citizens Nominating Com., Gt. Neck, 1972-75. Mem. Am. Soc. Journalists and Authors, Coun. Wis. Writers (pres. 1982-85), Authors Guild, Authors League, Nat. Press Club, Pen & Brush Club (Madison, publ. chmn. 1978—). Home and Office: 3006 Gregory St Madison WI 53711-1847

KU, CECILIA CHOU YUAN, analytical chemist, researcher; b. Peking, China, Jan. 9, 1942; came to U.S., 1966; naturalized, 1974; d. Hsiao-Hsing and Chin-Chung (Shih) Yuan; m. James Chen Ku, June 3, 1967; children—Grace, Philip. B.S., Nat. Taiwan Normal U., Taiwan, 1966; M.S., Carnegie-Mellon U., 1968. Cert. tchr., Pa. Chemist U. Pitts., 1969-71, Research Triangle Inst., N.C., 1974-75; chemist, scientist Carnegie-Mellon U., Pitts., 1971-73; analytical chemist, quality control chemist, US Dept. Labor Occupational Safety and Health Adminstrn., Salt Lake City, 1976—, cons., 1982—. Mem. Am. Indsl. Hygiene Assn. Mem. Evangelical Free Ch. Avocations: computers; statistical process control; cooking; piano. Office: US Dept Labor Occupational Safety & Health Adminstrn 1781 S 300 W PO Box 15200 Salt Lake City UT 84115

KUBE, BARBARA LOU, health facilities administrator; b. Cass City, Mich., July 7, 1939; d. James Roath and Catherine Elsie (Wallace) Gross; m. Kenneth Silvlon Kube, Apr. 22, 1961; children: Kimberly Kay Herrington, Brian James. Grad., Hurley Hosp. Sch. Nursing, Flint, Mich., 1960. RN, Mich. Staff nurse intensive care unit Hurley Hosp., 1960-61; pediatric nurse Cabrini Hosp., Alexandria, La., 1964-66; coordinator Friends for Life Hospice, Bad Axe, Mich., 1986—. Contbr. articles to religious newsletters. Vol. Bad Axe Sr. Citizens, 1978-87, ARC, 1970—; active Huron Meml. Hosp. Aux., Bad Axe, Interfaith Coun., Bad Axe, Huron County Med. Soc. Aux.; bd. dirs. Elkton(Mich.) Prayer Breakfast, 1978—, Interdenomination Community Bible Study, Bad Axe, 1988—. Mem. Mich. Hospice Nursing Assn. Baptist. Home: 945 S McMillan Rd Bad Axe MI 48413

KUBELA, JEANNINE VERYL, school system advisor; b. Wahpeton, N.D., Mar. 9, 1929; d. John and June Anna (Russell) kirkhus; m. Donald Dale Kubela, June 5, 1947 (dec. Apr. 1989); children: Karyn (dec.), Janelle, Donald Dale II, Gregory, Bradley, David, Todd. BS in Edn. summa cum laude, Minot (N.D.) State Coll., 1965; MA in Edn., Calif. State U., L.A., 1970. Cert. tchr., Calif. Tchr. West End Rural Sch., Wyndmere, N.D., 1948-49, Albion-L.A. Unified Sch. Dist., L.A., 1965-71, Vinedale-L.A. Unified Sch. Dist., Sun Valley, Calif., 1971-81; categorical program adviser L.A. Unified Sch. Dist., Sun Valley, 1981—; with reading lab. L.A. Unified Sch. Dist., 1981—. Mem. Phi Kappa Phi, Kappa Delta Pi. Republican. Lutheran. Home: 9912 Marnice Ave Tujunga CA 91042

KUBISTAL, PATRICIA BERNICE, secondary school principal; b. Chgo., Jan. 19, 1938; d. Edward John and Bernice Mildred (Lenz) Kubistal. AB cum laude, Loyola U., Chgo., 1959, AM, 1964, AM, 1965, PhD, 1968; postgrad. Chgo. State Coll., 1962, Ill. Inst. Tech., 1963, State U. Iowa, 1963, Nat. Coll. Edn., 1974-75. With Chgo. Bd. Edn., 1959—, tchr., 1959-63, counselor, 1963-65, adminstrv. intern, 1965-66, asst. to dist. supt., 1968-69, prin. spl. edn. sch., 1969-75, prin. Simpson Sch., 1975-76, Brentano Sch., 1975-87, Roosevelt High Sch., 1987, Haugan Sch., 1989, Jones Met. High Sch. Bus. and Commerce, 1988-89; supr. Lake View Evening Sch., 1982—; lectr. Loyola U. Sch. Edn., Nat. Coll. Edn. Grad. Sch., Mundelein Coll.; coord. Upper Bound Program of U. Ill. Circle Campus, 1966-68. Book rev. editor of Chgo. Prins. Jour., 1970-76, gen. editor, 1982—. Active Crusade of Mercy; mem. com. Ill. Constnl. Conv., 1967-69; mem. Citizens Sch. Com., 1969-71; mem. edn. com. Field Mus., 1971; ednl. advisor North Side Chgo. PTA Region, 1975; gov. Loyola U., 1961-87. Recipient Outstanding Intern award Nat. Assn. Secondary Sch. Prins., 1966, Outstanding Prin. award Citizen's Shc. Com. of Chgo., 1986; named Outstanding History Tchr., Chgo. Pub. Schs., 1963, Outstanding Ill. Educator, 1970, one of Outstanding Women of Ill., 1970, St. Luke's-Logan Sq. Community Person of Yr., 1977; NDEA grantee, 1963, NSF grantee, 1965, HEW Region 5 grantee for drug edn., 1974, Chgo. Bd. Edn. Prins.' grantee for study robotics in elem. schs.; U. Chgo. adminstrv. fellow, 1984. Mem. Ill. Personnel and Guidance Assn., NEA, Ill. Edn. Assn., Chgo. Edn. Assn., Am. Acad. Polit. and Social Sci., Chgo. Prins. Club (pres. aux.), Nat. Council Adminstrv. Women, Chgo. Council Exceptional Children, Chgo. Council Fgn. Relations, Chgo. Urban League, Loyal Christian Benevolent Assn., Kappa Gamma Pi, Pi Gamma Mu, Phi Delta Kappa, Delta Kappa Gamma (parliamentarian 1979-80, pres. Kappa chpt. 1988-90, Lambda state editor 1982—, chmn. internat. communications com.), Delta Sigma Rho, Phi Sigma Tau. Home: 5111 N Oakley Ave Chicago IL 60625 Office: Brentano Sch 2723 N Fairfield Chicago IL 60647

KUBLER-ROSS, ELISABETH, physician; b. Zurich, Switzerland, July 8, 1926; came to U.S., 1958, naturalized, 1961; d. Ernst and Emma (Villiger) K.; children: Kenneth Lawrence, Barbara Lee. M.D., U. Zurich, 1957; D.Sc. (hon.), Albany (N.Y.) Med. Coll., 1974, Smith Coll., 1975, Molloy Coll., Rockville Centre, N.Y., 1976, Regis Coll., Weston, Mass., 1977, Fairleigh Dickinson U., 1979; LL.D., U. Notre Dame, 1974, Hamline U., 1975; hon. degree, Med. Coll. Pa., 1975, Anna Maria Coll., Paxton, Mass., 1978; Litt.D. (hon.), St. Mary's Coll., Notre Dame, Ind., 1975, Hood Coll., 1976, Rosary Coll., River Forest, Ill., 1976; L.H.D. (hon.), Amherst Coll., 1975, Loyola U., Chgo., 1975, Bard Coll., Annandale-on-Hudson, N.Y., 1977, Union Coll., Schenectady, 1978, D'Youville Coll., Buffalo, 1979, U. Miami, Fla., 1976; D.Pedagogy, Keuka Coll., Keuka Park, N.Y., 1976. Rotating intern Community Hosp., Glen Cove, N.Y., 1958-59; research fellow Manhattan State Hosp., 1959-62; resident Montefiore Hosp., N.Y.C., 1961-62; fellow psychiatry Psychopathic Hosp., U. Colo. Med. Sch., 1962-63; instr. psychiatry Colo. Gen. Hosp., U. Colo. Med. Sch., 1962-65; mem. staff LaRabida Children's Hosp. and Research Ctr., Chgo., 1965-70; chief cons. and research liaison sect. LaRabida Children's Hosp. and Research Ctr., 1969-70; asst. prof. psychiatry Billings Hosp., U. Chgo., 1965-70; med. dir. Family Service and Mental Health Ctr. S. Cook County, Chicago Heights, Ill., 1970-73; pres. Ross Med. Assos. (S.C.), Flossmoor, Ill., 1973-77; pres., chmn. bd. Shanti Nilaya Growth and Health Ctr., Escondido, Calif., 1977—; mem. numerous adv., cons. bds. in field. Author: On Death and Dying, 1969, Questions and Answers on Death and Dying, 1974, Death-The Final Stages of Growth, 1975, To Live Until We Say Goodbye, 1978, Working It Through, 1981, Living With Death and Dying, 1981, Remember The Secret, 1981, On Children and Death, 1985, AIDS: The Ultimate Challenge, 1988; contbr. chpts. to books, articles to profl. jours. Recipient Teilhard prize Teilhard Found., 1981; Golden Plate award Am. Acad. Achievement, 1980; Modern Samaritan award Elk Grove Village, Ill., 1976; named Woman of the Decade Ladies Home Jour., 1979; numerous others. Mem. AAAS, Am. Holistic Med. Assn. (a founder), Am. Med. Women's Assn., Am. Psychiat. Assn., Am. Psychosomatic Soc., Assn. Cancer Victims and Friends, Ill. Psychiat. Soc., Soc. Swiss Physicians, Soc. Psychophysiol. Research, Second Attempt at Living. Address: care Celestial Arts Pub PO Box 7327 Berkeley CA 94707*

KUBRICHT, DOTTIE MAE WEIDEMEYER, professor, nurse; b. Balt., Nov. 15, 1942; d. Lloyd Harvey and Catherine (Greninger) Weidemeyer; m. Aug. 6, 1966 (div. 1983); children: Kimberly, Dawn, William III. BSN, U. Fla., 1964; MS, U. Southern Miss., 1980. RN, Fla.; lic. profl. counselor. Staff and charge nurse Shands Teaching Hosp., Gainsveille, Fla., 1964-66; instr. Coll. Nursing Tex. Women's U., Houston, 1966-71; instr. Emory U., Atlanta, 1973-76, Our Lady of the Lake, Baton Rouge, 1977-79; asst. prof. Southeastern La. U., Baton Rouge, 1980—; part-time staff nurse OLOL Tau Ctr., Baton Rouge, 1985—; part-time family counselor Olde Tan Ctr., Baton Rouge, 1983-85; part-time staff nurse BR Rehab. Ctr., Baton Rouge, 1989—; cons. in field; apptd. La. State Bd. Nursing, 1990. Mem. Baton Rouge Dist. Nurses Assn. (bd. dirs., sec. 1989—), La. State Nurses Assn. (dist. rep. 1989—), Nat. Chem. Dependency Nursing Assn., La. Counseling Assn., Baton Rouge C. of C., Nat. League Nursing, Chi Omega (bd. dirs. house corps 1988—, treas. 1989—). Republican. Episcopalian. Office: Southeastern La U 4849 Essen Ln Baton Rouge LA 70809

KUBSCH, KIM KAREN, commercial real estate consultant; b. Milw., Dec. 24, 1956; d. David Eugene and Jo Ann Myrtle (Fischer) K. BS in Home Econs., Silver Lake coll., 1979; postgrad., U. Wis., Stevens Point, 1980. Mall mgr., property mgr. Weingarten Realty, Inc., Houston, 1981-83; sr. property mgr. Stanley J. Williams Interests, Houston, 1983-84; regional property mgr. Patrician Group, Inc., N.Y.C., 1984-85; dir. property mgmt. Lincor Properties Ariz., Phoenix, 1985-87, Carmel-Givol Mgmt. Group, Hollywood, Calif., 1987-88; prin. cons. KK Consulting, L.A., 1988—; founder, pres. Networking for Phoenix Female Property Mgrs., 1986-87. Bd. dirs. Planned Parenthood, Wisconsin Rapids, Wis., 1979-80; Am. mktg. Assn., Houston, 1981-84. Mem. Inst. Real Estate Mgr. (cert. property mgr. candidate), Bldg. Owners Mgrs. Assn. (bd. dirs.), Nat. Assn. Women in Comml. Real Estate (hospitality chairwoman Houston chpt. 1981-84). Republican. Roman Catholic. Home: 340 S Cloverdale #106 Los Angeles CA 90036 Office: 3921 Wilshire Ste 505 Los Angeles CA 90010

KUBY, BARBARA ELEANOR, personnel executive, management consultant; b. Medford, Mass., Sept. 1, 1944; d. Robert William and Eleanor (Frasca) Asdell; m. Thomas Kuby, July 12, 1969. BS in Edn./Psychology, Kent State U., 1966, MEd, 1987. Tchr. Nordonia/Euclid (Ohio) Pub. Schs., 1966-78; mgr. tng. and devel. United Bldg. Factories, Manama, Bahrain, 1979-81, Norton Co., Akron, Ohio, 1981-85; v.p. Kuby and Assocs. Inc., Chagrin Falls, Ohio, 1973—; corp. dir. human resource devel. and systems TransOhio Savs. Bank, Cleve., 1985-88; asst. v.p. human resources and adminstrv. systems Leasing Dynamics, Inc., Cleve., 1988-90; dir. human resources, organizational devel. Go-Jo Industries, Akron, 1990—; adj. faculty, cons. Buffalo State U., 1972—, Lake Erie Coll., Cleve., 1985—; lectr., cons. Cleve. State U., 1978—; program dir. Ctr. Profl. Adv., East Brunswick, N.J., 1978—. cons., lectr. Girls Scouts Am., Cleve., 1981-90; trustee Vocat. Info. Program, Cleve., 1970-85, Colleague of Creative Edn. Found. Mem. Am. Mgmt. Assn., Human Resource Planning Soc., Soc. for Human Resource Mgmt., Orgnl. Devel. Network, Gestalt Inst. of Cleve., Greenpeace, Cleve. City Club. Home: 7236 Chagrin Rd Chagrin Falls OH 44022

KUCHAK, JOANN MARIE, management research executive; b. Scranton, Pa., Dec. 27, 1949; d. John J. and Rose T. Kuchak; m. George A. Kettner; children: Kimberly, Kevin. AB, Marywood Coll., 1971; MA, ED.S., U. Pitts., 1973. Project analyst Applied Mgmt. Scis., Silver Spring, Md., 1974-75, sr. analyst, 1975-76, tech. mgr., 1976-77, div. dir., 1977-79, v.p., 1979-90; v.p. Macro Systems, Silver Spring, 1990—; adv. panel mem. Urban Inst., Washington, 1988-90; reviewer grant proposals HHS, Washington, 1986-87; cons. U.S. Depts. Agr., Edn., Labor, HUD, HHS, Washington, 1979—. Mem. Am. Soc. for Quality Control, Am. Evaluation Assn. Office: Macro Systems Inc 8630 Fenton St Silver Spring MD 20910

KUCK, MARIE ELIZABETH BUKOVSKY, retired pharmacist; b. Milw., Aug. 3, 1910; d. Frank Joseph and Marie (Nozina) Bukovsky; Ph.C., U. Ill., 1933; m. John A. Kuck, Sept. 20, 1945 (div. Nov. 1954). Pharmacist, tchr. Am. Hosp., Chgo., 1936-38, St. Joseph Hosp., Chgo., 1938-40, Ill. Masonic Hosp., Chgo., 1940-45; chief pharmacist St. Vincent Hosp., Los Angeles, 1946-48, St. Joseph Hosp., Santa Fe, 1949-51; dir. pharm. services St. Luke's Hosp., San Francisco, 1951-76; pharmacist Mission Neighborhood Health Center, San Francisco, 1968-72; mem. peer rev. com. Drug Utilization Com., Blue Shield Calif. and Pharm. Soc. San Francisco. Recipient Bowl of Hygeia award Calif. Pharm. Assn., 1966. Mem. No., Calif. (legis. chmn. aux. 1967-69, chmn. fund raising luncheon 1953-71, pres. San Francisco aux. 1974), Nat., Am., No. Calif. (pres. 1955-56, pres. San Francisco aux. 1965-66, editor ofcl. publ. 1967-70), San Francisco (sec. 1977-79, treas. 1979-80, pres. 1982-83; Pharmacist of Yr. award 1978) pharm. socs., Am. Pharm. Assn. (pres. No. Calif. br. 1956-57, nat. sec. women's aux. 1970-72, hon. pres. aux. 1975—), Calif. Council Hosp. Pharmacists (organizer 1962, sec.-treas. 1962-66), Am. Soc. Hosp. Pharmacists, Assn. Western Hosps. (gen. chmn. hosp. pharmacy sect. conv. San Francisco 1958), Internat. Pharmacy Congress (U.S. del. Brussels 1958, Copenhagen 1960), Fedn. Internationale Pharmaceutique, Lambda Kappa Sigma. Home: 2261 33d Ave San Francisco CA 94116

KUCZAK, SOPHIE MARIE, small business owner; b. Wroclaw, Poland, Aug. 18, 1952; came to U.S., 1960; d. Walter and Janina (Pudlo) K. AS, Wright Coll., 1972; student, U. Ill., Chgo., 1972-73; BA in Mktg. Mgmt., Northeastern Ill. U., 1989. Lab. and radiocardiogram technician N.W. Hosp., Chgo., 1970-73; owner, mgr. Kuczak Sausage Shoppe, Inc., Chgo., 1973—. Mem. Internat. Deli and Cheese Assn., NAFE, Nat. Assn. Women Bus. Owners, Roundtable for Women, Polish-Am. Congress (Ill. chpt.), Young Polish Women's Alliance (gen. mem.), Norwood Park C. of C. (bd. dirs. 1986). Republican. Roman Catholic.

KUDENHOLDT, SHARON SUE, freelance author; b. Chgo., Aug. 2, 1942; d. Harold Gustavus Adolphus and Thelma (Geen) Soderling; m. John Bernhardt Kudenholdt, Aug. 15 , 1970; children: Mara, Kristian, Hannah, Paul. BS, Concordia Coll., River Forest, Ill., 1964; MA, Loyola U., Chgo., 1968. Cert. tchr., Ill. Art tchr. Walther High Sch., Melrose Park, Ill., 1964-67; asst. tchr. Vogue-Wright Art Studio, Chgo., 1967; English tchr. Kennedy High Sch., Chgo., 1967-72; tchr. Steinmetz High Sch., Chgo.; freelance resumée writer Park Ridge, Ill., 1976—. Contbr. short story "motif" Lit. Jour. 1967; columnist Park Ridge "Advocate" 1985-87. Active Ill. Coun. for the Gifted, Irish Children's Fund, North Suburban Chgo.; contbr. Action on Smoking and Health, Washington, 1971—, Cameron-Kravitt Found., Glencoe, Ill.; Christian Home Educators Coalition. Mem. LWV (editor, bd. dirs., chmn. news/pub. relations). Home and Office: PO Box 58 Park Ridge IL 60068

KUEBLER, PATRICIA IRENE, nurse; b. New Iberia, La., Nov. 17, 1942; d. Kirby Joseph and Beverley Irene; m. Walter Joseph Kuebler; children: Stephen Michael, Michelle Irene. Diploma, Hotel Dieu Sch. Nursing, 1963; cert. modeling, Vogue of Lexington, 1987. RN, La. Staff nurse Hotel Dieu Hosp., New Orleans, 1963-66; head nurse Charity Hosp., 1966-69; med. bus. mgr. Bowling Green, Ky., 1989—. Leader, coord. Boy Scouts Am., Lafayette, La., 1976-79; active women's club Cath. women's group, Community Greeters, Arts Alliance, Med. Aux., 1983—; fundraiser Arthritis Found., Lafayette, 1977-84; vol. Med. Ctr. Hosp. ARC, Bowling Green, 1984—. Named Hon. Ky. Col., 1986. Roman Catholic. Home: 1010 Grider Pond Rd Bowling Green KY 42104 Office: 250 Park St Bowling Green KY 42104

KUEHL, NANCY LOUISE, shorthand agency executive; b. Lufkin, Tex., May 22, 1947; d. Vance DeVille Ethridge and Sally Viola (Seale) Loggins; m. Jack B. Ely, Mar. 13, 1966 (div. 1967); 1 child, Robert Sterling; m. William Albert Kuehl Jr., Sept. 23, 1972 (div. 1989); children: Kristofer Jason, Kerry Elissa. BA, Stephen F. Austin State U., 1981. Paralegal asst. Harvill & Hardy, Houston, 1976-77; litigation supr. Fenley & Bate, Lufkin, 1976-77; legal asst. Forrest G. Braselton, Nacogdoches, Tex., 1977-78; owner, prin. Letter-Perfect, Nacogdoches, 1980-85, Kuehl Reporting Svc. Inc., Bryan, Tex., 1987—; ct. reporter Hill & Mace, Nacogdoches, 1982-87. Author: How to Set Up a Successful Typing Service, 1982, The Glass Staircase, 1982, A Seale Anthology, Vols. 1 and 2, 1985, 2nd edit., 1990, Henry Seale, The King's Bookseller, 1989. Mem. Nat. Assn. Legal Secs., Tex. Assn. Legal Secs., Houston Assn. Legal Secs., nat. Shorthand Reporters Assn., Tex. Shorthand Reporters Assn., Nacogdoches Writer's Group, Nat. Shorthand Verbatim Reporters Assn., Internat. Platform Assn., Phi Alpha Theta, Pi Sigma Alpha, Sigma Tau Delta. Democrat. Mem. Christian Church (Disciples of Christ). Office: Kuehl Reporting Svc PO Box 4165 Bryan TX 77805-4165

KUEHNE, MARGARET ANN, federal agency administrator; b. Balt., Nov. 12, 1939; d. Milton Woodrow and Marie Anna (Vain) Wilson; divorced; 1 child, Brian Scott Jeznach; m. Charles David Kuehne, Apr. 12, 1975; 1 child, Cheryl Anne. Grad. high sch., Dundalk, Md., 1957. Sec. Social Security Adminstrn. div. Dept. Health, Edn. and Welfare, Balt., 1957-58, asst. budget and reports, 1958-69; computer operator Woodlawn, Md., 1969-81, supervisory computer operator, instr. computer, 1981-82; mgr. computer operators Social Security Adminstrn. div. HHS (formerly HEW), Woodlawn, Md., 1982-85, specialist network control, 1985-89; computer systems programmer Social Security Adminstrn. div. Dept. Health Human Svcs., Woodlawn, Md., 1989—. V.p. Episc. Ch. Women, Sykesville, Md., 1987, 90, pres., 1988-89; mem. Alter Guild, St. Barnabas, Sykesville. Mem. Epsilon Sigma Alpha, Alpha Tau (v.p. Balt. chpt. 1970-71, pres. 1971-72). Democrat. Home: 7313 Brown St Sykesville MD 21784

KUEHNERT, DEBORAH ANNE, medical center administrator; b. Raleigh, N.C., Nov. 21, 1949; d. Eldor Paul and Lila Catherine (Gilbert) K. Student, Valparaiso (Ind.) U., 1967-69; BS in Biology, Lenior Rhyne Coll., Hickory, N.C., 1977. Cert. med. technologist. Rsch. asst. Strong Meml. Hosp., Rochester, N.Y., 1967-68; lab. technician Richard Baker Hosp., Hickory, N.C., 1969-76; med. technician, shift supr. Glenn R. Frye Hosp., Hickory, 1977-83; lab. tech. dir. Frye Regional Med. Ctr., Hickory, 1983-85, adminstrv. dir. lab. svcs., 1986—; instr. microbiology Catawba Valley Tech. Coll., Hickory, 1977—, Lenior Rhyne Coll., Hickory, 1978—; cons. Frye Physicians, Hickory, 1985—; lab. cons. Am. Med. Internat., New Orleans, 1986, Lake City, Fla., 1984-85; cons. Med. Lab. Observer, Chgo.,

1989. Mem. Am. Soc. Clin. Pathologists, N.C. Soc. Blood Bankers. Lutheran. Home: 34 Penny Ln Hickory NC 28601

KUENY, MARY ELLEN, English educator; b. Chillicothe, Mo., Apr. 13, 1955; d. David Encell and Janet Ethel (Guffey) Greenwood; m. James Vincent Kueny, Aug. 18, 1984; children: Robert Vincent, Joseph Edmund, Stephen James. BS, U. Mo., 1977, MEd, 1981. Cert. English tchr., libr. sci. English tchr./coach Warren County R-3 High Sch., Warrenton, Mo., 1977-80, Lexington (Mo.) High Sch., 1980-82; English/journalism tchr. Lebanon (Mo.) Jr. High, 1982-87, 88-89; chmn. Commn. on Jr. High Journalism, Manhattan, Kans.; judge Columbia Scholastic Press Assn., N.Y.C., 1987. Author: Curriculum Guide for Junior High Journalism, 1988; contbg. editor newsletter "Keeping Up With the Jones", 1990; advisor yearbook, 1983-89 (medalist 1989). Sec., treas. U. Mo. Alumni Bd., Laclede County., Lebanon, 1987—; mem. Youth-At-Risk Comprehensive Child Care Task Force, Laclede County, 1989—. Named to Outstanding Young Women of Am., Jaycees, 1981. Mem. U. Mo. Alumni Assn., Nat. Coun. Tchrs. of English, AAUW, Mo. State Tchrs. Assn., Journalism Edn. Assn. (chmn. 1985-87, workshop presenter, Chgo.), Veritas (pres. 1990), Zeta Tau Alpha, Phi Delta Kappa. Republican. Roman Catholic. Home: Rt 3 PO Box 25 Lebanon MO 65536

KUES, MARY CAROLYN, career counselor, educational administrator; b. Balt., Oct. 24, 1936; d. James Andrew and Jennie Frances (Robertson) Gaff-Becker; m. Irvin William Kues, Oct. 24, 1959; children: Pamela A., Janet M., Lynne P., Leslie F. BA, Mt. St. Agnes Coll., 1958; MS, Loyola U., Balt., 1979; cert. advanced study, Johns Hopkins U., 1988. Nat. cert. counselor, nat. cert. career counselor. Intelligence researcher Nat. Security Agy., Fort Meade, Md., 1958-60; career advisor asst. Loyola Coll., Balt., 1975-77, career cons., 1978, career advisor, 1979-83, asst. dir. career planning, 1983-87, assoc. dir career planning, 1987—; career counselor Balt. New Directions, 1978-79; part-time faculty Johns Hopkins U., Balt., 1988-89. Contbr. articles, reviews to profl. jours. Mem. AAUW, Am. Assn. for Counseling & Devel., Middle Atlantic Placement Assn. (com. mem.), Md. Career Devel. Assn. (sec. 1989—). Democrat. Roman Catholic. Office: Loyola Coll 4501 N Charles St Baltimore MD 21210

KUEVER, NANCY JEANNE, corporate professional; b. Cleve., Feb. 23, 1947; d. John Francis and Antoinette Marie (Nurre) Egan; m. Richard Philip Chepey, Dec. 30, 1967 (div. Feb. 1974); m. Gary William Kuever, Dec. 13, 1981. Student, John Carroll U., Cleve., 1966-67; BA cum laude, Ursuline Coll. for Women, 1968; postgrad., St. Louis U., 1969-71, Ch. of Scientology, Clearwater, Fla., 1978-80. Cert. secondary tchr.; ordained to ministry, 1976. Secondary sch. tchr. Augustinian Acad. for Boys, St. Louis, 1968-69, Lindbergh Sr. High Sch., St. Louis, 1969-75; dir. mktg. Rainbo Color Inc., St. Louis, 1981-86, pres., 1986—. Mem. Photo Mktg. Assn., St. Louis Regional Commerce and Growth Assn., St. Louis C. of C. Office: Rainbo Color Inc 1401 S Boyle Saint Louis MO 63110

KUFFNER-HIRT, MARY JANE, city manager; b. McKeesport, Pa., Aug. 26, 1951; d. Alan Eugene and Mary Elizabeth (Jeffries) Kuffner. BA, Ind. U. of Pa., 1973; MPA, U. Pitts., 1975, PhD, 1986. Community liaison Mon-Yough Justice Svcs. Ctr., McKeesport, Pa., 1974-76; coord. Steel Valley Coun. of Govts., Dravosburg, Pa., 1976-77; mcpl. rep. Allegheny County, Pitts., 1977-80; mgr. Borough of Forest Hills, Pa., 1980-86, Township of O'Hara, Pa., 1986—; adj. prof. Ind. U. of Pa., 1983—, U. Pitts., 1987—, Carnegie-Mellon U., Pitts., 1989; cons. Coalition to Improve State and Local Govt. Mgmt., 1988—. Treas. Beacon Hill Condominium Assn., Wilkinsburg, Pa., 1982-87; mem. Leadership Pitts., 1990. Recipient Mgmt. Innovation award, Pa. Dept. of Community Affairs, Harrisburg, 1985, Internship Suprs. award, Ind. U. Pa., 1987; nominee Nat. Schs. of Pub. Affairs and Adminstrn. Dissertation award, 1986. Mem. Internat. City Mgmt. Assn. (chmn. acad. com. 1988-90), Am. Soc. for Pub. Adminstrn. (bd. dirs. Pitts. chpt. 1980—), Assn. for Pa. Mcpl. Mgmt. (pres. 1986-87, chmn. ethics com. 1989-90), Govt. Fin. Officers Assn. (Disting. Budget award 1987). Methodist. Home: 210 St Charles Pl Pittsburgh PA 15215 Office: Township of O'Hara 325 Fox Chapel Rd Pittsburgh PA 15238

KUGLEN, FRANCESCA BERNADETTE, fashion manufacturing executive; b. Rahway, N.J., Mar. 5, 1961; d. Robert Riggs and Sarah Ann (Langford) K. BA, U. Calif., Berkeley, 1984. Pres., founder Jontee Accessories, Oakland, Calif., 1985—. Patentee hair accordian accessory, 1988. Mem. San Francisco Fashion Industries Assn. Democrat. Roman Catholic. Office: Jontee Accessories 3744 14th Ave Oakland CA 94602

KUHAR, JUNE CAROLYNN, retired fiberglass manufacturing company executive; b. Chgo., Sept. 20, 1935; d. Kurt Ludwig and Dorothy Julia (Lewand) Stier; m. G. James Kuhar, Feb. 5, 1953; children: Kathleen Lee, Debra Suzanne. Student William Rainey Harper Coll., Chgo. Engaged in fiberglass mfg., 1970—; sec.-treas. Q-R Fiber Glass Industries Inc., Rolling Meadows, Ill., 1970—. Mem. Multiple Sclerosis Soc., Nat. Fedn. Ileitis and Colitis, Bus. and Profl. Women N.W., Bus. and Profl. Woman's Club (pres. 1984—), Women in the Arts (charter). Home: 2303 Meadow Dr Rolling Meadows IL 60008

KUHL, MARGARET HELEN CLAYTON (MRS. ALEXIUS M. KUHL), banker; b. Louisville; d. Joseph Leonard and Maude (Mitzler) Clayton; student Loyola U. Home Study Div., Chgo., 1955—, Buena Vista Coll., Storm Lake, Iowa, summer 1964-65, 66; m. Alexius M. Kuhl, Apr. 21, 1936; children—Carol Lynn Ford Wassmuth, James Michael (adopted). Sales lady, buyer Silverberg, Akron, Iowa, 1924-34; owner dress shop, Fonda, Iowa, 1934-40; librarian, Fonda, 1940-43; bookkeeper, teller First Nat. Bank, Fonda, 1943-44; tchr. speech and drama, librarian asst. Our Lady Good Counsel Sch., Fonda, 1963-69; pres., chmn. bd. Pomeroy State Bank, 1975-83, also dir. Tel. counselor Christian TV Prayer Line. Recipient Adult Leadership award Catholic Youth Orgn., 1967, Pro Deo Juventute award, 1969. Mem. Cath. Daus. Am. (dist. dep. 1964-70, state chmn. ecumenism 1970-72, state treas. 1970-72), Diocesan Council Cath. Women (chmn. orgn. and devel. 1964-65), Nat. Council Cath. Women (diocesan pres. 1968-70, diocesan sec. 1966-67; chmn. Women in Community Service Sioux City Diocesan Bd. 1971-72), Women in Community Service (pres. Iowa bd. 1972-73), Legion of Mary (pres. curia 1964-66, 67-70), Sun City Country Club, Lakes Club, Fonda Golf Club. Home: 4th and Queen Sts Fonda IA 50540

KUHLER, DEBORAH G., state legislator; b. Moorhead, Minn., Oct. 12, 1952; d. Robert Edgar and Beverly Maxine (Buechler) Ecker; m. George Henry Kuhler, Dec. 28, 1973; children: Karen Elizabeth, Ellen Christine. BA, Dakota Wesleyan U., 1974; MA, U. N.D., 1977. Outpatient therapist Ctr. for Human Devel., Grand Forks, N.D., 1975-77; mental health counselor Community Counseling Services, Huron, S.D., 1978-88; owner, dir. bereavement svcs. Kuhler Funeral Home, Huron, 1978—; adj. prof. Huron U., 1979-83, 90—; mem. from dist. 23 S.D. Ho. Reps., Pierre, 1987—; mem. House Judiciary com., chair House Health and Welfare Com., Pierre, 1987-90. Active Beadle County Rep. Women, 1st United Meth. Ch. Named Young Alumnus of the Yr., Dakota Wesleyan U., 1989, Bus. and Profl. Women, 1989. Mem. Am. Mental Health Counselors Assn., Am. Assn. Counseling and Devel., AAUW (Achievement in Politics award 1987), Women Execs. and Adminstrs., Phi Kappa Phi. Home: 1360 Dakota Ave S Huron SD 57350

KUHN, ANNE NAOMI WICKER (MRS. HAROLD B. KUHN), educator; b. Lynchburg, Va.; d. George Barney and Annie (Hicks) Wicker; m. Harold B. Kuhn. Diploma Malone Coll., 1933, Trinity Coll. Music, London, 1937; A.B., John Fletcher Coll., 1939; M.A., Boston U., 1942, postgrad., 1965-70; postgrad. (fellow) Harvard U., 1942-44, 66-68; hon. grad. Asbury Coll., 1978. Instr., Emmanuel Bible Coll., Birkenhead, Eng., 1936-37; asst. in history John Fletcher Coll., University Park, Iowa, 1938-39; librarian Harvard U., 1939-44; tchr. adult edn. program U.S. Armed Forces, Fuerstenfeldbruck Air Base, Germany, 1951-52; prof. Union Bibl. Sem., Yeotmal, India, 1957-58; lectr. Armenian Bible Inst., Beirut, Lebanon, 1958; prof. German, Asbury Coll., Wilmore, Ky., 1962—, co-dir. coll. study tour to E. Ger. and W. Ger., 1976, 77, 78, co-dir. acad. tours, 1979, 80; dir. acad. tour, Russia, 1981, 85, Scandanavia, 1982, Indonesia, Singapore, 1983, Hong Kong and Thailand, 1983, 85, E.Ger., W.Ger., France and Austria, 1983, Russia and Finland, 1984, 85, 89, Peoples Republic China, 1984, 85, Estonia, Latvia, 1985, 89, Poland, 1989, Portugal, Spain, France, Ireland, Scotland, Norway, England, 1987; tchr. Seoul Theol. Sem., fall 1978. Author: (pamphlet) The Impact of the Transition to Modern Education Upon Religious Education, 1950; The Influence of Paul Gerhardt upon Wesleyan Hymnody, 1960, Light to Dispel Fear, 1987; transl. German ch. records, poems, letters; contbr. articles to profl. jours. Del. Youth for Christ World Conf., 1948, 50, London Yearly Meeting of Friends, Edinburgh, Scotland, 1948, World Council Chs., Amsterdam, 1948, World Friends Conf., Oxford, Eng., 1952, World Methodist Conf., Oslo, Norway, 1961, Deutscher Kirchentag, Dortmund, Germany, 1963, German Lang. Congress, Bonn, W. Ger., 1974, Internat. Conf. Religion, Amsterdam, Netherlands, Poland, West Berlin, Fed. Republic Germany, 1986, Internat. Missionary Conf., Eng., 1987, Congress on the Bible II, Washington, 1987; participant Internat. Congress World Evangelization, Lausanne, Switzerland, 1974; del., speaker Internat. Conf. on Holocaust and Genocide, Oxford and London, 1988; speaker Founders Week Malone Coll., Ohio, 1989, Nat. Quaker Conf., Denver; mem. acad. tour Poland, 1988. Recipient German Consular award, Boston, 1965, Thomas Mann award Boston U., 1967; named Ky. Col., 1978. Fellow Goethe-Institut für Germanisten, Munich, 1966-68, 70-71. Mem. AAUW, Am. Assn. Tchrs. German, NEA, Ky. Ednl. Assn., Lincoln Lit. Soc., Protestant Women of Chapel, United Daughters of the Confederacy, Delta Phi Alpha (award 1963, 65). Quaker. Club: Harvard Faculty. Home: 406 Kenyon Ave Wilmore KY 40390

KUHN, KATHLEEN JO, accountant; b. Springfield, Ill., Aug. 9, 1947; d. Henry Elmer and Norma Florene (Niehaus) Burge; m. Gerald L. Kuhn, June 22, 1968; children: Gerald Lynn, Brett Anthony. BS in Bus., Bradley U., 1969. CPA, Ill. Controller Byerly Music Co., Peoria, Ill., 1969-70; staff acct. Clifton Gunderson & Co., Columbus, Ind., 1970-71; acct. Dept. of Transp., State of Ill., Springfield, 1972-76; acct. Gerald L. Kuhn & Assocs., Springfield, 1976-78, ptnr., 1979—; grad. asst. in Dale Carnegie courses, 1979-80. Writer, editor co. policy guideline, 1979-80. Recipient Attendance award Continuing Profl. Edn. for Accts., 1977-79, 82—. Mem. Am. Inst. CPAs, Ill. Soc. CPAs, Am. Woman's Soc. CPAs. Lutheran. Clubs: Olympic Swim, Metro. Federated Jr. Women's. Home: 2511 Westchester St Springfield IL 62704 Office: 2659 Farragut Dr Springfield IL 62704

KUHN, LINDA M(ARIE), computer programming manager; b. Mineola, N.Y., May 9, 1953; d. Norbert Earl and Lillian Katherine (Jablonski) Gaylord; m. Larry A. Kuhn, July 13, 1974; children: Derek Scott, Brandon Alan. BA, SUNY, Albany, 1974; MBA, U. Rochester, 1982. Jr. programmer Xerox Corp., Rochester, N.Y., 1980-81; programmer IV Xerox Corp., 1981-83, programmer III, 1983-84, fin. analyst, 1984-85, systems analyst, 1985-86; mgr. tech. support svcs. Hillsborough Community Coll., Tampa, Fla., 1987-90; systems supr. GTE Communications Corp., Tampa, 1990—. Office: GTE Communications Corp 1907 US Hwy 301 N Tampa FL 33619

KUHN, LUCILLE ROSS, retired naval officer; b. Washington, July 19, 1927; d. Lilburn Joseph and Flora Lee (Perry) K.; A.A. with distinction, George Washington U., 1959, B.A., 1960. Ins. clk. Southwestern Life Ins. Co., Richmond, Va., 1945-48; joined U.S. Navy, 1949, advanced through grades to capt., 1975; woman officer rep. 2d Navy Recruiting Area, Washington, 1963-65; U.S. Naval Security Group, Washington, 1965-68; dir. mil. personnel 12th Naval Dist., San Francisco, 1968-70; mem. staff Office Asst. Sec. Def. for Legis. Affairs, Washington, 1971-74; dir. Officer Candidate Sch., Newport, 1975-77; dir. pay/personnel adminstrv. support system Bur. Naval Personnel, Washington, 1977-79; comdg. officer Recruit Tng. Command, Orlando, Fla., 1979-81; dep. comdr. Navy Recruiting Command, Washington, 1981-84. Aide de camp to Va. govs., 1960—. Decorated Legion of Merit with gold star, Meritorious Service medal with gold star, Nat. Def. Service medal with bronze star. Mem. Am. Sailing Assn., Naval Hist. Found., Naval Inst., Psi Chi. Home: 2302 Kenmore Rd Richmond VA 23228

KUHN, MARGARET (MAGGIE KUHN), organization executive; b. Buffalo, 1905; d. Samuel Frederick and Minnie Louise (Kooman) K. BA, Case-Western Res. U., 1926; hon. degree, Swarthmore Coll., Simmons Coll., Albright Coll., U. Pa., Beaver Coll., U. Mass., 1988, Case Western Res. U., 1989, No. Ill. U., 1990. Formerly with YWCA, Cleve., Phila.; Gen. Alliance Unitarian Women, Boston; later with United Presbn. Ch. U.S.A., N.Y.C.; editor, writer for ch. mag. Social Progress; alt. observer for Presbyns. at UN; ret., 1970; a founder Gray Panthers, Phila., 1971; now nat. convener; cons. nat. task force on women United Presbyn. Ch., past 3d v.p. health, edn. and welfare assn.; lectr.; mem. nat. adv. bd. Hospice, Inc.; adv. TV series Over Easy; former mem. Fed. Jud. Nominating Com. Pa. Author: Get Out There and Do Something about Injustice, 1972, Maggie Kuhn on Aging, 1977. Recipient 1st ann. award for justice and human devel. Witherspoon Soc., 1974, Disting. Service award in consumer advocacy Am. Speech and Hearing Assn., 1975, Freedom award Women's Scholarship Assn. Roosevelt U., 1976, ann. award Phila. Soc. Clin. Psychologists, 1976, Peaceseeker award United Presbyn. Peace Fellowship, 1977, Humanist of Yr. award Am. Humanist Assn., 1978.

KUHN, MARY CROUGHAN, educator; b. Rinard, Ill., Nov. 1, 1914; d. Ulysses Samuel and Susan Winnifred Croughan; m. Wolfgang E. Kuhn, Aug. 22, 1938; children: Suanna Breed, Elizbeth Bacchetti, Virginia Day. BA, U. Colo., 1958; Cert. d'etudes francaise, U. Tours, France, 1964; MA, Stanford U., 1968. Elem. tchr. cert. lifetime. Reading specialist. Tchr. supr. Kindergarten Co-op, Urbana, Ill., 1945-55; tchr. Kindergarten Co-op., Boulder, Colo., 1955-57, Cupertino (Calif.) Sch. Dist., 1959-82; bd. dirs. Co-op Kindergarten, Urbana, Ill., 1949-55, Boulder, Colo., 1955-57; mem. Children's Theatre Group, Urbana, 1950-55; master tchr., supr. student tchrs. Cupertino, Calif., 1971-81. Author: Second Harvest, 1987. Girl scout leader, Urbana, Ill., 1949-55, Boulder, Colo., 1958. Named Tchr. of Year PTA and Calif. Tchrs. Assn., Cupertino, 1964. Mem. AAUW (bd. dirs. 1968-90), LWV, Writer's Club (Los Altos, Calif.). Home: 612 Alvarado Row Stanford CA 94305

KUHN, NANCY ZELENY, bookkeeper; b. Mpls., Mar. 10, 1931; d. Lawrence and Olive Mary (Lowen) Zeleny; m. Richard J. Kuhn, July 3, 1964 (dec. 1984); children: Paul L., Stephanie M. BA, U. Md., 1952, MA, 1954. Rsch. psychologist U.S. Govt., Washington, 1954-65; bookkeeper The Ins. Exchange, Inc., Rockville, Md., 1978—. Mem. Assn. Former Intelligence Officers, Parents Without Partners. Democrat. Episcopalian.

KUHRT, SHARON LEE, nursing administrator; b. Denver, July 20, 1957; d. John Wilfred and Yoshiko (Ueda) K. BS in Nursing, Loretto Heights Coll., 1982. RN, Colo., Hawaii; cert. sch. nurse, Colo. RN level III Porter Meml. Hosp., Denver, 1981-87; transport supr. Kapiolani Med. Ctr. for Women & Children, Honolulu, 1987-89; dir. patient care unit Aspen Valley Hosp., Colo., 1989—. Mem. Am. Assn. Critical Care Nurses, Nat. Flight Nurses Assn., Colo. Soc. Nurse Mgrs. Home: 1165 Cemetery Ct Aspen CO 81612

KUKEC, ANNA MARIE, public information officer, writer; b. Chgo., Feb. 3, 1958; d. Ernest P. and Angeline Kukec. AA with honors, Moraine Valley Community Coll., Palos Hills, Ill., 1978; BA in Mass Communications and Journalism, St. Xavier Coll., Chgo., 1983. Columnist, editor TV/radio Pulitzer Community Newspapers, Chgo., 1977-89; speech writer, pub. info. officer Ill. Atty. Gen., Chgo., 1989—; guest lectr. on radio and cable TV various schs.; judge TV div. Chgo. Internat. Film Festival, 1982-83. Vol. telethon March of Dimes, Chgo., 1983, judge AIR awards, 1987; vol. Muscular Dystrophy Assn., 1985-87; mem. college board Mademoiselle mag., 1979. Winner Nat. Piano Playing Auditions, Nat. Guild Piano Tchrs., 1968-78; recipient Paderewski Meml. award, 1978; named Woman of Yr., Village of Evergreen Park and Evergreen Park High Sch., 1985. Mem. Women in Communications, Nat. Fedn. Press Women, Ill. Women's Press Assn., Chgo. Headline Club (bd. dirs.), Suburban Press Club (various news awards), Sigma Delta Chi. Office: State of Ill Ctr 100 W Randolph St Chicago IL 60601

KUKUK, KAREN ELOISE, educational coordinator; b. Burlingame, Kans., May 21, 1938; d. Charles Alfred and Elva Nadine (Dorman) Smith; m. Jim L. Sells, Sept. 13, 1958 (div. Oct. 1975); children: Leslie A. Sells Danborg, Amy J., Anna Renee; m. Francis L. Kukuk, June 4, 1976. B Elem. Edn., Washburn U., 1969; cert. reading specialist, U. Kans., 1978; MA in Adult Edn., Kans. State U., 1989. Cert. tchr., reading specialist, Kans. Sec. Eureka (Kans.) Credit Bur., 1963-65, Eureka C. of C., 1965-66; elem. tchr. Unified Sch. Dist. 450, Tecumseh, Kans., 1969-73; Chpt. I tchr. Unified Sch. Dist. 425, Highland, Kans., 1975-76; tchr. ESL, Am. U. Alumni Lang. Ctr., Bangkok, 1978-81; Title I tchr. Unifed Sch. Dist. 340, Meriden, Kans., 1981-82; coord. support svcs., ESL reading specialist Am. Sch. Found. Monterrey (Mex.), 1983-86; ESL coord. Unified Sch. Dist. 453, Leavenworth, Kans., 1987—; workshop presenter, 1984, 86; program planner, implementor ESL Vol. Group, Leavenworth, 1987-89. Mem. Leavenworth Arts Coun., 1987-89, Operation Internat., Leavenworth, 1987-89. Mem. NEA, Nat. Staff Devel. Assn., Assn. for Psychol. Type, Kans. Tchrs. Assn., Kans. Assn. Tchrs. ESL, AAUW, Am. Volkssport Assn., O.C.W.C. Republican. Presbyterian. Home: 2807 S 16th St Leavenworth KS 66048

KUKURA, RITA ANNE, educational administrator; b. Tulsa, July 18, 1947; d. James Albert and Carmen Alberta (Parsons) Hayden; m. Joel Richard Graft, Oct. 28, 1967 (dec. Apr. 1969); m. Raymond Richard Kukura, Dec. 18, 1971 (div. 1981); children: Tiffany Carmen Noel, Austin Raymond. BS, Kent. State U., 1971; MS, Okla. State U., 1990. Cert. early childhood, nursery, elem. tchr., Okla. Tchr. kindergarten Southlyn Elem. Sch., Lyndhurst, Ohio, 1971-73; elem. tchr. Wakefield Acad., Tulsa, 1981-83, tchr. kindergarten, 1983-87; reg. early intervention coord. Okla. Dept. Edn., Tulsa, 1990—; manuscript reviewer for profl. orgns., 1989—; presenter confs. in field; lectr. in field. Den leader Cub Scouts Am., Tulsa, 1984-88; com. mem. Boy Scouts Am., Tulsa, 1984-88; vol., officer worker Met. Tulsa Citizen Crime Commn., 1986; adv. com. Latchkey Project, Tulsa County, 1985; ad hoc task force on daycare Interagy. Coordinating Council, 1989-90. Recipient Den Leader Tng. award Boy Scouts Am., 1988. Mem. NAFE, Nat. Coun. on Family Rels. (cert. family life educator), Assn. for Childhood Edn. Internat., Am. Home Econs. Assn., Fedn. of Families for Children's Mental Health, Nat. Assn. Early Childhood Tchr. Educators, Parent to Parent of Fla., Friends of Spl. Children, Nat. Tourette Syndrome Assn. (state pres. 1987—), assn. for Care Children's Health, Southwestern Soc. for Rsch. in Human Devel., LWV, Kappa Delta Pi, Omicron Nu. Roman Catholic. Home: 3720 E 43d St Tulsa OK 74135-2743 Office: Tulsa City/County Health 4616 E 15th St Tulsa OK 74112

KULCZYNSKI, EDWINA MARY, education educator; b. Camden, N.J., May 15, 1935; d. Witold and Florence (Praiss) Zebrowski; m. Henry Theodore Kulczynski, Sept. 29, 1957; children: Mark, Damian, Edwina, Karen. BS, Immaculata Coll., 1957; student, Rutgers U., 1958. cert. tchr., Phila., 1958. Tchr., dept. head St. Joseph's Sch., Camden, 1958-63; buyer Jacob Reed's Mens Clothing, Cherry Hill, N.J., 1975-78; tchr., dept. head Paul VI High Sch., Haddonfield, N.J., 1978-88; co-owner Flories Inc., Westmont, N.J.; chairperson Middle States Evaluation of Paul VI High Sch., Westmont, 1986-88. Author: Second Chance, Cookbook; producer: gourmet product, Flories, 1983--. bd. dir. Parent Tchrs. Assn., Westmont, 1975-77. mem. Am. Assn. of U. Women, Camden County Home Econs. Home: 504 Stratford Ave Westmont NJ 08108

KULICK, FLORENCE OLIVIA POST, publisher; b. Bklyn., Sept. 17, 1923; d. Jacob Abraham and Emily (Mendis) Post; married Feb. 14, 1942; children: Spencer Lee, Fredda Pam, Matthew Post. BS, Stony Brook U., 1978. Pub. rels. officer U.S. Mcht. Marine Acad., N.Y.C., 1966-67; bd. dirs. East End Counseling Project, Southampton, N.Y., 1983--, adv. bd. East Hampton Town, 1983--. Editor: Danger, Insurance Fraud In Progress, 1987. Mem. Democratic Com., East Hampton, N.Y. Mem. AAUW (pres. 1987), Friends of Guild Hall (pres.), Hadassah (pres.). Office: Carriage House Press Carriage Ln Barnes Landing East Hampton NY 11937

KULL, BARBARA ANNE, small business owner; b. Cin., Sept. 11, 1946; d. Robert David and Naomi (Hail) Reese; m. Tony M. Horn, June 27, 1964 (div. Mar. 1976); children: Lauren, Scott, Jodi. Student, U. Cin., 1976-80. Sec. JMG Film Co., Cin., 1964-75; with real estate sales Signature Realtors, Cin., 1975-77; legal clk. Office of Hearings and Appeals, Cin., 1976-80; wholesale distbr. Barb's Aviary Supply, Marco, Fla., 1982—. Mem. Marco C. of C., Nat. Assn. Female Execs. Republican. Mem. Dutch Reformed Ch.

KULP, EILEEN BODNAR, social worker; b. Glens Falls, N.Y., Sept. 25, 1941; d. Joseph and Bertha (Choquette) Bodnar; m. Randolph Heath Kulp, June 5, 1961; children: Kimberly, Randolph Heath II, Kevin Joseph. B in Sociology, Hampton (Va.) U., 1978; MSW, Norfolk (Va.) State U., 1981. Lic. clin. social worker, Va.; diplomate in clin. social work Nat. Bd. Examiners. Social worker II adult chem. dependency Peninsula Hosp., Hampton, 1981-82, leader treatment team adolescent chem. dependency unit, 1982-84, sr. clinician adult chem. dependency unit, 1984-86, program coord. adult chem. dependency unit, 1986-88, dir. adult treatment programs, 1988—; pvt. practice Newport News, Va., 1986—; mem. addictions profls. team People to People Exchange Program, Norway, Sweden, Germany, 1989—. Bd. dirs. Hampton Coun. PTA's, pres., 1979-80; bd. dirs. Hampton City Schs. Bd. Edn., 1981-85; chmn. advisory bd. Hampton Juvenile and Domestic Rels. Ct., bd. dirs., 1984—; bd. dirs. Commonwealth Va. Citizens Adv. Bd. Youth and Family Svcs., Dept. Corrections, 1989—. Mem. Va. Coun. Social Welfare (pres. Tidewater chpt. 1987-88), Nat. Assn. Social Workers, Va. Assn. Alcoholism and Drug Abuse Counselors, Am. Coun. Alcoholism, Hampton Mental Health Bd. (pres. 1988-89), Va. Soc. Clin. Social Workers, Va. Coun. PTA's (life), Acad. Cert. Social Workers (cert.), Alpha Kappa Mu. Roman Catholic. Home: 26 Sarfan Dr Hampton VA 23664 Office: Peninsula Hosp 2244 Executive Dr Hampton VA 23664

KULP, NANCY JANE, comedienne; b. Harrisburg, Pa., Aug. 28, 1921; d. Robert Tilden and Marjorie (Snyder) K.; m. Charles Malcolm Dacus, Apr. 1, 1951. B.A. in Journalism, Fla. State U., 1943; postgrad., U. Miami, 1950. Publicity dir. radio sta. WGBS, 1946-47; continuity dir. radio sta. WIOD, Miami, 1947-49; continuity dir.-performer TV Sta. WTVJ, Miami, 1949-50; prof. TV and motion picture history Juniata Coll., Huntingdon, Pa., 1985, artist in residence, 1985. Began acting career in Hollywood, Calif., 1952; motion pictures include Model and the Marriage Broker, 1952, A Star is Born, 1953, Sabrina, 1954, Three Faces of Eve, 1955, The Parent Trap, 1957, A Wilder Summer, 1983; appeared on: TV shows Playhouse 90, 1956, Lux Video, 1955, Lucy Show, 1956, Bob Cummings Show, 1955-60, Beverly Hillbillies, 1961-71 (Emmy nomination 1967), Brian Keith Show, 1973, Sanford and Son, Return of the Beverly Hillbillies, 1981, Scarecrow and Mrs. King, 1986, Simon and Simon, 1986, Quantum Leap, Arsenio Hall, 1989; Broadway play Mornings at Seven, 1982; play Accent on Youth, Long Wharf Theatre, 1983, appeared in Romeo and Juliet, Ga. Shakespeare Festival, 1987, also London retropsective Showboat, Carnegie Hall, Angel Records. Hon. chmn. Humane Soc., 1965—; co-chmn. Roosevelt Coachella Valley March of Dimes, Valley March of Dimes; Dem. candidate for Congress, 9th dist. Pa., 1984. Served to lt. (j.g.) WAVES, USNR, 1943-45. Mem. Acad. Motion Pictures Arts and Scis., Actors and Others for Animals, LWV, Pi Beta Phi. Democrat.

KULPA, KAREN JOAN, benefit analyst; b. Chgo., Dec. 5, 1965; d. Alexander P. and Corinne A. (Gallagher) K. Student, dePaul U. Cert. employee benefit specialist. Benefit analyst Quaker Oats Co., Chgo. Mem. NAFE. Home: 5044 S LaCrosse Chicago IL 60638

KULZER-HOLLEN, REGINA DYANNE, business owner, counselor; b. Orange, N.J., May 8, 1951; d. Henry E. and JoAnn Crawford (Kieffer) Kulzer; m. L.A. Hollen II (div. 1988); 1 child, L. Adam III. BS in Home Econs. Edn., Bridgewater (Va.) Coll., 1973; MEd in Rehab. Counseling, James Madison U., 1981. Food svc. dir. Camelot Hall Nursing Home, Harrisonburg, Va., 1974-77; instr. Woodrow Wilson Ctr. for Ind. Living and Rehab., Fishersville, Va., 1977-82; owner, mgr. Victuals & Viands Catering, Harrisonburg, 1984-90; counselor students with disabilities Blue Ridge Community Coll., Weyers Cave, Va., 1986-89; counselor, learning disabled students Ga. So. U., Statesboro, 1989—; state appointee project VAST, Va. State Dept. Edn., Richmond, 1981—; disabilities cons., community cons. Va. Community Coll. System, Richmond, 1988—. Mem. Dem. Party, Harrisonburg, 1986-90; bd. dirs. Shenandoah Valley chpt. March of Dimes, Harrisonburg, 1975-80, Spl. Olympics Area IV, Harrisonburg, 1986-88. Mem. AAUW, Nat. Rehab. Assn., Va. Assn. Rehab. Instrs. (pres. 1977-81), Assn. on Handicapped Student Svc. Programs in Post Secondary Edn. Home: 131 Olde Towne Dr Statesboro GA 30458 Office: Ga So Univ Landrum Box 8011 Statesboro GA 30460-8011

KUMAR, PAMELA EILEEN, certified public accountant; b. Elkin, N.C., Oct. 22, 1944; d. Dennis Clemont and Mary (Adams) Brown; m. Cidambi Krishna Kumar, Aug. 17, 1968; children: Ramanathan, Gita. BA in Anthropology, U. N.C., 1967; postgrad., U. Mich., 1967-68, U. Balt., 1990—. CPA, Md. Staff acct. Russell Coburn & Co, PA, Columbia, Md., 1976-84; tax mgr. Russell Coburn & Co, PA, Columbia, 1984-89, tax ptnr., 1989—; sec. Columbia (Md.) Time Sharing, Inc., 1989—, Russell Coburn & Co., PA, Columbia, 1989—. Vol. Howard County Office on Aging, 1990—. Mem. AICPAs (tax div. 1989—), Md. Assn. CPAs (estate tax com. 1990—), Columbia Bus. Exchange (rep.), Howard County C. of C. (legis. com. 1989—, subcom. chmn. 1989—). Democrat. Home: 4281 Bright Bay Way Ellicott City MD 21043 Office: Russell Coburn & Co PA PO Box 832 Amer City Bldg Columbia MD 21044

KUMAR, SMITA RAJEEV, allergist, immunologist, pediatrician; b. Chengannur, Kerala, India, Apr. 12, 1959; came to U.S., 1982; d. Chandra and Shashikala (Pillai) Sekhar; m. T. Rajeev Kumar, Jan. 13, 1981; children: Akash, Anisha. MB, BS, S. Gujarat U., Surat, India, 1982. Diplomate Am. Bd. Pediatrics, Am. Bd. Allergy-Immunology. Intern in pediatrics N.Y. Med. Coll.-Met. Hosp. Ctr., 1982-83, resident in pediatrics, 1983-84, chief resident in pediatrics, 1984-85; fellow in allergy, immunology and pulmonary diseases Med. Coll. Cornell U., N.Y.C., 1985-87, instr. dept. pediatrics Med. Coll., 1987-88, asst. prof. pediatrics Med. Coll., 1988-89; staff allergist Our Lady Mercy Hosp., Bronx, 1989—. Contbr. articles to profl. jours. Fellow Am. Acad. Pediatrics; mem. Am. Acad. Allergy and Immunology, Am. Coll. Allergists. Home: 153 Ferndale Rd Scarsdale NY 10583 Office: Our Lady Mercy Hosp Med Ctr 600 E 233d St Bronx NY 10466

KUMIN, LIBBY BARBARA, speech pathologist, educator; b. Bklyn., Nov. 11, 1945; d. Herbert H. and Berniece (Shuch) K.; m. Martin J. Lazar, Jan. 18, 1969; 1 child, Jonathan Kumin. BA summa cum laude, LIU, 1965; MA, NYU, 1966, PhD, 1969. Lic. speech pathologist, Md. Asst. prof. speech pathology U. Md., College Park, 1972-76; cons., 1976-80; adj. prof. Loyola Coll., Balt., 1976-80, assoc. prof., 1980-88, chmn. dept. speech and lang. pathology, 1983—, prof., 1988—; mem. Speech/Lang./Hearing Commn., Howard County Bd. Edn., Columbia, Md., 1982-89; specialist in speech and language in Down Syndrome; assoc. profl. adv. bd. Nat. Down Syndrome Congress. Author: Aphasia, 1978; author articles on Down Syndrome, others. Vol. cons. Howard County Office on Aging, 1977-83. Recipient Outstanding Individual of Year award Howard County Assn. Retarded Citizens, Nat. Meritorious Service award Nat. Down Syndrome Congress, 1987. Aaron and Lillie Straus Found. grantee, 1983-89; Columbia Found. grantee; recipient summer research award Loyola Coll., 1983. Mem. Am. Speech/Lang./Hearing Assn. (cert.), Md. Speech and Hearing Assn., Nat. Down Syndrome Congress, ARC, Sigma Tau Delta, Pi Lambda Theta. Office: Loyola Coll Dept Speech Pathology 4501 N Charles St Baltimore MD 21210

KUMIN, MAXINE WINOKUR, author, poet; b. Phila., June 6, 1925; d. Peter and Doll (Simon) Winokur; m. Victor Montwid Kumin, June 29, 1946; children—Jane Simon, Judith Montwid, Daniel David. A.B., Radcliffe Coll., 1946, M.A., 1948. Cons. in poetry Library of Congress, 1981-82. Author: (poems) Halfway, 1961, The Privilege, 1965, The Nightmare Factory, 1970, Up Country, 1972 (Pulitzer prize for poetry 1973), House, Bridge, Fountain, Gate, 1975, The Retrieval System, 1978, Our Ground Time Here Will Be Brief, 1982, The Long Approach, 1985, In Deep: Country Essays, 1987, Nurture, 1989; (novels) Through Dooms of Love, 1965, The Passions of Uxport, 1968, The Abduction, 1971, The Designated Heir, 1974; (essays) To Make A Prairie, 1979; (short stories) Why Can't We Live Together Like Civilized Human Beings?, 1982; author 20 children's books; contbr. poems to nat. mags. Recipient Am. Acad. and Inst. Arts and Letters award, 1980, Levinson award Poetry Mag., 1987; Woodrow Wilson vis. fellow, 1979-80; Acad. Am. Poets fellow, 1985. Mem. Poetry Soc. Am., PEN Am., Authors Guild, The Writers Union. Address: Curtis Brown Assoc 10 Astor Pl New York NY 10003-6903

KUNDSIN, RUTH BLUMFELD, microbiology educator, epidemiologist; b. N.Y.C., July 30, 1916; d. John David and Emily Anna (Krumin) Blumfeld; m. Edwin Stanley Kundsin, June 17, 1935; children: Andrea Ruth, Dennis Edwin. BA, Hunter Coll., 1936; MA, Boston U., 1949; ScD in Pub. Health, Harvard U., 1958; ScD (hon.), Lowell (Mass.) U., 1975. Diplomate Am. Med. Microbiology. Microbiologist Brigham and Women's Hosp., Boston, 1951-58, asst. to surgery, 1958-64, assoc. staff mem., 1964-70, hosp. epidemiologist, 1970—, lab. dir., 1976—; founder Kundsin Lab., Boston, 1981—; assoc. prof. microbiology and molecular genetics Harvard Med. Sch., Boston, 1976—; mem. adv. panel U.S. Pharmacopeia, Rockville, Md., 1981-86. Editor: Women and Success, 1974; contbr. numerous articles to profl. jours. Named to Hall of Fame Hunter Coll.; neonatology grantee NIH, 1978-85. Fellow N.Y. Acad. Scis., Am. Acad. Microbiology, Phi Beta Kappa. Home: 71 Pratt Rd Squantum MA 02171 Office: Kundsin Lab 75 Francis St Boston MA 02115

KUNIN, MADELEINE MAY, governor of Vermont; b. Zurich, Switzerland, Sept. 28, 1933; came to U.S., 1940, naturalized, 1947; d. Ferdinand and Renee (Bloch) May; m. Arthur S. Kunin, June 21, 1959; children—Julia, Peter, Adam, Daniel. B.A., U. Mass., 1956; M.S., Columbia U., 1957; M.A., U. Vt., 1967; several hon. degrees. Newspaper reporter Burlington Free Press, Vt., 1957-58; guide Brussels World's Fair, Belgium, 1958; TV asst. producer Sta. WCAX-TV, Burlington, 1960-61; freelance writer, instr. English Trinity Coll., Burlington, 1969-70; mem. Vt. Ho. of Reps., 1973-78; lt. gov. State of Vt., Montpelier, 1979-82, gov., 1985-90; fellow Inst. Politics, Kennedy Sch. Govt., Harvard U., 1983; lectr. Middlebury Coll., St. Michael's Coll., 1984; mem. Vt. Commn. on Adminstrn. of Justice, 1976-77, Vt. Joint Fiscal Com., 1977-78; mem. exec. com. Nat. Conf. Lt. Govs., 1979-80. Author: (with Marilyn Stout) The Big Green Book, 1976; contbr. articles to profl. jours., mags. and newspapers. Mem. exec. com. Dem. Policy Council. Named Outstanding State Legislator, Eagleton Inst. Politics, Rutgers U., 1975. Mem. Nat. Gov.'s Assn. (mem. exec com.), Nat. Govs.' Conf. (chair com. on energy and the environ.), New Eng. Gov.'s Conf. (chairperson). Democrat. Office: Office Gov Pavilion Bldg 5th Fl Montpelier VT 05602

KUNKEL, GEORGIE MYRTIA, retired school counselor; b. Seattle; d. George Riley and Myrtia (McLaughlin) Bright; m. Norman C. Kunkel, June 25, 1946; children: N. Joseph D.C., Stephen Gregory, Susan Ann, Kimberly Jane. BA in Edn., Western Wash. U., 1945; MEd, U. Wash., 1968. Typist, clk. FHA, Seattle, 1940; tchr. pub. schs. Vadar, Centralia, Wash., Seattle, 1941-67; pvt. cons., Seattle, 1970-85; counselor Highline Pub. Schs., Seattle, 1967-82; sch. counselor rep. State of Art Conf., Balt., 1980; cons. Project Equality, Highline Sch. Dist., Seattle, 1975-76. Editor Women and Girls in Edn., 1972-75. Contbr. articles to profl. jours. Organizer Women and Girls in Edn., Wash. state, 1971; pres. Wash. State NOW, 1973; mem. West Seattle Community Council, 1980. Grantee Women Adminstrs. Wash. State, 1971, Edn. Service Dist., Seattle, 1980. Mem. NEA (sec. pub. relations), Am. Assn. Counseling and Devel. (pres. state br. 1982-83), Am. Sch. Counseling Assn. (pres. state div. 1980-81), Seattle Assn. Counseling and Devel. (organizer), Holmes Harbor Homeowners Assn. (organizer and pres.). Democrat. Unitarian Universalist. Club: Past Presidents (Seattle). Avocations: writing, singing. Home and Office: 3409 SW Trenton St Seattle WA 98126

KUNKLE, SANDRA LEE, brokerage house executive, sales executive; b. Park Ridge, Ill., June 20, 1960; d. Arland Blaine Kunkle and Judith (Spyrison) Carpenter. BS in Fin., U. Ky., 1982. Cert. fin. planner. Acct. exec. Paine Webber and Co., Chgo., 1982-84; v.p., mut. fund coordinator Bear Stearns and Co., Chgo., 1984—; sales mgr. Gruntal & Co., Chgo., 1989—; instr. "Successful Investing" Chgo. Bar Assn., 1985—. Contbr. articles to women's mags., 1985. Mgr. campaign Rep. com., Chgo., 1985-87. Mem. Am. Horse Show Assn. (Chgo. and Ky. chpts.). Office: Gruntal & Co 135 S LaSalle Ste 4200 Chicago IL 60603

KUNS, NANCY LEE, office manager, pharmacist; b. Ashtabula, Ohio, Apr. 16, 1960; d. Frank Joseph Jr. Nappi and Wanda Gay (Britton) Mackey; m. Bryan P. Kuns, July 30, 1983; 1 child, Kaitlyn. BS, U. Toledo, 1983. Office mgr. Kuns Family Medicine, Inc., Castalia, Ohio, 1987—; pharmacist Firelands Community Hosp., Sandusky, Ohio, 1989—, Pharmacy Support Systems, Cleve., 1989—. Com. chmn. Aux. to 5th Dist. of Ohio Osteo. Assn., 1990—, treas., 1987—. Mem. Ohio Pharmacist's Assn., N.W. Ohio Hosp. Pharmacists, Ohio Soc. Hosp. Pharmacists, Beta Sigma Phi (v.p. Pi Eta chpt. 1990-91). Roman Catholic. Home: 4710 Bellevue Castalia Rd Castalia OH 44824

KUNSTADTER, GERALDINE S., foundation executive; b. Boston, Jan. 6, 1928; d. Harry Herman and Nettie Sapolsky; m. John W. Kunstadter, Apr. 23, 1949; children: John W., Lisa, Christopher, Elizabeth. Student, MIT, 1945-48. Draftsman U. Chgo. Cyclotron Project, 1948; engring. asst. Gen. Electric Corp., Lynn, Mass., 1948-49; chmn., dir. A. Kunstadter Family Found., N.Y.C., 1966—; host family program dir. N.Y.C. Commn. for UN, 1971-86; pres. Nat. Inst. Social Scis., 1979-81. Bd. dirs. Ptnrs. of Ams. Found., Washington, Menninger Clin., Topeka, Yale-China Assn., Inst. Current World Affairs, English-Speaking Union, Feld Ballet, N.Y.C., Ctr. U.S.-China Arts Exch., N.Y. Regional Assn. Grantmakers, Inst. World Affairs, East Side Internat. Community Ctr., Am. Forum; mem. resource coun. Ptnrs. of Ams., Washington; mem. adv. coun. Bridges to China Found., East Asian studies program MIT Sch. Architecture; mem. nat. com. U.S.-China rels.; mem. Peace Links Leadership Network, Nat. Coun. of Women (internat. hospitality com.), Overseas Devel. Coun., Atlantic Coun., N.Y.-Beijing Friendship City Com., MIT Corp. Devel. Com.; hon. bd. dirs. Govs. of Nat. Women's Employment and Edn., Inc.; trustee, chmn. bd. Windham Coll., Putney, Vt. Recipient Windham award, 1970, silver medal Nat. Inst. Social Sci., 1981. Mem. Am. Women's Club, Hurlingham Club, Lansdowne Club (London).

KUNTZ, MARY M. KOHLS, corporate treasurer; b. Chgo., Nov. 25, 1928; d. George William and Myrtle Hansen K.; m. Earl Jeremy Kuntz, July 28, 1957; children: Karen A., Bradford G. Student, Northwestern U., 1946-50. Pvt. practice acctg. Chgo., 1951-63; owner Chgo. Tax Service, 1954-63; controller Gen. Bus. Services, Chgo., 1960-68; v.p., treas. Gen. Tele-Communications, Inc., Chgo., 1968—. Leader Girl Scouts Am., 1968-71; pres. Wilmette (Ill.) PTA, 1971-75. Mem. Assn. Telemessaging Svcs. Internat., Nat. Soc. Pub. Accts., Chgo. Soc. Clubs, Women's Club Wilmette (bd. dirs. 1975). Office: Gen Tele-Communications Inc 69 W Washington St Chicago IL 60602

KUNTZ, NOELLA MAE, pharmacist; b. Harvey, N.D., Dec. 20, 1950; d. John Martin and Kathleen Otillia (Senger) K. BS, N.D. State U., 1974. Registered pharmacist, Wis., Ill., Colo., Ariz. Pharmacist intern Severson Drugs, Pelican Rapids, Minn., 1974-75, Walgreen Drugs, Milw., 1975-76; staff pharmacist Walgreen Drugs, Chgo., 1977-79; chief pharmacist Walgreen Drugs, Naperville, Ill., 1979-82; chief pharmacist Walgreen Drugs, Chgo., 1982-84, dist. pharm supr., 1984-87; pharmacy mgr. Walgreen Drugs, Sun City West, Ariz., 1987-89; dist. pharm. supr. Walgreen Drugs, Phoenix, 1989—. Contbr. articles to profl. jours. Group speaker Walgreens, Chgo., 1979-87; bd. dirs. St. Luke's Cath. Ch., Phoenix, 1988. Mem. Am. Pharmacist Assn., Ill. Pharmacist Assn. (v.p. 1984-85), Ariz. Pharmacist Assn., Walgreen's Ambassador Club, Kappa Epsilon (v.p.). Home: 1010 E Rosemonte Dr Phoenix AZ 85024 Office: Walgreen Drug Co 4545 N 27th Ave Phoenix AZ 85017

KUNZ, JANET ALICE, university accounting administrator; b. Great Falls, Mont., July 21, 1956; d. George A. and Frances I. (Kuich) Kunz. BA, BS, U. Mont., 1987. Mgr., designer Flowers by Roll, Great Falls, 1984; brand transition asst. Black & Decker/Dery Ptnrs., N.Y.C., 1985-87; adminstrv. aide U. Mont., Missoula, 1985-89, acctg. technician, 1989-90; pvt. practice Automated Merchandising, Helena, Mont., 1990—. Mem. Am. Inst. Econ. Rsch., NAFE. Home and Office: 1020 Wilder Helena MT 59601

KUO, LOUISE RAMONA, insurance company executive; b. N.Y.C., May 28, 1963; d. Larry Han-Ching and Lilian Li-Cheng (Chou) K. BA, MA with distinction and honors, Stanford U., 1985; cert. with honors, Inst. Polit. Studies, Paris, 1983; postgrad., Inter-U. Ctr. Japanese Lang. Studies, Tokyo, 1985-86. Cons. Bain & Co., San Francisco, 1986-89; gen. ptnr. Vision Investments, real estate, San Francisco, 1987-89; mgr. enterprise plannning unit The Prudential Ins. Co. Am., Newark, 1989—. Vol. homelessness study Bain & Co., San Francisco, 1988. T.J. Watson Meml. scholar IBM, 1981-85, Japan Found. scholar, 1985, World Affairs Coun. scholar, 1985. Mem. Pi Sigma Alpha., Phi Beta Kappa. Office: The Prudential Ins Co Am Enterprise Planning Unit 22 Prudential Pla 751 Broad St Newark NJ 07102

KUPCINET, ESSEE SOLOMON, performing arts producer; b. Chgo., Dec. 7; d. Joseph David and Doris (Schoke) Solomon; PhB, Northwestern U., 1937; m. Irv Kupcinet, Feb. 12, 1939; children: Karyn (dec.), Jerry S. Asst. to dir. psychology dept. Michael Reese Hosp., Chgo., 1939-41; exec. producer eight Jefferson Award Shows; producer 1st Literary Arts Ball, Cultural Center, Chgo., 1979; talent coordinator Kup's Show, Chgo., 1964-84; producer for spl. events, 1978—. Mem. adv. bd., bd. dirs. Free St. Theater; prodn. chmn. Acad. Honors, 1984-87; chmn. bd. trustees Acad. Sch. Performing Arts, 1984-86, hon. lifetime chair, 1986—; prodn. chmn. Variety Club Telethon, 1984, 85; bd. dirs. Mus. Broadcasting Commn.; exec. com. Chgo. Tourism Council, 1984-88; exec. bd. Internat. Theatre Festival, 1985-86; mem. sponsors com. Chgo. Pub. Library, 1985-86. Decorated Knight of Orange Nassau (The Netherlands); recipient Spl. award Jefferson Com., 1976; Cliff Dwellers award, 1975; Emmy award CBS, 1977, 79; Artisan award Acad. Theatre Arts and Friends, 1977; Prime Minister's medal for service to Israel, 1974; Woman of Yr. award Facets Multimedia, 1982, Mass Media award NCCJ, 1988, others; named (with Irv Kupcinet) Mr. and Mrs. Chgo., Greater North Michigan Ave. Assn., 1987, Chgo. Acad. for the Arts, 1988, Woman of Yr., Variety Club #26, 1988. Mem. Nat. Acad. TV Arts and Scis. (governing bd., program chmn. 1982—, Govs. award 1986), Arts Club. Jewish.

KUPIETZ, ROBERTA, psychologist; b. N.Y.C., Mar. 14, 1953; d. Julius Nathan and Blanche (Gorelick) K.; m. Paul J. Shapiro, Feb. 26, 1989. BA, SUNY, Albany, 1975; MA, Hofstra U., 1977, PhD, 1980. Lic. clin. psychologist, N.Y. Sch. psychologist Wantagh (N.Y.) Pub. Sch., 1980—; pvt. practice Merrick, 1982—; lectr. United Synagogue Youth, N.Y.C., 1987-90, City Vols. Corps, N.Y.C., 1989. Dance leader, choreographer Folk Dance Group, 1976-89; dance cons. Israel Folk Dance Festival, 1990. Psychologist Com. on Spl. Edn., Wantagh, 1983-90. Mem. Am. Psychol. Assn., Nassau County Psychol. Assn., Phi Beta Kappa. Jewish. Office: 1955 Merrick Rd 204 Merrick NY 11566

KUPPERMAN, HELEN SLOTNICK, lawyer; b. Boston; d. Morris Louis and Minnie (Kaplan) Slotnick; B.A., Smith Coll.; postgrad. Royal Acad. Dramatic Art, London; J.D., Boston Coll., 1966; m. Robert H. Kupperman, Dec. 23, 1967; 1 dau., Tamara. Bar: Mass. 1966, D.C. 1986. Atty., advisor NASA, Washington, 1966-73, sr. atty., 1973-77, asst. gen. counsel for gen. law, 1977-86, assoc. gen. counsel, 1986, spl. asst. gen. counsel space station, 1986-87, chairperson contract adjustment bd., 1974-87, exec. v.p. Robert H. Kupperman & Assocs. Inc., 1987—; adj. fellow space policy study Ctr. Strategic and Internat. Studies, 1987-88; rep. on U.S. delegation to legal subcomittee of UN Com. on Peaceful Uses of Outer Space, 1977-87. Recipient NASA Sustained Superior Performance award, 1977, Exceptional Service medal, 1983, NASA Ses Bonus, 1980, 85, Space Station Task Force Group Achivement award NASA, 1984. Mem. U.S. Assn. of Internat. Inst. Space Law (sec. 1981, bd. dirs. 1989—), ABA, Fed., Mass., D.C., Boston bar assns., Internat. Women Lawyers Assn., Am. Astronautical Assn. (gen. counsel 1986-87). Jewish. Bus. editor Boston Coll. Indsl. and Comml. Law Rev., 1965-66. Home: 2832 Ellicott St NW Washington DC 20008

KUPST, MARY JO, psychologist, researcher; b. Chgo., Oct. 4, 1945; d. George Eugene and Winifred Mary (Hughes) K.; m. Alfred Procter Stresen-Reuter Jr., Aug. 21, 1977. BS, Loyola U., 1967, MA, 1969, PhD, 1972. Lic. clin. psychologist, Ill., Wis. Postdoctoral fellow U. Ill. Med. Ctr., Chgo., 1971-72; rsch. psychologist Children's Meml. Hosp., Chgo., 1972-89; assoc. prof. psychiatry and pediatrics Northwestern U. Med. Sch., Chgo., 1981-89; prof. pediatrics Med. Coll. Wis., Milw., 1989—; practice clin. psychology, Chgo., 1975-89, McHenry, Ill., 1987-89; assoc. prof. pediatrics and psychiatry, Northwestern U. Med. Sch., Chgo., 1980-89. Editor: (with others) The Child with Cancer, 1980; contbr. articles to profl. jours. Mem. Am. Psychol. Assn., Ill. Psychol. Assn. Office: Dept of Pediatrics Med Coll Wis 8701 Watertown Plank Rd Milwaukee WI 53226

KURAS, JEAN MARY, educator; b. Jersey City, Jan. 30, 1944; d. Stanley Gregory and Ann (Tyra) K. BA, N.J. State Tchrs. Coll., 1960, MA, 1966. Tchr. Bloomfield (N.J.) Bd. Edn., 1962—. Pres. Big Bros.-Big Sisters Essex and Newark, Bloomfield, 1982-84, Bloomfield Hist. Soc., 1989-91; vol. office staff Senator Bradley of N.J., 1984; trustee League for Family Svc., Bloomfield, 1988-90. Art for Kids grantee Sta. WOR-TV, N.J., 1990. Mem. NEA, N.J. Edn. Assn., Essex County Edn. Assn., Bloomfield Edn. Assn. (sec. 1987-90, v.p. 1990-91). Home: 11 Hawthorne Ave Glen Ridge NJ 07028 Office: Oak View Sch 150 Garrabrant Ave Bloomfield NJ 07003

KUREK, DOLORES BODNAR, physical science professor; b. Toledo, Dec. 14, 1935; d. James J. and Veronica Clara (Gorajewski) Bodnar; m. Arnold John Kurek, Aug. 30, 1958; children: Kerry Ellyn, Darrah Jeanne, Michele Marie, James Dominic, Ursula Elisabeth. BS, Mary Manse Coll., 1958; MEd, U. Toledo, 1968, postgrad. Chemistry, physics and math. tchr. St. Ursula Acad., Toledo, 1961-75; sci. tchr. McAuley High Sch., Toledo, 1975-78; chemistry tchr. St. Francis de Sales High Sch., Toledo, 1978-83; instr. math. and chemistry Owens Tech. Coll., Toledo, 1980-86; instr. chemistry and physics Lourdes Coll., Sylvania, Ohio, 1983-86, asst. prof. phys. sci., 1986—; instr. math. U. Toledo, 1986—; pres. judging chair N.W. Dist. Sci. Day, Toledo, 1975—; regional dir. Women in Sci., Toledo, 1987—; bd. dirs. Toledo Jr. Sci. Humanities Symposium, Toledo; v.p. edn. Tech. Soc. Toledo, 1989—. Inventee in field; contbr. articles to profl. jours. Mem. Toledo Mus. of Art, 1987—, Toledo Zool. Soc., 1988—. Named One of 100 Women Sci. Exemplars in Ohio Women in Sci., Engring. and Math. Consortium of Ohio, 1988, Woman of Toledo St. Vincent Med. Ctr., 1988; Mary Manse scholar, 1954-58. Mem. Am. Chem. Soc. (James Conant Bryant award 1980, 81), Ohio Acad. Sci. (Acker award 1980), Nat. Sci. Tchrs. Assn., Soc. for Coll. Sci. Tchrs., Am. Assn. Physics Tchrs., MENSA, Phi Delta Kappa (newsletter editor 1984-86). Roman Catholic. Home: 624 Arcadia Ave Toledo OH 43610 Office: Lourdes Coll 6832 Convent Blvd Sylvania OH 43560

KURIANSKY, JUDY, talk show host, psychologist, writer; b. N.Y.C., Jan. 31, 1947; d. Abraham and Sylvia (Feld) Brodsky; m. Edward Kuriansky, Aug. 24, 1969. BA, Smith Coll., 1968; MEd, Boston U., 1970; PhD, NYU, 1980. Reporter WABC-TV, N.Y.C., 1980-86, WBZ-TV, Boston, 1981-82, CBS-TV, N.Y.C., 1986-88, WPIX-TV, N.Y.C., 1987—, CNBC-TV, Ft. Lee, N.J., 1989—; host Wellness for Women program WDBB-TV, Birmingham, Ala., 1988-89; program host Sta. WARC-AM, N.Y.C., 1980-87, Sta. WOR-AM, 1987-88, ABC Talk Radio, N.Y.C., 1988-90, J.C. Penney Golden Rule Network, Dallas, 1988—; cons. Lily of France, Val Mode Lingerie, Charles of the Ritz, The Rolland Co., Taylor-Gordon Arons Advt.; tchr. Columbia U. Med. Sch., 1974-79, Inst. for Health and Religion, 1980-82; prof. psychology NYU, 1989—; adv. bd. Woman mag., 1989—. Author: Sex, Now That I've Got Your Attention, Let Me Answer Your Questions, 1984, How to Love A Nice Guy, 1990; columnist Family Circle mag., 1984-89, Whole Life Times, 1986-87; contbg. editor Beauty Mag., 1989-90. Named Most Unforgettable Woman, Revlon, 1990; recipient Civilian Commendation, N.Y.C. Police Dept., 1984, Cert., AWRT, 1984, Maggie award Planned Parenthood, 1985, Freedoms Found. award Children for a Better Soc., 1986, Olive award Coun. of Chs., 1986, Mercury award Larimi Communications, 1987. Mem. Am. Women in Radio and TV of N.Y. (pres. 1988-89, found. vice chair 1988-90—), TV Acad. of N.Y. (gov. 1987—). Office: CNBC 2200 Fletcher Ave Fort Lee NJ 07024

KURKE, KATHLEEN TIGHE, owner executive search company, consultant; b. Bronx, N.Y., Nov. 14, 1958; d. Donald W. and Catherine (Connolly) Tighe; m. David S. Kurke, Feb. 22, 1986. BA, Dickinson Coll., 1986. Assoc. dir. United Way Am., Alexandria, Va., 1980-84; account exec. The Forum Corp., Boston, 1984-86; v.p. sales Quicksoft Corp., Seattle, 1986-87; nat. account mgr. Weber and Assocs., Reston, Va., 1987-88; pres. Skills Cons., Fairfax, Va., 1988—. Mem. Am. Soc. Tng. and Devel. (program chmn. 1978-80). Home: 9695 Stanton Dr Fairfax VA 22031 Office: Skills Cons 10565 Lee Hwy #102 Fairfax VA 22030

KUROPAT, ROSEMARY LOUISE, marketing executive; b. Waterbury, Conn., Apr. 12, 1958; d. Stanley A. and Mildred A. (Harrigan) K. AA, Hartford Coll. for Women, 1978; AB, Smith Coll., 1980. Writer, editor Fed. Reserve Bank N.Y., N.Y.C., 1980-81; editor Chase Manhattan Bank, N.Y.C., 1981-82, v.p, 1982-83, internat. mktg. officer, 1983-84; ptnr. Soho Lexigraphics, N.Y.C., 1984-86; v.p., mktg. State of N.Y. Mortgage Agy., 1986-88; sr. v.p. Fin. Svc. Corp., N.Y.C., 1988-90; chief of staff Office of N.Y.C. Dep. Mayor for Fin. and Econ. Devel., 1990—; mktg. cons. Nat. Women & The Law Assn. N.Y., 1986—, mktg. writer, cons. for internat. devel. Author: Challenge Bigotry, 1986, Making NY The Home Advertising Campaign, 1987-88, Reaper Madness, 1989. Fundraiser Community Svc. Ctr., N.Y.C., 1986, God's Love We Deliver N.Y.C., 1988, Tom Duane for City Council, N.Y.C., 1988-89; bd. dirs. GLAAD, N.Y.C., 1986. Recipient Writing Excellence Internat. Assn. Bus. and Profl. Communicators, 1982-84. Mem. Regional Plan Assn., Women in Housing and Fin., N.Y. Advt. Network, Coun. Indsl. Devel. Bond Issuers. Democrat. Home: 80 Varick St Apt 4C New York NY 10013 Office: City Hall Rm 1B New York NY 10007

KURTH, CAROL LYNN, business project analyst; b. Balt., July 27, 1948; d. Richard Harvey and Lena Augusta (Mueller) Shackelford; m. David Julius Kurth, Dec. 30, 1967; children: Carl, Todd. AA in Acctg., Community Coll. Balt., 1968; student, U. Md., 1977-79; BA in Bus. Mgmt., Stats. summa cum laude, N.C. State U., 1984. Acctg. asst. 1st Nat. Bank Md., Balt., 1968-71; statis. analyst Comml. Credit Corp., Balt., 1972-75; fin. reporting mgr. Control Data Corp./Comml. Credit Corp., Balt., 1975-77; new product intro. specialist No. Telecom, Inc., Research Triangle Park, N.C., 1984-85, prodn. and inventory mgr., 1986-87, bus. process adminstr., 1988—; internal cons. No. Telecom, U.S. and Can., 1989—, Bell No. Rsch. Corp., Research Triangle Park, 1989—. Contbr. articles to profl. publs. Mem. Am. Prodn. and Inventory Control Soc., Am. Legion Aux., Omicron Delta Epsilon. Office: No Telecom 4001 E Chapel Hill Nelson Hwy Research Triangle Park NC 27522

KURTH, JULIETTE ELIZABETH, actress; b. Madison, Wis., July 22, 1960; d. Richard Herbert and Barbara Joan (Frampton) K. BFA with honors, SUNY, Purchase, 1983. Appeared on Broadway and nat. tour La Cage Aux Folles, off-Broadway works include The Miser, The Majestic Kid, Man and Superman, Loves Labours' Lost, La Ronde, Burn This; TV appearances include One Life To Live, All My Children, Monsters, also numerous commls.

KURTH, TAMMIE ELAINE, lawyer; b. Kansas City, Mo., Oct. 1, 1960; d. George Washington and Betty Lou (Heger) Lee; m.Gerald Lee Kurth, Aug. 16, 1986; 1 child, Brandee Elise. AA, Seward County Community Coll., 1981; BS, Fort Hays State U., 1983; JD, Washburn U., 1986. Bar: Kans., U.S. Dist. Ct. Kans. 1986, Okla. 1987, Colo. 1988; lic. real estate agt. Law clk. Neubauer, Sharp, McQueen, Dreiling & Morain, P.A., Liberal, Kans., 1984-85, assoc., 1986—; rsch. editor Washburn Law Jour. Bd. Editors, Topeka, 1985-86. Mem. Washburn Nat. Moot Ct. Team, Washburn Moot Ct. Coun.,Topeka, 1985-86. Mem. ABA, Kans. Bar Assn., Okla. Bar Assn., Kans. Trial Lawyers Assn., Am. Trial Lawyers Assn., Soroptimists. Republican. Baptist. Home: 509 N Western Ave Liberal KS 67901 Office: Neubauer Sharp McQueen Dreiling & Morain PA PO Box 2619 Liberal KS 67905-2619

KURTZ, BARBARA BRANDON, educational administrator; b. Hillsdale, Mich., Jan. 17, 1941; d. Robert Dale and Dortha May (Bird) Brandon; m. Robert Roger Kurtz, June 20, 1964; children—Kevin, Christopher, Kathryn. B.S. in Music Edn., Western Mich. U., 1963; M.A. in Edn., Mich. State U., 1969; postgrad. John Carroll U., 1979-80; Ph.D. in Early Childhood Edn., Clayton U., 1983. Pres. adminstrn. U. Iowa Coop. Preschool, Iowa City, 1972-75; dir. Coral Nursery, Iowa City, 1975-77; head tchr. Covenant Early Childhood Programs, Cleve., 1977-79, dir., 1979—; supr. practicum Case Western Res. U., Cleve., 1977—; adj. faculty Lakeland Community Coll., Kirtland, Ohio, 1981—; project coordinator Child Day Care Planning Project of Cuyahoga County, Cleve., 1985—. Author: Center-Sponsored Family Day Care Homes, 1984. Editor: (with Brenda Boyd) Student Aide Training Packet, 1978. Contbr. articles to profl. jours. Mem. adv. panel Beginnings jour., 1984—; mem. day care adv. council Ohio Dept. Human Services; pres. elect Ohio Assn. for Edn. Young Children; Ohio rep. Nat. Assn. Hosp. Affiliated Child Care Ctrs.; mem. nat. adv. panel on health regulations in day care Ctr. for Disease Control. Recipient Gov.'s Spl. Recognition award State of Ohio, 1985. Mem. Nat. Assn. for Edn. of Young Children, Nat. Coalition for Campus Child Care, Ohio Assn. for Edn. of Young Children, Cleve. Assn. for Edn. of Young Children (pres., Early Childhood award 1984), Nat. Assn. Hosp. Affiliated Child Care Programs. Democrat. Roman Catholic. Avocations: cross-country skiing; snowshoeing; hiking; travel; reading. Home: 8856 Kirtland-Chardon Rd Kirtland OH 44060 Office: Covenant Early Childhood Programs 11205 Euclid Ave University Circle Cleveland OH 44060

KURTZ, CAROL DEANNE, chamber of commerce executive; b. Sacramento, Apr. 2, 1956; d. Edward Allwyn and Myrna Joan (Meng) K. BA in Polit. Sci., San Diego State U., 1978; grad. paralegal, U. San Diego, 1978. Paralegal Abramson, Church & Stave, Salinas, Calif., 1979; field rep. Calif. Assembly, Salinas, 1979-82; field coord. Calif. Lt. Gov. Campaign, Sacramento, 1982; adminstrv. asst. to chmn. Monterey County Bd. Suprs., Monterey, Calif., 1982-84; legis. cons. Cen. Coast Agrl. Task Force, Salinas, 1984-89; exec. dir. Ind. Growers Assn., Greenfield, Calif., 1986-89; exec. v.p. Salinas Area C. of C., 1989—; dir. Monterey County Econ. Devel. Corp. Bd. dirs. Monterey Bay Coalition Labor, Agr. and Bus., Salinas, 1986-89, AgHelp, Salinas, 1987-89; chmn. adopt-a-legislator Calif. Women for Agr., Salinas, 1988; v.p. Sportsfest, Salinas, 1984-87; alt. Monterey County Grand Jury, 1986; participant numerous local, state and fed. polit. campaigns; mem. bus. devel. com. United Way Salinas Valley. Recipient Disting. Alumni Leadership award Nat. Assn. Community Leadership Orgns., 1988. Mem. Salinas Jaycees, Univ. and Profl. Women, Salinas Area C. of C. (chmn. Agribus. Bay 1985-89, Athena award 1988), Pi Sigma Alpha. Republican. Presbyterian. Office: Salinas Area C of C 119 E Alisal St Salinas CA 93902

KURTZ, DOLORES MAY, civic worker; b. Reading, Pa., Oct. 27, 1933; d. Harry Claude and Ethel Gertrude (Fields) Filbert; m. William McKillips Kurtz, Oct. 26, 1957. Cert. secretarial program, Pa. State U., 1980. Legal sec. Snyder, Balmer & Kershner, Reading, 1951-53; head teletype operator E.I. duPont de Nemours, Reading, 1953-56; exec. sec. Ford New Holland (Pa.) Inc. (formerly Sperry New Holland div. Sperry Corp.)., 1956—. Mem. Lancaster County Rep. Com., 1983-85; pres. New Holland Area Woman's Club, 1982-84; bd. dirs. Lancaster County Fedn. Women's Clubs, 1982—, 2d v.p., 1984-86, 1st v.p., 1986-88, pres. 1988-90; founding mem. Summer Arts Festival, New Holland, 1980—, bd. dirs., 1985—; membership chmn. S.E. dist. Pa. Fedn. Women's Clubs, 1984-86; bd. dirs. Community Meml. Park Assn., New Holland, 1957-82; area rep., bd. dirs. Woman's Rep. Club Lancaster County, 1982-84; committeewoman New Holland Boro 1983-85. Recipient Outstanding Vol. for Pa. award Pa. Fedn. Women's Clubs, 1984. Methodist. Avocations: arts and crafts, travel, photography, boating.

KURTZ, KAREN BARBARA, editor, grants writer; b. Ft. Dodge, Iowa, July 21, 1948; d. Clifford Wenger and Eleanor Marie (Ulrich) Swartzendruber; m. Mark Allen Kurtz, June 25, 1977. AA, Hesston Coll., 1968; BA in Edn., Goshen (Ind.) Coll., 1970; MA in Elem. Edn., Ind. U., 1975. Lifetime cert. elem. tchr. First grade tchr. Fairfield Community Sch., Goshen, 1970-79; asst. editor and advt. copywriter Barth and Assocs., Middlebury, Ind., 1986-87; free-lance writer Kurtz Lens and Pen, Goshen, 1979—; asst. dir.. info. services Goshen (Ind.) Coll., 1987-89; dir. sponsored programs, 1990—. Author: Paper, Paint and Stuff, 1984, More Paper, Paint and Stuff, 1989; asst. editor: Heritage Country Mag., 1986-87; contbr. articles to various mags. Ch. bd. dirs. Goshen City Ch. of Brethren, 1977, also chmn. stewardship dr., coordinator art in the ch. Mem. NEA, Ind. State Tchr.'s Assn., Fairfield Educators Assn. Republican. Club: Bayview.

KURTZ, MAXINE, personnel services executive, lawyer; b. Mpls., Oct. 17, 1921; d. Jack Isadore and Beatrice (Cohen) K. BA, U. Minn., 1942; BS in Govt. Mgmt., U. Denver, 1945, JD, 1962; postdoctoral student, U. Calif., San Diego, 1978. Bar: Colo. 1962. Analyst Tri-County Regional Planning, Denver, 1945-47; chief rsch. and spl. projects Planning Office, City and County of Denver, 1947-66, dir. tech. and evaluation Model Cities Program, 1966-71; pers. rsch. officer Denver Career Service Auth., 1972-86, dir. pers. svcs., 1986-88, sr. pers. specialist, 1988—; expert witness nat. com. on urban problems U.S. Ho. of Reps., U.S. Senate. Author: Law of Planning and Land Use Regulations in Colorado, 1966; co-author: Care and Feeding of Witnesses, Expert and Otherwise, 1974; bd. editors: Pub. Adminstrn. Rev., Washington, 1980-83, 88—; editorial adv. bd. Internat. Pers. Mgmt. Assn.; prin. investigator: Employment: An American Enigma, 1979. Active Women's Forum of Colo.; Denver Dem. Com.; chair Colo. adv. com. to U.S. Civil Rights Commn., 1985-89, mem. 1989—. Sloan fellow, U. Denver, 1944-45; recipient Outstanding Achievement award U. Minn., 1971. Mem. ABA, Am. Inst. Planners (sec. treas. 1968-70, bd. govs. 1972-75), Am. Soc. Pub. Adminstrn. (nat. council 1978-81, Donald Stone award), Colo. Bar Assn., Denver Bar Assn., Order St. Ives., Pi Alpha Alpha. Jewish. Home: 2361 Monaco Pkwy Denver CO 80207 Office: Denver Career Service Authority 414 14th St Denver CO 80202

KURTZ, MYRA BERMAN, microbiologist; b. N.Y.C., July 20, 1945; d. Milton Robert and Shirley (Letzter) Berman; m. Stuart Jacob Kurtz, Aug. 16, 1970; 1 child, Rachel Linda. AB, Goucher Coll., 1966; PhD, Harvard U., 1971. Rsch. assoc. SUNY, Albany, 1971-72; assoc. prof. microbiology Universidade Fed. de Sao Carlos, Brazil, 1972-74; rsch. assoc. Waksman Inst. Microbiology, Piscataway, N.J., 1975-76, asst. rsch. prof., 1976-82; sr. rsch. scientist E.R. Squibb & Sons, Princeton, N.J., 1982-87; sr. rsch. fellow Merck, Sharp & Dohme Rsch. Labs., Rahway, N.J., 1987-89, dir., 1989—; reviewer various jours. and granting orgns. Editor: Genetics of Candida; assoc. editor: Expl. Mycology Jour., 1988—; contbr. articles to profl. jours. Del. Dem. Nat. Conv., Miami, Fla., 1970. Mem. AAAS, Am. Soc. for Microbiology.

KURTZ, OLGA BECHKOWIAK, small business owner; b. Serednica, Lesko, Poland, Mar. 30, 1929; came to U.S., 1932; d. Joseph and Julia (Molohoskey) Bechowiak; div.; children: Christopher, Melissa. Teaching cert., U. Akron, 1952; BS in Elementary Edn., Buffalo State Tchrs. Coll., 1958. Tchr. Copley (Ohio) Schs., 1952-54; records libr. N.Mex. State Hosp., Las Vegas, N.Mex., 1955-56; tchr. West Seneca (N.Y.) Cen. Schs., 1958-64; alumni sec. The Gow Sch., South Wales, N.Y., 1975-76; owner & founder OK Fast Print, Akron, Ohio, 1978—. Youth Motivator, Pvt. Industry Coun., Akron Pub. Schs., 1988-89; counselor Sr. Corps of Retired Execs. Mem. Women's Network, Nat. Fed. Ind. Bus. Eastern Orthodox. Office: OK Fast Print 943 E Wilbeth Rd Akron OH 44306

KURTZ, SWOOSIE, actress; b. Omaha; d. Frank and Margo (Rogers) K. Student, Acad. Music and Dramatic Arts, London, U. So. Calif. Appeared on TV series Mary, 1978, Love, Sidney, 1981-83; TV films include Uncommon Women and Others, Ah, Wilderness!, Fifth of July, The House of Blue Leaves, The Visit, Guilty Conscience, A Time to Live, Walking Through the Fire, The Mating Season; film appearances include Slap Shot, 1977, The World According to Garp, 1982, Against All Odds, 1984, Wild Cats, 1986, True Stories, 1986, Vice Versa, 1988, Bright Lights, Big City, 1988, Baja, Oklahoma, 1988, Dangerous Liaisons, 1988, Stanley and Iris, 1989, A Shock to the System, 1989, The Image, 1989; theatrical appearances include: Ah, Wilderness!, 1975, Tartuffe, 1977, A History of the American Film, 1978 (Drama Desk award), Fifth of July, 1980-81 (Tony award, Drama Desk award, Outer Critics Circle award), Michael Bennett's Scandal, 1985, The House of Blue Leaves, 1986 (Tony award, Obie award), The Effect of Gamma Rays on Man in the Moon Marigolds, Uncommon Women and Others, 1977 (Obie award), Who's Afraid of Virginia Woolf?, 1980, Children, 1976, Summer, 1980, Beach house, 1986, The Middle Ages, 1980, Hunting Cockroaches, 1987 (Drama League award), Love Letters, 1989. Office: Internat Creative Mgmt care Sam Cohn 40 W 57th St New York NY 10019*

KURTZE, CRYSTAL CATHERINE, creative director; b. Sioux City, Iowa, Dec. 30, 1949; d. Lowell Emery and Frances Mary (Gasink) G.; m. John Wiliam Kurtze, Sept. 18. 1969; Div. 1972; 1 Child: Jennifer Kurtze. Student, Wayne State Coll., 1968-69; BFA, Morningside Coll., Sioux City, Neb., 1972-75. Artist Fairall & Co., Sioux City, 1972-74; advt. mgr. Tompkins Constrn., Sioux City, 1974-78; prin. Crystal Kurtze Advt., South Sioux City, Iowa, 1978-81, Creative Design & Mktg., Valley, Nebr., 1981-87; gen. mgr. Meta Mktg., Omaha, 1987—. Creative dir. Eagle Window, 1988 (Addy and Merit award 1988); contbr. articles to profl. jours. Mem. Am. Soc. Advt. and Promotion. Republican. Methodist. Office: META Mktg 3640 N 90th Omaha NE 68134

KURTZIG, SANDRA L., software company executive; b. Chgo., Oct. 21, 1946; d. Barney and Marian (Boruck) Brody; children: Andrew Paul, Kenneth Alan; B.S. in Math., UCLA, 1967; M.S.in aeronaut. engring., Stanford U., 1968. Math analyst TRW Systems, 1967-68; mktg. rep., Gen. Electric Co., 1969-72; chmn. bd., chief exec. officer, pres. ASK Computer Systems, Mountain View, Calif., 1972-85, chmn. bd., 1986-89, chmn., pres., chief exec. officer, 1989—. Cited one of 50 most influential bus. people in Am., Bus. Week, 1985. Office: ASK Computer Systems Inc 2440 W El Camino Real Mountain View CA 94039-7640

KURZROCK, RAZELLE, internist, educator; b. Toronto, Ont., Canada, Sept. 29, 1954; d. David and Matilda K.; m. Philip Cohen, Sept. 28, 1985; 1 child, Benjamin A. BS with honors, U. Toronto, 1974, MD, 1978. Asst. prof. U. Tex. M.D. Anderson Cancer Ctr., Houston, 1984-89, assoc. prof. medicine, 1989—; asst. prof. Grad. Sch. Biomed. Scis. U. Tex., Houston, 1987—; vis. prof. The Wistar Inst., Phila., 1987-88. Contbr. articles on molecular biology and cancer treatment to profl. jours. Mem. ACP. Office: U Tex MD Anderson Cancer Ctr 1515 Holcombe Blvd Houston TX 77030

KURZWEIL, EDITH, sociology educator, editor; b. Vienna; d. Ernest W. and Wilhelmine M. (Fischer) Weiss; m. Charles H. Schmidt, June 24, 1945 (div. 1958); children: Ronald J., Vivien A.; m. Mr. Kurzweil, Aug. 2, 1958 (dec. 1966); 1 child, Allen J. B.A., Queens Coll., CUNY, 1967; M.A., New Sch. Social Rsch., 1969, Ph.D., 1973. Asst. prof. sociology Hunter Coll., N.Y.C., 1972-75, Montclair State Coll., Upper Monclair, N.J., 1973-78; assoc. prof. sociology Rutgers U., Newark, 1979-85, prof. sociology, chmn., 1985—; vis. prof. Goethe U., 1984. Author: The Age of Structuralism, 1980, Italian Entrepreneurs, 1983, The Freudians: A Comparative Perspective, 1989; editor: (with others) Literature and Psychoanalysis, 1983, Writers and Politics, 1983, Cultural Analysis, 1984; exec. editor Partisan Rev., Boston, 1978—. Rockefeller Humanities fellow, 1982-83, NEH fellow, 1987-88; NEH grantee, 1989. Mem. Am. Sociol. Assn., Tocqueville Soc., Internat. Assn. History of Psychoanalysis, Internat. Sociol. Assn., Eastern Sociol. Assn., P.E.N. Home: One Lincoln Plaza New York NY 10023 Office: Partisan Review 236 Bay State Rd Boston MA 02215

KUSEK, CAROL JOAN (JOAN KUSEK), genealogist, publisher; b. Ottawa, Kans., Feb. 1, 1955; d. Ronald Eugene and Veda Doris (Geiss) Elliott; m. Gary Gerard Kusek, Sept. 10, 1977; children: Jacquelyn Ruth, David Michael. Student, Johnson County Community Coll., Overland Park, Kans., 1973-76, 88. Office mgr. Lenexa (Kans.) Animal Hosp., 1973-82; journeyman, sign painter Elliott Custom Signs, Overland Park, 1982—; owner Family Search, Overland Park, 1985—; instr. Johnson County Community Coll., Overland Park; researcher; contbr. gen. publs. Home: 9640 Walmer Overland Park KS 66212

KUSHNAR, DENISE MARGARET, marketing professional; b. Cleve., Sept. 3, 1957; d. Edward Jerome and Margaret Irene (Krisfaluski) Kushnar; m. Brian Thomas Dorr, May 5, 1979; 1 child, Margaret Ana. Student, Cuyahoga Community Coll., 1976-77, Troy State U., 1978-82. Asst. mgr. Marlborough Hotel, Suffolk, Eng., 1981-83; sales mgr. Cleve. Airport Marriott, 1983-84; dir. sales Cleve. Hilton South, 1984-85; dir. sales and mktg. Cleve. Marriott East, 1986-87, Louisville Marriott, Cleve., 1985-86, Cleve. Marriott West, 1987-88; mktg. mgr. Boykin Mgmt. Co., Cleve., 1988-89; dir. mktg. Sheraton Suites, Akron, Ohio, 1989—. Mem. Hotel Sales and Mktg. Assn. (v.p. membership 1984-85), Ohio Soc. Assn. Execs. Office: Sheraton Stes 1989 Front St Akron OH 44221

KUSHNER, EVA, educator, author; b. Prague, Czechoslovakia, June 18, 1929; d. Josef and Anna (Kafkova) Dubsky; m. Donn Jean Kushner, Sept. 15, 1949; children: Daniel Peter, Roland Joseph, Paul Joel. B in Philosophy, Coll. Marie de France, Montreal, 1946; BA, McGill U., 1948, MA in Philosophy, 1950, PhD in French Lit., 1956. Lectr. French, McGill U., Montreal, 1952-55, instr. French, summers 1956, 58, 61-62, 67-69, prof. French lang. and lit., 1976-87; pres., vice chancellor Victoria U. in the U. Toronto, 1987—; sessional lectr. philosophy Sir George Williams U., 1952-53; lectr. Univ. Coll., London, 1958-59; lectr. Carleton U., 1961, asst. prof. French and comparative lit., 1963, assoc. prof., 1965, prof., 1969-76, chmn. comparative lit., 1965-69, 70-72, 75-76, adj. prof. lit., 1976-79; mem. exec. com. Can. Coun., mem., 1975-81; v.p. Social Scis. and Humanities Rsch. Coun. Can., 1983-86; mem. adv. bd. Nat. Libr. Can.; pres. Humanities Rsch. Coun. Can., 1970-72. Author: Patrice de La Tour de Pin, 1961; Le mythe d'Orphée dans la littérature française contemporaine, 1961; Chants de Bohême, 1963; Rina Lasnier collections Ecrivains canadiens d'aujourd'hui, 1964; Poètes d'aujourd'hui, 1969; Saint-Denys Garneau, 1967; François Mauriac, 1972, Japanese transl., 1976; co-author anthology Que. poetry, transl. into Hungarian, 1978, Polish, 1985; editor Renewals in the Theory of Literary History; co-editor/co-author: L'avènement de l'esprit nouveau (1400-80), Théorie littéraire: problèmes et perspectives, 1989, and proc. XIth Congress; co-dir research Renaissance vols. Histoire comparée des littératures de langues européennes; mem. editorial com. Can. Comparative Lit. Rev., Dalhousie French Studies; mem. internat. adv. bd. Comparative lit. Studies. Contbr. articles to profl. publs. Fellow Royal Soc. Can. (v.p. 1980-82); mem. Academie Européenne des lettres, des sciences et des arts, Am. Comparative Lit. Assn. (adv. bd.), Internat. Comparative Lit. Assn. (pres. 1979-82), Internat. Fedn. for Modern Langs. and Lits. (v.p. 1987—), MLA (del. assembly, chmn. 16th century French lit. div., mem. exec. coun. 1983-86, nominating com. 1986-88), Assn. internat. des études françaises, Assn. des profs. de français des univs. canadiennes, Assn. canadienne de littérature comparée (v.p. 1969-71), Internat. Assn. Neo-Latin Studies, Soc. canadienne d'études de la Renaissance, Assn. des littératures canadienne et québecoise, Can. Soc. Semiotic Research. Office: Victoria U in U Toronto, 73 Queen's Park Crescent, Toronto, ON Canada M5S 1K7

KUSISTO, KATHRYN HAAS, marketing executive; b. Midland, Mich., Sept. 7, 1958; d. Paul Robert and Donetta Mae (Dean) Haas; m. Raymond Neil Kusisto, Oct. 4, 1986. BBA, Cen. Mich. U., 1981; MBA, Northwestern U., 1986. Mgmt. trainee Gerber Products Co., Fremont, Mich., 1981-82, method and procedures analyst, 1982-83, systems analyst, 1983-85; mktg. analyst Lithonia Lighting, Conyers, Ga., 1986-88, mgr. adminstrn. and sales promotion, 1988—. Rsch. coord. Optimax in trade jours. and Cable News Network, 1988. Mem. Bus. Profl. Advt. Assn. Office: Lithonia Lighting 1400 Lester Rd Conyers GA 30207

KUSKIE, PATRICIA LYNN, county services administrator; b. Traverse City, Mich., July 21, 1953; d. John Robert and Edith Mae (Butts) Kerrigan; m. John Edward Kuskie, Dec. 24, 1977 (div. 1987); children: John Kerrigan, Kristen Noel. AA, Delta Coll., University Center, Mich., 1971; BS, Cen. Mich. U., 1974; MPA, U. Colo., 1990. Counselor Youth Svcs. Bur., Harrison, Mich., 1975; juvenile officer State of Mich., Gladwin, 1975-76; with Arapahoe County Employment and Tng. Div., Littleton, Colo., 1977—, dir., 1983—; pres. Colo. Tng. Partnership Assoc., Englewood, 1990. Author: (newspaper articles) Labor Force Issues, 1988, Work Ethic, 1990. Vice chair Arapahoe/Douglas Community Coll. Adv. Bd., 1987-89; mem. Arapahoe County Placement Alternatives Commn., 1984—, Douglas County Placement Alternatives Commn., 1990; bd. dirs. Women's Crisis Ctr. Douglas County, 1989—. Recipient Women at Work award Gov. Richard Lamm, Denver, 1984, Innovation in Govt., Nat. Assn. Counties, Washington, 1984, 85, 90. Mem. Aurora C. of C. (bd. dirs. 1989-92). Home: 335 Helena Circle Littleton CO 80124-2710 Office: Arapahoe County Employment 11059 E Bethany Dr Ste 201 Aurora CO 80014-2617

KUSSMAN, ARDYS ANN, apparel manufacturing company executive; b. Pawnee City, Nebr., Jan. 22, 1948; d. Edmund Fangman and Evelyn Louise (Runnebaum) Lackey; m. Elbert Dale Kussman, Sept. 2, 1967 (div. July 1976); 1 child, Angela. Grad. high sch., Seneca, Kans. Prodn. planning analyst Lee Co., Merriam, Kans., 1972-73, supr. prodn. planning, 1974-75, mgr. prodn. planning, 1976-78, mgr. material control, 1979-80, mgr. forecasting, 1981, dir. forecasting and planning, 1982-84, v.p. ops. planning, 1985; v.p. ops. VF Corp., Wyomissing, Pa., 1986-87; sr. v.p. ops. Lee Co., Merriam, 1988—. Republican. Roman Catholic. Home: 12809 Cedar Leawood KS 66209 Office: Lee Apparel Co Inc 9001 W 67th St Merriam KS 66201

KUSTRON, KONNIE GERLYN, transportation company executive; b. Detroit, Oct. 19, 1954; d. Edward John and Margaret Helen (Kicinski) K.; m. Larry Raymond Belzak, Aug. 3, 1979; children: Christopher James, Bethany Jean, Katrina Margarite. BS with honors, Mich. State U., 1975; JD, Detroit Coll. Law, 1978. Bar: Mich. 1978, U.S. Dist. Ct. (ea. dist.) Mich. 1978. Pvt. practice Farmington Hills, Mich., 1978-81; dist. mgr. instrnl. svc. Mead Data Cen., Detroit, 1981-83, mktg. rep., 1983-84, br. mgr., 1985-88; v.p. Transerv, Inc., Southfield, Mich., 1988—, also bd. dirs.; asst. prof. Oakland Community Coll., Bloomfield Hills, Mich., 1978-81; instr. Wayne State U., 1980. Vol. Lansing (Mich.) Com. for Equal Justice, 1974. Blue Water charter chpt. Am. Bus. Women's Assn. scholar, 1975-77. Mem. ABA, State Bar Mich. Roman Catholic. Office: Transerv Inc 20700 Boening Southfield MI 48042

KUTASI, KATALIN ERZSEBET, banker; b. Ann Arbor, Mich., Sept. 7, 1956; d. Karoly and Margaret (Vidonyi) K. BA in Acctg., Mich. State U., 1978; MBA in Fin., DePaul U., 1983. Cost acct. Continental Ill. Nat. Bank and Trust Co. Chgo., 1978-80, banking officer trade fin., 1980-85, 2d v.p., 1985-88, v.p., 1988; workout specialist FDIC, Chgo., 1989; sr. investment mgr. Equitable Capital Mgmt. Corp., N.Y.C., 1989—; Bd. dirs. White Wave Rising Dance Co. Active Am. Coun. for Arts, Chgo. Coun. for Arts, Bus. Vol. for Arts. Mem. Am. Coun. for the Arts, Gamma Phi Beta.

KUYKENDALL, CRYSTAL ARLENE, educational consultant, lawyer; b. Chgo., Dec. 11, 1949; d. Cleophus Campbell and Ellen (Campbell) Logan; m. Roosevelt Kuykendall, Apr. 10, 1969 (dec. Aug. 1972); children: Keisha, Rasheki, Kashif. BA, Southern Ill. U., 1970; MA, Montclair State U., 1972; EdD, Atlanta U., 1975; JD, Georgetown U., 1982. Bar: D.C. 1988. Instr. Seton Hall U., South Orange, N.J., 1971-73; adminstrn. intern D.C. Pub. Schs., 1974-75; dir. citizens tng. inst. Nat. Com. for Citizens in Edn., Washington, 1975-77; dir. urban and minorities rels. dept. Nat. Sch. Bd. Assn., Washington, 1977-79; edn. dir. PSI Assocs., Inc., Washington, 1979-80; exec. dir. Nat. Alliance of Black Sch. Educators, Washington, 1980-81; dir. mktg. Roy Littlejohn Assoc., Inc., Washington, 1983—; pres., gen. counsel KIRK, Inc. (Kreative and Innovative Resources for Kids), Washington, 1981—; chmn. U.S. Pres. Nat. Adv. Coun. on Continuing Edn., Washington, 1978-81; cons. U. Pitts. Race Desegregation Assistance Ctr., 1982-87, J.H. Lowry Assn., Chgo., 1982, U.S. Dept. of Edn. Transition Team, Washington, 1980. Author: Developing Leadership for Parent/Citizen Groups, 1975, You & Yours: MAking the Most of this School Year, 1987, Improving Black Student Achievement by Enhancing Self Image, 1989. Mem. adv. bd. Inst. of the Black World, Atlanta, 1975-81; steering com. Nat. Conf. on Parental Involvement, Denver, 1977-78; mem. edn. task force Martin Luther King Jr. Ctr. for Social Change, Atlanta, 1978-80. Named Honorary Citizen of New Orleans, Mayor's Office, 1976; Ford found. fellow, 1973-74. Mem. Nat. Alliance of Black Sch. Edn., Alpha Kappa Alpha. Democrat. Baptist. Office: KIRK Inc PO Box 41397 Washington DC 20018

KUYPER, JOAN CAROLYN, foundation administrator; b. Balt., Oct. 22, 1941; d. Irving Charles and Ethel Mae (Pritchett) O'Connor; B.A. in Edn., Salisbury State U., 1963; postgrad. Columbia U., 1978; MA in Arts Mgmt. and Bus., NYU, 1988; m. L. William Kuyper, Dec. 20, 1964; children: Susan Carol, Edward Philip. Elem. sch. tchr. Prince Georges County Schs., Md., 1963-68; free lance singer, opera, oratorio, chamber music Amato Opera, N.Y.C., 1967-80; owner, mgr. Privette Artists' Registry, Placement Service for Singers, Teaneck, N.J., 1969-78; exec. dir. Teaneck Artists Perform-Chamber Music Series, 1975-80; program dir. Vols. in Arts & Humanities, Vol. Bur. Bergen County, N.J., 1978-81; dir. Bergen Mus. Art and Sci., 1981-83; cons. Am. Soc. Prevention Cruelty to Animals, 1984, Am. Council for the Arts, 1987; dir. ops. Isabel O'Neil Found. and Studio, 1984-85. Dir. vol. services March of Dimes Birth Defects Found. of Greater N.Y., 1985-88; dir. chpt. devel. Huntington's Disease Soc. Am., 1988—; bd. dirs Pro Arte Chorale and adv. bd. on the arts, Teaneck, 1976-81. Mem. Am. Assn. Mus., Mus. Council N.J., Am. Mktg. Assn., Assn. for Vol. Adminstrn. (author handbook). Democrat. Presbyterian. Clubs: Altrusa (bd. dirs. 1984-86, 90—, pres. 1986-88), P.E.O., Phi Alpha Theta. Home: 501 Rutland Ave Teaneck NJ 07666 Office: 140 W 22d St New York NY 10010-2420

KUZINA, JAN CELESTE, aeronautical engineer; b. Winnipeg, Man., Can., Oct. 30, 1956; d. John and Iris Alice (Huziak) K. BSC in physics with honors, U. Manitoba, 1982; M in Aero. Engring., Carleton U., 1985. Flight instr. Winnipeg Flying Club, 1975-77; charter pilot Aero Trades Western Ltd., Winnipeg, 1977; research officer Nat. Research Council Can., Ottawa, Ont., Can., 1981, Low Speed Aerodyns. Lab., Ottawa, Ont., Can., 1982-83, Nat. Research Council Can. Unsteady Aerodyns. Lab., Ottawa, Ont., 1984-85; aerodyn. flight test coordinator de Havilland div. Boeing Aircraft Co., Toronto, Ont., 1986—; speaker in field. Contbr. articles to profl. jours. Recipient Female Pvt. Pilot of Yr. award Royal Can. Flying Clubs Assn., 1973, Allister R. Gillespie Meml. award, 1975; S.F. Kay scholar in sci., 1980; Amelia Earhart fellowship Zonta Internat., 1984. Mem. Canadian Aeros. and Space Inst., Fedn. Engring. and Scientific Assns. Office: Boeing Aircraft Co, de Havilland Aircraft div, Garratt Blvd, Toronto, ON Canada M3K 1Y5

KUZNECOFF, IRENE CECILIA, company executive; b. Humboldt, Sask., Can., Dec. 1, 1937; came to U.S., 1957, naturalized, 1964.; d. George John and Maria (Bittner) Kosokowsky; m. Walter Michael Kuznecoff, Dec. 30, 1961; 1 child, Gregory Walter; 1 stepchild, Michael Kent. Student, Bulmer Bus. Coll., Windsor, Ont., Can., 1956-57; cert., Wayne State U., 1987. Teller Bank of Commerce, Humboldt, 1956; sec., acct. Poole Electronics and Fisher Electronics, Windsor and London, Ont., 1956-57; exec. sec. Goodbody & Co., Detroit, 1957-58; exec., sales sec. Wickwire Spencer Steel div. Colo. Fuel & Iron Corp., Detroit, 1958-62; sec.-treas. Kuznecoff & Assocs., Union Lake, Mich., 1963—, Mid-Pacific Comml. Window Reps., Detroit, 1976-86, Nu-Systems, Inc. (formerly Nu-Sash So. Mich.), Union Lake, 1976—. Sec., treas. Fox Bay Civic Assn., Union Lake, 1969, Douglas Houghton Sch. PTA, Union Lake, 1970-75; pres. West Point Parents Club Mich., Novi, 1982-84; mem. Rep. Nat. Com., 1986—; admissions rep. for S.E. Mich., U.S. Mil. Acad., 1982—; vice chmn. local bd. 323, SSS, 1982—; formerly active Boy Scouts Am., Pontiac, Mich. Recipient svc. award U.S. Mil. Acad., 1988. Mem. NAFE, Greater Detroit C. of C., Founders Soc. Detroit Inst. Arts, Drayton Plains Nature Ctr., Russian Am. Assn. Detroit, Res. Officers Ladies Assn. Methodist. Home and Office: 8883 Woodshire Dr Union Lake MI 48085-1041

KWANDT, JOANNE, nursing unit administrator; b. Camden, N.J., Mar. 23, 1944; d. John Joseph and Frances Ann (Robinson) Mahady; m. Dennis Charles Kwandt, May 30, 1969; children: Charann, Dennis Charles II. Student, Woman's Coll. Ga., Milledgeville, 1962-63; diploma in nursing, Grady Meml. Hosp., Atlanta, 1966; student, Ga. State Coll., Atlanta, 1963-67; AA, Merced (Calif.) Jr. Coll., 1972; BS in Social Psychology, Park Coll., 1979; MA in Psychology, U. No. Colo., 1980; cert. secondary sch. tchr., Boise (Idaho) State Coll., 1981; EdS, Coll. William and Mary, 1987, postgrad., 1989—. RN, Ga., Calif., Oreg. Va.; cert. clin. specialist; cert. secondary sch. counselor, Idaho. Grad. nurse Grady Meml. Hosp., Atlanta, 1966-67; staff RN Piedmont Hosp., Atlanta, 1967-68; RN vis. and office Home Health Service Agy., Eugene, Oreg., 1970-71; aide learning disabilities Lajes AFB Elem. Sch., Azores, 1973-77; intern in counseling Boise State Coll., 1980; psychiatric RN child and adolescent units Charter Colonial Inst., Newport News, Va., 1983-85, lectr., 1985; supr. nursing Ea. State Hosp., Williamsburg, Va., 1985-87; nurse mgr., clin. specialist Psychiat. Inst. Richmond, Va., 1987—; pvt. duty nurse, instr. pre-natal classes USAF Hosp., Lajes AFB; adj. instr. regional ctr. Park Coll., Mt. Home AFB, Idaho, 1980-82, Boise State Coll., Mt. Home AFB, 1981-82; counselor in field. Vol. children's unit Ea. State Hosp., Williamsburg, Va., 1985-87. Mem. Va. Nursing Assn., Non-Commd. Officers Assn. Aux. (bd. dirs. 1980—, treas. internat. aux. bd. 1981, sec. 1983, 2d v.p. 1984-87, pres. 1987-88). Democrat. Home: HCR01 Box 118 West Point VA 23181 Office: Psychiat Inst Richmond 3001 5th Ave Richmond VA 23222

KWAN-KISAICHI, SHIRLEY, writer, producer; b. Madrid, Oct. 2, 1958; d. Hon Cheun and Kazuko (Yoshioka) Kwan; m. Kazuhiro Kisaichi, 1988. BA, Wash. State U., 1980; MS in Journalism, Columbia U., 1982; student, Columbia U. Internat. Fellows Program, 1982. Acting edn. editor Sta. WNET-TV, N.Y.C., 1980, cons., 1980-81; newswriter Satellite News Channel, Stamford, Conn., 1982-83, Newsday, Melville, N.Y., 1983-84; nat.

copyreader Dow Jones & Co., N.Y.C., 1984-85; ind. multi-media writer/producer N.Y.C., 1985—; cover story corr. Cross and Talk mag., Tokyo, 1986-89; cons./assoc. producer Sta. WETA-TV, Washington, 1986-87; cons. ALC Press Inc., Tokyo, 1986-88. Investigative reporter/prodn. mgr. Who Killed Vincent Chin?, 1986 (Acad. award nominee); producer (feature film) Soho Murder, 1988; screenplays include Time of Your Life, Bourgeois Blues, Mail Order Matchup; contbr. to periodicals, films and video prodns. Mem. Asian Am. Journalist Assn. (treas. 1987-89), Asian Cine-Vision (vol. staffer/editor 1982-85, mem. Asian Am. Internat. Film Festival com. 1988, 90). Home and Office: 244 Dean St Brooklyn NY 11217

KWEI, GLORIA YUNG CHING, personnel official; b. Macao, June 26, 1943; came to U.S., 1950; d. Yu Chang and Lim Tsing (Poon); m. George Hsing; children: Lawrence K., Erica H. BA In History, Cum Laude, Radcliffe Coll., Cambridge, 1965. Program coordinator SUNY, Stony Brook, 1968-72; office mgr. Three Village Herald, Stony Brook, N.Y., 1973-74, Med. Office, Los Alamos, 1976-78; benefits rep. Los Alamos Nat. Lab., dep. grp. ldr., benefits, 1980-82, deputy grp. lrd., comp & benefits, 1982-85, group leader, compensation & benefits, 1985-86, div. leader, personnel services, 1987—, mem. mid. mgmt. coun., 1987-89; middle mgmt. council Los Alamos Nat. Lab., 1987--. Bd. dirs. Los Alamos Arts Coun., 1975-76, program chmn., 1977-79; mem. adv. bd. Los Alamos Sr. Ctr., 1981-85; mem. J. Robert Oppenheimer Meml. Com., 1987—. Mem. Harvard-Radcliffe Club N.Mex. (bd. dirs., officer 1985—). Office: Los Alamos Nat Lab PO Box 1663 Los Alamos NM 87545

KWIATKOWSKI, ANNE SUSAN, lawyer; b. Chgo., Dec. 20, 1955; d. Alois and Barbara Julia (Krajewski) K.; m. Frank Gee Leong, July 9, 1977. BA, Northwestern U., 1977; MBA, DePaul U., 1984; JD, Loyola U., Chgo., 1987. Bar: Hawaii 1987. Blood gas technician, sr. technologist, supr., asst. dir. Northwestern Meml. Hosp., Chgo., 1978-8l; gen. mgr. Leong Assocs., Inc., Chgo., 198l-86; assoc. Char, Hamilton, Campbell & Thom, Honolulu, 1987—. Mem. ABA, Hawaii Bar Assn., Hawaii Women Lawyers. Office: Char Hamilton et al 737 Bishop St Ste 2100 Honolulu HI 96813

KWIATKOWSKI, DEBORAH ANN, registered nurse, physical fitness consultant; b. Jersey City, Aug. 21, 1965; d. Edward Joseph and Dorothy Mary (Filipkowski) Kwiatkowski. BS in Nursing, Fairleigh Dickinson U., 1987. Women's health counselor Women's Med. Ctr., Howell, N.J., 1985-87; permanent charge nurse St. Peters Med. Ctr., New Brunswick, N.J., 1989-90; staff nurse Jersey Shore Med. Ctr., Neptune, N.J., 1987—. Mem. Am. Assn. Critical Care Nurses, Nat. Assn. Neonatal Nurses, Sigma Theta Tau. Republican. Roman Catholic. Home: 275 White St Howell NJ 07731

KYLE-WHITE, BARBARA LOUISE, real estate executive; b. Gloucester, Mass., July 11, 1945; d. Roland Parsons and Margaret (Stickney) Kyle; m. Asher Abbott White, Jr., Sept. 22, 1979; children: Anna, Andrew. RN, U. Pa., 1966, BSN, 1970; CRNA, U. Wash., 1978. Staff nurse U. Pa., Phila., 1966-69; intensive care nurse to mental health counselor U. Calif., San Francisco, 1969-72; sales assoc. Lord and Taylor, Chgo., 1974-75; anesthetist Group Health Hosp. Valley Gen., Seattle, 1975-79; adminstrv. exec. Am. Corp. Overseas, Oxford, Eng., 1979-84; owner catering company London and Seattle, 1984-85; sales mgr., mdse. mgr. Talbots, Seattle, 1985-87; real estate sales, investment counselor Windermere Real Estate/JL Inc., Bellevue, Wash., 1987—; lectr. in field. Editor Upper Heyford Cookery Book, 1983. Hostess Medina Home and Garden Tour, Wash., 1988; organizer Upper Heyford Arts and Crafts Fair, Oxford, Eng., 1981. U. Pa. Senatorial scholar. Mem. Assn. Cooking Profls., Master Chefs Inst. London, Nat. Assn. Female Execs., Real Estate Bd. of Seattle, Nat. Assn. Nurse Anesthetists. Republican. Episcopalian. Home: PO Box 194 Medina WA 98039 Office: Windermere Real Estate/JL Inc 2955 80th Ave SE Mercer Island WA

KYMAN, WENDY, sex therapist, health educator; b. N.Y.C., Mar. 29, 1947; d. Jack and Tess (Starman) K.; 1 child, Jesse. BS, CCNY, 1968; MS, Bklyn. Coll., 1971; PhD, NYU, 1984. Diplomate, cert. sex therapist and educator Am. Bd. Sexology. Tchr. N.Y.C. Bd. Edn., 1968-74; coord., supr. YWCA Women's Ctr., 1977-78; instr. health edn. SUNY, Old Westbury, 1980-81; instr. allied health SUNY, Nanuet, 1982; family planning counselor NYU Health Svc., N.Y.C., 1984; asst. prof. health edn. CUNY Hunter Coll., 1984-85; sr. pub. health educator Gouverneur Hosp., 1984-87; asst. prof. health edn. CUNY Baruch Coll., 1985—; pvt. practice sex therapy and sex educator, cons., N.Y.C.; teaching fellow NYU, 1980. Contbr. articles to profl. jours. Profl. Staff Congress of CUNY rsch. grantee, 1988-89. Mem. Am. Assn. Sex Educators, Counselors and Therapists (cert. sex educator), Nat. Coun. Women in Medicine, Am. Pub. Health Assn., Nat. Women's Health Network.**. Home: 272 6th Ave Brooklyn NY 11215 Office: CUNY Baruch Coll Box 330 17 Lexington Ave New York NY 11210

KYRIAKOU, LINDA GRACE, diversified manufacturing executive; b. N.Y.C., Dec. 5, 1943; d. Frank Thomas and Dolores Helen (Coscia) LaGamma; B.A., Hunter Coll., 1965; m. Konstantinos Kyriakou, May 7, 1967; 1 dau., Christina Elena. Info. editor Nat. Bur. Econ. Research, N.Y.C., 1967-69; dir. research/account officer Booke & Co., N.Y.C., 1969-75; mgr. communications services C.I.T. Fin. Corp., N.Y.C., 1975-79; dir. corp. communications Sequa Corp., N.Y.C., 1979-87, v.p. communications, 1988—. Mem. Public Relations Soc. Am., Nat. Investor Relations Inst. (dir. N.Y. chpt. 1981-82), Women's Bond Club N.Y. (bd. govs. 1978-80). Office: Sequa Corp 200 Park Ave New York NY 10166*

KYZAR, OLLIE JEANETTE, educator; b. Brookhaven, Miss., Oct. 7, 1933; d. Marcel Wooden and Annie Leona (Brister) Grice; m. Reese Eugene Kyzar, June 16, 1953. B.S. in Edn., Delta State U., 1960, postgrad., 1972-74, 79-81, 88—; postgrad. U. So. Miss., 1960-61, 65-66, 69-70, U. Miss., 1961-63. Tchr. English, Fielding L. Wright High Sch., Rolling Fork, Miss., 1960-61; tchr. Fielding L. Wright Elem. Sch., Rolling Fork, 1961-70; homebound tchr. Rolling Fork Elem. Sch., 1970-73, tchr. reading and math., 1973-84, resource tchr. computer assisted instrn., 1984-88, asst. prin., 1988—; evaluator Nat. Council Accreditation Tchr. Edn., Washington, 1982—, Miss. Accreditation Schs.; mem. supt.'s adv. bd., Rolling Fork, 1981-83; mem. steering com. on sch. evaluation So. Assn. Colls. and Schs., 1962-73. Sunday sch. tchr., former dir. Acteens, mem. Womens Missionary Union, 1st Baptis Ch. Rolling Fork, 1959; bd. dirs. Adult Bapt. Tng. Union, 1989—. Mem. Smithsonian Instn. (assoc.), Nat. Trust Historic Preservation, Fielding L. Wright Tchrs. Assn. (pres. 1966-67), Rolling Fork Assn. Educators (pres. 1977-78, 81-82, Disting. Service award 1978, 82), Miss. Assn. Educators (workshop presenter 1982-84), NEA, Miss. Ednl. Computing Assn., Assn. Supervision and Curiculum Devel., Miss. for Ednl. Broadcasting, Internat. Reading Assn., Miss. Reading Assn., Kappa Delta Pi. Avocations: reading; listening to music; walking; riding bicycle. Home: 105 N 2nd St Rolling Fork MS 39159 Office: Rolling Fork Elem Sch 600 S Pkwy Rolling Fork MS 39159

LABADIE, BARBARA LEE, financial analyst; b. Detroit, Apr. 26, 1943; d. Arthur W. and Elsie E. (DeBruyne) Boyden; m. Dwight D. Labadie, Sept. 5, 1964; children: Dwight, Barbara, Monique. BS, Wayne State U., 1966; MEd, Marygrove Coll., 1975; postgrad., Walsh Coll., 1988—. Sci. coord. Gross Pointe (Mich.) Acad., 1971-76; pres. Labadie Assoc. Inc., Harper Woods, Mich., 1976-85; investment specialist Plante & Moran CPA, Southfield, 1985-86; portfolio mgr. Mfrs. Bank, Detroit, 1986-89; v.p., shareholder Cooper, Van Dyke Assocs., Birmingham, Mich., 1989—. Sec., mem. bd. dirs. Rep. Women's Forum, Troy, Mich., 1984—; state chair Nat. Women's Polit. Caucus. Mem. Fin. Analysts Soc., Acad. Polit. Sci., Women's Econs. Club, Bus. Ptnrs. Home: 1193 Roslyn Grosse Pointe MI 48236

LABAGUIS, ROSE-MARIE QUIBILAN, laboratory professional; b. Santa Maria, Ilocos Sur, Philippines, June 21, 1942; came to U.S., 1967; d. Guillermo Q. and Asuncion (Arreola) Quibilan; m. Yodel J. Labaguis, June 21, 1969; children: Reynard, Jason. BS in Chemistry, Centro Escolar Univ., Manila, 1962; MS in Sci. Info., Ill. Inst. Tech., 1974. Quality control chemist Procter & Gamble, Manila, 1962-67, Milani Foods, L.A., 1968-69, E.J. Brach & Co., Chgo., 1969-70; biochemist, toxicologist Cook County Hosp., Chgo., 1970-79; toxicology mgr. MetPath Labs., Teterboro, N.J., 1979-84, client svc. mgr., 1984—. Grantee NIH, 1972-74,. Office: MetPath Labs 1 Malcolm Ave Teterboro NJ 07608

LABANT, CYNTHIA JEAN, ceramic engineer; b. St. Marys, Pa., July 7, 1963; d. Wayne George and Aletha Jane (Harrison) Schauer; m. Joseph William Labant Jr., Apr. 4, 1987. BS in Ceramic Sci. and Engring., Pa. State U., 1985. Lab. technician Keystone Carbon Co., St. Marys, 1983, 84, Materials Rsch. Lab., University Park, Pa., 1985; ceramic devel. engr. inorganic chems. div. Mobay Corp., Balt., 1985—. Contbr. articles to sci. publs. Fellow Am. Ceramic Soc., Nat. Inst. Ceramic Engrs., Porcelain Enamel Inst. Democrat. Roman Catholic. Home: 7380 Jennifer Way Sykesville MD 21784 Office: Mobay Corp Inorganic Chems 5601 Eastern Ave Baltimore MD 21224

LABARGE, MARGARET WADE, medieval history educator; b. N.Y.C., July 18, 1916; arrived in Can., 1940; d. Alfred Byers and Helena (Mein) Wade; m. Raymond C. Labarge, June 20, 1940 (dec. May 1972); children: Claire Labarge Morris, Suzanne, Charles, Paul. BA, Radcliffe Coll., 1937; LittB, Oxford (Eng.) U., 1939; LittD (hon.), Carleton U., Ottawa, Ont., Can., 1976. Lectr. history U. Ottawa, Carleton U., 1950-62; adj. prof. history Carleton U., Ottawa, 1983—. Author: Simon de Montfort, 1962, A Baronial Household, 1965, Gascony, 1980, A Small Sound of the Trumpet, 1987, others; contbr. articles to profl. jours. Chmn., bd. dirs. St. Vincent's Hosp., Ottawa, 1969-81; pub. rep., bd. dirs. Canadian Nurses Assn., 1980-83; bd. dirs. Carleton U., 1984—, Council on Aging, 1986—, pres. 1989—. Recipient Alumnae Recognition award Radcliffe Coll., 1987. Fellow Royal Soc. Can.; mem. Medieval Acad., Order of Can., Phi Beta Kappa. Roman Catholic. Home: 402-555 Wilbrod St, Ottawa, ON Canada K1N 5R4

LABEDZ, BERNICE R., state legislator; b. Omaha, Sept. 19, 1919; m. Stanley J. Labedz, May 9, 1942; children—Terry, Jan, Toni, Frank. Former businesswoman, employee Nebr. State Dept. Revenue, then mayoral, senatorial asst., pub. relations dir.; mem. Nebr. State Legislature, 1976—. Recipient community service awards. Office: Nebr State Capitol Bldg Lincoln NE 68509 also: 4417 S 40th St Omaha NE 68107

LA BIANCA, CORY JANE, public relations executive, journalist; b. L.A., Apr. 4, 1948; d. Leno Anthony and Mildred Alice (Skofield) La Bianca; children: Tony, Michael. BA in Communications, Calif. State U., Fullerton, 1984; MS in Mass Communications, Utah State U., 1987. Advt. copywriter Temme Advt., Newport Beach, Calif., 1980-81; stringer Newport Ensign, Newport Beach, 1983-84; grad. teaching asst. dept. communication Utah State U., Logan, 1985-87, instr. dept. communication, 1987-88; di. pub. relations Logan Regional Hosp., 1987—. Author: (for children) Legend of Snowshoe Thompson, 1989; contbr. articles. Deseret News grantee, 1987. Mem. Women in Communications Inc., Internat. Assn. Bus. Communicators, Soc. for Healthcare Pub. Relations and Advt., Utah Hosp. Assn., LWV (dir. pub. relations Cache County 1988-89). Office: Logan Regional Hosp 1400 North 500 East Logan UT 89321

LABOTA, DOLORES BERNADETTE, critical care nurse; b. Shamokin, Pa., Aug. 29, 1954; d. John Anthony and Rose Marie (Darrup) L. BSN, Villanova (Pa.) U., 1976; MD, Jefferson Med. Coll., Phila., 1981. RN, Pa. Staff nurse o.r. Hershey (Pa.) Med. Ctr., 1976-77; resident in gen. surgery Allegheny Gen. Hosp., Pitts., 1981-82; staff nurse Geisinger Med. Ctr., Danville, Pa., 1983-84; patient care mgr. asst. Geisinger Med. Ctr., 1984-86; critical care coord. Pottsville (Pa.) Hosp. and Warne Clinic, 1987—. Prog. com. mem. Am. Heart Assn., Schuylkill County, Pa., 1988—. Mem. Pa. Eastern Region Orgn. of Nurse Execs., Sigma Theta Tau. Democrat. Roman Catholic. Home: 133 S Willow St Mount Carmel PA 17851 Office: Pottsville Hosp & Warne Cli 420 S Jackson St Pottsville PA 17901

LABOTT, SUSAN MARIE, psychology educator; b. Milw., Dec. 14, 1956; d. Robert James and Arlene Elizabeth (Pahl) L. BS, U. Wis., 1981; MA, No. Ill. U., 1983, PhD, 1986. Lic. psychologist, Ohio. Asst. prof. psychology U. Toledo, 1986—; mem. admissions com. clin. psychology area U. Toledo, 1986—, mem. undergrad. scholarship com. dept. psychology, 1988—, mem. human subjects rsch. com., 1987—. Mem. Am. Psychol. Assn., Midwest Psychol. Assn., Eastern Psychol. Assn., Internat. Soc. for the Study of Multiple Personality and Dissociative States, Phi Beta Kappa. Office: U Toledo 2801 W Bancroft Toledo OH 43606

LABRY, ROBBIE SHIRLEY, administrative coordinator tv station; b. Ashtabula, Ohio, May 27, 1957; d. Gabriel and Phyllis (Kresin) L. Assoc. in Bus., Kent State U., 1977; postgrad., Lakeland Coll., Mentor, Ohio, 1985. Sec. Ashtabula Rubber Co., 1977-80, Ashtabula Forge Co., 1980-82; pers. asst. Reliance Electric Co., Ashtabula, 1982-87; adminstrv. coord. Sta. WEWS-TV, Cleve., 1987—; realtor Gordon Real Estate Co., Ashtabula, 1985—. Mem. Cleve. Bd. Realtors. Home: 1630 E 29th St Ashtabula OH 44004 Office: Sta WEWS-TV 3001 Euclid Ave Cleveland OH 44115

LACER, KATHRYN LORENE, corporate assistant secretary; b. Cromwell, Okla., Oct. 20, 1930; d. William Alfred and Beulah Addie (Hankins) Hopkins; m. Orland G. Lacer, May 27, 1951. Student, Amarillo Coll., 1983-85. Sec. Mansur-Campbell Ins. Agy., Wewoka, Okla., 1948-51, Phillips Petroleum Co., Borger, Tex., 1951-52; with Southwestern Pub. Svc. Co., Amarillo, Tex., 1952—, corp. asst. sec., 1983—. Participant Leadership Amarillo, 1985; participant Leadership Tex., 1984, regional chmn., 1987-90. Recipient Achievement award Amarillo Women's Network, 1984; named Woman of Yr. Am. Bus. Women's Assn., 1969. Mem. Amarillo C. of C. (chmn. com. women's coun., chmn. civic beautification com. 1987-88), Nat. Investor Rels. Inst., S.W. Securities Transfer Assn., Leadership Amarillo Alumni Assn. (bd. dirs. 1988-90, pres. 1990-91), Amarillo Club, Tascosa Country Club. Office: Southwestern Pub Svc Co Tyler at Sixth Amarillo TX 79101

LACEY, BEATRICE CATES, psychophysiologist; b. N.Y.C., July 22, 1919; d. Louis Henry and Mollie (Libowitz) Cates; m. John I. Lacey, Apr. 16, 1938; children: Robert Arnold, Carolyn Ellen. Student, Columbia U., 1935-38; A.B. with distinction, Cornell U., 1940; M.A., Antioch Coll., 1958. Mem. staff Fels Research Inst., Yellow Springs, Ohio, 1953-82; sr. investigator Fels Research Inst., 1966-72, sr. scientist, 1972-82; instr. Antioch Coll., Yellow Springs, 1956-63; clin. prof. psychiatry Antioch Coll., 1963-68; Fels prof. emeritus psychiatry Wright State U., 1968-73; prof. Antioch Coll., 1973-82; Fels prof. psychiatry Wright State U. Sch. Medicine, 1977-82, clin. prof. psychiatry, 1982-89, Fels prof. emeritus, 1989—; acting sci. dir. Fels Research Inst., 1979-82. Assoc. editor Psychophysiology, 1975-78; reviewer Jour. Abnormal Psychiatry, Psychophysiology, Biol. Psychology, Cognitive Psychology, Sci.; contbr. articles to profl. jours.; researcher, author numerous publs. in psychophysiology of the autonomic nervous system. Recipient Disting. Sci. Contbn. award, Am. Psychol. Assn., 1976, Psychol. Sci. Gold Medal award, Am. Psychol. Found., 1985; William James fellow, Am. Psychol. Soc., 1989. Fellow Acad. Behavioral Medicine Research, Soc. Exptl. Psychologists, Am. Psychol. Soc. (William James fellow 1989); mem. Soc. Psychophysiol. Research (dir. 1972-75, pres. 1978-79), Soc. Neurosci., Phi Kappa Phi. Home: 1425 Meadow Ln Yellow Springs OH 45387

LACH, ALMA ELIZABETH, food and cooking writer, consultant; b. Petersburg, Ill.; d. John H. and Clara E. (Boeker) Satorius; diplome de Cordon Bleu, Paris, 1956; m. Donald F. Lach, Mar. 18, 1939; 1 dau., Sandra Judith. Feature writer Children's Activities mag., 1954-55; creator, performer TV show Let's Cook, children's cooking show, 1955; hostess weekly food program on CBS, 1962-66, performer TV show Over Easy, PBS, 1977-78; food editor Chgo. Daily Sun-Times, 1957-65; pres. Alma Lach Kitchens Inc., Chgo., 1966—, dir. Alma Lach Cooking Sch., Chgo.; lectr. U. Chgo. Downtown Coll., Gourmet Inst., U. Md., 1963, Modesto (Calif.) Coll., 1978, U. Chgo., 1981; resident master Shoreland Hall, U. Chgo., 1978-81; food cons. Food Bus. Mag., 1964-66, Chgo.'s New Pump Room, Lettuce Entertain You, Bitter End Resort, Brit. V.I., Midway Airlines, Flying Food Fare, Inc., Berghoff Restaurant, Hans' Bavarian Lodge, Unocal '76, Peer Foods, Univ. Club Chgo.; columnist Modern Packaging, 1967-68, Travel & Camera, 1969, Venture, 1970, Chicago mag., 1978, Bon Appetit, 1980, Tribune Syndicate, 1982, The World & I, 1988-90. Recipient Pillsbury award, 1958; Grocery Mfrs. Am. Trophy award, 1959, certificate of Honor, 1961; Chevalier du Tastevin, 1962; Commanderie de l'Ordre des Anysetiers du Roy, 1963; Confrerie de la Chaine des Rotisseurs, 1964; Les Dames D'Escoffier, 1982. Mem. U. Chgo. Settlement League, Am. Assn. Food Editors (chmn. 1959). Clubs: Tavern, Quadrangle (Chgo.). Author: A Child's First Cookbook, 1950; The Campbell Kids Have a Party, 1953; The Campbell Kids at Home, 1953; Let's Cook, 1956; Candlelight Cookbook, 1959; Cooking a la Cordon Bleu, 1970; Alma's Almanac, 1972; Hows and Whys of French Cooking, 1974, The World and I, 1988. Contbr. to World Book Yearbook, 1961-75, Grolier Soc. Yearbook, 1962. Home and Office: 5750 Kenwood Ave Chicago IL 60637

LACH, EILEEN MARIE, lawyer; b. Mpls., June 27, 1950; d. Andrew Anthony and Adeline Florence (Smuda) L. Student Osmania U., Hyderabad, India, 1971-72; B.A. in Internat. Relations magna cum laude, U. Minn., 1973; M.P.A. in Internat. Affairs, Princeton U., 1976; J.D., NYU, 1977. Bar: N.Y. 1978, Pa. 1986, U.S. Dist. Ct. (so. dist.) N.Y. 1982, U.S. Dist. Ct. (ea. dist.) N.Y. 1982. Assoc. Lord, Day & Lord, N.Y.C., 1977-79; corp. atty. Wender, Murase & White, N.Y.C., 1979-82; assoc. Boulanger, Finley & Hicks, P.C., N.Y.C., 1982-83; ptnr. Drinker Biddle & Reath, 1984-89; spl. counsel-internat. Am. Home Products Corp., N.Y.C., 1989—. gen. counsel Amnesty Internat., 1977-84. Co-author/editor: New York Practice Guide: Business and Commercial, 1987. Minn. chmn. Young Democrats., 1968-69. McConnell fellow, 1973-76. Mem. ABA, N.Y. State Bar Assn., Assn. of Bar of City of N.Y., Internat. Law Assn., Phi Beta Kappa. Office: Am Home Products Corp 685 3rd Ave New York NY 10017

LACHANCE, JANICE RACHEL, labor union executive, lawyer; b. Biddeford, Maine, June 17, 1953; d. Ralph L. and Rachel A. (Desnoyers) L. BA, Manhattanville Coll., 1974; JD, Tulane U., 1978. Bar: Maine 1978, D.C. 1982. Staff dir. subcom. on antitrust Ho. of Reps., Washington, 1982-83; adminstrv. asst. Congresswoman Katie Hall, 1983-84; asst. pres. sec. Mondale-Ferraro Campaign, Washington, 1984; press sec. Congressman Tom Daschle, 1985; ptnr. Lachance and Assocs., Washington, 1985-87; dir. communications and polit. action Am. Fedn. Govt. Employees (AFL-CIO), Washington, 1987—; vis. scholar Cornell U., 1972-73. Editor newsletter Govt. Standard, 1987—. Mem. Alexandria (Va.) Dem. Com. Mem. Delta Delta Delta, Phi Alpha Delta. Democrat. Roman Catholic. Office: Am Fedn Govt Employees 80 F St NW Washington DC 20001

LACHENICHT, ANGELA MARIE, marketing professional; b. St. Louis, Feb. 3, 1955; d. Bernard J. and Dolores B. (Vaughn) L.; m. David L. Fuller, Sept. 6, 1974 (div. Mar. 1987). A in Bus. Adminstrn., Meremac Community Coll., St. Louis, 1983; Cert of Tng. in Employment Law, U. Mo.-St. Louis, 1989. P.B.X. operator Arthur Enterprises, St. Louis, 1971-73; credit mgr. Watson Furniture, St. Louis, 1973-80; owner, operator Action Video World, St. Louis, 1980-85; regional telemarketing mgr. Cencom Cable TV, St. Louis, 1985—; coord. Am. Cablevision, St. Louis, 1988; cons. Thomas Construction, St. Louis, 1987-90. Author, editor: (guide) Cencom Insider, 1989. Telemarketing coord. Comic Relief/Health Care for the Homeless Coalition, St. Louis, 1987-89; cons. Non-Profit Employment Liaison Com., St. Louis, 1989. Recipient Emmy award, St. Louis chpt. NATAS, 1988, Civic Commendation, Health Care for the Homeless Coalition, St. Louis, 1989, 90. Mem. Women in Cable, Nat. Cable TV Assn. Democrat. Roman Catholic. Office: Cencom Cable TV 9358 Dielman Ind Dr Saint Louis MO 63132

LACHER, CAROLYN HARPER, realty company executive; b. Paoli, Pa., July 10, 1959; d. John Franklin Harper and Katherine (Johnson) Holman; m. George Stuart Lacher, Oct. 4, 1986. B City Planning, U. Va., 1981, MBA, 1985. Analyst Johns Hopkins Health System, Balt., 1985-87; dir. rsch. Manekin Corp., Balt., 1987-88; v.p. Alex Brown Kleinwort Benson Realty Advisors, Balt., 1988—; mem. adv. bd. Nat. Real Estate Index, 1988-89. Treas. Riverdale Community Assn., Severna Park, Md., 1985-86; del. Magothy River Assn., Severna Park, 1986-87. Mem. Comml. Real Estate Women, Real Estate Market Analysts Assn. Republican. Episcopalian. Home: 1504 Maywood Ave Baltimore MD 21204 Office: Alex Brown Kleinwort Benson Realty Advisors 2 N Charles St Baltimore MD 21201

LACHER, MIRIAM RISE, neuropsychologist; b. Bronx, N.Y., Dec. 30, 1942; d. Philip and Ruth Frieda (Rabinowitz) Browner; m. Maury Lacher, Aug. 17, 1963. AB, Cornell U., 1963; PhD, U. Mich., 1970; postgrad., Columbia Coll., 1981. Asst. prof. psychology Carleton Coll., Northfield, Minn., 1970-77; vis. rsch. assoc. U. Calif., Berkeley, 1976-77; vis. lectr. Vassar Coll., Poughkeepsie, N.Y., 1978-79; assoc. neuropsychology Columbia-Presbyn. Med. Ctr., N.Y.C., 1980-81; cons. N.Y. State Psychiat. Inst., N.Y.C., 1981; chief cognitive rehab. Children's Specialized Hosp., Westfield, N.J., 1982-84; cons. Vassar Coll. Counseling Svc., Poughkeepsie, 1984-90, First Step Nursery Sch., Hyde Park, N.Y., 1988; pvt. practice Poughkeepsie, 1984—. Contbr. articles to profl. jours. Sci. advisor on bd. dirs. Parents of Children with Delicit Disorders, Mid-Hudson chpt., 1989—. Woodrow Wilson fellow, U. Mich., 1963-64. Mem. Am. Psychol. Assn., Internat. Neuropsychol. Soc., Eastern Psychol. Assn., Hudson Valley Psychol. Assn. (sec. 1984-85, 86-87, program chair 1985-86), N.Y. State Psychol. Assn., N.Y. Neuropsychol. Group. Office: 37 Alda Dr Poughkeepsie NY 12603

LACKRITZ, BARBARA BANK, speech and language pathologist, alderman; b. N.Y.C., July 16, 1938; d. Mac Albert and Lucy (Kublanow) Bank; m. Irving Lackritz, June 27, 1959; children: Pamela Ilene Lackritz Moehle, Hilary Sue Lackritz Hampsch, Neal Matthew. BA in Speech Correction, Communications, U. Mich., 1959; MA in Spl. Edn., Columbia U. Tchrs. Coll., 1962. Cert. tchr. speech/lang., secondary English, speech/drama, Conn., Mich., Mo., N.Y. Speech pathologist Stratford (Conn.) Pub. Schs., 1959-60; speech/lang. pathologist Garden City (N.Y.) Pub. Schs., 1960-63, 64-67; speech clinician Bklyn. Jewish Hosp. Speech Clinic, N.Y.C., 1963-64; pvt. practice Great Neck, N.Y., 1964-71; speech/lang. pathologist Kinnelon (N.J.) Pub. Schs., 1971-72; speech/lang. cons. La Petite Presch., Ballwin, Mo., 1973-75; tchr. Parkway Community Schs., St. Louis, 1975-78; cons. gifted programs Parkway, Ferguson, and Florissant Pub. Schs., St. Louis, 1975-78; speech/lang. pathologist Francis Howell Pub. Schs., St. Charles, Mo., 1980—; mem. legis. com. Mo. Speech/Lang. Assn., St. Louis, 1983-86; mem. steering com. Conf. on Edn. "Coalition for Vol. Sch. Desegregation", St. Louis, 1984-86; mem. com. on women Mo. NEA, Columbia, 1986-87. Author: Communication in the Language Arts, 1962. Mem. Planning Commn. City of Town and Country, Mo., 1983—; mem. Nat. Women's Polit. Caucus, 1983—; speaker Vol. Desegregation Program Network, St. Louis, 1985-86; chmn. Pub. Health and Sanitation Commn., Town and Country, 1985-89; alderman City of Town and Country, 1985—. Mem. AAUW (state bd. dirs., Edn. Found. chmn. 1985-89, com. on women chmn. 1985-87, peace and nat. security chmn. 1983-85, edn. chmn. 1983-84, chmn. met. interbr. coun. 1980-82, pres. creve coeur br. 1978-80, Mo. Woman of Distinction 1984, community leadership program for tchrs. 1990—). Home: 1779 Bradburn Dr Town and Country MO 63131

LACLUYSE, LINDA MARIE, pharmaceutical sales trainer; b. South Bend, Ind., Sept. 30, 1959; d. Joseph Paul and Geraldine Adelaide (Healy) LaC. BS in Pharmacy, Purdue U., 1982; MS in Indsl. Adminstrn., Krannert Grad. Sch. Mgmt., 1983. Registered pharmacist. Staff pharmacist Kroger, Elkhart, Ind., 1983; pharmacy mgr. Kroger, Frankfort, Ind., 1983-84; sales rep. Schering Labs., Muncie, Ind., 1984-85, SmithKline & French Labs., Chgo., 1986-89; sales trainer SmithKline & French Labs., Phila., 1989—. Mem. Nat. Soc. Pharm. Sales Trainers. Lutheran. Office: SmithKline & French Labs 1500 Spring Garden E-52 Philadelphia PA 19101

LACOMBE, RITA JEANNE, bank consultant; b. Panama City, Fla., Sept. 28, 1947; d. Robert Rosairio and Virginia May (Mauldin) L. AA, Los Angeles Pierce Coll., 1967; BSBA, Calif. State U., Northridge, 1969; postgrad., Stanford U., 1986. Br. mgr. Security Pacific Nat. Bank, San Fernando Valley, Calif., 1970-78; bankcard compliance officer, asst. v.p. Security Pacific Nat. Bank, Woodland Hills, Calif., 1978-82; sect. mgr., v.p. Security Pacific Nat. Bank, Los Angeles, 1982-87; sr. sales rep. corp. microcomputer sales ComputerLand, L.A., 1987-88; corp. sales rep. microcomputer sales ComputerLand, Northridge and Laguna Hills, Calif., 1988-89; sr. mgmt. cons. fin. industries group Deloitte & Touche, CPA, L.A., 1989—. Membership chair Sierra Club, Los Angeles, 1982. Mem. Nat. Assn. Female Execs. Democrat. Roman Catholic.

LACOUNTE, CHERYL DEWERFF, campus director, instructor; b. Long Beach, Calif., Aug. 13, 1961; d. Duane Lee DeWerff and Margery Carol (Plumb) Singer; m. Christopher Thomas LaCounte, Aug. 27, 1983; 1 child: Brendan Alexander. BBA with honors, Ea. N.Mex. U., 1983. Cert. hotel mgr., housekeeping supr. Bridal cons. Jordan Marsh, Framingham, Mass.,

1983-84; exec. asst. Sheraton Tara Hotel, Framingham, 1984-85, pers. dir., 1985-87; coll. instr. Newbury Coll., Brookline, Mass., 1987—; campus dir. Newbury Coll., Framingham, 1990—. Counselor Parental Stress Hotline, Mass., 1987—. Mem. NAFE, Acad. Women Achievers, Delta Mu Delta. Republican. Office: Newbury Coll 24 Myrtle St Framingham MA 01701

LACOUR, CARON ANN, accountant; b. Springfield, Mass., Oct. 13, 1963; d. Edward R. Jr. and Andrea F. (Caron) LaC. BSBA, Western New Eng. Coll., 1985. Acct. A.J. Hirschfeld & Co., West Hartford, Conn., 1985—; tax preparer, Vol. I*ncome Tax Assistance, Springfield, 1984, 85. Mem. Acctg. Assn. Western New Eng. Coll. (treas. 1985). Home: 84 Meadowbrook Rd Agawam MA 01001 Office: AJ Hirschfeld & Co 7 N Main St West Hartford CT 06107

LACROIX, MURIEL CLAIRE, business analyst; b. Woonsocket, R.I., July 20, 1939; d. Rene A. and Regina S. (Recore) L. BEd, Rivier Coll., 1971; BSBA, Bryant Coll., 1980, MBA, 1989. Tchr. jr. high pvt. and pub. schs., Mass. and R.I., 1964-74; student loan rep. Eastland Savs. Bank, Woonsocket, 1974-78; acct. Data Gen. Corp., Westboro, Mass., 1978-83; bus. analyst support svcs. sect. Data Gen. Corp., Milford, Mass., 1983—; prof. acctg. Newbury Coll., Boston, 1988—. Mem. adv. bd. Assumption Parish Renewal Program. Mem. NAFE, Bryant Coll. Alumni Assn., River Coll. Alumni Assn. Roman Catholic. Home: 301 Wrentham Rd Bellingham MA 02019

LACY, CAROL ANGELA, insurance executive; b. Watford, Eng., July 15, 1943; came to U.S., 1967, naturalized, 1976; d. Thomas and Winifred Joan (Stromberg) Carney; m. Floyd Raymond Lacy, May 25, 1968 (dec. July 1988); children: Susan, Timothy. Claims adjuster Central Mut. Ins. Co., Toronto, Can., 1964-68; exec. sec. TransFresh Corp., Salinas, Calif., 1968-70; claims examiner Monterey Bay Found., Salinas, 1972-78; pres., account mgr. ABC Med. Claims Services, Salinas, 1978—; chmn. bd. dirs. Monterey County Spl. Health Care Authority, Salinas, 1982-85. mem. adv. bd. Natividad Hosp., Salinas, 1979-82, North Monterey County Bd. Edn., Salinas, 1977-83; mem. 101 Bypass com., 1983—, chmn. exec. bd. 1986—; treas. Monterey County Bds. Assn., Salinas, 1981-83; mem. Monterey County Grand Jury, Salinas, 1984-85; pres. Prunedale PTA, Salinas, 1976; founding trustee Med. Ctr. Found. Monterey County, 1988; co-chmn. Yes on Measure B Com., 1989; chmn. Com. to elect Judy Pennycook, 1989; chmn. Com. to Elect Flip Baldwin, 1989; mem. tech. adv. com. 101 Bypass, 1989. Recipient Honorary Service award Prunedale PTA, 1982. Mem. Monterey Bay Life Underwriters Assn. Republican. Baptist. Avocations: stamp collecting; fishing; gardening.

LACY, ELIZABETH BERMINGHAM, state judge; b. 1945. BA, St. Mary's Coll., Notre Dame, Ind.; JD, U. Tex. Admitted to bar, 1969. Past commr. Va. State Corp. Commn.; justice Supreme Ct. Va., 1989—. Office: Va Supreme Ct 100 N 9th St PO Box 1315 Richmond VA 23210*

LADANYI, BRANKA MARIA, chemist, educator; b. Zagreb, Yugoslavia, Sept. 7, 1947; came to U.S., 1969; d. Branko and Nevenka (Zilic) L.; m. Marshall Fixman, Dec. 7, 1974. BSc, McGill U., Montreal, Can., 1969; M in Philosophy, Yale U., 1971, PhD, 1973. Vis. prof. of chemistry U. Ill., 1974; postdoctoral research assoc. Yale U., 1974-77, research assoc., 1977-79; asst. prof. chemistry Colo. State U., Ft. Collins, 1979-84, assoc. prof. chemistry, 1985-87, prof. chemistry, 1987—. Referee and contbr. articles to profl. jours. Fellow Sloan Found., 1982-84, Dreyfus Found., 1983-87; NSF grantee, NATO grantee 1983-89. Mem. AAAS, Am. Chem. Soc. (PRF grantee 1979-82, 1989—), Am. Phys. Soc., NOW, Sigma Xi. Home: 1100 E Pitkin St Fort Collins CO 80524 Office: Colo State U Dept Chemistry Fort Collins CO 80523

LADD, ROBERTA KAY, horsebreeder, marketing executive; b. Clearwater Beach, Fla., July 24, 1953; d. F. Robert and Marguerite Elizabeth (Ethier) L. BA in Indsl. Psychology, Calif. State U., Long Beach, 1975. Lic. seminar facilitator. Sales trainer western region GTE Directories Corp., Los Alamitos, Calif., 1977-84; breeder, mktg. dir. Liberty West Arabians, Calif., 1978—; dir. mktg., tng. and promotions Guam Cable TV. Pub. Desert Horse Directory, 1984-86; editor Arabian Horse Jour., 1982-83, Animal Air Transport mag., 1988-89; contbr. articles to trade jours. and newspapers. Dir. promotions Ride Across Am. Benefit, Tucson, 1988-89; fund raiser Rainforest Action Network, San Francisco, 1988-89; supporter Orange County Riders, 1980-81, Therapeutic Riding Orgn. Tucson, 1988-89. Mem. Internat. Arabian Horse Assn. (conf. del. 1987, 88), Am. Horse Shows Assn., Arabian Racing Assn. Calif. (Top 10 Arabian Race Mare award for LWA Khlassy Lady 1988, 89, Can. Top 20 Mare 1989), Arabian Jockey Club (vice chmn., mem. exec. com. 1988—), So. Ariz. Arabian Horse Assn. (racing chmn. Tucson chpt. 1988-89), Sierra Pacific Arabian Racing Coun. (pres. 1987-88). Methodist. Home: 1501 Palos Verdes Dr N Harbor City CA 90710 Office: 970 S Marine Dr #10-303 Tamuning GU 96911-3403

LADDUSAW-LANE, LISA ANN-MICHAEL, publisher, editor; b. Remsen, Iowa, July 18, 1954; d. Richard Paul and Doris Marie (Frank) Laddusaw; m. Daniel Joseph Lane, Apr. 12, 1953. BA, Calif. State U. at Fullerton, 1977. Asst. art dir. Wolsey Co., 1972-79; advt. mgr. Holman's Dept. Store, 1979-85; art dir. The Vaughn Orgn., 1985-86; prodn. mgr. Bus. Research and Communications, Monterey, Calif., 1986-87, prodn. dir., 1987-88, mng. editor, 1988—. Democrat. Roman Catholic. Home: 26193 Paseo Del Sur Monterey CA 93940

LADER, WENDY FRIEDMAN, psychologist; b. NYC, May 10, 1952; d. Jerome and Shirley Roslyn (Scheiner) F.; m. Michael Arlen Lader, Aug. 19, 1978. Syracuse U., 1974; MEd, Lesley Coll., Cambridge, Mass., 1975; MS, Nova U., Davie, Fla., 1982; PhD, Nova U., 1984. Dir. women's program Nat. Program for Treatment Self-Injury Hartgrove Hosp., Chgo., 1985--; dir., girls program. Mercy Hosp., Chgo., 1987-89; pvt. practice Chgo., 1987-- . Author: assessment scale, The Lader Attitudes Towards Violence Against Wives Scale, 1983. Vol. therapist, Loop YWCA, 1979-82, mem. State's Attorney's Task Force on Women's Issues, Chgo., 1986--. Mem. American Psychological Assn., Assn. of Women in Psychology, Assn. for the Advancement of Behavior Therapy. Democrat. Jewish. Office: 151 N Michigan Ave #904 Chicago IL 60601

LADEROUTE, LINDA DODD, energy consulting company executive; b. Berkeley, Calif., June 11, 1948; d. James LeRoy and Mary Jane (Sico) Dodd; m. Andrew O. Stortroen, Aug. 12, 1968 (div. 1972); 1 child, Erik Walter; m. Charles David Laderoute, June 8, 1985. Student, San Francisco State U., 1966-69; BA in Geography, Sonoma State U., Rohnert Park, Calif., 1975, cert. in mgmt. and supervision, 1984; lic. in real estate, Anthony Schs., San Francisco, 1978. Cert. in energy utilization analysis, Calif.; lic. resident and conservation auditor, Calif. Clk. various law firms, San Francisco, Santa Rosa, Calif., 1966-73; coach Santa Rosa Gymnastic Ctr., 1976-81; customer svc. rep. Pacific Gas & Electric Co., San Rafael, Calif., 1981-82; residential conservation auditor Pacific Gas & Electric Co., Ukiah, Calif., 1982-83, energy mgmt. rep., 1983-84; rate analyst Pacific Gas & Electric Co., San Francisco, 1984-85; v.p. Charles D. Laderoute, Ltd., Topsfield, Mass., 1985—; real estate agt. Vintage Properties, also other cos., Santa Rosa, 1978-81; lectr. computer tng. Ctr. for Profl. Advancement, East Brunswick, N.J., 1986. Mem. Assn. for Women in Computing (newsletter dir. Greater Boston chpt. 1986-88, membership dir. 1989-91, nat. sec. 1988), LWV, Boston Mus. Fine Arts, Mass. Hort. Soc. Republican. Office: PO Box 376 Topsfield MA 01983

LADINSKY, JUDITH LOUISE, preventive medicine educator; b. L.A., June 16, 1938; d. Irving and Eva (Freiden) Byers; m. Jack Ladinsky, July 16, 1961; children: Morissa, Mark. BS, U. Mich., 1960; MS, U. Wis., 1964, PhD, 1968. Project assoc. dept. genetics U. Wis., Madison, 1961-68, instr. preventive medicine, 1968-69, asst. prof. preventive medicine, 1969-75, assoc. prof. preventive medicine, 1975—; chmn. U.S. Com. for Scientific Cooperation with Vietnam, 1985—; cons. Ministry of Health Vietnam, Laos; bd. dirs. Office Internat. Health Officers Med. Schs., 1986—. Contbr. articles to profl. jours. Bd. dirs. Community Action Commn., Wis., 1975-80, Madison Community Health Ctr., Group Health Cooperative - HMO, 1980-85. Recipient rsch. grants, Rockefeller Found. and others., 1968—. Mem. Am. Pub. Health Assn. (chmn. sect., various offices), Am Soc. for Cell Biology, Assn. of Tchrs. of Preventive Medicine, Nat. Assn. Pub. Health Policy, Nat. Coun. Tchrs. of Preventive Medicine, Phi Kappa Phi (faculty award 1988), Sigma Xi. Office: Dept Preventive Medicine Univ Wis 1300 University Ave Madison WI 53706

LAFAVE, LEANN LARSON, lawyer; b. Ramona, S.D., May 31, 1953; d. Floyd Burdette and Janice Anne (Quist) L.; m. Richard Curtis Finke, May 19, 1973 (div. Jan. 1978); 1 child, Timothy; m. Dwayne Jeffery LaFave, May 31, 1981; children: Jeffrey, Allison. BS, U. S.D., 1974, JD with honors, 1977. Bar: S.D. 1977, U.S. Dist. Ct. S.D. 1977, U.S. Ct. Appeals (8th cir.) 1977, N.D. 1978, U.S. Dist. Ct. N.D. 1978. Asst. atty. gen. State of S.D., Pierre, 1977-78, 79-81; assoc. Bjella, Neff, Rathert & Wahl, Williston, N.D., 1978-79, Tobin Law Offices, P.C., Winner, S.D., 1981-83; assoc. dean, asst. prof. U. S.D. Sch. Law, Vermillion, 1983-86, dir. continuing legal edn., 1983-89, assoc. prof. law, 1986-89; ptnr. Aho & LaFave, Brookings, S.D., 1990—; cons. S.D. Coalition Against Domestic Violence, 1983-84; cert. hearing officer S.D. Div. Elem. and Secondary Edn., Pierre, 1982—; mem. S.D. Bd. Pardons and Paroles, 1987-90, chmn., 1989-90; comml. arbitrator Am. Arbitration Assn., 1985—; reporter S.D. State and Local Legal Ctr., Washington, 1984-89. Contbr. articles to profl. jours. Mem. planning council Nat. Identification Program for Advancement of Women in Higher Edn. Adminstrn., Am. Council on Edn., S.D., 1984—; bd. dirs. Mo. Shores Womens Resource Ctr., Pierre, 1980, W.H. Over Mus., Vermillion, 1986-87, S.D. Vol. Lawyers for the Arts, 1987—, Brookings Interagency Coun., 1990—, Brookings Womens Ctr., 1990—. Named S.D. Woman Atty. of Yr. Women in Law U. S.D., 1985. Mem. ABA, AAUW, S.D. Bar Assn. (bd. govs. young lawyers sect. 1983-84), S.D. Bd. Pardons & Paroles, Pierre, Nat. Assn. of Counsel for Children, Rotary Internat., Epsilon Sigma Alpha (S.D. council sec. 1985-86). Republican. Episcopalian. Home: 402-13th Ave Brookings SD 57006 Office: Aho & LaFave 518 Main Ave PO Box 767 Brookings SD 57006-0767

LAFAYE, CARY DUPRE, librarian; b. Horry County, S.C., June 22, 1945; d. Moffatt Barmore and Helen Elizabeth (Cappelmann) DuPre; m. Angus Bird Lafaye, Mar. 21, 1970; 1 dau., Helen Cary. B.A. cum laude, U.S.C., 1967, M. Librarianship, 1973. Reading, history tchr. Moultrie Jr. High Sch., Mount Pleasant, S.C., 1967-69; tchr. French, history Irmo High Sch. (S.C.), 1969-71; library asst. U.S.C., Columbia, 1971-72; librarian Richland County Pub. Library-Cooper Br., Columbia, S.C., 1973-74; reference librarian Midlands Tech. Coll., Beltline Library, Columbia, 1975—. Mem. Ala, S.C. Library Assn., Southeastern Library Assn., U. S.C. Coll. Library and Info. Sci. Assn. (v.p. 1987-88), Phi Beta Kappa, Beta Phi Mu (chpt. pres. 1983-84), Kappa Delta. Home: 1412 Haynsworth Rd Columbia SC 29205 Office: Midlands Tech Coll Beltline Library PO Drawer 2408 Columbia SC 29202

LAFFITTE-REGUERA, MARY E., finance executive; b. N.Y.C., June 13; d. Juan and Maria (Camilo) Laffitte; m. Aldo Manuel Reguera, June 14, 1985. AA, Miami Dade Community Coll., 1981; BS, Barry U., 1983; Cert. in Internat. Bus., St. Thomas U., 1989. Cert. real estate assoc. Fgn. exch. teller Fla. Fgn. Exch., Miami, 1979-81; internat. asst. head teller Southeast Bank Internat. Bldg., Miami, 1981-83; asst. loan adminstr. First Palm Beach Internat. Bank, Coral Gables, 1983-85; fin. analyst Internat. Funds Transfer Amex, Miami, 1985-90; supr. fin. control internat. div. Am. Express, Miami, 1990—. Active Alliance Francaise, Miami, 1979-81, 89—, Coalition of Hispanic Am. Women, Miami, 1983-86. Mem. NAFE. Home: PO Box 65-0564 Miami FL 33265 Office: American Express 14261 Commerce Way Miami Lakes FL 33265

LAFOND PICCOLOMINI, BERNADETTE, network television news executive; b. Menominee, Mich., Sept. 8, 1953; d. Cletus Anthony and Anne (de Beaussier) L.; m. Manfredi Piccolomini, Dec. 14, 1987. BA in French Lit., U. Mich., 1975. Assoc. dir. news Sta. ABC TV, N.Y.C., 1981—. Office: Sta ABC News 7 W 66th St New York NY 10023

LAFONTANT, JEWEL STRADFORD, lawyer; b. Chgo., Apr. 28, 1922; d. Cornelius Francis and Aida Arabella (Carter) Stradford; 1 son, John W. Rogers III. AB, Oberlin Coll., 1943; JD, U. Chgo., 1946; LLD (hon.), Cedar Crest Coll., 1973; D Humanitarian Svc. (hon.), Providence Coll., 1973; LLD (hon.), Ea. Mich. U., 1973; LHD (hon.), Howard U., 1974; LLD (hon.), Heidelberg Coll., 1975, Lake Forest Coll., 1977, Marymount Manhattan Coll., 1978, Oberlin Coll., 1979; LHD (hon.), Governor's State U., 1980, LLD (hon.), 1980; citation for pub. svc., U. Chgo., 1980; LLD (hon.), Chgo. Med. Sch., 1982, Loyola U. of Chgo., 1982. Bar: Ill. bar 1947. Asst. U.S. atty., 1955-58; sr. ptnr. Vedder, Price, Kaufman & Kammholz, Chgo., 1983-89; dep. solicitor gen. U.S. Washington, 1972-75; dir. Midway Airlines, Chgo., 1988-89; ambassador-at-large, U.S. Coord. for Refugee Affairs, 1989—; bd. dirs. Mobil Corp., Continental Bank, Foote, Cone & Belding, Equitable Life Assurance Soc. U.S., Trans World Corp., Revlon, Inc., Ariel-Capital Mgmt., Harte-Hanks Communications, Inc., Pantry Pride, Inc., Revlon Group, Howard U.; past dir. Jewel Cos., Inc., TWA, Hanes Corp.; past mem. U.S. Adv. Commn. Internat. Edn. and Cultural Affairs, Nat. Coun. Minority Bus. Enterprises, Nat. Coun. on Ednl. Rsch.; past chmn. adv. bd. Civil Rights Commn.; mem. Pres.'s Pvt. Sector Survey Cost Control; pres. Exec. Exchange; past U.S. rep. to UN. Bd. editors: Am. Bar Assn. Jour. Former trustee Lake Forest (Ill.) Coll., Oberlin Coll., Howard U., Tuskegee Inst.; bd. govs. Ronald Reagan Presdl. Found.; mem. Martin Luther King, Jr., Fed. Holiday Commn.; dir. Project Hope. Fellow Internat. Acad. Trial Lawyers; mem. Chgo. Bar Assn. (bd. govs.). Home: 2700 Virginia Ave NW Apt 4004 Washington DC 20037 Office: US Dept State Washington DC 20525 also: Mobil Corp 150 E 42d St New York NY 10017*

LAFORCE, TINA HORTON, legal information specialist; b. Washington, June 12, 1961; d. Forest W. Jr. and Karin J. (Dangel) Horton; m. Rollin D. Laforce, Apr. 29, 1988. Student, Am. U.; BA in Govt. and Politics, U. Md., 1983, postgrad., 1983-84; postgrad., Pepperdine U., 1984-85, U. So. Calif., L.A., 1985-86. Ind. contractor L.A.; law clk. Law Offices of Gordon P. Gitlen, Santa Monica, Calif., Law Offices of Berglund and Johnson, Granada Hills, Calif., Beverly Stone, Greenbelt, Md.; chief legal information officer Law Offices of R. Michael Wainman, West L.A.; legal asst. to various attys.; appearance on cable show The Silent Network. Contbr. articles to quarterly newsletter. Vol. West L.A. Animal Shelter, 1986-87. Mem. So. Calif. Assn. Law Librs., Sierra Club (legal def. fund), Animal Legal Def. Fund, Humane Farming Assn., In Def. of Animals, Defenders of Wildlife, Phi Alpha Delta. Home: 7651 Reseda Blvd #T-4 Reseda CA 91335 Office: Law Offices R Michael Wainman 11500 W Olympic Blvd Ste 441 Los Angeles CA 90064

LA FOREST, RACHEL JAMISON, protective services professional; b. Phila., Mar. 9, 1954; d. Alfred Roberts and Alma (Stowe) Jamison. Student, Calif. State U., Chico, 1972-75; cert., Mission Coll., 1983. Cert. firefighter and emergency med. technician. Designer circuit bds. Calif., 1975-83; firefighter, acting apparatus operator Palo Alto (Calif.) Fire Dept., 1982-90, also acting fire insp. Guest speaker at numerous schs. and fire depts., San Francisco and San Jose. Mem. Women in Fire Suppression, Internat. Assn. Firefighters (exec. bd. local 1319). Democrat. Office: Palo Alto Fire Dept 250 Hamilton Ave Civic Ctr Palo Alto CA 94301

LAFORGE, MARY CECILE, marketing educator; b. Mobile, Ala., Dec. 31, 1945; d. Siegfried Cecil and Nona Francis (Cardwell) Brutkiewicz; m. Robert Lawrence LaForge, June 10, 1972; children: Ryan Christopher, Scott Lawrence. BBA, Samford U., 1965, MBA, 1968; PhD in Mktg., U. Ga., 1980. Asst. mktg. research mgr. Progressive Farmer/So. Living Mags., Birmingham, Ala., 1965-67; asst. prof. mktg. James Madison U., Harrisonburg, Va., 1977-81; assoc. prof. mktg. Clemson U. (S.C.), 1981—. Fellow Acad. Mktg. Sci.; mem. Am. Mktg. Assn., So. Mktg. Assn., Assn. Consumer Research, Beta Gamma Sigma. Baptist. Home: 108 Knight Circle Clemson SC 29631 Office: Dept Mktg Clemson U Sirrine Hall Clemson SC 29631

LAFOUREST, JUDITH ELLEN, editor, publisher, writer, educator; b. Indpls., Jan. 10; d. Edward Elston and Dorothy Jeanette (Parker) LaFourest; B.A., Ind. U.-Purdue U., Indpls., 1972; M.A.T., Ind. U., 1980; m. William E. Lugar; 1 dau., Beth Anne Gruner; 1 son, Paul Christopher Stewart Pitts Lugar LaFourest. Lead pre-vocat. instr., ednl. adminstr. Opportunities Industrialization Ctr., Indpls., 1972-76; part-time English and human rels. instr. Profl. Careers Inst., Indpls., 1975-78; editor, pub. Womankind, Indpls., 1977-83; co-dir. Womankind Ctr., 1981-82; editor, creative writer, photographer Bio-Feed-Back Bio Dynamics/BMC, Indpls., 1977-80; mem. assoc. faculty, creative writing inst. and composition Ind.U.-Purdue U., Indpls., 1979—, supr. student tchrs. of English, 1983—; adj. faculty dept. English, Butler U., 1984—; also lectr., free-lance editor. Ind. sec. NOW, 1978-80. Recipient Disting. Alumni award Ind. U.-Indpls., 1980; Jessamyn West scholar. Mem. Nat. League Am. Pen Women, Ind. U.-Indpls. Liberal Arts Alumni Assn. (pres. 1982), Sigma Tau Delta. Office: Butler U Dept English 4600 Sunset Ave Indianapolis IN 46208

LA FROSCIA, ELIZABETH JEANNE, banker; b. Bklyn., May 24, 1942; d. Philip and Anna (Sirico) Deffina; m. Hannibal Frances La Froscia, July 30, 1966; children: Louis, Christine, Stephanie, Bruce; foster children: Skelly, Donald, Nhu, Nhan, Nghia Nguyen. BA in English, Polit. Sci. cum laude, Queens Coll., 1981; postgrad., St. John's U., 1983-84. Adminstrv. asst. Chem. Bank, L.I., N.Y., 1975-79; project leader, sr. trainer Citibank, Forest Hills, N.Y., 1979-88; dir. tng., officer Dime Savs. Bank, Valley Stream, N.Y., 1986—; asst. vice dir. corp. tng. Apple Bank for Savs., Valley Stream, N.Y., 1989—. Tchr. liaison N.Y.C. Pub. Sch. Bd. Edn., Bklyn., 1968; den leader Boy Scouts Am., Bklyn., 1970; foster parent Cath. Guardian Soc., Bklyn., 1986—, Vietnamese Refugee Program, Bklyn., 1986—. Recipient award Cath. Archdiocese of Bklyn., 1973. Mem. Am. Bus. Womens Assn., Am. Soc. Trainers and Devel., Club for Adoptive Parents (pres. 1978-80). Democrat. Office: Apple Bank for Savs 205 E 42nd St New York NY 10017

LAGANGA, DONNA BRANDEIS, rental and fabrication business executive; b. Bklyn., June 27, 1949; d. Sidney L. and Sylvia (Herman) Brandeis; B.S. in Bus. Edn., Central Conn. State Coll., New Britain, 1972, M.S., 1975; m. Thomas LaGanga, Aug. 11, 1974. Various secretarial positions, 1969-72; tchr. bus. Lewis S. Mills Regional High Sch., Burlington, Conn., 1972-78; cons. Southwestern Pub. Co., Pelham Manor, N.Y., 1978-84, dist. sales mgr., 1984-89; pres. DBL Industries, Inc., 1989—; co-owner Colonial Welding Svc.; seminar condr., 1980—; pres. DBC Industries, Inc. Adv. bd. secretarial sci. dept. LaGuardia Community Coll., Long Island City, N.Y., 1982—; adv. bd. Krissler Bus. Inst. EDPA grantee, 1973; mem. non-partisan ednl. reform task force Pres. George Bush; cert. profl. sec. Mem. NAFE, Assn. Info./Systems Profls., Am. Mgmt. Assn., Nat. Bus. Edn. Assn., Profl. Secs. Internat., Eastern Bus. Edn. Assn., Conn. Bus. Edn. Assn., New Eng. Bus. Edn. Assn., Profl. Secs. Assn. N.Y., Nat. Assn. Cert. Profl. Secs., U.S. Golf Assn., Delta Pi Epsilon. Avocations: knitting, sewing, reading, bicycling, golfing. Home: 2929 Torringford St Torrington CT 06790 Office: DBL Industries Inc 612 S Main St Torrington CT 06790

LAGASSEY, ELIZABETH W., real estate professional; b. New Britain, Conn., Jan. 28, 1955; d. John William and Helen Nadja (Demko) Wilkel; m. Donald Henry Lagassey, Mar. 10, 1978. Student, Hartford (Conn.) Hosp. Sch. Nursing, 1973-75, Manchester (Conn.) Community Coll., 1980-88. Supr. customer service Gen. ElectricCorp., East Hartford, Conn., 1980-81; sr. adminstrv. asst. Fotomat Corp., East Hartford, 1981-83; contract adminstr. Nat. Telephone Co., South Windsor, Conn., 1982-84; div. adminstr. Marshall Erdman and Assocs., Inc., East Windsor, Conn., 1984-88; broker River's Edge Realty, Coventry, Conn., 1987-88, Elizabeth W. Lagassey Real Estate, Walden, Vt., 1988—. Author: Computer System Primer, 1986. Mem. Realtors Polit. Action com., Conn., 1975—. Mem. Nat. Assn. Realtors, N.W. Kingdom Bd. Realtors (pres. 1990—), Vt. Assn. Realtors, Inc. (state dir.). Republican. Russian Orthodox.

LAGORE, CAROL ELAINE, real estate professional; b. Chillicothe, Ohio, Sept. 1, 1950; d. Robert Franklin and Zella Elizabeth (Titus) Bartlett; m. John David LaGore, Apr. 11, 1970. Assoc. in Real Estate, Ohio U., 1983, BBA in Mgmt., 1984. Asst. merchandising mgr. Buckeye Mart, Chillicothe, 1972-77; constrn. field adminstr. Multicon Communities, Chillicothe and Lancaster, Ohio, 1977-79; real estate agt. Adena Homes Century 21, Chillicothe, 1979-88; prin., real estate appraiser LaGore's Residential Appraisal, Chillicothe, 1984-88; designated fee appraiser VA, Cleve., 1985-88; regional farm appraiser Farm Credit Svcs., Chillicothe, 1988—. With USNR, 1979-83. J.R. Freeland scholar Ohio U., 1981-82. Mem. Nat. Real Estate Inst., Profl. Assn. Women Appraisers, Nat. Assn. Real Estate Appraisers (cert.), Certified Underwriters and Appraisers, Soc. Real Estate Appraisers (mem. data service com. 1985—), Nat. Assn. Realtors, Ohio Bd. Realtors, Ross County Bd. Realtors, Nat. Fedn. Bus. and Profl. Women's Club (pres. Chillicothe chpt. 1987—, regional v.p. 1988-89, regional pres.-elect 1989—), Chillicothe-Ross C. of C., Am. Soc. Farm Mgrs. and Rural Appraisers. Home: 3233 Three Locks Rd Chillicothe OH 45601 Office: Farm Credit Svcs 14 S Paint St Chillicothe OH 45601

LAGRONE, LAVENIA WHIDDON, chemist, real estate broker; b. Conroe, Tex., Feb. 27, 1940; d. James Lewis and Cora Lee (DeLuish) Whiddon; A.A., Kilgore Coll., 1960; B.S., North Tex. State U., 1962; grad. med. tech. Baylor U. Med. Center, 1962; m. Doyle W. LaGrone, June 26, 1959 (div. Sept. 1965); 1 child, Russell Randal. Sr. technologist in spl. chemistry Baylor U. Med. Center, Dallas, 1962-63; research chemist, supr. labs., cardiovascular surgery Southwestern Med. Sch., Dallas, 1964-69, Upstate Med. Center, SUNY, Syracuse, 1969-70; research assoc., supr. lab., dept. surgery U. Tex. Med. Br., Galveston, 1970-74, research assoc., supr. labs., pediatric nephrology, 1974—, mem. chem. safety com., 1984-87; real estate broker DeLanney & Assocs., realtors, 1979-83; owner La Grone & Assocs., Realtors, 1983—. Chmn. student activities PTA Galveston, Tex., 1976-77. Recipient Top Real Estate Sales award, Top Real Estate Producer award, DeLanney & Assocs., 1979, also named Broker's Excellence award and Top Real Estate Commn. award, 1980, also Million Dollar Producer 1980-88. Mem. Am. Soc. Clin. Pathologists (registered med. technologist), Nat. Assn. Realtors, Tex. Assn. Realtors, Galveston Bd. Realtors, Multiple Listing Service (budget com.), Phi Theta Kappa. Club: Bus. and Profl. Women's (pub. relations officer 1985-86, chmn. Young Careerist Award 1987, chmn. Woman of Yr. Award 1989, scholarship com. 1988). Contbr. articles to chemistry and med. jours. Home: 142 San Fernando St Galveston TX 77550 Office: U Tex Med Br 301 University Blvd Galveston TX 77550

LAHAYE, PAM MATERA, infosystems company executive; b. San Antonio, Nov. 19, 1955; d. William A. and Esther V. (Granizo) Matera; m. Philip A. LaHaye, Mar. 1, 1980. BS cum laude, Trinity U., 1977. Mfg. mgr. Johnson & Johnson, Sherman, Tex., 1977-79, Vicra div. Baxter Travel, Dallas, 1979-80; cost. acct. Gen. Portland, Inc., Dallas, 1980; mgr. sales, fin. Ionicron/Hydronics, Dallas, 1980-83; v.p. leasing Delta Bus. Systems, Orlando, Fla., 1983—; bd. dirs. Pure WAter Systems, Orlando, Fla.; owner, Abracadabra Jewelry. Scholar Trinity U., 1973-77. Mem. Sunshine Club. Republican. Episcopalian. Home: 732 Summerland Dr Winter Springs FL 32708 Office: Delta Bus Systems 4150 John Young Pkwy Orlando FL 32804

LAHM, DIANE CHESLEY, lawyer; b. Norwood, Mass., Sept. 27, 1942; d. Casimir Peter and Christine (Zabelle) Chesley; m. Wen-hsien Wu, Dec. 26, 1964 (div. July, 1973); children: Wendi Ann, Lisa Marie; m. Gunther Karl Lahm, Dec. 14, 1973; children: Michael Christopher, Gregory Andrew. AB, Trinity Coll., 1964; postgrad., Temple U., 1973-74; JD, Capitol U., 1976. Bar: Ind. 1976, U.S. Dist Ct. (so. dist.) Ind. 1976, Ohio 1977. Pvt. practice Richmond, Ind., 1976, Columbus, Ohio, 1977; asst. atty. gen. Office Atty. Gen. Ohio, Columbus, 1977; counsel, exec. Ohio Dental Assn., Columbus, 1977-79; dir. Continuing Legal Edn. Capital U. Law Sch., Columbus, 1980-88; sec. to commn. on Continuing Legal Edn. Columbus, 1988—. Leader Green Circle Program, Phila. Human Relations Com., 1969-71; Brownie leader Girl Scouts U.S., Morgantown (W.Va.) Pub. Schs. 1972-73; leader study group PTA, Morgantown, 1973; panelist Ohio State U. Continuing Edn. Forum, Columbus, 1976; team cons. Ohio Mock Trial Program, Columbus, 1985-86. Mem. ABA, Ohio State Bar Assn., Columbus Bar Assn. Lutheran. Office: Supreme Ct Commn on Continuing Legal Edn 30 E Broad St Columbus OH 43266-0419

LAHOOD, MARY ANNE, real estate investor; b. Grosse Pointe Farms, Mich., Aug. 23, 1947; d. Tom and Melania (Simon) LaH.; children: Lila, Michael. BA, Wayne State U., 1972. Ptnr. LaHood Lanes, Inc., St. Clair Shores, Mich., 1972-89, LaHood Properties, Grosse Pointe Shores, Mich., 1972—. Mem. Founders Soc. Detroit Inst. Arts, Women's Assn. Detroit Symphony, Scarab Club, Yacht, Club. Avocations: fiction writing, art collecting, long distance running, sailing, tennis. Home: 20 Stillmeadow Ln Grosse Pointe Shores MI 48236

LAHTI, CHRISTINE, actress; b. Detroit, Apr. 5, 1950; d. Paul Theodore and Elizabeth Margaret (Tabar) L.; m. Thomas Schlamme, Sept. 4, 1983; 1 child, Wilson Lahti. BA in Speech, U. Mich., 1972; postgrad., Fla. State U., 1972-73; studies with William Esper, Uta Hagen, Herbert Berghof Studios. Actress: (stage prodns.) The Woods, 1978 (Theater World award 1979), Division Street, 1980, Loose Ends, 1981, Present Laughter, 1983, Landscape of the Body, 1984, Little Murders, 1987, The Heidi Chronicles, 1989; regular mem. cast (TV series) The Harvey Korman Show, 1978; (TV films) The Last Tenant, 1978, The Executioner's Song, 1982, The Henderson Monster, 1980, Amerika, 1987, All Washed Up, Love Lives On, Single Bars, Single Women, No Place Like Home, 1989; (feature films) And Justice For All, 1979, Whose Life Is It, Anyway?, 1981, Swing Shift, 1984 (N.Y. Film Critics Circle award for best supporting actress 1985, Acad. award nomination 1985, Golden Globe award nomination 1985), Ladies and Gentlemen: The Fabulous Stains, 1985, Just Between Friends, 1986, Housekeeping, 1987, Season of Dreams, 1987, Stacking, 1988, Running on Empty, 1988, Gross Anatomy, 1989, Funny About Love, 1990. Office: care Triad Artists Inc 10100 Santa Monica Blvd 16th Fl Los Angeles CA 90067*

LAIDLAW, MELINDA KATHERINE, nurse; b. Cold Spring, N.Y., Jan. 9, 1955; d. Heinz Eugene and Catherine Rita (Miano) Ulrich; m. John Stewart Laidlaw, Sept. 30, 1979; children: Jacqueline Catherine, Michael Stewart; stepchildren: Kelly Ann, John Scott. BSN, Keuka Coll., Keuka Park, N.Y., 1977. Registered Nurse, N.J. Nurse Columbia Presbyn. Hosp., N.Y.C., 1977-78; nurse critical care Hackensack Hosp. & Med. Ctr., N.J., 1978-82; nurse St. Joseph's Hosp. & Med. Ctr., Paterson, N.J., 1983—; adminstrv. supr. nursing Chilton Hosp., Pompton Plains, N.J. Treas. North Blvd. Home & Sch. Assn., Pompton Plains N.J., 1987-88, pres. 1988-90. Lutheran.

LAIKEN, NORA DAWN, medical educator; b. Chgo., June 28, 1946; d. Reinhard Helmut and Selma (Liff) Lesser; m. Stuart Leslie Laiken, June 18, 1967; children: Hannah Joy, Ariella Ronit. SB, U. Chgo., 1967; PhD, Rockefeller U., 1970. Rsch. assoc. U. Oreg., Eugene, 1970-71; rsch. assoc. U. Calif., San Diego, 1971-72, sci. curriculum adviser, 1972-73, lectr. in medicine, 1973—, dir. tutorial program Sch. Medicine, 1973—, asst. dean for curriculum, student affairs Sch. Medicine, 1983—; mem. undergrad. teaching project com. Am. Gastroent. Assn., 1986—. Author: The Interpretation of Electrocardiograms: A Self-Instructional Approach, 1988; section editor: Best & Taylor's Physiological Basis of Medical Practice, 1985. Mem. Phi Beta Kappa. Jewish. Office: M-006 Univ Calif San Diego La Jolla CA 92093

LAINE, CLEO (CLEMENTINA DINAH DANKWORTH), singer; b. Southall, Middlesex, Eng., Oct. 28, 1927; d. Alexander and Minnie (Bullock) Campbell; m. George Langridge, 1947 (div.); m. John Philip William Dankworth, 1958; children: Stuart, Alec, Jackie. MA (hon.), Open U., 1975; MusD (hon.), Berkee Coll. Music, 1982. Vocalist Dankworth Orch., 1953-58; lead role in Seven Deadly Sins, Edinburgh, Scotland Festival and Sadlers Wells, 1961, in Showboat, 1972; acting roles Edinburgh Festival, 1966, 67, Colette, 1980; appeared in A Time to Laugh, Hedda Gabler, The Women of Troy, The Mystery of Edwin Drood, 1986 (Theatre World award, Tony award nomination, Drama Desk award nomination), Into the Woods, 1989 (L.A. Drama Critics award nomination); guest appearances symphony orchs. Eng. and abroad; numerous TV appearances and record albums; most recent albums That Old Feeling, 1985, Cleo Sings Sondheim, 1988, Woman to Woman, 1989; gold records: Feel The Warm, I'm a Song, Live at Melbourne; Platinum records: Best Friends, Sometimes When We Touch. Decorated Order Brit. Empire, 1979; recipient Golden Feather award Los Angeles Times, 1973, Edison award, 1974, Grammy award for best female jazz vocal, 1985, Theatre World award, 1986; named Show Bus. Personality of Yr., Variety Club, 1977, Singer of Yr., TV Times, 1978; Tony nominee, 1986; Theatre World award, 1986. Address: care Sonoma-Hope Inc PO Box 239 Hope NJ 07844

LAINE, KATIE MYERS, political campaign manager; b. Bluffton, Ohio, Oct. 2, 1947; d. George Emerson and Elanore (Keeney) Myers; m. Donald Edward Laine (div. Feb. 1990); 1 child, Brett Edward. BS in Edn., S.W. Tex. State U., 1970. Dir. vols. Austin (Tex.) Ctr. for Attitudinal Healing, 1983-86; talk show host Austin Cablevision, 1986—; community rels. officer Laguna Gloria Art Mus., Austin, 1989-90; spl. events mgr. Ann Richards for Gov. Campaign, Austin, 1990—. Mem. Mayor's Adv. Coun., Austin, 1989—, Austin Women's Polit. Caucus, 1989—, Emily's List, 1989—; vol. Mayor Lee Cooke Campaign, 1988, Ann Richards Campaign for Gov., 1989. Mem. NOW, Women in Communications, Nat. Assn. for Corp. Speaker Activities, Paramount Producers. Home: 3510 A Wendel Cove Austin TX 78731 Office: Ann Richards for Governor Campaign Headquarters Austin TX 78711

LAING, JOAN RAE, psychologist; b. Delta, Iowa, Dec. 10, 1938; d. George and Dorothea (Walker) Jones; m. Earl John Laing, Aug. 12, 1961 (div. July 1979); children: Catherine, John, Patricia. BA with honors, Cen. Coll., Pella, Iowa, 1958; MA, U. Iowa, 1960; MS, Iowa State U., 1977, PhD, 1979. Lic. psychologist, Iowa. Teaching asst. U. Iowa, Iowa City, 1958-60; tchr. Iowa Pub. Schs., 1960-63; rsch. asst. U. Iowa, Iowa City, 1964-67; intern in psychology U. Cin., 1978-79; psychologist Vassar Coll., Poughkeepsie, N.Y., 1979-80; rsch. psychologist Am. Coll. Testing, Iowa City, 1980-88; dir. psychol svcs. behavioral scis. dept. St. Anthony Regional Hosp., Carroll, Iowa, 1988—. Editor: Newsnotes, Assn. for Measurement and Evaluation in Counseling and Devel., 1984-87, mem. editorial bd., 1986-89; mem. editorial bd. Jour. nat. Assn. Women Deans, Adminstrs. and Counselors, 1983-87; contbr. articles to profl. jours. Mem. Friends Iowa City Pub. Libr., 1980-88, Friends Carroll Pub. Libr., 1988—. Mem. Assn. for Measurement and Evaluation in Counseling and Devel. (mem. exec. coun.), Am. Psychol. Assn., Iowa Psychol. Assn. (pres. 1991, sec. div. 1990-91). Episcopalian. Office: St Anthony Regional Hosp South Clark St Carroll IA 51401

LAING, KAREL ANN, magazine publishing executive; b. Mpls., July 5, 1939; d. Edward Francis and Elizabeth Jane Karel (Templeton) Hannon; m. G. R. Cheesebrough, Dec. 19, 1959 (div. 1969); 1 child, Jennifer Read; m. Ronald Harris Laing, Jan. 6, 1973; 1 child, Christopher Harris. Grad., U. Minn., 1960. With Guthrie Symphony Opera Program, Mpls., 1969-71; account supr. Colle & McVoy Advt. Agy., Richfield, Minn., 1971-74; owner The Cottage, Edina, Minn., 1974-75; salespromotion rep. Robert Meyers & Assocs., St. Louis Park, Minn., 1975-76; cons. Webb Co., St. Paul, 1976-77, custom pub. dir., 1977-89; pres. K.L. Publs., Inc., Bloomington, Minn., 1989—. Contbr. articles to profl. jours. Community vol. Am. Heart Assn., Am. Cancer Soc., Edina PTA; charter sponsor Walk Around Am., St. Paul, 1985. Mem. Bank Mktg. Assn., Fin. Instn. Mktg. Assn., Advt. Fedn. Am., Am. Bankers Assn., Direct Mail Mktg. Assn., St. Andrews Soc. Republican. Presbyterian. Office: KL Publs 2001 Killebrew Dr Bloomington MN 55425

LAIRD, DORIS ANNE MARLEY, humanities educator, musician; b. Charlotte, N.C., Jan. 15, 1931; d. Eugene Harris and Coleen (Bethea) Marley; m. William Everette Laird Jr., Mar. 13, 1964; children: William Everette III, Andrew Marley, Glen Howard. MusB, Converse Coll., Spartanburg, S.C., 1951; opera cert. New Eng. Conservatory, Boston, 1956; MusM, Boston U., 1956; PhD, Fla. State U., 1980. Leading soprano roles S.C. Opera Co., Columbia, 1951-53, Plymouth Rock Ctr. of Music and Art, Duxbury, Mass., 1953-56; soprano Pro Musica, Boston, 1956, New Eng. Opera Co., Boston, 1956; instr. Stratford Coll., Danville, Va., 1956-58, Sch. Music Fla. State U., Tallahassee, 1958-60, dept. humanities, 1960-68; asst. prof. Fla. A&M U., Tallahassee, 1979-89, assoc. prof., 1990—; vis. scholar Cornell U., 1988. Author: Colin Morris: Modern Missionary, 1980; contbr. articles to profl. jours. Soprano Washington St. Meth. Ch., Columbia, S.C., 1951-53, Copley Meth. Ch., Boston, 1953-56, Trinity United Meth. Ch., Tallahassee, 1983—; mem. Saint Andrews Soc., Tallahassee, 1986—; judge Brain Bowl, Tallahassee, 1981-84. Recipient NEH award, 1988; Phi Sigma Tau scholar, 1960. Mem. AAUP, AAUW, Nat. Art Educators Assn., Tallahassee Music Tchrs. Assn., Tallahassee Music Guild, Am. Guild of Organists, DAR (mus. rep. 1984-85), Colonial Dames of 17th Century (music dir. 1984-85). Democrat. Club: University Wy Women's. Avocations: traveling, dancing. Home: 1125 Mercer Dr Tallahassee FL 32312 Office: Fla A&M U Dept Humanities Tallahassee FL 32307

LAIRD, EVALYN WALSH, lawyer; b. Chgo., Feb. 6, 1902; d. Edward Joseph and Mae E. (Tarr) Walsh; m. Charles Hamilton Laird, Aug. 8, 1925; children: Lois Hillmann, Betty Ann Hillmann (dec.), Charles Hamilton Laird, Jr. (dec.), Edward J. Laird, Jane Glynn. JD, DePaul U., Chgo., 1926. Bar: Mich. 1982. Estate planner Prudential Ins. Co., Chgo., 1945-48; mgr. Edward J. Walsh Reporting Svcs., Chgo., 1948-60; owner Pvt. Law Practice, 1926; environ. chmn. Vilage of Grand Bch. Mem. personnel com. Girl Scouts of Chgo.; pres. 7th dist. Archdiocesan Coun. Cath. Women. Recipient 45th Yr. Citation for uninterrupted service Girl Scouts U.S., 1990. Mem. ABA, Ill. State Bar Assn., Chgo. Bar Assn., Mich. State Bar, Ill. Women's Bar, Mich. Women's Bar, Berrien County Bar Assn., Skokie Valley Skating Club, Mich. City YMCA, Grand Beach Golf & Country Club. Democrat. Office: 6 N Michigan Ave #1417 Chicago IL 60602 Home and Office: 47104 Pine Ave Grand Beach New Buffalo MI 49117

LAIRD, JEAN ELOUISE RYDESKI (MRS. JACK E. LAIRD), author, educator; b. Wakefield, Mich., Jan. 18, 1930; d. Chester A. and Agnes A. (Petranek) Rydeski; m. Jack E. Laird, June 9, 1951; children: John E., Jayne E., Joan Ann P., Jerilyn S., Jacquelyn T. Bus. Edn. degree Duluth (Minn.) Bus. U., 1948; posgrad. U. Minn., 1949-50. Tchr. Oak Lawn (Ill.) High Sch. Adult Evening Sch., 1964-72, St. Xavier Coll., Chgo., 1974—; lectr., commencement address cir. Writer newspaper column Around The House With Jean, A Woman's Work, 1965-70, Chicagotown News column The World As I See It, 1969, hobby column Modern Maturity mag., travel column Travel/Leisure mag., beauty column Ladycom mag., Time and Money Savers column Lady's Circle mag., consumerism column Ladies' Home Jour. Mem. Canterbury Writers Club Chgo. (past. pres.), Oak Lawn Bus. and Profl. Women's Club (Woman of Yr. award 1987), St. Linus Guild, Mt. Assisi Acad., Marist, Queen of Peace parents clubs. Roman Catholic. Author: Lost in the Department Store, 1964; Around The House Like Magic, 1968; Around The Kitchen Like Magic, 1969; How To Get the Most From Your Appliances, 1967; Hundreds of Hints for Harrassed Homemakers, 1971; The Alphabet Zoo, 1972; The Plump Ballerina, 1971; The Porcupine Story Book, 1974; Fried Marbles and Other Fun Things To Do, 1975; Hundreds of Hints for Harassed Homemakers; The Homemaker's Book of Time and Money Savers, 1979; Homemaker's Book of Energy Savers, 1981; also 348 paperback booklets. Contbr. numerous articles to mags. Home: 10540 S Lockwood Ave Oak Lawn IL 60453 also: 1 Magnificent Mile Bldg Chicago IL also: Lake Geneva WI 53147

LAIRD, MARGARET, auditor; b. Mpls., Dec. 26, 1954; d. Neal Frederick Johnson and Margaret (Brenneman) Laird; m. James W. Buck, Sept. 29, 1979 (div. Apr. 1984). BA in Internat. Studies, Miami U., Oxford, Ohio, 1976; MBA, So. Ill. U., 1984. Credit analyst Bank of N.J., Camden, 1977-79; with FMC Corp[., 1979—; auditor FMC Corp[., Chgo., 1987-89; sr. internal auditor FMC Corp[., Santa Clara, Calif., 1989—. Vol. Youth for Understanding, San Jose, 1990—; bd. govs. Homeowners Assn., Los Gatos, 1990—. Mem. Inst. for Internal Auditors (bd. govs. San Jose, Calif. chpt. 1990—). Office: FMC Corp 2830 De La Cruz Blvd Santa Clara CA 95052

LAIRD, MARY See WOOD, LARRY

LAITINEN, LINDA JEAN, sales executive; b. Milw., July 9, 1955; d. Robert Duane and Doris Gene (Gilbertson) L. BA cum laude, Carroll Coll., Waukesha, Wis., 1978. Tchr. Franklin (Wis.) High Sch., 1978-81; sales rep. Freedom Communications, Wauwatosa, Wis., 1981-82; customer svc. rep. Nat. Telecom, Milw./Chgo., 1982-83; mktg. mgr. Chgo. Bd. Trade, 1983-85; dist. mgr No. Telecom, Inc., Schaumburg, Ill., 1985—. Judge Wis Forensics Assn., Milw., 1980, Wis. Theatre Festival, Milw., 1980. Mem. NAFE, Ill. Orgn. Women in Telecommunications (officer 1984-85), Alpha Psi Omega, Kappa Delta Pi, Sigma Epsilon Sigma. Office: Northern Telecom Inc 475 N Martingale Rd Schaumburg IL 60173

LAITNER, LINDA DEMAREST, marketing executive; b. Columbus, Ohio, Nov. 24, 1947; d. Charles L. and Harriet Betty (Varner) DeMarest. BS, N.Mex. State U., Las Cruces, 1969, MS, 1971; cert., Purdue U., 1981. Exec. dir. Dreyer HMO, Aurora, Ill.; chief exec. officer Health Plan of Mid Am., Kansas City, Mo.; mktg. dir. Blue Cross/Blue Shield, Kansas City; instr., adminstr. Metro Jr. Coll. System, Kansas City. Mem. AMCRA, GHAA, Ill. Assn. HMOs. Home: 4400 NW 65th St Kansas City MO 64151

LAKE, BARBARA LEE, vocational administrator; b. Cleve., Feb. 8, 1934; d. Byron Edwin and Eva Maria Melissa (Kays) Ice; children: Melissa Lee, Ellen Maria. Student, Colby Coll., 1952-53; BS in Edn., Wheelock Coll., Boston, 1956; postgrad., Pacific Luth. U., Tacoma, Wash., 1973. Elem. tchr. Oxnard (Calif.) Sch. Dist., 1956-58, Army Am. Sch. System, Heilbronn, Fed. Republic Germany, 1958-59, Wayne (N.J.) Sch. Dist., 1959-61, Cleve. Sch. Dist., 1961-62, Peru (Ind.) Sch. Dist., 1962-64; kindergarten tchr. Puyallup (Wash.) Sch. Dist., 1966-67; asst. dir. Puyallup PlayCare Ctr., 1969; tchr. Tacoma Sch. Dist., 1969-71; day care coordinator Clover Park Vocat. Tech. Inst., Tacoma, 1972—; cons. Dept. of Def., Washington, 1977-79; advisor Child Devel. Assn. Credential, Washington, 1980—; validator Nat. Assn. for Edn. Young Children, Washington, 1985—; mem. exec. bd. Puyallup Play-Care Ctr., 1985—, Lakewood Community Ctr., Tacoma, 1980-83. Named Disting. Educator Clover Park Found., 1984. Mem. Tacoma Assn. for Edn. Young Children (pres. 1983-84), Wash. Assn. Edn. Young Children, Nat. Assn. Edn. Young Children, Am. Vocat. Assn., Wash. Vocat. Assn., Phi Delta Kappa. Office: Clover Park Vocat Tech Inst 4500 Steilacoom Blvd SW Tacoma WA 98499

LAKE, BLAIR MOODY, nursing educator; b. Nashville, June 14, 1932; d. Marlin Sheridan and Sara Alice (Blair) Moody; m. Richard Harrington Lake, July 17, 1954 (dec. May 1987); children: Richard Moody, Mary Anne (dec.), William Moody, Sara Blair. Cert., U. Neuchatel, Switzerland, 1950; Diploma, U. Paris (Sorbonne), 1951; BA, U. Tenn., 1952; AAS, No. Va. Community Coll., 1971; MS in Nursing, Cath. U. Am., 1978; cert. oncology nursing edn. Georgetown U. Sch. Nursing, 1978. Personnel adminstr. U.S. Civil Service, Fort Sheridan, Ill., 1952-53; office mgr. U.S. Navy Exchange, Bangkok, 1955-56; staff and charge nurse, Fairfax Hosp., Va., 1971-72; econ. cons. R.H. Lake Assocs., 1970-87, Thailand, 1972; primary nurse oncology Arlington Hosp., Va., 1979-80; oncology clin. practitioner Georgetown U. Hosp., Washington, 1980-82; assoc. prof. nursing Brevard Community Coll., Cocoa, Fla., 1982-85. Vol. sch. nurse Fairfax County Public Schs., 1974-76; crisis intervention counselor Haven of No. Va., Annandale, 1977-78; vol., pub. and profl. edn. Am. Cancer Soc., Fairfax County, Va., Brevard County, Fla., 1978-85; nursing vol. free clinic, Clearwater, Fla., 1990. Mem. Am. Nurses Assn., Fla. Nurses Assn., Oncology Nursing Soc., Sigma Theta Tau, Alpha Delta Pi. Episcopalian. Clubs: Daus. of U.S. Army, Soc. Mil. Widows, Ret. Officers Wives & Widows, Palm Harbor Newcomers. Avocations: equitation, swimming, historical research, current affairs. Office: 3098 Landmark Blvd #2102 Palm Harbor FL 34684-5002

LAKE, CAROL LEE, anesthesiologist, educator; b. Altoona, Pa., July 14, 1944; d. Samuel Lindsay and Edna Winifred (McMahan) L. BS, Juniata Coll., 1966; MD, Med. Coll. Pa., 1970. Intern Mercy Hosp., Pitts., 1970-71, resident in anesthesiology, 1971-73; staff anesthesiologist Pitts. Anesthesia Assocs., 1973-75; asst. prof. anesthesiology U. Va., Charlottesville, 1975-80, assoc. prof., 1980-89, prof. anesthesiology, 1989—; sr. assoc. examiner Am. Bd. Anesthesiology, Hartford, Conn., 1981—. Author: Cardiovascular Anesthesia, 1985; editor: Pediatric Cardiac Anesthesia, 1988, Clinical Monitoring, 1990. Fellow Am. Coll. Cardiology; mem. Assn. Cardiac Anesthesiologists (pres. 1987-88), Soc. Cardiovascular Anesthesiologists (bd. dirs.), Assn. U. Anesthetists, Alpha Omega Alpha. Presbyterian. Office: Univ Va Box 238 Dept Anesthesiology Charlottesville VA 22908

LAKE, R. ELAINE, optics technician; b. San Jose, Calif., June 18, 1954; d. Charles Gregory and Beverly June (Beaudoin) Attarian; m. David B. Lake, Feb. 14, 1986; 1 child, Michael. Student, Calif. State U., Fresno; cert. with honors, San Joaquin Valley Coll., 1988. Optical lab. technician Peggy's Optical Svc., Fresno; instr. in dispensing optics San Joaquin Valley Coll., Fresno; dispensing optician Frame-N-Lens, Clovis, Calif. Mem. CSCLA, OAA, FNAO, OAA, RSLD. Home: 568 W San Jose Ave Clovis CA 93612

LAKE, SUZANNE PHILENA, singer, teacher; b. Palisade, N.J., June 26, 1929; d. Mayhew Lester and Suzanne Louise (Robin) L.; m. George A. De Vos, Nov. 19, 1974. pvt. tchr., Oakland, Calif., 1976-86, univ. extension U. Calif., Sacramento State U., 1981-84. Featured roles opera, N.Y.C., 1948-61; appeared in Broadway plays The King and I, 1952-54, Flower Drum Song, 1960-61; concert appearances in U.S., Can., and Carribbean, 1955-86, also Tel. appearances. Mem. Actors Equity, AFTRA, Am. Guild Mus. Artists, Am. Guild Variety Artists. Home: 2835 Morley Dr Oakland CA 94611

LAKEBRINK, CYNTHIA, accountant; b. Huntsville, Ala., Nov. 9, 1963; d. Robert T. and Ruby (Hodges) L. BSBA, U. Ala., Huntsville, 1987. CPA, Ala. Auditor Arthur Andersen & Co., Birmingham, Ala., 1987—. Vol. ARC, Birmingham, 1988—; Sunday sch. tchr. Roman Cath. Ch. Recipient Wall St. Jour. award, 1987; named Outstanding Young Woman of Am., 1989. Fellow Assn. Women Accts.; mem. Nat. Assn. Accts. Republican. Home: 3709 Inverness Cliffs Birmingham AL 35242

LAKIN, DEBORAH ANNE, documentation specialist; b. Brookline, Mass., Oct. 30, 1947; d. Jack and Esther Gail (Koll) Eastein; m. Irwin Arnold Lakin, Sept. 2, 1968 (div. 1973); 1 child, Joshua Michael. AS, Newton Jr. Coll., 1967; Cert. dental nurse, Beth Israel Hosp., Boston, 1968; BA, Simmons Coll., Boston, 1986. Clinic mgr. Case Western Res. Dental Sch., Cleve., 1968-70; head dental nurse various dental practices, Boston, 1973-82; project mgr. RBN Corp. Tng., Boston, 1986-87; dir. ops. RBN Corp. Tng., 1987-88; systems analyst, documentation specialist, cons. Documentation Devel., Inc., Cambridge, Mass., 1988—. Author: (with other), editor MRP II-A Course for Certification, 1986. Mem. Am. Prodn. Inventory Control Soc., NAFE, B'nai B'rith (pres. Greater Boston coun. 1987-88, internat. Hillel commr. 1982—, adminstrv. bd. 1988—). Home: 88 E Side Pkwy Newtonville MA 02160 Office: Documentation Devel Inc 125 Cambridge Park Dr Cambridge MA 02140

LAKIN, JUDY SHELTON, insurance agent; b. Richmond, Va., Oct. 24, 1958; d. Vernon Clyde and Margie (Aistrop) Shelton; m. Robert Ralph Lakin, Apr. 30, 1988. BS in Journalism, U. Kans., 1982. Proshop asst. Alvhmar Country Club, Lawrence, Kans., 1979-81; intern McGavern Guild Radio Rep., Dallas, 1982; sec. Bloom Agy. (Advt.), Dallas, 1982; account exec. asst. Selcom, Inc. Radio Rep., Dallas, 1982-83; advt. cons. Keymarket, Inc. (Sta. KKMJ-FM), Austin, Tex., 1983-89; agt. N.Y. Life Ins. Co., Austin, 1989—. Vice pres. Cen. Tex. chpt. Cystic Fibrosis Found., 1987, pres., 1988—. Recipient Human Relations award Dale Carnegie Sales Course, Austin, 1985; named Sales Talk Champion Dale Carnegie Sales Course, Austin, 1985. Mem. Austin Women's Coun. Realtors, Austin Women's Art Guild, Nat. Assn. Life Underwriters, Austin Assn. Life Underwriters, Toastmasters (v.p. West Austin chpt. 1987). Baptist. Office: NY Life Ins Co 1250 Capital of Tex Hwys Bldg 3 Ste 200 Austin TX 78759

LAKIN, SANDRA FISHER, computer software developer; b. Tulsa, July 9, 1953; d. Robert Landis and Wanda Arlene (McDonald) Fisher; m. Allan William Lakin, Aug. 24, 1974; children: Paul Robert, Andrew Michael. SB in Aeronautics, MIT, 1975; MS in Computer Sci., U. So. Calif., L.A., 1981. Mem. tech. staff Rockwell Internat., Canoga Park, Calif., 1975-80; rsch. asst. U. So. Calif., L.A., 1981-83; engring. mgr. Edu-Ware Svcs., Inc., Agoura Hills, Calif., 1983-84; sr. programmer Quadratron, Inc., Sherman Oaks, Calif., 1985-86, Blue Chip Software, Canoga Park, 1984-85, 86; mgr. research & devel. Blue Chip Software, 1986-87; project leader Microcosm, Inc., Torrance, Calif., 1987-88; self-employed software developer Sherman Oaks, 1988—; cons. Britannica Software, Inc., San Francisco, 1987-89, Genoa Technologies, Inc., Simi Valley, Calif., 1988-89; free-lance programmer John Boeschen & Co., San Rafael, Calif., 1988-89. Author (comml. computer programs) Joshua's Reading AII, Millionaire II Aii; co-author: Am. Investor. Republican. Methodist. Office: 18034 Ventura Blvd #262 Encino CA 91316

LAKOS, MARCILLE HARRIS, clinical psychologist; b. Ontario, Oreg., Dec. 10, 1917; d. Marvin and Una Leota (Smith) Hurst; B.S. in Psychology, U. Oreg., 1947, M.S. in Psychology, 1949; m. Eugene A. Lakos, Mar. 3, 1957; 1 son, John Stuart. Co-therapist, Nathan W. Ackerman, Family Inst., N.Y.C., 1955-60, 62-72; pvt. practice clin. psychology, N.Y.C., 1972—. Mem. Am. Psychol. Assn., Fedn. Am. Scientists, AAAS, N.Y. State Psychol. Assn., N.Y. Acad. Scis., Nat. Register Health Service Providers in Psychology (cert., council), Sigma Xi. Home and Office: 201 E 66th St New York NY 10021

LA LIBERTE, ANN GILLIS, graphic designer, artist; b. St. Paul, Nov. 10, 1942; d. Edward Robert and Frances Caroline (Sullivan) Gillis; m. Paul Henry La Liberte, Aug. 22, 1964; children: Paul E., Elizabeth A., Stephen A., Helen C., Peter N., Marc H. Student, Am U., 1963-64, Cardinal Stritch Coll., Milw., 1960-63; BA, Coll. St. Catherine, St. Paul, 1985. Artist, owner Ann La Liberte Papers and Posters, Minnetonka, Minn., 1968-71, A.L. Graphic Design and Drawings, Minnetonka, Minn., 1983—; vis. artist Arts in the Schs., Mpls., 1985—. Liturgical designer Christian Chs., Mpls., St. Paul, 1977—; paintings, photography and sculptures exhibited Mpls., St. Paul area, 1983—; sculpture Life Exhibit, Paul VI Inst. for the Arts, Washington, 1988, on tour Vt., Ohio, Mo., Ill., Wis., 1988. Del. Minn. Ind. Reps., 1969, v. chair, 1970; promotional artist, Soc. Preservation Human Dignity, Palatine, Ill., 1973, Minn. Citizens Concerned for Life, 1980-88, Secular Franciscans, St. Paul, 1985; deanery rep. Pastoral Coun. Archdiocese of St. Paul, Mpls., 1978-82; chair devel. task force Out-Reach program Resurrection Ch., Mpls., 1980-81, cons. artist 1983—. Mem. Nat. Assn. Liturgical Ministers, Mpls. Soc. Fine Arts, Walker Art Ctr., Coll. St. Catherine Alumna Assn., Artists for Life Nat. Slide Registry, Delta Phi Delta. Roman Catholic. Home: 13418 Excelsior Blvd Minnetonka MN 55345

LALLIER, ERNA L., management; b. Lynn, Mass., Mar. 21, 1946; d. Clarence R. and Elizabeth T. (Moss) Rosendahl; m. Thornton E. Lallier, Apr. 30, 1976; children: T. Edward, Matthew T. Assoc., Burdett Coll., 1964; postgrad., Merrimack Coll., 1988. Legal sec. Hannah & Mayo, Lynn, Mass., 1964-71, Sears & Plunkett, Salem, Mass., 1971-72; judge's sec. Commonwealth Mass., Probate Court, Salem, Mass., 1972-78; paralegal office mgr. Lallier & Anderson, Amesbury, Mass. Mem. Bartlett Mus., Amesbury Mass. 1986—. Recipient Nat. Honor Soc. Liberal Arts Continuing Edn. award, Beta Iota Chpt., Merrimack Coll., 1985. Charter mem. Kiwanis (dir. 1988--); mem. Rowley Mass. C. of C. (sec. 1983-84). Home and Office: One Moody St PO Box 689 Amesbury MA 01913

LALLY, ANN MARIE, retired educational administrator; b. Chgo., Sept. 23, 1914; d. Martin J. and Della (McDonnell) L. AB, Mundelein Coll., 1935; AM, Northwestern U., 1939, PhD, 1950; postgrad., Chgo. Tchrs. Coll., Chgo. Art Inst., 1935-36. Tchr. Amundsen High Sch., 1935, Lindblom and Von Steuben High Schs., Chgo., 1936-38; chmn. art dept. Schurz High Sch., 1938-40; supr. art Chgo. Pub. Elem. Schs., 1940-48, dir. art Chgo. Pub. Schs., 1948-57; prin. John Marshall High Sch., 1957-63; supt. Dist. 16, Chgo. Pub. Schs., 1963-64, Dist. 5, 1964-80; lectr. Wright Jr. Coll., 1948; instr. creative drawing Chgo. Acad. Fine Art, 1941; instr. interior design Internat. Harvester Co., 1946-48; lectr. in edn. DePaul U., 1952-74; lectr. in edn. and art U. Chgo., 1956-59; lectr. edn. Chgo. Tchrs. Coll., 1960-62; trustee Pub. Sch. Tchrs. Pension and Retirement Fund Chgo., 1957-71, sec.-treas., 1960-65, pres., 1965-70. Contbr. articles to art and ednl. jours. Charter mem. women's bd. Loyola U., Art Inst. Chgo.; mem. Big Sisters, 1985—, bd. dirs. 1989—. Mem. Am. Assn. Sch. Adminstrs., Ill. Assn. Sch. Adminstrs., NEA (life), Ill. Edn. Assn., Dist. Supts. Assn. (pres. 1973-75), Ill. Women Adminstrs. Assn. (award 1979), Nat. Coun. Adminstrv. Women in Edn. (chmn. profl. relations com. 1958-62), Assn. Supervision and Curriculum Devel., Chgo. Area Women Adminstrs. in Edn. (Outstanding Adminstrn. award 1981), Nat. Art Edn. Assn. (mem. council 1956-60), Western Arts Assn. (pres. 1956-58), Internat. Soc. Edn. in Art, Ill. Art Edn. Assn. (pres. 1955), Chgo. Art Educators Assn. (founder, past v.p., sec. and treas), Ill. Club Cath. Women (bd. dirs. 1981—, rec. sec. 1982-86), Chgo. Pub. Sch. Art Soc., Chgo. Hist. Soc., LWV (Chgo. chpt.), AAUW (Chgo. chmn. elem. and secondary edn. 1966—, dir.-at-large 1962-66, 78-80, mem. Ill. div. promoting individual liberties task force, centennial com. Chgo. br. 1988-89, tech. dir. centennial celebration 1989), Chgo. Area Reading Assn. (bd. dirs. 1963-69), Nat. Assn. Secondary Sch. Prins., Ill. Assn. Secondary Sch. Prins., Chgo. Prins. Assn., Artists Equity Assn. of Chgo., Council on Fgn. Relations, Mundelein Coll. Alumnae Assn. (past pres., chmn. bd., Magnificat medal 1964), Pi Lambda Theta, Delta Kappa Gamma (chmn. legis. com. 1985—),

Chgo. Woman's Club (chair legacy com. 1987—), Univ. Guild. Home: 307 Trinity Ct Evanston IL 60201-1906

LALLY, NORMA ROSS, federal agency administrator; b. Crawford, Nebr., Aug. 10, 1932; d. Roy Anderson and Alma Leona (Barber) Lively; m. Robert Edward Lally, Dec. 4, 1953 (div. Mar. 1986); children: Robyn Carol Murch, Jeffrey Alan, Gregory Roy. BA, Boise (Idaho) State U., 1974, MA, 1976; postgrad., Columbia Pacific U., 1988—. With grad. admissions Boise State U., 1971-74; with officer programs USN Recruiting, Boise, 1974; pub. affairs officer IRS, Boise and Las Vegas, 1975—; speaker in field, Boise and Las Vegas, 1977—. Contbr. articles to newspapers. Mem. task force Clark County Sch. Dist., Las Vegas. Staff sgt. USAF, 1950-54. Mem. Mensa, Toasmasters (Las Vegas). Home: 7303 Coffeyville Las Vegas NV 89117 Office: IRS 4750 W Oakey Blvd Las Vegas NV 89102

LAMANQUE, SUSAN LYNN, service executive, business owner; b. Pitts., Jan. 8, 1952; d. George M. Jr. and Mary Jane (Menard) Clark; m. Timothy A. LaManque, May 6, 1983; children: Maggie Lauren, Wendy Marie. BA, VVSCS, 1969; postgrad., MVCC, 1970, Munson William Proctor Art Inst., Utica. Prin. Kelly Day Co., Verona, N.Y.; gen. ptnr. Creative Svcs., New Hartford, N.Y.; photographer Fraternal Composite, Yorkville, N.Y. Author: Trail Pac. Bd. dirs. Soc. for Prevention of Cruelty to Animals. Mem. Rome C. of C., Utica C. of C. Home: 5469 Vernon St Verona NY 13478

LAMARCHE, GERALDINE VENORA, editor; b. Birmingham, Ala., Sept. 16, 1942; d. Jim and Oneida Olivia (Kirksey) Johnson; m. Dwaine Coverson, Jan. 19, 1970 (div. Jan. 1972); children: Cherrl, Traci; m. Rene' Albert LaMarche Sr., Apr. 18, 1974; 1 child, Rene' Albert III. Student, Seattle Community Coll., 1964; cert., U. Wash., Seattle, 1984; cert. in arts, Inst. Children's Lit., 1984; AA, Highline Coll., 1986. Various data processing positions Seattle, 1970-80; reporter North Cariboo News, Quesnel, B.C., Can., 1984; dir. Svc. Technicians & Cons., Federal Way, Wash., 1976-86; co-editor Svc. Bus. Mag., Seattle, 1987—. Author poetry. Mem. NAFE (dist. bd. dirs. 1990—). Democrat. Home: 135 S 316th Pl Federal Way WA 98003 Office: Cleaning Bus Mag Svc Bus Mag 1512 Western Ave Box 1273 Seattle WA 98111

LA MARCHE, JUDITH ANN, neuropsychologist; b. Oak Park, Ill., May 11, 1947; d. Austin White and Margaret Hamilton (Bryant) La M.; m. Paul Newcomb Lydolph, June 8, 1968 (div. Oct. 1978); children: Paul Newcomb Jr., Tamara Bryant; m. Robert Dale Stainback, Oct. 7, 1983. BA in Psycology, U. Wis., 1968, MS in Edn., 1970; PhD in Psychology, Utah State U., 1984. Lic. psychologist, Ala. Tchr. Milton (Wis.) Union High Sch., 1968-69, Irving Crown High Sch., Carpentersville, Ill., 1969-70; instr. Harper Coll., Palatine, Ill., 1977-79, Coll. of Lake County, Grayslake, Ill., 1977-79; counselor, facilitator Utah State U., Logan, 1979-80, dir. Info.-Referral Helpline, 1980-81; rsch. asst. Neuropsychology Lab. Salt Lake City VA Med. Ctr., 1982-84; clin. psychologist Mental Health Mgmt. Heritage Ctr., Lloyd Noland Hosp., Fairfield, Ala., 1984-85; instr. U. Ala., Birmingham, 1985-87, neuropsychology fellow, 1989—; cons. Hoffman Estates (Ill.) Youth and Family Svcs., 1978-79; saleswoman La Marche Mfg. Co., Des Plaines, Ill., 1982-85, co-chmn. bd. dirs., 1985—; pres. Judaulf Co., Des Plaines, 1985—; presenter in field; mem. Am. Bd. Med. Psychotherapists, 1987—; mem. adv. bd. Kid's Country Presch., Palatine, 1978-79, Vol. Action Ctr., Logan, 1980-81, The Growing Place, Logan, 1980-81; mem. med. staff Lloyd Noland Hosp., 1984—. Contbr. articles to profl. jours. Mem. Logan Hospice, 1980-81, Logan Inter-Agy. Coun., 1980-81; mem. human resources coun. Bear River Assn. Govts., Logan, 1980-81; pastoral cons., mem. long-range planning com. Christ United Meth. Ch., Birmingham, 1987—. Mem. Assn. for Advancement Psychology, Am. Psychol. Assn., Ala. Psychol. Assn., Birmingham Regional Assn. Lic. Psychologists, Birmingham Mus. Art, Ala. Ballet. Home: 3304 Tartan Circle Birmingham AL 35242 Office: U Ala Neuropsychology Lab PO Box 109 University Sta 1501 6th Ave S Birmingham AL 35294

LA MARRE, MILDRED HOLTZ, business executive; b. Phila., May 10, 1917; d. Philip and Dora H.; student George Washington U., 1939-40; B.A., U. Md., 1966; m. Jack Understein, Dec. 25, 1938 (dec.); children—Robert, Norma Lisa, Norman, Gary; m. 2d, John La Marre, Feb. 14, 1981. With Jack Understein Co., Washington, 1960-71; exec. asst. Muskie for Pres., Washington, 1971-72; researcher Carnegie Endowment Internat. Peace, Washington, 1973-76; personal asst., adminstrv. asst. to Under Sec. Lucy Wilson Benson, U.S. Dept. of State, 1977-78; exec. asst. Mike Barnes for Congress, 1978; pres. Internat. Personal Shopping Service, Ltd., N.Y.C., 1980-84; exec. asst. John La Marre Appraisers, 1982—; actress, print model, 1987—. Bd. dirs. Hebrew Home Greater Washington, 1970-83, Internat. Sickle Cell Anemia Research Inst., Washington, 1976-83. Democrat. Address: 880 5th Ave Apt 7A New York NY 10021

LAMB, MARILYN FREEMAN, educator; b. Freehold, N.J., Sept. 14, 1933; d. Frederick Gilday and Marion (Rhodes) Freeman; m. Vincent P. Lamb, June 24, 1956 (div. Oct. 1975); children: Robert, Brian, Daryl Ann, Gregg, Marion, Dona. BS, Ursinus Coll., 1955. Health and phys. edn. tchr. Toms River (N.J.) Jr. High Sch., 1955-56, Freehold Boro High Sch., 1975—; advisor Freehold High Sch. Cheerleaders, 1975-79; detention proctor Freehold High Sch., 1979—; proctor Scholastic Aptitude Test, Monmouth County, N.J., 1979—. Rep. ARC, Lincroft, N.J., 1965-70; active Little League Com., Lincroft, 1965-75. Mem. NEA, N.J. Edn. Assn., Monmouth County Edn. Assn., Profl. Rels. Commn., Allaire Racquet Club. Roman Catholic. Home: 40 B Poplar Ct Brielle NJ 08730 Office: Freehold Regional High Sch Pine St Englishtown NJ 07726

LAMB, YANICK RICE, deputy editor, writer; b. Akron, Ohio, Sept. 27, 1957; d. William R. Rice and Carmelie (Laforest) Jordan; m. Michael Anthony Lamb, Jan. 16, 1988; 1 child, Brandon M. BA in Journalism, Ohio State U., 1980. Copy editor Toledo Blade, 1980-82, reporter, 1982-83; copy editor Atlanta Jour.-Constn., 1983-84; metropolitan copy editor N.Y. Times, 1985, asst. layout editor news desk, 1984-87, asst. editor Conn. Weekly, 1987-90, dep. editor home sec., 1990—. Mem. Nat. Assn. Black Journalists, N.Y. Assn. Black Journalists (pres. 1987-88, v.p. 1986-87, sec. 1985-86, adv. bd. mem. 1988—, profl. devel. chmn. 1990—, Svc. award 1988), Women in Communications (Newswriting 1st Pl. award 1983). Office: NY Times 229 W 43rd St New York NY 10036

LAMBERG, JOAN BERNICE, purchasing agent; b. St. Paul, July 5, 1935; d. Gustave William and Anna Marie (Steinhilpert) L.; 1 child, Mary Lamberg King. Student, U. Mo., Rolla, 1971. Payroll clk. Continental Baking Co., Mpls., 1953-54; with scheduling and inventory control Stewart Paint Mfg. Co., Mpls., 1954-72; with purchasing and sales dept. Horton-Earl Co., South St. Paul, Minn., 1972—. Mem. Northwestern Soc. for Coatings Tech. (treas. 1984-85, sec. 1985-86, v.p. 1986-87, pres. 1987-88, tech. com. 1985—, membership chmn. 1985—, advt. mgr. 1988—, Trigg award 1985-86), Fedn. of Socs. for Coatings Tech. (membership com. 1985-89, bd. dirs. 1985-89), Women in Coatings. Home: 6949 Macbeth Circle Woodbury MN 55125 Office: Horton-Earl Co 949 S Concord St South Saint Paul MN 55075

LAMBERT, CAROL ANN, audiologist; b. Easton, Pa., June 15, 1947; d. Harry and Clara (Miller) L.; B.A., U. Tulsa, 1972, M.A., 1977; m. Michael Read Minshall, Mar. 19, 1973; 1 child, Eugene Read. Lic. audiologist. Audiologist, Tulsa Otolaryngology, Inc., and U. Tulsa, 1977-78; speech reading instr. Tulsa Speech and Hearing Assn., 1977-78; audiologist Ear, Nose and Throat Consultants, Inc., Tulsa, 1978-83; audiologist U. Tulsa, 1983-89; pvt. practice audiology, Tulsa, 1987—; cons. audiologist Springer Clinic, 1979-80; cons. Okla. State Dept. Health, Tulsa Scottish Rite Ctr. for Childhood Lang. Disorders, 1979—; adj. asst. prof. U. Tulsa, 1981-82; bd. advisors coll. nursing and applied health scis., U. Tulsa. Sustaining mem. Jr. League of Tulsa; mem. Philbrook Art Ctr.; bd. mem. Coll. Nursing and Applied Health Scis. U. Tulsa. Mem. NAFE, Nat. Assn. Women Bus. Owners, Am. Prior to Speech and Hearing Assn. (cert. in audiology), Acad. Rehabilitative Audiologist, Okla. Speech and Hearing Assn. (past sec.), Acad. of Audiology (mem. exec. com.), Tulsa Assn. Speech Pathologists and Audiologists (past pres., bd. dirs. 1988), Tulsa Speech and Hearing Assn. (past dir.). Office: 6355 E Skelly Dr Tulsa OK 74135

LAMBERT, DEBORAH KETCHUM, public relations executive; b. Greenwich, Conn., Jan. 22, 1942; d. Alton Harrington and Robyna (Neilson) Ketchum; m. Harvey R. Lambert, Nov. 23, 1963 (div. 1985); children: Harvey Richard Jr., Eric Harrington. BS, Columbia U., 1965. Researcher, writer The Nowland Orgn., Greenwich, Conn., 1964-67; model Country Fashions, Greenwich, Conn., 1964-67; owner, mgr. Paper Collectables, McLean, Va., 1973—; freelance writer to various newspapers and mags., 1977-82; press sec. Va. Del. Gwen Cody, Annandale, Va., 1981-82; assoc. editor Campus Report, Washington, 1985—; adminstrv. asst. Accuracy in Media, Inc., Washington, 1983-84, dir. pub. affairs, 1985—; bd. dirs. Accuracy in Academia, Washington; film script cons. The Seductive Illusion, 1988-89. Columnist: The Eye, The Washington Inquirer, 1984—, Squeaky Chalk, Campus Report, 1985—; contbr. articles to various mags. Co-founder, mem. Va. Rep. Forum, McLean, 1983—. Mem. Pub. Rels. Soc. Am., DAR., World Media Assn., Am. Platform Assn. Republican. Presbyterian. Home: 1945 Lorraine Ave McLean VA 22101 Office: Accuracy in Media Inc 1275 K St NW Washington DC 20005

LAMBERT, DEBORAH SUE, data processing professional; b. Dayton, Ohio, Apr. 13, 1952; d. Walter Robert and Charlotte Marie (Rogers) L.; m. Thomas Ray Greer, Sept. 3, 1978 (div. 1980); children: Douglas Allen Byrd, Deborah Lynne Byrd. BA, Sinclair Coll., 1983. Teller Wright-Patt Credit Union, Fairborn, Ohio, 1977; auditor Wright-Patt Credit Union, Fairborn, 1977-78, interviewer sr. loan, 1978, loan officer, 1978-79, from asst. mgr. to mgr. remote mem. services, 1979-82, data coordinator, 1982-84; mgr. system quality assurance Summit Info. Systems Inc., Corvallis, Oreg., 1984-87; dir. product mgmt. Summit Info. Systems Inc., Corvallis, 1988-89, v.p. on-line svcs., 1989—. Mem. Nat. Credit Union Adminstrn. (cert.), Nat. Assn. Female Execs., Am. Bus. Women's Assn., Ohio Credit Union League (cert. ops.). Home: 572 SE Hathaway Pl Corvallis OR 97333 Office: Summit Info Systems 850 SW 35th St Corvallis OR 97333

LAMBERT, JEAN MARJORIE, health care consultant; b. Bay City, Mich., Mar. 19, 1943; d. Richard William and Fidelis Rena (LeVasseur) L. BA, Madonna Coll., Livonia, Mich., 1967; MA, Eastern Mich. U., 1975. Dir. religious edn. Archdiocese of Detroit, 1970-75, dir. of evaluation, 1975-77; assoc. dir. programming Intermedia Found., Santa Monica, Calif., 1977-78; acad. dean St. John Provincial Sem., Plymouth, Mich., 1978-84; asst. dir. quality mgmt. Sisters of Mercy Health Corp., Farmington Hills, Mich., 1984-87; sr. cons. Mercy Collaborative, Livonia., Mich., 1987-88; v.p. Mission Mercy Health System, Cin., 1988—; asst. prof. homiletics St. John Sem., Plymouth, Mich., 1978-85, St. Mary of the Woods Coll., Terre Haute, Ind., summer 1985, St. Meinrad Sem., Ind., summer 1984. Editor Religious Edn., 1975-77. Nat. Cath. Edn. Assn.-Assn. Theol. Schs. for U.S. and Can. grantee, 1983. Mem. Groundwork, Network, Nat. Assn. Female Execs., Am. Hosp. Assn., Am. Mgmt. Assn., Cath. Health Assn., Acad. Leadership in Cath. Health Care. Roman Catholic. Avocations: woodcarving, photography, continuing education. Office: Mercy Health System 2335 Grandview Cincinnati OH 45226

LAMBERT, JERLINE, real estate appraiser; b. Forrest City, Ark., July 16, 1938; d. Mack C. and Annie (Salley) Goins; m. Charles Lambert, Mar. 25, 1953 (div. Sept. 1977); children: Virginia, Charles, Kenneth, Herman, Patricia. AA, Cen. YMCA Coll., 1977; student, Northeastern U., 1983-88. Cert. real estate appraiser. Pres. Lambert Real Estate Corp., 1977—; mem. Ill. Gov.'s Commn. on Mortgage Practices, 1974. Mem. nat. bd. dirs. Operation Push, 1984-87; bd. dirs. Midwest Community Council, 1986-87, 3rd v.p. 1988. Recipient Chgo. 4-H Hero award, 1983, Efforts Beyond The Call of Duty award Midwest Community Council, 1983, various others. Mem. Nat. Assn. Real Estate Brokers (bd. dirs. 1972-78), Chgo. Real Estate Bd. (bd. govs. renting and mng. div. 1976-81), Dearborn Real Estate Bd. (pres. 1982, 83, Elmore Baker award 1986), Internat. Women's Econ. Devel. Corp. (v.p. 1983-86), Africare (pres., co-founder Chgo. chpt. 1986-87, Outstanding Svc. award 1987). Office: Lamberts Realty Inc 5361 W Madison St Chicago IL 60644

LAMBERT, JULIE LOUISE, psychologist; b. Altoona, Pa., Apr. 6, 1953; d. John Sylvester and Coletta Mary (Gill); m. John Arthur Jubala, May 20, 1978. BA, Point Park Coll., 1975; MA, Duquesne U., 1976, PhD, 1988. Lic. psychologist, Pa. Instr., asst. prof. Point Park Coll., Pitts., 1976-80; coord. women's resource ctr. YWCA of Greater Pitts., 1980-87; sr. rsch. assoc. Western Psychiat. Inst. Clin., Pitts., 1987, sr. clinician, program coord., 1987-89; pvt. practice Altoona, 1989—. Mem. Am. Psychol. Assn., Cen. Pa. Psychol. Assn. Democrat. Home: 2807 Edgewood Dr Altoona PA 16602 Office: 615 Howard Ave Altoona PA 16601

LAMBERT, LISA GAYE, sales professional; b. Roseville, Calif., Apr. 25, 1955; d. Lloyd Douglas and Dona (Holt) L. BS, Chico (Calif.) State U., 1977; MS, U. Conn., 1979. Clin. dietitian, mgr. L.I. Coll. Hosp., Bklyn., 1980-81; chemist Novo Labs., Wilton, Conn., 1981-83; applications chemist Varian Assocs., Houston, 1984-85; sales rep. Varian Assocs., Austin, Tex., 1985-86, Spectra Physics, San Jose, 1986-87; sales rep., magnetics rsch. Varian Assocs., Palo Alto, 1987—. Mem. Am. Chem. Soc., Am. Oil Chemist (pres., chmn. S. Cen. sect. 1985), Bay Area NMR Group. Republican. Mormon. Office: Varian Assocs 611 Hansen Way Palo Alto CA 94303

LAMBERT, MARTHA LOWERY, state legislator; b. Douglasville, Ga., Mar. 27, 1937; d. Edmond Davis and Mary (Daniel) Lowery; m. Paul Dean Lambert, June 13, 1959; children: Melanie Lynn, Kurt Phillip, Brett Cameron, Matthew Dean. Mem. N.Mex. Ho. of Reps., Santa Fe, 1981—; part-owner Premier Foods Inc., Albuquerque, 1989—. Pres. Albuquerque Dist. Dental Aux., 1971, Albuquerque Fed. Rep. Women, 1975; alt. del. Nat. Rep. Conv., Kansas City, Mo., 1976. Home: 616 Running Water Circle SE Albuquerque NM 87123 Office: Premier Foods Inc 3900 Second St NW Albuquerque NM 87107

LAMBERTH, ELLA RUTH WHEELER, principal; b. Pisgah, Ala., Apr. 28, 1927; d. Emmett Beeson and Nettie Mae (Lester) Wheeler; m. Ernest Lester Lamberth, Apr. 25, 1947; children: Ernest Lester, Lynda Renee Lamberth Vranek, Kristin Leigh. AS, Snead Jr. Coll., 1945; BS, Ala. A&M U., 1972, MEd, 1975. Cert. elem. tchr., Ala. Tchr. elem. Pisgah Elem. Sch., 1946-47, Dean's Chapel Elem. Sch., Henager, Ala., 1950-51, St. Matthew's Elem. Sch., Camden, S.C., 1967-68, 1968-69; tchr. Eden Elem. Sch., Pell City, Ala., 1969-70; tchr. Hebron Elem. Sch., Grant, Ala., 1970-73, prin., tchr., 1973-76; tchr. elem. L.W. Page Elem. Sch., Scottsboro, Ala., 1976-81, elem. prin., 1981—. Mem. Scottsboro-Jackson County Hist. Assn., 1978—. Mem. NEA, Ala. Edn. Assn., Nat. Assn. Elem. Sch. Prins., Ala. Coun. Sch. Adminstrs. and Suprs., Assn. Sch. Curriculum Devel., AAUW (sec. Scottsboro chpt. 1982- 83, program chmn. 1984-85), Alpha Delta Kapa. Democrat. Baptist. Home: Rte 4 Box 324G Scottsboro AL 35768 Office: LW Page Elem Sch 305 S Scott St Scottsboro AL 35768

LAMBERTI, JUDITH ANN, obstetrician-gynecologist; b. Oakland, Calif., Oct. 7, 1951; d. Antonio Aldo and Olga Catherine (Caviglia) L. BS, U. Calif., Davis, 1973; MD, U. Calif., San Francisco, 1978. Diplomate Am. Bd. Ob-Gyn. Resident in ob-gyn. U. Colo. Health Scis. Ctr., Denver, 1978-82; sr. physician The Permanente Med. Group, Inc., Oakland, 1982—; chair credentials and privileges, Kaiser-Permanente Med. Ctr., Oakland, 1986—. Fellow Am. Coll. Obstetricians and Gynecologists; mem. Am. Fertility Soc. Democrat. Roman Catholic. Office: Permanente Med Group Inc 280 W MacArthur Blvd Oakland CA 94611

LAMBERTI, MARILYN, nurse; b. Atlantic City, July 8, 1935; d. William and Betty (Meck) Abramoff; m. Elias, July 8, 1956; 1 child, Michael. BA, Jersey City State Coll., 1974; MA, Montclair State Coll., 1978; PhD, Calif. Pacific U., 1983. Registered nurse; lic. nursing home adminstr. Staff nurse Veterans Hosp., Bklyn., 1956-60, Irvington (N.J.) Gen. Hosp., 1960-65; head nurse Ivy Haven, Newark, 1965-69; from grad. nurse to asst. nursing dir. Essex County Geriatric Ctr., Belleville, N.J.; nursing dir. Essex County Geriatric Ctr., Belleville, 1976-88; acting div. dir. Essex County Geriatric Ctr., 1988—. Mem. Kappa Delta Pi, Omicron. Home: 32 Grove St Belleville NJ 07109 Office: Essex County Geriatric Ctr 125 Fairview Ave Cedar Grove NJ 07009

LAMBERTSEN, MARY ANN, human resources and information systems executive; b. Kane, Pa., Dec. 23, 1939; d. Arthur Nathaniel and Anna Marie (Peterson) Turnquist; m. John Franklin Lambertsen, Aug. 30, 1972. BS, Carnegie-Mellon U., 1961; MA, Columbia U., 1963; MS, Pace U., 1977. Tchr. math. Cleve. Pub. Schs., 1963-64; mgr. traffic Ohio Bell Telephone Co., Cleve., 1964-68, systems analyst, 1968-70, personnel analyst, 1970-71; specialist bus. systems Bell Telephone Labs., Piscataway, N.J., 1971-72; dist. mgr. personnel AT&T, N.Y.C., 1972-78; v.p. human resources Fisher-Price, East Aurora, N.Y., 1978-89, v.p. human resources and information systems, 1989—; chmn. bd. N.Y. Fed. Res. Bank, Buffalo. Vol. United Way of Buffalo and Erie County, 1980—; bd. dirs. Assn. for Retarded Children, Buffalo, 1985—; trustee D'Youville Coll., 1990—. Recipient award SUNY-Buffalo, 1986; named Mgr. of Yr. Ctr. for Women in Mgmt./D'Youville Coll., 1986, YWCA Leader award, 1988. Mem. Profit Sharing Council Am. (bd. dirs. 1983—), Profit Sharing Research Found. (trustee 1982—). Club: The Women's Group (Buffalo). Office: Fisher-Price 636 Girard Ave East Aurora NY 14052

LAMBIRD, MONA SALYER, lawyer; b. Oklahoma City, July 19, 1938; d. B.M., Jr. and Pauline A. Salyer; m. Perry A. Lambird, July 30, 1960; children: Allison Thayer, Jennifer Salyer, Elizabeth Gard, Susannah Johnson. B.A., Wellesley Coll., 1960; LL.B., U. Md., 1963. Bar: Okla. 1968, Md. Ct. Appeals 1963, U.S. Supreme Ct. 1967. Atty. civil div. Dept. Justice, Washington, 1963-65; sole practice law Balt. and Oklahoma City, 1965-71; mem. firm Andrews Davis Legg Bixler Milsten & Price, Inc. and predecessor firm, Oklahoma City, 1971—; cons. World Orgn. China Painters; minority mem. Okla. Election Bd., 1984—; mem. Profl. Responsibility Tribunal Okla. Supreme Ct., 1984—; Master of Bench, sec.-treas., Am. Inn of Ct. XXIII in Oklahoma City, 1986—. Editor: Briefcase, Oklahoma County Bar Assn., 1976. Profl. liaison com. City Oklahoma City, 1974-80; mem. Hist. Preservation of Oklahoma City, Inc., 1970—; del. Oklahoma County and Okla. State Republican Party Conv., 1971—; Okla. City Orch. League Inc., legal advisor, 1973—, bd. dirs., 1973—; incorporator, bd. dirs. R.S.V.P. of Oklahoma County, pres., 1982-83; bd. dirs. Congregate Housing for Elderly, 1978—, Vis. Nurses Assn., 1983-86, Oklahoma County Friends of Library, 1980—, The Support Ctrs., Inc., 1989—. Mem. ABA, Okla. Bar Assn. (pres. labor and employment law sect.), Oklahoma County Bar Assn. (bd. dirs. 1986—, pres. elect 1989), Oklahoma County Bar Found. (pres. 1988), Jr. League Oklahoma City (dir. 1973-76, legal adv.), Oklahoma County and State Med. Assn. Aux. (dir.). Methodist. Clubs: Seven Colls. (pres. 1972-76), Women's Econ. (steering com. 1981-86). Home: 419 NW 14th St Oklahoma City OK 73103 Office: 500 W Main Oklahoma City OK 73102

LAMBRECHT, SALLY BORCHER, pharmacist; b. Sidney, Nebr., Oct. 12, 1960; d. Arthur Junior and Marjorie Louise (Curlee) Borcher; m. Richard Dean Lambrecht, Apr. 30, 1988. BS in Pharmacy, U. Wyo., 1983. Registered pharmacist, Calif., Nebr. Pharmacist Gaston Pharmacy, Sidney, Nebr., 1983—. Sec. Cheyenne County Republican Com., Sidney, 1986—; mem. Holy Trinity Luth. Ch., Sidney. Recipient Cert. for Continuing Edn., Nebr. Coun. on Pharmacy Edn., 1986, 87, 88, 89. Mem. Am. Pharm. Assn., Nebr. Pharmacists Assn., U. Wyo. Alumni Assn., Cowboy Joe Club, Rho Chi, Kappa Epsilon, Beta Sigma Phi (pres. Alpha Nu chpt. 1987-88, city coun. treas. 1986-87, Girl of Yr. 1989).

LAMDEN, EVELYN OLSON, advertising executive; b. Akron, Ohio, Nov. 10, 1950; d. Myrle Mylo Olson and Luz (Talaña) Swartz; m. William Edward Lamden, Aug. 31, 1986. BA in Mass Media Communications magna cum laude, U. Akron, 1980. Sec. Goodyear Tire Co., Akron, 1968-74, field merchandiser, 1975-76, display coordinator, 1976-79, regional advt. mgr., 1979-83; ptnr., dir. Budji Corp., Los Angeles, 1983-85; sr. account exec. Internat. Communications Group, Los Angeles, 1985-87, account dir., 1987-88; ptnr. Lamden Property Mgmt., 1988—. Pres., Goodyear Community Theater, Akron, 1976-79; bd. dirs., Dallas Repertory Theater, 1980-83. Recipient Best Speaker award Toastmasters Internat., Akron, 1972. Mem. Women in Communications, Nat. Assn. Female Execs. Democrat. Roman Catholic. Office: Lamden Property Mgmt 233 A St Ste 1102 San Diego CA 92101

LAMDEN, JEAN SALLIE, editor; b. Olney, Ill., Apr. 10, 1927; d. Louis and Ida (Sack) Lopin; m. Robert Eugene Lamden, Dec. 26, 1954; children: Lawrence Alan, Andrew Maxwell, Susan Melissa. AA, UCLA, 1946, BA, 1948, MA, 1950. Asst. dir. pub. rels. Fedn. Jewish Welfare Orgns., L.A., 1953-54; contbg. editor Year, Inc., L.A., 1953-55; adminstrv. asst. Inst. for Study of Change in Higher Edn., Claremont, Calif., 1970; instr., lect. Calif. State U., Fullerton, Calif., 1971-75, Northridge, 1975-76; instr., lect. Calif. State Poly. U., Pomona, Calif., 1977-80; abstracts editor Comment, Claremont, 1971-86; pub. relations cons. China Health Inst., Beverly Hills, Calif., 1983-84; editor The Shofar, Covina, Calif., 1986—. Info. specialist Cancer Info. Svc. Nat. Cancer Inst., Los Angeles, 1979—; bd. dirs. Student-Faculty Publs. Calif. State U., Fullerton, 1971-75. Mem. Brandeis U. Nat. Women's Com., Covina Cycle. Jewish. Office: Jewish Fedn Coun 801 W San Bernardino Rd Covina CA 91722

LAMEL, LINDA HELEN, insurance company executive, former college president, lawyer; b. N.Y.C., Sept. 10, 1943; 1 child, Diana Ruth Sands. B.A. magna cum laude, Queens Coll., 1964; M.A., NYU, 1968; J.D., Bklyn. Law Sch., 1976. Bar: N.Y. 1977, U.S. Dist. Ct. (3d dist.) N.Y. 1977. Mgmt. analyst U.S. Navy, Bayonne, N.J., 1964-65; secondary sch. tchr. Farmingdale Pub. Sch., N.Y., 1965-73; curriculum specialist Yonkers Bd. Edn., N.Y., 1973-75; program dir. Office of Lt. Gov., Albany, N.Y., 1975-77; dep. supt. N.Y. State Ins. Dept., N.Y.C., 1977-83; pres., chief exec. officer Coll. of Ins., N.Y.C., 1983-88; v.p. Tchr.'s Ins. and Annuity Assn., N.Y.C., 1989—; dir. Seneca (N.Y.) Ins. Co. Contbr. articles to profl. jours. Campaign mgr. lt. gov.'s primary race, N.Y. State, 1974. Mem. ABA (tort and ins. sect. com. chmn. 1985-86), N.Y. State Bar Assn. (exec. com. ins. sect. 1984-88), Assn. of Bar of City of N.Y. (chair ad hoc com. on med. malpractice), Am. Mgmt. Assn. (ins. and risk mgmt. council), Fin. Women's Assn., Assn. Profl. Ins. Women (Woman of Yr. award 1988), Phi Beta Kappa, Kappa Delta Pi, Phi Alpha Theta. Office: 730 Third Ave New York NY 10017

LAMENDOLA, JENNIFER JOYCE, information systems specialist; b. Riverhead, N.Y., July 2, 1962; d. John B. and Hazel Irene (Conyers) L. BS, Indiana U. Pa., 1984; postgrad., Pace U., 1988—. Jr. personal computer analyst Combustion Engring., Stamford, Conn., 1984-85, personal computer analyst, 1985-87; coord. tech. edn. Dollar Dry Dock Bank, White Plains, N.Y., 1987-89; mgr. info. systems F.D. Rich Co., Inc., Stamford, 1989—. Mem. NAFE. Roman Catholic.

LAMISON-WHITE, LEATHA MAE, statistician; b. Courtland, Va., May 5, 1953; d. Winget and Beatrice Lamison; m. Michael Nathan White, May 25, 1985; children: Darren, Eric. BA in Sociology, Norfolk Va.) State U., 1974; postgrad., Va. Commonwealth U., 1974-76. Tchr. Richmond (Va.) Pub. Schs., 1974-77; social worker Richmond Dept. Welfare, 1978; tng. specialist Bur. of Census, Washington, 1979; regional technician Bur. of Census, Ft. Walton Beach, Fla., 1980, Mobile, Ala., 1980; survey statistician Bur. of Census, Washington, 1981—; real estate agt., investor Omega Properties, Lanham, 1986—. Researcher poverty sect. World Almanac, 1983-86. Mem. Commerce Com. for Black Concerns, Washington, 1987, NAACP. Mem. NAFE, Alpha Kappa Delta, Washington Investors, Ltd. Democrat. Mem. African Methodist Episcopal Zion Ch. Home: 9505 Vermell Pl Largo MD 20772

LAMM, CAROLYN BETH, lawyer; b. Buffalo, Aug. 22, 1948; d. Daniel John and Helen Barbara (Tatakis) L.; m. Peter Edward Halle, Aug. 12, 1972. BS, SUNY, Buffalo, 1970; JD, U. Miami (Fla.), 1973. Bar: Fla., 1973, D.C., 1976, N.Y. 1983. Trial atty. frauds sect. civil div. U.S. Dept. Justice, Washington, 1973-78, asst. chief comml. litigation sect. civil div., 1978, asst. dir., 1978-80; assoc. White & Case, Washington, 1980-84, ptnr., 1984—. Contbr. articles to legal publs.; mem. bd. editors Rev. Internat. Bus. Law; mem. Sec. of State's Adv. Com. on Pvt. Can.-U.S. Law. Fellow Am. Bar Found.; mem. ABA (chmn. young lawyers div., chmn. assembly resolution com., sec., chmn. internat. litigation com. sect. litigation, nominating com.), Fed. Bar Assn. (chmn. sect. on antitrust and trade regulation), Bar Assn. D.C. (bd. dirs., sec.), D.C. Bar (bd. govs., steering com. litigation sect.), Am. Law Inst., Women's Bar Assn. D.C., Am. Soc. Internat. Law, Internat. Bar Assn. (bus. law sect., internat. litigation com.), Am. Friends

Turkey (bd. dirs.), Washington Fgn. Law Soc., Nat. Women's Forum, City Tavern Club, Columbia Country Club. Democrat. Home: 2101 Connecticut Ave NW Washington DC 20008 Office: White & Case 1747 Pennsylvania Ave NW Ste 500 Washington DC 20006

LAMONT, ALICE, accountant, consultant; b. Houston, July 19; d. Harold and Bessie Bliss (Knight) L. BS, Mont. State U.; MBA in Taxation, Golden Gate U., 1982. Tchr. London Central High Sch., 1971-80; acct. Signetics, Sunnyvale, Calif., 1980-82, Metcalf, Frix & Co., Atlanta, 1983-84; propr. Alice Lamont Ltd., 1985—. Mem. Atlanta Hist. Soc., High Mus. Art, Atlanta Botanical Garden, Atlanta Zool. Soc., Friend of Zoo Atlant. Mem. AAUW (life), Ga. Soc. CPAs, EDP Auditors, Inst. Internal Auditors, English Speaking Union, Women Bus. Owners, Buckhead Bus. Assn., Atlanta Woman's Club (co-chair ways and means com. 1985-86, asst. treas. 1986-88, treas. 1990).

LAMONT, BARBARA, television executive; b. Paget, Bermuda, Nov. 9, 1939; came to U.S., 1949; d. Theophilus and Muriel (Aird) Alcántara; m. Ludwig Gelobter, Dec. 20, 1959; children: Michel, David, Elisabeth. BA in Internat. Law, Sarah Lawrence Coll., 1960; MPA, Harvard U., 1985. Reporter Sta. WINS, N.Y.C., 1971-73; reporter, anchor Sta. WNEW-TV, N.Y.C., 1973-76; writer, reporter CBS News, N.Y.C., 1976-82; dir. ops. Nigerian TV Authority, Lagos, Nigeria, 1982-84; writer ABC News, N.Y.C., 1985-86; pres., chief exec. officer New Orleans Teleport, 1987—; adj. assoc. prof. journalism Columbia U., N.Y.C., 1980-82, 82-86. Author: City People, 1976; mem. editorial bd. Amsterdam News, N.Y.C., 1986—; contbr. articles to the N.Y. Times. Dist. leader N.Y. County Dem. Com., N.Y.C., 1969-72; mem. Council Elected Black Dems., N.Y.C., 1969-72; bd. dirs. Planned Parenthood N.Y.C., 1971; mem. Nat. Women's Polit. Caucus, Washington, 1972; mem. exec. council Kennedy Sch. Alumnae Assn., Cambridge, Mass., 1985—; mem. parents com. Williams Coll., Williamstown, Mass., 1986—, fiscal reform com. Urban League. Recipient AP award, 1973, Ret. Detectives award N.Y.C. Detectives Assn., 1975. Mem. Nat. Assn. Broadcasters. Republican. Club: Harvard. Office: WCCL-TV 620 Desire St New Orleans LA 70117

LAMOUREUX, GLORIA KATHLEEN, nurse, military officer; b. Billings, Mont., Nov. 2, 1947; d. Laurits Bungaard and Florence Esther (Nielsen) Nielsen; m. Kenneth Earl Lamoureux, Aug. 31, 1973 (div. Feb. 1979). BS, U. Wyo., 1970; MS, U. Md., 1984. Staff nurse, ob-gyn DePaul Hosp., Cheyenne, Wyo., 1970; enrolled USAF, 1970, advanced through grades to lt. col.; staff nurse ob-gyn dept. 57th Tactical Hosp., Nellis AFB, Nev., 1970-71, USAF Hosp., Clark AB, Republic Philippines, 1971-73; charge nurse ob-gyn dept. USAF Regional Hosp., Sheppard AFB, Tex., 1973-75; staff nurse ob-gyn dept. USAF Regional Hosp., MacDill AFB, Fla., 1976-79; charge nurse ob-gyn dept. USAF Med. Ctr., Andrews AFB, Md., 1979-80, MCH coord., 1980-82; chief nurse USAF Clinic, Eielson AFB, Alaska, 1984-86, Air Force Systems Command Hosp., Edwards AFB, Calif., 1986-90; comdr., dir. base med. svcs. 7275th Air Base Group Clinic, Air Sta., San Vito Dei Normanni, Italy, 1990—. Named one of Outstanding Women Am., 1983. Mem. Nurses Assn. of Am. Coll. Obstetricians and Gynecologists (sec.-treas. armed forces dist. 1986-88, vice-chmn. armed forces dist. 1989—), Air Force Assn., Assn. Mil. Surgeons U.S., Bus. and Profl. Women's Assn. (pub. rels. chair Prince George's County chpt. 1981-82), Sigma Theta Tau. Republican. Lutheran. Office: PSC Box 674 APO New York NY 09240-5300

LAMPARD, CATHERINE ANN, lawyer, educator; b. New Orleans, Feb. 9, 1951; d. Robert Emmett and Catherine Rita (Hand) L.; m. Bruce E. Naccari, Dec. 8, 1984; 1 child, Paolo Atilio. BA in Anthropology, Tulane U., 1971; U. of Ams., Cholula, Puebla, Mex., 1972; postgrad., U. Rafael Landivar, Guatemala City, Guatemala, 1979, Escuela Libre Derechos, Mexico City, 1979; JD, Loyola U., New Orleans, 1982. Bar: La. 1982. Grants planning officer Office Health Svcs.-Environ. Quality La. Dept. Health and Human Resources, New Orleans, 1979-83; with Hand & Lampard, Metairie and Lacombe, La., 1982—; law clk. 24th Jud. Dist. Ct., Gretna, La., 1983; dir., staff atty. Ecumenical Immigration Svcs., Inc., New Orleans, 1983-89; supervising atty., dir. Immigration Clinic, adj. prof. law Tulane U., New Orleans, 1987—, speaker continuing legal edn., 1987—. Recipient Pro Bono award La. Bar Assn., 1986, svc. award Latin Am. Apostolate of Archdiocese of New Orleans, 1989; Loyola Law Clinic award, 1982. Mem. Am. Immigration Lawyers Assn. (treas. La. chpt. 1989—). Democrat. Roman Catholic. Office: 3200 N Turnbull Dr Metairie LA 70002

LAMPE, ANNACAROL, communications and training executive; b. Indpls., Sept. 30, 1951; d. William George and Helen Eleanor (Biddle) L.; m. Peter J. Florzak, Dec. 10, 1985; 1 child, Anna Eleanor. Student, Wroxton Coll., St. Mary, Eng., 1972, U. Hawaii, 1973; BS, Ind. U., 1973, MS, 1974; MBA, Rockhurst Coll., 1981. Tchr. speech, drama, English Eastside High Sch., Butler, Ind., 1974-77; dir. student activities Penn Valley Community Coll., Kansas City, Mo., 1977-79; mgr. tech. communications Martin Marietta Co., Oak Ridge, Tenn., 1983-84; assoc. dir. Kaleidoscope Hallmark Cards Inc., Kansas City, 1981-83, communications specialist, 1984—; speaker, presenter workshops stress mgmt., leadership, sex equity, 1977—; leader Midwest Conf. Women Bus., Kansas City, 1980. Mem. Kansas City Jr. League, 1986—; bd. dirs. Oak Ridge Arts Council, 1983, Tenn. Art Ctr., 1984, Westport Ballet, Kansas City, 1985. Recipient Key to City Mayor Love, Johnson City, Tenn., 1981, Young Careerist award Bus. Profl. Women No. Ind., 1977; named Outstanding Young Women Am., 1985, Outstanding Woman, Girl Scouts Am., Kansas City, 1987. Mem. Internat. Assn. Bus. Commnicators (Silver Quill Excellence 1986), Am. Soc. Tng. and Devel. Republican. Lutheran. Home and Office: 9627 NE Bradford Kansas City MO 64153

LAMPE, CAROL KARNELL, financial planner; b. Sacramento, Calif., July 31, 1945; d. Nick and Grace (Hadjis) Karnell; m. Paul J. Lampe, Sept. 12, 1970 (dec. 1987); children: Robert Grant, David Jason. BS, Carnegie Mellon U., 1967; MEd, U. Pitts., 1970; cert., Coll. for Fin. Planning, Denver, 1984. Tchr. Riverview High Sch., Oakmont, Pa., 1967-69, U. Pitts., 1969-70, Lakewood (Ohio) High Sch., 1970-71, W.Va. Career Coll., Wheeling, 1975; registered rep. IDS Fin. Svcs., Pitts., 1979-82, dist. mgr., 1982-85; registered rep. The Phoenix, Pitts., 1985-90; ptnr. Lampe Grimm DiCarlo Fin. Cons., Pitts., 1989—; cons. money mgmt. Am. Pension Benefits, Warrendale, Pa., 1989—; fin. spokesperson Sta. KDKA-TV Banking on Your Future, Pitts., 1988. Vice chmn. Ptnrs. With Youth, Pitts., 1988. Mem. Internat. Assn. Fin. Planning (chmn. pub. rels. Pitts. chpt. 1989-90, sec. 1988-89, bd. mem. at large 1987-88, spokesperson for TV 1987-88), Pitts. Life Underwriters Assn. Office: Lampe Asset Mgmt 3000 McKnight East Dr Pittsburgh PA 15237

LAMPEL, ANITA KAY, psychologist; b. L.A., May 25, 1946; d. Jack Murray and Rose (Maltun) L.; m. Stanley David Mishook, Dec. 21, 1975; children: Jacob, David. PhD, Stanford U., 1969. Diplomate Am. Bd. Profl. Psychology; lic. psychologist, Calif. Staff psychologist Children's Meml. Hosp., Chgo., 1970-73; mgr. children's program San Bernardino (Calif.) County Dept. of Mental Health, 1973-79; pvt. practice San Bernardino, 1979—; instr. various univs., Calif., 1973—. Author: (with others) Group Psychotherapy with Children and Adolescents, 1987; contbr. articles to profl. jours. Chair Gifted Edn. Adv. Commn., San Bernardino, 1988—; mem. Family Life Edn. Adv. Commn., San Bernardino, 1988—. Mem. Am. Psychology Assn., Calif. State Psychology Assn., Inland Counties Psychol. Assn. (sec. 1988-89), Am. Bd. Profl. Psychology (western regional bd. dirs. 1988—).

LAMPETER, KATHLEEN MARY, college system administrator; b. Manhattan, N.Y., Dec. 6, 1961; d. Robert Frederick and Mary Patricia (Crilley) L. BA, Ramapo Coll., New Jersey, 1983; MA, Columbia U., 1987. Summer intern Warner Communications, Manhattan, N.Y., 1982; summer conf. coordinator Ramapo Coll., Mahwah, NY, 1983; asst. dir. student activities Columbia U., NY, 1984; residence coordinator Pace U., Pleasantville, NY; dir. residence life Dominican Coll., Tappan, NY, 1987; advisor Resident Student Council, Dominican Coll., 1987, advisor, editor Residence Ctr. New Letter, Tappan, 1987, presenter, educator, Leadership Tng. Seminars, 1983. Coordinator Drive for Letters for Overseas Service Personal, mem. Green Peace, World Wildlife Fedn., Animal Rights Orgns., sponsor A Child in Africa World Vision, 1987. Mem. Assn. for Coll. Housing Orgns., Nat. Assns. Women Deans and Administrs., Assn. Coll. Personnel Adminstrs., Nat. Assn. Student Personnel Administrs. Office: Dominican Coll 10 Western Hwy Orangeburg NY 10984

LAMPHEAR, VIVIAN SHAW, psychologist, educator; b. Springfield, Ill., Feb. 4, 1954; d. Frank Shaw and Lois Eileen (Ziegler) Smith; m. Kenneth Allen Lamphear, Jan. 6, 1978; children: Ryan Michelle, Dylan Connor. BA in Psychology summa cum laude, Calif. State U., Long Beach, 1979, MA in Clin. Psychology, 1982; PhD in Clin. Psychology, SUNY, Stony Brook, 1987. Clin. intern Juv. Diversion Program U. Calif., Irvine, 1979-80; program coord. Child Care Worker Social Learning Program Children's Village, U.S.A., Beaumont, Calif., 1980-82; adult and child therapist Psychol. Ctr. SUNY, Stony Brook, 1984-85, therapist and program coord. Anger Control/Mgmt. Program, 1982-86; neuropsychol. assessment intern State Univ. of N.Y. Med. Sch. and Univ. Hosp., 1985-86; clin. psychology intern Psychol. Ctr. SUNY, Stony Brook, 1985-86; postdoctoral clin. tng. Family Stress Ctr., Juliann Singer Ctr., L.A., 1987-88; clin. psychologist, clin. dir. Child Devel. Clin. Fuller Grad. Sch. Psychology, Pasadena, Calif., 1986-89; clin. psychologist Christ-Centered Counseling Med. Group, Corona, Calif., 1989—; adj. asst. prof. psychology Fuller Grad. Sch. of Psychology, Pasadena, 1989—, asst. prof. 1986-89; instr. stats. psychology dep. SUNY, Stony Brook, 1985-86; co-prin. investigator fed. rsch. project in field, 1988—; initiator and project coord. Stony Brook Child Abuse Prevention Project, 1982-86, others. Contbr. numerous articles to profl. jours. Lectr., cons. community programs in field, 1986—. Recipient fellowships SUNY, Stony Brook, 1982, 86, Grad. Dean's Award for Outstanding Achievement in Psychology, Calif. State U., Long Beach, 1982, grants, Nat. Inst. Justice, 1988, Nat. Ctr. for Prevention of Child Abuse, 1988-91, others. Mem. Am. Psychol. Assn., Western Psychol. Assn., Assn. for the Advancement of Behavior Therapy, Soc. for Rsch. in Child Devel., Nat. Com. for the Prevention of Child Aubse, Calif. Profl. Soc. on the Abuse of Children, Long Beach Child Trauma Coun. Republican. Mem. Christian Ch. Office: Christ Centered Counseling PO Box 2594 Corona CA 91718

LAMPKIN, BARBARA JO, medical laboratory computer analyst, product manager; b. Lynn, Mass., Nov. 24, 1947; d. George James and Ella Margaret (Lunsford) L. BS in Med. Tech., Woman's Coll. of Ga., 1969; postgrad., Boston U., 1978-84. Med. technologist Med. Ctr. of Central Ga., Macon, 1969-71; hematology head tech. Coliseum Park Hosp., Macon, 1971-74; hematology chief tech. Boston City Hosp., 1974-76; satellite lab. supr. Smith-Klein Labs., Waltham, Mass., 1976-77; blood bank technologist ARC, Boston, 1977-78; hematology chief tech. Bioran Med. Labs., Cambridge, Mass., 1978-84; computer analyst and implementation specialist Collaborative Med. Sytems, Newton, Mass., 1984-86; product dir., computer analyst, Blood Bank, 1986—. Campaign vol. Dem. Nat. Com., Mass., 1980-86; bd. dirs. Mass. Choice, Boston, 1985-86, vol., 1983—; mem. Nat. Abortion Rights Action League, Washington, 1974—. Mem. Am. Soc. Clin. Pathologists (affiliate, registered med. technologist), Am. Soc. Profl. and Exec. Women, Boston Beanstalk Tall Club (bd. dirs. 1989-90, pub. rels. chmn. 1984-86, treas. 1989-90). Roman Catholic. Avocations: gourmet cuisine, skiing, travel, reading, knitting. Office: Co-Med div Mumps Collaborative 246 Walnut St Newton MA 02160

LAMPLEY, BIANCA SCHMIDT, computer programmer; b. Laurens, S.C., Dec. 30, 1964; d. Manfred Fritz and Rosemarie (Sagner) Schmidt; m. Charles Gordon Lampley IV, July 11, 1987. BS in Math. Scis., U. N.C., 1987. Computer programmer IBM Corp., Research Triangle Park, N.C., 1985-89, Charlotte, N.C., 1989—. Vol. Carolinas Med. Ctr., Charlotte, 1990—. Mem. N.C. Med. Assn. Aux. Office: IBM Corp 1001 W T Harris Blvd Charlotte NC 28257

LAMPLUGH, MARY BETH, accountant; b. Upland, Pa., May 31, 1948; d. Theodore Roosevelt and Margaret (Stewart) L. AS in Bus. Mgmt., Brandywine Coll., Wilmington, Del., 1970; BS in Acctg., Drexel U., Phila., 1974. Auditor Naval Audit Svc. NE Region, Camden, N.J., 1977-74, Naval Audit Svc. Capital Region, Falls Ch., Va., 1977-78, Def. Audit Svc., Rosslyn, Va., 1978-80, OIG U.S. Commerce Dept. Office Audits, Washington, Samuel M. Fisher Co., Broomall, Pa., 1984-86; tax examiner George S. May Co., Chgo., 1986; auditor Mitchell, Titus & Co., N.Y.C., 1986-87; acct. Foster Med. Corp., Blue Bell, Pa., 1988-89; tax examiner IRS, Phila., 1989; pres. Mary Kraft Corp., Claymont Del., 1986—. Mem. Assn. Govt. Accts., Toastmasters Club Va. Republican. Baptist. Office: PO Box 939 Linwood PA 19061

LAMPROS-KLEIN, FRANCINE DEMETRA, educational program director; b. Worcester, Mass., Mar. 12, 1948; d. James and Demetra (Pappanastos) Lampros; m. Robert Klein, Jan. 1, 1985. Student, local univs., Mex. and P.R., 1973, 75; BA, Worcester State Coll., 1970, MEd, 1980; paralegal cert., So. Career Inst., Boca Raton, Fla., 1988. Cert. bilingual and elem. sch. tchr., Mass., elem. prin., Mass. Tchr. ESL Birmingham (Ala.) Pub. Schs., 1985-86; tchr. Spanish/bilingual Worcester Pub. Schs., 1970-80, curriculum coord., 1980-85, 86-89, dir. bilingual edn., 1989—; mem. adv. bd. early childhood edn. Worcester Pub. Schs., 1988—, mem. adv. bd. gifted and talented program, 1989—. Mem. Worcester Human Rights Commn., 1984. Mem. Nat. Tchr.'s Assn., Mass. Tchr.'s Assn., Assn. Supervision and Curriculum Devel., Mass. Assn. Bilingual Educators, Edn. Assn. Worcester. Office: Worcester Pub Schs Bilingual Dept 20 Irving St Worcester MA 01609

LAMS, MONICA MARY, human resource executive; b. Bklyn., Feb. 10, 1947; d. Thomas McGoey and Mary Ursula (Murphy) Lamb. Assoc. Bus. Adminstrn., Dover Coll., 1968; AB in English Lit., Sussex Coll., 1975; student, Ladycliff Coll., 1965-67; postgrad., Morris Coll., 1972-74. Acctg. technician Selected Risks Ins. Co., Branchville, N.J., 1973-76; sr. acctg. technician S.B.E., Inc., Watsonville, Calif., 1976-77; benefits specialist E.F. Hutton Life Ins. Co., La Jolla, Calif., 1977-84, benefits adminstr., 1984-87; mgr. employee benefits 1st Capital Life Ins. Co., San Diego, 1987—. Mem. Pers. Mgmt. Assn., Compensation and Benefits Assn., NAFE, Soc. Human Resource Mgmt., Merchants and Mfrs. Assn. Roman Catholic. Office: 1st Capital Life Ins Co 10241 Wateridge Cir San Diego CA 92121

LANCASTER, ELAINE L., banker; b. Hennessey, Okla., July 20, 1935; d. Linley R. Krebs and Violet Elma Krebs Benson; B.S., U. Md., 1963; m. William Duval Lancaster, Apr. 30, 1977; children from previous marriage—Cameron Lakin, Jeffrey Lakin. with Calif. Fed. Savs. and Loan, Los Angeles, 1973-77; consumer loan mgr. Coast Fed. Savs. and Loan, Hawthorne, Calif., 1977-78; regional consumer loan officer Glendale Fed. Savs. & Loan, 1978-83, mktg. loan mgr., Riverside, Calif., 1983-86, statewide mgr. student loans, 1986—. Mary Hardin Baylor Coll. scholar, 1955: Ford Found. fellow, 1965-66. Mem. Nat. Assn. Student Fin. Aid Adminstrs., Calif. Assn. Student Fin. Aid Adminstrs., Wash. Assn. Student Fin. Aid Adminstrs., Savs. and Loan League, Am. Inst. Banking, Nat. Notary Assn., AAUW, Nat.Mgmt. Assn., YWCA, NOW. Democrat. Club: Toastmistresses. Office: Glendale Fed Savs & Loan 401 N Brand Ave Glendale CA 91304

LANCASTER, PEGGY, advertising agency executive. Prin., creative dir. Scott Lancaster Mills Atha, L.A., 1976—. Recipient numerous creative awards; named Woman of Yr., Am. Advt. Fedn., 1973. Office: Scott Lancaster Mills Atha 2049 Century Pk E Ste 860 Los Angeles CA 90067*

LANCASTER, SUZANNE CORBIN, medical technician; b. Washington, Oct. 23, 1947; d. William Boggs and Nadine (Kennedy) Corbin; m. James Harrison Lancaster, June 20, 1969 (div. 1973); 1 child, Martha Elizabeth. AA, DeKalb Community Coll., Clarkston, Ga., 1976, AS, 1982. Cert. advanced emergency med. technologist. Police officer Emory U., Atlanta, 1978-82; paramedic, firefighter DeKalb City Fire Dept., Decatur, Ga., 1982-83, Henry City Fire Dept., McDonough, Ga., 1983-84; physical measurements technician Equifax Services, Atlanta, 1984—. Instr., vol. ARC, Atlanta, 1978—; ski patroller Nat. Ski Patrol, Denver, 1980—, instr. winter emergency care, supr. Dixie Region; instr. advanced life support Am. Heart Assn., 1983-84; v.p. program and edn. bd. Parents Without Ptnrs., Jonesboro, Ga., 1984. Mem. Emergency Med. Technologists Assn., Exec. Womens Assn. Republican. Presbyterian. Club: Atlanta Ski. Home: 281 Northern Ave #4G Avondale Estates GA 30002 Office: Equifax 2536 Century Pkwy Atlanta GA 30345

LANCOUR, KAREN LOUISE, educator; b. Cheboygan, Mich., June 2, 1946; d. Clinton Howard and Dorothy Marie (Passeno) L. AA, Alpena Community Coll., 1966; BA, Ea. Mich. U., 1968, MS, 1970. Teaching asst. Ea. Mich. U., Ypsilanti, 1968-70; tchr. sci. Utica (Mich.) Community Schs., 1970—. Nat. event supr. Sci. Olympiad, 1986—, nat. rules com., 1987—, state event supr., 1986—, regional dir., 1987. Mem. Nat. Sci. Tchrs. Assn., Nat. Assn. Biology Tchrs., Met. Detroit Sci. Tchrs. Assn., Smithsonian Inst., Nat. Wildlife Assn., Nat. Geographic Soc., Edison Inst., Mortar Bd., Internat. Biographical Soc., Dep. Governor Am. Biographical Inst. Rsch. Assn., Phi Theta Kappa, Kappa Delta Phi. Home: 8378 18 Mile Rd 202 Sterling Heights MI 48313 Office: Henry Ford II High Sch 11911 Clinton River Rd Sterling Heights MI 48313

LAND, DOROTHY NADINE, billing specialist; b. Oakley, Kans.; d. Kenneth Freeman and Laure Mae (Nixon) Shaw; m. William Land Jr., Nov. 30, 1973; children: Sharon Ann Druse, Kenneth William Barnes. Student, Emily Griffith Opportunity Sch, 1956-58, Belleville (Ill.) Area Coll., 1989. Progress billing specialist LaBarge Electronics, St. Louis; civilian payroll and accounts maintenance supr. Scoff AFB, Belleville, Ill.; corp. bookkeeper payroll and bookkeeping dept. Lon W. Harlow Ins. Co., St. Louis; owner Peter Pan Nursery Sch., Royal Heights Beauty Salon, Artistic Styling Salon, Barnes Fence Co., 1963-75. Recipient Pub. Svc. award Nat. Grange Washington, Advanced Achievement award Redken Labs., Congratulatory Letter, Pres. Ronald Reagan. Mem. Nat. Hairdressers Assn., Profl. Womens Club, NAFE, Belleville C. of C. Democrat. Baptist. Home: 725 Royal Heights Rd Belleville IL 62223 Office: 707 N 2nd Saint Louis MO 63102

LAND, JUDY M., real estate developer; b. Phoenix, Oct. 6, 1945; d. Sanford Karl Land and D. Latanne (Hilburn) Land Krauss; divorced; children: Neal McNeil III, Latanne Tahnee. Student, Geneva Sch., 1965; AA in Econs., Merritt Coll., 1967; MBA, Brklyn Bus. Sch., 1984. Cert. real estate developer, broker and appraiser. Gen. mgr. ACE Rent-A-Car, San Francisco, 1967-71; with real estate sales dept. Odmark/Welch Co/Mesa Realty, San Diego, 1971-76; v.p. Brehm Communities, San Diego, 1977; mgr. investment div. Ayers Realty, Encinitas, Calif., 1978-79; asst. v.p. Harry L. Summers Inc., La Jolla, Calif., 1982-85; pres. The Land Co., Carlsbad, Calif., 1979—. Fundraiser Hunger Project, 1979-86, Youth at Risk, 1984-86, Multiple Sclerosis Soc., 1984; mem. exec. com. U.S. Olympics, 1984; bd. dirs. Polit. Policies Com., San Diego, 1986. Mem. Nat. Assn. Real Estate Appraisers, Nat. Assn. Women Execs., Nat. Assn. Home builders, Home Builders Council (pres. 1985), Building Industry Assn. San Diego (bd. dirs. 1985, sale and mktg. coun.), Econ. Devel. Corp. San Diego (membership com. 1984), Women Comml. Real Estate, Life Spike Club. Office: The Land Co 4225 Executive Sq Ste 1200 La Jolla CA 92037

LAND, JULIE KAY, collections representative, consultant; b. Dubuque, Iowa, Jan. 19, 1967; d. Gail and Mildred Thelma (Sandbothe) Douglas; m. Jeffrey Brian Land, Sept. 14, 1985. Grad. high sch., Liberty, Mo.; student, Maple Woods Community Coll. Office clk. Wal-Mart Inc., Liberty, Mo., 1984-87; customer svc. rep. Wolferman's English Muffins, North Kansas City, Mo., 1987-88; lead collector Citicorp, North Kansas City, Mo., 1988—. Democrat. Roman Catholic. Home: 2211 N Pursell Rd Gladstone MO 64118 Office: Citicorp 2900 Rockcreek Pkwy North Kansas City MO 64116

LAND, RHONDA MAE, banker; b. Rolla, Mo., Aug. 9, 1956; d. George Everett and Olive Berniece (Ratliff) L. Grad. high sch. (Valedictorian), Salem, Mo., 1974; student, Southwest Baptist U., to date. Bookkeeping clk. First Nat. Bank, Salem, Mo., 1973-75, computer operator, 1975-78; data processing mgr. First Nat. Bank, Salem, 1978-83, asst. v.p., 1983-84, v.p., 1984—. Advisor Salem R-80 Sch. Vo-Tech. Adv. Bd., 1985-87; mem. stewardship com. Pleasant Valley Bapt. Ch., Salem, 1986—. Republican. Baptist. Office: First Nat Bank 301 W 4th St Salem MO 65560

LANDA, MARIA COSTABILE, school psychologist; b. Havana, Cuba, Aug. 12, 1935; came to U.S., 1960; d. Francisco Andres and Ernestine (Landa) Morales; m: Duilio Costabile, April 22, 1961 (div. 1981); 1 child, Maurice. BA in Psychology magna cum laude, Montclair State Coll., 1984; MA, Columbia U., 1986; PD, Fordham U., 1989; postgrad., Howard U. Cert. sch. psychologist, Md., N.Y., Washington. Tchr. of autistic children Forum Sch., Waldwick, N.J., 1985-86; reading diagnostician adult edn. program LaGuardia Community Coll, Queens, N.Y., 1985; lang. and learning therapist St. Luke's/Roosevelt Hosp., N.Y.C., 1985-86; adj. prof. language arts Boricua Coll., Bklyn., 1987; counselor methadone maintenance and AIDS prevention program Montefiore Medical Ctr., Bronx, N.Y., 1987-88; pvt. practice, 1986-88; sch. psychologist Washington Pub. Schs., 1988—. Treas. Bergen County Assn. for Children with Learning Disabilities, 1982-84. Mem. Am. Psychol. Assn. (assoc.), Nat. Assn. Sch. Psychologists, Kappa Delta Pi (v.p. 1986-88), Phi Kappa Phi, Psi Chi. Office: Washington DC Pub Sch Iowa Ave and Webster NW Macfarland Assessment Ctr Washington DC 20001

LANDA, MICHELLE ANNETTE, marketing professional; b. Elkhart, Ind., Jan. 9, 1955; d. Robert Lee and Delphine Antoinette (Dosmann) Wirt; m. Randall P. Holtzinger, Aug. 27, 1971 (div. 1980); children: Corri Ann, Chad Jacob; m. John F. Landa, Oct. 3, 1981; 1 child, Bradley Jon. Student, Ind. U., 1988—. Sec. Coachmen Caravan div. Coachmen Industries, Middlebury, Ind., 1978-79; sales sec. Shaum Electric Co., Inc., Elkart, 1979-80; adminstrv. asst. SMI, Elkhart, 1980-81, advt. coord., 1981-83, adminstrv. supr., 1983-85, mktg. mgr., 1985—. Mentor Elkhart Community Schs., 1988, 89; adv. Ind. Ptnrs. in Edn., Elkhart, 1988, 89. Republican. Home: 26828 Bridgewater Ct Elkhart IN 46514 Office: SMI 1127 N Nappanee St Elkhart IN 46514

LANDAU, LAURI BETH, accountant, tax consultant; b. Bklyn., July 21, 1952; d. Jack and Audrey Carolyn (Zuckernick) L. BA, Skidmore Coll., 1973; postgrad., Pace. U., 1977-79. CPA, Oreg. Mem. staff Audrey Z. Landau, CPA, Suffern, N.Y., 1976-78; mem. staff Ernst & Whinney, N.Y.C., 1979-80, mem. sr. staff, 1980-82, supr., 1982-84; mgr. Arthur Young & Co., N.Y.C., 1984-87, prin., 1987-89; sr. mgr. Ernst & Young, N.Y.C., 1989—; speaker World Trade Inst., N.Y.C., 1987—, Nat. Fgn. Trade Coun., N.Y.C., 1989—. Composer songs. Career counselor Skidmore Coll., Saratoga Springs, N.Y., 1977—, mem. leadership com. Class of 1973, 1983-85, pres., 1985—, fund chmn., 1987-88, mem. planned gift com., 1989—. N.Y. State Regents scholar, 1970. Mem. AICPA, N.Y. State Soc. CPAs, Skidmore Coll. Alumni Assn. (mem. nominating com. 1989—). Democrat. Clubs: Skidmore Alumni (N.Y.C.); German Shepherd Dog Am. Office: Ernst & Young 277 Park Ave New York NY 10172

LANDAU, SHELLY, screenwriter; b. Englewood, N.J., Dec. 19, 1956; d. Gilbert William and Miriam (Friedman) L. BA in Biology, UCLA, 1978, JD, 1981; MFA in Profl. Writing, U. So. Calif., 1983, MA in Applied Linguistics, 1985. Bar: Calif. 1981. Researcher, aide bur. Consumer Protection FTC, Washington, 1980; teaching asst. freshman writing U. So. Calif., Los Angeles, 1981-85; staff writer TV show Double Trouble, Los Angeles, 1983; story editor TV show Rocky Road, Los Angeles, 1985-86; exec. script cons. TV show Webster, Los Angeles, 1986-89, Growing Pains, Los Angeles, 1989—. Mem. Writers Guild Am. West. Office: c/o Growing Pains 3701 W Oak St Burbank CA 91505

LANDAU-CRAWFORD, DOROTHY RUTH, local government executive; b. S.I., N.Y., Oct. 5, 1957; d. Robert August and Dorothy Faith (Schaut) Landau; m. John W. Crawford, Oct. 21, 1989. AS in Applied Sci., SUNY-Farmingdale, 1977; BS in Biology, Wagner Coll., 1979. Sci. tchr. Bais Yaakov, S.I., 1979-81; dental asst. Dr. Marvin Freeman, S.I., 1981-82; office mgr. Dr. Bennett C. Fidlow, S.I., 1982-85; polit. aide to S.I. Borough Pres., 1985—. Environ. chmn. S.I. League for Better Govt., 1984—; pres. Tottenville Improvement Council Inc., Staten Island, 1985—; exec. dir. Richmond Sr. Svcs. Project Share, 1990—; Dem. candidate for N.Y. State Assembly 60th dist., 1986, dist. leader; dir. community bds. S.I. Borough Pres.' Office; founder, pres. environ. group S.I.L.E.N.T., S.I., 1985; 1st v.p. 123d Community Council, S.I., 1986; social chmn. S. Shore Democratic Club; founding mem. Friends of Clay Pit Pond Park; mem. Protectors of Pine Oak Woods Inc., Roserio Alliotta Dem. Club, Dem. Orgn. of Richmond; trustee S.I. Bd. Leukemia Soc. Am., 1988—, dir., chair Celebrity Waiters Luncheon. Recipient Community Activist Award Office of Pres. S.I. Borough, 1987. Mem. NAFE, Bus. and Profl. Women (Young Careerist for

S.I.). Roman Catholic. Avocations: photography, sports, ceramics, youth programs. Home: 168 Bedell Ave Staten Island NY 10307 Office: S I Borough Pres Office Borough Hall Staten Island NY 10301

LANDBERG, ANN LAUREL, psychotherapist; b. Chgo., June 20, 1926; d. Carl Ryno and Ebba Sadie Elvira (Engstrom) Granlund; m. Harry Morton Landberg, Apr. 1, 1953 (dec. Feb. 1967); stepchildren—Rosabel, Marcene. R.N., Swedish Hosp. Sch. Nursing, Seattle, 1948. Asst. head nurse Halcyon Hosp., Seattle, 1948; doctor's asst. Office of H.M. Landberg, M.D., Seattle, 1948-50, psychotherapist, 1950-67; pvt. practice psychotherapy, Seattle, 1967—; cons. Good Shepherd Sch. for Disturbed Girls, Seattle, 1954—, bd. dirs., 1954-60. Mem. Am. Psychotherapy Assn., King County Med. Aux., Stevens Hosp. Aux. (life), Swedish Hosp. Alumni (pres. 1952-53), Nat. Council Jewish Women, City of Hope, Edmonds Arts Assn. (life patron), Seattle Forensic Inst. (charter). Club: Swedish (Seattle). Home: 16900 Talbot Rd Edmonds WA 98020 Office: 1007 Spring St Seattle WA 98104

LANDE, GAIL RUTH, lawyer; b. Phila., Mar. 18, 1962; d. Milton Jay and Nadine (Kurash) L. BS with distinction and magna cum laude, U. Del., 1984; JD cum laude, U. Richmond, 1987. Bar: Ariz. 1987. Law clk. to judge Ariz. Ct. Appeals, Phoenix, 1987-88; assoc. O'Connor, Cavanagh, Anderson, Westover, Killingsworth & Beshears, P.A., Phoenix, 1988—. Counselor, hotline vol. rape crisis program YWCA, Richmond, Va., 1985-87; hotline vol. Ctr. Against Sexual Assault, Phoenix, 1989—. Mem. ABA, Ariz. Bar Assn., Maricopa Bar Assn., Phi Beta Kappa, Alpha Kappa Delta, Phi Kappa Phi. Democrat. Jewish. Office: O'Connor Cavanagh Et Al 1 E Camelback Rd Ste 700 Phoenix AZ 85012

LANDE, SARAH DUNKERTON, cultural organization administrator; b. Marshalltown, Iowa, June 7, 1938; d. Wendell Charles and Margaret Louise (Stevens) Dunkerton; m. Roger Lee Lande, Aug. 20, 1960; children: Margaret Lande Minor, Roger Christopher. Student, Lindenwood Coll., 1956-57; BA, U. Iowa, 1960, MBA, 1983. Cert. tchr. Registered rep. Piper Jaffray & Hopwood, Bettendorf, Iowa, 1984-87; exec. dir. Iowa Sister State Com., Des Moines, 1988—; mem. Gov.'s Internation Work Group, Des Moines, 1989; culture com. chair Iowa Commn. on Fgn. Lang. and Internat. Edn., Des Moines, 1988-91; quality com. Legis. Higher Edn. Task Force, Des Moines, 1988-89; tchr. Jr. Great Books Program, 1973-75. Columnist Muscatine Jour. Trustee Drake U., Des Moines, 1988-91; bd. dirs. Blue Cross Blue Shield of Iowa, Des Moines, 1987-91, Iowa Peace Inst., Des Moines, 1988-91; pres. Iowa Sister State Friendship Com., Iowa, 1986-88; chairperson Citizen Adv. Com. for Improvement Muscatine (Iowa), 1978-79; mem. LWV, pres., 1976-78; pres. Musser Pub. Libr., 1978-79, Friends of Iowa Pub. Broadcasting Network, 1979-80; bd. dirs. YMCA, 1982-88. Recipient Disting. Svc. award Gov. of Iowa, 1989, Gov.'s Vol. award Gov. of Iowa, 1988; named Outstanding Vol., City of Muscatine, 1979. Mem. AAUW (internat. rels. chair 1988), Muscatine C. of C. (bd. dirs. 1988-89), Rotary (world svc. chair 1990). Republican. Lutheran. Home: 515 W 2d St Muscatine IA 52761 Office: Iowa Sister States 312 8th St Ste 230 Des Moines IA 52761

LANDERDAHL, BRENDA HUSCHKA, company executive; b. Billings, Mont., Dec. 11, 1161; d. William F. and Darlene Jeanne (Frank) Huschka.; m. Steven Arnell, May 22, 1962. BS in Bus. Mgmt., Montana State U., 1985. Mgmt. trainee (expeditor) Copac, Inc., Spartanburg, S.C., 1986-88, prodn. scheduler, 1988--.

LANDERS, ANN (MRS. ESTHER P. LEDERER), columnist; b. Sioux City, Iowa, July 4, 1918; d. Abraham B. and Rebecca (Rushall) Friedman; m. Jules W. Lederer, July 2, 1939 (div. 1975); 1 dau., Margo Lederer Howard. Student, Morningside Coll., 1936-39, LHD (hon.), 1964; hon. degree, Wilberforce (Ohio) Coll., 1972, Am. Coll. Greece, 1979, Meharry Med. Coll., 1981, Jacksonville U., 1983, St. Leo Coll., 1984, Fla. Internat. U., 1984, Med. Coll. Pa., 1985, New Eng. Coll., 1985, U. Wis., 1985, Lincoln Coll., 1986, Nat. Coll. Edn., 1986, Southwestern Adventist Coll., 1987, Duke U., 1987, Rosary Coll., 1989, U. Hartford, 1989, L.I. U., 1989, Med. Coll. Ohio, 1989. Syndicated columnist Chgo., 1955—; pres. Eppie Co., Inc., Chgo. Author: Since You Asked Me, 1962, Teen-agers and Sex, 1964, Truth is Stranger, 1968, Ann Landers Speaks Out, 1975, The Ann Landers Encyclopedia, 1978; syndicated columnist Los Angeles Times-Creators Syndicates. Chmn. Eau Claire (Wis.) Gray-Lady Corps, ARC, 1947-53; chmn. Minn.-Wis. council Anti-Defamation League, 1945-49; asst. Wis. chmn. Nat. Found. Infantile Paralysis, 1951-53; hon. nat. chmn. 1963 Tb Christmas Seal Campaign; bd. sponsors Mayo Clinic, 1970; mem. sponsors com. Mayo Found.; nat. adv. bd. Dialogue for the Blind, 1972; adv. com. on better health services AMA; county chmn. Democratic Party Eau Claire; bd. dirs. Rehab. Inst. Chgo.; nat. bd. dirs. Am. Cancer Soc., Nat. Cancer Inst.; vis. com. bd. overseers Harvard Med. Sch.; mem. Pres.'s Commn. Drunk Driving; trustee Menninger Found., Nat. Dermatology Found., Am. Coll. Greece, Deree-Pierce Coll., Athens, Meharry Med. Sch., Hereditary Disease Found.; dirs. adv. bd. Yale Comprehensive Cancer Ctr. Recipient award Nat. Family Service Assn., 1965, Adolf Meyer award Assn. Mental Health N.Y., 1965, Pres.'s Citation and nat. award Nat. Council on Alcoholism, 1966, 2d nat. award, 1975, Golden Stethoscope award Ill. Med. Soc., 1967, Humanitarianism award Internat. Lions Club, 1967; plaque of honor Am. Friends of Hebrew U., 1968, Gold Plate award Acad. Achievement, 1969; Nat. Service award Am. Cancer Soc., 1971, Robert T. Morse award Am. Psychiat. Assn., 1972; plaque recognizing establishment of chair in chem. immunology Weizmann Inst., 1974, Jane Addams Public Service award Hull House, 1977, Health Achievement award Nat. Kidney Found., 1978, Nat. award Epilepsy Found. Am., 1978, James Ewing Layman's award Soc. Surg. Oncologists, 1979, citation for disting. service AMA, 1979, Thomas More medal Thomas More Assn., 1979, NEA award, 1979, Margaret Sanger award, 1979, Stanley G. Kay medal Am. Cancer Soc., 1983, 1st William C. Menninger medal for achievement in mental health, 1984, Albert Lasker pub. service award, 1985, Edwin C. Whitehead award, 1988, Community Svc. award Gateway Found.'s Citizen's Coun., 1989, Pub. Svc. award NIMH, 1989, award for outstanding pub. edn. Nat. Alliance for the Mentally Ill, 1990. Fellow Chgo. Gynecol. Soc. (citizen hon.); mem. LWV (pres. 1948), Brandeis U. Women (pres. 1960). Clubs: Chgo. Econs. (dir. 1975), Harvard, Sigma Delta Chi. Office: Chgo Tribune 435 N Michigan Ave Chicago IL 60611

LANDERS, SUSAN MAE, sales representative; b. Houston; d. James Edward and Frances Pauline (Braunagel) L. BS in Advt., U. Tex.; postgrad., U. Houston; cert. in sales, Dale Carnegie Inst. Mktg. rep. K.C. Products, Houston, 1981-83; account exec. Williamson County Express, Austin, Tex., 1984, Sasser Outdoor Display, Austin, 1985; advt. cons. Stas. KMMM/KOKE, Austin, 1985; key account sales rep. GranTree Furniture Rental, Austin, 1986-89. Mem. NAFE. Home: 9000 Fondren #216 Houston TX 77074

LANDERS, VERNETTE TROSPER, educator, author; b. Lawton, Okla., May 3, 1912; d. Fred Gilbert and LaVerne Hamilton (Stevens) Trosper; m. Paul Albert Lum, Aug. 29, 1952 (dec. May 1955); 1 child, William Tappan; m. 2d, Newlin Landers, May 2, 1959; children: Lawrence, Marlin. AB with honors, UCLA, 1933, MA, 1935, EdD, 1953; Cultural doctorate (hon.) Lit. World U., Tucson, 1985. Tchr. secondary schs., Montebello, Calif., 1935-45, 48-50, 51-59; prof. Long Beach City Coll., 1946-47; asst. prof. Los Angeles State Coll., 1950; dean girls Twenty Nine Palms (Calif.) High Sch., 1960-65; dist. counselor Morongo (Calif.) Unified Sch. Dist., 1965-72, coordinator adult edn., 1965-67, guidance project dir., 1967; clk.-in-charge Landers (Calif.) Post Office, 1962-82; ret., 1982. V.p., sec. Landers Assn., 1965—; sec. Landers Vol. Fire Dept., 1972—; life mem. Hi-Desert Playhouse Guild, Hi-Desert Meml. Hosp. Guild; bd. friends Copper Mountain Coll., 1990—; bd. dirs., sec. Desert Emergency Radio Service; mem. Rep. Senatorial Inner Circle, 1990, Regent Nat. Fedn. Rep. Women, 1990, Nat. Rep. Congl. Com., 1990, Presdl. Task Force, 1990. Recipient internat. diploma of honor for community service, 1973; Creativity award Internat. Personnel Research Assn., 1972, award Goat Mt. Grange No. 818, 1987; cert. of merit for disting. svc. to edn., 1973; Order of Rose, 1978, Order of Pearl, 1989, Alpha Xi Delta ; poet laureate Center of Internat. Studies and Exchanges, 1981; diploma of merit in letters U. Arts, Parma, Italy, 1982; Golden Yr. Bruin UCLA, 1983; World Culture prize Nat. Ctr. for Studies and Research, Italian Acad., 1984; Golden Palm Diploma of Honor in poetry Leonardo Da Vinci Acad., 1984; Diploma of Merit and titular mem. internat. com. Internat. Ctr. Studies and Exchanges, Rome, 1984; Recognition award San Gorgonio council Girl Scouts U.S., 1984-90; Cert. of appreciation Morongo Unified Sch. Dist., 1984, 89; plaque for contribution to postal service and community U.S. Postal Service, 1984; Biographee of Yr. award for outstanding achievement in the field of edn. and service to community Hist. Preservations of Am.; named Princess of Poetry of Internat. Ctr. Cultural Studies and Exchange, Italy, 1985; community dinner held in her honor for achievement and service to Community, 1984; Star of Contemporary Poetry Masters of Contemporary Poetry, Internat. Ctr. Cultural Studies and Exchanges, Italy, 1984; named to honor list of leaders of contemporary art and lit. and apptd. titular mem. of Internat. High Com. for World Culture & Arts Leonardo Da Vinci Acad., 1987; ABI medal of honor 1987; other awards and certs. Life fellow Internat. Acad. Poets, World Lit. Acad.; mem. Am. Personnel and Guidance Assn., Internat. Platform Assn., Nat. Ret. Tchrs. Assn., Calif. Assn. for Counseling and Devel., Am. Biog. Research Assn. (life dep. gov.), Internat. Biog. Ctr. Eng. (dep. dir. gen. of the Ams. 1987), Nat. Assn. Women Deans and Adminstrs., Montebello Bus. and Profl. Women's Club (pres.), Nat. League Am. Pen Women (sec. 1985-86), Leonardo Da Vinci Acad. Internat. Winged Glory diploma of honor in letters 1982), Landers Area C. of C. (sec. 1985-86, Presdl. award for outstanding service), Desert Nature Mus., Phi Beta Kappa. Clubs: Whitter Toastmistress (Calif.) (pres. 1957); Homestead Valley Women's (Landers). Lodge: Soroptimists (sec. 29 Palms chpt. 1962, life mem., Soroptimist of Yr. local chpt. 19, Woman of Distinction local chpt. 1987-88). Author: Impy, 1974, Talkie, 1975, Impy's Children, 1975; Nineteen O Four, 1976, Little Brown Bat, 1976; Slo-Go, 1977; Owls Who and Who Who, 1978; Sandy, The Coydog, 1979; The Kit Fox and the Walking Stick, 1980; contbr. articles to profl. jours., poems to anthologies. Guest of honor ground breaking ceremony Landers Elem. Sch., 1989. Home: 632 Landers Ln PO Box 3839 Landers CA 92285

LANDGRAF, SUSAN MANNING, marketing manager; b. Detroit, Nov. 16, 1961; d. Donald Richard and Lou Ann (Sempsrote) L. BA, DePauw U., 1983; MBA, DePaul U., 1988. Supr. customer svc. dept. John Nuveen & Co., Inc., Chgo., 1983-85; spl. cashier Midwest Securities Trust Co., Chgo., 1985-86; ops. coord. Mortgage Backed Securities Clearing Corp., Chgo., 1986-89; mktg. mgr. Chgo. Bd. Trade, 1989—. Mem. Alpha Phi Internat. Sorority (Pinckley scholar 1982). Republican. Roman Catholic. Home: 2336 N Commonwealth #207 Chicago IL 60614 Office: Chgo Bd of Trade LaSalle St at Jackson Ste 2280 Chicago IL 60604

LANDMAN, BETTE EMELINE, academic administrator; b. Piqua, Ohio, July 18, 1937; d. Wilson Richard and Lois (Wilson) L. BS, Bowling Green State U., 1959; MA, Ohio State U., 1961, PhD, 1972. From instr. to asst. prof. anthropology Springfield (Mass.) Coll., 1962-67; asst. prof. Temple U., 1967-71; asst. prof. anthropology Beaver Coll., Glenside, Pa., 1971-76, dean, 1976-85, v.p. acad. affairs, 1980-85, acting pres., 1982-83, 85, pres., 1985—. Bd. dirs. Abington Meml. Hosp., Pa., 1986—; chair higher edn. com., blood donor campaign ARC Blood Svcs., Pa. and N.J. area, 1989—. Recipient Disting. Teaching award Christian R. and Mary F. Lindback Found., 1973; NSF fellow, 1961-63, Wenner-Glen Found. for Anthrop. Research fellow, 1965-66. Mem. Am. Coun. on Edn. (state coord. 1980-84, commn. on leadership devel. 1989—), Assn. Am. Coll. (bd. dirs. 1986—, v.p. 1989-90, pres. 1990—), Assn. Presbyn. Colls. and Univs. (exec. com. 1988—, sec. 1989-90, v.p. 1990—), Commn. for Ind. Colls. and Univs. (2d v.p. 1990—), Pa. Pres's. Ind. Colls. and Univs., Sigma Xi. Office: Beaver Coll Church & Easton Rds Glenside PA 19038

LANDOLFI, JENNIE L., nursing educator, critical care nurse; b. Warren, Ohio, Apr. 19, 1955; d. Gregory A. and Antoinette (Cervone) Landolfi. Student, Kent State U.; paramedic cert., Brentwood Hosp., Warrensville, Ohio; diploma Sch. of Nursing, Trumbull Meml. Hosp. RN, Ohio; cert. emergency nurse, ACLS provider and instr., BLS instr., prehospital trauma life support provider, instr. and coord., Ohio. Staff nurse Trumbull Meml. Hosp., Warren, 1978-82, charge nurse, 1982, coord. emergency med. svc. edn., 1986—; coord. emergency med. svc. Kettering (Ohio) Med. Ctr., 1982-83; staff nurse Warren Gen. Hosp., 1984-86; home health care nurse Nurses House Call, Warren, 1987—. Contbr. articles to publs. 1st Responder com. chair Trumbull County AIDS Task Force; mem. Trumbull County Local Emergency Planning Com., County Fire Chiefs Assn., Joint Com. Emergency Med. Svc., Prehospital Trauma Life Support. Mem. Ohio Assn. Emergency Med. Svcs., Nat. Assn. Emergency Med. Technicians, Emergency Nurses Assn. Democrat. Roman Catholic. Home: 114 Morningside Dr Niles OH 44446-2112 Office: 1350 E Market St Warren OH 44482

LANDOVSKY, ROSEMARY REID, director figure skating school, coach; b. Chgo., July 26, 1933; d. Samuel Stuart and Audrey Todd (Lyons) Reid; m. John Indulis Landovsky, Feb. 20, 1960; children: David John, Linette. BA in Psychology, Colo. Coll., 1956. Profl. skater Holiday on Ice Touring Show, U.S., Mex., Cuba, 1956-58; skating dir. and coach Paradice Arena, Birmingham, 1958-62, Les Patineurs, Huntsville, Ala., 1960-62; coach competitive (Ice Skating Inst. Am., U.S. Figure Skating Assn.) Michael Kirby and Assocs., River Forest, Chgo., Ill., 1962-63; rink mgr., skating dir. Lake Meadows Ice Arena, Chgo., 1963-68; coach (ISIA, USFSA) Rainbo Arena, Chgo., 1968-73; skating dir. Northwestern U. Skating Sch., Evanston, Ill., 1968-73, Robert Crown Ice Ctr., Evanston, 1973-75; dir. instl. programs Skokie (Ill.) Park Dist., 1975-87; competition dir. ISIA All America Competition, 1985-86. Dir., producer, choreographer Ice Show: Nutcracker Ballet, 1973, Ice Extravaganza III, 1985, Ice Lights '86, '87. Election judge, worker, Ind. Dems., Chgo., 1964-68. Mem. Profl. Skaters Guild, Ice Skating Inst. Am., Coll. Coll. Alumni Assn. (mem. Chgo. area com.), Gamma Phi Beta. Office: Skokie Skatium 9300 Bronx Skokie IL 60077

LANDRAM, CHRISTINA LOUELLA, librarian; b. Paragould, Ark., Dec. 10, 1922; d. James Ralph and Bertie Louella (Jordan) Oliver; m. Robert Ellis Landram, Aug. 7, 1948; 1 child, Mark Owen. BA, Tex. Woman's U., 1945, B.L.S., 1946, M.L.S., 1951. Preliminary cataloger Library of Congress, Washington, 1946-48; cataloger U.S. Info. Ctr., Tokyo, Japan, 1948-50, U.S. Dept. Agr., Washington, 1953-54; librarian Yokota AFB, Yokota, Japan, 1954-55; librarian St. Mary's Hosp., West Palm Beach, Fla., 1957-59; librarian Jacksonville (Ark.) High Sch., 1959-61; coord. Shelby County Libraries, Memphis, 1961-63; head catalog dept. Ga. State U. Library, 1963-86, librarian, assoc. prof. emeritus, 1986—. Contbr. articles to library jours. Mem. Ga. Library Assn. (chmn. resources and tech. services sect. 1969-71), Metro-Atlanta Library Assn. (pres. 1967-68), ALA (chmn. cataloging norms 1979-80, nominating com. 1977-78), Southeastern Library Assn. (mem. govtl. rels. com. 1975-78, intellectual freedom com. 1984-86, mem. Rothrock awards com. 1987—). Presbyterian. Home: 1478 Leafmore Ridge Decatur GA 30033

LANDRIEU, MARY, state treasurer; b. Nov. 23, 1955; m. E. Frank Snellings. BA, La. State U. Real estate agt., La. state rep. from dist. 90, 1979-89, La. state treas., 1987—; del., Dem. Nat. Conv., 1980. Mem. LWV, Women Execs. in State Govt., Fedn. Dem. Women, Delta Gamma. Roman Catholic. Office: Treasury Dept PO Box 44154 Baton Rouge LA 70804*

LANDRIGAN, PENELOPE SAVAGE, museum executive; b. Indpls., Oct. 14, 1939; d. Bruce Charles and Marabeth (Thomas) Savage; m. Richard Landrigan (dec.), Nov. 12, 1960; children: George Bruce, Sarah Anne. Student, Northwestern U., 1957-59, The Tudor Hall Sch., Indpls., 1957. Bd. dirs. Savage Landrigan Inc. Realtors, Indpls., 1975-84; personnel asst. Indpls. Mus. Art, 1983—. Sustain mem. Aux. Children's Bur., Indpls. 1960—, form. com. Learning Disabilities Coun., del. Nat. Child Welfare Conf., Pitts. 1969, Jr. League Indpls., 1969-74, Juvenile Diabetes, Pub. TV, United Way; vol. Am. Cancer Soc., Meridian Ind. Bloom Tour. Mem. NAFE, Am. Assn. Mus., Park-Tudor Alumni Assn., Nat. Wildlife Fedn., Chili, Chowder and Spaghetti Literary Soc., Kappa Kappa Gamma. Republican. Episcopalian. Home: 7434 King George Dr Indianapolis IN 46260 Office: Indianapolis Mus of Art 1200 W 38th St Indianapolis IN 46208

LANDRUM-BRUMMUND, FRANCES ANN, choreographer, dance instructor; b. N.Y.C., Apr. 5, 1918; d. Edmond Charles and Mary Elizabeth (Lannon) Lourie; student Vestoff-Serova Sch. of Dance, 1927-35, Tarasoff Sch. of Dance, 1929-31, Martha Graham Sch. Dance, 1935-36; m. Theodore Wayne Brummund, July 27, 1979; children by previous marriage: Elizabeth Ann Phelps, Robert Bascom Landrum II. Ballet dancer Russian Opera Co., 1930, Lee Schubert Prodns., 1931; soloist Corps de Ballet, Radio City Music Hall, N.Y.C., 1933-42; founder, owner, dir. Landrum Sch. of Dance, N.Y.C., 1948-80; active Old Island Restoration Soc., 1987—, founder Young People's Dance Group of L.I., 1964—; artistic dir. Ballet Repertory of L.I.; producer R.K.O. Keith's Flushing Theatre, 1960-80, also Andre Eglevsky Ballet Co. Active, Concerned Citizens for the Arts.; pres. DePoo Hosp. Sunshine Aux., 1986-88, dir. 1988—. Recipient merit award N.Y. State Commn. on World's Fair, 1964. Mem. Am. Assn. Dance Cos. (charter), N.Y. Dance Alliance, Marathon Garden Club (Florida Keys), Key West Garden Club, Key West Women's Club, Beta Sigma Phi. Presbyterian.

LANDRY, ELAINE G., educator; b. Brattleboro, Vt., July 23, 1943; d. Lester and Linda Lydia (Hiiva) Georgina; m. Lyn Edward Landry, Feb. 22, 1942; children: Jill Elizabeth, Scott Andrew, Karen Alicia. BEd, Keene State Coll., N.H., 1966. Tchr. Keene (N.H.) High Sch., 1966-69, tchr. English, 1978—; adult tutor Cheshire County Tutorial Adult Tutorial Prog., 1976. Active various charitable orgns. in past. Nat. Endowment for Humanities grantee, 1987. Mem. Keene Edn. Assn., N.H. Edn. Assn., NEA, Nat. Council Tchrs. English, Delta Kappa Gamma. Democrat.

LANDRY, KAREN EREMIN, hospital administrator; b. Queens, N.Y., June 2, 1959; d. Alan Noel and Kathleen Ellen (Finn) Eremin; m. Michael Joe Landry, June 25, 1983; children: Elizabeth Kathleen, Julianne Alexandra. BA, St. Lawrence U., 1981; MBA, Northwestern U., Evanston, Ill., 1983. Grad. fellow Rush-Presbyn. St. Luke's Med. Ctr., Chgo., 1983-84; assoc., cons. APM, Inc., mgmt. cons., N.Y.C., 1984-85; performance cons. Empire Blue Cross & Blue Shield, Albany, N.Y., 1985-86; project specialist Empire Blue Cross & Blue Shield, Albany, N.Y., 1986—, dir. mktg. support, 1987—; dir. planning St. Mary's Hosp., Troy, N.Y., 1988—; adj. prof. Union U. Grad. Inst., Schenectady. Mem. Health Care Mgrs. Assn. Northeastern N.Y., Phi Beta Kappa. Democrat. Roman Catholic. Home: 11 Putnam St Troy NY 12180 Office: St Mary's Hosp 1300 Massachusetts Ave Troy NY 12180

LANDRY, MONIQUE, Canadian government official; b. Montreal, Que., Can., Dec. 25, 1937; m. Jean-Guy Landry; four children. Grad., U. Montreal. With Montreal Children's Hosp.; mem. parliament Govt. Can., 1984—; former parliamentary sec. to Sec. of State and Minister of Internat. Trade; Minister of State for External Relations Govt. Can., 1986—; former mem. Standing Com. on Communications and Culture, Joint Com. on Ofcl. Langs. Policy and Programs, Standing Com. on Fin., Trade and Econ. Affairs, Cabinet Coms. on Fgn. and Def. Policy, Legis. and House Planning; alt. mem. Treas. Bd. Com.; v.p., co-founder Cordevin Internat., 1981—. Named Woman of the Yr. Montreal Salon de la femme, 1988. Mem. Can.-Europe, Can.-NATO Parliament Assns., Can.-France Inter-Parliament Assn., Que. Arthritis Soc. (pres. 1988—). Office: Ministry External Rels, Internat Devel, Hull, PQ Canada K1A 0G4*

LANDSKE, DOROTHY SUZANNE, state senator; b. Evanston, Ill., Sept. 3, 1937; d. William Gerald and Dorothy Marie (Drewes) Martin; m. William Steve Landske, June 1, 1957; children: Catherine Suzanne, Jacqueline Marie Basilotta, Pamela Florence Snyder, Cheryl Lynn Boisson, Eric Thomas. Student St. Joseph's Coll., Ind. U., U. Chgo. Receptionist Cedar Lake Med. Clinic (Ind.) 1959-62; owner, operator Sues Bridal House, 1967-75; dep. clk.-treas., Cedar Lake, 1975; chief dep. twp. assessor Center Twp., Crown Point, Ind., 1976-78, twp. assessor, 1979-84, mem. Ind. Senate, 1984—, majority whip. Vice-chmn. Lake County Rep. Cen. Com., 1978-89. Mem. Council State Govts., Nat. Order Women Legislators, Nat. Council State Legislators, Bus. and Profl. Women, League Women Voters, Grange Ind. Farm Bur. Roman Catholic.

LANE, ANDREA NEAL, auditor; b. N.Y.C., Jan. 18, 1957; d. Donald and Julie (Neal) Lane. BSFS, Georgetown U., 1978, postgrad., 1979-81. Asst. fin. advisor Sanford C. Bernstein & Co., Inc., N.Y.C., 1983-85; office mgr., acct. Don Lane Pictures, N.Y.C., 1985-86; accts. receivable mgr. AVR Mgmt. Inc., Yonkers, N.Y., 1986-88; auditor John F. Davie Co., Maspeth, N.Y., 1988—. Mem. Am. Massage Therapy Assn., Nat. Assn. Female Execs. Democrat. Home: 135 Rosedale Ave Hastings-on-Hudson NY 10706 Office: John F Davie Co 57-57 63d St Maspeth NY 10591

LANE, ANN JUDITH, history educator; b. N.Y.C., July 27, 1931; d. Harry A. and Elizabeth (Brown) Lane; children: Leslie Patricia, Joni Alexandra. BA, Bklyn. Coll., 1952; MA, NYU, 1958; PhD, Columbia U., 1968. Mng. editor Challenge Mag., N.Y.C., 1953-56; asst. prof. Douglass Coll., Rutgers U., New Brunswick, N.J., 1968-71; assoc. prof. CUNY, 1971-83; vis. prof. Wheaton Coll., Norton, Mass., 1981-82; prof. history, dir. women's studies Colgate U., Hamilton, N.Y., 1983-90, U. Va., Charlottesville, 1990—. Author: To Her Land and Beyond, 1990, Mary Ritter Beard: A Soucrsbook, 1977, 2d edit. 1988; editor: Charlotte Perking Gilman Reader, 1980, Herland: A Lost Utopian Novel, 1979; author: The Brownsville Affair, 1971. Dir. History Tchr. Inst., N.Y. Coun. for Humanities, summer 1985; mem. historians adv. com. Nat. Women's Hall of Fame, 1986—; bd. dirs. Louis M. Rabinowitz Found., 1972-76. Fellow, Berkshire Conf. Women Historians, 1988, Ford Found., 1981-82, Nat. Endowment for Humanities, 1980-81, Lilly Endowment, Inc., 1977-79, AAUW, 1959-60. Mem. AAUP (mem. com. on women 1987—), Orgn. Am. Historians (mem. Frederick Jackson Turner prize com. 1979), Women in Hist. Profession (exec. bd., coordinating com. 1971-74). Home: 2603 Jefferson Park Circle Charlottesville VA 22903

LANE, CONSTANCE CARMICHAEL RENICK, educational administrator; b. Rockford, Ill., Nov. 9, 1921; d. James Alexander and Nozella (Oda) Carmichael; m. Andrew J. Lane, June 20, 1964; children: Betty Anne Renick (Mrs. Flynn Jefferson), James Renick. BS in Edn. magna cum laude, W.Va. State Coll., 1943; MA, Northwestern U., 1962. Tchr., Rockford Pub. Schs., 1954-62, helping tchr. elementary math., 1962-63; prin. Henrietta Primary and Intermediate Schs., Rockford, 1963-66; prin. W. Ray McIntosh Sch., Rockford, 1966—; Area IV coordinator Rockford Pub. Schs., after 1971, asst. supt. elem. edn., 1979-85, spl. asst. to supt., 1989—; part-time instr. Rockford Coll., evenings 1964-79. Mem. Taus, Inc. (pres. 1960-63, 74-78, treas. 1972-74), Ill., Rockford edn. assns., NEA, AAUW, Nat. Council Tchrs. Math., Assn. Supervision and Curriculum Devel., Rockford Prins. Assn., Nat. Elementary Prins. Assn., Kiwanis Alpha Kappa Alpha, Delta Kappa Gamma, Phi Delta Kappa. Episcopalian. Contbr. articles to profl. jours. Home: 2224 Clover Ave Rockford IL 61102 Office: Rockford Bd Edn 201 S Madison St Rockford IL 61101

LANE, GLORIA JULIAN, foundation administrator; b. Chgo., Oct. 6, 1932; d. Coy Berry and Katherine (McDowell) Julian; m. William Gordon Lane (div. Oct. 1958); 1 child, Julie Kay Rosewood. BS in Edn., Cen. Mo. State U., 1958; MA, Bowling Green State U., 1959; PhD, No. Ill. U., 1972. Cert. tchr. Assoc. prof. William Jewell Coll., Liberty, Mo., 1959-60; chair forensic div. Coral Gables (Fla.) High Sch., 1960-64; assoc. prof. No. Ill. U., DeKalb, 1964-70; prof. Elgin (Ill.) Community Coll., 1970-72; owner, pub. Lane and Assocs, Inc., San Diego, 1972-78; prof. Nat. U., San Diego, 1978-90; pres., chief exec. officer Women's Internat. Ctr., San Diego, 1982—; founder, dir. Living Legacy Awards, San Diego, 1984—. Author: Project Text for Effective Communications, 1972, Project Text for Executive Communication, 1980, Positive Concepts for Success, 1983; editor Who's Who Among San Diego Women, 1984, 85, 86, 90—, Systems and Structure, 1984. Named Woman of Accomplishment, Soroptimist Internat., 1985, Pres.'s Coun. San Diego, 1986, Center City Assn., 1986, Woman of Yr., Girls' Clubs San Diego, 1986, Woman of Vision, Women's Internat. Ctr., 1990; recipient Independence award Ctr. for Disabled, 1986. Home and Office: 6202 Friars Rd 311 San Diego CA 92108

LANE, IRIS MARY, teacher; b. Kellogg, Idaho, June 24, 1934; d. Ivan John and Dorothy Vivian (McKinney) Green; m. C. Clayton, Dec. 19, 1959 (div. 1962); 1 child, Mark Andrew. AA, N. Idaho Jr. Coll., 1955; BS, U. Idaho, Moscow, 1964; postgrad., Whitworth Coll., Spokane, 1967, Eastern Wash. U., Cheney, 1967. Tchr. Sch. Dist. #391, Kellogg, Idaho, 1955-57, Sch. Dist. #81, Spokane, Wash., 1958-89; master tchr. Local Colls., Spokane, 1962-85. Supporter Republican Party, Spokane, 1958-89; Vol. Am. Heart Assn., Spokane, 1988-89, orphan and foster children assns., iliteracy improvement programs; Fin. Supporter Local Food Bank, Spokane, 1975-89, Local Goodwill, Spokane, 1975-89, United Crusade, Spokane, 1970-89.

Recipient Golden Acorn award Garfield Parent Tchrs. Assn., Spokane, 1978. Mem. Spokane Edn. Assn., Wash. Edn. Assn., Nat. Edn. Assn., Parent Tchr. Assn., Alpha Delta Kappa Honorary, Alpha Delta Kappa. Republican. Lutheran. Home: 3405 W Francis Spokane WA 99205

LANE, JANET ANN, accountant; b. Fort Campbell, Ky., May 14, 1959; d. Charles David and Carolyn Ann (Henderson) Barney; m. Richard Edward Lane, Oct. 3, 1982; children: Matthew Richard, Amy Sarah. BS in Acctg., Bentley Coll., 1981. Cert. Mgmt. Acct. Constrn. cost analyst Riley Stoker Corp., Worcester, Mass., 1981-82; mgr. contract acctg. Riley Stoker Corp., Worcester, 1982, sr. acct., 1982-83; mgr. contract acctg. Riley Consol., Inc., Worcester, 1983-88, project coord., 1988—. Mem. Nat. Assn. Accts. Home: 436 S Meadow Rd Lancaster MA 01523 Office: Riley Consol Inc Box 15040 Worcester MA 01615-0040

LANE, JEANNIE MAE, graduate school administrator; b. Charleston, Miss., Jan. 20, 1959; d. Perry Joe and Mary Yvonne (Pollan) Lane. BS in Edn., Miss. Coll., 1981, MEd, 1987, postgrad., 1989. Cert. secondary tchr., Miss. Student asst. Miss. Coll. libr., Clinton, 1977-78; clk. Gibson's Discount Store, Grenada, Miss., summer 1978; student asst. Miss. Coll. grad. sch., Clinton, 1978-81, sec., 1981-83, asst. to v.p. for grad. and spl. programs, 1983--; test ctr. supr. Nat. Tchr's. Exam., Grad. Record Exam., Clinton, 1988--. Bd. dirs. Arts Coun. of Clinton, Inc., 1985—, newsletter editor, 1987—, v.p. membership, 1989; tchr. Sunday Sch. 1st Bapt. Ch., Clinton, 1986-88, libr. media worker, 1989—. Mem. AAUW (v.p. Clinton chpt. 1986-87), Miss. Assn. Women in Higher Edn., Miss. Staff Club (hospitality chmn. 1986-87, sec. 1988-89), Olde Towne Civitan. Republican. Office: Miss Coll Grad Sch PO Box 4185 200 W College Clinton MS 39058

LANE, JULIA A., nursing educator; b. Chgo., June 29, 1927; d. James and Julia (Ivins) L. BSN, DePaul U., 1956; MSN, Cath. U. Am., 1961; PhD, Loyola U., Chgo., 1974. Cert. midwife. Staff nurse St. Joseph Hosp., 1954-55, Chgo. Bd. of Health, 1955-57; instr. South Chgo. Hosp. Sch. Nursing, 1957-58, dir. edn., 1960-63; assoc. prof. Loyola U. Sch. Nursing, 1963-74, dean, 1974—. Home: 300 N State #4532 Chicago IL 60610 Office: Loyola U Marcella Nehoff Sch Nursing 6525 N Sheridan Rd Chicago IL 60626

LANE, KATHLEEN MARGARET, optical company administrator; b. Mpls., Oct. 25, 1946; d. Bernard Melvin and Margaret (Beck) Aanerud; m. Kenneth LeRoy Lane, Sept. 1, 1979; 1 child, Dennis Leon. Cost acct. Honeywell, Mpls., 1964-66; bank bookkeeper Columbia Heights State Bank, Minn., 1968-71; inventory control mgr. Hodes Optical Inc., Torrance, Calif., 1972-75, office mgr., 1975-79; lens supr. Coburn Optical Industries, Inc., Carson, Calif., 1979-85, br. mgr., St. Paul, 1985; customer rels. Opti Fair, Aneheim, Calif., 1978-83. Mem. Am. Inst. Banking, NAFE. Avocations: restoring old furniture, camping, knitting. Office: Coburn Optical Industries Inc 1375 Wolters Blvd Ste 110 Vadnais Heights MN 55110

LANE, MARGARET BEYNON TAYLOR, librarian; b. St. Louis, Feb. 6, 1919; d. Archer and Alice (Jones) Taylor; B.A., La. State U., 1939, J.D., 1942; B.S. in Library Sci., Columbia U., 1941; m. Horace C. Lane, Jan. 6, 1945; children—Margaret Elizabeth, Thomas Archer. Reference and circulation asst. Columbia Law Library, N.Y.C., 1942-44; law librarian, asst. prof. U. Conn. Sch. Law, Hartford, 1944-46; law librarian La. State U. Law Sch., Baton Rouge, 1946-48; recorder documents La. Sec. of State's Office, Baton Rouge, 1949-75; law librarian Lane Fertitta, Lane & Tullos, 1976—. Author: State Publications and Depository Libraries, 1981, Selecting And Organizing State Government Publications, 1987. Mem. depository library council to Pub. Printer, 1972-77; mem. plan devel. com. La. Fed. Depository Library, 1982-83. Treas. Delta Iota House Bd. of Kappa Kappa Gamma, 1965-68. Inducted into La. State U. Law Ctr. Hall of Fame, 1987. Mem. ALA (interdivisional com. public documents 1967-74, chmn. 1967-70; govt. documents round table, state and local documents task force 1972—, coordinator 1980-82; James Bennett Childs award 1981), La. Library Assn. (Essae M. Culver Disting. Service award 1976; chmn. documents com. 1982-83, Lucy B. Foote award subject specialist sect. 1986), La., Baton Rouge Bar Assns., Mortar Bd., Phi Delta Delta, Kappa Kappa Gamma. Club: Baton Rouge Library. Home: 7545 Richards Dr Baton Rouge LA 70809 Office: PO Box 3335 Baton Rouge LA 70821

LANE, MARIE IRENE, librarian; b. East Stroudsberg, Pa., Mar. 5, 1944; d. Robert Fulton and Margureite Irene (Melhin) Chamberlain; m. John Marcus Lane, Mar. 24, 1965; 1 child, Jennifer Marie. Student, U. Fla., 1962-64; BA, U. Hawaii, 1968, MLS, 1971. Asst. br. libr. Fairfax County (Va.) Pub. Libr., 1971-78; asst. libr. George Mason U. Sch. Law Libr., 1978-82; media specialist Fairfax Hosp., 1990. Vol. Camelot Nursing Home, Arlington, Va., 1984-90, Arlington Ministering to Emergency Meals, 1984-90, Hope Counseling for Women, Falls Church, Va., 1989-90; asst. ch. libr. Clarenton United Meth. Ch., Arlington, 1982-90; mem. libr. adv. com. Arlington Sch. Bd., 1987, adv. com. home econs., 1989-90. Recipient Scribner Sons award, N.Y., 1972. Mem. DAR, AAUW, Arlington Extension Home-Makers, Network Biblical Storytellers, Ch. Women United. Republican. Methodist. Home: 3730 N Pershing Dr Arlington VA 22203

LANE, MARION SUE, editor, writer; b. N.Y.C., Sept. 16, 1944; d. Burton Russell and Lillian Marie (Reilly) Ln. AB, Harpur Coll., 1965. Asst. to pres. Rockefeller Found., N.Y.C., 1975-80; adminstrv. asst. Am. Kennel Club, N.Y.C., 1981-85, exec. editor, 1986—. Editor: Pure-Bred Dogs/American Kennel Gazette, 1986— (Best All Breed mag. 1989, 90); contbr. articles to profl. jours. Mem. Dog Writers Assn. Am. (bd. of govs. 1990—), People for the Ethical Treatment of Animals, Dog Fanciers Club. Home: 35-15 Leverich St #409 Jackson Heights NY 11372 Office: Am Kennel Club 51 Madison Ave New York NY 10010

LANE, MARY FRANCES, physical education specialist; b. Lakeland, Fla., Jan. 25, 1955; d. Steve Joseph and Dorothy Jean (Giamaresi) Forgach; m. Charles Edwin Lane Jr., June 23, 1984. AA, U. South Fla., 1975; BS magna cum laude, U. Fla., 1977, MA in Phys. Edn., 1978. Cert. tchr., Fla. Phys. edn. tchr. Pinellas Cen./Walsingham Sch., Pinellas County, Fla., 1978-80, Wekiva Elem. Sch., Seminole County, Fla., 1983-84, Spring Lake Elem. Sch., Seminole County, 1984-87; adapted phys. edn. tchr. Walsingham Elem. Sch., Pinellas County, 1980-83; adaptive phys. edn. specialist Seminole County Sch. Bd., Sanford, Fla., 1987—; speaker, lectr. to edn. and healthcare orgns.; cons. summer inst., Fla. Dept. Edn., Tallahassee, 1985, 90; tng. chair, Spl. Olympics, Sanford, 1987—. Author curriculum materials; contbr. articles to profl. jours. Mem. Morton F. Plant Hosp. Found., Clearwater, Fla., 1980-83. Grantee, Found. for Advancement of Community Through Schs., Seminole County, 1989, grantee Internat. Spl. Olympics, 1989. Mem. Coun. Exceptional Children, Fla. Assn. Health, Phys. Edn., Recreation and Dance (bd. dirs., treas. 1979-82, chair 1985-88), Phi Kappa Phi. Republican. Roman Catholic. Office: Seminole County Schs 1096 North St Altamonte Springs FL 32701

LANE, MARY HILL, personnel executive; b. Concord, N.C., Feb. 13, 1943; d. Cletus DeBerry and Buena Elizabeth (Winecoff) Hatley; m. James Wyles Peeples, Dec. 30, 1964 (div. 1977); children: James D., Emily Ann; m. John Edward Lane, Dec. 16, 1988. Student, Converse Coll., 1961-63; BA, U. N.C., 1964; MEd, Winthrop Coll., Rock Hill, S.C., 1980. Math. tchr. various high sch., Oreg., N.C., 1964-67, Cen. Piedmont Community Coll., 1968-70; math tchr. Fayetteville (N.C.) Acad., 1975-76; math tchr. Carmel Acad., Charlotte, N.C., 1976-77, chmn. dept. math, 1977-79; prin. upper sch. Carmel Acad.-Charlotte Country Day Sch., 1979-80; acct., analyst NCNB Corp., Charlotte, 1980-82, supr., CPA control div., 1982-84, mgr. trust adminstrn. svcs., 1984-85, mgr. compensation and relocation, 1985—. Mem. Charlotte adv. com. City of Charlotte, 1988-89; elder Good Shepherd Presbyn. Ch., Charlotte, 1985-89. Mem. Am. Mgmt. Assn., Am. Compensation Assn., Toastmasters (chpt. pres. 1986), Windyrush Country Club, Wessex Sq. Homeowners Assn., Phi Kappa Phi. Home: 4801 Deanscroft Dr Charlotte NC 28226 Office: NCNB 1 NCNB Plaza T12-3 Charlotte NC 28255

LANE, NANCY LEE, health products executive; b. Boston, Sept. 3, 1938; d. Samuel M. and Gladys (Pitkins) Lane. Student U. Oslo, 1961; BS, Boston U., 1962; MPA, U. Pitts. Grad. Sch. Pub. and Internat. Affairs, 1967; cert. program for mgmt. devel. Harvard U. Grad. Sch. Bus. Adminstrn., 1975. Project mgr. Westinghouse Broadcasting Co., 1964-66; dep. dir. personnel Nat. Urban League, N.Y.C., 1967-72; 2d v.p. Chase Manhattan Bank, N.Y.C., 1972-73; v.p. personnel Off Track Betting Corp., N.Y.C., 1973-75; v.p. personnel and adminstrn., dir. Ortho-Diagnostic Systems, Inc., Raritan, N.J., 1976-88; corp. affairs dir. world hdqrs. Johnson & Johnson, New Brunswick, N.J., 1988—. Chair bd. trustees Bennett Coll.; trustee Rutgers U. Recipient Disting. Alumni award Boston U. Coll. Communication, 1987. Mem. Harvard Bus. Sch. Club of Greater N.Y. Inc. (pres. 1990—). Home: 37 W 12th St New York NY 10011 Office: Johnson & Johnson World Hdqrs New Brunswick NJ 08933

LANE, PATRICIA LOUISE, nursing educator; b. Houston, Mar. 3, 1950; d. Harland Richard Lane and Elsie Agnes Puttman. BSN, U. Tex., 1972; MSN, Med. Coll. Ga., 1979; PhD, U. Tex., 1986. Staff nurse Meth. Hosp., Houston, 1972-74; clinic nurse Haleiwa Med. Clinic, Haleiwa, Hawaii, 1975-76; staff nurse Med. Ctr., Columbus, Ga., 1976; instr. assoc. degree program Columbus Coll., 1976-79; asst. prof. baccalaureate nursing program La. State U. Med. Ctr., New Orleans, 1979-86; assoc. prof. grad. nursing program La. State U. Med. Ctr., 1987—; liaison mem. nursing rsch. com. Charity Hosp., New Orleans, 1987—; expert witness orthopaedic malpractice cases, La., 1983—. Author: Development of a Nursing Questionnaire, 1989, Nursing of Musculo-Skeletal Problems, 1990. Instr. basic life support Am. Heart Assn., New Orleans, 1981—. La. All-State scholar S. La. League Nursing, 1985. Mem. So. Nursing Rsch. Soc., Nat. Assn. Orthopaedic Nurses, Am. Nurses Assn., Sigma Theta Tau (pres. Epsilon Nu chpt. 1987-89). Office: La State U Med Ctr Sch Nursing 1900 Gravier St New Orleans LA 70112

LANE, SARAH MARIE, newspaper correspondent, writer; b. Conneaut, Ohio, July 27, 1946; d. Robert George and Julia Ellen (Sanford) Clark; m. Ralph Donaldson Lane, May 28, 1977; children: Richard, Laura. Student, Muskingum Coll., 1964-66; BS in Edn., Kent (Ohio) State U., 1977; MA in Edn., Coll. Mt. St. Joseph, 1988. Cert. tchr., Ohio. Columnist News Herald, Conneaut, 1963-64; tchr. 1st grade Mesopotamia (Ohio) Local Schs., 1968; chpt. one aide Maplewood Local Schs., Cortland, Ohio, 1983-85; corr. Warren (Ohio) Tribune Chronicle, 1986-89, coord. newspaper in edn., 1988-89; chpt. I/Reading Recovery tchr. Cortland (Ohio) Elem. Sch., 1989—; cons. newspaper-in-edn. Warren (Ohio) Tribune Chronicle, 1989—; adj. prof. Kent State U., Trumbull Campus, Warren, 1989—. Tutor MacArthur Found. Early Literacy Intervention, Warren, 1988-89. George Record scholar, 1964. Mem. Bazetta-Cortland His. Soc. (v.p.1984-87). Republican. Mem. Christian Ch. (Disciples of Christ). Home and Office: 298 Corriedale Dr Cortland OH 44410

LANE, SHARI LEA, distribution company executive; b. Carmel, Calif., Oct. 20, 1950; d. Joseph Reynolds and Joan Martha (McBride) McElrath Lane. B.A., U. Va.-Fairfax, 1972; postgrad., U. Phoenix, 1988—. Notary pub.; real estate broker; grad. Realtors Inst. Asst. dir. personnel Mayflower Hotel, Washington, 1972-73; personnel adminstr. PRC Planning Research Corp., McLean, Va., 1973-75; dir. sales 1928 Jewelry Co., Burbank, Calif., 1975-78; dir. new home sales Sterpa Realty Register, Glendale, Calif., 1978-82; nat. accounts mgr. Bekins Moving & Storage, Glendale, Calif., 1982-83; mgr. Internat. Sales adminstrn. Applause Inc., Woodland Hills, Calif., 1983-88; owner Flowers by Cina of Garden Grove (Calif.), 1988—; mgr. FTD Master Florist, 1989. Mem. Nat. Assn. Female Execs. (assoc.), Womens Assn. Realtors (sec. treas. 1980-82), Am. Telemktg. Assn., Garden Grove C. of C. (bd. dirs. 1989—). Republican. Episcopalian. Avocations: swimming (Ala. state champion 1966 breastroke); gourmet cooking; travel. Home: 14331 Ward St Garden Grove CA 92643

LANG, BARBARA ANN, educator; b. Bklyn., Sept. 19, 1950; d. Peter Luke and Anita (Falconite) Della Pietra; m. William Joseph Lang, Jan. 1952; children: Jonathan William, Jeanine Ann. BS cum laude, SUNY, Brockport, 1972; MLS, SUNY, Stony Brook, 1975. Cert. elem. tchr., in physical edn. Physical edn. tchr. Sachem Cen. Sch. Dist., Holbrook, N.Y., 1972-80, 84—; state official field hockey sect. XI Suffolk Bd. Women's Officials, Setauket, N.Y., 1972-80, state/nat. official volleyball, 1974-80, state/nat. official basketball, 1972-80, local official softball. Co-chairperson blood drives St. James (N.Y.) PTA, 1986—, chairperson Blue & Gold Dinner, Pack 228, Boy Scouts Am., St. James, 1988—; mem. citizen adv. com. Smithtown Sch. Dist. Roman Catholic. Home: 44 Hitherbrook Rd Saint James NY 11780

LANG, DEBBIE DAVIS, psychologist; b. Jersey City, N.J., Jan. 14, 1956; d. Melvin Ira and June (Streisand) Davis. BS, U. Vt., 1977; MA, Queens Coll., 1980; PhD, CUNY, 1986. Research asst. Queens Coll. CUNY, Flushing, N.Y., 1980-82, graduate fellowship in tching., 1982-83; research asst. Meml. Sloan-Kettering Cancer Ctr., N.Y., 1983-85; cons. Scarsdale (N.Y) Family Counseling, N.Y., 1988; pvt. practice psychologic counseling and family therapy N.Y., 1988-; pvt. practice psychologist Somers, N.Y., 1988-9089. Contbr several articles to prof. mags. Mem. Am. Psychologist Assn., Assn. for Advancement of Behavior Therapists, Phobia Soc. of Am. Jewish. Office: Somers Profl Pk PO Box 582 Somers NY 10589

LANG, DEBORAH ODOM, educator; b. Greenville, S.C., July 12, 1953; d. Melburn and Lila Mae Odom; m. William Steve Lang, July 29, 1978; children: Steven Mark, William Scott. MusB, Furman U., 1975, MA, 1977; MEd, U. Ga., 1984; EdS, Ga. So. Coll., 1989. Tchr. music Pickens County Schs., Easley, S.C., 1976-79; tchr. reading Ware Shoals (S.C.) Schs., 1979-81; tchr. George Walton Acad., Monroe, Ga., 1982-84, Pine St. Elem. Sch., Spartanburg, S.C., 1984-86, Tattnall Elem. Sch., Reidsville, Ga., 1986-89. Author: Tale of Little Bittle, 1987. Recipient scholarship music North Greenville Coll., 1972-73. Mem. Children's Lit. Conf. (hostess 1983), Internat. Reading Assn., Phi Delta Kappa (sec. 1988). Republican. Presbyterian. Home: 15 Wimbledon Ct Statesboro GA 30458

LANG, GLORIA HELEN, tool engineer; b. N.Y.C., Mar. 15, 1932; d. Michael and Elizebeth (Snyder) L.; student Kent State U., 1957-61, Youngstown State U., 1977; A.A., SUNY, 1982. Retail salesman, 1947-51; owner, operator tax service, Tampa, Fla., 1954-55; tool and die maker Gen. Motors Corp., Warren, Ohio, 1955—; tool and die apprentice Ohio State U., 1972-76; tooling engr., cutting tool cons., pres., chief exec. officer Lang Industries, Inc., Warren, 1977—; lectr. on females in modern machine trades. Served with U.S. Army, 1951-54. Mem. Nat. Assn. Female Execs., Nat. Tool, Die and Precision Machining Assn., Nat. Small Bus. Assn., NOW, Internat. Platform Assn., Am. Mgmt. Assn., Am. Soc. Bus. and Profl. Women, Am. Legion (past comdr. post 748 Warren). Home: 4793 Ardmore Ave Youngstown OH 44505 Office: Lang Industries Inc PO Box 8135 Youngstown OH 44505

LANG, JEAN MCKINNEY, editor, educator; b. Cherokee, Iowa, Nov. 6, 1921; d. Roy Clarence and Verna Harvey (Smith) McKinney; BS, Iowa State U., 1945; MA, Ohio State U., 1969; postgrad. U. South Fla., 1972; m. Thomas E. Greef; 1 dau., Barbara Jean Wilcox; step-children: Mary McDonald, Daniel A. Greef. Merchandiser, jewelry buyer Rike-Kumler Co., Dayton, Ohio, 1952-59, Met. Co., Dayton, 1959-64; tchr. DeVilbiss High Sch., Toledo, 1966-67; chmn. dept. retailing Webber Coll., Babson Park, Fla., 1967-72; asso. editor Wet Set Illustrated, 1972-75; sr. editor Pleasure Boating, Largo, Fla., 1975-84; tchr. bus. adminstrn. St. Petersburg (Fla.) Jr. Coll., 1974-88; editor Suncoast Woman, 1986-88. Mem. U.S. Senatorial Bus. Adv. Bd.; mem. Nat. Boating Safety Adv. Council, 1979-81; Recipient recognition Nat. Retail Mchts. Assn., 1971, certs. of appreciation U.S. Power Squadron, 1976, Webber Coll., 1972. Mem. AAUW, Fla. Women's Alliance, Greater Tampa C. of C., Tampa Aux. Power Squadron, USCG Aux., Sales and Mktg. Execs. of Tampa (pres.'s award 1973), Fla. Freelance Writers Assn., Am. Mktg. Assn., Gulf Coast Symphony, Internat. Platform Assn., The Fashion Group, Fla. Coun. Yacht Clubs, Toledo Yacht Club (hon.), Tampa Yacht and Country Club, Chi Omega. Republican. Presbyterian. First woman to cruise solo from Fla. to Lake Erie in single-engine inboard, 1969, to be accepted into Fla. Council Yacht Clubs; yachting accomplishments published in The Ensign, Lakeland Boating, Yachting, Boote mags. Office: PO Box 402 Largo FL 34649

LANG, K. D. (KATHERINE DAWN LANG), country music singer, composer; b. Consort, Alta., Can., 1961; d. Adam and Audrey L. Lang. Mem. Tex. swing fiddle band, 1982—; formed band The Reclines. Albums include A Truly Western Experience, 1984, Angel with a Lariat, 1986, Shadowland, 1988, Absolute Torch and Twang, 1990 (Can. Country Music Awards album of the yr.). Recipient Can. Country Music awards, including Entertainer of Yr., 1989. Office: care Sire Records 75 Rockefeller Pla New York NY 10019*

LANG, KATHERINE ANNE, counseling psychologist; b. Benson, Minn., Jan. 22, 1947; d. Howard James and Barbara Anne (Bennett) L. B.A. in Art History, Smith Coll., Northampton, Mass., 1969; M.A., Bethel Theol. Sem., St. Paul, 1973; M.Ed., U. Mo.-Columbia, 1978, Ph.D., 1982. Lic. psychologist, Calif. Tchr., Am. Sch., Barcelona, Spain, 1970-71; campus ministry Univ. Reformed Ch., East Lansing, Mich., 1973-76; counselor Univ. Counseling Ctr., U. Mo., Rolla, 1978-79; coordinator Ctr. for Student Vols. Action, 1979-81; counseling psychologist U. Calif., Davis, 1982—; pvt. practice counseling psychologist, Sacramento, Calif., 1986—; cons. in field. Mem. Am. Psychol. Assn. Avocations: workshops on prayer; skiing; tennis; racquetball; writing. Office: U Calif Counseling Ctr Davis CA 95864

LANG, NANCY, communications executive; b. N.Y., Mar. 15, 1929; d. Carl and Annette Irma (Crystal) Lang. BMus, Skidmore Coll., 1950; MA, Columbia U., 1951. Music supr. String Music & Vocal System Pub. Sch., Sayville, N.Y., 1951-52; program guide editor, lib. info. WQXR Radio Station, N.Y. Times, N.Y., 1952-59; asst. editor Hi Fi Stereo Review, N.Y., 1959; music dir. Station WTFM, N.Y., Station WIFM, N.Y., 1961-62; publicity dir. Command Records, 1962-63; music specialist Record Ctr., Washington, 1963-65; music specialist Voice of Am., Wash., 1965-82, special events, arts coord., 1982--; Bd. dirs. Am. Women in Radio, TV., judge, Outstanding Young Women's Awards, Wash. 1978, Md. State Music Competitions, Montgomory, 1979. Mem. Women in Communication Inc., Am. Music Critics Assn., Am. News Women's Club (pres. 1976-78). Home: 5903 Frazier Ln McLean VA 22101

LANG, PHYLLIS JEAN, mass communication educator; b. Norfolk, Nebr., Oct. 31, 1938; d. Ross Raymond and Gladys Alma (Riggs) Martin; m. Wayne Wilson Lang, Aug. 23, 1959. AB with distinction, Nebr. Wesleyan U., 1960; MA, U. Nebr., 1962; PhD, U. Ill., 1972. Instr., asst. prof., then prof. English MacMurray Coll., Jacksonville, Ill., 1962-79; asst. editor The Arts Jour., Asheville, N.C., 1980-81, editor, 1981-86, pub., 1986-87; lectr. in mass communication U. N.C., Asheville, 1989—, dir. honors program, 1990—. Contbr. articles to arts jours. Bd. dirs. Penland (N.C.) Sch. Crafts, 1982—; pres. W.N.C. Creative Arts Hall of Fame, 1989—. Mem. Altrusa Club, Pub. Rels. Assn. Western N.C. Office: UNC Asheville 1 University Heights Asheville NC 28804

LANG, VICTORIA WINIFRED, television producer; b. Glen Cove, N.Y., May 13, 1955; d. Jack and Winifred Helen (Sabine) L.; m. Joseph Thomas McAuliffe, Jr. (div. 1982). Student, Emerson Coll., 1973-74; BFA, C.W. Post Coll., 1977. Asst. mgr. John Drew Theatre, East Hampton, N.Y., 1976-77; asst. to producer P.A.F. Playhouse, Huntington Sta., N.Y., 1976-77; asst. to v.p. merchandising Nat. Screen Svc., N.Y.C., 1977-79; media coord. Am. Cinema, Cardiff, Calif., 1979; asst. to dir. pub. relations CBS Newsradio 88, N.Y.C., 1979-80; asst. gen. mgr. Theatre Now, Inc., N.Y.C., 1980-82; assoc. producer Zev Bufman Prodns., N.Y.C., 1982-85; talent coord. Music Fair Group, N.Y.C., 1986-88; segment producer Live with Regis and Kathie Lee WABC-TV, N.Y.C., 1988—. Creative cons. (film) Jewish Humor in America, 1988; producer benefit shows, 1983, 87. Nominated for Emmy award Acad. TV Arts and Scis., N.Y.C., 1989. Mem. Drama Desk Assn., Comml. Theatre Inst., Post Theatre and Film Soc. (pres. 1976-78), Alpha Psi Omega (pres. 1977-78). Democrat. Roman Catholic.

LANG, VIVIAN LUEVENIER, secondary school educator, retired; b. Sarasota, Fla., Mar. 3, 1927; d. Joe Henry and Jessie Bell (Gadson) Elkins; m. Elijah Larry Lang, Sept. 16, 1947 (div. Nov. 1964); children: Nathaniel Cooper, Enrique G. Larrion. BS, Fla. A&M U., 1948; Cert., Ala. State U., 1951, Springhill Coll., 1974, U. So. Ala., 1975. Cert. tchr., bus. edn.; cert. real estate sales assoc. Sec., libr. Booker High Sch., Sarasota, 1948-49; tchr. Whitley Elem. Sch., Mobile, Ala., 1950-51, Theodore Jr. High Sch., Mobile, Ala., 1952, Williamson High Sch., Mobile, Ala., 1957-89; sales assoc. Ala. Real Estate, Mobile, 1989; instr. Heart of Mary Head Start, Mobile, 1969, Adult Edn., Mobile, 1968. Active Black Women's Resource Network, Mobile, 1985. Named Tch. of Yr., faculty Williamson High Sch., Mobile, 1985. Mem. Eastern Star (Marie V. Dixon chpt.), Retired Tchrs. Assn., Future Bus. Leaders of Am., Elks (daughter, trustee 1977), Fla. A&M Alumni Assn., Ala. Computer Career Educators. Methodist. Home: 557 E Downing St Mobile AL 36617

LANGAN, MARGARET ANN, investment manager; b. Hartford, Conn., Apr. 29, 1963; d. Richard Thomas and Dorothy (Gallligan) L. BA in Polit. Sci., Boston Coll., 1985; postgrad., Harvard U., 1990—. Assoc. credit tng. program Chase Manhattan Bank, N.Y.C., 1985-86, asst. treas. fin. analysis div., 1986-87, asst. treas. N.Am. corp. fin. div., 1987-88; investment officer MONY Capital Mgmt., N.Y.C., 1988-89, investment v.p., 1989—. Mem. Book Discussion Group, Boston Coll. Alumni (N.Y.C. chairperson admissions program 1986-90), Phi Beta Kappa. Democrat. Roman Catholic. Home: 2 Soldiers Field Pk #703 Boston MA 02163 Office: MONY Capital Mgmt 1740 Broadway New York NY 10019

LANGAN, MARIE A., public housing specialist; b. Cohoes, N.Y., June 5, 1943; d. Armand Rosario Thyot and Marie Rose (Lemay) Malonson; m. Daniel Noel Langan, July 27, 1963 (div. Dec. 1974); children: Judith Marie Langan, Daniel Noel II, Theresa Marie, Amanda Marie Estrada. Student, Asnuntuck Community Coll., Enfield, Conn., 1980, 82, N.H. Coll., 1986. Environ. health asst. town specialist Town of Manchester, Conn., 1975-78; code enforcement officer Town of Enfield, Conn., 1978-82; housing code enforcement officer Town of Wallingford, Conn., 1982-83; housing specialist jud. dept. State of Conn., New Haven, 1983—; mem. uniform relocation assistance act interim study subcom. of planning and devel. com. Conn. Gen. Assembly, Hartford, 1985-86, mem. uniform statewide housing code, interim study com. and planning and devel. com., 1989-90. Mem., head coach Enfield Lancers, 1977-78; bd. dirs., mem. Big Bros. & Big Sisters Enfield, Inc., 1978-82; before and after sch. chairperson, pres. parents group Enfield Day Care Ctr., Inc., 1978-82, co-chmn., bd. dirs., sec., 1973-76. Recipient Plaque of Appreciation, Enfield Lancers, 1978, Plaque in Recognition Community Mediation, Inc., 1990. Mem. Conn. Assn. Housing Code Enforcement Officers (sec. 1978-80, pres. 1980-84, bd. dirs. 1984-86, treas. 1986—, Placque of Appreciation 1984). Office: Superior Ct Housing Session 121 Elm St New Haven CT 06510

LANGBORT, POLLY, publishing executive; b. N.Y.C., June 29, 1938; d. Julius and Nettie (Berman) L. BA, Adelphi U., 1954. Sec. Young & Rubicam, Inc., N.Y.C., 1956, media buyer, 1956-60, media planner, 1960-65, planning supr., 1965-70, v.p. group supr., 1970-75, v.p. dir. planning devel., 1975-80, sr. v.p., dir. planning, 1980-85, sr. v.p. direct mktg. and media services Wunderman, Worldwide div., 1985-86, exec. v.p. dir. mktg. & media services Wunderman, Worldwide div., 1985-90; assoc. pub. Lear's Mag., N.Y.C., 1990—. Author: DMA Factbook, 1986; contbr. articles to profl. jours. Spl. gifts chairperson Am. Cancer Soc., N.Y.C., 1985—. Jewish. Home: 35 Sutton Pl New York NY 10022 Office: Lear's Publishing 655 Madison Ave New York NY 10022

LANGDON, DIANE STONE, market research executive; b. Walnut Creek, Calif., May 14, 1957; d. Donald Eugene and Beverly Lou (Larson) Stone; m. William Albert Langdon Jr., July 7, 1986. BA in Chemistry, Duke U., 1979; MBA, U. Houston, 1986. Mgmt. trainee Conoco Chemicals, Houston, 1979-80; market analyst Magna div. Baker Oil Tools Co., Houston, 1980-83; corp. market analyst Baker Oil Tools, Houston, 1983-84; ind. cons. Langdon Interests, Houston, 1986-87; investment analyst Retzloff Capital Corp., Houston, 1984-86, Acorn Ventures, Houston, 1987-88; mgr. market rsch. ENSR Corp., Houston, 1988—; cons. Small Bus. Devel. Ctr., Houston, 1987-88. Active Jr. League of Houston, 1988—. Mem. The Profl. Group (bd. dirs. 1987-88), Tex. Exec. Women (v.p. programs 1987-88), U. Houston Alumni Assn. (bd. dirs. 1987-88), Beta Gamma Sigma. Home: 10811 Greenwillow Houston TX 77035 Office: ENSR Corp 3000 Richmond Ave Houston TX 77098

LANGDON, MARILYN JAMISON, marketing company executive; b. S.I., N.Y., Mar. 13, 1962; d. William and Jacqueline (Beyers) Jamison; m. Scott

A. Langdon, Aug. 26, 1989. BA, U. New Haven, 1982; MBA, Boston Coll., 1988. Pres. William Leigh Co., Groton, Conn. Home: 1 Friar Tuck Dr Gales Ferry CT 06335 Office: Box 153 Groton CT 06340

LANGE, JANE LOUISE, state agency administrator; b. Platteville, Wis., Sept. 16, 1947; d. Ervin W. and Marian B. (Salzmann) L. BS in Nursing, Viterbo Coll., LaCrosse, Wis., 1971; MPH, U. N.C., 1978. RN, Ariz. Nurse various hosps., Wis., 1971-75; nurse Dept. Pub. Health County of Dane, Madison, Wis., 1975-77; instr. community health nursing Ariz. State U. Coll. Nursing, Tempe, 1978-81; pub. health cons. Dept. Health Svcs. State of Ariz., Phoenix, 1981-84, dir. patient care svcs. Ariz. Hosps. Home Health Agy., 1984-85, mgr. med. rev. program Div. Motor Vehicles Dept. Transp., 1985—; mem. Profl. Adv. Bd. Am. Nursing Resources, Inc., Phoenix, 1987—, Task Force Adolescent Injury Prevention Dept. Health Svcs. State of Ariz., Phoenix, 1987—, MEDPACT Steering Com. Dept. Transp. State of Wis., Madison, 1988—. Author self-instructional learning modules, 1980. Mem. Am. Pub. Health Assn., Ariz. Pub. Health Assn. (chmn. nursing sect. 1979-81), Assn. Advancement Automotive Medicine, Am. Nurses' Assn., Ariz. Nurses' Assn., Sigma Theta Tau. Office: Ariz Dept Transp 1801 W Jefferson St 512M Phoenix AZ 85007

LANGE, JESSICA, actress; b. Minn., Apr. 20, 1949; d. Al and Dorothy Lange; m. Paco Grande, 1970 (div. 1982); dau. with Mikhail Baryshnikov, Alexandra; children with Sam Shepard: Hannah Jane, Samuel Walker. Student, U. Minn.; student mime, with Etienne DeCroux, Paris. Dancer Opera Comique, Paris; model Wilhelmina Agy., N.Y.C. Film appearances include King Kong, 1976, All That Jazz, 1979, How to Beat the High Cost of Living, 1980, The Postman Always Rings Twice, 1981, Frances, 1982 (Acad. award nominee for best actress 1982), Tootsie, 1982 (Acad. award for best supporting actress 1982), Country, 1984, Sweet Dreams, 1985, Crimes of the Heart, 1986, Everybody's All American, 1988, Far North, 1988, Men Don't Leave, 1988, Music Box, 1989; star Showtime TV prodn. Cat on a Hot Tin Roof, 1984; in summer stock prodn. Angel on My Shoulder, N.C., 1980. Office: Creative Artists Agy care Ron Meyer 1888 Century Pk E 14th Fl Los Angeles CA 90067*

LANGE, KATHERINE JOANN, writer; b. Wyandotte, Mich., Feb. 8, 1957; d. James DiDi and Margaret Ann (Kirk) Putman. Student, Normandale Coll., 1980-82. V.p., artist mgr. The T.S.J. Prodns. Inc., Richfield, Minn., 1975—; mgr., agt. The T.S.J. Booking Agy., Richfield, 1980—; asst. editor, author Songwriter U.S.A. mag., Atlanta, 1986-87; staff writer Music Mgmt. and Internat. Promotion mag., Copenhagen, 1983—. Contbr. articles to Sun Newspapers, Songwriter Connection, Woman's Press. Mem. ASCAP, NAFE, Am. Fedn. Musicians. Democrat. Lutheran. Home and Office: The TSJ Prodns Inc 422 Pierce St NE Minneapolis MN 55413

LANGE, PHYLLIS LOUISE, educator; b. Lapeer, Mich., Feb. 11, 1942; d. Samuel Virgil and Gladys Gertrude (Evans) Hartgrove; m. Duane Albert Lange, June 23, 1962; children: Deborah, Kelly, Patricia, Christian, Timothy, Nicholas. BA, U. Mich., 1967; M. Spl. Edn., Ea. Mich. U., 1971. Cert. edn., spl. edn. Tchr. Imlay City Schs., Imlay City, Mich., 1965-69; tchr. Lapeer Community Schs., 1970—; organizer young authors day and read-a-thon day Irwin Elem. Sch., Lapeer, 1980-89. Chmn. Mardi Gras Day Bishop Kelley Sch., Lapeer, 1977-78, carnival fairs, 1979-80. Mem. NEA, Mich. Edn. Assn., United Univ. Am. Women, Nat. Campers and Hikers Assn. (chmn. camping youth bazaars Corunna, Mich., chpt., 1979, 81). Roman Catholic. Office: Irwin Elem Sch 250 2nd St Lapeer MI 48446

LANGENBERG, PATRICIA WARRINGTON, biostatistics educator, consultant; b. Des Moines, Sept. 10, 1931; d. Harold Paris and Rose Marie (Thompson) Warrington; m. Donald Newton Langenberg, June 20, 1953; children—Karen, Julia, John, Amy. B.S. in Math. Stats., Iowa State U., 1953; M.S. in Math., Temple U., 1975, Ph.D. in Math., 1978. Asst. prof. math. LaSalle Coll., Phila., 1977-80; asst. prof. biostats. Temple U., Phila., 1980-83; asst. prof. biostats. Sch. Pub. Health, U. Ill., Chgo., 1983-86, assoc. prof., 1986—; treas. Com. of Pres of Statis. Socs., 1981-86. Contbr. articles to biometric jours. Mem. Am. Statis. Assn., Biometric Soc., Assn. Women in Math., Caucus for Women in Stats. Democrat. Home: 6100 Westchester Park Dr Apt 1213 College Park MD 20740 Office: U Ill m/c 922 Box 6998 Chicago IL 60680

LANGENHEIM, JEAN HARMON, biology educator; b. Homer, La., Sept. 5, 1925; d. Vergil Wilson and Jeanette (Smith) H.; m. Ralph Louis Langenheim, Dec. 1946 (div. Mar. 1961). BS, U. Tulsa, 1946; MS, U. Minn., 1949, PhD, 1953. Rsch. assoc. botany U. Calif., Berkeley, 1954-59, U. Ill., Urbana, 1959-61; rsch. fellow biology Harvard U., Cambridge, Mass., 1962-66; asst. prof. biology U. Calif., Santa Cruz, 1966-68, assoc. prof. biology, 1968-73, prof. biology, 1973—; academic v.p. Orgn. Tropical Studies, San Jose, Costa Rica, 1975-78; mem. sci.adv. bd. EPA, Washington, 1977-81; chmn. com. on humid tropics U.S. Nat. Acad. Nat. Research Council, 1975-77; mem. com. floral inventory Amazon NSF, Washington, 1975-87. Contbr. articles to profl. jours. Grantee NSF, 1966-88; recipient Disting. Alumni award U. Tulsa, 1979. Fellow AAUW, Bunting Inst., Calif. Acad. Scis.; mem. Botanical Soc. Am., Internat. Soc. Chem. Ecology (pres. 1986-87), Ecol. Soc. Am. (pres. 1986-87), Assn. Tropical Biology (pres. 1985-86). Home: 191 Palo Verde Terr Santa Cruz CA 95060 Office: U Calif Sinsheimer Labs Thimann Labs Santa Cruz CA 95064

LANGER, ELLEN JANE, psychologist, educator, author; b. N.Y.C., Mar. 25, 1947; d. Norman and Sylvia (Tobias) L. BA, NYU, 1970; PhD, Yale U., 1974. Cert. clin. psychologist. Asst. prof. psychology The Grad. Ctr. CUNY, 1974-77; assoc. prof. psychology Harvard U., Cambridge, Mass., 1977-81; prof. Harvard U., 1981—; cons. NAS, 1979-81, NASA; mem. div. on aging Harvard U. Med. Sch., 1979—, mem. psychiat. epidemiology steering com., 1982—; chair social psychology program Harvard U., 1982—, chair Faculty Arts and Scis. Com. of Women, 1984-88. Author: Personal Politics, 1973, Psychology of Control, 1983, Mindfulness, 1989; editor: (with Charles Alexander) Higher Stages of Human Development, 1990; contbr. articles to profl. and scholarly jours. Guggenheim Fellow, grantee NIMH, NSF, Soc. for Psychol. Study of Social Issues, Milton Fund, Sloan Found., 1982. Fellow Computers and Soc. Inst., Am. Psychol. Assn. (Disting. Contributions to Psychology in the Public Interest award 1988); mem. Soc. Expl. Social Psychology, Phi Beta Kappa, Sigma Xi. Democrat. Jewish. Office: Harvard Univ Dept Psychology 33 Kirkland St Cambridge MA 02138

LANGER, MARIAN MARTHA, sales executive; b. Pittsburgh, July 4, 1936; d. Joseph and Martha (Volz); m. Henry Jay, Aug. 9, 1959 (dec. Mar. 1988); 1 child, David. Postgrad., St. Joseph's Hosp. Sch. of Nur, Pittsburgh, 1957; BS in Communication, Arts Lindenwood Coll., St. Charles, 1976; MA in Edn., Wash. U., St. Louis, 1980. Head nurse Allegheny Gen. Hosp., Pittsburgh, 1959-62; instr. Barnes Hosp., St. Louis, 1962-70, officer of the day, 1973-84; instr. St. Johns Mercy Med. Ctr., St. Louis; profl. rep. Lifescan, Inc., St. Louis, 1984-86; sr. profl. rep. Lifescan, Inc., 1986-. Contbr. articles to profl. jours. Mem. Am. Assn. of Diabetes Edn. Educators, Am. Diabetes Assn. Home: 23845 Arroyo Park Dr Valencia CA 91255 Office: Lifescan Inc 2443 Wyandotte St Mountain View CA 94043

LANGER, SUSANNE M., cosmetics executive; b. Red Wing, Minn., Aug. 19, 1955. Diploma Cosmetology, Ritter St. Paul Coll., 1974; grad., Bruno's, 1978. Instr. Ritter's St. Paul Coll., 1974-75; asst. mgr., mgr. Scot Lewis Inc., Bloomington, Minn., 1975-79; edn. dir. My Kind of Place, St. Paul, 1979-80; pres., co-owner Someone's Looking (formerly Charpentier's Inc.), St. Paul, 1980-86, owner, 1986—; co-owner, pres. SuPro, Inc., St. Paul; styles dir. women's sect. Minn. Cosmetology Edn. Com. Fundraiser, chairperson Battered Women's Shelter, St. Paul, 1984, Children's Home Soc., St. Paul, 1985; vol. St. Paul Food Shelves Food Dr., 1985, 88; vol., model United Arts Fashion Show, 1986; vol. fundraiser pub. TV Action Auction, Ronald McDonald House, Food Shelf Drives Someone's Looking, St. Paul, MS Walkathon, 1988. Recipient numerous hairstyling awards. Mem. Nat. Cosmetologists Assn., Minn. Hairdressers and Cosmetologists Assn., St. Paul Cosmetologists Assn. (dir. 1981-83, pres. 1983-85), Hair Am., Minn. Hair Fashion Com. Home: 1150 Cushing Circle Saint Paul MN 55108 Office: Someone's Looking Inc 151 Endicott Arcade Saint Paul MN 55101

LANGFELD, MARILYN IRENE, creative art company director; b. St. Louis, Apr. 28, 1951; d. Norman Max and Celeste (Brown) L. Student, Vanderbilt U., 1968-70; B.A. cum laude, Sonoma State U., 1978-80. Printer, Sojourner Truth Press, Altanta, 1971-73; carpenter apprentice Housebuilders Union, Atlanta, 1973-74; self employed housebuilder, Perry, Me., 1974-75; graphic artist Cuthberts Printing, San Rafael, Calif., 1976-77; graphic Designer Community Type & Design, Fairfax, Calif., 1977-80; owner, creative dir. Langfeld Assocs., San Francisco, 1980—. Recipient Am. Corp. Identity award, 1986, Type Dirs. Club award, 1987, Desi award, 1987, Simpson Paper Co. award, 1987, Printing Industries of Am. award, 1987. Mem. People Speaking Adv. Bd., 1979-84. Sonoma State scholar, Bank of Sonoma County, 1979-80; Vanderbilt U. scholar, 1968-69, 69-70; bd. dirs. Horizons Found. Mem. San Francisco C. of C., Am. Inst. Graphic Artists, San Francisco Art Dirs. Club, Western Art Dirs. Club. Art Dirs. and Artists of Sacramento, San Francisco Better Bus. Bur. Clubs: San Francisco Ad, City, Advertising (San Francisco). Democrat. Jewish. Office: 381 Clementina St San Francisco CA 94103

LANGFORD, ELLA HUNT, licensed clinical social worker; b. Dinwiddie, Va., Aug. 26, 1944; d. James Daniel and Luevinia (Parham) Hunt; m. Samuel Martin Langford Jr., Dec. 16, 1967 (div. 1975); 1 child, Samuel Martin III. BA, Va. State U., 1963-67; MS, Columbia U., N.Y.C, 1971-73. Prog. dir. Three Rivers Youth, Pitts., 1976-77; dir. Ettrick Mental Health Clinic, 1973-76; prog. dir. Family & Children's Service, Richmond, Va., 1977-81; adj. profr. Va. Union U., Richmond, 1982-82; dir. social work Barrow Geriatric Treatment Ctr., Petersburg, Southsde Va. Training Ctr., Petersburg, 1983-84; chief clin. social worker Med. Coll. Va., 1984-85; LCSW Metropolitan Clinic of Counseling, Richmond, 1985; psychotherapist Pvt. Practice, Richmond, 1984--; cons. Va. State U. Petersburg, 1979--, Trinity Bapt. Ch. Richmond, 1982--Metropolitan Clinic of Counseling Richmond 1988--, State Chpt. NAACP Richmond, 1989--. Chairperson Mental Health Com. Richmond 1985-88. Recipient Acad. Scholarship Columbia U. N.Y.C., 1971-72, STipend Vet. Administrn. N.Y.C., 1972-73, Juevenile Deliquency Prevention Grant Fed. Govt., 1978, Service Award Richmond Communiy Services Bd. Richmond, 1988. Mem. Nat. Assn. Social Work, Acad. Certified Social Workers, Nat. Assoc. Social Workers, Am. Assn. State Social Work Bds. (del.), Va. Bd. Social Work, Richmond County Svcs. Bd. Democrat. Baptist. Home: 3030 Montrose Ave Richmond VA 23222 Office: 1001 W Brookland Park Blvd Richmond VA 23220

LANGFORD, LORRAINE, state legislator; b. Monroe, Nebr.; m. Jack Langford, 1946; 3 children. Ed., U. Nebr., U. So. Calif. Mem. Nebr. Legislature; mem. Nat. Bd. Rep. Women. Home: 1717 W 26th St Kearney NE 68847*

LANG-GRUNDLER, MARY JANE, business educator; b. Wentworth, Mo., Oct. 26, 1919; d. Charles Fremont and Angeline Rose (Baker) Lang; m. Francis Edward Grundler, Dec. 26, 1963. BS, U. Mo., 1944, MEd, 1947, EdD, 1960. Tchr. Shiloh Sch., Carthage, Mo., 1940-41, Duenweg (Mo.) Elem. Sch., 1941-42; bus. tchr. Duenweg High Sch., 1942-43, Seneca (Mo.) High Sch., 1943-45, Lindenwood Coll., St. Charles, Mo., 1945-47; instr. U. Mo., Columbia, 1947-60, asst. prof., 1960-67, assoc. prof., 1967-76, prof., 1976-85, prof. emeritus, 1985—; coord. bus. edn. coll. edn. U. Mo., Columbia, 1968-80. Contbr. articles to profl. bus. edn. jours. Bd. dirs. Koinonia House, Columbia, 1988—. Named Outstanding Bus. Educator, Mo. Bus. Edn. Assn., 1979; recipient Recognition award Nat. Assn. Tchr. Educators for Bus. Edn., 1982, Disting. Svc. award U. Mo. Alumni Assn., 1986, Outstanding Alumnus award Mo. State So. Coll., 1988. Mem. Nat. Bus. Edn. Assn., AAUW (state treas. 1988-90), Ret. Tchrs. Assn. Mo. (newsletter editor 1988-90), Pi Lambda Theta (sponsor Alpha chpt. 1989—). Roman Catholic. Home: 106 E Stewart Rd Columbia MO 65203

LANGHAM, NORMA, educator, author, composer; b. California, Pa.; d. Alfred Scrivener and Mary Edith (Carter) L. BS, Ohio State U., 1942; B in Theatre Arts, Pasadena Playhouse Coll. Theatre Arts, 1944; MA, Stanford U., 1956; postgrad., Summer Radio-TV Inst., 1960, Pasadena Inst. Radio, 1944-45. Tchr. sci. Light High Sch., 1942-43; asst. office pub. info. Denison U., Granville, Ohio, 1955; instr. speech dept. Westminster Coll., New Wilmington, Pa., 1957-58; instr. theatre. California U. of Pa., 1959, asst. prof., 1960-62, assoc. prof., 1962-79, prof. emeritus, 1979—, co-founder, sponsor, dir. Children's Theatre, 1962-79; founder, producer, bd. dirs. Food Bank Players, 1985, Patriot Players, 1986. Writer: (plays) Magic in the Sky, 1963, (text) Public Speaking, John Dough (Freedoms Found. award 1968), Who Am I?, Hippocrates Oath, Gandhi, Clementine of '49, Soul Force, Esther, Music in Freedom, The Day the Moon Fell; composer-lyricist (plays) Why Me, Lord?, (text) Public Speaking. Mem. Community Choir., Calif., Pa. Recipient award exceptional acad. svc. Pa. Dept. Edn., 1975, Appreciation award Bicentennial Commn. Pa., 1976; Henry C. Frick Ednl. Commn. grantee. Mem. Theatre Assn. Pa., Internat. Platform Assn., Calif. U. of Pa. Assn. Women Faculty (founder, pres. 1972-73), AAUW (co-founder Calif. br., 1st v.p. 1971-72, pres. 1972-73, Outstanding Woman of Yr. 1986), Dramatists Guild, DAR, Alpha Psi Omega, Omicron Nu. Presbyterian (elder). Home: Box 455 California PA 15419

LANGHORNE, KATHRYN PAYNE, teacher; b. Norfolk, Va., Aug. 24, 1905; d. Charles Anton and Alma Gennette (Burton) Smith; m. Maurice Bilisoly Langhorne, Apr. 8, 1944 (dec. 1986). BS, Radford U., 1928; MA, Columbia U., 1941. Tchr. Sch. Bd. Norfolk City, Norfolk, Va., 1930-72, Substitute Mathews County Sch., 1973-78. Mem. choir Kingston Parish Christ Ch., 1974—. Republican. Episcopalian.

LANGLEY, ANN, nurse, navy officer; b. San Antonio, Nov. 1, 1942; d. John Thomas and Ruth Elaine (Gregoor) L. BS in Nursing, U. Tex., Galveston, 1964; MS in Bus., Naval Postgrad. Sch., Monterey, Calif., 1971. RN, Tex. Commd. ensign USN, 1964, advanced through grades to capt., 1985; head nurse Naval Hosp., Phila., 1972-74; various positions Bur. Medicine and Surgery, Washington, 1975-81; nursing supr. Naval Hosp., Portsmouth, Va., 1981-82; br. head Office Navy Surgeon Gen., Washington, 1982-85; exec. officer Naval Hosp., Jacksonville, Fla., 1985-87; comdr. officer Naval Hosp., Okinawa, Japan, 1987-89; officer-in-charge Naval Healthcare Support Office, Barbers Point, Hawaii, 1989—. Mem. Assn. Mil. Surgeons U.S., Sigma Theta Tau. Office: Naval Healthcare Support Office Naval Air Sta Barbers Point HI 96862

LANGLEY, CYNTHIA MURRAY, dentist; b. Elgin, Tex., Feb. 10, 1954; d. Robert O. Jr. and Juanita (Briggle) Murray; m. J.D. Langley, Mar. 19, 1978; children: Melissa Sue, Travis James. BS, Tex. A&M U., 1976; DDS, Baylor Coll., 1978. Dental officer Gorgas Hosp. Dental Clinic, Panama Canal Zone, 1978; practicing dentistry Balboa, Panama Canal Zone, 1978-79; assoc. prof. Dept. Gen. Practice U. Tex. Dental Branch, Houston, 1980-81; practicer, asst. adminstr. L.L. Gregory D.D.S. Inc., Houston, 1981-82; assoc. dentist C.C. Sullivan D.D.S., Houston, 1980-82; practicing dentistry Bryan, Tex., 1982—; bd. dirs. Baylor Coll. of Dentistry Century Club, Death, Disability and Retirement Trust, 1988-90, Better Bus. Bur. Contbr. articles to profl. jour. Del. Rep. St. Conv. 1986, 88, 90; co-mgr. J.D. Langley campaign 1985-86, 90; bd. dirs. Opera and Performing Arts Soc., 1984-87, A&M United Meth. Ch., 1986-88; bd. dirs., spl. events chmn. Rep. Women of the Brazos Valley, 1988, mem., 1985—; v.p. Brazos County Programs LWV, 1989, mem., 1985—. Mem. ADA, Tex. Dental Assn., Am. Assn. Women Dentists, Am. Assn. Univ. Women, Brazos Valley Dist. Dental Soc. (judicial com. 1986-87), Acad. Gen. Dentistry, Houston Dist. Dental Soc & Brazos Valley Acad. Gen. Dentistry, Am. Bus. Women Assn. (bd. dirs. 1985-89), Women's Small Bus. Owners Assn. Bryan and Coll. Station. Office: 3131 Briarcrest Dr E Ste 508 Bryan TX 77802

LANGLEY, MARGARET CAROL, advertising agency official; b. N.Y.C., Mar. 30, 1965; d. William Corey and Patricia Joyce (Smith) L. BA in Internat. Affairs, Lafayette Coll., 1987. Asst. press sec. Nickerson for Congress Campaign, Greenwich, Conn., 1987; asst. network buyer BBDO, N.Y.C., 1987-89, network buyer, 1989-90, network supr., 1990—. Mem. Sigma Kappa. Democrat. Presbyterian. Home: 640 Park Ave Hoboken NJ 07030 Office: BBDO 1285 Ave of Americas New York NY 10019

LANGLEY, PATRICIA ANN, lobbyist; b. Butler, Pa., Feb. 13, 1938; d. F.J. and Ella (Serafine) Piccola; m. Harold D. Langley, June 12, 1965; children: Erika, David. BA, U. Pitts., 1961; postgrad., Georgetown U., 1967, Cath. U. Am., 1985. Legis. staff U.S. Congress, Washington, 1961-63; dir. social studies Am. Polit. Sci. Assn., Washington, 1963-65; legis. specialist U.S. Congress, Washington, 1965-67, caseworker, 1967-68; polit. staff Dem. Study Group U.S. Congress, Washington, 1969; Washington rep. Family Services Am., 1975-82, dir. Washington hdqrs., 1982-89, v.p. for govt. rels., 1990—; bd. dirs. Coalition for Children and Youth, Washington, 1977-78; chmn. steering com. for the Coalition on White House Conf. on Families, 1979-80, Ad Hoc Coalition on A.F.D.C., 1981-82. Mem. Donaldson Run Civic Assn., Arlington, Va., 1980—. Recipient Service Recognition U.S. Dept. Health and Human Services, 1980. Mem. Am. Soc. of Assn. Execs., AAUW, Women in Govt. Relations. Roman Catholic. Home: 2515 N Utah St Arlington VA 22207 Office: Family Svcs Am 1319 F St NW Ste 606 Washington DC 20004

LANGSTAFF, ELEANOR MARGUERITE, library science educator; b. Washington, June 21, 1934; d. William Truman and Bernice Louise (Tharpe-Mecum) De Selms; m. David Knox Langstaff, June 19, 1970 (dec. 1984). B.A., Colo. State U.-Ft. Collins, 1958; M.A., Fordham U., 1961; M.S., Catholic U. Am., 1970; postgrad. CUNY, 1979—; cert. in tropical edn. U. London/Makerere Coll., Uganda. Mem. Tchrs. for East Africa program Columbia U., N.Y.C., 1961-64; fgn. service officer USIA, 1965-69, acting country pub. affairs officer, Bangui, Central African Republic, 1967-68, regional books officer, Lagos, Nigeria, 1968-69; librarian Sch. Library and Info. Sci., Pratt Inst., N.Y.C., 1970-72; assoc. prof. library sci. Bernard M. Baruch Coll., CUNY, 1973—; cons. on info. Langstaff-French Assocs., Manchester, Vt., 1982-88; dir. hypermedia devel. project Libr. Svc. and Constrn. Act, U.S. Dept. Edn., 1989-90. Author: Andrew Lang, 1978; (with Thomas V. Atkins) Access to Information: Library Research and Demonstration Methods, 1979; Panama, 1982; co-author Access Information: Business, 1986, 90, Access Information: Social Sciences and Humanities, 1990; (with others) British Women Writers, 1988. Vol., ARC, Bklyn., 1972—. Recipient excellence in French lit. award French Govt., 1958. Mem. ALA, Library Assn. CUNY (v.p. 1974-75, pres. 1975-76), Assn. Coll. and Research Libraries, Phi Beta Mu. Episcopalian. Home: 100 Remsen St Brooklyn NY 11201 Office: CUNY 317 Baruch Coll 156 E 25th St New York NY 10010

LANGUM, W. SUE, civic worker; b. Kennett, Mo., Jan. 10, 1934; d. Howard S. and Lucille (Hubble) Walker; m. Norman H. Nelson, June 22, 1957 (dec. Sept. 1969); 1 child, Kirby Walker Nelson; m. John K. Langum, Dec. 28, 1972. Student, Northwestern U., 1952-53, Crane Jr. Coll., 1953-54. Svc. rep. Ill. Bell Tel. Co., Chgo., 1956-57; receptionist Tri-City Animal Hosp., Elgin, Ill., 1967-69; rsch. asst. Bus. Econs. Inc., Chgo., 1969-73, dir., 1973—. V.p. Elgin Coun. PTA, 1969-73; bd. dirs. OEO, 1972-73, Meals on Wheels, Elgin, 1972—, Coloquy Coffee House, 1968-70, Judson Coll. Friends, 1976—, Elgin Hist. Soc., Elgin Symphony Orch. Assn., 1984—, Elgin Symphony League, 1982—, pres., 1984-86; bd. dirs. United Meth. Women, 1978—, pres., 1980-84; vol. Fish, 1974-76; bd. dirs., treas. Easter Seal Assn. for Crippled Children, 1977—; mem. Elgin Beautification Commn., 1986-88, Tuesday Morning Bible Study Club. Mem. LWV (v.p. Elgin Club 1965—), Elgin Women's Club, Current History Forum Club. Republican. Home: 1186 Duncan Ave Elgin IL 60120

LANGWORTHY, AUDREY HANSEN, state legislator; b. Grand Forks, N.D., Apr. 1, 1938; d. Edward H. and Arla (Kuhlman) Hansen; m. Asher C. Langworthy Jr., Sept. 8, 1962; children: Kristin H., Julia H. BS, U. Kans., 1960, MS, 1962. Tchr. jr. high sch. Shawnee Mission Sch. Dist., Johnson County, Kans., 1963-65; councilperson City of Prairie Village, Kans., 1981-85; mem. Kans. State Senate, 1985—; del. Midwestern Conf. State Legislatures, 1989; alt. del. Nat. Conf. State Legislatures, 1985-87, del., 1987—; mem. subcom. Nat. Conf. of State Legislatures Govt. Ops. and Pensions Assembly. City co-chmn. Kassebaum for U.S. Senate, Prairie Village, 1978; pres. Jr. League Kansas City, Mo., 1977, Kansas City Eye Bank, 1982-85; mem. bd. Greater Kansas City ARC, 1975—, pres., 1984, chmn. midwestern adv. coun., 1985-86, nat. bd. govs. ARC, 1987—, Johnson County Community Coll. Found., 1989—. Recipient Outstanding Vol. award Community Services Award Found., 1983, Confidence in Edn. award Friends of Edn., 1984. Mem. Nat. Rep. Legislator's Assn., LWV, Women's Pub. Svc. Network, U. Kans. Alumni Assn. Episcopalian. Home: 6324 Ash Prairie Village KS 66208

LANIER, ANITA SUZANNE, piano educator; b. Talladega, Ala., May 21, 1946; d. Luther Dwight and Elva (Hornsby) L. BS in Music Edn., Jacksonville (Ala.) State U., 1969. Elem. music tchr. Talladega City Schs., 1969-81; librarian, elem. tchr. Talladega Acad., 1981-84; tchr. piano and organ Talladega, 1981—. Organist Trinity United Meth. Ch., Talladega, 1981, Talladega Community Chorus; mem. rsch. bd. advisors ABI. Recipient Commemorative medal of Honor World Decoration of Excellence. Mem. NAFE, Nat. Guild Piano Tchrs., Music Tchrs. Nat. Assn., World Inst. Achievement, Women's Inenr Circle Achievement, Pilot Club (sec. 1977-78), Delta Omnicron. Home: 601 North St Talladega AL 35160

LANIER, CATHY GIBSON, data processing company executive; b. Chester, S.C., Feb. 8, 1957; d. James A. and Estelle G. (Grant) Gibson; m. Randy D. Lanier, 1980. BS in Psychology, Math with honors, Converse Coll., 1979; MS in Psychology, U. S.C., 1981. Freelance data processing recruiting cons. Columbia, S.C., 1981-83; recruitment mgr. Blue Cross and Blue Shield S.C., Columbia, 1983-85; area mgr. Am. Computer Profl., Columbia, 1985-88; regional mgr., recruiting and mktg. services CSX Tech., Columbia, 1988; div. mgr. profl. svcs. SCANA Software Svcs., Inc., Columbia, 1988-89; pres. Tech. Solutions, Inc., Columbia, 1989—. Rep. officer S.C. State Student Legis., Columbia, 1976-81. U. S.C. Experimental Psychology Unit grantee, 1979-81. Mem. Data Processing Mgmt. Assn. Home: 211 Lake Villa Rd Lexington SC 29072 Office: Tech Solutions Inc PO Box 212098 Columbia SC 29221-2098

LANIER, VIOLA WILSON, teacher; b. Lincoln, Ala., Dec. 16, 1927; d. Phillip and Lera B. (Montgomery) Wilson; m. Isiah Williams, July 28, 1945 (div. 1973); children: Curtis L., Quensetta D. Williams Lucas; m. Lavert D. Lanier, June 27, 1974. BEd, Ala. State U., 1952; MEd, Ind. U., 1960. Cert. tchr., Ind. Tchr., prin. Talladega County Schs., Ala., 1947-50; tchr. Montgomery (Ala.) County Schs., 1952-53, Indpls. Pub. Schs., 1959—; supr. instruction Shelby and Autauga County Schs., Ala., 1954-59; asst. dir. Nat. Coll. Bus., Indpls., 1977-80; exec. dir. Enrichment Learning Ctr. and Mus., Indpls., 1984—. Adv. com. ERIC Global Issues Project, Indpls., 1986-88, Indpls. Jr. High Improvement Com., 1986-88. Recipient Community Service award Indpls. Mayor's Office, 1982; U.S. Edn. Found. grantee, 1985. Fellow NEA; mem. Hist. Landmarks Found., Ind. Council Social Studies (sec. 1986—), Freedoms Found. (v.p. Indpls. chpt. 1981—, honor medal 1982), Indpls. C. of C., Nat. Trust Hist. Preservation, Internat. Platform Assn., Delta Sigam Theta, Phi Delta Kappa. Democrat. Mem. Christian Ch. Home: 209 Buckingham Dr Indianapolis IN 46208 Office: Indpls 400 Indianapolis IN 46236

LANIEWSKI, LAURA ANN, telecommunications company executive; b. Detroit, Feb. 25, 1961; d. Leonard W. and Joanne C. (Uhl) L. BSBA cum laude, Montclair State Coll., 1983; MBA, NYU, 1989. Telemarketing account exec. N.J. Bell Telephone Co., Parsippany, 1983-84, regional account exec., 1984-86, account exec. upstate devel. dept., 1986-88, account mgr., 1988—. Roman Catholic. Home: 182 Robertson Way Lincoln Park NJ 07035 Office: NJ Bell Telephone Co 700 Lanidex Plaza Parsippany NJ 07054

LANIS, VIOLET ANN, business educator; b. Gary, Ind., Sept. 10, 1948; d. Steve and Danica (Arbutina) Bayus; m. Barry S. Lanis, Dec. 1, 1973. BS, Ball State U., 1970, MEd, 1972. Tchr. Thornton Twp High Schs., Harvey, Ill., 1970-73; lectr. Katharine Gibbs Secretarial Sch., Norwalk, Conn., 1974-78, Sacred Heart U., Bridgeport, Conn., 1974-79; adj. asst. prof. U. Bridgeport, 1974-81; tchr. Darien (Conn.) Pub. Schs., 1981-83; instr. Norwalk Community Coll., 1983-87, Dekalb Coll., Dunwoody, Ga., 1988, Ind. U. N.W., Gary, 1989—. Author secretarial procedures manual, 1979. Mem. NEA, Norwalk J. Women's Club (v.p. 1980-81), Delta Pi Epsilon. Roman Catholic. Office: Ind U NW Div Edn 3400 Broadway Gary IN 46408

LANKFORD, LINDA MARIE, construction executive; b. Lubbock, Tex., Aug. 24, 1947; d. Jimmie and Maryann Florence (Jones) Smyth; m. Bobby

Ray Lankford, July 31, 1964 (div. 1974); children: Jimmie, Bobby, Michael. Grad. high sch.; student, Antelope Valley Coll., Lancaster, Calif. Cert. pvt. pilot. Haistylist, 1963-75; adminstrv. asst., controller Pagosabode, Inc., Pagosa Springs, Colo., 1975-80; office mgr. Aspen Homes, Pagosa Springs, 1978-80; adminstrv. asst. Teroco Constrn., Pagosa Springs, 1980-85; site supt. Teroco Constrn., Lake Arrowhead, Calif., 1985-86; mgr. Mission Bell Inc., Ventura, Calif., 1986-87; quality control inspector Quality Cons., Inc., Federal Way, Wash., 1987-88; quality control supt. Kaufman and Broad Inc., Los Angeles, 1988-90; pvt. as gen. contractor, 1990—. Pres. PTO, Pagosa Springs, 1983; sec.-treas. Aspen Springs Owners Assn., 1979; founder Ennis Youth Soccer Assn., Ennis and Archuleta County Soccer Assn. Mem. Nat. Assn. Female Execs., Archuleta County Builders Assn. Republican. Baptist. Office: 318 Kidder Ln Gross Valley CA

LANNING, JUDITH ANN, music teacher; b. Racine, Wis., Feb. 9, 1936; d. Leo Conrad and Eleanor Christine (Jensen) Draves; m. Norman V. Lanning, Dec. 2, 1955; children: Lise Dawn, Paul Norman. BA with highest distinction, Ohio U., 1954-57, U. Wis., Kenosha, 1973. Pvt. practice dog grooming, 1965-70, pvt. practice show dogs, 1970-80, pvt. practice violin, viola and voice instr., 1973-89; substitute tchr. Racine Unified Schs., 1974-75; asst. dir. Racine Sweet Adeline Chorus, 1974—; reporter, newscaster Sta. WRJN, Racine, 1978-81; area coord. Seminars Internat., Chgo., 1979-84; tutor German students U. Wis., Parkside, 1982-87; coord. gifted and talented St. Mary Grade Sch., Kenosha, Wis., 1987—; music dir. Racine Theatre Guild, 1989—. Translator: Der Schimmelreiter (Theodor Storm, 1989. Concertmistress Washington Pk. High Orch.; violinist Racine Musicians Union Little Symphony, U. Wis.-Milw. Summer Opera Orch., Racine Symphony Orch., RAcine Sweet Adelines. Mem. Am. String Tchrs. Assn., Racine Arts Coun., Racine Theatre Guild, Nat. Music Tchrs. Assn., Zertificat Deutsch als Freindsprache Goethe Inst., Wis. Music Tchrs. Assn., Theodor Storm Gesellschaft, Alpha Mu Gamma, Sigma Alpha Iota.

LANPHEAR, SHAWNA RAE, computer company professional; b. Bozeman, Mont., July 7, 1957; d. Donald Douglas and Dona Aline (McNeil) L. BA in Bus. Mgmt., Mont. State U., 1979; JD, Calif. Western Sch. Law, 1985. Asst. gen. mgr. Lanphear Ins. Agy., Bozeman, 1969-79; specialist compliance, registrar Gt. Global Assurance Co., Scottsdale, Ariz., 1980-83; adminstr. mktg. Millidyne Inc., San Diego, 1983-86; rep. contracts Computer Scis. Corp., San Diego, 1986-87; contracts mgr. Informaties Legal Systems, Phoenix, 1987-89; contracts negotiator NCR Corp., San Diego, 1989—. Mem. ABA, Contracts Mgmt. Assn., Nat. Assn. Female Execs., Alpha Gamma Delta (corr. sec. 1981, asst. rush 1982), Tau Pi Phi. Republican. Home: 2383 Cardinal Dr Apt 20 San Diego CA 92123

LANSBURY, ANGELA BRIGID, actress; b. London, Oct. 16, 1925; came to U.S., 1940; d. Edgar and Moyna (Macgill) L.; m. Peter Shaw, Aug. 12, 1949; children: Anthony, Deirdre. Student, Webber-Douglas Sch. Drama, London, 1939-40, Feagin Sch. Drama, N.Y.C., 1940-42; LHD (hon.), Boston U., 1990. Actress with Metro-Goldwyn-Mayer, 1943-50; films include: Gaslight, 1944, National Velvet, 1944, The Picture of Dorian Gray, 1944, The Harvey Girls, 1946, Till the Clouds Roll By, 1946, If Winter Comes, 1947, State of the Union, 1948, Samson and Delilah, 1949, Kind Lady, 1951, The Court Jester, 1956, The Long Hot Summer, 1957, Reluctant Debutante, 1958, Summer of the 17th Doll, 1959, A Breath of Scandal, 1959, Dark at the Top of the Stairs, 1960, Blue Hawaii, 1961, All Fall Down, 1962, Manchurian Candidate, 1963, In the Cool of the Day, 1963, The World of Henry Orient, 1964, Out of Towners, 1964, Something for Everyone, 1969, Bedknobs and Broomsticks, 1970, Death on the Nile, 1978, The Lady Vanishes, 1979, The Mirror Crack'd, 1980, The Pirates of Penzance, 1982; star TV series Murder She Wrote, 1984— (Golden Globe awards 1984, 86); appeared in TV mini-series Little Gloria, Happy at Last, 1982, Lace, 1984, Rage of Angels, part II, 1986; other TV movies include: Gift of Love, 1982, Shootdown, 1988, The Shell Seekers, 1989, Company of Wolves, 1983, Wings of the Water; appeared in plays Hotel Paradiso, 1957, A Taste of Honey, 1960, Anyone Can Whistle, 1964, Mame (on Broadway), 1966, 83 (Tony award for Best Mus. Actress 1966), Dear World, 1968 (Tony award for Best Mus. Actress 1969), All Over (London Royal Shakespeare Co.), 1971, Gypsy, 1974 (Tony award for Best Mus. Actress 1975), The King and I, 1978, Sweeney Todd, 1979 (Tony award for Best Mus. Actress 1979), Hamlet, Nat. Theatre, London, 1976 (Sarah Siddons award 1974, 80). Named Woman of Yr., Harvard Hasty Pudding Theatricals, 1968; inducted Theatre Hall of Fame, 1982. Office: William Morris Agy care Jerry Katzman 151 El Camino Beverly Hills CA 90212

LANSDOWNE, KAREN MYRTLE, retired English language and literature educator; b. Twin Falls, Idaho, Aug. 11, 1926; d. George and Effie Myrtle (Ayotte) Martin; B.A. in English with honors, U. Oreg., 1948, M.Ed., 1958, M.A. with honors, 1960; m. Paul L. Lansdowne, Sept. 12, 1948; chilren—Michele Lynn, Larry Alan. Tchr., Newfield (N.Y.) High Sch., 1948-50, S. Eugene (Oreg.) High Sch., 1952; mem. faculty U. Oreg., Eugene, 1958-65; asst. prof. English, Lane Community Coll., Eugene, 1965-82, ret., 1982; cons. Oreg. Curriculum Study Center. Rep., Cal Young Neighborhood Assn., 1978—; mem. scholarship com. First Congl. Ch., 1950-70. Mem. MLA, Pacific N.W. Regional Conf. Community Colls., Nat. Council Tchrs. English, U. Oreg. Women, AAUW (sec.), Jaycettes, Pi Lambda Theta (pres.), Phi Beta Patronesses (pres.), Delta Kappa Gamma. Co-author: The Oregon Curriculum: Language/Rhetoric, I, II, III and IV, 1970. Home: 15757 Rim Rd La Pine OR 97739

LANSING, SHERRY LEE, motion picture production executive; b. Chgo., July 31, 1944; d. Norton and Margo L. BS summa cum laude in Theatre, Northwestern U., 1966. Tchr. math. public high schs. Los Angeles, 1966-69; model TV commls. Max Factor Co., 1969-70, Alberto-Culver Co., 1969-70. Appeared in movies Loving, 1970, Rio Lobo, 1970; exec. story editor movies, Wagner Internat., 1970-73; v.p. prodn., Heyday Prodns., Universal City, Calif., 1973-75; exec. story editor, then v.p. creative affairs, MGM Studios, Culver City, Calif., 1975-77; sr. v.p. prodn., Columbia Pictures, Burbank, Calif., 1977-80, pres., 20th Century-Fox Prodns., Beverly Hills, Calif., 1980-83; ind. producer., Jaffe-Lansing Prodns., Los Angeles, 1983—; producer Racing With the Moon, 1984, Firstborn, 1984, Fatal Attraction, 1987, The Accused, 1988, Black Rain, 1989; TV (exec. producer) When the Time Comes, Mistress. Office: Jaffe-Lansing Prodns 5555 Melrose Ave Los Angeles CA 90038*

LANSKA, MARY JO, pediatric neurologist, educator; b. Burlington, Wis., Dec. 30, 1958; d. Roman Theodore and Catherine Jane (Navratil) Brook; m. Douglas John Lanska, June 26, 1982; 1 child, Joseph Thomas. BS, U. Wis., Milw., 1980; MS, Med. Coll. Wis., 1984, MD, 1984. Diplomate Am. Bd. Pediatrics, Nat. Bd. Med. Examiners. Resident physician U. Hosps. Cleve., 1984-86; staff physician Health Hill Hosp., Cleve., 1985-86; pediatric neurology fellow U. Hosps. Cleve., 1986-89; attending neurologist VA Med. Ctr., Lexington, Ky., 1989—; asst. prof. U. Ky. Med. Ctr., Lexington, 1989—; physician Ky. Physicians Care Program, Lexington, 1989—. Editorial reviewer Neurology Editorial Office, Cleve., 1988—; contbr. articles to med. jours. Recipient Doctors' Houghton award Wis. State Med. Soc., 1984, Janet Glasgow Meml. Achievement award Am. Med. Women's Assn., 1984; Knapp scholar U. Wis., 1979. Mem. AMA, Am. Acad. Pediatrics, Child Neurology Soc., Am. Acad. Neurology, N.Y. Acad. Scis., World Fedn. Neurology, Phi Kappa Phi, Alpha Omega Alpha. Roman Catholic. Office: Univ Ky Med Ctr Dept Neurology, 800 Rose St Lexington KY 40536-0084

LANT, NANCY JANE, school psychologist; b. Waterbury, Conn., Apr. 5, 1930; D. Samuel Merwin and Jane Hawley (Pearl) Main; m. Robert Carter Hayden, 1952 (div. 1958); children: Karen Carter Hayden Morton, Sharon Gale; m. Weston Franklyn Lant, 1962 (div. 1971); children: Weston Franklyn Jr., Craig Merwin. BA, Brown U., 1952; MEd, Bridgewater State Coll., 1971; cert. advanced grad. study, Boston U., 1974. Cert. tchr., guidance counselor, guidance dir., gen. supr., sch. psychologist, Mass.; nat. cert. sch. psychologist. Tchr. English City of New Bedford (Mass.) Sch. Dept., 1969-71, guidance counselor, 1971-75, sch. psychologist, 1975—; vis. lectr. II Bridgewater (Mass.) State Coll., 1978-81; part-time faculty Mass. Maritime Acad., Buzzards, Mass., 1971-77. Contbr. poems to several small jours. Treas. local Boys Scouts Am., Carver, Mass., 1965-69; sec. Community Action Coun., Plymouth, Mass., 1967-69. Fellow New Bedford Educators Assn. (bd. dirs. 1985—), Mass. Sch. Psychologists Assn., Nat. Assn. Sch. Psychologists; mem. Mass. Tchrs. Assn. (local rep. to annual meeting 1984—), NEA (life, local rep. to representation 1984—). Democrat. Buddhist. Home: 114 E Clinton St New Bedford MA 02740 Office: City of New Bedford Sch Dept 455 County St New Bedford MA 02740

LANTIERI, BRENDA JEAN, water utility official; b. Pen Argyl, Pa., Dec. 13, 1944; d. George and Mildred (Confalone) Striba; m. Joseph Charles Lantieri, June 27, 1970; 1 child, Joseph Anthony. AA, Glendale (Calif.) Coll., 1977; BS cum laude, West Coast U., L.A., 1986; postgrad., U. So. Calif., 1990. Adminstrv. asst. Met. Water Dist. So. Calif., L.A., 1966-76, contracts adminstr., 1976-88, facility mgr., 1988—. Recipient award Burbank Bus. and Profl. Women's Club, 1980. Mem. Internat. Facility Mgmt. Assn., Am. Water Works Assn. (affiliate), NAFE, Mgmt. Devel. Club Met. Water Dist. (pres. 1990), Affirmative Action Assn. for Women (pres. 1978-79), Toastmasters (club pres. 1984, 88, Outstanding and Competent Toastmaster award 1983), Alpha Chi. Republican. Roman Catholic. Office: Met Water Dist So Calif 1111 Sunset Blvd Los Angeles CA 90012

LANTRIP, KAY LYNN, civil engineer; b. Herrin, Ill., Aug. 25, 1953; d. Robert F. and Pauline K. Osowski; student So. Ill. U., 1971-73; m. Bruce M. Lantrip, Aug. 3, 1974; children: Emily Katherine, David Michael. BS in Civil Engring., U. Ill., 1975. Civil engr., Old Ben Coal Co., Benton, Ill., 1975-77, Bechtel Power Corp., Gaithersburg, Md., 1977; civil engr. Ralph M. Parsons Co., Balt. Regional Rapid Transit System, Balt., 1977-80; sr. project mgr. George Hyman Constrn. Co., 1980—. Registered profl. engr. Mem. Chi Epsilon. Home: 5452 Thunder Hill Rd Columbia MD 21045

LANTRY, MARILYN MARTHA, state legislator; b. St. Paul, Oct. 28, 1932; d. Louis Leonard and Josephine (Cermak) Kunz; m. Jerome Horton Lantry, 1953; children: Jacqueline, Kathleen. Grad. high sch. Legislative aide to city councilman Tedesco, Minn., 1973-80; mem. Minn. State Senate, 1981—. Democrat. Roman Catholic. Office: 2169 Beech Saint Paul MN 55119*

LANTTO, MARCIA MABEL, county official; b. Buffalo, Minn., Nov. 30, 1944; d. Byron Glenn and Ferne Geraine (Nelson) Peterson; m. Joseph Robert Lantto, Apr. 11, 1964. Student, St. Cloud U., 1962-63. Operator Northwestern Bell Telephone Co., Buffalo, 1963-64; cost auditor Honeywell Co., Mpls., 1965-66; dep. register deeds Wright County, Buffalo, 1966-74, recorder, registrar titles, 1975—; chartermem. uniform comml. code task force Sec. of State, Minn. Vol. ARC, St. Paul, 1988—; mem. pub. rels. com. Buffalo Mcpl. Airport Bd., 1989-90; mem. Buffalo Strategic Planning Com., 1990; mem. adv. task force on uniform conveyancing blanks Minn. Dept. Commerce, 1989—. Mem. Minn. Assn. County Officers (bd. dirs. or alt. 1978—, conf. liaison 1985—), Minn. Assn. County Recorders (cert., treas. 1978-85), Wright County Officers Assn. (sec.-treas. 1989—), Airplane Owners and Pilots Assn., Minn. 99's. Lutheran. Home: 702 4th Ave NW Buffalo MN 55313 Office: Wright County Recorder 10 NW 2d St Buffalo MN 55313

LANTZ, BILLIE JOANNE, nurse; b. Jacksonville, Fla., Sept. 26, 1956; d. William Albert and Sybil Rowena (Malone) L. BSN with honors, U. Fla., 1978; MS, U. South Fla., 1987. RN, Fla. Med.-surg. nurse North Fla. Regional Hosp., Gainesville, 1978-79; asst. supr. nursing Anheuser Busch, Tampa, Fla., 1979-86; mgr. occupational health Bapt. Med. Ctr., Jacksonville, 1986-90; exec. dir. Physical Restoration Ctr., Jacksonville, 1990—. Mem. Assn. Employee Health Profls., Occupational Health Nurses Assn. (cert.). Democrat. Roman Catholic. Home: 2311 L'Atrium Circle N Pointe Vedra Beach FL 32082 Office: Physical Restoration Ctr 7037 Commonwealth Ave #100 Jacksonville FL 32220

LANTZ, JOANNE BALDWIN, university chancellor; b. Defiance, Ohio, Jan. 26, 1932; d. Hiram J. and Ethel A. (Smith) Baldwin; m. Wayne E. Lantz. BS in Physics and Math., U. Indpls., 1953; MS in Counseling and Guidance, Ind. U., 1957; PhD in Counseling and Psychology, Mich. State U., 1969; LittD (hon.), U. Indlps., 1985. Tchr. physics and math. Arcola (Ind.) High Sch., 1953-57; guidance dir. New Haven (Ind.) Sr. High Sch., 1957-65; with Ind. U.-Purdue U., Fort Wayne, 1965—, interim chancellor, 1988-89, chancellor, 1989—. Contbr. articles to profl. jours. Mem. Fort Wayne Econ. Devel. Adv. Bd. and Task Force, 1988—, Corp. Coun., 1988—; bd. advisors Leadership Fort Wayne, 1988—; mem. adv. bd. Ind. Small Bus. Devel. Ctr., 1988—; bd. trustees Ancilla System, Inmc., 1984-89, chmn. human resources com., 1985-89, exec. com., 1985-89, bd. trustees St. Joseph's Med. Ctr., 1983-84, personnel advf. com. to bd. dirs. 1978-84, chmn., 1980-84;l bd. dirs. United Way Allen County, Sec. to the Bd., 1979-80; bd. dirs. Anthony Wayne Vocat. Rehab. Ctr., 1969-75. Mem. Fort Wayne Alumni Soc. (hon. mem. 1987), Am. Psychol. Assn., AAUW (internat. fellowship com. 1986-88, prog. com. 1981-83, Am. women fellowship com. 1978-83, chmn. 1981-83, trust rsch. grantee 1980), Southeastern Psychol. Assn. (referee conv. papers 1987, 88), Ind. Sch. Women's Club (v.p. prog. chair 1979-81), Pi Lambda Theta, Sigma Xi, Delta Kappa Gamma (editorial bd. 1986-88, gen. chair conv. 1985-86, dir. N.E. region 1982-84, adminstrv. bd., exec. bd. 1982-84, leadership devel. com.). Office: Ind U-Purdue U 2101 Coliseum Blvd E Fort Wayne IN 46805

LANTZ, KAREN MARIE, trade association administrator; b. Tucson, Nov. 22, 1946; d. Roy Fredrick and Carmelita Ann (Cessna) L. BA, Stephens Coll., 1968; MS in Indsl. and Labor, Cornell U., 1984. Flight attendant Trans World Airlines, Jamaica, N.Y., 1969—; with Ind. Fedn. Flight Attendants, 1979—; contract adminstr. Ind. Fedn. Flight Attendants, N.Y.C., 1983-84, v.p., 1984—. Mem. Nat. Women's Polit. Caucus, N.Y.C., 1985, 89; v.p. Mid-Manhattan New Dem. Club, N.Y.C., 1989—, female dist. leader, 1990; mem. N.Y. State Dem. Women's Leadership Coun. Mem. Coalition of Labor Union Women (del. nat. exec. bd. 1984—), Cornell U. Alumni Assn. (bd. dirs. 1987—), Indsl. Rels. Rsch. Assn., NOW, Crowley Inst. (bd. dirs. 1989—). Democrat. Episcopalian. Home: 320 E 46th St #9B New York NY 10017 Office: Ind Fedn Flight Attendants 630 Third Ave New York NY 10017

LANTZ, LOUISE KALAMAN, author, teacher; b. Balt., Nov. 22, 1930; m. Curtis Edward Lantz, June 9, 1951; children: Mark Edward, Monica Lantz Hauswald,. Student, U. Md., 1948-50; BA in Art History with honors, Goucher Coll., 1977; cert. in Md. decorative arts, Balt. Mus. Art, 1976. Freelance author, writer, 1961—, cons. to mus., 1961—; tchr. Balt. County Dept. Edn., 1963—; tchr. Goucher Coll., Towson, Md., 1977—, art slide libr., 1977—; tchr. Loyola Coll., Balt., 1980; cons. Mystic (Conn.) Seaport, 1973, Valentine House Mus., Richmond, Va., 1971, Cloisters Children's Mus., Balt., 1986, Peale Mus., Balt., 1981—, Time Life Books Ency. of Collectibles, 1979. Author: Old American Kitchenware 1725-1925, 1970-88 (17 eds.), Price Guide to Old American Kitchenware, 1965, subsequent eds. 1970, 72, 77, 80, Dictionary and Price Guide to Kitchenware Collectibles, 1981, contbr. chpts. to Spinning Wheel's Complete Book of Antiques, 1972, Spinning Wheel's Antiques for Women, 1974, Spinning Wheel's Collectible Iron, Tin, Copper and Brass, 1974; contbr. articles to profl. jours., newspapers, mags. Mem. Am. Assn. for State and Local History, Balt. County Hist. Soc., Am. Friends of English Heritage, Nat. Women's Studies Assn., Md. Horticultural Soc. Home: 5703 Williams Rd Hydes MD 21082 Office: Goucher Coll Dulaney Valley Rd Towson MD 21204

LANTZ, PEGGY SIAS, editor; b. Coral Gables, Fla., Aug. 8, 1933; d. Frederick Ralph and Mildred Lee (Hogg) Sias; m. James Donald Lantz, June 7, 1958; children: Linda Marie, Janet Katherine, Philip Ralph, Carolyn Sias. MusB, Rollins Coll., 1955. Music tchr. Elem. Schs. Leesburg, Winter Garden, Fla., 1955-58; editor Horse Country Newspaper, Orlando, Fla., 1980-83; editor The Palmetto Fla. Native Plant Soc., Orlando, 1981—; editor Fla. Naturalist The Fla. Naturalist Fla. Audubon Soc., Maitland, Fla., 1985—; Editor: (newsletter) Fellowship of United Meth. Musicians, Fla., 1988-89. Author, editor: Wekiva River-Scenic and Wild, 1988; contbr. 100 articles to mags. Dir. music various chs., Fla. and Minn., 1961-88; dir. various choruses, Mpls., 1973-79. Recipient Addy-2nd pl. Am. Advt. Fedn., Fla., 1988, Publ. in Paradise-Silver, Fla. Mag. Assn., 1989. Mem. Fla. Native Plant Soc. (bd. dirs., pubs. chair 1981—), Fla. Audubon Soc., Orange Audubon Soc. (bd. dirs. 1981-86, editor newsletter 1982-85, pres. 1989—), Nat. League Am. Pen Women (editor, sec. Orlando br. 1989—). Republican. Presbyterian. Home: 2020 Red Gate Rd Orlando FL 32818

LANWEHR, HELEN, retired educator; b. Nanty-Glo, Pa., Mar. 12, 1918; d. Michael and Anna (Gmiter) Kalenak; m. Frederick Herman Lanwehr, June 30, 1945; children: Bernhard Herman, Lawrence Michael. BS, Columbia U., 1945, MEd, 1946; postgrad., St. Peters Coll., Jersey City, N.J., Jersey City State Coll. Cert. bus., coop. office tchr., placement dir., N.J. Tchr. bus. Rhodes Prep. Sch., N.Y.C., 1945-50; tchr. bus. placement advisor Hoboken High Sch., 1961-87; ret., 1987; cons. Hoboken Free Sch., St. Peter's Coll., Hoboken, 1965-75. Fund raiser Jersey City Philharm., 1951; tchr. Literacy Vols. Am., Kearny, N.J., 1987—; coord. Search Bible Study, Kearny, 1988—; Sunday sch. tchr. 1st Luth. Ch., Kearny, 1988—; chmn. scholarship com. St. Mary Hosp. Aux., Hoboken, 1988. N.Y. State Regents scholar, 1939; N.J. Coop. Office Edn. grantee, 1984. Mem. NEA, N.J. Edn. Assn., N.J. Ret. Edn. Assn., Hudson County Ret. Educators Assn., Hoboken Edn. Assn. Ret. Tchrs. and Staff (organizer, pres. 1987—), AAUW (v.p. 1955-60), LWV (charter com. Jersey City 1952), Rotary.

LANZKRON, CAROLYN KAHN, software design engineer; b. Boston, Dec. 5, 1964; d. William Martin and Phyllis Irene (Brown) K.; m. Paul Joshua Lanzkron, Aug. 23, 1987. BEE, Boston U., 1987. Engr. BNR, Inc., Research Triangle Park, N.C., 1988-89, No. Telecom, Inc., Research Triangle Park, 1989—. Program v.p. Durham (N.C.) chpt. Hadassah, 1987-90, pres., 1990—; bd. dirs. Beth-El Synagogue, Durham, 1990—. Mem. IEEE (bull. editor, bd. dirs. 1987-89). Office: BNR Inc Dept 3T92 35 Davis Dr Research Triangle Park NC 27709

LAO, MARY ANN, financial analyst; b. Manila, The Philippines, Dec. 13, 1959; came to U.S.A., 1976; d. Benjamin and Esther (Kohtiao) L. BS in Acctg., State U. NY, 1981; MBA, Boston Coll., 1986. Acct. Translantic Reinsurance, NYC, 1981-82, Anders Services Co., NYC, 1982-84; sr. fin. analyst Gen. Foods, USA, White Plains, NY, 1986-87, fin. assoc., 1987-89, fin. specialist, 1989—. Roman Catholic. Office: Gen Foods USA 250 North St White Plains NY 10625

LAPADOT, SONEE SPINNER, automobile manufacturing company official; b. Sidney, Ohio, Apr. 19, 1936; d. Kenneth Lee and Helyn Kathryn (Hobby) Spinner; m. Jan. 13, 1955 (div. Apr. 1970); 1 child, Douglas Cameron; m. Robert Stephen Lapadot, May 4, 1974. Student, U. Cin., 1954-56, U. Akron, 1966, Spring Arbor Coll., 1989-90. Mgr. engring. change implementation Terex div. GM, Hudson, Ohio, 1975-77, mgr. prodn. scheduling, 1977-78, gen. adminstr. product purchasing, 1978-79; sr. staff asst. non-ferrous metals GM, Detroit, 1979-80, mgr. tires and wheels, 1980-83, mgr. staff purchasing, 1983-85, mgr. corp. constrn. contracting, 1985-86; mfg. techs. adminstr. Chrysler Motors, Detroit, 1986-87, mgr. mfg. prodn. control adminstrn. and svcs., 1988, mgr. advanced planning and prodn. systems, 1988-89, mgr. advanced planning and control power trains, 1989-90, mgr. Mound Rd. engine prodn. control, 1990—. Active fund-raising Boy Scouts Am., Grosse Pointe, Mich., 1980-82, Detroit, 1985-89, United Fund, Detroit, 1980-89, Jr. Achievement, Detroit, 1984, 90. Mem. NAFE, Soc. Automotive Engrs., Am. Soc. Profl. and Exec. Women, Am. Prodn. and Inventory Control Soc., Automotive Industry Action Group (schedule process mgmt. com.), Mensa, Women's Econ. Club of Detroit. Home: 1941 Squirrel Rd Bloomfield Hills MI 48013 Office: Chrysler Motors Corp Mound Rd Engine Plant 20300 Mound Rd Detroit MI 48234

LAPCZYNSKI, SUSAN AGNES, systems consultant; b. Somerville, N.J., Apr. 19, 1960; d. George Matthew and Agnes Patricia (Welch) L. BA, Rutgers U., 1982. Typesetter Targum Pub. Co., New Brunswick, N.J., 1978-82, prodn. dir., 1981-82; bilingual sec. Soc. Génerale, N.Y.C., 1982-83; applications specialist Investment Support Systems, Bloomfield, N.J., 1983-85; sr. systems analyst Merrill Lynch, N.Y.C., 1985-88; freelance graphic artist, Hoboken, 1988—; systems cons. Sycamore Cons. Group, Chatham, 1989—. Mem. Ventura Users Group N.Y., Alliance Francaise N.Y., Rutgers U. Alumni Club N.Y.C. (sec. 1988—). Roman Catholic. Home: 207 14th St Apt 2R Hoboken NJ 07030

LAPELLE, DIANE MCDONNELL, banker; b. Chgo., June 22, 1952; d. George F. and Mary M. (Merrick) McDonnell; m. William J. Lapelle, June 19, 1976. BA, U. Notre Dame, 1974. With staff ops. and mgmt. services Continental Ill. Nat. Bank, Chgo., 1974-76, cash position sr. analyst, 1976-79, mgr. cash position, 1979, ops. officer, 1980, mgr. cash position and ops. control, 1981, 2d v.p., 1982-85, relationship mgr. money ctr. banks, 1985-86, v.p., 1986—. Treas. Assocs. St. Joseph Hosp., Chgo., 1979—. Club: Notre Dame (bd. govs. 1986-87, 89—). Office: Continental Ill Nat Bank 231 S LaSalle St Chicago IL 60697

LAPID-BOGDA, GINGER SNAPP, management consultant; b. Salt Lake City, Apr. 18, 1946; d. Martin Maxwell and Edith Bearice (Cohen-Carter) Snapp Green; m. Gary George Lapid, Aug. 9, 1969 (div. 1971); m. Russell Wallace Bogda, Oct. 4, 1987. BA, U. Calif., 1968; MS in Edn., U. Pa., 1970; PhD, U. Calif., 1979. Tchr. Phila. Pub. Schs., 1970-72, Springside Sch., Chestnut Hill, Pa., 1972-74, Santa Barbara Community Sch., 1974-76; supr. U. Calif.; adminstr. Nat. Coll. Edn., Evanston, Ill., 1978-79, Elmhurst Coll., 1979-80, U. Phoenix, 1980; cons. Kaiser-permanente Med. Care Program, Oakland, Calif., 1981-86, Los Angeles, 1986--; teaching U. Redlands, 1977-78; adv. faculty Sonoma State, 1987--; teaching U. Phoenix, 1980-81. Bd. dirs. U Calif. Santa Barbara Womens Ctr., 1977-78, Domestic Violence Project, Santa Barbara, 1977-78; cons. Woman's Bldg. Arts Orgn., Los Angeles, 1988—, pro-choice orgns. Mem. Orgn. Devel. Network, Assn. Training and Devel., Cert. Cons. Internat. Democrat. Jewish. Home: 15322 Mulholland Dr Los Angeles CA 90077

LAPIN, SHARON JOYCE VAUGHN, interior designer; b. Lagrange, Mo., July 28, 1938; d. John Nolan and Wilma Emma (Huebotter) Vaughn; BA summa cum laude, U. Wash., Seattle, 1960; m. Byron Richard Lapin, Oct. 14, 1972. Appeared in various Broadway shows, TV commls. and TV shows, 1962-72; owner Sharon Lapin Designs St. Louis. Bd. dirs. St. Louis conservatory and Schs. for Arts, 1977—, v.p., 1982-87 ; chmn. bd. Studio Set, 1978-81, pres., 1975-78, bd. dirs., 1975-83; bd. dirs. Friends of Sci. Mus., 1980-90, v.p., 1984-85; pres. Assocs. Bd. Dirs., St. Louis Sci. Ctr., Inc., 1986-87; bd. dirs. Jr. Div., St. Louis Symphony Women's Assn., 1973-75; bd. dirs. Womens Assn. St. Louis Symphony, 1988-90. Mem. AFTRA, Screen Actors Guild, Actors Equity Assn., Am. Soc. Interior Designers, Pi Beta Phi, Mu Phi Epsilon.

LAPOINTE, CYNTHIA RUTH, public relations executive; b. Menominee, Mich., Jan. 2, 1962; d. Carl Wilfred and Ruth Ann (Schauer) LaPointe. AS, Washtenaw Community Coll., Ypsilanti, Mich., 1982. Respiratory therapist U. Mich. Hosp., Ann Arbor, 1981-82, Virginia Mason Hosp., Seattle, 1982-84, Children's Orthopedic Hosp., Seattle, 1984-86; asst. mgr. pub. relations Neiman Marcus, San Francisco, 1986-88; mgr. pub. relations Neiman Marcus, Dallas, 1988-89; dir. pub. relations Neiman Marcus, Palo Alto, Calif., 1989—. Event producer Valle Monte League, San Jose, Peninsula Children's Ctr., Palo Alto, Ronald McDonald House, 1988, 89, Chinese Hist. and Cultural Soc., 1990. Mem. Women in Communications. Republican. Roman Catholic. Office: Neiman Marcus 400 Stanford Shopping Ctr Palo Alto CA 94304

LAPOINTE, DAWN DUNAWAY, personnel executive; b. Watertown, N.Y., Sept. 25, 1955; d. Gordon Paul and Grovene Marie (Champion) Dunaway; 1 child, Gerard Jr. AAS, Jefferson Community Coll., Watertown. Exec. dir., co-founder N.E. Placement Svcs., Eastford, Conn., bus. mgr.; dir. Vocat. Svcs./Mental Retardation, Eastford; vocat. instr. County Industries, Coventry, Conn. Recipient Supported Employment Recognition award. Mem. NAFE, Assn. for Persons in Supported Employment. Home: 662 Phoenixville Rd Chaplin CT 06235

LAPP, ALICE WEBER, educator, editor; b. Lititz, Pa., July 29, 1931; d. Benjamin Franklin and Sarah (Hostetter) Weber; m. John Allen Lapp, Aug. 20, 1955; children: John Franklin, Jennifer W., Jessica W. BA, Eastern Mennonite Coll., 1955; MA, James Madison U., 1970. Tchr. English Brownell Jr. High Sch., Cleve., 1955-56; tchr. English Elkton (Va.) High Sch., 1956-58, Eisenhower Sr. High Sch., Norristown, Pa., 1958-60; art tchr. Eastern Mennonite High Sch., Harrisonburg, Va., 1962-64; lectr. English Eastern Mennonite Coll., Harrisonburg, 1964-69; substitute tchr. Ephrata (Pa.) Pub. Schs., 1970-72; lectr. English Bethlehem U., West Bank, Israel,

1978-79, Goshen (Ind.) Coll., 1983; substitute tchr. Lancaster (Pa.) Mennonite High Sch., 1987—; copy editor Lancaster Mennonite Hist. Soc., 1988—. Contbr. book revs. and articles to church mags. Sec. adv. bd. Salvation Army, Goshen, 1975-85; mem. bd. ARC, Elkhart County, Elkhart, Ind., 1975-85, vol., Goshen, Ephrata, 1975—. Mem. AAUW (v.p. Va. chpt. 1965-68, pres. Ind. chpt. 1981-84). Mennonite. Home: 13 Knollwood Dr Akron PA 17501

LAPP, MARY KLEMM, quality specialist; b. Clarkson, N.Y.; d. William E. and Helen (Bodnar) Klemm; m. Daniel S. Lapp, Apr. 10, 1974; children: Jeffrey, D. Schuyler, Spencer. BA, U. Rochester, N.Y., 1973; MS, Alfred (N.Y.) U., 1989. Quality specialist Corning (N.Y.) Inc., product engr.; supr. Glass and Refractory Tech. Mem. Nat. Assn. Purchasing Mgrs., Am. Ceramic Soc., Keramos, Phi Kappa Phi. Office: HP ME 1 13 Corning NY 14831

LAPP, SUSAN BOLSTER, learning disability educator; b. Washington, Nov. 23, 1945; d. Robert Fay and Nona (Peifly) Bolster; m. Richard Gordon Lapp, Apr. 22, 1967. BS in Edn., Miami U., Oxford, Ohio, 1967; MEd, Xavier U., Cin., 1977. Cert. tchr. English; cert. in learning disabilities and behavior disorders K-12. Sec. Penta Tech. Coll., Perrysburg, Ohio, 1065-67; tchr. 7th, 8th grades Toledo Pub. Schs., Perrysburg, 1965-67; tchr. 3d grade Toledo Pub. Schs., 1966-67; thcr. 7th and 8th grades Fairfield (Ohio) City Schs., 1967-78, 6th, 7th and 8th grade learning disabilities tchr., 1978—, spl. svcs. coordinator, 1984—, career edn. coordinator, 1987—; career edn. coordinator Butler County Joint Vocat. Sch., Hamilton, Ohio, 1987—; student vol. dir. Fairfield Middle Sch., 1990—. Named Spl. Edn. Tchr. of Yr., S.W. Ohio Spl. Edn. Regional Resource Ctr., 1989. Mem. NEA, S.W. Ohio Edn. Assn., Fairfield Classroom Tchrs. Assn., Nat. Assn. for Female Execs., Career Edn. Assn., Orton Soc. Home: 900 Harrison Ave Hamilton OH 45013 Office: Fairfield Middle Sch 255 Donald Dr Fairfield OH 45014

LAPPE, FRANCES MOORE, author, lecturer; b. Pendleton, Oreg., Feb. 10, 1944; d. John and Ina (Skrifvars) Moore; m. Marc Lappe, Nov. 11, 1967 (div. 1977); children: Anthony, Anna; m. J. Baird Callicott, Dec. 1, 1985. BA in History, Earlham Coll., 1966; PhD (hon.), St. Mary's Coll., 1983, Lewis and Clark Coll., 1983, Macalester Coll., 1986, Hamline U., 1987, Earlham Coll., 1988, Kenyon Coll., 1989. Co-founder, mem. staff Inst. for Food and Devel. Policy, San Francisco, 1975—. Author: Diet for A Small Planet, 1971, 75, 82, Now We Can Speak, 1982, What To Do After You Turn Off the TV: Fresh Ideas for Enjoying Family Time, 1985; co-author: (with Joseph Collins) What Can We Do?, 1980, Aid as Obstacle, 1980, Nicaragua: What Difference Could a Revolution Make?, Food and Farming in the New Nicaragua, 1982, World Hunger: Ten Myths, 1982, World Hunger: Twelve Myths, 1986, (with Joseph Collins) Mozambique and Tanzania: Asking the Big Questions, 1980, (with Adele Beccar-Varela) Casting New Molds: First Steps Toward Worker Control in a Mozambique Factory, 1980, (with Peter Sketchley) Food First: Beyond the Myth of Scarcity, 1977, rev. (with Joseph Collins), (with Rachel Schurman and Kevin Danaher) Betraying the National Interest, 1987, Rediscovering America's Values, 1989, (with Rachel Schurman) Taking Population Serioully, 1990. Named to Nutrition Hall of Fame Ctr. for Sci. and Pub. Interest, 1981; recipient Mademoiselle Mag. award, 1977; World Hunger Media award, 1982, Right Livelihood award, 1987. Office: Inst for Food and Devel Policy 145 9th St San Francisco CA 94103

LAPTAD, MARIA NITA RAMERIEZ, counselor; b. San Pablo, Philippines, Apr. 18, 1947; arrived in U.S., 1975; d. Joaquin Villanueva and Elpidia (Magpantay) Ramirez; m. Raymond Alan Laptad, Oct. 27, 1979. BA cum laude, St. Theresa's Coll., Manila, 1963, BS in Edn. magna cum laude, 1964; MA in Ednl. Adminstrn., Ateneo de Manila, 1965, MA in Edn. and Counseling, 1966; MA in Sociology, Asian Social Inst., 1972; PhD in Computer Edn. and Design, 1990. Asst. prin., head lit. and English dept. St. Theresa's Coll., Manila, 1963-65; dean student affairs, dir. lang. arts Ateneo de Manila Grade Sch., 1967-79; with St. Paul's Coll., Manila, 1967-69; dir. pastoral sociology research, project prof. Research Ctr., Manila, Asian Social Inst. Grad. Sch., Manila, 1969-76; chief exec. officer, counselor Shadow Hills Samaritan, Inc., Lakewood, Calif., 1976-90; gen. mgr. Brighten Data Inc., Newport Beach, 1990—; pres. Power Cube, Inc., Orange, Calif., 1987—; cons. George Basil & Assocs., Montreal, 1983-86; mgr. S.H.S., Inc., Las Vegas, 1986—. Campus counselor Asian-Am. Students Orgn., U. Calif., Davis, 1976-78; cons. Prison Ministries, Las Vegas, 1978-79; cons.internat. del. Vatican II, Rome, 1976—. Mem. Nat. Assn. Female Execs. Republican. Roman Catholic. Club: Commander's. Home: PO Box 1070 Lakewood CA 90711-3249 Office: Shadow Hills Samaritan Inc 4228 Lakewood Blvd Long Beach CA 90808

LAQUATRA, LISA ANN, advertising executive; b. Pitts., Mar. 26, 1962; d. Carl Jacob and Virginia Mae (Hause) Walpusk; m. Scott James Laquatra, Aug. 20, 1988. BS, California (Pa.) U., 1984. Asst. mktg. analyst McGraw-Edison Co., Coraopolis, Pa., 1984-85; advt. mgr. Nat. Draeger, Inc., Pitts., 1985—. Mem. Bus./Profl. Advt. Assn., Soc. for Tech. Communication, Am. Soc. Advt. & Promotion, Women in Communication Inc. Republican. Presbyterian. Office: Nat Draeger Inc 101 Technology Dr Pittsburgh PA 15230

LARACH, MARILYN GREEN, physician; b. Phila., Apr. 7, 1952; d. Philip and Fred (Rubin) Green; m. David Ross Larach, Aug. 8, 1976; 1 child, Daniel Benjamin. AB, Princeton U., 1973; MD, NYU, 1978. Diplomate Nat. Bd. Med. Examiners, Am. Bd. Anesthesiology, Am. Bd. Pediatrics. Resident in pediatrics Jacobi Hosp-Albert Einstein Coll. Medicine, Bronx, N.Y., 1978-80; intern in pediatrics Bronx Mcpl. Hosp. Ctr., Phila., 1978-79; resident in pediatrics Bronx Mcpl. Hosp. Ctr., 1979-80; resident in anesthesia Hosp. of U. Pa., 1980-83; fellow in anesthesiology Children's Hosp. Phila., 1982-83; chief of anesthesia service U. Hosp. for Rehab., Elizabethtown, Pa., 1983—; asst. prof. Pa. State U. Medicine, Hershey, 1983—; dir. N.Am. Malignant Hypertension Registry, Hershey, 1988—, bd. mem. Contbr. articles to profl. jours. Mem. Princeton U. Schs. and Scholarship Com., Cen. Pa., 1985—. Named Woodrow Wilson scholar, Princeton U., 1973; recipient McConnell fellowship, Princeton U., 1972. Mem. Malignant Hyperthermia Assn. of U.S. (profl. adv. coun. 1989—), Am. Acad. Pediatrics, Am. Soc. Anesthesiologists. Office: Dept Anesthesia PO Box 850 Hershey PA 17033

LARACH, RANDA ISELL, chemical engineer; b. San Pedro Sula, Honduras, Nov. 2, 1960; came to U.S., 1976; d. Salomon and Marlene Widad (Sansur) L. BS magna cum laude, U. Md., 1982. Process engr. Union Carbide Corp., Charleston, W.Va., 1982-84, advanced process engr., 1984-86; plant engr. Union Carbide Corp., Texas City, Tex., 1986-89; sr. process engr. Stone and Webster Engrng. Corp., Houston, 1989—. Senatorial scholar State of Md., 1978. Mem. Am. Inst. Chem. Engrs. Roman Catholic. Office: 330 Barker Cypress Rd Houston TX 77094

LARAR, JEANETTE G., insurance executive, fund raiser; b. N.Y., Dec. 7, 1934; d. Abraham and Ida (Breslin) Gittleman; m. Michael E. Larar, May 28, 1957 (div. 1970); children: Leslie Ann, Gerald Neil, Allen Maurice. Student, Hunter Coll., 1952-53, Geo. Wash. U., 1953, Winter Pk. Sch. of Real Estate Law, 1964, St. Leo Ext. Coll., 1970. Asst. underwriter Met. Life Ins. Co., N.Y.C, 1952-53; asst. office mgr. Met. Life Ins. Co., Washington, 1953-54; fund raiser Albert Einstein Coll. of Med., N.Y.C, 1954-56, Fedn. Jewish Philanthropies, N.Y.C, 1956-57; code enforcement clk. Dept. of H.E.W., Washington, 1957-58, pers. interviewer, 1959-60; realtor Orlando, Fla., 1964-66; pvt. practice San Antonio and Miami, Fla., 1966-77; ins. agent Ind., Miami, Fla., 1978-86; gen. agt., mktg. v.p. The Brennan Companies, Hollywood, Fla. and Atlanta, 1987—; non-profit endowment specialist, 1985—; freelance mktg. cons., fundraising campaign mgr., 1987—. Vol., Urban League, Israel Bonds, N.Y., 1950-52, Comm. Chest Fed. and U.J.A., Wash. 1954-57, Am. Cancer Soc., Miami, 1970-74, Muscular Distrophy & Cystic Fibrosis, Miami, 1980--, mem. Area Beautification Comm., Wash. 1953-54. Mem. NAFE, Natl. Assn. of Life Underwriters, Am. Soc. of Notaries. Republican. Jewish. Office: The Brennan Co 309 Morris Ave Suite J Spring Lake NJ 07762

LARAYA-CUASAY, LOURDES REDUBLO, pediatric pulmonologist, educator; b. Baguio, Philippines, Dec. 8, 1941; came to U.S., 1966; d. Jose Marquez and Lolita (Redublo) Laraya; m. Ramon Serrano Cuasay, Aug. 7, 1965; children: Raymond Peter, Catherine Ann, Margaret Rose, Joseph Paul. AA, U. Santo Tomas, Manila, Philippines, 1958, MD cum laude, 1963. Diplomate Am. Bd. Pediatrics. Clin. instr. Tulane U., New Orleans, 1967-68; asst. prof. pediatrics Temple Health Scis. Ctr., Phila., 1972-77; assoc. prof. pediatrics Thomas Jefferson Med. Sch., Phila., 1977-79; assoc. prof. pediatrics U. Medicine & Dentistry N. J., Robert Wood Johnson Med. Sch., New Brunswick, 1980-85, prof. clin. pediatrics, 1985—; dir. pediatric pulmonary and cystic fibrosis program U. Medicine and Dentistry, Robert Wood Johnson Med. Sch., New Brunswick, 1981—. Co-editor: Interstitial Lung Diseases in Children, 1988. Recipient Pediatric Rsch. award Mead Johnson Pharm. Co., Manila, 1965. Fellow Am. Coll. Chest Physicians (steering com., chmn. cardiopulmonary diseases in children 1976—), Am. Acad. Pediatrics (tobacco free generation rep. 1986—); mem. Am. Ambulatory Pediatric Soc., N.J. Thoracic Soc. (chmn. pediatric pulmonary com. 1986—), Lung Club. Home: 100 Mercer Ave Spring Lake NJ 07762 Office: Robert Wood Johnson Med Sch CN19 New Brunswick NJ 08903

LARBALESTRIER, DEBORAH ELIZABETH, writer; b. Pitts., July 17, 1934; d. Theron Benjamin and Granetha Elizabeth (Crenshaw) Cowherd; m. Dec. 25, 1969 (div.). AB, Storer Coll., 1954; student, Robert H. Terrell Law Coll., 1954-58, Woodbury Coll., 1959-60; certs., Univ. W. Los Angeles, 1971-73. Cert. legal asst., paralegal specialist. Author Prentice-Hall Inc., Englewood Cliffs, N.J., 1975—; prof. Southland Career Inst., L.A., 1985—; paralegal mgr. Lynberg & Watkins, L.A., 1988—; bd. dirs. Am. Paralegal Assn., Los Angeles, 1975-80, exec. dir., 1980—; nat. chmn. Am. Inmate Paralegal Assn., 1984—; cons. Fed. Bur. Prisons, 1983—. Mem. Los Angeles Police Dept. (Wilshire div.) Community Police Council, 1985—, Harbor Human Relations Council, Wilmington, Calif., 1985—; vol., crime prevention specialist Los Angeles Police Dept. (Wilshire div.), 1985—. Recipient gold plaque Am. Paralegal Assn. Chpt. Pres., Los Angeles, 1975, Nat. Notary Assn., Hawaii, 1979, cert. of acknowledgment Los Angeles Police Dept., 1985, Humanitarian Award of Spl. Merit, So. Calif. Motion Picture Council, 1987. Mem. U. of W. Los Angeles (adv. bd. 1980, 88), Am. Paralegal Assn. (exec. dir. 1975), Am. Inmate Assn. (nat. chmn. 1983), U. W. Los Angeles Paralegal Alumni Assn. Republican. Jewish. Home: 1321-1/2S Sycamore Ave Los Angeles CA 90019 Office: Lynberg & Watkins 888 S Figueroa St Los Angeles CA 90017

LAREAU, MARYBETH BASS, marketing professional; b. N.Y.C., July 12, 1941; d. James Gordon and Marjorie (Mestell) B.; m. Gerard Arthur Lareau, June 6, 1970 (div. Nov. 1984). AB in Biology, Bucknell U., 1963. V.p., creative group head Dancer Fitzgerald Sample, Inc., N.Y.C., 1966-78; sr. v.p., creative dir. Norman Craig & Kummel, N.Y.C., 1978-79; creative dir., pres. Lareau & Assocs., N.Y.C., 1980—; guest lectr. St. John's U., N.Y.C., 1980-83; adj. instr. Fashion Inst. Tech. SUNY, N.Y.C., 1982-84, 87—. Contbr. articles to mags., jours.; prin. works include L'eggs Pantyhose, 1974-78, corp. advt. campaign Gen. Electric Corp., 1981. Recipient ANDY award Advtg. Club N.Y., 1975, EFFIE award Am. Mktg. Assn., 1976. Mem. Internat. Wine and Food Soc., Advt. Women N.Y. (chair pub. svc. com. 1986-88), Women's Direct Response Group. Episcopalian. Home and Office: 140 West End Ave New York NY 10023

LARGE, DARLENE DINTINO, association executive, art educator; b. New Brunswick, N.J., Mar. 31, 1935; d. Albert William Dintino and Sophia (Terbovich) Terrill; m. Bruce Derr Large, June 16, 1956; children—Dirk, Letti, Todd, Rajakumari. B.S., Pa. State U., 1959; postgrad. Centro Venezuelano Americano, Caracas, Venezuela, 1956-57, Colinas des Bellas Artes, Caracas, 1957-58, Millersville State U., Pa., 1973-75. Cert. art tchr., Pa. Tchr. art Haven Jr. High Sch., Evanston, Ill., 1969-70; founder, pres. Homes of the Indian Nation, South India, 1972—, Mex., 1989; tchr. art Ephrata Area Sch. Dist., Pa., 1973-78; lectr. Pa. State U.-Grove City Coll., 1979—; tchr. art Dist. of Manheim Twp., Lancaster, Pa., 1984-85. Den mother Boy Scouts Am., Evanston, 1967-69; chmn. programs PTO Clay Elem. Sch., Ephrata, Pa., 1977; coordinator vols. Spanish Ctr., Lancaster, Pa., 1972-73; chmn. Cancer Drive, West Earl Twp., Pa., 1973. Named Woman of the Yr., Soroptomists, Lancaster, Pa., 1979; recipient Disting. Alumna award Pa. State U., 1982, Coll. of Edn. award Pa. State U., 1986. Democrat. Avocations: reading, stitchery, painting, ceramics, batik, writing, walking. Home: 41 N Hershey Ave Box 115 Leola PA 17540 Office: Homes of Indian Nation 41 N Hershey Ave Box 302 Leola PA 17540

LARGEN, CHERYL RENEE, insurance broker, agent; b. Yucaipa, Calif., Jan. 17, 1957; d. Joseph Henry and Inez Mae (Fister) L. BA, Calif. State U., Hayward, 1979. Cert. tchr. multiple subjects, Calif. Tchr. Empire (Calif.) Union Sch. Dist., 1979-81; insur. agt. The Equitable Life Assurance Co., N.Y.C., 1981-84, Provident Mutual Life, Phila., 1984-88, Central Life Assurance, Des Moines, Iowa, 1988—; prin. Cheryl R. Largen Ins. & Employee Benefits, 1988—. Mem. Cen. Life Assurance Assn. (Top One award 1988-89, qualifying mem. Million Dollar Round Table). Republican. Roman Catholic. Office: Cheryl Largen Insur & Employee Benefits 152 N Third St #504 San Jose CA 95112

LARKIN, JACQUELINE LEE, sales manager; b. Framingham, Mass., Aug. 29, 1948; d. Livio Charles and Genevieve (Ward) Costa; m. Jay V. Larkin, Mar. 12, 1971 (div. Aug. 1974). Student Framingham State U., 1966-69, Sch. Practical Arts, Boston, 1969-71. Mgr. adminstrn. TEE, Inc., Boston, 1978-81; telemktg. mgr. Warren Gorham & Lamont, Boston, 1982-85; communications cons. Larkin Communications, Boston, 1985—; telemktg. mgr. R.S. Means, Inc., Kingston, Mass., 1985-89, Desktop Data, Inc., Waltham, Mass. Author: Good Connections: Successful Telephone Selling, 1984; co-author: Telemarketing Operations Handbook, 1985. Mem. Nat. Assn. Female Execs., Nat. Assn. Women in Sales, Profl. Pubs. Mktg. Group (steering com. 1983-85), DMA Telephone Mktg. Council, Am. Telemktg. Assn. Democrat. Unitarian. Avocations: photography; writing. Home: 7 Oakley St Dorchester MA 02124 Office: Larkin Communications 7 Oakley St Dorchester MA 02124

LARKIN, KAREN LYNN, city official; b. Chgo., July 30, 1943; children: Ken, Tim, Tina, Cheryl. Student, St. Mary's Coll. Nursing; AA, Pima Community Coll., 1983; student, U. Ariz. Second v.p. Nat. Orgn. Mothers of Twins Clubs, Inc., 1979-80; recreation aide Marana Recreation Ctr., 1980; sr. recreation ctr. coord. Pima County Parks and Recreation, 1980-83; supr. I Tucson Parks and Recreation, 1983, coord. II, 1983-88, program mgr., 1988—. Trustee Ariz. Parks and Recreation Found., 1987-89. Mem. Nat. Recreation and Parks Assn., Ariz. Parks and Recreation Assn. (Outstanding Profl. award 1987). Home: 217 E Hyde St Tucson AZ 85704

LARKIN, MARY SUE, financial planner; b. Kansas City, Kans., Sept. 29, 1948; d. Claude Dewey Jr. and Mildred Elaine (Foster) Wyrick; m. James Donald Larkin, June 5, 1971; children: Michael James, David Kirk. BA in Elem. Edn., Baker U., 1970; MA in Edn., Ariz. State U., 1980. Tchr. Bonner Springs (Kans.) Unified Sch. Dist., 1970-71, Finney County Unified Sch. Dist., Garden City, Kans., 1971-73, Deer Valley Unified Sch. Dist., Phoenix, 1974-80; fin. planner Larkin & Assocs., Sun City, Ariz., 1980—. Co-author: The Larkin Guide-Enjoying the Riches of Retirement, 1987. Mem. Internat. Assn. for Fin. Planning, Inst. Cert. Fin. Planners, Altrusa (pres. Sun City club 1987-89), Sun City Ambassadors, Inc. (sec. 1987-89). Republican. Roman Catholic. Office: Larkin & Assocs 17220 Boswell Blvd Ste L200 Sun City AZ 85373

LARKIN, NELLE JEAN, computer programmer, analyst; b. Ralston, Okla., July 4, 1925; d. Charles Eugene and Jennivea Pearl (Lane) Reed; m. Burr Oakley Larkin, Dec. 28, 1948 (div. Aug. 1969); children: John Timothy, Kenneth James, Donald Jerome, Valerie Jean Larkin Rouse. Student, UCLA, 1944, El Camino Jr. Coll., 1946-49, San Jose (Calif.) City Coll., 1961-62. Sr. programmer, analyst III Santa Clara County, San Jose, Calif., 1963-69; sr. analyst, programmer Blue Cross of No. Calif., Oakland, 1971-73; sr. programmer, analyst Optimum Systems, Inc., Santa Clara, Calif., 1973-75, Crocker Bank, San Francisco, 1975-77, Greyhound Fin. Service, San Francisco, 1977-78, TRW Vidar, Mt. View, Calif., 1978-79; sr. program analyst Memorex, Santa Clara, 1979-80; staff mgmt. cons. Am. Mgmt. System, Foster City, Calif., 1980-82; sr. programmer, analyst, project leader Tymeshare, Cupertino, Calif., 1982-83; sr. programmer, analyst Beckman Instruments, Palo Alto, Calif., 1983-89, U.S. Postal Svc., San Mateo, Calif., 1989—. Mem. Calif. Scholarship Fedn. (life mem. 1943), Alpha Sigma Gamma. Home: 3493 Londonderry Dr Santa Clara CA 95050 Office: US Postal Svc 2700 Campus Dr San Mateo CA 94403

LARMOUR-GOLDIN, GIGI, realtor; b. Bloomington, Ind., Oct. 13, 1958; d. John Jack and Harriett (Walker) Larmour; m. Jeffrey Allen Goldin, July 10, 1982; children: Griffin Chaztopher, Gray Walker Joseph, Madison Teirrah. Student, Ind. U., 1981. Realtor Dilbeck Realtors, Glendale, Calif.; pvt. practice rehab. and speculator Glendale. Mem. Glendale Bd. Realtors, Ind. U. Alumni Assn. (pres.), Big Ten Club of So. Calif., Women's Coun. Realtors. Home: 3100 Autum Ct Bloomington IN 47401

LAROCHE, GLORIA ROSEMARIE, pilot; b. Pitts., June 17, 1946; d. William Edward and Lillian Marie (Brovchuk) LaR.; 1 child, Kathryn Alexandra. Student, George Peabody Coll., Nashville, 1966-70, Mountain View Coll., Dallas, 1974-76, Dallas Bapt. Coll., 1977. Lic. flight instr., ground instr., airline transport pilot, flight engr. Chief flight instr., FAA pilot examiner, safety counselor Piper S.W., Inc., Dallas, 1973-77; simulation instr. Mountain View Coll., Dallas, 1977; DC-3 1st officer Airgo Airlines, Dallas, 1977-78; 1st officer Evergreen Airlines, Marana, Ariz., 1978-79, Transam. Airlines, Oakland, Calif., 1979-80, Zantop Airlines, Ypsilanti, Mich., 1980-81; Convair capt. Interstate Airlines, Little Rock, 1981-82, Boeing 727 capt., 1983-85; Boeing 727 capt. Connie Kalitta Svcs., Ypsilanti, 1985-89; instr. B-727 flight engr. Flight Internat., Atlanta, 1982-83; Boeing 727 pilot instr. United Airlines, Denver, 1989—. Mem. Internat. Soc. Women Airline Pilots (Capt.'s Club), Archeaological Inst. Am., Mensa, Ukrainian Nat. Women's League Am. Democrat. Ukrainian Orthodox. Home: 1740 S Monaco Pkwy Denver CO 80224 Office: United Airlines Flight Tng Ctr Stapleton Airport Denver CO 80207

LAROCHELLE, PAULINE JOAN, controller; b. Lewiston, Maine, Jan. 13, 1958; d. Paul H. and Jeannette D. (Jean) L. BS in Acctg., Bentley Coll., 1980; cert. in Hotel Adminstr., Ednl. Inst. of Am. Hotel & Motel Assn., 1986. Asst. contr. Marriott Hotels, St. Louis, Raleigh, 1980-82; contr. Sonesta Hotels, Portland, Maine, 1982-87; asst. gen. mgr., contr. The Simsbury (Conn.) Inn, 1987-90; comptr. Am. Radio Relay League, Newington, Conn., 1990—. Republican. Roman Catholic. Home: 76 Silo Way Bloomfield CT 06002 Office: Am Radio Relay League 225 Main St Newington CT 06111

LA ROCQUE, MARILYN ROSS ONDERDONK, public relations executive; b. Weehawken, N.J., Oct. 14, 1934; d. Chester Douglas and Marion (Ross) Onderdonk; B.A. cum laude, Mt. Holyoke Coll., 1956; postgrad. N.Y. U., 1956-57; M. Journalism, U. Calif. at Berkeley, 1965; m. Bernard Dean Benz, Oct. 5, 1957 (div. Sept. 1971); children: Mark Douglas, Dean Griffith; m. 2d, Rodney C. LaRocque, Feb. 10, 1973. Jr. exec. Bonwit Teller, N.Y.C., 1956; personnel asst. Warner-Lambert Pharm. Co., Morris Plains, N.J., 1957; editorial asst. Silver Burdett Co., Morristown, 1958; self-employed as pub. rels. cons., Moraga, Calif., 1963-71, 73-77; pub. relations mgr. Shaklee Corp., Hayward, 1971-73; pub. rels. dir. Fidelity Savs., 1977-78; exec. dir. No. Calif. chpt. Nat. Multiple Sclerosis Soc., 1978-80; v.p. pub. rels. Cambridge Plan Internat., Monterey, Calif., 1980-81; sr. account exec. Hoefer-Amidei Assocs., San Francisco, 1981-82; dir. corp. communications, dir. spl. projects, asst. to chmn. Cambridge Plan Internat., Monterey, Calif., 1982-84; dir. communications Buena Vista Winery, Sonoma, Calif., 1984-86, asst. v.p. communications and market support, 1986-87; dir. communications Rutherford Hill Winery, St. Helena, Calif., 1987-88; pres. LaRocque/Hannaford Pub. Rels. and Pub. Affairs, Napa, Calif., 1988—; instr. pub. rels. U. Calif. Extension, San Francisco, 1977-79. Mem. exec. bd., rep-at-large Oakland (Calif.) Symphony Guild, 1968-69, Napa County Landmarks, Inc.; co-chmn. pub. rels. com. Oakland Mus. Assn., 1974-75; cabinet mem. Lincoln Child Ctr., Oakland, 1967-71, pres. membership cabinet, 1970-71, 2d v.p. bd. dirs., 1970-71; bd. dirs. Calif. Spring Garden and Home Show, 1971-77, 1st Agrl. Dist., 1971-77, Dunsmuir House and Gardens, 1976-77; mem. Calif. State Rep. Cen. Com., 1964-66; v.p. Piedmont coun. Boy Scouts Am., 1977. Mem. U. Calif. Alumni Assn., Pub. Rels. Soc. Am. (chpt. dir. 1980-82; accredited), Sonoma Valley Vintners Assn. (dir. 1984-87), Internat. Wine and Food Soc. (Marin chpt.), San Francisco Mus. Soc., Smithsonian Assocs., Sonoma Valley C. of C. (bd. dirs. 1984-87), Am. Inst. Wine and Food, W.I.N.O. (San Francisco chpt.), Napa C. of C., Napa Valley Symphony Assn., Friends of Napa Opera House, Knights of the Vine (master lady 1985—), Mount Holyoke Coll. Alumnae Club, Silverado Country Club. Office: LaRocque/Hannaford Pub Rels 1804 Soscol Ave Ste 200 Napa CA 94559

LAROUNIS, MARY GEORGE, clinical social worker, clinical psychologist; b. Cefalonia, Greece, Dec. 21, 1934; came to U.S., 1953, naturalized, 1960; d. George P. and Stamatia O. (Razis) Efthymiatos; m. George P. Larounis, Jan. 13, 1958; 1 child, Daphne H. Student, Pierce Coll., Athens, Greece, 1951-53; BA, Hunter Coll., 1955; MSW, Columbia U., 1957; AESA, U. Paris VII; PhD in Clin. Psychology, U. Paris, 1987. Case worker Community Service N.Y., 1957-60; caseworker Am. Aid Soc., Paris, 1964-66, asst. dir., 1966-79; dir. Am. Student and Family Counselling Service, 1979—; pres. Internat. Counseling Service, Paris, 1979—. Mem. Nat. Assn. Social Workers, Acad. Cert. Social Workers, Am. Psychol. Assn., N.Y. Acad. Scis., Polo Club (Paris).

LARRIMORE, PATSY GADD, nurse; b. Knoxville, Tenn., Feb. 18, 1933; d. Harry Collins and Frances (Irwin) Gadd; m. Walter Eugene Larrimore, Jan. 29, 1954; children: Patricia J. Titus, Walter Eugene Jr., Beverly Ann Calderon. BS, Johns Hopkins U., 1976, MEd, 1977. RN. Pediatric supr. Johns Hopkins Hosp., Balt., 1960-68; supr. critical care South Balt. Gen. Hosp., 1968-78; dir. nursing Hosp. for Sick Children, Washington, 1978-84; field rep. Joint Commn. Accreditation Hosp., Chgo., 1984-87; dir. nursing Bon Secours Hosp., Balt., 1987-88; assoc. dir. clin. affairs Paralyzed Vets. Am., Washington, 1989—; asst. prof. nursing, Catonsville Community Coll., 1974-78; cons. Joint Commn. Accreditation Hosp., 1987—. Contbr. articles to profl. jours. Leader Girl Scouts U.S.; bd. dirs. Christian Relief Svcs., Alexandria, Va., 1987—. Mem. Am. Heart Assn. (bd. dirs. Balt. chpt. 1972-84, Md. chpt. 1978-85, Bronze Service award Md. affiliate 1981, Silver Disting. Service Cen. Md. chpt. 1980, Bronze Service Recognition award, 1979), Am. Assn. Critical Care Nurses, Am. Nurses Assn., Advanced Nursing Adminstrn., Assn. Care Children's Health (bd. dirs. 1981-82), Am. Soc. Nursing Service Adminstrs., Am. Assn. Spinal Cord Injury Nurses, Phi Delta Kappa. Home: 108 Mountain Rd Linthicum MD 21090

LARSEN, DONNA KAY, public relations consultant; b. Anniston, Ala., Feb. 14; d. James Murray and Lucille H. Bible. BA, U. Ala., 1977; cert. in pub. rels., UCLA Extension. Feature writer L.A. Times, 1970-73; pres. Donna Larsen Pub. Rels., L.A., 1975—; pub. rels. cons. Pub. Broadcasting Svc., L.A., 1987—, Am. Pet Soc., South Pasadena, Calif., 1989—. Contbr. feature articles to various newspapers. Mem. NOW, NAFE, Am. Women in Radio and TV (rec. sec. So. Calif. chpt. 1989—), NAFE, People for Ethical Treatment of Animals, L.A. World Affairs Coun. Home and Office: Donna Larsen Pub Rels 720 S Plymouth Blvd Los Angeles CA 90005

LARSEN, ELIZABETH B. (LIBBY LARSEN), composer; b. Wilmington, Del., Dec. 24, 1950; m. James Reece, Sept. 6, 1975; 1 child. BA, U. Minn., 1971, MA, 1975, PhD, 1978. Composer-in-residence Minn. Orch., 1983-87; co-founder Minn. Composers Forum. Composer operas Some Pig, 1973, The Words upon the Windowpane, Silver Fox; orchestral and chamber works Symphony: Water Music, Four on the Floor, Overture: Parachute Dancing; choral and solo vocal works. Recipient Outstanding Achievement award U. Minn., 1987; named Minn. Woman of Yr. in Arts, 1981. Address: care EC Schirman 138 Ipswich St Boston MA 02215*

LARSEN, ETHEL PAULSON, retired educator; b. Superior, Wis., Jan. 24, 1918; d. Ole Peter Paulson and Petra Marie (Boardsen) Gilbertson; m. James Eugene Larsen, June 13, 1943; children: Robert, Karen Larsen DePalermo, Deborah Larsen Farmer, Candice Larsen Herrera. AA, Kendall Coll., 1940; BS, U. Wis., Madison, 1944; postgrad., Southwest Tex. U., 1960, U. Tex., Austin, 1961-67. Tchr. Lakefield (Minn.) Pub. Schs., 1944-46; credit mgr. Sagebiel's Automotive Parts, Seguin, Tex., 1948-49; supervisory clk. supply Edward Gary AFB, San Marcos, Tex., 1951-56; property/acctg. chief Gary Army Air Field, San Marcos, 1956-59; tchr. Seguin High Sch., 1960-80; substitute tchr. Seguin Pub. Schs., 1981-83; reporter, photographer Seguin Citizen newspaper, 1981; now ret.; developer speech-journalism curriculum, Minn. State Bd. Edn., 1945; pres. AAUW, Seguin, 1965-66, Seguin Classroom Tchrs., 1971-72; del. to Tex. State Tchrs. Assn., Austin, 1970. Founding mem. York Creek Flood Prevention Dist. for Hays, Comal and

Guadalupe counties, 1953-54; Voice of Democracy chair VFW Aux., Geronimo, Tex., 1970-78; writer radio scripts for improved farm-city rels., 1956; vol. tax aide, Seguin, 1987-90; Circle leader 1st United Meth. Ch., Seguin, 1989—; mem. T.B. Bd. Guadalupe County, 1954-57. Mem. Seguin Garden Club, Seguin-Guadalupe County Ret. Tchrs. (pres. 1990—), Order Eastern Star. Home: 1619 Driftwood St Seguin TX 78155

LARSEN, JANET JULIA, counselor education educator; b. St. Joseph, Mo., May 17, 1913; d. Harry Lee and Jessie (Armstrong) Seger; m. merwin John Larsen, Dec. 11, 1935; children: Mernet Palmer, Lyndell Millecchia, Janeen Larsen. BA, U. Iowa, 1935; MEd, U. Fla., 1957, EdS, 1967, EdD, 1969. Lic. sch. psychology, Fla.; cert. learning disabilities, elem. edn., counseling. Tchr. spl. edn. Alachua County Sch. Bd., Gainesville, Fla., 1958-61, coord. exceptional child program, 1962-65, coord. psychol. svcs., 1966-67; asst. prof. dept. English U. Fla., Gainesville, 1970-74, assoc. prof. dept. English, arts and scis. coll., 1975-77, assoc. prof. arts and scis. Grad. Sch., 1977-81, prof. dept. counselor edn. coll. edn., 1982-87, prof. emeritus dept. edn., 1988—; cons. in reading pvt. schs., Bogota, Columbia, 1978, Internat. Assn. Sch. Psychology, Southhampton, Eng., 1985; chmn. 20 doctoral dissertations U. Fla., Gainesville, 1978-90; bd. dirs. Nat. Reading Assn., N.Y.C., 1972-75; co-developer Nat. Exemplary Reading Program, 1978; dir. reading and personality workshops, Fla., Ga., Tex., Conn., 1979—; invited speaker UN Decade Women conf., Nairobi, Kenya, 1985, World Congress of Reading, Singapore, 1976. Contbr. articles to profl. jours. Bd. dirs. (nat.) AAUW, Washington, 1974-77; pre., chmn. bd. dirs. North Fla. Retirement Corp., Gainesville, 1989—; adminstrv. bd. 1st United Meth. Ch., Gainesville, 1984-91. Grantee congenital reading disabilities Coll. Medicine U. Fla, 1969-74, preventive devel. disabilities of children State of Fla., 1980-89; scholar AAUW, 1982. Mem. AAUW (pres. Fla. chpt. 1984-86), Am. Psychol. Assn., Am. Assn. Counseling and Devel., Nat. Reading Assn., Myers-Briggs Type Indicator Assn., U. Iowa Alumni Assn., Pi Lambda Theta (sponsor U. Fla. 1979-90, trustee Bloomington, Ind. chpt. 1987-92), Delta Kappa Gamma. Home: 805 NW 20th Terr Gainesville FL 32603 Office: Coll Edn Office Rm 175 Gainesville FL 32611

LARSEN, JEANETTE LENORE, insurance safety consultant; b. Fresno, Calif., Mar. 3, 1955; d. William Hans and Barbara Jean (Busch) L.; m. David Wagenleitner, Nov. 8, 1980. BA, Calif. State U., Fresno, 1977; A in Risk Mgmt., Ins. Inst. Am., Malvern, Pa., 1986, A in Loss Control Mgmt., 1988. Cert. safety profl., 1987. Health planner City of San Joaquin, Calif., 1977-78; safety cons. Fireman's Fund Ins. Co., Fresno, 1978—; bd. dirs. San Joaquin Health, 1978—. Mem. Am. Soc. Safety Engrs., Cen. Calif. Safety Soc. (pres. 1980-81), Fresno Art Mus., Phi Mu Alumnae (scholarship chmn., del. 1987-88). Republican. Club: Toastmasters (chpt. pres. 1985-86). Home: 3098 W Indianapolis Fresno CA 93722 Office: Fireman's Fund Ins Co 2490 W Shaw Fresno CA 93705

LARSEN, MOLLIE FITZGERALD, small business owner; b. Columbus, Ohio, Feb. 25, 1963; d. William Michael and Susan (Burt) Fitzgerald; m. Douglas Gaylord Larsen, Sept. 10, 1988. BA cum laude, Duke U., 1985. Owner Speciality Svcs. by Tres Bonne, Wexford, Pa., 1979—; v.p., co-owner Frontiers Internat. Travel, Wexford, 1985—. Author: The On-Campus Cookbook, 1984. Bd. dirs. Lawnvue Acres Shelter for Women, Wexford, 1989; com. chmn. Am. Mus. Fly Fishing, Manchester, Vt., 1986-88, Trout Unltd. Living Brightwater Trusts, Vienna, Va., 1987; jr. com. Vincent T. Lombardi Cancer Rsch. Ctr. Benefit, Washington, 1986, 87. Mem. Author's Guild, Rolling Rock Club, Kappa Kappa Gamma. Republican. Presbyterian. Office: Frontiers Internat Inc Pearce Mill & Logan Rds Wexford PA 15090

LARSON, BETTY JOAN, nurse, civic worker; b. Buffalo County, Wis., Dec. 8, 1931; d. Bennie Gilbert and Johanna (Hovey) Erickson; m. Ray A. Larson Jr., May 17, 1953; children: Eric Jon, Ingrid Jo, Christopher Ray, Andrea Beth. Diploma, Luther Hosp. Sch. Nursing, 1953. R.N., Wis. Staff nurse Luther Hosp., Eau Claire, Wis., 1953-54; vol. nurse ARC, Eau Claire, 1954—. Pres., Luther Hosp. Aux., 1973-74, Northwest Wis. Home Care, Eau Claire, 1989—; bd. dirs., Luther Hosp., 1982—, U. Wis. Found., Eau Claire, 1983-87. Mem. Vocat. Nurses Assn. (past pres. combined nursing peer rev. com., consumer rep. to Northwest Dist. Dental Soc., mem. com. for protection of human subjects), Eau Claire Svc. League, Luther Samaritan Club, Eau Claire Regional Arts Ctr. Republican.

LARSON, DIANE LAVERNE KUSLER, principal; b. Fredonia, N.D., July 28, 1942; d. Raymond Edmund and LaVerne (Mayer) Kusler; m. Donald Floyd Larson, Aug. 14, 1965. BS, Valley City (N.D.) State U., 1964; MS, Mankato (Minn.) State U., 1977; EdS, U. Minn., 1987. Cert. tchr., Minn. Tchr. elem. Cokato (Minn.) Elem. Sch., 1962-64, Lakeview Elem. Sch., Robbinsdale, Minn., 1964-66; vocal tchr. Wheaton (Minn.) High Sch., 1966-67; tchr. Owatonna (Minn.) Elem. Sch., 1967-88, prin., 1988—; v.p. Cannon Valley Uniserv, Mankato, 1981-83; NEA del. World Confederation of Orgns. of the Teaching Professions, Melbourne, 1988. Mem. NEA (bd. dirs. 1986-88), Minn. Edn. Assn. (bd. dirs. 1983-88, Outstanding Women in Leadership award 1983), Minn. Reading Assn. (bd. dirs. 1983—, Pres.'s award 1984), Minn. Elem. Prins. Assn., Delta Kappa Gamma (legis. chair 1986—). Congregationalist. Home: 19654 Bagley Ave Faribault MN 55021 Office: Lincoln Sch 747 Havana Rd Owatonna MN 55060

LARSON, EMILIE GUSTAVA, retired educator; b. Northfield, Minn., Apr. 28, 1919; d. Melvin Cornelius and Frieda (Christiansen) L. A.B., St. Olaf Coll., 1940; M.A., Radcliffe Coll., 1946; student U. Chgo., 1951-52. Tchr. Hanska (Minn.) High Sch., 1940-42, Two Harbors (Minn.) High Sch., 1942-45; tchr. J.W. Weeks Jr. High Sch., Newton, Mass., 1946-56, guidance counselor, 1956-79; counselor Warren Jr. High Sch., Newton, 1979-81. Deacon, Univ. Luth. Ch., 1979; bd. dirs. Bus. History and Econ. Life Program, Inc., Northeastern U.; mem. UN Rally Bd., 1984—. Mem. AAUW (state v.p. for program devel., topic chmn. Mass. div. 1975-76; corp. rep., area rep. for internat. rels. Minn. div. 1984-86), Mass. Tchrs. Assn., Newton Tchrs. Assn., St. Olaf Coll. Alumni Assn. (bd. dir. 1982-85), PEO, Va. Gildersleeve Internat. Fund for Univ. Women Inc. (membership com., bd. dirs.), Pi Lambda Theta. Lutheran. Contbr. articles to profl. jours. Address: 1008 W 1st St Northfield MN 55057

LARSON, JULIA LOUISE FINK, land use planner; b. Bethesda, Md., July 11, 1950; d. James A. and Helen J. (Grubb) Fink; m. Louis C. Larson, May 27, 1978 (div. Dec. 1981). BS, Radford Coll., 1972; MS, Oreg. State U., 1975; postgrad., Ga. State U., 1986-88. Geography tchr. Rappahannock County High Sch., Washington, Va., 1972-73; rsch. asst./sec. Oreg. Natural Area Preserves Adv. Com., 1974-75; energy conservation specialist Oreg. Dept. Energy, Salem, 1976-77; mem. Oreg. Fire Protection Master Planning Com., 1978-79, Oreg. State Environ. Edn. Adv. Com., 1977-80; growth mgmt. planner Salem Fire Dept., 1978-79; land use planner Salem Dept. Community Devel., 1979-83; field rep. Data Rsch. & Applications, Inc., Atlanta, 1983-84; land use coord. Ga. Mfd. Housing Assn., Atlanta, 1984-86; owner, The Planning Edge, Atlanta, 1986-87; project mgr., land use planner EDAW, Inc., Altanta, 1987-89; sr. planner Office Coordinated Planning Ga. Dept. Community Affairs, Atlanta, 1989—; editor: Summary of 1987 Energy and Environ. Legis., So. States Energy Bd.; cons. contbg. editor: 1979 Sun Calendar; co-editor: 1976 Energy Calendar. Co-author: Regulating Mobile Home Placement, 1988. V.p. Liberty Jaycee Women, Salem, 1981; land use adv. Northside Neighbors, Salem, 1979. Recipient cert. of appreciation City of Salem, 1983. Mem. ABA, AAUW (group leader 1987-88, newsletter editor 1987—, bd. dirs. 1987—), Am. Inst. Cert. Planners, Ga. Planning Assn. (editor Ga. Planner, 1986-87, chmn. growth strategies com. 1989—), Am. Mgmt. Assn., Am. Assn. Geographers, Am. Assn. Women Law Students, Ga. Assn. Zoning Adminstrs. and Bldg. Ofcls. (editor newsletter 1989—), High Mus. Art, Smithsonian Assocs., Ga. Conservancy, Delta Theta Phi. Avocations: backpacking, writing, wine tasting. Home: 3236 Mercer University Dr #309 Chamblee GA 30341

LARSON, KAREN ELAINE, business owner; b. Ft. Worth, Dec. 19, 1947; d. William Edelen and Eloise Marie (Gavin) Naylor; m. Keith Alan Larson, June 23, 1979; children: Mathew David, Joshua Ryan, Brandon Eric. BS, Eastern Mich. U., 1972; postgrad., Washtenaw U., 1973. Cert. respiratory technician; registered respiratory therapist. Charge and staff therapist St. Joseph's Mercy Hosp., Ann Arbor, Mich., 1968-73; instr. respiratory care U. Detroit, 1973; asst. dir. respiratory care Harper Hosp., Detroit, 1973-75, adminstrv. dir. cardiopulmonary and neurology svcs., 1976-89; dir. cardiopulmonary and neurology svcs. Riverside Hosp., Trenton, Mich., 1975-76; adminstrv. dir. cardiopulmonary and neurology svcs. MediTech Assoc., Livonia, Mich., 1988—; owner Larson's Farmers Ins. Agy., Livonia, 1989—; instr. Henry Ford Community Coll., Dearborn, Mich., 1982-83, Marygrove Coll., Detroit, 1972—. Editor: Mich. Jour., 1978; mem. editorial bd. Current Revs. for Pulmonary and Critical Care, 1979-88. Mem. forum on clin. specialties Joint Commn. on Health Care Orgn., Chgo., 1987-89. Recipient H. Allen Barth award Blue Cross, 1980. Mem. Am. Assn. for Respiratory Therapy (sec. 1974—), Am. Soc. Repiratory Care Adminstrn., Am. Lung Assn. (dir. 1985-88), Met. Soc. Cystic Fibrosis Found. (dir. 1977-80), Detroit Zool. Soc., Toledo Zool. Soc., Fairlane Club, Renaissance Club. Home: 34576 Fairfax Livonia MI 48152 Office: 32401 W 8 Mile Livonia MI 48152

LARSON, KARI MICHELLE, sales professional; b. Boston, Jan. 1, 1966; d. Russell Allen and Delores Gwendolyn (Nelson) L. BS, U. Maine, 1988. Tour guide Salem (Mass.) Witch Mus., 1986-87; sales mgr. Jordan Marsh Co., Peabody, Mass., 1988-89; asst. buyer Jordan Marsh Co., Boston, 1989—. Mem. NAFE, Met. Boston Alumni Assn., Am. Mktg. Assn., U. Maine Alumni Assn., Birka Lodge, Delta Zeta. Home: 20 Wiley Rd Belmont MA 02178

LARSON, LOIS IONE, small business owner, nurse; b. Eaw Claire, Wis., Apr. 3, 1922; d. Richard Sprague and Margaret Pearl (Best) Price; m. Neilus Ralph Larson, Dec. 25, 1943; (wid. 1979); children: Gary Allen, Darell Lee Larson. Student, Methodist Hosp., Madison, 1943. RN. Gen. duty nurse Stanley (Wis.) Hosp., 1943-44; emergency rm. nurse Viroqua (Wis.) Hosp., 1945-46; charge nurse Vernon County Hosp., Viroqua, 1961-67; head nurse Sauk County Hosp., Reedsburg, Wis., 1968-70; dir. nursing Maplewood Nursing Home, Sauk City, Wis., 1971-75; bus. owner Knit N Purl Ltd., Sauk City, 1976—.

LARSON, LYNN DIANE, customer service professional; b. Chgo., Apr. 22, 1960; d. Roger Gordon and Zelda Mae (Kurrack) Larson. AA, Wilbur Wright Community Coll., Chgo., 1986; BA, N.E. Ill. U., 1988. Customer svc. asst. Indian Summer Inc., Des Plaines, Ill.; mgmt. info. systems libr., mktg. assoc. Wilson Jones Co., Niles, Ill.; mktg. asst. Lane Telecommunications Inc., Chgo. Mem. Am. Soc. Profl. and Exec. Women, Chgo. Herpetological Soc., NAFE, Alpha CHi. Home: 5685 W Goodman Chicago IL 60630 Office: 606 Potter Rd Des Plaines IL 60016

LARSON, MARLENE LOUISE, educator, hotel consultant; b. Racine, Wis., Oct. 15, 1952; d. Louis Charles Larson and Mollie Esther (Mauther) Larson Bertana. BS, U. Wis., Whitewater, 1974, U. Nev., Las Vegas, 1982; M.S., U.Wis., Whitewater, 1978. Cert. wine steward, restaurant organizational exec.; nat. front desk cert. Tchr. Gilman (Wis.) High Sch., 1974-75, Head Start Child Devel., Kenosha, Wis., 1975-78, U. Wis., Whitewater, 1977-78; librarian, tchr. Kenosha Unified Schs., 1978-80; editor U. Nev.-Las Vegas Fedn. Hoteliers, 1981-83; food and beverage clk. MGM Casino & Hotel, Las Vegas, 1983-84; food and beverage controller Congress Hotel, Chgo., 1984-89; tchr. Mt. Mary Coll., Milw., 1990—; cons. Congress Hotel, Chgo., 1990—. Mem. Nat. Restaurant Assn., Coun. on Hotel, Restaurant, and Instl. Edn. Office: Mt Mary Coll 2900 N Menomonee River Milwaukee WI 53222

LARSON, MERIA ELLENA, lawyer; b. Independence, La., July 3, 1942; d. Nicholas B. and Helen (Frindik) Petho; m. Richard M. Larson, Dec. 21, 1968. BS in Chemistry, Southeastern La. U., 1964; postgrad., Georgetown U., 1968; JD, Detroit Coll. Law, 1979. Bar: Mich. 1979, U.S. Dist. Ct. (ea. dist.) Mich. 1979. Analytical chemist chem. div. Pitts.-Plate Glass Co., Lake Charles, La., 1964-66; forensic chemist FDA, Detroit, 1966-69, 72-80; analytical chemist Parke-Davis & Co., Holland, Mich., 1970; dir. crime lab. Grand Rapids (Mich.) Police Dept., 1971; trial atty. Barbier & Tolleson, P.C., Detroit, 1980—; spl. mediator Macomb County, 1988; mediator Macomb County Cir. Ct., 1989; seminar speaker on Mich. tort reform Inst. Continuing Legal Edn., 1988. Mem. Mich. Bar Assn., Assn. of Def. Counsel, Def. Rsch. and Trial Lawyers Assn., Women Lawyers Assn. Mich., Wayne County Bar Assn., Macomb County Bar Assn., Grosse Pointe Hunt Club (dir., past mem. various coms.). Office: Barbier & Tolleson PC 2020 Buhl Bldg Detroit MI 48226

LARSON, NANCY CELESTE, computer systems analyst, music educator; b. Chgo., July 17, 1951; d. Melvin Ellsworth and Ruth Margaret (Carlson) L. BS in Music Ed., U. Ill., 1973, MS in Music Edn., 1976; postgrad., Purdue Univ., 1982-86. Vocal music educator Consol. Sch. Dist., Gilman, Ill., 1975-77; elem. vocal music tchr. Sch. Dist. #161, Flossmoor, Ill., 1977-87; instr. Vander Cook Coll., Chgo., 1980-88; systems programmer analyst Sears, Chgo., 1987-89, tech. instr., 1989—; computer tchr. Homewood-Flossmoor High Sch., 1986-90, project leader, 1990—. Chmn. Faith Luth. Ch., 1982-87, pres. bd., 1988—, vocal soloist. Mem. Ill. Music Educators Assn., Music Educators Nat. Conf., Ill. Educators Assn., Nat. Educators Assn., Am. ORFF Schulwerk Assn., Flossmoor Edn. Assn. (negotiator 1983-86). Republican. Lutheran. Office: Sears Roebuck & Co Sears Tower Dept 704 Chicago IL 60684

LARSON, PHYLLIS JEAN, sales professional, educator; b. Lohrville, Iowa, Oct. 22, 1947; d. Lawrence Patrick and Margaret Florence (Miller) Cronin; m. Lyle Gene Larson, Sept. 5, 1981. BA in Elem. Edn., U. No. Iowa, 1970, postgrad., 1973, 75. Cert. elem. tchr., Iowa. Tchr. elem. Cedar Rapids (Iowa) Community Sch., 1970-81; substitute tchr. Eagle Grove (Iowa) Community Sch., 1981-87; proofreader Eagle Grove Newspaper, 1984-88, printer's asst., 1985-87; mgr. office supply sales div. Eagle Grove Office Supplies, 1987—; faculty rep. Tchrs. Salary Com., Cedar Rapids, 1973-75, Tchrs. Rep. Coun., Cedar Rapids, 1977-78. Mem. NEA, Iowa Edn. Assn., Cedar Rapids Edn. Assn., AAUW (treas. 1983-84, v.p. 1986-87, pres. 1987-89). Roman Catholic.

LARSON, PHYLLIS SHEPHERD, librarian; b. Winston-Salem, Sept. 19, 1933; d. John Ervin and Annie Jay (Walters) Shepherd; m. Carl Erik Larson, Jr., June 14, 1958; children: Douglas Alan, Brian Edward. AB in Chemistry, U. N.C., 1955, BSLS, 1956. Librarian Am. Cyanamid Co., various cities, 1956-60. Chmn. Citizens for Libraries, Delaware County, Pa., 1974-76; mem. Phila. Free Library, Dist. Adv. Com., 1974-77, Delaware County Planning Commn., Library Svcs. Task Force, Media, Pa. 1975; chmn. Del. County Delegation to Gov.'s Conf. on Libraries and Info. Svcs., Harrisburg, 1977; pres. Del. County Bd. Library Dirs., Media, 1980-88; mem. steering com. White House Conf. on Libraries and Info. Svcs.Task Force, 1987—; mem. Pa. Gov.'s Adv. Council on Library Devel./Fed. Adv. Council, Harrisburg, 1986—; del. Penn. Gov's. Conf. on Librs. and Info. Svcs. Harrisburg, 1990. Named Woman of Achievement Dela. County Girl Scouts, 1989. Mem. ALA, Pa. Library Assn. (cert. of merit 1977), Delta Phi Alpha, Beta Phi Mu. Republican. Methodist. Address: 239 Deer Run Media PA 19063

LARSON, TERESA JEANNE, public relations consultant; b. Scottsbluff, Nebr., Dec. 31, 1959; d. Delbert Leon and Nancy Jo (Johnson) L. BA in Journalism, Kans. State U., 1982. Asst. for legis. matters Kans. Sec. of State, Topeka, 1979-81; adminstrv. asst. Sen. Merrill Werts, Topeka, 1982; legis. corr. U.S. Sen. Bob Dole, Washington, 1982-84; dir. spl. events Nat. Rep. Sen. Com., Washington, 1984-86; fundraising cons. ARCO, L.A., 1986; cons. pub. relations and spl. events Merrill Lynch Co., Inc., N.Y.C., 1987—; regional dir. alumni assn. Hugh O'Brien Youth Found., Washington, 1982-84, state dir. leadership seminar, Washington, 1984, 86, event dir., 1988—; cons. The Main Event, Reno, 1989. Vol. Dole for Pres. campaign, 1988; cons. Giuliani campaign, 1989. Named one of Outstanding Young Women Am., 1988. Mem. Nat. Assn. Female Execs., Jaycees (v.p. Manhattan chpt. 1988—). Methodist. Home: 231 E 89th St #1FE New York NY 10128

LARTER, JANE MARIE, nurse consultant, nurse; b. Benson, Minn., Feb. 27, 1954; d. Lloyd Ervin and Deloris Lorraine (Gronseth) Hanson-Wanberg; m. Robert Allen Larter, Mar. 23, 1974; children: Christopher Michael, Jason Lloyd. AA, North Hennepin Community Coll., 1975; BA, Met. State U., 1988. RN, Minn. Staff nurse Monterrey Nursing Inn, Osseo, Minn., 1975-76; primary care and charge nurse Met. Med. Ctr., Mpls., 1976-77; health svc. specialist Osseo Pub. Sch. Dist., Brooklyn Park, Minn., 1981-85; pub. health nurse Meeker County Pub. Health, Litchfield, Minn., 1987-88; pub. health and sch. nurse McLeod County Pub. Health, Glencoe, Minn., 1988-89; cons. nurse Aveyron Home, Inc., Hutchinson, Minn., 1986—; mem. Child Abuse and Neglect Team, Edgewood Elem. Sch., New Hope, Minn., 1981-85; cons. Hutchinson Area Vocat. Tech. Inst., 1986-87. Mem. Christian Family and Life Com., Hockey Moms, Hutchinson, 1985-88, Befriender Ministry Program, Hutchinson, 1988-89; chairperson Luth. Social Svc. Bd., Hutchinson, 1988—; vol. ARC, Mpls. and Hutchinson, 1977-85, 87-89. Home: 1235 7th Ave NW Hutchinson MN 55350 Office: Aveyron Home 851 Dale St PO Box 176 Hutchinson MN 55350

LARTIGUE, SUSANA, travel agency executive; b. Orizaba, Mex., Apr. 19, 1942; came to U.S., 1964; d. Alfredo and Susana (Becerra) Lartique; divorced; children: Susan, Lizette, Monique. Student, Instituto Veracruz, 1961, La Salle U., Chgo., 1969, Pan Am. U., 1978-81, U. Tex., 1982. Asst. acct. Seguro Social Hosp., Orizaba, Mex., 1962-64; asst. export mgr. A. Torres Export Co., Chgo., 1964-65, Goss Co., Cicero, Ill., 1970-76; asst. acct. Julio Guzman, CPA, McAllen, Tex., 1977-78; with pub. rels., sales and mktg. depts. Tex. Tradewinds Travel, Austin, Tex., 1982-84; owner, mgr. Susana's Travels, Austin, 1985—. Contbr. articles on travel to various publs. Vol. Psychiat. Hosp., Orizaba, 1961-64, McAllen Gen. Hosp., 1970-74, Seton Hosp., Austin, 1982-83, Ctr. Battered Women, 1989—; room mother St. Louis Cath. Sch., Austin, 1981-85. Recipient cert. Austin Office Minority Bus. Affairs, 1989. Mem. Internat. Airlines Travel Agt. Network (cert.), Austin C. of C., Hispanic C. of C., Our Daus. Am. Republican. Roman Catholic. Office: 8440 Burnet Rd Ste 170 Austin TX 78758

LARUE, JANICE NADINE, editor-in-chief, consultant; b. Beloit, Wis., July 10, 1936; d. Harlow Stanley and Faye Leona (Dillree) Burtness; m. Donald Joseph LaRue, Aug. 11, 1957 (div. Dec. 1977); children: Harlo Burton, Michelle Fay LaRue Zimmerman, Londa Layne LaRue-Folstad, Joseph Matthew, William Alan. AA, Madison (Wis.) Bus. Coll., 1957; cert., Deltak, Inc., 1973, U. Wis., 1981; diploma in communcations, U. Wis., 1986. Continuity dir. Sta. WBEL, Beloit, 1954-56; traffic dir. Sta. WGEZ, Beloit, 1956-58; legal sec. Senator Thomas McEwen, Ogdensburg, N.Y., 1958-60; traffic dir. Sta. WMTV, Madison, Wis., 1966-68; continuity dir. Sta. WISC-TV, Madison, 1968-69; traffic dir. Sta. WCOW, Sparta, Wis., 1969-70; reporter, features writer LaCrosse (Wis.) Tribune, 1970-76; audit sec. Tolley Internat. Cons., Madison, 1976-77; editor-in-chief Wis. Restaurant Assn., Madison, 1977—; cons., advisor Fla. Restaurant Assn., Miami, 1987; cons. Hire Midwest, Stillwater, Minn., 1988—; advisor Wis. Architect mag., Madison, 1989-90; writer Culinary Trends Mag., Orange, Calif., 1990—. Author, editor: History of WRA, 1983; editor, writer: Wis. Restaurateur mag., 1977—. Canvasser Clark for Assembly, Tomah, Wis., 1976; hon. mem. Tomah C. of C., 1975-76; ward chmn. Monroe County Caucus, Sparta, 1975-76; bd. dirs. Monroe County Assn. Retarded Citizens, Sparta, 1974-75. Mem. Am. Soc. Assn. Execs., Nat. Writers Club, Madison Publs. Coop, NAFE. Democrat. Lutheran. Home: 616 Morningside Ave Madison WI 53716 Office: Wis Restaurant Assn 125 W Doty Madison WI 53703

LA RUSSO, MARIANNE ELIZABETH, construction executive; b. Bronx, Oct. 22, 1949; d. Michael Angelo and Anna Maria (Morena) Baviello; m. Anthony Carl LaRusso, Apr. 4, 1971; children: Anne Elizabeth, Tony Michael. AA, Elizabeth Seton Coll., 1969; BS, Mercy Coll., 1970; MEd, Coll. of New Rochelle, N.Y., 1971; cert. in constrn. mgmt., NYU, 1986. Asst. project mgr. Kreisler Borg Florman Constrn. Co., Scarsdale, N.Y., 1981-88, project mgr., 1988; asst. project mgr. Con Dev Constrn. Co., Mamaroneck, N.Y., 1988; project mgr. York-Hunter, Inc., Elmsford, N.Y., 1988—; mem. Archtl. Rev. Bd., Mahopac, N.Y., 1983-84. Mem. ASCE (affiliate), Profl. Women in Constrn., Nat. Assn. Women in Constrn. (v.p. Conn. and N.Y. chpts. 1985-86,. pres. 1986-87). Roman Catholic. Home: Carey St Mahopac NY 10541 Office: York Hunter Inc 570 Taxter Rd Elmsford NY 10541

LARWOOD, LAURIE, psychologist; b. N.Y., 1941; PhD, Tulane U., 1974. Pres., Davis Instruments Corp., San Leandro, Calif., 1966-71, cons., 1969—; asst. prof. organizational behavior SUNY, Binghamton, 1974-76; assoc. prof. psychology, chairperson dept., assoc. prof. bus. adminstrn. Claremont (Calif.) McKenna Coll., 1976-83, Claremont Grad. Sch., 1976-85; prof., head dept. mgmt. U. Ill.-Chgo., 1983-87; dean sch. bus. SUNY, Albany, 1987-90; dean Coll. Bus. Adminstrn., U. Nev., Reno, 1990—; mem. western regional advisory coun. SBA, 1976-81; dir. The Mgmt. Team; pres. Mystic Games, Inc. Mem. Acad. Mgmt. (editorial rev. bd. Rev. 1977-82, past chmn. women in mgmt. div., chmn. managerial consultation-tech. and innovation div.), Am. Psychol. Assn., Assn. Women in Psychology. Author: (with M.M. Wood) Women in Management, 1977; Organizational Behavior and Management, 1984, Women's Career Development, 1987, Strategies-Successes-Senior Executives Speak Out, 1988, Women's Careers, 1988, Managing Technological Development, 1988; mem. editorial bd. Sex Roles, 1979—, Consultation, 1986—, Occupational Behavior, 1987—, Group and Orgn. Studies, 1982-84, editor, 1986—; founding editor Women and Work, 1983, Jour. Mgmt. Case Studies, 1983-87; contbr. numerous articles, papers to profl. jours. Office: U Nev Coll Bus Adminstrn Reno NV 89557

LASA, MADELAINE IVETTE, dietitian, educator; b. Humacao, P.R., Aug. 6, 1954; d. Miguel Angel and Margarita (Silva) Hernandez; m. Ivan Lasa, Jan. 24, 1976; children: Marlene, Astrid. BS in Nutrition and Dietetics, U. P.R., Rio Piedras, 1975. Lic. dietitian, F.L. Intern San Juan VA Med. Ctr., Rio Piedras, 1975-76; clin. dietician P.R. Dept. Health, Humacao, 1977-78; chief adminstrv. dietitian P.R. Dept. Health, Cayey, 1978-79; dir. food and nutrition svc. P.R. Dept. Health, Guayma, 1979-81; clin. dietitian VA Med. Ctr., Gainesville, Fla., 1983-84, mem. nutrition support team, 1983—, clin. nutrition specialist, 1984—, team leader cardiac rehab. teaching program, 1986—; adj. clin. instr. dietetics U. Fla., Gainesville, 1983—. Author: Handbook of Clinical Nutrition, 1986, (with others) Gainesville Veterans Administration Medical Center Diet Manual, 1984, 87, 89. Sec. Partido Nuevo Progresista, Caquas, P.R., 1976-80; active Girl Scouts Am.; bd. dirs. Am. Heart Assn. Alachua County. Mem. Am. Dietetic Assn., Fla. Dietetic Assn., Gainesville Dist. Dietetic Assn., Nat. Kidney Found. Council on Renal Nutrition (sec. 1987-88, pres.-elect 1988-89, pres. 1989-90), Coll. Nutritionists and Dietitians P.R. Republican. Roman Catholic. Office: VA Med Ctr 1601 SW Archer Rd Gainesville FL 32602

LASALLE, PATRICIA S., corporate executive; b. Ft. Wayne, Ind., Nov. 22, 1955; d. Alfred and Florine (Dunn) Flennery; m. Keith LaSalle, Dec. 6, 1986; 1 child, Shayla. Grad., Ind. U., Ft. Wayne; postgrad., Montgomery Coll., Germantown, Md. Mgr. adminstrn. EDI, Inc., Gaithersburg, Md. V.p. Save Our Streams of Md. Experiment in Internat. Living scholar. Mem. NAFE, VAFE, SHRM. Address: 19936 Cedar Bluff Dr Germantown MD 20874

LASCHENSKI, MATHILDA JANE, art educator, sculptor; b. Drexel Hill, Pa., Oct. 3, 1942; d. Joseph Edward and Mathilda Diana (Gates) L. BS, Phila. Coll. of Art, 1964; MEd, Temple U., 1970, Columbia U., 1986; EdD, Columbia U., 1987. Tchr. art Phila. Sch. Dist., 1965—; freelance ceramist Phila., 1965—. One-woman exhibition Columbia U., N.Y.C., 1985; sculptures exhibited at Phila. Art Alliance, Phila. Civic Ctr. Mus., Fleisher Art Meml. at Phila. Mus. Art, Phila. U. of Arts, Tyler Sch. Art at Temple U., Trenton (N.J.) Mus. Art. Mem. Girl Scouts U.S., Phila., 1986—. Mem. Pa. Art Edn. Assn., Women's Caucus for Art, Phila. Fedn. Tchrs., Women in Edn.

LASHER, DONNA MARIA, lawyer; b. N.Y.C., Mar. 1, 1948; d. Thomas Earl and Angela (Canora) Fleming; m. Burton John Lasher, Aug. 21, 1976 (div. May 1982); 1 child, John Thomas. BS in Secondary Edn., Fordham U., 1969; JD, SUNY, Buffalo, 1972. Bar: N.Y. State, 1974. Asst. corp. counsel N.Y.C. Corp. Counsel Office, 1972-79; asst. dist. atty. Office Queens County Dist. Atty., N.Y.C., 1979-83; dep. insp. gen./ dept. advocate N.Y.C. Dept. Correction, 1983-86; prin. law asst. to acting superior ct. judge N.Y. State Ct. System, N.Y.C., 1986—; arbitrator N.Y.C. Small Claims Ct. Bd. dirs. Hilltop Village Coop. No. 4, N.Y.C. Mem. N.Y. State Bar Assn., Queens County Bar Assn. Roman Catholic. Office: N.Y. State Supreme Ct 88-11 Sutphin Blvd Jamaica NY 11435

LASHLEE, JOLYNNE VAN MARSDON, army officer, nurse, administrator; b. Asheville, N.C., May 22, 1948; d. William Reid and Frances (Furey) Van Marsdon. BS in Nursing, U. Fla., 1971; M Health Care Adminstrn., Baylor U., 1982. Team leader surg. specialties Shand Teaching Hosp., Gainesville, Fla., 1971; commd. lt. U.S. Army Nurses Corps, 1971, advanced through grades to lt. col., 1986; asst. head nurse organ transplant service unit Walter Reed Hosp., Washington, 1972; staff nurse surg. ICU, head nurse multi-service nursing unit Nurnberg, W. Ger., 1972-75; head nurse recovery room William Beaumont Army Med. Center, Ft. Bliss, El Paso, Tex., 1975-76, dep. dir. patient care specialist course, 1976-78; ednl. coordinator, project officer U.S. Lyster Hosp., Ft. Rucker, Ala., 1978; adminstrv. resident Madigan Army Med. Center, Tacoma, 1981-82; chief nurse methods div. Walter Reed Hosp., 1982-85; mem. Army Surgeon Gen.'s Task Force on Health Care, 1985-86; insp. gen. U.S. Army, 1986-89; asst. chief nurse Ireland Army Hosp., Ft. Knox, Ky., 1989—; pvt. image marketer Color 1 Assocs. Mem. Am. Hosp. Assn., Am. Coll. Healthcare Execs., Assn. Health Care Adminstrs. Nat. Capital Area, Am. Assn. Critical Care Nurses, Baylor U. Healthcare Adminstrs. Alumni. Home: 120 Durbin Way Vine Grove KY 40175-6008 Office: Ireland Army Hosp Asst Chief Nurse Fort Knox KY 40121-5520

LASIECKA, IRENA M., university professor; b. Warsaw, Poland, Feb. 4, 1948; came to U.S., 1978; d. Antoni and Yanina (Krzeminska) Lech; m. Stanislaw Lasiecki, June 22, 1971 (div. 1979); 1 child, Paul; m. Roberto Triggieni. BA, U. Warsaw, 1971, MS, 1972, PhD, 1975. Researcher Polish Acad. of Sciences, Warsaw, Poland, 1975-78; postdoctoral student UCLA, 1978-79, visiting asst. prof., 1979-81; assoc. prof. U. Fla., Gainesville, 1981-84; prof. U. Fla., 1984-87, U. Va., Charlotteville, 1987—; editor SIAM Jour. on Control, Phila., 1982—, Applied Math., N.Y.C., 1984—, Internat. Jour. of Math., Orlando, Fla., 1985—. Recipient Creative Extension award NSF, 1986, Award of Polish Acad. of Sciences, 1976. Mem. Internat. Fedn. Imfo. Processing. Roman Catholic. Office: U Va Dept Applied Math Charlottesville VA 22901

LASITER, ELEANOR JANET, nurse, director rehabilitation facility; b. Wadena, Sask., Can., Dec. 10, 1934; d. Reginald Clarence and Ellen Mae (Morton) Svedberg; m. Carl William Lasiter, Dec. 16, 1955; children: Tamara Lasiter Rundle, Kim Lasiter Cain, Susan Lasiter Hammer, John Lasiter. RN, Deaconess Sch. Nursing, 1955; BS in Health Sci., Chapman Coll., 1979. RN. Staff nurse Home of Guiding Hands, Lakeside, Calif., 1968-69, coordinator staff devel., 1969-70, dir. residential services, 1970-75, exec. dir., 1982—, also bd. dirs.; nurse clinician San Diego Regional Ctr. Developmentally Disabled, 1977-80, project coordinator, 1980-82; nurse educator Merric Coll., San Diego, 1975-77, mem. adv. com., 1983—; mem profl. adv. com., 1985—. Named Service Provider of Yr., Sen. Ellis Adv. Com., 1985; named one of Women of Accomplishment, Soroptimist Internat., 1986; recipient Clair Burgener Found., 1987. Mem. Am. Assn. Mental Deficiency (sec. region II 1985—), Calif. Assn. Residential Resources (bd. dirs., Adminstr. of Yr. 1985, pres. 1987-89), Nat. Assn. Private Residential Resources (bd. reps. 1989). Democrat. Lutheran. Home: 5359-29 Aztec Dr La Mesa CA 92041 Office: Home of Guiding Hands 10025 Los Ranchitos Rd Lakeside CA 92040

LASKI, KAREN ELAINE, psychologist; b. Hollywood, Calif., Aug. 28, 1944; d. George William and Lois H. (Lagergren) Gardiner; m. Mortimer Leon Laski, Mar. 17, 1978. BA in History, Calif. State U., Northridge, 1966; MA in Psychology, Calif. State U., L.A., 1982; PhD in Psychology, Claremont (Calif.) Grad. Sch., 1986; postgrad., UCLA, 1986-88; PhD, New Sch. for Social Rsch., 1948. Lic. psychologist, Calif. Mgr., rev. officer IRS, L.A., 1972-82; pvt. practice behavior therapist, 1982-89; pvt. practice psychologist Downing and Pasadena, Calif., 1989—; psychol. cons. Calif. Regional Ctrs. for Developmentally Disabled, L.A., 1989—. Mem. Am. Psychol. Assn., Assn. for Behavior Analysis, Assn. for Behavior Analysis of So. Calif., Am. Bus. Women's Assn. Office: Affiliated Counselors 9530 E Imperial Hwy Ste L Downey CA 90242

LASKOW, LYNDA THERESE, health care management executive, educator; b. Mpls., Oct. 3, 1947; d. Lucian Stanley and Henrietta Marcella (Malicki) L. BS, Coll. St. Catherine, St. Paul, 1969; postgrad., Met. State U., St. Paul. Cert. pub. health nurse. Staff nurse St. Barnabas Hosp., Mpls., 1969-70; nursing care coord. Met. Med. Ctr., Mpls., 1970-84, staffing coord., 1984, dir. acute care nursing, 1984-85, dir. surg. svcs., 1985-89; internal cons. continuous quality improvement Health One Corp., Mpls., 1990—; creator, speaker nursing workshops, 1981, 83. Mem. Mpls. Fine Arts Soc., Women's Assn. of Minn. Orch., Mpls. Mem. Assn. Oper. Rm. Nurses, NAFE, Sigma Theta Tau. Home: 405 Shelard Pkwy St Louis Park MN 55426 Office: Health One Corp 2810 57th Ave N Minneapolis MN 55430-2496

LASKOWSKI, IRMA WILLIAMS, hospice administrator; b. Chgo., June 4, 1943; d. Charles F. and Catherine (Hurter) Williams; m. Michael B. Laskowski, Jan. 23, 1965; children: Catherine, Marie, Elizabeth, Paul. BS in Biology, Loyola U., Chgo., 1965; BSN, St. Louis U., 1980. RN. Rsch. assoc. U. Okla., Oklahoma City, 1967-70; staff nurse St. Joseph Hosp., St. Louis, 1980-85; field nurse St. Joseph Home Health, St. Louis, 1985-88; patient care coord. Hospice of the Palouse, Moscow, Idaho, 1988-89; dir. Gritman Home Health/Hospice of the Palouse, Moscow, 1989—; cons. home health Idaho Hosp. Assn. Mem. Idaho Assn. Home Health Agencies (sec. 1990), Idaho Nurses Assn., AAUW, Idaho Faculty Women's Club (pres. 1989-90), Sigma Theta Tau. Roman Catholic. Home: 3382 Blaine Rd Moscow ID 83843 Office: Gritman Home Health 715 S Washington Moscow ID 83843

LASKY-LANGFORD, MARGARET ROLEEN, registered nurse; b. St. Louis, Dec. 21, 1936; d. Steven Joseph and Mildred Louise (Vallentine) Lasky; m. Harry Joe Langford, May 26, 1956 (div. 1967); children: Lesek Roleen Langford-Bellamy, Michael Joe. AA magna cum laude, Columbia State Community Coll., Tenn., 1974. RN, Tenn. Sec. Firth-Sterling, L.A., 1953-54; company clk. USMC, Parris Island, S.C., 1954-56; with materials control dept. Douglas Aircraft, El Segundo, Calif., 1957-59; printing control editor U.S. Army Infantry Sch., Fort Benning, Ga., 1959-66; exec. sec. Hamilton Nat. Bank, Chattanooga, 1967-69; dir. nurses Nat. Health Corp., Columbia, 1976-78; adminstr., owner Maury Home Health Agy., Columbia, 1978—; cons. I Can Cope Maury County Cancer Assn., Columbia, 1981—, nursing dept. Columbia State Community Coll., 1978—, Make Today Count, Columbia, 1981—; ombudsman South Cen. Tenn. Devel. Dist., Columbia, 1988—; speaker on home care, 1978—. Contbr. articles to profl. jours. Chaperone Cen. High Sch. Band, Columbia, 1978-84; health svcs. com. Maury County C. of C., Columbia, 1987-88; adv. com. Columbia State Community Coll., 1982—; campaigner Rep. Cen. Com., Columbia, 1968-80; den mother Boy Scouts Am., Columbia, 1972-76; active PTA, Columbia, 1964-78. Cpl. USMC, 1954-56. Mem. Nat. Assn. for Home Care, Middle Tenn. Home Care (v.p. 1987-90), Tenn. Assn. for Home Care (legis. com. 1987-88), Tenn. Hospice Assn., Nat. Hospice Assn., Am. Cancer Assn. Methodist. Home: 2411 Pulaski Pike Apt H66 Columbia TN 38401 Office: Maury Home Health 1620 S Main Columbia TN 38401

LASNIER, RINA, writer; b. St.-Gregoire d'Iberville, Que., Can., Aug. 6, 1910; d. Moise and Laura (Galipeau) Lasnier; Docteur Honoris Causa, U. Montreal (Que., Can.), 1977. Author 24 books of prose, poetry, and on theater; mem., v.p. Council of Arts Que. Recipient Prix Duvernay, 1957, Prix Molson, 1964, Smith prize U. Mich., 1974, Prix France-Can., 1974, Prix David, Province Que., 1974, Prix Edgar-Poe, France, 1979. Mem. Academie canadienne francaise, Societe royale du Canada, Institut Gracian, academie internationele. Roman Catholic.

LASON, SANDRA WOOLMAN, English educator, gifted and talented children's educator; b. Chgo., July 30, 1934; d. Irwin Robert and Annette (Hassman) Woolman; m. Marvin Mitchell Lason, Feb. 8, 1959 (dec. 1972); children: Caryn Anne, Joel Steven, Scott David. BS with highest distinction, Northwestern U., 1956; MA, Northeastern Ill. U., 1976; postgrad., U. Okla., 1982—. Cert. K-12 tchr. Tchr. Sch. Dist. 69, Skokie, Ill., 1956-60, tchr., dir. gifted students, 1972-76; tchr., adminstr. MONACEP, Morton Grove, Ill., 1964-76; freelance writer-editor, 1976—; curriculum writer-editor The Economy Co., Oklahoma City, 1978-80; instr., assoc. dir. English dept. U. Okla., Norman, 1980-83; prof., ESL coord. Oklahoma City Community Coll., 1983—; ptnr. Communications Cons.; adj. prof. English as a second lang. Austin Coll., Sherman, Tex., 1977; judge Okla. Olympics Mind, Mensokie Essay Contest; chmn. com. for English as a second lang. Okla. State Regents, 1985-86; speaker presentations on writing, English as a second lang. and educating the gifted. Writer, editor: K-8 Language Arts Series Expressways, 1980; author (with others) Resource Book, Oklahoma Gifted Galaxy; editor numerous books; contbr. numerous articles to profl. jours. Officer Karen Brown Chpt. Bobs Roberts Hosp., Skokie, 1964-74, Children's Meml. Hosp., Chgo., 1960-71; bd. dirs. Okla. Hillel Found., 1984-87, Women's Resource Ctr., Norman, 1982-83; officer Kenton PTA. Mem. Tchrs. English as Second Lang., Okla. Tchrs. English as Second Lang., Mensa (gifted child coord. Ill. chpt., 1973-76), Pi Lambda Theta, Alpha Epsilon Phi(officer alumnae chpt.). Home: 2103 Melrose Dr Norman OK 73069 Office: Oklahoma City Community Coll 7777 S May Ave Oklahoma City OK 73159

LASS, KATHERINE ANN, sales executive; b. Chgo., Sept. 29, 1951; d. David Richard and Dorothea Virginia (Dean) McKiernan; m. Kenneth John Lass, Aug. 19, 1972 (div. Jan. 1982). BS in Home Econs., Valparaiso U., 1973; MEd, Loyola U., New Orleans, 1980. Registered dietitian. Staff dietitian Charity Hosp., New Orleans, 1973-75; chief clin. dietitian St. Charles Gen. Hosp., New Orleans, 1975-79; mgr. health care Conco Food Svc., New Orleans, 1979-82; mgr. health care mktg. CFS Continental Food Svc. Co., Indpls., 1982-87; dir. health care sales CFS Continental Food Svc. Co., L.A., 1987-88; dir. multi-unit health care sales Sysco Corp., Houston, 1988—. Named one of Recognized Young Dietitians, La. Dietetic Assn., 1980. Mem. NAFE, Am. Dietetic Assn., Dietitians in Bus. and Industry. Office: Sysco Corp 1390 Enclave Pkwy Houston TX 77077

LASSABE, ALESSANDRA CRAIN, owner perfume company; b. New Orleans, Oct. 11, 1954; d. Alfred Charles Crain and Miriam Marguerite (Caro) Crain-Boyce; m. John Edward Bonvillain, Aug. 19, 1977 (div. June 1982); 1 child, Alessa Caron Bonvillain; m. Warren Justin Lassabe, July 3, 1982; 1 child, Ryan Joseph Lassabe. Student, U. New Orleans, 1974. Owner, pres., perfumer Bourbon French Perfume Co., Inc., New Orleans, 1973—; v.p. French Quarter Bus. Assn., New Orleans, 1987-89. Mem. La. Hemophilia Found. (bd. dirs. 1985-86), French Quarter Bus. Women's Network. Home: 900 Orlando Dr Pearlington MS 39572 Office: Bourbon French Perfume 525 St Ann St New Orleans LA 70116

LASSITER, BARBARA ANN, company executive; b. Harriman, Tenn., Feb. 14, 1960; d. Grady Earl and Patricia Ann (Basler) L. BS, Tenn. Tech. U., 1983. Staff acct. Home Health Cons., Inc., Crossville, Tenn., 1984; reimbursement cons. Health Care Mgmt. Cons., Inc., Jacksonville, Fla., 1985-88; dir. fin. Miss. Reg. Home Health Care, Inc., Hollandale, Miss., 1988; reimbursement cons. Southwell, Bellamy, Bridges & Lassiter, Jacksonville, 1989—. Baptist. Home: 3100 Lake Brook Blvd Apt 157 Knoxville TN 37909 Office: Southwell Bellamy et al 2938 Dupont Ave Jacksonville FL 32217

LAST, MARIAN HELEN, social services administrator; b. L.A., July 2, 1953; d. Henry and Renee (Kahan) Last. BA, Pitzer Coll., 1975; postgrad., U. So. Calif., 1975-84; MS, Long Beach State U., 1980. Lic. marriage therapist. Coordinator City of El Monte, Calif., 1975-76, project dir., 1976—; pvt. practice psychotherapist Long Beach, Calif., 1982—; dir. mgr. City of El Monte, 1982—; cons. U. So. Calif. Andrus Ctr., L.A., 1977-78; bd. dirs. Coordinating Council, City of El Monte, Sr. Pres.'s Council, Com. on Aging. Co-author rape survival guide, 1971. Dir., founder Rape Response Program, Pomona, San Gabriel, Calif., 1971-80; cons. sexual assault Pitzer Coll., Claremont, Calif., 1975-78; chair Sr. Conf. Com., San Gabriel Valley, 1984—. Recipient Susan B. Anthony award NOW, Pomona, 1976. Mem. Am. Soc. Aging, Calif. Assn. Sr. Svc. Ctrs. Dirs., Calif. Parks and Recreation Soc., Calif. Assn. Marriage and Family Therapists, Civitan, Chi Kappa Rho Gamma. Democrat. Jewish. Club: Women's, Civitan. Office: City of El Monte 3120 N Tyler Ave El Monte CA 91731

LAST, SONDRA CAROLE, public relations consultant, freelance writer; b. Bklyn., Nov. 6, 1932; d. Irving B. and Lynn (Freedman) L.; m. S. Rosenberg, July 15, 1951 (div. 1958); m. R. Prits, Apr. 14, 1961 (div. 1965); 1 child, Mikel Eve Renner. BS, UCLA, 1955, BA, 1956; MA, U. So. Calif., 1958, U. Fla., 1982. Dir. adminstrn. Escuela las Nereidas, Santurce, P.R., 1960-65; del. to Conf. on Poverty, Unemployment and Edn. UN, San Juan, P.R., 1965; acad. cons. Irwin W. Katz, Inc., Miami Beach, Fla., 1966-74; polit. and social commentator Sta. LOVE-AM, Miami, Fla., 1974-75; legis. aide, adminstrv. asst. Fla. Senator Gwen Margolis, Miami, 1974-85; coord. Conf. Former U.S. Secs. of State, Miami, 1985; legis. aide, adminstrv. asst. Fla. Rep. Irma Rochlin, Miami, 1986; exec. dir. Greater Biscayne Blvd. C. of C., Miami, Fla., 1988, Miami Commn. on Status of Women, 1989; owner, pres. Last Enterprises, Inc., Grand Island, Nebr., 1989—, The Last Word, Ink., Grand Island, Nebr., 1989—; adviser on normalization, Peoples Republic China, Beijing, 1978, coord. trade show participation at Caribbean Conf., 1987; bd. dirs. The Phoenix Plan, Inc., Lyons Communications, Inc.; ptnr. LDW, Inc., Pub. Rels. and Advt.; cons. to small bus. Scriptwriter The Loretta Young Show, Peter Gunn, Elmer Gantry, other TV prodns.; contbr. numerous articles to various nat. and regional publs.; author: Live and Work in South Florida, 1987, The Menopause Manual. Lobbyist Fla. Freelance Writers and Transition, Inc. Recipient Outstanding Achievement award Nat. Coun. Jewish Women, 1974, Trail Blazer award Federally Employed Women, 1975, Susan B. Anthony award Dade County NOW, 1976, Pub. Svc. award Federally Employed Women, 1978; Sondra C. Last Day proclaimed by City of North Miami Beach, Fla., 1979; named Community Leader North Miami Beach Commn. on Status of Women, 1979. Mem. Fla. Motion Picture/TV Assn., Internat. Women Writer's Guild, Fla. Freelance Writer's Assn., Screen Writers Guild Calif., Women in Communication, Adult and Continuing Edn. Assn. Nebr. Democrat. Home and Office: 4210 Kay Ave Grand Island NE 68803

LASTICK, MARJORIE ALICE, communications executive; b. Hartford, Conn., Sept. 3, 1948; d. Morton and Felicia Mildred (Goldberg) Garmise; m. Stanley Marcus Lastick, Dec. 22, 1968; children: Thomas Colby, Alice Heather. BA, Northwestern U., 1970; postgrad., U. Colo., 1974-75, MA in Journalism, 1980. Cert. tchr., Colo. Tchr. English St. Vrain Valley Sch. Dist., Longmont, Colo., 1975-78; newspaper reporter Longmont Daily Times-Call, 1979-81, news and copy editor, 1981-83; editor The Longmont Mag., 1983; pub., editor Network Pub., INc., Longmont, 1983-87; communications mgr. Nat. Environ. Health Assn., Denver, 1988—; pres., founder Network Pub., Inc., Longmont, 1983-87; edtoral advisor Colo. Woman News, Denver, 1988-89; newsletter editor Longmont Coalition for Women in Crisis, 1988—. Editor: Mag. for Colo. Women, Jour. Environ. Health. Sec. Longmont Coalition for Women in Crisis, 1988—. Recipient Cert. of Commendation, Women in Media, 1985, Women at Work award Colo. Coun. on Working Women, 1985, 86. Mem. Assn. for Rsch. and Enlightment, About Women and Fitness, Women in Communication, Inc. (treas. Denver chpt. 1987—), NOW, Women Bus. Owners Assn., St. Vrain Women's Connection, Kappa Alpha Theta. Home: 1331 S Lincoln St Longmont CO 80501 Office: Nat Environ Health Assn 720 S Colorado Blvd #970 Denver CO 80222

LATHAM, ALICE FRANCES PATTERSON, public health nurse; b. Macon, Ga., Dec. 18, 1916; d. Frank Waters and Ruby (Dews) Patterson; R.N., Charity Hosp. Sch. Nursing, New Orleans, 1937; student George Peabody Coll. Tchrs., 1938-39; BS in Pub. Health Nursing, U. N.C., 1954; M.P.H., Johns Hopkins U., 1966; m. William Joseph Latham, July 21, 1940 (dec. Apr. 1981); children: Jo Alice (Mrs. Phillip Schmidt), Marynette (Mrs. Charles Stephens), Lauryby Cathleen; m. Sidney Dumas Herndon, Apr. 26, 1985. Staff pub. health nurse assigned spl. venereal disease study USPHS, Darien, Ga., 1939-40; county pub. health nurse Bacon County, Alma, Ga., 1940-41; USPHS spl. venereal disease project, Glynn County, Brunswick, 1943-47; county pub. health nurse Glynn County, 1949-51, Ware County, Waycross, 1951-52; pub. health nurse supr. Wayne-Long-Brantley-Liberty Counties, Jesup, 1954-56 dist. dir. pub. health nursing Wayne-Long-Appling-Bacon-Pierce Counties, Jesup, 1956-70; dist. chief nursing S.E. Ga. Health Dist., 1970-79, organizer mobile health services, 1973—. Exec. dir. Wayne County Home Health Agy., 1968-80; exec. dir. Ware County Home Health Agy., 1970-79, mem. exec. com., 1978-85; mem. governing bd. S.E. Ga. Health Systems Agy., 1975-82; mem. governing bd. Health Dept. Home Health Agy., 1978—, also author numerous grant proposals. Bd. dirs. Wayne County Mental Health Assn., 1959, 60, 61, 81, 82, Wayne County Tb Assn., 1958-62; a non-alcoholic organizer Jesup group Alcoholics Anonymous, 1962-63; mem. adv. council Ware Meml. Hosp. Sch. Practical Nursing, Waycross, Ga., 1958; mem. Altar Guild, St. Paul's Episcopal Ch., 1979—, vestrywoman, 1981-82. Recipient recognition Gen. Service Bd., Alcoholics Anonymous, Inc. Fellow Am. Pub. Health Assn.; mem. Am. Nurses Assn., 8th Dist. (pres. 1954-58, sec. 1958-60, dir. 1960-62, 1st v.p. 1962), Ga. Nurses Assn. (exec. bd. 1954-58, program rev. continuing edn. com. 1980-86), Ga. Pub. Health Assn. (chmn. nursing sect. 1956-57), Ga. Assn. Dist. Chiefs Nursing (pres. 1976). Contbr. to state nursing manuals, cons. to Home Health Service Agys. Home: Route 6 Box 46 Brunswick GA 31520

LATHAM, ELEANOR RUTH EARTHROWL, neuropsychology therapist; b. Enfield, Conn., Jan. 12, 1924; d. Francis Henry and Ruth Mary (Harris) Earthrowl; m.Vaughan Milton Latham, July 20, 1946; children: Rebecca Ann, Carol Joan, Jennifer Howe, Vaughan Milton Jr. BA, Vassar Coll., 1945; MA, Smith Coll., 1947, Clark U., Worcester, Mass., 1974; EdD, Clark U., Worcester, Mass., 1979. Lic. psychologist, Mass. Guidance counselor Worcester Pub. Schs., 1967-74, sch. psychologist, 1975-80; pvt. practice neuropsychology Worcester, 1981—; postdoctoral trainee Children's Hosp.-Harvard Med. Sch., Boston, 1980-81; med. staff Hahnemann Hosp., Worcester, St. Vincent Hosp., Worcester; assoc. in pediatrics U. Mass. Med. Ctr. and Med. Sch., Worcester, 1982—. Author: Neuropsychological Impairment in Duchene Muscular Dystrophy, 1985. Mem. Internat. Neuropsychology Soc., Am. Psychol. Assn. Republican. Unitarian. Home: 59 Berwick St Worcester MA 01602 Office: Vernon Med Ctr 10 Winthrop St Worcester MA 01604

LATHAM, MARY ELIZABETH, clergywoman; b. Cin.; d. Lawrence Lorenzo and Eugenia (Peters) Latham; B.A. cum laude, Asbury Coll., 1929. Tchr. math. and Latin, McAfee High Sch., Mercer County, Ky., 1929-32; entered ministry of evangelism Ch. of the Nazarene, 1933, ordained to ministry, 1937; traveled in work of evangelism and Christian edn., 1937-48; internat. dir. vacation Bible schs. Dept. Ch. Schs., Kansas City, Mo., 1948-67; dir. audiovisuals Ch. of the Nazarene, 1962-74; chmn. audiovisual com. Council of Chs. Greater Kansas City, 1955-58, chmn. com. on communications edn., 1966-67; chmn. Latham Communications, 1975—; also lectr. Recipient Albert F. Harper award Adult Ministries, Ch. of Nazarene, 1980. Author: Vacation Bible School, Why, What, and How, 1954, 9th rev. edit., 1968; Adventures with Jesus, 1948, rev. edits., 1951, 54, 57, 60, 63; Teacher, You Are an Evangelist, rev. edit., 1977; contbr. numerous covers and articles to periodicals; dir. prodn. films The Great Transition, motion picture of Nazarene Colls., 1964; Sing His Wonderful Name, 1965; Would You Believe It?, 1967; The Debtors and They Do Not Wait, 1968; The Way Out and God's Word for Today's World, 1969; Moving Ahead, 1970; Just for the Love of It, 1971; To Make a Miracle, 1972; To New Worlds, 1972; The Church of the Nazarene, 1974 (Disting. Svc. award 1990); The Alabaster Story, 1974; dir. filmstrips with cassettes How Young Is Our Welcome? and What Made the Orange Go Away?, 1976; producer videotape Roy T. Williams-The Man, The Leader, 1983. Address: 10268 Cedarbrooke Ln Kansas City MO 64131

LATHAM, ROBIN LYNNE, chemical engineer; b. Tuscaloosa, Ala., Nov. 29, 1964; d. Walter Willard and Norma Faye (Findley) L. BSChemE, U. Ala., Tuscaloosa, Ala., 1986, MBA, 1988. Cert. engr.-in-tng., Ala. Environ. engr. E.I. Du Pont de Nemours, Inc., Aiken, S.C., 1988-89; property acct. Westinghouse Savannah River Co., Aiken, 1989, recruiter in profl. staffing, 1990—. Mem. Augusta Profls. Assn. Baptist. Office: Westinghouse Savannah River Bldg 742-A Aiken SC 29808

LATHROP, GERTRUDE ADAMS, chemist, consultant; b. Norwich, Conn., Apr. 28, 1921; d. Williams Barrows and Lena (Adams) L. B.S., U. Conn., 1944; M.A., Tex. Woman's U., 1953, Ph.D., 1955. Devel. chemist on textiles/Alexander Smith & Sons Carpet Co. Yonkers, N.Y., 1944-52; research assoc. textiles Tex. Woman's U., 1952-56; chief chemist Glasgo Finishing Plant div. United Mchts. & Mfrs., Inc., Conn., 1956-57; chief chemist Old Fort Finishing Plant div. United Mchts. & Mfrs., Inc., N.C., 1957-63; research chemist United Mchts. Research Ctr., Langley, S.C., 1963-64; lab. mgr. automotive div. Collins & Aikman Corp., Albemarle, N.C., 1964-78; chief chemist, lab. mgr. Old Fort Finishing Plant div. United Mchts., 1979-82. Treas. 1st Congl. Ch., Asheville, N.C., 1985-87; tax-aide counselor IRS, 1984—, Am. Assn. Ret. Persons; pub. rels. com. Swannanoa Valley, N.C., 1984—. Recipient Disting. Alumni award U. Conn. Sch. Family Studies, 1980-81. Mem. (emeritus) Am. Chem. Soc., Am. Assn. Textile Chemists and Colorists (sect. rsch. chmn., treas., vice-chmn. 1962-64; chmn. edn. com. Piedmont sect. 1977-78), ASTM (chmn. transp. fabrics on flammability com. 1973-75), AARP (recipient Community Svc. award 1989), Bus. and Profl. Women's Club (pres. chpt. 1974-76, Woman of Yr. 1979, 80), Iota Sigma Pi. Home and Office: Box 1166 Black Mountain NC 28711

LATHROP, JOYCE KEEN, civic worker; b. Los Angeles, Nov. 25, 1939; d. William Lavern Trewin and Therese (Wenig) Keen; B.A., U. So. Calif., 1961; m. Mitchell Lee Lathrop, June 29, 1959 (div. 1977); children—Christin Lorraine, Alexander Mitchell, Timothy Trewin Mitchell. Dir. Assistance League Glendale, 1964-70, Pasadena (Calif.) Sr. Center, 1966-68; dir. jrs. Los Angeles Orphanage Guild, 1966-78, 83-89, pres., 1974-75, treas., 1972-73, v.p., 1973-74; mem. Symphonians Los Angeles Philharm. Orch., 1969-73, Opera Assocs. Music Center, 1965-77, Met. Opera Assocs., 1967-78, 85-90, Aux. Hosp. Good Samaritan, Los Angeles; mem. Nat. Council Met. Opera, N.Y.C., 1970-77; bd. dirs. Los Angeles Music Center Opera Assn., 1973-74; bd. dirs. Calif. Mus. of Sci. and Industry Council, 1979-90, pres., 1981-83, chmn. bd., 1983-85. Recipient vol. service award Huntington Meml. Hosp., Pasadena, 1967; vol. service award Calif. Mus. Sci. and Industry, 1984, 85, 86, 87, 89; decorated officer Mil. and Hospitaller Order St. Lazarus of Jerusalem. Episcopalian. Club: Valley Hunt (Pasadena). Home: 601 E Del Mar Pasadena CA 91101

LATIMER, MARGARET PETTA, nutrition and dietetics educator; b. Sacramento, Aug. 17, 1932; d. Rosario and Helen (Sclafani) Petta; m. Westford Ramos Latimer, June 18, 1978. BS, U. Calif., Berkeley, 1954; MA, Calif. State U., Sacramento, 1982. Registered dietitian, Calif.; life teaching credential, Calif. Therapeutic dietitian U. Calif. Med. Ctr., San Francisco, 1955-65; dietitian Roseville (Calif.) Community Hosp., 1966-67, Mercy San Juan Hosp., Carmichael, Calif., 1967-69; substitute tchr. San Juan Unified Sch. Dist., Sacramento, 1970-75, tchr. adult edn., 1971-74; instr. dietetics American River Coll., Sacramento, 1975-77, San Joaquin Delta Coll., Stockton, Calif., 1975—; cons. dietitian, Sacramento, 1973-78. Mem. Am. Dietetic Assn., Soc. for Nutrition Edn., Nutrition Today, Calif. Dietetic Assn. (pres. Golden Empire dist. 1974-75), AAUW (gourmet chmn. 1981-82, editor AAUW Book of Favorite Recipes 1982). Republican. Roman Catholic. Office: San Joaquin Delta Coll 5151 Pacific Ave Stockton CA 95207

LATSHAW, PATRICIA JOAN HERGET, public relations professional; b. Lakewood, Ohio, Oct. 4, 1930; d. Walter Clyde and Helen Naomi (Jones) Herget; m. George Tarrant Latshaw, May 24, 1958; children: Christopher Herget, Michael Kevin. BA, Principia Coll., 1951; MA, U. Chgo., 1953; PhD, U. Iowa, 1957. Asst. to bus. mgr. Goodman Theatre, Chgo., 1951-53; instr. English U. Nebr., Lincoln, 1953-55; instr. communications skills U. Iowa, Iowa City, 1955-57; staff writer Ill. Bell Telephone Co., Chgo., 1957-58; pub. relations dir. Cleve. Area YWCA, 1958-59, Ursuline Coll., Pepper Pike, Ohio, 1970-72; dir. communications Univ. Svcs. Inst., Mayfield, Ohio, 1972-74; dir. community relations Akron (Ohio)-Summit County Pub. Libr., 1974—; co-editor Puppetry Jour., Macedonia, Ohio, 1983—. Contbr. articles to libr. jours. Dem. councilwoman, Macedonia, 1969-70. Mem. Pub. Rels. Soc. Am. (accredited, assn. del. 1977), ALA (John Cotton Dana Pub. Rels. award 1983, mem. intellectual freedom com., 1987—), Libr. Adminstrn. and Mgmt. Assn. (chmn. pub. rels. sect. 1989-90), Ohio Libr. Assn. (pres.-elect 1990—, chmn. mem. com. 1976, chmn. community rels. div. 1980, intellectual freedom com. 1981-84). Mem. United Ch. of Christ. Home: 8005 Swallow Dr Macedonia OH 44056 Office: Akron-Summit County Pub Lib 55 S Main St Akron OH 44326-0001

LATSIOS, BARBARA LYNN, federal agency administrator; b. Phila., Jan. 25, 1954; d. Stephen and Helen Valentina (Matweychuk) Samereck; m. George Latsios, Aug. 29, 1976. Clk., stenographer Nat. Park Svc., Phila., 1971-

72, park ranger, 1972-79, supervisory park ranger, 1979-85, purchasing agt., 1985-87; contract specialist EPA, Phila., 1987—. Mem. Nat. Contract Mgmt. Assn., AFL-CIO (sec. Local 2058 Phila. 1973-75, 2d v.p. 1976-79). Republican. Russian Orthodox. Office: US EPA 841 Chestnut Bldg Region III Philadelphia PA 19107

LATTA, JEAN CAROLYN, financial analyst, chemist; b. Chgo., Oct. 11, 1943; d. John Oscar and Katherine Helen (Schnitzer) Latta. BS in Chemistry, U. Ill., 1966; MS in Chemistry, IIT, 1970; MBA, U. Chgo., 1976. chemist, Gillette Co., Chgo., 1966-67; asst. research chemist, 1969-73; product designer Bunker-Ramo Corp., Chgo., 1973-75; staff exec. George S. May Internat. Co., Park Ridge, Ill., 1977; controller, ind. cons. Bayou City Service Co., Houston, 1978; staff acct. Chemtrust Industries, Franklin Park, Ill., 1979; fin. analyst U. Chgo., 1979-84; sr. price/cost analyst Northrop Corp., Pico Rivera, Calif., 1984-85, pricing coord., Hawthorne, Calif., 1989—. Patentee in electronic field. Democrat. Roman Catholic. Home: 17821 Heidi Cir Yorba Linda CA 92686

LATTA, JENNIE DAVIDSON, lawyer; b. Memphis, Jan. 9, 1961; d. Minor Lee and Sandra (Heath) Davidson; m. James Burr Latta, Sept. 6, 1980; children: Robert Wherry, John Burr, Kenneth Spicer, David Stuart. BA, Memphis State U., 1981, JD, 1986. Bar: Tenn. 1986, U.S. Dist. Ct. (we. dist.) Tenn. 1986. Assoc. McDonnell Boyd, Memphis, 1986—. Mem. ABA (bus. law sect., bus. bankruptcy com.), Tenn. Bar Assn. (comml. bankruptcy & banking law sect.), Memphis Bar Assn. (bankruptcy sect.). Republican. Presbyterian. Office: McDonnell Boyd 6075 Poplar Ave Ste 623 Memphis TN 38119

LATTAL, ALICE DARNELL, clinical psychologist, consultant; b. Chico, Calif., Apr. 8, 1943; d. Wendell Austin and Pearl (Jones) Hammer; m. Kennon Andy Lattal, Apr. 16, 1965; children: Kennon Matthew, Anna Rachel, Laura Ashley. BA, U. Ala., 1965, MA, 1968; C.A.S.E., Johns Hopkins U., 1970; PhD, W.Va. U., 1980. Lic. psychologist. Psychologist I Bryce State Hosp., Tuscaloosa, Ala., 1965-67; tchr. spl. edn. Tuscaloosa Bd. Edn., 1967-69; children's specialist Harford Mental Health Clinic, Bel Air, Md., 1969-70, Valley Community Mental Health Ctr., Morgantown, W.Va., 1972-75; coord. children's svcs. Valley Community Mental Health Ctr., Morgantown, 1975-79, asst. dir. prevention edn., 1980-81, dir. prevention edn., 1981-82; asst. to v.p. acad. affairs W.Va. U., Morgantown, 1982-85; pvt. practice Inst. for Behavioral Studies, Morgantown, 1985-86, pres., 1987—; cons. Corp. Behavior Analysts, Chgo., 1986—; pres. Learning Enhancement Ctrs. Inc., W.Va., 1988—; v.p. Psychol. Resources Inc., Morgantown, 1989—. Founder, Youth Svcs. Ctr., Morgantown, 1976-80. Mem. W.Va. Psychol. Assn. (pres. 1984-85), Am. Psychol. Assn., Orgn. Behavior Mgmt., Assn. Behavior Analysts, Am. Mgmt. Assn.

LATTERELL, MARI JEAN, marketing director; b. Cottage Grove, Oreg., Jan. 27, 1965; d. Cecil Arthur and Eleanor Pauline (Wolf) L. BA, Stanford U., 1985, Stanford U., 1985. Owner Innovative Thought and Design, Incline Village, Nev., 1983-89; product mgr. Intuit, Palo Alto, Calif., 1989—; cons. EF Hutton and Co., Palo Alto, Calif., 1985-87; dir. mktg. Migent, Inc., Incline Village, Nev., 1987-89. Mem., vol. Incline Village C. of C., Catholic Charities, Sparks, Nev., 1988. Mem. Nat. Assn. for Female Execs., Nat. Assn. for Desktop Publishers. Republican. Home: 909 Exmoor Way Sunnyvale CA 94087 Office: Intuit Inc 66 Willow Pl Menlo Park CA 94205

LATURNO, DEAN MARILYN, executive; b. Brunswick, Ga., Nov. 6, 1937; d. Willie B. and Lola M. Lane; m. William K. LaTurno, Aug. 15, 1956 (div. 1971). Student, U. Houston, 1988. Cert. credit union exec. designation, 1989. Office mgr. Harris County Boys Sch., Houston, 1959--66; pres. Dist. 12 Highway Employees Credit Union, Houston, 1968--. Mem. Credit Union Mgrs. Assn. SE Tex., Houston Chpt. Credit Unions, State Employees Credit Union Assn. Office: Dist 12 Highway Employees PO Box 2248 Houston TX 77252

LAU, CHERYL, state official. BM, Ind. U.; JD, U. San Francisco. Bar: 1986. Formerly dep. atty. gen. Nev. Motor Vehicles and Pub. Safety Dept., Carson City, Nev.; sec. of state, State of Nev. Carson City, Nev., 1991—. Address: Office of Sec of State Capitol Complex Carson City NV 89710*

LAU, ELIZABETH MARTINEZ, sales, public relations and marketing executive, researcher; b. Bayamo, Oriente, Cuba, Nov. 17, 1951; came to U.S., 1967; d. Jose Ramon and Roselvi Kathy (Lau) M.; m. Jose Ramon Argiz, Aug. 9, 1952 (div.); m. Justo Ernesto Montero, Nov. 7, 1950 (div. Aug. 1987); m. Rolando Orts Dec. 2, 1989. Student Miami Dade Jr. Coll., 1973-75, U. Miami, 1985—. Exec. sec. Union Fin., Miami, Fla., 1972-75; export sales mgr. Inter City Auto Stores, Miami, 1975-80; salesman A.G.E. Paper, Miami, 1982—. Mem. NAFE, Pacific Inst. Alumni Assn. Republican. Roman Catholic.

LAU, MICHELE DENISE, advertising consultant, television personality; b. St. Paul, Dec. 6, 1960; d. Dwyane Udell and Patricia Ann (Yri) L. Student, U. Minn., 1979-82. Pub. rels. coord. Stillwater (Minn.) C. of C., 1977-79; asst. mgr. Salkin & Linoff, Mpls., 1982, store merchandiser, sales trainer, 1982-83; rental agt. Sentinel Mgmt. Co., St. Paul, 1983-84; account exec. Community Svc. Publs., Mpls., 1984-85, frwy. news supr., 1985, asst. sales mgr., 1985-86; real estate advt. coord. St. Paul Pioneer Press Dispatch, 1986-89, display advt. sales rep., 1989—; on-air personality Sta. WCCO II Cable TV, Mpls., 1988-89, co-host afternoons midwest, 1989—; cons. U. Minn. Alumni mag., 1986-89. Author mechandising and sales tng. manuals. Fundraiser sustaining program YMCA, Mpls., 1986, Jr. Achievement, St. Paul, 1988; cons. Muscular Dystrophy Assn., St. Paul, 1988-89; bd. dirs. St. Paul Jaycees. Mem. NAFE, Nat. Assn. Home Builders, Mpls. Builder Assn. (amb.), Metro-East Profl. Builders Assn. (spl. events com.), Advt. Fedn., The Newspaper Guild, Speakeasy Club. Lutheran. Home: 8033 Belair Ln Eden Prairie MN 55347 Office: St Paul Pioneer Press Dispatch 345 Cedar St Saint Paul MN 55101

LAUBACH, SUSAN ANN, health and physical education educator; b. Bound Brook, N.J., June 13, 1940; d. Charles Paden and Mary Ella (Van-Fleet) L. BS, Douglass Coll., 1962; MEd, Rutgers U., 1966; EdD, Columbia U., 1975. Cert. health and phys. edn. tchr., coach and offl. in basketball, field hockey, lacrosse, softball. Health and phys. edn. tchr., coach Westmorris Regional High Sch., Flanders, N.J., 1962-63, Glen Rock (N.J.) Schs., 1963-66, William Paterson Coll., Wayne, N.J., 1966—; speaker in field. Contbr. articles to profl. jours. Mem. Jacksonville Band. Mem. AAHPER, N.J. Assn. Health Phys. Edn. and Recreation, Hudson Valley Orienteering Assn., Internat. Rels. Coun., Internat. Coun. Health, Phys. Edn. Recreation, Kimmelon Camera Club, Nordic Ski Club, Fayson Lakes Tennis Club. Office: William Paterson Coll Pompton Rd Wayne NJ 07405

LAUBE, LOIS RUTH, librarian; b. St. Peter, Minn., Oct. 23, 1946; d. Richard H. and C. Ruth (Rosel) Laube. BA, Valparaiso U., 1968; postgrad., George Washington U., 1968-69; MLS, Ind. U., 1971. Cert. librarian, Ind. Adminstrv. asst. Am. Hist. Assn., Washington, 1969-70; libr. social scis. div. Indpls.-Marion County Pub. Libr., 1971-80, div. mgr., 1981—; chmn. profl. relations com. Cen. Ind. Area Library Svcs. Authority, Indpls., 1989—. Contbr. articles to profl. jours. Mem. Valparaiso U. Guild, 1980—, Eiteljorg Mus. Am. Indian and Western Art, Indpls., 1989—. Mem. ALA, Ind. Library Assn., Beta Phi Mu. Office: Indpls-Marion County Public Library PO Box 211 Indianapolis IN 46206

LAUBER, MIGNON DIANE, food processing company executive; b. Detroit, Dec. 21; d. Charles Edmond and Maud Lillian (Foster) Donaker. Student Kelsey Jenny U., 1958, Brigham Young U., 1959; m. Richard Brian Lauber, Sept. 13, 1963; 1 child, Leslie Viane (dec.). Owner, operator Alaska World Travel, Ketchikan, 1964-67; founder, owner, pres. Oosick Soup Co., Juneau, Alaska, 1969—. Treas., Pioneer Alaska Lobbyists Soc., Juneau, 1977—. Mem. Bus. and Profl. Women, Alaska C. of C. Libertarian, Washington Athletic Club. Author: Down at the Water Works with Jesus, 1982; Failure Through Prayer, 1983, We All Want to Go to Heaven But Nobody Wants to Die, 1988. Home: 321 Highland Dr Juneau AK 99801 Office: PO Box 1625 Juneau AK 99802

LAUBER, PATRICIA GRACE, writer, juvenile prose; b. N.Y.C., Feb. 5, 1924; d. Hubert Crow and Florence (Walker) L.; m. Russell Frost III, Apr. 11, 1981. BA, Wellesley Coll., 1945. Rsch., writer Look Mag. Book Dept., N.Y.C., 1945-46; staff writer Scholastic Mags., N.Y.C., 1946-48, editor, 1948-54, freelance editor, 1954-56; freelance editor Challenge Books, Coward-McCann, N.Y.C., 1955-59; founding editor, editor-in-chief Science World, Street & Smith, N.Y.C., 1956-59; chief editor Science and Mathematics, The New Book of Knowledge, Grolier, N.Y.C., 1961-67; freelance editor Good Earth Books, Garrard, Scarsdale, N.Y., 1973-79. Author: Numerous children's books including Dinosaurs Walked Here and Other Stories Fossils Tell, 1987, Snakes Are Hunters, 1988, Lost Star, the Story of Amelia Earhart, 1988, Meteors and Meteorites: Voyagers from Space, 1989, The News About Dinosaurs, 1989 (N.Y. Acad. Scis. Hon. Mention 1990), Volcano: The Eruption and Healing of Mount St. Helens, 1986 (Newbery Honor Book 1987, N.Y. Acad. Scis. Hon. Mention 1987), From Flower to Flower: Animals and Pollination, 1986 (N.Y. Acad. Sci. Hon. Mention 1988) and others. Recipient award for Overall Contbn. to Children's Lit., The Washington Post/Children's Book Guild award, Washington, 1983, Eva L. Gordon award, The Am. Nature Study Soc., 1988, Lit. award Cen. Mo. State U., 1987. Mem. The Authors Guild (children's book com.), PEN, Soc. Children's Book Writers. Democrat. Congregationalist. Office: c/o Bradbury Press 866 Third Ave New York NY 10022

LAUCIUS, STEPHANIE EVE, retired teacher, director; b. Elizabeth, N.J., Dec. 16, 1915; d. Bruno Alexander and Eva Veronica (Gavelis) L. BS, Douglass Coll., New Brunswick, N.J., 1936; MA, NYU, 1945, postgrad., 1945-55. Cert. tchr., ednl. adminstr., supr. With Elizabeth pub. schs., 1936-80, gen. sci. tchr., dir. audio-visual aids, 1936-51; guidance counselor, 1951-54; supr. sci. and math. Elizabeth pub. schs., 1954-64, supr. of sci., 1964-67, prin. summer high sch., 1965, dir. summer sci. curriculum, 1966, dir. instrn., 1967-75, dir. secondary curriculum and instrn., 1975-80; vis. prof. aviation edn. workshop U. Tenn., Knoxville, 1956, vis. lectr. univ. edn. courses; mem. evaluation teams Middle States Sch. Evaluations; cons. in field. Editor Jour. St. Elizabeth Hosp. Guild, 1986—; editor FLASH, the newsletter of Garden State chpt. Myasthenia Gravis Found., 1983—; contbr. articles to profl. publs. Pres., bd. dirs. St. Elizabeth Hosp. Guild, Elizabeth, 1980—; pres., bd. dirs. Union County Hist. Soc., Elizabeth, 1980—, pres. 1989—; vice chmn. bd. dirs. Garden State chpt. Myasthenia Gravis Found., 1983—. Mem. NEA, N.J. Edn. Assn., Nat. Retired Educators, AAUW (bd. dirs. 1965—, scholarship chmn. Elizabeth br. 1965—), Douglass Coll. Alumnae Assn. (v.p., bd. dirs. 1984—), Elizabeth Edn. Assn. (past mem. exec. bd.), Elizabeth Schoolwomen's League (past bd. dirs.), Am. Assn. Sch. Adminstrs., Cen. Adminstrv. Coun. (officer, bd. dirs. 1954-75), Urban League (past bd. dirs.), Citizens' League of Elizabeth, Secondary Sch. Women's Club Elizabeth (exec. bd. 1975—, scholarships chmn. 1980—, bd. dirs. 1970—), Kappa Delta Pi. Roman Catholic. Home: 521 Chilton St Elizabeth NJ 07208

LAUDER, ESTEE, cosmetics company executive; b. N.Y.C.; m. Joseph Lauder; children: Leonard, Ronald. LLD (hon.), U. Pa., 1986. Chmn. bd. Estee Lauder Inc., 1946—. Author: Estee: A Success Story, 1985. Named One of 100 Women of Achievement Harpers Bazaar, 1967, Top Ten Outstanding Women in Business, 1970; recipient Neiman-Marcus Fashion award, 1962; Spirit of Achievement award Albert Einstein Coll. Medicine, 1968; Kaufmann's Fashion Fortnight award, 1969; Bamberger's Designer's award, 1969; Gimbel's Fashion Forum award, 1969; Internat. Achievement award Frost Bros., 1971; Pogue's Ann. Fashion award, 1975, Golda Meir 90th Anniversary Tribute award, 1988; decorated chevalier Legion of Honor France, 1978; medaille de Vermeil de la Ville de Paris, 9, 1979; 4th Ann. award for Humanitarian Service Girls' Club N.Y., 1979; 25th Anniversary award Greater N.Y. council Boy Scouts Am., 1979; L.S. Ayres award, 1981; Achievement award Girl Scouts U.S.A., 1983; Outstanding Mother award, 1984; Athena award, 1985; honored Lincoln Ctr., World of Style, 1986; 1988 Laureate Nat. Bus. Hall of Fame. Office: 767 Fifth Ave New York NY 10153*

LAUDER, VALARIE ANNE, editor, educator; b. Detroit, Mar. 1, 1926; d. William J. and Murza Valerie (Mann) L. AA, Stephens Coll., Columbia, Mo., 1944; postgrad. Northwestern U. With Chgo. Daily News, 1944-52, columnist, 1946-52; lectr. Sch. Assembly Service, also Redpath lectr., 1952-55; freelance writer for mags. and newspapers including N.Y. Times, Yankee, Ford Times, Travel & Leisure, Am. Heritage, 1955—; editor-in-chief Scholastic Roto, 1962; editor U. N.C., 1975-80, lectr. Sch. Journalism, 1980—; gen. sec. World Assn. for Pub. Opinion Rsch., 1988—; gen. sec. nat. chmn. student writing project Ford Times, 1981-86;pub. rels. dir. Am. Dance Festival, Duke U., 1982-83, lectr., instr. continuing edn. program, 1984; contbg. editor So. Accents mag., 1982-86. Mem. nat. fund raising bd. Kennedy Ctr., 1962-63. Recipient 1st place award Nat. Fedn. Press Women, 1981; 1st place awards Ill. Women's Press Assn., 1950, 1951. Mem. Pub. Rels. Soc. Am. (treas. N.C. chpt. 1982, sec. 1983, v.p. 1984, pres.-elect 1985, pres. 1986, chmn. council of past pres., chmn. 25th Ann. event 1987, del. Nat. Assembly 1988—), Women in Communications (v.p. matrix N.C. Triangle chpt. 1984-85), N.C. Pub. Rels. Hall of Fame Com., DAR, Soc. Mayflower Desc. (bd. dir. Ill. Soc. 1946-52), Chapel Hill Hist. Soc. (bd. dir. 1981-85, chmn. publs. com. 1980-85), Chapel Hill Preservation Soc., N.C. Press Club (3d v.p. 1981-83, 2d v.p. 1983-85, pres. 1985, 1st pl. awards 1981, 82, 83, 84), Univ. Woman's Club (2d v.p. 1988-89, Women's Press N.C. Club (2d v.p. 1989-90, Nat. 1st pl. awards 1981). Office: U NC Sch Journalism CB 3365 Chapel Hill NC 27599-3365

LAUDICINA, ELEANOR V., educator; b. Newark, Oct. 11, 1942; d. Anthony J. and Eleanor (S.) Veglia; m. Robert A. Laudicina, June. BA, Allegheny Coll., 1964; MA, Rutgers U., 1965, PhD, 1974. Asst. prof. Newark State Coll., Union, N.J., 197-9; asst., assoc. prof. pub. adminstrn. Kean Coll., Union, 1976-82, dir. MPA program, 1982-89. Contributor: The Political State of New Jersey. Mem. Nat. Asssoc. Schs. Pub. Affairs Adminstrn. (pres. 1989-90), Am. Soc. Pub. Adminstrn., Pi Alpha Alpha.

LAUENSTEIN, ANN GAIL, librarian; b. Milw., Nov. 8, 1949; d. Elmer Lester Herbert and Elizabeth Renatta (Bovee) Zaeske; m. Mark Lauenstein, Aug. 16, 1986; 1 child, Maria. BA, U. Wis.-Madison, 1971, MA, 1972. Asst. libr. U. Wis.-Wausau, 1972-73; cataloger, libr. MacMurray Coll., Jacksonville, Ill., 1973-76; corp. libr. Anheuser-Busch Co., Inc., St. Louis, 1976—; facilitator Anheuser-Busch Quality Circle, St. Louis, 1984—; treas. Friends of Kirkwood Libr., 1986—; mem. adv. coun. Sch. Info. Sci. U. Mo., 1987—. Mem. Spl. Libraries Assn. (network liason 1981-83, chmn. employment com. 1983-84, chmn. hospitality com. 1984-85, membership chmn. 1988-89), St. Louis Regional Libr. Network (coun. 1981-83), St. Louis Online Users Group, AAUW (editor jour. 1981-84, publicity chmn. 1985-87, scholar 1984), Women in Bus. Network (adv. panel 1980-82, 86-87, programs planner 1987-88, asst. coord. 1988-89), Ohio Coll. Libr. Consortium Acquisitions Users Coun. Avocation: stamp collecting. Office: Anheuser-Busch Co Inc 1 Busch Pl Saint Louis MO 63118

LAUER, ELIZABETH, composer; b. Boston, Mass., Dec. 2, 1932; d. Henry Sofus and Elizabeth Sarah (Fitch) Larsen; m. Louis Lauer; children: Amy, Katharine, Erik. BA, Bennington Coll., Vt., 1953; MA, Columbia U., N.Y.C., 1955; postgrad, Staatliche Hochschule Fur Mus., Hamburg, 1955-57. Asst. pres. Columbia Records, N.Y.C., 1957-62, assoc. producer, 1962-63; lectr. pvt. practice, Fairfield County, 1978; composer-in-residence various programs seminars, N.Y.C.; performer-opera New Eng. Opera, Fairfield County, 1980-84; performer/author on video Reading & O'Reilly, 1988—. Music published by Carl Fischer, Kjos & Galaxy, recorded on Newport Classics. Recipient Fulbright scholarship, 10 Pen Women awards. Mem. Am. Composers Alliance, Conn. Composers, Inc. (bd. dirs.). Home and Office: 26 Juniper Place Wilton CT 06897

LAUER, JEANETTE CAROL, history educator, author; b. St. Louis, July 14, 1935; d. Clinton Jones and Blanche Aldine (Gideon) Pentecost; m. Robert Harold Lauer, July 2, 1954; children: Jon, Julie, Jeffrey. BS, U. Mo., St. Louis, 1970; MA, Washington U., St. Louis, 1973, PhD, 1975. Assoc. prof. history St. Louis Community Coll., 1974-82; assoc. prof. history U.S. Internat. U., San Diego, 1982-90, prof., 1990—. Author: Fashion Power, 198l, The Spirit and the Flesh, 1983, Til Death Do Us Part, 1986, Watersheds, 1988. Woodrow Wilson fellow, 1970, Washington U. fellow, 197l-75. Mem. Am. Hist. Assn. (co-editor teaching column), Orgn. Am. Historians. Democrat. Presbyterian. Home: 13949 Davenport Ave San Diego CA 92129

LAUFENBERG, TERRE LYNN, insurance company executive; b. Madison, Wis., Dec. 26, 1951; d. Roy Charles and Ruth Marie (McCloskey) Pierstorff; m. Gary Peter Laufenberg, Feb. 15, 1969; children: Amie, Monte, Tawna. Sales agt. Bankers Life and Casualty, Madison, 1977-80, mgr., 1981-84; br. mgr. Bankers Life and Casualty, Peoria, 1984—. Office: Bankers Life and Casualty 4300 N Brandywine Peoria IL 61614

LAUFER, BEATRICE, composer; b. N.Y.C.; d. Samuel and Fanny (Silverman) L.; m. Theodore Lassoff, Oct. 2, 1940 (dec. 1955); 1 child, Samuel; m. Seymour H. Rinzler, Oct. 19, 1969 (dec. 1970). Student Julliard Sch. Music, 1944. Composer: Symphony No. 1 (performed by Eastman-Rochester Symphony Orch., 1945-46, performance Germany and Japan under auspices of State Dept., 1948, performed by Nat. Gallery Orch., Washington, 1982), Dance Festival (performed by Eastman-Rochester Symphony, 1946-47); choral compositions include: Under the Pines, Spring Thunder performed Tanglewood, 1949, Song of the Fountain, inter-racial chorus, UN Freedom celebration, 1952; Small Concerto for Chamber Orch. performed McMillan Theatre, Columbia, 1949-50; Ile, opera, world premiere Royal Opera Co., Stockholm, Sweden, 1958, recorded by Yale U. Orch. 1978, Broadcast Nat. Pub. Radio, 1980, 87, performed in Chinese at Nanjing U. World Conf. on O'Neill, Shanghai Opera House, June 1988; Second Symphony performed by Oklahoma City Orch., 1961; premiere concerto at Donnell Library Ctr., 1962; premiere performance Prelude and Fugue for Orch., Brevard Music Ctr., N.C., 1964, Cry! orchestral prelude, Orch. of Am., Town Hall, 1966, Lyric string trio, Bowdoin Coll. Contemporary Music Festival, 1966, performed with Eastman-Rochester Symphony, 1968, Shreveport Symphony Orch., 1978, Berkshire Symphony Orch., 1981; In the Throes performed Shreveport Symphony, 1980, New Orleans Symphony Orch., 1982, Berkshire Symphony Orch., 1985; Conn. Found. of Arts grantee for performance And Thomas Jefferson Said (symphonic version performed by S.W. Floridan Symphony Orch., 1987), Norwalk Symphony Orch., 1976, 3 excerpts performed by USAF Chamber Players, Washington, 1985, premiere version for concert band baritone solo performed by The Goldman Meml. Band, 1986, also at the Aspen (Colo.) Music Festival, 1987, orchestral performance We Hold These Truths, S.w. Fla. Symphony, Nov. 1987; premiere opera Ile performed by Shanghai (Peoples Republic of China) Opera House, 1988; master ceremonies Young Am. Artists, radio sta. WNYC; hostess The Conductor Speaks series sta. WNYC. Mem. ASCAP, Am. Symphony Orch. League, Am. Music Ctr. Address: PO Box 3 Lenox Hill Sta New York NY 10021

LAUFFENBURGER, SANDRA KAY, body movement educator, fitness consultant; b. Elgin, Ill., Nov. 10, 1951; d. Harold Arthur and Lois Geraldine (Ottinger) L.; m. Peter Bathurst Edwards, Sept. 29, 1978. BEd in Phys. Sci., U. Ill., 1973; MSc in Geology, U. Cin., 1975; cert. movement analyst, Laban Inst. Movement Studies, Seattle, 1985. Cert. massage therapist N. Winters Acad.; cert. fitness leader. Rsch. geologist Exxon Prodn. Rsch. Co., Houston, 1975-83; dir., founder Fitness Movement Tng., Houston, 1986—; instr. phys. edn. Houston Community Coll., 1989—, advisor dept. phys. edn., 1989-90; lectr. anatomy and physiology N. Winters Acad., Houston, 1989—; fitness cons. Clark Hatch Fitness Internat., Jakarta, Indonesia, 1988—; pvt. practice movement edn., U.S., Asia, Australia, 1986—; movement educator tennis team Rice U., Houston, 1988—; v.p., bd. dirs. Laban Inst. Movement Studies, N.Y.C., 1989—; advisor Guangdong Aerobics Fedn., Canton, People's Republic China, 1986-87. Contbg. author: Exercise Technique, 1989, Dance Injuries, 1990; contbr. numerous articles on exercise and Laban movement analysis to profl. publs. Mem. Internat. Dance Exercise Assn., Somatics Soc. for Bodily Arts, Am. Massage Therapy Assn., AAHPER and Dance, Alliance Profl. Fitness Instrs. (2d v.p., advisor Houston 1988—).

LAUGHLIN, JEAN WILLOUGHBY, jeweler, gemologist, small business owner; b. Tabor City, N.C., June 21, 1935; d. Benny Bruce Willoughby and Grace (Herring) Hatch; m. Marion Joseph Fontenot, Dec. 5, 1953; children: Marion Joseph Fontenot, Randall B. Fontenot, Shari Alaine Fontenot; m. Scott W. Laughlin, June 5, 1976 (div. 1979). Student, U. S.W. La., 1954-58; cert., Paris Jr. Coll., Paris, Tex., 1978. Cert. jeweler, gemologist, stone setter. Sales rep. Texchron/Texgems, San Antonio, 1978-80; mgr. Lavender & Co., Jacksonville, Fla., 1980-83; instr. jewelry dept. Paris Jr. Coll., 1983-86; owner, mgr. First Coast Jewelers & Mfrs., Inc., Atlantic Beach, Fla., 1986—. Mem. NAFE. Democratr. Roman Catholic. Office: First Coast Jewelers Inc 1007 Atlantic Blvd Atlantic Beach FL 32233

LAUGHLIN, NAOMI MYERS, real estate professional; b. Oliver, Ill., Mar. 11, 1913; d. Jesse and Mary Grace (Macke) Myers; m. Otis Alton Worthington, July 24, 1936 (dec. Apr. 1948); m. Cyril James Laughlin, Feb. 19, 1955. BA, George Washington U., 1934. Cert. assn. exec. Realtor Silver Spring, Md., 1943-50, 70—. Mem. AAUW (past pres.), Realtors Land Inst. (pres. 1976-77), Montgomery County (Md.) Bd. Realtors (exec. v.p. 1950-70, pres. fed. credit union 1981-84). Democrat. Roman Catholic. Home: 13716 New Hampshire Ave Silver Spring MD 20904

LAUPER, CYNDI, musician; b. Queens, N.Y., June 20, 1953. Studied with Katie Agresta, N.Y., 1974. Toured with Doc West's Disco Band Flyer; mem. musical group Blue Angel, N.Y.C., 1980. Featured in German TV music program; rec. artist: (album) She's So Unusual, 1983, A Night To Remember, 1989; co-writer: (songs) Girls Just Want to Have Fun, She Bop, Money Changes Everything, Time After Time, Goonies R Good Enough, 1985, A Night to Remember, 1989; star: (videos) Girls Just Want to Have Fun, Time After Time, others; film debut: Vibes, 1988; TV appearances include The Tonight Show, The David Letterman Show; concert tours in Japan, Australia, Hawaii and Eng. Named one of Women of Yr., 1984, Best Female Video Performer, MTV Video Music Awards, 1984, Best Female Performer, Am. Video Awards, 1985; recipient 6 Grammy awards, 1985, 2 Am. Video awards, 1985. Office: care Dave Wolff 853 7th Ave New York NY 10019*

LAURENT, SUSAN ELIZABETH, food products executive; b. Two Rivers, Wis., Sept. 2, 1962; d. Claude Elwyn and Audrey Jean (Schnorr) L. AS in Bus. Adminstrn., U. Wis., Manitowoc, 1983; BS in Food Sci., U. Wis., Green Bay, 1985. Shift mgr., cashier Super Am. Gas Station, Two Rivers, Wis., 1980-84; rsch devel. asst. Schreiber Foods, Inc., Green Bay, Wis., 1984-85; quality control and process engr. Geo. Hormel & Co., Ottumwa, Iowa, 1985-86; production supr. Hillshire Farm Co., New London, Wis., 1986-87; quality control rep. Gold Bond Ice Cream, Inc., Green Bay, Wis., 1987—; instr. Tae Kwan Do, YMCA, Manitowoc, Wis., 1981-85. Mem. Dairy Tech. Soc., Wis. Lab. Assn. (regional coord.). Home: 3614 Columbus St Two Rivers WI 54241 Office: Gold Bond Ice Cream Inc 909 Packerland Dr #19007 Green Bay WI 54307-9007

LAURICELLA, JANET MAY, association administrator; b. Fitchburg, Mass., Dec. 9, 1944; d. Ronald George and Pauline Janet (Perodeau) LeClair; m. David Lauricella, Apr. 3, 1987; children: Thomas II, Kristine, Beth, Robert, Heather, Cheryl. BA in Biology, Fitchburg State Coll., 1974, postgrad., 1974-80. Owner, operator Mrs. Connell's Nursery Sch., Westminster, Mass., 1980-82; assoc. dir. Mental Health Assn. North Cen. Mass., Fitchburg, 1982-83; job specialist Jobs for Bay State Grads., Fitchburg, 1983-84; state dir. student activities Jobs for Bay State Grads., Boston, 1984-87; exec. dir. United Way Greater Gardner, Mass., 1987—; pres., bd. dirs. Mental Health Assn. North Cen. Mass., Fitchburg, 1985—. Contbr. articles to profl. jours. Mem., past pres. Oakmont Music Parents Assn., Ashburnham, Mass.; bd. dirs. Montachusett coun. Girl Scouts U.S., 1987-90. Mem. NAFE, Bus. and Profl. Women, Rotary. Lutheran. Office: United Way of Greater Gardner 161 A Chestnut St Gardner MA 01440

LAURIE, MARILYN, telecommunications company executive; b. N.Y.C.; d. Abraham and Irene Gold; m. Robert Laurie; children: Amy, Lisa. BA in English, Barnard Coll., 1959; MBA, Pace U., 1975. Responsible for environ. programs AT&T, N.Y.C., 1970-75, established electronic media program, 1975-78, exec. speeches, policy statements, 1978-79, advt. mgr., 1979-80; exec. dir. AT&T Bell Labs., 1980-83; v.p. AT&T Bell Labs., N.J., 1983-84, AT&T, N.J., 1984-85; group v.p. AT&T, 1986-87; sr. v.p. AT&T, Basking Ridge, N.J., 1987—; chmn. AT&T Found., N.Y.C. Author articles on environ. issues. Co-founder Environ. Action Coalition, 1970; co-originator Earth Day, 1970; bd. dirs. N.Y.C. Ballet, N.Y.C. Pub. Edn. Fund; bd. visitors Medill Sch. Journalism Northwestern U. Recipient Tribute to Women in Internat. Industry award YWCA, 1981, Gold Key award Pub. Relations News, 1985, 87, 88, WEAL award Women's Equity Action League, 1985, Women in Communications Matrix award, 1988; named to YWCA Acad. Women Achievers, 1984. Mem. Pub. Relations Soc. Am., Arthur W. Page Soc., Catalyst (bd. dirs.). Office: AT&T 295 N Maple Ave RM 434213 Basking Ridge NJ 07920

LAURIE, PIPER (ROSETTA JACOBS), actress; b. Detroit, Jan. 22, 1932; m. Joseph Morgenstern, 1962; 1 child. Acted in sch. plays; motion picture debut in Louisa; other motion pictures include The Milkman, Francis Goes to the Races, Prince Who Was A Thief, Son of Ali Baba, Has Anybody Seen My Gal, No Room for the Groom, Mississippi Gambler, Kelly and Me, Golden Blade, Dangerous Mission, Johnny Dark, Dawn at Socorro, Smoke Signal, Ain't Misbehavin', Until They Sail, The Hustler, Carrie, 1976, Tim, 1978, Return to Oz, 1985, Children of a Lesser God, 1986, Appointment with Death; TV appearances include Days of Wine and Roses, Playhouse 90, The Deaf Heart, The Ninth Day, G.E. Theatre, Play of the Week, Hallmark Hall of Fame, Nova: Margaret Sanger, The Woman Rebel, In the Matter of Karen Ann Quinlan, Rainbow, Skag, The Thorn Birds, 1983; TV films include The Bunker, 1981, Love, Mary, 1985, Mae West, 1985, Promise, 1986, Toughlove, 1985; TV series: Twin Peaks, 1990; appeared Broadway play Glass Menagerie, 1965, off-Broadway plays Rosemary and the Alligators, 1961. Acad. award nominee for the Hustler, 1962, Carrie, 1976; recipient Emmy award Acad. TV Arts and Scis., 1987. Mem. Acad. Motion Picture Arts and Scis. Address: care Triad Artists Inc 10100 Santa Monica Blvd 16th Fl Los Angeles CA 90067*

LAURIMORE, ANN, educator; b. Cleve., Dec. 16, 1943; d. Burley and Mary Meister Laurimore (Knierim) Cooke. BA, Western Mich. U., 1965; MEd, U. Ariz., 1968. Cert. tchr., Mich.; ordained deacon Presbyn. Ch., 1984, as elder, 1987. Tchr. Midland Pub. Sch., Mich., 1965-66, Royal Oak Pub. Schs., Mich., 1966-67, Tucson Unified Sch. Dist., 1968-70; dept. def. dependent schs. Solars Elem. Sch., Misawa Air Base, Japan, 1970-71; dept. def. schs. dependent Wrutsmith Elem. Sch., Clark Air Base, The Philippines, 1971-72, Goeppingen Elem. Sch., Fed. Republic of Germany, 1972-73; reading specialist Mannheim Elem. Sch., Fed. Republic of Germany, 1973-76; reading tchr., cons., chpt. I coord. Traverse City (Mich.) Area Publ Schs., 1977—; pres. Northwestern Mich. Reading Coun., Traverse City, 1988, young authors, founder and chmn., 1983-88; spl interest coun. mem. Mich. Chpt. I; regional rep. region 2 Mich. Reading Assn., 1988; mem. Internat. Reading Assn.; mem. critical rev. com. Traverse City Area Pub. Schs., Reading. Lit. com. mem. Traverse City Pub. Schs. Mich. Dept. of Edn. Recipient Commendation award U.S. Army, Germany, 1976, Lit. award Northwestern Mich. Reading Coun., 1987. Mem. NEA, AAUW (v.p. in charge of programs), Nat. Coun. Tchrs. Maths., Mich. Coun. of Tchrs. Maths., Nat. Coun. Tchrs. English, Assn. Supr. and Devel., Traverse City Edn. Assn., Mich. Edn. Assn., Mich. Coun. Tchrs. English, Alpha Omicron Pi, Delta Kappa Gamma Soc. Internat. Presbyterian.

LAURITSEN, JILL ANN, registered nurse; b. Sheboygan, Wis., Jan. 10, 1959; d. Lyle Eugene and Sheila Faye (Nack) Watson; m. Keith Edward Lauritsen, July 10, 1982; children: Christopher, Robyn. BSN, U. Wis., Oshkosh, 1983. Grad. nurse Sheboygan Meml. Ctr., 1984-85; ins. nurse Am. Profl. Systems, Milw., 1984-85; nurse coord. wellness program Sheboygan Clinic, 1985; staff nurse Valley View Med. Ctr., Plymouth, Wis., 1985; floating nurse St. John's NE Hosp., Maplewood, Minn., 1986-88, St. Mary's Hosp., Green Bay, Wis., 1988—. Vol. ARC, Sheboygan, Stillwater, Minn., Oshkosh, Wis. and Green Bay, 1982—; mem. Sheboygan Y's Women, 1984-85. Mem. AAUW (membership chairperson 1989—), Sheboygan Svc. Club, Green Bay Newcomers (golf chairperson 1989). Lutheran. Home: 2077 Autumn Leaves Circle Green Bay WI 54313 Office: St Marys Hosp 1726 Shawano Ave Green Bay WI 54313

LAUTERBACH, SHIRLEY SUSAN PFEIFFER, principal; b. Louisville, Ky., Feb. 8, 1955; d. David Allen and Mary Elaine (Bevins) Pfeiffer; m. Steven Michael Lauterbach, Aug. 21, 1976; children: Christopher Michael, Kara Noelle. BA with high honors, U. Louisville, 1976, MEdn., 1979. Cert. secondary adminstr., Ky. Tchr. Oldham County Mid. Sch., Buckner, Ky., 1976-88; asst. prin. Oldham County Mid. Sch., 1988—; tchr. Nat. Sch. of Excellence, 1984-85; tchg. asst. U. Louisville, fall 1978; tchr. Horizons Unltd., fall 1981, SPREE Dimensions, LaGrange, Ky., Summers 1982, 83, Ky. Career Ladder Project Pilot, Frankfort, 1986-87; supr. tchr. U. Louisville Student Teaching Program, 1980-88. Contbr. articles to profl. jours. Recipient Presdl. Award for Excellence in Sci. Teaching, Washington, 1984; named to Order of Ky. Cols.; named Oldham County Tchr. of Yr., 1988. Mem. Nat. Assn. Secondary Sch. Prins., Ky. Assn. Sch. Adminstrs., Nat. Sci. Tchrs. Assn., Ky. Middle Sch. Assn., Ky. Sci. Tchrs. Assn. (pres.-elect 1989, pres. 1990), Ky. Inst. for Women Sch. Adminstrn., Ky. Acad. Assn. (Gov.'s Cup coach 1986-88), Chi Omega, Phi Delta Kappa. Democrat. Baptist. Office: Oldham County Mid Sch 2720 Old Cedar Point Rd PO Box 157 Buckner KY 40010

LAUTZENHEISER, BARBARA JEAN, insurance executive; b. LaFeria, Tex., Nov. 15, 1938; d. Fred E. and Verna V. L. B.A. with high distinction, Nebr. Wesleyan U., 1960. Actuarial trainee Bankers Life Ins. Co. Nebr., Lincoln, 1960-64, programmer and systems analyst, 1964-65, asst. actuary, 1965-69, assoc. actuary, 1969-70, 2d v.p., actuary, 1970-72, v.p., actuary, 1972-80; sr. v.p. Phoenix Mut. Life Ins. Co., Hartford, Conn., 1980-84; pres. Montgomery Ward Life Ins. Co., Montgomery Ward Ins. Co., Forum Ins. Co., Schaumberg, Ill., 1984-85; prin. Lautzenheiser & Assocs., Hartford, 1986—; spokesperson for ins. industry, testifier U.S. Senate and Ho. of Reps. coms., commns. and state legislatures; featured on TV, nat. mags. and newspaper articles; mem. Interim Actuarial Standard Bd., 1985-88, Actuarial Standard Bd., 1988; chmn. Com. for Fair Ins. Rates, 1983—. Contbr. articles to profl. jours. Mem. Lincoln Electric System Adminstrv. Bd., 1977-79; bd. dirs. Nebr. Wesleyan U., 1977-82, 89—, Am. Coll., 1987—. Fellow Soc. Actuaries (pres. 1982-83, dir. 1975-80, 81-85, exec. com. 1981-84, chmn. adminstrn. and fin. com. 1981-82); mem. Am. Acad. Actuaries (dir. 1974-77, chmn. com. on publs. 1980-81), Nebr. Actuaries Club (dir. 1969-70, 71-74, chmn. 1973-74, pres. 1972-73, sec., treas. 1971-72), Life Office Mgmt. Assn. (corp. fin. planning com. 1974-81, chmn. 1976-78), Am. Council Life Ins. (risk classification com. 1973-81), Greater Hartford C. of C. (nat. policies panel 1980-84). Home: 17 Huntingridge Dr South Glastonbury CT 06073 Office: 1 Commercial Pla 22d Fl Hartford CT 06103-3599

LAVA, LESLIE MICHELE, lawyer; b. LaGrange, Ill., Mar. 18, 1957; d. James Edward and Ruth Jane (Hadraba) L. BA with honors, Vanderbilt U., 1978; JD with honors, U. Fla., 1981. Bar: Ill. 1981, U.S. Dist. Ct. (no. dist.) Ill. 1981, Fla. 1982, Calif. 1985, U.S. Dist. Ct. (no. dist.) Calif. 1985, D.C. Ct. Appeals 1987. Assoc. Chapman and Cutler, Chgo., 1981-84; assoc. Brown & Wood, San Francisco, 1984-89, N.Y.C., 1989—. Mem. Edgewood Children's Ctr., San Francisco, 1985—, Calif. Marine Mammal Ctr., San Francisco, 1985—. Mem. ABA, Fla. Bar Assn., Calif. Bar Assn., San Francisco Mcpl. Bond Forum, Nat. Assn. Bond Lawyers, Order of Coif, Phi Beta Kappa, Phi Kappa Phi, Pi Sigma Alpha. Republican. Office: Brown & Wood One World Trade Ctr New York NY 10048

LAVAIL, JENNIFER HART, neurobiologist, educator, researcher; b. Evansville, Ind., Apr. 2, 1943; d. L. Paul and Ruth (Lensing) Hart; m. Matthew M. LaVail, July 25, 1970; children: Matthew H., Katherine H. BA, Trinity Coll., Washington, 1961-65; PhD, U. Wis., 1970. Postdoctoral fellow dept. neuropathology Harvard Med. Sch., Cambridge, Mass., 1970-73, instr., 1973-74, asst. prof., 1974-76; assoc. prof. anatomy U. Calif., San Francisco, 1976-83, prof., 1983—; bd. sci. counsellors Nat. Inst. Neurol. and Communicative Disorders and Stroke, NIH, 1988—. Woodrow Wilson fellow Ford Found., 1965-66; Alfred P. Sloan fellow Sloan Found., 1976-79. Mem. Am. Assn. Anatomists (v.p. 1988-90, Charles Judson Herrick award 1975). Office: U Calif Dept Anatomy Box 0452 San Francisco CA 94143

LAVALLE, EDITH, arbitrator, consultant; b. New Haven, Dec. 24, 1919; d. Joseph and Mary Ann (Rapuano) Zuccarelli; m. Francis LaValle, July 1, 1944; children—Fern LaValle Julianelle, Gary R. A.A. in Bus. Adminstrn., Larson Jr. Coll., 1939; B.A. in Human Services, Franconia Coll., 1977. Exec. dir. Conn. Laborers Health and Pension Funds, West Haven, 1961-83; arbitrator Am. Arbitration Assn., Hartford, Conn., 1983—; lectr. U. New Haven, 1980; cons. health and pension fund planning. Contbr. book revs. Bd. dirs. Youth Continuum, New Haven, 1976—(Community Service award 1985); fund raising program dir. Tng. Research Inst. Residential Youth Ctrs., New Haven, 1986—; counselor for aged St. John the Evanelist Ch., New Haven, 1981-84; vol. arbitrator Better Bus. Bur., New Haven, 1982—; pres. Baybrook Arms Housing Corp., West Haven, 1979—. Roman Catholic. Home: 41 Jones Hill Rd Apt 202 West Haven CT 06516

LAVALLEE, DEIRDRE JUSTINE, marketing professional; b. Woonsocket, R.I., June 14, 1962; d. Albert Paul and Margaret Justine (O'Brien) L. BS in Chem. Engring., U. R.I., 1984. Sales engr. NGS Assocs. Inc., Canton, Mass., 1985-87; mgr. dist. sales MKS Instruments Inc., Andover, Mass., 1987—. Mem. Balt. Coun. Fgn. Affairs; coord. west sect. Nat. Conf. Standards Labs. Mem. Am. Inst. Chem. Engrs. (sec. chpt.), Am. Soc. Materials, Am. Inst. Physics, Am. Vacuum Soc.(liason del. nat. conf. standards labs.). Home: 845 13th St Boulder CO 80302 Office: MKS Instruments Inc 5330 Sterling Dr Boulder CO 80301

LAVALLEE, LORRAINE DORIS, mathematics educator; b. Holyoke, Mass., May 31, 1931; d. Octavien Joseph and Annette Graziella (Labarre) L. AB, Mt. Holyoke Coll., 1953; MA, U. Mass., 1955; PhD, U. Mich., 1962. Instr. U. Mass., Amherst, 1959-60, asst. prof., 1960-70; assoc. prof. U. Mass., 1970—; assoc. head dept. math. and statistics U. Mass., Amherst, 1971-72, 77. Contbr. articles to profl. jours. Mem. Am. Math. Soc., Math. Assn. Am., Assn. for Women in Math., Sigma Xi, Phi Kappa Phi. Office: U Mass Dept Math and Statistics Lederle Grad Rsch Ctr Towers Amherst MA 01003

LAVELLE, BETTY SULLIVAN DOUGHERTY, legal professional; b. Omaha, Nov. 12, 1941; d. Marvin D. and Marie C. (Sery) Sullivan; children from previous marriage: Clayton B. Dougherty, Lance A. Dougherty; m. James S. LaVelle, 1986; 1 child, Lindsay L. A of Pre-Law, U. Nebr., 1960; student, U. Colo., 1964-66; BA in Philosophy, Metro State Coll., 1979; cert. legal assistant, U. San Diego, 1979. Teaching asst. Metro State Coll., Denver, 1978; paralegal Holland and Hart, Denver, 1979-85; litigation paralegal Rothgerber, Appel, Powers and Johnson, Denver, 1985-88; pres. Vivant, Inc., Boulder, 1987—; owner, adminstr. Homestead Group Home for Elderly, Longmont, 1987—; ptnr. LaVelle & McMillan, Boulder, 1989-90; water law paralegal Moses, Wittemyer, Harrison and Woodruff, p.c., Boulder, 1990—; mediator domestic relations 20th Jud. Dist., Boulder, 1984-85. Contbr. articles to profl. jours. Vol. legal aid Thursday Night Bar, Denver Bar Assn., 1979-86, paralegal coordinator, panelist, speaker, 1983-85; sr. paralegal Boulder County Legal Svcs., 1988-89; mediator landlord/tenant project City of Boulder, 1983-87; coach, trainer Ctr. for Dispute Resolution, Denver and Boulder, 1984-86; vol. Shelter for Homeless, Boulder, 1988. Recipient cert. U. Denver Coll. Law, 1981, Hoagland award Colo. Bar Assn., 1984. Mem. Colo. Bar Assn., Boulder Bar Assn. (assoc.), Soc. Profls. in Dispute Resolution, Rocky Mountain Legal Assts. (adv. bd. 1980-81, bd. dirs. 1983-85, dir. pro bono services 1984-85). Republican. Home: 1660 Bradley Dr Boulder CO 80303

LAVELLE, FAITH WILSON, retired anatomy educator, researcher; b. St. Johnsbury, Vt., Mar. 14, 1921; d. Theodore Halbert and Faith Evelyn (Harris) Wilson; m. Arthur LaVelle, Sept. 6, 1947; 1 child, Audrey. BA summa cum laude, Mt. Holyoke Coll., 1943, MA in Zoology, 1945; PhD in Biology, Johns Hopkins U., 1949. Administrv. asst. in zoology, instr. anatomy U. Pa., Phila., 1948-51; instr. U. Ill., Chgo., 1952-55, rsch. assoc., 1955-70; asst. prof. Stritch Sch. Medicine Loyola U., Maywood, Ill., 1970-76, assoc. prof., 1976-85, prof., 1985-87, acting chmn. dept., 1984-86, prof. emeritus, 1987—. Contbr. articles to profl. jours. Pres. Woman's Coll. Bd. Chgo., 1959-61, Camp Fire Girls, Inc., Kansas City, Mo., 1978-80, hon. mem., 1983—; trustee Mt. Holyoke Coll., South Hadley, Mass., 1960-65, trustee fellow, 1988—. Recipient Golden Apple Teaching award U. Ill. Med. Sch., 1953, Alumnae Medal of Honor, Mt. Holyoke Coll., 1965, preclin. teaching award Loyola U. Stritch Sch. Medicine, 1972, 73, 75, 76, 82, 86, 87, Wohelo Order award Camp Fire Girls, Inc., 1979. Mem. Am. Assn. Anatomists, Soc. for Neurosci. Office: Loyola U Stritch Sch Med 2160 S 1st Ave Maywood IL 60153

LAVENAS, SUZANNE, editor; b. Buenos Aires, Dec. 17, 1942; came to U.S., 1955; d. Carlos Fernando and Mary (Sharp) Lavenas; m. Wesley First, Jan. 9, 1982. Student, Antioch Coll., 1960-64, 65-66. Computer programmer N.Y. Telephone, N.Y.C., 1966-68; prodn. editor, then copy editor Travel Weekly, N.Y.C., 1968-76, chief copy editor, 1976-79; mng. editor Indsl. Chem. News, N.Y.C., 1981-82; editor, writer, cons. Consultant, N.Y.C., 1986—. Author numerous articles. Mem. Soc. of Silurians. Republican. Episcopalian. Home: 305 E 86th St Apt 20RW New York NY 10028

LAVENSON, SUSAN BARKER, consultant; b. L.A., July 26, 1936; d. Percy Morton and Rosalie Laura (Donner) Barker; m. James H. Lavenson, Apr. 22, 1973; 1 child, Ellen Ruth Stanclift. BA, Stanford U., 1958, MA, 1959. Cert. secondary tchr., Calif. Tchr. Benjamin Franklin High Sch., San Francisco, 1960; french dept. head Lowell High Sch., San Francisco, 1961-61; v.p. Monogram Co., San Francisco, 1963-73; creative dir. Monogram Co., N.Y.C., 1973-76; pres. SYR Corp., Santa Barbara, Calif., 1976-89; ptnr. Lavenson Ptnrs., Camden, Maine, 1989—; mem. commn. on co-edn. Wheaton Coll., Norton, Mass., 1985-87; cons. European Inst. Tourism Mgmt., Paris; mem. Relais et Chateaux, Paris, 1978-89. Author: Greening of San Ysidro, 1977 (Conf. award 1977). Trustee Camden Pub. Libr., 1989—; bd. dirs. Community Human Intelligence Project, Santa Barbara, 1986-88; mem. Native Daugs. of the Golden West, Santa Barbara, 1977-87; founding mem. Maine Women's Forum, 1990. Mem. Camden Yacht Club, Stanford Alumni Assn., Com. of 200 (treas. 1985-86), Phi Delta Kappa. Home and Office: 158 Chestnut St Camden ME 04843

LAVETT, DIANE K., biology educator, geneticist, consultant, writer; b. Ft. Benning, Ga., Feb. 29, 1944. BS, Emory U., 1969, PhD, 1973; MS, So. Conn. State Coll., New Haven, 1980; postgrad., Yale U., 1975-80. Asst. prof. Emory U., Atlanta, 1974-75, 1980-83; assoc. prof. biology SUNY, Cortland, 1986—; genetics cons. Scottish Rite Hosp., Atlanta, 1983-86, Xytex Corpo., Atlanta, 1985—, Forensic Use of Genetics, 1980—. Aukthor: Student Companion to An Introduction to Genetic Analysis, 1989; co-author: The Myofascial Release Manual, 1989, The Self-healing Body, 1989. Fellow NSF, 1969-72, NIH, 1975-76, Am. Cancer Soc., 1976-77. Mem. Phi Beta Kappa, Sigma Xi. Office: SUNY Cortland Dept Biology Cortland NY 13045

LAVID, JEAN STERN, superintendent of schools; b. Roanoke, Va., Jan. 4, 1943; d. Ernest George and Marianne (Stamm) Stern; m. Aug. 26, 1968 (div. 1989); children: Nathan, Eric, Craig, Brian, Laura. BA, Coll. William and Mary, 1965; MA, Wichita State U., 1986, specialist degree, 1989. Cert. permanent tchr. German, N.Y.; cert. supt., bldg. adminstr., Kans. Rural community devel. vol. Peace Corps, Girveli, Kayseri, Turkey, 1965-67; tchr. German, Spanish and English Kenmore (N.Y.)-Tonawanda Sch. Dist., 1967-70; tchr. German Grand Island (N.Y.) Sch. Dist., 1978-82, coord. adult edn., prin., 1982; grad. rsch. asst. Wichita (Kans.) State U., 1984-86, instr. German, 1985; asst. prin. Unified Sch. Dist. 259, Wichita, 1986-88; supt., high sch. prin. Unified Sch. Dist. 314, Brewster, Kans., 1988—; mem. sch. community adv. coms., N.Y., Kans., 1975-86; chm. Com. To Revise Fgn. Lang. Curriculum, Grand Island, 1981-83; judge Kans. Fgn. Lang. Competition, 1987. Contbr. numerous articles on ednl. leadership to profl. jours. Pres. Grand Island Food Coop., 1978-83, Waterford Food Coop., Wichita, 1983-88. Mem. Am. Assn. Sch. Adminstrs., Assn. for Supervision and Curriculum Devel., Nat. Assn. Secondary and Elem. Sch. Prins., Am. Assn. Tchrs. German, Kans. Assn. Sch. Adminstrs., Kans. United Sch. Adminstrs., AAUW (active local, regional and state levels 1973—), Phi Kappa Phi, Phi Delta Kappa. Home: Box 57 Brewster KS 67732 Office: Unified Sch Dist 314 Box 220 Brewster KS 67732

LAVIER, ANNABELLE THERESA, computer science educator; b. Hillsboro, Oreg., Aug. 6, 1947; d. Emil William and Ellen Florence (Englund) Egger; m. Bruce Edward Lavier, Dec. 16, 1969; children: Kristen, Jack. Student, Schiller Coll., Kleiningsheim, Germany, 1967-68; BA in German and History, Linfield Coll., McMinnville, Oreg., 1969; MEd in Reading, Oreg. State U., 1972. Tchr., lang. coordinator Castle Rock (Wash.) Upper Elem., 1970-71; acad. advisor Treaty Oak Community Coll., The Dalles, Oreg., 1979-83; coord. Adult Basic Skills Tech. Project, The Dalles, 1984—; instr. computer sci. Treaty Oak Community Coll., The Dalles, 1979—; cons. Apple Computer, Inc., Northwest Regional Labs., Cupertino, Calif., 1987—; editor software guides Dept. Edn., Olympia, Wash., 1985—; English-as-second-lang. coord. USN-Navy Relief, San Diego, 1972-74. Editor Buyer's Guide to Saftware, 1987, 88. Bd. chmn. Wasco County Sch. Bd., The Dalles, 1987—; mem. bd. East Cascade Nat. Pub. Radio, Wenetchee, Wash., 1987—, Mid Columbia Hops., The Dalles, 1986, Congl. Ch., The Dalles, 1988—; mem. steering com. Wasco County Dem. Party, The Dalles, 1986. Recipient Disting. Svc. award Treaty Oak Community Coll., The Dalles, 1984, Appreciation award Calif. Lit. Assn., Sacramento, 1987, award Oreg. Lit., Portland, 1987. Mem. AAUW (pres. 1984-86), PEO, Western Adult Basic Assn., Am. Assn. Adult and Continuing Edn., Oreg. Devel. Edn., Oreg. Reading and Learning Assn., Northwest Coun. Computer Edn. (bd. dirs. 1987—). Office: Treaty Oak Community Coll 300 E 4th St The Dalles OR 97058

LAVIN, BERNICE E., business executive; b. 1925; m. Leonard H. Lavin, Oct. 30, 1947; children—Scott Jay, Carol Marie, Karen Sue. Student, Northwestern U. Sec., v.p., treas. Alberto-Culver Co., 1961—, also dir.; sec.-treas., dir. Alberto-Culver Export, Inc., Leonard H. Lavin & Co., Milani Foods, Inc., Draper Daniels Media Svcs., Inc., Sally Beauty Co.; sec.-treas. Pay-Less Beauty Supply Co. Home: Glencoe IL 60022 Office: Alberto-Culver Co 2525 Armitage Ave Melrose Park IL 60160

LAVIN, LINDA, actress; b. Portland, Maine, Oct. 15, 1937; d. David J. and Lucille (Potter) L. BA, Coll. William and Mary, Williamsburg, Va., 1959. Debut: (Off-Broadway) Oh, Kay!, 1960, (Broadway) A Family Affairs, 1962; appearances in revues Wet Paint, 1965, The Game Is Up, 1965, The Mad Show, 1966; with nat. touring company On a Clear Day You Can See Forever, 1966-67; mem. acting company Eugene O'Neil Playwrights' Unit, 1968; other stage appearances include It's a Bird... It's a Plane... It's Superman, 1966, Something Different, 1967, Little Murders, 1969, Cop-Out, 1969, The Last of the Red Hot Lovers, 1969 (Tony nominee), Story Theatre, 1970, The Enemy is Dead, 1973, Love Two, 1974, The Comedy of Errors, 1975, Dynamite Tonite!, 1975, Six Characters in Search of an Author, Am. Repertory Theatre, Cambridge, Mass., 1983-84 season, Broadway Bound, 1986 (Tony award 1987), Gypsy, 1990; film appearances: See You In The Morning, 1989, I Want to Go Home; star: (TV series) Alice, 1976-85 (Golden Globe award 1979); other TV appearances on Phyllis, Family, Rhoda, Harry O; TV movies include: The Morning After, 1974, Like Mom, Like Me, 1978, A Matter of Life and Death, 1981, Another Woman's Child, 1983. Recipient Sat. Rev., Outer Critics Circle awards for Little Murders, Theater World award for Wet Paint. Office: care Litke-Grossbart-Gale 10390 Santa Monica Ste 3300 Los Angeles CA 90025*

LAVIN, NANCY JEAN, manufacturer's representative; b. Montpelier, Vt., Dec. 27, 1952. BS, U. Vt., 1974. Account exec. Garber Travel, Brookline, Mass., 1978-79; v.p., co-owner LND Sales Co., Ashland, Mass., 1979-88; ptnr. LND Sales Co., Framingham, Mass., 1988—. Mem. New Eng. Sanitary Supply Assn. (sec., treas.), Internat. Sanitary Supply Assn., Mfrs. Reps. of Am. Office: LND Sales PO Box 2931 Framingham MA 01701

LAVINGTON, JOI BAUER, real estate executive; b. Wichita Falls, Tex., July 21, 1952; d. Robert Roland Bauer and Sharon (Bornhuetter) Billings; m. Charles Stephen Lavington III, Jan. 21, 1984; children: Kiel Chad, Mikaela Kendra. AA, Orange Coast Coll., 1972; BS, Woodbury U., 1974; postgrad., Coast Line Coll., 1978-80, Rancho Santiago Coll., 1981-83. Cert. real estate salesman. Designer S.O.G. of Calif., Los Angeles, 1975-76, Stuart Mann Calif., Los Angeles, 1976-84; owner, mgr. I-N-JOI Cloze, Garden Grove, Calif., 1979-81; asst. to pres. Bauer Realty & Investments, Irvine, Calif., 1985-86; mgr., v.p. Century 21 Profls., Irvine, Calif., 1986—, instr. tng., 1987—. Mem. Realty Investment Assn. Orange County, East Orange County Bd. Realtors (cert. real estate salesman), Irvine Bd. Realtors. Democrat. Unitarian-Universalist. Home: 3592 Redwood St Irvine CA 92714 Office: Century 21 Profls 4000 Barranca Pkwy #110 Irvine CA 92714

LAW, CAROL JUDITH, medical psychotherapist; b. N.Y.C., May 1, 1940; d. Aldo and Jennie (Feldman) Settimo; m. Perry J. Koll, Dec. 26, 1967 (div. Nov. 1974); 1 son, Perry J.; m. 2d, Edwin B. Law, June 1, 1979. BA, Upsala Coll., 1962; postgrad. Rutgers U., 1964-66; MA, Columbia Pacific, 1982, PhD, 1984. Diplomate Am. Bd. Med. Psychotherapy. Personnel dir. Hotel Manhattan, N.Y.C., 1961; supr. social work Essex County, Newark, 1962-67; exec. dir. USO, Vungtau, South Vietnam, 1967-68; dir. Dept. Health and Rehab. Svcs., Pensacola, Fla., 1968-79; therapist, tchr. Franciscan Renewal Ctr., Scottsdale, Ariz., 1982—; mem. state adv. bd. Parents Anonymous, Phoenix, 1982; chmn. Gov.'s Adv. Commn. Drugs and the Elderly, Tallahassee, 1978. Pres. Jaycettes, Pensacola, 1969; chmn. social com. United Way Fund, Pensacola, 1977; mem. adv. bd. USO, Pensacola, 1973; trustee ORME Sch. Fellow Am. Acad. Polit. and Social Sci.; mem. Am. Assn. Pub. Adminstrs. Republican. Roman Catholic. Club: Phoenix Country, Desert Highlands Country. Home: 8214 E Del Cadena St Scottsdale AZ 85258

LAW, INA FLORIENE, accountant; b. Salt Lake City, Jan. 3, 1924; d. Frank Andrews and Annie (Langley) Keith; m. Glenn F. Law, Sept. 4, 1945. Student, N.Y. Sch. Short Story Writing. CPA, Calif. Ret.; from bookkeeper to acct. E.L. Fink & Son, Patterson, Calif.; acct. Guerdon Industries, Inc.; bookkeeper Sims Renault Dealership, Modesto. Contbr. articles to profl. jours. With Women Accepted for Vol. Emergency Svc., USN, 1944-45. Mem. Guardian Jobs Daughters (pres.), Soroptimists. Home: 850 N 2d St #13 Patterson CA 95363

LAW, JANE HINTON, artist, small business owner; b. Dayton, Ohio, Dec. 26, 1928; d. William Guy and Nelle Grant (Royse) Hinton; m. Lillard E. Law, Feb. 5, 1928; children: Melinda Talbot, Laurie Jorgensen, Thomas W. Hinton, Jonathan S. BA, Otterbein Coll., 1947; MA, NYU, 1970. Art supr. Worthington (Ohio) Schs., 1947-51; tchr. Gambler Schs., Mt. Vernon, Ohio, 1954-59; asst. prof. fine arts Union Coll., Elizabeth, N.J., 1969-74; tchr. So. Regional High Sch., Manahawkin, N.J., 1975-78; instr. Ocean County Coll., Toms River, N.J., 1975-76; owner Jane Law Art Studio and Gallery, Surf City, N.J., 1976—; state judge Fed. Art Assn., Westfield, N.J., 1984—; bd. dirs. Internat. Miniature Exhibit, Surf City, Nat. Watercolor Exhibit, Surf City. Editor: Long Beach Island Cookbook, 1981; artist several featured articles in cultural events, art bus. news on show, calendar and cover photos. Judge Stafford Twp. Founders Day, Manahawkin, N.J., 1987, state contest posters Women's History Month, 1990. Recipient Outstanding Community Bus. award Tax Payers Assn., 1988; named one of Outstanding Artists Ocean County Cultural and Heritage Commn., 1989; named Woman of Yr. AAUW, 1990. Mem. AAUW (v.p. 1985—), N.J. Assn. Sch. Adminstrs. (aux. pres. 1972—), Island Singers (pres. 1984—), Soroptimists (pres. 1983-84), Phila. Watercolor Club, Internat. Soc. Marine Painters, N.J. Watercolor Soc. (assoc.). Republican. Episcopalian. Home: 2005 Long Beach Blvd Surf City NJ 08008 Office: Jane Law Art Studio & Gallery 20th St & Long Beach Blvd Surf City NJ 08008

LAW, MARGARET IRENE, scientist; b. Pitts., Mar. 20, 1954; d. John Robert and Patricia (Zazzara) L. BS with honors, Cornell U., 1976; MS, Princeton U., 1979, PhD, 1982. Rsch. asst. Cornell U., Ithaca, N.Y., 1976-77; teaching asst. Princeton (N.J.) U., 1978-79; NIH postdoctoral fellow U. Calif. Med. Sch., San Francisco, 1982-84; rsch. scientist U. Calif., Berkeley, 1984-87, lectr., 1985; lectr. dept. anatomy U. Calif., San Francisco, 1984; sr. scientist Exploratorium, San Francisco, 1987—; vis. researcher workshop on central nervous system Cold Spring Harbor, N.Y., 1978. Contbr. articles to profl. publs. Docent Audubon Canyon Ranch, Bolinas, Calif., 1985-87. Giannini fellow Bank of Am., 1982, Harold W. Dodds fellow, 1981; Alan Ladd scholar, 1974. Mem. Soc. for Neuroscis., AAAS. Home: 1510 Greene Dr San Jose CA 95129

LAW, TERESA MARIE, health facility administrator; b. Harrisburg, Pa., Oct. 3, 1954; d. Charles Casper and Helen Rita (Roach) L. AA, Harrisburg Community Coll., 1976; BS, Coll. St. Francis, Joliet, Ill., 1989. RN, Pa. RN Holy Spirit Hosp., Camp Hill, Pa., 1976-80, charge nurse, 1985-88, occupational health coord., 1988-89, dir. family and occupational health svcs., 1990—; territory mgr. Wyeth Labs., Radnor, Pa., 1980-85; cons. speaker Pa. Assn. Constructors, Harrisburg, 1989-90. Mem. NAFE, Employee Assistance Network, Pa. Hosp. Assn. of Employee Profls. Roman Catholic. Home: 268 Park Ave New Cumberland PA 17070 Office: Holy Spirit Hosp N 21st St Camp Hill PA 17011

LAWLER, ALICE BONZI (MRS. OSCAR T. LAWLER), retired college administrator, civic worker; b. Milan, Italy, Dec. 25, 1914; came to U.S. 1920, naturalized 1925; d. Ercole and Alice (Spalding) Bonzi; m. Morris Warner Mothershead, Sept. 15, 1935 (dec.); children: Warner Bonzi, Maria (Mrs. Andrei Rogers); m. Oscar Thom Lawler, May 1989. Pvt. pupil music and art; student Pasadena City Coll., 1956-60. Ptnr. Floal Toy Co., Pasadena, Calif., 1942-44; community adv. Fgn. Student Program, Pasadena City Coll., from 1952, past dir. Community Liaison Ctr. Chmn. Am. Field Service Internat. Scholarships, Pasadena, 1953-55; mem. West Coast adv. bd. Inst. Internat. Edn., San Francisco, 1957-70; v.p. San Rafael Sch. PTA, Pasadena, 1945-46; active Community Chest, ARC, Pasadena; chmn. Greater Los Angeles Com. Internat. Student and Visitor Services, 1962; mem. Woman's Civic League Pasadena, chmn. city affairs com., 1985, pres., 1986-87; bd. dirs. Fine Arts Club of Pasadena, 1983-85, Friends of Caltech Y, 1984-89, Pasadena City Coll. Found., 1983-85; commr. City of Pasadena Cultural Heritage Commn., 1984-89. Decorated knight Govt. of Italy, 1975. Fellow Nat. History Mus.; mem. Nat. Assn. Fgn. Student Affairs (life, chmn. community sect. and v.p. 1964-65, chmn. U.S. study abroad com. 1969-70), Am. Assn. UN (chpt. 2d v.p. 1964), Soc. Women Geographers, Am. Friends Middle East, Zonta Internat., Am. Women for Internat. Understanding, Omicron Mu Delta. Club: International (Pasadena). Author: Social Customs and Manners in the United States, 1957; Dining Customs Around the World, 1982; co-author: 15 Years of the Foreign Student Program at Pasadena City College, 1965. Editor: Students to People to Future, 1971. Lodge: Lions. Home: 5224 W 2nd St Los Angeles CA 90004

LAWLER, KAREN STRAND, communications company official; b. Chgo., Sept. 2, 1939; d. George Burton and Annarose (De Rosa) Strand; m. Fenton J. Lawler, Feb. 13, 1971 (div. Dec. 1975); stepchildren: Fenton J. Jr., Steven K., Karen S. Lawler Dwerlkotte. BS, Ind. U., 1984; postgrad., Ind. U.-Purdue U., Indpls., 1988—. Various positions Western Electric Co., Indpls., 1960-64, investigator sickness absenteeism, 1965-70, pub. rels. asst., 1970-83; asst. dir. pub. rels. Hough Folding Door Co., Janesville, Wis., 1964-65; editor in-house paper Customer Info. Ctr., AT&T, Indpls., 1983-85, mktg. assoc., 1985-87, mgr. hazardous materials, 1988—. Mem. Marion County Mental Health Assn., 1982—; gen. chmn. Area 8 Spl. Olympics, Indpls., 1984-87; state treas. Ind. Pro Choice Action League, Indpls., 1985-86. Mem. Ind. Soc. Hazardous Materials Mgrs., Tel. Pioneers (sec. Indpls. 1978-83), Daus. of Nile. Republican. Presbyterian. Office: AT&T Customer Info Ctr 2855 N Franklin Rd Indianapolis IN 46219

LAWLEY, KAREN R., safety coordinator; b. Lakehurst, N.J., July 24, 1947; d. Marsden Jr. and Ruth (Nichols) L.; m. Steven A. Coval, July 20, 1985; 1 child, Elick M. BS, Pa. State U., University Park, 1969. Facilities coord., safety officer Harvard U., Cambridge, Mass., lab. coord.; sr. rsch. technician Mass. Gen. Hosp., Boston. Contbr. articles to profl. jours. Office: 16 Divinity Ave Rm 151 Cambridge MA 02138

LAWLEY, SUSAN MARC, management consultant; b. N.Y.C., July 5, 1951; d. Romolo and Catherine (Giacalone) Marcucci; m. Robert Lawley, Feb. 11, 1978; 1 child, Gregory. BA with honors, Herbert H. Lehman Coll., N.Y.C., 1972; MBA, Fairleigh Dickinson U., 1982; postgrad., Fielding Inst., 1989—. With AT&T, N.Y.C. and Bedminster, N.J., 1972-80; v.p., head adminstrn. investment banking dept. Bankers Trust Co., N.Y.C., 1980-87; v.p. head planning and adminstrn. mortgage securities dept. Goldman, Sachs & Co., N.Y.C., 1987-89; pres., mgmt. cons. Camelot Con, N.Y.C. and Parsippany, N.J., 1989—; strategic planning dir. GAIN Communications, Inc., 1989—; co-founder New View Video, 1989—. Bd. dirs. Katherine Gibb Scholarship Found., N.Y.C., 1986—; v.p. Edith Imre Found., N.Y.C., 1985—. Mem. Am. Mgmt. Soc., Am. Soc. Personnel Adminstrn., AWED, NAFE, Women's Club of Fairfield. Republican. Roman Catholic. Office: Camelot Con Group Inc 3799 Rte 46 E Fl 3 Parsippany NJ 07054

LAWLIS, PATRICIA KITE, air force officer, computer consultant; b. Greensburg, Pa., May 5, 1945; d. Joseph Powell, Jr., and Dorothy Theresa (Allshouse) Kite; m. Mark Craig Lawlis, Sept. 17, 1976 (div. 1983); 1 child, Elizabeth Marie. BS, East Carolina U., 1967; MS in Computer Sci., Air Force Inst. Tech., 1982; PhD in Computer Sci., Ariz. State U., 1989. Cert. secondary math. tchr. Employment counselor Pa. State Employment Service, Washington, Pa., 1967-69; math. tchr. Fort Cherry Sch. Dist., McDonald, Pa., 1969-74; commd. 2d lt. USAF, 1974, advanced through grades to maj., 1986, data base mgr. Air Force Space Command, Colorado Springs, Colo., 1974-77, computer systems analyst, USAF in Europe, Birkenfeld, Germany, 1977-80, prof. computer sci. Air Force Inst. Tech., Wright-Patterson AFB, Ohio, 1982-86, 89—; computer cons. C.J. Kemp Systems, Inc., Huber Heights, Ohio, 1983—; Ada cons., Ada Joint Program Office, Washington, 1984—. State treas. NOW, Pa., 1973-74. Recipient Mervin E. Gross award Air Force Inst. Tech., 1982, Prof. Ezra Kotcher award, 1985. Mem. Computer Soc. of IEEE, Assn. Computing Machinery, Tau Beta Pi (v.p. Ohio Eta chpt. 1981-82), Upsilon Pi Epsilon. Office: Air Force Inst Tech Dept Elec & Computer C Engring Wright-Patterson AFB OH 45433

LAWLOR, HELEN ANNE, database publisher; b. Phila., July 20, 1944; d. Walter John and Nellie (Branka) Quinn; m. John Francis Lawlor, Nov. 10, 1967 (div. June 1985). BS, Chestnut Hill Coll., 1966; MS, St. Joseph's U., 1976; MBA, U. Pa., 1989. Chem. indexer Inst. for Sci. Info., Phila., 1967-74, mgr. chem. indexing, 1974-76, asst. dir., 1976-77, dir., 1977-82, v.p., 1982-85, sr. v.p., 1985-89, exec. v.p., 1989—; bd. trustees, fin. com. PALINET, 1989-92. Mem. Am. Chem. Soc. (chmn. div. chem. info. 1989, founder and recording sec. local chpt.'s chem. info. group 1980-82, editor Chem. Info. Bull. 1977-82), Pa. Inst. Chemists (sec. 1981-82), Chem. Notation Assn. (sec. 1976-79, v.p. 1979, pres. 1980), Nat. Fedn. Abstracting and Info. Svcs. (pres. 1989-90), Union League Phila. Republican. Roman Catholic. Office: ISI 3501 Market St Philadelphia PA 19104

LAWRENCE, AMY L., small business owner; b. Wagner, S.D., Sept. 12, 1941; d. Charles Chester and June Helen (Soulek) Wright; m. Britain Webb Lawrence, Sept. 9, 1959 (div. Jan. 1976); children: Rocklan Eugene, Michelle Renee. Grad. high sch., West Sacramento, Calif., 1959. Pres., owner Green Acres Nurseries, Albuquerque, 1965-89, Sun Country Garden Products, Bernalillo, N.Mex., 1977—. Bd. dirs. Anderson Found., U. N.Mex. Bus. Sch., Albuquerque, 1986—; gov.'s bus. adv. coun., Santa Fe, N.Mex., 1986—; del. White House Conf. on Small Bus., Washington, 1986. Named Bus. Woman of the Yr., State of N. Mex., Albuquerque, 1977. Mem. Assn. Commerce and Industry (chmn. 1986-87), Albuquerque C. of C. (bd. dirs. 1987-89). Republican. Mem. Christian Ch. Home: 3212 La Sala Cuadra NE Albuquerque NM 87111 Office: Sun Country Garden Products PO Box 1797 Bernalillo NM 87004

LAWRENCE, BARBARA, information manager; b. N.Y.C., Dec. 16, 1944; d. Seth and Aline (Greenberg) L.; m. Allen I. Laskin. BA in Chemistry, U. Vt., 1965; student, Yale U., New Haven, 1965-66. Jr. organic chemist Burroughs Wellcome & Co., Tuckahoe, N.Y., 1966-67; asst. documentation scientist Schering Corp., Bloomfield, N.J., 1967-69; info. chemist, group head, database mgmt. Exxon Research & Engring., Linden, N.J., 1969-79; head, info. service unit Exxon Corp, Research & Environ. Health Division, East Millstone, N.J.; adminstr. tech. info. service Am. Inst. Aeros. and Astronautics, N.Y.C., 1982—; U.S. del. NATO Adv. Group for Aerospace R & D, Paris 1984—; pres., dir. Nat. Fed. Abstract and Info. Svcs., Phila. 1988-90. Contbr. articles to pubs. Mem. Nat. Orgn. for Women, Princeton N.J. Mem. Am. Chem. Soc., Am. Soc. for Info. Sci., Spl. Librs. Assn., Assn. Info. Mgrs., Am. Inst. Aeronautics and Astronautics. Home: RD2 Box 392T Somerset NJ 08873 Office: Am Inst Aero & Astro 555 W 57th St New York NY 10019

LAWRENCE, BARBARA ANN, management educator; b. Balt., Jan. 14, 1951; m. Charles R. Lawrence, Oct. 9, 1971; 1 child, Michelle C. BM in Performance, Oberlin Coll., 1972; MA in Adminstrn. and Counseling, U. Md., 1973; PhD in Mgmt., MIT, 1983. Adj. faculty dept. music U. Md., Baltimore County, 1973-75; guidance counselor Gen. John Stricker Jr. High Sch., Baltimore County, Md., 1974-77; computer staff cons. info. svcs. MIT, 1980-83; asst. prof. orgn. and strategic studies group Anderson Grad. Sch. Mgmt., UCLA, 1983—; orgn. cons., group trainer, 1977—; presenter in field. Co-author: The Handbook of Career Theory, 1989; contbr. articles to profl. jours.; invited editor Jour. Occupational Behavior, 1985; reviewer for various publications. Recipient Ascendent Scholar award Western Acad. Mgmt., 1989; UCLA Acad. Senate grantee 1986-87, NIH grantee 1983-87, Doctoral Dissertation grantee Adminstrn. on Aging, HHS, 1980-81; Collamore-Rogers fellow MIT, 1979-80, Austin fellow MIT, 1978-79, Ida M. Green fellow MIT, 1977-78; Bezazian Competition scholar Oberlin Coll., 1969-71. Mem. Acad. Mgmt. (editorial bd. Acad. Mgmt. Jour. 1988—, profl. div. policy com. 1988—, chairperson careers div. 1988-89, program chairperson careers div. 1986-87, pre-conf. workshop chairperson careers div. 1985-86, steering com. careers div. 1983-86, program rev. com. careers div. 1983-84, history div. 1984), Am. Sociol. Assn., Am. Psychol. Assn., Soc. for Indsl. and Organizational Psychology. Office: UCLA Anderson Grad Sch Mgmt Los Angeles CA 90024

LAWRENCE, CRISTENNA LOUISSA, marketing executive; b. Bainbridge, Md., July 9, 1953; d. Norman David and Dolores Frances (LaPierre) Beausoleil; m. Joseph R. Lawrence, Apr. 29, 1979; children: Tiffany, Ashleigh, J. Ross. BA in Communications, Northeastern U., 1975; postgrad., Cath. U., 1971-73. Dept. mgr. Jordan Marsh, Framingham, Mass., 1975-76; rep. customer service Suburban Credit Union, Framingham, 1976-78; asst. fin. aid Harvard Med. Sch., Boston, 1978; sec. Digital Equip. Corp., Maynard, Mass., 1979-80; project planner Digital Equip. Corp., Marlboro, Mass., 1980-84, revenue analyst, 1984-85; mktg. mgr. Dun & Bradstreet Software, Framingham, Mass., 1985-87, brand mgr., 1987—. Mem. Am. Prodn. and Inventory Control Soc., Am. Mgmt. Assn., Nat. Assn. Female Execs. Office: Dun & Bradstreet Software 550 Cochituate Rd Framingham MA 01701

LAWRENCE, DEAN GRAYSON, retired lawyer; b. Oakland, Calif.; d. Henry C. and Myrtle (Grayson) Schmidt; A.B., U. Calif.-Berkeley, 1934, J.D., 1939. Admitted to Calif. bar, 1943, U.S. Dist. Ct., 1944, U.S. Ct. Appeals, 1944, Tax Ct. U.S., 1945, U.S. Treasury Dept., 1945, U.S. Supreme Ct., 1967; asso. Pillsbury, Madison & Sutro, San Francisco, 1944, 45; gen. practice Oakland, 1946-50, San Jose, 1952-60, Grass Valley, 1960-63, 66—; county counsel Nevada County, 1964-65. Nevada County Bd. Suprs., 1969-73, chmn., 1971. Sec. Nev. County Humane Animal Shelter Bd., 1966-86; state humane officer, 1966-82; pres. Nev. County Humane Soc., 1974-86, mem. Humane Soc. U.S., Fund for Animals; bd. dirs. Nevada County Health Planning Council, Golden Empire Areawide Health Planning Council, 1974, 75. Mem. Bus. and Profl. Women's Club, AAUW, Animal Protection Inst. Am. (Humanitarian of Yr. 1986), Animal Legal Defense Fund, Golden Empire Human Soc. Phi Beta Kappa, Sigma Xi, Kappa Beta Pi, Pi Mu Epsilon, Pi Lambda Theta. Episcopalian. Office: PO Box 66 Grass Valley CA 95945

LAWRENCE, DONNA MARIE, inventory coordinator; b. Paris, Ky., Jan. 31, 1953; d. Thomas Euclid Lawrence Jr. and Nora Frances (Harris) Downey; m. Ronald Dean Bradley, June 12, 1980 (div. Sept. 1984); 1 child, Ronald Dean Bradley II. AA, Midway Jr. Coll., 1973; BA, Morehead (Ky.) State U., 1976. Cert. secondary tchr., Ky. Mdse. mgr. Mile High Girl Scout Coun., Denver, 1976-77; admissions legal clk. Health Scis. Ctr. U. Colo., Denver, 1977-80; asst. mgr. Foxmoor Casuals, Kansas City, Mo., 1980-81; tchr. Lincoln Acad., Kansas City, Mo., 1980-81; medico-legal clk. St. Joseph Hosp., Kansas City, 1981-83; field customer svc. rep. Am. Express, Inglewood, Colo., 1984-85; inventory coordinator Adolph Coors Co., Golden, Colo., 1985-90; adminstrv. supr. media/field events Coors Brewing Co., Golden, 1990—; tchr. Red Shield Community Ctr., Denver, 1977-78; court rep. St. Joseph Hosp., Kansas City, 1980-83; speaker for release of confidential info. St. Joseph Hosp., Kansas City, 1980-83; sales trainer Am. Express, Inglewood, 1984-85; software trainer Adolph Coors Co., Golden, Colo., 1988—. Mem. Nat. Assn. Female Execs., Alpha Kappa Alpha. Democrat. Baptist. Office: Adolph Coors Co 1221 Ford St Golden CO 80401

LAWRENCE, ESTELENE YVONNE, transportation executive, musician; b. Lynch, Ky., Aug. 10, 1933; d. Samuel Coleridge and Florence Estelle (Gardner) Taylor; m. Otto Lee Lawrence, Sept. 14, 1957; children: Stuart, Neil, Adelbert. Student Fenn Coll., 1953-60, Cleve. Inst. Music, 1955-56, John Carroll U., 1977-78, Northeastern U., 1979-80, Cleve. State U., 1989—. Stenographer Cleve. Transit System/Regional Transit Authority, 1951-76, tng. asst., 1976-78, per. devel. asst., 1978-82, dist. adminstr., 1983-86; supr./mgmt. skills instr. RTA, 1976-86, dir. tng. and career devel., 1986-88; dir. music Friendly United Baptist Ch., 1947—; piano tchr., 1953-73; pianist/organist Nat. Bapt. Conv., 1971, 80. Publicity chmn. Moses Cleve. Sch. PTA, 1965-75; audit chmn. RTA Main Office Credit Union, 1980-83; dist. sec. Boy Scouts Am., 1982-83; chmn. adv. bd. Baldwin Wallace Coll., 1984-88; mem. adv. bd. Cleve. Mgmt. Devel. Consortium, 1985-88. Mem. Cleve. Mgmt. Seminars (treas. 1979-81, pres. 1981-83), Conf. Minority Transp. Ofcls., Phi Kappa Gamma (pres. 1966-69), Mu Phi Epsilon (historian 1990—). Mem. A.M.E. Ch. Clubs: East 153d St. (v.p. 1980—), East Ky. Social. Home: 4066 East 153d St Cleveland OH 44128

LAWRENCE, EUGENIA JEWELL, state official; b. Waco, Tex., Dec. 7, 1965; d. Vernon and Betty Joann (Lynn) L.; 1 child, Daniel Cotto, Jr. BBA, Baylor U., 1988. Asst. head cashier Target Stores, Waco, Tex., 1984-86; office dir. Dwyer Real Estate and Devel., Waco, 1987-88, asst. property supr., 1988-89; eligibility specialist Tex. Dept. Human Svcs., Waco, 1989—. Democrat. Baptist. Home: 2011 Colcord Waco TX 76707 Office: Tex Dept Human Svcs 504 N 6th St Waco TX 76707

LAWRENCE, JANICE ANNETTE MERRILL, real estate company executive; b. Watha, N.C., Mar. 2, 1938; d. David Brondell and Ersil Lizette (Willis) Merrill; m. Dalmon Earl Lawrence, Jan. 21, 1956 (dec. Oct. 1982); children: Melanie, Dalmon Earl Jr. Grad. high sch., Beaufort, N.C. Cert. real estate appraiser. Sec., bookeeper Mitchell's Carpenter Shop, Morehead City, N.C., 1957-75; owner, sec., bookkeeper Western Auto Assoc. Store, Morehead City, 1962-80; broker Tenney Realty, Morehead City, 1973-78; owner, broker Lawrence Realty, Morehead City, 1978—; co-owner Big Dal's Sports Grill and Restaurant; sec. A & D Builders, Inc., Morehead City, 1986—. Mem. Carteret County Econ. Devel. Coun., Morehead City, 1984—. Mem. Nat. Assn. Real Estate Appraisers, Nat. Assn. Realtors, N.C. Assn. Home Builders, N.C. Assn. Realtors, Women's Coun. Realtors, Carteret County Home Builders, Morehead City-Carteret County Bd. Realtors, Carteret County C. of C. Democrat. Baptist. Home: Country Club Rd PO Box 728 Morehead City NC 28557 Office: Hwy 70 W PO Box 728 Morehead City NC 28557

LAWRENCE, JEAN HOPE, writer, public relations consultant; b. Waukegan, Ill., Mar. 5, 1944; d. George Herbert and Hope Delinda (Warren) L.; 1 child, Kelsey Hope. BA, George Washington U., 1966. Tech. editor, Am. Chem. Soc., Washington, 1966; proposal writer Krohn-Rhodes Inst., Washington, 1966-67; legislative counsel Aerospace Industries Assn., Washington, 1967-82; v.p., co-owner Data Specific, Washington, 1985-86; editorial adviser Am. C. of C. Execs., Alexandria, Va., 1983-86, lectr., 1984—. Contbg. editor: Communications Concepts, 1983-86; editor, pub., creator: (newsletters) Get It Done!, 1987-88, Cheap Relief, 1988—. Contbr. numerous articles to mags. Mem. Washington Ind. Writers, Women's Direct Response Group. Democrat. Methodist. Avocation: essayist. Address: 3217 Connecticut Ave NW Washington DC 20008

LAWRENCE, LOIS VANA, personnel placement executive; b. St. Paul, Aug. 9, 1947; d. William Herald and Sophie Francis (Antos) Vana; children: Justin, Joelle, Jordan. Supr. engring. dept. Pacific Telephone Co., San Diego, until 1968; co-founder Career Personnel, Can., 1968—, Career Personnel Internat., Carmel, Calif., 1979—; now with Marshall Group. Mem. Am. Mgmt. Assn., Nat. Assn. Personnel Cons., Am. Soc. Personnel Adminstrs. (dir., bd. dirs.), Am. Soc. Personnel Cons., Internat. Franchise Assn., Calif. Assn. Personnel Cons. Office: PO Box 1662 Carmel Valley CA 93924

LAWRENCE, LOUISE, art historian; b. Washington, Nov. 19, 1952; d. Malcolm and Jacqueline Mary (Drullard) L. AA, Montgomery Coll., 1976; BA in Art History, U. Md., 1979; MALS in Art History, Keene State Coll., 1986. Rsch. coord. USIA, Washington, 1971-72; meeting coord. Nat. Assn. Furniture Mfrs., Chevy Chase, Md., 1974-81; group coord. Crotched Mountain Ski Area, Francestown, N.H., 1982-83; publicity dir. Sharon (N.H.) Arts Ctr., 1983-84; asst. to dir. Archive Ctr. Hist. Soc. of Cheshire County, Keene, N.H., 1985-86; mgr. Charles Rosinski Builders, Swanzey, N.H., 1987-90; guest curator Bowdoin Coll., Brunswick Maine, Nat. Mus. of Women in Arts. Contbr. articles to profl. jours. Md. Ho. of Dels. scholar, 1977, Keene State U. scholar, 1984. Mem. Nat. Mus. Women in Arts, NAFE, AAUW, Nat. Audubon Soc., Friends of Sea Otters, Sierra Club. Democrat. Roman Catholic. Home: 4649 89th Ave SE Mercer Island WA 98040 Office: Charles Rosinski Builders Rte 32 Box 261K Swanzey NH 03431

LAWRENCE, MARY GEORGENE WELLS (MRS. HARDING LAWRENCE), advertising executive; b. Youngstown, Ohio, May 25, 1928; d. Waldemar and Violet (Berg); m. Harding Lawrence, Nov. 25, 1967; children: James, State, Deborah, Kathryn, Pamela. Ed., Carnegie Inst. Tech., 1949; LL.D., Babson Coll., 1970. Copywriter McKelvey's Dept. Store, Youngstown, 1951-52; fashion advt. mgr. Macy's, N.Y.C., 1952-53; copy group head McCann-Erickson, N.Y.C., 1953-56; with Doyle, Dane, Bernbach, N.Y.C., 1957-64, v.p., assoc. copy chief, 1963-64; sr. ptnr., creative dir. Jack Tinker & Partners, N.Y.C., 1964-66; chmn. bd., chief exec. officer Wells, Rich, Greene, Inc., N.Y.C., 1966-90. Named to Copywriters Hall of Fame Copy Club, 1969; named Mktg. Stateswoman of Year Sales Execs. Club N.Y., 1970, Advt. Woman of Year Am. Advt. Fedn., 1971. Mem. Dallas Advt. Club. Office: Wells Rich Greene Inc 9 W 57th St New York NY 10019*

LAWRENCE, MARY JO B., small business owner; b. San Rafael, Calif., Mar. 15, 1931; d. W. Murray and Hazel Georgia (Clark) B.; m. Lloyd Byron Smith, Nov. 12, 1955 (div. 1966); m. John Lawrence, 1968 (div. 1975); children: Byron, Murray, Denise, Malcolm. BA, U.C. Berkeley, 1953, Post Grad., 1954. Art tchr. Coalinga Jr. High Sch., Calif., 1954-55; owner 2 Duplexes, 4 Plex, Ho., San Rafael, Roseville, Calif., 1957-65, Flamingo Motel & Apts., Roseville, Calif., 1965-76; owner, developer RV Storage, San Rafael; owner, landlord Warehouse Restaurant, Roseville, Calif., 1984; owner,landlord Fallcreek Office Bldg., 1984. pres. AAUW 1981, Roseville Art Center 1982-85; chmn. Personnel Bd. Roseville 1974-84, First Presbyn. Ch. Capital Bldg. Roseville 1985; dir., founder Placer Bank of Commerce Roseville 1983-88. Republican. Presbyterian. Home: 1004 Audrey Way Roseville CA 95661

LAWRENCE, NANCY ANN, company executive; b. Detroit, May 18, 1959; d. Joseph A. and Barbara L. (Purdy) Huber; m. Robert A. Lawrence, Jr., Oct. 25, 1980. Grad. high sch., Detroit. Receptionist Ex-Cell-o Corp., Troy, Mich., 1980-81, purchasing sec., 1981-82, sec., 1982-84; acct. sec. McCann-Erickson, Inc., Troy, 1984-85, regional sec., 1985-86; sr. sec. Lintas: Campbell-Ewald, Warren, Mich., 1986-87; asst. art design Lintas: Ceco Communications, Warren, 1987, project coordinator, 1987-89; regional mgr. The Image Bank, stock photography agy., Troy, 1988—. Mem. NAFE. Home: 3605 Durham Royal Oak MI 48073 Office: The Image Bank Detroit 3150 Livernois Ste 150 Troy MI 48083

LAWRENCE, PATRICIA ANN, obstetrician-gynecologist; b. Rocky Mount, N.C., Mar. 31, 1926; d. Graham Vance and Vera Lynn (Burnette) L. Student, Queens Coll., 1942-43, U. N.C., Chapel Hill, 1943-46; MD, U. Va., 1950. Diplomate, Am. Bd. Ob.-Gyn. Resident in ob.-gyn. Ind. U. Med. Ctr., Indpls., 1950-54; pvt. practice Charlotte, N.C., 1955—; mem. staff, Charlotte Meml. Hosp., exec. com. dept. ob.-gyn., 1983-87, chmn. search com., 1988. Contbr. articles to med. jours. Pres. Mecklenburg unit Am. Cancer Soc., Charlotte. Named Outstanding Career Woman, Cen. Charlotte Assocs., 1968. Fellow Am. Coll. Obstetricians and Gynecologists, South Atlantic Assn. Obstetricians and Gynecologists; mem. AMA, N.C. Med. Assn., Mecklenburg County Med. Soc., So. Med. Assn., N.C. Ob-Gyn Soc., Raintree Country Club, Tower Club, Jefferson Club, Farmington Country Club. Democrat. Baptist. Home: 1908 Sterling Rd Charlotte NC 28209 Office: Med Ctr Pla Ste 402 1001 Blythe Blvd Charlotte NC 28203

LAWRENCE, PAULA DENISE, physical therapist; b. Ft. Worth, May 21, 1959; d. Roddy Paul and Kay Frances (Spivey) Gillis; m. Mark Jayson Lawrence, Apr. 20, 1985. BS, Tex. Women's U., 1982. Lic. phys. therapist, Tex., Calif. Sales mgr. R. and K Camping Ctr., Garland, Tex., 1977-82; staff physical therapist Longview (Tex.) Regional Hosp., 1982-83, dir. phys. therapy, 1983-87, dir. rehab. svcs., 1987-88; staff phys. therapist MPH Home Health, Longview, Tex., 1983-84; pres. Phys. Rehabil. Ctr., Hemet, Calif., 1988—; mem. adv. com. div. health occupations Kilgore (Tex.) Coll., 1985-88; mem. profl. adv. bd. Hospice Longview, 1985-88. Mem. NAFE, Am. Phys. Therapy Assn., Tex. Phys. Therapy Assn., Am. Bus. Women's Assn. (v.p. 1987, 89, pres., 1990, Woman of Yr. 1988), Soroptimist, Psi Chi, Omega Rho Alpha. Home: 899 Kristin Ln Hemet CA 92343 Office: DRCA Phys Therapy Corp 850 E Latham Ste G Hemet CA 92343

LAWRENCE, SALLY CLARK, educational administrator; b. San Francisco, Dec. 29, 1930; d. George Dickson and Martha Marie Alice (Smith) Clark; m. Henry Clay Judd, July 1, 1950 (div. Dec. 1972); children: Rebecca, David, Nancy; m. John I. Lawrence, Aug. 12, 1976; stepchildren: Maia, Dylan. Docent Portland Art Mus., Oreg., 1958-68; gallery owner, dir., Sally Judd Gallery, Portland, 1968-75; art ins. appraiser, cons. Portland, 1975-81; interim dir. Mus. Art. Sch., Pacific Northwest Coll. Art, Portland, 1981, asst. dir., 1981-82, acting dir., 1982-84, dir., 1984—; bd. dirs. Art Coll. Exch. Nat. Consortium, 1982—, pres., 1983-84. Mem. Nat. Assn. Schs. Art and Design (bd. dirs. 1984—), Oreg. Ind. Coll. Assn. (bd. dirs. 1981—, exec. com. 1989). Office: Pacific NW Coll of Art 1219 SW Park St Portland OR 97205-2486

LAWRENCE, STEPHANIE, small business owner; b. Caracas, Venezuela, July 18, 1958; d. Hal Myers; m. Roland Lawrence. BS, Calif. State U., Long Beach, 1981. Mgr. mktg. Myers Enterprises, Long Beach, 1978-83; restaurant mgr. Tin Lizzy's, Aurora, Colo., 1983-86; chief exec. officer Customworks, Littleton, Colo., 1986—. Designer stained glass. Recipient Internat. Glaziers Design Conf. award, 1988. Mem. NAFE, Greater Denver C. of C. Republican. Presbyterian. Office: Customworks 7378 S Hudson Way Littleton CO 80122

LAWRENCE, SYLVIA YVONNE, nurse; b. Danville, Pa., July 11, 1937; d. John Jacob and Florence Rebecca (Fenstermacher) Tanner; m. Davey Leon House, Oct. 4, 1958 (div. 1980); children: Susan D., Gayle Y. House Troxell; m. William C. Lawrence (separated). Diploma, Thomas Jefferson U., 1958; postgrad., Lycoming Coll., 1987—. RN, Pa. Nurse various med. facilities, Pa., 1958-70; ho. supr. Sycamore Manor Nursing Home, Williamsport, Pa., 1970-71; gen. duty staff nurse Evangelical Community Hosp., Lewisburg, Pa., 1971-82, surg. staff nurse, 1983-87; surg. staff nurse Twelve Oaks Hosp., Houston, 1982-83; staff nurse emergency dept. Muncy Valley Hosp., 1985—, Geisinger Med. Ctr., Danville, 1987—. Republican. Home: PO Box 208 Lewisburg PA 17837

LAWRENCE, TELETÉ ZORAYDA, speech and voice pathologist, educator; b. Worcester, Mass., Aug. 5, 1910; d. James Newton and Cora Valeria (Hester) Lester; A.B. cum laude, U. Calif., Berkeley, 1932; M.A., Tex. Christian U., 1963; pvt. study voice with Edgar Schofield, N.Y.C., 1936-41, drama with Enrica Clay Dillon, N.Y.C., 1937-40; m. Ernest Lawrence, Oct. 9, 1939; children—James Lester, Valerie Alma. Lic. speech-lang. pathologist. Mem. Am. Lyric Opera Co., 1939—; instr. speech Sch. Fine Arts, Tex. Christian U., Fort Worth, 1959-66, asst. prof., 1966-71, assoc. prof., 1971-75, prof., 1975-76, emeritus, 1976—, speech pathologist specializing voice disorders Speech and Hearing Clinic, 1959—, faculty research leave, Gt. Britain, Western Europe, Hungary, 1968; pvt. practice speech and voice pathology, 1960—. Mem. bd. Sunshine Haven, home for retarded children, 1957-59; gen. chmn. Ft. Worth and Tarrant County, Nat. Retarded Children's Week, 1954; mem. family and child welfare div. Community Council Ft. Worth and Tarrant County, 1955-57, mem. health and hosp. div., 1959-60; mem. women's com. Ft. Worth chpt. NCCJ, 1956-59; exec. v.p. Fine Arts Found. Guild of Tex. Christian U., 1955-56, past exec. sec., past fin. sec. Recipient Faculty Research grant Tex. Christian U., 1961. Fellow Internat. Soc. Phonetic Scis.; mem. Nat. Council Chs. (bd. joint com. missionary edn. Pacific Coast area, 1952-55), United Ch. Women of Ft. Worth (chmn. Christian world missions dept. 1955-57, pres. 1957-59). Ft. Worth Area Council

Chs. (v.p. 1955-57, exec. com. 1957-59, bd. dirs. 1959-60), U. Calif. Alumni Assn. (life), Am. Speech-Lang.-Hearing Assn. (life; cert. clin. competence in speech pathology), Tex. Speech-Lang.-Hearing Assn. (cert.), Ft. Worth Council for Retarded Children, Speech Communication Assn. (sec. speech and hearing disorders interest group 1962-63, mem. com. 1961-64), Am. Dialect Soc., Internat. Assn. Logopodics and Phoniatrics, Phonetic Soc. Japan, AAUP (emeritus), Lambda Ma'ams of Lambda Chi Alpha (pres. Ft. Worth 1962-63), Phi Beta Kappa Assn. (Ft. Worth chpt.), Phi Beta Kappa (Alpha of Calif. chpt.; charter mem., v.p. Delta of Tex. chpt. 1971-73, pres. 1973-74), Delta Zeta, Psi Chi, Sigma Alpha Eta. Republican. Mem. Christian Ch. Clubs: Woman's of Fort Worth, Women of Rotary. Participant, 13th Congress of Internat. Assn. Logopedics and Phoniatrics, Vienna, 1965, 14th Congress, Paris, 1968, 15th Congress, Buenos Aires, 1971, 16th Congress, Interlaken, Switzerland, 1974, 17th Congress, Copenhagen, 1977, 18th Congress, Washington, 1980, 19th Congress, Edinburgh, Scotland, 1983; participant 10th Internat. Congress of Linguists, Bucharest, 1967; participant 6th Internat. Congress of The Internat. Soc. Phonetic Scis., Prague, 1967, 7th Internat. Congress, Montreal, 1971, 8th Internat. Congress, Leeds, Eng., 1975; participant 1st Congress Internat. Assn. Sci. Study Mental Deficiency, Montpellier, France, 1967, Semmelweis Ann. Week, Budapest Acad. Scis., 1968, 3d World Congress Phoneticians, Tokyo, 1976. Author: Handbook for Instructors of Voice and Diction, 1968; contbr. articles to profl. jours. Home: 3860 S Hills Circle Fort Worth TX 76109-2757

LAWS, JUDITH A., human resources consultant; b. St Louis, July 3, 1937; d. James C. and H. Idell (McIntyre) L. BA, Washington U., St. Louis, 1959; BS in Metaphysics, Claregate Coll., London, 1980. Mgmt. analyst U.S. Dept. of the Army, 1960-62; vol. Peace Corps, Cameroon, 1962-63; pers. generalist HEW, Washington, 1964-66; asst. to dir. 1970 White House Conf. Children and Youth, 1966-68; manpower devel. and tng. cons., Washington, 1969-73; alcohol edn. cons., Washington, 1974—; credential and communications specialist Assn. Labor-Mgmt. Adminstrs. and Cons. on Alcoholism, Arlington, Va., 1984-89. Contbg. editor Quarante, 1985-87; contbr. articles to The Beacon, Jour. Esoteric Psychology, The New Humanity Jour., 1987—; researcher publs. for asst. sec. for policy U.S. Dept. of Labor, 1988, office of adminstr. U.S. Alcohol, Drug Abuse and Mental Health Adminstrn., 1989, Nat. Clearing House for Alcohol and Drug Info., 1988. Mem. adv. coun. Alcoholism Treatment Ctr. Washington, 1976-78; bd. dirs. Whitman-Walker Clinic, Washington, 1979. Mem. Inst. Noetic Scis., Dramatists Guild. Avocations: playwriting, acting, psychospiritual rsch. Home: 2800 Woodley Rd NW Washington DC 20008

LAWS, PRISCILLA WATSON, physics educator; b. N.Y.C., Jan. 18, 1940; d. Morris Clemens and Frances (Fetterinan) Watson; m. Kenneth Lee Laws, June 3, 1965; children: Kevin Allen, Virginia. BA, Reed Coll., 1961; MA, Bryn Mawr Coll., 1963, PhD, 1966. Asst. prof. physics Dickinson Coll., Carlisle, Pa., 1965-70; assoc. prof. Dickinson Coll., Carlisle, 1970-79, prof. physics, 1979—, chmn. dept. physics and astronomy, 1982-83; cons. in field. Author: X Rays: More Harm than Good?, 1977, The X-Ray Information Book, 1983; contbr. numerous articles to profl. jours.; assoc. editor Am. Jour. Physics, 1989—. Vice-pres. Cumberland Conservancy, 1972-73, pres. 1973; bd. dirs. Pa. Alliance for Returnables, 1974-77; asst. sec., treas. Carlisle Hosp. Authority, 1973-76; pres. bd. Carlisle Day Care Ctr., 1973-74. Fellow NSF, 1963-64, J. Luetzelschwab and N.Wolf, 1989; grantee NSF, 1968, 89-92, Commonwealth of Pa., 1985-86, U.S. Dept. Edn. Fund for Improvement of Post-Secondary Edn., 1986, 89-92, AEC; recipient Innovation award Merck Found., 1989, Educom Inciptal awawrd for curriculum innovation in sci. labs., 1989, award Sears Roebuck Co., 1990. Mem. Am. Assn. Physics Tchrs., Fedn. Am. Scientist, Sigma Xi, Sigma Pi Sigma, Omicron Delta Kappa. Democrat. Home: 10 Douglas Ct Carlisle PA 17013 Office: Dickinson Coll Dept of Physics & Astronomy Carlisle PA 17013

LAWSON, ANN MARIE MCDONALD, librarian; b. Jersey City; d. William and Mary Agnes (Dolan) McDonald; student Columbia, 1947, N.Y. U., 1949, City Coll. N.Y., 1959, Pratt Inst., 1963; m. Philip James Lawson, Apr. 26, 1952. Methods analyst Rueben H. Donnelley Corp., N.Y.C., 1953-57; librarian chems. div. Union Carbide Corp., N.Y.C., 1957-65, Tatham Laird & Kudner, N.Y.C., 1965-67, Met. Transp. Authority, N.Y.C., 1967-80; cons., 1980—; active library tng. program Ballard Sch. (YWCA), 1949—; cons. WHO, Geneva, Switzerland, 1950; lectr. Pratt Inst. Grad. Library Sch., 1967. Mem. Assn. Records Mgrs. and Adminstrs. (pres. 1948-50); Spl. Libraries Assn. Republican. Contbr. articles to mags. Home and Office: 119 Washington Pl New York NY 10014

LAWSON, BARBARA ELLEN, accountant; b. Abington, Pa., June 12, 1963; d. Harry Elton and Elizabeth Estelle (Watson) L. BS in Acctg., Rutgers U., 1986. Fiber acctg. analyst Scott Paper Co., Phila., 1986-88, assoc. auditor internal audit dept., 1988—; instr. Camden County Coll., Blackwood, N.J., 1988. Mem. Am. Soc. Women Accts., Nat. Assn. Accts. (bd. dirs. South Jersey chpt. 1987-88). Republican. Episcopalian. Home: 311 Steeplechase Ct Deptford NJ 08096 Office: Scott Paper Co Internal Audit Pla I Philadelphia PA 19113

LAWSON, BETTY NOYES, state senator, academic administrator; b. Dayton, Ohio, Apr. 13, 1928; d. Paul W. and Hazel (Zumbrun) Noyes; m. Douglas Eugene Lawson, June 11, 1949; children: William D., Constance A. Mandy, Craig A. BS in Secondary Edn. and Social Studies, Ind. U., South Bend, 1971; MS in Counseling and Guidance, Ind. U., Bloomington, 1974, EdS, 1977. Cert. secondary tchr., sch. counselor, sch. adminstr., sch. supr. Tchr. South Bend (Ind.) Community Sch. Corp., 1972-73, counselor, 1973-76, asst. prin., 1976-81, counselor pupil pers., 1981—. Bd. dirs. First United Meth. Ch., South Bend, 1970s, YWCA, South Bend, 1979-84. Democrat. Home: 17444 Starlite Dr South Bend IN 46614

LAWSON, CHARLENE ANN, data processing executive; b. Findlay, Ohio, Dec. 15, 1948; d. Charles Dwight and Geraldine Marie (Blaksley) Shively; m. Terry Michael Lawson, Aug. 9, 1976; children: Shannon Monroe, Wesley Dwight. Diploma, Internat. Bus. Coll., Ft. Wayne, Ind., 1968; degree in real estate, So. Ohio Coll., 1978; AAS in Computer Sci., Sinclair Coll., Dayton, Ohio, 1984. Adminstrv. asst. Marathon Oil Co., Findlay, 1969-74; mktg. analyst Savin Bus. Machines, Irvine, Calif., 1974-75, Systems & Services, Inc., Greenville, S.C., 1975-76; owner, realtor Village Green Realty, Dayton, 1979-84; mgr. word processing MacDonald Creative Mktg., Dayton, 1981-82; mktg. analyst The Computer Shoppe, Louisville, 1984-85; bus. systems analyst Humana, Inc., Louisville, 1986, systems communications mgr., 1986-89; Systems Prima mgr. Bapt. Hosps. Inc., Louisville, 1989—. Mem. Assn. for Systems Mgmt. (symposium co-chair 1987, sec. 1987-88, bd. dirs. 1987-88), Data Processing Mgmt. Assn. (v.p. awards com. 1986-87, bd. dirs. 1986-88, v.p. programs com. 1987-88, exec. v.p. 1989-90, pres. 1990—), Kentuckiana Data Processing Assn. (chmn. bd. dirs. 1987-88), Dayton Downtown Am. Bus. Women's Assn. (pres. 1982-83, chair ways and means com. 1983-84, nat. chpt. del. 1982-84), Coffee Trees Am. Bus. Women's Assn. (edn. com. chair 1986-87, bus. assn. com. chair 1986-87, nat. chpt. del. 1986-87, Mem. of Month 1987, Woman of Yr. 1987-88, 88-89), Am. Bus. Women's Assn. (gen. chmn. dist. IV). Republican. Lutheran. Home: 1115 Creekview Circle New Albany IN 47150-2027 Office: Humana Inc 500 W Main St Louisville KY 40201-1438

LAWSON, JEAN KERR, fundraising executive, consultant; b. Chgo., Oct. 31, 1941; d. Andrew Leslie and Dorothy Helen (Hayes) L.; m. Thomas Edward Miller, Aug. 4, 1962 (div.); children: Galen Elizabeth Miller Block, Andrew C., Colin P. Student, U. Colo., 1959-61, Marquette U., 1962; MA, St. John's Coll., Annapolis, Md., 1979. Reorgn. analyst Office of the Gov. State of N.Mex., Santa Fe, 1976-78; litigation case supr. Kirkland & Ellis, Chgo., 1980; legal analyst Clausen, Miller, Gorman, Caffrey & Witous, Chgo., 1980-81; dir. alumni ann. fund U. Wis.-Milw. Found., Milw., 1983-88; dir. devel. and alumni programs U. Md., College Park, 1988-90; devel. cons. White Plains, N.Y., 1990—. Author: (with others) N.Mex. State Government Reorganization, 1976, Executive Branch of N.Mex. State Government, 1976, Responsive Government in New Mexico, 1977, 78. Vol. scholarship run U. Wis. Alumni Assn., Milw., 1984-87, Jr. League Am. 1967—; founder, pres. Iowa chpt. Nat. Cystic Fibrosis Found., Waterloo, 1968-70; bd. dirs. Am. Cancer Soc., No. N.Mex., 1978-79. St. John's Coll. fellow, 1978, 79. Mem. AAUW, Nat. Soc. Fundraising Execs., Coun. for Advancement and Support Edn. Episcopalian. Home: 35 Bowbell Rd White Plains NY 10607

LAWSON, JOYCE MARIE MOSES, business educator; b. Houma, La., July 25, 1955; d. Clarence Sr. and Mercedes (Beauty) Moses; m. Clyde H. Lawson, July 30, 1976; 1 child, Kimberly Deanna. BS in Bus. Edn., So. U., 1977. Sec. Baylor Coll. Med., Houston, 1977-78; acad. adv. Saudi Arabian Ednl. Mission, Houston, 1978-85; instr. Houston Independent Sch. Dist., 1986, Nat. Edn. Ctr., Houston, 1986-87; chief instr. Internat. Tel. and Tel. Tech. Inst., Houston, 1987—. Dues mother Girl Scouts Am., Missouri City, Tex., 1988—; mem. Pastor's Appreciation Com. Brentwood Baptist Ch., Houston, 1988—. Mem. NAFE, Profl. Secs. Internat., So. U. Alumni Assn., Social Lites (treas. 1986-87). Home: 1510 Quail Trace Missouri City TX 77489

LAWSON, MARY VIV, importer, business professional; b. Tallahassee, Fla.; d. Abram Venable Lawson and Julia Lee (Clark) Gwynn. AB, Stanford U., Calif., 1984. Mktg. asst. The Pacific Bank, San Francisco, 1984-85; copy editor Women of China Mag., Beijing, P.R.C., 1985-86; communications mgr. Essex Products Ltd., Taipei, Taiwan, ROC, 1987--; gen. mgr. China Tech., Atlanta; project mgr., China Internat. Trade Assocs., Ltd. Recipient Silver Medal award Nat. Road. Championship U.S. Cycling Fed., Louisville 1976, Bronze Medal award Time Trial Championship U.S. Cycling Fed., Milw. 1979. Democratic. Episcopalian. Office: China Internat Trade 710 Peachtree St NE Ste 219 Atlanta GA 30308

LAWSON, NANCY HELEN, city official; b. Shelbina, Mo., Dec. 10, 1925; d. Herbert Franklin and Kathryn (Collins) Acuff; m. George T. Lawson, Jr., June 6, 1948; children: Georgann Lawson Metheny, Janet Lea Lawson Allbaugh, Richard Franklin. BS, Cen. Mo. State U., 1946; postgrad., U. Mo., 1976-90. Sec. Mid-Continent Airlines, Kansas City, Mo., 1946-48, Fed. Land Bank, Nat. Farm Loan Assn., Harrisonville, Mo., 1948-50; dep. city clk. City of Harrisonville, 1973-87, city clk., 1987—. Del. Women's Agenda Conf., Kans. City, 1989; former officer Am. Legion Aux., VFW Aux., Music Study Club, Band-Aides, Harrisonville United Way; Sunday sch. tchr., ch. pianist Christian Ch. Mem. Mo. City Clks. and Fin. Officers Assn. (sec., v.p., pres. Western Mo. chpt. 1984-86, state sec., v.p., pres. 1987—), AAUW (pres. 1983-84, v.p. 1989—), Harrisonville Bus. and Profl. Womens Club (v.p. 1987-88, pres. 1988-89, Woman of Yr. 1989), Delvers Gen. Fedn. Womens Club (past pres.), Mo. Extension Club (past treas.), Acad. for Advanced Edn., Internat. Inst. Mcpl. Clks. (cert.), Delta Zeta. Home: 707 S Independence St Harrisonville MO 64701 Office: City of Harrisonville 300 E Pearl PO Box 367 Harrisonville MO 64701

LAWSON, PATRICIA ANN, educator; b. Lynch, Ky., July 30, 1945; d. L.A. and Anna R. (Gaines) L. BA, Del. State Coll., Dover, 1967; MA, Atlanta U., 1968; postgrad., Temple U., 1975, U. Pa., 1976. Asst. prof. Del. State Coll.; instr., dir. writing skills program South Cen. Community Coll., New Haven; sec. WFS Contractors, Inc. Maj. USAR, 1975—. Nat. Urban League fellow, 1980; recipient Svc. award. Mem. NAFE, NAACP, Delta Sigma Theta. Home: 34 Benning Rd Claymont DE 19703

LAWSON, WILMA JEAN, electrical engineer; b. William. County, Ill., Oct. 11, 1940; d. John Clifford and Grace Evelyn (Spiller) Hampton; m. Steven Thomas Lawson, Jan. 15, 1966 (dec. 1987); 1 child, Jeanie Lynn. BSEE, U. Tex., Arlington, 1980. Environmentalist Brazos Electric Power Cooop., Waco, Tex., 1980-81, systems design engr., 1981—. Troop leader Hallsburg (Tex.) Girl Scouts U.S., 1981. With USAF, 1959-61. Mem. IEEE, NSPE. Republican. Baptist. Home: Rt 1 Box 148 Mart TX 76664 Office: Brazos Electric Power Coop 2404 LaSalle St Waco TX 76706

LAWTON, JACQUELINE AGNES, retired communications company executive, management consultant; b. Bklyn., June 9, 1933; d. Thomas G. and Agnes R. (McLaughlin) Maguire; m. George W. Lawton, Feb. 14, 1954; children: George, Victoria, Thomas. With N.Y. Telephone, 1954-82, mktg. mgr. govt., edn. and med. Mid State, 1978-81, mktg. mgr. health care, N.Y.C., 1981-82; dist. field market mgr. health care and lodging; region 1 N.E. and Region 2 Mid Atlantic, AT&T-Am. Bell, N.Y.C., 1982-83; ea. region mgr. pers., mktg. and sales AT&T Info. Systems, Parsippany, N.J., 1983-86, pvt. practice mgmt. cons., Cornish Flat, N.H., 1986—. Republican. Roman Catholic. Home and Office: PO Box 163 Cornish Flat NH 03746

LAWTON, LAJOYCE CHATWELL, management consultant; b. St. Louis, Aug. 10, 1947; d. Farrell William Sr. and Lois Geneva (Holley) Chatwell; m. Billy Carl Lawton, June 24, 1983. BS, Lincoln U., 1972; MA, Mich. State U., East Lansing, 1977; postdoctoral, U. Okla. With Family Health Ctr., 1972-73, Dade County Schs., 1973-76, Overseas Dependent Schs. Dept. Def., 1976-80, Merck Sharp & Dohme, 1980-83; pvt. practice mgmt. cons., 1983-87; mgmt. cons. Bapt. Med. Ctr., 1987-89, Lawton Internat., Oklahoma City, 1989—; presenter at Internat. Fedn. Tng. and Devel. Orgns, Buenos Aires, Bus. and Profl. Women's state confs. Contbr. numerous articles to profl. jours. Named Disting. Alumna Lincoln U., 1979. Mem. NAFE, Cen. Okla. chpt. Am. Soc. for Tng. and Devel. (presenter, Bd. Mem. of Yr. 1988, James Wallace award 1988, Achievement award 1989), Delta Sigma Theta. Democrat. Methodist. Home: PO Box 21401 Oklahoma City OK 73156

LAWTON, LORILEE ANN, pipeline supply company owner, accountant; b. Morrisville, Vt., July 17, 1947; d. Philip Wyman Sr. and Margaret Elaine (Ather) Noyes; m. Lee Henry Lawton, Dec. 6, 1969; children: Deborah Ann, Jeffrey Lee. BBA, U. Vt., 1969. Sr. acct., staff asst. IBM, Essex Junction, Vt., 1969-72; owner, treas. Red-Hed Supply Inc, Colchester, Vt., 1972—. Apptd. bd. dirs. Colchester (Vt.) Community Devel. Assn., 1987 , Vt., Assoc. Gen. Contractors Vt.; v.p. Colchester Vt. Community Devel. Assn.; mem. Bus. Edn. Adv. Com. Colchester High Sch. Mem. Associated Gen. Contractors Am., Associated Gen. Contractors Vt. (bd. dirs.), Am. Water Works Assn., Vt. Waterworks Assn., New Eng. Waterworks Assn., No. Vt. Homebuilders Assn., Water and Sewer Distbrs. Am. (bd. dirs.). Republican. Home: 53 Middle Rd Colchester VT 05446

LAWTON, MARCIA JEAN, psychologist, educator; b. Pawtucket, R.I., May 21, 1937; d. Walter Lincoln and Jean Fraser (Baldwin) L. AB, Brown U., 1959; MA, Northwestern U., 1961, PhD, 1963. Lic. psychologist, Nebr., Colo., Va. In-patient coord. Nebr. Psychiat. Inst., Omaha, 1963-67; clin. psychologist Arapahoe Mental Health Ctr., Englewood, Colo., 1968-72; pvt. practice clin. psychologist Denver, 1972-73; mgr. Women's Halfway House, Arlington, Va., 1974-75; assoc. prof. Va. Commonwealth U., Richmond, 1975—; pres., supr. Growth and Recovery Opportunities, Richmond, 1976—; editor Addiction Letter, Manisses, Providence, 1985—. Contbr. articles to profl. jours. Founder, chmn. Greater Richmond Coun. on Alcoholism and Drug Abuse, Richmond, 1978—. Recipient Outstanding Teaching award Va. Commonwealth U., 1988. Mem. Am. Psychol. Assn., Va. Psychol. Assn., Va. Alcohol and Drug Abuse Counselors Assn., Nat. Alcohol and Drug Abuse Counselors Assn. (Mel Schulstad award 1983), Phi Beta Kappa, Sigma Xi (Outstanding Tchr. award 1988). Office: Va Commonwealth U 921 W Franklin Box 2030 Richmond VA 23284

LAWYER, VIVIAN JURY, lawyer; b. Farmington, Iowa, Jan. 7, 1932; d. Jewell Everett Jury and Ruby Mae (Schumaker) Brewer; m. Verne Lawyer, Oct. 25, 1959; children: Michael Jury, Steven Verne. Tchr.'s cert. U. No. Iowa, 1951; BS with honors, Iowa State U., 1953; JD with honors, Drake U., 1968. Bar: Iowa 1968, U.S. Supreme Ct. 1986. Home econs. tchr. Waukee High Sch. (Iowa), 1953-55; home econs. tchr. jr. high sch. and high sch., Des Moines Pub. Schs., 1955-61; pvt. practice law, Des Moines, 1972—; bd. dirs. Micah Corp.; chmn. juvenile code tng. sessions Iowa Crime Commn., Des Moines, 1978-79, coord. workshops, 1980; assoc. Law Offices of Verne Lawyer, Des Moines, 1981—; co-founder, bd. dirs. Youth Law Center, Des Moines, 1977—; mem. com. rules of juvenile procedure Supreme Ct. Iowa, 1981-87, adv. com. on costs of ct. appointed counsel Supreme Ct. Iowa, 1985-88; trustee Polk County Legal Aid Svcs., Des Moines, 1980-82; mem. Iowa Dept. Human Services and Supreme Ct. Juvenile Justice County Base Joint Study Com., 1984—. Mem. Iowa Task Force permanent families project Nat. Council Juvenile and Family Ct. Judges, 1984-88; mem. substance abuse com. Commn. Children, Youth and Families, 1985—; co-chair Polk County Juvenile Detention Task Force, 1988. Editor: Iowa Juvenile Code Manual, 1979, Iowa Juvenile Code Workshop Manual, 1980; co-editor 1987 Cumulative Supplement, Iowa Academy of Trial Lawyers Trial Handbook; author booklet in field, 1981. Mem. Polk County Citizens Commn. on Corrections, 1977. Iowa Dept. Social Svcs. grantee, 1980. Mem. ABA, Iowa Bar Assn., Polk County Bar Assn., Assn. Trial Lawyers Am., Purple Arrow, Phi Kappa Phi, Omicron Nu. Republican. Home: 5831 N Waterbury Rd Des Moines IA 50312 Office: 427 Fleming Bldg Des Moines IA 50309

LAXSON, SUSAN JENSEN OURAND, real estate professional; b. Albuquerque, N.M., Oct. 2, 1949; d. James Robert and La Verna (Jensen) Ourand; m. Daniel Calvin Laxson, Nov. 20, 1982; children: Christopher Daniel, Kimberly Susan. BA, U.S. Internat. U., San Diego, 1982; MEd, U.S. Internat. U., 1982. Escrow officer First Centennial Title Co., San Diego, 1975-78; store owner Kismet Enterprises, Mex. and Calif., 1978-82; tchr. Rancho Santa Fe (Calif.) Sch., 1982-86; real estate sales Merrill Lynch, La Jolla, Calif., 1986—. Author: The Soul Taker, 1982. Mem. San Diego Bd. Realtors, Calif. Bd. Realtors, San Diego Zoological Soc. Republican. Presbyterian. Club: Torrey Pines Women's Golf (La Jolla). Office: Prudential Calif Realty 1227 Prospect St La Jolla CA 92037

LAYBE, SUZANNE CRAMTON, state legislator; b. Phoenix, Jan. 25, 1956; d. Paul Carl Cramton and Marguerite (Sackman) Stahnke; m. Michael Rue Laybe, Apr. 1, 1978; 1 child, Adrienne Michelle. Student, Phoenix Coll. Precinct committeeman Ariz. Dem. Party, Phoenix, 1987-88, state committeeman, 1988; state legislator Arizona State Legislature, 1988—. Mem. governance com. Phoenix Futures Forum, 1988, Ariz. Citizens for Edn., Phoenix, 1988; dep. registrar Maricopa County, 1987; intern Babbitt for Pres., Phoenix, 1988; office coord. Gore for Pres., Phoenix, 1988. Mem. Nucleus club (Phoenix), HERE club (record sec., Phoenix). Roman Catholic. Home: 2443 E Indianola Ave Phoenix AZ 85016 Office: Ariz Ho of Rep 1700 W Washington Phoenix AZ 85007

LAYER, MEREDITH MITCHUM, financial services company executive, public responsibility professional; b. Rutherfordton, N.C., July 26, 1946; d. Lee Wallace and Ellie (Saine) Mitchum; m. Charles Layer, 1990. B.S., U. N.C.-Greensboro, 1968; M.S., U. Md., 1972. Tchr. home econs. Prince Georges County pub. schs., Md., 1968-72; assoc. dir. market research H.J. Kaufman Advt., Washington, 1972-74; dir. consumer edn. Washington Consumer Affairs Office, 1974-76; dir. consumer affairs U.S. Dept. Commerce, Washington, 1976-80; v.p. consumer affairs Am. Express Co., N.Y.C., 1980-82, sr. v.p.-pub. responsibility, 1982—; former mem. consumer adv. coun. Fed. Res. System, Washington; bd. dirs. Nat. Consumers League, Washington, N.Y. Met. Better Bus. Bur., N.Y.C. Mem. policy bd. Jour. Retail Banking; contbr. articles to profl. jours. Bd. dirs. Women's Forum N.Y., 1987-88, Inst. for the Future; mem. bd. overseers Malcomlm Baldrige nat. Quality Award; commr. Nat. Commn. Working Women, 1987—. Recipient Consumer Edn. award Nat. Found. Consumer Credit Fedn., 1981, Disting. Woman award Northwood Inst., 1985, Matrix award N.Y. Women in Communications, Inc., 1986, Acad. Women Achievers award N.Y.C. YWCA, 1989. Mem. Soc. Consumer Affairs Profls. (pres. 1985), Advt. Women N.Y. (Advt. Woman of the Yr. award 1987), Fin. Women's Assn., Women's Econ. Roundtable, Am. Home Econs. Assn., Internat. Credit Assn. (bd. dirs. 1984—), Am. Assn. for Internat. Aging (bd. dirs. 1989—). Office: Am Express Co Am Express Tower World Fin Ctr New York NY 10285-4725

LAYMAN, LINDA ANNE, owner, manager photography studio; b. Pierceton, Ind., Jan. 19, 1936; d. Walter J. and Phyllis (Trachsel) Ward; m. Daniel James Layman, May 29, 1954; children: Lori Layman Parker, Lisa Layman Williams, LuAnn Layman Schroder, Daniel James Jr. Bookkeeper Sears Roebuck, West Lafayette, Ind., 1954-55; sec. Logansport State Hosp., 1955-56; civil svc. sec. USN Pers., Jacksonville, Fla., 1956-57; bookkeeper Cochran Filling Sta., Logansport, Elks Cafe, Logansport, 1976-78; sec. Dave Reed Roofing, 1979-81; owner, mgr. Harrington Studio, Logansport, 1981—. Mem., Beta Sigma Phi Sorority (pres. 1966), Altrusa Club of Logansport, (dir. 1987). Home: 727 Lynnwood Dr Logansport IN 46947

LAYTON, DEBORAH SUTTON, lawyer, development executive; b. Wilmington, Del., Dec. 13, 1937; d. George Handy and Mary Rachel (Poole) Sutton; m. Richard Carl Layton, Sept. 14, 1957; children: Marcia, Jonathan. Student, Cornell U., 1955-57; BA, U. Pa., 1971; JD, Widener U., 1984. Bar: Pa. 1985, Del. 1986, U.S. Dist. Ct. Del. 1986. With security office Hercules, Inc., Wilmington, 1958-65; free-lance writer Del. Today, Wilmington, 1973-75; with admissions office Wilmington Friends Sch., 1975-79, adminstrv. asst., 1979-85; jud. law clk. to presiding judge Superior Ct. Del., Wilmington, 1985-86; assoc. Crompton & Gritz, Wilmington, 1986-87; devel. assoc. Peninsula United Meth. Homes, Inc., Wilmington, 1987—. Assoc. and copy editor Del. Jour. Corp. Law, 1982-84. Del. Law Sch. merit scholar, 1982-84. Mem. ABA, AAUW (numerous coms.), Del. Bar Assn. (women and law com. estates and trusts com.), Nat. Soc. Fund Raising Execs. Republican. Episcopalian. Office: Peninsula United Meth Homes 1013 Centre Rd Wilmington DE 19805

LAZAR, SUSAN GABER, psychiatrist, psychoanalyst, educator; b. Chgo., July 20, 1944; d. Martin and Lita (LeAnce) Gaber; m. Joel Lazar, June 9, 1965; children: Jessica, Joanna. AB, Radcliffe Coll., 1966; MD, Yeshiva U., 1970. Cert. psychiatrist, psychoanalyst. Intern U. Va. Sch. Medicine, 1970-71; resident in psychiatry Tufts U. Sch. Medicine, 1971-74; asst. prof. psychiatry U. Va. Sch. Medicine, Charlottesville, 1974-77, asst. clin. prof., 1977-82; pvt. practice Bethesda, Md., 1977—; staff psychiatrist Chestnut Lodge, Rockville, Md., 1977-80; mem. faculty extension div. Washington Psychoanalytic Inst., 1978, instr., 1983—; clin. prof. psychiatry George Washington U. Sch. Medicine, Washington, 1989; presenter in field to profl. orgns., 1978—. Mem. Am. Psychiat. Assn., Am. Psychoanalytic Soc., Am. Psychol. Assn., Va. Psychoanalytic Soc. (charter), Washington Psychoanalytic Soc., Alpha Omega Alpha. Home and Office: 9104 Quintana Dr Bethesda MD 20817

LAZAR, ZOE L., psychologist; b. N.Y.C., June 27, 1948; d. Ira Gerald and Charlotte (Silverstein) Levy; m. Ira Lazar, Apr. 5, 1970; children: Alexander David, Samantha Chloe, Damien Jacob. BA, Brandeis U., 1969; MEd, Boston U., 1972, EdD, 1974; cert. in psychoanalysis, William Alanson White Inst., N.Y.C., 1984. Lic. psychologist, N.Y. Intern in clin. psychology McLean Hosp./Harvard U. Med. Sch., Belmont, Mass., 1973-74; staff psychologist out-patient clinic Coney Island Hosp., Bklyn., 1974-75; pvt. practice psychology and psychoanalysis Scarsdale, N.Y., 1976—; instr. psychology in psychiatry Cornell U. Med. Coll., White Plains, N.Y., 1978-82, clin. asst. prof. psychology in psychiatry, 1982—; asst. attending psychologist N.Y. Hosp., White Plains, 1982—; profl. assoc. in psychology Westchester (N.Y.) div. N.Y. Hosp., Cornell Med. Coll., White Plains, 1978-82, asst. attending psychologist, 1982—. Contbr. articles to profl. jours. Cornell U. fellow, 1975-77. Mem. Am. Psychol. Assn. (div. psychoanalysis), Westchester Psychol. Assn., William Alanson White Soc.

LAZARETH, KAREN BETH, state agency administrator; b. Phila., Oct. 8, 1956; d. William Henry and Jacqueline (Howell) L. BS, U. Maine, 1977; MA, Webster U., Geneva, 1983. Registered profl. forester. Forester International Paper Co., Clayton Lake, Maine, 1977; forester Island Falls, Maine, 1977-78, Livermore Falls, Maine, 1978-80; project forester Lincoln, Maine, 1980-82; credit rep. N.Y.C., 1983; dir. Fin. Authority Maine, Augusta, 1983—; bd. dirs. Natural Resources Coun. of Maine. Mem. Soc. Am. Foresters (ednl. policies com. 1986-91, accreditation com. 1984-85). Office: Fin Authority Maine PO Box 949 Augusta ME 04332

LAZARIS, PAMELA ADRIANE, municipal agency administrator; b. Dixon, Ill., Oct. 13, 1956; d. Michael Constantine and Ellen Euridice (Eftax) L.; m. Eugene Dale Monson, Oct. 17, 1987; 1 child, Anthony Edward. BFA in Fine Arts, U. Wis., Milw., 1978; MS in Urban and Regional Planning, U. Wis., 1982. Analyst planning Wis. Dept. Natural Resources, Madison, 1979-82; asst. city planner City of Albert Lea, Minn., 1982-83; specialist community devel. City of Winona, Minn., 1983-85; coordinator community devel. City of Waseca, Minn., 1985—. Vol. spl. events Farmam.-Minn. Agrl. Interpretive Ctr., Waseca, 1985-86. Named one of Oustanding Young Women of Am., 1986. Mem. Am. Inst. Cert. Planners (cert.), Am. Planning Assn. (bd. dirs. so. dist. Minn. chpt. 1986-89), Minn. Planning Assn. (v.p. 1989-90, bd. dirs. so. dist. 1985-89), Minn. Indsl. Devel. Assn., Toastmasters (sgt.-at-arms Waseca cpt. 1987, ednl. v.p. 1988). Home: PO Box 325 110 6th Ave NE Waseca MN 56093 Office: City of Waseca 508 S State St Waseca MN 56093

LAZAROFF, BEATRICE J. STEIN, psychologist, instructor; b. N.Y.C., July 4, 1951; d. Herbert and Rae Rose (Raymond) Stein; m. Jerry Mark Lazaroff, July 29, 1973; children: Justin Michael, Jordan Matthew. BS, Temple U., 1973; MEd, Ga. State U., 1974, PhD, 1981. Lic. psychologist, Pa. Clin. psychologist Benjamin Rush Mental Health Ctr., Phila., 1980-82; pvt. practice Media, Pa., 1980—; instr. Jefferson Med. Ctr., Phila., 1982-83; clin. psychologist Crozer-Chester (Pa.) Med. Ctr., 1982-83; instr. Villanova (Pa.) U., 1983—; bd. dirs. Scleroderma Rsch. Found., Columbus, N.J., The Arthritis Found., Phila. Mem. Am. Psychol. Assn., Phila. Soc. Clin. Psychologists, Nat. Register Health Svc. Providers in Psychology, Assn. for the Advancement of Psychology, Delaware County C. of C. (mem. health and human svcs. com.). Democrat. Jewish. Office: 1029 N Providence Rd Media PA 19063

LAZARUS, BARBARA BETH, academic administrator; b. Chgo., Apr. 17, 1946; d. David and Betty (Ross) L.; m. Thomas Fifield Wilson, June 26, 1967 (div. 1977); m. Marvin Alan Sirbu, Jan. 6, 1979; 1 child, Margaret Ann. AB cum laude, Brown U., 1967; MA in Anthropology, U. Conn., 1969; EdD in Ednl. Anthropology, U. Mass., 1973. Instr. dept. anthropology U. Conn., Storrs, 1967-72; info. unit dir. Ednl. Devel. Ctr., Newton, Mass., 1972-75; dir. Ctr. for Women's Careers Wellesley (Mass.) Coll., 1975-85; assoc. dean, sch. pub. affairs Carnegie-Mellon U., Pitts., 1985-87, assoc. provost for acad. projects, adj. assoc. prof., 1988—; co-dir. Commn. on Women and Work, Asian Women's Inst., 1978-88; vis. staff mem. Oxford U., St. Hilda's Coll., Fall, 1980; speaker on women and work, Internat. Communications Agy., Japan, Hong Kong, Thailand, and others, 1979; vis. team, tng. activities, Carleton Coll., Colby Coll., Wheaton Coll., Fisher Jr. Coll., Bucknell, 1980-85. Author: A Call for Action, 1985; co-editor: Aspirations: Women and Work in Asia, 1985; contbr. articles to profl. jours. Bd. mem. Cancer Guidance Inst., Pitts., B'nai B'rith Hillel, Pitts., Criminal Justice Tng. Task Force, Pa. Commn. on Crime and Delinquency, Va. Gildersleeve Internat. Fund for U. Women; adv. bd. Women's Desk of New Voices Radio Pub. Internat Video Network; women's concerns com. United Bd. for Christian Higher Edn. in Asia; rev. com. United Way of Allegheny County. Grantee Doris Duke Found., 1968. Mem. Assn. N.Am. Cooperating Agys. of Overseas Women's Christian Coll. (cons.), Coun. on Anthropology and Edn., Assn. for Women in Devel., Am. Assn. Higher Edn., Phi Kappa Phi. Democrat. Jewish. Office: Carnegie-Mellon Assoc Pro St BOM B 209 Pittsburgh PA 15213

LAZARUS, SARA LOUISE, theatre director and educator; b. Bklyn., Apr. 15, 1948; d. Laurence and Bella (Sollender) L.; m. David Seader, June 5, 1988. BS, Northwestern U., 1968; cert. in acting, Royal Acad. Dramatic Art, London, 1975. Actress, singer Broadway, Off-Broadway, nat. tours, regional theatre, 1968-78; actor, instr. Durham (N.H.) Summer Theatre, U. N.H., 1978; announcer, moderator New Eng. Forum, Sta. WHEB-AM-FM, Portsmouth, N.H., 1979; dir. Hangar Theatre, Cornell U., Ithaca, N.Y., 1981; founder, tchr. Sara Lazarus Studio for Mus. Theatre Studies, N.Y.C., 1982—; dir. 137th and 138th Ann. Hasty Pudding Shows, Harvard U., Cambridge, Mass., 1985, 86, Centenary Stage Co., Hackettstown, N.J., 1987, 89, Yale U. Dramatic Assn., New Haven, 1988; instr. Am. Mus. and Dramatic Acad., N.Y.C., 1985-86. Dir. Babes in Arms concert, Avery Fisher Hall, Lincoln Ctr., N.Y.C., 1989, Carried Away: Jeff Harnar Sings Comden and Green, 1989 (Back Stage Mistro award 1989). Mem. Soc. Stage Dirs. and Choreographers, Am. Dirs. Inst., Actors Equity Assn., Manhattan Assn. Cabarets. Mem. Soc. Stage Dirs. and Choreographers, Am. Dirs. Inst., Actors Equity Assn. Home and Office: 535 Cathedral Pkwy New York NY 10025

LAZOR, PATRICIA ANN, interior designer; b. Bound Brook, N.J., Feb. 3, 1936; d. Charles A. and Grace E. (Siegrist) LaGattuta; m. E. Alexander Lazor, Aug. 22, 1959; children: Pamela A., Carolyn L., Charles L., Peter A. BA, Chestnut Hill Coll., 1957; MEd, Rutgers Coll., 1962; cert., N.Y. Sch. Interior Design, 1972. Tchr. Bridgewater (N.J.) Raritan Schs., 1958-69; designer Patricia A. Lazor Interior Design, Bernardsville, N.J., 1975-85; pres. Alexander Abry, Inc., Washington, 1985-87; owner, designer Patricia A. Lazor Interior Design Antiques, Inc., Bernardsville, N.J., 1985—. Com.-woman Rep. Party, Somerset County, N.J., 1978; chmn. Family Counseling Service Somerset County, 1972-78. Mem. Essex Hunt Club (Peapack, N.J.), Somerset Hills Country Club (Baernardsville), Garden Club Morristown, Kappa Delta Phi. Republican. Roman Catholic. Home and Office: Interior Design/Antiques Inc Roebling Rd Bernardsville NJ 07924

LAZORWITZ, ELAINE SHERRI, project specialist; b. Newark, Oct. 7, 1954; d. Roy and Pauline (Goldblat) L. BFA, Sch. Visual Arts, 1980; postgrad., Polytech. Inst. N.Y. Sr. project mgr. N.Y.C. Health and Hosps., 1989—; asst. resident engr. Hazen and Sawyer, N.Y.C., 1990—. Recipient Nikon award. Home: 143 Fairway Dr Carmel NY 10512

LAZZARA, BERNADETTE See PETERS, BERNADETTE

LEA, ELEANOR LUCILLE, state agency administrator; b. Diller, Nebr., Nov. 6, 1916; d. Edward Richard and Gertrude (Loock) Henrichs; m. Stanley Guy Lea, Mar. 6, 1936; children: Dianna Evenson, Cylesta Peters, Jeffrey, Chad. Student, Fairburg State Coll. Owner Modern Furniture Store, Fairbury, Nebr., 1945-80; dist. mgr. Field Enterprises, Chgo., 1966-80; library resource person Fairbury Pub. Library, 1982-85; job coordinator Blue River Area Agy. on Aging, Lincoln, Nebr., 1985-87; Bd. mem. Operation ABLE, Lincoln, 1987—, Nat. Grandparent Program, Beatrice, Nebr., 1985-87. Pres., dist. v.p. United Meth. Women; Sunday Sch. supt. Meth. Ch., Fairburg; v.p. sch. bd. Fairburg Pub. Sch. Bd., 1956-62; bd. mem. Girl Scouts U.S.A., 1950-56. Republican. Home: 6100 Vine St Apt S101 Lincoln NE 68505

LEA, F. KAY AMEND, optical company executive; b. Smithville, Tex., Apr. 24, 1941; d. Lorene Lundy and Frances (German) Amend; m. J. Davis Lea; children: Kimberly Kay, Anthony Jay. Student, Coll. William and Mary, 1960-61. Unit control clk. Miller & Rhoades Dept. Store, Richmond, Va., 1961-66; optical lab. technician Superior Optical Svc., St. Petersburg, Fla., 1967-72; optician's apprentice Regenhardt Optical Co., St. Petersburg, 1972-73; co-owner, exec. sec.-treas. Lea Optical, Inc., Clearwater, Fla., 1977—, also bd. dirs. Den leader Boy Scouts Am., Seminole, Fla., 1982-84; vol. Pinellas County Schs., St. Petersburg, 1979-85. Mem. Optical Labs. Assn. (exec. bd. wives' auxiliary 1987—).

LEA, PAULINE S., nursing consultant and educator; b. Shreveport, La., Aug. 3, 1942; d. Ervin Ernest and Anna Lee (Crenshaw) Sipes; children: Curtis, William. BSN, Northwestern State U., 1967; MS in Nursing, La. State U., 1983. Cert. advanced practitioner nursing. Clin. specialist Parkland Hosp., Baton Rouge; cons. Behavioral Health, Inc., Baton Rouge; instr. Baton Rouge Gen. Med. Ctr. Sch. Nursing. Author: Meeting the Needs of Family Members of Critically Ill Patients. gov. appointee La. State Adv. Com. on Hospice Care, 1989. Mem. ANA (cert. clin. specialist in adult psychiat. and mental health nursing), La. State Nurses' Assn., Baton Rouge Dist. Nurses' Assn. Address: 3616 North Blvd PO Box 2511 Baton Rouge LA 70821

LEACH, ELIZABETH A. BIERYLA, benefits consultant, seminar leader; b. Scranton, Pa., July 21, 1949; d. Henry Joseph and Helen Theresa (Switlinski) Bieryla; m. Donald J. Leach, July 16, 1971 (marriage dissolved); 1 child, Michael J. BS in Human Services, U. Scranton (Pa.), 1979, MS in Rehab. Counseling, 1980. Cert. rehab. counselor, ins. rehab. specialist. Adjuster Gallager Bassett Ins. Services, Scranton, Pa., 1975-79; grad. asst. U. Scranton, 1979-80; ptnr. Rehab. Mgmt. Group, Scranton, 1980-83; tng. dir., asst. risk mgr., rehab. counselor Commonwealth Telephone Enterprises, Wilkes-Barre, Pa., 1982-84; employee assistance program mgr. Avtex Fibers, Front Royal, Va., 1984-86; pres. Med. Benefits Mgmt. Svcs., Inc., Phoenixville, Pa., 1986—; guest presentor Bur. of Vocat. Rehab., Phila., 1982 and Mgmt. Edn. Ctr., ASPA chpts., Del. Mfg. Assn; chmn. Profl. Devel. Greater Valley ASPA, 1987-88. Bd. dirs., various com. chairs., Planned Parenthood of Lackawanna County, Scranton, 1977-80, Pa. Power & Electric, Scranton, 1979. Mem. NAFE, Nat. Rehab. Assn., Nat. Assn. of Rehab. Profls. in the Pvt. Sector, Nat. Rehab. Counseling Assn., Am. Assn. Pers. Adminstrs. , Delta Tau Kappa, Alpha Sigma Lambda. Home: 2912 Aspen Circle Blue Bell PA 19422 Office: Med Benefits Mgmt Services Inc 2912 Aspen Circle Blue Bell PA 19422

LEACH, SHEILA NORMA, real estate developer; b. Macon, Ga., Sept. 16, 1945; d. David Hyman Rudman and Florene Lily (Yaughn) Myers; m. Joshua R. Leach III, June, 1963 (div. Jan. 1970); 1 child, Samantha Jane. Cert. in real estate, Tuxedo Ctr., 1984. Rate clk. Sentry Ins., Atlanta, 1963-65; sec. sales svc. dept. Lithonia Lighting, Conyers, Ga., 1966-68; from adminstrv. asst. to advt. assoc. Wilding, Inc., Atlanta, 1968-74; corp. sec. First Equities Mgmt. Corp., Atlanta, 1974-80; exec. sec. to gen. mgr. Stadium Hotel, Atlanta, 1980-81; corp. sec. United Corners, Inc., Atlanta, 1981-87; v.p. Gipson Co., Atlanta, 1987—. Charter mem. Quota Club of Northside, Atlanta, 1976; fund chmn. Ga. Heart Assn., Atlanta, 1980. Mem. NAFE, Internat. Coun. Shopping Ctrs. Office: Gipson Co 8 Piedmont Ctr Ste 505 Atlanta GA 30305

LEACHMAN, CLORIS, actress; b. Des Moines, June 30, 1930; m. George England, 1953 (div. 1979); 5 children. Ed., Northwestern U. Actress: (films) including Kiss Me Deadly, 1955, Butch Cassidy and the Sundance Kid, 1969, W.U.S.A., 1970, The Steagle, 1971, The Last Picture Show, 1971 (Acad. award for best supporting actress 1971), Dillinger, 1973, Daisy Miller, 1974, Young Frankenstein, 1974, Crazy Mama, 1975, High Anxiety, 1977, The North Avenue Irregulars, 1979, Scavenger Hunt, 1979, Herbie Goes Bananas, History of the World, Part 1, 1982, Shadow Play, Walk Like a Man, Hansel and Gretel, Texasville, 1990; TV series including Lassie, 1957, Route 66, Laramie, Trials of O'Brien, Mary Tyler Moore Show, Phyllis, 1975-77, Facts of Life, The Nutt House, 1989; (TV movies) including Silent Night, Lonely Night, 1969, Brand New Life, 1973, The Migrants, 1974, A Girl Named Sooner, 1975, Ladies of the Corridor, The New Original Wonder Woman, 1975, It Happened One Christmas, 1977, Long Journey Back, 1978, Willa, 1979, S.O.S. Titanic, 1979, The Acorn People, 1981, Advice to the Lovelorn, 1981, Miss All-American Beauty, 1982, Dixie: Changing Habits, 1983, The Demon Murder Case, 1983, Ernie Kovacs, Between the Laughter, 1984, Deadly Intentions, 1985, Love is Never Silent, (TV miniseries) Backstairs at the White House, 1979; theater appearance in Grandma Moses: An American Primitive, Washington, 1990; guest appearance: The Love Boat, 1976. Recipient 6 Emmy awards. Address: care McCartt-Oreck-Barrett 10390 Santa Monica Blvd Ste 310 Los Angeles CA 90025*

LEADER, FRANCIE DEBRA, cable television sales and marketing executive; b. Detroit, May 19, 1955; d. David and Gloria (Slobin) L. BA in Communications, U. Mich., 1976. Prodn. asst. mgr. Sta. WXYZ ABC-TV Channel 7, Detroit, 1977-79; exec. producer franchise devel. Teleprompter/Group W Cable, Detroit, 1980-84; from nat. affiliate relations mgr. to S.E. region mktg. mgr. The Learning Channel, Washington, 1984; nat. cable mktg. mgr. Reuters, Ltd., N.Y.C., 1985; mgr. affiliate sales and mktg. Fin. News Network, N.Y.C., Washington, 1985-87; dir. affiliate sales S.E. region The Travel Channel, Washington, 1987-89; with up cable sales dept. Nucable Resources Corp., Washington, 1989-90. Co-author: People to People Television, 1982. Mem. Women in Cable (membership chair, bd. dirs. Washington chpt. 1989), Cable TV Adminstrn. & Mktg. Soc.

LEAGUE, ALICE FAY, community action administrator; b. Stroh, Ind., Mar. 5, 1945; d. Vernie and Fay Blanche (Williamson) Gray; m. Larry League, May 8, 1971. BA in Social Work, Anderson (Ind.) Coll., 1968; postgrad., U. Ill., 1968, Dickinson (N.D.) State U., 1975-76. Exec. dir. Saga Food Svc. Nazarene Coll., Olathe, Kans., 1968-70, St. Margarets Hosp., Kansas City, Kans., 1970-71; exec. dir. St. Francis Hosp., Topeka, Kans., 1971-74; personnel dir. Dickinson Nursing Ctr., 1974-75; exec. dir. Community Action & Devel. Program, Dickinson, 1976—. Del. N.D. Dem. Conv., Fargo, 1989; pres. Dickinson Food Buying Club, 1977-85, N.D. Commn. on Status of Women, Bismarck, N.D., 1985—, N.D. Women's Network, Dickinson, 1986—. Mem. AAUW (pres. N.D. div.), N. D. Community Action Assn. (pres. 1979-80, 83-85), Nat. Community Action Assn. (nat. rep. 1986—), Region VIII of Community Action Assn. (sec., treas. 1982-90). Home: 1574 13th St W Dickinson ND 58601 Office: Community Action & Devel Program 652 W Villard Dickinson ND 58601

LEAK, MARGARET ELIZABETH, insurance company executive; b. Atlanta, Sept. 9, 1946; d. William Whitehurst and Margaret Elizabeth (Whitsitt) L. BS in Psychology, Okla. State U., 1968; postgrad., U. Okla., 1960-69, Cornell U., 1976-78; grad. advanced mgmt. program, Harvard U., 1983. Editor communications Eastern State Bankcard Assn., N.Y.C., 1969-71; sr. edn. specialist Citibank, N.Y.C., 1971-73; adminstr. orgn. devel. NBC, N.Y.C., 1973-74; mgr. tng. and devel. Atlantic Mut. Cos., Property/Casualty Ins., N.Y.C., 1974-76, sec. human resources, 1976-78, v.p. human resources, 1978-86, v.p. human resources and corp. communications, 1984-86, sr. v.p. adminstrv. services, 1987—. Presbyterian. Office: Atlantic Mut Cos 45 Wall St New York NY 10005

LEAKE, BRENDA GAIL, nurse; b. Harriman, Tenn., Aug. 5, 1950; d. James Frank and Pauline Ruby (McGuffey) Judd; m. Lee Leake, Aug. 1, 1970 (div. Apr. 1974). AS in Nursing, U. Nev., Las Vegas, 1971, BN, 1986; cert. enterostomal therapist, U. Calif., San Diego, 1975. RN, Nev. Staff nurse Humana Hosp. Sunrise, Las Vegas, 1971-73, relief charge nurse, 1973-76, enterostomal therapist, 1976—; speaker Hospice Vol. program, Las Vegas, 1982—, I Can Cope program, Las Vegas, 1984—. Author instructional guide. Vol. Am. Cancer Soc., 1983—, mem. program devel. nurse edn. com. Mem. Intenat. Assn. Enterostomal Therapists (cert.), Am. Nurses Assn., So. Nev. Nurses Assn., World Council Enterostomal Therapists, Am. Urol. Assn. (cert.), So. Nev. Ostomy Assn. (med. advisor 1976—), Ileitis & Colitis Assn., Advanced practitioners Nursing (cert., program chmn. 1986—). Republican. Presbyterian. Office: Humana Hosp Sunrise 3186 Maryland Pkwy Las Vegas NV 89109

LEANA, CARRIE RENEE, educator; b. Mpls., Sept. 22, 1953; d. Ricco Joseph and Pauline (Burns) L.; m. David I. Goldman. BA, Baylor U., 1976, MBA, 1978; PhD, U. Houston, 1984. Asset analyst Bank of the S.W., Houston, 1978-80; asst. prof. Coll. of Bus. Adminstrn. U. Fla., Gainesville, 1984-87; asst. prof. Grad. Sch. of Bus. U. Pitts., 1987-90, assoc. prof. Grad. Sch. Bus., 1990—. Contbr. numerous articles to profl. jours. Mem. adv. bd. Steel Valley Authority, Pitts., 1987—; bd. dirs. Planned Parenthood No. Fla., Gainesville, 1985-87, Tri-State Conf. on Steel, 1987—, Nat. Abortion Rights Action League of Pa., Phila., 1988—, Housing Devel. Corp. Allegheny County, 1990—. Mem. Am. Psychol. Assn., Acad. of Mgmt., Decision Scis. Inst., So. Mgmt. Assn., Soc. Indsl. and Orgnl. Psychologists, Sigma Xi Sci. Rsch. Soc. Democrat. Office: U Pitts Grad Sch of Business Pittsburgh PA 15260

LEAR, FRANCES LOEB, writer; b. Hudson, N.Y., July 14, 1923; d. Herbert Adam and Aline (Friedman) Loeb; m. Norman Milton Lear, 1957 (div. 1985); children: Kate, Maggie. Grad. high sch., Northampton, Mass. Asst. buyer Bloomingdales, N.Y.C., 1945-51; buyer Lord & Taylor, N.Y.C., 1952-59; owner Woman's Pl., Inc., L.A., 1965-84; founder, editor-in-chief Lear's Mag., N.Y.C., 1985—. Contbr. articles to jours. Office: Lear Pub Co 655 Madison Ave New York NY 10022

LEARY, NANCY JANE, marketing professional; b. Natick, Mass., Mar. 25, 1952; d. Norman Leslie and Dorothy (Holmquist) Pidgeon; m. Patrick J. Leary, Sept. 17, 1977 (div. May 1984). AA, Mass Bay Coll., Wellesley, Mass., 1979; BS, Lesley Coll., Cambridge, Mass., 1988. Cert. tchr., Fla. Sec. GTE Corp., Needham, Mass., 1973-78; coord. edn. Cullinet Software Inc., Westwood, Mass., 1983-84, adminstrv. asst., 1984-85, mgr. adminstrn., 1985-86; specialist product mktg. Cullinet Co., Westwood, Mass., 1986-88; v.p. mktg. and adminstrn. Jonathan's Landscaping, Bradenton Beach, Fla., 1988-89; supr. tech. support staff A Plus Tax Product Group, Arthur Andersen, Inc., Sarasota, Fla., 1989-90; mktg. cons. Sarasota, Fla., 1990—. Mem. Fla. Community Assn. Mgrs., NAFE. Office: 2803 Fruitville Rd Sarasota FL 34239

LEASE, JANE ETTA, librarian; b. Kansas City, Kans., Apr. 10, 1924; d. Joy Alva and Emma (Jaggard) Omer; B.S. in Home Econs., U. Ariz., 1957; M.S. in Edn., Ind. U., 1962; M.S. in L.S., U. Denver, 1967; m. Richard J. Lease, Jan. 16, 1960; children—Janet (Mrs. Jacky B. Radifera), Joyce (Mrs. Robert J. Carson), Julia (Mrs. Earle D. Marvin), Cathy (Mrs. Edward F. Warren); stepchildren—Richard Jay II, William Harley. Newspaper reporter Ariz. Daily Star, Tucson, 1937-39; asst. home agt. Dept. Agr., 1957; homemaking tchr., Ft. Huachuca, Ariz., 1957-60; head tchr. Stonebelt Council Retarded Children, Bloomington, Ind., 1960-61; reference clk. Ariz. State U. Library, 1964-66; edn. and psychology librarian N.Mex. State U., 1967-71; Amway distbr., 1973—; cons. solid wastes, distressed land problems reference remedies, 1967; ecology lit. research and cons., 1966—. Ind. observer 1st World Conf. Human Environment, 1972; mem. Las Cruces Community Devel. Priorities Adv. Bd. Mem. ALA, Regional Environ. Edn. Research Info. Orgn., NAFE, P.E.O., D.A.R., Internat. Platform Assn., Las Cruces Antique Car Club, Las Cruces Story League, N.Mex. Library Assn. Methodist (lay leader). Address: 2145 Boise Dr Las Cruces NM 88001

LEASOR, JANE, religion and philosophy educator, musician; b. Portsmouth, Ohio, Aug. 10, 1922; d. Paul Raymond Leasor and Rana Kathryn (Bayer) Leasor-McDonald. BA, Wheaton Coll., 1944; MRE, N.Y. Theol. Sem., 1952; PhD, NYU, 1969. Asst. prof. Belhaven Coll., Jackson, Miss., 1952-54; dept. chmn. Beirut Coll. for Women, 1954-59; asst. to pres. Wheaton (Ill.) Coll., 1961-63; dean of women N.Y. Theol. Sem., N.Y.C., 1963-67; counselor CUNY, Bklyn., 1967-74; assoc. prof. Beirut U. Coll., 1978-80; tchr. internat. sch., Les Cayes, Haiti, 1984-85; pvt. tutor, 1985—. Author religious text for use in Syria and Lebanon, 1960; editor books by V.R. Edman, 1961-63, Time and Life mags. Mem. Am. Assn. Counselors, Am. Guild Organists. Republican. Episcopalian. Home: 4102 Fallam Dr Malden WV 25306

LEASURE, MARY LOUISE, sales executive; b. Corona, Calif., Sept. 5, 1956; d. William Lloyd and Mary Ann (Jacobi) L. BA Sociology/Psychology, Southwest Tex. State U., 1976. Field sales mgr. Leasure Assocs., Fremont, Calif., 1978-83; sales tng. specialist Intel Corp., Santa Clara, Calif., 1983-86; sales rep. Epson Am., Santa Clara, 1986-87; dir. sales and mktg. Visionics Corp., Santa Clara, 1987—. Mem. Am. Mgmt. Assn. (charter), Am. Bus. Women's Assn., Bus. Owner's Network. Democrat. Roman Catholic. Home: 667 Madrone Ave Sunnyvale CA 94086 Office: Visionics Corp 3032 Bunker Hill Ln Ste 201 Santa Clara CA 95054

LEASURE, VICKEY ANN, guidance counselor; b. Pancoast, Ohio, June 13, 1949; d. Millard Jr. and Annabelle (Webb) Houseman; m. Billy Lee Leasure, Oct. 6, 1967; children: Tiffany, Seth, Peter. BS, Ohio U., 1973; MED, Wright State U., 1977; post grad., Ohio State U., 1978-82, Columbus Coll. of Art Design, 1981. Tchr. career coord. Miami Trace Sch., Wash. C.H., 1972-83; tchr., counselor Fayette County Sch. Adult Educ., Wash. C.H., Ohio, 1978-81; tchr. counselor Nature's Classroon Alternative Educ., Ivoryton, Conn., 1981; tchr., counselor Fayette Co. Probate Court, Wash. C.H., Ohio; prof., counselor Southern State Community Coll., Wash. C.H., Ohio, 1980-84; teaching assoc. Ohio State U., OHio, 1982; guidance counselor Huntington Local Sch., Chillicothe, Ohio, 1983--; tchr., counselor Pike Co. Adult Educ., Waverly, Ohio, 1989--; Ross County child abuse coord., Child Abuse Prevention Program, Columbus, 1985-89. Author (poetry) The Spider, 1988; contbr. articles to profl. mags. Volunteer, Humane Soc., Wash., 1983-89, Hospice, Fayette County, Ohio, 1988-89. Grantee Martha Holden Jennings Found, Cleve., 1988, Ohio Children's Trust Fund, 1986-87, Paint Valley Mental Health Bd., Chillicothe, 1987-88, Meade-Massie Trust Fund, 1983. Mem. AAUW, Ohio Sch. Counselors Assn. (v.p. elect 1983), Ross County Guidance Assn. (pres., v.p.), Career Edn. Assn., Ohio Edn. Assn., Young Astronauts (coun. leader 1988-89). Republican. Presbyterian. Office: Huntington Local Sch 188 Huntsman Rd Chillicothe OH 45601

LEATHERBERRY, ANNE KNOX CLARK, interior designer, new home design consultant, entrepreneur, business consultant; b. Geneva, Ill., Jan. 19, 1953; d. Donald William and Margaret Lorraine (Johnson) Clark; m. David Boyd Leatherberry, Aug. 5, 1978; children: Elizabeth Anne, Laura Knox. BS in Bus., Miami U., Oxford, Ohio, 1975. With Carson, Pirie, Scott & Co., Chgo., 1975-77; health care sales specialist Gen. Foods Corp., Northlake, Ill., 1977-78; account mgr. Cin., 1978-79; pres., owner Annie's Originals/Kids Collectables, Ltd., Waukesha, Wis., 1979—; mktg. rep./demonstrator mktg. Waukesha, 1988—; owner Dreamhouse Designs, Waukesha, 1989—; cons. Lamb's Quarters, Hartford, Wis., 1982-83, Ungerwear, West Alexandria, Ohio, 1982-84, Little Bits, Waukesha, 1984—, Evelyn's Creations, East Troy, Wis., 1986—, The Queen's Empire Inc., Pitts., 1989—, others; student recruitment rep. Miami U., 1986—. Sec. bd. dirs. Waukesha Area Symphonic Band, 1987-89, mem., 1979—, Carroll Coll. Community Orch., Waukesha, 1985-86; vol. tchr.'s aide Clarendon Ave. Sch., Mukwondago, Wis., 1988—; asst. leader Girl Scouts U.S., 1988, leader, 1988-89; vol. staff aide Jim Thompson for Gov. campaign, 1975-76; dir. Children's Choir, 1986, summer music dir. Luth. Ch., 1986, 88; events chairwoman Edgewood Golf League, 1988—. Mem. Dir. Mktg. Assn., Soc. Craft Designers, NAFE, PEO (officer 1980-82), Kappa Kappa Gamma. Republican. Lutheran. Home and Office: W241 S 5910 Autumn Haze Ct Waukesha WI 53186

LEATHERBY, JOANN, lawyer; b. L.A., May 13, 1955; d. Ralph William and Eleanor Augustine (Samson) L.; m. Emroy L. Watson, Oct. 1, 1983 (div. 1988). BA in English, Iowa Wesleyan Coll., 1977; JD, UCLA, 1980. Bar: Calif., 1980. Exec. dir. Women's Legal Clinic, L.A., 1978-81; v.p. adminstrn. UniCare Ins., Irvine, Calif., 1981-82; pvt. practice Newport Beach, Calif., 1982-84; gen. counsel Ricoh Electronics, Inc., Tustin, Calif., 1984-88; dir. adminstrn. and legal dept. Ricoh Electronics, Inc., Tustin, 1988-89; sr. dir. human resources dept. Ricoh Electronics, Inc., 1989—; bd. dirs. UniCare Fin. Corp., Irvine. Bd. dirs. Children or Parents Emergency Svc. Mem. Calif. Women Lawyers Assn., Orange County Bar Assn. Democrat. Office: Ricoh Electronics Inc 1100 Valencia Ave Tustin CA 92680

LEATHERMAN, MERRILEE STREUN, medical editor; b. Shreveport, La., Sept. 10, 1942; d. John Edward and Memory Lee (Sullivant) Streun; m. Edward Hopkins Leatherman, May 8, 1965; children: Todd Hopkins, Lori Leigh. BA in English Lit., U. Ark., Fayetteville, 1964. From assoc. women's editor to med. editor Shreveport Jour., 1964-74; pub. rels. dir. Bossier Med. Ctr., Bossier City, La., 1974-79; pub. rels. cons. Union Meml. Hosp., El Dorado, Ark., 1975-79; freelance pub. rels./mktg. cons. Ark., La., Tex., 1975-80; med. pubs. coord., med. editor Schumpert Med. Ctr., Shreveport, 1981—; freelance editor Boots Pharm. Co., 1987-88; cons. med. bull. Shreveport Med. Soc., 1987-89. Editor Schumpert Med. Quar., 1982—, Focus, 1977, 79, 80, 82. Chmn. Alcohol/Drug Awareness Coalition, Shreveport, 1977-79, 88, State of La. Mental Health and Substance Abuse Coun., Baton Rouge, 1983-86; bd. dirs. State of La. Housing Corp. for Handicapped, Baton Rouge, 1982-84; sec. Mayor's Adv. Bd., Community Blood Bank, Shreveport, 1975-77; bd. dirs. Oakwood Home for Women, 1980-83; bd. sec. women's adv. bd. Nat. Bank of Bossier, 1980-82; co-chmn. mental health com. Shreveport Med. Aux., 1978; publicity chmn. benefit sytle show St. Mark's Episcopal Ch. Recipient Cert. of Appreciation, State of La. Dept. Health and Human Resources, Office Mental Health, 1983; Outstanding Community Svc. in Field of Alcoholism and Drug Abuse, Alcohol/Drug Awareness Coalition, Shreveport, 1977. Mem. Am. med. Writers Assn. (forum presenter 1989), Women in Communications (tech. awards 1985, 86), La. Hosp. Assn., Nat. Fedn. Press Women, Lambda Tau, Sigma Delta Chi (state, reg., nat. awards 1965-88). Democrat. Office: Schumpert Med Ctr 915 Margaret PO Box 21976 Shreveport LA 71120-1976

LEATHERS, BURGE ROBERTS, management specialist; b. Fayetteville, Okla., May 1, 1959; d. James David Jr. and Anne (Jackson) Roberts; m. John Edwin Leathers, June 23, 1984. BA, Cen. State U., Edmond, Okla., 1982; postgrad., Oklahoma City U., 1989—. Clerk USDA, Oklahoma City, 1977-80; clerk typist USAF, Tinker AFB, Okla., 1981-82, 83-84, sec., 1982, supply clk., 1984-85, inventory mgmt. specialist, 1985—; mktg. sales rep. NBI Oklahoma City, 1983; interior decorator Montgomery Ward, Midwest City, Okla., 1983; mgr. directorate Fed. Womens Program, Tinker AFB, 1987-89. Author: Corvus Concept Computer, 1983. Mem. AAUW (treas. 1988-89), Air Force Assn. (br. sec. 1989-90, state sec. 1990—, recipient Award 1990), Tinker Mgmt. Assn. Home: 904 Jollie Dr Choctaw OK 73020

LEATHERS, MARGARET WEIL, foundation administrator; b. Princeton, Ind., Dec. 22, 1949; d. Albert J. and Nora Jewel (Franklin) Weil; m. Charles L. Leathers, June 19, 1971 (div. Dec. 1987); children: Julianna L., Kevin Sean. AB, U. Ill., 1971; MS, Russell Sage Coll., 1979. Cert. tchr., N.Y., health edn. specialist. Employment counselor Snelling & Snelling, Schenectady, N.Y., 1972-76; substitute tchr. Monahasen High/Jr. High Sch., Schenectady, 1978-79; grant abstractor State of N.Y., Albany, 1979; program coordinator Am. Lung Assn. Santa Clara-San Benito Counties, San Jose, Calif., 1982-84, dir. programs, 1984-87, nat. clinic leader trainer, 1986—, acting exec. dir., 1987-88, exec. dir., 1988—. Author: Camp Superstuff Workbook and Teachers Manual, 1983; contbr. articles to profl. publs. and mags. Bd. dirs., officer Santa Clara Valley Council Parent-Participating Nursery Schs., 1980-81; resource vol. Lyceum Santa Clara Valley, 1983-87; leader Explorer post Boy Scouts Am., San Jose, 1988; mem. adminstrv. bd. council ministries United Meth. Ch.; vol. 1st asthma camp Young Tchrs. of Health, Soviet Union, 1989. Mem. Am. Pub. Health Assn., Soc. Pub. Health Educators, Am. Sch. Health Assn., Phi Beta Kappa, Phi Kappa Phi, Eta Sigma Gamma, Alpha Xi Delta (pres. Santa Clara Valley 1985-87). Democrat. Home: 341 Springpark Circle San Jose CA 95136 Office: Am Lung Assn 1469 Park Ave San Jose CA 95136

LEATON, MARCELLA KAY, insurance representative, business owner; b. Eugene, Oreg., Oct. 9, 1952; d. Robert A. and Wanda Jo (Garner) Boehm; m. Michael G. Schlegel, Aug. 9, 1975; children: Kaellen June, Krystalynn Michele. Grad. high sch., Springfield, Oreg. Sales rep. The Prudential, Novato, Calif., 1973—; bus. owner Marcella Enterprises, Novato, 1983—. Contbr. articles to profl. jours. Named one of Outstanding Young Women Am., 1979. Mem. Nat. Assn. Life Underwriters (Nat. Quality award 1978, 80, 84), Marin Life Underwriters, Nat. Assn. Profl. Saleswomen (founder Marin chpt. 1982, pres. 1982-85, chmn. 1985-86, nat. v.p. 1985-86, awards and recognition chmn. 1985-88, nat. pres. 1987-90), Leading Life Producers No. Calif., Million Dollar Round Table (qualifying). Clubs: President's, Western Star. Office: Marcella Enterprises 901 Reichert Ave Ste #100 Novato CA 94945

LEAVITT, DEBBIE, photographer; b. Chgo., July 31, 1954; m. George A. Castleberry, Jan. 23, 1983. Student, U. Wis., Madison, 1972-74; BFA, Brooks Inst. Photography, Santa Barbara, Calif., 1978. Prin. Debbie Leavitt Photography, L.A., 1978-84, Chgo., 1984—. Exhibited in one-woman and group shows, including The Exit, Chgo., 1982, Skokie (Ill.) Libr., 1985. Active NARAL, People for the Am. Way, EarthFirst!, Art Inst. Chgo. Mem. ASMP. Democrat. Jewish. Office: 2029 W Armitage Ave Chicago IL 60647

LEAVITT, DONNA MARZEE, systems anlayst; b. Texarkana, Ark., Mar. 18, 1958; d. Noah and Evelyn Louise (Morton) Higgins; m. Michael W. Miller, Aug. 31, 1979; m. Teddy C.J. Leavitt, Feb. 14, 1987; 1 child, Sarai Rae. Student, TCC, Texarkana, 1981, U. Tex., Arlington. Acct. Bill Moores, CPA, Texarkana, 1985-87; office asst. Texarkana Community Coll., 1975-76, Jim Walter Corp., 1976-77; mgmt. asst. Celotex, 1977-80; acct. Grier, Reeves & Lawley, 1980-81; writer Wordtrek, Dallas, 1981—; mgmt. asst. Red River Army Depot, Texarkana, 1981-85; systems analyst Bank One Tex., Dallas, 1985—; Community affairs coord. Bank One, Tex., Dallas, 1990. Author: Rise to Consciousness, 1990, On Being Human, 1989, Michel De Nostradame, 1989, 1990's Handbook for the Hip Kid, 1989, Anthology of Poetry, 1988, Anthology of Songs, 1987. Recipient Poets award World of Poetry, 1986. Mem. NAFE, Internat. Toastmasters (v.p. 1986—).

LEAVITT, JOAN KAZANJIAN, state health official, physician; b. Boston, Jan. 14, 1926; d. Varaztad Hovannes and Marion V. (Hanford) Kazanjian; m. Don K. Leavitt; children—Mark S., Lynda Donn. A.B., Radcliffe Coll., 1947; M.A., Smith Coll., 1949; M.D., Boston U., 1953. Intern in pediatrics Boston City Hosp., 1953-54, resident in pediatrics, 1954-55; resident in pediatrics Mass. Gen. Hosp., Boston, 1955-56, 57-58; pediatrician Comanche County (Okla.) Guidance Center, 1959; practice medicine specializing in pediatrics Altus, Okla., 1959-64; med. dir. Jackson County (Okla.) Health Dept., 1960-67, Kay County (Okla.) Health Dept., 1967-76; chief maternal and child health service Okla. Health Dept., Oklahoma City, 1976; dep. commr. for personal health services Okla. Health Dept., 1976-77, commr. of health, 1977—. Mem. AMA, Okla. State Med. Assn., Okla. Public Health Assn., Oklahoma County Med. Soc., Assn. State and Territorial Health Ofcls. (pres. 1985-86), Sigma Xi. Office: 1000 NE Tenth St PO Box 53551 Oklahoma City OK 73152

LEAVITT, MARY JANICE DEIMEL, civic worker, educator; b. Washington, Aug. 21, 1924; d. Henry L. and Ruth (Grady) Deimel; B.A., Am. U., Washington, 1946; postgrad. U. Md., 1963-65, U. Va., 1965-67, 72-73, 78-79, George Washington U., 1966-67; m. Robert Walker Leavitt, Mar. 30, 1945; children: Michael Deimel, Robert Walker, Caroline Ann Leavitt Snyder. Tchr., Rothery Sch., Arlington, Va., 1947; dir. Sunnyside, Children's House, Washington, 1949; asst. dir. Coop. Sch. for Handicapped Children, Arlington, 1962, dir., Arlington, Springfield, Va., 1963-66; tchr. mentally retarded children Fairfax (Va.) County Pub. Schs., 1966-68; asst. dir. Burgundy Farm Country Day Sch., Alexandria, Va., 1968-69; tchr., substitute tchr. specific learning problem children Accotink Acad., Springfield, Va., 1970-80; substitute tchr. learning disabilities Children's Achievement Center, McLean, Va., 1973-82, Psychiat. Inst., Washington and Rockville, Md., 1976-82, Home-Bound and Substitute Program, Fairfax, Va., 1978-84; asst. info. specialist Ednl. Research Service, Inc., Rosslyn, Va., 1974-76; docent Sully Plantation, Fairfax County (Va.) Park Authority, 1981-87, 88—, vol. Honor Roll, 1987; sec. Widowed Persons Service, 1983-85, mem., 1985—. Mem. edn. subcom. Va. Commn. Children and Youth, 1973-74; Den mother Nat. Capital Area Cub Scouts, Boy Scouts Am., 1962; troop fund raising chmn. Nat. Capitol council Girl Scouts U.S.A., 1968-69; capt. amblyopia team No. Va. chpt. Delta Gamma Alumnae, 1969; vol. Prevention of Blindness, 1980—; fund raiser Martha Movement, 1977-78; mem. St. John's Mus. Art, Wilmington, N.C., 1989—, Corcoran Gallery Art, Washington, 1989—, Brunswick County Literacy Coun., N.C., 1989—. Recipient award Nat. Assn. for Retarded Citizens, 1975, Sully Recognition gift, 1989. Mem. AAUW (co-chmn. met. area mass media com. D.C. chpt. 1973-75, v.p. Alexandria br. 1974-76, fellowship co-chmn. Springfield-Annandale br. 1979-80, name grantee ednl. found. 1980, historian 1980-82, 88-90, cultural co-chmn. 1983-84), Assn. Part-Time Profls. (co-chmn. Va. local groups, job devel. and membership asst. 1981), Older Women's League, Nat. Trust for Historic Preservation, Nat. Mus. of Women in the Arts (charter mem.), Smithsonian Resident Assoc. Program, Delta Gamma (treas. No. Va. alumnae chpt. 1973-75, pres. 1977-79, found. chmn. 1979-81, Katie Hale award 1989). Roman Catholic. Club: Mil. Dist. of Washington Officer's Clubs (Ft. McNair, Ft. Myer). Home: 7129 Rolling Forest Ave Springfield VA 22152

LEAVITT, VIRGINIA CRAWFORD, nurse; b. Tallahassee, Dec. 21, 1948; d. Albert Lawrence and Patricia Ruby (Weeks) Crawford; m. John Joseph Leavitt. A in Nursing, Miami (Fla.) Dade Community Coll., 1975; BS in Nursing, U. Fla., 1982, MS in Nursing, 1984. Staff nurse Hosp. Corp. Am., North Miami Beach, 1975-76, head nurse intensive care unit, 1976-78; nurse hemodialysis North Fla. Kidney Ctr., Gainesville, 1979-80; staff nurse VA Med. Ctr., Gainesville, 1978-79, nurse hemodialysis, 1981-83, coord. Inpatient Monitoring program, 1984-85, head nurse, 1985-88; clin. nurse specialist VA Outpatient Clinic, Kauai, Hawaii, 1988-90; nursing care coord. VA Med. Ctr., Tampa, Fla., 1990—. Bd. dirs. Alachua County Commn., Gainesville, 1984; pres. Gainesville Jr. Woman's Club, 1985-86. Mem. Am. Nurses Assn. (cert.), Fla. Nurses Assn. (mem. coun., chmn. 1985-87), Hawaiian Nurses Assn., Am. Heart Assn. (bd. dirs. Kauai div.), Sigma theta Tau (co-editor newsletter), Phi Kappa Pi. Republican. Methodist. Home: 4800 S Westshore Blvd Apt 707 Tampa FL 33611 Office: VA Med Ctr Tampa FL 33611

LEBELL, JUNE, radio producer, announcer, writer; b. N.Y.C., Apr. 29, 1944; d. Irving and Harriet (Adler) LeB. Student, Mannes Coll. Music, 1961-63; Diploma in vocal music, U. Hartford, 1965. Mgr. visitor's services Lincoln Ctr., N.Y.C., 1974-76; staff announcer Sta. WQXR-AM & FM, N.Y.C., 1973—, writer, announcer, producer Today in N.Y., 1973—, writer, commentator, producer Program Notes, 1975-77, writer, commentator, producer IBM's Salute to the Arts, 1977—, programmer, announcer C.D. Preview, 1988-89; producer Kitchen Classics Sta. WQXR-AM, N.Y.C., 1989—. Mem. council N.Y. Philharmonic, N.Y.C., 1978—; pres. Alumni and Friends of LaGuardia High Sch., N.Y.C., 1982-86, v.p. fundraising, 1986-88. Recipient Angel award, 1986, 87, Gabriel award, 1987. Mem. Dutch Reformed Ch. Office: WQXR AM & FM 122 Fifth Ave New York NY 10011

LEBEY, BARBARA SYDELL, lawyer, artist; b. Newark, Feb. 28, 1939; d. Jacob and Edith Jean (Kligman) Sydell; m. Russell Julian Bent (div. 1974); m. Christian David LeBey, Jr., Feb. 3, 1975; children: Pamela, Daniel. Student, Sarah Lawrence Coll., 1955-58; BA, Montclair State Coll., 1959; JD, Emory U., 1970; studies with Roman and Constantine Chatov, 1979-80. Bar: Ga. 1970. Staff lawyer Atlanta Legal Aid Soc., 1970-71; assoc. Arnall, Golden & Gregory, Atlanta, 1971-74; adminstrv. law judge Ga. Bd. Worker's Compensation, Atlanta, 1974—; appointed vice chmn. Ga. Personnel Bd., 1971-74; artist contemporary impressionist paintings. One-man and group shows include The Swan Coach House Art Gallery, The Atlanta Art Gallery, Cen. Pl. Galleries, The Lowe Gallery, The Lagerquist Gallery, The Shirley Fox Gallery, The Little Acorn Gallery, Gallery 300 at Galleria Arts and Cultural Ctr., Decorators Showhouse Art Gallery, Leon Loard Gallery of Fine Arts; represented in permanent collections The Carter Presdl. Ctr. (pvt. collection of Pres. and Mrs. Jimmy Carter), The Princeton U. Art Mus., The Hunter Mus., The Albany Mus., The Robert P. Coggins Collection, The Vanderbilt Collection, Mr. and Mrs. Pat Conroy Collection, Mrs. Anne Rivers Siddons Collection, Mrs. Walter B. Ford Collection, 1989, The Hunter Mus., 1989, Chattanooga, Tenn., 1989, The Albany (Ga.) Mus., 1989; featured in Southern Homes Gardens of Painted Delights, 1987, Impressionism for the Eighties, 1988, The Virginian, 1988, Veranda Mag., 1987. Appointed artist Atlanta/Buckhead Sesquicentennary, 1988. Recipient Award for Dogwood Art Competition, 1986. Mem. Ga. State Bar Assn. Republican. Home: 3065 E Pine Valley Rd NW Atlanta GA 30305 Office: Ga Bd Workers Compensation 1000 S Tower CNN Bldg Atlanta GA 30335

LEBLANC, LILLIAN MARY, credit representative; b. Framingham, Mass., Nov. 20, 1959; d. Roland M. and Louise C. (Fitzgerald) LeB. Student, Worcester (Mass.) State Coll., Fitchburg (Mass.) State Coll. Credit rep. Southworth Machinery Inc., Milford, Mass.; asst. controller H. Hill and Sons, Inc., Milford. Mem. Assn. for Women.

LEBO, MARIE, mortgage broker; b. Newark, Jan. 22, 1941; d. Frank Joseph and Anna (Ferrara) Vumbaca; lic. in real estate Profl. Sch. Bus., Union, N.J., 1973; student NYU, 1973-74; m. Richard Lebo, Apr. 4, 1959; children—Corey Allen, Linda Marie. Sec. to pres. J.I. Kislak Mortgage Co., Newark, 1962-72, mortgage loan originator sales dept., 1973-77, asst. v.p., 1977-81; owner, sr. v.p. Mortgage Brokerage Services Co., East Orange, N.J., 1981-82; v.p. Supreme Fin. Services, Inc., Somerville, N.J., 1982-84, J.I. Kislak Mortgage Corp., 1984-85, 87—, exec. v.p. Premier Fin. Group, 1985-86; sr. v.p. GAF Fin., 1986—, v.p. J.I. Kislak Co., 1987-89. Mem. Nat. Assn. Female Execs., Am. Soc. Profl. and Exec. Women, Nat. Assn. Rev. Appraisers and Mortgage Underwriters. Office: 1000 Rte 9 Woodbridge NJ 07095

LEBOVITZ, MARCY, financial manager, accountant; b. Wilmington, Del., May 20, 1955; d. Benedict and Myra (Cutler) L. BA in Polit. Sci., Ind. U., 1976; postgrad., U. Pa., 1977-78; MBA in Acctg., Temple U., 1982. CPA, Del. Acct., cons. Lebovitz & Assocs., Wilmington, 1974—; various positions Chase Manhattan Bank, N.A., Wilmington, 1982-86; asst. treas., fin. analyst Chase Manhattan Bank, N.A., N.Y.C., 1986; asst. v.p., internal cons. First Fidelity Bancorp, Newark, 1986-90; asst. treas. Joyce Internat., N.Y.C., 1990—; treas. Hamilton Pk. Condominiums, Inc., Jersey City, 1988—. Fin. advisor, gen. vol. Theater by the Blind, N.Y.C., 1987—; vol. Operation Happy Child, Jaycees, N.Y.C., 1989. Mem. AICPA, Del. State Soc. CPAs, N.Y. State Soc CPAs. Home: 264 Ninth St #3J Jersey City NJ 07302

LEBOWITZ, CATHARINE KOCH, state legislator; b. Winchester, Mass., June 30, 1915; d. William John and Carolyn Sophia (Kistinger) Koch; m. Murray Lebowitz, Sept. 21, 1971 (dec. Oct. 1978). Student Northeastern U., 1948-49, Boston Coll., 1949-52. Sec. ERA, Bangor, Augusta, Maine, 1935-38, WPA, Portland, Maine, 1938-42; personnel officer, exec. sec. USN, Portland, 1942-47; exec. sec. Clark Babbitt, Boston, 1947-48; adminstrv. asst. Moore Bus. Forms, Boston, 1948-52; apt. mgr., wholesale appliance div. Coffin-Wimple Inc., 1952-62; sec. Portland Credit Bur., 1980-86; mem. Bangor City Council, 1985-87; mem. Maine State Legislature, 1982—; bd. dirs. Eastern Transportation, 1989—. Sec. Symphony Women, Bangor, 1964-84; bd. dirs. Opera House Com., Bangor, 1978; mem. Bangor C. of C. Consumer Rels. Coun., 1981-90, coord. 150th Anniversary Prodn. Music Man, 1984; del. Rep. Nat. Conv., 1984, 88; mem. Spl. Task Force to Study Child Abuse, 1985—; legis. com. United Way, 1988—; adv. com. Maine Devel. Found., 1984—; adv. bd. Aftercare, 1990, St. Joseph Hosp. Planning bd., 1987—, Bangar City Hosp. Aux., 1988—; bd. dirs. Penobscot Theater, 1990; accredited Beauty Pageant judge, 1986—. Recipient Civilian Meritorious Service award USN, Portland Maine, 1946; named Hon. Alumnus Secretarial Sci., Husson Coll., 1980. Mem. Credit Women Internat. (treas. 1975-77, Credit Woman of Yr. 1969), Credit Profls., Bangor Community Theater (treas. 1973—, award 1973), U. Maine Maine Masque Theater (judge 1983—), Maine N.G. Assn. (hon.), Maine Air N.G. (hon.), Credit Women Bangor (sec. 1965-67), Bangor Dist. Nursing Assn. (corp. mem. at large), Bangor Hist. Soc., Penobscot County Republicans, Penobscot County Rep. Women's Club (sec. 1979), Newcomb Soc., Zonta Club (pres. Bangor 1962-64, 80-82), Mgmt. Club. Office: State Ho Reps Augusta ME 04330

LEBSACK, PHYLLIS JEAN, county clerk; b. McCook, Nebr., July 22, 1921; d. George and Katherine Elizabeth (Kechter) Gettman; m. Samuel Lebsack, Aug. 8, 1942 (dec. Mar. 1981); children: Julie Ann, Christy Jean, Todd Douglas. Ct. clk. Red Willow County Ct., McCook, 1944-45, 1947-48, dep. county clk., 1970-77, county clk., 1977—; clk. City of McCook, 1948-50; sec. Red Willow County Health Bd., 1977-88, Red Willow County Health Bd., 1977—; county registrar Bur. Vital Statistics, Red Willow County, 1977-85; bd. dir. Election Registration Bd., McCook, 1952-67; vice chmn. clerks West Cen. Dist., Nebr., 1984-85, chmn., 1986-87, sec., 1990—. Democrat. Avocations: crafts, bridge, golf. Home: 911 E 3d St McCook NE 69001 Office: Ct House Norris Ave McCook NE 69001

LECKER, LISA JOY, management consultant; b. Chgo., Nov. 16, 1958; d. Abraham and Minnie (Kamenetzky) L. BS in BA, Washington U., St. Louis, 1980; MBA, U. Chgo., 1984. With Arthur Andersen & Co., Chgo., 1980-82; project mgr. Am. Mgmt. Sys., Inc., Arlington, Va., 1984—. Mem./vol. Arthritis Found., Arlington, 1987—; advisor/vol. B'nai B'rith Youth Orgn., Rockville, Md., 1985-89. Mem. U. Chgo. Bus. Sch. Club of Washington (pres. 1987-88), U. Chgo. Women's Bus. Group (sec.-treas. 1985—). Democrat. Jewish. Office: Am Mgmt Systems Inc 1777 N Kent St Arlington VA 22209

LECKIE, CAROL MAVIS, state government administrator; b. Watertown, Wis., Feb. 25, 1929; d. Arthur Walter Bessel and Effie Vada (Squires) Downs; m. Ralph Junior Judd, Sept. 27, 1947 (div. Dec. 1952); children: Russell Howard, Barbara Rae; m. Leonard John Leckie, Sept. 30, 1977; stepchildren: Leonard John, Gordon Armstrong, Lorna Jean. Grad. high sch. Madison, Wis. Mgr. data processing Dept. Justice, State of Wis., Madison, 1971-79, mgr. Records Mgmt. Program, 1979-83, mgr. Typography Sect., 1983—. Mem. com. State of Wis. Employees Combined Campaign, Madison, 1986, 88, 89, co-chair, 1987. Mem. Assn. Records Mgrs. and Adminstrs. (pres. 1983-84), Nat. Assn. Female Execs., Bus. Forms Mgmt. Assn., Internat. Assn. Printing House Craftsmen. Lutheran. Avocations: travel, aerobics. Home: 810 Ziegler Rd Madison WI 53714 Office: State of Wis 1 W Wilson St Suite B-355 Madison WI 53702

LECKIE, SHIRLEY ANNE, historian, educator; b. Claremont, N.H., June 15, 1937; d. Edward James Howard and Hazel Enola (Rahlston) Casillo; m. William H. BA in History, U. Mo., 1967, MA in History, 1969; PhD in history, U. Toledo, 1981. Grad. asst. Univ. Toledo, Ohio, 1969-72; adviser Univ Toledo, 1972-73; dir. adult liberal studies Univ. Toledo, 1973-80; asst. dean, cont. edn. Univ. Toledo, Jackson, Miss., 1980-81; assoc. dean, continued edn. Millsaps Coll., Jackson, Miss., 1981-82; dir. continued edn. Univ. N. C., Ashville, 1983-85; asst. prof. history Univ. Cen. Fla., Orland, 1985-88; assoc. prof. history Univ. Cen. Fla., Orlando, 1988--; co-chmn. adv. council, Ctr. Women, Toledo, 1977-78. Co-author: Unlikely Warriors, 1984; author, Colonel's Lady On The Western Frontier, 1989. Mem. state bd. Ohio Program in Humanities, 1977-80, Alumnae Leadership Ashville, 1984-85; recording sec. Orlando Met. Women's Polit. Caucus, 1989. Mem. AAUW, Orgn. Am. History, So. Hist. Assn. Democrat. Office: Univ Cen Fla University Ave Orlando FL 32817

LECKY, RENEE JEANNE, corporate executive; b. Tacoma, Apr. 24, 1927; d. Francis J. and Genevieve (Hewitt) Payette; m. James Burpee, Mar. 13, 1947 (dec. 1950); children: James, Victoria; m. Orville D. Hansey (div. 1987); children; Dan, Terri, John, Bill; m. Ralph Edward Lecky Sr., June 26, 1989; stepchildren: Ralph Edward Jr., Brent. Student in Layout and Design, Art Inst. Chgo., 1943; BS in Psychology, St. John's U., 1988; postgrad. in Graphics, U. Alaska, 1985. Copy writer Sta. KIT, Yakima, Wash., 1942-44; program mgr. Sta. KING, Seattle, 1945-47; advt. mgr. Sequim (Wash.) Press, 1967-70, editor, 1970-76; TV producer Municipality of Anchorage, 1976-86; pub. Voice, Port Angeles, Wash., 1986-89; cons. on media rels. and sr. citizens; founder Widowed Persons Svc., Anchorage, 1983-85; owner Frontier Pub., Anchorage, 1983-85; dir. Far North Network, Anchorage, 1982-86. Author: Go to the Source, 1977, One Way to the Funny Farm, 1978; producer (TV show) Opportunities for Seniors, 1981-86 (TV Prodn. award, 1982-85). Sec. Dem. Cen. Com. Clallam County, Wash., 1965-76; founder Olympic Women's Resource Ctr., Port Angeles, 1966-75; councilwoman City Sequim, 1973-76; active Affirmative Action Clallam County, Wash., 1974, Sr. Companions, Elder Abuse Task Force; bd. dirs. Port Angeles Sr. Ctr. With WAC, 1944. Mem. Alaska Press Women (pres. 1981-82, 85-86), Nat. Fedn. Press Women, Alaska Press Club. Roman Catholic. Home: 15206 Emory Ct Bowie MD 20716

LE COUNT, VIRGINIA G., communications company executive; b. Long Island City, N.Y., Nov. 22, 1917; d. Clifford R. and Luella (Meier) LeCount. BA, Barnard Coll., 1937; MA, Columbia U., 1940. Tchr. pub. schs. P.R., 1937-38; supr. HOLC, N.Y.C., 1938-40; translator Guildhall Publs., N.Y.C., 1940-41; office mgr. Sperry Gyroscope Co., Garden City, Lake Success, Bklyn. (all N.Y.), 1941-45; billing mgr. McCann Erickson, Inc., N.Y.C., 1945-56; v.p., bus. mgr., bd. dirs. Infoplan Internat, Inc., N.Y.C., 1956-69; v.p., bus. mgr. Communications Affiliates Ltd., Communications Affiliates (Bahamas) Ltd., N.Y.C., 1968-71; bus. mgr. Jack Tinker & Ptnrs., Inc., N.Y.C., 1969-70; mgr. office services Interpublic Group of Cos., Inc., N.Y.C., 1969-70, corp. records mgr., 1972-83, mktg. intelligence data mgr., 1978-83. Mem. Alumnae Barnard Coll. Mem. Marble Collegiate Ch. Club: Atrium. Home: 136 E 55th St Apt 10Q New York NY 10022

LECUYER, ELLEN DELPHINE, publishing company junior executive; b. Montreal, Que., Can., May 10, 1956; d. Lucien and Doris (Daly) L.; m. Michael S.L. Levesque, Dec. 30, 1983. B in Commerce, Concordia U., Montreal, 1977. Research analyst Reader's Digest, Montreal, 1977-79, asst. mgr. mktg. research, 1979-81, mgr. mktg. research, 1981-87, asst. product mgr., 1987—, mgr. spl. books div., 1987-88, mgr. list acquistion, new subscriber mailings mag. div., 1988—. Mem. Am. Mktg. Assn., Canadian Direct Mktg. Assn., Profl. Market Research Soc. Avocations: cross country skiing, curling. Home: 4554 Royal Ave, Montreal, PQ Canada H4A 2M8 Office: Reader's Digest Assn Can, 215 Redfern Ave, Westmount, PQ Canada H3Z 2V9

LECUYER-COONS, GEORGEIDA CELENE, nurse, small business owner; b. Clifton, Kans., Jan. 4, 1926; d. George and Ida Marie (Savoie) L.; m. Roger James Freeman (div. 1971); children: George W., Kathryn A., Margaret J., John M.; m. Merlyn D. (Tony) Coons (dec. 1985). BA, Park Coll., Parkville, Mo., 1980; RN, Avila Coll., Kansas City, Mo., 1948. RN, Kans. Med.-surg. staff nurse Research Hosp., Kansas City, Mo., 1966-67; anesthetist Oral Surgeons, Inc., Kansas City, 1967-70; instr. practical nursing Kansas City Bd. Edn., Mo., 1972-75; oncology staff nurse U. Kans. Med. Ctr., Kansas City, Kans., 1975-78; mental health staff nurse VA Hosp., Leavenworth, Kans., 1978-82; gerontology staff nurse VA Hosp., Topeka, 1982-85; ret. VA Hosp., 1985; owner Baby Boomer Hdqrs. of Kans., Salina, 1986—; ednl. cons. VA Hosp. In-Service dept., Topeka. 1982-85; conductor workshops on behaviors, team concept, alcoholism and ageism. Local leader Boy Scouts Am., Girl Scouts U.S., Kansas City, Mo., 1962-66. Served with U.S. Cadet Nursing Corps, 1944-47. Recipient Excellent Bedside Caregiver award U. Kans. Med. Ctr., 1977, Spl. Advancement award VA, 1982. Mem. Nat. Assn. Ret. Fed. Employees, Am. Assn. Ret. Persons. Republican. Roman Catholic. Club: Salina (Kans.) Christian Women's. Office: Baby Boomer Hdqrs of Kans PO Box 1454 Salina KS 67402-1454

LECZYNSKI, BARBARA ANN, statistician, consultant; b. Lowell, Mass., Aug. 27, 1954; d. Walter A. and Stella M. (Glod) L. BS in Math., U. Lowell, Mass., 1976; MS in Stats., U. Conn., 1978. Math. statistician Bur. Labor Stats., Washington, 1978-80; applied mathematician Eastman Kodak Co., Rochester, N.Y., 1980-84; project mgr. Battelle Meml. Inst., Washington, 1984-89; sr. statistician Washington Cons. Group, Washington, 1989-90; sr. cons. David C. Cox and Assocs., Washington, 1990—. Co-author: International Agency for Research on Cancer: Monograph on Hexachlorobenzene. Mem. Am. Statis. Assn., Am. Soc. Quality Control. Home: 8497 Lazy Creek Ct Springfield VA 22153 Office: David C Cox and Assocs 1620 22d St NW Washington DC 20008

LEDBETTER, SHARON FAYE WELCH, state education compliance monitor; b. L.A., Jan. 14, 1941; d. James Herbert and Verdie V. (Mattox) Welch; m. Robert A. Ledbetter, Feb. 15, 1964; children: Kimberly Ann, Scott Allen. BA, U. Tex.-Austin, 1963; learning disabilities cert. Southwestern U., Tex., 1974; MEd, Southwest Tex. State U., 1979, prin. cert., 1980, supt. cert., 1984. Speech pathologist Midland Ind. Sch. Dist., Tex., 1963, Austin Ind. Sch. Dist., Tex., 1964-72; speech pathologist, asst. prin. Round Rock Ind. Sch. Dist., Tex., 1972-84; prin. Hutto Ind. Sch. Dist., 1984-88; compliance monitoring of sch. dists. Tex. Edn. Agy., 1989—. Pres. Berkman PTA, 1983-84; sponsor Jr. Woman's Club, 1980-82; mistress ceremonies Hutto Beauty Pageant, 1986, 87. Recipient Appreciation award Round Rock Sch. Dist., 1984, St. Judes Children's Research Hosp., 1985, Soc. Disting. Am. High Sch. Students, 1985, 2000 Notable Women, 1988. Mem. Adminstrv. Women in Edn., Nat. Assn. Female Execs., Tex. Assn. Community Schs., Gen. Fedn. Women's Club, Tex. Fedn. Women's Clubs (com. chair), Round Rock Women's Club (pres.), Hutto C. of C., Phi Delta Kappa, Delta Kappa Gamma. Avocations: horses, spectator sports. Home: 1429 Windcrest Dr Round Rock TX 78664

LEDBETTER-STRAIGHT, NORA KATHLEEN, insurance company executive; b. Gary, Ind., May 11, 1934; d. Jacob F. and Nora I. (Bollen) Moser; student U. Houston, 1954-58; m. Robert L. Straight, Aug. 9, 1975; 1 dau., Cindy Kathleen Ledbetter Baurax. V.p. Hindman Mortgage Co., Inc., Houston, 1960-70, also mng. partner Assocs. Ins. Agy.; corp. sec. N.Am. Mortgage Co., Houston, 1970—; mng. partner N.Am. Ins. Agy., 1970—, now also pres. and mng. officer; ins. counselor Houston Apt. Assn., 1978—, dir. product service council, 1981—; mem. adv. bd. for continuing edn., State Bd. Ins.; v.p., sec. Better Bodies of Tex., Inc. CPCU; cert. Ins. Inst. Am., Soc. Cert. Ins. Counselors. Mem. Ind. Ins. Agts. Am., Soc. Cert. Ins. Counselors, Soc. C.P.C.U.s, Community Assos. Inst. (dir. 1976-80), Ind. Ins. Agts. Tex., S.W. Assn. Affiliated Agts (v.p., bd. dirs.), Tex. Assn. Affiliated Agts. (v.p., bd. dirs.), Ind. Ins. Agts. Houston (dir. 1974-78). Republican. Methodist. Author curriculum materials in field. Office: 14825 St Mary's Ln Houston TX 77079

LEDBURY, DIANA GRETCHEN, educator; b. Denver, Mar. 7, 1931; d. Francis Kenneth and Gretchen (Harry) Van Ausdall; m. Chander Parkash Lall, Dec. 26, 1953 (div. Aug. 1973); children—Anne, Neil, Kris; m. Eugene Augustus Ledbury, Sept. 13, 1976; stepchildren—Mark, Cindy, Rob. B.A. in Sociology, Colo. U., 1953. Instr. Home, and family life Community Coll., Seattle, 1957-71; asst. tchr. Renton Sch. Dist., Wash., 1974-83; adult edn. tchr. Mental Health Network, Renton, 1984—; coordinator Inter-Study, Renton, 1985—, program dir. Crossroads Child Care, 1985-86, family services coordinator , 1986-87, program supr. Candyland Too Child Care Ctr., 1987—. Mem. Renton Area Youth Services Bd., Sch. and Community Drug Prevention Program, Renton dist. council PTA, Renton Citizen's Com. on Recreation; vol. Griffin Home for Boys; coordinator Modern Dance Prodn., Carco Theater; adult leader Camp Fire Girls' Horizon Club; mem. bd. Allied Arts of Renton; mem. Bicentennial Com. for a Cultural Arts, Edn. and Recreation Ctr.; PTA rep. Dimmit Jr. High Sch.; mem. Sch. and Community Recreation Com.; founder Handicapped Helping Themselves, Mental Health Network; precinct committeeperson 11th dist. Republican party, Wash., 1976-85. Recipient Golden Acorn award Wash. State Congress PTA, Renton, 1972. Mem. Assn. Social and Health Services (mem. com. 1984-85), AAUW (legis. chair 1983-87). Episcopalian. Club: Campfire Horizon (leader). Avocations: arts; culture; recreation; child and family advocate.

LEDDY, SUSAN, nursing school dean; b. N.J., Feb. 23, 1939; d. Bart B. and Helen (Neumann) Kun; children: Deborah, Erin. BS, Skidmore Coll., 1960; MS, Boston U., 1965; PhD, NYU, 1973; cert., Harvard U., 1985.

Chair dept. nursing Mercy Coll., Debbs Ferry, N.Y.; dean sch. nursing U. Wyo., Laramie, dean coll. health scis.; dean sch. nursing Widener U., Chester, Pa., 1988—. Co-author: (with M. Pepper) Conceptual Bases of Professional Nursing, 1985, 2d edit., 1989. Mem. NLN (bd. dirs. and 1st v.p. 1985-87).

LEDERBERG, EDITH SCHAFFER, social services administrator; b. Mineola, N.Y., Oct. 26, 1929; d. Peter and Fanny (Kramer) Schaffer; m. Jack D. Lederberg, Nov. 10, 1950 (div. Nov. 1978); m. Carol Susan Cooperman, Peter, Joel. Student, U. Vt., 1947-49; BA in Spanish, Hofstra U., 1951, MS in Edn., 1956. Cert. elem. tchr., N.Y. Tchr. Freeport Sch. System, L.I., N.Y., 1951-52, Lindenhurst/Freeport Pub. Sch. System, L.I., 1955-61; tchr. Wantagh Union Free Sch. Dist., L.I., 1973-75, with pub. relations dept., 1975-77; community coordinator Area Agy. on Aging of Broward County, Ft. Lauderdale, Fla., 1977-86, exec. dir., 1986—; participant Gov.'s Conf. on Aging, 1980; media rep. White Ho. Conf. on Aging, 1981; conf. presenter Am. Soc. on Aging, 1988. Contbr. articles on aging to local publs., 1980—; contbr. poetry to Blue Mountain Arts, 1980—. Mem. Outreach com. Broward Aging Network, Broward Alzheimer Coordinating Coun., 1987—, Broward County Leadership-The GROUP, 1986—, Broward Coun. Exec. Dirs., 1986—; mem. Broward County Sch. Bd. Facilities Task Force; pres. Wantagh Sch. PTA, 1972-73; chmn. music com. Wantagh High Sch., 1969-72; chairperson pub. relations Wantagh Youth Coun., 1968-72; mem. adv. com. Foster Grandparents, Ft. Lauderdale, 1986—, Ctr. on Aging and Devel. Disabilities, Nova Gerontology Program. Recipient Award of Merit, Sr. Found. N.W. Broward, 1986, Disting. Community Svc. award Alzheimer Assn. of Broward, 1988; named Citizen of Yr., Broward chpt. Nat. Assn. Social Workers, 1981, Citizen of Day, Sta. WJOY-FM, 1981. Mem. Nat. Assn. Area Agys. on Aging (presenter ann. conf. 1988), Fla. Coun. on Aging (presenter ann. conf. 1988), Fla. Assn. Social Svcs., Fla. Assn. Area Agys. on Aging (v.p. 1989), Women in Communications, B'nai Brith Women, Kappa Delta Pi, Sigma Delta Pi. Democrat. Jewish. Home: 2870 NW 55th Ave Apt 2-D Lauderhill FL 33313 Office: Area Agy on Aging 5345 NW 35th Ave Fort Lauderdale FL 33309

LEDERBERG, VICTORIA, state legislator, lawyer, psychology educator; b. Providence, July 7, 1937; d. Frank and Victoria (Marzilli) Santopietro; m. Seymour Lederberg, 1959; children: Tobias, Sarah. AB, Pembroke Coll., 1959; AM, Brown U., 1961, PhD, 1966; JD, Suffolk U., 1976. Mem. R.I. Ho. of Reps., 1975-82, chmn. subcom. on edn., fin. com., 1975-82, subcom. on mental health, retardation and hosps. and health, spl. legis. commns pub. sch. funding and funding handicapped edn. programs; mem. Dem. Nat. Exec. Com.; mem. R.I. State Senate, 1985—, chmn. fin. com. subcom. on social svcs., 1985-89, dep. majority leader, 1989—; prof. psychology R.I. Coll., 1978—; pvt. practice, Providence. USPHS fellow physiol. psychology, 1964-66. Mem. New Eng. Bd. Higher Edn.; trustee Brown U., 1983-89, Roger Williams Coll., 1980—, Butler Hosp., 1985—, also sec. of corp. Mem. New Eng. Psychol. Assn., R.I. Psychol. Assn., Women Educators, New Eng. Edn. Rsch. Orgn., ABA, R.I. Bar Assn., Sigma Xi. Office: 190 Slater Ave Providence RI 02906

LEDERER, LUCY KEMMERER, retired artist; b. Milton, Pa., Oct. 8, 1892; d. William Benjamin and Katherine Elizabeth (Krumrine) Kemmerer; m. Eugene Herman Lederer, June 29, 1918 (dec. Oct. 1960); 1 child, Eugene William. Student, Pratt Inst., 1912; student, Simmons Coll., 1913; BA, Pa. State U., 1914; postgrad., Arts Students League, N.Y.C., 1943-45. Tchr. Bellefonte (Pa.) Sch. System, 1914-15; tchr. Lower Merion Sch. Dist., Wayne, Pa., 1916-18; artist State College, Pa., 1930—; real estate developer, State College, 1920-88. Mem. AAUW, Arts Students League N.Y. (life), DAR, Daus. Am. Colonists, Am. Legion Aux. Lutheran. Home: 1236 Penfield Rd State College PA 16801

LEDERMAN, CINDY SHELLENBERGER, judge, lawyer; b. Phila., Mar. 2, 1954; d. Donald Lee and Dolores Marie (Patton) Shellenberger; m. Robert Elliot Lederman, July 3, 1976. BA, U. Fla., 1976; JD, U. Miami, Fla., 1979. Bar: Fla., 1979, N.Y., 1986. Assoc. Mitchell L. Perlstein P.A., Miami, Fla., 1979-81, Brown, Huysman, Matthews & Singer, Miami, 1981-82; asst. city atty. North Miami Beach, Fla., 1982-84, dep. city atty., 1984-89; judge Dade County, Coral Gables, Fla., 1989—. Vice chmn. Dade County Commn. on Status of Women, 1987—; mem. Coalition Hispanic Am. Women, 1987—, Forum of North Dade, Fla. Supreme Ct. Racial and Ethic Bias Study Commn., 1989; chmn. Mediation Pilot Project Com., 1987-88; bd. dirs. Mental Health Assn. Dade County Inc., 1989. Named Outstanding Women of Yr. North Dade C. of C., 1988. Mem. ABA, Fla. Bar Assn. (vice chmn. govt. lawyer com. 1987—, chmn. grievance com. 1988), Acad. Fla. Trial Lawyers, Dade County Bar Assn. (bd. dirs. 1987—), Fla. Assn. for Women Lawyers (pres. 1986-87, pres.'s award 1986), Fla. Council of Bar Assn. Presidents, AAUW. Office: Dade County Courthouse 2801 Salzedo St Coral Gables FL 33134

LEDERMAN, FLORENCE, teacher; b. Toronto, Ontario, Canada, Sept. 11, 1932; Came to USA 1933.; d. Sam and Rose (Portnoy) Krinsky; m. Leonard L. Lederman, Nov. 23, 1931; children: Hugh Daniel, Steven Mark, Michael J. BSED (with hons.), U. Md., 1974; MS, Mont. City Pub. Sch., 1982. Tchr. Mont County Pub. Sch., Bethesda, Md., 1975--. Mem. Natl. Educ. Assn., Md. State Tchr. Assn., Montgomery County Edn., Council for Exceptional Children. Office: Montgomery County Pub Sch 850 Hungerford Dr Rockville MD 20853

LEDET, GRACE DOMINQUE, director; b. Lafayette, La., Sept. 17, 1943; d. Phillip and Hortense (Guillot) Dominique; m. Sheldon M. Ledet; children: Dawn Angel, Freddie Paul II, Phillip Keenan. Student Arts & Life Scis., U. South La., Lafayette, La., 1961-63, Nichols U., 1975—; student acctg., Young Mem. Vocat. Tech. Sch., Morgan City, La., 1976-77; student grant writing, Grantsmanship Ctr., Washington, 1987. Office mgr. Sheldon's Hair Studio, Morgan City, La., 1975-80; social svc. dir. Holy Cross Parish; dir., 1st adminstr. St. Mary Outreach, Morgan City, La., 1986—; cons. Emergency Aid, Franklin, La., 1987, Ministerial Alliance, Houston. Mo., 1989. Mem. Catechist, Morgan City, La., 1986, Adult Children of Alcohol, Morgan City, 1989, Acadiana Coalition for the Homeless, 1988-89, Mayoral Coun. Hire the Handicapped, 1989, United Way Community Assessment; organizer 3 polit. campaigns, Morgan City, 1970-74. Named Humanitarian Morgan City-Berwick Bus. & Profl. Women's Club, 1977. Mem. Am. Bus. Women Am., Am. Assn. Retired Persons. Home: 2312 Elm St Mogan City LA 70380 Office: St Mary Outreach Inc 1012 Seventh St Morgan City LA 70380

LEDFORD, TONI DANDRIDGE, computer scientist; b. New Orleans, La., Oct. 10, 1942; d. Willie Walter Dandridge Jr. and Odeal Johnson; m. Gerald Al Theriot, May 10, 1970 (div. Oct. 1973); m. Robert Howard Ledford, Feb. 1977 (div. Mar. 1978); 1 child, Anjanette Nicole Theriot. BS magna cum laude, So. U., New Orleans, 1964; MS in Computer Sci., W. Coast U., Los Angeles, 1981. Assoc. sci. Lockheed Missiles & Space Co., Palo Alto, 1965-67; Assoc. engr. The Boeing Co., New Orleans, 1967-70; computer programmer Naval Aerospace Med. R.L., New Orleans, 1973; programmer 3M Co., St. Paul, 1973-75; EDP analyst/programmer Ingalls Shipbuilding, Pascagoula, Ms., 1975-76; sr. programmer/analyst System Devel. Corp., 1976-81; asst. professor So. U., New Orleans, 1982-84; assoc. software engr. Norden Serv. Co., Gaithersburg, Md., 1985-86; analyst/programmer sr. Ingalls Shipbuilding, Pascagoula, Ms., 1987-89; owner/software cons. Toni Dandridge Ledford, Chula Vista, Calif., 1990—; Author: Presentation 9th Internat. Codata Conf. 1984. Recipient Zero Defects The Boeing Co. New Orleans 1968-69, Apollo/Saturn V Roll of Honor The Boeing Co. 1969. mem. Math. Assn. of Am., Assn. for Computing Machinery, IEEE Computer Soc. Democrat. Roman Catholic.

LE DUC, ELIZABETH ANN, systems engineer, consultant; b. Bronx, Nov. 22, 1963; d. Harold Joseph and Elizabeth Francis (Wosiski) Le D. BS in Nautical Sci., U.S. Merchant Marine Acad., 1985; M in Enging. Adminstrn., Va. Polytech. Inst., 1988—. Deck cadet U.S. Flag Merchant Vessels, 1983-84; intern Maritime Adminstrn., N.Y.C., 1984; asst. staff mem. Advanced Tech., Inc., Arlington, Va., 1985-87, assoc. staff mem., 1987—. Lt. USNR, 1985—. Named one of Outstanding Young Women in Am., Outstanding Young Women Am., 1985. Mem. U.S. Naval Inst., Navy League U.S., NAFE. Republican. Roman Catholic. Office: Advanced Tech Inc 2121 Crystal Dr Ste 200 Arlington VA 22202

LEE, ALEXIS ANNE, business owner, computer consultant; b. Boulder, Colo., Aug. 10, 1956; d. Robert Henry and Stella (Chuba) L. BS in Journalism, U. Colo., 1978. Computer operator Leanin' Tree Pub., Boulder, 1979, programmer, analyst, 1980-84; programmer, analyst Frontier Airlines, Denver, 1984-85; pvt. practice Denver, 1986-87; owner, cons. Alexis Lee & Assocs., San Francisco, Calif., 1988-89; pres., ptnr. Eclipse Data, Inc., Pembroke Pines, Fla., 1989—. Mem. NAFE, NASE, PETA, Greenpeace. Democrat. Roman Catholic.

LEE, ALISON ANN, education director; b. Holyoke, Mass., June 30, 1950; d. Robert Keating and Audrey Ethel (Emery) L.; student Russell Sage Coll., 1968-70; BA, Mt. Holyoke Coll., 1975; MA, Cen. Mich. U., 1985. Lab. technician Holyoke Hosp., 1969-72; research asst. U. Mass. Health Services, Amherst, 1972-73; med. technologist Wesson unit Baystate Med. Center, Springfield, Mass., 1973-78; cons. Tulsa City-County Health Dept., 1979-81, Moton Health Center, Tulsa, 1980-84; lead med. technologist St. Francis Hosp., Tulsa, 1978-86, dir. edn. Springer Clinic, 1986—; mem. adv. bd. Okla. Jr. Coll. Alumnae admissions rep. for Greater Tulsa, Mt. Holyoke Coll.; past public edn. chmn., mem. profl. edn. com., bd. dirs. Am. Cancer Soc.; mem. adv. bd. Am. Heart Assn.; vol. various community activities. Mem. Am. Soc. Clin. Pathologists, Am. Soc. Clin. Chemistry, Nat. Mgmt. Assn., Am. Soc. Med. Tech., Profl. Women Tulsa, Am. Coll. Healthcare Execs., Alumnae Assn. Mt. Holyoke. Home: 6370 H South 80 East Ave Tulsa OK 74133 Office: 6160 S Yale Tulsa OK 74136

LEE, AMY ELAINE, software company administrator; b. Knoxville, Tenn., June 7, 1960; d. Forrest Columbus and Mary Christine (Smith) L. AS, Cumberland Coll., 1979; student, U. Tenn., 1979-81. With Am. Software, Inc., Atlanta, 1982—, project mgr., 1984-87, sr. project coordinator, 1987—; cons., coord. Faberge/Elizabeth Arden Internat., Acton, Eng., 1988-89; analyst, cons. PTT Telecommunications, Hague, The Netherlands, 1987; sr. coord. Faberge, Inc., Mahwah, N.J., 1986-89; sr. project coord. Dennison Stationery Products Co., 1989-90. Mem. Nat. Assn. Female Execs., French Elephants. Republican. Mem. Ch. of Church. Office: Am Software Inc 470 E Paces Ferry Rd Atlanta GA 30305

LEE, AMY SHIU, biochemist, educator; b. Canton, Peoples Republic of China, Aug. 5, 1947; d. Chi To and Siu Yu (Wong) Shiu; m. Paul L. Lee, Jan. 15, 1972; children: May, Andrew. BA, U. Calif., Berkeley, 1970; PhD, Calif. Tech. Inst., Pasadena, 1975. Asst. prof. biochemistry sch. medicine U. So. Calif., L.A., 1980-83, assoc. prof., 1984-87, prof., 1988—; group leader gene regulation program comprehensive cancer ctr. U. So. Calif., 1987—; mem. study sects. NIH, Washington, 1981—. Mem. AAAS, Am. Soc. Biol. Chemist, Am. Soc. Microbiologists, Am. Cancer Soc. Office: U So Calif Sch Medicine 1441 Eastlake Ave Los Angeles CA 90033

LEE, ANNE NATALIE, nurse; b. Bklyn.; d. Taras Pavlovich and Maria (Jukovskaya) Dubovick; B.A., Hunter Coll., 1940; M.A., N.Y.U., 1948; R.N., McLean Hosp. Sch. Nursing, Waverly, Mass., 1946; M.S., Boston U., 1958; m. Henry Lee, Feb. 20, 1945; adopted children: Alice, Jennifer, Philip. Pvt. duty nurse, N.Y.C., 1946-48; staff nurse Vis. Nurse Service, 1947-48; staff nurse health dept. Schoharie Co., N.Y., 1948-51; supervising nurse N.Y. Dept. Health, Syracuse, 1951-53, cons. hosp. nursing, Albany, 1958-63, cons. nurse in svc. edn., 1963-75, dir. Bur. of Hosp. Nursing Svcs., 1975-80; cons. nursing svcs. and adminstrn., 1980—; dir., coord. nursing service instr. program co-sponsored N.Y. State Dept. Health, N.Y. State Hosp. Assn., N.Y. State League Nursing, N.Y. State Nurses Assn., 1954-57; sometimes lectr. Mem. Am. Nurses Assn. (cert. advanced nursing adminstrn.), Sigma Theta Tau. Contbr. articles to profl. jours. Home and Office: 1149 Hillsboro Mile Hillsboro Beach FL 33062

LEE, BETTY REDDING, architect; b. Shreveport, La., Dec. 6, 1919; d. Joseph Alsop and Mary (Byrd) Redding; student La. State U., 1936-37, 37-38, U. Calif. War Extension Coll., San Diego, 1942-43; student Centenary Coll., 1937; grad. Roofing Industry Ednl. Inst., 1980, 81, 82, 84, 86, 87, 88; m. Frank Cayce Lee, Nov. 22, 1940 (dec. Aug. 1978); children: Cayce Redding, Clifton Monroe, Mary Byrd (Mrs. Kent Ray). Sheetmetal worker Consol.-Vultee, San Diego, 1942; engrng. draftsman, 1943-45; jr. to sr. archtl. draftsman Bodman & Murrell, Baton Rouge, 1945-55; sr. archtl. draftsman to architect Post & Harelson, Baton Rouge, 1955-58; asso. architect G. Ross Murrell, Jr., Baton Rouge, 1960-66; staff architect Charles E. Schwing & Assos., Baton Rouge, 1966-71, Kenneth C. Landry, Baton Rouge, 1971, 73-74; design draftsman Rayner & McKenzie, Baton Rouge, 1972-73; cons. architect and planner, div. engrng. and cons. svcs., La. Dept. Health and Human Resources, Baton Rouge, 1974-82; architect La. Dept. Facility Planning and Control, 1982—. Author Instructions to Designers for Roofing Systems for Louisiana Public Buildings; co-author: Building Owners Guide for Protecting and Maintaining Built-Up Roofing Systems, 1981; designed typical La. country store for La. Arts and Sci. Ctr. Mus. Recipient Honor award Manville Group, 1989, 90, Better Understanding Roofing Systems Inst., 1980, 84, 89. Mem. La. Assn. Children with Learning Disabilities, 1970-71, Multiple Sclerosis Soc., 1963-82, CPA Aux., 1960-69, PTA, 1953-66; troop leader Brownies and Girl Scouts U.S.A., 1959-60; asst. den mother Cub Scouts, 1955-57. Licensed architect, Mem. ASTM, AIA (first women mem. Baton Rouge chpt.), La. Architects Assn., Nat. Fire Protection Assn., Constrn. Specifications Inst. (charter mem. Baton Rouge chpt.), Miss. Roofing Contractors Assn. (first woman hon.), Nat. Roofing Contractors Assn., So. Bldg. Code Congress Internat., La. Inst. Bldg. Scis. (founding mem. 1980), Architect and Engrng. Performance Info. Ctr., Jr. League Baton Rouge. Baton Rouge Caledonian Soc., DAR, Kappa Delta. Democrat. Episcopalian. Clubs: Fais Do Do, Le Salon du Livre. Home: 1994 Longwood Dr Baton Rouge LA 70808 Office: Capitol Sta Box 94095 Baton Rouge LA 70804-9095

LEE, BEVERLY ING, educational administrator; b. Honolulu, Oct. 10, 1932; d. Tim Sheu and Helen (Heu) Ing; m. Daniel David Lee, June 21, 1962; children: Helen Ann, Terence Daniel, Scott David. BA, Coll. of the Pacific, Stockton, Calif., 1954; MA, Columbia U., 1957. Officer Honolulu Police Dept., 1957-61; adminstr. Dept. Edn. State of Hawaii, Honolulu, 1961-88; contr., v.p. Classic Travel, Honolulu, 1988—; bd. dirs. Hawaii State Employee's Credit Union, Honolulu, 1986—, John Howard Assn., Honolulu, 1985—. Mem. Gov.'s Commn. on Child Abuse, Honolulu, 1985-89; bd. dirs. Hawaii Family Stress Ctr., Honolulu, 1975-89, Nat. Com. on Child Abuse, Honolulu, 1983—; mem. Casey Family Program Advisory Com. Mem. AAUW (life), Delta Kappa Gamma, Tri Delta. Office: Classic Travel 1413 S King St Ste 201 Honolulu HI 96814

LEE, BOK SIN See POWELL, JOY LEE

LEE, BRENDA (BRENDA MAE TARPLEY), singer, entertainer; b. Lithonia, Ga., Dec. 11, 1944; m. Ronnie Shacklett; children: Julie, Jolie. First appeared on Red Foley Ozark Jubilee Show, 1956; appeared in Opryland USA Show, Nashville, Music! Music! Music! Starring Brenda Lee, 1988; appeared in film Smokey and the Bandit II, 1980, in cable TV spl. Legendary Ladies, 1986, in PBS spl. Shake Rattle and Roll, 1988; recs. include Brenda Lee, 1960, Sincerely, 1961, All Alone Am I, 1962, By Request, 1964, Bye Bye Blues, 1966, 10 Golden Years, 1966, Memphis Portrait, 1970, Now, 1975, and many others. Recipient Gov.'s award Nat. Acad. Rec. Arts and Scis., 1984. Address: Brenda Lee Entertainments care Ronnie Shacklett PO Box 101188 Nashville TN 37210-1188*

LEE, CHARLEME ESMA, management analyst; b. Battle Creek, Mich., May 6, 1949; d. Charles Emanual and Iva Manester (Corlew) Henry; m. Robin David Parker, Jan. 20, 1968 (div. 1971); 1 child, Melanie Rochelle; m. Ivory Lee Jr., Feb. 1, 1974; 1 child, Yvonne Vernell. AA, Kellogg Community Coll., 1989; student, Cen. Mich. U. Key punch operator Dept. Mental Health, Agusta, Mich., 1969-72; acctg. receivable Ralston Purina, Battle Creek, Mich., 1973-75; computer aid Dept. Defense, Battle Creek, 1976-77; communication operator Dept. Defense Logistics Svc. Ctr., Battle Creek, 1977-80; mgmt. asst. reutilization and mktg. svc. Dept. Def., Battle Creek, 1980-82, mgmt. analyst, 1976-88, mgmt. analyst, supr., 1988—. Mem. Urban League Guild, Battle Creek, 1984—. Mem. Negro Bus. & Profl. Women, NAACP, Council Negro Women, Eta Phi Beta. Home: 211 Calico Ln Battle Creek MI 49017

LEE, CHUI-CHUN, librarian; b. Canton, People's Republic of China; came to U.S., 1967; BA, The Chinese U., Hong Kong, 1966; MS in Libr. Sci., Syracuse U., 1969; MA in Eng. Lit., NYU, 1973, MA in Edn., 1978. Instr. Chinese Lang. Ctr. New Asia Coll., Chinese U. of Hong Kong, Kowloon, 1966-67; asst. libr. SUNY, New Paltz, 1969-74, assoc. libr., 1974-81, libr., 1981—; cons. Orange County Community Coll. Libr., Middletown, N.Y., 1990. Author computer-assisted libr. instruction program, 1987; contbr. reviews and articles to profl. jours. Recipient grants SUNY, New Paltz, 1986, 89, Chancellor's Award for Excellence in Librarianship, SUNY, 1989. Mem. SUNY Librs. Assn. (del. 1980-84, automation and info. tech. com. 1982—), ALA (planning and evaluation libr. svcs. com. 1984-88, using stats for libr. planning and evaluation com. 1989-91), Beta Phi Mu, Delta Kappa Gamma. Office: SUNY Coll at New Paltz Sojourner Truth Libr New Paltz NY 12561

LEE, CONNIE SMITH, history educator; b. Charlotte, N.C., Nov. 12, 1930; d. Austin Edmund Smith and Hilda (Everist) Barnett; m. Richard Vincent Lee, Jan. 29, 1949 (div. Jan. 1972); children: Richard Vincent Jr., David Everist, Thomas Edmund, Marian Lee Wilson. BA in History, U. N.C., Charlotte, 1971; MAT in History, Winthrop Coll., Rock Hill, S.C., 1972; PhD in Social Scis., U. S.C., 1974. Cert. secondary tchr., S.C. Dir. admissions Winthrop Coll., 1974-76, asst. v.p. student affairs, 1976-77, asst. v.p. for devel., 1977-78, asst. dean Sch. Edn., interim dean, 1978-80, v.p. for devel., 1980-82; prof. history and polit. sci. York Tech. Coll., Rock Hill, 1982—; owner, mgr. family real estate and rental bus., Rock Hill, 1977—; condr. numerous workshopsfor mil. women U.S. and abroad; speaker to bus. clubs, honor socs., coll. and high sch. students, polit. groups in U.S. Mem. Def. Adv. Com. on Women in the Svcs., Washington, 1986-88, chair, 1989; mem. at-large S.C. Commn. on Women, Columbia, 1990—; resource panelist Total Force Policy Sec. Def., Washington, 1990; mem. Rock Hill Human Rels. Commn., 1988—, former chair. Recipient Pres.'s award for Teaching York Tech. Coll., 1990, Outstanding Pub. Svc. medal Sec. Def., 1989. Mem. LWV, DAR, AAUW (bd. dirs. 1985-87, 89-90, State award for Women's Issues 1990, edn. scholarship 1990), S.C. Tech. Edn. Assn., S.C. Coalition for Choice, S.C. Fedn. Bus. and Profl. Women (bd. dirs. 1986-88), 17th Century Colonial Dames, Phi Delta Kappa, Phi Kappa Phi. Republican. Episcopalian. Home: 1537 Clarendon Pl Rock Hill SC 29732 Office: York Tech Coll Anderson Rd Rock Hill SC 29730

LEE, CORINNE ADAMS, retired educator; b. Cuba, N.Y., Mar. 18, 1910; d. Duston Emery and Florence Eugenia (Butts) Adams; m. Glenn Max Lee, Oct. 30, 1936 (dec. Feb. 1964). BA, Alfred U., 1931. Cert. tchr., N.Y. Tchr. English Lodi (N.Y.) High Sch., 1931-36, Ovid (N.Y.) Cen. Sch., 1936-67. Author: (light verse) A Little Leeway, 1983, (anecedotes, light verse, quips) A Little More Leeway, 1984, (essays, short stories, poems) Still More Leeway, 1986. Mem. life PTA. Mem. Nat. Ret. Tchrs. Assn., N.Y. State Ret. Tchrs. Assn., Schuyler County Ret. Tchrs. Assn., Elmira and Area Ret. Tchrs. Assn., LWV. Avocations: reading, travel, writing.

LEE, DIANA BELINDA, banker; b. Florence, S.C., July 2, 1953; d. Henry Barker and J Jeannine (Berry) L. AB, Coker Coll., 1973; AA, Fashion Inst. Am., 1973; diploma retail banking Am. Inst. Banking, 1983; postgrad Coker Coll. Customer service rep. 1st Nat. Bank S.C., Columbia, 1974-79; with S.C. Nat. Bank, Florence and Columbia, 1979-82; with S.C. Fed., various locations, 1982-87, br. mgr., Columbia, 1983-85, asst. sec., br. mgr., Hartsville, 1985-87, br. mgr. Security Fed. Savs. Bank, Columbia, 1987—; br. mgr. Security Fed., 1986-89, asst. v.p., 1989—. Bd. dirs. Am. Cancer Soc., 1985—, chmn. regional edn. funds crusade, 1985—, regional dir., 1987-88; chmn. Hartscapades parade, 1986; co-chmn. Richland County First Lady Cookbooks. Mem. C. of C. Columbia (Community Achievement award 1989), Forest Acres Area Coun. C. of C. (pres. 1985, bdr. dirs. 1987—), Nat. Assn. Bank Women, Am. Bus. Womens Assn. (chmn. fund raising 1984-85), Am. Inst. Banking. Republican. Presbyterian. Avocations: reading, sewing, dance, crafts, designing. Office: Security Fed 1440 Broad River Rd Columbia SC 29210

LEE, EDNA PRITCHARD, education educator; b. Windsor, N.C., Oct. 6, 1923; d. Peter Bernard and Edna (Smith) Pritchard; m. Mack Lloyd Lee Sr., May 17, 1945 (dec. Nov. 1970); 1 child, Mack Lloyd Jr. BS, State U. N.C., Elizabeth City; MA, NYU, N.Y.C. Tchr. elem. schs. Windsor, N.C., 1944-61; tchr. elem. schs. Mohegan Lake, N.Y., 1961-68, asst. prin. elem. sch., 1968-82; dir. basic edn. Peekskill (N.Y.) High Sch., 1969-80; adj. prof. Mercy Coll., Peekskill, 1985—; vice chmn. bd. dirs. Peekskill Area Health Ctr., 1985—. Co-author: Syllabus for 4th Grade Social Studies, 1972. Named Woman of Yr., NAACP, Peekskill, 1976, Woman Engr. of Yr., Bus. and Profl. Women, Peekskill, 1980; recipient Louis Gregory award Bahai Religion, Peekskill, 1988. Mem. AAUW (v.p. 1970-72), Blacks in Govt., Delta Kappa Gamma, Alpha Kappa Alpha, Tee-Ettes (sec. 1982-88). Home: 101 Dutch St Montrose NY 10548

LEE, ELEANOR M., state legislator; b. Elgin, Ill., July 17, 1931; d. Earl H. and Catherine (Goldback) Selle; m. David H. Lee, 1951; children: Virginia Boylan, Phyllis Kenworthy, Marcia. BA, Evergreen State Coll., 1973. Bus. mgr. Fairman B. Lee Co., Inc., Burien, Wash., 1969—; state rep. State of Wash., Olympia, 1975-77; senator State of Wash., 1977—; mem. State Land Planning Commn., Wash., 1971-73; chair Jt. Adminstrv. Rules Com., 1982, Econ. Devel. and Labor Com., 1989; mem. exec. bd. and conv. com. SeaTac Task Force; founder, past chair Puget Sound Air Quality Coalition. Past chair Fire Dist. Civil Svc. Bd.; mem. Community Econ. Revitalization Bd. Mem. Bus. and Profl. Women (Woman of Yr. 1986), LWV (former pres.), S.W. King C. of C., Soroptomists (Women Helping Women award 1982, 86), The Mountaineers. Republican. Office: Wash State Senate 102 Institutions Bldg Olympia WA 98504

LEE, ELIZABETH BOBBITT, architect; b. Lumberton, N.C., July 9, 1928; d. William Osborne and Catharine Wilder (Bobbitt) Lee. Student Salem Coll., 1945-47; B.Arch. with honors, N.C. State Coll., 1952. Registered architect, N.C., 1955, S.C., 1964. Assoc. William Coleman, Architect, Kinston, N.C., 1952-55; Skidmore, Owens & Merrill, N.Y.C., 1955-56; prin. Elizabeth B. Lee, FAIA, Architect, Lumberton, N.C., 1956-73, 82—; sr. ptnr. Lee & Thompson, Architects, Lumberton, 1973-82. Bd. dirs. Robeson Little Theatre, Lumberton, 1977-80, N.C. Dance Theatre, Winston-Salem, N.C., 1980-85, Robeson County Community Concerts, Lumberton, 1980-87; trustee N.C. State U., Raleigh, 1983-92. Recipient cert. recognition Randolph E. Dumont Design Program, 1970, Disting. Alumna award, Salem Coll., 1989. Fellow AIA (nat. dir. 1983-85; officeholder N.C. chpt., 1959, v.p., 1978, pres. 1979, bd. dirs. 1980, pres. eastern sect. N.C. chpt., 1975, bd. dirs. S. Atlantic Regional Council, 1977-79); Fellow AIA; mem. Jr. League (pres. Lumberton chpt., 1968), Robeson County Heart Assn. (pres. 1970), N.C. Design Found., N.C. Archtl. Found. (pres. 1982-83), Lumberton Jr. Service League (pres. 1968), N.C. State Alumni Assn. (bd. dirs. 1982-85, chmn. Robeson county chpt.), Phi Kappa Phi. Democrat. Presbyterian. Home: 906 Chestnut St Lumberton NC 28358 Office: 407 Elm St PO Box 1067 Lumberton NC 28359

LEE, EVELYN MARIE, teacher; b. Germantown, Ohio, Dec. 17, 1931; d. Robert Orlandus and Edna Cathern (Durr) Stump; m. John Henry Lee, Dec. 16, 1956; children: Mark Douglas, David Matthew, Lori Ann Lee Delehoy. BS in Edn., Otterbein Coll., 1954; MA in Reading, U. Alaska, 1979. Dept. store tng. supr., asst. mdse. mgr. The Home Store, Dayton, Ohio, 1954-55; tchr. Parma (Ohio) Pub. Schs., 1955-56; math aide civil svc. Nat. Adv. Com. for Aeros. Ames Lab., Moffett Field, Calif., 1956-57; substitute tchr. Warren (Ohio) Pub. Schs., 1957-59, tchr., 1969-60; tchr. Gwinn (Mich.) Pub. Schs., 1960-64; tchr. Anchorage Sch. Dist., 1964-65, 68-87, substitute tchr., 1987—. Life mem. Alaska PTA; vol. Ushering in the Arts; performer Anchorage Community Theatre and Opera Co. Mem. Anchorage Concert Assn., Alaska Hist. Soc. (life). United Methodist. Home: 541 Donna Dr Anchorage AK 99504

LEE, FRANCES HELEN, editor; b. N.Y.C., Jan. 6, 1936; d. Murray and Rose (Rothman) Lee; BA, Queens Coll., 1957; MA, NYU, 1962. Editorial asst. Christian Herald Family Bookshelf, N.Y.C., 1957-62; with Gordon and Breach Sci. Pubs., Inc., N.Y.C., 1964-66, Am. Electric Power Svc. Corp. AEP Operating Ideas, N.Y.C., 1966-69, Indsl. Water Enging. Mag., N.Y.C., 1969-71; directory editor Photographic div. United Bus. Publs., N.Y.C., 1971-80; editor Am. Druggist Blue Book, Hearst Books/Bus. Publs. Group,

1980-81, spl. projects coord. motor manuals Hearst Book div., 1981-82, editor New Price Report, 1982-84; editor Am. Druggist Blue Book, 1982-88; freelance editor, cons., 1988—. Supr. Bronx div. N.Y. State CD, 1953-59. Mem. com. on N.Y.C. charter revision Citizens Union, 1975, com. on city personnel practices, 1975-76, com. on city mgmt., 1977—, bd. dirs., 1978—, co-chmn. com. on N.Y.C. Cultural Concerns, 1979—. Recipient cert. of honor NYU Alumni Fedn., 1985, Meritorious Serv. award, 1986 . Mem. N.Y. Bus. Press Editors (bd. dirs. 1988—, sec. 1990—), Women's Equity Action League (chmn. rsch. com.), Vill-Lobos Music Soc., Inc. (sec. 1989—), NYU Alumnae Club (dir. 1976-78, rec. sec. 1978-80, v.p. 1980-82, pres. 1982-84, rep. to bd. dirs. fedn. 1984-86), NYU Alumni Fedn. (dir.-at-large 1986—), N.Y. Bus. Pres. Editors (bd. dirs. 1988—), Villa-Lobos Music Soc. (sec. 1989—), NYU Club (bd. govs. 1987-88, bd. trustees 1988-89). Home: 170 2d Ave New York NY 10003

LEE, JANET WASHBURN, investment consultant; b. Tucson, Apr. 2, 1955; d. Benton Charles and Thelma Louise (Pritchett) Washburn. BA, Ariz. State U., 1976. Electronics buyer Motorola SG, Phoenix, 1976-78; mgr. communications and tng. Honeywell PMSD, Phoenix, 1978-80; stockbroker Kidder, Peabody and Co., Phoenix, 1980-88; banker Comml. Bus. Mktg. Valley Bank, Phoenix; cons., pres. Desert West, Ltd., Phoenix, 1990—; instr., conducts bus. and fin. seminars. Bd. mem. YMCA Fin. Devel., Phoenix, 1986--, mem. Phoenix Art Museum, Phoenix, 1984--, past chmn. Spina Bifida Celebrity Tennis, Scottsdale, 1984; com. mem. Symington for Gov. Campaign. Named Women of the Year Bus. and Profl. Women, Phoenix 1981, Young Career Woman , 1979. Mem. Phoenix C. of C., Glendale C. of C., Scottsdale C. of C., Phoenix City Club. Republican. Home: 11025 N 111th Way Scottsdale AZ 85259 Office: Desert West Ltd 2020 W Glendale Ave Ste 2097 Phoenix AZ 85021

LEE, JANIS, state legislator; b. Kensington, Kans., July 11, 1945; m. Lyn Lee; children: David, Brian, Daniel. BA, Kans. State U., 1970. Mem. from dist. 36 Kans. State Senate, 1988—. Mem. Kappa Delta Pi, Phi Kappa Phi. Democrat. Home: RR 1 Box 145 Kensington KS 66951*

LEE, JEANNE KIT YEW, administrative assistant; b. N.Y.C., July 31, 1959; d. Tat Yuen and Yow Seum (Chu) Lee. BBA, Baruch Coll., 1982. Clk. typist U.S. Dept. Health and Human Svcs., N.Y.C., 1980-83; clk. typist U.S. Consumer Product Safety Commn., N.Y.C., 1983-85, adminstrv. asst., 1985—; systems adminstr. U.S. Consumer Product Safety Commn., 1986—. Recipient Superior Performance award, 1986-89, Meritorious Svc. award, 1984. Mem. NAFE, Humane Soc., Nat. Wildlife Fedn. (assoc.), Am. Humane, DAV (Commanders Club 1988—).

LEE, JUDITH C., publishing executive; b. Myrtle Point, Oreg., 1936; d. Ralph F. and Lola M. (Greene) Milne; m. Myron E. Lee, 1967. BA, U. Oreg., 1959; MLS, San Jose State U., 1981. Tech. writer GTE Sylvania, Mountain View, Calif., 1962-66, sr. tech. writer, 1968-73; sr. tech. writer Microelectronics div. Philco-Ford, Santa Clara, Calif., 1966-67; sr. publs. writer Lockheed Corp., Sunnyvale, Calif., 1974; mgr. tech. communications Catalytica Assocs., Santa Clara, 1977-80; mgr. info. resources Hydro Research Sci., Santa Clara, 1982-83; staff editor Bus. Software Mag., Redwood City, Calif., 1984-85, mng. editor, 1985-86; mng. editor Sand-Castles, Inc., Mountain View, 1986-87; editorial cons. Alcatel Info. Systems, Milpitas, Calif., 1987-88; mng. editor NewsFaces, Inc., Los Gatos, Calif., 1988; sr. tech. writer, editor SRI Internat., Menlo Park, Calif., 1989—; mem. steering com. Silicon Valley Tech. Communications Conf., 1985. Book reviewer Sci. and Tech. Ann. Ref. Rev., 1989—. Recipient Award of Merit No. Calif. Tech. Communication Competition, 1979, Distinction in Corp. Advt. award, 1989. Mem. IEEE, AAUW (com. chmn. 1970), Soc. Tech. Communication (sec. Silicon Valley chpt. 1968), Assn. Tchrs. Tech. Writing, Spl. Libraries Assn., Sigma Delta Pi, Alpha Lambda Delta, Beta Phi Mu. Home: 3322 Saint Michael Dr Palo Alto CA 94306 Office: SRI Internat 333 Ravenswood Ave Menlo Park CA 94025

LEE, JUNE WARREN, dentist; b. Boston, Feb. 24, 1952; d. Earl Arnold and Rosemary Regina (Leary) Warren; m. William Lee, July 25, 1976; children: Jaime Michelle, Daniel William. BA, Brandeis U., 1973; DDS, Georgetown U., 1977; student, U.S. Dental Inst., 1985-87. Ptnr. June Warren Lee, DDS, William Lee, DDS, Boston, 1977—. Mem. Altrusa Club of Quincy, Mass., 1979—, Cunningham Sch. PTO, Milton, Mass, 1987—, Parent-Adv. Coun., Collicot Elem. Sch., Milton, 1986-87; dental instr. Cunningham Sch., 1987—; dental screening, Healthworks, Neponset Health Ctr., Boston, 1981-84. Mem. ADA, Mass. Dental Soc., South Shore Dist. Dental Soc. (vice chmn. elect 1990), Acad. Gen. Dentistry, Am. Orthodontic Soc., Am. Acad. Gnathologic Orthpedics, Am. Assn. for Functional Orthodontics, Am. Assn. Women Dentists (sec. 1987, v.p. 1988, pres. elect 1989, pres. 1990, A.T. Cross Co. Woman of Achievement award 1985), Women's Dental Soc. Mass. (sec. 1978, v.p. 1979-81, pres. 1981-83), Mass. Dentists Interested in Legislation, Chestnut Hill Rsch. Study Club. Roman Catholic. Office: June Warren Lee DDS 383 Neponset Ave Boston MA 02122

LEE, JUNG JA, chemist; b. Kang Nung, Korea; came to U.S., 1957; d. Tae Byuk and Soo Ahm (Park) L.; m. Henry G. Cohn, Sept. 17, 1962; 1 child, Richard G. Cohn-Lee. BS, Ewha Woman's U., Seoul, Korea, 1955; MS, Columbus U., 1959; postgrad., U. Wis., 1960-62; PhD, Rutgers U., 1966. Tchr. Kang Nung Girls' High Sch., 1955-56; assoc. scientist Warner-Lambert Rsch. Inst., Morristown, N.J., 1957-60; postdoctoral rsch. assoc. div. labs. and rsch. N.Y. State Dept. Health, Albany, 1966-70, rsch. scientist, 1981-87; rsch. asst. prof. Albany Med. Coll., 1971-75, rsch. assoc. prof., 1989—; rsch. scientist chem. dept. Rensselaer Poly. Inst., Troy, N.Y., 1988—; adj. asst. prof. chemistry SUNY, 1975-87; vis. fellow Princeton (N.J.) U., 1980. Contbr. articles to profl. jours. N.Y. State Health Rsch. Coun. grantee, 1986; fellow Johnson & Johnson, 1963, AAUW, 1980. Mem. Am. Chem. Soc., AAAS, Am. Inst. Chemists, N.Y. Acad. Sci., Am. Soc. Photobiologists, Sigma Xi, Rho Chi. Democrat. Methodist. Home: 69 S Manning Blvd Albany NY 12203 Office: Rensselaer Poly Inst Dept Chem Troy NY 12180-3590 also: Albany Med Coll Dept Immunology Albany NY 12208

LEE, KATHERINE ANN, human services administrator; b. Rosewell, N.Mex., Aug. 7, 1947; d. Merle Chester and Elta Frances (Eggert) Sims; m. Edward D. Lee, Aug. 30, 1975. BS, Tex. Woman's U., 1969. Club dir. Spl. Svcs. Dept. U.S. Army, Korea, 1969-70; unit mgr. Presbyn. Hosp., Albuquerque, 1970-76; program dir. Office of Sr. Affairs, Albuquerque, 1976-77; asst. dir. Retired Sr. Vol. Program, Albuquerque, 1978-79, dir., 1979-80; project coord. Trans., Albuquerque, 1979-80; ctr. dir. Human Svcs., Albuquerque, 1981—; mem. Multi-Svc. Ctr. Planning Commn., Albuquerque, 1990—, Human Svcs. Task Force, Albuquerque, 1988—; exec. dir. North Valley Adv. Coun., Albuquerque, 1984—. Active various polit. campaigns. Recipient Cert. of Appreciation Sec. of State, N.Mex., 1983, Indian Pueblo Cultural Ctr., 1989. Mem. Friends of the Indian Cultural Ctr., N.Mex. Crime Prevention Assn. (trustee 1990). Democrat. Methodist. Home: 1811 Tramway Ter Lp Albuquerque NM 87122

LEE, KATHRYN ADELE BUNDING, chemist; b. Chgo., Mar. 26, 1949; d. Irby Maedel and Ruth Lenore (Eisenstein) Bunding; m. Shu M. Lee, May 24, 1986. BA, U. Chgo., 1971; PhD, CUNY, 1980. NRC postdoctoral fellow Nat. Bur. Standards, Gaithersburg, Md., 1980-82; vis. scientist IBM Rsch., San Jose, Calif., 1982-84; rsch. chemist Naval Rsch. Lab., Washington, 1984-87; sr. rsch. scientist S.C. Johnson & Son, Inc., Racine, Wis., 1987—. Mem. Am. Chem. Soc., Soc. Applied Spectroscopy (chair Wis. sect. 1990), Electrochem. Soc. (chair So. Wis. sect. 1990). Office: S C Johnson & Son Inc 1525 Howe St MS 56 Racine WI 53403

LEE, LILY KIANG, scientific research company executive; b. Shanghai, China, Nov. 23, 1946; came to U.S., 1967, naturalized, 1974; d. Chi-Wu and An-Teh (Shih) Kiang; B.S., Nat. Cheng-Chi U., 1967; M.B.A. (scholar), Golden Gate U., San Francisco, 1969; m. Robert Edward Lee; children—Jeffrey Anthony, Michelle Adrienne, Stephanie Amanda, Christina Alison. Acct., then acctg. supr. Am. Data Systems, Inc., Canoga Park, Calif., 1969-73; sr. acct. Pertec Peripheral Equipment div. Pertec Corp., Chatsworth, Calif., 1973-76; mgr. fin. planning and acctg., then mgr. fin. planning and program control Sci. Center div. Rockwell Internat. Corp., Thousand Oaks, Calif., 1976—. Mem. Am. Mgmt. Assn., Nat. Mgmt. Assn., Nat. Property Mgrs. Assn., Nat. Assn. Female Execs. Republican. Baptist. Office: Rockwell Internat Corp PO Box 1085 1049 Camino Dos Rios Thousand Oaks CA 91360

LEE, LUCILLE, delivery service owner; b. Newark, N.J., Feb. 5, 1942; d. Ollie and Deana (Hall) Richardson; m. James William Johnson, Sept. 15, 1963 (div. 1975); m. Theodore Robert Lee Sr., Dec. 5, 1980; stepchildren: Theodore Jr., David Edgar. Grad. high sch., Newark, N.J. Clk. typist Newark Health Dept., 1971-72, Alston's Carpet Installation, Montclair, N.J., 1972-73; secretarial asst. Newark Bd. Edn., 1974-76; sec. New Hope Minority Contractors, Newark, 1976-78, Maplewood (N.J.) Bank and Trust Co., 1978-79; prin. acctg. clk. Irvington (N.J.) Town Hall, 1980-81; adminstrv. asst. Upsala Coll., East Orange, N.J., 1981-82; prin. Ed's News Delivery Svc., South Orange, N.J., 1985—. Sec., New Point Missionary Bapt. Ch., Newark, 1979, Ch. of Christ, 1982; nurse U. Hosp., 1987; tchr. Literacy Vols. Am., East Orange, 1983; vol. Project Return Players, Montclair, 1988. Mem. Mt. Tabor Club. Republican. Mem. Ch. of Christ. Home: 275 Prospect St East Orange NJ 07017 Office: Eds News Delivery Svc 33 1/2 Church St South Orange NJ 07079

LEE, LYNDA MILLS, librarian; b. Shreveport, La., Mar. 3, 1944; d. Donald Clarle and Eva Dell (Wooley) Mills; divorced; 1 child, Jennifer Lynn Netherland; m. Billy Ray Lee, Nov. 2, 1979. BA, Northwestern La. State U., 1966; MLS, La. State U., 1968. Cert. libr., La. Libr. Westlake (La.) High sch., 1966-67; ref. libr. East Tex. State U., Comniere, Tex., 1968-70; tchr. Morehouse Parish, Bootrop, La., 1970-71; br. libr. Ouachita Parish Pub. Libr., Monroe, La., 1971-72; dir. Bossier-Red River Parish Pub. Libr., Benton, La., 1972-78, Calcasieu Parish Pub. Libr., Lake Charles, La., 1978—. Named Outstanding Young Women, Bossier Jaycees, 1975. Mem. AAUW, Bus. and Profl. Women, Family and Youth Counseling Bd. (pres. 1986-87), Children's Mus. Bd., La. Libr. Assn. (Mid-Career award 1979, coord. legisl. network 1975-78, 83-86, pres. 1978-79), Art. Humanities Counsel (adv. bd., pres. 1986-88), Quota Club Lake Charels (pres. 1978-79). Methodist. Office: Calcasieu Parish Libr 411 Pujo St Lake Charles LA 70601

LEE, MAGGIE VIRGINIA, personnel director; b. Nottingham, Md., Dec. 25, 1941; d. Geary Cornelious and Myrtle Rose (Holland) Wiseman; m. Charles Dudley Lee, Jr., Mar. 25, 1962; children: Charles Dudley III, Christopher Michael, Anthony David. BBA, Calif. State U., Long Beach, 1979. Instr. High Sch./Jr. Coll., Yokohama, Japan, 1968-70; fashion/photo model various agcys/Hitachi, Tokyo, Japan, 1960-70; instr.-Ikebana U.S. Naval Base, Yokosuka, Japan, 1969-70; credit mgr. Bullocks Wilshire, LaJolla, Calif., 1983-84; asst. pers. dir. Bullocks, LaMesa, Calif., 1984-85; pers. dir. May Co., Carlsbad, Calif., 1985—. Recipient Letter Commendation Gov. Kanagawa Prefecture Japan, 1970. Mem. Pers. Mgmt. Assn. San Diego, No. County Pers. Assn. San Diego. Democrat. Roman Catholic. Home: 16643 Maverick Ln Poway CA 92064

LEE, MARGARET ANNE, psychotherapist; b. Scribner, Nebr., Nov. 23, 1930; d. William Christian and Caroline Bertha (Benner) Joens; m. Robert Kelly Lee, May 21, 1950 (div. 1971); children: Lawrence Robert, James Kelly, Daniel Richard. AA, Napa Coll., 1949; student, U. Calif., Berkeley, 1949-50; BA, Calif. State Coll., Sonoma, 1975; MSW, Calif. State U., Sacramento, 1977. Diplomate clin. social worker; lic. marriage and family counselor, Calif.; tchr. Columnist, stringer Napa (Calif.) Register, 1946-50; eligibility worker, supr. Napa County Dept. Social Services, 1968-75; instr. Napa Valley Community Coll., 1978-83; practice psychotherapy Napa, 1977—; oral commr. Calif. Dept. Consumer Affairs, Bd. Behavioral Sci., 1984—; bd. dirs. Project Access, 1978-79. Trustee Napa Valley Community Coll., 1983—, v.p. bd., 1984-85, pres. bd., 1986, 90, clk., 1988-89; bd. dirs. Napa County Coun. Econ. Opportunity, 1984-85, Napa chpt. March of Dimes, 1957-71, Mental Health Assn. Napa County, 1983-87, mem., 1983—; vice chmn. edn. com. Calif. Community Coll. Trustees, 1987-88, chmn. edn. com., 1988-89, legis. com., 1985-87, bd. dirs., 1989—. Recipient Fresh Start award Self mag., award Congl. Caucuson Women's Issues, 1984. Mem. Nat. Assn. Social Workers, Mental Health Assn. Napa County, Calif. Assn. Physically and Handicapped, Women's Polit. Caucus, Calif. Elected Women's Assn. Edn. and Rsch., Am. Assn. Women in Community and Jr. Colls. Democrat. Lutheran. Office: 1100 Trancas PO Box 2099 Napa CA 94558

LEE, MARGARET NORMA, artist; b. Kansas City, Mo., July 7, 1928; d. James W. and Margaret W. (Farin) Lee; PhB, U. Chgo., 1948; MA, Art Inst. Chgo., 1952. Lectr., U. Kansas City, 1957-61; cons. Kansas City Bd. Edn., Kansas City, Mo., 1968-86; guest lectr. U.Mo.-Columbia, 1983, 85, 87, 89; one-woman shows Univ. Women's Club, Kansas City, 1966, Friends of Art, Kansas City, 1969, Fine Arts Gallery U. Mo. at Columbia, 1972, All Souls Unitarian Ch. Kansas City, Mo., 1978; two-Woman show Rockhurst Coll., Kansas City, Mo., 1981 exhibited in group shows U. Kans., Lawrence, 1958, Chgo. Art Inst., 1963, Nelson Art Gallery, Kansas City, Mo., 1968, 74, Mo. Art Show, 1976, Fine Arts Gallery, Davenport, Iowa, 1977; represented in permanent collections Amarillo (Tex.) Art Center, Kansas City (Mo.) Pub. Library, Park Coll., Parkville, Mo. Mem. Coll. Art Assn. Roman Catholic. Contbr. art to profl. jours.; author booklet. Home and Studio: 4109 Holmes St Kansas City MO 64110

LEE, MARIANNE HOLLINGSWORTH, political activist and volunteer; b. Atlanta, May 30, 1930; d. Fred Law and Florence Elizabeth (Adams) Hollingsworth; m. Raymond William Lee Jr., June 21, 1952; children: Lelia Lee McGregor, Carol Lee Wilkerson, Raymond William III, Sally Anne. AB, Duke U., 1952. Cert. Ga. Real Estate Bd. Child welfare worker Richmond (Va.) Social Svcs. Bur., 1952-53; real estate agt. Warren Schmitz Agy., Atlanta, 1975-79, Buckhead Brokers Inc., Atlanta, 1979-88. Active Sandy Springs Hist. Community Found., 1988—; founder, bd. dirs. Sandy Springs Soc., 1988—, Sandy Springs Arts and Heritage Soc., 1986-87; charter mem. Rep. Women of Northside, 1978—; vice chmn. 5th dist. Rep. Party, Atlanta, 1985-89, chmn. 5th dist., 1989—; del. to nat. conv. New Orleans, 1988, chmn. ho. dist. 22, Fulton County, Ga., 1981-85, mem. state exec. com., 1989—; pres. Episcopal Churchwomen, St. martin in the Field Ch., 1974. Recipient Sight Saver award Ga. Soc. to Prevent Blindness, Atlanta, 1980. Mem. Delta Gamma (pres. Atlanta alumnae chpt. 1958-59, 86-87, Shield award 1964). Home: 6265 Riverside Dr NW Atlanta GA 30328

LEE, MARIETTA Y.W.T., biologist, educator; b. China, Mar. 3, 1943; came to U.S. 1961; d. Michael and Marion (Lo) Tsang; m. Ernest Y.C. Lee, Nov. 1, 1969; 1 child, Patrick. BS, Nazareth (Ky.) Coll., 1965; MS, NYU, 1968; PhD, U. Miami, Fla., 1973. Postdoctoral fellow U. Miami, 1975-78, fellow Howard Hughes Med. Inst., 1978-80, rsch. asst. prof., 1978-81, asst. prof. biology, 1981-86, assoc. prof. biology, 1986—. NIH predoctoral fellow 1970-73; NIH hematology trainee 1978-81; NIH grantee, 1983—, Am. Heart Assn. established investigator grantee, 1984-89. Mem. NIH (Biochemistry study sect. 1990—), Am. Soc. Biochemistry and Molecular Biology (com. on equal opportunity for women). Roman Catholic. Office: University of Miami R57 PO Box 016960 Miami FL 33101

LEE, MARVA JEAN, counselor, physical education educator, consultant; b. Cleveland, Miss., Feb. 16, 1938; d. Henry Davis and Willie Mae (Caver) Hardy. B.S., George Williams Coll., 1960; M.A., Northeastern Ill. U., Chgo., 1972; M.Edn., Loyola U., Chgo., 1978. Child care worker Inst. Juvenile Research, Chgo., 1960-61; phys. educator Chgo. Bd. Edn., 1961-69; instr. George Williams Coll., Downers Grove, Ill., 1969-73; phys. educator Chgo. Bd. Edn., 1973-86, counselor, 1986—, tchr. trainer family life edn., 1983—. Chmn. Chgo. Pub. Sch. campaign United Negro Coll. Fund, Chgo., 1981, 82, chmn. profl. women's aux., 1983—; bd. dirs. Chgo. com. NAACP Legal Defense and Edn. Fund, 1980—; sec. bd. dirs. Treshan Youth Found., Chgo., 1977-86; fin. sec. Chgo. Links Found., 1988—; mem. Com. to Elect/Re-elect Roland Burris State Comptroller, 1978—, Com. to Elect Harold Washington Mayor Chgo., 1982-83. Named Outstanding Vol., Mid-Am. chpt. ARC, Chgo., 1976, Outstanding Vol., United Negro Coll. Fund, N.Y.C., 1982; recipient Image award Fred Hampton Found., 1979, Svc. to Family Life Edn. award Chgo. Bd. Edn., Leadership Contbn. award United Negro Coll. Fund, 1990. Mem. AAHPERD, Ill. Assn. Health, Phys. Edn. and Recreation (mem. exec. com. Chgo. dist.), Ill. Council Family Relations, Am. Assn. Counseling and Devel., Chgo. Guidance and Personnel Assn. Inc., Council Coll. Attendance, Secondary Sch. Counselors Council, Alpha Kappa Alpha. Avocations: community vol.; community fundraiser; travel. Home: 8300 S Peoria St Chicago IL 60620 Office: Percy L Julian High Sch 10330 S Elizabeth Chicago IL 60643

LEE, MAY DEAN-MING LU, chemist; b. Fukian, China, May 14, 1949; came to U.S. 1972; d. John Chuan-Tzeng and Anna Tzas-Chyn (Liu) Lu; m. Ving Jick Lee, Aug. 24, 1974; children: Adrianne, Derric. BSc, U. B.C., Vancouver, 1972; MS, U. Ill., 1974, PhD, 1976. Postdoctoral fellow dept. chemistry Harvard U., Cambridge, 1976-77; rsch. chemist Med. Rsch. div. Am. Cyanamid, Pearl River, N.Y., 1977-81; sr. rsch. chemist Med. Rsch. div. Am. Cyanamid, 1981-87, group leader, 1987—. Contbr. articles to profl. jours.; patentee in field. Recipient Sci. Achievement awad, Am. Cyanamid Co., 1987. Mem. Am. Chem. Soc., Am. Soc. Microbiology, AAAS. Office: American Cyanamid Co Med Rsch Div Lederle Labs Pearl River NY 10965

LEE, MICHELE, actress; b. Los Angeles, June 24, 1942; d. Jack and Sylvia Helen (Silverstein) Dusick; m. James Farentino, Feb. 20, 1966 (div. 1983); 1 son, David Michael; m. Fred Rappoport, Sept. 27, 1987. Appeared in Broadway play How To Succeed in Business Without Really Trying, 1962-64; Broadway play Seesaw, 1973; movies How To Succeed in Business Without Really Trying, 1967, The Love Bug, 1969, Dark Victory, 1975, Bud and Low, 1976, A Letter to Three Wives, 1985, Single Women, Married Men, 1989; TV series Knots Landing, 1979—. Recipient Top Star of Tomorrow award Motion Picture Exhibitors of U.S. and Can., 1967; recipient Drama Desk award Broadway Critics, 1973, Outer Critics Circle award, 1973; nominated for Antoinette Perry award, 1973-74, Emmy for Knots Landing, 1981-82.

LEE, MIRANDA, advertising agency executive; b. Hong Kong, July 12, 1952; came to U.S., 1959BA, Sarah Lawrence Coll., 1973. Acct. exec. BBDO, N.Y.C., 1973-77, Grey Advt., N.Y.C., 1977-79; mgmt. supr. Rosenfeld, Sirowitz & Lawson, N.Y.C., 1979-82; v.p., mgmt. rep. Needham Harper & Steers, N.Y.C., 1982-84; sr. v.p. J. Walter Thompson, N.Y.C., 1984—. Office: Brouillard Communications 420 Lexington Ave New York NY 10017

LEE, NANCY ELLEN, quality assurance professional; b. Chgo., Aug. 23, 1944; d. William George and Marcella Mary (Werner) L. Grad., St. Mary of Nazareth Sch. Nursing, 1965; BS in Health Adminstrn., Coll. of St. Francis, Joliet, Ill., 1979. Cert. quality assurance profl. RN, cons. Sovereign Home, Chgo., 1975—; quality assurance and utilization rev. coord. Bohemian Home, Chgo., 1979—; dir social svc. utilization rev. and quality assurance dept. N.W. Hosp., Chgo., 1981-85; mgr. UR dept., coord. John F. Kennedy Med. Ctr., Chgo., 1985-87; with DON Reliable Home Health Care, Elmwood Park, Ill., 1987-88; patient care coord. mktg. dept. ABC Home Health of Ill, Inc., River Forest, 1988-89; pres., founder InfoData, Inc., 1988—. Contbr. articles to profl. jours. Recipient Red Cross pin N.W. Hosp., 1979. Mem. NAFE, Ill. Nurses Assn., Interdivisional Nursing, Specialty Coun. on Quality Assurance (chair), Am. Bd. Quality Assurance Utilization Review (credential com. 1983-86, 90—), Ill. chpt. Am. Coll. of Utilization Review Physicians (exec. com. 1988—). Office: 5061 N Pulaski Rd Chicago IL 60630

LEE, NAOMI PEARL, academic administrator; b. Moorhead, M.N., Nov. 28, 1948; d. Cecil Allen and Marcella Ester (Tweten) B.; m. Gary Ralph Lee, Jan. 6, 1968; 1 child, Laura Annabelle. BA, Wash. State U., 1976, MA, 1981, PhD, 1984. Counselling asst. Career Devel. Prog./WSU, Pullman, Wash., 1981-83; visiting asst. prof. WSU, Pullman, 1984-85; acad. counselor Dept. Athletics, Wash. State U., Pullman, 1983-87, Coll. Liberal Arts & Sci., U. Fla., Gainesville, 1987—; cons. Wash. State Dept. Labor, 1983. Editor: Research & Pub. Service with the Rural Elderly, 1980. Gen. mgr. Palouse Empire Cougars Semi-pro Baseball Team, Pullman, 1985-87. Mem., Nat. Acad. Adv. Assn., Am. Coll. Pers. Assn., Commn. XVI, Phi Kappa Phi. Democrat. Lutheran.

LEE, NELDA S., art appraiser and dealer, film producer; b. Gorman, Tex., July 3, 1941; d. Olan C. and Onis L.; A.S. (Franklin Lindsay Found. grantee), Tarleton State U., Tex., 1961; B.A. in Fine Arts, N. Tex. State U., 1963; postgrad. Tex. Tech. U., 1964, San Miguel de Allende Art Inst., Mexico, 1965; 1 dau., Jeanna Lea Pool. Head dept. art Ector High Sch., Odessa, Tex., 1963-68. Bd. dirs. Odessa YMCA, 1970, bd. dirs. Am. Heart Assn., Odessa, 1975; fund raiser Easter Seal Telethon, Odessa, 1978-79; bd. dirs. Ector County (Tex.) Cultural Center, 1979—, Tex. Bus. Hall of Fame, 1980-85; bd. dirs., mem. acquisition com. Permian Basin Presdl. Mus., Odessa, 1978; bd. dirs., chairperson acquisition com. Odessa Art Mus., 1979—; pres. Mega-Tex. Prodns., TV and movie producers; pres. Ector County Democratic Women's Club, 1975. Recipient Designer-Craftsman award El Paso Mus. Fine Arts, 1964. Mem. Am. Soc. Appraisers, Appraisers Assn. Am., Appraisers of Fine Arts Soc., Nat. Soc. Lit. and the Arts, Tex. Assn. Art Dealers (pres. 1978—), Odessa C. of C. Contbr. articles to profl. jours.

LEE, PAMELA ANNE, accountant; b. San Francisco, May 30, 1960; d. Larry D. and Alice Mary (Reece) L. BS in Bus., San Francisco State U., 1981. CPA, Calif. Typist, bookkeeper, tax acct. James G. Woo, CPA, San Francisco, 1979-85; tutor bus. math. and statistics San Francisco State U., 1979-80; teller to ops. officer Gibraltar Savs. and Loan, San Francisco, 1978-81; sr. acct. Price Waterhouse, San Francisco, 1981-86; corp. acctg. mgr. First Nationwide Bank, Daly City, Calif., 1986-89, v.p., 1989—; acctg. cons. New Performance Gallery, San Francisco, 1985, San Francisco Chamber Orch., 1986. Founding mem., chair bd. trustees Asian Acctg. Students Career Day, 1988—. Mem. Am. Inst. CPA's, Calif. Soc. CPA's, NAFE, Nat. Assn. Asian-Am. CPA's (bd. dirs. 1986, news editor 1987, pres. 1988). Republican. Avocations: reading, music, travel, personal computing. Office: First Nationwide Bank 3951 Lennane Dr Sacramento CA 95834

LEE, PATRICIA ANN, real estate broker; b. Des Moines, Jan. 16, 1939; d. Samuel Ellis and Grace LaNell (Ford) Campfield; m. Wylie Samuel Lee, Dec. 31, 1958; children: Daniel Ellis, Laura Clair Lee Anderson, John McKinley. Grad. high sch., Des Moines, 1957. Real estate broker Andrews Realty, Des Moines, 1972-78; real estate broker, owner Lee & Lee, Realtors, Des Moines, 1978-82; real estate broker, ptnr. Hallmark Realty, Des Moines, 1982-85; real estate broker 1st Realty, Better Homes & Gardens, 1985-87, real estate broker, mgr., 1987—. Chair bldg. com. Windsor United Meth. Ch., 1985-88. mem. Iowa Assn. Realtors (v.p. 1988—, chair legis. com. 1989, 90—), Greater Des Moines Bd. Realtors (pres. 1988, Realtor of Yr. 1981), Cert. Residential Specialist (pres. Iowa chpt. 1989-90), Women Coun. Realtors (pres. 1981, Woman of Yr. 1982). Republican. Methodist. Office: 1st Realty Better Homes & Gardens 5601 Douglas Des Moines IA 50310

LEE, R. MARILYN, personnel director/human resources specialist. BA in Polit. Sci., U. Calif., Santa Barbara, 1969; JD, U. Pacific, 1977. Dep. city atty. City of L.A., 1977-82; corp. dir. human resources The Times Mirror Co., L.A., 1982—; regent U. Calif. Bd. Regents, 1986-88. Mem. United Way Task Force on AIDS, chair subcom.; v.p. Timm Hackley Meml. Scholarship Found.; sec. Alliance of Bus. Childcare Devel.; bd. trustees U. Calif. Santa Barbara Found., Legis. aide congl. offices, Washington, 1970-74. Mem. ABA, Am. Newspaper Pubs. Assn. (task force on minorities in newspaper bus.), Newspaper Pers. Rels. Assn., Calif. State Bar Assn., L.A. County Bar Assn., McGeorge Sch. Law (alumni rep.), Alumni Assn. U. Calif. (pres. 1987-88. bd. dirs. 1983-89). Office: The Times Mirror Co Times Mirror Square Los Angeles CA 90053

LEE, RAMONA CARMEN, mathematician; b. Hinsdale, Ill., Oct. 14, 1959; d. David Nicholas and Joan H. Lee. Student, No. Ill. U., 1976-78, Konan U., 1981-82; BS in Maths., U. Ill., 1983. Actuarial trainee intermediate Security Casualty Co., Chgo., 1978-81; actuarial asst. Martin E. Segal Co., Chgo., 1983-84; sr. actuarial asst. Woodward & Fondiller, N.Y.C., 1986-87; analyst Constitution Reinsurance Corp., N.Y.C., 1987-89, Chubb & Son, Warren, N.J., 1987--; pntr. Blue Ibis, Vt., 1989--; ptnr. David's Pl. in Bethlehem, N.H., Dave's Other Place, N.H., 1989—. Flotilla staff officer USCG Auxiliary, Hackensack, N.J., 1987--. Mem. Mathematical Assn. Am. Home: PO Box 636 Saint Johnsbury VT 05819-0636 Office: Blue Ibis PO Box 668 Bethlehem NH 03574-0668

LEE, RENEE MCENTIRE, municipal official; b. Exeter, Calif., Sept. 11, 1949; d. Robert Ernest McEntire and Dorothy Odell (White) Alfred; m. Patrick Michael Lee, June 16, 1973 (div. 1977); 1 child, Bryan. Student, U. Calif., Davis, 1967-69; BA, Calif. State U., Hayward, 1980; postgrad., Stanford U., 1990. Flight attendant World Airways, Inc., Oakland, Calif., 1971-73; sr. sec. City of Oakland, 1973-78, zoning tech., 1978-79; pres. United Pub. Employees Local 390 Svc. Employees Internat. Union, Oakland, 1978-79, bus. agt. United Pub. Employees Local 790, 1980-84; personnel analyst City of Mountain View (Calif.), 1984-85; chief adminstrv. officer Menlo Park (Calif.) Fire Protection Dist., 1985—. Contbr. articles to numerous jours. and mags. Active Vols. City of Oakland, 1989—; mem. Oakland Citizens for Change, 1989—. Mem. Indsl. Rels. Rsch. Assn., Internat. Found. Employee Benefits, Internat. Personnel Mgmt. Assn., Nat. Safety Mgmt. Soc., Western Govtl. Rsch. Assn., San Mateo County Employers Adv. Coun., Nat. Coalition of Labor Union Women (mem. nat. exec. bd. 1980-84), Svc. Employees Internat. Union (first female pres. of local union 1978-79). Democrat. Office: Menlo Park Fire Protection Dist 300 Middlefield Rd Menlo Park CA 94025

LEE, RUTH MIKKELSON, personnel administrator; b. Pitts., Mar. 2, 1936; d. Eric Carl and Amelia Suzanne (Agle) Malte; children: Greg, Rick, Jeff. BA, Allegheny Coll., 1958; MA, U. Wis., 1963; Edn. Specialist, U. Kans., 1983. Tchr. Lutheran West High Sch., Rocky River, Ohio, 1958-61, Madison West High Sch., Wis., 1963-65; instr. English U. Kans., Lawrence, 1975-78, assoc. dir. residential programs, 1978-86; dean of students Baker U., Baldwin, Kans., 1986-88; pers. mgmt. specialist State of Kansas, Topeka, 1989—. Author: Contemporary Literature/Contemporary Problems 1973, Scarlet Ties That Bind, 1989, Images of God the Holy Spirit/Woman, 1989; editor: Staff Resource Book, 1979-86, Curbing Campus Violence, 1987. Pres. Good Shepherd Luth. Ch., Lawrence, 1971-72, 88-89; pres. PTA, Lawrence, 1978-79. Recipient Pan-Hellenic Svc. award 1958, Disting. Svc. award Am. Coll. Pers. Assn. Mem. Am. Assn. Counseling & Devel., AAUW (Outstanding Sr. Woman 1958), Nat. Assn. Student Personnel Adminstrs., Nat. Assn. for Women Deans, Adminstrs. and Counselors, Phi Delta Kappa.

LEE, SUSAN, dentist, microbiologist; b. Jellico, Tenn., June 2, 1943; d. Roy Pickerell and Florida Maybell (Weaver) Savage; m. Joseph James Lee, Dec. 30, 1969 (dec. Dec. 1980); 1 child, Susan. BS, Cumberland Coll., 1965; DMD, U. Louisville, 1976. Asst. head dept. microbiology Norton Children's Hosp. (formerly Norton Meml. Infirmary, Louisville, 1964-69; head dept. microbiology St. Anthony's Hosp., Louisville, 1969-72; mgr. office, cons. Drs. Med. Plaza, Louisville, 1976-82; dentist Office of Richard S. Bonn, DMD, Louisville, 1982-86; hygienist, dentist, cons. Office of James Lewis, DMD, Louisville, 1986—; cons. in field, 1982—. Named Hon. Order Ky. Cols. Mem. Louisville Soc. Physicians and Surgeons (sec., treas.), So. Med. Soc., Fraternal Order Police. Republican. Baptist. Home: 6303 Crest Creek Ct Louisville KY 40241

LEE, SUSAN PREVIANT, newspaper editor and writer; b. Milw., Aug. 7, 1948; d. David Spencer and Lois (Huebner) Previant; m. Kenneth R. Weisshaar, Sept. 4, 1988; 1 child, Spencer. BA, Sarah Lawrence Coll., 1965; MA, Columbia U., 1972, PhD with distinction (John Jay fellow), 1975. Assoc. editor Fortune mag., N.Y.C., 1980-81; editorial bd. The Wall Street Jour., N.Y.C., 1981-83; sr. writer Bus. Week mag., N.Y.C., 1983-84; sr. editor, columnist Forbes mag., N.Y.C., 1984-88; dep. editor Op-Ed Page The N.Y. Times, N.Y.C., 1988—; adj. asst. prof. econs. Columbia U., N.Y.C., 1977-80, adj. prof., 1980-84; cons. Nightline TV program, 1987—; frequent TV guest Good Morning, America. Columnist Vogue mag., 1982-84; regular guest editor Ind. Network News "From the Editor's Desk", 1981-85; author: The Signet Book of Inexpensive Wine, 1977, 2d edit., 1979, The Cotton Economy: Perceptions and Realities, 1977, A New Economic View of American History, 1979, revised edit., 1987, Susan Lee's ABZ's of Economics, 1987, Susan Lee's ABZ's of Money and Finance, 1988; contbr. articles to mags., newspapers, profl. jours., including The New York Times, Barron's, The New Republic, The Washington Post. Bd. visitors U. Calif. Grad. Sch. Bus., Davis, 1985—. Recipient NCFE award in editorial writing for Wall Street Journal, 1982, Amos Tuck Columnist award Dartmouth Coll., 1984.

LEE, TONÏA RENEÉ, government agent; b. Colorado Springs, Mar. 27, 1963; d. Ernest and Claudine (Brunt) L. BA in Oral Communication, Cen. (Okla.) State U., 1983; postgrad., Tex. So. U., 1983, Oral Roberts U., 1984-85; MPA, U. So. Calif., 1987, cert. in jud. adminstrn., 1987; doctoral studies, Saybrook Inst., 1989—, postgrad., 1988—. Spl. agt. U.S. Dept. Def., Gardena, Calif., 1986—; vol. cons. Tulsa County Juvenile Bur., 1985; black per rep. counselor, Cen. State U., 1982-83; libr. asst., 1981; admission and records clk., 1982, mem. High Sch.-Coll. rels. bd. (award of merit for outstanding svc. 1981), student senate 1981-83, student senate housing chmn. 1981-82, recruiter, 1981-83; housing mayor Oral Roberts U., 1982. Author: Slavery Without Chains and Other Selected Poems. Vol. ARC, 1980; mem. Young Democrats, 1981-83, NAACP (L.A. chpt.). Named one of Outstanding Young Women of Am., 1985. Mem. Assn. Trial Lawyers Am., Am. Judicature Soc., Am. Bus. Woman's Assn., NAFE, Women in Communication, Pre-Law Club (sec.-treas. 1982-83), Afro-Am. Soc., NCO Wives Club (ednl. scholarship 1980), Cen. State U. Alumni Assn., NAACP, Kappa Delta Pi, Delta Sigma Theta (golden life mem., ednl. scholarship 1980). Democrat. Baptist.

LEE, VICKI, corporate professional; b. Monroe, La., Oct. 20, 1944; d. Robert Leonard and Kathryn Marshall (Hall) Balfanz; m. Darrell Eugene Lee, June 1, 1968; children: Tiffani, Brittani, Derek, Austin. BS, McMurray U., 1966; MS, Portland State U., 1974, postgrad., 1979—. Sec. Bert Chapman Oil Co., Abilene, Tex., 1964-66; tchr. Austin (Tex.) Ind. Sch. Dist., 1966-68, Lake Washington Sch. Dist., Kirkland, Wash., 1968-70, Longview (Wash.) Sch. Dist., 1970-73; tchr., counselor, adminstr. Evergreen Schs., Vancouver, Wash., 1973-77; legal adminstr. Lee Law Office, Vancouver, 1977—; corp. officer 1st Hill, TLR Inc., Vancouver, 1979—; owner Victoria's World Trade, Vancouver, 1979—. Patentee in field. Mem. Women in Action (treas.), AAUW. Republican. Roman Catholic. Office: Lee Mitchelson et al 9102 NE Hwy 99 Vancouver WA 98665

LEEDER, ELLEN LISMORE, language and literature educator; b. Vedado, Havana, Cuba, July 8, 1931; came to U.S., 1959; d. Thomas and Josefina (Jorge) Lismore; m. Robert Henry Leeder, Dec. 20, 1957; 1 child, Thomas Henry. Doctora en Pedagogia, U. Havana, Cuba, 1955; MA, U. Miami, 1966, PhD, 1973. Lang. tchr. Emilia Azcárate Sch., Havana, 1950-52, St. George's Sch., Havana, 1952-59; from part-time instr. to full prof. Spanish Barry U., Miami Shores, Fla., 1960-75, prof. Spanish, 1975—; chmn. fgn. langs. dept. Barry U., 1975-76, fgn. lang. coord., 1976-78, acting chair dept. English and modern langs., 1983, coord. fgn. langs., 1984-89, dir. Spanish immersion program, 1986-88; prof. Miami-Dade Community Coll., Fla., 1974-75; vis. prof. U. Madrid, Spain, 1982, 89, 90; cons. NEH, Miami, 1981-83; judge Asociación Criticos y Comentaristas del Arte, Miami, 1985-90; oral examiner, juror Dade County Pub. Schs., Miami, 1986-87. Author: El Desarraigo en Las Novelas de Angel Maria de Lera, 1978, Justo Sierra y el Mar, 1979. Mem. MLA, South Atlantic MLA, Am. Council Teaching Fgn. Lang., Am. Assn. Tchrs. of Spanish and Portuguese (v.p. southeastern Fla. chpt. 1984-87), Visiting Nurse Assn. (bd. dirs. 1978-80), Phi Alpha Theta, Kappa Delta Pi, Sigma Delta Pi, Alpha Mu Gamma. Club: Coral Gables Country. Home: 830 SW 101 Ave Miami FL 33174 Office: Barry Univ 11300 NE 2 Ave Miami Shores FL 33161

LEEDS, ELIZABETH LOUISE, miniature collectibles executive; b. L.A., July 24, 1925; d. Charles Furnival and Etta Louise (Jackson) Mayes; m. Walter Albert Leeds, Jan. 20, 1973 (dec.); children: Pam Ravey Lewis, Linda Ravey McCallam, Diane Ravey Lathrop, Tom Ravey. Student pub. sch., Prescott, Ariz. Lic. real estate agt., Ariz., cert. motel mgr. Real estate agt., Prescott, Ariz., 1962-64; sec. to mgr. Kon Tiki Hotel, Phoenix, 1964-65; draftsman Goleta Water Dist., Calif., 1965-68; asst. to vp research and design House of Mosaics, Santa Barbara, Calif., 1968-69; exec. chmn. poster design, dept. music U. Calif.-Santa Barbara, 1969-74; v.p. Colorform West, Inc., Santa Barbara, 1974-75; pres. Leeds Miniatures, Inc., Lincoln City, Oreg., 1975-86, Leed's Co., Inc., 1989—; cert. instr. Technologies for Creating, DMA, Inc., 1986—; lamp and silk screen designer Colorform West, Inc.; ind. assoc. The Environ. Network. Illustrator: Just A Story by Gustav Coenod, 1964. Mem. Hobby Industry Am., Miniatures Industry Assn. Am., Nat. Assn. Female Execs., Eugene C. of C., Eugene Bus. and Profl. Women. Republican. Clubs: Assn. Humanistic Psychology, Internat. New Thought Alliance, Assn. Transpersonal Psychology. Home: 2290 Arthur Ct Eugene City OR 97405

LEEDS, NANCY BRECKER, sculptor, lyricist; b. N.Y.C., Dec. 22, 1924; d. Louis Julius and Dorothy (Faggen) Brecker; m. Richard Henry Leeds, May 9, 1945; children: Douglas Brecker, Constance Leeds Bennett. Student Pine Manor Jr. Coll., 1942-44. Pres. Roseland Ballroom, N.Y.C., 1977-81. One-woman shows: Andrew Crispo Gallery, N.Y.C., 1979, Jeannette McIntyre Gallery Fine Arts, Palm Springs, Calif., 1987-88; exhibited in group shows at Bond Street Gallery, Great Neck, N.Y., Gallery Ranieri, N.Y.C., 1978, Country Art Gallery, 1984, Nature Conservatory Show, Country Art Gallery, 1985, Bonwit Teller, Manhasset, N.Y., 1985, Jeanette C. McIntyre Gallery, Palm Springs, Calif., 1987, The Empire Collection, N.Y.C., 1988, 89. Writer lyrics for musical Great Scot, 1965, score for Scrooge Musical Theatre of Ariz., 1989; lyricist for popular music. Trustee The Floating Hosp., N.Y.C., 1975—, v.p. Mem. ASCAP, The Dramatist Guild, The Songwriters Guild. Avocations: tennis; skiing.

LEEDY, EMILY L. FOSTER (MRS. WILLIAM N. LEEDY), educational consultant; b. Jackson, Ohio, Sept. 24, 1921; d. Raymond S. and Grace (Garrett) Foster; MEd, Ohio U., 1957; postgrad. Ohio State U., 1956, Mich. State U., 1958-59, Case Western Res. U., 1963-65; m. William N. Leedy, Jan. 1, 1943; 1 son. Dwight A. tchr. Frankfort (Ohio) schs., 1941-46, Ross County Schs., Chillicothe, Ohio, 1948-53; elem. and supervising tchr. Chillicothe City Schs., 1953-56; dean of girls, secondary tchr. Berea City Schs., 1956-57; vis. tchr. Parma City Schs., 1957-59; counselor Homewood-Flossmoor High Sch., Flossmoor, Ill., 1959-60; teaching fellow Ohio U., 1960-62; asst. prof. edn., 1962-64; assoc. prof., counselor Cuyahoga Community Coll., 1964-66; dean of women Cleve. State U., 1966-67, assoc. dean student affairs, 1967-69; guidance dir. Cathedral Latin Sch., 1969-71; dir. women's service div. Ohio Bur. Employment Svcs., 1971-83; cons. in edn., 1983—. Mem. adv. com. S.W. Community Info. Svc., 1959-60; youth com. S.W. YWCA, 1963-70, chmn., 1964-70, bd. mgmt., 1964-70; group svcs. coun. Cleve. Welfare Fedn., 1964-66; chmn. Met. YWCA Youth Program study com., 1966, bd. dirs., 1966-72, v.p., 1967-68; chmn. adv. coun. Ohio State U. Sch. Home Econs., 1977-80. Named Cleve. area Woman of Achievement, 1969; named to Ohio Women's Hall of Fame, 1979, Chillicothe Ross Women's Hall of Fame, 1988; recipient Outstanding Contbn. special award Nat. Assn. Commns. for Women, 1983, Meritorious Svc. award Nat. Assn. Women Deans, Adminstrs. and Counselors, 1984. Mem. AAUW, Am., Northeastern Ohio (sec. 1958-59, exec. com. 1963-64, pub. rel. chmn. 1962-64, newsletter chmn., editor 1963-64, del. nat. assembly 1959-63) personnel and guidance assns., LWV, Am. Assn. Retired Persons (Ohio women's initiative spokesperson 1987-89, state legis. com. 1989—), Nat. Assn. Women Deans and Counselors (publs. com. 1967-69, profl. employment practices com. 1980-82, Meritorious Svc. award 1984), Ohio (program chmn. 1967, editor Newsletter 1968-71), Cleve. Counselors Assn. (pres. 1966), Zonta Internat. (exec. bd. 1968-70, treas. 1970-72, chmn. dist. V Status of Women 1980-81), Nat. Assn. Commns. for Women (dir. 1980-81, sec. 1981-83), Rio Grande Coll. Alumni Assn. (Atwood Achievement award 1975), Bus. and Profl. Women's Club (Nike award 1973), Ohio Retired Tchrs. Assn., Svc. Corps of Retired Execs. Delta Kappa Gamma, Women's City Club (Cleve.). Home: 580 Lindberg Blvd Berea OH 44017 Office: 699 Rocky Rd Chillicothe OH 45601

LEEF, AUDREY V., mathematics educator, minister; b. Hoboken, N.J., July 15, 1922; d. Chester Arthur and Lucile Francine (Guilloud) Vincentz; m. George Robert Leef, June 21, 1947; children: Eric David, Janet Lucile, Mark Jonathan, Carol Audrey. BA, Montclair (N.J.) State Coll., 1943; MS, Stevens Inst. Tech., Hoboken, N.J., 1947; MDiv, Drew U., Madison, N.J., 1985; EdD, Rutgers U., New Brunswick, N.J., 1976. Chmn. dept. math. Millburn (N.J.) High Sch., 1943-48; assoc. prof. math. Montclair State Coll., Upper Montclair, 1966—; assoc. minister First Congl. Ch., Irvington, N.J., 1985—; lectr. in field. Contbr. articles to profl. jours. Recipient Outstanding Alumni Citation, Montclair State Coll., 1985. Mem. AAUW (pres. state div. 1972), Montclair State Coll. Alumni Assn. (pres. 1976), Nat. Council Tchrs. Math., Research Council of Diagnostic and Prescriptive Math. (nat. bd.). Republican. Home: 24 Overlook Rd Mountain Lakes NJ 07046 Office: Montclair State Coll Normal Ave/Valley Rd Upper Montclair NJ 07043

LEEMAN, SHARON LYNN, employee benefits representative; b. Natrona Heights, Pa., Dec. 5, 1956; d. Fred Howard and Edith Irene (Brubaker) Leeman. AAS in Bus. Mgmt., Westmoreland County Coll., 1982; BA in Bus. Mgmt., Seton Hill Coll., 1987. Cert. employee benefits specialist. With Allegheny Power Svc. Corp., Greensburg, Pa., 1974—; employee benefits studies rep. Allegheny Power Svc. Corp., Greensburg, 1988—. Reporter West Penn News, Greensburg, 1983-85. Vol. coord. Westmoreland Arts & Heritage Festival, Greensburg, 1986-89; sec. West Penn Explorer's Post Com., Greensburg, 1983-84. Named Outstanding Young Women of Am., 1988. Mem. Nat. Mgmt. Assn., AAUW (editor newsletter 1988-90, Honored Woman award 1989), Greater Greensburg Jaycees (sec. 1988-89, v.p. 1989-90, Jaycee of Month award 1989), West Penn VA, Sigma Lambda. Democrat. Office: Allegheny Power Svc Corp 800 Cabin Hill Dr Greensburg PA 15601

LEE-MANN, ALLISON ANN, communications company personnel official; b. Washington D.C., Jan. 16, 1957; d. Edward H. and Shirley M. (Sandidge) Lee; m. A. Kenneth Mann, Aug. 27, 1983. BA, Duquesne U., Pitts., 1978. Cert. compensation profl. Form mgmt. trainee to compensation adminstr. Equibank, Pitts., 1978-84; personnel asst. Intec Systems, 1984; from sr. compensation analyst to mgr., benifit communication Mellow Bank, Pitts., 1984-89; pers. exec. Ketchum Communications Inc., Pitts., 1989—. Mem. alumni bd. govs. Duquesne U., 1984. Mem. Pitts. Personnel Assn., Am. Compensation Assn., Pitts. Assn. Human Resources Profls., Nat. Assn. Negro Bus. and Profl. Women Clubs (fin. sec. 1986-88, 2d v.p. 1988—), Jr. League Pitts. Democrat. Roman Catholic. Home: 2342 Orlando Pl Pittsburgh PA 15235 Office: Ketchum Communications Inc Six PPG Pl Pittsburgh PA 15222

LEE-MCDONALD, CYNTHIA ANN, psychologist, lawyer; b. Bethesda, Md., Apr. 28, 1954; d. Carl E. and Marceline (Harrow) Lee; m. Thurman David McDonald, Sept. 28, 1985. BA, Emory U., 1975; MA, U. Miss., 1976, PhD, 1979, JD, 1981. Bar: Mo., Miss.; lic. psychologist Mo., Miss. Account exec. Ferris & Co., Washington, 1981-85; dir. equities and estate planning Acadia Mut. Life, Washington, 1986-88; psychologist Great Oaks Ctr., Silver Spring, Md., 1988—; mem. adv. bd. Montgomery County Crisis Ctr., Bethesda, 1984-85; bd. dirs. Lee Assocs., Chevy Chase, Md.; psychologist Gaithersburg (Md.) Guidance-Evaluations, 1989—. Vol. Developmentally Disabled, Silver Spring, 1988—, Humane Soc., State of Md. Mem. Am. Psychol. Assn., Md. Psychology Assn., Md. Bar Assn., Miss. Bar Assn. Republican. Episcopalian. Home: 4905 Bradley Blvd Chevy Chase MD 20815

LEEMING, E. JANICE, venture capitalist; b. Central Falls, R.I., June 12, 1941; d. Edward A. and Estalle C.(Choiniere) L.; m. Arthur D. Little, Sept. 6, 1974; children: Cameron Royal, Kimberley Murray. BS, U. R.I., 1977; MBA, Babson Coll., 1980. Staff acct. Narragansett Capital, Providence, 1964-73; sr. assoc., v.p. Venture Capital Fund New Eng., Boston, 1981-88; pres., chief exec. officer Leeming Investment, Boston, 1988—; pub., chmn. bd. Mktg. to Women, Boston, 1990—; bd. dirs. Body Dynamics, 1990. Trustee, Little Family Found., 1980, Boston Ballet Co., 1987, Dance Umbrella, 1990, The Wellness Community, 1990; trustee, vice chmn. Boston Ballet Sch., 1988. Mem. Nat. Orgn. Female Entrepreneurs, New Eng. Venture Capital, Lyford Cay Club, Dunes Club. Home: 100 Fulton St Boston MA 02109 Office: Mktg to Women Inc 33 Broad St Boston MA 02109

LEESON, JANET CAROLINE TOLLEFSON, cake specialties company executive; b. L'Anse, Mich., May 23, 1933; d. Harold Arnold and Sylvia Aino (Makikangas) Tollefson; children by previous marriage: Warren Scott, Debra Delores; m. Raymond Harry Leeson, May 20, 1961; 1 child, Barry Raymond. Student Prairie State Coll., 1970-76; master decorator degree Wilton Sch. Cake Decorating, 1974; grad. Cosmopolitan Sch. Bus., 1980. Mgr., Peak Svc. Cleaners, Chgo., 1959; co-owner Ra-Ja-Lee TV, Harvey, Ill., 1961-66; founder and head fgn. trade dept. Wilton Enterprises, Inc., Chgo., 1969-75; tchr. cake decorating J.C. Penney Co., Matteson, Ill., 1975; office mgr. Pat Carpenter Assocs., Highland, Ind., 1975; pres. Leeson's Party Cakes, Inc., cake supplies and cake sculpture, Tinley Park, Ill., 1975—; lectr. and demonstrator cake sculpture and decorating; lectr. small bus. and govt. Sec., Luth. Ch. Women; active worker Boy Scouts Am. and Girl Scouts U.S., 1957-63; bd. dirs. Whittier PTA, 1962-70, South Suburban Parkinson's Support Group, 1989-90; active Bremen Twp. Rep. Com. Recipient numerous awards for cake sculpture and decorating, 1970—. Mem. Internat. Cake Exploration Soc. (charter, Outstanding Mem. Ill. 1984), Retail Bakers Am., Chgo. Area Retail Bakers Assn. (1st pl. in regional midwest wedding cake competition 1978, 80, 1st pl. nat. 1982, others), Am. Bus. Women's Assn. (chpt. publicity chmn., hospitality chmn. 1982-83, membership chmn. 1988-90, named Woman of Yr. 1986), Ingalls Meml. Hosp. Aux., Lupus Found. Am. (hot line girl Tuesdays Ill. chpt.). Lutheran. Home and Office: 6713 W 163d Pl Tinley Park IL 60477

LEET, MILDRED ROBBINS, corporate executive, consultant; b. N.Y.C., Aug. 9, 1922; d. Samuel Milton and Isabella (Zeitz) Elowsky; m. Louis J. Robbins, Feb. 23, 1941 (dec. 1970); children: Jane, Aileen; m. Glen Leet, Aug. 9, 1974. BA, NYU, 1942; LHD (hon.), Coll. Human Svcs., 1988. Pres. women's div. United Cerebral Palsy, N.Y.C., 1951-52; bd. dirs. United Cerebral Palsy, 1953—, chmn. bd., 1953-55; rep. Nat. Coun. Women U.S. at UN, 1957-64, 1st v.p., 1959-64, pres., 1964-68, hon. pres., 1968-70; sec., v.p. conf. group U.S. Nat. Orgns. at UN, 1961-64, 76-78, vice chmn., sec., 1962-64, mem. exec. com., 1961-65, 75—, chmn. hospitality info. svc., 1960-66; vice chmn. exec. com. NGO's UN Office Public Info., 1976-78, chmn. ann. conf., 1977; chmn. com. on water, desertification, habitat and environment Conf. NGO's with consultative status with UN/ECOSOC, 1976—; mem. exec. com. Internat. Coun. Women, 1960-73, v.p., 1970-73; chmn. program planning com., women's com. OEO, 1967-72; chmn. com. on natural disasters N.Am. Com. on Environment, 1973-77; N.Y. State chmn. UN Day, 1975; ptnr. Leet & Leet (cons. women in devel.), 1978—; co-founder, dir. Trickle Up Program, 1979—. Contbr. articles to profl. jours.; editor UN Calendar & Digest, 1959-64, Measure of Mankind, 1963; editorial bd.: Peace & Change. Co-chmn. Vols. for Stevenson, N.Y.C., 1956; vice chmn. task force Nat. Dem. Com., 1969-72; commr. N.Y. State Commn. on Powers Local Govt., 1970-73; chmn. Coll. for Human Svcs., 1985—; former mem. bd. dirs. Am. Arbitration Assn., New Directions, Inst. for Mediation and Conflict Resolution, Spirit of Stockholm; bd. dirs. Hotline Internat.; v.p. Save the Children Fedn., 1986—; rep. Internat. Peace Acad. at UN, 1974-77, Internat. Soc. Community Devel., 1977—; del. at large 1st Nat. Women's Conf., Houston, 1977; chmn. task force on internat. interdependence N.Y. State Women's Meeting, 1977; mem. Task Force on Poverty, 1977—; chmn. Task Force on Women, Sci. and Tech. for Devel., 1978; U.S. del. UN Status of Women Commn., 1978, UN Conf. Sci. and Tech. for Devel., 1979, co-dir. Trickle Up Program, Inc, 1979—; Brazzaville Centennial Celebration, 1980; mem. global adv. bd. Internat. Expn. Rural Devel., 1981—; mem. Coun. Internat. Fellows U. Bridgeport, 1982-88; trustee overseas edn. fund LWV, 1983—; v.p. U.S. Com. UN Devel. Fund for Women, 1983—; mem. Nat. Consultative Com. Planning for Nairobi, 1984-85; co-chmn. women in devel. com. Interaction, 1985—; mem. com. of cooperation Interam. Commn. of Women, 1986; bd. dirs. Nat. Women's Conf. Com., 1986-87; adv. com. Am. Assn. Internat. Aging, 1986—; mem. Overseas Devel. Bd., 1988—. Recipient Crystal award Coll. Human Svcs., 1983, ann. award Inst. Mediation and Conflict Resolution, 1985, Woman of Conscience award Nat. Coun. Women, 1986, Temple award Inst. Noetic Scis., 1987, Presdl. End Hunger award, 1987, Giraffe award Giraffe Project, 1987, Woman of the World award Eng.'s Women Aid, 1989; co-recipient Rose award World Media Inst., 1987, Human Rights award UN Devel. Fund for Women, 1987, (with Glen Leet) Pres.'s medal Marymount Manhattan Coll., 1988, Leadership award U.S. Peace Corps, Woman of Vision award N.Y.C. NOW, 1990, Matrix award Women in Communications, Inc., Spirit of Enterprise award Rolex Industries, 1990. Mem. AAAS, Women's Nat. Dem. Club, Cosmopolitan Club, Princeton Club. Home and Office: 54 Riverside Dr New York NY 10024

LEFEVRE, CAROL BAUMANN, psychologist; b. Pierron, Ill., Nov. 26, 1924; d. Berhard Robert and Eunice Leone Hoyt (Heston) Baumann; m. Perry Deyo LeFevre, Sept. 14, 1946; children: Susan LeFevre Hook, Judith Ann LeFevre-Levy, Peter Gerret. AA, Stephens Coll., 1944; MA in Sociology, U. Chgo., 1948, MST, 1965, PhD in Human Devel., 1971. Registered psychologist, Ill. Tchr. Chgo. Theol. Sem. Nursery Sch., 1962-63, U. Chgo., Lab. Sch., 1965-66; asst. prof. psychology St. Xavier Coll., Chgo., 1970-74, assoc. prof., 1974-86, acting chmn. dept. psychology, 1970-71, chmn. dept. psychology, 1971-77, asst. dir. Inst. Family Studies, 1973-82, dir., 1982-85; intern in clin. psychology with Adlerian pvt. practitioner, Chgo., 1973-75; pvt. practice clin. psychology, Chgo., 1975—; mem. staff Logos Inst. Chgo. Theol. Sem., 1973-76; speaker in field. Author, researcher on subjects including returning women grad. students' changing self-conceptions, women's roles, inner city children's perceptions of sch., aging and religion. Pub. Health Service tng. grantee NIMH, 1969. Mem. Am. Psychol. Assn., Ill. Psychol. Assn., N.Am. Soc. Adlerian Psychology, Phi Beta Kappa. Mem. United Ch. of Christ. Home and Office: 1376 E 58th St Chicago IL 60637

LEFF, LISA AMY, executive search company consultant; b. Bridgeport, Conn., Apr. 14, 1958; d. Martin Jan Leff and Arden (Weckstein) Costanzo. BS in English Lit., San Francisco State U., 1981. Mgr. Joshua Simon, San Francisco, 1979-82; ptnr. Myrone, Inc., San Francisco, 1982-85; assoc. Allied Search, Inc., San Francisco, 1985-87; ptnr. Berger & Assocs., San Francisco, 1987—. Big sister Big Bros./Big Sisters, San Francisco, 1988-89. Mem. The Investing Women Investment Club (sec. 1989—). Democrat. Jewish. Home: 1859 Broadway San Francisco CA 94109 Office: Berger & Assocs 50 California Ste 460 San Francisco CA 94111

LEFFELL, MARY SUE, educator; b. Knoxville, Tenn., Oct. 12, 1946; d. W.O. and Katherine (Warren) L. BS with highest honors, U. Tenn., 1968; PhD, U. N.C., 1973. Diplomate Am. Bd. Med. Lab. Immunology. Asst. prof. Dept. Microbiology/Immunology Eastern Va. Med. Sch., Norfolk, 1979-83, assoc. prof., 1983-85; assoc. prof. Med. Coll. Ga., Augusta, 1985-89, dir. histocompatibiity/immunology lab, 1985-89; assoc. prof. Dept. of Medicine, Johns Hopkins U. Sch. of Medicine, 1989—; co-dir. Immunogenetics Labs, 1989—. Contbr. articles to profl. jours. Woodrow Wilson fellow, 1968. Mem. Am. Soc. for Histocompatibility/Immunogenetics (chair accreditation program 1988—), United Network for Organ Sharing (bd. dirs.), Southeastern Organ Procurement Found., Am. Soc. of Transplant Physicians, Am. Coll. of Allergy and Immunology, Am. Assn. Immunologist. Office: Johns Hopkins U Sch Medicine Immunogenetics Lab Baltimore MD 21205

LEFFERTS, MELISSA BRIGGS, English teacher; b. Worcester, Mass., Apr. 4, 1962; d. Loring Greene and Priscilla Lorena (Pratt) Briggs; m. Edward Leedom Lefferts, May 31, 1965. BA in English and Music, Worcester State Coll., 1984. Cert. secondary English tchr., Mass. Nursing personnel cons. Med. Resources, Worcester, 1984-85; tchr. English Worcester Pub. Schs., 1986-88; substitute tchr. East Windsor (Conn.) High Sch., 1988—; make-up cons. Wachusett Regional High Sch. Mus., Holden, Mass., 1985. Mem., soprano I Worcester Chorus, 1980—; bd. dirs. Doherty HIgh Drama Club, Worcester, 1986. Democrat. Congregationalist. Home: 52 N Main St East Longmeadow MA 01028

LEFKOWITZ, BARBARA MELVILLE, travel program executive; b. State Coll., Pa., Mar. 4, 1945; d. S. Donald and Ella (Maguire) Melville; m. Theodore H. Lefkowitz; children: Kathryn, Margaret. BA, Mt. Holyoke, 1967. Trip dir. Am. Youth Hostels, N.Y.C., 1967-70; founder, owner/dir. Student Hosteling Program, Conway, Mass., 1970—. Home: Ashfield Rd Conway MA 01341

LEFLER, SALLY GENE, management consultant; b. St. Louis, Apr. 8, 1936; d. James I. Lefler and Gene (Heitman) Tripodi. B.A., Lindenwood Coll., St. Charles, Mo., 1957; postgrad. honors program, Am. U., Case Western Res. U., Harvard U. Trainee U.S. Dept. State, 1957-58; tchr., counselor Fairfax Hall Coll. Prep., Waynesboro, Va., 1958-60; buying exec. Famous-Barr, May Co., St. Louis, 1960-63; devel. dir. St. Louis Carondelet YWCA, 1963-66, exec. dir., 1966-70; fin. and devel. cons. Nat. Bd. YWCA of USA, Atlanta, San Francisco and N.Y.C., 1970-73; real estate broker Holiday Builders, St. Simons Isle, Ga., 1973-74; freelance cons., Chgo., Conn., 1975-79; mgmt. cons., N.Y.C., 1979—; dep. support coordinator world conf. World Assn. of Girl Guides/Girl Scouts, London, Eng., 1984; dir. Office Nat. Bd. dirs., Girl Scouts U.S.; mem. Internat. Tng. Inst. World YWCA, nat. bd., 1969; lectr. in field. Author, organizer: A Social History of Art in Missouri, 1969; asst. editor: Finance Administration Manual, Nat. Bd. YWCA, 1974-75. Mem. Press Club (Brunswick, Ga.), Zonta (treas., bd. dirs., sec. St. Louis County chpt.). Avocations: international travel, exploration of cultures through music and the arts. Home: 5 Orchard Hills New Canaan CT 06840

LEFOND, MICHELE M., social services administrator; b. Wyandotte, Mich., Apr. 26, 1955; d. Gerald J. Sr. and Mary Ann (Schlachter) S.; children: Susan, Elizabeth. BA, Mercy Coll. Detroit, 1977; MSW summa cum laude, U. Mich., 1984. Cert. child and family specialist. Dir. social work Advanced Profl. Home Health Care, Troy, Mich., 1986; project coord. Hegira Programs, Inc., Westland, Mich., 1987; program dir. Ea. Mich. U., 1988; chief operating officer Target Enterprises, Ypsilanti, Mich., 1989—. Past bd. pres. Downriver Anti-Rape Effort, 1986; active Mich. Coalition of Substance Abuse Educators, 1986—. Mem. NAFE, Southeastern Mich. Info. and Referral Alliance (bd. dirs.), Substance Abuse Prevention Edn. Network, Golden Key Soc. Home: 4860 Woodside Ypsilanti MI 48197 Office: Eastern Mich U Snow Health Ctr Ypsilanti MI 48197

LEGALLET, MARY MARGUERITE, automotive company executive; b. Burlingame, Calif., Oct. 27, 1962; d. Jon Simon and Martha Marguerite (Sullivan) L. BA in Journalism, U. So. Calif., L.A., 1984. Account mgmt. asst. DDB Needham Worldwide, L.A., 1985-86, account coord., 1986-87; asst. account exec. Saatchi & Saatchi DFSI Pacific, Torrance, Calif., 1988-89; bus. adminstr. Volvo Monitoring and Concept Ctr., Camarillo, Calif., 1989—. Vol. John Tracy Clinic, L.A., 1983, Ed Zschau senatorial campaign, L.A., 1986, Bob Dole presdl. campaign, L.A., 1988. Mem. Sunset Young Reps. (charter), Jr. League L.A. (asst. chair provisional com. 1989-90, chair mktg./pub. rels. com. 1990-91), L.A. Spinsters (chmn. membership 1989-90, 1st v.p. 1990-91). Roman Catholic.

LEGENDRE, LAURETTE MICHELE, architect; b. N.Y.C., July 4, 1954; d. Henri A. and Ruth Esther (Mills) LeG. BArch, Howard U., 1977. Registered architect, N.Y. Ptnr. LeGendre, Johnson, McNeil Architects/Planners, N.Y.C., 1984—, The LJM Group, Architects/Interior Designers, N.Y.C., 1987—, Henri A. LeGendre and Assocs., N.Y.C., 1984—. Vice pres. bd. dirs. Westchester-Putnam coun. Girl Scouts U.S.A., 1988. Mem. AIA, N.Y. Soc. Architects, Howard U. Alumni Assn. (pres. 1982-89), Delta Sigma Theta. Episcopalian. Office: LJM Group-Architects- Interior Designers 175 W 126th St New York NY 10027

LEGGETT, SONYIA ELIZABETH, treasurer, secretary; b. Bennettsville, S.C., June 16, 1936; d. Henry J. and Annie Bell (Spears) Moore; m. Early Leggett, May 12, 1956; children: Gregory, Michael, Reginald, Gwendolyn. Student, Empire State Coll., U. Mich., Cornell U. Sec., treas. N.Y. Metro Area Postal Union, N.Y.C. Mem. labor adv. com. Empire State Labor Coll., Black Unionist Leadership Com.; active N.Y.C. Cen. Labor Coun. Recipient Matron of the Yr. award. Mem. NAACP, Nat. Coun. Negro Bus. Women. Home: 460 W 34th St New York NY 10001

LEGGIO, BEVERLY CHAMBERS, small business owner; b. Houston, Oct. 11, 1953; d. A. Pat and Beverly (Coates) Chambers; m. Johnnie Leggio Jr., May 13, 1977 (div. 1987); children: Peter, Gina, Margaret, Jonice. Student, U. St. Thomas, 1972-73; AAS in Nursing, Alvin Community Coll., 1976-77; postgrad., Houston Bapt. U. RN, Tex. Lic. vocat. nurse Tex. Children's Hosp., Houston, 1974-76, RN, 1976-77; RN Frierson and Wolf Clinic, Houston, 1977-78, Meml. City Gen. Hosp., Houston, 1978-79; dir. Houston ops. Nurses, PRN, Inc. subs. Ventilation Assocs., Houston, 1979-81; v.p. OMNA Corp., Houston, 1981-84; cons. Pep, Inc. subs. Datalab, Inc., Houston, 1984; pres. ProCare Cos., Inc., Houston, 1984—. Mem. Tex. Assn. Home Health Agencies (v.p. 1989—), Oncology Nurse Soc., Intravenous Nurse Soc., Nat. Assn. Home Care, Tex. Assn. Home Health Agys. (govt. affairs com. 1988—), Coun. on Aging (chmn. home care com.), Am. Acad. Home Care Physicians (exec. dir., co-founder 1987—, outstanding contbn. to physician involvement in home care 1989). Office: Procare Cos 3715 Dacoma Houston TX 77092

LEGRANDE, MARGARET ESTELLA, school system administrator; b. Richmond, Va., May 28, 1931; d. Samuel Patrick LeGrande and Lula Estella LeGrande (Coxe) Groome; m. Floyd Posby, Aug. 20, 1960 (div. 1987); children: Floyd, Margaret LeGrande. Student, Va. Union U., 1952-54, 56; BS in Nursing, Va. Commonwealth U., 1957; postgrad., Columbia U., 1972, Pace U., 1974, Yeshiva U., 1985; MS, New Sch. Social Research, 1987. RN., N.Y.; cert. tchr., N.Y. Supr. Mt. Sinai Hosp., N.Y.C., 1958; pvt. duty nurse Hosp. for Joint Diseases, N.Y.C., 1959-65; head nurse Dept. Health, N.Y.C., 1965-66; dir. staff devel. Coll. View Nursing Home, N.Y.C., 1966-72; supr. Jewish Home and Hosp. for Aged, N.Y.C., 1972-77; supr. Concord Nursing Home, Bklyn., 1977-78, dir. nursing, 1978-80; tchr., clin. instr. N.Y.C. Bd. Edn., 1982-85, tchr., coordinator, 1985—; health planner Health Systems Agy., N.Y.C., 1974-76; adj. prof. physical/health edn. Borough of Manhattan Community Coll., N.Y.C., 1988; lectr. in field. Bd. dirs. Citizen Care Day Care, N.Y.C., 1986—, Citizen Care Com., N.Y.C., 1986—, N. Manhattan Credit Union, N.Y.C., 1987—; chmn. program com. Harlem Teams for Self Help Inc., N.Y.C., 1987—; mem. task force Harlem Hosp. Community Bd., N.Y.C. Recipient Sojourner Truth award Harlem Women's Com. New Future Found., 1988, Spl. Mother Yr. award ABG Cable TV, 1988, Recognition award Med-Manhattan Soc. Practical Nursing., 1988. Mem. Am. Coll. Health Care Adminstrs., Assn. Supv. and Curriculum Devel., Am. Mgmt. Assn., Nat. Assn. Female Execs., Chi Eta Phi, Alpha Kappa Alpha. Democrat. Episcopalian. Home: 626 Riverside Dr #24G New York NY 10031

LEGROS, SUSAN LEBLANC, bank executive; b. Lake Charles, La., Jan. 9, 1952; d. John Ozeme and Lila Mae (Thomas) LeBlanc; m. Andy Joseph Legros Jr., Mar. 6, 1976. Student, La. State U., 1970-72, McNeese State U., 1972-74, 89—; diploma real estate fin., Am. Bankers Assn. and Ohio State U., 1981. Sales assoc. Reinauer Real Estate, Lake Charles, 1976-77; note clk. Am. Bank of Commerce, Lake Charles, 1977-79, mgr. real estate, 1979-81, officer personal banking, 1981-83, asst. v.p., 1983-85, v.p., 1985-87; spl. assets officer Farm Credit Banks, Jennings, La., 1988—, sr. credit analyst, 1989—. Treas. opposition com. F.E.M.A., Calcasieu Parish, 1984-87; v.p. S.W. La. chpt. ARC, Lake Charles, 1986—, bd. dirs., 1984-87; bd. dirs. McNeese U. Rodeo Team Devel. Found, 1988—. Mem. Nat. Assn. Bank Women (treas. Lake Charles chpt. 1982-83, v.p. 1983-84, pres. 1984-85, program chmn. state conv. 1987), Home Builder Assn. Southwest La. (bd. dirs. 1983-87), La. Farm Bur., Am. Bankers Assn. (instr. real estate fin. SW La. chpt. 1988, 90). Democrat. Roman Catholic. Office: Farm Credit Banks PO Box 318 Jennings LA 70546

LE GUIN, URSULA KROEBER, author; b. Berkeley, Calif., Oct. 21, 1929; d. Alfred Louis and Theodora (Kracaw) Kroeber; m. Charles A. Le Guin, Dec. 22, 1953; children: Elisabeth, Caroline, Theodore. B.A., Radcliffe Coll., 1951; M.A., Columbia, 1952. Vis. lectr. or writer in residence numerous workshops and univs., U.S. and abroad. Author: Rocannon's World, 1966, Planet of Exile, 1967, City of Illusion, 1967, A Wizard of Earthsea, 1968, The Left Hand of Darkness, 1969, The Tombs of Atuan, 1971, The Lathe of Heaven, 1971, The Farthest Shore, 1972, The Dispossessed, 1974, The Wind's Twelve Quarters, 1975, A Very Long Way from Anywhere Else, 1976, Orsinian Tales, 1976, The Language of the Night, 1978, Leese Webster, 1979, Malafrena, 1979, The Beginning Place, 1980, Hard Words, 1981, The Eye of the Heron, 1981, The Compass Rose, 1982, King Dog, 1985, Always Coming Home, 1985, Buffalo Gals, 1987, Wild Oats and Fireweed, 1988, A Visit from Dr. Katz, 1988, Catwings, 1988, Solomon Leviathan, 1989, Fire and Stone, 1989, Catwings Return, 1989, Dancing at the Edge of the World, 1989, Tehanu, 1990; also numerous short stories, poems, criticism, screenplays. Recipient Boston Globe-Hornbook award for excellence in juvenile fiction, 1968; Nebula award (novel) 1969, 75, (story) 1975; Hugo award (novel), 1969, (story) 1973, (novella) 1973, (novelette) 1988; Gandalf award, 1979; Kafka award, 1986; Newbery honor medal, 1971; Nat. Book award, 1973; Fulbright fellow France, 1953-54. Mem. Sci. Fiction Research Assn., Sci. Fiction Writers Assn., Authors League, PEN, Writers Guild West, NOW, NARAL, Phi Beta Kappa. Office: Lit Agt Virginia Kidd PO Box 278 Milford PA 18337 also: Dramatic Agt Ilse Lahn 5300 Fulton Ave Van Nuys CA 91401

LEHMAN, CLARA MAY HILEMAN, physician; b. Sharon, Pa., Oct. 30, 1901; d. Mayberry and Clara May (Keasey) Hileman; B.S., Pa. State U., 1924; postgrad. Columbia, 1927-28, Marine Biol. Lab., 1930-31; M.D., Woman's Med. Coll., Pa., 1935; m. Robert N. Lehman, Apr. 24, 1938; 1 dau., Mary Dorcas. Intern Lancaster (Pa.) Hosp., 1935-36, resident, 1936-37; practice gen. medicine, Pa., 1936-47; practice staff geriatrics U.S. Army Hosp., Ft. Meyer, Va., 1948-51, VA Hosp., Aspinwall, Pa., 1955-57, Woodville State Hosp., Carnegie, Pa., 1957-68. Mem. AMA, Pa. County Med.Soc., Allegheny County Med. Soc., Royal Soc. Health, Alpha Omega Alpha, Alpha Epsilon Iota. Address: 801 Washington Ave Tyrone PA 16686

LEHMAN, PAMELA KAY, physical therapist, athletic trainer; b. Danbury, Conn., May 26, 1963; d. Ernest Alfred and Gail Louise (Henderson) L. BS in Phys. Therapy, U. Conn., 1985, postgrad. Registered physical therapist; cert. CPR instr., rape crisis counselor. Phys. therapy aide Danbury (Conn.) Hosp., 1979-81, 84, Danbury (Conn.) Orthopedic Assocs., summers 1981-85; phys. therapist, athletic trainer, dept. athletic medicine U. Conn., Storrs, 1981-87; asst. dir., med. supr. Conn. Soccer Sch., Storrs, 1981—; phys. therapist, athletic trainer Western Conn. Phys. Therapy and Sports Medicine Ctr., Danbury, 1987—, New Milford (Conn.) Orthopedic Assocs., 1989—; cons. dance medicine Eglevsky Ballet, New Hyde Park, N.Y., 1986-88, Sch. Performing Arts, New Milford, 1988—; phys. therapist, ahtletic trainer U.S. Olympic Tng. Ctr., Colorado Springs, Colo., 1987; mem. med. staff N.Y.C. Marathon, 1985—. Contbr. articles to profl. jours. CPR instr. ARC, Danbury, 1987—; counselor, chaperone Missouri Synod Internat. Youth Conf., Washington, 1986; counselor Greater Danbury Women's Ctr., 1988—; coord. prayer chain Prince of Peace Ch., Brookfield, Conn., 1990—; vol. Am. Ballet Theatre, N.Y.C., 1988—. Named Vol. of Yr. Danbury Hosp, 1978. Mem. Conn. Athletic Trainer's Assn. (pub. rels. chmn. 1987—), Ea. Athletic Trainer's Assn., Nat. Athletic Trainer's Assn. (examiner 1989—), Am. Coll. Sports Medicine, Am. Phys. Therapy Assn.-Sports Sect. Republican. Lutheran. Office: Western Conn Phys Therapy & Sports Medicine Ctr 73 Sandpit Rd Danbury CT 06810

LEHMAN, SHERELYNN, psychotherapist; b. Cleve., June 27, 1941; d. Marvin and Esther (Morgenstern) Friedman; m. Theodore Gary Falcon, Aug. 19, 1962 (div. Apr. 1971); 1 child, Michael Aaron Falcon; m. Paul James Lehman, Apr. 21, 1974 (div. Nov. 1984); 1 child, Jonathan Paul. BS, Ohio U., 1963; postgrad., UCLA, 1970-72; MA, Loyola U., Los Angeles, 1974. Cert. sex therapist; lic. marriage, family and child counselor. Instr. psychology Cuyahoga Community Coll., Cleve., 1977-82; pvt. practice marriage, family and sex therapy Cleve., 1978—; instr. psychology St. Thomas of Villanova, Miami, Fla., 1980-81; clin. mem. Gender Team Case Western Res. U., Cleve., 1983—. Author: Love Me, Love Me Not: How to Survive Infidelty, 1985; TV personality . Cleve., Sta. WKYC-AM (NBC), Cleve., 1981—; talk show host Sta. WJW, Cleve., 1983-85, The Sherry Lehman Show, Sta. WHK, 1989—, Morning Exch., WEWS-AM, 1990—. Fellow Internat. Council of Sex Edn. and Parenthood; mem. Am. Assn. for Marriage and Family Therapy (clin.), Nat. Com. on Values and Sexuality (v.p.), Am. Assn. Sex Educators, Counselors and Therapists (adv. bd., nat. pub. relations com.), Am. Fedn. TV and Recording Artists, NATAS, Assn. for Retarded Citizens, Assn. for Children with Learning Disabilities, Phi Beta Kappa, Pi Gamma Mu, Kappa Delta Pi, Alpha Lambda Delta. Office: 3619 Park E Ste 213 S Beachwood OH 44122

LEHMANN, BARBARA LOWIS, farmer; b. Taylorville, Ill., Sept. 20, 1934; d. Frank Ashton and Dorothy Jane (Beaty) Lowis; m. John Richard Lehmann, June 24, 1956; children: Nancy, Richard (dec.). BS, U. Ill., 1955, MS, 1958. Tchr., advisor Champaign High Sch., Ill., 1958-61; mgr. Walnut Lake Farms, Morrisonville Ill., 1964-81; pres., mgr. Walnut Lake Farms, Inc., Morrisonville, 1981—; bd. mem., program initiator Girl Scout Coun. of Nation's Capital, Washington, 1966-81, pres. 1981-87. Active PTA, Rockville, Md., 1966-75; docent chmn. Nat. Mus. of Am. History, Smithsonian Inst., Washington, 1978-79; docent, program initiator history Smithsonian Instn., 1970—. Recipient Thanks Badge, Girl Scouts U.S., 1975. Mem. AAUW. Methodist. Avocations: needlework, bicycling, stained glass, gardening, reading.

LEHMANN, ESTHER STRAUSS, investment company executive; b. Binghamton, N.Y., Apr. 19, 1944; d. Julius and Betty (Lind) Strauss; m. Aaron Lehmann, Feb. 27, 1966; children: Shanna, Shira, Marc, David. BS, Cornell U., 1966; cert. in vol. and non-profit orgn. mgmt., U. Conn., 1976; cert. employee benefits specialist, U. Pa., 1983. V.p. Fairway Mgmt., West Hartford, Conn., 1976-80; investment exec. Herzfeld & Stern, Paramus, N.J., 1980-86, Gruntal & Co., Inc., Ft. Lee, 1988—. Home: 1632 Dover Ct Teaneck NJ 07666

LEHMANN-CARSSOW, NANCY BETH, educator, coach; b. Kingsville, Tex., Sept. 9, 1949; d. Valgene William and Ella Mae (Zajicek) Lehmann; m. William Benton Carssow, Aug. 1, 1981. B.S., U. Tex., 1971, M.A., 1979. Free-lance photographer, Austin, Tex., 1971—; geography tchr., tennis coach Austin Ind. Sch. Dist., Tex., 1971-78, 79—; salesperson, mgr. What's Going On-Clothing, Austin, 1972-78; area adminstr. Am. Inst. Fgn. Study, Austin, 1974-81; area rep. World Encounters, Austin, 1981—, tour guide, Egypt, Kenya, 1977, 79, 81, 87; participant 1st summer inst. Nat. Geog. Soc., Washington, 1986, tchr., 1986—; tchr. Leader for People in Soviet Union, 1989, 90. Author curriculum materials. Photographer for book: Bobwhites, 1984. Recipient Merit award Nat. Council Geog. Edn., 1975, Creative Teaching award Austin Assn. Tchrs., 1978, Teaching Excellence award U. Tex. Ex-Student's Assn., 1987; Fulbright scholar, Israel, 1983. Mem. Nat. Council Social Studies, NEA, Nat. Council Geog. Edn., East African Wildlife, Earthwatch (participant archaeol. dig. in Swaziland 1984), Delta Kappa Gamma (pres. 1986-88), Phi Kappa Phi. Democrat. Roman Catholic. Avocations: stained glass; photography; tennis; gardening; needlepoint. Home: 1025 Quail Park Dr Austin TX 78758 Office: Lanier High Sch 1201 Peyton Gin Rd Austin TX 78758

LEHRMAN, ELA-JOY, nurse, researcher; b. Orange City, Iowa. A in Nursing, Kirkwood Community Coll., 1973; BSN, Ariz. State U., 1977; MS, U. Utah, 1980; PhD, U. Ariz., 1988. RN, cert. nurse midwife, Ariz., Ohio. Staff nurse Mercy Hosp., Iowa City, Iowa, 1973-74, Drs. Hosp., Phoenix, 1974-77, Kaiser Found. Hosp., San Diego, 1978; nurse midwife Phoenix Meml. Hosp., 1980-82; mem. faculty U. Ariz., Tucson, 1983-85, U. Phoenix, 1985-88; asst. prof. Case Western Res. U., Cleve., 1989—; cons. maternal child health March of Dimes, Tucson, 1985; rsch. cons. Tucson Med. Ctr., 1987-88. Mem. rules and regulations adv. com. on revision nurse practitioner Ariz. State Bd. Nursing, Phoenix, 1983; mem. profl. adv. com. March of Dimes, Tucson, 1985-88. Mem. Am. Coll. Nurse-Midwives, Am. Nurses Assn., Nat. Assn. Childbearing Ctrs., Sigma Xi, Sigma Theta Tau. Office: Case Western Res Univ Sch of Nursing 2121 Abington Rd Cleveland OH 44106

LEHRMAN, EMILY ROSENSTEIN, librarian; b. Kuibyshev, USSR, Mar. 1, 1923; came to U.S.A., 1935; d. Joseph L. Rosenstein and Sima B. (Glashow) Yaffe; m. Nathaniel S. Lehrman, June 18, 1944; children: Leonard, Paul, Betty. BS, Simmons Coll., Boston, 1945; MA, Columbia U., 1947; MLS, Long Island U., Brookville, N.Y., 1967. Profl. Librarian. Asst. to editor American Review of Soviet Medicine, N.Y.C., 1946-48; instr. of Russian Columbia U., N.Y.C., 1948, Adelphi U., Garden City, N.Y., 1962-66; librarian Hofstra U., Hempstead, N.Y., 1969-73, SUNY, Farmingdale, N.Y., 1974, Kingsboro Psychiatric Ctr., Bklyn., 1975-78; staff editor Macmillan Pub. Co., N.Y.C., 1980; librarian C.W. Post Campus, Long Island U., Brookville, N.Y., 1980—. Translator Folktales of the Amur, 1980, Novella, appeared in Mass. Rev., "A Week Like Any Other Week", 1974. Mem. ALA, Nassau County Library Assn., Acad. and Spl. Library Div., Assn. Coll. and Research Libraries, Beta Phi Mu. Home: 10 Nob Hill Gate Roslyn NY 11576

LEIBEL, SHELLEY JOY, lawyer; b. Bklyn., Jan. 24, 1957; d. Sol and Lee (Kornbluth) L.; m. Ben J. Szwalbenest, Nov. 8, 1981. BA summa cum laude, Queens Coll., Flushing, N.Y., 1978; JD, Temple U., 1981. Bar: Pa. 1981. Law clk. to presiding judge Pa. Ct. Common Pleas, Phila., 1980; assoc. Law offices of Elaine Smith, Phila., 1980-82; ptnr. Smith and Leibel, Phila., 1982—; instr. Inst. Paralegal Tng., Phila., 1986—. Vol., advisor United Way Southeastern Pa., 1985—. Mem. Pa. Bar Assn., Phila. Bar Assn., Phi Beta Kappa. Home: 1107 Bryn Mawr Ave Bala Cynwyd PA 19004 Office: Smith & Leibel 1420 Locust St Suite 110 Acad House Philadelphia PA 19102

LEIBOVITZ, ANNIE, photographer; b. Conn., Oct. 2, 1949. Student, San Francisco Art Inst. Chief photographer Rolling Stone, from 1973, photographer, 1970-83; photographer Vanity Fair, 1983—; photographer for advertisements, 1987—; proprietor Ann Leibovitz Studio, N.Y.C. Works exhibited various galleries; author: Annie Leibovitz: Photographs, 1983. Recipient Innovation in Photography award Am. Soc. Mag. Photographers, 1987. Office: Annie Leibovitz Studio 55 Vandam St New York NY 10013*

LEIBOW, LOIS MAY, educator; b. Newark, Jan. 4, 1937; d. Samuel and Sada (Rothman) Applebaum; m. Sheldon G. Leibow, Aug. 11, 1963; children: Philip, Frances, Brian. BA, Douglass Coll., 1959; MA in Sociology, CCNY, 1962. Substitute tchr. Monmouth County Registry, N.J., 1983—; telemarketer Denco-Kirby Co., Eatontown, N.J., 1985—. Newspaper columnist Atlanticville, Long Branch, N.J., 1984—; contbr. Am. String Tchr., 1979. Mem. Hadassah (life, program v.p. Woodbridge, N.J. chpt. 1972-74), Sisterhood of Temple Beth El (bd. dirs.), Jewish War Vets., Woman's Club Perth Amboy N.J. Republican. Office: Denco Distbrs 30 South St Eatontown NJ 07724

LEIBOWITZ, ANITA ZOE, computer science educator; b. Wash., D.C., Dec. 21, 1934; d. Mark Rawson and Camille (Prato) Bullock; m. Samuel Harold Lewis, 1956, (div. 1962); m. Gerald Martin Leibowitz, Feb. 17, 1936; children: Sarah Joy, Thomas Jacob, Neal Marev, Alice Roberta. BS, D.C. Tchrs Coll., 1956; MS, Northwestern U., 1966, U. Conn., 1981. Math, software engr. U.S. Army Map Svc., Washington, 1956-61; rsch. asst., software engr. George Washington U. Biometric Lab., Washington, 1961-62; math. programmer IBM, Cambridge, Mass., 1962-63; vis. lectr. Northwestern U., Evanston, Ill.; tchr. Windham Sch. System, Willimantic, Conn., 1973-75; instr. Ea. Conn. State Coll., Willimantic, 1978-80; rsch. asst., software engr. U. Conn., Storrs, 1980-81; asst. prof. Cen. Conn. State U., New Britain, 1981—; cons. George Washington U. Biometric Lab., 1962, U. Conn. 1984. Contbr. articles to prof. jours. Pres. Women's Club of Storrs, 1988-90. Mem. AAUW, Mansfield LWV, Assn. for Computing Machinery, Windham Whirlers Square Dance Club (pres. 1979-81, 86-88), Upsilon Pi Epsilon. Democrat. Office: Cen Conn State U 1615 Stanley St New Britain CT 06050

LEIDICH-ROSS, LOIS JEAN, controller; b. El Pao, Venezuela, July 20, 1952; came to U.S., 1953; d. Peter Weimer and Georgia (Beamer) Leidich; m. Thomas Frances Ross, Nov. 8, 1980; children: Julie Marie, Teresa Lynn. BS, U. Colo., 1976. Billing clk. Western States Machinery, Denver, 1971-76; acct. James O. Mc, CPA, Denver, 1977; accounts payable clk. Power Motive Corp., Denver, 1977-79, staff acct., 1979-81, contr., 1981-87, contr., sec., officer, 1987—. Mem. Nat. Assn. Accts. Roman Catholic. Home: 43393 Livermore Common Fremont CA 94539

LEIDIG-REED, CHERYL SUE, sales executive; b. Moline, Ill., May 25, 1947; d. Guy Ken Hoefle and Betty Jane (Ishmael) Sheil; m. Lareth Gayle Leidig, Dec. 10, 1967 (div. Mar. 1973); m. Shedrick Reed, Oct. 4, 1987; childrne: January, Terry, Elijah, Nikita. AA, Cypress (Calif.) Coll., 1985; BA in Advt., Calif. State U., Fullerton, 1989. With real estate sales dept. Century 21-Ben Hansen, Buena Park, Calif., 1978-80; advt. sales exec. Seattle Time Newspaper, 1989—; mktg. cons. Seattle Times Newspaper, 1989-90. Author poems. Vol. Victims of Incest Emerge Successful, Anaheim, Calif., 1985; leader Nat. Girl Scouts U.S., Brea, Calif., 1983. Recipient Tng. award Soroptimists, 1983; State of Calif. grantee, 1984. Mem. Women in Communications, Inc. Republican. Baptist. Home: 13904 4th Ave NE Seattle WA 98125 Office: Seattle Times Newspaper Seattle WA 98125

LEIDNER, SUZANNE CAROLYN, lawyer; b. Summit, N.J., Feb. 7, 1942; d. Preston P. and Elvera D. (Meiele) Burnett; m. Edmund W. Arthur, Mar. 17, 1961 (div. 1966); m. Joel D. Leidner, Dec. 24, 1966; 1 child, David C. BS, U.C.L.A, Los Angeles, 1970; JD, Peoples Coll. of Law, Los Angeles, 1979. Atty. Weiser, Kane, Ballmer & Berkman, Los Angeles, 1980-82; atty. (pres) Leidner & Leidner, Los Angeles, 1982--. Mem. ABA, Calif. Bar Assn., Nat. Lawyers Guyild, Nat. Orgn. Social Security Claims Rep.; chairperson Social Security Sect. Los Angeles Coounty Bar. Democrat. Jewish. Office: Leidner & Leidner 4622 Hollywood Blvd Los Angeles CA 90027

LEIFERMAN, SILVIA WEINER (MRS. IRWIN H. LEIFERMAN), artist, civic worker, sculptor; b. Chgo.; d. Morris and Annah (Kaplan) Weiner; m. Irwin H. Leiferman, Apr. 20, 1947. Student, U. Chgo., 1960-61; studied design and painting, Provincetown, Mass. Organizer, charter mem. women's div. Hebrew U. Chgo., 1947; Head Pres. Accessories by Silvia, Chgo., 1964; organizer women's div. Edgewater Hosp., 1954; chmn. bd. Leiferman Investment Corp.; chairwoman spl. sales and spl. events greater Chgo. Com. for State of Israel; originator, organizer Ambassador's Ball, 1956, Presentation Ball, 1963; met. chmn. numerous spl. events Nat. Council Jewish Women, Nathan Goldblatt Soc. Cancer Research, Chgo.; now life mem., trustee; chmn. numerous spl. events North Shore (Ill.) Combined Jewish Appeal; chmn. women's com. Salute to Med. Research City of Hope, 1959; founder Ballet Soc. of Miami; Bd. dirs. Jewish Children's Bur., North Shore Women's Aux., Mt. Sinai Hosp., George and Ann Portes Cancer Prevention Center Chgo., Nat. Council Jewish Women, Fox River (Ill.) Sanitorium, Edgewater Hosp., Greater Chgo. Bonds for Israel, Orgn. of Rehab. and Tng. Exhibited one-woman shows, Schram Galleries, Ft. Lauderdale, Fla., 1966, 67, D'Arcy Galleries, N.Y.C., 1964, Stevens Annex Bldg., Chgo., 1965, Miami (Fla.) Mus. Modern Art, 1966, 72, Contemporary Gallery, Palm Beach, Fla., 1966, Westview Country Club, 1968, Gallery 99, 1969; exhibited group shows, Ricardo Restaurant Gallery, Chgo., 1961, 62, Bryn Mawr (Chgo.) Country Club, 1961, 62, Covenant Club Ill., Chgo., 1963, D'Arcy Galleries, 1965, Internat. Platform Assn., 1967, Miami Mus. Modern Art, 1967, Bacardi Gallery, 1967, Hollywood Mus. Art, 1968, Gallery 99, Miami, Lowe Art Mus., Crystal Ho. Gallery, Miami Beach, 1968; represented in numerous pvt. collections. Bd. dirs. Brandeis U., Art Inst. Chgo., Miami Mus. Modern Art; co-founder, v.p. Silvia and Irwin Leiferman Found.; donor Leiferman award auspices City of Hope; internat. co-chairwoman Ball Masque; mem. pacesetter/trustee com. Greater Miami Jewish Fedn., 1976-77; founder Mt. Sinai Hosp. Greater Miami, Fla.; donor Michael Reese Hosp., 1978; benefactress Miami Heart Inst., 1979, St. Joseph Hosp., 1979, Mt. Sinai Med. Center, 1979. Recipient citations for def. bond sales U.S. Govt., for Presentation Ball State of Israel, 1965; Pro Mundi Beneficio Gold medal Brazilian Acad. Humanities, 1976; numerous awards Bonds for Israel; numerous awards Combined Jewish Appeal North Shore Spl. Gifts; Keys to cities Met. Miami area; named Woman of Valor State of Israel, 1963; donor award Miami Heart Inst. Fellow Royal Soc. Arts and Scis.; mem. Internat. Council Mus., 1st Ann. Cultural Conf. Chgo., Am. Fedn. Arts, Artist's Equity Assn., Fla. Poetry Soc., Miami Art Center, Miami Beach Opera Guild Com., Greater Miami Cultural Art Center, Guild Com. Greater Miami Cultural Art Center, Sculptors of Fla., Royal Acad. Arts, Internat. Platform Assn., Lowe Art Mus., Am. Contract Bridge League, Friends of U. Haifa. Jewish (mem. bd.). Clubs: Standard, Bryn Mawr Country, Covenant, Green Acres, International, Boye, Whitehall, Key (Chgo.); Jockey, Westview Country, Tower (Miami Beach, Fla.); Brickell Bay. Home: 10155 Collins Ave Bal Harbour FL 33154 Office: Harbor Island Spa Villa 44 Miami Beach FL 33144*

LEIGH, IRENE WOLFF, psychologist; b. London, Oct. 20, 1944; came to U.S., 1948; d. Paul and Hilde (Faber-Drucker) Wolff; m. David Israel Leigh, Aug. 19, 1965; children: Serena Jean, Darby Jared. BS in Deaf Edn. with honors, Northwestern U., 1966; MA in Rehab. Counseling, NYU, 1969, PhD in Clin. Psychology, 1986. Lic psychologist, N.Y. Tchr. Lexington Sch. for Deaf, N.Y.C., 1966-67, dir. guidance svcs., 1969-71, counselor, therapist, 1978-80; psychologist Lexington Ctr. for Mental Health, N.Y.C., 1985-89, asst. dir., 1989—. Contbr. articles to profl. jours. Mem. Am. Psychol. Assn., Am. Deafness and Rehab. Assn., N.Y.C. Civic Assn. of Deaf, AG Bell Assn. for Deaf, Nat. Assn. of Deaf. Office: Lexington Ctr Mental Health 30th Ave & 75th St Jackson Heights NY 11370

LEIGH, JANE ELLEN, veterinarian; b. Clinton, Iowa, Jan. 23, 1958; d. Robert Edward and Barbara Jane (Thomsen) Leigh. BS in Animal Sci., Iowa State U., 1980, DVM, 1984. Intern Cen. Hosp. for Animals, Marion, Ill., 1983; assoc. veterinarian Clinton Vet. Clinic, 1984-89, ptnr., 1990—; vol. lectr. Clinton Community Sch. Dist., 1989—; cons. Clinto Jr. Humane Soc., 1988—. Vol. Republican Party Com., Clinton, 1984—, Adult Literacy Campaign, Clinton, 1988—. Mem. AVMA, Iowa Vet. Med. Assn., Ill. Vet. Med. Assn. Republican. Methodist. Home: 2826 Pershing Blvd Clinton IA 52732 Office: Clinton Vet Clinic 1574 Main Ave Clinton IA 52732

LEIGH, MARLISA KAY MACLEOD, engineer; b. Bad Kreuznach, Fed. Republic Germany, Mar. 22, 1965; came to U.S., 1967; d. Jon Harold and Marian Harriette (Batdorff) MacLeod; m. Michael James Leigh, Aug. 20, 1988. BS in Physics, Mich. Technol. U., 1988; postgrad., Case Western Res. U., 1990. Office asst. Cen. Mich. U., Mt. Pleasant, summer 1984, 85; inventory analyst Morbark Industries, Winn, Mich., summer 1986; rsch. asst. Nat. Solar Obs., Sunspot, N.Mex., summer 1987; receptionist Mich. Technol. U., Houghton, 1983-85, resident asst., 1985-86, 86-87, CAD-CAM operator, 1987-88; Edison engr. GE Lighting, East Cleveland, Ohio, 1988—. Mem. Soc. Physics Students (v.p. 1987-88), Toastmasters (Richmond Heights, Ohio), Sigma Pi Sigma.

LEIGH, SHARI GREER, software consulting firm executive; b. Reading, Pa., Mar. 1, 1959; d. Martin and Francine Rita (Gross) Rothenstein; m. Martin Brad Greer, Dec. 31, 1979; children: Shannon Leigh, Krista Heather. BA in Biochemistry, Wellesley Coll.-MIT, 1980; postgrad. in bus. adminstrn., Colo. State U., 1982-83. Lead thermal engr. Rockwell Internat. Space div., Downey, Calif., 1980-81; systems engr. Martin Marietta Aerospace, Denver, 1981-82, aerospace new bus. analyst, 1982-84; v.p. Miaco Corp. (Micro Automation Cons.), Englewood, Colo., 1984-87, pres., 1987—. Co-designer life systems monitor for Sudden Infant Death Syndrome, 1980. Recipient Recog. award for satellite work Martin Marietta Aerospace, 1982; VIP at 1st Space Shuttle landing, Rockwell Internat., Vandenberg, Calif., 1981; nominated Entrepreneur of Yr. 1989 Inc. 500 and Arthur Young Entrepreneur program. Mem. Intermountain Humane Soc., MIT Enterprise Forum of Colo. Democrat. Office: Miaco Corp 6300 S Syracuse Way Ste 430 Englewood CO 80111

LEIGH, SUSAN JANE, lobbyist; b. Winchester, Va., June 7, 1951; d. Louis Henry and Barbara Jane (Stephens) L.; divorced; children: Erin Brunner, Kristin Brunner, Matthew Ross. BA, Fla. State U., 1974; MS, Okla. State U., 1978. Design cons. Higdon Furniture, Paducah, Ky., 1976; instr. Murray State U., Ky., 1976-77, Okla. State U., Stillwater, 1977-78; mgr. research and communications Homes and Land, Tallahassee, 1979-83; dir. legis. and tech. affairs Fla. Home Builders Assn., Tallahassee, 1983-87, bond devel. mgr. Fla. Housing Fin. Agy., 1987—, mgr. bond devel. Mem. Fla. Weatherization Adv. Council, Tallahassee, Fla. Collaborative Elderly Housing Initiative, Tallahassee, Onsite Sewage Disposal Systems Research Adv. Council. Editor, dir.: Housing Reference Manual, 1985, Energy Update, 1986. Contbr. articles to Homebuilder mag., 1983—. Chmn. Tallahassee Housing Found., 1984-86; bd. mem. Fla. Low Income Housing Coalition, Tallahassee, 1986. Mem. Am. Assn. Housing Educators (govtl. affairs chmn. 1985-86), Nat. Assn. Women in Constrn., So. Bldg. Code Congress, Bldg. Ofcl. Assn. Fla., Nat. Assn. Housing and Redevel. Ofcls. Democrat. Methodist. Office: Fla Housing Fin Agy 2570 Centerview Dr Tallahassee FL 32399

LEIGHTON, MIRIAM, artist, consultant; b. N.Y.C.; d. Nathan and Rose (Unger) Kaback; m. Bruce Leighton, Feb. 22, 1965 (dec.); children: Elayne Joyce, Jo-Ann Helene. Student, NYU, 1934, 45. Cons. Saks Fifth Ave., N.Y.C., 1954-56; free lance cons. Ft. Lee, N.J., 1973-80; cons. in field; rep. Artists and Sculptors, N.J., 1984—. Active vol. various charitable orgns. Honored by Am. Cancer Soc., Technion, Univ. of Tech., United Jewish Community of Bergen County, Holly Ctr. (adv. for abused children), others.

LEIMER, PHYLLIS HANCOCK, personnel consultant; b. Kansas City, Mo., June 27, 1936; d. Kenton L. and Lois (Post) Hancock. BA, Coll. of Wooster, Ohio, 1958; postgrad., NYU. Pers. cons. Girl Scouts U.S.A., N.Y.C.; pers. adminstr. Rsch. Hosp. and Med. Ctr., Kansas City; speaker in field. Tutor Lenox Hill Neighborhood; vol., shelter for homeless; elder, deacon Fifth Ave. Presbyn. Ch. Mem. Soc. for Human Resource Mgmt., N.Y. Personnel Mgmt. Assn. Home: 405 E 54th St Apt 7G New York NY 10022

LEIN, HEBE BEATRIZ, psychologist; b. Rosario, Argentina, Mar. 18, 1945; came to U.S., 1979; d. Adolfo and Debora (Slepoy) L.; m. Leonardo Berezovsky, Nov. 13, 1968 (div. Nov. 1987); children: Karen, Sonia. M in Psychology, U. Rosario, 1967; PhD in Psychology, U.S. Internat. U., San Diego, 1982. Lic. psychologist, Calif. Cons. psychologist Regional Ctrs., L.A., 1985-87; mem. panel of experts L.A. Superior Ct., Calif., 1986—; pvt. practice psychologist L.A., 1986—; cons. psychologist Mc Laren Hall, El Monte, Calif., 1990—. Mem. Am. Psychol. Assn. Office: 3407 W 6th St #800 Los Angeles CA 90020

LEINBERGER, JOAN SCHMIDT, mental health business manager; b. Bay City, Mich., Nov. 28, 1942; d. Alvin H. and Linda K. (Kernstock) Schmidt; m. Kenneth Edgar Leinberger, Oct. 14, 1961; children: Kelly Jean, David Alan. AS, Bay de Noc Community Coll., 1971; BS, No. Mich. U., 1973, MS, 1977. Sec. The Dow Chem. Co., Midland, Mich., 1960-61, 62-68, Briggs Mfg., Warren, Mich., 1961-62; purchasing asst. Rust Engring., Escanaba, 1973; substitute tchr. Gladstone (Mich.) Area Schs., 1974-76; coll. instr. Bay de Noc Community Coll., Escanaba, 1974-76; bus. mgr. George D. Maniaci Ctr., Escanaba, 1976—. Planning commr. Escanaba City Planning Commn., 1985—; bd. dirs. Delta County Community Concert Assn., Escanaba, 1985-89, mem. 1982—; mem. William Bonifas Fine Arts Ctr., Escanaba, 1987—; bd. dirs., sec. Pub. Service Employees Fed. Credit Union, Escanaba, 1986-88. Mem. AAUW (v.p. 1985-86, chair program edn. com. 1986-87, local chpt.), Am. Soc. Pub. Adminstrn., Kiwanis, Phi Kappa Phi. Lutheran. Office: George D Maniaci Ctr 2920 College Ave Escanaba MI 49829

LEINO, DEANNA ROSE, educator; b. Leadville, Colo., Dec. 15, 1937; d. Arvo Ensio Leino and Edith Mary (Bonan) Leino Malenck; adopted child, Michael Charles Bonan. BSBA, U. Denver, 1959, MS in Bus. Adminstrn., 1967; postgrad. Community Coll. Denver, U. No. Colo., Colo. State U., U. Colo., Met. State Coll. Cert. tchr., vocat. tchr., Colo. Tchr. Jefferson County Adult Edn., Lakewood, Colo., 1963-67; tchr. bus., coordinator coop. office edn., Jefferson High Sch., Edgewater, Colo., 1959—; sales assoc. Joslins Dept. Store, Denver, 1978—; instr. Community Coll. Denver, Red Rocks, 1967-81, U. Colo. Denver, 1976-79, Parks Coll. Bus. (name now Parks Jr. Coll.), 1983—; dist. adviser Future Bus. Leaders Am. Active City of Edgewater Sister City Project Student Exchange Com.; pres. Career Women's Symphony Guild; treas. Phantoms of Opera, 1982—; active Opera Colo. Assocs. & Guild, I Pagliacci; ex-officio trustee Denver Symphony Assn., 1980-82. Recipient disting. service award Jefferson County Sch. Bd. 1980; Jefferson High Sch. Wall of Fame 1981. Mem. NEA (life), Colo. Edn. Assn., Jefferson County Edn. Assn., Colo. Vocat. Assn., Am. Vocat. Assn., Colo. Educators for and about Bus., Profl. Secs. Internat., Career Women's Symphony Guild, Profl. Panhellenic Assn., Colo. Congress Fgn. Lang. Tchrs., Wheat Ridge C. of C. (edn. and scholarship com.), Delta Pi Epsilon, Phi Chi Theta, Beta Gamma Sigma, Alpha Lambda Delta. Republican. Roman Catholic. Club: Tyrolean Soc. Denver. Avocations: decorating wedding cakes, crocheting, sewing, music, world travel. Home: 3712 Allison St Wheat Ridge CO 80033

LEIPZIG, LIBBY BLACK (MRS. FRED LEIPZIG), state official, automotive products company executive; b. Easton, Pa.; d. Benjamin and Mary (Bizar) Black; student Paterson Normal Sch., N.J., 1928, Rutgers U., 1943-44, Fairleigh Dickinson U., 1962; m. Fred Leipzig, Apr. 12, 1940; 1 dau., Marta Beth Leipzig Berman; 1 stepson, Howard A. Leipzig. With N.J. State Employment Service, Passaic, 1941—, supr. profl. comml. dept., Paterson, N.J., 1962-69, supr. indsl. services dept., Passaic, 1969-72; v.p. Major Automotive Products Co., Inc., Clifton, N.J. 1945-69, sec.-treas., 1969—. Home: The Promenade 5225 Pooks Hill Rd Bethesda MD 20814

LEIS, WINOGENE B. (MRS. HENRY PATRICK LEIS, JR.), professional association executive; b. Clay, W.Va., Feb. 27, 1919; d. Gruder L. and Daisy M. (Young) Barnette; R.N. cum laude, Kanawha Valley Hosp., 1939; m. Henry Patrick Leis, Jr., Jan. 8, 1944; children: Henry Patrick III, Thomas Federick. Nurse, Kanawha Valley Hosp., 1939-43. Decorated lady comdr. Equestrian Order Holy Sepulchre Jerusalem. Mem. Woman's Aux. Internat. Coll. Surgeons (corr. sec. N.Y. State surg. div. 1955-57, v.p. 1961-63, pres. 1963-67; pres. U.S. sect. 1970, dir. 1970—, pres. Internat. Body 1977-78, bd. govs. 1978—, chariperson rsch. and scholarship com. 1990—), Flower Fifth Avenue Hosp. Woman's Aux. (dir. 1956-59, 69—), Woman's Aux. N.Y. Acad. Scis., Woman's Aux. N.Y. State Med. Soc., Woman's Aux. Internat. Coll. Surgeons (corr. sec. 1972-74, pres. 1977-78, dir. 1978—, chairperson rsch. scholarship com. 1990), Woman's Aux. Cabrini Med. Ctr., Woman's Aux. Westchester County Med. Ctr., Woman's Aux. Lenox Hill Hosp., Woman's Aux. So. Med. Assn. Republican. Roman Catholic.

LEISING, JEAN, state legislator. Farm owner and operator; indls. nurse Good Samaritan Hosp. Sch. Nursing; state senator from dist. 42 Ind. Senate, 1988—. Trustee Cath. Community Found. Mem. Ind. Corn Growers Assn., Batesville (Ind.) C. of C., Soybean Assn., Pork Producers and Cattlemen's Assn. Republican. Home: Star Rte Oldenburg IN 47036*

LEIST, ELISABETH PASEK, retailer; b. Hastings, Nebr., July 1, 1927; d. Joseph Edwin and Ethel (Anderson) Pasek; m. Frederick Morris Leist Sr., Nov. 26, 1949 (dec. 1976); children: Frederick Morris, Laurette Elisabeth. AA, Stephens Coll., 1947; BS, Ind. U., 1949. Ordained elder Presbyn. Ch., 1984. Electronics and camera merchandiser treasury div. J.C. Penney, Niles, Ill., 1974-79; with K-Mart, Des Plaines, Ill., 1979—, camera and jewelry dept. mgr., 1981-88, jewelry and cosmetic dept. mgr., 1988—. Chmn. pub. rel. coun. Girl Scouts Am., LaPorte, Ind., 1950-52, from organizer to svc. unit chmn., Ill., 1968-84, alt. del., publicity chmn., 1984-88. Office: K-Mart 4227 8500 Dempster Des Plaines IL 60016

LEITH, LINDA JOAN, automobile dealership executive, accountant; b. Wellesley, Mass., Aug. 12, 1959; d. Michael J. and Carolyn Ruth (Sperry) L.; m. David Sean Naber, May 24, 1980 (div. May 1987). BS in Acctg., U. N.C., 1981. CPA, N.C. Staff acct. Deloitte Haskins & Sells, Raleigh, N.C., 1981-83; contr. Leith, Inc., Raleigh, 1983-86; chief fin. officer Leith Mgmt. Co., Raleigh, 1986—. Mem. Am. Mgmt. Assn., N.C. Assn. CPA's. Republican. Presbyterian. Office: 5601 North Blvd Raleigh NC 27604

LEITHWOOD, DOREEN MARJORY, personnel director; b. North Battleford, Sask., Can., Aug. 25, 1930; d. Hugh Scott and Maude Christina (Ficken) Loudfoot; m. Robert Parker Leithwood, Mar. 27, 1948; children: David Robert, Brian Richard. Cert. Personnel Mgmt., Humber Coll., 1976. Cashier T. Eaton Co. Ltd., Toronto, 1948-49; cashier Dominion Stores, Toronto, 1955-57, bookkeper, personnel dir., 1957-60; sales, area mgr. Beauty Counselor, Brampton, Ont., 1961-65; with payroll, personnel dept. A.J. Jackson Constrn., Toronto, 1965-67, Kenting Aviation, Toronto, 1967-69; tng., sales mgr. Ashton Promotions, Toronto, 1969-72; sales, customer services Cameo Careers, Toronto, 1972-76; chief exec. officer Bramalea Personnel Inc., Brampton, 1976—. Bd. dirs. YMCA, Brampton, 1983-84, Peel Children's Found., Mississauga, Ont., 1984-86; exec. Brampton Liberal Assn., 1978-79; del. Liberal COnvention, Ottawa, Ont., 1978-79. Mem. Fedn. Temporary Help Services (bd. dirs. 1985-88, pres. Toronto chpt. 1985-87, Leadership award 1986), Personnel Assn. of Peel (sec., treas. 1987—), Assn. Profl. Placement Agencies and Cons., Brampton Indsl. Assn. (pres. 1981-82),Toronto Ad and Sales Club (chmn. sales courses, 1969-74), Brampton Bd. Trade (bd. dirs. 1978-86). Progressive Conservative. Anglican. Lodge: Zonta (v.p. 1987). Office: Bramalea Personnel Inc, 73B Bramalea Rd, Brampton, ON Canada L6T 2W9

LEITNER, CYNTHIA MADDEN, museum executive; b. Omaha, Mar. 22, 1951; d. John Worthington and Marjorie Ann (Putt) Madden; m. Roger D. Leitner; children: Schuyler, Blair, Paul. Student, U. Nebr., 1969-70, Creighton U., 1971-73. Leasing assoc. John Madden Co., Englewood, Colo., 1977-79; owner, dir. Cynthia Madden Galleries, Denver, 1979-82; dir. The Museum Outdoor Arts, Englewood, 1982-86, pres., 1986—; dir. John Madden Co., Englewood, 1987—; advisor Colo. Bus. Com. for the Arts, Englewood, 1986—; hon. dir. Nat. Museum Women in the Arts, Denver, 1988—. Editor: Portrait of a Museum, 1986. Mem. 50 for Colorado, Denver, 1986. Mem. Am. Assn. Museums, Nat. Assn. for Female Execs., Internat. Council Museums. Home: 1301 Cherryville Rd Littleton CO 80121 Office: The Museum of Outdoor Arts 6312 S Fiddler's Green Cir Englewood CO 80111

LEITNER, R. ELAINE, lawyer; b. Vineland, N.J., Sept. 29, 1953; d. Harry and Barbara Leitner; m. Steven G. Zieff, Jan. 3, 1987; 1 child, Ariel Hana. BS in Psychology, Tufts U., 1975; JD, Georgetown U., 1978. Bar: Calif. 1978. Law clk. to presiding judge U.S. Dist. Ct. (no. dist.) Calif., San Francisco, 1978-79; assoc. Morrison & Foerster, San Francisco, 1980; ptnr. Keker & Brockett, San Francisco, 1980—. Mem., bd. dirs. Legal Aid Soc. San Francisco, 1988—. Mem. ACLU (mem. atty.'s coun. 1989—), Calif. State Bar Assn. (mem. women in the law com. 1986-89), Nat. Assn. Criminal Def. Lawyers, Calif. Atty.'s for Criminal Justice, San Francisco Women Lawyers' Alliance (founding pres. 1983-85). Home: 5922 Almaden Ln Oakland CA 94611 Office: Keker & Brockett 710 Sansone St San Francisco CA 94111-1704

LEITSCHUH, CHERYL ANN, psychologist; b. Stevens Point, Wis., Apr. 30, 1955; d. Alvin Ellsworth and Francis Louise (Voet) McGonigle; m. Patrick Michael Leitschuh, Apr. 30, 1977; children: Christopher, Emily. B, U. Minn., 1976; M, S.D. State U., 1984; EdD in Psychol. Counseling, U. S.D., 1987. Lic. psychologist, Minn. Counselor Cath. Family Svc., Sioux Falls, S.D., 1984-85, Family Svc., Sioux Falls, 1985-87; psychologist Burnsville (Minn.) Counseling Clinic, 1987—; cons. Leitschuh & Assocs., Burnsville, Minn., 1987—; prof. Augsburg Coll., Mpls., 1989—. exec. bd. YMCA, Eagan, Minn., 1989-90. Mem. Am. Psychol. Assn., Am. Assn. Counseling and Devel. Office: Burnsville Counseling Clinic 14050 Nicollet Ave S #312 Burnsville MN 55337

LEITZINGER, SANDRA MAYES, artist, journalist; b. Philipsburg, Pa., Feb. 29, 1936; d. Kenneth Frank and Louise (Kirby) Mayes; m. Charles T. Kurtz III, June 4, 1960 (dec. 1964); children—Karen Elizabeth Earl, Charles Kenneth; m. Robert Frederick Leitzinger, July 8, 1967; 1 child, Robert Franklin. B.S. in Home Econs. and Journalism, Pa. State U., 1957. Home economist Pa. Power and Light Co., Williamsport, Pa., 1957-60; auto racing columnist Clearfield Progress, Pa., 1963-67, Centre Daily Times, State College, Pa., 1982—; freelance automotive artist, 1972—. One-woman shows include: Pa. State U., 1981, Interlaken Inn, Lakeville, Conn., 1987, 88; exhibited in group shows at l'art et l'automobile, N.Y.C., 1980, 88, Painters of Central Pa., Pa. State U., 1983, Alleghenies Mus. Art, Loretto, Pa., 1987, 88; represented in permanent collections at Mus. of Our Nat. Heritage, Lexington, Mass., Auto Art, West Cornwall, Conn., Auto Sport Gallery, Raleigh, N.C., also in pvt. and corp. collections U.S. and Europe; artist poster, program covers Watkins Glen (N.Y.) Internat., 1984-85, l'art et l'automobile, N.Y.C., Auto Art, West Cornwall, Conn., Auto Sport Gallery, Raleigh, N.C., Automotive Emporium, Dallas. Recipient Merit award Strathmore Paper Co., 1980, Bronze award for art display Am. Orchid Soc., 1977, Outstanding Regional Pub. award Antique Automobile Club Am., 1959. Mem. Pa. Watercolor Soc. (signature), Internat. Motor Press Assn., Sports Car Club Am., Antique Automobile Club Am., Internat. Motorsports Assn., Ea. Motorsports Press Assn. Republican. Avocations: travel; gardening; photography. Home: 130 West Outer Dr State College PA 16801 Office: Leitzinger Imports Inc 3220 W College Ave State College PA 16801

LEKAS, MARY DESPINA, otolaryngologist; b. Worcester, Mass., May 13, 1930; d. Spyridon Peter and Merciny S. (Manoliou) L.; m. Harold William Picozzi. BA, Clark U., 1949; MD, Athens (Greece) U., 1957; MA (hon.), Brown U., 1986; student, Boston U. Diplomate, Am. Bd. Otolaryngology. Sci. instr. Hahnemann Hosp. Sch. Nursing; rotating intern Meml. Hosp., Worcester, 1957-58; resident in otolaryngology R.I. Hosp., Providence, 1958-62; surgeon in chief, dept. otolaryngology R.I. Hosp., 1984—; pvt. practice Providence, 1962—; chmn. dept. otolaryngology, Brown U., Providence, 1984—; cons., Cleft Palat Clin. and Craniofacial of R.I. Hosp., 1964—, VA Hosp., Providence, 1967—, St. Joseph Hosp., Providence, 1983—, Miriam Hosp., Providence, 1984—; lectr. profl. orgns., Europe, U.S. Editorial bd., Am. Jour. Rhinology, 1987—; contbr. to profl. publs. Mem. alumni coun. Clark U. Fellow Soc. Univ. Otolaryngologists-Head and Neck Surgeons, Triological Soc. (ea. sect. sec.), ACS, Am. Acad. Otolaryngology-Head and Neck Surgeons, Am. Acad. Facial Plastic and Reconstructive Surgeons, Am. Acad. Broncho-Escophalogy (treas., v.p. 1990); mem. Assn. Acad. Dept. Otolaryngology-Head and Neck Surgery, AMA, Deafness Rsch. Found., Am. Cleft Palate Assn., Am. Med. Women's Assn., Centurian Club, New Eng. Otolaryng. Soc. (pres. 1980-81), Providence Med. Assn. (pres. 1987-88). Greek Orthodox. Home: 129 Terrace Ave East Providence RI 02915 Office: Physicians Office Bldg 110 Lockwood St Providence RI 02903

LEKUS, DIANA ROSE, librarian; b. Washington, Feb. 5, 1948; d. Max and Eleanor (Kruger) L. Student, Hofstra U., 1965-66; BA, Emerson Coll., 1969; MLS, U. Pitts., 1970. Asst. dept. head. search dept. Temple U., Phila., 1970-71; cataloging supr. weekly record sect. R.R. Bowker, N.Y.C., 1972-75; cataloger, asst. prof. U. Ill., Champaign-Urbana, Ill., 1975-78; customer svc. rep. Res. Fund, N.Y.C., 1979-81; list libr. Kleid Co., N.Y.C., 1981—. Sr. editor Am. Book Pub. Record, 1974; book reviewer Libr. Jour., 1979. Mem. So. Poverty Law Ctr., Montgomery, Ala., 1989—, Simon Wiesenthal Ctr., L.A., 1987—; charter mem. Nat. Mus. for Women in the Arts, Washington, 1988. Mem. Hadassah (recording sec. 1986-88), Manhattan Assn. Cabarets. Democrat. Jewish. Home: 28-05 37th St Astoria NY 11103 Office: Kleid Co 530 Fifth Ave 17th Fl New York NY 10036-5101

LELAIDIER-JAMES, PAULA CLAIRE, educator; b. N.Y.C., Mar. 22, 1947; d. Joseph Walfried and Pauline Ann (Butz) LeLaidier; m. Alan William James, Apr. 29, 1978; children: Sean Lawrence Smith, Adam Lawrence Smith. BS in Elem. Edn., St. John's U., 1968; postgrad., various univs. Cert. elem. tchr., N.Y., Ind. Tchr. New Hyde Park (N.Y.) Pub. Schs., 1970-71, Taylor Community Schs., Kokomo, Ind., 1971-75; tchr. Emanuel Lutheran Early Childhood Program, Patchogue, N.Y., 1979-83, dir., 1981-83; tchr. Emanuel Lutheran Day Sch., Patchogue, 1983-86; dir. Emanuel Lutheran After-Sch. Program, Patchogue, 1985-86; tchr. South Country Cen Schs, Brookhaven, N.Y., 1986—; instr. Suffolk County Coordinated Council for Gifted and Talented, Oakdale, N.Y., 1978-79; mem. staff devel. day planning com. South County Cen. Schs., 1988, policy bd. Tchr. Ctr., 1988. Author Hist. Time Capsule elem. sch. play, 1985; directorial asst. Playcrafters Children's Theatre, 1981; editor Cub Scout Pack newsletter, 1978-81. Mem. exec. bd. PTA, Bellport, N.Y., 1978-79; mem. adv. bd. Brookhaven (N.Y.) Elem. Sch., 1987-88, social studies textbook com., 1988; newsletter editor Boy Scouts Am., 1979-81. Mem. N.Y. State United Tchrs. Clubs: Bellport Yacht (exec. bd. 1986-88), Bellport Garden (house tour, flower show chair 1983-86). Lodge: Soroptomists. Office: Brookhaven Elem Sch Fireplace Neck Rd Brookhaven NY 11719

LELAND, PAULA SUSAN, school system administrator, educator; b. Duluth, Minn., Feb. 10, 1953; d. Clarence Henry and Agnes Gudrun (Feiring) L. BS in Elem. Edn. and Music with honors, U. Minn., Duluth, 1975, BS in English, Lang. Arts and Sec. Edn., 1979; MS in Edn. Adminstrn. and Edn. cum laude, U. Wis., Superior, 1982, MEd in Profl. Devel., English and Language Arts summa cum laude, 1984, Spl. Cert. Edn. Adminstrn. summa cum laude, 1988, postgrad., 1988; postgrad., Coll. St. Thomas, 1989, U. Minn., Mpls. Elem. tchr., profl. educator Hermantown Community Schs. #700, Duluth, Minn., 1975—, subs. adminstr., 1982—, mem. staff devel. com., 1987-89; dir. mus. and choir Zion Luth. Ch., Duluth, 1980—, dir./coord. music and handbell, 1983—; dist. coord. and chairperson, planning, evaluating and reporting com., adminstrv. rep. State Dept. of Edn. for Minn. #700, Duluth, 1984-86; student tchr., 1977-90, supr. for U. Wis., Superior; student tchr. supr. faculty community adv. com., community adv. com. U. Minn., Duluth; supr. tchr. aide, parent vols., 1980—. Writer: Hermantown Star Newspaper, 1978; mus. arranger, composer: Compositions, sch. and Zion Ch. activities; architectural planner: floor plans, Edn. Facilities and Creative Activity, 1984; vocalist and soloist community, univ. and Zion Ch. activities, spl. events, 1970; author: reading curriculum Hermantown Community Schs., 1981-82. Mem. Dem. Nat. Conv. supporter, Dem. Party Local Affiliation, Duluth, 1972-90; choir dir., co-chair music and co-author music tape for Centennial Celebration, 1988, mem. nominating and worship coms., recorder, sec. and choir sec. pastor-selected com., 1980—; Sunday sch. tchr., Bible sch. tchr. Zion Luth. Ch., 1970—; supporter Reading is Fundamental, 1975—, United Way of Greater Duluth; mem. Dairy Coun., Hermantown Arts Coun. Named Alworth Scholar. Mem. AAUW, Future Tchrs. Orgn., Red Cross Club (pres, former v.p., svc. award), Sons of Norway (viking ship project), Arrowhead Reading Coun., Minn. Reading Assn., Minn. Edn. Assn. (cert. of appreciation 1990), Hermantown Fedn. of Tchrs., Hermantown Sch. Dist. Cont. Edn. (co-chair, former sec.), Minn. Hist. Soc., Midwest Fed. Banking Consortium, U. Minn.-Duluth Alumni Assn., U. Wis.-Superior Alumni Assn., Minn. Naturalists Assn., Tweed Mus. Art, Mpls. Soc. of the Arts, Mpls. Soc. of Fine Arts, Minn. Inst. Art, Smithsonian Inst., Midwesterners Club, Alpine Club, Zoofari Club, Queen Mary and Spruce Goose Voyager Club, Kappa Delta Pi, Sigma Alpha Iota, Phi Kappa Phi, Phi Delta Kappa, Delta Kappa Gamma, Beta Sigma Phi. Home: 2237 W 11th St Duluth MN 55806

LELYVELD, GAIL ANNICK, actress; b. Boston, May 22, 1948; d. Edward I. and Beatrice Elizabeth (Hewitt) L. BA in Polit. Sci., Boston U., 1970; MA in Polit. Sci., Goddard Coll., 1974; studies with Paul Barry, Peter Donat, Ray Reinhardt, Darrell Laver, others. Actress, 1970—; tech. staff USA Prodns. and Midseason, Hempstead, N.Y., 1986-87, prodn. stage mgr., 1987—; tech. staff Gray Wig, Hempstead, 1986, 87; cons. Talking With prodn. M.A., C.W. Post. Appeared in numerous films including Frances, Halloween III, Children on Their Birthdays, Project 1917, Rocky II, Happy Endings, Seeds of Innocence, Bonfire of the Vanities, 1986, TV show Archie Bunker's Place; actor Alice in Wonderland, Not So Grimm Fairytale Players; actress (theatre) Toby Tyler, Marmelade Gumdrops, Bohemian Lights; singer Musicum Collegium, Hofstra U.; stage mgr., sound asst. Wings; sound asst. Danton's Death. Mem. AFTRA, Nat. Soc. Fund Raising Execs., Freeport Arts Coun. Jewish. Home: care Dennehy 464 Macatee Pl Mineola NY 11501 Office: USA Prodns/Midseason care Hofstra Cultural Ctr Hofstra Univ Hall Hempstead NY 11550

LEMAIRE, CATHY LOUISE, sales account executive; b. N.Y., Oct. 30, 1951; d. Felix Edward and Thelma (Walton) Johnson; m. John Peter LeMaire, May 11, 1974 (div. 1981). Student, Transylvania U., 1969-71. Prodn. control inside salesperson Iris Electonics, Farmingdale, N.Y., 1979-83; corporate prodn. mgr. Arrow Electronics, Melville, N.Y., 1983-84; prodn. mktg. mgr. Schweber Electronics, Westbury, N.Y., 1984-85; acct exec. The Burndy Corp., Norwalk, Conn. Mem. NAFE, Internat. Inst. for Connector and Interconnection Tech. (sec. N.Y. chpt. 1989—), Women in Electronics. Republican. Roman Catholic. Home: 1113 Washington Dr Centerport NY 11721

LEMANEK, KATHLEEN LYNN, pediatric psychologist; b. Sept. 24, 1958; d. Frank Edward and Dorothy Kathryn (Hedrick) Lemanek. BS, U. Pitts., 1980; MA, La. State U., 1983, PhD, 1985. Postdoctoral intern Kennedy Inst./Johns Hopkins U. Sch. Medicine, Balt., 1984-85; asst. prof. pediatrics and psychology U. Miami (Fla.) Sch. Medicine, 1985-89, co-dir. div. clin. psychology, acting internship dir., 1988-89; asst. prof. psychology in pediatrics U. Pa. Sch. Medicine, Phila., 1989—. Mem. editorial bd. Jour. Pediatric Psychology, 1989—, Clin. Child Psychology Newsletter, 1989—; contbr. chpts. to books, articles to profl. jours. Mem. Am. Psychol. Assn., Soc. Pediatric Psychology, Assn. for Advancement of Behavior Therapy, Greenpeace, Sierra Club, Omicron Delta Kappa, Phi Kappa Phi. Office: Div Child Devel/CHOP 34th and Civic Center Blvd Philadelphia PA 19104

LEMASTER, SHERRY RENEE, fund raising administrator; b. Lexington, Ky., June 25, 1953; d. John William and Mary Charles (Thompson) LeM. BS, U. Ky., 1975, MS, 1984. Cert. fund raising exec., real estate agt. Lab. technician in virology, serology Cen. Ky. Animal Disease Diagnostic Lab., Lexington, 1975-76; grant coord., environ. specialist Commonwealth Ky. Dept. for Natural Resources and Environ. Protection, Frankfort, 1976-78; coord. residence hall program Murray (Ky.) State U., 1978-80; dean students Midway (Ky.) Coll., 1980-81, v.p. devel., alumnae affairs, 1981-86; dir. devel. Wilderness Road Coun. Girl Scouts U.S., Lexington, 1986-88, Coll. of Agr. and Life Scis. Va. Poly. Inst. and State U., Blacksburg, Va. 1988—; amb. U. Ky. Coll. Agr.; field reader U.S. Dept. Edn., 1987—; chmn.

Midway chpt. Am. Heart Assn., 1981, Woodford County chpt., 1983; mem. adminstrv. bd. First United Meth. Ch., Lexington, 1982-84, 87; mem. Coun. for Advancement and Support Edn., 1981—, chmn. Ky. conf., 1982; planning com. Nat. Disciples Devel. Execs. Conf., 1984; mem. East Ky. First Quality of Life Com., 1987-88. Recipient Young Career Woman award Bus. and Profl. Women's Club, Frankfort, 1981; named to Hon. Order of Ky. col., 1977, hon. sec. state, 1984. Mem. Am. Coun. on Edn., Nat. Soc. Fund Raising Execs. (bd. dirs. Lexington chpt. 1986), Greater Lexington Area C. of C. (accreditation com. 1982), Advancement Women in Higher Edn. Adminstrn. (former state planning com.), Ky. Assn. Women Deans Adminstrs. and Counselors (editor Newsletter 1981), U. Ky. Alumni Assn. (life), Gen. Fedn. Womens Clubs, P.E.O. (charter), Ninety-Nines Internat. Assn. Women Pilots (vice chmn. Ky. Bluegrass chpt. 1986-87, chmn. and chmn. bd. 1987-88), Lexington Jaycees, N.Y. Found. Ky. Women, Kentuckians N.Y., Pi Beta Phi Nat. Alumnae Assn. (alumnae province pres. 1980-81, sec. bd. dirs. Ky. Beta chpt. 1982-84), Alpha Kappa Psi Alumnae Assn. (charter Murray chpt.). Avocations: private pilot, needlecrafts, swimming, equitation, racquetball. Home: 1404 Locust Dr Blacksburg VA 24060 Office: Va Poly Inst and State U Coll Agrl Blacksburg VA 24061-0402

LEMASTER, SUSAN M., marketing consultant, writer; b. Cody, Wyo., May 9, 1953; d. Floyd Morris and Virginia Kristena (Renner) LeM.; B.A., U. Wyo., Casper, 1979; A.A., Casper Coll., 1977. Reporter, night editor Casper Star Tribune, 1972-76; copy editor, editor In Wyo. mag., Casper, 1979; info. dir. Wyo. Rural Electric Assn., Casper, 1980-81; story editor Wyo. Horizons mag., Casper, 1981-82; asst., instr. English lab. Casper Coll., 1982-84; mktg. mgr. Chen & Assocs., Inc., 1984-87; mktg. cons., 1987-90; mgr. bus. devel. KaWES and Assocs., Inc., 1990—; freelance writer and editor, 1982—; night sch. instr. Casper Coll., 1983-84, summer sch. instr., 1984; editor Casper Jour., summers 1983-84. Recipient First Place News Story, Wyo. Press Assn., 1973; first pl. Editing award Wyo. Press Women, 1980. Democrat. Home: 1940 N Highland Ave #21 Hollywood CA 90068

LEMAY, HELEN LILLIAN SCHNEIDER, advertising and public relations executive; b. Stamford, Conn., July 10, 1947; d. George William and Wilhelmina Helen (Bellmar) Meier; m. Lester G. Lemay; children: Christopher Mitchell, Mark Robert. AA, Brian McMahon Community Coll., 1965-67; student, U. Wash., 1967-69. Asst. personnel mgr. W. H. Brady Co., Milw., 1976-78; mgr. mktg. Cornwell Services, Milw., 1978-80; owner Schneider & Assocs., Waco, Tex., 1981—. Dir. Assn. Locally Involved Vols., Waco, 1980—. Named one of Outstanding Young Women Am., Jr. Woman's Clubs Am., 1984, 85, Outstanding Vol. of Yr., Tex. Jr. Woman's Clubs, 1985. Mem. Advt. Club Am., Pub. Rels. Soc. Am., Am. Soc. for Quality Control, Waco Advt. Club (bd. dirs. 1984—), Waco C. of C. (communications com. 1986—), Rotary, Jr. Woman's Club (pres. 1983-84), Brown Deer Jr. Women's Club (Milw., pres. 1979-80). Lutheran. Home: 4458 Cabot Dr Grand Prairie TX 75052 Office: 6701 Sanger Ave Ste 106 #255 Waco TX 76710

LEMBERGER, COLEEN F., ; b. Oshkosh, Wis., Mar. 23, 1952; d. William A. and Emma M. (Hoffman) L. Student, U. Wis., Oshkosh, 1970-76. Sec. Mogul-Ed, Oshkosh, 1970-72, Lemberger Co., Oshkosh, 1968-70; lab. technician William A. Lemberger Assn., Germantown, Wis., 1977-82; mgr. William A. Lemberger Co., Inc., Oshkosh, 1982—. Office: William A Lemberger Co Inc 2500 Waukau Ave PO Box 2482 Oshkosh WI 54903

LEMBERGER, NANCY LEE, small business owner; b. Manitowoc, Wis., Mar. 27, 1947; d. William Osuld and Elizabeth Helen (Tuschl) Bredesen; m. Patrick A. Grad. high sch., Valderss, Wis., 1961-65. Archtl. drafts person Brandt & Brandt Architects, Manitowoc, Wis., 1965-66; elec. drafts person Primm Elec. Engring, Manitowoc, Wis., 1967; mech. drafts person Paragon Electronics, Two Rivers, Wis., 1968; drafts person Parks Constrn. Co., Dallas, 1977; sr. designer Vantage Cos., Dallas, 1977-85; owner, operator, designer NL Designs & Constrn., Nacogdoches, Tex., 1985--. Mem. Nacogdoches Women's Investment Network, 1985-88. Mem. Nat. Council Interior Designers, Am. Soc. Interior Design, Inst. Bus. Designers, Newcomers Club, Pilot Club, C. of C. Roman Catholic. Home: 2950 Shady Acres Nacogdoches TX 75961 Office: NL Designs & Constrn 2950 Shady Acres Nacogdoches TX 75961

LEMBERGER, NORMA, financial executive; b. Monticello, N.Y., July 21, 1944; d. Joe J. and Ellen Anna (Rosman) L. BS summa cum laude, Bklyn. Coll., 1965. With IBM, Armonk, N.Y., 1965—; dir. spl. fin. IBM Credit Corp., Stamford, Conn., 1985—; gen. mgr. Rolm Credit Corp. IBM, Santa Clara, Calif., 1985-87; pres. Rolm. Credit Corp. and dir. financing programs IBM Credit Corp., Stamford, Conn., 1987-88; treas. IBM Americas Group, Mt. Pleasant, N.Y., 1988-89; program dir. investor rels. IBM Corp., Armonk, 1989—. Mem. Women's Econ. Round Table.

LEMIEUX, ANNETTE ROSE, artist; b. Norfolk, Va., Oct. 11, 1957; d. Joseph and Margaret (Merci) L. BFA, Hartford Art Sch., 1980. One-woman shows U. Hartford, 1980, Artists Space, N.Y.C., 1984, Cash/Newhouse, N.Y.C., 1984, 86, 87, Josh Baer Galley, N.Y.C., 1987, 89, Daniel Weinberg Gallery, L.A., 1987, Lisson Gallery, London, 1988, Wadsworth Atheneum, 1988, Rhona Hoffman Gallery, Chgo., 1988, John and Mable Ringling Mus., 1989, Ctr. for Fine Arts, Miami, 1989; exhibited in numerous group shows, 1979—; represented in permanent collections Mus. Modern Art, N.Y.C., Mus. Fine Arts, Boston, Wadsworth Atheneum, Hartford, Conn. Bd. trustees Hartford Art Sch., 1989—. N.Y. fellow, 1987, others.

LEMIEUX, MARJORIE DIX, educator; b. Laurel, Mont., Nov. 11, 1921; d. Dale C. and Cora Jerome (Bradley) Dix.; m. Andrew Wear Elting, 1940 (div. 1962); children: Clayton Ross, Paula Jan; m. Archie L. Lemieux, 1967. Student, Wash. State Coll., Pullman, 1940-42, Fullerton Jr. Coll., 1945-46, Colo. State Coll., Ft. Collins, 1955-60. Lease clk. Carter Oil Co., Miles City, Mont., 1956; ins. agt. Western Life, Miles City, 1956-60; copy writer Women's News div. Sta. KGO, Missoula, Mont., 1961-63; sales woman Sta. KMSO-TV, Missoula, 1963-64; sec. Hilton Inn, San Francisco, 1964-66; exec. housekeeper trainee Hilton Hotels, 1966-67; exec. housekeeper Huntington Hotel, San Francisco, 1967-74, Oakland (Calif.) Hosp., 1974-83; asst. dir. housekeeping and laundry Peralta Hosp., Oakland, 1983-85; tchr. UAW-Learning Edn. Tng. Corp. and H.I.T.P., San Francisco, 1988—. Vassar Summer Inst. scholar, 1954. Mem. Nat. Exec. Housekeepers Assn. (past pres. Oakland Bay area chpt., past sec. Pacific Southwest dist.), Internat. Tng. in Communication (life, past club and coun. pres.). Republican.

LEMKE, CORRINE LARUE, university grants official; b. Sabin, Minn., May 25, 1934; d. Oswald Edward and Ida M. (Krabbenhoft) L. BA in Philosophy, Moorhead State U., 1972, MA in Liberal Arts, 1989. Notary pub., Minn. With WDAY radio and TV sta., Fargo, N.D., 1953-67; fin. aid grant coordinator Moorhead State U., 1967—, mem. task force study of changing student mix, 1983-84. Vol. Comstock Hist. House, Moorhead. Recipient cert. Gov. Minn., 1976, 20 yr. Svc. award Moorhead State U., 1988, letter of commendation U.S. Dept. Edn., 1983. Mem. Minn. Assn. Fin. Aid Adminstrs., Midwest Assn. Student Fin. Aid Adminstrs., Minn. Hist. Soc., State Hist. Soc. North Dakota, State Hist. Soc. Wis., Concordia Hist. Inst. of St. Louis, Phoenix Soc. of Moorhead, Concordia Coll. Alumni Assn., Moorhead State U. Alumni Assn. Lutheran. Author pvt. family history publs. Home: 3209 Village Green Dr E Moorhead MN 56560 Office: Moorhead State U Moorhead MN 56560

LEMKE, JUDITH A., lawyer; b. New Rochelle, N.Y., Sept. 28, 1952; d. Thomas Francis and Sara Jane (Blish) Fanelli; m. W. Frederick Lemke, Apr. 1, 1980. Student, Manhattanville Coll., Purchase, N.Y., 1970-72; BA, Case Western Res. U., Cleve., 1974, MA, 1975, JD, 1978. Sr. cert. pub. acct. Price Waterhouse, Cleve., 1978-81; assoc. Benesch Friedlander Coplan & Aronoff, Cleve., 1981-85; adjunct faculty Cleve. Marshall Coll. Law, 1982-86; ptnr. Benesch Fried lander Coplan & Aronoff, Cleve., 1986—. Recipient Elijah Watt Sells award for highest distinction AICPA, N.Y.C. 1979. Mem. Ohio State Bar Assn., Am. Bar Assn., Cuyahoga County Bar Assn., Cleve. Bar Assn., Cleve. Tax Club, Western Res. U. Alumni Assn. (exec. com. 1987—, trustee 1987—, chmn. spl. events com. 1987-90, pres. 1990—), Keelhaulers Club Cleve. Home: 2629 Exeter Rd Cleveland Heights OH 44118 Office: Benesch Friedlander Coplan 850 Euclid Ave Ste 1100 Cleveland OH 44114

LEMMA, ANNMARIE, teacher, publisher; b. Freeport, N.Y., Jan. 7, 1962; d. Cosmo Richard and Rose Marie (Tarantino) L. BS, L.I. U., 1984, MS, 1986. Cert. spl. edn. and elem. edn. tchr., N.Y. Tchr. presch. spl. edn. Nassau Ctr. for the Developmentally Disabled, Woodbury, N.Y., 1984-85; tchr. spl. edn. North Merrick (N.Y.) Union Free Sch. Dist., 1985—; freelance desktop pub. North Merrick, 1988—; learning resource specialist D.R.S., North Merrick, 1987—; tchr. pre-kindergarten Manhasset (N.Y.) Union Free Sch. Dist., summers 1984—; judge Creative Writing Com., North Merrick, 1986-88; mem. Mainstream Com., North Merrick, 1986-87. Photographer mag. Billboard Video Fast Forward, 1989—; set-up and layout artist newsletters Billboard Video and Music, 1988. Tchr. rep. N. Merrick PTA, 1988—; child sponsor Children Internat., 1989—. Mem. N.Y. State United Tchrs. Assn. Home: 2288 Sherman Ave North Merrick NY 11566 Office: N Merrick Union Free Sch 1775 Old Mill Rd North Merrick NY 11566

LEMMEY, TARA LYNN, marketing professional; b. Bayonne, N.J., Feb. 4, 1964; d. Robert Lemmey and Diana M. (Lorenston) Caldarola. BA, Rutgers U., 1987. Mktg. staff People Express Airline, Newark, 1983-87; account mgr. Douglas Turner Advt., Newark, 1987; dir. communications United Way, Newark, 1987-88; account mgr. Hammond Farrell, Inc., N.Y.C., 1988. Account exec. print campaign, Corning telecommunications, Benjamin Moore paint. Mem. N.Y. Ad Club, Bus. and Profl. Advt. Assn., Rutgers Alumni Assn. Office: Hammond Farrell Inc 257 Park Ave S New York NY 10010

LEMMON, MARILYN SUE, advertising executive; b. Avon, Ill., Nov. 2, 1939; d. Morrison Huffman and Rose Ellen (McElwee) Eslinger; m. James Marcus Lemmon, Aug. 31, 1957; children: J. Craig, Stephanie S. Lemmon DeVrieze, JoEllyn R. Lemmon Larrison. Student, U. Houston, 1958-59, So. Ill. U., 1965-66; AA in Bus. Adminstrn., Black Hawk Coll., 1978; BA in Bus. Adminstrn., Western Ill. U., 1983. Sec. H.J. Porter & James W. Porter Ind. Oil Operators, Houston, 1957-61; office mgr. Joseph A. Holland, DDS, Godfrey, Ill., 1968-69; counseling sec. guidance dept. United Twp. High Sch., East Moline, Ill., 1969-74; word processing sec. IBM, Moline, Ill., 1974-75; adminstrv. sec. Deere & Co. Corp. Hdqrs., Moline, 1975-84, mgr. advt. adminstrn., 1984—; career speaker, chmn. Profl. Secs. Internat., Moline, 1979; career speaker pers. dept. Deere & Co., Moline, 1979—. Adminstrv. asst. to chmn. Quad City Unification Project, Moline, 1988; treas. Kennedy Dr. Bapt. Ch., Moline, 1981-83. Mem. Romance Writers Am. (pres. Quad City chpt. 1990—), Bapt. Women's Club (pres. 1974). Republican. Office: Deere & Co Advt Dept John Deere Rd Moline IL 61265

LEMMONS, MIRIAM ELISE, nurse, social worker, rehabilitation counselor; b. New Orleans, Jan. 3, 1932; d. Walter Simpson and Ola Adele (Carruth) Weathersby; Asso. Nursing, Iowa Lakes Community Coll., 1977; B.A., Buena Vista Coll., 1978; M.S., Mankato State U., 1981; m. Ronald Lemmons, June 22, 1962; children: Robert, Linda, Mark, Kevin, Robin. RN, Holy Family Hosp., Estherville, Iowa, 1977-82, dir. home health dept., hospice, med. social services, 1981-86; mem. city coun., City of Kingsville, Tex., mayor, 1988-90; mem. Bd. dirs. Good Samaritan Nursing Home; mem. Estherville City Coun., 1984-86—. Named Citizen of Yr., Estherville C. of C., 1984. Mem. Nat. Hospice Assn., Am. Nurses Assn., Nat. League Nursing, Assn. Rehab. Nurses, Nat. Rehab. Assn., NOW, Social Workers in Health Facilities, Am. Soc. Profl. and Exec. Women, Nat. Assn. Rehab. Profls., Am. Pub. Health Assn., Iowa Hospice Orgn. (bd. dirs., mem. exec. com.), AAUW, LWV, Am. Nurses Found., Tex. Med. Soc. Aux., ACS Aux., Internat. Coll. Surgeons Aux., Bus. and Profl. Women's Club, Leadership Tex. Democrat. Methodist. Club: Century. Home: 1930 Shelly Kingsville TX 78363

LEMON, VERNA M., development specialist; b. Pontiac, Mich., Sept. 23, 1950; d. Henry and Maxine V. (Neil) Katip; 1 child, Jeffery L. BS, Western Mich. U., 1972; postgrad., Ind. State U., Wayne State U., Detroit, NYU. Practice devel. specialist Friedman, Fuller and Blewitt, Inc., Tysons Corner, Va.; ops. mgr. Phone Am. Corp., Birmingham, Mich., activity dir.; prin. Lemon-Aide Tax Preparation. Contbr. articles to profl. jours. Recipient Youth award. Home: 8354 Shady Grove Circle Manassas VA 22110

LEMOS, GLORIA ELLIOTT, soft drink company executive; b. Royston, Ga., Apr. 29, 1946; d. Richard F. and G. Maxine (Brown) Elliott; divorced; 1 child, Joseph David. A.A., Emmanuel Jr. Coll., Franklin Springs, Ga., 1966; postgrad. Oglethorpe U., 1966-68. With Coca-Cola Co., 1967—, mem. exec. staff group, Atlanta, 1972-77, asst. to chmn. bd., Washington, 1977-79, v.p. internat. govt. affairs, Washington, 1979—. Bd. dirs. Inst. for Study of Diplomacy, Georgetown U., Community Found. Greater Washington, 1980—, Am. Com. for East-West Accord; trustee Fed. City Council, 1978—, Am. U., 1983—, Meridian House Internat. Mem. Washington Internat. Bus. Council, UN Internat. Bus. Council, Internat. Mgmt. and Devel. Inst. So. Ctr. for Internat. Studies, Internat. Women's Forum. Episcopalian, International Club, World Trade Club. Office: Coca Cola Co 1627 K St NW Ste #800 Washington DC 20006 other: Coca-Cola Co 1 Coca-Cola Pla NW Atlanta GA 30313*

LENCHIN, JULIANNE MARIE, national account manager; b. St. Clair, Pa., Feb. 5, 1956; d. Joseph John and Julia Ann (Franco) L.; m. Thomas Howard Chetrick, Feb. 24, 1990. BS in Food Sci., Pa. State U. Chemist Nat. Starch & Chem. Co., Bridgewater, N.J., 1978-81, project supr., 1981-84, tech. mgr., 1984-86; asst. mktg. product dir. McNeil Specialty Products Co. (Johnson & Johnson), Skillman, N.J., 1986-88, sales account mgr., 1988-90; nat. sales acct. mgr. McNeil Specialty Products Co. (Johnson & Johnson), New Brunswick, N.J., 1990—. Inventor cowcockle starch, aseptic batter system, imitation cheese, microwave batter. Mem. NOW, Inst. of Food Technologists. Democrat. Roman Catholic. Home: 37-3 Potters Pl Holland PA 18966 Office: McNeil Specialty Products Co 501 George St New Brunswick NJ 08903

LENDACKI, SANDRA ELAINE, resource planning manager; b. Reading, Pa., May 25, 1955; d. Cyril J and Pauline (Levengood) L. BS in Acctg., Kutztown U., Pa., 1981. Office adminstr. Reitech Corp., Laureldale, Pa., 1976-80; site support mgr. General Public Utilities, Parispanny, N.J., 1981—. Mem. Nat. Honor Soc. Roman Catholic. Office: 100 Interpace Pkwy Parsippany NJ 07054

L'ENGLE, MADELEINE (MRS. HUGH FRANKLIN), author; b. N.Y.C., Nov. 29, 1918; d. Charles Wadsworth and Madeleine (Barnett) Camp; m. Hugh Franklin, Jan. 26, 1946; children: Josephine Franklin Jones, Maria Franklin Rooney, Bion. A.B., Smith Coll., 1941; postgrad., New Sch., 1941-42, Columbia U., 1960-61. Tchr. St. Hilda's and St. Hugh's Sch., 1960—; mem. faculty U. Ind., 1965-66, 71; writer-in-residence Ohio State U., 1970, U. Rochester, 1972, Wheaton Coll., 1976—, Cathedral St. John the Divine, N.Y.C., 1965—. Author: The Small Rain, 1945, Ilsa, 1946, Camilla Dickinson, 1951, A Winter's Love, 1957, And Both Were Young, 1949, Meet the Austins, 1960, A Wrinkle in Time, 1962, The Moon by Night, 1963, The 24 Days Before Christmas, 1964, The Arm of the Starfish, 1965, The Love Letters, 1966, The Journey with Jonah, 1967, The Young Unicorns, 1968, Dance in The Desert, 1969, Lines Scribbled on an Envelope, 1969, The Other Side of the Sun, 1971, A Circle of Quiet, 1972, A Wind in the Door, 1973, The Summer of the Great-grandmother, 1974, Dragons in the Waters, 1976, The Irrational Season, 1977, A Swiftly Tilting Planet, 1978, The Weather of the Heart, 1978, Ladder of Angels, 1979, A Ring of Endless Light, 1980, Walking on Water, 1981, A Severed Wasp, 1982, And it was Good, 1983, A House Like a Lotus, 1985, Trailing Clouds of Glory, 1985, A Stone for a Pillow, 1986, Many Waters, 1986, Too Part Invention, 1987, A Cry Like a Bell, 1987, Sold Into Egypt, 1988, From This Day Forward, 1988, An Acceptable Time, 1988, The Glorious Impossible, 1990. Pres. Crosswicks Found. Recipient Newbery medal, 1963; Sequoyah award, 1965; runner-up award Hans Christian Andersen Internat. award, 1965; Lewis Carroll Shelf award, 1965; Austrian State Lit. award, 1969; Bishop's Cross, 1970; U. South Miss. medal, 1978; Regina medal, 1984; Alan award Nat. Council Tchrs. English, 1986, Kerlan award, 1990; collection of papers at Wheaton Coll. Mem. Authors Guild (pres., mem. council, mem. membership com.), Authors League (mem. council), Writers Guild Am., Colonial Dames. Episcopalian. Home: Crosswicks Goshen CT 06756 Office: care Farrar Straus & Giroux Inc 19 Union Sq W New York NY 10003

LENGYEL, LAURA LA FORET, artist; b. Bridgeport, Conn., 1946. Student, Bridgeport (Conn.) Art Mus., 1963, Stanford U., Palo Alto, Calif., 1964-66, Mills Coll., 1964-67; BA in Art, Mills Coll., Oakland, Calif., 1967; postgrad., Aspen (Colo.) Art Sch., 1965, Humboldt State U., 1971, Mendocino Art Ctr., 1972, Coll. of the Redwoods, 1974, Acad. of Art, San Francisco, 1975, Calif. Coll. Arts & Crafts, Oakland, 1976. Bldg. renovation & design project mgmt. Fairfax, Calif., 1975-84, Church Studio, Fairfax, Calif., 1979-84; freelance and commissioned Carden Marin Sch., San Anselmo, Calif., 1968—, Marin County Studios, San Rafael, Calif., 1984—. One woman shows include Fairfax Libr., 1980, Design Period, Inc., San francisco, 1981, Sch. Pla. Restaurant, Fairfax, 1982, The Winery, San Anselmo, 1983, Point Marina Inn, Richmond, Calif., 1983, Health & Harmony Festival, Santa Rosa, Calif., 1983, Senator Milton Mark's Office, San Rafael, 1984, Marin Soc. Artists, Ross, Calif., 1984, Citicorp Savs., San Rafael, 1987, 88, Cafe Renoir, Mill Valley, Calif., 1988, Market St., San Francisco, 1988, The Richard Burton Gallery, L.A., 1989; exhibited in group shows at Nathan Galleries, Larkspur, Calif., 1986, Craftsfaire, Sausalito, Calif., 1986-88, Internat. Alumni Invitational, Oakland, 1987, Mills Coll., Oakland, 1987, Artiques, San Francisco, 1988, Am. Zephyr Gallery, 1988, Alliance Women Artists, San Francisco, 1988, Marin County Civic Ctr., Mendocino, Calif., 1989, Bay Gallery, Mendocino, 1989, Projects Gallery, San Rafael, 1989; represented in numerous pub. and pvt. collections. Mem. Bay Area Art Conservationists Guild, Marin Arts Guild; donated art paintings to various local charities. Recipient numerous awards and commns. Mem. Internat. Sculpture Soc., San Francisco Art Mus. Soc., San Rafael C. of C., Mills Coll. Alumni Assn. (pres. 1988—), Artists Equity Assn., Alliance of Women Artists. Home: 193 Mill St San Rafael CA 94901

LENHART, JULIE BROWN, advertising executive, graphic designer, consultant; b. San Francisco, Nov. 2, 1950. AA in Inhalation Therapy, Foothill Coll., 1970; AA in Promotion Graphics, Shasta Coll., 1983; postgrad., San Jose (Calif.) State U., 1974-77, St. Joseph's Coll., Windham, Maine. Cert. respiratory care practitioner, Calif. Respiratory care practitioner, instr. students Stanford (Calif.) U. Hosp., 1970-79; respiratory care practitioner Redding (Calif.) Med. Ctr., 1980-83; quality assurance reviewer for respiratory care St. Elizabeth Hosp., Red Bluff, Calif., 1983-89; adv. account exec. for Quality Digest publ. QCI, Internat., Red Bluff, 1990—; freelance graphic designer, Red Bluff, 1975—; regional site coord. instrl. television for students Calif. State U., Chico, 1989-90; cons. in field. Contbr. articles to profl. jours. Mem. NAFE, Calif. Soc. Respiratory Care, Christian Broadcasting Network, Toastmasters. Home: 340 David Ave Red Bluff CA 96080 Office: QCI Internat Airport Indsl Pk 1425 Vista Way Red Bluff CA 96080

LENHART, PAULINE JUNE HOUSE, teacher; b. Johnson City, N.Y., Apr. 13, 1929; d. Wendell Lester and Alice May (Van Winkle) House; m. Robert Eugene Lenhart, Apr. 9, 1955; children: Stephen John, Jennifer Louise. BS in Music Edn., SUNY, Potsdam, 1951. Elem. tchr. music Van Antwerp Sch., Schenectady, N.Y., 1951-55; music supr. South Butler County Joint Schs., Butler, Pa., 1956-57; tchr. elem. sch. Ridgefield., Crystal Lake, Ill., 1967-69; elem. tchr. Pine Ave. Sch., Alma, Mich., 1970-74; office mgr. Hull & Hull, Attys.-at-Law, Cleve., 1975-77; elem. sch. tchr. Steele Sch., Galesburg, Ill., 1986-87; remedial reading, writing, math. tchr. Florence (S.C.) Career Ctr., 1989—. Mem. AAUW (Muskegon, Mich.) (pres. 1978-79, 80-81) (Galesburg, Ill.) (pres. 1985-87). Republican. Home: 424 Guildford Cir Florence IL 29501

LENNING, DIANE ADELE BENGE, financial services executive; b. Long Beach, Calif., Dec. 28, 1946; d. Clyde Lomon and Elizabeth N. (Rohrig) Benge; m. Gerald Lynn Lenning, May 20, 1967; children: Geoffrey Sheldon, Tanya Roschelle. AA, Orange Coast Coll., 1966; BA, Calif. State U., San Luis Obispo, 1970; MA, Calif. State U., Long Beach, 1976. Cert. tchr., Calif. Substitute tchr. pub. schs., Calif., 1976-77, 78-80; tchr. music. Downey (Calif.) Unified Sch. Dist., 1977-78; office mgr. Gerald Lenning, CPA, Seal Beach, Calif., 1980-82; computer mgr. Gerald Lenning, CPA, 1982-88; pres. Fin. Svcs. Ctr., Seal Beach, 1988—; tchr. Nelles High Sch., Whittier, Calif., 1989—; pvt. music tchr., LaPalma, Calif., 1975-88. Dir. children's church, musicals, Christian Life Ch., Long Beach, 1975-80, violinist, ch. orch., 1984—, adult tchr., 1985-87; coach, Ayso Soccer, La Palma, 1980-83; instr., Cypress (Calif.) Community Youth Orch., 1982-87; supr. food lines and spiritual renewal, Christian Outreach Appeal, Long Beach, 1986-88; counselor, Calif. Youth Authority, Norwalk, 1986—. Mem. NAFE, Calif. Assn. for Safety Edn., MADD, One-A-Chord, Sacret Pals. Republican. Office: Fin Svcs Ctr Ste C 13924 Seal Beach Blvd Seal Beach CA 90740

LENNON, AMELIA OLES, government contracting consultant, trainer; b. Youngstown, Ohio, May 2, 1949; d. Henry J. and Amelia (Borak) Oles; m. John B. Lennon, Apr. 7, 1972; children: John Clark, Blake. BA, U. Miami, 1970; MA Specialist summa cum laude, U. Pitts., 1972; MEd, Cen. State U., Edmond, Okla., 1978; PhD, U. Okla., 1984. Rsch. asst. U. Pitts., 1971-72; psychology technician FAA, Oklahoma City, 1972-76, guidance counselor, 1976-79, edn. specialist, 1979-81; mgr. small bus. Glarecon, Inc., Oklahoma City, 1981-82; instr. trainer Jordan DeLaurentie Inc., Oklahoma City, 1987—; adj. prof. Cen. State U., Edmond, Okla., 1988-89. Active Oklahoma City Orch. League, 1981—; chmn. Easter Seal Golf Tournament, Oklahoma City, 1987. Acad. fellow U. Pitts., 1970-72. Mem. Am. Soc. for Tng. and Devel., Delta Zeta (pres. alumnae Oklahoma City 1986-88). Republican. Roman Catholic. Home: 12804 Williams Ct Oklahoma City OK 73142

LENNOX, GLORIA (GLORIA DEMEREE), real estate executive; b. Baden, Pa., Feb. 14, 1931; d. Gilbert and Marion (Slosson) Whetson; m; William Lennox, June 19, 1954 (div. 1985); children: Cheryl Lennox Watson, Lynda Lennox Huerta, Jim; m. Philip Demeree, July 4, 1985. BS in Edn., Kent State U., 1954; MA in Spl. Edn., Ariz. State U., 1968. Tchr. Maple Leaf Sch., Garfield Heights, Ohio, 1954-55, Madison (Ind.) Dist. Elem. Sch., 1958, Scottsdale (Ariz.) Schs., 1961-68, Devereux Sch., 1968-70, Tri-City Mental Health Sch., Mesa, Ariz., 1970-71; br. mgr. M. Leslie Hansen, Scottsdale, 1972-74; v.p., gen. mgr. John D. Noble and Assocs., Scottsdale, 1974-83; pres., broker Gloria Lennox & Assocs., Inc., Scottsdale, 1983—. Chmn. bd. Interfaith Counseling Svc., 1988, 89; trustee Scottsdale Congl. United Ch.of Christ, 1986-88. Kent State U. scholar, 1950-54. Mem. Nat. Assn. Realtors, Ariz. Assn. Realtors (Realtor Assoc. of Yr. 1975), Women's Coun. Realtors, Realtor Nat. Mktg. Inst., Scottsdale Bd. Realtors (pres. 1981-82, Realtor of Yr. 1982, GRI, CRS, CRB), Ariz. Town Halls, Ariz. Country Club. Republican. Home: 7561 Via Camello Del Sur Scottsdale AZ 85258 Office: Gloria Lennox and Assocs 4533 N Scottsdale Rd 200 Scottsdale AZ 85258

LENNOX, SHIRLEY ANN (AKALANI), artist, educator, consultant; b. San Francisco, Nov. 8, 1931; d. James Joseph and Mildred Mae (Hall) Amos; m. Arthur James Lennox, Jan. 6, 1951 (div. Oct. 1990); children: Sharron Kay, Kathleen Melanie, Bonnie Marie, Colleen Leta. Student pub. schs., South Glens Falls, N.Y. Cert. hypnotherapist. Window display artist Fowlers' Inc., Glens Falls, 1948-51; owner, operator Discovery House Gallery, Palo Alto, Calif., 1969-71; owner, operator, tchr. porcelain painting Lennox Art Sutdio, Santa Maria, Calif., 1972—; cons. art, Santa Maria, 1985—; owner, operator Gallerie 272, Morton, N.Y., 1979-81; resident artist, gallery mgr. Options Gallery, Shell Beach, Calif., 1985; mem. staff, ofcl. artist Gateway of Light Found., Soquel, Calif., 1989; prin. Lennox Specialty Mdse., 1989—; crystal carver, assoc. Frank Dorland Pioneer Biocrystallographer, Terra Found., Santa Marguerita, Calif. Exhibited paintings in one-woman shows Village Gallery, Hilton, N.Y., Lake George Inst. History and Art, N.Y., 1974, Swan Gallery, Albion, N.Y., 1979, Options Gallery, Shell Beach, Calif., 1984, Morro Bay Mus. Natural History, 1985, marine ppaintings Gallery 912 1/2 also Artists' At Work Day, 1989; group shows include The Calif. Scene (with Ansel Adams and others), Foothill Coll., Los Altos, Calif., 1970, Suburban Rochester Art Group shows, N.Y., 1976-80, Santa Ynez Art Shows, Calif., 1983-84, Los Padres Artists Guild Shows, 1983-86, Faulkner Gallery, 1985, Gallery 113, Santa Barbara, 1987, Sheldon Swope Art Gallery, Terre Haute, Ind., 1987, Internat. Soc. Marine Painters Exhibit, San Luis Obispo (Calif.) Art Ctr. Gallery, Aquarius XIII, 1990; represented in permanent collections Old Courthouse Mus., Lake George, N.Y., Shelter Cove Lodge, Pismo Beach, Calif.; represented by Haloti, Kilauea, Hawaii, The Sandpiper Art Gallery, Pismo Beach, Calif., Calif., Cambria (Calif.) Coast Gallery; executed background painting, recreated wildlife display Early Lompoc, Calif., Lompoc Mus., 1990. Active Santa Maria Arts Coun., 1988-

89. Mem. Internat. Soc. Marine Painters Inc. (juried profl. mem., west coast rep.), Nat. Soc. Painters in Casein and Acrylic (assoc.), Santa Maria Women's Network, Santa Barbara Art Assn. (juried), Cen. Coast Watercolor Soc., San Luis Obispo Art Assn., Artists Guild of Santa Ynez Valley, Porcelain Portrait Soc., Nat. Mus. Women in the Arts (charter mem.), NAFE. Republican. Mem. Unity Ch. Avocations: photography, camping. Address: Lennox Art Studio 4869 S Bradley Rd 18B-281 Santa Maria CA 93455

LENNOX FISCH, CAROL JEANINE, writer, marketing consultant; b. Wichita Falls, Tex., Sept. 13, 1952; d. Johnny Melvin and Betty Joy (Chastain) Cole; m. Scott Michael Lennox, Mar. 25, 1972 (div. Oct. 1979); m. Elliot Ronald Fisch, Apr. 26, 1986; stepchildren: Julie Ellen, Kendra Elissa. BS, Tex. Christian U., 1975; grad. Tex. Wesleyan U., 1979, 80. Cert. tchr., Tex. Tchr. learning disabled Ft. Worth Ind. Sch. Dist., 1975-78; fundraiser, editor, coll. rels. Tex. Wesleyan Coll., Ft. Worth, 1978-81; account exec., account supr. DBG & H, Inc., Ft. Worth, 1981-84, mgmt. supr., 1984-85; pres. The Lennox Group, Arlington, Tex., 1985-87; v.p. Synergy Works, 1984-87, pres., 1987—; v.p. Diversified Media Reps., Arlington, 1985—; lectr. local univs.; adj. prof., jouranlism Tex. Christian U., Ft. Worth, 1989-90; cons. Ft. Worth Opera, 1986, mem. mktg. com., 1986—; Contbr. articles to profl. jours. Vol. People for Am. Way, Windstar Found.; ct. apptd. spl. advocates. Recipient Coun. for Advancement and Support of Edn. award, 1981, Addy award, 1988. Mem. Network of Exec. Women, Advt. Club Ft. Worth (bd. dirs. 1983-85), Internat. Platform Assn. Democrat. Mem. Christian Ch. (Disciples of Christ). Avocations: reading, writing, dancing, aikido, windjammer cruises, metaphysics.

LENOIR, GLORIA CISNEROS, small business owner, business manager; b. Monterrey, Nuevo Leon, Mex., Aug. 18, 1951; came to U.S., 1956, naturalized; d. Juan Antonio and Maria Gloria (Flores) Cisneros; m. Walter Frank Lenoir, June 6, 1975; children: Lucy Gloria, Katherine Judith. Student, Inst. Am. Univs., 1971-72; BA in French Art, Austin Coll., 1973, MA in French Art, 1974; MBA in Fin., U. Tex., 1979. French tchr. Sherman (Tex.) High Sch., 1973-74; French/Spanish tchr, dept. chmn. Lyndon Baines Johnson High Sch., Austin, 1974-77; legis. aide Tex. State Capitol, Austin, Tex., 1977-81; stock broker Merrill Lynch, Austin, 1981-83, Schneider, Bernet and Hickman, Austin, 1983-84; bus. mgr. Holleman Photographic Labs., Inc., Austin, 1984-87, 88—; account exec., stock broker Eppler, Guerin & Turner, 1987-88; group counselor, organizer Inst. Fgn. Studies, U. Strasbourg, France, summer 1976; mktg. intern IBM, Austin, summer 1978; mktg. cons. Creative Ednl. Enterprises, Austin, 1980-81; hon. speaker Mex.-Am. U. of Tex., Austin, 1984; speaker various orgns., bus. classes, Austin, 1981-84; speaker, coordinator small bus. workshops, 1985. Photographs pub. in Women in Space, 1979, Review, 1988; exhibited in group shows throughout Tex., 1979, 88-89. Neighborhood capt. Am. Cancer Soc., Austin, 1982-86, 89, Am. Heart Assn., 1989; mem. PTA, 1989—, chair of 50th anniversary celebration com., 1990; hospitality chmn., first grade coord. PTA, Austin, 1986; pres. Bryker Woods Elem. PTA, 1990—; vol. liaison leads program Austin Coll., Austin, 1983—; mem. Advantage Austin, 1988; peer panelist Major Art Insts. of Austin, 1989-90; co-chairwoman fin. Cen. Presbyn. Ch., elder, 1988—, session clk., 1989, chair membership com., 1990. Recipient Night on the Town award IBM, 1978. Mem. Photo Mktg. Assn., Internat. Platform Assn. Republican. Presbyterian. Home: 1202 W 29th St Austin TX 78703 Office: Holleman Photog Labs Inc 3018 N Lamar Austin TX 78705

LENOX, CORA CLINKSCALES, retired pediatrician, cardiologist, educator; b. Troy, S.C., July 20, 1908; d. Cleon Curtis and Bertie Louise (Hix) Clinkscales; m. John E. Lenox; children: Marilyn, Jacquelyn, Don Allyn. BA, Winthrop Coll., Rockhill, S.C., 1929; M.D., West China U., Chengdu, Sichuan, China, 1936, Woman's Med. Coll., Phila., 1948. Diplomate Nat. Bd. Med. Examiners, 1938, W.Va., 1948-81, Pa., 1964; cert. Am. Bd. Pediatrics, 1963, Subbd. Pediatric Cardiology, 1971. Intern West China Union U., Chengdu, Sichuan, 1935-36, instr. medicine, 1938-45; resident in pediatrics Children's Hosp. Pitts., 1960-61, staff in pediatrics, 1968, emeritus staff, 1978; staff in pediatrics Myers Clinic and Broaddus Hosp., Phillipi, W.Va., 1946-64; from instr. to prof. pediatrics, then prof. emeritus U. Pitts. Sch. Medicine, 1968-87; ret., 1987; dir. cardiac outpatient svc., 1971-76; spl. work in cardiac morphology, 1976—; active in pediatric cardiology, patient care and teaching of cardiology fellows, pediatric house staff and med. students, 1968-87; lectr., demonstrator of cardiac morphology to med. staff, house officers and students, 1987—. Contbr. articles to numerous medical publs. Recipient Grant-in Aid-award for Computerization of Heart Mus. Pa. Heart Assn., 1979, Commonwealth Bd. award of Med. Coll. Pa. for Disting. Svc. in Medicine, 1976, Mary Mildred Sullivan award, 1979; Nat. Fedn. Women's Clubs scholar, 1929-30, PHS grantee, 1970. Fellow AAUP, Am. Acad. Pediatrics, Am. Coll. Cardiology; mem. AMA (coun. on cardiology disease in the young), Pa. Heart Assn., Allegheny County Med. Soc., Pitts. Pediatrics Soc., Western Pa. Heart Assn., Mended Hearts, Inc. (nat. adv. coun. 1977-80). Democrat. Baptist. Office: Children's Hosp Pitts 3705 Fifth at DeSoto Pittsburgh PA 15213

LENTS, ANN, lawyer; b. Houston, Sept. 4, 1949; d. Max Richey and Mary Frances (Hunsicker) L.; m. James David Heaney II, Aug. 11, 1973; children: J. David, Mary Elizabeth. BA, Wellesley Coll., 1971; JD, U. Tex., 1974. Bar: Tex. 1974, U.S. Dist. Ct. (so. dist.) Tex. 1975, U.S. Ct. Appeals (5th, 10th and 11th cirs.) 1981, U.S. Supreme Ct. 1982. Assoc. Vinson & Elkins, Houston, 1974-81, ptnr., 1981—. Bd. dirs. Houston Child Guidance Ctr., 1988—, Houston Bus. Forum, 1982, Trees for Houston, 1989—. Fellow Tex. Bar Found., Houston Bar Found.; mem. ABA, Tex. Bar Assn., Houston Bar Assn. (bd. dirs. antitrust sect. 1977-79), Ex-editors Assn. Tex. Law Rev., U. Tex. Law Sch. Assn. (bd. dirs. 1981-82), Fed. Energy Bar Assn. (antitrust com. 1987-88). Presbyterian. Office: Vinson & Elkins 1001 Fannin 3300 First City Tower Houston TX 77002

LENTZ, CHRISTINE MARIE ANDERSON, academic program director; b. Madison, Wis., Nov. 17, 1958; d. Wilbur R. and Lorraine K. (Schufletowski) Wiessinger. BSBA, U. Wis., 1980; MBA, Boston U., 1983, postgrad. Mgr. mgmt. info. systems Econ. Devel. and Indsl. Corp., Boston, 1981-82; asst. dir. info. resources Boston U., 1983-84, dir. info. resources, 1985-88, mgr. spl. projects, 1989—; cons. City of Boston, 1984; instr. MBA program Boston U., 1987—. Tchr. Sunday sch. 1st Luth. Ch., Boston, 1983-85. Mem. Soc. for Info. Mgmt., Data Processing Mgmt. Assn. Republican. Office: Boston U 111 Cummington St Boston MA 02215

LENZ, CYNTHIA LOWE, nursing educator; b. Titusville, Pa., Mar. 31, 1951; d. Glenn M. Lowe and Susan J. Budzinski; m. F.T. Lenz, June 2, 1973. BSN, U. Pitts., 1973; MS in Nursing, Ohio State U., 1978, PhD, 1982. Nurse Bethesda Hosp., Zanesville, Ohio; asst. prof. sch. nursing Ohio U., Zanesville; assoc. prof. sch. nursing Ohio U., Athens; assoc. prof., assoc. dean acad. programs of sch. nursing Clemson (S.C.) U.; dean sch. nursing East Tenn. State U., Johnson City, 1988—. Contbr. articles to profl. publs. Mem. ANA, Nat. League Nursing, Soc. Rsch. Nursing. Office: East Tenn State U Coll Nursing Johnson City TN 37614*

LEO, CHRISTY LYNN, financial executive; b. Harrisburg, Pa., Mar. 18, 1960; d. Clement A. and Ruby E. (Starr) L. AA, Harrisburg Area Community Coll., 1988. Sec., sales rep. C.A. Leo Real Estate, Camp Hill, Pa., 1978-81; sec. to pres. Consumers Life Ins. Co., Camp Hill, 1981-84, adminstrn. asst. pub. rels., 1984-88; mgr. investor, pub. rels. exec. Consumers Fin. Corp., Camp Hill, 1988—. Mem. Corp. Rels. Soc., Internat. Assn. Bus. Communicators. Home: 3870 Dawn Mar St Harrisburg PA 17111 Office: Consumers Fin Corp 1200 Camp Hill By-Pass Camp Hill PA 17011

LEON, JUANA AURORA, investment executive; b. Las Villas, Cuba, Feb. 14, 1940; came to U.S., 1971; d. Fernando and Isora R. (Hernandez) Medina; children: Jesus M., Isora A., Joan C. Cert. in acctg., Profl. Sch. Commerce, Gamaguey, Cuba, 1959, cert. in bookkeeping, 1973; cert. in gen. office, The English Ctr., Miami, Fla., 1972. CPA, Fla. V.p., sec. Sosa Leon Investments Corp., Miami; counselor Meml. Sales, Miami; group leader Stanley Home Products, Inc., Westfield, Mass. Mem. ARC, vocat. prayer group; choir mem. Sts. Peter and Paul Cath. Ch., 1986. Mem. Assn. Pub. and Pvt. Accts. of Cuba, NAFE, Euterpe Lyrid Sociely (treas. 1989), Cuban Acct. Assn., Cuban Women's Club.

LEON, MARGARET ADELE, financial service marketing company executive; b. Boston, Mar. 19, 1948; d. Richard and Florence (Hattub) L. B.S., Boston State Coll., 1969; M.A. in Counseling, Salem State Coll., 1977. Tchr. Chelsea Schs., Mass., 1969-76, guidance counselor, 1977-82; group therapist Behavioral Assocs., Brookline, Mass., 1977-79; real estate agt. Gen. Devel., Peabody, Mass., 1979-81; ins. and securities agt. A.L. Williams, Lynn, Mass., 1981-83, regional v.p., 1983-87, sr. v.p., 1987—. Avocations: photography, sewing, cooking, skiing, martial arts. Office: A L Williams Corp 679 Western Ave Ste 4 Lynn MA 01905

LEON, MARJORIE ROTH, psychology educator; b. Cheverly, Md., Feb. 29, 1952; d. Norman Raphael and Bettie Grace (Garelick) Roth; m. Jeffrey Samuel Leon, July 1, 1979; 1 child, Michael Jason. BA in Anthropology, U. Calif., Davis, 1974; MS in Edn., Syracuse U., 1975; MS in Psychology, Northwestern U., 1983, PhD in Psychology, 1985. Media dir. Elisabeth Ludeman Developmental Disabilities Ctr., Park Forest, Ill., 1975-76; instr. U. Ill., Carbondale, 1976-79; asst. prof. Barat Coll., Lake Forest, Ill., 1985-87; asst. prof. psychology Nat. Louis U., Evanston, Ill., 1987—; cons. theater dept. Columbia Coll, Chgo., 1988; cons. acad. affairs Barat Coll., 1987; presenter papers at profl. confs. Contbr. articles to profl. jours. Vol. Chiaravalle Montessori Sch., Evanston, 1989-90. Recipient rsch. award Conf. on Individualized Instrn., Waco, Tex., 1979; grantee Barat Coll., 1987, Nat. Coll. Edn., 1990. Mem. Am. Psychol. Assn., Am. Ednl. Rsch. Assn. Democrat. Jewish. Office: Nat Louis U 2840 Sheridan Rd Evanston IL 60201

LEONARD, CHERYL MARTSCHINK, speech/language pathologist; b. Charleston, S.C., Nov. 8, 1952; d. John Henry and Mary Edna (Parler) Martschink; m. Gary Owen Leonard, Aug. 23, 1975; children: Callie Camille, Jennie Marie. BS in Psychology, Coll. Charleston, 1974; MSP in Speech Pathology, U. S.C., 1975. Speech pathologist Charleston County Schs., 1975—; speech pathologist Tri County Home Health Assn., Charleston, 1976-80. Home: 2134 Eve Circle Charleston SC 29414 Office: Charleston County Schs Jenkins Avenue North Charleston SC 29406

LEONARD, DEBI LYNN (DELYN KYNTA LEONARD), manufacturing company marketing executive; b. Dodge City, Kans., May 6, 1955; d. Harold Duane and Kynta Lov (Kennedy) L. Student, Marymount Coll., 1972-76, Vo-Tech. U., Salina, Kans. 1976-78. Comml. art sales rep. Shoppers Guide, Salina, 1977-81; sales rep. Sta. KYEZ-AM, Salina, 1981-82, Freedom News, Denver, 1982-83; designer Delyns Fashions, Denver, 1983-86; mktg. mgr. Lenko Enterprises, Cripple Creek, Colo., 1981-88, Cellular One Mobile Communications, 1988—; product devel., fashion designer, sr. sales mgr., Silver-Mine, Cripple Creek, Colo., 1988—. Vol. Annual Bridal Show, Salina, 1985; active Am. Cancer Soc., membership drive YMCA. Mem. Life Underwriters Assn., Am. Bus. Womens Assn. Midwest Corvette Assn., Nat. Assn. Female Execs.; Denver Advt. Assn. Avocations: windsurfing; skiing; swimming; hot air ballooning. Office: Lenko Enterprises PO Box 16 Cripple Creek CO 80831

LEONARD, DOROTHY LOUISE, environmental analyst; b. Newark, Aug. 30, 1932; d. Joseph Peter and Charlotte Mary (Dinkel) L.; m. Gary Lawrence Fellows, Sept. 4, 1954 (div. Mar. 1978); children: Mark Leonard, Paige Charlotte Wright, Scott Lawrence, Joy Dorothy. BA, Syracuse U., 1954; postgrad., SUNY, Brockport, 1976, George Washington U., 1982-84. Asst. planner Monroe County Dept. Planning, Rochester, N.Y., 1975-77; specialist coastal resources N.Y. Dept. State, Albany, 1977-80; program analyst Office Coastal Zone Mgmt. Nat. Oceanic & Atmospheric Adminstrn. div. U.S. Dept. Commerce, Washington, 1980-83, specialist fisheries devel. Nat. Marine Fisheries Svc., 1983-86, program mgr. shellfish water quality projects, 1986—; pres. Dorothy Leonard Assocs., Washington, 1985—. Mem. com. N.Y. Legis. Com. on Women, Albany, 1975-77; pres. Washington Area Waterfront Action Group, 1986—; mem. bd. advisors Inst. for Coastal and Marine Recovery, 1988—. Mem. Am. Fisheries Soc., Nat. Fisheries Assn., World Aquaculture Soc., Am. Soc. Limnology and Oceanography, AIA (urban design com. 1986—), Chesapeake Bay Citizen Adv. Com., Waterfront Washington Assn., Survival of the Sea Soc. (bd. advisors 1987-89), LWV, Phi Kappa Phi. Republican. Presbyterian. Home and Office: 14337 Long Green Dr Silver Spring MD 20906

LEONARD, EILEEN ANN, motion picture trust fund executive; b. N.Y.C., Oct. 4, 1941; d. Errol Thomas and Marjorie (Cleary) Connelly; m. Wayne Leonard, Jan. 28, 1967 (div. Mar. 1975); 1 dau., Kimberly Anne; m. 2d Kenneth Paul Vensel, Sept. 6, 1980. B.A., Fairleigh Dickinson U., 1963. French sec. French Railroads, N.Y.C., 1964-65; legal sec. W.R. Grace Co., N.Y.C., 1965-67; exec. sec. Internat. Industries, Los Angeles, 1968-70; adminstr. Contract Services Adminstr. Trust Fund, Los Angeles, 1974-76, dir., 1976—. Pub. relations chairperson Los Angeles Basin Equal Opportunity League, 1975-84; bd. dirs. Internat. Inst., Los Angeles, 1983-86, Inroads, Los Angeles. Mem. Dir. Guild Am., Women in Film. Roman Catholic. Home: 12431 Landale St Studio City CA 91604 Office: Contract Services Adminstr Trust Fund 14144 Ventura Blvd Sherman Oaks CA 91604

LEONARD, ELLEN MARIE, physicist; b. N.Y.C., Nov. 28, 1944; d. Eberhard F. and Anne M. (Bazzone) Dullberg; m. Thomas A. Leonard, Nov. 24, 1965 (div.); m. John L. Kammerdiener, June 28, 1975; children: Susan, Michael. BS, U. Mich., 1966, MS, 1968, PhD, 1973. Staff mem. to project leader Los Alamos (N.Mex.) Nat. Lab., 1973—; adj. asst. prof. U. N.Mex., Albuquerque, 1977. Contbr. numerous articles to profl. jours. Mem. AAAS, IEEE, Am. Physical Soc., Am. Nuclear Soc. Home: 102 Monte Rey N Los Alamos NM 87544 Office: Los Alamos Nat Lab Mail Stop B230 Los Alamos NM 87545

LEONARD, JANET TONKA, management consultant; b. Indpls., July 31, 1952; d. Clarence and Marjorie (Tuley) Tonka; m. Kenneth Carl Leonard, Mar. 7, 1981. BA, Duke U., 1974; MBA, Columbia Grad. Sch. of Bus., 1983. Sales rep. to dist. account mgr. to asst. nat. account mgr. Gen. Foods Corp., Atlanta, Dallas and White Plains, N.Y., 1974-81; mgmt. cons. Touche Ross, N.Y.C., 1983-85; corp. planning mgr. PepsiCo, Purchase, N.Y., 1985-86; sr. mgmt. cons. The Alexander Group, Inc., N.Y.C., 1987-89; pres., founder Canaan Fin. Mgmt., Inc., New Canaan, Conn., 1989—, JTL Enterprises, New Canaan, Conn., 1988—. Site coordinator IRS Vol. Income Tax Assistance Program, New Canaan, 1989; alumni admissions adv. bd. Duke U., Fairfield County, Conn., 1988-89. Mem. Young Women's League (New Canaan chpt.), Assn. of Am. Univ. Women, Kappa Kappa Gamma (Delta Beta chpt.). Home: 213 Old Stamford Rd New Canaan CT 06840

LEONARD, JENNIFER CLARE, environmental protection specialist; b. Evansville, Ind., Sept. 20, 1952; d. William Thomas and Audrey Jean (Weidner) L. BA in Biology, St. Ambrose U., 1975. Environ. protection specialist Rock Island (Ill.) Arsenal Dept Army, 1980-84, Munitions and Chem. Command Dept Army, Rock Island, 1984-86, Army Materiel Command Dept Army, Alexandria, Va., 1986—; contbg. mem. Strategic Def. Command's Environ. Rev. panel, Alexandria, 1986—; staff mem. Environ. Quality Coun. C hdqrs. Army Material Command, 1989—. Mem. Nat. Assn. Environ. Profls. Roman Catholic. Home: 219 S Payne #202 Alexandria VA 22314-3542 Office: Hdqrs AMC Attn: AMC EN-A 5001 Eisenhower Ave Alexandria VA 22333-0001

LEONARD, JUANITA LOUISE EVANS, theology educator; b. Louisville, May 9, 1939; d. Walter Perry and B. Gertrude (Collins) Evans; m. Lawrence Samuel Leonard, June 24, 1961. BA in Sociology, Anderson U., 1961; MA in Social Services, U. Ind., 1963; postgrad., U. Minn., 1969; MA in Cross Cultural Stud, Fuller Theo. Seminary, 1987. Marriage therapist Family Service Madison County, Anderson, Ind., 1963-65; instr. sociology Anderson U., 1965-68, assoc. prof., 1987--; chief marriage therapist Dept. of Psychiatry, Ind. U. Med. Sch., 1969-72; inservice dir. Pastoral Counseling Inst., Indpls., 1972-73; instrn. materials dir. family life Nat. Christian Council of Kenya, 1973-76; assoc. in marriage and family Inst. of Pastoral Counseling, Indpls., 1976-78; assoc. pastor family ministries Ch. of God, Indpls., 1978-85; founding dir. Counseling Ctr. Ch. at the Crossing, Indpls., 1978-85; assoc. cross cultural relations Women of the Ch. of God, Anderson, Ind., 1987--; cons. Women Network of La. II Internat. Congress on World Evangelization, Manila, Philippines, 1989; urban ministry cons. Nat. Assn. Ch. of God, West Middlesex, Pa., 1988--, bd. mem. Wesleyan Urban Coalition, Chgo., 1987--. Editor: Youth are Saying..., 1976, Called to Minister Empowered to Serve, 1989; contbr., editor to local mags. Mem. AAUW, Nat. Assn. Social Workers, Acad. Cert. Social Workers, Am. Assn. Marriage Family Therapist (pres. 1978-82),. Office: Anderson U Sch Theology Anderson IN 46012

LEONARD, LORRAINE, marketing executive; b. N.Y.C., Oct. 3, 1954; d. Vincent Francis and Mary Theresa (Chianchiano) L. BA, St. John's U., Jamaica, N.Y., 1976. Regional sales mgr. Grand Met. Hotels, N.Y.C., 1982-84; corp. sales mgr. Forum Hotels Internat., N.Y.C., 1984-85, nat. sales mgr., 1985-86; mktg. mgr. Orient-Express Hotels, N.Y.C., 1986-87; dir. mktg. Venice Simplon-Orient-Express, N.Y.C., 1987—. Mem. Am. Soc. Travel Agts., Hotel Sales Mktg. Assn., Sales Exec. Club, Meeting Planners Internat., Soc. Incentive Travel Execs. Home: 1073 Maple Ave South Hempstead NY 11550 Office: Venice Simplon Orient Exp 1 World Trade Ctr Ste 2565 New York NY 10048

LEONARD, LUCINDA ELAINE, information management company executive; b. Winthrop, Mass.; d. Ernest W.J. and G. Elinor (Smith) L. BA, Northeastern U., 1966; MSLS, Drexel U., 1967; MBA, George Washington U., 1977. Systems analyst Bibliogrphic Systems Office, Libr. of Congress, Washington, 1969-76; project mgr. Automated Systems Office, Libr. of Congress, Washington, 1976-78; coord. FLICC/Fedlink, Washington, 1978-82; v.p., gen. mgr. Sterling Software Inc./Informatics, Rockville, Md., 1982-86; sr. info. mgr. Solutions by Design, Vienna, Va., 1986-89; pres. TriLeon, Inc., info. mgrs., Potomac, Md., 1989-90; v.p. libr. and info. svcs. ATLIS Fed. Svcs., Inc., Rockville, Md., 1990—; cons. Dept. of State/OFM, Washington, 1986—, J. Paul Getty Trust/FDA, Washington, 1989—. Contbr. articles to profl. jours. Office: ATLIS Fed Svcs Inc Rockville MD 20852

LEONARD, MARTHA FRANCES, pediatrician; b. New Brunswick, N.J., May 10, 1916; d. George Ferree and Jessie Rowe (Williams) L. BS, N.J. Coll. for Women, New Brunswick, 1936; MD, Johns Hopkins Med. Sch., 1940; MS, Yale U., 1979. Intern Balt. City Hosp., 1940-41; resident Vanderbilt U. Hosp., Nashville, 1943-43, N.Y. Hosp., N.Y.C., 1943-44, 45-46; pvt. practice Highland Park, N.J., 1946-60; fellowship Yale Child Study Ctr., New Haven, Conn., 1960-62, instr. to prof., 1962-86, prof. emerita, sr. rsch. soc., 1986—; cons. Aces, North Haven, Conn., 1978—. Contbr. scientific papers in field. Recipient Voorhees fellowship N.J. Coll. for Women, New Brunswick, N.J., 1936, Winslow award Conn. Pub. Health Assn. Mem. Am. Acad. Pediatrics (treas. Conn. chpt. 1987—), Am. Women's Med. Assn., World Assn. Infant Psychiatry and Allied Disciplines, New Haven Pediatrics Soc., Assn. Ambulatory Pediatrics, Conn. Pub. Health Assn. Democrat. Home: 20 Dorr St Branford CT 06405

LEONARD, MARTHA REED, academic administrator; b. Mpls., May 1, 1938; d. William Chester and Elizabeth (Martin) Reed; m. William E. Hostetler, Dec. 19, 1959 (div. Apr. 1975); children: Jane Elizabeth, Paul Andrew, Julie Marie; m. Frederic E. Leonard, July 18, 1975 (div. Apr. 1987). BA, U. Minn., 1960; MBA, Rutgers U., 1982. Jr. scientist U. Minn., Mpls., 1960-61, asst. to dean grad. sch., 1961-65, asst. to dean biol. scis., 1965-66; asst. to dean nursing Seton Hall U., South Orange, N.J., 1976-79; asst. to pres. Seton Hall U., 1979-82; v.p. student affairs Seton Hall U., South Orange, N.J., 1980; exec. asst. to pres. Poly. U., Bklyn., 1982-85, v.p. univ. rels., 1985-88; sr. v.p. univ. rels. Poly. U., 1988-90; v.p. for devel. Montefiore Med. Ctr., Bronx, N.Y., 1990—. Mem. Nat. Soc. Fund Raising Execs., U. Minn. Alumni Assn., Rutgers U. Alumni Assn. Office: Montefiore Med Ctr 111 E 210th St Bronx NY 10467

LEONARD, RUTH ANN, educational administrator; b. Lodi, Calif., May 23, 1946; d. Raymond and Wilma Ruth (Haverly) Nichols; m. Lewis D. Leonard, June 14, 1975 (div.). BA, Calif. State U., Long Beach, 1970; MA, Calif. State Coll., Turlock, 1984. Elem. tchr. Golden Hill Sch., Fullerton, Calif., 1970-7l; kindergarten tchr. Richman Sch., Fullerton, 1971-73; tchr. reading Sonora (Calif.) Elem. Sch., 1973-74; tchr. Curtis Creek Elem. Sch., Standard, 1974-85, dir. spl. projects, 1985-86, asst. prin., 1986-89; prin. Copperopolis (Calif.) Sch., 1989—; cons. Heart and Heart Drug Abuse Prevention, Sonora, 1977-80; mem. Tuolumne County Program Quality Rev. teams, 1986-88, Tuolumne County Mid. Sch. Task Force, 1988-89. Mem. Assn. Calif. Sch. Adminstrs., Calif. League Mid. Schs., Phi Delta Kappa. Democrat. Home: 349 Lyons St Sonora CA 95370 Office: Copperopolis School 217 School St Copperopolis CA 95228

LEONARD, SELINA PHYLLIS, computer-aided design specialist; b. N.Y.C., Oct. 17, 1963; d. William Franklin and Janice Inez (Jacobs) Woodard; m. Reginald Mendell Leonard, June 10, 1988. Diploma, ITT Tech. Inst., 1982. Computer-aided designer Gibbs & Cox Inc., N.Y.C., 1984-88, Rosenblatt & Sons, N.Y.C., 1988-89; computer-aided design coord. BJLJ Engrs. and Architects, P.C., Garden City, N.Y., 1989—. Mem. NAFE. Democrat. Episcopalian. Home: 1165 E 54th St Apt 4S Brooklyn NY 11234

LEONARD, SHAREN CRUMRINE, law librarian; b. Ashland, Ohio, Feb. 24, 1953; d. Walter Leroy and Charlene Isabell (Phillips) Crumrine; m. Andrew Donham Leonard, June 11, 1977; 1 child, Michael Donham. BA, Mt. Union Coll., Alliance, Ohio, 1975; MLS, Kent (Ohio) State U., 1976. Head tech. svcs. Rocky River (Ohio) Pub. Library, 1976-78; cataloger Bostonian Soc., Boston, 1979-81; asst. librarian Goodwin, Procter & Hoar, Boston, 1981-82; asst. librarian for tech. svcs. U.S. Ct. Appeals (1st cir.), Boston, 1982-84; head librarian Palmer & Dodge, Boston, 1984—. Mem. Am. Assn. Law Libraries, Spl. Libraries Assn., Assn. Boston Law Librarians, Law Librarians of New Eng. Methodist. Home: 95 Ronald Rd Arlington MA 02174 Office: Palmer & Dodge 1 Beacon St Boston MA 02108

LEONARD, SHERON RENA, computer analyst, air force officer; b. Jonesboro, La., Jan. 22, 1959; d. Ervin Leonard and Lizzie Davis. BS (computer science), Grambling U., Grambling, 1981; MBA, Central St. U., Edmond, 1988. Substitute tchr. Jackson Parish Sch., Jonesboro, La., 1981—; receptionist, loan officer CFI Federal Credit Union, Jonesboro, 1980-82; computer devel. officer U.S. Air Force, Tinker AFB, Okla., 1982-84; advanced through grades to capt. USAF; participant with industry US Air Force - Logicon, Inc., San Diego, Calif.; trainer & communications systems officer USAF, Tinker AFB, 1986-87; chief analysis software devel. section USAF, Okla., 1987-88; project mgr. block 4B Space Def. Ops. Ctr. USAF, Hanscom AFB, Mass., 1989—; Chair, Dining Out Com., Co. Grade Officer Coun., Tinker AFB, Okla., 1982—. Author: Concerns the 1st Black Flying Squadron, 1988. Blood Dr. Chair, Okla. Blood Inst., 1984-86. Recipient Certificate of Achievement, Cavanah Clark Scholastic Award, Cen. State U., 1987; named Distinguished Grad., USAF Reserve Officer Tng. Corp, 1981, Outstanding Young Women of Am., Montgomery, Ala., 1987-85. Democrat. Baptist.

LEONARD, SUSAN RUTH, psychologist, consultant; b. Mineola, N.Y., June 15, 1955; d. Donald Edward Leonard and Jane (Solomon) Hertzberg. BA, L.I. U., 1977; MA, U. N.C., 1980, PhD, 1985. Lic. psychologist, N.C. From instr. to asst. prof. psychology dept. Wake Forest U., Winston-Salem, N.C., 1984-86, staff psychologist counseling ctr., 1985-89; clin. psychologist Manoogian Psychol. Assocs., Winston-Salem, 1986—; cons. Ctr. for Creative Leadership, Greensboro, N.C, 1985—. Vol. United Way, Winston-Salem, 1989—; mem. adv. com. Family Svcs. Family Violence, Winston-Salem, 1987-89; trustee Resource Ctr. for Women & Ministry in the South, 1989—; bd. dirs. AIDS Task Force, Winston-Salem, 1986-90, Cancer Svcs. Inc., Winston-Salem, 1989—, Crisis Control Ministry, Winston-Salem, 1990—. Mem. Am. Psychol. Assn., Assn. of Women in Psychology, N.C. Psychol. Assn. Office: Manoogian Psychol Assocs 1338 Ashley Sq Winston-Salem NC 27103

LEONARD, VIRGINIA KATHRYN, budget officer; b. Street, Md., Aug. 31, 1944; d. Elbert Monroe and Mildred Rudolph (Patrick) Joines; m. James Richard Leonard, Aug. 31, 1963; children: James Richard II, Raymun Bradley. Student, Ea. Nazarene Coll., 1962-63; AA, Harford Community Coll., 1976; BS in Bus. Mgmt., U. Md., 1983; grad., U.S. Army Mgmt. Staff Coll., 1988. Sec. with U.S. Army, Aberdeen Proving Ground, Md., 1965-75; program analyst Facilities Engring., Aberdeen Proving Ground, Md., 1976-79; budget analyst Aberdeen Proving Ground Command, 1980; program analyst officer Facilities Engring., Aberdeen Proving Ground, Md., 1981;

budget analyst Test and Evaluation Command, Aberdeen Proving Ground, Md., 1982-83; budget officer test and evaluation command U.S. Army, Aberdeen Proving Ground, Md., 1985-89; fin. mgr. test and evaluation command U.S. Army, Aberdeen Proving Ground, 1989—; budget analyst Dept. of Army, Washington, 1984. Mem. Am. Soc. Mil. Comptrollers, Assn. U.S. Army. Office: Test and Evaluation Command AMSTE-RM AMSTE-RM-B Aberdeen Proving Ground MD 21005

LEONARD-BARTON, DOROTHY, business educator; b. Elsah, Ill., Mar. 18, 1942; d. Edwin Stanley and Gladys Eugenia (Lee) L.; m. Ronald Bruce Barton; children: Gavin B., Michelle A. BA, Principia Coll., 1963; MA, U. Va., 1968; PhD, Stanford U., 1979. Peace corp vol. Bangkok, Thailand, 1965-67; journalist freelance, Bangkok, 1968-70, Jakarta, Indonesia, 1970-75; research analyst S.R.I. Internat., Menlo Park, Calif., 1979-80; asst. prof. Sloan Sch. Mgmt. MIT, Cambridge, Mass., 1980-83; asst. prof. Harvard Grad. Sch. Bus., Boston, 1983-89, assoc. prof., 1989—; cons. in field. Contbr. many articles to profl. jours. Com. mem. Nat. Research Council, Washington, 1981-83; panel mem. Nat. Research Council, 1982. Recipient Kaiser Found. Grant, 1982, Whitaker Health Sciences Fund, 1981. Mem. Technology Innovation Div. Acad. Mgmt. Home: 20 Leslie Rd Winchester MA 01890 Office: Harvard Bus Sch Soldiers Field Boston MA 02163

LEONARDO, ANN ADAMSON, marketing and sales executive, consultant; b. Hamilton, Lanark, Scotland, Jan. 4, 1944; d. James Walker and Margaret Patterson (Burnside) Adamson; m. John Constantine Leonardo, Jr., Mar. 29, 1975; 1 child, Elizabeth Margaret. BS in Mktg. and Bus., Ryerson Coll., 1970. Market research mgr. MacLaren Advt., Toronto, Can., 1965-70; group product mgr. Menley & James, Montreal, 1970-74; mktg. mgr. Maybelline Div.-Plough, Toronto, 1974-75; v.p. mktg. Van De Kamp's Bakery, Glendale, Calif., 1976-80; v.p. mktg. and sales Cal West Periodicals, Oakland, 1980-84; mktg. cons., Novato, Calif., 1984—; dir., pres. Family House Inc., San Francisco; dir. Marin Services for Women, Larkspur, Calif. Mem. Am. Mktg. Assn., Smithsonian Inst. Home: 102 La Merida Ct Novato CA 94945

LEONDAR, BARBARA, academic administrator; b. N.Y.C., Jan. 19, 1928; d. Marcy and Pauline (Spiwack) L.; m. Aaron Reuben Cohn, Dec. 21, 1947 (div. 1962); children: D'Vera, Daniel Charles, Joel Jacob. BA, NYU, 1947; MA, Calif. State U., Northridge, 1964; EdD, Harvard U., 1968. English tchr. Taft High Sch., Woodland Hills, Calif., 1960-64; asst. prof. Harvard U., Cambridge, 1967-68, 1969-72, U. Mass., Boston, 1968-69; asst. dean, assoc. prof. Rutgers U., New Brunswick, N.J., 1972-74; assoc. dean Boston U., 1974-80; v.p. acad. affairs Worcester (Mass.) State Coll., 1980-86; pres. U. Maine, Ft. Kent, Maine, 1986-89; sr. assoc. presdl. search consultation svc. Assn. of Governing Bds. of Univs. and Colls., Washington, 1989—. Editor: The Arts and Cognition, 1977; contbr. articles to prof. jours. Kent fellow Danforth Found., 1966-68, Fulbright fellow, 1984. Mem. Modern Lang. Assn., Am. Soc. for Aesthetics, Nat. Council Tchrs. of English, New England Assn. Schs. and Colls. (mem. various accreditation teams 1978-84). Office: AGB 1 Dupont Circle Washington DC 20036

LEONE, CAROLE ANNE, teacher, consultant; b. London, Jan. 3, 1946; d. James Robert and Eleanor Mary (Gray) Peterson; m. Alfred Joseph Leone Jr., July 25, 1976; 1 child, Christopher Vincent. BS in Home Econs., Ohio State U., 1968; MEd, Rutgers U., 1973. Tchr. home econs. Perth Amboy (N.J.) High Sch., 1968—, tchr., coord. coop. home econs., 1977—; dir. project turn-around/focus on you home econs. curriculum N.J. Dept. Edn., Trenton, 1987-89. Contbg. tchr.: N.J. Cooperative Home Economics Education Handbook, 1988. Treas. Vocat. Home Econs. Edn. Assn., N.J., 1989—. Mem. Vocat. Home Econs. Edn. Assn. (treas. N.J. chpt. 1989—), Jr. Women's Club Westfield (N.J.) (sec. 1985, treas. 1986). Republican. Lutheran. Home: 166 Harrison Ave Westfield NJ 07090 Office: Perth Amboy High Sch Eagle Ave and Francis St Perth Amboy NJ 08861

LEONE, IDA A., retired plant pathology educator; b. Elizabeth, N.J., Apr. 28, 1922; d. Joseph and Josephine (Aprigliano) L. BS, N.J. Coll. for Women, 1944; MS, Rutgers U., 1946. Rsch. asst. Cook Coll., Rutgers U., New Brunswick, N.J., 1946-61, asst. rsch. specialist, 1961-71, assoc. rsch. prof. plant pathology, 1971-76, rsch. prof. I., 1976-86, prof. II, 1986-88, prof. II emerita, 1988—; expert witness N.Y. State Dept. Environ. Conservation, Albany, 1975-76; mem. siting com. Atlantic Electric Co., Atlantic City, 1979; mem. rsch. adv. com. Lake Erie Generating Sta., Niagara Mohawk Power Corp., Syracuse, N.Y., 1985-88. Contbr. over 175 articles to sci. jours., chpts. to books. Mem. Rahway (N.J.) Air Pollution Commn., 1970-80; commr. Cen. Jersey Air Pollution Control Agy., Woodbridge, N.J., 1970-80; trustee Amateur Astronomers, Inc., Cranford, N.J., 1984-86, St. John the Apostle Ch., Linden, N.J., 1985—. Recipient AMITA award Nat. Italian-Am. Found., 1966, Disting. Prof. award Rutgers U., 1987; scholar State of N.J., 1940-44. Mem. Am. Soc. Plant Physiologists, Am. Phytopath. Soc., Air and Waste Mgmt. Soc. (chmn. ecology com. 1986-88), N.J. Acad. Sci. (bd. dirs. 1988—), Audubon Soc. Roman Catholic. Home: 876 Rayhon Terr Rahway NJ 07065 Office: Rutgers U Cook Coll Dept Plant Pathology New Brunswick NJ 08903

LEONE, JUDITH GIBSON, educational media specialist, video production company executive; b. Toms River, N.J., Sept. 27, 1945; d. James Delaney and Louise Gertrude (Eberhardt) Gibson; m. Stephan Robert Leone, Nov. 27, 1971; stepchildren: Cheryl, Debra. BA, Kean Coll., 1970; MLS, Rutgers U., 1980. Cert. edn. media specialist. Tchr. Toms River Schs., 1970-84, media specialist, 1984-89; v.p., owner Prodn. House, Toms River, 1985—; libr. coord. Amb. Christian Acad., Toms River, 1989—; mem. region 5 book evaluation com. N.J. State Libr. System, 1986—. Sec., bd. dirs. The Shelter, Inc., Bricktown, N.J., 1979—; corr. sec. Open Arms, Inc.; trustee Harbor House. Mem. N.J. Ednl. Assn., Ednl. Media Assn. N.J., Ocean County Libr. Assn., Internat. TV Assn., Internat. Assn. Sch. Librarianship, Open Arms, Toms River Country Club. Democrat. Home: 143 Cranmoor Dr Toms River NJ 08753 Office: Prodn House PO Box 1076 Island Heights NJ 08732

LEONG, CAROL JEAN, electrologist; b. Sacramento, Jan. 9, 1942; d. Walter Richard and Edith (Bond) Bloss; m. Oliver Arthur Fisk III, Apr. 12, 1964 (div. 1973); 1 child, Victoria Kay. BA in Sociology, San Jose (Calif.) State Coll., 1963; degree, Western Bus. Coll., 1964; cert. in electrolysis, Bay Area Coll. Electrolysis, 1978. Registered and cert. clin. profl. electrologist, Calif. Model various orgns., Calif., 1951-64; employment counselor Businessmen's Clearinghouse, Cin., 1966-67; dir. personnel Kroger Food Corp., Cin., 1967-68; prin. Carol Leong Electrolysis, San Mateo, Calif., 1978—; prin. Designs by Carol, San Mateo, 1987—; mem. Profl. Women's Forum, 1988—. Contbr. articles to profl. publs. Recipient Cert. of Appreciation San Francisco Lighthouse for the Blind, 1981-82, 83. Mem. Internat. Guild Profl. Electrologists (mem. continuing edn. com.), NAFE, Profl. Women's Forum, Peninsula Humane Soc., San Francisco Zool. Soc., Friends of Filoli, Am. Electrologists Assn., Electrologists Assn. Calif., Internat. Platform Assn, Chi Omega. Republican. Methodist. Home: 3339 Glendora Dr San Mateo CA 94403 Office: Carol Leong Electrolysis 36 S El Camino Real Ste 205 San Mateo CA 94401

LEONG, JANET MEE, restaurant manager; b. Fallon, Nev., June 2, 1961; d. Frank and Lai Wah (Tang) L. BA, Brooks Inst., Santa Barbara, Calif., 1984. Cashier Rice Bowl Restaurant, Sparks, Nev., 1971-79; freelance photographer Los Angeles, 1984-87; restaurant mgr. Rice Bowl Restaurant, Sparks, Nev., 1987--.

LEONG, JO-ANN CHING, microbiologist, educator; b. Honolulu, May 15, 1942; d. Raymond and Josephine Ching; m. Oren T.H. Leong; children: Kara Elise, Jonathan Raymond. BA in Zoology, U. Calif., Berkeley, 1964; PhD in Microbiology, San Francisco Sch. Medicine, 1971. Postdoctoral rsch. assoc. dept. biochemistry U. Calif., San Francisco, 1971-75, asst. rsch. virologist Cancer Rsch. Inst., 1975; asst. prof. Oreg. State U., Corvallis, 1975-80, assoc. prof., 1980-86, prof., 1986—; grant reviewer Sea Grant, NSF, CRIS, NIH; cons. Am. Microscan, 1986. Co-author: Retroviruses and Differentiation, 1982, Molecular Approaches to Bacteria and Viral Diseases of Fish, 1983, Fish Vaccination, 1988. Coord. Women in Sci. Career Workshop, Portland (Oreg.) State U., 1977. Recipient Dernham Rsch. Fellowship, Am. Cancer Soc., 1973-75, fellowship Giannini Found. for Med. Rsch., 1973; named NORCAS prof. Batelle NW Labs., 1976. Fellow Am. Acad. Microbiology; mem. Am. Soc. Microbiology, Am. Soc. Virology, AAAS, Am. Fisheries Soc. (fish health sect.), Assn. Women in Sci., Am. Assn. Cancer Rsch., AAUP (exec. bd. 1982). Office: Dept Microbiology Oreg State U Corvallis OR 97331-3804

LEONIDOW, NATASHA MATRINA, nursing administrator; b. Nyack, N.Y., June 12, 1958; d. Paul and Matrina (Butich) L. AAS, Rockland Community Coll., 1979; BS in Nursing cum laude, SUNY Coll. Technology, Utica, 1982; MS in Nursing magna cum laude, Syracuse U., 1985. RN, N.Y.; cert. nurse adminstr. Staff nurse Englewood Hosp., N.J., 1979-80; charge nurse Mary Imogene Bassett Hosp., Cooperstown, N.Y., 1980-82, nursing service coordinator, 1983-86, asst. dir. systems devel., 1986-87; assoc. nursing practice coord. Strong Meml. Hosp.-U. Rochester, N.Y., 1987-88, asst. dir. nursing Bayfront Med. Ctr., St. Petersburg, Fla., 1989—. Translator: Excellence in Russian Language, 1976 (Otrada award). Served as 1st lt. USAR, 1987—. Mem. Nat. League of Nursing, Fla. Orgn. Nurse Execs., Sigma Theta Tau. Office: Bayfront Med Ctr 701 6th St S Saint Petersburg FL 33701

LEOPOLD, ANNA MARIE, visual sociologist; b. Altoona, Pa., June 17, 1925; d. William Plummer and Anna Eliza Shaefer; m. Louis Emanuel Leopold, June 12, 1947; children: John William and Louise Marie. PhB, U. Chgo., 1944, MA, 1962. Instr. Sociology Penn State U., Altoona, 1957-66, asst. profr., 1966-68; visual sociologist Ind., Altoona, 1968—; exhibitor more than 70 exhibits and progs. for Coll., Mus., profl conf. and art and photo salons, U.S., 1970—. Co-author: Photographic Soc. Am. Jour., 1984. Cultural com. Heritage Project Nat. Park, Svc. U.S. Replacement Delegate Nat. Dem. Conv., Memphis, 1978. Recipient Best of Show Slide Arts, Blair County, Pa., 1987; named Photographer of the Yr. Altoona Blair County Photo Soc., 1976-77, 77-78, 87-88. Mem. Photographic Soc. Am. (co-sec. Anglo Am. cur.) Penn. Ea. & Am. Sociol. Soc., Soc. for Indsl. Archaeology, Am. Assn. U. Women (past br. pres.), Indsl. Rels. Rsch. Assn. (charter mem.). Democrat. United Ch. of Christ. Home and Office: 101 Halleck Pl Altoona PA 16602

LEPOME, PENELOPE MARIE, rehabilitation counselor, educator; b. Buffalo, Dec. 17, 1945; d. Raymond Arthur and Mildred Evelyn (Johnson) Kramer; m. Robert Charles LePome, May 26, 1966 (div. Jan. 1982); children: Lisa Anne, Kathryn Jane, Robert Charles II. BA in Biology, SUNY, Buffalo, 1967; MS in Vocat. Rehab., U. Nev., Las Vegas, 1984. Cert. rehab. counselor; cert. substitute tchr., Nev.; cert. substance abuse counselor, Nev. Co-owner, salesman Flamingo Realty, Las Vegas, Nev., 1974-76; substitute tchr. Clark County Sch. Dist., Las Vegas, 1969-74, 1982-84; adj. faculty Clark County Community Coll., Las Vegas, 1984-86, Truckee Meadows Community Coll., Reno, 1987; bus. and industry field specialist, Tng. Inst. Clark County Community Coll., 1985-86; probation officer on call Clark County Juvenile Services, Las Vegas, 1984; counselor Nike House, Las Vegas, 1984; mental health techician III, State of Nev., 1984-86 ; rehab. coordinator I, Nev. Bur. Vocat. Rehab., Reno, 1986—; pvt. practice rehab. counseling, 1984-86. Active Nev. Womens Polit. Caucus, Las Vegas, 1983-85 ; carnival chmn. Rex Bell PTA, Las Vegas, 1974-75, treas., 1975-76; leader Frontier Area Girl Scouts, Las Vegas, 1975-76, cookie sale chmn., 1980; treas., bd. dirs. Young Audiences, Las Vegas, 1979-80. N.Y. State Regents scholar, 1963. Mem. Am. Assn. Counseling & Devel., AAUW (div. officer Nev. 1983-85, pres. 1982-83, v.p. programming 1981-82, v.p. membership 1980-81, life mem.), Assn. Part-time Profls. (bd. dirs.), Nat. Rehabilitation Assn. Republican. Lodge: Toastmasters. Office: 1050 Matley Ln Reno NV 89502

LEPOW, GLORIA KANTOR, meat packing company executive; b. Houston, Sept. 16, 1955; d. Howard and Celia Jean (Collector) Kantor; m. Gary Michael Lepow, Mar. 5, 1989; 1 child, Lauren Alyse; stepchildren: Denise and Brian (twins), Michelle, David. BS cum laude, C.W. Post Coll., 1979. Cert. elem. edn. and bus. tchr., Tex. Substitute elem. tchr. Ft. Bend County Sch. Dist., Ft. Bend, Tex., 1979-80; saleswoman Circle Art Gallery, Houston, 1979-80; exec. v.p. Kay Meat Co., Houston, 1980—, sec.-treas., 1982—. Co-chairperson Shoes for Houston's Homeless and Needy; career advisor L.I. U. Mem. S.W. Meat Packing Assn. Jewish. Office: Kay Meat Co PO Box 385 Houston TX 77001

LEPPERT, PHYLLIS CAROLYN, obstetrician-gynecologist; b. Phila., July 7, 1938; d. Walter Jennings and Alice (Brubach) L. BS, Columbia U., 1961, MS, 1964; MD, Duke U., 1973; PhD, Columbia U., 1986. Diplomate Nat. Bd. Med. Examiners, Am. Bd. Obstetrics and Gynecology. Clin. scholar Duke U., Durham, N.C., 1973-74; resident in pediatrics Duke U. Med. Ctr., Durham, 1974-76; resident in obstetrics/gynecology Yale U. Med. Sch., New Haven, 1976-79; assoc. in ob-gyn. Columbia U., N.Y.C., 1979-81, asst. prof. ob-gyn., 1981-88; visiting prof. Tokyo (Japan) Coll. of Pharmacy, Hachioji, Tokyo, Japan, 1989; chmn. dept. ob-gyn., assoc. prof. Rochester (N.Y.) Gen. Hosp., U. Rochester, 1989—; bd. dirs. Maternity Ctr. Assn., N.Y.C., 1988—, Riverdale Mental Health assn., 1986-89, St. Luke/Roosevelt Hosp., N.Y.C., 1986-88. Contbr. numerous articles to profl. jours. Vestry Christ Ch. Riverdale, Bronx, N.Y., 1984-86; adv. com. Office of Technology U.S. Congress, 1984. Recipient Berlex Found. Internat. Research Fellowship, 1989, Irving Friedman Award in Ob-Gyn. Yale U., 1978. Fellow Am. Coll. Obstetrics/Gynecology; mem. N.Y. Obstetrical Soc., Soc. for Exptl. Medicine, AAAS. Episcopalian. Office: Rochester Gen Hosp 1425 Portland Ave Rochester NY 14621

LERMA, ROSANNA, electrical engineer; b. Santa Maria, Calif., Nov. 17, 1963; d. Anselmo Israel and Rebeca (Cardenas) L. BSEE, U. Pacific, 1986. Engrng. asst. Port Hueneme (Calif.) Naval Base, 1981-82; engr. IBM, San Jose, 1983-84, Santa Barbara (Calif.) Research Ctr., 1985; teaching asst. Oxnard (Calif.) High Sch., 1986-87; electrical engr. Belden Inc., San Leandro, Calif., 1987--. Speaker Expanding Your Horizons, Livermore, 1989—. Mem. Soc. Women Engrs., IEEE, Calif. Maths. Council. Democrat. Home: 1465 Allman St Oakland CA 94602

LERMA, VICKI GAYLE WHITE, counseling specialist; b. Austin, Tex., Oct. 12, 1953; d. Ralph and Frances (May) White. BS in Edn. of Deaf, U. Tex., 1974, MEd in Vocat. Rehab. Counseling, 1979. Cert. tchr. of the deaf, interpreter for deaf; licensed profl. counselor. Tchr. Tex. Sch. for the Deaf, Austin, 1974-78; vocat. rehab. counselor Tex. Rehab. Commn., Austin and Ft. Worth, 1979-85, 87-88; rehab. specialist Regional Rehab. Exchange of S.W. Ednl. Devel. Lab., Austin, 1985-86; pvt. practice Austin, 1986-88; project coord. supported employment Vaughn House, Inc., Austin, 1987; with psychol. svcs./mental health svcs. for the deaf U. Tex./Callier Ctr. Communication Disorders, Dallas, 1988—; vocat. communication specialist, TRC. Council mem. Travis County Council for Deaf, Austin, 1980-85; mem. Pub. Responsibility Com. Travis State Sch., Austin, 1985; alt. Pvt. Industry Council, Austin, 1988. Fellow U. Tex. 1978-79; recipient Spl. Merit award Tex. Rehab. Commn., 1984. Mem. NAFE, Nat. Assn. for Deaf, Am. Deafness and Rehab. Assn., Registry Interpreters for the Deaf, Childrenof Deaf Adults, AACD, ARCA. Office: U Tex Callier Ctr Communication Disorders 1966 Inwood Rd Dallas TX 75235

LERMAN, EILEEN R., lawyer; b. N.Y.C., May 6, 1947; d. Alex and Beatrice (Kline) L. BA, Syracuse U., 1969; JD, Rutgers U., 1972; MBA, U. Denver, 1983. Bar: N.Y. 1973, Colo. 1976. atty. FTC, N.Y.C., 1972-74; corp. atty. RCA, N.Y.C., 1974-76; corp. atty. Samsonite Corp. and consumer products div. Beatrice Foods Co., Denver, 1976-78, assoc. gen. counsel, 1978-85, asst. sec., 1979-85; ptnr. Davis, Lerman, & Weinstein, Denver, 1985—; bd. dir. Legal Aid Soc. of Met. Denver, 1979-80. Bd. dirs., vice chmn. Colo. Postsecondary Ednl. Facilities Authority, 1981-89; bd. dirs., pres. Am. Jewish Com.; mem. Leadership Denver, 1983. Mem. ABA, Colo. Women's Bar Assn. (bd. dir. 1980-81), Colo. Bar Assn. (bd. govs.), Denver Bar Assn. (trustee), N.Y. State Bar Assn., Rutgers U. Alumni Assn. Lodge: Soroptimists. Home: 1018 Fillmore St Denver CO 80206 Office: Davis Lerman & Weinstein 50 S Steele St Ste 420 Denver CO 80209

LERMAN, HANNAH, psychologist; b. N.Y.C., Mar. 7, 1936; d. Ephraim and Lillian (Harris) L.; m. Bartin T. Smith, Jan. 17, 1957 (div. 1960). BA, CCNY, 1957; MA, Mich. State U., 1961, PhD, 1963. Lic. Psychologist, Calif. Clin. psychology intern VA Hosps., Mich., 1958-61; counselor Mich. State U., East Lansing, 1961-63; clin. psychologist II Topeka State Hosp., Kans., 1963-66, L.A. County-So. Calif. Univ. Med. Ctr., 1966-70; dean academic affairs Calif. Sch. Profl. Psychology, L.A., 1970-73; pvt. practice L.A., 1973—. Author: A Mote in Freud's Eye, 1986; editor: Ethics in Feminist Therapy, 1990; contbr. articles on women's psychology to numerous publs. CCNY fellow, 1957-58. Mem. L.A. Soc. Clin. Psychologists (pres. 1979), Am. Psychol. Assn. (pres. div. 35 psychology of women 1984-85), Am. Psychol. Assn. (fellow 1986, leadership award 1987). Home: 1543 Oakhurst Dr Los Angeles CA 90035

LERMAND, BARBARA PATRICIA, foundation administrator, fundraiser; b. N.Y.C., Nov. 15; d. Oliver Raymond and Carmen Millicent (Guy) L. BFA, Hofstra U., 1980; MA, Pa. State U., University Park, 1982. Membership dir. Jamaica Arts Ctr., 1986-88; chmn. theatre-dance panel Queens ReGrants Program, Jamaica, N.Y., 1988; grant adminstr. Juvenile Diabetes Found. Internat., N.Y.C., 1988—; grant wisher Starlight Found., 1989; cons. in resumé preparation. Author: Centerview. Drama Hon. scholar Hofstra U., 1977. Mem. NAFE, Soc. Rsch. Adminstrs., Am. Soc. for Profl. and Exec. Women, Alpha Psi Omega. Office: Juvenile Diabetes Found Internat 432 Park Ave #206 New York NY 10016

LERNER, BARBARA, public policy consultant, researcher, writer; b. Chgo., Mar. 31, 1935; d. Jacob Israel and Mary (Turen) L. BA with honors, U. Ill., 1956; MA, U. Chgo., 1961, PhD, 1965, JD, 1977. Bar: Ill. 1977; registered psychologist, Ill. Intern U. Chgo. Hosp. and Clinic, 1962-63; instr. Coll. Medicine U. Ill., 1963-64; clin. psychologist Ill. Mental Health Ctr., Chgo., 1965-68; assoc. prof. Ohio U., Athens, 1968-70; pvt. practice clin. psychologist Chgo., 1970-78; assoc. prof. Roosevelt U., Chgo., 1972-74; study dir. Nat. Acad. Scis., Washington, 1977-78; pres. Lerner Assocs., Princeton, N.J., 1981—; vis. scholar Ednl. Testing Svc., Princeton, 1978-79, sr. rsch. scientist, 1980-81; expert witness fed. cts. Debra P. vs. Turlington, Tampa, Fla., Marshall vs. Ga., 1983; vis. prof. U. Tex., Austin, 1989. Author: Therapy in the Ghetto, 1972, Minimum Competence, Maximum Choice, 1980; assoc. editor U. Chgo. Law Rev., 1975-77; contbr. articles to profl. jours. Pres. nominee U.S. Dept. Edn., Washington, 1986; mem. adv. com. U.S. Commn. Civil Rights, N.J., 1985-87. Recipient Cert. of Appreciation award for outstanding service U.S. Dept. Edn., 1985. Mem. Am. Psychol. Assn., ABA, Nat. Council Measurement in Edn., Am. Ednl. Research Assn., Phi Beta Kappa, Sigma Xi. Jewish. Office: Lerner Assocs 111 Carter Rd Princeton NJ 08540

LERNER, CAROLE JEAN, occupational therapist; b. Detroit, Aug. 28, 1938; d. Andrew B. and Maxine Curtis (Scudder) Sutyak; m. Paul Marvin Lerner, May 6, 1967; 1 child, Brett Andrew. BS, Ea. Mich. U., 1960. Lic. occupational therapist, N.C. Dir. occupational therapy Lenawee County Spl. Edn., Adrian, Mich., 1960-64; dir. psychiat. occupational therapy Sinai Hosp., Detroit, 1964-68, Mt. Sinai Hosp., Toronto, Ont., Can., 1973-86; lectr. faculty of medicine U. Toronto, 1978-86; cons. occupational therapy Asheville, N.C., 1988—; freelance graphic designer, Asheville, 1988—. Contbr. articles to profl. jours., chpts. to books; reviewer Can. Assn.Occupational Therapists, 1986-88. Mem. AAUW, N.C. Occupational Therapy Assn. (sec. western dist. 1989—), Am. Women's Club of Toronto (bd. dirs. 1986-88). Democrat. Home: 20 Buena Vista Rd Asheville NC 28803

LERNER, INA ROSLYN, executive administrator; b. Woodbury, N.J., Jan. 19, 1938; d. Jacob and Reba Docktor (Goodman) Goldman; m. Norman C. Lerner, Sept. 6, 1959; children: Sheila Beth, Julie Anne. BA, Marymount U., 1975. Pres. Ina R. Lerner Cons., Fairfax, Va., 1978-85; assoc. Fac Technology Inc., Vienna, Va., 1985—; exec. adminstr. Black & Decker/Planning Rsch. Corp., McLean, Va., 1987—; career advisor Women's Ctr. of No. Va., 1988. Mem. ambassador com. Fairfax C. of C., Vienna, 1988—. Mem. Va. Assn. Female Execs. (adv. com., 1989), NAFE, Sailing Club of Washington. Home: 4527 Pickett Rd Fairfax VA 22032

LERNER-LAM, EVA I-HWA, transportation executive; b. N.Y.C., Dec. 27, 1954; d. Sau-Wing and Jean (Lu) Lam; m. Arthur Lawrence Lerner-Lam, Sept. 4, 1977; children: Timothy Chi-Wen, Matthew Ta-Wen. AB, Princeton U., 1976; MS, MIT, 1978. Asst. planner County of San Diego, San Diego, 1977-78; dir. transp. planning group PRC Toups/Voorhies, La Jolla, Calif., 1978-79; assoc. planner Orange County Transit Dist., Garden Grove, Calif., 1979-80; assoc. planner San Diego Met. Transit Devel. Bd., 1980, sr. planner, 1981, dir. planning and ops., 1982-84; gen. mgr. Regency Motors, Montclair, N.J., 1984-85; asst. v.p., dir. planning and adminstrn. The Dah Chong Hong Trading Corp., N.Y.C., 1985-88; prin., cons. The Palisades Group, Tenafly, N.J., 1988—; bd. dirs. N.J. Transit Corp., Newark. Founder, coord. Asian-Am. Admissions Vols. Group, Princeton, N.J., 1985—; chmn. bd. dirs. Si-Yo Music Soc. Found., N.Y.C., 1988—; bd. dirs. Princeton U., 1984-88, founder, bus. mgr. and condr. Princeton U. Jazz Ensemble, 1973-76. Outstanding student fellow State Farm Cos., Princeton, 1974; recipient Outstanding Achievement award Tribute to Women in Industry, San Diego, 1983. Mem. NSF (transp. rsch. bd.), ASCE (vice chmn. planning com. urban transp. div. 1987—, sec. exec. com. 1988—), Am. Planning Assn., Inst. Transp. Engrs., Asian Alumni of Princeton (Outstanding Achievement award 1988), Campus Club (bd. dirs. 1984—), San Diego Princeton Club (pres. 1983-84). Office: The Palisades Group 85 Palmer Ave Tenafly NJ 07670

LEROY, ISABEL HERNANDEZ, library specialist; b. Tempe, Ariz., Nov. 4, 1951; d. Luis Molina and Brigida (Alcantar) Hernandez; m. Scott W. LeRoy, Aug. 17, 1974; children: Jesse Alejandro, Nicholas Andres. Student, Ariz. State U., Tempe. Libr. outreach coord. Maricopa Community Colls., Phoenix; dir. project read Phoenix Pub. Libr. Recipient Community Svc. award Girl Scouts U.S., 1989, Youth Recognition award, 1989. Memm. ALA, Libr. Pub. Rels. Coun.. Home: 6829 S 16th Way Phoenix AZ 85040 Office: South Moutain Community Coll 7050 S 24th St Phoenix AZ 85040

LESCHINSKI, SUSAN VIRGINIA, teacher; b. Chehalis, Wash., Mar. 15, 1954; d. Donald Lester and Dorothy Louise (Riley) Smith; m. Darwin Dale Pag; m. 2d John Leschinski, July 9, 1988. AA in Liberal Arts, Walla Walla Community Coll., Wash., 1972-74; BA in Edn., Eastern Wash. U., Cheney, Wash., 197579; M Ed., Eastern Wash. U., Cheney, 1983-84. Cert. Tchr., Wash. Tchr. aide Cheney Sch. DIst., Wash., 1975-79; substitute tchr. Cheney Sch. Dist., Wash, 1979-80; devel. pre sch. tchr. Liberty Sch. Dist., Spangle, Wash., 1980-81; piano tchr. Cheney, Wash., 1976-87; graduate asst. Eastern Wash. U., Cheney, Wash., 1983-84; pre sch. facilitator, parent educator Spokane Falls Community Coll., Wash., 1984-87; univ. instr. Eastern Wash. U., Cheney, Wash., 1985-87; devel. pre tchr. Aberdeen Sch. Dist., Wash., 1987--; devel. presch. tchr. N. Franklin Sch. Dis., Connell, Wash., 1988--; parent educator Liberty Sch. Dist., Spokane Wash., 198081, Spokane Falls. Researcher: Research, Incidence of Child Abuse ar EWU 1984. Named Vol. Yr., State of Wash., Walla Walla Community Coll., 1975. Mem. Council for xceptional Children (Pres. 1988---), Phi Kappa Phi Honor Soc. Democrat. Metodist. Office: N Franklin Sch Dist E 600 Adams Connell WA 99326

LESHANE, PATRICIA ROLAND, lobbyist, public relations consultant; b. Binghamton, N.Y., July 19, 1954; d. Ralph M. and Cecelia M. (Gearon) R.; m. Patrick J. Sullivan, Sept. 5, 1986. BS in Urban Planning, Springfield (Mass.) Coll., 1976; M. in Health Care Adminstrn., Hartford (Conn.) Grad. Ctr., 1983. Youth dir. Middlesex YMCA, Middletown, Conn., 1975-77; extension 4-H agt. U. Conn., Storrs, 1977-79; dir. planning Easter Seal Soc. of Conn., Hebron, 1979-83; ptnr. Sullivan & LeShane, Inc., Hartford, 1983—, Sullivan & LeShane Pub. Rels., Inc., Hartford, 1988—; corporator Springfield (Mass.) Coll. Mem. Hartford Rehab. Ctr., 1986; bd. dirs. Sister City Hartford; govt. rels. com. United Way of Greater Hartford. Recipient Young Alumni award Springfield Coll., 1986; named one of Women of the Time, Hartford Advocate, Women to Watch Hartford Women, 1988. Mem. Assn. of Entrepreneurial Women, 1985—. Democrat. Roman Catholic. Home: 14 Essex Ct Farmington CT 06032 Office: Sullivan & LeShane 287 Capitol Ave Hartford CT 06106

LESIAK, LUCILLE ANN, graphic designer; b. Chgo., Dec. 31, 1946; d. Walter Joseph and Anna (Cachur) L. BS, Ill. Inst. Tech., 1968. Designer Scott, Foresman & Co., Glenview, Ill., 1968-79, McDougal, Littell & Co., Evanston, Ill., 1979-80; prin. Image Concepts Ltd., Chgo., 1980-82; pres. Lucy Lesiak Design Ltd., Chgo. Mem. Am. Inst. Graphic Arts, Nat. Assn. Women Bus. Owners, Chgo. Book Clinic (Cert. of award 1974, 78, 79, 85-90, Desi award 1987, 89). Roman Catholic. Office: 445 E Illinois St Chicago IL 60611

LESIGER, ILENE GLORIA, paralegal, purchasing agent; b. Bklyn., Feb. 23, 1943; d. Abraham B. and Sarah (Kaufman) Wolf; m. Lawrence R. Lesiger, June 17, 1967; children: Alana Stacey, Nicole Michelle, Samantha Tara. Student, CCNY, 1961-63, Omega Inst., 1989—. Sec. to advt. mgr. Columbia Pictures Corp., N.Y.C., 1960-63; media buyer Don Kemper Advt. Agy., N.Y.C., 1963-68; media buyer Dodge car account Batten, Barton, Durstine & Osborne, Atlanta, 1969-72; legal asst., purchasing agt. First Mut. Corp., Pennsauken, N.J., 1974—. Leader Girl Scouts U.S., Haddonfield, N.J., 1980-86; co-chmn. Am. Field Svc. Exch. Program, Haddonfield, 1987-89. Mem. Paralegal Assn. So. N.J. Home: 212 Rhoads Ave Haddonfield NJ 08033 Office: First Mut Corp 5525 S US Hwy 130 Pennsauken NJ 08110

LESJAK, LISA MARY, marketing executive; b. Milw., June 18, 1963; d. Richard Joseph and Mary Barbara (Lezala) L. BA in Journalism/Polit. Sci., U. So. Calif., 1985. Asst. Peter S. Greenberg, L.A., 1984-85; mktg. asst. Mt. Carmel healthcare Ctr., Milw., 1986; dir. devel. St. Mary's Acad., Milw., 1986—. Coordinator Oak Creek Young Woman of the Yr. Prog., Oak Creek, 1986—; com. mem. Wis. Young Woman of the Yr. Prog., West Allis, 1989—. Newcomers scholar, 1987. Mem. Coun. for Advancement and Support of Edn., Cath. Sec. Sch. Devel. Assn. (pres. 1989-90), Women in Communications, Oak Creek Jaycees (Spl. Lady 1988). Republican. Roman Catholic. Home: 440 E Parkway Estates Dr Oak Creek WI 53154

LESLIE, CHERYL LEES, architectural illustrator; b. Pitts., Aug. 13, 1947; d. Joseph Meredith and June Elizabeth (Stinedorf) L.; m. Bruce Harper, June 14, 1969; children: Sean, Kirsten, Adam. AAS, Monticello Coll., 1967; BA, Baldwin-Wallace Coll., 1969; MEd., Houston State U., 1972; postgrad., Harvard U. Cert. in Teaching. Coord. community edn. Austin Ind. Sch. Dist., 1974-77; account rep. IBM, Chgo., 1982-84; art teacher Crete (Ill.) Sch. Dist., 1983-84; freelance architectural illustrator Skaneateles, N.Y., 1985—. Bd. dirs. Cultural Resource Coun., Syracuse, 1985, v.p. Skaneateles Symphony Guild, 1986. Methodist. Home: 9 Heatherwoods Skaneateles NY 13152

LESLIE, VICTORIA HALL, retail executive; b. Evanston, Ill., Dec. 3, 1954; d. John Hampton and Virginia Hall (Andersen) L.; m. Robert Adamy Duisberg; 1 child, Robyn Elizabeth. BA, U. Wis., 1977. Zool. researcher African Wildlife Found., Tanzania, Africa, 1978-79, NOAA, Seattle, 1979-80; founder, owner Flying Shuttle, Seattle, 1982—. Mem. Am. Craft Enterprise, African Wildlife Found. (coun. mem. 1989—). Office: Flying Shuttle 607 1st Ave Seattle WA 98104

LESSARD, LYNN MARIE, health insurance company administrator; b. Laconia, N.H., Nov. 19, 1953; d. Rene Arthur and Jane Marie (Gingras) Lessard; m. Robert Raymond Simoneau, Sept. 1978 (div. Sept. 1987); 1 child, Ryan Robert. BA, U. N.H., 1975. Staff writer-editor Daily Breeze, Torrance, Calif., 1976-81; news. corr. Union Leader-N.H. Sunday News, Manchester, 1982-83; communications coordinator Blue Cross Blue Shield of N.H., Concord, 1984—. Bd. dirs. The Friends Program, Concord, 1987-89. Mem. Women in Communications (v.p. membership N.H. chpt. 1989-90, pres. N.H. chpt. 1988-89), Healthcare Pub. Relations Exchange N.H. (v.p. 1989-90, sec.-treas. 1988-89). Roman Catholic. Home: 11-A Badger St Concord NH 03301 Office: Blue Cross Blue Shield NH 2 Pillsbury St Concord NH 03306

LESSE, ETTA GORDON (MRS. S. MICHAEL LESSE), psychiatric social worker; b. Trenton, N.J.; d. H. Charles and Rose (Miers) Gordon; B.A., Beaver Coll.; M.Social Sci., Smith Coll.; postgrad. Bryn Mawr Coll. Sch. Social Economy; U. Pa. Sch. Social Work; m. S. Michael Lesse; children—Toni Gordon and Cathy Ross (twins). Exec. sec. Clinic for Child Psychiatry, Temple U. Med. Sch., Phila.; psychiat. social worker Bur. Family Service, Orange, N.J., Family Welfare Soc., Newport, R.I.; intake worker Bur. Family Service, Orange, N.J.; case supr., asst. to chief social worker VA, Phila.; consultant for social agys. and ct. Social and health counsellor to Draft Bd., Orange, N.J.; organizer steering com. for establishment case work sect. Council Social Agys., Newport, R.I.; chmn. Workshop for Profl. Social Workers Lehigh Valley; group chmn. regional conf. pub. edn. Gov.'s Commn. Pub. Edn., Pa. Gov.'s Commn. on Aging; cons. foster home devel. Northampton County Children's Aid Soc.; profl. participant in religion and psychiatry seminars, Easton, Pa.; interviewer Easton-Phillipsburg (Pa.) Commn. Human Relations; mem. adv. bd. Northeastern region Pa. Dept. Pub. Welfare. Lectr. to child study group PTA, Easton, Pa. Bd. dirs. Lehigh Valley Center Performing Arts Assn., v.p.; bd. dirs. Lehigh Valley Community Council, 1975—, Planned Parenthood of Northampton County; exec. bd. Am. Heart Assn., 1978—; mem. adv. bd. Jr. League of Lehigh Valley. Mem. Nat. Assn. Social Workers, Acad. Certified Social Workers, AAUW (past br. pres., dir. Eastern br., chmn. career advancement loan fund, named Outstanding Woman of Yr. 1981-82, founder, chair meml. fund 1987—), Lehigh Valley Mental Health Assn. (dir., chmn. com. on personnel and nominating), Allentown Art Mus., Women's Com. Phila. Assn. Psychoanalysis, Northampton County Med. Soc. Aux., (dir. 1980—, v.p., pres., chmn. scholarships, chmn. med. and profl. nursing students loan fund), Phila. Orch. Assn., Met. Opera Assn., Smith Coll. Alumni Assn. Contbg. author Two Hundred Years of Life in Northampton County, Pa. Home: 2768 Stephens St Easton PA 18042

LESSENDEN, EDITH ANN FLEMING, writer, monologist; b. Garden City, Kans., Jan. 21, 1922; d. Arthur Milo and Edith Ann (Hambleton) Fleming; m. Chester Merral Lessenden, June 1, 1943; children: Sandra L. Lessenden; Marged L. Amend, Eve L. Supica, Mark Charles. A.B., Kans. U., 1946, M.A., 1952. Editor-writer Med. Aux. News, Kans., 1958-60, Allegro, Topeka Symphony, 1970-86; writer, dir. musical revues; contbr. articles to various publs. Organizer, chmn. Symphony League, Topeka, 1966-70, bd. dirs., 1966—; bd. dirs. Kans. Med. Aux., 1958—, pres., 1964-65; bd. dirs. AMA Aux., 1970-77, fund-raiser, 1973-75, regional v.p. 1975-77. Recipient Charles Marling award Topeka Symphony Soc., 1984. Mem. Nat. League Am. Pen Women (Roller award 1985, pres. Topeka br. 1986-88, pres. Kans. chpt. 1988-90), Kans. Authors Club, P.E.O. (chpt. pres. 1959-60, coop. bd. pres. 1961-62), Mortar Bd. Republican. Methodist. Clubs: Minerva (pres. 1963-64), Western sorosis (pres. 1980-81). Avocations: French conversation; sewing; needlepoint; reading.

LESSICK, MIRA L., nursing educator; b. Hazleton, Pa., Jan. 25, 1949; d. Jack H. and Shirley E. (Frumkin) L. Diploma in nursing, Albany (N.Y.) Med. Ctr., 1969; BSN, Boston U., 1972; MS, U. Colo., 1973; PhD, U. Tex., 1986. Staff nurse Boston City Hosp. and Mass. Gen. Hosp., 1969-72; instr. to asst. prof. nursing, genetics clinician U. Rochester, N.Y., 1973-79; asst. prof. nursing, practitioner Rush U., Chgo., 1986—. Contbr. articles to profl. jours. Recipient Bd. of Govs. award, Excellence in Pediatric Nursing award Albany Med. Ctr., 1969. Mem. AAAS, ANA, Chgo. Nurses Assn. (legis. com. 1990—), Nat. Assn. Ob-Gyn. and Neonatal Nurses, Am. Pub. Health Assn., Am. Soc. Human Genetics, N.Y. Acad. Scis., Midwest Nursing Rsch. Soc., Sigma Theta Tau, Phi Kappa Phi. Home: 4180 N Marine Dr Apt 610 Chicago IL 60613 Office: Ruch U Coll Nursing 1743 W Harrison St 30155H Chicago IL 60612

LESSOR, EDITH SCHROEDER, education educator; b. Chgo., Aug. 5, 1930; d. William and Hanna Maria (Ingwersen) S.; m. Arthur Eugene Lessor Jr., Nov. 20, 1955 (dec.); children: Ralph Arthur, Karen Lessor Moran. BS, Valparaiso U., 1952; PhD, Ind. U., 1955. Instr. Ulster County Community Coll., Kingston, N.Y., 1965-66, SUNY, Binghamton, 1966-68; from instr. to assoc. prof. Mt. St. Mary Coll., Newburgh, N.Y., 1968-76, prof. Mem. League of Women Voters, 1969-89, Dutchess County Coun. for Women. Mem. AAAS, Am. Chem. Soc., Nat. Orgn. for Women, AAUW, Sigma Xi. Home: 7F Knightsbridge Rd Poughkeepsie NY 12603 Office: Mt St Mary Coll 330 Powell Ave Newburgh NY 12550

LESUEUR, JOAN KAVANAUGH, librarian; b. Mt. Sterling, Ky., Nov. 16, 1929; d. Joe Miller and Nancy Hall (Clay) Kavanaugh; m. Alexander Armand Lesueur, Sept. 7, 1960; 1 child, Alexander Armand Jr. AB in Edn., U. Ky., 1951, MA in Spanish, 1954, MS in Library Sci., 1971. Tchr. Douglas County High Sch., Douglasville, Ga., 1951-52, Pinkerton High Sch. and Midway (Ky.) Jr. Coll., 1953-55, 1956-59; tchr. Coll. High Sch., Bartlesville, Okla., 1955-56; asst. prof. Spanish Morehead (Ky.) State U., 1959-61, 62-63, 64-65; inst. library sci. Western Carolina U., Cullowhee, N.C., 1968-78; librarian Canton (N.C.) Jr. High Sch., 1978—. Pres. Jackson County and Haywood County Cancer Soc., Sylva and Waynesville, N.C., 1982-83, 85-86; bd. dirs. N.C. div. Am. Cancer Soc., Raleigh, 1982-86; vestryman, lector local Episc. Ch. Recipient Terry Sanford award, Haywood County N.C. Educators, 1989; named Tchr. of Yr. Haywood County N.C. Educators, 1984. Mem. Am. Assn. Sch. Librs. (presenter media programs 1986, 89), N.C. Assn. Sch. Librs. (presenter media programs 1984, 86), N.C. Assn. Educators (state pres. support personnel div. 1982-83, bd. dirs. 1982-83, Outstanding Mem. award 1987), Nat. Cathedral Assn. Diocese Western N.C. (co-chmn. 1978-81), Phi Delta Kappa (sec.-treas., pres. Western Carolina chpt. 1990, Outstanding Tchr. award Western Carolina chpt. 1981), Delta Kappa Gamma, Beta Phi Mu, Blue Grass Soc. Colonial Daughters 17th Century, others. Home: 209 Pigeon St Waynesville NC 28786 Office: Canton Jr High Sch 60 S Penland Canton NC 28716

LETERNEAU, SUSAN MARIE, marketing director, educator; b. Detroit, Aug. 24, 1945; d. Daniel Lewis and Regina Elisabeth (Hohman) Bowers; m. Lawrence G. Rowland; children: John Andrew, Robert Daniel. BSBA, Regis Coll., 1982; MBA, U. Denver, 1984. Credit mgr. McBride Electric Inc., Englewood, Colo., 1973-76; office mgr. Monitor II Inc., Lakewood, Colo., 1976-78; purchasing asst. King Soopers, Inc., Denver, 1978-82; research asst. U. Denver, 1982-83; mktg. dir. Citicorp Diners Club Inc., Englewood, 1983-89; spl. asst. to pres. Regis Coll., Denver, 1989—; adj. prof. prodn. and ops. mgmt. Loretta Heights Coll., Denver, 1983—. Mem. exec. bd. S.W. Denver YMCA, 1982-84; bd. dirs. Bros. Redevel., Inc, 1986—. Named one of Top 15 Colo. Bus. Sch. Grads., Denver Bus. Mag., 1984; acad. scholar U. Denver, 1982-83. Mem. Am. Prodn. and Inventory Control. Soc., Rocky Mountain Assn. Credit Mgmt., Sigma Iota Epsilon. Office: Regis Coll W 50th Ave and Lowell Blvd Denver CO 80221

LETT, SHERRI J., health facility administrator; b. Winamac, Ind., Jan. 30, 1949; d. Herbert and Helen (Budd) Whiteman; m. Ronald Lett, May 26, 1979; children: Teresa Troutman, Andrea Troutman. Student, St. Elizabeth Hosp., Lafayette, Ind., 1968; postgrad., AMRA, 1986-89. Surgery technician Pulaski Meml. Hosp., Winamac, Ind., 1969-78, clinic asst., 1978-79, quality assurance, 1979-85, dir. patient affairs. Mem. Ind. Assn. Quality Profls. (treas. 1988-90), Hosp. Risk Mgrs., Ind. Assn. Quality Assurance Profls. (chmn. fin. 1985-88). Office: Pulaski Meml Hosp 616 E 13th St Winamac IN 46996

LETTS, CHRISTINE WEBB, state government official; b. Canton, Ohio, Sept. 26, 1948; d. Homer Dansby Jr. and Edna Mae (Winkler) W.; m. David Raymond Letts, Dec. 23, 1979; 2 children. BA, Conn. Coll., 1970; MBA, Harvard U., 1976. Mgmt. analyst N.Y.C. EPA, 1970-73, N.Y. State Charter Revision Commn., N.Y.C., 1974; mfg. mgr. Cummins Engine Co., Columbus, Ind., 1976-82, plant mgr., 1983-86, v.p., 1987-88; commr. Ind. Dept. Transp., Indpls., 1989—. Dir. Quinco Cons. Ctr., Columbus, 1983-86, Bartholomew County United Way, Columbus, 1988, Columbus Area Arts Coun., 1988. Recipient Tribute to Women in Internat. Industry. Mem. Women Execs. in State Gov. Democrat. Office: Ind Dept Transp 100 N Senate Indianapolis IN 46204

LEULIETTE, CONNIE JANE, secondary educator; b. Buckhannon, W.Va., Mar. 7, 1941; d. Audie Nelson and Sadie Laura (Gregory) Ware; m. Charles Benjamin Leuliette, Jr., Sept. 5, 1964; 1 child, Eric Wesley. BS, W.Va. U., 1963, MA, 1965. Tchr. grades 1-4 Point Mountain Elem. Sch., Webster Springs, W.Va., 1959-60; tchr. gen. sci. Webster Springs (W.Va.) High Sch., 1963-64; tchr. 2d grade Norwood Elem. Sch., Clarksburg, W.Va., 1965-66, tchr. 6th grade, 1966-67; circulation clk., librarian Clarksburg-Harrison Pub. Library, 1981-83, reference librarian, 1983-89; tchr. sci. South Harrison High Sch., Lost Creek, W.Va., 1989-90, Roosevelt-Wilson Jr. High Sch., Nutter Ft., W.Va., 1990—. Mem. AAUW (sec. W.Va. div. 1981-83, br. pres. 1983-85, conv. chmn. W.Va. 1978-80), NEA, Nutter Fort PTA (pres. 1978-79), W.Va. Assn. Parliamentarians (unit sec. 1986—), W.Va. Fedn. Woman's Clubs (chmn. edn. dept. 1982-86, chmn. contg. edn. div. 1990—, chmn. dist. edn. dept. 1990—), Womans Club of Nutter Fort (pres. 1990—), LWV, Alpha Delta Kappa. NSF grantee, 1964-65. Mem. AAUW (sec. W.Va. div. 1981-83, br. pres. 1983-85, conv. chmn. W.Va. 1978-80), NEA, Nutter Fort PTA (pres. 1978-89), W.Va. Assn. Parliamentarians (unit. sec. 1986—), W.Va. Fedn. Woman's Clubs (chmn. edn. dept. 1982-86), Woman's Club of Nutter Fort (pres. 1990—), LWV, Alpha Delta Kappa. Democrat. Presbyterian. Home: 107 Arbutus Dr Clarksburg WV 26301

LEUNG, JACQUELINE M., anesthesiologist, educator; b. Hong Kong, Jan. 9, 1958; came to U.S., 1982; d. Chung Ching and Jane Hing-Chun (Lau) Leung; m. David W. Sretavan, June 30, 1981. BSc with honors, McGill U., 1980; MD, Stanford U., 1984. Diplomate Nat. Bd. Med. Examiners. Intern Stanford (Calif.) U. Sch. Medicine, 1984-85; resident in anesthesia U. Calif., San Francisco, 1985-87, rsch. fellow, 1987-88, instr., 1988-89, asst. prof., 1989—. Cons. reviewer Anesthesiologist, 1988—; contbr. chpts. to books, articles to profl. jours. Mem. AMA, Am. Soc. Anesthesiologists (2d prize in residents rsch. essay contest 1988), Calif. Soc. Anesthesiologists, No. Calif. Soc. Anesthesiologists, Internat. Anesthesia Rsch. Soc. Office: VA Med Ctr Anesthesia (129) 4150 Clement St San Francisco CA 94121

LEUNG, LINA LEE, real estate developer; b. Macau, July 5, 1932; came to U.S., 1956; d. Chu Ho and Fok Yee (Leung) Lee; m. Kamman Francis Leung, July 26, 1959; children: Eileen, Elaine, Wing, Wesley. BA in Lit., U. Hong Kong, 1954; AA, Glendale Coll., 1959, Calif. State U., L.A., 1962. Cons. Li Chung Shing Tong Patent Medicine Manufactury, Hong Kong, 1950—, internat. mktg. cons., 1956—; owner, pres. Kam Co., Los Angeles, 1952—, Chang Shu-Chi Art Studio, Los Angeles, 1963—; owner, founder South Sea Investment and Mgmt., Los Angeles, 1978—; chmn., chief exec. officer Golden Capital Enterprise, Los Angeles, 1982—; founder Ea. Savs. Bank, Alhambra, Calif., 1984—; chmn. Golden Summit Enterprises, Inc., Los Angeles, 1986—; ptnr., treas. Seven Star Investment Group, Los Angeles, 1973—. Bd. dirs. Leong Family Assn. So. Calif., Los Angeles, 1984. Mem. Hong Kong Assn. So. Calif., Apt. Owners Assn. So. Calif., Apt. Assn. Greater Los Angeles, Chinese C. of C. Los Angeles. Democrat. Buddhist. Home: 1260 Mill Ln San Marino CA 91108 Office: South Sea Investment and Mgmt Co 767 N Hill St Suite 304 Los Angeles CA 90012

LEUSCHEN, MARY PATRICIA, research director; b. Iowa, June 3, 1943; d. Franklin G. and Genevieve J. (Stessman) Oppold; m. James W. Leuschen; children: Susan M., Paul A., Kathleen A., James P. BS, Creighton U., 1965, MS, 1967; MS, U. Nebr. Med. Ctr., 1974, PhD, 1976. NIH postdoctoral fellow Dept Physiology U. Nebr. Med. Coll., Omaha, 1976-80; asst. prof. Dept. Pediatrics U. Nebr. Med. Coll., Omaha, 1980—, Dept. Pediatrics Creighton U., Omaha, 1989—; rsch. dir. Newborn Medicine Creighton, U. Nebr. Med. Ctr., Omaha, 1988—. Chair Midlands chpt. Multiple Sclerosis Soc., Omaha, 1988-90. Office: U Nebr Med Ctr 600 S 42nd Ave Omaha NE 68198

LEUTHARD, JOY LYNNE, state agency administrator, social worker; b. Denver, Mar. 28, 1952; d. John Joseph and Garnett Edwana (Ferry) L.; m. Thomas Wayne Gillock, Nov. 9, 1985. B.A., Colo. State U., 1974; M.S., Okla. State U., 1976. Lic. social work assoc. Okla. Juvenile diversion counselor Ponca City Police, Okla., 1976-78; youth and family counselor Kay County Youth Services, Ponca City, 1978-81; program dir. YWCA Rape Crisis Ctr., Oklahoma City, 1981-82; sexual assault program dir. Women's Resource Ctr., Norman, Okla., 1982-85; state rape prevention coordinator Okla. Dept. Mental Health, 1982-85; exec. dir. Tri-City Youth and Family Ctr., Choctaw, Okla., 1985-89; state perinatal program dir. Okla. Dept. Health, Oklahoma City, 1989—; instr. Okla. State U., Stillwater, 1982-83. Author and editor: (with others) Sexual Assault: A Guide for Professionals, 1983. Editor directory Oklahoma Directory of Sexual Assault Services, 1983. Bd. dirs. Okla. Assn. Youth Svcs., 1985-86; mem. women's adv. council Okla. Dept. Mental Health, chairwoman, 1989-90; mem. local adv. coun. March of Dimes. Mem. Nat. Assn. Female Execs., NOW, Nat. Assn. Social Workers, Am. Assn. Counseling and Devel., Am. Mental Health Counselors Assn., Okla. Assn. D.U.I. Sch. Adminstrs. (pres. elect 1987-88). Democrat. Avocations: horses; music; theater; ballet; reading; gardening. Office: Okla Dept Health Maternal & Child Health Svcs PO Box 53551 1000 NE 10th St Oklahoma City OK 73152

LEV, JUDITH WILKENS, financial consultant; b. N.Y.C., Feb. 7, 1944; d. Samuel and Ruth (Ross) Wilkins: children: Russell, Corey. BS in Art Edn., Hofstra U., 1968; MS in Art Edn., L.I. U., 1971; MBA, Aldephi U., 1982. V.p., fin. cons. Shearson Lehman Bros., Manhasset, N.Y., 1983—. Mem. Delta Mu Delta. Republican. Jewish. Office: Shearson Lehman Hutton 1165 Northern Blvd Manhasset NY 11030

LEVALLEY, JOAN CATHERINE, accountant; b. Decatur, Ill., Nov. 27, 1931; d. Clarence and Pearl Mae (McClure) Krall; m. Charles R. LeValley, Apr. 13, 1958 (div.); children: Curtis Ray, Cara Marie. BA in Bus., Manchester Coll., 1957. Accredited tax advisor, Ill. Acct. with various firms, 1960-76; pvt. practice acctg., Park Ridge, Ill., 1964-79; pres., dir. LeValley & Assocs., Inc., Park Ridge, 1979—; mem. tax adv. com. Chgo. IRS Dirs. Mem. Nat. Assn. Pub. Accts., Ind. Acct. Assn. Ill. (2d woman pres. 1987-88, Person of Yr. award 1990), Bus. and Profl. Women Park Ridge (pres. 1974-75, Bus. Woman of Yr. 1983), Park Ridge C. of C. (treas. 1985-87). Baptist. Avocations: baking; sewing; gardening. Home: 2200 Bouterse #101 Park Ridge IL 60068 Office: LeValley & Assocs Inc 841 W Touhy Ave Park Ridge IL 60068

LEVANDOWSKI, BARBARA SUE, educational administrator; b. Chgo., Mar. 16, 1948; d. Earl F. and Ann (Klee) L. BA in Edn. and Spanish, North Park Coll., 1970; MS in Elem. Edn., No. Ill. U., 1975, degree in curriculum and supervision/instruction, 1977, EdD, 1979. Cert. elem. tchr.; cert. secondary tchr. Tchr. Round Lake (Ill.) Sch. Dist., 1970-75; tchr. Schaumburg (Ill.) Sch. Dist., 1975-87, asst. prin., 1977-87; prin. Dist. 200 Northwood Elem. Sch., Woodstock, Ill., 1987—; curriculum cons. Spring Grove (Ill.) Sch. Dist., 1980-81; instr. various courses, Schaumburg, 1984-86; dir. Einstein Sch. Writing Project; presenter various confs. Mem. editorial bd. Ill. Sch. Research and Devel. Jour., 1981—; contbr. articles to profl. jours. Mem. staff Round Lake Park Dist., 1973—. Recipient numerous awards for excellence in teaching, Those Who Excel award State of Ill., 1979; fed. grantee. Mem. NAESP, NAFE, Am. Biog. Inst. Research Assn. (research bd. dirs. 1985—, publs. com. 1983), Nat. Staff Devel. Coun., Assn. for Supervision and Curriculum Devel. (inservice presenter 1984-86, presenter state and nat. conv. 1989—), Nat. Coun. of States for InSvc., Ill. Staff Devel. Coun., Ill. Assn. for Supervision and Curriculum Devel. (chairperson. research com. 1982), Ill. Computer Educators, Inst. for Ednl. Rsch. (Omega award), Ill. Prin. Assn., Phi Delta Kappa, Delta Kappa Gamma. Home: 426 Normandie Ln Round Lake IL 60073 Office: Northwood Elem Sch 2045 N Seminary Ave Woodstock IL 60098

LEVASSEUR, PAULA ANN, medical technologist; b. Bay City, Mich., Dec. 10, 1961; d. Michael Henry and Loretta Germaine (Olenijczak) Sullivan; m. Eric James LeVasseur, Aug. 10, 1984; children: Jaqqi Marie, Kelly Ann. BS, Mich. State U., 1984. Intern med. technologist San Bernardino (Calif.) County Med. Ctr., 1985-86; med. technologist Jerry L. Pettis VA Hosp., Loma Linda, Calif., 1986-87, Desert Hosp., Palm Springs, Calif., 1987—; p.m. supr. Desert Hosp., Palm Springs, 1989—. Mem. Am. Soc. Clin. Pathologists. Office: Desert Hosp 1150 N Indian Ave Palm Springs CA 92263

LEVBARG, DIANE, fashion industry executive; b. Mar, 18, 1950; d. Morrison Levbarg and Ann-Louise Lewis; m. Martin I. Klein, May 23, 1974. Cert. in retail studies Coll. for Distributive Trades, London; student Vassar Coll., 1972. Exec. Trainee Harrods, London, 1970-71; exec. trainee, asst. dept. mgr., asst. buyer Saks Fifth Ave, N.Y.C., 1971-73; asst. buyer, buyer Bonwit Teller, N.Y.C., 1973-75; merchandise mgr. Bloomingdale's, N.Y.C., 1975-82; pres., fashion cons. Diane Levbarg & Assocs. Inc., N.Y.C., 1982—; exec. v.p. Missoni U.S.A.; v.p., chief operating officer U.S. devel. Nina Ricci; cons. Daniel Hechter, Christian Dior U.S.A., Bogner U.S.A.; adv. bd. Lab Inst. of Merchandising. V.P., James Beard Affiliate, City Meals-on-Wheels; cons. Irvington Inst. Med. Rsch. Named One of 100 Women of Promise, Good Housekeeping.

LEVENSON, JUDY ANN, lawyer; b. Haverhill, Mass., Mar. 25, 1951; d. Russell and Shura (Simon) L. BA, Wellesley Coll., 1973; MCP, MIT, 1976; JD, Yale U., 1982. Bar: Mass. 1983, U.S. Dist. Ct. Mass. 1984. Rsch. analyst MIT-Harvard Joint Ctr. for Urban Studies, Cambridge, Mass., 1975-76; dir. of policy analysis Mass. Advocacy Ctr., Boston, 1977-79; law clk. Justice, U.S. Dist. Ct., Bklyn., 1982-83; assoc. Hill & Barlow, Boston, 1983-87, Goodwin, Procter & Hoar, Boston, 1987—; bd. dirs. Farnsworth Housing Corp., Jamaica Plain, Mass., 1988—. Mem. Civil Liberties Union Mass., 1983—; mem. nominating com. Boston YWCA, 1988—. Named Wellesley Pendleton Scholar, 1970, Durant Scholar for Highest Acad. Achievement, 1973. Mem. Nat. Health Lawyers Assn., Mass. Bar Assn., Boston Bar Assn., Women's Bar Assn., Phi Beta Kappa. Office: Goodwin Procter & Hoar Exchange Pl Boston MA 02109

LEVENTHAL, CYNDI, vending executive; b. HollisHills, N.Y., July 20, 1963; d. Donald D. and Frances (Kaiser) Jordan; m. Mitchell Leventhal; children: Liza, Dani. BSBA, Hofstra U., 1985. Asst. mgr. Pearle Vision Ctr., Massapequa, N.Y., 1981-84; systems analyst Berliner Computer Corp., New Hyde Pk., N.Y., 1984; vending exec. Miro Amusements Corp., Melville, N.Y, 1985—. Office: Miro Amusements Corp PO Box 1519 Melville NY 11747

LEVENTHAL, RUTH, university provost and dean, educator; b. Phila., May 23, 1940; d. Harry Louis Mongin and Bertha (Rosenberg) Mongin Blai; children—Sheryl Anne, David Alan. B.S., U. Pa., 1961, Ph.D., 1973, M.B.A., 1981. Cert. med. technologist, clin. lab. scientist. Trainee NSF, 1971; trainee USPHS, 1969-70, 73; asst. prof. med. tech. U. Pa., Phila., 1974-77; acting dean U. Pa., 1977-81; dean Hunter Coll., N.Y.C., 1981-84; provost, dean, prof. biology Capitol Coll. Pa. State U., Middletown, 1984—; site visitor Middle State Assn. Colls. and Secondary Schs., Phila., 1983—. Author: (with Cheadle) Medical Parasitology: A Self Instructional Text, 1979, 2d edit., 1985; contbr. chpt. to book and articles to profl. jours. Chmn. pub. service div. Tri-County United Way, South Central Pa., 1985—; mem. health found. bd. Harrisburg Hosp., Pa., 1984—; bd. dirs. Tri-County Planned Parenthood, 1984—, Harrisburg Acad., Wormleysburg, Pa., 1984—, Metro Arts of Harrisburg, 1984—. Recipient Alice Paul award Women's Faculty Club, U. Pa., 1981; Recognition award NE Deans of Schs. of Allied Health, 1984; fellow U. Pa., 1972. Mem. Am. Soc. Parasitologists, Am. Assn. Higher Edn., N.Y. Soc. Tropical Medicine, N.J. Soc. Parasitology, AAUW (bd. dirs. Pa. br. 1985—), Sigma Xi. Office: Pa State U-Harrisburg Capital Coll Rte 230 Middletown PA 17057

LEVENTHAL, SHEILA SMITH, educator; b. Raymondville, Tex., May 4, 1941; d. M. C. and Jessie Mae (Sansom) Smith; m. Ira Yale Leventhal, Aug. 5, 1966; 1 child, Adam Yale. BS, N. Tex. State U., 1963, MEd, 1965; postgrad. Nova U., 1972, MIT, 1979. Elem. tchr. Grapevine Pub. Schs. (Tex.), 1963-65; tchr., team leader Lamplighter Sch., Dallas, 1965—, mem. steering com., computer staff, 1979-84. Staff mem. Episcopal Sch. of Spirituality, Dallas, 1983, dir., 1989-91. Mem. NEA, Tex. Tchrs. Assn., Women of St. Francis (v.p. Dallas 1983), Phi Delta Kappa. Home: 2947 Talisman Dr Dallas TX 75229 Office: Lamplighter Sch 11611 Inwood Rd Dallas TX 75229

LEVENTHAL, TERI V., communications executive; b. N.Y.C., Feb. 23, 1932; d. Solomon Edward and Lillian Francis (Taub) Feldman; m. Herbert Leventhal, May 29, 1957; children: Lawrence George, Sheryl Ann, Neil Richard. BS, Bridgeport U., 1953; postgrad., CCNY, 1979-82. Dental hygienist Dept. Health, N.Y.C., 1953-59; market researcher Market Research Inc., N.Y.C., 1971-73; tchr. Bd. Cooperative Edn., N.Y.C., 1973-82; pres. All Media Communication Corp., N.Y.C., 1982-84, TVL Media Assocs. Inc., N.Y.C., 1984—; telemktg. cons. Saslow, N.Y.C., 1983-86, Econodent, N.Y.C., 1984-86, Island Dental, N.Y.C., 1986-89, Met. Life, L.I.; instr. Hofstra U., 1988—. Pres. chpt. Hadassah, Baldwin, N.Y., 1971-73; rep. Civic Assn., Baldwin, Freeport, N.Y., 1981-85; bd. dirs. YMHA, Baldwin, 1978-82. Named Woman of Yr. Hadassah, N.Y.C., 1969; recipient Pres.' award Hadassah, N.Y.C., 1973, Service awards, 1964-84. Mem. Nat. Assn. Female Execs., Am. Soc. Tng. Devel. (advt. com.), Long Island Assn., Pres. Club. Jewish. Office: TVL Media Assocs 223 Jericho Turnpike Mineola NY 11501

LEVERE, JANE LOIS, magazine editor; b. Hackensack, N.J., Sept. 17, 1950; d. Bernard and Zelda (Gordon) L. BA, Smith Coll., 1972. Editorial, publicity asst. Doubleday & Co., Inc., N.Y.C., 1972-73; assoc. editor Editor & Publisher mag., N.Y.C., 1973-78; editor The Fairchild Syndicate, N.Y.C., 1978-79; dep. pub. affairs dir. White House Conf. on Families, Washington, 1979-80; sr. editor Travel Weekly newspaper, N.Y.C., 1980-87; mng. editor Frequent Flyer mag., N.Y.C., 1987—. Contbr. articles to Travel & Leisure mag., Advt. Age, Working Woman mag., N.Y. Daily News, Chgo. Tribune, Houston Chronicle, San Francisco Examiner, and others. Recipient Gene Dubois award N.Y. Airlines Pub. Relations Assn., N.Y.C., 1986. Mem. Am. Soc. Mag. Editors, N.Y. Travel Writers' Assn. (sec. 1987-88, v.p. 1988-89), Soc. Am. Travel Writers, N.Y. Fin. Writers' Assn., Women in Communications (pres. N.Y.C. chpt. 1978-79). Office: Frequent Flyer Mag 1775 Broadway New York NY 10019

LEVETIN AVERY, ESTELLE, botany educator, researcher; b. Boston, Mar. 24, 1945; d. Myer and Pauline (Miller) Levetin; m. Allan Avery, June 1, 1974; children: Deborah Gail, Jason Aaron. BS in Edn., Boston State Coll., 1966; PhD, U. R.I., 1971. Rsch. assoc. U. R.I., Kingston, 1971-72; asst. prof. botany U. Tulsa, 1972-80, assoc. prof. botany, 1980—. Editor Internat. Aerobiology Newsletter, 1986—; contbr. articles to profl. jours. NIAID-NIH grantee, 1986-89. Mem. Bot. Soc. Am., Mycological Soc. Am., Internat. Aerobiology Assn., Brit. Mycology Soc., Pan Am. Aerobiology Assn. Office: Faculty Biol Science U Tulsa 600 S College St Tulsa OK 74104

LEVI, BARBARA GOSS, physicist, editor; b. Washington, May 5, 1943; d. Wilbur H. and Mildred C. (Wallin) Goss; m. Ilan M. Levi, Sept. 10, 1966; children: Daniel S., Sharon R. BA, Carleton Coll., 1965; MS, Stanford U., 1967, PhD, 1969. Assoc. editor Physics Today Am. Inst. Physics, N.Y.C., 1969-70, cons. editor Physics Today, 1970-89, assoc. editor Physics Today, 1987-88, sr. assoc. editor Physics Today, 1989—; mem. rsch. staff ctr. Energy & Environ. Studies Princeton U., N.J., 1981-87; mem. tech. staff Bell Labs, Holmdel, N.J., 1982-83; mem. rsch. staff Ctr. for Energy and Environ. Studies Princeton U., 1981-82, 83-87; lectr. Ga. Tech, Atlanta, 1976-80, Fairleigh Dickinson U., Madison, N.J., 1970-75; vis. prof. Rutgers U., Piscataway, N.J., 1988-89; cons. U.S. Office Tech. Assessment, Washington, 1976—. Editor: (with others) Energy Sources: Conservation and Renewables, 1985, The Future of Land-Based Strategie Missiles, 1989. Troup leader Girl Scouts Am., Stone Mountain, Ga., 1979-80; treas. LWV, Holmdel and Colts Neck, N.J., 1983—. Mem. Am. Phys. Soc. (edn. com. 1989—, chmn. forum on physics and soc. 1988-89), Fedn. Am. Scientists (gov. bd. 1985-89), Am. Assn. Physics Tchrs., AAUW (mem. nuclear energy task force 1975-77).

LEVI, SUZANNE EVANS, business forms company executive; b. Gainesville, Tex., Oct. 28, 1938; d. Gilbert Warren and Jessica Earlyne (Lowe) Evans; m. William C. Thurston; 1 child, Steven L.; m. Richard Joseph Levi, Nov. 4, 1967; 1 child, James Stanford. Student, Barnard Coll., 1956, Columbia U., 1957-60, U. Ill., Chgo., 1970. Asst. banquet dept. Waldorf Astoria, N.Y.C., 1957-60; exec. asst. Hewitt Assocs., Libertyville, Ill., 1963-70; supr. Washington Nat. Ins. Co., Evanston, Ill., 1970-81; supr. office info. systems Moore Bus. Forms and Systems div. Moore Corp. Ltd., Glenview, Ill., 1981—. Contbr. articles to profl. jours. Mem. office systems adv. bd. Triton Coll., River Grove, Ill. Mem. Assn. Info. Systems Profls., Internat. Soc. Wang Users, Women Mgmt. Unitarian. Home: 25 Fox Trail Lincolnshire IL 60069

LEVI, TAMARA, marketing executive; b. Belgrade, Yugoslavia, Feb. 7, 1947; came to U.S., 1953, naturalized, 1967; d. Jakov M. and Slava Levi. AB in English, Clark U., 1968; tchr. cert. Hunter Coll., 1971; postgrad. Columbia Tchr.'s Coll., 1973-74, Bank St. Coll., 1975-78. Cert. tchr., N.Y. Tchr. East Harlem Block, N.Y.C., 1973-78; mem. adj. faculty Bank St. Coll., N.Y.C., 1976-78; direct mkgt. svcs. mgr. Flaghouse, Inc., N.Y.C., 1980-87 , pres. Clean Lists Assocs., N.Y.C., 1987—; prin. SBI Advt. and Mktg., 1984—, N.Y.C. and S. Lee, Mass., 1986-89; assoc. Classic Printers Ltd., N.Y.C., 1987—; instr. direct mkgt. Marymount Manhattan Coll., 1985-87; instr. direct mktg., Baruch Coll., 1987—; devel. cons. Conn. Women's Edn. and Legal Fund, Hartford, Conn., 1983-86; In Touch Networks, N.Y.C., 1982-88. Adaptor script for film, staging The Only Jealousy of Emer, 1968. Bd. dirs. Berkshire Pub. Theater, Pittsfield, Mass., 1979-81; active career resources com. Clark Alumni Assn., 1980-89. Mem. Am. Women Entrepreneurs, Women's Direct Response Group, Direct Mktg. Club of N.Y., Mcpl. Arts Soc. (co-chair membership com. fellows program 1989—), B'nai B'rith. Home: 531 E 72d St New York NY 10021 Office: Classic Printers Ltd 54 W 21st St New York NY 10010

LEVIN, BETTY BERGMAN, publicist, business owner; b. Burlington, Vt., July 20, 1941; d. George John and Molly Bessie (Perelman) Bergman; m. Amos Levin, Sept. 19, 1969. BS in Edn., U. Vt., 1963. Cert. tchr., Vt., Mass. Prodn. asst., researcher, assoc. producer, producer Sta. WHDH-TV, Boston, 1963-72; freelance writer, publicist, 1972-73; writer-producer Sta. WCVB-TV, Needham, Mass., 1973-78; mgr. pub. relations and promotion Crimson Travel Svc., Cambridge, Mass., 1978-85; mgr. pub. rels. and promotion Crimson Travel Svc., Boston, 1978-85; pres. Re:Sources, Newton, Mass., 1982—; continuity dir. Sta. WCAX, Burlington, Va., 1962; assoc. producer Consumer's Quiz, Sta. WHDH-TV, 1972. Author: Good Sense, 1000 Helpful HInts, 1977, Entertaining—A Personal Record, 1977, Apple Orchard Cook Book, 1978, Victorian Secrets, 1987. Bd. trustees Nat. Multiple Sclerosis Soc., Mass. 1979-84. Recipient Emmy nomination for best pub.-svc. programming, 1979, Gabriel awards, 1979, Emmy nomination for best locally produced program, 1976, Action for Children's TV award, 1972, UPI Award for Best Documentary in New Eng., 1972. Jewish. Home and Office: Re:Sources 194 Grant Ave Newton Centre MA 02159

LEVIN, CAROL ARLENE, educator; b. Los Angeles, Apr. 4, 1945; d. Harold Allen and Sally (Salter) L. AA, Santa Monica Coll., 1965; BA, UCLA, 1967; MS, Pepperdine U., 1990. Cert. tchr., 1969, bilingual tchr., 1977. Tchr. L.A. Unified Sch. Dist., 1969—, bilingual tchr., 1977—; master tchr. UCLA, 1985—; pres., v.p. Calif. Assn. Childhood Edn., Los Angeles, 1977-81; chmn. workshop Calif. State Assn. for Childhood Edn. Internat. Conf., Universal City, 1979; invited observer Assn. for Childhood Edn. Internat. White House Conf.-Families, Los Angeles, 1980; tchr., adviser elem. news Sta. KTTV, Los Angeles, 1980-82. Editor: (with others) Our Los Angeles, 1976; tchr. adviser, bilingual editor newsletter D.A.R.E. to Read, 1989—; contbr. articles to profl. jours. Treas. Dickens Towers Homeowners Assn., Sherman Oaks, Calif., 1978-80; sec. Sherman Villas Homeowners Assn, Sherman Oaks, 1981-83; mem. Sherman Oaks Homeowners Assn., 1986—, Palm Springs (Calif.) Tennis Club Owners Assn., 1981—; mem. Los Angeles Music Ctr. Theatre Group Vols., 1987—. Recipient P.I.E. award Los Angeles Schs., 1978, 79, 80, 81. Mem. Nat. Edn. Assn., Calif. Tchrs. Assn., United Tchrs. L.A., Women Ednl. Leadership. Office: Los Angeles Unified Sch Dist Office of Instrn 450 N Grand Ave Rm A-319 Los Angeles CA 90012

LEVIN, DEBBE ANN, lawyer; b. Cin., Mar. 11, 1954; d. Abram Asher and Selma Ruth (Herlands) L. BA, Washington U., St. Louis, 1976; JD, U. Cin., 1979; LLM, NYU, 1983. Bar: Ohio 1979. Staff atty. U.S. Ct. Appeals (6th cir.), Cin., 1979-82; assoc. Schwartz, Manes & Ruby, Cin., 1983—; lectr. tax conf. U. Cin., 1984-86, adj. prof. coll. of bus., 1987-89. Editor: U. Cin. Law Rev., 1972-79. Mem. ABA, Ohio Bar Assn., Cin. Bar Assn., Women Entrepreneurs, Inc., Cin. Bus. & Profl. Women's Club, Order of Coif. Jewish. Office: Schwartz Manes & Ruby 2900 Carew Tower Cincinnati OH 45202

LEVIN, DIANA PHYLLIS KARASIK, educational administrator; b. Chgo., July 4, 1938; d. Harry Archie and Rachel (Kirshbaum) Karasik; m. Richard Levin, July 22, 1962; 1 child, Laura Rae. BA, Lake Forest Coll., 1960. Pub. rels. officer Freedomland, Inc., Bronx, N.Y., 1960; adminstrv. asst. Albert Jay Rosenthal & Co. Advt., Chgo., 1961-62; tchr. English Chgo. City Schs., 1962-63; exec., buyer, bookkeeper Couture, Ltd., Chgo., 1963-80; adminstr., v.p. Lake Shore Teaching and Learning Ctr., Chgo., 1981—. Pres., 1st v.p. Girl Scouts U.S., Chgo., nominating com. 1990—; mem. women's bd. Am. Cancer Soc., Chgo., 1987—. Mem. Nat. Ind. Pvt. Sch. Assn., Nat. Assn. Edn. Young Children (validator early childhood programs 1990—), Nat. Assn. Child Care Mgmt., East Bank Club, Latin Sch. Chgo. Alumni Assn. (sec.-treas. 1987—). Office: Lake Shore Teaching and Learning Ctr 300 W Hill St Chicago IL 60610

LEVIN, EDITH WEGNER, cost analyst; b. Gary, Ind., Jan. 10, 1939; d. Henry Edward and Mary Elizabeth (Gobrecht) Wegner; m. Mark David Levin, Apr. 13, 1963; children: David Fredrick, Eric Joel, Rebecca Ann. BS in Psychology, Purdue U., 1959; MLS, Fla. State U., 1970; BS in System Sci., U. West Fla., 1981, MBA, 1989. Libr. Leon County Sch. System, Tallahassee, 1970-78, Okaloosa County Sch. System, Crestview, Fla., 1978-80; trainee cost technology team Cost Analysis Directorate, Munitions Systems Div., Eglin AFB, Fla., 1980-81, ops. rsch. analyst, 1981-84, cost analyst, 1984-85; team leader cost estimating div. Dep. for AMRAAM, Munitions System Div., Eglin AFB, Fla., 1985-86, chief cost estimating div., 1986-87; chief counter air advanced concepts Cost Analysis Directorate, Munitions Systems Div., Eglin AFB, Fla., 1987—; student Profl. Mil. Comptroller Sch., Air Univ., Maxwell AFB, Fla., 1987. Troop leader Okaloosa County area Girl Scouts U.S., 1980-87. Mem. AAUW (publicity chair 1983-85, scholarship chair 1985-87, program v.p. 1986-89), Am. Soc. Mil. Comptrollers (edn. chair 1989—), Internat. Soc. Parametric Analysts, Panhellenic Assn. Home: 7 Poplar Ave Shalimar FL 32579 Office: MSD/ACCE Eglin AFB FL 32542

LEVIN, IRENE STAUB, librarian; b. Bklyn., Sept. 30, 1928; d. Harry and Regina (Klein) Staub; B.A., Hunter Coll., CUNY, 1949; M.L.S., L.I.U., 1969; m. Harold E. Levin, Nov. 19, 1950; children—Alan, Leslie, Kim, Paula. Reference librarian and young adults Henry Waldinger Library, Valley Stream, N.Y., 1969-87, program coordinator public relations, 1976-87; free-lance info. specialist, Boynton Beach, Fla., 1988—; cons. on Jewish books and libraries; librarian Judaica Libr. Temple Emanu El, Palm Beach., Fla., 1988—; lectr. books with Judiac themes. Trustee, Sisterhood Temple B'nai Israel of Elmont, 1969-71, 87, Temple B'nai Israel of Elmont, 1982; libr. Temple Emanuel, Palm Beach, Fla., 1988—. Recipient Library Public Relations Council award, 1973. Mem. Assn. Jewish Libraries (editor Bull., 1973-83, Newsletter, 1978—), Am. Mizrachi Women, Hadassah. Contbr. to Contemporary Literary Criticism, Vol. 13, 1979.

LEVIN, JANE SUSAN, psychologist; b. N.Y.C., Aug. 30, 1948; d. Lawrence M. and Frances M. (Minowitz) L. BA, Queens Coll., 1970; MA in Edn., Washington U., St. Louis, 1975, PhD, 1981. Lic. cons. psychologist. Clin. assoc. Washington U., St. Louis, 1975-84; post-doctoral fellow Mo. Inst. Psychiatry, St. Louis, 1982-84; clin. dir. Lesbian and Gay Community Services, Mpls., 1984-85; dir. clin. svcs. Northland Therapy Ctr., Mpls., 1985—; adj. assoc. prof. St. Mary's Coll., Mpls., 1985—; cons. Pride Inst., Eden Prairie, Minn., 1986—, The Wayside House, Mpls., 1986-87, Model Women's Treatment Program, St. Paul, 1986—; trainer Bur. Criminal Apprehension, St. Paul, 1985-86. Contbr. articles to profl. jours. V.p., bd. dirs. Crossroads Counseling Ctr., St. Louis, 1975-76; midwest organizer March on Washington for Lesbian/Gay Rights, Washington, 1979; organizer Take Back the Night, St. Louis, 1982; co-founder Community Liaison for Edn. and Research, St. Louis, 1981-84; author funding grants United Way of Hennepin County, Mpls., 1984. Mem. Am. Psychol. Assn. (task force co-chairperson), Assn. Lesbian and Gay Psychologists, Assn. for Women in Psychol. Jewish. Office: Northland Therapy Ctr 2233 University Ave W Ste 430 Saint Paul MN 55114

LEVIN, LOIS ANN, psychologist; b. Boston, Dec. 1, 1941; d. Sidney and Pearl (Koufman) L. BA, Brandeis U., Waltham, Mass., 1964; EdM, Harvard U., 1965; MA, Boston U., 1966, PhD, 1973. Lic. psychologist, Mass.; diplomate Am. Bd. Profl. Psychology. Dir. psychoedn. Boston U. Med. Ctr., Dept. Child psychiatry, 1972-73, staff psychologist, 1973-76; rsch. psychologist Boston U. Sch. Medicine, 1974-76; chief psychologist Westborough State Hosp./Cambridge-Somerville unit, 1976-80; dir. inpatient psychology The Cambridge Hosp., 1976-82, rsch. psychologist, 1977-82; cons. in psychology Newton-Wellesley Hosp., Newton Lower Falls, Mass., 1983—; asst. attending psychologist McLean Hosp., Belmont, Mass., 1984—; pvt. practice psychology Waban, Mass., 1977—. Editor: Facilitating Psychotherapy: Selected Papers of Sidney Levin, M.D., 19878. Corporator, All Newton Music Sch., 1987—. Mem. Am. Psychol. Assn., Mass. Psychol. Assn., Mass. Soc. Clin. Psychologists. Home and Office: 497 Chestnut St Waban MA 02168

LEVIN, M. PENNY, clinical psychologist, consultant; b. Phila., June 7, 1956; d. Bernard Rice and Goldie (Kauffman) Levin; m. Philip David Rosenberg, July 3, 1978; children: Sarina Claire, Brenna Michelle. BA, Northwestern U., 1977; MA, Temple U., 1983, PhD, 1987. Lic. psychologist. Counselor Jewish Employment and Vocat. Svcs., Phila., 1977-78; resettlement counselor Jewish Family Svc., Phila., 1978-80; psychology intern Friends Hosp., Phila., 1983-84; staff psychologist St. Gabriel's Hall, Audobon, Pa., 1984-85, Achievement and Guidance Ctrs. in Am., Bensalem, Pa., 1985-87; clin. dir. Phila. Inst. for Rational-Emotive Therapy, Phila., 1988-90; pvt. practice Phila., 1986—; counselor Childbirth Edn. Assn., Phila., 1987-89; psychologist Human Svcs. Ctr., Phila., 1990. Temple U. fellow, 1980-81, 82-83. Mem. Am. Psychol. Assn., Pa. Psychol. Assn. (chmn. internal communications 1989-90), Phila. Soc. Clin. Psychologists, Delaware Valley Group Psychotherapy Soc. Jewish. Home: 144 Harrison Ave Glenside PA 19038 Office: 1831 Chestnut St Ste 301 Philadelphia PA 19103

LEVIN, MARLENE, human resource executive, educator; b. Detroit, Oct. 7, 1934; d. Louis and Cele (Drapkin) Bertman; m. Jerome J. Goodman, Apr. 4, 1954 (dec. Mar. 1962); children: Bennett J., Marc R.; m. Herbert R. Levin, June 7, 1967. Student U. Miami, 1952-53; BA, Coll. of New Rochelle, 1975; MPA, NYU, 1978. Cert. human resource mgr. Asst. administr. Richmond Children Ctr., Yonkers, N.Y., 1973-74; research assoc. Westchester Country Dept. Mental Health, N.Y., 1975-80, clinic adminstr., 1980-82; founder, pres. The Phoenix Group, Armonk, N.Y., 1982-88; v.p. human resources and adminstrn. Ensign Bank, N.Y.C., 1988—; adj. prof. Iona Coll., New Rochelle, N.Y., 1978-88; cons. Social Area Research, Scarsdale, N.Y., 1983-84; lectr./trainer Volvo of Am., Inc., Rockleigh, N.J., 1983-84, Lederle Labs., Spring Valley, N.Y., 1984-88. Contbr. articles on sociol. subjects to profl. jours. Mem. Mental Health Council, Mount Kisco, N.Y., 1981-83, Council for Youth, Armonk, 1984-85; mem. legis. adv. com. N.Y. State 37th Dist., 1984. Mem. Nat. Staff Devel. Council, NOW (v.p. White Plains 1978-80). Democrat. Jewish. Avocation: stamp collecting. Home: 14 Day Rd Armonk NY 10504 Office: Ensign Bank FSB 1185 Ave of Americas New York NY 10036

LEVIN, VEDA MARA, middle school educator, writing consultant; b. Miami Beach, Fla., Aug. 10, 1949; d. Louis Levin and Lynne Helen (Jaffe) Levin Martin. BA, U. Miami, 1970; MS, Fla. Internat. U., 1984. Cert. secondary sch. tchr. Occupational specialist Model Cities Manpower Agy., Miami, Fla., 1971-72; tchr. Brownsville Jr. High Sch., Miami, 1972-76, McMillan Jr. High Sch., Miami, 1976-77; tchr. English Southwood Middle Sch., Miami, 1977—; supt. Dade County Youth Fair Creative Writing, Miami, 1987—; judge Columbia Scholastic Press Assn., 1986—. Editor, adviser mag. Illusions, 1981-90. Nat. Endowment for Humanities grantee, 1984. Mem. United Tchrs. of Dade, Columbia Scholastic Press Assn., So. Interscholastic Press Assn., Ind. Order of Foresters, Delta Kappa Gamma. Democrat. Jewish. Office: Southwood Middle Sch 16301 SW 80th Ave Miami FL 33157

LEVINE, BERYL JOYCE, state supreme court justice; b. Winnipeg, Man., Can., Nov. 9, 1935; came to U.S., 1955; d. Maurice Jacob and Bella (Gutnik) Choslovsky; m. Leonard Levine, June 7, 1955; children: Susan Brauna, Marc Joseph, Sari Ruth, William Noah, David Karl. BA, U. Man., Winnipeg, 1965; JD with distinction, U. N.D., 1974. Assoc. Vogel, Branther, Kelly, Knutson, Weir & Bye, Ltd., Fargo, N.D., 1974-85; justice N.D. Supreme Ct., Bismarck, 1985—, chmn. jud. planning com. Bd. dirs. Fargo Youth Commn., 1974-77, Hospice of Red River Valley, Fargo; chmn. Gov.'s Commn. on Children at Risk, 1985. Named Outstanding Woman in N.D. Law, U. N.D. Law Women's Caucus, 1985. Mem. Cass County Bar Assn. (pres. 1984-85), N.D. State Bar Assn., Burleigh County Bar Assn., Order of Coif. Office: ND Supreme Ct State Capitol Bismarck ND 58504*

LEVINE, DIANA MAISEL, journalist; b. N.Y.C., May 10, 1914; d. Isaac and Celia (Davis) Maisel; m. Jack E. Levine, May 28, 1933 (dec.). BA, NYU, 1931; MA, Columbia U., 1935. Pres. Hadassah Bus. and Profl., N.Y.C., 1950-52, conf. chmn., 1960-62; dist. dept. Free Sons of Israel, N.Y.C., 1978-81; dep. grand master Free Sons of Israel, Fla., 1981—; Am. affairs chmn. Hadassah Fla. Attache, West Palm Beach, 1986-89, program coord., 1989—; educator social studies, adminstr. high sch. div., N.Y.C., 1940-70. Author: Economics for the Slower Student, 1970; contbr. articles to profl. jours. Chmn. women's div. City Fusion party, N.Y.C., 1934-65. Home: 295 W Sheffield West Palm Beach FL 33417 Office: Free Sons of Israel 180 Varick St New York NY 10014

LEVINE, EILEEN BLANCHE, retired employee benefits specialist; b. Bklyn., Oct. 7, 1934; d. George Joseph and Ethel (Doctor) L. BA in Psychology, Bklyn. Coll., 1956; MA in Liberal Studies, New Sch. for Social Rsch., 1986. Cert. employee benefit specialist. Unit supr. Equitable Life, N.Y., 1961-65, sr. tech. cons., 1965-70, actuarial cons., 1970-75, acct. cons., tech. assoc., 1984-88; investigator 14th St. Bus. Improvement Dist., 1989—; adminstrv. asst. to bd. dirs. 16 W. 16th St Tenants Corp., N.Y.C., 1989-90. Corr. sec. Union Square Park Community Coalition, N.Y., 1986—. Mem. Internat. Soc. of Employee Benefit Plans. Democrat. Jewish. Home: 16 W 16th St Apt 10P New York NY 10011

LEVINE, ELIZABETH P., non-profit organization administrator; b. Tallahassee, Dec. 23, 1954; d. David Lawrence and Laura (Kaplan) L. BS in Edn. summa cum laude, U. Ga., 1975; M in City Planning, San Diego State U., 1980; MA in Organizational Psychology, Columbia U., N.Y.C., 1988. Talk show hostess Sta. WGTV (PBS Affiliate), Athens, Ga., 1974; film editor Sta. XETV, San Diego, 1976-77; mgmt. analyst N.Y.C. Dept. Investigation, N.Y.C., 1980-82; ops. analyst Columbia U., N.Y.C., 1982-83, mgr., 1983-85, dep. dir., 1986-87; dep. auditor gen. N.Y.C. Bd. Edn., Bklyn., 1987—. Bd. dirs. Calif. Feminist Fed. Credit Union, San Diego, 1976-78. N.Y.C. Dept. Personnel fellow, 1978-79, Inst. Ednl. Leadership fellow, 1988-89. Mem. Assn. Internal Mgmt. Cons. (assoc.), Acad. of Mgmt., Nat. Assn. Local Govt. Auditors, Adminstrv. Women in Edn., N.Y.C. Urban Fellows Alumni Assn. Office: NYC Bd Edn 65 Court St Rm 900 Brooklyn NY 11201

LEVINE, ELLEN GAIL, clinical psychologist; b. Castro Valley, Calif., Mar. 31, 1961; d. Julius and Clara (Kerekes) L. BA, U. of the Pacific, 1982; MA, U. Ala., Birmingham, 1986, MPH, 1988, PhD, 1990. Predoctoral intern VA Med. Ctr., Palo Alto, Calif., 1988-89; postdoctoral fellow VA Med. Ctr., Martinez, Calif., 1989-90. Contbr. articles to profl. jours. Mem. Soc. Behavioral Medicine, Am. Psychol. Assn., Assn. Internat. Coun. Psychologists, Am. Psychol. Soc., VFW Ladies Aux., Alpha Phi Omega. Office: VA Med Ctr 116B 150 Muir Rd Martinez CA 94542

LEVINE, FAITH LAUREL, educational administrator; b. Richmond Hill, N.Y., May 10, 1939; d. Henry and Pearl (Freedman) Brofman; children: Debra Sue Goldberg, Heidi Beth Levine. BA, Queens Coll., 1960; MS in Early Childhood Edn., Bklyn. Coll., 1965; postgrad., St. John's U., NYU, Pace U. Lic. elem. sch. tchr., prin., dir. early childhood edn., N.Y. Head tchr. Headstart, Bklyn., 1965; tchr. English as second lang. Hato Rey, P.R., 1966-67; tchr. early childhood N.Y.C. Bd. Edn., Bklyn., 1960-79, coord. early childhood, 1979—, coord. dist. 23 mentor tchr. internship program, 1989—; dir. nursery unit Jewish Community Ho., Bklyn., 1985-86; tchr. English ASL Sta. WIPR-TV, P.R., 1966-67. Contbr. to manuals. N.Y. State grantee, 1978; N.Y.C. Sch. Human Rels. prize, 1978. Mem. Flatlands Civic Assn. (rec. sec.), N.Y. Pub. Sch. Early Childhood Assn. (v.p. 1984—), United Fedn. Tchrs. (chpt. leader 1967-69), Nat. Assn. Adminstrv. Women Edn., Brownsville Boys Alumni Assn. (chpt. pres. 1975-79), Hadassah Club (program chmn. 1968-70), Kings Sq. Dance Club (rec. sec. 1987-88). Democrat. Jewish. Home: 2775 E 16th St Apt 2F Brooklyn NY 11235 Office: Dist Office 23 2240 Dean St DO 23 Brooklyn NY 11233

LEVINE, JANIS E., financial analyst; b. Akron, Ohio, Apr. 7, 1953; d. Paul and Sarah (Levin) L.; student U. Cin., 1971-73; B.S. in Acctg., U. Akron, 1975; M.B.A., Xavier U., 1978. Acctg. intern Price Waterhouse & Co., Cleve., 1974-75; systems acct. Mead Corp., Cin., 1975-77; internal auditor, sr. capital expenditures analyst Champion Internat. Corp., Stamford, Conn., 1977—. Vol., Headstart and ARC; adv. Jr. Achievement; mem. Young Republicans. Recipient Young Citizens Achievement award for Headstart, 1969. Mem. Women in Mgmt., Bus. and Profl. Women, Young Leadership Council, Nat. Assn. Female Execs., Stamford Forum for World Affairs, Westport-Weston Arts Council, Assn. M.B.A. Execs., Nat. Assn. Accts. (community programs dir.), AAUW, Am. Jewish Congress, B'nai B'rith Women, Beta Alpha Psi (sec.). Office: Champion Internat Corp 1 Champion Plaza Stamford CT 06921

LEVINE, MARILYN MARKOVICH, lawyer, arbitrator; b. Bklyn., Aug. 9, 1930; d. Harry P. and Fannie L. (Hymowitz) Markovich; m. Louis L. Levine. June 24, 1950; children: Steven R., Ronald J., Linda J. Morgenstern. BS summa cum laude, Columbia U., 1950; MA, Adelphi U., 1967; JD, Hofstra U., 1977. Bar: N.Y. 1978, U.S. Dist. Ct. (so. and ea. dists.) N.Y. 1978, D.C. 1979, U.S. Supreme Ct. 1982. Sole practice Valley Stream, N.Y., 1978—; contract arbitrator Bldg. Service Industry, N.Y.C., 1982—; panel arbitrator Retail Food Industry, N.Y.C., 1980—; arbitrator N.Y. Dist. Cts., Nassau County, 1981—. Panel arbitrator Suffolk County Pub. Employee Relations Bd., 1979—, Nassau County Pub. Employee Relations Bd., 1980—, Nat. Mediation Bd., 1986—, N.Y. State Pub. Employee Relations Bd., 1984—; mem. adv. council Ctr. Labor and Industrial Relations, N.Y. Inst. Tech., N.Y., 1985—; counsel Nassau Civic Club, 1978—. Mem. ABA, N.Y. State Bar Assn., D.C. Bar Assn., Nassau County Bar Assn., N.J. Bd. Mediation (panel arbitrator), Am. Arbitration Assn. (arbitrator 1979—), Fed. Mediation Bd. (arbitrator 1980—). Home and Office: 1057 Linden St Valley Stream NY 11580

LEVINE, RHEA JOY COTTLER, anatomy educator; b. N.Y.C., Nov. 26, 1939; d. Zachary Robert Cottler and Hildreth (Abramson) Cottler Rosenfeld; m. Stephen Maxwell Levine, June 16, 1960; children: Elizabeth, Michael Gordon, Zachary Thomas. AB summa cum laude, Smith Coll., 1960; MS, NYU, 1963, PhD, 1966. Lab. instr. NYU Sch. Commerce, N.Y.C., 1963-64; postdoctoral fellow, instr. histology Yale U. Sch. Medicine, New Haven, 1966-68; rsch. assoc. U. Pa. Sch. Medicine, Phila., 1968-69; asst. prof. anatomy Med. Coll. Pa., Phila., 1969-74, assoc. prof. anatomy, 1974-80, prof. anatomy, 1980—, vice chmn., 1988-89; manuscript reviewer numerous sci. journals, Washington and N.Y.C., 1975—; reviewer grant proposals NSF, Washington, 1975—, mem. NIH Study Sect., 1980-84. Contbr. sci. articles to profl. jours. Trustee Stockton State Coll., Pomona, N.J., 1983—; bd. dirs. The Hollybush Festival, Glassboro, N.J., 1987—, Smith Coll. Friends of Library, Northampton, Mass., 1968-72. NYU Sch. Medicine summer research fellow, 1960, Nat. Sci. Found. grad. fellow, 1960-65, A.H. Robins research fellow, 1966, USPHS fellow, 1966-68; grantee Women's and Program project grants, NIH, NSF, 1973—; recipient NYU Founder's Day award, 1966. Mem. Coalition Jewish Profl. Women South N.J. (steering com.), Am. Assn. Anatomists, Am. Assn. Advancement Sci., Am. Soc. Cell Biology, Biophysical Soc., Histochem. Soc., Soc. Gen. Physiology, Wilderness Med. Soc., N.Y. Acad. Sci., Phi Beta Kappa, Sigma Xi. Jewish. Clubs: Smith Coll. (Phila.), Woodcrest Country (Cherry Hill, N.J.) (house chair 1983-84). Office: Med Coll of Pa Dept Anatomy EPPI Div 3200 Henry Ave Philadelphia PA 19129

LEVINE, SANDRA JOY, retail store executive; b. Phila., Oct. 6, 1937; d. Leon M. and Leonore (Freilick) Bardfeld; m. Jerome Paul Levine, 1958; children: Laura E., Michael R., Jeffrey R. BS, Boston U., 1959; MA, Lesley Coll., 1979. Cert. remedial reading tchr., counselor, Mass. Kindergarten tchr. Kingston (N.J.) Pub. Schs., 1959-61; grad. practicum tchr. Winchester (Mass.) Schs., 1979; tchr. remedial reading Billerica (Mass.) Pub. Schs., 1979-80; tchr. social studies and English, Newton (Mass.) Pub. schs., 198l, tchr. remedial reading, 198l-82; cons. House of Zodiac, Framingham, Mass., 1982-84, mgr., 1984-87, owner, co-dir., v.p., 1987—; tchr. Newton Adult Community Schs., 1983-86, 89—, Dover Sherborn Adult Community Schs., 1990—. Tchr. Newton Adult Community Schs., 1983-86. Jewish. Office: House of Zodiac Shoppers World Framingham MA 01701

LEVINE, SANDRA MARY, marketing agency executive, lecturer, author; b. Newark, May 30, 1935; d. Samuel P. and Josephine E. (Sinisgalli) Marzano; student, Rutgers U.; divorced; children: Joseph B. Martinez, Samuel A. Martinez. Exec. v.p. Staflex Co., N.Y.C., 1968-83; prin. SML Levine Enterprises, Inc., N.Y.C., 1983-86; owner, mgr. Sinisgalli's, Ocean City, N.J., 1986-89; exec. ACWA/Joint Powers Assn., Fair Oaks, Calif., 1989—. Mem. Internat. Assn. Clothing Designers (exec. dir.), Women's Bus. Club. N.Y. (founder, pres.), Women in Apparel Related Industries (founder, pub.), N.J. Bus. Women's Assn. Office: ACWA/Joint Powers Assn 2620 El Camino Sacramento CA 95825

LEVINE, YARI, artist, jewelry designer; b. Minsk, Russia; came to U.S. 1927; d. Samuel and Lillian (Lapidus) Turboff; m. Samuel S. Levine, June 10, 1945; children—Steven Robert, Mark Eric. Cert. in Fine Arts, Pratt Inst., 1939; student Am. Artists Sch., 1941, New Sch. Social Research, 1942-43. One-woman shows at: Ward Egleston Galleries, 1964, Washington Hebrew Congregation, N.Y.C., 1959, Brandeis U., 1966, U. Wis., 1969, Union of Am. Hebrew Congregations, 1953, 66, Nassau Community Coll., 1970, Art and Design Atelier, 1980, Hebrew Tabernacle, 1981; exhibited in group shows at: Creative Gallery, John Myers Gallery, 1952, A.C.A. Gallery, 1954, 55, 56, Nat. Acad. Galleries, 1953-78, Internat. Jewish Conf. Exhibit, Los Angeles, 1955, Suffolk Mus., 1957, 300th Houston Commemorative Exhibit, 1957, Art League of L.I., 1957, Heckscher Mus., 1962, Lido Gallery, 1970, Harbor Gallery, 1974, Hudson Guild Gallery, 1980, Artists Equity of N.Y., 1980, Lever House, 1983, Jacob K. Javits Fed. Bldg., 1984, 85; works represented in permanent collections at House of Living Judaism of Union of Am. Hebrew Congregations, N.Y.C., Westchester Reform Temple, Temple Sinai of Washington, U. Wis., others. Named Artist of Jewish Yr., Union of Am. Hebrew Congregations, 1966. Fellow Internat. Inst. Arts and Letters; mem. Artists Equity of N.Y., Nat. Assn. Women Artists, Jewish Visual Artists Assn. of Nat. Council on Arts in Jewish Life, Internat. Platform Assn. Address: 63 Hamlet Rd Levittown NY 11756 Studio: 24 Fifth Ave Suite 214 New York NY 10011

LEVINE-GOFFMAN, LAURA AMY, bank executive; b. N.Y.C., May 3, 1959; d. Aaron and Florence (Chaiter) Levine; m. Steven Zachary Goffman, Sept. 24, 1989. AS, Temple U., 1980, BA magna cum laude, 1981; MBA, Georgetown U., 1983. Project mgr. Small Bus. Adminstrn., Washington, 1982-83; fin. analyst R.H. Macys Inc., Newark, 1983-85; cons. Computer Horizens Corp., Parsippany, N.J., 1985-87; asst. v.p. Citibank Global Fin., N.Y.C., 1987—. Jewish.

LEVINS, ILYSSA, public relations executive; b. New Hyde Park, N.Y., Dec. 3, 1958; d. Jack and Marlene (Newman) L. BA, NYU, 1980. Asst. account exec. Gross, Townsend, Frank, Hoffman, N.Y.C., 1982, account exec., 1983, sr. account exec., 1984, account supr., 1985, group account supr., 1986, v.p., dir. pub. rels., 1987-88, sr. v.p., dir. pub. rels., 1988—. Mem. Pub. Rels. Soc. Am., Am. Soc. for Hosp. Mktg. and Pub. Rels., Women in Communications, Pharm. Advt. Coun., Food and Drug Law Inst., Am. Med. Writer's Assn. Jewish. Office: Gross Townsend Frank Hoffman 149 Fifth Ave New York NY 10011

LEVINSON, ANNE, lawyer, municipal official; b. Topeka, Kans., Feb. 1, 1958; d. Harry and Roberta Gloria (Freiman) Levinson. BA, U. Kans., 1980; JD, Northeastern U., 1983. Bar: Wash. Exec. dir. Wash. Environmental PAC, Seattle, 1983-84; policy analyst office of mgmt. and budget City of Seattle, 1986, spl. asst. to the Mayor, 1986-88, legal counsel Mayor's Office, 1988; dir. pub. affairs O'Neill & Co., Inc., Seattle, 1988-89; dep. chief of staff, legal counsel to the Mayor City of Seattle, 1990—; bd. dirs. Privacy Fund, Seattle, 1987-89. Mem. campaign staff senatorial campaign, Seattle, 1983, presdl. campaign, Cedar Rapids, Iowa, 1984, Mayoral campaign, Seattle, 1985; advisor Mayor of Seattle, 1985—; cons. incumbent Seattle City Coun. Mems., 1985—, non-profit orgns.; mem. Dem. Nat. Com.; v.p. N.W. Women's Law Ctr.; bd. dirs. N.W. AIDS Found. Named to 100 Up and Coming in Seattle, Seattle Weekly, 1989. Mem. ACLU, Wash. State Bar Assn., Nat. League of Cities, Women's Polit. Caucus (bd. dirs. 1985-86). Office: Office of the Mayor 600 4th Ave 12th Fl Seattle WA 98104

LEVINSON, RABIAH, gallery director; b. Norfolk, Va., Dec. 24, 1952; d. George Ernest and Geraldine (Maples) Smith; m. Michael Haim Levinson, Nov. 25, 1988 (div. June 1990). Student, Tidewater Community Coll., 1974. Tchr. art Virginia Beach (Va.) Art Ctr., 1977-78; prodn. asst. Record Plant Recording Studio, N.Y.C., 1978-82, Live Oak Sound Recording Studio, Norfolk, Va., 1982-84; v.p. Musicians Referral Svc., Norfolk, Va., 1984-85; program dir., air personality Sta. WVAB AM Radio, Virginia Beach, 1985-86; air personality Sta. WNUZ FM Radio, Virginia Beach, 1986-87; promotions-mktg. dir. Virginia Beach Omni Plaza Hotel, 1987-88; dir., founder The Working Gallery, Virginia Beach, 1988—; lectr. Virginia Beach Ctr. for the Arts, Norfolk State U., other orgns. Artist (water color painting) Thirty Pieces of Silver, 1988, (mixed media paintings) Dawn's Early Light, 1989, The Calling, 1989, Poppies, 1989. Commr. Virginia Beach Adv. Commn., 1990-93; liaison com. mem. resort area adv. commn. City of Virginia Beach Spl. Events, 1990—; vol. tchr. severly and profoundly retarded Princess Ann High Sch. West Wing, 1990—. Grantee Virginia Commn. for the Arts, 1978. Mem. Virginia Beach Ctr. for the Arts, Nat. Artists Equity (Washington), Art and Co., Artists Svcs. Network, Richmond Slide Registry, Tidewater Artists Assn. (bd. dirs.), Working Gallery Artist Assn. (bd. dirs. 1989—). Home: 124 Pinewood Rd Virginia Beach VA 23451 Office: The Working Gallery 2407 Pacific Ave 202 Virginia Beach VA 23451

LEVINSON, RIKI, art director; b. Bklyn.; d. Samuel Eliezar and Anna Sarah (Blau) Friedberg; m. Morton Levinson. BA, Cooper Union Sch. Arts, N.Y., 1943. Graphic designer Riki Levinson Design Studio, N.Y.C., 1945-69; art dir. edn. div. Western Pub. Co., N.Y.C., 1970, dir. design, mfg. edn. div., 1970-72; art dir. E. P. Dutton Inc., N.Y.C., 1972-85; asst. pub., art dir. E.P. Dutton Inc., N.Y.C., 1986-87, assoc. pub., art dir., 1987—. Author: Watch the Stars Come Out, 1985, I Go With My Family to Grandma's, 1986, Dinnie Abbie Sister-r-r-!, 1987, Touch! Touch!, 1987, Our Home Is The Sea, 1988. Mem. Am. Inst. Graphic Arts, Authors Guild.

LEVINSON, ROCHELLE FOX, cleaning company executive; b. Chattanooga, May 30, 1949; d. Isaac Israel and Bertha (Klempner) Fox; m. Morton Allen Levinson, July 12, 1970 (dec. 1982); children: Jason Franklin, Lori Anne. Student Memphis State U., 1967-68, Draughon's Bus. Coll., 1968-69. Pres. Clean Team, Inc., Arlington, Tex, 1978—. Active Arlington Women's Shelter Aux., Mid-Cities Jewish Community Ctr.; mem. nat. panel consumer arbitrators Better Bus. Bur. Mem. Arlington C. of C., NAFE, Network for Exec. Women, . Clubs: Altrusa (info. chmn. 1985-87, yearbook editor 1984-86, editor 1984-86), The Arlington Girls Club (Wildflower aux.). Lodge: B'nai Brith (charter pres. Mid-Cities Couples). Avocations: dancing, traveling, photography. Office: Clean Team Inc 3630 Pioneer Pkwy Suite 116 Arlington TX 76013

LEVINSON, SUNNI ROBERTA, health education consultant; b. Bklyn., Feb. 28, 1949. R.N., St. Johns Episcopal Sch. Nursing, 1968; B.S., St. Joseph's Coll., North Windham, Maine, 1989. Asst. head nurse emergency svcs. St. John's Episcopal Hosp., Bklyn., 1968-69; psychiat. nurse Interboro Gen. Hosp., Bklyn., 1969-70; team leader medicine/surgery/orthpedics and gynecology N.Y. Med. Coll., Flower Fifth Ave Hosp., N.Y.C., 1970-72; head nurse communications N.Y.C. Health and Hosp. Corp. Emergency Med. Svcs., 1972-73, supr. nurses emergency med. svcs. tng. div., Maspeth, N.Y., 1973-85, dir. edn. program emergency med. svcs. tng. div., Queens Hosp. Ctr., N.Y.C., 1980-81, exec. adminstr. Emergency Med. Svcs. Acad., Queens Hosp. Ctr., 1981-85; co-founder, exec. dir. Sungail Assocs., health edn. cons., 1986—; cons. health svcs. div. N.Y.C. Emergency Med. Svc., Maspeth, 1983-85; cons. med. systems devel. St. Joseph Children's Svcs., Bklyn., 1985-88, asst. med. dir., 1988-90; liaison from emergency med. svc. to Bur. Emergency Health Svcs., N.Y. State Dept. Health, Albany, 1981-85; childcare edn. cons. AUPAIR Homestay USA, Washington, N.Y. region, 1988—. Mem. Coffca Aids Task Force, Albany; chairperson dept. child care Cath. Archdiocese, N.Y.C., Health Coordinates Group; com. mem. Child Medicaid Rate Methodology, 1989. Mem. N.Y. State Nurses Assn., N.Y. Acad. Scis. Democrat.

LEVIT, EDITHE JUDITH, physician, medical association administrator; b. Wilkes-Barre, Pa., Nov. 29, 1926; m. Samuel M. Levit, Mar. 2, 1952; children: Harry M., David B. BS in Biology, Bucknell U., 1946; MD, Woman's Med. Coll. of Pa., 1951; DMS (hon.), Med. Coll. Pa., 1978; DSc (hon.), Wilkes U., 1990. Grad. asst. in psychology Bucknell U., 1946-47; intern Phila. Gen. Hosp., 1951-52, fellow in endocrinology, 1952-53, clin. instr., asso. in endocrinology, 1953-57, dir. med. edn., 1957-61, cons. med. edn., 1961-65; asst. dir. Nat. Bd. Med. Examiners, Phila., 1961-67; assoc. dir., sec. bd. Nat. Bd. Med. Examiners, 1967-75, v.p., sec. bd., 1975-77, pres., chief exec. officer, 1977-86, pres. emeritus, life mem. bd., 1987—; cons. in field, 1964—; mem. coun. Coll. Physicians of Phila., 1986—, adv. coun. Inst. for Nuclear Power Ops., Atlanta, 1988—; bd. dirs. Phila. Electric Co., Germantown Savs. Bank, Phila. Contbr. articles to profl. jours. Bd. dirs. Phila. Gen. Hosp. Found., 1964-70; bd. dirs. Phila. Council for Internat. Visitors, 1966-72; bd. sci. counselors Nat. Library Medicine, 1981-85. Recipient award for outstanding contbns. in field of med. edn. Commonwealth Com. of Woman's Med. Coll., 1970; Alumni award Bucknell U., 1978; Disting. Dau. of Pa. award, 1981; Spl. Recognition award Assn. Am. Med. Colls., 1986; Disting. Service award Fedn. State Med. Bds., 1987; Master A.C.P. Fellow Coll. Physicians of Phila.; mem. Inst. Medicine of Nat. Acad. Scis., AMA, Pa., Phila. County med. socs., Assn. Am. Med. Colls., Phi Beta Kappa, Alpha Omega Alpha, Phi Sigma. Home and Office: 1910 Spruce St Philadelphia PA 19103

LEVITAS, MIRIAM C. STRICKMAN, realtor associate; b. Phila., Aug. 3, 1936; d. Morris and Bella (Barsky) Cherrin; m. Bernard Strickman, June 3, 1956 (dec. 1975); children—Andrew, Brian, Craig, Deron; m. Theodore Clinton Levitas, Apr. 25, 1976; children—Steven, Leslie, Anthony. Student Temple U., 1953-56, LaSalle U., Chgo., 1968. Cert. in Gerontology Ga. State U., 1987, coord. intergenerational network. V.p. programming interior design Nat. Home Fashions League, Atlanta, 1974-75; Ga. Bd. Realtors, 1971; adminstr. Stanley H. Kaplan Ednl. Ctr., Atlanta, 1974-84; owner, pres. Levitas Services, Inc. (Internat. Destinations), Atlanta, 1984—; owner, v.p. Nat. Travel Services and Internat. Destinations, Atlanta, 1984-85; realtor Philip White Properties, Inc./Sotheby's Internat. Realty, 1985—. Exec. producer, host local TV programs, Atlanta; solo pianist Paul Whiteman TV, Phila. Youth Orch., Frankford Symphony Orch., 1950. Pres. Ahavath Achim Sisterhood, Atlanta, 1977-79; bd. dirs. Jewish Family Svcs.; chmn. Tea at the Ritz Scottish Rite Children's Med. Ctr., women's div. Israel Bond, Atlanta, 1987, 88, 89; mem. Young Women of the Arts Atlanta, Atlanta Symphony, High Mus. Art, Nat. Mus. of Women in Arts (charter), Alliance Theater Atlanta. Phila. Bd. Edn. scholar, 1952. Mem. Nat. Assn. Health Professions, Atlanta Bd. Realtors, Nat. Osteoporosis Found., Internat. Furnishings and Design Assn., Nat. Com. for Prevention of Child Abuse, Brandeis Nat. Women (life), Hadassah (life), Nat. Council Jewish Women (life), B'nai Brith (life). Democrat.

LEVITAS, TAMARA B., training coordinator; b. Balt., May 31, 1948; d. Frederick Bernard and Bertha (Scheinin) Rudo; m. Alan Harvey Levitas, June 30, 1970; 1 child, Michelle Bobbie. BA, U. Md., 1970; MA, Loyola Coll., 1974; postgrad., U. Md., 1981. Edn. specialist U.S. Dept. Army, Aberdeen, Md., 1986-89; tng. coord. Nat. Naval Med. Ctr., Bethesda, Md., 1989-90; prof. Catonsville (Md.) Community Coll., Towson (Md.) State U.; edn. specialist USCG, Washington, 1990—. Exec. bd. Franklin Sr. High PTA, 1989—; bd. dirs. U.S. Against Muscular Dystrophy, 1989—, Reistertown-Owings Mills-Glyndon Assn., 1989—. Mem. NEA, NAFE, Assn. for Supervision and Curriculum Devel., Speech and Communication Assn., Soc. for Tng. and Devel., Toastmasters Internat.

LEVITON, ADINA PLATT, rehabilitation consultant; b. N.Y.C., July 9, 1962; d. George L. and Naomi D. Platt. BA, SUNY, Albany, 1983; MA, George Washington U., 1985; postgrad., U. Md. Cert. rehab. counselor, cert. profl. counselor, Md. Crisis hotline counselor SUNY, Albany; rehab. counselor Va. DRS, Alexandria, U. D.C.; pvt. practice Alexandria, Va. Mem. Am. Assn. Counseling and Devel., Am. Rehab. Counseling Assn., Nat. Rehab. Assn., Nat. Rehab. Counseling Assn., Chi Sigma Iota. Home: 523 Coral Reef Dr Gaithersburg MD 20878

LEVITT, MIRIAM, pediatrician; b. Lampertheim, Germany, June 10, 1946; came to U.S., 1948; d. Eli and Esther (Kingston) L.; m. Harvey Flisser, June 25, 1967; children: Adam, Elizabeth, Eric. AB, NYU, 1967; MD, Albert Einstein Coll. Medicine, Yeshiva U., 1971. Diplomate Am. Bd. Pediatrics. Intern Montefiore Hosp., Bronx, N.Y., 1970-71, resident in pediatrics, 1971-73, attending pediatrician, 1975—; dir. outpatient svcs. pediatrics Bronx-Lebanon Hosp., N.Y.C., 1973-77, med. dir. women, infants and children nutrition program, 1974—; instr. pediatrics Albert Einstein Coll. Medicine, N.Y.C., 1973-76, asst. prof. clin., 1976—; med. staff Lawrence Hosp., Bronxville, N.Y., 1978—, dir. pediatrics, 1988—; instr. pediatrics Albert Einstein Coll. Medicine, N.Y.C., 1973-76, asst. prof., 1976—; sch. physician Bronxville Bd. Edn., 1983; Human Sexuality Adv. Com., Scarsdale (N.Y.) Union Free Sch. Dist., 1985, Health Edn. Adv. Coun., 1988. Fellow Am. Acad. Pediatrics; mem. Westchester County Med. Soc. Office: 1 Pondfield Rd Bronxville NY 10708

LEVITT, NANCY GAIL, marketing executive; b. Detroit, Dec. 19, 1954; d. Monte Abraham and Brenda (Burton) L. BA, U. Mich., 1976, MPH, 1979. Researcher Inst. Social Rsch., Ann Arbor, 1978; rsch. specialist S.W. Detroit Community Mental Health Ctr., 1978-79; sr. health research analyst Market Opinion Rsch., Detroit, 1980-83; v.p. Iowa Meth. Health System, Des Moines, 1983—; adj. instr. Coll. St. Francis, Joliet, Ill., 1988. Vol. Iowa Jewish Home, Des Moines, 1987—; bd. dirs. Am. Diabetes Assn., Des Moines, 1989, Jewish Family Svcs., Des Moines, 1989; mem. Leadership Inst. Greater Des Moines, 1988-89. Donald W. Cordes fellow Iowa Meth. Health System, Des Moines, 1983. Mem. Am. Hosp. Assn., Am. Mktg. Assn. (bd. dirs., v.p., sec. 1983—), Iowa Assn.-SPME (bd. dirs. 1983-89), Am. Mktg. Assn., Am. Coll. Healthcare Mktg. Jewish. Home: 4105 Woodland Plaza Apt 11 West Des Moines IA 50265 Office: Iowa Meth Health System 1200 Pleasant St Des Moines IA 50309

LEVREAULT, ROSEMARY BOWERS, school counselor; b. Beaucoup, Ill., Aug. 21, 1927; d. Raymond Ellsworth and Mary Bertha (Schwind) Bowers; m. Lionel Paul Levreault,June 22, 1957. BS, So. Ill. U., 1949; MA, Ohio U. Resident counselor U. Ill., Urbana, 1953-57; social worker Charles V. Chapin Hosp., Providence, 1957-61; sch. counselor Cumberland Valley Sch. Dist., Mechanicsburg, Pa., 1962-65, West Shore Sch. Dist., Lemoyne, Pa., 1965—. Mem. DAR (regent Cumberland County chpt. 1989—).

LEVY, CORNELIA Y., English and writing educator; b. Matamoros, Mexico, Oct. 19, 1939; came to U.S., 1957; d. Ramon Ernesto and Marise Genevieve (Tetreau) Gonzalez; m. Leon B. Levy, Feb. 17, 1968; children: Elizabeth, Joseph. BA, Tex. Woman's U., 1961; MA, Tex. A&I U., 1966; supr. cert., Corpus Christi State U., 1982. Speech and drama tchr. Christen Jr. High Sch., Laredo, Tex., 1963-66; English tchr. Miller High Sch., Corpus Christi, Tex., 1966-68; English and drama tchr. Calallen High Sch., Corpus Christi, 1979-80; honors English tchr. Incarnate Word High Sch., Corpus Christi, 1980-84; lang. arts tchr. Shannon Jr. High Sch., Corpus Christi, 1984-85; honors English and creative writing tchr. Carroll High Sch., Corpus Christi, 1985—; adj. prof. English Del Mar Coll., Corpus Christi, 1987—; in-svc. presenter Corpus Christi Ind. Sch. Dist., 1987, curriculum writer, 1983, acad. decathlon sponsor, 1989-90, UIL ready writing coach, 1986—. Playwright: Bicentennial Celebration, 1976, Rainbow Theatre Festival, 1990. Block chmn. Lloyd Bentsen for V.P. Campaign, Tex., 1989, Am. Heart Assn., Corpus Christi, 1986-88; dir. Community Theatre, Corpus Christi, 1979-90; active Temple Beth El Sisterhood. Recipient Bicentennial award Bicentennial Commn., Tex., 1976, All-Tex. Star Rating Tex. High Sch. Press Assn., 1986. Mem. Nat. Coun. Tchrs. English (award of excellence 1986-89), Tex. Joint Coun. Tchrs. English, Corpus Christi Classroom Tchrs. Assn., Hadassah. Democrat. Home: 6130 Coralridge Dr Corpus Christi TX 78413

LEVY, ELAINE GRACE, quality assurance professional; b. Newark, July 27, 1957; d. Robert John and Barbara Rose (Davis) Celentano; m. Ethan Levy, Oct. 9, 1983. BS, Rutgers U., 1979. Assoc. scientist Carter-Wallace, Cranbury, N.J., 1979-81; data analyst, clin. monitor Warner-Lambert Co., Morris Plains, N.J., 1981-85; quality assurance adminstr. R&D dept. Berlex Labs. Inc., Wayne, N.J., 1985—; co-dir. Micra Biotechs. Inc., N.J., 1989—. Mem. Drug Info. Assn., N.Y. Acad. Sci. Office: Berlex Labs Inc 300 Fairfield Rd Wayne NJ 07470

LEVY, ELINOR MILLER, immunologist, researcher; b. N.Y.C., Mar. 18, 1942; d. Louis and Tillie (Shepeton) Miller; m. Charles Joseph Levy, July 11, 1962; children: Benjamin, Rebecca. BA, Brandeis U., 1963; PhD, Emory U., 1972. Postdoctoral fellow U. B.C., Vancouver, Can., 1973-75; rsch. assoc. Sch. of Medicine Boston U., 1975-79, asst. prof. microbiology, 1979-84, assoc. prof. microbiology, 1984—. Mem. Am. Assn. Immunologists, ADAMHA/NIAA (study sect. Washington chpt. 1990—). Office: Boston U Sch of Medicine 80 E Concord St Boston MA 02118

LEVY, JANET CAPLAN, technical search firm executive; b. Scranton, Pa., Dec. 30, 1936; d. Sidney Max Caplan and Henrietta Toby (Morrison) Frankel; m. Saul Y. Levy, June 16, 1957; children: Linda Levy Raydo, Jonah. BA, Hunter Coll., 1958; MA, Rutgers U., 1968. Asst. to dir. South Brunswick Twp. Migrant Program, Kendall Park, N.J., 1969-70; freelance writer, editor Paris, 1970-71; writer, editor Transaction, Inc., New Brunswick, N.J., 1971-73; freelance writer N.Y., N.J., 1973-74; staff writer Rutgers U., New Brunswick, 1974-75; mgr. mktg. communications Mathematica Inc., Princeton, N.J., 1975-82; mktg. dir. Data Decisions, Cherry Hill, N.J., 1982-85; pres. TechniConnection Inc., Phila., 1985—. Contbr. articles to profl. jours. mem. Nat. Assn. Women Bus. Owners, Independent Computer Consultants Assn., Assn. Personal Computer Profls., Data Processing Mgmt. Assn., MidAtlantic Assn. Personnel Cons., Oracle Users Group, Greater Phila. C. of C. Home: 228 Monroe St Philadelphia PA 19147 Office: TechniConnection Inc 525 S 4th St Philadelphia PA 19147

LEVY, JERRE MARIE, psychobiology educator; b. Birmingham, Ala., Apr. 7, 1938; d. Jerome Milton and Marie (Ullman) L.; m. Thomas Andrew Nagylaki, Jan. 30, 1969; children: Marie Basch, Todd Basch. BA, U. Miami, 1962, MS, 1966; PhD, Calif. Inst. Tech., 1970. Postdoctoral fellow U. Colo., Boulder, 1970-71, Oreg. State U., 1971-72; asst. to assoc. prof. U. Pa., Phila., 1972-77; assoc. prof. to prof. U. Chgo., 1977—. Cons. editor Jour. Exptl. Psychology: Human Perception and Peformance, 1972-84; assoc. editor Brain and Cognition, 1982—, Neuropsychologia, 1988—, The Journal of Neuroscience, 1990—; editorial bd. Human Neurobiology, 1985-87; contbr. articles to profl. jours. and books. Grantee Spencer Found. 1979—, NIMH, 1979—. Mem. Internat. Neuropsychol. Symposium, Soc. Exptl. Psychologists. Avocations: reading, traveling. Home: 1441 E 54th St Chicago IL 60615 Office: U Chgo Dept Psychology 5848 S University Ave Chicago IL 60637

LEVY, JOANNA SUE, voice educator; b. N.Y.C., Sept. 14, 1951; d. Leonard Saul and Geraldine (Plush) L. BS, Ithaca Coll., 1972; MFA, Hofstra U., 1974. Cert. music tchr., N.Y. Prin. solo artist N.Y.C. Opera, Washington Opera, Pitts. Opera, St. Louis Opera, 1978-85; also numerous appearances throughout U.S.; pvt. voice tchr. N.Y.C., 1984; bd. edn. officer N.Y.C., 1985-89; instr. voice SUNY, Purchase, 1986—; assoc. voice faculty Curtis Inst. Music, 1989—. Mem. Nat. Assn. Tchrs. Singing, Am. Guild Music, Sigma Alpha Iota. Jewish. Office: NYC Bd Edn 131 Livingston St Brooklyn NY 11201

LEVY, JULIA, immunology educator, researcher; b. Singapore, May 15, 1935; came to Can. 1940; d. Guillaume Albert and Dorothy Frances (Brown) Coppens; m. Howard Bernard Gerwing, Oct. 8, 1955 (div. 1962); children—Nicholas, Benjamin; m. Edwin Levy, June 13, 1969; 1 child, Jennifer. B.A. with honors, U. B.C., 1955; Ph.D., U. London, 1958. Asst. prof. U. B.C., Vancouver, 1959-65, assoc. prof., 1965-72, prof. immunology, 1972—; dir., v.p. research and devel. Quadra Logic Technologies, Vancouver, 1980—; cons. Monsanto Chems., Mo., 1978-80; mem. Prime Minister's Nat. Adv. Bd. on Sci. and Tech., 1987—. Fellow Royal Soc. Can.; mem. Am. Soc. Immunology, Can. Soc. Immunology (pres. 1983-85), Can. Fedn. Biol. Sci. (pres. 1983-84). Home: 2034 W 36th Ave, Vancouver, BC Canada V6M 1K9 Office: U BC, 300-6174 University Blvd, Vancouver, BC Canada V6T 1W5

LEVY, KATHY ANN, nurse educator; b. Lynchburg, Va., Dec. 13, 1951; m. Paul Bruce Levy, Feb. 19, 1978. Diploma in Nursing, Va. Bapt. Hosp., 1973; BSN, U. N.C., 1977; MSN, Med. Coll. of Ohio, 1987. Certified gerontol. nurse. Med./surgical staff nurse Va. Bapt. Hosp., Lynchburg, Va., 1973-74; neurosurgery staff nurse Duke U. Med. Ctr., Durham, N.C., 1974-76; RN U. Hosp. of Jacksonville, Fla., 1978-79; nurse counselor St. Vincent's Med. Ctr., Jacksonville, 1979; inservice edn. instr. Meth. Hosp., Jacksonville, 1979-80; staff devel. coord. Americare Nursing Ctr., Oregon, Ohio, 1981; nursing lab instr. Monroe County Community Coll., Monroe, Mich., 1981-88; research asst. Med. Coll. of Ohio, Toledo, 1987-89; asst. prof. Lourdes Coll., Sylvania, Ohio, 1988—; clin. nurse specialist gerontology St. Vincent's Med. Ctr., Toledo, 1990—. Mem. Ohio Nurses Assn., Toledo Nurses Assn., Am. Nurses Assn., Nat. Gerontol. Nurses Assn., AAUW (pres. 1988-89), Nurse Specialists in Gerontology , Sigma Theta Tau. Office: Lourdes Coll 6832 Convent Blvd Sylvania OH 43560-2898

LEVY, ROCHELLE FELDMAN, artist; b. N.Y.C., Aug. 4, 1937; d. S. Harry and Eva (Krause) Feldman; m. Robert Paley Levy, June 4, 1955; children: Kathryn Tracey, Wendy Paige, Robert Paley, Angela Brooke, Michael Tyler. Student Barnard Coll., 1954-55, U. Pa., 1955-56; BFA, Moore Coll. Art, 1979. Mgmt. cons. Woodlyne Sch., Rosemont, Pa., 1983-84; sr. ptnr. DRT Interiors, Phila., 1983—; ptnr. Phila. Phillies, 1981—. One-woman shows: Watson Gallery, Wheaton Coll., Norton, Mass., 1977, U. Pa., 1977, Med. Coll. Pa., Phila., 1982, Aqueduct Race Track, Long Island, N.Y., 1982, 68, Phila. Art Alliance, 1983, Moore Coll. Art, Phila., 1984. Pres., League of Children's Hosp., Phila., 1969-70; chmn. bd. trustees Moore Coll. Art, 1988—. Recipient G. Allen Smith Prize, Woodmere Art Gallery, Chestnut Hill, Pa., 1979; Woman honoree Samuel Paley Day Care Ctr., Phila., 1990. Trustee Moore Coll. Art, 1988—; mem. selections and acquisitions com. Pa. Acad. Fine Arts, 1979—; bd. mgrs., 1975—, chmn. exec. com., 1982—. Mem. Allied Artists Am., Artist's Equity, Phila. Art Alliance, Phila. Print Club.

LEVY, (ALEXANDRA) SUSAN, construction company executive; b. Rockville Centre, N.Y., Apr. 26, 1949; d. Alexander Stanley and Anna Charlotte (Galasieski) Jankoski; m. William Mack Levy, Aug. 12, 1977. Student, Suffolk Community Coll., Brentwood, N.Y., 1976. Cert. constrn. assoc. Supr. N.Y. Telephone Co., Babylon, 1970-74; v.p. Aabbacco Equipment Leasing Corp., Lindenhurst, N.Y., 1974-81; pres., owner Femi-9 Contracting Corp., Lindenhurst, 1981—. Mem. affirmative action adv. coun. N.Y. State Dept. Transp., Albany, 1984—, human resources adv. panel Long Island Project 2000; mem. Presdl. Task Force, Washington, 1982—. With U.S. Army, 1967-69. Recipient Henri Dunant Corp. award ARC Suffolk County, 1986. Mem. Nat. Assn. Women in Constrn. (founder L.I. chpt., pres. 1983—, regional chmn. woman-owned bus. enterprise com., nat. chmn. pub. rels. and mktg. com., nat. dir. Region 1 1988—, Mem. of Yr. L.I. chpt. 1987, nat. dir., 1988—), Nassau Suffolk Contractors Assn. (sec. 1984-87, sec.-treas. 1987—, bd. dirs.), Nat. Assn. Women Bus. Owners (charter), Am. Plat form Assn. Republican. Roman Catholic. Avocations: reading, writing, golf. Home: 133 Hollins Ln East Islip NY 11730 Office: Femi-9 Contracting Corp 305 E Sunrise Hwy Lindenhurst NY 11757

LEW, KAREN LESLIE, writer; b. Washington, Feb. 19, 1942; d. Lyman Littlefield and Betsy Mae (Dekema) Woodman; m. Dan Wing Lew, Jan. 12, 1962 (div. 1970); children: Kent Charles, Danika Leslie, Mark Daren. Student, San Francisco State Coll., 1960-61, El Camino Jr. Coll., 1966, UCLA, 1967, U. Alaska, Anchorage, 1971, 75, 77, Sheldon Jackson Coll., 1979, Anchorage Community Coll., 1980, 81, 82, 83Info. specialist ITT Arctic Svcs., Inc., Anchorage, Alaska, 1969-71; adminstrv. asst., Mike Ellis Advt., Anchorage, 1971; copywriter, continuity dir. Sta. KYAK, Anchorage, 1971-72; copywriter, media buyer Graphix West, Anchorage, 1972-73; classified advt. mgr. Anchorage Daily News, 1973-74; media specialist Alaska Native Commn. on Alcoholism/Drug Abuse, 1974-75; copywriter, continuity dir. Sta. KYAK/KGOT, Anchorage, 1976-77; advt. mgr. Alaska Advocate, Anchorage, 1977-78; advt. rep., writer Alaskafest mag., Anchorage, 1979; info. officer Dept. Natural Resources, State of Alaska, Anchorage, 1979-83, Dept. Fish and Game, 1983-85; writer, editor Kripalu Ctr. for Yoga and Health, Lenox, Mass., 1987-89; freelance writer, 1969—; adj. lectr. composition Anchorage Community Coll., 1982; speaker in field ednl. and community groups. Editor newsletter Alaska State Coun. on the Arts, 1979-82; arts colunist Alaskafest mag., 1979-84. First v.p. Anchorage Coun. on Alcoholism, 1976-77; vol. arts writer; adv. bd. Independence Mine State Historic Park, 1984-85. Recipient various state and nat. awards for writing, 1969-86. Mem. Nat. Fedn. Press Women, Alaska Press Women (v.p., 1973, 85, rec. sec. 1982), Pub. Rels. Soc. Am., Fireweed Mountaineers Ltd. (pres. 1983-84), Anchorage Chess Club, U.S. Chess Fedn. Club, Theatre Guild Club, Anchorage Community Theatre Club, Audubon Soc., Anchorage Community Chorus Club. Unitarian-Universalist. Home: # 306-900 Central Ave Albany NY 12206

LEWANDOWSKA, BARBARA EWA, designer; b. Bydgoszcz, Poland, Oct. 5, 1959; came to U.S., 1986; d. Ryszard Czeslaw and Halina Wanda

(Korejwo) L. BA, Tech. Coll. Bldg. Engring., Gdansk, Poland, 1979; postgrad., Tech. U. Gdansk, 1979-80, Tech. U. Gdansk, 1984, Rhein-Westf Technische Hoch., Aachen, West Germany, 1985-86. Designer Iwashiro Assocs., N.Y.C., 1986-87, Stephanie Mallis, Inc., N.Y.C., 1987-89, I.M. Pei and Ptnrs., N.Y.C., 1989—; cons. Der Scutt Architect, N.Y.C., 1986, Giblin Currier Assocs. P.C. Architects and Engrs., N.Y.C., 1988-89. Prin. works include summer house, Wudzyn, Poland, 1985, Pershing Sq., L.A., 1986, U.S. Chancery, Dacca, Bangladesh, 1987, Bank of China, Hong Kong, 1988, Yerba Buena, San Francisco, 1989, U. Ala. Health Care Facilities, Birmingham, 1989, St. Triadas Ch., Long Island City, N.Y., 1989. Mem. Pilsudski Inst. Am., N.Y.C., 1988—, Ind. Polish News Service, N.Y.C., 1988—. Grantee Tech. U. Gdansk, 1983, 84. Mem. Mcpl. Art Soc. N.Y. Roman Catholic. Office: IM Pei & Ptnrs 600 Madison Ave New York NY 10022

LEWANDOWSKI, VICTORIA THERESA, educator; b. Pound, Wis., Nov. 7, 1935; d. Frank O. and Otillia (Malecki) L. BS, U. Wis., Oshkosh, 1961; MS, U. Wis., Milw., 1970. Cert. tchr., Wis., Ill. With gen. office Northwestern Mut. Life Ins., Milw., 1953-54; elem. tchr. Fairfield Sch., Pound, 1956-58, Bethesda Sch., Waukesha, Wis., 1958-60, Elm Brook Schs., Brookfield, Wis., 1961-65, Marcy Sch., Sussex, Wis., 1965-66, Whitefish Bay (Wis.) Schs. (Cumberland), 1966-69, Racine (Wis.) Schs., 1969-70, North Chicago (Ill.) Dist. 187 Schs., 1970—; curriculum com. North Chicago Dist. 187 Schs., 1984-85. Mem. Waukegan (Ill.) Hist. Soc., 1988—, Cath. Women's Club, Lake County, Ill., 1985—; bldg. rep. North Chicago Tchrs. Assn., 1970-71; mem. Ill. Tchrs. Assn., 1980-88. Mem. Am. Fedn. Tchrs.

LEWENT, JUDY C., pharmaceutical executive; b. 1948. BA, Goucher Coll., 1970; MBA, MIT, 1972. With corp. fin. dept. E.F. Hutton & Co., Inc., 1972-74; asst. v.p. for strategic planning Bankers Trust Co., 1974-75; sr. fin. analyst dept. corp. planning Norton Simon, 1975-76; contr. Pfizer, Inc., 1976-80; dir. acquisitions, capital analyst Merck & Co., Inc., Rahway, N.J., 1980-83, asst. contr., 1983-87, v.p., treas., 1987-90, v.p. fin., chief fin. officer, 1990—. Office: Merck & Co Inc PO Box 2000 Rahway NJ 07065*

LEWIN, ELIZABETH SAMELSON, financial planner; b. Bridgeport, Conn., Feb. 26, 1938; d. Lester and Edith Hecht Samelson; B.A., N.Y. U., 1959; A.S., Sacred Heart U., 1977; cert. fin. planner, Adelphi U., 1980; children: Valerie, Eric. With Hirsch Travel, 1974-76; founder, dir. Budget Adv. Svc., Westport, Conn., 1977; sr. v.p. Black & Nash Assocs., Wilton, Conn., Mineola, N.Y. and N.Y.C., 1984-86; fin. planning officer, Soc. for savs., Hartford, Conn., 1985-89; lectr. on money mgmt., fin. planning. Mem. Internat. Assn. Fin. Planners (v.p. 1980-83, pres. 1983-84), Women's Place, Author's Guild, Nat. Assn. Female Execs. Author: Your Personal Financial Fitness Program, 1983; Financial Fitness for Newlyweds, 1984, Financial Fitness Through Divorce, 1987, Financial Fitness For New Families, 1989. Contbr. articles to money mgmt. publs.

LEWIN, PEARL GOLDMAN, psychologist; b. Bklyn., Apr. 25, 1923; d. Frank and Anna (Simon) Goldman; m. Seymour Z. Lewin, Oct. 17, 1943; children: David, Jonathan. BA, Hunter Coll., 1943; MS, U. Mich., 1947; PhD, NYU, 1980. Lic. psychologist, N.Y. Inspector chemist quarter master corps U. S. Army, 1943-45; chemist chem. warfare U. S. Army, Edgewood Arsenal, Md., 1945; asst. psychologistBur. Psychol. Svcs. U. Mich., Ann Arbor, 1947-48; rsch. asst. chemistry U. Mich., N.Y.C., 1955-71; adj. lectr. CUNY, Bklyn., 1973-74, instr., 1974-79, asst. prof., 1979-80; psychologist Creedmore Psychiat. Ctr., N.Y.C., 1980-82; sr. psychologist Manhattan Family Ct., N.Y.C., 1982—; mentor Peer Counseling Orgn., Bklyn. Coll., 1976-80, coord. student svcs. New Sch. Liberal Arts, 1974-76, adminstr. acad. regulations, 1974-76. Author: Sexist Humor, 1979. Mem. Am. Psychol. Assn., Pi Lambda Theta, Phi Kappa Phi. Home: 110 Bleecker St New York NY 10012

LEWIN, SUSAN GRANT, creative director advertising and public relations; b. Phila., Feb. 25, 1939; d. Benj Gerald Wing and May (Lipsky) Feman; m. Chester Grant, Aug. 7, 1960 (div. 1966); m. Harold F., June 4, 1967; children: Adam, Gabrielle. BA, U. Penn., Phila. Reporter and columnist Home Furnishing Daily, 1962-65, design editor, 1965-70; sr. editor architecture House Beautiful Mag. Hearst Publs., 1970-82; creative dir. Formica Corp., N.Y.C., 1982—; pres. design Communications Internat., N.Y.C., 1988—; exhibition curator Surface & Ornament, 1983-88, Material Evidence, Smithsonian, 1984-87; bd. dirs. Archtl. League. Recipient Disting. Editorial award A.S.I.D., 1967, Nat. Endowment for Arts, 1978, Pres.' award Inst. Bus. Designers, 1983, Nominee Inst. Honor award Am. Inst. Architecture, 1985-87, Interiors Mag. award Chgo. chpt., 1986-87. Mem. AIA, Archtl. League, World Design, Am. Inst. Graphic Arts, Indsl. Designers Soc., Mcpl. Arts Soc., IFDA. Office: Formica Corp 1501 Broadway New York NY 10036

LEWIS, ANNE MCCUTCHEON, architect; b. New Orleans, Oct. 15, 1943; d. John Tinney and Susan (Dart) McCutcheon; m. Ronald Burton Lewis, Oct. 2, 1971; children: Matthew, Oliver. B.A. magna cum laude, Radcliffe Coll., 1965; M.Arch., Harvard U., 1970. Registered architect, D.C. Designer and planner Skidmore, Owings & Merrill, Washington, 1969-72, Keyes, Lethbridge & Condon, Washington, 1972-75; prin. Anne McCutcheon Lewis AIA, Washington, 1976-81; ptnr. McCartney Lewis Architects, Washington, 1981—. Mem. Harvard U. Grad. Sch. Design Alumni Coun., Cambridge, Mass., 1979-82; bd. dirs. Friends Non-Profit Housing, Washington, 1981—, Washington Humane Soc., 1990—. Mem. AIA (historic preservation awards 1979, 83, dir.-at-large Washington chpt. 1982-84, Mayor's award 1989). Mem. Soc. of Friends. Office: McCartney Lewis Architects 1503 Connecticut Ave NW Washington DC 20036

LEWIS, ANNEBEL VICTORIA, healthcare administrator; b. Tillamook, Oreg., Mar. 26, 1935; d. Jens Stenhus and Ragna Laursetta (Christensen) Brondom; m. Stanley Keith Lewis, Nov. 17, 1956; children: Stanley Keith Jr., Roxanne Michelle, Renée Marie. AA in Social Sci., Mira Costa Coll., Oceanside, Calif., 1978; BA in Anthropology magna cum laude, San Diego State U., 1981, MA in Anthropology, 1985. Ct. reporter USMC, San Diego, 1956-57; bus. mgr. Tri-City Dental Group, Vista, Calif., 1971-80; adminstr. Grossmont Dental Group, San Diego, 1980-82; asst. dept. adminstr. Kaiser Permanente Med. Ctr., L.A., 1982-83, dept. adminstr., 1983-88; asst. dir. quality of svc. Kaiser Permanente Med. Group, Pasadena, Calif., 1988—; multicultural mgmt. cons., L.A., 1980—; overseas living skills and travel cons., L.A., 1987—; guest lectr. anthropology Mira Costa Coll.; workshop presenter in field. Contbr. articles to profl. jours. Mem. spl. projects com. Bd. County Suprs., San Diego, 1979; literacy tutor; vol. worker San Diego Archaeol. Soc.; treas. Sierra Club, San Diego, 1978, mem. exe c. bd., 1978-80. Recipient svc. award Sierra Club, 1980. Mem. Am. Anthropology Assn., Soc. for Applied Anthropology, Nat. Assn. for Practicing Anthropologists, Am. Inst. Archaeology, Soc. Intercultural Edn., Tng. and Rsch., Southwestern Anthropology Assn., So. Calif. Applied Anthropology Network. Home: 1890 E Covina Blvd Covina CA 91724 Office: Kaiser Permanente Med Care Dept Clinical Services 393 E Walnut Pasadena CA 91188

LEWIS, ARLENE JANE QUIRING, music educator; b. Mt. Lake, Minn., Aug. 19, 1934; d. Emil Quiring and Mary (Schmidt) Quiring; m. James Edgar Lewis, Dec. 30, 1936; children: Brenda Janelle, Barry Jonathan, Bethamy Janine. BS, Bob Jones U., 1952-57; postgrad., S.D. State U., 1964-65, Mankato State U., 1970-72. Accredited piano tchr. Nat. Guild Musicians. Tchr. English and music Huron (S.D.) Pub. Sch., 1962-63, tchr. elem. music supr., 1963-64; tchr., music supr. Forestburg S.D. Sch., 1968-69; tchr. music edn. Pillsbury Coll., Owatonna, Minn., 1969-84; pvt. piano tchr. Nat. Piano & Omta, Enid, Okla., 1984—; music cons. and workshops Am. Christian Sch. Internat., Dallas, Tex., 1986-88. Editor Compiler: Hymns with Classical backgrounds Resource, 1982, Literacy Works found in Hymnals Resource, 1986. Mem. Chmn. Nat. Fedn. Muscians (chmn. 1971-84). Republicans. Home and Office: 1410 W Thompson Enid OK 73703

LEWIS, BARBARA, psychiatrist; b. N.Y.C., Feb. 22, 1954; d. Jack Marshall and Barbara Jane (Silverman) L. BA, U. Calif., 1985. Lic. psychiatric techician. location scout various advt. and film cos. Home: 1133 Fell St Apt 12 San Francisco CA 94117

LEWIS, BARBARA ANN, writer, public relations consultant, computer software company executive; b. Buffalo, July 8, 1945; d. Earl and Rose (Galante) Spellburg; m. Knoxie Henry Lewis, Sept. 6, 1975 (div. 1982). B.S., Daemen Coll., 1966; postgrad. SUNY, 1967-69. Exec. sec., sci. instr. Erie Community Coll., Buffalo, 1966-69; beauty and fashion dir., v.p. U.S. Universal, 1971-73; originator, pres. Magic of Venus Internat., Inc., Chgo., 1971-73; writer, producer, narrator The Beauty of It All radio show (nationwide), 1973-75; writer charm curriculum Erie Community Coll., 1968-69; author, producer charity benefit play: The City of Hope, 1972; pub. relations cons. Chgo., 1974-76, Houston, 1982—; co-owner Teddy Bear Software, Inc. Syndicated newspaper columnist The Beauty of It All, 1970-73; contbr. articles to profl. jours. Adoptive parent World Vision, Nairobi, Kenya, 1980—; campaigner Whale Protection Fund, 1978—; mem. Middlebrook Community Assn., Houston, 1978—; charter mem. Statue of Liberty-Ellis Island Commn. Recipient Outstanding Achievement in Bus. Edn. award Nat. Assn. Bus. Tchr. Edn., 1966. Mem. AAUP, Nat. Bus. Edn. Assn. (student tchr. of yr. 1966), N.Y. Assn. Jr. Coll. Tchrs., Am. Fedn. Tchrs., Faculty Senate of Erie Community Coll., Tex. Mariners Cruising Assn., Alumni Assn. Daemen Coll., Clear Lake Rowing Club. Roman Catholic. Office: 15815 Stonehaven Dr Houston TX 77059

LEWIS, BARBARA ANN, cellular communications company official; b. Bklyn., Apr. 6, 1953; d. Irving and Ethel Lewis. BA, NYU, 1974, M Profl. Studies, 1988. Prodn. mgr. Floor Covering Weekly, N.Y.C., 1975-77, asst. editor, 1977-78; advt. prodn. mgr. IEEE Spectrum mag., N.Y.C., 1978-86; ops. mgr. The Equity Group, N.Y.C., 1986-88; adminstrv. mgr. Exponents Mktg. Resource Group, San Diego, 1988-89; gen. mgr. Nutek Cellular, San Diego, 1989—. Rcipient award Nat. Mag. Pubs. Assn., 1978, 85, Ned Murphy Good Fellowship award IEEE Spectrum, 1985. Mem. Greater San Diego C. of C., World Wildlife Fedn., Japan Soc. 5:01 Club.

LEWIS, BARBARA JIMMIE, artist; b. El Paso, Tex., Mar. 14, 1932; d. Frederick Howard and Mildred (Neilson) Cushing; m. Rollin C. Lewis, Oct. 27, 1951; children—Lynn, Bradley, David. Student, U. Tex.-El Paso, 1950-70, U. Nev., 1982—. Tchr., El Paso Pub. Schs., 1954-69; condr. various art classes, workshops; Exhibited in group shows in Salt Lake City, Las Vegas, Nev., Farmington, N.Mex., Ann Original Gallery, Tucson; nat. and regional shows in Calif., Utah, Tex., Nev., N.Mex. (first prize watercolor 1982) Mem. N.Mex. Watercolor Soc., Nev. Watercolor Soc., Nat. League Am. Penwomen, Santa Cruz Valley Art Assn., So. Ariz. Watercolor Guild.

LEWIS, CLIDIE REBECCA HARVEY, construction executive; b. Pulaski County, Va., Feb. 16, 1947; d. Staples and Sarah (Stigger) Harvey; 1 child, Carla D Pretlow. AS, NRCC, 1974; BS in Mgmt., Radford (Va.) U., 1990. Pres. Lewis Constrn., Inc., New River, Va., v.p.; bookkeeper Long's Pump Svc., Radford; credit mgr. Radva Corp., Inc., Radford. Supt. Sunday sch. Mem. NAFE. Home: PO Box 43 New River VA 24129

LEWIS, CYNTHIA LYNNE, financial analyst; b. Pitts., Apr. 25, 1962; d. Lynn Lorain and Ruth (Carter) L. BA, Alma Coll., 1984; MBA, Ind. U., 1987. Cost analyst Comerica Bank, Detroit, 1983; mktg. asst. CMI Corp., Bloomfield Hills, Mich., 1984-85; fin. analyst Xerox Corp., Rochester, N.Y., 1986, Ford Motor, Detroit, 1987—; treas. Fin. Guild-Ind. U., Bloomington, 1985-86. Mem. Orientation Com. Ind. U., Bloomington, 1986, Dean's Assocs., Ind. U. Mem. Am. Youth Hostels.

LEWIS, DARLENE D., manufacturing company executive; b. Milw., May 4, 1938; d. William John and Agnes Mary (Funk) Gengler; m. Lynn Ernest Lewis, May 29, 1961; children: Tracy Lee, Kelley Jean. Cert. mgmt., Marquette U., 1982. Sales asst. Kimberly-Clark Corp., Neenah, Wis., 1956-66; sr. v.p. Cheney Co., New Berlin, Wis., 1970-87, pres., 1987—, also sec., 1980—. Mem. Assn. Sales and Mktg. Execs. (Exec. of Yr. 1986). Republican. Clubs: Westmoor Country (Brookfield, Wis.), Tumblebrook Country (Waukesha, Wis.). Office: The Cheney Co 2445 S Calhoun Rd New Berlin WI 53151

LEWIS, DIANE, entrepreneur; b. Chgo., Jan. 24, 1936; d. George W. and Kathryn (McKinnen) W.; divorced; children: William Brosius, Dwight Scott. Student, U. Ill., Chgo., 1953-57. Exec. officer, founding dir. Interviewing Technicians, Inc., Chgo., 1959-69; exec. officer, founding dir. Interviewing Dynamics, Inc., Chgo., Atlanta and Houston, 1969—, London, 1980—; cons. IDI Profl. Recruitment, Inc., Chgo., 1988—, Indyna Pub. & Pub. Rels., Inc., Chgo., 1988—, Internat. Cons., Inc., Chgo., 1978—; owner I.D. Mgmt., Chgo., 1981—; lectr., pub. speaker TV. Authors: Insider's Guide to Finding the Right Job, 1987, Equal to the Challenge, 1988. Speaker Inner Cir. Rep. Com. Job Seminars, U.S. & Can., 1984—. Trustee Adv. Bd. City Univ. Mem. Am. Mgmt. Assn., Ill. Employment Assn., Aircraft Owners & Pilots Assn., Equal to the Challenge Assn. (pres., founder 1988—).

LEWIS, DIANE PATRICIA, finance executive; b. Elizabeth, N.J., Oct. 9, 1956; d. Walter Charles and Ethel Alida (Worth) L. Assocs. of Bus., Union Coll., 1976; B of Psychology, Rutgers Coll., 1979. Br. mgr. Household Fin. Corp., Wayne, N.J., 1979-85; asst. treas., budget coord. instl. banking Chase Manhattan Bank, N.Y.C., 1985-90; FHA fund retriever, raiser Fanwood, N.J., 1990—; dir. seminars, workshops, classes Eckankar, Rahway, N.J., 1979-89; lectr. in field. Mem. Phi Theta Kappa.

LEWIS, ELLEN, psychiatrist; b. Oberlin, Ohio, Mar. 19, 1948; d. John Donald and Ewart (Kellogg) L.; m. Steven C. Lawrence, Apr. 21, 1986. AB, Oberlin Coll., 1970; MD, Ohio State U., 1975. Cert. Bd. Am. Acad. Pediatrics, 1980, Am. Acad. Psychiatry, 1984. Intern Univ. Colo. Dept. Pediatrics, resident; resident Univ. Colo. Dept. Psychiatry, Univ. Colo. Dept. Child Psychiatry; cons. psychiatrist S.W. Denver Mental Health Ctr., 1983-86; cons. psychiatrist student health svc. dept. U. Denver, 1983—; cons. psychiatrist Pediatric Group Practice, Denver Gen. Hosp., 1988—; supervising child psychiatrist U. Colo. Health Scis. Ctr., Denver, 1988—. Mem. Am. Psychiatric Assn., Am. Acad. Child Psychiatry, Alpha Omega Alpha. Office: 425 S Cherry St #700 Denver CO 80222

LEWIS, ELLEN TERRY, psychologist; b. Queens, N.Y., Mar. 12, 1959; d. Sam and Muriel (Nadel) L. BA in Psychology, SUNY, Albany, 1980; MA in Psychology, So. Ill. U., 1984, PhD in Psychology, 1988. Lic. psychologist, Md. Family health worker Carver Community Health Ctr., Schenectady, 1980-81; teaching asst. So. Ill. U., Carbondale, 1981-82, 84-85, rsch. asst., 1982-84; therapist House of Ruth, domestic violence intervention ctr., Balt., 1986-89; psychologist outpatient psychiatry dept. Sinai Hosp. Balt., 1989—; therapist Rape Crisis Intervention Svc. Carroll County, Westminster, Md., 1988-89, North Balt. Ctr., Inc., 1988-89; vol. group facilitator HERO, Balt., 1987-88. Contbr. articles to profl. jours. Vol. therapist Chase-Brexton Clinic, Balt., 1988-89. Office: Sinai Hosp Balt Belvedere and Greenspring Aves Baltimore MD 21215

LEWIS, EVELYN, management consultant; b. Goslar, Germany, Sept. 19, 1946; came to U.S. 1952, naturalized 1957; d. Gerson Emanuel and Sala (Mendlowicz) L. BA, U. Ill.-Chgo., 1968; MA, Ball State U., 1973, PhD, 1976. Rsch. analyst Comptr. State Ill., Chgo., 1977-78; lectr. polit. sci. dept. Loyola U., Chgo., 1977; asst. to commr. Dept. Human Svcs., Chgo., 1978-81; group mgr. communications Arthur Andersen & Co., Chgo., 1981-84; dir. communications and pub. rels. Heidrick and Struggles, Inc., Chgo., 1984-88; mgr. change mgmt. svcs. practice Andersen Cons., 1989—; adj. faculty sch. bus. adminstrn. Roosevelt U., 1988. Mem. Children of the Holocaust, Chgo., 1982; bd. dirs. Child Abuse Prevention Svcs. Mem. Internat. Communication Assn., Internat. Assn. Bus. Communicators, Publicity Club Chgo., Chgo. Coun. Fgn. Rels., Coun. of Communication Mgmt, NAFE, B'nai Brith. Jewish. Avocations: writing, poetry, bicycling, hiking. Office: Anderson Cons. Arthur Anderson & Co S C 69 W Washington Chicago IL 60606

LEWIS, FLORA, journalist; b. Los Angeles; d. Benjamin and Pauline (Kallin) L.; m. Sydney Gruson, Aug. 17, 1945 (div.); children—Kerry, Sheila, Lindsey. B.A., UCLA, 1941; M.S., Columbia U., 1942, LHD (hon.), 1984; LL.D., Princeton U., 1981; hon. doctorate, Mt. Holyoke Coll., Bucknell U., Muhlenberg Coll., Manhattan Marymount. Reporter Los Angeles Times, 1941, A.P., N.Y., Washington, London, 1942-46; free lance or contract for Observer, Economist, Financial Times, France-soir, Time Mag.; free lance or contract for N.Y. Times Mag., London, Warsaw, Berlin, Hague, Mexico City, Tel Aviv, 1946-54, Prague, Warsaw, 1956-58; editor McGraw-Hill, N.Y.C., 1955; bur. chief Washington Post, Bonn, London, N.Y.C., 1958-66; syndicated columnist Newsday, Paris, N.Y.C., 1967-72; bur. chief N.Y. Times, Paris, 1972-80; European diplomatic corr. N.Y. Times, 1976-80, fgn. affairs columnist, 1980—. Author: Case History of Hope, 1958, Red Pawn, 1964, One of Our H-Bombs is Missing, 1967, Europe: A Tapestry of Nations, 1987; contbr. to anthologies, books, mags. Arthur D. Morse fellow in communications and society Aspen Inst. for Humanistic Studies, 1977; decorated chevalier Legion d'Honneur; recipient awards for best interpretation fgn. affairs, 1956, best reporting fgn. affairs, 1960; Overseas Press Club award; Columbia Journalism Sch. 50th Anniversary Honor award, 1963; award for disting. diplomatic reporting George Washington U. Sch. Fgn. Service, 1978, Carr Van Anda award Ohio State U. Sch. Communications, 1982, Fourth Estate award Nat. Press Club, 1985, Matrix award for Newspapers N.Y. Women in Communications Inc., 1985, Elmer Holmes Bobst award in Arts and Letters NYU, 1987, Internat. House award, 1990; named hon. fellow UCLA Coll. Arts and Scis. Mem. Coun. on Fgn. Rels., Internat. Inst. for Strategic Studies (coun.), Inst. for East-West Security Studies, Phi Beta Kappa. Office: NY Times Foreign News Desk 229 W 43rd St New York NY 10036 also: NY Times, 3 Rue Scribe, Paris 9e France

LEWIS, FLORENCE WIRSCHING, mathematics educator; b. Hoboken, N.J., Dec. 25, 1924; d. Otto Julius and Kathe Anna (Luedecke) Wirsching; m. Richard Lowell Lewis, June 17, 1951 (dec. Oct. 1974); children: Martha, Jonathan, Ruth, Paul. BA summa cum laude, Montclair State Coll., 1944; MA, Northwestern U., 1949. Instr. math. Purdue U., West Lafayette, Ind., 1946-51, 53-55; supt. Julian (Nebr.) Pub. Schs., 1951; tchr. Fitzgerald High sch., Detroit, 1952; instr. algebra An Indsl. Corp., Benton Harbor, Mich., 1957-58; tchr. St. Joseph (Mich.) High Sch., 1962-63; instr. Lake Mich. Coll., Benton Harbor, 1963-66; pvt. tutor South Bend, Ind., 1978—; cons. South Bend Sch. Corp., 1986. Tuition scholar Montclair State Coll., 1942-44, grad. scholar Northwestern U., 1945; NSF fellow Vanderbilt U., 1966. Mem. AAUW (chmn. excellence in ed. study group), Pi Mu Epsilon. Lutheran. Home and Office: 6236 Chaucer Ct South Bend IN 46614

LEWIS, GAIL DIANNE, pharmacologist; b. Denver, Sept. 9, 1956; d. John Burdette and Caroline Hope (Drabing) L. BA cum laude, U. Tex., 1978; MA, U. TEx., 1984. Rsch. assoc. Genentech, Inc., South San Francisco, 1985—. Mem. AAAS, Soc. for Leukocyte Biology, Am. Assn. for Cancer Rsch. Republican. Methodist. Home: 710 Guildford Ave San Mateo CA 94401 Office: Genentech Inc 460 Point San Bruno Blvd South San Francisco CA 94080

LEWIS, GLADYS SHERMAN, nurse, educator; b. Wynnewood, Okla., Mar. 20, 1933; d. Andrew and Minnie Elva (Halsey) Sherman; R.N., St. Anthony's Sch. Nursing, 1953; student Okla. Bapt. U., 1953-55; A.B., Tex. Christian U., 1956; postgrad. Southwestern Bapt. Theol. Sem., 1959-60, Escuela de Idiomas, San Jose, Costa Rica, 1960-61; M.A. in Creative Writing, Central (Okla.) State U., 1985; m. Wilbur Curtis Lewis, Jan. 28, 1955; children—Karen, David, Leanne, Cristen. Mem. nursing staff various facilities, Okla., 1953-57; instr. nursing, med. missionary Bapt. mission and hosp., Paraguay, 1961-70; vice-chmn. edn. commn. Paraguay Bapt. Conv., 1962-65; sec. bd. trustees Bapt. Hosp., Paraguay, 1962-65; chmn. personnel com., handbook and policy book officer Bapt. Mission in Paraguay, 1967-70; trustee Southwestern Bapt. Theol. Sem., 1974-84, chmn. student affairs com., 1976-78, vice-chmn. bd. 1978-80; ptnr. Las Amigas Tours, 1978-80; writer, conference leader, campus lectr., 1959—. Active Democratic com., Evang. Women's Caucus, 1979-80; leader Girl Scouts U.S.A., 1965-75; Okla. co-chmn. Nat. Religious Com. for Equal Rights Amendment, 1977-79; tour host Meier Internat. Study League, 1978-81. Mem. AAUW, Internat. and Am. colls. surgeons women's auxiliaries, Okla. State, Okla. County med. auxiliaries, Am. Nurse Assn., Nat. Women's Polit. Caucus, 1979-80. Author: On Earth As It Is, 1983; Two Dreams and a Promise, 1984; also religious instructional texts in English and Spanish; editor Sooner Physician's Heartbeat, 1979-82; contbr. articles to So. Bapt. and secular periodicals. Home: 14501 N Western Ave Edmond OK 73013

LEWIS, GWEN ANN, educational administrator; b. Desoto, Mo., Mar. 3, 1941; d. Earl Edward Lewis and Ruth Virginia (Maness) Beatte. BS in Edn., Southeast Mo. State U., 1963, MA in Adminstrn., 1981. Cert. tchr., adminstr., Mo. Coach varsity volleyball Fox High Sch., Arnold, Mo., 1963-67; girls' athletic dir., dir. student activities Desoto High Sch., 1967-87; asst. prin. Desoto Jr. High Sch., 1987—; tchr. phys. edn., coach varsity volleyball, 1967-79; dir., program developer, City of Desoto Parks Program, 1972-88. Speaker, civic fund raiser, 1981. Outstanding Young Woman, Desoto Jaycees, 1975. Mem. Mo. State Tchrs. Assn., Desoto Community Tchrs. Assn. (pres. 1986-87), Ellis Island Found., Southeast Mo. Secondary Prins. Assn., Phi Delta Kappa. Democrat. Roman Catholic. Home: 1201 Rock Rd Desoto MO 63020 Office: Desoto Jr High Sch 815 Amvets Dr Desoto MO 63020

LEWIS, HELEN ELIZABETH, theatre arts educator; b. Memphis, Oct. 21, 1951; d. Mansel Bill and Esther Adine (Marsh) Rodgers; m. Jerry R. Lewis, May 26, 1979; children: Tiffany, Tara, Justin. BA, North Tex. State U., Denton, 1973. Cert. theater arts, speech and English tchr., Tex. Tchr. theatre arts Keller (Tex.) Ind. Sch. Dist.; tchr. 4th grade Jacksboro (Tex.) Ind. Sch. Dist.; tchr. theatre arts Ft. Bend Ind. Sch. Dist., Missouri City, Tex.; tchr. speech and English Hurst-Euless-Bedford (Tex.) Ind. Sch. Dist. Mem. textbook proclamation com. State of Tex. Named Tchr. of the Yr., VFW. Mem. Theatre Educators Am., Tex. Ednl. Theatre Assn., Tex. Classroom Tchrs. Assn., Internat. Thespian Soc. Home: 7104 Stonybrooke North Richland Hills TX 76180

LEWIS, HELEN NATALIE, visual arts advisor; b. St. Louis, Oct. 2, 1946; d. Robert Alameda and Sylvia Krevin; m. Roy Lee Lewis (div.); m. Marvin Burton Meyer, Aug. 1, 1982. BA, Calif. State U., L.A., 1972, MA, 1974. Asst. curator Parsons Sch. Design, Otis Art Inst., L.A., 1974-79, asst. dir., curator, 1979-82, acting dir., 1982; dir. L.A. Louver Gallery, Venice, Calif., 1983; prin. Helen N. Lewis, Beverly Hills, Calif., 1982-88; ptnr. Lucoff/Lewis, Beverly Hills, 1988—; ind. curator L.A. Mcpl. Gallery, L.A. Inst. Contemporary Art, 1977, Mt. St. Mary's Coll. Art Gallery, L.A., 1977. Jury mem. Angel City Links, L.A. City Sch. System, 1977, Bill of Rights Commemorative Com., L.A. Schs., 1977; bd. dirs. L.A. Mcpl. Art Gallery, 1988—; docent Venice Family Clinic Art Walk, 1990; founding mem. Mus. Contemporary Art, L.A. Nat. Endowment Arts Saab grantee L.A. Inst. Contemporary Arts, 1977; Fellows of Contemporary Art grantee, Otis Art Inst., 1982. Home: 704 N Beverly Dr Beverly Hills CA 90210

LEWIS, HELEN PHELPS HOYT, association executive; b. Lakewood, N.J., Dec. 27, 1902; d. John Sherman and Ethel Phelps (Stokes) Hoyt; m. Byron Stookey, May 11, 1929 (dec. Oct. 20, 1966); children: John Hoyt, Lyman Brumbaugh, Byron; m. Robert James Lewis, Aug. 5, 1971 (dec. May 17, 1988). A.B., Bryn Mawr Coll., Pa.) Coll., 1923; M.A., Union Theol. Sem. of Columbia U., 1925. Bd. mgrs. Christodora Settlement House, N.Y.C., 1927-38; 1st v.p. Christodora Settlement House, 1929-38; nat. bd. YWCA, 1927-30; mem. women's adv. council N.Y. Bot. Garden, 1952—; mem. nursing com. Columbia Presbyn. Med. Center, N.Y.C., 1944-54; trustee Columbia Presbyn. Med. Center, 1969-78, hon. trustee, 1978—; mem. women's aux. Neurol. Inst., N.Y.C., 1939—, chmn., 1949-54; mem. women's exec. com., chmn. com. hosp. auxs. United Hosp. Fund, 1951-64, vice chmn. women's campaign com., 1961-62, chmn. women's subcom. distbn., 1963-65, vice chmn. women's exec. com., 1963-64. Mem. Colonial Dames Am. (dir. 1951-56, chmn. scholarship com. 1949-51, pres.-gen. 1953-56), Daus. Cincinnati. Republican. Presbyterian. Clubs: Darien (Conn.); Garden (pres. 1935-38), Millbrook Garden (past pres.), Garden Club Am; Colony (N.Y.C.) (gov. 1954-76, sec. 1956-59, sec., v.p. 1969-71, pres. 1972-76, chmn. membership com. 1956-71). Address: 580 Park Ave New York NY 10021

LEWIS, JANET RUTH, purchasing executive; b. Weymouth, Mass., May 11, 1952; d. Edward Anthony and Margaret Emily (Knight) Daniele; m. John David Lewis, Aug. 24, 1975 (dec. Apr. 1989). BS in Human Devel., U. Mass., 1973. Cert. tchr., Mass. Asst. purchasing mgr. Hendrie's Ice Cream, Milton, Mass., 1985-87, purchasing mgr., 1987-89; purchasing mgr. ice cream div. H.P. Hood, Milton, 1989—. Mem. New Eng. Dairy Tech. Soc. (pres. 1984). Home: 122 Mountain Ave Pembroke MA 02359

LEWIS, JOAN MENDENHALL, spice company executive, researcher; b. Aberdeen, Wash., Dec. 7, 1929; d. William Swartz and Verna Bernice (Rader) Mendenhall; m. Robert John Lewis, July 28, 1950 (div. 1971); children: James Rader, Michael Steven, Tamara Jean. B.A., U. Wash., 1950; M.S., Calif. State U.-Hayward, 1970. Cert. secondary tchr. and coll. instr., Calif. Mem. guided missile team Boeing Aircraft Co., Seattle, 1950-51; importer Custom Bldg. Products, Moraga, Calif., 1961-65; program coordinator Martinez Sch. Dist., Calif., 1965-68; research dir. Contra Costa Coll., San Pablo, Calif., 1968-69; dir. Experiential Research Assocs., Emeryville, Calif., 1969-79; founder, pres. Bayseng, Orinda, Calif., 1979—; cons. Nat. Alliance Businessmen, Washington, 1969; researcher Manaman Enterprises, Seattle, 1983—. Author: Counseling for Employment, 1969. Film producer: Complete and Unabridged Job Guide for Serious Dreamers, 1972. Inventor vacuum dehydration equipment, Participant Cannes Film Festival, France, 1982-84. Organizer Neighborhood Youth Corps, San Francisco, 1965-68; mem. No. Calif. Industry Edn. Council, 1964-75, San Francisco Symphony Assn., 1976-77, Mental Health Assn. Contra Costa, 1980-81. NDEA grantee, 1965; Calif. Dept. Vocat. Edn. grantee, 1966, 67, 68, 72, 73; Calif. Dept. Rehab. grantee, 1970; Calif. Community Colls. grantee, 1973. Mem. AAUW, Moraga C. of C., Delta Zeta. Republican. Mem. Christian Ch. Avocations: home and landscape design; travel; art. Home: 9 Archer Circle Moraga CA 94556

LEWIS, JOSEPHINE VICTORIA, marketing executive; b. Chgo., Dec. 3, 1936; d. Wincenty and Helena (Francyszczak) Gurbacki; m. Laurence Warren Lewis, Jan. 8, 1955; children: Laurence Michael, Michaleen Kay, Gregory Michael. AS, Triton Coll., 1979. Sec. Marsh & McLennan, Chgo., 1953-57; with factory prodn. Motorola, Franklin Park, Ill., 1969-70; with inventory control Reflector Hardware, Melrose Park, Ill., 1970-71; distbn./inventory supr. Jewel Imports (Osco Drug, Inc.), Oakbrook, Ill., 1971-83; Midwest regional mgr. Port of Seattle, 1983—. Leader, Dupage Coun. Girl Scouts U.S.A., 1968-71; den mother Thatcher Coun. Boy Scouts Am., 1974-75; fundraiser United Way Northlake, Ill., 1972-74. Mem. Women in Internat. Trade, Internat. Trade Assn. Greater Chgo., Customs Brokers and Fgn. Freight Forwarders Assn., Ocean Freight Agts. Piggyback Assn. Chgo., Midwest Fgn. Commerce Club, Chgo. Transp. Club. Office: Port of Seattle Midwest 122 W 22nd St Ste 102 Oak Brook IL 60521

LEWIS, JOYCE MARIE KIENZLE, tax assessor; b. Utica, N.Y., Jan. 20, 1926; d. Gordon Edward and Sarah Frances (Adams) Kienzle; m. Albert James Lewis, Sept. 7, 1946; children: Timothy Mead, Lorri Jenks Lewis. Cert., Katherine Gibbs Sch., Providence, 1946; Credits, U. R.I, Rhode Island, 1954, U. R.I., Rhode Island, 1974-75. Reporter E. Bay Newspapers, Bristol, R.I., 1960-65; sec. Town Hall Assessor's Office, Barrington, R.I., 1965-74; tax assessor Town Barrington, 1974-90. Author: Brown Univ. $10,000 Exemption from Eng. 1764. Mem. R.I. Assoc. Assessing Officers (pres. 1981-82), Internat. Assoc. Assessing Officers, Soc. Profl. Appraisers, N.E. Regional Assoc. Assessing Officers, R.I. Govt. Fin. Officers Assn., Tax Officials Assn., Repub. Women's Club, Episcopal Club. Republican Episcopalian. Home: 45 Lamson Rd Barrington RI 02806 Office: Town of Barrington 283 County Rd Barrington RI 02806

LEWIS, JOYCE STAAT, lawyer; b. Chgo., Apr. 6, 1952; d. George Richard and Eleanor Lucille (Schuck) Staat; m. Charles Britton Lewis, July 21, 1950; children: Jessica Joyce, Charles Britton Jr., Elizabeth Blair. AB, Mount Holyoke Coll., 1974; JD, Boston U., 1977. Bar: Ill. 1977, U.S. Dist. Ct. (no. dist.) Ill. 1977. Assoc. Clausen, Miller, Gorman, Caffrey & Witous, P.C., Chgo., 1977-86, ptnr., 1986—. Bd. dirs. United Cerebral Palsy, Chgo., 1988—. Mem. Ill. Bar Assn., Ill. Assn. Hosp. Attys., Def. Rsch. Inst., Chgo. Bar Assn., Trial Lawyers Club Chgo. (bd. dirs. 1979—), Chgo. Soc. of Clubs. Republican. Mem. United Ch. of Christ. Home: 305 S Garfield Hinsdale IL 60521 Office: Clausen Miller Gorman et al 10 S LaSalle St Chicago IL 60603

LEWIS, JULIANNE, pharmacist, consultant; b. Orangeburg, S.C., Mar. 27, 1949; d. Henry Jefferson and Wilkie Effie (Dantzler) L. BS in Pharmacy, U. S.C., 1972, MS, 1983. Pharmacist-in-a-charge Forest Hills Nursing Ctr., Columbia, S.C., 1972-75; pharmacist Swanse (S.C.) Drug Co., 1975-76; controlled substance insp. div. investigation S.C. Dept. Social Svcs., Columbia, 1976-79; pharmacy cons. div. certification S.C. Dept. Health and Environ. Control, Columbia, 1979-81, pharmacy supr., 1986—; pharmacist Midlands ctr. S.C. Dept. Mental Retardation, Columbia, 1981-86; cons. pharmacist S.C. Dept. Youth Svcs., Columbia, 1985-86, Vanguard Residential Facility, Manning, S.C., 1986, Sandlapper Pharmacy Cons., Columbia, 1987—; instr. Clemson (S.C.) U. Coll. of Nursing, 1987-88. Mem. Riverbanks Zool. Soc., Columbia. U. S.C. Ednl. Found. fellow. Mem. Am. Pharm. Assn., Am. Pub. Health Assn., S.C. Pharm. Assn., S.C. Soc. Hosp. Pharmacists, S.C. Pub. Health Assn., U. S.C. Alumni Assn., S.C. State Employees Assn., Alpha Delta Pi. Baptist. Home: 111 Steeplechase Rd Lexington SC 29072 Office: SC Dept Health & Envrion 2600 Bull St Columbia SC 29201

LEWIS, KAREN CALLIS, accountant; b. Batesville, Ark., Aug. 13, 1951; d. Tommy Lee Callis and Alloween (Bradley) Turner; m. H. Bert Lewis, Feb. 26, 1972; children: Margaret Allison, Zachary Bert. BSE summa cum laude, U. Ark., 1979. CPA, Ark. Bus. tchr. Decatur (Ark.) High Sch., 1979-80; dir. acctg. Sparks Regional Med. Ctr., Ft. Smith, Ark., 1980—; mem. adv. com. Westark Community Coll., Ft. Smith, Ark. Pres. Sparks Good Neighbor Found., Ft. Smith, 1986—. Mem. Am.Inst. CPA's, Ark. Soc. CPA's, Healthcare Fin. Mgmt. Assn., Beta Sigma Pi (treas. 1986—), Phi Beta Lambda (Phi Xi chpt. historian 1978), Kappa Delta Pi. Republican. Methodist. Home: 5620 Free Ferry Rd Fort Smith AR 72903 Office: Sparks Regional Med Ctr 1311 South I St Fort Smith AR 72901

LEWIS, KATHRYN MONICA, nurse educator; b. Youngstown, Ohio, Sept. 20, 1936; d. Peter Paul and Mary (Slosar) Janic; m. Charles Edward Lewis, Aug. 23, 1969; children: Michelle Marie, Mark Paul. Diploma in nursing, St. Elizabeth Hosp., Youngstown, 1957; B in Nursing, Ariz. State U., 1972, MEd, 1975. RN, Ohio, Ariz., Calif.; cert. tchr., Ariz. Charge nurse polio ward St. Elizabeth Hosp., Youngstown, 1957-59, surg. staff nurse, 1959-60; office nurse Leonard Caccamo, MD, FACC, Youngstown, 1959-60; staff nurse Alta Bates Hosp., Berkley, Calif., 1960; charge nurse med.-surg. Good Samaritan Hosp., Phoenix, 1960-69, coordinator surg. nursing care, 1969-74, instr. critical care, 1974-85; ind. instr. nursing, paramedicine, cardiovascular and electrocardiography, critical care nursing Am. Heart Assn. Ariz., Samaritan Health Services, Phoenix, Tempe, Mesa, Chandler and Glendale Fire Depts. Paramedic Tng.; parttime clin. instr. Mesa Community Hosp., 1985-89; instr. com. on trauma Am. Coll. Surgeons. Contbr. articles to profl. jours; author pre-operative instructional mans.; producer numerous ednl. videotapes. Active various coms. Am. Heart Assn. Maricopa County, Ariz., 1984—; chair Emergency Med. Tech. and Fire Sci. Dept. Phoenix (Ariz.) Coll. Recipient Merit award City of Phoenix and Phoenix Fire Dept., 1984. Mem. Am. Trauma Soc., Am. Nurses Found., Am. Nurses Assn., Am. Assn. Critical Care Nurses (cert., past mem. cert. com., past pres. Phoenix chpt., past bull. chairperson, past edn. com. chairperson, recording sec.), Nat. Critical Care Inst. Edn., Ariz. State Nurses Assn. (mem. continuing edn. com.), Assn. Advancement Instrumentation, St. Elizabeth Hosp. Alumni Assn., Sigma Theta Tau, Phi Kappa Phi. Roman Catholic. Home: 5801 E Windsor Scottsdale AZ 85257 Office: Phoenix Coll 1202 W Thomas Rd Phoenix AZ 85013 also: Kacel Inc PO Box 8627 Scottsdale AZ 85252 also: Phoenix Coll 1202 W Thomas Rd Phoenix AZ 85013

LEWIS, KRISTIN ANITRA, architect; b. Dallas, Jan. 31, 1949; d. Louis Wilson Lewis and Barbara Ann (Moen) Renton; m. Charles Stanley Forsman, June 10, 1972. BS, U. Calif., Davis, 1971; MArch., U. Calif., Berkeley, 1975. Licensed architect, Colo., N.Y. Designer, drafting Dominick Assocs., Denver, 1976; project architect Everett, Zeigel, Tumpes and Hand, Boulder, Colo., 1977-79, James, Stewart, Polshek and Ptnrs., N.Y.C., 1979-81, Midyette Assocs., Boulder, 1981-82; prin. Kristin Lewis & Assocs., Boulder, 1982—; bd. dirs. Colo. Chautauqua Assocs., Boulder, Friendship City Projects, Boulder; pres. Architects and Planners of Boulder, 1983; vis. lectr. U. Colo., Boulder, 1983-86. Contbr. chpts. to books, photographs to profl. pubs. Mem. AIA, Women in Architecture, Nat. Trust Hist. Preservation, Soc. Comml. Archaeology, Architects & Planners Boulder, (pres. 1983), Chatauqua Assn. (bd. dirs. 1986), Soc. Comml. Archeology, Historic Boulder. Democrat. Office: 2033 11th St #2 Boulder CO 80302

LEWIS, LINDA ELLEN, venture capitalist; b. Norwich, Conn., Oct. 30, 1958; d. Richard Forest and Frances Amelia (Stankiewicz) L.; m. Iain Hay Bruce, Sept. 30, 1989. BS, Purdue U., 1980; MBA, U. Chgo., 1984. Med. technologist Assocs. in Internal Medicine, Chgo., 1980-82; mktg. analyst Joint Commn. on the Accreditation Health Care Facilities, Chgo., 1983; cons. Laventhol & Horwath, Phila., 1984-85; assoc. Cain Bros., Shattuck & Co., N.Y.C., 1985-88; asst. v.p. Elf Technologies, Inc., Stamford, Conn., 1988—. Mem. U. Chgo. Women's Bus. Group. Club: Chgo. Bus. Sch. (N.Y.C.). Office: Elf Techs Inc High Ridge Park PO Box 10037 Stamford CT 06904

LEWIS, L(INDA) MAUREEN, publishing company executive; b. Culver City, Calif., May 22, 1948; d. Richard Harold and Nada Maureen (Kimball) Eastwood; m. James T. Mayer, Apr. 29, 1970 (div. Mar. 1985); children: Theodore Duke, Kirk Ryan; m. John S. Lewis, July 23, 1988. BA, UCLA, 1969; elem. teaching credential, Calif. State U., Northridge, 1972; postgrad., Calif. State U., Fullerton, 1986. Instr. journalism Saddleback Community Coll., Mission Viejo, Calif., 1981-83; mgr. advt. and mktg. communications Kim Lighting, Industry, Calif., 1985-87; adminstr. mktg. dir. Approved Products, Santa Ana, Calif., 1987-88; asst. to pres., mgr. advt. and spl. projects Republic Capital Holding Corp., Burbank, Calif., 1988-89; exec. dir. The Dalton Press, Corona del Mar, Calif., 1989—; assoc. editor Preface mag., Laguna Hills, Calif., 1982, Saddleback Alive mag., Laguna Hills, 1983. Mem. AAUW (publs. editor Mission Viejo br. 1979-80, chmn. pub. info. 1980-81, 1st v.p. 1981-82, pres. 1982-83, named grante honoree 1981, communications officer publs. and pub. info. Calif. div. 1981-83).

LEWIS, LUCIE KAYE, academic program director; b. Springfield, Mass., July 28, 1951; d. John Henry and Meta Leona (Postell) Thomas; m. James Edward Lewis, June 28, 1980; children: Michael Thomas Cromwell Lewis. BS in Elem. Edn., Am. Internat. Coll., Springfield, Mass., 1973; MEd, Springfield (Mass.) Coll., 1987. Claims adjuster Allstate Ins., Farmington, Conn., 1973-77; comml. loan officer BayBank Valley, Springfield, 1977-84; econ. devel. specialist community devel. office City of Springfield, 1984-87; dir. instl. rsch. Springfield Tech. Community Coll., 1987—; asst. treas. Primus Mason Devel. Corp., Springfield, 1984-86. Recording sec. Winchester Sq. Task Force, Springfield, 1986-87; soprano Springfield Symphony Chorus, 1988—. Mem. Assn. for Instl. Rsch. Office: Springfield Tech Comm Coll 1 Armory Sq Springfield MA 01101-9000

LEWIS, MARGARET MARY, marketing professional; b. Bridgeport, Conn., Sept. 27, 1959; d. Raymond Phillip and Catherine Helen (Gayda) Palovchak; m. William A. Lewis Jr., Oct. 4, 1980. BS summa cum laude, Sacred Heart U., 1986; postgrad., U. Bridgeport; AS, Katherine Gibbs Sch., 1980. Asst. project mgr. sales promotion Mktg. Corp. of Am., Westport, Conn.; mgr. mktg. support, sales adminstr. Supermarket Communication Systems Inc., Norwalk, Conn.; program mgr. sales svc. group Newspaper Coop. Couponing, Inc., Westport. Mem. NAFE, Direct Mktg. Assn., Am. Mgmt. Assn. Democrat. Roman Catholic. Home: 26 Heather Hill Rd Huntington CT 06484 Office: 355 Riverside Ave Westport CT 06880

LEWIS, MARIAN V., state representative, real estate corporation officer; b. Bloomsburg, Pa., Jan. 2, 1929; m. Thomas F. Lewis; children: Michele Bowman, Thomas F. Jr., Nancy Heins. Grad., Palm Beach Jr. Coll. Owner real estate co., North Palm Beach, Fla., 1967—; state rep. Fla.; mem. adv. bd. Flagler Nat. Bank, West Palm Beach. Mem. adv. bd. Comprehensive Alcoholic Rehab. Program, West Palm Beach; bd. govs. Big Brother/Big Sisters, West Palm Beach; bd. dirs. Deaf Svcs., West Palm Beach; mem. adv. bd. Palm Beach Community Coll. Named Realtor of Yr., North Palm Beach, 1973, Bus. Person of Yr., West Palm Beach, 1977; recipient Women in Leadership award North Palm Beach, 1985. Mem. Bus. Execs. (pres. 1976-77), No. Palm Beach County Bd. Realtors (pres. 1975), No. C. of C. (pres. 1979). Republican. Methodist. Office: 721 US Hwy 1 Ste 111 North Palm Beach FL 33408

LEWIS, MARTHA ANNE, nurse executive; b. New Orleans, May 13, 1942; d. William West and Eulala (Estes) Miller; m. Carl E. Lewis (div.); children: Carl Jr., Timothy. Diploma, Gilfoy Sch. Nursing, Jackson, Miss., 1963; BS in Nursing, U. So. Miss., 1980, MS in Nursing Adminstrn., 1985. Staff nurse Miss. Hosp. Sch. for Cerebral Palsy, Jackson, 1963; staff nurse Lafayette County Hosp., Oxford, Miss., 1964; clinic nurse U. Miss. Student Infirmary, Oxford, 1964-65; pediatric head nurse, pediatric/nursery supr. Miss. Bapt. Hosp., Jackson, 1965-67; staff nurse-operating room psychiatry and obstetrics Miss. Bapt. Hosp., 1967; from pediatric clinic nurse to charge nurse ICU-burn unit Univ. Med. Ctr., Jackson, 1967-68; head nurse pediatric endocrine pulmonary, oncology Univ. Med. Ctr., 1969-71; asst. dir. nursing svc. Riley Meml. Hosp., Meridian, Miss., 1971-75; from dir. nursing svc. to asst. exec. dir. Riley Meml. Hosp., Meridian, 1976—; mem. adv. com. Meridian Community Coll., 1980-89, MHA-MNA-MSMA-MHCC liaison com, 1982-84, Deans and Dirs. Liaison Com., 1982-84. Bd. dirs. Meridian Symphony League, 1983-88, hon. bd., 1988-89; mem. Ednl. Coun.-Concern for Dying, Meridian, 1985, Lauderdale County Interagency Coun., Meridian, 1985-87, Meridian Indsl. Found., 1989, ARC. Mem. Am. Orgn. Nurse Execs., Mental Health Assn., Am. Nurses Assn. (In Search of Excellence award 1989), Miss. Hosp. Assn.-Orgn. Nurse Execs. (chmn. communications com. 1980-84, 88—, East Cen. coun. 1987-89, pres. 1982-83), bd. dirs. 1980-84, 88-89, chmn. recognition com. 1984), Miss. Nurses Assn. (state health affairs com. 1985-86, del. to confs., membership com., program com. v.p., bd. dirs. dist. 16, Nurse of Yr. award dist. 16, 1983, Adminstrv. Nurse of Yr. award 1987). Republican. Baptist. Home: 4918 Skyland Dr Meridian MS 39301 Office: Riley Meml Hosp 1102 Constitution Ave Meridian MS 39301

LEWIS, MARY ETTA, special education teacher; b. Ontario, Calif., Oct. 23, 1928; d. Franklin Carr and Marguerite Mae (Wood) McMakin; m. Charles Jesse Lewis, Dec. 15, 1946; children: Kenneth Arnold, Linda Marie. AA, Chaffey Coll., Alta Loma, Calif., 1963; BA, LaVerne Coll., 1965; MA, Calif. State U., L.A., 1979. Cert. elem. tchr., learning handicapped specialist. Tchr. Chino (Calif.) Unified Sch. Dist., 1965-67; tchr. Ontario-Montclair Sch. Dist., 1967-79, spl. edn. tchr., 1979-80, resource specialist, 1980-88; resource specialist, math cadre Morongo Unified Sch. Dist., Yucca Valley, Calif., 1988—. Tchr. Presby. Ch., Upland, CAlif., 1956-78, deacon 1976-79, Alta Loma, Calif., 1980-83. Recipient Delta Kappa Gamma award Teaching Colleagues, 1982-88. Mem. AAUW (sec. 1967-69), NEA, Pilot's Internat. Assn., Calif. Tchrs. Assn., Coun. for Exceptional Children, ZONTA, Calif. Assn. Resource Specialists (co-chmn. Hi-Desert chpt.), 99er's Club, Assitance League Club. Republican. Home: PO Box 2349 Yucca Valley CA 92286 Office: Mels Learning Sta 56020 Santa Fe Tr Ste Q Yucca Valley CA 92284

LEWIS, MARY FRANCES, media director; b. Ft. Lauderdale, Fla., May 12, 1956; d. Robert J. and Josephine Mary (Saladino) Durham; m. Robert Lewis, Jan. 20, 1979. BS in Mass Communications, Fla. State U., 1977. Traffic mgr., copywriter Nusskern Communications, Ft. Lauderdale, 1978-80; copywriter Advt. Internat., Hollywood, Fla., 1980-81; freelance copywriter and media specialist Ft. Lauderdale, 1981-82; media dir., copywriter, account rep. PL&P Advt., Pompano Beach, Fla., 1982—. Office: PL&P Advt 1280 SW 36th Ave Ste 101 Pompano Beach FL 33069

LEWIS, MAYMO BERYL, retired college director; b. Brookhaven, Miss., Dec. 14, 1931; d. Jimmie B. and Lillian R. (Ford) Hoskins; m. James Julius Lewis, Dec. 27, 1953; children: Natalie Blackburn, Jay Roger Lewis. BS, U. So. Miss., 1953; MEd, U. Houston, 1968, EdD, 1974. Cert. tchr., Miss., Tex. Tchr., coach Guifport (Miss.) High Sch., 1953-55; tchr., drill squad Ball High Sch., Galveston, Tex., 1955-56; tchr., coach Houston Independent Sch. Dist., 1957-67; tchr., coach, coord. continuing edn. and student svcs. San Jacinto Coll. Dist., Pasadena, Tex., 1967-84. Mem. Clean City Commn., Baytown, Tex., 1989—; bd. dirs. Welfare League, Baytown, 1990—; bd. trustees St. James House, Baytown, 1989—. Mem. AAUW (Baytown br. membership v.p. 1987-88, program v.p. 1988-89, pres. 1989-90). Republican. Episcopalian. Home: 3406 Creekbend Baytown TX 77521

LEWIS, NANCY WHYTE, English educator; b. Waukegan, Ill., July 17, 1937; d. Charles Lewis and Helen Glenn (Kottcamp) Whyte; m. Robert Gean Lewis, Aug. 18, 1962; 1 child, Cynthia Whyte. AB, Stanford U., 1959; MA, U. Wis., 1961, PhD, 1976. Tchr. Hellenic-Am. Union, Athens, Greece, 1963-65; instr., asst. prof. English, U. Wis., Whitewater, 1967-83, assoc. prof., 1983—; vis. prof. Bristol (Eng.) Poly., 1986, Lund (Sweden) U., 1988. Contbr. articles to profl. jours. Pres. Wis. Intellectual Freedom Coalition, Madison, 1980-81. Grantee U. Wis. System, Madison, 1987, Bendigo, Victoria, Australia, 1990. Mem. Nat. Coun. Tchrs. English, Wis. Coun. Tchrs. English, Lawrence Durrell Soc. (v.p. 1984-86, pres. 1986-88), James Joyce Found., ACLU, Wis. Civil Liberties Union. Democrat. Home: N 1119 Cold Spring Rd Fort Atkinson WI 53538 Office: U Wis Dept English Whitewater WI 53190

LEWIS, P. HELEN, education educator; b. Freeport, Mich., Nov. 29, 1930; d. Minard and Ruby Marion (Adams) Lewis Hammond. BA, Houghton Coll., 1951; MA, Western Mich. U., 1964; PhD, Ohio State U., 1972. Cert. tchr., Mich. Asst. dir. child evangelism Mich. Conf., Wesleyan Meth. Ch., 1951-55; tchr. Northview Pub. Schs., Grand Rapids, Mich., 1955-64; assoc. prof. edn. Houghton (N.Y.) Coll., 1964-68; EPDA fellow Ohio State U., Columbus, 1968-69, teaching assoc., 1969-71; prof. edn. Ind. U., South Bend, 1971—; instr. English, United Christian Coll., Hong Kong, 1980-82; supr. new overseas workers teaching English, OMS Internat., Hong Kong, summers 1984, 90. Author: (with S. Smilansky and J. Hagan) Clay in the Classroom, 1989. Mem. St. Joseph County Literacy Coalition, South Bend, 1985—; bd. dirs. El Campito Day Care Ctr., South Bend, 1986—; asst. chaplain Westville (Ind.) Correctional Ctr., 1990. Mem. Nat. Coun. Tchrs. English (citation for promising rsch. 1973), Internat. Reading Assn., Nat. Conf. for Rsch. in English, Nat. Assn. for Edn. Young Children, Assn. Childhood Edn. Internat., Ind. Reading Profs. Assn. (pres. 1977-78), Phi Delta Kappa (pres.-elect 1979-80), Pi Lambda Theta. Home: 1002 S 21st St South Bend IN 46615 Office: Ind U 1700 Mishawaka Ave South Bend IN 46634

LEWIS, PADDY SANDRA, clinical psychologist; b. Pretoria, South Africa, Dec. 5, 1945; d. Jack Jonas and Sylvia (Hofman) Greenwall; m. Nolan Lewis (div. Jan. 1980); 1 child, Peter Lewis. PhD, U. Chgo., 1974. Lic. psychologist, Ill. Counselor Orthogenic Sch., Chgo., 1968-69; intern Michael Reese Hosp., Chgo., 1972; chief psychologist Siegel Inst. Michael Reese Hosp., Chgo., 1974-83; attending profl. staff Michael Reese Hosp., Chgo., 1983—; pvt. practice Chgo., 1976—. Mem. Am. Psychol. Assn. Office: 111 N Wabash #822 Chicago IL 60602

LEWIS, PATRICIA FIELDS, sales executive, consultant; b. Cleve., Sept. 3, 1946; d. Irving Lincoln and Corinne Adelle (Davis) Fields; m. John D. Lewis, Oct., 1982 (div. Jan. 1985). Student, Bradley U., 1964-66; BA in Elem. Edn., Parsons Coll., 1968. Asst. fleet adminstr. Leaseway Transp., Cleve., 1968-71; office mgr., dir. PGA tournament J. Edwin Carter, Inc., Cleve., 1971-72; student program coord. Vocat. Info. Program, Cleve., 1976-77; with sales, designer Becht & Co., Cleve., 1978-81; editor Harshaw Chem. Corp. div. Gulf Oil Corp., Cleve., 1981-83; account exec. SEI Pub. Corp., Denver, 1984-87, Westinghouse Group-Sta. KOSI/KEZW, Denver, 1987-88, Sta. KOSI/KEZW, D&D Broadcasting, Denver, 1989-90; owner advt. agy. Impact Impressions, Denver, 1990—; mktg. cons. Pointe Devel. River Pointe, Denver, 1987-88, Dayton Pl., Denver, 1989—; sales cons. MJ Designs, Denver, 1989—. Youth advisor Vocat. Info. Program, Cleve., 1976-79; bd. dirs. Sr. Housing Options, 1989; active fundraising com. Big Sisters, Denver, 1988; with publicity com. Polo Cup, Denver, 1988. Mem. Denver Advt. Fedn., Sigma Delta Tau. Republican. Home and Office: Impact Impressions 1300 S Monaco Pkwy Denver CO 80224

LEWIS, PATTY JEAN, communications company executive; b. Omaha, Oct. 1, 1952; d. Harlan Gale and Mildred Olive (Noyes) L.; m. James Morgan Holden, Apr. 15, 1974 (div. 1977); m. Leonard Val Pollreis, Dec. 8, 1978. BA in Psychology, Bellevue Coll., 1984. Sales rep. Northwestern Bell Tel. Co., Omaha, 1976-78, account exec. industry cons., 1978-82, 84-85, mgr. real estate design and constrn., 1985-88; account mgr. USWest Communications, 1988—; account exec. industry cons. AT&T Info. Systems, Omaha, 1982-83. Trustee Sanitary Improvement Dist. 1, Union Nebr., 1984-86. Mem. NAFE. Democrat. Mem. Christian Ch. (Disciples of Christ). Avocations: skiing, water skiing, snowmobiling, reading. Office: USWest Communications MBC 2130 1801 California 7th Fl Denver CO 80202

LEWIS, REBECCA L., education educator; b. Darlington, S.C., June 12, 1938; d. Hazel and Carrie (Williams) L.; children: Glenda, Regina, Blondell, Terence Pamela, David, Monica. BA, William Paterson U., Wayne, 1974; Master of Urban Edn. Comm, William Paterson U., 1977. Social worker Div. of Youth & Family, Paterson, N.J., 1968-71; tchr. Paterson Bd. of Edn., 1974-83, guidance counselor, 1983—; youth program dir. Young Women Christian Assn., Paterson, N.J.; summer camp dir. Young Women Christian, Paterson, N.J., 1987-88; summer camp counselor Foster Home for Children Residential, Hackensack, 1978-79, Young Women Christian Assn., Paterson, 1987-88. Pres. A. Phillip Randolph Inst. Passaic County Chpt., 1980—; Researcher Am. Fedn. of Labor and Congress of Industrial Orgn. Passaic County, 1984. Recipient Special Recognition Paterson Edn. Found., 1988, Cert. of Appreciation Supt. of Schs., Paterson, 1987, Achievement award Nat. Council of Negro Women, N.Y., 1980-86, Community Orgn. Nat. Assn. Advancement of Colored People, 1987—. Mem. Assn. for Supervision & Curriculum, Nat. Council of Negro Women Chairperson, N.J. Passaic Edn. Assn. (chairperson), Passaic Guidance Assn. Minority Affairs, Black Educator Assn. (v.p.), Eastside Home Sch. Council (pres.). Home: 541 E 25th St Paterson NJ 07514 Office: Pub Sch #20 500 E 37th St Paterson NJ 07504

LEWIS, REGINA MARIE, lawyer; b. L.A., Nov. 3, 1954; d. David Martin and Charlotte Frances (Bride) Rudd; m. Paul Lewis, Oct. 2, 1982; children: Rachel, Phoebe. BA, San Francisco State U., 1981; LLD, New Coll. of Calif., 1983. Bar: Calif. 1984, U.S. Tax Ct. 1989. Pvt. practice San Francisco, 1984—; bd. dirs. United Cellular Minorities, Redwood City, Calif., U.S. Ind. Cellular Tele. Assn., Washington. Editor: San Francisco Eviction Defense Manual, 1980, Calif. Supreme Court Service, 1982-85. Mem. Community Adv. Coun. for Spl. Edn., San Francisco, 1989—. Mem. Calif. State Bar Assn., Lioness Club. Democrat. Roman Catholic. Home and Office: 920 Stanyan St San Francisco CA 94117

LEWIS, RITA HOFFMAN, plastic products manufacturing company executive; b. Phila., Aug. 6, 1947; d. Robert John and Helen Anna (Dugan) Hoffman; 1 child, Stephanie Blake. Student Jefferson Med. Coll. Sch. Nursing, 1965-67; Gen. mgr. Sheets & Co., Inc. (now Flower World, Inc.), Woodbury, N.J., 1968-72; dir., exec. v.p., treas. Hoffman Precision Plastics, Inc., Blackwood, N.J., 1973—; ptnr. Timber Assocs.; commr. N.J. Expressway Authority, 1990—; guest speaker various civic groups, 1974; poetry editor SPOTLIGHTER Innovative Singles Mag. Author: That Part of Me I Never Really Meant to Share, 1979; In Retrospect: Caught Between Running and Loving; columnist Innovative Singles mag., 1989—. Mem. Com. for Citizens of Glen Oaks (N.J.), 1979—, Gloucester Twp. Econ. Devel. Com., 1981—, Gloucester Twp. Day Scholarship Com., 1984—; chairperson Gloucester Twp. Day Scholarship Found., 1985—; bd. dirs. Diane Hull Dance Co. Recipient Winning Edge award, 1982, Mayor's award for Womens' Achievement, 1987, Outstanding Community Service award Mayor, Council and Com., 1987. Mem. NAFE, Sales Assn. Chem. Industry, Blackwood Businessmen's Assn., Soc. Plastic Engrs. Roman Catholic.

LEWIS, SABRINA LAVERNE, environmental engineer; b. Mar. 7, 1963; d. Frank William and Kathleen Marie (Clark) L.; m. Kevin Donell Johnson, Oct. 8, 1985. Grad., MIT, 1984; postgrad., Northeastern U., Boston. Assoc. CSI Resource System, Inc., Boston; environ. engr. Foxboro (Mass.) Co., project engr. Recipient J.R. Stewart award. Mem. NAFE. Home: 66 Dinsmore Ave Apt 609 Framingham MA 01701

LEWIS, SANDRA COMBS, research psychologist, writer; b. Troup County, Ga., Oct. 8, 1939; d. Robert Milton and Imogene (Richardson) Combs; children: Virginia Susan Lewis Salvo, Charles James III. AB, Wesleyan Coll., 1961; MEd, Mercer U., 1972; Ga. State U., 1976; PhD, U. Ga., 1980. Personnel asst. Sears Roebuck & Co., Atlanta, 1961-62; rsch. asst. U. Ga., Atlanta, 1962-63; asst. psychol. svcs. Bibb County Bd. Edn., Macon,

Ga., 1972-73; instr. Macon (Ga.) Jr. Coll., 1973, 82, Wesleyan Coll., Macon, 1973-75, 81; psychometrist Middle Ga. Psychoednl. Ctr., Macon, 1975-76; instr. Mercer U., Macon, 1980-82; presenter at profl. confs. Officer Women's Aux. to Cen. Dist. Dental Soc., Macon, 1971-73; pres. Macon Wesleyan Alumnae Club, 1973-74; bd. dirs. Family Counseling Ctr., Macon, 1975-76; ruling elder, clk. of session Northminster Presbyn. Ch., Macon, 1988-90, vice moderator, 1989-90, moderator, 1990—. Mem. Am. Psychol. Assn., Ga. Psychol. Assn. Home: 184 Buford Pl Macon GA 31204

LEWIS, SHEILA ELLIAN, banker; b. Niles, Mich., Apr. 8, 1958; d. Robert James and Virginia Jo (Kelly) L. BSBA, Washington U., St. Louis, 1980; MBA, Atlanta U., 1986. With Saks Fifth Ave., Troy, Mich., 1980-81; asst. dir. admissions Washington U., St. Louis, 1981-84; mktg. intern Ralston Purina Co., St. Louis, 1985; mktg. asst. The Quaker Oats Co., Chgo., 1986-87, asst. brand mgr., 1987-88; asst. v.p. new product devel. First Nat. Bank Chgo., 1988-89; v.p. new product devel. CoreStates Bank of Dela., Wilmington, 1989—. Chmn. subcom. Young Alumni Exec. Coun. Washington U., Chgo., 1986-88; mem. Coun. on Student Life, St. Louis, 1988—; mem. leadership inst. Urban League, Phila., 1990. Mem. NAFE, Nat. Assn. Urban Bankers, Nat. Black MBA Assn., Phila. Assn. Direct Mail, Young Alumi Exec. Coun., Alpha Mu Alpha. Baptist. Office: CoreStates Bank Dela NA FC 05-002-03-50 PO Box 8924 Wilmington DE 19879-8924

LEWIS, SYLVIA GAIL, journalist; b. N.Y.C., Apr. 8, 1945; d. Ben and Clara Lewis. BA, Cornell U., 1967; MA, U. Wash., Seattle, 1968; MS in Journalism, Northwestern U., 1974. Reporter Seattle-Post Intelligencer, 1968-69; asst. editor Cowles Book Co., N.Y.C., 1969-70; with Am. Planning Assn., Chgo., 1974—, mng. editor Planning mag., 1975-77, dir. pubs., editor, assoc. pub. Planning mag., 1977—. Contbr. articles to profl. jours. Mem. Soc. Profl. Journalists, Chgo. Headline Club (bd. mem. 1989—), Soc. Nat. Assn. Publs. (pres. Chgo. chpt. 1986-87), Northwestern U. Alumni Assn., Cornell Club of Chgo., Phi Beta Kappa. Office: Am Planning Assn 1313 E 60th St Chicago IL 60637

LEWIS, VERNITA ANN WICKLIFFE, beauty culturist, fast food restaurant executive; b. Chgo., Apr. 6, 1955; d. Kernett Henry and Clara Lillian (Wells) Robinson; m. Lloyd Maurice Wickliffe, Sr., Jan. 31, 1976 (dec. 1982); children: Calvin Earl, Nicole Latrice, Lloyd Maurice Jr.; m. Kenneth Lewis, Feb. 17, 1985. Student William Jones Comml. Bus. Sch., 1971-72; degree Pivot Point Inst., 1982-83; student Prairie State Coll., 1987-88. Lic. cosmetology tchr. Clerk Typist I & II State Dept. Pub. Aid., Chgo., 1972-74, caseworker I, 1975-77, med. caseworker II, 1978-79, med. caseworker III, 1979-83; cosmetology student instr. Lyndon Beauty Acad., Steger, Ill., 1985—; owner Kenny's for Ribs and Pizza, Chgo., 1985—, MS VE's Profl. Skin Care Salon, Park Forest, Ill.; lectr., cons. Huth Jr. High Sch., Matteson, Ill., 1985—; with child devel. pre-school program Prairie State Jr. Coll., 1988—; underwriter drug abuse program Jesse James Lloyd Wickliffe Meml. Scholarship Fund; asst. to prof. Coll. Bus. and Pub. Adminstrn., 1989-90. Recipient 2d and 3rd place trophies Unique Beauty Sch. Competition, 1982, Morris Acad., 1982; 4th and 3rd place trophies Pivot Point Beauty Sch., 1983; Creative Service award Environ. Conservation Commn., 1984; nomination for acad. achievements USAA. Bd. govs. BA degree program Govs. State U., University Park, Ill., 1989-90, student orgn. coun.-BOG, 1989-90. Mem. Nat. Assn. Female Execs., Nat. Hair Dressers and Cosmetologists Assn., Nat. Cosmetology Assn. (educator esthetics div. 1986—), Ill. Cosmetology Assn. (educator aesthetics div. 1986), Nat. Assn. Nail Artists, Sno Goffers Ski Club, Child Devel. Club (student govt. treas. 1989-90), Phi Kappa Theta. Democrat. Avocations: music, bowling, gardening.

LEWIS, VIRGINIA MARIE, psychologist; b. San Rafael, Calif., June 21, 1942; d. Lyle C. Lewis and Juanita Marie (Nelson) Smith. BA, Calif. State U., San Francisco, 1968, MA, 1971; PhD, Pacific Sch. of Psychology, Palo Alto, Calif., 1986. Lic. psychologist, ednl. psychologist, marriage, family and child counselor; cert. sch. psychologist, Calif. Counselor Haight Ashbury Med. Clinic, San Francisco, 1969-71; counselor/edn. coord. EOC Program, San Francisco, 1971-72; sch. psychologist San Francisco Unified Sch. Dist., 1972-78; clin. and rsch. assoc. Mental Rsch. Inst., Palo Alto, 1978—; pvt. practice psychologist/therapist Palo Alto, 1980—; instr. dept. edn. psychology Calif. State U., Hayward, 1985-87, Western Grad. Sch. of Psychology, Palo Alto, 1987—; cons., com. mem. doctoral dissertations, 1987—; cons. Evergreen Ctr., San Leandro, Calif., 1983-85; founding mem. Soterial Alt. Family Edn. Clin., 1978-80; external assessor, State of Calif. Commn. for Tchr. Prep and Licensing, 1979; co-prin. investigator Rsch. on the Recovery Process of Alcholoic Families, 1989—; prin. investigator, author Devel. of the Family Goal Attainment Scales, 1980—; co-author grants in field. Contbr. articles to profl. jours. Resource Cons. Friends for Youth, Redwood City, Calif., 1989—. Recipient Don D. Jackson Meml. award Mental Rsch. Inst., Palo Alto, 1980. Mem. Am. Psychol. Assn., Calif. State Psychol. Assn., Santa Clara County Psychol. Assn., Calif. Assn. Sch. Psychologists and Psychometrists, Psychologist Assn. San Francisco (exec. sec., editor 1974-77). Office: 555 Middlefield Rd Palo Alto CA 94301

LEWIS, YVONNE FAY, administrative assistant, educator; b. Corpus Christi, Tex., Aug. 2, 1946; d. Raymond R. Sr. and Willie F. (Johnson) Henderson; m. Apr. 2, 1967 (div. 1976); 1 child, Kevin I. AA in Bus. Adminstrn., Coll. of Ala., 1978; BA in Mgmt., St. Mary's Coll., Moraga, Calif., 1986. Exec. sec. Kaiser Engrs., Inc., Oakland, Calif., 1968-76; exec. sec. Laney Coll., Oakland, 1976—, adminstrv. asst., 1990—, instr. in bus., 1981—; instr. in bus. Coll. of Alameda, Calif., 1979-80; mem. retirement com. Laney Coll., 1982—; mem., chairperson Classified Staff Devel. Com., Oakland, 1982-86; speaker Oakland Youthworks, 1987-89. Mem. Oakland Mus., 1987—; bd. dirs. Oakland Citizens Com. for Urban Renewal, 1989—. Recipient Outstanding Svcs. award Coun. on Black Am. Affairs, 1983. Mem. Am. Mgmt. Assn. (assoc.), Peralta Fedn. of Tchrs., NAFE. Democrat. Baptist. Office: Laney Coll Pres' Office 900 Fallon St Oakland CA 94607

LEWIS CONGDON, REBECCA ANN, television station executive; b. Whiteville, N.C., Dec. 8, 1942; d. Benjamin Brinson and Marjory Johnson (Powell) Lewis; m. Frederick Voorhees Congdon, Dec. 31, 1978; children: Suanne, Christopher, Jon. AB in Polit. Sci., U. N.C., 1965. Traffic mgr. WGXI Radio, Atlanta, 1965-70, WAGA-TV, Atlanta, 1970-74; nat. sales coordinator WXIA-TV, Atlanta, 1974-80; traffic mgr. WGNX-TV, Atlanta, 1980—. Mem., ERA, Ga., 1978—, NOW, 1979—, Nat. Women's Polit. Caucus, 1983—, LWV, Atlanta, 1985; vol. Wayne Fowler Senate campaign, 1988, others. Recipient Golden Mike award Coll. Students in Broadcasting, U. Ga., 1978. Mem. Am. Women in Radio and TV (pres. Atlanta chpt. 1978-79, 84-85, S.E. conf. chair 1985), Nat. Acad. TV Arts and Scis. Democrat. Methodist. Avocations: reading; crossword puzzles; bridge. Office: Sta WGNX-TV 1810 Briarcliff Rd Atlanta GA 30329

LEWIS-JENSON, SANDRA M., insurance company executive; b. Nampa, Idaho, Feb. 26, 1950; d. Grover Henry and Ethlyn M. Lewis; m. Dwight R. Jenson, Sept. 3, 1989. BA, De Paul U., 1987. Mgr. comml. dept. Susman Agy., Dallas; asst. v.p. and mgr. personal accounts Marsh & McLennan, Chgo. and N.Y.C.; v.p. Rollins Burdick Hunter, Chgo.; adv. com. RBH Nat. Personal Lines; coun. mem. Firemans Fund Agy. active various civic and ch. orgns. Mem. Nat. Assn. Ins. Women, Ins. Distaffs Execs. Assn. Address: 1951 W Cornelia Chicago IL 60657

LEWIS-KOLBUS, MELINDA ANNE, risk manager, corporate safety administrator; b. Arlington, Va., Oct. 25, 1958; d. Jack Collins and Jacqueline Lucille (Allen) L.; married. Grad., Largo Sr. High, 1973-76. Policy typist Marsh & McLennan Ins. Agy., Washington, 1977-79; account rep. Frank B. Hall & Co., San Antonio, 1979-80, regional mgr., 1980-81; account exec. Charles R. Myers Ins. Agy., San Antonio, 1981-84; risk mgr. James E. Strates Shows, Inc., Orlando, Fla., 1984-85, Reithoffer Shows, Inc., Gibsonton, Fla., 1985—; ins. cons. various outdoor amusement bus., 1984—; pub. relations Boys and Girls Clubs of Am. Mem. Tampa Showmen's Ladies Aux., Miami Showmen's Ladies Aux., Nat. Assn. Female Execs., Outdoor Amusement Bus. Assn. Office: Reithoffer Shows Inc 9022 Wiggins Rd Gibsonton FL 33534

LEWITZKY, BELLA, choreographer; b. Los Angeles, Jan. 13, 1916; d. Joseph and Nina (Ossman) L.; m. Newell Taylor Reynolds, June 22, 1940; 1 dau., Nora Elizabeth. Student, San Bernardino Valley (Calif.) Jr. Coll., 1933-34; hon. doctorate, Calif. Inst. Arts, 1981; PhD (hon.), Occidental Coll., 1984, Otis Parsons Coll., 1989. Chmn. contemporary dance dept. U. So. Calif., Idyllwild, 1956-72; adv. panel U. So. Calif., 1972—; founder Sch. Dance, Calif. Inst. Arts, 1969, dean, 1969-72; vice chmn. dance adv. panel Nat. Endowment Arts, 1974-77, mem. artists-in-schs. adv. panel, 1974-75; mem. Nat. Adv. Bd. Young Audiences, 1974—, Joint Commn. Dance and Theater Accreditation, 1979—; com. mem. Am. chpt. Internat. Dance Council of UNESCO, 1974—; bd. dirs. Am. Arts Alliance, 1977-82, Arts, Edn. and Americans, 1978—; trustee Nat. Found. Advancement Arts, 1982—, Lake Placid Ctr. for Arts, 1982-84, Calif. Arts Council, 1983-86, Calif. Assn. Dance Cos., 1976-81, Nat. Found. Advancement in Arts; trustee Idyllwild Sch. Music and the Arts, 1986—. Co-founder, co-dir., Dance Theatre, Los Angeles, 1946-50; founder, dir., Dance Assocs., Los Angeles, 1951-55; founder 1966, since artistic dir., Lewitzky Dance Co., Los Angeles; choreographer, 1948—; founder, artistic dir. The Dance Gallery, Los Angeles; contbr. articles in field. Mem. adv. com. Actors' Fund of Am., 1986—, Women's Bldg. Adv. Council, 1985—, Calif. Arts Council, 1983-86, City of Los Angeles Task Force on the Arts, 1986. Recipient ann. award Dance mag., 1978, Dir.'s award Calif. Dance Educators Assn., 1978, achievement award YWCA, 1982, Disting. Svc. award Western Alliance Arts Adminstrs., 1987, 1st recipient Calif. Gov.'s award in arts for individual lifetime achievement, 1989, honor in dance L.A. Arts Coun., 1989; grantee Mellon Found., 1975, 81, 86, Guggenheim Found., 1977-78, Nat. Endowment for Arts, 1969-86. Mem. Am. Arts Alliance (bd. dirs. 1977), Internat. Dance Alliance (adv. council 1984—), Dance/USA (bd. dirs. 1988).

LEWNES, TULA, translator; b. Bklyn., May 25, 1921; d. Peter and Pauline (Karambellas) L. BA in Romance Langs., NYU, 1943; postgrad., Ecole Libre Des Hautes Etudes, N.Y.C., 1945-47, Alliance Francaise, N.Y.C., 1950. Translator Office Censorship, N.Y.C., 1943-45; translator, interpreter Immigration and Naturalization, N.Y.C., 1944-45; translator Cen. Hanover Bank, N.Y.C., 1949-51, Chase Manhattan Bank, N.Y.C.; demonstrator Linguaphone Inst., N.Y.C., 1956-57; reporter, translator Dun & Bradstreet, 1962-70; bus. devel. officer U.S. Small Bus. Adminstrn., N.Y.C., 1970-84; publs. dir. organized and conducted workshops, N.Y.C.; mgmt. officer seminars, symposia, 1980-84. Author: How to Succeed in Business; contbr. articles to profl. jours. corr. Greater N.Y. Fund, 1960; fund raiser United Hosp. Fund, N.Y., 1962; vol. Prospect Park Environ. Ctr., Bklyn, 1989; contributor Am. Museum Immigration Statue of Liberty, N.Y.; tutor Acad. of Languages, N.Y. Mem. Hellenic U. Club, Am. Lit. Translators Assn., Poetry Soc. Am. Republican. Greek Orthodox. Home: 186 Prospect Park W Brooklyn NY 11215

LEYDA, MARGARET LARUE, retired educator, bed and breakfast owner; b. Bloomfield, Iowa, Aug. 25, 1923; d. Ray and Pearl Larue (Coffman) Carey; m. Robert Leyda, June 7, 1940 (div. 1975); children: Constance, Carolyn, Richard, Rodney. BA, McKendree Coll., 1965; MA, So. Ill. U., 1976. Cert. elem. and secondary tchr., media specialist. Tchr. 3d, 4th and 5th grades Wolf Branch Sch., Belleville, Ill., 1960-61; kindergarten tchr. Lebanon (Ill.) Grade Sch., 1961-62; tchr. 5th grade gifted Mascoutah (Ill.) Grade Sch., 1963-68; media ctr. coordinator Triad High Sch., St. Jacob, Ill., 1969-84; owner, operator Maggie's Bed and Breakfast, Collinsville, Ill., 1985—; cons. bed and breakfast workshops U. Ill., Champaign, 1990. Author: (cookbook) Wake Up and Smell the Coffee, 1987. Election judge Dem. Party, Collinsville, 1985—. Mem. Ill. Edn. Assn. (bd. dirs. 1977-84, state legis. com. 1988—), Ret. Tchrs. Assn. (legis. chmn. 1986—), Ill. Bed and Breakfast Assn., AAUW, C. of C., Bus. and Profl. Women. Home: 2102 N Keebler Ave Collinsville IL 62234 Office: Maggie's Bed & Breakfast 2102 N Keebler Collinsville IL 62234

L'HEUREUX-DUBÉ, CLAIRE, judge; b. Quebec City, Que., Can., Sept. 7, 1927; d. Paul H. and Marguerite (Dion) L'H.; m. Arthur Dubé (dec. 1978); children: Louise Dubé, Pierre Dubé. BA magna cum laude, Coll. Notre-Dame de Bellevue, Que., 1946; LLL cum laude, Laval U., Que., 1951, LLD (hon.), 1984; LLD (hon.), Dalhousie U., 1981, Montreal U., 1983, Ottawa U., 1988, U. Que., 1989. Bar: Que. 1952. Ptnr. Bard, L'Heureux & Philippon, 1952-73; sr. ptnr. L'Heureux, Philippon, Garneau, Tourigny, St.Arnaud & Assocs., from 1969; Puisne judge Superior Ct. Que., 1973-79, Ct. Appeal of Que., 1979-87, Supreme Ct. Can., Ottawa, 1987—; commr. Part II Inquiries Act Dept. Manpower and Immigration, Montreal, 1973; del. Gen. Council Bar of Que., 1968-70, com. on adminstrn. justice, 1968-73, others; pres. family law com., Family Ct. com. Que. Civil Code Revision Office, 1972-76; pres. Can. sect. Internat. Commn. Jurists, 1981-83; participant Internat. Invitational Conf. on Matrimonial and Child Support, Inst. Law Research and Reform, Edmonton, Alta., 1981; adminstr., mem. Que. founding com. of Judges' Conf., 1982-83; lectr. in family law. Editor: (with Rosalie S. Abella) Family Law - Dimensions of Justice, 1983; chmn. editorial bd. Can. Bar Rev., 1985-88; author articles, conf. proc., book chpt. Bd. dirs. YWCA, Que., 1969-73, Ctr. des Loisirs St. Sacrement, 1969-73, Ctr. Jeunesse de Tilly-Ctr. des Jeunes, 1971-77; v.p. Can. Consumers Council, 1970-73; v.p. Vanier Inst. of the Family, 1972-73; lifetime gov. Fondation Univ. Laval, 1980, bd. dirs., 1984-85; mem. Comité des grandes orientations de l'Univ. Laval, 1971-72; mem. nat. council Can. Human Rights Found., 1980-82, 82-84; mem. Can. del. to Peoples Republic China on Status of Women, 1981. Apptd. Queen's Counsel, 1969; recipient Medal of the Alumni, U. Laval, 1986, Medaille du Barreau de Que., 1987. Mem. Can. Bar Assn., Can. Inst. Adminstrn. Justice, Internat. Soc. Family Law (bd. dirs. 1977-88, v.p. 1981-88), Internat. Fedn. Woman Lawyers, Fedn. Internat. des Femme Juristes, L'Assn. des Femmes Diplômées d'Univ., Assn. Québécoise pour l'Étude Comparative du Droit (pres. 1984—), Phi Delta Phi. Roman Catholic. Office: Supreme Ct Can, Wellington St, Ottawa, ON Canada K1A 0J1

L'HOMMEDIEU, TONI ROBIN, psychologist; b. Manhasett, N.Y., June 24, 1942; d. Kenneth Edward and Nancy Cormany (Robinson) L'Hommedieu; m. Abolghasem Shamsi, Oct. 13, 1979; children: kenneth, Tod, Laila, Parveen. BS, Springfield Coll., 1964; MEd, U. Pitts., 1969, PhD, 1981. Asst. buyer Gimbels Dept. Store, Pitts., 1964-66; reading specialist Pitts. Pub. Schs., 1966-68; reading instr. Community Coll. Allegheny County, West Mifflin, Pa., 1968-69; chmn. devel. studies dept. Community Coll. Allegheny County, West Mifflin, 1969-72, chmn. behavioral sci. dept., 1973-75, assoc. prof., 1979, prof., 1982—; cluster coordinator Nova U., Ft. Lauderdale 1986—; proposal reviews Henry A. Murray Ctr. for Human Studies, Radcliffe Coll., Cambridge, 1986—. Author: The Divorce Experience of Working and Middle Class Women 1984, Survival Manual for Introduction to Psychology, 1989, Survival Manual for Psychology of Health and Dying, 1989; editor Resource Directory for Sr. Senior Citizens Fayette County. Mem. Bd. Dirs. Women's Resouce Ctr., Uniontown, Pa., Albert Gallatin Sch. Dist. Adv. Council Fairchance, Pa.; leader Girl Scouts Am., Hickory, Pa., 1969-72; lectr. Albert Gallatin Sch. Dist. Gifted Class, Fairchance, 1988. Mem. AAUW. Democrat. Quaker. Office: Community Coll Allegheny County Rte 885 West Mifflin PA 15122

LI, REBECCA MEI-HUEY, automotive company executive; b. Taipei, Taiwan, China, July 29, 1942; came to U.S., 1966; d. Deng-Tsai and Swan (Chen) Chang; m. Chin-Hsiu Li, Jan. 25, 1969; children: Albert, Karen. BA in Bus. Adminstrn., Nat. Taiwan U., 1964; MBA in Mktg., Central Mich. U., 1967. Sec. to pres. Cathay Constrn. Co., Taipei, 1964-66; adminstrv. asst. to pres. Cathay Constrn. Co, Taipei, 1968; lectr. Nat. Chen-Kung Univ., Tainan, Taiwan, 1971-72; coll. grad. in tng. Detroit Diesel Allison Div., Gen. Motors Corp., 1974-75; market analyst Detroit (Mich.) Diesel Allison Div., Gen. Motors Corp., 1975-79, mktg. specialist, 1979-84, sr. staff asst., 1984-87, adminstr., market research & econ. analysis, 1987; staff asst. Chevrolet Motor Div., Gen. Motors Corp., Warren, Mich., 1988-89; sr. staff asst. Chevrolet Motor Div., Gen. Motors Corp., Warren, 1989-90, mktg./product planner, 1990—. Substitute tchr. Chinese Sch. of Greater Detroit, Bloomfield Hills, Mich., 1981-82. Mem. Am. Mktg. Assn. Home: 4281 Ramsgate Lane Bloomfield Hills MI 48302 Office: Chevrolet Motor Div Gen Motors Corp 30007 Van Dyke Ave Warren MI 48090

LI, TU LEUNG, management executive; b. N.Y.C., Nov. 10, 1948; d. Gum Ming and Toa Moy (Wong) Lee; m. Ta M. Li, Dec. 31, 1969; 1 child, Ta Ming. B.S., U. Utah, 1977. Sr. cons. Aetna Ins. Co., Salt Lake City, 1977-78; advt. mgr. Assn. Surg. Technologist, Littleton, Colo., 1978-80; research mgr. MET-Research Co., Lakewood, Colo., 1980-82; pres., chief exec. officer Tatum & Assocs., Littleton, 1982-85; sr. acct. Martin Marietta Data Systems, Colo., 1985—; dir. Asian X-M Ltd, Loveland, Colo. Contbr. articles on computer mgmt. techniques to publs. Sec., Friends of Littleton Library, 1984. Mem. AAUW (bd. dirs. 1983-84). Club: Argonauts Investment (pres. 1982-83) (Littleton).

LIADRA KIS, FLORENCE, educator; b. Constantinople, Turkey, Sept. 21, 1914; came to U.S., 1923; d. Constantine and Mary (Marmas) Vipoulou; m. Emaniel Liadrakis, Aug. 21, 1939; children: Crete Maria, Constantine (dec.). BS, Coll. St. Scholastica, 1934; MS, Marywood Coll., 1968. Instr. St. Louis County, Duluth, Minn., 1936-39; clinician speech and hearing Carbon County, Jim Thorpe, Pa., Schuylkill County, Pa., 1970—. Mem. Pa. Tchrs. Assn. (pres. 1969), Pa. Assn. Sch. Retirees, Pa. Speech and Hearing Assn., Caus Penelope (dist. gov. 1949), Mcht. Assn. (Mahanoy City, Pa. chpt.). Greek Orthodox. Home: 29 E Centre St Mahanoy City PA 17948

LIAKOS, SHIRLEY ATCHISON, data managment consultant; b. Nyack, N.Y., Oct. 4, 1953; d. Allan Edward and Anna (Bernat) Atchison; m. Peter A. Liakos, May 6, 1978. BA, Rutgers U., 1975; M Engring., U. Va., 1977. Mfg. systems engr. Corning (N.Y.) Glass Works, 1977-78; systems engr. The Mitre Corp., Bedford, Mass., 1978-79; prin. systems analyst Digital Equipment Corp., Maynard, Mass., 1979-80; sr. mgmt. scis. cons. Digital Equipment Corp., Stow, Mass., 1980-83, standards mgr., 1983-84; planning mgr. Digital Equipment Corp., Chelmsford, Mass., 1984-86, reference architecture program mgr., 1986-88, reference adminstrn. mgr., 1988-90, data mgmt. cons., 1990—. Author conf. procs. Am. Inst. Decision Scis., 1981. Mem. Soc. Women Engrs., Phi Beta Kappa. Home: 4 Betty Ln Westford MA 01886-1571 Office: US Info Mgmt & Tech 129 Parker St Maynard MA 01754

LIANG, ELISA LEE, lawyer; b. N.Y.C., Nov. 18, 1961; d. Benjamin and Jane (Lee) L. BA cum laude, Amherst Coll., 1981; JD cum laude, Boston Coll., 1986. Bar: N.Y. 1987, Mass. 1987. Legal asst. Choate, Hall & Stewart, Boston, 1981-83; assoc. Shearman & Sterling, N.Y.C., 1986-88, O'Melveny & Myers, N.Y.C., 1988—; mem. faculty program on mus. adminstrn. Al. Law Inst., Boston, 1987. Mem. ABA, N.Y. State Bar Assn., Mass. Bar Assn. Democrat. Home: 111 4th Ave Apt 5G New York NY 10003 Office: O'Melveny & Myers Citicorp Ctr 153 E 53d St New York NY 10022

LIANTONIO, JULIA ANN MARY, communicatons executive; b. Bklyn., Mar. 15, 1950; d. Joseph John and Grace Joan (Russo) L. Grad. high sch., New Hyde Park, N.Y. Press rep. Mineola (N.Y.) Playhouse, 1967-68; asst. to art dir. Washington Sch. of Art, Port Washington, 1968-73; asst. to store mgr. Gimbel's Dept. Store, Garden City, N.Y., 1973-74; promotions mgr. Trade Wind Tours, Great Neck, N.Y., 1975-83; account exec. Howard Blankman Inc., Hicksville, N.Y., 1983-84; mktg. coord. L.I. Jewish Hosp., New Hyde Park, 1985-87; prin. JAL Communications, Albertson, N.Y., 1987—; cons. Hapag-Lloyd Tours, East Meadow, N.Y., 1985—, Hapag-Lloyd Travel, Inc., East Meadow, 1989—, Pro Fairs, East Meadow, 1989—. Mem. Am. Cancer Soc., Albertson and Williston Park, N.Y., 1990—, Dem. Campaign Com., Washington, 1990—, NARAL and Planned Parenthood, Washington, 1989, Am. Film Inst., L.A., 1990—. Mem. NAFE. Roman Catholic. Home and Office: 97 Sampson Ave Albertson NY 11507

LIAPAKIS, PAMELA ANAGNOS, lawyer; b. Queens, N.Y., Jan. 26, 1947; d. Charles G. and Mary (Andriakos) Anagnos; m. John Liapakis, Nov. 9, 1969 (div. 1981). BA, Bklyn. Coll., 1967; JD, St. John's U. Sch. of Law, 1970. Bar: N.Y., U.S. Supreme Ct. Assoc., Harry H. Lipsig, P.C., N.Y.C., 1969-72, Berman & Frost, N.Y.C., 1972-75; pvt. practice law, Bklyn., 1975-76; sr. ptnr. Lipsig, Sullivan & Liapakis, P.C., N.Y.C., 1976-89; sr. ptnr. Sullivan & Liapakis P.C., N.Y.C., 1989—. Author: Appellate Advocacy, Trial Diplomacy Jour., Sept. 1987, Feb. 1988, other jours. Bd. trustees Civil Justice Found., 1989—. Recipient Freedom award Inst. Jewish Humanities, 1988. Mem. ABA, N.Y. Women's Bar Assn. (rec. sec. 1974-75, 3d v.p. 1976-77, treas. 1975-76), Assn. Trial Lawyers Am. (bd. govs. 1986-88), Assn. of City Trial Lawyers (bd. dirs. 1987—, co-chair membership and state support coms. 1989—, trustee 1989—), N.Y. State Trial Lawyers Assn. (bd. dirs. 1985-86, dep. treas. 1987-88, pres. elect 1988-89, pres. 1989—, liaison to Alliance for Consumer Affairs trustee 1988—), Assn. of Bar of City of N.Y (ad hoc com. on med. malpractice), Nat. Conf. Women Attys., NOW. Greek Orthodox. Office: Lipsig Sullivan & Liapakis 100 Church St New York NY 10007

LIBBY, GWYNNE MARGARET, dietitian, writer; b. Santa Rosa, Calif., Dec. 14, 1958; d. Edward E. and Lorene Ann (Helmberger) L. BS, U. Calif., Davis, 1982; MEd, Vanderbilt U., 1988. Outreach nutritionist Sonoma County Indian Health Project, Santa Rosa, 1984-85; clin. dietitian Sonoma State Devel. Ctr., Eldridge, Calif., 1985—. Mem. Am. Dietetic Assn., Calif. Dietetic Assn., Redwood Empire Dietitians. Office: Sonoma Devel Ctr PO Box 39 Eldridge CA 95431

LIBBY, JULIANNA, naval architect; b. Westbrook, Maine, Mar. 10, 1956; d. Clifford Emery and Elizabeth Phipps (Bennett) L. BCE, U. N.H., 1978; MS in Ocean & Marine Engring., George Washington U., Washington, 1982. Naval architect David Taylor Rsch. Ctr., Bethesda, Md., 1978-88; with Bath (Maine) Iron Works Corp., 1988—. Assoc. mem. Am Soc. Naval Engrs., Am. Soc. Civil Engrs. Republican. Mem. United Ch. of Christ. Office: Bath Iron Works Corp Bath ME 04530

LIBBY, PAMELA JOANNE, nurse, naval officer; b. Portland, Oreg., Mar. 28, 1955; d. Alan Robert and Vesta Joanne (Schmid) L. BS in Nursing, U. Portland, 1977. RN, Oreg., Fla., Wash., Va. Staff nurse St. Charles Med. Ctr., Bend, Oreg., 1977, Holliday Park Hosp., Portland, 1977-82, USAF, Tampa, Fla., 1983-86; asst. charge nurse maternity unit Providence Med. Ctr., Seattle, 1987-89; commd. ensign USN, 1989; asst. charge nurse ear, nose and throat unit US Naval Hosp., Portsmouth, Va., 1989—. Home: 5914 SW Gunther Ln Portland OR 97219

LIBBY, SANDRA CHIAVARAS, educator; b. Clinton, Mass., Apr. 8, 1949; B.S. in Spl. Edn., Fitchburg (Mass.) State Coll., 1970, M.Ed. in Reading, 1976; postgrad. (fellow) Clark U., 1981-83; 2 children. Tchr. spl. class Webster (Mass.) Schs., 1970-73, asst. coord. program materials, resource room, 1974, tchr./coord. primary spl. needs program, 1975-78, tchr. jr. high English, 1978-79, reading tchr. jr. high, 1979-80 adminstrv. asst. intern Shepherd Hill Regional Sch., Dudley, Mass., 1980-81; dir., owner Teddy Bear Day Care Ctr., Dudley, Mass., 1983-85; devel. specialist Ft. Devens Post Learning Ctr., Shirley, Mass., 1985-86; resource room tchr. Murdock High Sch., Winchendon, Mass., 1986; tchr. behavioral modification Middle Sch., Winchendon, 1986-87; coord., tchr. gifted and talented Lancaster Pub. Schs., 1987—. Mem. Nat. Edn. Assn., Mass. Tchrs. Assn., Lancaster Tchrs. Assn., Webster Emblem Club (pres. 1984-85), Phi Delta Kappa (Horace Mann grant 1989-90). Cert. in elem. and spl. edn., reading, reading supervision, learning disabilities, English (secondary), Mass. Home: 54 Green St Leominster MA 01453

LIBER, HILLARY SELESE JACOBS, foundation administrator; b. Balt., Apr. 25, 1953; d. David Paul and Claire Beth (Kuff) Jacobs; m. Jeffrey Robert Liber, Aug. 5, 1972; children: Reuben Raphael, Seth Avram. BS in Edn., Kent State U., 1973; MS, SUNY, Buffalo, 1979. Intensive edn. instr. Cleveland Heights/University Heights Sch. Dist., Cleve., 1973-75; instr. for multi-handicapped Orleans Niagara BOCES, Lockport, N.Y., 1975-76; sales cons. Economy Co. Publishers, So. Calif., 1979-82; instr. gerontology sr. adult edn. Palomar Coll., San Marcos, Calif., 1979-86; instr. creative writing and current events sr. adult edn. Mira Costa Coll., Oceanside, Calif., 1979-88; regional dir. City of Hope, San Diego, 1989—; prin. Congregation Beth Am, Solana Beach, Calif., 1984-86; nat. field cons. supr. Hadassah, 1986-89. Contbg. author: Motivation, Career Striving and Aging, 1982. Office: City of Hope 5090 Shoreham Pl #10 San Diego CA 92122

LIBERATI, SHARI LYNN, television producer; b. Pitts., May 30, 1961; d. Joseph James and Margaret (Laird) L. BA, Dickinson Coll., Carlisle, Pa., 1983. Pub. relations assoc. Metro-Arts, Harrisburg, Pa., 1982-83; prodn. asst. Pa. Ho. Reps., Harrisburg, Pa., 1983; TV producer WHTM-TV, Harrisburg, Pa., 1983-86; continuity dir., producer WHP-TV, Harrisburg, Pa., 1986—; advt. cons., free-lance writer cen. Pa. area businesses, 1983—;

producer corp. videos. Recipient Alumni award, Dickinson Coll., 1983. Cen. Pa. Advt. Fedn., Nat. Assn. Exec. Women. Home: 623 State St #4 Lemoyne PA 17043 Office: WHP-TV 3300 North Sixth St Harrisburg PA 17110

LIBERATORE, MARCIA ANTOINETTE, emergency physician; b. Buffalo, N.Y., Jan. 7, 1954; d. Donato F. and Liese L. (Medele) Liberatore. BA in Molecular, Cellular and Devel. Biology, Psychology magna cum laude, U. Colo., 1977; MD, U. Colo., Denver, 1981. Cert. in emergency medicine. Intern sch. medicine Marshall U., Huntington, W.Va., 1982-83; resident health sci. ctr. U. Okla., Oklahoma City, 1983-85; attending physician South Suburban Hosp., Hazel Crest, Ill., 1985-87; mem. emergency com. South Suburban Hosp., Hazel Crest, 1986-87; attending physician Resurrection Hosp., Chgo., 1985-87; physician emergency medicine Alaska, 1987—. Contbr. articles to profl. jours., 1978—. Mem. Am. Coll. Emergency Physicians (Alaska chpt.), AMA. Club: 99's (Chgo.).

LIBERMAN, GAIL JEANNE, editor; b. Neptune, N.J., Feb. 26, 1951; d. Si and Dorothy (Gold) L. BA, Rutgers U., 1972. Youth editor AP, N.Y.C., 1972-73; writer United Feature Syndicate, N.Y.C., 1973; reporter, broadcast editor UPI, Phila. and Hartford, Conn., 1973-75; reporter Courier-Post, Camden, N.J., 1976-80, Bank Advt. News, North Palm Beach, Fla., 1981-82; editor Bank Rate Monitor, North Palm Beach, 1982—.

LIBERMAN, LEE SARAH, lawyer, educator; b. N.Y.C., Aug. 19, 1956; d. James Benjamin and Deen (Freed) L. BA, Yale U., 1979; JD, U. Chgo., 1983. Bar: N.Y. Law clk. U.S. Ct. Appeals (D.C. cir.), Washington, 1983-84; spl. asst. to asst. atty. gen., civil div. U.S. Dept. Justice, Washington, 1984-86; dep. assoc. atty. gen. U.S. Dept. Justice, 1986, assoc. dep. atty. gen., 1986; law clk. to Justice Antonin Scalia U.S. Supreme Ct., Washington, 1986-87; asst. prof. law George Mason U., Arlington, Va., 1987-89; assoc. counsel to the Pres. Exec. Office of the Pres., Washington, 1989—. Mem. ABA (adminstrv. law sect.), Inns of Ct. Republican. Jewish. Office: 115 Old Exec Office Bldg Washington DC 20500

LIBERTI, KELLY S., television news producer; b. San Antonio, July 22, 1967; d. David C. Liberti and Susan J. (Butler) Hill. BS in Journalism, Ohio U., 1989. News anchor, reporter WOUB AM-FM-TV, Athens, Ohio, 1985-89; news producer WOWK-TV, Huntington, W.Va., 1989-90, WHIO-TV, Dayton, Ohio, 1990—. Vol. Big Bros. and Sisters, United Way, Huntington, 1989. Mem. Radio-TV News Dirs. Assn. Democrat. Roman Catholic. Office: WHIO-TV 1414 Wilmington Ave Dayton OH 45401

LIBROS, MAXINE, clinical psychologist; b. Bklyn., May 28, 1924; d. Charles Silverstein and Dora Poberesky; m. Harold Libros, May 1, 1946 (div. 1982); children: Tracy, Randy, Brad; m. William Cooper Davidon, 1987. BA in Econ., Bklyn. Coll., 1944; MA in Psychology, Bryn Mawr Coll., 1963. Lic. psychologist, Pa. Asst. prof. child care dept. Temple U., Phila., 1970-89, chmn. child care dept., 1978-83; pvt. practice Pa., 1974—; prof. emeritus Sch. Social Adminstrn. Temple U., 89—; cons. group therapy N.E. Community Mental Health Ctr., 1970-75. Bd. dirs. S.E. Pa. chpt., Americans for Dem. Action, 1982-88. Fellow Am. Orthopsychiat. Assn.; mem. Am. Psychol. Assn., Am. Group Psychol. Assn., Pa. Psychol. Assn., Soc. Rsch. Psychotherapy, Del. Valley Group Psychotherapy Soc. (past pres.). Home: 4 College Ln Haverford PA 19041

LICHT, JANICE B., critical care nurse; b. North Tonawanda, N.Y., Mar. 9, 1954; d. Alexander William and Alice Patricia (Berringer) Bennett; m. Keith Lawrence Licht, Sept. 6, 1980. A in Nursing, Sinclair Community Coll., 1977; BS in Nursing, Minot State U., 1988. Cert. critical care nurse, advanced cardiac life support instr., emergency nurse. Head nurse emergency room Greene Meml. Hosp., Xenia, Ohio; staff nurse, unit mgr. ICU Trinity Med. Ctr., Minot, N.D.; head nurse emergency room Midlands Community Hosp., Papillion, Nebr., hosp. supr.; nurse staff relief emergency and critical care Kimberly Quality Care; staff nurse emergency dept. Archbishop Began Mercy Hosp. Mem. Am. Nursing Assn., Am. Assn. Critical Care Nurses, Emergency Nurse Assn. Republican. Address: 7637 Emiline La Vista NE 68128-8000

LICHTENAUER, DIXON ANN, contractor, music educator; b. Houston, Jan. 11, 1934; d. Jasper Henry and Elsie M. (Rehm) Yarbrough; m. Donald Eugene Smith, Dec. 12, 1955 (div. 1974); children: Michael Wayne, Mark Alan; m. William Louis Lichtenauer, July 22, 1977. BS, U. Houston, 1956. Cert. tchr., Tex. Dir. youth choir 1st Unitarian Ch., Houston, 1956-58; elem. music tchr. Houston Ind. Sch. Dist., 1958-68, choral music instr., 1970-71; instr. music Good Hope Sch., St. Croix, U.S.V.I., 1972-73; choral music instr. Queens Intermediate Sch., Pasadena, Tex., 1973-74; sec. 1st Am. Title Co., Houston, 1974-75; owner Kerne Properties, Houston, 1975-78, Music Studio I, Houston, 1979—, Bilda Cos., Bilda Environ. Services Tex., Inc., Houston, 1981—. Dir., singer Sweet Adelines, Inc., 1963-69. Recipient awards in field. Mem. Houston Music Tchrs. Assn. (bd. dirs. 1984—, yearbook editor 1986-88). Mem. Tex. Music Tchrs. Assn., Music Tchrs. Nat. Assn., Am. Coll. Musicians, Nat. Honor Roll Guild Tchrs., Associated Gen. Contractors Am., Nat. Asbestos Coun., Better Bus. Bur. Met. Houston, Nat. Assn. Women Bus. Owners. Home and Office: Bilda Cos & Music Studio I 12226 Fairpoint Houston TX 77099

LICHTENBERGER, DORIS L., accountant, educator; b. Memphis, Mar. 5, 1925; d. John D. and Angela I. (Grenough) Longhill; m. H. Davis Lichtenberger, Aug. 21, 1948; children: John, Kathleen, Laurel, Grayce. BS, Rollins Coll., 1978; MBA, Stetson U., 1980; MS in Systems Mgmt., Fla. Inst. Tech. Mem. faculty Fla. Inst. Tech., Melbourne, 1980—. Mem. Am. Acctg. Assn., Nat. Trust for Hist. Preservation, Lombard Svc. League (1st v.p. 1962-63), St. Peter's Women's Guild (pres. 1972-73), Cocoa Beach Women's Club (1st v.p. 1983-84). Republican. Roman Catholic. Address: 1404 Parkside Pl Indian Harbour Beach FL 32937

LICHTI, BARBARA JEAN, accountant; b. Corydon, Ind., Jan. 14, 1942; d. Lester and Evelyn Rose Ferguson; diploma acctg. Bryant and Stratton Bus. Coll., Louisville, 1962; enrolled to practice before IRS; m. Marvin Lichti, Dec. 20, 1963; 1 dau., Diana. Acct., Sta. WLKY, Louisville, 1962-64; head dept. grain storage Dept. Agr., Champaign, Ill., 1964-68; acct. Larry Buhrmester, Champaign, 1968-73, Armstrong & Acord, C.P.A.s, Champaign, 1973-75; self-employed acct., Champaign, 1976—. Mem. Twin Cities Bus. and Profl. Women's Club, Nat. Assn. Tax Practioners, Assn. Bus. Accts., Nat. Assn. Enrolled Agts., Nat. Soc. Pub. Accts., Ill. Ind. Accts. Assn. Address: 909 Devonshire St Champaign IL 61821

LICHTMAN, JUDITH, lawyer, organization administrator. Pres. Women's Legal Def. Fund, Washington. Office: Women's Legal Def Fund 2000 P St NW Washington DC 20036*

LICK, SHERRY LEE, hotel executive; b. St. Paul, Apr. 1, 1940; d. Joseph Percy and Rachel (Wahl) DeMars; m. Dennis Allen Lick (div. 1983); 1 child, John Patrick Cullen. Student, U. Wis., 1958-61, Vocat. Sch., Eau Claire, Wis., 1961-62. Mgr. Stuart Levine Group, Chgo., 1976-82; speakers bur. Chgo. Bears Football, 1976-82; spl. agent Backyard Travel, Highland Pk., Ill., 1981-82; mktg. exec. L.A. Raiders Football, El Segundo, Calif., 1982-87, Trop World, Arlington, Va., 1987-90; br. mgr. Taj Mahal, Atlantic City, 1990, Mirage Hotel, Las Vegas, 1990—; pub. relations dir. Chgo. Bears Wives Aux., 1979-82. Mgr. Jack Kemp for pres., L.A., 1987. Republican. Roman Catholic. Office: Mirage Hotel 9465 Wilshire Blvd Beverly Hills CA 90212

LIDDELL, CYNTHIA ANN, corporate administrator, psychologist; b. San Rafael, Calif., Nov. 11, 1951; d. James Nelson and Bettyjane (Hambridge) Liddell; children: Danielle René, Justin Bryan. B.S. cum laude, U. Calif.-Davis, 1973; M.A. summa cum laude, Calif. State U.-Sacramento, 1975. Cert. psychologist, community coll. tchr., Calif.; lic. contractor, Calif. Asst. prof. Calif. State U.-Sacramento, 1972-74; adminstr. State of Calif., Sacramento, 1974-79; mng. ptnr. Liddell & Assocs., 1979-81; chmn. bd. Carefree Greens, Inc. Mem. Calif. Gov.'s Roundtable, Sacramento, 1975. Calif. State scholar 1969. Nat. scholar Alcoa Co. Mem. Internat. Erosion Control Assn., AAUW, Calif. Scholarship Fedn. (life), Psi Chi, Mu Alpha Theta, Calif. Women in State Service (founder, pres.).

LIDDELL, JANE HAWLEY HAWKES, civic worker; b. Newark, Dec. 8, 1907; d. Edward Zeh and Mary Everett (Hawley) Hawkes; A.B., Smith Coll., 1931; postgrad. in art history, Harvard U., 1933-35; M.A., Columbia U., 1940; Carnegie fellow Sorbonne, Paris, 1937; m. Donald M. Liddell, Jr., Mar. 30, 1940; children: Jane Boyer, D. Roger Brooke. Pres., Planned Parenthood Essex County (N.J.), 1947-50; trustee Prospect Hill Sch. Girls, Newark, 1946-50; mem. adv. bd., publicity and public relations chmn. N.J. State Mus., Trenton, 1952-60; sec., then v.p. women's br. N.J. Hist. Soc.; women's aux. prodn. chmn. Englewood (N.J.) Hosp., 1959-61; pres. Dwight Sch. Girls Parents Assn., 1955-57; v.p. Englewood Sch. Boys Parents Assn., 1958-60; mem. Altar Guild, women's aux. bd., rector's adv. council St. Paul's Episcopal Ch., Englewood, 1954-59; bd. dir. N.Y. State Soc. of Nat. Soc. Colonial Dames, 1961-67, rep. conf. Patriotic and Hist. Socs., 1964—; bd. dirs. Huguenot Soc. Am., 1979-86, regional v.p., 1979-82, historian, 1983-84, co-chmn. Tercentennial Book, 1983-85; bd. dirs. Soc. Daus. Holland Dames, 1965-82; nat. jr. v.p. Dames of Loyal Legion, USA; bd. dirs., mem. publs. com. Daus. Cin., 1966-72; bd. dirs. Ch. Women's League Patriotic Service, 1962—, pres., 1968-70, 72-74; bd. dirs., chmn. grants com. Youth Found., N.Y.C., 1974—; chmn. for Newark, Smith Coll. 75th Ann. Fund, 1948-50; pres. North N.J. Smith Club, 1956-58; pres. Smith Coll. Class 1931, 1946-51, 76-81, editor 50th anniversary book, 1980-81. Author: (with others) Huguenot Refugees in the Settling of Colonial America, 1985. Recipient various commendation awards. Republican. Mem. Colonial Dames Am. (N.Y.C. chpt.). Clubs: Colony, City Gardens, Church (N.Y.C.); Jr. League Bergen County; Needle and Bobbin, Nat. Farm and Garden; Englewood Woman's, Englewood Field; Hillsboro (Pompano Beach, Fla.). Editor: Maine Echoes, 1961; research and editor asst., Wartime Writings of American Revolution Officers, 1972-75.

LIDE, NEOMA JEWELL LAWHON (MRS. MARTIN JAMES LIDE, JR.), poet; b. Levelland, Tex., Apr. 1, 1926; d. Charles Samuel and Juel (Yeager) Lawhon; Secretarial cert. Draughon's Bus. Coll., 1943; student U. Tex., 1944-46; R.N., Jefferson-Hillman Sch. Nursing, 1950; m. Martin James Lide, Jr., Nov. 12, 1950; children—Martin James, III, Brooks Nathaniel, Gardner Lawhon. Writer column Baldwin Times, Bay Minette, Ala., 1964-68, Shades Valley Sun newspapers, Birmingham, Ala., 1974-75; v.p., sec. Martin J. Lide Assocs., Inc., Birmingham, 1977-81; R.N. supr. St. Martin's in the Pines, 1984. Mem. def. adv. com. Women in Services, for Ala., 1961-63; coordinator women's activities Nat. Vets. Day, Birmingham, 1961-68; mem. exec. com., 1968-70; exec. bd. Women's Com. of 100 for Birmingham, 1964-65. Mem. Gorgas bd. U. Ala., Tuscaloosa, 1959. Recipient citation Merit, Muscular Dystrophy Assn. Am., 1961. Author: (poetry) Instead of Sunset, 1973; (narrative) Life of Service-These are My Jewels, 1979; Music in the Wind - The Story of Lady Arlington, 1980; Brother James Bryan-Hope Lives Eternal, 1981; Music of the Soul, 1982; The Past and Psyche of Arlington, 1983, The Light Side of Life in the American Colonies, 1988, The American Woman, 1989. Home: 3536 Brookwood Rd Mountain Brook Birmingham AL 35223

LIDESTRI, PAULA ANN, freelance artist; b. N.Y.C., July 27, 1965; d. Joseph Carmine and Paula (Italia) L. BA in Architecture, Columbia U., 1989. Draftsperson Voorsanger & Mills Assocs., Architects, N.Y.C., 1988-89; freelance artist May Merchandising Co., N.Y.C., 1990—. Recipient Marcia Mead Design award honorable mention Barnard Coll., 1989.

LIDON, JEAN SIH, lawyer; b. Bethlehem, Pa., June 27, 1961; d. George Charles and Jennice C. (Jen) Sih; m. James Peter Lidon, Mar. 21, 1960. BS, Lehigh U., 1983; JD, Duke U., 1986. Bar: N.J., 1986. Assoc. Porzio, Bromberg & Newman, Morristown, N.J., 1986-88; staff atty. com. on character N.J. Supreme Ct, Trenton, 1988—; candidate interviewer Duke Law Alumni, Durham, N.C., 1986—. Vol. Spl. Olympics, Somerset, N.J., 1987—. Bell scholar, 1983-86. Mem. Delta Gamma. Republican. Roman Catholic. Home: 47 Arapaho Trail Branchburg NJ 08876 Office: Supreme Ct N.J CN 973 Hughes Justice Complex Trenton NJ 08625

LIDTKE, DORIS KEEFE, computer science educator; b. Bottineau County, N.D., Dec. 6, 1929; d. Michael J. and Josephine (McDaniels) Keefe; m. Vernon L. Lidtke, Apr. 21, 1951. BS, U. Oreg., 1952; MEd cum laude, Johns Hopkins U., 1974; PhD, U. Oreg., 1979. Programmer analyst Shell Devel. Co., Emeryville, Calif., 1955-59, U. Calif., Berkeley, 1960-62; asst. prof. Lansing (Mich.) Community Coll., 1963-68; ednl. specialist Johns Hopkins U., Balt., 1968; assoc. program mgr. NSF, Washington, 1984-85; sr. mem. tech. staff Software Productivity Consortium, Reston, Va., 1987-88; asst. prof. Towson State U., Balt., 1968-80, assoc. prof., 1980-90, prof. computer sci., 1990—. Named Outstanding Educator, Assn. for Ednl. Data Systems, 1986; recipient Outstanding Contbn. award IEEE Computer Soc., 1986. Mem. Assn. for Computing Machinery (coun. 1984-86, SIG bd. 1985—, edn. bd. 1980—, Recognition Svc. award 1978, 83, 85, 86, 90), Computer Soc. IEEE, Nat. Ednl. Computer Conf. (steering com., chair 1985-89, vice chair 1983-85, Recognition award 1988). Home: 4806 Wilmslow Rd Baltimore MD 21210 Office: Towson State U Computer & Info Scis Baltimore MD 21204

LIEBAN, IRENE STAHOVICH, psychologist; b. London, Nov. 9, 1942; came to U.S., 1949; d. Alexander Stahovich and Marina (Struve) Lieban; m. Harvey E. Wheeler, June 6, 1964 (div. 1979); children: Kevin, Meredith, Jessica, Geoffrey; m. Douglas Logan Dunlap, May 16, 1981. BA in French, U. Houston, 1977, MSW, 1980; D in Psychology, Hahnemann U., 1987. Lic. psychologist Wash., Oreg. Clin. social worker MacGregor Clinic, Houston, 1980, Family Svc. Ctr., Houston, 1980-82; intern in psychology Phila., 1982-87; resident in psychology Longview (Wash.) Psychol. Group, 1987-88; clin. psychologist, neuropsychologist Emanuel Hosp., Portland, 1988—; cons. in neuropsychology Vocat. Rehab. Div., Portland, 1989—, Dammasch State Hosp., Wilsonville, Oreg., 1990—. Alliance Francaise scholar, 1975; Fulbright fellow France, 1977. Mem. Am. Psychol. Assn., Nat. Assn. Neuropsychologists, Oreg. Psychol. Assn., Internat. Neuropsychol. Soc. Home: 4304 SW 36th Pl Portland OR 97221

LIEBELER, SUSAN WITTENBERG, lawyer; b. New Castle, Pa., July 3, 1942; d. Sherman K. and Eleanor (Klivans) Levine; BA, U. Mich., 1963, postgrad. U. Mich., 1963-64; LLB (Stein scholar), UCLA, 1966; m. Wesley J. Liebeler, Oct. 21, 1971; 1 child, Jennifer. Bar: Calif. 1967, Vt. 1972, D.C. 1988. Law clk. Calif. Ct. of Appeals, 1966-67; assoc. Gang, Tyre & Brown, 1967-68, Greenberg, Bernhard, Weiss & Karma, L.A., 1968-70; assoc. gen. counsel Rep. Corp., L.A., 1970-72; gen. counsel Verit Industries, L.A., 1972-73; prof. of law law sch. Loyola U., L.A., 1973-84; spl. counsel, chmn. John S. R. Shad, SEC, Washington, 1981-82; commr. U.S. Internat. Trade Commn. Washington, 1984-88, vice chmn., 1984-86, chmn., 1986-88; ptnr. Irell & Manella, Washington, 1988—; vis. prof. U. Tex., summer 1982; cons. Office of Policy Coordination, office of Pres.-elect, 1981-82; cons. U.S. Ry. Assn., 1975, U.S. EPA, 1974, U.S. Price Commn., 1972. Mem. editorial adv. bd. Regulation mag. CATO Inst. Mem. State Bar Calif., L.A. County Bar Assn., D.C. Bar Assn., ABA, ITC Trial Lawyers Assn., Washington Legal Found. (acad. adv. bd.), Asia Pacific Lawyers Assn., Internat. Bar Assn., Computer Law Assn. , Order of Coif. Jewish. Sr. editor UCLA Law Review, 1965-66; contbr. articles to legal publ.

LIEBELER, VIRGINIA MARY MAYER, writer, educator, lecturer; b. Great Falls, Mont., May 23, 1900; d. John Henry and Sophia Julia (Sosnick) Mayer; m. Rae E. Liebeler, 1922 (dec. 1976); children: Yvonne, Natalie (dec.), John Rae. BA in Edn., U. Minn., 1922, MA, 1950. With promotion, pub. rels. dept. Mpls. Soc. Fine Arts and Mpls. Symphony Orchestra, 1928-35; promotion editor, state dir. enrollment Minn. Hosp. Service Assn. (Blue Cross of Minn.), 1935-44; co-dir. NW Hosp. Service Plan (Portland, Oreg. Blue Cross), 1944-45; tchr. English, creative writing evening div. Minn. Voc. Sch. Adults, 1945-54; instr. creative writing, English and office practices U. Minn., tchr. tng. specialist, 1946-68; writer Hosp. Mgmt. Mag. U. Modern Hosp., 1942-54. Author: (novel and radio program) Kid Galahad, 1936; (novel) You, the Jury, 1944; also wrote 12 tng. manuals for tchrs., numerous textbooks; numerous articles, poetry and short stories; writer, editor, Blue Cross News, 1935-44. Campaigner Hubert Humphrey for Mayor, 1940's. Mem. Writers' Workshop (pres. 1938-40), Novel Workshop (pres. 1946-48), U. Minn. Alumni Assn., Nat. League Am. Penwomen (chmn. scholarship for mature womrn com. 1978-80, v.p., pres.) (recipient numerous awards 1968-80), Internat. Poetry Soc. (honorary), Beta Sigma Phi (honorary). Roman Catholic. Home: 4805 NW 47th Terr (Tamarac) Fort Lauderdale FL 33319 also (summer): 758 Highlands Rd Franklin NC 28734

LIEBEL-WECKOWICZ, HELEN PAULINE GRIT, historian, educator, political analyst; b. N.Y.C., June 17, 1930; d. Frederick Emil and Anna Wilhelmina Johanna (Bonk) Liebel; m. Thaddeus E. Weckowicz, July 11, 1966. B.A. summa cum laude, Bklyn. Coll., 1952; M.A., Northwestern U., 1953, Ph.D., 1959. Assoc. editor Chgo. Consol. Publ., 1954-55; mem. Am. Hist. Assn. microfilming project of captured German war documents, 1958-59; Sessl lectr. Bklyn. Coll., 1959-62; mem. faculty U. Alta, Edmonton, Can., 1962—, prof. history, 1972—; mem. Can. nat. com. Internat. Congress, 1967-70, 77-80; research dir. Can. Council grants, 1969-71, 73-74. Author books, articles in field; mem. editorial bd. Can. Jour. History, Austrian Hist. Yearbook; research editorial bd. Am. Biog. Inst., 1986-88. Recipient Commemorative Gold medal Am. Biog. Inst., 1986, World Decoration award, 1990; Fulbright grantee, W. Ger., 1955; AAUW scholar, 1956-57; grantee Carnegie Fund., 1957-58, U. Alta., 1962-82, Am. Com. Promotion of Hapsburg Studies, 1984-88. Mem. Am. Hist. Assn., Am. 18th Century Studies Assn., Can. 18th Century Studies Assn., Can. Hist. Soc., German Studies Assn., Conf. Group Central European History, Internat. Econ. Hist. Soc., Internat. Soc. 18th Century Studies, Bicentaire French Rev. U. Rene Descartes. Democrat. Club: U. Alta. Faculty. Office: U Alta, Dept History, Edmonton, AB Canada T6G 2H4

LIEBERMAN, ANNE MARIE, financial executive; b. Jersey City, Aug. 28, 1946; d. Ralph Norman and Kathleen Celestine (Dooris) L.; m. Stephen Bruce Oshry, Sept. 21, 1986. BA, Sonoma State U., 1968; MLS, U. Calif., 1970, MBA, 1977. Cert. fin. planner. V.p. Bank of Am., San Francisco, 1977-81, Lawrence A. Krause & Assocs., San Francisco, 1982-86; dir. Lieberman Assocs., Larkspur, Calif., 1986—. Author: Marketing Your Financial Planning Practice, 1986, Mastering Money, 1987; contbg. author: Financial Planning Can Make You Rich, 1987, The Expert's Guide to Managing a Successful Financial Planning Practice, 1988, About Your Future, 1988. Mem. Inst. Cert. Fin. Planners (Fin. Writer's award 1986), Internat. Assn. Fin. Planning, Rotary. Office: Lieberman Assocs 100 Larkspur Landing Circle Ste 214 Larkspur CA 94939

LIEBERMAN, BETH WEINSTEIN, obstetrician, gynecologist; b. N.Y.C., Dec. 1, 1947; d. Harry and Miriam (Klein) W.; m. Carl Marc Lieberman, Feb. 4, 1968; children: Stefanie Elaine, Andrew Barrett. BA, CUNY, 1968; MD, NYU, 1973. Resident ob-gyn. Med. Ctr., Bellevue Hosp. NYU, N.Y.C., 1973-77, asst. clin. prof. dept. ob-gyn. Sch. Medicine, 1977—; dir. abortion svcs. Bellevue Hosp., N.Y.C., 1977-78. Recipient Founder's Day award NYU, N.Y.C., 1973, Glasgow Achievement award Am. Med. Woman's Assn., N.Y.C., 1973. Fellow Am. Bd. Ob-Gyn., Am. Coll. Ob-Gyn.; mem. N.Y. County Med. Soc. Jewish. Office: 333 E 30th St New York NY 10016

LIEBERMAN, DANA KAPLAN, human resource specialist; b. Miami Beach, Fla., Dec. 2, 1964; d. Ronald M. and Barbra (Breakstone) Kaplan; m. Eric H. Lieberman, Nov. 29, 1986. BBA, U. Miami, 1986. Assoc. compensation analyst Cordis Corp., Miami, Fla., 1986-87; recruiter Neponset Valley Health System, Norwood, Mass., 1987-88; recruiter Krupp Cos., Boston, 1988-89, mgr. personnel and benefits adminstrn., 1989—. Mem. NAFE.

LIEBERMAN, GAIL FORMAN, financial executive; b. Phila., May 26, 1943; d. Joseph and Rita (Groder) Forman. BA in Physics and Math., Temple U., 1964, MBA in Fin., 1977. Dir. internat. fin. Standard Brands Inc., N.Y.C., 1977-79; staff v.p. fin. and capital planning RCA Corp., 1979-82; chief fin. officer, exec. v.p. Scali McCabe Sloves, Inc., 1982—; bd. dirs. Elmer Little Glove Co., Johnstown, Pa., 1983-86. Mem. Fin. Execs. Inst. Office: Scali McCabe Sloves Inc 800 3rd Ave New York NY 10022

LIEBERMAN, ILENE, performing arts adminstrator; b. N.Y.C., Oct. 13, 1956; d. Jason Harold and Adrienne (Kavelle) L.; m. Jon H. Sprance, Sept. 24, 1989. MusB, Marymount Coll., 1977; postgrad., Adelphi U., 1981. Cultural affairs coord. City of Yonkers, N.Y., 1977-80; devel. officer Lehman Ctr. for the Performing Arts, Bronx, N.Y., 1980-83; dir. devel. Queens (N.Y.) Symphony Orch., 1983-85; dir. corp. and found. support N.Y. Philharm., N.Y.C., 1985-89, assoc. dir. devel., 1989—; pres. Bang on a Can Festival, N.Y.C., 1989—; freelance mgmt. cons. Mem. Am. Symphony Orch. League. Office: NY Philharmonic 132 W 65th St New York NY 10023

LIEBERMAN, SHARI, clinical nutritionist; b. Brklyn., June 24, 1958; d. Mort and Sheila (Kolchin) L. BS, N.Y.U., 1979, MA, 1981. Registered Dietition. Pvt. practice N.Y.C., 1982—; lectr. Health and Med. Conf., 1981—; nutritional cons. and product devel. Garden State and Windmill Vitamins, N.J., 1987—, Home Shopping Club, USA, Can., 1988—, Books Mag. Prod. USA, 1987—. Author: Design Your Own Vitamin and Mineral Program, 1987; contbg. editor Better Nutrition, Today's Living, 1988-. Mem. Nat. Acad. of Sci., Internat. Coll. Applied Nutriton. Office: 100 Lehigh Dr Fairfield NJ 07006

LIEBERMAN-NISSEN, KAREN, nutrition and food service executive; b. Bklyn., Mar. 1, 1950; d. Sidney and Shirley Phyllis (Greff) Lieberman; m. Bruce A. Nissen, Apr. 26, 1978; cihldren: Jared Abraham, Leif Andrew. BA, NYU, 1973; MS, Purdue U., 1986. Registered dietitian, Ind. Mem Family Food Svc. Operation, L.I., N.Y., 1966-74; sr. compliance officer N.Y.C. Mayor's Office for Contract Compliance, 1974-79; contract asst. Dist. Coun. 1l99, N.Y.C., 1980-8l; food svc. lab. technician Ind. U.-Purdue U., Indpls., 1982; instr. Ivy Tech. Coll., Indpls., 1983; program chmn. culinary arts Ivy Tech. Coll., Hammond, Ind., 1984-85; dietetic intern St. Catherine's Hosp., East Chicago, Ind., 1986-87; dietitian Children and Youth Clinic, Gary, Ind., 1988; dir. restaurant, hotel and instnl. mgmt. program Purdue U. North Cen., Westville, Ind., 1988—; nutrition scientist, food svc. cons., Gary, 1986—; mem. Comml. Food Svc. Adv. Bd.; Heinz Meml. lectr./fellow, 1970-71. Health columnist The Times, Hammond, 1989—. Fund raising chmn. Miller Little League, Gary, 1985—; bd. dirs. Temple Israel Sisterhood, Gary. Statler Found. scholar, 1982-84. Mem. Am. Dietetic Assn., Inst. Food Technologists, Nat. Restaurant Assn., N.W. Ind. Chefs Assn. (edn. chmn. 1984-86, Outstanding Assistance award 1985), N.W. Ind. Hotel-Motel Assn. (edn. chmn. 1988—), Tau Alpha Pi. Democrat. Office: Purdue U North Cen l40l S US 42l Westville IN 46391

LIEBES, RAQUEL, import/export company owner, lecturer; b. San Salvador, El Salvador, Aug. 28, 1938; came to the U.S., 1952, naturalized, 1964; d. Ernesto Martin and Alice Bella Juliane (Philip) L.; m. Richard Paisley Kinkade, June 2, 1962 (div. 1977); children: Kathleen Paisley, Richard Paisley Jr., Scott Philip. BA, Sarah Lawrence Coll., 1960; MEd, Harvard U., 1961; MA, Yale U., 1962, postgrad., 1961-65. Instr. Spanish Sarah Lawrence Coll., Bronxville, N.Y., 1958-60, admissions rep., 1963-68; teaching fellow Yale U., New Haven, 1964-65, instr. Spanish, 1964-66; exec. stockholder, ptnr., owner Import Export Co., San Salvador, 1968—, St. Ann's Coll. Oxford (Eng.) U., 1989; lectr. Am. U., Washington, 1989—; lectr. Dept. Fgn. Lang. and Linguistics. Georgetown U., Washington, 1990—. Contbr. glossary of Spanish med. terms. Hon. consul Govt. of El Salvador, 1977-80; docent High Mus. of Art, Atlanta, 1972-77; vol. Grady Hosp., Atlanta, 1966-71; instr. Spanish for med. drs. Tucson Med. Ctr., 1966-71; chmn. Atlanta Coun. for Internat. Visitors, 1966-71; mem. Outreach Group on Latin Am., Washington, 1982-86; founding mem. John Kennedy Ctr. for Performing Arts, 1980—; mem. Folger/Shakespeare Libr., Smithsonian Inst., Agape, El Salvador. Fellow Yale U., 1963, econ. fellow Yale U., 1964-65; fellow Corcoran Mus. of Art, 1984-85. Mem. Jr. League of Washington, Harvard Club (Washington, Boston, N.Y.C.), Yale Club (Washington). Republican. Home: 700 New Hampshire Ave Washington DC 20037

LIEBICH, MARCIA TRATHEN, community volunteer; b. Troy, N.Y., Mar. 10, 1942; d. Roland Henry and Ida Mae (Horsfall) Trathen; m. Donald Herbert Liebich, May 13, 1941; children: Kurt Roland, Mark Christian. BA, Elmira Coll., 1964. Co-founder Parents' Anonymous Lay Therapy, Schenectady, 1974-80; trustee Elmira (N.Y.) Coll., 1978—; bd. dirs. United Way, Schenectady, 1980—, pres. 1985; bd. dirs. Sunnyview Rehab. Hosp., Schenectady, 1982—, pres. 1988—; social svcs. Women's Legis. Forum, Albany, 1984—; bd. dirs. Leadership Schenectady, 1987—,

Schenectady C. of C., 1987-90; pres. Samaritan Counseling Ctr., Schenectady, 1988—; bd. dirs., treas. Bridge Ctr./Drug Treatment, Schenectady, 1988-91. Recipient YWCA Community Vol. award, 1986, K.S. Rozendaal award Community Svc. Schenectady, 1987, Liberty Bell award Schenectady BAr Assn., 1990. Mem. AAUW (pres. 1978), Jr. league Schenectady (Vol. of Yr. award 1981), Phi Beta Kappa. Republican. Lutheran. Home: 6 Brian Dr Rexford NY 12148

LIEBZEIT, ANDREA CLARA, trade association administrator; b. Caracas, Venezuela, July 9, 1960; d. Jochen K. and Elsa R. (Moravek) Wagner; m. Gregory Ray Liebzeit, Sept. 14, 1985. BA in Marine Affairs, BA in Econs., U. Miami, Coral Gables, Fla., 1982; MA in Marine Policy, U. Del., 1984. Rsch. assoc. Coastal Fisheries Inst., La. State U., Baton Rouge, 1984-87; rsch. dir. Atlantic Offshore Fisheries Assn., Newport, R.I., 1988-89; exec. dir. R.I. Lobstermen's Assn., Newport, 1990—; adminstr. Atlantic Offshore Fishermen's Assn., Newport, 1990—. Home: 309 Corey Ln Middletown RI 02840 Office: RI Lobstermens Assn 221 3rd St Newport RI 02840 also: Atlantic Offshore Fishermen's Assn 221 3d St Newport RI 02840

LIEM, ANNIE, pediatrician; b. Kluang, Johore, Malaysia, May 26, 1941; d. Daniel and Ellen (Phuah) L. BA, Union Coll., 1966; MD, Loma Linda U., 1970. Diplomate Am. Bd. Pediatrics. Intern Glendale (Calif.) Adventist Hosp., 1970-71; resident in pediatrics Children's Hosp. of Los Angeles, 1971-73; pediatrician Children's Med. Group, Anaheim, Calif., 1973-75, Anaheim Pediatric Med. Group, 1975-79; practice medicine specializing in pediatrics Anaheim, 1979—. Fellow Am. Acad. Pediatrics; mem. Los Angeles Pediatric Soc., Orange County Pediatric Soc., Adventist Internat. Med. Soc., Chinese Adventist Physicians' Assn. Office: 1741 W Romneya #D Anaheim CA 92801

LIFKA, MARY LAURANNE, history educator; b. Oak Park, Ill., Oct. 31, 1937; d. Aloysius William and Loretta Catherine (Juric) L. B.A., Mundelein Coll., 1960; M.A., Loyola U., Los Angeles, 1965; Ph.D., U. Mich., 1974; postdoctoral student London U., 1975. Life teaching cert. Prof. history Mundelein Coll., Chgo., 1976-84, coordinator acad. computer, 1983-84, prof. history Coll. St. Teresa, Winona, Minn., 1984-89, Lewis U., Romeoville, Ill., 1989—; chief reader in history Ednl. Testing Service, Princeton, N.J., 1980-84; cons. world history project Longman, Inc., 1983—; cons. in European history Coll. Bd., Evanston, Ill., 1983—; mem. Com. on History in the Classroom. Author: Instructor's Guide to European History, 1983; contbr. articles to publs. Mem. Am. Hist. Assn., Ednl. Testing Service Devel. Com. of History. Democrat. Roman Catholic. Office: Lewis U Rte 53 Romeoville IL 60441

LIGENZA, ANDREA ANGELA, nurse; b. Lansford, Pa., Apr. 7, 1952; d. Stanley Walter and Mary (Porambo) L. Diploma in Nursing, Hosp. of U. Pa., 1973; BS in Nursing, U. Pa., 1976. RN; cert. nurse practitioner, Pa. Staff nurse Hosp. of U. Pa., Phila., 1973-79, nurse practitioner cardiothoracic surgery sect., 1979-88; pvt. practice nurse practitioner, 1988—; preceptor nursing students U. Pa., 1985—; founder, group leader Self Esteem Workshops, 1986—; nurse practitioner Cardiothoracic Surg. Assocs. Pa. Hosp., 1988—. Vol. Gary Hart for Pres. campaign, Phila., 1984. Mem. People for Am. Way, Puccini Inst., Sigma Theta Tau. Democrat. Roman Catholic. Club: Center City Running. Avocations: classical music, tennis, travel, writing poetry. Office: Univ of Pa Hosp 3400 Spruce St Philadelphia PA 19104

LIGGINS, ISABELLE G., union official; b. Charleston, S.C., Sept. 8, 1928; d. George W. and Isabelle (Lucas) German; m. John W. Liggins, Jan. 8, 1955; children: Stacy, John. BS in English, Ft. Valley State U., 1955; MA, U. R.I., 1969; postgrad., U. Md., U. So. Calif. Cert. in preservation law, leadership, guidance and counseling. Tchr. English and reading Sch. Dist. 20, Charleston; dir. edn. Mission of Community Concern Inc., Washington; asst. dir. reading D.C. Pub. Sch. System, Washington; sec.-treas. Local 1422, ILA, Charleston; conducter labor rels. workshop Bur. Nat. Affairs, Washington, 1990—. Recipient Mission Moton Ednl. Opportunity award, Community Svc. award; NDEA grantee. Mem. NAFE, Nat. Trust for Hist. Preservation, Smithsonian Assocs., Daus. of Isis, Alpha Kappa Alpha, Delta Sigma Theta (community svc. award). Address: 153 Queen St Charleston SC 29401

LIGGIO, JEAN VINCENZA, artist, teacher; b. N.Y.C., Nov. 5, 1927; d. Vincenzo and Bernada (Terrusa) Verro; m. John Liggio, June 6, 1948; children: Jean Constance, Joan Bernadette. Student, N.Y. Inst. Photography, 1965, Elizabeth Seton Coll., 1984, Pasons Sch. of Design, 1985. Hairdresser Beatuy Shoppe, N.Y.C., 1947-65; freelance oil colors and portraits N.Y.C., 1958-75; instr. watercolor N.Y. Dept. Pks., Recreation and Conservation, Yonkers, 1985-89, Bronxville (N.Y.) Adult Sch., 1989—; substitute tchr. cosmetology Yonkers Bd. Edn., 1988-89. Recipient numerous awards. Mem. Mt. Vernon Art Assn. (bd. dirs. membership com. 1983—), Mamaroneck Artist's Guild, Hudson River Contemporary Artists, Scarsdale Art Assn. (publicity chmn. 1984-89), New Rochelle (N.Y.) Art Assn., Italian Club. Home and Office: 166 Helena Ave Yonkers NY 10710

LIGHT, MARION JESSEL, retired educator; b. San Antonio, Dec. 5, 1915; d. Marion Jackson and Kate Jessel (Cox) Parr; m. Marion Russell Light, Nov. 8, 1958 (dec. July 1983); children: Russell Jeffers, Paul Love. BA, So. Meth. U., 1936; MA, U. Tex., 1947. Cert. elem. and secondary sch. tchr., Tex. Elem. tchr. Dalls Independent Sch. Dist., 1936-72. Del. to the county conv. Dem. Party, Dallas, 1986; moderator Presbyn. Women, 1st Ch. Dallas, 1989-90. Mem. Dallas Retired Tchrs. Assn. (corr. sec. 1984-90), Dallas Womans Forum (rec. sec. Friday study 1987-89), AAUW (chmn. hobbies and crafts Dallas br. 1970s), Bay View Century Club (corr. sec. 1988-89), Dallas Symphony Orch. League, Delta Kappa Gamma (pres. Delta Sigma chpt. 1956-58, Chpt. Achievement award 1979, Marion Parr Light Recruitment Grant named in her honor Delta Sigma chpt. 1958). Democrat.

LIGHT, PATRICIA KAHN, psychologist; b. Elizabeth, N.J., Mar. 29, 1939; d. Perry M. Kahn and Thelma Kurtz; m. Richard J. Light, June 27, 1965; children: Jennifer Susan, Sarah Elizabeth. AB, Bennington (Vt.) Coll., 1960; EdM, Harvard U., 1966, EdD, 1973. Lic. psychologist, Mass. Tchr. math. Elizabeth pub. schs., 1961-65; counselor Newton (Mass.) High Sch., 1967-68; staff psychologist Powell Assocs., Cambridge, Mass., 1969-74, Harvard Bus. Sch., Boston, 1974-76; dir., chief psychologist Harvard Bus. Sch., 1976—; cons., invited speaker in field. Author: Let the Children Speak, 1975; author casette: Dual Career Families, 1979. Mem. advisory com. Radcliff Coll., 1987-90; parent advisor Buckingham, Browne & Nichols Sch., 1980—. Fellow Mass. Psychol. Assn.; mem. Am. Psychol. Assn., Pi Lambda Theta. Office: Harvard Bus Sch Counseling Service Boston MA 02163

LIGHTFEATHER, MELODY, artist, educator; b. Nov. 18, 1951; d. G.P. II and Janet Josephine Wiston (Ferst) Velasco; children: Virginia, Loralea. BA, Glenville (W.Va.) State Coll., 1978; MA, Glenville U., 1981. Tchr. pub. schs. and Indian schs., N.Mex., Ariz., Conn., W.Va.; owner Am. Indian Mktg. Svcs., Albuquerque, Lightfeather Prodns. Inc., Albuquerque; lectr. Native Am. arts and crafts; mem. Nat. Minority Supplier Devel. Coun. Recipient Gold medal Internat. Le Salon Competition of Art of Nations, 1984, Nat. Thorpe Meml. Competition of Arts, 1984, Internat. Congress on Arts and Scis., 1988; Nepenthe Munde Internat. Arts Competition award, 1987; named Poster Artist of Yr., Am. Cancer Soc., 1985. Mem. Nat. Found. in Arts, Native Am. Arts Found. (chair), N.Mex. Indian Bus. Assn., N.Mex. Watercolor Soc. Address: 2412 Venetian Way SW Albuquerque NM 87105

LIGHTFOOT, JAN LINDA, artist, photographer; b. Middletown, Conn., Dec. 3, 1949; d. Francis St. Martin and Isabella Carta-Fairfield Me. AS, U. Maine at Orono, 1977. Freelance artist, photographer Maine, 1978-83; bd. coordinator Hospitality House Inc., Fairfield, Maine, 1982—; program coordinator Hospitality House Inc., Hickley, Maine, 1986—; speaker in field. Impressionistic artist; photographer wildlife. Office: Hospitality House Inc PO Box 62 Hinckley ME 04944

LIGHTFOOT, TEDDI, music school director, composer, singer; b. Poteau, Okla., Apr. 29, 1946; d. Charles Fredrick and Frances Mary (Stucin) Zirbel; m. Jon Charles Lightfoot, Feb. 5, 1970 (div. June 1978). MusB, San Francisco State Coll., 1968, MA, 1972; postgrad., Conservatorio, Florence, Italy, 1968-69. Designer mfg. Lightfoot Fyne Leather Clothing, San Francisco, 1970—; supr. Police Fire Communications, South San Francisco, Calif., 1977-85; dir., tchr. Yamaha Music Sch., South San Francisco, 1986—; owner, dir. Yamaha Music Sch., San Francisco, 1989—; choral dir. Bayside Middle Sch., San Mateo, Calif., 1985-86; coach voice and composition Lightfoot Studio, South San Francisco, 1984—; actress in commercials and TV, San Francisco, 1978—, Italy, 1968-69; dir. Razzle Dazzle Kids Performance Troupe, South San Francisco, 1985—; creative/mus. cons. schs. and orgns., Bay ARea, Calif., 1984—. Composer, arranger shows, original works, prodns., San Francisco, 1978—; composer, singer: Let Me Sing, 1989; music dir. (rock opera) Love's Destiny, 1990. Dir. Barbara Neal Prodns., San Francisco, 1987; lay minister Unity Christ Ch., San Francisco, 1988—, choir dir., 1985—. Named State Grand Champion, Calif. State Talent Assn., 1986, 87, 88, 89, 90. Mem. Music Tchrs. Assn. Calif., No. Calif. Songwriters Assn., Theatre Bay Area, Internat. New Thought Music Alliance Com., Nat. Assn. Singing Tchrs., Nat. Assn. Unity Chs. (contemporary music com.). Democrat. Office: Lightfoot Studio 574 Commercial Ave South San Francisco CA 94080

LIGHTNER, CANDY LYNNE, advocate, consultant, author; b. Pasadena, Calif., May 30, 1946; d. Dykes Charles and Katherine (Karrib) Doddridge; children: Serena, Travis. Student pub. schs., Fairfield, Calif.; hon. D.Humanities, St. Francis Coll., Johnstown, Pa., 1984; D in Pub. Service (hon.), Kutztown U., Johnstown, Pa., 1987; HHD (hon.), Marymount Coll., Johnstown, Pa., 1987. Dental asst., various pvt. offices, 1964-70; real estate salesperson Calif., 1972-80; founder, pres., chmn. bd. Mothers Against Drunk Driving, Hurst, Tex., 1980-85; cons. Mothers Against Drunk Driving, Arlington, Tex., 1985-87. Contbr. articles to profl. jours. Mem. Sacramento County Task Force on Drunk Driving, Presdl. Commn. on Drunk and Drugged Driving; bd. dirs. Nat. Commn. on Drunk Driving, 1984—, Nat. Partnership for Drug Free Use, Nat. Hwy. Safety Adv. Com., Love is Feeding Everyone (LIFE), 1988—, Found. Mideast Communication, 1988, others. Named to Good Housekeeping's Most Admired Woman's Poll, 1986; ranked in top 25 of Am. Most Influential Women World Almanac and Book of Facts, 1986; recipient Pres.'s Vol. Action award, 1983, Jefferson award Am. Inst. Pub. Service, 1983, Testimonial award Civitan Internat., 1984, Epilespy Found. award, 1984, Woman of Year award Mortar Bd. Soc., Baylor U., 1985, Anti-discrimination award Am. Anti-discrimination Com., 1985, YWCA Woman of Year award, 1986, Commonwealth award U. Del., 1986, Black and Blue award Thomas Jefferson U. Hosp. Emergency Medicine Soc., Human Dignity award Kessler Inst. for Rehab., Woman of Distinction award Third Nat. Congress Coll. Women Student Leaders and Woman of Achievement, 1987, Disting. Leadership award World Congress of Victimology, 1987, Living Legacy award Women's Internat. Ctr., 1988, Friends of Children award Assn. Childhood Edn. Internat., 1988; selected by Johns Hopkins U. to participate in Anglo-Am. Successor Generation program, 1985; honored as one of Seven Who Succeeded, Time Mag., 1985; honored by Esquire mag. as mem. Am.'s New Leadership Class, 1985, others. Office: 22653 Pacific Coast Hwy Ste 1-289 Malibu CA 90265

LIGHTNER, RUTH H., transportation executive; b. N.Y.C., Mar. 9, 1940; d. William Weir and Ruth May (Hayes) McLoughlin; m. John N. Lightner; children: Ruth Marie, Kelly Rachael. Grad. high sch. With NYPA Sand & Gravel, Buffalo, 1964-69, Idamont Ind., Lolo, Mont., 1969-71, Amoco Oil, Missoula, Mont., 1971-74; owner Lightner Brokerage, Missoula, 1974-84; ops. mgr. Bronco Trucking, Downey, Calif., 1984-85; term mgr. Federal Transport, Chino, Calif., 1986—. Mem. Women's Traffic Club of L.A., L.A. Transp. Club, Am. Businesswomen (pres. 1980-82), Delta Nu Alpha. Office: Fed Transport Box 1658 Chino CA 91708

LIGHTWOOD, CAROL WILSON, writer; b. Tacoma, Wash., Oct. 2, 1941; d. Harry Edward and Cora H. Wilson; m. Keith G. Lightwood (div. Dec. 1968; children: Miles Francis, Clive Harry. BA, Smith Coll., 1963. Writer various advt. agencies, 1968-82; v.p. Wakeman & DeForrest, Newport Beach, Calif., 1985-86; owner Lightwood & Ptnrs., Long Beach, Calif., 1986—. Author: Malibu, 1984; contbr. articles to profl. jours. Chair mus. coun. Long Beach Mus. Art, 1989. Mem. Sierra Club, Sisters in Crime. Episcopalian.

LIGLER, FRANCES SMITH, biochemist; b. Louisville, June 11, 1951; d. George Frederick and Mary Frances (Hagan) Smith; m. George Todd Ligler, Aug. 19, 1972; children: Amy Elizabeth, Adam George. BS, Furman U., Greenville, S.C., 1972; PhD, Oxford (Eng.) U., 1977. Postdoctoral fellow U. Tex. Health Sci. Ctr., San Antonio, 1975-76; instr., asst. instr. Southwestern Med. Sch., Dallas, 1976-80; group leader cellular immunology DuPont, Glenolden, Pa., 1980-85; supervisory chemist Naval Rsch. Lab., Washington, 1985—; cons. Potomac (Md.) Biotech, 1985—. Contbr. articles to profl. jours. Recipient Alan Berman Rsch. Publ. award, 1988, Manuscript award 3M/Am. Assn. Med. Instrumentation Ann. Meeting, 1988, Chemistry Div. award Superior Tech. Publ., 1989. Mem. Am. Assn. Immunologists, Am. Assn. Pathologists, Am. Chem. Soc., Chem. Soc. Washington (bd. dirs. 1988—), FASEB Internat. Interest Group in Biorecognition Tech., Dept. of Def. Tech. Working Group, Dept. of State Tech. Task Group L. Office: Naval Rsch Lab Code 6090 Washington DC 20375-5000

LIGNELLI, ELENA MARIA, loan officer; b. Phila., Jan. 1, 1958; d. George Francis and Amelia (Forgione) L. BA in Communications cumn laude, Temple U., 1979. Urban homesteading coord. City-wide Devel. Corp., Dayton, Ohio, 1980-82; loan adminstrv. asst. Tex. Investment Bank, Houston, 1982-85, Allied Bank, Houston, 1985-87; personal bank promotion officer First Interstate Bank of Tex., Houston, 1987-88; exec. asst. Century Nat. Bank, Washington, 1988-89, loan officer, 1989—. Editor, author newspaper articles. Vol. Multiple Sclerosis Soc. (Movers and Shakers) D.C. chpt., 1990. Recipient Community Recognition award Dayton (Ohio) Area Women Realtors, 1981. Mem. NAFE, Robert Morris Assocs. (assoc.). Republican. Roman Catholic. Home: 4311A Ramona Dr Fairfax VA 22030 Office: Century Nat Bank 1875 Eye St N W Washington DC 20006

LIGON, PATTI-LOU ELSIE, real estate investor, educator; b. Riverside, Calif., Feb. 28, 1953; d. Munford Ernest and Patsy Hazel (Bynum) L. BS, San Diego State U., 1976; BBA, Nat. U., San Diego, 1983, MA in Bus. Adminstrn., 1984; Clear Profl. Credential, Nat. U., 1986. Cert. profl. counselor. Escrow asst. Cajon Valley Escrow, El Cajon, Calif., 1978-79; escrow asst. Summit Escrow, San Diego, 1979-81; escrow officer Fidelity Nat. Title, San Diego, 1982-84, Dawson Escrow, San Diego, 1984; owner, property mgr., investment adviser Ligon Enterprises., San Diego, 1980—, cons., 1982—. Chmn. com., alumnae and assocs. San Diego State U., 1983, 84, 85; com. chmn. San Diego Zool. soc., 1985; pres. Friends of Symphony, Riverside, Calif., 1978. Recipient commendation City and County of Honolulu, 1981. Mem. Nat. Notary Assn., Calif. Escrow Assn., Am. Home Econs. Assn., Nat. Assn. Female Execs, Internat. Platform Assn., Calif. Bus. Edn. Assn., Jr. League of San Diego, Sigma Kappa (pres. 1974, v.p. sorority corp. 1976—). Republican. Methodist. Club: Spinster (pres. 1981), Univ. (San Diego). Avocations: racquetball; clothing design; photography; travel. Home: 7937 Wetherly St La Mesa CA 92041 Office: Ligon Enterprises 4545 Collwood Blvd San Diego CA 92115

LIKINS, JEANNE MARIE, educational administrator; b. Atlanta, Apr. 8, 1953; d. William Henry and Martha Ann (Grant) L.; m. Joseph Flood, May 19, 1984. BA, Baldwin-Wallace Coll., Berea, Ohio, 1975; MA in Edn., George Washington U., 1978; PhD, Am. U., 1981; student, U. Western Australia, Perth, 1976. Asst. to dean of students Am. U., Washington, 1977-79, asst. dean of students, 1979-82, dir. student services, 1982-84; ednl. cons. Columbus, 1984-86; dir. commuter student affairs Ohio State U., Columbus, 1986—, interium dir. student orgns., activities, 1988-89, dir. student life svcs., 1990—. Author: A Stepping Stone: The History of Anne Arundel Community College, 1982; contbr. articles to profl. jours. Bd. dirs. German Village Found., Columbus, 1986-89, pres. 1988-89; trustee The Fraternity and Sorority Found., Columbus, 1987—, sec., 1989-90; project coordinator Heritage America: The First Nat. Symposium of Historic Communities, 1985-86. Rotary fellow, 1976. Mem. Am. Coll. Personnel Assn. (v.p. commns. 1990-92, chmn. conf. 1987-88, Outstanding Service award 1986, vice-pres. elect for commns. 1988-90), Am. Assn. Counseling and Devel., D.C. Coll. Personnel Assn. (founding mem.), Ohio Coll. Personnel Assn. Democrat.

LILAGAN-SCHAEDEL, MARIA NIEVES, educator, consultant, school counselor; came to U.S., 1967; d. Ignacio Rodrigo and Ester (Bumanlag) Lilagan; children: Rena M. Heinrich, Aaron J. Heinrich; m. William John Schaedel, Apr. 4, 1985. BS in Edn., Santa Isabel Coll., Manila, 1964, BA, 1965; MA in Teaching, Bilingual/Multicultural Edn., Alaska Pacific U., 1984; MEd in Counseling and Guidance, U. Alaska, Anchorage, 1990. Cert. tchr., Alaska. Scriptwriter G. Miranda & Sons Pub. Co., Manila, 1961-62; instr., tchr. Santa Isabel Coll., 1964-66; tng. instr. Cen. Tng. Inst. U.S. Army, Saigon, Vietnam, 1966-67; tchr. St. Mary's High Sch., Salem, S.D., 1967-69; math tchr. T.B. Livaudais Mid. Sch., Gretna, La., 1969-70, St. Joseph's Indian Sch., Chamberlain, S.D., 1970-71; math lab. tchr. Anchorage Sch. Dist., 1971-72, bilingual tutor, 1977-79, bilingual resource tchr., 1979-81, multicultural tchr. expert, ESL/bilingual resource tchr., 1982-85, math tchr., 1985-86; sr. program specialist N.W. Regional Ednl. Lab., Anchorage, 1987—; ind. cons. bilingual/multicultural edn. Anchorage, 1988—; mem. multicultural edn. program adv. com. Anchorage Sch. Dist., 1982—. Mem. St. Elizabeth A. Seton Sch. Bd., Anchorage, 1981-82; v.p. Filipino Community of Anchorage, Inc., 1986—. NSF grantee, 1968, 71. Roman Catholic. Office: 3211 Montpelier Ct Anchorage AK 99593-4635

LILEIKA, LAIMA T., accountant; b. Munich, Germany, Jan. 8, 1947; came to U.S., 1948; d. Peter and Eugenia (Gelazius) Minkunas; m. Alfonse George Lileika, Nov. 18, 1967; children: Andrew, Alex. BA, CUNY, 1967. Enrolled agent with IRS. Assoc. acct. Vebeliunas Tax Counselor, Richmond Hill, N.Y., 1972-80; ptnr. Vebeliunas-Lileika Accts., Richmond Hill, 1980—; treas. Kasa-Lithuanian Fed. Credit Unioin, Richmond Hill, 1980-84, gen. mgr., 1984-86. Mem. Nat. Soc. Pub. Accts., Nat. Assn. Enrolled Agents. Home: 16 Factory Pond Rd Lattingtown NY 11560 Office: Vebeliunas-Lileika 8601 114th St Richmond Hill NY 11418

LILJESTRAND, KATHRYN EILEEN, marketing professional; b. Chgo., Sept. 27, 1956; d. Henry A. McCormack and Kathryn Barry Dobbs; m. Bengt Anders Liljestrand, Sept. 13, 1980; children: Kristin Eileen, Kaitlin Elizabeth. BA, Siena Coll., Loudonville, N.Y., 1979; student, J. Hagen Sch. Bus., New Rochelle, N.Y., 1979-82. Ops. mgr. Motif Designs, Inc., New Rochelle, 1979-82; sales rep. U.S. Surg. Corp., Norwalk, Conn., 1982-84; product mgr. U.S. Surgical Corp., Norwalk, Conn., 1984-85; internat. market specialist mgr. Med. Device Div. Davis and Geck Internat., Wayne, N.J., 1985-89; critical care mktg. mgr. Datascope Corp., Montvale, N.J., 1989-90; product mgr. Becton Dickinson Vacutainer Systems, Rutherford, N.J., 1990—. Mem. Am. Mktg. Assn., Nat. Assn. Working Women, Nat. Assn. Female Execs. Democrat. Roman Catholic. Home: 39 Sagamore Trail Sparta NJ 07871 Office: 1 Stanley St Rutherford NJ 07070

LILLEY, MILI DELLA, entertainment management consultant, insurance company executive; b. Valley Forge, Pa., Aug. 29; d. Leon Hanover and Della Beaver (Jones) L. MBA, Tex. Christian U., 1957, PhD, 1959. Various positions G & G Cons. Inc., Ft. Lauderdale, Fla., 1971-75; v.p. AMEX, Inc., Beverly Hills, Calif. and Acapulco, Mex., 1976-80; pres. The Hanover Group, Ft. Lauderdale, 1981—, mgr. entertainers Ink Spots, Del-Vikings, Moonglows, and Mario Kinsey; dist. agt. Farmers & Traders Life Ins. Co. and other leading cos.; officer, bd. dirs. Arline's World of Travel, Tamarac, Fla.; dist. agt. Farmers & Traders Life Ins. Co. and other leading companies. Named to All Stars Honor Roll Nat. Ins. Sales Mag., 1989. Mem. Fla. Assn. Theatrical Agents, Fla. Guild of Talent Agts., Mgrs., Producers and Orchestras. Office: The Hanover Group 1001 W Cypress Creek Rd Ste 314 Fort Lauderdale FL 33309 also: 3 Sloane Gardens Club, Sloane Sq, London SWI England

LILLIE, CHARISSE RANIELLE, lawyer, educator; b. Houston, Apr. 7, 1952; d. Richard Lysander and Vernell Audrey (Watson) L.; m. Thomas L. McGill, Jr., Dec. 4, 1982. B.A. cum laude, Conn. Wesleyan U., 1973; J.D., Temple U., 1976; LL.M., Yale U., 1982. Bar: Pa. 1976, U.S. Dist. Ct. (ea. dist.) Pa. 1977, U.S. Ct. Appeals (3d cir.) 1980. Law clk. U.S. Dist. Ct. (ea. dist.) Pa., Phila., 1976-78; trial atty., honors program, civil rights div. Dept. Justice, Washington, 1978-80; dep. dir. Community Legal Services, Phila., 1980-81; asst. prof. law Villanova U. Law Sch., Pa., 1982-83, assoc. prof., 1983-84, prof., 1984-85; asst. U.S. atty. U.S. Dist. Ct. (ea. dist.) Pa., 1985-88; gen. counsel Redevel. Authority City of Phila., 1988-90; city solicitor Law Dept. City of Phila., 1990—; mem. 3d Cir. Lawyers Adv. Com., 1982-85, legal counsel Pa. Coalition of 100 Black Women, Phila., 1983—; bd. dirs. Juvenile Law Center, Phila., 1982—; trustee Women's Law Project, Phila., 1984—; mem. Mayor's Commn. on May 13 MOVE Incident, 1985—. Bd. dirs. Women's Way, Phila. Davenport fellow, 1973; Yale Law Sch. fellow, 1981. Mem. ABA, Nat. Bar Assn., Fed. Bar Assn. (1st v.p. Phila. chpt. 1982-84, pres. Phila. chpt.1984-86), Nat. Conf. Black Lawyers (pres. 1976-78, Outstanding Service award 1978), Phila. Bar Assn., Hist. Soc. U.S. Dist. Ct. (ea. dist.) Pa. (dir. 1983—). Home: 6748 Emlen St Philadelphia PA 19119 Office: City Solicitor's Office 1520 Mcpl Svcs Bldg Philadelphia PA 19102

LILLY, ELIZABETH GILES, mobile park executive; b. Bozeman, Mont., Aug. 5, 1916; d. Samuel John and Luella Elizabeth (Reed) Abegg; m. William Lilly, July 1, 1976; children: Samuel Colborn Giles, Elizabeth Giles. RN, Good Samaritan Hosp., Portland, Oreg., 1941; student, Walla Walla Coll., Lewis and Clark Coll. Bus., Portland. ARC nurse area high schs., Portland; with Welton Studio Interior Design, Portland; in pub. rels. Chas. Eckelman, Portland; owner, builder Mobile Park Plaza, Inc., Portland. Recipient Svc. award Multnomah County Commrs., 1984. Mem. Soroptimist Internat. (local bd. dirs.), Rep. Women's Club (pres.), C. of C., World Affairs Coun., Toastmistress (pres.) Oreg. Logging Assn. (bd. dirs.). Address: 19825 SE Stark Portland OR 97233

LILLY, LESLIE BJERG, realtor, sales executive; b. San Antonio, Jan. 29, 1953; d. John Cunningham and Elisabeth Christine (Bjerg) Lilly; m. David Hart Wollins, Apr. 1, 1989. BA in Polit. Sci., Columbia U., 1982; MBA, U. Miami, Coral Gables, Fla., 1990. High fashion model Mannequin Fashion Models, N.Y.C., 1976-82; high fashion model Glamour Models, Paris, 1976-82, Cosa Nostra, Milan, 1976-82; real estate asst. Zimmer, Fishback & Hertan, N.Y.C., 1983; sr. real estate asst. Skadden Arps, N.Y.C., 1983-86, Steel, Hector & Davis, Miami, Fla., 1986-88; realtor Coldwell Banker, Miami, 1988—; v.p. Marine Rsch. & Devel., Miami, Westportls, Maine, 1986—; Skadden Arps, Westport, Maine, 1986—. Officer, bd. dirs. Coconut Grove (Fla.) Civic Club, 1988-90; active Land Trust of Dade County Com., Miami, 1990; bd. dirs. South Grove Homeowners Assn., Coconut Grove, 1989. Republican. Home: La Solana LaSolana 3670 Hibiscus St Coconut Grove FL 33133 Office: Coldwell Banker 2960 Oak Ave Miami FL 33133

LIM, TERRY, law firm administrator; b. Houston, June 21, 1959; d. Harry H. and Molly (Lo) L. Student, U. St. Thomas, Houston, 1977; BBA, U. Houston, 1981. CPA. Staff acct. G.J. Schafer, CPA, Houston, 1976-82; staff acct. Price Waterhouse, Houston, 1982-84, sr. acct., 1984-85; sr. acct. Sonat Offshore Drilling, Inc., Houston; CPA Terry L. Phillips, Houston, 1985-87; law firm administrator Caddell & Conwell, 1987–. Mem. Am. Inst. of CPA's, Tex. Soc. of CPA's, Houston Chpt. of TSCPA, Assn. of Legal Adminstras. Phi Mu Fratnerity. Republican. Roman Catholic. Home: 15 Greenway Pla E #6A Houston TX 77046

LIMKEMANN, MARGARET ALICE, music director; b. Cleve., July 1, 1941; d. Ralph Eugene and Alice (Rosenjack) Poulson; m. William O. Limkemann, June 22, 1963; children: Susan Margaret, Brian William. MusB, Coll. Wooster (Ohio), 1963. Dir. music Trinity Luth. Ch., Canton, Ohio, 1961-64; organist 1st Presbyn. Ch., Mansfield, Ohio, 1969-71; organist, dir. music Lakewood (Ohio) Presbyn. Ch., 1971—. Recipient Outstanding Tchr. of Organ award Michelson-Morley Centennial Celebration Competition, 1988. Mem. Am. Guild Organists (dean bd. dirs. 1984-86, chmn. edn. and exams 1985-87, co-chmn. region convention 1987—), Hymn Soc. Am., Presbyn. Assn. Musicians, Three Arts Club Lakewood (chmn. scholarship com. 1984-87). Home: 589 Debbington Dr Bay Village OH 44140 Office: Lakewood Presbyn Ch 14502 Detroit Lakewood OH 44107

LIMMROTH, KARIN LEIGH, graphic designer, consultant; b. New Orleans, Oct. 4, 1949; d. Weldon Eugene and Cora Elizabeth (Graby)

L. BA, So. Meth. U., 1968; BFA, Sch. Visual Arts, N.Y.C., 1970. Designer RCA Records, N.Y.C., 1970-73, Fantasy Records & Filmworks, Berkeley, Calif., 1975-76; designer, assoc. art dir. Essence mag., N.Y.C., 1973-75; design cons. U.S. Olympic Com., Boulder, Colo., 1978-79; asst. art dir., set designer CBS TV, L.A., 1979-81; art dir. CBS Entertainment, N.Y.C. and L.A., 1981-83; art dir., design cons. various advt. agys., N.Y.C. and L.A., 1983-87; assoc. creative dir. E&J Gallo Winery, Modesto, Calif., 1987-89; design cons., ptnr. Image, N.Y.C. and Paris, 1989—; design cons. San Francisco Opera, 1975-76, Internat. Olympic Com., Barcelona, Spain, 1989—. Fundraiser Martha Graham Dance Co., N.Y.C., 1985, Amnesty Internat., Paris, 1989. Recipient award N.Y. Art Dirs. Club, 1977-78. Mem. NARAS (bd. govs. 1976-78, Grammy nomination 1973), Am. Film Inst. (art direction fellow 1976, 77), Am. Inst. Graphics Arts. Office: Image, 5 Rue du Foin, 75003 Paris France

LIMONCELLI, BARBARA MARIE, nurse; b. N.Y.C., Aug. 24, 1936; d. Francis Joseph and Flora Gertrude (Weber) Springer; m. Frank Michael, Sept. 12, 1959; children: Susan, Carole, Barbara, Frank M. Jr. Student, Bklyn. Coll., 1954-57; Assoc. degree, Middlesex Communtiy Coll., Mass., 1982. RN, Mass. Staff nurse N.E. Meml. Hosp., Stoneham, Mass., 1982-83; staff nurse, nursing supr. North End Community Nursing Home, Boston, 1983-90; community health nurse Mystic Valley Elder Svcs., Malden, Mass., 1990—. Roman Catholic. Office: Mystic Valley Elder Svcs Main St Malden MA 02148-9804

LIN, ALICE LEE LAN, physicist, researcher, educator; b. Shanghai, China, Oct. 28, 1937; came to U.S., 1960, naturalized, 1974; d. Yee and Tsing Tsing (Wang) L.; m. A. Marcus, Dec. 19, 1962 (div. Feb. 1972); 1 child, Peter A. Lin-Marcus. AB in Physics, U. Calif., Berkeley, 1963; MA in Physics, George Washington U., 1974. Statis. asst. dept. math. U. Calif., Berkeley, 1962-63; rsch. asst. in radiation damage Cavendish Lab. Cambridge (Eng.) U., 1965-66; info. analysis specialist Nat. Acad. Scis., Washington, 1970-71; teaching fellow, rsch. asst. George Washington U., Catholic U. Am., Washington, 1971-75; physicist NASA/Goddard Space Flight Ctr., Greenbelt, Md., 1975-80, Army Materials Tech. Lab., Watertown, Mass., 1980—. Contbr. articles to profl. jours. Mencius Ednl. Found. grantee, 1959-60. Mem. AAAS, N.Y. Acad. Scis., Am. Phys. Soc., Am. Ceramics Soc., Am. Acoustical Soc., Am. Men and Women of Sci., Optical Soc. Am. Democrat. Home: 28 Hallett Hill Rd Weston MA 02193 Office: Army Materials Tech Lab Mail Stop MRS Bldg 39 Watertown MA 02172

LIN, MAYA, architect; b. Athens, Ohio, Oct. 5, 1959; d. Henry H. and Julia (Chang) L. BA, Yale U., 1981, MArgr., 1986, PhD in Fine Arts, 1987. Architectural designer Peter Forbes & Assocs., N.Y.C., 1986-87; pvt. practice N.Y.C., 1987—; mem. Batey & Mack, San Francisco, 1983, Fumihiko Maki Assoc., Tokyo, 1985. Prin. work include Vietnam Veterans Meml., Washington, 1981, Civil Rights Meml., Montgomery, Ala., 1986.

LINCOLN, YVONNA SESSIONS, education educator; b. Tampa, FL, May 25, 1944; d. Edgar Eugene Sr. and Mary Bond (Brown) Sessions; m. Clark E. Lincoln, May 6, 1971 (div. 1977); m. Egon G. Guba, Aug. 7, 1980. BA, Mich. State U., 1967; AM, U. Ill., 1970; EdD, Ind U., 1977. Resident Hall Coord. Ind. U., Bloomington, Ind., 1971-73; research asst. Ind. U., Bloomington, 1973-77; asst. to the v.p. Ind. U., Bloomington, 1976-77; asst. prof. U. Kans., Lawrence, Kans., 1981-86; assoc. prof. Vanderbilt U., Nashville, 1986—. Author (with others): book, Effective Evaluation, 1981, Naturalistic Inquiry, 1985, Fourth Generation Evaluation, 1989; editor: book, Orgn. Theory & Inquiry, 1985. Mem. Am. Evaluation Assn. (pres. 1989-90, Lazarsfeld prize 1987), Assn. for Study Higher Edn. (exec. bd. 1987-90), Am. Ednl. Rsch. Assn. (nat. program chmn. div. J 1988-89). Democrat. Office: Vanderbilt U Box 514 Peabody Coll Nashville TN 37203

LIND, DEBORAH STOEPPELWERTH, interior designer; b. St. Louis, Feb. 28, 1943; d. Russel William and Betty Jayne (Owen) Stoeppelwerth; m. Richard Conner Lind, Feb. 1, 1964; children: Dana Christine, Derek Justin. BA, UCLA, 1965. Interior designer Tarzana Falls Devel., 1986-87, Darien for E & K Assocs., Tarzana, Calif., 1986-89, White Oak Ranch Estates Devel., 1988-89; prin., interior designer Lind Interiors, Woodland Hills, Calif., 1974-86, 89—; cons. Calif. Contractors, Chatsworth, Saddletree Devel., Calabasas, Calif., 1988-89, M. Fagan-Homeward Devel., Studio City, Calif., 1988-89, San Marino (Calif.) Residence for M/M Korompis of Jakarta, Indonesia. Mem. Am. Soc. Interior Design (profl.), Nat. Kitchen and Bath Assn., Bldg. Industry Assn. Home and Office: Lind Interiors 20929-47 Ventura Blvd Ste 201 Woodland Hills CA 91364

LIND, KENDRA JOHNSON, materials and safety executive; b. Whitefish, Mont., Nov. 3, 1947; d. Harold Norman and Laura Beryl (Schooley) Johnson; m. L. Harold Lind, July 3, 1976; 1 child, Toni Lynn Carnahan. BS, No. Mont. Coll., 1972; postgrad., Flathead Valley Community Coll., 1984—. Instr. sci. Powell County High Sch., Deer Lodge, Mont., 1972-74; with ins. sales N.Am. Life & Casualty, Billings, Mont., 1975; dir. pub. rels. Mid Yellowstone Areawide Planning Orgn., Billings, Mont., 1976; mill maintenance clk. W.R. Grace & Co., Libby, Mont., 1976-80, warehouse clk., 1981, warehouse supr., 1982-89, safety dir., warehouse supr., 1989—; mem. adv. com. Kellogg Found.for Lincoln County Intermountain Communication, Learning & Info. System, 1988—; bd. dirs. Zonolite Employees Credit Union, sec. 1978—. Editor-producer: MYAPO Newsletter, 1976, Grace Safety Newsletter, 1977-81; author-illustrator: Field Guide to Alpine & Subalpine Flora of the Deer Lodge Valley, 1973; author: Coloring Book Guide to Endangered Species, 1973. Campaign coord. L.H. Lind for Nat. Jr. Commdr. in chief VFW, 1985-88; vice-chmn. Lincoln County Crimestoppers, bd. dirs. 1989—; mem. Wyo. Safety Coun., Evergreen Safety Coun. Mem. VFW Aux. (#7311 dist. 3 chmn. bicentennial celebration 1975-76, convention credentials com. 1976, encampment planning com. 1988, coord. nat. campaign), DAV Aux. (#21 life, adj.-treas. 1984—), Mont. Mining Assn. (sec., treas. Lincoln County chpt. 1983-85), Sigma Tau Sigma, Order Ea. Star (worthy matron Libby chpt. 1986-87, treas. 1988—, unit 1 chmn. ESTARL 1987-88, grand teller 1988-89), Women of the Moose (Libby chpt.). Republican. Home: PO Box 1317 Libby MT 59923 Office: WR Grace & Co PO Box 609 Libby MT 59923

LINDAMAN, LOIS JANE, social worker; b. Phila., Dec. 11, 1940; d. Raymond Howard and Anna Mae (O'Neill) Peltz; m. Arnold David Lindaman, Oct. 5, 1963; children: Kevin, David, Matthew, Brian. BS, Iowa State U., 1961, MS, 1972. Cert. permanent profl., Iowa, Mo. Tchr. Johnston (Iowa) High Sch., 1961-63, Bettendorf (Iowa) High Sch., 1963-65, Rock Port (Mo.) Jr. High Sch., 1969-70; med. social worker Story County Hosp., Nevada, Iowa, 1975-76, St. Luke's Hosp., Davenport, Iowa, 1977-80, Davenport Good Samaritan Ctr., 1982-88, Mercy Hosp., Davenport, 1988-89; social work cons. Ridgecrest Retirement Ctr., Davenport, 1980-82, Davenport Luth. Home, 1980-82; med. social worker St. Francis Hosp., Maryville, Mo., 1990—; bd. dirs. Nodaway County Theater Co. Sec., v.p., pres. Countryside Community Theatre, Eldridge, Iowa, 1984-89; mem. Dependent Adult Abuse Task Force, Davenport, 1988-89, Coordinating Com. for Case Mgmt. Pilot Project, Davenport, 1988-89.

LINDAMOOD, JUDY BETH, education educator; b. Champaign, Ill., Sept. 26, 1948; d. Noland Leroy and Beda Alta (Basinger) VanDemark; m. Robert Lee. BS, Ohio State U., 1969, MS, 1977; postgrad., U. Md., 1978, Tchrs. Coll., Columbia, 1989—. Tchr. Maple Grove Preschool, Columbus, Ohio, 1969-72; adminstr. Creative Play Ctr., Worthington, Ohio, 1972-77, Silver Spring (Md.) Child Care, 1977-78, Day Care Lic., State of Ohio, Columbus, 1978-81; v.p. Familiae Inc., Columbus, 1981-84; coord. dept. Early Childhood N.Mex. Jr. Coll., Hobbs, N.Mex., 1984-87; faculty coord. Early Childhood Bunker Hill Community Coll., Boston, 1987—; various consulting jobs. Contbr. articles to profl. jours. Mem. Nat. Assn. Edn. Young Children, Assn. Childhood Edn. Internat., New. Recipient Vocat. Ednl. Grants, 1984-89. Office: Bunker Hill Community Coll New Rutherford Ave Boston MA 02129

LINDAUER, LOIS LYONS, weight control company executive; b. N.Y.C., Feb. 6, 1933; d. Ken and Rose (Schneidman) Lyons; A.B., Brandeis U., 1953; m. William Seltz, Nov. 12, 1972; children by previous marriage—Karen Lyons, Amy Hope. Copywriter, Herbert Frank Advt. Agy., Boston, 1956-57; pres. Paisley workshop, handmade plaques and wall decor, N.Y.C., 1962-65; nat. dir. Diet Workshop, Inc., Boston, diet cons. Jana Brands, Inc., Chalet Products, Inc., The Astor Group, Inc., STOKELY, USA, Cumberland Packing, Ladies Home Jour. Author: It's In to Be Thin, 1971; The Diet Workshop Restaurant Manual, 1972; The Fast and Easy Teenage Diet, 1973; The Success Diet, 1978, The Wild Weekend Diet, 1982. Home: One Longfellow Pl Boston MA 02114 Office: Ten Brookline Pl W Brookline MA 02146

LINDBERG, GAIL BOWMAN, hospital official; b. Ruleville, Miss., Aug. 12, 1959; d. Lloyd and Joy (Alexander) Bowman; m. William Allen Lindberg II, May 11, 1985. BS, Miss. U. for Women, 1981; postgrad., Dallas Bapt. U. Mem. office staff McGehee (Ark.)-Desha County Hosp., 1981-83; bus. office mgr. Ennis (Tex.) Community Hosp., 1983-85; dir. bus. svcs. Charlton Meth. Hosp., Dallas, 1985-89, Zale Lipshy Univ. Hosp., Dallas, 1989—. Mem. Am. Guild Patient Accounts Mgrs., Healthcare Fin. Mgmt. Assn., North Tex. Hosp. Admitting Mgrs. Office: Zale Lipshy Univ Hosp 5151 Harry Hines Blvd Dallas TX 75235

LINDBOM, DIXIE DARLENE, shop owner; b. Unionville, Mo., May 7, 1939; d. Emmett and Zelta Irene (Rex) Norton; m. Kenneth Eugene Valentine, Feb. 7, 1956 (div. 1965); children: Gregory, Kenneth Eugene, Joan Annette; m. Jerry Frederick Lindbom, Mar. 11, 1966. Grad. high sch., Bettendorf, Iowa, 1958. Bookkeeper Johnson Mfg. Co., Princeton, Iowa, 1968-76; office mgr. Davenport Country Club, Pleasant Valley, Iowa, 1976-79; owner, mgr. Horse 'n' Halter, Princeton, 1974-77, Darlene's Collectibles, Paris, Tenn., 1986—; bd. dir. for corp. Mem. Downtown Bus. Assn., Paris C. of C. Office: Darlenes Collectibles 102 N Market St Paris TN 39242

LINDE, LUCILLE MAE (JACOBSON), motor-perceptual therapist; b. Greeley, Colo., May 5, 1919; d. John Alfred and Anna Julia (Anderson) Jacobson; m. Ernest Emil Linde, July 5, 1946 (wid. Jan. 1959). BA, U. No. Colo., 1941, MA, 1947, EdD, 1974. Cert. tchr. Calif., Colo., Iowa, N.Y.; cert. ednl. psychologist; guidance counselor. Dean of women, dir. residence C.W. Post Coll. of L.I. Univ., 1965-66; asst. dean of students SUNY, Farmingdale, 1966-67; counselor, tchr. West High Sch., Davenport, Iowa, 1967-68; instr. grad. tchrs. and counselors, univ. counselor, rsch. Nor. Ariz. U., Flagstaff, 1968-69; vocat. edn. and counseling coord. Fed. Exemplary Project, Council Bluffs, Iowa, 1970-71; sch. psychologist, counselor Oakdale Sch. Dist., Calif., 1971-73; sch. psychologist, intern Learning and Counseling Ctr., Stockton, Calif., 1972-74; pvt. practice, rsch. in motor-perceptual tng. Greeley, 1975—; researcher ocumeter survey, Lincoln Unified Sch. Dist., Stockton, 1980, Manteca (Calif.) High Sch., 1981, motor perceptual tng./ocumeter rsch. Lincoln Unified Sch. Dist., 1981-82, YMCA, Stockton, 1983, others; presenter seminars in field. Author: Psychological Services and Motor Perceptual Training, 1974; author guidebook, manual and monographs in field; inventor instrument for measuring ocular tracking ability, 1989. Mem. Rep. Presdl. Task Force, 1990, Greeley Rep. Women's Club, 1990. Recipient medallion World Declaration of Excellence, 1989; named to Hall of Fame Internat. Cultural Diploma Honor, 1990. Mem. NAFE, Nat. Assn. Sch. Psychologists and Psychometrists (speaker at conf. 1976), Nat. Fedn. Rep. Women, The Smithsonian Assocs., Nat. Trust for Hist. Preservation, Am. Personnel and Guidance Assn., Nat. Assn. Student Personnel Adminstrs., Nat. Assn. Women Deans and Counselors, AAUP, Calif. Tchrs. Assn., Internat. Platform Assn., Independence Inst., Learning Disabilities Assn. (speaker internat. conv. 1976), Pi Omega Pi, Pi Lambda Theta. Home: 1954 Eighteenth Ave Greeley CO 80631

LINDEGREN, CECILE KEYSER, music educator; b. DeFuniak Springs, Fla., July 1, 1946; d. Charles Renshaw and Ouida (Higdon) Keyser; m. John Emory Lindegren, Feb. 14, 1981; children: Erica Kristen, Jason, Jeremy. AA, Pensacola (Fla.) Jr. Coll., 1967; B in Mus. Edn., Fla. State U., 1969; M in Mus. Edn., U. South Miss., 1979. Cert. elem. and secondary tchr., Fla. Choral dir. Pryor Jr. High Sch., Ft. Walton Beach, Fla., 1969-77, 86—; dir. music and youth Mary Esther (Fla.) United Meth. Ch., 1977-81; owner, instr. Lindegren Music Studio, Ft. Walton Beach, 1981—; children's choir dir. Trinity United Meth. Ch., 1983-87. Dir. Ft. Walton Beach Community Chorus, 1976—. Mem. Okaloosa County Music Tchrs. Assn. (pres. 1981-83), Fla. Vocal Assn. (chmn. local dist. 1973-74, 76-77), Fla. State Music Tchrs. Assn., AAUW (chmn. fine arts com. 1978-80), Kelly Fine Arts Coun. (arts festival co-chmn. 1986), Playground Mut. Concert Assn. (sec. 1984-86, 88-89), Music Educators Nat. Conf., Am. Coll. Musicians, Ft. Walton Beach Woman's Club (music dir. 1984-87, 2d v.p. 1984-86), Choctaw Bay Music Club (pres. 1985-86). Democrat. Methodist. Clubs: Ft. Walton Beach Woman's (music dir. 1984-87, 2d v.p. 1984-86), Choctaw Bay Music (pres. 1985-86). Home: 206 Vicki Leigh Ave Fort Walton Beach FL 32548

LINDELL, ANDREA REGINA, college dean, nurse; b. Warren, Pa., Aug., 21, 1943; d. Andrew D. and Irene M. (Fabry) Lefik; m. Warner E. Lindell, May 7, 1966; children—Jennifer I., Jason M. B.S., Villa Maria Coll., 1970; M.S.N. Catholic U., 1975, D.N.Sc., 1975; diploma R.N., St. Vincent's Hosp., Erie, Pa. Instr. St. Vincent Hosp. Sch. Nursing, 1964-66; dir. Rouse Hosp., Youngsville, Pa., 1966-69; supr. Vis. Nurses Assn., Warren, Pa., 1969-70; dir. grad. program Cath. U., Washington, 1975-77; chmn., assoc. dean U. N.H., Durham, 1977-81; dean, prof. Oakland U., Rochester, Mich., 1981-90, U. Cin., 1990—; cons. Moorehead U., Ky., 1983. Editor; Jour. Profl. Nursing, 1985; contbr. articles to profl. jours. Mem. sch. bd. Strafford Sch. Dist., N.H., 1977-80; Gov.'s Blue Ribbon Commn. Direct Health Policies, Concord, N.H., 1979-81; vice chmn. New England Commn. Higher Edn. in Nursing, 1977-81; mem. Mich. Assn. Colls. Nursing, 1981—. Named Outstanding Young Woman Am., 1980. Mem. Nat. League Nursing, Am. Assn. Colls. Nursing, Sigma Theta Tau. Democrat. Roman Catholic. Avocations: water skiing; roller skating; reading; fishing; camping; Office: U Cin Procter Hall Cincinnati OH 45267

LINDELL, DEBORAH KAY, data processing analyst; b. Newark, Del., Nov. 24, 1959; d. Randolph Dickinson III and Kay Annette (Golt) L.; m. Donald Lee Butler, Apr. 25, 1986. BA, U. Del., 1981. Cade operator E.I. duPont de Nemours & Co., Inc., Newark, 1981-82; dir. mktg. Custom Computer Svc., Inc., Wilmington, Del., 1982-85; sr. account exec., nat. accounts ADP, Inc., Balt., 1985-89; human resources info. specialist Himont USA, Inc., Wilmington, 1989—; cons. Computer Solutions, Inc., Newark, 1990. Mem. Wilmington Women in Bus., NAFE. Office: Himont USA Inc 2801 Centerville Rd Wilmington DE 19808

LINDEMAN, JANET CLAIRE, psychologist; b. Dumaguette City, The Philippines, Dec. 8, 1941; (parents Am. citizens); d. Paul Raymond and Clara (Malbon) Lindholm; m. Michael John Lindeman, Dec. 27, 1966; 1 child, Christopher Paul. BA in History, Oberlin (Ohio) Coll., 1963; MA in Teaching, Harvard U., 1964; MS in Psychology, U. Alaska, 1973; PhD in Guidance and Counseling, Wash. State U., 1977. Lic. psychologist, Alaska. Tchr. Episcopal Deanery Day Sch., San Francisco, 1965-66; social worker, tchr. Alaska Div. Social Svcs. and Dept. Edn., Bethel, 1966-68; vol. U.S. Peace Corps, Manila, 1968-69; social worker Head Start Program, Anchorage and Chugiak, Alaska, 1970-73; counselor intern Wash. State U. Student Counseling Ctr., Pullman, 1974-77; family therapist Alaska Clinic, Anchorage, 1977-79; psychologist Langdon Psychiat. Clinic, Anchorage, 1979-81; pvt. practice Anchorage, 1981-84; psychologist Fireweed Therapy Ctr., Anchorage, 1984—; adj. instr. U. Alaska, 1979—; cons. Standing Together Against Rape, Anchorage, 1980—, Soldatna (Alaska) Family Recovery Ctr., 1990. Contbr. chpt. to book. Treas., sec. Meditation-in-Motion, Inc., Anchorage, 1985—; foster parent Dept. Corrections, Anchorage, 1982-86. Mem. Am. Psychol. Assn., Alaska Psychol. Assn. (sec. 1978-80).

LINDEN, PATRICIA, controller; b. L.A., Mar. 2, 1955; d. Seymour Leon and Ruth Martha (Hyman) L.; m. Jeffrey A. Altman, Aug. 10, 1975 (div. Dec. 1979); m. Fred Arnold Gysi, Jr., May 27, 1984; children: Elissa Linden Gysi, Madeleine Linden Gysi. BS, UCLA, 1976, MBA, 1979. CPA. Accountant, mgr. Coopers & Lybrand, L.A., 1979-88; controller Gladden Entertainment, L.A., 1988—; v.p., controller The Athena Fund, L.A., 1988—, The Athena Fund II, L.A., 1988—, The NFA World Coin Fund, L.A., 1988—. Mem. Jewish Fedn. Bus. and Profl. Women, AICPA, Calif. Soc. CPAs, Anderson Grad. Sch. of Mgmt. Alumni. Office: Gladden Entertainment Corp 10100 Santa Monica Blvd Ste 600 Los Angeles CA 90067

LINDENFELD, LORE, fiber artist; b. Wuppertal, Germany, Apr. 27, 1921; came to U.S. 1939; d. Alfred and Frieda (Roos) Kadden; m. Peter Lindenfeld, May 31, 1953; children: Thomas, Naomi. Grad. Cert., Black Mt. (N.C.) Coll., 1948; MEd in Creative Arts Edn., Rutgers U., 1982. Fabric designer Herbert Meyer, Inc., John Walther Fabrics, others, N.Y.C., 1948-58; faculty mem. Visual Arts dept. Middlesex County Coll., Edison, N.J., 1968-86; with Newark Mus., 1990—. Numerous exhibits of textiles and fiber art including N.J. State Mus., Grey Art Gallery, NYU, Walker Art Ctr., Mpls., Phila. Coll. Textiles & Sci., Am. Craft Gallery, N.Y.C., Circle Gallery, Detroit, Rutgers U., Rider Coll. Art Gallery, others; numerous articles in profl. and craft publs. including Craft Internat., Fiber Arts, Surface Design, Craft Horizons (now Am. Craft), others; works in collections of the N.J. State Mu., Rider Coll. Art Collection. N.J. State Coun. on the Arts craft fellow, 1985. Mem. Am. Craft Coun., N.J. Designer-Craftsmen (contbg. editor), Textile Study Group. Home and Office: 121 Harris Rd Princeton NJ 08540

LINDENSTEIN, JOAN KATHRYN, hospital administrator; b. Pipestone, Minn., May 20, 1953; d. Robert Gregory and Camilla Jean (Jackley) Degen; m. Kevin D. Lindenstein, Nov. 8, 1975; children: Joshua George, Kristen Suzanne, Alex Joseph. BS in Med. Record Adminstrn., Coll. St. Mary, Omaha, 1975; MHA, U. Minn., 1989. Dir. med. records Good Samaritan Hosp., Kearney, Nebr., 1979-85; dir. med. records and quality assurance Richard H. Young Hosp., Kearney, Nebr., 1985-87, interim chief operating officer, 1987-88, chief operating officer, 1988-89, asst. adminstr., 1989—; asst. med. record adminstr. Bergan Mercy Hosp. Omaha, 1975-77; asst. dir. med. records. St. Francis Hosp., Grand Island, Nebr., 1977-78; utilization rev. coord. Good Samaritan Hosp., Kearney, 1979-88. Mem. Am. Coll. Healthcare Execs., Am. Med. Record Assn., Bus. and Profl. Women's Assn., Nebr. Med. Record Assn., Rotary, Kearney C. of C. Roman Catholic. Office: Richard H Young Hosp PO Box 1750 Kearney NE 68848

LINDERMAN, JEANNE HERRON, priest; b. Erie, Pa., Nov. 14, 1931; d. Robert Leslie and Ella Marie (Stearns) Herron; m. James Stephens Linderman; children: Mary Susan, John Randolph, Richard Webster, Craig Stephens, Mark Herron, Elizabeth Stewart. BS in Indsl. and Labor Rels., Cornell U., 1953; MDiv magna cum laude, Lancaster Theol. Sem., 1981; postgrad., clin. pastoral edn., Del. State Hosp., New Castle, 1981. Ordained priest, Episcopal Ch. Mem. personnel staff Hengerer Co., Buffalo, 1953-55; chaplain Cathedral Ch. St. John, Wilmington, Del., 1981-82; priest-in-charge Christ Episcopal Ch., Delaware City, Del., 1982-87; vicar Christ Episcopal Ch., 1987—; mem. human sexuality taskforce, Diocese of Del., 1981-82, mem. clergy compensation com. 1982-86, mem. standing com., 1988—, com. on constitution and canons, 1989. Author, editor hist. study papers. Bd. dirs., St. Michael's Day Nursery, Wilmington, 1985-88; mem. Cornell Univ. Secondary Schs. Com. Mem. Episcopal Women's Caucus, Del. Episcopal Clergy Assn., Nat. Assn. Episcopal Clergy, DAR, Mayflower Soc., Dutch Colonial Soc. Del., Stoney Run Questers, Cornell Women's Club Del., Women of St. James the Less. Republican. Home: 307 Springhouse Ln Hockessin DE 19707 Office: Christ Episcopal Ch PO Box 4122 Delaware City DE 19706

LINDER-VICTOR, MIRA, cosmetics company executive; b. Gostynin, Poland, Dec. 25, 1921; came to U.S., 1965; d. Zelig and Sala (Koren) Hodes; m. David Linder, Mar. 1941 (dec. 1975); 1 child, Lily; m. Arthur Van Victor, Apr. 1977. Student pharmacology and cosmetology, Poland and Belgium, 1938-39; student cosmetology, Geneva, Paris, Munich, N.Y.C., 1965-68. Founder, pres. Esthetics of Mira Linder, Inc., Southfield, Mich., 1968—, Mira Linder Inc., Toronto, Ont., Can., 1973—, Mira Linder Spa in City, Palm Beach, Fla., 1983—. Author: Beauty Begins at 60, 1989; columnist Michigan Woman mag. Active Founders Soc. Detroit Inst. Arts, Am. Cancer Soc., Archives Am. Art; com. chmn. Am. Lung Assn., Detroit; trustee Mich. Opera Theatre, Detroit; bd. dirs. Fashion Group. Mem. Com. Internat. Esthetics and Cosmetology, Franklin Hills Country Club (Franklin, Mich.). Office: 29935 Northwestern Hwy Southfield MI 48034

LINDNER, ERNA CAPLOW, educator, choreographer, movement therapist; b. N.Y.C., May 26, 1928; d. Abraham Murray and Mildred T. (Farb) Caplow; A.B., Bklyn Coll., 1948; M.S., Smith Coll., 1950; Ph.D., Columbia Pacific U., 1986; m. Norman Lindner, June 18, 1950 (dec. Sept. 1981); 1 dau., Amy Beth. Instr. dance Brown U., 1950-54, Rutgers U., 1954-55; dance specialist Samuel Field YM-YWHA, Queens, N.Y., 1962-68; dance specialist N.Y.C. Bd. Edn., 1963-69; asst. dance dir., choreographer Martin de Porres Center, Queens, 1967-70; dir. Saturday Cultural Program, Rochdale Village Nursery Sch., Queens, 1964-73; dir.-choreographer Danceabouts Co., N.Y.C., 1966-80; prof. health, phys. edn. and recreation Nassau Community Coll. SUNY, L.I., 1968—; adj. prof. phys. edn. and dance Adelphi U., 1979—; lectr. and tng. cons. on dance for spl. populations. Charter mem. Queens Council on Arts, exec. bd. dirs., 1970-74; sec., mem. exec. com. Nat. Ednl. Council Creative Therapies. Mem. Am. Dance Guild (charter mem., past nat. pres., nat. exec. bd.), Am. Dance Therapy Assn., Am. Assn. Sex Educators, Counselors and Therapists (cert. sex educator, sex counselor), Heritage Com. Nat. Dance Assn. Contbr. chpts on dance to Fun for Fitness; interviewer on dance Sta. WHPC-FM; (with others) selected music and wrote manual for Special Music for Special People, Ednl. Act Rec. Co., 1977; Special Dancing on Your Feet and in Your Seat, 1982; Come Dance Again, 1987. Author: (with others) Therapeutic Dance/Movement, 1979; (monograph) Use of Dance in Sex Education and Counseling, 1974; also articles on geriatric dance therapy. Home: PO Box 993 Woodside NY 11377 Office: Nassau Community Coll Stewart Ave Garden City NY 11530

LINDNER, SISTER MARY JOHN, school superintendent; b. Cumberland, Md., Dec. 24, 1923; d. John Howard and Teresa Louise (Lehman) L. AB, Fontbonne Coll., 1951; MEd, St. Louis U., 1956; PhD, St. John's U., Jamaica, N.Y., 1966. Tchr. elem. St. Theresa's Sch., New Orleans, 1946-52; tchr. secondary edn. Laboure High Sch., St. Louis, 1953-57; tchr. Marillac Coll., Normandy, Mo., 1957-61, 66-71; edn. councillor Daughters of Charity of St. Vincent de Paul, Normandy, Mo., 1971-74; provincial for community Daus. of Charity of St. Vincent de Paul, Normandy, 1974-83; with religious edn. div. St. Joseph's Ch., Odessa, Tex., 1983-85; supt. schs. Diocese of Amarillo, Tex., 1985—; head edn. dept. Marillac Coll., St. Louis, 1966-71; chairperson supt.'s dept. Tex. Cath. Conf., Austin, 1988, 89. Mem. Nat. Cath. Ednl. Assn., Chief Adminstrs. Cath. Edn., Assn. for Supervision and Curriculum Devel. Roman Catholic. Office: Diocese of Amarillo 1800 N Spring Amarillo TX 79117

LINDQUIST, JANE INGRID, marketing professional; b. Worcester, Mass., Oct. 11, 1953; d. Gustaf Berg and Ingrid Virginia (Berglund) L. BA, Randolph-Macon Woman's Coll., 1975. Pub. rels. asst. Garfinckel's, Washington, 1980, dir. special events, 1980-85; ind. cons. Washington, 1985-86; dir. special events, fundraising Easter Seal Soc. of Va., Inc., Fairfax, 1986-87; dir. mktg. Mktg. and Media Solutions, Inc., Fairfax, 1987-89; customer svc. mgr. Sutton Pl. Gourmet, Alexandria, 1989—. Bd. dirs. Arlington (Va.) Symphony Orchestra Assn., 1987-90; council del. Arlington United Way, 1986-87; com. mem. The Mayor's Festival Cherry Blossom Com., Washington, 1982-83; vol. Greater Washington Chpt. Lupus Found. Am., 1985—; mem. Hexagon, Inc., 1983-90.

LINDQUIST, LINDA JANETTE, city official; b. Jonesboro, Ark., May 31, 1951; d. Davis Edward and Reba (Eades) Thomas; m. Harry A. Lindquist; children: Jeffrey, Julie, Michael. BA, Gov.'s State U., Ill. Cert. mcpl. treas., Ill. Market analyst Time-Life Inc., Chgo., 1969-71; account rep. Coca-Cola, Atlanta, 1974-77; acct. Deltaco (W.R. Grace), Atlanta, 1980-81; asst. treas. village of Romeoville, Ill., 1982-83, fin. dir., 1983-89, village mgr., 1989—; treas. Police Pension Bd., Romeoville, 1983—. Vol. Romeoville Parade Assn., 1984—, Romeoville Beautification Com., 1984; tabulator Miss Romeoville Pageant, 1984—. Mem. Govt. Fin. Officers Assn., Exec. Women Nat. Assn., Ill. Treas. Assn. Home: 39 Abbeywood Dr Romeoville IL 60441 Office: Village of Romeoville 13 Montrose Dr Romeoville IL 60441

LINDQUIST, MARGARET CHARLOTTE, retired secondary educator; b. Gary, Ind., Mar. 1, 1917; d. Edvard and Minnie Matilda (Johansson) L. BS in Edn., Ind. U., 1946, MS in Edn., 1951. Tchr. Luther Inst., Chgo., 1946-51, Luther High Sch. South, Chgo., 1951-78; ret., 1978; supr. bus. dept. Luther High Sch. South, 1956-78. Mem. AAUW, AARP (bd. dirs. 1987-89, chpt 679), Profl. Secs. Internat.

LINDSAY, CAROLYN PATRICIA, social service administrator; b. Hartford, Conn., Mar. 17, 1953; d. Robert Lee and Catherine (Delaney) Seay; children: Joseph A., Sean J. Student, San Diego State Coll. Adminstr. Beach Area Community Clinic, San Diego, 1975-77; project dir., econ. devel. asst. project Community Congress of San Diego, 1978-79; planning mgr. Dept. Social Svcs., County of San Diego, 1983-85; asst. div. chief employment preparation div. Dept. Social Svcs. County San Diego, 1985—; cons. Western Ctr. for Health Planning, Nat. Coun. on Altenative Health Care Policy, San Diego Coun. Community Clinics, Calif. State Dept. Health; project dir. youth self sufficiency project. Co-author: Fund Raising and the Community Based Human Services Agency; contbg. editor Calif. Health Coalition Newsletter. Preceptor U. Calif. at San Diego Sch. Medicine, Dept. Community Medicine; chair San Diego Youth 2000 Project, 1988—; mem. Univ. Hosp. Community Adv. Bd., 1978-79, Pathways Drug Program Community Adv. Bd., 1978, Zool. Soc. San Diego; treas. Community Congress San Diego, Inc., 1978; mem. program and budget rev. panel United Way, San Diego, 1977-79. Recipient 4 awards for programs Nat. Assn. Counties. Mem. Nat. Assn. Exec. Women, Am. Pub. Health Assn., Positive Parenting. Office: County of San Diego 1027 10th Ave San Diego CA 92101

LINDSAY, DIANNA MARIE, principal; b. Boston, Dec. 7, 1948; d. Albert Joseph and June Hazelton (Mitchell) Raggi; m. James William Lindsay III, Feb. 14, 1981. BA in Anthropology, Ea. Nazarene Coll., 1971; MEd in Curriculum and Instrn., Wright State U., 1973, MEd in Social Studies Edn., 1974, MEd in Edn. Adminstrn., 1977; EdD in Edn. Adminstrn., Ball State U., 1976. Supr. social edn. Ohio Dept. Edn., Columbus, 1976-77; asst. prin. Orange City Schs., Pepper Pike, Ohio, 1977-79; prin. North Olmsted (Ohio) Jr. High Sch., 1979-81; dir. secondary edn. North Olmsted City SChs., 1981-82; supt. Copley (Ohio)-Fairlawn City Schs., 1982-85; prin. North Olmsted High Sch., 1985-89, New Trier High Sch., Winnetka, Ill., 1989—; bd. dirs. Harvard Prins. Ctr., Cambridge, Mass. Contbr. articles to profl. jours. Bd. dirs. Nat. PTA, Chgo., 1987-89 (Educator of Yr. 1989). Named Prin. of Yr. Ohio Art Tchrs., 1989, one of 100 Up and Coming Educators, Exec. Educator Mag., 1988; recipient John Vaughn Achievements in Edn. North Cen. Assn., 1988. Mem. AAUW, Ill. Tchrs. Fgn. Lang., Rotary Internat., Phi Delta Kappa. Methodist. Office: New Trier High Sch 385 Winnetka Ave Winnetka IL 60093

LINDSAY, ELENA MARGARET, nurse; b. Evansville, Ind., Oct. 6, 1941; d. Gordon Graham and Irma Louise (Berkemeier) Kuhn; m. Robert Dean Lindsay Jr., Dec. 29, 1988; children: Maria, Robert. BS in Nursing, U. Evansville, 1963. RN. 0vening coord., head nurse Wellborn Meml. Bapt. Hosp., Evansville, 1969-74; dir. nurses Warrick Hosp., Boonville, Ind., 1975-76; head nurse St. Mary's Med. Ctr., Evansville, 1980-82; staff nurse VA Med. Ctr., Salt Lake City, 1987—. 2d lt. U.S. Army, 1961-64. Mem. DAV (life aux. mem.), Soc. Orthopedic Nurses (past pres.). Republican. Mem. United Ch. of Christ. Home: 5064 S Heath Ave Kearns UT 84118-6972 Office: 500 Foothill Blvd Salt Lake City UT 84148

LINDSAY, JACQUELINE MAE, freelance writer and designer; b. Pitts., July 25, 1959; d. Raymond A. and Juanita M. (Davis) L. BA, Merrimack Coll., 1981. Sec. Digital Equipment Corp., Maynard, Mass., 1977, employment coord., 1979-80; with mktg. communications dept. Omtool Corp., Tewksbury, Mass., 1983-84; freelance writer, editor, publs. designer Phoenix, 1986—. Columnist, contbg. editor PC-AI, 1988—; contbr. articles to profl. jours. Vol. Kidney Transplant Dialysis Assn., Boston, 1985-89; vol. homebound program Mesa (Ariz.) Pub. Libr., 1986; tchr., vol. ednl. dept. Phoenix Zoo, 1986-89. Mem. Am. Assn. for Artificial Intelligence, Computer Profls. for Social Responsibility. Democrat. Unitarian. Home: 1 DeMauro Dr Tyngsboro MA 01879

LINDSAY, KATHERINE ANN, principal; b. Decatur, Ill., Apr. 18, 1946; d. Frank Merrill and Margery (Crawford) L. BS, Millikin U., Decatur, 1968; MEd, U. Ill., 1969. Cert. ednl. adminstr., guidance counselor, Ill. Tchr. Decatur Pub. Sch. Dist., 1969-75, adminstrv. intern, 1975-76, prin. Pershing Sch., 1976-82, prin. South Shores Elem. Sch., 1982—; ednl. adv. com. Millikin U., Decatur, 1976—. Co-author, illustrator: (book) Decatur, Today and Yesterday, 1979. Pres. Mental Health Assn. of Macon County, Decatur, 1972; bd. dirs. ARC, Macon County chpt., Decatur, 1981-84, 85-88, YWCA, Decatur, 1986-88, Am. Cancer Soc., Macon County chpt., Decatur, 1988—; deacon, elder Cen. Christian Ch., Decatur, 1986—. Named Outstanding Young Educator award Decatur Jaycees, 1972, Young Alumnus of Yr. Millikin U., 1973, Outstanding Educator Alpha Delta Kappa, 1982, Adminstr. of Yr. Decatur Assn. Ednl. Office Personnel, 1983; recipient Those Who Excel award Ill. Bd. Edn., 1985. Mem. Assn. Supervision and Curriculum Devel., Decatur Assn. Bldg. Adminstrs. (past pres.), Delta Kappa Gamma, Phi Delta Kappa. Lodge: Zonta. Home: 1580 Lynnwood Dr Decatur IL 62521 Office: South Shores Elem Sch 2500 S Franklin St Decatur IL 62521

LINDSAY, LESLIE, packaging engineer; b. Amsterdam, N.Y., Oct. 30, 1960; d. R. Gardner and Dorothy (Loucks) L. BA in Advt., Mich. State U., 1981, BS in Package Engring., 1982. Cert. profl. engr. in packaging. Constrn. inspector N.Y. State Dept. Transp., Albany, 1983; sr. package design engr. Wang Labs., Inc., Lowell, Mass., 1983-90; packaging engr. Apple Computer, Santa Clara, Calif., 1990—. N.Y. state Regents scholar, 1977. Mem. Soc. Packaging Profls., Boston Women's Rugby Club (tour chmn. 1985), Wang Ultimate Frisbee (social chmn. 1986-89). Home: 1761 Bucknall Rd Campbell CA 95008 Office: Apple Computer 3565 Monroe St MS67A Santa Clara CA 95051-5207

LINDSAY, MARIA THERESA, human resources executive; b. N.Y.C., Nov. 4, 1950; d. John F. and Mary T. (Schuster) Richter; m. John Bruce Lindsay, Oct. 11, 1980; children: John William, James Richter. BA in History, Coll. of Mt. St. Vincent, Bronx, N.Y., 1972; MA in Reading, Manhattan Coll., Bronx, 1975. Tchr. Annunciation Sch., Yonkers, N.Y., 1972-79; adminstrv. asst. McCall's mag., N.Y.C., 1979-81; various positions U.S. Surg. Corp., North Haven, Conn., 1981-88, mgr. human resources, 1989—. Mem. Am. Compensation Assn., Working in Employee Benefits. Republican. Presbyterian. Office: US Surg Corp 195 McDermott Rd Fairfield CT 06473

LINDSEY, ANN KENDRICK, management educator, consultant; b. Columbia, S.C., May 25, 1945; d. James Robert and Glennie Sared (Johnson) Kendrick; m. Harold Eugene Lindsey Jr., Nov. 15, 1963 (div. 1983); children: H. Eugene, Bruce K. BA, U. S.C., 1967; postgrad. in psychology, Harvard U., 1974-75; MBA, Simmons Coll., 1977. Tchr. English Newman Jr. High Sch., Needham, Mass., 1967-70; substitute tchr. Newman and Wellesley Jr. High, 1971-73; liaison position Gen. Motors Assembly div. GM Corp., Detroit and Boston, 1977-79, human resources staff assoc., 1979-82; asst. prof., adj. assoc. prof. mgmt. Grad. Sch. Mgmt. Simmons Coll., Boston, 1982—; ptnr., sr. cons. Gumpert, Lindsey & Smith, Boston, 1984—; individual cons. women in bus.; co-developer tng. prog. work culture change. Mem. Simmons Coll. Grad. Sch. Mgmt. Alumnae Assn., Phi Beta Kappa. Democrat. Home: 90 Fairlee Rd Newton MA 02168 Office: Simmons Coll Grad Sch Mgmt 409 Commonwealth Ave Boston MA 02215

LINDSEY, BARBARA ANN, publishing executive, dress designer, government official; b. Corry, Pa., Sept. 11, 1940; d. Melvin C. and Madge Jeanette (Peterson) Gable; children: Melody Layne, Merry Lee, Lorrie Ann, Jewel Lynne, Mona Louise. Student, U. Palm Beach, Indian River Jr. Coll., USDA Grad. Sch., Washington. Head librarian, dept. sec. RCA, Palm Beach Gardens, Fla., 1960-63; legal sec. Thurlow & Thurlow, Stuart, Fla., 1963-64; v.p. R.C. Lindsey Plumbing, Inc.; dress designer Candi Lin, 1958—; pres. Lindsey, Gable, Conroy & Assocs., Inc., Stuart, 1979-82; pres. Am. Advt. Agy.; spl. asst., pres.-gen. Nat. Soc. DAR, Washington, 1985-86; confidential asst. to assoc. dir. by presdl. appointment Fed. Emergency Mgmt. Agy., Washington, 1987—. Editor, pub. Prominent People in Fla. Govt. Apptd. dir. info. services Visitor's Ctr., Bicentennial Commn. on U.S. Constn., 1985-87; Rep. state committeewoman Martin County; mem. exec. bd. Rep. Party of Fla., 1976-80; Rep. nominee for commr. agr. and consumer affairs State of Fla., 1982; alt. vice chmn. 10th Congl. Dist.; mem. Rep. Nat. Com. Congl. Adv. Bd.; bd. advisors Am. Security Soc.; mem. Nat. Congl. Adv. Com. Named Sec. of Yr., Palm Beach Profl. Secs., 1968, Mem. of Yr., Treasure Coast Home Builders Aux., 1979. Mem. Profl. Secs. Internat., Nat. Home Builders Aux., Women for Responsible Legislation, Internat. Entrepreneurs Assn., Fla. Direct Markets Assn., Fla. Farm Bur., Stuart C. of C., Gold Coast Direct Mktg. Assn., Internat. Platform Assn. Baptist. Clubs: United Women's Rep. (pres.), Rep. of Fla., Arlington Women's Rep., Women's Rep. of Martin, Fla. Fedn. Rep. Women., Fla. State Soc., Conservative Network, Citizens for Am., Forum, Delphi, Renissance Women, Combined Internat. Philippine-Am. Assn., Nat. Press Club. Office: Fed Emergency Mgmt Agy 500 C St SW Washington DC 20024

LINDSEY, BONNIE JOAN, vocational educator; b. Oklahoma City, May 4, 1935; d. David DeWitt and Genevieve Catherine (Rucinski) Bevans; m. Donald G. Lindsey, Apr. 3, 1963 (div. 1974): 1 child, Jon Erik. AS, Mt. San Jacinto Coll., 1973; BA Vocat. Edn., Long Beach State U., 1975, MA Vocat. Edn., 1977. Tchr. Riverside (Calif.) Regional Occupation program, 1972-74, mem. adv. com., 1983-85; supr. Colton-Redlands-Yucaipa Regional Occupation Program, Redlands, Calif., 1974-75; assoc. prof. Riverside Community Coll., 1975-89, prof. emeritus, 1989—. Author: Medical Assisting, 1974, 75, 89; co-author Professional Medical Assistant: Clinical Assisting, 1990. Mem. Am. Assn. Med. Transcription (pres. Orange Empire chpt. 1985-88), Am. Assn. Med. Assts., Calif. Assn. Med. Assisting Instrs., Vocat. Indsl. Clubs of Am. (named Advisor of Yr. 1974), Epsilon Pi Tau. Democrat. Roman Catholic. Home: 1705 Euclid Ave Boise ID 83706 Office: Riverside Community Coll 4800 Magnolia Ave Riverside CA 92506

LINDSEY, D. RUTH, educator; b. Kingfisher, Okla., Oct. 26, 1926; d. Lewis Howard and Kenyon (King) L. BS, Okla. State U., 1948; MS, U. Wis., 1954; PEd, Ind. U., 1965. Cert. kinesiotherapist, 1970. Instr. Okla. State U., Stillwater, 1948-50, Monticello Coll., Alton, Ill., 1951-54, DePauw U., Greencastle, Ind., 1954-56; prof. Okla. State U., Stillwater, 1956-75; vis. prof. U. Utah, Salt Lake City, 1975-76; prof. phys. edn. Calif. State U., Long Beach, 1976-88; prof. emeritus phys. edn. Calif. Sate U., 1988—. Co-author: Fitness for the Health of It, 6 edit., 1989, Concepts of Physical Fitness, 1990, Fitness for Life, 3 edits. 1990, The Ultimate Fitness Book, 1984, Survival Kit for Those Who Sit, 1989; editor Perspectives: Jour. of Soc. Phys. Edn. for Coll. Women, 1988—. Amy Morris Homans scholar, 1964, Meritorious Performance award, Calif. Sate U., 1987, Julian Vogel Meml. award, Am. Kinesiotherapy Assn., 1988. Fellow AAHPER (chmn. com. on workshops Coun. on Aging and Adult Devel. 1987-88), Am. Coll. Sports Medicine (emeritus mem.), Am. Kinesiotherapy Assn., Calif. Assn. Health, Phys. Edn., Recreation and Dance (chmn. older adult task force), Nat. Coun. Against Health Fraud, Orange County Nutrition Coun., Phi Kappa Phi. Republican. Baptist. Office: Calif State Univ 1250 Bellflower Blvd Long Beach CA 90840

LINDSEY, DOTTYE JEAN, educator; b. Temple Hill, Ky., Nov. 4, 1929; d. Jesse D. and Ethel Ellen (Bailey) Nuckols; m. Willard W. Lindsey, June 14, 1952 (div.). BS, Western Ky. U., 1953, MA, 1959. Owner, Bonanza Restaurant, Charleston, W.Va., 1965; tchr. remedial reading Alice Waller Elem. Sch., Louisville, 1967-75, tchr., 1953-67, 1975-84, contact person for remedial reading, 1968—; regional v.p. A.L. Williams Fin. Mktg. Co., 1988—; profl. model Cosmo/Casablancas Modeling Agy., Louisville, 1984—; with A.L. Willams Fin. Svcs., Louisville, 1988—. Treas. Met. Louisville Women's Polit. Caucus, 1980-88, Ky. Women's Polit. Caucus, 1988—; bn. sponsor ROTC Western Ky. U., 1950; local precinct capt., 1987—; election officer, 1984—. Named Miss Ky., 1951. Mem. NEA, Ky. Edn. Assn., Jefferson County Tchrs. Assn., various polit. action coms., Internat. Reading Assn., Am. Childhood Edn. Assn. Democrat. Baptist.

LINDSEY, RIKI SUE, real estate agent; b. Longview, Wash., Apr. 11, 1953; d. Ralph Virgil and Clara Ferol (Loper) L.; m. Kurt Michael Thoma, May 13, 1978 (Feb. 1986). AA, Chamberlyne Coll. Jr. Coll., 1973; BFA, Roger Williams Coll., 1976. Retail mgr. Apogee, Boston, 1973; retail buyer T. Edwards, Atlanta, 1974; retail mgr. T. Edwards, Chgo., 1976; dist. mgr. Jaeger Internat., Chgo. and Hartford, N.J., 1976-78; retail mdse. mgr. Peter Wittman, Wellesley, Mass., 1978; pres. Confetti Inc., Newport, R.I., 1978—, Riki Jewelers, Boston, 1984—; real estate The Kaplan Group, Newton, Mass., 1986—; cons. in field. Bd. dirs. Tifobet Theatre Co., Newport, 1979-83; pres. Downtown Mchts., Newport, 1981; mem. R.I. State Commn. on Arts, Newport, 1982-84. Mem. NOW, Nat. Assn. Female Execs., Bus. and Profl. Women. Home: 84 Prospect St Wellesley MA 02181 Office: 5609 SW 34th St Topeka KS 66614

LINDSKOG, MARJORIE OTILDA, educator; b. Rochester, Minn., Oct. 13, 1937; d. Miles Emery and Otilda Elvina (Hagre) L. BA, Colo. Coll., 1959, MA in Teaching, 1972. Field advisor/camp dir. Columbine council Girl Scouts U.S., Pueblo, Colo., 1959-65; staff mem. Wyo. Girl Scout Camp, Casper, 1966, dir., 1967; tchr. Sch. Dist. 60, Pueblo, 1966—; asst. dir. camp Pacific Peaks Girl Scouts U.S., Olympia, Wash., 1968, dir., 1969; instr. Jr. Gt. Books Program, 1981—; mem. adv. bd. Newspapers in Edn., 1988—; chmn. credit com. Pueblo Tchr.'s Credit Union; lectr., instr. edn. U. So. Colo., 1990—. Author: (series of math. lessons) Bronco Mathmania, 1987, 88, 89, 90; area co-chair Channel 8 Pub. TV Auction, Pueblo, 1983-87; contbr. articles to profl. jours. Bd. dirs. Columbine Girl Scout Council, 1983-85, Dist. #60 Blood Bank, 1985—; mem. Pueblo Greenway and Nature Ctr., 1981—. Recipient Thanks badge Girl Scouts U.S. Mem. Colo. Archeol. Soc., Assn. for Supervision and Curriculum Devel., Nat. Council for Tchrs. Math., Colo. Coun. Tchrs. Math. (Outstanding Elem. Math Tchr. of Yr. 1989), Intertel, Mensa, Phi Delta Kappa (treas. 1989—), Alpha Phi. Lutheran. Club: Pueblo Country. Lodge: Sons of Norway. Home: 2810 7th Ave Pueblo CO 81003 Office: Sunset Park Sch 110 Univ Circle Pueblo CO 81005

LINDSLEY, CYNTHIA WOODS, legal assistant; b. Dallas, Tex., June 17, 1962; d. Richard Simms and Virginia (Price) W.; m. Don Dickinson Lindsley, Nov. 28, 1987. BS, U. Tex., 1984. Cert. paralegal. Paralegal Thompson and Knight, Dallas, Tex., 1984--. vol. North Dallas Legal Clinic., 1986--. Mem. Susan G. Komen Ambs., Dallas Symphony Innovators, Jr. League of Dallas, Chi Omega Alumni Night Club (mem. Christmas market steering com.), Dallas Theater Ctr. Backstager, Dallas County Heritage Soc., Cotillion (v.p. 1989-90, pres. 1990), Slipper Club. Republican. Presbyterian. Office: Thompson and Knight 3300 First City Ctr Dallas TX 75201

LINDSLEY, JULIE LYNN, microbiologist; b. Anderson, Ind., May 29, 1959; d. Richard Farrell and Wilda Jean (Baines) McFadden; m. Mark Edward Lindsley, June 26, 1982; children: Megan Ellen, Matthew Sean. BA in Botany, Bacteriolog, Depauw U., Greencastle, Ind., 1981. Med. technologist Veteran's Adminstrn. Med. Ctr., Indpls., 1982-86; supr. microbiology VA Med. Ctr., Indpls., 1986--. Mem. Am. Soc. for Microbiology, South Cen. Assn. for Microbiology, American Soc. Clin. Pathologists. Republican. Roman Catholic. Office: VA Med Ctr 1481 W 10th St Indianapolis IN 46202

LINDSTEDT-SIVA, (KAREN) JUNE, marine biologist, oil company executive; b. Mpls., Sept. 24, 1941; d. Stanley L. and Lila (Mills) Lindstedt; m. Ernest Howard Siva, Dec. 20, 1969. Student, U. Calif.-Santa Barbara, 1959-60, U. Calif.-Davis, 1960-62; B.A., U. So. Calif., 1963, M.S., 1967, Ph.D., 1971. Asst. coordinator Office Sea Grant Programs U. So. Calif., 1971; environ. specialist So. Calif. Edison Co., Rosemead, 1971-72; asst. prof. biology Calif. Luth. U., 1972-73; sci. advisor Atlantic Richfield Co., Los Angeles, 1973-77, sr. sci. advisor, 1977-81, mgr. environ. scis., 1981-86, mgr. environ. protection, 1986—; mem. Nat. Sci. Bd., 1984—; mem. biology adv. council Calif. State U.-Long Beach; bd. dirs. So. Calif. Acad. Scis., 1983—; mem. Marine Scis. adv. council Univ. So. Calif. Inst. Coastal and Marine Scis.; trustee Bermuda Biol. Sta. for Research.; chmn. Oil Spill Conf., San Antonio, 1989, API Oil Spills Com. Contbr. articles to profl. jours. Bd. dirs. Irene McCulloch Found., Los Angeles Devel. Com. Internat. Med. Corps. Recipient Calif. Mus. Sci. and Industry Achievement award, 1976, Trident award for Marine Scis., 11th Ann. Rev. Underwater Activites, Italy, 1970, Achievement award for Advancing Career Opportunities for Women, Career Planning Council, 1978; research grantee; distg. scholar biology Calif. Lut. U. Colloquim Scholars, 1988. Fellow ASTM (award of merit 1990); mem. AAAS, Soc. Petroleum Industry Biologists (pres. 1976-80), Marine Tech. Soc., U. So. Calif. Oceanographic Assocs. (bd. dirs.), Conejo Valley Audubon Soc., Calif. Native Plant Soc., Am. Inst. Biol. Sci., Western Soc. Naturalists, Phi Beta Kappa, Sigma Xi, Phi Kappa Phi. Office: Atlantic Richfield Co 515 S Flower St Los Angeles CA 90071

LINDSTROM, LYDIA SALUCKA, lawyer; b. Rockford, Ill., Jan. 15, 1960; d. Vytautas V. and Silvia Virginia (Zauka) Salucka; m. Jeffery Alan Lindstrom, Mar. 9, 1985. BS in Edn., Rockford Coll., 1982; JD, No. Ill. U., 1985. Bar: Ill. 1985, U.S. Dist. Ct. (no. dist.) Ill. 1987. Assoc. Kostantacos Law Office, Rockford, 1986-87, Gilbert, Natale & Meyer, Rockford, 1987—. bd. dirs. United Cerebral Palsy, Rockford. Mem. ABA, Ill. Bar Assn., Winnebago County Bar Assn. Republican. Roman Catholic. Office: Gilbert Natale & Meyer 3106 N Rockton Ave Rockford IL 61103

LINDSTROM, MARY LOU, psychologist; b. Billings, Mont., Apr. 23, 1928; d. Harold Matheson and Violet Winefred (Cantrell) L.; m. Louis Arthur Reinken, Aug. 3, 1951 (div. Dec. 1969); children: Louis Arthur, Dirk Christian; m. Robert William Stickelberger, Oct. 23, 1981. BS in Speech, Syracuse U., 1951; MA in Psychology, Furman U., 1970; PhD in Psychology, U. S.C., 1977. Lic. counseling psychologist S.C. Psychologist I & II A-O-P- Mental Health Ctr., Anderson, S.C., 1969-75; psychologist III Orangeburg (S.C.) Mental Health Ctr., 1977-85; psychologist IV Lexington County Mental Health Ctr., West Columbia, S.C., 1985—; human rels. cons. U.S. Army, Columbia, 1976, Bamberg County, Denmark, S.C., 1978-79. Contbr. articles to profl. jours. Recipient Child & Adolescent Staffing grant NIMH, Anderson, S.C., 1974, doctoral scholarship S.C. Dept. Mental Health, Columbia, 1975-77. Mem. AAUW, Assn. for Counselor Edn. and Supervision, Am. Psychol. Assn., S.C. Acad. Profl. Psychologists, S.C. Psychol. Assn., Am. Personnel and Guidance Assn., S.C. Personnel and Guidance Assn. Episcopalian. Home: 204 Cannondale Rd Columbia SC 29214 Office: Lexington County MHC 138 N Hospital Dr West Columbia SC 29169

LINDSTROM, NINA LUCILLE, school administrator, director; b. Cleveland, Tenn., Dec. 9, 1940; d. Noah Haskins Jones and Grace (Mae) Burke; m. Larry Lance Lindstrom, June 26, 1966; children: Anton Lee, Kristina Mae. BS in Edn., Biology, U. Tenn., 1963; MS in Edn., Portland (Oreg.) State U., 1970. Cert. tchr., Oreg., Calif. Tchr. sci. Hudson Sch. Dist., LaPuente, Calif., 1963-64, Baldwin (Calif.) Park Dist., 1964-67; tchr. biology Beaverton Sch. Dist. 48, Portland, 1968-70; student tchr. supr. Portland State U., 1971; tchr. Portland Community Coll., 1971-72; prin., dir., founder Belmont Sch., Portland, 1973—; co-owner Riverview Properties, Portland, 1973—; v.p. Mt. Park Vet. Clinic, Lake Oswego, 1978—. Chmn. Sunnyside Neighborhood, Portland, 1987; childcare advisor Portland Pub. Schs., 1976-87. Mem. Portland C. of C. (distinguished service award 1985), Belmont Bus. Assn. (treas. 1985-86, sec. 1986-87, pres. 1989—), Oreg. Fedn. Pvt. Schs. (pre-sch. com. 1986-87, treas. 1988-89, sec. 1989—). Republican. Baptist. Office: Belmont Sch 3841 SE Belmont Portland OR 97219

LINE, KIMBERLY CAMPBELL, administrator-retirement village; b. Sioux Falls, S.D., Oct. 31, 1961; d. Mark George and Janet Rae (Campbell) L. BS, Gustavus Adolphus Coll., 1983. Lic. nursing home adminstr., Hawaii, Kans. Adminstr.-in-tng. Nemeha County Good Samaritan Ctr., Auburn, Nebr., 1983-84; adminstr. nursing home Good Samaritan Soc., Wamego, Kans., 1984-87; adminstr. retirement village Good Samaritan Soc., Honolulu, 1987—. Tutor Hawaii Literacy Program, 1989—; mem. Elder Abuse-Hawaii, 1989—. Mem. Hawaii Long-Term Care Assn., Jr. League Honolulu. Democrat. Lutheran.

LINEHAN, HELEN M., paralegal; b. N.Y.C., Sept. 4, 1939; d. Timothy Finbar and Emma Louise (deLuis) O'Callaghan; m. William Linehan, Nov. 14, 1958 (div. 1979); children: M.E. Linehan, Sarah L. Linehan. Student, Fordham U., 1976-79. Asst. adminstr. Rudolf Steiner, N.Y.C., 1972-76; dir. sales adminstrn. Boris Kroll Fabrics Inc., N.Y.C., 1976-87, asst. v.p., 1986-87; edn. com. ACT, N.Y.C., 1986-87; paralegal bankruptcy Horwitz & Assocs., N.Y.C., 1988—. Democrat. Roman Catholic. Avocations: Marine life, communications with mammals, swimming, writing. Office: Horwitz & Assocs 276 Fifth Ave New York NY 10001

LINERT, SUSAN MARIE, oil company executive; b. Seattle, May 18, 1949; d. Edwin Joseph and Gilda Leah (Taylor) L. Diploma, Skagit Valley Coll., Mt. Vernon, Wash., 1969; BS, N.Mex. Inst. Mining and Tech., 1984. Rsch. and devel. equipment operator Petroleum Tech. Corp., Redmond, Wash., 1977-79; well completion supr. William Perlman Co., Ignacio, Colo., 1985; asst. dept. mgr. Best Products, Lynnwood, Wash., 1986-87; prodn. supt. Kimbell Oil Co. Tex., Farmington, N.Mex., 1987—. Mem. Soc. Petroleum Engrs., DAR, Am. Saddlebred Horse Assn., Nat. Geographic Soc. Home: 1218 N McCoy Ave Aztec NM 87410 Office: Kimbell Oil Co Tex 112 N Behrend Farmington NM 87401

LINFORD, MARY SUZANNE (SUE LINFORD), food distibrution executive; b. Indpls., Apr. 15, 1935; d. Robert William and Mary Catherine (Madden) Schmutte; widowed; children: Christopher, Douglas, Mark, Paul, Julie. Student, U. Alaska, 1959-80. Lic. real estate agt., Alaska. Various positions Indpls. and Anchorage, 1949-1973; acct., treas., gen. mgr., pres. Linford of Alaska Wholesale Food Distbr., Anchorage, 1973-83; pres., gen. mgr. Linford of Alaska, Anchorage, 1985—; exec. dir. Common Sense for Alaska, Anchorage, 1984-86; property mgr. Sue Linford Investments, Anchorage, 1983—; pvt. practice real estate, Anchorage, 1985—. Editor State PTA Bulletin, 1969-71. Mem. Alaska State Blue Ribbon Commn., 1979-80, various city commns. City of Anchorage, 1979—, budget commr., 1988—89; commr. Port of Achorage, 1989—; chmn. library bds. City of Anchorage/Greater Anchorage Borough/Municipality of Anchorage, 1969-77; founding mem., officer Anchorage Arts Council, 1971-74; pres. Anchorage Sch. Bd., 1974-77; bd. dirs. Alaska Zoo, 1989—; active Anchorage PTA. Mem. Alaska State C. of C., Anchorage C. of C. (sec.-treas., v.p., bd. dirs. 1977-81, Outstanding Community Service Gold Pan award 1981), Anchorage Bd. Realtors, Ruralcap (Cert. of Appreciation 1981, Outstanding Contbn. award 1985), Chaîne Des Rôtisseurs, Bailliage of U.S.A. Roman Catholic. Clubs: Petroleum of Anchorage, Anchorage Aquanaut Swim (pres. 1980-81), Alaska-Anchorage U.S. Swimming (publicity com. 1977-78, vice-chairperson tech. com. 1980-81); San Francisco Tennis (life), Capt. Cook Athletic. Lodge: Zonta (bd. dirs. 1968-80), Rotary. Office: Linford of Alaska Inc 4551 Fairbanks St Suite D Anchorage AK 99503

LING, KATHRYN WROLSTAD, health association administrator; b. Watertown, Wis., Aug. 3, 1943; d. Jeffery Harold and Constance Devina (Egre) Wrolstad; m. Cyril Curtis Ling; step-children: Renee Rainey, Roz Harper. BS in History, Polit. Sci., U. Wis., 1965. Supr. recreation ARC, DaNang, Cam Ran Bay, VietNam, 1968; assoc. exec. dir. Am. Cancer Soc., Evanston, Ill., 1968-71, exec. dir., 1971-73; exec. dir. Montgomery County Unit Am. Cancer Soc., Md., 1973-76, cons. income devel., 1976, dir., profl. edn. cancer incidence and end results, 1976-78, dir. income devel., 1978-82; exec. dir. Am. Cancer Soc., Chgo., 1982-84; assoc. exec. dir. Alzheimer's Disease and Related Disorder Assn., Chgo., 1985—, v.p. community service; cons. Nat. Aphasia Assn. Home: 1255 Sandburg Terr Chicago IL 60610

LING, MARIAN MING HO, educator; b. Hong Kong, Aug. 15, 1930; arrived in U.S., 1963; m. Edward Shang-Yi Ling, Dec. 1, 1956; 1 child, Lawrence Tsung-Lun. BA in Edn., Chu Hoi Coll., Hong Kong, 1953, BS in Sociology, 1953. Cert. tchr., Hong Kong. Data entry staff SCE & G Co., Columbia, S.C., 1969—. Vol. United Way, Columbia, S.C., 1970—, Columbia Action Coun., 1985—, ARC, Columbia, Hugo and Charleston, S.C., 1989; foster parent Holyland Christian Mission Internat., Kansas City, Mo., 1983—. Recipient Vol. Svc. award Providence Hosp., 1986, 88. Mem. Am. Inst. for Cancer Rsch., Nat. Arbor Day Found. Baptist. Home: 108 Westport Dr Columbia SC 29223 Office: SCE & G Co PO Box 764 Columbia SC 29202

LINGENFELSER, CATHERINE THERESA, computer operator, accounting technician; b. Savannah, Ga., June 30, 1952; d. William Francis Jr. and Catherine Elizabeth (Moore) L. AA, Armstrong State Coll., 1983. Bookkeeper, asst. office mgr. Valenti Volkswagen Inc., Savannah, 1970-74; cost acctg. clk. Great Dane Trailers, Savannah, 1974-81; acctg. clk. Savannah Foods and Industries, 1981-82; computer operator, acctg. technician U.S. Postal Svc., Savannah, 1982—. Contbg. author: History of Fayette County, Tennessee, 1986, Moore Family Register, 1986; editor: (quar. newspaper) The Flashback, 1980-83, (monthly computer newspaper) Byts and Bytes, 1987-89. Rec. sec. Women's Adv. Council for So. Region Postal Service, Savannah, 1987-89; bd. dirs. St. Vincent's Acad., Savannah, 1980-85, v.p.

alumnae assn., 1980-82; vol. tour guide Historic Savannah Found., 1980-88. Recipient Community Service award La Sertoma Orgn., 1970, Community Service award Historic Savannah Found., 1984. Mem. Savannah Commodore User's Group (pres. 1987-89), Ga. Hist. Soc., Savannah Area Geneal. Assn. (lectr. 1987, editor newsletter 1989), Monroe County (Ohio) Hist. Soc., DAR (rec. sec. Lachlan McIntosh chpt. 1986-90), UDC, Order of Crown Charlemagne, Daus of Ireland (bd. dirs. 1987-90, historian 1989-90). Roman Catholic. Home: 26 Broadmoor Circle Savannah GA 31406-2268 Office: US Postal Svc 2 N Fahm St Savannah GA 31402-9511

LINGLE, KATHLEEN MCCALL, marketing executive, entrepreneur; b. Berea, Ohio, Aug. 24, 1944; d. Arthur Vivian McCall and Mary M. (Maxwell) Miller; m. John Hunter Lingle, Sept. 3, 1968; 1 child, Michael Cameron. BA, Occidental Coll., 1966; MS, Ohio State U., 1977. Project dir. Ohio State U. Hosp., Columbus, 1977-78; rsch. assoc. Ednl. Testing Service, Princeton, N.J., 1978-82; mgr. mktg. services Gulton Industries, Princeton, 1982-84; rsch. dir. Rsch. 100, Princeton, 1984-85; dir. mktg. planning and rsch. Applied Data Research, Princeton, 1985-88; Western European sales mgr. Heuristics Software, Inc., Sacramento, 1988-89; pres., chief exec. officer Princeton Leadership Dynamics, 1989—. Vice pres. ops. Unitarian Ch. of New Brunswick (N.J.), 1983-84; served with Peace Corps, Chile and Venezuela, 1966, 69-72. Mem. NAFE, Am. Mktg. Assn., Am. Mgmt. Assn., Bus. and Profl. Women (co-chairperson membership com.), N.J. Assn. Women Bus. Owners, Princeton Network Profl. Women, Princeton Area C. of C. (mem. membership com.), Am. Field Svc. (Princeton chpt.). Democrat. Home: 988 Princeton Kingston Rd Princeton NJ 08540

LINGLE, MARILYN FELKEL, freelance writer; b. Hillsboro, Ill., Aug. 16, 1932; d. Clarence Frederick and Anna Cecelia (Stank) Felkel; m. Ivan L. Lingle, Oct. 4, 1950; children: Ivan Dale, Aimee Lee Lingle Galligan, Clarence Craig. Sec. Ill. State Police, 1950; with welfare dept. Ill. Pub. Aid, Hillsboro, 1951-52; researcher Small Homes Council, Champaign, 1952-53; sec. Hillsboro Schs., 1954; office, payroll clk. Eagle Picher Zinc, Hillsboro, 1955-56; continuity dir. Sta. WSMI, Litchfield, Hillsboro, 1966-87; active family bus. Church Street Pub/Restaurant; adv. bd. Am. Savs. Bank/Eagles Club, 1986-87, vice chmn., 1988—. Contbr. poetry to profl. jours. Fin. chmn. Hillsboro Hosp. Aux., 1972; literacy lifeline vol. Graham Correctional Ctr., Hillsboro, 1986—; pres., bd. dirs. Montgomery Players and Encore Play Theatre, 1954-70; child sponsor through World Vision. Mem. Cousteau Soc., Internat. Wildlife Fedn., Nat. Wildlife Fedn., Greenpeace. Democrat. Lutheran. Club: Hillsboro Country. Avocations: bridge, golf, gardening, travel, reading.

LINGLE, MURIEL E., elementary school educator; b. Sundown Twp., Minn.; d. Harold O. and Carrie H. (Ewald) Anderson; m. Dale A. Lingle, Aug. 21, 1946; children: Barbara Jean, Tamara Jane. BS with distinction, Union Coll., Lincoln, Nebr., 1968; MA, U. Nebr., Lincoln, 1976. Cert. tchr., Nebr. Elem. tchr. Hallam, Nebr., 1950-62; tchr. Cen. Elem. and High Sch., Sprague-Martell, Nebr., 1963-67, Helen Hyatt Elem. Sch., Lincoln, 1968-69; elem. tchr. Crete (Nebr.) Sch. System, 1969—. Mem. NEA, Nebr. State Edn. Assn. Democrat. Seventh Day Adventist. Home: 4730 Hillside Lincoln NE 68506 Office: Crete Pub Sch 920 Linden Ave Crete NE 68506

LINGO, HAZEL ISABEL, retired secondary educator; b. Topeka, Jan. 1, 1911; d. George Henry and Cicily Neva (Johnson) Fleischer; m. Robert M. Lingo, June 12, 1940. BA, Washburn U., Topeka, 1932; MS, Kans. U., 1957. Tchr. Soldier (Kans.) High Sch., 1932-36, Ellsworth (Kans.) High Sch., 1937-40, Coun. Grove (Kans.) High Sch., 1943-44, Neodesha (Kans.) High Sch., 1944-46; instr. Washburn U., Topeka, 1946-51; tchr. Topeka High Sch., 1951-73. Mem. local YWCA, 1946—, nominating com., 1980-84; benefactor to Ward-Meade Hist. Home, vol., 1985—; contbr. to Friends of Topeka Libr. Fellow Rotary; mem. AAUW (bd. dirs. 1947-51), Kans. Assn.s Tchrs. English (liaison officer 1955-70), Topeka Area Ret. Tchrs. (pres. 1979-80), Philanthropic Ednl. Orgn. Sisterhood (pres. local chpt. 1979-80), Order Eastern Star, Masons (pres. social order Beauceant 1979), Delta Kappa Gamma (pres. 1964-66, hon. tchr.)Phi Kappa Phi. Republican. Methodist.

LINGO, PATRICIA MARIE SAWYER, government official; b. Milw., Mar. 27, 1950; d. Kenneth John and Helen Elizabeth (Janicek) Sawyer; m. Ed Lee Lingo, Jr., Jan. 18, 1969 (div. Jan. 1986); children: Jacqueline Susanne, Patricia Louise. Student, La. State U., 1968-70, U. S.W. La., 1977-80, 89—. Clk. U.S. Postal Svc., Shreveport, La., 1973-76; clk. U.S. Postal Svc., Lafayette, La., 1983-86, supr. mails, 1986-88; officer-in-charge U.S. Postal Svc., Lake Arthur, La., 1986, Jennings, La., 1987; acting tour supr. U.S. Postal Svc., Lafayette, 1987-88; postmaster U.S. Postal Svc., Lake Arthur, 1988—. Mem. Jefferson Davis Task Force on Chem. Health. Mem. Nat. Assn. Postmasters U.S., Nat. League of Postmasters of the U.S., Kiwanis. Republican. Roman Catholic. Home: PO Box 540 Lake Arthur LA 70549-0540 Office: US Postal Svc 302 Kellogg St Lake Arthur LA 70549-9998

LINHART, DIANE SUE, social services administrator; b. Natrona Heights, Penn., Mar. 27, 1953; d. Robert McCrea and Henrietta Helen (Baker) L. BS, U. Pittsburgh, 1971-75; MS, U. Arizona, Tucson, 1977-79. Resident counselor Transitional Services, Pittsburgh, 1975; volunteer social worker VISTA, Bardwell, 1975-76; dormitory supr. Az. Sch. for Deaf & Blind, Tucson, 1977; counselor SW Center Hearing Impaired, San Antonio; various positions, presently dean of students South West Collegate Inst. for Deaf, Big Spring, Tex., 1980—. Mayor's panel C. of C. Christmas in Apr.; bd dirs. Highland Coun. for the Deaf, Rape Crisis Svcs., Am. Heart Assn., Big Spring, 1981-89. Mem. Leadership Big Spring, Am. Deafness & Rehab. Assn., Junior Coll. Student Personnel Assn. Tex., Nat. Assn. of Deaf, Tex. Jr. Coll. Teachers Assn., Tex. Assn. the Deaf, Tex. Assn. Coll. & U. Student Personnel Adminstra, Big Spring Kennel Club (v.p.). Democrat. Home: 1501 Runnels St Big Spring TX 79720

LINK, DEBORAH SHAW, psychiatrist, psychoanalyst; b. Boston, Apr. 19, 1933; d. Lawrence and Helen Louise (Fernald) Shaw. BA, Smith Coll., 1955; MA, Yale U., 1956; MD, Albert Einstein Coll. Medicine, 1971; grad., N.Y. Psychoanalytic Inst., 1984. Diplomate Am. Bd. Psychiatry and Neurology, Am. Psychoanalytic Assn. Researcher Newsweek Mag., N.Y.C., 1956-60; adminstr. Sarah Lawrence Coll., N.Y., 1964-67; resident Bronx Mcpl. Hosp., 1971-74; pvt. practice New Canaan, Conn., 1974—. Mem. Am. Psychiat. Assn, Am. Psychoanalytic Assn., N.Y. Psychoanalytic Soc., Am. Coll. Psychoanalysts. Home and Office: 97 Marvin Ridge Rd New Canaan CT 06840

LINK, MAE MILLS (MRS. S. GORDDEN LINK), space medicine historian and consultant; b. Corbin, Ky., May 14, 1915; d. William Speed and Florence (Estes) Mills; m. S. Gordden Link, Jan. 11, 1936. B.S., George Peabody Coll. for Tchrs., Vanderbilt U., 1936; M.A., Vanderbilt U., 1937; Ph.D., Am. U., 1951; grad., Air War Coll., 1965. Instr. social sci. Oglethorpe U., 1938-39; instr. English Drury Coll., 1940-41; asso. dir. edn. Ga. Warm Springs Found., 1941-42; mil. historian Hdqrs. Army Air Forces, 1943-45, Office Mil. History, Dept. of Army, 1945-51; spl. asst. to surgeon gen., sr. med. historian U.S. Air Force, Washington, 1951-62; cons. in documentation and space medicine historian NASA, Washington, 1962-64; coordinator documentation, life scis. historian NASA, 1964-70; research asso. Ohio State U. Found., 1970-72. Author: Medical Support of the Army Air Forces in World War II, 1955, Annual Reports of the U.S. Air Force Medical Service, 1949-62, Space Medicine in Project Mercury, 1965; (with others) USA/USSR Joint Publ. Foundations of Space Biology and Medicine, 1976; Editor: U.S. Air Force Med. Service Digest, 1957-62; Contbr. to profl. jours.; Collier's Ency., Ency. Brit.; contbr. to Funk and Wagnall's New Ency. Recipient Meritorious Service award U.S. Air Force, 1955, Ann. Outstanding Performance awards, 1956-62, Outstanding Alumna award Sue Bennett Coll., 1977. Fellow Am. Med. Writers Assn. (past pres. Middle Atlantic region); mem. Aerospace Med. Assn., Air Force Hist. Found. (charter), Internat. Congress History Medicine, Societe International d'Histoire de la Medecine, Planetary Soc. (charter). Republican. Episcopalian. Club: Garden of Va.

LINKEY, HELEN ELINOR, psychology professor; b. Toledo, Sept. 26, 1938; d. Myrle and Helen Jean (Ordas) L. BS, Siena Heights Coll., 1965; MA, Bowling Green State U., 1969, U. Detroit, 1977, Wayne State U., 1986. Tchr. Detroit, 1965-82; grad. student Wayne State U., Detroit, 1982-88; asst. prof. Marshall U., Huntington, W. Va., 1988—. Contbr. articles to profl. jours. Mem. Am. Psychol. Assn., Midwestern Psychol. Assn., Soc. Personality and Social Psychology, Sigma Xi. Office: Marshall U Dept Psychology Huntington WV 25755

LINN, CAROLE ANNE, dietitian; b. Portland, Oreg., Mar. 3, 1945; d. James Leslie and Alice Mae (Thorburn) L. Intern, U. Minn., 1967-68; BS, Oreg. State U., 1963-67. Nutrition cons. licensing and cert. sect. Oreg. State Bd. Health, Portland, 1968-70; chief clin. dietitian Rogue Valley Med. Ctr., Medford, Oreg., 1970—; cons. Hillhaven Health Care Ctr., Medford, 1971-83; lectr. Local Speakers Bur., Medford. Mem. ASPEN, Am. Dietetic Assn., Am. Diabetic Assn., Oreg. Dietetic Assn. (sec. 1973-75, nominating com. 1974-75, Young Dietitian of Yr. 1976), So. Oreg. Dietetic Assn., Alpha Lambda Delta, Omicron Nu. Democrat. Mem. Christ Unity Ch. Office: Rogue Valley Med Ctr 2825 Barnett Rd Medford OR 97504

LINN, JO WHITE, genealogist, lecturer; b. Chattanooga, Sept. 11, 1930; d. Franklin Turner and Lena (George) White; m. Stahle Linn, Dec. 12, 1953; children: Stahle III, Sarah Arrington. AB, Randolph-Macon Woman's Coll., 1952; student, U. N.C., 1952-53, Oxford (Eng.) U., 1980. Pvt. practice genealogy Salisbury, N.C., 1969—. Author: The Gray Family and Allied Lines, 1979 (Historians award 1977), People Named Hanes, 1980 (Historians award 1980), Drake-Arrington, White-Turner, Linn-Brown, 1984 (Robert Bruce Cook award 1984), A Holmes Family of Rowan and Davidson Counties, 1987 (Historians award); advisor Va. Genealogy mag., 1984—; editor, pub. Rowan County Register, 1986—. Recipient Hist. Preservation award Hist. Salisbury Found., 1988. Mem. Nat. Genealogical Soc. (regional rep.), DAR (regent 1968-70, state register 1974-77), DAC (regent 1970-75), N.C. Genealogical Soc. (pres. 1979-81), Country Club Salisbury, Fairyland Lookout Mountain (Tenn.). Democrat. Presbyterian. Home and office: 403 Idlewood Dr PO Box 1948 Salisbury NC 28144

LINNANSALO, VERA, engineer; b. Helsinki, Finland, Oct. 9, 1950; came to U.S., 1960, naturalized, 1969; d. Boris and Vera (Schkurat-Schkuropatsky) L. BS in Computer and Info. Sci., Cleve. State U., 1974, BME, 1974; MBA, U. Akron, 1983. Engring. assoc. B.F. Goodrich Co., Akron, Ohio, 1974-75, assoc. product engr., 1975-77, tire devel. engr., 1977-79, advanced tire devel. engr., 1979-84, quality devel. engr., 1984-85, sr. quality devel. engr., 1985-86; coordinator GM-10 Uniroyal Goodrich Tire Co., Akron, 1986-88, sr. tire devel. scientist, 1988-89; mgr. design and product quality Pirelli Armstrong Tire Corp., New Haven, 1989—; mem. Akron Rubber Group Inc. Mem. ASME, Am. Soc. Quality Control (sr., cert. quality engr.), Soc. Automotive Engrs. Home: 9 Stone Ridge Ln Branford CT 06405 Office: Pirelli Armstrong Tire Corp 500 Sargent Dr New Haven CT 06536

LINOFF-THORNTON, MARIAN GOTTLIEB, retired psychologist; b. Mpls., Feb. 17, 1937; d. Jack and Anne (Meirowitz) Gottlieb; m. Alan Lee Linoff, June 17, 1956 (div. 1968); children: Joseph, Deborah, Gordon; m. Thomas Elton Thornton, July 8, 1984. BA cum laude, U. Minn., 1961, MA, 1963; PhD, U. Miami, Fla., 1972. Lic. psychologist, Fla. Psychologist VA Med. Ctr., Miami, 1971-89; cons. Nat. Humanities Faculty, U. Miami Ctr., 1976-79, Nat. Drug Abuse Tng., 1974-78; specialist in geropsychology and aging. Mem. County Employ Handicapped, Miami, 1980-85. NIMH fellow, 1969-71; recipient Outstanding Performance award VA, 1983, 84, 85, Outstanding Handicapped Employee award Dept. Vet. Affairs, 1986. Mem. Am. Psychol. Assn., Gerontol. Soc. Am., Biofeedback Soc. Am., Fla. Psychol. Assn. (Dade County chpt.), Jewish. Research on geropsychological care of the chronically and terminally ill, psychological assessement of the elderly and medically frail. Home: 7450 SW 140 Dr Miami FL 33158 Office: VA Med Ctr 116B Miami FL 33158

LINQUIST, CINDY RAYE, lawyer; b. Topeka, Oct. 10, 1955; d. Edwin Ray and Rita Lee (Haydel) L. BS, U. No. Colo., 1978; JD, U. Kans., 1987. Bar: Colo. 1987, U.S. Dist. Ct. Colo. 1987. Tchr., coach Weldon Valley Sch. Dist., Weldona, Colo., 1978-79; tchr., coach St. Vrain Valley Sch. Dist., Longmont, Colo., 1979-83; assoc. Calkins, Kramer, Grimshaw & Harring, Denver, 1987—. AAU Jr. Olympic Nat.-Track and Field, 1972, Nat.-Basketball, 1989. Basketball scholar U. No. Colo., 1975-78. Mem. Colo. Bar Assn., Denver Bar Assn., Women's Bar Assn. Office: Calkins Kramer et al 1700 Lincoln St 3800 Denver CO 80203

LINSMEIER, MARY THERESE, educational administrator, family therapist; b. Peshtigo, Wis., Feb. 13, 1928; d. Franklin Benjamin and Martha (Archambault) Newbury; m. Francis G. Linsmeier, Aug. 27, 1955; children: Thomas, David, William, Alice, Nancy, Patricia, James, Mark. PhB, Marquette U., 1950; MS, U. Wis., Milw., 1974. Tchr. Notre Dame High Sch., Rochester, Minn., 1951-52, Union Free High Sch., Campbellsport, Wis., 1952-54, St. Augustine Grade Sch., Milw., 1954-56; tchr. remedial math and reading area schs., Milw., 1956-64; ednl. dir. Mary Linsmeier Schs. and Children's Edu-Care, Milw., 1964—; instr. in early childhood edn./Linsmeier method of edn. Mount Mary Coll., Milw., 1969—; pvt. practice specializing in marriage and family therapy Milw., 1984—. Author various ednl. materials. Vol. therapist Milw. Counseling Ctr., 1989—. Recipient Alumni Merit award Marquette U., Milw., 1982. Mem. Am. Assn. Marriage and Family Therapists (clin.). Roman Catholic. Home: 2615 Mayfair Dr Brookfield WI 53005 Office: Childrens Programs Inc 4445 N 124th St Brookfield WI 53005

LINZER, ESTELLE, program consultant; b. N.Y.C.; d. Martin M. and Lottie (Peist) L. BS in Mktg. and Journalism, N.Y.U. Field asst., field dir., assoc. dir. Am. Assn. for the UN, N.Y., 1945-66; con. The Johnson Found., Racine, Wis., 1966—; prog. con. N.Y., 1966—; adminstr. World Assembly for Human Rights, Montreal, 1968; adminstr. U.S del. Dartmouth Talks, Kiev, USSR, 1971; exec. dir. Albert Schweitzer Fellowship, N.Y., 1978—. Organizing com. mem. Eleanor Roosevelt Centenary of Friends and Admirers of Eleanor Roosevelt, 1984; chmn. exec. Non-govtl. Organs. Associated with the UN, N.Y., 1976-78. Mem. UN Assn. (vice chmn. 1977—, chmn. So. N.Y. State div. 1977-81, Arnold Goodman Leadership award 1983), Assn. for Internat. Practical Tng. (gen. bd. 1987—). Office: 866 United Nations Pla New York NY 10017

LION, STEPHANIE ANN, music educator; b. Alpena, Mich., Oct. 22, 1937; d. Anthony Henry and Marguerite Alicia (Tripp) Koch; children: Christopher, Tamara. BA in Music, Mich. State U., 1959, MA, 1961. Lic. kindermusik tchr. Ind. piano tchr. North Syracuse, N.Y., 1973—; cons. in organ restoration to chs.; cons. Mary Kay Cosmetics. Developed several manuals for young students. Mem. Nat. Guild Piano Tchrs., Am. Coll. Musicians (faculty), Cen. N.Y. Assn. Music Tchrs. (bd. dirs.), Nat. Fedn. Music Clubs, N.Y. State Fedn. Music Clubs, Nat. Piano Guild (judge, demonstrator, workshop clinician). Home and Office: 211 Volney Dr North Syracuse NY 13212

LIONTOS, ANTHEA LINDA, public relations executive; b. Montreal, Que., Can., May 19, 1961; came to U.S., 1988; d. Theodore Nicholas and Margaret Stewart (Cairns) L. BA in English, McGill U., 1982. Promotional dir. Boutique Quinto Ontario Ltd., Montreal, 1983-86; pub. relations dir. La Coupe/Charles Booth Haircare Products, Montreal, 1986-88, La Coupe/Charles Booth Co., Inc., N.Y.C., 1988—. Active Montreal Museum of Fine Arts, Met. Museum of Art, N.Y.C. Mem. Fashion Group Internat., Montreal Amateur Athletic Assn., Can. Club of N.Y. (chmn. jrs. com., co-chmn. events com.). Office: LaCoupeCharles Booth Co Inc 694 Madison Ave New York NY 10021

LIPE, LINDA BON, lawyer; b. Clarksdale, Miss., Jan. 10, 1948; s. William Ray and Gwendolyn (Strickland) Lipe; m. Larry L. Gleghorn, Feb. 15, 1983 (div. Feb. 1988). BBA in Accountancy, U. Miss., 1970, JD, 1971. Bar: Miss. 1971, Ark. 1976, U.S. Dist. Ct. (no. dist.) Miss. 1971, U.S. Dist. Ct. (ea. dist.) Ark. 1976, U.S. Ct. Appeals (8th cir.) 1985. Sr. tax acct. Arthur Young & Co., San Jose, Calif., 1971-74, A.M. Pullen & Co., Knoxville, Tenn., 1975; legal counsel to gov. State of Ark., Little Rock, 1975-79; dep. pros. atty. 6th Jud. Dist. Ark., Little Rock, 1979-80; chief counsel Ark. Public Service Commn., Little Rock, 1980-83; asst. U.S. atty. Eastern Dist. Ark., Dept. Justice, Little Rock, 1983—. Mem. ABA, Miss. State Bar, Ark. State Bar Assn., Ark. Bar Assn. Episcopalian. Office: US Atty's Office 600 W Capitol PO Box 1229 Little Rock AR 72203

LIPELY, KIM RENEE, television personality; b. Alliance, Ohio, Apr. 27, 1955; d. Bruce Leroy and Barbara Ann (Foltz) Brewer; m Gary Bruce Lipely, Mar. 22, 1975. Cert., Barbizon Sch. of Modelling, New Orleans, 1986. Info. operator Ohio Bell, Ohio, 1973-74; dental asst. J. F. Kelleher DDS, Inc., Alliance, Ohio, 1974-85; fashion model Freelance, Biloxi, Miss., 1986-; television hostess Singing River Hosp., Pascagoula, Miss. Republican. Presbyterian. Home: 2559 Audubon Pl Biloxi MS 39531

LIPHAM, MARY CATHERINE, infosystems specialist; b. Bowdon, Ga., Sept. 16, 1947; d. James Cliff and Mildred Elizabeth (Garrett) L.; m. H. Brooks Handy, Oct. 28, 1990. BA, W. Ga. Coll., 1969; MA, U. Ga., 1971. Archivist Md. Hall of Records, Annapolis, 1972-79; residential assessor Md. State Dept. of Assessments and Taxation, Annapolis, 1978-84; mem. task force Md. State Dept. of Assessments and Taxation, 1983-84; comml. indsl. trainee Md. State Dept. of Assessments and Taxation, Upper Marlboro, 1984-86; instr. telecommunications procedures Md. State Dept. of Assessments and Taxation, 1986-87; comml. indsl. assessor Md. State Dept. of Assessments and Taxation, Annapolis, 1986. Mem. Condominium Covenants Com., 1980-82, bd. dirs. 1982-83. Ford Found. fellow, 1969-70. Mem. Internat. Platform Assn., Nat. Trust for Hist. Preservation, Md. Assn. Assessing Officers (parliamentarian), Davidsonville Ballroom Dance Club. Home: 1552 Crofton Pkwy Crofton MD 21114 Office: Md Dept Assessments and Taxation 301 W Preston St Baltimore MD 21201

LIPINSKI, ANN MARIE, newspaper reporter. Reporter Chgo. Tribune. Recipient Pulitzer prize for series on politics and conflicts of interest Chgo. City Coun., 1988. Office: Chgo Tribune 435 N Michigan Ave Chicago IL 60611*

LIPINSKI, JANE LYNN, medical-surgical equipment sales representative; b. Columbia City, Ind., Aug. 20, 1953; d. Wilbur Demoines and Ruth Lucille (Cordill) Bennett; m. James Martin Lipinski, Oct. 26, 1983. B.A. in Bus., Purdue U., 1976. Orthopedic sales rep. Zimmer Co., Mpls., 1978-81; asst. to orthopedic physician, Clearwater, Fla., 1981-82; asst. dir. materials mgmt., Mease Hosp., Dunedin, Fla., 1982-84, sterile processing supr., 1982-84; med./surg. sales rep., surg. instrument specialist Edward Weck & Co., Inc., Research Triangle Park, N.C., 1984—. Mem. Nat. Assn. Female Execs., Assn. Operating Room Nurses, Assn. Hosp. Central Supply Mgrs. Republican. Avocations: scuba diving; underwater photography; tennis. Home: 12525 56th Pl N Royal Palm Beach FL 33411 Office: PO Box 16539 West Palm Beach FL 33416

LIPKIN, MARY CASTLEMAN DAVIS (MRS. ARTHUR BENNETT LIPKIN), retired psychiatric social worker; b. Germantown, Pa., Mar. 4, 1907; d. Henry L. and Willie (Webb) Davis; student Acad. Fine Arts, Pa., 1924-28, grad. sch. social work U. Wash., 1946-48; m. William F. Cavenaugh, Nov. 8, 1930 (div.); children: Molly C. (Mrs. Gary Oberbillig), William A.; m. 2d, Arthur Bennett Lipkin, Sept. 15, 1961 (dec. June 1974). Nursery sch. tchr. Miquon (Pa.) Sch., 1940-45; caseworker Family Soc. Seattle, 1948-49, Jewish Family and Child Service, Seattle, 1951-56; psychiat. social worker Stockton (Calif.) State Hosp., 1957-58; supr. social service Mental Health Research Inst., Fort Steilacoom, Wash., 1958-59; engaged in pvt. practice, Bellevue, Wash., 1959-61. Former mem. Phila. Com. on City Policy. Former diplomate and bd. mem. Conf. Advancement of Pvt. Practice in Social Work; former mem. Chestnut Hill women's com. Pa. Orch. Mem. AAAS, ACLU, Acad. Cert. Social Workers, Nat. Assn. Social Workers, Linus Paul Inst. Sci. and Medicine, Inst. Noetic Scis., Menninger Found., Union Concerned Scientists, Physicians for Social Responsibility, Center for Sci. in Pub. Interest, Jr. League, Asian Art Council, Nature Conservancy, Wilderness Soc., Sierra Club, Cosmopolitan Club Phila., Women's Univ. Club, Friday Harbor Yacht Club (Washington). Home: 10022 Meydenbauer Way SE #202 Bellevue WA 98004

LIPMAN, WYNONA M., state legislator; b. Ga.; children—Karen Anne, William (dec.). BA, Talladega Coll.; MA, Atlanta U.; Ph.D., Columbia U.; LL.D. (hon.), Kean Coll., Bloomfield Coll. Former high sch. tchr., lectr. Seton Hall U., Assoc. prof. Essex Community Coll.; mem. N.J. State Senate, 1971—, chmn. state govt. com., mem. joint appropriations com., revenue, fin. and appropriations com. vice-chmn., Commn. on Sex Discrimination in the Statutes. Mem. NAACP, Nat. Coun. Negro Women, Women's Polit. Caucus, Essex County Urban League. Recipient Outstanding Woman award Assn. Women Bus Owners, 1983. Democrat. Home: 50 Park Pl Ste 1035 Newark NJ 07102 Office: N J State Senate Trenton NJ 08625*

LIPPA, LINDA SUSAN MOTTOW, ophthalmologist; b. Boston, Apr. 9, 1951; d. George and Edith Etelka (Farcas) Mottow; m. Erik Alexander Lippa, Mar. 6, 1980; 2 children. BA magna cum laude, Harvard U., 1973; MD, Columbia U., 1977. Diplomate Am. Bd. Ophthalmology. Intern St. Luke's Hosp. Med. Ctr., N.Y.C., 1977-78; resident in ophthalmology Albert Einstein-Montefiore Hosp., Bronx, N.Y., 1978-81; fellow ophthalmol. pathology Ill. Eye and Ear Infirmary, Chgo., 1981-82; attending ophthalmologist, ophthalmic pathologist Cook County Hosp., Chgo., 1982-84, St. Paul (Minn.) Ramsey Med. Ctr., 1984-85; practice medicine specializing in ophthalmology Phila., 1985—; clin. asst. prof. Thomas Jefferson Med. Coll., Phila., 1986—; with Med Eye Care Assocs., Norristown, Pa., 1990—; asst. surgeon Wills Eye Hosp., Phila., 1985—; clin. instr., then clin. asst. prof. Loyola U.-Hines VA Hosp., Maywood, Ill., 1982-84; clin. asst. prof. U. Minn., Mpls., 1984-85, Jefferson Med. Coll., Phila., 1986—; clin. investigator in ocular pharmacology Thomas Jefferson Univ., Phila., 1987. Contbr. to profl. publs. Fellow Soc. Heed Fellows; mem. AMA, Am. Assn. Ophthalmic Pathologists, Midwestern Ophthalmic Pathology Soc., Phila. County Med. Soc., Pa. Med. Soc. Office: Med Eye Care Assocs McShea Hall 15 W Wood St 5th Fl Norristown PA 19401

LIPPE, PAMELA TOWEN, communications consultant; b. N.Y.C., Mar. 28, 1952; d. Vincent Stuyvesant and Barbara (Crane) Lippe. BA, Hampshire Coll., 1977. Legis. assoc. Friends of the Earth, Washington, 1976-79; found. dir. MUSE Found., N.Y.C., 1979-81; creative dir. Nat. Com. for an Effective Congress, N.Y.C., 1981-87; exec. dir., N.Y. State Dem. Assembly Campaign Com., 1987-88; New York regional fin. dir. U.S. Dem. Senate Campaign Com., 1988; communications cons., 1988—; sec., treas. Citizens Vote, Inc., N.Y.C., 1982—, also bd. dirs. Celebrity liaison Mondale-Ferraro campaign, 1984.

LIPPINCOTT, BARBARA BARNES, microbiology researcher, educator; b. Raleigh, Ill., Oct. 27, 1934; d. James Ward and Helen Mae (Dawes) Barnes; m. James Andrew Lippincott, June 2, 1956; children: Jeanne Marie, Thomas Russell, John James. AB, Washington U., St. Louis, 1955, MA, 1957, PhD, 1959. Postdoctoral fellow Nat. Ctr. Sci. Rsch., Gif-sur-Yvette, France, 1959-60; rsch. assoc. dept. biol. scis. Northwestern U., Evanston, Ill., 1960-81, rsch. assoc. dept. biochemistry, molecular biology and cell biology, 1981—, lectr., 1972-73, 80—; vis. scientist U. Calif., Berkeley, 1970-71, U. Heidelberg, Fed. Republic Germany, 1974. Contbr. numerous articles to profl. jours., chpts. to books. Fellow Jane Coffin Childs Meml. Fund for Med. Rsch., 1959-60. Mem. Am. Soc. for Microbiology, Phi Beta Kappa, Sigma Xi. Office: Northwestern U Dept Biochem Molecular and Cell Biology Evanston IL 60208

LIPPINCOTT, JANET, artist, art educator; b. N.Y.C., May 16, 1918. Student Emil Bisttram, Taos., N.Mex., Colorado Springs Fine Art Ctr., Art Students League N.Y.C., San Francisco Art Inst. Artist in residence, Durango, Colo., 1968; guest artist Tamarind Inst., Albuquerque, 1973; participant TV ednl. programs, Denver, Albuquerque; art instr. Santa Fe Community Coll., N.Mex., 1984—. Participant juried exhbns. including: Denver Mus., 1968, N.Mex. Arts Commn. traveling shows, 1967, Chautauqua Exhbn. Am. Art, N.Y., 1967, High Mus., Atlanta, Butler Inst. Am. Art, Springfield, Ohio, Dallas Mus. Fine Art, Mid Am. Exhbn., Nelson Atkins Mus., Kansas City, Kans., Mus. Fine Arts, Houston, Denver Art Mus., U. N.Mex. Art Gallery, Albuquerque, Ball State Tchrs. Coll., Muncie, Ind., N.Mex. Painting Invitational, 1968, Colorado Springs Fine Art Ctr., 1968, N.Mex. Biennial, Santa Fe, 1969, 72, 73 (award 1962), Tyler Mus. Art, Tex, 1977, Santa Fe Arts Festival, 1978, 79, 80, Enthios Gallery, Santa Fe, 1987; participant invitation exhbns. including: Albuquerque Mus. Art, 1977, Bethune & Moore, Denver, 1969, Yellowstone Art Ctr., Billings, Mont., 1967, Tucson Fine Art Ctr., 1965, Hockaday Sch., Dallas, 1965, Hayden Calhoun Galleries, Dallas, 1966, Leone Kahl Gallery, Dallas, 1965, U. Utah,

Salt Lake City, 1966, Roswell Mus. and Art Ctr., N.Mex., 1963, Lucien Labaudt Gallery, San Francisco, 1963, Denver U.S. Nat. Ctr., 1963, Muse d'Art Moderne, Paris, 1962, Instituto Cultural, Mexico City, 1957, Colo. State Coll., Greeley, 1961, Highland U., Las Vegas, N.Mex., 1960-70, St. John's Coll., Santa Fe, 1965, 75, 80, Coll. Santa Fe, 1968, 81, 4748 Galleries, Oklahoma City, 1965, Owen Gallery, Denver, 1970, New West Gallery, Albuquerque, 1970, 71, 72, 73, 74, Columbia Fine Arts Mus., S.C., 1972, Arts and Crafts Mus., Columbus, Ga., 1972, Dubose Gallery, Houston, 1972, Jamison Gallery, Santa Fe, 1972, Tex. Tech U., Lubbock, 1973 (award), Triangle Gallery, Tulsa, 1973, Gallery 26, Tulsa, 1974, West Tex. Mus., Lubbock, 1976, Britton Gallery, Denver, 1975, 77, 78, 79, 80, Osborne Gallery, Winnipeg, Ont., Can., 1979, Blair Gallery, Santa Fe, 1979, 80; works represented in pvt. and mus. collections; represented by Fletcher Gallery, Santa Fe, 1989-90, Day Star Internat. Galleries, Albuquerque, 1990. With WAC, 1943-45, ETO. Purchase awards and prizes include: Southwestern Biennial, Santa Fe, 1966, N.Mex. Mus. Fine Arts, 1957, Roswell Mus., 1958, Okla. Art Ctr., Oklahoma City, 1962, Atwater Kent award, Palm Beach, Fla., 1963, Chautauqua Art Award Assn. prize, 1963, El Paso Mus. prize, 1962, 76. Home: 1270 Canyon Rd Santa Fe NM 87501 Office: PO Box 2970 Santa Fe NM 87504

LIPPITT, ELIZABETH CHARLOTTE, writer; b. San Francisco; d. Sidney Grant and Stella L. Student Mills Coll., U. Calif.-Berkeley. Writer, performer own satirical monologues, nat. and polit. affairs for 85 newspapers including Muncie Star, St. Louis Globe-Dem., Washington Times, Utah Ind., Jackson News. Singer debut album Songs From the Heart; contbr. articles to 85 newspaper including N.Y. Post, L.A. Examiner, Orlando Sentinel, Phoenix Rep. Mem. Commn. for Free China, Conservative Caucus, Jefferson Ednl. Assn., Presdl. Adv. Commn. Recipient Congress of Fredom award, 1959, 71-73. Mem. Amvets, Nat. Trust for Hist. Preservation, Am. Security Coun., Internat. Platform Assn., Am. Conservative Union, Nat. Antivivisection Soc., High Frontier, For Our Children, Childhelp U.S.A., Free Afghanistan Com., Humane Soc. U.S., Young Ams. for Freedom, Coun. for Inter.-Am. Security, Internat. Med. Corps, Assn. Vets for Animal Rights, Met. Club, Olympic Club, Commonwealth Club. Home: 2414 Pacific Ave San Francisco CA 94115

LIPPS, CAROLYN S., healthcare risk manager; b. Gibson, N.C., June 2, 1943; d. Charles E. and Myrtle (Freeman) Skipper; 1 child, Rhonda Lipp Laxton. Grad. high sch., Garner, N.C.; diploma, Am. Med. Record Assn., Chgo., 1975; student, U. S.C., 1979. Cert. risk mgr.; accredited record technician. Assoc. exec. dir. S.C. Med. Card Found., Columbia; exec. dir. Del. Rev. Orgn., Wilmington; dir. utilization systems Humana, Inc., Louisville; dir. quality and resource mgmt. Humana Hosp., Aventura, Fla. Named Bus. Woman of Yr., 1971. Mem. Am. Med. Peer Rev. Assn. (bd. dirs.), Am. Soc. Exec. Women, Am. Assn. Quality Assurance Profls. Address: 1201 S Ocean Dr Apt 1109N Hollywood FL 33019

LIPSCOMB, ANNA ROSE FEENY, arts organizer, fundraiser b. Greensboro, N.C., Oct. 29, 1945; d. Nathan and Matilda (Carotenuto) L. Student langs., Alliance Francaise, Paris, 1967-68; BA in English and French summa cum laude, Queens Coll., 1977; diploma advanced Spanish, Forester Instituto Internacional, San Jose, Costa Rica, 1990. Reservations agt. Am. Airlines, St. Louis, 1968-69, ticket agt., 1969-71; coll. rep. CBS, Holt Rinehart Winston, Providence, 1977-79, sr. acquisitions editor Dryden Press, Chgo., 1979-81; owner, mgr. Taos (N.Mex.) Inn, 1981-89, fundraiser Taos Arts Celebrations, 1989—; bd. dirs. N.Mex. Hotel and Motel Assn., 1986—; sem. leader Taos Women Together, 1989. Editor: Intermediate Accounting, 1980; Business Law, 1981. Contbr. articles to profl. jours. Bd. dirs., 1st v.p. Taos Arts Assn., 1982-85; founder, bd. dirs. Taos Spring Arts Celebration, 1983—; founder, dir. Meet-the-Artist Series, 1983—; bd. dirs. and co-founder Spring Arts N.Mex., 1986; founder Yuletide in Taos, 1988, A Taste of Taos, 1988; bd. dirs. Music from Angel Fire, 1988—; founding mem. Assn. Hist. Hotels, Boulder, 1983—; organizer Internat. Symposium on Arts, 1985; bd. dirs. Arts in Taos, 1983, Taoschool, Inc., 1985—. Recipient Outstanding English Student of Yr. award Queens Coll., 1977; named Single Outstanding Contbr. to the Arts in Taos, 1986. Mem. Millicent Rogers Mus. Assn., Taos Lodgers Assn. (mktg. task force 1989), Taos County C. of C. (1st v.p. 1988-89, bd. dirs. 1987—, advt. com. 1987-90, chmn. nominating com. 1989), Internat. Platform Assn., Phi Beta Kappa. Democrat. Home: Talpa Rte Taos NM 87571 Office: PO Drawer N Taos NM 87571

LIPSCOMB, SALLY T., healthcare administrator; b. Owensboro, Ky., Oct. 30, 1948; d. Jack Edward and Martha Ann (Moors) Threlkeld; m. Jay Lipscomb, Feb. 1, 1969. BS in Nursing, Murray (Ky.) State U., 1970; M in Pub. Health, U. Ill., 1977. RN; cert. employee assistance profl. Asst. head nurse Our Lady Mercy Hosp., Owensboro, Ky., 1971; nurse researcher clin. rsch. ctr. NIMH, Lexington, Ky., 1971-73; drug abuse cons.region 5 HEW, Chgo., 1973-76; adminstr.legal div. Nat. Assn. State Mental Program Dirs., Wash., D.C., 1977-78; instr.pub. health U. Ill., 1977-79; clin. dir. Interventions, Chgo., 1979-84, dir. program devel., 1984-85, dir. spl. health programs, 1985—; cons. Nat. Inst. Drug Abuse, Rockville, Md., 1977-81. Contbr. articles to profl. jours. Mem. Employee Asst. Profls. Assn. (bd. dirs. chair benefits com. 1986—, HMO com. 1981-86, Employee Assitance Profl. of Yr. 1989), Ill. Alcoholism Drug Dependence Assn. (chair ins. com. 1980-81), Delta Omega Soc. Democrat. Office: Interventions 1234 S Michigan Ave Chicago IL 60605

LIPSKI, C. J., company official, computer consultant; b. Durham, N.C., Aug. 17, 1943; d. William Allen Sr. and Mamie Jane (Lemmons) Neal; m. Arthur Harold Lipski, Jr., Nov. ll, 1967; children: Christian Allen, Kevin Arthur. AB in English, High Point Coll., 1965; postgrad., Ea. Ky. U., 1976-77, U. Ala., Birmingham, 1981-83, Fairleigh Dickinson U., 1983. Cert. info. processor. Tchr. English Cen. High Sch., Lexington, N.C., 1965-66; equipment engr. Pacific Tel. Co., San Jose, Calif., 1966-68; tchr. Lexington Ave. Presch., Danville, Ky., 1975-78, St. Andrew's Cath. Sch., Harrodsburg, Ky., 1978-81; adminstrv. asst. U. Ala. Grad. Sch., 1982-83; tchr. computer St. Joseph's Cath. Sch., Mendham, N.J., 1983-84, Carden Sch. Moraga (Calif.), 1985-86; mgr. end-user computing Cetus Corp., Emeryville, Calif., 1986-88, mgr. customer svc. dept., 1988-90; owner, mgr. CJ Lipski, Computer Cons., Long Valley, N.J., 1983-85. Trustee Boyle County Libr., Danville, 1978-80; co-chmn. Ky. Pro-ERA Alliance, Danville, 1981; v.p. Moraga Playhouse Found., 1988-89, pres., 1989-90. Named Outstanding Young Bus. Woman, Bus. and Profl. Womens Club, Salisbury, N.C., 1965; recipient cert. of appreciation Town of Moraga, 1988; nominated for Shellie award best supporting actress in a play Bay Area Theatres, 1989. Mem. Infoholics Anonymous, AAUW (v.p. Danville 1980-8l). Democrat. Methodist. Office: 6374 E Calle de Mirar Tucson AZ 85715

LIPSKY, LINDA ETHEL, business executive; b. Bklyn., June 2, 1939; d. Irving Julius and Florence (Stern) Ellman; m. Warren Lipsky, June 12, 1960 (div. Sept. 1968); 1 child, Phillip Bruce; m. Jerome Friedman, Jan. 17, 1988. BA in Psychology, Hofstra U., 1960; MPS in Health Care Adminstrn., Long Island U., 1979. Child welfare social worker Nassau County Dept. Social Service, N.Y., 1960-64; adminstr. La Guardia Med. Group of Health Ins. Plan of Greater N.Y., Queens, 1969-72; cons. Neighborhood Service Ctr., Bronx, N.Y., 1973-78; dir. ODA Health Ctr., Bklyn., 1978-82; pres. Millin Assocs., Inc., Nassau, N.Y., 1982—. Mem. Health Care Fin. Mgmt. Assn., Nat. Assn. Community Health Ctrs., Nat. Assn. Female Execs., Hofstra U. Alumni Assn. (mem. senate 1984—, chairperson membership com. 1985—), Pi Alpha Alpha. Republican. Jewish. Avocations: cooking, writing, reading. Office: Millin Assocs Inc 521 Chestnut St Cedarhurst NY 11516

LIPSMAN, PAULEE, legislative staff administrator; b. Davenport, Iowa, July 19, 1947; d. Victor and Zita (Siev) L. BS, Northwestern U., 1969. Tchr. Balt. Pub. Schs., 1969-70; news reporter Sta. KSTT/WXLP, Davenport, 1972-77, sales rep., 1978-81, sales mgr., 1981-84; fin. dir. Harkin for Senate, Des Moines, 1984; polit. cons. Fitzpatrick & Assocs., Des Moines, 1985-86; dep. Sec. of State, Des Moines, 1987-89; dir. Ho. Dem. rsch. staff Iowa Ho. of Reps., Des Moines, 1989—. Bd. dirs. Iowa Dem. State Cen. Com., Des Moines, 1988—, Jewish Community Rels. Commn., Des Moines, 1988—, Iowa Network for Women, Des Moines, 1988—. Named Mentor of the Yr., Iowa Young Dems., 1989. Mem. NOW, Iowa Civil Liberties Union (bd. dirs. 1989—). Home: 2880 Grand Ave #106 Des Moines IA 50312

LIPSON, AVIS RUTH, management information systems director; b. Elmira, N.Y., June 20, 1951; d. Leonard LeRoy and Ruth Belle (Green) Grippin; m. John L. Bogart, June 26, 1971 (div. Mar. 1982); 1 child, Jeremy Bogart; m. Andrew W. Lipson, June 11, 1988. Assoc. Applied Sci., Corning Community Coll., N.Y., 1971. Cooperative edn. cert. computer sci., 1969. Keypunch operator St. Joseph's Hosp., Elmira, N.Y., 1969-71; audit clk. St. Joseph's Hosp., 1971-73, patient acctg. mgr., 1973-75, office mgr. rehab., 1975-76, data processing coord., 1976-82; dir. data processing Mercy Community Hosp., Port Jervis, N.Y., 1983-86; dir. info. systems St. Mary's Hosp., Rochester, N.Y., 1986—; cons., Rochester, 1986-88. Den leader Boy Scouts Am., Elmira, 1972-74. Mem. Am. Hosp. Assn. Info. Systems Soc., NAFE. Methodist. Home: 110 Old Scottsville Chili Churchville NY 14428 Office: St Marys Hosp 89 Genesee St Rochester NY 14611

LIPSTATE, JO ANN, cemetery executive, public relations consultant; b. San Antonio, Aug. 4, 1930; d. Herbert and Beatrice (Adelman) Davis; m. Eugene J. Lipstate, Feb. 26, 1950; children—James Mitchell, Betsy Ann Lipstate Horner. Student in fine arts and English, U. Tex., 1947-49. Copywriter Sta.-KATC-TV, Lafayette, La., 1970-73; pres. Lipstate Creative Services, Lafayette, 1973-80; pub. relations cons. N.W. Oil Co., Lafayette, 1979—; v.p. Eugene J. Lipstate, Inc., 1979; pres. Eterna, Inc., dba Fountain Meml. Gardens and Mausoleum, Lafayette, 1983—, chmn. bd., 1988; bd. dirs. Mid La. Health Systems Agy., Lafayette, 1980-83, chmn. project, 1982-83; found. mem. Women's Hosp. Acadiana, Lafayette, 1982—; trustee Women's and Children Hosp., Lafayette, 1987. Bd. dirs. Lafayette Juvenile and Young Adult Program, 1969, art therapist, 1970. Mem. Ad Club Acadiana (pres. 1978-79, 3 TV comml. awards 1972). Republican. Jewish. Clubs: City, Oakbourne Country (Lafayette). Avocations: golf; tennis; fishing; painting; gardening. Home: 401 Shelly Dr Lafayette LA 70503 Office: Bldg 12 Oil Center Dr at Heyman Blvd PO Box 52421 Lafayette LA 70505

LIPSTONE, JANE N., producer video industrials, syndication, cable; b. Chgo., Jan. 9, 1931; d. Sol and Ruth (Cohen) Nudelman; m. Howard H. Lipstone, Apr. 7, 1957; children: Lewis, Gregory. BA, Purdue U., 1952. Publicist The Landsburg Co., L.A., 1977-87, producer, 1987—; publicist Reeves Entertainment Group, Burbank, Calif., 1984. Mem. Blue Ribbon Bd. L.A. Philharmonic, 1980—; bd. of govs. Cedars Sinai Med. Ctr., L.A., 1986—, mem. exec. bd., 1990—. Named Best Home Video, USDA, 1989.

LIPTAK, IRENE FRANCES, retired business executive; b. Clifton, N.J., Feb. 22, 1926; d. George J. and Anna J. (Strelec) L. Student, U. Newark, 1944-45; BS, Rutgers U., 1950, MBA, 1955, EdM, 1964; postgrad., Montclair State Coll., 1960-61, Fairleigh Dickinson U., 1963-64. Exec. sec., adminstrv. asst. to pres. and chmn. bd. Botany Mills, Inc., Passaic, N.J., 1942-53; treas., sec. Rowland-Johnson Co., Clifton, 1953-80; exec. sec. to chief exec. officer Edison Parking Corp., Newark, 1983; bldg. adminstr. Hippodrome Bldg., N.Y.C., 1984; office mgr. Decor Structure, Inc., Carlstadt, N.J., 1984-85. Editor: Ch. News, 1958-68. Mem. conf. planning com. N.J. Commn. on Women, 1972; treas. Slovak Nat. Cath. Cathedral, Passaic, 1976-77; sec., dir., trustee Charles Jr. and Dorothy Johnson Found., 1957-80. Mem. Grad. Sch. Edn. Alumni Assn. Rutgers, Rutgers U. Coll. Honor Soc.(life), Rutgers U. Coll. Alumni Assn. (life, mem. cen. coun. 1971-74, v.p. Paterson regional coun. 1986-90), AAUW (corr. sec. Nutley br. 1972-74, treas. 1974-76, pres. 1979-81, dir. N.J. div. 1975-76), Am. Soc. Notaries, Am. Friends Arts, S.W. Bergen Stroke and Disabled Club (founder, pres. 1987-88), Phi Chi Theta (chmn. nat. conv. 1972). Republican. Home: 106 Ridge Rd Rutherford NJ 07070

LIPTON, BARBARA, museum director, curator; b. Newark, N.J.; m. Milton Lipton; children: Joshua, Sara, Beth. BA, U. Iowa; MA, U. Mich.; MLS, Rutgers U. Library dir. Newark Mus., 1970-75, spl. projects cons., 1975-82; asst. dir. Castle Gallery Coll. of New Rochelle, N.Y., 1982-83; guest curator Dept. Indian and No. Officers, Ottawa, Ont., Can., 1983-85; dir. Jacques Marchais Mus. Tibetan Art, S.I., N.Y., 1985—; tchr., lectr. various schs. and mus. including Mus. Natural History, N.Y.C., Smithsonian Inst., Washington, 1976—; former guest curator many mus. Author: (catalogs) Arctic Vision, 1984, Survival Art Life of the Alaskan Eskimo, 1976; (bibliography) Westerners in Tibet, 1972; exec. producer, writer documentary film: Village of No River, 1981. Trustee Planned Parenthood, Essex County, N.J., 1976—. NEH grantee, 1976, 79, 80, 87. Mem. Am. Assn. Mus., Mid-Atlantic Assn. Mus. Home: 282 Scotland Rd South Orange NJ 07079 Office: Jacques Marchais Mus Tibetan Art 338 Lighthouse Ave Staten Island NY 10306

LIPTON, LEAH, art historian, educator; b. Kearny, N.J., Mar. 22, 1928; d. Abraham and Rose (Berman) Shneyer; m. Herbert Lipton, Sep. 19, 1951 (dec. 1979); children: David, Ivan, Rachel. BA, Douglass Coll. Rutgers U., New Brunswick, N.J., 1949; MA, Harvard U., Cambridge, Mass., 1950; postgrad., Harvard U., 1970-73, Wellesley Coll., 1970-73. Photo, library researcher Mus. Fine Arts, Boston, 1950-53, lectr., division edn., 1965-70; instr. Boston Coll., 1968-69; faculty, full prof. Framingham State Coll., Mass.; mem. bd. trustees Danforth Mus. Art, Framingham Mass., 1975--; adjunct curator Am. art Danforth Mus. Art, Framingham Mass. 1987--; chair exhibitions Com.; Collections Com. Danforth Mus., Framingham Mass. 1980--; guest curator Nat. Portrait, Wash. 1985. Author: Book, 1985, Exhibition Catalogue 1988, Contbr. articles to profl. jours. 1981-88. Mem. Chmn. Planning Bd. Wayland, Mass. 1966-69; Cons. Framingham Planning Bd., Mass. 1977-79; Co-Founder Danforth Mus. Art., Mass. 1973-75. Recipient Distinguished Service award Framingham State Coll., Mass. 1978, 87. Mem. Coll. Art Assn., Soc. Archl. Historians, Am. Assn. Mus. Office: Framingham State Coll 100 State St Framingham MA 01701

LIPTON, LORIAN, computer professional; b. Mineola, N.Y., Mar. 16, 1957; d. David and Florence (Abby) L. BA, SUNY, Binghamton, 1978. Microcomputer mgr. Milton Bradley Co., East Longmeadow, Mass.; dir. networks, edn. and systems support Command Performance Computers, Windsor, Conn.; dir. tech. svcs. JWP Info. Systems, Windsor; dir. tech. svcs. Computerland of Hartford. Pres. Hartford Women's Ctr., Inc. Mem. NAFE, Boston Computer Soc., Conn. Computer Soc., Local Area Network Dealer Assn. Home: 49 Oxford St Hartford CT 06105

LIPTON, MILDRED CERES, child psychologist; b. Bklyn., May 21, 1921; d. Salvatore and Josephine (Nicotra) Ceres; m. Edmond Lipton, Aug. 2, 1963; stepchildren: Richard Lipton, Judith Hodson. BA, Douglass Coll., 1943; MA, State U. Iowa, 1946. Clin. psychology intern Rockland State Hosp., Orangeburg, N.Y., 1943-44, clin. psychologist children's unit, 1945-48; clin. psychologist VA Mental Health Clinic, Bklyn., 1948-50, Erie (Pa.) Guidance Ctr., 1950-51; chief clin. psychologist Westchester Guidance Ctr., White Plains, N.Y., 1951-63; instr. psychology Mills Coll. of Edn., N.Y.C., 1963-67; pvt. practice clin. child psychology Bklyn., 1967—; instr. psychology St. John U., Jamaica, N.Y., 1983; Ikenobo instr. of Ikebana Bklyn. Botanic Gardens, 1984—. Mem. Am. Psychol. Assn., Bklyn. Mental Health Assn. (bd. dirs., chair com. for emotionally disturbed children, 1967-71), Ikenobo Soc. of Eastern Seaboard (pres. 1986—). Home: 132 Argyle Rd Brooklyn NY 11218 Office: 132 Argyle Rd Brooklyn NY 11218

LISA, ISABELLE O'NEILL, law firm, mergers-acquisitions company executive; b. Phila., Mar. 12, 1934; d. Thomas Daniel and Margaret Marie (Hayes) O'Neill; m. Donald Julius Lisa, June 15, 1957; children: Richard Allan, Steven Gregory. Student, Harper Community Coll., Rolling Meadows, Ill., 1976, Scottsdale Community Coll., 1980, Ariz. State U., 1981-82. Cost control clk. Curtis Pub. Co., Phila., 1952-56; sec. United Ins. Co., Annapolis, Md., 1956-57; firm adminstr., legal sec. Law Offices Donald J. Lisa, Bloomingdale, Ill., 1987; legal sec. Lisa & Kubida, P.C., Phoenix, 1987-88, firm adminstr., 1987-89; firm adminstr. Lisa & Assocs., Phoenix, 1989-90, Lisa & Lisa, Phoenix, 1990—; v.p. adminstrn. Lisa & Co., Phoenix, 1987—. Den mother Cub Scouts Am., Millburn, N.J., 1965; founder, pres. Pro-Tem Rutgers U. Law Wives Assn., 1962-63. Mem. NAFE, Assn. Legal Adminstrs., Rotary, Rotary Anns. Republican. Roman Catholic. Home: 10935 E Tierra Dr Scottsdale AZ 85259 Office: 2200 N Central Ave Ste 1225 Phoenix AZ 85004

LISBOA-FARROW, ELIZABETH OLIVER, public and government relations consultant; b. N.Y.C., Nov. 25, 1947; d. Eleuterio and Esperanza Oliver; student pvt. schs., N.Y.C.; m. Jeffrey Lloyd Farrow, Dec. 31, 1980; 1 son, Hamilton Oliver Farrow; 1 stepson, Maximillian Robbins. With Harold Rand & Co. and various other public relations firms, N.Y.C., 1966-75; dir. public relations N.Y. Playboy Club and Playboy Clubs Internat., 1975-79; pres. Lisboa Assocs., Inc., N.Y.C., 1979—. Sec. Nat. Acad. Concert and Cabaret Arts; mem. nat. adv. council SBA, 1980-81; exec. dir. Variety Club of Greater Washington, Inc., Children's Charity. Mem. U.S. Hispanic C. of C., Hispanic Bus. and Profl. Women's Assn. Office: 1317 F St NW Washington DC 20004

LISI, PENELOPE LEITNER, university official; b. Milw., Feb. 2, 1951; d. Gordon Frank and Jessie Virginia (Hartill) Leitner; m. Peter Waterman Lisi, Dec. 11, 1982. BA with honors, DePauw U., 1973; MS, U. Wis., Milw., 1977; PhD, U. Wis., Madison, 1982. Cert. tchr., adminstr., Ariz., Wis. Tchr. Peoria (Ariz.) Pub. Schs., 1973-76, St. John's Mil. Acad., Delafield, Wis., 1976-77, Stavanger (Norway) Am. Sch., 1977-79, Copenhagen Internat. Jr. Sch., 1979-80; supr. sch. svcs. Mystic (Conn.) Seaport Mus., 1983-87; exec. dir. Ctr. for Ednl. Excellence, Conn. State U., New Britain, 1987—; vis. instr. Conn. Coll., New London, 1986—; Kellogg resident Smithsonian Instn., Washington, 1986. Editor Seaport Signal, 1986-87, EXCEL, 1987-89. Mem. communications bd., pastoral care team Asylum Hill Congl. Ch., Hartford, Conn., 1989—. Mem. Nat. Assn. Women Deans, Adminstrs. and Counselors, Am. Assn. for Counseling and Devel., AAUW (membership v.p. Conn. div. 1989—). Office: Conn State U PO Box 2008 New Britain CT 06050

LISICKI, BERNICE MARIE, computer resourecs coordinator; b. Phila., Feb. 8, 1963; d. Stephen Joseph and Alberta Jean (Pote) L. BA, Holy Family Coll., Phila., 1985; postgrad., LaSalle U., 1988—. Jr. acct. Reliance Life Cos., Phila., 1985-86, Cameo Stores, Inc., Phila., 1986-87; fin. aid counselor Northeastern Hosp. Sch. Nursing, Phila., 1987; computer lab. asst. Holy Family Coll., Phila., 1987-88, computer resources coord., 1988—; cons., Phila., 1988—, Andalusia, Pa., 1988—. Named one of Outstanding Young Women Am., 1987, 88, 89. Mem. NAFE, Assn. for Info. Mgmt. Republican. Roman Catholic. Office: Holy Family Coll Grant and Frankford Aves Philadelphia PA 19114

LISK, JOANNE ESTELLE JACKSON, nurse, educator, consultant; b. Beaumont, Tex., Mar. 4, 1933; d. Claude Leonard and Frances Nietta (Campbell) Jackson; m. Richard Arlen Lisk, Dec. 17, 1955; children: Lynn, Richard Joe, Nietta (dec.). Student, North Tex. State U., 1949-52; BS in Nursing, Baylor U., 1956; MS in Nursing, U. Cen. Ark., 1981. RN, La., Miss. Staff nurse various hosps., Okla., 1956-68; instr. lic. practical nurse program O.T. Autry Vocat. Tech. Sch., Enid, Okla., 1973-75; dir. out-patient program Cen. Ark. Mental Health Ctr., various cities, 1977-80; asst. prof. nursing Alcorn State U., Natchez, Miss., 1981—; cons. psychiat. nursing, South Miss. Home Health and Rehab., Natchez, 1982—; co-leader, cons., Talk Line teen crisis line, Natchez, 1987—. Contbr. articles to various publs.; author curriculum materials. Pres. European Bapt. Conv., Women's Missionary Union, So. Bapt. Conv., 1971-73, Ark. v.p., 1979. Mem. Miss-Lou Mental Health Assn., Am. Nurse's Assn., Miss. Nurse's Assn., Am. Psychiat. Nurse's Assn., Orgn. for Advancement of Assoc. Degree Nursing, Nat. League of Nursing, PEO, Sigma Theta Tau, Delta Kappa Gamma. Republican. Home: 504 N Oak St Vidalia LA 71373 Office: Alcorn State U Div Nursing PO Box 1830 Natchez MS 39120

LISKA, EILEEN MARGUERITE, lobbyist; b. Chgo., Nov. 28, 1948; d. Louis Joseph and Elizabeth (Fojtik) L.; m. Philip Edward Stevens, Mar. 1, 1975. Student, Mich. State U., 1966-68, Leningrad (USSR) State U., 1967, Middlebury Coll., 1968; BA in Russian Lang./Lit. with honors, U. Mich., 1970. Ref. libr., translator, editor Mathematical Review, Ann Arbor, Mich., 1972-74; tech. libr., NIH and NSF grant proposal editor Dept. Physiol. Chemistry, U. Wis. Med. Sch., Madison, 1974-75; personnel mgr. in-patient admissions dept. U. Wis.-Madison Hosps., 1975-76; legis. aide to state assemblyman Wis. State Capitol, Madison, 1977-80; writer, editor, devel. officer, community rels. office U. Mich. Hosps. and Med. Sch., Ann Arbor, 1980-81; dir. edn. and community rels. Humane Soc. of Huron Valley, Ann Arbor, 1981-82; legis. aide to state senator Mich. State Senate, Lansing, Mich., 1982-84; dir. rsch. and legislation Mich. Humane Soc., Detroit, 1984—. Scholarship Mich. State U., 1966-68, Leningrad State U., 1967, Middlebury Coll., 1968, U. Mich., 1968-70. Office: Mich Humane Soc 7401 Chrysler Dr Detroit MI 48211

LISKIN, BARBARA ANN, psychiatrist; b. Englewood, NJ, Nov. 24, 1952; d. Louis and Anita (Merker) L.; m. Vincent Robert Bonagura, June 3, 1982; children: Elizabeth, Rebecca. AB, Smith Coll., Northampton, 1974; MS, Columbia U., N.Y.C., 1974, MD, 1979. Boarded in Pediatrics and Psychiatry. Research asst. Columbia U., N.Y.C., 1974-75; asst. psychiat. instr. Columbia U., 1985-87, asst. clin. prof. pediatrics and psychiatry, 1987—, dir. young adult psychiatry, 1987—; clin. dir. Barnard Coll. Mental Health Svcs., 1988—. Recipient NIMH Jr. Faculty award 1985; Resident Research award 1985. Mem. Am. Psychiatry Assn. Office: Barnard Coll Health Svcs 3009 Broadway New York NY 10027

LISKOV, BARBARA HUBERMAN, software engineering educator; b. Los Angeles, Nov. 7, 1939. BA in Math., U. Calif., Berkeley, 1961; MS in Computer Sci., Stanford U., 1965, PhD, 1968. With applications programming sect. Mitre Corp., Bedford, Mass., 1961-62, mem. tech. staff, 1968-72; with Harvard U., Cambridge, Mass., 1962-63; grad. research asst. dept. computer sci. Stanford U., Palo Alto, Calif., 1963-68; prof. computer sci. and engring. MIT, Cambridge, 1972—, NEC prof. software sci. and engring., 1984—. Author: (with others) CLU Reference Manual, Lecture Notes in Computer Science 114, 1981; (with J. Guttag) Abstraction and Specification in Program Development, 1986; assoc. editor Transactions on Programming Langs. and Systems; contbr. articles to profl. jours. Mem. IEEE , Assn. Computing Machinery (spl. interest groups on microprogramming and oper. systems programming langs.), Nat. Acad. Engring.

LISONI, GAIL MARIE LANDTBOM, lawyer; b. San Francisco, Mar. 11, 1949; d. William A. and Patricia Ann (Cruden) Landtbom; m. Joseph Louis Lisoni, Mar. 24, 1984. B.A., Dominican Coll., Calif., 1971; J.D., U. West Los Angeles, 1978, cert. paralegal, 1974. Bar: Calif. 1979. Campaign treas. Calif. for Lisoni, Arcadia, 1979-81; assoc. Joseph Lisoni, Esq., Los Angeles, 1981, Arnold S. Malter, Esq., Los Angeles, 1982; ptnr. Lisoni & Lisoni, Los Angeles, 1983—. Mem. Assn. Trial Lawyers Am., Calif. Trial Lawyers Assn., Los Angles Trial Lawyers Assn., ABA, Italian Am. Lawyers Assn. Democrat. Roman Catholic. Lodge: Sons of Italy. Office: Lisoni & Lisoni 35 N Lake Ave Ste 700 Pasadena CA 91101

LISSANT, ELLEN MARIE, retired biology educator, artist; b. St. Louis, Nov. 4, 1922; d. Walter C. V. and Hedwig C. (Stroh) Kern; m. Kenneth Jordan Lissant, June 14, 1947; children: Joyce Ellen, Keith Jordan, Nathan Kern. AB, Washington U., St. Louis, 1944, MA, 1946, PhD, 1968. Lab. instr. Washington U., 1943-45, lab. asst., 1946-47; tchr. biology Webster Groves (Mo.) High Sch., 1945-46; herbarium asst. Stanford U., Palo Alto, Calif., 1947; from instr. to prof. biology Fontbonne Coll., Clayton, Mo., 1960-79, chmn. dept., 1977-79; instr. biology St. Louis Community Coll.-Meramec, Kirkwood, Mo., 1982-86, ret., 1986. Illustrator: Corn & Corn Growing (Edgar Anderson), Corn Plant Today (Edgar Anderson), Sacred Plume (Edgar Anderson), Studies in Paleobotany (Henry Andrews), Traite De Palebotanique (Henry Andrews); artist cover design Science mag., 1963; contbr. articles on botany to sci. publs. Mem. Bot. Soc. Am., Phycological Soc. Am., Internat. Phycological Soc., Sigma Xi, Phi Beta Kappa, Alpha Lambda Delta, Pi Mu Epsilon, Kappa Delta Pi, Sigma Lambda Epsilon. Lutheran. Home: Rte 1 Box 251A Clever MO 65631

LIST, DIANE RUTH, psychologist; b. Saginaw, Mich., Aug. 8, 1948; d. Wilfred James and Ruth Ida (Miller) Dunn; m. Donald Richard List, June 14, 1969); children: Jeffery James, Jacqueline Diane. BA, Sophia U., 1970; MA, Ball State U., 1975, PhD, 1984. Lic. psychologist, Mich. Tchr. Bridgeport (Mich.) Schs., 1971-72; counselor Caro (Mich.) Community Schs., 1975-82; dir. psychology Caro Regional Mental Health Ctr., 1984-88; pvt. practice Caro, 1988—; co-owner, cons. Human Resources Unltd., Caro, 1988—. Trustee, Caro Community Hosp. Bd., 1987-88. Mem. Am. Psychol. Assn., Bus. and Profl. Women Assn. Democrat. Lutheran. Home: 1580 Oakwood Caro MI 48723

LISTER, PRISCILLA M., publishing company executive; b. La Jolla, Calif., Oct. 31, 1949; d. Keith F. and Margaret Jean (Boman) L.; m. Robert Olds Schupp, Nov. 18, 1982 (div. Sept. 1988). BA in English, Northwestern U., 1971; postgrad. U. Wash., 1973-74, Western Wash. State U., 1974-75. Cert. secondary sch. tchr., Wash. Asst. account exec. Cole & Weber, Inc., Seattle, 1975-77; catalog copy chief Recreational Equipment, Inc., Seattle, 1978-80; editor La Mesa (Calif.) Courier, 1980-84, pub., 1981-85; city editor San Diego Daily Transcript, 1984—. co-founder, dir. Seattle Women in Advt.; 1976. Office: San Diego Daily Transcript 2131 3d Ave San Diego CA 92101

LISTER, SUE ANN, editor, publisher, genealogical researcher; b. Newton, Iowa, June 17, 1950; d. Robert Bradley and Norma Lee (Clymer) L.; m. Merlyn J. Pollock, Dec. 19, 1981; 1 child, Milissa Kristeen Burch. BA summa cum laude, Drake U., 1986; postgrad., So. Meth. U. Adminstrv. asst. Iowa Optometric Assn., Des Moines, 1978-80; site interpreter, curations asst. Living History Farms, Des Moines, 1985; grad. teaching asst. Iowa State U., Ames, 1986-87; geneal. researcher, freelance editor Dallas, 1987—. Recipient Keach Johnson award. Mem. NAFE, NOW, Am. Hist. Assn., Orgn. Am. Historians, Phi Beta Kappa, Omicron Delta Kappa, Delta Phi Alpha, Phi Alpha Theta. Democrat. Methodist. Office: PO Box 9145 Dallas TX 75209

LITCHARD, MARY JANE, artist; b. Kotzebue, Alaska, Jan. 3, 1951; d. Harvard Brewster and Orella (Walluk) Brown; m. Ronald Hopson Brower, July 14, 1970 (div. July 1975); children: Audrey Marie, Dale Robert; m. Robert Onalik Tevuk, Apr. 1, 1978 (dec. 1979); children: Demarus Robin, Dwight David; m. Milton Edward Litchard, Dec. 17, 1980; children: Loren Harvard, Vincent Thomas. AAS, Northwest Comm. Coll., 1979, AA, 1984; student, Mary Baldwin Coll., 1989--. Nurses aide Pub. Health Service Hosp., Barrow, Alaska, 1969-70; special educ. aide Barrow Elem. Sch., Alaska, 1972-73; posting machine operator North Slope Borough, Barrow, 1973-75; exec. sec. NANA Environmental Services, Anchorage, Alaska; insurance billing clerk Norton Sound Regional Hosp., Nome, Alaska, 1977; materials developer Nome Pub. Sch., 1977-79, bilingual instr., materials developer, 1979-80, bilingual instr., 1980-82; substitute tchr. Various Orgn., 1982--; Eskimo art instr, Northwest Comm. Coll, Nome, Alaska, 1983. Artist, Museum Quality Basket, Baleen Basket, 1985, contbr. poems to prof. jours. president, Alaska Federation of Natives Youth Council, 1977. Mem. Inst. of Alaska Native Arts. Bahai. Home: PO Box 982, Iqaluit, NT Canada

LITCHFIELD, JEAN ANNE, nurse; b. Gary, Ind., Oct. 6, 1942; d. Donald Kleine and Helen Louise (Sweet) Eller; m. Norman E. Stone, Dec. 27, 1965 (div. Aug. 1973); children: Diana, David, Julie; m. Frank Litchfield, Jan. 26, 1979. Lic. practical nurse, Ind. U. Vocat. Tech. Coll., 1973. Nurse asst. St. Anthony Hosp., Terre Haute, Ind., 1960-73, nurse, 1973-74; nurse St. Mary's Hosp., Decatur, Ill., 1974—. Recipient 2d place Art award, 1984, 85, 2d place County Fair, 1985, Silver Poet award World of Poetry, 1990; named Most Caring Nurse St. Mary's Hosp., 1990. Mem. Barn Colony Artists (treas. 1986-88), Beta Sigma Phi (treas. 1976-78). Home: 1680 N 30th St Decatur IL 62526

LITMAN, RUTH ANN, systems analyst, engineer; b. Oak Ridge, Tenn., Nov. 20, 1959; d. Arnold Powell and Beatrice (Lazaroff) L. BSME, Ga. Tech. Inst., 1982; postgrad., U. Redlands, Calif., 1988—. Engrng. intern IBM Corp., Gaithersburg, Md., 1980-81; packaging engr. Hughes Aircraft Co., El Segundo, Calif., 1982-85; field engr. Spectrum Control, Inc., Valencia, Calif., 1985-86; pres. Precision Jaunt, El Segundo, 1986-87; sr. systems analyst Marquardt Co., Van Nuys, Calif., 1987—. Mem. Whitehead Leadership Soc., NAFE, Phi Tau Sigma, Tau Beta Pi. Office: Marquardt Co 16555 Saticoy St Bldg #109 Van Nuys CA 91409

LITRENTA, FRANCES MARIE, psychiatrist; b. Balt., June 25, 1928; d. Frank P. and Josephine (DeLuca) L. AB, Coll. Notre Dame Md., 1950; MD, Georgetown U., 1954. Diplomate Am. Bd. Psychiatry and Neurology. Rotating intern St. Agnes Hosp., Balt., 1954-55, asst. resident in psychiatry, 1955-56; fellow in psychiatry Univ. Hosp., Balt., 1956-57; fellow in child psychiatry Georgetown U. Hosp., Washington, 1957-59; clin. instr. psychiatry Med. Ctr. Georgetown U., Washington, 1959-63; clin. asst. prof. Med. Ctr. Georgetown U., 1963-72, clin. assoc. prof. psychiatry Med. Ctr., 1972-87; pvt. practice Balt., 1959—; cons. St. Vincent's Infant Home, Balt., 1965-75. Mem. coun. to dean Georgetown U. Sch. Medicine, 1977—. Fellow Am. Acad. Child and Adolescent Psychiatry, Am. Orthopsychiat. Assn.; mem. Am. Psychiat. Assn., Md. Psychiat. Soc., Georgetown Med. Alumni Assn. (nat. communications chmn. 1987—, bd. dirs. 1989—, co-chmn. Med. Class of 1954 1974-87, communications chmn. Med. Class of 1954 1988—). Office: 6110 York Rd Baltimore MD 21212

LITRIDES, LINDY, marketing and fundraising executive; b. Bethlehem, Pa., Feb. 23, 1952; d. Stephen James and Stella (Axas) L. BA, Franklin and Marshall Coll., Lancaster, Pa., 1974. From copywriter to asst. direct mail mgr. Jordan Marsh Co., Boston, 1974-77; mktg. communications mgr. Epsilon Data Mgmt., Inc., Burlington, Mass., 1977-80; from mktg. communications mgr. to v.p. corp. mktg. Endata Inc., Nashville, 1980-89; v.p. mktg Unique Mktg. Inc., Brentwood, Tenn., 1989; v.p. direct response mktg. Arthritis Found., Atlanta, 1990—; cons. Found. for Christian Living, Pawling, N.Y., 1986-90, United Cerebral Palsy of Mid. Tenn., 1987-89, Dream Makers, Inc., Nashville, 1989, Tenn. Soc. to Prevent Blindness, 1987-90, Nashville Songwriters Assn. Internat., 1989-90. Chair project bus. adv. com., cons. Jr. Achievement, 1987-89, mem. U.S. English, Washington, 1989—. Mem. Direct Mktg. Assn., Nat. Soc. Fund Raising Execs. Republican. Office: Arthritis Found 1314 Spring St NW Atlanta GA 30309

LITTELL, GAYELIN GRAY, manager; b. Milw., Nov. 16, 1961; d. Willis Guy and Mary Rogers (Wirth) L. BA, Miami U., 1985. Div. sec. Marine Bank N.A., Milw., 1986; asst. box officer mgr. Summerfest, Milw., 1987—. Bd. dirs. Milw. Dance Theatre, 1988—; co-chair Friends of Easter Seals, 1989. Republican. Congregationalist.

LITTELL, PATRICIA L., contracting corporation executive; b. Albuquerque, May 28, 1954; d. Birnie Glenn and Eleanor Marie (Maloney) Hammock; student U. N.Mex., 1972-73, Coll. Santa Fe, 1984—; m. E. Austin Littell, Nov. 19, 1979; 4 stepchildren. Exec. sec. to v.p. systems integration BDM Corp., Albuquerque, 1976-80; pres., treas., co-founder Littell and Assocs., Albuquerque, 1979—; civil rights specialist legal dept. City of Albuquerque, 1987—. cons. small bus. firms. Recipient Corp. safety award Associated Gen. Contractors Am., 1980. Mem. Nat. Assn. Female Execs., Nat. Assn. Legal Assts. Rebuplican. Methodist. Home: 1605 Camino Rosario NW Albuquerque NM 87107 Office: Kirtland AFB PO Box 5596 Albuquerque NM 87185

LITTELL, VICKI C., realtor; b. Flushing, N.Y., Dec. 23, 1946; d. George Austin Crockett and Ingrid (Moberg) Russell; m. William S. Littell, Sept. 19, 1975; children: Kevin J., William S. Jr. BS, So. Conn. State Coll., 1980. Claims analyst Aetna Life & Casualty Co., Hartford, Conn., 1970-75; realtor The Hull Agy., Inc., Madison, Conn., 1975—, sales mgr., 1981—. Chmn. Bd. Tax Rev., Town of Madison, 1985—; pub. rels. chmn. Rep. Town Com., Madison, 1984-90, fundraiser E.C. Scranton meml. Libr., Madison, 1982-85; deacon John Grave House, Madison, 1990; mem. Madison Hist. Soc., 1975—, fundraiser, 1980. Mem. AaUW (v.p. fundraiser Ednl. Found. Prog. 1987-90, honoreed 1989), Shoreline Bd. Realtors (chmn. coms. 1975—), Women's Club Madison (pres. 1988-90), Duck Island Yacht Club, Madison Beach Club. Republican. Congregationalist. Home: 20 North Ave Madison CT 06443 Office: The Hull Agy Inc 14 Wall St PO Box 487 Madison CT 06443

LITTERER, KAREN SUE, performing company executive; b. Columbus, Ohio, July 19, 1962; d. James Eaton and Phyllis Ann (Mittermaier) L. MusB, Ohio State U., 1984; MA, U. Cin., 1988. Sales and acctg. asst. Cin. Symphony Orch., 1985-86; dir. mktg. and pub. rels. Kalamazoo Symphony Soc., 1986-88, gen. mgr., 1988—. Bd. dirs. Kalamazoo Bach Festival Soc., 1988—. Mem. Am. Symphony Orch. League, Mich. Orch. Assn. (v.p., bd. dirs. 1986—), West Mich. Assn. Mktg. Adminstrs., Rotary. Home: 634 W Kalamazoo Ave Kalamazoo MI 49007 Office: Kalamazoo Symphony Soc 426 S Park St Kalamazoo MI 49007

LITTLE, ANGELA CAPOBIANCO, nutritional science educator; b. San Francisco, Jan. 12, 1920; d. Alfredo Agosto and Elizabeth (Kruse) Capobianco; m. George Gordon Little, Nov. 8, 1947; 1 child, Judith Kristine. BA, U. Calif., Berkeley, 1940, MS, 1954, PhD, 1969. Specialist jr. to asst. to assoc. U. Calif., Berkeley, 1958-69, food scientist, 1969-85, assoc. prof. to prof, 1977-85, prof. emeritus, 1985—, acad. ombudsman, 1985-87, 89-91; cons. in field; v.p., bd. dirs. Math/Sci. Network, Berkeley; vis. scholar U. Wash., Seattle, 1976-77, Kans. State U., Manhattan, 1972. Author: Color of Foods, 1962. Nutritional adv. bd. Project Open Hand, San Francisco, 1989—, vol., 1988—, UNICEF, San Francisco, 1986-89. Rsch. grantee Robert Woods Johnson Found., 1989-90, others 1960-85. Mem. Am. Soc. of Wine and Food (bd. editors), N.Y. Acad. Sci., Am. Women in Sci., San Francisco Acad. Sci., San Francisco Mus. Soc., Sigma Xi. Home: 85 Cleary Ct #3 San Francisco CA 94109 Office: U Calif Dept Nutritional Scis Berkeley CA 94720

LITTLE, ANNA DENISE, marketing professional; b. Montclair, N.J., May 2, 1954; d. Jethro Craven and Verneader (Wright) L. BA, Fla. State U., 1980. Researcher, tech. asst. Sta. WFSU-TV, Tallahassee, 1979-80; with editorial staff Burrelle's Press Clipping Service, Livingston, N.J., 1981-82; customer service and sales rep. Funk and Wagnalls, Inc., L.I., 1982-84; editor, media coordinator Murdoch Mags., N.Y.C., 1984-86; promotional and editorial mgr. Direct Response Group div. Hearst Mags., N.Y.C., 1986-88; sales rep. Good Housekeeping Mag., Hearst Mag., 1988-89; key account specialist The Faxon Co., N.Y.C., 1989; pvt. practice J & L Assocs., Montclair, N.J., 1989—. Vol. homeless shelter Isaiah House, East Orange, N.J. Mem. NAFE, Acad. TV Arts and Scis. (mem. Blue Ribbon Panel), Internat. Platform Assn., Am. Biog. Inst. (rsch. bd. advisors). Democrat. Mem. Pentecostal Ch. Home and Office: J & L Assocs E 8th Mission St Montclair NJ 07042-4518 Office: Isaiah House 85-87 N 14th St East Orange NJ 07107

LITTLE, DEBRA KRUEGER, process engineer; b. Eunice, La., Apr. 23, 1960; d. Edward A. and Bonnie R. (Morris) Krueger; m. James Stephen Little, Mar. 24, 1984. BS in Engring. Mgmt., U. Mo., Rolla, 1982. Process engr. Internat. Paper, Mansfield, La., 1982-88; shift supr. James River Corp., St. Francisville, La., 1988—. Republican. Southern Baptist. Office: James River Corp PO Box 218 Saint Francisville LA 70775

LITTLE, EMILY BROWNING, architect; b. Austin, Tex., June 4, 1951; d. Betty (Browning) L. BA in Cultural Anthropology, U. Tex., 1973, MArch, 1979. Registered architect, Tex. Archtl. apprentice Austin Design Assocs., 1980-81; project architect Nutt, Walters & Assocs., Austin, 1981-84; prin. Emily Little/Architect, Austin, 1984—. Prin. works include numerous residences, hist. restorations and comml. bldgs. Mem. citizens adv. com. Travis County Juvenile Ct., Austin, 1984-86; mem. adv. bd. Deborah Hay Dance Co., Austin, 1984—; chmn. Austin Design Commn., 1987-89. Recipient Archtl. Merit award Austin Bd. Realtors, 1989. Mem. AIA (commr. Austin chpt. 1987-88), Tex. Soc. Architects, Austin Women in Architecture (pres. 1985-86), Nat. Trust for Hist. Preservation, Tex. Fine Arts Assn., Heritage Soc. Austin (bd. dirs. 1989—, Bldg. award (2) 1988, 90). Democrat. Office: 1001 E 8th St Austin TX 78702

LITTLE, HAZEL MARIE, educator; b. Monroe, N.C., May 4, 1934; d. Ervin and Ruby Cureton; m. James Eugene Little, Nov. 30, 1957; 1 child, Cynthia. BA in Edn., Livingstone Coll., Salisbury, N.C., 1955; postgrad., Newark State Coll., Union, N.J., 1956, Bank Street Coll., N.Y.C., 1977. Elem. tchr. Madison Sch., Franklin Twp., N.J., 1956-58, Avon Ave. Sch., Newark, 1959-62, Sch. 24, 11, 12 and 4, Paterson, N.J., 1962—; instr. Tech. for Children, 1986-87, Paterson Edn. Found., Inc., 1985, Dept. Spl. Svcs., 1982-83, 88-89. Chmn. Arra Porter Goode Scholarship Com., Newark, 1982—; mem. phone alert United Way, Montclair, N.J., 1984-85; chmn. Sr. Citizen Com., Montclair, 1986-88; mem. Nat. Polit. Congress Black Women, 1987. Mem. NEA, N.J. Edn. Assn., Paterson Edn. Assn. (sch. rep. 1964-66), NAACP (life), Lambda Kappa Mu (nat. pub. rels. com. 1978-82, nat. recommendations com. 1983-84, epistoleus 1984-86). Home: 45 Cambridge Rd Montclair NJ 07042

LITTLE, JULIA ELIZABETH, medical technologist, educator; b. Canton, Ohio, Aug. 23, 1932; d. Nicholas Charles and Julie Ella (Boldizsar) Psenka; children: Linda Marie, Lori Elizabeth. BS, Mt. Union Coll., 1954. Registered med. technologist Am. Soc. Clin. Pathologists, Calif. Med. technologist Aultman Hosp., Canton, 1955-56; supr. chemistry Barberton (Ohio) Citizens Hosp., 1956-57; supr. bacteriology Massillon (Ohio) City Hosp., 1957-63; chief technologist Lynwood (Calif.) Clin. Lab., 1964-65; med. technologist Los Altos Hosp., Long Beach, Calif., 1966-70, Newhall (Calif.) Community Hosp., 1973-79; med. technologist, hemotology and urinalysis educator Eisenhower Med. Ctr., Rancho Mirage, Calif., 1980—. Mem. C.A.M.L.T. State Conv. Com. Mem. Am. Soc. Clin. Pathology, Calif. Assn. Med. Lab. Technologists (pres. Palms to Pines chpt. 1988—, treas. 1986-88, state mem. com. 1989-90). Republican. Home: 34161 Linda Way Cathedral City CA 92234 Office: Eisenhower Med Ctr 39000 Bob Hope Dr Rancho Mirage CA 92270

LITTLE, SYLVIA FORD, oil industry executive. Student, So. Meth. U., Scottsdale Community Coll., Ariz. Owner, operator gas and oil properties San Juan Basin, N.Mex., 1977—; pres. Little Oil & Gas, Inc., San Juan Basin, N.Mex. Founder Farmington (N.Mex.) Totah Festival of Authentic Indian Art; chmn. residential com. of Town Forum 2000, 1980; mem. Mayor's Census Com. 1980; exec. com., state cen. com., N.Mex. Rep. party, 1984-86; bd. dirs. N.Mex. Fed. Rep. Women, 1984-90, Farmington League of Women Voters. Mem. Ind. Petroleum Assn. N.Mex. (pres.-elect 1990), N.Mex. Oil and Gas Assn., Assn. Commerce and Industry N.Mex. (bd. dirs. 1988—), Farmington C. of C. (redcoats amb. com.), Rotary, San. Juan Federated Rep. Women's Club, Four Corners Federated Rep. Women's Club. Office: 2346 East 20th St Farmington NM 87499

LITTLEDALE, FREYA LOTA BROWN, writer, editor; b. N.Y.C., d. David Milton and Dorothy (Passloff) Brown; B.S., Ithaca Coll., 1951; postgrad. N.Y. U., 1952; 1 son, Glenn David. Tchr. English, Pub. Schs. Willsboro (N.Y.), 1952-53; editor South Shore Record, L.I., N.Y., 1953-55; asso. editor Maco Mag. Corp., N.Y.C., 1960-61, Rutledge Books and Ridge Press, N.Y.C., 1961-62; juvenile book editor Parents' Mag. Press, N.Y.C., 1962-65; free-lance writer-editor, 1965—; writer Silver Burdett div. Time-Life Corp., 1965; editor, anthologist Arrow Book Club div. Scholastic Book Services; adj. prof. Fairfield U., 1984, 86-90. Author: The Magic Fish, 1967, rev. edit., 1985; (with Harold Littledale) Timothy's Forest, 1969; King Fox and Other Old Tales, 1971; The Magic Tablecloth, The Magic Goat, and The Hitting Stick, 1972; The Boy Who Cried Wolf, 1975; The Elves and the Shoemaker, 1975; Seven at One Blow, 1976; The Snow Child, 1978, rev. edit., 1989; The Magic Plum Tree, 1981, The Farmer in the Soup, 1987, Peter and the North Wind, 1988, The Twelve Dancing Princesses, 1988; editor: A Treasure Chest of Poetry, 1964; Fairy Tales by Hans Christian Andersen, 1964; Aesop's Fables, 1964; Grimm's Fairy Tales, 1964; 13 Ghostly Tales, 1966; Ghosts and Spirits of Many Lands, 1970; Ghosts, Witches, and Demons, 1971; Strange Tales from Many Lands, 1975; (poetry) I Was Thinking, 1979; (plays) The King and Queen Who Wouldn't Speak, 1975; Stop That Pancake, 1975; The Giant's Garden, 1975; The Magic Piper, 1978; adapter: Pinnochio, 1979; Snow White and the Seven Dwarfs, 1981; The Wizard of Oz, 1982; Frankenstein, 1983; The Sleeping Beauty, 1984; The Little Mermaid, 1986, The Twelve Dancing Princesses, 1988, King Midas and the Golden Touch, 1989; contbr. to Scribner's Anthology for Young People, 1976; A New Treasury of Children's Poetry, 1984. Mem. Soc. Children's Book Writers, Authors Guild, PEN. Address: care Curtis Brown Ltd 10 Astor Pl New York NY 10003

LITTLEFIELD, JOAN KOHLER, instructor; b. N.Y.C., Dec. 16, 1936; d. Michael Julius and Mary Belle (Barnes) Kohler; m. William Nelson Littlefield; children: Kathleen Susan, Sharon Elizabeth. BA in Psychology, Pomona Coll., 1958; postgrad., Stanford U., 1958-60. Life credential elem. edn. and jr. coll. home decorative arts, Calif., gen. elemn. credential, Va. Various teaching positions Calif., 1959-67; instr. quilting Orange Coast Coll., Costa Mesa, Calif., 1978-86, Coastline Community Coll., Costa Mesa, 1980-82; instr. computers Orange Coast Coll., Costa Mesa, 1985-87; instr. quilting and computers Irvine (Calif.) Valley Coll., 1986—; elem. sch. tchr. Va., 1990—; lectr. Fabric Fair, Costa Mesa, 1977-87, mem. steering com., 1985-87; cons. Orange (Calif.) Patchwork Pubs., 1980-86; mem. steering com. Irvine Valley Coll. Emeritus Inst., 1989—; tutor computer sci., 1988—; lectr., workshop presenter on parliamentary procedure. Pres. Irvine chpt. Orange County Philharm. Soc., 1973-75; pres. Nat. Charity League, Irvine, 1987-88, nat. parliamentary, 1988—. Mem. AAUW (pres. Irvine chpt. 1979-81, various state coms. 1979-84, grant honoree 1978, 81), Pomona Coll. Alumni Assn. (bd. dirs. Orange County br.), DAR (Clara Barton Huntington Beach, Calif. chpt., chmn. Am. Heritage com.), Orange County Geneal. Soc., Orange County Computer Club. Republican. Methodist. Home: 18822 Via Palatino Irvine CA 92715 Office: Irvine Valley Coll 5500 Irvine Ctr Dr Irvine CA 92720

LITTLEFIELD, VIVIAN MOORE, nursing educator, administrator; b. Princeton, Ky., Jan. 24, 1938; d. Willard Anson and Hester V. (Haydon) Moore; children—Darrell, Virginia. B.S. magna cum laude, Tex. Christian U., 1960; M.S., U. Colo., 1964; Ph.D., U. Denver, 1979. Staff nurse USPHS Hosp., Ft. Worth, Tex., 1960-61; instr. nursing Tex. Christian U., Ft. Worth, 1961-62; nursing supr. Colo. Gen. Hosp., Denver, 1964-65, pvt. patient practitioner, 1974-78; asst. prof. nursing U. Colo., Denver, 1965-69, asst. prof., clin. instr., 1971-74, asst. prof., 1974-76, acting asst. dean, assoc. prof. continuing edn., regional perinatal project, 1976-78; assoc. prof., chair dept. women's health care nursing U. Rochester Sch. Nursing, N.Y., 1979-84; clin. chief ob-gyn., nursing U. Rochester Strong Meml. Hosp., N.Y., 1979-84; prof., dean U. Wis. Sch. Nursing, Madison, 1984—; cons. and lectr. in field. Author: Maternity Nursing Today, 1973, 76; Health Education for Women: A guide for Nurses and Other Health Professionals, 1986. Contbr. articles to profl. jours. Bur. Health Professions Fed. trainee, 1963-64; Nat. Sci. Service award, 1976-79. Mem. Am. Nurses Assn., Health Care for Women Internat. (editorial bd. 1984—), Midwest Nursing Research Soc., Sigma Theta Tau (v.p.). Avocations: golf; tennis. Office: U Wis-Sch Nursing 600 Highland Ave H6/150 Madison WI 53792

LITTLEJOHN, LINDA LOU, corporate communication specialist, educator; b. Hopkinsville, Ky., Apr. 18, 1952; d. James Edwin and Mary Magdalene (Oakley) L.; children: Charles Edwin-Ashley Haak, Meridith Oakley Haak. BS, Western Ky. U., 1974, MA, 1977; postgrad., Murray (Ky.) State U., 1987. Cert. elem. adminstrn. Substitute tchr. Somerset (Ky.) and Pulaski County Bd. Edn., 1974-76; tchr. Logan County Bd. Edn., Russellville, Ky., 1977-79, Calloway County Bd. Edn., Murray, 1979-82; student activities coord., acad. counselor Paducah (Ky.) Community Coll., 1982-84; tchr. Marshall County Bd. Edn., Benton, Ky., 1984-87; asst. staff mgr. mktg. support dept. Bell South Svcs., Birmingham, Ala., 1987-89, asst. staff mgr. carrier access svcs., 1990—. Mem. Shelby County Rep. Women, Pelham, Ala., 1987—. Mem. Network Birmingham (chairperson career enhancement com. 1988—). Baptist. Home: 924 Willow Bend Rd Pelham AL 35124 Office: Bell South Svcs South S611 3535 Colonnade Birmingham AL 35243

LITTLE-MARENIN, IRENE RENATE, astronomy educator; b. Pilsen, Czechoslovakia, May 4, 1941; came to U.S., 1957; d. Myron Andreas and Maria Franziska (Kraus) Marenin; m. Stephen J. Little, Feb. 24, 1973; children: Erika, Kevin. BA, Vassar Coll., 1964; MA, Ind. U., 1966, PhD, 1970. Postdoctoral fellow Ohio State U., Columbus, 1970-72; vis. asst. prof. U. Western Ontario, London, Can., 1972-73; asst. prof. Ferris State Coll., Big Rapids, Mich., 1973-74; researcher Am. Sci. & Engring., Cambridge, Mass., 1976-77; assoc. prof. Wellesley (Mass.) Coll., 1977—; vis. scientist Air Force Geophysics Lab/Optical Physics Infrared, Bedford, Mass., 1986-88; vis. fellow Joint Inst. Lab. Astrophysics, Boulder, Colo., 1984-85; vis. prof. U. Victoria (B.C., Can.), 1980; NSF vis. prof. for women U. Colo., 1990—. Contbr. articles to profl. jours. Fellow Am. Astronomy Soc. Democrat. Home: PO Box 37 Glen Haven CO 80532 Office: Wellesley Coll Whitin Obs Wellesley MA 02181

LITTMAN, LYNNE, film director; b. N.Y.C., June 26, 1941; d. Carl and Yetta (Abler) L.; m. Taylor Hackford, May 7, 1977; 1 child, Alexander Littman; 1 stepson Rio Hackford. B.A., Sarah Lawrence Coll., 1962; student The Sorbonne, Paris, 1960-61. Researcher for CBS News, 1965; assoc. producer Nat. Ednl. TV, 1966-69; dir. NIMH film series on drug abuse UCLA Media Center, 1970; producer, dir. documentary films, news and pub. affairs series KCET Community TV So. Calif., 1971-77; dir. WNET Ind. Filmmakers Series, 1979; co-producer, dir. TV spl. Rick Nelson, It's All Right Now, 1978, (documentary) In Her Own Time, 1985; films include: Till Death Do Us Part (CPB award), 1976, In The Matter of Kenneth (Los Angeles Emmy award), 1974, Wanted: Operadoras (Los Angeles Emmy award), 1974, Women in Waiting, 1975; dir. film Testament, 1983, short films, Number Our Days (1977 Academy award, best short documentary), Once a Daughter, 1979, Running My Way, (1982 Cine Golden Eagle award). Recipient numerous awards including Los Angeles Press Club award, 1977, San Francisco Internat. Film Festival award, 1977, Corp. for Public Broadcasting award, 1977, Los Angeles Emmy award, 1972, 73, 74, 77; Columbia/Dupont Journalism award, 1977; Ford Found. grantee, 1978. Mem. Dirs. Guild Am. Address: 6620 Cahuenga Terr Los Angeles CA 90068*

LITTMAN, WENDY P., fund raising professional; b. Providence, R.I., Dec. 19, 1946; d. Cyrus Ransom and Roberta Marguerite (Northrup) Pangborn; m. Marcel Rosenberg, June 15, 1969 (div. 1975); m. C. Arthur Littman, June 9, 1976; children: Karl Arthur, Robert Richard. BA, Douglass Coll./Rutgers State U, New Brunswick, N.J., 1968. Cert. fundraising exec. Case worker Dept. of Social Svcs., Bronx, N.Y., 1968-69; assoc. dir. Assoc. Alumnae of Douglass Coll., New Brunswick, N.J., 1969-76; dir. pub. relations Am. Leprosy Missions, Elmwood Park, N.J., 1976-83; pres. Littman Assocs., Belle Mead, N.J.; editor and pub. The N.J. Mitchell Guide to Found., Corp. and Their Mgrs., Belle Mead, 1987--; dir. devel. Carrier Found., Belle Mead, N.J., 1985--. Choir dir. Children's Choir, Hillsborough Presbyn. Ch., 1986—. Mem. Nat. Soc. of Fund Raising Executives N.J. Chpt. Democrat. Home: 3 Riverview Terr Belle Mead NJ 08502 Office: Carrier Found County Rte 601 Belle Mead NJ 08502

LITWACK, ARLENE DEBRA, psychotherapist, psychoanalyst, consultant, educator; b. Brookline, Mass., July 18, 1945; d. Hyman and Bessie Litwack. BA cum laude, Boston U., 1967; MS, Columbia U., 1969; postgrad. Ctr. for Mental Health, N.Y.C., 1981, Inst. for Psychoanalytic Tng. and Rsch., 1980—. Diplomate Am. Bd. Psychiatry and Neurology. Caseworker Pride Treatment Ctr., Douglaston, N.Y., 1969-73, supr., 1973-78, sr. worker, 1978-80; pvt. practice psychotherapy and psychoanalyst, N.Y.C., 1980— mem. faculty Inst. for Mental Health Edn., Englewood, N.J., 1983-89; clin. cons. N.Y. Spaulding for Children, 1989; bd. dir. child therapy dept. L.I. Consultation Ctr., Rego Park, N.Y., 1980-85; faculty workshop leader Human Svcs. Workshops, N.Y.C.; adj. faculty Columbia U., 1977—. Contbr. articles to profl. jours. Mem. Psychoanalytic Study Ctr. Mem. N.Y. State Soc. of Clin. Social Worker, Nat. Assn. of Social Workers. Home: 115 4th Ave Apt 3E New York NY 10003

LIU, ALICE YEE-CHANG, biology educator; b. Hunan, China, July 12, 1948; came to U.S., 1970; d. Tin-Kai and Te-Ming (Young) L.; m. Kuang Yu Chen, Aug. 26, 1978; children: Andrew T-H, Winston T-C. BS, Chinese U., Hong Kong, 1969; PhD, Mount Sinai Sch. Med., 1974. Postdoctoral fellow Yale U. Med. Sch., New Haven, Conn., 1974-77; asst. prof. Harvard Med. Sch., Boston, 1977-84; assoc. prof. Rutgers U., Piscataway, N.J., 1984-89; prof. Rutgers U., Piscataway, 1989; mem. pharmacological scis. review com. NIH, 1984-88; mem. cell biology panel, NSF, 1989 --. Author: Receptors Again, 1985. Recipient N.Y.C. Bd. of Higher Edn. award, 1972, Am. Cancer Soc. Scholar award, Boston, 1982-85; NIH postdoctoral fellow, 1974-77, Medical Found. fellow, Boston, 1977-79. Mem. Am. Soc. Biochemistry and Molecular Biology, Am. Soc. Pharmacology and Experimental Therapeutics. Home: 20 Woodlake Dr Piscataway NJ 08854 Office: Rutgers U PO Box 1059 Nelson Biology Labs Piscataway NJ 08855-1059

LIU, FONG YU MARY, importer-export company executive; b. Szechwan, China, May 4, 1948; d. Li Hsjung and Ling Chu (Wang) L.; 1 child, Lisa Wang. BS, Nat. Cheng Chi U., 1971; MBA, U. La Verne, 1980. V.p. Lasonic Electronic Corp., Alhambra, Calif., 1980-82; mgr. import, export Kunnan Tackle Co., Westminister, Calif., 1982-84; pres. KNL Internat. Corp., Monterey Park, Calif., 1984—; bd. dirs. P C Warehouse, Monterey Park, Calif., M.J.S. Lindbrook Corp., Monterey Park; corp. sec. Lotus Inc.,

City Industry, Calif., 1989. Home: 630 E Winnie Way Arcadia CA 91006 Office: KNL Internat Corp 428 S Atlantic Blvd #203 Monterey Park CA 91754

LIVELY, CAROL A., association executive; b. Chgo., Sept. 2, 1935; d. William Mann and Lillian (Juske) Haycock; m. Olin A. Lively, June 9, 1954 (div.); children: Richard B., Laura Jean. L.P.N., Los Angeles Sch. Nursing, 1953; student, Columbia U., 1954, Boston U., 1956-57. Program dir. United Fund, Pittsfield, Mass., 1966-71; exec. dir. Western Mass. Health Council, 1971-74; asst. exec. dir. Genesee Health Council, Rochester, N.Y., 1974-76; dir. devel. Shimer Coll., Mt. Carroll, Ill., 1976-77; assoc. dir. Am. Hosp. Assn., Chgo., 1977-80; dir. health div., v.p. Smith Bucklin Assn., Washington, 1980—; mem. Achievement Rewards Coll. Scientists, Washington, 1980—; cons. Dept. Health Rep. Haiti, Washington, 1976—. Contbg. author: Politics of Health Planning, 1962; contbr. articles to profl. jours. Bd. dirs. Jacobs Pilba Dance Theatre, Pittsfield, 1968; bd. dirs. Albany Regional Med. Program, N.Y., 1971-74; active Jr. League, Washington, 1965—; mem. Commn. Drug Abuse Council, Boston, 1971-74. Recipient Woman of Yr. award Bus. and Profl. Women, 1971. Mem. New Eng. Pub. Health Assn., Mass. Council on Aging, Am. Soc. Hosp. Planning, Am. Pub. Health Assn. Home: 2138 California St NW Washington DC 20008 Office: Smith Bucklin Assn 1101 Connecticut Ave NW Washington DC 20036

LIVINGSTON, LAURIE ANNE, psychologist, consultant; b. Bloomington, Ill., Feb. 5, 1951; d. Aaron Edward and Zelona Lurie (Worden) L. BA, Drake U., 1973; MS, Ill. State U., 1976; EdD, Boston U., 1983. Lic. clin. and counseling psychologist. Dir. Career Devel. Ctr., Norwood (Mass.) CETA Consortium, 1976-78; prin. psychologist Fernald State Sch., Waltham, Mass., 1978-79; dir. behavior therapy svcs. Coastal Community Counseling, Braintree, Mass., 1984-86; co-dir. stress disorders program Beth Israel Hosp, Boston, 1982-84; psychologist Agoraphobia Treatment Ctr., Boston, 1982-83, co-dir., 1983-88; behavioral cons. Fenway Community Health Ctr., Boston, 1986—; psychologist, dir. Agoraphobia Svcs., Brookline, Mass., 1988—; teaching asst. psychology dept. Ill. State U., Normal, 1974-76; Bd. dirs. Greater Boston Phobia Soc.; group developer Fenway County Health Ctr., 1988—. Vol. mental health subcom. AIDS Action Com., Boston, 1984-86, dir., vice chmn. bd. dirs., 1986-88. Mem. Am. Psychol. Assn., Mass. Psychol. Assn., Assn. Advancement of Behavior Therapy, New England Soc. Behavior Analysis & Therapy, Phobia Soc. Am., Assn. Women in Psychology. Office: 1131 Beacon St Ste 1 Brookline MA 02146

LIVINGSTON, MARGARET MORROW GRESHAM, civic leader; b. Birmingham, Ala., Aug. 16, 1924; d. Owen Garside and Katherine Molton (Morrow) Gresham; m. James Archibald Livingston, Jr., July 16, 1947; children: Mary Margaret, James Archibald, Katherine Wiley, Elizabeth Gresham. Grad. The Baldwin Sch., Phila., 1942; AB, Vassar Coll., 1945; MA, U. Ala., 1946. Acting dir. Birmingham Mus. Art, 1978-79, 81, chmn. bd. dirs., 1978-86; bd. dirs. Birmingham Civic Ctr. Authority, 1988—, U. Ala. Art Gallery, Birmingham, 1978—; bd. dirs. Altamont Sch., Birmingham, 1959-89, chmn. bd. 1986. Named Woman of Yr., Birmingham, 1986. Mem. Am. Assn. Mus. (edn. com., pub. rels. com.). Episcopalian. Clubs: Jr. League, English Speaking Union, Colonial Dames of Commonwealth of Va., Ala. State Tennis Assn. Home: 12 Country Club Rd Birmingham AL 35213

LIVINGSTON, MYRA COHN, poet, writer, educator; b. Omaha, Nebr., Aug. 17, 1926; d. Mayer L. and Gertrude (Marks) Cohn; m. Richard Roland Livingston, Apr. 14, 1952; children: Joshua, Jonas Cohn, Jennie Marks. B.A., Sarah Lawrence Coll., 1948. Profl. horn player, 1941-48; book reviewer Los Angeles Daily News, 1948-49, Los Angeles Mirror, 1949-50; asst. editor Campus Mag., 1949-50; various public relations positions and pvt. sec. to Hollywood (Calif.) personalities, 1950-52; tchr. creative writing Dallas (Tex.) public library and schs., 1958-63; poet-in-residence Beverly Hills (Calif.) Unified Sch. Dist., 1966-84; sr. instr. UCLA Extension, 1973—; cons. to various sch. dists., 1966-84, cons. poetry to publishers children's lit., 1975—. Author: Whispers and Other Poems, 1958, Wide Awake and Other Poems, 1959, I'm Hiding, 1961, See What I Found, 1962, I Talk to Elephants, 1962, I'm Not Me, 1963, Happy Birthday, 1964, The Moon and a Star and Other Poems, 1965, I'm Waiting, 1966, Old Mrs. Twindlytart and Other Rhymes, 1967, A Crazy Flight and Other Poems, 1968, The Malibu and Other Poems, 1972, When You Are Alone/It Keeps You Capone: An Approach to Creative Writing with Children, 1973, Come Away, 1974, The Way Things Are and Other Poems, 1974, 4-Way Stop and Other Poems, 1976, A Lollygag of Limericks, 1978, O Sliver of Liver and Other Poems, 1979, No Way of Knowing: Dallas Poems, 1980, A Circle of Seasons, 1982, How Pleasant to Know Mr. Lear!, 1982, Sky Songs, 1984, A Song I Sang to You, 1984, Monkey Puzzle, 1984, The Child as Poet: Myth or Reality?, 1984, Celebrations, 1985, Worlds I Know and Other Poems, 1985, Sea Songs, 1986, Earth Songs, 1986, 1987, Higgledy-Piggledy, 1986, Space Songs, 1988, There Was a Place and Other Poems, 1988, Up in the Air, 1989, Birthday Poems, 1989, Remembering and Other Poems, 1989, My Head is Red and Other Riddle Rhymes, 1990, Climb Into the Bell Tower: Essays on Poetry, 1990; co-editor: The Scott-Foresman Anthology, 1984; author: The Writing of Poetry; film strips; editor 25 anthologies of poetry; contbr. articles on children's lit. to ednl. publs., contbr., essays on lit. and reading in edn. to various books; mem. editorial adv. bd. The New Advocate. Officer Beverly Hills PTA Council, 1966-75; pres. Friends of Beverly Hills Public Library, 1979-81; bd. dirs. Poetry Therapy Inst., 1975—, Reading is Fundamental of So. Calif., 1981—. Recipient Honor award N.Y. Herald Tribune Spring Book Festival, 1958, Excellence in Poetry award Nat. Council Tchrs. of English, 1980, Commonwealth Club award, 1984, Nat. Jewish Book award, 1987. Mem. Authors Guild, Internat. Reading Assn., Soc. Children's Book Writers (honor award 1975), Tex. Inst. Letters (awards 1961, 80), So. Calif. Council on Lit. for Children and Young People (Comprehensive Contribution award 1968, Notable Book award 1972, Poetry Quartet award 89), PEN. Address: 9308 Readcrest Dr Beverly Hills CA 90210

LIVINGSTON, PAMELA ANNA, corporate image and marketing management consultant; b. Richmond Hill, N.Y., Nov. 21, 1930; d. Paul Yount and Anna Margaret (Altland) L.; B.A., Adelphi U., 1951; postgrad. NYU, 1952, Columbia U., 1959, Am. Acad. Dramatic Art, 1954, IBM Systems and Mktg. Schs., 1967-70, Brandon Sch. Electronic Data Processing, 1973. Personnel and public relations depts. Am. Can Co., N.Y.C., 1951-60; exec. sec. to pres. York (Pa.) div. Borg-Warner Corp., 1962-65; freelance writer, 1965-67; mktg. ofcl. IBM Corp., 1967-70; research analyst, dir. new EDP bus. Ins. Co. N. Am., 1971-74; asst. to v.p. corp. affairs IU Internt., Phila., 1974-75; communications and mktg. mgmt. cons. specializing in corp. identity, 1975—; corp. image cons., 1984—. Recipient various journalism awards, award in mktg. and sales IBM, 1969-70, award for innovative product application, 1969. Mem. Sales/Mktg. Execs. Internat., Art Alliance, Public Relations Soc. Am., Econs. Club of York C. of C., Phila. Club Advt. Women, AAUW, Phila. Acad. Fine Arts, World Affairs Council, English-Speaking Union, Kappa Kappa Gamma. Contbr. articles to tech. jours. Home and Office: 108 S Rockburn St York PA 17402-3467

LIVINGSTONE, CHARLEEN THOMPSON, furniture manufacturer; b. Utica, N.Y., Dec. 13, 1929; d. Charles Alva and Edith Elizabeth (Wagner) Thompson; m. James Richard Livingtone, Apr.12, 1952; children: Charleen E. Steers, Edith A., Jane Roberts. Grad., Mohawk Valley Community Coll., 1949. Asst. prodn. Time Inc., N.Y.C., 1951-52; advt. prodn. Hoag & Provandie, Boston, 1953-55; sales cons. Guy P. Livingstone Co., Winchester, Mass., 1964-89; v.p. Livingstone Mfg. Co. Mass. Inc., Winchester. Apptd. mem. Wellington Sch. Bldg. Com., Belmont, Mass., 1968, elected sec., 1969, elected. chmn. Pro Tem, 1972. Mem. Gardner Mass. C. of C., Associated Industries of Mass. Episcopalian. Home: 90 Agassiz Ave Belmont MA 02178 Office: Livingstone Mfg Co Mass Inc 28 Church St Winchester MA 01890

LIVINGSTONE, TRUDY DOROTHY ZWEIG, dancer, instructor; b. N.Y.C., June 9, 1946; d. Joseph and Anna (Feinberg) Zweig; m. John Leslie Livingstone, Aug. 7, 1977; 1 child, Robert Edward. Student, Charles Lowe Studios, N.Y.C., 1950-52, Nina Tinova Studio, N.Y.C., 1953-56, Ballet Russe de Monte Carlo, N.Y.C., 1956-57, Bklyn. Coll., 1964-66; BA in Psychology cum laude, Boston U., 1968, MEd, 1969; postgrad., Serena Studios, Carnegie Hall Ballet Arts, N.Y.C., 1973-74. Tchr. Millis (Mass.) Pub. Schs., 1969-72; instr. Hebrew Acad. Atlanta, 1974-76; profl. dancer various orgns. including Rivermont Country Club, Jewish Community Ctr., Callanwolde Performing Arts Ctr., Atlanta, 1974-84; founder, owner, instr. dance Sasha Studios, Atlanta, 1974-77; owner Trudy Zweig Livingstone Studios, Wellesley, Needham, Mass., 1987-88, Palm Beach, Fla., 1989—; judge dance competition Atlanta Council Run-Offs, 1976. Vol. League Sch., Bklyn., 1965, Kennedy Meml. Hosp., Brighton, Mass., 1969, Nat. Affiliation for Literacy Advances, Santa Monica, Calif., 1982. Mem. L.A. Athletic Club, Wellesley Coll. Club, Governor's Club (West Palm Beach). Jewish.

LIVIO, ANNE MARIE SULLIVAN REHER, civic worker; b. Denver, Dec. 25, 1915; d. Dennis Francis and Mary Ellen (Malone) Sullivan; m. Sven Helge Reher, Apr. 11, 1942 (div. 1984); children—Thomas, Kathleen, David, Vincent, Mary Regina; m. Joseph Anthony Livio, June 29, 1986. B.A. in History and Philosophy, Loretto Heights Coll., 1937; B.A. in Music, UCLA, 1942; M.A. in Music, Mt. St. Mary's Coll., 1952. Concert pianist, 1942—; accompanist for Sven Reher, concert violist, goodwill ambassador Gen. Petroleum Corp., Union Bank; tchr. Graland Country Day Sch., Denver, Marymount Grade and High Sch., Los Angeles; community coordinator Adult Edn. Programs UCLA; founder women's com. Braille Inst.; commr. Dept. Municipal Arts, City of Los Angeles, 1974-80. Bd. dirs. Community Relations Conf. So. Calif., NCCJ, Am. Jewish Com., Urban League, NAACP, Christian Friends of Palestine; pres. UN Assn. Beverly Hills; v.p. UN Assn. Los Angeles; founder Christines, The Commonweal Club, Catholic Peace Assn.; founding bd. dir. Catholic Human Relations Council, Loyola Human Relations Workshop, Friendship Day Camp; mem. Clergy and Laity Concerned, Blue Ribbon Com. of Music Ctr., Assistance League, Women's Com. of Los Angeles Philharm. Orch., Women's Internat. Com. of UCLA, Faculty Wives of UCLA, Los Angeles County Mus. Assn., Friends of CalTech, Westwood Community Plan Adv. com., Girl Scouts USA, PTA. Recipient Los Angeles City Council Commendation, 1980; named Calif. Child Study Found. Woman of Yr., 1984. Mem. Sigma Alpha Iota, Delta Omicron. Roman Catholic. Clubs: Immaculate Heart College Mothers'; Loyola Mothers'; Paulist Mothers'. Avocations: music, drama, art, writing, politics. Home: 911 Malcolm Ave Los Angeles CA 90024

LIVOUS-MCDOWELL, KAREN MICHELLE, insurance company executive; b. San Francisco, Dec. 30, 1956; d. James Otis Gray and Christine (Muldrow) Tillman; m. Charles Livous Jr., Jan. 30, 1974 (div. 1980); 1 child, Charles Allen; m. Nathan Bancroft McDowell, Feb. 24, 1983; 1 child, Ruby Sherise. AA, Diablo Valley Coll., Pleasant Hill, Calif., 1974. Tchr., rsch. specialist Pittsburg (Calif.) Unified Sch. Dist., 1974-76; splicer Johns-Manville, Pittsburg, 1975-79; cable splicer Pacific Gas & Electric, Merced, Calif., 1979-80; security supr. Silks-Disco, Emeryville, Calif., 1980-85; inventory gen. clk. Williams-Sonoma, Emeryville, 1982-84; steelworker Judson Steel, Emeryville, 1984-86; purchasing adminstr. Insurnet, Inc., Emeryville, 1986—. Democrat. Baptist. Home: 5724 Gaskill St Oakland CA 94608

LIZENBY, LINDA LEE, hospital finance and personnel director; b. Logansport, Ind., May 11, 1956; d. Robert Pike and Naomi May (Stellter) L. BS in Vocat. Edn., Purdue U., 1978; cert. in pub. mgmt., Ind. U., 1983, MPA, 1987. Control desk supr. Pulaski Meml. Hosp., Winamac, Ind., 1978-88; dir. fin. and personnel Community Hosp. Bremen, Bremen, Ind., 1988—. Mem. Pulaski Meml. Hosp. Aux. (Winamac, sec. 1985-87), Order Eastern Star, Pi Alpha Alpha. Republican. Baptist. Home: 511 W Plymouth Bremen IN 46506 Office: Community Hosp of Bremen 411 S Whitlock Bremen IN 46506

LIZOTTE, SHIRLEY GUICE, insurance sales agent, underwriter; b. Carpenter, Miss., Oct. 2, 1935; d. Malcolm Gilchrist and Emma Audrey (Linton) Guice; m. Charles Joel Lizotte, Oct. 8, 1961. Student U. Tex.-Arlington 1982-83. CLU Sec. First Nat. Bank, Jackson, Miss., 1954-61; office mgr., trainee, supr. MONY, Dallas, Ft. Worth, Jackson, 1961-84; adminstrv. asst. Thomas M. Dunning Ins., Dallas, 1984-85; ins. salesman Gen. Am., Ft. Worth, 1986-87, MONY, Ft. Worth, 1987—. Sec. bd. edn. Most Blessed Sacrament Ch., Arlington, Tex., 1985. Mem. Am. Soc. C.L.U., Nat. Assn. Female Execs., Beta Sigma Phi, Life Ins. Co. Office Mgrs. Assn. (sec. 1982-84), Am. Bus. Women's Assn. (pres. 1961), DAR, First Families of Miss. Roman Catholic. Club: Altrusa PM (Arlington, v.p. 1989—); CLU (Ft. Worth). Avocations: reading, knitting, travel. Home: 2015 Elmridge Dr Arlington TX 76012 Office: Mony Fort Worth TX

LIZUT, NONA MOORE PRICE, retired state health official; b. Quay, N.Mex., Aug. 8, 1923; d. Charley W. and Alba Moore; student N.Mex. State U., 1941-42; m. Charles P. Price, Jr., 1944; 1 son, Charles P. III; m. 2d, William J. Lizut, May 27, 1970. Sec., N.Mex. Health Dept., Santa Fe, 1942-44: sec. environ. div., 1951-68; adminstrv. sec. environ. div. N.Mex. Health and Social Services Dept., Santa Fe, 1968-74, adminstrv. asst. to dep. dir., 1974-78; adminstrv. asst. to dep. sec. N.Mex. Health and Environ. Dept., Santa Fe, 1978-82, adminstr. office of dir. health services div., 1982-84; owner, mgr. Secretarial Services, Santa Fe, 1984-87. Mem. N.Mex. Water Pollution Control Assn. (life, adminstrv. officer 1956-71), N.Mex. Pub. Health Assn. (sec.-treas. 1962-68, pres. elect 1969), Nat. Secs. Assn. (v.p., program chmn. rec. sec., corr. sec.), Santa Fe C. of C. (women's div.), Santa Fe Women's Club and Library Assn., 1987—, N.Mex. Round Dance Assn. (co-pres. 1981-82, newsletter editor 1979-82), Retired Pub. Employees of N.Mex. (bd. dirs.), DAR (Stephen Watts Kearny chpt.). Club: Capitol City Bus. and Profl. Women's (v.p., program chmn.). Home: 1408 Santa Rosa Dr Santa Fe NM 87501

LJUNG, GRETA MARIANNE, statistician, educator; b. Jakobstad, Finland; d. Paul Johannes and Ellen Alina L. M.S. in Psychology, Abo Acad., Turku, Finland, 1968; M.S. in Stats., U. Wis., 1972, Ph.D. in Stats., 1976. Instr. in stats. Abo Acad., 1967-69; research and teaching asst. U. Wis., Madison, 1970-74, research assoc. Math. Research Ctr., 1975-77; asst. prof. stats. U. Denver, 1977-79; asst. prof. quantitative methods Boston U. Sch. Mgmt., 1979-86; vis. assoc. prof. applied math. MIT, 1986—; cons. in field; presentations at nat. confs. Research, numerous articles, tech. revs. and reports in time series analysis and forecasting; assoc. editor Jour. Forecasting, Internat. Jour. Forecasting. Research grantee U. Uppsala (Sweden), 1968. Mem. Am. Statis. Assn., Inst. Math. Stats., Internat. Inst. Forecasters. Office: MIT Dept Math 2-332 Cambridge MA 02139

LLEWELLYN, BETTY HALFF, archivist; b. Midland, Tex., June 12, 1911; d. Henry Mayer and Rose (Wechsler) Barnet; m. Martin Zinn, Jr., Nov. 12, 1935 (div. 1947); children: Martin III, Henry Harold, Mary Elizabeth Zinn Stewart; m. 2d, George W. Llewellyn, Nov. 9, 1948 (div. 1966). B.A., So. Meth. U., 1934; grad. Gemological Inst. Am., Santa Monica, Calif., 1968. Dir., New Theater, Dallas, 1936-40; exec. dir. McCord Theater Collection, Dallas, 1968—; ptnr. Halff Interests, Dallas, 1934—; pub. Walnut Hill Pub., Dallas, 1983—; contbr. to numerous schs. and museums, 1978—. Author: (with A.C. Greene) I Can't Forget, 1984. Officer, Lake Charles (La.) LWV, 1946-47; bd. dirs. Lake Charles ARC, 1941-45. Recipient James Smithson Bronze medal Smithsonian Instn., 1978, James Smithson Silver medal, 1980. Mem. So. Meth. U. Alumni Assn., Circus Fans Am., Circus Hist. Assn., Clowns of Am., Mineral. Assn. Dallas, Lone Star Showmans Club, James Smithson Soc., Dallas Gem and Mineral Soc., B'nai B'rith Women, Zeta Phi Eta. Jewish. Club: Pleasant Oaks Gem & Mineral (Tex.).

LLEWELLYN, JULIA ANN WAGNER, dentist; b. Harrisonburg, Va., Aug. 1, 1950; d. Thomas Elmer and Betty Ann (Holloway) Wagner; m. Richard Eaton Llewellyn, July 12, 1975. BS in Dental Hygiene, U. Md., Balt., 1972, DDS, 1980. Resident in gen. practice Johns Hopkins Hosp., Balt., 1980-81; clin. asst. prof. spl. patient clinic Dental Sch., U. Md., 1981-86; pvt. practice dentistry Columbia, Md., 1982—; cons. Dental aux. dept. Essex Community Coll., Balt., 1984-86. Mem. ADA, Les Amis Du Vin, Gorgas, Omicron Kappa Upsilon, Gamma Pi Delta. Republican. Methodist. Office: Berne Edelstein Llewellyn & Bowman PA 6395 Dobbin Rd Ste 210 Columbia MD 21045

LLOYD, CAROLYN PROVAN, state agency administrator; b. Amsterdam, Ohio, Feb. 25, 1936; d. William McMaster and Eleanore (Steffens) Provan; m. Paul Caine Moore; children: Jim, Jeff, Mike, Scott, Jon. BS in Bus. Edn., Brigham Young U., 1976, MPA, 1979. Cert. vocat. tchr., Utah. Ind. provider secretarial svcs. Provo, Utah, 1960-76; instr. Utah Tech. Coll. Bus. Dept., Provo, 1973-77; dep. commr. Dept. Agriculture State of Utah, Salt Lake City, 1978-82, dir. adminstrv. svcs. Dept. Agriculture, 1982-85, adminstrv. officer Dept. Adminstrv. Svcs., 1985-87, asst. dir. Dept. Adminstrv. Svcs., 1987, exec. dir. Dept. Adminstrv. Svcs., 1987—; bd. dirs. Utah Workers' Compensation. Mem. Am. Soc. Pub. Adminstrn., Ouelessbougou Alliance (bd. dirs. 1987—), Salt Lake City Track Club (pres. 1986). Office: Dept Adminstrv Svcs State of Utah 3120 State Office Bldg Salt Lake City UT 84114

LLOYD, ELIZABETH ELLEN, community education coordinator; b. Munich, June 7, 1949; (parents Am. citizens); d. Betty Ellen (Cox) Ramey; m. William Taylor Lloyd, June 12, 1971; children: Stefanie, Kathryn. BS, Ball State U., 1971; MS, Nat. Coll. of Edn., 1986. Adult edn. instr. Shelby Twp. Schs., Shelbyville, Ind., 1971-73; adminstrv. asst. Ind. Ins. Co., Indpls., 1973-74; bus. edn. instr. Clark Coll., Indpls., 1976-78; community edn. coord. Ill. State Bd. of Edn., Springfield, Ill., 1983-87. Co-pres. LWV, Joliet, Ill., 1983-85; bd. dirs. DuPage Twp. Com. on Youth, Bollingbrook, Ill., 1983-85; chmn. Juvenile Justice Task Force, Bollingbrook, 1982-84; adv. bd. mem. Parent Anonymous, Will County, Ill., 1982-84. Mem. Ill. Community Edn. Assn. (sec. 1987-89, spl. events coord. 1984-87, state membership chmn. 1983-85, regional membership chmn. 1982-83, Outstanding Membership Svc. award, 1983, Outstanding Young Women, 1984, Svc. award 1984, 88). Home: 1825 Talbot Ct Lawrenceville GA 30244

LLOYD, ELIZABETH JEANINE, insurance rehabilitation specialist; b. Terre Haute, Ind., Sept. 17, 1936; d. Raymond Eugene Vaughn and Evelyn Hudson (Neel) O'Dell; m. John Edward Mullen, Dec. 5, 1959 (dec. June 1960); 1 child, Shawna Marie; m. Harold Chester Lloyd, Sept. 4, 1964; 1 child, Jeffrey Roger. Cert. nurse, Leominster (Mass.) Hosp., 1958; BS in Health Studies, Anna Maria Coll., 1978; MA in Rehab. Counseling, Assumption Coll., 1980; MS in Nursing, Anne Maria Coll., 1986. RN, cert. ins. rehab. specialist. Pediatric staff nurse Worcester (Mass.) City Hosp., 1958-59; camp nurse Boy Scouts Am., ME, N.H., 1960-62; med., surg. staff and head nurse Clinton (Mass.) Hosp., 1960-70; pub. health nurse Clinton Health Dept., 1965-66; pvt. duty nurse various hosps., Central, Mass., 1970-71; head nurse Quaboag Nursing Home, West Brookfield, Mass., 1972-73; indsl. nurse William E. Wright Com., West Warren, Mass., 1973-74; rehab. coordinator Travelers Ins. Co., Worcester, Mass., 1974—; speaker various colls., med. programs, Mass., 1980-85, Gov.'s Council Mass. Rehab. Com., Boxboro, 1983; coordinator Workers Compensation Job Fair, Worcester, 1982. Author: Rehabilitation: Nursing Management Model, 1986. Mem. Lake Lashaway Assn., North Brookfield, Mass., 1987. Mem. NAFE, Insurance Rehab. (coordinator nurses 1978—, continuing edn. coordinator 1978—), Nat. Rehab. Assn., Occupational Heatlh Nurses Assn. (program developer 1973-75), Assumption Coll. Alumni Assn., Anna Maria Coll. Alumni Assn., Leominster Hosp. Alumni Assn. Congregationalist. Clubs: Worcester Mineral; Southeast Fedn. Office: Travelers Ins Co 120 Front St Worcester MA 01608

LLOYD, HORTENSE COLLINS, English language educator; b. Houston; d. Jephtha D. and Sallie (Shepherd) Collins; m. Raymond G. Lloyd, Sept. 18, 1943; 1 child, Jacqueline Michele. AB, Prairie View Coll., 1942; MA, Columbia U., 1946. English tchr. Pub. Sch. #42, N.Y.C., 1944-46; instr. English Wiley Coll., Marshall, Tex., 1947, Agrl. and Tech. Coll., Greensboro, N.C., 1947-48, Orangeburg (S.C.) State Coll., 1951-52; English tchr. Alfred Beach High Sch., Savannah, Ga., 1953-58; asst. prof. Tenn. State U., Nashville, 1958-72; asst. prof. Edward Waters Coll., Jacksonville, Fla., 1972-77, prof., dir. honors program, 1977—; field-tested essays for Ednl. Testing Service, Princeton, N.J. Book rev. editor Negro Ednl. Review, 1950—. Pres. Clara White Mission, Jacksonville, 1986—; bd. dirs. Northeast Fla. Camp Fire Girls. Named a Disting. Faculty Mem. Edward Waters Coll., 1988; Danforth fellow, 1970. Mem. AAUW, Nat. Council Tchrs. English, Conf. of College Composition and Communication, Alpha Kappa Alpha. Presbyterian. Home: 5006 Andrew Robinson Dr Jacksonville FL 32209 Office: Edward Waters Coll 1658 Kings Rd PO Box 73 Jacksonville FL 32209

LLOYD, MARILYN, congresswoman; b. Ft. Smith, Ark.; d. James Edgar and Iva Mae (Higginbotham) Laird; children: Nancy Lloyd Smithson, Mari, Mort II. Student, Shorter Coll., 1963. Mem. 94th-102nd Congresses from 3d Tenn. dist., Washington, 1975—. Office: US Ho of Reps 2266 Rayburn Washington DC 20515

LLOYD-CALDWELL, MARIAN JEAN, business owner; b. Detroit, June 19, 1942; d. Junius and Ada Mae (Thomas) L.; m. Julius James Caldwell. BA, U. Windsor, Ont., Can., 1978; cert., Marygrove Coll., 1987; grad. Dale Carnegie course, 1987. Employment recruit State of Mich., Detroit, 1981-82; job developer Greater Orgn. Indsl. Ctr., Detroit, 1982-83; dist. mgr. State of Mich. Bur. of Lottery, Detroit, 1984—; owner J. Brandon Co., Detroit, 1986—; lectr. Lakeview High Sch., St. Clair Shores, Mich., 1972; TV producer Employment Svcs. of Mich., St. Clair Shores, 1981; producer, writer J. Brandon Co., Detroit, 1986—, pub. rels com., 1986—. Author: MARJEAN, 1977; editor: newsletter The Calvary Advocator, 1980; playwright play Not Yet Lord, 1989. Founder. Library Tribute to Black Am., Detroit, 1975; campaign mgr. Dem. candidate for office, Detroit, 1982; pres. local sch. community orgn., Detroit, 1986-89. Recipient Outstanding Recognition, 1986, 87, 90. Mem. NAFE, Gamma Phi Delta. Office: 19410 Livernois ave Detroit MI 48221

LLOYD-JONES, JEAN, state legislator; b. Washington, Oct. 14, 1929; d. John and Lucille Thurston Hall; m. Richard Lloyd-Jones, 1951; children: Richard A., Mary, John D., Jeffrey. Student, U. N.Mex., 1946-49; BA, Northwestern U., 1951; MA, U. Iowa, 1970. Formerly mem. Iowa Ho. of Reps.; now mem. Iowa Senate. Mem. LWV (pres. Iowa state league 1972-76), NOW, Iowa Assn. R.R. Passengers, UN Assn., Iowa Peace Inst. Democrat. Home: 160 Oakridge Ave Iowa City IA 52240*

LLOYD-MURIE, ROSEMARIE, graphic arts equipment executive; b. Trenton, Mich., Aug. 23, 1960; d. Edward Robert and Cynthia Mary (Christie) Lloyd; m. John Thomas Murie, Oct. 20, 1984. BBA in Mgmt., Ea. Mich. U., 1988. Sec. Finazzo Constrn. Co., Wyandotte, Mich., 1977-79; payroll clk. Babcock and Wilcox, Wyandotte, 1979; sec. Kelly Services, Trenton, 1980; sec. Heidelberg Ea., Inc., Taylor, Mich., 1981-82, adminstrv. asst., 1982-84, regional adminstrv. mgr., 1984—. Mem. Nat. Assn. Female Execs., Beta Gamma Sigma, Golden Key Hon. Soc. Democrat. Roman Catholic. Home: 10201 Cherokee Taylor MI 48180 Office: Heidelberg Ea Inc 24500 Northline Rd Taylor MI 48180

LO, ELIZABETH SHEN, organic chemist; b. Tokyo, Feb. 24, 1926; came to U.S., 1946; d. Zee and She-Ven (Huang) Shen; m. Arthur W. Lo, Aug. 24, 1950; children: Katherine, James. BS with honors, St. John's U., 1946; MS, U. Ill., 1947, PhD, 1949. Rsch. chemist Johnson & Johnson Rsch. Ctr., New Brunswick, N.J., 1957-60; staff rsch. chemist IBM Corp., Poughkeepsie, N.Y., 1960-63; sr. rsch. chemist Thiokol Chem. Corp., Trenton, N.J., 1965-70; vis. fellow Princeton (N.J.) U., 1972-74; mem. tech. staff RCA David Sarnoff Rsch. Ctr., Princeton, 1975-77; chief chemist Refac Electronics Corp. Optel Div., Edison, N.J., 1978-81; polymer materials mgr. Electro-Sci. Lab., King of Prussia, Pa., 1982—; Patentee in field. Fellow Am. Inst. Chemists; mem. Am. Chem. Soc., Internat. Soc. Hybrid Microelectronics, Sigma Xi. Home: 102 Maclean Circle Princeton NJ 08540 Office: Electro-Sci Lab Inc 416 E Church Rd King of Prussia PA 19406

LO, THERESA NONG, health science administrator; b. Hai Phong, Vietnam, Mar. 16, 1945; d. Dang Van and Boi Thuy (Lam) Nong; m. Chu Shek Lo, Dec.27, 1969; 1 child, Francesca Che Lo. Student, Ottumwa Heights Coll., 1964-65; BA, Clarke Coll., 1968; PhD, Ind. U., Indpls., 1974. Lab. asst. Clarke Coll., Dubuque, Iowa, 1966-68; teaching/rsch. asst. Med. Ctr. Ind. U., Indpls., 1968-73; USPHS postdoctoral trainee U. Calif., San Francisco, 1973-75; vis. fellow Nat. Heart, Lung & Blood Inst., Bethesda, Md., 1975-77; vis. fellow Nat. Cancer Inst. NIH, Bethesda, 1977-78; rsch. chemist Lab. of Cellular Metabolism, Nat. Heart, Lung & Blood Inst., Bethesda, 1979-82, Lab. Chem. Pharmacology, Nat. Heart, Lung & Blood Inst., Bethesda, 1982-88; health sci. adminstr. div. blood diseases and resources Nat. Heart, Lung & Blood Inst., Bethesda, 1988-89; health sci. adminstr. rev. logistics br. Nat. Cancer Inst. NIH, Bethesda, 1989—; liaison to Drug Enforcement Adminstrn., U.S. Dept. Justice, lab. chem. pharmacology, Nat. Heart, Lung and Blood Inst., Bethesda, 1982-83; coord. sci. seminar program lab. chem. pharmacology Nat. Heart, Lung & Blood

Inst., Bethesda, 1982-83; role model NIH career day div. equal opportunity NIH, Bethesda, 1988, 90; U.S. savs. bond canvasser, 1989; invited speaker Chinese Acad. Med. Scis., Beijing, 1982; invited speaker The Ottumwa (Iowa) Quota Club, 1964, Div. Drug Biology, FDA, Washington, 1983. Contbr. articles and abstracts to profl. jours. Sec. Orgn. Chinese Ams., Inc., Greater Washington, 1984, woman rep. White House briefing, Washington, 1985; participant women's mgmt. tng. initiative HHS Personnel Adminstrn., 1987-88. Ottumwa Quota Club scholr, 1965, Clarke Coll. scholar, 1965-68; named hon. citizen City of Indpls., 1968, hon. speedway ambassador Civil Town of Speedway (Ind.), 1972; recipient Spl. Achievement award Nat. Cancer Inst., div. extramural activities, 1990. Mem. Am. Soc. for Biochemistry and Molecular Biology, Am. Soc. for Pharmacology and Exptl. Therapeutics, Am. Soc. for Cell Biology, Inflammation Rsch. Assn., Cardiovascular Rsch. Inst. Alumni Assn., Ind. U. Alumni Assn., Clarke Coll. Alumni Assn. Home: 5304 Elsmere Ave Bethesda MD 20814 Office: Nat Cancer Inst Dea Rev Logistics Br WW/838 5333 Westbard Ave Bethesda MD 20892

LOBENE, JOYCE ANNE, real estate corporation executive; b. Rochester, N.Y., Oct. 17, 1939; d. James John and Flora (Anasimele) Nuccitelli; m. Thomas Robert Lobene, May 6, 1961 (dec. July 1988); children: James, Mary, Michael, Thomas J. Lic. real estate broker, N.Y. Sec. Stromberg Carlson, Rochester, N.Y., 1958-59; sec. Xerox Corp., Rochester, 1959-61, customer relations rep., 1961-62; sales assoc. John T. Nothnagle, Inc., North Chili, N.Y., 1978-83, br. mgr., 1983—; cons. in field. Active Ogden Rep. Club, Spencerport, N.Y., 1982—, Bd. Assessment & Rev., 1983—. Recipient numerous profl. awards. Mem. Nat. Realtors Assn., Women's Council Realtors (pres. 1983-85), N.Y. State Bd. Realtors, Real Bd. Rochester, Gallery of Homes (chmn. N.Y. Upstate regional coun.). Republican. Roman Catholic. Home: 28 Kresswood Dr Rochester NY 14624 Office: 4156 Buffalo Rd Rochester NY 14624

LOBER, HOLLY HENDERSON, small business owner; b. Bloomington, Ill., Jan. 16, 1951; d. Jerry M. and Ellen E. (Jones) Henderson; m. Arnie Lober, Nov. 4, 1982; children: Heather Nord, Brent Nord, Kristin Nord. Cert. profl. employment counselor. Co-owner, sec., treas. Halo, Inc., 1982—, Bloomington Bowling Enterprises, Inc., 1983—; co-owner, pres. Champaign Bowling Enterprises, Inc., 1988—. Mem. NAFE, WESRA (bd. dirs. PEERS chpt.), Ill. State Bowling Proprs. (v.p. east cen. region), Ill. State Young Ams. Bowling Alliance (bd. dirs.). Home: RR1 Box 226 Towanda IL 61776 Office: 804 N Hershey Rd Bloomington IL 61704

LOBIG, JANIE HOWELL, special education educator; b. Peoria, Ill., June 10, 1945; d. Thomas Edwin and Elizabeth Jane (Higdon) Howell; m. James Frederick Lobig, Aug. 16, 1970; 1 child, Jill Christina. BS in Elem. Edn., So. Ill. U., 1969; MA in Spl. Edn. Severely Handicapped, San Jose State U., 1989. Cert. elem. tchr., Calif., Mo., Ill., handicapped edn., Calif., Mo.; ordained to ministry Presbyn. Ch. as deacon, 1984. Tchr. trainable mentally retarded children Spl. Luth. Sch., St. Louis, 1967-68; tchr. trainable mentally retarded and severly handicapped children Spl. Sch. Dist. St. Louis, 1969-80, head tchr., 1980-83; tchr. severly handicapped children San Jose (calif.) Unifed Sch. Dist., 1983-86; tchr. multihandicapped students Santa Clara County Office Edn., San Jose, 1986—. Vol. Am. Cancer Soc., San Jose, 1986-89, St. Louis Reps., 1976-82; troop leader Camp Fire Girls, San Jose, 1984-85; moderator of bd. deacons Evergreen Presbyn. Ch., 1986-89; exec. bd. Norwood Creek Elem. Sch. PTA, 1983-86. Mem. Council for Exceptional Children, Assn. for Severly Handicapped, Nat. Edn. Assn., Calif. Tchrs. Assn. Republican. Home: 3131 Creekmore Way San Jose CA 95148 Office: Fred Marten Spl Sch 14265B Story Rd San Jose CA 95127

LOCHHEAD, LOUISE P., business educator; b. Salt Lake City, Sept. 10, 1940; d. Joseph John and Helen Anna (Habiger) Keiser; m. Donald G. Lochhead, Nov. 21, 1964; children: Laura Marie, Donna Victoria, Mark Joseph. BS, U. Utah, 1964; postgrad., various schs., 1964-89. Cert. tchr., Utah. Bus. tchr. Skyline High Sch., Salt Lake City, 1963-66; tchr. English USIA English Sch., Tripoli, Libya, 1966-67; tchr. Davis High Sch., Kaysville, Utah, 1967—, chair dept. bus., 1979—; mem. state com. for acctg. and free enterprise standards and objectives, 1986-90; presenter profl. confs. Coauthor: Open for Business, 1989; contbr. articles to Forum mag. Vol. local polit. campaign, 1986; mem. parish coun., Bountiful, Utah, 1990-92. Recipient Utah Bus. Edn. Action award, 1986, Disting. Teaching award Utah acad. Scis., Arts and Letters, 1987. Mem. AAUW (rights and responsibilities chair 1987-88), NEA, Davis Edn. Assn., Nat. Bus. Edn. Assn., Utah Bus. Edn. Assn. (v.p. 1988-89), Utah Edn. Assn. Roman Catholic. Office: Davis High Sch 325 S Main St Kaysville UT 84037

LOCKARD, PEGGY LOU, publisher, publishing company executive; b. Denver, Mar. 23, 1931; d. Jerry Hamilton and Hazel Margaret (Schroeder) Morehead; m. Douglas Neil Gieske, Aug. 19, 1950 (div. Feb. 1969); children: Sandra Gieske Larriva, David Brian; m. William Kirby Lockard, Dec. 9, 1972. Legal sec. Royal and Carlson, Tucson, 1964-68; legal sec. Bilby, Thompson, Shoenhair, Tucson, 1968-69, Waterfall, Economidis Falk, Tucson, 1969; with real estate sales Denton Real Estate, Tucson, 1969-70, Ariz. Enterprises, Tucson, 1970-71; real estate broker Pepper Properties, Tucson, 1971—; pres. Pepper Pub., Tucson, 1973—. Author: This is Tucson, 1983, 2nd edit., 1985, 3rd edit., 1988; editor, designer: Where the Desert Meets the Sea, 1988; editor: Comme je Trouve: I Take Things as I Find Them. Chmn. Tucson Sign Code Adv. and Appeals Bd., 1989; mem. Tucson Citizens Sign Code Com., 1984-88, Tucson Sign Code Revision Com., 1977-80, Tucson Bd. Adjustment, 1970-77, chmn., 1972, 1974-75, Tucson Tomorrow, Friends of Coll. Architecture; mem. centennial com. Coll. Architecture; vice chmn. Blenman Elm Neighborhood Assn., Tucson, 1988-89; mem., vice chmn. Tucson Planning and Zoning Commn., 1971-72; bd. dirs. Tucson Festival Soc. Named Distig. Citizen, U. Ariz. Alumni Assn., 1985, Young Republican Woman of Yr. Ariz. Young Republicans, 1966. Mem. Tucson Book Pub. Assn. (vice chair 1990—), Rocky Mountain Book Pub. Assn. (chair 1984-85). Democrat. Office: Pepper Publishing 433 N Tucson Blvd Tucson AZ 85716

LOCKE, VIRGINIA OTIS, textbook editor, behavioral sciences writer; b. Tiffin, Ohio, Sept. 4, 1930; d. Charles Otis and Frances Virginia (Sherer) L. BA, Barnard Coll., 1953; MA in Psychology, Duke U., 1972. Program officer, asst. corp. sec. Agrl. Devel. Coun., N.Y.C., 1954-66; staff psychologist St. Luke's-Roosevelt Med. Ctr., N.Y.C., 1973-75; freelance writer and editor N.Y.C., 1976-85; writer-editor Cornell U. Med. Coll./N.Y. Hosp. Med. Ctr., N.Y.C., 1986-89; sr. editor coll. book editorial devel. coll. div. Prentice Hall, Englewood Cliffs, N.J., 1989—. Co-author: (coll. textbook) Introduction to Theories of Personality, 1985, The Agricultural Development Council: A History, 1989. Founder Help Our Neighbors Eat Year-round, H.O.N.E.Y., Inc., N.Y.C., chmn., 1983-87, vol., 1987—; reader Recording for the Blind, N.Y.C., 1978-84; vol. Reach to Recovery program Am. Cancer Soc., Bergen County, N.J., 1990—. Recipient Our Town Thanks You award, N.Y.C., 1984, Mayor's Vol. Svc. award, N.Y.C., 1986, Cert. of Appreciation for Community Svc. Manhattan Borough, 1986, Jefferson award Am. Ins. Pub. Svc., Washington, 1986. Democrat. Episcopalian. Office: Prentice Hall Coll Book Coll Book Div Prentice Hall Bldg Englewood Cliffs NJ 07632

LOCKETT, BARBARA ANN, librarian; b. Northampton, Mass., Feb. 21, 1936; d. William M. and Anna A. (Vachula) Prabulos; m. Richard W. Rice, June 2, 1957 (div. Feb. 1966); 1 child, Annamarie Louise; m. Benjamin B. Lockett, June 7, 1985. BS, U. Mass., 1957; MLS, U. Calif., Berkeley, 1967. Documents librarian Knolls Atomic Power Lab., Schenectady, N.Y., 1968-74; coordinator bibliog. devel. SUNY, Albany, 1974-81; prin. librarian reference services N.Y. State Library, Albany, 1981-85; dir. libraries Rensselaer Poly. Inst., Troy, N.Y., 1985—; cons. Office Mgmt. Svcs., Assn. Rsch. Librs., Washington, 1981—. Contbr. articles on collection devel., mgmt. to profl. jours. Mem. ALA (cons. collection mgmt. and devel. com., Resources and Tech. Svcs. div. 1983-87), Assn. Coll. and Rsch. Librs. (chair standards and accreditation com. com. 1988-90), N.Y. State Edn. and Rsch. Network Inc. (chair info. resources com. 1988-89), Spl. Librs. Assn. (pres. Upstate N.Y. chpt. 1981-82), Sigma Xi, Phi Kappa Phi, Beta Phi Mu. Mem. Unitarian Ch. Home: 6 Broderick St Albany NY 12205 Office: Rensselaer Poly Inst Folsom Libr 110 8th St Troy NY 12180-3590

LOCKETT-EGAN, MARIAN WORKMAN, advertising executive; b. Murray, Ky., May 5, 1931; d. Otis H. Workman and Myrtle A. (Jones) Jordan; m. Gene Potts, Jan. 6, 1947 (div. Feb. 1963); children: Reed Nasser, Jennifer Potts, George M., Cynthia Klenk; m. Barker Lockett, Oct. 11, 1963 (div. Dec. 1972); 1 child, Stephen R.W.; m. Douglas S. Egan Jr., Feb. 14, 1981. BA Murray State U., 1962. Asst. media dir. Noble-Dury & Assocs., Nashville, 1963-64; asst. research dir. Triangle Publs. Phila., 1964-66; assoc. media dir. Lewis & Gilman, Phila., 1966-72; v.p. advt. media, Scott Paper Co., Phila., 1972-83; pres. DMS Communications Inc., Ardmore, Pa., 1983—; faculty adviser The Media Sch., N.Y.C., 1983-85, 87—, exec. dir. Mktg. and Media Edn., 1985-87, exec. dir., 1990—; mem. TV com. Assn. Nat. Advertisers, N.Y.C., 1977-83; guest lectr. Wharton U., Phila., 1981-82, 85, 86, 87; Gannet vis. prof. Sch. Journalism U. Fla., Gainesville, 1982. Guest editor Media Decisions, 1981. Trustee Meth. Hosp. Found., Phila., 1973-87. Mem. Broadcast Pioneers, TV and Radio Advt. Club (pres. 1973). Republican. Episcopalian. Avocations: sailing, tennis. Home: 45 Llanfair Circle Ardmore PA 19033 Office: DMS Communications PO Box 110 Ardmore PA 19033

LOCKHART, ANN JUNE, public relations executive; b. Elkader, Iowa, Dec. 9, 1945; d. Frank Wesley and Phylis Marie (Kramer) L. AA, N. Iowa Area Community Coll., Mason City, Iowa, 1966; BA, U. Iowa, 1968; postgrad., Denver U., 1988-90. Advt. sales rep. San Marcos (Tex.) Record, 1968-69; tchr. Refugio (Tex.) Ind. Sch. Dist., 1969-71; from receptionist Englewood (Colo.) to editor Wheat Ridge Community Publs. Co., 1971-75; editor, med. ctr. U. Colo. Health Scis. Ctr., Denver, 1975-78; pub. rels. asst. Nat. Jewish Hosp./Nat. Asthma Ctr., Denver, 1978; pub. rels. dir. Colo. Dept. Health, Denver, 1978—. bd.dirs. Womanschool Network, pub. rels. com. Colo. Energy Asst. Found., 1990. mem. Nat. Pub. Health Info. Coalition, Inc. (pres. 1990-91, steering com. (1989-90), Colo. State Mgrs. Assn., Denver, 1989-90. Named Disting. Toastmaster, Toastmasters Internat., Denver, 1990, Toastmaster of Yr., Body Shops Toastmasters, Denver, 1986, Woman Achievement, Colo. Press Women, Denver, 1985, writing awds. Colo. Press Women, Nat. Fedn. Press Women. Mem. Colo. Press Women (pres. 1978-80, program, bylaws com.), Colo. Press Assn., Colo. Coun. Govt. Communicators. Democrat. Office: Colo Dept Health 4210 E 11th Ave Denver CO 80220

LOCKHART, COLLEEN MARIE, forensic scientist; b. Yonkers, N.Y., June 15, 1964; d. William Thomas and Alice Wilma (Davis) L. BS, John Jay Coll., 1987, postgrad., 1988—. Analytical chemist Purdue Frederick Rsch., Yonkers, N.Y., 1984-88; forensic scientist Yonkers Police Forensic Lab., 1988—. Candystripper Yonkers Gen. Hosp., 1974-78; participant Multiple Sclerosis Readathon, Yonkers, 1978. Named Vol. of Yr., Yonkers Gen. Hosp., 1979, East Yonkers Rotary Club, 1982. Mem. Northeastern Assn. Forensic Scientists (provisional), N.Y. Micros. Soc., Am. Mus. Natural History (assoc.), Smithsonian Assocs., KC. Democrat. Lutheran. Home: 279 N Broadway Yonkers NY 10701

LOCKHART, MADGE CLEMENTS, educator; b. Soddy, Tenn., May 22, 1920; d. James Arlie and Ollie (Sparks) Clements; m. Andre J. Lockhart, Apr. 24, 1942 (div. 1973); children: Jacqueline, Andrew, Janice, Jill. Student, East Tenn. U., 1938-39; BS, U. Tenn., Chattanooga and Knoxville, 1955, MEd, 1962. Elem. tchr. Tenn. and Ga., 1947-60, Brainerd High Sch., Chattanooga, 1960-64, Cleveland (Tenn.) City Schs., 1966-88; owner, operator Lockhart's Learning Ctr., Inc., Cleveland and Chattanooga, 1975—; co-founder, pres. Hermes, Inc., 1973-79; co-founder Dawn Ctr., Hamilton County, Tenn., 1974; apptd. mem. Tenn. Gov.'s Acad. for Writers. AuthAor poetry, short stories and fiction; contbr. articles to profl. jours. and newspapers. Pres. Cleveland Assn. Retarded Citizens, 1970, state v.p., 1976; pres. Cherokee Easter Seal Soc., 1973-76, Cleveland Creative Arts Guild, 1980; bd. dirs. Tenn. Easter Seal Soc., 1974-77, 80-83; chair Bradley County Internat. Yr. of Child. Recipient Service to Mankind award Sertoma, 1978, Gov.'s award for service to handicapped, 1979; mental health home named in her honor, Tenn., 1987. Mem. NEA (life), Tenn. Edn. Assn., Am. Assn. Rehab. Therapy, Cleveland Edn. Assn. (Service to Humanity award 1987). Mem. Ch. of Christ. Clubs: Byliners, Fantastiks. Home: 3007 Oakland Dr Cleveland TN 37312

LOCKHART, MARY GUY, nurse; b. Jackson, Miss., Feb. 15, 1947; d. Jim Bishop and Louise (Turner) L. Student, Miss. Coll., 1965-67, Millsaps Coll., 1966; BS in Nursing, U. Tenn., 1970; grad. with honors, Sch. Aerospace Medicine, Brooks AFB, Tex., 1981. RN, Miss., Tenn. Staff nurse John Hosp., Memphis, 1970-72, Sanyati Bapt. Hosp., Sanyati Rhodesia (Zimbabwe) Fgn. Mission, Richmond, Va., 1972-74, VA Hosp., Jackson, 1975-90; commd. USAF, 1977, advanced through grades to maj.; stationed at Rhein Main-Frankfort, Fed. Republic Germany, 1990—. Named to Outstanding Young Women Am., 1977. Mem. Am. Assn. Critical Care Nurses (critical care RN), Assn. Mil. Surgeons of U.S., Am. Heart Assn., Salvation Army Med. Fellowship, Assn. Air Nat. Guard Nurses, Nurses Orgn. Vets. Affairs, Cousteau Assn., World Wildlife Fund. Republican. Baptist. Home: 1602 Myrtle St Jackson MS 39202-1333

LOCKHART, THELMA, marketing professional; b. Jonesville, Va., Apr. 22, 1942; d. Robert H. and Georgia Orr. AAS, Mountain Empire Comm. Coll., 1972; BA, Calif. Coast Coll., 1990; MA, Calif. Coast Univ., 1990. Prin. USDA, Jonesville, Va., 1962-72, Mountain Empire Community Coll., Big Stone Gap, Va., 1972-85, Draughton Jr. Coll., Kingsport, Tenn., 1985-89; mktg., mgmt. Oak Hill Funeral Home, Kingsport, 1989—; cons. in field. Mem. NAFE, Kingsport C. of C., Downtown Kingsport Assn., Rotary. Methodist. Home: 421 Eastley Ct Apt F Kingsport TN 37660 Office: PO Box 1068 Kingsport TN 37660

LOCKLEAR, JEANNE MARIE, retail security executive; b. Wood River, Ill., May 28, 1953; d. Carl Henry Locklear and Virginia Mae (Smith) Torbitt; m. David Leroy Bedwell, July 20, 1970 (div. 1975); children: Craig Curtis Bedwell Brown, Rebecca Jean Bedwell Brown; m. Steven Ray Brown, May 7, 1977 (div. 1984). Cert., U.S. Army Inst., 1975, Mo. Hwy. Patrol Acad., 1981; BS, Drury Coll., 1982. Factory worker, union rep. Owens Ill. Glass, Glass Bottle Blowers Assn., Alton, 1971-75; personnel specialist U.S. Dept. of Army, Ft. Leonard Wood, Mo., 1975-77, West Point, N.Y., 1977-79; security officer Famous Barr Co., St. Louis, 1980; police officer Rolla (Mo.) Police Dept., 1981; correctional officer U.S. Dept. Justice Bur. Prisons, Springfield, Mo., 1982; instr. Belleville (Ill.) Area Coll., 1988—, Lewis & Clark Community Coll., Godfrey, Ill., 1985—; security exec. Famous Barr Co., St. Louis, 1982—; guest speaker on retail security, Vocat. Tng. Ctr., St. Louis, 1986, Fairview Heights (Ill.) Police Dept., 1986. Asst. Brownie troop leader Godfrey area Girl Scouts U.s., 1979-80, fund raiser, New Windsor, N.Y., 1977-78. Mem. Security Adv. Com., Mo. Crime Prevention Assn., Nat. Assn. Female Execs., Assn. Bus. and Indsl. Security. Democrat. Greek Orthodox. Office: Famous Barr Co 200 St Clair Square Fairview Heights IL 62208

LOCKWOOD, DORIS HOFFMANN, clinical psychologist; b. Berlin; came to U.S., 1934; d. Jakob Hoffmann and Rose Ruth (Mandowsky) Goldschmidt; m. Lewis Lockwood, Dec. 26, 1953; children: Alison, Daniel. PhD, Rutgers U., 1963. Lic. psychologist, N.J., Mass. Staff psychologist Mercer County Guidance Clinic, Princeton, N.J., 1971-80; sr. staff Trinity Counseling Svc., Princeton, 1975-80; sr. family therapy supr. Kennedy Meml. Hosp. for Children, Brighton, Mass., 1980-83; dir. family svcs. and dir. tng. Newton (Mass.) Guidance Clinic, 1983-86; asst. prof. Dept. Psychology Emmanuel Coll., Boston, 1989—; pvt. practice Brookline, Mass., 1973—; asst. attending psychologist McLean Hosp., Belmont, Mass., 1988—. Fellow Mass. Psychol. Assn.; mem. Am. Psychol. Assn., Am. Family Therapy Assn., Am. Orthopsychiat. Assn. Office: Emmanuel Coll 400 The Fenway Boston MA 02215

LODGE, MICHELLE, journalist; b. Philippi, W.Va.; d. John Woodford Lodge and Patricia (Lalley) Mazurek. Student, Randolph-Macon Woman's Coll., 1970-71, U. Pontificia Bolivariana, 1973; BA, W.Va. U., 1974. Editor-in-chief Apalachicola (Fla.) Times, Carrabelle Times, 1976-77; reporter, arts writer The Day, New London, Ct., 1978-83; editor Ziff-Davis Pub. Co., N.Y.C., 1983-85; asst. news editor Sch. Libr. Jour., N.Y.C., 1985; freelance journalist numerous periodicals, N.Y.C., 1983—; adj. prof. mag. writing NYU, 1989—; judges panel best books of 1988 Libr. Jour. 1988-89. Book rev. editor: Library Journal, 1988-89. Mem. N.Y. Women in Communications (bd. dirs., v.p. communications 1990—, scholarship com. 1990), Nat. Writers Union, Editorial Freelancers Assn.

LODGE, PATRICIA GRACE, public relations executive, commercial photographer; b. Wilmington, Del., Mar. 16, 1934; d. James Francis and Grace Lyda (Veazey) Kearney; m. Joseph Howard Lodge, Dec. 31, 1970 (div. Apr. 1990); children: Susan Lynn Proth, Linda Kay Delp, Deborah Gail Wrye, William Craig Fisher. Student, Ann Arundel Community Coll., 1976-80, Willsey Inst. Art, Miami, Fla., 1980-81, Fla. Internat. U., 1986-88. Mktg. and pub. rels. rep. Minn. Mining and Mfg. Co., Wilmington, 1964-66; mktg. and pub. relations rep. Minn. Mining and Mfg. Co., Miami, 1966-68; account exec. Wometco, Inc., Miami, 1968-70; photographer Visitor Pub. Co., Miami Beach, Fla., 1980-82; co-founder, exec. v.p. Corp. Security Advisors, Inc. (merged Bus. Risks Internat., Inc.), Miami Beach, 1982-87; founder, pres. PGL Enterprises, Miami Beach, 1987-90, pub. rels. exec., comml. photographer, 1990—; pub. rels. cons. Photographer for various mags. Mem. NAFE (network dir.), Friends Japanese Garden (bd. dirs., pub. relations and publicity chmn., tour guide), Am. Soc. Mag. Photographers (pub. rels. and promotions chmn.), Zoolog. Soc. Fla., South Fla. Hist. Soc., , Tropical Audubon Soc., Japan/America Soc., Greater Miami C. of C. (drug free workplace and culture coms., Navy League U.S., Sierra Club, Miami Beach Garden Club, Jockey Club Miami, Toastmasters. Home: 1601 W 28th St Sunset Island #1 Miami Beach FL 33140 Office: PGL Enterprises PO Box 402891 Miami Beach FL 33140

LODMELL, MARILYN MAKI (LYNN LODMELL), director state correctional industries; b. Proctor, Vt., Oct. 2, 1937; d. Viljo Richard and Marion (Keenan) Maki; m. Dean S. Lodmell, Jan. 25, 1958 (div. May 1982); children: Dean W., Kimberly, Richard. BSBA cum laude in Acctg., Fairleigh Dickenson U., 1977. Ins. supr. Nat. Grange Ins. Co., Rutland, Vt., 1959-61; with actuary dept. N.Y. Life Ins. Co., Pasadena, Calif., 1961-63; with mktg. and sales Columbia U. Press, N.Y.C., 1963-65; bus. mgr., contr. Balo Precision Parts, Franklin Lakes, N.J., 1971-77; chief acct. Dlisa Electronics, Franklin Lakes, 1977-78; auditor Wash. State Dept. Social & Health, Olympia, 1978-79; fin. system analyst Wash. State Office Fin. Mgmt., Olympia, 1979-80; asst. supr., program mgr. Wash. State Dept. Corrections Instl. Industries, Olympia, 1980-88; dir. div. correctional industries Wash. State Dept. Corrections, Olympia, 1988—; cons. Fin. Svcs., N.J., Wash., 1978—, correctional field, Md., Wash., 1988—, Am. Inst. Internat. Edn., Dacca, Bangladesh, 1969-71. Mem. Jr. Club, Walla Walla, Wash., 1964-68, WCHS Wash. Children Home Soc., Walla Walla, 1964-68; mem., treas. St. Peter Hosp. Aux., Olympia, 1978—. Mem. NAFE, Am. Correction Assn. (bd. dirs. 1988—, Wash. State Gov's. Disting. Mgmt. award), Western Correctional Industries Assn. (v.p. 1988-90, pres. 1990—), Nat. Community Svc. Sentencing Assn. (founding mem.), Nat. Assn. Vols. in Corrections., Wash. Corrections Assn. Office: Wash State Dept Corrections 423 4th Ave Olympia WA 98504

LODOWSKI, RUTH ELLEN, physician; b. Dallas, Feb. 15, 1951; s. Charles Harry and Genevieve (Gowaty) L. BS, U. Tex., 1972; MBA, North Tex. State U., Denton, 1976; MD, U.Tex.-San Antonio, 1986. Resident asst., then head resident Castilian Dormitory, Austin, Tex., 1971-73; singer self-employed band, Austin, 1972-74; teller Greenville Ave. Bank, Dallas, 1974-75; employment interviewer Tex. Employment Commn., Grand Prairie, 1975-76; personnel intern U.S. Dept. Justice, Seagoville, Tex., 1976-77; personnel asst. Army and Air Force Exchange Service, San Antonio, 1977-78; staffing adminstr., personnel adminstr. Tex. Instruments Inc., Dallas, 1978-81, U. Tex. Med. Sch. at San Antonio, 1982-86; intern, then resident Parkland Meml. Hosp., Dallas, 1986—. Active, YWCA, ARC. Recipient Top 10 Medal of Honor Kiwanis Internat., 1969. Mem. AMA, Tex. Med. Assn., Dallas Area Women Psychiatrists, Tex. Exes Club.

LODWICK, SHEILA ANNE RAMERMAN, lawyer; b. Annapolis, Md., Dec. 15, 1956; d. Herbert Clare and Mary Alice (McNally) Ramerman; m. David P. Lodwick, Sept. 3, 1983. BA in Pub. Adminstrn., Miami U., Oxford, Ohio, 1978; JD, Cleve. State U., 1981. Bar: Ohio 1982, U.S. Dist. Ct. (no. dist.) Ohio, 1982, U.S. Ct. Appeals (6th cir.) 1989. Assoc. Shapiro, Turoff, Gisser & Belkin, Cleve., 1982—; vol. legal cons. Jewish Family Svc. Assn., Cleve., 1986—. Mem. Assn. for Retarded Citizens, Cleve., 1986—. Mem. Ohio Bar Assn., Greater Cleve. Bar Assn. Democrat. Roman Catholic. Office: Shapiro Turoff et al 1200 Standard Bldg Cleveland OH 44113

LOEB, FRANCES LEHMAN, civic leader; b. N.Y.C., Sept. 25, 1906; d. Arthur and Adele (Lewisohn) Lehman; student Vassar Coll., 1924-26; L.H.D. (hon.), NYU, 1977; m. John L. Loeb, Nov. 18, 1926; children: Judith Loeb Chiara, John L., Ann Loeb Bronfman, Arthur Lehman, Deborah Loeb Brice. N.Y.C. commr. for UN and Consular Corps, 1966-78. Exec. com. Population Crisis Com., Washington; life mem. bd. Children of Bellevue, Inc., 1974—; bd. dirs. Bellevue Assn., Internat. Presch., Inc., N.Y. Landmarks Conservancy; chmn. bd. East Side Internat. Community Ctr., Inc.; mem. UN Devel. Corp., 1972—; life trustee Collegiate Sch. for Boys, N.Y.C.; trustee Cornell U., 1979-88, trustee emeritus, 1988—; trustee Vassar Coll., 1988—; bd. overseers Cornell U. Med. Coll., 1983-88 (life mem. 1988—), Inst. Internat. Edn. (life). Mem. UN Assn. (dir.). Clubs: Cosmopolitan, Vassar, Women's City (N.Y.C.). Home: 730 Park Ave New York NY 10021 also: Anderson Hill Rd Purchase NY 10577 other: Lyford Cay, New Providence The Bahamas

LOEB, JANE RUPLEY, university administrator, educator; b. Chgo., Feb. 22, 1938; d. John Edwards and Virginia Pentland (Marthens) Watkins; m. Peter Albert Loeb, June 14, 1958; children: Eric Peter, Gwendolyn Lisl, Aaron John. BA, Rider Coll., 1961; PhD, U. So. Calif., 1969. Clin. psychology intern Univ. Hosp., Seattle, 1966-67; asst. prof. ednl. psychology U. Ill., Urbana, 1968-69, asst. coord. rsch. and testing, 1968-69, coord. rsch. and testing, 1969-72, asst. to vice chancellor acad. affairs, 1971-72, dir. admissions and records, 1972-81, assoc. prof. ednl. psychology, 1973-82, assoc. vice chancellor acad. affairs, 1981—, prof. edn. psychology, 1982—. Author: College Board Project: the Future of College Admissions, 1989. Chmn. Coll. Bd. Coun. on Entrance Svcs., 1977-82; bd. govs. Alliance for Undergraduate Edn., 1988—. HEW grantee, 1975-76. Mem. APA, Am. Ednl. Rsch. Assn., Nat. Coun. Measurement in Edn., Harvard Inst. Ednl. Mgmt. Home: 1405 N Coler Urbana IL 61801 Office: U Ill 601 E John St Champaign IL 61820

LOEB, JOYCE LICHTGARN, interior designer, civic worker; b. Portland, Oreg., May 20, 1936; d. Elias Lichtgarn and Sylvia Amy (Margulies) Freedman; m. Stanley Robinson Loeb, Aug. 14, 1960; children: Carl Eli, Eric Adam. Student U. Calif.-Berkeley, 1954-56; B.S., Lewis and Clark Coll., 1958; postgrad. art and architecture, Portland State U., 1976. Tchr. art David Douglas Sch. Dist., Portland, 1958-59, 61-64; tchr., chmn. art dept. Grant Union High Sch. Dist., Sacramento, 1959-60; designer, pres. Joyce Loeb Interior Design, Inc., Portland, 1976—; cons. designer to various developers of health care facilities. Chairperson fundraisers for civic orgns. and Jewish orgns.; mem. women's com. Reed Coll.; bd. dirs. Met. Family Services, Portland, 1968-71, Inst. Judaic Studies, 1989—, Young Audiences, Inc., Portland, 1970-76, 78-80, Portland Opera Assn., 1978-84, Arts Celebration, Inc., Portland, 1984—, Congregation Beth Israel, 1986—; chmn. Artquake Festival, 1985, Operaball, 1987, Children's Charity Ball Com., 1989; v.p. Beth Israel Sisterhood, 1981-83; trustee Congregation Beth Israel, 1986—, chmn. art interior design com.; trustee Robison Home, 1990—. Mem. Am. Soc. Interior Design, Nat. Council Jewish Women. Democrat. Club: Multnomah Athletic. Home: 1546 SW Upland Dr Portland OR 97221

LOEB, MARCIA JOAN, research physiologist; b. N.Y.C., Mar. 26, 1933; m. George I. Loeb, Aug. 30, 1953; children: Alex, Daniel. BA in Biology, Bklyn. Coll., 1953; MS in Physiology, Cornell U., 1957; PhD in Comparative Physiology, U. Md., 1970. Rsch. asst. dept. zoology Cornell U., Ithaca, N.Y., 1956-57; rsch. asst. Sch. of Nurtition Cornell U., Ithaca, 1957-59; rsch. asst. NIH, Bethesda, Md., 1961-62, Natural Resources Inst., U. Md., College Park, Md., 1968-70; post-doctoral rsch. assoc. Nat. Rsch. Coun.-Naval Rsch. Lab., Washington, 1970-72; rsch. assoc. NERC unit Marine Sci. Labs., U. Coll. North Wales, Menai Bridge, Wales, 1973-74; rsch. physiologist chem. and bio-phys. control lab. USDA, Beltsville, Md., 1978-80, rsch. physiologist insect reproduction lab., 1980—; vis. asst. prof. invertebrate zoology Am. U., Washington, 1977-78; vis. asst. prof. invertebrate zoology, comparative physiology Wesstern Md. Coll., Westminster, 1976-77; adj. prof. invertebrate zoology, anatomy and physiology Am. U., Washington, 1975-76; instr. biology, human anatomy and physiology No. Va. Community Coll., Annandale, 1972-73. Co-author: Insect Neurochemistry and Neurophysiology, 1984; contbr. articles and abstracts to profl. jours. Recipient Best Poster award for established investigator Chesapeake Soc. for Electron Microscopy, 1987. Mem. Am. Soc. Zoologists (div. comparative endocrinology and invertebrate zoology), Internat. Soc. Invertebrate Reproduction, Am. Microscopical Soc., Entomological Soc. Am., Tissue Culture Assn., Sigma Xi. Home: 6920 Fairfax Rd Bethesda MD 20814 Office: USDA Insect Reproduction Lab Bldg 306 Rm 319 BARC East Beltsville MD 20705

LOEB, MARGARET ANN, college administrator; b. Plainfield, N.J., Dec. 2, 1940; d. Edward Loeb and Lillian (Slocum) Whitman. BS, Simmons Coll., 1962. Editor Jerome Press Publs., Boston, 1962-70; dir. pub. info. Simmons Coll., Boston, 1971—, editor Simmons Rev., 1979—. Office: Simmons Coll 300 The Fenway Boston MA 02115

LOEB, NACKEY SCRIPPS, publisher; b. Los Angeles, Feb. 24, 1924; d. Robert Paine and Margaret (Culbertson) Scripps; m. William Loeb, July 15, 1952 (dec. 1981); children—Nackey Loeb Scagliotti, Edith Loeb DuBuc. Student, Scripps Coll. Pub. Union-Leader Corp., Manchester, N.H., 1981—. Republican. Baptist. Home: Paige Hill Rd Goffstown NH 03045 Office: Union Leader Corp 35 Amherst St Manchester NH 03105*

LOEB, NANCY HILL, educator; b. Highland, Ill., June 17, 1949; d. Lawrence Andre and Mary Elizabeth (Scheeler) Hill; m. Allan David Loeb, May 25, 1974; children: Andrew T., Emily E. BS in Edn., Culver-Stockton Coll., 1971; MA in Remedial Reading, Western Ill. U., 1981. Cert. reading tchr., Ill. Tchr. Springfield (Ill.) Sch. Dist. 186, 1971—; tchr. gifted edn. Sch. Dist. 186, Springfield, 1984—. Mem. AAUW, Springfield, 1986-88. Recipient Recognition award Nat. Pk. Svc., 1989. Mem. Jr. League Springfield (active child abuse hotline 1982-90, tour guide 1987-89), P.E.O., Jr. Federated Women's Club (corr. sec. Springfield chpt. 1978-79), Alpha Xi Delta. Episcopalian. Home: 16 Birch Lake Dr Sherman IL 62684 Office: J Addams Elem Sch 10 Babiak Ln Springfield IL 62702

LOEDY, ANN, real estate development executive; b. Poughkeepsie, N.Y., Mar. 31, 1941; d. William Luke and Anne Louise (Moore) Lawlor; m. Edmond G. Loedy, Aug. 4, 1963; children: Lisa, Brant, Roark. BS in Nursing, Hunter Coll., 1963; diploma, Cornell U., 1975. Nurse practitioner Sharon Clinic, Millbrook, N.Y.; in comml. and residential real estate devel. and constrn. Dutchess County (N.Y.) Legislature. Contbr. articles to newspapers and mags. Mem. Coalition of Organized Practitioners of N.Y. State (co-founder). Republican. Home: Altamont Rd Millbrook NY 12545 Office: 27 Garden St Poughkeepsie NY 12601

LOEFFLER, CHERYL, systems analyst; b. Shamrock, Tex., May 18, 1944; d. Charles Boone and Dorothy (Palmer) McClure; m. Samuel J. Brenner, May 18, 1968 (div. 1982); children: Catherine Megan, Samantha Lauren; m. David H. Loeffler Jr., Feb. 8, 1983. BS, Tex. Tech. Coll., 1965; MBA, U. Tulsa, 1982. Lic. real estate assoc., Fla. Instr. MIS U. Tulsa, 1981-85, asst. to provost, 1983-84; computer cons., ptnr. Systems 3, Tulsa, 1982-85; sr. systems analyst The Williams Cos., Tulsa, 1985-88; sales assoc. Mt. Vernon Realty Co., Inc., Sarasota, Fla., 1989—. Pres., Jr. Assn. Tulsa Boys' Home, 1974-75, Alliance of Arts and Humanities, Jr. League Tulsa, 1975-76; mentor, gifted program Tulsa Jr. High Schs., 1980-82; bd. dirs. Tulsa Community Svc. Coun., 1985-88; active local polit. campaigns; corp. commr., Okla. State Treas. for ERA; mem. Sarasota Film Festival Com., 1989, 90. Mem. Sarasota Bd. Realtors (fin. com. 1989—), Kappa Alpha Theta, Beta Gamma Sigma, Daus. of Nile. Democrat. Jewish. Home: 1145 Gulf of Mexico Dr Longboat Key FL 34228

LOEFGREN, GAIL PITCHFORD, mayor; b. St. Louis, Sept. 16, 1942; d. Milburn Calvin and Lillian (Niles) Pitchford; m. H. Michael Loefgren, July 25, 1964; children: Michael, Kristin. BEd in History and French, Bradley U., 1964. Mem. Flagg-Rochelle (Ill.) Park Dist. Bd., 1979-87, pres., 1983-85; exec. dir. Rochelle C. of C., 1985-87; mayor City of Rochelle, 1987—. Bd. dirs. Rochelle Community Hosp.; chmn. Rochelle United Way; founder Oktoberfest Celebration; co-chmn. Farmer's Picnic, Rochelle; overseer Youth Adv. Coun., Rochelle; local chmn. Muscular Dystrophy Telethon, 1987; past mem., sec. Ogle County Civic Ctr. Authority. Recipient Merit citation Ill. Assn. Park Dists., 1982, Resolution of Honor Ill. Assn. Park Bds., 1985; named Community Leader of Yr., Kiwanis, Rotary, Lions, C. of C., 1984. Mem. LWV, Rotary. Presbyterian. Home: 1040 Calvin Rd Rochelle IL 61068 Office: City of Rochelle PO Box A Rochelle IL 61068

LOEHR, SISTER MARLA, college president; b. Cleve., Oct. 7, 1937; d. Joseph Richard and Eleanore Edith (Rothschuh) L. BS, Notre Dame Coll., South Euclid, Ohio, 1960; MAT, Ind. U., 1969; PhD, Boston Coll., 1988. Joined Sisters of Notre Dame, Roman Cath. Ch., 1956. Cert. high sch. tchr., counselor, Ohio. Mem. faculty Notre Dame Acad., Cleve., 1960-64, John F. Kennedy High Sch., Warren, Ohio, 1964-66; adminstrn. asst., dir. residence halls Notre Dame Acad., Chardon, Ohio, 1966-72; dean students Notre Dame Coll., So. Euclid, 1972-85, acting acad. dean, 1988, pres., 1989—; cons. Nat. Cons. Network, Washington, 1978-85; facilitator Coun. for Ind. Colls., Washington, 1980-84. Author: Mentor Handbook, 1985; co-author: Notre Dame College Model for Student Development, 1980. Mem. United Way Planning Commn., Cleve., 1989—, No. Ohio Gives, Cleve., 1989—, Leadership Cleve. Class of 90; team leader Women in Ch. and Soc., Cleve., 1988—; chairperson edn. com. Diocesan Pastoral Coun., Cleve., 1980-85. Grantee Cleve. Found., 1980, Title VIII - Office Edn., Washington, 1981-83. Mem. Am. Assn. Higher Edn., Assn. Governing Bds., Pax Christi, Alpha Sigma Nu. Office: Notre Dame Coll 4545 College Rd South Euclid OH 44121

LOEHRKE, CHRISTINE CAROL, rehabilitation facility administrator; b. Dayton, Ohio, June 9, 1950; d. Eugene Max and Carol Jean (Showalter) L. BA in Psychology, Wittenberg U., 1973. Psychology asst. Vocat. Guidance & Rehab. Services, Cleve., 1973-76, program mgr., 1976-79, tng. specialist, 1979-81; dir. rehab. and planning Goodwill Industries Inc., Dayton, Ohio, 1981-84; assoc. dir. Youth Enrichment Services Inc., Cleve., 1984-87, Epilepsy Found. N.E. Ohio, Cleve., 1987—; instr. Cuyahoga Community Coll., Parma, Ohio, 1979-81; co-founder Westside Guidance Ctr., Lakewood, Ohio, 1974-76; vol. counselor Third Legacy Alcoholism Ctr. Inc., Lakewood, 1974-76. Co-author: (bus. plan) Implementation of a Prime Manufacturing subsidiary in a Sheltered Workshop, 1985. Recipient cert. appreciation Council Exceptional Children, 1977, cert. appreciation, Kiwanis, 1978; named Disting. Rehab. Profl., Nat. Disting. Service Registry Med. and Vocat. Rehab. Div., 1987. Mem. Nat. Rehab. Assn., Nat. Rehab. Adminstrs. Assn., Ohio Rehab. Adminstrs. Assn. (bd. dirs. 1982-84, 88—), N.E. Ohio Rehab. Assn. (bd. dirs.), NAFE. Democrat. Lutheran. Home: 1034 E 171st St Cleveland OH 44119 Office: Epilepsy Found of NE Ohio 2800 Euclid Ave #450 Cleveland OH 44115

LOESCH, JUDITH ANN, registered nurse; b. Camden, S.C., Sept. 23, 1946; d. Thomas Vardell and Elizabeth (Campbell) Young; m. Laurence Michael Loesch, May 24, 1969 (div. May 30, 1978); children: Timothy Michael, Kevin Joseph, Brian Michael (dec.). Diploma, Med. U. S.C., 1967; BA in Applied Behavioral Scis., Nat. Coll. Edn., 1989. RN.; cert. chem. dependency nurse, 1988; cert. assoc. addictions counselor, Ill., 1989. Staff nurse Roper Hosp., Charleston, S.C., 1967-68; staff RN Highland Park (Ill.) Hosp., 1978—. Club's sec.-treas. Highland Park Jaycee Mates, 1976-77; active pack 39 Cub Scouts, troop 150 Northeast Ill. coun. Boy Scouts Am., Highland Park, 1988. Capt. USAF, 1968-72. Named Jaycee Mate of Yr. Highland Park Jaycee Mates, 1977. Mem. Med. U. S.C. Alumni, Luth. Ch. Women (sec.-treas. Zion Luth. Ch., Deerfield, Ill. 1984-85), Order Ea. Star. Democrat. Home: 813 W Park Ave S Highland Park IL 60035

LOESCHER, BARBARA ANN, fraud auditing executive; b. Mauston, Wis., Aug. 20, 1953; d. Arnold John Loescher and Carol Jeanne (Vinopal) Gross. BS in Bus. and Acctg., Edgewood Coll., 1988. CPA, Wis; cert. internal auditor, fraud examiner. Acct. Harco Ins. Co., Milw., 1977-78; corp. acct. Blunt Ellis and Loewi, Milw., 1978-79; fin. technician Cumis Ins. Soc., Inc., Madison, Wis., 1979-81; budget, tax and cost specialist Cumis Ins. Soc., Inc., Madison, 1981-83, risk mgmt. investment specialist, 1983-84, fraud auditing mgr., 1984—; lectr. seminars on risk mgmt. and fraud auditing. Author of numerous articles in field. Mem. AICPA, Wis. Inst. CPAs, Inst. Internal Auditors (sec. 1987), Nat. Assn. Cert. Fraud Examiners. Republican. Roman Catholic. Home: 7009 Carnwood Rd Madison WI 53719 Office: Cumis Ins Soc Inc 5910 Mineral Pt Rd Madison WI 53705

LOEW, PATRICIA ANN, small business owner; b. Farmville, Va., Aug. 28, 1943; d. Joseph Leo and Delores (McGurk) Dooley; m. Hubert Victor Loew; children: Moritz, Franz. BA, Clarke Coll., Dubuque, Iowa, 1965; MA, Pius XII Inst. Fine Arts, Florence, Italy, 1966. Chmn. fine arts dept. Little Flower High Sch., Chgo., 1966-68; staff painter Otto Galleries, Vienna, Austria, 1968-71; retail store owner Austrian Ski & Sports Haus, Country Club Hills, Ill., 1971—; fashion coord. Marshall Field & Co., Chgo., 1966-67; recreational therapist State of Ill. Mental Health Ctr., Tinley Park, 1966-68; asst. translator Richard Neutra Architect, Vienna, 1971; wholesale importer Franz Klammer USA, Ltd., 1986—. Active Frankfort, Ill. chpt. PTA; mem. Friends of the Libr. Frankfort. Asst. Art Award scholar Pius XII Inst. Grad. Studies, 1966. Mem. Nat. Sporting Goods Owners Am., Ski Industries Am. Democrat. Roman Catholic. Clubs: Prestwick Country, Frankfort Women's. Home: 567 Aberdeen Rd Frankfort IL 60423 Office: The Austrian Ski & Sport Haus 19001 S Cicero Ave Country Club Hills IL 60477

LOEWEN, IRENE LEONA, psychologist; b. Winkler, Manitoba, Mar. 16, 1945; d. David Jacob Reimer and Katherina (Derksen) Friesen; m. Howard John. BA, Fresno Pacific Coll., 1980; PhD, Calif. Sch. Profl. Psychology, Fresno, 1984. Asst. head nurse Huntington Meml. Hosp., Pasadena, Calif., 1968-72; prof. Mennonite Brethren Biblical Sem., Fresno, 1984-88; clin. psychologist Fresno, 1988—; chmn. Women's Concern, 1984—. Contbr. articles to profl. jours. Mem. Am. Psychol. Assn., Calif. State Psychol. Assn., San Joaquin Psychol. Assn. Home: 5182 E Braly Ave Fresno CA 93727 Office: 6315 N Fresno #103 Fresno CA 93710

LOEWENSTEIN, MARTHA J(OSEPHINE), retired financial executive; b. N.Y.C., Mar. 8, 1913; d. Solomon and Frieda (Abelson) L. BA, Barnard Coll., 1933. Statistician Coun. Jewish Fedns. and Welfare Funds, N.Y.C., 1938-40; adminstrv. asst. to exec. dir. Nat. Hadassah, 1940-41; exec. asst. to exec. dir. Jewish Welfare Bd., N.Y.C., 1941-47; adminstr., controller, chief protocol Consulate Gen. of Israel and Israel Mission to UN, N.Y.C., 1949-53; chief fiscal officer, sec. governing bodies Am. Com. for Weizmann Inst. Sci., N.Y.C., 1953-78, bd. dirs., 1978—. Class pres. Barnard Coll., 1988—, co-chair fund raising, 1980-88. Mem. Am. Jewish Pub. Rels. Soc. (sec., exec. com. 1982—), Community Svc. Soc./Ret. Sr. Vol. Program (chmn. Ret. Profl. Placement Com. 1982-89, treas. N.Y.C. adv. bd. 1988—, sec. 1982-88, exec. com. 1985—), Friends of Ret. Sr. Vol. Program (bd. dirs. 1990—), Nat. Coun. Jewish Women (founder Norma Loewenstein Drabkin scholarship fund), Hadassah (life). Democrat.

LOEWENSTEIN, RUTH, import production manager; b. Munich; d. Willy and Anny (Cahen) L. BA, Hunter Coll., 1951; MA, New Sch. for Social Rsch., 1953. Treas. Willy Loewenstein Corp., N.Y.C.; v.p. sales/imports Davide Schwab & Co., N.Y.C.; with design/sales David E. Schwab & Co., N.Y.C.; import prodn. mgr. Mirage, N.Y.C., 1984—. Trustee R.P.J.C., N.Y.C., 1983—, chmn. 1980—, chmn. adult edn.; sisterhood pres. Rego Park Jewish Ctr., N.Y.C.; bd. dirs. N.S.L.I.W.L. for Conservative Judaism, N.Y.C.-Long Island. Named Woman of Achievement, Jewish Theol. Sem. Am., 1985; recipient honor award United Jewish Appeal. Mem. Hedassah, N.C.J.W., Alpha Chi Alpha. Democrat. Jewish. Home: 63 60 98th St Rego Park NY 11374

LOEWENTHAL, NESSA PARKER, educator; b. Chgo., Oct. 13, 1930; d. Abner and Frances (Ness) Parker; m. Martin Moshe Loewenthal, July 7, 1951 (dec. Aug. 1973); children: Dann Marcus, Ronn Carl, Deena Miriam; m. Gerson B. Selk, Apr. 17, 1982 (dec. June 1987). BA in Edn. and Psychology, Stanford U., 1952. Faculty Stanford Inst. for Intercultural Communication, 1973-87; dir. Transcultural Svcs., San Francisco, 1981—; dir. dependent svcs. and internat. edn. Bechtel Group, San Francisco, 1973-81, internat. edn. cons., 1981-84; mem. adv. com. dept. internat. studies Leslie Coll., Cambridge, Mass., 1986—; mem. Bay Area Ethics Consortium, Berkeley, 1989—; chmn. ethics com. Sietar Internat., Washington, 1987—; mem. faculty Summer Inst. for Internat. Communications, Portland, Oreg., 1987—. Author: Professional Integration, 1987; author, editor: (series of books) Your International Assignment, 1973-81; contbr. articles to profl. publs. Mem. Lafayette (Calif.) Traffic Commn., 1974-80; bd. dirs. Ctr. for Ethics and Social Policy; mem. exec. bd., planning com. Temple Isaiah, Lafayette, 1978-82; bd. dirs. Calif. Symphony, Orinda, 1988—; mem. exec. com. overseas schs. adv. com. U.S. State Dept., 1976-8. Named Sr. Interculturalist, Sietar Internat., 1986. Mem. Am. Soc. for Tng. and Devel., World Affairs Coun. (co-chmn. 1989-90), Soc. for Intercultural Edn., Tng. and Rsch. (chmn. 1986-87, nominating com. 1985-86, co-chmn.1989-90), Am. Women for Internat. Understanding, Commonwealth Club. Democrat. Jewish. Office: Trans Cultural Svcs 1967 Pine St San Francisco CA 94109

LOEWY, JOANNE VICTORIA, music therapist, educator; b. Phila., Feb. 13, 1961; d. Robert Gustav and Lila Myrna (Spinner) L.; m. Anthony Antoniello, Aug. 14, 1988. MusB, SUNY, Potsdam, 1983; MA, NYU, 1985, postgrad., 1990—. Pvt. practice music therapist Albany, N.Y., 1981-83, N.Y.C., 1983—; music therapist Lifeline Ctr. for Children, Queens Village, N.Y., 1985—; dir. children's choirs Village Temple Choir and Cen. Synagogue Choir, 1990—. Rep. Dem. Club of Greenwich Village, N.Y.C., 1989—. Mem. Am. Assn. Music Therapy (cert. and ethics com. 1989—). Jewish. Office: Lifeline Ctr for Children 80-09 Winchester Blvd Queens NY 11427

LOF, CAROL MURIEL, professional association executive; b. N.Y.C., Sept. 14, 1941; d. Henning George and Ethel Muriel (Soderstrom) L. BA, Hartwick Coll., 1963; diploma, Italian U. at Perugia, 1968; postgrad., NYU, 1983-84. Rsch. analyst Library of Congress, Washington, 1964-67; asst. dir. Cahners Travel Group, N.Y.C., 1968-73; sales mgr. Haley Corp., N.Y.C., 1973-77; market mgr. Fiat Ventana, N.Y.C., 1977-79; exec. dir. IEEE Communications, N.Y.C., 1979—; guest lectr., Rensselaer Poly. U., Troy, N.Y., 1985. Mem. Soc. Tech. Communications (pres. 1983-85), Soc. Scholarly Pubs. (chmn. tech. programs 1986), IEEE (program com. 1986—). Office: IEEE 345 E 47th St New York NY 10017

LOFF, BETTY GARLAND, religious administrator and educator; b. L.A., Aug. 18, 1932; d. Lewis Michael and Bernice (Siberz) Hohenthaner; m. Daniel David Loff, May 1, 1951; children: Dana Elizabeth, Tamra Marie. Grad., Lamson Dental Coll., L.A., 1950-51; M in Catechist, Diocese Phoenix, 1971; M in Pastoral Ministry, U. San Francisco, 1986, postgrad., 1986—. Dental asst. various offices L.A., 1952-53; office mgr. Supply Co, Phoenix, 1968-71; adminstrv. asst. Diocese Phoenix Religious Edn., 1971-75; adminstrv. asst., intern religious edn. St. Theresa Ch., Phoenix, 1975-79; dir. religious edn. St. Paul Ch., Phoenix, 1979—; chmn. Catechetical Congress Diocese, 1971-89, Diocesan Religious Edn. Adv. Bd., Phoenix, 1983-86; mem. steering & formation com., co-chmn., spirituality com. CADRE-Profl. Orgn. for Dirs. & Coords. Religious Edn., Phoenix, 1986—; insvc. facillitator Retreat Team. Author-editor Catechetical Congress Job Description booklet, 1974; contbr. articles to profl. jours. Mem. Ariz. Masterworks Chorale (affiliate Phoenix Symphony Orch., 1989—). Recipient Concern for Kids in the Community award Gen. Fedn. Women's Clubs, 1985. Mem. Nat. Cath. Edn. Assn., Religious Edn. Assn. Phoenix (sec. 1972-83). Office: St Paul Cath Ch 330 W Coral Gables Dr Phoenix AZ 85023

LOFFICIER, RANDY JOANNE, writer; b. Phila., Feb. 3, 1953; d. Max Apfelbaum and Irene Marcia (Rosenberg) Gerken; m. Jean-Marc Lofficier, May 5, 1979. Grad. high sch., Rosemont, Pa. Cert. x-ray technologist. Free-lance writer, 1979—; v.p. prodn. Starwatcher Graphics, Encino, Calif., 1985—. Author: The Best Video Films, 1984, Your Movie Guide to Musicals on Videotape, 1985, Basil, the Great Mouse Detective, 1986 (with Jean-Marc Lofficier) Doctor Who Programme Guide 1 and 2, 1981, 89, Les Maitres de L'Insolite, 1985; (comic books) Fury of Firestorm #32, 1984, Arak #45-50, 1985, Action #579, 1986, Teen Titans #44, Dr. Strange #6; (screenplays) Mayday 1982, Royal Flush, 1984, Terminus Four, 1985, The Airtight Garage, 1988, Arzach, 1989 (TV screenplays) Science-Fiction Plus!, 1983, The Real Ghostbusters, 1986, Duck Tales, 1986, Bionic Six, 1987, others; contbg. and cons. editor L'Anee du Cinema Fantastique, 1983, The Official Explorers Moviebook, 1985, others; contbr. to Am. Cinematographer, Starlog, Heavy Metal, Twilight Zone mag., Weekly Reader, numerous others in U.S., France and Eng.; translator: Moebius, 1987, The Incal, 1988, French Ice, 1987-88, 89, Lt. Blueberry, Cheval Noir, 1989. Mem. Animation Writers Am., Women in Film. Home: 6539 Jamieson Ave Reseda CA 91335 Office: Starwatcher Graphics Inc PO Box 17270 Encino CA 91416

LOFGREN-LAUDENSCHLAGER, SANDRA, retired musician, educator; b. Mpls., Aug. 15, 1937; d. Rudolf Justus and Janet (Hedlund) Lofgren; m. Rohn M. Laudenschlager, Aug. 6, 1958; children: Elizabeth Siporin, Robert, Jennifer, Peter. BA summa cum laude, L.I. U., 1979, MA, 1981. Percussionist Mpls. Symphony Orchestra, Min., 1956-58, Rochester Min. Symphony Orchestra, 1957-59; percussion soloist Various, Mpls., 1954-59; percussion instr. Pvt., Mpls.; research U. Min., 1959; sec. Northwestern Natl. Bank, 1962-64; corporate wife Irving Trust Co., N.Y., 1964-87; dog breeder Pvt., Port Wash., N.Y., 1980-84; pvt. dog breeder Northfield, Minn., 1989—. Precinct worker, Presidential Campaign, Pt. Wash., 1976, publicity chair, PTA, 1977-78, animal activist various local, nat. Humane Soc., 1980—. Mem. Belgian Sheep Dog Club Am., Voyageur Belgian Sheep Dog Club, Kappa Delta, Sigma Alpha Iota.

LOFTON, OTMARA (MAGGIE LOFTON), teacher; b. Havanna, Cuba, Mar. 13, 1959; d. Jose and Mirta (Fernandez) Hernandez; m. Donald Douglas Lofton. AA in Liberal Arts, Queensborough Community Coll., Bayside, N.Y., 1978; BA in Edn. and Fine Arts, Queens Coll., Flushing, N.Y., 1980; cert., Calif. Community Coll., 1989. Cert. tchr., N.Y., Calif. Tchr. kindergarten St. Nicholas of Tolentine, Flushing, 1981-83; tchr. secondary Piru Sch. and Fillmore (Calif.) Sch. Dist., 1984—. Mem. Calif. Tchrs. Nat. Edn. Assn. Home: 21653 Farmington Ln Saugus CA 91350

LOFTUS, RITA CELESTINE, educator; b. Wilkes-Barre, Pa., July 28, 1938; d. John and Eleanor (Davis) Toole; m. John Joseph Loftus, June 4, 1960; children: John Augustine, Patrick Joseph. BS in Edn., Coll. Misericordia, Dallas, 1972; MS in Edn., Wilkes Coll., 1975. Cert. elem. sch. tchr., Pa. Educator St. Jude's Elem. Sch., Mountain Top, Pa.; math. tchr. Wilkes-Barre Area Sch. Dist., 1972—. Mem. Wyoming Hist. & Geol. Soc., Wilkes-Barre, 1989—, Friends of Osterhout Free Libr., Wilkes-Barre, 1989—. Mem. NEA, Wilkes-Barre Area Edn. Assn., Pa. State Edn. Assn., Coll. Misericordia Alumni Assn., Wilkes Coll. Alumni Assn. Democrat. Roman Catholic.

LOGAN, BARBARA AIMAR, pharmacist; b. Charlotte, N.C., Dec. 20, 1941; d. Malcolm Noyes and Barbara (Aimar) Goodwin; m. Richard Akers, July 22, 1962 (div. 1971); children: Richard, Matthew; m. Thomas Logan (div. Oct. 1988); children: Elizabeth, Mary, Barbara. BS in Pharmacy, U. N.C., 1964; MS in Biology, U. S.C., 1978. Lic. pharmacist, S.C. Intern Duke U. Hosp. Pharmacy, Durham, N.C., 1964-65; pharmacist Eckerds, Beaufort, S.C., 1966-80; cons. pharmacist Area Health Edn. Ctr., Med. U. S.C., Charleston, 1980-84; owner, pharmacist Med. Specialties, Beaufort, 1984—; cons. in continuing pharm. edn. Lowcountry Area Health Edn. Ctr., chmn. statewide pharmacy coun., 1982-84; organizer intravenous mfg. co. for Presbyn. ch., Haiti, 1989; clin. prof. Sch. Pharmacy, Med. U. S.C., 1988-89. Host community tours of hist. homes, Beaufort; deacon, Sunday sch. tchr. 1st Presbyn. Ch., Beaufort, 1988—; flutist Beaufort Chamber Ensemble, 1980-85. Named Woman Pharmacist of Yr., U. S.C. Sch. Pharmacy, 1982. Mem. AAUW, S.C. Pharm. Assn. (pres. 1985-86, bd. dirs. 1982-86), S.C. Bd. Pharmacy, S.C. Assn. Durable Med. Equipment Dealers (bd. dirs.), Zonta, Phi Lambda Sigma. Republican. Home: 24 Burkmeyer Beach Beaufort SC 29902 Office: Med Specialties 159 Ribault Sq Beaufort SC 29902

LOGAN, CHRISTINE LYNNE, manufacturing engineer; b. Indpls., Jan. 16, 1961; d. James Paul and Jane Lynne (Phillips) Henry; m. Patrick Joeseph Logan, Mar. 22, 1986. BS, Purdue U., 1983. Prodn. supr. Square D. Co., Peru, Ind., 1984—, prodn. planner, 1986; prodn. supr. Square D. Co., Seneca, S.C., 1986—, mfg. engr., unit mgr., 1988—; mfg. engr. Stolle Corp., Sidney, Ohio, 1989—. Mem. NAFE, Soc. Mgr. Engring., Am. Prodn. and Inventory Control Soc. Republican. Methodist. Office: Stolle Corp 1501 Michigan St Sidney OH 45365

LOGAN, GRACE ELEANOR MILLER (MRS. HENRY WHITTINGTON LOGAN), English educator; b. Valencia, Pa., June 22, 1908; d. Alvah John and Lillian (Gibson) Miller; B.S., Temple U., 1930, M.S., 1931; postgrad., 1955-56; m. Henry Whittington Logan, Mar. 16, 1940; 1 son, Henry Whittington III. English instr. Temple U., 1930-33; asst. prof. to dept. head Moravian Coll., Bethlehem, Pa., 1933-42; assoc. prof. edn. and philosophy Widener U., Chester, Pa., 1956-67, prof. English, 1967-85, prof. emeritus, adj. prof. 1985—; dir. Coll. Reading Services, 1958-85; dir. Fed. Office of Edn. Equal Opportunities Tng. Br. Insts., 1965—; bd. dirs. 1683 Caleb Pusey House, Upland, Pa., dir. bd. of friends, 1986—, Emergency Aid Found.; cons., lectr. in biblical studies, 1985—; only woman on faculty any mil. coll. U.S. for 8 yrs. Elder, Presbyn. Ch.; mem. Emergency Aid Pa. Found.; mem. adv. bd. Pa. Inst. Tech. Mem. AAUP, Delaware County Hist. Soc. (dir.), Nat. Council Tchrs. English, Coll. English Assn., Coll. Reading Assn., Internat. Reading Assn., Pa. Council of Tchrs., Am. Acad. Religion, Questers Potpourri, Kappa Delta Epsilon, Pi Delta Epsilon. Home: 201 Sykes Ln Wallingford PA 19086 Office: Widener U Chester PA 19013

LOGAN, JANET RUTH, art specialist; b. Artesia, Calif., Nov. 22, 1941; d. Anthony Arthur and Ruth Marcia (Ellis) Flores; m. Gerard Anthony Logan, Apr. 11, 1939; children: Michelle Ruth Phillips, Julianna Marie. BA in Fine Arts Edn., Fresno State U., 1966; postgrad., Otis Parsons Sch. Design, L.A., 1981-86, Otis Parsons Sch. Design, Paris, 1982-83, NYU, 1989. Arts and crafts tchr. Kings Canyon Jr. High Sch., Fresno, Calif., 1966-67; arts and crafts tchr. Nueva Vista Continuation Sch., Riverside, Calif., 1969-71, Smedley Jr. High Sch., Santa Ana, Calif., 1971-73; freelance designer Chelsea Designs, Fountain Valley, Calif., 1974-77; comml. artist Pacific Flyway Editions, Rancho Cucamong, Calif., 1984-90, Toluca Lake Galleries, Burbank, Calif., 1984—, Zola Fine Art, L.A., 1984—; art specialist Irvine Unified Sch. Dist., Irvine, Calif., 1977—; art edn. instr. Calif. State U., Fullerton, 1987—; art edn. cons. Ventura Sch. Dist., Ventura, Thousand Oaks, Calif., 1980-81, K.C.E.T. TV Festival Art, L.A., 1982, Fountain Valley (Calif.) Sch. Dist., 1982, 86, Anaheim (Calif.) Sch. Dist., 1984, Westminster (Calif.) Sch. Dist., 1984, Magnolia Sch. Dist., Anaheim, Calif., 1990, Little Lake Sch. Dist., Santa Fe Springs, Calif., 1990, U. Calif., Irvine, 1990. Art exhbns.: (group show/faculty) The Edge, 1988, (group show/NYU) Palazzo Pema, Venice, Italy, 1987, 88, Art Expo N.Y., 1987, 88, 90, Art Expo L.A., 1987, 89, Washington Sq. East Galleries, N.Y.C., 1989; represented in permanent collections Hilton Hotels, Las Vegas, Nev., Santa Maria, Calif., San Francisco, Sheraton Hotels, Stanford, Conn., Dorado Beach, P.I., Trumps Castle Hotel and Casino, Atlantic City, Union Bank, Century City, Calif., El Monte, Calif., Irvine, L.A., Oxnard, Calif. Recipient Outstanding Fine Arts Educator Irvine Unified Sch. Dist., 1989. Mem. Calif. Art Edn. Assn., Nat. Art Edn. Assn., Orange County Art Edn. Assn. (pres. 1979). Democrat. Roman Catholic. Office: Irvine Unified Sch Dist 5050 Barranca Irvine CA 92714

LOGAN, JEAN SHIPLEY, management consultant; b. Richmond, Va., Feb. 9, 1943; d. Oliver Henry and Louisa (Brookes) Johnson; m. John Edward Logan, May 16, 1966 (div. 1975); 1 child, Brooke Telaryn Logan. BS in Journalism, U. Wis., 1965. Pub. info. dir. U. Wis. Ctr. System, Madison, 1965-66; publs. editor Wis. Dept. Pub. Instrn., Madison, 1967-68; mng. editor Press Tech, Inc., Madison, 1969; account exec. Barkin, Herman & Assocs., Milw., 1969-74; pub. rels. dir. Curative Rehab. Ctr., Milw., 1975-81; assoc. dir. Milw. County Dept. Health & Human Svcs., 1981-88; dep. asst. sec. Fla. Dept. Health & Rehab. Svcs., Tallahassee, 1988—; pres. Jean S. Logan Mgmt. Group, Inc., Tallahassee, 1988—. Bd. dirs., exec. com. Govs. Com. for People with Disabilities, Madison, 1975-83; bd. dirs., v.p. Nat. Spinal Cord Injury Assn., Newton, Mass., 1978—; bd. dirs. Community Care Orgn., Milw., 1982-88; mem. community options adv. com. Wis. Dept. Health & Social Svcs. Madison, 1983-88; mem. Milw. County Transit Bd., 1977-78; chmn. 504 adv. com. Milw. County, 1979-82, Com. for Barrier Free Environments, Madison, 1974-78; mem. planning com.

Internat. Yr. Disabled Persons, 1981. Recipient James Smittkamp award Nat. Spinal Cord Injury Assn., 1983, Timothy Nugent award, 1980; Pub. Interest Award, Ctr. for Pub. Representation, 1988. Mem. Wis. Hosp. Pub. Rels. Soc., Milw. Area Soc. Pub. Adminstrs., U. Wis. Alumni Assn., Ctr. for Pub. Representation, Am. Pub. Welfare Assn., Nat. Assn. Pub. Child Welfare Adminstrs. Democrat. Home: 2001 Trescott Dr Tallahassee FL 32312 Office: Florida Dept HRS 1317 Winewood Blvd Tallahassee FL 32399

LOGAN, KATHRYN VANCE, research engineer; b. Atlanta, June 12, 1946; d. Charles Monroe Vance and Lucille (James) Evitt; m. William Stephen Logan, Sept. 9, 1967; children: Stephanie Anne, William Stephen Jr. B Ceramic Engring., Ga. Inst. Tech., 1970; MS in Ceramic Engring., Ga. Tech. U., 1980. Registered profl. engr., Ga. Rsch. engr. Ga. Tech. Rsch. Inst., Atlanta, 1970—, head thermite processing, 1985—, head ceramics br., 1988—; dir. materials sci. and tech. lab. Ga. Tech. Rsch. Inst., 1990—; bd. dirs. Powder Technologies, Inc., Roswell, Ga. Contbr. articles to engring. jours.; patentee in field. Instr. ARC, Ga., 1980-82. Mem. Am. Ceramic Soc., Keramos, Materials Rsch. Soc., Nat. Soc. Profl. Engrs., Sigma Xi, Alpha Xi Delta. Episcopalian. Office: Ga Tech Rsch Inst Baker Bldg Rm 116 Atlanta GA 30332

LOGAN, LACEY ALEXIS, public relations executive; b. Corning, Calif., Oct. 28, 1958; d. Joseph Dee Logan and Maralee (Ogle) Logan-Taylor. BA in Pub. Rels. and Journalism, Calif. State U., Long Beach, 1981. Staff asst. Rogers & Cowan, L.A., 1978-79; party coord. The Moveable Feast, L.A., 1977-81; events mgmt. cons. O'Malley & Co., Chgo., 1981-82; mktg. events specialist Herman Miller, Inc., Zeeland, Mich., 1982-83; sr. account exec. Anthony M. Franco, Inc., Detroit, 1983-85; mgr. corp. communications The Stroh Brewery Co., Detroit, 1985-87, nat. mgr. corp. communications and pub. rels., 1987—; cons. Boy Scouts Am., Detroit, 1990. Fundraiser The Music Hall, 1989, Detroit Symphony Orch., 1990. Mem. Pub. Rels. Soc. Am., Internat. Assn. Bus. Communicators, Women in Communications Internat., Jr. League Detroit, Delta Delta Delta. Home: 1153 Bishop Ave Grosse Point MI 48230 Office: The Stroh Brewery Co 100 River Pl Detroit MI 48207

LOGAN, LIZ, magazine editor; b. Fontainebleau, France, Nov. 23, 1957; came to U.S., 1960; d. Robert Joseph and Marianne (De Smidt) L. BA, U. Tex., 1979. Asst. editor Dallas Morning News, 1983-85; restaurant critic Orlando (Fla.) Sentinel, 1985; assoc. editor Tex. Homes, Dallas, 1985-86; sr. editor D Mag., Dallas, 1986-87; sr. writer Washingtonian, Washington, 1987; life editor 7 Days, N.Y.C., 1987-88; features editor House and Garden Mag., N.Y.C., 1989; sr. editor Cosmopolitan Mag., N.Y.C., 1989; articles editor Mademoiselle Mag., N.Y.C., 1990—. Columnist: 7 Days Restaurant Rotation, 1988-90, New York, Underground Gourmet, 1990. Home: 51 Bank St #9 New York NY 10014 Office: Mademoiselle 350 Madison Ave New York NY 10017

LOGAN, NESTA ADEAN, medical technologist; b. Pearissburg, Va., Apr. 1, 1951; d. John Hamilton and Ruby Lear (VanDyke) Wickline. BS in Biology, Concord Coll., 1974. Dir. tech. lab. Summers County Hosp., Hinton, W.Va., 1975—. Mem. choir Christian Ch., Peterstown, W.Va. 1975—, camp counselor. Mem. Am. Soc. Med. Tech., Am. Soc. Clin. Tech. Home: Rte 1 Box 73 Ballard WV 24918 Office: Summers County Hosp PO Box 940 Hinton WV 25951

LOGAN, SANDRA JEAN, economics and business educator; b. Dayton, Ohio, Jan. 3, 1940; d. Max B. and Edna E. (Sanderson) Parrish; m. John E. Logan, Apr. 25, 1964. BA, Drew U., 1962; MBA, Columbia U., N.Y.C., 1964; PhD, U. S.C., 1976. Piano tchr. Whippany, N.J., 1957-64; lab. analyst Bear Creek Mining Co., Morristown, N.J., summer 1957, 58; rsch. asst. Drew U., Madison, N.J., summer 1962; staff asst. N.J. Bell Telephone Co., Newark, summer 1963, 64-67; instr. bus. U. Toledo, 1967-69; asst. prof. econs. and bus. S.C. State Coll., Orangeburg, 1970-76; prof. econs. and bus. Newberry (S.C.) Coll., 1976—; cons. econs., Ohio and S.C., 1967—, N.J. Bell Telephone Co., Newark, 1968; lectr. bus. Ea. Mich. U., Ypsilanti, spring 1969. Active Coldstream Home Owners Assn., Columbia, S.C., 1972-80; officer St. Andrews Woman's Club, Columbia, 1969-76. Rsch. grantee U. S.C. and S.C. State Coll., 1974-75. Mem. Am. Econs. Assn., Atlantic Econs. Assn., So. Econs. Assn., So. Mgmt. Assn. Republican. Presbyterian. Home: 112 Smiths Market Ct Columbia SC 29212 Office: Newberry Coll College St Newberry SC 29108

LOGAN, SHARON BROOKS, lawyer; b. Easton, Md., Nov. 19, 1945; d. Blake Elmer and Esther N. (Statum) Brooks; children: John W. III, Troy Blake. BS in Econs., U. Md., 1967, MBA in Mktg., 1969; JD, U. Fla., 1979. Bar: Fla. 1979. Ptnr. Raymond Wilson, Esq., Ormond Beach, Fla., 1980, Landis, Graham & French, Daytona Beach, Fla., 1981, Watson & Assocs., Daytona Beach, 1982-84; prin. Sharon B. Logan, Esq., Ormond Beach, 1984—; legal advisor to paralegal program Daytona Beach Community Coll., 1984—. Sponsor Ea. Surfing Assn., Daytona Beach, 1983—, Nat. Scholastic Surfing Assn., 1987—. Recipient Citizenship award Rotary Club, 1962-63; Woodrow Wilson fellow U. Md., 1967. Mem. ABA, Fla. Bar Assn. (real property and probate sect.), Volusia County Bar Assn. (bd. dirs.), Volusia County Real Property Council, Inc. (bd. dirs. 1987—, sec. 1987-88, v.p. 1988-89, pres. 1989-90, sec. 1990-91) , Fla. Assn. Women Lawyers, Volusia County Estate Planning Council, Daytona Beach Area Bd. Realtors, Ormond Beach C. of C., Gator Club, Beta Gamma Sigma, Alpha Lamba Delta, Phi Kappa Phi, Omicron Delta Epsilon, Delta Delta Delta (Scholarship award 1964), Sigma Alpha Epsilon. Democrat. Episcopalian. Avocations: cooking, sewing, golf, tennis, aerobics. Office: Sharon B Logan Esq 400 S Atlantic Suite 110 Ormond Beach FL 32176

LOGAN, VERYLE JEAN, retail executive, realtor; b. St. Louis, Oct. 24; d. Benjamin Bishop and Eddie Mae (Williams) Logan. BS, Mo. U., 1968; postgrad. Wayne State U., 1974, 76, U. Mich.-Detroit, 1978, 80. Cert. residential specialist. With Hudson Dept. Store, Detroit, 1968-84, Dayton Hudson, Mpls., 1984-86, div. mdse. mgr., 1983-84, retail exec. div. mdse. mgr. Coats and Dresses, 1984-86; pres. Ultimate Connection, Inc., Mpls., 1987—. Mem. Pilgrim Bapt. Ch., Golden Valley Black History Month Com., 1987—, also bd. dirs. Trustee Harry Davis Found., 1988—, mem. exec. bd., 1990. Named Woman of Yr., Am. Bus. Women, 1984. Mem. Grad. Realtors Inst., Am. Bus. Womens Assn. (v.p. 1983-84, named Woman of Yr. 1984), Minn. Black Networking (exec. bd. 1985—), Delta Sigma Theta Mpls.-St. Paul Alumnae Assn. (life mem., recording sec. 1985-87, chmn. arts and letters, corresponding sec. 1987-88, chmn. heritage and archives 1988-89, named Delta of the Yr., 1988). Mem. Grad. Realtors Inst., M.L. King Tennis Buffs Club. Office: PO Box 16438 Minneapolis MN 55416

LOGUE, PEGGY KING, accounting manager; b. Washington, Oct. 30, 1958; d. Lloyd Lee and Barbara (Allen) King; m. Stephen Andrew Logue, Aug. 28, 1982 (div. Sept. 1989); 1 child, Travis Stephen. BS in Acctg., Tenn. Tech. U., 1981; MBA with hons. Southeastern U., Washington, 1987. Cert. in mgmt. acctg. Asst. fin. mgr. Associated Real Estate Mgmt., McLean, Va., 1981-84; collection adminstr. Rolm Corp., Vienna, 1984; jr. acct. Verdix Corp., Chantilly, Va., 1984-85, acctg. supr., 1985-86, fin. acct. Airbus Service Co., Herndon, Va., customer acct. adminstr., 1988—. Mem. NOW, NAFE. Avocations: running, bicycling, softball, swimming. Home: 713 Brethour Ct Sterling VA 22170 Office: Airbus Industrie of NAm Inc 593 Herndon Pkwy Herndon VA 22070

LOGUE-KINDER, JOAN, public relations executive; b. Richmond, Va., Oct. 26, 1943; d. John T. and Helen (Harvey) Logue; m. Lowell A. Henry Jr., Oct. 6, 1963 (div. Sept. 1981); children: Lowell A. Henry III, Catherine D. Henry, Christopher Logue Henry; m. Randolph S. Kinder, Dec. 13, 1986. Student, Wheaton Coll., 1959-62; BA in Sociology, Adelphi U., 1964; cert. in edn., Mercy Coll., Dobbs Ferry, N.Y., 1971; postgrad., NYU, 1973; cert. in edn., St. John's U., 1974. Asst. to dist. mgr. U.S. Census Bur., N.Y.C., 1970; tchr. and adminstr. social studies Yonkers (N.Y.) Bd. Edn., 1971-75; dir. pub. relations Nat. Black Network, N.Y.C., 1976-83; corp. v.p. NBN Broadcasting, N.Y.C., 1984-90; sr. v.p. The Mingo Group/Plus, N.Y.C., 1990—; cons. in field. Mem. alumnae recruitment council Wheaton Coll.; mem. Nigerian-Am. Friendship Soc., 1978-81; bd. dirs. Westchester Civil Liberties Union, 1974-77, Greater N.Y. Council, Girl Scouts U.S., 1985—, Operation PUSH, 1985—; del. White House Conf. on Small Bus.; active Morris Udall for Pres. Campaign, Howard Samuels for Gov. Campaign; sr. black media advisor Dukakis/Bentsen 1988; state del. nat. conv. N.Y. State Women's Polit. Caucus, 1975, pres. Black caucus, 1976-77. Recipient Excellence in Media award Inst. New Cinema Artists, 1984. Mem. World Inst. Black Communications (bd. dirs. 1983—), Women in Communications, Inc., Nat. Assn. Market Developers, Advt. Women of N.Y., 100 Black Women. Home: 1800 7th Ave New York NY 10026 Office: The Mingo Group/Plus 228 E 45th St New York NY 10019

LOHMAN, LORETTA CECELLIA, social scientist, consultant; b. Joliet, Ill., Sept. 25, 1944; d. John Thomas and Marjorie Mary (Brennan) L. BA in Polit. Sci., U. Denver, 1966, postgrad., 1985—; MA in Social Sci., U. No. Colo., 1975. Lectr. Ariz. State U., Tempe, 1966-67; survery researcher Merrill-Werthlin Co., Tempe, 1967-68; edn. asst. Am. Humane Assn., Denver, 1969-70; econ. cons. Lohman & Assocs., Littleton, Colo., 1971-75; rsch. assoc. Denver Rsch. Inst., 1976-85; rsch. scientist Milliken Chapman Rsch. Group, Littleton, 1986-89; owner Lohman & Assocs., Littleton, 1989—; affiliate Colo. Water Resources Rsch. Inst., Ft. Collins, Colo., 1989—; cons. Constrn. Engring. Rsch. Lab., 1984—; peer reviewer NSF, 1985-86; manuscript referee Social Studies Jour.; mem. adv. team Denver Reuse Demonstration Plant. Contbr. articles to profl. jours. Researcher legis. campaigns Arapahoe County, Colo., 1988; vol. Metro Water Conservation projects, Denver, 1986—. Recipient Huffsmith award Denver Rsch. Inst., 1983; Nat. Ctr. for Edn. in Politics grantee, 1964-65. Mem. ASCE (social and environ. objectives com.), Am. Water Works Assn., Am. Water Resources Assn., Water Pollution Control Fedn., Freshwater Found., Colo. Water Congress, Am. Hist. Assn., Sigma Xi, Phi Gamma Mu, Phi Alpha Theta. Democrat. Home and Office: 3375 W Aqueduct Ave Littleton CO 80123

LOHR, MRS. BENJAMIN FRANKLIN See DAVIS, RUTH MARGARET

LOHR, JUDITH KAUFER, educator; b. Chgo., Feb. 15, 1944; d. Stanley Charles and Norma (Wolf) K.; m. John Allen Lohr, Aug. 10, 1969 (div. Apr. 1971). BA, Purdue U., 1965; MS in Edn., Purdue U., Hammond, Ind., 1970; adminstrv. cert., Chgo. State U., 1983; MA in Edn., Gov. State U., 1987. Cert. in secondary edn., guidance and counseling, adminstrn., Ill. Tchr. Crete (Ill.)-Monee Sch. Dist., 1965-66; tchr. Thornton Fractional Sch. Dist., Calumet City, Ill., 1966—, dept. chmn., 1986-90; adj. prof. Gov. State U., University Park, Ill., 1987—, Prairie State Coll., 1989—; sec., pres. Speed Coop., Chicago Heights, Ill., 1976—; mem. South Met. Assn., Flossmoor, Ill., 1976-87, pres., 1989—. Mem. Rich Twp. High Sch. Bd., Park Forest, 1976—, Congregation Beth Sholom; bd. dirs. LWV, Park Forest, 1985-87. Mem. Nat. Coun. Tchrs. English, Assn. Supervision & Curriculum Devel., Ill. Assn. Tchrs. English, Ill. Assn. Supervision & Curriculum Devel., Nat. Assn. Sch. Bds., Ill. Assn. Sch. Bds., South Suburban Juvenile Officers Assn., Phi Delta Kappa. Office: Thornton Fractional S High Sch 18500 Burnham St Lansing IL 60438

LOHRY, JANET SUE, accountant; b. Paonia, Colo., May 15, 1941; d. Dana Norman and Helen Anita (Davison) Peitersen; m. Charles S. Lohry, Oct. 5, 1959 (div. May 1967); children: Christine Ann, Gary Charles. Grad. high sch., Ft. Collins, Colo., 1959. Receptionist, operator PBX Forney Industries, Ft. Collins, 1959-60; sec. Hooper & Assocs., Ft. Collins, 1967-68; sec., bookkeeper Barker & Collins, P.A., Sheridan, Wyo., 1968-69; bookkeeper Kenneth Cox, CPA, Sheridan, Wyo., 1969-70; adminstr. fin. Burroughs Corp., Casper, Wyo., 1970-80, Stuart Shop, Ltd., Casper, Wyo., 1980-81; controller Sta. KCWY-TV subs. Chrysostom Corp., Casper, Wyo., 1981-84; data operator, accountant Cyclone Well Service, West Winds Trucking, Triple J Oil Resources, Casper, Wyo., 1984—; also sec. bd. dirs. Cyclone Well Service, Casper, Wyo.; cons. Sandy Cordoba Advt., Casper, 1978-82; pres. Burnett Livestock, Buffalo, Wyo., 1987—; sec., bd. dirs. Triple J. Oil Resources. Den mother Boy Scouts Am., Casper, 1972-75; vol. mgr. Zipay for Sheriff, Casper, 1982; campaign mgr. Simmons for State House, 1986; vol. Literacy Vols. of Am., 1987, Spl. Olympics, 1986-87; chmn. mobilization for women's lives com. Nationa County Coalition for Choice, 1989. Mem. NOW. Republican. Lutheran. Home: 419 W 13th St Casper WY 82601 Office: Cyclone Well Service Ltd 100 N Center #205 Casper WY 82601

LOKEY, IRENE RAYE, association representative; b. Cin., Feb. 26, 1946; d. Clarence Fredrick and Clara Belle (Matthews) Millies; m. Christopher G. Lokey, Nov. 23, 1967 (div. 1983); children: Christopher, Thor. BBA, So. Meth. U., 1968; MS, Tex. A&I U., 1974. Svc. rep. Southwestern Bell Telephone, Dallas, 1966; receptionist Summers Metals, Dallas, 1967-68; stocks and bonds clk. Ling & Co., Dallas, 1969; tchr. Brownsville (Tex.) Ind. Sch. Dist., 1969-77, supr., 1977-83, tchr., 1983-85; Uniserv rep. Tex. State Tchrs. Assn., Austin, 1985—; trainer Performance Learning Sys., Emerson, N.J., 1990—. Precinct chmn. Rep. Party, 1986—, county sec., 1987—; mem. Planning and Zoning Com., City of Los Frensos, 1987—; mem. pastor parish rels. com. Los Fresnos United Meth. Ch., 1984-85, 1990—; mem. Pan Am. Round Table II. Recipient Human Rels. award, Assn. Brownsville Edn., 1982; Kappa Kappa Iota scholarship award, 1974. Mem. NEA, AAUW (chpt. founder), Nat. Staff Assn., Tex. Profl. Staff Assn., Assn. Brownsville Educators (pres. 1983-85), Tex. State Tchrs. Assn. (dist. I chmn. of profl. rights and responsibilities com. 1974-75), Tex. Assn. Supervision and Curriculum Devel. (pres. 1981-82), Internat. Reading Assn. (Dena J. Gallic coun. founder), Alpha Delta Kappa (pres. 1978-80), Kappa Kappa Iowa (pres. 1981-82), Delta Kappa Gamma. Republican. Methodist. Home: 106 E Resaca Dr Los Fresnos TX 78566 Office: Tex State Tchrs Assn 2202 S 77 Sunshine Strip Harlingen TX 78550

LOKKEN, EVA TRYTI, communications executive; b. Aardalstangen, Norway, Feb. 18, 1964; d. Anders and Gudny (Aase) Tryti; m. Norton Charles Lokken, June 10, 1989. Student, U. Oslo, Norway, 1984, 86; BA in Pub. Rels., U. South Fla., 1988. Journalist Valdres (Norway) Newspaper, 1983-84; pub. rels. specialist IBM Corp., Oslo, 1986, Ted Bates, Oslo, 1987; dir. pub. rels. Melbourne (Fla.) Eye Assocs., 1988-90; v.p. communications Broward Econ. Devel. Bd., Ft. Lauderdale, Fla., 1990—. Mem. Pub. Rels. Soc. Am., Ft. Lauderdales Sister Cities Internat., Sons of Norway. Office: Borward Econ Devel Bd 1 E Broward Blvd Ste 1604 Fort Lauderdale FL 33301

LOMAN, DIANE LOUISE MOORE, nurse, educator; b. Connellsville, Pa., Feb. 22, 1948; d. Glenn and Dorothy May (Eager) Moore; m. Terry Eugene Loman, Apr. 4, 1970; children: Kimberly Joan, Kathy Lynn. Diploma in Nursing with honors, Mercy Hosp. Sch. Nursing, Johnstown, Pa., 1969; AA with high honors, U. S.C., 1978; student, Wilson Coll., 1988—. Staff nurse Brunswick Hosp. and Clinic, Memphis, 1972, Ochsner Hosp. Stress Unit, New Orleans, 1981; nurse supr. New River Nursing Home, Jacksonville, N.C., 1973-77, Willowwood Home for Jewish Aged, New Orleans, 1979-80; dir. nursing Elderlodge (formerly New River Nursing Home), Jacksonville, N.C., 1981-84; sales rep. E.F. Hutton Life, N.Y. Life, Jacksonville, 1984-85; nurse specialist, br. mgr., dir. nursing PORTAMEDIC Health Care/Surveys, Camp Hill, Pa., 1986-89; AIDS edn. coord. Pa. Dept. Corrections, 1990—; bd. dirs. Health Am., 1990—, Pa. AIDS Task Force, 1990—. Mem. Johnstown Community Chorus, 1968-69; mem. svc. and rehab. com. Am. Cancer Soc., 1986—. Served to lt. (j.g.) USNR, 1969-71. Recipient letter of appreciation USNR, 1971. Mem. N.C. Nurses Assn. (pres. dist. 1977), Life Underwriters Assn., Am. Bus. Women's Assn., Assn. Rehab. Nurses, Phi Theta Kappa, Gamma Beta Phi (coord. tutoring). Republican. Roman Catholic. Home: 101 Fetrow Ln New Cumberland PA 17070 Office: Pa Dept Corrections Tng Acad PO Box 598 Camp Hill PA 17001-0598

LOMAN, M. LAVERNE, mathematics educator; b. Stratford, Okla., June 10, 1928; d. Thomas D. and Mary Ellen (Goodwin) Glass; m. Coy E. Loman, Dec. 23, 1944; 1 child, Sandra Leigh Loman Easton. BS, U. Okla., 1956, MA, 1957, PhD, 1961. Grad. asst., then instr. U. Okla., Norman, 1956-61; asst. prof. Cen. State U., Edmond, Okla., 1961-62; assoc. prof. Cen. State U., 1962-66, prof. math., 1966—, chmn. dept. math., 1988-89. NSF fellow, 1965-67. Mem. Math. Assn. Am., Nat. Coun. Tchrs. Math., Okla. Coun. Tchrs. Math. (v.p. 1972-76), Higher Edn Alumni Coun. Okla., VFW Aux., Delta Kappa Gamma. Home: 2201 Tall Oaks Trail Edmond OK 73034 Office: Cen State U Math Dept Edmond OK 73034

LOMBARDO, BONNIE JANE, film company executive; b. Akron, Ohio, Jan. 25, 1941; d. George Mayfield Reed and Grace Jane (Gercevic) Morrison; m. Joseph Stanley Wrobel, Jan. 28, 1959 (div. July 1971); children: Vicki Leopold, Eric Wrobel, Teri Jo Huston; m. Richard Lombardo. AA in Bus. Law, L.A. Valley Coll., 1974; BA in Bus. Adminstrn., U. Akron, 1964. Sec. L.A. Valley Coll. Businesswomen's Assn., 1973-74; ops. mgr. TV bus. affairs dept. Columbia Pictures Industries, Burbank, Calif., 1981—. Recipient award of Merit Columbia Pictures Industries, 1977, 87. Mem. Women in Film, Women of Motion Picture Industry, NAFE, Kappa Kappa Gamma (sec. 1962-64). Democrat. Roman Catholic. Avocation: interior design. Home: 248-G Cameron Rd Sequim WA 98382 Office: Columbia Pictures Industries 3300 Riverside Dr Burbank CA 91505

LOMELI, MARTA, bilingual educator; b. Tijuana, Baja Calif, Mexico, Oct. 28, 1952; came to U.S. 1954; d. Jesus and Guadalupe (Ascencio) Lomeli; m. Rudolph Benitez, 1978 (div. 1982); children: Pacual Lomeli Benitez. BA, San Diego State U., 1977. With M & N Tree Nursery, Vista, Calif., 1957-70; libr. Vista Boys Club, 1969-70; vol. tutor MECHA U. Calif. San Diego, La Jolla, 1971-73; tchr. aide San Diego City Schs., 1976-77; bilingual educator National City (Calif.) Schs., 1978—; pres./acct. Lomeli, Lopez & Lyte, San Diego, 1980-90. Mem. Lincoln Acres Com. to Advise, National City, 1986-88, com. to advise supt., National City, 1986-88; art editor Lincoln Jr. Hi, Vista, Calif., 1964-65, Third World U. Calif., San Diego, 1970-73; faculty advisor Cool Sensations Dance Group, National City, 1988—. Mem. Calif. Tchrs. Assn., Calif. Assn. Bilingual Edn. (sec. 1986), Nat. Assn. Bilingual Edn., Assn. of Mexican Am. Educators, La Raza Club (pres. 1970). Democrat. Home: 6920 Alsacia St San Diego CA 92139-2101

LOMPA, SUSAN JOYCE, printing and lithograph company owner, concert artist; b. Albany, Calif., Apr. 25, 1941; d. Coulter Morgan and Zorah Alice (Bassett) Bowers; m. Richard M. Lompa, Feb. 17, 1962 (div. Oct. 1989); children: Ernest Frederic, John Paul. Grad. high sch., Oakland, Calif., 1959. Catalog clk. Montgomery Ward & Co., Oakland, 1959-61; underwriting clk. Blue Cross/No. Calif., Oakland, 1961-64; owner Lompa Printing and Lithograph Co., Albany, 1967—; soloist, concert artist D&S Music Ministry, No. Calif. Soloist, profl. Christian concert artist at chs. of numerous denominations and prisons, No. Calif.; recorded Someone Up There Loves Me, 1989. Affiliate mem. Live Oak Br., Children's Hosp., Oakland, Calif.; mem. Richmond (Calif.) Art Ctr., 1967—. Mem. Printing Industries of No. Calif., Printing Industries Am., Soroptimist Internat. of the Ams. (founder region, pres., dist. dir., regional sec., gov., Woman of Distinction, 1984, numerous certs.), Richmond Club. Republican. Methodist. Office: Lompa Printing & Lithograph 600 Cleveland Ave Albany CA 94710

LONDON, CHERYL ANN, communications executive; b. Albuquerque, Apr. 14, 1957; d. Roger William and Barbara Jean (Olendorf) Greer; m. Kim Brian London, June 24, 1978. BA in Biology with honors, U. Calif., Santa Cruz, 1979. Teller, loan processor Monterey Savs. and Loan Co., Watsonville, Calif., 1979-80; data processing acct. rep. Monterey Savs. and Loan Co., Calif., 1980-82; mktg. tech. specialist Tymshare, Inc., Cupertino, Calif., 1982-83; acct. rep. Tymnet, Inc., Irvine, Calif., 1983, assoc. communications cons., 1984; communications cons. Tymnet-McDonnell Douglas, Inc., Irvine, 1984-85, sr. communications cons., 1985, tech. mgr., 1985-88, tech. sales mgr. SE region, 1988-90; nat. account mgr. BT Tymnet, Inc., 1990—. Mem. Nat. Assn. Female Execs. Office: Tymnet-McDonnell Douglas Inc 2070 Chainbridge Rd Ste 200 Vienna VA 22018

LONDON, JILL ABBEY, neurophysiology research scientist; b. Chgo., Feb. 18, 1953; d. Samuel Abraham and Ellen (Berg) L. BS, U. Ill., 1975, MS, 1980, PhD, 1983. Post-doctoral fellow Dept. Physiology Yale U. Sch. Medicine, New Haven, Conn., 1983-87; asst. prof. Dept. Bio Structure and Function U. Conn., Farmington, 1987—. Contbr. articles to profl. jours., 1973-88; creator workshops on neurophysiology, 1985, 88. Fellow Grass Found., 1986; post-doctoral fellow NIH, 1984-87; Klingstein fellow, 1990. Mem. Soc. for Neurosci., Assn. for Chem. Senses, Women in Neurosci., Conn. Chemosensory Clin. Research Ctr. Office: Dept Bio Structure Function U Conn Health Ctr Farmington CT 06032

LONDON, MARINA, psychiatric social worker; b. N.Y.C., Mar. 31, 1956; d. George London and Nora (Shapiro) L.; m. John Norman Wollberg, June 26, 1983; 1 child, Jamie London Wollberg. BA, Yale U., 1977; MS, Columbia U., 1980. Med. social worker The N.Y. Hosp., N.Y.C., 1981—; pvt. practice psychotherapist N.Y.C., 1987—; sr. psychiat. social worker Payne Whitney Clinic, N.Y.C., 1986—. Mem. Acad. Cert. Social Workers, Nat. Assn. Social Workers. Democrat. Jewish. Home: 1675 York Ave Apt 22K New York NY 10128 Office: Payne Whitney Clinic Dept Social Work 525 E 68th St New York NY 10021

LONDON, ROBIN SIGMAN, compensation consultant; b. Phila., Sept. 17, 1963; d. Bernard N. and Barbara (Lieberman) Sigman; m. Jay Michael London, Nov. 19, 1989. BA, U. Del., 1985. Sr. compensation analyst RCA Svc. Co., Cherry Hill, N.J., 1985-87; sr. cons. asst. Wm. M. Mercer Meidinger Hansen, Phila., 1987-89; compensation cons. MacLean Assocs., Inc., New Hope, Pa., 1989—. Mem. Am. Compensation Assn., Phi Beta Kappa. Jewish. Office: MacLean Assocs Inc 20C S Main St New Hope PA 18938

LONDON, SHERI FAITH, financial planner; b. Hackensack, N.J., Dec. 6, 1955; d. Julius and Millie (Dier) L. BA, Rutgers U., 1977; postgrad., Emory U., 1978-80, Cardozo Sch. Law, 1990—. Cert. fin. planner. Research asst. grad. sch. Emory U., Atlanta, 1978-79; registered rep. Donald & Co. Securities Inc., Jersey City, 1980—, v.p., registered options prin., 1984—, gen. prin., 1986—; researcher, office mgr. Pub. Citizen's Congress Watch, Washington, 1982-83; pres. S.F.L. Fin. Planning, Inc., Hackensack, 1985—; life, health ins. rep. Berger Agy., Neptune, N.J., 1987—; sr. v.p. Donald & Co. Securities, inc., 1989—; fin. planner seminars for orgns. and high schs.; cons. in field, 1986—. Contbr. articles to profl. jours.and mags. Bd. dirs. Bergen County chpt. ACLU, N.J., 1983—. Emory U. Grad. Sch. grantee, 1978. Mem. No. N.J. Inst. Cert. Fin. Planners. Office: SFL Fin Planning Inc 15F Coles Ave Hackensack NJ 07601

LONDON, SHERRI SUE, communications executive; b. Bklyn., Apr. 25, 1960; d. Carl and Mildred Barbara (Blitstein) L.; m. Michael Edward Pastolove, Nov. 27, 1988. BFA, N.Y.U., 1982. Asst. media buyer Media Buying Svcs., N.Y.C., 1982; prodn. asst. Drossman Yustein Clowes, N.Y.C., 1983; adminstrv. asst. Janklow Bender Inc., N.Y.C., 1983-85; sales asst. Arts & Entertainment Cable Network, N.Y.C., 1985-86, account rep., 1987, account mgr., 1988-89. Judge NY Emmy awards, N.Y.C., 1983.

LONEY GALLEGOS, JACQUELINE A., advertising executive; b. Ft. Walton Beach, Fla., Aug. 28, 1961; d. Carlos T. and Mavis (Durden) Gallegos; m. Clayton Wayne Loney,. BA, U. West Fla., 1983. With advt. dept. Pensacola (Fla.) News Jour., 1983; with cable advt. Warner Cable Communications, Ft. Walton Beach, 1983; TV advt. TV WEAR, Pensacola, 1984-86; cons. Sta. WYZB, Mary Esther, Fla., 1986; publicity chmn. Stage Crafters Community Theatre, FWB, Fla., 1989--. Fund raising project Cystic Fibrosis. Mem. AAUW, Omicron Delta Kappa.

LONG, ANNE WILLIAMS, teacher; b. Syracuse, N.Y., June 6, 1943; d. Howard Frederick and Florence Eloise (Frank) Williams; m. Robert Arthur Long; 1 child, Gregory Christopher. BA, SUNY, Potsdam, 1965. Cert. tchr. Pa. Tchr. DeForest (Wis.) Union High Sch. Dist., 1966-67, Edmonton (Alta.) Pub. Sch. Dist., 1967-69, Wyalusing (Pa.) Sch. Dist., 1970—. Bd. dirs. Children's Cultural Program Trust, Towanda, Pa., 1975—, Towanda Area Schs., 1987—, Bradford County Vocat.-Tech. Bd., 1987-89, Boy Scouts Am., Towanda, 1979—; pres. Jay-N-Cees, Towanda, 1978, Cen. Bradford County United Way, 1979, bd. dirs. 1979—. Mem. AAUW (pres. 1973-75), NEA, Pa. Edn. Assn., Wyalusing Edn. Assn., Order of Eastern Star, Delta Kappa Gamma. Republican. Methodist. Home: RD 3 Box 34 Towanda PA 18848 Office: Wyalusing Elem Sch RD4 Box 8 Wyalusing PA 18853

LONG, CHERYL LYNN, marketing executive; b. Chgo., May 3, 1946; d. Louis Russell and Catherine Lois (Schumann) Fritz; m. Thomas David Brown, Jan. 25, 1969 (div. Nov. 1982); m. Gregory David Long, July 3, 1985; 1 child, Nathan Alan. BA, Cornell Coll., Des Moines, 1968. Advt., promotions specialist Better Homes & Gardens, Des Moines, 1974-75, mktg.

specialist, 1975-77, consumer panel mgr., 1977-82, mktg. services mgr., 1982—. Mem. Advt. Fedn. Des Moines (pres. 1974-75, Advt. Woman of the Yr. 1977), Nat. Assn. Profl. Saleswomen (sec. 1984-85).

LONG, CYNTHIA ANN, high school educator, newspaper reporter; b. Torrance, Calif., Mar. 31, 1961; d. Roger Whitney and Jocelyn Ann (Muller) Gilbert; m. Michael Gregory Long. AB in Polit. Sci. cum laude, Occidental Coll., 1983; MA in Internat. Affairs, George Washington U., 1986; postgrad., Yale U., 1983; teaching cert., San Jose State U., 1988. Adminstrv. asst. AID, Washington, 1985-86; underwriter Gt. Am. Ins. Co., San Francisco, 1987; high sch. instr. Met. Adult Edn. Program, San Jose, Calif., 1988—; reporter Sanat Clara (Calif.) Am. Weekly, 1989—. Fundraiser Cen. Am. Refugee Ctr., L.A., 1984; document asst. Father Moriarity Cen. Am. Refugee Ctr., San Francisco, 1987; precinct capt. Dukakis for Pres. Campaign, San Jose, 1988. Mem. Calif. Coun. Soc. Studies, Doris Day Animal League, Tau Delta Phi. Democrat. Office: Met Adult Edn Program 1149 E Julian St San Jose CA 95116

LONG, DOROTHY VALJEAN, personnel management company executive; b. Paducah, Ky., Mar. 10, 1928; d. Athel Sr. and Lora Bea (Vaughn) Shepherd; m. Earl Wallace Long; children: Robert Earl and Stephen Howard. Grad. high sch., Chgo.; various certificates in acctg., computing and control data mgmt. Keypunch supr. IBM Corp., Houston, 1950-54; terminal service mgr. SW region Control Data Corp., Houston, 1966-80; pres., chief exec. officer Keypeople Resources, Inc., Houston, 1980—. Pres. PTA, Houston, 1962-63; cons. Mission Bend UMC, 1986; social service vol. Sheltering Arms, 1986-87; mem. Temporary Help Services of Tex., Houston Bus. Council, City of Houston Certification; life mem. Women's Soc. of Christian Service, PTA State of Tex. Mem. Tex. Assn. Personnel Cons., Am. Bus. Women Assn. Republican. Office: Keypeople Resources Inc 2000 W Loop St #1620 Houston TX 77027

LONG, ERNESTINE MARTHA JOULLIAN, educator; b. St. Louis, Nov. 14, 1906; d. Ernest Cameron and Alice (Joullian) Long; A.B., U. Wis., 1927; M.S., U. Chgo., 1932; Ph.D., St. Louis U., 1976; postgrad. Washington U., St. Louis, 1932-68, Eastman Sch. Music, 1956, (NSF fellow) So. Ill. U., 1969-70. Tchr. scis. pub. schs. Normandy dist., St. Louis, 1927-66, Red Bud, Ill., 1966-70, St. Louis, 1970-75; coordinator continuing edn. U. Mo., St. Louis, 1976-79; ednl. cons. Area IV, St. Louis Pub. Schs.; dir. Project Think, Mo. and Ill., 1976-88; apptd. adv. com. to U.S. Senate adv. commn. Recipient Community Service award St. Louis Newspaper Guild, 1978-79, Sci. Edn. Commendation award, 1978; named One of the Most Outstanding Contributors to 20th Century Science, 1987. Mem. AAAS, Am. Physics Tchrs. Assn., Am. Personnel and Guidance Assn. (treas. St. Louis br. 1954), Am. Chem. Soc., Cen. Assn. Sch. Sci. Math. Tchrs. (chmn. chemistry sect.), Am. Soc. for Microbiology, LWV, St. Louis Symphony Soc. (women's div., docent), Am. Guild Organists, NEA, Nat. Sci. Tchrs. Assn. Home: 245 N Price Rd Ladue MO 63124-1916

LONG, EVELYN MARGARET, academic official; b. Spangler, Pa., Apr. 3, 1964; d. Cletus Robert and Bernetta Mary (Veneskey) L. BA, Point Park Coll., 1986. Freelance writer Pitts., 1986-87; with mktg. dept. J.L. Sullivan Inc., Carnegie, Pa., 1987; asst. dir. pub. rels. Duquesne U., Pitts., 1988—. Mem. Pub. Rels. Soc. Am.

LONG, JILL, congresswoman; b. Warsaw, Ind., July 15, 1952. BS, Valparaiso U.; MBA, Ind. U., PhD. Prof. various colls. and univs.; mem. 101st, 102nd Congresses from 4th Ind. dist., 1989—; cons. in small bus. mgmt. Councilwoman City of Valparaiso, Ind. Democrat. Methodist. Office: US Ho of Reps Office House Mems Washington DC 20510*

LONG, KATHLEEN PETTEBONE, publishing executive; b. Louisville, Apr. 28, 1945; d. John Elliott II and Elsie Mae (Gyles) Pettebone; m. John Darrieulat Weidmann, Nov. 2, 1968 (div. Sept. 1972); m. R. Eugene Long Jr., June 29, 1974. Student, Meredith Coll., Raleigh, N.C., 1963-65; BA, U. Md., 1967; postgrad., Harvard U., 1972-73, U. Pa., 1977-79. Guest lectr. Publs. Specialist Program George Washington U., Washington, 1977-82; dir. pub. activities Nat. Inst. Child Support Enforcement Univ. Research Corp., Washington, 1979-81; mng. editor BioScience Mag. Am. Inst. Biol. Sci, Arlington, Va., 1981-84; exec. editor Computer Graphics News Mag. Scherago Assocs. Pub., Inc., N.Y.C., 1984—; pres., chief exec. officer KPL and Assocs., Annapolis, Md., 1976—. Author: The History and Fundamentals of Child Support Enforcement, Paternity Establishment: Who Does it Benefit, 1981; author: (with Patricia Semler-Carlson) (filmstrip) Child Support Enforcement: Program Basics, 1980; editor numerous books; contbr. articles to profl. jours. Mem. AAUW, NOW, Soc. Scholarly Pub. (com. budget and fin. 1986—), Coun. Biology Editors (chmn. pub. affairs com. 1984-86), Am. Soc. Tng. and Devel., Washington Book Pubs., Balt. Pubs. Assn., Meredith Coll. Alumni Assn., Jr. League of Balt., Chesapeake Bay Yacht Racing Assn., Indian Landing Boat Club (bd. govs. 1985—). Democrat. Methodist. Home: 7875 Americana Cir Glen Burnie MD 21061 Office: 11 Bladen St Annapolis MD 21401

LONG, KERRY JEAN, pharmaceutical company executive; b. Joliet, Ill., Oct. 28, 1948; d. Robert Armand and Marilyn Jean (Burt) L. BS in Chemistry, St. Mary's Coll., Notre Dame, Ind., 1970; MBA, U. Chgo., 1978. Analytical chemist Gillette Co., Chgo., 1970-74, Cen. Soya Co., Chgo., 1974-75; analytical chemist G. D. Searle, Skokie, Ill., 1975-78, supr. quality control, 1978-81; mgr. quality control Skokie and San Juan, P.R., 1981-82, University Park, Ill., 1982-84; dir. quality assurance Skokie, 1984-87, sr. dir. quality assurance, 1987—. Mem. St. Mary's Coll. Alumnae (v.p. 1984-87), U. Chgo. Women's Bus. Group. Democrat. Roman Catholic. Office: G D Searle & Co 5200 Old Orchard Rd Skokie IL 60077

LONG, LINDA ANN, federal government official; b. Phila., Oct. 26, 1953; d. Charles Haydn and Sophie (Musick) White; m. George Howard Long, May 12, 1979. BA, Shippensburg U., 1975; postgrad., Temple U., 1980. Benefit authorizer Social Security Adminstrn., Phila., 1975-81, claims rep., 1981-88; manpower devel. specialist U.S. Dept. Labor, Phila., 1988—; U.S. Dept. Labor rep. Fed. Women's Program Com., Phila., 1988-89. Author: (children's book) Dragon Dinwittie's Kingdom, 1988; staff artist (bi-monthly newsletter Frontier Dist. Communicator, Boy Scouts., Am. 1979—. Recording sec. troop 168 Boy Scouts Am., Phila., 1983-86, vice-chairperson troop 168, 1986—; parish rep. Espisc. Community Svcs., Phila., 1979-84. Lt. USNR. Recipient Chapel of the Four Chaplains award Four Chaplains Legion of Honor, Phila., 1985. Republican.

LONG, LINDA JEAN, veterinarian; b. Wichita Falls, Tex., June 7, 1953; d. William Floyd Jr. and Libby Jean (Allen) Rozell; m. James Roy Long, Feb. 24, 1974 (div. May 1975); m. Robert Hugh Thurston Jr., July 4, 1987 (div. June 1989). Student, Tyler (Tex.) Jr. Coll., 1972-73, 75-76; BS, Tex. A&M U., 1979, Tex. A&M U., 1984; DVM, Tex. A&M U., 1986. Veterinarian Riverside Vet. Clinic, Austin, Tex., 1986-87, Vet. Relief Svcs., Austin, 1987-88, Southpark Animal Clinic, Austin, 1988-89, Westgate Pet & Bird Clinic, Austin, 1989—. Mem. Am. Vet. Med. Assn., Am. Vet. Dental Assn., Am. Animal Hosp. Assn., Tex. Vet. Med. Assn., Capitol Area Vet. Med. Assn., Tex. A&M Archery, Phi Kappa Phi, Gamma Sigma Delta, Am. Bus. Women's Assn. (scholar 1984). Republican. Episcopalian. Office: Westgate Pet & Bird Clinic 4534 Westgate Blvd Ste 103 Austin TX 78745

LONG, LORNA ERICKSON, human resources executive; b. Worcester, Mass., Nov. 18, 1944; d. Roland Axel and Roxie Sophie Erickson; divorced; children: Christopher Carson, Jessica Erickson. AB, Mt. Holyoke Coll., 1966. Various positions in personnel and mgmt., 1966-69; systems analyst Paul Revere Life Ins. Co. subs. Avco Corp., Worcester, Mass., 1970-71, pers. asst., 1971-74, mgr. compensation and benefits, 1974-78, v.p., 1980-84; corp. dir. compensation, corp. hdqrs. Avco Corp., Greenwich, Conn., 1978-79, corp. dir. compensation and benefits, 1979-80, exec. dir. human resources, 1984-85; v.p. human resource devel. and adminstrn. Textron, Inc., Providence, 1985-89, v.p. human resources, 1989—. Bd. dirs., chmn. pers. com. Montachusett council Girl Scouts U.S.A., Worcester, 1976-78, mem. nominating com. Montachusett coun., 1982-83; mem. coun., vice chmn. subcom., manpower planing coun. CETA adminstrn. City of Worcester, 1977-78. Mem. Human Resource Planning Soc. (bd. dirs. 1987—). Republican. Office: Textron Inc 40 Westminster St Providence RI 02903

LONG, LUCINDA HERRON, account specialist; b. Columbus, Ohio, Feb. 26, 1946; d. Leo James Pyle and Ethel (Toth) Pyle Markham; m. Donald J. Herron, Jan. 14, 1972 (div. Nov. 30, 1979); 1 child, Kimberly Dawn; m. Don E. Long, Mar. 18, 1989. Customer svc. officer Flagship Nat. Bank, Coral Gables, Fla., 1965-79; mktg. support rep. Lanier Bus. Products, Miami, Fla., 1979-82; account exec. Clarke Am., Ft. Lauderdale, Fla., 1982—. Contbr. articles to profl. jours.; owner, handler, trainer world's most titled Am. Pit Bull Terrier. Pres. Keep-In-Step Dancers. Mem. Am. Inst. Banking, Nat. Dog Owner's Assn., Nat. Assn. for Am. Pit Bull Terriers, Everglades Pit Bull Club (founder, 1st pres.), Miami Obedience Club (trial chmn. 1978), South Fla. Schutzhund Club., Greater Miami C. of C., Jaycees. Democrat. Presbyterian. Home: 14240 SW 96th Terr Miami FL 33186

LONG, MARJORIE JEAN, lawyer; b. Elmhurst, Ill., June 15, 1950; d. Kenneth A. and June M. (Dudgeon) L.; m. Walter J. Downing, Aug. 6, 1983; children: Leigh Anne, Kellan. BA, U. Colo., Boulder, 1972, JD, 1982. Bar: Colo. 1983. Editorial asst. Sphere Mag., Chgo., 1972; asst. registrar U. Colo., Boulder, 1975-79; sr. editor Shepard's/McGraw-Hill Inc., Colorado Springs, 1982-84; staff atty. Children's Legal Clinic, Denver, 1984-85; adj. prof. Regis Coll., Colorado Springs, Colo., 1982—; sr. atty The Legal Ctr., Denver, 1985—; guardian ad Litem Juvenile Ct., Denver, 1985—; faculty Continuing Legal Edn., Denver, 1988; cons. Colo. Dept. Edn., Denver, 1988. Author: Rights to Special Education in Colorado, 1988. Vol. Aurora (Colo.) Assn. for Retarded Citizens, 1987—. Recipient Best Performance in Legal Aid Clinic award U. Colo. Law Sch., Boulder, 1982. Mem. ABA, Colo. Bar Assn. (co-chmn. juvenile law forum com. 1990—), Bernese Mountain Dog Club Am. (OFA chmn. 1977-80). Democrat. Home: 455 Sherman St Denver CO 80203 Office: The Legal Ctr 455 Sherman St Denver CO 80203

LONG, NANCY K., psychotherapist; b. Chester, Pa., Sept. 12, 1938; d. Paul John and Anne (Jeffers) Klotz; m. Donald Max Long, June 29, 1957 (div. 1977); children: Gregory Paul, Kerry Kathleen, Kevin Lyle. BS, So. Oreg. State Coll., Ashland, 1976; MS, U. Oreg., 1980. Guidance counselor Ashland (Oreg.) pub. schs., 1976-77; voc. counselor The Job Council, Medford, Oreg., 1977-78; instr. So. Oreg. State Coll., Ashland, 1977; research asst. U. Oreg., Eugene, 1979-80; prog. mgr. U. Oreg., 1980-82; pvt. practice Emerald Counseling Svcs., Eugene, 1980-82; dir. R. Joseph Assocs., Boston, 1983-85; clinic dir. Human Resource Inst., Boston, 1986-88; mktg. dir. Kimberly Quality Care, Medford, Oreg., 1989—; lectr. in field; psychotherpaist Jackson County Community Human Svcs., 1989. Co-producer TV series: Generations, 1985; founder: Extended Circle Theatre Co., 1989. Com. mem. Gov.'s Commn. on Vietnam Vets., Boston, 1984; pres. adv. bd. Lindemann Mental Health Ctr., Boston, 1984-85; sec. So. Oreg. Mental Health Task Force on Women, Eugene, 1975-76. Omnibus grantee, 1976; named Outstanding Woman in Psychology, AAUW, 1976. Democrat. Home: 1301 Iowa St #16 Ashland OR 97520

LONG, NICHOLA Y., technical writer; b. Walnut Creek, Calif., Jan. 4, 1955; d. Shogo and Elizabeth (Hughes) Yamaguchi. BS in Indsl. Tech./Electronics, Tuskegee U., 1978. From spl. tech. asst. to tech. writing specialist Western Electric Corp., Winston-Salem, N.C., 1977-86; sr. tech. documentation specialist AT&T Network Systems, Winston-Salem, 1986—. Friend, The Arts Council, Inc., Winston-Salem, 1984-86. Mem. Am. Mgmt. Assn., Am. Soc. Profl. and Exec. Women, Tuskegee Nat. Alumni Assn. (pres. Winston-Salem chpt. 1984-85), Alliance Black Telecommunications Employees, Alpha Kappa Mu. Home: 168 Carrisbrooke Ln Winston-Salem NC 27104 Office: AT&T Network Systems 2400 Reynolda Rd Winston-Salem NC 27106

LONG, SARAH ANN, librarian; b. Atlanta, May 20, 1943; d. Jones Lloyd and Lelia Maria (Mitchell) Sanders; m. James Allen Long, 1961 (div. 1985); children: Andrew C., James Allen IV; m. Donald J. Sager, May 23, 1987. BA, Oglethorpe U., 1966; M in Librarianship, Emory U., 1967. Asst. libr. Coll. of St. Matthias, Bristol, Eng., 1970-74; cons. State Libr. of Ohio, Columbus, 1975-77; coord. Franklin County Pub. Libr., Columbus, 1977-79, dir. Fairfield County Dist. Libr., Lancaster, Ohio, 1979-82, Dauphin County Libr. System, Harrisburg, Pa., 1982-85, Multnomah County Libr., Portland, Oreg., 1985-89; system dir. North Suburban Libr. System, Wheeling, Ill., 1989—; chmn. Portland State U. Libr. Adv. Coun., 1987-89. Contbr. articles to profl. jours. Bd. dirs. Dauphin County Hist. Soc., Harrisburg, 1983-85, ARC, Harrisburg, 1984-85; pres. Lancaster-Fairfield County YWCA, Lancaster, 1981-82; vice-chmn. govt. and edn. div. Lancaster-Fairfield County United Way, Lancaster, 1981-82; sec. Fairfield County Arts Coun., 1981-82; adv. bd. Portland State U., 1987-89. Recipient Dir.'s award Ohio Program in Humanities, Columbus, 1982; Sarah Long Day established in her honor Fairfield County, Lancaster, Bd. Commrs., 1982. Mem. ALA, Pub. Libr. Assn. (pres. 1989-90)., Ill. Libr. Assn. Office: N Suburban Libr System Wheeling IL 60015

LONG, SHELLEY, actress; b. Fort Wayne, Ind.; m. Bruce Tyson; 1 child, Juliana. Student, Northwestern U. Writer, assoc. producer, co-host Chicago TV program Sorting It Out, 1970's (3 local Emmys 1970); mem. Second City, Chgo.; guest TV appearances various shows; regular TV series Cheers, 1982-87, M.A.S.H., Love Boat, Family; motion pictures include A Small Circle of Friends, 1980, Caveman, 1981, Night Shift, 1982, Losin' It, 1983, Irreconciliable Differences, 1984, The Money Pit, 1986, Outrageous Fortune, 1987, Hello Again, 1987, Troop Beverly Hills, 1989, Don't Tell Her It's Me, 1990; TV films include The Cracker Factory, 1979, The Promise of Love, 1980, The Princess and the Cabbie, 1981; TV mini-series Voices Within The Lives of Trudy Chase, 1990. Recipient Emmy award Outstanding Actress in a Comedy Series for Cheers, 1983. Office: care William Morris Agy 151 El Camino Beverly Hills CA 90212

LONG, SUSAN WEBB, financial consultant; b. Binghamton, N.Y., Feb. 28, 1946; d. Hyle Fuess and Mary Elizabeth (Harrison) Webb; m. Robert R. Adams, Feb. 10, 1968 (div. Mar. 10, 1969); m. Clayton Shiel Long Jr., Dec. 21, 1974; children: Clayton S. III, Susan H. BS, Syracuse U., 1971; MBA, U. S.C., 1975, PhD, 1976. Asst. prof. fin. East Carolina U., Greenville, N.C., 1975-78; cons. C&S Rsch. Assoc., Ypsilanti, Mich., 1978-82; assoc. prof. fin. Ea. Mich. U., Ypsilanti, 1978-82; pvt. practice cons. Tampa, Fla., 1982-88; assoc. prof. fin. U. South Fla., Tampa, 1982-89; prin. Whitestone Cons. Group, Tampa, 1988—; v.p., treas., owner Whitestone Consulting Group, Tampa, 1988—; pres., owner C&S Research Assoc., Ypsilanti, 1978-82; treas. Am. Med. Support Flight Team, Lake Wales, Fla., 1985—. Contbr. various articles to profl. jours. Treas. St. Marks Episc. Ch., Tampa, 1986-88. Recipient Grace Vedder Fellowship Syracuse U., 1970. Mem. Fin. Mgmt. Assn., Inst. Bus. Appraisers, NAFE (treas. Tampa Bay Network 1989—). Office: Whitestone Cons Group Inc 1502 W Fletcher Ste 105 Tampa FL 33612

LONGACRE, LILIAN T., personnel services company executive; b. London, Aug. 5, 1928; d. Charles J. and Amelia E. (Hicks) Brackenbury; m. William T. Longacre, Sept. 8, 1984; children: Raymond Baga, David Baga, Peter Baga, Gregory. Cert. in basic electronics and electronic calculatons; cert. inst. on placement svcs. Owner, pres. Network Pers. Svcs., Carmel, Calif.; pers. cons. to doctors. Mem. Monterey and Salinas C. of C., U.S. C. of C. Office: 26624 Fisher Dr Carmel CA 93923

LONGNECKER, BETH ANNE, audiologist; b. Hamilton AFB, Calif., Dec. 17, 1956; d. David Earl and Myrtle Ethel Elizabeth (Bock) L. BA cum laude, Wash. State U., 1978; M Speech Pathology and Audiology, U. Wash., 1980. Cert. audiologist. Trainee VA Med. Ctr., Seattle, 1979-80; clin. fellow in audiology Porterville (Calif.) State Hosp., 1981-82; audiologist El Paso Rehab. Ctr., 1982-85; clin. audiologist El Paso Ear, Nose and Throat Assocs., 1985—; pvt. practice, El Paso, 1982—; workshop presenter, 1982, 86. Mem. NAFE, NOW, Am. Speech-Language-Hearing Assn. (continuing edn. award 1987, 90), Tex. Speech-Language-Hearing Assn. (hearing impaired task force 1987-88, infant task force 1983-87, hospitality chmn. annual convention 1989), Am. Auditory Soc., Am. Acad. Audiology, El Paso Speech-Language-Hearing Assn., Rio Grande Group Self Help for Hearing Impaired Persons (chmn. steering com., profl. adv. com.), Gamma Tau (Mortar Bd. 1978). Home: 734 Mesa Hills #184 El Paso TX 79912 Office: El Paso Ear Nose Throat 5959 Gateway W #160 El Paso TX 79925

LONGO, DIANE, business administrator; b. Bklyn., June 18, 1957; d. Ralph Francis and Teresa Marie (Scotto) Longo. Cert. grad. Katharine Gibbs Sch., 1976. Exec. sec. Allstate Ins. Co., Farmingville, N.Y., 1977-80, Torrance, Calif., 1980-81; adminstrv. asst. Pepperdine U. Sch. Law, Malibu, Calif., 1981-83, asst. to dean, 1984-86; sales ops. mgr. Herman Miller, Inc., Dallas, 1986—; cons. Law Offices Ronald R. Helm, Oakland, Calif., 1986—. Mem. Meeting Planners Internat., Nat. Assn. Female Execs. Republican. Roman Catholic. Club: Jr. Women's (Woodland Hills, Calif.). Avocations: skiing; tennis; cooking. Office: Herman Miller Inc 300 Crescent Ct Suite 1750 Dallas TX 75201

LONGO, PATRICIA LACY, deputy mayor, advertising company executive; b. Anderson, Ind., Sept. 24, 1927; d. Flay Samuel and Arla Robbins (Begeman) Lacy; m. Charles Rudolph Longo, Jan. 19, 1952; children: Stephen, Christopher, Tracy. Student Brevard Coll., 1945, Ventura Coll., 1964-67, 75-76. Dir. pub. rels. Gallaudet Coll. for the Deaf, Washington, 1958-61; field cons. Am. Nat. Red Cross, San Francisco, 1966-68; fund cons. Fiesta delas Rosas, San Jose, Calif., 1968-69; mgr. San Jose Symphony, 1969-71; mem. Ventura City Coun., Calif., 1981—, dep. mayor; mem. community, econ. and human devel. com., 1981-86, mem., transp. and communication com., 1981-86; with Impact Advt., Ventura, 1987—. Commr. Ventura Redevel. Agy., 1981-86; bd. dirs. South Coast Area Transit, 1981-86, chmn., 1983—; chmn. Ventura County Repub. Cen. Com., 1982—; assoc. dir. Calif AARP/VOTE, AARP Congl. Contact Com.; Calif. spokesperson AARP Womens Iniative; pres. Ventura Rep. Assembly; bd. dirs. Rape and Sexual Abuse Ctr. Ventura County; mem. Calif. Rep. exec. com., 1983—. Mem. Calif. Elected Women Assn. Edn. and Rshc., Ventura County Profl. Womens Network, So. Calif. Assn. Govts. (community devel. com.), Ventura C. of C. Club: PEO. Lodges: DAR, Am. Legion. Office: 501 Poli St PO Box 99 Ventura CA 93002

LONGOBARDI, ANITAROSE TERESA, economist; b. Bklyn., June 5, 1961; d. Raphael Francis and Anna (Bellone) L. BS in Bus., Fordham U., 1982, MA in Econs., 1985, PhD in Economics, 1989. Rsch. asst. Morgan Guaranty Trust Co., N.Y.C., 1982-83; rsch. asst. econs. dept. Fordham U., Bronx, N.Y., 1983-86; instr. econs. dept. Fordham U., 1986-87; assoc. economist econs. dept. Marine Midland Bank, N.Y.C., 1989—. Dissertaion fellow Richard D. Irwin Found., 1988-89, Fordham U., 1988-89. Mem. Am. Econs. Assn., Beta Gamma Sigma, Phi Kappa Phi.

LONGOBARDI, LAURA ELIZABETH, lawyer; b. Bklyn., Sept. 1, 1962; d. Raphael F. and Ann M. (Bellone) L. BA, Fordham U., 1983, JD, 1986. Bar: N.Y. 1987, Conn. 1986, U.S. Dist. Ct. (ea. and so. dists.) N.Y.1987. Law clk. to judge U.S. Dist. (Ea. Dist.) N.Y., Bklyn., 1988; assoc. Reid & Priest, N.Y.C., 1990. Contbr. articles to profl. jours. Mem. Am. Bar Assn., N.Y. State Bar Assn. (mem. comml. and def. litigation sect., com. on antitrust), 2d Cir. Fed. Bar Coun., Phi Beta Kappa, Phi Kappa Phi, Alpha Sigma Nu. Office: Reid & Priest 40 W 57th St New York NY 10019

LONGSTREET, DONNA MAE, librarian; b. Covington, Ky., Jan. 8, 1937; d. Albert and Ola (Jones) L. BS in Commerce, U. Cin., 1962; MLS, U. Denver, 1964; MBA, Calif. State U., Dominguez Hills-Carson, Calif., 1975; JD, Am. Coll. Law, 1980. Cert. Jr. Coll. Educator. Abstracting librarian Standard Oil Co., San Francisco, 1964-65; adult reference librarian Anaheim (Calif.) Pub. Library, 1965-68; law librarian Orange County Law Library, Santa Ana, Calif., 1967-68; bus. law librarian Calif. State U., Long Beach, 1968—; cons. in field. Editor, contbr.: Locating the Law: A Handbook for Non-Law Librarians, 1988; contbr. articles to profl. jours., chpts. to books. Asst. coordinator Area Employees Polit. Info. Ctr., Sacramento, 1987—; gen. del. Calif. Faculty Assn., 1981, 89. Recipient Gold lKey award Dem. Women Orange County, 198l, 85. Mem. Calif. Libr. Assn. (v.p. govt. documents chpt. 1974, pres. 1975, bd. dirs. 1974-76, newsletter editor, 1975-76), So. Calif. Assn. Law Librs. (pub. access to legal info. com. 1987—, cons. com. 1988—, inst. com. 1989—, bibliography com. 1989—). Democrat. Office: Calif State U 1250 Bellflower Blvd Long Beach CA 90840

LONGSTRETH, SUSAN, academic administrator; b. Tacoma, May 9, 1946; d. Charles Magruder and Betty Jane (Foreman) L. AA, Coll. of the Desert, Palm Springs, Calif., 1970; B in Vocat. Edn., Calif. State U., Sacramento, 1980; MA in Edn., Colo. State U., Palm Springs, 1984. Shift leader respiratory therapy dept. Desert Hosp., Palm Springs, Calif., 1969-71; staff therapist Sutter Hosp., Sacramento, 1971-73, inservice coord. respiratory therapy dept., 1973-75; clin. coord. Am. River Coll Respiratory Program, Sacramento, 1975-79; administr., program dir. Healthcare Inst., Sacramento, 1979-80; staff therapist Kaiser Hosp., Sacramento, 1980-82, Poudre Valley Hosp., Ft. Collins, Colo., 1982-83; administrv. asst. Larimer County Voc-Tech. Ctr., Ft. Collins, 1983-86; mgr. evening program Front Range Community Coll./Larimer County Ctr., Ft. Collins, 1986-89, assoc. dean, 1989—. Mem. study group future Larimer County Voc.-Tech., Ft. Collins, 1987. Mem. AAUW, Am. Vocat. Assn., Colo. Vocat. Assn., Omicron Tau Theta. Home: 2501 Powell Pl Fort Collins CO 80526

LONGSWORTH, EILEEN CATHERINE, library director; b. N.Y.C., Feb. 7, 1950; d. Francis L. and Maurine E. (Romkey) Brannigan; m. Laurence S. Woodworth, June 16, 1970 (div. 1982); 1 child, David; m. Bruce Todd Longsworth, May 28, 1983. Student, Dunbarton Coll., 1966-68; BA, U. Md., 1970; MS in Libr. Sci., Cath. U., Washington, 1973. Dept. head Anne Arundel County Pub. Libr., Annapolis, Md., 1974-75, br. librarian, 1975-79; adult services specialist Enoch Pratt Free Libr., Balt., 1979-84; asst. dir. Salt Lake City Pub. Libr., 1984-87; dir. Salt Lake County Libr. System, 1987—. Mem. ALA (chmn. tech. com. 1985-87), Utah Libr. Assn. (chmn. legis com. 1987—, 1st v.p.-pres.-elect 1989-90). Democrat. Home: 860 N Terrace Hills Salt Lake City UT 84103 Office: Salt Lake County Libr System 2197 E 7000 S Salt Lake City UT 84121

LONGSWORTH, ELLEN LOUISE, art historian; b. Auburn, Ind., Aug. 21, 1949; d. Robert Smith and Alice Louise (Whitten) L.; m. Frederic Sanderson Stott, Sept. 1, 1973 (div. 1981). BA, Mt. Holyoke Coll., 1971; MA, U. Chgo., 1976; PhD, Boston U., 1987. Trainer, designer Polaris Enterprises Corp., Quincy, Mass., 1981-82, asst. v.p., 1982-84, cons., 1989—, also bd. dirs.; asst. prof. Merrimack Coll., N. Andover, Mass., 1985—, assoc. prof., 1990—; adj. instr. art and art history Bradford Coll., Haverhill, Mass., 1975-80; visiting lectr. in art history Lowell (Mass.) U., 1981-82, Boston U., 1982-86, 88, Babson Coll., Wellesly, Mass., 1984-85. Mem. Merrimack Valley Coun. on the Arts and Humanities, Haverhill, 1975-78, Friends of Kimball Tavern, Bradford Coll., Haverhill, 1975-80. Grantee Faculty Devel., Merrimack Coll., 1989-90, 90—, Kress Summer Travel, Boston U., summers 1980, 86; fellowship Boston U., 1980-82, 85; recipient internship Isabella Stewart Gardner Museum, Boston, 1979-80. Mem. Coll. Art Assn., Midwest Art History Soc., South-Cen. Renaissance Conf., Am. Assn. Italian Studies, Italian Art Soc. Republican. Methodist. Home: 62 Arlington St Haverhill MA 01830 Office: Merrimack Coll North Andover MA 01845

LONKART, GEORGIA FAITH, banker; b. Trenton, N.J., Jan. 17, 1947; d. George W. and Laura L. (Tilghman) Balles; m. Robert S. Lonkart, Apr. 8, 1967; children: Kevin. L., Scott C. Student, Rutgers U., Camden, 1972-75; BA in English, U. R.I., 1982. Fin. aid officer Brown U., Providence, 1980-84; ops. mgr. R.I. Hosp. Trust Nat. Bank, Providence, 1984-85, ops. officer, 1985-86, asst. v.p., 1986-87, v.p., 1987-89; mgr. sr. ops. Bank of Boston, 1989-90; 1st v.p. R.I. Hosp. Trust (subs. Bank of Boston), Providence, 1990—. Mem. Am. Inst. Bankers, R.I. Assn. Fin. Aid Adminstrs., NAFE, Consumer Bankers Assn. Home: 62 Carue Dr North Scituate RI 02857 Office: RI Hosp Trust 15 Westminster St Providence RI 02903

LOOK, VIVIAN ANN, management assistant, consultant; b. San Francisco; d. Hing Mon and Dor Fook Look; m. Scott Stephen Krieger, Mar. 25, 1988. BS with honors, U. Calif., Berkeley, 1972; MPH, U. Mich., 1980; MPA, Ariz. State U., Tempe, 1984. Trainer, nutritionist Community Nutrition Inst., Washington, 1973-74; tchr. spl. vocat. edn. Springfield (Oreg.) Pub. Schs., 1974-75; asst. prof. Lane Community Coll., Eugene, Oreg., 1974-75; nutritionist Lane County Dept. Health and Social Svcs., Eugene, 1975-79; project cons. Ariz. Dept. Health Svcs., Tempe, 1980-83; rsch. asst. Ariz. State U., Tempe, 1983-84; performance auditor State of Ariz., Phoenix, 1984-87; mgmt. analyst Maricopa County Mgmt., Phoenix, 1987-88; adminstrv. asst. to dep. city mgr. City of Barstow, Calif., 1988-89; asst. exec. officer local agy. formation commn. Sonoma County Adminstr's. Office, 1989—;

mem. task force Western Oreg. Health Systems Agy., Eugene, 1978-79; program chairperson Lane Nutrition Coun., Eugene, 1978-79. Mem. Am. Soc. for Pub. Adminstrn., Calif. Mgmt. Assts. Assn., Cen. Ariz. Dist. Dietetic Assn. (mem. exec. bd. 1982-83, mem. community nutrition sect. chairperson 1981-82, Phi Kappa Phi. Democrat. Presbyterian. Office: 575 Administration Dr Rm 104A Santa Rosa CA 95403

LOOKEBILL, GAYLENE LUCILE, pharmacist, educator; b. Oklahoma City, Mar. 7, 1941; d. ElRoy Charles and Lucile (Hawker) Neely; m. Gary D. Lookebill, Aug. 26, 1960 (div. July 1977); children: Misha, Lauri, Kelly, Paige. BS in Pharmacy, U. Okla., 1967. Registered pharmacist, Okla., Ark. Relief pharmacist Gene Allen Pharmacy, Oklahoma City, 1967-68, Muldrow (Okla.) Pharmacy, 1969-77, Key Drug, Ft. Smith, Ark., 1969-71, Clinic Pharmacy, Poteau, Okla., 1970-75, Wal-Mart Pharmacy, Sallisaw, Okla., 1970-76, City Drug, Van Buren, Ark., 1975-77; pharmacist, mgr. G.B. Pharmakon, Oklahoma City, 1977-81; pharmacist, store asst. mgr., mgr. Revco DS Inc., Edmond, Okla., 1981-90; staff pharmacist VA Hosp., Oklahama City, Okla., 1990—; adj. instr. U. Okla. Coll. Pharmacy, Oklahoma City, 1989—; transistional advisor health care profls. Active rural troop organizer Girl Scouts U.S.A., Muldrow, 1970-77; active wives auxs. for mens orgns., Muldrow, 1970-77; local and regional coach Odyssey of Mind, Edmond, 1981-89. Mem. Am. Pharm. Assn., Acad. Pharmacy Practice and Mgmt., Am. Inst. Practicing Pharmacists (legisl dir. Oklahoma City 1989—, pres. 1989-90), Okla. Pharm. Assn. (employer-employee com., profl. rels. com.), Am. Arbitration Assn., NAFE, Am. Biog. Inst. (rsch. bd. advisors). Democrat. Methodist. Home: 1207 N Washington Ave Edmond OK 73034 Office: Am Inst Practicing Pharms PO Box 4036 Edmond OK 73083-4036

LOOMIS, CAROL J., journalist; b. Marshfield, Mo., June 25, 1929; d. Harold and Mildred (Case) Junge; m. John R. Loomis, Mar. 19, 1960; children: Barbara, Mark. Student, Drury Coll., 1947-49; B in Journalism, U. Mo., 1951. Editor Maytag News, Maytag Co., Newton, Iowa, 1951-54; rsch. assoc. Fortune mag., N.Y.C., 1954-58, assoc. editor, 1958-68, mem. bd. editors, 1968—. Office: Fortune Mag 1271 Ave of Americas New York NY 10020

LOOMIS, JACQUELINE CHALMERS, photographer; b. Hong Kong, Mar. 9, 1930 (parents Am. citizens); d. Earl John and Jennie Bell (Sherwood) Chalmers; m. Charles Judson Williams III, Dec. 2, 1950 (div. Aug. 1973); children: Charles Judson IV, John C., David F., Robert W.; m. Henry Loomis, Jan. 19, 1974; stepchildren: Henry S., Mary Loomis Hankinson, Lucy F., Gordon M. Student, U. Oreg., 1948-50, Nat. Geog. Soc., 1978-79, Winona Sch. Profl. Photography, 1979, Sch. Photo Journalism, U. Mo., 1979. Pres. J. Sherwood Chalmers Photographer, Jacksonville, Fla., 1979—, Windward Corp., Washington, 1984—. Contbr. photos to Nat. Geog. books and mag., Fortune mag., Nat. Newspapers, Ducks Unltd., Living Bird Quar., Orvis News, Frontiers Internat., others, also calendars; one-woman show Woodbury-Blair Mansion, Washington, 1980; rep. in pub. and pvt. collections. Trustee Sta. WJCT-TV, Jacksonville, Fla., 1965-73, mem. exec. com., chmn., 1965-66; co-chmn. Arts Festival, Jacksonville, 1970, chmn., 1971; bd. dirs., mem. exec. com. Nat. Friends Pub. Broadcasting, N.Y.C., 1970-73; bd. dirs. Washington Opera, 1976—, Pub. Broadcasting Svcs., Washington, 1972-73, Planned Parenthood of North Fla., 1968-70; bd. dirs. Jacksonville Art Mus., 1968-70, treas., 1968; bd. dirs. Jacksonville Symphony Assn., 1988—, Home Soc. of Fla., 1988—; bd. womens coun. Cummer Gallery of Art, 1988—. Recipient Cultural Arts award Jacksonville Coun. Arts, 1971, award Easton Waterfowl Festival, 1982, 1st and 2d prizes, 1984. Mem. Profl. Photographers Am. (Merit award 1982), Photog. Soc. Am., Am. Soc. Picture Profls., Jr. League Jacksonville Inc., Fla. Yacht Club (Jacksonville), Amelia Island Plantation Club (Fla.), Ctr. Harbour Yacht Club (Brooklin, Maine). Republican. Presbyterian. Avocations: travel, golf, sailing, skiing, riding., riding. Home and Office: 4661 Ortega Island Dr Jacksonville FL 32210

LOONEY, J. ANNA, corporate affairs officer; b. Winnemucca, Nev., Oct. 22, 1951; d. Robert Holland and Gladys Frances (Shovelin) Raring; m. James E. Looney, May 13, 1978; 1 child, Emily Claire. BA, Ursinus Coll., 1973; MA, SUNY, Stony Brook, 1986. Pub.. policy research Va. Power, Richmond, 1983-87; asst. corp. sec., mgr. corp. affairs Black & Decker Corp., Towson, Md., 1987—. Co-author: Middle Scots Poets Reference Guide, 1985. Mem. Am. Soc. Corp. Secs., Assn. Balt. Area Grantmakers. Republican. Presbyterian. Office: Black & Decker 701 E Joppa Rd Towson MD 21204

LOONEY, MARLENE DE JESUS, marketing professional; b. Havana, Cuba, Aug. 19, 1959; came to U.S., 1965; d. Armando and Maria Luisa (Lastra) Parra; m. Greg A. Looney, May. 31, 1986. BS, Loyola U., Chgo., 1982; postgrad., Lamar U., 1982-84; MBA in Mktg., U. Mo., 1990. Rsch. assoc. U. Tex. Med. Sch., Houston, 1984-85; rsch. asst. U. Kans. Med. Ctr., Kans. City, 1986-87; profl. rep. Merck, Sharp & Dohme, Kansas City, 1987—; invited speaker in field. Active ad hoc com. on recycling, Roeland Park, Kans., 1990; team capt. Neighborhood Watch, Roeland Park, 1990; vol. Fan Club Greater Kans. City, 1988. Latin Am. Student scholar Loyola U., 1978. Mem. Am. Mktg. Assn. Democrat. Roman Catholic.

LOOS, JACKIE JAYNINE, psychologist; b. Marshalltown, Iowa, Mar. 30, 1960; d. Gerald Otis and Arlene Ruby (Tychsen) Navara; m. Paul Eugene Loos, May 26, 1984; 1 child, Ashley. BA in Psychology, Cen. Coll., 1982; EdS in Sch. Psychology, U. No. Iowa, 1985. Cert. psychology tchr., Iowa. Sch. psychologist Arrowhead Area Edn. Agy., Ft. Dodge, Iowa, 1985—. Mem. Nat. Assn. Sch. Psychologists, Iowa Sch. Psychology Asns., Iowa State Edn. Assn., NEA (rep. 1986—). Office: Arrowhead Area Edn Assn 628 Geneseo Storm Lake IA 50588

LOOSLEY, JANINE ELISABETH, chemist; b. Albuquerque, Sept. 15, 1962; d. Donald James and Gwendolin Charlotte (Hammitzsch) L. BS in Chemistry, Mary Washington Coll., 1984; MS in Pharm. Sci., U. Cinn., 1986. Sales clk. Instant Replay, Reston, Va., 1978-81, Woodward and Lothrop, Fairfax, Va., 1981-82; waitress, hostess Caruso's Ristorante, Reston, 1982; waitress Internat. Town & Country Club, Fairfax, 1983; lab. tech. Automata, Inc., Reston, 1983; lab. asst. Mary Washington Coll., Fredericksburg, Va., 1983-84; sales clk. The Hecht Co., McLean, Va., 1984; cosmetic chemist Cosmair, Inc., Clark, N.J., 1986--. Mem. YMCA, Scotch Plains, 1988--, The Deutscher Club, Clark, 1987--. Mem. Soc. Cosmetic Chemists, NAFE, North Jersey Assn. Female Execs. Republican. Lutheran. Office: Cosmair Inc 285 Terminal Ave Clark NJ 07066

LOOTS, BARBARA KUNZ, writer; b. Kansas City, Mo., Sept. 30, 1946; d. William Ellis and Doris Karcher (Schuerman) Kunz; m. Larry Rolfe Loots, July 20, 1969. BA, Winthrop Coll., 1967. Writer Hallmark Cards, Kansas City, 1967-70, 85—, editor, 1970-79, mgr., 1979-85; writing workshop cons. Jewish Community Ctr. and pub. sch., Kansas City, 1972--. Author: The Bride's Mirror Speaks, 1985, Sibyl and Sphinx, 1988; author numerous poems. Recipient Hanks award-2nd St. Louis Poetry Ctr., 1988. Mem. Poets and Writers, Inc. Presbyterian. Home: 7943 Charlotte Kansas City MO 64131

LOPACKI, JOAN MARIE, marketing professional; b. Toledo, Mar. 23, 1957; d. John Thaddeus and Margie Ann (Weiland) Szaroleta; m. Edwin Anthony Lopacki Jr., Sept. 3, 1983; children: Margaret Anna, Mitchell Edwin. BFA, Bowling Green State U., 1978; MBA, U. Toledo, 1983. Art dir. Thomas Hart Assocs., Toledo, 1979-83; mgr. advt. Am.-Lincoln, Bowling Green, Ohio, 1983-84, W.S. Jenks & Son, Washington, 1984-88; mgr. mktg. The Source, Springfield, Va., 1988—. Office: The Source 7305 Boudinot Dr Springfield VA 22150

LOPATO, ESTHER WOLF, psychologist; b. N.Y.C., Aug. 29, 1920; d. Philip and Rose (Herman) Wolf; married 1950; children: Leslie Lopato-Getz, David Lopato. BS, City Coll. N.Y., N.Y.C., 1948, MA, 1949; PhD, NYU, 1961. Lic. psychologist, N.Y. Psychologist NYU, 1961-88; pvt. practice N.Y.C., 1988—; adj. asst. prof. NYU, 1971-72, Bklyn. Coll., N.Y.C., 1973-75; psychologist, cons. N.Y.C. Bd. Edn., 1975-81. Bd. dirs. community planning, Bklyn., 1972—; trustee Bklyn. Pub. Libr., 1973—; mem. Community Sch. Bd., Bklyn., 1970-72. Mem. N.Y. State Assn. Libr. Bds. (bd. dirs. 1974—, Velma K. Moore award 1984, NYLA, Outstanding Contbns. 1989), ALTA (bd. dirs. 1982—, Outstanding Contbns. 1981). Home and Office: 1231 E 21 St Brooklyn NY 11210

LOPER, CANDICE KAY, computer analyst; b. Sublette, Kans., Oct. 29, 1953; d. Robert Franklin and Marion Joyce (Sooby) L. Student, McPherson (Kans.) Coll., 1971-72; lic. in cosmetology, Crums Beauty Sch., Manhattan, Kans., 1974; student, Garden City (Kans.) Community Coll., 1975-76, Diablo Valley Coll., 1988-89. Owner, operator Candi's For Beautiful Hair, Garden City, 1974-78; systems project librarian Bank of Am., San Francisco, 1980, analyst, 1981, systems analyst, 1981-82, sr. systems analyst, 1982-83, cons., 1983-84, systems cons., team leader, 1984; project mgr. Wells Fargo Bank, Concord, Calif., 1984-86; systems analyst 1st Nationwide Bank, San Francisco, 1986-88; adv. systems engr. Bank Am., Concord, Calif., 1988-89; owner Loper Comp-U-Pix, Independence, Mo., 1988—; systems analyst Policyholder Svc. Corp., Kansas City, Mo., 1989—. Home: 3419 S Home Ave Independence MO 64052 Office: Policyholder Svc Corp 1004 Baltimore Kansas City MO 64105

LOPER, CHARLENE M., military officer; b. Allentown, Pa., Mar. 11, 1958; d. Henry Noe and Pauline E.L. (Hubbard) Magnon; m. Leonard J. Loper, Mar. 29, 1985; 1 child, John W. BS, N.E. La. U., 1979; MS, U. So. Calif., 1989. Commd. 2d lt. U.S. Army, 1979, advanced through grades to capt.; platoon leader to exec. officer 101st M.I. Bn. U.S. Army, Ft. Riley, Kans., 1979-81, assignments officer 1st Inf. Div., 1981-83; with pers. staff office 184th Transp. Brigade Miss. Army N.G. U.S. Army, Laurel, 1983-86; from tng. officer to brigade electronic warfare officer to bn. ops. officer then co. comdr. 103d M.I. Bn. U.S. Army, Wurzburg, Fed. Republic Germany, 1986-90; chief ops. and resource mgmt. Field Sta. Berlin U.S. Army, 1990—. Decorated Army Achievement medal, Army Commendation medal, Meritorious Svc. medal. Mem. Marne Assn., Assn. Old Crows, Phi Kappa Phi. Roman Catholic. Address: HHS OPS BN FSB APO New York NY 09742

LOPER, JANET SWANSON, data processing executive; b. Dunkirk, N.Y., Sept. 17, 1934; d. Ralph Edwin and Isabel Spencer (Emerson) Swanson; B.S. in Sales Mgmt., Syracuse U., 1956; m. Lyle C. Loper, Oct. 15, 1971. Systems engr. IBM, Rochester, N.Y., 1956-58, tech. writer, product planner, Endicott, N.Y., 1959-66, planner instruction systems devel. dept., Los Gatos, Calif., 1966-70, mem. R.B. Johnson fellow program, 1970-72, communications analyst, gen. systems div., 1972-79, application devel. cons., 1975-79; v.p., dir. communications Citibank, N.Y.C., 1979-84; pres. Info. Integrators, Inc., 1984—; cons. U.S. Office Edn., 1970. Co-chmn. higher edn. com. Collier Cultural and Ednl. Ctr., 1989—. Recipient Outstanding Contbn. award IBM, 1975. Mem. Am. Bus. Women's Assn. (pres. Binghamton chpt. 1964-66), Soc. Tech. Communications (past program dir.), Data Processing Mgmt. Assn. (past internat. dir.), Naple's C. of C. (chmn. higher edn. com. 1989—).

LOPES, MYRA AMELIA, educator; b. Nantucket, Mass., Sept. 7, 1931; d. Leo Joseph and Mary Ellen (Moriarty) Powers; m. Curtis Linwood Lopes, June 25, 1955; children: Dennis, Sherry, Kathy, Curtis, Becky. BS, Bridgewater, 1954; diploma, Inst. Children's Lit., 1982, N.Y. Inst. Journalism, 1984. Cert. elem. educator, Mass. Tchr. Fairhaven (Mass.) Sch. System, 1954-58; prin. Sheri Ka Kindergarten, Fairhaven, 1960-76; market promotion Store Systems, Greater New Bedford, Mass., 1976-82; writer Fairhaven Sch. System, 1987—, fund raiser, reading promoter, 1987—. Author: Look Around You, 1990. Pres. Fairhaven Improvement Assn., 1990-91, bd. dirs., 1986-90, chmn. membership, 1986-89, chmn. beautification, 1988-89. Recipient Nat. award 1989 Outstanding Community Vol., 1989, Outstanding Svc. award YWCA, 1985. Mem. YWCA (chmn. personnel bd. 1984-88, nominating chmn. 1983-84, community relations chmn. 1982-83, bd. dirs. 1982-88). Democrat. Roman Catholic. Home: 71 Fort St Fairhaven MA 02719

LOPEZ, ELIZABETH JEANNETTE, pyhsician; b. Merced, Calif., Sept. 11, 1958; d. Refugio and Vera (Melgoza) Lopez; m. Cesar Pablo Velaquez, May 6, 1988. BA in Physiology, U. Calif., 1980; postgrad., U. Minn., 1986. Research asst. Univ. Calif., Berkeley, Calif., 1977-80, teaching asst., 1979; research asst. San Francisco Gen. Hosp., 1980--81; family practice resident San Bernardino County Med. Ctr., 1986—. Mem. Mpls. Community Forum, 1985; vol. Inland Diabetes Control Program. Mem. Am. Acad. Family Physicians, Calif. Med. Assn., San Bernardino County Med. Soc., Calif. House Officer Med. Soc., Am. Med. Assn. Democrat. Roman Catholic. Office: San Bernardino County Med Ctr 727 W Childs Ave Merced CA 95341

LOPEZ, GERALDINE JEAN, food services professional; b. New Orleans, Mar. 11, 1968; d. Charles Ivy and Iceline Ann (Conner) L. Grad. high sch., 1986. Gen. mgr. Gulf Coast Food Svc. Inc., New Orleans, 1983-86; sr. mgr. Rax Restaurant, New Orleans, 1986-88, mktg. dir., 1987-88; gen. mgr. Al Copeland Enterprises, New Orleans, 1988—. Mem. NAFE. Democratic. Catholic. Home: 1300 W Esplande Apt 20 Ste F Kenner LA 70065

LOPEZ, KATHLEEN ANNE, dietitian; b. New Haven, Dec. 25, 1957; d. Joseph Anthony and Gladys Marie (Schneider) Roderick; m. Alcides Lopez Jr., Aug. 1, 1987. BS in Dietetics with highest honors, Calif. Poly. U., 1980. Registered dietitian. Dietetic intern Mass. Gen. Hosp., Boston, 1980-81; chief clin. dietitian ARA Svcs., Eureka, Calif., 1982-83; asst. dir. food svcs. ARA Food Svcs., Riverside, Calif., 1983-85; asst. food svc. mgr. Food Dimensions Inc., San Jose, Calif., 1985-87; chief clin. dietitian Food Dimensions Inc., Vallejo, Calif., 1987-88, dir. food svcs., 1987-88; mgr. nutritional svcs. Sonoma Valley Hosp., Calif., 1988-90; nutrition cons. Mem. NAFE, Am. Dietetic Assn., Sonoma Valley Cuisine Soc., Phi Kappa Phi, Phi Upsilon Omicron. Home: 114 W Aqua Caliente Rd Sonoma CA 95476 Office: 347 Andrieux St Sonoma CA 95476

LOPEZ, KAY STRICKLAND, company executive; b. Meridian, Miss., Aug. 20, 1946; d. Wilburn Clayton and Winifred Craven (Meador) Moncrief; m. James Wilburn Strickland, May 17, 1968 (div. Apr. 1985); children: Cherie Dail, Jamie Kay; m. James Lopez, July 18, 1987. Student, Annual Ednl. Workshop, 1976-86. V.p. co-owner Rain-Flow of Houston, Inc., Stafford, Tex., 1972-87; pres., owner Landscape Maintenance of Tex., Ft. Worth, 1988—, Tex. Gutters, Inc., Ft. Worth, 1987—. Named Credit Woman of Yr. Houston Credit Women's Group, 1982, Credit Exec. of Yr. Houston Assn. Credit Mgmt., 1985-86; recipient Presdl. award., Houston, 1986. Fellow Nat. Inst. Credit; mem. Nat. Assn. Credit Mgmt. (cert. credit exec., bd. dirs. Ft. Worth div. 1986-87), Tex. Assn. Builders, Tarrant County Builders Assn., Houston Credit Women's Group (sec. 1978-79, treas. 1981-82, v.p. 1983-84, pres. 1984-85, counselor 1985-86), Order of Eastern Star. Republican. Methodist. Home: 2324 Field Fort Worth TX 76117 Office: Tex Gutters Inc Po Box 14066 Fort Worth TX 76117

LOPEZ, MICHELINE BRIERRE, artist, designer; b. Jeremie, Haiti, June 9, 1943; came to U.S., 1981; d. Luc H. and Simone (Lataillade) Brierre; divorced; children: Charles, Lisa. Studied at Nehemie-Jean Art Acad., Haiti, Ramponeau Art Sch., Haiti, Miraflores Art Ctr., Lima, Peru. Owner All Things Beautiful, Miami, Fla., 1985—; conductor lectures and workshops/seminars on creativity, personal devel. and metaphysics. Numerous exhibits of paintings, jewelry and drawings include Haiti, P.R., Colombia, Miami; author: Soy Eva; contbr. articles to mags., profl. jours. Regional dir. Inner Peace Program, Haiti, 1976-80. Address: PO Box 570-577 Miami FL 33257

LOPEZ, NANCY, professional golfer; b. Torrance, Calif., Jan. 6, 1957; d. Domingo and Marina (Griego) L.; m. Ray Knight, Oct. 25, 1982; children: Ashley Marie, Erinn Shea. Student, U. Tulsa, 1976-78. Profl. golfer Ladies Profl. Golf Assn., 1978—. Author: The Education of a Woman Golfer, 1979. First victor at Bent Tree Classic, Sarasota, Fla., 1978; Named AP Athlete for 1978; admitted to Ladies Profl. Golf Assn. Hall of Fame, 1987, to PGA World Golf Hall of Fame, 1989. Mem. Ladies Profl. Golf Assn. (Player and Rookie of Yr. 1978). Republican. Baptist. Office: 1 Erieview Pla Cleveland OH 44114

LOPEZ, PIA, paralegal; b. Jovellano, Matanzas, Cuba, July 11, 1937; came to U.S., 1969; d. Francisco Perez and Ramona Cabrera; m. Carlos Martin Lopez, Sept. 16, 1960; children: Marcia, Maruchy, Carlos. PhD in Pedagogy, U. Havana, Havana, Cuba, 1963; BA, Montclair State Coll., 1974. Cert. sch. adminstr., N.J. Social worker Jersey City, 1974-75; bilingual tchr. Jersey City Bd. Edn., 1975-82; Hispanic affairs dir., mayor's aid City of Union City, N.J., 1982-86; paralegal Pena & Ahl, Esqs., Union City, N.J., 1987—. Founder Assn. Cuban Am. Women, Union City, 1981; mem. League of Women Voters, N.J., 1989—, Hudson County Rep. Party, 1989—. Named Woman of the Year Art & Culture Assn., 1985, Woman of the Year, Fontana de Treve, 1988. Mem. Salvadorians Assn. (pres. 1985—), Dominican Rep. Assn. (pres. 1984—), Fedn. Hispanic Am. Students (founder 1980—), Caballero de la Luz (founder 1975-89), Odd Fellows, Masonic Order. Republican. Roman Catholic. Home: 4700 New York Ave Union City NJ 07087 Office: Pena & Ahl Esqs 314 48th St Union City NJ 07087

LOPEZ, ROSEMARY, electrical engineer; b. Gary, Ind., Mar. 21, 1963; d. Daniel and Maria (Canchola) Lopez. BSEE, Purdue U., 1987. Mgmt. assoc. midwest div. Nat. Steel Corp., Portage, Ind., 1988-89, engr. midwest div., 1989—. Co-founder, pres. Hispanic Alumni Soc., 1988-90; mem. N.W. Ind. Hispanic Coordinating Coun., 1987—; sec. League of United Latin Am. Citizens Coun., Merrillville, Ind., 1989, Los Latinos of Purdue U., 1987; advisor Jr. Achievement, Portage, Ind., 1988. Mem. Soc. Hispanic Profl. Engrs., Soc. Women Engrs. (pres.). Democrat. Roman Catholic. Home: 842 Delaware St Gary IN 46402 Office: Nat Steel Corp Midwest div US Rte 12 Portage IN 46368

LOPEZ, WILMA IDA, temporary employment company executive; b. Santurce, P.R., June 9, 1938; d. Angel Luis and Verania (Morales) L.; children: Rene Luis Aviles, Angel Luis Aviles. BA in Psychology, U. P.R., 1959. Sales mgr. Empresas Diaz, Rio Piedras, P.R., 1964-67; real estate broker Mackle Bros., Daytona, Fla., 1967-70; record mgr. San Juan (P.R.) City Hall, 1970-73; mgr. P.R., Kelly Svcs., Inc., Hato Rey, 1973—, v.p. regional offices, 1988—. Mem. Am. Soc. Pers. Adminstrs., P.R. C. of C., P.R. Mfrs. Assn. (bd. dirs.), Sales and Mktg. Execs. Assn., Am. Bus. Women Assn., Zonta Internat. Republican. Roman Catholic. Office: Kelly Temp Svcs Inc Scotiabank Pla Ste 107 Hato Rey PR 00917

LOPEZ-FALKOWSKI, SONIA MILAGROS, teacher; b. San Juan, P.R., Oct. 25, 1942; d. Luis and Milagros (Duran) Lopez; m. Daniel Carl Falkowski; children: Tanya Marynka, James Daniel. High Sch. diploma, Bayridge High Sch., Bklyn., 1960; BA, New York U., 1964; MA in Modern Lang., Middlebury Coll., Vt., 1971. Permanent New York State Cert. in Teaching Spanish Levels. English tchr. Ciudad Satelite, Mex., 1962; Spanish tchr. Patchogue Sr. High Sch., N.Y.C., 1965-66; Modern Lang. instr. Northwestern U., Boston, 1969-72, Canisius Coll., Buffalo; Systems analyst, programmer M&T Bank, Williamsville, N.Y.C., 1980-84; Spanish tchr. Depew High Sch., 1986-87, Cleve. Hill High Sch., Cheektowaga, N.Y.C., 1987-89; Translator Dresser Industries, Inc., Sports Services Inc. Buffalo 1975-79; Tchr. Canisius Coll. Buffalo 1975-79. Contbr. poems, articles to profl. jours. 1968-89. Vol. Leukemia Soc., Am. Cancer Soc. Buffalo, N.Y.C. 1987-89. Recipient Medal award Pan Am. Orgn. N.Y.C. 1958. Mem. Judge Western New York Fgn. Lang. Educators Coun., Ill. Circolo. Roman Catholic. Office: Cleveland Hill High Sch Mapleview Drive Cheektowaga NY 14226

LOPEZ-GOMEZ, SUSANA, controller; b. San Salvador, El Salvador, Apr. 8, 1955; came to U.S. 1980, naturalized 1987; d. Mario H. and Esther C. (Gomez) Lopez; m. Efrain R. Lara, Oct. 1, 1980; children: Francisco, Carlos. BA in Econs. summa cum laude, CCNY, 1984, MA in Bus. Adminstrn. and Econs., 1984. Analyst programmer Planning Ministry, El Salvador, 1974-79; acct. Showstoppers..., N.Y.C., 1980-84; acctg. mgr. Standard Enterprises, N.Y.C., 1984-85; contr. Comint Leather Goods, Inc., Saddle Brook, N.J., 1985. Editor, reporter: Our Bulletin, 1990. Mem. Saddle Brook C. of C. Democrat. Roman Catholic. Home: 26 Wolffe St Yonkers NY 10705

LOPEZ-MUNOZ, MARIA ROSA P., land development company executive; b. Havana, Cuba, Jan. 28, 1938; came to U.S., 1960; d. Eleuterio Perfecto and Bertha (Carmenati Colon) Perez Rodriguez; m. Gustavo Lopez-Munoz, Sept. 9, 1973. Student, Candler Coll., Havana, 1951-53; Sch. Langs., U. Jose Marti, Havana, 1954-55. Lic. interior designer, real estate broker. Pres. Fantasy World Acres, Inc., Coral Gables, Fla., 1970-84, pres., dir., 1984—; sec. Sandhills Corp., Coral Gables, Fla., 1978-85, dir., 1978—. Treas. Am. Cancer Soc., Miami, Fla., 1981, sec. Hispanic Bd., 1987, pres. Hispanic div., 1989, bd. dirs., aux. treas.; bd. dirs. Am. Heart Assn., Miami, 1985, chmn. Hispanic div.; bd. dirs. YMCA, Young Patronesses of Opera, Miami, 1985, Lowe Mus. of U. Miami, 1986—, Linda Ray Infant Ctr.; trustee Ronald McDonald House. Recipient Merit award Am. Cancer Soc., 1980, 81, 82, 83, 84; Woman with Heart Award, Am. Heart Assn., 1985, Merit awards, 1980-84, Women of Yr., 1986; named to Gt. Order of José Marti, 1988. Mem. Real Estate Commn. Republican. Roman Catholic. Clubs: Ocean Reef (Key Largo, Fla.); Opera Guild (Miami); Key Biscayne Yacht; Regine's International (Paris), Jockey. Avocations: yachting, snow skiing, scuba diving, guitar, piano. Office: Fantasy World Acres Inc 147 Alhambra Circle Suites 220-21 Coral Gables FL 33134

LOPKER, ANITA MAE, psychiatrist; b. San Diego, May 25, 1955; d. Louis Donald and Betty Jean (Sayman-Campbell) L. BA magna cum laude, U. Calif., San Diego, 1978; MD, U. Rochester, 1982. Diplomate Nat. Bd. Med. Examiners. Intern in internal medicine Yale U. Sch. Medicine-Greenwich Hosp., 1982-83; resident in psychiatry Yale U. Sch. of Medicine, 1983-86; postdoctoral fellow Yale U. Sch. Medicine, New Haven, Conn., 1982-86; clin. instr. Yale U. Sch. Medicine, New Haven, 1986-88; pvt. practice Westport, Conn., 1987—; cons. psychiatrist, Yale-New Haven Hosp. Lyme Disease Study Clinic, 1987—, Yale U. Lyme Disease Rsch. Project, 1986—, Alcoholism and Drug Dependency Coun., Inc., 1989—. Contbr. articles to profl. jours. Founding mem. Nat. Mus. for Women in the Arts, Washington, 1987; mem. Menninger Found. Mem. AAAS, N.Y. Acad. Scis., Am. Psychiat. Assn., Conn. Psychiat. Soc., World Fedn. Mental Health, Menninger Found., Alpha Omega Alpha, Phi Beta Kappa. Home: 27 Strathmore Ln Westport CT 06880 Office: 21 Bridge Sq Westport CT 06880

LOPO, ALINA CONCEPCION, developmental biologist; b. Havana, Cuba, June 14, 1951; came to U.S., 1960; d. Armando Jesus and Emma (Gonzalez) L.; m. Stephen Landis Wolfe, July 30, 1982; 1 child, Christopher Thomas. AA, Miami Dade Community Coll., 1970; BS, U. Miami, 1972, MS, 1974; PhD, U. Calif., Davis, 1979. Postdoctoral researcher U. Calif. Med. Ctr., San Francisco, 1979-81, Davis, 1981-85; asst. prof. Biomed. Sci. dept. U. Calif., Riverside, 1985—. Author: Lab Tex Developmental Biology, 1982; contbr. articles to profl. jours. Numerous postdoctoral fellowships, 1979-85. Mem. AAAS, Nat. Network of Hispanic Women, Am. Soc. Cell Biology, Soc. for Deve. Biology, Am. Soc. Biochemistry and Molecular Biology. Home: PO Box 5520 Riverside CA 92517

LORBER, CHARLOTTE LAURA, publisher; b. Bklyn, Apr. 11, 1952; d. Morris and Libby (Slatsky) L. BBA in Fin., U. Miami, 1975. Dir. special events Third Century U.S.A. Dade County Bicentenial Orgn., Miami, Fla., 1975-76; promotion dir. Donato Advt. Co., Coral Gables, Fla., 1977-78; pres. Towne Pub. & Advt. Co., Inc., Coral Gables, Fla., 1979—. Publisher: (directories) View of our City, 1985-86 (Excellence award), Greater Miami Chamber, 1986-87 (Merit award), (brochure) Big Does Mean Better, 1986-87 (Merit award). Recipient Merit award City of Hialeah, 1977. Mem. Am. C. of C. Execs., Greater Miami C. of C. (trustee), Coral Gables C. of C., Miami Beach C. of C. (trustee), South Miami C. of C., North Dade C. of C., World Trade Ctr. Lodge: Rotary. Office: Towne Pub & Advt 4203 Salzedo St Coral Gables FL 33146

LORD, BETTE BAO, writer; b. Shanghai, China, Nov. 3, 1938; came to U.S., 1946, naturalized, 1964; d. Sandys and Dora (Fang) Bao; B.A., Tufts U., 1959, M.A., 1960, hon. doctorate, 1982; hon. doctorate, U. Notre Dame, 1985; m. Winston Lord, May 4, 1963; children: Elizabeth Pillsbury, Winston Bao. Asst. to dir. East-West Cultural Center, Honolulu, 1961-62; program officer Fulbright Exchange Program for Sr. Scholars, 1962-63; dancer, tchr. modern dance, Geneva and Washington, 1964-73; conf. dir. Assoc. Councils of the Arts, N.Y.C., 1970-71; writer, lectr., 1982—; author: (non-fiction) Eighth Moon, 1964 (Readers' Digest Condensed Books), (novel) Spring Moon, a novel of China (Lit. Guild selection), 1981, In the Year of the Boar and Jackie Robinson (named one of best books for children AIH), 1984, Legacies: A Chinese Mosaic, 1990. Mem. selection bd. White House Fellows, 1979-81; bd. dirs. Nat. Com. U.S.-China Rels., Inc., N.Y.C., 1982. Named

Woman of Yr., Chinatown Planning Council, 1982; recipient Nat. Geographic Art prize, 1974, Disting. Ams. Fgn. Birth award, 1984, Disting. Am. award Internat. Ctr., 1984. Mem. Asia Soc. (Pres.'s council), Asia Found., Coun. on Fgn. Rels., PEN, Authors Guild. Address: 740 Park Ave #2A New York NY 10021

LORD, JACQUELINE WARD, accountant, photographer, artist; b. Andalusia, Ala., May 16, 1936; d. Marron J. and Minnie V. (Owen) Ward; m. Curtis Gaynor, Nov. 23, 1968. Student U. Ala., 1966, Auburn U., 1977, Huntingdon Coll., 1980, Troy State U., 1980; B.A. in Bus. Adminstrn., Dallas Bapt. U., 1985. News photographer corr. Andalusia (Ala.) Star-News, 1954-59, Sta. WSFA-TV, Montgomery, Ala., 1954-60; acct., bus. mgr. Reihardt Motors, Inc., Montgomery, 1962-69; office mgr., acct. Cen. Ala. Supply, Montgomery, 1969-71; acct. Chambers Constrn. Co., Montgomery, 1972-75; pres. Foxy Lady Apparel, Inc., Montgomery, 1973-76; acct. Rushton, Stakely, Johnston & Garrett, attys., Montgomery, 1975-81; acctg. supr. Arthur Andersen & Co., Dallas, 1981-82; staff acct. Burgess Co., C.P.A.s, Dallas, 1983; owner Lord & Assocs. Acctg. Service, Dallas, 1983—; tax acct. John Hasse, C.P.A., Dallas, 1984-86; Dallas Bapt. Assn., 1986—. Vol. election law commr. Sec. of State of Ala. Don Siegelman, Montgomery, 1979-80; mem. Montgomery Art Guild, 1964-65, Ala. Art League, 1964-65, Montgomery Little Theatre, 1963-65, Montgomery Choral Soc., 1965. Recipient Outstanding Achievement Bus. Mgmt. award Am. Motors, 1968. Mem. Am. Soc. Women Accts. (pres. Montgomery chpt. 1976-77, area day chmn. 1978, del. ann. meeting 1975-78). Home: 5209 Meadowside Dr Garland TX 75043

LORD, SALLY ANN, business consultant; b. Pitts., Nov. 25, 1966; d. Winston William and Georgetta Ann (Oravec) L. Grad. high sch., Gibsonia, Pa. Personnel mgmt. cons. Vincent J. Marsico Co., Valencia, Pa., 1984—; v.p., treas. Fin. Analysis Group, Valencia, 1985—; treas. Affiliated Leasing Personnel, Gibsonia, 1986—. Mem. Nat. Soc. Female Execs., Pitts. Life Underwriters. Republican. Roman Catholic. Home: Rte 4 Box 242 Valencia PA 16059 Office: Fin Analysis Group RD #3 Box 84B Valencia PA 16059

LORDI, SUSAN LOUISE, nurse educator; b. N.Y.C., Dec. 15, 1937; d. Cornelius Francis and Eileen (Fox) Schilo; m. Vincent John Lordi, Nov. 12, 1960; children: Dena, John. AA, Diploma in Nursing, Pasadena (Calif.) City Coll., 1957; BS in Nursing, Cath. U. Am., Washington, 1959; MS, Calif. State U., Long Beach, 1979. Cert. pediatric nurse practitioner. Pub. health nurse L.A. County Health Dept., L.A., 1959-60; sch. nurse L.A. Unified Sch. Dist., 1960-63, Pomona (Calif.) Unified Sch. Dist., 1967-80; instr. Calif. State U., Long Beach, 1979-88; coord. health, edn. and health svcs. Pasadena Unified Sch. Dist., 1980-83; cons. health svc. div. evaluation, attendance and pupil svc. L.A. County Office Edn., Downey, Calif., 1983—; mem. Statewide Nursing Program Adv. Com., Calif. State U., 1985-89; mem. Health Careers Adv. Com., Hosp. Coun. So. Calif., 1988—; mem. AIDS Edn. Adv. Com., Calif. Dept. Edn., 1988—; project dir. L.A. County AIDS Tchr. Tng. Grant, 1988—; mem. Task Force on Specialized Phys. Health Care Svcs., 1987—; mem. Credential Consortium Task Force on Revision of Criteria for Evaluation of Profl. Sch. Nurse Eddn. Programs in Calif., 1986-88; mem. Sch. Health Svcs. Adv. Com., 1984-85. Mem. East Area Maternal, Child and Adolescent Adv. Com., L.A., 1980—, County Task Force on Proposition 99 Implementation, 1989—. Fellow Nat. Assn. Pediatric Nurse Assocs., Practitioners (Svc. award 1983, standards of practice task force 1980-87, chair task force on sch. nurse evaluation), Am. Sch. Health Assn. (mem. CE conf. rev. com. 1990, pres. 1990—; CE chmn. 1986-89), Nat. Assn. Sch. Nurses (pres. 1990-91), Calif. Sch. Nurse Orgn. (exec. bd. 1983-89, recognition and svc. award 1983-89), Pi Gamma Mu, Phi Kappa Phi. Roman Catholic. Home: 303 Spinnaker Way Seal Beach CA 90740 Office: LA County Office Edn 9300 Imperial Hwy Rm 210 Downey CA 90247

LORENTSON, HOLLY JEAN, health facility executive; b. Mpls., Nov. 27, 1956; d. Leslie Arnold and Mary Ann Jean (Anderson) L. BA in Nursing, Coll. St. Catherine, St. Paul, 1978; MPH, U. Minn., 1986. RN, Minn.; registered pub. health nurse. Nurse Abbott/Northwestern Hosp., Mpls., 1978-79; acting dir. community nursing services Ebenezer Soc., Mpls., 1979-81, pub. health nurse supr., 1981-82; charge nurse Ebenezer Hall nursing Home, Mpls., 1982-84; patient services coordinator San Diego Hospice Corp., 1984-85, exec. dir., 1985-88, pres., 1988—; mem. fiscal intermediary provider task force Region X Health Care Financing Adminstrn., 1984-88. Mem. Nat. Hospice Orgn., Internat. Soc. Pres. Non-Profit Orgn., Calif. Hospice Assn. (v.p. 1985-88), Calif. Assn. Health Svcs. at Home (com. mem.), Rotary, Sierra Club, Soroptimists. Office: San Diego Hospice Corp 9797 Aero Dr Ste B San Diego CA 92123

LORENTZEN, MARIANNE LOUISE, television executive; b. Mpls., June 10, 1949; d. Anthony Joseph and Marcella (Myszka) Bury; m. Robert Roy Lorentzen, Sept. 21, 1973; children: Brian, Kristin. AA, North Hennepin Coll., Mpls., 1971. Sec. treas. Interlachen, Inc., Brainerd, Minn., 1973—, Video Techniques, Inc., Bradenton, Fla., 1980—. Contbr. to profl. publ. Mem. adv. bd. Kind Med. Sch., Bradenton, 1986, 87, 89; facilitator Leadership Manatee, 1989-90, sec.; Bd. dirs. Red Carpet Sch. Award; mem. Dist. Adv. Bd. Com. for Schs. Recipient Marie Abel award for best show Fla. State Fair, 1986. Mem. Burka Art Assn. (corr. sec. 1984-86, 2d v.p. 1986-88, first place award Am. Japanese chpt. 1986). Roman Catholic. Office: Video Techniques Inc 600 US 301 Blvd W Ste 188 Bradenton FL 34205

LORENZ, CAROL ELAINE, customer service manager; b. San Antonio, Dec. 15, 1946; d. Arthur August and Olga Meta (Schmidt) L.; m. M. David Preston, Apr. 29, 1989. BA, Tex. Tech., 1968; MS, Duke U., 1975; PhD, N.C. State U., 1986. lic. physical therapist, N.C. Field svcs. dir. Girl Scouts U.S., Wichita Falls, Tex., 1968-70, Agana, Guam, 1971-73; dir. physical therapy Hillhaven Nursing Home, Durham, N.C., 1975-76; dir. physical, occupational therapy Murdoch Ctr. Mentally Retarded, Butner, N.C., 1976-80; pres., owner Triangle Therapy Assocs., Hillsborough, N.C., 1980-84; coord. productivity programs Northern Telecom, Rsch. Triangle Pk., N.C., 1984-86; mgr. mfg. Northern Telecom, Rsch. Triangle Pk., 1986-87, Creedmoor, N.C., 1987-88; mgr. materials Northern Telecom, Creedmoor, 1988-89; mgr. customer liason Northern Telecom, Rsch. Triangle Park, 1989—. Past chief, life mem., Orange County Rescue Squad, Hillsborough, N.C., 1981—; mem. Altrusa Wichita Falls, Tex., 1970. Recipient Leadership award Orange County Rescue Squad, 1988. Mem. Am. Production and Inventory Control Soc., Internat. Assn. of Quality Circles (pres. Durham N.C., 1984-85) Inst. Indusl. Engrs., N.C. Physical Therapy Assn. (chmn. pub. relations 1977). Democrat. Lutheran. Home: 124 Murdock Rd Hillsborough NC 27278

LORENZ, KATHERINE MARY, banker; b. Barrington, Ill., May 1, 1946; d. David George and Mary (Hogan) L. BA cum laude, Trinity Coll., 1968; MBA, Northwestern U., 1971; grad., Grad. Sch. for Bank Adminstrn., 1977. Ops. analyst Continental Bank, Chgo., 1968-69, supr. ops. analysis, 1969-71, asst. mgr. customer profitability analysis, 1971-73, acctg. officer, mgr. customer profitability analysis, 1973-77, 2d v.p., 1976, asst. gen. mgr. controller's dept., 1977-80, v.p., 1980, controller ops. and mgmt. services dept., 1981-84, v.p., sector controller retail banking, corp. staff and ops. depts., 1984-88, v.p., sr. sector controller pvt. banking, centralized ops. and corp. staff, 1988-90, v.p., sr. sector controller bus. analysis group, 1990—. Mem. Nat. Assn. for Bank Cost and Mgmt. Acctg., Fin. Women Internat., Execs. Club Chgo. Office: Continental Bank 231 S LaSalle St Chicago IL 60697

LORENZEN, HEIDI CHRISTINE, editor; b. N.Y.C., Dec. 20, 1963; d. Carsten Christian Lorenzen and Susan Claire (Johnson) Bormolini. Student, Taipei Lang. Inst., 1984; BA in East Asian Studies, Middlebury U., 1985; postgrad., Chinese U. Hong Kong, 1988; MBA in Internat. Bus., NYU, 1989. With Irving Trust, N.Y.C., 1982; editor United Pacific Internat. Inc., Taipei, Taiwan, 1985-86; co-founder, dir. bus. devel. Larco Internat. Ltd., Taipei, 1986—; cons. Urban Bus. Assistance Corp., N.Y.C., 1987-88; asst. program dir. Bus. Week Exec. Programs, N.Y.C., 1989, program dir., 1989—; interpreter World Trade Inst., Washington, 1988; mktg. cons. Passion Food and Music, Taipei, 1986. Mem. NAFE, Asia Soc., Women's Career Forum (co-pres. 1987-89), Mgmt. Cons. Assn., Phi Beta Kappa. Democrat. Lutheran. Office: Bus Week 1221 6th Ave 36th Fl New York NY 10021

LORIMER, LINDA KOCH, college president, educator; M. Ernest McFaul Lorimer; children: Katharine Elizabeth, Peter Brailler. AB, Hollins Coll., 1974; JD, Yale U., 1977; DHL, Green Mountain Coll., 1981. Bar: N.Y., Conn. Assoc. Davis Polk and Wardwell, N.Y.C., 1977-78; asst. gen. counsel Yale U., New Haven, 1978-79, assoc. gen. counsel, 1979-84, assoc. provost, 1983-87, acting assoc. v.p. human resources, 1984-85; prof. law, pres. Randolph-Macon Woman's Coll., Lynchburg, Va., 1987—; lectr. Yale Coll. Undergrad. Seminars, 1980, 83; bd. dirs. Centel Corp.; mem. com. on responsible conduct rsch. Inst. Medicine, NAS, 1988; cons., counsel Women's Coll. Coalition; mem. Corp. of Yale U. Editor, chair editorial bd. Jour. Coll. and Univ. Law, 1983-87. Former trustee Hollins Coll., Berkeley Div. Sch.; bd. dirs. Norfolk Acad.; cabinet mem. United Way of Greater New Haven. Fellow Yale Corp.; mem. Nat. Assn. Coll. and Univ. Attys. (exec. bd. 1981-84), Assn. Am. Colls. (bd. dirs.), Am. Assn. Theol. Schs. (bd. dirs.), Mory's Assn., Phi Beta Kappa. Episcopalian. Home: 3115 Rivermont Ave Lynchburg VA 24503 Office: Randolph-Macon Woman's Coll 2500 Rivermont Ave Lynchburg VA 24503

LORING, MEREDITH SUSAN ELLIOTT, communications consultant; b. Charleston, S.C., Dec. 24, 1945; d. Elliott Legare Loring and Lillian Marsha (Rosman) Loring Selby; m. Eugene William Goffin, June 7, 1966 (div. Aug. 1976). BA, Stanford U., 1965; MA, NYU, 1967, PhD, 1973. Researcher U.S. State Dept., Rio de Janeiro, 1972-75; mgr. Dushkin Pub. Group, Guilford, Conn., 1975-77; acquisitions editor CBS Coll. Pub., Phila., 1977-79; editorial dir., sr. editor Acad. Press Coll. Dept., N.Y.C. and Orlando, Fla., 1979-84; dir. sales Ea. Phone Corp., Hackensack, N.J., 1984-88; area sales mgr. TSI, Montgomery, N.Y., 1988—; div. sales mgr. TIE Systems, Inc., Tri-State div., Pine Brook and Marlton, N.J., 1989-90; cons. telecommunications div. Laventhol & Howath, 1990—; freelance cons. editor 1984—. Committeewoman Buffalo Dem. Com., 1972-73; del. Dem. Nat. Convention, Miami, 1972. Grantee NDEA, 1965-68. Mem. Am. Soc. Criminology, Am. Econ. Assn. Democrat. Episcopalian. Office: 605 Third Ave New York NY 10017

LORMAN, BARBARA K., state senator; b. Madison, Wis., July 31, 1932; 3 children. Student U. Wis., Whitewater and Madison. Pres. Lorman Iron and Metal Recycling Co., 1979-87; mem. Wis. State Senate from 13th Dist., 1980—, mem. coms. on Agriculture, Health and Human Services, Senate Judiciary and Consumer Affairs, Joint Retirement Systems, Edn. and Govt. Ops., others. Bd. dirs., mem. exec. com. Forward Wis.; bd. dirs. Ft. Atkinson Meml. Hosp.; mem. Retirement Research Com., Transpn. Projects. Commn.; past pres. Ft. Atkinson Devel. Council, Wis. Mem. Jefferson County Bus. and Profl. Women, New Rep. Conf., Dodge County Fedn. Rep. Women. Office: Wis State Capitol Bldg Madison WI 53702 also: 1245 Janette St Fort Atkinson WI 53538*

LORTON, MARY MANNING, psychotherapist, consultant; b. Kansas City, Kans., Apr. 20, 1948; d. F. Howard and Katherine (Arcury) Manning; m. Philip Clive Lorton, Feb. 14, 1969 (div. Mar. 1974); 1 child, Joe. BA, U. Mo., Kansas City, 1970, MA, 1972, PhD, 1976. Cert. employee assistance profl. Asst. prof. Aquinas Coll., Grand Rapids, Mich., 1976-79; vis. prof. McGill U., Montreal, 1977, No. Ill. U., DeKalb, 1980; adj. lectr. U. Mo., Kansas City, 1982; project specialist U. Kans. Med. Ctr., Kansas City, 1981; cons. EAP Systems, Inc., Kansas City, Kans., 1988—; counselor Lathrop (Mo.) Elem.Sch., 1982; psychotherapist Raphael Ctr. Hosp., Nevada, Mo., 1983. Author monograph. Bd. dirs. Mayor's Youth Council, Kansas City, Mo., 1983-86. Mem. Am. Assn. Counseling and Devel., Greater Kansas City Mental Health Assn., Greater Kansas City Psychol. Assn., Pi Lambda Theta, Phi Delta Kappa. Home: 7300 Wyoming Kansas City MO 64114

LOSADA-PAISEY, GLORIA, psychologist; b. Havana, Cuba, Apr. 20, 1957; came to U.S., 1962; d. Manuel Benito and Maria del Pilar (Fernandez) Losada; m. Timothy John Henry Paisey, June 4, 1983 (div. June 1989); 1 child, Monica Leigh. BA, Fla. Internat. U., 1980; D Psychology, Nova U., 1984. Lic. psychologist, Conn. Pre-doctoral pyschology fellow Yale U., New Haven, 1983-84; clin. psychologist State of Conn. Dept. Mental Retardation Southbury Tng. Sch., Southbury, Conn., 1984-86, State of Conn. Dept. Mental Retardation New Haven Ctr., New Haven, 1986-88; dir. psychol. svcs. State of Conn. Dept. Mental Retardation Region 6, Waterford, Conn., 1988—; pvt. practice psychology, Waterbury, 1986—; dir. treatment program for mentally retarded offenders Southbury Tng. Sch., State of Conn., 1984-86. Mem. Am. Psychol. Assn., Am. Assn. Mental Retardation, Assn. for the Advancement Behavior Therapy. Democrat. Roman Catholic. Office: State of Conn DMR Region 6 36 Shore Rd Waterford CT 06385

LOSAPIO, KATHLEEN (TONI LOSAPIO), technical editor; b. Rochester, N.Y., July 3, 1955; d. Anthony and Grace (Castiglione) L. AAS in Profl. Photography, Rochester Inst. Tech., 1975, BS with honors in Profl. Photography and Communications, 1979. Photographer Eastman Kodak Co., Rochester, 1975-78, specialist customer svc., 1978-84, tech. editor, 1984—; adj. faculty Rochester Inst. Tech., 1982-84. Vol. Wesley-on-East Home for Elderly; mem. Young Leadership div. Jewish Community Fedn. Fellow Kodak Camera Club (pres. 1987-88, pres. elect 1986-87, trustee 1983-86; mem. Soc. Tech. Communicators (3 achievement awards 1987, Merit award 1988, 90, achievement award 1989, Disting. Tech. Communication award 1990, Merit and Acheivement awards Internat. Competition 1990), Soc. Photographic Scientists and Engrs., Photographic Soc. Am. (area rep., ranked 7th of Top Ten Nature Print Exhibitors in World 1984), Women in Communications, Writers and Books, Internat. Platform Assn., Rochester Singles Network (membership chair 1987-88). Home: 273 Barrington St Rochester NY 14607 Office: 343 State St Rochester NY 14650

LOSSE, ARLYLE MANSFIELD, retired librarian; b. Sheboygan, Wis., Apr. 15, 1917; d. Truman Roy and Emilie (Hildebrandt) Mansfield; m. Carl H. Losse, Jan. 20, 1962. BS, Milw. State Tchrs. Coll., 1939; MS in Libr. Sci., U. Wis., 1960. Asst. to reference libr. Mead Pub. Libr., Sheboygan, 1958-59; libr. Milw. (Wis.) Pub. Libr. System, 1960-82. Contbr. articles and poetry to publs. and jours. Active mem. Sheboygan (Wis.) Community Players, 1957-58; leader Great Books Discussion Group, Milw., 1963-64. Mem. ALA, Spl. Librs. Assn., Art Librs. Soc. of N.Am., (com. standards for art librs., 1973-75), Wis. Fellowship Poets, Nat. League Am. Pen Women, Acad. Am. Poets, Inc., Beta Phi Mu. Presbyterian. Home: 7240 W Burleigh St Apt 2 Milwaukee WI 53210-1185

LOSTY, BARBARA PAUL, dean; b. Norwich, N.Y., June 16, 1942; d. Henry Edward and Mary Frances (Crowell) Paul; m. Thomas August Losty, Nov. 23, 1965; children: Ellen Christine, Amanda Elizabeth. BA, Wellesley Coll., 1964; MA, U. Conn., 1969, PhD, 1971. Asst. prof. psychology Westminster Coll., Fulton, Mo., 1971-73; asst. prof. psychology Stephens Coll., Columbia, Mo., 1973-75, assoc. dir. sch. liberal and profl. studies, 1975-79, assoc. dean of faculty, 1979-85; dean U. Wis. Ctr.-Sheboygan County, Sheboygan, 1985—. Pres. Altrusa Club, Sheboygan, 1987-89; sec. U Wis./Sheboygan County Found., Inc., 1985—. Mem. Sheboygan County C. of C. (bd. dirs. 1988—). Home: 1218 N 1st St Sheboygan WI 53081 Office: U Wis Ctr Sheboygan County One University Dr Sheboygan WI 53081

LOTAS, JUDITH PATTON, advertising executive; b. Iowa City, Apr. 23, 1942; d. John Henry and Jane (Vandike) Patton; children: Amanda Bell, Alexandra Vandike. BA, Fla. State U., 1964. Copywriter Liller, Neal, Battle and Lindsey Advt., Atlanta, 1964-67, Grey Advt., N.Y.C., 1967-72; creative group head SSC&B Advt., N.Y.C., 1972-74, asso. creative dir., 1974-79, v.p., 1975-79, sr. v.p., 1979-82, exec. creative dir., 1982-86; founding ptnr. Lotas Minard Patton McIver, Inc., N.Y.C., 1986—. Active scholarship fund raising; bd. dirs. Samuel Eaxman Cancer Rsch., Found., N.Y.C., 1981-88; fundraiser Nat. Coalition for the Homeless, N.Y.C., 1986—. Recipient Clio award, Venice Film Festival award, Graphics award Am. Inst. Graphic Artists, 1970, Effie award; named Woman of Achievement, YWCA, One of Advt. Agys 100 Best Women Ad Age, 1989. Mem. Advt. Women N.Y. (1st v.p. 1984-87, bd. dirs. 1981-87), Kappa Alpha Theta. Democrat. Home: 45 E 89th St New York NY 10028

LOTEMPIO, JULIA MATILD, accountant; b. Budapest, Hungary, Oct. 14, 1934; came to U.S., 1958, naturalized 1962; d. Istvan and Irma (Sandor) Fejos; m. Anthony Joseph, Mar. 11, 1958. AAS in Lab. Tech. summa cum laude, Niagara County Community Coll., Sanborn, N.Y., 1967; BS in Tech. and Vocat. Edn. summa cum laude, SUNY, Buffalo, 1970; MEd in Guidance and Counseling, Niagara U., 1973, BBA in Acctg. summa cum laude, 1983. Sr. analyst, researcher Great Lakes Carbon Co., Niagara Falls, N.Y., 1967-71; tchr. sci. Niagara Falls Schools, 1973-75; tchr. sci. and English Starpoint Sch. System, Lockport, N.Y., 1975-77; instr. applied chem. Niagara County Community Coll., Sanborn, N.Y., 1979, instr. acctg. principles, 1989—; club adminstr., acct. Twinlo Racquetball, Inc., Niagara Falls, 1979-81; bus. cons. Twinlo Beverage, Inc., Niagara Falls, 1981-85; staff acct. J.D. Elliott & Co. PC, CPAs, Buffalo, 1986-87; acct., Lewiston, N.Y., 1988—; instr. acctg. prins. Niagara County Community Coll., Sanborn, N.Y., 1989—; bd. dirs. Niagara Frontier Meth. Home Inc., Niagara Frontier Nursing Home Inc., The Blocher Homes Inc., Buffalo. Mem. faculty continuing edn., speaker, chairperson fin. and community rels. coms. United Meth. Ch., Dickersonville, N.Y., 1985-90; guest speaker, counselor, tchr. Beechwood Service Guild, Buffalo, 1987—; bd. dirs. Niagara Frontier Meth. Home, Inc., Getzville, N.Y., 1988—; bd. dirs., mem. fin., investment, pension, ins., and community rels. coms. Niagara Frontier Nursing Home Co., Inc., Getzville, 1988—, Blocher Homes, Inc., Williamsville, N.Y., 1988—; asst. sec., bd. dirs., mem. exec., quality and assurance coms., chmn. community rels. com. Beechwood/Blocher Community, Buffalo, 1990—. Mem. Nat. Assn. Accts., Nat. Assn. Female Execs., Nat. Fedn. Bus. and Profl. Women's Club, Internat. Platform Assn., Niagara U. Alumni Assn., SUNY Coll. at Buffalo Alumni Assn., Niagara County Community Coll. Alumni Assn. Home and Office: 1026 Ridge Rd Lewiston NY 14092

LOTHARIUS, SUSAN MOECKER, controller; b. Waukegan, Ill., Nov. 11, 1950; d. Harold Joseph and Dorothy Esther (Bode) Moecker. BS, Towson State U., 1985. Dir. personnel Kidde Cons., Inc., Balto, Md., 1977-85; controller, dir. personnel Devel. Engr. Cons., Inc., Balto, 1985--. Mem. Am. Soc. Personnel Adminstra., Women's Exec. Network Club. Democrat. Roman Catholic. Office: Devel Engring Cons Inc 6603 York Rd Baltimore MD 21212

LOTT, BRENDA LOUISE, insurance company executive; b. Clinton, Ind., July 29, 1955; d. John and Thelma Louise (Anderson) Pastore; m. Robert Ralph Rundle, June 16, 1974 (div. July 1985); children: Danielle Marie Rundle, John Robert Rundle; m. Mark Lee Lott, July 4, 1985. Student, Colo. Women's Coll., Denver, 1973-74, Ins. Inst. of Am. Claim adjuster Allstate Ins. Co., Englewood, Colo., 1973-83; field claim adjuster Transamerica Ins. Co., Englewood, 1983-86; claim examiner Colonial Ins. Co., Denver, 1986-87, examiner/supr., 1987-89, regional claim mgr., 1990—; staff speaker Western Ins. Info. Svc., Denver, 1983-85; participant, invited faculty mem. 5-day lecture series Colonial Univ., Anaheim, Calif., 1990. Sponsor Plan Internat. foster parents program, 1989—. Mem. NAFE, LWV, NAACP (mem.-at-large), Ins. Women of Denver, Colo. Claims Assn. (bd. dirs. 1986-88), Claim Mgrs. Coun., Denver Claims Assn.

LOTZ, JOAN THERESA, public relations company executive; b. N.Y.C., Feb. 22, 1948; d. Andrew J. and Joan (McCartney) L. BA, Lehman Coll., 1969. Libr. asst. Met. Mus. Art, N.Y.C., 1969-74; office mgr. York Cable Corp., Inc., N.Y.C., 1974-77, Mobile Communications, Inc., N.Y.C., 1977-78; lease mgr. Major Muffler Ctrs., Inc., N.Y.C., 1978-81; v.p., asst. to chmn. Rowland Worldwide, N.Y.C., 1981—. N.Y. State Regent's scholar, 1965-69. Mem. Nat. Scholastic Soc. Democrat. Roman Catholic. Office: Rowland Worldwide 415 Madison Ave New York NY 10017

LOTZ, VIVIAN EVELYN, school counselor; b. Paterson, N.J., Sept. 30, 1943; d. George Henry Lotz and Evelyn Elizabeth (Manger) Mulvihill. AB, Rutgers U., 1965; MEd, Temple U., 1968, Temple U., 1972; PhD, Temple U., 1984. Cert. spl. edn. tchr., counslor, Pa. Pers. asst. Ford Found., N.Y.C., 1965-66; tchr. spl. edn. Sch. Dist. Phila., 1966-72, counselor, 1972—; counselor Episcopal Hosp. Nursing Sch., Phila., 1972-77; supr. Temple U., Phila., summer 1983. Bd. dirs., v.p. SW Community Action Group, Inc., Phila., 1972-79. Recipient commendation Sch. Dist. Phila., 1973, 75, 87, 88, award Assn. Retarded Children, Phila., 1967. Mem. Phila. Fedn. Tchrs., Phila. Counseling Assn., Jean Piaget Soc., Assn. Severely Handicapped, Poverty Law Ctr. Democrat. Mem. Reformed Ch. of America. Office: William Penn High Sch Broad and Master Sts Philadelphia PA 19122

LOTZE, BARBARA, physicist; b. Mezokovesd, Hungary, Jan. 4, 1924; d. Matyas and Borbala (Toth) Kalo; came to U.S., 1961, naturalized, 1967; Applied Mathematician Diploma with honors, Eotvos Lorand U. Scis., Budapest, Hungary, 1956; PhD, Innsbruck (Austria) U., 1961; m. Dieter P. Lotze, Oct. 6, 1958. Mathematician, Hungarian Cen. Statis. Bur., Budapest, 1955-56; tchr. math., Iselsberg, Austria, 1959-60; asst. prof. physics Allegheny Coll., 1963-69, assoc. prof., 1969-77, prof., 1977-90, prof. emeritus, 1990—, chmn. dept., 1981-84; lectr. in history of physics; speaker to civic groups. Mem. Am. Phys. Soc., Am. Assn. Physics Tchrs. (coun., sect. rep. Western Pa., chmn. nat. com. on women in physics 1983-84, Disting. Svc. award 1986, cert. of appreciation 1988), AAUP, AAUW, N.Y. Acad. Scis., Am. Hungarian Educators Assn. (pres. 1980-82), Wilhelm Busch Gesellschaft (Hanover, Fed. Republic Germany). Editor: Making Contributions: An Historical Overview of Women's Role in Physics, 1984; co-editor The First War Between Socialist States: The Hungarian Revolution of 1956 and Its Impact, 1984; contbr. articles to profl. jours. Home: 462 Hartz Ave Meadville PA 16335 Office: Allegheny Coll Dept Phsyics Meadville PA 16335

LOUCKS, NANCY J., association executive; b. Lansing, Mich., Mar. 21, 1957; d. John Robert and Marian Elizabeth (Lemmon) L. BS in Edn., Cen. Mich. U., 1980. Therapeutic counselor Hope Ctr. for Youth, Houston, 1981-82; recreation therapist Mental Health/Mental Retardation Assn., Houston, 1983-86; case mgr. Mental Health/Mental Retardation Assn., 1986-87; area dir. Tex. Spl. Olympics, Houston, 1988—; cons. YMCA, Houston, 1985-87; event dir. Internat. Spl. Olympic Games, Baton Rouge, 1983. Vol. Mental health/Mental Retardation Assn. of Houston, 1988—; spl. friend Tex. Spl. Olympics, 1988. Mem. Assn. Retarded Citizens, Lambda Chi Alpha.

LOUGHLIN, BEVERLY ANNE, accountant; b. Frederick, Md., June 4, 1944; d. Joe Edwin and ruth Elizabeth (Thrasher) Craven; m. Eugene J. Loughlin, Jr.; children: Brian Christopher, Melissa Elizabeth. Student, Frostburg (Md.) State Coll., 1962-64, Hartford Community Coll., Bel Air, Md., 1981-86; BS in Acctg., U. Balt., 1988. Classroom aide Hartford County Schs., Navre de Grace, Md., 1978-84; bookkeeper Art Builders Inc., Bel Air, Md., 1984-86; acct. J.P. Seisman & Assocs., CPA, Bel Air, 1986-89; pres. Loughlin Fin. Svcs. Ltd., Bel Air, 1989—. Mem. Aberdeen (Md.) Jaycee Women, 1978-79. Office: Loughlin Fin Svcs Ltd 23 Ellendale St Bel Air MD 21014

LOUGHLIN, KATHI PUGLISE, advertising agency executive; b. Bridgeport, Conn., July 16, 1958; d. Thomas and Lucille (Verrilli) Puglise; m. Thomas Patrick Loughlin, Oct. 10, 1981. BS in Mktg., Fairfield U., 1980. Mktg. assoc. GTE, Stamford, Conn., 1980-81, mktg. specialist, 1981-84; sr. mgr. MCI, Washington, 1984-88; pres. Loughlin Creative, Inc., Washington, 1988—. Recipient 2 Best of Category awards Printing Industry Met. Washington, 1988, 1st place Immy Mktg. Achievement award Info. Industry Assn., 1990. Mem. Direct Mail Mktg. Assn., Advt. Club Washington. Office: 1918 18th St NW Ste 24 Washington DC 20009

LOUIE, ALEXINA DIANE, composer; b. Vancouver, B.C., Can., July 30, 1949. MusB, U. B.C.; MA, U. Calif., San Diego. Profl. solo pianist Vancouver, 1966-71, profl. music copyist, 1970-73; instr. music Pasadena (Calif.) City Coll., 1974-80. Compositions include Molly, 1972, O Magnum Mysterium: In Memoriam Glenn Gould, 1982, Songs of Paradise, Music for a Thousand Autumns, Concerto for Piano and Orchestra, Love Songs for a Small Planet, The Eternal Earth, Winter Music, Music for Heaven and Earth. Named Composer of the Yr., Can. Music Coun., 1986; composition grantee Can. Coun. for the Arts, 1974, 80, 81; recipient Juno award, 1988, best recorded classical composition. Address: care Can League Composers, 20 St Joseph St, Toronto, ON Canada M4Y 1J9

LOUISON, DEBORAH FINLEY, federal agency administrator; b. Aberdeen, S.D., Sept. 20, 1951; d. Donald S. and Barbara F. (Lowenstein) Finley; 1 child, Stacey Renee. BA, Nat. Coll. Edn., 1987. Asst. to sec. Dept. Edn. & Cultural Affairs State of S.D., Pierre, 1973-77; program dir. forestry div. State of S.D., Pierre, 1978-81; legisl. dir. Congressman Clint

Roberts, Washington, 1981-83, Congresswoman Barbara Vucanovich, Washington, 1983-84; assoc. dir. fed. affairs Nat. Conf. State Legisl., Washington, 1984-89; dir. govt. affairs Nat. Conf. State Legisl., 1989; gost. asst. sec. U.S. Dept. of Energy, 1989—. Contbr. articles to profl. jours. Planning and devel. com. Pierre C. of C., 1974-76; campaign asst. Clint Roberts for Congress, 1979-80; coordinator for state legisl. Bush/Quayle Campaign, Washington, 1988. Mem. NAFE, Women in Govt. Relations (com. chair), Am. Soc. Assn. Execs. Republican. Roman Catholic.

LOUP, JEAN L., librarian; b. Council Bluffs, Iowa, Apr. 18, 1941; d. Carl Henry and Kathryn Lorraine (Wells) Zimmerman; m. Roland J., June 4, 1966 (div. Jan., 1984); children: Kathryn Althe, Thomas John. BS, Iowa State U., Ames, 1963; MA, U. Okla., Norman, 1965, MLS, 1965. Reference librarian Iowa State Traveling Library, Des Moines, 1965-66; acquistions librarian Iowa State U. Library, Ames, 1966-67, catalog librarian, 1967-70; veterinary med. librarian Iowa State U. Libr., Ames; head, processing U. Mich. Libr., Ann Arbor, 1971-74; reference librarian U. Mich. Library, 1974-78; library sci. librarian U. Mich. Library, Ann Arbor, 1978-82, head documents ctr., 1982-89; mem. task force Govt. Info. in Electronic Format, Assn of Research Libraries, Wash., 1986-88; chmn. Budget Priorities Com. U. Mich., 1989. Author (with others): Acquisitions, Budgets and Material Costs, 1988. Grantee Librarian Cooperative Research grant with Helen L. Snoke Council on Library Resources, Wash., 1985. Mem. ALA, Beta Phi Mu, Sigma Alpha Iota. Home: 14 Donegal Ct Ann Arbor MI 48104 Office: Hatcher Grad Libr Ann Arbor MI 48109

LOVALLO, PATRICIA GAFFNEY, corporate executive; b. Rochester, N.Y., Jan. 23, 1957; d. Patrick Raymond and Janet Marie (Kivell) Gaffney; m. Joseph Dante Lovallo III, Sept. 20, 1986. BSBA, Bucknell U., 1979; MBA, Harvard U., 1985. CPA. Internal auditor CBS, Inc., N.Y.C., 1979-80; audit asst. Arthur Andersen and Co., N.Y.C., 1980-81, experienced asst. auditor, 1981-82, sr. auditor, 1982-83; assoc. capital markets group Mfrs. Hanover, N.Y.C., 1985-86, asst. sec., 1986, asst. v.p., 1986-87; mgr. corp. fin. Gen. Signal Corp., Stamford, Conn., 1987-89, asst. treas., 1989—. Active jr. com. Inner City Scholarship Fund, N.Y.C., 1985—. Mem. AICPA, Fairfield County Treasury Mgmt. Assn., Nat. Corp. Cash Mgrs. Assn. Roman Catholic.

LOVAN, JOAN DENISE, contracts administrator; b. Kansas City, Kans., Sept. 4, 1954; d. Richard Michael Sr. and Mildred Marie (Monroe) Everard; (div. Mar. 1985); children: Brandon Erick, Garrett Andrew. BS, Cen. Mo. State U., 1975. Acctg. asst. Tex. A&M Rsch. Found., College Station, 1977-78, 79-80, budget asst., 1980-84, budget mgr., 1984-89; purchaser, buyer Milbank Mfg. Co., Kansas City, Mo., 1978-79; contracts mgr. Metrica, Inc., Bryan, Tex., 1989—. Fellow Nat. Coun. Univ. Rsch. Adminstrs.; mem. Nat. Contracts Mgr. Assn. (v.p.). Office: Metrica Inc 3833 Texas Ave Ste 207 Bryan TX 77802

LOVE, BONNIE, marketing executive; b. Rochester, N.Y., Feb. 19, 1948; d. Victor John and Cora Louise (Amico) L.; m. Alexander J. DiPasquale, Aug. 26, 1989. BA in English, SUNY, Oswego, 1970; MS in Ednl. Adminstrn., SUNY, Brockport, 1975. Cert. tchr., N.Y. Tchr. English Rush-Henrietta (N.Y.) Central Schs., 1970-82; asst. dir. pub. info. County of Monroe, Rochester, N.Y., 1983-88; communications asst. Rochester City Sch. Dist., 1988-89; mktg. communications mgr. SUNY, Brockport, 1990—; sr. counselor, speaker Planned Parenthood Rape Crisis, Rochester, 1980-85; pub. rels. cons. Respite Cares, Rochester, 1989—; adj. prof. Rochester Inst. Tech., 1989. Mem., pub. rels. coord. Rochester Area Women's Polit. Caucus, 1985-88. Mem. Women in Communications, Inc. (membership directory chair 1989-91), NOW. Republican. Home: 270 Woodmill Dr Rochester NY 14626

LOVE, EDITH HOLMES, theater producer; b. Boston, Oct. 17, 1950; d. Theodore Rufus and Mary (Holmes) L. Student, Denison U., 1968-72; BFA, U. Colo., 1973. Freelance designer various orgns., Atlanta, 1974-75; costumer Atlanta Children's Theatre, 1975-77; prodn. acct. David Gerber Co., L.A., 1980-81; bus. mgr. Alliance Theatre/Atlanta Children's Theatre, 1977-79, adminstrv. dir., 1981-83, gen. mgr., 1983-85, mng. dir., 1985—; bd. dirs. Midtown Bus. Assocs.; mem. adv. bd. Stage Hands, Inc., Atlanta, 1983-89; exec. com. Prodn. Valves, Inc., Atlanta, 1985-89. Bd. advisors Bus. Vols. for the Arts, 1988—. Mem. League Resident Theatres (treas. 1987—), Atlanta Theatre Coalition (exec. com. 1987—, pres. 1989). Office: Alliance Theatre Co 1280 Peachtree St NE Atlanta GA 30309

LOVE, EMMA LOUISE, educational administrator; b. Minden, La., Apr. 15, 1944; d. Henry and Annie (Johnson) Allums; divorced; 1 child, Bryan Earl. BA, Calif. State U., Long Beach, 1966, MA, 1976; postgrad., U. So. Calif., 1985. Cert. secondary tchr., counselor, adminstr., Calif. Tchr. secondary schs. Los Angeles Unified Sch. Dist., 1967-74, secondary counselor, 1974-80, asst. prin. secondary counseling services, 1980-84, 88—, adviser integration compliance, 1984-88; cons. English Med-Core, U. So. Calif., 1980. Dean's Acad. Leadership scholar U. So. Calif., 1985, Verna B. Dauterive scholar, 1986, Educare scholar, 1988; recipient Gladys M. Byram award Calif. Community Found., 1988. Mem. NAACP, Assn. for Supervision and Curriculum Devel., Calif. Assn. for Supervision and Curriculum Devel., Assn. Adminstrs. Los Angeles, Council Black Adminstrs., Black Women's Forum, Urban League, Calif. Afro-Am. Mus. Found., Phi Delta Kappa. Democrat. Baptist.

LOVE, LOIS MARIE, psychologist; b. Putnam County, Ind., Apr. 4, 1931; d. Orville Odus and Nancy Jane (McCloud) Elliott; m. John R. Love, June 19, 1949 (div. 1979); children: Stephen, Joseph, John, David; m. Al A. Rizzo, Apr. 21, 1984. BEd, Duquesne U., Pitts., 1971, MEd, 1973; PhD, U. Pitts., 1984. Lic. psychologist, Pa., W.Va.; cert. sch. psychologist, Pa., W.Va.; cert. tchr., Pa. Office mgr. J.R. Love Co., Pitts., 1964-73; tchr. Plum Borough Sch. Dist., Pitts., 1971-73; psychologist Pace Sch. for Disordered Students, Pitts., 1975-80; staff psychologist A.A. Rizzo, 1980-85; pvt. practice Pitts. and Murrysville, 1985—; psychologist, cons. Forbes Regional Health Ctr., Monroeville, Pa., 1985—; chairperson psychology dept. Forbes Regional Health Ctr., Monroeville, 1989—, program coord. adolescent unit, 1986, developer women's program Affective Disorders Program, 1989; cons. Ctr. for Assessment and Treatment of Youth, Pitts., Nat. Learning and Resource Ctr., Gibsonia, Pa., Easter Seal Soc., Pitts., 1975-80; instr. Duquesne U., LaRoche Coll., Carlow Coll.; bd. dirs. Youth Svcs. Tng. Ctr., 1988—. Pres. Parent Tchr. Orgn.; vol. Boy Scouts Am., YMCA Swim Team; vol. Mentally Handicapped Children's Program, 1968; leader Cub Scouts Am., Pitts., 1965, Indpls., 1957-60. Mem. Am. Psychol. Assn., Bd. Med. Psychotherapists, Nat. Assn. Sch. Psychologists, Assn. for Advancement of Behavior Therapy, Pa. Psychol. Assn., Greater Pitts. Psychol. Assn., Pa. Sch. Psychology Assn. Democrat. Unitarian-Universalist. Office: 4251 Old William Penn Hwy Murrysville PA 15668

LOVE, MILDRED ALLISON, retired teacher, historian, writer, volunteer; b. Moultrie, Ga., Mar. 12, 1915; d. Ulysees Simpson Sr. and Susie Marie (Dukes) Allison; m. George Alsobrook Love, Aug. 24, 1956 (dec. 1978). BSEd, U. Tampa (Fla.), 1941; MS in Home Econs., Fla. State U., 1953; MA in History, U. Miami, Coral Gables, Fla., 1969. Cert. tchr., Fla. Vocat. home econs. tchr. Hamilton County Pub. Schs., Jasper, Fla., 1941-43, Pinellas County Pub. Schs., Tarpon Springs, Fla., 1946-51; vocat. home econs. tchr. Dade County Pub. Schs., Miami, Fla., 1951-61, history tchr., 1961-73; supr. food svcs. Ft. Jackson (S.C.), 1944-46. Chmn. subcoun. for crime prevention Brickell Area, City of Miami, 1983-87; mem. Crisis Response Team, Miami Police Dept., 1983—; vol. VA Hosp., Miami, 1987—; historian, vol. vets affairs VFW Auxiliary, Miami, 1988-89; precinct worker presdl. election, 1976, 80; sponsor history honor soc. Miami Edison Sr. High Sch., 1961-73; mem. Mus. of Sci., St. Stephen's Episc. Ch., Coconut Grove, Fla. Mem. AAUW, VFW ((aux. post 471 Miami, Fla.), Inst. for Retired Profls., Hist. Assn. S. Fla., U. Miami Alumni Assn., Fla. Ret. Educators Assn., Nat. Wildlife Fedn., Am. Legion (aux. post 29 Miami, Fla.), Nat. Trust Hist. Preservation, Coll. of Arts and Scis. Assn. U. Miami, Fla. Vocat. Home Econs. Tchrs. (pres. 1947), Woman's Club of Miami Beach, Sierra Club, Phi Alpha Theta. Democrat. Episcopalian. Home: 1824 Brickell Ave Miami FL 33129

LOVE, MILDRED LOIS (JAN LOVE), public relations executive; b. Iowa City, July 9, 1928; d. Joseph R. and Gladys M. (Parsons) Casey; BS in Bus. Adminstrn., U. Iowa, 1951; m. Gerald Dean Love, Apr. 4, 1952; children: Laura Anne Love Parris, Cynthia Love-Hazel, Gregory Alan, Linda Love Mesler, Geoffrey Dare. Vocal soloist Sta. KXEL, Waterloo, Iowa, 1944-46; sec. to lawyer, La Porte City, Iowa, 1944-46; administrv. aide Office of Supt., La Porte City High Sch., 1947-48; office mgr. Minn. Valley Canning Co., Iowa div. offices, LaPorte City, 1947-48; sec. dept. mktg. U. Iowa, 1948-51; asst. dept. pub. rels. Chgo. Bd. Trade, 1949-51; exec. sec. patent dept. Collins Radio Co., Cedar Rapids, 1951-52; vol. VA Hosp., Albany, N.Y., 1965-73; adminstrv. dir. Tri-Village Nursery Sch., Delmar, N.Y., 1960-61; participant Internat. Lang. Teaching Exch., Cambodia, 1961; vol. hosps. in Concord, N.H., 1963-64; vol. Chgo. Maternity Center, 1973-74; mgr. Wolf Trap Assocs. Gift Shop, Vienna, Va., 1975-80; gen. mgr. Travelhost of Washington, 1980-81; cons. mgmt., 1980—; chmn. Nat. Cherry Blossom Festival, Washington. Participant community pageants on local and dist. levels, Iowa, 1950-51; Sunday sch. tchr. Meth. Ch., 1941-61; mem. Flossmoor (Ill.) Planning and Zoning Commn., 1973-74, McLean (Va.) Planning and Zoning Commn., 1975—; precinct worker in Iowa, 1946-52, N.Y., 1956-61, N.H., 1963-64, Va., 1979—; pres. I.O.W.A. Inc., Washington, 1980-81; active various community fund raising drives; mem. LWV, Ladies Aux., McCosh Infirmary, Princeton, N.J. Mem. AAUW, Am. Mkgt. Assn., NAFE, Nat. Conf. State Socs. (pres. 1983), Ariz. Opera League, Princeton Club, Can. Club, Normanside Country Club, Olympia Fields Winter Club, Kenilworth Club, Delta Zeta. Republican. Home: 1167 Blanc Ct The Vintage Hills Pleasanton CA 94566

LOVE, SANDRA RAE, information specialist; b. San Francisco, Feb. 20, 1947; d. Benjamin Raymond and Charlotte C. Martin; B.A. in English, Calif. State U., Hayward, 1968; M.S. in L.S., U. So. Calif., 1969; m. Michael D. Love, Feb. 14, 1971. Tech. info. specialist Lawrence Livermore (Calif.) Nat. Lab., 1969—. Mem. Spl. Libraries Assn. (sec. nuclear sci. div. 1980-82, chmn. 1983-84, bull. editor 1987-89), Beta Sigma Phi. Democrat. Episcopalian. Office: Lawrence Livermore Nat Lab PO Box 808 L-389 Livermore CA 94550

LOVE, SUSAN DENISE, accountant, consultant, small business owner; b. Portland, Oreg., Aug. 5, 1954; d. Charles Richard and Betty Lou (Reynolds) Beck; m. Daniel G. Oliveros, Dec. 21, 1979 (div. Nov. 1983); m. Michael Dean Love, Aug. 24, 1984 (div. Mar. 1989); m. Michael Eugene Watson, July 28, 1990. BA in Graphic Design, Portland State U., 1976. Office mgr. Rogers Machinery Co., Portland, 1972-77; exec. sec. Creighton Shirtmakers, N.Y.C., 1977-80; dir. adminstrn. Henry Grethel div. Manhattan Industries, N.Y.C., 1980-81; exec. asst. S.B. Tanger and Assocs., N.Y.C., 1981-83; exec. asst., bookkeeper M Life Ins. Co., Portland, 1983-84; acct. cons., owner Office Assistance, Portland, 1984—; owner WE LOVE KIDS Clothing Store, Portland, 1985—; owner, pres. Oreg. Music and Entertainment, 1989—; sec./treas. Designers' Roundtable, Portland, 1985-88. Mem. Oreg. State Pub. Interest Research Group, Portland, 1985-90, Oreg. Fair Share, Salem, 1987, adv. bd. program for displaced homemakers and single parents Clackamas Community Coll., 1989—. Mem. Women Entrepreneurs of Oreg. (bd. dirs. 1988-90), North Clackamas County C. of C. Democrat. Home: 8106 SE Lake Rd #407 Milwaukie OR 97267 Office: Oregon Music and Entertainment PO Box 772 Clackamas OR 97015

LOVEC, ROSITA BORUNDA, counselor, educator; b. Alamogordo, N.Mex., June 5, 1935; d. Francisco Baca and Clementina Rivera (Garcia) Borunda; m. Gary Edward Lovec, July 16, 1957; children: David Wayne, Denise Elaine Lovec Elkins. AA, Mesa Community Coll., 1975; BA magna cum laude, San Diego State U., 1983; PhD, Am. Inst. of Hypnotherapy, 1988. Exec. and personal sec. comdr. of installation USAF, Hollman AFB, N.Mex., 1956-60; dept. head sec., supr., mgr., sec. to dept. dir. Honeywell, Inc., San Diego, 1964-69; asst. to prof. Psychology Dept. Mesa Community Coll., San Diego, 1973—; pvt. counselor San Diego, 1983—; presenter active parenting ednl. programs. Lectr., educator, cons., organizer and leader of workshops, classes and seminars for PTA's, schs., ch. orgns., civic clubs and others. Mem. Am. Inst. of Hypnotherapy, Am. Bd. of Hypnotherapy, Friends of Jung, Am. Assn. of Women, Nat. Assn. for Children of Alcoholics, Phi Beta Kappa, Clairemont Woman's Club (San Diego). Home: 5280 Canning Ct San Diego CA 92111

LOVEJOY, JEAN HASTINGS, teacher; b. Battle Creek, Mich., July 1, 1913; d. William Walter and Elizabeth (Fairbank) H.; m. Allen Perry, March 27, 1912; children: Isabel L. Best, Linda L. Ewald, Elizabeth L. Fulton, Margaret L. Baldwin, Helen L. Battad. BA, Mt. Holyoke Coll., So. Hadley, Mass., 1935. Traveling sec. Student Volun. Movement, N.Y.C., 1935; bookkeeper Hartford Consumers Co-operative, Conn., 1944; tchr. Pre-School, Congl. Ch., W Hartford, Conn., 1944-45; instr. St. John's U., Shanghai, China; tchr. Edn., 1st Congl. Ch., Berkeley, Calif., 1958-59; instr. Tunghai U., Taiwan, 1960-63; sec. Pres. Tunghai U., Taichung, Taiwan, 1960-63;, -. Pres. Ecumenical Assn. for Housing, San Rafael, 1971, 78-80; founding mem. Hospice of Havasu, 1982—, bereavement coord., 1989—. Mem. LWV (program v.p. Pierce county chpt., Tacoma 1967, pres. cen. Marin county chpt., San Rafael, Calif. 1973-75, legis. analyst land use Sacramento chpt. 1979-80), Witherspoon Soc. Presbyterian. Home: 3125 Desert Palm Dr Lake Havasu City AZ 86403

LOVELACE, DONNA LANDON, registered nurse; b. Palmer, Tenn., Mar. 16, 1947; d. George Edward and Clara Augusta (Bone) Landon; m. Larry Ray Lovelace, Aug. 25, 1967; children: Chanda Darlene, Larry Heath. RN, Baroness Erlanger Sch. Nursing, Chattanooga, 1968. R.N., Tenn. Charge nurse orthopedics Baroness Erlanger Hosp., Chattanooga, 1968-69; dir. nursing Cumberland Hgts. Hosp., Coalmont, Tenn., 1969-70; weekend supr. Grundy Gen. Hosp., Coalmont, 1983-84; staff nurse Mountain Care Home Health, Sewanee, Tenn., 1984-86, adminstr., 1986-87; staff nurse Meth. Hosp. Home Care, Winchester, Tenn., 1987-88, asst. dir. nursing, 1988; supr. Emerald Hodgson Health Care Ctr., Sewanee, 1988-89, unit mgr., 1989—. Sec. Tracy City Elem. Parent Tchrs. Aux., Tenn., 1980-83. Democrat. Home: Box 513 Tracy City TN 37387

LOVELAND, HOLLY STANDISH, information systems executive; b. Slater, S.C., Aug. 28, 1947; d. Albert C. and Lucille E. (Standish) L. AA, Macomb Coll., 1974; BA Siena Heights Coll.,1985. Applications analyst Burroughs Corp., Detroit, 1977-79; programmer analyst Ford Hosp., Detroit, 1979-80, project leader applications support, 1980, project mgr. applications support, 1980-82, mgr. systems svcs., 1982-84; dept. exec. VI, info. svcs. Wayne County, Detroit, 1984-86, dir. data svcs. City of Milw., 1986—; computer cons. mem. MIS adv. bd. Marquette U. Mem. Soc. for Info. Mgmt. (Wis. chpt. sec.). Home: 2538 S Wentworth Ave Milwaukee WI 53207 Office: 809 N Broadway Rm 400 Milwaukee WI 53202

LOVELL, EMILY KALLED, journalist; b. Grand Rapids, Mich., Feb. 25, 1920; d. Abdo Rham and Louise (Claussen) Kalled; student Grand Rapids Jr. Coll., 1937-39; B.A., Mich. State U., 1944; M.A., U. Ariz., 1971; m. Robert Edmund Lovell, July 4, 1947. Copywriter, asst. traffic mgr. Sta. WOOD, Grand Rapids, 1944-46; traffic mgr. KOPO, Tucson, 1946-47; reporter, city editor Alamogordo (N.Mex.) News, 1948-51; Alamogordo corr., feature writer Internat. News Service, Denver, 1950-54; Alamogordo corr., feature writer El Paso Herald-Post, 1954-65; Alamogordo news dir., feature writer Tularosa (N.Mex.) Basin Times, 1957-59; co-founder, editor, pub. Otero County Star, Alamogordo, 1961-65; newscaster KALG, Alamogordo, 1964-65; free lance feature writer Denver Post, N.Mex. Mag., 1949-69; corr. Electronics News, N.Y.C., 1959-63, 65-69; Sierra Vista (Ariz.) corr. Ariz. Republic, 1966; free lance editor N.Mex. Pioneer Interviews, 1967-69; asst. dir. English skills program Ariz. State U., 1976; free-lance editor, writer, 1977—; part-time tchr., lectr. U. Pacific, 1981-86; part-time interpreter Calif., 1983—, Interpreters Unlimited, Oakland, 1985—; sec., dir. Star Pub. Co., Inc., 1961-64, pres., 1964-65. 3d v.p., publicity chmn. Otero County Community Concert Assn., 1950-65; mem. Alamogordo Zoning Commn., 1955-57; mem. founding com. Alamogordo Central Youth Activities Com., 1957; vice chmn. Otero County chpt. Nat. Found. Infantile Paralysis, 1958-61; charter mem. N.M. Citzens Council for Traffic Safety, 1959-61; pres. Sierra Vista Hosp. Aux., 1966; pub. relations chmn. Ft. Huachuca chpt. ARC, 1966. Mem. nat. bd. Hospitalized Vets. Writing Project, 1972—. Recipient 1st Pl. awards N.Mex. Press Assn., 1961, 62. Pub. Interest award Nat. Safety Council, 1962. 1st Pl. award Nat. Fedn. Press Women, 1960, 62; named Woman of Year Alamogordo, 1960. Editor of Week Pubs. Aux., 1962, adm. N.Mex. Navy, 1962, col. a.d.c. Staff Gov. N.Mex., 1963, Woman of Yr., Ariz. Press Women, 1973. Mem. N.Mex. (past sec.), Ariz. (past pres.) press women, N.Mex. Fedn. Womens Clubs (past dist. pub. relations chmn.), N.Mex. Hist. Soc. (life), N.Mex. Fedn. Bus. and Profl. Womens Clubs (past pres.), Pan Am. Round Table Alamogordo, Theta Sigma Phi (past nat. 3d v.p.), Phi Kappa Phi. Democrat. Moslem. Author: A Personalized History of Otero County, New Mexico, 1963; Weekend Away, 1964; Lebanese Cooking, Streamlined, 1972; A Reference Handbook for Arabic Grammar, 1974, 77; contbg. author: The Muslim Community in North America, 1983. Home: PO Box 7152 Stockton CA 95267-0152

LOVELY, CANDACE WHITTEMORE, artist; b. Springfield, Vt., Mar. 15, 1953; d. John Whittemore and Sally (Reck) L.; m. Donald R. Korst, Sept. 7, 1980. BA, U. Vt., 1975, edn. cert., 1978. Artist student Boston Sch., Fenway Studios, 1980-84, artist, 1983—; artist Am. Impressionist, Boston, 1984—, Copley artist, 1986, Copley master, 1988. Paintings exhibited at Salamagundi Club, N.Y.C., 1983—, Am. Artist Profl. League, N.Y.C., 1983—. Recipient award Salamagundi Club, N.Y.C., Am. Artist Profl. League, N.Y.C., Fitchburg (Mass.) Art Mus. Show. Mem. Copley Soc., Art Guild of the Kennebunks, Rockport (Mass.) Art Assn. (Most Popular Painting 1987, 88). Home and office: Fenway Studio 110 30 Ipswich St Boston MA 02211

LOVELY, MARY RUTH, beverage products executive; b. Bridgeport, Conn., May 4, 1961; d. Edward Coughlin and Nancy Ann (Michalka) L. BS in Chemistry, St. Joseph Coll., 1983; postgrad., U. R.I., 1983-84; MBA in Mgmt., Indsl. Relations, U. Bridgeport, 1988. Grad. asst. chemistry dept. U. R.I., Kingston, 1983-84; quality assurance asst. chemist Clairol, Inc., Stamford, Conn., 1984-85, package devel. sr. chemist, 1985-87; assoc. quality specialist quality svcs. hdqrs. PepsiCo, Inc., Valhalla, N.Y., 1987-88, supr. quality svcs. hdqrs., 1988-89; mgr. quality svcs. Cadbury Schweppes Beverages, Trumbull, Conn., 1989—. Recipient research fellowship Hartford Hosp., 1982. Mem. Am. Chem. Soc., NAFE, Soc. Soft Drink Technologists, St. Joseph Coll. Alumnae (sec. Fairfield County club 1986-88, co-pres. 1988—), Am. Mgmt. Assn., Inst. Food Technologists. Roman Catholic. Home: 6C Ann Dr Danbury CT 06810 Office: Cadbury Schweppes Beverages 30 Trefoil Dr Trumbull CT 06611

LOVERING, LORELI, nurse practitioner, secretary; b. Renton, Pa., Dec. 28, 1934; d. Harry and Mary (Romanco) Federoff; m. Francis J. Piekarski, May 4, 1957 (dec. Mar. 1973); children: Jill C., Beth S. Hammack, Karen, James; m. Larry J. Lovering. Diploma in nursing, West Pa. Hosp. Sch. Nursing, 1955; cert. nurse practitioner, U. Pitts., 1969, Russellton Med. Group, 1973. Staff and rehab. nurse Angelus Rehab. Ctr., Pitts., 1955-56; psychiat. nurse Vets. Hosp., Pitts., 1956-58; nurse part-time Citizen Gen. Hosp./Columbia Hosp., New Kensington, Pa., 1958-63; from nurse to nurse practitioner Penn Plum Med. Bldg. (merged with Miners Clinic, Inc., New Kensington, 1963-78; nurse practitioner VA Nursing Home Care Unit, Phoenix, 1978—; chair nursing com. VA, 1988-89; pres. Nat. Assurance Svcs., Inc., Phoenix, 1986—; owner, pres. Interiors by Loreli, 1987—. Mem. Ariz. Gerontol. Soc. (assoc.), Women's Bus. Clubs (scholar 1952), Toastmaster. Republican. Home: 2745 E Winchcomb Dr Phoenix AZ 85032 Office: Carl T Hayden Vets Med Ctr 7th St and Indian Sch Rd Phoenix AZ 85012

LOVETRI, JEANNETTE LOUISE, voice educator; b. Southampton, N.Y., Apr. 2, 1949; d. James John and Aline Rita (Zimmer) L. Student, Manhattan Sch. Music, 1967-68, Juilliard Sch., 1971-72; pvt. dance, piano and vocal study. Singer opera, cabaret, summer stock, oratorios, jazz, 1966-80; owner voice studio, Greenwich, Conn., 1970-75, N.Y.C., 1975—; tchr. voice music dept. Upsala Coll., East Orange, N.J., 1976-81; founder, dir. The Voice Workshop, pub. speaking seminar, 1983—; guest lectr. Boston Conservatory of Music, 1987-89, Internat. Symposium Care of Profl. Voice, N.Y., 1987-90; lectr., workshop leader, various U.S. cities, Amsterdam, and Copenhagen; numerous appearances with Bklyn. Contemporary Chorus, Chapman Roberts Singers, Mid-Hudson Opera, others; former chmn. Music Theatre Com. Ann. Symposium. Mem. N.Y. Singing Tchrs. Assn. (bd. dir., pres.), Nat. Assn. Tchrs. Singing.

LOVETT, JUANITA PELLETIER, clinical psychologist; b. Youngstown, Ohio, Mar. 9, 1937; d. Joseph Acadia and Alice Beatrice (Davis) Pelletier; B.A. with honors in Psychology summa cum laude, Fairleigh Dickinson U., 1975; M. Phil. Tchrs. Coll., Columbia U., 1978, M.A., 1979; Ph.D., Columbia U., 1980; children: Laura Ann, James Emmett. Free lance fashion cons., 1958-70; psychology fellow Westchester Div. N.Y. Hosp.-Cornell Med. Center, White Plains, 1977-80; program dir. inpatient service Fair Oaks Hosp., Summit, N.J., 1980-82; pvt. practice, 1980—; asst. dir. med. research CIBA-GEIGY Pharms., Summit, 1982-83; cons. AT&T Bell Labs., Murray Hill, N.J., 1983; adj. asst. prof. psychology and edn., dept. psychology, Tchrs. Coll., Columbia U., N.Y.C., 1980-84; field supr. grad. sch. applied profession psychology Rutgers U., 1981-83; assoc. prof. Polytechnic, N.Y., 1988—. Union County Mental Health Bd. mem., 1974-76; coll. companion Overbrook Hosp., Cedar Grove, N.J., 1972-75. Mennen scholar, 1975; recipient Laurie Shavel award, 1975. Mem. Am. Psychol. Assn., N.Y. State Psychol. Assn., Soc. Personality Assessment, N.J. Acad. Psychology, N.Y. Acad. Scis., N.J. Psychol. Assn., Sigma Xi, Phi Omega Epsilon. Contbr. articles to profl. publs. Home: 38 D Elm St Apt 5B Summit NJ 07901 Office: 86 Summit Ave Summit NJ 07901

LOVINGER, SOPHIE LEHNER, child psychologist; b. N.Y.C., Jan. 15, 1932; d. Nathaniel Harris and Anne (Rosen) Lehner; m. Robert Jay Lovinger, June 18, 1957; children: David Fredrick, Mark Andrew. BA, Bklyn. Coll., 1954; MS, City Coll., N.Y.C., 1959; PhD, NYU, 1967. Sr. clin. psychologist Bklyn. State Hosp., 1960-61; grad. fellow NYU, N.Y.C., 1961-67; psychotherapy trainee Jamaica (N.Y.) Ctr., 1964-67; asst. prof. Hofstra U., Hempstead, N.Y., 1967-70; prof. Cen. Mich. U., Mt. Pleasant, 1970—; psychotherapist, psychoanalyst N.Y.C. and Mt. Pleasant, Mich., 1964—. Author: Learning Disabilities and Games, 1978; contbr. articles to profl. jours. Fellow Am. Orthopsychiat. Assn.; mem. Am. Psychol. Assn., Nat. Register Health Svc. Providers. Office: 405 S Main St Mount Pleasant MI 48858

LOVINS, SHARRON JOYCE, data processing executive, consultant; b. Malden, Mass., Mar. 8, 1946; d. Max and Gladys (Singer) L. BA, U. Mass., 1967; postgrad., Boston Coll., 1969-70, Boston U., 1970-72, 89—. Tchr. English Malden (Mass.) Pub. Schs., 1967-80; sr. ednl. mktg. specialist, customer ednl. mgr. Honeywell Info. Systems, Waltham, Mass., 1980-84; sr. ednl. planning specialist Wang Labs., Inc., Burlington, Mass., 1984-86; edn. design cons., program product mgr. Wang Labs., Inc., Lowell, Mass., 1986-89; mktg. cons. Database Mktg. Systems, Woburn, Mass., 1989—; mktg., ednl., writing, mktg. and media cons., 1981-84. Contbr. articles to high tech. jours. Fundraiser WGBH Pub. TV, Boston, 1970, 71, Mondale-Ferraro election com., Brookline, Mass., 1984; Tanglewood Festival Chorus singer, Boston Symphony Orch., 1974-81. Mem. NAFE, Am. Soc. Tng. and Devel., Am. Jewish Congress, Combined Jewish Philanthropies. Democrat. Home: 200 Bedford Rd 21A Glenbrook Estates Woburn MA 01801

LOVVORN, JOELLA, newspaper editor; b. Pep, Tex., Mar. 20, 1934; d. Alford Marion and Emma (Daniel) L. B.S., Wayland Bapt. Coll., 1969. Ch. news editor Plainview (Tex.) Daily Herald, 1957-60, typesetter, proofreader, 1965-67; offset printer, photographer Muleshoe (Tex.) Jours., 1960-64; asst. editor Ariz. Bapt. Beacon, Phoenix, 1964-65; society editor Lamb County Leader-News Littlefield, Tex., 1967-69, editor, 1969—. Bd. dirs. United Way Fund, 1979-88, Salvation Army, 1976—; dir. Lamb County Spelling Bee, Littlefield, 1980—; judge Regional Spelling Bee, Lubbock, 1980—; chmn. public info. Am. Cancer Soc., 1968—, Am. Heart Assn., 1976-79; chmn. publicity county chpt. ARC, 1976, retail trade com., 1987—. Recipient appreciation cert. Am. Cancer Soc., 1974, 80, 83, 86-89, Am. Heart Assn., 1974, appreciation plaque Distributive Edn. Classes Am., 1983-85, appreciation plaque Future Farmers Am., 1985. Mem. Soc. Profl. Journalists, Nat. Press Photographers Assn., Tex. Press Assn., West Tex. Press Assn. (contest chmn. 1970), West Tex. Competitive Shooters, Nat. Rifle Assn., Littlefield C. of C. (chmn. publicity, named Woman of the Yr. 1988). Republican. Lodge: Woodmen of World. Office: Lamb County Leader-News 313 W 4th St Littlefield TX 79339

LOW, BOBBI S., biologist; b. Louisville, Dec. 4, 1942; d. James B. and Roberta (Henry) Middendorf; m. William A. Low, Jan. 29, 1965 (div. 1980); 1 child, Michael Muir. BA with hons., U. Louisville, 1960; MA, U. Tex., 1962, PhD, 1965; postgrad., U. B.C., Vancouver, 1965-67. Rsch. scientist Commonwealth Sci. & Industry Rsch. Orgn., Alice Springs, Australia, 1967-72; asst. prof. U. Mich., Sch. Natural Resources, Ann Arbor, 1972-75; assoc. prof. U. Mich., Sch. Natural Resources, 1975—; mem. com. developing rangelands strategies Nat. Acad. Sci., 1980-81; cons. in field. Contbr. articles to profl. jours. Recipient Mich. Teaching Excellence award, 1990. Mem. AAAS, Am. Soc. Naturalists, Am. Inst. Biol. Scis., Sigma Xi, Phi Kappa Phi. Office: Univ Michigan 430 N University Ann Arbor MI 48109-1115

LOW, MARISSA EVA, sales executive; b. San Francisco, Mar. 3, 1960; d. Fred and Winifred (Quan) L. AA, Fashion Inst. of Design and Mdse., 1979; Cert. Corp. Communications, Calif. State U.-Long Beach, 1987; student, U. of Redlands. Assoc. area mgr. Buffums, Glendale, Calif., 1979-80; asst. buyer Buffums, Long Beach, Calif., 1981-83; mdse. control mgr. Buffums, Long Beach, 1983-86, advt. mgr., 1987-89; account rep. CompuMed, Culver City, Calif., 1989—. Judge Miss Lakewood Pageant of Beauty, 1987; vol. Long Beach Conv. and Visitors Coun., 1987; pub. rels. chmn. March of Dimes, Calif., 1986; v.p. programs, spl. projects chmn., bd. dirs. nomination chmn. Women's Coun., 1985—; sec. Women Bus. Conf., 1985. Mem. NAFE, Long Beach C. of C. Women's Coun., Am. Mktg. Assn., Med. Mktg. Assn. Office: CompuMed 8549 Higuera St Culver City CA 90232

LOW, MERRY COOK, civic volunteer; b. Uniontown, Pa., Sept. 3, 1925; d. Howard Vance and Eleanora (Lynch) Mullan; m. William R. Cook, Dec. 27, 1947 (div. May 1979); m. John Wayland Low, July 8, 1979; children: Karen, Cindy, Bob, Jan. RN, Allegheny Gen. Hosp., Pitts., 1946; BS, Colo. Women's Coll., 1976. RN, Colo. Dir. patient edn. Med. Care and Rsch. Found., Denver, 1976-78; cons. Core Communications in Health, N.Y.C., 1976-78. Contbr. chpt. to Pattern for Distribution of Patient Education, 1981. Bd. dirs. Women's Libr. Assn., U. Denver, 1982—, vice chmn., 1985-86, chmn., 1986-87; chmn. Am. ind. docents Denver Art Mus., 1984-86, chmn. collector's choice benefits, 1988, pres. vols., trustee, 1988-90; trustee ch. coun., chmn. invitational art show 1st Plymouth Congl. Ch., Englewood, Colo., 1981-84; pres. PEO Colo. chpt. DX, 1982-84. Recipient Disting. Svc. award U. Denver Coll. Law, 1988, King Soopers Vol. of Week award, 1989. Mem. Am. Assn. of Mus. (vol. meeting coord. 1990—), Colo. Symphony Guild, Opera Colo. Guild. Republican. Home: 2552 E Alameda #11 Denver CO 80209 Office: Denver Art Mus 100 W 14th Ave Pkwy Denver CO 80204

LOWD, CATHERINE ANN, hospital administrator; b. Scranton, Pa., Aug. 1, 1943; d. John Francis and Margaret Thomas (Hosfeld) Radle; m. Harry Mosher Lowd III; children: Kristen A. Stevens, Kathalie M. Diploma in mursing, Geisinger Med. Ctr., Danville, Pa., 1964; BS in Nursing, U. N.H., 1983, MS in Nursing Adminstrn., 1989. RN, Pa., N.H. Supr. Tyler Meml. Hosp., Tunkhannock, Pa., 1972-76; dir. health svcs. Colby-Sawyer Coll., New London, N.H., 1976-88; nurse mgr. Cath. Med. Ctr., Manchester, N.H., 1988-89; asst. adminstr. patient svcs. Monadnock Community Hosp., Peterborough, N.H., 1989—; cons. N.H. Coll. and Univ. Coun., 1983-84; mem. Gov.'s Task Force on Health Manpower, Concord, N.H., 1987-88. Mem. Am. Nurses Assn. (del. 1985-89), N.H. Nurses Assn. (pres. 1985-87), Sigma Theta Tau. Republican. Home: Box 47 North Sutton NH 03260 Office: Monadnock Community Hosp Old Street Rd Peterborough NH 03458

LOWE, ADELE VIRGINIA (MRS. ALBERT ST. CLAIR LOWE), retired pharmacist; b. Indpls., June 27, 1919; d. Michael Angelo and Ivy Opal (Wilson) Lobraico; B.S. Indpls. Coll. Pharmacy, 1941; m. Albert St. Clair Lowe, Dec. 10, 1942; 1 dau., Judith A. (Mrs. Robert Frank Campbell). Chemist, E.I. duPont de Nemours & Co., Pryor, Okla., 1942-43; registered pharmacist Lobraico's Broad Ripple Pharmacy, Indpls., 1943-90, ret. Mem. Nat. Assn. Retail Druggists, Womens Orgn. Nat. Assn. Retail Druggists (pres. chpt. 20, 1977-79, chmn. legis. com.) Indpls. Assn. Pharmacists, Broad Ripple Bus. and Profl. Womens Club, Lambda Kappa Sigma (mem. grand council, supr. Midwest region 1948-50, 66-68, supr. So. region 1958-60, 4th v.p. 1950-54, grand v.p. 1968-70, grand pres. 1970-74, mem.-at-large 1974-78, chmn. ednl. trust com. 1975—, hon. adv. 1978-84, Disting. Service citation 1982). Clubs: Order Eastern Star, Daus. of Nile. Home: 12610 Brookshire Pkwy Carmel IN 46032 Office: 902 E Westfield Blvd Indianapolis IN 46220

LOWE, ETHEL BLACK, artist; b. Kiowa County, Olka., Jan. 30, 1904; d. Benjamin Alonzo and Harriet Ann (Heaton) Black; m. William Glenn Lowe, June 5, 1939 (dec. 1942). BA, Cen. State U., Okla., 1926; MA, U. Tulsa, 1937; postgrad., U. Okla., U. Colo., Columbia, U. Hawaii. Tchr. pub. schs. Okla., 1922-39, N.Y., 1942-49, 50-68; ret.; teaching prin. Dragon Sch., Sasebo, Kyushu, Japan, 1949-50. Exhibits include Nat. Assn. Women Artists, 1953, 55, 71, 75, 77, Terry Nat. Art Exhibit, 1952, Provincetown Art Assn., 1952-53, Nassau Community Coll., 1971; represented in schs. and pvt. collections; reproductions of works in newspapers, mags, paintings in schs. and pvt. homes. Mem. N.Y. State Ret. Tchrs. Assn., Nat. Assn. Women Artists, Am. Watercolor Soc., Nat. Ret. Tchrs. Assn., Delta Kappa Gamma. Home: 48-50 44th St Woodside NY 11377

LOWE, FLORENCE SEGAL, public relations executive; b. N.Y.C.; d. Samuel I. and Rose (Cantor) Segal; BS in Edn., U. Pa., 1930; postgrad. Sch. Social Svc., 1935-36; m. Herman Albert Lowe, June 27, 1935; children: Lesley Ellen Lowe Israel, Roger Bernard. Guidance counsellor Phila. Pub. Schs., 1935-41; Washington corr. Variety and Daily Variety, Phila. Daily News, Manchester Union Leader, TV Guide, 1942-58; spl. pub. rels. Radio Sta. WIP, Phila. and Metromedia, 1958-60; coord. spl. projects Metromedia, 1960-70; spl. asst. to chmn. pub. affairs Nat. Endowment for Arts, Washington, 1970-86; sr. cons. arts and cultural communications Kamber Group, 1986—. Mem. pub. rels. and advt. com. Nat. Symphony, 1952-56; mem. Sec. State's Commn. on Travel, 1970-71; mem. Coordinating Com. for Ellis Island, 1982-87; mem. Com. for Nancy Hanks Endowment for Arts, Duke U. Recipient All-Army Entertainment Contest award, 1958; spl. achievement award Nat. Endowment for Arts Chmn., 1983; Spl. Merit award Fed. Govt., 1981, Spl. Achievement award, 1983, Disting. Svc. award, 1985. Mem. Am. Women in Radio and TV (founder, pres. 1954-55), Am. News Women's Club, Coun. Jewish Women, Women in Communications (citation for meritorious reporting 1962), Nat. Press Club, Women's Nat. Press Club (treas. 1954, v.p. 1956, Washington Press Club (bd. dirs. 1968-71, 83-84), Am. News Women's Club (v.p. 1969-70), Washington Press Club Found. Republican. Home: 2801 New Mexico Ave NW Washington DC 20007 Office: Kamber Group 1920 L St NW Washington DC 20037

LOWE, JANET, financial writer; b. Santa Rosa, Calif., May 15, 1940; d. David W. and Celesta (Lisle) L.; m. Edward Husmann, 1960 (div. 1968); children: Elizabeth, Rise; m. H. Austin Lynas, Sept. 6, 1976. U. Nevada, Las Vegas, 1968; MS, San Diego State U., 1982. Writer, instr. San Diego Community Coll., 1972-79; fin. writer The Daily Transfer, San Diego, 1980-81, The Tribune, San Diego, 1981-89; Co-author: "Dividends Don't Lie, A Search for Value in Blue Chip Stocks", 1988. Co-author: Dividends Don't Lie, A Search for Value in Blue Chip Stocks, 1988, paperback, 1990; author: The Super Saver: Fundamental Principles of Building Wealth, 1990. Mem. Soc. Profl Journalists, San Diego Press Club.

LOWE, KATHLEEN ORBAN, learning disabilities specialist; b. Colorado Springs, Colo., Apr. 2, 1947; d. Henry Albert and Jacqueline Lucile (Krogh) Orban; m. Robert N. Lowe, May 24, 1969; children: Matthew, Timothy. BA in Social Studies, So. Meth. U., 1969; MEd in Learning Disabil., Ga. State U., 1975. Learning disabilities resource tchr. Peachtree Elem. Sch., Norcross, Ga., 1973-75, Barton Chapel Elem. Sch., Augusta, Ga., 1975-77, Sweetwater Middle Sch., Lawrenceville, Ga., 1978-80, Trickum Middle Sch., Lilburn, Ga., 1980-81; interrelated resource tchr. S. Columbia Elem. Sch., Martinez, Ga., 1977-78; learning disabilities specialist Brevard Community Coll., Cocoa, Fla., 1982-88; curriculum and learning disabilities specialist for continuing edn. Brevard Community Coll., Cocoa, 1988—; cons., presenter workshops in field. Mem. Assn. for Children and Adults with Learning Disabilities, Fla. Assn. for Children with Learning Disabilities, Titusville Jr. Women's Club (bd. dirs. 1987-88), Titusville Soccer Club (bd. dirs. 1984-87), Phi Beta Kappa. Republican. Presbyterian. Home: 3713 Chiara Dr Titusville FL 32796

LOWE, MARGARET B., personnel director; b. Phila., Aug. 14, 1927; d. Horace Willard and Ellen (Gallagher) Breece; m. E. Nobles Lowe, Dec. 1, 1961; 1 child, James. BS, Pa. State U., 1949; MA, Columbia U., 1972. Pers. asst. Pa. State U., 1949-51, Westvaco, 1951-53; group ins. rep. N.Y. Life Ins. Co., 1953-55; mgr. employee benefits Warner Lambert Pharm. Co., 1955-62; pers. dir. Barnard Coll., 1972-78, Inst. of Internat. Edn., 1978-81, Ford Found., 1981—. Co-chmn. League of Women Voters, East Manhattan, N.Y. 1966-70 (mem. Legal Aid Women's Com 1970-72); pres. YWCA NYC, 1987— (bd. dirs. 1976—). Mem. Gipsy Trail Club (Carmel, N.Y.). Office: The Ford Found 320 E 43rd St New York NY 10017

LOWE, MARY JOHNSON, federal judge; b. N.Y.C., June 10, 1924; children by previous marriage: Edward H., Leslie H.; m. Ivan A. Michael, Nov. 4, 1961; 1 child, Bess J. Michael. BA, Hunter Coll., 1952; JD, Bklyn. Law Sch., 1954; LLM, Columbia U., 1955. Bar: N.Y. 1955. Pvt. practice law N.Y.C., 1955-71; judge N.Y.C. Criminal Ct., 1971-73; acting justice N.Y. State Supreme Ct., 1973-74, justice, 1977-78; judge Bronx County Supreme Ct., 1975-76; justice 1st Jud. Dist., 1978; judge U.S. Dist. Ct. (so. dist.) N.Y., 1978—. Recipient award for outstanding service to criminal justice system Bronx County Criminal Cts. Bar Assn., 1974, award for work on narcotics cases Asst. Dist. Attys., 1974. Mem. Women in Criminal Justice, Harlem Lawyers Assn., Bronx Criminal Lawyers Assn., N.Y. County Lawyers Assn., Bronx County Bar Assn., N.Y. State Bar Assn. (award for outstanding jud. contbn. to criminal justice Sect. Criminal Justice 1978), NAACP, Nat. Urban League, Nat. Council Negro Women, NOW. Office: US Dist Ct US Courthouse Foley Sq New York NY 10007*

LOWE, RITA K., healthcare professional; b. Louisville, Aug. 8, 1966; d. Gordon Fields and Mary Lilly (Grissom) L; m. Jeffrey A. Bowen, May 21, 1988. BA with distinction, Hanover (Ind.) Coll., 1987; student, Centre Coll., Danville, Ky., 1984. Br. support Citizen Fidelity Bank, Louisville; asst. dir. planning and placement Ind. Vocat. Tech. Coll., Madison; placement dir., work study coord. Watterson Coll., Louisville; patient rep. Humana Hosp-Audubon, Louisville. Mem. Nat. Soc. for Patient Reps. (sec. Ky. chpt.), Ky. Soc. Patient Representation and Consumer Affairs, Mortar Board. Address: 7101 Shibley Ave Louisville KY 40291

LOWE, RUTHE MEEKINS, guidance counselor; b. Vicksburg, Miss., Jan. 1, 1945; d. Charles Alvin and Nicie (Flowers) Meekins; m. Harrison Lowe, Aug. 20, 1966; children: Sheila Dionne, Tracey M., Toni Tinese. BEd, Talladega Coll., 1965; MS in Guidance, Jackson State U., 1972; Specialist Degree in Edn., Miss. State U., 1975. Math. tchr Vickburg Pub. Schs., 1965-67; exec. sec. Child Devel. Group Miss., Edwards, 1965; tchr. Warren County Schs., 1967-69, Warren City Schs., Vicksburg, 1969—; guidance counselor Vicksburg Warren Sch. Dist., 1978—; counselor for single parents and displace homemakers Vicksburg Warren Schs., 1989—; chmn. Vickburg Warren Credit Union 1984—. Author: EEO (Equal Edn. Opportunity) Newsletter, 1987. Mem. Am. Personnel Guidance Assn., Miss. Counseling Assn., Capitol Area Counseling Assn. (pres. 1984-85), Am. Fedn. Tchrs., Paramount Civic and Social Club. Democrat. Baptist. Home: 1927 Martin Luther King Dr Vickburg MS 39180 Office: Sch Adminstrv Bldg Annex A Hwy 27 Vicksburg MS 39180

LOWE, SUE ESTHER, optometrist; b. Scottsburg, Ind., July 22, 1954; d. Donald and Etta (Helton) L.; m. Eric Stephen Lundell, May 24, 1953. BA, U. Wyoming, 1976; OD, Pacific U., Forest Grove, Oreg., 1980. Rsch. asst. Pacific U. Coll. of Optometry, Forest Grove, Oreg., 1976-77; pvt. practice optometrist, 1980—; assoc. Snowy Range Vision Ctr., Laramie, Wyo., 1980-82, ptnr. Trustee Albany County Hosp. Dist., 1985-88, mem. Episcopal Ch., 1983—, bd. dirs. LWV, 1981—, Wyoming Infant Stimulation, 1982—, Precinct Com. Woman, 1983-84; interviewer Albany County Oral History Project, 1983-86. Named One of the Outstanding Young Women of Am, 1976, 1978, Outstanding Greek Woman, 1976. Fellow Acad. of Optometry, Coll. Optometrists in Vision Devel.; mem. Am. Optometric Assn., Wyoming Optometric Assn., Calif. Optometric Assn., Colo. Optometric Assn., Am. Pub. Health Assn., Infant Stimulation Edn. Assn., Am. Optometric Found., Zontas Internat. Lioness, Omega Epsilon Phi, Alpha Epsilon Delta, Alpha Chi Omega Alumna Club. Democrat. Home: 1704 Skyline Rd Laramie WY 82070 Office: Snowy Range Vision Ctr 301 S 8th Laramie WY 82070

LOWELL, JACQUELINE PETERS, advertising agency executive. With Lewis, Gilman & Kynett, Inc., Phila., 1980—, v.p., sr. v.p., now sr. v.p., exec. creative dir. Recipient numerous creative awards. Office: Lewis Gilman & Kynett Inc 200 S Broad St Philadelphia PA 19103*

LOWENGARD, MARY BEAR, public relations executive; b. Phila., July 15, 1953; d. Jerome Harry and Elaine (Title) Lowengard. BA with honors, NYU, 1974; MA, Columbia U., 1977; MBA, UCLA, 1986. Tchr., adminstr. Dalton Sch., N.Y.C., 1974-78; edn. coord. Info. Builders, Inc., N.Y.C., 1981-82; cons. Peat, Marwick, Mitchell, N.Y.C., 1982-83, QAD Systems (Hewlett Packard), Santa Barbara, Calif., 1983-84; mgr. investor rels. Continental Corp., N.Y.C., 1987-88; ind. cons. N.Y.C., 1988—. Author: Investor Relations, 1988; contbr. articles to Pub. Rels. jour. Mem. Nat. Investor Rels. Inst. Democrat. Office: 300 Grand St #421 Hoboken NJ 07030

LOWENTHAL, JUDITH NELSON, psychologist; b. Phila., Nov. 15, 1945; d. Sidney David and Pauline (Taksey) Nelson; m. Rodger Lowenthal; m. Alan Robert Morgenstein; children: Jessica, Eric, Ariel. BA, Penn State U., 1966; MA, Temple U., 1969; PhD, U. Pa., 1974. Cert. psychologist. Psychologist Diagnostic & Rehab. Ctr., Phila., 1967-69, Phila. Gen. Hosp., 1969-70, Cope Ctrs., Ambler, Pa., 1972-75; pvt. practice psychotherapy Elkins Park, 1975—; lectr. U. Pa., Phila., 1981—, Community Coll. Phila., 1985—, Coll. Allied Health, Thomas Jefferson U., 1989—; cons. in field. Pres. Del. Valley AHP, Phila., 1978-80. Mem. Am. Psychol. Assn., Assn. Humanistic Psychology (pres. Phila. chpt. 1978-80). Democrat. Jewish. Home and Office: 530 Elkins Ave Elkins Park PA 19117

LOWENTHAL, SUSAN, finance company executive; b. Munich, Nov. 30, 1946; came to U.S., 1949; d. Jerry and Gertrude (Wiestreich) L.; m. Alex J. Stolitzka, Oct. ll, 1987. BA, Bklyn. Coll., 1969. Exec. dir. Manhattan Girls Club, N.Y.C., 1969-73; conf. coord. Orton Soc., N.Y.C., 1973-77; v.p. Gemtique, N.Y.C., 1977-81; broker Prudential Bache, N.Y.C., 1981-83, Smith Barney, N.Y.C., 1983-85; pres., chief exec. officer Lowenthal Fin. Svcs., Inc., N.Y.C., 1985-89, ind. fin. cons., 1990—. Jewish.

LOWER, DOROTHY MARGARET, editor, retired librarian; b. Monroeville, Ind., Feb. 5, 1914; d. Allen Virgil and Cleo Marguerite (Edwards) L. AB, Western Coll., 1936; MA, Ind. U., 1960. Mem. staff Ft. Wayne (Ind.) Pub. Libr., 1957-60, mgr. genealogy dept., 1961-84; editor Gale Rsch. Co., Detroit, 1985—; tchr. genealogy adult edn. dept. Purdue U., Ft. Wayne, 1968-69. Author: The Patriots, 1976, Basic Bibliography for a Genealogy Collection, 1982; editor: (series) Passenger and Immigration Lists Index, 1986—. Vol. receptionist Allen County Hist. Mus., Ft. Wayne, 1984—. Recipient Cert. of Appreciation, State of Ind., 1984, Disting. Svc. award Fedn. Geneal. Socs., 1987. Mem. Ind. Geneal. Soc., Soc. Ind. Pioneers, Colonial Dames XVII Century (registrar 1987-89), DAR (1st vice-regent 1987-89). Republican. Home: 1310 3 Rivers E Fort Wayne IN 46802

LOWERS, GINA CATTANI, physicist; b. Evanston, Ill., Oct. 16, 1961; d. Lawrence F. and Arlene Bernice (Phillips) Cattani; m. Robert Judson Lowers, Oct. 10, 1984. BS in Math., U. Calif., Riverside, 1984; BS in Physics, Carnegie-Mellon U., 1987, MS in Physics, 1989; postgrad., W.Va. U. Test systems engr. Aerojet Electrosystems Co., Azusa, Calif., 1983-85; instr. calculus Carnegie Mellon U., Pitts., 1986-88; product devel. engr. Philips Lighting Co., Fairmont, W.Va., 1988—; lectr. physics Fairmont State Coll., 1990—. Judge physics and math. orals and presentations W.Va. State Sci. and Engring. Fair, 1989-1990, judge physics projects, 1989. Mem. Am. Phys. Soc., Electrochem. Soc., Soc. Mfg. Engrs., Soc. Tech. Communication. Office: Philips Lighting Co Rt 3 Box 505 Fairmont WV 26554

LOWERY, SHARON A., travel industry executive; b. Chgo., Sept. 27, 1943; d. James William and Alice Dorothy (Buckley) L. BA, Knox Coll., 1965. Owner Expert Visa Svc., Chgo. Mem. Nat. Assn. Women Bus. Owners, Nat. Bus. Travel Assn., Ohio Valley Bus. Travel Assn. Home: 1430 Sandstone Dr Wheeling IL 60090 Office: 203 N Wabash Ave Chicago IL 60603

LOWERY-PAYNTER, MARION MARGARET, rehabilitation counselor; b. Phila., Dec. 19, 1934; d. Harry Galleghar and Margaret (Sauer) R.; m. James E. Paynter, Aug. 29, 1989; children from previous marriage: Pamela A., James D., Stephen L. BA, U. North Colo., Greeley, 1967-70; EdM magna cum laude, Oreg. State U., 1974. Coord.-adult basic Edn. Rogue Com. Coll., Grants Pass, 1971-75; dir.-loaves and fishes Fed. Title VII Programme, Medford, 1975-79; child abuse caseworker State Oregon, Medford, 1979-81; adult caseworker State of Oregon, Medford, employment spec., 1982-87; rehabilitation counselor State Oregon, 1987—. Author: (pub. rsch.) Changing Status of Women in Middle East. Bd. dirs. Crisis Intervention Svc., Parents Anonymous, Supported Work Coun., Interagy. Coun., Medford, 1980-90, Crisis Intervention Coun. Democrat. Home: 830 Carol Rae Medford OR 97501 Office: Vocat Rehab 201 W Main Ste 2A Medford OR 97501

LOWEY, NITA M., congresswoman; b. July 5, 1937; m. Stephen Lowey, 1961; children: Dona, Jacqueline, Douglas. BS, Mt. Holyoke Coll., 1959. Community activist, prior to 1975; asst. sec. state State of N.Y., 1975-87; mem. 101st, 102nd Congresses from 20th N.Y. dist., 1989—. Democrat. Office: US Ho of Reps Office House Mems Washington DC 20515*

LOWMAN, MARY BETHENA HEMPHILL (ZELVIN D. LOWMAN), civic worker, realtor; b. Lewis, Kans., Feb. 10, 1922; d. Frederick William and Gladys (Follin) Hemphill. A.B., Western State Coll., Colo., 1945; m. Zelvin D. Lowman, Oct. 24, 1943; children: Freda Ruth (Mrs. Neal Frink), James Fredrick, William Martin, Elizabeth June (Mrs. Joseph Herbst) (dec.). Tchr. Stout Creek Sch., Colo., 1942-43, San Diego City Sch. Dist., 1944-45, L.A. City Sch. Dist., 1948-50; pvt. sch. tchr. So. Inst. Music, 1956-57. Troop leader Frontier coun. Girl Scouts U.S., 1957-70, mem. exec. bd., 1961-73, 2d v.p., 1962-63, pres., 1968-71, chmn. established camp com., 1963-67, dir. Camp Foxtail, 1965, 67, chmn. Gold award com., 1986-87; mem. Calico Task Group, 1986-89, chmn., 1988-89; mem. Girl Scouts U.S. Region VI Com., 1973-75, chmn. Region VI Com., mem. nat. bd., mem. exec. com. and couns. com., 1975-78; mem. Am. Field Svc. Exchange Student Bd. So. Nev., 1961. Parliamentarian, West Charleston PTA, 1957-59, Nev. Congress, 1960-61; elder, trustee Presbyn. Ch., 1964-67, 90—; chmn. Christian Edn. Commn., 1964-65; chmn. Commn. on Mission of Ch., 1966; chmn. exec. com. Clark County Bicentennial Commn., 1974-76; chmn. bd. First Presbyn Pre-Sch. Day Care Ctr., 1982-85. Family chosen as Nev. All-Am. Family, 1960. Recipient Thanks Badge U.S. Girl Scouts U.S., 1963, Thanks Badge II, 1989. Mem. Gen. Fedn. Women's Clubs (dir. 1958-60, 62-64, 72-78, chmn. scholarships and student aid 1974-76, chmn. family living div., 1976-78; treas. Western States Conf. 1968-70, sec. 1970-72, pres. 1972-74), Nev. Fedn. Women's Clubs, (past pres.), Md. fedn. women's Clubs (past jr. dir.), Clark County Pan-Hellenic Assn., So. Nev. Alumni Club (pres. 1961-62), Internat. Platform Assn. Presbyn. (elder, dir. capital stewarship canvas program, 1987-88), Las Vegas Bd. Realtors (chmn. membership com. 1988-90, vice chmn. bylaws com. 1990—, memberships com. 1990—), Las Vegas Mesquite Club (past pres.), Jr. Women's Club (past pres., College Park, Md.), Newcomers Club (past pres.), Nat. Presbyn. Mariners Club (past pres.), Nevada-Sierra District Mariners Club, Las Vegas Nautilus Mariners Club. Home: 1713 Rambla Ct Las Vegas NV 89102

LOWMAN, MEREDITH ANN, executive assistant; b. Bklyn., Oct. 7, 1950; d. Jules and Ann Meredith (Buckley) Honig; m. John M. Sweeney, Feb. 15, 1970 (div. Feb. 1972); m. James Charles Lowman, Aug. 7, 1976; children: Erin Meredith, Joshua Craig. Student, Western Ill. U., 1983, Howard Community Coll., 1990—. Sec. to exec. v.p. Compton Co., N.Y.C., 1972-78; asst. to sales mgr. Inc. Mag., N.Y.C., 1980; sec., bookkeeper Sta. WJEQ div. McDonough Broadcasting Co., Macomb, Ill., 1983-84; sec. III Coll. Fine Arts Western Ill. U., Macomb, 1984-85; adminstrv. asst. The Ryland Group, Columbia, Md., 1985-86; word processing adminstr. Bon Secours Health System, Columbia, 1986-87; system adminstr. The Enterprise Found., Columbia, 1987-89; office mgr. Nucletron Corp., Columbia, 1989—. Asst. to dir., bookkeeper Two Rivers Arts Coun., Macomb; former leader Girl Scouts U.S.; den leader Boy Scouts Am., Columbia. Mem. NAFE, Mid-Atlantic Notary Assn. (notary). Democrat. Jewish. Home: 5772 Flag Flower Pl Columbia MD 21045

LOWMAN, PATRICIA J., controller; b. Dearborn, Mich., Nov. 28, 1941; d. Albert F. and Edith V. (Trombley) Frost; children: Daniel, Erin. Student, U. Utah. Cert. in mgmt. and mktg. Internat. Coun. Shopping Ctrs. Mgr., leasing agt., controller Horman & Sons, Salt Lake City; controller, corp. office mgr. Conely Co., Salt Lake City; systems analyst Info Now, Inc., Salt Lake City; asst. controller Jardine Petroleum, North Salt Lake City; controller Al Park Petroleum, Elko, Nev. 2nd lt. Civil Air Patrol, cadet leader 1989—; girls' dir. United Youth Soccer Assn., vol. coach 1980-85. Mem. Am. Soc. Women Accts., Mensa. Home: 690 E Patriot Blvd #373 Reno NV 89511

LOWRANCE, MURIEL EDWARDS, program specialist; b. Ada, Okla., Dec. 28, 1922; d. Warren E. and Mayme E. (Barrick) Edwards; B.S. in Edn., East Central State U., Ada, 1954; 1 dau., Kathy Lynn Lowrance Gutierrez. Accountant, adminstrv. asst. to bus. mgr. East Central State U., 1950-68; grants and contracts specialist U. N.Mex. Sch. Medicine, Albuquerque, 1968-72, program specialist IV, dept. orthopaedics, 1975-86; asst. adminstrv. officer N.Mex. Regional Med. Program, 1972-75. Bd. dirs. Vocat. Rehab. Center, 1980-84. Cert. profl. contract mgr. Nat. Contract Assn. Mem. Am. Bus. Women's Assn. (past pres. El Segundo chpt., Woman of Yr. 1974), AAUW, Amigos de las Americas (dir.). Democrat. Methodist. Club: Pilot (Albuquerque) (pres. 1979-80, dir. 1983-84, dist. treas. 1984-86, treas. S.W. dist., 1984-86, gov.-elect S.W. dist. 1986-87, gov. S.W. dist. 1987-88). Home: 3028 Mackland Ave NE Albuquerque NM 87106

LOWRIE, KATHRYN YANACEK, recruiting service executive; b. Midland, Mich., Nov. 23, 1958; d. Frank Joseph and Jacqueline Ann (Sipko) Yanacek; m. David Bruce Lowrie, Mar. 14, 1987. BA in Psychology, Northeastern U., 1980. Psychology tech. Research Inst. of Environ. Medicine, U.S. Army, Natick, Mass., 1980-81, computer programmer, 1981-83; assoc. recruiter Mgmt. Adv. Services, Burlington, Mass., 1983-85, v.p. mgmt. info. systems, 1985-86, exec. v.p., 1986-89; chief exec. officer Computer Careers, Raynham, Mass., 1989—. Mem. NAFE. Roman Catholic. Office: 9 Sarah Ln Raynham MA 02767

LOWRY, CONSTANCE KEENAN, science teacher; b. Olean, N.Y., July 11, 1956; d. Leo Edward Jr. and Ann (Finlay) Keenan; m. Joseph Patrick Lowry, Dec. 29, 1984. BS, St. Bonaventure (N.Y.) U., 1977; M Sport Mgmt., U. Ga., 1984. Cert. tchr., Tex., N.Y., Okla., Ga. Residence sales rep. N.Y. Telephone Co., Olean, 1980-81; tchr., coach Ellicottville (N.Y.) Central Sch., 1981-83, Hefner Jr. High Sch., Oklahoma City, 1985-87, Creekwood Middle Sch., Kingwood, Tex., 1988—; teaching asst. U. Ga., Athens, 1983-84; asst. sports promotion intern U.S. Mil. Acad., West Point, N.Y., 1984; tchr. Stovall Jr. High Sch., Houston, 1987-88. Sch. chmn. United Way, Oklahoma City, 1986-87. 2d lt. U.S. Army, 1977-79. Mem. Nat. Sci. Tchrs. Assn., Delta Epsilon Sigma. Roman Catholic.

LOWRY, JEAN, retired geology educator; b. Indpls., Feb. 7, 1921; d. Ellsworth and Ethel (Stryker) L. BS in Geology, Pa. State U., 1942; PhD in Geology, Yale U., 1951. Jr. economist non-metallic minerals sect. Office Price Adminstrn., Washington, 1942-43; cons. quartz crytsal sect. Bd. Econ. Warfare, Washington, 1943; from jr. to asst. geologist groundwater sect. U.S. Geol. Survey, Jamaica, N.Y., and New Haven, 1943-49; dist. geologist Va. Geol. Survey, Wytheville, 1949-57; prof. geology East Carolina U., Greenville, N.C., 1958-83, prof. emeritus, 1983—; vis. prof. U. Concepción, Chile, 1962-63. Sec. Greenville Bi-Racial Com., 1972-74; pres. Pitt County chpt. ACLU, Greenville, 1973-75. Democrat. Unitarian. Home: 211 S Eastern St Greenville NC 27858

LOWRY, JOAN MARIE DONDREA, broadcaster; b. Weirton, W.Va., June 8, 1935; d. Rudolph and Mary (Telmanik) Dondrea; m. Robert William Lowry, June 15, 1957; 1 child, Christopher Scott. B.S. in Edn., Baldwin-

Wallace Coll., 1956; student Ohio Sch. Broadcasting, 1977-79. Gen. mgr., news dir. Sta. WLRO, Lorain, Ohio, 1980-82; host 35 Live, Cinemavidio TV, Elyria, Ohio, 1980-83; TV show host Continental Cable, Cleve., 1983—; pub. relations dir. Sta. WZLE, Lorain, 1982-83; broadcaster, community relations dir. Sta. WRKG, Lorain, 1983—, news dir., 1988—; performer commls.; speaker in field. Appeared in motion pictures: Those Lips Those Eyes, 1982, One Trick Pony, 1982. Mem. nat. steering com. Better Hearing and Speech, 1985—, Lorain County coun., 1986—; mem. community resource council Leadership Lorain County, 1988-89; nat. pres. Delta Zeta Sorority and Found., 1980—, trustee, 1980—, nat. found. pres., 1987—; mem. Lorain Litter Control Bd., 1981-83, communications and mktg. com. United Way, 1987—; bd. dirs. Lorain Conty Sr. Citizens Assn., 1982-85, Lorain Consumers Council, 1980—; v.p. Bay Village PTA Council, 1973-75; mem. Martin Luther King Steering Com., 1987—; chmn. adv. bd. Lorain County Heart Assn., 1988; mem. Am. Heart Assn. Leadership Council, 1988—; active Multiple Sclerosis Soc., Am. Cancer Soc., Muscular Dystrophy Assn., Founders Meml. Found, others; chair Lorain County Mothers March of Dimes, 1988; grand marshal numerous parades. Named Woman of Achievement, Nat. YWCA and Lorain County Bus. and Industry Assn., 1983, Ohio Delta Zeta Alumnae Woman of Yr.; recipient USAF award, 1982, USN award, 1981, Media award Am. Cancer Soc., 1982, Communication award Easter Seals Soc., 1981, Community Service award Lorain County chpt. Am. Heart Assn., 1981, Service to Mankind award Sertoma Internat., 1988; ofcl. hostess for U.S. Army in Lorain County, 1980-83; Mayor's Proclamation, 1982; hon. recruiter award U.S. Army, 1981; recognition award Ohio House Reps. Mem. Bus. and Profl. Women, Lorain County Arts Council, Baldwin-Wallace Alumni Assn. (nat. pres. 1979-81), LWV (chpt. pres. 1966-67), Cleve. Amateur Fencers (pres. 1965-67), Internat. Platform Assn. Byzantine Catholic. Home: 578 Yarmouth Ln Bay Village OH 44140

LOWRY, MARLENE FAYE, special education teacher; b. Hays, Kans., June 23, 1950; d. Ruben Harold and Viola Elnora (Timken) Grose; m. Ronald Ivan Lowry, Nov. 5, 1983; 1 child, Bennett Alan. AA, Hutchinson Community Coll., 1970; BS, Kans. State U., 1972, MS, 1973; postgrad., Kansas State U., 1973—, Emporia State U., 1973—, Ft. Hays State U., 1973—. Cert. elem. tchr. Educable mentally handicapped tchr. Washington Grade Sch., Independence, Kans., 1972-73; emotionally disturbed tchr. South Breeze Grade Sch., Newton, Kans., 1973-74; educable mentally handicapped tchr. Rex Grade Sch., Haysville, Kans., 1974-78; second grade tchr. Udall (Kans.) Grade Sch., 1978-81; at-risk tchr. Ellsworth (Kans.) High Sch., 1988—; CPR instr., Am. Heart Assn., 1979-81; cons. Mary Kay Cosmetics, 1989—. Designer wheat waving display Nat. Mus. Am. History, Washington, 1986. Mem. NEA, Kansas NEA, Internat. Twins Assn., Kans. State Twins Assn. (co-founder 1979, co-pres. 1979-81, 88), Twins Found., Nat. Assn. of Wheat Weavers (numerous awards), Nat. Campers and Hikers Assn., Smoky Hill Campers Extention Homemakers Unit, Kappa Delta Pi. Republican. United Methodist. Home: 807 Charles Ellsworth KS 67439 Office: Ellsworth High School Unified School Dist #327 Ellsworth KS 67439

LOWRY, PATRICIA See **HOFF, KATHLEEN PATRICIA**

LOWSON, KATHLEEN, motion picture and television producer; b. Bklyn., Aug. 26, 1953; d. Harry John Lowson and Frances Sicari. MA in Bus. and Psychology, SUNY, Stony Brook, 1971. Vice pres. VJL & Assocs., Inc., N.Y.C., 1972-82; pres., owner Lowson Entertainment Internat., L.A., 1983—; cons. in field. Exec. producer theme song and feature film Room Enough to Dance, The Armageddon File; creator, writer, exec. producer TV series Teenage America, feature film screenplay Spelling on the Stone, 1989. Office: 7130 Hollywood Blvd Los Angeles CA 90046

LOY, MYRNA, actress; b. Helena, Mont., Aug. 2, 1905; d. David Franklin and Della Williams. Grad., Venice (Calif.) High Sch., Westlake Sch. Girls. Appeared in numerous motion pictures, including Best Years of Our Lives (award World Film Festival, Brussels), 1946, The Bachelor and the Bobby Soxer, 1947, Mr. Blanding Builds His Dream House, 1948, If This Be Sin, Cheaper by the Dozen, 1950, Airport 75, The End, 1979, Just Tell Me What You Want, 1980, others; appeared in stage plays Relative Speaking; TV appearances in Death Takes a Holiday, also, Do Not Fold, Spindle or Mutilate, Indict and Convict, Columbo, Ironsides, Family Affair, The Virginian, The Couple Takes a Wife, It Happened at Lakewood Manor, Summer Solstice, 1981. Organizer Hollywood Film com. U.S. Nat. Commn. for UNESCO, 1948, mem. commn., 1950-54; asst. head welfare activities ARC, N.Y. area, 1941-45; Mem. Am. Assn. UN, Nat. Commn. Against Discrimination in Housing. Recipient Kennedy Ctr. Honor, 1988. Address: 229 S Orange Dr Los Angeles CA 90036

LOYLESS, BONNIE WAINRIGHT, educator; b. Macon, Ga., Apr. 12, 1954; d. Walter Matthew and Helen (Bazemore) Wainright; m. Kirk G. Loyless, Feb. 3, 1973 (div. 1982); 1 child, Deborah Kirk. BSEd, Ga. State U., 1977; MEd, Ga. So. Coll., 1984, EdS, 1987. Cert. tchr., Ga. Libr. asst. Ga. State U., Atlanta, 1973-76; tchr. Valdosta (Ga.) City Sch. System, 1977-78, Jefferson County Sch. System, Louisville, Ga., 1978-80, Burke County Sch. System, Sardis, Ga., 1981-82, Jeff Davis County Sch. System, Hazlehurst, Ga., 1982—. Adviser Y Clubs, State YMCA Ga., 1982—; mem. Jeff Davis County Libr. Bd., Hazlehurst, 1989—; pres. Circle VI, United Meth. Women, Hazlehurst, 1990. Mem. Profl. Assn. Ga. Educators, Phi Delta Kappa, Phi Kappa Phi. Home: 402 Wilson St Hazlehurst GA 31539 Office: Jeff Davis High Sch Broxton Rd Hazlehurst GA 31439

LU, ALLENA FONG, computer software executive; b. San Francisco, Nov. 9, 1941; d. Allen Teng and Abbie (Lau) Fong; m. David S. Lu, June 19, 1965; children: Gene, Donhald, Bonnie. BA, U. Calif., Berkeley, 1963; postgrad., U. Calif., Irvine, 1980-81. Computer programmer Aeronutronic/Ford Motor Co., Newport Beach, Calif., 1963-65; mathematician Lockheed-Calif. Co., Burbank, 1965-66; software engr. Aerojet Gen. Corp., Azusa, Calif., 1967-68; programming supr. McDonnell Douglas Automation, Carson, Calif., 1974-79; programming mgr. Calcomp, Anaheim, Calif., 1979-84; from software mgr. to pres. Systonetics, Inc., Fullerton, Calif., 1984—. Mem. Project Mgmt. Inst., U.S. Power Squadron. Republican. Office: Systonetics Inc 1561 E Orangethorpe Fullerton CA 92631

LU, MARY CHAO, chemistry educator; b. Liaoyang, China, Sept. 6, 1935; came to U.S., 1956; d. Yun Ti and Pin Ru (Chang) Chao; m. Paul H. Lu; children: William Yaun-Hai, Henry Yaun-Huang. BS, Notre Dame Coll., 1959; MS, U. Detroit, 1962; PhD, U. Tenn., 1968. Chemist U.S. Testing Co., Hoboken, N.J., 1961-62; asst. prof. chemistry Morris Coll., Sumter, S.C., 1963-64; prof. chemistry and math Lincoln Meml. U., Harrogate, Tenn., 1968-78; prof. chemistry Walter State Community Coll., Morristown, Tenn., 1978—; rsch. participant Dept. Energy, Oak Ridge Nat. Lab., 1980, 83. Mem. Am. Chem. Soc., Tenn. Acad. Sci. Home: 4297 Henrietta Dr Morristown TN 37814 Office: Walters State Community Col Morristown TN 37814

LUALLEN, SALLY CAROL SHANK, director college programs; b. Liberal, Kans., July 4, 1938; d. Albert Isaac and Maxine A. (Long) Shank; m. Donald C. Luallen, June 24, 1964; children: Stacy Carol, Amy Joan, Molly Dawn. B Music Edn., Wichita State U., 1960. Tchr. music Wichita (Kans.) Pub. Schs., 1960-62, Liberal Pub. Schs., 1963-64, 66-67; instr. music edn. Dodge City (Kans.) Community Coll., 1964-65, mgr. spl. projects, coord. arts and humanities, 1988—. Co-founder, past pres. Dodge City Area Arts Coun.; bd. dirs. Dodge City Community Concerts Assn., 1970—, pres., 1983-86; past pres., v.p. region II, PTA; chmn. coun. on ministries, mem. edn. com., dir. youth choir 1st United Meth. Ch., Dodge City; bd. dirs. Mid-Am. Arts Alliance, 1979-80; bd. dirs. Sta. KANZ, PBS, 1983-89, also mem. exec. bd., sec.; mem. Kans. Arts Commn. Adv. Bd., 1983—, Kans. Citizens for Arts, 1984—, Kans. Adv. Com. for Art with Handicapped. Named one of Outstanding Young Women Am., 1967; Wichita Symphony Assn. scholar, 1955-60. Mem. AAUW (v.p., program chmn., Woman of the Yr. 1990), Dodge City Area Women's C. of C. (program and community svc. com.), Assn. Community Arts Agys. Kans. (bd. dirs. 1976—, pres. 1978-80), Wichita State U. Alumni Assn. (bd. dirs. 1984-86), Soroptimists (Athena award 1986, Making a Diffrence for Women award 1989), Mortar Bd., Mu Phi Epsilon, Kappa Delta Pi. Republican. Home: 2020 Windsong Way Dodge City KS 67801 Office: Dodge City Community Coll 2501 N 14th St Dodge City KS 67801

LUBBEN, LYNN-ALISON, flight attendant; b. Danbury, Conn., Oct. 12, 1964; d. Thomas Joseph and Evelyn Ann (Miklaszewski) Evagash; m. Paul Allan Lubben, Oct. 10, 1987. AS in Travel and Tourism, Fisher Jr. Coll., 1985. Flight attendant N.Y. Air/Continental Airlines, 1985—. Mem. Union Flight Attendants. Home: 3302 Glen Springs Kingwood TX 77339 Office: Continental Airlines 2929 Allen Pkwy Houston TX 77210

LUBBERS, LAURA LEE, marketing and advertising executive; b. Grand Rapids, Mich., Mar. 23, 1962; d. Robert and Lorna (Groters) L. BA in Telecommunications, Mich. State U., 1984. Acct. exec. Grand Rapids Mag., 1984-86, WZZM TV-13, Grand Rapids, 1986-88; mktg. mgr. Brooks Shoe Inc., Rockford, Mich., 1988-89, dir. mktg. and advt., 1989—. Mem. NAFE. Office: Brooks Shoe Inc 123 N Main St Rockford MI 49351

LUBECK, SALLY, education educator; b. St. Louis, May 12, 1945; d. Lambert Walter and Erma Jean (Gilbert) Roy; children: Julie Rebecca, Aaron David. BA, Washington U., St. Louis, 1967, MAT in English, 1969, MA in Edn., 1969; EdD, U. Mo., St. Louis, 1984. Postdoctoral felloww Grad. Sch. Edn., Harvard U., 1984-85; postdoctoral fellow U. N.C., Chapel Hill, 1985-86, coord. Bush Inst. for Child & Family Policy, 1986-88, sr. investigator Frank Porter Graham Child Devel. Ctr., 1988—; asst. prof. Sch. Edn. U. N.C., 1988—. Author: Sandbox Society, 1985 (Outstanding Acad. Book award 1987); cons. editor Internat. Jour. Qualitative Rsch. in Edn., 1987—; editor Theory into Practice, winter 1989. Recipient Disting. Alumni award U. Mo., St. Louis, 1988; Spencer fellow, 1986-88. Mem. Am. Ednl. Rsch. Assn. (asst. chmn. div. D 1989-90, Am. Anthrop. Assn. (bd. dirs. coun. on anthropology and edn. 1987-90). Office: 300 NCNB Plaza CB #8040 Chapel Hill NC 27599

LUBIC, RUTH WATSON, association executive, nurse, midwife; b. Bucks County, Pa., Jan. 18, 1927; d. John Russell and Lillian (Kraft) Watson; m. William James Lubic, May 28, 1955; 1 son, Douglas Watson. R.N., Sch. Nursing Hosp. U. Pa., 1955; B.S., Columbia U., 1959, M.A., 1961, Ed.D. in Applied Anthropology, 1979; C.N.M.,M.C.A., SUNY, Bklyn., 1962; LL.D. (hon.), U. Pa., 1985; D.Sc. (hon.), U. Medicine and Dentistry, N.J., 1986. Mem. faculty Sch. Nursing, N.Y. Med. Coll.; mem. faculty Maternity Center Assn., SUNY Sch. Nurse-Midwifery, Downstate Med. Center; staff nurse through head nurse Meml. Hosp. for Cancer and Allied Disease, N.Y.C., 1955-58; clin. assoc. Grad. Sch. Nursing N.Y. Med. Coll., N.Y.C., 1962-63; parent educator, cons. Maternity Ctr. Assn., N.Y.C., 1963-67, gen. dir., 1970—; bd. dirs., v.p. Am. Assn. for World Health U.S. Com. for WHO, 1975—, pres., 1980-81; mem. bd. maternal child and family health research NRC, 1974-80; mem. Commn. on Grads. Fgn. Nursing Schs., 1979-83, v.p., 1980-81, treas., 1982-83; bd. govs. Frontier Nursing Service, 1982—; bd. dirs. Pan Am. Health and Edn. Found., pres. 1987-88. Author: (with Gene Hawes) Childbearing: A Book of Choices, 1987; contbr. articles to profl. jours. Recipient Letitia White award, Florence Nightingale medal, 1955, Alumnae award Sch. Nursing U. Pa., 1986, Rockefeller Public Service award, 1981, Hattie Hemschemeyer award, 1983, R. Louise McManus award Dept. Nursing Alumni Assn. Tchrs. Coll., Columbia U., 1989; named Maternal-Child Health Nurse of Yr., Am. Nurses Assn., 1985. Fellow Am. Acad. Nursing, AAAS, N.Y. Acad. Medicine (assoc.); mem. Am. Coll. Nurse-Midwives (v.p. 1964-66, pres.-elect 1969-70), Am. Pub. Health Assn. (com. internat. health, MCH coun. sec. 1982, governing coun. 1986-89, nominating com. 1987, action bd. 1988-90), Soc. Applied Anthropology, Inst. Medicine of NAS, Nat. Assn. Childbearing Ctrs. (pres. 1983—), Herman Biggs Soc. (sec., treas. 1989-90), Cosmopolitan Club, Sigma Theta Tau. Office: 48 E 92nd St New York NY 10128

LUBIN, JOY KATHLEEN, human resources executive; b. Elizabeth, N.J., July 20, 1943; d. Joseph Andrew and Mary Elizabeth (Hajicek) Silvoy; children: James David, Dawn Marie. Grad. high sch., Clark, N.J. Asst. to pers. mgr. Boyle-Midway div. Am. Home Products Corp., Cranford, N.J., 1961-68; sales rep. Avon Products, Inc., N.Y.C., 1976-81; supr. human resources Glass Products, Inc. subs. AFG Industries, Carbondale, Pa., 1981—; rep. AFG Employee's Credit Union, Kingsport, Tenn., 1986—. Mem. Pa. Employers Adv. Coun. Recipient Outstanding Personal and Profl. Achievement plaque Lackawanna County Pvt. Industry Council, 1986. Mem. Nat. Fedn. Bus. and Profl. Women's Club. Democrat. Roman Catholic. Office: Glass Products Inc Clidco Dr PO Box 313 Carbondale PA 18407

LUBKIN, GLORIA BECKER, physicist; b. Phila., May 16, 1933; d. Samuel Albert and Anne (Gorrin) B.; m. Yale Jay Lubkin, June 14, 1953 (div. Apr. 1968); children: David Craig, Sharon Rebecca. AB, Temple U., 1953; MA, Boston U., 1957; postgrad., Harvard U., 1974-75. Mathematician Fairchild Stratos Co., Hagerstown, Md., 1954, Letterkenny Ordnance Depot, Chambersburg, Pa., 1955-56; physicist TRG Inc., N.Y.C., 1956-58; acting chmn. dept. physics Sarah Lawrence Coll., Bronxville, N.Y., 1961-62; v.p. Lubkin Assocs., electronic cons., Port Washington, N.Y., 1962-68; assoc. editor Physics Today, Am. Inst. Physics, N.Y.C., 1963-69; sr. editor Physics Today, Am. Inst. Physics, 1970-84, editor, 1985—; cons. in field; mem. Nieman adv. com. Harvard U., 1978-82; co-chmn. search/adv. com. Theoretical Physics Inst., U. Minn., 1987-89, co-chmn. oversight com., 1989—; mem. mng. com. Westinghouse Sci. Writing Prizes, 1988—; mem. selection com. Knight Fellowships, 1990—. Contbr. articles to profl. publs. Nieman fellow, 1974-75. Fellow AAAS (mem. nominating com. for sect. B physics 1987-89, chair 1989), Am. Phys. Soc. (exec. com. history of physics div. 1983-86, exec. com. forum on physics and society 1977-78); mem. Nat. Assn. Sci. Writers, Sigma Pi Sigma. Jewish. Office: Am Inst Physics 335 E 45th St New York NY 10017

LUBORSKY, ELLEN B., clinical psychologist; b. Topeka, Nov. 14, 1948; d. Lester B. and Ruth O. (Samson) L.; m. James L. Outman, Oct. 27, 1970 (div. June 1985); children: Miranda, Alexander. BA, Sarah Lawrence Coll., 1970; MA, NYU, 1978, PhD, 1987. Lic. profl. psychologist, N.Y. Intern N.Y. Hosp Cornell Med. Ctr., White Plains, 1983-85; staff psychol. N.W. Guidance Clinic, Mt. Kisco, N.Y., 1985-87; staff psychotherapist Riverdale (N.Y.) Mental Health Ctr., 1987-89; pvt. practice psychologist Mt. Kisco, N.Y., 1987—, Rye, N.Y., 1988—; dir. Early Childhood Ctr., Riverdale, N.Y., 1989—; cons. Country Children's Ctr., Katonah, N.Y., 1985—, Riverdale Neighborhood House, 1987—, Purchase (N.Y.) Children's Ctr., 1989—; speaker various civic groups and day care ctrs.; lectr. Roosevelt Hosp., N.Y.C., 1989. Contbr. articles to profl. jours. Mem. Am. Psychol. Assn., Weschester County Psychol. Assn., Women in Transition (co-founder). Democrat. Jewish. Office: 105 Theodore Fremd Ave Rye NY 10580 Also: 275 Main St Mount Kesco NY 10549

LUCAS, BARBARA B., electrical equipment manufacturing executive; b. 1945. BA, U. Md., 1967; MA, Johns Hopkins U., 1968. V.p., sec. Equitable Bancorp, 1977-85; v.p. Black & Decker Corp., from 1985, now v.p. pub. affairs and corp. sec. Office: Black & Decker Corp 701 E Joppa Rd Baltimore MD 21204*

LUCAS, CAROL ANN, public relations executive; b. Cleve., Feb. 11, 1941; d. Louis Leo and Elizabeth Rose (Leuenberger) L. BA in Communications, Kent State U., 1977; postgrad., Baldwin Wallace Coll., 1989—. Adminstrv. asst. Carney & Assocs., Cleve., 1958-63, Walston & Co., Inc., Cleve., 1963-67, Sta. WKYC-TV News, NBC, Cleve., 1967-74; asst. producer Sta. WJW-TV News, Cleve., 1978-79; adminstrv. asst. Cleve. State U., 1977-79, recruitment and communications coord., 1979-82; dir. mktg. communications Akron (Ohio) Gen. Med. Ctr., 1982-86; mgr. pub. rels. Cleve. Advanced Mfg. Program, 1986—; pub. rels. cons.; pub. speaker on pub. rels., communications, career planning, Cleve. Mem. pub. rels. adv. task force United Way Summit County, Akron, 1984-85; mem. communications adv. bd. Work in N.E. Ohio Coun., Cleve., 1988-89. Recipient 1st place award Internat. Assn. Bus. Communicators, 1981, 84; 1st place award Ohio Hosp. Assn., 1984, award of excellence, 1986; MacEachern 1st place award Am. Hosp. Assn., 1985, 1st place award Women in Communications, 1988. Mem. Pub. Rels. Soc. Am. (pres. Akron chpt. 1985), Cleve. Press Club. Democrat. Roman Catholic. Home: 6703 Virginia Ave Parma OH 44129 Office: Cleve Advanced Mfg Program 17325 Euclid Ave Cleveland OH 44112

LUCAS, ELIZABETH COUGHLIN, teacher; b. Youngstown, Ohio, May 5, 1918; d. Joseph Anthony and Gertrude Elizabeth (Handel) Coughlin; m. Charles Edward Lucas, Apr. 7, 1945. BS magna cum laude, Notre Dame Coll. of Ohio, 1940; Diploma, Harvard U., 1944; MA in Edn., Calif. State Poly U., 1980. Cert. tchr., Calif. (life), secondary tchr., Pa., Ohio. Tech. sec. for v.p. engring and purchasing Patterson Foundry and Machine Co., East Liverpool, Ohio, 1941-42; tchr. chemistry Point Marion (Pa.) High Sch., 1942, Lincoln High Sch., Midland, Pa., 1942-44; radar specialist Thunderstorm Project U.S. Weather Bur., St. Cloud, Fla., 1946, Wilmington, Ohio, 1947; substitute tchr. math, sci. Chaffey (Calif.) Union High Schs., 1971-75; tchr. math Claremont (Calif.) High Sch., 1975-80; tchr., counselor, head sci. dept. San Antonio High Sch., Claremont, 1980-88; substitute tchr. Claremont Unified Sch. Dist., Claremont, 1988—; dist. adv. com., math, sci., Claremont, 1983-85; subsititute tchr. San Antonio (Calif.) High Sch., 1988—, Upland (Calif.) High Sch., 1988—, Hillside High Sch., 1988—. Author, editor: A Descriptive Study of the Effects of the New Math Syndrome on the Average High School Student, 1980. Lt. (j.g.) USNR, 1944-48. Mem. NAFE, Nat. Coun. of Tchrs. of Math., Nat. Sci. Tchrs. Assn., Assn. for Supervision and Curriculum Devel., Cath. Daus. of the Ams. (regent 1975-77, diocesan chmn. 1979-81). Republican. Roman Catholic. Home: 9185 Regency Way Alta Loma CA 91701 Office: Claremont Unified Sch Dist 2080 N Mountain Ave Claremont CA 91711

LUCAS, ELIZABETH HELENE, artist, calligrapher, educator; b. Pasadena, Calif., Aug. 21, 1936; d. Edward A. and Anona Marie (Snyder) Buse; m. Justice Campbell M. Lucas, Dec. 17, 1960; children: Scott, Stephen, Lisanne. AA, Long Beach City Coll., 1956; BA, Whittier Coll., 1958, MA, 1984. Cert. gen. secondary tchr., Calif. Chmn. dept. sci. Bolsa Grande High Sch., Garden Grove, Calif., 1960-65; ind. tchr. calligraphy Long Beach, Calif., 1976—; instr. Sch. for Adults, Long Beach, 1978-80; assoc. prof. calligraphy Calif. State U.-Long Beach, 1979—, coord. cert. in calligraphy program, 1982—; instr. calligraphy and bookbinding U. Calif.-Riverside, 1982—; instr. calligraphy Whittier Coll., Calif., 1984-85; designer bokks for great quotations; free-lance calligrapher and graphic designer, 1976—; designer, pub. line of calligraphy greeting cards, 1978—, owner Elizabeth Lucas Designs. Author: Calligraphy, The Art of Beautiful Writing, 1984; one-Woman calligraphy shows Long Beach Mus. Art Bookshop/Gallery, 1981, 84, Sr. Eye Gallery, Long Beach, 1982, 85, Gt. Western Savs. and Loan, Long Beach, 1983, David Scott Meier Gallery, Mendocino, Calif., 1983, Whittier Coll. Mendenhall Gallery, 1983; also group shows. Active, past mem. bd. dirs. Long Beach Law Aux., 1960—, Jr. League, Long Beach, 1968—; pres. Lowell Sch. PTA, Long Beach, 1972. Named Sci. Tchr. of Yr., So. Calif. Edison Co., 1963; recipient art awards, including First Place award Calif. State Lawyers' Wives, 1984. Mem. Soc. for Calligraphy (past pres. 1982-83), Soc. Scribes and Illuminators, Friends of Calligraphy, Soc. Scribes, Profl. Writers League, Calif. State PTA (hon. life 1973—), Long Beach Mus. Art Found. (co-chairperson dir.'s circle 1985), Long Beach Art Assn., Pub. Corp. for Arts, Fine Art Affiliates of Calif. State U. at Long Beach. Republican. Lodge: Soroptimists (com. chairperson local club 1981—), Rotary (Long Beach). Home: 518 Monrovia Ave Long Beach CA 90814 Office: Elizabeth Lucas Designs 2501 E 28th St Ste 110 Signal Hill CA 90806

LUCAS, GEORGETTA MARIE SNELL, retired educator, artist; b. Harmony, Ind., July 25, 1920; d. Ernest Clermont and Sarah Ann (McIntyre) Snell; m. Joseph William Lucas, Jan. 29, 1943; children—Carleen Anita Lucas Underwood-Scrougham, Thomas Joseph, Joetta Jeanne Lucas Allgood. BS, Ind. State U., 1942; MS in Edn., Butler U., 1964; postgrad. Herron Sch. of Art, Indpls., 1961-65, Ind. U., Indpls. and Bloomington, 1960, 61, 62, 65. Music, art tchr. Jasonville City Schs., Ind., 1942-43, Van Buren High Sch., Brazil, Ind., 1943-46, Plainfield City Schs., Ind., 1946-52, Met. Sch. Dist. Wayne Twp., Indpls., 1952-56, 1959-68; art tchr. Met. Sch. Dist. Perry Twp., Indpls., 1968-81. Illustrator: (book) Why So Sad, Little Rag Doll, 1963; artist (painting) Ethereal Season, 1966, (lithograph) Bird of Time, 1965-66: represented in permanent collections Ind. State U., Ind.-Purdue U.-Indpls.; lectr. Art Educators Assn. Ind., Ind. U.-Bloomington, 1976. Mem NEA, Nat. Assn. Women Artist, Ind. Artist-Craftsmen, Inc. (pres. 1979-85, 87, 88), Ind. Fedn. Art Clubs (pres. 1986-87), Hoosier Salon, Art Edn. Assn. Ind., Nat. League Am. Pen Women (Ind. state art chmn. 1984—, Best of Show award 1983), Fine Art for State Ind. (Internat. Women's Yr. fine art chmn. 1977), Internat. Platform Assn. (bd. dirs. 1983—, chmn. art com. 1987—, lectr. 1975, 78, 82, 84, Silver award 1978, appointed gov. 1983—), Cen. Ind. Artists (hon.), Mortar Bd., Alpha Delta Kappa (Ind. state chmn. of art 1973-77, pres. 1972-74, represented by painting in nat. hdqrs.-Kansas City, Mo.), Order of Eastern Star. Republican. Methodist. Avocations: genealogy, travel, numismatics. Home and Office: 9702 W Washington St Indianapolis IN 46231

LUCAS, SHARRON RIESSINGER, director development; b. Mt. Sterling, Ky., Apr. 4, 1961; d. George and Reniva (Rogers) Riessinger; married; 1 child, Elspeth Kathleen. Student, David Lipscomb U., 1978; BA, U. Tenn., 1984; cert. filmmaking, NYU, 1986. Tng. dir. The Leader, Inc., Chattanooga, 1982-83; workshop coord. McKenzie Coll., Chattanooga, 1983-84; mfg. rep., owner Pine Mountain Prodns., Chattanooga, 1983-85; devel. coord. Sta. WUTC-FM, Chattanooga, 1986-87; asst. dir. devel. U. Tenn., Chattanooga, 1987—. Editor: film Day by Day, 1986. Mem. devel. bd. Cadek Conservatory; mem. adv. bd. Children's Ctr., U. Tenn., Chattanooga; v.p. Hamilton County Young Dems., Chattanooga, 1982. Mem. NAFE, Coun. for Advancement and Support Edn., Nat. Soc. Fundraising Execs. (sec. S.E. Tenn. chpt. 1990). Office: U Tenn 615 McCallie Ave Chattanooga TN 37403

LUCAS, SHIRLEY AGNES HOYT, management executive; b. Chgo., Aug. 21, 1921; d. Howard L. and Lucille P. (Von Krippenstapel) Hoyt; m. William H. Lucas, Feb. 2, 1952; 1 child, Lucille Shirley. Student, Northwestern U., 1941-42. V.p. Lucas Co., Chgo., 1980-90. Mem. Ill. Hosp. Assn. (Leadership award 1975), Aux. Christ Hosp. and Med. Ctr. (life, past bd. dirs., cotillion chmn., housewalk chmn.). Republican. Lutheran. Office: Lucas Co 9127 S Kedzie Evergreen Park IL 60642

LUCAS, VALERIE PATRICIA, minister, writer; b. Bridgeport, Conn., Apr. 1, 1951; d. Alexander and Kathleen Pearl (Golding) L. Student, Cen. Conn. State U., 1969-71, Light of Christ Sem., 1985-89. Mgr., account rep. News Publ. Co., Statford, Conn., 1971-77; ins. sales person Mutual of Omaha, Westport, Conn., 1978-80, ins. sales mgr., 1980-82; mktg. assoc. Mutual of Omaha, Omaha, 1982-83, advt. copywriter, 1983-85; dir. Indwelling Christ Ctr., Omaha, 1986—, Rev., 1989—; field rep. Light of Christ Ch., Tahlequah, Okla., 1989—. Mystical Christian. Home and Office: 10682 Hamilton Plz #713 Omaha NE 68114

LUCCHETTI, LYNN L., advertising executive, military officer; b. San Francisco, Calif., Aug. 21, 1939; d. Dante and Lillian (Bergeron) L. AB, San Jose State U., 1961; MS, San Francisco State U., 1967; grad. U.S. Army Basic Officer's Course, 1971, U.S. Army Advanced Officer Course, 1976, grad. U.S. Air Force Command and Staff Coll., 1982, U.S. Air Force War Coll., 1983, Sr. Pub. Affairs Officer Course, 1984. Media buyer Batten, Barton, Durstine & Osborn, Inc., San Francisco, 1961-67; producer-dir. Sta. KTVA-TV, Anchorage, 1967-68; media supr. Bennett, Luke and Teawell Advt., Phoenix, 1968-71; commd. 1st lt. U.S. Army, 1971; advanced through ranks to lt. col., 1985, col., 1989; officer U.S. Army, 1971-74, D.C. N.G., , 1974-78, U.S. Air Force Res., 1978—, program advt. mgr. U.S. Navy Recruiting Command, 1974-76; exec. coordinator for the Joint Advt. Dirs. of Recruiting (JADOR), 1976-79; dir. U.S. Armed Forces Joint Recruiting Advt. Program (JRAP), Dept. Def., Washington, 1979—. Author: Broadcasting in Alaska, 1924-1966. Decorated U.S. Army Meritorious Svc. medal, Nat. Def. medal, U.S. Air Force Longevity Ribbon, U.S. Navy Meritorious Unit Commendation, Dept. Def. Joint Achievement medal, 1984. Sigma Delta Chi journalism scholar, 1960. Mem. Women in Def., Nat. Coun. Career Women, Va. Real Estate Bd. Home: 5416 Barrister Pl Alexandria VA 22304 Office: Dir US Armed Forces JRAP Dept of Def 1600 Wilson Blvd Ste 400 Arlington VA 22209-2593

LUCCHITTA, BAERBEL KOESTERS, geologist; b. Muenster, Westfalia, Fed. Republic of Germany, Oct. 2, 1938; came to U.S., 1959; d. Bernhard and Frida (Muehleisen) Koesters; m. Ivo Lucchitta, Apr. 17, 1964. BS, Kent (Ohio) State U., 1961; MS, Pa. State U., University Park, 1963, PhD, 1966. Geologist U.S. Geol. Survey, Flagstaff, Ariz., 1967—; coord. Jupiter satellite mapping program NASA and U.S. Geol. Survey, Flagstaff, 1980—; assoc. chief br. astrogeology U.S. Geol. Survey, Flagstaff, 1987—; lectr. Sigma Xi, 1990-91. Contbr. articles to profl. jours. Recipient Spl. Recognition Group award NASA, 1979, Spl. Achievement award U.S. Geol. Survey, 1983; NASA grantee, 1970—. Mem. Assn. Women in Sci., Assn. Women Geoscientists, Geol. Soc. Am. (sec., treas. planetary div. 1988-89, 2d vice chmn. 1990—), Am. Geophys. Union, Internat. Glaciol. Soc. Office: US Geol Survey 2255 N Gemini Dr Flagstaff AZ 86001

LUCE, MRS. HENRY, III See HADLEY, LEILA ELIOTT-BURTON

LUCENTE, ROSEMARY DOLORES, educational administrator; b. Renton, Wash., Jan. 11, 1935; d. Joseph Anthony and Erminia Antoinette (Argano) Lucente; B.A., Mt. St. Mary's Coll., 1956, M.S., 1963. Tchr. pub. schs., Los Angeles, 1956-65, supr. tchr., 1958-65, asst. prin., 1965-69, prin. elem. sch., 1969-85, 86—, dir. instrn., 1985-86; nat. cons., lectr. Dr. William Glasser's Educator Tng. Ctr., 1968—; nat. workshop leader Nat. Acad. for Sch. Execs.-Am. Assn. Sch. Adminstrs., 1980; Los Angeles Unified Sch. Dist. rep. for nat. pilot of Getty Inst. for Visual Arts, 1983-85, site coordinator, 1983-86. Recipient Golden Apple award Stanford Ave. Sch. PTA, Faculty and Community Adv. Council, 1976, resolution for outstanding service South Gate City Council, 1976. Mem. Nat. Assn. Elem. Sch. Prins., Los Angeles Elem. Prins. Orgn. (v.p. 1979-80), Assn. Calif. Sch. Adminstrs. (charter mem.), Assn. Elem. Sch. Adminstrs. (vice-chmn. chpt. 1972-75, city-wide exec. bd., steering com. 1972-75, 79-80), Asso. Adminstrs. Los Angeles (charter), Pi Theta Mu, Kappa Delta Pi (v.p. 1982-84), Delta Kappa Gamma. Democrat. Roman Catholic. Home: 6501 Lindenhurst Ave Los Angeles CA 90048 Office: Roscomare Rd Sch 2425 Roscomare Rd Los Angeles CA 90077

LUCHT, SONDRA MOORE, state senator; b. Stumptown, W.Va., Dec. 12, 1942; d. Arthur Jackson and Lucille (Cain) Moore; m. William Lucht; 1 child, Carl Joseph. B.A., Glenville State Coll., M.A., Marshall U.; postgrad. James Madison U. Cert. sch. psychologist. Mem. W. Va. State Senate from Dist. 16, 1982—, re-elected, 1986; speaker, lectr. on women in politics, other women's issues, child abuse, other youth issues. Co-founder Shenandoah Women's Ctr. Mem. NOW (pres. 1977-82, chair task force on pay equity 1983—, chair commn. on juvenile law 1985—). Democrat. Episcopalian. Office: 1013 Mill Race Dr Martinsburg WV 25401*

LUCID, SHANNON W., biochemist, astronaut; b. Shanghai, China, Jan. 14, 1943; d. Joseph O. Wells; m. Michael F. Lucid; children: Kawai Dawn, Shandara Michelle, Michael Kermit. BS in Chemistry, U. Okla., 1963, MS in Biochemistry, 1970, PhD in Biochemistry, 1973. Sr. lab. technician Okla. Med. Rsch. Found., 1964-66, rsch. assoc., from 1974; chemist Kerr-McGee, Oklahoma City, 1966-68; astronaut NASA Lyndon B. Johnson Space Ctr., Houston, 1979—; mission specialist flights STS-51G and STS-34 NASA Lyndon B. Johnson Space Ctr. Address: NASA Johnson Space Ctr Astronaut Office Houston TX 77058*

LUCIUS, ERNETTE KAY, chemical dependency nurse; b. Alliance, Nebr., Oct. 15, 1944; d. Earnest Earl and Christina (Van Egdom) Stevens; m. Michael Allen Lucius, Oct. 13, 1979. AS, U. Biola, LaMirada, Calif., 1966; BSN, U. Wis., 1970. RN, Minn. Nurse cons. psychiatry U. Wis., 1970-72, U. Ariz., 1972-74; intensive care nurse St. Mary Hosp., Tucson, 1974-81; chem. dependency nurse Riverside Med. Ctr., Mpls., 1981—; profl. beauty cons. Mary Kay Cosmetics, Mpls., 1990—; chem. dependency cons. Hennepin County, Minn.; psychiat. cons. Riverside Med. Ctr.; lectr. in field. Author: rsch. jour. Cause/Effect of MI/CD, 1987. Treas. Nurses for Peace, Madison, 1969-70. Winner various swimming trophies, speech trophy Salvation Army, Chgo., 1959. Mem. Minn. Nurses Assn. (mem. nominating com.), NAFE. Democrat. Jewish.

LUCKEY, ALICE DAVISON, retired educational administrator; b. Fairmont, W.Va., Apr. 6, 1930; d. Asa Jerry and Frederica (Calloway) Davison; m. Howard Tracy Luckey, Sept. 30, 1954; 1 child, Howard Tracy. BA in Edn., W.Va. State Coll., 1953; postgrad., U. Md., 1956; MA in Edn., George Washington U., 1969. Tchr. Prince Georges County (Md.) Pub. Schs., 1956-67; asst. elem. prin. Prince Georges County (Md.) Pub. Schs., Fairmount Heights, Md., 1967-70; prin. Carmody Hills Elem. Sch. Prince Georges County (Md.) Pub. Schs., 1970-83; prin. Apple Grove Elem. Sch. Prince Georges County (Md.) Pub. Schs., Ft. Washington, 1984-86; mem. middle sch. instrnl. team Prince Georges County (Md.) Pub. Schs., 1983-84; ret., 1986; reading cons. Ency. Brit. Edn. Corp., Washington, 1968-70. Scoutleader Boy Scouts Am., Washington, 1963-64; mem. Brightwood Park Concerned Citizens Assn., Washington, 1964—; vol. Mental Health Assn., Washington, 1987—; bd. dirs. Phyllis Wheatly YWCA, 1990-91; Sixteenth St. Heights Civic Assn., 1988—; chmn. council of ministries Brightwood Park Methodist Ch., 1989-91. Recipient numerous awards, including cert. of appreciation Boy Scouts Am., Girl Scouts U.S.A., Carmody Hills, 1970-83, Mental Health Assn., 1988, Outstanding Vol. Svc. award Project Head Start, 1980; letter of commendation Prince Georges County Bd. Edn., 1984, cert. of recognition, 1986. Mem. Md. Ret. Tchrs. Assn., W.Va. State Coll. Alumni Assn. (v.p. Met. Washington chpt. 1989), Alpha Kappa Alpha (charter Iota Gamma Omega chpt., program coord. 1970). Methodist. Home: 1633 Madison St NW Washington DC 20011

LUCKEY, IRENE, social worker, educator; b. N.Y.C., May 29, 1949; d. Miles Calvin and Ollie Faye (Brevard) L.; m. Robert Lewis Cook, June 23, 1973 (div. Dec. 1983). BA, N.C. A&T State U., 1971; MA, U. Chgo., 1973; D Social Work, CUNY Grad. Sch. and Univ. Ctr., 1982. Med. social worker Met. Hosp., N.Y.C., 1973-76; asst. prof. social work N.C. Agrl. and Tech. State U., Greensboro, 1976-78; dir. ednl. programs Brookdale Ctr. on Aging of Hunter Coll., N.Y.C., 1979-81; vis. prof. social work, gerontology LeMoyne-Owen Coll., Memphis, 1981-82; asst. prof. social work Clark Coll., Atlanta, 1982-84; assoc. dir. Ctr. on Aging U. West Fla., Pensacola, 1985-89, asst. prof. social work, 1985-89; Nat. Inst. on Aging postdoctoral fellow U. Mich., Ann Arbor, 1987-89; asst. prof. social welfare SUNY, Albany, 1989-90, faculty rsch. assoc. Ringel Inst. on Aging, 1989-90; asst. prof. Rutgers U., New Brunswick, N.J., 1990—; cons. Regional Adminstrn. on Aging, N.Y.C., 1981; cons. Atlanta Regional Commn. on Aging, 1984; bd. dirs. Geriatric Residential Treatment Services Inc., Fla., 1986-87; mem. State of Fla. Long-Term Care Dist. I Ombudsman council, 1986-87; chairperson Ednl. Programs Assn. of Black Social Workers, Pensacola, 1985-88; adv. council cons. Mental Health Assn. of Escambia County 1985-87; trainer, workshop developer Escambia County Council on Aging, 1986-88, (adv. council mem. 1987); organizer, coordinator Black Family in Rural Am. symposium, 1987; mem. Social Research Planning and Practice Task Force on Minority Issues subcom. on Policy and Service/Practice, Gerontological Soc., 1987—; Nat. Inst. on Aging postdoctoral rsch. fellow U. Mich., 1987-89. Bd. dirs. N.W. Fla. Area Agy. on Aging, 1985-86; mem. Escambia County Coalition of the Homeless, 1986-87. Brookdale fellow. Mem. Council of Social Work Edn., Gerontol. Soc., Assn. for Gerontology and Human Devel. in Hist. Black Univs. and Colls., Alpha Kappa Alpha, Phi Alpha, Alpha Kappa Mu. Home: 117 Benner St C6 Highland Park NJ 08904 Office: Rutgers U Sch Social Work 536 George St New Brunswick NJ 08901-5058

LUCZAK, JANET WILLIAMS, biopharmaceutical testing laboratory executive; b. Pitts., July 6, 1955; d. Owen and Beatrice Loretta (Ernst) Williams; m. Raymond Walter Luczak, Oct. 11, 1980. BS, Carlow Coll., Pitts., 1977; M Gen. Adminstrn., U. Md., 1986. Lab. technician Children's Hosp., Pitts., 1975; med. technologist Mercy Hosp., Pitts., 1976-77, Am. Med. Labs., Fairfax, Va., 1977-80; med. technologist Microbiol. Assocs., Bethesda, Md., 1981-85, lab. supr., 1985-86; assoc. study dir. Microbiol. Assocs., Rockville, Md., 1986-87, study dir., 1987-89, assoc. div. dir., 1989—. Contbr. poetry to anthologies. Recipient Golden Poet award World of Poetry Press, 1989, 90. Mem. Am. Soc. Clin. Pathologists (cert. med. technician), Soc. Mycoplasmologists, Nat. Honor Soc., Phi Kappa Phi, Delta Epsilon Sigma. Roman Catholic. Home: 605 E Franklin Ave Silver Spring MD 20901 Office: Microbiol Assocs 9900 Blackwell Rd Rockville MD 20850

LUCZKOWSKI, BARBARA JEAN, business, finance administrator; b. Lorain, Ohio, Apr. 30, 1958; d. Frank Allen Luczkowski and Aloha Jean (Beachler) Kuzniar. BSBA in Mktg., Bowling Green (Ohio) State U., 1980. New account rep. CCP Coffee Plan div. Farmer Bros., Houston, 1981-84; nat. account exec. Endicot Over Seas Express, Houston, 1984-85; bus. mgr. Rick Case Honda, Cleve., 1985-88, Fred Stecker Olds, Inc., Euclid, Ohio, 1988—; dir. fin. Credit Mgmt. Concepts, Inc. Big Sister Project Friendship, Cleve. 1990. Mem. NAFE. Roman Catholic. Home: 27900 Bishop Pk #108F Willoughby Hills OH 44092 Office: Fred Stecker Olds Inc 25200 Euclid Ave Euclid OH 44117

LUDEL, JACQUELINE, biology and psychology educator, writer; b. Boston, Mar. 17, 1945; d. William and Corinne (Goldberg) L. BA, Queens Coll., 1966; PhD, Ind. U., 1971. Asst. prof. Jacksonville (Fla.) U., 1971-73, Stockton State Coll., Pomona, N.J., 1973-76; prof. Guilford Coll., Greensboro, N.C., 1976—; staff psychologist FAA, Atlantic City, N.J., 1974-75; chairperson psychology dept. Guilford Coll., 1981-84; sci. corr. Event Alert Network-Smithsonian Inst., Washington, 1976-82; bd. dirs. Marine Mammal Standing Ctr., Brigantine, N.J., 1979—. Author: Introduction to Sensory Processes, 1978, Margaret Mead (An Impact Biology), 1984; reviewer in field. Co-organizer Guilford Coll., Focus, South africa, 1989; organizer Relief Drive for Cambodia, Guilford Coll., 1979; mem. Coalition of Voices, 1987—. NSF grad. fellow Ind. U., 1966-71; Kenan grantee Guilford Coll., 1977; recipient Excellence in Teaching award, Guilford Coll. Mem. Psychologists for Social Responsibility, Educators for Social Responsibility, Phi Beta Kappa, Beta Beta Beta, Psi Chi, Sigma Delta Epsilon. Office: Guilford College 5800 W Friendly Ave Greensboro NC 27410

LUDLOW, CHRISTY LESLIE, speech pathologist, scientist; b. Montreal, June 7, 1944; came to U.S., 1967; d. Forester Wilcox and Margaret Helen (Sweet) Leslie; m. Gregory Ludlow, Sept. 7, 1968. BSc, McGill U., 1965, MSc, 1967; PhD, NYU, 1973. Cert. speech pathologist. Speech pathologist NYU Med Ctr., N.Y.C., 1967-70, doctoral fellow, 1970-73; project mgr. Am. Speech Lang. Hearing Assn., Bethesda, Md., 1973-74; speech pathologist NIH, Bethesda, 1974-86; rsch. speech pathologist Nat. Inst. Deafness and Other Communication Disorders, Bethesda, 1986—. Author: Assessment of Vocal Pathology, 1981, Genetic Aspects of Speech and Language Disorders, 1983. Recipient Editor's award Am. Speech-Lang.-Hearing Assn., 1987, Achievement awardMd. Speech-Lang.-Hearing Assn., 1990. Mem. Assn. for Rsch. in Otolaryngology, Soc. for Neurosci., Acad. of Aphasia, Internat. Neuropsychology Soc., Am. Acad. Otolaryngology and Head and Neck Surgery (assoc.). Office: NIDCD-NIH Bldg 10 Room 5C218 Bethesda MD 20892

LUDTKE, MARY ALICE, mental health administrator; b. Mt. Clemens, Mich., Oct. 2, 1950; d. Stanley Otto and Ruth Rose Lydia (Appel) L. BS in Edn., Cen. Mich. U., 1972, MA, 1975. Head resident advisor Cen. Mich. U., Mt. Pleasant, 1972-75; with mental health staff Saginaw (Mich.) County Community Mental Health Svcs., 1975; counselor Interlochen (Mich) Ctr. for the Arts, 1975-78; clinican St. Clair County Community Mental Health, Port Huron, Mich., 1978-80, clin. supr., 1980-85, prevention/spl. projects officer, 1985—; interim dir. Blue Water Ctr. for Ind. Living, Port Huron, 1989; bd. dirs. Cornell Ctr., Port Huron. Mem. Great Lakes Regional Partial Hospitalization Assn. (sec. 1984-86, pres.-elect 1987-88, pres. 1988-90). Lutheran. Office: St Clair Comm Mental Health 3415 28th St Port Huron MI 48060

LUDWICK, ANDREA MARIE, hospital official; b. Lansing, Mich., July 30, 1962; d. Norman Keith and Alice Lorraine (Varey) Jones. AA, Ferris State U., 1982, MS, 1984; MPA, U. Mich., 1989. Health record analyst Riverside Osteo. Hosp., Trenton, Mich., 1982; supr. med. records Flint (Mich.) Osteo. Hosp., 1984-90; health care cons. Coopers & Lybrand, 1990—. Mem. Am. Med. Record Assn., Mich. Med. Record Assn. (ednl. com. 1986), East Cen. Med. Records Assn. (chmn. nominating com. 1987). Lutheran. Home: 524 Neff Ln Grosse Pointe MI 48230 Office: Flint Osteo Hosp 400 Renaissance Ctr Detroit MI 48243

LUDWIG, MARGARET G., state legislator; m. Leland Ludwig; 3 children. BA, Colby Coll. Mem. Maine State Senate. Mem. Maine State Sch. Bd. Assn. Republican. Home: 3 Rogers Rd Houlton ME 04730 Office: Maine State Senate Augusta ME 04330*

LUEB, LOUISE ESTELLE, budget analyst; b. N.Y.C., Apr. 13, 1947; d. Morris and Ruth L. (Soskin) Eskenazi; m. Daniel F. Lueb, Mar. 11, 1965 (div. Sept. 1985); children: Mechelle R., Ronald M., Rhonda L.; m. Kevin R. Warner, May 27, 1988. BS in Bus. Mgmt., Southland U., 1986; MBA, Calif. Coast U., 1988, PhD in Bus. Adminstrn., 1989. Civil svc. comptroller Comptroller Orgn., USAF, 1965-89; budget analyst Sec. of Air Force, Washington, 1990—. Mem. San Antonio (Tex.) Singles Network, 1988-89, San Antonio (Tex.) Profl. Soc., 1983-89. Mem. Am. Soc. Mil. Comptrollers (budget chair 1988-89), NAFE. Republican. Roman Catholic. Office: SAF/FMBOS Pentagon Washington DC 22312

LUECK, THERESE LOUISE, communications educator; b. Wilmington, Del., Aug. 8, 1956; d. Charles Henry and Sheila (Branchaud) L; m. Thomas Michael LaPlante, Nov. 4, 1988. AA in Art, BA in English, Thomas More Coll., Crestview Hills, Ky., 1983; M in English, Bowling Green (Ohio) State U., 1985, PhD in Am. Culture, 1989. Sect. editor The Tennessean, Nashville, 1976-78; freelance writer newspapers, tabloids, Nashville, 1978-80; copy editor The Blade, Toledo, Ohio, 1984; GED tchr. No. Ky. Community Action Commn., Newport, Ky., 1981-83; teaching asst. Sch. Journalism, Bowling Green State U., 1983-85, teaching fellow, 1985-87; fgn. expert Xi'an (China) Fgn. Langs. U., 1987-88; teaching fellow Bowling Green State U., 1988-89; asst. prof. communications U. Akron (Ohio), 1989—; seminar leader Great Lakes Interscholastic Press Assn., Bowling Green, 1984-86, 88; judge Ohio Newspaper Assn., Hooper Newspaper Show, 1986, Nebr. Press Woman Competition, 1985; workshop leader Newspaper Feature Seminar, Ohio Newspaper Assn., 1985. NEH summer rsch. grantee, 1985. Mem. Am. Culture Assn., Am. Journalism Historians Assn., Assn. Educators in Journalism and Mass Communication, Nat. Women's Studies Assn., Women in Communications, Inc. Office: Dept Communication U Akron Guzzetta Hall Akron OH 44325-1003

LUEDKE, JANET LOUISE, systems engineer; b. Fremont, Nebr., Oct. 14, 1962; d. William Barr and Beverly Jean (Kemerling) L. BS, Kearney State U., 1984. Quality assurance cons., systems engr. Electronic Data Systems, Dallas, 1984-90, Lakewood, Colo., 1990—. Mem. Beta Sigma Phi, Chi Omega. Home: 10687 W Darmouth Ave Lakewood CO 80215 Office: 12600 W Colfax Ave Lakewood CO 80215

LUEGER, SUSAN ANN, psychologist; b. Rantoul, Ill., Oct. 27, 1953; d. Leonard Joseph and Haline Theresa (Ostojski) Borkowski; m. Robert Joseph Lueger, May 29, 1977; children: Michael Joseph, Emma Jane. BS, Western Ill. U., 1974; MA, Loyola U. Chgo., 1980, PhD, 1983. Intern Office State Planning and Rsch., State of Kans., Topeka, 1977-78; analyst Dept. Social and Rehab. Svcs., State of Kans., Topeka, 1978-79, supr. program evaluation, 1979-81; instr. dept. psychology Washburn U., Topeka, 1980-81, Marquette U., Milw., 1982; mgr. tng. and orgn. devel. Inryco, Inc., Milw., 1983-85; sr. specialist placement Wis. Electric Power Co., Milw., 1985-88, project specialist placement, 1988-90, mgr. compensation and benefits, 1990—; bd. dirs. Employees' Mut. Savs. Bldg. & Loan Assn., Milw., 1990—; cons. Devel. Disabilities Coun., 1981. Mem. Shorewood Wis. Civil Svc. Commn., 1986—, chair, 1989—. Leadership grantee Western Ill. U., 1973; recipient Leadership award YWCA, Milw., 1988. Mem. Am. Psychol. Assn., Midwest Psychol. Assn., Milw. Area Psychol. Assn. (program chair 1986-87, pres. 1987-88, bd. dirs. 1988-89), Human Resource Planning Soc. Office: Wis Electric Power Co 333 W Everett St Rm A128 Milwaukee WI 53203

LUEKEN, SISTER MARY JUDEANN, hospital administrator; b. Cin., Sept. 16, 1942; d. Ferdinand John and Helen Catherine (Kammer) L. AS in Nursing, Lexington (Ky.) Tech. Inst., 1969; BSN, U. Cin., 1971; MSN, U. Ky., 1981. Tchr. elem. Parochial Sch. System, Covington, Ky., 1962-67; staff nurse St. Claire Med. Ctr., Morehead, Ky., 1971-74, dir. nursing svcs., 1977-79, asst. adminstr., 1979—; dir. nursing St. Charles Nursing Home, Covington, 1974-77; mem. adv. bd. Rowan County Vocat. Sch. Health Occupations, Morehead, 1981—, Morehead State U., N.E. Ky. Area Health Edn. Ctr., Morehead; mem. voluntary faculty U. Ky. Coll. Nursing, 1986—. Adminstr., provider nursing continuing edn. St. Claire Med. Ctr., Morehead, 1980—. Mem. Ky. Orgn. Nurse Execs. Democrat. Roman Catholic.

LUENZ, PAMELA MARIE, educator; b. Dec. 16, 1947; d. August S. and Ethel A. (Franklin) Weisler; m. John V. Grabel (div. 1974); m. Michael F. Luenz. BA, Bradley U., Peoria, Ill., 1973, MS, 1974. Cert. spl. edn. tchr., Ill., Ind. Tchr. Loucks Sch., Peoria, 1974-77, W. Wilson Sch., Peoria, 1977, C. Lindbergh Sch., Peoria, 1978-80; staff devel. specialist Peoria Dist. 150, 1980; tchr. Glen Acres Sch., Lafayette, Ind., 1980-81, 1981-87; tchr. Sunnyside Mid. Sch., Lafayette, 1987-89. Vol. Indpls. Zoo, 1988-89, Glen Oak Zoo, Peoria, 1976-80; sec. Friends of The Lafayette Zoo, 1981-84; treas. Greater Lafayette Reading Coun., 1988-89; vol. in spl. edn. classes Bethany High Sch., 1989-90. Mem. Overseas Women's Club (sec. 1989—).

LUEPKE, GRETCHEN, geologist; b. Tucson, Nov. 10, 1943; d. Gordon Maas and Janice (Campbell) Luepke; B.S., U. Ariz., 1965, M.S., 1967; U. Colo., summer, 1962. Geol. field asst. U.S. Geol. Survey, Flagstaff, Ariz., 1964; with U.S. Geol. Survey, Menlo Park, Calif., 1967—, geologist, Pacific Br. of Marine Geology, 1976—. Registered geologist, Ore. Mem. U.S. Congress Office Tech. Assessment Workshop, Mining and Processing Placers of EEZ, 1986. Mem. Soc. Econ. Paleontologists and Mineralogists (chmn. com. libraries in developing countries 1988—), Geol. Soc. Am., Ariz. Geol. Soc., Peninsula Geol. Soc., Bay Area Mineralogists (chmn. 1979-80), History of the Earth Scis. Soc., Internat. Assn. Sedimentologists, Internat. Marine Minerals Soc. (charter), Sigma Xi. Editor: Stability of Heavy Minerals in Sediments; Econ. Analysis of Heavy Minerals in Sediments; editor book rev. Earth Scis. History, 1989—. Contbr. articles on heavy-mineral analysis to profl. jours. Office: 345 Middlefield Rd Menlo Park CA 94025

LUERS, WENDY WILSON WOODS, management consultant; b. Ann Arbor, July 16, 1940; d. Ward Wilson and Patricia (Fay) Woods; m. William Turnbull, Jr., Apr. 1, 1967, (div. 1979); children: Connor, Ramsay; m. William Henry, Oct. 18, 1979. Postgrad, U. Madrid, 1961; BA, Stanford U., Paol Alto, Calif., 1962. Asst. editor San Francisco Mag., 1965-67; asst. producer Film Bullett, San Francisco, 1970; stringer Time Mag., San Francisco, 1964-71; commentator KOED TV, San Francisco, 1974-79; dir., special project Amnesty Internat., San Francisco; cultural correspondent Venevision TV, Caracas, 1982-83; dir. special projects Human Rights Watch, 1987-89; lectr. Nancy Nelson (Agent), N.Y., 1987-89. Contbr. articles to mags., newspapers and profl. jours. Founder/Pres. Friends of Art & Preservation Embassies, Wash., Bd. dir. Nat. Council on Children & TV, Los Angeles. Mem. Nat. Coun. on the Arts, Luce Scholars Program (ind. com. on arts policy). Democrat. Roman Catholic. Home: 993 Fifth Ave New York NY 10028

LUETH, FAITH M., music educator; b. Washington, Feb. 13, 1943; d. Francis and Ellen D. (Parsons) Musker; m. Richard A. Lueth, Dec. 26, 1968; 1 child, Rachel. BA, Boston U., 1964; MA, MM, Boston Conservatory, 1986. Cert. music tchr. K-12. Dir. music Wellesley Park Ch., Wayland, Mass.; choral dir. Pollard Middle Sch., Needham, Mass.; asst. prof. music edn. Berklee Coll. Music, Boston, choral clinician adolescent voice; guest condr. Contbr. chpt. to book. Recipient Disting. Tchr. award Ednl. Coop. Supts.; Mann grantee. Mem. Am. Choral Dirs. Assn., Music Educators Nat. Conf., Mass. Music Edn. Assn., Mu Phi Epsilon. Address: 8 Irving Dr Walpole MA 02081

LUETKEMEYER, MARY JANE, french educator; b. St. Charles, Mo., July 18, 1951; d. Harold Karl and Cecilia Elizabeth (Vomund) L. BA, Fontbonne Coll., 1974; Lic. es Lettres, U. Nantes, France, 1976; MA in Teaching, Webster U., 1982. French tchr. Parkway South High Sch., St. Louis, 1976-83, French tchr., dept. chairperson, 1983—. Bd. dirs. Friends of Steinberg Meml. Skating Rink, St. Louis, 1985—. Mem. Am. Assn. Tchrs. French. Home: 480 Longfellow Saint Louis MO 63122 Office: Pkwy South High Sch 801 Hanna Rd Manchester MO 63021

LUJAN, CLEO CHARLOTTE, psychologist; b. Trinidad, Colo., June 30, 1946; d. Joseph Tobias and Annie (Lopez) Baca; m. Toby I. Lujan, July 10, 1965; 1 child, Maria Lynn. AA, Met. State Coll., Denver, 1973; BA, Loretto Heights Coll., Denver, 1976; D in Psychology, U. Denver, 1980. Lic. clin. psychologist, Colo. Psychologist Denver Mental Health Clinic, 1980-82; pvt. practice Denver, 1982—; sch. psychologist Denver Pub. Schs., 1985; staff psychologist Lowry AFB, Denver, 1985-86, Ft. Logan Mental Health Ctr., Denver, 1986; psychologist Met. State Coll., 1987-88; psychologist examiner State Bd. Psychologist Examiners, Denver, 1987-90; cons. Profl. Examination Svcs., Denver, 1990. Centennial Bi-Centennial scholar Loretto Heights Coll., 1976. Mem. Am. Psychol. Assn., Colo. Psychol. Assn. Office: 360 S Monroe #350 Denver CO 80209

LUKA, CONCETTA GERTRUDE, corporate administrator; b. Chgo., Dec. 24, 1939; d. Joseph P. and Josephine (Marino) Minutello; m. Daniel R. Luka, Jan. 28, 1967; children: Lauren Sue, Theresa Jo, Kenneth, Michael Joseph, Mary Kathleen. AS in Bus. Adminstrn., Bliss Coll., 1980; BSBA, Urbana (Ohio) Coll., 1981. Instr. part-time Bliss Coll., Columbus, Ohio, 1981-83; supr. medicare billing Mt. Carmel Med. Ctr., Columbus, 1981-83; patient account mgr. Martha Washington Hosp., Chgo., 1983-84, Ravenswood Hosp., Chgo., 1984-85; outpatient accounts mgr. Columbus-Cuneo Cabrini Med. Ctr., Chgo., 1985-88; corp. adminstr. Hand Therapy Ltd., Hand Surgery, Hand Rehab. Svcs., Chgo., 1988-90; mgr. client svcs. Medaphis Physician Svcs., Atlanta, Ga., 1990—. Mem. Healthcare Fin. Mgrs. Assn., Am. Guild Patient Account Mgrs. Office: Medaphis Physician Svcs Corp 210 Interstate N Ste 601 Atlanta GA 30339

LUKAS, ELAINE KOZLOWICZ, health care administrator; b. Milw., Jan. 3, 1954; d. Richard Matthew and Helen Christine (Wysocki) Kozlowicz; m. Todd Richard Lukaszewski, Aug. 21, 1976. BS, U. Wis., Milw., 1976, MS, 1977; bus. mgmt. cert., Alverno Coll., Milw., 1983. Lic. nursing home adminstr., Wis. Speech pathologist Milw. Pub. Schs., 1977-78, Wis. Spl. Edn. Needs Project, Milw., 1978-79, Waukesha County Spl. Edn., Brookfield, Wis., 1979-81, Jewish Vocat. Svc., Milw., 1981-83; adminstr. nursing home Beverly Enterprises, Milw., 1983-87, Wheaton Francsican System, Milw., 1987-89, Unicare Health Facilities, Milw., 1989—; cons., guest lectr. U. Wis., Milw., 1978-79; external assessor Alverno Coll., Milw., 1984—. Gov.'s appointment to Wis. Nursing Home Study Com., Madison, 1987; treas. Milw chpt. Wis. Women's Political Caucus, 1989—, Gubernatorial appointments chair, 1989—. Named 1 of 3 Women Honored, Mil.'s Outstanding Women, 1982; U.S. Office Edn. fellow, 1976. Mem. NOW (Milw. chpt. co-chair polit. action task force 1980-88, treas. 1985-89), Am. Speech/Language Hearing Assn., Wis. Assn. Nursing Homes (co-chair pub. affairs com. 1985-87, 90—, bd. dirs. 1985-87, pres. dist. 5 1986-87), Wis. Assn. Homes and Svcs. for Aging, Catholic Health Care (bd. dirs. 1988-89). Democrat. Home: 4204 W Mequon Rd Mequon WI 53092

LUKE, PATRICIA ANN, management and communications consultant; b. Putnam, Conn., May 28, 1934; d. Edward Elmer and Florence Margaret (Collins) Brenn; m. Donald Joseph Luke, Dec. 28, 1956; children: Melanie A., Richard B., Ivy S. Student, U. N.C., Greensboro, 1952-53; BS in Edn., Central Conn. State U., New Britain, 1957, MS in Edn., 1968. Lectr. communications dept. Central Conn. State U., New Britain, 1965-80; legis. liaison Conn. Assn. Bds. Edn., Hartford, 1973-74, dir. legis. svcs., 1980-84, assoc. exec. dir., 1984-89; owner, cons. Quality Solutions Cons., Hartford, 1989—; dir. Nat. Sch. Bds. Assn., Washington, 1978-80; mem. policy bd. Nat. Assessment of Edn. Progress, Denver, 1978-80; resource person Conn. Edn. Equity Study com., Hartford, 1984-89; mem. blue ribbon commn. Conn. State Dept. Edn., Hartford, 1988-89; co-chmn. truancy adv. com. Conn. State Dept. Edn., Hartford, 1988-89. Co-author: Summary and Analysis of School Finance Legislation in Connecticut, 1986; contbr. articles on sch. fin. and legis. issues to profl. jours. Recipient Disting. Svc. award Radio Sta. WRCH, Farmington, 1974, Disting. Svc. award City of New Britain, 1977, Meritorious Svc. award Nat. Assessment Edn. Progress, Edn. Commn. of States, Denver, 1980; named Involved Woman of Yr. YMCA New Britain, 1977, Outstanding Community Vol., Community Coun., 1979. Mem. NAFE, Am. Mgmt. Assn., Conn. Assn. Bds. Edn. (life, pres. 1977-78, disting. svc. award 1988), Phi Delta Kappa. Office: Quality Solutions 111 Charter Oak Ave Hartford CT 06106

LUKEMAN, KAREN CALMON, purchasing specialist; b. New London, Conn., July 24, 1953; d. Morris and Lillian (Nasser) Calmon; m. Joseph F. Lukeman, Feb. 23, 1975. 2d degree, U. Rouen, France, 1974; BA, U. Conn., 1975; MBA, N.H. Coll., 1990. With Advent Corp., Cambridge, Mass.,

1975-77; buyer, purchasing mgr., then materials mgr. Kurzweil Computer Products, Inc., Cambridge, 1977-84; materials mgr. Imagitex, Inc., Nashua, N.H., 1984-88; purchasing mgr. Data Translation, Inc., Marlborough, Mass., 1988—. Vol. helping Russian immigrants adapt to American culture. Mem. Am. Prodn. and Inventory Control Soc. Jewish. Office: Data Translation Inc 100 Locke Dr Marlborough MA 01752

LUKSIC, CYNTHIA LEE, human resources research and development assistant; b. Springville, N.Y., July 27, 1965; d. Kenneth Joseph and Charlotte Sharon (Anzalone) Luksic. Student, George Mason U., 1989. Office mgr. Hechinger Co., Landover, Md., 1983-85; tax mgr. Assoc. Tax Svcs., Inc., McLean, Va., 1985-86; supr. tech. svcs. Prison Fellowship Ministries, Reston, Va., 1986-90. Mem. Nat. Assn. for Female Execs. Home: 1600 N Brandon Ave Sterling VA 22170

LUM, JEAN LOUI JIN, nurse educator; b. Honolulu, Sept. 5, 1938; d. Yee Nung and Pui Ki (Young) L. BS, U. Hawaii, Manoa, 1960; MS in Nursing, U. Calif., San Francisco, 1961; MA, U. Wash., 1969, PhD in Sociology, 1972. Registered nurse, Hawaii. From instr. to prof. Sch. Nursing U. Hawaii-Manoa, Honolulu, 1961—, acting dean, 1982, dean, 1982-89; project coordinator Analysis and Planning Personnel Services, Western Interstate Commn. Higher Edn., 1977; extramural assoc. div. Research Grants NIH, 1978-79; mem. mgmt. adv. com. Honolulu County Hosp., 1982—; mem. exec. bd. Pacific Health Research Inst., 1980-88; mem. health planning com. East Honolulu, 1978-81. Contbr. articles to profl. jours. Recipient Nurse of Yr. award Hawaii Nurses Assn., 1982; USPHS grantee, 1967-72. Fellow Am. Acad. Nursing; mem. Am. Nurses Assn., Am. Pacific Nursing Leaders Conf. (pres. 1983-87), Council Nurse Researchers, Nat. League for Nursing (bd. rev. 1981-87), Western Council Higher Edn. for Nurses (chmn. 1984-85), Western Soc. for Research in Nursing, Am. Sociol. Assn., Pacific Sociol. Assn., Assn. for Women in Sci., Hawaii Pub. Health Assn., Hawaii Med. Services Assn. (bd. dirs. 1985—), Mortar Bd., Phi Kappa Phi, Sigma Theta Tau, Alpha Kappa Delta, Delta Kappa Gamma. Episcopalian. Office: U Hawaii-Manoa Sch Nursing Webster 409 2528 The Mall Honolulu HI 96822

LUM, LINDA LI CHING, government administrator; b. Mt. Vernon, N.Y., Apr. 23, 1957; d. Joseph and Kew (Chan) L. BA, Yale U., 1979; MA, U. Chgo., 1981. Conf. specialist Ctr. for Study of Fgn. Affairs U.S. Dept. State, Washington, 1984-88, staffing mgmt. officer Bur. Internat. Orgns., 1988-90, fgn. affairs officer Bur. Politico-Mil. Affairs, 1990—. Author monographs. Mem. Yale Club of Washington, U. Chgo. Club of Washington. Office: Dept State PM Room 7815 Main State Washington DC 20520-7815

LUMADUE, JOYCE ANN, hobby company executive; b. New London, Conn., Oct. 21, 1941; d. James E. and Camilla (Romeo) Hayes; student U. Conn.; m. Donald Dean Lumadue, June 28, 1958; children—Dawnia Jean, Donald Dean, Robert Ryan, Ronald Jeffrey. Partner, Joydon's Coin Shop, New London, 1958—, House of Leisure, New London, 1967—, Hobby Crafts, New London, 1969—; v.p. New Eng. Internat. Inc., New London, 1969-85, Lumadue Inc., New London, 1978—. Mem. Hobby Industry Assn. Am., Internat. Mgmt. Council, Nat. Assn. Female Execs., NOW. Methodist. Contbr. articles to profl. jours. Office: 78-88 Captains Walk New London CT 06320

LUMBA, GRACIA NAVARRO, retired educator; b. Calbayog, Philippines, July 23; came to U.S. 1970; d. Constancio Miciano and Sabina Carmen (Mendoza) Navarro; m. Gerardo Foronda Lumba, June 29, 1942; children: Ellen Guanlao, Roberto, Carol Thompson, Maria Halliday, Gerardo Jr. BSE, U. Santo Tomas, 1943, MA in English, 1947, PhD, 1952. Prof. U. Santo Tomas, Manila, 1947-72; lectr. grad. and undergrad. U. Santo Tomas, 1974-76; cons., dir. social svcs. John Randolph Hosp. and Nursing Home, Petersburg, Va., 1977-78; lectr. Assumption Convent, Manila, 1960-63, Chapman Coll., Ft. Lee, Va., 1976-78; vis. observer Melbourn U., Australia, summer 1959. Contbr. articles to profl. jours. Recipient Gold medal Philippine Normal Sch. Alumni Assn., 1988, Vol. of Yr. award Nat. Mental Hosp.; named Disting. Alumna Coll. of Edn. Alumni Assn., U. St. Tomas, 1989. Mem. AAUW, Philippine Assn. Univ. Women (pres. N.S.T. chpt. 1968-69). Democrat. Roman Catholic. Home: 1766 Berkeley Ave Petersburg VA 23805

LUMPKIN, ANNE CRAIG, television company executive; b. DeValls Bluff, Ark., Apr. 3, 1919; d. Claude Cleo and Lou (Craig) L. Student, Little Rock Bus. Sch., 1938-39, Patricia Stevens, 1953. Adminstrv. asst. to pres. Sta. KVLC (S.W. Broadcasting), Little Rock, 1948-52, Sta. KGKO (Lakewood Broadcasting), Dallas, 1952-54, Sta. KTLN, Inc., Denver, 1954-58; asst. mgr. Sta. KLRA, Inc., Little Rock, 1958-83; asst. dir. fin. affairs KLRT-TV, Little Rock, 1983—. Mem. Ark. Arts Ctr., Little Rock, 1989—, Fine Arts Club, Little Rock, 1989—, Nat. Audubon Soc., 1989—, Pulaski County Hist. Soc., Little Rock, 1989—. Mem. ABA, Am. Women in Radio-TV, Am. Bus. Womens Assn., Little Rock Club. Baptist.

LUMPP, KAREN EVE, accountant; b. Paterson, N.J., June 9, 1951; d. John A. and June (McHardy) L. BS in Mgmt., Babson Coll., Wellsley, Mass., 1973. CPA, N.J. Ptnr. Deloitte & Touche, Short Hills, N.J., 1973—. Mem. Subcom. on Credit and Collection procedures for the Uninsured, Trenton, N.J., 1989. Mem. AICPA, N.J. Soc. CPA's, Exec. Women N.J. (bd. dirs. 1982-84), Healthcare Fin. Mgmt. Assn. (pres. N.J. chpt. 1985-87, region III liaison 1988-89, William G. Follmer award 1983, Robert Reeves award 1987). Office: Deloitte & Touche 51 John F Kennedy Pkwy Short Hills NJ 07078

LUNA, CAROLYN F., nursing administrator; b. Nauvoo, Ala., Dec. 6, 1945; d. Barney V. and Claudine (Atkins) Lawson; m. Carl M. Luna, Jr., Aug. 19,1967 (dec. 1988); 1 child, Alisa. RN, San Jose Hosp., 1967; BSN, NYU, 1982; MSN, U. N.Mex., 1985. Staff nurse Tempe (Ariz.) Hosp., 1969-72; with San Jose Hosp., 1967-69; nursing supr. Morenci (Ariz.) Hosp., 1972-75; infection control nurse U. Ariz., Tucson, 1975-76; head nurse ICU St. Vincent Hosp., Santa Fe, N.Mex., 1976-78; dir. staff devel. St. Vincent Hosp., 1978-84, clin. dir., 1984-87; nurse adminstr. Los Alamos (N.Mex.) Med. Ctr., 1987—. Exec. dir. LaLuz de Santa Fe Family Shelter, 1987—; bd. dirs. Bible Life Community Ch., Santa Fe, 1986—. Sigma Theta Tau grantee, 1984. Mem. Am. Orgn. Nurse Execs., Am. Acad. Med. Adminstrs., Sigma Theta Tau. Republican. Assemblies of God. Home: Route 19 Box 90-4 Santa Fe NM 87505 Office: Los Alamos Med Ctr 3917 West Rd Los Alamos NM 87544

LUNA, ELIZABETH J(EAN), cell biologist, educator, researcher; b. Poplar Bluff, Mo., Oct. 18, 1951; d. William Marion and Frieda L (Phillis) Luna; m. Alonzo H. Ross, June 24, 1974. BA with highest honors, So. Ill. U., 1972; PhD in Phys. Chemistry, Stanford U., 1977. Postdoctoral fellow dept. cell and molecular biology Harvard U., Cambridge, Mass., 1977-81; asst. prof. dept. biology Princeton (N.J.) U., 1981-88; sr. scientist Cell Biology group Worcester Found. for Exptl. Biology, Shrewsbury, Mass., 1988—; assoc. prof. dept. cell biology U. Mass. Med. Sch., Worcester, 1989—; mem. adv. com. on personnel for rsch.-B, Am. Cancer Soc., Atlanta, 1989—. Contbr. chpts. to books, articles to profl. jours. Mem. profl. adv. com. March of Dimes Birth Defects Found., Cen. N.J. chpt., 1983-88. Recipient Borden award, Merck award So. Ill. U., 1971; grantee Am. Cancer Soc., NIH, others. Mem. AAAS, Am. Chem. Soc., Am. Soc. for Cell Biology, Am. Women in Sci., Biophys. Soc., Protein Soc., Sigma Xi. Office: Worcester Found Exptl Biol 222 Maple Ave Shrewsbury MA 01545

LUNA, PATRICIA ADELE, marketing executive; b. Charleston, S.C., July 22, 1956; d. Benjamin Curtis and Clara Elizabeth (McCrory) L. BS in History, Auburn U., 1978, MEd in History, 1980; MA in Adminstrn., U. Ala., 1981, EdS in Adminstrn., 1984, PhD, ABD in Adminstrn., 1986. Cert. tchr., Ga., Ala. History tchr. Harris County Middle Sch., Ga., 1978-79, head dept., 1979-81; residence hall dir. univ. housing U. Ala., 1981-83, asst. dir. residence life, 1983-85; intern Cornell U., Ithaca, N.Y., 1983; dir. of mktg. Golden Flake Snack Foods, Inc., Birmingham, Ala., 1985-89; sr. v.p. Quest U.S.A., Inc., Atlanta, 1989—; cons., lectr. in field. Author: Specialization: A Learning Module, 1979, Grantsmanship, 1981, Alcohol Awareness Programs, 1984; University Programming, 1984; Marketing Residential Life, 1985; The History of Golden Flake Snack Foods, 1986; Golden Flake Snack Foods, Inc., A Case Study, 1987. Fundraiser, U. Ala. Alumni Scholarship Fund, Tuscaloosa, 1983, Am. Diabetes Assn., Tuscaloosa, 1984, Urban Ministries, Birmingham, 1985-88; fundraiser, com. chmn. Spl. Olympics, Tuscaloosa, 1985; fundraiser Am. Cinema Soc., 1988; chmn. Greene County Relief Project, 1982-89; bd. dirs. Cerebral Palsy Found., Tuscaloosa, 1985-86; lay rector and com. chmn. Kairos Prison Ministry, Tutwiler State Prison, Ala., 1986—; lobbyist, com. chmn. task force Justice Fellowship, 1988-89; bd dirs. Internat. Found. Ewha U., Seoul, Korea, 1988—. Recipient Dir. of Yr. award U. Ala., 1982, 83; Skeets Simonis award, U. Ala., 1984, nat. award Joint Council on Econ. Edn., 1979, rsch. award NSF, 1979; named to Hon. Order Ky. Cols. Commonwealth of Ky., 1985—, Rep. Senatorial Inner Circle, 1986; Mem. Sales and Mktg. Execs. (chmn. com. 1985-86), Leadership Ala. (pres. 1982-83), Am. Mktg. Assn. (Disting. Leadership award 1987, Commemorative Medal of Honor 1988), Assn. Coll. and Univ. Housing Officers (com. chmn. 1983-85), Nat. Assn. Student Personnel Officers, Snack Food Assn. (mem. mktg. com. and conf. presenter), Commerce Exec. Soc., Emmaus Club (chmn. com. 1985-89), Snow Skiing Club, Sailing Club, Omega Rho Sigma (pres. 1983-84), Omicron Delta Kappa, Phi Delta Kappa, Kappa Delta Pi, Phi Alpha Theta. Republican. Methodist. Avocations: skiing, racquetball, tennis, community work, public speaking. Home: 11 Vestavia Hills Northport AL 35476 Office: Quest USA Inc 5500 Roswell Rd Atlanta GA 30303

LUNA PADILLA, NITZA ENID, university director; b. San Juan, P.R., Mar. 13, 1959; d. Luis and Carmen Iris (Padilla) Luna. BFA, Pratt Inst., 1981; MS, Brooks Inst., 1985. Instr. U. P.R., Carolina, 1981-82; libr. asst. Brooks Inst. Libr., Santa Barbara, Calif., 1982-84; instr. Cultural Inst., San Juan, 1988, U. Sagrado Corazón, Santurce, P.R., 1987-89; assoc. dir. communication ctr. U. Sacred Heart Sagrado Corazón, Santurce, P.R., 1989—; juror Avco Fin. Svcs., San Juan, 1988. MacDowell Colony grantee, 1989. Mem. Friends of Photography, New Pictorialist Soc., Soc. for Photographic Edn. Roman Catholic. Office: U Sagrado Corazón Correo Calle Loiza Apt 12383 Santurce PR 00914

LUNA SMITH, CARLA MARIE, publicist, editor; b. Santa Fe, May 15, 1960; d. Tony Jr. and Doris Jeanne (Gaussoin) Luna; m. Steven Gregory Smith, Feb. 15, 1986. BA in Journalism, U. Okla., 1983. News editor Sta. KTVY-TV, Oklahoma City, 1983-84; news reporter Sta. KTSM-TV, El Paso, Tex., 1984-85; editor/sports reporter Sta. KVUE-TV, Austin, Tex., 1986-88; publicist-editor Frank Erwin Ctr./Applause Mag., Austin, 1988—. Co-chair communications com. Am. Cancer Soc., 1987—, slogan creator, 1989; publicity chmn. Tex. Athletic Equity Project, Austin, 1986-88. Mem. Women in Communications (editor newsletter 1988-89, sec. 1989-90, vol. chair 1990—), Sooner Club (dir., mem. founding bd.), Austin Music Industry Coun., Kappa Alpha Theta. Republican. Roman Catholic. Office: Frank Erwin Center 1701 Red River St Austin TX 78701

LUNBURG, DEBRA ANN, health insurance executive; b. Weehawken, N.J., Oct. 18, 1952; d. Joseph Charles and Laura Christine (Larson) Dealessi; m. Robert Mark Bociulis, Dec. 19, 1948; children: Erik, Ryan. BA, Montclair State Coll., 1974; cert. paralegal, Caldwell Coll., 1979. Systems project mgr. Mut. Benefit Life Ins Co., Newark, N.J., 1979-82; computer systems exec. Seligman and Latz Inc., N.Y.C., 1982-84; health ins. exec. Blue Cross Blue Shield of N.J., Newark, 1984—. Bd. dirs. Am. Diabetes Assn.; trustee Health and Welfare Coun.; mem. child placement bd. Bergen County Superior Ct., Rep. Nat. Com., Washington, 1987—; pres., bd. dirs. Am. Diabetes Assn.; pres. Nat. Found. for Diabetes. Mem. NAFE, Am. Mktg. Assn. (exec.), NAFE, Smithsonian Instn., Essex Council, Nat. Railway Hist. Soc. Home: 475 Colonial Terr Hackensack NJ 07061 Office: 15 Vreeland Rd Florham Park NJ 07932

LUNCEFORD, LAURA, sales and marketing executive; b. Provo, Utah, July 24, 1954; d. Wayne Jack and Gloria (Snell) L. BA in Philosophy, U. Utah, 1976. Product mgr., mgr. advt. and mktg. svcs. Quanta Corp., Salt Lake City; mgr. mktg. and communications Chyron Corp., Melville, N.Y., dir. mktg.; dir. sales and mktg. Cubicomp Corp., Hayward, Calif.; cons. in video products sales and mktg. Home: 404 Mendocino Way Redwood Shores CA 99065

LUND, JO LYNN, human resource professional; b. Okinawa, Oct. 7, 1954; d. Dale Leroy and Catherine Lorraine (Donovan) L. BA in Psychology, U. Notre Dame, 1976; MS in Indsl. & Labor Rels., U. Wis., 1978. Coord. safety & tng. Am. Can Co., Neenah, Wis., 1978-80, James River Corp., Neenah, 1980-83; employee rels. assoc. Frito Lay, Inc., Wooster, Ohio, 1983-84; rep. Parallel Svcs. Inc., Indpls., 1984-86; tng. coord. Bd. Pub. Utilities, Kansas City, Kans., 1986-88; human resource devel. specialist Farmland Industries, Kansas City, Mo., 1988—; speaker Profl. Secs. Internat., Kansas City, Kans., 1989. Mem. Nat. Soc. for Performance & Instrn., Nat. Soc. for Tng. & Devel. Office: Farmland Industries PO Box 7305 Kansas City MO 64116

LUND, LOIS ANN, economics educator; b. Thief River Falls, Minn., Aug. 9, 1927; d. Robert J. and E. Luella (Tosdal) L. B.S., U. Minn., 1949, M.S., 1954, Ph.D., 1966. Instr. foods U. Iowa, 1951-55, U. Minn., 1955-63; assoc. prof., dir. core studies program, asst. dir. Sch. Home Econs., 1966-68; research fellow U.S. Dept. Agrl., 1963-66; assoc. dean, dir. Sch. Home Econs. Ohio State U., 1969-72; dean Coll. Human Ecology Mich. State U., East Lansing, 1973-85, prof. food sci. and human nutrition, 1985—; bd. dirs. Consumres Power Co., CMS Energy, Jackson, Mich. Contbr. articles to profl. jours. Recipient Betty award for excellence in teaching U. Minn., 1958, 63, 68, Hon. Alumni award Mich. State U., 1977, Outstanding Achievement award U. Minn. Alumni Assn., 1977. Mem. Am. Coun. on Consumer Interest, Am. Dietetic Assn., Am. Pub. Health Assn., Inst. Food Technologists, Gerontol. Soc. Am., Am. Home Econs. Assn. (nat. treas. 1980-82, Disting. Leader award 1984), Am. Agrl. Econs. Assn., Soc. for Nutrition Edn., Pi Lambda Theta, Phi Kappa Phi, Phi Upsilon Omicron, Omicron Nu, (nat. treas. 1971-74, 84-86), Sigma Delta Epsilon. Lutheran. Home: 5927 Shadow Lawn Dr East Lansing MI 48823 Office: Mich State Univ Dept Food Sci and Human Nutrition East Lansing MI 48824

LUND, MIREYA VALENCIA, psychologist; b. Santiago, Chile, Sept. 8, 1936; came to U.S., 1960; naturalized, 1982; d. Luis Alberto Valencia and Sara Rosa Gutierrez; m. Victor Lund, Dec. 22, 1975. Tchr. cert., U. Chile, 1963; MEd, U. Tex., 1962; PhD, UCLA, 1970. Lic. psychologist, Calif. Teaching asst. U. Tex., Austin, 1961-62; vocat. and psychol. counselor U. Chile, Santiago, 1963-67; rsch. asst. UCLA, 1968-70, psychologist, 1973—; prof. U. Chile, Santiago, 1971-73; tchr. Westlake Sch. for Girls, Brentwood, Calif., 1969-70; pvt. practice psychotherapist Pacific Palisades, Calif., 1980-89; corp. exec. MVL Properties, Inc., Pacific Palisades, Calif., 1989—; lectr. schs., women's groups, internat. orgns., 1960—; chief exec. MVL Properties, Inc., 1989—. Author poetry and various books, 1980— (awards 1987-90). Founding mem. Women's Resource Ctr., UCLA, 1970; sponsor Children Internat., 1988—. Recipient PEO Sisterhood, Tex. Chapel, 1961, Fullbright Commn., 1967; IEE grantee, Washington, 1960. Volleyball team champion, Santiago, 1953-54. Mem. Am. Psychol. Assn., Soc. Clin. and Exptl. Hypnosis, Internat. Soc. Hypnosis, Inst. Noetic Scis., UCLA Faculty Women's Club.

LUND, PAULINE KAY, physiology, pediatrics, educator; b. Golborne, Eng., Apr. 20, 1955; came to U.S., 1979; d. Leonard and Doris Margaret (Bolton) L.; m. Mark Smith, Feb. 25, 1980; children: Emma Terese Lundsmith, Alice Patricia Smithlund. BS with honors, U. Newcastle Upon Tyne, 1975, PhD, 1979. Demonstrator in medicine U. Newcastle Upon Tyne, 1978-79; postdoctoral fellow Mass. Gen. Hosp./Harvard Med. Sch., Boston, 1979-82; asst. prof. in physiology U.N.C., Chapel Hill, 1982-88, assoc. prof. in physiology, 1988—, assoc. prof. in pediatrics, 1989—; cons. Glaxo, Inc., Raleigh, N.C., 1989; study section mem. NIH, Bethesda, Md., 1989—. Contbg. author several books; contbr. articles to profl. jours. Recipient Fogarty postdoctoral fellowship, NIH, 1979, British SERC postdoctoral fellowship Sci. and Engring. Rsch. Coun., 1980, Rose Sidgewick Meml. fellowship, AAUW, 1979, Career Devel. award Juv. Diabetes Found., 1982-85, rsch. grants, NIH. Mem. Endocrine Soc. Office: Univ NC/Dept Physiology Chapel Hill NC 27514

LUND, RITA POLLARD, telecommunications executive; b. Vallscreek, W.Va., Aug. 28, 1950; d. Willard Garfield and Faye Ethel (Perry) Pollard; m. James William Lund, Dec. 30, 1969. Student, Alexandria Sch. Nursing, 1968-70, Columbia Pacific U., 1989—. Confidential asst. U.S. Ho. of Reps., Washington, 1975-76; exec. asst. White House Domestic Policy Staff, Washington, 1977-82, White House Sci. Office, Washington, 1982-83; asst. to pres. Telecom Futures Inc., Washington, 1983-84; v.p., internat. accounts mgr. Telecom Futures Inc., McLean, Va., 1985-89; ind. cons. telecommunications Washington, 1989—. Republican. Home: 9020 Patton Blvd Alexandria VA 22309

LUNDBERG, BARBARA JEAN, investment banker; b. Oslo, Sept. 30, 1952; d. Eugene Daniel and Doris Jean (Mercer) L.; m. Robert Brian Oley, Aug. 24, 1974 (div. 1984); 1 child, Erika Lundberg Oley; m. Frank W. Snyder, May 18, 1985; 1 child, Logan Lundberg Snyder; stepchildren: Keirith Ann Snyder, Devin Alan Snyder. BA in Polit. Sci., Tufts U., 1973; MBA in Fin., U. Pa., 1975. Auditor Ernst & Whinney, Hartford, Conn., 1975-76; fin. analyst TWA, N.Y.C., 1976-77; with bus. devel. Exxon Enterprises, N.Y.C., 1977-81, McGraw-Hill, 1981-83; venture capitalist Alan Patricof Assocs., Sunnyvale, Calif., 1983-86; v.p. Kidder Peabody, N.Y.C., 1986—. Home: 8 Old Farm Rd Darien CT 06820 Office: Kidder Peabody 10 Hanover Square New York NY 10005

LUNDBERG, LOIS ANN, public relations professional; b. Tulsa, Sept. 21, 1928; d. John T. and Anna M. (Patterson) McQuay; m. Ted W. Lundberg, Sept. 30, 1954; children: Linda Ann, Sharon Lynn. Student, Long Beach City Coll. With Pacific Telephone, 1950-65; gen. ptnr. McLund Co. Property Mgmt., 1972—; realtor Morgan Realty, 1974—; with Nason, Lundberg and Assoc., Orange, Calif., 1983-85, pres., campaign cons., 1985—. Bd. dirs. Luth. Ch. of the Master, La Habra, Calif., 1970-75, v.p. of congregation, 1986-87; mem. bd. trustees Nixon Law Office Preservation, Inc., 1972-75, Regional Ctr. of Orange County, 1982; bd. dirs. UCI Med. Ctr./Burn Ctr., 1982; apptd. Council on Criminal Justice Com., 1983—; mem. adv. bd. KOCE-TV, 1976—, La Habra Children's Mus., 1985—. Recipient Gov. Ronald Reagan award, 1967, Woman of Achievement award City of La Habra, 1979; named Outstanding Rep. of Orange County, 1978. Lutheran. Home: 1341 Carmela Ln La Habra CA 90631 Office: Nason Lundberg and Assocs 777 S Main St Ste 206 Orange CA 92668

LUNDE, DOLORES BENITEZ, educator; b. Honolulu, Apr. 12, 1929; d. Frank Molero and Matilda (Francisco) Benitez; m. Nuell Carlton Lunde, July 6, 1957; 1 child, Laurelle. BA, U. Oreg., 1951, postgrad., 1951-52; postgrad., U. So. Calif., L.A., 1953-54, Colo. State U., 1957-58, Calif. State U., Fullerton, 1967-68. Cert. gen. secondary tchr., Calif.; cert. lang. devel. specialist. Tchr. Brawley (Calif.) Union High Sch., 1952-55; tchr. Fullerton (Calif.) Union High Sch., 1955-73; tchrs. aide Placentia (Calif.) Unified Sch. Dist., 1983-85; tchr. continuing edn. Fullerton Union High Sch. Dist., 1985—; tchr. Fullerton Sch. Dist., 1988, Fullerton Union High Sch. Dist., 1989—; presenter regional and state convs., so. Calif., 1986-88. Innovator tests, teaching tools, audio-visual aids. Vol. Luth. Social Svcs., Fullerton, 1981-82, Messiah Luth., Yorba Linda, Calif., 1981-88. Recipient Tchr. of Yr. award Fullerton Union High Sch. Dist., 1989. Mem. NEA, AAUW (life, bull. editor 1979-80, corr. sec. 1981-83, program v.p. 1983-84, gift honoree Fullerton br. 1985), Calif. State Tchrs. Assn., Fullerton Secondary Tchrs. Assn., Internat. Club/Spanish Club (La Habra, Calif. advisor 1965-72). Office: Buena Park High School 8833 Academy Dr Buena Park CA 90621

LUNDE, KATHERINE L., educational administrator; b. Kankakee, Ill., May 3, 1947; d. James Armond and Frances Elizabeth (Maas) LaMontagne; m. Walter Arne Lunde Jr., June 15, 1969; children: Lisa Christine, Walter James. BS, No. Ill. U., 1969; postgrad., Jacksonville (Fla.) U., 1972. Cert. elem., secondary and early childhood educator. Tchr. 1st grade Kenwood Elem. Sch., Ft. Walton Beach, Fla.; kindergarten tchr., supr. Orange Park (Fla.) Kindergarten; asst. dir. Stoneway Sch., Stoneway Pvt. Sch., Plano, Tex.; dir. Westminster Preschool and Kindergarten, Dallas; v.p., bd. dirs. MiEscuelita Presch., Inc., Dallas; leader design team for early childhood seminar, Plano, Tex., 1990. Track coach Spl. Olympics, 1981-83; learning disabilities tutor, 1978-85. Sewell Funding grantee. Mem. Nat. Assn. Edn. Young Children, Dallas Assn. Edn. Young Children, Assn. for Curriculum Devel., Kappa Delta Pi. Office: 8200 Devonshire Dallas TX 75209

LUNDEN, JOAN, television personality; b. Sept. 19, 1950; m. Michael Krauss; children: Jamie Beryl, Lindsay Leigh, Sarah Emily. Student, Universidad de Las Americas, Mexico City, U. Calif., Calif. State U., Am. River Coll., Sacramento, Calif. Began broadcasting career at Sta. KCRA-TV and Radio, Sacramento; with Sta. WABC-TV, N.Y.C., 1975-80, co-anchor, 1976-80; co-host Good Morning America, ABC-TV, 1980—; host nat. syndicated TV show Everyday; spokesperson Beechnut Baby Food. Recipient Outstanding Mother of Yr. award, Nat. Mother's Day Com., 1982. Office: ABC-TV Good Morning Am 1965 Broadway New York NY 10023*

LUNDGREN, CLARA ELOISE, public affairs professional, journalist; b. Temple, Tex., Mar. 7, 1951; d. Claude Elton and Klara (Csirmaz) L. AA, Temple Jr. Coll., 1971; BJ, U. Tex., 1973; MA, Columbia Pacific U., 1986. Reporter Temple Daily Telegram, 1970-72; news editor Austin (Tex.) Am.-Statesman, 1972-75; mng. editor Stillhouse Hollow Pubs., Inc., Belton, 1975-77; pub. affairs officer Darnall Army Community Hosp., Ft. Hood, Tex., 1978-80; editor Ft. Hood Sentinel III Corps, 1980-85; command info. officer Pub. Affairs Office III Corps, Ft. Hood, 1985-87, community relations officer, 1987-88, dep. pub. affairs officer, 1988—. Recipient Nat. Observer Journalistic Achievment award Dow Jones and Co., 1971, Superior Civilian Svc. award Dept. of Army, 1989. Mem. NOW, TEx. Press Women, Fed. Women's Program, Assn. U.S. Army (sec. Cen. Tex.-Ft. Hood chpt.), Tex. Sheriff's Assn., Army Aviation Assn. Home: 1305 S 13th Temple TX 76504 Office: III Corps Pub Affairs Office Fort Hood TX 76544-5056

LUNDGREN, RUTH WILLIAMSON WOOD (RUTH LUNDGREN WILLIAMSON WOOD), public relations executive, writer; b. Bklyn.; d. William and Hanna (Carlson) L.; m. W.F. Williamson, Dec. 17, 1949 (dec.); children: John Ross (dec.), Mark Ward; m. John Earle Wood, Aug. 27, 1988. Student, Bklyn. Coll., 1936-41, Columbia U., 1942. Assoc. editor Everywoman's mag., 1940-42; pub. relations staff exec. J.M. Mathes Advt. Agy., 1942-45; dir. pub. relations Pan-Am. Coffee Bur., 1945-48; pres. Ruth Lundgren Ltd., N.Y.C., 1948—. Pub. Ruth Lundgren Newsletter, 1950-58; writer daily column St. Petersburg (Fla.) Times, 1956-60; contbg. editor, writer monthly column Motor Boating and Sailing mag., 1962-80; contbr. to popular profl. publs. Home: 3319 Bay Front Dr Baldwin Harbor NY 11510 also: 1111 Crandon Blvd Apt A1008 Key Biscayne FL 33149 Office: PO Box 184 Baldwin NY 11510

LUNDGREN-WEBER, GAIL, lawyer; b. Tacoma, June 14, 1955; d. Arthur Dean and Vera Martha (Grimm) L.; married, 1989. AB cum laude, Vassar Coll., 1977; JD cum laude, U. Puget Sound., 1980. Bar: Wash. 1981. Legal intern Reed, McClure, Moceri & Thonn, Seattle, 1979; Burgess & Kennedy, Tacoma, 1979-80; legal intern Lee, Smart, Cook, Martin & Patterson, P.S., Inc., Seattle, 1980-81, assoc., 1981—. Vestry com. Queen Anne Luth. Ch., 1983-86, v.p. of congregation, 1988, 89, mem. worship and music com., 1982-83, 84-86, parish edn. com., 1983-84. Recipient Am. Jurisprudence Book awards, 1980. Mem. ABA, Fed. Bar Assn., Wash. State Bar Assn., Seattle-King County Bar Assn., Wash. Def. Trial Lawyers Assn., Order of Barristers, Wash. State Vassar Club (chmn. alumni admissions 1983-85, rep. 1986—). Democrat. Avocations: scuba diving, tennis, classical music, needlepoint and stitchery. Office: Lee Smart Cook Martin & Patterson 1325-4th Ave Ste 800 Seattle WA 98101

LUNDQUIST, LINDA ANN JOHNSON, insurance professional; b. Iowa City, Iowa, Aug. 15, 1945; d. Elmer Clinton and Georgia Joan (Molloy) L.; m. Scott Arthur Johnson, Sept. 26, 1981. BA, U. Iowa, 1968. Civil engring. drafter firm Shive-Hattery & Assocs., Iowa City, 1968-78; dir. drafting svcs. firm Shoemaker & Haaland, Profl. Engrs., Coralville, Iowa, 1978-82; mktg. rep. Veenstra & Kimm, Inc., Engineers and Planners, Iowa City and West Des Moines, 1982-86; mktg. support dept. Stanley Cons. Inc., Muscatine, Iowa, 1986-87; age. State Farm Ins. Cos., 1988—. mem. spl. appointments Urban Environment Ad Hoc Com., Iowa City, 1985-86, groundwater protection ad hoc adv. com. State Iowa, 1987-88. Recipient Spl. Merit award Cedar Rapids Mus. Art, Iowa, 1979. Mem. Greater Iowa City Area C. of C. (environ. concerns com. 1982-87, chair 1984-86, govt. affairs com. 1988—), Iowa Groundwater Assn. (bd. dirs. 1986-89), Nat. Assn. Life Underwriters, Iowa Assn. Life Underwriters, Nat. Wildlife Fedn., Iowa Wildlife Fedn. (conservation issues com. 1987-88), Internat. Fund Animal Welfare, Wilderness Soc., World Wildlife Fund, Alpha Gamma Delta (bd. dirs. house assn. 1986—). Avocations: drawing, watercolors, dance, painting. Office: 407 K-Plaza Hwy 1 W Iowa City IA 52246

LUNDQUIST, MARY ELIZABETH, insurance agency principal; b. Detroit, Dec. 28, 1954; d. Benjamin Albert and Loretta Rose (Dyki) Purcott; m. Dennis Ray Lundquist, July 28, 1978; 1 child, Mark Ryan. AA in Criminal Justice, BA in Music Edn., Madonna Coll., 1976. Cert. ins. counselor; lic. resident agt., Mich.; lic. ins. counselor. Mktg. clk. John Thomas Agy., Birmingham, Mich., 1970-76; mktg. rep. Nickel Agy. Inc., Birmingham, 1976-78, Republic-Hogg-Robinson, Inc., Southfield, Mich., 1978-80; corp. officer Ins. Guaranty Internat., Southfield, 1980-83, Able/Atlantic Ins., Inc., Southfield, 1983-85; pres., owner Atlantic Ins. Assoc., Inc., West Bloomfield, Mich., 1983—; mem. State of Mich. Ins. Commr.'s Agts. Adv. Coun. Mem. Mothers Against Drunk Drivers; cons. Mich. Cheerleading Coaches Assn., Lansing, 1987—; pres. concerned citizens for West Bloomfield League of Women Voters. Mem. Gt. Am. Agts. Adv. Council, Profl. Ins. Agts. of Am., Nat. Assn. of Life Underwriters, Metro Detroit Ins. Club. Office: Atlantic Ins Assocs Inc 6346 Orchard Lake Rd Suite 202 West Bloomfield MI 48322

LUNDQUIST, VIOLET ELVIRA, state agency administrator; b. Bristol, Conn., Jan. 28, 1912; d. Otto Nimrod and Mabel Elvira (Lindeen) Ebb; m. Vernon Arthur Lundquist, May 14, 1935; children: Karen Ebb, Jane Christine. Diploma music Augustana Coll., Rock Island, Ill., 1932; postgrad. mgmt. systems U. Mo., 1969. Cert. vocat. rehab. adminstr. Tchr. music pub. schs., Olds, Iowa, 1932-35; editor Warsaw (Mo.) Times, 1935-45, Anthon (Iowa) Herald, 1945-57; field dir. Iowa Heart Assn., Des Moines, 1957-66; exec. dir. S.E. Iowa Community Action Program, Burlington, 1966-74; adminstrn. dir. S.E. Ariz. Govts. Orgn. Community Svcs., Bisbee, Ariz., 1975-77; statewide advocate developmentally disabled adults, 1977—; adminstr. Arizona City Med. Ctr., part-time, 1979-80; adminstr. Dist. V Coun. on Devel. Disabilities, 1980-87. Bd. dirs. Cen. Ariz. Health Systems Agy., 1979—, chmn., 1986—; chmn. Arizona City Home and Property Owners Assn., 1979-82; bd. dirs. Ariz. State Health Planning Coun., 1986—; mem. Ariz. Statewide Health Coordinating Coun., 1986—, Ariz. Dist. V Human Rights Com., 1986—; pres. Pinal County Assn. for Retarded Citizens, 1987—, v.p., vice chmn. state assn.; co-organized Adults for Self-Advocacy in Soc., assn. for high functioning retarde young persons, 1988-89. Recipient Carol Lane award Nat. Safety Coun., 1956, 1st place award Nat. Fedn. Press Women, 1952, 53, 55, 57; USPHS scholar, Columbia U., 1963, 64. Mem. Nat. Soc. Community Action Program Dirs. (dir. 1966-75), Ariz. Fedn. Press Women, Zonta (area dir. 1984-86), Women of Moose. Lutheran. Home and Office: 15686 S Reef PO Box 2265 Arizona City AZ 85223

LUNDRY, VIOLA DELIGHT, retired educator; b. Jesup, Iowa, Mar. 7, 1924; d. Floyd R. and Mary Elizabeth (Keckler) Caldwell; m. Raymond Headley, July 8, 1972; stepchildren: Bess, Larry, Pat, Lou Ann, Barbara, Raymond, Sharon. BS in Edn., Marion Coll., 1948; MA, U. Northern Iowa, 1968. Cert. tchr., Iowa. Elem. sch. tchr. Arlingotn (Iowa) Independent Sch. Dist., 1943-46; jr. high tchr. Fayette (Iowa) Consolidated Sch. Dist., 1948-57, Waverly (Iowa) Sch. Dist., 1957-72. Former pres. Waverly-Shell Rock Tchr. Assn., Waverly; Sunday sch. tchr. Wesleyan Meth. Ch., Fayette, 1938—; Bible sch. tchr. First Bapt., Oelwein, Iowa, 1974—, 1974—; mem. Ch. Women United, Oelwein, 1972—. Mem. NaEA (life), Delta Kappa Gamma (former chpt. v.p., former chpt. pres., state scholar). Home: 801 2nd Ave NE Oelwein IA 50662

LUNDY, KATHRYN RENFRO, retired librarian; b. Horse Cave, Ky., Aug. 15, 1918; d. Edmund Lovell and Rose (Strader) Renfro; m. Frank Arthur Lundy, Nov. 12, 1971 (dec. May 1975). Student, Colo. Coll., 1935-38; AB in LS, U.Denver, 1939. Catalog reviser U. Denver, summer 1939; asst. cataloger Stephens Coll., Columbia, Mo., 1939-42; head cataloger Utah State Agrl. Coll., Logan, 1942-43; cataloger Iowa State Coll., Ames, 1943-46; sr. asst. librarian catalog dept., catalog librarian U. Nebr., Lincoln, 1946-50, tech. svc.librarian to assoc. dir. libraries for tech. svc., 1950-68, assoc. dir. libraries for gen. svcs., 1968-74, acting dir.libraries, summer 1973, library rsch. analyst, 1974-77, prof. planning and rsch., 1977-80; cons. on centralized processing Nebr. Pub. Library Commn., Lincoln, 1967-70; cons. Eastern Iowa Community Coll. Libraries at Clinton and Muscatine, 1970. Author: Women View Librarianship: Nine Perspectives, 1980; contbr. articles to library jours. Mem. ALA, Nebr. Libr. Assn. (pres. 1963-64, Meritorious Svc. award 1980), AAUW, U. Nebr. Emeriti Assn., Kappa Kappa Gamma, Beta Phi Mu. Democrat. Unitarian. Home: 1913 Monterey Dr Lincoln NE 68506

LUNDY, LISA GAIL, leasing agent; b. Dallas, Apr. 2, 1962; d. Clarence Harold Lundy. BS in Home Econs., Stephen F. Austin Coll., 1984. Lic. real estate, Tex. With sales Foley's, Dallas, 1979-88; owner, renovator Lisa Lundy, Inc., Dallas, 1984-87; asst. property mgr. Vantage, Dallas, 1986-87; interior designer Pate-Lundy Systems, Dallas, 1987-89; leasing assoc. Tom Thompson & Co., Dallas, 1988-89; leasing agt. Kelley-Lundeen, Inc., Dallas, 1989-90, A.E.M.C., 1990—. Mem. Comml. Real Estate Women (social com. Dallas 1989-90, vol. Dallas-Golf Tour for charity 1990), Delta Delta Delta, Am. Soc. Interior Designers (assoc.). Republican. Baptist. Office: AEMC 16775 Addison Rd Ste 103 Dallas TX 75248

LUNDY, SADIE ALLEN, small business owner; b. Milton, Fla., Mar. 29, 1918; d. Stephen Grover and Martha Ellen (Harter) Allen; m. Wilson Tate Lundy, May 17, 1939 (dec. 1962); children: Wilson Tate Jr., Houston Allen, Michael David, Robert Douglas, Martha Jo-Ellen. Degree in acctg., Graceland Coll., 1938. Acct. Powers Furniture Co., Milton, Fla., 1939-40, Lundy Oil Co., Milton, 1941-52; controller First Fed. Savs. & Loan, Kansas City, Mo., 1953-55, Herald Pub. Co., Independence, Mo., 1956-58; mgr. Baird & Son Toy Co., Kansas City, Mo., 1959-62; regional mgr. Emmons Jewelers of N.Y., Kansas City, 1963-65; owner, pres. Lundy Tax Service, Independence, 1965-85; acct. Optimation, Inc., Independence, 1974-85, mgr., 1985—; v.p. Lundy Oil Co., Milton, 1941-52. Contbr. articles to profl. jours. Mem. com. Neighborhood Council, Independence, 1985. Mem. Am. Bus. Women's Assn., Independence C. of C. (mem. com. 1965-85). Republican. Mem. Reorganized Ch. of Jesus Christ of Latter Day Saints. Club: Independence Women's. Home: PO Box 520238 Independence MO 64052 Office: Optimation Inc 645 N Powell Rd Independence MO 64050

LUNIAK, RHONDA JEAN, downtown revitalization organization executive; b. Appleton, Wis., Aug. 14, 1965; d. Joseph William and Joelene Ann (Brantmeier) Luniak; m. Eldon Guy Walker, June 23, 1989. BS in Communication Studies, Northwestern U., 1987. Cert. in downtown mgmt. Mktg. mgr. City of Omro, Wis., 1987-88; program mgr. Sheboygan Falls (Wis.) Main St., 1989—; v.p. Wis. Downtown Action Council, Madison, 1989—. Mem. Sheboygan Area Bus. and Profl. Women (Young Careerist 1990), Nat. Trust for Hist. Preservation, Sheboygan Falls Jaycees (v.p. community devel. 1989-90). Democrat. Roman Catholic. Office: Sheboygan Falls Main St 110 Pine St Sheboygan Falls WI 53085

LUNIN, LOIS FRUMKIN, information scientist, fiber artist; b. Schenectady; d. Hyman and Sophie Jane (Tauber) Frumkin; m. Martin Lunin, June 22, 1947. AB, Radcliffe Coll., 1945; MS, Drexel U., 1966. Editorial asst. C.V. Mosby Co., St. Louis, 1947-48, Washington U. Sch. Dentistry, St. Louis, 1948-50; editorial asst., rsch. asst. Columbia U. Faculty Medicine, N.Y.C., 1950-55; rsch. adminstr. William Douglas McAdams, N.Y.C., 1955-58; rsch. assoc. U. Tex. M.D. Anderson Hosp. and Tumor Inst., Houston, 1958-64; co-dir., program dir. Info. Ctr. for Hearing, Speech and Disorder of Human Communication Johns Hopkins Med. Instns., Balt., 1965-76; instr. Sch. Medicine and Sch. Hygiene and Pub. Health Johns Hopkins U., Balt., 1966-79; dir. info. sci. Environ. Programs, Inc., Balt., 1977-78; v.p. Herner & Co., Arlington, Va., 1978-89; adj. assoc. prof. Cornell U. Med. Sch., N.Y.C., 1982—; cons. WHO, Pan Am. Health Orgn., various univs., fed. govt., 1974—; rsch. project evaluator NSF, 1983—; mem. nat. adv. bd. U. Md. Campus for Professions, 1988—. Co-author: Index-Handbook of Ototoxic Agents, 1973; author: Health Sciences and Services, 1979 (One of Best Reference Books of Decade award Am. Reference Books Ann. 1980); mem. editorial bd. Jour. Med. Practice Mgmt., 1986—; contbr. articles to profl. jours. and mags., chpts. to books; exhibited fiber art in regional and nat. group shows. Founding mem., bd. dirs. James Renwick Alliance for Renwick Gallery, Smithsonian Instn., Washington, 1983-88, mem. adv. bd., 1988—. Fellow AAAS, Inst. Info. Scientists, N.Y. Acad. Medicine; mem. Am. Soc. Info. Sci. (bd. dirs., coun., chmn. spl. interest groups and coms. 1966—, editor-in-chief Bull. 1973-80, editor Perspectives Jour. of the Am. Soc. for Info. Sci. 1981—, mem. planning com. 1988—, Watson Davis award 1976), ASTM (com. mem.), Fiber Art Study Group (co-founder, co-dir.), Textile Study Group, Phi Kappa Phi, Beta Phi Mu. Home and Office: 922 24th St NW Washington DC 20037

LUONGO, LUCILLE FRANCESCA, communications company executive; b. N.Y.C., May 29, 1948; d. Carmine and Jean (Gubitosi) Ariniello. BA in English and Speech, Hofstra U., 1970, MA in Communications, 1975. Tchr. Roosevelt (N.Y.) High Sch.; exec. sec. Katz Communications, Inc., N.Y.C., 1978-79, asst. dir. corp. communications, 1979-81, dir. communication svcs., 1981-82, dir. corp. rels., 1982-85, v.p. corp. rels., 1985—. Mem. Internat. Radio and TV Soc., Am. Women in Radio and TV (pres. N.Y. chpt.), NAFE, Broadcast Promotion and Mktg. Execs. Office: Katz Communications Inc 1 Dag Hammarskjold Pla New York NY 10017

LUPONE, PATTI, actress; b. Northport, L.I., N.Y., Apr. 21, 1949; d. Orlando Joseph and Angela Louise (Patti) LuP. BFA, The Juilliard Sch., 1972. Off-Broadway prodns. include: The Woods, School for Scandal, The Lower Depths, Stage Directions; appeared in Broadway prodns.: Next Time I'll Sing to You, The Time of Your Life, The Three Sisters, The Robber Bridegroom (Tony award nominee), The Water Engine, The Beggar's Opera, Edward II, The Baker's Wife, 1976, The Woods, 1977, Working, 1978; Catchpenny Twist, 1979, As You Like It, 1981, The Cradle Will Rock, 1982, Stars of Broadway, 1983, Edmond, 1983, Oliver, 1984 star Broadway play Evita, 1979, Anything Goes, 1987; London prodn. Les Miserables, 1987; films include: King of the Gypsies, 1978, 1941, 1980, Striking Back, 1981, Fighting Back, 1982, Witness, Driving Miss Daisy, 1989; TV Appearances include: Kitty, The Time of Your Life; TV series, Life Goes On, 1989. Recipient Antoinette Perry award, 1980. Office: care Gersh Agy Inc 130 W 42d St Ste 1804 New York NY 10036*

LUPTON, DEBBIE ANN, health facility administrator, consultant; b. Kingwood, W.Va., Jan. 4, 1962; d. Paul Lee and Ruth Elaine (Jeffreys) Loar; m. Forest Richard Lupton, Aug. 30, 1985; 1 child, Nicole Elizabeth. AAS, Fairmont (W.Va.) State Coll., 1983. Records technician Culpeper (Va.) Meml. Hosp., 1984-85, Sacred Heart Hosp., Cumberland, Md., 1985-86; med. records dir. Hampshire Meml. Hosp., Inc., Romney, W.Va., 1986—; cons. long care unit Hampshire Meml. Hosp., Romney, 1986—. Mem. Am. Med. Record Assn., W.Va. Med. Record Assn., Am. Legion Aux. (mem.-at-large Kirby, W.Va. chpt. 1987-89, sgt.-at-arms 1988-89, 2d v.p. 1989-90). Democrat. Methodist. Home: Rt 2 Box 34 Kirby WV 26729 Office: Hampshire Meml Hosp Inc 549 Center Ave Romney WV 26757

LUPTON, MARY HOSMER, retired owner, operator rare book search service; b. Olympia, Wash., Jan. 2, 1914; d. Kenneth Winthrop and Mary Louise (Wheeler) Hosmer; student Gunston Hall Jr. Coll., 1932-33; BS in Edn., U. Va., 1940; m. Keith Brahe Wiley, Oct. 12, 1940 (dec. Apr. 1955); children: Sarah Hosmer Wiley Guise, Victoria Brahe Wiley; m. Thomas George Lupton, Nov. 27, 1965 (dec. Feb. 1989); 1 stepson, Andrew Henshaw. Ptnr., Wakefield Press, Earlysville, Va., 1940-55; owner, operator Wakefield Forest Bookshop, Earlysville, 1955-65, Forest Bookshop, Charlottesville, 1965-85, Wakefield Forest Tree Farm, 1955-85. Contbr. articles to profl. mags. Corr. sec. Charlottesville-Albemarle Civic League, 1963-64; sec. Instructive Vis. Nurses Assn., Charlottesville, 1961-62; chmn. pub. info. Charlottesville chpt. Va. Mus. Fine Arts, 1970-77; mem. writers' adv. panel Va. Center for Creative Arts, 1973-75, chmn. pub. info., 1976-77; mem. Albemarle County Forestry Com., 1961-62; bd. dirs. Charlottesville-Albemarle Mental Health Assn., 1980-82, 89—. Mem. AAUW, DAR (Am. Heritage com. chmn. 1983-85, 89—), Assns. of U. Va. Libr., New Eng. Hist. Geneal. Soc., Conn. Soc. Genealogists, Geneal. Soc. Va., Albemarle County hist. socs., Va. Soc. Mayflower Descs. (asst. state historian 1979-82), LWV, Soc. Mayflower Descs., Am. Soc. Physical Research, Brit. Soc. Psychical Research, Nature Conservancy, Chi Omega. Unitarian. Address: La Casita Blanca PO Box 5206 Charlottesville VA 22905-0206

LURIE, ALISON, author; b. Chgo., Sept. 3, 1926; children: John, Jeremy, Joshua. AB, Radcliffe Coll., 1947. Lectr. English Cornell U., 1969-73; adj. assoc. prof. English Cornell U., Ithaca, N.Y., 1973-76, assoc. prof., 1976-79, prof., 1979—. Author: V.R. Lang: A Memoir, 1959, Love and Friendship, 1962, The Nowhere City, 1965, Imaginary Friends, 1967, Real People, 1969, The War Between the Tates, 1974, Only Children, 1979, The Language of Clothes, 1981, Foreign Affairs, 1984, The Truth About Lorin Jones, 1988, Don't Tell the Grownups, 1990. Recipient award in lit. Am. Acad. Arts and Letters, 1978, Pulitzer prize in fiction, 1985; fellow Yaddo Found., 1963-64, 66, Guggenheim Found., 1965, Rockefeller Found., 1967. Office: Cornell U Dept English Ithaca NY 14853

LURIE, MAXINE NEUSTADT, historian; b. N.Y.C., Dec. 28, 1940; d. Harrison and Dora (Goldstein) Neustadt; m. Jonathan Lurie; children: David, Deborah, Daniel. BA, Alfred U., 1962; MA, U. Rochester, 1963; PhD, U. Wis., Madison, Wis., 1968. Asst. prof. Marquette U., Milw., 1967-69; coadutant Rutgers U., Newark and New Brunswick, N.J., 1969—; asst. prof. Rutgers U. Libraries, New Brunswick, 1980-89. Editor Minutes East Jersey Proprietors, 1985; contbr. various articles to profl. jours. Mem. Friends of Library, Piscataway, N.J., 1975—, Curriculum Com. Sch. Bd., Piscataway, 1986—. Recipient N.J. Hist. Commn. Research Grant, 1985, Folger Inst. Fellowship, 1987. Mem. Orgn. Am. Historians, Am. Hist. Assn., MidAtlantic Regional Archive Conf., N.J. Hist. Soc., N.Y. Hist. Soc. Democrat. Jewish. Home: 6 Rye St Piscataway NJ 08854 Office: Rutgers Univ History Van Dyck Hall New Brunswick NJ 08854

LUSCOMB, KAREN MARIE, sales executive; b. Highland Park, Mich., Oct. 24, 1942; d. Nicholas J. CAntor and Catherine (Karlicko) Mazzorana); m. Ronald A. Kipp, June 30, 1962 (div. Mar. 1975); 1 child, David C.; m. Robert C. Luscomb, Jr., Oct. 11, 1985; children: Mark, Roberta, Philip, James. Student, San Diego State U., 1960-61. Sales Internat. Telephone & Telegraph, Livonia, Mich., 1978-80, Commerce Clearing House, Detroit, 1983—.

LUSHIS, STELLA ANNE, academic counselor; b. Easton, Pa., June 16, 1958; d. John Francis and Dora Katherine (DeMonte) L. BA in Sociology, E. Stroudsburg (Pa.) U., 1980; MA in Counseling, Marywood Coll., Scranton, Pa., 1983; postgrad., LaSalle U., Phila., 1980. Cert. counselor. Primary therapist Lourdesmont Good Shepherd Adolescent Svcs., Clarks Summit, Pa., 1984-86; acad. counselor Marywood Coll., Scranton, Pa., 1987-88; assertiveness tng. instr. and community rep. programming Community Med. Ctr., Scranton, 1988—; acad. counselor Coll. Misericordia, Dallas, Pa., 1988—; asst. individual and marital counselor Office of Thomas Fiume, Scranton Ctr., Scranton, 1989—; cons. in field; cert. trainer Temple U. Child Welfare Tng. Inst., Phila., 1988—; cert. AIDS course instr. ARC, Scranton, 1988—; conductor workshops in field. Vol. ann. ch. bazaar Immaculate Conception Ch., Scranton, 1982—. Mem. AAUW, Am. Assn. Counseling and Devel., Northeastern Pa. Counseling Assn. (exec. bd. 1986—). Democrat. Roman Catholic. Home: 411 Mortimer St Dunmore PA 18512 Office: College Misericordia Dallas PA 18612

LUSK, GLENNA RAE KNIGHT (MRS. EDWIN BRUCE LUSK), librarian; b. Franklinton, La., Aug. 16, 1935; d. Otis Harvey and Lou Zelle (Bahm) Knight; m. John Earle Uhler, Jr., May 26, 1956; children: Anne Knight, Camille Allana; m. 2d, Edwin Bruce Lusk, Nov. 28, 1970. BS, La. State U., 1956, MS, 1963. Asst. librarian Iberville Parish Library, Plaquemine, La., 1956-57, 1962-68; tchr. Iberville Parish Pub. Schs., Plaquemine, 1957-59, Plaquemines Parish Pub. Schs., Buras, La., 1959-61; dir. Iberville Parish Library, Plaquemine, 1969-89; chmn. La. State Bd. Library Examiners, 1979-89; pres. Camille Navarre Gallery, Ltd., Zachary, La., 1989—. Mem. Iberville Parish Econ. Devel. Council, Plaquemine, 1970-71; sec. Iberville Parish Bicentennial Commn., 1973—; mem. La. Bicentennial Commn., 1974. Named Outstanding Young Woman Plaquemine, La. Jr. C. of C., 1970. Mem. La. (sect. chmn. 1967-68), Riverland (sec. 1973-74) libraries assns., Capital Area Libraries (chmn. com. 1972-74). Democrat. Episcopalian. Author: (with John E. Uhler, Jr.) Cajun Country Cookin' 1966; Rochester Clarke Bibliography of Louisiana Cookery, 1966; Royal Recipes from the Cajun Country, 1969; Iberville Parish, 1970. Home: 22756 Plainsland Dr Zachary LA 70791 Office: 5145 Main St Zachary LA 70791

LUST, ELENORE, artist; b. Chgo.; d. Herbert and Dora (Koumas) Lust; m. Robert Eising, Jan. 7, 1932 (div.). Student, Smith Coll., 1929-30; BA, NYU, 1935, MA, 1957. Cert. tchr., N.Y., N.J. Dir., co-founder Norlyst Art Gallery, N.Y.C., 1940-49; art tchr. Cape of Good Hope Seminary, Capetown, South Africa, 1952-55; St. Siprian's Sch., Capetown, 1952-55, N.J. High Schs., 1957-79; art lectr. Herald Tribune, N.Y.C., 1944-49; art tchr. Little Red Sch. House, N.Y.C., 1944-46, Bklyn. Mus. Art Sch., 1947-49. Exhibited in one-woman shows at Norlyst Art Gallery, 1944, Stuttaford's Gallery, Capetown, 1952, Cafe Gallery, Burlington, N.J., 1988, Ft. Dix, Pemberton, N.J., 1988; Nat. Mus. Women in Arts, Washington; represented in 75 private and corporate collections. Docent Burlington County Cultural and Heritage Commn., Smithville, N.J., 1984—; vol. Pavilion Gallery Meml. Hosp., Mt. Holly, N.J., 1985—, Chatsworth (N.J.) Festival, 1988—. Mem. Burlington County Art Guild (pres. 1983-85, v.p. 1989), Atlantic City Art Ctr., Trenton Artisits' Workshop Assn., So. N.J. Advocates for Arts. Democrat. Episcopalian. Studio: PO Box D Mount Holly NJ 08060

LUSTER, MICHELLE, distribution of mails, insurance producer; b. Chgo., Mar. 16, 1955; d. Nokomis Luster and Ella Mae (Johnson) Richard. AA, Cen. YMCA Coll., Chgo., 1974; BA, No. Ill. U., 1975; student, U. Ill., Chgo., 1979-81, 88—. Youth counselor Chgo. Boys Clubs of Am., 1973-75; distbn. of mails U.S. Postal Svc., Chgo., 1977—; tchr. Chgo. Bd. of Edn., 1985-87; ins. producer Mass. Indemnity & Life Ins. Co., Duluth, Ga., 1987—; registered rep. First Am. Nat. Securities, Duluth, Ga., 1987—. Democrat. Baptist. Home: 6724 S Ada St Chicago IL 60636-2920 Office: AL Williams Inc 8232 S Western Chicago IL 60620

LUSTIG, ILANA DENISE, obstetrician-gynecologist; b. N.Y.C., July 15, 1951; d. Oscar and Felicia (Mitz) L.; m. Eugene Robert Gillman, Feb. 20, 1982; children: Jeffrey Ross, Jennifer Alexis. BS, Fairleigh Dickinson, 1973; MD, George Washington U., 1977. Diplomate Am. Bd. Ob-Gyn., Am. Bd. Ob-Gyn. Maternal Fetal Medicine. Intern Yale U. Med. Sch., New Haven, 1978, resident in ob-gyn, 1978-81; fellow in maternal fetal medicine NYU Med. Sch., N.Y.C., 1981-83; dir. perinatal diagnostic unit Bellevue Hosp., N.Y.C., 1983-89, asst. prof. ob-gyn., 1983—; asst. prof. ob-gyn. N.Y. U., 1983—. Mem. Soc. Perinatal obstet., N.Y. Soc. of Periatology, N.Y. Art Sudents Leaque (Concour Art award, 1963). Jewish. Home: 46-14 197th St Flushing NY 11358

LUTCHI, DOINA PEANA, advertising agency official; b. Bucharest, Romania, Sept. 11, 1967; came to U.S., 1980; d. Ion and Nina (Tcaciuc) P. Student advt., Fla. Internat. U., 1986—. Typesetter, mech. artist Mason Distbrs., Inc., Hialeah, Fla., 1986-89; media dir. Creative Advantage, Miami, Fla., 1989; freelance artist Hollywood, Fla., 1989. Exec. sec. Romanian Bapt. Youth Assn. U.S.A., Can. and Australia, Hollywood, Fla., 1986. Advt. Fedn. Greater Miami scholar, 1989. Mem. Women in Communications. Republican. Home and Office: 1247 Harrison St Hollywood FL 33019-1511

LUTERS, AINA, librarian; b. Freudenstadt, Schwartz., Fed. Republic Germany, Dec. 9, 1944; came to U.S., 1962; d. Vladimirs and Vera (Lielbiksis) L. BA in Anthropology, U. of the Ams., Mexico, 1969; MA equivalent/Anthropology, U. Calif., Riverside, 1972; MLS, U. Ariz., 1976. Photo archivist, libr. EQE, San Francisco; libr. Riverside (Calif.) Pub. Libr.; indexer Office of Arid Land Studies, Tucson; photo editor Follett Pub. Co., Chgo.; researcher Capital Times, Madison, Wis.; rsch. asst. PIMA Alcoholism Consortium; field rsch. supr. Elrick & Lavidge, Inc., San Francisco; social sci. researcher U. Ariz.; researcher R & D dept. EQE Engring., San Francisco; cons. in field. Mem. Am. Assn. Ind. Info. Profls., Spl. Librs. Assn., ALA, Am. Anthropol. Assn., Soc. for Med. Anthropology, Soc. for Psychol. Anthropology, Soc. for Visual Anthropology.

LUTHER, DORIS EVELYN, organist, choir director; b. Blanchard, La., Dec. 25, 1933; d. William Carl and Annie Marie (Barker) Barham; m. William Harold Luther, Sr., July 27, 1958; children: Deborah Elaine, William Harold Jr., Ola Marie. MusB, La. Poly. Inst., Ruston, 1954; MusM, Union Theol. Sem., N.Y.C., 1956. Cert. dir. music Meth. Ch., 1957. Minister of music Mt. Vernon Meth. Ch., Danville, Va., 1956-60; tchr., dept. music Averett Coll., Danville, 1960-67, Converse Coll., Spartanburg, S.C., 1967-69, Spartanburg Meth. Coll., 1969-84; organist, choir dir. Prince of Peace Luth. Ch., Huntsville, Ala., 1984-85; organist First Presbyn. Ch., 1985-88; organist, choir dir. Ghent United Meth. Ch., Norfolk, Va., 1988—; recitals presented in Danville, Va., in connection with position at ch. and colls. in Spartanburg; dir. recitals presented in Huntsville area in Feb. 1983, Sept. 1986, Nov. 1986, 87, Mar. 1988. Vol. bd. mem. Hunstville Hosp. Aux., 1981-87, Hist. Huntsville Found., 1983-86, Hospice of Huntsville, 1985-88; pres. bd. Hospice Hunstville, 1988. Mem. Am. Guild of Organists, Cosmopolitan Club Huntsville, Rotary (chmn. Huntsville-Ann chpt. 1983-85). Home: 40 Rader St Unit 501 Norfolk VA 23510 Office: Ghent United Meth Ch Stockley Gardens at Raleigh Norfolk VA 23507

LUTHER, FLORENCE JOAN (MRS. CHARLES W. LUTHER), lawyer; b. N.Y.C. June 28, 1928; d. John Phillip and Catherine Elizabeth (Duffy) Thomas ; J.D. magna cum laude, U. Pacific, 1963; m. William J. Regan (dec.); children—Kevin P., Brian T.; m. 2d, Charles W. Luther, June 11, 1961. Admitted to Calif. bar; mem. firm Luther, Luther, O'Connor & Johnson, Sacramento, 1964—. Mem. faculty McGeorge Sch. Law, U. Pacific, Sacramento, 1966—, prof., 1968—. Judge Bank Am. Achievement awards, 1969-71. Bd. dirs. Sacramento Suicide Prevention League, 1969-70. Mem. ABA, Calif., Sacramento County bar assns., AAUP, Womens Legal Groups, Am. Judicature Soc., Order of Coif, Iota Tau Tau. Mem. bd. advisors Community Property Jour., 1974—, state decision editor, 1974—. Home: 11101 Fair Oaks Blvd Fair Oaks CA 95628 Office: PO Box 1030 Fair Oaks CA 95628

LUTHER, LOUISE ELLEN, medical group administrator; b. Endicott, N.Y., Nov. 19, 1943; d. Edward Paul and Margie E. (Devine) Ryan; m. Bernard J. Luther, Aug. 31, 1963 (div. 1981). AAS, Cazenovia Coll., 1963. Adminstr. dept. anesthesiology U. Mich., Ann Arbor, 1965-80; mgr. medicine U. Tex. Health Sci. Ctr., San Antonio, 1980—; cons. U. Tex. Southwestern, Dallas, U. N.C., Chapel Hill, 1979. Chmn. fundraiser Muscular Dystrophy Assn., San Antonio, 1990. Mem. Med. Group Mgmt. Assn. (acad. practice bd. 1981-82), Am. Coll. Med. Group Adminstrs., Med. Adminstrs. Tex., San Antonio Med. Mgrs. (pres. 1987). Office: U Tex Health Sci Ctr 7703 Floyd Curl Dr San Antonio TX 78284

LUTHER, LUANA MAE, editor; b. L.A., Mar. 7, 1939; d. Chester Harry and Mildred P. (Knight) L.; m. O. Solorzano, Sept. 6, 1958 (div. 1974); children: Suzanne, Troy, Stephanie, Paul; m. Edwin J. Salzman, Apr. 4, 1981. BA, Calif. State U., Sacramento, 1974. Law indexer, legis. counsel State Calif., Sacramento, 1975-80, analyst, adminstrv. law, 1981-84; communications dir. Townsend & Co., Sacramento, 1985-87; adminstrv. asst., dept. justice State of Calif., Sacramento, 1987-88; editorial asst. Golden State Report Mag., Sacramento, 1986—; mktg. cons. Lake Oswego, Oreg., 1989—; editor Doral Pub., Wilsonville, Oreg., 1990—. Author: Red Mack Truck Massacre, 1981; contbr. articles to numerous publs.; columnist: Sacramento Bee, 1982-84; editor: (newsletter) Sacramento Youth Band, 1985. Dir. pub. rels., newsletter editor LWV, West Clackamas County, Oreg., 1989; vol. numerous polit. campaigns, Sacramento; fundraiser Dem. Women's Com., Sacramento, 1986. Mem. Mex.-Am. Ednl. Assn. (treas. 1964, Cert. Appreciation 1971). Democrat. Home: 17701 Blue Heron Way Lake Oswego OR 97034

LUTHER-LEMMON, CAROL LEN, educator; b. Waverly, N.Y., May 8, 1955; d. Carl Ross and Mary Edith (Auge) Luther; m. Mark Kevin Lemmon, June 21, 1986; children: Matthew C., Cathryn M. BS, Ithaca Coll., 1976; MS inlEdn., Elmira Coll., 1981. Cert. elem. and secondary tchr., Pa. Reading aide Waverly (N.Y.) Central Schs., 1978-80; tchr. reading N.Y. State Div. for Youth, Lansing, 1980-81; tchr. chpt. I reading Athens (Pa.) Area Sch. Dist., 1981—; physical activities specialist USAR, 1978-80. Author exercise guide, 1978. Basketball coach Youth Activities Dept.,

Athens, 1981-85, asst. softball coach, 1990—; active Girls Softball League, Waverly, 1978-80, commr., 1990—; bd. dirs. Waverly Community Ch., 1976-78; choir mem. Meth. Ch., Waverly, 1976-90, adminstrv. bd., trustee; mem. Valley Chorus, Pa. and N.Y., 1983-86. Mem. AAUW (v.p. 1982-83), Am. Legion Aux. (girl's state chmn. 1976-80). Republican. Home: 490 Waverly St Waverly NY 14892 Office: Athens Area Sch Dist Pennsylvania Ave Athens PA 18810

LUTKENHOUSE, ANNE, administrator; b. S.I., N.Y., Feb. 18, 1957; d. Emile Anthony and Jane Anne Lutkenhouse. BA magna cum laude, Wagner Coll., 1979; cert. Goethe Inst., N.Y.C., 1981. Supr. Credit Suisse, N.Y.C., 1979-85; dist. office adminstr. N.Y. City Council, 1985-86; asst. dir., Appalachian Trail Field asst., N.Y.-N.J. Trail Conf., N.Y.C., 1986—; contbg. cons. Wagner Coll. Study Program, Bregenz, Austria, 1978—. Photographer, producer photography show, 1984. Swimming instr. ARC, S.I., 1977; campaign aide council member Fossella, N.Y. City Council, S.I., 1985; pres., bd. dirs. S.I. Chamber Music Players, 1984-86; co-chmn. Flag Day Parade, Tottenville Improvement Council, Inc., 1986; producer Appalachian Trail 50th Anniversary celebration, N.Y., 1987. Contbr. travel articles to mags; contbg. writer Appalachian Trailway News, 1987—. Mem. Nat. Assn. Female Execs., Norwegian-Am. C. of C. Democrat. Roman Catholic. Avocations: needlecrafts, ballet, skiing, travel. Home: 399 Yetman Ave Staten Island NY 10307 Office: NY-NJ Trail Conf 232 Madison Ave New York NY 10016

LUTZ, JULIE HAYNES, astronomy educator; b. Mt. Vernon, Ohio, Dec. 17, 1944; d. Willard Damon and Julia Awilda (Way) Haynes; m. Thomas Edward Lutz, July 8, 1967; children: Melissa, Clea. BS, San Diego State U., 1965; MS, U. Ill., 1968, PhD, 1971. Asst. prof. astronomy Wash. State U., Pullman, 1972-78, asst. dean sci., 1978-79, assoc. prof., 1978-84, assoc. provost, 1981-82, prof., 1984—; rsch. fellow Univ. Coll. London, England, 1976-77, 82-83; vis. resident asronomer Cerro Tololo Inter-Am. Observatory, 1988-89; dir. Div. of Astron. Scis. NSF, 1990-91. Contbr. articles on astron. research to profl. jours. Dir. div. astron. scis. NSF, 1990-91. Fellow Royal Astron. Soc.; mem. AAAS (mem. com. 1982-85), Am. Astron. Soc. Pacific (bd. dirs. 1988—, v.p., pres.-elect 1989, pres. 1990-92), Internat. Astron. Union, Astron. Soc. Pacific. Home: NE1200 McGee Way Pullman WA 99163 Office: Wash State U Program in Astronomy Pullman WA 99164-2930

LUZURIAGA, ADEL, realtor, investment counselor, developer; b. The Philippines, Oct. 31, 1949; came to U.S., 1970; d. Laurie Trinidad; student Maryknoll Coll., U. Madrid, Glendale Coll.; m. Apr. 1, 1970 (div.). With Kramer Wilson Co., 1971-74, Barnes Ins. Agy., 1974-75; salesperson PRO Realty, 1975-80; assoc. Famous Real Estate Co., 1980; pres. Realty Benefit Systems Inc., 1980—. Mem. Nat. Assn. Realtors (cert. comml. investment, gov. 1987-88), Calif. Assn. Realtors (bd. dirs. 1989-90), Glendale Bd. Realtors (bd. dirs. 1990, pres. 1991, Pres.'s award 1985, realtor of the Yr. award 1986,), Women's Coun. Realtors (pres. Glendale chpt. 1985, gov. nat. chpt. 1987, 88), Glendale C. of C. Roman Catholic. Club: Zonta (bd. dirs.). Office: 413 E Glenoaks Blvd Glendale CA 91207

LYBARGER, ADRIENNE REYNOLDS (MRS. LEE FRANCIS), college administrator; b. Boston, Mar. 8, 1926; d. Joseph Anthony and Albertine (Mouton Drevet) Reynolds; B.A., Mills Coll., Calif., 1947; cert. Katharine Gibbs Sch., 1948; m. Lee Francis Lybarger, Jr., Sept. 15, 1955 (dec); children: Linda, Lauretta, James (dec.), Lisa, Leslie (dec.), Jeffrey (dec.), Lucia, Lana. Asst. to dir. Mid-Century convocation M.I.T. Cambridge, 1949, asst. to dir. West Coast regional office Mid-Century devel. program, 1949-50, asst. dir. So. regional office, 1950-51; asst. to dir. convocation devel. program Ithaca (N.Y.) Coll., 1951; asst. to dir., devel. program U. Buffalo, 1951-52; asst. to dir. Diamond Jubilee program Case Inst. Tech., Cleve., 1952-54; asst. to dir., expansion and improvement program John D. Archbold Hosp., Thomasville, Ga., 1955-61; ptnr. Lybarger Prodns., comml. films, N.Y.C.; asst. dir., dir. regional campaigns, Ohio, Boston, Mass., N.Y.C., also supr. all other nat. regional campaigns Mount Holyoke Coll. Fund for Future, South Hadley, Mass., 1961-63; fund-raising cons. to capital programs, Vocation Service Center and Bronx-Westchester YMCA, YMCA Greater N.Y., 1963-65; dir. devel. and public relations Bank St. Coll. Edn., N.Y.C., 1965-79; cons. S. Bronx Overall Econ. Devel. Corp., 1978-79; v.p. devel. Wells Coll., 1979—, dir. Wells Capital campaign; cons. capital campaign Borough of Manhattan Community Coll., 1979-80; Realtor assoc./mktg. cons. Century 21, Clinton, N.J., 1978-81; Pres., Birch Island (Maine) Corp., 1979; trustee Nat. Women's Hall of Fame, 1987—. Author: (with L.F. Lybarger) Proven Guides to Effective Soliciting (slide film), 1950, rev., 1960, 81; exec. producer, Scriptwriter Now More than Ever, Wells Coll. Home: Kings Manor Pittstown NJ 08867 Office: Wells Coll Aurora NY 13026

LYCAN, REBECCA TATUM, professional dog handler; b. Atlanta, Oct. 10, 1960; d. Clement Marduke and Ruth (Davenport) Tatum; m. Glenn Eugene Lycan, July 14, 1984. BS in Microbiology, U. Ga., 1982. Lab. technician Optimal Systems, Inc., Norcross, Ga., 1982-84; asst. dog handler Canine Country Club, Chattanooga, 1984-86; prof. dog handler Leading Edge Kennel, Griffin, Ga., 1986—. Mem. Profl. Handlers Assn., Griffin Kennel Club (show chmn. fall shows 1990—). Office: Leading Edge Kennel PO Box 849 Griffin GA 30224

LYCZKO, JUDITH ELIZABETH, academic administrator; b. Amsterdam, N.Y., Oct. 13, 1947; d. William Francis and Helen Ann (Butkus) L. AB in Art History, Barnard Coll., 1969; MA in Art History, Bryn Mawr Coll., 1971, PhD in Art History, 1976; MFA in Arts Adminstrn., Columbia U., 1982. Asst. prof. art history Bates Coll., Lewiston, Maine, 1973-77, 78-80; dir. devel. Artists Space, N.Y.C., 1982-86, Strawbery Banke, Portsmouth, N.H., 1986-87; govt. affairs assoc. Bklyn. Mus., 1987-88; dir. devel. Nat. Acad. Design, N.Y.C., 1988-89; sr. devel. officer Cooper Union, N.Y.C., 1989—; cons. Princeton (N.J.) Hist. Soc., 1989, Fabric Workshop, Phila., 1985-89, Chase Manhattan Bank, N.Y.C., 1981-82, Exxon Corp., N.Y.C., 1981-82. Recipient rsch. fellowship, Samuel H. Kress Found., Bryn Mawr Coll., 1970-72, Bates Coll., 1976-80, postdoctoral fellowship, Nat. Endowment for the Arts, Columbia U., 1977-78, doctoral fellowship, Samuel H. Kress Found., Bryn Mawr Coll, 1972-73. Mem. Coll. Art Assn., Am. Assn. Mus. Home: 304 W 109th St #1-C New York NY 10025

LYERLY, MELIA LYNN, advertising executive; b. Charlotte, N.C., July 29, 1956; d. Junius M. and Annie Mary (Myrick) L.; m. Richard Stephen Fox, May 20, 1984. AS, N.Y. State, 1987; postgrad, Western Ill U., 1987-89. Cert. Bus. Communicator (CBC). Mgmt. mktg. specialist Country Kitchen, Charlotte, 1978-79; exec. v.p. Eve Communication Svcs., Inc., Charlotte, 1979-85, Lyerly Agency, Inc. (formerly Eve Communication Services, Inc.), Charlotte, 1985—; mktg. advisor To Life, Charlotte, 1980—; speaker Charlotte C. of C., 1983, Internat. Assn. Bus. Communicators, 1984-89; advisor R.S. Fox Mktg., Charlotte, 1986—; bus. advisor Space Mktg. Assocs., Charlotte, 1988—. Contbr. articles to profl. jours. chairperson To Life Mktg. Com., Charlotte, 1980-84; Communications Com., Am. Red Cross, Charlotte, 1982-84; bd. advisors, To Life, Charlotte, 1981—. Recipient "I Dare You Award", West Meckleburg High Sch., Charlotte, 1974; named one of Outstanding Teenagers of Am., 1974. Mem. Bus. Profl. Advt. Assn. (bd. dirs. 1982—, v.p. mem. 1985-86, adminstrv. v.p., 1987-89, pres. 1988-89, internat. bd. dirs. 1988—, internat. v.p. of publs. 1988—), Carolinas Assn. Bus. Communicators. Office: Lyerly Agy Inc 1015 East Blvd Charlotte NC 28203

LYFORD, CAROL GRAY, insurance company executive; b. Marietta, Ga., Oct. 30, 1956; d. Loyd and Mary Frances (Ferguson) Gray; m. John Edward Lyford, Sept. 18, 1976 (div. Aug. 1984). AS in Bus. Adminstrn., Kennesaw Coll., 1982, BBA in Mgmt., 1987. FLMI. Claims mail/file clk. Ga. Internat. Life, Atlanta, 1973-74, claims examiner, 1974-81, claims supr., 1981-83, mgr. billing, 1983-84, sales coord., credit adminstrn., 1986-89; dept. project coord. Creditor Resources, Inc., Atlanta, 1989-90, project mgr., 1990—. Treas. Elizabeth United Meth. Ch., Marietta, 1989—. Fellow Life Office Mgmt. Assn.; mem. NAFE, Zoo Atlanta, Cobb County Jaycees (Jaycee of the Month 1985). Republican. Home: 4816 Highpoint Dr Marietta GA 30066 Office: Creditor Resources Inc 1100 Johnson Ferry Rd Ste 300 Atlanta GA 30342

LYLES-ANDERSON, BARBARA DUNBAR, civil engineer; b. Columbia, S.C., June 2, 1954; d. Thomas McDonald and Barbara Ann (Dukes) L.; m. John Bristow Anderson, Feb. 20, 1988. BSCE magna cum laude, Clemson (S.C.) U., 1976. Registered profl. engr., S.C. Engr. Davis & Floyd Engrs., Inc., Greenwood, S.C., 1976-80; project mgr. Life Cycle Engring., Inc., Charleston, S.C., 1980-88; corp. mgr. Jordan, Jones & Goulding Engrs. and Planners, Inc., Atlanta, 1988—. V.P. Greenwood Ballet Guild, 1978. Recipient John M Ford Meml. award, Walter Lowry award. Mem. ASCE (Charleston chpt. co-chmn. Mathcounts 1986), NSPE (bd. dirs.), S.C. Soc. Profl. Engrs. (Charleston chpt. bd. dirs. 1986-87), Soc. Women Engrs., Am. Waterworks Assn. (com. 1980—), Water Pollution Control Fedn. (com. 1980—), Lords Proprietors Soc., Jr. League of Atlanta. Republican. Presbyterian. Home: 4111 N Stratford Rd Atlanta GA 30342 Office: Jordan Jones & Goulding Inc 2000 Clearview Ave NE Atlanta GA 30340

LYMAN, ELISABETH REED, educator; b. Bklyn., Sept. 13, 1912; d. Carl Sweetland and Florence Irene (Bemis) Reed; BA, Smith Coll., 1933; postgrad. U. Calif.-Berkeley, 1933-38; m. Ernest McIntosh Lyman, June 12, 1934; children: Nancy Lyman Repp, Elisabeth Lyman Rachal, Richard, Jerome, Carl. Instr., Smith Coll., 1941; research asst. Mass. Inst. Tech., 1941, staff mem. Radiation Lab., 1942-46; research asst. prof. Computer-based Edn. Research Lab., U. Ill., Urbana-Champaign, 1962-84, emerita, 1984—. Mem. Urbana Bd. Edn., 1950-65, pres., 1955-60; chmn. Dist.-Wide Sch. Com., Urbana, 1969-70; mem. Urbana Park Dist. Adv. Com., 1971-73, chmn., 1972-73; mem. Urbana Park Bd. Commrs., 1973-79; mem. Boneyard Creek Commn., 1976-87, pres., 1978-81; treas., exec. bd. Univ. YWCA, 1964-77, endowment com., 1987—; bd. dirs. Champaign County United Way, 1974-78. Named Mother of Year, Champaign News Gazette, 1962. Mem. Am. Soc. for Engring. Edn., LWV, Soc. Women Engrs., Ill. Assn. Sch. Bds., U. Ill. Athletic Assn. (bd. dirs. 1976-79, sec. 1977-78, vice chmn. 1978-79), Assn. Devel. Computer-Based Instructional Systems, Assn. for Women in Sci., Crystal Lakeshore Assn. (pres. 1986-90, bd. dirs. 1983—), Urbana C. of C. (Women's Bus. Council), Phi Beta Kappa, Sigma Delta Epsilon, Alpha Lambda Delta. Republican. Congregationalist. Contbr. numerous articles to profl. jours. Home: 1009 S Orchard St Urbana IL 61801 Office: U Ill Engring Rsch Lab 103 S Mathews Urbana IL 61801

LYMAN, ELLYN ELIZABETH, communications executive; b. Albuquerque, Sept. 3, 1951; d. Robert Joseph and Mary Coletta (Burkhardt) L. BA, Purdue U., 1973; MBA, Keller Grad. Sch., Chgo., 1980. With AT&T, 1975-90; market mgr. Long Lines div. AT&T, Bedminster, N.J., 1980-83; employment mgr. Am. Transtech div. AT&T, Jacksonville, Fla., 1983-84, product devel. mgr. Am. Transtech div., 1984-86, nat. accounts mgr. Am. Transtech div., 1986-88; telemarketing applications mgr. Bus. Markets Group AT&T, San Francisco, 1988—; instr. Kripalu Hatha yoga, 1985—. Mem. Am. Telemarketing Assn., Direct Mktg. Assn., Purdue U. Alumni Assn. Democrat. Home: 1957 Beacon Ridge Ct Walnut Creek CA 94596 Office: Present Moment Greeting 2941 Telegraph Ave Ste A Berkeley CA 94705

LYMAN, PEGGY, dancer, choreographer, educator; b. Cin., June 28, 1950; d. James Louis and Anne Earlene (Weeks) Morner; m. David Stanley Lyman, Aug. 29, 1970 (div. 1979); m. Timothy Scott Lynch, June 21, 1981; 1 child, Kevin Kynch. Grad. high sch., Cin. Solo dancer Cin. Ballet Co., 1964-68, Contemporary Dance Theater, 1970-71; chorus dancer N.Y.C. Opera, 1969-70; chorus singer and dancer Sugar, Broadway musical, N.Y.C., 1971-73; prin. dancer Martha Graham Dance Co., N.Y.C., 1973-89, rehearsal dir., 1989—; head dance div. No. Ky. U., 1977-78; artistic dir. Peggy Lyman Dance Co., N.Y.C., 1978-89; asst. prof. dance, guest choreographer Fla. State U., Tallahassee, 1982-89; guest choreographer So. Meth. U., Dallas, 1986; adjudicator Nat. Coll. Dance Festival Assn., 1983—; co-host To Make a Dance, QUBE cable TV, 1979; mem. guest faculty Am. Dance Festival, Durham, N.C., 1984; site adjudicator Nat. Endowment for Arts, 1982-84. Prin. dancer Dance in America, TV spls., 1976, 79, 84; guest with Rudolph Nureyev, Invitation to the Dance, CBS-TV, 1980; guest artist Theatre Choregraphique Rennes, Paris, 1981, Rennes, France, 1983. Founding mem. Cin. Arts Coun., 1976-78. Mem. Am. Guild Mus. Artists. Office: Martha Graham Dance Co 316 E 63d St New York NY 10021

LYNAM, JILL A., accountant; b. Englewood, N.J., May 30, 1958; d. John Joseph and Peggy Jane (McCann) L. BS in Acctg. magna cum laude, Fordham U., Bronx, N.Y., 1980. Audit mgr. Arthur Young Co., N.Y.C., 1980-85; dir. real estate, mortgage acctg. MONY Finl. Services, N.Y.C., 1985-87, asst. v.p. investment acctg., 1987--. Mem. N.Y. State Soc. CPA's, AICPA, LOMA, Beta Alpha Psi, Beta Gamma Sigma. Office: MONY Finl Svcs Glenpointe Center W Teaneck NJ 07666

LYNCH, ANNETTE KAY, marketing and public relations executive; b. Ponca City, Okla., Feb. 6, 1958; d. Anthony Blaise and Carol Kay (Albee) Carter; m. Fred Louis Grill, Feb. 22, 1974 (div. May 1982); children: Michael Anthony, Leslie Anne; m. B. Kevin Lynch, July 25, 1986. AA in Journalism, Oklahoma City Community Coll., 1984; BA Journalism-Pub. Rels., U. Okla., 1986. Clk. appropriations com. Okla. Senate, Oklahoma City, 1982-84; news clk. AP, Oklahoma City, 1984; legis. bill tracker Okla. Pub. Co., Oklahoma City, 1984-86; dir. communications Okla. Pub. Employees Assn., Oklahoma City, 1986-87; asst. mktg. dir. Ednl. Employees Credit Union, St. Louis, 1987-89; exec. asst., pub. rels. cons. Philip Samuels Fine Art, St. Louis, 1989—. Vol. Ams. for Hart, Oklahoma City, 1984, also local campaigns, Oklahoma City, 1986, 87. Recipient Bronze Derrick award Pub. Rels. Soc. Am., 1987; Oklahoma City Gridiron Club scholar, 1984, 85, McMahon Found. scholar, 1986. Mem. Internat. Assn. Bus. Communicators (Black Gold award 1987), NAFE, St. Louis Advt. Club, Kappa Tau Alpha. Democrat. Presbyterian. Home: 1449 Edgar Rd Saint Louis MO 63119

LYNCH, BEVERLY PFEIFER, library science educator; b. Moorhead, Minn., Dec. 27, 1935; d. Joseph B. and Nellie K. (Bailey) Pfeifer; m. John A. Lynch, Aug. 24, 1968. B.S., N.D. State U., 1957, L.H.D. (hon.); M.S., U. Ill., 1959; Ph.D., U. Wis., 1972. Librarian Marquette U., 1959-60, 62-63; exchange librarian Plymouth (Eng.) Pub. Library, 1960-61; asst. head serials div. Yale U. Library, 1963-65, head, 1965-68; vis. lectr. U. Wis., Madison, 1970-71, U. Chgo., 1975; exec. sec. Assn. Coll. and Research Libraries, 1972-76; univ. librarian U. Ill.-Chgo., 1977-89; dean Grad. Sch. Libr. and Info. Sci. UCLA, 1989—. Author: Management Strategies for Libraries, 1985, (with Thomas J. Galvin) Priorities for Academic Libraries, 1982, Academic Library in Transition, 1989. Named Acad. Librarian of Yr., 1981. Mem. Acad. Mgmt., ALA (pres. 1985-86), Am. Sociol. Assn., Bibliog. Soc. Am., Phi Kappa Phi. Clubs: Caxton, Grolier, Arts (Chgo.). Office: UCLA Grad Sch Libr & Info Sci 405 Hilgard Ave Los Angeles CA 90024

LYNCH, CANDACE KRAFFT, laboratory technologist; b. Augusta, Ga., Nov. 12, 1952; d. Emil Edward and Eugenie Alice (Paull) Krafft; m. Brian Stephen Lynch, Sept. 19, 1950; 1 child, Michael Stephen. BS, U. Southwestern La., 1975. Cert. med. technologist. Med. technologist Bapt. Med. Ctr., Little Rock, 1975-76, Ochsner Found. Hosp., Jefferson, La., 1976-78; med. technologist, microbiology supr. Slidell (La.) Meml. Hosp., 1978-81; med. technologist Nat. Health Lab., Lafayette, La., 1981-89; chemist, lab. technologist Petroleum Lab., Inc., Lafayette, 1983-89; lab. technologist, biology rsch. asst. U. Southwestern La., Lafayette, 1989—. Author: Procedure Microbiology, 1980, Serology, 1980, Urinalysis Parasitology, 1980, Radioimmunoassay, 1982. Roman Catholic.

LYNCH, CATHERINE GORES, social work administrator; b. Waynesboro, Pa., Nov. 23, 1943; d. Landis and Pamela (Whitmarsh) Gores; BA magna cum laude and honors, Bryn Mawr Coll., 1965; Fulbright scholar, Universidad Central de Venezuela, Caracas, 1965-66; postgrad. (Lehman fellow), Cornell U., 1966-67; m. Joseph C. Keefe, Nov. 29, 1981; children: Shannon Maria, Lisa Alison, Gregory T. Keefe, Michael D. Keefe. Mayor's intern, Human Resources Adminstrn., N.Y.C., 1967; rsch. asst. Orgn. for Social and Tech. Innovation, Cambridge, Mass., 1967-69; cons. Ford Found., Bogotá, Colombia, 1970; staff Nat. Housing Census, Nat. Bur. Statistics, Bogotá, 1971; evaluator Foster Parent Plan, Bogotá, 1973; rsch. staff FEDESARROLLO, Bogotá, 1973-74; dir. Dade County Advocates for Victims, Miami, Fla., 1974-86; asst. to dep. dir. Dept. Human Resources, Miami, 1986-87, computer liaison, 1987-88, asst. adminstr. placement svcs. program, 1988-89; exec. dir. Health Crisis Network, 1989—; guest lectr. local univs. Participant, co-chmn. various task forces rape, child abuse, incest, family violence, elderly victims of crime, nat., state, local levels, 1974-86; developer workshops in field; mem. gov.'s task force on victims and witnesses, gov.'s task force on sex offenders and their victims; cert. expert witness on battered women syndrome in civil and criminal cts. Recipient various public svc. awards including WINZ Citizen of Day, 1979, Outstanding Achievement award Fla. Network Victim Witness Svcs., 1982, Pioneer award Metro-Dade Women's Assn., 1989; cert. police instr. Mem. Nat. Orgn. of Victim Assistance Programs (bd. dirs. 1977-83; Outstanding Program award 1984). Fla. Network of Victim/Witness Programs (bd. dirs., treas., 1980-81), Nat. Assn. Social Workers, Am. Soc. Public Adminstrs., Dade County Fedn. Health and Welfare Workers, Fla. Assn. Health and Social Svcs. (Dade County chpt., treas., 1979-80), LWV (bd. dirs. Dade County chpt. 1989—). Contbr. writings in field to publs. Office: Health Crisis Network PO Box 42-1280 Miami FL 33242-1280

LYNCH, ELIZABETH ANN, banker; b. Norwalk, Conn., Nov. 24, 1965; d. Kenneth Michael and Mary Louise (Kilcoyne) L. BSBA, U. Denver, 1987. Sr. assoc. M.B.I., Norwalk, 1987-88; mortgage asst. Barclays Bank, Scarsdale, N.Y., 1988-89, Apple Bank, Scarsdale, 1990—. Assoc. producer Fairfield County Student Operetta Workshop, Wilton, Conn., 1987-88. Mem. NAFE, Am. Mgmt. Assn.

LYNCH, ERIN YVETTE, communications executive; b. Schenectady, N.Y., Aug. 22, 1963; d. Patrick Hugh and Lois Sanford (Helwig) L. BA in Communications, Va. Poly. Inst., 1986. Spl. events asst. Va. Poly. Inst. Pub. Affairs, Blacksburg, 1986; editorial asst. TRW, Fairfax, Va., 1987-88; communications dir. Fed. Mgrs. Assn., Washington, 1988—; editor Fed. Mgrs. Quarterly, 1988—. Contbr. articles to mags. and newspapers. Active Alexandria Vol. Program, 1989—. Mem. Women in Communications, Am. Soc. Assn. Execs. Roman Catholic. Home: 5840 Berkshire Ct Alexandria VA 22303 Office: Fed Mgrs Assn 1000 16th St NW Ste 701 Washington DC 20036

LYNCH, FRAN JACKIE, real estate development executive; b. Bklyn., Dec. 15, 1948; d. William R. and Ruth (Slaiman) Diamondstein; m. James P. Lynch, Jan. 8, 1969; children: Cheryl Ann, Christopher, Kevin. BA, Bklyn. Coll., 1969; student, Suffolk Community Coll., Brentwood, N.Y., 1980-82; postgrad, L.I. U., 1983. V.p. Castle Capital Corp., N.Y.C., 1971-74; agt. Jerome Castle Found., N.Y.C., 1970-74; dir. office services Penn-Dixie Industries, N.Y.C., 1970-74; exec. asst. Med. Fin. Advisor, N.Y.C., 1974; v.p. Sept. Capital Corp., Glen Cove, N.Y., 1977-80; controller Bobgar Inc., Wallweaves Inc. and N.Y. Twine, Syosset, N.Y., 1980-86, The Kapson Group, Commack, N.Y., 1987—; cons. Women's Times, Queens, N.Y., 1987. Sec. Elwood Booster Club, East Northport, N.Y., 1987; mem. Harley Ave. PTA, 1980-87; coach Northport Youth Soccer, 1982; tchr. Confraternity Christian Doctrine Project St. Elizabeth's Ch., 1972-80, bd. dirs. Parish council, S. Huntington, N.Y., 1978-80. Home: 25 Hooper Ct East Northport NY 11731

LYNCH, KAREN RENZULLI, lawyer; b. Bridgeport, Conn., Feb. 4, 1946; d. Lidizio Amerigo and Cynthia Maria (Scott) Renzulli; m. Eugene Patrick Lynch Jr., Apr. 12, 1969; children: Tracy Regina, Kevin Anthony. BA, Manhattanville Coll., Purchase, N.Y., 1967; MPA, U. Hartford, West Hartford, Conn., 1975; JD, Western New Eng. Coll., Springfield, Mass., 1981. Bar: Conn. 1981, U.S. Dist. Ct. Conn. 1981. Mgmt. intern U.S. Army Chief of Staff, Washington, 1967-68; intelligence analyst U.S. Army for Sci. and Tech. Ctr., Washington, 1968-69; admnistr. N.Y. State Bd. Equalization, Albany, N.Y., 1969-70, U. Conn. Health Ctr., Farmington, 1971-76; pvt. practice West Hartford, 1981—; law clk. U.S. Dist. Ct., Hartford, 1980; law intern Conn. Superior Ct., Hartford, 1981. Editor Constabar News of Gen. Practice, 1985-88. Mem. Jewish Family Svc. Greater Hartford Task Force on Conservatorship, West Hartford, 1988. Mem. ABA (coun. sect. gen. practice div. 1987—, bd. dirs. 1990-91), Conn. Bar Assn. (exec. com. gen. practice sect. 1982—, chmn. legal svcs. com. Old Am. Day 1986), Hartford County Bar Assn., Hartford Assn. Women Attys. (dir. 1984-86). Office: PO Box 270715 West Hartford CT 06127-0715

LYNCH, KELLE ELIZABETH, construction engineer; b. Buffalo, Aug. 12, 1966; d. Earl Morris and Marice Berndette (Taylor) L. BS in Constrn. Engring., U. D.C., 1990. Asst. engr. Gilbane Constrn. Co., Washington, 1986-87; intern Archtl. Rsch. Inst., Washington, 1987-89, constrn. engr., 1989—. Scholar U. D.C., 1988-90, Presdl. scholar, 1989-90. Mem. ASCE, AIA, Washington Women in Architecture, NAFE, Am. Women's Econ. Devel. Coun., Union Internat. Fenne Architects. Roman Catholic. Office: Archtl Rsch Inst PO Box 6241 Washington DC 20015

LYNCH, LINDA LA REAU, marketing professional; b. York, Pa., Mar. 25, 1947; d. Albert Frederick La Reau and Mary Ann (Madia) Casciato; m. David Lewis Lynch, Jan. 8, 1983. Student, Orange County Community Coll., Middletown, N.Y.; grad. 1st in class, Peninsula Acad. Criminal Jus., Hampton, Va., 1976; student, Christopher Newport Coll., 1976-82. Exec. dir. Girl's Club Hampton, 1979-81; program dir. Knight-Ridder Sta. WTKR-TV, Norfolk, Va., 1981-83; sr. account exec. TVX Corp., Sta. WCAY-TV, Nashville, 1984-85; gen. mgr. Green River Broadcasting Sta. WGRB-TV, Campbellsville, Ky., 1985-86; local sales mgr. Odessy Ptnrs., Sta. WPCQ-TV, Charlotte, N.C., 1986-87; nat. sales mgr. Sta. WNYB-TV, Niagara Frontier Hockey, Buffalo, N.Y., 1987, gen. sales mgr., 1987-88, dir. sports mktg. and sales, 1988-89; sales mgr. Tak Communications, Sta. WGRZ-TV, Buffalo, 1989-90; account exec. Sta. WRKO, Boston, 1990—. V.p. pub. rels. com. 65 Roses Sports Club, Cystic Fibrosis Found., 1989, bd. dirs. Western N.Y. chpt. Mem. Buffalo Bisons Booster Club. Roman Catholic. Home: 665 Main St Hanover MA 02339 Office: Sta WRKO 3 Fenway Pla Boston MA 02215

LYNCH, MARTHA SCHIESZ, management consultant; b. Columbia, S.C., Oct. 23, 1962; d. Donald Frederick and Letty Ann (Pratt) Schiesz; m. Paul Scott Lynch, June 3, 1989. BS, Auburn U., 1984, MS, 1986. Grad. rsch. asst. Coll. Bus., Auburn (Ala.) U., 1984-85; cons. Am. Assn. State Psychology Bds., Montgomery, Ala., 1985-86; sr. cons. Andersen Cons., Arthur Andersen & Co., Atlanta, 1986—; cons. to telecommunications cos., 1986—. Auburn U. Coll. Bus. scholar, 1985. Mem. Pi Beta Phi. Home: 8390-S Rowsell Rd Dunwoody GA 30350 Office: Andersen Cons 133 Peachtree St NE Atlanta GA 30303

LYNCH, SISTER MARY DENNIS, librarian; b. Phila., Apr. 23, 1920; d. J. Raymond and Ida A. (Teal) L. A.B., Temple U., 1941; B.S. in L.S., Drexel U., 1942; M.S. in L.S., Cath. U., 1956; M.A., Villanova U., 1970, St. Charles Sem., 1980. Joined Soc. Holy Child Jesus, 1942; tchr., libr. Sch. Holy Child Jesus, Sharon Hill, Pa., 1942-45, 53-62, Summit, N.J., 1945-47; tchr. social studies West Phila. Cath. Girls High Sch., 1947-53; libr. Rosemont (Pa.) Coll., 1962—, lectr. methods of social studies, 1963-71, chmn. Am. studies com., 1970-73, lectr. polit. sci., 1973-87, lectr. New Testament, 1987—; instr. libr. sci. dept. Villanova U., 1964-65; mem. ednl. adv. bd. St. Charles Borromeo Sem., 1968-76, 78-87; bd. dirs. Tri-State Coll. Libr. Coop., 1967—, pres., 1980-81, exec. sec., 1967-70; trustee PALINET, 1978-81, 83-86, 90—, v.p., 1986; mem. Pa. State Libr. Bibliog. Access Study Adv. Com., 1977-78. Mem. ALA, Cath. Libr. Assn. (nat. exec. coun. 1975-79, 81-87, pres. 1983-85, adv. coun. 1985—), Pa. Libr. Assn. (chairperson coll. and rsch. sect. 1975-76, parliamentarian 1977-88), Assn. Coll. and Rsch. Librs. (pres. Del. Valley chpt. 1987-88), Cath. Libr. Assn. (v.p. Newman chpt. 1987-89, pres. 1989—), OCLC Users Coun. (del. 1978-83, 88-89, exec. com. 1982-83, del. 1988-89), Am. Acad. Polit. and Social Scis., Acad. Polit. Sci., Am. Studies Assn., Nat. Cath. Ednl. Assn., Nat. Coun. Social Studies, Beta Phi Mu. Office: Rosemont Coll Libr Rosemont PA 19010-1699

LYNCH, MARY PATRICIA, insurance sales executive; b. Chgo., Oct. 31, 1932; d. Thomas and Nora Marie (Cooney) Lavelle; m. Terrence Brons Lynch, Oct. 9, 1954 (div. 1985); children: Patrice M., Michael J., Thomas F., Teresa J. Student, Loyola U., Chgo., 1951-53, U. Calif., Sacramento, 1956, Rollins Coll., 1981, Valencia Community Coll., 1982; cert., Am. Coll., Bryn Mawr, Pa., 1980-86. CLU, chartered fin. cons. Office mgr. Guardian Life Ins. Co. Am., Orlando, Fla., 1971-80; ptnr. Macsay, Lynch & Assocs., Casselberry, Fla., 1980-85; owner, operator Mary "Pat" Lynch, CLU, Chartered Fin. Cons. & Assocs., Longwood, Fla., 1985—; moderator Life Underwriter Tng. Course, Orlando, 1989—. Mem. Internat. Assn. Fin. Planning, Women's Life Underwriters Confdn. (bd. dirs. 1985—), Soc. CLU (chmn. Huebner Sch. 1983-84), Cen. Fla. Life Underwriters, Cen. Fla. Soc. CLU (bd. mem. 1983-84), Seminole County C. of C. Democrat. Roman Catholic. Home: 436 Evesham Pl Longwood FL 32779 Office: 2917 W SR 434 Ste 141 Longwood FL 32779

LYNCH, MONIKA FEHRMANN, German language educator; b. Dresden, Sachsen, Germany, July 5, 1932; came to U.S., 1956; d. Franz Rudolf and Maria Antonie (Weissbach) Fehrmann; m. James Walter Lynch, May 2, 1959; children: Steve Allen, David Bryant, Judith Colleen. AB, Ga. So. U., Statesboro, 1969; MA, U. Ga., 1972; postgrad., Fla. State U., 1978. Asst. prof. German Ga. So. U., 1972—. Recipient German Am. Friendship award Fed. Republic Germany, 1989. Mem. Am. Assn. Tchrs. German (editor Ga. chpt. newsletter 1986—, named Ga. German Prof. Yr., Ga. chpt. 1988), Fgn. Lang. Assn. Ga., Phi Kappa Phi (sec. 1984-87). Lutheran. Office: Ga So U Dept Fgn Langs LB 8081 Statesboro GA 30460

LYNCH, PATRICIA A., production engineer; b. N.Y., Feb. 18, 1958; d. Thomas and Mary Theresa (Costsello) McCormack; m. Michael John Lynch, May 15, 1982. BS, Columbia U., 1979; MBA, St. Johns U., 1989. Lic. stationary engr., N.Y. Ops. supt., prodn. engr. Consol. Edison Co. N.Y., Staten Island; plant mgr. Consol. Edison Co. N.Y., Bklyn. Mem. Am. Mgmt. Assn. Address: 19 Quincy St Merrick NY 11566

LYNCH, PATRICIA GATES, organization executive, former ambassador; b. Newark, Apr. 20, 1926; d. William Charles and Mary Frances (McNamee) Lawrence; m. Mahlon Eugene Gates, Dec. 19, 1942 (div. 1972); children: Pamela Townley Gates Sprague, Lawrence Alan; m. William Dennis Lynch. Student, Dartmouth Inst., 1975. Broadcaster Sta. WFAX-Radio, Falls Ch., Va., 1958-68; pub. TV host Sta. WETA, Washington, 1967-68; broadcaster NBC-Radio, Europe, Iran, USSR, 1960-61; internat. broadcaster, producer Voice of Am., Washington, 1962-69; staff asst. to First Lady The White House, Washington, 1969-70; host Breakfast Show, Morning show, 1970-86; U.S. ambassador to Madagascar and the Comoros, 1986-89; dir. corp. affairs Radio Free Europe/Radio Liberty, Washington, 1989—; worldwide lectr., 1968-86; adv. com. Ind. Fed. Savs. and Loan Assn., Washington, 1970-86. Author stories on Am. for English teaching dept. Radio Sweden, 1967-68, others on internat. broadcasting. Chairperson internat. svc. com. Washington chpt. ARC, 1979-86. Grantee USIA, 1983; recipient Pub. Service award U.S. Army, 1960. Mem. Coun. Am. Ambs., Am. Women in Radio and TV (pres. 1966-67), Am. News Women's Club, Sulgrave Club. Republican. Episcopalian. Office: Radio Free Europe/Radio Liberty 1201 Connecticut Ave NW Washington DC 20036

LYNCH, PAULINE ANN, trust company executive; b. Saginaw, Mich., Mar. 19, 1939; d. Frank H. and Marie A. (Gaertner) Krueger; m. Ralph T. Lynch, Jan. 17, 1959; children: Patrick Thomas, Michael F., Terri Marie. Cert., Am. Inst. Paralegal, Detroit, 1985, Nat. Trust Sch./Northwestern U, 1988. Sec. Sun Life Ins. Co., Saginaw, 1956-57; exec. sec. Mich. Bell Telephone, Saginaw, 1957-60; paralegal/probate Polasky, Meisel, Rosenbaum & McLeod, Saginaw, 1964-83; bus. owner Saginaw, 1983-86; asst. v.p., trust officer Second Nat. Bank of Saginaw, 1986—; instr. legal asst. program, Delta Coll., Saginaw, 1987—. Vol. United Way, Saginaw, 1987—, Voluntary Action, Saginaw, 1987—; commentator communion distributor Holy Spirit Cath. Ch., Saginaw, 1980—. Mem. Networking of Saginaw, Northeastern Estate Planning Coun., Zonta Club (various offices), Nat. Assn. Bus. Women. Home: 1200 Curwood Saginaw MI 48603 Office: Second Nat Bank of Saginaw 101 N Washington Saginaw MI 48607

LYNCH, ROBYN DELPHINE, insurance company official; b. Harrisburg, Pa., May 9, 1960; d. William Clyde and Delphine (Baird) L. BA, Duquesne U., 1982. Exec. asst. U.S. Parachute Assn., Alexandria, Va., 1982-83; dir. investment products The Underwriters Group, Harrisburg, 1983-87; mem. profl. staff Wolper Ross & Co., Miami, Fla., 1987-88; mktg. coord. 1st Equity Corp., Miami, 1988; mgr. annuity mktg. and client mgmt. system Home Life Ins. Co., Piscataway, N.J., 1988—. Contbr. articles on mkgt. to profl. publs. Mem. NAFE, Am. Mktg. Assn. Home: 8508 Timberline Ct Monmouth Junction NJ 08852 Office: Home Life Ins Co One Centennial Ave Piscataway NJ 08855

LYNCH, SHERRY KAY, counselor; b. Topeka, Kans., Nov. 20, 1957; d. Robert Emmett and Norma Lea Lynch. BA, Randolph-Macon Woman's Coll., 1979; MS, Emporia State U., 1980; PhD, Kans. State U., 1987. Vocat. rehab. counselor Rehab. Services, Topeka, 1980-81, community program cons., 1981-86. Mem. exec. com. Sexual Assault Counseling Program, Topeka, 1983-86, recruitment coordinator, 1983-86, counselor, 1981-86, Nat. Singles Conf. Planning Com., Green Lake, Wis., 1987—; area admissions rep. Randolph-Macon Woman's Coll., Lynchburg, Va., 1981-87; counseling intern, Winthrop Coll., Rock Hill, S.C., 1986-87; counselor Ripon (Wis.) Coll., 1987—; mem. adv. bd. dirs. Student Outreach Svcs. Coun. Northbrooke Hosp.; bd. dirs., sec. Ripon Chem. Abuse and Awareness program, 1987—. Recipient Kans. 4-H Key award Extension Service of Kans. State U., 1974; named Internat. 4-H Youth Exchange Ambassador to France, 1977. Mem. Nat. Rehab. Counseling Assn. (bd. dirs. 1982-88, chairperson br. devel. subcouncil 1982-87, chairperson policy and program council 1987-88), Gt. Plains Rehab. Counseling Assn. (newsletter editor 1982-85, bd. dirs. 1983-87, pres. 1984-85, sec. 1986-87), Gt. Plains Rehab. Assn. (bd. dirs. 1983-85, awards chairperson 1984-85), Kans. Rehab. Counseling Assn. (bd. dirs. 1983-86, pres. 1984-85), Kans. Rehab. Assn. (bd. dirs. 1982-85, advt. chairperson 1983-85), Topeka Rehab. Assn. (bd. dirs. 1982-85, sec. 1982-83, pres. 1983-84), Am. Assn. Counseling and Devel., Am. Coll. Personnel Assn., Wis. Coll. Personnel Assn. (bd. dirs. 1988—), Assn. for Specialists in Group Work, Wis. Assn. for Counseling and Devel., Wis. Assn. of Profl. Counselors in Higher Edn. Republican. Methodist. Avocation: tennis. Home: 799 Hillside Terrace #9 Ripon WI 54971 Office: Ripon Coll Counseling Ctr PO Box 248 Ripon WI 54971

LYNCH, SONIA, data processing consultant; b. N.Y.C., Sept. 17, 1938; d. Espriela and Sadie Beatrice (Scales) Sarreals; m. Waldro Lynch, Sept. 18, 1981 (div. Oct. 1983). BA in Langs. summa cum laude, CCNY, 1960; cert. in French, Sorbonne, 1961. Systems engr. IBM, N.Y.C., 1963-69; cons. Babbage Systems, N.Y.C., 1969-70; project leader Touche Ross, N.Y.C., 1970-73; sr. programmer McGraw-Hill, Inc., Hightstown, N.J., 1973-78; staff data processing cons. Cin. Bell Info. Systems, 1978-89; sr. analyst AT&T, 1989—. Mem. bd. fellowship St. Andrew Luth. Ch., Silver Spring, 1987—. Downer scholar CUNY, 1960, Dickman Inst. fellow Columbia U., 1960-61. Mem. Assn. for Computing Machinery, Phi Beta Kappa. Democrat. Home: 13705 Beret Pl Silver Spring MD 20906

LYNCH, STEPHANIE NADINE, clinical psychologist; b. Cambridge, Mass., Apr. 11, 1951; d. Jeremiah and Irma C. (Gauntt) L.; m. Rickey Bernard Silverman, Apr. 17, 1983; children: Jason Frederick, Leonard Jeremiah, Rachel Elizabeth. PhD in Clin. Psychology, Case Western Res. U., 1977. Lic. psychologist, Mass., cert. psychologist, N.H. Staff psychologist Reading (Pa.) Hosp. & Med. Ctr., 1977-79, St. Elizabeth's Hosp., Brighton, Mass., 1979-81; pvt. practice Silverman & Assocs., Plaistow, N.H., 1981—; clin. instr. Tuft U. Sch. Medicine, Boston, 1980-89; cons. Parkland Hosp., Derry, N.H., 1990—, Cath. Med. Ctr., Manchester, N.H., 1990—, St. Elizabeth's Hosp., Brighton, Mass., 1980—, St. John of God Hosp., Brighton, 1981—, Bon Secours Hosp., Methuen, Mass., 1981—. Co-author: (chpt.) Handbook of Innovative Psychotherapies, 1981. Pres. No. New England Down Syndrome Congress, Maine, N.H., Vt., 1988-90. Mem. Am. Psychol. Assn., Mass. Psychol. Assn., Biofeedback Soc. New England. Office: Silverman & Assocs 31 Main St Plaistow NH 03865

LYNCH, VIVIAN ELIZABETH, lawyer; b. Detroit, June 17, 1940; d. Edward Winemac and Winifred (Grant) L.; m. Robert L. Rubin, Sept. 18, 1963 (div. Aug. 1973); children: David B., Edward A., Ruth L. BA, Wayne State U., 1960, JD, 1962. Bar: Nev. 1985, U.S. Dist. Ct. Nev. 1985, U.S. Ct. Appeals (9th cir.) 1986. Ptnr., exec. dir. Club Tahoe, Incline Village, Nev., 1978-81; exec. adminstr. Harbor/Depoe Bay, Oreg., 1982; ptnr. Hamilton and Lynch, Reno, 1985—; cons. Oreg. Real Estate Div., Salem, 1982-83; conv. speaker Western Regional Assn. Regulatory Agys., Incline Village, 1983; lead trial counsel Vance vs. Judas Priest, Reno, Nev., 1990; speaker in field. Editor Survey/Mich. Law Rev., 1961. Wayne State U. scholar, 1961-62. Mem. Washoe County Bar Assn., Am. Trial Lawyers Assn., Nev. Trial Lawyers Assn. (mem. Amicus Curiae com., lectr.). Republican. Roman Catholic. Office: Hamilton and Lynch 321 S Arlington Ave Reno NV 89501

LYNCH-BRENNAN, MARGARET ELIZABETH, educational administrator; b. Rockville, N.Y., Aug. 16, 1950; d. Daniel Joseph and Margaret Evelyn (Murphy) Lynch; m. John David Brennan, Oct. 9, 1987; stepchildren: David, Kathleen. BA cum laude, Coll. of St. Rose, Albany, N.Y., 1972; MA, SUNY, Albany, 1976. Cert. nursery, kindergarten, elem., and social studies tchr., N.Y. Tchr. social studies St. John's Acad., Rensselaer, N.Y., 1972-73, New Lebanon Cen. Sch. Dist., West Lebanon, N.Y., 1977-78; legal researcher, law clk. Community Legal Rights Found., Albany, 1973-74; tchr. St. Piux X Sch., Loudonville, N.Y., 1974-77; proofreader, legis. bill clk. rsch. svc. N.Y. State Senate, Albany, 1978-79; edn. aide N.Y. State Edn. Dept., Albany, 1979-80, asst. in edn. rsch., 1980, asst. in occupational edn. civil rights, 1980-81, assoc., 1981—, also vice chmn. Info. Dissemination Coun.; vol. tutor N.Y. State Office Gen. Svcs., 1986. Mem. Sweet Adelines, Steuben Athletic Club. Roman Catholic. Office: NY State Edn Dept EBA Rm 481 Albany NY 12234

LYNE, DOROTHY-ARDEN, educator; b. Orangeburg, N.Y., Mar. 9, 1928; d. William Henry and Janet More (Freston) Dean; m. Thomas Delmar Lyne, Aug. 16, 1952 (div. June 1982); children: James Delmar, Peter Freston, Jennifer Dean. BA, Ursinus Coll., 1949; MA, Fletcher Sch. Law and Diplomacy, 1950. Assoc. editor World Peace Found., Boston, 1950-51; editorial assoc. Carnegie Endowment Internat. Peace, N.Y.C., 1951-52; dir. Assoc. of Internat. Rels. Clubs, N.Y.C., 1952-53; editor The Town Crier, Westport, Conn., 1966-68; editorial assoc. Machinery Allied Products Inst., Wash., 1959-63; tchr. Helen Keller Mid. Sch., Easton, Conn., 1967-89; vice chmn. Cooperative Ednl. Svcs., Fairfield, 1983-85. Editor: Documents in American Foreign Rels., 1950, Current Rsch. in Internat. Affairs, 1951. Chmn. Westport Zoning Bd. of Appeals, 1976-80, Westport Bd. of Edn., 1985-87; vice chmn. Westport Bd. of Edn., 1980-85; mem. Westport Charter Revision Commn., 1966-67. Mem. NEA, Assn. Supervision and Curriculum Devel., Coop. Ednl. Svcs., Westport Charter Commn. Republican. Episcopalian.

LYNN, DONNA MARIA, public relations and advertising executive, writer; b. Hollywood, Calif., Oct. 4, 1945; d. Kane Wallace Lynn and Rita (Piazza) Maxwell; m. Dennis D. Schreffler, 1965 (div. 1973); children: Scott G. Schreffler, Susan M. Schreffler. Student, UCLA, 1963-65, U. Utah, 1965-68; BA, U. Ark., 1970; postgrad. in law, U. Balt., 1973-74. Lobbyist, UniServ dir. NEA, Washington, 1970-77; pres., chief exec. officer Lynn Assocs., Inc., Westport, Conn., 1977—; mgr. media rels. Perrier/Great Waters of France, N.Y.C., 1978-79; sr. cons. The Nestle Co., Washington and White Plains, N.Y., 1979-83; dep. dir. sports div. Hill & Knowlton, N.Y.C., 1983-85; mgr. pub. relations Avon Products, Inc., N.Y.C., 1985-86; supr. account group Daniel J. Edelman, N.Y.C., 1979-81. Features editor: Flight Attendant mag., 1986-87; contbr. numerous articles to newspapers and mags. Founder, dir. Earth Day in Ark., 1970; del. White House Conf. on Children and Youth, Washington, 1970; liaison White House Press Office, Dem. Nat. Conv., N.Y.C., 1979; mem. Md. Commn. for Women, Annapolis, 1976-77; pres. Annapolis Summer Garden Theatre, 1976-78; mem. bus. adv. bd. Nat. Down Syndrome Soc., N.Y.C., 1985-89. Mem. Am. Mgmt. Assn., Boating Writers Internat., Pub. Rels. Soc. Am., NEA (life, legis. chair Ark. chpt. 1970-73), Phi Alpha Theta. Office: 103 King's Hwy N Westport CT 06880-3103

LYNN, DONNA MARIE, copywriter; b. Bklyn., Sept. 10, 1960; d. Michael J. and Violet J. (Bellestri) Romano; m. Marshall W. Lynn, Feb. 19, 1989. BA in English cum laude, Manhattan Coll., 1982. Asst. account exec. Sawdon & Bess Advt., N.Y.C., 1982-83; account exec. Non-Ferrous Internat., N.Y.C., 1983-85; promotion mgr. Delta Communications, Chgo., 1985-87; promotion dir. Putman Pub., Chgo., 1987-88; promotion mgr. Frost & Sullivan, N.Y.C., 1989-90; sr. copywriter Prentice Hall, Englewood Cliffs, N.J., 1990—. Mem. Chgo. Advt. Club, 1986-88. Republican. Home: 119 Reldyes Ave Leonia NJ 07605

LYNN, KATHRYN LOUISE, nurse; b. Ft. Ord, Calif., Aug. 3, 1953; d. George Anthony and Lenore Grace (Roeltgen) L. BS, Towson State U., Balt., 1975; MS, U. Md., Balt., 1981. RN, Md.; cert. clin. specialist psychiat. nurse, advanced nursing adminstr. Sr. staff nurse Balt. City Hosps., 1975-77; nurse clinician Regional Inst. for Children, Balt., 1977-79, Highland Health Facility, Balt., 1979-83; head psychiat. nurse Fallston (Md.) Gen. Hosp., 1983-87, adminstrv. dir. psychiat. svcs., 1987-89; nurse SRT Med. Staff, Balt., 1989—; v.p. Productivity Systems Inc., Joppa, Md., 1990—; asst. dir. nursing mental health div. North Arundel Hosp., Glen Burnie, Md., 1990—; pvt. pracitce Bel Air, 1990—. Mem. NAFE. Home: 3437 Howell Ct Abingdon MD 21009 also: 1203 Churchville Rd Bel Air MD

LYNN, LORETTA WEBB (MRS. OLIVER LYNN, JR.), singer; b. Butcher Hollow, Ky., Apr. 14, 1935; d. Ted and Clara (Butcher) Webb; m. Oliver V. Lynn, Jr., Jan. 10, 1948; children—Betty Sue Lynn Markworth, Jack Benny (dec.), Clara Lynn Lyell, Ernest Ray, Peggy, Patsy. Student pub. schs. Sec.-treas. Loretta Lynn Enterprises; v.p. United Talent, Inc.; hon. chmn. bd. Loretta Lynn Western Stores. Country vocalist with MCA records, 1961—(numerous gold albums); most recent album Just a Woman, 1985, (with Conway Twitty) Making Believe, 1988. Author: Coal Miner's Daughter, 1976. Hon. rep. United Giver's Fund, 1971. Named Country Music Assn. Female Vocalist of Year 1967, 72, 73, Entertainer of Year, 1972, named Top Duet of 1972, 73, 74, 75; recipient Grammy award 1971, Am. Music award 1978, named Entertainer of Decade, Acad. Country Music 1980; inducted into Country Music Hall of Fame, 1988; first country female vocalist to record certified Gold album. Office: care MCA Records Inc 70 Universal City Pla North Hollywood CA 91608*

LYNN, MARY, sales executive; b. Rochelle, Ill., Apr. 26, 1951; d. Walter and Lois (Harms) Tigan; m. Roger Lynn, Oct. 6, 1975; children: Jenny, Lucy, Sofie. AA, DeAnza, Cupertino, Calif., 1972. Sales rep. Terminals Unltd., Hayward, Calif.; sr. sales rep. RC Data Inc., San Jose, Calif., PSI, San Jose; regional sales mgr. Peripheral Systems, Inc., San Jose. Address: 1429 Weaver Dr San Jose CA 95125

LYNN, NANCI C. KOPERSKI, registered nurse; b. Omaha, Sept. 14, 1962; d. William S. Jr. and Ethel A. (Friday) Koperski; m. Scott B. Lynn, Apr. 29, 1989. Student, Marquette U.; BS in Nursing cum laude, Creighton U., 1980. RN; cert. in advanced fetal monitoring, cert. childbirth educator, cert. neonatal resuscitation instr./provider. Nurse Phoenix Meml. Hosp., Phoenix Gen. Hosp.; staff nurse Phoenix Indian Med. Ctr. Mem. Nurses Assn. of Am. Coll. Ob-Gyn., Nat. League for Nursing, Am. Nurses Assn., Ariz. Nurses Assn., Sigma Theta Tau. Roman Catholic. Home: 11230 N 49th Dr Glendale AZ 85304 Office: 4212 N 16th St Phoenix AZ 85014

LYNN, NANNE JOYCE, educator; b. Muncie, Ind., Sept. 27, 1938; d. Hal Paul and Rose Mary (Femyer) Duffey; divorced;children: Joel Robert, Michael Charles, Lorry Rose. BA, Ball State U., 1960, MA, 1974. Cert. secondary tchr. Dir. child welfare Del. County Dept. of Welfare, Muncie, 1958-63; tchr. Coachella Valley Unified Sch. Dist., Thermal, Calif., 1978—; student travel coord., guide Europe and Soviet Union tours, 1987, 88; freelance reporter Desert Sun, Palm Springs, Calif., Palm Desert Post, Palm Desert, Calif., 1978-80. Vol. Birch Bayh for Pres. campaign, Ind., 1970-71. Mem. Palm Desert C. of C. (pub. relations 1980-83), Bus. Profls. Women (ednl. chmn. 1973-74), Phi Delta Kappa, Alpha Phi Gamma. Office: Coachella Valley High Sch 83-800 Airport Blvd Thermal CA 92274

LYNN, PATRICIA ANITA, postal service official; b. Newark, July 17, 1943; d. Mario Russo and Concetta Marie (Stella) Macaluso; m. Ronald Lee Lynn (div. May 1969); children: Valerie Jean, Veronica Lee (dec.). Student, Cortland (N.Y.) State Coll., 1961-63, Broward Community Coll., Ft. Lauderdale, Fla., 1975-78, Biscayne Coll., Miami, Fla., 1978-82. Customer svc. rep. Goodyear Tire & Rubber Co., Ft. Lauderdale, Fla., 1965-69; acct. Ben Clair Automotive Co., Oakland Park, Fla., 1969-71; customer svc. mgr. Sunny South Aircraft Svc., Ft. Lauderdale, 1971-74; police officer, dispatcher Ft. Lauderdale Police Dept., 1974-81; letter carrier U.S. Postal Svc., Pompano Beach, Fla., 1981—. Recipient Hidden Hero award Fla. Sheriff's Youth Ranches, 1988. Mem. Nat. Assn. Letter Carriers (shop steward Miami 1985—, Humanitarian of Yr. award 1987). Democrat. Baptist. Home: 3125 SW 16th St Fort Lauderdale FL 33312-3709 Office: US Postal Svc PO Box 1852 Pompano Beach FL 33061-1852

LYNN, PAULINE JUDITH WARDLOW, lawyer; b. Columbus, Ohio, Nov. 14, 1920; d. Charles and Helen P. (Christman) Wardlow; student Wellesley Coll., 1938-40; B.A., Ohio State U., 1942, J.D., 1948; m. Arthur D. Lynn, Jr., Dec. 29, 1943; children—Pamela Wardlow, Constance Karen, Deborah Joanne, Patricia Diane. Admitted to Ohio bar, 1948; practiced in Columbus, 1948-49. Troop leader Girl Scouts U.S.A., 1969-71. Mem. ABA, Columbus Bar Assn., Phi Beta Kappa, Kappa Kappa Gamma (mem. research com. Heritage mus. 1981-87), Pi Sigma Alpha. Republican. Episcopalian. Home: 2679 Wexford Rd Columbus OH 43221

LYNN, SHEILAH ANN, service executive, consultant; b. Anderson, Ind., Jan. 28, 1947; d. John Benton and Kathleen (Taylor) Bussabarger; m. John Hoftyzer, Dec. 21, 1968 (div. June 1982); children: Melanie Kay, John Theo; m. Guy C. Lynn, May 20, 1984. BS, Ind. U., 1969; postgrad., U. N.C., Greensboro, 1972-74, U. Cen. Mich., 1988-89; diploma, Data Processing Inst., Tampa, Fla., 1983; postgrad., Cen. Mich. U. Lic. in real estate. Bookkeeper John Hancock Life Ins. Co., Greensboro, 1970-72; freelance seminar leader and devel. Dhahran, Saudi Arabia, 1978-82; dir. programming Fla. Tech. Inst., Jacksonville, 1983-84, instr. in computer sci., 1984-85; real estate sales assoc. Fla. Recreational Ranches, Gainesville, 1985; coord. informational program Fla. Community Coll., Jacksonville, 1986—; handwriting analyst, cons. Sheilah A. Lynn & Assocs., Jacksonville, 1989—; cons. programmer, analyst Postmasters Co., Jacksonville, 1986—; pres. Acad. Options Cons., Jacksonville, 1986-89, Sheilah A Lynn & Assocs., handwriting analysts, cons., Jacksonville, 1989—. Mem. Jacksonville Community Council, Inc., 1986-87, Fla. Literacy Coalition, 1986-87. Mem. NAFE, Fla. Assn. Ednl. Data Systems, Bus. and Profl. Women, Jacksonville C. of C. (bd. dirs. south coun. 1987, internat. devel. bd. 1987, sec. 1989). Democrat.

LYNN, SYLVIA KREIN, educator; b. Langdon, N.D., Aug. 25, 1944; d. Alvin R. and Grace I. (Duncan) Krein; m. Jerry Jacob Lynn, Dec. 19, 1965; children: Angela Grace, Brian Kenneth Alvin, Jonathan Jerry. BS, N.D. State U., 1965; MS in Edn., No. Ill. U., 1972. cert. tchr. Tchr. home econs. St. Louis Bd. Edn., 1966-70, Fenton High Sch., Bensenville, Ill., 1970-71, Glenbard North High Sch., Carol Stream, Ill., 1972-73; tchr. adult edn. Newport News (Va.) Pub. Schs., 1975-78; tchr. A.W. Beattie Voc-Tech, Allison Park, Pa., 1980-82, St. Paul Preschool, Allison Park, 1983-89, No. Area Sub Svc., Allison Park, 1989—; Christian edn. coordinator Berkeley Hills Luth. Ch., Pitts.; mem. long range planning com. for elem. sch. coms. North Hills High Sch. and Sch. Dist.. Neighborhood chmn., leader, outdoor planning team troop organizer Girl Scouts U.S.A. Named Outstanding Vol., Girl Scouts, 1990. Mem. AAUW (treas. hospitality, program leader), Am. Home Econs. Assn., Nat. Tchrs. Assn., PTA. Republican. Lutheran.

LYNNE, JANICE C., sales executive; b. Eugene, Oreg., Feb. 4, 1954; d. Ralph L. and Mary Ann (McFarlane) Nafziger; m. Glenn R. Caddy, July 30, 1977 (div. Feb. 1989); stepchild: Gavin David. BA, Wash. State U., Bellingham, 1976. Probation counselor Snohomish County, Everett, Wash., 1974-76; substitute tchr. Norfolk (Va.) Pub. Schs., 1976; probation and parole officer State of Va., Norfolk, 1977-78; account exec. Cruise Internat., Norfolk, 1978-80; mgr. sales Carnival Cruise Line, Miami, Fla., 1981-87, dir. sales, 1987—; adv. bd. Fla. Atlantic U., 1984—, South Fla. Travel Acad., 1989—; speaker in field, Fla., 1981—. Mem. Bons Vivants (1st v.p. 1988, bd. dirs. 1986-87, pres. 1989), Thespians. Lutheran. Office: Carnival Cruise Lines 5225 NW 87th Ave Miami FL 33178

LYON, BERENICE IOLA CLARK, civic worker; b. Westfield, Pa., June 4, 1920; d. Stephen Artemus and Ruth Gertrude (Tubbs) Clark; m. Robert Louis Lyon, May 28, 1944. Pres., Twin Tiers Geneal. Soc., N.Y. and Pa., 1976-88, pub. jour. Gemini; Pa. state pres. Colonial Dames XVII Century, 1981-83, state chmn. heraldry, 1977-79, hon. state pres., 1983—, organizer-pres. Tyoga Gateway chpt., 1973-75, Treaty Elm chpt., 1975-77, state yearbook-directory compiler, 1979-81, Pa. state chmn. 1988—; N.Y. state chmn. DAR, 1968-71, pres. N.Y. coun. of regents, 1968-71, regent Corning (N.Y.) chpt. 1965-68, Wellsboro (Pa.) chpt., 1977-80, Pa. state vice chmn., 1980-83, Pa. dist. dir., 1983-88, Pa. state chmn., 1987—; N.Y. state chmn. Daus. Am. Colonists, 1965—, Atlantic Coast chmn., 1970-79, organizer-regent Forbidden Trail chpt., 1967-76, regent, 1974-76, 83-88, Pa. state chmn. 1987—; condr. geneal. seminars; speaker to convs., meetings, TV, radio; contbr. articles on heraldry to 17th Century Rev., 1978-79. Recipient medal of appreciation SAR, 1966. Mem. Ams. of Royal Descent, Descs. Knights of Garter, Magna Carta Dames, Old Plymouth Colony Descs., Order of Crown, Order of Washington, Plantagenet Soc., Mansfield Friends of Library (pres. 1980-81). Clubs: Kiwanis Ladies, Clionian Circle (Corning); Mansfield (Pa.) Garden (pres. 1979-80), N.Y. Fedn. Garden Clubs (sect. chmn. 1969-73). Home: Lowenhof 168A Bailey Creek Rd Millerton PA 16936

LYON, MARTHA SUE, naval officer, research engineer; b. Louisville, Oct. 3, 1935; d. Harry Bowman and Erma Louise (Moreland) Lyon. B.A. in Chemistry, U. Louisville, 1959; M.Ed. in Math., Northeastern Ill. U., 1974. Cert. tchr. Ill., Ky. Research assoc. U. Louisville Med. Sch., 1959-61, 62-63; commd. ensign, USNR, 1965, advanced through grades to comdr., 1983; instr. instrumentation chemistry Northwestern U., Evanston, Ill., 1968-70; tchr. sci., chemistry, gifted math. Waukegan (Ill.) pub. schs., 1970-75; phys. scientist Library of Congress, Washington, 1975-76; research engr. Lockheed Missiles & Space Co., Sunnyvale, Calif., 1976-77; instr., assoc. chmn. dept. physics U.S. Naval Acad., Annapolis, Md., 1977-80; analyst Systems Analysis Div., Office of Chief of Naval Ops. Staff, Washington, 1980-81; comdg. officer Naval Res. Ctr., Stockton, Calif., 1981-83; mem. faculty Def. Intelligence Coll., 1983-85; program mgr. Space and Naval Warfare Systems Command, 1985-86, commanding officer PERSUPPACT Memphis, 1986-88; program mgr. Space and Naval Warfare Systems Command, 1988—. Grantee Am. Heart Assn., 1960-62, NSF, 1971, 72. Mem. Soc. Women Engrs., Am. Statis. Assn., Am. Soc. Photogrammetry, Internat. Conf. Women in Sci. Engring. (protocol chair), Mensa, Zeta Tau Alpha, Delta Phi Alpha. Club: Order of Ea. Star. Developer processes used in archival photography, carbon-14 analyses; presenter of papers at profl. confs.

LYON, NORMA DUFFIELD, sculptor, agriculturist; b. Nashville, July 29, 1929; d. Benton J. and Elsa (Walburn) Stong; m. Gaylord Joe Lyon, July 22, 1950; children: Emily, Mark, Eric, Michelle, Gregory, Valerie, Lori, Kurt, Douglas. BS, Iowa State U., 1951. annual sculptor Iowa State Fair, Des Moines, Ill. State Fair, Springfield, Kans. State Fair, Hutchinson, Nat. Cattle Congress, Waterloo, 1960—; cattle judge, 1960—; art tchr. gifted and talented, South Tama (Iowa) Sch., 1986—; elem. nutrition tchr., Toledo, Iowa, 1986. Prin. works include numerous temporary and permanent sculptures in Iowa, Calif., Wis., Ariz., Can.; illustrator pen and ink drawings for books. Mem. County Dem. Cen. Com., Tama. Named Disting. Grad. Dairy Sci. Club, 1990, Hon. mem. 4-H, 1990, World Dairy Expo Woman of Yr., 1990. Mem. AAUW (treas. 1987—), Iowa 4-H Found. (trustee 1986—), Arts Coun. Tama-Toledo Area, Iowa Jersey Cattle Club, Am. Jersey Cattle Club, Dairy Shrine (state membership chmn.), Alpha Delta Pi. Roman Catholic. Home: Rte 2 Box 100 Toledo IA 52342

LYON, VIRGINIA ROSE, volunteer worker; b. Mishawaka, Ind., June 11, 1928; d. Irving and Genevieve Harriet (Kunce) Baim; m. Robin Loss Lyon, Apr. 15, 1951; children: Jennifer Susan, Sharon Ann, Robin Bruce. BS, Purdue U., 1950. Intern U. Wis., Madison, 1951. First pres. adv. com., organizer vol. program and community bd. (info. ctr. dedicated in honor 1979, Silver Tray award 1985); adv. com. Big Brothers/Big Sisters (Montgomery County/North Harris County, Tex. chpts.); beautification com. chmn. Northampton Subdiv.; vol. coord. pub. schs.; pres. elem. and jr. high PTA; troop leader, cadette program adv. bd. Girl Scouts U.S.; active Am. Cancer Soc., Am. Heart Assn., United Way. Named Outstanding Woman of Yr. North Harris County, 1980. Mem. AAUW (Tex. div. ednl. found. v.p., dist. coord., bylaws com., North Harris County br. pres. ednl. found. programs, various coms., Gift honoree to Ednl. Found 1978-79, named unit in name of, 1984-85, finalist for Disting. Svc. award 1990, 3 awards for fund raising efforts), Northampton Garden Club (pres. and various other offices, resource book donated to libr. in honor of). Home: 6222 Allentown Dr Spring TX 77389

LYONS, HEIDI HELD, creative analyst, illustrator; b. Mansfield, Ohio, Mar. 26, 1962; d. Michael and Margaret (Wroblewske) Held; m. Milton Dean Lyons. Aug. 8, 1988. BA in English, U. Calif., Davis, 1983. Creator, writer Heidi's Funshoppe, Hemet, Calif., 1975-88; writer, photographer Lake Elsinore (Calif.) Valley Sun -Tribune & Rancho News, 1984-87, Moreno Valley (Calif.) News, 1987-88; creator/writer Lyons Den Enterprises, Yakima, Wash., 1988—; freelance writer various mags. and newspapers. Author: (with others) 7 poetry anthologies. Mem. task force Bus. Devel. Council, Yakima, 1989—, Econ. Devel. Council, Yakima, 1989—, Inventor's Fair Council, Yakima, 1989—. Mem. Cen. Wash. Inventors Assn., Cascadians, Franklin Mint Collectors Assn., I. Calif. Davis Alumni Assn., Internat. Wildlife Fedn., Nat. Wildlife Fedn., Worl Wildlife Fund, Smithsonian Instn. (assoc.) Greater Yakima C. of C., The Gorilla Foundation. Lutheran. Office: Lyons Den Enterprises PO Box 8208 Yakima WA 98908

LYONS, LINDA MARY, lawyer; b. Buffalo, Oct. 25, 1949; d. Harry Gustave and Evelyn (Simon) Lyons; m. Thomas C. Warren, Dec. 10, 1988. BA, U. Calif., Santa Barbara, 1971; JD, Hastings Coll., San Francisco, 1976. Bar: Calif. 1976. Ptnr. Howell & Hallgrimson, San Jose, 1978-89. Mem. Calif. Bar Assn., N.Y. State Bar Assn. Home: 245 W 104th St Apt 10C New York NY 10025

LYONS, MARGARET J., electrical engineer; b. Plainfield, N.J., June 10, 1964; d. Edwin William and Teresa (Murphy) L. BSCEE, Purdue U., 1986. Registered profl. engr., N.J. Systems engr. RAM Communications Consultants, Woodbridge, N.J. Mem. IEEE, Soc. Women Engrs. (pres. N.J. sect. 1989-90). Address: 188 Tillotson Rd Fanwood NJ 07023

LYONS, MARGARET V., public relations executive; b. U.K., Jan. 17, 1942; came to U.S., 1967, 1988.; d. Fred and Elizabeth (Higgins) Flower; m. Herbert Lyons, 1971 (div. 1983); 1 child, Gavin Lyons. BA honors, U. Wales, U.K., 1964. ATCL (Assoc. of Trinity Coll. of Music/London). Asst. to cultural attache British Embassy, Bucharest, Romania, 1965-66; music adminstr. Nat. Symphony Orch., Washington, 1968-76; concert mgr. City of Oxford (Eng.) Orch., 1983-86; devel. mgr. Mansfield Coll. Oxford U., U.K., 1986-88; publs. dir. Nat. Coffee Svc. Assn., Fairfax, Va., 1989—; dir. Theater Chamber Players, Washington, 1990—, Mt. Vernon (Va.) Chamber Orch., 1989—; instr. piano and music theory; lectr. on music; graphic artist. Author: (program notes) Nat. Symphony Orch. programs, 1968-76, Delos recording; freelance writer and graphic artist. Vol. Sen. Warner campaign, 1990. Recipient Surrey County Coun. scholarship London/Trinity Coll., 1953, grant U. Wales, 1960. Mem. Pub. Rels. Soc. Am., Women in Communications (pub. rels. com.), Nat. Soc. of Fundraising Execs., Music Tchrs. Nat. Assn., Am. Symphony Orch. League. Episcopalian. Home: 7919 Jackson Rd Alexandria VA 22308

LYONS, VICTORIA MARY, psychologist; b. Washington (D.C.), Dec. 18, 1953; d. Victor Herbert and Angela Justine (Walinsky) L. BA, Coll. Notre Dame of Md., 1975; MA, U. Md., 1977, PhD, 1979. Lic. psychologist, Md., Va.; cert. sch. psychologist, Va. Part-time psychometrist Prince George's County Schs., Upper Marlboro, Md., 1978-79; part-time lectr. U. Md., College Park, 1979; sch. psychologist Loudoun County Pub. Schs., Leesburg, Va., 1979—; testing practicum supr. George Mason U., Fairfax, Va., 1987. Contbr. articles to profl. jours. Treas. Heritage Sq. Homeowner's Assn., Leesburg, 1984-87, Loudoun County Youth Suicide Prevention Coalition, Leesburg, 1988—; mem. Community Svcs., Bd., Leesburg, 1987-89. Mem. Am. Psychol. Assn., Nat. Assn. Sch. Psychologists, Va. Psychol. Assn. Democrat. Roman Catholic. Home: 1011 Clymer Ct NE Leesburg VA 22075 Office: Loudoun County Pub Schs 102 North St NW Leesburg VA 22075

LYOU, KEITH WEEKS (KAY LYOU), editor; b. Los Angeles, Aug. 2, 1930; d. Howard Keith Weeks and Ruth Manson (Day) Wood; m. Joseph Lyou, Mar. 26, 1955 (div. 1972); children: Tracy Ann, Joseph Keith. BS, Lindenwood Coll., 1977, MA, 1979. Cert. community coll. instr., Calif. Editorial asst. Annals of Biomed. Engring., Culver City, Calif., 1971-76; exec. asst. Biomed. Engring. Soc., Culver City, 1974-81; editor Inkslingers, Culver City, 1974—; editor biotechnology lab. UCLA, 1974-81, campus advisor theses and dissertations , 1983-86; exec. asst. Biomed. Engring. Soc., Culver City, 1974-81; instr. adult sch. Culver City Unified Sch. Dist., 1979-81. Mng. editor Am. Intra-Ocular Implant Soc. Jour., Santa Monica, 1982-83. Trustee Culver City Bd. Edn., 1981—, pres. bd., 1987; counselor Adv. Ctr. for Edn. and Career Counseling, Santa Monica, Calif., 1981-82; vice chair project area com. Project and Redevel., Culver City, 1975-77, 85, chair 1979-82; bd. dirs. Culver City Foster Children's Assn., 1981—; mem. Culver City Coun. PTA (hon. svc. award 1988). Recipient Citizen Recognition award Culver City C. of C. Mem. LWV, Bus. and Profl. Women, Biomed. Engring. Soc., Calif. Elected Women's Assn. for Edn. and Research, UCLA Grad. Students Assn. (outstanding adminstrv. award 1970). Democrat. Office: Inkslingers PO Box 2160 Culver City CA 90230

LYSEIGHT, CYNTHIA ANNA MARIA, nurse; b. St. Louis, May 4, 1950; d. Frederick Douglas and Margret (Knox-Watson) Crawford; m. Errol Constantine Lyseight, Sept. 20, 1975 (div. May 1988). Student, Highland Park (Mich.) Jr. Coll., 1968-69, U. Tex., 1969-71; BS in Nursing, Tex. Christian U., 1974; cert. in coronary care, El Paso Community Coll., 1974; postgrad., Tex. Woman's U., 1975. Critical care RN Nurse Finders, El Paso, Tex., 1975-81; staff nurse telemetry Sun Towers Hosp., El Paso, 1978-79; relief charge telemetry Sierra Med. Ctr., El Paso, 1978-79; sch. nurse El Paso Ind. Sch. Dist., 1979-85; staff nurse N.W. Tex. Hosp., Amarillo, 1987—; sch. nurse Canyon (Tex.) Ind. Sch. Dist., 1986—; with Kimberly Nurse Travelers, Kansas City, Mo., 1981-88, Splty. Care, L.A., 1988, Med. Help, Long Beach, Calif., 1988—; staff nurse N.W. Tex. Hosp., Amarillo, 1987—. Mem. NAFE, Nat. Assn. Sch. Nurses, Tex. Assn. Sch. Nurses, Post Anesthesia Care Nurse Assn., Amarillo Women's Network (Profl. Woman's Aux.), Alpha Kappa Alpha. Home: 6703 Green Haven Rd Amarillo TX 79110

LYSTER, SHIRLEY ANN, educator; b. Columbus, Ind., Sept. 6, 1929; d. Oren Russell and Mabel Ruth (Hoffman) L. AB in English, Franklin Coll., 1951; BS in Edn., Ind. U., 1958; postgrad., Purdue U., 1967, 68, 71. Tchr. English, Bartholomew Consol. Sch. Corp. North High Sch., Columbus, 1951—; chmn. dept. North High Sch., Columbus, 1972—. Contbr. articles to profl. jours. Named Hoosier Tchr. of Yr., Ind. Council Tchrs. English, Indpls., 1982, Ind. Acad. All-Star Tchr. Inpls. Star newspaper, 1990; recipient Edna Folger Outstanding Tchr. award, Arvin Industries, Columbus, 1983. Mem. NEA, Nat. Coun. Tchrs. English (Ctr. of Excellence award 1985-87, L.A. 1988-90, CSSEDC Outstanding Writer award 1989), Ind. Coun. Tchrs. English, Coun. Sect. English Dept. Chmns., Ind. Tchrs. Assn., Columbus Educators Assn. (sec. 1962-64), Columbus Sch. Found. (sec. 1959-62), Delta Kappa Gamma (sec. 1972-73), Delta Theta Tau, Delta Zeta (pres. alumni 1952-55). Democrat. Methodist. Home: 609 Lafayette Ave Columbus IN 47201 Office: North High Sch English Dept Chmn 1400 25th St Columbus IN 47201

LYTLE, VICTORIA ELIZABETH, communications executive; b. Miami Beach, Fla., Aug. 25, 1951; d. Reginald Vivian and Antoinette (Whitfield) L.; m. Edward Hula, Apr. 5, 1975 (Div. Aug. 1979). BA in English, Fla. State U., 1971-74; postgrad., Georgetown U., 1988. Asst. pub. rels. dir. Marco Beach Hotel, Marco Island, Fla., 1975-76; assoc. editor Career Edn. Ctr., Tallahassee, 1976-78; writer, editor Am. Vocat. Assn., Alexandria, Va., 1978-80, 81-83; sr. writer, editor Azen, Kaplan & Assocs., Ft. Lauderdale, Fla., 1989; staff writer NEA Today, Washington, 1983-88, 89—; newsletter editor Nat. Urban Coalition, Washington, 1980-81. Assoc. editor Fla. Vocat. Jour., 1976; contbr. articles to profl. jours. and popular publs. Mem. Women in Communications, Washington Ind. Writers, Toastmasters (v.p. Alexandria 1986-87). Home: 1200 N Nash St Arlington VA 22209 Office: NEA 1201 16th St NW Washington DC 20036

MAAS, JANE BROWN, advertising executive; b. Jersey City; d. Charles E. and Margaret (Beck) Brown; m. Michael Maas, Aug. 30, 1957; children: Katherine, Jennifer. BA, Bucknell U., 1953; postgrad., U. Dijon, France, 1954; MA, Cornell U., 1955; LittD, Ramapo Coll., 1986, St. John's U., 1988. Assoc. producer Name That Tune TV Program, N.Y.C., 1957-64; v.p. Ogilvy and Mather Inc., N.Y.C., 1964-76; sr. v.p. Wells, Rich, Greene, Inc., N.Y.C., 1976-82, Muller Jordan Weiss Inc., N.Y.C., 1982-89; pres. Earle Palmer Brown Cos., N.Y.C., 1989—. Co-author: How to Advertise, 1975, Better Brochures, 1981, Adventures of a Advertising Woman, 1986. Trustee Bucknell U., Lewisburg, 1976-86, Fordham U., N.Y., 1983—; mem. bd. govs. com. Scholastic Achievement, 1985—; active Girl Scouts U.S. Greater N.Y., 1970-76. Recipient Matrix award Women in Communications, 1980, N.Y. Advt. Woman of Yr., 1986. Mem. Am. Assn. Advt. Agys. (bd. govs.). Home: 300 E 93d St New York NY 10128

MAASS, VERA SONJA, psychologist; b. Berlin, July 6, 1931; came to U.S., 1958; d. Willy Ernst and Wally Elizabeth (Reinke) Keck; m. Joachim Adolf Maass, Dec. 24, 1954 (div.). BA, Monmouth Coll., 1971; MA, Lehigh U., 1974; PhD, U. Mo., 1978. Diplomate, clin. supr. Am. Bd. Sexology; cert. family life educator. Tutor in adult basic edn. Teaching Asst. Edn., Kansas City, Mo., 1973-74; clin. intern U. Ky. Med. Sch., Lexington, 1975-76; psychologist, therapist Dunn Mental Health Ctr., Richmond, Ind., 1976-80; psychology br. dir. Dunn Mental Health Ctr., Winchester, Ind., 1980-83; psychology outpatient clin. supr. Tri-County Mental Health Ctr., Indpls., 1983-85; psychology cons. Disability Determination Div., Indpls., 1985—; pres. clin. dir. Living Skills Inst., Inc., Indpls., 1982—; divorce and child custody mediator, 1990—; lectr. internat. confs., 1973—. Mem. adv. bd. Sta. WXTZ, Indpls., Indpls. Mus. Art, Indpls. Art League. Mem. Am. Psychol. Assn., Am. Assn. Counseling Devel., Am. Assn. Sex Educators, Counselors and Therapists (cert.), Internat. Acad. Profl. Counseling and Psychotherapy, Ind. Psychol. Assn. Home and Office: 8204 Westfield Blvd Indianapolis IN 46240

MABIE, RUTH MARIE, realtor; b. Pueblo, Colo., Feb. 7; d. Newton Everett and Florence Ellen Allen; M.B.A., La Jolla U., 1980, Ph.D., 1981; m. Richard O. Mabie, Nov. 29, 1946; 1 son, Ward A. Mgr., LaMont Modeling Sch., San Diego, 1962; tchr. Am. Bus. Coll., San Diego, 1964-66; fashion modeling, 1960-72; owner, broker Ruth Mabile Realty, San Diego, 1972—; asst. v.p. Skil-Bilt, Inc., 1976—; dir. Mabie & Mintz, Inc. Bd. dirs. Multiple Sclerosis Dr., 1971—. Mem. San Diego Bd. Realtors, Nat. Assn. Female Execs. Republican. Office: 2231 Camino del Rio So #302 San Diego CA 92108-3605

MAC, PAULA MARIE, accountant; b. Dearborn, Mich., June 5, 1961; d. Frank Stanley and Helen Theres (Ulanowski) M. BS in Fin., U. Mich., Dearborn, 1985. Customer svc. rep. Security Bank & Trust, Birmingham, Mich., 1980-85; bus. asst. GM, Warren, Mich., 1985-86; cost acct., consolidations acct., bus. devel. analyst Masco Corp., Taylor, Mich., 1986-89; cash mgmt. analyst, bus. devel. analyst, staff acct. TriMas Corp., Ann Arbor, Mich., 1989—. Universal Oil Products merit scholar, 1979. Mem. Am. Mgmt. Assn., NAFE, Nat. Corp. Cash Mgmt. Assn., Detroit Treasury Mgmt. Assn., U. Mich. Alumnae Assn. Roman Catholic. Office: TriMas Corp 315 E Eisenhower Pkwy Ann Arbor MI 48180

MACALISTER, KIM PORTER, advertising executive; b. Providence, Oct. 25, 1954; d. Bruce Barnes and Jeanne Marie (Cahill) Macalister; m. Bruce Phillip Person, Dec. 29, 1979 (div. June 1984); m. Arthur Gene Quinby, Feb. 19, 1988. BS, Skidmore Coll., Saratoga Springs, N.Y., 1976. Media planner, account exec. J.H. Dietz Advt., Providence, 1976-79; media planner Della Femina, Travisano, L.A., 1979-80; media planner J. Walter Thompson, L.A., 1980-82, assoc. media dir., 1982-83, v.p., media dir., 1983-85; v.p., media dir. Thompson Recruitment Advt. subs. J. Walter Thompson, 1985-86, mgr.and v.p., 1986-89, pres., chief oper. officer, 1989-90, pres., chief exec. officer, 1990—; mem. AAAA Inst. Advanced Advt. Studies. Mem. L.A. Media Dirs. Coun., L.A. Advt. Club. Republican. Office: Thompson Recruitment Advt 6500 Wilshire Blvd #2100 Los Angeles CA 90048

MACALPINE, LORETTA, editor; b. Bryn Mawr, Pa., Oct. 7, 1960; d. James L. Sr. and Milda Patricia (Baltadonis) Womer; m. David William MacAlpine, May 7, 1988. BA, Hollins (Va.) Coll., 1982. Mng. editor Video Insider Mag., Wayne, Pa. Freelance writer nat. mags. and local newspapers, Kennett Square, Pa. Mem. Pub. Rels. Soc. Am.

MACARTHUR, DIANA TAYLOR, business executive; b. Santa Fe, July 7, 1933; d. Antonio J. and Elizabeth (Steele) Taylor; student U. Geneva, 1953-54, B.A., Vassar Coll., 1955; children—Elizabeth, Alexander Tschursin; m. Donald Malcolm MacArthur, Mar. 31, 1962 (dec. 1988). Cons. economist Checchi & Co., Washington, 1957-61; v.p. Thomas J. Deegan Co., dir. Washington office, 1961-62; dep. chief W. Africa, Peace Corps, 1963, regional program officer N. Africa, Near East, South Asia, 1964, dir. div. pvt. and internat. orgns., 1965-66; coordinator Nat. Youth Conf. on Natural Beauty and Conservation, 1966-68; self-employed cons. public affairs to corps., assns., govt., Washington, 1968-76; pres. Consumer Dynamics, Inc., 1976-81; dir. Dynamac Internat., Inc., 1978-88, v.p., dir., 1980-88; chmn., chief exec. officer Dynamac Internat., Inc., 1988—; chmn., chief exec. officer Rsch., Analysis and Mgmt. Corp., 1988—; pres. Fgn. Traders, Inc., 1980-86 . Mem. citizens adv. bd. Pres.'s Council on Youth Opportunity, 1968-69; trustee Menninger Found., Topeka, 1972—; bd. dirs. The Sante Fe Opera, 1990—, Washington Area Council Alcoholism and Drug Abuse, chmn. bd., 1974. Mem. Phi Beta Kappa. Home: 5103 Cape Cod Ct Bethesda MD 20816 Office: Dynamac Bldg 11140 Rockville Pike Rockville MD 20852

MACARTHUR, SANDRA LEA, financial services executive; b. Springfield, Mass., July 21, 1946; d. John J. MacArthur and Catherine E. (Lantry) Mason; m. Edgar A. Dunn, June 23, 1973 (div. Mar. 1980); 1 child, Jonathan H.; m. Robert M. Cruickshank, Sept. 15, 1984. AA, Bradford Coll., 1966; BA, Simmons Coll., 1973; MBA, Babson Coll., 1983. Asst. dir. rental properties Wintergreen Resort, Charlottesville, Va., 1978-79; treas., ptnr. Elan, Inc., Boston, 1983-84; agt. State Mut. Am., Newton Center, Mass., 1985-86; sr. account officer Fidelity Investments Instl. Svcs., Boston, 1986-87, mgr. client svcs., 1987-88, assoc. market mgr., 1988-89; market mgr. Fidelity Instl. Retirement Svcs. Co., Boston, 1989-90, v.p., 1990—. Fundraiser Babson Coll., Wellesley, Mass., 1988. Mem. New Eng. Employee Benefits Coun., Beta Gamma Sigma. Democrat. Episcopalian. Home: 47 Westchester Rd Jamaica Plain MA 02130 Office: Fidelity Instl Retirement Svcs Co 82 Devonshire St Boston MA 02109

MACARTNEY, MICHELLE LYNN, trust company executive; b. Lorain, Ohio, Sept. 8, 1963; d. Thomas Robert and Linda Kay (Evansco) M. BA, Baldwin-Wallace Coll., 1985, MBA, 1989. Ops. analyst Ameritrust Co. N.A., Cleve., 1985-86, analytical supr., 1986-87, project controller, 1987-88, mgr. retail system devel., 1988-89, bus. systems analyst, 1989, mgr. platform automation support, 1989—. Class rep. Baldwin-Wallace Coll. Annual Fund, Berea, Ohio, 1988-89; flutist St. Peter's Contemporary Choir, 1988-89; gen. and fin. advisor Zeta Tau Alpha Fraternity Delta Delta chpt., Berea, Ohio, 1987—. Home: 11738 Lake Ave #303 Lakewood OH 44107 Office: Ameritrust Co NA 900 Euclid Ave Cleveland OH 44115

MACAULAY, ALICE ITTNER, physician; b. Bklyn.; d. William and Anna (Holzman) Ittner; B.A. cum laude, Barnard Coll., postgrad., 1944-46; M.D., N.Y. Med. Coll., 1950; postgrad. N.Y. U., 1952-53; M Med. Sci., L.I. U. at Mercy Coll., 1982, M in Guidance and Counseling; cert. in gerontology, 1983; m. David Harvard Macaulay, July 10, 1936 (dec. 1971). Tchr. N.Y.C. high schs., until 1946; actress Columbia Lab. Players, 1928—, Summer Stock, Roxbury, Conn., 1932-34, Old Vic, London, 1934-35; intern and resident Grasslands Hosp., Valhalla, N.Y., 1950-56, hosp. practice internal medicine Grasslands Hosp., 1956-74, dir. outpatient services, 1956-74, asso. attending internal medicine, 1958-76, chmn. pharmacy and therapeutics com., 1967-74, mem. adminstrv. team, 1961-74, named to Nat. Disting. Service Registry for Med. and Vocat. Rehab., 1987—; hon. attending in internal medicine Westchester County Med. Center, 1976-84, attending emeritus, 1984—; liaison hosp. officer for devel. of Neighborhood Health Centers; chmn. med. adv. bd. Westchester County Public Health Nursing; med. cons., dir. med. affairs Westchester Community Coll.; cons. Office of Vocat. Rehab. and State Med. Programs; cons. hypertension, 1956—; med. adv. bd. Westchester Heart Assn., chmn. com. on hypertension, 1973-75; prof. medicine Pace U. Grad. Sch. Nursing, 1974-77; vocat. rehab. specialist, 1975—; adv. bd. Columbia U. Ctr. for Geriatrics. Bd. dirs., med. cons. Donald Reed Speech Center, 1976—. Mem. AMA, Westchester Acad. Medicine, N.Y. State Med. Soc., Westchester, Am. heart assns., AAAS Cor et Manus, Contin, Am. Lung Assn., N.Y. Trudeau Soc., Alpha Epsilon Iota, Sigma Phi Omega (award 1984). Clubs: Soroptimists; Ardsley Country. Address: Hudson House Ardsley-on-Hudson NY 10503

MACAULAY, ANN SAUNDERS, research animal scientist; b. New Orleans, Dec. 29, 1958; d. George Raymond and Betty Jean (Anders) M. BS, La. State U., 1981, MS, 1983; PhD, Tex. A&M U., 1989. Lab asst., grad. rsch. asst. La. State U., Baton Rouge, 1982-83; grad. rsch. asst., teaching asst. Tex. A&M U., College Sta., Tex., 1983-87; sub. tchr. Bryan (Tex.) Ind. Sch. Dist., 1987-88; rsch. animal sci. Agrl. Rsch. Svc. of USDA, Logan, Utah, 1989—; adj. asst. prof. animal, dairy and vet. scis. dept. Utah State U. Contbr. articles to profl. jours. Bd. dirs. ARC, Brazos County, Tex., 1986-88, Cache County, Utah, 1989—; vol., coord. pet therapy program Sunshine Terr. Found., Logan, Utah. Mem. Am. Soc. Animal Sci., Am. Dairy Sci. Assn., Humane Soc. U.S., Treehouse Animal Found., No. Utah Assn. for Women in Sci. (founder, pres.), Delta Soc., Alpha Zeta, Beta Sigma Phi (treas. Alpha Chi Tau chpt. 1987-88), Delta Gamma (Gamma Zeta chpt.). Republican. Presbyterian. Office: Utah State U UMC 4815 Logan UT 84322

MACAVINTA-TENAZAS, GEMORSITA, family physician; b. Numancia, Aklan, Phillippines, Dec. 18, 1938; came to U.S., 1967; d. Dominador Zalazar and Georgina Estrada (Tabanera) Macavinta; m. Salvador Torrefiel Tenazas Jr., Apr. 18, 1963; children: Alan, Alex, Albert, Alfred. BA, Far Ea. U., Manila, 1959, D of Medicine, 1964. Diplomate Am. Bd. Family Practice, recert., 1985. Intern North Gen. Hosp., Manila, 1963-64; pvt. practice Manila, 1965-67; extern Chinese Gen. Hosp., Manila, 1965-67; with St. Joseph Med. Ctr., Burbank, Calif., 1967-69; chief cytotechnologist Cancer Screening Svcs., North Hollywood, Calif., 1969-73; resident in family practice medicine Health Scis. Ctr., Tex. Tech. U., Lubbock, 1974-75; staff physician VA Outpatient Clinic, L.A., 1975—. Recipient physician recognition awards AMA, 1973-85. Fellow Am. Acad. Family Physicians; mem. Calif. Acad. Family Physicians, Filipino Asian-Pacific VA Employees Soc. (pres. L.A. chpt. 1988—), Aklanons of Am. (pres. 1988—, 1st Mrs. Aklan 1986-89), Far Ea. U. Med. Alumni Assn. (asst. sec. 1988—). Roman Catholic. Office: VA Outpatient Clinic 425 S Hill St Los Angeles CA 90013

MACBRIDE, TERI J., marketing director; b. Waynesboro, Pa., Sept. 21, 1957; d. Thomas James and Yvonne (Holthau) MacB. BA, Am. U., 1979; MS, Shippensburg (Pa.) U., 1982. Export mgr. SEDA-COG, Lewisburg, Pa., 1984-88; mktg. dir. Chromagraphic Processing Co., Williamsport, Pa., 1988—. Mem. LWV (bd. dirs. Lewisburg chpt. 1987—). Office: Chromagraphic Processing Co 2475 Trenton Ave Williamsport PA 17701

MACCALLUM, (EDYTHE) LORENE, pharmacist; b. Monte Vista, Colo., Nov. 29, 1928; d. Francis Whittier and Berniece Viola (Martin) Scott; m. David Robertson MacCallum, June 12, 1952; children: Suzanne Rae MacCallum Barslund and Roxanne Kay MacCallum Batezel (twins), Tracy Scott, Tamara Lee MacCallum Johnson, Shauna Marie MacCallum Bost. BS in Pharmacy U. Colo., 1950. Registered pharmacist, Colo. Pharmacist Presbyn. Hosp., Denver, 1950, Corner Pharmacy, Lamar, Colo., 1950-53; rsch. pharmacist Nat. Chlorophyll Co., Lamar, 1953; relief pharmacist, various stores, Delta, Colo., 1957-59, Farmington, N.Mex., 1960-62, 71-79, Aztec, N.Mex., 1971-79; mgr. Med. Arts Pharmacy, Farmington, 1966-67; cons. pharmacist Navajo Hosp., Brethren in Christ Mission, Farmington, 1967-77; sales agt. Norris Realty, Farmington, 1977-78; pharmacist, owner, mgr. Lorene's Pharmacy, Farmington, 1979-88; tax cons. H&R Block, Farmington, 1968; cons. Pub. Svc. Co., N.Mex. Intermediate Clinic, Planned Parenthood, Farmington. Advisor Order Rainbow for Girls, Farmington, 1975-78. Mem. Nat. Assn. Bds. Pharmacy (com. on internship tng., com. edn., sec., treas. dist. 8, mem. impaired pharmacists adv. com., chmn. impaired pharmacists program N.Mex., 1987—, mem. law enforcement legis. com.), N.Mex. Bd. Pharmacy (first woman pres. 1987-88), Nat. Assn. Retail Druggists, N.Mex. Pharm. Assn. (mem. exec. coun. 1977-81), Order Eastern Star (Farmington). Methodist. Home and Office: 1301 Camino Sol Farmington NM 87401

MACCINI, MARGARET AGATHA, county official; b. N.Y.C., Dec. 6, 1931; d. Camillo and Mary (Varca) Vergano; m. Arthur Maccini, Sept. 25, 1955; children—Mark Robert, Alan Arthur, Deirdre Rose. Student NYU, 1949-51, CCNY, 1952. Cert. mcpl. clk. Exec. sec. Universal Pictures Inc., N.Y.C., 1952-55, Chipman Chem. Co., Bound Brook, N.J., 1956-57; corp. treas. Pyramid Bindery Inc., N.Y.C., 1957-73, pres., 1979-82; adminstrv. asst. Somerset County Bd. Chosen Freeholders, Somerville, N.J., 1973-75, dep. clk. of bd., 1975-76, clk. of bd., 1976—; ptnr., corp. sect. Branchburg Assocs., 1987—; ptnr. PVC Assocs., 1983—; co-adj. instr., mem. edn. com. Rutgers U. Dept. of Govt. Services, New Brunswick, N.J., 1983—. Bd. dirs. Voluntary Action Ctr., Somerville, 1977-80, N.J. Ctr. for the Performing Arts, Somerville, 1980-83, Camp Okee Sunokee, Bridgewater, N.J., 1980—; dir. Adult Day Care Ctr., Finderne, N.J., sec., 1977-84, commr., sec., treas. Somerset County Cultural and Heritage Commn., Somerville, 1983—, sec. 1983, treas. 1987-88; del. N.J. Counties Cultural and Heritage Assn., 1981—; co-founder, chmn. Van Wickle Dames, Somerset, 1977—; trustee Meadows Found., Inc., Somerset, 1977—, fin. chmn., grantsman, 1982—, pres. 1983-84-89, v.p. 1987, initiator, supporter Vergano Nature Conservancy; dep. registration clk. Franklin Township Election Bd., Somerset, 1970-75; mem. Somerset County Office on Aging Adv. Council, Raritan, N.J., 1978-83, LWV, 1970-71, St. Matthias Rosary Altar Soc., Somerset, 1975-83, Franklin Township Republican Club, Somerset, 1970-84, Hillsborough Township Rep. Club., Somerville, 1985; campaign sec. N.J. Assembly Candidate B. Williams, 1973. Mem. N.J. Assn., Somerset County Governing Officials Assn. (legis. com. 1987-89), Freeholder Bd. Clks. (sec. 1977-78, v.p. 1979-80, pres. 1981-89), Somerset County Mcpl. Clks. Assn. (treas. 1980-81, sec. 1982, v.p. 1983, pres. 1984), Mcpl. Clks. Assn. of N.J. (county rep., alternate 1984—, county membership chmn. 1985, consn. com. 1988), Internat. Inst. Mcpl. Clks. (mem. records mgmt. com. 1984, vice chmn. records mgmt. com. 1985), N.J. Assn. Counties (legis., pub. works and environ. coms. 1982—), Internat. Platform Assn. Somerset County 4-H Assn. (established 1987-88 and funds Vergano Agriculture Scholarship). Roman Catholic. Club: Zonta Internat. (sec. 1977-78). Avocations: cooking, traveling, gardening, farming. Home: 38 Murrary Dr Neshanic NJ 08853 Office: Somerset County North Bridge and High Sts PO Box 3000 Somerville NJ 08876

MACCOBY, ELEANOR EMMONS, psychology educator; b. Tacoma, May 15, 1917; d. Harry Eugene and Viva May (Johnson) Emmons; m. Nathan Maccoby; Sept. 16, 1938; children: Janice Maccoby Carmichael, Sarah Maccoby Bellina, Mark. BS, U Wash., 1939; MA, U. Mich., 1949, PhD, 1950. Study dir. div. program surveys USDA, Washington, 1942-46; study dir. Survey Research Ctr. U. Mich., Ann Arbor, 1946-48; lectr., research assoc. dept. social relations Harvard U., Cambridge, Mass., 1950-58; from assoc. to full prof. Stanford (Calif.) U., 1958-87, chmn. dept. psychology, 1973-76, prof. emeritus, 1987—. Author: (with R. Sears and H. Levin) Patterns of Child-Rearing, 1957, (with Carol Jacklin) Psychology of Sex Differences, 1974, Social Development, 1980; editor: (with Newcomb & Hartley) Readings in Social Psychology, 1957, The Development of Sex Differences, 1966. Recipient Gores award for Excellence in Teaching Stanford U., 1981, Disting. Contbn. to Ednl. Research award Am. Ednl. Research Assn., 1984, Disting. Sci. Contbn. to Child Devel. award Soc. for Research in Child Devel., 1987, Disting. Sci. Contbns. award Am. Psychol. Assn., 1988; named to Barbara Kimball Browning professorship Stanford U., 1979—. Fellow Soc. for Rsch. in Child Devel. (pres. 1981-83, mem. governing coun. 1963-66), Am. Psychol. Assn. (div. 7 pres. 1971-72, G. Stanley Hall award 1982), Ctr. for Youth Studies; mem. Western Psychol. Assn. (pres. 1974-75), Inst. for Rsch. on Women and Gender, Social Sci. Rsch. Coun. (chmn. 1984-85), Carnegie Counc. on Adolescence, Inst. of Medicine, Am. Acad. Arts and Scis. Democrat. Home: 729 Mayfield Stanford CA 94305 Office: Stanford U Dept Psychology Stanford CA 94305

MACCONKEY, DOROTHY I., academic administrator; b. New Brunswick, N.J.; d. Donald Thurston and Dorothy Bennett (Hill) Ingling; m. Joseph W. MacConkey, June 19, 1949 (dec. Aug. 1975); children: Donald Franklin, Diane Margaret, Dorothy Frances. BA, Beaver Coll., 1947; MA, Wichita State U., 1953; PhD, U. Md., 1974; LLD (hon.), Beaver Coll., 1988. Lectr. Wichita (Kans.) State U., 1950-51; research-campaign assoc. United Fund and Council, Wichita, 1951-62; research-com. coordination Health and Welfare Council of Nat. Capital Area, Washington, 1963-65; exec. dir. multiprogram agy. Prince Georges County Assn. for Retarded Children, Hyattsville, Md., 1965-66; prof. George Mason U., Fairfax, Va., 1966-76, asst. vice pres., acting dean, 1976-82; v.p., dean of coll. Hiram (Ohio) Coll., 1982-85; pres. Davis & Elkins (W.Va.) Coll., 1985—; bd. dirs. Davis Trust Co., Elkins, 1987—; adv. bd. George Mason U. Fdn., Fairfax, 1976—; trustee Beaver Coll., Glenside, Pa., 1971-87; cons., evaluator North Cen. Assn., Chgo., 1985—. Recipient Citizen award for service to handicapped, Fairfax County, 1981, Goddin Women Alumni award, 1985, Woman of Yr. in Edn. award W.Va. Fedn. Women's Clubs, 1986. Mem. Coun. of Pres.', Nat. Assn. Intercollegiate Athletics, Coun. Ind. Colls. (bd. dirs.). Office: Davis & Elkins Coll 100 Sycamore St Elkins WV 26241-3996

MACCRACKEN, MARY JO, physical education teacher; b. Akron, Ohio, Oct. 6, 1943; d. Joel Milton and Mary Ellen (Frame) Weaver; m. Alan Lemuel MacCracken Jr., Aug. 23, 1969; 1 child, Alan Lemuel III. BA, Coll. of Wooster, 1965; MA, U. Akron, 1969; PhD, Kent State U., 1980. Tchr., coach Hudson (Ohio) Pub. Schs., 1965-68; instr. U. Akron, 1968-78, asst. prof., then assoc. prof., 1978-88, prof., 1988—, dir. Motor Behavior Lab., 1986—; collaboration tchr. Ritzman Sch., Mason Sch., Akron, 1978—; presenter at profl. confs. Contbr. articles to refereed jours. Sunday sch. tchr. Christ Ch. Episcopal, Hudson, 1979—; vol. Liltin' Leaguers, Jr. League Cleve., 1979—; faculty mentor Akron High Sch. Drop-Out program, 1989. Grantee Ohio Bd. Regents, 1987—. Mem. AAHPERD (v.p. health Midwest dist. 1990-92; meritorious honor award Ohio assn. 1988), Am. Psychol. Assn., N.Am. Soc. for Psychology of Sport and Phys. Activity, Nat. Assn. Phys. Edn. in Higher Edn., Delta Kappa Gamma (Annie Webb Blanton award 1980). Republican. Home: Box 631 431 N Main St Hudson OH 44236 Office: U Akron Motor Behavior Lab MH 81 Akron OH 44325-5103

MACDONALD, ANNA KAY, nurse; b. Grahn, Ky., Dec. 18, 1950; d. Eaph and Cleo (Nolen) Lowe; m. Ronald Jerry MacDonald, Sept. 3, 1977 (div. 1982). B.S. in Nursing and Behavioral Sci., Loretto Heights Coll., 1983. Staff nurse intensive care unit and cardiac care unit King's Daus. Hosp., Ashland, Ky., 1971-73; commd. officer USAF, 1973, advanced through ranks to maj., 1984; med. surg. staff nurse Rickenbacker AFB Hosp., Ohio, 1973-74; charge nurse intensive care unit and cardiac care unit USAF Hosp., Colo., 1974-78, USAF Med. Ctr., Wright-Patterson AFB, Ohio, 1978-80, cardiac catheterization lab. and rehab. coordinator, 1980-82; chief nurse internal medicine br. USAF Sch. Aerospace Medicine, Brooks AFB, Tex., 1984-87; charge nurse intensive care and spl. care units USAF Med. Ctr., Keesler AFB, Miss., 1987—; instr. Am. Heart Assn., San Antonio, 1983—. Vol. United Way, San Antonio, 1985, UNICEF, Muscular Dystrophy Assn., 1985—. Mem. Am. Assn. Critical Care Nurses, Sigma Theta Tau. Democrat. Baptist. Club: Barry's San Antonio Very Strange Manifans (pres. 1985—). Avocations: piano; macrame. Home: 421 Inverness Ct Ocean Springs MS 39564 Office: USAF Med Ctr Keesler/SGHNI Keesler AFB MS 39534

MACDONALD, KAREN CRANE, occupational therapist, geriatric counselor; b. Denville, N.J., Feb. 24, 1955; d. Robert William and Jeanette Wilcox (Crane) M. BS, Quinnipiac Coll., 1977; MS, U. Bridgeport, 1982; postgrad., NYU, 1983—. Cert. occupational therapist. Occupational therapist, coord. of spl. care unit Jewish Home for the Elderly, Conn., 1987—, N.Y. Inst., N.Y.C., 1984-86; pvt. practice Fairfield County, Conn., 1977-88; instr. NYU, 1985-89, Quinnipiac Coll., 1986—; lectr., cons. in field. Contbr. articles to profl. jours. Youth leader, deacon Union Meml. Ch., Stamford, Conn., 1980-88. Teaching fellow NYU, 1983-86. Mem. World Fedn. Occupational Therapy, Am. Occupational Therapy Assn. (scholar 1985, coun. edn.), Conn. Occupational Therapy Assn. (gerontology liaison 1980-83). Home: 2600 Park Ave #3Y Bridgeport CT 06604 Office: Jewish Home for Elderly 175 Jefferson St Fairfield CT 06430

MACDONALD, KATHARINE MARCH, reporter; b. Los Angeles, Nov. 12, 1949; d. Ian G. and Eve (March) M. Grad. high sch., Beverly Hills, Calif.; student, Santa Monica Coll., 1971-73, Whittier Law Sch., Los Angeles, 1975-76. Scheduling asst. Jess Unruh for Gov., Los Angeles, 1969-70; dep. press. sec. Jess Unruh for Mayor, Los Angeles, 1973; polit. cons. various local campaigns, Los Angeles, 1973-78; researcher Washington Post-Los Angeles Bur., 1978-86; spl. corr. Washington Post-Los Angeles Bur., Washington, 1980-86; reporter State Capitol Bur. San Francisco Examiner, 1986-89; press dep. to L.A. City Councilman Zev Yaroslavsky, 1990—; guest lectr. journalism and polit. sci. various colleges and universities, 1984—. Office: City Hall Room 318 200 N Spring St Los Angeles CA 90012

MAC DONALD, SISTER MATTHEW ANITA, college president; b. N.Y.C., June 15, 1938; d. Matthew John and Jean (Ottobre) MacDonald. A.B., Chestnut Hill Coll., Phila., 1960; M.A., U. Pa., 1970, Ph.D., 1973. Cert. tchr. in English and social studies, Pa. Joined Sisters of St. Joseph of Chestnut Hill, Roman Catholic Ch., 1962; fellow in acad. adminstrn. Bryn Mawr Coll., 1974-75; assoc. prof. Chestnut Hill Coll., Phila., 1974—, dir. continuing edn., 1975-80, pres., 1980—; cons.; mem. Phila. Archdiocesan Speakers Bur., 1977—; evaluator Middle States Assn.; chairperson exec. com. Sisters of St. Joseph Coll. Consortium, 1986-88. Bd. dirs. Chestnut Hill Community Assn., 1980—; mem. Mayor's Commn. on Women, Phila., 1981-83; dir. NCCJ, 1980-82; nat. adv. bd. commn. social justice Order Sons of Italy; vice chair Pa. Commn. for Women, 1987—; trustee U. Scranton, 1989—. Fellow Philosophy of Edn. Soc., Am. Council Edn.; mem. Am. Inst. Italian Culture, Commn. Ind. Colls. and Univs. (pres.), Nat. Cath. Edn. Soc., Teilhard de Chardin Soc., Assn. Continuing Higher Edn., Found. for Ind. Colls. (exec. com. 1986-90). Democrat. Home and Office: Chestnut Hill Coll Philadelphia PA 19118-2695

MACDONALD, SHARON ETHEL, dancer; b. Pittsfield, Mass., Mar. 24, 1952; d. Harry and Angeline (Saracco) MacD. BA, Skidmore Coll., 1974; postgrad., Smith Coll., 1974-76. Faculty Smith Coll., Northampton, Mass., 1974-76; dancer, tchr. Berkshire Ballet, Pittsfield, 1976-77; dance dir. Becket (Mass.) Arts Ctr., Mass., 1977-80; faculty mem. Williams Coll., Williamstown, Mass., 1979-80; co-artistic dir., owner N.E. Am. Ballet, Northampton, 1980-85; devel. dir., tchr. Berkshire Ballet, Pittsfield, 1984-85; adminstr., tchr. Hartford (Conn.) Ballet, Inc., 1985—; asst. choreographer Easthampton Mass. Community Theatre Assn., 1981-83, Project Opera, 1982; bd. dirs. Jacob's Pillow Dance Festival, Becket, 1978-81; bd. trustees Becket Arts Ctr., 1979-80; tchr. Trinity Coll., Hartford, Conn., 1990—; guest artist numerous pub. schs., pvt. studios, colls., and univs. Pres. Friends of Jacob's Pillow, Becket, 1978-81; mem. Berkshire County (Mass.) Hist. Soc., 1989—, Friends of the Hartford Ballet, 1988—, Jacob's Pillow Almanac/Archives Com., 1988—, Dance History Scholars, 1976-79. Mass. Arts Lottery Grantee Mass. Arts Coun., 1984, Arts Lottery Grantee Northampton Arts Coun., 1984; Smith Coll. Fellow. Democrat. Baptist. Home: PO Box 697 Stockbridge MA 01262

MACDONALD, SHEILA DE MARILLAC, energy company executive; b. Santa Monica, Calif., Jan. 17, 1952; d. William Alan and M. Jane (Crotty) M. BS, Stanford U., 1975; BA, U. San Francisco, 1976; MBA, Harvard U., 1980. Fin. analyst CBS, N.Y.C., 1980-82; cons. pvt. practice Colombia, 1982-83; cons. Columbine Enterprises, Houston, 1983-88; v.p. acquisitions PSI Energy Resources, Houston, 1988-90; with Tex. Transaction Mgmt. Co., Houston, 1990—. Producer (album) Lullaby, 1984. Active Mus. of Fine Arts Guild, Contemporary Arts Mus., Houston Ballet, 1983—. Mem. Houston Assn. of Petroleum Landmen, Harvard Club of N.Y., Houston Club, Metropolitan Club. Home: 2700 Revere Apt 150 Houston TX 77098 Office: Tex Transaction Mgmt Co 5100 Westheimer Ste 1400 Ste 200 Houston TX 77056

MACDONALD, THERESA PELLEGRINO, advertising agency executive; b. Port Reading, N.J., Nov. 10, 1927; d. Matthew and Maria (DePalma) Pellegrino; m. Edward B. MacDonald, Aug. 14, 1975. BA, Bucknell U., 1949. Research asst., supr. sampling Young & Rubicam Inc., N.Y.C., 1949-59, supr. media analysis, 1959-64, asst. to media dir., 1964-70, v.p., dir. plan. devel., 1970-74, v.p., mgr. communications services, 1974-81, v.p., dir. communications devel., 1978-81, sr. v.p., 1981—; adminstrv. mgr. Young & Rubicam Inc., N.Y., 1983—. Named Woman Achiever in Bus. YWCA, 1979. Mem. Acad. Women Achievers in Bus., Cath. Assn. Radio and TV Advt. (co-chmn., dir. exec. com.), Advt. Info Services (dir., exec. com. 1975—, v.p. 1978), Am. Assn. Advt. Agys. (chmn. newspaper com.). Republican. Roman Catholic. Home: 350 W 57th St New York NY Office: Young & Rubicam 285 Madison Ave New York NY 10017*

MACDONALD, VIRGINIA B., state senator; b. El Paso, Tex.; d. Wendell Holmes and Dorothy (White) Blue; student U. N.Mex.; m. Alan Hunter MacDonald, 1941; children: Susan, Alan H. Mem. Ill. Ho. Reps., 1973-83, sec. Ho. Republican Caucus in Gen. Assembly, 1972; mem. Ill. Senate, 1983—. Del. 6th Ill. Constl. Conv., 1970; co-chmn. Cook County Rep. Cen. Com., 1964-68; co-chmn. Ill. Assembly Coun. on Women; mem. adv. com. Wheeling Twp. Rep. Com.; chmn. Statewide Women's div. Everett McKinley Dirksen's Campaign, 1968; mem. adv. council Resource Ctr. for the Elderly, Community Counciling Ctr., Suburban Br. Salvation Army; past pres. Ill. Fedn. Republican Women, 1972-74. Mem. Mt. Prospect Bus. and Profl. Women. Episcopalian.

MACDONNELL, JOANNE THERESA, writer/editor; b. Santa Rosa, Calif., Jan. 26, 1937; d. Joseph Lawrence and Mabel Alida (Strome) Capella; m. S.J. Cogliandro, Feb. 23, 1957 (div. 1963); 1 child, Cory; m. Ignacio Plancarte Lopez, June 2, 1964 (dec. 1971); children: Kenneth Lopez, Lauren Lopez; m. John Faust MacDonnell, Sept. 6, 1981. Student, U.C. Berkeley, 1955-56; BA in Eng., Journalism, San Jose State U., Calif., 1956-57. Advt. Palo Alto Times, Calif., 1960-62; columnist San Jose Mercury News, Calif., 1962-83; editor Santa Clara County Supr. Court, San Jose, Calif., 1984—; author, fund raising brochure Valley Med. Ctr., San Jose Calif. 1964; vol. Alexian Brothers Hosp. San Jose Calif. 1967; tv appearances Local Pub. TV., San Jose 1967-70. Author six-part series on unsafe toys, 1968; humor columnist San Jose Mercury News, 1977-81. Recipient 2nd Place feature series award San Francisco Press Club 1968, Achievement in writing award Santa Clara County Pen Women Los Gatos Calif. 1965. Mem. San Francisco Press Club, San Jose Newspaper Guild. Democratic. Roman Catholic. Home: 3514 El Grande Dr San Jose CA 95132

MACDOUGALL, GENEVIEVE ROCKWOOD, journalist, educator; b. Springfield, Ill., Nov. 29, 1914; d. Grover Cleveland and Flora Maurine (Fowler) Rockwood; m. Curtis D. MacDougall, June 20, 1942; children: Priscilla Ruth, Bonnie MacDougall Cottrell. BS, Northwestern U., 1936, MA, 1956, postgrad., 1963—. Reporter, Evanston (Ill.) Daily News Index, 1936-37; assoc. editor Nat. Almanac & Yearbook, Chgo., 1937-38, News Map of Week, Chgo., 1938-39; editor Springfield (Ill.) Citizens' Tribune, also area supr. Ill. Writers Project, 1940-41; reporter Chgo. City News Bur., 1942; tchr. English, social studies Skokie Jr. High Sch., Winnetka, Ill., 1956-68, coordinator TV, 1964-68; tchr. English Washburne Sch., Winnetka, 1968-81; editor Winnetka Public Schs. Staff Newsletter, 1981-87; dir. Winnetka Jr. High Archeology Field Sch., 1971-83; cons., lectr. in field. Author: Grammar Book VII, 1963, 68; (with others) 7th Grade Language Usage, 1963, rev. 1968; also articles. Winnetka Tchrs. Centennial Fund scholar, 1964, 68; named Tchr. of Year, Winnetka, 1976, Educator of Decade Northwestern U. and Found. Ill. Archeology, 1981. Mem. Winnetka Tchrs. Council (pres. 1971-72), NEA, Ill. Edn. Assn., Ill. Assn. Advancement Archeology, Women in Communications (pres. N. Shore alumni chpt. 1949-53), Pi Lambda Theta. Home: 537 Judson Ave Evanston IL 60202

MACDOUGALL, MARY KATHERINE, minister-counselor, author; b. Mt. Auburn, Ill., May 30; d. Fay Dudley and Kittie Mae (Alexander) Slate; m. Wayne Fox McMeans, Apr. 6, 1929 (dec. May 1938); children: David Fox, Nancy McMeans Richey; m. Harold Alexander MacDougall, Aug. 31, 1940 (dec. July 1949); children: Alexander, Kent, Alan; m. Lynn Gregory Schneider, Aug. 17, 1989. BA, U. Mich., 1930. Ordained minister Unity Ch., 1978. Tchr. Sandusky (Mich.) High Sch., 1939-42; editor Abilene (Tex.) Reporter News, 1950-54, Tex. Mut. Ins. Assn. Mag., Austin, 1956-57; tchr. William B. Travis High Sch., Austin, 1957-58; editor Austin Am. Statesman, 1958-59; tchr. S.F. Austin High Sch., 1959-70; adj. prof. U.Tex., Austin, 1972-74; minister Unity Ctr. Positive Prayer, Austin, 1975-90. Author: (children's) Black Jupiter, 1960; What Treasure Mapping Can Do For You, 1968; Prosperity Now, 1969; Healing Now,. 1970; Making Love Happen, 1970; Happiness Now, 1971; Dear Friend, I Love You, 1980; Sē Prosper-o...Ahora, 1982, Sē Sano... Ahora, 1983; Dear Me, I Love You, 1986, others. Del., State Dem Conv., Austin, 1990. Recipient minor journalistic awards. Mem. Women in Communication Inc., Delta Kappa Gamma. Home: 2511 Hartford Rd Austin TX 78703

MACDOWELL, ANNE KATHERINE, healthcare professional; b. Boston, Oct. 28, 1956; d. William Dunlap and Jane Mollie (Kemmerer) MacD.; m. Martin Rae Quigley, July 2, 1988. AB in Music, Swarthmore (Pa.) Coll., 1978; MBA, Harvard U., 1986. Mktg. rep. HMO of Pa., Willow Grove, 1979-81, sr. mktg. rep., 1981-82; physician coord. HMO of Pa. and N.J., Willow Grove, 1982-83; dir. provider rels. HMO of Fla., Jacksonville, 1983-84; intern healthcare dept. Booz, Allen & Hamilton, Chgo., summer 1985; asst. to the pres. Glasrock Home Health Care, Atlanta, 1986-87; gen. mgr. Glasrock Home Health Care, Kansas City, Kans., 1987-88, field reimbursement mgr., 1988-89; dir. ops. standards Glasrock Home Health Care, Rosemont, Ill., 1989—. Contbr. articles to profl. jours. Home: 3223 N Racine Chicago IL 60657 Office: Glasrock Home Health Care 10275 W Higgins Rosemont IL 66103

MACE, MARY ALICE, coal company administrator; b. Charleston, W.Va., Nov. 21, 1949; d. John Robert Leake and Georgia Alice (Wilhelm) Crist; m. Charles Michael Mace, May 20, 1968; 1 child, Christina Michelle. Student, U. Charleston, East Bank, W.Va., 1967; student, U. Charleston, 1990—. Sec. Capitol Paper Supply, Inc., Charleston, 1967-68, Persingers, Inc., Charleston, 1968-77; benefits coordinator Elk Run Coal Co., Inc., Sylvester, W.Va., 1981—; notary public. Sec. PTA, Pettus, W.Va., 1981-83, pres. 1983-85. Mem. Health Benefits Group, NAFE. Democrat. Home: 2741 Roselane Dr Charleston WV 25302 Office: Elk Run Coal Co Inc PO Box 497 Sylvester WV 25193

MACEACHERN-CONDON, LAURA, nurse, medical facility marketing executive; b. Pontiac, Mich., Dec. 27, 1954; d. Steve James and Dorothy Mae (Polasek) Condon; 1 child, Stevie James. Lic. Practical Nurse, St. Clair County Community Coll., Port Huron, Mich., 1977; postgrad., Oakland Community Coll., Union Lake, Mich., 1979; AA, NYU, 1986. RN, Calif. Owner, founder Procare I Obstetrics Nurses Registry; mktg. dir. obstretrics FHP, Fountain Valley, Calif.; dir. profl. svcs. MedStar Home Care, Beverly Hills, Calif. Recipient Rose Griffin award; Acad. scholar. Mem. ANA, NAFE, PAC Perinatal Outreach, Irvine (Calif.) C. of C. Office: 18662 MacArthur Blvd Ste 310 Irvine CA 92715

MACEDO, CHERYL A., industrial engineer; b. New Bedford, Mass., Apr. 12, 1964; d. John Manual and Gladys Elaine (Correia) Macedo. BSME, Worcester Poly. Inst., 1986, postgrad., 1986-87. Teaching asst. Worcester Poly. Inst., 1986-87; volleyball ofcl. Southeastern Mass. Volleyball Ofcls., New Bedford, Mass., 1987-88; pkg. car driver UPS, Brockton, Mass., 1987-88; indsl. engr. UPS, Norwood, 1988—; voice recognition team mem. UPS, Balt., 1988-89. Admissions liaison Worcester Poly. Inst. Admissions Office, 1986—, co-chmn. Alumni Club, Boston, 1988—. Mem. ASME, Prince Henry Soc.

MACEDONIA, MARGARET ANNE, educator; b. Dayton, Ohio, Apr. 21, 1955; d. James William and Sarah Wyatt (Clement) Tisdale; m. David Louis Macedonia, Feb. 18, 1984; children: David Michael, Nicholas James, Margaret Anne and Anna Marie (twins). B of Psychology, Coll. of William and Mary, 1977, M of Edn., 1979. Cert. tchr., Va. Spl. edn. tchr. Arlington (Va.) County Pub. Schs., 1979—, tchr. summer sch., 1980-83, 85, 87; tchr. coord. Oakridge Sch., Arlington, 1980-89, workshop presenter, 1982, ednl. diagnostician, 1983—, contact tchr. spl. edn. team, 1988-89; mem. evaluation team Arlington County Spl. Edn. State Procedures Check, 1981-82; sec. Spl. Edn. Coordinating Com., Arlington, 1981-83; tchr. rep. Kennedy Ctr. Workshop, Washington, 1982; Arlington Schs. rep. Nat. Assn. Children with Learning Disabilities Conv., 1983; mem. PTA, 1979—. Co-author: Testing Resources for Special Education Teachers, 1982. Music minister New Creation Cath. Community, Newport News, Va., 1977-79, tchr. Sunday sch., 1977-79; interpretive dancer St. Bede's Cath. Ch., Williamsburg, 1978-79; parent coordinator, coach, athletic trainer Oakridge Spl. Olympics, Arlington, 1980-85; election day campaigner Rep. Party, Arlington, 1980-83; coordinator, tchr. Lamb of God Cath. Community, Arlington, 1980-83, Christ House Food Provider, 1981-84, lectr., 1982-83; campaign worker Tribble for Senator, Arlington, 1982. Recipient Excellence in Edn. award U.S. Dept. Edn., 1986, Cert. of Appreciation Spl. Edn. Adv. Com., 1987. Mem. NEA, Arlington Edn. Assn., Arlington County Assn. Adults and Children with Learning Disabilities, Internat. Platform Assn., No. Va. Parents of Multiples Club, Nat. Mothers of Twins Clubs, Inc., William and Mary Alumnae Assn., Kappa Kappa Gamma Alumnae Assn. Home: 6000 Wilson Blvd Arlington VA 22205

MACERO, JEANETTE DIRUSSO, academic administrator; b. Somerville, Mass., Feb. 21, 1931; d. Pietro and Alessandria (Pennacchio) Dirusso; m. Daniel J. Macero, June 14, 1952; children: Diana, Peter. BA, Barnard Coll., N.Y.C., 1952; MA, Columbia U., N.Y.C., 1955; student, U. Mich., Ann Arbor, 1957. Asst. prof. Syracuse U., 1970-76, assoc. prof., 1977—; cons. Laubach Lit. Internat., Syracuse, 1980—. Author: Laubach Way to English, 1977-86. Mem. N.Y. State Tchrs. to Speakers of other Languages, Internat. TESOL (chairperson, pres., chair publs. com. 1989—), Nat. Assn. Fgn. Student Advisors, Nat. Coun. Tchrs. of English. Office: Syracuse U Dept of Fgn Langs and Lit Syracuse NY 13244

MACER-STORY, EUGENIA ANN, writer, artist; b. Mpls., Jan. 20, 1945; d. Dan Johnstone and Eugenia Loretta (Andrews) Macer; divorced; 1 child, Ezra Arthur Story. BS in Speech, Northwestern U., 1965; MFA, Columbia U., 1968. Writing instr. Polyarts, Boston, 1970-72; theater instr. Joy of Movement, Boston, 1972-75; artistic dir. Magik Mirror, Salem, Mass., 1975-76, Magick Mirror Communications, Woodstock, N.Y., 1977—. Author: Congratulations: The UFO Reality, 1978, Angels of Time, 1982, Project Midas, 1986; (plays) Fetching the Tree, Archeological Politics, Strange Inquiries, Divine Appliance, 1989, The Zig Zag Wall, 1990, The Only Qualified Huntress, 1990, others; philosophy writer; contbr. articles to profl. jours.; author poetry in Woodstock Times, Lamian Ink!, Golden Dawn, Anomalous Encounters, Manhattan Poetry Rev., others; feature writer, editorial cons. Body, Mind, Spirit mag., Golden Dawn mag., Magical Blend, others. Shubert fellow, 1968. Mem. AAAS, Dramatists Guild, N.Y. Acad. Sci., U.S. Psychotronics Assn., Ctr. for UFO Studies. Democrat. Office: Magick Mirror Communications Box 741 JAF Bldg New York NY 10116

MACGILLIVRAY, LOIS ANN, academic administrator; b. Phila., July 8, 1937; d. Alexander and Mary Ethel (Crosby) MacG. BA in History, Holy Names Coll., 1966; MA in Sociology, U. N.C., 1971, PhD in Sociology, 1973. Joined Sisters of Holy Names of Jesus and Mary, 1955. Research asst. U. N.C., Chapel Hill, 1969-70, 71-72, instr. sociology, 1970-71; sociologist Rsch. Triangle Inst., Durham, N.C., 1973-75, sr. sociologist, 1975-81; dir. Ctr. for Population and Urban-Rural Studies, Research Triangle Inst., Durham, N.C., 1976-81; pres. Holy Names Coll., Oakland, Calif., 1982—; mem. steering com. Symposium for Bus. Leaders Holy Names Coll., 1982—; mem. policy bd. Oakland Met. Univ. Forum; bd. dirs. Bay Area Bioscience Ctr., 1989. Bd. dirs. Oakland Coun. Econ. Devel., 1984-86, Bay Area Bioscience Ctr., 1989—; mem. Coconvenar Panel on Edn. and Youth, 1988—. Mem. Am. Sociol. Assn., Assn. Ind. Calif. Colls. and Univs. (exec. com. 1985—, vice chmn. 1989—), Regional Assn. East Bay Colls. and Univs. (past pres., bd. dirs. 1982—). Home: 3500 Mountain Blvd Oakland CA 94619-9989 Office: Holy Names Coll 3500 Mountain Blvd Oakland CA 94619-9989

MACGILLIVRAY, MARYANN LEVERONE, marketing consultant; b. Mpls., Oct. 18, 1947; d. Joseph Paul and Genevieve Gertrude (Ozark) Leverone; B.S., Coll. of St. Catherine, St. Paul, 1969; Med. Technologist, Hennepin County Gen. Hosp., 1970; M.B.A., Pepperdine U., 1976; m. Duncan MacGillivray, Apr. 28, 1973; children—Duncan Michael, Catherine Mary and Monica Mary (twins), Andrew John. Med. technologist Mercy Hosp., San Diego, 1970-72; with Diagnostics div. Abbott Labs., South Pasadena, Calif., 1972-79, tech. service rep., 1972-74, sr. tech. service rep., 1974-75, product coordinator, mktg., 1975-77, mktg. product mgr., 1977-79; clin. diagnostic mktg. cons., Sierra Madre, Calif., 1979-88; founder, mktg. dir. Health Craft Internat., Pasadena, Calif., 1988—. Recipient Pres.'s award Abbott Diagnostics Div., 1975. Mem. Biomed. Mktg. Assn., Am. Assn. Clin. Chemistry, Am. Assn. Clin. Pathologists, Am. Soc. Med. Tech., Calif. Assn. Med. Lab. Technologists. Roman Catholic. Home: 608 Elm Ave Sierra Madre CA 91024

MACGREGOR, BONNIE LYNN, academic administrator; b. Buffalo, Apr. 18, 1948; d. John Stevenson and Sylvia Marie (Bailey) MacG.; m. Franklin H. McCulloch, July 28, 1976. AAS, Erie County Tech. Inst., Buffalo, 1968; BS, SUNY, Buffalo, 1971, MS, 1976. Cert. bus. and distributive edn. and workstudy tchr., N.Y. Asst. bus. mgr. Sta. WKBW-TV-AM, Buffalo; tchr., chmn. dept. bus. Cheektowaga Cen. High Sch., Buffalo; lectr. D'Youville Coll., Buffalo; curriculum coord. Bryant and Stratton Bus. Schs., Buffalo. Contbr. numerous articles to profl. jours. Mem. BTANYS (pres.), Am. Vocat. Assn., BEAWNY (Post-Secondary Tchr. of Yr. 1986), NYSOEA, ASTD, PSI, NYSCEA, EBEA, NBEA, Assn. Supervision and Curriculum Devel., NAFE, Alpha Lambda. Address: 633 Delaware Ave Buffalo NY 14202

MACGREGOR, MELISSA ANN, telecommunications specialist; b. Orange, N.J., Feb. 9, 1959; d. Robert John and Marie Adele (Malone) MacG. BS, Lynchburg Coll., 1981. Project analyst Merrill Lynch, N.Y.C., 1981-83, cons., 1983-85, project mgr., telecommunications, 1985-88, asst. v.p., systems mgr., 1988—. Mem. Nat. Assn. Female Execs., Lynchburg Coll. Alumni Club (pres. 1987—). Republican. Roman Catholic. Office: Merrill Lynch World Fin Ctr New York NY 10080-0515

MACHAJ-SCHUTZ, JANICE LYNN, nuclear medicine technologist; b. Chgo., June 18, 1953; d. George Eugene and Leona Rosemary (Mocny) Machaj; m. Ernest A. Schutz, Aug. 9, 1987; children: Brian Edward, Eric Allen (twins). BS in Physics, DePaul U., 1976; Cert. in Nuclear Medicine, Hines (Ill.) Ja Hosp., 1976. Cert. clin. pathologist, radiologic tech., nuclear med. tech. Med. tech. in radioimmunoassay Foster McGaw Hosp./Loyola Univ. Med. Ctr., Maywood, Ill., 1977-88. Mem. Chgo. Clin. Radioassay Soc. (sec. 1980-81), Soc. Nuclear Medicine, Am. Registry Radiologic Techs.

MACHTIGER, HARRIET GORDON, psychoanalyst; b. N.Y.C., July 27, 1927; d. Michael J. and Miriam D. (Rand) Gordon; B.A., Bklyn. Coll., 1947; dipl. with distinction, U. London, 1966, Ph.D., 1974; m. Sidney Machtiger, Feb. 7, 1948; children: Avram Coleman, Marcia Gordon, Bennett Rand. Tchr., Phila. Pub. Schs., 1962-64; ednl. therapist Child Guidance Tng. Center, London, 1966-68; ednl. therapist Sch. Psychol. Svc., Inner London Edn. Authority, 1968-70; therapist Paddington Day Hosp., London, 1970-71, London Centre for Psychotherapy, 1971-74, Staunton Clinic, U. Pitts., 1974-78; pvt. practice psychoanalysis, Pitts., 1976—; pres. C.G. Jung Ctr., Pitts., 1976-81; cons. in field. Mem. S.W. Pitts. Community Mental Health, 1976-78; past dir. Pitts. program Inter-Regional Soc. Jungian Analysts, 1975-85. Recipient award for Disting. Contributions to Advancement in Edn., Pa. Dept. Edn., 1962; Social Sci. Rsch. Coun. award, 1973; cert. psychologist, Pa. Fellow Am. Orthopsychiat. Assn.; mem. Am. Psychol. Assn., N.Y. Assn. Analytical Psychologists, Internat. Assn. Group Psychotherapists, Pa. Psychol. Assn., Brit. Psychol. Soc., Brit. Assn. Psychotherapists, Assn. Child Psychology and Child Psychiatry, Western Pa. Group Psychotherapy Assn., Nat. Assn. for Advancement Psychoanalysis, NOW. Home: 207 Tennyson Ave Pittsburgh PA 15213 Office: 123 Cathedral Mansions 4716 Ellsworth Ave Pittsburgh PA 15213

MACIA, SYLVIA, banker; b. Columbus, Ga., May 24, 1964; d. Roberto and Maria del Carmen (Gutierrez) M. BA, Fla. Internat. U., 1988. Mcht. banking officer Pvt. Bank & Trust, N.A., Miami, Fla., 1988—. Campaign worker various local and nat. Rep. candidates, Miami, 1982-87. Mem. Coalition Hispanic Am. Women, Mortar Bd., Kappa Kappa Gamma. Roman Catholic. Office: Pvt Bank & Trust NA 1438 Brickell Ave Miami FL 33131

MACIAS, VERONICA DENISE, systems analyst; b. West Plains, Mo., Jan. 21, 1958; d. Kenneth Walter and Dorys Ann (Downen) Wilson; m. Mark Tadeusz Dec, July 10, 1976 (div. 1981); 1 child, Autumn Rose Dec; m. Jose Carlos Macias, Aug. 5, 1988. Student, Kans. City Art Inst., 1976-77; AA, Longview Coll., 1988. Cert. technician cons. Xerox laser printers. Carhop Dog-N-Suds, Independence, Mo., 1971; from waitress to asst. mgr. Sizzler Family Steakhouse, Independence, 1973-75; broiler chef York Steakhouse, Independence, 1975-77; sales clk. Children's Palace, Independence, 1977-78; asst. mgr. Burger King Am., Independence, 1980-81; membership sec. Bd. Realtors Kansas City, Kansas City, Mo., 1981-82; data processing assoc.

IRS, Kansas City, 1981-83; computer tape libr. U.S. Dept. Agr., Kansas City, 1983-85; sr. computer operator analyst AT&T Microelectronics Inc., Lee's Summit, Mo., 1985-89; sr. computer equip. analyst and telecommunications cons. AT&T Microelectronics, Mesquite, Tex., 1989—; cons. Santa Fe Computer Club, Independence, 1987-88; speaker Single Parents' Coping, 1987, Women's Equal Credit Rights, 1987. Canvasser Dem. Party, Kansas City, 1988, telephone assoc, Independence, 1988; aerobics instr. Greater Kansas City Community Workshop on Aging, N. Kansas City, Mo., 1987-88; activist Am. Hispanics Rights Group, Kansas City, 1989. Mem. Nat. Forensic League (treas. 1975-76), Thesbians Soc., Friends of the Zoo, DECA (pres. Independence chpt. 1974-76), Nat. Assn. Female Execs., Am. Bus. Women's Assn. Baptist. Home: 834 W 30th St Independence MO 64055 Office: AT&T Microelectronics 3000 Skyline Mesquite TX 75149-1802

MACINNES, MARGO, writer; b. Troy, N.Y.; d. Harold Boyce and Julia (Storr) MacI.; m. Richard Shackson (div. 1971); children: Carol Ann Luongo, Russell Mark. BA in Am. Studies, U. Mich., 1971. Asst. dean U. Mich., Ann Arbor, 1970-80; pres. MacInnes & Assocs., Inc., Ann Arbor, 1980-85; editor Henry Ford Mus. and Greenfield Village, Dearborn, Mich., 1985—; cons., judge Internat. Assn. Bus. Communicators, 1986—; writer, photographer. Bd. dirs. Soundings, Ann Arbor, 1985—. Recipient Exceptional Achievement and Merit awards Coun. for Advancement and Support of Edn. Mem. Internat. Assn. Bus. Communicators. Home: 1125 Newport Rd Ann Arbor MI 48103

MACIUSZKO, KATHLEEN LYNN, librarian, educator; b. Nogales, Ariz., Apr. 8, 1947; d. Thomas and Stephanie (Horowski) Mart; m. Jerzy Janusz Maciuszko, Dec. 11, 1976; 1 child, Christinia Alexsandra. BA, Ea. Mich. U., 1969; MLS, Kent State U., 1974; PhD, Case Western Res. U., 1987. Reference libr. Baldwin-Wallace Coll. Libr., Berea, Ohio, 1974-77, dir. Conservatory of Music Libr., 1977-85; dir. bus. info. svcs. Harcourt Brace Jovanovich, Inc., Cleve., 1985-89; staff asst. to exec. dir. Cuyahoga County Pub. Libr., Cleve., 1989-90; dir. Cleve. Area Met. Library System, Beachwood, Ohio, 1990—. Author: OCLC: A Decade of Development, 1967-77, 1984; contbr. articles to profl. jours. Named Plenum Pub. scholar, 1986. Mem. Spl. Librs. Assn. (pres. Cleve. chpt. 1989-90, v.p. 1988-89, editor newsletter 1988-89), Baldwin-Wallace Coll. Faculty Women's Club (pres. 1975),. Office: Cleve Area Met Libr System 3645 Warrensville Center Rd Beachwood OH 44122

MACIVOR, HAZEL JUDITH ARNOLD, retired teacher, genealogist; b. Holly Creek, Ga., Nov. 18, 1921; d. Charles Dewey and Vergia Plummer Paralee (Teem) Arnold; m. Lenwood Wilson Elliott, Sept. 24, 1938 (div. 1940); m. Angus Stewart MacIvor Jr., Dec. 7, 1940; children: Angus Stewart III, Sandra Susan, Charlene Margaret MacIvor Burns, Victoria Dion MacIvor Carson, Catherine Jane. BEd, Wayne State U., 1958, MA, y. Cert. secondary edn. tchr., Mich. History tchr. Detroit Bd. Edn., 1958-63, S. Macomb Community Coll., Warren, Mich., 1961-62, Oak Park (Mich.) Bd. Edn., 1963-66; sec., cons. MacIvor Cons., Inc., Marshfield, Mass., 1984-87; pvt. practice genealogy Marshfield, 1971—. Author: Benjamin Arnold of New Kent County, Va. and Greenville, S.C., 1974; editor Arnold Family of the South jour., 1971-84; contbr. articles on genealogy to profl. publs. Chmn. Dem. Party, Royal Oak, Mich., 1953, fundraiser, 1950's; active Oakland County coun. Camp Fire Girls, 1950's, leader, 1958-59; sponsor Future Tchrs. of Am., Chadsey High Sch., Detroit, 1962-63; vol. tchr. Adult Illiteracy Program, Gainesville, Ga., 1989—. Recipient Red Feather award Father Weinman Settlement Ho., Detroit, 1949. Mem. Nova Scotia Genealogical Soc., United Daus. of Confederacy, U.S. Daus. of War of 1812, DAR (vice regent Ezra Parker chpt. 1976-78, regent Col. Thomas Lothrop chpt. 1982-83, regent Col. William Candler chpt. 1989—, chmn. bicentennial com. 1976-78), United Daus. of the Confederacy, U.S. Daus. War of 1812, Daus. of Founders and Patriots, Nat. Huguenot Soc., London Huguenot Soc., Soc. Descents Colonial Clergy, Daus. Colonial Wars, Daus. of Am. Colonists, Colonial Dames of XVII Century, Flagon and Trencher, Order of Soc. of Colonial Physicians and Chirurgiens, Magna Carta Dames, Order of Ams. of Armorial Ancestry, Order of the Crown of Charlemagne, Nat. Soc. Ams. Royal Descent, Pi Lambda Theta. Episcopalian. Home: 2358 Thompson Bridge Rd NE #3 Gainesville GA 30501

MACK, BRENDA LEE, sociologist, public relations consulting company executive; b. Peoria, Ill., Mar. 24; d. William James and Virginia Julia (Pickett) Palmer; m. Rozene Mack, Jan. 13 (div.); 1 child, Kevin Anthony. AA, L.A. City Coll.; BA in Sociology, Calif. State U., L.A., 1980. Ct. clk. City of Blythe, Calif.; partner Mack Trucking Co., Blythe; ombudsman, sec. bus facilities So. Calif. Rapid Transit Dist., L.A., 1974-81; owner Brenda Mack Enterprises, L.A., 1981—; lectr., writer, radio and TV personality; cons. European community; co-originator advt. concept View/Door Project; pub. News from the United States newsletter through U.S. and Europe. Past bd. dirs. Narcotic Symposium, L.A. With WAC, U.S. Army. Mem. Women For, Calif. State U. L.A. Alumni, German-Am. C. of C., European Community Studies Assn. Home: 8749 Cattaraugus Ave Los Angeles CA 90034 Office: Brenda Mack Enterprises PO Box 5942 Los Angeles CA 90055

MACK, CRISTINA IANNONE, accountant; b. Olean, N.Y., Sept. 25, 1940; d. Angelo M. and Rose M. (Sirianni) Iannone; m. John O. Mack, Nov. 19, 1967; children—Elizabeth, Andrew. B.A. in Math., U. Calif.-Santa Barbara, 1962; postgrad. U. San Francisco, 1978—, Golden Gate U., 1983. Exec. dir. Bar Assn. San Francisco, 1966-68; owner, acct. CIM Assocs., San Francisco, 1978—; pres. Pacific Staff Inc., 1987—. Treas. Mothers Milk Bank, 1977-87; bd. dirs. Am. Paralysis Assn. Aux., 1984; precinct adminstr. Rep. County Central Com., 1964-66; Coro Found. fellow, 1963. Mem. Calif. Agrl. Assn. (bd. dirs. dist. 1-A 1986—), Chi Omega Sorority (pres. 1962, treas. 1984-89), Calif. Dist. 1-A Agrl. Assn. (bd. dirs.). Roman Catholic. Club: San Francisco Lawyers Wives (pres. 1974, auditor 1978—). Lodge: Little Sisters of Poor Aux. Avocations: hunting; tennis. Home: 2963 23d Ave San Francisco CA 94132 Office: 114 Sansome St Suite 1205 San Francisco CA 94104

MACK, DEBRA KAYE, lawyer; b. New Orleans, Mar. 29, 1955; d. Willie Bell Mack and Dorothy (Maples) Watson. BA, Dillard U., 1976; JD, Loyola Law Sch., 1979. Bar: La. 1979. Recreational asst. New Orleans Recreation Dept., 1973-79; pub. defender Orleans Indigent Defender Program, New Orleans, 1979-81; staff atty. Larry P. Williams Law Firm, New Orleans, 1979-81; part-time instr. bus. law Ga. State U., Atlanta, 1982; spl. agt. atty. FBI, Newark, 1985-89; supervisory spl. agt., atty. FBI, Washington, 1989—; part-time instr. bus. law Dillard U., New Orleans, 1981; EEO counselor FBI, Newark, 1986—; legal advisor FBI, Newark, 1986—; gen. police instr. FBI, 1986—; target selection interviewer FBI, 1986—, mem. speaker's bur. Mem. Coalition of Black Women, Newark, 1989. Mem. Nat. Bar Assn., La. Bar Assn., Garden State Bar Assn., Assn. Black Women Lawyers, Nat. Orgn. Black Law Enforcement. Democrat. Office: FBI 10th and Pennsylvania Ave Washington DC 20535

MACK, JULIA COOPER, appellate judge; b. Fayetteville, N.C., July 17, 1920; d. Dallas L. and Emily (McKay) Perry; m. Jerry S. Cooper, July 30, 1943; 1 dau., Cheryl; m. Clifford S. Mack, Nov. 21, 1957. B.S., Hampton Inst., 1940; LL.B., Howard U., 1951. Bar: D.C. 1952. Legal cons. OPS, Washington, 1952-53; atty.-advisor office gen. counsel Gen. Svcs. Adminstrn., Washington, 1953-54; trial appellate atty. criminal div. Dept. Justice, Washington, 1954-68; civil rights atty. Office Gen. Counsel, Equal Employment Opportunity Commn., Washington, 1968-75; assoc. judge Ct. Appeals, Washington, 1975-89; sr. judge, 1989—. Mem. Am., Fed., Washington, Nat. Bar Assns., Nat. Assn. Women Judges. Home: 1610 Varnum St NW Washington DC 20011 Office: DC Ct Appeals 500 Indiana Ave NW 6th Fl Washington DC 20001

MACK, MARY ELIZABETH, advertising agency executive. Reporter Am. Statesman, Austin, Tex.; with mktg. ops. Pizza Inn Restaurants, Dallas; account exec. Tracy-Locke, Bozell & Jacobs, Dallas; account exec. Bloom Agy., Dallas, from 1981, v.p., then sr. v.p. Office: Bloom Agy 3500 Maple Dallas TX 75219*

MACK, MOLLY ANN, university professor; b. Portland, Oreg., July 19, 1950; d. Robert Smith and Gretchen Ann (Sutter) M.; m. Gary Thomas Whitmer, May 10, 1985. BA in English, Willamette U., 1972; MA in English, U. Vt., 1976; PhD in Linguistics, Brown U., 1983. Instr. summer enrichment program U. Vt., Burlington, 1975; teaching asst. Dept. Linguistics, Brown U., Providence, 1978-80; instr. English as a Foreign Lang. Program, Brown U., Providence, 1978-82; rsch. asst. Dept. Linguistics, Brown U., Providence, 1980-82; asst. prof. Dept. Psychology, Wellesley (Mass.) Coll., 1984; post-doctoral rsch. fellow Dept. Linguistics, Brown U., 1984; speech researcher MIT Lincoln Lab., Lexington, Mass., 1983-85; now cons. MIT Lincoln Lab., Lexington; asst. prof. div. English as internat. lang. U. Ill., Urbana, 1985—; also asst. prof. dept. linguistics U. Ill.; cons. in field. Contbr. numerous articles to profl. jours. Recipient Univ. Fellowship Brown U., 1977, Summer Linguistics Inst. Fellowship, 1980, Helen Swallow Richards Endowed Fellowship AAUW, 1982, Dean's Fund Travel Grant U. Ill., 1988, Internat. Research Support Grant in the Humanities and Arts U. Ill., 1988, Research Bd. awards U. Ill., 1987, 88, 89, 90; named Fellow in the Ctr. for Advanced Study U. Ill., 1988. Mem. AAUW, Acoustical Soc. Am., Am. Assn. Applied Linguistics, Linguistic Soc. Am., N.Y. Acad. Sci., Delta Gamma, Alpha Lambda Delta. Democrat. Home: 2004A Eagle Ridge Ct Urbana IL 61801 Office: U Ill Div English as Int Lang 707 S Mathews Ave Urbana IL 61801

MACK, SARA ROHRBACH, librarian, educator; b. Topton, Pa., Nov. 20, 1921; d. Jonathan H. and Alda S. (Heffner) Rohrbach; m. George Mack, June 26, 1943 (wid. Jan. 1949); 1 child, Carol Mack Foy. BS, Kutztown State Tchrs. Coll., 1943; MS in Libr. Sci., Columbia U., 1955; postgrad., Temple U. and U. Pa. Elem. tchr. Chalfont (Pa.) Pub. Sch., 1943-45; libr. Mt. Penn Jr.-Sr. High Sch., Reading, Pa., 1949-58; prof. libr. sci. Kutztown (Pa.) State Coll., 1958-82, dept. chmn., 1977-82; retired, 1982; adj. prof. Drexel U., Phila., 1968; bd. dirs. Friends of the Reading-Berks Pub. Librs., pres., 1983-84, exec. bd., 1985—. Compiler: Inspirational Readings for Elementary Grades, 1964; contbr. articles to profl. jours, book reviewer; contbg. author: American Reference Books Annual, Along the Saucony. Trustee Kutztown U. Council, 1983—; com. chmn. Kutztown Area Hist. Soc., 1983—; church libr. Trinity Lutheran Ch., Topton, 1966—; del. to Penn. Govs. Conf. onLibrs., 1990. Recipient Superior Teaching award Kutztown State Coll., 1962, Alumni Citation, 1980, 88, Award of Merit, Pa. Libr. Assn., 1969; named Outstanding Contbr. to Sch. Libr. Programs, Pa. Sch. Librs. Assn., 1981. Mem. ALA (com. mem. 1945), Pa. Libr. Assn., Pa. Sch. Librs. Assn. (pres. 1963-65, exec. bd. 1977-80), Ch. and Synagogue Libr. Assn. (speaker and book reviewer), Pa. Citizens for Better Librs., Emeriti Faculty Kutztown U. (coord. 1989—), Phila. Children's Reading Roundtable, Am. Assn. Univ. Women, Delta Kappa Gamma. Home: 44 A South Elm St Kutztown PA 19530

MACKAY, PATRICIA MCINTOSH, counselor; b. San Francisco, Sept. 12, 1922; d. William Carroll and Louise Edgerton (Keen) McIntosh; A.B. in Psychology, U. Calif., Berkeley, 1944, elem. teaching credential, 1951; M.A. in Psychology, John F. Kennedy U., Orinda, Calif., 1979; Ph.D. in Nutrition, Donsbach U., Huntington Beach, Calif., 1981; m. Alden Thorndike Mackay, Dec. 15, 1945; children—Patricia Louise, James McIntosh, Donald Sage. Elem. tchr. Mt. Diablo Unified Sch. Dist., Concord, Calif., 1950-60; exec. supr. No. Calif. Welcome Wagon Internat., 1960-67; wedding cons. Mackay Creative Services, Walnut Creek, Calif., 1969-70; co-owner Courtesy Calls, Greeters and Concord Welcoming Services, Walnut Creek, 1971—; marriage, family and child counselor, nutrition cons., Walnut Creek, 1979—; coordinator Alameda and Contra Costa County chpts. Parents United, 1985—, pres. region 2; bd. dirs. New Directions Counseling Center, Inc., 1975—, founder, pres. aux., 1977—. Bd. dirs. Ministry in the Marketplace, Inc.; founder, dir. Turning Point Counseling; bd. dirs. counseling dir. Shepherd's Gate-shelter for homeless women and children, 1985—. Recipient Individual award New Directions Counseling Center, 1978, awards Neo-Life Co. Am. Prestige Club, yearly, 1977-86. Mem. Assn. Marriage and Family Therapists, C. of C., Prytanean Alumnae, Delta Gamma. Republican. Mem. Zion Fellowship. Club: Soroptomist (dir. 1976, 86) (Walnut Creek). Home: 1101 Scots Ln Walnut Creek CA 94596 Office: 1399 Ygnacio Valley Rd Suite 12 Walnut Creek CA 94598

MACKECHNIE, LINDA ALLEN, special education administrator; b. Morgantown, W. Va., Feb. 16, 1950; d. Virgil I. and Gwendolyn M. (Tucker) Allen; m. Allan C. Mackechnie, Nov. 23, 1973; children: Candice, Elizabeth, Robynn. BS in Edn., U. Ala., 1972; MA in Vocat. Rehab., Auburn U., 1975; postgrad in Edn., U. S.C., 1985. Cert. tchr. 5 areas, S.C. Tchr. Lee County Bd. of Edn., Opelika, Ala., 1972-73, Chambers County Bd. of Edn., Lafayette, Ala., 1973-74; coord. spl. svcs. Chambers County Bd. of Edn., Lafayette, 1974-77; supr. adult svcs. Charles Lea Ctr., Spartanburg, S.C., 1977-79; tchr. S.C. Sch. Deaf & Blind, Spartanburg, 1980-81, pre-vocat. tchr., 1981-85, edn. supr., 1985-87, edn. specialist, 1987-88, asst. prin., 1988—. Regional organizer Spl. Olympics, Area 12 Coun., Spartanburg, S.C., 1981; pres. Coun. for Exceptional Children, 1986-88; bd. dirs. United Cerebral Palsy, Raleigh, N.C., 1989-91; pres. Tri-County Cerebral Palsy Support Assn., Spartanburg, 1990-91; mem. chmn. Assn. Retarded Citizens, Spartanburg, 1987. Mem. AAUW. Democrat. Unitarian. Home: 7908 Valley Falls Rd Spartanburg SC 29303 Office: SC Sch Deaf & Blind Cedar Springs Station Spartanburg SC 29302

MACKENZIE, DIANNE VERONICA, computer programmer, systems analyst; b. Providence, Mar. 3, 1947; d. John Domenic and Angelina Loretta (Di Pasquali) Lombardi; m. David Mackenzie, July 4, 1968 (div. Oct. 1981); children: Heather Nicole, Joshua Morgan. BS, Boston U., 1969. Programmer Media Records, N.Y.C., 1981; programmer analyst Savs. Bank Trust Co., N.Y.C., 1981-82, Guardian Life Ins. Co., N.Y.C., 1982-83; sr. programmer analyst Chase Manhattan Bank, New Hyde Park, N.Y., 1983-85; programming mgr. Doubleday Book Clubs, Garden City, N.Y., 1985-86; cons. Merrill Lynch, N.Y.C., 1986-87; tech. officer Chem. Bank, N.Y.C., 1987-88; cons. L.I. Savs. Bank, East Northport, N.Y., 1988, Mfrs. Hanover Trust, 1989; tech. dir., sec.-treas. Brosis Enterprises, Inc., East Northport, N.Y., 1989—; cons. East Northport, N.Y., 1988—; cons. L.I. Savs. Bank, 1987-88, Mfrs. Hanover Trust, 1988—; bd. dirs. Arrow Electronics. Sec. Northport/East Northport Youth Ctr. Soccer Club, 1981-85; bd. dirs. Katrina Trask Nursery Sch., Saratoga Springs, N.Y., 1976-78. Mem. Ind. Computer Cons. Assn., NAFE. Home: 281 Laurel Rd East Northport NY 11731 Office: Brosis Enterprises Inc 281 Laurel Rd East Northport NY 11731

MACKENZIE, JULIANNE SCHLASS, computer software executive, international marketing executive; b. Darby, Pa., Aug. 9, 1953; d. Jerome J. and Patricia (Cullen) Schlass; m. John Edward Mackenzie, Aug. 12, 1989. BA in Mgmt./Computer Sci., Boston Coll., 1975. Lead programmer, analyst New Eng. Life Ins. Co., Boston, 1975-80; product cons. Ins. Systems Am., Atlanta, 1980-82, adv. systems cons., 1982-85, mng. fin. cons., 1985-86, mgr. internat. cons., 1986-88, mgr. global markets, 1989—. Fellow Life Office Mgmt. Assn.; mem. Nat. Assn. Female Execs., Data Processing Mgmt. Assn., Beta Gamma Sigma. Home: 3107 Queen Anne Ct Dunwoody GA 30350 Office: Info Systems Am 500 North Ridge Rd Atlanta GA 30350

MACKENZIE, LINDA ALICE, computer company executive, consultant telecommunications; b. Bronx, N.Y., June 24, 1949; d. Gino Joseph and Mary J. (Damon) Arale; m. John Michael Lassourreille, Aug. 7, 1968 (div. 1975); 1 child, Lisa Marie Lassourreille; m. Donald John Mackenzie, July 2, 1978 (div. 1982). Student Richmond Coll., 1967-68, West L.A. Community Coll., 1978-81. Spl. rep. N.Y. Telephone Co., White Plains, 1968-71; asst. mgr. Paul Holmes Real Estate Inc., Richmond, N.Y., 1974-77; telcom applications specialist engring. Continental Airlines, L.A., 1977-83; data transmission specialist Western Airlines, Los Angeles, 1983-87; owner Computers on Consignment, El Segundo, Calif., 1984—; cons. Farwest Brokers, L.A., 1984-85, Caleb Feb. Credit Union, Las Vegas, Nev., 1985, Nat. Dissemenators, Las Vegas, 1985, Vega & Assocs. Prodn. Div., 1987, Uptech/Downtech, 1986, Dollar Rent-a-Car, 1987, Pomona Sch. Dist., 1987, Advanced Digital Networks, 1987; mktg. cons. AT&T, L.A., 1984-85. Author: The World Within, 1983. Active Calif. Lobbyists for Conservation, 1986. Contbr.: Am. Anthology Poetry, 1987, 88., Poetic Voices of America, 1988. Recipient Alexander award Met. Mus. Art, N.Y., 1967. Mem. Nat. Assn. Female Execs., El Segundo C. of C., Mgmt. Assocs. (assoc.). Republican. Clubs: Marina City, Manhattan Beach Women's. Avocations: painting, creative writing, aerobic dance, skiing, travel. Office: Computers on Consignment 531 Main St Suite 426 El Segundo CA 90245

MACKENZIE, MARY HAWKINS, hospitality placement company executive; b. St. Louis, July 27, 1936; d. Henry Goodheart and Elizabeth Cummings (Collins) Hawkins; m. Robert S. McGregor, Sept. 3, 1956 (div. May 1973); children—Robert B., Mary Catherine McGregor Ryan, Susan Leigh; m. Kenneth W. MacKenzie, Jr., Apr. 24, 1976; 1 son, Kenneth W. III. B.A., So. Methodist U., 1957. Ctr. dir. YWCA, Dallas, 1966-67; profl. cons. in personnel M. David Lowe, Houston, 1973-75; employment mgr. St. Joseph Hosp., Houston, 1976-78; personnel dir. Greater Houston Hosp. Council, 1978; personnel dir. exec. com. Dunfey Hotel, Houston, 1978-81; pres. The Hotelier Inc., Houston, 1981—; adj. prof. Sch. of Hotel Restaurant Mgmt. Houston Community Coll., 1989-90; industry adv. bd. High Sch. for Restaurant and Travel Careers, 1986-87; guest columnist The Houston Chronicle and The Houston Post, 1987, 88, 89, Houston Busches Jour., 1990. Chmn. bd. dirs. Houston Jazz Ballet, 1979; mem. vestry Ch. of the Epiphany, Houston, 1979-82; judge Houston Women on the Move, 1987; mem. adv. bd. hotel restaurant mgmt. div., Houston Community Coll., 1988—, mem. 8 for '88 bd. Am. Lung Assn. Mem. Houston Hotel Motel Assn. (assoc.), Tex. Assn. Personnel Cons., Tex. Exec. Women (pres. 1984-85), Houston Women on the Move (chmn. 1985), Houston Hotel Personnel Dirs. (founder, exec. 1980-81), Am. Inst. Wine and Food, Delta Gamma. Episcopalian. Avocation: Running. Office: The Hotelier Inc 6776 Southwest Frwy Ste 150 Houston TX 77074

MACKERELL, KERRY, marketing professional; b. Lansdale, Pa., Oct. 11, 1959; d. William Jr. and Susan (Myers) MacKerrell. BA in Psychology, Dickinson Coll., 1981. Child care counselor Silver Springs-Martin Luther Sch., Plymouth Meeting, Pa., 1982-84; mgr. office Nat. Hosp. Equipment Report, Inc., Ft. Washington, Pa., 1984-86; v.p. Nat. Hosp. Equipment Report, Inc., Montgomeryville, Pa., 1988-89; mkt. rsch. prodn. dir. med. device register div. Hosp. Equip. Report, Inc., Stamford, Conn., 1989—. Mem. NAFE, Environ. Coun. Stamford, Nat. Wildlife Fedn., Nat. Parks and Conservation Assn. Democrat. Presbyterian. Office: Hospital Equipment Report 655 Washington Blvd Stamford CT 06901

MACKETY, CAROLYN J., operating room nurse; b. Chgo., Feb. 27, 1932; d. Gerald J. and Minnette (Buis) Kruyf; m. Robert Martin, Oct. 3, 1952 (div.); m. Armand Mackety, Apr. 15, 1972 (div.); children: Daniel, David, Steven, Martin, Laura Fitzgerald. RN, Hackley Hosp., Muskegon, Mich., 1969; BA, Coll. St. Francis, Joliet, Ill., 1977; MA, Columbia Pacific U., San Rafael, Calif., 1987. Dir. surg. svcs. Grant Med. Ctr., Columbus, Ohio; pres. Laser Cons., Inc., Chgo.; v.p. Laser Ctrs. Am., Cin.; nursing adminstr. Med. Ctr. Hosp., Burlington, Vt. Contbr. articles to profl. jours. Mem. Assn. Operating Rm. Nurses, Am. Soc. Laser Medicine, Internat. Laser Soc. (bd. dirs.). Home: 1 Bay Rd #5 Shelburne VT 05482

MACKEY, DOROTHEA MARGARETTE, professional sports team manager; b. N.Y., Nov. 1, 1925; d. Harold and Dorothy (Cinnamon) Warner; m. John Edward George, Nov. 6, 1943; m. Daisley, Oct. 24, 1945; children: Roger, Ronald, Dawn Dorothy. Profl. skater N.Y., 1942—, profl. sports team exec.; N.Y. state champion Am. Roller Skating Assn., 1942-43, 46-47; U.S. Champion, 1943-44, 46-47. Featured films include Bingo Madness, 1986, The Steps, 1987. Elected Com. Republican, Islip, 1971-81. Recipient Medal of Merit Rep. Pres. Task Force, Bronze medal, 1942; runner-up Ladies Pairs, 1942, 3rd pl. runner-up Sr. Singles, 3rd pl. pairs, 1946. Mem. Am. Security Council. Republican. Episcopalian. Home: 124 Drake Ct West Islip NY 11795

MACKEY, MRS. JAMES A. See BRYAN, BILLIE MARIE

MACKEY, LENORA JARVIS, social services administrator, social worker; b. Powells Point, N.C., Oct. 14, 1944; d. William Columbus and Martha Ann (Case) Jarvis; m. Claudie James Mackey, May 28, 1966; 1 child: Hasani Jabari Mackey. B.S., Elizabeth City State U., 1966; Cert. in Community Orgn., Columbia U. Sch. Social Work, 1973. Cert. social worker, N.C. Caseworker, N.Y.C. Dept. Social Sevices, Bklyn., 1966-72; community organizer N.Y. Dept. Social Services, 1972-74; protective services worker Spl. Services for Children, Jamaica, N.Y., 1975-77; living-learning specialist Elizabeth City State U., N.C., 1978-79, coordinator living-learning program, 1979-82, human resources dir., Ctr. Rural and Coastal Living, 1989—; dir. Correlation of Youth Services program, Currituck County Involvement Council, N.C., 1983—; bd. dirs. Friends of the Court/One-on-One Program, 1987—; v.p. N.C. Peer Helpers Assn. Editor: (newspaper) Viking Yard, 1980-82. Bd. dirs. Elizabeth City Boys Club, 1983—, Am. Cancer Soc., Elizabeth City, 1984— ; mem. Pasquotank Action Council, Elizabeth City, 1984—, NAACP, 1985—. Recipient Outstanding Services award Elizabeth City State U. Gen. Alumni Assn., 1981, Meritorious Achievement award Jack & Jill of Am. Inc., 1982, Gov.'s Vol. award State of N.C., 1984, 85, 86, 87, Outstanding Service award Community Based Alt. Region VII, 1987, Cert. Appreciation for Vol. Services St. Jude's Childrens Research Hosp., 1982-87. Mem. Assn. Black Social Workers, Am. Assn. Counseling and Devel., Nat. Assn. Univ. Women, Elizabeth City Bus. and Profl. Women's Club, Alpha Kappa Alpha. Democrat. Clubs: Elizabeth City State U. Booster (pres. 1979-82, Most Outstanding Booster award 1982), Jack & Jill of Am. Inc. (pres. 1980-82), Pasquotank County Homemakers Extension Assn. (2d v.p. 1982-84). Home: 2213 Meads St Elizabeth City NC 27909 Office: Ctr Coastal and Rural Living ECSU PO Box 913 Elizabeth City NC 27909

MACKIE, CAROLYN LEE, lawyer; b. Lower Merion, Pa., May 11, 1962; d. Donald Alan and Clara Leedom (Buffum) M. BA, U. Pa., 1984; JD cum laude, U. Ga., 1987. Bar: Ga., 1987. Law clk. to judge U.S. Ct. Appeals (11th cir.), Newnan, Ga., 1987-88; assoc. Long, Aldridge & Norman, Atlanta, 1988-90; asst. regional counsel Office Gen. Counsel HHS, Atlanta, 1990—. Mem. ABA, State Bar Ga., Atlanta Bar Assn. Democrat. Episcopalian. Office: HHS Office Gen Counsel 101 Marietta Tower Ste 521 Atlanta GA 30323

MACKIE, DIAN BOYCE, electronics company executive; b. Piedmont, Ala., Oct. 11, 1950; d. Wesley and Jeannette (Herod) Boals; 1 child, Jamie Heatherton Boyce; m. Bruce Russell Mackie, 1990; children: Shaina, Jordan. BSBA, U. Cen. Fla., 1976. Dist. sales mgr. MDB Systems, Orlando, Fla., 1980-85; owner Sensations Inc., Winter Park, Fla., 1985-86; sr. sales engr. Emulex Corp., Orlando, 1986-87; regional sales mgr. Datacube, Inc., Orlando, 1988-89; standard products mgr. Automatix Inc., Orlando, 1989-90; pres. Dimac, Inc., Orlando, 1990—. Past pres. Orlando PTA; chmn. local sch. adv. com. Mem. NAFE. Baptist. Home: PO Box 691046 Orlando FL 32869-1046

MACKIE, DIANA JANE, management consultant; b. Oak Park, Ill., Sept. 29, 1946; d. Charles George and R. Carol (Bauersfeld) M. BS, U. Ill., 1968; MS, MIT, 1970, MBA, 1979. Chemist Nyanza, Ashland, Mass., 1970-71; tech. brand mgr. Procter & Gamble Co., Cin., 1972-77, asst. advt. brand mgr., 1977-78; assoc. McKinsey & Co., Inc., N.Y.C., 1979-85, prin., 1986—. Contbr. articles to profl. publs. Bd. govs. MIT Alumni Ctr., N.Y.C., 1989—. Named best advisor of yr. Jr. Achievement, Cin., 1978. Mem. Rockefeller Club. Presbyterian. Office: McKinsey & Co Inc 55 E 52d St New York NY 10022

MACKIE, SHIRLEY M., composer; b. Rockdale, Tex., Oct. 25, 1929; d. John Ransom and Marie (McLean) M. BM, La. State U., 1949, MusM, 1950; studies with, Darius Milhaud, Paris, 1953, Nadia Boulanger, Paris, 1959, 68. Freelance composer Waco, Tex., 1950—; dir. music McLennan County Dept. Edn., Waco, 1959-78; assoc. prof. music U. of Mary Hardin-Baylor, Belton, Tex., 1954-57; founder/condr. Chamber Orch. Waco, 1961-69; prin. clarinetist Waco Symphony, 1962-64. Composer solos for soprano, bassoon, flute, clarinet, including Five Moods, 1965, Three Movements, 1968, ballet Gemini's Journey, 1967, Opera Mister Man, 1963, Dance in the Brazos Brakes, 1973, symphony orch. Symphony for the Bicentennial, 1976, synthesizer, chorus and orch., Comments, 1976; contbr. articles to profl. jours. Mem. Cen. Tex. Zool. and Bot. Soc., Tex. Composers Forum. Episcopalian. Address: 100 Wilderness Rd Rte 12 Box 430 Waco TX 76712

MACKIEWICZ, ANNE LISA, computer company official; b. Scituate, Mass., Sept. 25, 1950; d. Henry Michael and Martha Mary (Lavoine) M. BA cum laude, Salem State Coll., 1972; postgrad., North Adams State

Coll., 1974, Leslie Coll., 1975, Wesleyan U., Middletown, Conn., 1975. Cert. secondary English, French and history tchr., Mass. Tchr. English, Drury High Sch., North Adams, Mass., 1972-76, Silver Lake Jr. High Sch., Halifax, Mass., 1977-78, Marlboro (Mass.) High Sch., 1978-81; substitute tchr. South Shore area Mass., 1976-78; tchr. drama Braintree (Mass.) High Sch., summer 1977; tech. writer Digital Equipment Corp., Littleton, Mass., 1982-89; product tng. mgr. Digital Equipment Corp., Stow, Mass., 1989—. Recipient merit award Soc. for Tech. Communications, 1985; Mass. Bd. Higher Edn. scholar, 1970. Mem. Sterling Inst. (team leader 1988), Smithsonian Assocs., Ea. Interclub Ski League (race mem. 1978-89, club rep. 1979-81), Wedeln Ski Club (Lowell, Mass., social chmn. 1978, tri-club sec. 1984-86, 89-90, editor yearbook 1978, 79). Office: Digital Equipment Corp 40 Old Bolton Rd Stow MA 01775

MACKIEWICZ, LAURA, advertising agency executive. Formerly with D'Arcy Advt.; with BBDO, Chgo., 1973—, v.p., now sr. v.p. and dir. ops. Office: BBDO Chgo 410 N Michigan Ave Chicago IL 60611*

MAC KIMM, MARGARET PONTIUS (MARDIE), public relations executive; b. Chgo., July 14, 1933; d. Guy Victor and Jane H. (Irvine) Pontius; children—Thomas J., Daniel C., David G. B.A., Coll. William and Mary, 1955. Chgo. editor Gifts and Decorative Accessories, 1966-69; dir. public relations and sales promotion Gen. Fire Extinguisher Corp., Northbrook, Ill., 1969-72; sr. staff writer Kraftco Corp., Glenview, Ill., 1972-74; v.p., dir. public relations Kraftco Corp., 1974-76, Kraft, Inc., Glenview, 1976-80; sr. v.p. public affairs Kraft, Inc., 1980-81; v.p. public affairs Dart & Kraft, Inc., Northbrook, Ill., 1981-86; sr. v.p. corp. communications Kraft, Inc., Glenview, Ill., 1986—; dir. E.I. du Pont de Nemours & Co., F.W. Woolworth Co.; exec. com. Chgo. Community Trust. Trustee, nat. council 4-H, 1978—; dir. Chgo. United Way-Crusade of Mercy, 1980—; chair Chgo. Network, 1981-84. Clubs: Women's Athletic Economic, Commercial (Chgo.). Office: Kraft Inc Kraft Ct Glenview IL 60025

MACKINNON, MARION ELIZABETH, sales executive; b. Providence, Sept. 9, 1952; d. Gordon Henry and Marion Joanna (Taylor) MacK. BA, Emerson Coll., 1972; cert. in teaching, Mass. Maritime Acad., 1973; postgrad., Hyannis (Mass.) Coll., 1972-73. Salesperson Sta. WJAR subs. Outlet Broadcasting Co., Providence, 1974-80, Sta. XTRA subs. Noble Multimedia Broadcasting, San Diego, 1980-81; sales mgr. Sta. KLAV sub. Korngold Broadcasting, Las Vegas, 1981-82; gen. sales mgr. Sta. KLAU subs. Corngold Broadcasting, Las Vegas, 1982-84; cons. direct mktg. response Sta. KABC, Los Angeles, 1982-88; gen. sales mgr. Sta WRQX, Cap Cities ABC, Washington, 1988—; tchr. Smithfield (R.I.) High Sch., 1978-84; gen. sales mgr. Kottcom Broadcasting, San Bernardino, Calif., 1981-82; freelance sales trainer. Youth dir. Girls Friendly Soc., Providence, 1970-74; dir. Falmouth (Mass.) Theatrical Dept., 1972-74, Episcopal Diocese Youth Group; asst. dir. Smithfield Theatrical Group; youth dir. Girls Friendly Soc., Providence, 1970; supporter YMCA, Los Angeles, 1982—; creative cons. Jewish Community Ctr. Hope High Sch., Providence. Recipient Honorary Plaque YMCA, L.A., 1985, Commendation award Fairfax Rels. Coun., L.A., 1987. Mem. So. Calif. Broadcasting Assn., Los Angeles Ad Club, Long Beach C. of C. (com. 1985—); chairwoman R.I. Women Advt. Home and Office: 5708 Aberdeen Rd Bethesda MD 20814

MACKINNON, MAUREEN ELIZABETH, banker; b. Malden, Mass., Jan. 16, 1966; d. John Angus and Geraldine Pauline (Shomph) MacK. Cert. culinary arts, Assabet Valley Regional Vocat. High Sch., Marlboro, Mass. Teller to asst. mgr. Bay Bank Middlesex, Marlboro, Mass., 1985-86; asst. mgr. N. Middlesex Savs. Bank, Littleton, Mass., 1986-88, mgr., asst. treas., 1988—. Mem. Nat. Assn. Female Execs. Office: North Middlesex Savs Bank 225 Great Rd Littleton MA 01460

MACKINNON, NANCY WILLIAMS, retired educator, state legislator; b. Boston, July 18, 1925; d. Nathaniel White and Rose Francis (Bates) Williams; m. Gerald Langtry MacKinnon Jr., Apr. 3, 1948 (dec. 1967); children: Marcia MacKinnon Calabro, Geoffrey W. BS in Edn., Boston U., 1947; M in Edn. and Human Resources, New Eng. Coll., 1982. Cert. tchr., N.H. Sec. Boston Navy Yard, Charlston, Mass., 1944-45; tchr. Derry (N.H.) Sch. Dist., 1967-88; mem. N.H. Ho. of Reps., Concord, 1988—. Mem. Derry Budget Com., 1978-82; mem. fin. com. Derry Sch. Dist., 1986-88. Mem. N.H. Retired Tchrs. Assn., Orgn. Women Legislators, P.E.O. (chaplain Derry chpt. 1988—). Home: PO Box 117 71 Hampstead Rd East Derry NH 03041

MACKLER, JUDITH ANN, real estate developer; b. Evansville, Ind., June 22, 1945; d. Samuel Davis and Emma Louetta (Carter) Stooksberry; m. Donald Franklin Mackler, Jan. 14, 1979; children: Joshua Reuben, Jacob Isaac. BS, Nebr. Wesleyan U., 1968. Lab. mgr. Kerbs Meml. Hosp., St. Albans, Vt., 1974-78; lab. mgmt. cons. St. Albans (Vt.) Hosp., 1976-78; office mgr. Donald F. Mackler M.D., Chattanooga, 1979-82; residential comml. sales Fletcher Bright Co., Chattanooga; comml. sales Darlene Brown Inc., Realtors, Chattanooga, 1988--; mgmt. cons. Interiors by Lynn Love, 1986—, comml. edn. com. Chattanooga Assn. Realtors, comml. multiple listing com., 1989. Co-founder, bd. mem. Chattanooga chpt. for Ileitis and Colitis, co-founder, chmn. Neighbors Against Crime, v.p. Walker-Catoosa-Dade County Med. Aux., Northwest Ga., buyer qualification Chattanooga Neighborhood Enterprise, Religious Sch. Bd. Mizpah congreg. Mem. Nat. and Local Assn. Realtors. Home: 312 S Crest Rd PO Box 3612 Chattanooga TN 37404 Office: 3496 Brainerd Rd Chattanooga TN 37411

MACKNIGHT, CAROL BERNIER, educational administrator; b. Quincy, Mass., Apr. 12, 1938; d. Harold Nelson and Marguerite (Norris) Bernier; m. William J. MacKnight, July 19, 1967. BS, Ithaca Coll., N.Y., 1960; MM, Manhattan Sch. Mus., N.Y.C., 1961; Dipl., Fontainebleau Sch. Music/Art, France, 1963; EdD, U. Mass., 1973. Asst. to supt. Falmouth (Mass.) pub. schs., 1975-76; dir. bus., mgmt., engring. prog. Sch. Bus. Adminstrn. U. Mass., Amherst, 1976-79; assoc. dir. continuing edn. U. Mass., 1979-82, dir. Office Instructional Tech., 1982—; bd. trustees New Eng. Reg. Computing Prog., Inc., 1986—. Editor Jour. Computing in Higher Edn., 1988—; author/editor computer progs.; contbr. articles to profl. jours. CDC grantee, 1986, Regents of Boston grantee, 1988. Mem. ACM, Assn. for Computing Machinery, Soc. Applied Learning Tech., Assn. for Devel. of Computer Based Instructional Systems. Home: 127 Sunset Ave Amherst MA 01002 Office: Office Instructional Tech A115 Lederle Grad Res Ctr Amherst MA 01003

MACKO, HELEN ANN, architect, interior designer; b. Bratislava, Czechoslovakia, Aug. 16, 1937; came to U.S., 1969; d. Ludovit L. and Barbara E. Lednar; m. Vlado Macko, July 20, 1930; 1 child, Daniel. BArch, Tech. U., Bratislava, 1964, MArch, 1966. Lic. architect, N.Y., N.J., Conn.; lic. interior designer. Designer Project Orgn. for Health Facilities, Bratislava, 1966; prin. Bauform Architecture, Brauschweig, Fed. Republic of Germany, 1968-69; assoc. Switzer & Zegler Architects, Bronxville, N.Y., 1970-76; prin. Helen Macko Interior Design, White Plains, N.Y., 1977-81; ptnr. Ballantyne Macko Architects, White Plains, 1982-85; prin. Helen Macko Architect, White Plains, 1985-87; ptnr. Bauform Cima Architects & Engrs., White Plains, 1988-90; prin. Bauform Architecture & Interiors, White Plains, 1989—. Mem. AIA (chairperson pub. rels. com. 1984-85), Am. Soc. Interior Designers. Republican. Roman Catholic. Office: Bauform Architecture 9 Pinewood Circle North White Plains NY 10603

MACKOWIAK, ELAINE DECUSATIS, pharmacist, educator; b. Hazleton, Pa., Apr. 28, 1940; d. Stanley Joseph and Veronica Marie (Zabrosky) DeCusatis; m. Robert C. Mackowiak, Sept. 5, 1964 (wid. Sept. 1984); children: Jeffrey, Lisa. BS in Pharmacy, Temple U., 1962, MS in Radiation Health, 1965; PhD in Pharmacology, Thomas Jefferson U., 1974. Registered pharmacist. Asst. chief pharmacist Holy Redeemer Hosp., Huntingdon Valley, Pa., 1962-63; lectr. Sch. Dist. Phila., 1964-68; instr. Temple U., Phila., 1964-73, asst. prof., 1973-77, assoc. prof., 1977-86, prof., 1986—; vis. prof. Montgomery County Community Coll., Blue Bell, Pa., 1974—; radiation cons. AIRCO, Rare and Speciality Gases, Riverton, N.J., 1982-88, N.J. Bur. of Environ. Labs., Trenton, 1985. Author: (book chpt.) Sterile Dosage Forms, 1987; contbr. articles to profl. jours. Active parent's bd. Mt. St. Joseph Acad., Flourtown, Pa., 1987—. Recipient several awards Temple U. Sch. Pharmacy, 1962. Mem. Am. Pharm. Assn., Pa. Pharm. Assn., Am. Assn. Colls. of Pharmacy, Health Physics Soc., Pharmacy Alumni Assn. of Phila. (bd. dirs. 1965—, cert. honor 1979),Temple U. Alumni Assn. (bd. dirs. 1977—), Thomas Jefferson U. Grad. Sch. Alumni Assn. (bd. dirs. 1980-86), Rho Chi, Sigma Xi, Magnet Honor Soc. Roman Catholic. Home: 189 E Hillcrest Ave Philadelphia PA 19118 Office: Sch of Pharmacy/Temple Univ 3307 N Broad St Philadelphia PA 19140

MACLACHLAN, PATRICIA, author; b. Cheyenne, Wyo.. Tchr. English. Author: The Sick Day, 1979, Arthur, For the Very First Time, 1980, Moon, Stars, Frogs, and Friends, 1980, Through Granda's Eyes, 1980, Mama One, Mama Two, 1982, Tomorrow's Wizard, 1982, Cassie Binegar, 1982, Seven Kisses in a Row, 1983, Unclaimed Treasure, 1984, Sarah, Plain and Tall, 1985 (Newbery medal). Office: care Harper Jr Books 10 E 53rd St New York NY 10022*

MACLAINE, SHIRLEY, actress; b. Richmond, Va., Apr. 24, 1934; d. Ira O. and Kathlyn (MacLean) Beaty; m. Steve Parker, Sept. 17, 1954; 1 dau., Stephanie Sachiko. Ed. high sch. Broadway plays include Me and Juliet, 1953, Pajama Game, 1954; films: The Touble With Harry, 1954, Artists and Models, 1954, Around the World in 80 Days, 1955-56, Hot Spell, 1957, The Matchmaker, 1957, The Sheepman, 1957, Some Came Running, 1958 (Fgn. Press award 1959), Ask Any Girl, 1959 (Silver Bear award as best actress Internat. Berlin Film Festival), Career, 1959, Can-Can, 1959, The Apartment, 1959 (Best Actress prize Venice Film Festival), Children's Hour, 1960, The Apartment, 1960, Two for the Seesaw, 1962, Irma La Douce, 1963, What A Way to Go and, Yellow Rolls Royce, 1964, John Goldfarb Please Come Home, 1965, Gambit and Woman Times Seven, 1967, The Bliss of Mrs. Blossom, Sweet Charity, 1969, Two Mules for Sister Sara, 1969, Desperate Characters, 1971, The Possession of Joel Delaney, 1972, The Other Half of the Sky: A China Memoir, 1975, The Turning Point, 1977, Being There, 1979, A Change of Seasons, 1980, Loving Couples, 1980, Terms of Endearment, 1983 (Acad. award 1984), Madame Sousatzka, 1988 (Best Actress Venice Film Festival), Steel Magnolias, 1989, Waiting For the Light, 1990, Postcards From the Edge, 1990; TV shows Shirley's World, 1971-72, Shirley MacLaine: If They Could See Me Now, 1974-75, Gypsy in My Soul, 1975-76, Where Do We Go From Here?, 1976-77, Shirley MacLaine at the Lido, 1979, Shirley MacLaine . . . Every Little Movement, 1980; producer, co-dir.: documentary on China The Other Half of the Sky; star U.S. tour stage musical Out There Tonight, 1990; author: Don't Fall Off the Mountain, 1970, The New Celebrity Cookbook, 1973, You Can Get There From Here, 1975, Out on a Limb, 1983, Dancing in the Light, 1985, It's All in the Playing, 1987, Going Within: A Guide for Inner Transformation, 1989; editor: McGovern: The Man and His Beliefs, 1972. Office: MacLaine Enterprises 1900 Ave of the Stars #760 Los Angeles CA 90067

MACLEOD, CHARLOTTE, author; b. Bath, N.B., Can., Sept. 12, 1922; d. Edward Philips and Mabel Maude (Hayward) MacL. Mem. advt. firm N.H. Miller & Co., Inc., Boston, 1952-82. Author: Astrology for Skeptics, 1972, Rest You Merry, 1978, The Family Vault, 1979, The Luck Runs Out, 1979, The Withdrawing Room, 1980, The Grub-and-Stakers Move a Mountain, 1981, The Palace Guard, 1981, Murder Goes Mumming, 1981, A Pint of Murder, 1982, Wrack and Rune, 1982, Cirak's Daughter, 1982, The Bilbao Looking Glass, 1982, Something the Cat Dragged In, 1983, The Terrible Tide, 1983, The Convivial Codfish, 1984, Maid of Honor, 1984, The Grub-and-Stakers Quilt a Bee, 1985, The Curse of the Giant Hogweed, 1985, The Plain Old Man, 1985, The Corpse in Oozak's Pond, 1987, Vane Pursuit, 1989, (works for juveniles) Mystery of the White Knight, 1964, Next Door to Danger, 1965, The Food of Love, 1965, Headlines for Caroline, 1967, The Fat Lady's Ghost, 1968, Mouse's Vineyard, 1968, Ask Me No Questions, 1971, Brass Pounder, 1971, King Devil, 1978, We Dare Not Go A-Hunting, 1980; contbr. articles and stories to mags. Office: ICM care Ted Mathes 40 W 57th St New York NY 10019*

MACLEOD, MILLIE EVELYN, city council member; b. Larimore, N.D., Dec. 16, 1933; d. Selmer and Elsie (Amanda) Moen; m. Robert Nathan MacLeod, June 9, 1956; children: Barbara Ann, Mary Lee, Robert Bruce. BS, Concordia Coll., Moorhead, Minn., 1955; student, Iowa State U., 1953-54; postgrad., Phys. Edn. Inst., U. Oslo, Norway, 1956. Tchr. Brainerd (Minn.) High Sch., 1956-57, Concordia Coll., Moorhead, Minn., 1957-59, Brainerd High Sch., 1959-62; substitute tchr. Roseville (Minn.) Sch. Dist., 1962-65; reg. mgmt. cons. Camp Fire Inc., Kansas City, Kans., 1974-77; council mem. City of Moorhead, 1977—; policy mem. N.L.C. energy environ. and natural resources com., Washington, 1985-86, steering com. fin., adminstrn. and intergovtl. relations com., 1986—. Vice chmn. fed. legis. com. Luth. Ch., St. Paul, 1985—; mem. Mayors-Citizens Adv. Com., Moorhead, 1973-77; bd. dirs. Plains Art Mus., 1979—. Recipient Ernest Seton award, Camp Fire, Inc., 1969, Luther Gulick award, 1975, others. Mem. Nat. League Cities, Minn. League Cities (v.p. 1988-89, pres. 1989-90), Minn. Planning Assn., Women's Athletic Assn. (pres. 1971-72), PEO. Home: 1111 23rd Ave S Moorhead MN 56560

MACMANUS, SUSAN ANN, political science educator, researcher; b. Tampa, Fla., Aug. 22, 1947; d. Harold Cameron and Elizabeth (Riegler) MacM. BA cum laude, Fla. State U., 1968, PhD, 1975; MA, U. Mich., 1969. Instr. Valencia Community Coll., Orlando, Fla., 1969-73; rsch. asst. Fla. State U., 1973-75; asst. prof. U. Houston, 1975-79, assoc. prof., 1979-85, dir. M of Pub. Adminstrn. program, 1983-85, rsch. assoc. Ctr Pub. Policy 1982-85; prof., dir. PhD program Cleve. State U., 1985-87; prof. pub. adminstrn. and polit. sci., U. South Fla., Tampa, 1987—, chairperson dept. govt. and internat. affairs, 1987—; vis. prof. U. Okla., Norman, 1981—; field rsch. assoc. Brookings Instn., Washington, 1977-82, Columbia U., summer 1979, Princeton (N.J.) U., 1979—, Nat. Acad. Pub. Adminstrn., Washington, summer 1980, Cleve. State U., 1982-83, Westat, Inc., Washington, 1983—. Author: Revenue Patterns in U.S. Cities and Suburbs: A Comparative Analysis, 1978, (with others) Governing A Changing America, 1984, (with Francis T. Borkowski) Visions for The Future: Creating New Institutional Relationships Among Academia, Business, Government, and Community, 1989; writer manuals in field; mem. editorial bds. various jours.; contbr. articles to jours. and chpts. to books. Bd. dirs. Houston Area Women's Ctr., 1977, past pres., v.p. fin., treas.; mem. LWV, Gov.'s Coun. Econ. Advisers, 1988—, Harris County (Tex.) Women's Polit. Caucus, Houston; bd. dirs. USF Rsch. Found., Inc. Recipient U. Houston Coll. Social Scis. Teaching Excellence award, 1977, Herbert J. Simon Award for best article in 3d vol. Internat. Jour. Pub. Adminstrn., 1981; Ford Found. fellow, 1967-68; grantee Valencia Community Coll. Faculty, 1972, U. Houston, 1976-77, 79, 83; Fulbright Rsch. scholar, Korea, 1989. Mem. Am. Polit. Sci. Assn. (program com. 1983-84, chair sect. intergovtl. rels., award 1989), So. Polit. Sci. Assn. (v.p.-elect 1989, V.O. key award com. 1983-84, best paper on women and politics 1988), Midwest Polit. Sci. Assn., Western Polit. Sci. Assn., Southwestern Polit. Sci. Assn. (local arrangements com. 1982-83, profession com. 1977-80), Am. Soc. Pub. Adminstrn. (nominating com. Houston chpt. 1983), Policy Studies Orgn. (mem. editorial bd. jour. 1981—, exec. coun. 1983-85), Women's Caucus Polit. Sci. (portfolio predecision rev. com. 1982-83, projects and programs com. 1981, fin.-budget com. 1980-81), Acad. Polit. Sci., Mcpl. Fin. Officers Assn., Phi Beta Kappa, Phi Kappa Phi, Pi Sigma Alpha. Republican. Methodist. Home: 746 Collier Pkwy Land O'Lakes FL 34639 Office: U South Fla Dept Govt and Internat Affairs Soc 107 Tampa FL 33620

MACMILLAN, CATHERINE COPE, restaurant owner; b. Sacramento, Mar. 3, 1947; d. Newton A. Cope and Marilyn (Jacobs) Combrink; m. Thomas C. MacMillan, Dec. 18, 1967 (div. Jan. 1984); children: Corey Jacobs, Andrew Cope. BA, U. Calif., 1969; MBA, Calif. State U., Sacramento, 1978. Pub. health microbiologist County of Sacramento, 1969-74; pres., gen. mgr. The Firehouse Restaurant, Sacramento, 1980—; bd. dirs. Westamerica Bank, San Rafael, Calif., Am. Recreation Ctrs., Sacramento. Chmn. Sacramento Conv. and Visitors Bur., 1987-88; pres. Old Sacramento Propery Owners Coun., 1987; mem. Sacramento Sports Commn, 1988-89. Mem. Calif. Restaurant Assn. (bd. dirs.), Sacramento Restaurant Assn. (Restaurateur of Yr. 1983), Old Sacramento Citizen's and Mchts. Assn. (chmn. bd. 1984), Sacramento Met. C. of C. Office: The Firehouse Restaurant 1112 Second St Sacramento CA 95814

MACMILLAN, JOANN LAWLER, hospital executive; b. Pitts., June 25, 1926; d. Albert Michael and Lucylle (Nye) Lawler; m. Francis Williams MacMillan Sr., Dec. 27, 1952; children: Francis Williams Jr., Lucylle Lynn, Sandra Nye. AA, Va. Intermont Coll., 1945; BA, U. N.C., 1947; MEd, N.C. State U., 1970. Dir. pub. info. Fayetteville (N.C.) Tech. Inst., 1969-79; v.p. Acclaim! Artists' Assocs., Ltd., Fayetteville, 1979-84; dir. mktg. Cumberland Hosp., Fayetteville, 1984-86, asst. adminstr. market devel., 1986—; pres. NETWORTH, Fayetteville, 1988—; bd. dirs. 1st Union Nat. Bank, Fayetteville. Co-author: (play) Infamous Love, 1979. Mem. Fayetteville Mus. Art. Named Vol. of Yr., Fayetteville YMCA, 1979, Fayetteville Mental Health Assn., 1987. Mem. Nat. Assn. Corp. Speakers of Am. (N.C. chpt.), Nat. Dramatists' Guild, NOW, Highland Country Club. Democrat. Presbyterian. Home: 2707 Bennington Rd Fayetteville NC 28303 Office: Cumberland Hosp 3425 Melrose Rd Fayetteville NC 28304

MACMILLAN, TRACY MARIE, sales and marketing executive; b. Cleve., May 20, 1953; d. Norman P. and Geraldine A. (Heintz) Ladd; m. Howard C. MacMillan, Feb. 22, 1986. BA, Nazareth Coll., 1975. Account exec. Hutchins/Young and Rubicam, Rochester, N.Y., 1979-85, Roberts Communications, Rochester, 1985-86; account mgr. LML & P Advt., Providence, 1986-87; mgr. spl. accounts North Safety Equipment, Cranston, R.I., 1987—. Recipient Achievement award Sherwin-Williams Co., Cranston, 1988. Mem. NAFE. Home: 72 Pheasant Dr Cranston RI 02920

MACMULLEN, JEAN ALEXANDRIA STEWART, nurse, administrator; b. N.Y.C., Feb. 21, 1945; d. John Douglas and Isabella Stewart (Park) MacM. Diploma in nursing, Lenox Hill Hosp., N.Y.C., 1965; BS in Nursing, Adelphi U., 1969, MS in Nursing, 1971; MA in Anthropology, U. South Fla., 1978. Nurse renal disease unit N.Y. Hosp., N.Y.C., 1971-72; clin. nurse specialist VA Hosp., Tampa, Fla., 1972-76, med./surg. coord., 1976-82; assoc. chief nurse VA Med. Ctr., Gainesville, Fla., 1982—. Jour. editor Am. Assn. Nephrology Nurses, Pitman, N.J., 1980-82, referee, adviser, 1983—; contbr. numerous articles to profl. publs. Mem. Fla. Nurses Assn., Fla. Orgn. Nurse Execs. Republican. Episcopalian. Office: VA Med Ctr 1601 Archer Rd Gainesville FL 32608

MACNAMARA, SUSAN ELIZABETH, psychologist; b. Mpls., Dec. 6, 1955; d. Harold Charles and Alice Louise (Needham) M.; m. Alan Barker Hayes, Aug. 14, 1983. BA, St. Olaf Coll., Northfield, Minn., 1979; MA, U. Utah, 1981, PhD, 1985. Lic. psychologist, Utah. Coord. cognitive stimulation project Salt Lake VA Med. Ctr., Salt Lake City, 1984-86; coord. directions employee asst. program Intermountain Health Care, Salt Lake City, 1986-87; psychologist Quinney Rehab. Inst., Salt Lake City, 1987-88, Assessment and Psychotherapy Assocs., Inc., Salt Lake City, 1988—, Intermountain Rehab. Ctr. at LDS Hosp., Salt Lake City, 1988—; data analysis cons., Salt Lake City, 1981-87. Contbr. articles to profl. jours. Vol. tutor Literacy Action Ctr., Salt Lake City, 1987—. Mem. Am. Psychol. Assn., Utah Psychol. Assn. Home: 940 E Laird Ave Salt Lake City UT 84105 Office: Intermountain Rehab Ctr LDS Hosp 8th Ave and C St Salt Lake City UT 84143

MACO, TERI R., consumer products company professional, child placement firm executive; b. Allentown, Pa., Nov. 4, 1953; d. Francis M. and Jacqueline K. (Becker) Regan; m. Bruce F. Maco, Oct. 1, 1983; children: Adam S., Alex M. BSChemE with honors, Lehigh U., 1975; MBA with distinction, U. New Haven, 1979. Supr. Ivory, Procter & Gamble Mfg. Co., S.I., N.Y., 1975-77; asst. mgr. processing Chesebrough-Ponds, Inc., Clinton, Conn., 1977-81, sec. and bd. dirs. credit union, 1980; group supr. Johnson & Johnson, Ft. Washington, Pa., 1981-83, mgr. processing, 1983-84, mgr. nat. planning, 1984-87; group mgr. acctg. McNeil Computer Products, Inc., Ft. Washington, 1987—; pres. Child Placement Network, Inc., Norristown, Pa., 1989—; developer computer-based tng. program. Author: Capital Asset Pricing Model: Capital Budgeting Applications (NAA Manuscript award 1979). Mem. INA, NAA, CCAC, NACCRRA, MDCPA, Nat. Assn. for Family Day Care. Democrat. Roman Catholic. Home: 4183 Ironbridge Dr Collegeville PA 19426 Office: McNeil Consumer Products Inc Camp Hill Rd Fort Washington PA 19034 also: Child Placement Network Inc 2720 Potshop Rd Norristown PA 19403

MACON, IRENE ELIZABETH, designer, consultant; b. East St. Louis, Ill., May 11, 1935; d. David and Thelma (Eastlen) Dunn; m. Robert Teco Macon, Feb. 12, 1954; children: Leland Sean, Walter Edwin, Gary Keith, Jill Renee Macon Martin, Robin Jeffrey, Lamont. Student Forest Park Coll., Washington U., St. Louis, 1970, Bailey Tech. Coll., 1975, Lindenwood Coll., 1981. Office mgr. Cardinal Glennon Hosp., St. Louis, 1965-72; interior designer J.C. Penney Co., Jennings, Mo., 1972-73; entrepreneur Irene Designs Unltd., St. Louis, 1974—; vol. liaison Pub. Sch. System, St. Louis, 1980-82; cons. in field. Inventor venetian blinds for autos, 1981, T-blouse and diaper wrap, 1986; author 26th Word newsletter, 1986. Committeewoman Republican party, St. Louis, 1984; vice chair 4th Senatorial Dist. of Mo., 1984, vol. St. Louis Assn. Community Orgns., 1983; instr. first aid Bi-State chpt. ARC, St. Louis, 1984; cubmaster pack #80 Keystone dist. Boy Scouts Am.; block capt. Operation Brightside, St. Louis, 1984; co-chair status and role of women Union Meml. United Meth. Ch., 1986—, program resource sec., 1990—; trustee Wofit Found., 1989. Named One of Top Ladies of Distinction St. Louis, 1983. Mem. Am. Soc. Interior Designers (assoc.), NAACP, Nat. Mus. Women in the Arts (charter), Internat. Platform Assn., Nat. Council Negro Women (1st v.p. 1984), Invention Assn. of St. Louis (subcom. head 1985), Coalition of 100 Black Women, St. Louis Assn. Fashion Designers, Pres. Club. Methodist. Avocations: reading; designing personal wardrobe; modeling; horseback riding; boating. Home and Office: PO Box 20370 Saint Louis MO 63112-0370

MACON, MYRA FAYE, library director; b. Slate Springs, Miss., Sept. 29, 1937; d. Thomas Howard and Reba Elizabeth (Edwards) M. BS in Edn., Delta State U., 1959; MLS, La. State U., 1965; postgrad., U. Akron, Ohio; EdD, Miss. State U., 1977. Librarian Greenwood (Miss.) Jr. High Sch., 1959-62, Greenwood High Sch., 1962-63, Grenada (Miss.) High Sch., 1963-64; library supr. Cuyahoga Falls (Ohio) City Schs., 1964-71; assoc. prof. U. Miss., Oxford, 1971-83; dir. libraries Delta State U., Cleve., 1983—. Editor: School Library Media Services for Handicapped; editor: ANRT Newsletter, Miss. Libraries; contbr. articles to profl. jours. Mem. ALA, Southeastern Library Assn., Miss. Library Assn., Phi Delta Kappa, Beta Phi Mu, Delta Kappa Gamma, Omicron Delta Kappa. Home: 307 S Fifth Ave Cleveland MS 38732 Office: Delta State U WB Robers Library Cleveland MS 38733

MACPHERSON, ALEXA ZIVLEY BINNION, communication executive; b. Dallas, June 26, 1956; d. Robert Charles and Janie Wood (Cotten) Binnion; m. Frank Becker MacPherson, Feb. 14, 1985; children: Jennifer Ryan, Ian Becker. BA, Wells Coll., Aurora, N.Y., 1978; MBA, Temple U., Phila., 1982. Fin. writer Fidelity Bank, Phila., 1978-81; writer, sr. cons. The Mader Group Fin. Tech., Narbeth, Pa., 1981-82; asst. to pres. communication Sunshine-Jr. Stores, Panama City, Fla., 1983-85; copy chief, account exec. Fin. Communications, Wash.; corp. communications cons. Milford, Mass., 1987-89. Vol. The Jr. League, Phila. 1982, Panama City Fla. 1983-85, Wash. 1986, Boston 1987-89. Mem. Phi Beta Kappa. Republican. Episcopal. Home: 406 Reading Ave Pennington NJ 08534

MACRAE, MARY JENKINS, career and motivation speaker, trainer and workshop leader; b. Nashville, Jan. 6, 1954; d. George T. Sr. and Mary Ellen (Barnes) Jenkins; m. Johnny MacRae, Dec. 6, 1984. BBA summa cum laude, Tenn State U., Nashville, 1986; postgrad., Vanderbilt U., Nashville. Asst. dir. Office Patient Affairs Vanderbilt Med. Ctr., Nashville, 1972-83; dir. mktg. Venture Tek, Inc., Nashville, 1986-87; owner, sr. cons. First Impressions, Ashland, Tenn., 1987—. Author: Get a Job...No, Get a Great Career, The American Dream 101: or, How to Start and Manage Your Own Small Business, The Winner's Attitude: Choose It or Lose It!. Vol. speaker, instr. for disadvantaged high sch. students; bd. dirs, co-chair United Way of Middle Tenn.; mem. Crisis Intervention Ctr., telephone counselor, 1978-80. Named Disting. Prof. Tenn. State U. Small Bus. Devel. and Tng. Programs, one of Outstanding Young Women Am., 1981; recipient cert. appreciation 101st Airborne Div. and Ft. Campbell Mil. Base, 1990, Voice of Democracy award, 1972. Mem. ASTD (pres. Middle Tenn. chpt. 1990—). Office: 1102 N Main St PO Box 579 Ashland City TN 37015

MACROE-WIEGAND, VIOLA LUCILLE, psychiatrist, psychoanalyst; b. Indiana, Pa., May 17, 1920; d. Joseph Cyprian and Lucy E. (Colson) Macro; BA, St. Joseph's Coll. for Women, 1941; MA, Columbia U., 1942, PhD, 1958; MD, U. Hamburg (Germany), 1962; m. Thomas F. Gordon, Nov. 23, 1977. Instr. and chief psychologist Manhattan Eye and Ear Hosp., N.Y.U. Med. Sch., N.Y.C., 1952-58; lectr. dept. psychiatry SUNY Downstate Med.

Ctr., Bklyn., 1962-63; psychiat. fellow Creedmore State Hosp., Queens, N.Y. 1962-63; intern U. Hamburg, 1962-63; resident St. Georg's Hosp., Hamburg, 1963-64; research fellow in neurology Mt. Sinai Hosp., 1963-64; resident in psychiatry P.R. Inst. of Psychiatry, 1976-79; practice internal medicine and psychiatry, San Juan, P.R., 1974—; psychologist geriatrics Little Sisters of Poor Hosp., Bklyn., 1965-67; mem. staff dept. neurology Kingsbrook Med. Ctr., Bklyn., 1967-68; asst. prof. psychology Kingsborough Community Coll., N.Y., 1966-67, CCNY, summer, 1968; mem. staff psychiatry Rio Piedras State Hosp., San Juan, 1974-82, P.R. Inst. of Psychiatry, San Juan, 1976-82: psychiatrist dept. mental health Knud Hansen Meml. Hosp., St. Thomas, V.I., 1979-82; neurol. and psychol. research dir., adminstr. Humboldt Med. Arts Bldg., 1987-88. Fellow Am. Assn. Mental Deficiency; mem. Am. Psychol. Assn., Ea. Psychol. Assn., N.Y. State Psychol. Assn., AMA, Am. Psychiat. Assn., P.R. Med. Assn., Associación Hermandad en las Carreteras de P.R. (v.p. 1975—), Pi Lambda Theta, Kappa Delta Pi. Roman Catholic. Avocation: speaking fgn. langs. (German, Spanish, French, Italian, Russian). Contbr. articles on physiol. psychology to profl. jours.; research in visual and auditory perception. Office: 185 Clinton Ave Brooklyn NY 11205 also: Michael Balint Inst für, Psychoanalysis, 62 Hamburg Federal Republic of Germany

MACULAITIS, JEAN D'ARCY, language educator, researcher, consultant; b. N.Y.C.; d. Peter Anthony D'Arcy and Lillie (Tossas) Favorito; m. Joseph Patrick Maculaitis, Dec. 10, 1966 (div. 1985); children: Martine, Alexis, Maria Elena; foster children: Matthew, David; 1 adopted child, Theresa; m. John W. Cooke, June 7, 1986; 1 stepchild, John Jr. BA in English magna cum laude, Jersey City State Coll., 1966; MA in TESOL, NYU, 1973, PhD, 1978; postdoctorate in neurolinguistics, Princeton U., 1986—. Tchr. English, ESL pub. schs., N.J., 1966-77; adj. instr. tchr. training, ESL, bilingual edn. colls. and univs., N.Y., N.J., P.R., 1978—; leader workshops in ESL, tchr. training pub. schs., Calif., Nev., Ill., N.Y., P.R., 1987—; pres. Career Wise Inc., Sea Bright, N.J., 1986—, MAC Testing and Cons. Inc., Sea Bright; ednl. cons. Prentice Hall, Oxford U. Press, Macmillan Pubs., Longman Pubs., Georgetown Bilingual Svc. Ctr., others; Coll. Commencement speaker, Georgian Ct., 1989. Author: Desarollando Habilidades de Comprehensión en la Lectura: Lectura de Interpretación, 1981, MAC Guidelines for Evaluating, Designing and/or Improving ESL and BE K-12 Programs, 1981, MAC Checklist for Evaluating, Preparing and/or Improving Standardized Tests for Limited English Speaking Students, 1981, Standards for the Preparation and Certification of International Studies Teachers in the United States, 1983, Maculaitis Assessment Program: A Coordination Series of Test Batteries for ESL Students in Grades K-12 (Mac:K-12), 1985, rev. edit., 1990, Centennial Celebration of the Death of Venerable Father Ludovico, 1985, Odyssey: Assessment Component, 1986, Hello, English: Assessment Component, 1988, Viva el Español!: Assessment Component, 1989, Exciting Writing Workbook: Discovering, Imagining and Navigating Series, 1989; (with Mona Scheraga) What to Do Before the Books Arrive (and After), 1982, Declaration of Rights of the Limited English Proficient Child, 1988, (with Mona Scheraga) The Complete ESL/EFL Resource Book: Strategies, Activities and Units for the Classroom, 1988, MAC S.A.T. Grammarworks, 1990; contbr. articles to profl. jours. Trustee Georgian Ct. Coll., 1982, Dominican Acad., 1988—; active Bd. Edn. Holy Cross Sch., 1986—. Miss America contestant, State of N.J., 1964; Dayton Ball scholar Jersey City State Coll., 1964; named An Outstanding Am. Educator NCCJ, 1978. Mem. International Assn. Tchrs. English to Speakers of Other Langs. (chair secondary sch. spl. interest sect., 1972-78, 82-84, bd. execs., 1972-78), NYU Alumnae Assn. (fund raiser, rep. local chpt., 1980-85), Assn. for Supervision and Curriculum Devel., Acad. Guidance Svcs., Am. Entrepreneurs Assn., N.J. Assn. Women Bus. Owners, Nat. Assn. Women Bus. Owners, Nat. Assn. Women Cons. Inc., Am. Booksellers Assn., Soroptimist Internat., Phi Delta Kappa, Kappa Delta Pi. Home: 103 S Ward Ave Rumson NJ 07760 Office: MAC Testing & Cons Inc PO Box 3056 Sea Bright NJ 07760

MACUR, PATRICIA A., computer programmer, analyst; b. Chgo.; d. Alexander J. and Alice Mary (Styburski) Mackiewicz; m. George J. Macur, 1960; children: Alexander, Cindy Macur Conti. BS, SUNY, 1978; MS, Thomas J. Watson Sch. of Engring., 1984. System control analyst IBM Corp., Endicott, N.Y., 1977; programmer trainee intelligent systems NCR, Ithaca, N.Y., 1978-79, assoc. programmer software integration, 1980, assoc. programmer I gen. purpose systems, 1980-81, programmer, analyst terminal software div., 1981-84; applications analyst material mgmt. systems Eastman Kodak Co., Rochester, N.Y., 1984-86, applications analyst planning and control systems, 1986—; sr. programmer, analyst mfg. systems Ingersoll-Rand Systems, Athens, Pa., 1986-88; sr. assoc. programmer copics packaging and DDS, applications system div. IBM, Atlanta, 1988—. Mem. IMC, AMA (assoc.). Home: 3441 Alexander Pl Smyrna GA 30082 Office: IBM 1500 River Edge Pkwy Atlanta GA 30328

MACUT, SHARON NICKOLENE, newspaper art director; b. Toledo, Ohio, Nov. 10, 1951; d. Nick M. and Nancy (Macut) Petkovich; m. Donald Fredrick Green, July 10, 1981 (div. May 2, 1985). Student, Eastern Mich. U., 1971-73. Dept. sec. Eastern Mich. U., Ypsilanti, 1974-75; fin. mgr. Domestic Violence Project, Ann Arbor, Mich., 1976-81; personal sec. Can.-Am. Investments, Inc., Key Largo, Fla., 1982-83; sales rep. Islamorada (Fla.) Trolley Co., 1984—; art dir. The Reporter, Tavernier, Fla., 1984—; exec. bd. Transp. Planning Adv. Com., Monroe County, Fla., 1985—. Fundraiser Key Largo Pub. Library Bldg., 1985—, Florida Keys Children Shelter, Monroe County, 1985—, Domestic Abuse Shelter, Monroe County, 1986—; mem. Monroe County Commn. on the Status of Women, 1987—. Mem. NOW (pres. Upper Keys chpt. 1984-86, fundraiser Fla. chpt. 1983—), jaycees, NARAL. Democrat. Serbian Orthodox. Office: The Reporter PO Box 1197 Tavernier FL 33070

MACY, DAYNA ALISON, publishing executive, writer, singer; b. Spring Valley, N.Y., Oct. 22, 1960; d. Gilbert and Estelle (Bogoff) M. BA, Drew U., Madison, N.J., 1981; MA in Philosophy, Brown U., Providence, 1983. Art coord. Clinique Estee Lauder, N.Y.C., 1983-84; publicity mgr. Ten Speed Press, Berkeley, Calif., 1985-89; publicity dir. Mercury House Pub., San Francisco, 1989—; mem. faculty dept. profl. pub. Stanford (Calif.) U., 1989—. Subject of interviews on pub. to major newspapers. Mem. Women's Nat. Book Assn. (bd. dirs. 1986—, program chair 1990—). Democrat. Office: Mercury House Pub 201 Filbert St Ste 400 San Francisco CA 94133

MACY MARCY, SUZANNE KAY, behavioral ecologist, educator, biologist; b. Seattle, Oct. 24, 1951; d. Marshall Eugene Macy and Kathleen Mae (Lobb) Macy Costello; m. Scott Colson Marcy, May 2, 1981. A.A., Shoreline Community Coll., 1971; B.S., U. Wash., 1974, Ph.D., 1981; postgrad. Sangamon State U., 1984-85. Research asst. dept. psychology U. Wash., Seattle, 1974-75, teaching asst. dept. psychology, 1976-79, instr. psychology, 1979-81, also instructional cons. Ctr. for Instructional Devel. and Research, 1979-81; biol. technician Nat. Marine Fisheries Service, Seattle and Pribilof Islands, Alaska, 1975-77; dir. graphic arts Leisure Press, Highland Falls, N.Y., 1982; writer, editor West Point Mus., N.Y., 1983; mem. vis. faculty in biology Vassar Coll., Poughkeepsie, N.Y., 1984; sci. researcher, sci. office Ill. Legis. Research Unit, Springfield, 1984-85; mem. adj. faculty biology Northwestern State U. of La. Fort Polk Ctr., Leesville, 1986; legis. sci. intern Sangamon State U., Springfield, 1984-85; mem. sr. faculty, leader Sch. for Field Studies, affiliate Northeastern U., Cambridge, Mass., 1985-87; biologist Office of Water U.S. EPA, Washington, 1988—. First author booklet: Alzheimer's Disease: Activity of the 84th Illinois General Assembly and appendix, 1985. Rep., Nat. Mil. Family Assn., Washington, 1986. Nat. Marine Fisheries Service dissertation grantee, 1976, 77. Mem. AAAS, Am. Inst. Biol. Scis. (congl. liaison 1985-87), Animal Behavior Soc., N.Y. Acad. Scis., Phi Beta Kappa, Sigma Xi, Phi Theta Kappa. Clubs: PEO (chpt. corr. sec. and ednl. loan fund chairperson 1983-84) (New City, N.Y.). Avocations: reading; book collecting; painting; drawing; crafts. Home: 7905 Morning Ride Ct Alexandria VA 22310 Office: US EPA CSD/OWRS WH-585 401 M St SW Washington DC 20460

MACZULSKI, MARGARET LOUISE, coporate executive; b. Detroit, Apr. 1, 1949; d. Bohdan Alexander and Olga Louise (Martinuick) M. BS, Mich. State U., 1972. Mgr. meetings Nat. Assn. Realtors, Mktg. Inst., Chgo., 1977-82, mgr. mktg., 1982-83; regional sales mgr. Fairmont Hotels, Chgo., 1982; dir., mgr. trade shows and confs. Am. Broadcasting Co./Pub. Div., Wheaton, Ill., 1983-85; mgr. meeting and conf. planning Am. Soc. Personnel Adminstrn., Alexandria, Va., 1985-90; mgr. meeting and conv. planning Kraft Gen. Foods, Glenview, Ill., 1990—. Mem. Meeting Planners Internat., Greater Washington Soc. Assn. Execs. (past chmn. site inspection com.), Am. Soc. Assn. Execs., Nat. Assn. Exposition Execs., Mich. State U. Alumni Assn. (treas. D.C. chpt. 1987-90). Republican. Roman Catholic. Avocations: piano, swimming. Home: 9670 Dee Rd #202 Des Plaines IL 60016 Office: Kraft Gen Foods 1 Kraft Ct Glenview IL 60025

MADDALENA, LUCILLE ANN, management executive; b. Plainfield, N.J., Nov. 8, 1948; d. Mario Anthony and Josephine Dorothy (Longo) M.; m. James Samonte Hohn, Sept. 7, 1975; children: Vincent, Nicholas, Mitchell. AA, Rider Coll., 1968; BS, Monmouth Coll., West Long Branch, N.J., 1971; EdD, Rutgers U., 1978. Newscaster, dir. pub. relations Sta. WBRW, Bridgewater, N.J., 1971-73; editor-in-chief Commerce mag., New Brunswick, N.J., 1973-74; dir. pub. relations Raritan Valley Regional C. of C., New Brunswick, N.J., 1973-74; aide pub. relations to mayor City of New Brunswick, 1974; dir. communications United Way Cen. Jersey, New Brunswick, 1974-77; mgmt. cons. United Way Am., Alexandria, Va., 1977-78; pres., owner Maddalena Assocs., Chester, N.J., 1978—; sr. cons. United Research Co., Morristown, N.J., 1980-81; sr. ptnr., dir. OCD Group, Parsippany, N.J., 1984-87; chmn. bd. dirs. OCD Group (subs. Xicom Inc.), Morristown, N.J., 1988; pres. Morris Bus. Group, 1989—; adj. faculty Somerset County Coll., Bridgewater, N.J., 1970, Fairleigh Dickinson U., 1980; guest lectr. Rutgers U., New Brunswick, N.J., 1975-80. Author: A Communications Manual for Non-Profit Organizations, 1980; editor New Directions for Instl. Advancement, 1980-81. Mem., chmn. personnel com., police com. Chester Borough Council, 1984-87. Recipient Mayor's Commendation City of New Brunswick, 1973. Mem. AAUW, LWV, Nat. Assn. Press Women, N.J. Elected Women Officials, Kappa Delta Pi. Republican. Roman Catholic. Club: N.J. Sled Dog Assn. Home: 75 Melrose Dr Chester NJ 07930 Office: Morris Bus Group 530 E Main St Suite 4B Chester NJ 07930

MADDEN, EMMA FAE, special education educator; b. Tulsa, Jan. 18, 1931; d. Nolan Frank and Raye (Stacy) Brock; m. Marion Leroy Madden, July 17, 1949; children: Howard, Rebecca, Ruth, Robin, Michael. BS in Edn., Ark. State U., Jonesboro, 1965, MS in Edn., 1969. Cert. elem. and learning disabilities tchr., Ark., Mo. Tchr. Clover Bend Sch. Dist., Hoxie, Ark., 1963-65, Walnut Ridge (Ark.) Pub. Sch., 1965-66, Spl. Sch. Dist. of St. Louis County, Town and Country, Mo., 1966—, Mo. Bapt. Coll., Creve Coeur, Mo., 1974-82. Ark. State Dept. Edn. grantee, 1966, Mo. State Dept. Edn. grantee, 1968. Mem. Coun. of Exceptional Children, Bus. and Profl. Women's Assn., Kappa Delta Pi. Republican. Baptist. Home: 6 Rendina Ct Ellisville MO 63011

MADDEN, MARSHA LOUISE, nuclear medicine professional; b. Chicopee, Mass., Aug. 25, 1952; d. David Alexander Staples and Patricia Ruth (Webb) Carter; m. John David McCaughey, Nov. 7, 1967 (div. 1970); m. Michael John Madden, Apr. 4, 1975; children: John David, Shelley Ann. AS, Springfield Community Coll., 1985. Cert. pharmacy technician, 1985. Pharmacy technician Rite Aid Pharmacy, Ware, Mass., 1978-85, Baystate Med. Ctr., Springfield, Mass., 1984-85; nuclear med. technician Wing Meml. Hosp., Palmer, Mass., 1985-86; chief of nuclear medicine Ludlow (Mass.) Hosp., 1985-89; supr. nuclear medicine Providence Hosp., Holyoke, Mass., 1989—; cons. Siemens Med. Systems, Aston, Pa., 1989—. Mem. Soc. Nuclear Medicine (continuing edn. dir. 1989-90), New Eng. Technicians of Nuclear Medicine (chair 1987-89), Aircraft Owners and Pilots Assn., Order of Eastern Star. Home: 20 Westbrook Ave Ware MA 01082 Office: Providence Hosp 1233 Main St Holyoke MA 01040

MADDICKS, NONA MIHR, production planning administrator; b. Rochester, N.Y., July 20, 1942; d. Norman Carl and Geraldine Helen (Hoffman) Mihr; divorced; 1 child, Shana L. AAS, Rochester Inst. Tech., 1962; BS in Psychology, U. Rochester, 1974. Prodn. asst. Eastman Kodak Co., Rochester, 1969-76, prodn. specialist, 1976-83, supervising prodn. specialist, 1983-86, supr. estimating, scheduling, planning and monitoring, 1986-90, printing prodn. specialist, 1990—. Mem. Rochester Club of Printing House Craftsmen (dinner chmn. 1976-78, club printer 1983-85, treas. 1987—). Home: 54 Larkwood Dr Rochester NY 14626 Office: Eastman Kodak Co 343 State St Rochester NY 14650

MADDOCK, ROSEMARY SCHROER, administrator, researcher; b. Coldwater, Ohio, Dec. 19, 1919; d. Henry Herman and Rose Elizabeth (Schlagheck) Schroer; m. Ernest A. Maddock, May 28, 1942 (div. 1951); children: Ernest H., Barbara A., Rosemary E. BS, Bowling Green State U., 1941; MS in Adminstrn., Cen. Mich. State U., 1976; postgrad., U. Ariz. Tchr. math. and sci. Ohio Pub. Schs., Spencerville, Grafton, and Coldwater, 1941-45; radio-chemistry rsch. asst. U. Mich., Ann Arbor, 1952-63; tech. info. specialist Analytical Chemistry div. Nat. Bur. Standards, Washington, 1963-79, writer-editor tech. pubs., specialist Nat. Measurement Lab. NIST, 1979-81; asst. to curator of collections Ariz. State Mus. U. Ariz., Tucson, 1982-86, film libr. adminstr. and researcher, 1986-88; adminstr. NSF-Ariz. Accelerator Mass Spectrometer Facility, Tucson, 1988—. Author, editor: Radiochemistry Monographs, 1959-62; asst. editor: Ultrasonic Imaging, 1979-81; contbr. articles to profl. jours. Vol. Archeology dept. Ariz. State Mus., 1982-87; program coord. Nuclear Chemistry Monographs, 1963-65. Recipient Bronze award U.S. Dept. Commerce, 1973; Spl. Act award Nat. Bur. Standards, 1980. Mem. Soc. for Tech. Communications (Spl. Merit award 1980), Soc. for Scholary Pub., Juror, CINE Film Festival (mem. Coun. on Internat. Nontheatrical Events-Secondary Edn.). Office: U Ariz Physics and Atmospheric Scis Tucson AZ 85721

MADDOX, CATHARINE PATRICK, state agency administrator; b. Mobile, Ala., Nov. 3, 1948; d. Benjamin Franklin and Ethellene (Nall) Patrick; m. R. Bruce Maddox; children: Ami Catharine, Natalie Nicole, Bradley Patrick, Allison Paige. BS in Edn., Auburn U., 1970; MBA, U. South Ala., 1982; cert. in health care adminstrn., U. Ala., Birmingham, 1984. Lic. nursing home adminstr. Chemistry and physics tchr. Greystone Christian Sch., Mobile, 1971-73; math. and algebra tchr. Cen. Bapt. Sch., Mobile, 1974-75; coordinator staff devel. Albert Brewer Devel. Ctr., Mobile, 1975-81, asst. ctr. dir., 1981-84; regional dir. J.S. Tarwater Devel. Ctr., Wetumpka, Ala., 1984-88; dir. Bur. MR Quality Assurance Ala. Dept. Mental Health/Mental, Montgomery, Ala., 1988—; tng. assoc. Paige Mktg. and Mgmt., Montgomery, 1988—. Editor: Mobile, City by the Bay, 1968. Loaned exec. United Way, Mobile, 1982, 83, del. assembly, 1984—, mem. community coun., del. assembly, Montgomery, 1984—; grad. Leadership Mobile, 1982. Fellowship recipient Inst. Exec. Women, 1982-83. Mem. Am. Soc. Tng. and Devel. (chpt. pres. 1982, leadership award 1982), Am. Assn. Mental Retardation, S.E. Am. Assn. Mental Retardation, Montgomery Assn. Retarded Citizens, Nat. Assn. Quality Assurance Profls., Capital City Club. Republican. Episcopalian. Home: 4431 Eley Ct Montgomery AL 36106

MADDOX, MICHELE, data processing executive; b. Kirksville, Mo., May 7, 1946; d. Delbert E. and Louise (Surbeck) M.; children: Dana, Channing, Shann. BA, William Jewell, Liberty, Mo., 1974; postgrad., U. Mo., Kansas City, 1976-77. Mgr. trainee Radio Shack, Opolis, Kans., 1981; asst. mgr. Video Concepts, Opolis, 1981-83; mgr. Computer Land, Opolis, 1983-84; personal computer coord. Marley Cooling Tower, Mission, Kans., 1984—. Mem. Micro Mgrs. Assn. (A86 standardization com.), NAFE, Kans. Hist. Soc. Club, Kans. Wildflower Soc. Office: Marley Cooling Tower Co 5800 Foxridge Dr Mission KS 66202

MADER, PAMELA BEILE, fitness administrator; b. Chgo., Dec. 15, 1939; d. Walter Carl and Marjorie Eveline (Gasprich) Beile; m. Ronald Edward Mader, Apr. 4, 1964 (div. 1980); children: Todd Anthony, Tammy Ann; m. Frank Allen Roberts, June 20, 1987. BA, Butler U., 1962. Cert. exercise tchr. Choreographer Russell Sch. Ballet, Falls Church, Va., 1975-86; master tchr. Jazzercise and Dance, U.S., Va., 1983—; instr. Jazzercise and Dance, U.S., Fairfax, Va., 1980—, N.E. regional adminstr., 1985—; weight mgmt. instr. Jazzercise, U.S., Fairfax, Va., 1989—; asst. staging dir. Jazzercise Performance Internat. Exhbn. YES '89, Yokohama, Japan; dir. opening show Jazzerjam '89, Arie Crown Theater, Chgo. Coreographer numerous jazz ballets and routines. Home and Office: 10702 Zion Dr Fairfax VA 22032

MADERA, MARIE LOUISE, magazine publishing executive; b. Los Angeles, June 11, 1955; d. Leroy James and Helen Jean (Clark) M. BA, Calif. State U., Long Beach, 1978. Art dir. Keyboard World mag., Downey, Calif., 1978-79, Popular Ceramics mag., Glendale, Calif., 1980; mgr. prodn. Creative Age Pubs., Van Nuys, Calif., 1980-86; dir. prodn. High Tech Pubs., Torrance, Calif., 1986; dir. pubs. Family Living mag., Buena Park, Calif., 1986—; cons. Affluent Target Mktg., La Mirada, Calif., 1986—. Choreographer community theatres, 1981—. Mem. Nat. Assn. Female Execs., Western Pubs. Assn., Advt. Prodn. Assn. So. Calif., Pubs. Prodn. Mgr. Club So. Calif. Roman Catholic. Office: Affluent Target Mktg 6280 Manchester Blvd #219 Buena Park CA 90621

MADEY, CANDICE WHITMORE, advertising agency executive; b. Gardena, Calif., May 30, 1958; d. Harry Joseph and Inez Mary (Ressler) Chick; children from previous marriage: Alyson Whitmore, Chase Whitmore; m. Joseph Leonard Madey, Nov. 30, 1985; 1 child, Monica. Student, U. Ark., 1977-80. Rsch. assoc. Greater Little Rock (Ark.) C. of C., 1981-84; pres. Advice and Art Plus, Inc., North Little Rock, Ark., 1984—. Mem. North Little Rock C. of C. (bd. dirs. 1985-89, v.p. 1989), Assn. of Ark. Entrepreneurs (co-founder). Democrat. Roman Catholic. Office: Advice and Art Plus Inc 1920 N Main St Ste 229 North Little Rock AR 72114

MADHERE, MARIE IMMACULEE MAGALY, microbiologist; b. Port-Au-Prince, Haiti, Nov. 29, 1953; came to U.S., 1972; d. Gerard L. and Francesca (Remy) Jacques; divorced; children: Serge, Maxime. AAS, N.Y.C. Tech. Coll., 1975; BS, Hunter Coll., 1979; MA, Bklyn. Coll., 1988. Asst. supr. sci. ctr. SUNY, Brooklyn, 1979—; part-time microbiologist Brookdale Med. Ctr., Bklyn., 1981-82. Mem. Am. Soc. Microbiology, Am. Acad. Microbiologists (registered), United Univ. Profls. Democrat. Roman Catholic. Office: SUNY Health Sci Ctr 450 Clarkson AVe Brooklyn NY 11203

MADIGAN, AMY, actress; b. Chgo., 1957; m. Ed Harris. With rock music group, 10 yrs. Appeared in films Love Child, 1982, Streets of Fire, 1984, Places in the Heart, 1984, Alamo Bay, 1985, Twice in a Lifetime, 1985, Nowhere to Hide, 1987, The Prince of Pennsylvania, 1988, Uncle Buck, 1989, Field of Dreams, 1989, (TV films) Crazy Times, 1981, The Ambush Murders, 1982, Victims, 1982, Travis McGee, 1983, The Day After, 1983, Roe vs. Wade. Office: care Alan Somers Mgmt 8335 Sunset Blvd Los Angeles CA 90069*

MADISON, ROBERTA ELEANOR, epidemiologist, educator, consultant; b. Bklyn., Feb. 10, 1932; d. A.I. and Grace (Weinstein) M.; children: Jerry Solomon, Sue Vann. AB in History, UCLA, 1966, MA, 1969, MSPH in Environ. Health, 1972, DrPH, 1974. Chief epidemiological analyst Los Angeles County, L.A., 1972-75; from asst. prof. to assoc. prof. Calif. State U., Northridge, 1975-83, prof. epidemiology and biostatistics, 1983—; part-time epidemiologist City of Hope, Duarte, Calif., 1977-85; instr. biostatistics UCLA Sch. Pub. Health, 1978-84; cons., biostatistician Northridge Hosp., 1983—; cons. epidemiology and biostatistics Thrasher & Assocs., Northridge, 1988—, Cytosystems, Cupertino, Calif., 1988-90; cons. epidemiology Warner Day Care Ctr., Woodland Hills, Calif., 1988—. Mem. editorial rev. bd. Alzheimers Disease and Assoc. Disorders, 1985—; contbr. articles to profl. jours. Bd. dirs. Basehart Theatre, Woodland Hills, 1986—. Grantee Am. Lung Assn., others. Fellow Am. Coll. Epidemiology, Cancer Rsch. Ctr.; mem. Am. Statis. Assn. (sec. state edn. sect. 1982), Golden Key Honor Soc. (hon.), Sigma Xi (sec. chpt. 1982). Office: Calif State U Northridge 18111 Nordhoff St Northridge CA 91330

MADLENER, ELIZABETH W., horse trainer; b. Hattiesburg, Miss., Sept. 6, 1941; d. David Jesse and Betty June (Jackson) Wilson. BA, Old Dominion U., Norfolk, Va., 1964; MA, U. Wash., 1974. Cert. tchr., Va., Wash. Tchr. English Norfolk City Schs.; chmn. dept. English Bellevue (Wash.) Pub. Schs.; horse trainer EM Dressage Assocs., Clarksburg, Md.; pres. Md. Horse Ctr., Inc., Gaithersburg; researcher on psychology of tng. Author: Putting Your Horse on the Bit, 1980; contbr. articles to Chronicle of the Horse, Practical Horseman, Equus mags. Recipient numerous Horse of Yr. awards, German Bronze medal in riding, 1957. Mem. U.S. Dressage Fedn. (examiner judge, judges com., instr. trainers com.), U.S. Equestrian Team, Am. Horse Shows Assn. (cert. "I" Judge rating, grass roots com.), Am. Horse Coun., U.S. Dressage Fed. (judges and trainers com.), Md. Horse Coun., Potomac Valley Dressage Assn., NAFE, Am. Youth Horse Coun., Md. C. of C. (edn. com. 1990—), Md. SBA (advocate), Rockville C. of C. Republican. Address: 14211 Quince Orchard Rd Gaithersburg MD 20878

MADORE, SISTER BERNADETTE, college president; b. Barnston, Que., Can., Jan. 24, 1918; came to U.S., 1920, naturalized; d. Joseph George and Mina Marie (Fontaine) M.; A.B., U. Montreal, 1942, B.Ed., 1943; M.S., Cath. U. Am., 1949, Ph.D., 1951. Instr. math. and English, Marie Anne Coll., Montreal, Que., 1943-44; prof. biology, dean of coll. Anna Maria Coll., Paxton, Mass., 1952-76, v.p., 1975-77, pres., 1977—; fund-raising cons.; corporator YWCA. Bd. dirs. Central Mass. chpt. ARC; bd. dirs. Worcester Coll. Consortium; trustee Worcester Boys Club. Mem. AAAS, AAUW, Am. Soc. Microbiology, Nat. Assn. Biology Tchrs., Am. Assn. Higher Edn., Worcester C. of C. Roman Catholic. Lodge: Soroptimist. Home & Office: Anna Maria Coll Sunset Ln Paxton MA 01612-1198

MADRID, DONNA KAY, personnel executive; b. Mt. Ayr, Iowa, May 29, 1937; d. Clete Hewitt and Murice Marjorie (Cornwall) Madison; married; children: Murice Elaina Scanlon, Cathy Lynne Carlson. AA, Interior Designers Guild, Sherman Oaks, Calif., 1987. Owner Home Cleaning Service, Canoga Park, Calif., 1970-79; designer Beam Interiors, Northridge, Calif., 1979-80; owner, mgr. Innovative Interiors, Chatsworth, Calif., 1980-81; office mgr. Jardine Emett & Chandler, Los Angeles, 1981—, asst. v.p., 1988—; mem. Ins. Personnel Mgmt. Forum. Mem. Personnel and Indsl. Rels. Assn., NAFE, Women Referral Svc. Office: Jardine Emett & Chandler LA Ins Brokers 11835 W Olympic Blvd Los Angeles CA 90021

MADRON, BEVERLY BROWN, university computer center director; b. Ft. Smith, Ark., Dec. 17, 1937; d. Elmus C. and T. Ernestine (Brown) Brown; m. Thomas William Madron, Mar. 26, 1960. BA, Hendrix Coll., 1959; MA, Tulane U., 1970; PhD, George Peabody Coll., 1979. Cert. in data processing. Dept. mgr. C.A. Reed Co., Williamsport, Pa., 1964-66; asst. prof. Western Ky. U., Bowling Green, 1967-80; programmer, analyst Tex. Instruments, Dallas, 1980-81; mgr. systems support Tex. Instruments, 1981-82, systems supr., 1982, curriculum mgr., 1982-84, coord. people and asset effectiveness, 1984-87; assoc. dir. Rutgers U., Newark, 1987-90, Piscataway, N.J., 1990—. Trustee United Meth. Ch., New Brunswick, N.J., 1989; bd. adjustments City of Bowling Green, 1980. Mem. Data Processing Mgmt. Assn. (pres. Edn. Found. 1988-89, bd. dirs., individual performance awards 1974, 80, 84), Data Processing Mgmt. Assn. (spl. interest groups), Assn. Inst. for Certification of Computer Profls. Democrat. Office: Rutgers U Hill Ctr Busch Campus PO Box 879 Piscataway NJ 08854

MADSEN, DOROTHY LOUISE (MEG MADSEN), writer, career counselor; b. Rochester, N.Y.; d. Charles Robert and Louise Anna Agnes Meyer; B.A., Mundelein Coll., Chgo., 1968; m Frederick George Madsen, Feb. 17, 1945. Public relations rep. Rochester Telephone Corp., 1941-42; feature writer Rochester Democrat & Chronicle, 1939-41; exec. dir. LaPorte (Ind.) chpt. ARC, 1964; dir. adminstrv. services Bank Mktg. Assn., Chgo., 1971-74; exec. dir. Eleanor Assn., Chgo., 1974-84; founder Meg Madsen Assocs., Chgo., 1984-88; women's career counselor; founder, Clearinghouse Internat. Newsletter; founder Eleanor Women's Forum, Clearinghouse Internat., Eleanor Intern Program Coll. Students and Returning Women. Served to lt. col. WAC, 1942-47, 67-70. Decorated Legion of Merit, Meritorious Service award. Mem. Res. Officers Assn., Mundelein Alumnae Assn., Central Eleanor Club, Phi Sigma Tau (charter mem. Ill. Kappa chpt.). Home and Office: 1030 N State St Chicago IL 60610

MAEDA, J. A., data processing executive; b. Mansfield, Ohio, Aug. 24, 1940; d. James Shunso and Doris Lucille (Moore) M.; m. Robert Lee Hayes (div. May 1970); 1 child, Brian Sentaro Hayes. BS in Math., Purdue U., 1962, postgrad., 1962-63; postgrad., Calif. State U., Northridge, 1968-75; cert. profl. designation in tech. of computer operating systems and tech. of info. processing, UCLA, 1971. Cons., rsch. asst. computer ctr. Purdue U., West Lafayette, Ind., 1962-63; computer operator, sr. tab operator, mem. faculty Calif. State U., Northridge, 1969, programmer cons., tech. asst. II, 1969-70, supr. acad. applicatons, EDP supr. II, 1970-72, project tech. support coord. programmer II, office of the chancellor, 1972-73, tech. support coord. statewide timesharing tech. support, programmer II, 1973-74, acad. coord., tech. support coord. instrn., computer cons. III, 1974-83; coord. user svcs. info. ctr., mem. tech. staff IV CADAM INC subs. Lockheed Corp., Burbank, Calif., 1983-86, coord. end user svcs., tech. specialist computing dept., 1986-87; v.p., bd. dirs. Rainbow Computing, Inc., Northridge, 1976-85; pres. Akiko Maeda Tech./Design Cons., Northridge, 1980—; mktg. mgr. thaumaturge Taro Quipu Tech./Design Cons., Northridge, 1987—; tech. cons. Digital Computer Cons., Chatsworth Calif., 1988; cons. computer tech., fin. and bus. mgmt., systems integration, 1988—. Author 100 user publs., 1969-83, 98 computer user publs., 1983-87, basic computer programming language; contbr. articles and papers and photos to profl. jours. Mem. IEEE, SHARE, Digital Equipment Computer Users Soc. (author papers and presentations 1977-81, ednl. spl. interest group 1977-83, steering com. Resource Sharing Timesharing System/Extended (RSTS/E), 1979-82). Office: 18257 Shepley Pl Northridge CA 91326

MAEHL, AUDREY ELLSWORTH, higher education consultant; b. Saratoga Springs, N.Y., Aug. 20, 1930; d. Ray Grippin and Genevieve Irene (Geil) Ellsworth; m. William Henry Maehl, Aug. 25, 1962; 1 child, Christine Amanda. BS magna cum laude, St. Lawrence U., 1952; MA in Philosophy, U. Okla., 1955. Asst. dir. Presbyn. campus ministry U. Tex., 1955-57; dir. Presbyn. campus ministry So. Meth. U., Dallas, 1957-60; edn. dir. 1st Presbyn. Ch., Norman, Okla., 1960-63; program coord. S.W. Ctr. for Human Rels., Norman, 1963-65; adminstrv. sec. Okla. United Ministries, Norman, 1972-81; assoc. dir. Scholar-Leadership Enrichment, Norman, 1978-87; cons. on higher edn. Maehl Assocs., Santa Barbara, Calif., 1987—; cons. U. Redlands (Calif.), 1988—, Fielding Inst., Santa Barbara, 1988, Presbyn. Ch., U.S.A., Louisville, 1989. Mem. com. on 1990's, U. Calif., Santa Barbara, 1987—, chmn. United Campus Ministry, 1987—, Univ. Calif., Santa Barbara. Kingfisher fellow U. Okla., 1953-55. Mem. AAUW, Phi Beta Kappa. Democrat. Presbyterian. Home and Office: 817 E Anapamu St Apt 2 Santa Barbara CA 93103

MAEL, BOBBIE LOUISE, hospital sales executive; b. Lockport, N.Y., Dec. 12, 1955; d. Robert U. and Margaret L. (Heath) M. AA, U. South Fla., 1976; BS in Bus. Adminstrn., East Carolina U., 1978. Sales rep. Sandoz Pharm. Co., Wilmington, N.C., 1978-83, USV Labs., Buffalo, 1983-85, Purdue Frederick Co., Buffalo, 1985-86, O'Brien Pharms., Buffalo, 1986-88, Kendall McGaw Labs., Inc., Buffalo, 1988-89; hosp. sales mgr. Kendall McGaw Labs., Inc., Washington, 1989—. Contbr. photographs to regional newspapers and mags. Active Emmanuel Meth. Ch., Amherst Women's Suburban Softball League. Mem. Bus. Women's Assn., Nat. Assn. for Profl. Sales Women. Republican. Clubs: Amherst Bus. and Profl. Women's; Up Downtown of Buffalo, Bali Matrix Health and Fitness. Home: 6121 Summer Park Ln Alexandria VA 22310

MAFFEI, DOROTHY J., theatre manager; b. Syracuse, N.Y., Dec. 25, 1951; d. Neil Carmine and Leona (Howland) M. BA, Carleton Coll., Northfield, Minn., 1974. Prodn. mgr. Playwrights Horizons, N.Y.C., 1977-81, Hartford (Conn.) Stage Co., 1981-83, Pepsico Summerfare, Purchase, N.Y., 1981, 85; project coordinator Amnesty Internat. "A Conspiracy of Hope" Tour, 1986; adminstrv. dir. NYU-Tisch Sch. of the Arts, 1987; mng. dir. Second Stage Theatre, N.Y.C., 1987—; adj. faculty NYU/Tisch Sch. Arts, Grad. Acting Prog., 1989—. Assn. of Non-Profit Theatre in N.Y. (treas. 1989—). Office: PO Box 1807 Ansonia Sta New York NY 10024

MAGAD, LINDA MAUREEN, real estate association executive, writer, editor; b. Chgo., May 9, 1940; d. Louis Arthur and Faye (Mann) Bloom; m. Irwin A. Magad, Aug. 20, 1961; children: Arlene Levin (Jeffrey), Howard, Joel. BA, Roosevelt U., 1962. Corr. Lerner Newspapers, Skokie, Ill., 1978-79; prodn. editor Nelson Pub., Highland Park, Ill., 1979-84; staff writer Am. Soc. Real Estate Counselors, Chgo., 1984-86, dir. communications, 1986-89, staff v.p., 1989—; cons. Bloom, Bloom & Magad, Skokie, Ill., 1988—, Concept 1, Inc., Libertyville, Ill., 1989. Editor: How to Perform an Economic Feasibility Study of a Hotel/Motel, 1988; Real Estate Analyses, 1989; editor newsletter and jour. Sch. bd. rep. Dist. 65, Skokie/Evanston, 1979; troop leader Girl Scouts U.S., Skokie/Evanston, 1971-73. Recipient Excellence in Journalism award Ill. Community Colls. Journalism Assn., 1979; Blue Ribbon award Assoc. Coll. Press, 1979. Mem. Am. Soc. Assn. Execs., Hadassah (chmn. coms. 1973-78). Home: 3850 Enfield Skokie IL 60076 Office: Am Soc Real Estate Counsel 430 N Michigan Ave Chicago IL 60611

MAGAFAN, ETHEL, artist; b. Chgo., Aug. 10, 1916; d. Peter J. and Julie (Bronick) M.; m. Bruce Currie, June 30, 1946; 1 dau., Jenne Magafan. Student, Colorado Springs Fine Arts Center. guest artist-in-residence Syracuse U., 1976. Painter of 8 murals including Social Security Bldg (now HEW bldg.), Washington, Recorder of Deeds Bldg., Washington, Fredericksburg (Va.) Nat. Mil. Park, 1978; paintings exhibited Carnegie Inst., Corcoran Gallery, Pa. Acad. Fine Arts, NAD, Met. Mus., Denver Art Mus., San Francisco Mus., N.Y. Exhbn., 1950-51, 53, 55, 56, 59, 61, 63, 66, 69, 70, 73, 79, 81, Art Gallery, SUNY, Albany, 1981, Midtown Galleries, N.Y.C., 1984, Smithsonian, 1988, Colo. Springs Fine Arts Ctr., 1989 Nat. Mus. Am. Art, Arvada Ctr. for Arts and Humanities, 1989; represented in permanent collections, including, Springfield (Mo.) Art Mus., Provincetown Art Assn., Met. Mus. Art, Denver Art Mus., Del. Soc. Fine Arts, Des Moines Art Center, Norfolk Mus., Columbia Mus., Butler (Ind.) Inst. Art, Nat. Mus. Women in the Arts, 1987, Albany Inst. of Art & History, Wichita Art Mus., Nat. Mus. Am. Art, Smithsonian Instn.; one-man show Midtown Galleries, N.Y.C., 1987, others; also pvt. collections. John Stacey scholar, 1947; Tiffany fellow, 1949; Fulbright grantee, 1951; Recipient Collectors Am. Art award, 1947, 48; Adele Hyde Morrison prize San Francisco Mus., 1950; hon. mention Am. Painting Today exhbn., Met Mus. Art, 1950; 1st Hallgarten prize NAD, 1951; Ida Wells Stroud award, Am. Watercolor Soc., 1955; purchase prize Nat. Exhbn. Contemporary Arts, 1956; Altman prize for landscape NAD, 1956; Hallmark Art award, 1952; Purchase award, Ball State Tchrs. Coll. Art Gallery, 1958; Columbia (S.C.) Mus., 1959; Portland (Maine) Mus., 1959; 1st award Albany Inst. Art, 1962; Benjamin Altman award NAD, 1964, 73; Andrew Carnegie prize, 1977; award Conn. Acad. Fine Arts, 1965; purchase award Watercolor, U.S.A., Springfield Mus., 1966; Kirk Meml. award NAD, 1967; Berkshire Art Assn. award, 1966, 67, 68, 75; jurors prize Albany Inst. Art, 1969; Grumbacher award, 1970, 75; Hassam Fund purchase, 1970; Arches Paper award Am. Watercolor Soc., 1973; Zimmerman award Phila. Watercolor Soc., 1973; Pres.'s award Audubon Artists, 1974; Emily Lowe award, 1979; Stefan Hirsch Meml. award Audubon Artists Ann., 1976; award Rocky Mountain Nat. Watermedia Exhbn., 1976; Condec award Silvermine Guild Artists, 1978; award, 1979; Silver medal Audubon Artists, 1983; Cooperstown Art Assn. award, 1978, 83; Highwinds award and medal Am. Watercolor Soc., 1983; drawing award Ball State U., 1981; Art of Northeast USA exhibit award Silvermine Guild, 1984; John W. Taylor award Woodstock Artist's Assn. for Drawing, 1985, Harrison Cady award Am. Water Color Soc., 1987, Adirondacks Brobock prize, 1988, Robert Philipp Meml. award Audubon Artists, 1989, The Grumbacker award and Gold medal Audubon Artists, 1990, Martin Family award Adirondacks Nat. Exhbn. Am. Watercolors, 1990. Mem. NAD (2d v.p. 1975, Benjamin Altman award 1980), Am. Water Color Soc.

MAGALLANES, DEBORAH JEAN, business consulting company executive; b. Gary, Ind., May 22, 1951; d. Ray Daniel and Courtney Ann (Manders) M.; m. Gary Allen DeBardi, 1975. Student pub. schs., Crown Point, Ind. Adminstrv. asst. Fasfax Corp., Nashua, N.H., 1971-75; adminstrv. asst. Advanced Tech. Labs., Bellevue, Wash., 1975, part-time, 1975-77; sales asst. VMC Corp., Woodinville, Wash., 1975-76; cons. personnel Bus. Men's Clearing House, Bellevue, 1976-79; salesperson, gen. mgr. Cypress Steel, Inc., Bellevue, 1979, part-time, 1979-80; pres. Magallanes, Inc., Bellevue, 1979—; cons., project mgr. in field; founder Hug'M Messengers, 1979, Ace Entertainment, 1980. Author: (with others) Guide to Better Relationships Through Dealmaking, 1985. Mem. Up With People, Seattle-King County Conv. and Visitors Bur.; bd. dirs. Friends of Youth, Renton, Wash., 1984-90, v.p., 1986-90, vol., 1990—, Save the Elephants Campaign, Seattle, 1984-87; mem. Bellevue Leaders, 1982—, bd. dirs., 1983—, pres., 1984, sec./treas., 1990—. Mem. Women's Bus. Exchange (bd. dirs. 1981-85, Networker of Yr. 1983), MIT Alumni Assn. (hon. nat. officer 1984). Club: Briefcase Brigade (Bellevue), Hetty Green Partnership (pres. 1986-88, treas. 1988-89). Lodge: Soroptimists (bd. dirs. 1986, 88, 90, corr. sec. 1990). Avocations: investments, canoeing, fishing, snow skiing, drill team. Office: 405 114th Ave SE #300 Bellevue WA 98004

MAGEE, M. ANN SHEEN, insurance consultant; b. Lima, Peru, Sept. 22, 1939; came to U.S., 1960; d. C.A. and Esther T. (Gallesse) Sheen; m. Don Perry W. Magee, Dec. 8, 1961; 1 child, Marcus. AA, Santa Monica (Calif.) Coll., 1985; BS, U. Redlands, Calif., 1987. Mgr. workers compensation GTE, Thousand Oaks, Calif.; pres. Consultation Svcs. for Mgmt., L.A.; cons. workers compensation Arter, Hadden, Lawler, Felix & Hall, L.A.; mem. adv. com. CCR, W.C. Forum, C. of C.; workers' compensation instr. UCR Ext. Developer tng. program for med. field in writing worker compensation reports; contbr. articles to profl. publs. Mem. Workers Compensation Claims Adminstrn. (instr. UCR extension, cert., 1990). Home: 2239 Veteran Ave Los Angeles CA 90064

MAGEE, SHARON LYNN, teacher, director; b. Tucson, Ariz., Jan. 6, 1952; d. Alwin James and Marjorie Jo (Wilson) Girdner; m. Fred Ira Magee Jr., Aug. 21, 1971; children: Heather Lynn, Glen Ira. BS, U. N.Mex., 1974; postgrad., Perkins Sch. Theology, Dallas, 1978. Tchr. Albuquerque Pub. Schs., 1974-76; dir. Youth Ministries Cen. United Methodist, Albuquerque, 1977-78; dir. children's Day Out St. John's United Methodist, Albuquerque, 1983—; tchr. Hands on Sci. Outreach, Albuquerque. Leader Girl Scouts of Am., Albuquerque, 1980-88; v.p. Parent Faculty Club of Zuni Elem., Albuquerque, 1988-89. Named Life Membership, United Methodist Women, 1984. Mem. Am. Assn. U. Women (recording sec. 1985-86), Sweet Adelines (com. chair 1989—, bd. dirs. 1990—). Republican. Home: 7125 Dellwood NE Albuquerque NM 87110 Office: St. John's United Methodist 2626 Arizona Albuquerque NM 87110

MAGERS, JANE F., food service executive; b. Bluffton, Ind., Feb. 10, 1943; d. John W. and Dorothy L. (Loney) M. Student, Ball State U., Muncie, Inc.; cert., LaSalle Inst., Chgo., 1973. Lifeguard, water instr. Hartford Mcpl. Pool, Hartford City, Ind.; store mgr. William E. Bowman, Hartford City; bookkeeper One Hour That's Just Yours, Pellston, Mich.; gen. mgr. The Pancake Chef Restaurant, Mackinaw City, Mich. Exec. dir. Miss Teen Ft. Michilimackinac Pageant; pres. Concerned Citizens for Better Community; sec., treas., parade co-chair Ft. Michilimackinac Meml. Day Weekend Pageant. Recipient Disting. Citizen award Mackinaw City C. of C., 1988-89. Mem. NAFE, Women of the Moose (Coll. Regents, Star Recorders degree).

MAGGIORE, SUSAN, geophysical oceanographer; b. Newark, Mar. 14, 1957; d. John James and Marietta Nancy (Testa) M.; m. Stephen P. Garreffa, Oct. 21, 1989. BS in Geosci., Montclair State Coll., 1978; postgrad., U. So. Miss., 1981-84. Supr. research and communications The Cousteau Soc., N.Y., 1979-81; geophysicist Naval Oceanographic Office, Bay St. Louis, Miss., 1981-85, NE Consortium Oceanographic Research, Narragansett, R.I., 1985-86; mem. tech. staff AT&T Bell Labs., Whippany, N.J., 1986—; writer, creative cons. The Cousteau Soc., Los Angeles, 1981-89. Researcher book The Cousteau Almanac of the Environment, 1981; contbr. articles to profl. jours. Vol. Dover (N.J.) Gen. Hosp., 1987-88. Mem. Am. Geophys. Union, Marine Tech. Soc., Nat. Assn. Female Execs. Roman Catholic. Office: AT&T Bell Labs 1 Whippany Rd Whippany NJ 07981

MAGIE, PATRICIA CRANE, publishing executive; b. Trenton, N.J., May 10, 1961; d. Stuart Gerald and Barbara Joyce (Cohen) Crane; m. Robert MacGregor Magie, Sept. 27, 1987. BA, Lake Forest Coll., 1983; MEd, Tufts U., 1987. Editor Crane Pub Co., Trenton, 1983-89, ednl. cons., 1985—, v.p., 1988—. Home: 22 Elmwood Ave Watertown MA 02172 Office: Crane Pub Co 1301 Hamilton Ave Trenton NJ 08629

MAGLIOLA, GERTRUDE LOUISE, educator; b. Jamestown, N.Y., May 2, 1933; d. Frank and Frances R. (Ricotta) M. BE, SUNY, Buffalo, 1955; MEd, SUNY, Fredonia, 1961; postgrad., SUNY, U. Pitts., 1979, Pa. State U., 1962-64; cert. adv. studies spl. edn., Syracuse U., 1966; postgrad., Edinboro State Coll., U. Pitts, 1979. Tchr. elem. sch. Jamestown (N.Y.) Pub. Schs., 1955-65, tchr. spl. edn., 1966—; cons. tchr. tng. insvc. Dunkirk Pub. Schs., 1975-77. Chmn. com. exceptional children Jamestown City Coun. PTA; life mem. Carlyle Ring PTA,; mem. adv. bd. State Univ. Coll., Fredonia, 1978-80; bd. dirs. Jamestown Area Learning Ctr., 1972-76, Jamestown Gen. Hosp., 1980, United Cerebral Palsy Chautauqua County, 1980. Mem. ACLD (charter mem., v.p. Chautauqua County chpt.), N.Y. State Assn. for Handicapped Coun. for Learnig Disabilities, Phi Delta Kappa, Delta Kappa Gamma (v.p. 1988-90, pres. 1990—). Home: 153 S Main St Jamestown NY 14701 Office: Rogers Sch 41 Hebner St Jamestown NY 14701

MAGNELLI, ANDREA DALE, behavior therapist; b. Bellevue, Pa., July 29, 1959; d. Anthony Frank and Lillian (Berie) M.; 1 child, Rachel Elizabeth Hills. BA, Carlow Coll., Pitts., 1981; MSW, U. Pitts., 1983. Lic. social worker, Pa. Prog. monitor Assn. for Retarded Citizens, Coraopolis, Pa., 1981-88; cons. 3 Rivers Ctr. for Ind. Living, Pitts., 1984-86; instr. Community Coll. Allegheny County, Pitts., 1987-88; behavior specialist Staunton Clinic, Sewickley, Pa., 1988-89; cons. Staunton Clinic, Sewickley, 1989, outpatient psychotherapist, 1989—. Democrat. Roman Catholic. Home: 726 Ferree St Coraopolis PA 15108 Office: Staunton Clinic Sewickley PA 15143

MAGNER, RACHEL HARRIS, banker; b. Lamar, S.C., Aug. 5, 1951; d. Garner Greer and Catherine Alice (Cloaninger) Harris; B.S. in Fin., U. S.C., 1972; postgrad. UCLA, 1974, Calif. State U., 1975; m. Fredric Michael Magner, May 14, 1972. Mgmt. trainee Union Bank, Los Angeles, 1972-75, comml. loan officer, 1975-77; asst. v.p. comml. fin. Crocker Bank, Los Angeles, 1978, asst. v.p., factoring account exec. subs. Crocker United Factors, Inc., 1978-81; v.p. comml. services div. Crocker Bank, 1981-82, v.p., sr. account mgr. bus. banking div., 1982-83; v.p. corporate banking Office of Pres., Sumitomo Bank Calif., 1983—. Home: 2200 Pine Ave Manhattan Beach CA 90266 Office: Sumitomo Bank of Calif 101 S San Pedro Ste 500 Los Angeles CA 90012

MAGNESS, CARLA LOUISE, pharmaceutical company administrator; b. Camden, Ark., Nov. 18, 1957; d. Charles Ross and Roberta (Leake) M. BA, Hendrix Coll., 1979; postgrad., U. Ark. Med. Sch., 1979-81. Microbiology and genetics lab. technician Hendrix Coll., Conway, Ark., 1977-79; quantitative analysis asst. U. Ark. Sch. Pharmacy, Little Rock, 1979-80, pathology rsch. assoc., 1979-81; pharm. rep. McNeil Pharm., Springhouse, Pa., 1982-83; market cons. mgr. Ciba-Geigy Pharm., Summit, N.J., 1986—, clin. conf. mgr., 1986—; skills trainer Ciba-Geigy Pharm., Summit, 1988—. Mem. Human Soc., Washington, 1988; mem. vol. Alpha-K (Child Abuse Shelter), Fayetteville, Ark., 1989. Recipient scholarship, U. Ark. Med. Sch., Little Rock, 1980, 81, grantee, 1980. Mem. Women of the N.W. Ark. Pharm. Industry, AAAS, Bus. and Profl. Women's Club. Republican. Methodist. Home: 14 Greenbriar Dr Fayetteville AR 72703 Office: Ciba-Geigy Pharm 1825 S Grant St San Mateo CA 94401

MAGNUSSON, KATHY RUTH, veterinarian; b. Owatonna, Minn., Aug. 26, 1957; d. Arthur Bror and Mary Ella (Gilmore) M. Student, Utah State U., 1975-76, U. Mont., 1977; BS, U. Minn., 1980, DVM, 1982, PhD, 1989. Veterinarian Nordic Vet. Svc., Hoffman, Minn., 1982-84; vet. med. assoc., teaching asst. U. Minn., St. Paul, 1984-86; research fellow U. Minn., 1986-89; asst. prof. Colo. State U., 1989—. Contbr. articles to profl. jours. NIH Physician Scientist award, 1986—; Louise Dosdall fellow, U. Minn., 1986. Mem. Am. Assn. Vet. Anatomists, Soc. for Neurosci., Phi Zeta, Gamma Sigma Delta. Office: Colo State U Dept of Anatomy and Neurobiology Fort Collins CO 90523

MAGRUDER, MARION REILEY, office equipment company executive; b. Danville, Ky., July 31, 1918; d. Thomas Marion and Hallie Kirtley (Helm) Reiley; m. Jerry Buren Magruder, Jr., Oct. 23, 1945; children: Robert Scott, Patricia Ann, Bruce Franklin. BA in Music, Miami U., Oxford, Ohio, 1940; grad. Moser Bus. Coll., Chgo., 1940. Sec. to dir. pub. rels. United Airlines, Chgo., 1941, Union League Club, Chgo., 1942; sec. to chmn. R.R. Retirement Bd., Chgo., 1946-48; exec. sec. to pres., office mgr., sec., bd. dirs. Media Methods Pub. Rels., Montville, N.J., 1971-83; v.p. J.B. Magruder & Assocs., Sparta, N.J., 1986—. Co-founder Youth Employment Svc., Sparta, also vol.; elder, chmn. worship and sacraments commn. and Christian edn. commn., pres. bd. deacons, pres. ch. women, Sunday sch. tchr., mem. choir 1st Presbyn. Ch., Sparta; past pres. United Ch. Women; vol. Newton (N.J.) Meml. Hosp.. Aux., also past membership chmn. and pres. Sparta br., past v.p. overall aux.; hon. mem. Commn. on Ecumenical Mission and Rels., United Presbyn. Ch. U.S.A., 1969. Lt. WAVES, USNR, 1943-46. Recipient hon. cert. of appreciation plaque Newton Meml. Hosp. Aux., 1969. Mem. AAUW (past corr. sec., chmn. nominating com., 2d v.p. membership, pres. Sussex County br. 1989—, N.J. Membership award 1988, Ednl. Found. gift in her name Sussex County br. 1988), P.E.O. (chaplain, publicity chmn., courtesy chmn. Sparta chpt. C), Sparta Woman's Club (past 1st v.p., music chmn.), Lake Mohawk Country Club, Lake Mohawk Golf Club, Delta Omicron, Chi Omega. Home and Office: 7 Alpine Trail Sparta NJ 07871

MAGUIRE-KRUPP, MARJORIE ANNE, corporate executive, developer; b. Stamford, Conn., Apr. 29, 1955; d. Walter Reeves and Jean Elisabeth (Cook) Maguire; m. Joseph Michael Krupp, Jr., Nov. 26, 1983; children: Parnell Joseph Maguire Krupp; stepchildren: Theresa Margaret, Donna Marie, Maura Elizabeth. BA in Acctg. cum laude, Franklin and Marshall Coll., 1977; MBA in Fin. with honors, NYU, 1983, cert. in real estate, 1986; cert. in French, U. Strasbourg, France, 1971. CPA, Conn. Real estate sales person, Stack and Stack, N.J.; supervisory auditor Arthur Young & Co., Stamford, 1976-80; mgr. fin. planning Combustion Engring., Stamford, 1980-84; asst. v.p., mgr. fin. planning and analysis Kidder Peabody & Co., N.Y.C., 1984-87, fin. cons. to brokerage industry, 1988—; pres. Parnell Devel. Corp., 1987—; v.p. fin. Jeremiah Devel. Co., 1987-89; mem. bd. realtors Hudson County. Advisor Jr. Achievement, Stamford, 1979-80; mem. Met. Opera Guild, N.Y.C., 1985-89, Met. Mus. Art, N.Y.C., 1983—, Mus. Modern Art, N.Y.C., 1983—; treas., bd. dir. Cliffhouse Condo Assn., Cliffside Park, N.J., 1983-85. Mem. AICPA, Stamford Jaycee Women Club (pres. 1980-81, chmn. bd. 1981-82, Stamford Disting. Svc. award, Outstanding Young Woman of Yr. award, 1980), Phi Beta Kappa (honor soc.), Beta Gamma Sigma (bus. honor soc.). Republican. Presbyterian. Avocations: travel, skiing, sailing, gourmet cooking, golf. Home: 107 Shearwater Ct Port Liberte NJ 07305

MAGUIRE-ZINNI, DEIRDRE, federal community development administrator; b. Bklyn., Oct. 21, 1954; d. James Michael and Dorothy Ursula (Gronske) Maguire; m. Nicholas A. Zinni, Aug. 27, 1977. BA with honors, SUNY, Stony Brook, 1976; MS, Fla. State U., 1981. Housing specialist Suffolk Community Devel. Corp., Coram, N.Y., 1977-78; planner Palm Beach County Housing and Community Devel., West Palm Beach, Fla., 1980-83, sr. planner, 1983-84, mgr. adminstrn. and ops., 1984-87; fed. community planning and devel. rep. HUD, Jacksonville, Fla., 1987-88; community planning and devel. specialist HUD, Washington, 1988—; staff liaison Affordable Housing Task Force, West Palm Beach, 1985-86, Fla. Community Devel. Assn., 1985-87. Named one of Outstanding Young Women of Am., 1985. Democrat. Roman Catholic.

MAHAFFEY, MARCIA JEANNE HIXSON, school administrator; b. Scoby, Mont.; d. Edward Goodell and Olga Marie (Frederickson) Hixson; m. Donald Harry Mahaffey (div. Aug. 1976); 1 child, Marcia Anne. BA in English, U. Wash.; MA in Secondary Edn., U. Hawaii, 1967. Cert. secondary and elem. tchr. and adminstr. Tchr. San Lorenzo (Calif.) Sch. Dist., 1958-59; tchr. Castro Valley (Calif.) Sch. Dist., 1959-63, vice prin., 1963-67; vice prin. Sequoia Union High Sch. Dist., Redwood City, Calif., 1967-77, asst. prin., 1977—; tchr. trainer Project Impact Sequoia Union Sch. Dist., Redwood City, 1986—; mem. supr.'s task force for dropout prevention, 1987—, Sequoia Dist. Goals Commn. (chair subcom. staff devel. 1988); mentor tchr. selection com., 1987—; mem. Stanford Program Devel. Ctr. Com., 1987—; chairperson gifted and talented Castro Valley Sch. Dist.; mem. family services bd., San Leandro, Calif. Vol. Am. Cancer Soc., San Mateo, Calif., 1967, Castro Valley, 1965; Sunday sch. tchr. Hope Luth. Ch., San Mateo, 1970-76; chair Carlmont High Sch. Site Council, Belmont, Calif., 1977—. Recipient Life Mem. award Parent, Tchr., Student Assn., Belmont, 1984, Svc. award, 1989, Exemplary Svc award Carlmont High Sch., 1989; named Woman of the Week, Castro Valley, 1967, Outstanding Task Force Chair Adopt A Sch. Program San Mateo (Calif.) County, 1990. Mem. Assn. Calif. Sch. Adminstrs. (Project Leadership plaque 1985), Sequoia Dist. Mgmt. Assn. (pres. 1975, treas. 1984, 85), Assn. for Supervision and Curriculum Devel., Met. Mus. Art, Smithsonian Inst., AAUW, DAR, Animal Welfare Advocacy, Commonwealth Club of Calif., Delta Kappa Gamma, Alpha Xi Delta. Office: Carlmont High Sch 1400 Alameda De Las Pulgas Belmont CA 94002

MAHAN, CLARE MAUREEN, biostatistician; b. Boston, Apr. 7, 1941; d. J. Victor and Josephine C. (Gillis) M. AB, Emmanuel Coll., 1962; MA, Boston U., 1970; PhD, U. Calif., Berkeley, 1979. Rsch. asst. Harvard U., Cambridge, Mass., 1960-62; statistician Sch. Medicine Boston U., 1962-63, 72-73, epidemiologist, biostatistician, 1978-79; math. statistician chronic diseases div. USPHS, Boston, 1963-72; asst. prof. biostatistics Tufts U., Medford, Mass., 1979-86; sr. biostatistician Am. Health Found., N.Y.C., 1986-88; biostatistician Mass. Dept. Pub. Health, Boston, 1988—; pres. Cardiovascular Risk Assessments, Marblehead, Mass., 1985—; cons. in field. Author: Cancer Incidence in Massachusetts 1982-86, 1990; contbr. 35 articles to profl. jours. Bd. dirs. Diabetes and Arthritis Found., Wellesley, Mass., 1971—; mem. com. Am. Cancer Soc., Boston, 1988—. NIH fellow, 1973-77. Mem. AAUP, Am. Coll. Epidemiology (assoc.), Am. Diabetes Assn. (coun. epidemiology and statistics), Am. Statistical Assn., Biometric Soc., Internat. Diabetes (epidemiology group), Internat. Epidemiol. Assn. (elected mem.), Soc. Epedemiol. Rsch. Roman Catholic. Home: 15 Goodwins Ct Marblehead MA 01945 Office: Dept Pub Health 150 Tremont St 5th Fl Boston MA 02111

MAHANEY, ELIZABETH FLORENCE, police officer; b. New Rochelle, N.Y., Nov. 16, 1962; d. William J. and Helen Mary (Walsh) Wood; m. William Philip Mahaney, June 17, 1989. BA in English, Washington and Jefferson Coll., 1984. Police officer spl. ops. div. N.Y.C. Transit Police Dept., 1985—. Mem. N.Y.C. Transit Police Benevolent Assn., Transit Policewomen's Assn., Transit Police Emerald Soc. Roman Catholic. Office: NYC Transit Police Dept 370 Jay St Brooklyn NY 11201

MAHAR, SHERRY LYNN, elementary educator; b. Madisonville, Ky., Mar. 29, 1954; d. Paul Lynwood and Rose Frances (Cunningham) Mahar; m. Hugh David Stacey, Aug. 10, 1977 (div. 1982); children: Carmen, Joseph, Joshua; m. John Frederick Berggren, Sept. 8, 1984; 1 child, John Jacob. BS summa cum laude, Middle Tenn. State U., 1976, MA, 1984; postgrad. in law, U. Tenn., 1990—. Cert. Elem. and Secondary Educator; cert. Sch. Psychologist. Clk., buyer Vogue Shoppe, McMinnville, Tenn., 1969-84; tchr. Warren County Schs., McMinnville, 1976-89; intern, sch. psychologist Multi County Mental Health Ctr., Shelbyville, Tenn., 1977; elem. tchr. North Elem. Sch., McMinnville, 1989; sponsor Adopt-A-Grandparent Program, McMinnville, 1985-89; in-service com. Warren County Schs., McMinnville, 1989; retirement chmn. Exec. Bd. Warren County Educators Assn., McMinnville, 1988-89; sponsor/adult dir. Just Say No Club, McMinnville, 1986-89. Mem. membership drive com. Community Concert Assn., McMinnville, 1988-89; bd. dirs. Black House Hist. Soc., McMinnville, 1989; fundraising chmn. Found. for Geriatric Edn., McMinnville, 1987-89; grad. Leadership McMinnville, 1989. Named Outstanding Member AAUW, 1984, Outstanding Young Woman of the Year Jaycees, 1988. Mem. NEA, Tenn. Assn. Sch. Psychologists, Tenn. Assn. Mid. Schs., Assn. for Supervision and Curriculum Devel., AAUW, McMinnville Jaycees. Home: 301 Woodlawn Pk Apt G7 Knoxville TN 37920

MAHARRY, SHARON SCOTT, advertising executive; b. Roanoke, Va., Sept. 30, 1949; d. Conrad Young and Mildred (Altice) Scott; m. Robert H. Maharry, July 26, 1986. BA, Roanoke Coll., 1971. Copywriter Creative Advt., Roanoke, 1971-72; prin. Image Advt., Roanoke, 1972-79; copywriter Lawler-Ballard Advt., Richmond, Va., 1979-81; sr. writer Young and Rubicam/Zemp, St. Petersburg, Fla., 1981-82, sr. v.p., creative dir., 1982-84; exec. v.p., creative dir. Johanesson, Kirk and Maharry, Clearwater, Fla., 1984-85, I.C.E. Communications, Rochester, N.Y., 1985-86; sr. v.p., creative dir. Hutchins/Young and Rubicam, Rochester, 1986—. Recipient Clio awards, 1978, 82, 84, 85, 87, 88, 89, IBA award Hollywood Radio and TV Soc., 1981, 87, 88, 89, Andy awards Advt. Club N.Y., 1980-85, Addy awards Am. Advt. Fedn., 1977, 82, 83, 87, 88, 89, One Show award N.Y. Art and Copy Club, 1982, Creativity awards Art Dirs. Mag., 1982, 83, 86, 88, 89, Mobius award U.S. TV and Radio Commls. Festival, 1985, 87, Art Dirs. Merit awards The Art Dirs. Club N.Y., 1985, 86, Gold medals Internat. TV and Radio Festival N.Y., 1985, 87, 88, Gold medal award

London Internat. Advt., 1987. Office: Hutchins/Young & Rubicam 400 Midtown Tower Rochester NY 14604

MAHER, FRAN, advertising agency executive; b. Chgo., June 22, 1938; d. Edward Stephan and Virginia Rose (Harrington) M.; m. Anthony Peter Petrella, Sept. 17, 1957; children: Roland, Louis, Marcus. Student (univ. scholar) U. Minn., 1956-57; student Spectrum Inst., 1968-71; BA summa cum laude, Kean Coll. N.J., 1979. Office mgr. Lead Supplies, Inc., Mpls., 1957-59; freelance artist and writer, Warren, N.J., 1968-72; prin. Visuals, Warren, N.J., 1974-79; pres. Fran Maher, Inc., Stirling, N.J., 1980—; dir. Parent Edn. Advocacy Tng. Center, Alexandria, Va., 1979-85. Officer Friends of Weigand Farm, Milton, N.J., 1977-80, Somerset County Assn. for Retarded Citizens, 1982—, pres., bd. dirs. 1987-89; officer, bd. dirs. Assn. Retarded Citizens N.J., 1989, 90—; trustee Peoplecare Ctr., Inc., 1990—; founding mem. Flintlock Boys' Club. Recipient N.J. Art Dirs. Show award, 1978, 1st place award in graphics Watchung Art Center, 1980. Mem. Art Dirs. Club N.J., Am. Women's Econ. Devel. Corp., Advt. Agy. Network Internat., Internat. Platform Assn., Somerset County C. of C. (bd. dirs. 1989—). Office: 1390 Valley Rd Stirling NJ 07980

MAHER, JEAN ELIZABETH, school counselor; b. Cortland, N.Y., Aug. 13, 1953; d. Russell Edgar and Frances Mae (MacGregor) Owen; m. Kevin John Maher, Aug. 6, 1983. BA, Houghton Coll., 1975; MS, SUNY, Oneonta, 1979, cert. of advanced study, 1980. Tchr. English Monticello (N.Y.) High Sch., 1975-80, dir. gifted program, Sr. Hon. Soc. advisor, 1978-79; sch. counselor Lounsberry Hollow Mid. Sch., Vernon, N.J., 1980—; coord. spl. svcs. Lounsberry Hollow Mid. Sch., Vernon, 1982—; tchr. Gen. Equivalency Diploma program Port Jervis (N.Y.) High Sch., 1985-86. Leader Youth Group, Port Jervis, 1982; editor ch. newsletter Port Jervis, 1986—. Named Vernon Twp. Tchr. of Yr., 1989-90. Mem. NEA, Am. Assn. Counseling and Devel., N.J. Edn. Assn., Sussex County Sch. Counselors Assn. (sec. 1983-85, treas. 1985-87, pres. 1987-88), N.J. Profl. Counselors Assn. (ethics com. 1988—). Home: RD 5 Box 720 Montague NJ 07827 Office: Lounsberry Hollow Mid Sch Sammis Rd PO Box 219 Vernon NJ 07462

MAHER, KIM LEVERTON, museum administrator; b. Washington, Feb. 25, 1946; d. Joseph Wilson and Helen Elizabeth (Bell) Leverton; m. William Fredrick Maher, June 12, 1965 (div. 1980); 1 child, Lauren Robinson. Student Duke U., 1963-65, George Washington U., 1966; B.A. in English, U. Fla., 1969. Social worker Fla. Health and Rehab. Service, Gainesville, 1969-71, Delray Beach, 1972-74, fraud unit supr., West Palm Beach, 1974-76, direct service supr., 1977-78; ctr. dir. Palm Beach County Employment and Tng. Adminstrn., West Palm Beach, 1979-81; exec. dir. Discovery Ctr., Inc., Ft. Lauderdale, Fla., 1981—. Bd. dirs. Singing Pines Mus., Boca Raton, Fla., 1984—, Broward Art Guild, Ft. Lauderdale, 1985—; mem. Leadership Broward II, Ft. Lauderdale, 1983-84. Recipient Cultural Arts award Broward Cultural Arts Found., 1985, Woman of Yr. award Women in Communications, 1990. Mem. Am. Assn. Museums, Assn. Sci. and Tech. Ctrs., Southeastern Museums Conf., Fla. Sci. Tchrs. Assn. (bd. dirs.), Leadership Broward Alumnae (curriculum com. 1984—), Fort Lauderdale Downtown Council, Ft. Lauderdale C. of C. (cultural affairs task force 1983—), Women's Exec. Club, Phi Kappa Phi. Republican. Methodist. Avocations: scuba diving; piano; creative writing; collecting art and antiques; painting. Office: Discovery Ctr Inc 231 SW 2d Ave Fort Lauderdale FL 33301

MAHER, MARY ANN, infosystems specialist; b. Kingston, N.Y., Sept. 19, 1949; d. Thomas Emmett and Antionette (Menge) M.; m. Peter John McCourt, June 25, 1977 (div. 1983). BA in Edn. and Social Sci, Mt. St. Mary Coll., Newburg, N.Y., 1971; MS in Edn., SUNY, New Paltz, 1975. Cert. elem. and jr. coll. tchr., N.Y., Ariz., Fla. Tchr. Highland (N.Y.) Central Schs., 1971-78, Amphitheater Schs., Tucson, 1978-79; computer sci. tchr. Lamson Bus. Coll., Tucson, 1980-83, Spencer Bus. Inst., Schenectady, N.Y., 1985; bus. tchr. Tucson Coll. Bus., 1980; programmer Computational Analysis Corp., Tucson, 1980; systems adminstr. Greenberg Chin Cons., Tucson, 1986-87; info. systems dir. Kino Community Hosp., Tucson, 1987—; cons. in field; tchr. ITT Tech. Inst., Tucson, 1985. Mem. NAFE, Data Processing Mgmt. Assn., Border Area Mid-range Users' Group, Am. Hosp. Assn., Healthcare Info. and Mgmt. Systems Soc., Greenpeace. Roman Catholic.

MAHER, PATRICIA MARIE, lawyer; b. Bklyn., June 26, 1954; d. Joseph Francis and Margaret (O'Keefe) M. BA, Siena Coll., 1976; JD, St. John's U., 1983. Bar: N.Y. 1983. Social worker Charlton Sch., Burnt Hill, N.Y., 1977-78; ptnr. Maher & Lawrence, N.Y.C., 1983—. Mem. ABA, N.Y. State Bar Assn. Office: Maher & Lawrence 40 Broad St 7th Fl New York NY 10004

MAHER, SYLVIA ARLENE, nurse executive; b. Kansas City, Mo., Nov. 12, 1946; d. Elmer Newton and Enid Louise (Olson) McKinley; m. A.C. Amborn Jr., 1969 (div. 1971); m. Mark Edward Maher, Oct. 14, 1977. Diploma in Nursing, Trinity Luth. Hosp., Kansas City, Mo., 1967; BSN, U. Kans. Med. Ctr., 1971, MA in Nursing, 1975. Nurse Trinity Luth. Hosp., Kansas City, Mo., 1967-71; head nurse emergency svcs. Baptist Meml. Hosp., Kansas City, Mo., 1971-77; clinical nurse specialist Bethany Med. Ctr., Kansas City, Mo., 1977-78, critical care div. dir., 1978-80, v.p. for nursing svcs., 1980—; adj. faculty William Jewell Coll., Liberty, Mo., 1975-77, U. Kans. Med. Ctr., Kansas City, 1979—, Avila Coll., Kansas City, 1981-82. Editorial bd. Jour. of AACN, 1978-84. Mem. Kansas City Nursing Asminstrs. (pres. and pres. elect 1987, 88), Kans. Forum Women Execs., Am. Nurses Assn., Sigma Theta Tau. Home: 262 Lakeshore W Lake Quivira KS 66106 Office: Bethany Med Ctr 51 N 12th St Kansas City MO 66102

MAHEU, SHIRLEY, Canadian legislator; b. Montreal, Que., Can., Oct. 7, 1931; d. George William Johnson and Bertha Hunt; m. René Albert Maheu, Sept. 5, 1953; children: Ronald, Richard, Daniel, Marc. Ed., O'Sullivan Bus. Coll., Vanier Coll. Ins. broker; mcpl. councillor City of Saint-Laurent, Que., 1982-88; mem. from Saint-Laurent Ho. of Commons, 1988—. Pres. Saint-Laurent br. Red Cross Soc. Mem. Ins. Brokers Assn. Que., Saint-Laurent C. of C. Roman Catholic. Office: House of Commons, Parliament Bldgs, Ottawa, ON Canada K1A 0A6*

MAHL, OLGA BERDE, lawyer, real estate developer, financial consultant; b. Bucharest, Rumania, June 25, 1946; B.A., CCNY, 1967; J.D., St. John's U., N.Y.C., 1970. Bar: N.Y. 1971, U.S. Supreme Ct. 1972. Assoc. various law firms, N.Y.C., 1970-74; sole practice, N.Y.C., 1974—; mem. legal com. Real Estate Bd. N.Y., N.Y.C., 1982—. Author numerous pieces of legislation on artist housing, renovation of comml. to residential properties, and real estate taxation in N.Y. State. Adviser ARTPAC, N.Y.C.; bd. advisers various artist-related orgns., including Pub. Art Fund, Pub. Art Council. N.Y.C. Mem. Assn. Bar City N.Y., N.Y. Women's Bar Assn., N.Y. State Bar Assn., ABA. Office: 16 Desprosses St New York NY 10013

MAHLER, ELLA SWARTZ ZONIS, music educator; b. Boston, Mar. 19, 1936; d. Edward Swartz and Lena (Rothman) Zion; m. Marvin Zonis, Dec. 21, 1958 (div. 1973); children: Nadia Eleanor, Leah Hya Sarah. BA, Wellesley (Mass.) Coll., 1957; M in Music, New Eng. Conservatory, Boston, 1961; MDiv., Harvard U., 1985; PhD, Brandeis U., 1968. Prof. U. Chgo., 1969-73, U. Hawaii, Oahu, 1976, MIT, Cambridge, 1976-80. Author: (book) Classical Persian Music, 1973; contbr. articles to numerous musical publs. Unitarian. Home: 7A Walnut Ave Cambridge MA 02140

MAHLUM-HENEGAR, RHONDA LYNN, accountant, realtor; b. Crookston, Minn., Apr. 25, 1959; d. Werner Conway and Darlene Harriet (Benson) M. B.S. in Acctg., Moorhead State U., 1981. CPA, N.D. Resident asst. Moorhead State U., 1979-81; cons. Small Bus. Inst., Moorhead, 1980-81; auditor Tax Dept. State of N.D., Bismarck, 1981-84; Realtor Bianco Realty, Bismarck, 1984-88; acct. Puklich & Eckroth, P.C., Bismarck, 1985-87; contr. N.D. State Treas. Office, 1987—; asst. mgr. Capt. Kit's Lake Sakakawea Concessions, Pick City, N.D., 1989; sec.-treas. Lake Sak, Inc., Riverdale, N.D., 1989—. Officer Heart Butte Water Ski Shows, Lake Tschide, 1982-84. Mem. N.D. Soc. CPAs (Bismarck-Mandan chpt.), N.D. Assn. Realtors (chmn. edn. 1985-86), Bismarck-Mandan Bd. Realtors (chmn. edn. 1985-86), N.D. Pub. Employees Assn., River Women's Golf Club League (Bismarck). Home: PO Box 1812 Bismarck ND 58502 Office: ND Treas Office Capitol Bldg Bismarck ND 58505

MAHON, FLORENCE LUCY, psychologist; b. New Bedford, Mass.; d. Michael J. and Inez (Miller) Collins; m. Frank W. Mahon, July 8, 1935; children: Judith Bolton, Lois Beedy. BS, Boston U., 1956, MEd, 1958, EdD, 1962. Cert. clin. psychologist, speech pathologist. Instr. Boston U., 1961-62; prin. New Bedford (Mass.) Pub. Schs., 1962-67, dir. Headstart, 1965-67, curriculum coord., 1967-70, asst. supt., 1970--76; clin. psychologist State of Mass., New Bedford, 1982--; supr. Right to Read, S.E. Mass., 1970-74; instr. Southeastern Mass. U., Dartmouth, 1964-77; instr. Bristol Community Coll., Fall River, Mass., 1980-81; dir. bilingual program, coord. tchr. aides., dir. Model Cities program, cons. ONBOARD Day Care, New Bedford Schs. Author: Little Listening Boy, 1973; Mahon Kindergarten Test, 1971; Let's Streamline Reading, 1973; English Pronunciation Guide, 1987. Trustee New Bedford Pub. Libr., 1979-86; dir. Office for Children, 1978-79; pres. New Bedford YWCA, 1979; pres. Friends of the Libr., 1980-85. Mem. Am. Psychol. Assn., Acad. Am. Educator, Who's Who Biog. Assn., Delta Kappa Gamma, Pi Lamba Theta, Internat. Reading Assn., Catholic Women's Club (pres. 1962-63). Home and Office: 196 Reed St New Bedford MA 02740

MAHON, RITA, physicist; b. Golborne, Eng., Sept. 23, 1949; came to U.S., 1975; d. Thomas A. and Ellen H. Mahon; m. Richard Conn Henry, May 10, 1975; children: George William, Mark Winston. BS, Imperial Coll., 1970, PhD, 1973. Postdoctoral fellow Ctr. for Rsch. in Exptl. Sci., York U., Toronto, Ont., Can., 1974-75; rsch. assoc. Inst. for Phys. Sci. and Tech. U. Md., College Park, 1975-80, 86—, rsch. assoc. dept. physics and astronomy, 1980-84, rsch. assoc. Lab for Plasma and Fusion Energy, 1984-86; cons. Plasma Fusion Ctr. MIT, College Park, 1985-86; scientist Laser Physics br. optical scis. div. Jaycor, Vienna, Va., 1985—; scientist Laser Physics Br., Optical Scis. Div., Naval Rsch. Lab, Washington, 1985—; assoc. Inst. for Phys. Sci. and Tech., U. Md., 1986—. Mem. Am. Phys. Soc. (life), Optical Soc. Am. Home: 12515 Meadowood Dr Silver Spring MD 20904

MAHONEY, DOROTHY REED, photojournalist; b. Chgo., July 1, 1919; d. Earl Howell and Edith (Lobdell) Reed; m. Edward Ansel Mahoney, Aug. 13, 1960 (div. Nov., 1980). BA, Conn. Coll., 1941. Assoc. editor Esquire Magazine, Chgo., 1944-45; youth editor Woman's Home Companion, NYC, 1946; freelance writer, photojournalist Chgo., 1947-60; photojournalist Roanoke, Va.; developer First Roanoke (Va.) Crafts Festival, k, 1971; developer, dir. Va. Mountain Crafts Guild, Claytor Lake, Va., 1975-79; developer Va. Mountain Crafts Guild Fair, Claytor Lake, Va., 1979; cons. on crafts Roanoke, Va., 1979--; cons. Richmond Crafts Fair, 1978. Author: A Farm for Andy, 1951, Zippy's Birthday, 1954; writer, photographer, sound film, Barbara's Christmas, 1956. Democrat. Home: 1865 Elbert Dr SW Roanoke VA 24018

MAHONEY, IRENE JACOBSON, pensions and benefits specialist, actuary; b. Long Beach, N.Y., Mar. 13, 1954; d. Lester Herbert and Audrey Sara (Koss) Jacobson; m. Daniel P. Mahoney, Sept. 6, 1974 (div. Dec. 1986). BS in Maths., SUNY, Albany, 1974; MBA, Coll. of William and Mary, 1982. Sr. compensation analyst Newport News (Va.) Shipbuilding, 1982-83; pension adminstr. fibers div. BASF Corp., Williamsburg, Va., 1983-86; dir. employee benefits Reynolds Metals Co., Richmond, Va., 1986—. N.Y. State Regents scholar, 1971. Mem. Soc. Actuaries, Middle Atlantic Actuarial Club, Beta Gamma Sigma, Alpha Mu Alpha. Republican. Jewish. Office: Reynolds Metals Co 6603 W Broad St Richmond VA 23230

MAHONEY, KAREN RENEE, marketing communications executive; b. Clarion, Iowa, Oct. 14, 1960; d. Robert Dale and Marlene Maxine (Campbell) M. Student, U. Cape Town, 1982; BS, Iowa State U., 1983. Mktg. analyst Weyerhaeuser Co., Tacoma, 1984-85, sourcing mgr., 1986-87, mgr. mktg. communications, 1987—. Rotary Found. scholar, 1982. Roman Catholic. Home: 733 Summit Ave E Apt 309 Seattle WA 98102

MAHONEY, LAURA STEPECK, insurance executive; b. East Haven, Conn., Dec. 17, 1926; d. Edward J. and Esther (Karbowski) Stepeck; m. Robert F. Lorch, Sept. 17, 1949 (dec. Mar. 1968); children: Robert F. Jr., Christopher Edward, Pamela Sue, Amy Lorch Lombard; m. Kevin Mahoney, July 28, 1970 (dec. July 1977). Student, Bates Coll., 1943-44; BA, U. Conn., 1947, MEd, 1968. Employment specialist Aetna Life & Casualty Cos., Hartford, Conn., 1947-52; tchr. Granby (Conn.) Bd. Edn., 1966-74, adminstr., 1974—. Mem. Rep. Town Com., Rocky Hill, Conn., 1988—, Econ. Devel. Commn., Rocky Hill, 1989; commr. Rocky Hill Housing Authority, 1989, chmn., 1990—; del. Rep. State Conv., Hartford, 1990. Roman Catholic. Home: 36 Fernwood Dr Rocky Hill CT 06067 Office: Aetna Life & Casualty Cos 151 Farmington Ave Hartford CT 06457

MAHONEY, MARGARET ANN, lawyer; b. Alliance, Nebr., Apr. 22, 1949; d. John Charles and Grace Margaret (Hoban) M.; m. Peter B. Ogren, June 28, 1980. BA, Coll. of St. Catherine, 1971; JD cum laude, U. Minn., 1974. Bar: Minn. 1974, Fla. 1975, Tex. 1988. Ptnr. Stringer, Courtney & Rohleder, Ltd., St. Paul, 1974-84; U.S. bankruptcy judge Dist. Minn., Mpls., 1984-87, So. Dist. Tex., Houston, 1987-89; ptnr. Weil, Gotshal & Manges, Houston, 1989—. Nat. Merit scholar Coll. of St. Catherine. Mem. State Bar Tex., Houston Bar Assn., Houston Bankruptcy Conf., Nat. Conf. Bankruptcy Judges (bd. dirs. 1989, adv. com. to adminstrv. office of cts. bankruptcy div. 1988-89), Minn. Bar Assn., Fla. Bar Assn., Sigma Delta Phi, Phi Beta Kappa. Office: Weil Gotshal & Manges 1600 NCNB Center 700 Louisiana Houston TX 77002

MAHONEY, MARGARET ELLERBE, foundation executive; b. Nashville, Oct. 24, 1924; d. Charles Hallam and Leslie Nelson (Savage) M.; BA magna cum laude, Vanderbilt U., 1946; LHD (hon.), Meharry Med. Coll., 1977, U. Fla., 1980, Med. Coll. Pa., 1982, Williams Coll., 1983, Smith Coll., 1985, Beaver Coll., 1985, Brandeis U., 1989. Fgn. affairs officer State Dept., Washington, 1946-53; exec. assoc., assoc. sec. Carnegie Corp., N.Y.C., 1953-72; v.p. Robert Wood Johnson Found., Princeton, N.J., 1972-80; pres. Commonwealth Fund, N.Y.C., 1980—. Contbr. articles to profl. jours. Trustee John D. and Catherine T. Mac Arthur Found., 1985—, Hosp. Rsch. and Ednl. Trust, 1983-87, Dole Found., 1984—, Smith Coll., 1988—; vis. fellow Sch. Architecture and Urban Planning, Princeton U., 1973-80; bd. dirs. Council on Found., 1982-88; mem. N.Y.C. Commn. on the Yr. 2000, 1985-87, MIT Corp., 1984-89, Jackson Lab. Corp., 1988—; bd. govs. Am. Stock Exchange, 1987—; adv. com. The Robert Wood Johnson Found. Minority Med. Edn. Program, 1987-89; adv. bd. Office of the Chief Med. Examiner, N.Y.C., 1987—, Barnard Coll, Inst. Med. Research, 1986—; bd. dirs. Alliance for Aging Rsch., 1987—, Overseas Devel. Coun., 1988—; mem. vestry Parish of Trinity Ch., 1982-89; trustee Smith Coll., 1988—. Recipient Frank H. Lahey Meml. award, 1984. Mem. AAAS, Inst. Medicine, Council Fgn. Rels., Fin. Women's Assn. N.Y., N.Y. Acad. Medicine, Am. Acad. Arts. and Scis., NY Acad. Scis., Alpha Omega Alpha (award 1985). Office: Commonwealth Fund 1 E 75th St New York NY 10021

MAHONEY, MARGARET ELLIS, advertising executive; b. Detroit, Mar. 17, 1929; d. Seth Wiley and Mildred Elizabeth (Hill) Ellis; m. Stephen Bedell Smith, Mar. 15, 1956 (div. Oct. 1962); 1 child, Laura Elizabeth; m. Patrick John Mahoney, Sept. 1, 1972 (dec.). BA, Butler U., 1953. Copywriter Hook Drugs Inc., Indpls., 1953; continuity dir. Sta. WXLW, Indpls., 1954-57; ptnr. Steve Smith and Assocs. Advt., Indpls., 1956-62; account mgr. Sive Advt., Cin., 1963-64, Associated Advt., Cin., 1964-65; copywriter SupeRX Drugs Inc., Cin., 1965-72; promotion writer U.S. News and World Report, Washington, 1974; asst. mgr. advt. Drug Fair, Alexandria, Va., 1975-82; dir. advt. Cosmetic and Fragrance Concepts Inc., Beltsville, Md., 1982-89; cons. Woodbridge, Va., 1989—. Hosp. chairperson Sleepy Hollow Citizens Assn., Falls Church, Va., 1973; vestry mem. St. Matthews Episc. Ch., Cin., 1969-71; vol. Resident Assoc. Program Smithsonian Inst., Washington, 1989—. Mem. Potomac Valley Aquarium Soc. (past treas., past sec., editor jour.), Am. Cichlid Assn. (nat. pub. rels. chair 1985-90), Delta Delta Delta. Republican. Home and Office: 12094 Stallion Ct Woodbridge VA 22192

MAHONEY, MARY DZURKO, teacher; b. McKeesport, Pa., Apr. 5, 1946; d. William Thomas and Anne Cecelia (Basarab) Dzurko; m. Thomas Francis Mahoney; 1 child, David. BA in Eng. Lit., U. Pitts., 1968; MA in Teaching in Elem. Edn., George Washington U., 1969; postdoctoral, Johns Hopkins U. Tchr. Seven Locks Elem. Sch., Bethesda, Md., 1970-73, Tuckerman Elem. Sch., Potomac, Md., 1973-78, Stedwick Elem. Sch., Gaithersburg, Md., 1976-78; sub. tchr. Barnesville (Md.) Sch., 1985-86; home instr. Montgomery County Pub. Schs., Rockville, Md., 1984—; tchr. English Montgomery Coll., 1990. Active PTA, Poolesville, Md., 1985. Mem. Woman's Club Upper Montgomery County (sec. 1986, scholarship com. 1988), Phi Delta Gamma (historian 1974-75, newsletter editor 1975-76). Democrat. Roman Catholic.

MAHONEY, SUZANNE MATTHEWS, sales executive; b. Pitts., Apr. 18, 1963; d. John Patrick and Naomi Ruth (O'Neil) M. BS in Elec. Engr., Pa. State U., 1985; MS in Indsl. Adminstrn., Carnegie Mellon U., Pitts., 1990. Project mgr. Otis Elevator Co., Pitts., 1986, svc. sales rep., 1986-89, new equipment sales rep., 1989—. Dir. Canevin High Sch. Musical, Pitts. 1987. Mem. Am. Mktg. Assn., Western Pa. Soc. Engrs., Pitts. Ski Club, Pa. State Alumni Assn., Delta Delta Delta Alumni Assn. Democrat. Roman Catholic. Home: 2257 Old Oak Dr Pittsburgh PA 15220 Office: Otis Elevator Co 50 Thirteenth St Pittsburgh PA 15222

MAHOOD, HELEN MAYNARD, advertising executive; b. Summit, N.J., Nov. 16, 1953; d. Joseph and Mildred Evelyn (Thompson) MaH. BA, Bates Coll., 1975; MBA, U. Conn., 1984. Staff mgr. Advt. So. New England Tel., 1979-83; acct. supr. Young & Rubicam, L.A., 1983-84; dir. of mktg. Geneva Corp., Costa Mesa, Calif., 1984-85; v.p. Tracy-Locke, Dallas, 1985-86; div. sales mgr. GTE Directories Corp., 1986—; owner, pres. Maynards Mix Co., Houston, 1986—. group instr. Dale Carnegie, Dallas; founder ADRDA S. Cen. Conn. Chpt., New Haven, 1983. Office: GTE Directories Corp 233 Benmar Houston TX 77060

MAHOOD, JANICE H., marketing professional; b. Glen Cove, N.Y., Oct. 1, 1940; d. John Randolph Bricker and Margaretta Ruth (Davey) Hermsted; m. Gary D. Mahood, Sept. 14, 1963; children: Scott Elizabeth Bricker, Grant Davey. BA, Syracuse U., 1962; postgrad., U. Chgo., 1977-78; MBA, Adelphi U., 1988. Exec. trainee, writer McGraw-Hill Inc., N.Y.C., 1962-64; journalist Hartford (Conn.) Times, 1964-66, Richmond (Va.) News Leader, 1966-69; editorial prodn. dir. Cap Cities/ABC Mags., Chgo., 1974-77; mktg. dir., v.p. Storer Communications, Chgo., 1978-81; mktg. cons. Cablevision, Woodbury, N.Y., 1982-85; prin. Mahood & Powell, Glen Head, N.Y., 1985-89; v.p. Unity Mgmt., Inc., 1989-90, fin. svcs. mktg. cons., 1990—. Contbr. articles to profl. publs. Dir., exec. com. Cold Spring Harbor (N.Y.) Whaling Mus., 1986—. Mem. N.Y. Fin. Writers Assn., Soc. Profl. Journalists, L.I. Cable Assn. (founder 1984), Fin. Women's Assn. N.Y. (bd. dirs. 1990—), Profl. Communicators of N.Y. Episcopalian.

MAIDLOW, DOLORES MARY, federal agency executive; b. Westphalia, Mich., Apr. 19, 1934; d. Joseph Ludwig and Ida Veronica (Spitzley) Fox; m. Donald Eugene Maidlow, July 25, 1953; children: Thomas O., Randolph E., Fredric P., Nicholas D., Geoffrey J., Sarah E. Postal clk. U.S. Postal Svc., 1962-77; supr. U.S. Postal Svc., Okemos, Mich., 1977-80; postmaster U.S. Postal Svc., Howell, Mich., 1980—. Bd. dirs., Livingston County United Way, Howell, 1985—, sec., 1987, treas., 1989, v.p., 1990; bd. dirs., United Way Mich., 1987—. Mem. Nat. Assn. Postmasters (area dir. 1982-84), Nat. Mus. Women in Arts, Smithsonian Instn. Home: 2806 Forest Rd Lansing MI 48910 Office: US Postal Svc 325 S Michigan Ave Howell MI 48843

MAIDON, CAROLYN HOWSER, academic officer; b. Chgo., May 13, 1946; d. Lloyd Earl and Esther Lillian (Beck) Howser; m. Charles Randall Maidon, Nov. 21, 1970; children: Randall Scott, April Janel. BS in Edn., Okla. State U., 1968; MS in Edn., N.C. State U., 1984, postgrad., 1987—. Tchr. biology and English Cary (N.C.) High Sch., 1968-71; grad. instr. N.C. State U., Raleigh, 1984-85, asst. affirmative action officer, 1985-89, asst. dir. univ. undesignated program, 1989—. Home: 311 Hemlock St Cary NC 27511 Office: NC State U Box 7105 Raleigh NC 27695-7105

MAIER, DONNA JANE-ELLEN, history educator; b. St. Louis, Feb. 20, 1948; d. A. Russell and Mary Virginia Maier; m. Stephen J. Rapp, Jan. 3, 1981; children: Alexander John, Stephanie Jane-Ellen. BA, Coll. of Wooster, 1969; MA, Northwestern U., 1972, PhD, 1975. Asst. prof. U. Tex. at Dallas, Richardson, 1975-78; asst. prof. history U. No. Iowa, Cedar Falls, 1978-81, assoc. prof., 1981-86, prof., 1986—; cons. Scott, Foresman Pub., Glenview, Ill., 1975-90; editorial cons. Children's Press, 1975-76, Macmillan Pubs., 1989-90. Co-author: History and Life, 1976, 4th edit., 1990; author: Priests and Power, 1983; contbr. articles to profl. jours., essay to book. Mem. Iowa Dem. Cen. Com., 1982-90, chmn. budget com., 1986-90; chmn. 3d Congl. Dist. Cen. Com., 1986-88. Fulbright-Hays fellow, Ghana, 1972, Arab Republic Egypt, 1987; fellow Am. Philos. Soc., London, 1978. Mem. Am. Hist. Assn., African Studies Assn., AAUW (fellow Ghana 1973), Quota Club. Home: 219 Highland Blvd Waterloo IA 50703 Office: U No Iowa Dept History Cedar Falls IA 50614

MAILANDER, CAT MARGARET, operations manager; b. Phila., Nov. 24, 1957; d. Edward O'Rourke and Catherine (Drumm) Juhline; m. James Lee Mailander, Nov. 1, 1983. Grad., Phila. Performed various musical groups, U.S., 1976-77; co-founder, v.p. Big Deal Records, Inc., N.Y.C., 1979-81; performer various musical groups, N.Y.C., 1981-82; mgr., performer with husband The Immortals Musical Group, N.Y.C., 1982-85; operations mgr. Skidmore, Owings & Merrill Architects, N.Y.C., 1986-89, Goelet Corp., N.Y.C., 1989—; cons. Sharon Pursell Inc., N.Y.C., 1987—; bus. mgr. Outlaw Gypsy Musical Group, N.Y.C., 1988—. Composer: Rock N' Roll is Alive, 1980, Waiting for the Bus to Japan, 1979; composer, performer Artificial Stimulation Album, 1983. Active mem. People for the Ethical Treatment of Animals, N.Y.C., 1979—, The Humane Soc. N.Y., 1989—. Mem. ASCAP, Am. Fedn. Musicians. Democrat. Roman Catholic. Office: Goelet Corp 22 E 67th St New York NY 10021

MAIN, ALICE LEE, municipal administrator; b. St. Louis, Mar. 11, 1941; d. George and Lillie (Poleos) M.; m. Waldemar Schimming, June 1, 1974 (div. 1988); 1 child, Nicole Maria. BA, Webster U., 1963, U. Mo., 1967; MA, U. No. Colo., 1981; arts mgmt. cert., N.C. State U., 1981. Dept. mgr., buyer Famous-Barr, St. Louis, 1957-64; asst. rsch. librarian Fed. Res. Bank, St. Louis, 1964-66; tchr. drama and English Riverview Gardens Sch. Dist., St. Louis, 1966-69; div. fashion specialist Helene Curtis, Inc., Chgo., 1969-70; asst. buyer Fashion Bar, Denver, 1970-72; credit mgr. Montgomery Wards, Aurora, Colo., 1973; cultural arts adminstr. City of Aurora, 1973—. Founder, treas., v.p. Aurora Arts and Humanities Council, 1978—; theater cons. renovation bd., Fox Arts Ctr., Aurora, 1982-85; cons. Colo. Council Arts and Humanities, Denver, 1979-84; speech judge Voice of Dem., VFW, Colo., 1980-81, 90; coach Aurora Girls' Softball Assn., 1987-89; chmn. com. Colo. Parks and Recreation Assn., 1979-82; bd. dirs. Colo. Dance Alliance, 1985-89; mem. Denver Ballet Guild, 1988-89. Named Woman of Yr. Aurora Bus. and Profl. Women, 1984; recipient Svc. award Aurora Dance Arts, 1987. Mem. AAUW, Aurora C. of C. (chmn. arts com. 1988-89), Assn. Coll. U. and Community Arts Adminstrs., Zonta Internat. (treas. 1989-90). Democrat. Roman Catholic. Home: 11661 E Colorado Dr Aurora CO 80012 Office: City of Aurora Bicentenn Art Ctr 13655 E Alameda Ave Aurora CO 80012

MAIN, EDNA DEWEY, educator; b. Hyannis, Mass., Sept. 1, 1940; d. Seth Bradford and Edna Wilhelmina (Wright) Dewey; m. Donald John Main, Sept. 9, 1961 (div. Dec., 1989); children: Alison Teresa Main Ronzon, Susan Christine Main Leddy, Steven Donald. Degree in Merchandising, Tobe-Coburn Sch., 1960; BA in Edn., U. North Fla., 1974, MA in Edn., 1979, M in Adminstrn. and Supervision, 1983; postgrad. U. Fla., 1986—. Asst. buyer Abraham & Straus, Bklyn., 1960-61; asst. mdse. mgr. Interstate Dept. Stores, N.Y.C., 1962-63; tchr. Holiday Hill Elem. Sch., Jacksonville, Fla., 1974-86; mem. adv. council Coll. Edn., U. North Fla., 1982—, instr. summer sci. inst., 1984—; instr. U. South Fla., 1981, U. North Fla., 1984—, U. Fla., 1987—. Co-author: Developing Critical Thinking Through Science, 1990. Rep. United Way, 1981-86; tchr. rep., chpt. leader White House Young Astronaut Program, 1984-85; mem. supervisory com. Ednl. Community Credit Union; team leader Nat. Sci Found's. Shells Elem. Sci. Project, 1988—. Mem. Nat. Sci. Tchrs. Assn. (sci. tchrs. achievement recognition award 1983), Assn. Supervision and Curriculum Devel., Council Elem. Sci. Internat., Fla. Assn. Sci. Tchrs., Phi Kappa Phi, Phi Delta Kappa, Delta Kappa Gamma, Kappa Delta Pi. Republican. Episcopalian. Office: U North Fla Coll Edn Curriculum and Instrn 4567 Saint Johns Bluff Rd Jacksonville FL 32216

MAIN, NANCY LILLIAN, lawyer, artist; b. Flint, Mich., Sept. 30, 1946; d. Harold Sherman Reamer and Harriet Mae (Burroughs) Durkee; m. James Main (div. 1976); 1 child, Rodney. BA in Anthropology, Colo. State U., 1976; MBA, Ariz. State U., 1981, JD, 1982. Bar: Calif. 1982. Dist. dir. CETA, Phoenix, 1978; instr. Maricopa Community Colls., Phoenix, 1979-81; law clk. to Speaker Ariz. Ho. of Reps., Phoenix, 1981, lobbyist, 1982; ptnr. Horwich & Main, L.A., 1983-89; of counsel Fleischman & Rigdon, L.A., 1989—. Bd. dirs. New Dem. Channel, L.A., 1985-89; bd. dirs., past chmn. Connections Unltd., L.A., 1986—, L.A. Women's Campaign Fund, 1987—; trustee, vice chmn. Odyssey Theatre, L.A., 1988—; instr. Chrysalis Ctr. for Homeless, L.A., 1988-89. Recipient commendation Vol. Lawyers Project, Pasadena, Calif., 1984. Mem. Los Angeles County Bar Assn. (del. Calif. Bar conf. 1985-88), Beverly Hills Bar Assn., Century City Bar Assn., Women's Caucus for Art, Mus. Contemporary Art, Los Angeles County Art Mus. Democrat. Office: Fleischman & Rigdon 1900 Ave of Stars Ste 2450 Los Angeles CA 90067

MAIOCCHI, CHRISTINE, lawyer; b. N.Y.C., Dec. 24, 1949; d. George and Andreina (Toneatto) M.; m. John Charles Kerecz, Aug. 16, 1980; children: Charles George, Joan Christine. BA in Polit. Sci., Fordham U., 1971, JD, 1974; postgrad., NYU, 1977—. Bar: N.Y. 1975, U.S. Dist. Ct. (so. and ea. dists.), N.Y. 1975, U.S. Ct. Appeals (2nd cir) 1975. Law clk. to magistrate U.S. Dist. Ct. (so. dist.) N.Y., N.Y.C., 1973-74; atty. corp. legal dept. The Home Ins. Co., N.Y.C., 1974-76; asst. house counsel corp. legal dept. Allied Maintenance Corp., N.Y.C., 1976; atty. corp. legal dept. Getty Oil Co., N.Y.C., 1976-77; v.p., mgr. real estate Paine, Webber, Jackson & Curtis, Inc., N.Y.C., 1977-81; real estate mgr. GK Techs., Inc., Greenwich, Conn., 1981-85; real estate mgr., sr. atty. MCI Telecommunications Corp., Rye Brook, N.Y., 1985—. Bd. dirs. League Women Voters, Dobbs Ferry, N.Y., 1988. Mem. ABA, Nat. Assn. Corp. Real Estate Execs. (pres. 1983-84, treas. 1985-86, bd. dirs. 1986), Indsl. Devel. Rsch. Coun. (program v.p. 1985, Profl. award 1987), N.Y. Bar Assn., Women's Bar Assn. Manhattan, Westchester Fairfield Corp. Counsel Assn. (sec. real estate div. 1987-89, chmn., 1990—), Jr. League Club (Tarrytown, N.Y.), Dobbs Ferry Womens Club (program dir. 1981—). Home: 84 Clinton Ave Dobbs Ferry NY 10522 Office: MCI Telecommunications 5 International Dr Rye Brook NY 10573

MAIORANO, ISABELLE J., librarian; b. N.Y.C., June 26, 1922; d. Peter and Mary (Balsamo) M. BA summa cum laude, Wagner Coll., 1944, MS in Edn., 1956; MLS, Pratt Inst., 1961. From sr. br. libr. to asst. coord. N.Y. Pub. Lib., 1963—. Scholar N.Y. Pub. Lib. Sch. 1958-61. Mem. AAUW, ALA, N.Y. Lib Club, N.Y. Librn. Assn., Beta Phi Mu (Theta chpt.). Republican. Roman Catholic. Home: 86 Kirshon Ave Staten Island New York NY 10314

MAIRS, CANDYCE WENBORG, manufacturing company executive; b. Mpls., June 29, 1958; d. Glen Roger and Mary Ann (Bishop) Wenborg; m. Todd Partridge Mairs, Mar. 22, 1980; children: Tealina Partridge, Bryant Wenborg. BA, U. Minn., 1980. Profl. tchr. figure skating Mpls. and St. Paul, 1977-80; import and traffic clk. George S. Bush, Seattle, 1982; import mgr., v.p. Far Ea. Marine Transp., Oakland, Calif., 1982-87; owner, pres. Candyce and Co., Alameda, Calif., 1985-88, Mpls., 1988—; designer, mfr. CaryCrib, CaryClose. Patentee Cot'n Cary infant carrier. Recipient Gold medals Am. Gold Figure and Free Style, 1977, Can. Gold Figure and Free Style, 1977, European Gold Figure and Free Style, 1977, numerous Silver medals, 1973. Mem. NAFE, Dungeness Diver Club (Bremerton, Wash., v.p. 1982). Episcopalian.

MAJORS, SHIRLEY FANELLE, lawyer; b. Spencer, W.Va., Aug. 17, 1934; d. Don and Lexi Oleta (Moss) DePue; m. Gene Majors, Dec. 20, 1952; children: Linda Majors, John Philip Majors. BA summa cum laude, Kent State U., 1975; JD, U. Akron, 1978; student, Aultman Hosp. Sch. Nursing, Canton, Ohio. RN; bar: Ohio 1978. Pvt. practice Akron, Ohio. Mem. Akron Bar Assn., Ohio State Bar Assn., Delta Theta Phi. Home: 5999 Canterbury NW Canton OH 44708

MAJUMDAR, SHARMILA, education educator; b. Calcutta, W. Bengal, India, Nov. 23, 1961; d. Anil Kumar and Sipra (Roy) M. BSc., U. Delhi, India, 1979-82; MS, Yale U., 1984, MPhil, 1985, PhD, 1987. Assoc. rsch. scientist Yale U., New Haven, Conn., 1987—, asst. prof., 1988-89; asst. prof. U. Calif., San Francisco, 1989—; mem. alumni sch. com. Yale U., 1988—. Contbg. author; contbr. papers in field. Recipient BRSG Fluid Funds NIH in collaboration with Yale, 1988; Engrng. award Whittaker Found., 1990—, Radiology Rsch and Edn. award U. Calif., 1990. Mem. AAPM, Am. Phys. Soc., Soc. Magnetic Resonance in Medicine, Sigma Xi. Home: 244 Diapian Bay Alameda CA 94501 Office: U Calif Dept Radiology 533 Pannassus St San Francisco CA 94143

MAKAROVA, NATALIA, ballerina; b. Leningrad, Russia, Nov. 21, 1940; m. Edward Karkar, 1976; 1 child, Andrei Michel. Grad., Vaganova Ballet Sch., Leningrad Choreographic Sch., 1959. assoc. artist London Festival Ballet, 1984. Formerly ballerina with Leningrad Kirov Ballet, performed at Royal Opera House, Covent Garden, London, 1961; toured U.S., 1961, 64; roles include Giselle, Swan Lake, Les Sylphides, Sleeping Beauty, Cinderella, Raymonda, La Bayadere, Onegin (London Evening Standard award 1985), others; joined Am. Ballet Theatre, 1970; guest appearances in U.S. and Europe, 1972—; presented Makarova & Co., 1980 (one season); staged full-length prodn. of La Bayadere for Am. Ballet Theatre, 1980; appeared in Broadway prodn. On Your Toes, 1983 (Tony award 1984, Olivier award); appeared in TV and film prodns.: Makarova: Class of her Own, Channel 4, 1984, Natasha Special, BBC, 1985, (4-part documentary) Ballerina, BBC, 1987; author: A Dance Autobiography, 1979; defected from Russia, 1970. Recipient Gold medal 2d Internat. Ballet Competition, Varna, Bulgaria 1965. Office: care Herbert Breslin Inc 119 W 57th St New York NY 10019 also: Am Ballet Theatre 888 7th Ave New York NY 10019*

MAKER, JANET ANNE, author, lecturer; b. Woburn, Mass., Feb. 13, 1942; d. George Walter and Margaret Anna (Kopasz) M.; children: Thomas Walter, Jane McKinley. BA, UCLA, 1963; MS, Columbia U., 1967; PhD, U. So. Calif., 1978. lectr. in psychology and edn., 1979—. Author: Get It All Together, 1979, Interpretive Reading Comprehension, 1984, Keys to a Powerful Vocabulary, Leval I, 1981, 88, Level II, 1983, 90, Keys to College Success, 1980, 85, 90, College Reading, Book 1, 1984, 88, Book 2, 1982, 86, 89, Book 3, 1985. Home and Office: 925 Malcolm Ave Los Angeles CA 90024

MAKOWSKI, KAREN RAECHAL, banker; b. Buffalo, May 14, 1956; m. Leonard V. Makowski. BS, Canisius Coll., Buffalo, 1977; diploma banking, Grad. Sch. Banking, U. Wis., 1984. Mgmt. trainee to dist. loan officer Marine Midland Bank, Buffalo, 1977-83; asst. treas., corp. loan officer Bank N.Y., Buffalo, 1983-84; asst. v.p. to v.p. commercial lending Key Bank Western N.Y., Buffalo, 1984-86, sr. v.p., exec. officer bank adminstrn., 1986—. Bd. mem., officer Leadership Buffalo, Inc., 1988—, Amherst Saxaphone Quartet Soc., Buffalo, 1988—; bd. mem. Meals on Wheels Buffalo and Erie County, 1989—. Named Profl. Woman of Yr., Sibleys, Buffalo, 1989, Buffalo Ambassador, Conv. and Tourism Bd., 1988. Mem. Fin. Women Internat. (adv. to bd. 1988-90, N.Y. state pres. 1987), Buffalo 2000, Buffalo C. of C. (Athena award 1989). Office: Key Bank Western NY NA 17 Court St Buffalo NY 14202

MAKUPSON, AMYRE PORTER, television station executive; b. River Rouge, Mich., Sept. 30, 1947; d. Rudolph Hannibal and Amyre Ann (Porche) Porter; m. Walter H. Makupson, Nov. 1, 1975; children: Rudolph Porter, Amyre Nisi. BA, Fisk U., 1970; MA, Am. U., Washington, 1972. Asst. dir. news Sta. WGPR-TV, Detroit, 1975-76; dir. pub. rels. Mich. Health Maintenance Orgn., Detroit, 1974-76, Kirwood Gen. Hosp., Detroit, 1976-77; mgr. news and pub. affairs, news anchor Sta. WKBD-TV, Southfield, Mich., 1977—. Mem. adv. com. Mich. Arthritis Found., Co-Ette Club, Inc., Met. Detroit Teen Conf. Coalition, Cystic Fibrosis Soc., Alzheimers Disease and Related Disorders Assn.; mem. exec. com. March of Dimes; pres. bd. dirs. Detroit Wheelchair Athletic Assn.; bd. dirs. Sickle Cell Assn., Kids In Need of Direction, Drop-out Prevention Collaborative, Merill-Palmer Inst. Recipient numerous svc. awards including Arthritis Found. Mich., Mich. Mchts. Assn., DAV, Jr. Achievement, City of Detroit, Salvation Army. Mem. Pub. Rels. Soc. Am., Am. Women in Radio and TV (Outstanding Achievement award 1981), Women in Communications, Nat. Acad. TV Arts and Scis., Detroit Press Club, Ad-Craft. Roman Catholic. Office: 26955 W 11 Mile Rd Southfield MI 48034

MALACH, JANICE TONI, health facility administrator; b. Detroit, Sept. 18, 1959; d. Reuben and Dorothy (Gell) Sherman; m. Leonard Marvin Malach, Mar. 29, 1987; 1 child, Daniel Jacob. BA, Wayne State U., 1981. Med. cons. 50 Pvt. Physician Clinics, Southfield, Mich., 1974-85; group mgr. Sinai Hosp., Detroit, 1985-86, dir., 1986-88, assoc. adminstr., 1988—; cons. in field. Mem. Mich. Group Mgmt. Assn., NAFE. Jewish. Office: Sinai Hosp 6767 W Outer Dr Detroit MI 48235

MALACHOWSKI, CARLA, products company executive; b. Southington, Conn., Nov. 26, 1953; d. Carl Raymond and Jeanette Ann (Zoni) Malachowski. AA, Endicott Jr. Coll., 1973; BA in History, Newton Coll./Boston Coll., 1975. Admissions rep. Katharine Gibbs Sch., Boston, 1977-79, cons., 1981; mgr. sales tng. and devel. Katharine Gibbs Sch. subs. Macmillan Inc., N.Y.C., 1979-81; mgr. mgmt. info. systems Fidelity Investments, Boston, 1982-85, dir. market mgmt., 1985-86, asst. v.p. 1986-88, v.p. new bus. devel., 1989—; speaker, panelist profl. assn. Mem. Am. Soc. Tng. and Devel., Nat. Assn. Securities Dealers. Office: Fidelity Investments 82 Devonshire St LIIC Boston MA 02109

MALAMUD, JUDITH REVA, medical librarian; b. Detroit, Dec. 25, 1940; d. Sol and Dorothy (Lifshitz) Disner; m. Daniel F. Malamud, Mar. 5, 1961; children: Randy, Lisa. BS, We. Mich. U., 1962; MLS, Simmons Coll., 1971. Chem. libr. Ventron Corp., Beverley, Mass., 1971-72; med. libr. Lawrence Meml. Hosp., Medford, Mass., 1972-77; veterinary libr. U. Pa., Phila., 1977-83, asst. dir. Biomed. Libr., 1983-88, assoc. dir. Biomed. Libr., 1989; dir. Med. Libr. Albert Einstein Coll. Medicine, Bronx, N.Y., 1989—. Mem. Am. Libr. Assn., Med. Libr. Assn., Assn. Coll. and Research Librs.

MALAMUD, PHYLLIS CAROLE, journalist, magazine editor; b. Bklyn., Sept. 15, 1938; d. Louis and Hannah (Unterman) Malamud; m. Matthew A. Clark, Jr., Nov. 9, 1986. BA, CCNY, 1960; postgrad. (Russell Sage Found. fellow), Washington U., St. Louis, 1968-69. Publicity asst. Newsweek mag., N.Y.C., 1960-62, researcher, 1962-64, feature reporter, 1964-74, N.Y. polit. reporter, 1975-77; chief New Eng. bur. Newsweek mag., Boston, 1977—; editor My Turn column Newsweek mag., N.Y.C., 1983-88; freelance writer N.Y.C., 1989—. Contbr. articles to various publs. Trustee Actor's Temple, N.Y.C., 1985—. Recipient Gavel award ABA, 1968, award for article Am. Psychol. Assn., 1975, Page One award N.Y. Newspaper Guild, 1977. Mem. Coffee House Club. Jewish. Home: 1199 Park Ave New York NY 10128

MALANAPHY-SORG, MARIE A, management consultant; b. Rochester, Minn., Aug. 29, 1955; d. James Joseph and Jean H. (Holien) Malanaphy; m. Michael Sorg, Nov. 4, 1989. BA, Rockhurst Coll., 1977. Sect. mgr. Hallmark Cards, Inc., Lawrence, Kans., 1977-79; sales mgr., asst. buyer Macy's Midwest, Kansas City, Mo., 1980-81; chief of installation Alexander Proudfoot Co., Chgo., 1982-86; mgmt. cons. St. Paul, 1986—; dir. Cons. Svcs., The Worker Group, L.A. Chmn. citizens panel St. Paul United Way, 1987-88, chmn. task force, 1990, mem. fund distbn. com., 1987, 88, 90. Mem. Freedom Writers, Amnesty Internat.

MALCHON, JEANNE K(ELLER), state senator; b. Newark, June 17, 1923; d. Leslie Stafford and Edith Katherine (Marcelle) Keller; m. Richard Malchon, 1946 (dec.); 1 child, Richard Jr. A.A., Va. Intermont Coll., 1943. Draftsman, Curtis-Wright Propeller div., Caldwell, N.J., 1943-44; civilian employee U.S. Army, Hickam Field, Hawaii, 1944-45; merchandising rep. L. Bamberger & Co., Newark, 1946-49; with Office of Tech. Assessment Task Force, 1971; mem. Gov.'s Commn. on Criminal Justice Standards and Goals, 1981-82, Fla. Jud. Council, 1972-82; commr. Pinellas County (Fla.), 1975-82; mem. Supreme Ct. Dispute Resolution Alternatives Com., Nat. Com. and Nat. Air Quality Commn., 1978-82; mem. Fla. State Senate from Dist. 18, 1982—, chmn. Senate Select Com. on Aging, vice chmn. Senate Health and Rehab. Services Com., 1985-86, Mem. exec. com. Am. Lung Assn., 1977-85, nat. pres., 1982-84; chmn. Nat. Air Conservation Com. 1978-83, mem. Fla. Cancer Control and Research Adv. Bd., 1986—, bd. dirs. Ctr. for Govtl. Responsibility. Recipient women in govt. award Soroptimists, 1979, outstanding equal opportunity efforts award Pinellas County Urban League, 1980, most effective sen. for law enforcement Fla. Sheriff's Assn., 1983, environment award, Fla. Sierra Club, 1984, outstanding legislator of the yr. Fla. Nurses Assn., 1985, legislator of the yr. Fla. Psychol. Assn., 1985, disting. service award Pinellas County Assn. Respiratory Care Mgrs., 1985, Human Service award United Way Pinellas County, 1986, Legislator of Yr. Fla. Consumer Fedn., 1986. Mem. State Assn. County Commrs. (dir. 1975-80, chmn. urban affairs com. 1979-80), Nat. Assn. Counties (criminal justice steering com. 1975-80 , chmn. law enforcement subcom. 1979-80). Democrat. Home: 2400 Pinellas Point Dr S Saint Petersburg FL 33712 also: 424 Central Ave Ste 804 Saint Petersburg FL 33701*

MALCOLM, GAIL BAUMGAERTEL, information systems executive; b. Philadelphia, Oct. 15, 1954; d. G. George and Margery Ann (Mansfield) Baumgaertel; m. Lawrence Reid Malcolm, Apr. 18, 1981; 1 child, Christine Alison. Student, Albright Coll., 1972-73; BSBA, The King's Coll., 1973-76; MA/Health Care Adminstrn., George Washington U., 1976-78. Adminstrv. resident Shared Med. Systems, King of Prussia, Pa., 1977-78, product mgr., 1978, supr. mktg. svcs., 1978-79; installation dir. Shared Med. Systems, Boston, 1979-80; data base adminstr. Hosp. of the U. Pa., Phila., 1980-82; dir. info. systems Paoli (Pa.) Meml. Hosp., 1982-84, Med. Coll. Pa., Phila., 1985; asst. exec. dir. Thomas Jefferson U. Hosp., Phila., 1985—. Mem. The King's Coll. Alumni Assn. (pres.-elect 1986-88, pres. 1988—), Am. Coll. Healthcare Execs., Am. Hosp. Assn. Healthcare Info. Mgmt. Systems Soc., Del. Valley Hosp. Info. Mgmt. Systems Soc. Republican. Episcopalian. Home: 1870 Black Rock Lane Paoli PA 19301 Office: Thomas Jefferson U Hosp 11th and Walnut Sts 2024NH Philadelphia PA 19107

MALDEN, JOAN WILLIAMS, physical therapist; b. Bayshore, N.Y., Apr. 14; d. Sidney S. and Myrtle L. (Williams) Siegel; B.S., N.Y. U., 1957; m. Alan A. Chasnov, Jan. 20, 1951; children—Marc, Robin, Debra and David (twins); m. 2d, Miroslav Mladenovic, Sept. 14, 1967; 1 dau., Kristine. Phys. therapist hosps. and orgns. in N.Y.C. area, 1956-57; phys. therapist Brunswick Hosp. Center, Amityville, N.Y., 1968-69; pvt. practice phys. therapy, Wantagh, N.Y., 1968—; licensure examiner, N.Y. State; cons., tchr. in field; lectr. L.I. U., NYU; clin. coord. Hunter Coll., L.I. Coll., L.I. U., Daemon Coll., NYU, Columbia U., SUNY at Stony Brook, Touro Coll., Springfield Coll. Contbr. articles to profl. jours. Pres. internat. scholarships com. Massapequa chpt. Am. Field Service, 1962-64. Mem. Am. Acad. Cerebral Palsy, Am. Phys. Therapy Assn. (chmn. polit. action com. N.Y. chpt., chmn. L.I. dist.), AAUW (pres. Massapequa chpt. 1962-64), N.Y. State Soc. Continuing Edn. in Phys. Therapy, Airplane Owners and Pilots Assn., Ninety-Nines, Exptl. Aviation Assn., Farmingdale Flyers (officer). Democrat. Unitarian. Home: 35 S Bay Ave Massapequa NY 11758 Office: Wantagh Med Bldg 1228 Wantagh Ave Wantagh NY 11793 also: 161 E Main St Huntington NY 11743

MALDONADO-BEAR, RITA MARINITA, economist, educator; b. Vega Alta, P.R., June 14, 1938; d. Victor and Marina (Davila) Maldonado; B.A., Auburn U., 1960; Ph.D., N.Y.U., 1969; m. Larry Alan Bear, Mar. 29, 1975. With Min. Wage Bd. & Econ. Devel. Adminstrn., Govt. of P.R., 1960-64; asso. prof. fin. U. P.R., 1969-70; asst. prof. econs. Manhattan Coll., 1970-72; assoc. prof. econs. Bklyn. Coll., 1972-75; vis. assoc. prof. fin. Stanford (Calif.) Grad. Bus. Sch., 1973-74; assoc. prof. fin. and econs. Grad. div. Stern Sch. Bus. NYU, 1975-81, prof., 1981—; cons. Morgan Guaranty Trust Co., N.Y.C., 1972-77, Bank of Am., N.Y.C., 1982-84, Res. City Bankers, N.Y.C., 1978-87, Swedish Inst. Mgmt., Stockholm, 1982—, Empresas Master of Puerto Rico, 1985— ; dir. Medallion Funding Corp., 1985-87. P.R. Econ. Devel. Adminstrn. fellow, 1960-65; Marcus Nadler fellow, N.Y.U., 1966-67, Phillip Lods Dissertation fellow, 1967-68. Mem. Am. Econs. Assn., Am. Fin. Assn., Metro. Econ. Assn. N.Y., Assn. for Social Econs. Author: Role of the Financial Sector in the Economic Development of Puerto Rico, 1970; contbr. articles to profl. jours. Home: 95 Tam O'Shanter Dr Mahwah NJ 07430 Office: 40 W Fourth St New York NY 10003

MALEC, JUDITH MARY, management services company executive, consultant; b. Jersey City, June 21, 1955; d. Frank and Irene (Bilan) M. Student, Pa. State U., 1976-78; BS in Econs., U. Pitts., 1980. Asst. buyer Joseph Horne Co., Pitts., 1980-81; sales rep. Budget Uniform, Pitts., 1981-83, Allnet, Pitts., 1983-84; sales rep. Dictaphone Co., Pitts., 1984, sr. sales rep., 1985-86; nat. acct. mgr. Lizardy Assocs., Pitts., 1986; nat. sales dir. Lizardy Assocs., San Diego, 1986-88; v.p. G.M.W. Mgmt. Svcs., Inc., Pitts., 1988—; cons. Southwestern Bell Corp., St. Louis, 1987—. Mem. Am. Soc. for Tng. and Devel. (cons.-on-call 1987—), Vectors of Pitts. (pres. pioneer 1987), Greater Pitts. C. of C., Toastmasters. Roman Catholic. Club: Toastmasters. Office: PO Box 15251 Pittsburgh PA 15237

MALECKI, JEAN MARIE, medical director; b. Miami, Mar. 27, 1953; d. Raymond Edward and Patricia Ann (Diehl) Mortimer; m. Peter John Malecki, Apr. 11, 1981; 1 child, Heather Marie. BS, Fairfield U., 1971; MD, N.Y. Med. Coll., 1975; MPH, U. Miami Sch. Medicine, 1985. Diplomate Nat. Bd. Medical Examiners, Am. Bd. Preventive Medicine and Pub. Health. Acting med. dir. HRS Palm Beach County Pub. Health Unit, Lake Worth Br., Lake Worth, Fla., 1983—; dir. Grad. Programs in Pub. Health, 1989—; med. dir. HRS/Palm Beach County Pub. Health Unit, West Palm Beach, Fla., 1989—; vice-chairperson Residency Adv. Com. Palm Beach County Pub. Health Unit, 1989—; adj. asst. prof.Dept. Epidemiology & Pub. Health, U. Miami Sch. Medicine, 1988—; chairperson Residency Adv. Com. Gen. Preventive Medicine & Pub. Health, 1986-89; lectr. in field. Contbr. articles to profl. jours. Recipient Up and Comer award, 1990, Citation for Scholastic Achievement Am. Med. Women's Assn., 1979, Cor Et Manus award N.Y. Med. Coll., 1979. Mem. AMA, Palm Beach County Med. Soc., Am. Cancer Soc., Fla. Med. Assn., Fla. Pub. Health Assn., Am. Pub. Health Assn., Alpha Omega Alpha. Office: HRS Palm Beach County PO Box 29 Pub Health Unit West Palm Beach FL 33402

MALEK, DIANA GAIL, teacher; b. San Marcos, Tex., Oct. 16, 1953; d. Frank Byrd and Margaret (Ewing) Hoch; m. Lawrence LeRoy Malek, June 14, 1975 (div.); children: Macy Lynn, Wesley Lyle. Cert. in cosmetology, San Marcos Beauty Sch., 1973; BS, S.W. Tex. State U., 1976; cert., Tex. Tech. U., 1979, U. Houston, 1980. Cert. tchr. Tex. Clk. Hays County Tax Office, San Marcos, 1972-73; cosmetologist Sylvia's Hair Fashions, San Marcos, 1973-77; agt. life ins. A.L. Williams, Austin, Tex., 1983-84; tchr. San Marcos Ind. Sch. Dist., 1978-90, vocat. edn. adminstr., 1990—; sponsor Future Homemakers Am., 1978-90, San Marcos, 1978—; mem. Home Econs. Adv. Coun., 1979—; chairperson Goodnight Jr. High Electives, 1980-90. Asst. leader troop 272 Girl Scouts U.S., 1987-89. Named one of Outstanding Young Women of Am. 1988. Mem. Vocat. Home Econs. Tchrs. Assn. Tex., San Marcos Classroom Tchrs. Assn. (faculty rep. 1987-89, pres. 1989—), Phi Upsilon Omicron Alumni (sec. 1985-87), Alpha Delta Kappa. Methodist. Home: PO Box 1442 San Marcos TX 78667 Office: San Marcos High Sch 1301 St Hwy 123 San Marcos TX 78666

MALEK, MARLENE ANNE, nurse, foundation executive; b. Oakland, Calif., June 22, 1939; d. William Alexander and Yolanda Katherine (Stella) McArthur; m. Frederic Vincent Malek, Aug. 5, 1961; children: Frederic William, Michelle Ann. AA, Armstrong U., 1959; AS in Nursing, Marymount U., 1979; cert. in hospice tng., Arlington, Va., 1980. Dir. Psychiat. Inst. Found., Washington, 1982—; women's bd. Am. Heart Assn., 1973—, bd. treas., chmn. ann. luncheon, 1988. Bd. dirs. Nat. Fed. Rep. Women, Washington, 1972-74, Marymount U., Arlington, Va., 1974— ; chmn. Eisenhower Meml. Found., Washington, 1972-74; cons. hospitality Presdl. Inaugural Com., Washington, 1988; mem. adv. bd. Second Genesis Drug Rehab. Program, Bethesda, Md., 1983—, chmn. Second Genesis Benefit, 1968, 84-85; founding mem. Arena Stage Guild, Washington; bd. dirs. Nat. Mus. Women in Arts, 1987, Claude Moore Colonial Farm, 1986—. Episcopalian. Avocations: skiing, collecting antiques, painting, running.

MALEMUD, LEE L., operations executive; b. Syracuse, N.Y., Oct. 10, 1948; d. Wylford Howard and Mary Louise (Hondorf) Lepinske; m. Charles Jay Malemud, Dec. 22, 1986; 1 child, Gabriel Abraham. BA in Humanities, Ursuline Coll., 1971; MA in Mgmt., Cen. Mich. U., 1979; MS in Orgn. Devel. and Analysis, Case Western Reserve U., 1983; postgrad., Sch. Applied Social Scis. Instr. adult edn. Mayfield City Schs., Ohio, 1971-82, South Euclid-Lyndhurst, Ohio, 1975; cons. Allied Health Profl. Edn. Program N.E. Ohio Multipurpose Arthritis Ctr., Cleve., 1979-81; sr. rsch. asst. Case Western Res. Sch. Medicine, Cleve., 1971-83; facilitator Arthritis Support Groups, Cleve., 1981-83; coord. Revco Arthritis Rsch. Lab., Cleve., 1982; cons. Human Resources Internat., Beachwood, Ohio, 1984; dir. edn. Jostens Ednl. Systems/Career Com., Cleve., 1984-88; dir. edn., corp. dir. faculty devel. and tng., corp. curriculum cons. Vocat. Tng. Ctrs., Inc., Cleve. and St. Louis, 1988-90; v.p. ops., gen. mgr. The Brentley Inst., Inc., Cleve., 1990—. Editor in chief Jour. Histotechnology, 1980-82; contbr. articles to profl. jours. Mem. adv. bd. Lakeland Community Coll., 1978-80; affiliate mem. Am. Soc. Clin. Pathologists, Chgo., 1978-83; mem. Atty. Gen.'s Task Force, Ohio, 1988—, Community Rels. Bd., Cleve., 1990—; instr. ARC, Ednl. Found. Office: The Brentley Inst PO Box 20724 Cleveland OH 44120

MALESKI, CYNTHIA MARIA, lawyer; b. Natrona Heights, Pa., July 4, 1951; d. Richard Anthony and Helen Elizabeth (Palovcak) M.; m. Andrzej Gabriel Groch, Aug. 7, 1982; 1 child, Elizabeth Maria. B.A. summa cum laude, U. Pitts., 1973; student U. Rouen (France), 1970; J.D., Duquesne U., 1976. Bar: Pa. 1976, U.S. dist. ct. (we. dist.) Pa. 1976, U.S. Supreme Ct. 1980, U.S. Ct. Appeals (3d cir.) 1984. Indsl. relations adminstr. Allegheny Ludlum Industries, Inc., Brackenridge, Pa., 1972-74; law clk. Conte, Courtney, Tarasi & Price, Pitts., 1974, Paul Hammer, Pitts., 1974-76; sole practice Natrona Heights, Pa., 1978—; gen. counsel Mercy Hosp., Pitts., 1976—; spl. master Allegheny County Ct. Common Pleas, 1989; candidate for judge Pa. Ct. Common Pleas; bd. dirs. legal adv. bd. Catholic Health Assn., 1980-82; gen. counsel, vice chmn. nat. assembly of reps. Nat. Confedn. Am. Ethnic Groups, 1980—; health law cons. and lectr.; task force on Pa. Med. Malpractice Reform, Hosp. Assn. Pa. Co-author: The Legal Dimensions of Nursing Practice (Nurses' Book of Month Club award 1982), 1982; contbr. articles to publs. Corp. sec., legal counsel Tamburitzan Nat. Folk Arts Ctr., Pitts., 1979—, pres., 1987—; mem. Council Self-Insured Hosps. of Pa.; vice chmn. Czechoslovak room com. Nationality Rooms Program, U. Pitts., 1983; elected mem. Allegheny County Dem. Com., 1986-89; candidate for del. Dem. Nat. Conv. 20th Pa. Congl. Dist., 1984; chmn. Com. to Re-elect U.S. Congressman Doug Walgren, 1982; Ethnic Com. for Pa. Atty. Gen., 1980, Ethnic Com. for Judge Peter Paul Olszewski, 1983; U.S. del 4th Slovak World Congress, 1981; mem. adv. bd. Children's and Youth Services, Allegheny County, 1984—; soloist, speaker various groups, Pitts. Slovakians. Scholar U. Rouen, 1970; Allegheny Ludlum Industries scholar, 1969-73; Andrew Mellon scholar, 1969; tuition scholar U. Pitts., 1969-73; tuition remission grantee Duquesne U., 1975, 76; recipient acad. excellence award Duquesne U., 1976; Mem. ABA (forum com. on health law, tort and ins. sect.), Am. Soc. Hosp. Attys., Nat. Health Lawyers Assn., Soc. Hosp. Attys. of Hosp. Assn. Pa. (v.p.), Soc. Hosp. Attys. Western Pa., Pa. Bar Assn. (med.-legal com., long range planning com., jud. reform com.), Allegheny County Bar Assn. (chmn. med.-legal com., council civil litigation sect., council tax. exempt orgns. and professionalism, chmn. interprofl. code com. Allegheny County Bar Assn.-Allegheny County Med. Soc.), Slavic Edn. Assn. (nat. treas. 1981-86), St. Thomas More Soc. (bd. govs. 1980—), First Cath. Slovak Union, 1st Cath. Slovak Women's Assn., Civic Club Allegheny Valley, Bus. and Profl. Women Allegheny Valley, Phi Beta Kappa. Roman Catholic. Home: 137 Oak Manor Dr Natrona Heights PA 15065 Office: Mercy Hosp of Pitts 1400 Locust St Pittsburgh PA 15219-2413

MALES-MADRID, SANDRA KAY, medical facility administrator; b. South Gate, Calif., Aug. 1, 1942; d. Albert Odus and Evelyn Louise (Corbett) Males; m. James O. Spurbeck, Apr. 15, 1963 (div. Nov. 1967); m. Miguel Madrid Jr., Feb. 9, 1980; stepchildren: Priscilla, Betty, Dru, Rachel. BA, U. Redlands, Calif., 1987. Payroll clk. Lever Bros. Co., Los Angeles, 1961-69; med. asst. William Stafford, M.D., Fullerton, Calif., 1969-71; mgr. office David H. Armstrong, M.D., Inc., Fullerton, 1971-79; mgr. office Med. Ctr. for Women, Fullerton, 1977-79, adminstr., 1986—; owner Sandy's Discount Boutique, Hemet, Sun City, Calif., 1979-83; asst. adminstr. Fullerton Cardiovascular Med. Group, 1983-86; cons., tchr. Riverside (Calif.) Community Coll., 1984—; bd. dirs. No. Orange County Regional Occupational Ctr., Anaheim, Calif., 1985—. Vol. Riverside Rape Crisis Ctr., 1984—. Republican. Club: Fullerton. Lodge: Soroptimist (Sun City) (sec.

1982-83, Women Helping Women award 1985). Office: Fullerton Cardiovascular Med Group 2720 N Harbor Blvd #210 Fullerton CA 92635

MALEY, PATRICIA ANN, preservation planner; b. Wilmington, Del., Dec. 25, 1955; d. James Alfred and Frances Louise (Fenimore) M. AA, Cecil Community Coll., 1973; BA, U. Del., 1975, MA, 1981. Cert. secondary tchr., Del. Analyst econ. devel. City of Wilmington, 1977-78, evaluation specialist, 1978-80, planner II mayor's office, 1980-86, cons. preservation, 1986-87; dir. Belle Meade Mansion, Nashville, 1987-88; dir. planning, devel. Children's Bur. of Del., Wilmington, 1988; prin. preservation planner Environ. Mgmt. Ctr., Brandywine Conservancy, Chadds Ford, Pa., 1988—; prin. operator rsch. sect. The History Store, 1989—; cons. cultural resources M.A.A.R. Inc., Newark, Del., 1987, ITC Cons., Wilmington, 1985-86. Contbg. photographer America's City Halls, 1984; author numerous Nat. Register nominations, 1980-86; 88—. Pres., founder Haynes Park Civic Assn., Wilmington, 1977-80; photographer Biden U.S. Senate campaign, New Castle County, Del., 1984; sec. parish council Our Lady Fatima Roman Cath. Ch., 1985-86, choir dir., 1983-87; bd. dirs. Del. Children's Theatre; music dir. St. Elizabeth Ann Seton parish, Bear, Del., 1988—. U. Del. fellow, 1976-77. Mem. Nat. Trust Hist. Preservation, Am. Planning Assn., Nat. Assn. Pastoral Musicians, Del. Soc. Architects, Del. Archeol. Soc., Del. Hist. Soc., Pi Sigma Alpha. Democrat. Office: Brandywine Conservancy Environ Mgmt Ctr PO Box 141 Chadds Ford PA 19317

MALGIERI, KATHRYN DRISCOLL, elementary educator; b. N.Y.C., Apr. 4, 1951; d. Daniel Joseph and Anne (O'Connor) Driscoll; m. John Joseph Malgieri, June 9, 1973; children: Kathleen, John Driscoll, Peter James, Robert Francis. BA, Coll. Mt. St. Vincent, 1973; postgrad., Ashland U., 1987—. Cert. elem., secondary tchr., Ohio. Libr. U. Hosps., Cleve., 1973-74; adminstrv. asst. dean's office Sch. Medicine Case Western Res. U., Cleve., 1974-75; tutor Coll. of Wooster (Ohio), 1984-85; libr. St. Mary's Sch., Wooster, 1986-89, tchr. 2d grade, 1989—; aquatics instr. Wooster YMCA, 1980—. Aquatics instr. ARC, Wooster, 1981—; adv. bd. Wayne County coop. extension office, Wooster, 1988—; bd. dirs. Wooster Swim Club, 1988—. Mem. AAUW. Roman Catholic. Home: 965 Greensview Dr Wooster OH 44691 Office: St Mary's Sch 535 Bowman St Wooster OH 44691

MALIK, HELEN THERESA, corporate officer; b. Owosso, Mich., Jan. 23, 1943; d. Anthony Joseph and Helen Ann (Kleinedler) Sovis; m. Frederick Malik, May 22, 1965; 1 child, Frederick Fabian. Student, Charles Stewart Mott Community Coll., Flint, Mich., 1975, Gen. Motors Inst., Flint, Mich., 1985, Lansing (Mich.) Community Coll., 1988. Cert. payroll profl. Clk. accts receivable Mitchell Corp. of Owosso, Mich., 1964-67, sec. purchasing dept., 1967-70, clk. payroll dept., 1970-72, sr. clk. payroll and ins. benefits, 1972-82, asst. corp. sec., adminstr. pension, benefits, payroll, 1982-89, corp. sec., adminstr. pension and benefits, 1989—, sec. bd. dirs., 1990—. Treas. Corunna Band Boosters, Corunna, Mich., 1981-83; mem. Owosso Personnel Group, 1986. Mem. Am. Compensation Assn., Am. Payroll Assn., Bar Code User's Group. Roman Catholic. Home: 1425 New Lothrop Rd Lennon MI 48449 Office: Mitchell Corp of Owosso 123 N Chipman St Owosso MI 48867

MALIK, JOSIE M. MEZA, psychologist; b. Brawley, Calif., Nov. 29, 1947; d. Johnnie Villegas and Elvera (Ramirez) Meza; m. Sherkhan Malik, Aug. 12, 1976; children: Tarig Joshua, Shaunna Yasmin. AA, San Joaquin Delta Coll., 1968; BS, U. The Pacific, 1973, MA, 1975. Cert. sch. psychologist, Calif. Psychologist Lincoln Unified Sch. Dist., Stockton, Calif.; mem. learning disability adv. bd. San Joaquin Delta Coll., Stockton, Calif., 1990. Mem. Internat. Assn. Sch. Psychologists, Nat. Assn. Sch. Psychologists, Calif. Assn. Sch. Psychologists, San Joaquin County Mental Health Assn., Calif. Assn. Bilingial Educators.

MALIN, EVANGELINE MAY, social services case worker, retired; b. L.A., Dec. 19, 1928; d. Ray and Mary Alice (Yandell) Wheeler; m. Robert E. Zipperer, Feb. 6, 1953 (div. 1973); 1 child, Robert Eugene.; m. Sigmund John Malin, Sept. 9, 1976. AA, Pasadena City Coll., 1950; BA, Pasadena Coll., 1952; cert. in social svcs., U. Calif., Berkeley, 1969; 2 certs. in social work, Ethel Percy Andrus Gerontology Ctr. U. So. CAlif., 1971, 72. Social worker San Bernardino (Calif.) Co. Social Svcs., 1953-56; med. social worker Santa Clara County Valley Med. Ctr., San Jose, Calif., 1956-66; social worker Santa Clara Dept. Social Svcs., San Jose, Calif., 1966-81; ret. Santa ClaraDept. Social Svcs., San Jose, Calif., 1981. Mem. Pasadena & Point Loma Alumni Assn., Santa Clara Co. Employees Assn., Castle Med. Ctr. Aux., Mid-Pacific Country Club. Republican. Methodist. Home: 998 Iopono Loop Kailua HI 96734 also: 2308 Back Nine Oceanside CA 92056

MALIN, RONI SUE, author; b. Denver, Nov. 26, 1939; d. William and Fredella (Brilliant) Friedman; m. Ronald H. Malin; children: Andrea Malin DeBre, Allison, Gregory. BA, U. Wis., 1959; postgrad., U. Geneva, 1960. Lectr. numerous orgns. and colls.; condr. of seminars on entertaining, 1983—. Co-author: Only in Los Angeles, 1980, Beverly Hills Hostess Survival Kit, 1984. Mem. visitors adv. bd. 1984 Olympics; trouble shooter for Olympic Press, L.A., 1984.

MALINA-MAXWELL, CHRISTINE YVONNE, publishing executive; b. Maisons Laffitte, France, Aug. 16, 1950; came to U.S., 1979; d. Robert and Elisabeth (Meynard) Maxwell; m. Roger Frank Malina; children: Xavier Jan, Yuri. BA in Latin Am. Studies and Sociology, Pitzer Coll., Claremont, Calif., 1972. Current awareness editor World Devel. Jour., Pergamon Press, Oxford, Eng., 1972-73; tchr. Shephards Hill Middle Sch., Oxford, 1974-76; editor sch. book div. A. Wheaton & Co., Exeter, Eng., 1976-78; pres. Sci./Tech. Pub. Svcs., Inc., Berkeley, Calif., 1979—; chief exec. officer Info. on Demand, Inc., Berkeley, 1982-88, pres., 1985-88; dir. mktg. Pergamon Press, Inc., N.Y.C., 1983-85; v.p., dir. internat. mktg. SRA, Chgo., 1988-89; pres. Rsch. on Demand, Berkeley, 1989—; bd. dirs. Jossey-Bass Pubs., San Francisco, Sphere Corp., Alameda, Calif., Molecular Design San Leandro, Calif., Macmillan Pubs., N.Y., Pergamon Press Pubs. Author: Pergamon Dictionary of Perfect Spelling, 1977, Practice Your Spelling, 1977; editor ednl. programs. Bd. dirs. Marimed Found., Honolulu, 1984—, San Francisco Vols., 1989. Mem. Internat. Soc. Arts, Scis. and Tech. (dir. mktg.), Spl. Library Assn. Democrat. Office: Sci/Tech Pub Svcs Inc 2030 Addison St Ste 400 Berkeley CA 94704

MALKOFF, EILEEN WEIDER, small business owner; b. Beachwood, Ohio, Feb. 2, 1954; d. Benjamin and Bertha (Yaeger) Weider; m. Robert Jules Malkoff, Nov. 6, 1982. Student, Ohio State U., Cleve., 1972-74; grad., Cleve. Fashion Inst., 1974. Sales rep. Donna Lee Shop, Beachwood, 1969-76; mgr. Hahn Shoes, Beachwood, 1976-79; sales rep. Boris Shoes, Beachwood, 1979-80; fin. advisor Ohio Savs. & Loan, Pepper Pike, 1980-82; owner Gold Masters Jewelers, Inc., Cleve., 1982—. Fund raiser F.O.P.; mem. Cleve. Better Bus. Bur., Cleve. Growth Assn. Mem. Consumers Union, Nat. Fedn. Ind. Bus., Ind. Jewelers Orgn. Democrat. Jewish. Office: Gold Masters Jewelers Inc. 1747 Randall Park Mall Cleveland OH 44128

MALLARY, GERTRUDE ROBINSON, civic worker; b. Springfield, Mass., Aug. 19, 1902; d. George Edward and Jennie (Slater) Robinson; student, Bennett Coll., 1921-22, U. Conn., 1941-42; m. R. DeWitt Mallary, Sept. 15, 1923; children: R. DeWitt, Richard Walker. Co-owner, ptnr. Mallary Farm, Bradford, Vt., 1936—; mem. Vt. Ho. of Reps., 1953-56, sec. agr. com., 1953, mem. appropriations com., 1955; mem. Vt. Senate, 1957-58, mem. appropriations com., clk. pub. health com., vice chmn. edn. com. Pres., Jr. League, Springfield, 1931-33; trustee Wesson Meml. Hosp., Springfield, 1937-42, chmn. nursing services, 1939-42; chmn. Springfield Council Social Agys., 1938-40; mem. Mass. Commn. Pub. Safety, 1941-42; pres. Vt. Holstein Club, 1951-53; mem. Vt. Bd. Recreation, 1959-65; trustee Fairlee (Vt.) Public Library, 1953-84, Asa Bloomer Found., 1963-71, Orange County 4-H Found., 1969-71; trustee Justin Smith Morrill Found., 1964-71, pres., 1968-71; chmn. Fairlee Bicentennial Com., 1974-77; mem. Com. for New Eng. Bibliography, 1971-84, vice chmn. for Vt., 1977; Orange County chmn. Vt. Achievement Ctr., 1985-89. Recipient Theresa R. Brungardt award, 1979, Master Breeders award Vt. Holstein Assn., 1979, Master Breeders award New Eng. Holstein Assn., 1969, co-recipient with husband Disting. Svc. award, 1989. Mem. Vt., Bradford (pres. 1965-69), Fairlee hist. socs., Am. Antiquarian Soc. Editor New Eng. Holstein Bull., 1947-50. Address: Mallary Farm RR1 Box 620 Bradford VT 05033

MALLECK, DIANE ELIZABETH, home economist; b. Benkelman, Nebr., Nov. 15, 1954; d. Clinton Stuart and Mary Lou (Nighswonger) Munn; m. Philip Keith Malleck, July 21, 1974. BS, U. Nebr., 1976; MS, Kansas State U., 1977. Cert. home economist. Social svcs. worker Nebr. Dept. Social Svcs., McCook, 1978-79; extension home economist U. Idaho Coop. Extension Svc., Soda Springs, Idaho, 1980—; office chmn. Coop. Extension Svc., Soda Springs, 1983—. Author: You Can Do It, 1986, The Family Gardener, 1985. Co-chmn. Community Resource Council, Soda Springs, 1987-89; mem. Caribou County Task Force on Sexual Abuse, Soda Springs, 1983-87. Mem. Idaho Assn. Extension Home Economists (sec. 1984-86, 82, v.p. 1983), Idaho Home Economist Assn. (newsletter editor 1987). Roman Catholic. Home: 371 McLean Soda Springs ID 83276 Office: Coop Extension Svc 159 S Main Soda Springs ID 83276

MALLIN, DEA ZUCKERMAN, English educator; b. Phila., Apr. 1, 1942; d. Hyman Zuckerman and Henriette (Wolodin) Zuckerman-Landis; m. Michael David Mallin, Dec. 30, 1977 (dec. 1980); 1 child, Clio Alexandra. BA magna cum laude, U. Pa., 1964, MA, 1969. Tchr. Akiba Acad., Merion, Pa., 1964-68; instr., supr. U. Pa. Grad. Sch. Edn., Phila., 1968-70; assoc. prof. Community Coll. Phila., 1970—; anchorwoman WPVI-TV, ABC affiliate, 1976-78; founding mem. Galleryspace, 1976-78; cons. in field. Author: Clio Remembers, 1988; contbr. articles to newspapers and mags. Field rep. Earthwatch, Watertown, Mass., 1982—; bd. dirs. Phila. Theater Festival for New Plays, 1984-86, YMHA Arts Coun., Phila., 1974-80, Young Widow and Widower Assn., Phila., 1982—; docent Internat. Vis. Ctr., Phila., 1986—, Pa. Acad. Find Arts, 1972-80. Women's Way grantee, 1986-87. Fellow AAUW; mem. Phila. Writers Orgn., Phi Beta Kappa (coun. mem. Del. Valley 1989—), Pi Delta Theta. Home: 2200 Benjamin Franklin Pkwy Philadelphia PA 19130 Office: Community Coll Phila 1700 Spring Garden St Philadelphia PA 19130

MALLORY SILLIERE, JUDITH ESTHER, chief operating officer; b. N. Kingston, R.I., Feb. 7, 1961; d. Arthur Lorenzo and Mary Patricia (York) M. BA, Eisenhower Coll., 1983. Legal asst. Bell, Kalnick, Beckman, Klee & Green, N.Y.C., 1983-85; adminstrv. asst. Nutmeg Real Estate Svcs., West Port, Conn., 1985; dir. operations Nutmeg Real Estate Svcs., West Port, 1986, asst. v.p., 1986, asst. v.p., chief operating officer, 1988—. Co-author: Computer Literacy, 1982. Nurses aide Good Samaritan Hosp., West Islip, N.Y., 1975-79; library vol. West Islip Pub. Library, 1976-79; instr. Conn. Chpt. Vols. for Literacy, Norwalk, Conn., 1988—. Mem. NAFE, Real Estate Bd. N.Y. Democrat. Roman Catholic. Home: 51 Seaview Ave E Norwalk CT 06855 Office: Nutmeg Real Estate Svcs Inc 1 Morningside DrN Westport CT 06880

MALLOUK, ANN MARMON, clinical social work; b. Memphis, Sept. 1, 1923; d. Jeff Audrey and Naomi (Merrell) Marmon; m. George Elias Mallouk, July 6, 1945; children: John, Jeff, William, James, Thomas. Student, Tulane U., 1942-45; BA, Hofstra U., 1972; MSW, Adelphi U., 1980. Diplomate Clin. Soc. Workers. Asst. to pres. Hofstra U., Hempstead, N.Y., 1974-76, asst. to dir. devel., 1976-77; asst. dir. admissions Adelphi U., Garden City, 1980-81; exec. dir. Family Life Ctr., Garden City, 1981-88; supv. Interfaith Nutrition Network, Hempstead, 1989—; cons. Interfaith Nutrition Network, Hempstead, 1988-89, Family Life Ctr., Garden City, 1988—; field instr. Adelphi U., Garden City, 1990—, SUNY, Stony Brook, 1990—. Bd. dirs. Planned Parenthood Nassau County, Mineola, N.Y., 1989—; nat. bd. dirs. United Ch. Christ, 1986-89, chmn. ch. coun. Community Ch., Garden City, 1975-76; mem. adv. bd. Family Life Ctr., 1988—, Sch. Social Work Adelphi U., 1982-88; trustee Hofstra U., 1972—; chair adv. bd. Hofstra Family Ctr. and Child Care. Recipient Beatrice McClintock award Planned Parenthood, 1989, George M. Estabrook Disting. Svc. award Hofstra U., 1990; Ann Mallouk Day proclaimed by Nassau County, Mar. 22, 1987. Mem. AAUW, LWV, Acad. Cert. Social Workers. Democrat. Office: Interfaith Nutrition Network 148 Front St Hempstead NY 11530

MALLOW, MARISA GALE, management executive; b. Wichita Falls, Tex., Aug. 5, 1959; d. John Ben and Elsie Mae (Ramsey) M. BS, Tex. Woman's U., 1981. Pvt. practice Mallow Oil Co., McKinney, Tex.; office mgr. Johnsons Furniture, McKinney; ops. asst., office mgr. First State Bank, McKinney; beauty cons. Mary Kay. Recipient numerous scholarships. Mem. NAFE. Baptist. Home: 201 Dove Creek McKinney TX 75069 Office: PO Box 478 McKinney TX 75069

MALLOY, BETSY BROWNRIGG, semiconductor process engineeer; b. Pryor, Okla., June 7, 1952; d. John Henry and Ruth M. (Beckett) B. BS in Chemistry, U. of Tulsa, 1974; PhD in Analytical Chemistry, Baylor U., Waco, Tex., 1979. Process engr. Mostek, Carrollton, Tex., 1979-83; tech. mgr. ITT GaAs Tech. Ctr., Roanoke, Va., 1983-86; sr. engr. Microwave Semiconductor, Somerset, N.J., 1986-89; section head TRW, Redondo Beach, Calif., 1989—. Vol. Recording for the Blind, L.A., 1989—. Mem. Am. Soc. for Quality Control, IEEE.

MALLOY, GRACE LOUISE, actuary; b. Denver, Nov. 8, 1959; d. John Francis Jr. and Janet Margaret (Green) M. BS, Mass. Inst. of Tech., Cambridge, 1982. Actuarial asst. John Hancock Mutual Life Ins. Co., Boston, 1982-85, actuarial assoc., 1986-88, actuarial fellow, 1989, asst. actuary, 1989—; instr. Boston Actuaries Club, 1989—. Mem. Natick Town meeting, 1990—. Fellow Soc. Actuaries; mem. Am. Acad. Actuaries, Boston Actuaries Club.

MALLOY, KATHLEEN SHARON, lawyer; b. Evergreen Park, Ill., Apr. 7, 1948, d. Clarence Edmund and Ruth Elizabeth (Petrini) M.; m. Randall Kleinman, Aug. 5, 1978; children: Brighid, Ellena, Grant. BA in Psychology, St. Louis U., 1970; JD, Loyola U., Chgo., 1976. Bar: Ill. 1976, Calif. 1977. CPCU. Account exec. Complete Equity Mkts., Wheeling, Ill., 1970-76, corp. counsel, 1976-80, v.p., gen. counsel, 1980-83, exec. v.p., gen. counsel, 1983, chief operating officer, gen. counsel, 1984-85, vice chmn. bd., gen. counsel, 1986—; founding ptnr. firm Malloy & Kleinman, P.C., Des Plaines, Ill., 1985—. Vol. atty. legal aid orgns., Calif., 1976-79. Mem. ABA, Calif. State Bar Assn., Mensa, Women's Bar Assn., Nat. Legal Aid and Defender Assn. (ex-officio mem. ins. com. 1986—), Am. Soc. Chartered Property Casualty Underwriters. Office: Malloy & Kleinman PC 640 Pearson St Ste 206 Des Plaines IL 60016

MALLOY, PHEOBE SMALLS, educator; b. Charleston, S.C., Oct. 9, 1954; d. James and Evelina (Jenkins) Singleton; m. Edward Lamar Smalls, July 9, 1977 (div. Dec. 1983); 1 child, Ashanti Lamar; m. Frank Walter Malloy Jr., Mar. 10, 1984; 1 child, Maggie Blythwood. BA, Johnson C. Smith U., Charlotte, N.C., 1976; MEd, The Citadel, 1979. Cert. tchr. educable mentally handicapped. Intern Ctr. for Human Devel., Charlotte, 1975-76; tchr. for educable mentally handicapped Bapt. Hill High Sch., Charleston, 1976-81; resource tchr. for students with learning disabilities, corr. pub. relations Burke High Sch., Charleston, 1981—, chair exceptional children's month, 1982-86, chair black history month, 1982-86, co-chair sch. based mgmt. team, 1985—, co-chair self-study team for So. Assn. Accreditation, 1986—; est. Spanish program James Simmons Elem. Sch., Charleston, 1985; co-owner Malloy's Ctr. for Desktop Pub. Liaison editorial staff Handbook for Tchrs., 1982; contbr. articles to profl. jours. Mem. pub. relations com. Burke PTA, 1985-87, co-chair ways and means com., 1986-87; sec. dist. 20 City Council PTA, Charleston, 1986-87. Named Disting. Corr., Burke High Sch., 1986-87, Disting. Vol., Charleston County Schs., 1987, Disting. Vol., James Simons Elem. Sch., 1987. Mem. Council for Exceptional Children, Div. for Learning Disabilities, Cath. Women Orgn., Eta Phi Beta (sec. 1983-84, 1st v.p. 1984-86). Home: 804 Sprague St Charleston SC 29412 Office: Burke High Sch 244 President St Charleston SC 29403

MALM, RITA P., securities executive; b. May 8, 1932; d. George Peter and Helen Marie (Woodward) Pellegrini; student Packard Jr. Coll., 1950-52, N.Y. Inst. Fin., 1954, Wagner Coll., 1955; m. Robert J. Malm, Apr. 19, 1970. Sales asst. Dean Witter & Co., N.Y.C., 1959-63, asst. v.p., compliance dir., 1969-74; v.p., dir. Securities Ind. Assocs., N.Y.C., 1969-72; chief exec. officer Muriel Siebert & Co., Inc., N.Y.C., 1981-83; pres., founder Madison-Chapin Assocs., N.Y.C., 1984-89; pres. Hayward Malm Securities, Ltd., 1989—; art mktg. cons. Mem. Women's Bond Club N.Y. (dir., v.p., program chmn., pres. 1980-82). Home: 1300 Ocean Way Jupiter FL 33477 Office: 2000 PGA Blvd Palm Beach Gardens FL 33408

MALMGREN, RENÉ LOUISE, academic arts administrator; b. Mpls., Nov. 14, 1938; d. Albert William and Hildegarde Ann (Topel) Erickson; m. Donald Elwin Malmgren, Dec. 27, 1958; D. Gustaf, Ericka Susan, Tavus Val, Beret Kristina. BA in Theatre, Speech and English, Colo. Women's Coll., 1966; MA in Ednl. Adminstrn and Curriculum Devel., U. Colo., 1981. Cert. supt., Ariz.; cert. type D adminstr., Colo. Cons. creative drama Cultural Arts Program Denver Pub. Schs., 1970-72; tchr. APS Crawford Elem. Sch., Aurora, Colo., 1972-78; instr. Colo. Women's Coll., Denver, 1974-75; tchr. English Hinkley High Sch., Aurora; ednl. dir. Colo. Children's Theatre Co., Denver, 1977-86; adminstrv. intern Aurora Pub. Schs., 1981-82, coord. curriculum, 1982-85; asst. dir. instrn. fine arts Tucson Unified Sch. Dist., 1985-90; external auditor lang. arts Jefferson County Pub. Schs., Littleton, Colo., 1984; curriculum evaluator North Cen. Assn., Grand Junction, Colo., 1985; editor dramatic arts curriculum Ariz. Dept. Edn., Phoenix, 1989; rev. panelist Ariz. Commn. on Arts, Phoenix, 1986-87. Co-author satellite TV curriculum, 1987; appeared in premier of play The Only Woman Awake, 1984. Del. Colo. Dem. Conv., Denver, 1980; peacekeeper Take Back the Night March-Rape Assistance and Awareness Program, Denver, 1982-84; mem. policy com. Tucson Cable Arts Channel, 1986-87; mem. edn. com. Tucson Symphony Orch., 1988—; mem. So. Ariz. Opera Guild, 1988—; mem. corp. bd. Ariz. Arts Alliance 1988—; bd. dirs. Arts Genesis, 1990—. Colo. Council on Arts and Humanities grantee, 1978. Mem. Nat. Art Edn. Assn., Assn. for Supervision and Curriculum Devel., Arts in Edn. Coun., Nat. Adminstrv. Women in Edn., Ariz. Arts Supervisory Coalition, Ariz. Theatre Educators Assn. (bd. dirs. 1985-89, pres. 1988-89), Nat. Soc. for Arts and Letters, Phi Delta Kappa. Home: 2612 E La Cienega Dr Tucson AZ 85716

MALONE, BETTE JUNE, real estate broker, interior designer, small business owner; b. Seattle, June 29, 1950; d. Harry Louis and Emma (Jeske) Cohn; m. Jon L. Malone, Mar. 13, 1980, (div. Nov. 1981); children: Christine Lynn, Robert Lee. AA in Arts, U. Md. Extension, Naples, Italy, 1977. Paralegal JAG, Naples, 1974-76; mktg. rep. Polaroid Corp., Timex Corp., Naples, 1976-78; broker Norwood Group Inc., Nashua, N.H., 1978-81; pres. G. Ea. Properties Corp., Nashua, N.H., 1981-90, One of a Kind Jewelry, Edmonds, Wash., 1990—. Bd. dir. United Way, Nashua, 1985; chmn., vip panelist, Easter Seal Soc., Manchester, 1982-87. Named Disting. Woman Leader YWCA, Nashua, 1982. Mem. Greater Nashua Bd. Realtors, (pres. 1986-87, v.p. 1985, Realtor Yr.), New Eng. Chpt. Cert. Real Estate Brokerage Mgrs., Sales and Mktg. Coun., Nashua Jaycee Women (chmn. project yr. 1980-81, Outstanding Chmn. Yr. 1980-82), Mensa, Profl. Assn. Diving Instrs., Realtors Inst. (cert.). Clubs: MENSA, Profl. Assn. Diving Instrs. Home: 13026 Fourth Ave W Everett WA 98204 Office: One of a Kind Jewelry 114 Fourth Ave N Edmonds WA 98020

MALONE, DOROTHY ANN, life underwriter, marketing executive, consultant, lecturer; b. Logansport, Ind., June 19, 1931; d. Harry and Lena Estella Malone. BBA, McKendree Coll., Radcliff, Ky., 1981; postgrad. in humanities Webster Coll., 1981-84; M. Pub. Service Adminstrn., Western Ky. U., 1984, M. Pub. Counseling, 1985. Lic. life and health agt. Joined U.S. Army, 1952, advanced through grades to master sgt., 1972, ret., 1975; ind. life underwriter, Elizabethtown, Ky., 1977—; dir. mktg. and sales Dixie Rabbit, Inc., Ekron, Ky., 1981—; sr. counselor, tchr. Southeastern Tng. Corp., Elizabethtown, 1987—; sr. instr., counselor AJS Enterprises, Inc., Tng. Corp. Am.; v.p. S.T.E.M. Concepts, Inc.; cons., lectr. minority and women's subjects. First v.p. Hardin County (Ky.) chpt. NAACP, 1975; mem. Hardin County Human Relations Com., 1977-78; chairperson Hardin County Blue Ribbon Com., 1977; trustee Embry Chapel AME Ch., Elizabethtown, 1983—; mem. Ky. Gov.'s Council on Volunteerism. Decorated Army Commendation medal with 5 oak leaf clusters; recipient numerous letters of commendation and appreciation and awards, including cert. of appreciation NAACP, 1976, others. Mem. Federally Employed Women (chairperson program Ft. Knox Area chpt. 1978-79, v.p. Ft. Knox Area chpt. 1978-79), Ky. Assn. Ret. Mil., Nat. Assn. Exec. Women, Ky. Cen. Assn. Life Underwriters, Life Investors' Pacer Club, Am. Defender Life Ins. Co., NAACP (life), Am. Soc. Profl. and Exec. Women. Lodge: Order Eastern Star.

MALONE, ELQUIN LEA, civil engineer; b. Springfield, Mo., Sept. 18, 1956; d. James Scott Malone and Lucille Marie (Newberry); m. Frederick Earl Turner, Sept. 18, 1973; (div. Aug. 1978). BA in Psych., So. Mo. State U., Springfield, 1978; BS in Civil Engring., U. Mo., Rolla, 1981. Cert. profl. engr. Asst. civil engr. U. S. Forest Svc., Rolla, 1979-81; design engr. Texaco, Port Arthur, 1981-84; civil engr. Texas Hwy. Dept., Port Arthur, 1985, Black & Veatch, Austin, 1985-86; sr. constrn. engr. Parson's Brinckerhoff, Austin, 1986-88; sr. civil engr. Parson's Brinckerhoff, Herndon, Va., 1988--. Mem. ASCE. Home: 5851 Rock Forest Ct Centreville VA 22020 Office: Parson's Brinckerhoff 460 Spring Park Pl Herndon VA 22070

MALONE, JEAN HAMBIDGE, educational administrator; b. South Bend, Ind., Nov. 23, 1954; d. Craig Ellis and Dorothy Jane (Piechorowski) Hambidge; m. James Kevill Malone, July 8, 1978; children: Julia Mae, James Kevill III. BS in Edn., Butler U., 1976, MS in Edn., 1977. Tchr. Indpls. Pub. Schs., 1977-78; dir. student center and activities Butler U., Indpls., 1978-87. Trustee Eisenhower Meml. scholarship, 1977-80; bd. dirs. Heritage Place of Indpls., 1983-88, Ind. Office Campus Ministries, Intercollegiate YMCA Indpls., 1985-87, 89—, Campfire of Cen. Ind. 1980-84, 86-87, Urban Parish Coop., 1987—, Indpls. Jr. League, 1989—, Indpls. Urban Parish Coop., 1987—, St. Thomas Aquinas Bd. Edn., 1990, v.p. Recipient Outstanding Faculty award, Butler U., 1980. Mem. Ind. Assn. Women Deans (v.p. bd. dirs. 1987-88), Adminstrs. and Counselors (bd. dirs. 1982-83), Ind. Assn. Coll. Personnel Adminstrs., Nat. Assn. Women Deans, Adminstrs. and Counselors, Kappa Delta Pi, Phi Kappa Phi, Alpha Lambda Delta, Kappa Kappa Gamma. Roman Catholic. Home: 5256 N Illinois Indianapolis IN 46208-2636

MALONE, KAREN SELLARS, accountant; b. Gilmer, Tex., Apr. 3, 1951; d. Everett and Ruby Faye (Nix) Sellars; m. James Douglas Coleman, Jan. 17, 1970 (div. Nov. 1977); m. Don Michael Malone, Jan. 2, 1981; children: Ramona Rene, Joshua Douglas. BS, U. Tex., 1988, postgrad., summer 1989. From receptionist to exec. sec. Tex. Bank & Trust, Dallas, 1969-73; exec. sec., bookkeeper Campbell Co., Dallas, 1973, Thompson Mng. Co., Dallas, 1973-76; staff acct. Bright & Bright, Dallas, 1976-82; controller Robert M. Edsel, Dallas, 1982-87; pvt. practice acct. Dallas, 1987—. Mem. AICPAs, Tex. Soc. CPAs, Nat. Assn. Investment Club (treas.), Phi Theta Kappa. Republican. Home and Office: 9608 Vista Oaks Dr Dallas TX 75243

MALONE, LINDA SUE, nurse; b. Shelby, N.C., Sept. 19, 1944; d. Garther Albert and Lucille (Smith) Whisnant; m. Gary P. Malone, Jan. 7, 1965; children: Mark Patrick, Gary Michael, Christopher Matthew. Diploma in nursing Charlotte Presbyn., N.C., 1965; BS, St. Joseph's Coll., 1986. RN, N.C., N.J., Hawaii; cert. profl. in quality assurance. Nurse Heilbronn Elem. Sch., Germany, 1967-68; nurse pvt. duty Long Branch Nurses Registry, N.J., 1972-73; staff nurse Cape Fear Valley Med. Ctr., Fayetteville, N.C., 1975-78, coordinator quality assurance, 1978-85, dir. quality assurance, 1985—; cons., lectr. quality assurance. Vol. nurse Westover Jr. High Sch., Fayetteville, 1979; pres. Paramed. Service, Fayetteville, 1982-85. Republican. Methodist. Avocations: crafts, gourmet cooking, water sports. Home: 426 Dunmore Rd Fayetteville NC 28303 Office: Cape Fear Valley Med Ctr Fayetteville NC 28302

MALONE, LUCY WAGGONER, conference coordinating executive; b. Nashville, Oct. 17, 1947; d. Melburn James and Thelma Louise (Yates) Waggoner; m. Michael Blair Malone, Feb. 10, 1963 (div. Jan. 1983); children: Lisa Ann, Mary Elizabeth. AS in Bus. Edn., Vol. State (Tenn.) Coll., 1976, AS in Bus. Mktg., 1988. Motor carrier registration coordinator Tenn. Pub. Service Commn., Nashville, 1969-74; adminstrv. asst. Ted Wynne & Assocs., Nashville, 1976-79; office mgr. Malones Market, Nashville, 1980; exec. asst. Blevins Home Parts Distributor, Nashville, 1981; adminstr. tech. transfer Aladdin Industries, Nashville, 1982-87; exec. dir., bd. dirs. Tech. Transfer Confs., Nashville, 1984—. Tchr. 8th grade girls Baptist Ch., Goodlettsville, Tenn., 1980-82, 7th and 8th grade dept. head, 1983-84; coach girls softball and basketball, 1975-78; newletter editor Pathfinders Class, Brentwood, Tenn., 1986-87. Mem. Licensing Exec. Soc., Tech. Transfer Soc., Meeting Planners Internat., High Tech. Initiative (edn. com.). Baptist. Home: 2001 Sunnyslope Ln Goodlettsville TN 37072 Office: Tech Transfer Confs 325 Plus Park Blvd #108 Nashville TN 37217

MALONE, MARY FRANCES ALICIA, academic administrator; b. N.Y.C., Sept. 24, 1946; d. James Patrick and Mary Theresa (McGarry)ú Hoban; m. Kieran Malone, May 10, 1985. BA in History, Molloy Coll., 1967; MA in Am. History and Lit., Fordham U., 1969; PhD in Organizational Behavior/Adminstrn, NYU, 1977. Placement dir. Molloy Coll., Rockville Centre, N.Y., 1969-71; doctoral rsch. fellow NYU, N.Y.C., 1971-74, exec. asst. to dean of librs., div. of libr., 1974-77; mgr. profl. devel. Spl. Librs. Assn., N.Y.C., 1977-83; asst. dean, grad. sch. of communication Fairfield (Conn.) U., 1983-89, asst. acad. v.p., 1989—; task force facilitator Fairfield 2000 Regional Plan Assn., Greenwich, Conn., 1987; facilitator Assn. for Mgmt., "Mgmt. Survival Kit,", Greenwich, 1987; contract reviewer U.S. Dept. Edn., Washington, 1982. Editor Profl. Devel. Series; contbr. articles to profl. jours. Recipient citation, Bd. dirs. Spl. Librs. Assn., 1983, Challenge Grant, NEH, 1977; named to 1st worldwide conf. on spl. librs., H.W. Wilson Fedn., Exxon Edn. Found., Honolulu, 1979. Mem. Advt. Women of N.Y. (chmn. com. 1981—), Women in Communication (bd. dirs. 1984-86, 88-89), White House Conf. on Libr. and Info. Sci. (facilitator), Continuing Libr. Edn. Network and Exch. (bd. dirs. 1980-82), Pi Lambda Theta. Roman Catholic. Office: Fairfield Univ Canisius 312 Fairfield CT 06851

MALONE, MONICA, psychologist; b. Camden, N.J.. BA, La Salle Coll., Phila., 1975; MA, U.S. Internat. U., San Diego, 1976. Lic. psychologist, Pa. Drug abuse counselor Rehab. A.I.D., Phila., 1976-77; drug abuse social worker Camden County Drug Abuse Clinic, Camden, N.J., 1977-78; mental health cons. Atlantic Mental Health Ctr., Atlantic City, 1978-83; weight loss counselor Nutrisystem Weight Loss Ctrs., Northfield, N.J., 1983-84; psychologist Woodbine (N.J.) Devel. Ctr., 1984—; pvt. practice, Phila., 1986—; developer, presenter tng. workshops Internat. Lifeline Conv., Melbourne, Australia, tng. programs for other hotlines and adult edn. classes, 1977-84. Pres. Environ. Action Group, Cherry Hill, N.J.; coord. Cherry Hill Recycling Program. President's scholar La Salle Coll., 1971. Mem. Am. Psychol. Assn., Brigantine Yacht Club. Office: 230 S Broad St 11th Fl Philadelphia PA 19102

MALONE, PERRILLAH ATKINSON (PAT MALONE), state official; b. Montgomery, Ala., Mar. 17, 1922; d. Odolph Edgar and Myrtle (Fondren) Atkinson. BS, Oglethorpe U., 1956; MAT, Emory U., 1962. Asst. editor, then acting editor Emory U., 1958-64; asst. project officer Ga. Dept. Pub. Health, Atlanta, 1965-68; asst. project dir. Ga. Ednl. Improvement Coun., 1968-69, assoc. dir., 1970-71; dir. career svcs. State Scholarship Commn., Atlanta, 1971-74; rev. coord. Div. Phys. Health, Ga. Dept. Human Resources, Atlanta, 1974-79; project dir. So. Regional Edn. Bd., 1979-81; specialist Div. Family and Children Svcs., Atlanta, 1982—; mem. Gov.'s Commn. on Nursing Edn. and Nursing Practice, 1972-75, Aging Svcs. Task Force, Atlanta Regional Commn., 1985—; book reviewer Atlanta Jour.-Constn., 1962-79. Recipient Recognition award Ga. Nursing Assn., 1976, Korsell award Ga. Ga. League for Nursing, 1974, Alumni Honor award Emory U., 1964. Mem. Am. Pub. Health Assn., Am. Pub. Welfare Assn., N.Y. Acad. Scis., Ga. Gerontology Soc. Methodist. Home: 1146 Oxford Rd NE Atlanta GA 30306 Office: 878 Peachtree St Ste 503 Atlanta GA 30309

MALONE, SUE ANDERSON, medical records administration educator; b. Chattanooga, Apr. 18, 1930; d. Thomas E. and Camie M. (Dean) Anderson; widow; children: Mick Z., Tacea C., Kerry P. BS in Health Care Mgmt., Fla. Internat. U., 1977, BS in Med. Record Admin., 1979; MPA, U. Mo., Kansas City, 1981. Registered record administr. Dir. med. record dept. King's Daughters Hosp., Madison, Ind., 1967-70; dir. med. record svcs. Gwinnett County Hosp. Authority, Lawrenceville, Ga., 1970-72, Imperial Point Med. Ctr., Ft. Lauderdale, Fla., 1972-79; assoc. prof. med. record adminstrn. edn. Sch. Allied Health, U. Kans. Med. Ctr., Kansas City, 1979—, chmn. dept., 1981—; cons. Bottomley & Assocs., Duluth, Ga., 1987—; critical reviewer W.B. Saunders Co., 1988; cons. numerous health care facilities; speaker in field. Vol. Children's Miracle Network Telephon, 1987-88. Recipient Disting. Teaching award U. Kans. Amoco Found., 1984. Mem. NAFE, Am. Med. Record Assn., Kans. Med. Record Assn. (chmn. continuing edn.-program com. 1983-84), Kansas City Area Med. Record Assn., Am. Bus. Women's Assn. (v.p. Mo.-Kans. Star chpt. 1988-89, Woman of Yr. 1989). Baptist. Office: U Kans Med Ctr 39th and Rainbow Kansas City KS 66103

MALONEY, DOROTHY ANN GOSE, school system administrator; b. Long Beach, Calif., Mar. 13, 1933; d. Harold Marian and Rachel Nane (Dyer) Gose; m. John Calvin Maloney, Apr. 24, 1955; children: John Patrick, Richard S. BA, Calif. State U., Long Beach, 1953; MA, Calif. State U., Northridge, 1972. Cert. life gen./elem. tchr., life jr. high tchr., life gen./pupil personnel svcs. in counseling and psychometry, life gen. elem. adminstr., ryan adminstrv. svcs. K-12, reading specialist. Officer personnel office Commandant 11th Naval Dist., San Diego, 1956-60; tchr. Timber and San Diego, Thousand Oaks, Calif., San Diego, 1960-66; counselor Redwood intermediate Timber Sch. Dist., Thousand Oaks, 1966-69, coord. spl. edn., 1970-73; counselor Sequoia Intermediate, Conejo Valley Unified Sch. Dist., Thousand Oaks, 1969-79; prin. Ladera Elem., Conejo Valley Unified Sch. Dist., Thousand Oaks, 1979-81; dir. rsch., planning and assessment Conejo Valley Unified Sch. Dist., Thousand Oaks, 1981-87; lectr. grad. edn./adminstrn. Calif. Luth. U., Thousand Oaks, 1975—; dir. curriculum devel. Conejo Valley Unified Sch. Dist., Thousand Oaks, 1987—; mem. Calif. State Task Force on Assessment and Accountability, Sacramento, 1983-86, Calif. State Ad Hoc Com. Dir. Writing Assessment, Sacramento, 1983-87, Calif. State Ad Hoc Com. on Golden State Exams., Sacramento, 1983-87. Rep. ACT, Calif. Luth. U.; chair sch. site coun. Sequoia Intermediate, Thousand Oaks, 1979, Conejo/Moorpark/Simi Mental Health Adv. Com., Ventura County, Calif., 1976. Lt. USNR, 1954-60. Mem. Assn. Calif. Sch. Adminstrn., Am. Ednl. Rsch. Assn., Am. Assn. Curriculum Devel., Internat. Reading Assn., Calif. Assn. Curriculum Devel., Phi Delta Kappa (pres. East Valley chpt. 1987-89), Delta Kappa Gamma (Eta Psi chpt., Outstanding Educator 1985). Office: Conejo Valley Unified Sch Dist 1400 E Janss Rd Thousand Oaks CA 91362

MALONEY, JOAN ANN, bank executive; b. Mt. Kisco, N.Y., Dec. 29, 1942. BBA, Western Conn. State U., 1990. Asst. v.p., br. mgr. Mechanics and Farmers Savs. Bank FSB, Danbury, Conn. Mem. United Way-Allocations Sub-com., account exec. Mem. Fin. Women Internat., Women's Coun. Realtors, Am. Inst. Banking (area rep. Danbury chpt., instr. Daubury chpt. 1990)., Kiwanis Internat., Danbury Ski Club. Home: 1701 Village Sq Danbury CT 06810

MALONEY, LUCILLE TINKER, civic worker; b. Twin Falls, Idaho, Mar. 13, 1920; d. Edward Milo and Lillian (Schaefer) Tinker; Frank E. Maloney, Feb. 20, 1943 (dec.); children: Frank E., JoAnn Maloney Smallwood, Elizabeth Maloney Hurst. Tchr's cert., Idaho State U.; student Wash. State U., 1941. Pres., U. Fla. Women's Club, 1960-61, Gainesville Women's Club, 1974-75, Friends of Five Sta. WUFT-TV, Public Broadcasting, 1976-77; chmn., organizer Gainesville Spring Pilgrimage, 1976; founder, pres. Thomas Center Assocs., 1978-80; v.p. U. Fla. Art Gallery Guild, 1981, pres., 1982-84; mem. Fla. Gov.'s Challenge Program Com., 1981; trustee Fla. House, Washington, 1975-80; patron, organizer, trustee Hippodrome State Theatre; chmn. Santa Fe Regional Library Bd., 1980-81; pres. Gainesville Women's Forum, 1984-85; mem. Exec. Commn. Fla. for Statue of Liberty-Ellis Island Centennial; bd. dirs. Classic 89, Nat. Pub. Radio, 1987—; trustee Displaced Homemakers, Santa Fe Community Coll.; adv. bd. Gainesville for Thomas Ctr. Gardens, 1985—. Recipient Fla. Leadership pin Gov. LeRoy Collins, 1961, Disting. Svc. award Women in Communication, Inc., 1975, Appreciation plaque Sta. WUFT-TV, 1977, Community Svc. award Gainesville Sun, 1979, Appreciation cert. Rotary Club Gainesville, 1980, Paul Harris fellow Rotary Club, 1986, Gainesville Area Woman of Distinction award Sante Fe Community Coll., 1987, Outstanding Svc. award Jr. League, 1980, Bicentennial plaque Alachua County Bicentennial Com., 1976, plaque Gainesville City Beautification Bd., 1990; honoree Alachua County Girls' Club Bd. Roast and Toast, 1990. Mem. Friends of Libr., Fla. State Mus. Assocs. (pres. 1985-87), Friends of Music, Hist. Gainesville, Inc., Found. for Promotion Music, Civic Chorus, Fla. Trust for Hist. Preservation, Fla. League Conservation Voters (bd. dirs. 1983—), Gainesville C. of C. (pub. affairs com. 1983-84), Altrusa Internat., Internat. Platform Assn., Fla. Women's Network, Howe Soc. for Rare Books (bd. dirs.), U. Fla. Club, Gainesville Garden Club, Heritage Club (bd. govs.), Designer Club, Christmas Wreath So. Living Mag. Club. Home: 1823 N W 10th Ave Gainesville FL 32605

MALONEY, SUSAN YACHER, accountant; b. Youngstown, Ohio, May 1, 1954; d. Joseph Michael and Stella Sophie (Maslach) Yacher; m. John Franklin Maloney, Mar. 20, 1976. BSBA, Ohio State U., 1977. CPA, Ohio. Cost analyst Republic Steel Corp., Warren, Ohio, 1977-83; sr. fin. analyst Kimberly Clark Corp., Neenah, Wis., 1984-86; cost acct. Clermont Mercy Hosp., Batavia, Ohio, 1987-89; dir. decision support systems U. Cin. Hosp., 1989—. Advisor Jr. Achievement, Youngstown, Ohio, 1982-83. Mem. Health Care Fin. Mgmt. Assn. (newsletter editor 1990), Hosp. Mgmt. Orgn., Adminstrv. Mgmt. Orgn. Home: 3801 Linn Tree Dr Amelia OH 45102 Office: University of Cin. Hospital 234 Goodman St ML 702 Cincinnati OH 45267

MALONEY, THERESE ADELE, insurance company executive; b. Quincy, Mass., Sept. 15, 1929; d. James Henry and F. Adele (Powers) M. BA in Econs., Coll. St. Elizabeth, Convent Station, N.J., 1951; AMP, Harvard U. Bus. Sch., 1981. CPCU. With Liberty Mut. Ins. Co., Boston, 1951—, asst. v.p., asst. mgr. nat. risks, 1974-77, v.p., mgr. nat. risks, 1977-79, v.p., mgr. nat. risks, 1979-86, sr. v.p. underwriting mktg. and adminstrn. 1986-87, exec. v.p. underwriting, policy decision, 1987—, also bd. dirs.; pres. and bd. dirs. subs. Liberty Mut. (Bermuda) Ltd., 1981—, LEXCO Ltd.; bd. dirs., dep. chmn. Liberty Mut. (Mass.) Ltd., London; bd. dirs. Liberty Mut. Ins. Co., Liberty Mut. Fire Ins. Co.; mem. faculty Inst. Inst., Northeastern U., Boston, 1969-74; mem. adv. bd., risk mgmt. studies Ins. Inst. Am., 1977-83; mem. adv. coun. Suffolk U. Sch. Mgmt., 1984—; mem. adv. coun. to program in internat. bus. rels. Fletcher Sch. Law and Diplomacy, 1985—. Mem. Soc. CPCUs (past pres. Boston chpt.), Univ. Club, Algonquin Club (Boston). Office: Liberty Mut Ins Co 175 Berkeley St Boston MA 02117

MALONEY, TONI, corporate communications specialist. Sr. v.p. Ogilvy & Mather Advt., N.Y.C., 1987-90; v.p. corp. communications Am. Express Co., N.Y.C., 1990—. Office: Am Express Co Am Express Tower 200 Vessey St New York NY 10285*

MALOUF-CUNDY, PAMELA BONNIE, visual arts editor; b. Reseda, Calif., July 9, 1956; d. Jubert George and Marguerite I. (Llido) Malouf. AA in Cinema with honors, Valley Community Coll., 1976. Asst. film editor various film studios including Paramount, 20th Fox, CBS MTM, and others, 1976-80; post prodn. coordinator, supr. David Gerber Co., Culver City, Calif., 1981-82; post prodn. coordinator Paramount TV, Los Angeles, 1982-84; sole proprietor Trailers, Etc., North Hollywood, Calif., 1984-85, 88-89; film and video editor Paramount Pictures, Los Angeles, 1985-88; film editor Universal Studios, Universal City, Calif., 1986—. Film and video editor (TV) A Year in the Life, MacGyver, Family Ties on Vacation, Call to Glory, The Making of Shogun, Nightingales, Mission Impossible, Murder C.O.D., I'll Take Romance, others, (movies) Sweet Bird of Youth, Without You I'm Nothing, That Was Then, This Is Now, All in the Family, others; asst. film editor (movies) King of the Gypsies, Star Wars, others. Mem. Internat. Alliance of Theatrical Stage Employees and Moving Picture Machine Operators of the U.S. and Can., Tri-Network (pres. 1979-80), Acad. Magical Arts, Inc., Acad. TV Arts and Scis. Democrat. Roman Catholic.

MALSON, VERNA LEE, educator; b. Buffalo, Wyo., Mar. 29, 1937; d. Guy James and Vera Pearl (Curtis) Mayer; m. Jack Lee Malson, Apr. 20, 1955; children: Daniel Lee, Thomas James, Mark David, Scott Allen. BA in Elem. Edn. and Spl. Edn. magna cum laude, Met. State Coll., Denver, 1975; MA in Learning Disabilities, U. No. Colo., 1977. Cert. tchr., Colo. Tchr.-aide Wyo. State Tng. Sch., Lander, 1967-69; spl. edn. tchr. Bennett Sch. 29J, Colo., 1975-79, chmn. health, sci., social studies, 1977-79; spl. edn. tchr. Deer Trail Sch., Colo., 1979—, chmn. careers, gifted and talented, 1979-87; mem. spl. edn. parent adv. com. East Central Bd. Coop. Ednl. Services, Limon, Colo. Colo. scholar Met. State Coll., 1974; Colo. Dept. Edn. grantee, 1979, 81. Mem. Council Exceptional Children, Bennett Tchrs. Club (treas. 1977-79), Internat. Biographical Assn., Kappa Delta Pi. Republican. Presbyterian. Avocations: coin collecting; reading; sports. Home: PO Box 403 Deer Trail CO 80105 Office: Deer Trail Pub Schs 26J PO Box 129 Deer Trail CO 80105

MALUGEN, LOUISE D., federal judge; b. 1945. BA, Pa. Coll. Women, Pitts.; JD, Loyola U., Chgo. Admitted to bar, 1970. Bankruptcy judge U.S. Dist. Ct. (so. dist.) Calif., San Diego. Office: US Dist Ct 940 Front St San Diego CA 92189*

MALVEAUX, JULIANNE MARIE, economist; b. San Francisco, Sept. 22, 1953; d. Paul and Proteone Marie (Alexandria) M. BA, Boston Coll., 1974, MA, 1975; PhD, MIT, 1980. Jr. staff economist Council Econ. Advisor The White House, Washington, 1977-78; research fellow Rockefeller Found., N.Y.C., 1978-80; asst. prof. New Sch. Social Research, N.Y.C., 1980-81, San Francisco State U., 1981-85; vis. scholar U. Calif., Berkeley, 1985—, Stanford U., 1987-89; syndicated columnist King Features Syndicate, 1990—; cons. women's issues, labor, edn. devel., 1981—. Contbg. editor: Essence mag., 1984—; co-editor Slipping Through the Cracks: Status of Black Women; contbr. articles to profl. jours. Founder, chmn. San Francisco Anti-Apartheid com., 1985-86; bd. dirs. Coleman Advs. Children Youth, San Francisco, 1985—, Nat. Rainbow Coalition, Washington, 1986-89, NAACP, San Francisco, 1984, Dem. Women's Forum, San Francisco, 1986-88; pres. San Francisco Bus. and Profl. Women's Club, 1987-89, San Francisco Leadership Forum, 1987-89; pres. San Francisco Black Leadership Forum, 1989-90. Named one of Am.'s Top 100 Black Bus. and Profl. Women, Dollar and Sense Mag., 1985, one of 5 Black Women Who Make it Happen, Nat. Council Negro Women and Frito-Lay, 1987; postdoctoral fellow NRC, 1985-86. Roman Catholic. Home: 220 Kingston St San Francisco CA 94110 Office: U Calif Afro Am Studies Dwinelle Hall Berkeley CA 94570

MAMPRE, VIRGINIA ELIZABETH, communications executive; b. Chgo., Sept. 12, 1949; d. Albert Leon and Virginia S. (Joboul) M. BA with honors, U. Iowa, 1971; Masters degree, Ind. U., 1972; spl. cert., Harvard U., 1981. Cert. tchr. Harris Intern WTTW-TV Sta., Chgo., 1972, asst. dir., 1972-73; prod. and dir. WSIU/WUSI-TV Sta., Carbondale, Ill., 1973-74; instr. So. Ill. U., Carbondale, 1972-77; prog. and prod. mgr. WSIU/WUSI-TV, Carbondale, 1974-77; prog. dir. KUHT-TV Sta., Houston, 1977-83; pres. Victory Media, Inc., Houston, 1984-89, Mampre Media Internat., Houston, 1984—; cons. Corp. for Pub. Broadcasting, Washington, 1981-83; chmn. AWRT/YCOC, Houston (Texas) Metro Area, 1983-85; adv. coun. Pub. Broadcasting Svc., Washington, 1981-83; bd. & programming chmn., So. Edn. Communications, Columbia, S.C., 1978-83; bd. dirs. Interreg. Prog. Svc./EEN, Boston, 1980-83. Author: articles, Focus mag., 1989, News & Views mag., 1987-88; creator: report card campaign, Multi-media, U.S., 1985—; exec. producer: TV spls., Pub. affairs and info., 1977-83 (awards 1978-83). Pres. bd. dirs. Houston Fin. Coun., 1983—; pres. Child Abuse Prevention Coun., Houston, 1984—; officer Crime Stoppers, Houston, 1984—; chmn. exhbns. Mayor's 1st Hearing, Children and Youth, Houston, 1985-88; chmn. Evening Guild; rep. for Houston, 2d World Conf. of Mayors, Japan, 1989; com. chmn. SJD. Fellow W.K. Kellogg Found., Battle Creek, Mich., 1987-90; recipient Award for Excellence Pres. Pvt. Sector, White House, Washington, 1987, Ohio State U., Columbus, 1983, Feddersen Award for Excellence in Pub. TV Ind. U., Bloomington, Ind., 1981, Heritage award Child Abuse Prevention Con., 1990; named among Outstanding Women Vols. for community, civic and profl. contbns., 1989; finalist Woman on the Move, 1987, Rising Star, 1987. Mem. Am. Women in Radio and TV (nat. v.p. 1986-90, award 1987, pres. Houston chpt. 1990, bd. dirs. 1985—), Houston Fedn. Profl. Women (del. 1986-88), Nat. Assn. Ednl. Broadcasters (presenter nat. conv. 1975-76), NAPTE, Delphian's. Republican. Episcopalian. Office: Mampre Media Internat. 5123 Del Monte Ste 7 Houston TX 77056

MAMRAK, SANDRA ANN, computer science educator; b. Cleve., Sept. 8, 1944; d. Frank Joseph and Frances Mamrak; m. B. Chandrasekaran, Oct. 12, 1978; 1 child, Mallika. BS, Notre Dame Coll., 1968; MS, U. Ill., 1973, PhD, 1975. Prof. dept. computer and info. sci. Ohio State U., Columbus, 1975—; scientist Nat. Inst. for Sci. and Tech., Washington, summers 1975-79, Bell Labs., Columbus, summer 1980, Lawrence Livermore Nat. Labs., Livermore, Calif., summers 1981-83; dir. Chameleon Rsch. Lab., Columbus, 1986—. Contbr. articles to profl. jours. Home: 2053 Iuka Ave Columbus OH 43201 Office: Ohio State U 2036 Neil Ave Columbus OH 43210

MAN, EVELYN BROWER, retired biochemist, educator; b. Lawrence, N.Y., Oct. 7, 1904; d. Edward and Mary (Hewitt) M. BA in Chemistry, Wellesley Coll., 1925; PhD in Physiol. Chemistry, Yale U., 1932. Med. technician Yale U. Sch. Medicine, New Haven, 1928-29, rsch. asst., 1929-33, rsch. asst. dept. psychiatry and mental hygiene, 1933-49, asst. prof., 1949-61; fellow AAUW, 1933-34; with Inst. Life Scis. Brown U., Providence, 1961-70, emeritus, 1970—. Contbr. articles to sci. and med. jours. Vol. Westerly (R.I.) Hosp., 1970-88; officer North Stonington (Conn.) Hist. Soc., 1978-88; hon. life mem. Wheeler Sch. and Libr., North Stonington. Recipient award for rsch. on mental retardation of children United Cerebral Palsy Assn., 1966. Mem. Am. Soc. Biochemistry and Molecular Biology, AAAS, Am. Chem. Soc., N.Y. Acad. Scis., Am. Thyroid Assn. (disting. svc. cert. 1976), Endocrine Soc., Assn. Clin. Scientists (diploma of honor 1966), Am. Assn. Clin. Chemists, Royal Soc. Medicine, New Eng. Hypothyroidism, Phi Beta Kappa, Sigma Xi. Home: 275 Steele Rd Apt B407 West Hartford CT 06117

MANASC, VIVIAN, architect, consultant; b. Bucharest, Romania, May 19, 1956; d. Bercu and Bianca (Smetterling) M.; m. William A. Dushenski, Feb. 25, 1984; children: Peter Gabriel, Lawrence Alexander. BS in Architecture, McGill U., Montreal, Que., Can., 1977, BArch, 1979; MBA, U. Alta., Edmonton, 1982. Architectural insp. Transport Can., Edmonton, 1977-79; project architect Bell Spotowski Architects, Edmonton, 1980-82; asst. dir. design constrn. Edmonton Pub. Schs., 1982-84; mgr., prin. Ferguson, Simek, Clark Architects Ltd., Edmonton, 1985-88; mng. dir. FSC Groves Hodgson Manasc Architects Ltd., Edmonton, 1988—. Contbr. articles to profl. jours. Advisor YWCA, Edmonton, 1980-82; mentor RAIC Syllabus Program, Edmonton, 1982-88; bd. dirs. Design Workshop, Edmonton, 1983. Scholar McGill U., 1974. Mem. Alberta Assn. Architects, Royal Archtl. Inst. Can. (architecture for healthcare com.), Coun. Edn. Facility Planners. Office: FSC Groves Hodgson Manasc, 10417 Saskatchewan Dr, Edmonton, AB Canada T6E 4R8

MANASSE, ADRIENNE LORRI, organizational consultant; b. L.A., Oct. 24, 1941; d. Martin Sidney and Pearl Ida (Rankin) Obrand; m. Russell Misheloff, Jan. 2, 1982; 1 child, Matthew; 1 step child, Adrienne. BA, UCLA, 1962; MA, Calif. State U., Northridge, 1968; PhD, U. So. Calif., 1976; cert. in bus. adminstrn., Wharton Sch., 1982. Tchr. L.A. Unified Sch. Dist., 1963-72, English cons., 1970, dir. community centered classroom program, 1974-78; assoc. Nat. Inst. Edn., Washington, 1978-82; dir. organizational consulting Stanford Engring. and Mgmt. System Co., Arlington, Va., 1983-84; pres. Cortland Group, Washington, 1984—; adj. faculty sch. pub. adminstrn. U. So. Calif., 1974-80, sch. bus. adminstrn. Georgetown U., Washington, 1984-88; speaker in field. Author: Creating Conditions for Effective Principals, 1984, A Bankers Guide to Better Service, Bigger Profits, 1989; contbr. articles to profl. jours. bd. dirs. Washington Presch. Inc., Washington, 1981-82. Ednl. Policy fellow Inst. for Ednl. Leadership, Washington, 1978-79, Mellon Found. fellow U. So. Calif., 1972-75. Mem. Exec. Exch. (founder, bd. dirs. 1986), Am. Soc. for Tng. and Devel. (speaker), Acad. Mgmt., Orgnl. Devel. Network, World Future Soc., Fin. Women Internat., Am. Soc. Pub. Adminstrn. (nat. com. 1978-82). Jewish. Office: Cortland Group 2916 Cortland Pl NW Washington DC 20008

MANBURG, BARBARA RUTH, optometrist; b. Cleve., Jan. 3, 1953; d. Milton Harold and Sylvia Esther (Levitt) M.; m. Steven John Louie, Mar. 3, 1981. BS, Mass. Coll. Optometry, 1975; OD, New Eng. Coll. Optometry, Boston, 1977. Pvt. practice N.Y.C., 1978-81, Tampa, Fla., 1981-83, Delray Beach, Fla., 1984—; vol. Vol. Optometrists Serving Humanity, Durango, Mex., 1985. Mem. Am. Optometric Assn., Fla. Optometric Assn., Palm Beach County Optometric Assn., Palm Beach County Med. Aux., Assocs. of Am. Acad. Allergy and Immunology, Am. Coll. Allergy and Immunology Aux. Office: 1715 S Federal Hwy Delray Beach FL 33483

MANCHESTER, MELISSA TONI, singer, songwriter; b. Bronx, N.Y., Feb. 15, 1951; d. David and Ruth M.; m. Kevin DeRemer, May 1, 1982; 1 child, Nathan. Grad., High Sch. Performing Arts, N.Y.C., 1969. Pres., owner Rumanian Pickleworks Music. Singer with Bette Midler, 1971-72, rec. artist Bell and Arista records; recordings include Melissa (Gold Album award), For the Working Girl, Mathematics, 1985, Tribute, 1989; co-writer: Midnite Blue, Come in from the Rain, Whenever I Call You Friend; appeared in play: Song and Dance, 1987. Recipient Best New Female Vocalist of Year award Cashbox mag., 1974; New Female Vocalist of Year award Billboard mag., 1975; Wright award for Midnight Blue, Broadcast Music Inc., 1975; Grammy award for best female vocal, 1982. Mem. Broadcast Music Inc., AFTRA, Screen Actors Guild, Am. Fedn. Musicians. Office: care Triad Artists Inc 10100 Santa Monica Blvd 16th Fl Los Angeles CA 90067*

MANCUSO, MICHELE GERYL, communications executive; b. Cleve., July 19, 1956; d. Frank J. and Olga (Ujhelyi) M. AA, The Acad. Ct. Reporting, Cleve., 1975. Registered profl. reporter. Pres. M.G. Mancuso Reporting, Inc., Washington; ptnr. Johnson Waga Mancuso, Washington; official rep. U.S. Ho. Reps., Washington; seminars speaker. Recipient cert. of merit, 1976. Mem. Nat. Shorthand Reporter's Assn., D.C. Bar Assn. (chair pro bono com.), GWSRA (past pres., v.p.). Roman Catholic. Office: 1133 15th St NW Ste 1200 Washington DC 20005

MANCUSO, NANCY J., banker; b. N.Y.C., Apr. 26, 1957; d. Michael Robert and Marie Anne (Mosia) M. BS in French, Georgetown U., Washington, 1979; MBA in Fin., Pace U., N.Y.C., 1985. Adminstrv. asst. Am. Bankers Assn., Washington, 1979-82; cons. The Bond Buyer, N.Y.C., 1982; mktg. analyst Bankers Trust Co., N.Y.C., 1982-85; asst. v.p. mktg. Bankers Trust Co. Calif., San Francisco, 1986-89; asst. v.p., mgr. Bank of Am., San Francisco, 1985-86, v.p., mgr., 1989—. Mem. Sierra Club. Home: 3979 18th St San Francisco CA 94114 Office: Bank of Am 55 Hawthorne St San Francisco CA 94105

MANDEL, CAROLA PANERAI (MRS. LEON MANDEL), foundation trustee; b. Havana, Cuba; d. Camilo and Elvira (Bertini) Panerai; ed. pvt. schs., Havana and Europe; m. Leon Mandel, Apr. 9, 1938. Mem. women's bd. Northwestern Meml. Hosp., Chgo. Trustee Carola and Leon Mandel Fund Loyola U., Chgo. Life mem. Chgo. Hist. Soc., Guild of Chgo. Hist. Soc., Smithsonian Assos., Nat. Skeet Shooting Assn. Frequently named among Ten Best Dressed Women in U.S.; chevalier Confrerie des Chevaliers du Tastevin. Capt. All-Am. Women's Skeet Team, 1952, 53, 54, 55, 56; only woman to win a men's nat. championship, 20 gauge, 1954, also high average in world over men, 1956, in 12 gauge with 99.4 per cent; European women's live bird shooting championship, Venice, Italy, 1957, Porto, Portugal, 1961; European woman's target championship, Torino, Italy, 1958; woman's world champion live-bird shooting, Sevilla, Spain, 1959, Am. Contract Bridge League Life Master, 1987. Named to Nat. Skeet Shooting Assn. Hall of Fame, 1970. Mem. Soc. Four Arts. Club: Everglades (Palm Beach, Fla.), The Beach. Home: 324 Barton Ave Palm Beach FL 33480

MANDEL, KARYL LYNN, accountant; b. Chgo., Dec. 14, 1935; d. Isador J. and Eve (Gellar) Karzen; m. Fredric H. Mandel, Sept. 29, 1956; children: David Scott, Douglas Jay, Jennifer Ann. Student, U. Mich., 1954-56, Roosevelt U., 1956-57; AA summa cum laude, Oakton Community Coll., 1979. CPA, Ill. Pres., nat. bd. mem. Women's Am. Orgn. for Rehab. through Tng., 1961-77; pres. Excel Transp. Service Co., Elk Grove, Ill., 1958-78; tax mgr. Chunowitz, Teitelbaum & Baerson, CPA's, Northbrook, Ill., 1981-83, tax ptnr., 1984—; sec-treas. Lednam, Inc., Coffee Break, Inc.; mem. acctg. curriculum adv. bd. Oakton Community Coll., Des Plaines, Ill., 1987—. Contbg. author: Ill. CPA's News Jour. Recipient State of Israel Solidarity award, 1976. Mem. AICPA, Am. Soc. Women CPA's, Women's Am. ORT, Ill. CPA Soc. (vice chmn. estate and gift tax com. 1985-87, chmn. estate and gift tax com., 1987-89, mem. legis. contact com. 1981-82, pres.

North Shore chpt., award for Excellence in Acctg. Edn., bd. dirs. 1989—), Chgo. Soc. Women CPA's, Chgo. Estate Planning Council, Nat. Assn. Women Bus. Owners. Office: 401 Huehl Rd Northbrook IL 60062

MANDEL, LESLIE ANN, investment advisor, fundraiser, business owner, author; b. Washington, July 29, 1945; d. Seymour and Majorie Syble (Perlman) M. BA in Art History, U. Minn., 1967; cert., N.Y. Sch. Interior Design, 1969. Pres. Leslie Mandel Enterprises, Inc., N.Y.C., 1972—; sr. v.p. Maximum Entertainment Network, L.A. and N.Y.C., 1988—; pres. Rich List Co., 1989—; pres., chief exec. officer Mandel Airplane Funding and Leasing Corp., N.Y.C., 1990—; fin. advisor Osmed Inc., Mpls., 1986—, Devine Communication/Allen & Co., N.Y., Del., Utah, N.Mex., 1984—, Am. Kefir Corp., N.Y., 1983—, Sta. KVBC-TV, Los Vegas, 1983—, Shore Group (Internat., Guyana); owner The Rich List Co., 20 nationwide catologues, mags. and fundraising lists; pres., owner Mandel Airplane Funding and Leasing Corp. Photographer: Vogue, 1978, Fortune mag.; braille transcriber: The Prophet (Kalil Gibran), 1967, Getting Ready for Battle (R. Prawe Jhabuala), 1967; exec. producer film: Hospital Audiences, 1975 (Cannes award 1976); author: Hungry at the Watering Hole: Gardiners Island, 1636-1990, 1989, Apple Pie and 400 Years, 1990. Fin. advisor Correctional Assn., Osborn Soc., 1977—; founder, treas. Prisoners Family Transportation and Assistance Fund, N.Y., 1972-77; judge Emmy awards of Acad. TV Arts and Scis., N.Y.C., 1970; bd. dirs. Prisoners Assn., 1990; chmn. U.S.A. com. Violeta B. de Chamarro for Pres. of Nicaragua Campaign. Recipient Inst. for the Creative and Performing Arts fellowship, N.Y.C., 1966, Appreciation cert. Presdl. Inaugural Com., Washington, 1981. Fellow N.Y. Women in Real Estate, Explorers Club; mem. Com. on Am. and Internat. Fgn. Affairs, Lawyers Com. on Internat. Human Rels., Venture Capital Breakfast Club, Sigma Delta Tau, Sigma Epsilon Sigma. Democrat. Jewish. Home: 4 E 81st St Penthouse New York NY 10028 Office: IJL Realth Co 201 E 87th Ste 10-R New York NY 10028

MANDELBAUM, DOROTHY ROSENTHAL, psychologist; b. N.Y.C., May 18, 1935; d. Benjamin Daniel and Rachael (Osofsky) Rosenthal; A.B. cum laude, Hunter Coll., 1956; Ph.D., Bryn Mawr Coll., 1975; m. Seymour Jacob Mandelbaum, Aug. 19, 1956; children—David Gideon, Judah Michael, Betsy Daniella. Tchr., Valley Road Sch., Princeton, N.J., 1956-59; instr. ednl. psychology dept. Temple U., Phila., summer 1970; asst. prof. dept. edn. Rutgers, The State U., Camden, N.J., 1974-80, asso. prof., 1980—, dir. women's studies, 1981-86, chair edn. dept., 1986—. AAUW predoctoral fellow, 1973-74. Mem. Am. Psychol. Assn., AAUP, Soc. Research in Child Devel. Contbr. articles on psychology of women and med. edn. to profl. pubis. Author: Work, Marriage, and Motherhood: The Career Persistence of Female Physicians, 1981. Home: 2290 N 53d St Philadelphia PA 19131 Office: Rutgers U Camden NJ 08102

MANDELBAUM, JONNA LYNN KNAUER, education educator; b. Pottstown, Pa., Nov. 23, 1946; d. John Davis and Doris Mildred (Hartung) Knauer; m. John David Mandelbaum, Jan. 1, 1977. BS in Nursing, Lebanon Valley Coll., 1969; MPH, Johns Hopkins U., Balt., 1978; PhD, Ga. State U., 1986. Cert. pediatric nurse practitioner. Instr. pediatrics NE Wis. Tech. Inst., Green Bay, 1978-79; edn. adminstr. No. Wis. Tech. Inst., Green Bay, 1979-81; instr. nursing Ga. State U., Atlanta, 1981-83, grad. asst., 1983-85; curriculum advisor JHPIEGO Corp., Balt.; asst. prof. U. Md. Sch. Nursing, Balt.; asst. prof. nursing U. Md. Author: Missionary as Cultural Interpreter, 1989, Contbr. articles to profl. jours. Mem. Nat. Assn. Pediatric Nurse Assocs. and Practitioners, Am. Nurses Assn., Ga. Ptnrs. Am., Sigma Theta Tau. Methodist. Home: 1214 S Potomac St Baltimore MD 21224 Office: U Md 622 W Lombard St Baltimore MD 21201

MANDELBAUM, KATHY COONS, lawyer; b. Boston, Dec. 31, 1958; d. Richard Daniel and Nancy (Jacobs) Coons; m. David Gideon Mandelbaum, May 29, 1983; 1 child, Ruth Elizabeth. AB, Harvard U., 1980, JD, 1983. Bar: Pa. 1983, U.S. Dist. Ct. (ea. dist.) Pa. 1983. Assoc. Schnader Harrison Segal & Lewis, Phila., 1983—. Bd. dirs., sec. Alzheimer's Disease and Related Disorders Assn., Phila., 1985—. Mem. ABA, Pa. Bar Assn., Phila. Bar Assn. (exec. bd. sect. probate and trust law 1988—), Harvard-Radcliffe Club Phila. (exec. bd. 1986-89), Phi Beta Kappa. Jewish. Office: Schnader Harrison et al 1600 Market St Ste 3600 Philadelphia PA 19103

MANDELBLATT, JEANNE SUSAN, physician; b. L.A., Sept. 10, 1951; d. Seymour Mandelblatt and Gladys (Glassman) Mandelblatt Regins; m. Peter R.A. Frecknall, June 25, 1989. BA, U. So. Calif., 1972; MD, Columbia U., 1976. Diplomate Am. Bd. Family Practice. Intern then resident Montefiore Hosp., Bronx, N.Y., 1976-79; physician Boriken Health Ctr. East Harlem Coun., N.Y.C., 1979-81; physician Elmhurst City (N.Y.) Hosp., 1981-87; physician Community Medicine Dept. Mt. Sinai Hosp., N.Y.C., 1984-87; physician geriatrics Montefiore Hosp., Bronx, 1987-89; physician N.Y.C. Health and Hosp. Corp., 1987-89; physician Meml. Sloan-Kettering Cancer Ctr., N.Y.C., 1989—, asst. prof. dept. edpidemiology and biostatistics, 1989—; clin. instr. Mt. Sinai Sch. Medicine, N.Y.C., 1981-86, asst. clin. prof., 1986-87; cons. and presenter in field. Contbr. articles to profl. jours. Grantee NIH, Nat. Inst. on Aging, 1989-94, Nat. Cancer Inst., 1989-92, N.Y.C. Am. Cancer Soc., 1990-91. Fellow Am. Bd. Family Practice; mem. Am. Acad. Family Physicians, Soc. for Gen. Internal Medicine (chairperson task force on social responsibility), Am. Pub. Health Assn. Democrat. Jewish. Office: Meml Sloan Kettering Ctr 1275 York Ave New York NY 10021

MANDELL, ARLENE LINDA, writing and communications educator; b. Bklyn., Feb. 19, 1941; d. George and Esther Kostick; m. Lawrence W. Mandell, May 23, 1982; children by previous marriage: Bruce R. Rosenblum, Tracey B. Rosenblum. BA magna cum laude, William Paterson Coll., 1973; MA Columbia U., 1989. Newspaper reporter Suburban Trends, Riverdale, N.J., 1972-73; writer Good Housekeeping mag., N.Y.C., 1976-78; account exec. Carl Byoir & Assocs., N.Y.C., 1978-86; v.p. Porter/Novelli, N.Y.C., 1986-88; adj. prof. William Paterson Coll., Wayne, N.J., 1989—, Ramapo Coll., Mahwah, N.J. Contbr. articles to profl. jours. and newspapers, poetry to N.Y. Times and poetry jours. Recipient 1st place women's interest writing N.J. Press Assn., 1973; named John W. Stahr Writer of Yr., Carl Byoir & Assocs., N.Y.C., 1981. Mem. Women in Communications, Newswomen's Club.

MANDELL, BETTY ELLEN, clinical psychologist, consultant; b. Cin., Jan. 31, 1936; d. Robert Webster and Florence M. (McClure) Kehr; m. Richard D. Mandell; children: Victoria, Eleanor, Maximillian, Isabelle. BA, Reed Coll., 1957; MA, U. Colo., 1959; PhD, U. S.C., 1969, post-grad. in clin. psychology, 1983. Lic. clin. psychologist, S.C. Statistician Sch. Pub. Health, U. Calif., Berkeley, Calif., 1960-61; instr. U. S.C., Columbia, S.C., 1966-68; rsch. assoc. U. S.C., Columbia, 1968-82, dir. Title IX Tng. Inst., 1978-80; psychotherapist, owner Resource Assocs., Inc., Columbia, 1984—; cons. Commn. on Aging, Dept. Social Svcs., Dept. Corrections, S.C., 1975-89; expert witness Family Ct., Columbia, 1984—; cert. adoption investigator Dept. Social Svcs., S.C., 1986—. Photographer (photo exhbn.) Aging in S.C., 1982; writer monthly column The State called Mind Matters, 1988—; contbr. articles to profl. jours. Mem. bd. examiners in psychology, S.C., 1983-86; trustee sch. bd. Palmetto Unified Sch. Dist. I, S.C., 1981-89 (disting. svc. honor, 1989). Named Career Woman of Yr., Bus. and Profl. Women's Club, Columbia chpt. and statewide, 1981. Mem. Am. Psychol. Assn., S.C. Psychol. Assn., S.C. Acad. Profl. Psychologists, S.C. Gerontol. Soc. (founding pres. 1978-80, Rosamond Boyd award, 1982). Home: 1403 Summerville Ave Columbia SC 29201 Office: Resource Assocs Inc 2210 Devine St Columbia SC 29205

MANDES, ELLEN A., healthcare executive; b. Washington, Mar. 19, 1936; d. Hendrick and Hermione Bascom; children: George J., Sean P. BS, Am. U., 1958. Adminstrv. asst. Chief Personnel Ops., U.S. Army, Washington, 1958-63, Dep. Commr. on Aging, Washington, 1963-65; nat. dir. Home Care Svcs., Inc., New Haven, 1971-73; pres. Homecare, Inc., Wallingford, Conn., 1973—. Commr. Econ. Devel. Commn., Wallingford, 1988—, Wallingford Visitors Coun., 1988—; bd. dirs. YMCA, Wallingford, 1988—; bd. dirs. Boy Scouts Am., Hamden, 1988—, Wallingford Ctr., Inc., 1988; commr. Hist. Commn. Study Group, 1989—; bd. govs. Wallingford Hosp., 1988-91. Spl. honoree Meriden YWCA, 1988. Mem. Wallingford C. of C. (past pres., dir.), Rotary (bd. dirs. 1989—). Republican. Lutheran.

MANDICOTT, GRACE MARIE, health care center executive; b. Reading, Pa., Aug. 31, 1942; d. Dominick Adam and Angeline Grace (Carabino) M. Grad., Binghamton (N.Y.) Gen. Hosp., 1963; RN, BS, SUNY, Binghamton, 1976; MA, Cen. Mich. U., 1981; PhD in Philosophy and Healthcare Adminstrn., Walden U., 1983. Cert. nurse practitioner, physician's asst. Nurse various hosps., 1963-65, Lourdes Hosp., 1965-67, St. Peter's Hosp., Albany, N.Y., 1967-68, Gen. Electric Co., 1968, Dr. Janith S. Kice, Garden City, N.Y., 1968-69, E. H. Titchener & Co., Binghamton, 1970-72, Family Health Ctr., Johnson City, N.Y., 1972-74; nurse practitioner, physician's asst., adminstr. pvt. practice, Binghamton, 1975-83; dir., owner PMS and Menopause Health and Wellness Ctr., Binghamton, 1984-88, PMS & Menopause Health & Wellness Ctr., Tampa and Largo, Fla., 1988—; health care cons., N.Y., N.J., Pa., Fla., 1981—; cons. MICA Imaging Inc., Buffalo Grove, Ill., 1989—; coord. med. student clerkship SUNY, Binghamton, 1979-82, asst. instr. Sch. Nursing, 1980; dir. med. svcs. Adelaide Environ. Health Assocs., Binghamton, 1983-88; adj. prof. masters program New Sch. for Social Rsch. Sch. Mgmt., N.Y.C., 1985-87; speaker in field. Coordinator walkathon Am. Cancer Soc., 1976. Republican. Roman Catholic. Home: 1430 Gulf Blvd Apt 808 Clearwater FL 34630 Office: Centurion Hosp 7171 N Dale Mabry Tampa FL 33614 also: PMS and Menopause Health and Wellness Ctr 2401 W Bay Dr Largo FL 34640 also: 320 W Fletcher Ave Rear Tampa FL 33612

MANDLER, SUSAN RUTH, dance company administrator; b. Kew Gardens, N.Y., Feb. 11, 1949; d. Ernest and Clea (Reisner) M.; m. Howard Reed, July 3, 1975 (div. 1980); m. 2d, Robert Morgan Barnett, July 30, 1982. B.S., Boston U., 1971. Asst. mgr. Pilobolus, Inc., Washington, Conn., 1977-80, mgr., 1980—.

MANDRAVELIS, PATRICIA JEAN, nursing executive; b. Hanover, N.H., May 7, 1938; d. William J. and Ruth E. (Darling) Bartis; m. Anthony M. Mandravelis, Nov. 8, 1959; children: Michael A., Tracy J. Diploma in nursing, Nashua (N.H.) Meml. Hosp. Sch. Nursing; BS in Psychology, Sociology, New Eng. Coll., 1978; MBA, N.H. Coll., 1989. Cert. nursing adminstr. Staff nurse Nashua Meml. Hosp., 1959-60, obstet. nurse, 1962-65, charge nurse, 1969-71, supr., 1971-76, assoc. dir. nursing, 1976-81, dir. nursing, 1981-83, asst. exec. dir. nursing, 1983-87, v.p. nursing, 1987—. Contbr. articles to profl. jours. Bd. dirs. deNicola Women's Ctr., Nashua, 1987—, Nashua Vis. Nurse Program, 1986-88; v.p. Nashua chpt. ARC, 1985-87; bd. dirs. Home Health Hosp., 1988—; mem. citizen adv. bd. W.R. Grace, 1989—. Mem. Nat. League of Nursing, Am. Nurses Assn., Am. Orgn. Nurse Execs., N.H. Nurses Assn., N.H. Orgn. Nurse Execs., Sigma Theta Tau. Office: Nashua Meml Hosp 8 Prospect St Nashua NH 03061

MANDRELL, BARBARA ANN, singer, entertainer; b. Houston, Dec. 25, 1948; d. Irby Matthew and Mary Ellen (McGill) M.; m. Kenneth Lee Dudney, May 28, 1967; children: Kenneth Matthew, Jaime Nicole, Nathaniel. Grad. high sch. Country music singer and entertainer, 1959—, performed throughout U.S. and in various fgn. countries; mem., Grand Ole Opry, Nashville, 1972—; star TV series Barbara Mandrell and the Mandrell Sisters, 1980-82, Barbara Mandrell: Get to the Heart, 1987; albums include Midnight Oil, Treat Him Right, This Time I Almost Made It, This is Barbara Mandrell, Midnight Angel, Barbara Mandrell's Greatest Hits, Morning Sun, 1990. Author (with George Vecsey): Get To the Heart: My Story, 1990. Named Miss Oceanside, Calif., 1965; Named Most Promising Female Singer, Acad. Country and Western Music, 1971; Female Vocalist of Yr., 1978; Female Vocalist of Yr., Music City News Cover Awards, 1979; Female Vocalist of Yr., Country Music Assn., 1979; Entertainer of Yr., 1980, 81; People's Choice awards (6), 1982-84. Mem. Musicians Union, Screen Actors Guild, AFTRA, Country Music Assn. (v.p.). Mem. Order Eastern Star. Office: care World Class Talent 1522 Demonbreux Nashville TN 37203*

MANDUKE, RHONDA CAROL, computer scientist; b. Doylestown, Pa., Aug. 20, 1955; d. Raymond C. and Myra Taylor (Mercer) Rosenberger; m. Joseph Edgar II, May 20, 1985. BS, Gwynedd Mercy Coll., 1983. Sr. scientist Cincinatti Bell Info Systems, Vienna, Va.; pres. HTS-US, Columbia, Md.; sr. v.p. Hydrotech Group, Berlin, N.J., Reliance Cons. Svcs. Home: 14636 Mustang Path Glenwood MD 21738

MANERO, VICTORIA, educator; b. Las Tunas, Cuba, Mar. 23, 1942; came to U.S., 1966; d. Victoriano and Renee (Urquiola) M. Diploma in Music Edn., Internat. Conservatory of Music, Havana, Cuba, 1958; BA, Mercy Coll., 1970; MA, NYU, 1973; MS, Hunter Coll., 1977. Clk. Am. Express Co., N.Y.C., 1966-69; investigator internat. ops. The Chase Manhattan Bank, N.Y.C., 1969-72; tchr. N.Y.C. Bd. Edn., 1972-77, bilingual program coordinator, 1977-81, supr. bilingual and second lang. edn., 1981—; freelance editorial cons., 1975-77, adj. prof., CCNY, 1979. Mem. Assn. for Supervision and Instrn., Nat. Assn. for Bilingual Edn., Tchrs. English to Speakers of Other Langs., N.Y. State Assn. for Bilingual Edn. Office: Community Sch Dist #5 433 W 123d St New York NY 10040

MANEWITZ, SHARON F., investment officer; b. Bronx, N.Y., July 8, 1948; d. Frank Popovitz and Margaret (Klein) Harber; m. Mark Lee Manewitz, June 22, 1969; children: Samantha Alexandra, Thomas Franklin. BA, Hunter Coll., 1969; MBA, Pace U., 1976. Gifts libr. U. Chgo. (Ill.) Libr., 1969-70; writer, editor Encyclopaedia Britannica, Chgo., 1970; claims examiner Office of the Compt. City N.Y., N.Y.C., 1970-72; asst. dir. personnel Nat. Bd. YMCA's, N.Y.C., 1972-75; analyst Am. Can Co., Greenwich, Conn., 1975-76; trainee to v.p. Bankers Trust Co., N.Y.C., 1976-88; investment officer Tchrs. Ins. and Annuity Assn. Coll. Retirement Equities Fund, N.Y.C., 1988—. Andrew Mellon fellowship, 1975-76. Mem. Turnaround Mgmt. Assn. Office: Tchrs Ins Annuity Assn Coll Retirement Equity Fund 730 Thrid Ave New York NY 10017

MANFORD, BARBARA ANN, contralto; b. St. Augustine, Fla., Nov. 13, 1929; d. William Floyd and Margaret (Kemper) Manford; Mus.B. in Voice, Fla. State U., 1951, Mus.M., 1970; studied with L. Palazzini, A. Strano, Japelli, E. Nikolaidi, E. Joseph. Appearances in Europe, performing major roles in 12 leading opera houses, 1951-68, with condrs. including Alfredo Strano, Felice Cilario, Robert Shaw, Arnold Gamson, Giuseppe Patané, Ottavio Ziino, also numerous concerts and recitals in Paris and throughout Italy and Belgium; performed in world premiere Fugitives (C. Floyd), Fla. State U., Tallahassee, 1950; chosen by Gian Carlo Menotti for leading role in world premiere The Leper, Fla. State U., 1970; numerous radio, TV, and concert appearances, U.S., 1968—; artist-in-residence, assoc. prof. voice Ball State U., Muncie, Ind., 1970-90; numerous recs. Semi-finalist vocal contest, Parma, Italy, 1964; winner contest, Lonigo, Italy, 1965. Mem. Nat. Assn. Tchrs. Singing, Chgo. Artists Assn., Am. Tchrs. Nat. Assn., Sigma Alpha Iota, Pi Kappa Lambda. Christian Scientist. Home: 405 S Morrison Rd Apt 104 Muncie IN 47304 Office: Ball State Univ Muncie IN 47304

MANFRA-MARRETTA, SANDRA, veterinarian; b. S.I., N.Y., Nov. 19, 1949; d. Virgil Louis and Jean (Annear) Manfra; m. Joseph Salvatore Marretta, June 11, 1977; children: Jennifer, Joseph. BA, Hunter Coll., 1971; DVM, Cornell U., 1977. Diplomate Am. Coll. of Vet. Surgeons, Am. Vet. Dental Coll. (sec. 1988--). Intern The Animal Med. Ctr., N.Y.C., 1977-78, surg. resident, 1978-80, assoc. staff surgeon, 1980-81, sr. staff surgeon, 1983-90; staff vet. Hylan Animal Hosp., S.I., N.Y., 1981-83; asst. prof. in surgery and dentistry Coll. of Vet. Med., U. Ill., Urbana, 1990--. Editor: Problems in Veterinary Medicine (Dentistry), 1990; contbg. editor Jour. of Vet Dentistry, 1988—; contbr. articles to profl. jours. Fellow Acad. of Vet. Dentistry; mem. Am. Vet. Med. Assn., Am. Animal Hosp. Assn. Catholic. Office: U Ill Coll of Vet Medicine 1008 W Hazelwood Dr Urbana IL 61801

MANFREDONIA, CATHERINE CARMELA BERNITT, psychotherapist; b. N.Y.C., Apr. 5, 1946; d. Robert Otto and Carmela Catherine (Rachele) Bernitt; children: Michael, Andrew, Matthew, Rachele. BS, Cornell U., 1968; MA, NYU, 1975. Faculty Flushing (N.Y.) Med. Ctr. Sch. Nursing, 1969-71, SUNY Dept. Nursing, Farmindale, 1973; asst. prof. L.I. U., Dept. Nursing, Greenvale, 1975-81; chmn. L.I. U., Dept. Nursing, 1978-81; psychotherapist in pvt. practice Smithtown, N.Y., 1980—; adj. asst. prof. Suffolk Community Coll., 1990. Com. mem. Northpoint Civic Assn., Dix Hills, N.Y., 1980, Boy Scouts Am., Dix Hills, 1980-88; mem. L.I. Assn., Commack, 1988—; bd. dirs. Health Svcs. at Home, Commack, 1988—, del. at large, exec. bd., 1989—, 1st v.p., 1990—; part-time patient care coord., Lutheran Ctr. for the Aging, 1988—. Mem. Am. Assn. Reg. Hypnologists, Nat. Guild Hypnotists, N.Y. State Nurses Assn., Dist. 14 Psychiat. Conf. Group, Bus. and Profl. Women's Assn. (corres. sec. 1989—), AAUW. Office: 9 Brooksite Dr Smithtown NY 11787

MANGAN, PATRICIA ANN PRITCHETT, research statistician; b. Hammond, Ind., Feb. 4, 1953; d. Edward Clayton and Helen Josephine (Mills) Pritchett; m. William Paul Mangan, Aug. 30, 1980; 1 child, Ryan Christopher. BS in Maths. and Stats., Purdue U., 1975, MS in Applied Stats., 1977. Tobacco devel. statistician R.J. Reynolds Tobacco Co., Winston-Salem, N.C., 1978-82, R&D statistician, 1982-86, sr. R&D statistician, 1986-90, sr. staff R&D statistician, 1990—; cons. Lab. for Application of Remote Sensing, West Lafayette, Ind., 1976-77; statis. engr. Corning Glass Works, Harrodsburg, Ky., 1977. Contbr. articles to sci. jours. Rep. United Way, Winston-Salem, 1985. Recipient G.R. DiMarco award, 1990. Mem. Am. Statis. Assn., Wash. Statis. Soc., Nat. Assn. Female Execs., Smithsonian Assocs., Purdue Alumni Assn. Office: RJ Reynolds Tobacco Co BGTC 611-12/109 Winston-Salem NC 27102

MANGELSDORF, JENNY LYNN MOFFITT, communications specialist; b. Santa Monica, Calif., Nov. 5, 1957; d. William John Moffitt and Jane Ann Ayling; m. J. Hans Mangelsdorf, Sept. 6, 1986. BA, Calif. State U., Northridge, 1981. Asst. editor Daily News, Van Nuys, Calif., 1981-84, Computer Merchandizing, Encino, Calif., 1984-85; communications specialist Computer Sci. Corp., El Segundo, Calif., 1986—. Mem. Amigos De Bolsa Chica Huntington Beach Calif.; assoc. mem. Nat. Charity League L.A., 1970—. Mem. Internat. Assn. Bus. Coordinators. Office: Computer Scis Corp 2100 E Grand Ave El Segundo CA 90245

MANGINO, ANGIE THERESA, corporate executive; b. Bronx, N.Y., Aug. 4, 1949; d. Pasquale and Mary (Villani) Vassallo; m. Carmine Albert Mangino, Oct. 1, 1972; children; Joseph, Dominic, Jennifer. BA, Fordham U., 1971. Acctg. office mgr. Nat. Car Rental, Queens, N.Y., 1971-75; supr. Stanley Home Products, S.I., N.Y., 1979-85; regional mgr. House of Lloyd, S.I., N.Y., 1985—. Roman Catholic. Office: House of Lloyd PO Box 070111 Staten Island NY 10307

MANGINO, KRISTIN MIKALSON, teacher; b. Spokane, Wash., July 7, 1939; d. Norman Lillard and Mabel Mae (Lewis) Mikalson; m. Paul Angelo Mangino, Aug. 15, 1965; children: Kyle Aaron, Lisan Kristin. Student, Cottey Coll., 1957-58, Ea. Wash. Coll. Edn. (now Ea. Wash. U.), 1958-61; BS in Psychology, Wash. State U., 1961; student, Calif. State U., Fullerton, 1961-66; postgrad., U. Calif.Irvine, 1966; MS in Spl. Edn., Portland State U., 1983. Cert. elem. and secondary tchr., Calif., Wash., Oreg. Tchr. English and reading Jr. High Sch., Anaheim and Monterey, Calif., 1961-68; substitute tchr. Elma (Wash.) Sch. Dist., 1970-71, Evergreen Sch. Dist., Vancouver, Wash., 1974-75; tutor Evergreen Sch. Dist., Vancouver, 1975-84; tutor, substitute tchr. Vancouver and Evergreen Sch. Dists., 1984-88, tutor, 1988—; hostess with service sales City Welcome Service, 1986-87; co-pres. Spl. Edn. Adv. Council, Vancouver, 1986-87. Officer P.E.O., Vancouver, 1984-86; sec. Spl. Olympics, Evergreen Sch. Dist., 1989-90. Mem. NAFE, Berg Freunde Ski Club. Presbyterian. Home and Office: PO Box 5542 Vancouver WA 98668

MANGION, CARMEN MARGARET, management consultant; b. Qormi, Malta, Mar. 10, 1962; came to U.S., 1967; d. Saviour and Iris Mary (Theuma) M. BBA, U. Mich., 1983. CPA, Calif. Staff acct. C.H. Rubin & Co., CPA's, Ann Arbor, Mich., 1983-85; sr. acct. BDO Seidman, San Francisco, 1987-89, sr. mgmt. cons., 1989—. Mem. Nat. Assn. Accts. (treas. San Francisco chpt. 1989—). Office: BDO Seidman One Sansome St Ste 1100 San Francisco CA 94104

MANGUS, DEBBIE DEE, marketing executive; b. Fort Wayne, Ind., May, 1955; d. Kenneth R. and M. Irene Miller; m. Charles D. Lewis (div. 1981); children: David R., Carrie A.; m. John T. Mangus, Dec., 1981 (div. 1989). Store activities rep. McDonald's Systems, Newport News, Va., Fort Wayne, Ind., 1978, community relations rep. Fort Wayne, Columbus, Ohio, 1979-81; regional mktg. mgr. Arby's, Inc., Columbus, 1982-83; mktg. dir. McNeill Enterprises, Inc., Chillicothe, Ohio, 1984-86; project mgr. mktg. dept. Mid-Am. Fed., Columbus, 1987-88; dir. advt. Record Herald, Washington Court House, Ohio, 1988—; trainer regional mktg. mgrs. Arby's, Columbus, 1982-83; mktg. cons. MEI Franchisees, Inc. Franchisees, Ohio, Ill., Ky., 1984-86. Fund raiser Ronald McDonald House, Columbus, Indpls., 1980-81; mem. Alliance for a Prosperous Downtown Washington Ct. House, . Recipient Best Bets awards McDonald's-Indpls. region, 1980, 81. Mem. Ohio Newspaper Advt. Execs., Washington Ct. House Jaycees. Methodist. Avocations: reading, softball, bicycling, crafts. Office: Record Herald 138 S Fayette St Washington Court House OH 43160

MANHART, MARCIA Y(OCKEY), art museum director; b. Wichita, Kans., Jan. 14, 1943; d. Everett W. and Ruth C. (Correll) Yockey; m. Thomas Arthur Manhart; children: Caroline Amanda, Emily Alexandrea. BA in Art, U. Tulsa, 1965, MA in Ceramics, 1971. Dir. edn. Philbrook Art Ctr., Tulsa, 1972-77, exec. v.p., asst. dir., 1977-83, acting dir., 1983-84; exec. dir. Philbrook Mus. of Art (formerly Philbrook Art Ctr.), Tulsa, 1984—; instr. Philbrook Art Ctr. Mus. Sch., Tulsa, 1963-72; gallery dir. Alexandre Hogue Gallery, Tulsa U., 1967-69. Vis. com. Smithsonian Instn./Renwick Gallery, Washington, 1986; cultural negotiator Gov. George Nigh's World Trade Mission (Okla.), China., 1985; com. mem. State Art Coll. of Okla., 1985—; mem. Assocs. of Hillcrest Med. Ctr., 1983-88, exec. com., 1985-88; com. mem. Neighborhood Housing Services, 1985-87; mem. Mapleridge Hist. Dist. Assn., 1982—; steering com. Harwelden Isnt. for Aesthetic Edn., 1983; com. mem. River Parks Authority, 1976; mem. Jr. League of Tulsa Inc., 1974-78; adv. panel mem. Nat. Craft Planning Project, NEA, Washington, 1978-81; regional rep. Art Mus. Assn. Am., 1978—; craft adv. panel mem. Okla. Arts and Humanities Council, 1974-76; juror numerous art festivals, competitions, programs; reviewer Inst. Mus. Services, Washington, 1985, 88; auditor Symposium on Language & Scholarship of Modern Crafts, NEA and NEH, Washington, 1981; nominator MacArthur Fellows Program, 1988. Recipient Harwelden award for Individual Contbrn. in the Arts, 1989. Mem. Assn. Am. Mus., Assn. Art Mus. Dirs., Art. Mus. Assn. Am., Mountain Plains Assn. Mus., Am. Craft Council, Okla. Mus. Assn. Office: Philbrook Mus Art 2727 S Rockford Rd PO Box 52510 Tulsa OK 74114 :

MANIACI, ELIZABETH HOFFER, banker; b. Muncie, Ind., July 23, 1955; d. Robert Morrison and Martha Cathern (Quirk) Hoffer; m. Thomas Vincent Maniaci, June 21, 1980; 1 child, Alexander Morrison. BS in Math., Econs., Tufts U., 1977; postgrad., U. Ariz., 1978-79. Internal auditor Wis. Tel. Co., Milw., 1979-80; tax acct. Arthur Andersen and Co., Detroit, 1980-83; assoc. v.p. Fireman's Fund Mortgage Corp., Farmington Hills, Mich., 1983—. Author: (with others) Tax Bibliography for Mortgage Bankers, 1986. Bd. dirs. Pontiac (Mich.) Art Ctr., 1980-82. Mem. Nat. Assn. Accts., Jr. League of Birmingham (Mich.) (pub. rels. chmn. 1987-88), Women's Econ. Club. Home: 1751 Villa Birmingham MI 48009 Office: Firemans Fund Mortgage Corp 27555 Farmington Rd Farmington Hills MI 48018

MANKILLER, WILMA PEARL, principal chief Indian tribe; b. Stilwell, Okla., Nov. 18, 1945; d. Charley and Clara Irene (Sitton) M.; m. Hector N. Olaya, Nov. 13, 1963 (div. 1975); children—Felicia Marie Olaya, Gina Irene Olaya. Student Skyline Coll., San Bruno College, Calif., 1973, San Francisco State Coll., 1973-75; B.A. in Social Sci., Flaming Rainbow Coll., Okla., 1977; postgrad. U. Ark., 1979. Community devel. dir. Cherokee Nation, Tahlequah, Okla., 1977-83, dep. chief, 1983-85, prin. chief, 1985-87; pres. Inter-Tribal Council Okla.; mem. exec. bd. Council Energy Resource Tribes; bd. dirs. Okla. Indsl. Devel. Commn. Bd. dirs. Okla. Acad. for State Goals, 1985—. Recipient Donna Nigh First Lady award Okla. Commn. for Status of Women, 1985, Am. Leadership award, Harvard U., 1986; inducted Okla. Women's Hall of Fame, 1986. Mem. Cherokee County Democratic Women's Club, Nat. Tribal Chairmen's Assn., Nat. Congress Am. Indians. Avocations: reading; writing. Office: Cherokee Prin Chief PO Box 948 Tahlequah OK 74465*

MANLEY, AUDREY FORBES, physician; b. Jackson, Miss., Mar. 25, 1934; d. Jesse Lee and Ora Lee (Buckhalter) Forbes; m. Albert Edward

Manley, Apr. 3, 1970. A.B. with honors (tuition scholar), Spelman Coll., Atlanta, 1955; M.D. (Jesse Smith Noyes Found. scholar), Meharry Med. Coll., 1959; MPH, Johns Hopkins U.-USPHS traineeship, 1987. Diplomate: Am. Bd. Pediatrics. Intern St. Mary Mercy Hosp., Gary, Ind., 1960; from jr. to chief resident in pediatrics Cook County Children's Hosp., Chgo., 1960-62; NIH fellow neonatology U. Ill. Research and Ednl. Hosp., Chgo., 1963-65; staff pediatrician Chgo. Bd. Health, 1963-66; practice medicine specializing in pediatrics Chgo., 1963-66; assoc. Lawndale Neighborhood Health Center North, 1966-67; asst. med. dir., 1967-69; asst. prof. Chgo. Med. Coll., 1966-67; instr. Pritzker Sch. Medicine, U. Chgo., 1967-69; asst. dir. ambulatory pediatrics, asst. dir. pediatrics Mt. Zion Hosp. and Med. Center, San Francisco, 1969-70; med. cons. Spelman Coll., 1970-71, med. dir. family planning program, chmn. health careers adv. com., 1972-76; med. dir. Grady Meml. Hosp. Family Planning Clinic, 1972-76; with Health Services Adminstrs., Dept. Health and Human Services, 1976—; commd. officer USPHS, 1976—; chief genetic diseases services br. Office Maternal and Child Health, Bur. Community Health Services, Rockville, Md., 1976-81; acting assoc. adminstr. clin. affairs Office of Adminstr. Health Resources and Services Adminstrn., 1981-83, chief med. officer, dep. assoc. adminstr. planning, evaluation and legis., 1983-85; sabbatical leave USPHS JOhns Hopkins Sch. Hygiene and Pub. Health, 1986-87; dir. Nat. Health Service Corps.; asst. surgeon gen., 1988; dep. asst. Sec. for Health, 1989—; mem. U.S. del. UNICEF, 1990—. Author numerous articles, reports in field. Trustee Spelman Coll., 1966-70. Recipient Meritorious Service award USPHS, 1981, Mary McLeod Bethune award Nat. Council Negro Women, 1979; Disting. Alumni award Meharry Med. Coll., 1989; Spelman Coll. 108 Founder's Day Convocation, 1989; numerous service and achievement awards. Fellow Am. Acad. Pediatrics; mem. Nat. Inst. Medicine of Nat. Acad. Sci., Nat. Med. Assn., Am. Public Health Assn., AAUW, AAAS, Spelman Coll. Alumnae Assn., Meharry Alumni Assn., Operation Crossroads Africa Alumni Assn. Home: 2807 18th St NW Washington DC 20009 Office: 200 Independence Ave SW Washington DC 20201

MANLEY, BARBARA LEE DEAN, nurse, hospital administrator, safety and health consultant; b. Washington, Nov. 5, 1946; d. Robert L. Dean and Mary L. (Jenkins) Smallwood; m. Major Otis Manley, Nov. 16, 1969; 1 child, Laura Selena. B.S., St. Mary-of-the-Woods, Terre Haute, Ind., 1973; M.A., Central Mich. U., 1981. Indsl. nurse Ford Motor Co., Indpls., 1973-80; employee health nurse Starplex, Inc., Washington, 1981-84, Doctor's Hosp., Lanham, Md., 1984-85; regional occupational health nurse coordinator Naval Hosp., Long Beach, Calif., 1985-88; project mgr. Health Care Network, Inc., Washington, 1980-84; cons. Health and Human Services, Washington, 1980-84; occupational health and safety cons., mgr. FPE Group, Torrence, Calif., 1989—; pvt. practice contract nurse specialist, Washington, 1980-84; part-time lectr. Compton (Calif.) Coll. Vol. ARC, Ft. Lewis, Wash., 1974-76, Ft. Harrison, Ind., 1978-80; counselor Crisis Hot-Line, Laurel, Md., 1981-83, Laurel Boy's and Girls Club, 1981-84. Recipient Navy's Meritorious Civilian Svc. medal and cert., 1989, Women of Excellence award, 1990. Fellow Acad. Ambulatory Nursing Adminstrs. (Honor plaque 1981); mem. Assn. Exec. Females, Am. Pub. Health Assn., Am. Nurses Assn., Nat. Safety Mgmt. Soc., Am. Assn. Occupational Health Nurses, Assn. Hosp. Employee Health Profls. (sec. 1986-88, conf. chairperson 1988, Outstanding Nurse of Yr. 1987), Fed. Occupational Safety and Health Council, Cen. Mich. U. Alumni Assn. (sec. 1985-88), Chi Eta Phi (regional bd. dirs. 1978-81). Presbyterian. Avocations: reading; crocheting; traveling; roller skating. Office: FPE Group 3868 Carson St Ste 218 Torrance CA 90503

MANLEY, CATHEY NERACKER, interior design executive; b. Rochester, N.Y., Feb. 10, 1951; d. Albert John and Eleanor (Roberts) Neracker; m. Keith Howard Manley, Dec. 2, 1972 (div. Sept. 1977). AS, Endicott Jr. Coll., Beverly, Mass., 1971. Interior designer Bayles Furniture Co., Rochester, 1971-78, dir. mktg. and design, 1978-81; pres. Fabric PROTECTION Rochester, 1982—; bus. cons. Susanne Wiener & Assocs., Stamford, Conn., 1981—; owner Cathey Manley Assocs., Rochester and Clearwater, Fla., 1981—; cons. Womens' Career Ctr., Rochester, 1976—. Contbr. to book: What Do You Say To A Naked Room, 1981; designer TV show Great American Home; writer, hostess video How to Sell Accessories. Mem. bldg. com. Rochester Health Assn., 1978-83; dir. Family Service of Rochester at Greece (N.Y.), 1973-76, Town of Greece Youth Bd., 1973-77; founder "The Point", Greece, 1971. Fellow Interior Design Soc. (pres. Rochester chpt. 1977-78, nat. bd. dirs. 1977—, nat. pres. at Chgo. 1983-85). Home: 2255 Springrain Dr Clearwater FL 34623-2238

MANLEY, JOAN MARIE, occupational therapist; b. Buffalo, Dec. 19, 1955; d. William Joseph and Luella Pauleen (Schiltz) M. AS, U. Fla., 1975; BS, Fla. Internat. U., 1977; postgrad., Trenton State Coll., 1989—. Registered occupational therapist, N.J. Staff occupational therapist United Cerebral Palsy, Miami, Fla., 1978, Med. Ctr. Princeton, N.J., 1978-84; rehab. specialist Assn. Rehab. Cons., Cranbury, N.J., 1984-85; sr. occupational therapist St. Lawrence Rehab. Ctr., Lawrenceville, N.J., 1985-87; adminstrv. dir. Occupational Therapy Med. Ctr., Princeton, 1987—. Mem. Am. Occupational Therapy Assn., N.J. Occupational Therapy Assn., Princeton Folk Music Soc. (bd. dirs. 1988-89), YWCA. Democrat. Roman Catholic. Home: 169 Witherspoon St Princeton NJ 08542 Office: Med Ctr Princeton 79 Bayard Ln Princeton NJ 08540

MANLEY, KIM, geologist; b. Chgo., Apr. 28, 1943; d. John Henry and Kathleen (Baird) M.; m. Latimer Alan Epps, Apr. 2, 1983. BA, U. Colo., 1964; MEd, U. Tex., 1968; PhD, U. Colo., 1976. NSF rsch. participant Inst. Arctic & Alpine Rsch., Boulder, Colo., 1961; rsch. asst. Lab. of Anthropology, Santa Fe, N.Mex., 1965; prof., asst. Pan Am. Petroleum Corp., Denver, 1966; asst. prof. Western Wash. State Coll., Bellingham, 1970-74; geologist U.S. Geol. Survey, Denver, 1974-82; geologic cons. Los Alamos, N.Mex., 1983—; invited lectr. Geol. Soc. Am., 1974, U. Kans., 1977, Geol. Soc., Los Alamos, N.Mex., 1981; chmn. Penrose Conf., U.S. Geol. Survey seminars, Geol. Soc. Am., 1974, 75-77, 76. Contbr. articles to profl. jours. Field trip leader Internat. Symposium on Rio Grande Rift, Santa Fe, 1978. Grantee Warren Thompson, U. Colo., 1969, 71. Mem. Geol. Soc. Am. (Penrose grantee 1974), Geol. Soc. N.Mex. (field trip leader 1979, 84). Home and office: 4691 Ridgeway Dr Los Alamos NM 87544

MANLEY, NANCY JANE, civil engineer; b. Ft. Smith, Ark., Sept. 13, 1951; d. Eugene Hailey and Mary Adele (Chave) M. BSE, Purdue U., 1974; MSE, U. Wash., 1976; postgrad., U. Minn., 1976-77; grad., Air Command and Staff Coll., 1984, Exec. Leadership Devel. Program Dept. Def., 1988. Lic. profl. engr., Ga. Sanitary engr. Minn. Dept. Health, Mpls., 1976-77; sanitary engr. water supply EPA, Chgo., 1977; leader primacy unit water supply EPA, Atlanta, 1977-79, leader tech. assistance team, 1979-82; chief environ. and contract planning, project mgr. Grand Bay Range design USAF, Moody AFB, Ga., 1982-84; dep. base civil engr. USAF, Carswell AFB, Tex., 1984-86; dep. base civil engrs. USAF, Scott AFB, Ill., 1986-89; mem. tech. adv. com. Scott AFB master plan study USAF, Belleville, Ill., 1986-89; dep. base civil engr. USAF, Robins AFB, Ga., 1989—; mem. Fla. Tech. Adv. Com. for Injection Wells, Tallahassee, 1980-82, Nat. Implementation Team for Underground Injection Control Program, Washington, 1979-82, tech. panel Nat. Groundwater Protection Strategy Hearings, 1981; judge Internat. Sci. and Engring. Fair, 1986; was 1st woman assigned as dep. base civil engr. USAF, Carswell AFB. Active various ch. support activities, 1969-74; vol. Meals-on-Wheels, Girl Scouts U.S., and others, various towns, 1982—; founder, crisis intervention counselor Midwest Alliance, West Lafayette, Ind., 1970-74; active St. Louis Math. and Sci. Network Day, 1989, Adopt-a-Sch. Program, Lebanon, Ill., 1987-89; scientist by mail Boston Mus. Sci., 1989—. Recipient Disting. Govt. Svc. award Dallas/Ft. Worth Fed. Exec. Bd., 1986. Mem. NSPE, Soc. Women Engrs. (sr. mem. local offices 1979-82, 84-86), ASCE, Am. Women in Sci., Soc. Am. Mil. Engrs. (local membership and contingency engring. coms.), Internat. Platform Assn. Office: USAF Civil Engring 2853 CES/DE Robins AFB GA 31098-5000

MANN, CHELSEA See **HUSAK, SUSAN M. V.**

MANN, EDITH KERBY, social worker, educator; b. Camden, N.J., Jan. 2, 1946; d. Benjamin III and Elizabeth Lula (Coulborn) M.; children: Laura Lynne Miller, Benjamin Christian Miller. BSW summa cum laude, Keuka Coll., 1984; MSW, W.Va. U., 1985. Cert. social worker, N.Y. Adminstrv. asst. W.Va. U. Sch. Social Work, Morgantown, 1985-87; therapist Keuka Psychol. Svcs., Penn Yan, N.Y., 1987—; dir. Rape and Abuse Crisis Svc. Yates Community, Penn Yan, 1987—; adj. instr. Elmira Correctional Facility campus program and main campus Keuka Coll., Keuka Park, N.Y., 1988—; mem. Yates County Task Force for AIDS, Penn Yan, 1987—, Yates County Youth Bd., 1987—, Four County Domestic Violence Task Force, Geneva, N.Y., 1987—, Regional Coalition Against Sexual Assault, Ithaca, N.Y., 1987—; co-chmn. Victim Svc. Coalition So. Tier Region, Owego, N.Y., 1988-89. Founding mem. Yates County Domestic Violence Task Group, 1989—, Concerned Citizens Yates County, 1983—; trustee, bd. dirs. Soldiers and Sailors Meml. Hosp., Penn Yan, 1987-89, Keuka Mgmt., Inc., 1987—, Family Enrichment Resource Ctr., Penn Yan, 1988—; team mem. Drug-Free Schs. and Communities, Penn Yan, 1989; bd. dirs. Yates Concert Series, Inc. Recipient internat. students appreciation award W.Va. U., 1986; Bus. and Profl. Women's scholar, 1981; NIMH grantee, 1984-85. Mem. Nat. Assn. Social Workers, Alpha Mu Gamma. Democrat. Methodist. Home: 2962 Coates Rd Penn Yan NY 14527 Office: Rape and Abuse Crisis Svc 112 North Ave PO Box 624 Penn Yan NY 14527

MANN, ELIZABETH BROWN, library, educator; b. Yale, Okla., Mar. 6, 1924; d. Coleman T. and Bertha (Harrison) Brown; m. Robert Trask Mann, Dec. 27, 1947; children: Robert T. Jr., Margaret Mann Spencer. AB in History, Fla. State Coll. for Women, Tallahassee, 1945; BSLS, Carnegie Inst. of Tech., Pitts., 1946; AMD LS, Fla. State U., 1969, PhD LS, 1972. Children's libr. Pub. Library, Washington, 1946-48; sch. libr. Alachua County Pub. Schs., Gainesville, Fla., 1948-49, Hillsborough County Pub. Schs., Tampa, Fla., 1955-61; sch. libr. system coord. Polk County Pub. Schs., 1961-67; assoc. dir. Learning Resources Fla. Mental Health Inst., Tampa, Fla., 1973-74; asst. prof. Fla. State U. Sch. of Libr. Studies, Tallahassee, 1978-84, assoc. prof., 1984-89; vis. instr. U. Ga., Athens, Summer Sems. 1967, 68, 73, 74, 75, winter sems. 1974, 75; adj. asst. prof. U. Fla., Gainesville, 1975-78; vis. asst. prof. Fla. State U., Tallahassee, summer 1969, faculty senate mem. 1979-89. steering com., 1984-89. Co-author: The 21st Century, 1988; chpt., Sch. Libr. Media Annual, 1983-86. Mem. Cap. Tiger Bay, Tallahassee, 1983-89, Pres.' Club, Fla. State U., 1985—; bd. dirs. Friends of Leon County Libr., Tallahassee, 1986-87, Community Adv. Bd. Fla. State U., 1983-87. Recipient Fed. Fellowship for Adv. Study, U.S. Govt., Tallahassee, 1968-71, grant, Coun. of Libr. Resources, Washington 1986. Mem. Spl. Librs. Assn., ALA (coun. 1967-71, intellectual freedom com. 1971-73), Assn. Record Mgrs. and Adminstrs., Fla. Libr. Assn. (pres. 1966-67), Fla. Assn. Media in Edn. (pres. 1961-62, life), Fla. Women's Alliance (pres. 1984-87), Capital Women's Network (pres. 1979-83), Internat. Alliance (vice chair Pinellas County, bd. dirs. Libr. Coop., 1988—), Beta Pi Mu, Delta Kappa Gamma, Kappa Delta Pi, Phi Delta Kappa. Democrat. Methodist. Home: PO Box 907 Tarbon Springs FL 34688 Office: Fla State U Sch of Libr & Info Studies Tallahassee FL 32306

MANN, GENEVIEVE CORATTI, marketing professional; b. Meriden, Conn., Aug. 1, 1958; d. William J. and Gwen Ann (Gallanis) Bagley; m. Stephen E. Mann, Nov. 26, 1988; 1 child, Laura Elizabeth. BA, Morse Sch. Bus., Hartford, Conn., 1985. V.p., dir. mktg. Hartford Aviation Group, Inc.; model, Fla., Mich., Conn. Chairperson ARC; v.p. Special Needs, Antioch, Calif. Mem. NAFE, Phi Beta Lambda. Republican. Roman Catholic. Office: One Gold St Ste 18A Hartford CT 06103

MANN, JACINTA, educator, consultant; b. Pinckneyville, Ill., May 13, 1925; d. Bernard Albert and Magdalen Elizabeth (Ruppert) M. BS, So. Ill. U., 1946; MS, U. Wis., 1947, PhD, 1958. Statistician U. Wis., Madison, 1948-50; novitiate Sisters of Charity, Greensburg, Pa., 1950-53; tchr. secondary math. Altoona (Pa.) Cath. High Sch., 1953-56; with Seton Hill Coll., 1958—, dir. admissions, 1960-67, acad. dean, 1968-71, prof., 1971—; adminstrv. intern Scripps Coll., Claremont, Calif., 1967-68. Contbr. articles to profl. jours. Mem. Pa. Gov.'s Commn. on Women, 1979-89. Kemper K. Knapp fellow U. Wis., 1957-58, Am. Coun. on Edn. fellow, 1967-68; recipient Faculty award Seton Hill Coll., 1970-71, Medal of Honor, Inst. for Women Today, 1977, Teaching award Freedoms Found., 1987; named Prof. of the Yr., Seton Hill Coll., 1988. Democrat. Roman Catholic. Home: 10 Meadowbrook Ave Greensburg PA 15601 Office: Seton Hill Coll Greensburg PA 15601

MANN, JONNIE YVONNE, brokerage house executive; b. Ft. Worth, Dec. 7, 1939; d. Delbert W. and Florence Evalynne (Fuller) McAmis; children: Robert, Terry, Shawn. BBA in Acctg., Cleary Coll., 1986. Lic. securities, real estate broker, Tex. Contr., office mgr. J.L. Scott Enterprises, Irving, Tex., 1980-82, Ivan Brown, Inc., Houston, 1982-83; due diligence officer Mut. Svc. Corp., Detroit, 1983-88; v.p. Realty Income Corp., Escondido, Calif., 1988-90, 1st Pacific Capital Corp., Vancouver, Calif., 1990—. Mem. Internat. Assn. Fin. Planners, Am. Mgmt. Assn., Women in Action. Home: 4701 NE 72d Ave Apt 222J Vancouver WA 98661

MANN, KAREN, consultant, educator; b. Kansas City, Mo., Oct. 9, 1942; d. Charles and Letha (Anderson) M. BA, U. Calif.-Santa Barbara, 1964; MPA, Golden Gate U., 1975, postgrad., 1989—. Cert. lay minister Order of Buddhist Contemplatives. Tchr. Sisters of Immaculate Heart, Los Angeles, 1964-68; group counselor San Francisco and Marin County Probation Depts., parole agt. Calif. Dept. Corrections, Sacramento and San Francisco, 1970-86; researcher and cons. Non-profit Orgnl. Devel., 1986—, Computer Applications for Persons with Disabilities, 1986—; adj. faculty Grad. Theol. Union, Berkeley, 1984—; Compuserve Disabilities Forum, 1988—; asst. forum adminstr.; mem. faculty Golden Gate U., 1990. Co-author: Prison Overcrowding, 1979; Community Corrections: A Plan for California, 1980. Active Buddhists Concerned for Animals, San Francisco, 1983—, Fellowship of Reconciliation, N.Y., 1970—; co-founder Network Ctr. for Study of Ministry, San Francisco, 1982; pres. San Francisco Network Ministries, 1980-82; mem. Disabled Children's Computer Resource Group, 1988—, Springwater Ctr. for Meditative Inquiry and Retreats, 1986—. Office: PO Box 377 Lagunitas CA 94938

MANN, LISA, university administrator, psychologist; b. N.Y.C., Nov. 14, 1953; d. Robert Nathaniel and Lucy (Zeitlin) M.; m. Rocco Francis Marotta, Sept. 17, 1980; 1 child, Nicholas Charles. BA with honors, Radcliff Coll., Cambridge, Mass., 1975; PhD, NYU, 1986. Elem. tchr. Dalton Sch., N.Y.C., 1975-77; remedial therapist for learning disabled children Katrina de Hirsh and Jeanette Jansky Clinic, N.Y.C., 1977-79; supervising psychologist St. Luke's - Roosevelt Hosp. Ctr., N.Y.C., 1986-88, dir. tng., 1988—; assoc. in clin. psychology Columbia U., N.Y.C., 1989—. Co-author: Ethnotherapy: An Exploration of Italian American Identity, 1985; also researcher and coeditor of videotapes of same subject; contbr. numerous articles. Mem. Am. Psychol. Assn., N.Y. Psychol. Assn. Democrat. Office: Saint Lukes-Roosevelt Hosp Ctr 411 W 114th St New York NY 10025

MANN, MARYLEN, hospital administrator; b. St. Louis, Mar. 13, 1937; d. Morris and Ruth (Sobel) Lipkind; (widowed); children: Robert Gordon, John Douglas. BA in Philosophy, Washington U., St. Louis, 1957; MA in Edn., Washington U., 1959. Tchr. St. Louis Pub. Schs., 1961-62; supr. student tchrs. dept. edn. Washington U., 1969, rsch. instr. Med. Sch., 1984—; instr. edn. U. Mo., St. Louis, 1972-74, dir. Older Adult Service and Info. System, fellow Ctr. Metro Studies, lctr. Dept. Edn., 1983-84; instr. curriculum devel. Webster U., St. Louis, 1977-78; dir. various programs CEMREL Inc., St. Louis, 1974-82; exec. dir. Older Adults Svc. and Info. System Jewish Hosp., St. Louis, 1984—; mem. bd. trustees Fontbonne Coll., 1989—; bd. dirs. Gerontology Concentration Adv. Com. Washington U., 1987—, Jewish Hosp. Women's Adv. Council Women's Health Resources, 1986—. Contbr. articles to profl. jours. Bd. dirs. Jewish Ctr. Aged, 1984-87, St. Louis Psychoanalytic Inst., 1983—, Arts and Edn. Council St. Louis, v.p., 1986, chmn. membership com., exec. com., 1989—, Gov.'s Adv. Council Aging, Mo. exec. com., 1984-86, Gov.'s Task Force Alternative Care Elderly, 1982, Clayton (Mo.) Sch. Bd., 1970-84, pres., 1979-81, v.p., 1976, sec., 1975; bd. dirs. The Repertory Theatre, St. Louis, 1989. Recipient numerous grants on care of the elderly, Bronze medal award U.S. Surgeon Gen., 1988; named Woman of Yr. City of Clayton, 1981, Woman of Achievement St. Louis Globe Democrat, 1980. Mem. Nat. Council Aging Inc., Am. Soc. Aging, Western Gerontol. Assn., Jr. League of St. Louis (community adv. bd. 1990), Sigma Phi Omega. Home: 900 Audubon Dr Clayton MO 63105 Office: Older Adult Svc & Info System 7710 Carondelet Ave Ste 125 Saint Louis MO 63105

MANN, PEGGY, writer; b. N.Y.C.; d. Edna Brand and Harvey Theordore M.; m. William Horlton; children: Jennifer, Betsy. BA, U. Wis. Author: A Room in Paris, 1959, Golda: The Life Of Israel's Prime Minister, 1971, (with r. Kluger) The Last Escape: The Launching of the Largest Secret Rescue Movement of All Time, 1973, Ralph Bunche: UN Peacemaker, 1975, The Tell-tale Line: the Secrets of Handwriting Analysis, 1976, Luis Munoz Marin: The Man Who Remade Puerto Rico, 1976, (with Nina Brodsky) Israel in Pictures, 1979, Gizelle, Save the Children!, 1981, Marijuana Alert!, 1984, The Street of the Flower Boxes, 1966, That New Baby, 1967, The Boy with the billion Pets, 1968, Clara Barton: Battlefield Nurse, 1969, When Carlos Closed the Street, 1969, The Clubhouse, 1969, Amelia Earhart: Pioneer of the Skies, 1970, The Twenty-five-Cent Frien, 1970, How Juan Got Home, 1972, The Lost Doll, 1972, William the Watchcat, 1972, Whitney Young, Jr.: Crusader for Freedom, 1972, The Secret Dog of Little Luis, 1973, My Dad Lives in a Downtown Hotel, 1973, Now Is Now, 1974, Last Road to Safety, 1975, (with J. Houlton) Ghost Boy, 1975, Handwriting: A Secret Way to Look Inside, 1975, (with V. Siegal) The Man Who Bought Himself: The Story of Peter Still, 1975, A Present for Yanya, 1975, There Are Two Kinds of Terrible, 1976, Lonely Girl, 1976, The Secret Ship, 1977, Twelve Is Too Old, 1981; contbr. to mags. Men. PEN, Am. Soc. of Journalist, Am. Soc. Med. Writers. Home: 46 W 94th St New York NY 10025

MANN, SANDRA PEETE, elementary educator; b. Memphis, July 4, 1948; d. David and Katherine (Dabilia) Peete; m. Willie Aaron Mann, Aug. 22, 1987. BS in Sociology, Tenn. State U., 1970; MS in Mgmt. Pub. Service, DePaul U., Chgo., 1976. Cert. elem. tchr., Ill. Tchr. Chgo. Bd. Edn., 1970—, dist. cons. educator, 1988—; program evaluator Model Cities, Chgo., 1974; program dir. Project Girls Chgo. Commn. Human Relations, 1976. Active Dem. Cen. Com., Chgo., 1989, Polit. Action Com., Chgo., 1986. Named Master Tchr. State of Ill., 1984, Outstanding Sch. Educator Chgo. Black Alliance, 1985. Mem. NEA, Nat. Assn. Female Execs. Presbyterian. Home: 388 Woodhollow Ln Bartlett IL 60103

MANNERS, NANCY, mayor; b. Catania, Sicily, Italy; d. Gioacchino Jack and Maria Providenza (Virzi) Marasa; m. George Manners, Dec. 20, 1941; children: Gene David, Nancy Ellen Manners Sieh, Joan Alice. BA in Pub. Adminstrn., U. La Verne, 1979. Asst. city mgr. City of Covina, 1963-74; mcpl. mgmt. cons., 1975-85; mem. city coun. City of West Covina, Calif., 1984; pres. Ind. Cities Risk Mgmt. Authority, West Covina, 1988; mayor City of West Covina, 1988-89; pres. Ind. Cities Assn., 1989-90. Pres. San Gabriel Valley Planning Com., 1986; chmn. L.A. County Solid Waste Mgmt. Com., 1986-89; pres. Mid-Valley Mental Health Coun., 1988; foremen pro tem, L.A. County Grand Jury, 1980-81; trustee Covina-Valley Unified Sch. Dist., 1973-77; pres. East San Gabriel Valley Regional Occupation Program, 1974-76, Altrusa Club of Covina-West, 1971-72; regional chmn. San Gabriel Valley Lung Assn. 1971-73; pres. Covina Coordinating Council 1970-71. Named Covina Citizen of the Yr., 1977, West Covina Citizen of the Yr., 1983; recipient Woman of Distinction award Today's Woman Forum, 1988, Woman of Achievement award YWCA, 1987, 88, Community Svc. award West Covina C. of C., 1989, and others. Mem. Ind. Cities Assn. (v.p. 1988, pres. 1989), LWV (pres. San Gabriel Valley, 1978). Home: 734 N Eileen Ave West Covina CA 91791

MANNES, ELENA SABIN, television news and public affairs producer; b. N.Y.C., Dec. 3, 1943; d. Leopold Damrosch and Evelyn (Sabin) M. BA, Smith Coll., 1965; MA, Johns Hopkins U., 1967. Researcher Pub. Broadcast Lab. Nat. Ednl. TV, N.Y.C., 1967-68, 1968-70; writer Sta. WPIX-TV, N.Y.C., 1970-73; assignment editor Sta. ABC-TV, N.Y.C., 1973-76; producer, writer Sta. WCBS-TV, N.Y.C., 1976-80; producer CBS News, N.Y.C., 1980-87, Pub. Affairs TV/Bill Moyers PBS Documentaries, N.Y.C., 1987—; ind. documentary dir. and producer, 1987—. Recipient Emmy awards NATAS, 1984, 1985 (2), Peabody award 1985, Cine Golden Eagle award, 1988, 90, Robert F. Kennedy Journalism award, 1989. Mem. Writers Guild Am., Dirs. Guild Am., Am. Film Inst. (dir. workshop for women 1989-90).

MANNING, BONNIE LEE, sales executive; b. Delaware County, Pa., May 16, 1958; d. Frank J. Jr. and Cathryn (Murphy) Lee; m. Richard D. Manning Jr., Nov. 7, 1981; children: Richard III, Brandon. BA, Villanova U., 1982; postgrad., Widner U., 1983. Sr. sales rep. Honeywell Inc., Valley Forge, Pa.; regional mgr. Saf Am., Phila.; pres. Honeywell Sales Profl. Orgn. Mem. Jr. League of Phila. Recipient Sales award Summit Club, 1989.

MANNING, CATHERINE MARIE, health care administrator; b. Bradford, Pa., Nov. 10, 1938; d. James Joseph and Mary Magdalen (Chohrach) M. BS in Elem. Edn., Villa Maria Coll., Erie, Pa., 1966; MEd, Gannon U., Erie, 1971; MA in Theology, Boston Coll., 1981. Joined Sisters of St. Joseph, Roman Cath. Ch., 1956. Tchr. Erie Diocesan Sch. Sys., Erie, 1956-66; piano instr. Villa Maria Conservatory, Erie, 1957-58; prin. Erie Diocesan Sch. Sys., 1966-73; dir. admissions Villa Maria Coll., Erie, 1973-76; med. social svc. caseworker St. Vincent Health Ctr., Erie, 1976-79; sociology and psychology instr. Marian Ct. Bus. Coll., Swampscott, Mass., 1981-82; acad. dean Marymount Internat. Sch., Rome, Italy, 1982-85; v.p. patient affairs St. Vincent Health Ctr., Erie, 1985—; bd. trustees St. Mary's Home of Erie, 1986—; bd. dirs. Minority Health Edn. Delivery Sys., Inc., Erie, 1986—. Mem. AAUW, Am. Coll. Healthcare Execs., Erie Art Mus., Pax Christi USA. Democrat. Roman Catholic. Home: 1014 Weschler Ave Erie PA 16502 Office: Sisters of Saint Joseph 819 W 8th St Erie PA 16502-1650

MANNING, CYNTHIA RIETTE, structural engineer; b. N.Y.C., Nov. 26, 1925; d. Morris Leo and Florence (Alexander) Bergman; m. George Gross, Sept. 5, 1947 (div. 1955); m. John Pearce Manning, Dec. 5, 1956; children: Melanie Ann Brandston, Elizabeth Leona, Renee Adele. BCE, CCNY, 1945. Registered profl. engr., N.Y., Ariz., N.Mex. Structural draftsman Hardesty and Hanover, N.Y.C., 1945-47; structural designer Anaconda Co., N.Y.C., 1948-56, Werner Jensen and Adams, Stamford, Conn., 1956-72, Mountain States Mining Co., Tucson, 1973-74; civil designer Pima County Hwy. Dept., Tucson, 1975-77; structural engr. Miller Sales and Engring., Tucson, 1979-81; instr. civil and structural engring. Tucson Coll. Bus., 1982-84; civil designer Osborn, Peddersen and Walbert, Tucson, 1986-87; civil engr. Finical and Dombrowski Assocs., Tucson, 1987-90. Mem. CCNY Alumni Assn, Tucson Racquet Club, Singletarians (v.p.). Episcopalian. Home: 5390 E Francisco Loop Tucson AZ 85712-1386

MANNING, HELEN HARTON, retired theater educator; b. Albion, Mich., June 7, 1921; d. William C. and Mildred (Brown) Harton; m. George A. Manning, Mar. 21, 1958 (dec.); 1 child, Lora Annette Manning. BA, Albion Coll., 1943; MA, Northwestern U., 1950, PhD, 1956. Teaching fellow U. Iowa, Iowa City, 1944-46; tchr. theater Muskegon (Mich.) Sr. High Sch., 1946-50; dir. theatre Hope Coll., Holland, Mich., 1950-54; dri. teatre, chair dept. Albion Coll., 1956-85; sec.-treas. Mich. Speech Communication Assn., 1957-61, bd. dirs., 1980-84. Author, editor Julia, 1980; author script Passion of Jesus, 1977; actress several plays in Albion area, 1984—. Bd. dirs. Calhoun County Literacy Coun., Battle Creek, Mich., 1989—, Hist. Soc., Albion, 1989—, United Meth. Ch., Albion, 1989—; lay del. West Mich. Meth. Conf., 1985—. Recipient Disting. Svc. award Mich. Assn. Speech Com., 1984, Disting. Alumni award Albion Coll., 1987, Community Svc. award Festival of the Forks Com., Albion, 1989; named Community Minute Man, Albion City Coun., 1984. Mem. AAUW (v.p. 1969-72, historian 1985—, bd. dirs. Albion chpt. 1987—), Mich. Assn. Speech Communication (life mem., 1st. v.p. 1987-89, pres. 1989—), United Meth. Women (pres. 1986-88), Book Rev. Club (program chair 1990), Albion Coll. Alumni Assn. (bd. dirs. 1987—), Emitte Lucam Tuam Club (2nd v.p. 1985-87, 1st v.p. 1987-89, pres. 1989—). Democrat. Home: 415 Brockway Pl Albion MI 49224

MANNING, JOAN ELIZABETH, health service executive; b. Davenport, Iowa, July 7, 1953; d. George John and Eugenie Joan (Thomas) Stolze; m. Michael Anthony Manning, July 30, 1977. BA, U. No. Iowa, 1975; MPH, U. Minn., 1986—. Traveling collegiate sec. Alpha Delta Pi Nat. Sorority, Atlanta, 1975-76; recreational therapist Americana Healthcare Ctr., Mason City, Iowa, 1976-81; communication coord. Area Agy. on Aging, Mason City, 1981-83; exec. dir. United Way Cerro Gordo County, Mason City, 1983-85, Health Fair of the Midlands, Omaha, 1985-87; dir. health services ARC, Omaha, 1987-90, asst. exec. dir., 1990—. Bd. dirs. YMCA of U.S.A., Chgo., 1981-83, Mason City YMCA, 1980-84, Mason City Parks and

Recreation Bd., 1983-85, Camp Fire Coun., 1989—, Potters Therapy House, 1989—; mem. spl. adv. bd. Cerro Gordo County Human Svcs. Bd., 1983-85; mem. spl. activities com. Omaha Wellness Coun. of Midlands, 1986-89; chmn. wider opportunity task force Great Plains (Nebr.) Girl Scouts U.S., 1986-89. Mem. U. Minn. Alumnae Assn., Alpha Delta Pi. Republican. Roman Catholic. Office: ARC 3838 Dewey Omaha NE 68105

MANNING, JUDITH SUSAN, intercultural organization executive; b. N.Y.C., Oct. 4, 1941; d. Armin William and Anita Louise (Spnnagel) M. BA in Edn. and History, Valparaiso U., 1963; MA in Edn., Syracuse U., 1967. Tchr. L.I. Luth. High Sch., Brookville, N.Y., 1963-65, Solvay (N.Y.) High Sch., 1967-68; dir. Caribbean program Operation Crossroads Africa, Inc., N.Y.C., 1969-87; exec. dir. World Horizons Internat., Inc., N.Y.C., 1987—; cons., tour specialist Inter-Pacific Tours Internat., N.Y.C., 1984—. Mem. Soroptimists (v.p. N.Y.C., 1984—). Republican. Office: World Horizons Internat Inc 1427 2d Ave New York NY 10021

MANNING, KATHRYN ANN, police officer; b. Ft. Worth, Apr. 1, 1958; d. Roy Denton and Elizabeth Ann (Baker) Ward; m. Roy Mikel Manning, Sept. 22, 1984; children: Stephanie Renae, Kevin Mikel. Policewoman Ft. Worth Police Dept., 1981—. Office: Ft Worth Police Dept 350 W Belknap Fort Worth TX 76102

MANNING, LYDIA, customer service-converting scheduler; b. Linz, Austria, Nov. 12, 1948; came to U.S., 1951; d. John and Marie (Hexel) Nowak; m. Jack Dean Manning, Jan. 1, 1970; children: Dean, Brian. Student, Angelo State U., 1967-70, Howard Payne U., 1976, Tarleton State U., 1987. Office mgr. Zale's Jewelers, San Angelo, Tex., 1967-71; receptionist Minn. Mining & Mfg., Brownwood, Tex., 1971-72; order dept. clk. Minnesota Mining & Mfg., Brownwood, Tex., 1972-75, converting clk., 1975-76, finished goods scheduler, 1979, prodn. scheduler, 1979-83, order dept. analyst, 1983, customer service, 1983—. pres. Brownwood Freshman League, 1980; Chmn. Brownwood Freshman League, 1981. Mem. Nat. Assn. Female Execs., Pi Sigma Epsilon. Democrat. Roman Catholic, Baptist. Home: 113 Vick Dr Brownwood TX 76801 Office: Minniesota Mining & Mfg P O Box 1669 Brownwood TX 76804

MANNING, MARY (MARY WHITAKER), journalist, photographer; b. Marlboro, Mass., Apr. 2, 1947; d. John Francis and Mary Virginia (Bordeleau) Manning; m. Frank D. Whitaker, July 15, 1975 (div. May 1980); 1 child, Michelle. BA in English, U. Nev., 1970. Copy girl Las Vegas Sun, Nev., 1965, corr. for nature, 1966-71, Sunday editor, 1976-78, journalist, 1978—; info. officer Clark County Health Dist., Las Vegas, 1971-73; reporter AP Stanford, San Francisco, 1973-76. Mem. State and Las Vegas Pen Women (recording sec.), Sigma Delta Chi (bd. dirs. 1986-88). Democrat. Unitarian. Office: Las Vegas Sun 121 S Martin L King Blvd Las Vegas NV 89127

MANNING, PATRICIA KAMARAS, biochemist, process engineer, research scientist; b. Harlingen, Tex., May 26, 1953; d. Henry Julius and Audrey Marie (Klimas) Kamaras; m. Steven Allan Manning, Feb. 26, 1983. BS, U. Ariz., 1975, MS, 1978, PhD, 1987. Grad. rsch. asst. U. Ariz., Tucson, 1976-78, sponsor grad.rsch., 1986-88; rsch. scientist Armour Dial, Inc., Scottsdale, Ariz., 1978-79; sr. chemist Armour Rsch. Ctr., Armour Food Co., Scottsdale, Ariz., 1979-86; exec. v.p., tech. dir. Manning, Batson & Assocs., Inc., Seattle, 1986-90; pres. Manning & Assocs., Gilbert, Ariz., 1989—; v.p. Quality Assurance and Rsch. Oceantrawl, Inc., Seattle, 1990—. Inventor in field. Vol. Humane Soc Ariz., 1986—, Humane Soc. Am., 1987—. Mem. Inst. Food Technologists (profl.), Nat. Fisheries Inst. (tech. subcom. 1988—, govt. rels. com. 1988—), Assn. Ofcl. Analytical Chemists, Am. Oil Chemists Soc., Alaska Fisheries Devel. Found. (voting cons. 1986—, rsch & devel. grantee 1986-89), N.Y. Acad. Scis., So. Ariz. Runners Club. Roman Catholic. Office: Oceantrawl Inc 1200 Market Place Tower 2025 1st Ave Seattle WA 98121

MANNING, SANDRA KAY, small business owner; b. Toledo, June 21, 1951; d. Chester Leroy and Mildred (Obenour) Yawberg; m. John Lee Manning, Apr. 1, 1972; children: Michael, Kelly, Steven. BS in Edn., Bowling Green State U., 1972; postgrad., Ea. Mich. U., 1977, Western Mich. U., 1978, Cen. Mich. U., 1981-82. Tchr. Grant (Mich.) Schs., 1972-74, Charlevoix (Mich.)-Emmet Intermediate Sch. Dist., 1976-83; tchr. cons. Battle Creek (Mich.) Schs., 1974-75, Crestwood Schs., Dearborn Heights, Mich., 1975-76; owner, adminstr., editor newsletter Creative Connections, children's programs, Petoskey, Mich., 1988—; lectr., seminar condr. various orgns.; cons. to bus. on children's involvement. Area rep. Family Community Leadership Program, Lansing and Petoskey, 1988; v.p. Petoskey Sch. Bd., 1986—; elder 1st Presbyn. Ch., Petoskey, 1988—; pres. aux. bd. Little League, Petoskey, 1987-89. Named Woman of Yr., Petoskey Jaycees, 1983, Friends of Handicapped, Coalition Advs. for Impaired, Petoskey, 1984, Early Childhood Educator of Yr. Grand Traverse region Community Coordinated Child Care Coun., 1988. Mem. Nat. Assn. for Edn. Young Children, AAUW (internat. affairs rep., community involvement rep. 1978-80), Beta Sigma Phi (pres. Petoskey 1979-80). Home and Office: 1039 Lindell Ave Petoskey MI 49770

MANNING, TONI RUTH, food company executive; b. Greenfield, Mass., Oct. 17, 1946; d. Farley A. and Ruth (Koegel) Manning. BS, U. Mass., 1971; MBA, U. Balt., 1980. Home economist McCormick & Co., Inc., Balt., 1971-78; mgr. planning McCormick & Co., Inc., Hunt Valley, Md., 1978-80; asst. to v.p. sci. and tech. McCormick & Co., Inc., Hunt Valley, 1980-85; mgr. mktg. Hunt Cup, Ltd., Riderwood, Md., 1986-88; pres. Cristle Foods, Inc., Balt., 1989—; cons. in field, Balt., 1985—. Mem. Inst. Food Technologists (profl., Md. sect. chmn. 1976-77), Am. Home Econs. Assn., Am. Mktg. Assn. (bd. dirs. 1977-81). Democrat. Unitarian.

MANNING RUSSELL, MARLOU, psychotherapist; b. Tucson, June 2, 1956; d. William Herman and Carole Eleanor (Musgrove) McBratney; m. Jan Christophher Russell, Sept. 9, 1989. BA U. Ariz., 1981; MA Calif. Grad. Inst., 1983, PhD, 1987. Lic. marriage, family and child counselor. Asst. to pres. Western Psychol. Svcs., L.A., 1978-81; crisis counselor Cedars-Sinai Med. Ctr., L.A., 1980-84; counselor South Bay Therapeutic Clinic, Hawthorne, Calif., 1982-84; psychotherapist PMC Treatment Systems, L.A., 1984-85, Beverly Hills Counseling Ctr., 1984-85, Comprehensive Care Corp., L.A., 1985-86; pvt. practice, L.A., 1986—; counselor Brotman Med. Ctr., L.A., 1982-83, Julia Ann Singer Ctr., Los Angeles, 1984; bd. dirs. Los Angeles Commn. Assaults Against Women, 1987-89. Mem. Internat. Assn. Eating Disorders Profls, Nat. Assn. Women Bus. Owners, Women in Health, Women's Referral Svc., Am. Anorexia-Bulimia Assn., Calif. State Psychol. Assn., Calif. Assn. Marriage & Family Therapists. Democrat. Office: 9911 W Pico Blvd Ste 670 Los Angeles CA 90035

MANOBIANCO, PATRICIA ANN, nurse anesthetist; b. Hempstead, L.I., Nov. 27, 1959; d. Vincent J. and Joan M. (Toner) M.; m. Michael B. Puma, May 5, 1990. BS, Keuka Coll., 1981; MS, Columbia U., 1990. RN, N.Y., N.J. Staff nurse Valley Hosp., Ridgewood, N.J., 1981-85; head nurse Englewood (N.J.) Hosp., 1985-90; nurse practitioner Critical Difference, Inc., N.J., 1989-90; nurse anesthetist St. Luke's/Roosevelt Hosp., N.Y.C., 1990—. Mem. Am. Assn. Nurse Anesthetists. Republican. Roman Catholic. Home: 8 Trevor Lake Dr Congers NY 10920 Office: Roosevelt Hosp W 59th St New York NY

MANOFF, DINAH BETH, actress; b. N.Y.C.; d. Arnold and Lyova (Rosenthal) (Lee Grant) M. Student public schs., N.Y. and Calif. Appeared in: TV series Soap, 1977-78, Empty Nest, 1989—; TV movie appearances include Raid on Entebbe, 1977, High Terror, 1977, The Possessed, 1977, For Ladies Only, 1981, A Matter of Sex, 1984, The Seduction of Gina, 1984, Celebrity, 1984, Flight #90, 1984, Classified Love, 1986, Babies, 1990; stage performances include I Ought To Be In Pictures (Tony award), 1980 (Theatre World award), Leader of the Pack, 1985, Alfred and Victoria: A Life, Los Angeles Theatre Ctr., 1986-87; films include Grease, 1977, Ordinary People, 1979, I Ought To Be in Pictures, 1981, Gifted Children, 1983, Child's Play, 1988. Mem. Screen Actors Guild, Actors Equity, AFTRA. Jewish. Home: 140 W 23rd New York NY 10023 Office: care Gersh Agy 222 N Canon Dr Beverly Hills CA 90210*

MANOGUE, HELEN SMITH, banker; b. Bergen, N.J., Dec. 14, 1931; d. William Casper and Teresa Elizabeth (Wulftange) S.; m. Nov. 28, 1959; children: Joseph Mark, Stephen James, Philip William. BA, Rutgers U., 1975. Buyer Bonwit Teller, N.Y.C., 1956-61; curator Stevens Inst. Tech., Hoboken, N.J., 1973-75; project dir. Ctr. for Mcpl. Studies, Hoboken, 1975-77; program officer N.J. Mortgage Fin. Agy., Newark, 1977-79; v.p., community investment officer City Fed. Savs. Bank, Elizabeth, N.J., 1979-82, mgr. securities svcs., 1982-85; v.p., fin. officer City Savs. Bank, Somerset, 1985—. Founder, dir. waterfront Coalition of Hudson and Bergen, Hoboken, 1977—; bd. dirs. Liberty State Pk. Devel. Corp.; bd. advisors Waterfront Ctr. Wash.; chmn. Hoboken Environ. Com., 1970-85; reg. trustee Assn. N.J. Environ. Coms., Mendham, 1979—; chmn. Hoboken Hist. Dist. Com., 1978—. Recipient Spl. Merit award U.S. EPA, 1978; named one of Women of Achievement, Jersey Jour., 1971. Mem. Nat. Assn. Housing and Redevel. Ofcls., Phi Beta Kappa. Home: 1108 Park Ave Apt 6 Hoboken NJ 07030

MANSEAU, MELISSA MARIE, infosystems specialist; b. Exeter, N.H., Mar. 24, 1962; d. Stuart Wayne and Dorothy Edith (Follis) Cady; m. Gerald Vincent Manseau; 1 child, Lindsay Marie. AS in Electronic Engring. Tech., N.H. Tech. Inst., Concord, 1982; BS in Computer Sci., U. So. Maine, 1988. Assoc. system technician Nat. Semiconductor Corp. (formerly Fairchild Semiconductor), South Portland, Maine, 1982-83, system technician, 1983-85, sr. system technician, 1985, assoc. computer system engr., 1985-88, software engr., 1988—. Mem. IEEE, IEEE Computer Soc., Nat. Assn. Female Execs. Congregationalist. Home: 10 Pinecrest Dr Hollis Center ME 04042

MANSFIELD, MARGO, psychiatric occupational therapist; b. Chgo., Mar. 29, 1947; d. Howard and Anne (Goldberg) M. BS, U. Ill., 1970; MA, Roosevelt U., Chgo., 1975. Lic. therapist, Ill. Dir. psychiat. occupational therapy Rush Presbyn.-St. Luke's Med. Ctr., Chgo.; asst. prof. Rush U., Chgo.; adv. bd. Chgo. Citywide Colls. Contbr. articles to profl. jours. Bd. dirs. People Environments Programs, Inc., 1982-88. Mem. Am. Occupational Therapy Assn., Ill. Occupational Therapy Assn., Am. Occupational Cert. Bd., Acad. Content Experts, Roster Accreditation Evaluators, Accreditation Commn. Office: 1653 W Congress Chicago IL 60612

MANSFIELD, TOBI ELLEN, psychologist; b. Miami Beach, Fla., Oct. 4, 1949; d. Murray Irwin and Rose Turner (Plansky) Mantell; 1 child, Mia Michelle. BA, U. Miami, Fla., 1974; MA, Norwich U., Montpelier, Vt., 1982; PhD, Union Inst., Cin., 1987. Mental health counselor South Dade Crisis Intervention, Miami, Fla., 1978-80; adj. faculty Miami Dade Community Coll., 1977-80; clin. assoc. Miami Psychotherapy Inst., 1980-88; adj. faculty Nova U., 1984-87, U. Miami Med. Sch., 1988-90; psychologist, dir. Miami Wellness Ctr., 1987—. Contbr. articles to profl. jours. Mem. APA, Am. Bd. Med. Psychotherapists (assoc.), Royal Soc. Medicine. Office: Miami Wellness Center 1390 S Dixie Hwy #1208 Coral Gables FL 33146

MANSK, SHARON SUE, graphic designer; b. Elmhurst, Ill., Apr. 9, 1948; d. Robert William and Violet (Stamos) Conklin; m. Kenneth M. Mansk, Oct. 11, 1969; children: Jeffrey, Amanda, Bridget. Postgrad., Elmhurst Coll., Ill., 1989. Customer rep. Ill. Bell Tel., Elmhurst, 1964-67; collection correspondent Xerox Corp., Oak Brook, Ill., 1967-69; graphics technician Elmhurst Coll., Ill., 1984-. V.p. York High Sch. Choral Parents Assn., 1989—. Recipient Supreme Patriotism Essay award Internat. Order of Job's Daughters, 1966. Mem. Newcomers Club Elmhurst (Publicity Mgr. 1973-74), Young Women's Ch. Group Club Elmhurst (Pres. 1980). Lutheran. Office: Elmhurst Coll 190 Prospect Elmhurst IL 60126

MANSMANN, CAROL LOS, federal judge, educator; b. Pitts., Aug. 7, 1942; d. Walter Joseph and Regina Mary (Pilarski) Los; m. J. Jerome Mansmann, June 27, 1970; children: Michael, Casey, Megan, Patrick. B.A., J.D., Duquesne U.; LL.D., Seton Hill Coll., Greensburg, Pa., 1985. Asst. dist. atty. Allegheny County, Pitts., 1968-72; assoc. McVerry Baxter & Mansmann, Pitts., 1973-79; assoc. prof. law Duquesne U., Pitts., 1973-82; judge U.S. Dist. Ct. Pa., Pitts., 1982-85, U.S. Ct. Appeals, Phila., 1985—; mem. Pa. Criminal Procedural Rules Com., Pitts., 1972-77; spl. asst. atty. gen. Commonwealth of Pa., 1974-79; bd. dirs. Pa. Bar Inst., Harrisburg, 1984—. Mem. adv. bd. Villanova U. Law Sch., 1985—. Recipient St. Thomas More award, 1983. Mem. Nat. Assn. Women Judges, ABA, Pa. Bar Assn., Fed. Judges Assn., Am. Judicature Soc., Allegheny County Bar Assn., Phi Alpha Delta. Republican. Roman Catholic. Office: US Ct Appeals 402 US PO & Courthouse 7th & Grant Sts Pittsburgh PA 15219*

MANSOLINO, BARBARA ANN, human resources professional; b. Plainfield, N.J., Feb. 11, 1947; d. Harry W. and Anna (Susko) Leszchyn; m. Robert Mansolino, Sept. 17, 1983. BS, Rider Coll., 1986. Profl. staff recruiter St. Peter's Med. Ctr., New Brunswick, N.J.; personnel generalist Hunterdon Med. Ctr., Flemington, N.J.; staff scheduler, personnel asst. Coopers and Lybrand, Newark. Mem. NAFE. Home: 246 Laurel Ct Whitehouse Station NJ 08889 Office: St Peter's Med Ctr Dept Human Resources 254 Easton Ave New Brunswick NJ 08901

MANSUR, JULIANE LOUISE, urban planner; b. Detroit, June 17, 1957; d. George Alexander and Rachel Eloise (Anthony) Mansur. BA in Geography, U. Calif., Santa Barbara, 1979; MA in Urban & Regional Planning, U. Hawaii, 1985. Environ. reviewer State of Hawaii Environ. Ctr., Honolulu, 1984-85; urban planner City & County of Honolulu Dept. Land Utilization, 1984-85, Research Corp./Sea Grant Extension, Honolulu, 1985; environ. planner R.M. Parsons Co., Honolulu, 1985-89; planner Leo A. Daly, 1989—. Mem. Am. Planning Assn. (exec. com. 1985-89). Home: 59-510 Makana Rd Haleiwa HI 96712 Office: Leo A Daly 500 Ala Moana Blvd #500 Honolulu HI 96813

MANSUY, JANE WEBSTER, human resources professional; b. Norristown, Pa., Sept. 27, 1951; d. Eugene Duffield and Betty Ruth (Shuler) Webster; m. Bucky Patrick Mansuy, Jan. 22, 1983. BA, Dickinson Coll., 1973; MA, Beaver Coll., 1976. Cert. English and Spanish tchr., Pa. Dir. staff/community rels. Methacton Sch. Dist., Fairview Village, Pa.; Presenter in field. Mem. Nat. Sch. Pub. Rels. Assn., Pa. Sch. Pub. Rels. Assn., Am. Assn. Sch. Pers. Adminstrs., Pa. Assn. Sch. Pers. Adminstrs., Ea. Pa. Assn. Sch. Pers. Adminstrs., Am. Soc. Curriculum Devel. Home: 2144 Schultz Rd Lansdale PA 19446

MANTEL, WENDY LUISE, advertising firm executive; b. Indpls., Jan. 21, 1954; d. Thomas David and Flo Mary (Foreman) M.; m. Daniel Victor Garbowit, June 5, 1988. BA magna cum laude, Amerst Coll., 1976; MA, Columbia U., 1977. Asst. editor Am. Cancer Soc., N.Y.C., 1977-78; copy writer Springer-Verlag, Inc., N.Y.C., 1978-80; sr. med. writer Instructional Techniques, Manhasset, N.Y., 1980-83; account exec. William Douglas McAdams, N.Y.C., 1983-84; account supr. Sudler and Hennessey, N.Y.C., 1984-87, v.p., 1987—, now sr. v.p. Mem. Pharm. Advt. Council, Amherst Alumni Admissions Com. Office: Sudler & Hennessey Inc 1633 Broadway New York NY 10019*

MANTHE, CORA DE MUNCK, real estate company executive; b. Alton, Iowa, Oct. 10, 1928; d. Cornelius John and Bessie Bell (Miller) De Munck; m. Carl Robert Manthe, Apr. 5, 1952 (dec. Dec. 1987); children: Barry Paul, David Glenn. BA in Econs., U. Iowa, 1950; postgrad., U. Wis., Madison and Oshkosh; grad., Realtors Inst., 1972, 73, 74,75. Rsch. analyst Dept. Def., Washington, 1951-52; social work investigator Dane County, Madison, 1960-62; civic hostess Welcome Wagon, Beaver Dam, Wis., 1963-70; real estate broker "C" Manthe Realty, Ltd., Beaver Dam, 1979—, property mgr., pres., treas., 1982—. Deacon Grace Presbyn. Ch., 1974-77, elder, 1979-82, ruling elder, 1989—. Mem. Nat. Assn. Realtors, Am. Frat. Real Estate Appraisers (cert. residential appraiser), Beaver Dam C. of C., Waupun C. of C., AAUW (life), U. Iowa Alumni Assn. (life), Optimist. Home and Office: 404 De Clark St Beaver Dam WI 53916

MANTHORNE, JACKIE ANN, writer, adminstrator; b. Halifax, N.S., Can., Dec. 3, 1946; d. Ralph Eugene and Mildred Freda (Rhuland) M.; BA, Dalhousie U., 1968, BE, 1970. Teaching asst. Miriam Sch. for the Exceptional, Montreal, Que., Can., 1972-73; tchr. Peter Hall Sch. for the Exceptional, Montreal, 1973-75; info. officer Women's Ctr. of Montreal, 1975-78, asst. dir., 1978-86, dir. adminstrv. services, 1986—; pub., editor Les Editions Communiqu' Elles, 1981—. Mem. Internat. Women's Writing Guild, Women's Centre of Montréal, Federation des femmes du Quebec, Centre Investigative Journalism. Editor Communiqu' Elles. (French and English), 1975—, Montreal Women's Directory (French and English), 1977, 80, 82, 85, Canadian Women's Directory (French and English), 1987, Newcomer's Handbook (French, English, Greek, Portuguese, Hindi), 1979. Office: 3585 St-Urbain, Montreal, PQ Canada H2X 2N6

MANTICA, PAMELA ANN, nurse, consultant; b. Albany, N.Y., Nov. 12, 1956; d. Joseph Richard and Patricia Ann (Nunnally) M. ASin Bus. Adminstrn., Hudson Valley Community Coll., 1984; BBA, SUNY, 1987. Cert. in nursing, Albany Med. Ctr., 1977; RN, N.Y. Nurse St. Clare's Hosp., Schenectady, N.Y., 1978-81; critical care nurse Meml. Hosp., Albany, N.Y., 1981-88; nurse cons. Nounan, Trone, Gutermuth & O'Connor, Troy, N.Y., 1987—; profl. services rep. Upstate Imaging and So. Tier Imaging, Latham and Johnson City, N.Y., 1988—; rep. imaging svcs. Med. Resources, Inc., Teaneck, N.J. Mem. Nat. Assn. Female Execs., Beta Gamma Sigma, Phi Gamma Nu (recipient scholarship key). Home: 1155 Warburton Ave Yonkers NY 10701 Office: 955 Yonkers Ave Yonkers NY 10704

MANTIONE, SANDRA MARIE, financial company executive; m. Anthony DeFranco, June 7, 1985. BS in Econs., SUNY. Cert. fin. planner. Fin. planning coord. N.E. region Prudential-Bache Securities, Inc., Rochester, 1981-85; v.p. Personal Fin. Planners, Inc., Rochester, 1985-88; pres., co-founder Capital Designs of Rochester (N.Y.), Inc., 1988. Bd. mem. Rochester Internat. Friendship Coun. Mem. NOW, NAFE, Internat. Assn. of Cert. Fin. Planners, Western N.Y. Soc. of IACFP (pres. 1990—). Home: 27 Alameda St Rochester NY 14613 Office: 80 St Paul St Ste 512 Rochester NY 14604

MANTYLA, KAREN, sales executive; b. Bronx, N.Y., Dec. 31, 1944; d. Milton and Sylvia (Diamond) Fischer; m. John A Mantyla, May 30, 1970 (div. 1980); 1 child, Michael Alan. Student, Rockland Community Coll., Suffern, N.Y., 1962, NYU, 1967, Mercer U., 1981. Mktg. coordinator Credit Bur., Inc., Miami, Fla., 1973-79; dist. mgr. The Research Inst. Am., N.Y.C., 1979-80, regional dir., 1980-85, field sales mgr., 1985-86, nat. sales mgr., 1986-87; dir. mktg. TempsAmerica, N.Y.C., 1987-88; nat. accounts mgr. The Rsch. Inst. Am., N.Y.C., 1989; regional sales mgr., asst. v.p. Bur. Bus. Practice, Waterford, Conn., 1989—. Mem. Sales and Mktg. Execs. N.Y. (bd. dirs., v.p. Ft. Lauderdale chpt. 1979). Home: 3 Rockledge Dr Suffern NY 10901 Office: Bur Bus Practice 24 Rope Ferry Rd Waterford CT 06386

MANUELL, LYNN MARIE, cultural administrator, singer, actress; b. Grand Rapids, Mich., Apr. 17, 1961; d. Richard James and Barbara Ann (Reeves) M. AA, Prairie State Coll., Chicago Heights, Ill., 1983; BA with honors, Columbia Coll., Chgo., 1985; postgrad., Am. Acad. Dramatic Arts, N.Y.C., 1985-86, Wavendon Allmusic Plan, U.K., 1987-89. Singer, actress Ill. Theatre Ctr., Park Forest, Ill., 1975-83; singer Whaler/Madison Towers, N.Y.C., 1986; pub. relations photographer Columbia Coll., Chgo., 1983-84, Connie Zonka and Assocs., Chgo., 1984; mgr. Raymond Annlisa Promotional, N.Y.C., 1985; office coord. Nat. Shakespeare Co., N.Y.C., 1985-86; promotional sales agt. Cliff Steward & Assocs., N.Y.C., 1985; spl. events coord. Cultural Coun. Found., N.Y.C., 1986-89; asst. coord. Minority Arts Mgmt., N.Y.C., 1987; events coord. Soho Booking, N.Y.C., 1987, Community Literacy Rsch. Project, N.Y.C., 1987; singer in N.Y., London and Chgo. Clubs, Spirit of N.Y. Cruise Ship; intern Gatchell and Neufeld. Author: (poetry) Unicorns and Golden Traces, 1981; contbr. articles to profl. jours. Friend, Community Literacy Rsch. Project, N.Y.C., 1986-87; polit. worker NOW, Chgo., 1978-80. Mem. Nat. Orgn. Female Execs., Theatre Devel. Fund, Am. Friends of Royal Shakespeare Co., Dickens Fellowship of N.Y. Home: 110 Post Ave #507 New York NY 10034 Office: 165 W 46th #810 New York NY 10019

MANUTI, ANNABELLE THERESA, advertising agency financial executive; b. Bklyn., Sept. 11, 1928; d. Decio Dan and Anna Michelle (Vanacore) Assorto; m. John Thomas Manuti, Dec. 31, 1958. Student, Hunter Coll., 1950, postgrad. in real estate sch. Continuing Edn., 1980-82. Lic. real estate broker, N.Y. Statis. auditor Am. Fore Ins. Group, N.Y.C., 1950-55; bookkeeper Picard Advt., N.Y.C., 1955-60; supr. dept. acctg. Moquel Williams & Saylor Advt., N.Y.C., 1960-65; comptroller's asst. Frolich Advt., N.Y.C., 1965-70; supr. accounts payable Miller Advt., N.Y.C., 1970-80; v.p. fin. Jaffe Communications, N.Y.C., 1980-90; free-lance, 1990—; real estate sales mgr. Gen. Devel. Corp., 1980-85. Roman Catholic. Home and Office: 65-70 Booth St Rego Park NY 11374

MANYEN, SUSAN MARY GAGER, automotive executive; b. Rochester, N.Y., Feb. 14, 1956; d. D. Jerome and Carol (Brady) Gager; m. Douglas Paul Manyen, Jan. 20, 1979; children: Paul Douglas, 1 daughter. B in Indsl. Adminstrn., Gen. Motors Inst., 1979; MBA, Saginaw (Mich.) Valley State Coll., 1982. Employee benefits rep. Gen. Motors Corp., Saginaw, 1980-83, supr. tech. services Cen. Foundry Div., 1983-86, gen. supr. engring. adminstrv. services, 1986—. Advisor Jr. Achievement, Saginaw, 1982—. Mem. Am. Foundrymen's Soc. (Saginaw Valley chpt. vice chmn. 1985-86, chmn. 1987—). Roman Catholic. Club: Gen. Motors Women's. Home: 4442 Shattuck Rd Saginaw MI 48603

MANZ, BETTY ANN, nurse administrator; b. Paterson, N.J., Nov. 30, 1935; d. James Albert and Elsie (Basse) Brown; diploma Newark Beth Israel Hosp. Sch. Nursing, 1955; BSN, Seton Hall U., 1964; m. Roger A. Johnson, Feb. 1988; children: Laura, Richard, Garry. Staff nurse oper. room Newark Beth Israel Hosp., 1955-56, recovery room head nurse, 1956-57, oper. room head nurse, 1957-58, supr. oper. room, 1958-60; substitute tchr. pub. schs. Harding Twp., 1966-70; charge nurse St. Barnabas Med. Ctr., Livingston, N.J., 1965-70, head nurse emergency room, 1970-72; oper. room supr. St. Clares Hosp., Denville, N.J., 1972-77; asst. dir. for oper. rooms and post anesthesia rooms Newark Beth Israel Med. Ctr., 1977-82; asst. dir. nursing oper. room care program Thomas Jefferson U. Hosp., Phila., 1982-84; asst. dir./assoc. nursing dir. oper. room, anesthesia ICU, ambulatory surgery Univ. Hosp., SUNY-Stony Brook, 1984-87 dir. oper. room/post anestesia care ambulatory surgery Med. Ctr. Del., Wilmington and Christiana, Del., 1987-88; practice mgr. Orthopaedic Surgeons Facility, Wilmington, 1989—; faculty mem. postgrad. course in microsurgy for Am. Coll. Obstetricians and Gynecologists, Newark, 1982; profl. cons. oper. room products, also health cons. Henry E. Wessel Assos., Moraga, Calif.; profl. tech. cons., lectr. Surgicot, Inc., Smithtown, N.Y. Dep. dir. Harding Twp. CD, 1967-75. Recipient Service award Essex County Med. Soc., 1979. Mem. AAMI, Nat. Assn. Orthopaedic Nurses, Assn. Oper. Room Nurses, Am. Soc. Post Anesthesia Nurses, Newark Beth Israel Hosp. Nursing Alumnae Assn., Seton Hall U. Alumnae Assn., Harding Twp. Civic Assn., Am. Field Svc.. Republican. Club: Mt. Kemble Lake Community. Editor operating room sect. SCORE mag. Home: 2620 Lamper Ln Wilmington DE 19808 Office: 2501 Silverside Rd Wilmington DE 19810

MANZANO, J. MIA, air force official; b. Merrill, Wis., Nov. 11, 1952; d. Daniel H. Rusch and LaVine D. (Huehnerfuss) Larson; m. Leo N. Manzano, July 3, 1981 (div. May 1987); children: Daniel P. Manzano, Benjamyn Buchanan. BS in Edn., U. Wis., Eau Claire, 1974; postgrad., U. Wash., 1977-78. Cert. communications disorders tchr., Wis. Instr. English, Inlingua Sprachschule, Fulda, Fed. Republic Germany, 1975-76; instr. Pre-Discharge Edn. Program, Fulda, 1976; speech clinician Cochise County Schs., Bisbee, Ariz., 1976-77; pers. staffing specalist U.S. Office Pers. Mgmt., Seattle, 1979-81; chief spl. exam. unit Dept. Army, Ft. Hood, Tex., 1982-83, pers. staffing specialist, 1983-84; pers. staffing specialist Dept. Army, Ft. Lewis, Wash., 1984-86, Seattle Dist. C.E., 1986-89; personnel officer Air Force Plant Rep.'s Office, Boeing Co., Seattle, 1989—, advisor, cons. fed. women's program and EEO com., 1989-90; coll. rels. dir. Office Personnel Mgmt., Seattle, 1979-80, C.E., Seatle, 1986-89. Del. EEO com. Fed. Exec. Bd., Seattle, 1980, del. handicapped com., 1986-87, organizer handicapped conf., 1987. Mem. NAFE, Fed. Exec. Bd. Pers. Officers Assn. Home: 5129 S 173d Ct Seattle WA 98188 Office: Air Force Plant Rep Office Boeing Co PO Box 3707 M/S 3C-83 MSCF Seattle WA 98124-2207

MANZIEL, DOROTHY NOLAN, oil and gas, real estate company executive; b. Baton Rouge, June 28, 1920; d. Joseph N. and Victoria (Hannie) N.;

m. Bobby Joseph Manziel (dec.); children: Bobby Joseph II, Nolan Edward, N. Paul, Merigale Manziel Pyron, Dorothy Suzanne Manziel Frank, Victoria Lynn Manziel Heath. Student, La. State U., 1936-37. Owner, pres. Manziel Interests, Tyler, Tex., 1937—. Mem. altar soc., past v.p. Cathedral Immaculate Conception, Tyler; past city dir. Am. Lebanese Syrian Associated Charities, St. Jude Hosp., Tyler; bd. dirs. Mother Francis Hosp. Found., Tyler. Recipient Holy Trinity medal of honor, 1960. Mem. Tex. Ind. Producers and Royalty Owners Assn., Ind. Petroleum Assn. Am., AAUW, So. Fedn. Syrian Lebanese Am. Clubs (past bd. dirs., scholarship donor 1958—), Cath. Daus. Am., Cedars of Lebanon Club (past pres.), Tyler Petroleum Club, Willow Brook Country Club, Hollytree Country Club. Hme: 2630 Old Bullard Rd Tyler TX 75701 Office: 110 W 8th St Tyler TX 75701

MAPELLI, STEPHANIE D., wholesale food distribution executive; b. Denver, July 9, 1953; d. Eugene Mario and Velda (King) M.; m. John S. Beuchat (div. July 1976); 1 child, Melissa; m. David Ira Silverman (div. Oct. 1987). BA, U. Mont., 1982. Sales rep. Mapelli Meat Co., Las Vegas, 1977-79; v.p. Palm Springs, Calif., 1983—. Mem. Nat. Assn. Meat Purveyors (bd. dirs.). Democrat. Roman Catholic. Home: 36-066 W Ave de las Montana Cathedral City CA 92234 Office: Mapelli Meat Co 67 625 Highway 111 Cathedral City CA 92234

MAPLE, MARILYN JEAN, educational media coordinator; b. Turtle Creek, Pa., Jan. 16, 1931; d. Harry Chester and Agnes (Dobbie) Kelley; B.A., U. Fla., 1972, M.A., 1975, Ph.D., 1985; 1 dau., Sandra Maple. Journalist various newspapers, including Mountain Eagle, Jasper, Ala., Boise (Idaho) Statesman, Daytona Beach (Fla.) Jour., Lorain (Ohio) Jour.; account exec. Frederides & Co., N.Y.C.; producer hist. films Fla. State Mus., Gainesville, 1967-69; writer, dir., producer med. and sci. films and TV prodns. for six medically related colls. U. Fla., Gainesville, 1969—; pres. Media Modes, Inc., Gainesville. Recipient Blakslee award, 1969, spl. award, 1979, Monsour Lectureship award, 1979. Mem. Health Edn. Media Assn. (dir., awards, 1977, 79), Phi Delta Kappa, Kappa Tau Alpha. Columnist: Health Care Edn. mag.; contbr. Fla. Hist. Quar. Home: 6722 SW 53d Ave Gainesville FL 32608 Office: U Fla Box J-16 Gainesville FL 32610

MAPLE, OPAL LUCILLE, school psychologist; b. Canton, Ill., Nov. 15, 1935; d. Dwight Willard and Eileen Beatrice (Cadwalader) Beaty; m. Gilbert Roy Maple, June 30, 1967 (dec. 1985). BA, Wheaton (Ill.) Coll., 1958; MS, We. Ill. U., 1962. Cert. sch. psychologist, Ill. Tchr. Community Dist. #5, Cuba, Ill., 1958-60, Community Dist. #66, Canton, Ill., 1960-61; asst. dean women Moody Bible Inst., Chgo., 1961-64; sch. psychologist intern Chgo. Pub. Schs., 1964-65; sch. psychologist Peoria (Ill.) pub. schs., 1965-69, Waukegan (Ill.) pub. schs., 1969-81, Knox-Warren Spl. Edn., Galesburg, Ill., 1986—. Co-author pre-sch. test, 1975. Deaconess, treas. Antioch Evang. Free Ch., 1971-81; deaconess, fin. sec. Bethel Bapt. Ch., Galesburg, 1982—. Mem. Cen. Ill. Sch. Psychologists Assn. (pres. 1967-68), Ill. Psychol. Assn. (sec. 1977-79), DAR, Knox County Genealogical Soc., Nat. Assn. Sch. Psychologists, Ill. Sch. Psychologists Assn., Council Exceptional Children, Delta Kappa Gamma. Republican. Baptist.

MAPLES-PACHECO, ELIZABETH MAE, psychotherapist, counselor psychology; b. St. Petersburg, Fla., Nov. 22, 1941; d. Samuel Ernest Jr. and Mamie Belle (France) Maples; m. Henry Kenneth Camacho, June 27, 1959 (div. 1963); children: Michael D., Deborah C., Linda Louise; m. Joseph Felimon Pacheco, July 8, 1972; children: Joseph L., Alicia Maria. Student, U. Albuquerque, 1981-84, Sierra U., 1987-88; human devel. tng., Hypnotherapy Albuquerque, 1988. Field dir. Girl Scouts U.S., Albuquerque, 1984-86; counselor, therapist Westside Counseling Assocs., Albuquerque, 1987—, Counseling & Psychotherapy Inst., Inc., Albuquerque, 1987—; cons. N.Mex. Human Svcs., Albuquerque, Bernalillo and Rio Rancho, 1988—. Pres. AAU N.Mex., 1975-85, chmn. Women's Basketball, 1980-85, nat. men's bd. dirs. AAU, 1981-83. Mem. Am. Assn. Counseling & Devel., Am. Assn. Family Counselors & Mediators, Am. Coun. Hypnosis (cert.), SW Hypnotherapists Examining Bd. Democrat. Office: Westside Counseling Assocs PO Box 1222 Corrales Albuquerque NM 87048

MARANGIELLO, BETTY ANN, educator, travel consultant; b. Bronx, N.Y., May 23, 1942; d. Frank Anthony and Carmela (Miceli) M. BA, CUNY, 1965; postgrad. in edn., L.I. U., 1978-86; computer literacy cert., Dowling Coll., 1988. Cert. permanent tchr., N.Y. Lab. technician N.Y., 1965; elem. tchr. Smithtown (N.Y.) Sch. Dist., 1965-67, Three Village Schs., Stony Brook, N.Y., 1967-70, 72—; social worker Cath. Charities, N.Y.C., 1971-72; travel cons., N.Y. Vol. social worker InterChristian-Neuman Project, Tampico, Mex., 1963; vol. pre-literacy and literacy tchr., counselor; sch. rep. Muscular Dystrophy Assn., 1982, 84, 89; ch. youth counselor, leader, 1973-75; fund raiser Hauppauge Dem. Com., 1982-83; host Coun. Internat. Projects profl. exchange program, 1989—. Bethpage High Sch. scholar, 1960, Dowling Coll. scholar, 1988. Mem. Three Village Tchrs. Assn. (union rep. 1975, 86, 88-89), Alpha Delta Pi. Office: Three Village Schs Nichols Rd Stony Brook NY 11790

MARATTA, GRACE ELVIRA, volunteer; b. Jackson, Ohio, July 22, 1922; d. John William and Mary Ann (Lewis) Matthews; m. James Edward Maratta, Oct. 14, 1957 (div. May 1971). Student, Rio Grande Coll., 1940-41, Columbus Bus. U., 1941-42. Clk.-typist Ohio State Dept. Trans., Columbus, 1942-44; adminstrv. office mgr. Div of Police City of Columbus, 1944-77, ret., 1977; legis. agt. Police and Fire Retirees of Ohio, Columbus, 1978—; Bd. trustees Columbus Police Sub-Relief Fund, 1967—, Adult Life Care Ctr., Reynoldsburg, Ohio, 1990—; lobbyist Police and Fire Retirees of Ohio, Columbus, 1978—. Past pres. Reynoldsburg Womens Civic Club, 1979-81, Reynoldsburg Womens Rep. Club, 1982-84; pres. Reynoldsburg Sr. Citizens Ctr., 1988—. Recipient Disting. Svc. Ohio Gen. Assembly, 1970; named Outstanding Svc. Sr. Citizen Reynoldsburg Jaycees, 1987, Outstanding Eldercare Work, Ohio State Dept. Aging, 1989. Mem. Columbus Police Retirees Assn. (Outstanding Svc. 1981). Republican. Methodist. Office: Police & Fire Retirees 2101 S Hamilton Rd Ste 110 Columbus OH 43232

MARAVEL, PATRICIA, human services administrator; b. Bklyn., Sept. 29, 1949; d. James Peter and Lilliam (Xanthos) M.; children: Jessica Maravel Piccolo, Alex Maravel Piccolo. BA in Sociology, SUNY, Stony Brook, 1971, postgrad., 1972-77; postgrad., Hofstra U., 1977, St. Rose's Coll., 1977. Cert. secondary tchr., N.Y. Tchr. A. Fantis Sch., Bklyn., 1971-72, Commack (N.Y.) Pub. Schs., 1972-78; dir. adminstrn. L.I. Assn. for AIDS Care, Inc., Huntington Station, N.Y., 1986-89; exec. dir. Resurrection House, Inc., Wheatley Heights, N.Y., 1989—; cons. L.I. Assn. for AIDS Care, Huntington Station, 1989, hotline counselor and coord., 1985-86. Support group facilitator Village Parenting Ctr., Huntington, 1981-84, treas.; hotline counselor The Place, Northport, N.Y., 1982; mem. Nassau Suffolk Coalition for the Homeless, 1989—; mem. com. on hunger and homeless Suffolk Community Coun., 1989—; Women and AID subcom. SSuffolk County Dept. Health, 1990—, AIDS Resource Ctr., 1990—. Mem. NOW. Democrat. Home: 18 Frost Ln Greenlawn NY 11740

MARAVICH, MARY LOUISE, realtor; b. Fort Knox, Ky., Jan. 4, 1951; d. John and Bonnie (Balandzic) M. AA in Office Adminstrn., U. Nev., Las Vegas, 1970; BA in Sociology and Psychology, U. So. Calif., 1972; grad. Realtors Inst. Cert. residential specialist. Adminstrv. asst. dept. history U. So. Calif., L.A., 1972-73; asst. pers. supr. Corral Coin Co., Las Vegas, 1973-80; realtor, Americana Group div. Better Homes and Gardens, Las Vegas, 1980-85, Jack Matthews and Co., 1985—. Mem. Nev. Assn. Realtors (cert. realtors inst.), Las Vegas Bd. Realtors, Nat. Assn. Realtors, Women's Council of Realtors, Am. Bus. Women's Assn., NAFE, Million Dollar Club, Pres.'s Club. Office: Jack Matthews & Co 3100 S Valley View Blvd Las Vegas NV 89102

MARAZITA, ELEANOR MARIE HARMON, secondary school teacher; b. Madison County, Ind., Oct. 25, 1933; d. William Houston Harmon and Martha Belle (Savage) Hinds; m. Philip Marazita; children: Mary Louise, Frank, Dominic, Vincent, Elizabeth Faye, Candice Marie, Daniel William. BS in Home Econs., Cen. Mich. U., 1955; MA in Human Ecology, Mich. State U., 1971. Cert. vocat. home econs. tchr., K-Jr. Coll., cert. speech correction tchr. Tchr. adult edn. Mt. Pleasant, Mich., 1956; substitute tchr. North Branch (Mich.) Schs., 1961=64; tchr., coordinator Pied Piper Cooperative Nursery Sch., Lansing, Mich., 1964-69; tchr. Lansing Community Coll., 1971-81, Grand Ledge (Mich.) High Sch., 1969—; del. World Conf. of Teaching Profl., 1986. Vol. St. Lawrence Mental Health Hosp., 1972-73, Listening Ear Crisis Intervention Ctr., 1973-77, Capital City Convalescent Home; vol., chmn. Delta Twp. Libr. Study Com., 1969-73, Jr. League, 1969—; interviewer Youth for Understanding, 1978-83; active Exchange Student Orientation Program, Mich. State U., 1977, Exchange Student Trips, 1979-82; hosted nine exchange students; adv. bd. Mich. League Human Svcs., Eaton County Ext. Svcs., Mich. Women's Assembly; mem. Friends of Waverly Libr. Recipient State Tchr. Multicultural award, 1989. Mem. AAUW, Mich. Edn. Assn. (v.p. women's caucas), NEA, Delta Kappa Gamma, Phi Delta Kappa. Home: 214 Farmstead Lansing MI 48917

MARBACH, LOIS BETTY, political, marketing consultant; b. July 21, 1946; d. Joseph and Helen Ann (Weiner) M. Student, SUNY, New Paltz. Pres. Promotional Strategies, Bayside, N.Y., 1987—. Project coord. newsletters; producer videos Lexington Sch. for the Deaf, Mass Transit St. Theater. Candidate for pres. Queens Borough, N.Y., 1986; campaign mgr. Jerry Goldfeder City Coun. campaign, 1989, Pedro Espada Jr. Congl. campaign, 1988; Queens campaign coord. N.Y.C., Carol Bellamy for Mayor, 1985, David Dinkins for Mayor, 1989; chair Queens Coalition for Polit. Alternatives, Flushing, N.Y.; bd. dirs. N.Y. State, Nat. Abortion Rights Action League, Aaron Weiss Humanitarian Award Fund, Flushing, N.Y.; co-founder Womens Ctr., Flushing, N.Y., 1975. Recipient plaque Aaron Weiss Humanitarian Award Fund, 1986, Korean-Am. Small Bus. Svc. Ctr., 1987, Dems. for New Politics, 1990. Mem. NAFE, NAACP, ACLU, NOW, N.Y. Pub. Interest Rsch. Group, Queens Women's Polit. Caucus (mem. exec. bd., Plaque 1990), Queen's Women's Netowrk (bd. dirs.). Home and Office: 64-64 229th St Bayside NY 11364

MARCANTEL, SILVA COOPER, educational administrator, counselor; b. Portola, Calif., July 16, 1940; d. Clarence Laborn Alton and Vivian (Ratcliff) Cooper; m. Wesley Marcantel, Oct. 19, 1961; children—Dawn, Laura. B.A., McNeese State U., Lake Charles, La., 1963, M.Ed., 1967, Ed.D., 1981. Cert. in elem. edn., secondary social studies, guidance, sch. psychology, child welfare and attendance, adminstrn., supervision and counseling, La. Tchr. Calcasieu Parish Pub. Schs., Lake Charles, 1963-76; asst. dir. Health Counseling Service, Lake Charles, 1976; counselor Calcasieu Parish Pub. Schs., 1976-81, supr. guidance, 1983-85, dir. child welfare and attendance, 1985—; vis. lectr. McNeese State U., 1982. Bd. dirs. La. Epilepsy Assn., 1980-83; mem. scholarship com. McNeese State U., 1975-76. Acad. scholar, 1958; T.H. Harris scholar, 1958; Phi Delta Kappa research grantee. Mem. NEA (nat. conv. del. 1980), Calcasieu Counselors Assn. (pres. 1978-79), La. Assn. Suprs. Child Welfare and Attendance (pres. 1989—), La. Assn. Sch. Execs., Phi Delta Kappa (grantee 1983-84). Democrat. Baptist. Club: Lake Charles Quota.

MARCASIANO, MARY JANE, fashion designer; b. N.J., Sept. 23, 1955. Grad., Parsons Sch. Design, 1978. Designer under own label, 1979—. Recipient Cartier Stargazer award, 1981, Wool Knit award, 1983, DuPont award for most promising designer, 1984, Cutty Sark award for most promising men's wear designer, 1984. Office: Marcasiano Knitwear 138 Spring St New York NY 10012*

MARCELLO, JODY SMOTHERS, educator; b. Tomball, Tex., Nov. 19, 1956; d. Rufus Andrew and June (Davis) Smothers; m. Joseph Anthony Marcello, Aug. 20, 1977; 1 child, Laurinda Anne. BS, Tex. A&M U., 1978, MEd, 1981. Cert. secondary social studies tchr., Alaska, Tex. Admissions clk. Tex. A&M U., College Station, 1979, grad. asst., 1980-81; tchr. social studies St. Joseph's Sch., Bryan, Tex., 1979-80; rsch. assoc. IIC Western-Western Inst., Denver, 1981-82; program asst. Wash. State U., Pullman, 1982-86, coord. spl. programs Coll. Engring. and Architecture, 1986; instr., coord. Islands Coll., Sitka, Alaska, 1987; tchr. social studies Sitka Sch. Dist., 1987—, equity coord., 1989—; geography bee coord. Alaska Geog. Alliance, 1988—; participant Summer Geography Inst., Nat. Geog. Soc., Washington, 1989. Chmn. Presdl. Commn. on Status Women, Pullman, 1985-86; Nat. Coalition for Sex Equity in Edn. and Alaska Gender Equity Tng. Cadre. Alaska Dept. Edn. grantee, 1988, 89. Mem. Nat. Coun. Social Studies (Outstanding Secondary Tchr. Yr. 1990), Nat. Coun. Geographic Edn., Nat. Women's History Project, NEA (sec. Sitka 1988—), Alaska Coun. Social Studies (regional rep. 1989, sec. 1990—, Outstanding Secondary Tchr. of Yr. 1990), Sitka Hist. Soc., AAUW (sec. Sitka 1987-88), LWV (pres. Sitka 1987—, sec. Alaska chpt. 1987-90, v.p. 1990—, editor Voter 1988-89, Hazel Johnson award 1988), Sitka Women's Club, Phi Delta Kappa. Roman Catholic. Office: Blatchley Mid Sch 601 Halibut Point Rd Sitka AK 99835

MARCELLO, LINDA SUSAN, mental health therapist; b. Indpls., May 17, 1949; d. Kenneth Robert and Virginia Francis (Best) Nelson; m. Richard Peter Marcello, Aug. 12, 1972 (div. 1982); 1 child, Megan Elisabeth. BS, Millersville (Pa.) U., 1971; MEd, U. Ariz., 1982; postgrad., Temple U., 1975, U. Del., 1973-74. Tchr. English William Penn Sch. Dist., Yeadon, Pa., 1971-77; pvt. practice in clin. therapy Tucson, 1981-84; clin. therapist Camelback Hosp., Phoenix, 1984-87; patient rep. Camelback Hosp., Scottsdale, Ariz., 1987—; mem. community rels., edn. mktg. staff, 1989; pvt. practice in psychotherapy Phoenix, 1987—; host children's radio talk show Sta. KSUN, Phoenix, 1986. Author: (booklet): Back to School Survival Kit, 1988. Mem. Ariz. Counselors Assn. Democrat. Methodist. Office: Scottsdale Camelback Hosp 7575 E Earll Dr Scottsdale AZ 85251

MARCH, BERYL ELIZABETH, animal scientist, educator; b. Port Hammond, B.C., Can., Aug. 30, 1920; d. James Roy and Sarah Catherine (Wilson) Warrack; m. John Algot March, Aug. 31, 1946; 1 dau., Laurel Allison. B.A., U. B.C., Vancouver, 1942, M.S.A., 1962; D.Sc., U. B.C., 1988. Mem. indsl. research staff Can. Fishing Co. Ltd., 1942-47; mem. research staff, faculty U. B.C., 1947—, prof. poultry sci., 1970—. Recipient Poultry Sci. Assn.-Am. Feed Mfrs. award, 1969, Queen's Jubilee medal, 1977, Earle Willard McHenry award Can. Soc. Nutritional Sci., 1986. Fellow Agrl. Inst. Can., Royal Soc. Can., Poultry Sci. Assn.; mem. Profl. Agrologists, Agr. Inst. Can., Can. Soc. Nutritional Sci., AAAS, Poultry Sci. Assn., World's Poultry Sci. Assn., Am. Soc. Exptl. Biology and Medicine, Am. Inst. Nutrition, Can. Soc. Animal Sci., Aquaculture Assn. Can. Office: Dept Animal Sci U BC, Vancouver, BC Canada V6T 2A2

MARCH, JACQUELINE FRONT, chemist; b. Wheeling, W.Va. BS, Case Western Res. U., MA, 1939; Wyeth fellow med. rsch. U. Chgo.; postgrad. U. Pitts., Ohio State U., Wright State U.; m. A. W. March (dec.); children: Wayne Front, Gail Ann March Cohen. Clin. chemist, Mt. Sinai Hosp., Cleve.; med. rsch. chemist U. Chgo.; rsch. analyst Koppers Co., also info. scientist Union Carbide Corp., Mellon Inst., Pitts.; propr. March Med. Rsch. Lab., etiology of diabetes, Dayton, Ohio; guest scientist Kettering Found., Yellow Springs, Ohio; Dayton Found. fellow Miami Valley Hosp. Rsch. Inst.; mem. chemistry faculty U. Dayton, info. scientist Rsch. Inst. U. Dayton; prin. investigator Air Force Wright Aero. Labs., Wright-Patterson AFB Tech. Info. Ctr.; chem. info. specialist Standards Devel. & Tech. Transfer, Nat. Inst. Occupational Safety and Health HHS, Cin., 1979—; propr. JFM Cons., 1980—; designer info. systems, speaker in field. Recipient Recognition cert. U. Dayton, 1980. Mem. Am. Soc. Info. Sci. (treas. South Ohio chpt. 1973-75, 50 yr. mem. cert. 1988), Am. Chem. Soc. (50 yr. mem., pres. Dayton 1977), Dayton Engring. Soc. (hon.), Soc. Advancement Materials & Process Engring. (pres. Midwest chpt. 1977-78), Affiliated Tech. Socs. (Outstanding Scientist and Engr. award 1978), Am. Congress Govtl. Indsl. Hygienists (rev. com. toxic chems. 1983—, Dept. of Labor, Mine Safety & Health Adminstrn. 1989—), AAUP (exec. bd.), Sigma Xi (treas. Dayton 1976-79, Conrad P. Straub lectr. 1982, chmn. nominating com. 1989). Contbr. articles to profl. publs. Home: 154 Stillmeadow Dr Cincinnati OH 45245-2812 Office: 4676 Columbia Pkwy Cincinnati OH 45226

MARCHAK, MAUREEN PATRICIA, anthropology and sociology educator; b. Lethbridge, Alta., Can., June 22, 1936; d. Adrian Ebenezer and Wilhelmina Rankin (Hamilton) Russell; m. William Marchak, Dec. 31, 1956; children: Geordon Eric, Lauren Craig. BA, U. B.C., Vancouver, Can., 1958, PhD, 1970. Asst. prof. U. B.C., Vancouver, 1972-75, assoc. prof., 1975-80, prof., 1980—, head dept. anthropology, 1987-90, dean faculty arts, 1990—. Author: Ideological Perspectives on Canada, 1975, 2d edit., 1981, 3d edit., 1988, In Whose Interests, 1979, Green Gold 1983 (John Porter award 1985); author, co-editor: Uncommon Property, 1987; mem. editorial bd. Can. Rev. Sociology and Anthropology, Montreal, Que., 1971-74, Studies in Polit. Economy, Ottawa, Ont., Can., 1980-87, Current Sociology, London, 1980-86, Can. Jour. Sociology, 1986-90, B.C. Studies, 1988-90. Fellow Royal Soc. Can.; mem. Can. Sociology and Anthropology Assn. (pres. 1979-80, other offices), Internat. Sociol. Assn., Can. Polit. Sci. Assn., Assn. for Can. Studies. Mem. New Dem. Party (Can.). Home: 4455 W 1st Ave, Vancouver, BC Canada V6R 4H9 Office: U BC Faculty Arts Office of Dean, 1866 Main Mall, Vancouver, BC Canada V6T 1W5

MARCHAND, NANCY, actress; b. Buffalo, June 19, 1928; d. Raymond L. and Marjorie F. M.; m. Paul Sparer, July 7, 1951; children: David, Kathryn, Rachel. BFA, Carnegie Inst. Tech., 1949. Vol. actress Am. Theater Wing studio, N.Y.C.; TV appearances include A Touch of the Poet; series regular on TV show Lou Grant, 1977-82; theater engagements at Circle in the Sq., N.Y.C., Los Angeles Music Center, Lincoln Center, N.Y.C., Am. Shakespeare Festival, Goodman Theater, Chgo., Ahmanson Theatre, Los Angeles; appeared on Broadway in Mornings at Seven, 1988, 40 Carats, Octette Bridge Club; Off Broadway plays: Children, Sister Mary Ignatius, Cocktail Hour, The Balcony; films include Tell Me That You Love Me Junie Moon, Some Kind of Miracle, Sparkling Cyanide, North and South Book II, The Golden Moment--An Olympic Love Story, From the Hip, 1987, Naked Gun. Recipient Obie award, 1960; Emmy awards, 1978, 80, 81, 82. Office: William Morris Agy care Katie Rothacker 1350 Ave of the Americas New York NY 10019

MARCHETTI, KIMBERLY, intelligence research specialist; b. Pensacola, Fla., May 6, 1958; d. Donald Francis Marchetti and Bobby Jean (Walden) Haynes. BA in Chemistry, Troy State U., 1980; postgrad., Cen. Mich. U., 1988—. Intelligence rsch. analyst Naval Tech. Intelligence Ctr., Washington, 1987-88, head Space and Ocean Surveillance div., 1988—. Capt. USAF, 1980-87.

MARCHI, ROSEMARIE, rehabilitation counselor; b. Somerville, Mass., July 31, 1927; d. Nazzareno and Rose (Cimonetti) Tarabelli; m. Basil Vincent Marchi, Nov. 21, 1948; 1 child, Linda. Assoc. Sci. summa cum laude, Northeastern U., 1980; BS summa cum laude, Boston U., 1982; MS summa cum laude, 1985. Dir. elder-hire employment svcs. Cambridge (Mass.) Econ. Opportunity Com., 1979-82; vocat. rehab. counselor, intern McLean Hosp., Waltham, Mass., 1983, Mass. Rehab. Commn., Cambridge, 1984; vocat. rehab. counselor Mass. Rehab. Commn., Jamaica Plain, 1985-87, Gen. Rehab. Svcs., Inc., Waltham, 1987-89; case mgr. Morgan Meml. Goodwill Industries, Inc., Beverly, Mass., 1984-85; dir. vocat. cons. Tara Rehab, Arlington, Mass., 1989—. Mem. Nat. Assn. Rehab. Profls. in Pvt. Sector, Pro-Mass. Home: 45 Fairview Ave Arlington MA 02174 Office: Tara Rehab 45 Fairview Ave Arlington MA 02174

MARCHI, TERESA, editor, journalist; b. Boise, Idaho, Mar. 14, 1962; d. John Thomas and Julia (Walsh) Harding; m. Maximillion Marchi, Jan. 20, 1987 (dec. Mar., 1987); 1 child, Samuel Ackerson. BA in English, U. Notre Dame, 1986; MA in English Lang. and Lit., U. Chgo., 1988. Copyeditor U. Chgo. Mag., 1987-89; reporter Chgo. Tribune, 1989; corr., editor, columnist Boise Mountain News, 1990—. Author: Mistress of Arts, 1987; contbr. editor U. Chgo. Style Manual, 1989; contbr. articles to popular mags. Vol. Boise Youth Swim League, 1989—; active Young Widowed Mothers Found., Boise, 1989—. Recipient Golden Lute Poetry award Sand Lake Poetry Alliance, Phelps, Wis., 1986. Mem. DAR, AAUW, Nat. Assn. Widowed Mothers, U. Notre Dame Alumni Assn., Dames of Malta. Libertarian. Greek Orthodox. Home: 4235 N Ottawa #16 Oakland CA 94701 Office: Werik Office Bldg 936 Wisconsin St San Francisco CA 94107

MARCIL, DENISE MARY, literary agent; b. Troy, N.Y.; d. George B. and Dorothy H. (Connell) M. BA, Skidmore Coll., 1974. Editorial asst. Avon Books, N.Y.C., 1974-76; asst. editor Simon & Schuster, N.Y.C., 1976; pres. Denise Marcil Literary Agy., N.Y.C., 1977—. Trustee Skidmore Coll., Saratoga Springs, N.Y., 1985-89. Named to Top 10 Outstanding Young Working Women, Glamour Mag., N.Y.C., 1985; recipient Outstanding Alumni Svc. award, Skidmore Coll., 1989. Mem. Ind. Literary Agts. Assn. (council mem. 1977—, bd. dirs. 1988—), Women in Pub., Internat. Woman's Writing Guild (bd. dirs. 1983, Outstanding Svc. award 1984). Office: 685 West End Ave New York NY 10025

MARCINEK, JOYCE E., business executive; b. Nevada, Ohio, July 28, 1930; d. W. Frank and Bernice Marie McCallister; student Newark Coll. Engring., 1952-53, Sinclair Community Coll., 1968-69. With sales, service, public relations depts. Standard Oil Co., Canton and Akron, Ohio, 1957-63; with TRW Supermet, Dayton, Ohio, 1966-70, sales engr., 1972-75; acct. Texaco Inc., Atlanta, 1970-72; asst. to pres. Hot Sam div. Gen. Host, Troy, Mich., 1975-76; accounts rep. Kelly Services, Lexington, Ky., 1976-77, br. mgr., 1977-80; v.p. Career Mgmt., Inc., Lexington, 1980-82; dir. personnel EBS Inc., subs. Traveler's Ins. Co., Lexington, 1982-83; pres. Kelleher Wholesale Div., and Joymar Corp., Orlando, Fla., 1983-86, gen. mgr. Joymar Corp. Temp. Resources, Inc., Southfield, Mich., 1986-87, cons., personnel, 1987—. Active Urban League, Todd Trease Teddy Bear Fund; bd. dirs. Jr. Achievement, program chmn., 1981-82, also contest judge; sponsor, coordinator secretarial scis. Explorer troop Bluegrass council Boy Scouts Am.; team capt. United Way, 1978-81; mem. Better Bus. Bur. Recipient Distributive Edn. award Lexington Edn.-Work Council, 1978; adv. bd. Ken. Jr. Coll., 1982-83. Mem. Sales Mktg. Execs. (dir., coordinator seminar 1979), Adminstrv. Mgmt. Assn. (dir.), Lexington C. of C. (dir., mem. pres.'s council). Club: Zonta (regional dir. public relations). Home and Office: 46675 N Hills Dr Apt 53F Northville MI 48167

MARCINEK, MARGARET ANN, nursing educator; b. Uniontown, Pa., Sept. 29, 1948; d. Joseph Hugh and Evelyn (Bailey) Boyle; m. Bernard Francis Marcinek, Aug. 11, 1973; 1 dau., Cara Ann. R.N., Uniontown Hosp., 1969; B.S. in Nursing, Pa. State U., 1970; M.S., U. Md., 1973; Ed.D., W.Va. U., 1983. Staff nurse Presbyn. U., Pitts., 1970-71; instr. nursing W.Va. U., Morgantown, 1973-77, asst. prof., 1977-80, assoc. prof., 1980-83; assoc. prof. California U. of Pa., 1983-87, prof., 1987—, dept. chmn., 1985—. Contbg. author: Critical Care Nursing. Contbr. articles to profl. jours. Mem. adv. coun. Valley Home Health, Inc. Mem. Am. Nurses Assn., Am. Assn. Critical Care Nurses, Nat. League for Nurses, Sigma Theta Tau, Phi Kappa Phi. Office: California U of Pa Dept Nursing California PA 15419

MARCOPULOS, BERNICE ANNE, neuropsychologist; b. Washington, May 8, 1958; d. Donald Paul and Gizela Bernice (Domin) M. BA with high honors, U. Fla., 1980; MA, U. Victoria (B.C., Can.), 1982, PhD, 1986. Predoctoral intern Phila. Geriatric Ctr., Phila., 1985-86; rsch. health scientist VA Med. Ctr., Palo Alto, Calif., 1986-88; lectr. U. Md. European div., Heidelberg, West Germany, 1988-89; staff psychologist Western State Hosp., Staunton, Va., 1989—; asst. prof. behavioral medicine and psychiatry U. Va., Charlottesville, 1990—. U. Victoria grad. fellow, 1980-85. Mem. Internat. Neuropsychol. Soc., Am Psychol. Assn., Gerontol. Soc. Am., Phi Beta Kappa, Phi Theta Kappa, Golden Key. Democrat. Roman Catholic. Home: 120-4 Georgetown Rd Charlottesville VA 22901 Office: Western State Hosp PO Box 2500 Staunton VA 24401-1405

MARCOUX, MARIE CELESTE, lawyer; b. Hazleton, Pa., July 16, 1951; d. William Nicholas and Margaret Agnes (Lynch) M. BA in Journalism, Pa. State U., 1972, BA in Psychology, 1972; JD, Franklin Pierce Law Ctr., 1980; Diploma in Pub./Pvt. Internat. Law, InterAm. Judicial Com., Rio de Janeiro, 1982; cert. pub. and pvt. internat. law, Hague Acad. of Internat. Law, The Netherlands, 1984. Bar: D.C. 1981, Md. 1987. Conf. dir. Franklin Pierce Law Ctr., Concord, N.H., 1979-80; reporter, editor AP, Concord, N.H., 1978; assoc. Hanson, O'Brien, Birney and Butler, Washington, 1980-82; of counsel Robert M. Foley, Washington, 1986; proprietor Law Offices of Marie C. Marcoux, Washington, 1983—; of counsel Law Office of Donald L. Herskovitz, Washington, 1989-90; assoc. Law Offices of Philip J. Hare, Washington, 1988-90, of counsel, 1990—; legal counsel Borromeo Housing, Inc., Arlington, Va., 1988—; chief indexer Index to Recent N.H. Cases, Manchester, 1978-79. Editor, co-author conf. proceedings in internat. product liability law. Mem. DuPont Circle Citizens Assn., Washington, 1988—; vol. Peace Corps, Colombia, 1973, Peru, 1974, Tunisia, 1975. Recipient fellowship Inter-Orgn. of Am. States, Rio De Janeiro, 1982; named to Outstanding Young Women of Am., 1982. Mem. Am. Immigration Lawyers Assn., Inter-Am. Bar Assn., Womens Bar Assn., D.C. Bar

Assn., Md. State Bar Assn. Roman Catholic. Office: 1734 Seaton Place NW Washington DC 20009-2626

MARCUS, LEAH, writer; b. Chgo., Feb. 22, 1936; d. Lou and Betty (Bernstein) Nathanson;, m. Philip Alan Marcus, Jan. 22, 1961; children: Jonathan, Jessica, Sarah. BS, U. Wis., 1957. Assoc. editor Opportunity Pub. Co., Chgo., 1957-63; columnist Elmhurst (Ill.) Press, 1964-65, Pioneer Press, Oak Park, Ill., 1978-79; writer River Forest, Ill., 1980—. Mem. Oak Park and River Forest High Sch. Bd. Edn., 1979-85, pres., 1984-85; trustee West Suburban Edn. Svc. Ctr., River Grove, Ill., 1985-88, speaker, 1987; speaker Conn. Assn. for Supervision and Curriculum Devel., 1984; bd. dirs. Chgo. Regional Anti-Defamation League, 1984—, Community Chest of Oak Park and River Forest, 1985-90; speaker, panelist Chgo. Bd. Jewish Edn., 1987-89. Mem. Ill. Assn. Sch. Bds. (workshop leader 1980—, chair West Cook County chpt. 1980-85).

MARCUS, NANCY HELEN, oceangraphy educator; b. N.Y.C., May 17, 1950; d. Harold Theodore and Betty (Levy) M. BS, Goucher Coll., 1972; MPhil., Yale U., 1975, PhD, 1976. Postdoctoral scholar Wood Hole (Mass.) Oceanographic Inst., 1976-77, postdoctoral investigator, 1977-78, asst. scientist, 1978-82, assoc. scientist, 1982-87; assoc. prof. oceanography Fla. State U., Tallahassee, 1987—, dir. Marine Lab., 1989—; panel mem. biol. oceanography NSF, 1988—. Contbr. articles to sci. jours. Fellow AAAS (coun. del, 1986—); mem. Assn. Women in Sci. (pres. New Eng. chpt. 1985), Am. Soc. Zoologists (sec. div. ecology 1985-87), Am. Soc. Limnology and Oceanography. Office: Florida State U Dept Oceanography Tallahassee FL 32306

MARCY, ELONA G., dentist; b. Albertson, N.Y., July 3, 1941; d. Anthony Robert and Ellen (Barankovich) Marsicovetere. BA, U. Pitts., 1963; DDS, Balt. Coll. Dental Surgery, 1967. Dental intern The Wilmington (Del.) Med. Ctr., 1967-68; asst. dental surgeon The Johns Hopkins Hosp., Balt., 1968-71; asst. clin. dental dir. Ga. Retardation Ctr., Atlanta, 1971—; part-time pvt. practice Associatship, Atlanta, 1976—; clin. assoc. prof. dept oral medicine, Emory Sch. Dentistry, Atlanta, 1972-88; hon. faculty Med. Coll. Ga., Augusta, 1975—. Author: Clinical Delineation of Birth Defects Conference, 1971. Lt. col. (chief dental svcs.) Ga. Air NG, 1981—. Fellow No. Dist. Dental Soc.; mem. Acad. Air N.G. Dentists (sec. 1985-87, v.p. 1987-89, pres. 1989-91), Ga. Dental Assn. (alt. del. 1979-81), Am. Dental Assn., N.G. Assn. US, N.G. Assn. Ga. Roman Catholic. Home: 1587 Dogwood Terr Marietta GA 30066 Office: Ga Retardation Ctr 4770 N Peachtree Rd Atlanta GA 30338

MARCZYNSKI, KAREN KATHRYN, health care administrator; b. Ponca City, Okla., Feb. 26, 1943. BS, U. So. Colo., 1979; PhD, Union Inst., Cin. Dir. Sch. Vocat. Nursing Hale Ctr., 1966; pub. health nurse community health dept. County of Wichita-Sedgewick, Kans., 1966-68; with pediatric ambulatory services dept. U. Ark. Med. Ctr., Little Rock, 1968-69; pub. health nurse El Paso County Health Dept. of Colo. Springs, 1971-73, community nurse coord., 1973-78, program dir. vis. nurse assn., 1979-80; dir. profl. services Vis. Nurse Assn. Colo. Springs, 1980-83; exec. dir. Community Health Ctr. Colo. Springs, 1983—; cons. Region VIII Clin. Consultation Network. Mem. Med. Group Mgmt. Assn., Nat. Assn. Community Health Ctr. (edn. com.), Nat. Primary Care Assn. Bd., Am. Pub. Health Assn., Colo. Community Health Network (legis. award 1986, v.p., sec.), Colo. Pub. Health Assn. (v.p.), Colo. League Nursing (pres.), Future Soc. Office: Community Health Ctrs Inc 2828 International Circle Colorado Springs CO 80910

MARDIE See MAC KIMM, MARGARET PONTIUS

MARDIS, LINDA KEISER, music educator, consultant, author; b. New Haven, Jan. 9, 1937; d. Donald Eskil and Elizabeth Marie (Horwath) Hallsten; m. Gordon Delbert Craig, June 29, 1957 (dec. Jan. 1963); m. Harry Robert Keiser, June 11, 1964 (div.); children: Harry Rudolph, Robert Hungerford; m. Herbert Harold Mardis, Dec. 29, 1990. BA, Mount Holyoke Coll., 1957; MA, Yale U., 1958. Chmn. Dept. Foreign Langs. Walter Johnson High Sch., Bethesda, Md., 1960-65; music dir. Geneva United Presbyn. Ch., Rockville, Md., 1966-79; assoc. dir. ICM Tng. Seminars, Balt., 1979-85; Reiki master Archedigm, Inc., Kensington, Md., 1982—, pres., 1985—; founder, dir. The Archedigm Collection, 1990—; workshop, retreat leader, 1959—; bd. dirs. Well-Springs Found., Madison, Wis., 1980-88; cons. Lind Inst., San Francisco, 1988—. Author: Conscious Listening, 1986, Light Search, 1987, Teaching Guided Imagery & Music, 1989, (taped music series) Creativity I, II and III: Grieving, Expanded Awareness, Changing Patterns, 1984-88; contbr. articles to profl. publs. Deacon Christ Congregational Ch, Silver Spring, Md., 1981-84. Fellow Inst. Music and Imagery (bd. dirs. 1981-88, assoc. exec. dir. 1986-89); mem. Am. Assn. for Counseling and Devel., Assn Music and Imagery, The Reiki Alliance, Assn. Transpersonal Psychology, Internat. Arts Medicine Assn., Internat. Soc. for Study of Subtle Energies and Energy Medicine, Mt. Holyoke Coll. Alumnae Assn. (bd. dirs. 1978-83). Republican. Home: 17247 Sandy Knoll Dr Olney MD 20832 Office: Archedigm Inc PO Box 557 Garrett Park MD 20896

MARGED, JUDITH MICHELE, educator; b. Phila., Nov. 27, 1954; d. Bernard A. and Norma Marged. Student, Drexel U., 1972-73; AA in Biology, Broward Community Coll., Ft. Lauderdale, Fla., 1977; BA in Exceptional Edn., Fla. Atlantic U., 1980, BA in Biology, 1977, MEd in Counseling, 1984; postgrad. in early and mid. childhood, Nova U. Cert. tchr., Fla. Tchr. Coral Springs (Fla.) Mid. Sch., 1979-80, Am. Acad., Wilton Manors, Fla., 1980-83, Ramblewood Mid. Sch., Coral Springs, 1984—. Mem. Nat. Sci. Tchrs. Assn., Am. Sch. Counselor Assn., Am. Assn. for Counseling and Devel., Assn. for Supervision and Curriculum Devel., Fla. Assn. Sci. Tchrs., Fla. Assn. for Counseling and Devel. Democrat. Jewish. Home: 9107 NW 83d St Tamarac FL 33321 Office: Ramblewood Mid Sch 8505 W Atlantic Blvd Coral Springs FL 33071

MARGIOTTA, MARY-LOU ANN, programmer analyst; b. Waterbury, Conn., June 14, 1956; d. Rocco Donato and Louise Antoinette (Carosella) M. AS in Gen. Edn., Mattatuck Community Coll., Waterbury, 1982; BS in Bus. Mgmt., Post Coll., 1983; MS in Computer Sci., Rensselaer Polytech. Inst., 1989. Programmer analyst Travelers Ins. Co., Hartford, Conn., 1985-87; sr. programmer analyst Conn. Bank and Trust Co., East Hartford, Conn., 1987-88; programmer analyst The Torrrington Co., Torrington, Conn., 1990—; cons. Computer Assistance, Inc., Waterbury, 1983-84. Mem. social action com. St. Helena's Parish, West Hartford, Conn., 1988—; advisor Jr. Achievement, Waterbury, 1981-83; tutor Traveler's Ins. Co. Tutorial Program, West Hartford, 1986-87; trainer CPR, ARC, Hartford, 1986-87. Clayborn Pell grantee Post Coll., 1982-83, State of Conn. grantee, 1982-83; recipient Citation, Jr. Achievement, 1982. mem. IEEE, Assn. for Systems Mgmt., Am. Mktg. Assn., Women in Am. Bus., Tau Alpha Beta Gamma. Roman Catholic. Home: 210E Brittany Farms Rd New Britain CT 06053

MARGLY, VIOLET R., corporation lawyer; b. Chgo., Oct. 8, 1931; d. Steven and Katherine (Horvath) M. BA, U. Wis., Madison, 1953; JD, John Marshall Law Sch., 1977. Bar: Ill. 1977, U.S. Dist. Ct. (no. dist.) Ill. 1977. Corp. sec. Imperial Eastman, Niles, Ill., 1953-78; atty. sole practice, Wilmette, Ill., 1978-80; sr. v.p., gen. counsel Callaghan & Co., Deerfield, Ill., 1980—. Dir. TMA of Lake Cook Corridor, Deerfield, 1988—, Women in Mgmt., Skokie, Ill., 1978-80. Mem. Ill. State Bar Assn., Chgo. Bar Assn. Office: Callaghan & Co 155 Pfingston Deerfield IL 60015

MARGOLIS, ESTHER LUTERMAN, court administrator; b. Pitts., Jan. 12, 1939; d. Nathan and Belle (Fogel) Luterman; B.S., Ariz. State U., 1976, M.S., 1978; m. Herbert Marvin Margolis, Apr. 15, 1962; children: Ruth Lys, Judith Lyn. Statistician, court planners office Ariz. Supreme Ct., 1976-77; planner Ariz. Dept. Corrections, 1979; adminstrv. asst. planning and research bur. Phoenix Police Dept., 1979-82, police research analyst, 1982-83; ct. mgmt. analyst Calif. Jud. Council, Adminstrv. Office of Cts., San Francisco, 1983-84; asst. ct. adminstr., jury commr. Contra Costa County Superior Ct., 1984-89; ct. adminstr. El Dorado County Superior and Mcpl. Cts., Placerville, Calif., 1989—; instr. Phoenix Community Coll., 1980-82; presenter paper ann. meeting Acad. Criminal Justice Scis., Phila., 1981. Mem. textbook selection com. Roosevelt Sch. Dist., Phoenix, 1975; chmn. bd. YMCA, South Mountain br., 1977-81; bd. mgrs. Phoenix and Valley of the Sun YMCA, 1978-81; pres. bd. dirs. Do it Now Found., 1978-80; bd. dirs. Boys' Clubs Phoenix, 1982-83; fin. officer Pinole Ridge Homeowners Assn., 1986-87, pres., 1987-89. Mem. Am. Soc. Public Adminstrn. (program com., panel coordinator regional conf. 1983; panel discussant ann. meeting N.Y.C. 1983), Am. Soc. Criminology, Nat. Council Crime and Delinquency, Nat. Assn. Women in Criminal Justice, Profl. Women for Kennedy. Editor ann. report Phoenix Police Dept., 1979-82. Home: 3266 Cimmarron Rd #1 Cameron Park CA 95682 Office: El Dorado County Superior and Mcpl Cts 495 Main St Placerville CA 95667

MARGOLIS, GWEN LIEDMAN, state senator, developer; b. Phila., Oct. 4, 1934; d. Joseph and Rose Liedman; children: Edward, Ira, Karen, Robin. Student Temple U., 1951-54; AA (hon.), Miami Dade U., 1983. Owner, broker Gwen Margolis Real Estate, North Miami Beach, 1965— ; mem. Fla. Ho. of Reps., Tallahassee, 1974-80; mem. Fla. Senate, 1980—. Bd. dirs. Anti-Defamation League of B'nai Brith. Recipient Outstanding Woman in Politics award Bus. and Profl. Women's Assn.; Woman of Yr. award North Miami Beach C. of C.; awards Women in Communication, Fla. Women's Polit. Caucus, Profl. Firefighters of Fla.; Legis. Friend of Arts award Gov.'s Arts Com., 1982; Spirit of Life Humanitarian award City of Hope, 1974, 79, established Margolis Cancer Rsch. fellowship. Mem. North Miami C. of C. (dir.). Office: Fla State Senate Tallahassee FL 32301 also: 13899 Biscayne Blvd North Miami Beach FL 33181

MARGOLIS, TINA LOUISE, advertising executive; b. Bklyn.; d. Sidney and Edith Margolis; m. Arthur Rones, 1979; 1 child, Julie Lauren. BA, NYU, 1973, MA, 1981, PhD, 1990. Freelance writer, editor, researcher N.Y.C., 1973—; advt. mgr. The Drama Rev., Cambridge, Mass., 1977-82, U.S. Inst. Theatre Tech., N.Y.C., 1982-90; pres. Tina Margolis & Assocs., N.Y.C., 1990—; ad sales rep. theatre and film industries. Contbr. articles to profl. jours. NYU Drama Dept. grad. fellow, 1977-81. Mem. League Historic Am. Theatres, Am. Soc. Theatre Rsch., Theatre Hist. Soc. Office: Tina Margolis and Assocs 445 Broadway Ste 3J Hastings-on-Hudson NY 10706

MARGON, MARILYN SIMON, managed care administrator; b. Bklyn., June 5, 1947; d. Albert and Gertrude (Rosenthal) Simon; m. Arthur Margon, Mar. 23, 1969; children: Sarah, Andrew. BA, Middlebury Coll., 1968; MA, Roosevelt U., 1972. Instr. med. edn. So. Ill. U. Sch. Medicine, Springfield, Ill., 1971-73; coord. ednl. devel. Montefiore Hosp., Bronx, N.Y., 1973-77; mgr. pediatric protocol project Fund for City of N.Y., 1977-78; spl. asst. Health and Hosps. Corp., N.Y.C., 1978-80; assoc. dir. planning dept. Health Sci. Ctr., Bklyn., 1980-86; v.p. U.S. Healthcare, Lake Success, N.Y., 1987—. Bd. dirs. Park Slope Neighborhood Family Ctr., Bklyn., 1986-88. Nat. Def. Edn. fellow, 1971. Office: US Healthcare 1981 Marcus Ave Lake Success NY 11042

MARGOSIAN, LUCILLE K. MANOUGIAN (MRS. ERVIN M. MARGOSIAN), artist, educator; b. Highland Park, Mich.; d. George Krikor and Vera Varsenig (Jernukian) Manougian; B.F.A., Wayne State U., 1957, M.A., 1958; postgrad. Calif. State U., Fresno, 1959-60, U. Calif. at Berkeley, 1960-61; m. Ervin M. Margosian, Oct. 28, 1960; children—Rebecca L., Rachel L. One-man show at Jackson's Gallery, Berkeley, Calif., 1961; exhibited in group shows at Detroit Art Inst., 1958, Oakland (Calif.) Art Museum, 1961, Wayne State U. Community Arts Center, Detroit, 1965, San Francisco Ann. Art Festivals, 1967, 68, 69, Jack London Square Arts Festival, Oakland, 1969, 70, Judah L. Magnes Meml. Mus., Berkeley, 1970, Kaiser Center Gallery, Oakland, 1970, Oakland Mus. Changing Gallery, 1969, Olive Hyde Art Center, Fremont, 1971, 73, Richmond (Calif.) Art Center, 1972, Villa Montalvo Galleries at Phelan Estate, Saratoga, Calif., 1976, others; faculty Peralta Community Colls., Laney campus, Oakland, 1967—, prof. art, 1970—, chmn. dept., 1982-84, 89—. Charter mem. univ. art mus. council U. Calif. at Berkeley, 1965—. Recipient Certificate of Distinguished Achievement, Am. Legion, 1950; Best of Show 1st prize 5th Ann. Textile Exhbn., Fremont, Calif., 1973; Merit award City of Fremont, 1973, Zellerbach Bldg. Gallery, San Francisco, 1975. Mem. Calif. Art Edn. Assn., Oakland Museum Assn., Richmond Art Center, Women of Wayne, Wayne State U. Alumni Assn., East Bay Watercolor Soc., Internat. Platform Assn., Am. Fedn. Tchrs., Peralta Fedn. Tchrs. Office: Laney Coll Art Dept 900 Fallon St Oakland CA 94607

MARGOWSKI, MARILYN JOYCE, bank executive; b. Denver, Colo., Nov. 10, 1949; d. James C. and Lois M. (Roach) Metz; m. Jack W. Calabrese, Apr. 15, 1977 (div. 1981); m. Frank C. Margowski, Oct. 13, 1986. Student, Colo. State U., 1968-72; diploma, Colo. Grad. Sch. Banking, 1983. With First Interstate Bank Denver, 1972-83; v.p., mgr. United Banks Colo., Denver, 1983-88; v.p., area mgr. First Interstate Bank Oreg., Portland, 1988-89; v.p., dist. mgr. 5 brs. lst Interstate Bank Wash., Seattle, 1989—. Bd. dirs., Met. Child Dental Care Assn., 1985-87. Mem.Nat. Assn. Bank Women (state pres. Colo. 1986-87), Cherry Creek Commerce Assn. Republican. Office: lst Interstate Bank Wash 1763 4th Ave S Seattle WA 98134

MARGULIS, LYNN (LYNN ALEXANDER), biologist; b. Chgo., Mar. 5, 1938; d. Morris and Leone (Wise) Alexander; m. Carl Sagan, June 16, 1957; m. Thomas N. Margulis, Jan. 18, 1967; children: Dorion Sagan, Jeremy Sagan, Zachary Margulis, Jennifer Margulis. A.B., U. Chgo., 1957; A.M., U. Wis., 1960; Ph.D., U. Calif., Berkeley, 1965. Mem. faculty Boston U., 1966-88, asst. prof. biology, 1967-71, assoc. prof., 1971-77, prof., 1977-88, Univ. prof., 1986-88; Disting. Univ. prof. U. Mass., Amherst, 1988—; Sherman Fairchild Disting. scholar Calif. Inst. Tech., 1976-77; vis. prof. dept. microbiology U. Autónoma de Barcelona, Spain, 1986, 88; Disting. univ. prof. U. Mass. Author: Origin of Eukaryotic Cells, 1970, Symbiosis in Cell Evolution, 1981, Early Life, 1982, (with K.V. Schwartz) Five KIngdoms, 1982, 2nd edit., 1988, (with Dorion Sagan) Microcosmos, 1986, Origins of Sex, 1986, Garden of Microbial Delights, 1988, (with Dorion Sagan) Biospheres From Earth To Space, 1988, (with René Fester), Global Ecology, 1989; editor: Handbook Protoctista, 1990; contbr. articles to profl. jours. Guggenheim fellow, 1979. Fellow AAAS (pres. sect. G 1990—); mem. NAS, Soc. Environ. Protistology (co-founder). Office: Univ Mass Morrill Sci Ctr Amherst MA 01003

MARIANI, VERONICA JOAN, systems administrator; b. Washington, Oct. 20, 1960; d. Theodore Frank and Veronica Rose (Budrecki) M. BS in Gen. Sci., Villanova U., 1982; MBA in Info. Systems, George Washington U., 1984. Mktg. asst. Mariani & Assocs., Washington, 1984-85; systems analyst Integrated Microcomputer Systems, Rockville, Md., 1985-86; systems adminstr. Mariani & Assocs., Washington, 1986—. Chair, producer Wildwood Summer Theatre, Bethesda, Md., 1982; pres. Sandy Spring (Md.) Theatre Group, 1989—; visual arts coord. Villanova Student Union, 1981-82. Mem. Soc. Archtl. Adminstrs., Second Wind-Soccer Club. Republican. Roman Catholic. Office: Mariani & Assocs Inc 1600 20th St NW Washington DC 20009

MARIE, KATHY LOUISE, data systems executive; b. Denver, July 24, 1953; d. Johnny Santos and Anna Louise (Martinez) Vigil; m. Philip Randall Marie, Feb. 13, 1971; children: Lisa Jean, Danni Rae. Student, Colo. Women's Coll., 1980-81. Computer operator Western Electric, Aurora, Colo., 1971-75; sr. operator Samsonite Corp., Denver, 1975-77; supr., mgr. of ops. Sterns Roger, Denver, 1977-79; prodn. services mgr. Citicorp, Englewood, Colo., 1979-80; applications mgr. Citicorp, Englewood, 1980-81; computer ops. mgr. CIGNA, Thornton, Colo., 1981-83; sr. ops. mgr. CIGNA, Thornton, 1983-84, ops. section mgr., 1984-85, ops. asst. dir., 1985-87; owner, cons. SYSTEK, Aurora, Colo., 1986-89. Mem. Soc. Info. Mgmt., Data Processing Mgmt. Assn., NAFE, U.S. Postal Customer Coun. (exec. bd.), Beta Sigma Phi. Democrat. Roman Catholic. Home: 5778 S Laredo Ct Aurora CO 80015 Office: CIGNA 12396 Grant St Thornton CO 80241

MARIENCHILD, EVA, public relations, marketing, communications and management consultant; b. N.Y.C., Mar. 24, 1957; d. Benjamin Beauchamp de Jesus Rodriguez-Martinez and Marien (Engracia) Martinez-Ceberio. Student, Dominican Comml. Sch., 1976. Account mgmt. exec. sec. Warwick, Welsh & Miller, N.Y.C., 1978-80; chem. patent trademark paralegal Davis, Hoxie, Faithfull & Hapgood, N.Y.C., 1980-82; dir. publicity, exec. sec. Waring & LaRosa Advt., N.Y.C., 1981-82; assoc. account exec. Stiefel/Raymond Advt., N.Y.C., 1982-83; copy editor personal fin. E.F. Hutton, N.Y.C., 1983-84; account exec. Anderson Stone & Jason, N.Y.C., 1984-85; v.p. sales Computer Rsch. Tabs, N.Y.C., 1985-86; pres., chief exec. officer Collection Resource Team, N.Y.C., 1986—, Eva Marienchild Cons., N.Y.C., 1988—; dir. promotion Motion Picture & TV Media Registry, N.Y.C., 1983. Editor, pub. Sidelines mag., 1984, various newsletters; contbr. to Seventeen mag., others. Graphic artist fin. div. UNICEF, N.Y.C., 1983; collaborator sci. and tech. entry program Manhattan Coll. Mem. NAFE, Am. Women's Econ. Devel. Home: 172 Thompson St Ste 14 New York NY 10012 Office: 172 Thompson St #14 New York NY 10012

MARIKOS, KATHRYN ANN, communications executive; b. Astoria, Oreg., Nov. 18, 1947; d. Robert Ray and Hazel Kathryn (Magee) Vagt; m. John Fredrick Waterman, June 28, 1969 (div. Oct. 1976); m. John Michael Marikos, Aug. 12, 1979. BA, U. Oreg., 1968. Tchr. Glendale (Oreg.) Pub. Schs., 1969-70, St. Helens (Oreg.) Pub. Schs., 1970-72; with market rsch. div. U.S. Testing, Chgo., 1972-76, G.M.A. Rsch., Seattle, 1976-84; dir. mktg. and rsch. div. Sta. WPLG-TV, Miami, Fla., 1984-86; dir. client svcs. Marshall Mktg. & Communications, Pitts., 1986—; mem. retail mktg. bd. TV Advt. Bur., N.Y., 1984-86; mem. adv. coun. Target Dollars, Pitts., 1984-86. Bd. dirs. Eckankar, Seattle, 1980-82, dir. communications, Pa., 1988-89. Mem. Am. Mktg. Assn., World Future Soc., Pitts. Rose Soc. Democrat. Office: Marshall Mktg 1699 Washington Rd Pittsburgh PA 15241

MARIL, ELIZABETH JOAN, educator; b. Zanesville, Ohio, Feb. 17, 1943; d. Charles James and Mary Elizabeth (Young) Burgess; m. David Randel Maril, Aug. 21, 1965; children: Mary Katherine, Virginia Lynn. BS in Edn., Ohio U., 1965. Tchr. Oklahoma City Sch. Dist., 1965-67, Glendale (Ariz.) Sch. Dist., 1967-68, Caesar Rodney Sch. Dist., Dover, Del., 1968-70; owner/designer J. M. Creations, Austin, 1978-85; substitute tchr. Austin Ind. Sch. Dist., 1981-88. Vice pres. Austin City Council of PTA's, 1986-88;/ PTA rep. exec. bd. C. of C. Adlopt a Sch. Com., Austin, 1987-88; mem. Austin Ind. Sch. Dist. budget com., 1986-88, mem. citizens textbook com., 1984-88; bd. dirs. Kirby Hall, Austin, 1981-82; cons. in field. Mem. Officers Wives Club, Res. Officers Assn... Ladies. Democrat. Roman Catholic.

MARIN, CONNIE, health services administrator; b. Sonora, Tex., Dec. 8, 1939; d. Silverio and Concepcion (Rodriquez) Flores; 1 child, Alfonso. Diploma nursing, Bapt. Meml. Sch. Nursing, 1964. RN. Adminstr. spl. projects Ingham Med. Ctr., Lansing, Mich.; coord. health svcs. Cristo Rey Community Ctr., Lansing, coord. emergency svcs.; cons. in field. Bd. policy analyst Mich. Medicaid, 1979-89; treas., fundraiser, organizer PTA, 1973-87; fire commr. Fire Dept. City of Lansing, 1988—; tchr. Sunday Sch., 1968-86. Named an Outstanding Community Leader Lansing State Jour., Outstanding Vol. Ingham County. Mem. NAFE, Am. Bus. Women Assn. (edn. chmn., sec. fundraising, Bus. Advocate of Yr. Lansing chpt. 1986), Kiwanis (pres.). Home: 2039 Sunderland Rd Lansing MI 48911 Office: Ingham Med Ctr 401 W Greenlawn Lansing MI 48910

MARINAK, KATHLEEN LOUISE, insurance company official; b. Lebanon, Pa., Oct. 23, 1957; d. Edward John and Constance (Steckbeck) M. Student, James Madison U., 1977-79; BS in Nursing, Med. Coll. Va., Richmond, 1979, M Health Adminstrn., 1984. RN. Asst. nursing Winchester (Va.) Med. Ctr., 1974-78, Med. Coll. Va. Hosps., Richmond, 1978-79; charge nurse intensive care unit St. Mary's Hosp., Richmond, 1979-83; adminstrv. resident Hunter Holmes McGuire VA Med. Ctr., Richmond, 1983-84, specialist health systems, 1984-85; adminstrv. asst. to chief of staff Lebanon VA Med. Ctr., 1985-87; nat. corp. mgr. The Prudential Ins. Co., Roseland, N.J., 1987—. V.P. Washington Sq. Homeowners Assn., North Plainfield, N.J., 1988-89. Nominee Fed. Woman of Yr. Vets. Adminstrn., Richmond, 1985. Mem. NAFE, Am. Coll. Health Care Profls., Cen. Va. Young Adminstrs. (v.p. 1984-85), Richmond Jaycees (bd. dirs. 1984-85, 1st place speaking competition 1985, 1st place also in dist.-wide competition 1985). Roman Catholic. Office: The Prudential Ins Co 56 N Livingston Ave Roseland NJ 07068

MARINCOLA, DIAN ANGELA, data processing executive; b. Norristown, Pa., May 26, 1954; d. Dominic Peter and Mafalda Monica (D'Amore) M. BA, Shippensburg U. of Pa., 1976; MS in Info. Resource Mgmt., Syracuse U., 1983. Info. specialist Regional Resource Ctr. Pa. Info. Ctr. for Spl. Edn., King of Prussia, 1977-81; project supr. Informatics Gen. Corp., Rockville, Md., 1983-84, legal services mgr., 1984-85; user svcs. mgr. RMS Assocs. at NASA STI Facility, Balt.-Washington Internat. Airport, Md., 1985—; documentation cons. BRS, Latham, N.Y., 1981. Editor: (newsletter) Prise Wise, 1980-81; author: (newsletter) STI Bulletin, 1985—. Mem. Am. Soc. for Info Sci., Soc. of Profl. Journalists, Soc. for Advanced Learning Tech. Office: NASA STI Facility Balt-Washington Internat Airport Box 8757 Baltimore MD 21240

MARINELLI, ADA SANTI, government official, real estate company official; b. Borgo a Mozzano, Italy, July 27, 1942; came to U.S., 1953; d. Attilio and Maria Josephine (Biondi) Santi; m. Rudolph Marinelli, July 12, 1964; children: Gina Marie, Marisa Bianca. Student, Rivier Coll., 1962-63, George Washington U., 1963; AA with high honors, Prince Georges Community Coll., 1980. Sec. U.S. Post Office, Washington, 1963-70; adminstrv. sec. U.S. Postal Service, Washington, 1970-80, real estate specialist trainee, 1980-82, realty mgmt. and acquisition analyst, 1982-84; real estate specialist Washington, 1984—; realty mgmt. specialist U.S. Postal Service, Washington, 1989—; assoc. broker Larry Eul Realty, Inc., Camp Springs, Md., 1977-83, Alvin Turner Real Estate Upper Marlboro, Md., 1988—. Recipient spl. achievement award U.S. Postal Service, 1987. Mem. Fed. Real Property Assn., Alumnae Assn. Rivier Coll. Democrat. Roman Catholic. Club: Orsogna (Washington) (pres. 1965-66). Home: 7006 Sheffield Dr Camp Springs MD 20748

MARING, NORMA ANN, military academy official; b. Humboldt, Kans., Oct. 1, 1933; d. Edward Simon and Anna Agnes (Frederich) Breiner; m. L. Keith Maring, Dec. 27, 1951 (dec. July 1988); children: Stan, Steve, Scot, Ron. Grad. high sch., Chanute, Kans. Cert. swimming pool operator. Instr. dance, water safety courses Wentworth Mil. Acad., Lexington, Mo., 1968—, alumni dir., 1979—; operator Chanute Mcpl. Swimming Pool, 1956—; water safety trainer ARC, Kans., Mo., 1969—. Bd. dirs., chmn. water safety Neosho County unit ARC, Chanute, 1965-85; pres. Lexington PTA, 1960-64, Lafayette County PTA, 1965-70. Recipient Disting. Svc. award Nat. ARC, 1982; coll. scholarship in her name given by PTA Coun., Chanute, 1982. Mem. Kans. Swimming Pool Assn., Kans. PTA (hon. life), Gen. Fed. Women's Clubs (pres. Lexington 1970-72), Lexington Garden Club (v.p. 1969-70), Am. Contract Bridge League. Roman Catholic. Home: 1622 South St Lexington MO 64067 Office: Wentworth Mil Acad 18th and Washington Sts Lexington MO 64067

MARINKO, MONICA MARIE, psychologist; b. Cleve., Feb. 26, 1948; d. Fred Joseph and and Sophia Frances (Gornik) M. BA, U. Detroit, 1970; MA, John Carroll U., 1975. Cert. and lic. sch. psychologist, Ohio. Psychologist Ashtabula (Ohio) Area City Schs., 1975—; pvt. practice sch. psychology Chesterland, Ohio, 1985—. Mem. Nat. Assn. Sch. Psychologists, Ohio Sch. Psychologists Assn., Soc. for Personality Assessment (assoc.), Am. Chronic Pain Assn. (regional dir. No. Ohio, nat. dir. sponsor program, group leader Chesterland chpt.). Home: 12321 Norton Dr Chesterland OH 44026 Office: Ashtabula Area City Schs 401 W 44th St Ashtabula OH 44004

MARINO, JOANNE MARIE, psychotherapist, consultant; b. Greenwich, Conn., Feb. 15, 1951; d. Frank Dominic and Matilda (Salvatore) M. B.A., U. Conn., 1973, M.A. in Ednl. Psychology/Rehab. Counseling, 1975. Cert. nat. clin. mental health counselor, nat. cert. counselor. Counselor Ea. Ct. Drug Action Program, Inc., Willimantic Conn., 1974-77; sr. counselor Liberation Programs, Inc., Stamford, Conn., 1977-79, program dir. 1980-83, quality assurance coordinator, 1982-83; gen. practice psychotherapy, cons. counseling and vocat. assessment, 1983—. Mem. Am. Assn. Counseling and Devel., Am. Mental Health Counselors Assn., Assn. of Specialists in Group Work. Avocations: films, traveling, computers, gardening, reading. Office: The Learning Exch 21 Strickland Rd Cos Cob CT 06807

MARINO, SHEILA BURRIS, education educator; b. Knoxville, Nov. 24, 1947; d. David Paul and Lucille Cora (Maupin) Burris; m. Louis John Marino, Dec. 19, 1969; children: Sheila Noelle, Heather Michelle. BS, U.

Tenn., 1969, MS, 1971, EdD, 1976; postgrad., W.Va. U. Elem./early childhood tchr. Knoxville City Schs., 1969-71; cooperating tchr. U. Tenn., Knoxville, 1969-71; dir. early childhood edn./tchr. Glenville (W.Va.) State Coll., 1971-72, Colo. Women's Coll., Denver, 1972-73; asst. prof. edn. Lander Coll., Greenwood, S.C., 1973-75; instr., spl. asst. coordinator of elem./early childhood edn. U. Tenn., 1975-76; prof. edn., dir. clin. experiences Lander Coll., 1976—; cons. in field; dir. Creative Activities Prog. for Children, Lander Coll., 1979—; mem. W.Va. Gov.'s Early Childhood Adv. Bd., 1971-72, Gov.'s Team of Higher Edn. Profls. on Comprehensive Plan for S.C. Early Childhood Edn., 1982. Contbr. articles to profl. jours.; author: International Children's Literature, 1989. Pres.-elect Greenwood Literacy Coun., St. Nicholas Speech & Hearing Ctr., Greenwood; coord. Old Ninety-Six coun. Girl Scouts U.S., 1987—; vol. March of Dimes prog., Greenwood, 1987. Recipient Disting. Prof. award Lander Coll., 1976, Cert. Appreciation award Gov. S.C., 1979, Cert. Disting. Svc. and Leadership award NEA, 1984, Internat. Reading Assn., 1988. AAUW (pres. 1990—), Piedmont Assn. for Children and Adults with Learning Disabilities (pres. 1986—, mem. exec. bd.), S.C. Assn. for Children and Adults with Learning Disabilities (pres. 1990, exec. bd.), AAUP, S.C. Edn. Assn., NEA (state advisor 1981-88), S.C. Assn. for Children Under Six, So. Assn. for Children Under Six, S.C. Assn. Tchr. Educators, S.C. Assn. Early Childhood Tchr. Educators, Piedmont Reading Council (v.p. 1985-86, pres. 1986-88), S.C. Coun. of Internat. Reading Assn. (pres. 1986-88), Delta Kappa Gamma (pres. Epsilon chpt. 1984-88, mem. exec. bd.), Pi Lambda Theta, Kappa Delta Pi (pres. U. Tenn. chpt. 1974-75), Phi Delta Kappa (pres. Lander Coll. chpt. 1990—). Democrat. Presbyterian. Home: 103 Essex Ct Greenwood SC 29649 Office: Lander College Stanley Avenue Greenwood SC 29649

MARION, BEVERLY ANN, nurse; b. Lowell, Mass., July 10, 1962; d. Louis Emery Jr. and Patricia Marie (Lawlor) M.; 1 child, Houston Andre Green. Practical nurse diploma, Putnam Meml. Sch. Nursing, Bennington, Vt.; AS in Nursing, Middlesex Community Coll., Bedford, Mass., 1988. RN, Mass. Operator phototherapy equipment Chelmsford (Mass.) Med. Assocs., 1986-87; nurse Palm Manor Nursing Home, Chelmsford, 1987, MI Restorative Nursing Ctr., Lawrence, Mass., 1988, The Agy., nursing network, Beverly, Mass., 1988—. Democrat. Home: 8 Diamond St Apt 8 Lawrence MA 01843

MARION, GEORGETTE A. (GIGI MARION), editor, writer; b. Hollywood, Calif., Nov. 17, 1927; d. George Francis and Dorothy Whelan (Maldeis) M.; m. Robert P. Collier, Mar. 20, 1952 (div. 1974); children: Robert P. Collier Jr., Marion C. Collier. BA in History, Stanford U., 1949. Reporter, editor Mademoiselle Mag., N.Y.C., 1950-57; editor, writer Daily News, N.Y.C., 1959-61; news dir. Vogue, N.Y.C., 1962; columnist Caracas (Venezuela) Daily Jour., 1962-68; editor Glamour Mag., N.Y.C., 1971; v.p. creative svcs. Am. Cancer Soc., Atlanta, 1988—; freelance writer Seventeen Mag., Metro News, Leavitt Advt., 1971-73. V.p. bd. dirs. Older Women's League, N.Y.C., 1983-88; bd. dirs. Caracas Circulating Libr., 1962-68. Mem. Women in Communications (N.Y.C., Atlanta chpts.). Office: Am Cancer Soc 1599 Clifton Rd Atlanta GA 30329

MARISOL (MARISOL ESCOBAR), sculptor; b. Paris, May 22, 1930. Ed., Ecole des Beaux-Arts, Paris, 1949, Art Students League, N.Y.C., 1950, New Sch. for Social Research, 1951-54, Hans Hofmann Sch., N.Y.C., 1951-54; DFA (hon.), Moore Coll. Arts, Phila., 1969, R.I. Sch. design, 1986. One-woman shows at Leo Castelli Gallery, 1958, Stable Gallery, 1962, 64, Sidney Janis Gallery, N.Y.C., 1966, 67, 73, 75, 81, 84, 89, Hanover Gallery, London, 1967, Boymans-van Beuningen Mus., Rotterdam, Netherlands, 1968, Inst. Contemporary Art, London, 1968, Fondation Maeght, Paris, 1970, Moore Coll. Art, Phila., 1970, Worcester (Mass.) Art Mus., 1971, N.Y. Cultural Center, 1973, Columbus (Ohio) Gallery of Fine Arts, 1974, Makler Gallery, Phila., 1982, Hirshhorn Mus. and Sculpture Garden, 1984, Nat. Portrait Gallery, Washington, 1987, Boca Raton Mus. Art, Fla., 1988, Whitney Mus. at Philip Morris, N.Y.C., 1988, Galerie Tokoro, Tokyo, 1989, Hasagawa Gallery, Tokyo, 1989, Rose Art Mus., Waltham, Mass., 1990, numerous others; exhibited in group shows including Painting of a Decade, Tate Gallery, London, 1964, New Realism, Municipal Mus., The Hague, 1964, Carnegie Internat., Pitts., 1964, Art of the U.S.A, 1670-1966, Whitney Mus. Am. Art, N.Y.C., 1966, American Sculpture of the Sixties, Mus. of Art, Los Angeles, 1967, Biennale, Venice, 1968, Art Inst. Chgo., 1968; represented in permanent collections at Mus. Modern Art, N.Y.C., Whitney Mus. Am. Art, Albright-Knox Gallery, Buffalo, Hakone Open Air Mus., Tokyo, Nat. Portrait Gallery, Washington, Harry N. Abrams Collection, N.Y.C., Yale U. Art Gallery, Art Inst. Chgo., Met. Mus., N.Y.C., numerous others. Mem. Am. Acad. and Inst. Arts and Letters (v.p. art 1984-87). Address: care Sidney Janis Gallery 110 W 57th St New York NY 10019

MARITZEN, LYNN MARIE, data processing executive; b. Biddeford, Maine, Nov. 14, 1958; d. Joseph and Helen (Biemer) M. BS, Tex A&M U., 1981, postgrad., 1988—. Rsch. asst. Tex. A&M U., College Station, 1980-82; mgr. data processing dept. LGL Ecological Rsch. Assocs., Bryan, Tex., 1981-89, Tech. Mfg., Inc., Bryan, Tex., 1987-89; end user support mgr. Sun Microsystems, Inc., Mountain View, Calif., 1989—; tutor cons. Tex. A&M U., Bryan, 1982—, systems operator, College Station, 1984. Mem. Notable Women Tex., Tex. A&M U. Former Students Assn., Tex. A&M U. Microcomputer Club, SOS (Bryan) (pres. 1987-88). Office: Sun Microsystems Inc M/S M9-54 2550 Garcia Ave Mountain View CA 94043

MARK, ARLENE JOAN, psychologist, educational foundation worker; b. Johnstown, Pa., Nov. 4, 1940; d. Paul And Anna (Condor) Slobodzian; m. Reuben Mark, Jan. 10, 1963; children: Lisa, Peter, Stephen. Cert. in paraverbal therapy, Columbia U., N.Y.C., 1980; MA in Teaching, Manhattanville Coll., Purchase, N.Y., 1981; M in Sch. Psychology, Coll. New Rochelle, N.Y., 1985; BA in Music, Manhattanville Coll., Purchase, N.Y. Lic. sch. psychologist, N.Y.; cert. spl. edn. tchr., Conn., Mass. Psychoednl. diagnostician Eagle Hill Diagnostic Unit, Greenwich, Conn., 1981-84; sch. psychologist Lincoln Hall Residential Treatment Ctr., Somers, N.Y., 1985-87; Mem. exec. com., class sponsor I Have a Dream Found., N.Y.C., 1986—; co-chmn. N.Y.C. Mentoring adv. com., 1988—; mem. profl. adv. bd. Nat. Ctr. Learning Disabilities, N.Y.C., 1988—; bd. dirs. Sch. and Bus. Alliance, N.Y.C., 1988—; mem. adv. bd. Project Future, Bd. Edn., N.Y.C., 1987—; bd. trustees Bank St. Coll. of Edn., N.Y.C., 1990—; bd. citizens Union of City of N.Y., 1990—. Co-author: Not Through Words Alone Paraverbal Communication with Children, 1990; contbr. articles to profl. jours. and newspapers. Recipient Challenge award Found. for Children with Learning Disabilities, 1988, Disting. Leadership award Citizens Union of City N.Y., 1988, Volunteerism award Big Bros., Big Sisters N.Y.C., 1990. Mem. Am. Psychol. Assn., Am. Orthopsychiat. Assn.

MARK, BETSY YVONNE, educator, consultant; b. Ironwood, Mich., Aug. 25, 1947; d. Harold and Bernice Florence (Barnett) M.; m. H. Edward Pirtle, Sept. 1, 1984; stepchildren: Kimberly, Jeffrey, Michelle. BS in Edn., U. Mich., 1973, MA, 1978. Cert. tchr., Mich. Tchr./cons. Jackson (Mich.) Pub. Schs., 1973—. Bd. dirs. Genesis of Ann Arbor (Mich.), 1987-88, sec., 1988-89, v.p., 1989-90, pres. 1990—; speaker ann. conf. Mich. Coun. for Exceptional Children, 1977, 88. Named Most Inspirational Tchr. sr. class Jackson High Sch., 1988, 89. Mem. NEA, Mich. Edn. Assn., Jackson County Edn. Assn., Jackson Edn. Assn. (bd. dirs. 1989—), Am. Mensa (membership chmn. S.E. Mich. 1983-85, treas. 1985-86, Ann Arbor area steering com. 1989, proctor 1983—, gen. rep. 1990—). Jewish. Home: 3674 Oak Dr Ypsilanti MI 48197 Office: Parkside Jr High Sch 2400 4th St Jackson MI 49203

MARK, JANE ANNE, real estate investment executive; b. N.Y.C., Aug. 31, 1945; d. Laurence and Annette (Mark) M.; divorced; 1 child, Andrew; m. Frank John Visich, Dec. 31, 1980. BA magna cum laude, Brandeis U., 1967; MA in Psychology, New Sch. of Social Rsch., 1970. Exercise fitness trainer Women-Shape Up!, N.Y.C., 1972-79; pres. Jed Mgmt. Corp., N.Y.C., 1979—; mem. Real Estate Bd. N.Y., 1986—. Active community home improvement program, N.Y.C., 1982—; activist for property owners protection N.Y.C. civil and dist. cts., 1979—. Grad. study scholar Fed. Govt., New Sch. of Social Rsch., 1968. Mem. Small Property Owners N.Y. Democrat. Jewish. Home and Office: Jed Mgmt Corp 736 Broadway New York NY 10003

MARK, KATHLEEN MARY, real estate company executive; b. Chgo., Mar. 12, 1951; d. Michael and Lucille M. (Ciullo) Scotella; m. Al A. Fosco, 1971 (div. 1981); m. Robert Paul Mark, 1983; 1 child, Alan James. BA, Northeastern U., 1979. Broker Century 21 Village Sq., Arlington Heights, Ill., 1983-85; mng. broker Century 21 Village Sq., Palatine, Ill., 1985-87; v.p., mng. broker 1st United Realtors, Arlington Heights, 1987—. Producer video Hemingway's Michigan Adventure, 1978. Mem. N.W. Suburban Bd. Realtors (treas. 1988-89, pres. 1990), Women's Coun.

MARK, LESLIE DEAN, graphic artist, consultant, calligrapher; b. Geneva, Switzerland, Oct. 12, 1961; d. David Everett and Elisabeth Lewis (Lewis) M.; m. Mark David Eisemann, Apr. 5, 1987; 1 child, Emma Sophie. AB, Smith Coll., 1983. Artist Hallmark Cards, Inc., Kansas City, Mo., 1984-86, art dir., 1986-87; owner, freelancer Leslie D. Mark Designs, Leawood, Kans., 1987—. Designer, editor: Lying, 1983. Mem. NOW, Common Cause, Internat. Rels. Coun. Kansas City, Smith Coll. Alumni Assn. (candidate's chair 1985-89). Democrat. Jewish.

MARK, LILLIAN GEE, school founder and official; b. Berkeley, Calif., Mar. 18, 1932; d. Pon Gordon and Sun Kum (Wong) Gee; m. Richard Muin Mark, June 20, 1954; children: Dean, Kim, Faye, Glenn, Lynne. AB in Psychology, U. Calif., Berkeley, 1954; MS in Christian Sch. Adminstrn., Pensacola Coll., 1987. Sec., Western Life Ins. Co., San Francisco, 1944-54; child care tchr. San Diego Child Care Ctr., 1954-55; dir. pre-sch. ABC Nursery, San Mateo, Calif., 1969-76; founder, prin. Alpha Beacon Christian Sch., San Carlos, Calif., 1976—; pres. Alpha Beacon Christian Ministries. Author: Handbook for Parents and Students, 1983, How to Encourage Your Staff. Mem. Christian Ministries Mgmt. Assn., Nat. Christian Adminstrs. Assn., Christian Schs. Internat. (dist. rep.). Republican. Mem. Pentacostal Ch. Avocations: tennis, piano, Bible study. Home: 182 Exbourne Ave San Carlos CA 94070 Office: Alpha Beacon Christian Ministries 750 Dartmouth Ave San Carlos CA 94070

MARK, RONNIE JOAN, medical librarian; b. Bklyn., Mar. 10, 1941; d. Morris and Sylvia (Moskowitz) Horowitz; m. Steven Mark, June 1, 1969. BS in Biology, Fairleigh Dickinson U., 1963; MS in Library Info. Scis. summa cum laude, Palmer Grad. Library Sch. C.W. Post U., 1978. Med. librarian Ayerst Labs., N.Y.C., 1964-67; head librarian Med. World News, N.Y.C., 1967-77; librarian health scis., asst. prof. L.I. U., Bklyn., 1977-80; dir. med. library Coney Island Hosp., Bklyn., 1980—. Mem. Med. Library Assn., N.Y.-N.J. cpt. Med. Library Assn., Bklyn., Queens, Staten Island Health Scis. Librarians (pres. 1985-89), Beta Phi Mu, Beta Mu. Jewish. Office: Coney Island Hosp 2601 Ocean Pkwy Brooklyn NY 11235

MARKEE, KATHERINE MADIGAN, librarian, educator; b. Cleve., Feb. 24, 1931; d. Arthur Alexis and Margaret Elizabeth (Madigan) M. AB, Trinity Coll., Washington, 1953; MA, Columbia U., 1962; MLS, Case Western Res. U., 1968. Employment mgr., br. store tng. supr. The May Co., Cleve., 1965-67; assoc. prof. libr. sci., data bases libr. Purdue U. Libr., West Lafayette, Ind., 1968—. Contbr. articles to profl. jours. Mem. ALA, AAUP, Spl. Librs. Assn., Med. Libr. Assn., Am. Soc. Info. Sci., Ind. Online Users Group, Sigma Xi (Rsch. Support award 1986). Office: Purdue Univ Libr West Lafayette IN 47907

MARKEL, GERALDINE, psychologist, consultant; b. N.Y.C., Jan. 4, 1939; d. Charles and Anne (Handelman) Ponte; m. Sheldon Foster Markel, July 5, 1958; children: Laura, David, Stephen. BA in Social Scis., U. Mich., 1959, MA in Ednl. Psychology, 1964; EdS in Spl. Edn., George Washington U., 1968, PhD in Ednl. Psychology, 1974. With exec. edn. ctr. Grad. Sch. of Bus. U. Mich., Ann Arbor, 1972—, asst. prof. exec. edn. ctr. Grad. Sch. of Bus., 1974-82, sr. rsch. assoc. reading and learning skills ctr., 1982—, lectr. dept. prevention and health care Sch. of Dentistry, 1987—; mgmt. cons. Communication Systems Group, Oak Park, Mich., Gen. TV Network, Oak Park, Mich. Bell Telephone, Southfield, Mich., Schlumberger, Ann Arbor, Pitney-Bowes, Atlanta, Mfrs. Hanover Bank, N.Y.C., U.S. Customs Dept. Law Enforcement Tng. Ctr., Sea Isle, Ga., Olivia St. Press, Ann Arbor, Fin. Mgmt. Svcs., L.A., Domino's Pizza, Ann Arbor, Catherine McCauley Health Ctr., Ann Arbor; asst. psychologist Reading and Learning Skills Ctr., U. Mich., 1972; evaluator Office Rsch. and Evaluation, 1971. Contbr. numerous articles to profl. jours. Mem. Mich. Affiliate Assn. for Behavior Therapy (pres. 1989—). Democrat. Jewish. Home: 3975 Waldenwood Ann Arbor MI 48105 Office: U Mich 1014 School of Dentistry Ann Arbor MI 48105

MARKESSINI, JOAN, psychologist; b. N.Y.C., Aug. 14, 1942; d. John Demetrios and Diana (Vlahos) M.; m. Peter John Georges, Jan. 28, 1981. BA in English and French, U. Del., 1964, PhD in Cognitive Psychology, 1979; MA in Linguistics, U. Wash., 1966. Tng. analyst U.S. Dept. State, Washington, 1967-70; writer, editor-in-chief Edcom Systems, Inc., Princeton, N.J., 1970-72; ednl. psychologist U. Del., Newark, 1972-78; dir. corp. and found. rels. Cath. U. Am., Washington, 1978-84; asst. dir. resources devel. Nat. Trust for Hist. Preservation, Washington, 1984-85; sr. staff psychologist BDM Internat., Inc., McLean, Va., 1985-87; dir. publs. and communications Maxwell Communication Corp., McLean, 1987-90; psychologist Allen Corp., Alexandria, Va., 1990—. Author: The First Year of Life (13 vols.), 1971, The First Twelve Months of Life, 1973; producer (film) Death of a Giant, 1967; numerous reports. U. Wash. grad. fellow, 1965-66, U. Mich. fellow, 1965, U. Del. fellow, 1977-79. Mem. Am. Psychol. Assn., Assn. Psychol. Type (gen.), N.Y. Acad. Scis., Nat. Mus. Women in Arts (charter), Am. Film Inst. Club. Home: 2331 9th St S Arlington VA 22204

MARKEY, JOANNE ZINK, computer consultant; b. Phila., June 7, 1941; d. Albert Barnes and Mildred (Gerhab) Zink; 1 child from previous marriage, James A. Kenney; m. Owen Charles Markey Jr., Aug. 2, 1975; children: Stephen James, Janice M., Michael James. Cons. computer Ambler, Pa., 1978-83; owner, cons. computer Z-Mark Assocs., Ambler, 1983—. Home and Office: 112 Stout Rd Ambler PA 19002

MARKGRAF, ROSEMARIE, real estate broker; b. Grantsburg, Wis., Oct. 31, 1934; d. Helen Elizabeth Pribil. BS, U. Wis., 1957, MS, 1958. Cert. educator;. Tchr. High Schs., Wis., Conn, 1958-61; office mgr. Robert S. Palmer, Middletown, Conn., 1962-64; edn. adv. Girl Scouts U.S.A., N.Y.C., 1964-66; community relation assoc. Motion Picture Assn. Am., N.Y., 1967-69; mgr. The Chateau Inn, Stamford, N.Y., 1970-78; real estate salesman Atkins Realty, Ltd., Bklyn., 1979-80; real estate broker, prin. The Markgraf Group, Ltd., Bklyn., 1980--; cons. Real Estate Counseling Group Conn., Storrs, 1963—; pres. Tuff Transport, Inc. Mem. C. of C. (v.p.), Bklyn. Bd. Realtors. Roman Catholic. Home: 60 Remsen St Brooklyn Heights NY 11201 Office: The Markgraf Group Ltd 160 Montague St Brooklyn NY 11201

MARKHAM, ELIZABETH MARY, mathematics educator; b. New Haven, Oct. 12, 1929; d. James Joseph and Agnes Veronica (Manning) M. BA, St. Joseph Coll., West Hartford, Conn., 1951; MS, U. Notre Dame, 1960, PhD, 1964. Tchr. math. and sci. Cathedral High Sch., Hartford, Conn., 1954-59; math. instr. St. Joseph Coll., 1964-65, asst. prof., 1965-71, assoc. prof., 1971-81, prof., 1981—, chair math. dept., 1964—; dir. In-svc. Insts. for Tchrs., NSF, West Hartford, 1966-69, Cause Math/Sci. Project, NSF, West Hartford, 1978-80; evaluator proposal panels NSF, Washington, 1969-79; cons., lectr. in field. Contbr. articles to profl. publs. Mem. math. edn. task force State of Conn., Hartford, 1969-74, 78-80. Grantee NSF, 1957-60, 73-79, 80-81, Math. Assn. Am., 1967; Lilly fellow, 1975-76. Mem. Math. Assn., Assn. Tchrs. of Math. in New Eng., Women's Rsch. Inst. (adv. bd. 1983-84). Democrat. Roman Catholic. Office: St Joseph Coll 1678 Asylum Ave West Hartford CT 06117

MARKHAM, MARION M., writer; b. Chgo., June 12, 1929; d. William Joseph and Marion (Dammann) Bork; m. Robert Bailey Markham, Dec. 30, 1955; children—Susan Markham Andersen, Jane Markham Madden. B.S. in Speech, Northwestern U., 1953. Continuity dir. Sta. WTVP, Decatur, Ill., 1953-54; TV bus. mgr. Earle Ludgin Advt. Co., Chgo., 1955-58; free-lance writer, Northbrook, Ill., 1967—. Novels include: Escape from Velos, 1981, The Halloween Candy Mystery, 1982, The Christmas Present Mystery, 1984, The Thanksgiving Day Parade Mystery, 1986, The Birthday Party Mystery, 1989; contbr. articles and short stories to mags. and jours. Bd. dirs. Northbrook Pub. Library, 1976-86, pres. bd., 1981-83. Mem. Soc. Children's Book Writers, Authors Guild, Mystery Writers Am. (midwest regional v.p. 1977-78, dir. 1983-87), Soc. Midland Authors (dir. Chgo. 1983-86). Home and Office: 2415 Newport Rd Northbrook IL 60062

MARKHAM, SARA FRANCES NORRIS, municipal department manager; b. Ft. Worth, Oct. 9, 1947; d. William Oxford and Katherine Burton (Sydnor) Norris; m. Richard Charles Markham, Feb. 4, 1978; children: Katherine Elizabeth, Emily Frances. BA in Sociology, U. Tex., Arlington, 1970, MA in Urban Studies, 1977. Placement interviewer Tex. Employment Commn., Ft. Worth, 1971-74, 77-78; adult and youth program coord. Tarrant County Manpower Program, Ft. Worth, 1974-75, manpower planner, 1975-77; employment and tng. mgr. Hartford (Conn.) Employment and Tng. Adminstrn., 1978-81; mgmt. analyst ops. improvement div. City of Hartford, 1981-85; mgmt. analyst Office Mgmt. and Budget, 1985-87, chief mgmt. analyst, 1987-88; mgmt. svcs. officer Hartford Fire Dept., 1988—; chair employment com. Mayor's Coun. on Youth Opportunities, Ft. Worth, 1975-77; mem. Southwestern Assn. Manpower Planners, Ft. Worth, 1975-77. Bd. dirs. Tex. Employment Commn. Employee Credit Union, Ft. Worth, 1973-74; mem. Hartford Women's Network, 1987-89. Mem. Am. Soc. for Pub. Adminstrn., Alpha Kappa Delta. Democrat. Episcopalian. Office: Hartford Fire Dept 275 Pearl St Hartford CT 06103

MARKIJOHN, JUDY ANN, nurse; b. Conneaut, Ohio, Nov. 21, 1956; d. James David and Norma Ruth (Triplett) M. AS, Kent State U., 1982; BSN, Bowling Green State U., 1989; postgrad., Cleve. State U., 1989—. RN, Ohio. Office mgr. Clcogna Electric Co., Ashtabula, Ohio, 1978-82; nurse Cleve. Clin. Foun., 1982--, Bahman Guyuron M.D., Lyndhurst, Ohio, 1986--; clin. preceptor Cleve. Clin. Found., 1983—; CPR instr. Am. Heart Assn., 1988—. Mem. Sigma Theta Tau. Methodist. Home: 27600 Chardon Rd #953 Willoughby Hills OH 44092 Office: Cleve Clin Found 9500 Euclid Ave Cleveland OH 44195

MARKLE, ANN ELIZABETH, mental health clinic administrator; b. Terre Haute, Ind., June 12, 1952; d. Richard Theodore and Mary Elizabeth (Beach) M.; m. Arthur Douglas Ford, June 12, 1968 (div. Dec. 1971); 1 child, Eleanor Elizabeth; m. John Louis Shifflett, July 30, 1988. BS in Psychology, Ind. State U., 1976, MS in Clin. Psychology, 1978; MSW, SUNY, Buffalo, 1989. Cert. social worker, rehab. counselor, N.Y. Legal sec. Donald W. Reely, Terre Haute, 1972-74, Tofaute & Spelman, Terre Haute, 1974-77; crisis counselor Cen. Erie Mental Health Corp. III, Buffalo, 1978-79; outcare counselor NW Mental Health Corp. I, Buffalo, 1979-81; sr. counselor Horizon Human Svcs., Buffalo, 1981-89, program dir., 1989—. Editor: (anthology) Blatherskite, 1982, Buffalo Arts Rev., 1983-84, Faith...Works, 1990—; contbr. poetry and articles to various publs. Rachel Miller Manchester scholar SUNY, Buffalo, 1987-88, Welles V. Moot grad. scholar, 1987-88; grantee Buffalo Found., 1988-89. Mem. Nat. Assn. Social Workers, Am. Psychol. Assn. (assoc.), Ind. State U. Alumni Assn., SUNY-Buffalo Alumni Assn., NOW (pres. Terre Haute 1974), Niagara-Erie Writers (co-chmn. bd. dirs. 1984, chief exec. officer 1985). Democrat. Episcopalian. Office: Horizon Human Svcs 36 Delaware St Tonawanda NY 14150

MARKOVICH, LOIS ANN GIMONDO, automobile association executive; b. San Francisco, Jan. 13, 1947; d. Henry Mario and Theresa Marie (Posca) Gimondo; m. Thomas Richard Markovich, Nov. 25, 1973. BA, Loyola U.-Marymount Coll., L.A., 1971; MA in Adult Edn., San Francisco State U., 1980. CPCU. Personnel asst. Calif. Automobile Assn., San Francisco, 1971-75, tng. specialist, 1975-77, tng. dir., 1977-79, mgr. tng. devel., 1980-81, asst. v.p. human resources, 1981-83, v.p. human resources, 1983-87, v.p. human resources and adminstrv. svcs., 1987-89, v.p. pub. svcs., 1989—. Mem. Soc. CPCU, Ins. Ednl. Assn. (sec.-treas., trustee 1989—), Soc. Insurance Trainers and Educators (pres. 1985-86, Pres.'s award 1988), Tamalpa Runners. Republican. Roman Catholic. Office: Calif Automobile Assn 100 Van Ness Ave San Francisco CA 94102

MARKOVICH, OLGA, magazine editor; b. Toronto, Ont., Can., Feb. 24, 1940; d. Bozidar Marinko and Milica (Trumich) M. Diploma in Journalism, Ryerson Poly. Inst., 1965, B in Applied Arts in Journalism, 1973. Asst. editor Shoe and Leather Jour. Southam Communications Ltd., Don Mills, Ont., 1965-72, assoc. editor, 1972; editor Southam Bldg. Guide, Don Mills, 1972-82; mng. editor Can. Indsl. Equipment News, Don Mills, 1975-77, editor, 1977—, assoc. pub., 1990—. Author: Serbs in Canada--Their Immigration and Settlements, 1965, (with others) American Srbobran, Voice of Canadian Serbs; editor: Tributes to Mihailovich, 1966, Vinka Testimonial Book, 1977, Souvenir Book 35th Anniversary of the Circle of Serbian Sisters, 1976. Recipient Thomas Turner Meml. award Southam Communications Ltd., 1973, Mktg. award Southam Communications, 1977, Queen Elizabeth's Can. Silver Jubilee medal, 1977. Mem. Bus. Press Editors Assn., Am. Bus. Press, Soc. Serbian Writers and Artists Abroad (London), Serbian Nat. Shield Soc. Can., Serbian Nat. Fedn. (Person of Yr. award 1986). Progressive Conservative. Eastern Orthodox. Home: 254 Chine Dr, Scarborough, ON Canada M1M 2L8 Office: 1450 Don Mills Rd, Don Mills, ON Canada M3B 2X7

MARKOVICH-TREECE, PATRICIA HELEN, economist; b. Oakland, Calif.; d. Patrick Joseph and Helen Emily (Prydz) Markovich; BA in Econs., 1986, MS in Econs., U. Calif.-Berkeley; postgrad. (Lilly Found. grantee) Stanford U., (NSF grantee) Oreg. Grad. Rsch. Ctr., DD World Christian Ministries; children: Michael Sean, Bryan Jeffry, Tiffany Helene. With pub. rels. dept. Pettler Advt., Inc.; pvt. practice polit. and econs. cons.; aide to majority whip Oreg. Ho. of Reps.; lectr., instr., various Calif. instns., Chemeketa (Oreg.) Coll., Portland (Oreg.) State U. Commr., City of Oakland (Calif.), 1970-74; chairperson, bd. dirs. Cable Sta. KCOM, Piedmont; coord. City of Piedmont, Calif. Gen. Planning Commn.; mem. Piedmont Civic Assn., Oakland Mus. Archives of Calif. Artists. Mem. Mensa, Bay Area Artists Assn. (coord., founding mem.), Berkeley Art Ctr. Assn., San Francisco Arts Commn. File, Index for Contemporary Arts, Pro Arts.

MARKS, BARBARA HANNAH, magazine publisher; b. Carrollton, Ga., Dec. 23, 1956; d. Marshall Harrison Hannah and Pauline Ruth (Honadel) Chou; m. Henry William Marks, Dec. 18, 1981 (div. Jan. 1987). BS in Mktg., St. John's U., N.Y.C., 1978; postgrad., NYU, 1980-82. Promotion mgr. Playboy mag., N.Y.C., 1978-79; pub. TeenAge Mag., N.Y.C., 1982-84, 86-88, v.p., advt. dir., 1986-88; assoc. pub. Success! mag., N.Y.C., 1984-86; v.p. pub. CPS, Inc., Bedford, Mass., 1986-88; sr. v.p. group pub. Macfadden Holdings, Inc., N.Y.C., 1988—. Home: 7 Pioneer Rd Westport CT 06880 Office: Macfadden Holdings 233 Park Ave New York NY 10003

MARKS, BEATRICE GLASS, public relations and communications executive; children: Steven, Jamie, Claudia, Lindsey, Robin. AB in Psychology, U. Mich. Host radio and TV programs Albuquerque; editor, pub. Memo Mag.; asst. to pub. Portland (Oreg.) Mag.; with Botsford Ketchum, Inc., San Francisco, from 1965; now sr. v.p., dir. food, nutrition and health communications Ketchum Pub. Rels., N.Y.C.; former pres. Ctr. for Nutrition Edn.; mem. food and nutrition bd. of com. on dietary guidelines implementation NRC. Bd. visitors U. Md. Coll. Human Ecology. Mem. Am. Dietetic Assn. (found. corp. adv. coun.). Office: Ketchum Pub Rels 1133 Ave of the Americas New York NY 10036*

MARKS, CAROLYN ANN, management training consultant; b. Larchmont, N.Y., July 16, 1945; d. Ralph Silas and Harriet (Voloshin) M.; m. Steven D. Gratz, Dec. 27, 1975; 1 child, Joel Benjamin. BS, Boston U., 1967; MEd, U. Miami, 1970; EdD, Temple U., 1980. Tchr. Wilson Sch. Dist., Phoenix, 1967-69, Dade County Schs., Miami, Fla., 1969-70; coord. work experience Broward County Schs., Ft. Lauderdale, Fla., 1970-73; personnel asst. Temple U., Phila., 1973-74, mgr. employee rels., 1974-76, dir. communications and tng., 1976-79; exec. dir. Penjerdel Employee Benefits Assn., Phila., 1980-89; pres. Carolyn A. Marks & Assocs., Chalfont, Pa., 1989—; pres. Broward Tchrs. Union, 1970-72. Mem. Bucks County Commr.'s Women's Adv. Coun., Doylestown, Pa., 1987-88; del. Dem. Nat. Conv., 1988. Fellow U. Miami, 1969-70. Mem. Am. Soc. for Tng. and Devel., Human Resources Profl. Assn., Pa. Elected Women's Assn., Bus. and Profl. Women, NOW (pres. Bucks County 1986—), Phi Delta Kappa, Phi Delta Gamma (pres. 1982-84, editor jour. 1986). Address: PO Box 342 Chalfont PA 18914

MARKS, DOROTHY LIND, mathematics tutor; b. N.Y.C., Apr. 30, 1900; d. Alfred Daniel and Martha (Herzog) Lind; m. Norman Lincoln Marks, May 29, 1923 (dec. 1959); 1 son, Alfred Lind (dec. 1980). B.A., Barnard Coll., 1921. Substitute tchr. N.Y. high schs., 1921-28; math tutor The Brearley Sch., N.Y.C., 1953-62, The Marlborough Sch., Los Angeles, 1973—, pvt. and pub. secondary schs., Los Angeles, 1973—, NYU, 1965-72; chmn. math dept. The Lenox Sch., N.Y.C., 1960-70. Bd. dirs. women's orgn. Temple Rodeph Sholem, N.Y.C., 1925-50, fin. sec., 1925-47. Mem. Phi Beta Kappa (recipient Kohn Math. Prize 1921, sec.-treas. Barnard chpt. 1925-50, chartermem. alumnae in N.Y.). Republican. Jewish. Avocations: reading, music, theatre, concerts, ballet.

MARKS, JANET LYNN, computer engineer; b. Kingston, N.Y., May 7, 1963; d. John William and Marlene Mabel (Downing) M. BS in Computer Sci., N.C. State U., 1985; MBA, U. S.C., 1990. Project leader NCR Corp., Columbia, S.C., 1986—. Republican. Methodist.

MARKS, JANICE ELIZABETH, marketing professional; b. Britt, Iowa, June 21, 1960; d. Richard Stephen and Barbara Louise (Hauser) M. BS, Iowa State U., 1982; MS in Mktg. Research, U. Ga., 1984. Mktg. rsch. intern Ralston Purina, St. Louis, 1984; mgr. mktg. rsch. Vlasic Foods, West Bloomfield, Mich., 1988; acct. exec. Mktg. & Research Counselors, Irving, Tex., 1988-89; sr. mktg. rsch. analyst Hershey (Pa.) Chocolate USA, 1985-87, lead mktg. rsch. analyst, 1989—. Mem. Dallas Mus. of Art; vol. leader Pioneer Girls Clubs, 1986-87. Mem. Am. Mktg. Assn., Iowa State Alumni Assn., Order Ea. Star, Alpha Kappa Psi. Evangelical. Home: 107 E 2nd St Hummelstown PA 17036 Office: Hershey Chocolate USA 19 E Chocolate Ave Hershey PA 17033

MARKS, JUDITH FRANCINE See **CHUSID, JUDITH FRANCINE**

MARKS, LILLIAN SHAPIRO, education educator, author; b. Bklyn., Mar. 16, 1907; d. Hayman and Celia (Merowitz) Shapiro; B.S., N.Y. U., 1928; m. Joseph Marks, Feb. 21, 1932; children: Daniel, Sheila Blake, Jonathan. High sch. tchr., N.Y.C., 1929-30; tchr. Evalina de Rothschild Sch., Jerusalem, Palestine, 1930-31; social worker United Jewish Aid, Bklyn., 1931-32; tchr. Richmond Hill High Sch., 1932-40, Andrew Jackson High Sch., Cambria Heights, N.Y., 1940-71; mem. faculty New Sch. Social Rsch., N.Y.C., 1977-87; staff Vassar Summer Inst., 1946. Mem. Am. Fedn. Tchrs., English-Speaking Union, Inst. Ret. Profls. Democrat. Am. editor: Teeline, A System of Fast Writing, 1970; author: College Teeline, 1977; College Teeline Self-Taught, 1983; Touch Typing Made Simple, 1985. Home and Office: 117-16 Park Lane S Kew Gardens NY 11418

MARKS, LYNN WILSON, forensic document examiner; b. Dayton, Ohio, Feb. 1, 1955; d. John W. and Beatrice A. (Dorst) Wilson; m. Peter L. Marks, June 19, 1976; children: Erika, Wilson. Student, U. Cen. Fla. Forensic document examiner, owner Lynn Wilson Marks & Assocs., San Antonio; lectr., instr. for academic, legal and forensic disciplines U. Texas Grad. Sch., 1990, U. Texas Health Sci. Ctr. San Antonio, 1988, 90, U. Trier West Germany, 1990, St. Mary's Law Sch., Pan Am. Assn. Forensic Sci.; developer standards in forensic document exam. Contbr. articles to profl. jours. Mem. North San Antonio C. of C. speakers bureau, Greater Boerne Area C. of C. Mem. Assn. of Forensic Document Examiners (cert., sec., v.p. 1990), Forgery Investigators Assn. of Tex., Pan Am. Assn. of Forensic Sci. (co-chair questioned document sect. 1987-90). Office: PO Box 690526 San Antonio TX 78269

MARKS, ROBERTA BARBARA, artist, educator; b. Savannah, Ga.; d. Philip W. and Eleanore (Margolis) Dilner; children—Jeffery Allen, Steven Craig. B.F.A., U. Miami, Coral Gables, Fla., 1980; M.F.A., U. S. Fla., 1981. Instr., lectr. multi-media, lectr., vis. artist to numerous art schs., including U. S. Fla., Tampa, Chgo. Art Inst., Valparaiso U., Ind., Rochester Inst. Tech. Am. Sch. of Crafts, N.Y., Galerie de Koull, Murten, Switzerland, Santa Fe Community Coll., Gainesville, Brookfield Craft Ctr., Conn., Fla. Keys Community Coll., U. Wis.-Milw., Parson Sch. Design; juror Riverside Avondale Preservation Art Festival, Jacksonville, Fla., 1981, Ybor Square Art Festival, Tampa, 1980, Miami Lakes Art Festival, Fla., 1975. One woman shows include Brevard Community Coll., Melbourne, Fla., 1982, Cocoa, Fla., 1982, Coventry Galleries, Ltd., Tampa, 1983, Barbara Gillman Gallery, Miami, 1984, 87, Tennessee Williams Fine Arts Ctr., Key West, 1985, Garth Clark Gallery, N.Y.C., 1985, Fred Gros Gallery, Key West, 1985, Key West Art and Historical Soc. East Martello Mus. and Gallery, 1985, U. Miami New Gallery, Fla., 1987, Katie Gingrass Gallery, Milw., 1987, Zimmerman Saturn Gallery, Nashville, 1987, Bern, Zurich Switzerland, 1988, Galerie Alte Krone, Altstadt, Biel, Switzerland, 1990, Helander Gallery, N.Y.C., 1990, Gump's Gallery, San Francisco, 1990, many others; exhibited in group shows at Netsky Gallery, Miami, 1982, The Craftsman's Gallery, Scarsdale, N.Y., 1982, Garth Clark Gallery, Los Angeles, 1983, Nelson-Atkins Mus. Art, Kansas City, Mo., 1983, Am. Craft Mus., N.Y.C., 1984, N. Miami Mus. and Art Ctr., 1985, Joanne Lyon Gallery, Aspen, Colo., 1984, Key West Art and Hist. Soc. East Martello Mus. and Gallery, 1985, Garth Clark Gallery, N.Y.C. and Los Angeles, 1985, 24X24, Ruth Siegel Ltd., N.Y.C., 1987, Artforms Gallery, Louisville, 1986, The Pvt. Collection Women Artists, Ohio, 1987, East Martello Mus., Key West, Fla., 1990, many others; represented in permanent collections Smithsonian Instn., Renwick Gallery, Rochester Inst. Tech. Fine Arts Dept., U. Utah Mus., U. South Fla. Fine Arts Dept., Galerie du Manoir, La Chaux-de-Fonds, Switzerland, Valencia Community Coll., Okum Gallery, Victoria and Albert Mus., London, IBM, Jacksonville, Fla., AT&T, N.Y.C. , others. Recipient Regional Visual Artist fellowship, Miami, Fla., 1990, also numerous awards. Mem. World Craft Council, Artists Equity Assn., Internat. Sculpture Ctr.

MARKS, SHEILA HOFFMAN, apparel designer; b. N.Y.C.; d. David B. and Diana Hoffman. BFA, Pratt Inst., 1960; MA, Hunter Coll. Creative dir. Womenswear (Japan) Bill Blass Ltd., N.Y.C., designer; pres. Sheila Marks Enterprises, N.Y.C.; designer Anne Klein, N.Y.C. Mem. NAFE, Fashion Group Internat. (chairwoman membership com. 1987), Coll. Art Assn. Office: Bill Blass Ltd 550 Seventh Ave New York NY 10018

MARKS, STEPHANIE LYN, social services administrator; b. Boston, July 21, 1958; d. Wesley and (Hershenson) M. AA, U. Hartford, 1978, BA, 1980; MEd, U. Mass., Boston, 1988. Vol. Hartford (Conn.) Parole Bd, 1977-78; intern Hartford (Conn.) Correctional Ctr., 1978-79; housing administr. U. Hartford (Conn.), 1978-80; counselor Conn. Halfway Houses, Hartford; from correction social worker to asst. to assoc. commr. Mass. Dept. of Correction, Boston, 1980-83; asst. to warden, mgr. of inmate grievance program Walpole (Mass.) State Prison, 1983-87; asst. to supt., pub. affairs, community svcs. Old Colony Correctional Ctr., Bridgewater, Mass., 1987-90; staff assoc. counselor U. Mass., Boston, 1990—; v.p. criminal justice Assn., U. Hartford, 1978-80, trainer, U. Mass., 1987, presenter Nat. Conf. on Family and Corrections, N.Y.C., 1989. Author The Family Awareness Training Program, 1990. Chair Women's Internat.Zionist Orgn., Boston, 1988; active Jewish Philanthrophils, Little Bros., Friends of Elderly. Mem. Am. Correctional Assn., Mass. Correctional Assn., Internat. Student Assn., Publicity of Boston, Am. Soc. Tng. and Devel., Nat. Soc. Performance and Instrn., Nat. Family and Corrections Network, Internat. Assn. Pers. Women. Home: 357 Austin St West Newton MA 02165

MARKS, SUSAN JANE, banker; b. Detroit, Sept. 11, 1954; d. Richard Ellis and Mary Arthur (Johnson) M.; m. Douglas J. Stelsing, Sept. 26, 1987. B in Gen. Studies, U. Mich., 1976, MA, 1977. Product mgmt. officer 1st Chgo. Corp., 1978-83; v.p., group product mgr. Nat. Westminster Bank, U.S.A., N.Y.C., 1983—. Mem. N.Y. Jr. League, U. Mich. Club N.Y. (bd. dirs. 1983—). Republican. Office: Nat Westminster Bank USA 175 Water St New York NY 10038

MARKS, TAMARA ELIZABETH, electronic product representative; b. San Jose, Costa Rica, Dec. 12, 1962; came to U.S., 1968; d. Russell Edward and Patricia (Hunt) M. Student, Wheaton Coll., Norton, Mass., 1981-83; BA in Spanish Lang. and Lit., Boston U., 1985. Research analyst Coopers & Lybrand, N.Y.C., 1985-87; project coordinator Healthcare Communications, Inc., Princeton, N.J., 1987-88, product mgr., 1988-89; electronic product rep. Commerce Clearing House, Inc., Boston, 1990—. Pres. Boston U. South Campus Govt., 1984-85; mem. June Opera Festival N.J., Princeton, 1986-90. Mem. Am. Mus. of Natural History, Boston U. Alumni Assn., Wheaton Coll. Alumni. Republican. Episcopalian. Home: 7 Pond Ln Apt 3 Arlington MA 02174

MARKUSZKA, NANCY ANN, counselor; b. Cleve., Jan. 28, 1951; d. John Michael and Harriet Wanda (Klonowski) M. BS in Edn., Kent State U., 1973; cert. real estate agt., Cuyahoga Community Coll., 1977; cert. Employee BenefitsSpecialist, Cleve. State U. Substitute tchr. Ohio, 1972-73; personnel technican State of Ohio Dept. of Adminstrv. Svcs., Cleve., 1974-75; personnel officer Welfare Dept. Lake County, Painsville, Ohio, 1975-76; lic. real estate agt. Gerspacher Realty, Greater Cleveland, Ohio, 1978-79; dist. sales rep. Chanslor & Lyons Inc., Brisbane, Calif., 1981-82, TRW Replacement Div., Cleve., 1979-81; counselor, instr. Bur. of Employment Svcs. State of Ohio, Cleve., 1983—. Trustee Edn. Fund League of Woman Voters of Cleve., 1987—. Outstanding Service award State of Ohio Assembly, Columbus, 1987, Cert. of Merit LWV, Cleve., 1987,88, Carrier Chapman Catt award for Outstanding Service LWV, Cleve., 1989. Mem. Bd. dirs., 1st v.p. voter svcs., Internat. Assn. of Personnel in Employment Security, Am. Society of Profl. and Exec. Women, NAFE, LWV (bd. dirs. 1984-89, sec. 1985-86, 2d v.p. 1987-88.), Kent State U. Alumni. Home: 577 Tollis Pkwy Broadview Heights OH 44147

MARLAN, LORI J., real estate developer; b. Rochester, N.Y., Jan. 6, 1957; d. Morton William and Fern Mauya (Seeman) M. BA, Yale U., 1979; JD, SUNY, Buffalo, 1983. Assoc. Milbank, Tweed, Hadley & McCloy, N.Y.C., 1983-85, Salomon Bros., Inc., N.Y.C., 1985-88; v.p. Greenwich (Conn.) Capital Markets, Inc., 1988-89; project mgr. KG Land N.Y. Corp., N.Y.C., 1989—. Playwright: Firewaltz, 1981. Mem. Yale Club N.Y.C., Fin. Women's Assn., Yale Club Greenwich, Elizabethan Club. Republican. Office: KG Land NY Corp 4 Columbus Cir 3d Fl New York NY 10019

MARLAND, DOROTHY MARGARET, Canadian provincial official; b. St. Catherines, Ont., Can.; m. Kenneth Marland; children: Ruth, Donald, Robert. Mem. Ont. Legis. Assembly, 1985—; opposition critic for Housing and Women's Issues, 1985, opposition critic for Culture, 1985, opposition critic for Culture and Sr. Citizens Affairs, 1986, mem. edn. task force, 1986; mem. Progressive Conservative Task Force on Extended Shopping Hours, 1987; progressive conservative critic for Environment, Community and Social Svcs. and Disabled Persons, 1987, progressive conservative critic for Environment, Disabled Persons and Citizenship, 1988. Mem. Mississauga Hosp. Women's Aux.; chairwoman Progressive Conservative Conf. on Gender in Sports; mem. Standing Com. on Govt. Agys., Bds. and Commns.; mem. Resource Devel. Com., Gen. Govt. Com., Standing Com. on Procedural Affairs; councillor ward City of Mississauga; regional councillor Region of Peel; mem. adv. bd. St. Brides Anglican Ch.; bd. dirs. Peel Family Svcs., Peel Region United Way; trustee Peel Bd. Edn; bd. govs. Sheridan Coll., Oakville Trafalgar Hosp. Office: Ont Parliament, Parliament Bldgs, Toronto, ON Canada M7A 1A2

MARLEAU, DIANE, Canadian legislator; b. Kirkland Lake, Ont., Can., June 21, 1943; d. Jean-Paul and Yvonne (Desjardins) LeBel; m. Paul C. Marleau, Aug. 3, 1963; children: Brigitte, Donald, Stéphane. Student, U. Ottawa, Ont., 1960-63; BA in Econs., Laurentian U., Sudbury, Ont., 1976. Acct. Donald Jean Acctg. Svcs., Sudbury, 1971-75; receiver mgr. Thorne Riddell, Sudbury, 1975-76; treas. No. Regional Recovery Home for Women, Sudbury, 1976-80, Com. for the Industry and Labour Adjustment Program, Sudbury, 1983; chmn. Can. Games for the Physically Disabled, Sudbury, 1983; rep. Ont. Adv. Coun. on Women's Issues, Toronto, 1984-85; mem. transition team Ont. Premier's Office, Toronto, 1985; firm adminstr. Collins Barrow-Maheu Noiseux (formerly Desmarais, Arsenault & Co.), Sudbury, 1985-88; mem. of Parliament House of Commons, Ottawa, 1988—; councilor Regional Municipality of Sudbury, 1980-85; alderman City of Sudbury, 1980-85; mem. No. Devel. Coun., Sudbury, 1986-88; chmn. Cambrian Coll. Bd. Govs., Sudbury, 1987-88. Chmn. Canadian Cancer Soc., Sudbury, 1987-88; co-chmn. Laurentian Hosp. Cancer Care Svcs. Campaign, Sudbury, 1988. Mem. Sudbury Bus. and Profl. Women Club. (named Woman of the Day 1989). Office: House of Commons, Confederation Bldg, Rm 613, Ottawa, ON Canada K1A 0A6*

MARLER, LINDA SUSAN, microbiologist; b. Bloomington, Ind., May 28, 1951; d. Lynne Lionel and Lucille Elizabeth (Widman) Merritt; B.S. in Med. Tech., Ind. U., 1973, M.S. in Allied Health Edn., 1978; m. David William Marler, May 21, 1977 (div.); children—Brian David, Brittney Lynne. Med. technologist, then sr. med. technologist Ind. U. Med. Center, Indpls., 1973—, edn. coordinator dept. microbiology, 1974—, asst. prof. div. allied health Sch. Medicine, 1978-84, assoc. prof., 1984—; speaker in field. Mem. Am. Soc. Microbiology, Am. Soc. Med. Tech., South Central Assn. Clin. Microbiologists (teleconf. chairperson, assn. dir.). Methodist. Office: Fesler 416 1120 South Dr Indianapolis IN 46223

MARLETT, JUDITH ANN, professor; b. Toledo. BS, Miami U., Oxford, Ohio, 1965; PhD, U. Minn., 1972; postgrad., Harvard U., 1973-74. Registered dietitian. Therapeutic and metabolic unit dietitian VA Hosp., Mpls., 1966-67; spl. instr. in nutrition Simmons Coll., Boston, 1973-74; asst. prof. U. Wis., Madison, 1975-80; acting dir. dietetic program Dept. Nutritional Scis. U. Wis., 1977-78, assoc. prof., 1981-84, prof., 1984—; vis. prof. Oreg. State U., Corvallis, 1989; cons. grain, drug and food cos., 1985—; adv. bd. U. Ariz. Clin. Cancer Ctr., 1987—; sci. bd. advisors Am. Health Found.; NIH ad hoc reviewer; researcher in dietary fiber and gastrointestinal function. Contbr. articles to profl. jours.; editorial bd. Jour. of Sci. of Food and Agrl., 1989—; achievements include rsch. on dietary fiber and gastrointestinal function. Mem. sci. bd. advisors Am. Health Found.; ad hoc reviewer NIH. Mem. AAAS, Am. Inst. Nutrition, Am. Dietetic Assn., Wis. Dietetic Assn., Madison Dist. Dietetic Assn., Am. Soc. for Clin. Nutrition, Inst. of Food Technologists, Am. Assn. Cereal Chemists. Office: U Wis Dept Nutritional Sci 1415 Linden Dr Madison WI 53706

MARLETTO, JANET CHERYL, hotel management executive; b. Oakland, Calif., Jan. 28, 1946; d. Michael Louis and Marie Nina (Radonich) M. BA in French and History, U. Calif, Santa Barbara, 1967; postgrad. for secondary edn. certificate, U. Calif, 1968. Cert. secondary tchr., Calif. Asst. dir. housekeeping Hotel St. Francis Western Internat. Hotels, San Francisco, 1975-77; dir. housekeeping Galeria Plaza Hotel Western Internat. Hotels, Houston, 1977-79, Royal Sonesta Hotel, New Orleans, Four Seasons Hotel Houston Ctr., Houston, 1981-83; cons. Houston, Orlando, Tex., Fla., 1983—; dir. housekeeping Westin Houston, Walt Disney World Swan, Westin Hotels, Houston, Orlando, 1989—; dir. of housekeeping Chase-Park Plaza Hotel, St. Louis, 1979; adj. instr. Houston Community Coll., 1984-88; owner cons. svc. for homes, 1983—. Mem. AAUW (pres. Houston br. 1987-88), Nat. Exec. Housekeepers Assn.

MARLEY, ELFRIEDE, insurance company administrator; b. Germany, Apr. 21, 1943; came to U.S., 1963; d. Emil and Lydia (Rometsch) Wrede; m. Kenneth R. Marley, Sept. 18, 1964; 1 child, Shanon. AA, Columbia Coll., 1981; BBA summa cum laude, Ottawa U., 1984. Asst. sec., dir. benefit dept. Old Am. Ins. Co., Kansas City, Mo., mgr. health claims div. Mem. Life and Health Claim Assn. of Greater Kans. City (pres.), Old Am. Toastmasters (pres.). Office: Old Am Ins Co 4900 Oak St Kansas City MO 64112

MARLEY, MARY LOUISE, psychologist; b. Columbia, Pa., Apr. 18, 1923; d. William Edward and Carrie Cook (Lockard) M. BS in Edn., Millersville (Pa.) State U., 1944; MEd in Psychology and Audiology, Franklin & Marshall Coll., 1952. Lic. psychologist, speech pathologist, audiologist, Pa. Cons. remedial reading Dearborn (Mich.) Elem. Schs., 1944-49; tchr. spl. edn. Hershey (Pa.) Elem. Sch., 1949-52; speech pathologist York (Pa.) County Schs. Office, 1952-55, asst. psychologist, 1955-68; clin. psychologist stroke unit York Hosp., 1968-74; pvt. practice clin. psychology York, 1974—; cons. York City, York Twp., West York, Hazelton, Pa., Windsor Twp., Red Lion, Gettysburg, Springettsburg Twp., No. Regional, West Manchester, Hanover Boro, Wrightsville, Jackson Twp., Penn Twp. police depts., 1983—. Author: Organic Brain Pathology and the Bender Gestalt Test, 1982. Pres., cons. Loving Care Inc., York, 1984—. Mem. Pa. Psychol. Assn., Nat. Assn. Neuropsychology, Nat. Register Clin. Psychology, York County Psychol. Assn. Republican. Methodist. Home: 926 McKenzie St York PA 17403 Office: 1620 S Queen St York PA 17403

MARLIN, THERESE ROSE, supervisor; b. Camden, N.J., Apr. 7, 1938; d. Thomas Joseph and Rose Lucile (Dimuro) Puzzutelli; m. William Herbert Marlin, Dec. 22, 1973; 1 child, Richard Hillen. BA, Immaculata Coll., 1968; MA, Glassboro State U., 1977; EdD, Rutgers U., 1987. Tchr. Archidiocese of Phila., Phila., 1958-69, Villa Maria Acad., Lima, Peru, 1969-71; tchr. Camden City Pub. Sch., Camden, 1971-86, supr.; adj. faculty Glassboro State Coll. N.J., 1985-88, Camden County Coll. Blackwood, N.J., 1989—; cons. Rutgers U. Ednl. Resource Ctr. Cen. South, N.J., 1972—. Co-author: Teachertorium, 1984; Author: Cassocks in the Attic, 1983; Exec. Producer: Supervising Tchrs., 1987. Rec. Sec. Camden County Coun. Educators Haddonfield, N.J., 1973-75; Advisor 4-H Urban League Camden, N.J., 1986—, Ednl. Opportunity Fund Camden County Coll., 1987—, Jr. Achievement Camden County, 1989. Recipient Grant N.J. Historical Soc., 1982, Hilda Maeling Fellowship Nat. Edn. Assn. Phila., 1983, Outstanding Tchr. Award Camden City Bd. Edn. Camden, 1983. Mem. N.J. Edn. Assn., Assn. Curriculum and Supervision Devel., Nat. Council of Tchr. English, Internat. Reading Assn. Democrat. Roman Catholic. Home: 29 Euclid Ave Haddonfield NJ 08033

MARLING-GEORGE, LISA, executive search consultant; b. Fremont, Ohio, Apr. 20, 1964; d. Richard Alan and Shirley Ann (Trigg) Marling; m. David Lee George, Aug. 1, 1987. BSBA, Ohio State U., 1986, postgrad., 1989—. Trainee Sherwin Williams Co., Dublin, Ohio, 1986; asst. mgr. Sherwin Williams Co., Westerville, Ohio, 1986-87; cons. Splty. Recruiting Systems, Inc., Dublin, 1987-88, mgr., 1988—. Mem. Dublin Arts Coun. (bd. dirs., scholarship com, liason to Dublin Women in Bus. & Professions), Ohio, 1989—. Mem. Am. Mktg. Assn. (Career Day com., asst. v.p. mem.), Dublin Women in Bus. and Professions (bd. dirs., steering com., Miss Colleen com., co-chmn. Career Day). Republican. Methodist. Home: 2473 Shillingham Ct Powell OH 43220 Office: Splty Recruiting Systems 400 Metro Pl N Ste 350 Dublin OH 43017

MARMER, ELLEN LUCILLE, pediatrician; b. Bronx, N.Y., June 29, 1939; d. Benjamin and Diane (Goldstein) M.; m. Harold O. Shapiro, June 5, 1960; children: Cheri, Brenda. BS in Chemistry, U. Ala., 1960; MD, U. Ala., Birmingham, 1964. Cert. Nat. Bd. Med. Examiners, 1965; Diplomate Bd. Pediatrics, 1969, Bd. Qualified and Eligible Pediatric Cardiology, 1969. Intern Upstate Med. Ctr., Syracuse, N.Y., 1964-65, resident, 1965-66; fellow in pediatric cardiology Columbia Presbyn. Med. Ctr.-Babies Hosp., N.Y.C., 1967-69; pvt. practice Hartford, Vernon, Conn., 1969—; examining pediatrician child devel. program Columbia Presbyn. Med. Ctr.-Babies Hosp., N.Y.C., 1967, instr. pediatrics, 1967-69; dir. pediatric cardiology clinic St. Francis Hosp., Hartford, 1970-80; asst. state med. examiner, Tolland County, Conn., 1974-79; sports physician Rockville (Conn.) High Sch., 1976—; advisor Cardiac Rehab. com., Rockville, 1984—. Mem. Vernon Town Coun., 1985-89; bd. dirs. Child Guidance Clinic, Manchester, Conn., 1970—; life mem. Tolland County chpt. Hadassah, v.p., 1969-70, pres., 1970-72, bd. dirs., 1973-74; mem. B'nai Israel Congregation and Sisterhood, Vernon, Conn., 1969—, chmn. youth commn., 1970-72; bd. dirs. Heart Assn. Greater Hartford, 1970—, exec. com. bd. dirs. 1972-73, 79—, sec., 1978-80, v.p., 1980-82, pres. 1982-84). Recipient Outstanding Svc. award Indian Valley YMCA, 1985. Fellow Am. Acad. Pediatrics, Am. Coll. Cardiology; mem. Am. Acad. Sports Medicine, Conn. Med. Soc., Am. Heart Assn. (mem. coun. cardiovascular disease in young 1969—, chmn. elect New Eng. regional heart com. 1990-91), Conn. Heart Assn. (bd. dirs. 1974-75, 83-84, pres. 1986-88), Heart Assn. Greater Hartford (bd. dirs. 1970-89, mem. exec. com. 1972-73, 79-84, pres. 1982-84), Tolland County Med. Assn. (sec. 1971-72), Rockville Pub. Health Nursing Assn., LWV (state program chairperson Vernon chpt. 1971-73). Democrat. Jewish. Office: 351 Merline Rd Vernon CT 06066

MARMOR, DEBRA SUSAN, marketing professional; b. West Berlin, Fed. Rep. Germany, Feb. 17, 1958; came to U.S., 1976; d. Simon James and Ruth (Schmalzigaug) M. AB in History, Politics, Mount Holyoke Coll., 1980; MBA, U. Pa., 1983; MA in Law and Diplomacy, Fletcher Sch. Law & Diplomacy, Medford, Mass., 1984. Internat. analyst NASA, Washington, 1981; fin. analyst COMSAT, Washington, 1982; competitive analyst AT&T, Basking Ridge, N.J., 1983; brand asst. Procter and Gamble Co., Cin., 1984-85, asst. brand mgr., 1985-88, brand mgr., 1988-89; brand mgr. Blendex GmbH, Mainz, W. Ger., 1989—. Chmn. corp. letters Zoofari '89 Cin. Zoo, 1989, chmn. sponsor letters, 1988, chmn. ad sales, 1987; vol. Cin. Hist. Soc., 1988. Ruth Lawson fellow in politics Mount Holyoke Coll., 1980. Mem. Direct Mktg. Assn., Fgn. Policy Assn., Cin. World Affairs Coun.

MARNELL, MARJORIE ANN, hospital administrator; b. Wheeling, W.Va., Sept. 27, 1954; d. Edmund David and Marjorie Ann (Pearl) Mathieu; m. John James Marnell, July 27, 1986; children: Ann-Marie, Marissa. BS in Pharmacy, W.Va. U., 1977, MBA, 1983. Lic. pharmacist, W.Va., Ohio. Staff pharmacist W.Va. U. Hosp., Morgantown, 1977-78; staff pharmacist Ohio Valley Med. Ctr., Wheeling, 1978-84, materials mgr., 1984-86; dir. materials mgmt. and pharmacy svcs. Ohio Valley Health Svcs. and Edn. Corp., Wheeling, 1986-89; asst. adminstr. Ohio Valley Med. Ctr., Wheeling, 1989-90, assoc. adminstr., 1990—; chmn. W.Va. Materials Mgmt. Svcs. Com., Charleston, 1988—; nat. treas. League of Intervenous Therapy Edn., Pitts., 1983-85. Bd. dirs. Wheeling chpt. Am. Heart Assn., 1984-88; chmn. Holly Twig, Wheeling, 1988—; pharmacy selection com. Sisters of the Third Order of St. Francis, Peoria, Ill, 1986—. Mem. W.Va. Soc. of Hosp. Pharmacists, W.Va. Pharmacists Assn., Ohio Soc. of Hosp. Pharmacists, Am. Soc. of Hosp. Materials Mgmt., Ohio-Marshall County Pharmacy Assn., Soroptimist Internat. (ways and means chmn. 1988-89), Am. Soc. of Hosp. Pharmacy, Beta Gamma Sigma. Democrat. Roman Catholic. Office: Ohio Valley Med Ctr 2000 Eoff St Wheeling WV 26003

MAROHN, ANN ELIZABETH, hospital official; b. Grand Rapids, Mich., Feb. 26, 1946; d. Luther Alfonse and Mary Inez (Pinkstaff) M. BS, Ind. U., 1968; MS, SUNY, Buffalo, 1978. Asst. med. record dir. Highland Park (Mich.) Gen. Hosp., 1968-70; asst. dir. med. record svcs. Meml. Hosp., Elmhurst, Ill., 1970-73; dir. med. record tech. program Alfred (N.Y.) State Coll., 1974-76; mem. faculty med. record adminstrn. dept. Lincoln Coll., Melbourne, Australia, 1977-78, Kean Coll., Union, N.J., 1984-85, Med. U. S.C., Charleston, 1985-87; mem. faculty health record dept. Ferris State Coll., Big Rapids, Mich., 1979-80; dir. health info. mgmt. Armstrong State Coll., Savannah, Ga., 1980-84; dir. med. record dept. Tucson Gen. Hosp., 1988-89, N.D. State Hosp., Jamestown, 1990—; cons. Oglethorpe Ctr., Savannah, 1983-84. Columnist Australian Med. Record Jour., 1981-87, Communique, 1981-84, Palmetto Breeze, 1985-87, Progress Notes, 1984-85. Recipient disting. mem. award Ga. Med. Record Assn., 1984. Mem. Am. Med. Record Assn. (registered), Am. Hosp. Assn., Ariz. Med. Record Assn. (program chmn. 1988-89, sec. 1989—), Ariz. Assn. Quality Assurance Profls. Episcopalian. Home: 522 14th St NE Jamestown ND 58401 Office: ND State Hosp PO Box 476 Jamestown ND 58401

MAROIS, HARRIET SUKONECK, computer scientist; b. Newark, Jan. 30, 1945; d. Edward and Mae S.; m. George Marois, Oct. 18, 1986. B.A., Rutgers U., 1966; M.A., U. So. Calif., 1968, Ph.D. (NIMH fellow), 1971. NIMH clin. postdoctoral fellow, div. psychiatry Children's Hosp. of Los Angeles, 1971-73; lectr. Calif. State U., Los Angeles, 1971-76; core faculty research series Calif. Sch. Profl. Psychology, Los Angeles, 1973-78, clin. psychologist in pvt. practice, Santa Monica, Calif., 1973-78; vis. asst. prof. Loyola Marymount U., Los Angeles, 1976-78; research assoc. Neuropsychiat. Inst., UCLA, 1978-79, adminstrv. analyst office of vice chancellor UCLA, 1979; sr. mem. tech. staff, project leader Systems Sci. Corp., El Segundo, Calif., 1979-81; systems cons./project adminstr. First Interstate Services Co., El Segundo, Calif., 1981-83; dir. research and product planning Data Line Service Co., 1983-84; project mgr. Xerox Corp., El Segundo, 1984—; founder, bd. dirs. Brainstorms, Los Angeles, 1985—.Lic. psychologist, Calif. Mem. Assn. Computing Machinery, Am. Psychol. Assn., AAAS. Contbr. articles to profl. jours. Editor et al, social sci. jour., 1971-76. Bd. dirs. So. Calif. Hot Jazz Soc. Los Angeles, 1988.

MAROSCHER, BETTY JEAN, librarian; b. Ashland, Ky., Aug. 12, 1934; d. Raymond and Virginia Dell (Staten) Boggs; student Columbus Coll. (Ga.), 1963-64; B.S., Hardin-Simmons U., 1967; M.S. in L.S., Our Lady of Lake U., San Antonio, 1970; M.Ed., Trinity U., 1975; m. Albert G. Maroscher Mar. 21, 1955 (dec.). Tchr., McAllen (Tex.) Ind. Sch. Dist., 1967-68; tchr. Northside Ind. Sch. Dist., San Antonio, 1968-69, librarian, 1969-71; reference librarian ednl. media Trinity U., San Antonio, 1971-76; reference librarian St. Philip's Coll., San Antonio, 1976, audiovisual librarian, mgr. audiovisual dept., 1977-86; librarian, coordinator Learning Resources Ctr., 1986—; lectr., cons. in field; chmn. subcom. programming and scheduling Univ. and Fine Arts Cable TV Com., 1980-81, sec. 1984-85. Active ARC; sec., trustee Compañia de Arte Español, 1982-84; sec. Council of Research and Academic Libraries, 1988-89. Recipient Minter/Medal Hardin-Simmons U., 1965, 66. Mem. Tex. Library Assn., Bexar County Library Assn., ALA, Tex. Jr. Coll. Tchrs. Assn., Tex. Assn. Chicanos in Higher Edn. (sec. St. Philip's chpt. 1982-84), Instructional Media Services Group, Council Research and Acad. Libraries Coop. Circulation Group (sec.-treas. 1977-79), Pi Gamma Mu (sec. chpt. 1965-67), Alpha Chi (historian 1965-67), other orgns. Republican. Home: 5230 Galahad Dr San Antonio TX 78218 Office: 2111 Nevada St San Antonio TX 78203

MAROTTA, PRISCILLA VALERIE, psychologist; b. Chelsea, Mass., Aug. 28, 1946; d. Joseph Francis and Fleurdelis Valerie (Peluso) M.; 1 child, Christopher Joseph. BA, Am. Internat. Coll., 1968; MEd, Bridgewater State U., 1971; PhD, U. So. Miss., 1985. Lic. psychologist, Fla., Mass., Ga., Wis. Clin. psychologist Ctr. for Cognitive Behavior Therapy, Ft. Lauderdale, 1989—; rsch. asst. U. So. Miss., Hattiesburg, 1982; behavioral medicine coordinator Forrest Gen. Hosp., Hattiesburg, 1983; mgmt. devel. specialist Am. Express, Ft. Lauderdale, Fla., 1984; psychology assoc. Boston VA Med. Ctr., 1985; psychologist Wis. Dept. Corrections, Madison, 1986; med. cons. Social Security Disability Bur., Madison, 1986; program dir. Northeast Ga. Med. Ctr., Gainesville, 1986-87; clin. psychologist Affiliates Evaluation and Therapy, Pembroke Pines, Fla., 1988-89. Mem. com. Easton (Mass.) Recreation Commn., 1972. Named to Outstanding Young in Am., 1978. Mem. Am. Psychol. Assn., Assn. for Advancement Behavior Therapy, Soc. Prof. and Exec. Women, NOW, LWV, Delta Kappa Gamma. Democrat. Roman Catholic. Home: 591 E Lake Dasha Dr Plantation FL 33324 Office: 300 NW 70th Ave Ste 302A Plantation FL 33317

MARPLE, ELAINE NOEL, personnel company executive; b. Indpls., June 12, 1951; d. Edward and Marie (Randolph) Noel; m. Michael R. Marple, Aug. 1, 1970; 1 child, Michael Chad. Student, Wayne Community Coll., Mt. Olive Coll. Owner AAA Employment, Goldsboro, Greenville, N.C., AAA Profession Resume Svc., Goldsboro, Greenville, N.C. Pres. Ladie Ministries, 1989—; tchr. Sunday sch. Mem. NAFE, Women Bus. Owners (v.p.). Office: 652 N Spence Ave Goldsboro NC 27534

MARQUARDT, CHRISTEL ELISABETH, lawyer; b. Chgo., Aug. 26, 1935; d. Herman Albert and Christine Marie (Geringer) Trolenberg; children: Eric, Philip, Andrew, Joel. BS in Edn., Mo. Western Coll., 1970; JD with honors, Washburn U., 1974. Bar: Kans. 1974, U.S. Dist. Ct. Kans. 1974, U.S. Supreme Ct. 1979, U.S. Ct. Appeals (10th cir.) 1980. Tchr. St. John's Ch., Tigerton, Wis., 1955-56; personnel asst. Columbia Records, Los Angeles, 1958-59; ptnr. Cosgrove, Webb & Oman, Topeka, 1974-86, Palmer & Marquardt, Topeka, 1986—; mem. atty. bd. discipline Kans. Supreme Ct., 1984-86; lectr. in field. Contbr. articles to legal jours. Asst. treas., mem. exec. Rep. Party, Kans., 1983-87; dist. bd. adjudication Mo. Synod Luth. Ch., Kans., 1982-88; bd. dirs. Topeka Civic Symphony, 1983— ; hearing examiner Human Relations Com., Topeka, 1974-76; local advisor Boy Scouts Am., 1973-74; bd. dirs., nominating com. YWCA, Topeka, 1979-81; bd. govs. Washburn U. Law Sch., 1987—; bd. dirs. Brown Found., 1988—. Named Women of Yr., Topeka Mayor, 1982; Mabee scholar Washburn U., 1972-74. Fellow Kans. Bar Found. (trustee 1987—); mem. ABA (ho. of dels. 1988—, specilization com. 1987—, chmn. 1989-90, mem. labor law family sect. 1989—), Kans. Bar Assn. (sec., treas. 1981-82, 83-85, v.p. 1985-86, pres. elect 1986-87, pres. 1987-88, lectr. 1974—, Disting. Svc. award 1980), Kans. Trial Lawyers Assn. (bd. govs. 1982-86, lectr.), Topeka Bar Assn., Am. Bus. Women's Assn. (lectr., corr. sec. 1983-84, pres. career chpt. 1986-87, one of Top Ten Bus. Women of the Yr. 1985), Kans. C. fo C. and Industry, Nat. Coun. Bar Pres. (exec. coun. 1989—). Home: 3121 Briarwood Circle Topeka KS 66611 Office: Palmer & Marquardt 112 SW 6th St Topeka KS 66603

MARQUARDT, DIANA LEE, internist, allergy and immunology educator; b. La Crosse, Wis., Oct. 4, 1954; d. Jerome Charles and Beth Ann (Kohnstamm) M.; m. John Rodney Franklin, Dec. 15, 1984. BA in Chemistry, David Lipscomb Coll., 1975; MD, Washington U., St. Louis. Diplomate Am. Bd. Internal Medicine, Am. Bd. Allergy and Immunology. Medicine intern U. Calif. Med. Ctr., San Diego, 1979-80, resident in medicine, 1980-82, fellow in allergy and immunology, 1982-84, asst. prof. medicine and immunology, 1984-90, assoc. prof. medicine and immunology, 1990—; cons. Gensia Pharms., San Diego, 1985—. Mem. editorial bd. Jour. Allergy and Clin. Immunology, 1988—; contbr. articles on immunology rsch. to med. jours. Recipient nat. rsch. svc. award NIH, 198l, new investigator award, 1985; Am. Lung Assn. fellow, 1983, John and George Hartford Found. fellow, 1986. Fellow Am. Acad. Allergy and Immunology; mem. Am. Assn. Immunologists, Am. Fedn. for Clin. Rsch. (univ. rep. 1988—, trainee rsch. award 1983), Peninsula Women's Soccer League (sec. 1986-87). Democrat. Mem. Ch. of Christ. Office: U Calif Med Ctr H-8ll-G 225 Dickinson St San Diego CA 92103

MARQUARDT, KATHLEEN PATRICIA, business executive; b. Kalispell, Mont., June 6, 1944; d. Dean King and Lorraine Camille (Buckmaster) Marquardt; m. William Wewer, Dec. 6, 1987; children—Shane Elizabeth, Montana Quinn. Purser, Pan Am. World Airways, Washington, 1968-75; info. specialist Capital Systems Group, Kensington, Md., 1979-81; dir. pub. affairs Subscription TV Assn., Washington, 1981-83, exec. dir., 1983-86 ; pres. Internat. Policy Studies Orgn., 1983—, pres., designer Elizabeth Quinn Couture. Chmn. bd. Friends of Freedom, 1982—, Putting People First Found., 1990—. Mem. Nat. Women's Polit. Caucus, NOW, Women in Communications, Nat. Assn. Women Bus. Owners. Home: 6302 30th St NW Washington DC 20015 Office: 7201 Wisconsin Ave Ste 705 Bethesda MD 20814

MARQUES, DIANE MARIE, clinical psychologist; b. Newark, Mar. 9, 1958; d. Julio and Vitalina (Lopes) M.; m. William T. Oswald, Apr. 9, 1983; children: Elena Victoria, Andrew. BA, Seton Hall U., 1979; MA, U. R.I., 1983, PhD, 1986. Lic. psychologist, Mass. Intern Children's Hosp. Med. Ctr./Judge Baker Children's Ctr., Boston, 1984-85; staff psychologist South Shore Mental Health Ctr., Quincy, Mass., 1985-86, Alianza Hispana/Alianza Familiar, Roxbury, Mass., 1986-88; psychotherapist North Shore Children's Hosp., Salem, Mass., 1986-87; staff psychologist Children's Hosp. Med. Ctr., Boston, 1988—; sr. staff psychologist Alianza Hispana/Judge Baker Children's Ctr., Roxbury, 1986-88; instr. psychology dept. psychiatry Harvard U. Med. Sch., Boston, 1988—; instr. psychology Sch. Human Svcs. Springfield Coll., Manchester, N.H., 1989—; sch. cons. Human Resource Inst., Malden, Mass., 1987—; presenter workshops on children's responses to grief. Contbr. articles to various publs. Pres. bd. dirs. Alliance for Progress of Hispanic Ams., Manchester, 1990—; mem. Latin-Am. Ctr., Manchester, 1990—. Clin. fellow in family systems NIMH, U. R.I., 1979-80; clin. fellow in psychology, Harvard U. Med. Sch., 1984-85. Mem. Am. Psychol. Assn., Nat. Hispanic Psychol. Assn., Psi Chi. Office: Children's Hosp Med Ctr Dept Psychiatry 300 Longwood Ave Boston MA 02115

MARQUEZ, SYNTHIA LAURA, marketing manager; b. Tonawanda, N.Y., Aug. 29, 1963; d. Albert and Sydelle (Farber) Wachtel; m. Edward Gneier Marquez, Dec. 31, 1982. AS, Pomona Coll., Claremont, Calif., 1982; BS, U. La Verne, 1985; MBA, Claremont Grad. Sch., 1989. Microbiology technologist Iolab Corp. (div. Johnson & Johnson), Claremont, 1982-85; quality assurance supr., regulatory analyst Ioptex Rsch. Inc., Azusa, Calif., 1985-89; regulatory compliance adminstr. Hyland div., Baxter Healthcare Corp., Glendale, Calif., 1989-90; dir. market rsch. Reimbursement Dynamics, Inc., Orange, Calif., 1990—. Mem. LWV, Am. Soc. for Quality Control, Med. Mktg. Assn., Toastmasters, Peter F. Drucker Alumni Assn. Home: 2951 Rockmont Ave Claremont CA 91711 Office: 750 The City Dr Ste 210 Orange CA 92668 also: 2000 L St Ste 200 Washington DC 20036

MARQUIS, JANET, physical educator; b. St. Joseph, Mo., Apr. 7, 1948; d. Jay S. and Clara Lillian (Burkett) M. BS in Education, Cen. Mo. State U., 1970. Tchr., coach Lexington (Mo.) R-V Sch. Dist., 1970—; chmn. Phys. Edn. Curriculum Com., Lexington, 1987—, Health Edn. Com, 1988—. Co-author: Physical Education Curriculum Guide, 1988, Lexington Health Competency Guide, 1989. Named Coach of Yr., Mo. Assn. of Track Coaches, Columbia, Mo., 1982. Mem. Mo. State Tchrs. Assn., Lexington Community Tchrs. Assn. (treas. 1982-83, ins. chmn. 1986-89, wellness co-chmn. 1989—), Nat. Fedn. Interscholastic Coaches Assn., Mo. Assn. for Health, Phys. Edn., Recreation and Dance (Tchr. of Yr. award, St. Louis, 1989), Am. Alliance for Health, Phys. Edn., Recreation and Dance, Sweet Adelines (asst. dir. Lafayette Trails chpt. 1979—), Delta Kappa Gamma. Democrat. Methodist. Home: 2302 Aull Ln Lexington MO 64067

MARQUIS, JEANNE LORRAINE, marketing specialist; b. Nashua, N.H., Dec. 16, 1953; d. Edward Noel and Pearl Theresa (Lavoie) Fortin; m. Daniel Charles Marquis, June 9, 1973; 1 child, Jaime Lisa. Student, Emery Sch. Bus. Legal sec., asst. Leonard, Prunier et al, Nashua, 1971-81; engring. adminstrn. sec. Digital Equipment Corp., Merrimack, N.H., 1981-83, engring. ops. analyst, 1983-85; software specialist II and III Digital Equipment Corp., Nashua, 1985—; justice of peace, notary pub., N.H. Recipient Software Svcs. Excellence award, 1987, Mktg. Excellence award, 1990. Mem. NAFE, Nashua Country Club. Republican. Roman Catholic. Home: 15 Eagle Dr Bedford NH 03102 Office: Digital Equipment Corp 10 Tara Blvd TTBl-3/F10 Nashua NH 03062

MARR, ROSE MARIE, real estate broker, business owner; b. Mason City, Iowa, May 8, 1943; d. Clarence Wigg and Marie Jacobina (Faaborg) Peterson; m. William Angus Marr, Nov. 21, 1967; children: Christopher Angus, Samantha Marie. BA, U. Ariz., 1965, postgrad., 1966; postgrad., Ariz. State U., Tempe, 1967-68. Tchr. drama, speech coach various schs. Tucson and Phoenix, Ariz., 1965-70; owner, mgr. Tiffany's Bakery, Brea Mall, Calif., 1976-85; merger and acquisitions specialist Nat. Bus. Brokers, El Toro, Calif., 1985-89; real estate broker, owner RMM Realty, Irvine, Calif., 1989—. Mem. St. Paul's Episcopal Ch., Tustin, Calif., 1990—, AAUW, Irvine, 1988-89; sec. Irvine High Sch. Booster Club, 1989—; co-chmn. Irvine High Sch. Swim Parents Orgn., 1988-89. Mem. Irvine Assn. Realtors, Orange County Bus. Network, Irvine C. of C. Republican. Home: 3 Citadel Irvine CA 92720

MARRA, DOROTHEA CATHERINE, chemist; b. N.Y.C., Jan. 23, 1922; d. Salvatore and Maria (Faugiana) Polizzi; m. Michael D. Marra, Jan. 11, 1947 (dec.); 1 child, Jacques. BA, Bklyn. Coll., 1943. Chemist Matam Corp., N.Y.C., 1943-44, Foster D. Snell, Inc., N.Y.C., 1944-69, Omar Rsch., N.Y.C., 1969-81, Aerosol Product Tech., N.Y.C., 1981-84, Costech, Inc., N.Y.C., 1984—. Soc. Cosmetic Chemists, Sigma Xi. Home: 107 Fernwood Rd Summit NJ 07901

MARRERO, MAGALY VICTORIA, psychologist; b. Havana, Cuba, Mar. 10, 1952; came to U.S., 1961; d. Ignacio and Ciria (Rivero) M.; m. Edward A. Wagner Jr., June 3, 1988. BA in Psychology, U. Tex., 1980; PhD in Psychology, U. North Tex., 1986. Lic. psychologist, Tex. Dallas Psychiat. Assocs., 1982-85; Biofeedback therapist Psychol. Devel. Ctr., Dallas, 1980-84; postdoctoral fellow Tex. Back Inst., Plano, 1985-88; psychologist Med. Support Psychology, Dallas, 1988—; cons. Brookhaven Psychiat. Pavillion, Dallas, 1988—, Firra Therapeutics, Garland, Tex., 1989—. Co-chair Chem. Dependence in Hispanic Families, Dallas, 1989; chair com. Hispanic Issues in Bio-Feedback Therapy, Washington, 1990—. Mem. Am. Psychol. Assn., Tex. Biofeedback Soc. (bd. dirs. 1986-89), Assn. Latino-Am. Para La Salud Mental (founder, bd. dirs. 1988—), Assn. Applied Psychophysiology and Biofeedback. Office: Med Support Psychology 2915 LBJ Freeway #102 Dallas TX 75234

MARRINAN, SUSAN FAYE, lawyer; b. Vermillion, S.D., May 29, 1948; d. H. Lyal and Ada Myrtle (Hollingsworth) Abild; children: Molly, Cara. BA, U. Minn., 1969, JD, 1973. Bar: Minn. 1973. Atty. Carlson Cos., Plymouth, Minn., 1973-74, Prudential Ins. Co., Mpls., 1974-75; v.p., gen. counsel, corp. sec. H.B. Fuller Co., St. Paul, 1977—. Fundraiser Am. Cancer Soc., St. Paul, 1984—; bd. dirs. Family Services of St. Paul, 1985, Childrens Theatre Co. Mem. Corporate Counsel Assn. (pres. 1986—), Am. Assn. Corporate Counsel (bd. dirs. Minn. chpt. 1986—). Republican. Office: H B Fuller Co 8 Pine Tree Dr Saint Paul MN 55112

MARRIOTT, TERREZ S., controller; b. Balt., Jan. 15, 1961; d. David Small and Salima Louise (Siler) M. BS cum laude, Morgan State U., 1981. CPA, Ga, Md. Contr. Coca Cola Trading Co., Atlanta, acctg. mgr.; sr. acct., sr. auditor Price Waterhouse, Atlanta. Mem. AICPA, Ga. Soc. CPA, Nat. Assn. Black Accts., Delta Mu Delta. Office: Coca Cola One Coca Cola Pl Atlanta GA 30313

MARRON, DARLENE LORRAINE, real estate development executive, financial and marketing consultant; b. Auburn, N.Y., July 20, 1946; d. William Chester and Elizabeth Barbara (Gervaise) Kulakowski; m. Edward W. Marron, Jr., Apr. 28, 1973. BS cum laude, Rider Coll., 1968; MBA, NYU, 1970. Lic. securities broker. Dir. mktg. Am. Airlines, N.Y.C., 1970-79; asst. v.p. Merrill Lynch, N.Y.C., 1979-83; v.p. Kidder, Peabody & Co., N.Y.C., 1983-86; owner, principal, Marron Cos., Upper Saddle River, N.J., 1986—; fin. and mktg. cons. to real estate devel. industry. Avocations: pianist, flutist, skiing, fly fishing. Home: 743 W Saddle River Rd Ho-Ho-Kus NJ 07423 Office: Marron Cos 118 Hwy 17 Upper Saddle River NJ 07458

MARROW, DOROTHY COMBELLACK, nurse, educator; b. Gardiner, Maine, Mar. 8, 1937; d. James Henry and Esther Phoebe (Morang) Combellack; m. Norman Filmore Marrow, Nov. 27, 1958 (div. July 1982); children: Peter Ward, Gregory James, Jennifer Esther. Nursing diploma, Peter Bent Brigham Hosp., Boston, 1958. Staff nurse, kidney rsch. Peter Bent Brigham Hosp., 1958; staff nurse, psychiatry VA, Togus, Maine, 1958-59, staff nurse, med., surgery, 1960-64, staff nurse, CCU, ICU, 1967-77, nursing instr., 1977—; nursing instr. Mid-State Coll., Augusta, Maine, 1982-85; nursing cons. Loring Air Force Base, Limestone, Maine, 1987; nursing recruiter LPN schs., Maine, 1984-86. CPR instr. Am. Heart Assn., Augusta, 1975-90; nursing chairperson Combined Fed. Campaign, Togus, 1981-82; speaker Girl Scouts USA, Pittston, Maine, 1983, Westbrook (Maine) Community Coll., 1984; mem. bd. dirs. Motivational Svcs., Inc., Augusta, 1987-88. Recipient Makaria Club scholarship, Meth. Ch., Gardiner, Maine, 1955, Peter Bent Brigham Hosp. scholarship, Boston, 1955. Mem. Webber Pond Fish and Game Assn. (sec. 1979-81). Republican. Methodist. Home: Box 290 RFO #2 Gardiner ME 04345 Office: VA Togus ME 04330

MARRS, BARBARA JEANNE, human resources executive; b. Oklahoma City, Nov. 13, 1943; d. Corbin M. Opal (McMillan) Slagle; m. Donald E. Marrs, Jan. 15, 1972. Student, Okla. State U., 1963, Draughon's Bus. Sch., Oklahoma City, 1964. Mgr. human resources Gulfstream Aerospace Technologies, Oklahoma City; adminstrv. asst. to dir. advance tech. Rockwell Internat., Richardson, Tex.; counselor, exec. search profl. Lexington, Ky., sr. sec. Mem. Citizens Amb. Program for Human Resources Del. to U.S.S.R., 1990. Mem. NAFE, Am. Compensation Assn., Am. Soc. Tng. and Devel., Soc. Human Resource Mgmt., Employee Assistance Profls. Assn., Okla. Safety Assn., Oklahoma City Health Care Coalition, Oklahoma City Personnel Assn., Mgmt. and Profl. Assn. (pres.). Congregationalist. Home: 8000 Tammy Circle Oklahoma City OK 73132 Office: 7400 NW 50th Oklahoma City OK 73123

MARSH, CLARE TEITGEN, school psychologist; b. Manitowoc, Wis., July 7, 1934; d. Clarence Emil and Dorothy (Napiezinski) Teitgen; m. Robert Irving Marsh, Jan. 30, 1955; children: David, Wendy Marsh Tootle, Julie Marsh Domino, Laura Marsh Beltrame. MS in Ednl. Psychology, U. Wis., Milw., 1968. Sch. psychologist Milw. Pub. Schs., 1975-76, West Allis (Wis.)-West Milw. Pub. Schs., 1968—, Wauwatosa (Wis.) Pub. Schs., 1987-89; instr. Milw. Sch. Engring., 1989-90, Alverno Coll., 1990—. NDEA fellow, 1966-68. Mem. Nat. Assn. Sch. Psychologists, Suburban Assn. Sch. Psychologists (pres. 1976-77, 86-87), Wis. Assn. Sch. Psychologists (pres. 1990—, chmn. membership com. 1980-84, sec. 85-89, chmn. conv. 1987), Wis. Fedn. Pupil Svcs., AAUW, Phi Kappa Phi, Pi Lambda Theta, Kappa Delta Pi, Sigma Tau Delta, Alpha Chi Omega. Home: 14140 W Honey Ln New Berlin WI 53151 Office: West Allis Sch System 2930 S Root River Pkwy West Allis WI 53227

MARSH, COLLEEN BETH MEYLOR, product manager, educator; b. Milw., Nov. 29, 1957; d. Michael Bernard and Karole Joan (Kabbeck) M.; m. James W. Marsh, July 1, 1989. BSCE, U. Wis., Madison, 1979; MBA, Baldwin Wallace Coll., 1987. Devel. engr. Foseco, Inc., Cleve., 1980-82, foundry product specialist, 1982-85, sr. product devel. specialist, 1985-86, steelmill product specialist, 1986-88, product mgr. evaporative pattern casting products, 1988—; instr. Cast Metals Inst., Am. Foundry Soc., Chgo., 1984—; bd. dirs. Foseco Employees Fed. Credit Union, 1983—, treas. 1986. Mem. Profl. Engring. Soc., Am. Foundryman's Soc., Am. Women in Metal Industries, Nat. Assn. Female Execs., Iron & Steel Soc., U. Wis. Alumni Assn. Avocations: piano, water sports. Home: 4451 Pine Lake Dr Medina OH 44256 Office: Foseco Inc 20200 Sheldon Rd Cleveland OH 44142

MARSH, DOROTHY JANE, retired obstetrician-gynecologist; b. Monrovia, Calif., Oct. 16, 1915; d. Clark Herbert and Florence (Best) M. DO, Coll. Osteopathy, 1938; MD, U. Calif., Irvine, 1962. Intern residency L.A County Hosp., 1938-42; pvt. practice Specilizing OB Gyn, Glendale, Calif., 1952-88; chmn. OB Gyn Dept. Glendale Community Hosp., 1943-82; pres. Calif. Osteopathic Assn., Am. Coll. Osteopathic, 1951-52; dir. clin. obstretics Calif. Coll. Osteopathic, 1945-61; vice chmn. Dept. Ob-Gyn. Glendale Adventist Hosp., 1983-88; honorary clin. prof. ob-gyn. U. Calif., Irvine, 1985, chair Dorothy Marsh in Reproductive Endocrinology, 1988. Mem. AMA, L.A. County Med. Assn., Calif. Med. Assn. Republican. Home: 3017 Scotland St Los Angeles CA 90039

MARSH, JOAN KNIGHT, educational film, video and computer software company executive; b. Butler, Mo., Apr. 8, 1934; d. E. Lyle and Ruth (Hopkins) Knight; m. Alan Reid Marsh, Sept. 27, 1958; children: Alan Reid, Clayton Knight. BA, Tex. Tech. U., 1956. Owner, pres. MarshMedia, Kansas City, Mo., 1969—. Bd. dirs., Crittenton Ctr., Kansas City, 1983-88; mem. council Family Study Ctr., U. Mo., Kansas City, 1983-89, Children's Relief Assn. Mercy Hosp., Kansas City, 1984—, pres. 1989—, Gamma Phi Beta. Republican. Presbyterian. Club: Jr. League (sustaining chmn. 1982-84). Avocation: Egyptology.

MARSH, MARY ELIZABETH, librarian; b. Lowell, Mass., July 27, 1949; d. Michael Francis and Elizabeth Theresa (Erwin) Harrington; m. Geoffrey Thomas Marsh, Feb. 14, 1979. BA, Lowell State Coll., Mass., 1971; MLS, SUNY, Buffalo, 1972. Libr. Westford Acad., Westford, Mass., 1972-73; media specialist Billerica (Mass.) Pub. Schs., 1973-83; libr. Milford (N.H.) Mid. Sch., 1983—. Mem. Milford Area Br. of AAUW (pres. 1989—). Republican. Home: 54 County Rd Box 993 Amherst NH 03031 Office: Milford Middle School Osgood Rd Milford NH 03055

MARSHAK, HILARY WALLACH, owner, graphic arts executive, computer personalization; b. N.Y.C., May 27, 1950; d. Irving Isaac Wallach and Suni Fox; m. Harvey Marshak, Jan. 1, 1981; children: Emily Fox, Jacob Randall. BA, U. Conn., Storrs, 1973; postgrad., N.Y.U., 1990—. Tchr. English Glastonbury (Conn.) High Sch., 1973, U. Autonoma de Guerrero, Acapulco, Mexico, 1974; administrv. asst. 4M Pub. Svcs. Corp., N.Y.C., 1975, bus. mgr.; exec. v.p. Vitalmedia Enterprises Inc., N.Y.C., 1977-87, pres., chief exec. officer, 1987—; mktg. cons. Liederman, Lowy Enterprises, N.Y.C., 1988-89, Frana, Ltd., London, 1988-89. Editor: Before the Bar, 1978-80, Guide to Higher Edn., 1980. Founder Women's Radical Caucus, U. Conn., 1970; broadcaster Sta. WHUS: 1st Women's Programming, U. Conn., 1971. Recipient 2nd Place Flowers Ulster County Agrl. Fair, New Paltz, N.Y., 1987, 1st Place Herbs, 1988. Jewish. Office: Vitalmedia Enterprises Inc 80 80th Ave Ste 200 New York NY 10011

MARSHAL, NELLIE JEAN, financial executive; b. Pulaski, Tenn., Jan. 30, 1933; d. William Vernon and Elsie Beatrice (Glover) DeRamus; children: Jerami A., Roberta M. Goldstein. Student Baxter Sem. Owner, Trailestate Realty, Reno, 1957-60; v.p. Bank Mortgage Loan Co., Los Angeles, 1960-66; mgr. first trust deed dept. Union Home Loans, L.A., 1966-69; owner Marshal Plan, Inc., Santa Monica, Calif., 1969—; chmn. bd. Golden State Holding Co., Inc., 1980—; speaker in field. Named to Hon. Order of Ky. Cols. Gov. Commonwealth of Ky. Mem. Internat. Platform Assn., Santa Monica Bd. Realtors, Nat. Assn. Review Appraisers and Mortgage Underwriters (sr.), Women in Business, NAFE, Santa Monica C. of C., Thalians Club. Democrat. Office: Marshal Plan Inc 2701 Ocean Park Blvd Ste 131 Santa Monica CA 90405

MARSHALL, BEULAH MARIAN, children's theatre owner; b. Pt. Lavaca, Tex., Feb. 19, 1929; d. Harrison Carroll and Virginia Faye (Brecheen) Hartzog; m. Willie Clay Marshall, June 29, 1948 (dec. 1986); children: Marian Lei Harrison, Shirley Jo Cox Hobizal, Charles Ray Cox. Student, S.W. Tex. State Tchrs. Coll., San Marcos, 1948. Floral asst. Flowerland, Port Lavaca, 1953-54; tchr. substitute Calhoun County Ind. Sch. Dist., Port Lavaca, 1953-76; owner The Cottage, Port Lavaca; art instr.; V.P. Bush steering com., 1987-88; Pres. Regan's taskforce for Bush. Leader Brownies Girl Scouts U.S., 1956-64, leader adult scout coun. orgn., chmn. day camp dir.; den mother Cub Scouts local pack Boy Scouts Am., 1958-59. Mem. DAR, Puppeteers of Am., Tex. Parent Tchrs. Assn. (life), Jackson Puppeteers and Hobby Club, Inc., Lone Star Puppet Guild, Calhoun County Arts Coun. (founder, dir.). Methodist. Office: The Cottage 205 S Ann Port Lavaca TX 77979

MARSHALL, BRENDA FRAN, secondary school teacher; b. Bronx, N.Y., Nov. 18, 1954; d. George A. and Martha (Wallace) M. BS in Earth-Space Sci., SUNY, Stony Brook, 1977; MS in Rec. Adminstrn., Lehman Coll., 1981, MS in Phys. Edn., 1986; MS in Exercise Physiology, Queens Coll., 1989. Cert. secondary tchr., N.Y. Coach, dir. hockey, Yonkers (N.Y.) Parks and Recreation, 1979-85; asst. supr. community svc. Dept. Parks and Recreation County of Westchester, White Plains, N.Y., 1981-86; tchr., coach Eastchester (N.Y.) Pub. Schs., 1980-82, Mt. Vernon (N.Y.) Pub. Schs., 1982—; asst. dir. camp Greenburgh (N.Y.) Parks and Recreation, 1983-86; chief instr. N.Y., N.J. Nat. Novice Hockey Assn., Vienna, Va., 1986—. Contbr. articles on plyometrics and nutrition for skaters for the Nat. Hockey League and Darien Club Competition Jour. Asst. Dem. campaign coord. County of Westchester, 1985, 88-89. Mem. Am. Coll. Sports Medicine, USA Hockey Assn. (speaker 1988), U.S. Figure Skating Assn., Am. Alliance for Health, Phys. Edn., Recreation, Nat. Novice Hockey Assn., Darien Figure Skating Club So. Conn. (bd. dirs.). Home: 1 Sadore Ln Yonkers NY 10710

MARSHALL, BRENDA JOYCE, physical education educator; b. Corpus Christi, Tex., Aug. 11, 1955; d. Ernest Oce and Norma Lorene (Smith) M. BA in Phys. Edn., Health, English, U. Tex., Arlington, 1978; MS in Edn., Phys. Edn., Health, Baylor U., 1979; MS in Edn. Mid-Mgmt., Corpus Christi State U., 1990. Head softball coach, tchr. West Tex. State U., Canyon, 1979-83, Sam Houston State U., Huntsville, Tex., 1983-86; asst. athletic dir. Corpus Christi Ind. Sch. Dit., 1986—; nat. adv. staff Pro One Sporting Goods, Corpus Christi, 1987—; clinician area girls fast pitch orgns., Corpus Christi, 1986—. Recipient Olympic Gold medal, U.S. Softball team, 1979; named Coach of Yr. Gulf Star Conf., 1986; named to Outstanding Young Women of Am., 1980. Mem NAFE, Nat. Interscholastic Athletic Adminstrs. Assn., Tex. Assn. Health, Phys. Edn., Recreation, Tex. Girls Coaching Assn., Tex. High Sch. Coaches Assn., Tex. High Sch. Athletic Dirs. Assn., Corpus Christi C. of C. Baptist. Home: 6301 Meadow Vista #925 Corpus Christi TX 78414 Office: Corpus Christi Ind Sch Dist 3005 Leopard Corpus Christi TX 78408

MARSHALL, CAK (CATHERINE ELAINE MARSHALL), music educator, composer; b. Nashville, Nov. 24, 1943; d. Dean Byron and Petula Iris (Bodie) M. BS in Music Edn., Ind. U. Pa., 1965; cert., Hamline U., 1981, 82, 83, Memphis State U., 1985; postgrad., Duquesne U., 1988—. Cert. vocal music tchr., Pa. Tchr. music Mars (Pa.) Area Sch. Dist., 1965-66; music specialist Fox Chapel (Pa.) Area Sch. Dist., 1966—; Orff specialist Chatham Coll. Fine Arts Camp, Pitts., 1977—; instrn. rep. elem. curriculum Dist. I, Pitts., 1986—; arts curriculum project Pa. Dept. Edn., 1988. Author: (plays) The Rainbow Recorder, 1988, The Gift Disk Dilemma, 1989; composer, author: play Pittsburgh-The City With a Smile on Her Face, 1986, holiday mus. The Dove That Could Not Fly, 1986, book Seasons in Song, 1987. Actor North Star Players, Pitts., 1975-80; soloist Landmark Bapt. Ch., Penn Hills, Pa., 1981-86, Bible Bapt. Ch., 1987; performer Pitts. Camerata, 1977—; group leader Pitts. Recorder Soc., Pitts., 1985-86. Mem. NEA, Am. ORFF-Schulwerk Assn., Pitts. Golden Triangle Chpt. (pres. 1985—), Music Educators Nat. Confl., Pa. Music Educators Assn. (elem. jour. 1986—), Am. Recorder Assn., Delta Omicron. Baptist. Home: 1707

Kirk Dr Verona PA 15147 Office: O'Hara Elem Sch 115 Cabin Ln Pittsburgh PA 15238

MARSHALL, CONSUELO BLAND, federal judge; b. Knoxville, Tenn., Sept. 28, 1936; d. Clyde Theodore and Annie (Brown) Arnold; m. George Edward Marshall, Aug. 30, 1959; children: Michael Edward, Laurie Ann. A.A., Los Angeles City Coll., 1956; B.A., Howard U., 1958, LL.B., 1961. Bar: Calif. 1962. Dep. atty. City of L.A., 1962-67; assoc. Cochran & Atkins, L.A., 1968-70; commr. L.A. Superior Ct., 1971-76; judge Inglewood Mcpl. Ct., 1976-77, L.A. Superior Ct., 1977-80, U.S. Dist. Ct. Central Dist. Calif., L.A., 1980—. Contbr. articles to profl. jours.; notes editor Law Jour. Howard U. Mem. adv. bd. Richstone Child Abuse Center. Research fellow Howard U. Law Sch., 1959-60. Mem. State Bar Calif., Calif. Women Lawyers Assn., Calif. Assn. Black Lawyers, Calif. Judges Assn., Black Women Lawyers Assn., Los Angeles County Bar Assn., Nat. Assn. Women Judges, NAACP, Urban League, Beta Phi Sigma. Mem. Ch. Religious Science. Office: US Dist Ct 312 N Spring St Los Angeles CA 90012*

MARSHALL, CYNTHIA LOUISE, English educator, appraising company executive; b. Ellwood City, Pa., Aug. 16, 1956; d. Luther Harold and Elizabeth (Prescott) M.; m. William H. Smith, Dec. 30, 1985. BS in English summa cum laude, Slippery Rock (Pa.) U., 1978, MA in English, 1980; PhD in Edn., U. Pitts., 1987. Grad. asst. Slippery Rock U., 1978-80; owner, mgr. Whistler Enterprises, real estate and antique appraising, Butler, Pa., 1980—; adj. instr. English, Butler County Community Coll., Butler, 1988-90; instr. English Community Coll. of Beaver County, 1990—; mem. adj. faculty Slippery Rock U., 1990—; creator workshop Formal Writing in Workplace, VA Med. Ctr., Butler, 1989; presenter in field; lectr. on Am. quilts, antique trends and films, Shakespeare, 1986—. Contbr. articles and book revs. to various publs. Appraiser, vol. United Cerebral Palsy, Butler, 1987—, Ellwood City Hist. Soc., 1987—, Butler County Hist. Soc., 1987—; mem. Stratford Festival Friends; pres. Lending Hands Orgn., Butler, 1990-91; mem. Pa. Gov.'s Conf. on Librs., 1990—. Scholarship given in her name Butler County Community Coll., 1990; grantee Pa. Humanities Coun., 1990. Mem. MLA, Pa. Coll. English Assn., AAUW, Wintherthur Mus., Nat. Trust for Hist. Preservation, Smithsonian Assocs., Slippery Rock U. Alumni Assn. (life). Democrat. Presbyterian. Home: 603 N Main St Butler PA 16001 Office: Community Coll of Beaver County College Dr Monaca PA 15061

MARSHALL, DENISE JILL, biomedical photographer; b. Abington, Pa., Oct. 3, 1965; d. David G. and Sandra (Goldstein) Marshall. AS, Photog. BFA, Rochester Inst. Tech., 1988. Photographer Amerimar Reality, Phila., 1983-88, Mass. Gen. Hosp., Boston, 1988—; photographer, intern, dir. orthopaedic media dept. U. Pa., Phila., 1986. Photographer pamphlet The Ridings, 1984; book photo The Rittenhouse Views, 1988, cover N.Y. Times Mag., 1989. Photographer Jewish Community Ctr., Rochester, N.Y., 1987. Mem. Biol. Photographic Assn., B'nai B'rith (social dir. 1983). Republican. Jewish. Office: Mass Gen Hosp Media D Ortho Gray 6 Fruit St Boston MA 02114

MARSHALL, ELIZABETH EILEEN, cultural organization administrator, teacher; b. Houston, Dec. 2, 1942; d. Sterling Guy and Ruth (Burke) M. BS, North Tex. State U., 1965; D in Metaphysics, Esoteric Philosophy Ctr., 1985. Tchr. Houston Ind. Sch. Dist., 1965-71; adminstrv. sec. Sch. Nursing U. St. Thomas, Houston, 1972-74; project sec. Tellepson Constrn. Co., Houston, 1974-77; exec. dir. Tex. Nurses Assn. Dist. 9, Houston, 1977-80; owner Automotive Maintenance Systems, Houston, 1980-84; sales rep. So. Educators Ins., Dallas, 1984; ops. sec. Nelson-Westerberg of Tex., Inc., Dallas, 1984-85; admissions rep. United Tech. Inst., Nashville, 1986-87; exec. dir. Harmonious Alignment Edn. Ctr., Inc., Nashville, 1989—; cons. Harmonious Alignment Edn. Ctr., Inc., Nashville, 1989—; guest speaker Beyond Reason Teddy Bart Prodns., Nashville, 1988-90. Contbr. articles to profl. jours. Office: Harmonious Alignment Edn 1701 Portland Ave Nashville TN 37212

MARSHALL, JEANNE, data processing executive; b. Chgo., Aug. 30, 1945; d. William Herman and Mary Lou (Allen) Clendenin; m. Charles Morris Marshall, Apr. 4, 1967 (div. May 1981); children: Kimberly Ann, Kevin Luke. BS, U. Ill., 1967; MS, U. Wis., 1971. Textile technician Gillette Rsch. Inst., Rockville, Md., 1967-68; rsch. asst. U. Wis., Madison, 1970-71; sales rep. fabric mgr. Singer Co., Madison, 1971-75; data entry operator Profl. Mgmt. Systems Inc., Madison, 1975-79; data entry mgr. Wis. Dairy Herd Improvement Coop., Madison, 1979-84, systems analyst II, 1984-87, dir. computer svcs., 1987—. Troop com. chmn. 4 Lakes coun. Boy Scouts Am., 1986—, mem. at large Yahara Dist., 1987—; sec. Madison Area coun. for Gifted and Talented, 1989—; chmn. adminstrv. bd. Bashford United Meth. Ch., Madison. Mem. Data Processing Mgmt. Assn. (So. Wis. chpt. pres. 1987-88, Bronze IPA award1989, bd. dirs. 1985-89), Am. Soc. Quality Control, Optimist Club (bd. dirs. 1989—). Democrat. Office: Wis Dairy Herd Improvement 5301 Tokay Blvd Madison WI 53711-1027

MARSHALL, JOANNE ELLEN, state agency administrator; b. Harrisburg, Pa., Dec. 25, 1954; d. Dominick and Joan Marie (Wesner) Sgrignoli; divorced; 1 child, Jessica Ellen; m. James Brock Mercer, June 9, 1990. Clerical support state real estate commn. Commonwealth of Pa., Harrisburg, 1973-76, adminstr. state bd. accountancy, 1976-83, adminstrv. asst. to chief of law enforcement, 1984-85, adminstr. testing and contract mgmt. dept. state, 1985—. Democrat. United Methodist. Office: Dept State Bur Profl and Occupational Affairs Testing Contract Mgmt Unit 605 Transportation Bldg Harrisburg PA 17120

MARSHALL, LESLIE B., nursing educator; b. Mpls., Sept. 1, 1943; d. Orville Leonard Brusletten and Miriam Barry (Butler) Ramey; m. Keith Macdonald Marshall (div. Dec. 1988), 1 child, Kelsey Andrew. BA in Psychology, Grinnel Coll., 1965; PhD in Psychology and Physiology, U. Wash., 1973; BS in Nursing, Mt. Mercy Coll., 1990. RN. Elem. tchr. Namoluk (Micronesia) Sch., 1969-71; postdoctoral fellow Dept. Internal Medicine U. Iowa, Iowa City, 1973; asst. in instrn. Dept. Biology U. Iowa, Iowa City, 1974-75; assoc. prof. Dept. Physiology U. Iowa, Iowa City, 1976-78; asst. prof. Coll. Nursing U. Iowa, Iowa City, 1978-85, assoc. prof., 1985—; nursing pool staff U. Iowa Hosps. and Clinics, Iowa City, 1988—; tutor, rsch. officer U. Papua, New Guinea, 1981; cons. on infant feeding U. Iowa, 1982-85, Ross Labs., Columbus, Ohio, 1979, 82. Author: (with Mac Marshall) Silent Voices Speak: Women and Prohibition in Truk, 1990, (with Donald Denoon) Public Health in Papua New Guinea, 1990; editor: Infant Care and Feeding in the South Pacific, 1985; editorial bd. Qualitative Health Rsch., Social Devel. Issues, 1989—; manuscript reviwer for jours., 1980—; contbr. articles to profl. jours. Speaker for churches and community groups, Iowa City. Recipient Excellence in Teaching award Burlington No. Found., 1985. Fellow Am. Anthropol. Assn., Assn. for Social Anthropology in Oceania (exec. bd. 1989-92, bd. chair 1991-92), Woodrow Wilson Found. (hon.); mem. Coun. on Nursing and Anthropology (nominating com.), Mortar Bd., Phi Beta Kappa, Sigma Theta Tau. Democrat. Office: Coll Nursing U Iowa Iowa City IA 52242

MARSHALL, LINDA RAE, cosmetic company executive; b. Provo, Utah, Aug. 1, 1940; d. Arvid O. and Tola V. (Broderick) Newman; children—James, John. Student Brigham Young U., 1958-59, U. Utah, 1960-61. Buyer, Boston Store, 1961-62; sec. Milw. Gas & Light Co., 1962-64; mktg. rep. Elysee Cosmetics, Madison, Wis., 1971-75, pres., 1975—; v.p., Dionne, Inc., 1987—, ptnr. Pres. Falk Sch. PTA, Madison. Author: Discover the Other Woman in You; monthly beauty columnist Beauty Fashion mag.; contbg. author Cosmetic Industry Sci. and Regulatory Found., 1984. Mem. Aestheticians Internat. Assn. (adv. bd.), Cosmetic, Toiletry and Fragrance Assn. (exec. com., bd. dirs., chmn. voluntary program, chmn. small cosmetic com., membership com. task force), Cosmetic Exec. Women. Address: Box 4084 Madison WI 53711

MARSHALL, MARGUERITE MITCHELL, retired educator; b. Pittsburg, Kans., Oct. 5, 1911; d. Henry Levi and Emily (Fonchoser) Mitchell; m. Ulysses Marshall, Aug. 19, 1939 (dec. 1980). BS in Elem. Edn., Kans. State Tchrs. Coll., 1934; MA in English Lit., Howard U., 1950; postgrad., D.C. Tchrs. Coll., 1953. Cert. tchr., Va., Ga., D.C. Tchr. Va. Pub. Sch. System, Stapleton, 1934-37, Ga. Pub. Sch. System, Dawson, 1937-42; tchr. Washington, D.C. Pub. Sch. System, Washington, 1942-52, guidance counselor, 1952-72; asst. children's libr. Pittsburg Pub. Libr., 1974-89. Author: The Path to Peace, 1982, An Account of Afro-Americans in Southeast Kansas, 1884-1984, 1986, The Oral History of Marguerite Marshall, 1987, I Remember When..., 1990. Bd. dirs. Redbud Trail coun. Girls Scouts, 1975-79; treas. Pitts. Black Homecoming Club, 1975-85, ARC, Pitts., 1985-88; 1st v.p. Pitts. chpt. AAUW, 1975-79. Mem. Century Club Howard U., Assn. for Study of Afro-Am. Life and History, One Hundred Club, Carver League (v.p. 1987-90), D.C. Ret. Tchrs. Assn., Friends of Pittsburg Pub. Libr., La Petite Club (publicity chmn. 1973—). Republican. Baptist. Home: 302 S Warren St Pittsburg KS 66762

MARSHALL, MARIE ANNETTE, military petty officer; b. San Antonio, Jan. 1, 1958; d. John Andrew Jr. and June Marie (Adams) Fuschich; m. Deane Morris Marshall, Dec. 30, 1954; children: Charles Walter Deane, Catherine Marie. Cert., USN, 1985, USN, 1988; AS, SUNY, Albany, 1988. Enlisted USN, 1978; ward hosp. corpsman Naval Hosp., Patuxent River, Md., 1978-80; outpatient leading petty officer, ambulance dispatcher, tng. officer, career counselor Naval Hosp., Camp LeJeune, N.C., 1982-84; trauma rm., clin. asst. Naval Sta. Dispensary, Guam, 1980-82; tng. officer Naval Med. Clinic, Kings Bay, Ga., 1984-88; med. officer programs recruiter Navy Recruiting Area Seven Command, Dallas, 1988—; mem. Welfare and Recreation Com., Camp LeJeune, 1983-84, Honor Guard and Funeral Drill Team. Mem. ch. choir St. Paul's Ch., Garland, Tex., 1988—; helper Spl. Olympics, Kings Bay, 1988, Dallas, 1989; unit coord. Combined Fed. Campaign, Kings Bay, 1986; bd. dirs. Chateau Gardens Recreation Assn., St. Mary's, Ga., 1984-88. Fellow 1st Class Petty Officers Assn., Rotaract Club (pres. St. Mary's chpt. 1986). Republican. Office: Navy Recruiting Area Seven 1499 Regal Row Ste 501 Dallas TX 75247-3688

MARSHALL, MARY AYDELOTTE, state legislator; b. Cook County, Ill., June 14, 1921; d. John A. and Nell. A. Rice; B.A. with highest honors, Swarthmore Coll., 1942; m. Roger Duryea Marshall, Mar. 3, 1944; children: Nell Aydelotte, Jenny Winslow Marshall Davies, Alice Marie. Economist anti-trust div. Dept. Justice, Washington, 1942-46; mem. Va. Ho. of Dels., 1966-70, 72—, mem. privileges and elections com., appropriations com., rules com., chmn. counties, cities and towns com., chmn. Legis. Study Commn. on Needs Elderly Virginians, 1973-78; chmn. Legis. Commn. Monitoring Long Term Care, 1983-86; mem. No. Va. Transp. Commn., 1974-80; mem. exec. com. Nat. Conf. State Legislators, 1981-87, also chmn. human svcs. com., chmn. programs and svcs. to states com.; chmn. Task Force on Social Security for Women, Fed. Council on Aging, 1978-81, mem. exec. com., chmn. human resources com. So. Legis. Conf., 1988—; bd. dirs. Washington Met. Council Govts., 1978, 80, 87, 88, United Srs. Health Corp. Pres., Va. Assn. Mental Health, 1970-73, Va. Fedn. Democratic Women's Clubs, 1971-72; bd. dirs. Nat. Assn. Mental Health, 1972-78; mem. Dem. Central Com. Va., 1976-78. Recipient Achievement award Va. Assn. Mental Health, No. Va. Assn. Mental Health, Va. Fedn. Bus. and Profl. Women's Clubs, Va. Assn. Ind. Retail Gasoline Dealers, No. Va. Retarded Citizens Assn., Arthur Fleming Lecture, Nat. Assn. State Units on Aging, Gov.'s award for Child Care Legis.; named WETA Disting. Woman. Mem. AAUW, LWV. Congregationalist. Clubs: Bus. and Profl. Women's, Home Demonstration, No. Va. Dem., Downtown.

MARSHALL, MARY HEWITT, health care consultant; b. Florence, S.C., Nov. 18, 1939; d. Ralph Clement and Jacqueline (Spann) Hewitt; divorced; children: Mary Lynn, Malvin Hurst. BA, Columbia Coll., 1960; MEd, U. S.C., 1970; PhD, U. So. Miss., 1974. Lic. speech language pathologist, Ga., Calif. Pres. Mgmt. and Planning Svcs., Atlanta, 1982—; speech pathologist, tchr. Speech and Hearing Clin. Greater St. Petersburg, Fla., 1970-71; mem. faculty U. So. Miss., Hattiesburg, 1971-74; prin. Mary H. Marshall, PhD and Assocs., Miss. Gulf Coast, 1974-77, L.A., 1979-81; dir. speech/language pathology Irwin Lehrhoff, PhD and Assocs., Beverly Hills, Calif., 1977-79; coord. medicare/ancillary So. div. Beverly Enterprises, 1982-83; cons. Dynamics, Inc., Lake City, Fla., 1983-86; pres., ptnr. Marshall Rehab. Ctrs. Ga., Inc., Atlanta, 1983-86, pres., cheif exec. officer, 1986-87; adj. faculty U. So. Miss., Hattiesburg, 1974-77, Calif. State U., L.A., 1977-80. Author: Your Private Practice: Planning and Organization, 1982, (manual) Medicare! Resource Information and Guidelines, 1988; contbr. numerous articles to profl. jours. Dir. religious edn. 1st Meth. Ch., Laurens, S.C., 1960-62. Mem. Am. Speech Language Hearing Assn., Ga. Speech Language Hearing Assn., Am. Acad. Speech Pathologist and Audiologist in Pvt. Practice, Calif. Speech Pathologist and Audiologist in Pvt. Practice, Inst. Profl. Health Svcs. Adminstrs., Am. Health Care Assn. (assoc.), Ga. Health Care Assn. (assoc.), N.C. Health Facilities Assn. (assoc.), Tenn. Health Care Assn. (assoc.), Am. Coll. Helath Care Adminstrs. (assoc.). Office: 400 Cumberland Pkwy Bldg 800 B Atlanta GA 30359

MARSHALL, MARY JONES, civic worker; b. Billings, Mont.; d. Leroy Nathaniel and Janet (Currie) Dailey; m. Harvey Bradley Jones, Nov. 15, 1952 (dec. 1989); children: Dailey, Janet Currie, Ellis Bradley. Student, Carleton Coll., 1943-44, U. Mont., 1944-46, UCLA, 1959. Owner Mary Jones Interiors. Founder, treas. Jr. Art Council, L.A. County Mus., 1953-55, v.p., 1955-56; mem. costume council Pasadena (Calif.) Philharm.; cofounder Art Rental Gallery, 1953, chmn. art and architecture tour, 1955; founding mem., sec. Art Alliance, Pasadena Art Mus., 1955-56; benefit chmn. Pasadena Girls Club, 1959, bd. dirs., 1958-60; chmn. L.A. Tennis Patron's Assn. Benefit, 1965; sustaining Jr. League Pasadena; mem. docent council L.A. County Mus.; mem. costume council L.A. County Mus. Art., program chmn. 20th Century Greatest Designers; mem. blue ribbon com. L.A. Music Ctr.; benefit chmn. Venice com. Internat. Fund for Monuments, 1971; bd. dirs. Art Ctr. 100, Pasadena, 1988—; pres. The Pres.'s L.A. Children's Bur., 1989; co-chmn. benefit Harvard Coll. Scholarship Fund, 1974, steering com. benefit, 1987, Otis Art Inst., 1975; mem. Harvard-Radcliffe scholarship dinner com., 1985; mem. adv. bd. Estelle Doheny Eye Found., 1976, chmn. benefit, 1980; adv. bd. Loyola U. Sch. Fine Arts, L.A., Art Ctr. Sch. Design, Pasadena, Calif., 1987—; patron chmn. Benefit Achievement Rewards for Coll. Scientists, 1988; chmn. com. Sch. Am. Ballet Benefit, 1988, N.Y.C.; bd. dirs. Founders Music Ctr., L.A., 1977-81; mem. nat. adv. council Sch. Am. Ballet, N.Y.C., nat. co-chmn. gala, 1980; adv. council on fine arts Loyola-Marymount U.; mem. L.A. Olympic Com., 1984, The Colleagues; founding mem. Mus. Contemporary Art, 1986; chmn. The Pres.'s Benefit L.A. Children's Bur., 1990. Mem. Valley Hunt Club (Pasadena), Calif. Club (L.A.), Kappa Alpha Theta. Home: 10375 Wilshire Blvd Apt 8B Los Angeles CA 90024

MARSHALL, MARYAN L(ORRAINE), chemistry educator; b. New Haven, Jan. 18, 1940; d. Rush Porter and Lillian Louise (Merz) M. BA, Conn. Coll., 1960; PhD, Yale U., 1965. Instr. chemistry Randolph-Macon Woman's Coll., Lynchburg, Va., 1964-66, asst. prof. chemistry, 1966-72; assoc. prof. chemistry Cen. Va. Community Coll., Lynchburg, 1972-75, prof. chemistry, 1975—. Mem. AAAS, AAUW, Am. Chem. Soc., Va. Acad. Sci., Sigma Xi (sec. Lynchburg chpt. 1983-90), Phi Delta Kappa (treas. Lynchburg chpt. 1985-89). Presbyterian. Home: 5804 Navajo Circle Lynchburg VA 24502 Office: Cen Va Community Coll 3506 Wards Rd Lynchburg VA 24502

MARSHALL, MARYANN CHORBA, office administrator; b. Scranton, Pa., Apr. 18, 1952; d. Edward M. and Mildred (Polc) Chorba; m. Daniel V. Marshall III. BA, Emmanuel Coll., 1974. Personal, social sec. Jordan Embassy Mil. Office, Washington, 1974-76; exec. asst, office mgr. Jordan Embassy Info. Bur., Washington, 1976-81; asst. to pres. Nat. Press Club, Washington, 1981—. Mem. Nat. Fedn. Rep. Women, Washington, 1989. Mem. NAFE, Am. Soc. Profl. and Exec. Women, League Rep. Women. Republican. Roman Catholic. Home: 1140 23rd St NW Washington DC 20037 Office: Nat Press Club Nat Press Bldg Washington DC 20045

MARSHALL, MERYL CORINBLIT, broadcast production executive, lawyer; b. Los Angeles, Oct. 16, 1949; d. Jack and Nita (Green) Corinblit; B.A., UCLA, 1971; J.D., Loyola Marymount U., Los Angeles, 1974. Bar: Calif. 1974. Dep. pub. defender County of Los Angeles, 1975-77; sole practice, Los Angeles, 1977-78; ptnr. Markman and Marshall, Los Angeles, 1978-79; sr. atty. NBC, Burbank, Calif., 1979-80, dir. programs, talent contracts bus. affairs, 1980, asst. gen. atty., N.Y.C., 1980-82, v.p., compliance and practices, Burbank, 1982, v.p. program affairs, Group W Prodns., from 1987, now sr. v.p. future images. Treas. Acad. T.V. Arts and Scis., 1985-87; chmn., Nat. Women's Polit. Caucus, Westside, Calif., 1978-80; mem. Calif. Dem. Cen. Com., 1978-79; mem. Hollywood Women's Polit. Com., 1988. Mem. Acad. TV Arts and Scis. (treas. 1985), Women in Film. Democrat. Jewish. Office: Group W Productions Co One Lakeside Plaza 3801 Barham Blvd. Los Angeles CA 90068*

MARSHALL, NAVARRE, retired secondary educator; b. Stockton, Calif., Oct. 31, 1916; d. Winfield Scott and Elizabeth (Brophy) Baggett; m. Robert Frank Marshall, Aug. 10, 1947; 1 child, Roberta Navarre Marshall. BA, San Francisco State U., 1937; postgrad., U. Calif., Berkeley, 1945-47, U. Calif., Santa Cruz, 1970-72. Cert. elem.-jr. high tchr. Tchr. Pittsburg (Calif.) Sch. Dist., 1937-39, Martinez (Calif.) Sch. Dist., 1941-49, Pajaro Valley Sch. Dist., Watsonville, Calif., 1958-76; ret., 1976. Sec., sponsor Watsonville Friends of the Libr. Mem. AAUW (sec. 1963-64), Calif. Tchrs. Assn., Order Eastern Star, Delta Kappa Gamma Soc. (charter pres. 1961-62), Internat. Zeta Epsilon (chpt. pres. 1986-88). Democrat.

MARSHALL, PHILOMENA ANN, health care administration; b. Oak Park, Ill., Mar. 21, 2149; d. John and Marie (Desmond) Piscopo; m. Robert Paul Marshall, June 17, 1972. BS in Nursing, Loyola U., 1972; postgrad., U. Minn., 1989—. Registered Nurse. Staff nurse Rush Pres. St. Luke's Med. Ctr., Chgo., 1972-73; pub. health nurse Vis. Nurse Assn., Chgo., 1973-75, Lake County Health Dept., Waukegan, Ill., 1975-76; mem. faculty St. Francis Hosp. Sch. Nursing, Evanston, Ill., 1976-78; dir. home care and hospice St. Joseph Med. Ctr., Brainerd, Minn., 1978-83; dir. family home care Empire Health Svcs., Spokane, Wash., 1983-87; dir. sr. svcs. West Suburban Hosp. Med. Ctr., Oak Park, 1987-89, v.p. nursing, 1989—. Bd. dirs. United Way, Brainerd, 1980-82, Spokane, 1985-86; chmn. Ideal Community Svc. Orgn., Pequot Lakes, Minn., 1981-82. Mem. Am. Soc. Aging, Nat. Council on Aging, Nat. Assn. Home Care, Ill. Council Home Health Services, Alumni Assn. Minn. Roman Catholic.

MARSHALL, PHYLLIS, marketing and public relations executive; b. Phila., Aug. 26, 1933; d. Joseph Moses and Hannah (Schneider) Pulin; children: Carolyn Anne Mustopa, Jonathan David, Paul Andrew, Suzanne Leigh Mernyk. Student, Hunter Coll., 1954-55; AA, Am. Acad. Dramatic Art, N.Y., 1968; student, The New Sch., 1973-74. Asst. pub. rels. specialist Health Facilities Corp., N.Y.C., 1970-73; freelance pub. rels. and writing Wisdom's Child, N.Y.C., 1973-75; pub. rels. specialist Ideal Mut. Ins. Co., N.Y.C., 1977-85; dir. corp. communications N.Y. Ins. Exch., Inc., 1985-87; pres. Marshall Communication Group, Inc., N.Y.C., 1987—. Editor U.S. Reinsurance Report; contbr. articles to profl. jours. Mem. Nat. Ins. Industry Assn., Internat. Assn. Bus. Communicators (mem. bd. govs. U.S. Dist. I, asst. dir. 1986-88, dist. dir. 1988, chmn. literacy program, pres. N.Y. chpt. 1984-85, mem. bd. govs. 1983—). Democrat. Jewish. Home: 875 W End Ave Ste 1F New York NY 10025

MARSHALL, PHYLLIS ELLINWOOD, mental health system executive, consultant; b. Kansas City, Mo., Dec. 20, 1929; d. Herbert Dwight and Mildred (Gillham) Ellinwood; m. John D. Reich, July 1, 1950 (div. 1964); children: Martha Reich Millican, Michael David, Donald Martin; m. C. Randolph Marshall, Nov. 27, 1969. B.A., Washington U., St. Louis, 1951, M.S.W., 1969. Adult program dir. St. Louis YWCA, 1962-64, dir. decentralized programs, 1964-67; alcoholism caseworker Malcolm Bliss Mental Health Ctr., St. Louis, 1968; exec. dir. Cobb County YWCA, Ga., 1969-72; dir. Coastal Area Community Mental Health Ctr., Brunswick, Ga., 1973-77; dir. Mental Health Svcs., Ga. Dept. Human Resources, Atlanta, 1977-84; exec. dir. Integrated Mental Health, Inc., Rochester, N.Y., 1984—; cons. NIMH, Washington, 1979-84, So. Regional Ednl. Bd., Atlanta, 1979-84, N.Y. State Office Mental Health, Albany, 1980-84, State of Ill. Dept. Mental Health, 1988, WHO, 1989; co-chair Metro Atlanta Deinstitutionalization Task Force, 1983-85; bd. dirs. Children Have All Rights, Legal, Ednl. and Emotional, Menninger Found. project, Atlanta, 1983-84; mem. council Fingerlakes Health Systems Agy., Rochester, 1985-90; adviser WHO, 1989; mem. Monroe Couty Adv. Com. on Women's Issues. Contbg. author: Perspectives in Mental Health, 1980, New Directions for Mental Health Svcs., 1988, New Frontiers in Mental Heath, 1989; contbr. articles to profl. publs. Bd. dirs. Human Resources Credit Union, Atlanta, 1982-84. Recipient Boss of Yr. award Brunswick Jaycees, 1977, Good Friend award Brunswick Mental Health Assn., 1977, Community Mental Health award Atlanta U., 1980, Outstanding Achievement award Am. Soc. for Pub. Adminstrn., 1990. Mem. AAUW (chpt. pres. 1978), Assn. Mental Health Adminstrs., Ga. Assn. Community Mental Health Ctrs. (pres. 1975-77), Rochester Women's Network (bd. dirs.). Club: Midtown Tennis (Rochester). Avocations: ocean sailing, music, tennis. Office: Integrated Mental Health Inc Monroe Sq 259 Monroe Ave Rochester NY 14607

MARSHALL, SHIRLEY, data processing executive; b. Columbus, Ohio, Apr. 24, 1941; d. Edward and Mary (Hall) Williams; children: Julie, Ted. BA, Purdue U., 1964; MA, Trenton State, 1976. Cert. tchr., Ill., Ind., N.J. Dep. dir. Systems and Devel. Svcs., N.Y.C.; client svcs. mgr. Gelco Corp., Mpls., Mainstem Corp., Princeton, N.J.; tchr. English and history, Ind., Ill. Home: 4 Knollwood Dr West Windsor NJ 08520

MARSHALL, SUSAN LOCKWOOD, civic worker; b. Orange, N.J., Dec. 2, 1939; d. Richard Douglas and Helen Lockwood (Stratford) Nelson; B.E., Wheelock Coll., 1961; m. William Pendleton Marshall, Aug. 20, 1960; children: Jill, James. Vol., Newton-Wellesley (Mass.) Hosp., 1962-63, New Eyes for the Needy, Inc., 1963-64, amblyopia screening program, Short Hills, N.J., 1969-71; bd. dirs. Jr. League of Oranges and Short Hills, Inc., 1967-69, 70-72, corr. sec., 1970-72; fund raising vol. Children's Aid and Adoption Soc. N.J., 1969-73, dir., 1970-73, asst. sec., 1970-72, 1st v.p., 1972-73; bd. dirs. Jr. League Stamford-Norwalk (Conn.), 1974-78, asst. treas., 1976-77, treas., 1977-78; bd. dirs. Program One to One, Inc., 1975-76, also treas.; vol. Voluntary Action Center 1975-76; bd. dirs. Episcopal Churchwomen of St. Luke's Parish, 1974-75, 76-80, 2d v.p., 1976-77, asst. treas., 1977-78, treas., 1978-80, pres., 1980-81; bd. dirs. Lockwood Mathews Mansion Mus., 1979-88, 89—, vol., 1979, treas., 1979-88, 89—, v.p., 1983-88; mem. council Darien Sch. Parent Bd., 1978-83, recording sec. 1981-83; bd. dirs. Middlesex Jr. High Parents Assn., 1979-83, treas., 1982-83; mem. The Vol. Ctr., 1984—; mem. vol. mgmt. assistance program adv. comm. Darien Chpt. Am. Field Service, 1984-87; Darien High Sch. Parents Assn., 1982-85, chmn., 1984-85; bd. dirs. Darien United Way, 1984—, asst. treas., 1988—. Address: 358 Hollow Tree Ridge Rd Darien CT 06820

MARSHALL-NADEL, NATHALIE, artist, writer, educator; b. Pitts., Nov. 10, 1932; d. Clifford Benjamin and Clarice (Stille) Marshall; m. Robert Alfred Van Buren, May 1, 1952 (div. June 1965); children—Christine Van Buren Popovic, Clifford Marshall, Jennifer Van Buren Lake; m. David Arthur Nadel, Dec. 30, 1976. A.F.A., Silvermine Coll. Art, New Canaan, Conn., 1967; B.F.A., U. Miami, Coral Gables, 1977, M.A., 1982, Ph.D. in English and Fine Art, 1982. Instr. humanities Miami Ednl. Consortium, Miami Shores, Fla., 1977-79, Barry U., Miami Shores, 1979-81, U. Miami, Coral Gables, 1977-81; sr. lectr. Nova U., Ft. Lauderdale, Fla., 1981-84, assoc. prof. humanities, 1985-86; prof. art, chair dept. art. Old Coll., Reno, Nev., 1986-88; chief artist Rockefeller U., N.Y.C., 1973-75; asst. registrar Lowe Art Mus., Coral Gables, 1976-78; co-founder, dir. The Bakehouse Art Complex, Miami, 1984—; advisor, bd. mem. NAH YAH EE (Indian children's art exhibits), Weimar, Calif., 1984-86; mem. adv. bd. New World Sch. Arts, Miami, 1985—. One-woman shows: Silvermine Coll. Art, New Canaan, Conn., 1968, Ingber Gallery, Greenwich, 1969, Capricorn Gallery, N.Y.C., 1969, Pierson Coll. at Yale U., New Haven, 1970, The Art Barn, Greenwich, 1972, Art Unltd., N.Y.C., 1973, Benevy Gallery, N.Y.C., 1974, Richter Library, U. Miami, 1985, Nova U., Ft. Lauderdale, 1985, Ward Nasse Gallery, N.Y.C., 1985, Old Coll., Reno, 1986, Washoe County Library, Reno, 1987; group shows include: Capricorn Gallery, N.Y.C., 1968, Ingber Gallery, Greenwich, 1968, Compass Gallery, N.Y.C., 1970, Optimums Gallery, Westport, Conn., 1970, Finch Coll. Mus., N.Y.C., 1971, Town Hall Art Gallery, Stamford, Conn., 1973, 74, Jewish Community Ctr., Miami Beach, 1981, Continuum Gallery, Miami Beach, 1982, South Fla. Art Inst., Hollywood, Fla., 1984, Met. Mus., Coral Gables, Fla., 1985, Ward Nasse Gallery, N.Y.C., 1985, Brunnier Mus., Iowa State U., Ames, 1986, Nat. Mus. of Women in he Arts Libr., Washington, 1987, 89, Raymond James Invitational, St. Petersburg, Fla., 1989, 90. Author, artist: Vibrations on Revelations, 1973, The Firebird, 1982, numerous artist books, 1968—. Author: Be Organized for College, 1980. Artist: (children's book) The Desert: What Lives There?, 1972; editor, designer: Court Theaters of Europe, 1982; writer, dir. T.V. programs Moutain Mandala: Autumn, Mountain Mandala: Winter;

contbr. poems to poetry mags., articles to profl. jours. Recipient Sponsor's award for Painting Greenwich Art Soc., 1967; Steven Buffton Meml. award Am. Bus. Women's Assn., 1980. Mem. Coll. Art Assn., MLA, Nat. Women's Studies Assn., Women's Caucus for Art (nat. adv. bd. 1983-88, pres. Miami chpt. 1984-86, southeast regional v.p. 1986). Address: 6213 12th Ave S Saint Petersburg FL 33707

MARSHALL-REED, DIANE, psychologist, educator; b. Wyandotte, Mich., Feb. 28, 1950; d. Thomas Edward Mullett and Etta Mae (Morris) McCormick; m. Thomas O. Marshall, Feb. 3, 1968 (div. Nov. 1981); children: Michael, Jonathan; m. Edmond L. Reed III, Sept. 17, 1985. BS, Wayne State U., 1972, MEd, 1976, postgrad. Cert. psychologist, social worker. Counselor for family of terminally ill, 1972-82; tchr. homebound and hospitalized Wyandotte Pub. Schs., 1972-81, tchr. learning disabled, 1981, tchr. mentally retarded, 1981-84, ednl. therapist, 1984-87; pvt. practice Riverside Psychol. Svcs., Trenton, Mich., 1982-88, Hillsdale (Mich.) Psychol. Svcs., 1987—; prin. Hillsdale County Intermediate Sch. Dist., Mich., 1987—; therapist for abusive parents Dept. Social Svcs. contract, 1984—; cons. family matters Hillsdale, Branch, Wayne and Oakland Counties Cts., 1984—; instr. English for adult edn.; speaker in field; pvt. practice psychology Hillsdale Counseling Ctr., 1987—. Dept. Social Svcs. grantee, 1984-89; named Mother of Yr., News Herald, 1986. Mem. Am. Psychol. Assn., Women in Ednl. Adminstrn. (treas. 1978-80), Mich. Assn. Psychologists, Wayne County Homebound Assn. (past chmn.), Save the Whales, Gorilla Found., Exchange Club, Mensa, Phi Delta Kappa, Pi Lambda Theta. Home: 6340 Hudson Rd Osseo MI 49266 Office: Hillsdale Psychol Svcs 108 E Sharp St Hillsdale MI 49242

MARSZALEK, GEORGIA ANN, marketing consultant; b. Buffalo, Nov. 14, 1946; d. Edward S. and Helen (Rudick) M.; m. Peter Loranger, Jan. 15, 1989. BA, SUNY, Buffalo, 1969; MBA, Pepperdine U., 1979. Mktg. mgr. Nat. Semiconductor, Santa Clara, Calif., 1975-79; dir. mktg. Atari, Inc., Santa Clara, Calif., 1979-83, Convergent Technologies, Inc., Santa Clara, Calif., 1983-84, Tektronix, Inc., Santa Clara, Calif., 1984-85, Teradyne, Inc., Santa Clara, Calif., 1985-89; ind. mktg. cons. Foster City, Calif., 1989—. Mem. Bus. and Profl. Advt. Assn. Office: PO Box 4032 Foster City CA 94404

MARTAS, JULIA ANN, special education administrator; b. Bronx, N.Y., July 30, 1949; d. Julio and Emilia (Guerra) M. BS, CCNY, 1972, MS, 1975; postgrad., NYU. Cert. spl. edn. tchr., N.Y., sch. adminstrn. and supr. Regional coord. bil.-spl. edn. div. spl. edn. Manhattan N.Y.C. Bd. Edn., 1982-86, profl. assocs., div. personnel, 1986-87, chancellor's monitor spl. edn. office of monitoring, 1987-88, dist. adminstr. spl. edn., 1988—; Instr. grad. spl. edn. dept. Coll. of New Rochelle, L.I. U., Adelphi U., CCNY, 1984—; cons. sch. div. McGraw Hill Pub. Co., Globe Pub. Co., Bowmar Noble, Economy Pub. Co. Mem. Coun. of Exceptional Children, Assn. Supr. Curriculum Devel., Puerto Rican Educators Assn., N.Y. Archdiocese, Social Action, Grand Order Oddfellow, House of Ruth.

MARTEL, BONNIE GILLESPIE, real estate broker, educator; b. Elizabeth, N.J., Apr. 30, 1940; d. James Gregory Gillespie and Ellen Mae (Winter) Mangels; m. Richard Francis Martel, Apr. 16, 1966; children: Richard Francis Jr., Christopher Henri, Stephanie Winter, Olivia Dolbec. BA, Cabrini Coll., 1962. Cert. tchr., N.J., real estate salesperson. Tchr. elem. Eatontown (N.J.) Sch. System, 1962-64; tchr. English Wall Twp. (N.J.) High Sch., 1964-67; real estate agt. Marie Cox Agy., Oceanport, N.J., 1973-78, The Hickey Agy., Monmouth Beach, N.J., 1978-83; real estate broker Joan Parent Realtors, Monmouth Beach, 1983-90, Schlott Realtors, Fair Haven, N.J., 1990—; sec. Housing Info. Coun., Princeton, N.J., 1989-90. Chmn. entertainment com. Community Rels. Com. of Monmouth County, 1988-90. Named Realtor Assoc. of Yr., County of Monmouth and State of N.J., 1989. Fellow Grad. Realtor Inst. Roman Catholic. Office: Schlott Realtors 636 River Rd Fair Haven NJ 07704

MARTEL, EVA LEONA, accountant; b. Bristol, Conn., Feb. 14, 1945; d. Samuel L. and Irene A. (Beaulieu) Martel. BS in Acctg., N.H. Coll., 1986; MBA, Plymouth State Coll., 1990. Acccounts payable clk. Elliot Hosp., Manchester, N.H., 1971-79; bookkeeper Elliot Hosp., Manchester, 1979-84, dir. acctg., 1984—; speaker Daniel Webster Coun. Boy Scouts Am., Manchester, 1988. Treas. N.H. Indian Coun., 1980-84; vol. United Way, Manchester, 1988—, account exec. 1990; mem. adv. coun. health care adminstrn. N.H. Coll., 1990. Mem. Hosp. Fin. Mgmt. Assn., Exec. Female. Roman Catholic. Home: RFD 4 11 Medford Farms Goffstown NH 03045

MARTELL, CLARE EILEEN, psychologist; b. Jersey City, Jan. 5, 1945; d. William Joseph and Catherine Magdalene (Martell) Gantner; children: Janet Marie, Nicholas Jr., Stephen Robert, Carmen Michael. AA, Atlantic Community Coll., Mays Landing, N.J., 1971; BA, Stockton State Coll., Pomona, N.J., 1973; MA, Glassboro State Coll., 1975; PhD, Temple U., 1985. Lic. psychologist. Tchr. Mainland Regional High Sch., Linwood, N.J., 1974-75; profl. counselor Del. House Mental Health Agy., Burlington, N.J., 1975-76; psychology intern Gloucester County Mental Health and Ancora Psychiat. Hosp., 1976-77; from staff clin. psychologist to dir. quality assuran Ancora (N.J.) Psychiatric Hosp.; staff clin. psychologist Vineland (N.J.) Devel. Disabilities Ctr., 1977-78, New Lisbon (N.J.) Devel. Disabilities Ctr., 1978-79; staff psychologist Cumberland County Mental Health Clinic, Vineland, 1986-88; pvt. practice Medford, N.J., 1988—; clin. psychologist, cons., Medford, N.J., 1984—, Pa. Hosp. Counseling Progam, Marlton, N.J. Mem. League of Women Voters, Camden County, N.J., Nat. Women;s Health Network, Wash., 1989—. Mem. N.J. Psychol. Assn., South Jersey Psychol. Assn. Democrat. Roman Catholic. Office: Briarwood Med Ctr 25 Jackson Rd Medford NJ 08055

MARTELLA, JANET ELAINE, educator; b. Modesto, Calif., May 1, 1956; d. John William and Mildred Elaine (Honeywell) McConnell; m. Gregory Eugene Martella, Dec. 17, 1978. Student, Pacific Union Coll., 1974-78; student, Seminario Adventista, Sagunto, Spain, 1975-76; BA, Calif. State U., Sacramento, 1980; postgrad., Calif. State U., Fresno, 1982. Master tchr. Armona (Calif.) Elem. Sch. Dist., 1982-88; tchr. gifted and talented edn. Hanford (Calif.) Elem. Sch. Dist., 1988—. Trustee Hanford Community Med. Ctr., 1988—. Mem. AAUW. Democrat. Seventh-Day Adventist.

MARTELLO, LOIS PENN, social worker; b. N.Y.C., Oct. 7, 1951; d. Jack Ira and Evelyn (Peer) Penn; m. John Martello, May 5, 1977. BA in Speech and Theater, Trenton St. Coll., 1973; MA in Counseling, Montclair State Coll., 1978; M in Social Work, Fordham U., 1983. Cert. social worker, N.Y.; cert. employee assistance profl. Case mgr. N.J. Div. Pub. Welfare, Paterson, N.J., 1973-78; alcoholism counselor Long Island Coll. Hosp., Bklyn., 1978-82; social worker Lower Eastside Svc. Ctr., N.Y.C., 1983-84; employee assistance counselor Cen. Labor Rehab. Council, N.Y.C., 1984-85; program adminstr. The Human Resources Group, N.Y.C., 1985-87; employee assistance coordinator Exec. Health Examiners, N.Y. Stock Exchange Clinic, 1987—; speaker in field. Fellow Occupational Clin. Profls. Group, Assn. Labor-Mgmt. Adminstrs. and Cons. on Alcoholism; m. Toastmasters Internat. (adminstrv. v.p. 1988-89, sec. 1987-88), Nat. Assn. Social Workers (co-dir. Indsl. Social Work com., N.Y.C., 1985-87). Democrat. Jewish. Home: 206 E 9th St 5 New York NY 10003

MARTENEY, LOIRE, international sales executive; b. Phoenix, May 30, 1959; d. Conn Marteney West. Cert. in sales and mktg., U. So. Calif., 1985; postgrad. in law, Pacific Coast U., Fullerton, Calif., 1990. Internat. sales Indo-Atlantic, U.S.A., Los Angeles, 1980-83; area sales mgr. Meadows Airfreight, U.S.A., Los Angeles, 1983-86; account exec. DHL Airways, Los Angeles, 1988—; internat. account exec. Hellmann Internat. Ferwarders, 1986-87; dir. mktg. Opis, Inc., 1985—; dir. mktg. OPIS, Inc., Los Angeles, 1985—; owner Reach for Success Publs., 1985—. Author: Your Personal Sales Guide, 1984. Fundraiser Sr. Action Care Network, Los Angeles, 1983; fundraiser, chairperson Human Rights Awards Banquet, Newport Beach, Calif., 1983. Mem. Am. Profl. Assn., Internat. Law Soc. (sec. 1985-86), Internat. Mktg. Assn., Women in World Trade, U. So. Calif. Alumni Assn., Delta Theta Phi, Delta Nu Alpha. Democrat. Presbyterian. Clubs: Winston Polo (Anaheim, Calif.); John Wayne Tennis (Newport Beach, Calif.). Home: 195 Claremont Belmont Shores CA 90803

MARTENS, BARBARA COLWELL, computer programmer/analyst; b. Pawnee City, Nebr., July 24, 1932; d. Ervin Barr and Verna Alberta (Puls) Colwell; children: Craig, Eric, Douglas. BA cum laude, U. Nebr., 1954; AAS, Metro Community Coll., Omaha, 1983; MEd, Syracuse U., 1971, postgrad., 1972-73. Cert. tchr., N.Y. Health planner then dir. info. and edn. Health Planning Coun. of the Midlands, Omaha, 1976-81; programmer Mut. of Omaha, 1983-85; sr. programmr/analyst U. Nebr., Omaha, 1985-89, asst. dir. adminstrv. computing, 1987-89; programmer-analyst U. Nebr., Lincoln, 1989—; sr. programmer/analyst U. Nebr. Mem. NAFE, Phi Beta Kappa, Phi Sigma Iota, Alpha Lambda Delta. Home: 1300 G St #201E Lincoln NE 68508 Office: U Nebr 225 Nebraska Hall Lincoln NE 68588-0521

MARTENS, PATRICIA MARGARET, physician recruiter; b. St. Louis, Mar. 28, 1962; d. John Robert and Margaret June (Pederson) Cooper; m. Herman Henry Martens, Apr. 24, 1987. BS Health Svcs. Mgmt., U. Mo., 1984. Area dir. Arthritis Found., St. Louis, 1985-87; provider rels. coord. Sanus Health Plan, St. Louis, 1987-88; search cons., physician recruiter Jackson and Coker, St. Louis, 1988—. Mem. NAFE. Roman Catholic. Office: 502 Earth City Expwy Ste 307 Earth City MO 63045

MARTI, LORI LEE, account consultant; b. Seattle, Jan. 14, 1963; d. Fred Walter and Sherry Lee (Dahl) M. BSBA, U. Ariz., 1985. Asst. mgr. Gen. Novelty, Mesa, Ariz., 1985; mgr. Gen. Novelty, San Diego, 1985-86; asst. dist. mgr. Gen. Novelty, Westminster, Calif., 1986-87; mgr. MGA-Guess Products, Tucson, 1987-88; Tucson br. mgr Ryder Transp., Tucson, 1988-89; account exec. COM Systems, Tucson, 1989-90; account cons. MCI, Tucson, 1990—. Mem. NAFE. Republican. Roman Catholic. Home: 1 E River Rd #233 Tucson AZ 85704 Office: MCI 6369 E Tanque Verde Rd #160 Tucson AZ 85715

MARTIKAINEN, A(UNE) HELEN, retired health education specialist; b. Harrison, Maine, May 11, 1916; d. Sylvester and Emma (Heikkinen) M.; AB, Bates Coll., 1939, DSc (hon.), 1957, Smith Coll., 1969; MPH, Yale, 1941; DSc, Harvard U., 1964. Health edn. sec. Hartford Tb and Public Health Assn., 1941-42; cons. USPHS, 1942-49; chief health edn. WHO, Geneva, 1949-74; chair internat. rels. N.C. div. AAUW, 1986—. Trustee Bridgton Acad., North Bridgton, Maine; citizen councillor Atlantic Coun. U.S.A., 1987—; mem. N.C. Women's Forum, 1984—; N.C. Ctr. of Laws Affecting Women, Inc.; mem. adv. bd. Sch. Pub. Health, U. N.C., Chapel Hill; bd. dirs. N.C. Women's Resource Ctr., 1987-90, Orange and Durham Counties chpt. U.N. Assn. Recipient Delta Omega award Yale U.; Nat. Adminstrv. award Am. Acad. Phys. Edn.; Bates Key award; Internat. Service award, France, 1953; Prentiss medal, 1956; spl. medal, certificate for internat. health edn. service Nat. Acad. Medicine for France, 1959; Profl. award Soc. Pub. Health Educators, 1963, Benjamin Elijah Mays award Bates Coll. Alumni Assn., 1989. Fellow Am. Pub. Health Assn. (chmn. health edn. sect., Excellence award 1969); mem. AAUW, LWV (Chapel Hill, N.C. br. 1987—), Women's Internat. League for Peace and Freedom, U.S. Soc. Pub. Health Educators, Internat. Union Health Edn. (Parisot medal, tech. adviser), Acad. Phys. Edn. (assoc.), N.C. Coun. Women's Orgns. (mem. coun. assembly 1988—, Women of Distinction award 1989), Phi Beta Kappa. Home: PO Box 2315 Chapel Hill NC 27515

MARTIN, ANGELA MICHIKO, pediatrician; b. Tokyo, Nov. 14, 1957; d. Carnell Luther and Catherine (Farley) M. AA, Emory U., Oxford, 1977; BS in Biology, Emory U., 1979, MD, 1984; postgrad., Ga. So. Coll., 1979-80, Morehouse Sch. Medicine, 1980-82. Diplomate Am. Bd. Pediatrics. Pediatrician Etowah Quality of Life Coun., Inc., Gadsden, Ala., 1987—; cons. physician Head State Program, Gadsden, 1988—. Tutor Literacy Action Program, Atlanta, 1977; active in Feed-The-Hungry Campaign, Atlanta, 1977. Recipient scholarship Nat. Health Svc. Corps, 1981, Outstanding Citizenship citation Mayor and Citizens Dublin, Ga., 1984. Mem. AMA, Am. Acad. Pediatrics, Med. Assn. State of Ala., Med. Soc. State of Ala., Med. Soc. Etowah County, Dept. Human Resources (physician mem.). Mem. Ch. of God.

MARTIN, ANITA ELLEN, nurse; b. Chgo., Aug. 5, 1925; d. Cornelius James and Sophie Ann (Bruczyk) M.; diploma DePaul Hosp. Coll. Nursing, St. Louis, 1949; B.S.N., Mt. St. Mary's Coll., Los Angeles, 1955; postgrad. UCLA, 1955-56, Rutgers U., 1969. Supr. pediatrics St. Mary's Hosp., Evansville, Ind., 1950-52; supr. medicine St. Vincent's Hosp., Los Angeles, 1952-56; supr. pediatrics Hotel Dieu Hosp., El Paso, 1956-60; head nurse Hanson's Disease, USPHS Hosp., Carville, La., 1960-62; head nurse, night supr. gen. surgery Hines (VA) Hosp., 1962-65, head nurse oncolgy, 1965-68, head nurse Restoration Center, 1968-72, community health nurse hosp.-based home care, 1972-74, coordinator hosp.-based health care, 1974-85, counselor alcoholic treatment program Restoration Center, 1968-72, cons. palliative care com., 1979-85; Alzheimer's disease nurse Family Alliance Adult Day Care Ctr., Woodstock, Ill.; lectr. high schs., civic orgns. Mem. Am. Nurses Assn., Nat. Orgn. VA Nurses, Am. Assn. Rehab. Nurses, Ill. State Hospice Assn. (charter). Roman Catholic. Contbr. articles to profl. jours. Home: 1208 Manchester Mall McHenry IL 60050 Office: Family Alliance 248 N Throop St Woodstock IL 60098

MARTIN, BARBARA A., sales executive; b. N. Brunswick, N.J., Jan. 24, 1942; d. John Joseph and Stella (Florek) Kociolek; m. Raymond A. Mioduszewski, Feb. 9, 1963 (div. 1980); 1 child, Sandra Ann. Student, Kean Coll.; A in Mgmt. Sci., Middlesex Co. Coll.; Degree in Sectl. Sci., Berkeley Sectl. Sch., 1961; Cert. Paralegal, Am. Paralegal Inst., S. Orange, N.J. Adminstrv. sec. Benson and Benson, Princeton, N.J., 1961-62; mgr. customer svc. Middlesex Container Co., Inc., Milltown, N.J., 1962-65; mgr. purchasing East Side Hair Co., E. Brunswick, N.J., 1971-78; gen. mgr. Middlesex Container Co., Inc., 1978-87; v.p. ops., sales Rampac Industries, Livingston, N.J., 1987—. Active S. River Dem. Orgn., N.J., 1972; pres. St. Mary's PTA, S. River, 1974-76, 1st v.p., 1976-78; treas. Trenton (N.J.) Reg. PTA, 1976-77. Named Advisor of Yr., St. Peters Athletic Assn., 1974. Mem. Nat. Assn. Female Execs. Clubs: S. River Women's (publicity com. 1978-79), CYO. Home: 121 Heffernan St Piscataway NJ 08854

MARTIN, BARBARA BURSA, chemistry educator; b. Oak Park, Ill., Aug. 2, 1934; d. George and Bessie Z. Bursa; m. Dean F. Martin, Dec. 22, 1956; children: Diane, Bruce, John, Paul, Brian, Eric. BA, Grinnell (Iowa) Coll., 1956; MSc, Pa. State U., University Park, 1959. Teaching asst. Pa. State U., University Park, 1956-57, rsch. asst., 1957-58; adj. rsch. assoc. U. South Fla., Tampa, 1971-72, vis. lectr., 1972-75, asst. prof. courtesy chemistry, 1975—. Co-author: Coordination Compounds, 1964—; contbr. articles to sci. jours. Recipient Alumni award Grinnell Coll., 1981. Mem. Am. Chem. Soc., Fla. Acad. Sci. (co-editor quar. jour. 1984—), Aquatic Plant Mgmt. Soc., Sigma Xi. Home: 3402 Valencia Rd Tampa FL 33618 Office: U South Fla 4202 Fowler Ave Tampa FL 33620

MARTIN, BARBARA JO, healthcare administrator; b. Reedsburg, Wis., May 1, 1954; d. Julius J. and Mariel J. Moyer; m. Douglas Martin; children: Terra, Kale. BS in Nursing, Lewis U., 1977, MBA, 1985. BSN Ingalls Meml. Hosp., Harvey, Ill., 1977-78, team supr., 1978-79, house coord., 1979-81, pediatric unit coord., 1981-82, assoc. dir. maternal child nursing, 1982-85, dir. maternal child nursing, 1985, dir. nursing, 1985-87; v.p., patient svcs. St. Margaret Hosp. and Health Ctrs., Hammond, Ind., 1987-90; v.p. ambulatory svcs. St. Joseph Med. Ctr., Joliet, Ill., 1990—. Mem. Am. Orgn. Nurse Execs., Am. Coll. Healthcare Execs. (nominee), NW Ind. Orgn. Nurse Execs. (pres.). Home: 403 S Brookshore Shorewood IL 60436 Office: St Joseph Med Ctr Ambulatory Svcs 333 N Madison Joliet IL 60435

MARTIN, BARBARA LEE, computer programmer and analyst; b. Warsaw, N.Y., Feb. 11, 1941; d. Eldon Merritt Glor and Ora Elizabeth (Putney) Newton; m. Brent Robert Martin, July 7, 1962 (div. Jan. 1979); children: Dane Robert, Dale Eldon. BS, Otterbein Coll., 1962; postgrad., Marion (Ohio) Tech. Coll., 1977-78. Tchr. math. Avon (Ohio) High Sch., 1962, Taft Jr. High Sch., Marion, 1962-66; computer programmer Nationwide Ins. Co., Columbus, Ohio, 1968-70; lead programmer/analyst O.M. Scott & Sons Co., Marysville, Ohio, 1970—. Sec. bd. zoning appeals Delaware Twp., Delaware, Ohio, 1989, 90; chairperson outreach com. Olentangy River Valley Assn., Delaware, 1988-90, chairperson, 1990—. Mem. NAFE. Presbyterian. Office: OM Scott & Sons Co 14111 Scottslawn Rd Marysville OH 43041

MARTIN, BARBARA LYNNE, educator; b. Lynn, Mass., May 21, 1943; d. Edward M. and Margaret (Deacon) Kehoe; m. Gerald W. Weber (div. Dec. 1978); 1 child, Karen Michelle; m. E. Dale Martin, Dec. 26, 1982. BA, U. N.H., 1965. Tchr. Norwalk (Conn.) Sch. Dist., 1965-67, Fremont (Calif.) Unified Sch. Dist., 1967-68, Los Altos (Calif.) Sch. Dist., 1972—. Home: 22954 Longdown Rd Cupertino CA 95014 Office: Springer Sch 1120 Rose Ave Mountain View CA 94022

MARTIN, CAROL ANN, academic administrator, English educator; b. Niagara Falls, N.Y., Oct. 26, 1941; d. William E. and Anne Marie (Spiroch) M.; m. Lonnie L. Willis, Nov. 29, 1980; children: Anne Marie Mullaney, Matthew Mullaney. BA, Cath. U. Am., 1963, MA, 1965, PhD, 1971. Instr. Cath. U. of Am., Washington, 1971-72; with Boise (Idaho) State U., 1972—, prof., 1980—, chairperson English dept., 1988—. Editor Rocky Mountain Review of Language and Literature; contbr. articles to profl. jours. Bd. dirs. State Humanities Coun., Boise, 1978-82, YWCA, Boise, 1990—; pres. Women's Caucus for the Modern Langs., N.Y.C., 1989. Mem. Modern Lang. Assn., Rocky Mountain Modern Lang. Assn. (bd. dirs. 1977-79), Interdisciplinary 19th Century Studies Assn. Office: Boise State U English Dept Boise ID 83725

MARTIN, CAROLYN STEWART, administrator, counselor; b. Pitts., May 16, 1951; d. Robert Thomas and Mary (Schoenecker) Stewart; m. Bradley W. Ritter Feb. 14, 1973 (div. 1979); m. Scott Harwood Martin, July 29, 1983; 1 child, Carrie Lee Martin. BS, Calif. State U., 1972; MA, Ohio State U., 1978; postgrad., Stetson Univ., DeLand, Fla., 1985-87. Tchr. Garrett County Schs., Oakland, Md., 1972-74, Little Darlings Sch., Columbus, Ohio, 1974-75, Colegio Nueva Granada, Bogota, Colombia, 1978-80; bilingual tchr. Othello (Wash.) Sch. Dist., adminstr. title VII, 1981-82; primary specialist, counselor Lake County Sch. Dist., Fla., 1982-84; tchr. Volusia County Sch. Dist., Deltona, Fla., 1984-85; guidance counselor Volusia County Schs., Deltona, Fla., 1985—; self employed parenting instr. DeLand 1988, chairperson Volusia Mental Health Assn., Daytona 1987, mem. Fla. State Dept. Edn. Task Force, Orlando 1989. Co-author Survival Spanish for Teachers, 1982, presenter Nat. Jr. High and Middle Convention, 1986, Fla. Assn. Counseling and Devel. Convention, 1985, 1986, 1988, guest speaker Women Volusia Conf., 1989. Mem. exec. bd. S.W. Volusia YMCA, 1988-90. Mem. AAUW, Volusia Assn. Counseling and Devel., Assn. for Supervision and Curriculum Devel. Republican. Episcopalian. Home: 2449 Tracy Ln Deltona FL 32725

MARTIN, CECILIA ANN, educator; b. Broken Bow, Okla., Nov. 10, 1934; d. Cecil C. and Faye (Burks) Martin; B.S., Baylor U., 1955; M.Ed., North Tex. State U., 1962; Ed.D., U. No. Colo., 1975. Instr. phys. edn. Stripling Jr. High Sch., Ft. Worth, 1955-65; cons. in phys. edn. Ft. Worth Ind. Sch. Dist., 1965-74; dir. profl. preparation dept. phys. edn. Colo. State U., Fort Collins, 1974—, asst. dean Coll. Profl. Studies, 1979-80. Mem. Tex. Tchrs. Assn., Am., Tex. (asso. conv. mgr. 1970-71), Colo. (sec. elect) assns. health, phys. edn. and recreation, Nat., Central (membership chmn.) assns. phys. edn. in higher edn., Colo. Assn. Health, Phys. Edn., Recreation and Dance (sec., pres.), Phi Delta Kappa, Kappa Delta Pi, Delta Psi Kappa. Home: 1977 17th Ave Greeley CO 80631 Office: Colo State U Moby Gymnasium Fort Collins CO 80523

MARTIN, CHERI CHRISTIAN, health services administrator; b. Nashville, Mar. 9, 1956; d. Jesse Thomas and Eloise (McClain) Christian; m. George A. Martin, June 25, 1977; children: Matthew Alexander, Kristin Leigh. BS in Family Resources and Consumer Scis., U. Wis., 1977. Asst. buyer Dayton Hudson, Mpls., 1978-79, assoc. buyer, 1979-81; instr. Nat. Coll., Mpls., 1981-82; mgr. store Connco Shoes, Inc., Mpls, 1982-83; patient svcs. rep. Group Health, Inc., Mpls., 1984-89; dental supr. Group Health, Inc., 1989—. Facilitator seminar Non-Verbal Communication, 1986. Mem. Nat. Soc. Patient Representation and Consumer Affairs, Minn./Dakota Assn. Patient Reps. (v.p. 1989-90), U. Wis. Alumni Assn., Group Health Social Club Mpls. (pres. 1987-89). Home: 4640 Nevada Ave N Crystal MN 55428

MARTIN, CONNIE RUTH, sales executive; b. Kansas City, Kans., Nov. 5, 1963; d. Joe Bob and Mary Jo Martin; m. Mark T. Lord; children: Carissa Marie Washburn, Dylan Thomas Lord. AS, Mesa Coll., 1984. Account exec. Med. Surg. & Hosp. Supply Co., Phoenix, 1977-79, Health Care Resources, Phoenix, 1979-80, CIGNA Health Plan, Phoenix, 1980-85; sr. account exec. United Health Care, Phoenix, 1985-87; regional mktg. dir. Pharm. Card System, Scottsdale, Ariz., 1987; v.p. nat. and spl. accounts MEDCO Containment Svcs., Fair Lawn, N.J., 1987—. Home: 174 White Birch Rd New Canaan CT 06840 Office: MEDCO Containment Svcs 1900 Pollitt Dr Fair Lawn NJ 07410

MARTIN, DALE, vocational rehabilitation executive; b. N.Y.C., May 10, 1935; d. Byron Pink Molter and Ruth (Nobel) Gestram; m. Robert A. Wishart, Dec. 13, 1985; children by previous marriage: Elizabeth, Devon. BS, U. Conn., 1957. RN, cert. ins. rehab. specialist. Dental asst. Hempstead, N.Y., 1951; with Wesson Maternity Hosp., Springfield, Mass., 1957-58, Huntington Hartford Meml. Hosp., Pasadena, 1958-59; office mgr. Indsl. By Products Inc., Kalamazoo, 1969-72; controller Indsl. By Products Inc., Chgo., 1970-74; cons. Mgmt. Resources Inc., Broomall, Pa., 1978-81; cons., owner Martin-Collard Assn., Inc., Monmouth Beach, N.J., 1980-84; cons., owner, chmn. bd. dirs. MCA, Inc., Boston, 1984—; cons. Viewfinder, Old Chatham, N.Y., 1987—. Contbr. articles to profl. jours.; painter, sculptor. Mem. Nat. Assn. Rehab. Profls. in Pvt. Sector (rep. region I to bd. dirs.), Internat. Assn. Psychosocial Rehab. Specialists, Sigma Theta Tau, Alpha Delta Pi. Clubs: Town (v.p.), Ski (Mountain Lakes, N.J.) (founder), Jr. Women's, Jr. League. Office: MCA Inc PO Box 5438 Boston MA 02102 also: MCA Inc PO Box 789 Port Salerno FL 34992-0789

MARTIN, DEBORAH JONES, health care consultant; b. Hiawassee, Ga., Aug. 7, 1956; d. Robert Warren and Betty (Brown) Jones; m. Reynol Hamilton Martin, Jr., Apr. 25, 1981; 1 child, Christopher Reynol. BBA in Acctg., U. Ga., 1977, postgrad., 1977-79. Cons. McBee Assocs., Balt., 1980-82; sr. cons. Peat Marwick, Atlanta, 1982-84; HFR coord. Hosp. Corp. Am., Atlanta, 1984-86; reimbursement mgr. Norrell Health Care, Atlanta, 1986-89; prin. Heathcare Systems & Svcs., Atlanta, 1989—. Fellow Healthcare Fin. Mgmt. Assn.; mem. Ga. Assn. for Home Health Agencies (assoc.), Atlanta Healthcare Alliance. Democrat. Methodist. Office: Healthcare Systems & Svcs 1100 Johnson Ferry Rd NE Center One Ste 430 Atlanta GA 30342

MARTIN, DOROTHY ANNE, retired military officer, consultant; b. Bklyn., July 21, 1938; d. Chester Edward and Sophia Ann (Homontowski) Machulski. AA, Nassau County Community Coll., 1967; BBA, Hofstra U., 1969; MS, Jacksonville State U., 1974. Commd. 1st lt. U.S. Army, 1970, advanced through grades to maj., 1980, ret., 1988; chief mil. police investigations 24th Inf. Div. U.S. Army, Fort Stewart, Ga., 1974-75; staff advisor to comdg. gen. 24th Inf. Div. U.S. Army, Fort Stewart, 1975-77; chief security police Tripler Med. Ctr., Honolulu, 1977-80; dep. dir. indsl. security Def. Investigative Svc., Boston, 1980-82; orgnl. effectiveness cons. 3d Support Command U.S. Army, Frankfurt, Fed. Republic Germany, 1983-86; personnel war planner U.S. Army, New Orleans, 1986-87; staff officer Office of Dir. Personnel and Community Activities U.S. Army, Fort Polk, La., 1987-88; ind. cons., corp. trainer; pres., corp. trainer Martin Assocs., 1988—. Contbr. articles to profl. jours. Mem. NAFE, Women Marines Assn. (pres. 1987-90), Assn. U.S. Army Retired Officers Assn., Women Bus. Owners Assn. Democrat. Home: 4701 Robin Hood Dr New Orleans LA 70128 Office: PO Box 870117 New Orleans LA 70187

MARTIN, EDITH KINGDON GOULD (MRS. GUY MARTIN), pianist, civic worker; b. N.Y.C., Aug. 20, 1920; d. Kingdon and Annunziata (Lucci) Gould; student Barnard Coll., N.Y.C., 1939-40; pvt. study piano; m. Guy Martin, Oct. 12, 1946; children—Isaiah Guyman III, Jason Gould, Christopher Kingdon, Edith Maria Theodosia Burr. Actress, Barter Theater, 1941, Summer Stock, Nyack, 1942, A Young American, 1946, Louis Bromfield's West of the Moon, 1946, Agatha Christie's Hidden Horizons, 1946; guest pianist Werner Lywen Quartet, 1965—. Bd. dirs. Paul VI Inst. for Arts, 1979—; trustee, past pres. Washington Opera. Served with USNR, 1942-46. Decorated Navy Expert Pistol medal. Clubs: City Tavern, Sulgrave (Washington). Author: Poems, 1934. Composer: Song Cycle on Poems of Lenau and Schiller, 1968. Home: 3300 O St NW Washington DC 20007

MARTIN, EDITH WAISBROT, computer scientist, aerospace and electronics company executive; b. Chgo., June 25, 1945; d. Alexander Joseph and Helen Mae (Hance) Waisbrot; m. Charles Samuel Martin, Dec. 16, 1967 (div. Jan. 1982); children: William McNutt, Christine Katherine; m. Douglas Carter Montgomery, Sept. 2, 1982 (div. July 1986). B.A., Lake Forest Coll., 1967; postgrad., Universitat Karlsruhe, W. Ger., 1971-72; M.S. in Info. and Computer Sci., Ga. Inst. Tech., 1975-76, Ph.D., 1980. Dir. computer sci. tech. lab. Ga. Inst. Tech., Atlanta, 1976-80; corp. exec. dir. Control Data Corp., Atlanta, 1980-82; pres. EWM & Assocs., Inc., Atlanta, 1982; dep. under sec. Dept. Def. for Rsch. and Advanced Tech., Washington, 1982-84; U.S. prin. Non-Atomic Rsch. and Devel. Com., 1982, NATO Def. Rsch. Group, Brussels, Belgium, 1982; v.p., high tech. ctr. Boeing Aerospace and Electronics, Seattle, 1984—; bd. vis. U. Wash. Law Sch., 1990—. Contbr. articles to profl. jours.; editorial reviewer: Mil. Electronics Countermeasures, 1976-80; mem. editorial bd. IEEE Spectrum, 1983—. Nat. adv. bd. Ga. Inst. Tech., Atlanta, 1983; vis. com. U. Washington Coll. Engring.; bd. visitors Carnegie-Mellon Software Engring. Inst.; vis. com. Coll. Engring., Cornell U.adv. bd. for Women in Engring. Initiative U. Washington/NSF; nat. adv. com. Strategic Def. Initiative; bd. dirs. Washington Tech. Ctr.; trustee Pacific N.W. Ballet. Recipient numerous awards Dept. Def. including Disting. Pub. Svc. award Caspar Weinberg (1984); Susan B. Anthony award, 1987, Upward Mobility award Soc. Women Engrs., 1989. Fellow IEEE (exec. bd.dirs. tech. com. on software Computer Soc. 1982—, award of appreciation-recognition 1983); mem. Assn. Computing Machinery, Electronics Industries Assn. (subcom. chmn. 1981 recognition award), Air Force Assn., Assn. Old Crows, Sigma Xi (award of appreciation-recognition from Pres. Ronald Reagan 1983, Women in Communication award 1989). Republican. Presbyterian. Clubs: Army-Navy Country (Washington), Lakes (Bellevue, Wash.), Bellevue Athletic, Overlake Golf and Country (Medina, Wash.). Office: Boeing Aerospace & Electronics High Tech Ctr PO Box 3999 M/S 7J-20 Seattle WA 98124-2499

MARTIN, ELLEN FISHWICK, banker; b. Roanoke, Va., July 28, 1948; d. John Palmer and Blair (Wiley) Fishwick; m. Isaiah Guyman III, Sept. 2, 1972; children: Isaiah Guyman IV, John Blair Fishwick Martin. BA, Wellesley Coll., 1970; postgrad., Southwestern Grad. Sch. Banking, Dallas, 1981. Rep. Merrill Lynch Reg. Commodities Div., Boston, 1970-72; portfolio mgr., trust dept. Riggs Nat. Bank, Washington, 1973-75, trust investment officer, 1976-81, v.p., trust investment officer, 1981-89; v.p., sr. investment officer Chevy Chast Trust Group, Bethesda, Md., 1989—. Author: Trust Industry, Profitablity, the Status, the Regulatory Perception, the Obstacles, and the Challenges. Bd. dirs. The Madeira Sch., McLean, Va., 1983, chmn. fin. com., 1984, v.p., 1987-89, pres., 1989—; mem. investment com. Diocesan Investment Fund of Episcopal Diocese of Washington Christ Ch., 1984, 86—. Mem. Washington Soc. of Investment (v.p. 1982-83, pres. 1983-84, bd. dirs. 1989-90). Democrat. Episcopalian.

MARTIN, FRANCINE RENEE, personnel consultant; b. Bklyn., May 16, 1948; d. Charles Harrison and Shirley Mae (Siegel) Odom; m. James Allen Gebhardt, Aug. 25, 1967 (div. 1968); m. William Micajah Martin, May 15, 1972; 1 child, Sahndra Lynne Martin. Student, Calif. State Coll., L.A., 1966, Mt. San Antonio Coll., Walnut, Calif., 1966-68. Cert. employment specialist, personnel cons. Checker, clk. Longs Drug Store, West Covina, Calif., 1971-72; legal sec., bookkeeper Cletus J. Hanifin, Atty. at Law, Arcadia, Calif., 1972-73; office mgr., sales rep. Van Gott and Assocs., San Gabriel, Calif., 1973-74; cost acctg. analyst Howell Co. div. Burd, Inc., Azusa, Calif., 1974-78; office asst. level 2 Employment Devel. dept. State of Calif., West Covina, Long Beach, 1980-84; patient accounts rep. Harriman Jones Med. Group, Long Beach, 1985-86; patient accounts collecting mgr. Hirschman Eye Surgery Ctr., Long Beach, 1986-87; credit sec. Cessna Fin. Corp., Long Beach, 1987-88; asst. mgr., personnel cons. Abigail Abbott Personnel Cos., Long Beach, Torrance, Calif., 1988—; mktg. trainer Abigail Abbott Personnel Co., Newport Beach, 1989-90; speaker Torrance Small Bus. Coun., 1989-90. Adv. bd. Mt. San Antonio Coll., Walnut, Calif., 1973; mem. West Covina (Calif.) Sunshine Club, 1980-84; vol. to help disabled Am. vets. Mem. NAFE, Calif. Assn. of Personnel Cons. (cert.), Nat. Assn. Personnel Cons., Torrance C. of C., Redondo Beach C. of C., San Pedro C. of C., Carson C. of C., Palos Verdes C. of C. Democrat. Home: 930 Roswell Ave #6 Long Beach CA 90804 Office: Apple One Employment Svcs 3609 Long Beach Blvd Long Beach CA 90807

MARTIN, HELEN ELIZABETH, teacher; b. West Chester, Pa., Feb. 19, 1945; d. Thomas Edwin and Elizabeth Temple (Walker) M.; BA, The King's Coll., Briarcliff Manor, N.Y., 1967; MEd, West Chester U., 1970; postgrad. Goethe Inst., Freiberg, Fed. Republic Germany, 1979, Oxford U., 1979. Tchr. math. and sci. Unionville (Pa.) High Sch., 1967—; adj. prof. W. Chester (Pa.) U., 1989—; mem. Carnegie Forum on Edn. and the Economy. Mem. Pa. Rep. State Com., Rep. Com. of Chester County, 1987—. Named Alumna of the Yr. The King's Coll., 1987; recipient State Presdl. award, 1989, Frank G. Brewer Civil Air Patrol Meml. Aerospace award, 1989. Fellow Am. Sci. Affiliation; mem. AAAS, Nat. Bd. Profl. Teaching Standards, Nat. Sci. Tchrs. Assn., Nat. Council Tchrs. Math., History Sci. Soc., So. Chester County Rep. Women's Council, Red Clay Valley Assn., Brandywine Valley Assn. Clubs: Delaware Camera, Women's Rep. of Chester County, Nat. Sci. Tchrs. Assn. (internat. lectr. 1987), Assn. for Sci. Edn. in U.K. (internat. lectr. 1987). Home: 329 Lambortown Rd West Grove PA 19390 Office: Unionville High Sch Unionville PA 19375

MARTIN, HELENE GETTER, university development program director; b. Boston, May 24, 1940; d. Seymour Samuel and Doris Viola (Taylor) Getter; divorced; children: Lauren Renee, Susannah Taylor. AB in English Lit. with distinction, Wheaton Coll., 1962; MS, Columbia U., 1964; postgrad., U. Calif., Berkeley, 1981. Caseworker, cons. Mass. Dept. Mental Health, Milton, 1965-78; program analyst dept. nursing Ambulatory Care Ctr., U. Calif., San Francisco, 1980-81; cons. mental health, mem. faculty Boston Coll. Legal Assistance Bur., Waltham, Mass., 1978-80; mktg. assoc. Vesper Hosps., San Leandro, Calif., 1981-83; dir. resource devel. Am. Acad. Opthalmology, San Francisco, 1983-85; mgr. membership devel. The Mus. Soc., San Francisco, 1986-89; dir. devel. and alumni rels. Sch. Social Work Columbia U., N.Y.C., 1989—; case worker Mass. Dept. of Mental Health, 1965-78; programs dir. Mass. Mental Health Assn., 1978-80. Co-founder Marin PACT (Parents and Community Together), Marin County, Calif., 1987; bd. dirs., mem. exec. com. Oxfam-Am., Boston, 1973-79; mem. Com. to Aid East Pakistan, Cambridge, Mass., 1970; chairperson Bangladesh Emergency Relief Fund, Newton, Mass., 1972, Ad-Hoc Com. to Remove Asbestos, Newton, 1978; mem. Dem. City Com., Newton, 1978; chairperson welfare com. LWV, Newton, 1970. Mem. Nat. Soc. Fund Raising Execs. (Golden Gate chpt., bd. dirs 1989, chairperson Nat. Philanthrophy Day awards com. 1989). Home: 601 W 115th St #53 New York NY 10025 Office: Columbia U Sch Social Work Sch Social Work 622 W 113th New York NY 10025

MARTIN, IVA BERNIECE, elementary educator; b. Billings, Mont., May 17, 1929; d. Ross Adelbert and Gertrude Iva (Reifle) Coles; m. Edward Dean Martin, Sept. 2, 1950; children: Ross Harrison, Debbie DeAnne. BS, Ea. Mont. Coll., 1970, MS, 1976, postgrad., 1977-88. Cert. elem. educator; reading K-12 endorsement. Elem. tchr. Huntley Project, Worden, Mont., 1969-70, Sch. Dist. #2, Billings, Mont., 1970—. Mem. AAUW (program v.p. 1983-85, pres. 1985-87, mem. nat. conv. Columbus chpt. 1985, NW regional conv. Bellingham Wash., 1986, parliamentarian 1987-89, internat. rels. rep. 1989—,), Midland Empire Reading Coun., Delta Kappa Gamma. Home: 929 Lewis Ave Billings MT 59101

MARTIN, JACQUELINE BYRD, personnel administrator; b. McComb, Miss.; d. Geneva (Holmes) Brown; m. Donald E. Martin; 1 child, Donald Christopher. Student, Straight Bus. Coll., 1967; AA, S.W. Jr. Coll., 1974; student, U. So. Miss., 1985—. Operator N.Y. Telephone Co., N.Y.C., 1964-68; girl friday JC Penney Co., N.Y.C., 1968-70; instrn. supr. Learning Found., N.Y.C., 1970-71; clk. typist Greater N.Y. Blood Program, N.Y.C., 1971-72; posting clk. Deposit Guaranty Bank, McComb, 1972-73; dir. asst. operator South Cen. Bell, McComb, 1974-80; personnel office City of McComb, 1981—. Adv. coun. Drug Free Schs., McComb. Mem. NAFE, Miss. Assn. Personnel Administrs., Nat. Assn. Federated Clubs, Miss. State Fedn., Omicron Federated Club. Democrat. Baptist. Home: 705 N Live Oak St McComb MS 39648 Office: City of McComb 115 Third St McComb MS 39648

MARTIN, JEAN ANN, reading specialist; b. Omaha, June 27, 1942; d. Clarid Fee and Frances Catherine (Dugan) McNeil; m. Robert William Martin, Dec. 28, 1968. BS, Pa. State U., 1963; MEd, U. Del., 1968. Cert. English tchr., Pa., N.Y., Del., reading specialist, Va., N.Y., Del. Tchr. English Neshaminy Sch. Dist., Langhorn, Pa., 1963-65; tchr. English and reading Unionville (Pa.) Sch. Dist., 1965-68; tchr. reading Jamesville-DeWitt (N.Y.) Sch. Dist., 1968-69, South Colonie Sch. Dist., Albany, N.Y., 1969-70; tchr. English Bethlehem Cen. Sch. Dist., Delmar, N.Y., 1970-71, Smyrna (Del.) Sch. Dist., 1971-73; reading specialist, tchr. English Delmar Sch. Dist., 1973-88; reading specialist Accomack (Va.) County Schs., 1988—. Editor DSRA Reader Jour., 1986-90. Past pres. Lioness, Delmar; co-chair Harbor Festival Com., Onancock, Va., 1988—; mem. Onancock Parks and Recreation Coun., 1990—. Named Tchr. of the Yr., Delmar Sch. Dist., 1984. Mem. Internat. Reading Assn., Diamond State Reading Assn. (pres. 1985-86), Sussex. County Orgn. for Reading Excellence (pres. 1980-81), Va. State Reading Assn. (bd. dirs.), NEA, Eastern Shore Reading Coun. Va. (pres. 1989—), Accomack County Edn. Assn., Assn. for Supervision and Curriculum Devel., Va. Edn. Assn., Eastern Shore Yacht and Country Club. Home: 3 Market St Onancock VA 23417 Office: South Accomack Elem Sch Melfa VA 23410

MARTIN, JENNIFER MILLER, mechanical engineer; b. Alexandria, La., Nov. 10, 1962; d. Odis James and Ethel Juneau) Miller; m. Bruce Edwin Martin, May 23, 1987. BSME, La. Tech. U., 1984; MSME, Rensselaer Poly. Inst., 1986. Aerospace structural design engr. Gen. Dynamics, Ft. Worth, 1986—. Mem. Pi Tau Sigma, Tau Beta Pi. Republican. Roman Catholic.

MARTIN, JERRI WHAN, public relations executive; b. Aurora, Ill., Oct. 21, 1931; d. Forest Livings and Geraldeane Jeanette (Cutler) Whan; m. Charles L. Martin (div.); children: Vicki, Bill, Erica, Kevin. BMus, Wichita State U., 1952. Co-owner Sta. KCNY, San Marcos, Tex., 1957-70; correspondent Austin Am.-Statesman, 1959-85; co-owner Sta. KWFT, Wichita Falls, Kans., 1965—; cons. U.S. Office Econ. Opportunity, Austin, 1966-68, Tex. Ednl. Found., Inc., San Marcos, 1975—, State Bank and Trust Co., San Marcos, 1985—. Mem. ethics com. Hays Meml. Hosp., 1985—; pres. Hays County Women's Polit. Caucus, Tex., 1985—; del. State Dem. Convs., Dallas, Houston, 1982, 84; bd. dirs. Cen. Tex. Higher Edn. Authority, San Marcos, 1982—, Scheib Opportunity Ctr., San Marcos, 1983—, Edwards Underground Water Dist., San Antonio, 1985—, sec. Named Outstanding Reporter in Tex., Tex. Legis., 1960. Mem. Bus. and Profl. Women, Jr. Service League (sustaining), San Marcos C. of C. Office: Tex Ednl Found Inc PO Box 1108 San Marcos TX 78666

MARTIN, JOANN SPEER, military officer; b. Wurzburg, Federal Republic Germany, Sept. 1, 1955; came to U.S., 1957; d. James Daniel and Helyn (Baity) Speer; m. Garnel Martin, Dec. 20, 1986. BA, Grambling State U., 1977; MA, Ball State U., 1990. Commd. 2d. lt. USAF, 1977, advanced through grades to major, 1989; chief mgmt. and systems br. USAF, Spangdahlem AB, Fed. Republic Germany; chief ops. support br. USAF, Grissom AFB, Ind.; comdr. USAF, Grissom AFB. Named Disting. Alumni Nat. Assn. for Equal Opportunity in Higher Edn., 1988. Mem. NAFE, Tuskeegee Airmen, AF Sgts. Assn., Grissom AFB Officer's Club Adv. Coun., Grambling State U. Alumni Assn., Squadron Assn. (pres.). Democrat. Methodist. Home: 160 Woodland Hills Peru IN 46970

MARTIN, JUNE JOHNSON CALDWELL, journalist; b. Toledo, Oct. 6; d. John Franklin and Eunice Imogene (Fish) Johnson; A.A., Phoenix Jr. Coll., 1939-41; B.A., U. Ariz., 1941-43, 53-59; student Ariz. State U., 1939, 40; m. Erskine Caldwell, Dec. 21, 1942 (div. Dec. 1955); 1 son, Jay Erskine; m. 2d, Keith Martin, May 5, 1966. Free-lance writer, 1944—; columnist Ariz. Daily Star, 1956-59; editor Ariz. Alumnus mag., Tucson, 1959-70; book editor, gen. feature writer, tape audio rev. columnist Ariz. Daily Star, Tucson, 1970—; panelist, co-producer TV news show Tucson Press Club, 1954-55, pres., 1958. Contbg. author: Rocky Mountain Cities, 1949; contbr. articles to World Book Ency., and various mags. Mem. Tucson CD Com., 1961; vol. campaigns of Samuel Goddard, U.S. Rep. Morris Udall, U.S. ambassador and Ariz. gov. Raul Castro. Recipient award Nat. Headliners Club, 1959, Ariz. Press Club award, 1957-59, Am. Alumni Council, 1966, 70. Mem. Nat. Book Critics Circle, Jr. League of Tucson, Tucson Urban League, P.E.N. U.S.A. West, Pi Beta Phi. Democrat. Methodist. Club: Tucson Press. Home: PO Box 2631 Tucson AZ 85702 Office: PO Box 26807 Tucson AZ 85726

MARTIN, KAREN KRAUSCHE, social services administrator, clinical social worker; b. N.Y.C., Sept. 2, 1947; d. John Francis and Gladys Rose (Cure) K.; m. John Charles Martin, Oct. 16, 1977; children: Stacey Elizabeth, Sean Patrick. BA, Sacred Heart U., 1984; MSW, Fordham U., 1985; cert. family therapy, Smith Coll., 1989. Cert. social worker, N.Y., Conn.; cert. sch. social worker, Conn. Social worker United Cerebral Palsy, Bridgeport, Conn., 1983, Norwalk Sch. System, Norwalk, Conn., 1983-84, Cath. Family Services, Bridgeport, 1984-89; pvt. practice social work Ctr. Family Guidance, Stratford, Conn., 1986-90; cons. Apple Tree Nursery Sch., Trumbull, Conn., 1989-91. Cons. Shelton (Conn.) Bd. Edn., 1989—; bd. dirs. Trumbull (Conn.) Counseling Ctr., 1984-89; mem. Reg. Youth Substance Abuse Prevention Coun., Trumbull, 1988-89. Mem. Nat. Assn. Social Workers (register of clin. social work), Conn. Assn. Sch. Social Workers, Acad. Cert. Social Workers. Roman Catholic. Home: 50 Friar Ln Trumbull CT 06611 Office: Ctr Family Guidance 33 King St Stratford CT 06497

MARTIN, KATHLEEN ANN, executive secretary; b. Salt Lake City, Mar. 18, 1944; d. Wallace Lester and Helen Agnes (Stanford) M.; children: Jon, Kendal, Robert, Jill. Student, U. Utah. Sec. Reese C. Anderson Atty., Salt Lake City, 1963-70; personal sec. Asphalt Supply, Salt Lake City, 1970-83; office adminstr. Kidder, Peabody Inc., Salt Lake City, 1983-85; exec. sec., office supr. Salt Palace and Fine Arts, Salt Lake City, 1985-90, Ogden (Utah)-Weber Conv. and Visitors Bur., 1990—. Past pres. Jaycettes, Salt Lake City, 1968-70. Mem. NAEM, Salt Lake City C. of C. (women's forum). Office: Ogden Weber Conv and Visitors Bur 2501 Wall Ave Ogden UT 84401

MARTIN, KATHLEEN ANNE, information management consultant; b. Rochester, N.Y., Aug. 19, 1942; d. Edwin Wilkins and Hilda Ellen (Hartell) Martin; BA, Marygrove Coll., Detroit, 1964; MA in Libr. Sci. (Josenhans scholar 1965), U. Mich., 1965; advanced online tng. cert. Nat. Libr. Medicine, 1979; m. Oliver Kalman Peterdy, Oct. 15, 1971 (div. 1981); children: Elizabeth, Matthew. Libr. Detroit Pub. Libr., 1964-66; bibliographer, then asst. tech. svcs. libr. Edward G. Miner Med. Libr., U. Rochester, 1969-72; libr. lab. indsl. medicine Eastman Kodak Co., Rochester, 1966-69, libr. health, safety and human factors lab., 1972-78, tech. info. analyst, 1978-84, health and environment lab., 1978-86, Info Edge, 1987—; libr. Monroe Devel. Ctr., 1987-90, Park Ridge Hosp., 1990—. Mem. AAUW (treas. Rochester br. 1979-80), Spl. Librs. Assn., Med. Libr. Assn. Home: 37 Richsquire Dr Rochester NY 14626

MARTIN, KELLIE SUE, speech pathologist; b. Osage, Iowa, Jan. 12, 1961; d. Kenneth Cyril and Janice Rae (Lammers) M. BS, Iowa State U., 1983; MA, U. No. Iowa, 1984. Lic. speech pathologist, Iowa. Speech language pathologist Miss. Bend Area Edn. Agy., Bettendorf, Iowa, 1985—; speech language pathologist Mercy Hosp., Davenport, Iowa, summers 1986-89. Judge Iowa High Sch. Speech Assn. Mem. Am. Speech and Hearing Assn. (cert.), Iowa Speech and Hearing Assn., Quad City Speech and Hearing Assn. Roman Catholic. Home: 1835 Winding Hill Rd Apt 1418 Davenport IA 52807 Office: Miss Bend Area Edn Agency Bettendorf IA 52722

MARTIN, KENDRA LEIGH, data automation executive; b. Ft. Benning, Ga., Aug. 26, 1961; d. Norman Maynard and Violet (Pope) Smith; m. Fred Martin III, Mar. 18, 1989. BA, U. N.C., Greensboro, 1983. Graphics specialist Bruce W. Eberle & Assocs., Vienna, Va., 1983-85; dir. publs. Nat. Indsl. Transp. League, Washington, 1985-87, dir. computer and systems devel., 1987-90; mgr. airline industry data automation Air Transport Assn., Washington (D.C.), 1990—. Mem. Am. Nat. Standards Inst. (accredited standards com. X12), UN Electronic Data Interchange for Adminstrn., Commerce and Transport (N. Am. rapporteur adv. and support team), Washington Women in Pub. Rels. Home: 5335 Duke St Apt 603 Alexandria VA 22304 Office: Air Transport Assn 1709 New York Ave NW Washington DC 20006

MARTIN, LAURA BELLE, real estate and farm land manager, retired teacher; b. Jackson County, Minn., Nov. 3, 1915; d. Eugene Wellington and Mary Christina (Hanson) M. BS, Mankato State U., 1968. Tchr. rural schs., Renville County, Minn., 1937-41, 45-50, Wabasso (Minn.) Pub. Sch., 1963-81; pres. Renville Farms and Feed Lots, 1982—. Pres. Wabasso (Minn.) Edn. Assn., 1974-75, publicity chmn., 1968-74; sec. Hist. Renville Preservation Com., 1978—; publicity chmn. Town and Country Boosters, Renville, 1982-83. Mem. Genealogy Soc. Renville County, Am. Legion Aux. Democrat. Lutheran. Home and Office: Box 567 Renville MN 56284

MARTIN, LESLIE KAY, insurance management professional; b. Lafayette, La., Apr. 26, 1958; d. C. David and Alice Joyce (Chandler) M. BA, Stanford U., 1980; MBA, Duke U., 1984. CLU, Chartered Fin. Cons. Nongroup acct., sales rep. Blue Cross of Oreg., Portland, 1980-82; human resources intern Harris Corp., Melbourne, Fla., 1983; assoc. in human resources Eli Lilly Co., Indpls., 1984-86; asst. v.p. Intyon Corp., Winston-Salem, N.C., 1986—. Bd. dirs. Eastside Credit Union, Indpls., 1985, 86; host family N.C. Sch. of Arts, Winston-Salem, 1987, 88; cons. Jr. Achievement, Winston-Salem, 1989, 90; bd. dirs. Untitled Assocs., Reynolds House Mus. Am. Art, Winston-Salem, 1989—. Office: Integon Corp 500 W 5th St Box 3199 Winston-Salem NC 27104

MARTIN, LISA ANN, controller; b. Bridgeport, Conn., May 29, 1961; d. Aurele Joseph and Carmella (Cialdella) M. BA, U. South Fla., 1984; MPA, U. Hartford, 1990. Acct. City of Pinellas Park, Fla., 1984-87; controller Town of Glastonbury, Conn., 1987—. Mem. Govt. Fin. Officer Assn., Am. Soc. Pub. Adminstrs., Sons of Italy. Office: Town of Glastonbury 2155 Main St Glastonbury CT 06033

MARTIN, LORRAINE B., humanities educator; b. Utica, N.Y., Aug. 18, 1940; d. Walter G. and Laura (Bochenek) Bolanowski; m. Charles A. Martin; children: Denise, Tracy. Student, SUNY, Albany, 1958-60; BA in English and Edn. magna cum laude, Utica Coll. of Syracuse U., 1977; MS in Edn. and Reading, SUNY, Cortland, 1979, cert. of advanced studies, 1984. Cert. elem. tchr., secondary tchr., sch. adminstr. and supr., sch. dist. adminstr., reading specialist, N.Y. Tchr. Poland (N.Y.) Cen. Sch., 1972-80, reading specialist, 1980-84; instr. reading Utica Coll. of Syracuse U., summer 1982-84; adminstr. spl. edn. and chpt. 1 remedial program Little Falls (N.Y.) City Sch. Dist., 1984-85; adminstr. adult and continuing edn. Madison-Oneida Bd. Coop. Ednl. Svcs., Verona, N.Y., 1985-86; dir. gen. programs Herkimer (N.Y.) Bd. Coop. Ednl. Svcs., 1986-88; inst. humanities Herkimer County Community Coll., Herkimer, 1988—; trainer tchr. performance evaluation program N.Y. State Edn. Dept., Herkimer, 1984, facilitator effective schs. program, 1986-88, cons. Coll. Devel. Ctr., trainer writing process for tchrs., 1985—; cons. N.Y. State Edn. Dept. Two-Yr. Coll. Devel. Ctr. Author: A Pilot Project - The Bridge Program - Easing the Transition from High School to College, Teaching Writing to Adults, Tips for Teachers: An Idea Swap; conbr. to Teaching Writing. Active Myasthenia Gravis Found., 1984—, Muscular Dystrophy Assn., 1989—, Thyroid Found. of Am., 1988—. Recipient Leader Silver award for volunteerism 4-H Coop. Extension, Utica, 1980. Mem. Internat. Reading Assn., N.Y. State Reading Assn., Assn. Supervision and Curriculum Devel., Nat. Coun. Tchrs. of English, N.Y. State Coll. Learning Skills Assn., The Network for Effective Schs., Phi Kappa Phi, Alpha Lambda Sigma. Democrat. Home: RR2 Box 415B Crooked Brook Rd Utica NY 13502 Office: Herkimer County Comm Coll Reservoir Rd Herkimer NY 13350

MARTIN, LUCY Z., public relations executive; b. Alton, Ill., July 8, 1941; d. Fred M. and Lucille J. Kirk. BA, Northwestern U., 1963. Adminstrv. asst., copywriter Batz-Hodgson-Neuwoehner, Inc., St. Louis, 1963-64; news reporter, Midwest fashion editor Fairchild Publs., St. Louis, 1964-66; account exec. Milici Advt. Agy., Honolulu, 1967; publs. dir. Barnes Med. Ctr., St. Louis, 1968-69; communications cons. Fleishman-Hillard, St. Louis, 1970-74; communications cons. Lucy Z. Martin & Assocs., Portland, Oreg., 1974—, chief exec. officer, pres., 1987—. Feature in Entrepreneurial Woman mag.; contbr. articles to profl. jours. Chmn. women's adv. com. Reed Coll., Portland, 1977-79; mem. Oreg. Commn. for Women, 1984-87; bd. dirs. Ronald McDonald House Oreg., 1986, Oreg. Sch. Arts & Crafts, 1988-92; chmn. Good Samaritan Med. Ctr. Assocs. Recipient MacEachern Citation Acad. Hosp. Pub. Relations, 1978, Rosey awards Portland Advt. Fedn., 1979, Achievement award Soc. Tech. Communications, 1982, Disting. Tech. Communication award, 1982, Exceptional Achievement award Council for Advancement and Support Edn., 1983, Monsoon award Internat. Graphics, Inc., 1984; named Woman of Achievement Daily Jour. Commerce, 1980. Mem. Pub. Relations Soc. Am. (pres. Columbia River chpt. 1984, chmn. bd. 1980-84, Oreg. del. 1984-86, judicial panel N. Pacific dist 1985-86, exec. bd. health care sect. 1986-87, mem. Counselors Acad., Spotlight awards 1985, 86, 87, 88, nosimal exec. com. 1987-91), Portland Pub. Relations Roundtable (chmn. 1985, bd. dirs. 1983-85), Assn. Western Hosps. (editorial adv. bd. 1984-85), Best of West awards 1978, 80, 83, 87), Oreg. Hosp. Pub. Relations Orgn. (pres. 1981, chmn. bd. 1982), Acad. Health Service Mktg., Am. Hosp. Assn., Am. Mktg. Assn., Am. Soc. Hosp. Mktg. & Pub. Relations, Healthcare Communicators Oreg., Internat. Assn. Bus. Communicators (18 awards 1981-87), Oreg. Assn. Hosps. Oreg. Press Women, Nat. and Oreg. Soc. Healthcare Planning & Mktg., Women in Communications (Matrix award 1977). Office: 1881 SW Edgewood Rd Portland OR 97201-2235

MARTIN, LYNN MORLEY, congresswoman; b. Evanston, Ill., Dec. 26, 1939; d. Lawrence William and Helen Catherine (Hall) Morley; children from a previous marriage: Julia Catherine, Caroline; m. Harry D. Leinenweber, Jan. 1987. B.A., U. Ill., 1960. Former tchr. pub. schs.; mem. Ill. Ho. of Reps., 1977-79, Ill. Senate, 1979-81; mem. 97th-101st Congresses from 16th Ill. Dist., 1981-91. Nat. co-chmn. Bush-Quayle Presdl. campaign, 1988. Named one of Outstanding Young Women in Am., U.S. Jaycees; named Rep. Woman of the Yr., 1989. Mem. AAUW, C. of C. of Rockford, Jr. League. Republican. Office: US Ho of Reps 1214 Longworth Office Bldg Washington DC 20515

MARTIN, MARSHA ANN, social work educator; b. Iowa City, May 22, 1952; d. Fred Jr. and Helen (Paige) M. BA in Psychology, U. Iowa, 1974, MSW, 1975; DSW, Columbia U., 1982. Program specialist Willkie House Inc., Des Moines, 1976-77; cons. research Clark, Phipps, Clark and Harris Inc., N.Y.C., 1979-81; dir. Midtown Outreach Program, N.Y.C., 1981-86; assoc. prof. Sch. Social Work Hunter Coll., N.Y.C., 1986—; cons. Port Authority N.Y. and N.J., 1982—, NIMH, 1985—. Contbr. articles to profl. jours. Cons. U.S. Conf. Mayors, Five City Project 1986; co-chair, bd. dirs. Women Need Inc., 1984—, vice-chair, bd. dirs. N.Y. Coalition Homeless, 1982—; advisor Office Mayor Homeless Services, N.Y.C. 1987—; com. mem. N.Y. State Hands Across Am. 1987—; com. chair, bd. dir. N.Y.C. Coalition Mental Health, 1986—. Nat. Assn. Social Workers, Internat. Conf. Social Welfare, Council Social Work Edn. Democrat. Mem. United Ch. Christ. Office: Hunter Coll Sch Social Work 129 E 79th St New York NY 10021

MARTIN, MARY EVELYN, advertising executive; b. Lexington, Ky., Dec. 23, 1958; d. George Clarke and Georgann Elizabeth (Bovis) M. BA magna cum laude, Lindenwood Coll., 1980; postgrad, U. Ky., 1987—. Asst. to pres. The Hamlets, Ltd/Park Place Country Homes, Louisville, 1984-85; advt. designer, copywriter Park Place Country Homes, Anchorage, Ky., 1985-86; creative dir. of advt., mktg., v.p., treas. Park Place Country Homes/Park Place Properties, Anchorage, Ky., 1986—; founder, pres. Good Help Cons. Svc., Louisville, Lexington, Maison Marche Advt. & Promotions, Louisville, 1989—; instr. dept. English, U. Ky., 1989—. Editor: (poetry mag.) The Griffin, 1979-80. Mem. People for the Am. Way, Greenpeace. Recipient Haggin fellow, U. Ky., 1987, Spahmer Creative Writing award, 1979. Mem. Am. Film Inst., NAFE, Nat. Assn. Home Builders (affiliate), Internat. Platform Assn., Ky. Film Artists Coalition. Democrat. Home: PO Box 23282 Anchorage KY 40223 Office: Park Place Country Homes PO Box 23226 Anchorage KY 40223

MARTIN, MARY LEE, volunteer; b. Ft. Collins, Colo., Mar. 7, 1938; d. C.K. and Merle (Harrison) Collins; m. George G. Martin, June 4, 1960; children: Linda Gail, Thomas Brian. Student, Colo. State U., 1956-59. Instr. Albuquerque Gymnastic Sch., 1980-90. Sec., Albuquerque Bd. Edn., 1987-88, pres., 1988-89, budget and fin. clk., 1989-90; mem. steering comm., Urban Dist. Leadership Consortium, 1989-91. Mem. Nat. Assn. Women's Gymnastic Judges, N.Mex. Fedn. Women's Clubs (pres. 1986-88), Gen. Fedn. Women's Clubs (legis. chmn. 1988-90, resolutions com. 1990-92), N.Mex. Crime Prevention (treas. 1979—). Home: 10305 Chapala Pl NE Albuquerque NM 87111

MARTIN, MARY LOU, manufacturing company specialist; b. New Hampton, Iowa, June 4, 1953; d. Henry Herman and Elsie Alice (Thieman) Harnisch; m. Merl James Martin, May 10, 1980. Student, Gates Bus. Sch., 1973, U. No. Iowa, 1974-85; BS in Mgmt., Mktg., Upper Iowa U., 1987; MBA, U. Iowa, 1989. Sec. Law Offices John M. Warren, Waterloo, Iowa, 1973; sec. registrar's office, asst. recorder Upper Iowa U., Fayette, Iowa, 1973-74; mfg. systems planning specialist John Deere Tractor Works, Waterloo, 1974-80, mem MRP task force, 1980-81, supr. prodn. control, 1981-84, forecast analyst, master scheduler, 1984-89, gen. supr. tractor assembly prodn. control, 1989—. Mem. appropriations com. United Way, Waterloo, 1986; endowment com. and bd. mem. area VII Multiple Sclerosis. Mem. Am. Prodn. and Inventory Control Soc. (bd. dirs.), NAFE. Lutheran. Home: 4104 Ansborough Waterloo IA 50701

MARTIN, MONA HELEN, academic program director; b. Corning, N.Y., June 24, 1951; d. Clayton Arlinton II and Ramona Louise (Herbert) Teator; student Alfred U., 1981—; m. Thomas J. Martin, Dec. 21, 1968 (div. Mar. 1989); children: James H., Tina M. Univ. rels. records clk. Alfred U., 1974-75, supr. records, 1975-76, records clk., 1976-78, assoc. for devel. rsch., 1978, supr. rsch. and records, 1979-84, dir. devel. svcs., 1984—. Vol., CD Disaster Preparedness, Steuben County, United Way, Am. Heart Fund; instr. religious edn. program St. Ignatius Loyola Ch.; bd. dirs. Alfred/Allegany Ednl. Fed. Credit Union. Mem. Alpha Kappa Omicron. Republican. Roman Catholic. Home: 263 Grand St Hornell NY 14843 Office: PO Box 1165 Alfred NY 14802

MARTIN, NANCY LEE, research analyst; b. DuQuoin, Ill., Apr. 3, 1962; d. Charles Howard and Norma Lee (Pavletich) M. BS in Computational Maths, Eastern Ill. U., 1984. Research analyst SW Research Inst., San Antonio, Tex., 1984--. Mem. Assn. Computing Machinery, Spl. Interest Group Computer Human Interaction, Rsch. Recreation Assn. (chmn.). Roman Catholic. Home: 4400 Horizon Hill #4509 San Antonio TX 78229 Office: SW Research Inst 6220 Culebra San Antonio TX 78284

MARTIN, PAULA JEAN, educational administrator; b. N.Y.C, June 24, 1947; d. Frances C. Martin. BA, Syracuse U., 1968; MA, Columbia U., N.Y.C., 1969. Rsch. asst. Tchr. Coll., Columbia U., N.Y.C., 1970-71; academic counselor Columbia U., Project Double Discov, N.Y.C., 1973-74; asst. dir. Columbia U. Proj. Double Discov., N.Y.C., 1974-81; project dir. Columbia U., Double Discov. Ctr., N.Y.C., 1981-85; exec. dir. The East Harlem Coll. and Career Counseling Program, N.Y.C., 1985—; lectr., Malcolm King: Harlem Coll. Extension, N.Y.C., 1971-73; guest lectr., Champ Morningside Children's Ctr., N.Y.C., 1973-74; cons., The East Harlem Tutorial Program, N.Y.C., 1988--. Co-author: Relative Effectiveness of Various Letter Discrimination Procedures, 1974; Politics, Be All or End All, 1972. Workshop presenter: Overcoming the Traditional Female Role, 1985, 86, 88. Sec., Community Planning Bd. 9, Manhattan, 1975-77; Mem., West Harlem Inwood Community Neighborhood Family Care Ctr., N.Y.C., 1972--; Treas, West 148th St. Block Assn., Manhattan, 1973-77; Mem., Friends of Malcolm-King Coll: Harlem Extension, N.Y.C., 1972-76. Mem. Assn. for Equality and Excellence in Edn. (bd. dirs. 1978-82, 1983--; pres. 1983-84), Nat. Coun. Ednl. Opportunity Assns. (bd. dirs. 1983-85, 1988-89). Dem. Episcopalian.

MARTIN, REGINA MARIA ANITA, computer programmer/analyst; b. Rutland, Vt., Jan. 18, 1950; d. Eli L. and Blanche A. (Preseau) Quesnel; m. Raymond J. Martin, June 22, 1968; children: Scott Joseph, Jennifer Anne, Denise Marie. A in Computer Sci., Springfield (Mass.) Tech. Community Coll., 1986; student, Westfield Community Coll. Sr. programmer/analyst City of Springfield; instr. Springfield Tech. Community Coll.; prin. clk./typist City of Springfield Tchr. Payroll; asst. supr. transit Bank of Boston, Springfield.

MARTIN, ROSE KOCSIS, law librarian; b. Kiralyrev, Hungary, Aug. 25, 1928; came to U.S., 1949, naturalized, 1954; d. Ferenc and Zsuzsanna (Nehai Szabo) Kocsis; m. Donald L. Martin, Aug. 23, 1961; 1 child, Virginia Kim. Student Seton Hall U., 1960-61; BBA, Kensington U., Glendale, Calif., 1968-69; cert. Cath. U. Am. 1981, George Washington U., 1982. Documents librarian Seton Hall U., South Orange, N.J., 1958-61; mem. office staff Dept. Def., Washington, 1962-63, Dept. Agr., Washington, 1963-67; info. specialist law Office Adminstrv. Law Judges, Dept. Labor, Washington, 1976—. Active Rep. Club, Great Falls, Va., 1986—. Recipient Meritorious award Dept. Agr., 1966, Outstanding award Dept. Labor, 1977, Honorable Svc. to the Nation award Dept. Labor, 1988. Mem. Am. Assn. Law Libraries, NAFE, Nat. Mus. Women in Arts, Internat. Platform Assn., Great Falls Woman's Club, River Bend Golf and Country Club. Roman Catholic. Avocations: travel, tennis, reading, swimming, cooking. Home: PO Box 651 Middleburg VA 22117

MARTIN, SALLY NAN, nursing administrator; b. Potsdam, N.Y., Dec. 8, 1947; d. Arthur Ellsworth and Blanche Maryland (Henderson) M. Diploma in nursing, St. Luke's Hosp., N.Y.C., 1968; BS in Sociology, Marymount Manhattan Coll., 1973; EdM in Adult Edn., Columbia U., N.Y.C., 1976; M in Pub. Adminstrn., NYU, 1988. Asst. dir. critical care St. Luke's Roosevelt Hosp. Ctr., N.Y.C., 1980-85; asst. dir. operating room Maimonides Med. Ctr., Bklyn., 1985-86; assoc. dir. nursing The Meth. Hosp., Bklyn., 1986—; chmn. critical care policy and procedure com. nursing dept. St. Luke's/Roosevelt Hosp.; co-chmn. critical care administrv. com. nursing and med. dept.; chmn. ambience com.,also lectr., first line mgr., chmn. evaluation revision com., nursing care plan com.; preceptor for grad. students in nursing adminstrn., NYU; chmn. research on utilization of nursing knowledge workshop Woman's Hosp., N.Y.C. Home: 191 73rd St Apt 212 Brooklyn NY 11209 Office: The Meth Hosp 506 6th St Brooklyn NY 11215

MARTIN, SALLY SYKES, systems analyst, editor, audio-visual producer; b. St. Louis, Feb. 4, 1953; d. William Graham III and Winifred Estelle (Hamilton) M.; m. David Carlton Williams, May 15, 1977. B.A. in English Lit., Washington U., St. Louis, 1975; postgrad. U. Mo.-St. Louis, 1982-85, Washington U., St. Louis, 1987—. Data processing editor Emerson Electric Co., St. Louis, 1976-77; asst. editor Facts and Comparisons, St. Louis, 1977-78; procedures writer/analyst McDonnell Douglas, St. Louis, 1978-82; tech. writer Ralston Purina, St. Louis, 1982-84; supr. communications-product assurance McDonnell Douglas Astronautics Co., St. Louis, 1984-86, long range planning systems and procedures, 1987-88, adminstr. co. gain sharing plan, 1988-89; mgr. admstrn., policies, procedures McDonnell Douglas Missile Systems Co., St. Louis, 1989—; editor Catalyst newsletter Women in Bus., St. Louis, 1983. Mem. Lafayette Sq. Restoration Com., St. Louis, 1983—, editor Marquis newsletter, 1983-84; treas., mem. vestry, mem. worship com. St. Stephen's Episcopal Ch., St. Louis, 1984-86. Recipient 2d Place award Assn. for Multi-Image Festival, 1983, Elizabeth Cook award Lafayette Sq. Restoration Com., 1984. Mem. IEEE (assoc.), Soc. Tech. Communications (Achievement award for brochure 1984, achievement award for newsletter 1986), KETC, Zoo Friends. Avocation: piano (classical music). Home: #9 Girard Dr Webster Groves MO 63119 Office: McDonnell Douglas Missile Systems Co PO Box 516 Saint Louis MO 63166

MARTIN, SANDRA ARCHER, school psychologist; b. Memphis, Nov. 3, 1945; d. Robert Edward and Gloria Ellen (Lawhorn) Archer; m. George Denley Martin, June 24, 1967; children: Ellen Ashley, Andrew Denley. BA, Memphis State U., 1981, MA, 1988, EdS, 1990; BS in Nursing, U. Tenn., Memphis, 1985. Psychiat. nurse Meth. Hosp.-Cen., Memphis, 1985-87; grad. rsch. asst. Memphis State U., 1987-89; sch. psychologist Memphis City Schs., 1990—. Teaching leader Bible Study Fellowship, Memphis, 1983-85. Mem. Am. Psychol. Assn. (assoc.), Nat. Assn. Sch. Psychologists, Memphis Area Psychol. Assn., Tenn. Assn. Sch. Psychologists. Methodist. Office: Memphis City Schs MH Ctr 2597 Avery Ave Memphis TN 38112

MARTIN, SANDRA LOUISE, management executive; b. Elizabeth, N.J., July 13, 1956; d. Franklin Stewart and Alice Emily (Paulsen) M. BA in Hist., U. Ga., 1978; MS in Computer Sci., Memphis State U., 1983. News/sportswriter The Times, Gainesville, Ga., 1978-80; sportswriter The Memphis Press-Scimitar, Memphis, Tenn., 1980-82; teaching asst. Memphis State U., 1982-83; systems assoc. HBO and Co., Atlanta, 1983-84; tech. writing mgr. MBA Technology Devel. Corp., Vancouver, B.C., Can., 1984; tech. writer Apollo Computer, Inc. (now a div. Hewlett-Packard), Chelmsford, Mass., 1985-87, project mgr., nat. language support, 1987-89, sect. mgr. commands and internationalization, 1989; program mgr. Open Software Found., Cambridge, Mass., 1990—. Press intern U.S. Sen. Sam Nunn's office, Washington, 1978. Recipient lst place award for spot newswriting UPI, 1979. Mem. Internat. Spl. Interest Group (co-chmn.), Open Software Found., USR Group (tech. subcom. on internationalization), Groton Theater Group, Phi Beta Kappa, Phi Kappa Phi. Presbyterian. Office: Open Software Found 11 Cambridge Ctr Cambridge MA 02142

MARTIN, SHARON JAFFE, waterproofing company executive; b. Elyria, Ohio, June 20, 1944; d. Edward Gilbert and Sylvia Sophia (Werner) Jaffe; m. David Richard Martin, May 8, 1965; 1 child, Jeffrey Ross. Student Miami U., Oxford, Ohio, 1962-64, Lorain Community Coll., 1966, 73-74. Cashier Elyria Meml. Hosp., 1964-67; asst. tchr. Westshore Montessori Sch., North Ridgeville, Ohio, 1973-75, Montessori Cooperative of Vienna, Va., 1975-76; v.p., sec., treas. Reston Pressure Seal, Inc., Va., 1977—; pres. Dave Martin & Son, Inc., 1987-88; vol. fin. advisor Fairfax County Fin. Edu. Ctr., 1986—. Mem. Reston Community Players, Inc., treas., 1981-84. Nominated Reston Woman of Yr., 1983. Mem. No. Va. Builders Assn. (membership com. 1988—, outreach com. 1989—). Jewish. Avocations: dancing, acting, antiques, reading. Home: 11281 Spyglass Cove Ln Reston VA 22091 Office: Reston Pressure Seal Inc PO Box 2292 Reston VA 22090

MARTIN, SHELLY JO, small business owner; b. Abilene, Tex., Feb. 25, 1957; d. Kenneth Eugene and Mary Ellen (Smith) Roberts; m. Carl T. Martin, Oct. 11, 1975; 1 child, Carl Matthew. Student, Cabrillo Sch. Nursing, San Diego, 1977, Cisco Jr. Coll., Abilene, 1990—. Office mgr. Design Communications, Abilene, 1981-84; merchandiser McCatty-Curtis, Lubbock, Tex., 1984-86, GSC Distbg., Abilene, 1986-88; owner Shelly's Snack Bar, Abilene, Tex., 1988—. Home: 209 S Danville Bldg B #124 Abilene TX 79605

MARTIN, SHIRLEY, Canadian legislator; b. Nov. 20, 1932; m. Jack Martin; children: John, Christopher. Previously bus. service mgr. for Bell Can., mem. Can. House of Commons, 1984—, prin. del. U.N. 40th Gen. Assembly, vice chair Progressive Conservative Nat. Caucus, minister of state for transport, 1988-90, minister of state for Indian Affairs and No. Devel., 1990—, mem. Privy Coun., 1988—. Mem. United Ch. Canada. Office: Ho of Commons, Parliament Bldgs, Ottawa, ON Canada K1A 0A6*

MARTIN, SHIRLEY MARIE, insurance company executive; b. Tekamah, Nebr., Apr. 15, 1944; d. J. Clinton Martin and N. Marie (McKain) Grant; m. Michael P. Burnett, Apr. 19, 1963 (div. Oct. 1980); children: Todd Burnett, Tara Burnett. Student, Everett (Wash.) Jr. Coll., 1962-64; grad., Bell and Howell Sch. Acctg., Chgo., 1974. Fin. coordinator, collection mgr. The Continental Ins. Co., Seattle, 1963-70; audit reviewer The Home Ins. Co., Seattle, 1970-75, premium field auditor, 1975-80; owner Martin & Assocs., Bellingham, Wash., 1980—; author, pub. S.M. Martin Co., Bellingham, 1986—. Mem. Nat. Assn. Premium Auditors, Nat. Assn. Life Underwriters, Nat. Assn. Female Execs., Whatcom C. of C. Democrat. Roman Catholic. Home and Office: PO Box 5523 Bellingham WA 98227

MARTIN, STACEY LYNN, tax specialist; b. Dallas, Dec. 5, 1951; d. Orval Calvin and Della (Morgan) M.; m. Bryan Keith Ellis, Jan. 31, 1987. BA, Austin Coll., 1973; MBA, So. Meth. U., 1974. CPA, Tex. Jr. acct. MacIver & Bell, CPAs, Dallas, 1974-76; staff acct. Steak and Ale Restaurants, Dallas, 1976; internal auditor Columbia Gen. Corp., Dallas, 1976-80; asst. contr. M/A/R/C Inc., Dallas, 1981-86, tax specialist, 1986—; owner Sallie's Baby Infant & Toddler Knitwear, 1988—. Mem. Greenland Hills Neighborhood Assn., Dallas, 1983—. Mem. Am. Inst. CPA's, Tex. Soc. CPA's, Dallas Heritage Soc., Dallas Arboretum Soc., DAR. Presbyterian. Office: M/A/R/C Inc 7850 N Beltline Rd Irving TX 75063

MARTIN, SUSAN KATHERINE, librarian; b. Cambridge, Eng., Nov. 14, 1942; came to U.S., 1950, naturalized, 1961; d. Egon and Jolan (Schonfeld) Orowan; m. David S. Martin, June 30, 1962. BA with honors, Tufts U., 1963; MS, Simmons Coll., 1965; PhD, U. Calif., Berkeley, 1983. Intern libr. Harvard U., Cambridge, Mass., 1963-65, systems libr., 1965-73; head systems office gen. libr. U. Calif., Berkeley, 1973-79; dir. Milton S. Eisenhower Libr. Johns Hopkins U., Balt., 1979-88, exec. dir. Nat. Commn. on Libraries and Info. Sci., 1988-90; univ. libr. Georgetown U., Washington, 1990—; instr. U. Md., College Park, 1981; mem. library adv. com. Princeton (N.J.) U., 1987—; mem. vis. com. Harvard U. Libr., 1987—; mem. bd. overseers for univ. libr. Tufts U., 1988-90; univ. libr. Georgetown U., 1990—; cons. to various librs. and info. cos., 1975—; mem. adv. bd. ERIC, 1990—, History Assocs., Inc., 1990—. Author: Library Networks: Libraries in Partnership, 1986-87; editor: Jour. Libr. Automation, 1973-77; mem. editorial bd. Jour. Libr. Adminstrn., 1986—, Libr. Hi-Tech, 1989—; contbr. articles to profl. jours. Trustee Phila. Area Library Network, 1980-81; bd. dirs. Universal Serials and Book Exchange, 1981-82, v.p., 1983, pres., 1984. Recipient Simmons Coll. Disting. Alumni award, 1977; Council on Library Resources fellow, 1973. Mem. ALA (coun. 1988—), Research Libraries Group (gov., exec. com. 1985-87), Library and Info. Tech. Assn. (pres. 1978-79), Assn. Research Librs., Libr. of Congress (optical disk pilot project adv. com. 1985-89), Cosmos Club, Phi Beta Kappa. Home: 4709 Blagden Terr Washington DC 20011 Office: Georgetown Univ Lauinger Libr Washington DC 20057

MARTIN, SUSAN LORDE, law educator; b. N.Y.C., Feb. 19, 1943. AB, Barnard Coll., 1963; JD, Hofstra U., 1987. Bar: N.Y. 1988, U.S. Dist. Ct. (ea. dist.) N.Y. 1988, D.C. 1989. Assoc. Martin, Fallon & Mullé, Huntington, N.Y., 1987-88; asst. prof. bus. law Hofstra U., Hempstead, N.Y., 1988—. Contbr. articles to profl. jours. Bd. dirs. Massapequa (N.Y.) Philharm. Orch., 1987—. Rsch. grantee Hofstra U., 1990. Mem. ABA, N.Y. State Bar Assn., D.C. Bar Assn., Nassau County Bar Assn. Office: Hofstra U Sch Bus Dept Acctg and Bus Law Hempstead NY 11550

MARTIN, SYLVIA COOKE, human resources professional; b. Balt., May 2, 1938; d. Emanuel Levi and Clara Marie (Evans) Cook; m. Donald W.K. Martin, Sept. 8, 1957; div., Nov. 1970; children: Donald Eugene Kemp Martin, Marcia Lauren Martin. BA, U. Md., 1972; Cert. Execs. at Mid Career, U. Va., 1975; M of Policy Sci., U. Md., Baltimore County, 1978; postgrad., U. Md.; Cert. Human Resource Devel., Bowie (Md.) State U., 1987. File clk. Social Security Adminstrn., Balt., 1963-66, intern health ins., 1966-68, mgmt. intern, 1968-70; sr. career devel. specialist Social Security Adminstrn., Health Care Financing Adminstrn., Balt., 1970-78; faculty mem. Antioch Coll., Columbia, Md., 1975-79, cons., 1969—; chief staff tng. and devel. Library of Congress, Washington, 1978—; instr. human resources devel. Bowie State Coll., 1985—. Active United Negro Coll. Fund Job Fair, Washington, 1987, Md. Hist. Soc. Mem. NAACP, Oral History in Mid-Atlantic Region, Md. Geneal. Soc., Md. Hist. Soc., Nat. Assn. Negro Bus. and Profl. Women's Clubs, Afro-Am. Hist. and Geneal. Soc. (historian 1984-86, parliamentarian 1986-88, pres. 1988-90), Nat. Coun. Negro Womena, The Pierians (parliamentarian 1985-87, rec. sec. 1989-91), Daniel Murray Afro-Am. Culture Assn. (pres. 1988), Delta Sigma Theta. Democrat. Office: Library of Congress 100 Independence Ave Washington DC 20540

MARTIN, TAMELA SHEREE, lawyer; b. Russellville, Ala., Nov. 28, 1962; d. Jimmy Colin and Peggy Sue (Aycock) M. BA, U. Ala., 1984, JD, 1987; LLM in Taxation, U. Fla., 1989. Bar: Fla. 1987, Ala. 1988, U.S. Ct. Appeals (11th cir) 1988. Assoc. Blackwell, Walker, Fascell & Hoehl, Miami, 1987, Potts & Young, Florence, Ala., 1987-88, Tanner, Guin, Ely, Lary & Neiswender, P.C., Tuscaloosa, Ala., 1989; pvt. practice Florence, Ala., 1990—. Chmn. Young Reps., Muscle Shoals, Ala., 1988; mem. Colbert County Rep. Exec. Com., Tuscumbia, Ala., 1988; bd. dirs. Boys and Girls Clubs N.W. Ala., Inc., Univ. Ala. Alumni Assn., Lauderdale County chpt. Recipient Am. Jurist Book award Lawyer's Cooperative Publ. Co., 1986. Mem. ABA (exec. com. young lawyers div., vice chmn. lawyers and the arts com. 1989), Fla. Bar Assn., Ala. Bar Assn. Fla. Bar Assn. (sect. on entertainment and sports law, com. on music and recording), Farrah Law Soc., Fla. Track Club, Phi Delta Phi, Delta Zeta (U. Ala. social chmn. 1983). Baptist. Home: Rte 2 Box 381 Leighton AL 35646 Office: 409 N Court St Ste 120 Florence AL 35630

MARTIN, VICKI JEAN, educational administrator, educator; b. Milw., Mar. 26, 1954; m. Larry J. Martin; 1 child, Kendall. BA, U. Wis., Milw., 1977; MA, U. N.D., 1979; MS, Cardinal Stritch Coll., 1984. Counselor, advisor U. Wis., Milw., 1979-80; counselor Columbia Coll. of Nursing, Milw., 1980-84, asst. dean of students, 1984-86, dean of students, 1984-88; regional student svcs. adminstr. Milw. Area Tech. Coll., 1988—. Bd. dirs. Sojourner Truth House. Mem. Am. Assn. Counseling and Devel., Milw. Coun. Adult Learning (sec. 1986-87, bd. dirs. 1986—), Phi Lambda Theta. Office: Milw Area Tech Coll 6665 S Howell Ave Oak Creek WI 53154

MARTIN, VIRVE PAUL, counselor; b. Tallinn, Estonia, Nov. 19, 1928; came to U.S., 1949; d. Walter Gerhard and Alice (Haas) Paul; m. Albert Lynn Martin Jr., May 31, 1952; children: Lynda Lee, Elaine Lynne, Monique Louise. Student, U. Heidelberg, Germany, 1948-49; BA, Wesleyan Coll., Macon, Ga., 1952; MA, U. Minn., 1970. Cert. profl. counselor, Ga. Interpreter Internat. Refugee Orgn., Nuremberg, Frankfurt, Heidelberg, Fed. Republic of Germany, 1947-49; bookkeeper, receptionist DeKalb Nat. Bank, Atlanta, 1955-56; rsch. asst. Kenny Inst., Mpls., 1966-67; vocat. evaluator Dept. Human Resources, Atlanta, 1970-73, rehab. counselor, 1973—; interpreter Mpls. C. of C., 1963-65, Dem. Nat. Conv., Atlanta, 1988. Writer, editor World Pen Pals, 1964-66. V.p., bd. dirs. Ms. JCs, Minn., 1959-62; pres. Valley View Mothers' Club, Bloomington, Minn., 1961-62. Mem. Nat. Rehab. Assn., Ga. Rehab. Assn. (membership chair 1988). Home: 1106 Norwich Circle NE Atlanta GA 30324 Office: Dept Rehab Svc 1800 Peachtree St NW #444 Atlanta GA 30309

MARTIN, YVONNE CONNOLLY, pharmaceutical company executive; b. St. Paul, Minn., Sept. 13, 1936; d. Elvert Farrell and Irene Mildred (Aitken) C.; m. William Brady Martin, Dec. 14, 1964; children: Margaret Anne, Catherine Irene. BA, Carleton Coll., 1958; PhD, Northwestern U., Evanston, Ill., 1964. Pharmacology asst. Abbott Labs, North Chgo., Ill., 1958-60, sr. pharmacologist, 1964-67; sr. pharmacologist Abbott Labs, Abbott Park, Ill., 1968-70, assoc. rsch. fellow, 1970-74, rsch. fellow, 1974-85, sr. project leader, 1983—, sr. rsch. fellow, 1985—; instr. in chemistry Northwestern U., 1963-64; vis. instr. Pomona Coll., Claremont, Calif., 1967-68. Author: Quantitative Drug Design, 1978; Editor: Paths to Better and Safer Drugs, 1989; contbr. articles to profl. jours. Recipient predoctoral fellowship NSF, Northwestern U., 1960-63. Fellow, AAAS; mem. Am. Chem. Soc., Am. Crystall. Assn., Molecular Graphics Soc., Protein Soc., Phi Beta Kappa, Sigma Xi. Office: Abbott Labs 1 Abbott Park Rd Abbott Park IL 60064

MARTINAK, ROSEMARY, airline professional; b. East Chicago, Ind., Nov. 20, 1954; d. Paul and Emma (Gross) M. BA with highest distinction, Purdue U., 1976; M., U. Colo., 1980, PhD, 1985. Tchr. Washington High Sch., East Chicago, 1976-77; testing assistant Purdue U., West Lafayette, Ind., 1976; exec. housekeeper Highlander Motel, Boulder, Colo., 1978-84; teaching asst. U. Colo., Boulder, 1983-85, rsch. asst., 1984-85; rsch. assoc. Stanford (Calif.) U., 1985-86; rsch. fellow U. Aberdeen (Scotland), 1986-87; lead instl. designer McDonnell Douglas Co., Aurora, Colo., 1988-89; staff coord. flight tng. United Airlines, Denver, 1989—. Co-author: Teaching Knowledge and Intelligent Tutoring, 1989. Mem. Human Factors Soc., Phi Beta Kappa. Office: United Airlines Flight Ctr Stapleton Internat Airport Denver CO 80201

MARTINDALE, LUCY GENE, pharmaceutical company executive; b. Vincennes, Ind., Feb. 28, 1954; d. Webster Roy and Gertrude Louise (Dellinger) McGiffen; m. Allen R. Martindale, June 5, 1976; 1 child, Meredith Lynn. BS, Ind. U., 1976; MBA, Campbell U., 1987. Staff acct. Am. Hosp. Supply, McGaw Park, Ill., 1976-77; area fin. mgr. Am. Hosp. Supply, Columbus, Ohio, 1977-78; regional ops. mgr. Am. Hosp. Supply, Louisville, 1979-80; budget cons. Bristol Myers, Evansville, Ind., 1980-82, supr. gen. acctg. dept., 1982-83; with Glaxo, Inc., Research Triangle Park, N.C., 1984—, dir. fin. svcs., 1986-87, dir. planning and fin. svcs., 1988-89, v.p. fin. planning, 1989—. Mem. Durham (N.C.) Day Care Coun., 1987—; advisor Jr. Achievement, Evansville, 1981-82; bd. dirs. A Network for Evansville Women, 1982-83, Epworth United Meth. Ch., Durham, 1988—. Mem. Nat. Assn. Accts., Ind. U. Alumni Assn., North Hills Club (Raleigh, N.C., bd. dirs. 1986-87), Phi Kappa Phi. Republican. Methodist. Office: Glaxo Inc 5 Moore Dr Research Triangle Park NC 27709

MARTINEAU, DENISE CORY, physical chemist; b. Oakland, Calif., Mar. 27, 1954; d. Carl Pierre Martineau and Lucille (Cefalu) Swanson. AS in Chemistry, DeAnza Coll., 1985; BA in Chemistry, U. Calif., Santa Cruz, 1987; MS in Chemistry, U. Ill., 1989. Free-lance tech. writer San Jose, Calif., 1978-84; tech. coordinator Energy System Planning, Palo Alto, Calif., 1976-78; tech. intern NASA, Moffett Field, Calif., 1984-85; cons. rsch. asst. Stanford (Calif.) U., 1986-87; Ill. Consortium for Ednl. Opportunity Program fellow U. Ill., Urbana, 1986—; student rep. U. Calif. Faculty Commn., Santa Cruz, 1985-86; mem. bd. dirs. Math/Sci. Network. Editor: Voices: Women in Science, 1987. Chair fundraising student leadership panel YWCA, Urbana, 1987; bd. dirs. Urbana Girl's Club. Recipient scholarship Am. Bus. Women's Assn., 1985-88, minority grad. hon. mention NSF, 1987; Ford Found. alt. Nat. Research Council, 1987-88. Mem. Soc. of Women Engrs. (Excellence award 1985, 86, 87, 88), AAAS, Grad. Women in Sci., Assn. for Women in Sci., Am. Chem. Soc., Am. Phys. Soc. Democrat. Mem. Unity Ch. Office: 444 Central Ave Alameda CA 94501

MARTINELLI, ROSEMARY, public relations executive; b. Pitts., May 13, 1957. BA summa cum laude, Duquesne U., 1979, MA summa cum laude, 1988. News dir., reporter Sta. WDUQ-FM, Pitts., 1977-78; news and pub. affairs producer Sta. KDKA-AM/WPNT-FM, Pitts., 1978-80; news assignment mgr. and consumer producer WPXI-TV, Pitts., 1980-83, creative dir., publicist, 1983-85; dir. spl. events and publicity Gimbels, Pitts., 1985-86; mgr. community rels. Columbia Gas of Pa., Pitts., 1987—. Mem. young execs. com., corp. com. Pitts. Ballet Theatre, 1988—; mem. Pitts. Conv. and Visitors Bur., 1987—, Pitts. Attraction Assn. Recipient Community Rels. award of excellence Nat. Bellringer Awards, 1990, award for commitment to safety of children Pa. Chiefs of Police, 1990. Mem. NAFE, Women in Communications (profl. advisor 1987-88, v.p. programming 1990—, Matrix award 1989), Pub. Relations Soc. of Am., Am. Women in Radio and TV, Pitts. Radio and TV Club, Pitts. C. of C. (publicity chairperson celebrating women in sports com., 1987—), Women's Press Club Pa. (exec. women's coun.), Phi Kappa Phi, Kappa Tau Alpha, Sigma Delta Chi (Golden Quill award 1984), Omicron Delta Kappa. Office: Columbia Gas of Penn 1405 McFarland Rd Pittsburgh PA 15216

MARTINEZ, ABIGAIL, psychiatric social worker; b. N.Y., Feb. 11, 1953; d. Pedro Juan and Esther (Rodriguez) M.; children: Raquel Asheley Miranda, Eric Michael Miranda. AA, N.Y.C. Community Coll., 1975; BA, City Coll. of N.Y., 1977; MSW, Hunter Coll. Sch. of S.W, N.Y., 1986. Social Worker. Mental health worker Council's Ctr. for Problems in Living, N.Y., 1977-81; social worker asst. N.Y. State Psychiatric Inst., 1981-86, psychiatric social worker, 1986--.; clin. instr. in psychiat. social work Columbia Coll. of Physicians and Surgeons, 1988—. Mem. Nat. Assn. of Social Workers, Am. Orthopsychiatric Assn., Assn. of Hispanic Mental Health Profls., N.Y. Acad. of Scis. Democrat. Episcopalian.

MARTINEZ, BETTY ELNORA, chemical company executive; b. Oklahoma City, Jan. 7, 1947; d. Jim and Jewell Frances Smith; B.S., Oklahoma City U., 1974, M.B.A., 1975; divorced. Pvt. booking agt. and bus. mgr. local rock and roll bands, Okla., Colo., 1960-67; with Kerr McGee Corp., Oklahoma City, 1965-81, acct., 1974-76, solvent sales rep., from 1975, assoc. sales rep. until 1981; petrochems. sales rep. No. Petrochem. Co., Ramsey, N.J., 1981-85; Southern area sales rep. AC Polyethylene Allied/Signal Corp., Morristown, N.J., 1985—. Del. Okla. Democratic Conv., 1972; vol. Grady Hosp., Atlanta, Ga. Rape Crisis Ctr. Mem. M.B.A. Club

Oklahoma City U. (pres. 1975), ACLU, Soc. Plastic Engrs. (bd. dirs. 1987-88), Toastmasters (adminstrv. v.p., 1988). Home and Office: PO Box 70426 Marietta GA 30007

MARTINEZ, CINDY LEE, staff nurse; b. Alliance, Ohio, July 13, 1952; d. Harold L. and Edna Jane (Stultz) Becker; 1 child, Deborah. BA, Chapman Coll., 1988, postgrad., 1988—; AS, Victor Valley Coll., 1981. RN, Calif. Labor and delivery nurse Barstow (Calif.) Community Hosp., 1983—; co-facilitator Women's Group Therapy Marine Corps Logistics Base, Barstow, Calif.; sch. nurse St. Joseph's Sch., Barstow, 1982-89. Home: 34927 Norwich Ct Barstow CA 92311

MARTINEZ, DONNA LYNN, paving company executive; b. Warsaw, Ind., June 18, 1952; d. Donald Leroy Elder and Mary Emma (Plant) Dean; m. Mike Logan Haggard, Aug. 20, 1972 (div. 1973); 1 child, Mike Leroy; m. Manuel Herrera Martinez, Jan. 3, 1986. Student, Blinn Jr. Coll., 1970-72, Southwest Tex. State U., 1973-75, San Antonio Coll., 1988—. Cashier Wickes Lumber Co., New Braunfels, Tex., 1972-73; sales rep. So. Music Co., San Antonio, 1973-74; acctg. supr. Page Gulfstream, San Antonio, 1974-79; bookkeeper N.Am. Towns of Tex., San Antonio, 1978-79; acctg. supr. Schaefer-Burdick Homes, Inc., San Antonio, 1979-80; asst. to v.p. CFC Group, Inc., San Antonio, 1980-86; pres. Orion Systems, Inc., San Antonio, 1984—; co-owner Spike I, San Antonio, 1987—; v.p. San Antonio Interlocking Paving Systems, Inc., 1985—. Com. mem., San Antonio Livestock Exposition, 1987—; trustee, Miss Rodeo Tex., 1989-90; cnadidate for bd. trustees Alamo Community Coll. Dist. Mem. Am. Arbitration Assn. (mem. panel of arbitrators), Am. Coun. Constrn. Edn., Nat. Assn. Women in Constrn. (cert. constrn. assoc., bd. dirs. San Antonio chpt. 1986-87, pres.-elect 1988-89, newsletter editor, 1988-89, pres. 1989-90), Assoc. Subcontractors San Antonio (mem. mediation com., legislation com., edn. com.), San Antonio Conservation Soc., World Affairs Coun., U.S. C. of C. Home: 13811 Kingsbury Hill San Antonio TX 78217 Office: SA Interlocking Paving Sys 13811 Kingsbury Hill San Antonio TX 78217

MARTINEZ, ELENA, health sciences educator; b. Santiago, Oriente, Cuba, Aug. 18, 1940; came to U.S., 1962; d. Felipe Martinez Arango and Margarita C. Repilado. BS, Oriente U., Santiago, Cuba, 1962. Cert. Nat. Bd. Respiratory Care. Lab. technician U. Miami (Fla.), 1965-68, lab. technologist, 1968-70, chief pulmonary tech., 1970-87, dir. pulmonary lab., 1987-88, faculty mem., 1988—; cons. Children Med. Svcs., Miami, 1972-89; pres. EMPA Profl. Assocs., Miami, 1989; instr. U. Miami Sch. Medicine, 1970-89, respiratory therapy dept. Miami-Dade Community Coll., 1972-89. Contbr. articles to profl. jours. Fundraiser Cystic Fibrosis, Miami, 1968-89. Recipient Plaque of Appreciation, Sta. WPBT Pub. TV, Miami, 1976. Mem. Nat. Bd. Respiratory Care, Nat. Soc. Cardiopulmonary Technicians, Internat. Game and Fish Assn., League of Bus. Women, Cousteau Soc., Audubon Soc., Pine Island Boating Club. Democrat. Roman Catholic. Home: 800 West Ave Ste 710 Miami Beach FL 33139 Office: U Miami Sch Medicine Med Campus Miami FL 33136

MARTINEZ, HERMINIA S., banker, economist; b. Havana, Cuba; came to U.S., 1960, naturalized, 1972; d. Carlos and Amelia (Santana) Martinez Sanchez; B.A. in Econs. cum laude, Am. U., 1965; M.S. in Fgn. Service (Univ. fellow), M.S. in Econs., Georgetown U., 1967; postgrad. Nat. U. Mex. Instr. econs. George Mason Coll., U. Va., Fairfax, 1967-68; researcher World Bank, 1967-69, indsl. economist, industrialization div., 1969-71, loan officer, Central Am., 1971-79, loan officer, economist, Mex., 1973-74, Venezuela and Ecuador, 1973-77, sr. loan officer in charge of Panama and Dominican Republic, Washington, 1977-81, sr. loan officer for Middle East and North Africa, 1981-84, sr. loan officer for Western Africa region, 1985-87, sr. economist Africa Region, 1988—. Mid-Career fellow Princeton U., 1988-89. Mem. Am. Econ. Assn., Soc. Internat. Devel., Brookings Inst. Latin Am. Study Group. Roman Catholic. Contbg. author: The Economic Growth of Colombia: Problems and Prospects, 1973. Home and Office: 5145 Yuma St NW Washington DC 20016

MARTINEZ, JO ANN, dance educator; b. Tampa, Fla., Oct. 5, 1950; d. Joseph Buglione and Lillie Mae (Faulkner) Cueto; m. Walter Stone, July 18, 1972 (div. 1979); m. Peter Martinez, Jan. 17, 1988. Bachelor's, Fla. State U., 1972; Master's, Fla. Internat. U., 1975. Cert. tchr., Fla. Tchr. dance various pvt. studios, Miami, Fla., 1972—; tchr. spl. edn. Dade County Pub. Schs., Miami, 1972—, tchr. dance, 1983—; head talent programs dept. Southwood Jr. High Sch., Miami, 1984—. Mem. Profl. Dance Tchrs. Am., Dance Masters Am., Phi Delta Kappa. Roman Catholic. Office: Southwood Jr High S Ctr Arts 16301 SW 80th Ave Miami FL 33157

MARTINEZ, MARIA LEONOR, translator, hotel executive; b. Cali, Colombia, Mar. 12, 1948; came to U.S., 1960, naturalized, 1984; d. Alfonso Martinez-Arizabaleta and Angela Esther (Rengifo) Martinez. BA, Inst. Cath. Paris, Madrid, 1976, MA, 1978; postgrad., Barry U. Asst. to owner export-import firm Navios Madrid, 1978; med. staff coord. dept. oncology U. Miami, Fla., 1978-79; mgr. travel wholesale ops. OK Tours, Miami Beach, Fla., 1979-80; sec., pharmacist asst. Miami Heart Inst., Miami Beach, 1980-81; computer operator Investors', Inc., Coral Gables, Fla., 1981-82; asst. to pres. Barcelo Internat. Corp. subs. Fontes & Fontes Assocs. Inc., Miami, 1983-87; owner Polypholologie Trans. Svcs., Miami Beach, 1986—; legal sec. Alan M. Fisher Law Firm, South Miami, Fla., 1988; exec. officer, translator Servihotels Corp. subs. Fontes & Fontes Assocs. Inc., Miami, 1988—. Mem. AACD, Dade County Counselors' Assn., Club Campestre de Cali (hon.), Sacred Heart Alumni Assn. Roman Catholic. Home and Office: 3440 Garden Ave Miami Beach FL 33140-3824

MARTÍNEZ, YOLANDA R., social services administrator; b. San Bernardino, Calif., Feb. 11, 1936; d. Eduardo R. and Consuelo (Rincon) M.; A.A., San Bernardino Valley Coll., 1959; B.A., U. Wash., 1974; m. William Edward Hawkins, Mar. 27, 1963 (div. Mar. 1983); children—Ricardo, Eduardo, William T. Tchr. public schs., Calif., 1958-59; parole adviser, project dir., counselor Active Mexicanos, Seattle, 1972-76; instr. Everett Community Coll., Everett, Wash., 1975-76; research, translator Wash. State Council Crime and Delinquency, Seattle, 1977; program asst., minority affairs Seattle Central Community Coll., cons. to community offenders programs 1977-81; sr. community service rep. Seattle Dept. Human Resources, 1981—; cons. Chicano mental health. Democratic precinct committeeman, 1968, 70, 88—; vol. worker various local and state polit. campaigns; translator Am. Red Cross Lang. Bank, 1975—; chmn. Region 10 Chicano Task Force on Drug Abuse, 1977-79; mem. Seattle Women's Commn., 1977-81; mem. Seattle Cable Citizens Adv. Bd., 1988-90; v.p. Concilio for Spanish Speaking; state dir., mem. nat. exec. bd. League United Latin Am. Citizens, 1980-82; chmn. Hispanic adv. bd. Seattle Community Coll. Dist. 6, 1981-83, chair Seattle/Mazatlan Sister City Assn., 1981-83; v.p. Neighborhoods U.S.A., 1987, bd. dirs. 1986; bd. dirs. United Way of King County; dist. adv. com. group health Northgate Clinic; del. White House Conf. on Families, Los Angeles, 1980. Recipient Gov.'s citation, 1974, award for committment to higher edn. Seattle Community Coll. Dist., 1983; award as One of 10 Unsung Heroes in Seattle, Radical Women, 1983; Community Service award Am. G.I. Forum, 1984; named assoc. mem. Eastern Washington U. Found., One of 100 Women Role Models for Pub. Schs., State Office Pub. Instrn. Author: Usted y La Ley, 1977.Mem. Rotary. Home: 12018 17th Ave NE Seattle WA 98125

MARTIN-GERHARDS, REBECCA ANN, psychologist; b. Columbus, Ohio, July 21, 1949; d. Gerald Dale and Penelope Virginia (Kyne) Martin; m. Michael C. Gerhards, Aug. 14, 1976. BA, Gonzaga U., 1971; MA, Idaho State U., Pocatello, 1972, EdD, 1977. Sch. psychologist Rockwood Sch. Dist., Portland, Oreg., 1972-74; pvt. practice clin. psychologist Portland, 1977—. Mem. Am. Psychol. Assn., Oreg. Psychol. Assn. (bd. dirs. 1983-84), Oreg. Acad. Profl. Psychologists (bd. dirs. 1981-86, lpres. 1984-85). Office: 1020 SW Taylor Ste 740 Portland OR 97205

MARTINO, REZAN SOLMAZ, data processing executive; b. Wilmington, N.C., Feb. 14, 1961; d. Gungor Mustafa and Diana Marie (Patrick) Solmaz; 1 child, Cristina Marie Martino. BA in Bus. Adminstrn., Belmont Abbey Coll., 1988. Mail and file clk. Temp. Personnel Inc., Monroe, N.C., 1985-86; stenographer Yale Security, Inc., Monroe, 1986-87; underwriter U.S. Fidelity and Guaranty Co., Charlotte, N.C., 1988-89; intern Belmont (N.C.) Abbey Office Continuing Edn., 1988; temp. Kelly Temp., Inc., Charlotte, 1989; receptionist Belk Printing, Inc., Charlotte, 1989-90; with office/computer support G.S. Industries, Inc., Newton, N.C., 1990—. Pell grantee, 1987. Mem. NAFE, Nat. Congress Parents and Tchrs., Planetary Soc., Habitat for Humanity. Republican. Baptist. Home: 122 Lakeview Rd Denver NC 28037

MARTINSON, GENE(VIEVE) L., association editor; b. Coldwater, Kans., Mar. 23, 1923; d. John Harry and Louesa Marie (Stuhlmacher) Canfield; m. Donald Charles Martinson, Feb. 18, 1950; children: Susan Dianne, Donna Jeanne, James Alan, Dale Robert. Telephone operator Southwest Telephone Co., Coldwater, 1941-43; long-distance operator Southwestern Bell Telephone Co., Wichita, Kans., 1943-45; long-distance supr. Southwestern Bell Telephone Co., 1945-50; organizing editor Canfield Family Assn., Wichita, 1982—. Girl Scout leader Girl Scouts U.S., Wichita, 1960-70; cub scout leader Boy Scouts Am., Wichita, 1965-72; bd. dirs. Citizen Participation Orgn., Wichita. Mem. North High Sch. Faculty Wives Club (pres. 1959-60), Extension Homemakers Unit Club (past pres.). Presbyterian. Home: 1144 North Gordon Wichita KS 67203

MARTINSON, HELEN DELABAR, insurance agency executive; b. Van Lear, Ky., Dec. 18, 1939; d. Morris Martin and Carrie Beatrice (Holbrook) McCormick; m. Carl Bernard Delabar, Feb. 2, 1957 (div. June 1970); children: Carl Martin, Gregory Michael, Steven Edward, James Thomas; m. Warren Charles Martinson III, June 7, 1975 (div. May 1982); m. Yancy Bailey Spencer Jr., Apr. 9, 1988. Student, U. Ky., 1963. Cert. ins. counselor. Cashier, sec. So. Life Ins. Co., Lexington, Ky., 1965-66; service rep. Carpenter Warren Ins., Lexington, 1966-69; ins. agt., pres. Delmac Ins. Inc., Lexington, 1969-72; agt., office mgr. O'Leary Ins. Agy., Boyton Beach, Fla., 1972-75, Hayes & Assocs. Inc., Boyton Beach, 1975-77; prodn. mgr. Normandin Ins. Agy. Inc., West Palm Beach, Fla., 1977-80; sec., treas. Normandin-Martinson Ins., West Palm Beach, 1980-85; v.p., mgr. Raymond/Patterson Agy. Inc., West Palm Beach, 1985—. Bd. dirs. Palm Beach County Fire Code and Appeals, West Palm Beach, 1985—. Fellow Profl. Ins. Agts. Fla. (bd. dirs. 1987—, membership chmn. 1987-89, spl. Olympics chmn., 1984, Best Overall Individual Fundraiser award 1986, 87, Leadership award 1985, Agt. of Yr. 1986), Ind. Agts. the Palm Beaches (bd. dirs. 1979-86, 2d v.p. 1982-83, 1st v.p. 1983-84, pres. 1984-85, Chmn. award 1982, Agt. of Yr. 1985). Republican. Baptist. Home: 4956 Sable Pine Circle #B-2 West Palm Beach FL 33417 Office: Raymond/Patterson Agy Inc 2827 Exchange Ct West Palm Beach FL 33409

MARTINSON, IDA MARIE, nurse, physiologist, educator; b. Mentor, Minn., Nov. 8, 1936; d. Oscar and Marvel (Nelson) Sather; m. Paul Varo Martinson, Mar. 31, 1962; children—Anna Marie, Peter. Diploma, St. Luke's Hosp. Sch. Nursing, 1957; B.S., U. Minn., 1960, M.N.A., 1962; Ph.D., U. Ill., Chgo., 1972. Instr. Coll. St. Scholastica and St. Luke's Sch. Nursing, 1957-58, Thornton Jr. Coll., 1967-69; lab. asst. U. Ill. at Med. Center, 1970-72; lectr. dept. physiology U. Minn., St. Paul, 1972-82; asst. prof. Sch. Nursing U. Minn., 1972-74, asso. prof., research, 1974-77, prof., dir. research, 1977-82; vis. research prof. Nat. Taiwan U. Def. Med. Ctr., 1981; vis. prof. nursing Sun Yat-Sen U. Med. Scis., Guangchow, Republic of China; prof., chmn. family health care nursing U. Calif., San Francisco, 1982—. Author: Mathematics for the Health Science Student, 1977; editor: Home Care for the Dying Child, 1976, Women in Stress, 1979, Women in Health and Illness, 1986, The Child and Family Facing Life Threatening Illness, 1987, Family Nursing, 1989, Home Health Care Nursing, 1989; contbr. chpts. to books, articles to profl. jours. Active Am. Cancer Soc. Recipient Am. Bus. Press award, 1977; recipient various grants. Mem. Council Nurse Researchers, Nat. League for Nursing, Am. Acad. Nursing, Am. Nurses Assn., Inst. Medicine, Sigma Xi, Sigma Theta Tau. Lutheran. Office: U Calif Family Health Care Nursing San Francisco CA 94135-0606

MARTINSON, JUDITH ANN, city official; b. Dayton, Ohio, Apr. 2, 1951; d. Arthur L. and Helen E. (O'Connor) M. BA in Psychology, Miami U., Oxford, Ohio, 1973; postgrad. bus. adminstrn., Wright State U.; grad. exec. devel. program, Ind. U., 1987-89. Media specialist Dayton Bd. Edn., 1973-75; child care worker State of Ohio, Dayton, 1976; asst. dir. Dayton Recreation and Parks Dept., 1977-80, ctr. dir., 1980-8l, coord. recreation program, 198l—. Mem. spl. events com. Montgomery County Coun. on Aging; mem. Dayton Student Assistance Program Bd.; pres. adv. bd. New Directions, 1989. City of Dayton and U. Dayton urban fellow, 1989. Mem. Am. Soc. Pub. Adminstrs., Ohio Park and Recreation Assn. (cert., Youth Program award 1984). Roman Catholic. Home: 124 Maplelawn Dr Dayton OH 45405 Office: Dayton Recreation and Parks 2013 W 3d St Dayton OH 45417

MARTOGLIO, ALBERTA MARGARET, nursing educator, researcher; b. South Amboy, N.J., July 29, 1932; d. Walter Charles and Anna (Jakubczak) O'Brien; m. Charles Vincent Martoglio, June 11, 1955; children: Charles, Mary Ann, Christopher, Jeanne-Marie, Frances. BSN, Mt. St. Vincent Coll., N.Y.C., 1953; MEd, Cleve. State U., 1978; MSN, Case Western Res. U., 1988. Sch. nurse West Hartford (Conn.) Sch. System, 1971-72, Hartford (Conn.) Sch. System, 1972-74; staff nurse Newington (Conn.) Vets. Hosp., 1974-75; instr. Fairview Gen. Hosp., Cleve., 1975-88; asst. prof. nursing Cleve. State U., 1988—; dir., instr. workshops for mentors for nursing students Cleve. State U. Author: Marketing Evaluation of Classes, 1987, (with others) Community Assessment Diagnosis: Elderly of Cleveland, 1988. Liaison for nursing dept. United Way, Cleve., 1988. Mem. Nat. League for Nursing, Assn. for Care of Children's Health, Sigma Theta Tau, Catawba Island Club. Republican. Roman Catholic. Home: 28204 Osborn Rd Bay Village OH 44140 Office: Cleve State U Euclid Ave & 24th Sts Cleveland OH 44115

MARTSCHINK, SHERRY SHEALY, senator; b. Columbia, S.C., Oct. 26, 1949; d. Ryan and Elsie Shealy; m. Gustave Charles Martschink Jr., 1973; children: Tiffany Lynn, Gustave Charles III, Mandy Elizabeth. BA, U. S.C., 1976. Sch. tchr., 1970-71; mem. S.C. Ho. of Reps., 1970-74; senator S.C. State Senate, 1987—; exec. dir. Children at Risk; del. White House Conf. on Aging, 1971, Rep. Nat. Conv., 1972, 76. Recipient George Washington medal Freedoms Found., Valley Forge, Pa., 1974; named Woman of Yr., Charleston Fedn. Women's Clubs, 1986. Republican. Lutheran. Home: 723 Angus Ct Mount Pleasant SC 29464-3601*

MARTUCCI, SHERYL LEE, chemist; b. Troy, N.Y., Nov. 18, 1962; d. William LeRoy and Susanne Elaine (Sibbald) Blom; m. Ricky Anthony; 1 child, Amanda Lee. BS, Siena Coll., 1985. Chemist Adirondack Environ. Svcs., Inc., Rensselaer, N.Y., 1989—. Mem. Am. Chem. Soc., Nat. Physics Honor Soc., N.Y. Acad. Scis. Democrat. Methodist. Home: 556 Bloomingrove Dr Rensselaer NY 12144

MARTY, GEORGANNE SPURLING, publicity executive; b. Moberly, Mo., Nov. 16, 1933; d. George Omar and Fannie B. (Edwards) Spurling; m. Victor Garfield Marty, June 16, 1957; children: Philip Scott, Neil Steven. BJournalism, U. Mo., 1955; MS in Journalism, U. Ill., 1974. Editorial asst. AT&T, Kansas City, Mo., 1955-60; pub. info. asst. Wyo. Hwy. Dept., Cheyenne, 1963-64; editor U.S. Agy. for Internat. Devel., Ankara, Turkey, 1965-67; staff writer, copy editor Fla. Times-Union, Jacksonville, 1968-70; editor Office Internatl Programs & Studies U. Ill., Champaign, 1971-75, publicity, promotion specialist Assembly Hall, 1979—; lifestyle editor Morning Courier, Urbana, Ill., 1975-79. Mem. DAR (nat. chmn. mag. 1986—, regent local chpt. 1985-87), Daus. Am. Colonists, Colonial Dames 17th Century (Ill. 1st v.p. 1989—), Colonial Dames Am. (corr. sec. St. Louis chpt. 1988—), Colonial Daus. 17th Century, Nat. League Am. Pen Women (1st v.p. local br. 1975-77), U. Ill. Alumni Assn., Champaign County Geneal. Soc., Zonta, Phi Theta Kappa, Theta Sigma Phi. Republican. Presbyterian.

MARTYN, PAMELA PAGONES, human resource supervisor; b. Aberdeen, S.D., June 28, 1949; d. John Peter and Barbara Louise (Kullander) Pagones; m. William F. Martyn, Apr. 28, 1972; children: Molly K., William F. AA, NSC, 1972, BS, 1988, postgrad., 1988—. Sec. S.D. Dept. of Labor, Aberdeen, S.D., 1970-74; sec. 3M, Aberdeen, 1975-78, office coord., 1978-79, human resource asst., 1979-83, human resource supr., 1983—; clerical staff supervision 3M, 1983-86; social club advisor 3M, 1981—; cafeteria start up 3M, 1986—; founder outlet store for artists, Aberdeen, 1988—. Speaker's bur. Aberdeen C. of C., 1983-84; arts chairperson indsl. com. Aberdeen C. of C., 1984-87; loaned exec. United Way, Aberdeen, 1982; chairperson, mem. Vocat. Sch. Bd. (office occupations com.) 1984—; bd. mem. Hospice, 1987—. Mem. Pers. Assn., Pers. Accreditation Inst. Episcopalian. Home: 1424 North Lincoln St Aberdeen SD 57401

MARTZ, CINDY LYNNE, industrial engineer; b. Louisville, Sept. 24, 1965; d. William Merrill and Sandra Lynne (Seberger) M. BS in Indsl. Engring. and Ops. Rsch., Va. Poly Inst. and State U., 1988. Indsl. engr. Aluminum Co. Am., Alcoa, Tenn., 1988—. Coord., liason Alcoa Can Recyling Program for East Tenn. Boy Scouts Am., 1989; vol. Boy Scouts Am. Explorer Program, Alcoa, Tenn., 1989-90; vol. Big Bros./Big Sisters, 1989—, Knoxville Mus. Art, 1989—. Mem. NAFE, Inst. Indsl. Engrs., Kiwanis (co-chmn. ann. auction 1990-91, vol. Ronald McDonald House 1989—), Women in Tech. (co-chmn. career fair 1989—, mem. monitoring program 1990—), Delta Zeta (Golden Heart award 1986, Grace Mason Lundy award 1988). Office: Alcoa PO Box 9128 Alcoa TN 37701

MARTZ, DONNA KAY, financial consultant; b. Indpls., Oct. 7, 1959; d. Kenneth T. and V. Jean (Morris) M. BS, Purdue U., 1981. CPA, Ill, Ind. Acct. Arthur Andersen & Co., Chgo., 1981-83; sr. field staff auditor United Airlines, Chgo., 1983-85; owner, fitness cons., aerobic instr. Energize Aerobics, Indpls., 1985—; fin. cons. Shearson Lehman Hutton, Indpls., 1987—; fitness specialist AM Ind., WTHR-TV, Indpls., 1986-87; mem. adv. panel Reebok, Indpls., 1988—. Asst. choreographer aerobics Pan Am Games, Indpls., 1987; coord. Nat. Employee Health and Fitness Day, Indpls., 1990; Sunday sch. tchr. Pleasant Run United Ch.Christ, Indpls., 1987—. Mem. NAFE, Am. Coll. Sports Medicine, Internat. Dance Exercise Assn., Assn. Fitness and Bus., Aerobic and Fitness Assn., Ind. Soc. CPAs, Indy Runners, Indpls. Athletic Club, Phi Kappa Psi, Phi Mu. Home: 615 Phaeton Pl Indianapolis IN 46227 Office: Shearson Lehman Hutton 201 N Illinois Capital Ctr #400 Indianapolis IN 46204

MARUSKIN MOTT, JOAN, educator, writer; b. Rochester, Pa., Feb. 9, 1944; d. John Raymond and Dorothy (Oresconin) Maruskin; children: Artemas Mott, Titus Mott. BSEd, California (Pa.) State Coll., 1964; postgrad., Bucks County Community Coll., 1970-71, Trenton State Coll., 1971-73; MS, Johns Hopkins U., 1988. Drama tchr. Hopewell High Sch., Aliquippa, Pa., 1964-65, Pikesville (Md.) Sr. High Sch., 1967-69, Woodrow Wilson Sr. High Sch., Fairless Hills, Pa., 1969-71; tchr. English Laurence Twp. (N.J.) Sr. High Sch., 1971-73; ind. potter Shreasbury, Pa., 1973-77; instr. Adult Basic Edn./Gen. Edn. Diploma Lincoln Intermediate Unit 12, New Oxford, Pa., 1977-83; freelance writer Stewartstown, Pa., 1984-86; alternative sch. tchr. Lincoln Intermediate Unit 12, New Oxford, Pa., 1983-86; tchr. emotionally disabled adolescents Hannah More Ctr. Sch., Reisterstown, Md., 1986—; adult edn. cons., presenter workshops Pa. Dept. Edn., Harrisburg, 1977-83; cons. on gifted edn. 7th World Conf. on Gifted and Talented, Salt Lake City, 1987, Seng Conf., Pitts., 1988; cons. alternative edn. York County (Pa.) Edn. Soc., 1988. Author adult edn. text, 1987; author plays; contbr. articles to profl. jours. Youth leader Stewartstown United Meth. Ch., 1989—; rep. Hopewell Area Recreation and Park Bd., Stewartstown; bd. dirs. Friends of Mason Dixon Libr., Stewartstown. Grantee N.J. Dept. Edn., 1971. Mem. Md. Assn. Non-Pub. Sch. Edn. FAcilities, Coun. Exceptional Chidren, Dramatists Guild, Stewartstown Hist. Soc. Democrat. Home: 41 S Main St Stewartstown PA 17363 Office: Hannah More Ctr Sch Box 370 Reisterstown MD 21136

MARVIN, HELEN RHYNE, state senator; b. Gastonia, N.C., Nov. 30, 1917; d. Dane S. and Tessie (Hastings) Rhyne; B.A. magna cum laude, Furman U., 1938; M.A., La. State U., 1938; postgrad. Winthrop Coll., U. N.C.-Chapel Hill, U. N.C.-Charlotte, U. Colo., U. Vt., U. Oslo; m. Ned Marvin, Nov. 21, 1941; children—Kathryn Nisbet, Richard Morris, David Rhyne. Part-time instr. polit. sci. Gaston Coll.; pres. Gaston County Democratic Women, 1973-75; mem. Gaston County Dem. Exec. Com., 1973-76; mem. N.C. State Dem. Exec. Com., 1973-76; del. Nat. Dem. Conv., 1972, 84; mem. N.C. Senate, 1977—, vice chairperson edn. com., 1979-82, vice-chairperson law enforcement and crime control com., 1981-82, appropriations com., 1981—, chmn. congl. redistricting com., 1981-82, constl. amendment com., 1983-84, 89-90, chmn. legis. study com. on social, econ. and legal needs of women, 1981-86, chmn. pensions and retirement com., 1985-87, vice chmn. children and youth com., 1985-87, chmn. appropriations com. on jusitce and pub. safety, 1987—, vice chmn. P&R com., 1987—. Bd. dirs. N.C. Equity, Inc., Gaston County Mental Health Assn., Gaston County Family Svcs., Inc., Gaston County Council for Children with Spl. Needs, Gaston County Children's Council; past mem., sec. So. Piedmont Health Services Agy.; past mem. N.C. State Health Coordinating Council, N.C. State Textbook Commn.; past chairperson N.C. Council on Status of Women, N.C. State Social Services Commn., N.C. Day Care Adv. Council; mem. N.C. Commn. on Yr. 2000; former mem. Gov.'s Advocacy Council on Children and Youth; former mem. N.C. Apprenticeship Council; trustee Vagabond Sch. Drama, Flat Rock Playhouse; former mem. bd. N.C. Child Advocacy Inst.; active N.C. Child Support Council; elder 1st Presbyterian Ch., 1983—. Recipient N.C. Disting. Woman award, 1987, Valand award, 1980, 89, N.C. Mental Health Dir.'s award, 1988, Ham Stevens award for svc. to Pub. Health in N.C., 1988, Ellen Winston award for Social Svcs. Legislation, 1989, Svc. to Pub. Edn. award N.C. Assn. Educators, 1989, N.C. Pediatric award for Svc. to Children, 1990, 1990 Headstart award, 1990; named Gaston County Outstanding Woman, 1990. Mem. So. Polit. Sci. Assn., N.C. Polit. Sci. Assn. (pres. 1976-77), N.C. Assn. for Edn. Young Children, Altrusa, Delta Kappa Gamma. Office: N C State Senate Raleigh NC 27611 Other: 119 Ridge Ln Gastonia NC 28054*

MARVIN, SUSAN ISABELLE, sales/marketing executive; b. Warroad, Minn., Dec. 14, 1954; d. William Sibley and Margaret Isabelle (Wallen) Marvin; m. William Robert Kleckner. BA, U. Minn., 1979. With Am. Hoist & Derrick, St. Paul, 1979-81; mktg. comm. mgr. Marvin Windows, Mpls., 1981-86; v.p. sales & mktg. Marvin Windows, 1986—. Chmn. New Am. Home Com., Washington, 1991, co-chmn., 1990; trustee Nat. Council of the Housing Ind., Washington, 1987—. Mem. Nat. wood Window & Door Assn., Nat. Sash & Door Jobbers Assn., nat. Assn. Home Bldrs. Republican. Episcopalian. Office: Marvin Windows 8043 24th Ave South Minneapolis MN 55425

MARVIN, URSULA BAILEY, geologist; b. Bradford, Vt., Aug. 20, 1921; d. Harold Leslie and Alice Miranda (Bartlett) Bailey; m. Lloyd Burton Chaisson, June 28, 1944 (div. 1951); m. Thomas Crockett Marvin, Apr. 1, 1952. BA, Tufts Coll., 1943; MA, Harvard/Radcliffe Coll., 1946; PhD, Harvard U., 1969. Rsch. asst. dept. geology U. Chgo., 1947-50; mineralogist Union Carbide Corp., N.Y.C., 1952-58; instr. dept. geology Tufts U., Medford, Mass., 1958-61; geologist, sr. staff Smithsonian Astrophys. Obs., Cambridge, Mass., 1961—, fed. womens program coord., 1974-77; vis. prof. dept. geology Ariz. State U., Tempe, 1978; lectr. geology Harvard U., 1974—; trustee Tufts U., 1975—, U. Space Rsch. Assn., Columbia, Md., 1979-84. Author: Continental Drift, 1973; contbr. chpt.: Astronomy from Space, 1983, The Planets, 1985; assoc. editor Earth in Space, Am. Geophys. Union, 1988—; contbr. articles to profl. jours. Mem. Lunar and Planetary Sci. Coun., Houston, 1987—. Recipient Antarctic Svc. medal NSF, 1983, Group Achievement award NASA, 1984. Fellow AAAS, Meteoritical Soc. (pres. 1975-76), Geol Soc. Am. (History of Geology award 1986); mem. Assn. Women in Sci., Mineralogical Soc. Am., History of Earth Scis. Soc. (pres.-elect 1989—), Internat. Commn. on History Geol. Scis. (sec.-gen. 1989—). Office: Smithsonian Astrophys Obs 60 Garden St Cambridge MA 02138

MASCARENHAS, CELA MARGARET, pension fund administrator; b. Chakrata, India, June 10, 1935; came to U.S., 1962; d. Justin Wilfred and Florence Margaret (Peris) Albuquerque; m. Maurice John Mascarenhas, Sept. 8, 1960; children: Dinesh, Vijay. BA, Mysore (India) U., 1955; MA, Madras (India) U., 1957. Sec., treas. Mascarenhas Cons. Svcs. Inc., Sewickley, Pa., 1976-86, pension mgr., 1986—. Contbr. articles to profl. publs. Mem. AAAUW (pres. Coraopolis/Sewickley br. 1976-78), Woman's Club Sewickley Valley (bd. dirs. 1985-87), S.T.B. Investment Club (founding pres. 1984-86), Sewickley Music Club (pres. 1987-89). Democrat. Home and Office: 457 Maple Ln Sewickley PA 15143

MASCARENHAS, MARY-ANN HELEN, medical technologist; b. Karachi, Pakistan, Jan. 23, 1961; came to U.S., 1984; d. Dacian Stanislaus and Marie Bernadette (Cardoza) M.; m. Gemunu Sidath Samaranayake, July

15, 1989. BS, U. Karachi, 1980; BS summa cum laude, Marymount Coll., 1987. Med. technologist, supr. micro dept. Holy Family Hosp., Karachi, 1980-84; med. technologist hematology dept. Danbury (Conn.) Hosp., 1987-88; med. technologist White Plains (N.Y.) Hosp., 1988—. Mem. NAFE, Am. Soc. Clin. Pathologists, Nat. Cert. Agy., Delta Epsilon Sigma. Roman Catholic.

MASCI, CARMELA, sociologist; b. White Plains, N.Y., Sept. 4, 1964; d. Luigi and Anna Ida (Marrapodi) Campa m. John Charles Masci, Mar. 13, 1988. BA, Iona Coll., 1986. Teaching asst. Italian Lang. Dept., Iona Coll., New Rochelle, N.Y., 1985-86; interviewer, counselor Planned Parenthood of Westchester & Rockland, Mt. Vernon, N.Y., 1986-88; case mgr. Planned Parenthood of Westchester & Rockland, Port Chester, N.Y., 1987—. Mem. Psi Chi. Roman Catholic. Office: Planned Parenthood 111 S Ridge St Port Chester NY 10573

MASCOLL, DORIS WALKER, vice principal; b. Prentiss, Miss., July 11, 1936; d. George Henry and Queretta (Powell) Robinson; m. Lonnie C. Walker, Nov. 20, 1955 (div. 1980); children: Jacqueline, Sidney; m. Lester C. Mascoll, July 20, 1985. Student, U. Calif., 1972; BA, Calif. State U., 1971, MA, 1978, postgrad, 1981. Vice prin. Elementary Sch., Lynwood, Calif., 1989--. Fellowship, Robert Taft Found., 1979. Mem. Women Leaders in Edu., Calif. Alliance of Black Educ., Lynwood Tchrs. Assn., Calif Tchrs. Assn. Democratic. Catholic. Home: 16321 Visalia Ave Carson CA 90746

MASCOLO, DONNA MARIE, finance company executive; b. Lakewood, N.J., Jan. 13, 1955; d. James Vincent and Marilyn Ann (Gutzler) M. BA in Math and Econs., Susquehanna U., 1976; MBA in Mgmt. and Fin., Lehigh U., 1979. Credit mgr. comml. loans Midlantic Banks, Inc., West Orange, N.J., 1976-78; ops. rsch. analyst Air Products & Chems., Trexlertown, Pa., 1978-79; teaching asst. in econs. Lehigh U., Bethlehem, Pa., 1979; systems engr. Bell Labs., Holmdel, N.J., 1979-81; bus. planning advisor Exxon Corp., Coral Gables, Fla., 1981-85; dir. planning and reporting Burger King Corp. subs. Pillsbury Co., Miami, Fla., 1985-88; dir. planning and analysis Jack Eckerd Corp., Largo, Fla., 1988—. Dir. community devel. com. United Way, Miami, 1987-88. Mem. NAFE, Miami C. of C. (bd. dirs. strategic planning com. 1987), Am. Mgmt. Assn. Home: 757 Tomoka Dr Palm Harbor FL 34683 Office: Jack Eckerd Corp 8333 Bevan Dairy Rd Largo FL 34618

MASE, BARBARA ANN, academic official, educator; b. Phila., Nov. 5, 1950; d. Charles F. and Mamie E. (Stahler) M. BMusic, Boston Conservatory, 1972; MPA, U. Hartford, 1989. Special events coordinator Heritage House, Inc., Brockton, Mass., 1973-79; free-lance agt. Springhouse Assocs., Alexandria, Ind., 1978-81; acct. exec. WEZE Radio, Boston, 1979-80; tour/booking mgr. Linda Miller & Assocs., Nashville, Tenn., 1980-81; concert mgr., vis. lectr. music mgmt., interim chmn. dept. U. Hartford Hartt Sch. Music, West Hartford, Conn., 1982—; music dir. Bethany Covenant, New Britian, Conn., 1986-87; project coordinator Conn. Pub. TV documentary, Hartford, 1987. Mem. Women in Communications Assn., Am. Soc. for Pub. Adminstrs., Sigma Alpha Iota (pres. 1971-72), Sigma Alpha Iota (assoc. 1985—). Democrat. Mem. The Covenant Ch. Office: U Hartford Hartt Sch Music 200 Bloomfield Ave West Harford CT 06117

MASEY-AYUB, MARY OMA, small business owner; b. Laredo, Tex., Oct. 22, 1952; d. Willard Cecil and Guadalupe (De La Luna) Masey; m. Edward Ayub, Nov. 22, 1979; 1 dau. Nicole, 1 stepson, Joshua. Lic. real estate, Anthony Schs., San Diego, 1979; Lic. real estate broker, U. Oxnard Program, 1989. Mgr. Pantry Clothing Co., San Diego, 1974-77; real estate agt. Point Loma Real Estate, San Diego, 1979-89, Don Moffatt Enterprise, Atlanta, 1979-82; property mgr. Don Moffatt Enterprise, New Orleans, 1979-80; v.p. Source Enterprises, Lafayette, La., 1980-82; bus. mgr., owner Edward Ayub, Physical Therapist, San Diego, 1982—; real estate broker Masey Broker, San Deigo, 1989—; ptnr. Ayub & Ayub Property Mgmt., Sun Valley, Idaho, 1989—. Mem. Nat. Assn. for Women. Democrat. Methodist. Home: 4092 Bonita Rd Bonita CA 92002 Office: Edward Ayub Phys Therapist 120 Elm St San Diego CA 92101

MASHBURN, KIMBERLY JOY NEEDHAM, science association director; b. St. Charles, Mo., Mar. 10, 1957; d. Earl David and Marie Cecelia (Stahlschmidt) Needham; m. Douglas Newton Mashburn, Dec. 8, 1979; children: David Nicholas, Jennifer Marie. BS in Nursing, U. Tenn., 1979. RN, Tenn. Staff nurse U. Tenn. Hosp., Knoxville, 1979-80; pediatric nurse Dr. Donald Larmee, Knoxville, 1980-81; staff devel. coord. Ft. Sanders Regional Med. Ctr., Knoxville, 1981-85; dir. communication and edn. Thompson Cancer Survival Ctr., Knoxville, 1986—. Mem. Childcare adv. bd., Knoxville, 1987, Knoxville Jr. League, 1988. Mem. NAFE, Tenn. League for Nursing (chmn. 1984-86), AIDS Response Knoxville (bd. dirs. 1987-88), Am. Cancer Soc. (nursing edn. com. 1985—, pub. edn. chmn. 1988-89, bd. dirs. 1990—), Assn. Community Cancer Ctrs., Delta Delta Delta. Office: 1915 White Ave Knoxville TN 37916

MASHBURN, LILLIAN TAUXE, university official, consultant; b. Knoxville, Tenn., Feb. 12, 1943; d. Samuel Louis and Jean (Sitton) Tauxe; m. John Mashburn, Sept. 17, 1965; children: Samuel Louis, Laura Jean. BS in Edn., U. Tenn., 1965. Tchr. Knox County Schs., Knoxville, 1965-67; exec. dir. NCCJ, Knoxville, 1975-77; pub. rels. dir., corp. bank officer United Am. Bank, Knoxville, 1977-80; mktg. dir. GSCD Architects, Knoxville, 1980-82; owner, mgr. LTM Cons., Knoxville, 1982—; asst. to dean Coll. Engring. U. Tenn., Knoxville, 1986—; mem. exec. bd. WATTec Energy Conf., Knoxville, Oak Ridge, Tenn., 1985—. Com. chmn. 1982 World's Fair, Knoxville, 1976-82; bd. dirs. Knox County Child and Family Svcs., 1979-85, Planned Parenthood East Tenn., 1981-87; elder Presbyn. Ch., Knoxville. Recipient T.O. Gilliland Svc. award WATTec Conf., 1986. Mem. Am. Soc. Engring. Mgmt. (sec.-treas. 1988—), Am. Soc. Engring. Edn. (mem. bd. rels. with industry 1989—), Am. Nuclear Soc. (com. chmn. 1982—), Knoxville Tech. Soc. (sec.-v.p. 1989—), Venture Exchange Forum (bd. dirs. 1986-89), Tenn. Inventors Assn. (bd. dirs. 1986-89), Exec. Women's Assn. (founding pres. 1979-80), Knoxville C. of C. (hon. life), Optimist. Home: 920 Venice Rd Knoxville TN 37923 Office: U Tenn 121 Perkins Hall Knoxville TN 37996-2000

MASHEK, CAROL ANN MARTIN, historian, researcher, writer; b. RFD Lamont, Iowa, Aug. 6, 1937; d. James Theodore and Caroline Marie (Stauss) Martin; m. William August Mashek, July 3, 1960; children: Tarence Lynn, Timothy Lawrence. BA, Sioux Falls Coll., 1959; MA, U. Mo., 1964. Tchr. Kans. City, Reedsburg and Janesville Pub. Schs., Kans./Wis., 1959-69; edn. supr. and tchr. Sioux Falls (S.D.) Coll., 1973; writer Ctr. for Western Studies, Sioux Falls, 1974; community programmer Sioux Falls Bicentennial Commn., Sioux Falls, 1975-77; census taker U.S. Census Bur., Sioux Falls, 1975-77; researcher, writer, tour guide Sioux Falls Research Svcs., 1977-80; writer in res. Sioux Falls Coll., 1980-83; newspaper columnist Sioux Falls Tribune, 1983-85; researcher, writer, tour guide Sioux Falls Research Svcs., 1985—; dir. Sioux Valley Genealogical Soc., Sioux Falls, 1975-79; pres., life mem. Minnehaha County Hist. Soc., Sioux Falls, 1978-80; co-founder/dir. Forest Home Cemetery Assn., Sioux Falls, 1979—; founder/mem. Sioux Falls Hist. Coun., 1987-89. Author: mag. articles with religious themes, 1964-74; annual papers, Dakota History Conf. 1978-89; local history articles, Sioux Falls Host Mag., 1985-89. City Coord., City Govt. Internat. Women's Yr., Sioux Falls, 1975; bd. dirs. Sioux Falls Bd. of Hist. Preservation, Sioux Falls, 1975—; city organizer, Sioux Falls Bell Ringing Project, 1988; sec. S.D. United Nat. Assn., Sioux Falls, 1985—; bd. dirs. count gov. County Abandoned Cemetary Bd.; officer Ch. Women United, Sioux Falls; v.p. Am. Bapt. Women, 1962-87. Recipient Purple Feather, Sioux Falls Coll. 1959, Sioux Falls YMCA Leadership Award, 1989; named Women's Grant Hon., Am. Assn. of U. Women., Sioux Falls, 1981; Am. Assn. Women grantee, 1981. Mem. (life) S.D. State Hist. Soc., Nat. Trust for Hist. Preservation, Assn. for State and Local Hist., YWCA (Award for Disting. Contbr. to Hist., Dakota State Coll., Madison, S.D., 1989). Democrat. Home and Office: 1014 W 22nd St Sioux Falls SD 57105

MASHIN, JACQUELINE ANN COOK, federal agency consultant; b. Chgo., May 11, 1941; d. William Hermann and Ann (Smidt) Cook; m. Fredric John Mashin, June 7, 1970; children: Joseph Glenn, Alison Robin. BS, U. Md., 1984. Cert. realtor. Adminstrv. asst. CIA, Washington, 1963-66; asst. to mng. dir. Aerospace Edn. Found., Washington, 1966-74; exec. asst. to asst exec. dir. Air Force Assn., Washington, 1974-79; v.p., ptnrship. owner Discount Linen Store, Silver Spring, Md., 1979-81; asst. regional polit. dir. Office of Pres.-elect, Washington, 1980-81; confidential asst. to dir. Office of Personnel Mgmt. (US), Washington, 1981-83; spl. asst. to dep. dir. Office of Mgmt. and Budget, Washington, 1983-86; dir. internat. communications and spl. asst. to commr. Dept. of the Interior, Washington, 1986-89, cons., 1989—. Pres. Layhill Civic Assn., Silver Spring, Md., 1980; state chmn. Md.'s Reagan Youth Delegation, Annapolis, Md., 1980; state treas., office mgr. Reagan-Bush State Hdqrs. of Md., Silver Spring, 1980; mem. Women's Com. Nat. Symphony Orch. Mem. Air Force Assn. (life), Aux. Salvation Army (life), Am. League Lobbyists, Am. Soc. Pers. Adminstrn., Am. Soc. Pub. Adminstrn., Internat. Platform Assn., Chevy Chase Women's Club (Md.), Capitol Hill Club, Indian Spring Country Club, Touchdown Club. Republican. Jewish. Home and Office: 2429 White Horse Ln Silver Spring MD 20906

MASILOTTI, SHARYN ROSE, advertising executive; b. Vineland, N.J., Apr. 7, 1956; d. Angelo Robert and Catherine Ann (Taormina) M.; m. Joseph V. Bonanno, Sept. 23, 1978 (div. 1987); m. Randall W. Watson, Oct. 20, 1990. Student, Stockton State, 1975-78. Sec., receptionist Quality Litho Printing, Vineland, N.J., 1976-77; graphics specialist Wheaton Sci., Millville, N.J., 1978-80; designer, artist Wheaton Fine Glassware, Millville, N.J., 1980-81; advt. mgr. Bristolite Skylights, Santa Ana, Calif. Designer brochure, trade show booth, bristolite skylights, 1985, 88, Bristolite Catalog, 1986. Performer, Olympic Honor Choir, Los Angeles 1984. Recipient awards for various advt. projects. Republican. Christian. Home: 3095 B Cassia Ave Costa Mesa CA 92626 Office: Bristolite Skylights 401 E Goetz Ave Santa Ana CA 92707

MASKALL, MARTHA JOSEPHINE, executive recruiter; b. Kearny, N.J., Mar. 30, 1945; d. Charles Edgar and Mathilda (Comba) M. BA in Biology, Stanford U., 1966; MA, Duke U., 1969. Cert. data processor, 1979. Data base adminstr. Armco Steel, Ashland, Ky., 1972-74; project mgr. Rand Info. Systems, San Francisco, 1974-78; mgr. systems devel. Itel Corp., San Francisco, 1978-79; sales rep. Datacom ADR, San Francisco, 1980-81; systems engr. Four-Phase Systems, Sacramento, Calif., 1981-83; data processing recruiter Mgmt. Recruiters, Sacramento, 1983-86; executive recruiter Telos, Sacramento, 1983—; coord. data base series info sci. seminars Golden Gate U., 1979-80. NDEA fellow, 1966-68. Mem. Data Processing Mgmt. Assn. (program dir. 1980, 82, sec. 1983), NOW, Sierra, Toastmasters (v.p. 1985, pres. 1986, div. gov. 1987, speakers bur. 1988, Disting. Toastmaster award 1989). Democrat. Home: 8456 Hidden Valley Circle Fair Oaks CA 95628 Office: Marty Maskall & Assoc 8125 Sunset Ave Ste 258 Fair Oaks CA 95628

MASLOFF, SOPHIE, mayor; b. Pitts., Dec. 23, 1917; d. Louis and Jennie Friedman; m. Jack Masloff; 1 child, Linda. Grad. high sch., Pitts. Chief investigator Ct. of Common Pleas, Allegheny County, Pa., 1940—; mem. Pitts. City Council, 1976-88; mayor City of Pitts., 1988—. Alternate del. Dem. Nat. Conv., 1968; del. Dem. Nat. Conf., 1978. Mem. Allegheny County Dem. Women's Guild (sec. 1940—), Pa. Fedn. Dem. Women (sec. 1967—, formerly pres.). Jewish. Lodges: B'nai B'rith, Hadassah. Office: 414 Grant St Pittsburgh PA 15219*

MASLYK, CHERI A(NN), marketing professional, business consultant; b. Fort Wayne, Ind., Dec. 25, 1949; d. Van Watt Gardner and Margaret Joann (Little) Moore; m. Brian Joseph Maslyk, June 18, 1971. Cert. of Airline Op., Atlantic Sch., Kansas City, Mo., 1968; student, U. Ky., 1969, Ind. Inst. Tech., 1982-90. Owner Concept Advt. and Mktg., Kalamazoo, 1975-80; major accounts mgr., new product devel. mgr. Fort Wayne Newspapers, 1980-85; dist. mgr. Modern Metals, Chgo., 1985-87; dir. product devel. Rho Lyn Engring., Detroit, 1985; exec. dir. Small Bus. Devel. Ctr., Fort Wayne, 1987; acting dir. Ft. Wayne Enterprise Ctr. Found., 1990—; mem. adv. bd. Ind.-Purdue U. Mktg. Club, 1987-88, Young Entrepreneurs Success Program; instr. continuing edn. dept. Ind.-Purdue U.; speaker Entrepreneur's Day Conf., Ind. Inst. of New Bus. Ventures, Indpl., 1990. Event organizer Run Jane Run, 1983-84; fund raiser United Way, 1984, drive trainer, 1989; chmn. mktg. com. Ft. Wayne Ballet, 1988, v.p., 1990-91; mem. Leadership Ft. Wayne; mem. City of Ft. Wayne Citizen's Adv. Com., 1988-89; task force mem. Tech. Resource Assistance Ctr., 1989-90; facilitator City of Ft. Wayne Workforce Conf., 1990; Urban Land Inst. Task Force, 1990. Recipient Cert. of Recognition Crossroads Children's Home, Nat. Safety Council cert., 1988, Cet. of Profl. Contbn. Delta Sigma Pi. Mem. Women's Bur., Small Bus. Inst. Dirs. Assn., Friends of the Urban League, Women's Bus. Owners Assn. (speaker 1988-90). Republican. Roman Catholic. Home: 2330 Springmill Rd Fort Wayne IN 46825 Office: Small Business Devel Ctr 1830 Wayne Trace Fort Wayne IN 46803

MASON, AIMEE HUNNICUTT ROMBERGER, retired educator; b. Atlanta, Nov. 3, 1918; d. Edwin William and Aimee Greenleaf (Hunnicutt) Romberger; m. Samuel Venable Mason, Aug. 16, 1941 (dec. 1988); children: Olivia Elizabeth (Mrs. Mason Butcher), Christopher Leeds. BA, Conn. Coll., 1940; postgrad. Emory U., 1946-48; MA, U. Fla., 1979, PhD, 1980, MA, Stetson U., 1968. Jr. exec. merchandising G. Fox & Co., Hartford, Conn., 1940-41; air traffic contr. CAA, Atlanta, 1942; ptnr. Coronado Concrete Products, New Smyrna Beach, Fla., 1953-81; adj. faculty Valencia Jr. Coll., Orlando, Fla., 1969; instr. philosophy and humanities Seminole Community Coll., Sanford, 1969, ret. Area cons. ARC, 1947-50; del. Nat. Red Cross, Washington, 1949; founding mem. St. Joseph Hosp. Aux., Atlanta, 1950-53; v.p., treas. New Smyrna Beach PTA 1955-60; bd. dirs. Atlanta Symphony Orch., Fla. Symphony Orch., 1954-59. Lt. USCGR, 1943-46. Recipient award in graphics Nat. Assn. Women Artists, 1939, 41. Mem. AAUP, AAUW (founding mem. New Smyrna Beach, exec. bd. 1984-85, chmn. scholarship com. 1984-87, coll./univ. liaison 1987—), DAV, Am. Philos. Assn., Fla. Philos. Assn. (exec. coun. 1978-79), Collegium Phenomenologicum, Soc. Existential and Phenomenological Philosophy, Soc. Phenomenology in Human Scis., Merleau-Ponty Circle, Fla. Assn. Community Colls. Home: 511 N Riverside Dr Edgewater FL 32132

MASON, BARBARA ELLEN, plastics manufacturing company executive; b. Seattle, May 4, 1945; d. Joseph Reese and Mary Elizabeth (Jorgensen) Leonnig; m. Lee Bennett Mason, Feb. 27, 1970; children: Joseph Lynn, John Leslie, Glen Robert. Student, U. Wash., 1963-65, Oreg. Sch. Arts and Crafts, 1987-88, Portland State U., 1988—. Kitchen supr. Earl Kelly's Restaurant, Portland, Oreg., 1968-70; owner, mgr. Craft Factory, Portland, 1970-78; designer JJF Assocs., Portland, 1978-81; v.p., owner CF Plastics Inc., Hillsboro, Oreg., 1976—. Exhibitor prints local art shows, 1980—. Vol. Beaverton (Oreg.) Sch. Dist., 1976—; mem. Women's Caucus for Art, Portland, 1989—; mem. Speaker's Bur. Oreg. div. Nat. Mus. Women in Arts, Portland, 1989—. Republican. Lutheran. Office: CF Plastics Inc 2820 39th Loop Ste H Hillsboro OR 97123

MASON, BARBARA MENTZER, environmental specialist; b. Atlanta, Jan. 2, 1937; d. Maxwell Richardson and Martha Jean (Osborne) Mentzer; m. John Augustus Lee (div. 1978); children: George A., Martha J.A., Sara Lee Fernandez, Maxwell R.M., Rebecca D.C.; m. Edward Augustus Mason, Sept. 22, 1979. BS, Fla. State U., 1959. Tchr. sci. Atlanta Pub. Sch. System, 1959-60, tchr. home econs., 1960-62, 1967-70; specialist mktg. Ga. Egg Commn., Atlanta, 1976-77, coordinator consumer program, 1977-78; state dir. Ga. Clean and Beautiful Dept. Community Affairs State of Ga., Atlanta, 1978-89; exec. dir. Clean Fla. Commn., Tallahassee, 1989—. Tchr. Sunday sch., vacation Bible sch. St. Philips Episc. Cathedral, 1962-67; chmn. com. orgn. Atlanta Clean City Commn, 1976; pres. Peachtree Battle Alliance Civic Assn., 1974-76, v.p., 1975, chmn. beautification, 1977; mem. Council Vol. Adminstrs., Ga. Assn. Vol. Adminstrn., 1986—, Ga. Conservency, 1980—, Ga. Environ. Council, 1986—. Named Outstanding Citizen, Fultop County Bd. Commrs., 1986, Outstanding Citizen State Cobb County Clean Commn., Ga., 1987; recipient Profl. leadership award Keep Am. Beautiful Inc., 1983, leadership award State of Ga., 1989. Mem. NEA (Ga. chpt.), Am. Home Econs. Assn. (Ga. chpt.), Nat. Assn. Female Execs., Atlanta Womens' Network, DAR Jr. Com. (pres. 1963), Delta Gamma Alumnae (pres. 1963, chmn. recommendations 1959). Home: 975 Vistavia Cr Decatur GA 30033

MASON, BETTY GWENDOLYN, superintendent of schools; b. Tulsa, Mar. 3, 1928; d. Stacy Ervin and Carrie (McGlory) Hopkins; 1 child, Trena Janell Combs. BA, Bishop Coll., Marshall, Tex., 1949; MEd, Calif. State U., Haywood, 1974; EdD, U. Okla., 1986. Tchr. pub. schs., Kansas City, Mo., 1963-69; asst. Title I schs. Berkeley (Calif.) Unified Schs., 1970-71, asst. prin., 1971-72, dir. elem. edn., 1974-79; prin. Le Conte Elem. Sch., Berkeley, 1972-74; dir. elem. edn. Oklahoma City Pub. Schs., 1979-83, asst. supt., 1983-88; supt. Gary (Ind.) Pub. Schs., 1988—; mem. exec. bd. supt.'s initiative Nat. Urban League, N.Y.C., 1988—. Mem. exec. bd. YWCA, Gary, 1988—, N.W. Ind. chpt. Urban League, Gary, 1988—. Recipient Citizen of Yr. award Omega Phi Psi, 1985, Outstanding Woman in Edn. award Okla. Commn. in Edn., 1987, Youth Svc. award City and Mayor of Gary, 1988, Outstanding Educator award Ind. U. Dons, 1989. Mem. Am. Assn. Sch. Adminstrs., Nat. Assn. Black Educators, NW Ind. Supts. Coun., Phi Delta, Phi Delta Kappa (chpt. basileus, edn. chmn.), Alpha Kappa Alpha. Home: 7511 Harold Ave Gary IN 46403 Office: Gary Community Sch Corp 620 E 10th Pl Gary IN 46403

MASON, BOBBIE ANN, novelist, short story writer; b. Mayfield, Ky., 1940; married. BA, U. Ky.; MA, SUNY-Binghamton; PhD, U. Conn. Author: Nabokov's Garden, 1974; The Girl Sleuth, 1976; Shiloh and Other Stories, 1982 (Ernest Hemingway award, Nat. Book Critic's Circle award nominee, Am. Book award nominee, PEN Faulkner award nominee), In Country, 1985, Spence plus Lila, 1988, Love Life, 1989. Contbr. regularly: The New Yorker, 1980—. Contbr. fiction to: The Atlantic, Redbook, Paris Rev., Mother Jones, Harpers, N.Am. Rev., Va. Quar. Rev.,; contbr. works: Best American Short Stories, 1981; The Pushcart Prize: Best of the Small Presses, 1983; Best American Short Stories, 1983 (O. Henry awards, 1986, 88). Grantee Pa. Arts Council, 1983, 1989, Nat. Endowment Arts, 1983, Am. Acad. and Inst., 1984; Guggenheim fellow, 1984. Address: care Amanda Urban Internat Creative Mgmt 40 W 57th St New York NY 10019

MASON, CAROLINE FAITH VIBERT, chemist; b. Harrogate, Eng., Feb. 24, 1942; came to U.S., 1967; d. Thomas Vibert and Edith (Legerton) Pearce; m. Rodney Jackson Mason, Feb. 1, 1969; children: Vanessa, Rosalind. BSc, U. London, 1964, PhD, 1967. Postdoctoral fellow SUNY, Buffalo, 1967-68; analysis chemist Howmet Corp., Dover, N.J., 1969-70; synthesis chemist Ortho Rsch. Found., Raritan, N.J., 1970-72; rsch. chemist Los Alamos (N.Mex.) Nat. Lab., 1975—; vis. scholar cornell U., 1990-91. Mem. Am. Chem. Soc. Home: 148 Piedra Loop Los Alamos NM 87544 Office: Los Alamos Nat Lab IT-3 B230 Los Alamos NM 87545

MASON, ELIZABETH, historian, consultant; b. Washington, Jan. 1, 1919; d. Hilarion Noel and Ella Augusta (Moler) Branch; m. John Thomas Mason, Jr., May 8, 1954. BA, Mt. Holyoke Coll., 1940; MA, Columbia U., 1941. Press officer Brit. Embassy, Mexico City, Mex., 1941-47; analyst Office of Naval Intelligence, Washington, 1948-54; instr. U. Maine, Orono, 1955-57; asst. dir.oral history research office Columbia U., N.Y.C., 1959-68, assoc. dir., 1968-84, acting dir., 1980-82; lectr. sch. of library service Columbia U., N.Y.C., 1973-82, Barnard Coll., N.Y., 1978-79, Mt. Holyoke Coll., South Hadley, Mass., 1983; cons. oral history research office Columbia U., N.Y.C., 1985—. Editor: The Oral History Collection of Columbia University, 1979. Nat. officer exec. council Episc. Ch., N.Y.C., 1961-67. Mem. Oral History Assn. (council mem. 1978-81, 1983-84, v.p., pres. elect 1981-82, pres. 1982-83), Mt. Holyoke Coll. Alumnae Assn. (Sesquicentennial award 1988). Home: Amenia Union Rd Sharon CT 06069 Office: Columbia U Oral History Research Office Box 20 Butler Library New York NY 10027

MASON, JUDITH ANN, freelance writer; b. Newark, Dec. 27, 1945; d. Richard Algie and Mary Ann (Beneck) M. Diploma in legal sci., Spencerian Bus. Coll., 1965; BA, Northeastern Ill. U., 1984. Legal sec. Harney B. Stover, Atty., Milw., 1967-69, Robert P. O'Meara, Atty., Waukegan, Ill., 1969-70; sec. to pres. First Midwest Bank, Waukegan, 1970-72, asst. cashier, 1972-76; legal sec. Eugene M. Snarski, Atty., Waukegan, 1976-81; adminstrv. aide Lake County Forest Preserve Dist., Libertyville, Ill., 1981-89; freelance writer Tucson, 1989—; travel rep. Antioch (Ill.) Travel Agy., 1980-89, Advance Travel Agy., Zion, Ill., 1980-89; pub. speaker for various orgns., Lake County, Ill., 1984-89. Author: Why I Remember Yesterday, 1979, Haggadah (play), 1982; editor poetry column: Bank Man Magazine, 1972-75; contbg. article writer Compendum Mag. Tchr. Confraternity Christian Doctrine St. Patrick's Ch., Wadsworth, Ill., 1980-85; lector, eucharistic min. Prince of Peace Ch., Lake Villa, Ill., 1980-89; hospice vol. St. Therese Hosp., Waukegan, 1984; speech writer Grace Mary Stern lt. gubernatorial campaign, Lake County, 1984; voter registrar County of Lake, Ill., 1986-89; cons. pub. rels. Lake County Cir. Ct. Judge campaign, 1988, Presdl. Campaign Paul Simon. Recipient Brian F. Shehanhan Creative Writing award Am. Inst. Banking, 1972, 1st Place pub. speaking, 1974. Mem. AAUW (pub. rels. chair 1986, pres. Chain O'Lakes br., 1988-89, Ill. pub. info. award 1987), Northeastern Ill. U. Alumni Assn., NAFE, Pi Rho Zeta (pres. 1964-65). Democrat. Roman Catholic. Home and Office: 2255 W Orange Grove Rd #15106 Tucson AZ 85741

MASON, LINDA ANN, health company executive; b. Columbus, Ohio, Mar. 31, 1947; d. Lloyd Walter and Ann Elizabeth (Seely) M.; m. Clifford A. Bridges, Sept. 14, 1968 (div. Dec. 1982); 1 child, David Lloyd Bridges. BA summa cum laude, Ohio U., 1969; MA, Kutztown (Pa.) U., 1985. Ptnr. Thomas Brownback & Linda Mason, Allentown, Pa., 1982—; cons. Kutztown Crisis Pregnancy Ctr. Bd. dirs. Lehigh Valley Nursing Mothers. Mem. Internat. Soc. of Multiple Personality and Dissociation (co-presenter 1985, 86, 89), Christian Assn. Psychol. Studies, Lehigh Valley Psychol. Assn., Internat. Soc. Profl. Hypnosis, Mortar Bd., Phi Beta Kappa. Home: 1702 Walnut St Allentown PA 18104 Office: T Brownback and Linda Mason 1702 Walnut St Allentown PA 18104

MASON, LUCILE GERTRUDE, fund raiser, consultant; b. Montclair, N.J., Aug. 1, 1925; d. Mayne Seguine and Rachel (Entorf) M. AB, Smith Coll., 1947; MA, NYU, 1968, 76. Editor ABC, N.Y.C., 1947-51; asst. casting dir. Compton Advt., Inc., N.Y.C., 1951-55, dir. and head casting, 1955-65; conf. mgr. Camp Fire Girls, Inc., N.Y.C., 1965-66; exec. dir. Assn. of Jr. Leagues of Am. Inc., N.Y.C., 1966-68; dir. div. pub. affairs Girl Scouts U.S., N.Y.C., 1969-71; dir. pub. rels. YWCA of City of N.Y., 1971-73; dir. community rels. and devel. Girl Scout Coun. of Greater N.Y., N.Y.C., 1973-76; dir. devel. Montclair Kimberley Acad., Montclair, N.J., 1976-78, Ethical Culture Schs., N.Y.C. and Riverdale, N.Y., 1978-80; pres. Lucile Mason & Assocs., Montclair, 1980-83; devel. officer founds. and corps. Fairleigh Dickinson U., Rutherford, N.J., 1983-85; dir. devel. Whole Theatre, Inc., Montclair, 1985-86, YMWCA of Newark & Vicinity, 1986-88; v.p. adminstrn. and fin. devel. Inst. Religion and Health, N.Y.C., 1988—. Vol. bd. counselors Smith Coll., 1964-74, chmn. theatre com., mem. exec. com., 1969-74; vol. mem. Citizens Com. Presbyn Meml. Iris Garens of Montclair, 1980—; v.p. The Neighborhood Ctr., Inc., Montclair, 1987—; mem. fin. adv. com., fund devel. com. Girl Scout U.S. Coun. Greater Essex County, 1986—. Mem. Am. Women in Radio and TV (pres. N.Y.C. chpt. 1955-56), Community Agys. Pub. Rels. Assn. (membership chmn. 1973-76), Nat. Soc. Fund Raising Execs. (bd. dirs. N.J. chpt 1983-86), Pub. Rels. Soc. Am., Smith Coll. Club of Montclair (bd. dirs. 1986-90). Home: 142 N Mountain Ave Montclair NJ 07042 Office: Insts of Religion and Health 3 W 29th St New York NY 10001

MASON, MARILYN GELL, library administrator, writer, consultant; b. Chickasha, Okla., Aug. 23, 1944; d. Emmett D. and Dorothy (O'Bar) Killebrew; m. Carl L. Gell, Dec. 29 1965 (div. Oct. 1978); 1 son, Charles E.; m. Robert M. Mason, July 17, 1981. B.A., U. Dallas, 1966; M.L.S., N. Tex. State U., Denton, 1968; M.P.A., Harvard U., 1978. Librarian N.J. State Library, Trenton, 1968-69; head dept. Arlington County Pub. Library, Va., 1969-73; chief library program Metro Washington Council of Govts., 1973-77; dir. White House Conf. on Libraries and Info. Services, Washington, 1979-80; exec. v.p. Metrics Research Corp., Atlanta, 1981-82; dir. Atlanta-Fulton Pub. Library, Atlanta, 1982-86, Cleve. Pub. Library, 1986—; trustee Online Computer Library Ctr., 1984—; Evalene Parsons Jackson lectr. div. librarianship Emory U., 1981. Author: The Federal Role in Library and Information Services, 1983; editor: Survey of Library Automation in the Washington Area, 1977; project dir.: book Information for the 1980's, 1980. Bd. visitors Sch. Info. Studies, Syracuse U., 1981—, Sch. of Library and Info. Sci., U. Tenn.-Knoxville, 1983-85. Recipient Disting. Alumna award N. Tex. State U., 1979. Mem. ALA (mem. council 1986—), Am. Assn. Info. Sci., Ohio Library Assn., D.C. Library Assn. (pres. 1976-77). Home: 2888 Morley Rd Shaker Heights OH 44122 Office: Cleve Pub Libr 325 Superior Ave Cleveland OH 44114-1271

MASON, MARSHA, actress; b. St. Louis, Apr. 3, 1942; d. James and Jacqueline M.; m. Gary Campbell, 1965 (div.); m. Neil Simon, Oct. 25, 1973 (div.). Grad., Webster (Mo.) Coll. Mem.: cast Broadway and nat. tour Cactus Flower, 1968; other stage appearances include The Deer Park, 1967, The Indian Wants the Bronx, 1968, Happy Birthday, Wanda June, 1970, Private Lives, 1971, You Can't Take It With You, 1972, Cyrano de Bergerac, 1972, A Doll's House, 1972, The Crucible, 1972, The Good Doctor, 1973, King Richard III, 1974, The Heiress, 1975, Mary Stuart, 1982; one-woman show off-Broadway, The Big Love, Perry St. Theatre, 1988; film appearances include Blume in Love, 1973, Cinderella Liberty, 1973 (recipient Golden Globe award 1974, Acad. award nominee), Audrey Rose, 1977, The Goodbye Girl, 1977 (recipient Golden Globe award 1978, Acad. award nominee), The Cheap Detective, 1978, Promises in the Dark, 1979, Chapter Two, 1979 (Acad. award nominee), Only When I Laugh, 1981 (Acad. award nominee), Max Dugan Returns, 1982, Heartbreak Ridge, 1986; TV appearances include PBS series Cyrano de Bergerac, 1974, The Good Doctor, 1978, Lois Gibbs and the Love Canal, 1981, Surviving, 1985, Trapped in Silence, 1986, The Clinic, 1987, Dinner At Eight, 1989. Office: care Internat Creative Mgmt 40 W 57th St New York NY 10019*

MASON, MARTHA, elementary school teacher; b. Hope, Ark., Mar. 7, 1931; d. Sidney Rexford and Mattie Flora (Turrentine) McClung; m. James Luther Mason, Apr. 23, 1949; children: Carol Jean, Merry Lynn, Daniel Luther, Melody Ann. BA, U. Redlands, 1954; MEd in Sch. Mgmt., U. Laverne, 1986; postgrad., U. Calif., Berkeley. Cert. gen. elem., spl. edn./mental retardation, kindergarten, primary edn. tchr., Calif. Kindergarten tchr. Alvord Unified Sch. Dist., Riverside, Calif.; first grade tchr. McKinnely Sch., Redlands, Calif.; kindergarten tchr. Del Rosa Sch., San Bernardino, Calif.; elem. tchr. Vanalden Sch., Reseda, Calif.; guest lectr. U. Calif., Riverside, 1963-68, Riverside Community Coll., 1990—; mem. profl. orgn. educators Alvord Unified Sch. Dist. Adminstrv. mentor Tchr. Selection Com.; founding pres. Walter Knott PTA; past pres., officer Foothill Elem. Sch., Riverside, 1982-90; vol. drill team, co-advisor La Sierra High Sch., Riverside, 1956-58; vol. student tutor and parent counselor, 1955-90; mem. Raymond Temple PTA, Buena Park, Calif. Recipient 3 Drovla awards Alvord Unified Sch. Dist., 1983-89, also nominee Tchr. of Yr., 1985, 88, 89; Calif. State Tchr. ednl. sch. grantee, 1985-86. Republican. Baptist. Office: 8230 Wells Ave Riverside CA 92503

MASON, NANCY TOLMAN, state agency director; b. Buxton, Maine, Mar. 14, 1933; d. Ansel Robert and Kate Douglas (Libby) M. Grad., Bryant Coll., Providence, R.I., 1952; BA, U. Mass., Boston, 1977; postgrad., Inst. Governmental Services, Boston, 1985, Bryant Coll. The Auditor's Inst., Boston, 1987. Asst. to chief justice Mass. Superior Ct., Boston, 1964-68; community liaison Action for Boston Community Devel., Boston, 1968-73; mgmt. cons. East Boston Community Devel. Assn., Boston, 1973-78; asst. dir. Mass. Office of Deafness, Boston, 1978-86; dir. of contracts Mass. Rehab. Commn., Boston, 1986—; cons. Jos. A. Ryan Assocs., Boston and Orleans, Mass., 1981-86, WFCC Radio Sta., Chatham, Mass., 1987—. Author: Bromley-Heath Security Patrols, 1974, Reorganization of East Boston Community Development Corporation, 1976, How to Start Your Own Small Business, 1981. Vol. Am. Cancer Soc., Winchester, Mass., 1986—; cons. Boston Indian Council, 1972-73. Recipient Good Citizen award DAR, 1950, Community Service award Northeastern U.,1986 ;named one of Outstanding Young Women of Am. Montgomery Jr. C. of C., 1965. Mem. Nat. Assn. Female Execs., Mass. State Assn. of the Deaf. Democrat. Episcopalian. Office: Massachusetts Rehab Commn 20 Park Plaza Boston MA 02116

MASON, SHARON ANN, data processing search firm owner; b. Toledo, May 29, 1949; d. Donald Charles and Angeline (Walkowiak) M.; m. Charles Steven Kangas, June 13, 1970 (div. Aug. 1981); children: Sonja Kangas, Nicholas Kangas. Student, Mich. State U., 1967-70; student, U. Mich., 1970-71. V.p. northwest region Knauer Computer Consulting, Seattle, San Francisco, 1980-84; account mgr. The Manus Consulting Group, Seattle, 1985-86; profl. staffing specialist CAP GEMINI AM., Seattle, 1986-89; owner Mason Recruiting Group, Bellevue, Wash., 1989—. Mem. Soc. Info. Mgrs. Office: Mason Recruiting Group 1611 116th Ave NE Bellevue WA 98004-3094

MASQUELIER, SIBYL W., executive search consultant and executive; b. Canonsburg, Pa., July 8, 1946; d. David Jules and Grace Winston (Strickland) M.; m. John Ruffalo III, Aug. 31, 1968 (div. Apr. 1976); 1 child, Phaedra Danielle Ruffalo. BA, U. Pitts., 1967; MEd, U. Miami, 1969. Counselor, teaching asst. U. Miami, Coral Gables, 1967-69; personnel mgr. Div. Family Svcs., Miami, Fla., 1970-73; mgr. employment Miami Herald, 1974-76; v.p. Gordon Wahls Co., Media, Pa., 1976-85; pres. Exec. Resource Group, Portland, Maine, 1985—, Boston, 1985—; lectr. Cornell U., Ithaca, N.Y., 1979—, Soc. Women Engrs., Cherry Hill, N.J., 1980, New Eng. Newspaper Pubs., Providence, 1989, Poynter Inst. for Media Studies, 1989. Contbr. articles to profl. jours. Host mother EF Student Exchange, Cape Elizabeth, Maine, 1982—; mem. choir St. Albans Episcopal Ch., Cape Elizabeth, 1988—; mem. women's com. Portland Symphony Orch. Mem. Women in Communications, Computer Mus. (Boston) Fundraiser, Am. Newspaper Pubs. Assn. (affiliate), Boston C. of C., Portland (Maine) C. of C., Bangor C. of C. Republican. Office: Exec Resource Group PO Box 10257 Portland ME 04104

MASS, DONNA MARIE, occupational therapist, consultant; b. Montebello, Calif., May 4, 1954; d. Donald George and Lois Mae (Jacobson) M. Cert. emergency med. technician, Horry-Georgetown Tech. Sch., Conley, S.C., 1976; cert. occupational therapy asst., L.A. City Coll., 1979. Operating room technician Myrtle Beach (S.C.) Hosp., 1976-77, Conway (S.C.) Gen. Hosp., 1976-77, Presbyn. Intercommunity Hosp., Whittier, Calif., 1977-79; occupational therapist Del Amo Psychiat. Hosp., Torrance, Calif., 1979-80, Annette Levy & Assocs., Marina Del Rey, Calif., 1986-87, Universal Health Care Svcs., Santa Monica, Calif., 1987-88; occupational therapist, supr. outpatient therapy svcs. Casa Colina Rehab. Hosp., Pomona, Calif., 1980-86; owner, mgr., occupational therapist O.T. Connection, Crestline, Calif., 1988—; restorative feeding program cons. Med. Ctr. Convalescent Hosp., San Bernardino, Palm Terrace Convalescent Hosp., Riverside, Calif., 1988—. Trustee Unity Christ Ch., Riverside, Calif., 1987, pres., 1988, sec., 1989; facilitator A Course in Miracles study group, Riverside, Crestline, 1988—; sponsor Youth of Unity, Riverside, 1989. Sgt. USAF, 1972-76. Mem. Am. Occupational Therapy Assn., Calif. Occupational Therapy Assn., Women in Networking. Democrat. Home and Office: 170 Wylerhorn PO Box 531 Crestline CA 92325

MASSAR, R(UTH) LISA, cardiac nurse; b. N.Y.C., Dec. 14, 1962; d. Paul and Marilyn Iris (Koscis) Peskin; m. Robert C. Massar, June 26, 1988. AAS, Rockland Community Coll., Monsey, N.Y., 1982; diploma, Englewood Hosp. Nursing Sch., N.J., 1985; grad. summa cum laude, St. Peter's Coll., 1990. Staff nurse Cardiac Surgery Step Down Unit, Hackensack, N.J.; patient svcs. coord. Home Nutritional Support, Pinebrook, N.J.; staff nurse, per diem Hackensack Med. Ctr. Van Houten scholar St. Peter's Coll. 1986, 87, 88. Mem. NAFE, Onocology Nurses Soc., Nightingale Soc. Nursing, Sigma Theta Tau. Office: Hackensack Med Ctr Hackensack NJ 07631

MASSELINK, CARLA ANN, stockbroker; b. Holland, Mich., June 21, 1943; d. Vernon C. Reidsma and Ruth I. (Palmer) Meppelink; m. Bruce A. Masselink, June 18, 1966; children: Ilse K., Reid A., Braden J. BA magna cum laude, Hope Coll., 1965; postgrad., U. Mich., 1966-68. French tchr. Grosse Ile (Mich.) Public Schs., 1966-67, Ann Arbor Public Schs., 1967-69; stock broker/fin. planner Royal Alliance Assocs., Inc., Holland, 1984—. Pres. Holland Public Schs. Edn. Found., 1987; incorporator Edn. Found., Holland, 1984, chmn. publicity on edn., 1986-88. Music scholarship Hope Coll., 1961. Mem. Investment Dynamics Club (pres. 1989—). Republican. Home: 660 Graafschap Rd Holland MI 49423 Office: Royal Alliance Assocs Inc Corp 603 E 16th St Holland MI 49423

MASSENGALE, SHARI LOUISE, air force officer; b. Red Lodge, Mont., Dec. 3, 1958; d. John Leonard Korpela and Lorna May (Zook) Carlson; m. James Douglas Braden, Aug. 5, 1980 (div. 1984); m. Robert Michael Massengale, Aug. 9, 1985; stepchildren: Michael, Matthew; children: Benjamin, Meagan. BS magna cum laude, U. Md., 1982; MA in Human Resources, Webster U., 1987. Enlisted USAF, 1977, commd. 2d lt., 1983, advanced through grades to capt., 1987; aircraft maintenance supt. 922d Strategic Reconnaissance Squadron, Hellinikon AFB, Greece, 1981-83; aircraft maintenance officer 433d Field Maintenance Squadron, Altus AFB, Okla., 1983-86; resource mgr. Hdqrs. Mil. Airlift Command, Scott AFB, Ill., 1986—. Mem. St. Clair County Hist. Soc., Belleville, Ill., 1986—, St. Louis Zoo Friends, 1986—. Mem. Maintenance Officers Assn., Airlift Assn. Episcopalian.

MASSEY, DOROTHY BUTLER (MRS. GUY M. MASSEY), accountant; b. LaFayette, Ga.; d. R. Maihue and Cora (Sisemore) Butler; student U. Chattanooga, 1949; LL.B., Atlanta Law Sch., 1957, LL.M., 1958; B.B.A., Ga. State Coll., 1966; m. Guy M. Massey, Feb. 21, 1953. Accountant Gulf Oil Corp., Chattanooga, 1944-53, Crawford and Porter, Atlanta, 1953-54; accountant Baker Audio Assos., 1955-70, sec.-treas., 1955-70, also dir.; accountant Glenkaron Assos., Inc., 1955-68, sec.-treas., 1957-68; pres. Massey Co., 1971—, also dir.; pres. Profl. Credit Bur., Inc., 1977—; real estate agt. Shotz Assos. Mem. Am. Soc. Women Accountants (dir.), Ga. Soc. C.P.A.'s, Notaries Pub. Assn., Bus. and Profl. Women, Kappa Delta. Home: 1534 Peachtree Battle Ave NW Atlanta GA 30327

MASSEY, KATHY DIANE, designer; b. Chattanooga, June 5, 1964; d. Jack Travis and Marion Glenda (Clark) M. BS, U. Tenn., 1987. Mgr., contractor Kitchen and Bath Creations, Chattanooga. Mem. NAFE, Am. Soc. Interior Designers. Home: PO Box 90003 Chattanooga TN 37412

MASSIE, ELAINE CATHERINE, substance abuse treatment center administrator; b. Waukegan, Ill., Sept. 4, 1944; d. Casimir Frank and Sophia Elizabeth (Paluckis) Walczak; m. Stephen LeRoy Massie; Aug. 5, 1973; 1 child, Nicholas Evan. BS in Nursing, St. Xavier Coll., 1969; MBA, U. Phoenix, 1987. RN; cert. alcoholism counselor. Nurse clinician Parkside Luth. Hosp., Park Ridge, Ill., 1972-79; coord. substance abuse svcs. Luth. Gen. Hosp., Park Ridge, 1979-84; program dir. Parkside Lodge of Colo., Thornton, 1989—, youth program mgr., 1984-86, concurrent mgr., 1986-89; instr. Wester U., Aurora, Colo., 1990, Parks Jr. Coll., Thornton, 1989—; cons. ch. orgns., 1982—; trainer Addiction Orgns., Ill, Colo., 1979—, Parkside Med. Svcs., Ill., 1980—. Sec. Parks and Recreation Adv. Bd., Broomfield, Colo., 1988; mem. speakers bur. Luth. Ch., Colo., 1988—; vol. Mile High Coun. on Alcoholism, Colo., 1985; continuing edn. com. Ill. Alcoholism Cert. Bd., Ill., 1979. Mem. NAFE, Eating Disorders Profls. of Colo., Sigma Theta Tau. Home: 1270 E Third Ave Broomfield CO 80020 Office: Parkside Lodge Colo 8801 Lipan St Thornton CO 80221

MASSON, GAYL ANGELA, airline pilot; b. L.A., Feb. 5, 1951; d. Jack Watson and Margaret Jean (Evans) M.; m. Joseph Dominic Statuto, Apr. 18, 1987. BFA, U. So. Calif., 1970, MA, 1972, MPA, 1975, PhD, 1976. Lic. airline transport, seaplane, glider pilot, flight instr., flight engr. Pilot Antelope Valley Land Investment Co., Century City, Calif., 1972; ROTC flight instr. Claire Walters Flight Acad., Santa Monica, Calif., 1973; flight instr. Golden West Airways, Santa Monica, 1974; co-pilot Express Airways, LaMoore Naval Air Sta., Calif., 1975-76; charter pilot, instr. Shaw Airmotive, Orange County Airport, Calif., 1976; flight engr. Am. Airlines, Dallas, 1976-79, co-pilot, 1979-86, capt., 1986—. Contbr. articles to profl. publs. Participant Powder Puff Derby, Angel Derby, Pacific Air Race and others. First woman type-rated on Boeing 747; also type-rated on DC-10, DC-9, Boeing 767, Boeing 757. Mem. Airline Pilots Assn., Internat. Soc. Women Airline Pilots (charter), Ninety-Nines (past v.p. Smo Bay chpt.).

MASSY, PATRICIA GRAHAM BIBBS (MRS. RICHARD OUTRAM MASSY), social worker, author; b. Newbury, Eng., Mar. 21, 1918; came to U.S., 1963, naturalized, 1969; d. Oswald Graham and Dorothy (French) Bibbs; m. Richard Outram Massy, July 22, 1944 (dec. Aug. 1986); children: Patricia Lynn Massy Holmes, Julie Suzanne, Shaun Adele Massy Brink. BA, U. B.C., 1941, MSW, 1962. Lic. religious sci. practitioner. With B.C. Welfare Field Svc., Vancouver, Kamloops, Abbottsford, 1942-44; social worker Brandon Welfare Dept., Man., Can., 1945; with Children's Aid Soc., Vancouver, 1948-62; supr. Dept. Pub. Social Svc., L.A., 1963-70, staff devel. specialist-mgmt., 1970-77; lectr. colls. and seminars; author, publisher: A Study Guide for a Course in Miracles, 1984; One, 1985. Mem. AAUW (treas. 1970), Nat. Assn. Social Workers, Alpha Phi. Mem. Religious Sci. Ch. Home: 18936 Upper Cow Creek Rd Azalea OR 97410

MASTEN, ANN STRINGFELLOW, child development educator; b. Augusta, Ga., Jan. 27, 1951; d. Charles Chester and Ruth (Graham) Stringfellow; m. Stephen Bruce Masten, Dec. 30, 1971; children: Carrie Lowe, Madeline Russell. AB cum laude, Smith Coll., Northampton, Mass., 1973; PhD, U. Minn., Mpls., 1982. Lic. cons. psychologist. Rsch. asst. NIMH, Bethesda, Md., 1973-76; intern Neuropsychiat. Inst. UCLA, 1981-82; rsch. assoc. U. Minn., Mpls., 1983-86, asst. prof. Inst. Child Devel., 1986—, adj. asst. prof. dept. psychology, 1983—, McKnight-Land Grant prof., 1988-91; prin. investigator, dir. Project Competence, U. Minn., 1988—; cons. Wilder Child Guidance Clinic, 1989—, clin. child psychologist, 1983—; asst. program dir. residential treatment ctr. for mentally disabled adults Ramsey County, Lake Owasso Residence, 1978. Co-editor Risk and Protective Factors in the Development of Psychopathology, 1990; contbr. articles to profl. jours., chpts. to books. NIMH tng. fellow, 1976-79, Eva O. Miller fellow U. Minn., Mpls., 1979-80; grantee W.T. Grant Found., 1983-89, NIMH, 1983-91. Mem. Soc. Rsch. in Child Devel., Am. Psychol. Assn., Soc. Rsch. on Adolescence, Soc. Traumatic Stress Studies, Am. Psychol. Soc. Office: Inst Child Devel U Minn 51 E River Rd Minneapolis MN 55455

MASTER, LORI ELIZABETH, financial analyst; b. Camden, N.J., Apr. 30, 1962; d. Alan Harold and Barbara (Berezow) M. BA in Speech Communication and Internat. Politics, Pa. State U., 1984; postgrad., Fordham U., 1988—. Fl. mgr. Lord and Taylor, N.Y.C., 1984-85; group coord. Radio Page Am., N.Y.C., 1985-86; program coord. Pvt. Satellite Network, N.Y.C., 1986; cons. Goshow Assocs., N.Y.C., 1986-88; portfolio asst. Equitable Capital Mgmt. Corp., N.Y.C., 1987-88, internat. asst., 1988—. City chmn. alumni admissions com. Pa. State U., N.Y.C., 1986-89. Mem. NAFE, Penn State Alumni Club N.Y.C. (pres. 1988—), Internat. Platform Assn., Alpha Phi Omega, Beta Sigma Beta. Republican. Jewish. Club: Pa. State of N.Y.C. Home: 108 Willow Ave Apt 2R Hoboken NJ 07030 Office: Equitable Capital Mgmt Corp 1221 Ave of the Americas Fl 32 New York NY 10020

MASTERS, BEDA DORIS, elementary educator; b. McComb, Miss., Feb. 14, 1942; d. Robert C. and Selma Doris (Barksdale) Moak; m. Terry Labe Masters Sr., Oct. 12, 1940; children: Terry Labe Jr., Karen Denise Masters Ishee. AS, S.W. Miss. Jr. Coll., 1971; BS, U. So. Miss., 1975; M in Edn., William Carey Coll., 1981. Cert. elem. educator, Miss. Teller 1st Nat. Bank, McComb, 1971-72, Laurel, Miss., 1972-73; tchr. Jones County Schs., Laurel, 1975—; cons. Longaberger Baskets, Laurel, 1988—; presenter Miss. Reading Assn. Conf., 1986. Mem. YWCA. Mem. Internat. Reading Coun., Miss. Reading Coun., Laurel-Jones County Reading Coun. (pres. 1980-81, membership dir. 1988—), Assn. Excellence in Edn., Phi Theta Kappa, Phi Kappa Phi, Kappa Delta Pi, Delta Kappa Gamma (Zeta Mu state chpt., corr. sec. 1986-88). Baptist. Home: Rte 12 Box 590 Laurel MS 39440

MASTERS, ELAINE THERESE, audio-video business owner; b. Columbia, S.C., Sept. 8, 1951; d. Edward John and Emilie Therese (Nawrocki) M. AA in Psychology, Morris County Coll., 1971; BS in Bus. Mgmt., Union for Experimenting Colls. and Univs., 1988. Fin. asst. J.J. Newberry and Co., Dover, N.J., 1966-69; dept. rep. Dept. Drug Abuse Morris County, Morristown, N.J., 1970-71; asst. to head ednl. psychology dept. Ariz. State U., Tempe, 1971; supr. quality control Gen. Semiconductor, Tempe, 1972; mgr. personnel Los Compadres Restaurant, San Diego, 1973-80; office mgr. W.C. Matz Inc., Escondido, Calif., 1980-82; exec. asst. to pres. Gold Medal Pools Inc., Escondido, 1982-86; co-owner, mgr. Masters Video, San Diego, 1987-88; spl. projects coord. Constrn. Specifications Inst., 1988—; adminstrv. asst. Union for Experimenting Colls. and Univs., San Diego, 1988; coordinator spl. projects San Diego Constrn. Specifications Inst., author, originator Fair Procedures Manual. Mem. Zool. Soc. San Diego, 1980, Greenpeace, Washington, 1982, Cousteau Soc., Norfolk, Va., 1985, Amnesty Internat., N.Y.C., 1986. Recipient Record of Performance cert. San Diego County, 1983. Mem. Nat. Assn. Women Constrn. (cert.), NAFE. Republican. Roman Catholic.

MASTERSON, DEBORAH, financial services executive; b. N.Y.C., Sept. 14, 1953; d. C. Parke and Marie (O'Connor) Masterson; 1 child, Elizabeth. Student, Queensborough Coll., Coll. of Ins., N.Y.C. Mgr. CIGNA, N.Y.C.; asst. v.p. Bertholon Rowland Corp., N.Y.C. Mem. P.I.A., Nat. Bus. Honor Soc., Alpha Beta Gamma. Republican. Roman Catholic. Office: 16 Jay St New York NY 10013

MASTERSON, PATRICIA O'MALLEY, publications editor, writer; b. Worcester, Mass., May 15, 1952; d. Paul Francis and Dorothy M. (O'Malley) M. BFA, Emerson Coll., 1974; MA, Goddard Coll., 1980. Reporter, photographer Patriot Newspaper, Webster, Mass., 1975-78; pub. relations dir. Mt. Pleasant Hosp., Lynn, Mass., 1980-84; pubs. editor Ocean Spray Cranberries, Inc., Plymouth, Mass., 1984-89; mktg. communications coord. Groundwater Tech., Norwood, Mass., 1989—; freelance writer newspaper and mag. articles, 1974—. Mem. adv. bd. Ad Com mga.; contbr. numerous articles to newspapers, mags.; stringer Hanover (Mass.) Mariner Newspaper, 1987-89. Bd. dirs. Cambridge (Mass.) YWCA; publicity com. United Way, 1987, Healthworks; player Abington, Weymouth, Mass., Softball Leagues; vol. Rosie's Homeless Shelter, Boston, 1987—. Recipient Amy England award YWCA, 1986, Green Eyeshade award Internat. Assn. Bus. Communicators, 1987, Employee Pub. 2d Place award Cooperative Info. Fair, 1987, 88, Membership Mag. award Cooperative Info. Fair, 1988; named One of Outstanding Young Women in Am. Jaycees, 1983. Mem. South Shore Ad Club (publicity com., 9th Wave award 1987, 89), Women in Communications, Coop. Communicators Assn. (1st place employee publ. award 1987, 3d place mag. award 1989). Home: 132 Union St Rockland MA 02370

MASTROBERTE, VIOLET MARIE, nursing administrator; b. Englewood, N.J., Jan. 26, 1932; d. Dominick John and Alsista Viola (Krone) M. BS in Nursing, Fairleigh Dickinson U., 1961, MS in Pub. Adminstrn., 1983; postgrad., N.Y.U., 1979. RN, N.J., N.Y. Various positions Columbia Presby. Med. Ctr., N.Y.C., 1954-71, dir. nursing, assoc. dir., 1971-84, coord. nursing systems, instr., 1974-79; staff builder supplemental agys., Hackensack and Paramus, N.J., 1979-80; asst. dir. nursing Bergen Pines County Hosp., Paramus, 1980-86, assoc. dir. nursing, 1987-88, asst. exec. dir. nursing, 1988, also bd. dirs.; adj. instr. Grad. Sch. Nursing Seaton Hall U. Mem. Am. Nurses Assn., Am. Soc. Profl. Adminstrs., Internat. Pers. Mgmt. Assn., NAFE, Soc. Nursing Profls., N.J. Nursing Assn., Am. Hosp. Assn., N.J. Hosp. Assn., N.J. Nursing Execs., AONE, Sigma Theta Tau, Phi Alpha Alpha. Home: 43 Brook St Bergenfield NJ 07621 Office: Bergen Pines County Hosp East Ridge Paramus NJ 07662

MASURY, JULIA ANNE, daycare center and pre-school director; b. Tampa, Fla., Nov. 24, 1962; d. Werner Ludwig and Beryl Mary (Meakin) Bachmann; m. Mark Allen Masury, Aug. 19, 1984; 1 child, Meghan Brittany. AA, Farmingham (Mass.) State Coll., 1981; BS in Edn. cum laude, Framingham (Mass.) State U., 1984. Spl. needs counselor Camp Lymelight, Accord, N.Y., 1982; pre-sch. tchr. Bon Soigne Childrens Centres, Natick, Mass., 1983; head tchr. Raggedy Ann & Andy Pre-Sch., Framingham, 1984-86; dir. Clubhouse Day Care, Inc., Derry, N.H., 1987—; voting del. Kappa Delta Pi Convocation, Montreal, Can., 1984; program coord. Clubhouse Day Care, Inc., Derry, 1988—. Mem. team Pre-Can. Engagement Encounter, St. Bridge's Ch., Framingham, 1983-86; charity promoter Sunset Point Vacation House, Papa Gino's of Am., Dedham, Mass., 1984-86. Hillsborough Community Coll. scholar, 1980-82. Mem. Nat. Assn. for the Edn. Young Children (speaker 1989), Kappa Delta Pi (v.p. Kappa Chi chpt. 1983-85, Leadership Recognition award 1984, 86). Roman Catholic. Office: Clubhouse Day Care Inc 1 E Broadway Derry NH 03038

MASZKIEWICZ, RUTH AGNES, nursing educator, university administrator; b. Pitts., July 24, 1928; d. Sylvester Patrick and Alvina Ann (Munch) Conlogue; m. Steve J. Maszkiewicz, Feb. 2, 1954 (dec.); children: Stephen, Valli, Daniel, Mark, Suzanne, Amy. Nursing diploma, Braddock Gen. Hosp., Pitts., 1950; BS in Nursing Edn., Duquesne U., 1954, MEd, 1969; PhD, U. Pitts., 1977. Staff nurse Braddock Gen. Hosp., 1950; asst. head nurse Montefiore Hosp., Pitts., 1951, head nurse, 1952-54, supr. nursing, 1955; pvt. practice nursing Pitts., 1956-66; instr. nursing Presbyn.-Univ. Hosp., Pitts., 1967-72, chmn. dept. nursing, 1968-72; instr. nursing U. Pitts., 1972-73, asst. prof. nursing, 1973-77, assoc. prof., dir. grad. program med.-surg. nursing, from 1978; now dean coll. nursing Duquesne U., Pitts.; field dir. Appalachian Health Team Project, Ky., 1975-76, mem. fundraising and med. supplies com., Pitts., 1977-78; educator com. long-range planning Gateway Sch. Dist., 1981-82; chmn. Commn. on Nursing, Pitts., 1974-75. Author: The Presbyterian Hospital of Pittsburgh: A Critical Analysis of Its Early History, 1893-1927, The Continuing Heritage of a Hospital that Cares: Presbyterian University Hospital of Pittsburgh, 1928 to the Mid 70s. Mem. AACCN, ANA, Internat. History Nursing Soc., Nat. League Nursing, Pa. Nurses Assn., Carroll F. Reynolds Hist. Soc., Sigma Theta Tau (Leadership in Nursing Edn. award 1981), Alpha Tau Delta, Phi Delta Gamma. Democrat. Roman Catholic. Office: Duquesne U Coll Nursing 600 Forbes Ave Pittsburgh PA 15282*

MATALAMAKI, MARGARET MARIE, educator, consultant; b. Hampton, Iowa, May 10, 1921; d. Byron Jacob and Vera Margaret (Wheaton) Myers; m. William Matalamaki, Sept. 11, 1942 (dec. 1978); children—Judith Marie Gerlinger-Thiem, William Micheal. A.A., Itasca Community Coll., 1941; student U. Minn., 1941-42, 72. High sch. instr. Sch. Dist. 1, Bigfork, Minn., 1942-45, U. Minn. Sch. Agr., Grand Rapids, Minn., 1955-58; high sch. substitute Sch. Dist. 318, Grand Rapids, 1967-69; vocat. instr. Itasca Community Coll., Grand Rapids, 1970-78. bd. dirs. Blandin Found., Grand Rapids, trustee, 1981—, v.p., 1985-87, chmn. 1988—; bd. dirs. Christus Home, Grand Rapids; cons. to Keewatin Community Devel. Corp., Grand Rapids, 1985; mem. consumer adv. bd. Land of Lakes Inc., St. Paul, 1984-87, chmn. 1986-87; pres. Kooch-Itasca Action Council, Grand Rapids, 1981-84; adv. council mem. Women's Econ. Devel. Corp., Mpls., 1984-87; bd. dirs. Itasca Meml. Hosp., 1975-85, Itasca County Nursing Home, 1975-85, No. Itasca Nursing Home, 1982-85, Itasca County Social Services, 1975-85; county commr. Itasca County, 1981-85; legis. coordinator Luth. Ch. Am., 1983-86, staff, advocacy coordinator Minn. Synod, 1983-86; mem. adv. council Inst. Agr., Forestry and Home Econ. U. Minn., 1981-90; 4-H club leader, Esko, Minn., 1945-49, Grand Rapids, Minn., 1949-63; home extension leader, Esko, 1945-49, Grand Rapids, 1949-63; county fair judge No. Minn., 1950-84; bd. dirs. United Way Grand Rapids, 1980-84; mem. Grand Rapids Citizen's League, 1980—, Minn. Women for Agr., 1982-88, Joint Religious Legis. Coalition, Mpls., 1977-78, U. Minn. Nat. Alumni bd. dirs., 1987—, U. Minn. 4H Found. bd. dirs., 1987—, U. Minn. North Cen., Research Station Found./Fund, 1987— ; bd. dirs. Luth. Social Serives Minn., 1986—, vice chair, mem. adv. bd. Luth. Social Services North Eastern Minn., 1986-87 ; mem. Minn. Child Abuse Team, 1986-87; pres. Luth. Ch. Women, 1959-62, Luth. Ch. Women Synodical Bd., 1972-76, dist. chmn., 1964-65; com. mem. Commn. for a New Luth. Ch., 1985, chmn. transition team, 1986-87 , mem. exec. com. Synod Council, 1976-79; trustee Gustavus Adolphus Coll. Bd., 1988—; dir., clinic bd. govs. U. Minn. Hosp. and Clinic, 1990—. Recipient Good Govt. award Grand Rapids Jr. C. of C., 1977, Good Neighbor award WCCO Radio, 1976, Outstanding Achievement award U. Minn., 1989. Mem. Grand Rapids C. of C. (life). Mem. LWV. Club: PEO (pres., sec. 1964—). Avocations: cross country skiing, canoeing, traveling. Home and Office: 727 Mishawaka Shores Dr Grand Rapids MN 55744

MATANOSKI, GENEVIEVE MURRAY, physician, educator; b. Salem, Mass., Aug. 26, 1930; d. James J. and Genevieve E. (McNally) Murray; children: Gregory, Vincent, Dennis, Mary Katherine, Joseph. A.B., Radcliffe Coll., 1951; M.D., Johns Hopkins U., 1955, M.P.H., 1962, Dr.P.H., 1964. Diplomate: Am. Bd. Preventive Medicine. Research asst. Johns Hopkins Sch. Medicine, Balt., 1955; intern in pediatrics Johns Hopkins Hosp., Balt., 1955-56; asst. resident pediatrics Johns Hopkins Sch. Medicine, 1956-57, research asst. epidemiology, 1957-59, asst. prof. epidemiology sch. hygiene and pub. health, 1964-69, tng. fellow in pub. health, 1962-64, assoc. prof. epidemiology, 1969-76, coord., evaluator spl. projects, Evaluation and Biostats. Ctr. of Regional Med. Program, 1970-73; assoc. prof. sch. health svcs. Johns Hopkins U., 1973-76, prof. epidemiology sch. hygiene and pub. health, 1976—, program dir. occupational and environ. epidemiology sch. hygiene and pub. health, 1978—; pediatrician Out-Patient Dept. Johns Hopkins Hosp., 1957—; instr. preventive medicine U. Md., Balt., 1967-69, assoc. prof., 1970-76; instr. epidemiology U. Minn., Mpls., 1981-82; mem. teaching faculty Internat. Agy. for Research on Cancer, U. Occupational and

Environ. Health, Kitakyushu, Japan, 1982. Contbr. articles to profl. jours. Fellow Am. Coll. Preventive Medicine (cert. specialist 1973); mem. AAAS, Am. Coll. Preventive Medicine, Internat. Epidemiological Assn., Am. Epidemiol. Soc., Am. Pub. Health Assn., N.Y. Acad. Sci., Air and Waste Mgmt. Assn., Soc. Epidemiol. Rsch., Internat. Epidemiol. Assn., Assn. Tchrs. Preventive Medicine, Soc. Occupational and Environ. Health, Delta Omega. Office: Johns Hopkins Univ Sch Hygiene and Pub Health 615 N Wolfe St Baltimore MD 21205

MATASAR, ANN B., business educator, university dean; b. N.Y.C., June 27, 1940; d. Harry and Tillie (Simon) Bergman; m. Robert Matasar, June 9, 1962; children—Seth Gideon, Toby Rachel. A.B., Vassar Coll., 1962; M.A., Columbia U., 1964,, Ph.D., 1968; M.M. in Fin., Northwestern U., 1977. Assoc. prof. Mundelein Coll., Chgo., 1965-78; prof., dir. Ctr. for Bus. and Econ. Elmhurst Coll., Elmhurst, Ill., 1978-84; dean, prof. mgmt. Walter E. Heller Coll. Bus. Adminstrn. Roosevelt U., Chgo., 1984—; dir. Corp. Responsibility Group, Chgo., 1978-84; chmn. long range planning Ill. Bar Assn., 1982-83; mem. edn. com. Ill. Commn. on the Status of Women, 1978-81. Author: Corporate PACS and Federal Campaign Financing Laws: Use or Abuse of Power?, 1986; (with others) Research Guide to Women's Studies, 1974. Contbr. articles to profl. jours. Dem. candidate 1st legis. dist., Ill. State Senate, no. suburbs of Chgo., 1972; mem. Dem. exec. com., New Trier Twp., Ill., 1972-76; research dir., acad. advisor Congressman Abner Mikva, Ill., 1974-76; bd. dirs. Ctr. Ethics and Corp. Policy. Named Chgo. Woman of Achievement Mayor of Chgo., 1978. Fellow AAUW; mem. Am. Polit. Sci. Assn., Midwest Bus. Adminstrn. Assn., Acad. Mgmt., Women's Caucus for Polit. Sci. (pres. 1980-81), John Howard Assn. (bd. dirs.), Beta Gamma Sigma. Democrat. Jewish. Office: Roosevelt U Coll Bus Adminstrn 430 S Michigan Ave Chicago IL 60605-1394

MATASOVIC, MARILYN ESTELLE, business executive; b. Chgo., Jan. 7, 1946; d. John Lewis and Stella (Butkauskas) M. Student, U. Colo. Sch. Bus., 1963-69. Owner, pres. UTE Trail Ranch, Ridgway, Colo., 1967—; pres. MEM Equipment Co., Mokena, Ill., 1979—; v.p., treas. Marlin Corp., Ridgway, 1968—, Linmar Corp., Mokena, 1976—; ptnr. Universal Welding Supply Co., New Lenox, Ill., 1964—; v.p. OXO Welding Equipment Co, Inc., New Lenox, 1964—. Co-editor newsletters. U.S. rep. World Hereford Conf., 1964, 68, 76, 80, 84. Mem. Am. Hereford Aux. (charter, bd. dirs.), Am. Hereford Assn., Colo. Hereford Aux., Ill. Hereford Aux. (v.p. 1969-70), Internat. Hereford Orgn., U. Colo. Alumni Assn.

MATCHETTE, PHYLLIS LEE, editor; b. Dodge City, Kans., Dec. 24, 1921; d. James Edward and Rose Mae (McMillan) Collier; A.B. in Journalism, U. Kans., 1943; m. Robert Clarke Matchette, Dec. 4, 1943; children: Marta Susan, James Michael. Reporter, Dodge City Daily Globe, 1944; tchr. English, Dodge City Jr. High Sch., 1944-45; asst. instr. Coll. Liberal Arts, U. Kans., Lawrence, 1945-47; dir. Christian edn. Southminster United Presbyn. Ch., Prairie Village, Kans., 1963-65; editor publs., dir. communications, supr. in-plant printing Village United Presbyn. Ch., Prairie Village, 1965-86 ; freelance journalist, 1987—. Hon. mem. Commn. of Ecumenical Mission and Relations, hon. mem. Program Agy., Presbyn. Ch., U.S.A.; ordained elder Village Presbyn. Ch., 1964, elected elder, 1988—. Mem. Women in Communications, Kans. U. Dames (pres. 1946), Kansas City Young Matrons, P.E.O., Alpha Chi Omega (pres. edn. found. Phi chpt. 1951). Republican. Club: Order of Eastern Star. Home: 7405 El Monte Rd Prairie Village KS 66208

MATERIA, KATHLEEN PATRICIA AYLING, nurse; b. Jersey City, Nov. 7, 1954; d. Donald Anthony and Muriel Cecilia (Joyce) Ayling; m. Francis Peter Materia, June 5, 1983. BS in Nursing, Fairleigh Dickinson U., 1976. RN. Critical care nurse Palisades Gen. Hosp., North Bergen, N.J., 1976—, grad. nurse, 1976-77; nurse CCU, North Hudson Hosp., Weehawken, N.J., 1977-78. Mem. Alpha Sigma Tau. Democrat. Roman Catholic. Avocations: bowling, dancing.

MATEVICH, BRANISLAVA, pharmaceutical sales professional; b. Lingen/Ems, Germany, Mar. 28, 1949; came to U.S., 1954; d. Miodrag and Katarina (Sokačich) Todorovič; m. Peter Michael Matevich, Oct. 7, 1972; children: Sava, Elizabeta. BS in Psychology, Loyola U., Chgo., 1980. Med. technologist Skokie (Ill.) Valley Hosp., 1971-73; supr. clin. chemistry Ill. Masonic Med. Ctr., Chgo., 1973-80; sales rep. Worthington Diagnostics, Freehold, N.J., 1980-82, Sigma Chem., St. Louis, Mo., 1982—; insp. CAP, Chgo., 1981-82. Editor: Cookbook Sampler, 1985. Mem. Springfield Arts Coun., 1986-90; head Sunday sch. St. Anthony Hellenic Orthodox Ch., Springfield, 1987-89; bd. dirs. Springfield Schs. PTO, 1988-90. Mem. AAUW (bd. mem. 1987-89), Nat. Aphasia Orgn. Home: 1202 Vermont Ct Naperville IL 60540

MATHÉ, LYNDA ANNE PALOMA, educator; b. Hackensack, N.J., Mar. 25, 1948; d. Clarence Eugene and Rose (Heinz) M.; m. Richard Roy Zila (div. 1981). BA, Fairleigh Dickinson U., 1969; MA, Columbia U., 1971. Owner, dir. Mathé Dance Studio, Clifton, N.J., 1973—; program dir., tchr. Meadowlands Area YMCA, Rutherford, N.J., 1979-80; program coord., tchr. Cultural Homestay Inst., Roseville, Calif., 1981-84; tchr. Calif. Youth Authority, Nevada City, 1984—; program developer, instr. Nevada Union Adult Edn., Grass Valley, Calif., 1984—; adj. prof. Essex Community Coll., Newark, 1972-76, Dutchess Coll., Poughkeepsie, N.Y., 1974-76, Sussex County Coll., Peekskill, N.Y., 1975-76, Sullivan County Coll., 1975-76; publicity dir. Rainbow Theatre Co., Nevada City, 1986-89; publicity dir., instr. Dance Drum Workshop, Grass Valley, 1988—; organizer, performer STARS (Short Term Artists in Residency), Nevada City, 1987—; broadcaster Sta. KNCO, Grass Valley, 1988. Columnist Sr. Life, 1989. Guest broadcaster Sta. KYMR, Nevada City, and KOBO, Yuba City, Calif., 1984-88. Recipient award Nevada County Arts Coun., 1984, 85, 87, cert. of artistry Nat. Assn. Dance and Assoc. Artists, 1975. Mem. AAUW. Office: 529 Linden Ave Grass Valley CA 95945

MATHER, JENNIE POWELL, endocriniologist, cell biologist; b. Louisville, Feb. 8, 1948; d. John Robert and Hannah (Trigg) M. BA, Brandeis U., 1969; PhD, U. Calif., San Diego, 1975. Postdoctoral fellow U. Calif., San Diego, 1975-78; exch. scientist NIH INSERM, Lyon, France, 1978-79; scientist The Population Coun., N.Y.C., 1979-84; asst. prof. The Rockefeller U., N.Y.C., 1979-84; sr. scientist Genentech, Inc., South San Francisco, Calif., 1984-88, staff scientist, 1988—; industry cons., 1980-84. Author: Mammalian Cell Culture, 1984; editor Cytotechnology, 1989—, In Vitro Rapid Communications, 1987—; patentee in field; contbr. articles to profl. jours. Named Fohs Found. Fellow, 1969-70. Mem. Endocrine Soc., Tissue Culture Assn. (program com. mem.), Am. Soc. for Cell Biology (com. for women in cell biology), AAAS. Office: Genentech Inc 460 Point San Bruno Blvd South San Francisco CA 94080

MATHER, PATRICIA LYNN, psychologist, educator, lecturer; b. Glen Ridge, N.J., Mar. 20, 1950; d. Robert Isaac and Jocelyn Marie (Northfield) M. BA, U. Iowa, 1972; MS, Purdue U., 1975, PhD, 1979. Lic. psychologist, N.Y., Ill. Asst. tchr. Purdue Presch. Labs., West Lafayette, Ind., 1972-74; rsch. asst. Purdue U., West Lafayette, 1974-75, grad. lectr., 1975-78; vis. instr. Iowa State U., Ames, 1978-79; assoc. prof. Utica (N.Y.) Coll., Syracuse U., 1979-86, Northeastern Ill. U., Chgo., 1986-90; pvt. practice Arlington Child Psychology Ctr., Arlington Heights, Ill., 1989—; cons. Hospice Care, Inc., New Hartford, N.Y., 1985-86; psychologist Lewis County ARC, Inc., Turin, N.Y., 1985, Utica Head Start, 1985-86; lectr. in field to local schs., radio program and other orgns. Contbr. articles to profl. jours. Grantee Soc. for Psychol. Study Social Issues, 1976, Utica Coll., 1980, 82, 84, Northeastern Ill. U., 1988. Mem. Am. Psychol. Assn., Assn. Care of Children's Health, Child Life Coun. (exec. bd. 1984-86). Avocations: golf, reading, hiking. Office: Arlington Child Psychology Ctr 120 W Eastman Ste 207A Arlington Heights IL 60004

MATHERS, MARGARET, charitable agency administrator, consultant, political activist; b. Ada, Okla., Feb. 16, 1929; d. Robert Lee and Josiephine Margaret (Reed) Erwin; m. Coleman F. Moss, Sept. 1956 (div. 1966); children: Carol Lee Doria, Marilyn Frances; m. Boyd Leroy Mathers, Apr. 10, 1967. B.S. in Music, Tex. U., 1950. Svc. rep. Gen. Tel. Co., Santa Monica, Calif., 1955-58; tchr. pvt. sch., Santa Monica, 1958-60; computer program and data analyst System Devel. Corp., Santa Monica, 1961-66; computer programmer Inst. Def. Analyses, Arlington, Va., 1966-70; typist, transcriber, Edgewater, Md., 1971-80; dir. San Juan Cath. Charities, Farmington, N.Mex., 1984—; pres. San Juan Coun. Community Agys., 1986-87, treas., 1987-89, sec., 1989—; pres. Davidsonville-Mayo Health Assn., Edgewater, 1973-76, 77-80; cons. in field, 1983—. Chmn. county Libertarian Party of N.Mex.; San Juan County, 1985, sec. cen. com., 1988—; asst. sec. Our Lady of Perpetual Health, Parish Coun., Edgewater, 1979-82, Parish Coun. Sacred Heart, Farmington, 1987, sec., 1988—; sec. River Club Community Assn., Edgewater, 1975-82. Mem. Secular Franciscan Order. Roman Catholic. Avocations: nature study, birdwatching, reading, music, Indian studies. Office: San Juan Cath Charities 119 W Broadway Farmington NM 87401

MATHES, MARY LOUISE, retired educator; b. Williamstown, Ky., July 26, 1919; d. Joseph Edward and Omega Mae (Rodgers) Myers; m. John Seldon Steers, Mar. 3, 1939 (div. 1945); 1 child, Linda Steers Dorn; m. Forest Andrew Mathes, Mar. 27, 1959; children: Forest Alva, Bette Josephine. AA, San Angelo Jr. Coll., 1958; BS in Edn., Tex. Wesleyan Coll., 1961; MA in Edn., Libr. Sci., Ariz. State U., 1969, MA in Edn., Audio Visual, 1972. Cert. tchr., Tex., N.Mex., sch. libr., Ariz., master tchr. libr. sci., Ariz. Tchr. Arlington (Tex.) Sch. Dist., 1961-64; tchr. Scottsdale (Ariz.) Sch. Dist., 1964-66, sch. libr., 1966-78; now ret.; sec. Scottsdale Edn. Assn., 1967-68, Scottsdale unit NEA, 1966-67; chmn. Elem. Sch. Librs., Scottsdale Sch. Dist., 1973; treas. Ariz. State Libr. Assn., 1973-74; past pres. Maricopa County Libr. Assn.; mem. Ariz. State Reading Coun., Kiva Elem. Sch. PTA, Scottsdale. Contbr. articles, columns to various publs. Vol. USO-ARC, 1941-45, Shadow Mountain Health Care Ctr., Ariz., 1986—; mem. ptnrs. program Ariz. State U., 1985; organizer, mgr. support group for ret. tchrs., Scottsdale, 1986—. With WAF, 1951-54. Mem. Scottsdale Boys Club Aux., Scottsdale Meml. Hosp. Aux., Las Rancheras Rep. Women, McCormick Ranch Women's Club, Delta Kappa Gamma. Methodist. Home: 8214 E Morgan Trail Scottsdale AZ 85258

MATHESON, JANE GESELL, banker; b. Warwick, N.Y., Sept. 15, 1955; d. Garfield Eric and Doris (Bradner) Gesell; m. Allan F. Matheson, May 24, 1980 (div. 1989). BA, Gettysburg Coll., 1977. Personnel specialist Pfizer Med. Systems, Columbia, Md., 1977-78; personnel asst. domestic compensation Irving Trust Co., N.Y.C., 1978-82, asst. sec. internat. personnel, 1982-86; v.p. Middletown (N.Y.) Savs. Bank, 1986—. Mem. Orange County Bus. Day Care Task Force, 1990. Mem. AAUW (treas. 1989-91), N.Y. Savs. Banks Assn. Officers Forum (sec. 1988-89, treas. 1989-90, v.p. 1990-91). Republican. Office: Middletown Savs Bank 4 South St Middletown NY 10940

MATHESON, LINDA, clinical social worker; b. Martna, Estonia, Dec. 29, 1918; came to U.S., 1962, naturalized, 1969; d. Endrek and Leena Endrekson; m. Charles McLaren Matheson, Feb. 5, 1955. Diploma, Inst. for Social Scis., Tallinn, Estonia, 1944; MS, Columbia U., 1966; D in Social Work, Columbia U., 1974. Diplomate clin. social work. Social work officer UN Rehab. and Resettlement Assn., Germany, 1946-48; social worker Victorian Mental Hygiene, Australia, 1955-62; rsch. assoc., social work project dir. Arthritis Midway Ho., N.Y.C., 1966-68; researcher Columbia Presbyn. Med. Center, N.Y.C., 1971-75, now social worker; field instr. Columbia U. Sch. Social Work, 1977-79, Columbia Presbyn. Med. Ctr., NYU Sch. Social Work. Family Found. fellow, 1966; NIMH grantee, 1969-72. Mem. Nat. Assn. Social Workers, Am. Security Council, Nat. Wildlife Fedn., Center for Study of Presidency, Smithsonian Assn., English Speaking Union, Alliance Francaise, Columbia U. Alumni Assn., Internat. Platform Assn., Nat. Trust Historic Preservation, Met. Mus. of N.Y. Lutheran. Home: 30-95 29th St Astoria NY 11102

MATHEWS, BARBARA EDITH, gynecologist; b. Santa Barbara, Calif., Oct. 5, 1946; d. Joseph Chesley and Pearl (Cieri) Mathews; A.B., U. Calif., 1969; M.D., Tufts U., 1972. Intern, Cottage Hosp., Santa Barbara, 1972-73, Santa Barbara Gen. Hosp., 1972-73; resident in ob-gyn Beth Israel Hosp., Boston, 1973-77; clin. fellow in ob-gyn Harvard U., 1973-76, instr., 1976-77; gynecologist Sansum Med. Clinic, Santa Barbara, 1977—. faculty mem. ann. postgrad. course Harvard Med. Sch.; dir. ann. postgrad course UCLA Med. Sch. Bd. dirs. Meml. Rehab. Found., Santa Barbara, Channel City Women's Forum, Santa Barbara, Music Acad. of West, Santa Barbara; mem. citizen's continuing edn. adv. council Santa Barbara Community Coll. Diplomate Am. Bd. Ob-Gyn. Fellow ACS, Am. Coll. Obstetricians and Gynecologists; mem. AMA, Am. Soc. Colposcopy and Cervical Pathology (dir. 1982-84), Harvard U. Alumni Assn., Tri-counties Obstet. and Gynecol. Soc. (pres. 1981-82), Phi Beta Kappa. Clubs: Birnam Wood Golf (Santa Barbara). Author: (with L. Burke) Colposcopy in Clinical Practice, 1977; contbg. author Manual of Ambulatory Surgery, 1982. Home: 2105 Anacapa St Santa Barbara CA 93105 Office: 317 W Pueblo St Santa Barbara CA 93102

MATHEWS, JEAN ANN H., state legislator; b. Ogden, Utah, Oct. 17, 1941; d. Walter H. and Connie Laverne (Jorgenson) Holbrook; m. John Phillip Mathews, Sept. 8, 1960; children: Michael, Mark, Nanette. Student, Weber Coll., Ogden, Utah, 1959-61; AA, Florissant Community Coll., 1973; BS in Edn. magna cum laude, U. Mo.-St. Louis, 1980; MPA, U. Mo.-Columbia, 1988. Cert. tchr., Mo. Tchr., Mathews Vocal Studio, Florissant, 1964-80; profl. sales evaluator Edison Bros., Inc., St. Louis, 1971-73; mem. Mo. Ho. of Reps., 1981—. Author: Letting Go Is the Hardest, 1972; Repeat Drunken Driver Slips Through the System, 1982. Vice chmn. Florissant Bd. Appeals, 1976-80; committeewoman Florissant Twp., 1979—; sec. Mo. State Republican Party, Jefferson City, 1982-88 ; mem. Gov.'s Commn. on Crime, 1984—. Recipient Golden Gleaner award Ch. Jesus Christ Latter-day Saints, 1969; Rookie Legislator of Yr. award Capitol City Press Corp., Jefferson City, 1981; Eagle award Eagle Forum, 1982; Leadership in Mo. State Govt. award AAUW, 1982; Americanism award VFW, 1983; YWCA Women in Govt. award, 1988; inducted Alumni Hall of Fame, St. Louis Community Coll., Florissant Valley, 1987; named one of Outstanding Young Women of Am., 1974. Mem. Nat. Order Women Legislators, Am. Legis. Exch. Coun. (state chmn. 1982-88, nat. dir. 1988—, Outstanding State Legislator 1984), Nat. Fedn. Republican Women, Kappa Delta Pi. Club: Rep. Women North St. Louis County (pres. 1978-82).

MATHEWS, MARY KATHRYN, federal agency administrator; b. Washington, Apr. 20, 1948; d. T. Odon and Kathryn (Augustine) M. Student, Pa. State U., 1966-68; BBA, Am. U., 1970, MBA, 1975. Personnel mgmt. specialist, coordinator coll. recruitment program, GSA, Washington, 1971-75, adminstrv. officer, 1975-78; personnel mgmt. specialist Office of Personnel Mgmt., Washington, 1978; employee devel. specialist Office Sec. Transp., Washington, 1978-80, dep. chief operational services and spl. programs div., 1980-81; asst. dir. adminstrv. div. Farm Credit Adminstrn., Washington, 1981-84; dir. adminstrv. div. Farm Credit Adminstrn., McLean, Va., 1984-86; chief adminstrv. services div. Farm Credit Adminstrn., McLean, 1987-88; dep. staff dir. for mgmt. U.S. Commn. on Civil Rights, Washington, 1988-90, asst. staff dir. for mgmt., 1990—; chief spl. programs staff and Homebound Handicapped Employment Program GSA, Washington, 1973-74; mem. task force Presdl. Mgmt. Intern Program, Washington, 1977-78; coordinator Mgmt. Devel. Program for Women, Washington, 1979-81 Office of the Sec. of Transp. Mem. Nat. Assn. Mus. of Women in the Arts (charter), Am. Soc. Profl. and Exec. Women, Nat. Trust Hist. Preservation, Delta Gamma (pres. ho. corp. bd. local chpt. 1972-73, rush adv. 1971-73), Assn. Exec. Women in Govt. Home: 405 S Royal St Alexandria VA 22314 Office: Commn on Civil Rights 1121 Vermont Ave NW Washington DC 20425

MATHEWS, PATRICIA ANN, food and beverage company executive; b. North Tonawanda, N.Y., Oct. 20, 1945; d. Daniel and Elizabeth Marian (Kassay) Por; m. Gregory Robert Mathews, Nov. 20, 1966 (separated Aug. 1989); 1 child, Christopher Robert. B.A., SUNY-Fredonia, 1967; MBA, SUNY-Buffalo, 1982. Tchr., Wheelock Sch., Fredonia, 1967-68; library intern SUNY-Binghamton, 1968-73; office mgr. Bell and Howell, Buffalo, 1973-76; mgr. college rels. Occidental Chem. Co., Niagara Falls, N.Y., 1977-82; mgr. recruitment and devel. Rochester Telephone Co., N.Y., 1982-83; sr. career devel. specialist Anheuser-Busch Co., St. Louis, 1983-87, mgr. employee rels., 1987-89, dir. employee rels., 1989—; cons. in human resources, St. Louis, 1983—; coord. Women in Bus. Network at Anheuser-Busch. Chmn. spl. awards YWCA Leader Lunch, St. Louis, 1985-86. Mem. Personnel Assn. St. Louis (v.p. 1985-86). Internat. Assn. Personnel Women, Am. Soc. Personnel Adminstrs. Lutheran. Avocations: exercise; reading; women's issues. Home: 1013 Hollybend Dr Ballwin MO 63021 Office: Anheuser-Busch Co Inc 12855 Flushing Meadow Dr Saint Louis MO 63131

MATHEWS, RITA A., advertising executive; b. Ft. Wayne, Ind., Oct. 10, 1939; d. Homer Franklin and Betty Ann (Sessions) M. Cert., Am. Art Acad., Mpls., 1958; student, Dayton Art Inst., 1959, Bela Horvath, Dayton, Ohio, 1958-60. Staff artist McCall Pubs., Dayton, 1960-61; prod. art asst. Willis, Case, Harwood Advt., Dayton, 1961-62; designer, illustrator Standard Pubs., Dayton, 1962-69; v.p., art dir. Center Advt., Sarasota, Fla., 1969-74, Mathews & Clark Advt., Sarasota, 1974-87; pres. Mathews & Co. Advt., Sarasota, 1987—; cons. Spotlight Graphics, Sarasota, 1987—. Artist: (Book Lettering) Exploring the Film, 1968 (merit award 1968). Photographer Whitfield Congregation Jehovah's Witnesses, 1988, minister, 1989; speaker Sarasota Vo-Tech. Sch., 1988. Mem. Am. Advt. Fed. (Best of Show 1977, 78, 79, 1st pl. local newspaper campaign , musical concept, radio commercial, 4th dist. 1982), Sarasota C. of C. Office: Mathews & Company Advt 1501 Laurel St Sarasota FL 34236

MATHEWS, SHARON WALKER, ballet educator, artistic director; b. Shreveport, La., Feb. 1, 1947; d. Arthur Delmar and Nona (Frye) Walker; m. John William (Bill) Mathews, Aug. 14, 1971; children: Rebecca, Elizabeth, Anna. BS, La. State U., 1969, MS, 1971. Dance grad. asst. La. State U., Baton Rouge, 1969-71; 6th grade tchr. East Baton Rouge Parish, 1971-72, health phys. edn. tchr., 1972-74; dance instr. Magnet High Sch., Baton Rouge, 1975—; artistic dir. Baton Rouge Ballet Theatre, 1975—; dance dir. Dancers' Workshop, Baton Rouge, 1971—. Named Dance Educator of Yr., La. Alliance for Health, Physical Edn., Recreation and Dance, 1986-87. Mem. Southwestern Regional Ballet Assn. (bd. dirs. 1981—, treas., exec. bd. dirs. 1989—). Republican. Baptist. Office: Baton Rouge Ballet Theater 10689 Perkins Rd Ste C Baton Rouge LA 70810

MATHEWS, SUSAN MCKIERNAN, health care executive; b. N.Y.C., May 28, 1946; d. Thomas Joseph and Eileen Ann (Looschen) McK.; m. Robert Emmett Mathews, June 17, 1967; children: Colin Robert, Brendan Robert, Devin Robert, Kiernan Robert. Diploma in nursing, St. Francis Sch. Nursing, 1966; BS in Health Adminstrn., St. Joseph's Coll., 1979; MS in Pub. Svc. Adminstrn., Russell Sage Coll., 1983; PhD in Health Adminstrn., Columbia Pacific U., 1985. RN, N.Y. Utilization rev. analyst N.Y. State Office Mental Retardation & Devel. Disabilities, Albany, 1980-83; med. rev. analyst Empire Blue Cross & Blue Shield, Albany, 1983-84, mgr. cost containment programs, 1984-85, dir. instl. utilization rev., 1985-86, cons. in field, 1986-88; chief operating officer, ptnr. Corp. Health Dimensions, Troy, N.Y., 1988—; exec. v.p. Geriatric Health Resources, Troy, 1988—; sec. bd. dirs. Corp. Health Dimensions; speaker in field. Mem. exec. bd. New Scotland Neighborhood Assn., Albany, 1986—, Capital Leadership Program; active N.Y. State Bus. Coun.; mem. Capital Dist. World Trade Task Force, 1990—. Mem. Med. Group Mgmt. Assn., Albany-Colonie C. of C. Roman Catholic. Home: 63 Crescent Dr S Albany NY 12208 Office: Corp Health Dimensions 2001 5th Ave Troy NY 12180

MATHEWS, WILMA, public relations executive; b. Danville, Va., Dec. 23, 1945; d. Clarence Blanchard and Tina Collins (Powell) Kendrick; AA, Stratford Coll., 1966, BA, 1970; student East Carolina U., 1966-67, U. Md., European div., 1967-68, Guilford Coll., 1978-80. Asst. editor The Commonwealth Mag., Richmond, Va., 1970-72; news editor The Comml. Appeal, Danville, Va., 1972-73; pub. rels. mgr. Danville C. of C., 1973-74; publs. officer Bowman Gray Bapt. Hosp. Med. Ctr., Winston-Salem, N.C., 1974-78; sr. pub. rels. specialist Western Electric, 1978-82; mgr. pub. rels. AT&T Internat., Basking Ridge, N.J., 1982-84; media rels. mgr. AT&T Network Systems, 1985-87, mgr. pub. rels. field support, 1987—; sr. pub. rels. adv. N.C. Epilepsy Info. Svc., 1979-80. Co-author: On Deadline: Managing Media Relations, 1985; Inside Organizational Communications, 2d edit., 1985, Marketing Communications, 1987; Mem. Danville Bicentennial Commn., 1972-74; bd. dirs. Nat. Tobacco-Textile Mus., 1973-74; mem. Danville City Beautiful Com., 1973-74, Maplewood Cultural Commn., 1986-87. Fellow Internat. Assn. Bus. Communicators (dir. 1978-81, pres. N.C. chpt. 1977, 78, dir. Found. 1984-87, chmn. Found. 1987-90, accreditation bd. 1983-89; mem. Danville Hist. Soc. (dir. 1973-74), N.C. Zool. Soc., Smithsonian Instn., Internat. TV Assn. (sec. N.C. chpt. 1979-80), Internat. Pub. Rels. Assn., Coun. for Communications Mgmt. (bd. dirs. 1987-89), Friends of Maplewood Libr. (pres. 1985-86), Stratford Coll. Alumni Assn., Internat. Order Job's Daus. Republican. Baptist. Home: 65 Hudson Ave Maplewood NJ 07040 Office: 475 South St Morristown NJ 07962-1976

MATHIAS, ALICE IRENE, health plan company executive; b. N.Y.C., Mar 2, 1949; d. Murray and Charlotte (Kottle) M. B.S. in Math., Western New Eng. Coll., 1972. Programmer, Carnation Co., Los Angeles, 1973-78; programmer/analyst Cedars-Sinai Med. Ctr., Los Angeles, 1978-79, Union Bank, Los Angeles, 1979-81; group leader Kaiser Found. Health Plan, Pasadena, Calif., 1981—. Mem. Nat. Assn. Female Execs., Am. Mgmt. Assn., Kaiser Mgmt. Assn., Kaiser Women in Mgmt., Los Angeles County Mus. Art (patron), Los Angeles Philharm. Assn., Soc. Preservation Variety Arts. Home: 4210 Via Arbolada Unit 311 Los Angeles CA 90042 Office: Kaiser Found Health Plan Info Svcs Dept 393 E Walnut St Pasadena CA 91188

MATHIAS, BETTY JANE, communications and community affairs consultant, writer, editor, lecturer; b. East Ely, Nev., Oct. 22, 1923; d. Royal F. and Dollie B. (Bowman) M.; student Merritt Bus. Sch., 1941, 42, San Francisco State U., 1941-42; 1 dau., Dona Bett. Asst. publicity dir. Oakland (Calif.) Area War Chest and Community Chest, 1943-46; pub. relations Am. Legion, Oakland, 1946-47; asst. to pub. relations dir. Cen. Bank of Oakland, 1947-49; pub. relations dir. East Bay chpt. of Nat. Safety Council, 1949-51; propr., mgr. Mathias Public Relations Agy., Oakland, 1951-60; gen. assignment reporter and teen news editor Daily Rev., Hayward, Calif., 1960-62; freelance pub. relations and writing, Oakland, 1962-66, 67-69; dir. corp. communications Systech Fin. Corp., Walnut Creek, Calif., 1969-71; v.p. corp. communications Consol. Capital companies, Oakland, 1972-79, v.p. community affairs, Emeryville, Calif., 1981-84, v.p. spl. projects, 1984-85; v.p., dir. Consol. Capital Realty Services, Inc., Oakland, 1973-77; v.p., dir. Centennial Adv. Corp., Oakland, 1976-77; communications cons., 1979—; cons. Mountainair Realty, Cameron Park, Calif., 1986-87; pub. les. coord. Tuolumne County Visitors Bur., 1989—; lectr. in field; bd. dirs. Oakland YWCA, 1944-45, ARC, Oakland, So. Alameda County chpt., 1967-69, Family Ctr., Children's Hosp. Med. Ctr. No. Calif., 1982-85, March of Dimes, 1983-85, Equestrian Ctr. of Walnut Creek, Calif., 1983-84, also sec.; adult and publs. adv. Internat. Order of the Rainbow for Girls, 1953-78; communications arts adv. com. Ohlone (Calif.) Coll., 1979-85, chmn., 1982-84; mem. adv. bd. dept. mass communications Calif. State U.-Hayward, 1985; pres. San Francisco Bay Area chpt. Nat. Reyes Syndrome Found., 1981-86; vol. staff Columbia Actors' Repertory, Columbia, Calif., 1986-87, 89; mem. exec. bd., editor newsletter Tuolumne County Dem. Club, 1987; publicity chmn. 4th of July celebration Tuolumne County C. of C., 1988. Recipient Grand Cross of Color award Internat. Order of Rainbow for Girls, 1955. Order Eastern Star (publicity chmn. Calif. state 1955). Editor East Bay Mag., 1966-67, TIA Traveler, 1969, Concepts, 1979-83. Home: 20575 Gopher Dr Sonora CA 95370

MATHIAS, LYNDA ROWELL, educator; b. Orangeburg, S.C., Aug. 31, 1943; d. Harold Deland and Edna (Hancock) Rowell; m. Ervin McDonald Mathias Jr., June 26, 1965; children: Ervin M. III, Michael K. BA, Newberry Coll., 1964; MEd, U.S.C., 1985. Cert. tchr., S.C. Tchr. bus. edn. Orangeburg High Sch., 1964-65; tchr. English Saluda (S.C.) Middle Sch., 1965-67; tchr. econs. St. Andrews High Sch., Charleston, S.C., 1968; tchr. bus. edn. Allendale (S.C.) Vocat. Edn. Ctr., 1970-73; tchr. English, guidance counselor Allendale Acad., 1976-88; instr. continuing edn., adj. prof. Trident Tech. Coll., Charleston, 1989—; tchr. gifted and talented Charleston County Schs., 1989-90. Solo vocalist, various local church, sch. and civic functions. Tchr. Sunday sch., Ehrhardt Meml. Lutheran Ch., Trinity Luth. Ch.; active Am. Cancer Soc., Am. Heart Assn. Named S.C. Ind. Sch. Tchr. of Yr., 1988. Mem. S.C. Ind. Sch. Assn. (workshop presenter, mem. com. on tchr. improvement, advanced accreditation evaluator, judge for 1989 tchr. of yr. award). Republican. Home: 1112 Ocean Club Villas Isle of Palms SC 29451

MATHIAS, MARGARET GROSSMAN, manufacturing company executive, leasing company executive; b. Detroit, June 26, 1928; d. D. Ray and

Lila May (Skinner) Grossman; m. Robert D. Mathias, Oct. 1, 1955 (div. Feb. 1983); children: Deborah, Robert, Lesley, Jennifer, Mary. BA, Mt. Holyoke Coll., 1949; cert., Am. Acad. Art, 1951. Artist and co-mgr. Mary Chase Marionettes, N.Y.C., 1951-54; exec. v.p. L & J Press Corp., Elkhart, Ind., 1970—, also bd. dirs., sec., chmn. bd., 1985—; exec. v.p. Star Five Corp., Elkhart, 1978-85, pres., treas., chmn. bd., 1985—; chmn. MAGCo Inc., Elkhart, 1986—. Mem. fin. com. United Fund, Elkhart, 1960-64, parents adv. bd. Furman U., Greenville, S.C., 1978-83, art adv. bd. Mount Holyoke Coll., South Hadley, Mass., 1982—; pres. Tri Kappa Service Orgn., Elkhart, 1965-66; trustee Stanley Clark Sch., South Bend, Ind., 1977-87. Mem. Elkhart C. of C. Republican. Clubs: Elcona Country (Elkhart), Woman's Athletic (Chgo.), Thursday (Elkhart) (pres. 1976).

MATHIESEN, PAT HARMON, sculptor; b. North Hollywood, Calif., Jan. 15, 1934; d. Hilary and Dorothy Jean (Harmon) Beger; m. David Kay Mathiesen, June 29, 1959 (div. 1977); children: Susan Greenberg, Eric. G-rad. high sch. Ticket agt. Western Airlines, San Francisco, 1955-56; travel agt. Cahill Travel Svc., Phoenix, 1957-59; wildlife photographer Farewell Lake, Alaska, 1960-63; travel agt. Brad Phillips Travel, Anchorage, 1963-64; bd. dirs. Scottsdale (Ariz.) Artist Sch., 1983-85. Group exhbns. include: Nat. Cowboy Hall of Fame, Oklahoma City, 1975, Mont. Hist. Soc., Helena, 1978, Grand Cen. Galleries, N.Y.C., 1976; represented in permanent collections: Am. Quarter Horse Assn., Amarillo, Tex., Turf Paradise Race Track, Phoenix, The Estes Co., Tucson, The Symington Co., Phoenix; featured in Contemporary Western Artists, 1982, Contemporary American Women Sculptors, 1988. Mem. Phoenix Art Mus., Heard Mus., Scottsdale Artist Sch. Aux., Internat. Sculpture Ctr., Nat. Wildlife Fedn., Audubon Soc., Wilderness Soc., World Wildlife Fund, Mt. Oyster Club. Republican. Office: PO Box 13598 Scottsdale AZ 85267 also: PO Box 399 Gallatin Gateway MT 59730

MATHIEU-HARRIS, MICHELE SUZANNE, association executive; b. Chgo., Mar. 24, 1950; d. Joseph Edward Mathieu and Mary Ellen (Knapp) Fisher; m. Robert Steven Harris, May 1, 1988. Student DePaul U., 1971, 74-76, Regents Coll., Albany, N.Y., 1987—. Broadcast coord. Grey-North Advt., Chgo., 1967-71; head drama dept. Patricia Stevens Coll., Chgo., 1972; instr. beginning acting Ted Liss Sch. of Performing Arts, Chgo., 1973-75; project coord. grants and contracts Am. Dietetic Assn., Chgo., 1974-81, adminstr. govt. affairs, 1981-86, mgr. licensure communications, 1986-90, adminstr. nutrition svcs. payment systems, 1990—; grant proposal cons. various performance arts, Chgo., 1978—. Editor Legis. Newsletter, 1981-86; contbg. editor Nutrition Forum, 1986, Courier, 1987—; contbr. articles to profl. jours., mags., newspapers. Treas. Am. Dietetic Assn. polit. action com., Washington, 1981-86; adv. bd. Rejoice Repertory Theatre Company, Inc., Chgo.; mem. Chgo. Women in Govt. Rels. Ill. Arts Coun. grantee, 1981. Mem. Nat. Assn. Female Execs., Am. Soc. Assn. Exec.(award Excellence in Govt. Rels. 1989). Roman Catholic. Avocations: reading, jazzercise. Office: Am Dietetic Assn 216 W Jackson Blvd Chicago IL 60606

MATHIS, BETTY, public relations counsel; b. Atlanta, Oct. 5, 1918; d. Walter Rylander and Evelyn Battle (Epting) M.; student Agnes Scott Coll., 1934-36. Sports writer, columnist Atlanta Constitution, 1936-39; gen. news and feature writer, then editor spl. supplements, 1939-40; dir. public relations Atlanta Housing Authority, 1940; feature writer, asst. city editor, daily by-line columnist Atlanta Constitution, 1941-43; asst. regional info. exec. OPA, 1943-45; partner Mathis, Murphey & Bondurant public relations counsel, Atlanta, 1945-50; editor Sun Colony Mag., Fort Lauderdale, Fla., 1950-53; partner Mathis & Bondurant public relations, Ft. Lauderdale, 1953-82, owner, 1982—. Bd. dirs. ARC; mem. coms. United Way; sec. vestry All Saints Episcopal Ch., 1974-76, mem. vestry, 1978-80, 85-87, treas., 1979, sr. warden, 1980, del. Diocesan Conv., 1975, 79, 80. Nominee, Pulitzer prize, 1937. Mem. Public Relations Soc. Am., Am. Soc. Hosp. Public Relations (profl. advancement com. 1980), Public Relations Council Fla. Hosp. Assn. (dir. 1977-79, pres. 1977-78), Women in Communications (pres. county 1968, 69, Atlantic Fla. chpt. 1979, named Woman of Yr. 1979), Gold Coast Hosp. Public Relations Council (founding, pres. 1981-82), Am. Hosp. Assn. Democrat. Club: Tower. Home and Office: 1628 NE 15th Ave Fort Lauderdale FL 33305

MATHIS, JUNE GREEN, business office manager; b. Louise, Miss., June 12, 1941; d. Thomas Leo and Louella (Sanders) Green; m. P. Michael Mathis, Mar. 27, 1960; children: Jon Michael, Gregory D., Thomas Vincent. Student, Holmes Jr. Coll., Goodman, Miss., 1977-78. Operator South Cen. Bell. Telephone Co., Yazoo City, Miss., 1959-63; with King's Daughters Hosp., Yazoo City, 1963—, personnel adminstr., 1971-78, mgr. bus. office, 1978—; chmn. Health Fair, King's Daughters Hosp., 1986, 88. Chmn. Nat. Hosp. Week, Yazoo City, 1983—; v.p. Merry Gardeners Garden Club, Yazoo City, 1981. Mem. Miss. Hosp. Assn., Soc. Personnel Adminstrn., Ord. Ea. Star. Baptist. Home: 1605 Gaywood Ave Yazoo City MS 39194 Office: Kings Daughters Hosp 823 Grand Ave Yazoo City MS 39194

MATHIS, LAURELLE SHEEDY, entrepreneur, volunteer; b. Southampton, N.Y., Aug. 29, 1948; d. Edmund Sheedy and Tatiana (Widrin) Brooks; m. Robert Trimble Mathis, Oct. 20, 1979; children:Liliana Sheedy, Bronwyn Trimble, Kane Timberlake. B.A., Stephens Coll., Columbia, Mo., 1970; M.B.A., Harvard U., 1977. Spl. asst. Congressman Ed Foreman, Washington, 1970; staff asst. Senator James L. Buckley, Washington, 1971-72; staff asst. to pres. U.S., Washington, 1973-75; v.p. Blyth Eastman Paine Webber, N.Y.C., 1977-81; v.p. Merrill Lynch Capital Markets, N.Y.C., 1981-84. Bd. curators Stephens Coll., 1981-83; bd. dirs. Putnam Indian Field Sch., Greenwich, Conn., 1986—, chmn. auction, 1987; chmn. Christ Ch. Antiques Show, 1987, 88, 89; bd.dir. Episcopal Ch., Women of Christ Ch., Greenwich Acad. Mother's Bd. Recipient Alumni Achievement award Stephens Coll., 1980. Republican. Episcopalian. Home: 266 Stanwich Rd Greenwich CT 06830

MATHIS, MARGARET E. MYRICK, special education educator; b. Montgomery, Ala., June 13, 1932; d. Elives Westly and Lou Olive (Wilson) Myrick; m. William Franklin Mathis, July 16, 1955 (div. 1976); children: Margaret Victoria, William Jr., Christopher Myrick. BS in English and Music, U. Ala., 1953; MA in Guidance and Counseling, Peabody U., 1954; MA in Spl. Edn., U. Ala., 1978. English and history tchr. Bessemer (Ala.) Bd. Edn., 1953-55; speech tchr. Birmingham (Ala.) Bd. Edn., 1955-61; spl. edn. tchr. Jefferson County Bd. Edn., Birmingham, 1978-90; music tchr. Vestavia (Ala.) Bapt. Kindergarten, 1970-74. Vol. music tchr. Svc. League Aphasoid Children, Birmingham, 1965-67; leader Girl Scouts Am., Birmingham, 1967-71; vol. phone solicitor Gov.'s Campaign, Birmingham, 1990; campaign worker Atty. Gen., Birmingham, 1990; vol. fund solicitor Birmingham Symphony, 1964-66. Mem. Ala. Edn. Assn. (lobbyist 1986-90), Jefferson County Edn. Assn. (reporter, journalist newsletter 1988-90, exec. bd. 1988-90, faculty rep. Pittman Jr. High Sch. 1978-90), Pilot Club, Alpha Delta Pi (pres.), Phi Delta Kappa. Presbyterian. Home: 3700 Northcote Dr Mountain Brook AL 35223 Office: Jefferson County Bd Edn A-400 Court House Birmingham AL 35263 Also: Pittman Middle Sch 701 Sunrise Blvd Hueytown AL 35023-2798

MATHIS, MARILYN KELTY, organization executive director; b. Louisville, Feb. 18, 1958; d. John Martin and Marion (Seng) Kelty; m. Tony E. Mathis, Nov. 25, 1978. BS cum laude, Spalding U., 1989. Ins. clk. Norton Kosair Hosp., Louisville, 1976-77; receptionist Gist Piano Co., Louisville, 1978-79; treasury clk. Kahn & Co. Brokerage, Memphis, 1980; sec. Ratterman & Son, Louisville, 1981-82, office mgr., 1982-88; office mgr. Accord, Louisville, 1988, exec. dir., 1989—. Mem. NAFE, U.S. Fencing Assn. (sec.-treas. Louisville 1976-83), Nat. Bookkeeping Assn., Louisville Bus. & Profl. Women Assn., Louisville Dive Club (divemaster). Office: Accord 1930 Bishop Ln Ste 947 Louisville KY 40218

MATHIS, MARSHA DEBRA, software company executive; b. Detroit, Dec. 22, 1953; d. Marshall Junior and Anita Willene (Biggers) M. BS, Fla. State U., 1978; MBA, Miss. Coll., 1982. With telecommunications dept. Fla. State Dept. Safety, Tallahassee, 1973-76; asst. to chmn. Tallahassee Savs. and Loan Assn., 1976-78; sales engr. Prehler, Inc., Jackson, Miss., 1978-82; mktg. mgr. Norand Corp., Arlington, Tex., 1982-87; v.p. mktg. and sales Profl. Datasolutions, Inc., Irving, Tex., 1987-88; v.p. mktg. and sales, ptnr. Target Systems, Inc., Irving, 1988-89, also bd. dirs.; v.p. mktg. Profl. Datasolutions, Inc., Irving, 1990—. Contbr. articles in industry trade jours. Advisor Am. Diabetes Assn., Jackson, 1983—. Mem. Internat. Platform Assn., Nat. Adv. Group, Nat. Assn. Convenience Stores (Industry Task Force 1987-88). Republican. Roman Catholic. Home: 600 Eagle Nest Irving TX 75063 Office: Profl Datasolution Inc 5301 Knickerbocker Rd San Angelo TX 76904

MATHIS, SHARON ANN, mental health nurse; b. Normangee, Tex., Sept. 29, 1957; d. James Ezekiel Sr. and Rosie Mae (Stovall) M. BS in Nursing, Prairie View A&M U., 1980; MPA, Tex. So. U., 1987. RN, Tex.; cert. nurse adminstr. Nursing coord. West Oaks Hosp., Houston, 1984-86, unit dir., 1986-88, dir. nursing, 1988-89; adminstr. Directions of Nursing Svcs. HCA Beaumont (Tex.) Neurol. Hosp., 1989—. Mem. Am. Nurses Assn., Am. Evaluation Assn., S.E. Tex. Assn. Psychiat. Nurses, Tex. Nurses Assn., Houston Assn. Psychiat. Nurses, Impaired Nurse Advocate, Prairie View Agr. and Mechanical Alumni Assn. (life), Carter G. Woodson Alumni Assn. (pres. 1987), Sigma Theta Tau. Office: Box 741384 Houston TX 77274-1384

MATHIS, THELMA ATWOOD, artist; b. Creal Springs, Ill.; d. Hubert L. and Mima (Hutchison) Atwood; B.S., So. Ill. U., 1955, M.F.A., 1957; student Art Students League, 1957-59; m. John A. Mathis, Sept. 1, 1928 (div. 1950); children—John Atwood, Shirley (Mrs. Frank Woosley), James Stevens. One-man shows So. Ill. U., 1957, 59, Sparta (Ill.) Pub. Library, 1960, Art Mart, Inc., St. Louis, 1961, St. Louis Artists Guild, 1962, Midwestern Coll. (Iowa), 1967; two-man show Madison Galleries, N.Y.C., 1963; juried N.Y.C. Center, 1958, 59, Madison Sq. Garden, N.Y.C., 1958, Nat. Old Testament, St. Louis, 1961, 62, Mo. Art Show, St. Louis City Art Mus., 1954, 55, Nat. Arts & Crafts, Wichita, Kans., 1953, 55; instr., asst. prof. art dept. Midwestern Coll., Denison, Iowa, 1965-70. Recipient Grand prize oil and drawing DuQuoin State Fair, 1955, 56, 58, 59. Mem. St. Louis Artists Guild, AAUW, Pi Lambda Theta. Baptist.

MATHISEN, LILLIAN ALICE, television station executive; b. Bronx, N.Y., Nov. 16, 1941; d. Johann Nordell Bang and Alice (Kostka) M.; m. Thomas Joseph Conroy, July 3, 1965 (div. 1989); children: Christian, Eric, Brian. BA, Fairleigh Dickinson U., 1963. Instr. Fairleigh Dickinson U., Teaneck, N.J., 1963-64; market rsch. field supr. W.R. Simmons Assocs., N.Y.C., 1964-65; assoc. library dir. NYU, Tuxedo, N.Y., 1966-70; computer operator IBM Corp., East Fishkill, N.Y., 1978-79; sys. analyst Texaco, Inc., White Plains, N.Y., 1980-84; law firm adminstr. Jacobowitz & Gubits, Walden, N.Y., 1985-86; bus. mgr. Sta. WTZA-TV, Kingston, N.Y., 1986—. Mem. Broadcast Fin. Mgmt. Assn. Democrat. Lutheran. Home: RD 1 Box 180 DeLancey NY 13752 Office: Sta WTZA-TV 721 Broadway Kingston NY 12401

MATHISEN, RHODA SHARON, international communications consultant; b. Portland, Oreg., June 25, 1942; d. Daniel and Mildred Elizabeth Annette (Peterson) Hager; m. James Albert Mathisen, July 17, 1964 (div. 1977); m. James A. Reid Sr., Jan. 1, 1990. BA in Edn., Music, Bible Coll., Mich., 1964. Community Rels. officer Gary-Wheaton Bank, Wheaton, Ill., 1971-75; br. mgr. Stivers Temporary Personnel, Chgo., 1975-79; v.p. sales Exec. Technique, Chgo., 1980-83; prin. Mathisen Assocs., Downers Grove, Ill., 1983—; presenter seminars; featured speaker Women in Mgmt. Oak Brook Chpt., 1988; cons. Haggai Inst., Atlanta; adv. mem. Nat. Bd. Success Group, 1986. Pres. chancel choir Christ Ch. of Oak Brook, 1985-87. Mem. Bus. and Profl. Women (charter mem. Woodfield chpt.), Execs. Club Oak Brook, Internat. Platform Assn., NAFE, Sales & Mktg. Execs. Chgo., Chgo. Council Fgn. Relations, Chgo. Assn. Commerce and Industry (named Ambassador of Month N.W. suburban chpt. 1979), Oak Brook Assn. Commerce and Industry (mem. membership com.), Women Entrepreneurs of DuPage County (membership chmn., featured speaker Jan. 1988), Art Inst. Chgo., Internat. Platform Assn. Republican. Office: Mathisen Assocs Box 9208 Downers Grove IL 60515

MATLIN, MARLEE, actress; b. Morton Grove, Ill., Aug. 24, 1965. Attended William Rainey Harper Coll. Appeared in films Children of a Lesser God (Acad. award), 1986, Walker, 1987, Fox; TV film: Bridge to Silence, 1989. Office: care ICM 8899 Beverly Blvd Los Angeles CA 90048*

MATLOW, LINDA MONIQUE, photographic agency executive, periodicals publisher; b. Chgo., July 24, 1955; d. Charles and Milly (Labioso) M. Grad. high sch., Chgo.; student, Sch. Modern Photography, N.Y.C., 1977-79. Promotions and pub. relations staff Jaydee Enterprises, Chgo., 1971-73; mgr. First Venture, Inc., Chgo., 1973-77; photographer, pub. relations staff Bands & Mags., Chgo., 1977—; pres., photographer Pix Internat., Chgo., 1982—; photo-editor Beat. Chgo. Sounds; bur. chief. Prairie Sun. Contbr. photographs to publs. including N.Y. Times, Chgo. Tribune, Boston Globe. Vol. telethon Variety Club of Chgo., 1986, Spl. Childrens' Charities. Named Rock Photographer Night Rock newspaper, Chgo., 1980, 81, one of Chgo.'s Most Successful and Eligible Bachelorettes Today's Chgo. Woman mag., 1989. Mem. Nat. Press Assn., Nat. Acad. Rec. Arts and Scis., Internat. Freelance Photographers Orgn., Chgo. Women in Pub. Roman Catholic.

MATNEY, MARJORIE MAYE, educator; b. Rushville, Ind., Apr. 7, 1931; d. Herbert Garl and Ruth (Miller) Wagoner; m. Chester L. Matney, Aug. 11, 1951; children: Joan, Stephen. BS, Ind. U., Terre Haute, 1953; MA, Ball State U., 1971. Tchr. Milroy (Ind.) elem. sch., 1953-55, Moscow (Ind.) elem. sch., 1955-62, Sabina (Ohio) elem. sch., 1962-63, Shelbyville (Ind.) Cen. Kindergarten, 1968-73, dir. kindergarten, 1973—. Mem. AAUW, Ind. Assn. Edn. Young Children, Ind. State Tchrs. Assn., NEA, Shelbyville Cen. Schs. Assn., Alpha Delta Kappa (pres. 1986-88). Home: Rte 6 Box S147A Greensburg IN 47240 Office: Shelbyville Kindergarten Rte 1 Box 9 Shelbyville IN 46176

MATO, CHRISTINE YURIKO, marine geologist; b. Honolulu, May 13, 1950; d. G.K. and K. (Suehiro) M. BS, U. Hawaii, 1974. Supr. coring Hawaii Inst. Geophysics, Honolulu, 1976-84; supr. curation and repositories, Ocean Drilling Program Tex. Agrl. and Mech. U., College Station, 1984—. Home: 302 Dexter St College Station TX 77840 Office: Ocean Drilling Program 1000 Discovery Dr College Station TX 77845-9547

MATRE, SUSAN JANE, veterinarian; b. Cin., Oct. 13, 1952; d. Edward Emerson Jr. and Dorothy Jane (Bohlander) M. BS in Animal Nutrition, Ohio State U., 1973, DVM, 1978. Assoc. All Pets Animal Hosp., Cin., 1978-79, Columbine Animal Hosp., Littleton, Colo., 1979-83; assoc., ptnr. Parktown Vet. Clinic, Milpitas, Calif., 1984—. Mem. Am. Vet. Med. Assn., Santa Clara Valley Vet. Med. Assn., Sierra Club. Office: Parktown Vet Clinic 1393 S Park Victoria Milpitas CA 95035

MATSA, LOULA ZACHAROULA, social services administrator; b. Piraeus, Greece, Apr. 16, 1935; came to U.S., 1952, naturalized 1962; d. Eleftherios Georgiou and Ourania E. (Fraguiskopoulou) Papoulias; student Pierce Coll., Athens, Greece, 1948-52; B.A., Rockford Coll., 1953; M.A., U. Chgo., 1955; m. Ilco S. Matsa, Nov. 27, 1953; 1 son, Aristotle Ricky. Marital counselor Family Soc. Cambridge, Mass., 1955-56; chief unit II, social service Queen's (N.Y.) Children's Psychiat. Ctr., 1961-74; dir. social services, supr.-coord. family care program Hudson River Psychiat. Ctr., Poughkeepsie, N.Y., 1974—; field instr. Adelphi, Albany and Fordham univs., 1969—. Fulbright Exch. student, 1952-53; Talcott scholar, 1953-55. Mem. Internat. Platform Assn., Internat. Coun. on Social Welfare, Nat. Assn. Social Workers, Assn. Cert. Social Workers, Pub. Employees Fedn., Pierce Coll. Alumni Assn. Democrat. Greek Orthodox. Contbr. articles to profl. jours.; instrumental in state policy changes in treatment and court representation of emtionally disturbed and mentally ill. Home: 81-11 45th Ave Elmhurst NY 11373 Office: Hudson River Psychiat Ctr Br B Poughkeepsie NY 12601

MATSON, ARLENE MAE, principal; b. Brush Creek Twp., Minn., Mar. 3, 1926; d. Oscar Alfred and Constannia (Asmus) M. BA, Luther Coll., 1948; MS in Elem. Sch. Adminstrn., Mankato (Minn.) State U., 1961. Tchr. 4th grade Redwood Falls (Minn.) Pub. Schs., 1948-51, Fairmont (Minn.) Pub. Schs., 1951-56; tchr. 4th grade Albert Lea (Minn.) Pub. Schs., 1956-60, elem. sch. prin., 1956-86, ret., 1986; mem. adv. bd. Minn. Dept. Ednl. Adminstrn., 1980-87. Mem. Assn. for Retarded Citizens, Albert Lea, 1970—. Recipient Cert. of Appreciation, Albert Lea Pub. Schs., 1986. Mem. Nat. Assn. Elem. Sch. Prins., NEA, Minn. Elem. Prins. Assn. (state sec.), Ret. Educators Minn., AAUW, Sons of Norway (fin. sec. 1990—), Luth. Brotherhood (br. pres. 1980—), Delta Kappa Gamma (chpt. pres., state 2d v.p., state pres. 1987-89).

MATSON, FRANCES SHOBER, social worker; b. Cin., Mar. 21, 1921; d. Frank Lyford and Florence Leone (Bridgeford) Shober; student U. Cin., 1939-41, B.A., 1951, postgrad., 1951-52; M.S.W., U. Calif., 1956; Nat. Registry of Clin. Social Work; m. John Alan Matson, Dec. 2, 1942 (dec.). Diplomate Am. Bd. Examiners in Clin. Social Work. Councillor, County of San Mateo, 1956-57; therapist, supr. Center for Treatment and Edn. on Alcoholism, Oakland, Calif., 1957-63; pvt. practice social worker, Berkeley, Calif., 1960-64; supr. dept. social service County of Marin, Calif., 1966; psychotherapist Marin Inst., 1966-70, Oaknoll Naval Hosp., 1969; public health social worker Dept. Health County of Contra Costa (Calif.), 1972; psychotherapist Day Care Center for Schizophrenics, Contra Costa County Med. Services, 1972-74; dir. Martinez Mental Health Clinic, Contra Costa County Med. Services, 1974-81; coordinator adult outpatient services, edn., group therapy Contra Costa County Mental Health Center, 1981-88, ret., 1988. Amem. Nat. Assn. Social Workers, Acad. Cert. Social Workers, Internat. Transactional Analysis Assn., Marin Assn. Mental Health, Contra Costa County Mental Health Assn., Soc. Clin. Social Work. Home: Box 22012 Louisville KY 40252-0012 Office: 2025 Port Chicago Hwy Concord CA 94520

MATSON, MARIECHEN ANNE (MANDY MATSON), writer; b. Stamford, Conn., June 11, 1957; d. George Dutilh and Mariechen (Wilder) Smith; m. Randal B. Matson Jr., Oct. 13, 1979; 1 child, Julia Mariechen. BA in Speech-Communications, N.C. State U., 1979. Writer, producer intern Raleigh (N.C.) Dept. Human Resources, 1978; camera operator Sta. WRAL-TV, Raleigh, 1978, engring. ops. technician, 1978-81; host, producer part-time Sta. WYNA, Raleigh, 1980-81; client svcs. rep. Admix, Inc., Cary, N.C., 1981; freelance videographer and writer Cary, 1981-82; creative and video dir. Thorne & Trigg, Cary, 1982-83; writer, producer Carolina Power & Light, Raleigh, 1983-86; freelance writer Cary, 1986—. Author: Using Your Camcorder, 1989; contbr. articles to consumer mags.; writer newspaper column Cary News and TV scripts. Counselor Centre Stone Crisis Intervention, Darien, Conn., 1972-75; reader N.C. Library for the Blind Physically Handicapped, Raleigh, 1986. Recipient Communications Contest award United Way, 1985, Silver Reel award Internat. TV Assn., 1985. Mem. N.C. Writers Network (bd. dirs. 1989—). Methodist. Home and Office: 305 S Walker St Cary NC 27511

MATSON, MERRIDEE LYNN, sales and marketing executive; b. Storm Lake, Iowa; d. Donald C. and Kathryn B. (Ries) Berg; m. Wayne R. Matson, Aug. 27, 1966; children: Ann Marie, Matthew. BS, Northern Ariz. U., 1968; MEd, Cen. Washington U., 1983. Tchr. Frank Borman Jr. High Sch., Phoenix, 1968-69; asst. to dir. Sch. Journalism, Okla. State U., Stillwater, Okla., 1971-73, Nat. Civil Service League, Washington, 1974-76; v.p. adminstrn. Am. Soc. Aero. Edn., Washington, 1977-81; sr. editor edn. Aviation/Space Mag., Washington, 1979-88; IBM product mgr. Entre' Computer Ctrs., Inc., Vienna, Va., 1982-86, major account program mgr., 1986-88; nat. mgr. bus. devel. Intel Corp., Portland, Oreg., 1988-89, mgr. bus. devel. and channel mktg., 1989—; U.S. del. to annual world conf. Fedn. Aeronautique Internationale, Paris, 1975—. Contbr. articles to profl. jours. Mem. parade com. County of Fairfax, 1973-74. Named Companion of Honor, Fedn. Aeronautique Internationale, 1987. Mem. Am. Soc. Aero. Edn. (aero. ambassador Washington area 1981), Nat. Aero. Assn., Beta Sigma Phi (city council sec. Fairfax chpt. 1976-77, all offices including pres. 1973-81). Republican. Clubs: Aero of So. Calif., Fedn. Aeronautique Internat. Home: 13684 SW Ashley Ct Tigard OR 97224

MATSUI, DOROTHY NOBUKO, educator; b. Honolulu, Jan. 9, 1954; d. Katsura and Tamiko (Sakai) M. Student, U. Hawaii, Honolulu, 1972-76, postgrad., 1982; BEd, U. Alaska, Anchorage, 1979, MEd in Special Edn., 1986. Clerical asst. U. Hawaii Manoa Disbursing Office, Anchorage, 1974-76; passenger service agt. Japan Air Lines, Anchorage, 1980; bilingual tutor Anchorage Sch. Dist., 1980, elem. sch. tchr., 1980—. Vol. Providence Hosp., Anchorage, 1986, Humana Hosp., Anchorage, 1984, Spl. Olympics, Anchorage, 1981, Municipality Anchorage, 1978, Easter Seal Soc. Hawaii, 1975. Mem. NAFE, NEA, Alaska Edn. Assn., Smithsonian Nat. Assoc. Program, Nat. Space Soc., Smithsonian Air and Space Assn., World Aerospace Edn. Orgn., Internat. Platform Assn., Nat. Trust For Hist. Preservation, World Inst. Achievement, U.S. Olympic Soc., Women's Inner Circle Achievement, U. Alaska Alumni Assn., Alpha Delta Kappa (treas. Alpha chpt. 1988—). Office: Anchorage Sch Dist 7001 Cranberry Anchorage AK 99502

MATSUMURA, VERA YOSHI, pianist; b. Oakland, Calif.; d. Naojiro and Aguri Tanaka; B.A. in Piano Pedagogy, Coll. of Holy Names, Oakland, 1938; pvt. studies with F. Moss, M. Shapiro, L. Kreutzer, P. Jarrett; m. Jiro Matsumura, Aug. 8, 1942; 1 son, Kenneth N. Staff mem., pianist Radio Sta. KROW, Oakland, 1938-39; numerous concert performances in Far East (Japan, Thailand), 1940—; numerous teaching appointments, 1940—; dir. Internat. Music Council, Berkeley, Calif., 1969—. Named to Hall of Fame, Piano Guild, 1968. Mem. Music Tchrs. Nat. Assn., Music Tchrs. Assn. Calif., Internat. Platform Assn., Alpha Phi Mu. Methodist. Home: 2 Claremont Crescent Berkeley CA 94705

MATTEA, KATHY, vocalist, songwriter; m. Jon Vezner, Feb. 14, 1988. Student, W.Va. U. Former mem. bluegrass band. Albums include Walk the Way the Wind Blows, 1986, Untasted Honey, 1988, Willow in the Wind, 1989. Recipient awards for best single Acad. Country Music, 1988, Best Female Vocalist award Country Music Assn., 1989, 90, award for Eighteen Wheels and a Dozen Roses, 1989. Address: care Robert R Titley 1016 16th Ave S Nashville TN 37212*

MATTERSON, JOAN MCDEVITT, physical therapist; b. Bryn Mawr, Pa., Feb. 24, 1949; d. William J. and Wanda Jean (Edwards) McD.; children: Brian, Jennie, Kira. BS in Biology, St. Joseph's U., Phila., 1973; cert. in phys. therapy, U. Pa., 1974. Assoc. pharmacologist, researcher immunolotgy and arthritis Progressive Phys. Therapy, P.A., Wilmington, Del., 1968-73, pediatric phys. therapist, 1974-81, pres., 1976—; lectr. in field. Mem. AAUW, Am. Soc. Laser Medicine and Surgery, Nat. Inst. Inc., New Castle County C. of C. Office: Progressive Phys Therapy PA 2018 Naamans Rd Ste 9 Wilmington DE 19810

MATTES-KULIG, DEBRA ANN, owner gift basket business, dietitian; b. Erie, Pa., Mar. 22, 1954; d. Ford Stuart and Mary (Barber) Mattes; m. Michael L. Kulig, May 19, 1979; children: Allison, Ryan. BA, Mercyhurst Coll., 1976; MS, Pa. State U., 1979. Registered dietitian. Rsch. nutritionist Georgetown U. Med. Ctr., Washington, 1980-83; pres. Bite by Byte, Fairfax, Va., 1983—; owner, operator That Perfect Gift, Fairfax, 1989—. Author: The Four Star Health Club, 1976; contbr. articles to profl. jours. Treas. Annandale (Va.) Presch., 1988; bd. dirs. Meals on Wheels, Arlington, Va., 1987. Recipient Recognized Young Dietitian award Am. Dietetic Assn., 1984. Mem. Cons. Nutritionists of Am. Dietetics Assn. (treas., chair-elect), Va. Dietetic Assn. (pres. no. dist. 1987, Ross Profl. Devel. award 1983, newsletter editor 1989). Home and Office: 5205 Richardson Dr Fairfax VA 22032

MATTESON, PATRICIA ELY, bank executive; b. Iowa City, Feb. 1, 1945; d. Lawrence Orlo and Dorothy (Jenkins) Ely; m. Charles C. Matteson, Jr., May 9, 1970. BA, Northwestern U., 1967, postgrad., 1968; MBA, NYU, 1979. Personnel specialist Roland Cos., Chgo., N.Y.C., 1968-70; personnel asst. employment orgn., mktg. dept., product mgr. Dun and Bradstreet, N.Y.C., 1970-76; nat. accounts mgr., mktg. mgr., gen. mgr. UK, v.p. mktg. Merrill Lynch Relocation Mgmt., White Plains, N.Y., 1976-85; pres., chief exec. officer Matteson Cos. Internat., Inc., Norwalk, Conn., 1985-86; sr. v.p. mktg. People's Bank, Bridgeport, Conn., 1986—. Bd. dirs. Stamford (Conn.) Ctr. for the Arts, 1987—; pres., bd. dirs. Women in Mgmt., Stamford, 1979—. Recipient Boy Scouts Community award Exploring div. Boy Scouts Am., 1990. Mem. Women in Mgmt. (bd. dirs. 1981-82, 85, 90, Recognition award 1986). Home: 160 Rose Hill Rd Southport CT 06490 Office: Peoples Bank 850 Main St Bridgeport CT 06490

MATTEUCCI, MARGARET MARY, broadcast executive; b. Albuquerque, Oct. 17, 1940; d. Peter Lawrence and Margaret (Balduini) M.; m. Rodney Dale Dixon, Aug. 16, 1969 (div. 1980); 1 child, Richard Matthew. BA, Marymount Coll., 1963; postgrad., Ea. N.Mex. U., 1965, 67. Cert. tchr., Colo. Tchr. Denver Pub. Schs., 1963-71; stockholder rep. Richard Distbg. Co., Albuquerque, 1980-82; owner, mgr. Matteucci Broadcasting Co. (KDEF-AM/KMYI-FM), Albuquerque, 1984—. Bd. dirs., officer, St. Francis Healthcare, Albuquerque, 1984—, St. Francis Day Care Ctr.; troop chmn., Albuquerque area Boy Scouts Am., 1982, 83. Mem. Parent-Faculty Assn. (pres. 1977, 78), Parent Effectiveness Group. Office: Matteucci Broadcasting Co 2117 Menaul Blvd NE Albuquerque NM 87107

MATTHEW, LYN, art marketing consultant, educator; b. Long Beach, Calif., Dec. 15, 1936; d. Harold G. and Beatrice (Hunt) M.; m. Wayne Thomas Castleberry, Aug. 12, 1961 (div. Jan. 1976); children: Melanie, Cheryl, Nicole, Matthew. BS, U. Calif.-Davis, 1958; MA, Ariz. State U., 1979. Cert. hotel sales exec., 1988. Pres., Davlyn Cons. Found., Scottsdale, Ariz., 1979-82; cons., vis. prof. The Art Bus., Scottsdale, 1982—; pres., nat. sales mgr. Embassy Stes., Scottsdale, 1987—, bd. trustees Hotel Sales and Mktg. Assn. Internat. Found., 1989—; vis. prof. Maricopa Community Coll., Phoenix, 1979—, Ariz. State U., Tempe, 1980-83; cons. Women's Caucus for Art, Phoenix, 1983-88. Bd. dirs. Rossom House and Heritage Square Found., Phoenix, 1987-88. Author: The Business Aspects of Art, Book I, 1979, Book II, 1979; Marketing Strategies for the Creative Artist, 1985. Mem. Women Image Now (Achievement and Contbn. in Visual Arts award 1983), Women in Higher Edn., Nat. Women's Caucus for Art (v.p. 1981-83), Ariz. Women's Caucus for Art (pres. 1980-82, hon. advisor 1986-87), Ariz. Vocat. Edn. Assn. (sec. 1978-80), Ariz. Visionary Artists (treas. 1987-89), Hotel Sales and Mktg. Assn. Internat. (pres. Great Phoenix chpt. 1988-89, regional dir. 1989—), Meeting Planners Internat. (v.p. Ariz. Sunbelt chpt. 1989—, Supplier of Yr. award 1988, Chpt. Supplier of Yr. award 1988), Ariz. Soc. Govt. Meeting Planners (charter bd. dirs. 1987), Ariz. Visionary Artists (treas. 1987-88), Ariz. Acad. Performing Arts (v.p. bd. dirs. 1987-88, pres. 1988-89).

MATTHEWS, AGNES CYNTHIA, state senator; b. Washington, Pa., Feb. 1, 1924; d. Spero and Harriet Kosmas; m. Phathon James Matthews, Dec. 5, 1946; children: Denise, Spero. B.S., Barnard Coll., 1946. Dep. mayor (1 term) Wethersfield, Conn., mayor (2 terms), council woman, 1973-81; mem. Conn. Senate (representing 9th dist.), 1982—; v.p., dir. Pie-O-Neer Corp., East Hartford, Conn., 1980—, Sargent's Head Realty Corp., East Lyme, Conn., 1959—, The Stonington Co.; v.p. Out O' Mystic Schooner Cruises. Mem. Ch. Women United (nat. bd. dirs. 1977-80), LWV (former pres. Wethersfield/Rocky Hill chpt.), Civitans. Greek Orthodox. 1st woman mayor of Wethersfield. Office: Conn State Senate Hartford CT 06106*

MATTHEWS, ANNE LAMB, educational administrator, state official; b. Florence County, S.C., Nov. 3, 1942; d. Alex B. and Mettie (Nettles) L.; B.S. in Bus. Edn., Coker Coll., 1964; M.A. in Econs., Appalachian State U., 1968; Ed.D. in Ednl. Adminstrn., U. S.C., 1975; LHD Coker Coll., 1988; m. Glenny Jeff Matthews, Sept. 2, 1967. Tchr. bus. edn. dept. Hannah-Pamplico High Sch., Pamplico, S.C., 1964-67; instr. dept. bus. adminstrn. and secretarial sci. Florence-Darlington Tech. Edn. Coll., Florence, S.C., 1967-69; tchr.-counselor Youth Study Center, Greenville, S.C., 1970-71; dist. cons. Office Occupations Edn., Anderson (S.C.) Dist. Office, 1971-73; adj. prof. Coll. Bus. Adminstrn. U. S.C., Columbia, 1975-78; state supr. bus. and office edn. S.C. Dept. Edn., Columbia, 1973-80, chief supr. program planning and devel., 1980—, asst. dir., program dir., mem. various coms., 1975—; presdl. appointment Nat. Adv. Coun. for Career Edn.; mem. Nat. Commn. Employment Policy, Practitioners Task Force; nat. speaker over 1500 confs. Vol. Vets Hosp., Columbia, 1978—; trustee Coker Coll., Hartsville, S.C.; bd. dirs. Richland County Am. Cancer Soc. Recipient Hulda Erath award, 1978, 79, John Robert Gregg award McGaw-Hill Pub. Co., 1988. Mem. Nat. Bus. Edn. Assn. (chmn. policies com. on bus. and econ. edn. 1979-80, pres. elect 1984, pres. 1985-86, Outstanding Adminstr. 1980), So. Bus. Edn. Assn. (pres. 1984-85), Nat. Assn. State Suprs. of Bus. and Office Edn. (pres. 1977-79), S.C. Office Occupations Assn. (mem. exec. bd. 1973-76), Internat. Soc. for Bus. Edn., Am. Vocat. Assn. (mem. policy and planning com. 1977—), Adminstrv. Mgmt. Soc., S.C. Vocat. Dirs. Assn., S.C. Bus. Edn. Assn. (pres. 1969-70, mem. exec. bd. 1965-77), S.C. Vocat. Assn. (mem. program com. 1975-76), S.C. State Employees Assn., Internat. Word Processing Assn., S.C. Coun. for Adminstrv. Women in Edn., Nat. Speakers Assn., S.C. Hist. Soc., Found. for Future of Bus. Edn. (chmn. 1989), Nat. Fedn. Ind. Bus. (bd. dirs. 1989, mem. nat. edn. adv. bd.), Friends of State Mus., Rotary, Delta Kappa Gamma, Phi Delta Kappa. Baptist. Contbr. numerous articles to profl. jours.; author textbooks on word processing materials; editor and reviewer various manuals and instructional guides on bus. and office occupations programs. Office: 904 Rutledge Bldg State Dept Education Columbia SC 29201

MATTHEWS, BARBARA ANN, telecommunications executive; b. Columbia, S.C., Oct. 16, 1951; d. William Nathan and Lilly Ruth (Harvey) M.; BA, U. S.C., 1973, MBA, 1976. Dir. pub. rels. United Way, Columbia, 1973-75; S.C. Med. Assn., Columbia, 1975-76; mng. dir. Pi Sigma Epsilon, N.Y.C., 1976-78; account exec. AT&T, L.A., 1979-84; mgr. Amdahl Communications, Marina del Rey, Calif. and Richardson, Tex., 1984-86; owner Custom House, Ltd., L.A., 1987—. Mem. L.A. Transp. Club, Pi Sigma Epsilon (alumni v.p. 1983-85, bd. dirs. 1983—, pres. 1985-87), Delta Nu Alpha.

MATTHEWS, BARBARA JEAN, sales and marketing professional; b. Oakland, Calif., Sept. 8, 1936; d. Francis E. and Leila K. (Goold) McQuilkin; m. Jacob E. Kasten, Sept. 12, 1987; children: Carol, Kathleen, Kimberly, Terrance. Student, Armstrong Coll.; BS, Coll. San Mateo, 1969. Sales svc. mgr. Waste King Universal, San Mateo, Calif., 1957-60; asst. pers. mgr. MILPRINT Inc., South San Francisco, 1960-63; sales and mktg. rep. Polyvue Plastic, Petalumn, Calif., 1965-81; regional mgr. Automated Packaging Systems, Anaheim, Calif., 1981—. Mem. Bus. and Profl. Women (pres.), Internat. Bottled Water Assn., Nat. Soft Drink Assn., Petroleum Packing Inst., Dairy Assn. Home: 2 Carmel Ct Laguna Beach CA 92651 Office: 1350 N Knollwood Anaheim CA 92801

MATTHEWS, CAROLYN CROKER, nurse, director; b. Vernon, Tex., Mar. 7, 1938; d. Thomas C. and Myrtle (Renner) Croker; m. Edward Harold Matthews, Dec. 26, 1959; children: Thomas E., David H. BS in Profl. Arts, St. Joseph Coll., 1980; MS in Health Adminstrn., Columbia Pacific U., 1982, PhD in Health Adminstrn., 1983. Staff nurse Mobile (Ala.) Infirmary, 1959-62, head nurse woman's clinic, 1966-77, instr. operating room, 1977-78; asst. dir. surgery Mobile (Ala.) Infirmary, Mobile, 1978-89; dir. surg. and emergency svcs. Mobile (Ala.) Infirmary, 1989—. Aux. policewoman Saraland (Ala.) Police Dept., 1975-77. Mem. ANA, Assn. Operating Room Nurses (bd. dirs. Mobile chpt. 1978), Nat. League Nurses, Ala. Nurses Assn. Republican. Presbyterian. Home: 916 Leon St Saraland AL 36571 Office: Mobile Infirmary Med Ctr #5 Circle Mobile AL 36652

MATTHEWS, DARLENE THERESA, owner, manager employment agency; b. Jacksonville, Fla., May 11, 1953; d. Raymond H. and Lillian M. (Wilczewski) M.; m. James M. Waller, Feb. 25, 1987; 1 child, Thomas J. Freelance legal sec. Imperial Beach, Calif.; legal sec. Aguirre and Eckmann, San Diego; owner, mgr. Darlene's Referrals. Mem. NAFE.

MATTHEWS, DOMINA MARYL, counselor; b. Chillicothe, Ohio, Mar. 10, 1947; d. Wesley Smith and Ruth Marie (Fields) M. BS in Early Childhood, Wright State U., 1978, MS in Mental Health Counseling, 1988, postgrad., 1990—. Cert. sch. counselor. Therapist Montgomery Bd. Mental Retardation Adult Svcs., Dayton, Ohio, 1973-77; elem. sch. tchr. Monticello Elem., Huber Heights, Ohio, 1978-89; unit mgr. Juvenile Ct., Dayton, 1989—; coach Wayne High Sch., Huber Heights, 1986-87; adventure programs tchr. Aullwood Audubon Farm, Englewood, Ohio, 1988; cons. Ligonier Valley Treatment Ctr., Stahlstown, Pa., 1990—. Advisor Dist. Just Say No Program, Huber Heights, 1987—; mem. Miami Valley Citizens Against Substance Abuse, Dayton, 1988—, Youth 2000, Dayton, 1989—. Named Martha Holden Jennings Scholar, Dayton, 1983, WOEA Teach of the Year, 1987; recipient Grad. Studies Scholarship Wright State U., 1990. Home: 5543 Hummock Rd Trotwood OH 45426

MATTHEWS, EARNESTINE STROUD, educator; b. Memphis, July 16, 1943; d. Odell and Elsie (Hassell) Stroud. BS in Elem. Edn., Lincoln U., 1964; MA, U. Mo., Kansas City, 1974, Ednl. Specialist Degree, 1987. Tchr. Sch. Dist. Kans. City, 1964-72, reading and Math specialist, 1972-75, coordinator, 1975-83; prin. Manchester Sch., Kansas City. Co-author: (handbook) Remedial Teaching Strategies for Math., 1977,. Vol. Kansas City Tomorrow Program sponsored by Kansas City Civic Coun. Mem. Assn. for Curriculum and Supervision, Nat. Assn. Black Sch. Educators, Kansas City Assn. Elem. Sch. Prins. (pres.-elect), Mo. Assn. Elem. Sch. Prins., Phi Delta Kappa. Democrat. Baptist. Home: 724 E 122d Pl Kansas City MO 64146

MATTHEWS, ELIZABETH WOODFIN, law librarian, law educator; b. Ashland, Va., July 30, 1927; d. Edwin Clifton and Elizabeth Frances (Luck) Woodfin; m. Sidney E. Matthews, Dec. 20, 1947; 1 child, Sarah Elizabeth Matthews Wiley. BA, Randolph-Macon Coll., 1948, LLD (hon.), 1989; MS in Libr. Sci., U. Ill., 1952; PhD, So. Ill. U., 1972; LLD, Randolph-Macon Coll., 1989. Cert. law libr., med. libr., med. libr. III. Libr. Ohio State U., Columbus, 1952-59; libr., instr. U. Ill., Urbana, 1962-63, lectr. Grad. Sch. Libr. Sci., 1964; libr., instr. Morris Libr. So. Ill. U., Carbondale, 1964-67, classroom instr. Coll. Edn., 1967-70, med. libr., asst. prof. Morris Libr., 1972-74, law libr., asst. prof., 1974-79, law libr., assoc. prof., 1979-85, law libr., prof., 1985—. Author: Access Points to Law Libraries, 1984, 17th Century English Law Reports, 1986, Law Library Reference Shelf, 1988, Pages and Missing Pages, 1983. Mem. AAUW (pres. 1976-78, corp. rep. 1978-88), Am. Assn. Law Librs., Mid Am. Assn. Law Librs., Beta Phi Mu, Phi Kappa Phi. Methodist. Home: 811 Skyline Dr Carbondale IL 62901 Office: So Ill U Sch Law Libr Carbondale IL 62901

MATTHEWS, JANA B., management consultant; b. Chgo., Oct. 23, 1940; d. L. Emmet and Helen J. (Severson) Beauchamp; m. Samuel R. Matthews, June 1, 1963 (div. 1971); 1 child, Carolyn E.; m. Charles C. Halbower, May 13, 1975. BA, Earlham Coll., 1962; MA, U. R.I., 1970; EdD, Harvard U., 1979. Tchr. Portsmouth (N.H.) and Coventry (R.I.) Pub. Schs., 1963-68; asst. provost Mass. State Coll. System, Boston, 1970-73; sr. staff Arthur D. Little, Inc., Cambridge, Mass., 1973-76; div. dir. NCHEMS, Boulder, Colo., 1980-83; pres. NCHEMS Mgmt. Svcs., Inc., Boulder, Colo., 1983-85, M & H Group, Inc., Boulder and Herndon, Va., 1985—. Co-author: Managing the Partnership Between Higher Education and Industry, 1984; author: Effective Use of Management Consultants in Higher Education, 1983; contbr. articles to profl. jours. Appointed commr. Colo. Adv. Tech. Inst., 1988—. Mem. Assn. Univ. Related Rsch. Parks (dir. 1987—), Soc. Coll. & Univ. Planning (v.p. 1973-75), Assn. Instl. Researchers, Harvard Club. Home: 49 Alder Ln Boulder CO 80304 Office: M&H Group Inc PO Box 1888 Boulder CO 80306

MATTHEWS, KAY ANN BEAN, cash and investments manager; b. Winston-Salem, N.C., Oct. 30, 1955; d. Richard Carleton and Nancy Ann (Vaughn) Bean; m. Richard Alan Matthews, June 20, 1981; 1 child, Lisa Kay. BA in Econs., Calif. State U., Chico, 1978. Cert. cash mgr. Asst. ops. supr. County Bank Santa Cruz, Santa Cruz, Calif., 1978-80; cash and investment mgr. Bowman Gray Sch. Medicine, Winston-Salem, 1981—. Mem. Nat. Corp. Cash Mgmt. Assn. Office: Bowman Gray Sch Medicine 300 S Hawthorne Rd Winston-Salem NC 27103

MATTHEWS, LINDA LLEWELLYN FINK, professional association administrator; b. LaPort, Ind., Oct. 29, 1950; d. Omar Ray and Marianne Denham (Smith) Fink, Jr.; student U. N.C., Greensboro, 1968-70; B.A., George Washington U., 1973; m. Daniel G. Matthews, Oct. 25, 1975; children—Strelka Jamila, Francesca Alina. Admnstrv. asst. African Bibliog. Center, Washington, 1974-75, adminstrv. editor, 1975-79, adminstrv. dir., 1979—; adminstrv. dir. African Devel. Info. Assn. U.S.A., 1981-84; fin. analyst Martin Marietta Info. and Communications Systems, 1985—; treas., bd. dirs. African Communications Liaison Services, Washington, 1978-84. Asso. mem. Women's Inst. for Freedom of Press, Washington, 1977-80; coordinator communications liaison com. Washington Task Force on African Affairs, 1975-78; cons. article on Rhodesia, Nat. Geog. Mag., 1975. Mem. African-Am. Women's Assn. Editorial bd. and reviewer A Current Bibliography on African Affairs, 1974—; editor AMA: Women in African & American Worlds, An Outlook, 1975-80, HABARI Special Reports, 1978-84, (newsletter) Africa Catalyst, 1985—; asso. producer Film Leopold Sedar Senghor, 1975; cons., writer Changing Africa, NBC/WRC-TV, 1976; asst. editor Am-South African Relations: Bibliographic Essays, 1975; compiler, co-author: Burundi: A Selected Bibliography & Resource Guide, 1975. Pres. Operation Santa Claus East, 1988—. Mem. I.D.E.A. Home: 1921 S St NW Washington DC 20009 also: PO Box 53398 Temple Heights Station Washington DC 20009

MATTHEWS, PAMELA THORNTON, chef; b. Bridgeport, Conn., Feb. 6, 1954; d. Wesley Earl and Helen (Ficzere) Thornton; m. Wayne Michael Matthews. BA, Franklin Pierce Coll., 1976; grad., Culinary Inst. Am., 1978. With Omni Internat. Hotel, Atlanta, 1978-79; chef saucier Sonesta Beach Hotel, Key Biscayne, Fla., 1979; sous chef Fifth Ave. Restaurant, Miami, 1979-80; chef de partie Hotel Inter-Continental Four Ambassadors, Miami, 1980-81; sous chef Hotel St. Anthony Inter-Continental, San Antonio, 1981; area chef Walt Disney World Co., Orlando, Fla., 1981-85, sous chef, 1985-87, exec. sous chef, 1987—; pastry apprentice Sonesta Beach Resort, 1980-81. Alumni rep. ann. fund drive Franklin Pierce Coll. Mem. Culinary Inst. Am., Chaine des Rotisseurs, Franklin Pierce Coll. Alumni Assn. Home: 4150 Black Powder Way Kissimmee FL 34746 Office: Walt Disney World Co PO Box 10 150 Lake Buena Vista FL 32830-0150

MATTHEWS, ROWENA GREEN, biological chemistry educator; b. Cambridge, Eng., Aug. 20, 1938 (father Am. citizens); d. David E. and Doris (Cribb) Green; m. Larry Stanford Matthews, June 18, 1960; children: Brian Stanford, Keith David. BA, Harvard U., 1960; PhD, U. Mich., 1969. Instr. U. S.C., Columbia, 1964-65; postdoctoral fellow U. Mich., Ann Arbor, 1970-75, asst. prof., 1975-81, assoc. prof. biol. chemistry, 1981-86, prof. 1986—, assoc. chmn., 1988—; mem. phys. biochemistry study sect. NIH, 1982-86. Editorial adv. bd. Biochem. Jour., 1984—. Contbr. articles to profl. jours. Recipient Faculty Recognition award U. Mich., 1984; NIH grantee, 1978—. Mem. AAAS, Am. Soc. Biol. Chemists, Am. Chem. Soc. (program chmn. biochemistry div. 1985, sec. biochemistry div. 1990—), Phi Beta Kappa, Sigma Xi. Avocations: bicycling, snorkeling, cross country skiing, cooking. Home: 1609 S University St Ann Arbor MI 48104 Office: U Mich Biophysics Rsch Div 2200 Bonisteel Ann Arbor MI 48109-0606

MATTHEWS, VALERIE JO, development company executive; b. Omaha, June 6, 1947; d. Blaine Leroy and Betty Rae (Peterson) Rish; m. L. D. Matthews (div. 1975); children: Amy Lynne, Timothy Bryan. Grad. high sch., Omaha, 1965. Acct. various firms, Fremont, Nebr., 1967-78; sales assoc. Sunrise Home, Lincoln, Nebr., 1979-81, Lamb Realty, Thousand Oaks, Calif., 1981-82; rep. and mgr. sales Centex Homes, Oklahoma City, 1982-85; div. pres. Oklahoma City and Denver, 1985-87; with Lamb Realty, Thousand Oaks, Calif., 1988; dir. constrn. and land C.R. Wood Devel. Inc., Thousand Oaks, 1987—; pvt. practice tax and fin. cons. Vol. YMCA, Fremont, 1972, Vols. in the Arts, Oklahoma City, 1985; active Boy Scouts Am., Thousand Oaks, 1981-82. Mem. Calif. Assn. Realtors, Nat. Assn. Home Builders, Bldg. Industry Assn.

MATTHEWS, WESTINA L., finance and banking executive; b. Chillocothe, Ohio, Nov. 8, 1948; d. Wesley Smith and Ruth (Fields) M. BS, U. Dayton, 1970, MS, 1974; PhD, U. Chgo., 1980. Tchr. Mills Lawn Elem. Sch., Yellow Springs, Ohio, 1970-75; program officer The Chgo. Community Trust, 1982-83, sr. program officer, 1983-85; sec. Merrill Lynch & Co. Found., Inc., N.Y.C., 1985—, mgr.corp. contributions, 1985-86, asst. v.p., 1986-87; v.p. Merrill Lynch & Co., Inc., N.Y.C., 1987—; bd. dirs. Ms. Found.; chair Contributions Adv. Group, N.Y.C., 1989-90; guest editor rsch. jour. Columnist New Dawn. Mem. Gov. Adv. Com. on Black Affairs, Albany, N.Y., 1987; mem. NAACP; mem. Bd. Edn., N.Y.C., 1990—. Named Outstanding Svc. Nat. Urban Affairs Coun.m N.Y.C., 1989, Black Achiever in Industry Harlem YMCA, N.Y.C., 1989, Women In Industry Nat. Coun. Negro Women, N.Y.C., 1989; postdoctoral fellow Northwestern U., 1980-81, U. Wis., 1981-82. Mem. Mid. State Assn. (bd. dirs. 1990—), N.Y. Regional Assn. of Grantmakers (sec. 1988-89), Coalition of 100 Black Women, Assn. of Black Found. Exec. (bd. dirs. 1982-86), Women and Founds./Corp. Philanthropy. Office: Merrill Lynch & Co 225 Liberty St New York NY 10080

MATTHEWS-JOHNSON, CYNTHIA L., computer systems specialist; b. Queens, N.Y., Feb. 28, 1959; d. George E. Matthews and Patricia L. (Osburn) Matthews; children: Kenneth Lee II, Catherine LaVone, Elizabeth Lynette. AS in Data Processing, La Guardia Community Coll., Long Island City, N.Y., 1985; BS in Info. Systems Mgmt., York Coll., Jamaica, N.Y., 1990. Computer systems operator U.S. Postal Svc., Jamaica, 1989—; EDP systems ops. U.S. Postal Svc., Jamaica. Mem. NAFE. Democrat. Lutheran. Office: US Postal Svc AMF-JF Kennedy Bldg 250 Jamaica NY 11430

MATTHIES, EVELYN FERN, artist, art educator; b. Albert Lea, Minn., June 24, 1936; d. Kermit Rufus and Violet Idora (Nelson) Jensen; m. William N. Matthies Jr., Aug. 18, 1956; children: James, Jane, Todd. BS, Mankato (Minn.) State U., 1959; MS, St. Cloud (Minn.) State U., 1975. Tchr. North Mankato Elem., 1956-57, Rapidan (Minn.) Elem., 1957-59, Brainerd (Minn.) High Sch., 1959-63, Brainerd Sch. Dist. 181, 1963-65; art dir., instr. State Minn., Brainerd Community Coll., 1966—; co-owner Minn. Sch. Diving, Brainerd, 1961—, On the Other Hand, Nisswa, Minn., 1981-84; owner Evelyn Matthies Studio & Gallery, 1990—; dir. summer grants Minn. Sch. and Resource Ctr. for Arts, St. Paul, 1986, 87, 88, 89; art. dir. Minn. Community Colls., St. Paul, 1981-86; juror Minn. Natural Resources, Brainerd, 1988, 89; facilitator Minn. Faculty Devel., Mpls., 1988, 89, State Fine Arts Festival, Mpls., 1988, 89; chmn. Minn. Community Coll. Faculty Devel., State Minn., 1988—; mem. Nat. Coun. Staff, Profl., Orgn. Devel., 1978—. One woman show Madden's Resort, 1988; group shows include St. Cloud State Gallery, 1972, others. Named Outstanding Faculty Mem., Minn. Community Coll., St. Paul, 1985, Outstanding Instr. Brainerd Community Coll., 1988; recipient Gov.'s award Minn. Sch. and Resource Ctr. for Arts, St. Paul, 1986, Citizen for the Arts award Sch. Dist. 181, 1987, Rev. of Excellence Artist award Exchange Club, Brainerd, 1989. Mem. AAUW (v.p. 1966-70), NEA, Minn. Edn. Assns., Minn. Community Coll. Faculty Devel., Art Educators Minn., Alpha Delta Kappa (pres. 1970-74). Lutheran. Home: 418 N 3d St Brainerd MN 56401 Office: Brainerd Community Coll College Dr Brainerd MN 56401 also: Evelyn Matthies Studio & Gallery Brainerd MN 56401

MATTHIS, EVA MILDRED BONEY, educator; b. Waycross, N.C., Aug. 18, 1927; d. James Horace and Eva Alice (Merritt) Boney; m. George Clifton Matthis, Aug. 31, 1949; 1 child, George Clifton Jr. AA, Louisburg Coll., 1946; BS, East Carolina U., 1969, MLS, 1971. Advt. mgr. Efirds, Wilmington, N.C., 1946-49; syn. aviation instrument instr. Serv-Air Aviation, Kinston, N.C., 1950-57; advt. account exec. Kinston Free Press, 1959-64; libr. Caswell Ctr., 1965-66; history tchr. North Lenoir High Sch., 1969-70; libr. Sampson Elem. Sch., 1970-72; head libr. media program Lenoir Community Coll., 1972-76, dean, learning resources, 1976-89, dean, mktg. instl. devel., learning resources, 1989-90, dean, instl. advancement, 1990—; alumni rep. East Carolina U. LS SACS Self-study, Greenville, 1987-89. Family editor: Heritage of Lenoir County, 1981. Developer Local History Mus., Heritage Pl., 1988; pres. Jr. Women's Club, Kinston, 1960; dist. dir. N.C. Jr. Women's Club, N.C., 1961; mem. Mayor's All-Am. CityCom., Kinston, 1988; rep. Lenoir County Bicentennial Com., Kinston, 1987; parish chair Queen St. United Meth. Ch., 1988-90, bishop's coun., 1988-90, Sunday sch. tchr., mem. adminstrv. bd., 1984—. Recipient Merit award N.C. Hist. Soc., 1989, Award of Excellence Kinston C. of C., 1985. Mem. N.C. Community Coll. Learning Resources Assn. (pub. info. officer 1989-90, exec. bd., dir. dist. II 1986-89), Librarians of Lenoir County (pres. 1985), Lenoir County Hist. Assn., Coun. on Resource Devel., Historic Lenoir County-Kinston Celebration, East Carolina U. Alumni Assn., Phi Theta Kappa, Delta Kappa Gamma (yearbook editor). Home: 2312 Riley Rd Kinston NC 28501 Office: Lenoir Community Coll PO Box 188 Kinston NC 28501

MATTIS, NOEMI PERELMAN, psychologist; b. Lodz, Poland, Oct. 16, 1936; came to U.S., 1958; d. Chaim Pinchas and Fela Estera (Liwer) Perelman; m. Daniel Charles Mattis, Nov. 9, 1958; children: Michael, Olivia. BA, Free U., Brussels, 1955, JD, 1958; MA, Columbia U., 1963, PhD, 1973. Lic. psychologist, Utah. Instr. French lit. Briarcliff Coll., 1960-62; psychologist Cage Teen Ctr., White Plains, N.Y., 1973-76; pvt. practice, Scarsdale, N.Y., 1976-80, Salt Lake City, 1981—; psychologist, adj. asst. prof. dept. ednl. psychology, Women's Resource Ctr., U. Utah, Salt Lake City, 1980-83, clin. asst. prof. dept. psychology, 1980-85; vice-chair Utah Gov.'s Commn. for Women of Families, 1989—; chair Task Force on Ritual Abuse. Mem. Utah Women's Forum, 1987—, Utahns United Against Nuclear Arms Race, 1986—, Women Concerned about Nuclear War, 1985—; bd. dirs. YWCA, 1981-86, Salt Lake Acting Co., 1984-87. Mem. Am. Psychol. Assn., Utah Psychol. Assn. (bd. dirs. 1984), Soc. Psychol. Study Social Issues, Utah Psychologists in Pvt. Practice (pres. 1984), Internat. Soc. for the Multiple Personality & Dissociation, Psi Chi, Kappa Lambda Pi, Pi Lambda Theta. Address: 299 Federal Heights Circle Salt Lake City UT 84103

MATTISON, PRISCILLA JANE, film director and producer; b. Phila., July 28, 1960. Cert., Tech. U. Berlin, 1983; BA, Yale U., 1982; cert., Am. Film Inst., 1987. Coordinator prodn. office Eyris Prodns., Inc., N.Y.C., 1983-84; asst. producer LKL Prodns. Inc., N.Y.C., 1984-85; distbn. dir. Michael Blackwood Prodns. Inc., N.Y.C., 1985-86; asst. to pres. Concorde Pictures Inc., L.A., 1987-88, dir. acquisitions and devel., head casting, 1987-89, feature film dir., 1989—; free-lance assoc. producer, pub. relations, N.Y.C., 1985-86. Dir., editor music video, 1986; composer various songs, 1985—; asst. producer films and videos, 1985—; dir. feature film Slumber Party Massacre III, 1990. Fundraiser Cystic Fibrosis Found., Narberth, Pa., 1976-78; English tutor Internat. Ctr., N.Y.C., 1985. Recipient Eunice Pond Meml. award Pa. Poetry Soc., 1978; Fulbright scholar Inst. Internat. Edn., 1982. Mem. Greenpeace, Calif. Abortion Rights Action League, Zero Population Ggrowth, Nat. Assn. Female Execs., Nat. Acad. Songwriters, Fulbright Alumni Assn., Women in Film (ind. feature project). Democrat. Home: 2904 Broadway Santa Monica CA 90404

MATTMAN, LIDA HOLMES, microbiologist, educator; b. Denver, July 31, 1912; d. Eureka Spurgeon and Lillie Edith (Henry) Holmes; children: Sandra, Paul. BA, U. Kans., 1933, MA, 1934; PhD, Yale U., 1940. Head clin. labs. UN Relief and Rehab., 1944; sr. bacteriologist dept. pub. health Commonwealth of Mass., Boston, 1947-48; instr. Wayne State U., Detroit, 1949-85; instr. immunology Oakland U., Rochester, Mich., 1986; rsch. investigator, emeritus prof. Wayne State U., Detroit, 1986—; cons. immunology U.S. Dept. Justice, Detroit, NSF. Author: Cell Wall Deficient Forms, 1975; contbr. chpts. to books and numerous articles to profl. jours. AMA grantee, Am. Thoracic Soc. grantee, Damon Runyon Soc. grantee, Mich. Cancer Soc. grantee, Mich. Heart Assn. grantee, Detroit Tuberculosis Soc. grantee, Wayne County Tuberculosis Soc. grantee, USPHS grantee, Wayne State U. grantee, Yale U. scholar, U. Pa. rsch. fellow. Mem. Am. Soc. Microbiology (pres. Mich. br.), Mich. Acad. Scis. (chmn. med. div.). Home: 319 Rivard Grosse Pointe MI 48230 Office: Wayne State U Biology Dept Detroit MI 48202

MATTOON, SARA HALSEY (SALLY MATTOON), business consultant, educator; b. Bronxville, N.Y., July 8, 1947; Henry Amasa Jr. and Dorothy Ann (Teeter) M. AAS in Edn., Bennett Coll., 1967; BS in Edn. and Scis., So. Conn. State U., 1969; MA in Edn. and Humanistic Psychology, Calif. State U., Chico, 1976. Cert. tchr., Calif. Tchr. San Diego Unified Sch. Dist., 1969-72, Montgomery Creek Sch. Dist., Round Mountain, Calif., 1972-73; founder, tchr., dir. Chico Youth Devel. Ctr., Inc., 1973-80; pres. Exec. Excellence and Sunrise Communications, San Diego, Weston, Conn., 1973—; chmn. bd. dirs. Chico Youth Devel. Ctr., Inc., 1980—. Mem. Am. Assn. Profls. Practicing Transcendental Meditation Program (San Diego chpt. pres. 1985—), Greater San Diego C. of C., MIT Enterprise Forum (founding mem. San Diego chpt. 1985—), World Plan Exec. Council (bd. govs. 1978—, Info. and Inspiration award 1985). Office: Sunrise Communications 3566 Conrad Ave San Diego CA 92117-1702

MATTSON, CAROL LINNETTE, social services administrator; b. Frederic, Wis., Oct. 3, 1946; d. Clarence Waldemar and Lucille Anna Mathilda (Bengtson) Hedlund; m. Wesley Harlan Mattson, June 24, 1967; 1 child, Aaron Ray. BS, U. Wis., Menomonie, 1968. Home econs. tchr. Luck (Wis.) High Sch., 1968-72; clk. Daniels Twp., Siren, Wis., 1973-75; family living instr. Wis. Indianhead Tech. Inst., New Richmond, 1974-77; aging program dir. Polk County, Balsam Lake, Wis., 1977—; sec., bd. dirs. Polk

County Transp. for the Disabled and Elderly, Inc., Balsam Lake, 1978—; sec., mem. com. Long Term Support Com., Balsam Lake, 1985—. Mem. Community Edn. Coun. for Frederic (Wis.) Schs.; sec. Ch. Parish Bd. Mem. Wis. Assn. Nutrition Dirs., Wis. Assn. Aging Unit Dirs. Lutheran. Office: Polk County Aging Programs Courthouse Box 281 Balsam Lake WI 54810

MATTSON, GAIL, environmental engineer, consultant; b. Kansas City, Mo., Dec. 23, 1950; d. John Richard and Shirley Coleen (Standish) Giese; m. Peter Lawrence Mattson, Apr. 28, 1974. BS in Chemistry and Biology, Baker U., 1973; MS in Environ. Engring., U. Wash., Seattle, 1982. Registered profl. engr. Wash., Alaska, Wis., Ill., Ind. Project cost engr. Bechtel Power Corp., San Francisco, 1973-75; field cost engr. Can. Bechtel Ltd., Ft. Murray, Alta., Can., 1975-77; environ. engr. Envirosphere Co., Bellevue, Wash., 1983-86; pres. Mattson Environ. Engring., Seattle, 1986-87; Chgo. ops. mgr. Ebasco Environ., 1987—. Mem. Am. Soc. Civil Engrs., Ill. Water Pollution Control Assn., Cert. Hazardous Materials Mgrs. (pres. Chgo. chpt. 1990—), Soc. Women Engrs. (Chgo. sect. rep. 1990—), Phi Mu (pres. Chgo. chpt. 1990—). Lutheran. Home: 1518 Forest Ave River Forest IL 60305 Office: Ebasco Environ 111 N Canal St Ste 915 Chicago IL 60606

MATTSON, JEAN MURPHEY, microbiologist; b. Bklyn., Apr. 1, 1926; d. Fredxerick Albert and Elizabeth Frances (Henning) Odenwald; m. Daniel Forney Hoke Murphey, Aug. 14, 1971 (dec. 1974); m. Arthur Mattson, Apr. 16, 1979. BS, L.I. U., Bklyn., 1948. Cytotechnologist Cornell Med. Coll., N.Y.C., 1948-51; chief of microbiology Bayfront Med. Ctr., St. Petersburg, Fla., 1952-71; microbiologist Lab. of Ira C. Evans, M.D., St. Petersburg, 1975-79; registered rep. Anchor Financial, Brevard, N.C., 1984-89. Vol. Transylvania Community Hosp., Brevard, 1983—. Mem. Am. Soc. Clin. Pathologists, Nat. Assn. Securities Dealers. Republican. Episcopalian. Home: 6 Robin Cir Brevard NC 28712-4208 Office: Anchor Financial 6 Robin Cir Brevard NC 28712-4208

MATTSON, KAY ROBERTA, art consultant; b. Roseau, Minn., Feb. 22, 1950; d. James Chester and Mildred Udell (Larson) Robertson; m. Allan Leslie Mattson, Aug. 21, 1971. BS, U. Minn., 1972. Customer svc. rep. M.W. Lapidary Supply, Mpls., 1972-75; realtor assoc. East-West Realty, Grand Rapids, Minn., 1976-78; terr. mgr. Shulton, Inc., Indpls. and Wayne, N.J., 1978-83; pres. Classic Calligraphy, Zionsville, Ind., 1987—; art cons. Gallery Frame Designs, Indpls., 1989—; info. desk Indpls. Mus. Art, 1988-89, docent, 1989—. Vol., news media Pan-Am Games, Indpls., 1987. Mem. Indpls. Zool. Guild (patron; chmn. invitations and reservations 1987), Pi Beta Phi. Office: Gallery of Frame Designs 342 Massachusetts Ave Indianapolis IN 46204

MATULICH, ERIKA, marketing educator; b. Sacramento, Sept. 14, 1963; d. Serge and Margarete (Manderscheid) M. BBA, Tex. Christian U., 1984, MBA, 1986; postgrad., U. Wis., Madison, 1989—. Ops. officer M Bank Dallas, 1986-87; instr. Tex. Christian U., Ft. Worth, 1986-89; ops. analyst Bell Helicopter, Textron, Ft. Worth, 1987-89; teaching asst. U. Wis., Madison, 1989—; market researcher All Saints Episc. Hosp., Ft. Worth, 1984, Shakespeare in the Park, Ft. Worth, 1985, Infomart, Dallas, 1985; strategic planner Williamson-Dickie, Ft. Worth, 1985; presenter at conf. Am. Assn. Advances in Health Care, 1987, 88, 89. Mem. Am. Mktg. Assn., Am. Assn. Advances in Health Care Rsch., Beta Gamma Sigma. Office: Univ Wis Madison 1155 Observatory Dr Madison WI 53706

MATUSZAK, ALICE JEAN BOYER, pharmacy educator; b. Newark, Ohio, June 22, 1935; d. James Emery and Elizabeth Hawthorn (Irvine) Boyer; m. Charles Alan Matuszak, July 27, 1955; children: Matthew, James. BS summa cum laude, Ohio State U., 1958, MS, 1959; postgrad., U. Wis., 1959-60; PhD, U. Kans., 1963. Registered pharmacist, Ohio, Calif. Apprentice pharmacist Arensberg Pharmacy, Newark, 1953-58; rsch. asst. Ohio State U., Columbus, 1958, lab. asst., 1958-59; rsch. asst. U. Wis., Madison, 1959-60, U. Kans., Lawrence, 1960-63; asst. prof. U. of the Pacific, Stockton, Calif., 1963-67, assoc. prof., 1971-78, prof., 1978—. Contbr. articles to profl. jours. NIH grantee, 1965-66. Mem. Am. Assn. Colls. of Pharmacy (chmn. chemistry sect. 1979-80), Am. Pharm. Assn. (chmn. basic scis. 1990, Am. Inst. History of Pharmacy (exec. coun. 1984-88, 90-92, chmn. contributed papers 1990-92, Cert. of Commendation 1990), Am. Chem. Soc., Internat. Fedn. Pharmacy, Sigma Xi, Phi Kappa Phi, Kappa Epsilon, Lambda Kappa Sigma (hon.), Delta Zeta. Democrat. Episcopalian. Home: 1130 W Mariposa Ave Stockton CA 95204 Office: U of the Pacific Sch of Pharmacy Stockton CA 95211

MATZ, KAY ELAINE, savings and loan executive; b. Warren, Ohio, Apr. 18, 1946; d. Nick M. and Julia H. (Petrulak) Kovic. grad. bus. mgmt. Hiram Coll., 1987. Staff acct. R.M. Robbins & Assocs., Warren, 1964-73; with 1st Fed. Savs. & Loan Assn. Warren, 1973—, asst. treas., 1980-81, contr., 1982—; ann. fin. auditor Children's Rehab. Ctr., Warren, 1970-74. Mem. Am. Soc. Women Accts. (pres. Youngstown chpt. 1975-76), Fin. Mgrs. Soc. (pres. Pa.-Ohio chpt. 1983-84), Warren Area C. of C., Exec. Link of Warren, Emblem Club, Warren Women's Networking Club, Lions (Warren). Democrat. Avocations: travel, golf. Home: 2940 Reeves Rd NE Warren OH 44483 Office: 1st Fed Savs & Loan Assn Warren 185 E Market St PO Box 551 Warren OH 44481

MAUCH, BETTY L., construction executive; b. Long Beach, Calif., 1941; d. Walter Ray and Betty Jane (O'Malia) Pitts.; m. Harold R. Mauch, 1958; children: John Falkenhagen, Harold Jr., Betty. Ptnr. Swede's Roofing, Cheyenne, Wyoming. Home: 5501 Gateway Dr Cheyenne WY 82007

MAULE, CYNTHIA LEA, dental laboratory executive; b. Vienna, Austria, Apr. 26, 1949; came to U.S., 1952; d. Richard Haseltine and Jean Ardelle (Moore) Timmins; m. George Walter Maule, Oct. 17, 1986. Student fgn. studies, U. Vienna, 1971; BA, Coe Coll., 1971. Cert. secondary English tchr., Iowa, S.D., Minn. Field counselor Alpha Xi Delta Nat. Frat., Indpls., 1971-72; flight attendant Transamerica Airlines, Oakland, Calif., 1972-83, sr. flight attendant, 1983-86; exec. sec. Dexterity Dental Arts, Inc., Rosemount, Minn., 1987-89, mgmt. analyst, 1989—. Mem. Assn. Flight Attendants (sec.-treas. master coun., union local chairperson, negotiator grievance-arbitration, bd. dirs. 1983-86), PEO (philanthropic vol. 1968—), Rainbow Girls (life), Order of Eastern Star, Alpha Xi Delta (life, philanthropic vol. 1968-71, Outstanding Mem. award 1969, 70). Republican. Presbyterian.

MAUN, MARY ELLEN, communications company analyst; b. N.Y.C., Dec. 18, 1951; d. Emmet Joseph and Mary Alice (McMahon) M. BA, CUNY, 1977, MBA, 1988. Sales rep. N.Y. Telephone Co., N.Y.C., 1970-76, comml. rep., 1977-83, programmer, 1984-86; systems analyst Nynex Svc. Co., N.Y.C., 1987-89, sr. systems analyst, 1990—. Corp. chmn. United Way of Tri-State Area, N.Y.C., 1985; recreation activities vol. Pioneers Am., N.Y.C., 1982—; active Sleepy Hollow Hist. Soc. Recipient Outstanding Community Service award, Calvary Hosp., Bronx, N.Y., 1984. Mem. N.Y. Health and Racquet Club, Road Runners. Democrat. Home: 3 Farrington Ave Philipse Manor NY 10591-1302 Office: Nynex Svc Co 1166 Ave of the Americas New York NY 10036

MAUNSBACH, KAY BENEDICTA, financial analyst, consultant, real estate developer; b. N.Y.C., Apr. 25, 1933; d. Eric and Katherine M. BA, Hunter Coll., 1961; postgrad., NYU, 1961-64. CLU. Jr. fin. analyst Vilas and Hickey, N.Y.C., 1960-62; v.p. investment services Shearson Loeb, Rhoades and Co. Inc., N.Y.C., 1962-73; v.p., dir. corp. communications Manhattan Life Ins. Co., N.Y.C., 1974-80; pres. Atrium Group Ltd., 1979—; gen. ptnr. Prospero Properties, 1982—; gen. ptnr. Prospero Properties, 1982-89; pres. Atrium Holding Corp., 1982—, Prospero Prop., II and of N.Y., 1985-89, Pegasus Asset Mgmt. Corp., 1985—; v.p. Eaton St. Assoc. Fla., 1986—; ptnr. Rivers Edge Assn. Trustee Art Festival of Continents, Key West, Fla., 1988; commr. cultural affairs Soc. of Key West; adv. bd. Founders Soc. Fellow Fin. Analysts Fedn.; mem. Life Advertisers Assn., Nat. Assn. Bus. Economists, Pub. Relations Council, Am. Council Life Ins., Internat. Assn. Bus. Communicators, Fin. Communications Soc., Pub. Affairs Council, Women's Econ. Roundtable, Life Ins. Council N.Y., N.Y. Soc. Security Analysts, Chartered Life Underwriters, Life Underwriters Assn. N.Y., N.Y. Bd. Realtors, N.Y. Bus. Communicators, World Futurists Soc., N.Y. Soc. Security Analysts.

MAUPIN, CAROL GRINSTEAD, food consultant; b. Jan. 31, 1936; d. Randolph Henry and Mildred Asilee (Pfaff) Grinstead. B.A., U. Okla., 1958. Asst. to food dir. Neiman Marcus, Dallas, 1958-62; asst. to food dir. So. Meth. U., Dallas, 1963-64; asso. dir. food ops. Mut. of Omaha, Dallas, 1964-69; dir. tearoom, parties and spl. events Denver Dry Goods, Dallas, 1970-74; dir. food and party services Jr. League of Houston, Dallas, 1974-81; ptnr. Jackson and Co., catering service, Dallas, 1981-83; head food research and devel. Neiman Marcus, Dallas, 1983—; Entertaining columnist Dallas Morning News; food cons. Mus. Food Arts; cooking instr. Batterie de Cuisine Cooking Sch., Foleys, Gourmet Kitchens; food lectr.; food and party cons. protocol office City of Houston; food service cons., bd. dirs. Alley Theatre of Houston. Mem. Am. Home Econs. Assn., Nat. Assn. Cooking Schs., Internat. Food and Wine Soc., Houston Culinary Guild. Republican. Episcopalian. Office: Neiman Marcus Dallas TX 75201

MAURER, CAROL NELLIS, psychiatrist; b. Franklin, Pa., May 15, 1933; d. Charles N. and Grace W. Nellis; m. Kenneth O. Maurer, July 5, 1958; children: Timothy Charles, Kathleen Cynthia, Sabrina Lynn. AA, Colo. Women's Coll., 1953; BA, Goucher Coll., 1956; MD, Temple U., 1960. Rotating intern Nazareth Hosp., Phila., 1960-61; resident psychiatry Warren State Hosp., Warren, Pa., 1965-68; staff physician Polk State Sch. & Hosp., Polk, Pa., 1962-65; psychiatrist Warren State Hosp., 1968; staff psychiatrist Venango County Mental Health Clinic, Oil City, Pa., 1969-72; med. dir. Titusville Mental Health Clinic, Titusville, Pa., 1971-73; pvt. practice gen. psychiatry Oil City, 1972—; lectr. neurology sch. nursing Oil City Hosp., 1962; cons. staff Oil City Hosp., 1969-72, active staff, 1972-87, courtesy staff, 1987—; sec.-treas. med. staff, 1978-80, pres. med. staff, 1980-82, dept. head psychiatry, 1978-80, 82-87; cons. staff Franklin Hosp., 1969—, Titusville Hosp., 1971-86; cons. Clarion County Child Welfare, 1972-75, George Junior Republic, Grove City, Pa., 1981—; cons. psychiatry, med. dir. Family Svc. Agy., Oil City, 1975—; cons. psychiatry Decision House, Oil City, 1975—. Bd. dirs. Franklin chpt. ARC, 1964-65, Venango County chpt. Am. Cancer Soc., 1964-65, Venango County Diagnostic and Tng. Ctr., Family Svc. Agy., Oil City, 1974—; mem. Oil City Area Sch. Bd., 1971-85, v.p. 1976, bd. pres., 1979-81; mem. adult chpt. Am. Field Svc., Oil City Area, 1978—, pres. 1989—; mem. AAUW, 1961-62, Hasson Heights Home and Sch. Club, 1969-80, Zonta Internat., 1970-75, Venango County and Pa. Republican Women, social welfare com. Christ Luth. Ch., 1973-76; worship asst. Good Hope Luth. Ch., 1990—; mem. discipline com. N.W. Pa. Synod Luth. Ch. in Am. Mem. Am. Psychiat. Assn., Pa. Psychiat. Assn., Western Pa. Psychiat. Soc., Pa. Med. Soc. (bd. dirs. 1984-88, exec. com. 1987-88), Venango County Med. Soc. (pres. 1984-86), Pa. Med. Polit. Action Com. (bd. dirs. 1985-89, asst. treas. 1987-89, exec. com. 1987-89). Home and office: 15 Stewart Rd Oil City PA 16301

MAURER, JOANN DENICE, health science facility administrator; b. Bay City, Mich., Dec. 18, 1951; d. Phillip C. Maurer and Elsie (Etherington) McGowan. AS, Eas. Mich. U., 1979; BS in Pharmacy, Mercer U., 1982, PharmD, 1983. Registered Pharmacist, Ga., Fla. Pharmacy intern Drs. Meml. Hosp., Atlanta, 1979-82; pharmacist Egleston Hosp., Atlanta, 1982-84; clin. specialist Lee Meml. Hosp., Ft. Myers, Fla., 1984—; asst. clin. prof. U. Fla., 1989—. Lectr. Arthritis Found., Ft. Myers, 1984—. Mem. So. Gulf Soc. Hosp. Pharmacists (pres. 1988), Am. Soc. Parenteral Enteral Nutrition, Fla. Soc. Hosp. Pharmacists, Phi Theta Kappa. Republican. Episcopalian. Home: 1910 Viginia Ave Apt 502B Fort Myers FL 33901

MAURER, LUCILLE DARVIN, state treasurer; b. N.Y.C., Nov. 21, 1922; d. Joseph Jay and Evelyn (Levine) Darvin; m. Ely Maurer, Apr. 29, 1945; children: Stephen Bennett, Russell Alexander, Edward Nestor. Student, U. N.C., Greensboro, 1938-40; BA, U. N.C., Chapel Hill, 1942; MA, U. N.C., 1945; HLD (hon.), Hood Coll., 1984, U. Md., 1990. Economist U.S. Tariff Commn., 1942-43; econ. and market research for pvt. firms, 1957-60; cons. Nat. Center for Ednl. Stats., 1969-70; mem. Md. House of Dels., 1969-87, mem. ways and means com., 1971-87, chmn. joint com. on fed. relations, 1983-87; now state treas. State of Md.; mem. intergovtl. adv. council U.S. Dept. Edn., 1980-82. Del., Md. Constl. Conv., 1967-68; mem. Montgomery County Bd. Edn., 1960-68; trustee Montgomery Community Coll., 1960-68; vice chmn. nat. planning com., advanced leadership program of seminars on edn. and ednl. policy for state legislators Edn. Commn. of States, 1979-81; mem. exec. com. of edn. com. Nat. Conf. of State Legislatures, 1975-84, chmn., 1978-79, chmn. com. on taxes, trade and econ. devel., 1985-86; mem. adv. com. Servicemems. Opportunity Colls., 1978-82; mem. nat. adv. bd. Inst. for Ednl. Leadership, 1979-81; co-chmn. Md. Commn. on Intergovernmental Cooperation, 1976-82; mem. Nat. Com. on Postsecondary Accreditation, 1974-1979; bd. dirs. Montgomery United Way, 1971-76, 84—; mem. Commn. Higher Edn. of Middle States Assn., 1982-85; mem. Gov.'s Employment and Tng. Council, 1983—. Recipient Legislator of Yr. award Md. Assn. for Retarded Children, 1972, John Dewey award Montgomery County Fedn. Tchrs., 1972, Hornbook award Montgomery County Edn. Assn., 1972, Legislator of Yr. award Md. Assn. Counties, 1984, Willis award for outstanding service Md. Assn. Bds. Edn., 1984, Louis B. Brandeis Justice in Govt. award Am. Jewish Congress, 1988, Judge Sarah T. Hughes' award for disting. pub. svc. Goucher Coll., 1989, Disting. Pub. Svc. award Md. C. of C., 1989; inductee Md. Women's Hall of Fame, 1990. Mem. LWV (past dir. Montgomery County, past dir. Md.), AAUW (Internat. Women's Yr. award Silver Spring 1975), Bus. and Profl. Women's Club (Woman of Yr. 1984), NOW (Legis. Excellence award 1981), Nat. Assn. State Treas. (v.p. 1989—, chmn. legis. com. 1989—), Nat. Assn. State Auditors, Compts. and Treas. (exec. com. 1988—), Women Execs. State Govt. (bd. dirs. 1988—), Women's Equity Action League, Women's Polit. Caucus, Montgomery County Hist. Soc., Order Women Legislators, Delta Kappa Gamma. Jewish. Office: Goldstein Treasury Bdlg Annapolis MD 21401

MAURER, ROSALIE GRACE, credit and collections specialist; b. Balt., Feb. 25, 1945; d. Dominic Joseph and Josephine (Colluroffci) Pasta; m. Joseph Thompson Maurer, July 19, 1964; 1 child, Joseph C. Grad. high sch., Parkville, Md. Keypuncher Users Inc., Valley Forge, Pa., 1973-75, customer svc. rep., 1975-77; data entry clk. United Container Machinery Group Inc., Glen Arm, Md., 1977-83, accounts recievable clk., 1983-86, gen. acctg. clk., 1986—. Mem. Credit and Fin. Devel. Div. (bd. dirs. Balt. chpt. 1989—, editor monthly memo Kreditkrier 1988—). Office: United Container Machinery 5200 Glen Arm Rd Glen Arm MD 21057

MAURER, RUTH ALLENE, mathematics educator; b. Windsor, Colo., July 19, 1939; d. Allen B. and Lillian I. (Kolin) Lamb; m. Charles L. Maurer, Jan. 21, 1961; children: Mike, Barbara, Karl. BS in Phys. Sci., Colo. State U., 1961, MS in Math., 1963; PhD, Colo. Sch. Mines, 1978; postgrad., Harvard U., 1982. Assoc. prof. math. Colo. Sch. Mines, Golden, 1977—; vis. prof. engring. U.S. Mil. Acad., West Point, N.Y., 1987-89; chmn. planning comm. City of Golden, Colo., 1980-81; cons. energy economist First Interstate Bank, Denver, 1980-82; mayor City of Golden, Colo., 1982-85. Bd. dirs. Met. Denver Waste Water Treatment Dist., 1976-82; mem. community corrections bd. County of Jefferson, 1984-85, chmn. emergency telephone authority bd., 1984-87; com. mem. Buffalo Bill Days, 1990; founding mem. steering com. Leadership Golden, 1984-86, 90—; pres. Jefferson Symphony Guild, 1990. Recipient Outstanding Civilian Svc. medal U.S. Army, 1989; Boettcher scholar, 1957-61; Gates fellow, 1982. Mem. Inst. Mgmt. Sci., Ops. Rsch. Soc. Am., Internat. Inst. of Forecasting, Sigma Xi, Phi Kappa Phi. Republican. Home: 303 19th St Golden CO 80401 Office: Colo Sch Mines Dept Math and Computer Scis Golden CO 80401 Mailing: PO Box 736 Golden CO 80402

MAURER, TRACEY LYNN, pharmacist; b. Ft. Hood, Tex., Oct. 15, 1963; d. Robert William and Jean Ann (Canter) M. BS, Ohio No. U., 1986. Staff pharmacist St. Elizabeth Med. Ctr. South, Edgewood, Ky., 1986—. Mem. Greater Cin. Soc. Hosp. Pharmacists, Greenpeace, Nat. Parks and Conservation Assn. Home: 3400 Gerold Dr Cincinnati OH 45238 Office: St Elizabeth Med Ctr South One Medical Village Dr Edgewood KY 41017

MAURIN, GAYLE ELIZABETH, institution executive; b. Kans., 1950. BBA, So. Meth. U., 1972, MBA, 1977; postgrad. in drama, Yale U., 1984, 85. Assoc. product mktg. mgr., then project mgr. Hallmark Cards, Inc., Kansas City, Mo., 1977-84; assoc. dir. devel. Pub. Broadcasting Svc., Alexandria, Va., 1986-88; product mgr. product devel. and licensing Smithsonian Instn., Washington, 1988-89; dir. mktg., membership Am. Youth Hostels, Inc., Washington, 1990—. Coord. fundraising KERA TV & FM, Dallas; co-founder New Arts Theatre Co., Dallas, 1976-77; co-founder Renaissance Festival of Kansas City, 1978-82; bd. dirs. Am. Royal B.O.T.A.R.s, Nelson-Atkins Mus., Friends of Art Guild. NEA fellow, 1986. Mem. Am. Film Inst. (bd. dirs., co-founder Premiere vols.). Home: 411 Wolfe St Alexandria VA 22314

MAX, CAROL ANN, oil company executive; b. Chgo. Heights, Ill., Jan. 12, 1947; d. Martin H. and Lydia Fern (Moore) Graham; m. James L. Max (div. Mar. 1972); children: Martin L., Cynthia S., Christopher A. Fiscal officer State of Ind., Valparaiso, 1971-73; v.p. Steelco Indsl. Lubricants, Valparaiso, 1973—. Mem. NOW, Am. Bikers Aimed Toward Edn. of Ind., Valparaiso Bus. and Profl. Women, Eagles. Republican. Baptist.

MAX, CLAIRE ELLEN, physicist; b. Boston, Sept. 29, 1946; d. Louis William and Pearl (Bernstein) M.; m. Jonathan Arons, Dec. 22, 1974; 1 child, Samuel. AB, Harvard U., 1968; PhD, Princeton U., 1972. Postdoctoral researcher U. Calif., Berkeley, 1972-74; physicist Lawrence Livermore (Calif.) Nat. Lab., 1974—; dir. Livermore br. Inst. Geophysics and Planetary Physics, 1984—; cons. to women in sci., 1978—; mem. Jason Group, Mitre Corp., McLean, Va., 1983—; mem. adv. panel Women in Internat. Security, College Park, Md., 1987—. Editor: Particle Acceleration Mechanisms in Astrophysics, 1979; contbr. numerous articles to sci. jours. Mem. Math.-Sci. Network, Mills Coll., Oakland, Calif. Fellow Am. Phys. Soc. (exec. com. div. plasma physics 1977, 81-82); mem. Am. Astron. Soc. (exec. com. div. high energy astrophysics 1975-76), Am. Geophys. Union, Internat. Astron. Union, Phi Beta Kappa, Sigma Xi. Office: Lawrence Livermore Nat Lab 7000 East Ave Livermore CA 94550

MAXEY, CATHERINE ANNETTE, human resource executive, trainer, consultant; b. Carbondale, Ill., Dec. 12, 1938; d. J. Ellsworth and Catherine (Crossno) Tucker; m. James H. Maxey, Aug. 20, 1961; 1 child, Gregory Scott. B.A., Ill. Wesleyan U., Bloomington, 1960; M.A., U. Chgo., 1962. Dir. Gwinnett-Rockdale Mental Health Mental Retardation Services, Lawrenceville, Ga., 1973-76; supt. Ga. Regional Hosp., Decatur, 1977-82; exec. dir. Nat. Assn. Social Workers, Silver Springs, Md., 1982-83; instr. U. Ga., Athens from 1984; mem. exec. bd. Health Systems Agy., Atlanta, 1980-82; dir. Health Planning Agy., State of Ga., 1984-89, div. Mental Health, Mental Retardation and Substance Abuse Dekalb Bd. of Health, 1989—; mem. task panel Pres. Commn. on Mental Health, Washington, 1978; del. Internat. Fedn. Social Workers, 1982. Recipient Disting. Alumnus award Ill. Wesleyan U., 1978. Mem. Nat. Assn. Social Workers, Mental Health Assn., Assn. for Retarded Citizens, NOW, Acad. Cert. Social Workers. Democrat. Club: Ansly Golf (Atlanta). Office: DeKalb County Div Mental Health Mental Retardation and Substance Abuse 440 Winn Way Ste 318 Decatur GA 30030

MAXEY, ROBERTA GAY, nurse, coordinator; b. Princeton, W.Va., Jan. 21, 1947; d. Dewey I. and Lessie (Ellison) M.; m. children: Cherie Denise Justis, Angela Michelle Justis. AAS in Nursing, Wytheville Community Coll., Va., 1976. Psychiatric nurse Mental Health & Mental Retardation Svcs., Radford, Va., 1976-77; staff nurse Fed.-Mogul Corp., Blacksburg, Va., 1977-81; charge nurse emergency room Montgomery County Hosp., 1981-83; nursing supr. AT&T Techs., Radford, 1983-87; regional nursing svcs. coord. AT&T Corp. Hdqrs., Oakton, Va., 1987-90; mgr. clin. svcs. AT&T Corp. West/South Region, 1990—; tng. officer 343rd Med. Co., Galax, Va., 1982-87; med. surgical nurse 92d Field Hosp. Vol. ARC, Roanoke, Va., 1977, Fairfax County Pub. Shelter, 1987—. Capt. USAR. Mem. NAFE, Am. Mil. Surgeons U.S., Am. Occupational Health Nurses. Republican. Baptist. Home: 201 Pinnacle Ct Peachtree City GA 30269 Office: 1200 Peachtree St NE Rm 12060 Atlanta GA 30309

MAXMAN, SUSAN ABEL, architect; b. Columbus, Ohio, Dec. 30, 1938; d. Richard Jack Abel and Gussie (Brenner) Seiden; children: Andrew Frankel, Thomas Frankel, Elizabeth Frankel; m. William H. Maxman; children: Melissa, Abby, William Jr. Student, Smith Coll., 1960; MArch., U. Pa., 1977. Registered profl. architect, Pa., Ohio, N.J., Md. Project designer Kopple Sheward & Day, Phila., 1978-80; ptnr. Maxman & Sutphin, Phila., 1980-83; prin. Susan Maxman Architects, Phila., 1984—. Works include restoration Vernon House, Germantown, Robert Lewis House (recipient McArthur award 1985), Phila., interior architecture Criminal Justice Ctr., Phila. Participant community leadership seminars, Phila., 1986-87. Recipient Benjamin Franklin Bridge Lighting honor award, Phila., 1986, Am. Wood Coun. Honor award for Cmap Tweedale-Freedom coun. Girl Scouts U.S.A., 1989. Mem. AIA (Phila chpt. bd. dirs. 1980-87, nat. bd. dirs. 1988—, regional dir. nat. bd. 1988-90), Pa. Soc. Architects (bd. dirs. 1983-87, exec. com., sec. 1984-85, v.p. 1986, pres. 1987), Am. Archtl. Found. (bd. regents), Carpenters' Co. Office: 123 S 22nd St Philadelphia PA 19103

MAXSON, LINDA ELLEN, biologist, educator; b. N.Y.C., Apr. 24, 1943; d. Albert and Ruth (Rosenfeld) Resnick; m. Richard Dey Maxson, June 13, 1964; 1 child, Kevin. BS in Zoology, San Diego State U., 1964, MA in Biology, 1966; PhD in Genetics, U. Calif., Berkeley, 1973. Instr. biology San Diego State U., 1966-68; tchr. gen. sci. San Diego Unified Sch. Dist., 1968-69; instr. biochemistry U. Calif., Berkeley, 1974; asst. prof. zoology, dept. genetics and devel. U. Ill., Urbana-Champaign, 1974-76, asst. prof. dept. genetics and ecology, ethology & evolution, 1976-79, assoc. prof., 1979-84, prof., 1984-87, prof. ecology, theology and evolution, 1987-88; prof., head dept. biology Pa. State U., State College, 1988—; exec. officer biology programs Sch. Life Scis., U. Ill., 1981-86, assoc. dir. acad. affairs, 1984-86, dir. campus honor program, 1985-88; vis. prof. ecology and evolutionary biology U. Ill., 1988; chmn. external rev., dept. biol. scis., Knoxville, Tenn., 1989, dept. zoology, 1990—; mem. adv. panel rsch. tng. groups BBS, 1990—. Contbr. numerous articles to sci. jours. Recipient Disting. Alumna award San Diego State U., 1989. Fellow AAAS; mem. Am. Men and Women in Sci., Am. Genetics Assn., Inst. Molecular Evolutionary Penn State (charter), Soc. for Study of Amphibians and Reptiles (pres. elect), Internat. Herpetological Com., Soc. for Study of Evolution, Soc. Systematic Zoology, Assn. Tropical Biology, Am. Soc. Ichthyalogists and Herpetologists, Am. Soc. Zoologists, Herpetologists League, Societas Europaea Herpetologico, European Soc. Evolutionary Biology. Home: 403 Canterbury Dr State College PA 16803 Office: Pa State U 208 Mueller Lab University Park PA 16802

MAXWELL, BARBARA SUE, educator, consultant; b. Bklyn., Feb. 22, 1950; d. Vincent and Esther Alice (Hansen) M. BA in Math Edn., Rider Coll., 1972; postgrad., Montclair State U., 1973. Cert. secondary tchr., N.J. Math tchr. Westwood (N.J.) High Sch., 1973-80; programmer Prudential Ins. Co., Roseland, N.J., 1980-81; programmer, analyst Grand Union, Paramus, N.J., 1981-82; project mgr. Info. Sci., Montvale, N.J., 1982-84; cons. Five Techs., Montvale, N.J., 1985-87; cons., project mgr. Info. Sci., Inc., Montvale, N.J., 1987-90; pres. B. Maxwell Assoc., Inc., Westwood, N.J., 1990—; cons. in field, 1984—; guest speaker Info. Sci. Contbr. articles to profl. jours. Trustee Westwood Heritage Soc. Mem. Nat. Assn. Female Execs., N.J. Users of Payroll Personnel, Inform, Am. Payroll Assn. Republican. Lutheran. Office: PO Box 291 Westwood NJ 07675

MAXWELL, FLORENCE HINSHAW, civic worker; b. Nora, Ind., July 14, 1914; d. Asa Benton and Gertrude (Randall) Hinshaw; BA cum laude, Butler U., 1935; m. John Williamson Maxwell, June 5, 1936; children: Marilyn Maxwell Grissom, William Douglas. Coord., bd. dirs. Sight Conservation and Aid to Blind, 1962-73, nat. chmn., 1969-73; active various fund drives; chmn. jamboree, hostess coms. North Cen. High Sch., 1959, 64; Girl Scouts U.S., 1937-38, 54-56; mus. chmn. Sr. Girl Scout Regional Coun., 1956-57; scorekeeper Little League, 1955-57; bd. dirs. Nora Sch. Parents' Club, 1958-59, Eastwood Jr. High Sch. Triangle Club, 1959-62, Ind. State Symphony Soc. Women's Com., 1965-67, 76-79, Symphoguide chmn., 1976-79; vision screening Indpls. innercity pub. sch. kindergartens, pre-schs., 1962-69, also Headstart, 1967—; asst. Glaucoma screening clinics Gen. Hosp., Glendale Shopping Ctr., City County Bldg., Am. Legion Nat. Hdqrs., Ind. Health Assn. Conf., 1962-73; chmn. sight conservation and aid to blind Nat. Delta Gamma Found., Indpls., Columbus, Ohio, 1969-73; mem. telethon team Butler U. Fund, 1964; symphoguide hostess Internat. Conf. on Cities, 1971, Nat. League of Cities, 1972; mem. health adv. com. Headstart, 1976—, sec., 1980—, mem. social svcs. com., 1987—, assessment team of compliance steering com., 1978-79, 84, 86, 87, 88 (appreciation award 1983); founder People of Vision Aux., 1981, bd. dirs., 1981—, v.p., 1990, mem. coordinate vision and glaucoma screenings and office svcs.; initiated vision screening and eye safety education at Jameson Camp for Children:, 1987; trainer vision screening, 1988—. Recipient Key to City of Indpls., 1972, Those Spl. People award Women in Communication, 1980. Mem. Nat. Soc. to Prevent Blindness, Ind. Audubon Soc., Ind. Hist. Soc., Ind. Soc. to Prevent Blindness (dir. 1962—, exec. com. 1971—, v.p. 1983-86, sec., 1971-83, asst. sec.-treas., 1987—, Ind. del. to nat. 3-yr. program planning conf. 1985, internal analysis task force for svcs. 1987, Sight Saving award 1974, life hon. v.p. 1983—), Delta Gamma (chpt. golden anniversary celebration decade and communication chmn. 1975, treas. Alpha Tau house corp. 1975-78, nat. chmn. Parent Club Study Com. 1976-77, instr. province leadership seminar workshop 1989, Cable award 1969, Outstanding Alumna award 1973, Svc. Recognition award 1977, Shield award 1981, scholarship honoree 1981, Stellar award 1986). Republican. Address: 1502 E 80th St Indianapolis IN 46240

MAXWELL, JOANNE DUTCHER, public relations professional; b. Chgo., Apr. 27, 1931; d. William Rodney and Phoebe (Hirshey) D.; m. Donald Philip Maxwell, Oct. 6, 1956; children: Donna Ruscik, Barbara Cherep. BA, Monmouth (Ill.) Coll., 1953. Assoc. editor Glen News Publs., Glen Ellyn, Ill., 1953-55; pres. DuPage County News Svc., Naperville, Ill., 1955-64; editor, corp. officer Clarion Publs., Naperville, 1956-62; exec. asst. U.S. Rep. John Erlenborn, Ill., 1965-85; founder, corp. officer Attention! Inc., Naperville, 1965-79, pres., owner, 1979—. Contbr. articles and editorials to various publs. (several 1st Pl. awards Nat. Editorial Assn., Ill. Press Assn.). Cons. numerous mcpl., county and state polit. campaigns, various Rep. orgns. Named Editor of Yr., Ill. Press Assn., 1960. Mem. Am. Assn. Polit. Cons., Chgo. Pub. Affairs Group, Women in Communications (past chmn. nat. freedom of info. com.), Naperville C. of C. Episcopalian. Home: 40 Westmoreland Ln Naperville IL 60540 Office: Attention! Inc 127 W Aurora Ave Naperville IL 60540

MAXWELL, JUDITH, economist; b. Kingston, Ont., Can., July 21, 1943; d. James Ruffee and Marguerite Jane (Spanner) McMahon; m. Anthony Stirling Maxwell, May 8, 1970; children: David, Elizabeth Jane. B in Commerce, Dalhousie U., 1963; postgrad., London Sch. Econs., 1965-66. Researcher Combines Investigation Br. Consumer and Corp. Affairs, Ottawa, Can., 1963-65; econs. writer, mem. editorial bd. Fin. Times, Montreal, Que., Can., 1966-72; dir. policy studies C.D. Howe Inst., Montreal, 1972-80; cons. Esso Europe Inc., London, Eng., 1980-82, Coopers & Lybrand, Montreal, Que., 1982-85; chmn. Econ. Council Can., Ottawa, Ont., 1985—; dir. Can. Found. for Econ. Edn., 1985-88, Inst. for Rsch. on Pub. Policy, 1987-88. Author: Energy From the Arctic, 1973; (with C. Pestieau) Economic Realities of Contemporary Confederation, 1980; (with S. Currie) Partnership for Growth: Corporate University Education in Canada, 1984. Active Ont. Premier's Coun., 1988-90, Nfld. and Labrador Sci. and Tech. Adv. Coun., 1988-90. Mem. Can. Assn. Bus. Econs. (pres. 1976-77), Montreal Econs. Assn. (pres. 1975-76). Office: Econ Coun Can, PO Box 527, Ottawa, ON Canada K1P 5V6

MAXWELL, KAREN OLIVER, telecommunications consultant; b. Newark, July 19, 1960; d. Henderson Charles Oliver and Doris Eunice (Timmons) Dean; m. Robert Maxwell, June 12, 1982; 1 child, Melanie. BS in Mktg., Rutgers U., 1981; MBA, L.I. U., Bklyn., 1985. Account rep. ITT, Secaucus, N.J., 1982-84; account exec. Bell Atlanticom, Princeton, N.J., 1984-86; telecommunications analyst Port Authority of N.Y. and N.J., N.Y.C., 1986-88, mgmt. info. specialist, 1988; telecommunications cons. Oliver Maxwell & Assocs., Piscataway, N.J., 1988—. Sec. Prevention Intervention Crisis Ctr., Rahway, N.J., 1988-89. Mem. Nat. Assn. Female Execs., Assn. MBA Execs., Black Profl. Women's Network, Am. Cons. League. Office: Oliver Maxwell & Assocs PO Box 335 Piscataway NJ 08854

MAXWELL, KATHERINE GANT, school psychologist, educational consultant; b. El Paso, Tex., Nov. 27, 1931; d. Leslie and Lillian (Beard) Gant; B.S., Abilene Christian U., 1955; M.S., Miss. State U., 1967, Ph.D., 1974; m. Fowden Gene Maxwell, July 14, 1955; children—Steve, Becky Harvey, Randy. Teaching asst. Miss. State U., Starkville, 1969-72, practicum in sch. psychology, 1973-74; adminstr. psychol. tests Starkville Pub. Schs., 1974-75; sch. psychologist Dixie & Gilchrist (Fla.) County Schs., 1977-79; instr. continuing edn. dept. U. LaVerne (Calif.), 1979-80; sch. psychologist Bryan (Tex.) Ind. Sch. Dist., 1979-80; owner, dir. Reading Improvement Center, College Station, Tex., 1979-80, Assn. Interpersonal Devel., Inc., 1982-88; sch. psychologist, ednl. diagnostician Temple (Tex.) Ind. Sch. Dist., 1980-81; sch. psychologist Franklin (Tex.) Ind. Sch. Dist., 1981-82; ednl. cons., College Station, Tex., 1982-86; newsletter editor Friends Assn. of Symphony Orch., 1987-88, corr. sec., 1988-90. Author: What Makes Bosses Tick, 1986; 15 poems pub. in nat. poetry anthologies including Best New Poets of 1988, Selected Poets of the New Era, 1989; recipient Poet of Merit trophy, 1989. Cub Scout leader Boy Scouts Am., Starkville, 1960; Brownie leader Girl Scouts U.S.A., Starkville, 1961-64; pres. Starkville Overstreet PTA, 1962; sec. Starkville Civic League, 1962-65; active Mental Health Assn. Alachua County (Fla.), 1976-77; treas. Citizens Com. for Mental Health in Bryan, 1979-80, Humana Sunshine Hosp. Aux., 1984-86; sec.-treas. Am. Cancer Soc. Brazos Valley, 1988-89; vol. Crestview Retirement Home, Brazos Food Bank, 1986-88. Mem. Bryan-College Station C. of C. (OPAS gala program chmn. 1988-89), Bus. and Profl. Women's Club (Bryan/College Station br. newsletter editor 1986-87), Opera and Performing Arts Soc. (College Station/Bryan OPAS Gala Program chmn. 1988-89, yearbook chmn. 1988-89, chmn. OPAS gala children's Mardi Gras Mask contest 1988), Arts Council Brazos Valley, Am. Pen Women (assoc.), Phi Delta Kappa. Clubs: Sorosis (sec. 1962-65), Tex. A&M Faculty Wives (beginning bridge chmn. 1987-88, 1st v.p. 1987-88), Tex. A&M Newcomers, Altrusa, Extension Service (1st v.p. 1984, sec. 1987-88, pres. 1988-89, parliamentarian 1989-90), Campus Study (pres. 1988-89), Brazos Beautiful (sponsor), Tex. A&M U. Social (pres. fine arts sect. 1988-89, 3d v.p. 1988-89). Clubs: TAMU Social (v.p. 1988-89), Fine Arts (pres. 1988-89). Office: Redmond Terr Sta PO Box 10027 College Station TX 77842

MAXWELL, LORRAINE EDWYNA, environmental psychologist; b. N.Y.C., Aug. 26, 1946; d. Oscar Clay and Vivian Lorraine (Shaw) M. BA, Queens Coll. CUNY, 1968; M in City & Regional Planning, Rutgers U., 1974; PhD in Psychology, Grad. Ctr. CUNY, 1990. Lectr. Essex County Community Coll., Newark, 1970-72; rsch. asst. Queens Coll., CUNY, Flushing, N.Y., 1968-69; edn. planner N.J. State Dept. Edn., Trenton, 1969-70; asst. prof. rsch. Rutgers U., Newark, 1970-72; sr. planner Mayor's Policy and Devel. Office, Newark, 1972-77; lectr. Coll. New Rochelle, N.Y., 1980—; assoc., sr. planner Gruzen Samton Steinglass Architects/Planners, N.Y.C., 1977—; cons. Harlem Urban Devel. Corp., N.Y.C., 1982. Mem. Mission Coun. N.Y. City Presbytery, 1985—. Mem. N.Y. Assn. Black Psychologists (bd. dirs. 1984-90, Svc. Award 1988), Am. Psychol. Assn., Environ. Design Rsch. Assn., Black Presbyn. Caucus (Svc. Award 1989). Democrat. Presbyterian. Office: Gruzen Samton Steinglass 304 Park Ave S New York NY 10010

MAXWELL, MARCIA GAIL, insurance company executive; b. Polk County, Ga., Aug. 15, 1948; d. Morris Lee Sr. and Mildred Ruth (Head) Martin; m. Larry O. Maxwell, July 31, 1970; 1 child, Mischelle D. Sec., Ga. Income Tax Unit, Atlanta, 1969-72; sr. sales rep. Fed. Nat. Mortgage Assn., Atlanta, 1972-83; secondary mktg. acct. exec. GE Capital, Atlanta, 1983—; rep. GECC Capital Markets Group, Atlanta, 1985—. Recipient Outstanding Achievement award Pinnacle Club, 1990. Mem. NAFE, Am. Mgmt. Assn., Nat. Assn. Profl. Mortgage Women (mem. publicity com. 1985-86), Nat. Assn. Securities Dealers (registered rep.), SEC (registered rep.), Toastmasters Internat. Club (pres. 1976-77), Fed. Nat. Mortgage Assn. Recreation Club (pres. 1980-81), Summit Club. Democrat. Baptist. Avocations: camping, boating, flower arranging. Home: 652 Stillwaters Dr Marietta GA 30064 Office: GE Capital 400 Perimeter Ctr Terr Atlanta GA 30346

MAXWELL, MARGARET WITMER, musician, editor; b. Irwin, Pa., Jan. 9, 1918; d. Charles Kendrick and Winona (Harrison) W.; m. Paul Russell Maxwell, Jan. 8, 1954 (dec. Oct. 1973); 1 child, James Witmer. MusB, U. Rochester, 1939; MEd, Lehigh U., 1969. cert. music tchr., Pa., Mass., N.Y. Feature writer Gannett Newspapers, Rochester, N.Y., 1945-52; staff mem. Fred Waring Enterprises, Delaware Water Gap, Pa., 1952-55; editor Mus. Jour., N.Y.C., 1953-56; tchr. music, English various pub. schs., Stroudsburg, Pa., Cape Cod, Mass. and Rochester, N.Y., 1956-76, ret., 1976; organist, choir dir. various chs., Pa., N.Y., Mass., N.J. and Fla., 1940—. Contbr. numerous articles to mags., newspapers. Mem. Am. Guild Organists, Sigma Alpha Iota (nat. editor, nat. exec. bd. 1979—). Republican. Presbyterian. Home: 1518-A Stoeber Ave Sarasota FL 34232

MAXWELL, MELISSA FAYE, business owner; b. Pensacola, Fla., Sept. 19, 1939; d. James Crawford and Zadie Magdalene (Wise) Maxwell. Grad. high sch. Founder, owner Carburetor World, Inc., Miami, Fla., 1973—. Author: Gas Mileage for the Serious Tinkerer, 1982; patents and blueprints twenty known carburetors claiming 50-200 MPGs. Benefactor various youth orgns., 1976—; mem. coun. Carburetor World Rehab. for Troubled Youths, Miami, 1976-80. Home and Office: PO Box 13331 Saint Petersburg FL 33733

MAXWELL, PATRICIA ANNE, writer; b. Winn Parish, La., Mar. 9, 1942; d. John Henry and Daisy Annette (Durbin) Ponder; m. Jerry Ronald Maxwell, Aug. 1, 1957; children: Jerry Ronald Jr., Richard Dale, Delinda Anne, Katherine Leigh. GED, 1960. Author (as Patricia Maxwell): Secret of Mirror House, 1970, Stranger At Plantation Inn, 1971, The Bewitching Grace, 1974, Notorious Angel, 1977, Night of the Candles, 1978, numerous others; (as Elizabeth Trehearne): Storm At Midnight, 1973; (as Patricia Ponder): Haven of Fear, 1977, Murder For Charity, 1977; (as Maxine Patrick): The Abducted Heart, 1979, numerous others; (as Jennifer Blake): Love's Wild Desire, 1977, Golden Fancy, 1980, Embrace and Conquer, 1981, Royal Seduction, 1983, others. Recipient Hist. Romance Author of Yr. award Romantic Times Mag., 1985. Mem. Nat. League Am. Penwomen, Romance Writers of Am. (charter) (Golden Treasure award 1987). Home: Rte 1 Box 133 Quitman LA 71268

MAXWELL, ROBIN LEE, management executive; b. Camden, N.J., Apr. 7, 1956; d. Robert Elmer and Dorothy Rita (Camilli) M. BS, Phila. Coll., 1979. Registered pharmacist, Pa., N.J. Pharmacy intern Our Lady of Lourdes Hosp. Pharmacy, Camden, 1974-77; asst. mgr. Thrift Drug Co., Kutztown, Pa., 1978-82; mgr. Rite Aid Pharmacy, Easton, Pa, 1982-84, Chemist Shoppe Pharmacy, Lindenwold, N.J., 1984-85; territorial sales mgr. Glaxo, Inc., Central, N.J., 1985-88; ops. adminstr. Hoechst Roussel Pharm., Inc., Sommerville, N.J., 1988-89, purchasing agt. materials mgmt., 1989—; lectr. Glaxo Inc. Atlantic City, 1985-88, asst. trainer, 1986, guest trainer Research Triangle Park, N.C., 1986. Mem. Am. Pharm. Assn., N.J. Soc. Hosp. Pharm., Princeton Bus. Profl. Women, Inc., Am. Soc. Tng. and Devel., GMP Edn. and Tng. Assn., Pres.'s Club, Kappa Epsilon. Home: 62 Edgewater Pl Edgewater NJ 07020

MAXWELL, RUBY HOOTS, county official; b. Hendersonville, N.C., July 4, 1924; d. James Few and Nora Adlaide (Capps) Hoots; m. Foy Judson Maxwell, Apr. 24, 1944; 1 child, Terry Chandler. Supr. Spinning Wheel Rugs, Hendersonville, 1943-48; nurse aid ARC, Hendersonville, 1954-55; asst. Optician, Hendersonville, 1963-64; dep. register of deeds Henderson County, N.C., 1964-78, registrar, 1978—; instr. notary pub. edn. Blue Ridge Tech. Coll., Flat Rock, N.C., 1978—. Active Women's Dem. Club, Hendersonville, 1978—. Recipient award for disting. service to people of Henderson County, 1987, 88. Mem. N.C. Register of Deeds Assn., Am. Soc. Notaries. Avocations: art, music. Office: Register of Deeds Courthouse Hendersonville NC 28739

MAXWELL, SANDRA ROSE, speech and language pathologist; b. Stratton, Colo., Sept. 23, 1945; d. Daniel Frank and Rose Mary (Laffoon) Smith; m. Peter Arthur Malmberg, Aug. 20, 1965 (div.); children: Peter Arthur Jr., Heather; m. Dwight Maxwell, July 18, 1979. AA, Southwestern Community Coll., 1977; BS in Geology, N.W. Mo. State U., 1981, BS in Edn., 1983, MS in Communication Disorders, 1985. Speech-lang. pathologist Gentry County Sch. Dist. Region II, Stanberry, Mo., 1983-88, Midwest Rehab. Ctr., Inc., Kansas City, Mo., 1986-88, Elaine R. Stevens Assocs., Waterville, Mo., 1988, Maryville (Mo.) Region II Schs., 1988—. Mem. Am. Speech-Lang.-Hearing Assn., Mo. Speech-Lang.-Hearing Assn., Mo. Tchrs. Assn., Community Tchrs. Assn. (sec. 1987-88), AAUW (v.p. Maryville 1987-88, pres. 1988-89). Home: 622 W Halsey #4 Maryville MO 64468 Office: Eugene Field Elem Sch 418 E 2d Maryville MO 64468

MAXWELL-BROGDON, FLORENCE MORENCY, school administrator, educational adviser; b. Spring Park, Minn., Nov. 11, 1929; d. William Frederick and Florence Ruth (LaBrie) Maxwell; m. John Carl Brogdon, Mar. 13, 1957; children: Carole Alexandra, Cecily Ann, Daphne Diana. B.A., Calif. State U., L.A., 1955; MS, U. So. Calif., 1957; postgrad. Columbia Pacific U., San Rafael, Calif., 1982-86. Cert. tchr., Calif. Dir. Rodeo Sch., L.A., 1961-64; lectr. Media Features, Culver City, Calif., 1964—; dir. La Playa Sch., Culver City, 1968-75; founding dir. Venture Sch., Culver City, 1974—, also chmn. bd.; bd. dirs., v.p. Parent Coop. Preschools, Baie d'Urfe Que., Can., 1964—. Author: Let Me Tell You, 1973; Wet 'n Squishy; 1973; Balancing Act, 1977; (as Morency Maxwell) Framed in Silver, 1985; (column) What Parents Want to Know, 1961—; editor: Calif. Preschooler, 1961-74; contbr. articles to profl. jours. Treas. Democrat Congl. Primary, Culver City, 1972. Mem. Calif. Council Parent Schs. (bd. dirs. 1961-74), Parent Coop. Preschools Internat. (advisor 1975—), Pen Ctr. USA West, Mystery Writers of Am. (affiliate), Internat. Platform Assn. Libertarian. Home: 10814 Molony Rd Culver City CA 90230 Office: Venture Sch 5333 S Sepulveda Blvd Culver City CA 90230

MAY, ANNE CATHERINE, neuropsychologist; b. Phila., Nov. 25, 1940; d. William James and Mary Loretta (Philbin) Barrett; m. Robert Michael May, June 16, 1962; children: Laura, Karen. BA, Trinity Coll., Washington, 1962; MA, Ariz. State U., 1978, PhD, 1981. Cert. psychologist, Ariz. Exec. dir. Hope Ctr. for Head Injury, Phoenix, 1980-84; neuropsychologist Good Samaritan Med. Ctr., Phoenix, 1984-86, chief neuropsychology, 1985-87, chief psychology, 1987-88; program dir. NeuroCare Residential Rehab., Phoenix, 1988-89; pvt. practice Phoenix, 1989—; cons. NeuroCare, Inc., Phoenix, 1990—; co-chair, exec. com. Ariz. Head Injury Found. Profl. Group, Phoenix, 1990—; bd. chmn North Phoenix Behavior Health Ctr., 1981-82; bd. dirs. Ariz. Head Injury Found., Tucson, 1983-86. Recipient Leadership award North Community Behavioral Health Ctr., Phoenix, 1983, Appreciation award Hope Ctr. for Head Injury, Phoenix, 1987. Mem. Am. Psychol. Assn., Internat. Neuropsychol. Soc., Ariz. Psychol. Assn. (AIDS com. 1988—, ethics com. 1989—), NOW, Sierra Club. Democrat. Office: 301 E Bethany Home Rd A-125 Phoenix AZ 85012

MAY, AVIVA RABINOWITZ, educator, linguist, musician; b. Tel Aviv; naturalized, 1958; d. Samuel and Paula Pessia (Gordon) Rabinowitz; (divorced); children: Chelley Mosoff, Alan May, Risa McPherson, Ellanna May/Gassman. AA Oakton Community Coll., 1977; BA in Piano Pedagogy, Northeastern Ill. U., 1978. Folksinger, educator, musician Aviva May Studio/Piano and Guitar, 1948—; tchr. B'nai Mitzva, 1973; tchr., music dir. McCormick Health Ctrs., Chgo., 1978-79, Cove Sch. Perceptually Handicapped Children, Chgo., 1978-79; prof. Hebrew and Yiddish, Spertus Coll. Judaica, Chgo., 1980—; tchr. continuing edn. Northeastern Ill. U., 1978-80, also Jewish Community Ctrs.; with Office Spl. Investigations, Dept. Justice, Washington. Composer classical music for piano, choral work, folk songs; developer 8-hour system for learning piano or guitar; contbr. articles to profl. jours. Recipient Magen David Adom Pub. Service award, 1973; grantee Ill. State, 1975-79, Ill. Congressman Woody Bowman, 1978-79. Mem. Music Tchrs. Nat. Assn. (co-founder), North Shore Music Tchrs. Assn. (charter mem., sec.), Ill. Music Tchrs. Assn., Organ and Piano Tchrs. Assn., Am. Coll. Musicians, Ill. Assn. Learning Disabilities, Sherwood Sch. Music, Friends of Holocaust Survivers, Nat. Yiddish Book Exchange, Nat. Ctr. for Jewish Films, Chgo. Jewish Hist. Soc., Oakton Community Coll. Alumni Assn., Northeastern Ill. U. Alumni Assn. Democrat. Office: Aviva May Studio 410 S Michigan Ave Studio #527 Chicago IL 60605

MAY, ELAINE, entertainer, director; b. Phila., 1932; d. Jack Berlin; m. Marvin May (div.); 1 child, Jeannie Berlin; m. Sheldon Harnick, Mar. 25, 1962 (div. May 1963). Ed. high sch., studied Stanislavsky method of acting withMarie Ouspenskaya. Stage and radio appearances as child actor; performed with Playwright's Theatre, in student performance Miss Julie, U. Chgo.; appeared with improvisational theatre group in night club The Compass, Chgo., 1954-1957, (with Mike Nichols) appeared N.Y. supper clubs, Village Vanguard, Blue Angel, also night clubs other cities; TV debut on Jack Paar Show, 1957; also appeared in Omnibus, 1958, Dinah Shore Show, Perry Como Show, Laugh Line, Laugh-In, TV spls.; comedy albums include Improvisations to Music, An Evening with Mike Nichols and Elaine May, Mike Nichols and Elaine May Examine Doctors; weekly appearance NBC radio show Nightline; appeared (with Mike Nichols) NBC radio show, N.Y. Town Hall, 1959, An Evening with Mike Nichols and Elaine May, Golden Theatre, N.Y.C., 1960-61; theater appearances include The Office, N.Y.C., 1966, Who's Afraid of Virginia Woolf?, Long Wharf Theatre, New Haven, Conn., 1980; dir. plays The Third Ear, N.Y.C., 1964, The Goodbye People, Berkshire Theater Festival, Stockbridge, Mass., 1971, various plays at Goodman Theatre, Chgo., 1983; dir., author screenplay, actress film A New Leaf, 1972; dir. films The Heartbreak Kid, 1973, Mikey and Nicky, 1976 (writer, dir. remake 1985), Ishtar, 1987 (also writer); appeared in films Luv, 1967, California Suite, 1978 (Acad. award Best Supporting Actress 1978), In The Spirit, 1990; co-author screenplay Heaven Can Wait, 1978; author plays A Matter of Position, 1962, Not Enough Rope, 1962, Adaptation, 1969, Hot Line, 1983, Better Part of Valor, 1983; stage revue: (with Mike Nichols) Telephone, 1984; co-recipient (with Mike Nichols) Grammy award for comedy performance, Nat. Acad. Recording Arts & Scis., 1961. Office: Dirs Guild Am 7950 W Sunset Blvd Los Angeles CA 90046*

MAY, ELIZABETH THERESA, nursing educator; b. Fitchburg, Mass., Sept. 25, 1935; d. John and Mary (Ferrick) M. Diploma sch. of nursing, Burbank Hosp., Fitchburg, 1957; BS in Edn., Fitchburg State Coll., 1957; MS in Nursing, Boston Coll., 1964; postgrad., Columbia U., 1968-70, 75. RN, Mass. Instr. sch. of nursing Burbank Hosp., Fitchburg, 1957-61; dir. edn. sch. of nursing Henry Heywood Hosp., Gardner, Mass., 1962-68; assoc. prof. Fitchburg State Coll., 1970—. Mem. Am. Nurses Assn., Mass. Nurses Assn. (legis. com. 1958—), Sigma Theta Tau (charter). Democrat. Roman Catholic. Home: 129 Olin Ave Fitchburg MA 01420 Office: Fitchburg State Coll Pearl St Fitchburg MA 01420

MAY, ELVIRA MARGARITE, dental association administrator; b. Fitchburg, Mass., Mar. 22, 1927; d. Charles George and Elizabeth Margarite (Schott) Zink; m. Clarence Edward, May 8, 1948, (div. July 1975); children: Lance Douglas, Blair Dunton, Randall Dexter. DA, Boston Sch. of Dental Nursing, 1945; RDH, U. Pa., 1947; BA, Framingham St. Coll., 1981. Dental Hygienist. Community dental hygienist Nashoba Health Agy., Ayer, Mass., 1957-68; P.H. dental hygienist Mass. Dept. of Pub. Health, Boston, 1968-86; dental health cons. H.H.S. Pub. Health Service, Boston, 1976—; program coord. Mass. Dept. Pub. Health, Boston, 1986—; chmn. Wachusett D.H. Assn., Fitchburg, 1961; program coord. Mass. Pub. Health D.H. Assn., Boston, 1975-89; adj. prof. Quinsigamond Coll. Dental Hygine Sch., Worcester, 1978-89. Program coord. Coun. on Aging; chmn. Lunenburg Coun. on Aging, 1989; mem. Friends of Eagle House Sr. Ctr.; past worthy advisor Rainbow Girls. Recipient James N. Dunning award Mass. Pub. Health Assn., Boston, 1988. Mem. Am. Dental Hygiene Assn., Mass. Pub. Health Assn., Wachusett Dental Hygienists Assn., Mass. Pub. Health, Dental Hygienists Assn., Am. Assn. Pub. Health Dentistry, Maplewood Ladies Golf Assn., Lunenburg. Republican. Home: 121 Peninsula Dr Lunenburg MA 01462 Office: Cen Regional Health Office Rutland Heights Hosp Rutland MA 01543

MAY, JACQUELINE MARIE, electronics company executive, contract negotiator; b. Cin., July 26, 1961; d. Bobby May and Glenda Joyce (Bregen) May Poynter. BBA, Eastern Ky. U., 1983. Contract negotiator Air Force Logistics Command, Dept. Def., McClellan AFB, Calif., 1983-87, contracting officer, 1987-88; contracts mgr. Cin. Electronics Corp., 1988—. Mem. Nat. Contract Mgmt. Assn., Nat. Assn. Female Execs. Office: Cin Electronics Corp 2630 Glendale-Milford Rd Cincinnati OH 45241-3187

MAY, MARY DIANE, media specialist, educator, business owner; b. Detroit, May 1, 1930; d. Donald McIntosh and Mary Ann (Lambert) Dixon; m. Frank Owen May Jr., July 5, 1952 (dec. July 1957); children: Susan, Steven. Student, Hillsdale (Mich.) Coll., 1948-50; BS, Mich. State U., 1957; MEd, Wayne State U., 1968. Tchr. St. Clair Schs., Anchorville, Mich., 1950-51, Fresno (Calif.) Schs., 1953-54; tchr. 5th grade Berkley (Mich.) Schs., 1956-64, library coord., 1964-68; librarian Palm Beach Schs., Boca Raton, Fla., 1969-73, media specialist, 1974-84; library organizer Gondia (India) Pvt. Sch., 1973-74; media specialist Hernando County Schs., Brooksville, Fla., 1984—; owner Ednl. Media Prodns., Deerfield Beach, Fla., 1977—. Author: Wealth of Wholeness, 1989. Mem. Fla. Assn. Media in Edn., Fla. Assn. for Computers in Edn., Nat. Hon. Tchrs. Assn. (pres. Boca Raton chpt. 1972-74). Office: Cen High Sch 14075 Ken Austin Pkwy Brooksville FL 34613

MAY, MELANIE ANN, theologian; b. Wash., Jan. 6, 1955; d. Russell Junior and Arlene Virginia (Ringgold) May. AB, Manchester Coll, 1976; MDiv., Harvard Div. Sch., 1979; AM, Harvard U., 1982, PhD, 1986. Teaching fellow Harvard Univ., Div. Sch., Cambridge, Mass., 1981-83; asst. head tutor Harvard Univ., Cambridge, 1983-84; staff (program for women) Ch. Brethren Gen. Bd., Elgin, Ill., 1985—; ecumenical officer Ch. Brethren Gen. Bd., Elgin, 1985—; adj. faculty Bethany Theol. Sem., Oak Brook, Ill., 1986—; assoc., gen. sec. human resources Ch. Brethren Gen. Bd., Elgin, 1987—. Author: Bonds of Unity, Women, Theology and Worldwide Church, 1989, Women and Church: A Challenge of Solidarity in a Time of Turmoil, 1990, For All The Saints: The Practice of Ministry in the Church; assoc. editor Jour. Ecumenical Studies. Quality Ministerial candidates, 1987—, chmn. commn. Faith and Order, Nat. Council, N.Y., 1988. Mem. N.Am. Acad. Economists, Am. Acad. Religion. Home: 18 W 711 22nd St Lombard IL 60148 Office: Ch Brethren Offices 1451 Duncee Ave Elgin IL 60120

MAY, PHYLLIS JEAN, business executive; b. Flint, Mich., May 31, 1932; d. Bert A. and Alice C. (Rushton) Irvine; m. John May, Apr. 24, 1971. Grad. Dorsey Sch. Bus., 1957; cert. Internat. Corr. Schs., 1959, Nat. Tax Inst., 1978; MBA, Mich. U., 1970. Registered real estate agt. Office mgr. Comml. Constrn. Co., Flint, 1962-68; bus. mgr. new and used car dealership, Flint, 1968-70; contr. various corps., Flint, 1970-75; fiscal dir. Rubicon Odyssey Inc., Detroit, 1976-87, Wayne County Treas.'s Office, 1987—; acad. cons. acctg. Detroit Inst. Commerce, 1980-81; pres. small bus. specializing in adminstrv. cons. and acctg., 1982—; supr. mobile svc. sta., upholstery and home improvement businesses; owner retail bus. Pieces and Things. Pres. PTA Westwood Heights Schs., 1972; vol. Fedn. of Blind, 1974-76, Probate Ct., 1974-76; mem. citizens adv. bd. Northville Regional Psychiat. Hosp., 1988, sec. 1989-90. Recipient Meritorious Svc. award Genesee County for Youth, 1976, Excellent Performance and High Achievement award Odyssey Inc., 1981. Mem. Am. Bus. Women's Assn. (treas. 1981, rec. sec. 1982, v.p. 1982-83, Woman of Yr. 1982), NAFE (bd. dirs.), Womens Assn. Dearborn Orch. Soc., Mich. Mental Health Assn., Internat. Platform Assn., Pi Omicron (officer 1984-85). Baptist. Home: 12050 Barlow St Detroit MI 48205 Office: 1 Woodward City-County Bldg Detroit MI 48226

MAYBERRY, JANIS PETERSON, psychologist; b. Highland Park, Ill., June 28, 1957; d. Paul Anthony Peterson and Elizabeth Ann (Mueller) Coleman; m. Ross Lowell Mayberry, June 21, 1983; children: Erin, Rebecca, Caitlin. BA with honors in Psychology, Purdue U., 1978; MS in Clin. Psychology, Wash. State U., 1980; PhD in Clin. Psychology, U. Vt., 1982. Lic. psychologist, N.H., Wash. Postdoctoral trainee Primary Children's Med. Ctr., Salt Lake City, 1982-83; child and family psychologist West Cen. Svcs., Claremont, N.H., 1983-86; outpatient psychologist Plymouth (N.H.) Psychology Ctr., 1986-87, Southlake Profl. Group, Renton, Wash., 1988—; asst. clin. prof. Dartmouth Med. Ctr., Hanover, N.H., 1984-87; researcher in field. Contbr. articles to profl. publs. Mem. Am. Psychol. Assn., Wash. State Psychol. Assn., Nat. Register Health Care Providers Psychology, Phi Beta Kappa, Phi Kappa Phi, Psi Chi. Office: Southlake Profl Group 1400 Talbot Rd S Ste 203 Renton WA 98055

MAYEFSKY, CHERYL JOYCE, actuary; b. Syosset, N.Y., Mar. 26, 1966; d. Milton and Sylvia Mayefsky. BA in Econs., SUNY, Binghamton, 1988. Actuarial asst. Buck Cons., N.Y.C., 1988—. Mem. NAFE, Women's Tennis Assn., Omicron Delta Epsilon, Delta Gamma. Home: 30-2911 Newport Pkwy Jersey City NJ 07310 Office: Buck Cons 2 Pennsylvania Plaza New York NY 10121

MAYELL, SHARON LEE, city official; b. Boston, Mar. 21, 1953; d. Albert Jefferson and Patricia Ann (Henry) Mayell; m. David Harvey Waterman, Mar. 26, 1989; 1 child. BA, U. N.C., Greensboro, 1976; MA, U. So. Calif.,

1988. Dir. mktg. Warner Theatre/Washington Theatre League, Washington, 1978-84; mgr./v.p. Warner Theatre/Washington Theatre League, 1984-86; paralegal McCabe & Allen, Washington, 1986-87; head teaching asst. U. So. Calif., L.A., 1987-88; project mgr. City of Santa Monica - PEN Network, Calif., 1988—; lectr. in field. Contbr. articles to profl. jours. Recipient Appreciation award, Washington Area Music Assn., 1987, High Tech. award, Hewlett Packard Co., 1989. Mem. Women in Communications, Soc. Satellite Profls. Office: Info Sys City Hall 1685 Main St Santa Monica CA 90401

MAYER, BEATRICE CUMMINGS, civic worker; b. Montreal, P.Q., Can., Aug. 15, 1921; came to U.S., 1939, naturalized, 1944; d. Nathan and Ruth (Kellert) Cummings; BA in Chemistry, U. N.C., 1943; postgrad. U. Chgo., 1946; LHD (hon.), Spertus Coll. Judaica, 1983, Kenyon Coll., 1987; m. Robert Bloom Mayer, Dec. 11, 1947 (dec.); children: Robert N., Mrs. Ruth M. Durchslag. Mem. vis. com. Sch. Social Svc. Adminstrn. U. Chgo., 1964—, dept. art, 1972—; dir. women's bd., 1973—, Art Inst. Chgo. (life trustee) 1984—; bd. dirs. Michael Reese Hosp. Corp., Chgo., 1982—, bd. dirs. Spoleto Festival, 1980—; trustee Kenyon Coll., Gambier, Ohio, 1976-89, mem. adv. com. to bd. trustees, 1987-89, trustee emritus, 1989—; bd. fellows Brandeis U., Waltham, Mass., 1977—; mem. womens bd. Northwestern U., 1978-89; trustee Anshe Emet Synagogue, Chgo., 1974—; trustee Mus. Contemporary Art, Chgo., 1974—; mem. adv. com. N.C. Sch. of Arts, 1983-89, bd. visitors, 1984—; bd. visitors U. NC., 1987-89. Recipient Brandeis U. Disting. Community Service award, 1972, medallion Am. Jewish Com. Human Rights, 1976, Outstanding Achievement award in the Arts, YWCA Met. Chgo., 1979, Centennial Gold Medal for Disting. Community Service Jewish Theol. Sem., 1986, Alumni Laureate award Loyola Coll. Balt., 1984; named to Hall of Fame, Jewish Community Ctrs. Adult Services, 1987. Clubs: Tavern, Standard (Chgo.); Lake Shore Country (Glencoe, Ill.). Home: Hancock Apts 175 E Delaware Pl Apt 7403 Chicago IL 60611

MAYER, DEBORAH AMY, physician; b. Yonkers, N.Y., Dec. 7, 1947; d. David and Blanche (Eisnitz) M.; m. Edward J. Kosinski, July 19, 1976; children: Daniel, Julia, Benjamin. BA, U. Wis., 1968; MA, New Sch. for Social Rsch., 1971; MD, Columbia U., N.Y.C., 1977. Intern, then resident in internal medicine New Eng. Deaconess Hosp., Boston, 1977-80; pvt. practice Lexington, Mass., 1980-88.

MAYER, GAIL LYNNE, management; b. Chgo., May 2, 1952; d. Mack Paul and Rosa (Palmisano) Mayer. BA in English, Southern Ill. U., 1974, MS in Rehab. Counseling, 1980. Asst. dir. Hill House Residential Coop., Carbondale, Ill., 1975-77; founder, dir. Alpha Resdl. Cooperative Vienna (Ill.) Correctional Ctr. (all male), 1977-79; midwest regional mgr. Towers Fin. Corp., N.Y., 1987-88; founder, dir. comml. div. Malcam Gerald & Assoc., Chgo., 1988-89; v.p. Weybridge Assoc., Des Plaines, Ill., 1989—. Mem. Nat. Assn. Female Exec. Office: Weybridge Associates Des Plaines IL 60614

MAYER, KATHE, small business owner; b. N.Y.C., Dec. 23, 1940; d. Lawrence R. and Helen (Beling) K.; m. James H. Mayer, Jan. 1, 1965; children: Wayne E., Amy H. BA in History, U. Del., Newark, 1962; MA in History, Ohio State U., 1966. Libr. Ohio State U., Newark, 1966-67; spl. projects mgr. Ohio U., Athens, 1967-68; tchr. Jewish Community Ctr., Toledo, 1968-69, Cleve., 1978—; owner, v.p. Mayer Assocs. Mfrs. Agt. Inc., Cleve., 1983—; Com. Chmn. AESF Cleve. 1988-89. Free-lance writer and photographer Washington County Bull., 1973-77, Cleve. Jewish News, 1980—; contbr. articles to pubs. Active Lake Erie coun. Girl Scouts U.S. Mem. AAUW, Women Together, Jewish Secular Commn., Women's Bus. Owners Assn. Democrat. Home and Office: 2614 Charney Rd University Heights OH 44118

MAYER, LUCILLE MENDENHALL, realtor, sales agent; b. Whittier, Calif., Feb. 6, 1926; d. Warren D. and Esther L. (Lewis) Mendenhall; m. John C. Mayer, May 3, 1953 (dec. Dec. 1983); children: Lynn Ann, Kim Marie, Mark Raymond, Scott Thomas. MusB, Westminster Choir Coll., 1948; MusM, North Tex. State Coll., 1952. Minister of music Wesley Meth. Ch., San Diego, 1953-55; soloist asst. dir. 1st Presby. Ch., San Diego, 1955-64, 1st Meth. Ch., San Diego, 1964-69; voice tchr. Grossmont Coll., El Cajon, Calif.; minister of music St. Marks Meth., San Diego, 1973-77; tchr. Grossmont Sch. Dist., Calif., 1971-77; sales rep. Malmark Handbells, Riverside, Calif., 1982--; real estate agt. Century 21 Emery, Riverside, 1985-89; with The Jelley Real Estate Co., LaCosta, Calif., 1989—. Active pub. rels. Mayor's Ball for Riverside Arts Found., 1983-86; mem. Riverside Bd. Realtors; soloist San Diego Opera Co., San Diego Starlight Opera Co. Mem. Carlsbad Assn. of Realtors. Democrat. Home: 1843 Avenida Mimosa Encinitas CA 92024 Office: The Jelley Real Estate Co 7030 Avenida Encinas Ste 100 LaCosta CA 92009

MAYER, MARILYN GOODER, steel company executive; b. Chgo.; d. Seth MacDonald and Jean (McMullen) Gooder; m. William Anthony Mayer, Nov. 14, 1959; children—William Anthony Jr., Robert MacDonald. grad. Career Inst. Chgo., 1941; student Lake Forest Coll., Ill., 1942. Adminstrv. asst. Needham, Louis & Brorby, Chgo., 1949-53; v.p. RMB Corp., Chgo., 1963-71, Mayer Motors, Ft. Lauderdale, Fla., 1965-74, Gooder-Henrichsen, Chicago Heights, Ill., 1975—; dir. Barnett Bank, West Palm Beach, Fla. Trustee Gulf Stream (Fla.) Sch., St. Andrew's Sch., Boca Raton, Fla.; bd. dirs. Bethesda Hosp. Assn., Boynton Beach, Fla., pres. 1981-82; bd. dirs. Gulf Stream Civic Assn. Mem. Soc. Four Arts. Republican. Episcopalian. Clubs: Little, Gulf Stream Bath and Tennis. Avocation: travel. Home: 2925 Polo Dr Gulf Stream FL 33483

MAYER, NANCY JO HARMON, education educator; b. Columbia, S.C., Sept. 20, 1950; d. Royce Hamilton and Winnie (Seay) Harmon; m. Charles Albert Mayer, July 11, 1971; children: Carrie Elizabeth, Benjamin Evans. BA in Eng., U. S.C., 1971, MAT in Eng., 1979. Cert. Tchr., S.C. Tchr. Forest Acres Elem. Sch., Easley, S.C., 1971-73, Gaffney (S.C.) High Sch., 1973-75, Oak Grove Elem. Sch., Lexington, S.C., 1975-76, Lexington High Sch., Gilbert (S.C.) High Sch., 1977-89; tchr. Campus R Irmo Mid. Sch., Columbia, 1989—; mem. adv. bd. S.C. Scholastic Press Assn., Columbia, 1983-86; chmn. adv. bd. S.C. Scholastic Press Assn., Columbia, 1984-86; mem. adv. bd. S.C. Scholastic Press Assn., Columbia, 1988-89. Advisor: student newspaper, 1979-89, student mag. Sparkleberry, 1987-89; contbr. articles to profl. jours. Mem. Providence Lutheran Ch., Lexington S.C. 1950--. Recipient Master Tchr. award AP Summer Inst., Clemson U., 1987; named Tchr. of the Yr., Gilbert High Sch. of S.C., 1987. Mem. S.C. Coun. Tchrs. of English, Delta Kappa Gamma. Lutheran.

MAYER, PATRICIA JAYNE, financial officer; b. Chgo., Apr. 27, 1950; d. Arthur and Ruth (Greenberger) Hersh; m. William A. Mayer Jr., Apr. 30, 1971. AA, Diablo Valley Coll., 1970; BSBA, Calif. State U., Hayward, 1975. Staff acct., auditor Elmer Fox Westheimer and Co., Oakland, Calif., 1976; supervising auditor Auditor's Office County of Alameda, Oakland, 1976-78; asst. acctg. mgr. CBS Retail Stores doing bus. as Pacific Stereo, Emeryville, Calif., 1978-79; contr. Oakland Unified Sch. Dist., 1979-84; v.p. fin. YMCA of San Francisco, 1984-89, v.p. fin., chief fin. officer, 1984—; instr. acctg. to staff YMCA, San Francisco, 1984—, CBS Retail Stores, 1978-79. Draft counselor Mt. Diablo Peace Ctr., Walnut Creek, Calif., 1970-72; dep. registrar of voters Contra Costa County Registrar's Office, Martinez, Calif., 1972-77. Mem. Nat. Assn. Accts., Dalmatian Club No. Calif., Dalmation Club Am. Democrat. Jewish. Home: 2395 Lake Meadow Circle Martinez CA 94553 Office: YMCA 220 Golden Gate Ave 3d Fl San Francisco CA 94102

MAYER, RAMONA ANN, regulatory compliance manager; b. Algona, Iowa, May 9, 1929; d. William John and Esther (Wolf) M. B.A. in Chemistry, State U. Iowa, 1956. Library asst. State U. Iowa, Iowa City, 1954-56; info. specialist Battelle, Columbus, Ohio, 1956-59, research scientist, 1959-77, quality assurance dir., 1977-89, mgr. regulatory compliance, 1989—; lab. asst. U. Iowa Tb Hosp., Iowa City, 1952-53; abstractor Chem. Abstract Services, Columbus, 1958-79. Author: Spacecraft Coatings, 1969 (NASA Achievement award 1970), (with others) Advances in Petroleum Chemistry and Refining, 1963, Effects of Radiation on Materials and Components, 1964; contbr. articles to profl. jours. Fellow Am. Inst. Chemists; mem. Am. Soc. Quality Control (vice chmn. Columbus sect. 1982-84, Saddoris chmn. 1984-85), ASTM (chmn. com. 1984—), Am. Chem. Soc., Soc. Quality Assurance (bylaws com. 1985, nominating com. 1986, program com. 1987—, regulatory review com. 1988—). Avocations: golf, crafts, travel. Office: Battelle-Columbus 505 King Ave Columbus OH 43201

MAYER, RUTH ANN, human factors engineer; b. Ashtabula, Ohio, May 13, 1951; d. Martha C. Hutcheson; 1 child, Timothy A. Thielen; m. Dan E. Mayer. BA in Social Psychology, Fla. Atlantic U., 1987. Human factors lab. technician IBM Corp., Boca Raton, Fla., 1983-87, human factors engr., 1987—. Mem. Human Factors Soc., Math. Assn. Am. Office: IBM Corp 1000 NW 51st St Boca Raton FL 33432

MAYER, VIRGINIA ANNE, dietitian; b. Cortez, Colo., June 14, 1929; d. James Edward and Anna May (Coleman) Casey; m. Frederick Henry Mayer, Feb. 7, 1954; children: Jennifer, Valorie, Helen, Lydia. AS, Cottey Coll. for Women, Nevada, Mo., 1949; BS, U. Colo., 1951. Dietitian Columbia Presbyn. Med. Ctr., N.Y.C., 1952-55; food service dir. Luth. Sanitarium, Wheatridge, Colo., 1955-57; adminstrv. dietitian VA Hosp., Grand Junction, Colo., 1961-65; nutritionist Maricopa County Health Dept., Phoenix, 1965-68; food service dir. ARA Services, Phila., 1968-72, supr. dietitian, 1972-75, area exec. dietitian, 1975-76, dist. mgr., 1976-81; pres., chief exec. officer SunWest Services, Inc., Tempe, Ariz., 1981-89; pres. Vamcor, Inc., Tempe, 1989—. Alt. del. White House Conf. on Small Bus., Ariz., 1986; gov. adv. bd. Minority and Women Bus. and Econ. Devel. Named Pacesetter, Roundtable for Women in Food Service, Chgo., 1988. Mem. Am. Dietetic Assn., Ariz. Dietetic Assn. (bd. dirs., chm,n. 1987-88), Nat. Assn. Women Bus. Owners (pres. 1988-89, rep. nat. bd. dirs. 1990), The Exec. Com., PEO Sisterhood (pres. Tempe chpt. 1970-72), Dietitians in Bus. and Industry (nat. treas.). Office: Vamcor Inc 2163 E Aspen Dr Tempe AZ 85282

MAYES, LORENE ANDERSON, small business owner; b. Horn Lake, Miss., Nov. 3, 1939; d. Estes W. and Irene (Orange) Anderson; m. Jeff Mayes, Oct. 13, 1962; children: Samuel Terrell, Jeff Clifton, Hubert Raleigh. Diploma, Para Med. Inst., 1970; beautician, Sheriee's Cosmetology, Memphis, 1980; cert., Mr. Tax Income Tax Prep, 1972, Inst. for Leadership Skills, 1983. Owner, mgr. Beauty Salon, Memphis. Spl. dep. sheriff, Memphis; sunday sch. tchr., choir pres., pres. Ester Club. Recipient cert. Congresman Harold E. Ford, 1946, others. Mem. NAFE, OES Assoc. Matron. Office: 1459 S Trezevant St Memphis TN 38114

MAYFIELD, JUDITH ANN, financial manager; b. Shelbyville, Ky., Aug. 21, 1946; d. Harry Lee and Geneva Garret (Tingle) Ritchey; m. William Leslie Mayfield, Aug. 17, 1968 (div. July, 1982); 1 child, Kelly Lyn; m. Richard Allen Burge, Mar. 1, 1985. BS, U. Louisville, 1967; MBA, Bellarmine Coll., 1983. Cert. Info. Systems Auditor. Systems rep. Honeywell, Inc., Louisville, 1967-68; systems engr., analyst Regional Computer Ctr., Cin., 1968-72; systems engr. Space Age Computer Systems, Louisville, Ky., 1972-74, Standard Oil (Chevron), Louisville, 1974-77, Brown & Williamson (Batus), Louisville, 1977-79; supr., mgr. EDP Audit Batus, Inc., Louisville, 1979-84, supr. fin. analysts, 1984-87, mgr. fin. systems, 1987—. Mem. EDP Auditors Assn. (v.p. 1983-84), Louisville Jr. C. of C. (v.p. 1978). Republican. Office: Batus Inc 2000 Citizens Plaza Louisville KY 40202

MAYFIELD, LORI JAYNE, customer service representative; b. Newport Beach, Calif., Sept. 11, 1955; d. John Vincent and Marilyn Jane (Huish) M. Student Linn-Benton Community Coll., 1973-75, N.W. Coll., 1975-76. Gen. ins. cert. Ins. Inst. Am. Cashier Auto Club So. Calif., Anaheim, 1977-80, ins. clk., sec., Fullerton, 1980-81, ins. rep., 1981, field coord., Costa Mesa, Calif., 1981-86; auto. club sales rep., 1986-88; pres. LJM Enterprises; customer svc. rep. Roadway Express, Irvine, Calif. Recipient Outstanding Citizenship award YMCA, Santa Ana, Calif., 1984. Mem. NAFE. Office: Roadway Express 12 McLaren Irvine CA 92718

MAYFIELD, PEGGY JORDAN, psychologist; b. Atlanta, Aug. 4, 1934; d. Claude Emmett and Ruby Earnestine (Hutchison) Jordan; m. James Ronald Mayfield, June 14, 1953; children—Steven Jay, David Lee. BA with high honors, Agnes Scott Coll., 1956; MEd, Ga. State U., 1971, SEd, 1976, PhD, 1978. Lic. psychologist, Ga. Tchr. music, Atlanta, 1956-70; exec. dir. Hi Hope Ctr., Lawrenceville Ga., 1971-74; devel. service chief program dir. Gwinnett Rockdale Newton Mental Health and Mental Retardation Service, Lawrenceville, 1974-78; owner, dir. Gwinnett Mental Health Assocs., Lilburn, Ga., 1978-85; sec., treas. So. Clinic, Inc., 1985-87, pres., 1987-90; pvt. practice clin. psychologis in assessment counseling cons., Lawrenceville, 1982-90; cons. Creative Enterprises, Lawrenceville, 1978-82; adjudicator Nat. Guild Piano Tchrs., Austin, Tex., 1979—. Author community project reports, ednl. materials. Named to Hall of Fame, Nat. Guild Piano Tchrs., 1962-63; HEW fellow, 1969-71; recipient Community Program award Ga. Assn. Retarded Citizens, 1973, Nat. Tng. award, Nat. Assn. Retarded Citizens. Mem. Am. Psychol. Assn., Am. Assn. Marriage and Family Therapists, Ga. Psychol. Assn., Phi Beta Kappa. Avocations: music, writing, reading, fishing, travel. Office: So Clinic Inc 601-A Professional Dr Lawrenceville GA 30245

MAYFIELD, SANDRA JEANNE, recreational therapist, consultant; b. Mpls., Aug. 28, 1942; d. Glen Douglas and Ellynore (Kukko) M. BS in Recreation, San Jose State U., 1967, MS in Therapeutic Recreation, 1979. Cert. recreation therapist, Calif., therapeutic recreation specialist. Recreation asst. supr. Sunnyvale (Calif.) Park and Recreation Dept., 1960-67; dir. recreation Santa Clara Valley Med. Ctr., San Jose, Calif., 1967—; lectr. San Francisco State U., 1976-78; instr. San Jose State U., 1986-88, Tex. Women's U., Denton, 1989; cons. Western Med., Hayward, Calif., 1978-79; bd. dirs. Horizons West; chmn., presenter numerous local, state and nat. workshops and conf. sessions; mem. steering com. Coma to Community Bain Trauma Conf., 1988—. Author: Protocols in Therapeutic Recreation, 1989; co-author: Facilitating a Desired Leisure Lifestyle, 1987. Recipient Disting. Recreation Alumnus award San Jose State U., 1983, Alumnus of Yr. award dept. recreatin and leisure studies, 1988. Mem. Nat. Therapeutic Recreation Soc. (bd. dirs. 1983-89, pres. 1988-89), Calif. Park and Recreation Soc. (pres. therapeutic recreation sect. 1981-83, state bd. dirs. 1981-83, chmn. recreation therapy licensure task force 1983—, Outstanding Therapeutic Recreator award 1985, Citation 1988). Democrat. Office: Santa Clara Valley Med Ctr 751 S Bascom Ave San Jose CA 95128

MAYHEW, ELIZABETH WHITEHOUSE, art gallery executive, consultant; b. Bklyn., Apr. 24, 1951; d. John Henry and Elizabeth Caroline (Catlin) Whitehouse; m. Emil A. Kratzman, Oct. 10, 1975; (div. 1978); m. Timothy Peter Arnoldi Mayhew; 1 child, Caroline Elizabeth Mary. BA, Marietta Coll., 1973. Art dir. Benton & Bowles, N.Y.C., 1973-81; freelance N.Y.C., 1981-86; art cons. Images by Alan Spanier, Inc., Bklyn., 1986-88; pres., owner Picture This Corp. Art, Inc., N.Y.C., 1988—; pres. L.I. Coll. Hosp. Assoc. Bd. Regents, 1982—. Pres. bd. regents L.I. Coll. Hosp. Assn., 1981—; chair com. Grace Ch. Fair., 1984—; com. mem. landmarks house tours Bklyn. Heights Assn., 1989—; mem. Bklyn. Bot. Gardens. Democrat. Episcopalian. Office: Picture This Corp Art Inc 370 Court St Ste #24 Brooklyn NY 11231

MAYHEW-PEREZ, TERESA ANN, optometrist; b. L.A., June 11, 1960; d. Robert Jay and Helen (Burbeck) Mayhew; m. Randolph Collier Perez, June 25, 1983. AS, Antelope Valley Jr. Coll., 1980; BA in Chemistry, San Francisco State U., 1981; BA in Biology, Calif. State U., Northridge, 1983; OD, So. Calif. Coll. of Optometry, 1987. Sales rep. Home Shop, Northridge, Calif., 1981-83; chemist Andrew Jergens, Burbank, Calif., 1982-84; pvt. practice Carpinteria, Calif., 1987--; cons. Santa Barbara State U., 1988--. Mem. Am. Bus. Womans Assn., Calif. Optometric Assn., Tri-County Optometric Soc., Carpinteria C. of C. Office: Teresa A Mayhew, OD 5434 Carpinteria Ave Carpinteria CA 93013

MAYNARD, JOAN, educator; b. Louisa, Ky., Oct. 18, 1932; d. Macon Scott and Jeanette (Thompson) Chambers; m. Frank Maynard Jr., June 15, 1951 (dec. Nov. 1988); children: Mark Steven, Julia Beth Maynard McFann, Robert Blake. BA, Wittenberg U., 1977; MEd, Wright State U., 1980, Wright State U., 1984. Tchr., reading specialist Mechanicsburg (Ohio) Exempted Village Schs., 1976—; pres. TOTT Publs. Inc., Bellbrook, Ohio, 1988—; rep. Career Edn., Mechanicsburg, 1981-88, mem. Thompson Grant Com., Mechanicsburg, 1987-88. Author: Mud Puddles, 1988, Mud Pies, 1989. Vol. Mechanicsburg Schs. Levy, 1980, 82, 88, Congl. Race, Champaign County, Ohio, 1982, 84, 86, cons. Urbana U., Ohio, 1988—, tutor Laubach Literary Action, Urbana, 1989—. Recipient Thompson grant, 1982, 88. Mem. AAUW (ednl. chmn. 1988-89, treas. 1989—), Internat. Reading Assn., Champaign County Reading Coun. (treas. 1990—), Midwestern Assembly Lit. Young People (treas. 1989—), Kappa Delta Pi. Home: 1546 Parkview Rd Mechanicsburg OH 43044 also: Mechanicsburg Exempted Village Schs 60 High St Mechanicsburg OH 43044

MAYNARD, NANCY GRAY, biological oceanographer; b. Middleboro, Mass., Apr. 18, 1941; d. Thomas LaSalle and Clara (Gray) M.; m. Conrad Dennis Gebelein, Jan., 1969 (div. 1977); 1 child, Jennifer Lynn. BS, Mary Washington Coll., 1963; MS, U. Miami (Fla.), 1967, PhD, 1974. Rsch. assoc. Bermuda Biol. Sta., Ferry Reach, 1972-75; rsch. fellow Lamont-Doherty Geol. Obs. Columbia U. (CLIMAP), 1972-75; post-doctoral fellow Div. Engrng., Applied Physics Harvard U., Cambridge, Mass., 1975-76; field coord. environ. studies Alaska Outer Continental Shelf Office U.S. Dept. Interior, Anchorage, 1976-78; with oil spills sci. support Nat. Oceanic and Atmospheric Adminstrn., Alaska and S.E. U.S., 1978-81; policy analyst Exec. Office Pres. U.S. Office Sci. and Technology Policy, Washington, 1982-83; fellow Dept. of Commerce Sci. and Tech., 1982-83; staff dir. Bd. Ocean Sci. and Policy NAS, Washington, 1983-85; resident rsch. assoc. Nat. Rsch. Coun. Scripps Instn. Oceanography and Jet Propulsion Lab NASA, 1985-87; br. head Oceans and Ice Br. Goddard Space Flight Ctr. NASA, Greenbelt, Md., 1987-88, assoc. chief rsch. Lab. for Oceans, 1988-89—; asst. dir. for environment Exec. Office of Pres. Office Sci. and Tech. Policy, Washington, 1989—. Contbr. numerous articles profl. jours. Recipient Pub. Svc. Commendation USCG, 1979. Mem. AAAS, Assn. Women in Sci., The Oceanography Soc., Am. Geophys. Union, Women's Aquatic Network (bd. dirs.), Corp. Bermuda Biol. Sta. Rsch. Office: Office Sci and Tech Policy Exec Office of Pres Washington DC 20506

MAYNARD, VIRGINIA MADDEN, political organization executive; b. New London, Conn., Jan. 29, 1924; d. Raymond and Edna Sarah (Madden) Maynard; B.S., U. Conn., 1945; postgrad. Am. Inst. Banking, 1964-66, Cornell U., 1975. With Nat. City Bank (now Citibank), N.Y.C., 1954-79, asst. cashier, 1965-69, asst. v.p., 1969-74, v.p. internat. banking group, 1974-76, comptroller's div., 1976-79; v.p. First Women's Bank, N.Y.C., 1979-80; Internat. Fedn. Univ. Women rep. UN, 1982—; cons. in field. Trustee fellowships endowment fund AAUW Ednl. Found., Washington, 1977-80, Va. Gildersleeve Internat. Fund Univ. Women, Inc. (pres., 1987—). Mem. AAUW (fin. chmn. N.Y.C. br. 1976-79, bylaws chmn. 1979-83, adminstr. Meml. Fund 1983—, Woman of Achievement 1976). Republican. Congregationalist. Home: 601 E 20th St New York NY 10010

MAYO, CATHY METCALF, pharmacist; b. Tulsa, June 10, 1955; d. Earl William and Doris Alene (Maden) Metcalf; m. Dan Roper Mayo, Mar. 25, 1989. BS in Pharmacy, U. Fla., 1978. Registered pharmacist, Fla. Pharmacy mgr. Eckerd Drugs, Jacksonville, Fla., 1978-84; gen. mgr. Pharmacy Corp. Am., Longwood, Fla., 1984—; cons. in field; insvc. coord. Pharmacy Corp. Am., Longwood, Fla., 1984—; cons. pharmacist adult protection team Health and Rehabilitative Svcs. Dist. VII, 1988—. Editor: Monthly Newsletter For Long Term Care, 1988. Com. mem. Cen. Fla. Assn. Older Ams., Orlando, Fla., 1989; speaker in field. Fellow Am. Soc. Consultant Pharmacists; mem. Fla. Pharmacy Assn., Cen. Fla. Pharmacy Assn. Republican. Home: 5059 Knotty Pine Ct Sanford FL 32771 Office: Pharmacy Corp of Am 735A W Hwy 434 Longwood FL 32750

MAYO, JANICE, marketing professional, advertising executive; b. St. Paul, Minn., Sept. 15, 1952; d. Gail Myron and Alvina Marie (Rybaski) M.; m. Charles Surasky, Dec. 26, 1982; 1 child, Sarah. BA, Macalester Coll., St. Paul, Minn., 1974. Editor Twin Cities Courier, Mpls., 1974-79; writer Calhoun's Collector's Soc., Mpls., 1979-81; copy chief Smith, Hemmings & Gosden, El Monte, Calif., 1981-82, creative dir., 1984-87, gen. mgr., 1987-88, pres., chief exec. officer, 1989—; head of copy group Publisher's Clearing House, Port Washington, N.Y., 1982—. Mem. Direct Mktg. Assn. (recipient ECHO award 1985), Direct Mktg. Guild of So. Calif., Direct Mktg. Creative Guild (recipient Pioneer award 1982, 86). Democrat. Jewish. Office: Smith-Hemmings-Gosden 3360 Flair Dr El Monte CA 91731

MAYO, PAMELA ELIZABETH, fine arts appraiser; b. Richmond, Va., June 18, 1959; d. Robert Bowers and Margaret (Thomas) M. BFA, Longwood Coll., Farmville, Va., 1981. Asst. dir. Gallery Mayo, Inc., Richmond, Va., 1981-86, gallery dir., 1986--. Author: Lue Osborne and Cordray Simmons, 1980; editor: America: The Sporting View, 1985. Mem. Internat. Soc. of Appraisers. United Methodist.

MAYOR, HARRIET, foundation administrator; b. N.Y.C., Dec. 13, 1933; d. Brantz and Evelyn (Griswold) M.; m. William Watts, Aug. 4, 1954 (div. 1975); children: Evelyn G. Ward, Shelby S. Watts, Heidi H. Watts; m. J. William Fulbright, Mar. 10, 1990. BA, Radcliffe Coll., Cambridge, Mass., 1955; MFA, George Wash. U., 1975. Chair art dept. Maret Sch., Washington, 1975-80; asst. dir. Congl. Arts Caucus, Washington, 1980-82, Alliance of Ind. Coll. Art, Washington, 1982-84; exec. sec. Internat. Congress Art History, Washington, 1984-87; exec. dir. Fulbright Assn., Washington, 1987—; cons. Paul Hill Chorale, Wash. Music Ensemble. Author: How To Get Your Own Pre-School Play Group; editor: Fulbrighters Newsletter. Pres. Maret Sch. Bd. Office: Fulbright Assn 1307 New Hampshire Ave NW Washington DC 20036

MAYRON, MELANIE, actress, writer; b. Phila., Oct. 20, 1952. Ed., Am. Acad. Dramatic Arts, N.Y.C. Appeared in films Harry and Tonto, Girl Friends (British Acad. award nomination), Missing, Car Wash, Heartbeeps, You Light Up My Life, The Great Smokey Roadblock, Sticky Fingers (also co-writer, co-producer); TV prodns. include Hustling, 1975, Katie: Portrait of a Centerfold, 1978, The Best Little Girl in the World, 1981, Will There Really Be a Morning?, 1983, miniseries Wallenberg: A Hero's Story, 1985, Playing for Time, The Boss's Wife, series thirtysomething (Emmy award for best supporting actress in a drama series, 1989); co-writer several TV movies. *

MAYS, CLARA FLORENCE, insurance agent, consultant; b. Morenci, Ariz., Dec. 31, 1944; d. William Kilgo and Clara Edna (Hutson) Pryor; m. Herschel Raymond Mays, Oct. 26, 1963; children: Herschel D., Mark S., Kevin W. Student, Missoula Tech. Ctr., 1975. Cert. ins. counselor. Retail salesman East Gate Drug, Missoula, Mont., 1963-64; ins. underwriter, exec. sec. to pres. Glacier Gen. Assurance Co., Missoula, 1964-67; salesman Avon, Missoula, 1967-68; retail salesman Singer Co., Missoula, 1968-70; v.p. ops. Bishop Ins. Svc., Polson, Mont., 1977-88; sr. customer svc. rep. Terry Payne & Co., Missoula, 1988—. Den mother Boy Scouts Am., Arlee, Mont., 1972-73; vice-rector, speaker Cursillo, Missoula, Ronan, Mont., 1975-84; scorekeeper, bracketer Amateur Athletic Union, Wrestling Program, Ronan, 1973-80; scholarship judge Soroptimist Internat., Polson chpt., 1984-85; instr. baton twirling YMCA, Missoula, 1974; vol. United Way, 1989-90. Named Disting. Achiever Safeco Ins. Co. Edn. Dept., Seattle, 1979. Mem. Soc. CPCU, Soc. Cert. Ins. Counselors, Nat. Assn. Ins. Women (legis. com. Missoula chpt. 1985, chmn. social and program com. 1988-89, sec. 1989—, edn. com. 1989—, chmn. legis. com. 1990), Ins. Inst. Am. (coord., course instr. 1988—), Ind. Ins. Agts. Mont. Roman Catholic. Office: Terry Payne & Co Inc PO Box 8747 Missoula MT 59807

MAYS, JANICE ANN, federal agency administrator; b. Waycross, Ga., Oct. 21, 1951; d. William H. and Jean (Bagley) M. AB, Wesleyan Coll., Macon, Ga., 1973; JD, U. Ga., 1975; LLM in Taxation, U. Georgetown, 1980. Bar: Ga. 1976. Tax counsel com. on ways and means U.S. Ho. Reps., Washington, 1975-88, chief tax counsel com. on ways and means, 1988—. Mem. Tax Coalition (past chair). Office: 1135 Longworth House Office Bldg Washington DC 20515

MAYS, PENNY SANDRA, educator, radiologic technologist, academic administrator; b. Russellville, Ark., Dec. 23, 1940; d. William Haywood Sr. and Frances (Sanford) M. Cert. in radiologic tech., U. Tenn., 1961, cert. adv. radiologic, 1962. Dir. radiologic svcs. Huntsville (Ala.) Hosp., 1969-82; mgr. office Anesthesia Analgesia, Memphis, 1982-85; mem. faculty radiologic tech. program Shelby State Coll., 1985—. Contbr. Textbook Introduction to Fundaments of RAdiologic Technology. Recipient Govs. award State of

Ala., 1980, 71, 72, and others, John Cahoon award in radiology Southeastern Conf. Radiologic Technologists, 1979, Presentation award Southeast Radiology Conf., 1980; named Technologist of Yr., Ala. Radiologic Soc., 1983, Boss of Day, City of Huntsville, Ala., 1982. Mem. Am. Soc. Radiologic Tech., Ala. Soc. Radiologic Technologists (past v.p.), Am. Acad. Radiography, Assn. Educators in Radiography, Tenn. Soc. Radiologic Technologists. Home: 57 N Somerville #810 Memphis TN 38104

MAYSILLES, ELIZABETH, educator; b. Sleepy Creek, W.Va.; d. Evers and Rose (Scott) M. AB, W.Va. U.; MA, Hunter Coll., 1963; PhD, NYU, 1980. Announcer Radio Sta. WAJR, Morgantown, W.Va.; broadcaster Radio Sta. WGHF-FM, N.Y.C.; group leader GMAC, N.Y.C.; instr. NYU, N.Y.C.; prof. dept. speech communication Pace U., N.Y.C.; exec. adminstr. Am.-Scottish Found., N.Y.C.; cons. to hosps., acctg. and pubs. cos., 1971—; lectr. in field. Counselor Help Line, N.Y.C., 1971-75. Recipient Disting. Svc. award NYU Grad. Orgn., 1970, 71. Mem. Internat. Platform Assn. (bd. govs. 1980—), N.Y. Acad. Scis., Speech Communication Assn., Ctr. for Study of Presidency. Home: 155 E 77th St New York NY 10021 Office: Pace U 41 Park Row New York NY 10038

MAYSON, BETTY ANNE PEEPLES, medical consultant; b. Aiken, S.C., Dec. 23, 1943; d. Junius Black Peeples and Edna Earle (Sandifer) Peeples McKnight; m. Richard Grey Mayson, Sept. 23, 1959 (div. Sept. 1968); children—Richard Grey, Elizabeth Boatwright. Cert. operating room technician Adjust Edn., Augusta, Ga., 1973; Assoc. degree in Nursing with high honors, U. S.C., 1975, B.S. in Nursing cum laude, 1978. R.N., Ga., S.C. Mgr. car rental co., Augusta, Ga., 1966-70; ward clk. Plantation Gen. Hosp., Fla., 1970-72; staff nurse St. Joseph Hosp., Augusta, Ga., 1975-76; teaching assoc. U. S.C., Columbia, 1978; cons. O.F. Furr, Esquire, Columbia, 1977-82; med. cons. Solomon, Kahn, Smith & Baumil, attys., Charleston, S.C., 1982—; cons. Westinghouse Health System, Atlanta, 1977-80, Kirschner Assocs., Atlanta, 1979-80. Vol. Med. U. S.C., Charleston, 1985, Hospice, Charleston, 1986, Friends of Library, 1986. Panhellenic scholar, 1975; Bus. and Profl. Women's Found. Lady Clairol scholar, 1976-78; Lettie Mae Whitehead Meml. scholar U. S.C., 1976-78. Mem. Charleston C. of C., Sigma Theta Tau. Methodist. Home: 207 Hamlet Rd Summerville SC 29485 Office: Solomon Kahn Smith & Baumil 39 Broad St Charleston SC 29401

MAYSTEAD, SUZANNE RAE, optometrist; b. Hillsdale, Mich., Sept. 30, 1955; d. Marvin Charles and Helen Alberta (Glendenning) Patrick; m. Ivan Karl Maystead, III, June 4, 1977. OD, Ferris State Coll. Optometry, 1979. Research asst. to optometrist, Big Rapids, Mich., 1979-80; clin. assoc. Ferris State Coll. Optometry, Big Rapids, 1979-84; pvt. practice optometry, Portland, Mich., 1980—. Recipient Contact Lens Achievement award Bausch & Lomb, 1979. Mem. Mich. Optometric Assn., Portland C. of C. (Optometric Extension program, Am. Optometric Assn. contact lens sect.). Avocations: indoor gardening, piano. Club: Am. Chesapeake. Home: 7667 Peckins Rd Lyons MI 48851 Office: 1311 E Bridge St Portland MI 48875

MAYWEATHER, BILLIE JEAN FIELDS, counselor; b. Memphis, Nov. 17, 1938; m. Robert L. Mayweather Sr., June 17, 1961; children: Robert L. Jr., Robin F. BS, Tenn. State U., 1960; MEd, Memphis State U., 1969. Tchr. Memphis City Schs., 1960-70; tchr. adult edn., 1981-82, elem. guidance counselor, 1970—; tchr. Vacation Bible Sch., Memphis 1982—; bd. dirs. Christian Edn. Bd., Memphis. Active in Orgn. Dem. Women, 1970, Leath St. Day Care Ctr., Memphis, 1970. Mem. NEA, Memphis Edn. Assn., Tenn. Edn. Assn., West Tenn. Edn. Assn., West Tenn. Guidance Assn. Baptist. Home: 1895 Fairmeade Ave Memphis TN 38114 Office: 2597 Avery Ave Memphis TN 38112

MAZUR, STELLA MARY, former organization administrator; b. Lowell, Mass.; d. Stanley and Katherine (Cichowicz) M.; B.S. in Edn., U. Lowell; student ARC Mgmt. Tng. Sch., 1962, Nat. Tng. Lab. for Applied Behavioral Sci., 1963. USO club dir., Windsor Locks, Conn., 1942; gen. field rep. ARC, 1944, exec. dir., Waltham, Mass., 1944-79. Spl. assignment State Dept. USIA Graphic Arts Cultural Exchange Program, Eastern Europe, Poland, 1965. Mem. Pres.' Circle, Lowell U. Recipient Waltham Rotary Club spl. citation, 1952; Waltham Community 25 Year Service award, 1969; Recognition award Waltham chpt. ARC, 1971; Outstanding Woman, Waltham News Tribune, 1974; Woman of Today, Waltham Bus. and Profl. Women's Club, 1976; Outstanding Service award ARC New Eng., 1979; Disting. Alumni award U. Lowell, 1979. Mem. Internat. Platform Assn., ARC Retiree Assn., Am. Assn. Ret. Persons, Smithsonian Assos., Lowell U. Alumni Assn. (hon. life). Seton Guild Lowell, Lowell Hist. Soc., Lowell Mus. Corp. Clubs: Vesper Country (Tyngsboro, Mass.); Longmeadow Golf, Country, Lowell U. Pres.' Univ. Circle (Lowell). Author, pub.: Roots and Heritage of Polish People in Lowell, 1976. Home: 170 Andover St Lowell MA 01852

MAZURA, ADRIANNE C., lawyer; b. Detroit, Mar. 21, 1951; d. John G. and Marie (Schultz) Mazura; m. John Paul Ryan, Oct. 11, 1980; 1 child, Stephen John. BA, U. Mich., 1973; JD, Wayne State U., 1978. Bar: Ill. 1978, U.S. Dist. Ct. (no. dist.) Ill. 1978, U.S. Ct. Appeals (7th cir.) 1985. Bd. dirs., shareholder Pope, Ballard, Shepard and Fowle, Ltd. Chgo., 1978—. Author: Drug Testing in the Workplace, 1989, What to Do When the Union Calls, 1981, (with others) IICLE Handbooks, 1983-89; contbr. articles to profl. jours. Bd. dirs. Eleanor Assn., Chgo., 1985—. Fellow ABF; mem. ABA, Ill. Bar Assn., Chgo. Bar Assn., Women's Bar Assn., Nat. Health Lawyers Assn. Office: Pope Ballard Shepard Fowle 69 W Washington St Chicago IL 60602-3069

MAZZA, ARLENE JOAN, educator; b. Holyoke, Mass., Apr. 13, 1944; d. John Fenton and Adeline Rose (Banas) Ayers; m. Peter D. Mazza, Nov. 28, 1963; children: Karen Ann Mazza Costello, Peter John. BSBA, Am. Internat. Coll., 1970, MA in Teaching, 1976, Cert. Advanced Grad. Studies, 1980. Cert. tchr., Mass. Tchr. bus. Easthampton (Mass.) Pub. Schs., 1970-71; tchr. bus. Agawam (Mass.) Pub. Schs., 1971—, chmn. dept., 1972—; instr. word processing Springfield (Mass.) Tech. Community Coll., 1984-89. Horace Mann grantee, 1986. Mem. NEA, Mass. Tchrs. Assn., Agawam Edn. Assn. (sec. 1978-80), Mass. Bus. Edn. Dirs., Agawam C. of C. (mem. edn. com.), Delta Kappa Gamma (Springfield chpt. 1st v.p.). Home: 726 N West St Feeding Hills MA 01030-0294

MAZZA, CHRISTINE ELAINE, office manager; b. N.Y.C., Dec. 5, 1952; d. Joseph Anthony and Florence (Elbert) M.; m. Oliver A. Cromwell, Nov. 6, 1982. AAS, Burlington County Coll., Pemberton, N.J., 1986. Sr. office mgr. BA Managistics, Mt. Laurel, N.J.; sales asst. Gen. Sportcraft, Ltd., Bergenfield, N.J.; asst. to pres. Milo Reproductions, N.Y.C. Mem. NAFE. Roman Catholic. Office: 14000A Commerce Pkwy Mount Laurel NJ 08054

MAZZEI, DOREEN CHERYL, service executive; b. N.Y., June 28, 1956; d. James Q. and Sylvia E. (Holappa) M. A, Sullivan Community Coll., 1978; BA, N.Y. Inst. Tech., 1987; postgrad., Adelphi U., 1987—. Paraprofl. Nassau Ctr. for Disabled, Woodbury, N.Y., 1978-80; kitchen mgr., gen. mgr. Pointview Inn, Pt. Lookout, N.Y., 1980—. Reporter Community Outlook, Pt. Lookout, 1987. Trustee Pt. Lookout, 1987; sexton Community Ch., Pt. Lookout, 1987. Mem. NAFE, Rsch. Inst. for the Exec., Lookout Hist. Soc., Smithsonian Inst. Home: 60 Freeport Ave Point Lookout NY 11569

MAZZEO-MERKLE, LINDA L., legal administrator; b. Washington, Apr. 6, 1947; d. Robert Clifton, Shreeves II and Esther A. (Harrison) Cumming; m. John T. Mazzeo; children: Christina L., Regina L. Lic. real estate, Prince Georges Community Coll., Largo, Md., 1972. Various secretarial positions, 1964-65, 67-72; real estate saleswoman, 1973-74; div. sec. Prince Georges Community Coll., 1974-75; real estate saleswoman Harvest Realty Inc., Clinton, Md., 1974-75; legal adminstr., property mgr., investment mgr. firm Tucker, Flyer, Sanger, Reider & Lewis P.C., Washington, 1975-84; legal adminstr. Anderson, Heibey, Nauheim & Blair, Washington, 1984-85; v.p. fin. and adminstrn. Barnes, Morris & Pardoe, Inc., Washington, 1985—; dir. Md. Corp.; pres. Lawtabs Inc. Del. Corp.; cons., speaker Mem. Assn. Legal Adminstrs. (chmn. new adminstrs. and gen. adminstrn. sect. 1984-85), ABA (assoc.). Home: 4100 N River St Arlington VA 22207 Office: 919 18th St NW Washington DC 20006

MAZZOLA, MARY PAPAKYRIKOS, health care company executive; b. Lesvos, Greece, May 6, 1959; came to U.S., 1969; d. Stratis N. and Ariadni (Grossomanidis) Papakyrikos; m. Lawrence M. Mazzola, Aug. 16, 1986; 1 child, Mathew P. BS, Simmons Coll., 1982; MS, Mass. Coll. Pharmacy and Allied Scis., 1988. Primary nurse Beth Israel Hosp., Boston, 1982-85; nurse mgr. Faulkner Hosp., Jamaica Plain, Mass., 1985-86; nursing case mgr. Baxter Health Care Corp., Lexington, Mass., 1986, nat. product dir., 1986—, regional adminstr., 1988, mem. corp. product rev. bd., 1988-90; nat. product dir. CORE Mgmt. Inc., Lexington, Mass., 1990—; chmn. nursing liaison Simmons Coll., Boston, 1980-82; cons. HCFA, Balt., 1989-90. Campaign vol. Ray Shamie, Boston, 1980-82; v.p. Greek Orthodox Youth Am., Watertown, Mass., 1980-82. Mem. NAFE, Nat. Nurse Execs. Coun. Mid. Mgmt. (sec. 1985-86). Republican. Office: CORE Management Inc 20 Maguire Rd Lexington MA 02173

MAZZOTTA, DOROTHY, business owner; b. N.Y.C., Jan. 18, 1933; d. Gus and Katherine (Gannon) Cohen; m. Al Mazzotta; children: Joanne Mazzotta Greene, Elizabeth Mazzotta Aversa. Cert. broker, Pohs Inst. Ins., N.Y.C., 1954. Cert. travel cons. Owner, mgr. D. Mazzotta Ins., Bklyn., Friendly Holidays, Inc., Lake Success, N.Y., 1970—. Office: Friendly Holidays 1983 Marcus Ave Lake Success NY 11042

MAZZUCA, ROBIN LYNN, firefighter, paramedic; b. Berwyn, Ill., July 16, 1958; d. Robert Walter and June Emily (Tvrz) Hass; m. Dale Charles Mazzuca, Nov. 6, 1982. Student, Northland Coll., Ashland, Wis., 1976-77, Morton Coll., Cicero, Ill., 1978-79, U. Ill., Chgo., 1979. Apprentice pharmacist, asst. mgr. Golden Drugs, Berwyn, 1978-79; accounts payable, receivable clk. Transp. Engring., Inc., Oak Brook, Ill., 1979-80; adminstrv. asst. Chgo. Haulage, Inc., Schiller Park, Ill., 1980-84; emergency med. svc. coord. Lyons (Ill.) Fire Dept., 1980-90; owner, pres., instr. Phoenix Emergency Care Tng., Inc., Lyons, 1985—; code enforcement officer, paramedic, firefighter, pub. edn. Western Springs (Ill.) Fire Dept., 1987—; emergency med. svcs. coord. McCook (Ill.) Police and Fire Dept., 1985—; emergency med. svc. instr. Forest Park (Ill.) Fire Dept., 1985-90, Reynolds Metals, McCook, 1989—. Editorial bd. Jour. Emergency Care, 1987-89. Instr., trainer Am. Heart Assn., Westchester, Ill., 1981—, ARC, Westchester, 1985—; mem. standards com. Gov.'s EMS Adv. Coun., Ill., 1989—; mem. Task Force Focusing on Chem. Wastes in Schs., U.S. Fire Adminstrn., 1990. Mem. Ill. Emergency Med. Technician Inst. Coord. Soc. (sec. 1985-87), Nat. Assn. Emergency Med. Technicians, Nat. Fire Protection Assn., Am. Trauma Soc. Lutheran. Office: Western Springs Fire Dept 4353 Wolf Rd Western Springs IL 60558

MCABEE, ROBIN, emergency room nurse; b. Gaffney, S.C., Sept. 9, 1956; d. Paul and Faye (Robinson) McA. ADN, U. S.C., Spartanburg, 1979. Nursing supr. Upstate Carolina Med. Ctr., Gaffney, 1983-89; emergency rm. nurse mgr. Upstate Carolina Med. Ctr., Gaffney, S.C., 1989—. Mem. NAFE, Emergency Nurses Assn., USCS Alumni Assn. Baptist. Home: PO Box 902 Gaffney SC 29342

MCABEER, SARA CARITA, school system administrator; b. Logan, Utah, Aug. 19, 1906; d. Edward Thomas and Carrie Estelle (Martin) Harris; m. Frederick Alexander McAbeer, Dec. 24, 1929 (div. 1971); 1 child, Winifred. BA, Iowa State Tchr., Cedar Falls, 1929; postgrad., Sacramento (Calif.) Coll., 1956. Cert. high sch. adminstr. Clk., bookkeeper Curtis Jewelry, Kemmerer, Wyo., 1923-24; tchr. Miles High Sch., Miles, Iowa, 1929-30, Salinas (Calif.) High Sch., 1930-32; sec., supr. U. Calif., Berkeley., 1934-41; tchr. Vallejo (Calif.) Jr. High Sch., 1947-50, Napa (Calif.) Jr. High Sch., 1950-52; dean of girls Napa (Calif.) High Sch., 1952-72. Active Mem. Napa County Dem. Party, 1950-52, St. Thomas Altar Guild Napa, 1965—, Community Projects, Inc. Napa, 1968—; mem., vol. tchr., bd. dirs. North Bay Suicide Prevention, Inc. Napa, 1972—; leader Vallejo Girl Scouts, 1947-49; tchr. St. John's Cath. Ch., Napa, 1960-62. Recipient Vol. of Yr. North Bay Suicide Prevention Napa, 1986, Finalist continuing Svc. Vol. Ctr. Napa, 1988; Top Ten Ia. State Tchr. Cedar Falls scholar, 1929. Mem. AAUW, Delta Kappa Gamma. Democrat. Roman Catholic.

MCADAMS, MELINDA JEANNE, copy editor; b. York, Pa., July 23, 1959; d. William Arthur and Jeanne Elaine (Sipe) McAdams. BA, Pa. State U., 1981. Copy editor Dell Pub. Co., Inc., N.Y.C., 1982-84, MIS Week, Fairchild Publs., N.Y.C., 1984-87; copy chief, 1987-88; copy editor Time mag. Time-Warner Inc., N.Y.C., 1988—; press. sec. Am. Go Assn., N.Y.C., 1987—. Big sister Big Sisters Inc., N.Y.C., 1984-85. Mem. Soc. Profl. Journalists, Sigma Delta Chi. Democrat. Office: Time Mag Rockefeller Ctr New York NY 10020

MCADAMS, PATRICIA DANIELS, theatre educator, director; b. Hominy, Okla., Oct. 2, 1936; d. William Walter and Delpha Lee (Calico) Daniels; m. John Harris McAdams, June 4, 1964 (div. Aug. 1977); children: Ann Marie, William Thomas. BS, Okla. Bapt. U., 1958; postgrad., Yale U., 1958-60; MA, U. Denver, 1971; PhD, U. Colo., 1984. With Columbia Artists Mgmt., N.Y.C., 1963, Sta. NBC-TV, N.Y.C., 1963-64; with advt. dept. Henderson Bucknum, Denver, 1963-68; pub. rels. dir. Colo. Shakespeare Festival, Boulder, 1976, ticket office mgr., 1979-81, dramaturg, 1983; dir. theatre dept. Wayland Bapt. U., Plainview, Tex., 1983-85; chair theatre Hardin-Simmons U., Abilene, Tex., 1985—; intern acad. affairs U. Colo., Boulder, 1979-81, instr. drama and dance, 1977-80. Contbr. articles to profl. jours. Chair pulpit guest com. 1st Bapt. Ch., Abilene, 1989—; stage dir. benefit Abilene Girls Home, 1988; mem. textbook com. Abilene Ind. Sch. Dist., 1989—. Nat. Endowment for the Humanities grantee, 1985, Acad. Found. grantee, 1989. Mem. Assn. for Theatre in Higher Edn., S.W. Theatre Assn., Tex. Ednl. Theatre Assn., Alpha Psi Omega. Republican. Baptist. Office: Hardin Simmons U HSU Station Box 864 Abilene TX 79698

MCADOO, GAYLE A., marriage and family therapist, psychotherapist; b. Houston, Sept. 15, 1947; d. Walter Kenneth and Lucile Mae (Green) Kurtz; m. Stewart French McAdoo, Jr., Sept. 3, 1966. BS, U. Houston, 1969; MA, U. Houston, Clear Lake City, Tex., 1978; postgrad., Houston Family Inst., 1979-81. Lic. profl. counselor, Tex. Tchr. math. Hitchcock (Tex.) Ind. Sch. Dist., 1971-73, Clear Creek High Sch., Houston, 1973-76; teaching asst. U. Houston, Clear Lake City, 1978; family therapist Yough Shelter Galveston, Tex., 1978-81, Deer Park (Tex.) Hosp., 1984—; psychotherapist Clear Lake Psychiatry Assocs., Webster, Tex., 1985—; marriage and family therapist, psychotherapist, Houston, 1981—; contract therapist, cons. Sand Dollar, Inc., Pasadena, Tex., 1988—; contract therapist Alternative Paths/Hazelden EAP, Houston, 1989—; presenter in field. Pres. Clear Lake Jaycee-Ettes, 1978-79; state programming chmn. child abuse-operation peace of mind runaway hotline Tex. Jaycee-Ettes, 1979-80; mem. Bay Area Coun. on Druugs and Alcohol, Clear Lake City, 1981-88, pres., bd. dirs., 1982-83; v.p. social svcs. Gulf Coast chpt. Retinitis Pigmentosa Found., Houston, 1984-85. Mem. Am. Assn. for Marriage and Family Therapy (clin.), Houston Assn. for Marriage and Family Therapy (sec. 1985-87, pres. 1988-89), Am. Orthopsychiat. Assn., Mental Health Assn., Clear Lake Networking Group, Net-Bay Area Mental Health Providers Network (pres. 1987), Tex. Jaycee Women (hon. life, awards 1978-80). Office: 17629 El Camino Real Ste 400 Houston TX 77058

MC AFEE, JOYCE JANINE, electronics engineer; b. Joplin, Mo., Nov. 12, 1958; d. Gaylen Dwight Lauck and Mary Catherine (Reaves) Payne; m. Carl Marc Jensen, Aug. 19, 1978 (div.); 1 child, James Nicholas. Grad. high sch., Tulsa. Technician Teledyne Brown Engring., Huntsville, Ala., 1981-83; field rep. I, technician GTE Govt. Systems, Mountain View, Calif., 1983-86; assoc. engr. Ultrasystems Def. and Space, Inc., Sunnyvale, Calif., 1986-89; sr. technician Applied Signal Tech., Sunnyvale, 1989—. With U.S. Army, 1977-81. Republican. Baptist.

MCAFEE, NAOMI JONES, engineering executive; b. Hart County, Ky., Oct. 27, 1934; d. Charles Thomas and Emma Florence (Cobb) Jones; m. George Henry McAfee, Aug. 22, 1958. BS in Physics, Western Ky. State Coll., 1956. With electronic systems group Westinghouse Electric Corp., Balt., 1956—, dir. reliability, maintainability and supportability, 1987—. Editor: Reliability Training text, 1958; contbr. articles to profl. publs. Mem. Army Sci. Bd., Washington, 1983—; active Presidents Com. on the Nat. Medal Sci., 1981-84. Fellow Soc. Women Engrs. (nat. pres. 1972-74); mem. IEEE (pres. reliability soc. 1984-86), Am. Soc. Quality Control (electronic div. award 1977, Edwards medal 1980). Republican. Baptist. Home: 13 Seminole Ave Catonsville MD 21228

MCALINDON, MARY NAOMI, nursing administrator; b. Ebensburg, Pa., Oct. 16, 1935; d. S. David and Genevieve (Little) Solomon; m. James Daniel McAlindon, Nov. 25, 1961; children: Robert, Donald, James, Peter, M. Catherine. BS in Nursing, Georgetown U., 1957; MA, U. Mich., 1979. RN, Mich. Staff nurse Georgetown U. Hosp., Washington, 1957-59; instr. St. Joseph Hosp., Flint, 1959-62; clin. instr. Mott Community Coll., Flint, 1980-81; asst. dir. nursing McLaren Hosp., Flint, 1980—; cons. Nat. League for Nursing, N.Y. 1986, mem. exec. com., 1988. Active adv. coun. United Way Genesee County, Flint, 1988-89. Mem. Vis. Nurse Assn. (pres. bd. dirs. 1988-89), Am. Nurses Assn., Sigma Theta Tau. Roman Catholic. Office: McLaren Gen Hosp 401 S Ballinger Hwy Flint MI 48532

MCALLASTER, CLAUDIA, pediatrician; b. Kansas City, Mo., Feb. 10, 1952; d. Wendale E. and Donna Lee (Rhodes) McA.; m. William Pray, 1973; m. Pete Clagett, Dec. 24, 1986. BA, U. Kans., Lawrence, 1974; MD, U. Kans., Kansas City, 1977. Diplomate Am. Bd. Pediatrics. Resident in pediatrics Children's Mercy Hosp., Kansas City, Mo., 1977-80; pvt. practice Leavenworth, Kans., 1980—; coroner 1st Jud. Dist., Kans., 1980—; pres. med. staff St. John Hosp., 1987-88, chmn. pediatric dept., 1983-85, chmn. quality assurance com., 1987-90; fee-basis physician Eisenhower VA Hosp., Leavenworth, 1985-88, St. John Adolescent Chem. Dependency Ctr., 1986-89; assoc. chmn. pediatrics dept. Providence-St. Margaret Hosp., 1986-88; adviser Snow Creek Ski Patrol, 1988—; mem. adv. com. Leavenwroth Emergency Med. Svc., 1981—. Bd. dirs. Neighborhood House, Leavenworth, 1982-84, YWCA, Leavenworth, 1988-90; mem. choir Meth. Ch., Leavenworth, 1984-90, mem. fin. bd., 1990—. Maj. USAR, 1985-90. Fellow Am. Acad. Pediatrics; mem. Assn. Mil. Officers of U.S., Kans. Coroner's Assn., Soc. Adolescent Medicine, Greater Kansas City Pediatric Soc., Phi Beta Kappa, Alpha Chi Sigma. Republican. Office: 4500 S 4th St Leavenworth KS 66048

MCALLISTER, DIANNE ELAINE, author, poet, lyricist, information systems operator; b. Seneca, S.C., Feb. 21, 1951; d. Ray Harold and Clara Vivian (Cleland) McAllister. Info. sys. operator Coats & Clark Inc., Toccoa, Ga., 1980-90; customer svc. mgr. Coats & Clark Inc., 1990—. Author: (poetry) Gulls and Sea (Golden Poet award 1989), 1989; contbr.: American Poetry Association Anthology, 1989; author how-to manuals. Mem. Presdl. Task Force, 1989-90. Named to 2000 Notable Women Hall of Fame, 1990. Mem. Nat. Authors Registry, Pase Lit. Soc., Computer Zealists, Computer Enthusiasts, Nat. Assn. Female Execs., Poets Circle N, Authors Process. Republican. Baptist.

MCALLISTER, JULIA ANNE, recreational facility executive, consultant; b. Evanston, Ill., Nov. 21, 1962; d. Dale and Marlo (Dinsmore) McA. Student, William Smith Coll., 1980-82; BS, Fla. State U., 1986. Mgmt. trainee Hyatt Regency of Louisville, 1986-87; asst. club mgr. Atlanta Athletic Club, 1987-89; gen. mgr. Fairhope (Ala.) Yacht Club, 1989—. Chmn. fund drive United Way, Louisville, 1987. Mem. Internat. Spl. Events Soc., Am. Bus. Women's Assn., Club Mgrs. Assn. of Am., NAFE. Democrat. Presbyterian. Office: Fairhope Yacht Club 101 Volanta St PO Box 1327 Fairhope AL 36533

MCALLISTER, NANCY HARDACRE, music academy administrator; b. Highland Park, Ill., Feb. 24, 1940; d. Milton Joseph Jr. and Virginia Letitia (Engels) Hardacre; m. Claude Huntley McAllister, Sept. 5, 1970. MusB, B Music Edn., Denison U., 1962; MA, U. N.C., 1967, M Music Edn., 1968. Cert. in music edn., violin performance, composition. Organist, choir dir. St. Mark's Episcopal Ch., Barrington, Ill., 1957-58; orch. dir. Adrian (Mich.) Pub. Schs., 1964-66, Luther Coll., Decorah, Iowa, 1966-67; orch. dir., tchr. New Hanover Pub. Schs., Wilmington, N.C., 1964-87; dir., owner Wilmington Acad. Music, 1987—; grad. asst. U. N.C., Chapel Hill, 1962-66; violinist Columbus (Ohio) Symphony Orch., 1961-62, Acad. Music Chamber Trio, Wilmington, 1987—; concertmaster Wilmington Symphony Orch., 1986—; condr. Acad. Music Orch., 1987—. Composer: Sonata in A Major for violin and piano, 1961, Suite for Horn and Strings, 1961 (2d place Priz de Rome 1965). Mem. Am. String Tchrs. Assn. (sec. 1987-91), Music Educators Nat. Conv., Nat. Sch. Orch. Assn., Wilmington C. of C., P.E.O. Episcopalian. Office: Wilmington Acad Music 1635 Wellington Ave Wilmington NC 28401

MCALLISTER, ROMETTA, telemetry technician; b. Birmingham, Ala., Mar. 3, 1948; d. Gaines Terry Jr. and Helen (Morgan) Terry Rogers; m. Elijah Collins (div.); childen: Dane, Victoria; m. Fredrick McAllister (div.); children: Demetria, Fredrick, Veronica. Student, Pontiac Bus. Inst., 1988. Unit sec. Pontiac (Mich.) Gen. Hosp., 1067-69, Havenwyck Hosp., Pontiac, 1982-85; telemetry technician St. Joseph Hosp., Pontiac, 1985—. Tchr. cons. Jefferson Jr. High Sch., Pontiac, 1990. Office: St Joseph Mercy Hosp 900 Woodward Ave Pontiac MI 48053

MCANINCH, MARY KUNKLE, elementary education educator; b. Homer City, Pa., July 14, 1935; d. Lisle Henry and Mary (Harris) Kunkle; m. Victor E. Reinhold, Aug. 18, 1956 (div. 1983); children: Victor E. Jr., Lavern C.; m. Ivan Arthur McAninch, Feb. 16, 1990. BS, Roberts Wesleyan Coll., North Chili, N.Y., 1957; MA, Syracuse U.; postgrad., Buffalo State U., NYU. Cert. tchr., N.Y. Tchr. Falconer (N.Y.) Cen. Sch., 1961-64, Jamestown (N.Y.) Pub. Schs., 1965-90; ret. Mem. barbershop choir Zion Covenant Church, Jamestown. Mem. Christian Profl. Women, PTA (life), N.Y. State Tchrs. Assn., Jamestown Tchrs. Assn., Ret. Tchrs. Orgn. Republican. Swedish Covenant. Home: 217 Pinewood Dr Eustis FL 32726

MC ANULTY, MARY CATHERINE CRAMER (MRS. CHARLES GILBERT MC ANULTY), retired educator; b. Braddock, Pa., June 26, 1908; d. Albert R. and Sara (Kelly) Cramer; A.B., Fla. So. Coll., 1929; M.A., Tchrs. Coll. Columbia, 1937; postgrad. Fla. State U., 1946-50; m. Charles Gilbert McAnulty, Dec. 25, 1937. Elem. tchr. Lake Ann Sch., Lake Garfield, Fla., 1930-31, elem. prin., 1932-34; prin. South Winter Haven Elem. Sch., Winter Haven, Fla., 1935-55; adminstrv. asst. to supervising prin. Winter Haven Area Schs., 1956-60; prin. Fred Garner Elem. Sch., Winter Haven, 1961-68, Lake Alfred Elem. Sch., 1969-70. Asst. chmn. vols., asst. tng. chmn., local chpt. ARC, 1967-68, 2d v.p., also chmn. vols., 1969-70, bd. mem., chmn. service to mil. families, 1970-71, chmn. coll. youth, 1971-72; treas. Imperial Harbours Condominium, 1980-82, pres., 1984; v.p. Beymer United Methodist Women, 1973-75, pres., 1976-77, 89-90; lay del. ann. conf. Meth. Ch., 1978, 79; pres. Lake Region Extension Homemaker's Club, 1974, 75; bd. dirs. Winter Haven Hosp. Aux., rec. sec., 1985-86, corr. sec., 1986-88. Mem. Am. Assn. Supervision and Curriculum Devel., Internat. Reading Assn. (pres., Polk County chmn.), NEA, Fla. Edn. Assn. (dir. dept. elem. sch. prins. 1965-67), Polk County Elem. Prins. Assn. (sec.), LWV (local dir. 1962), AAUW (local br. chmn. status women com. 1963), DAR (chpt. treas. 1967-68, historian 1969-70, regent 1970-72, state chmn. jr. Am. citizens 1972—, dir. dist. VI 1973-74, parliamentarian 1986-90), Fla. So. Coll. Alumni Assn. (sec.), Internat. Platform Assn., P.E.O. (chpt. treas. 1970-74, 80-89, chaplain 1976, 77, chpt. pres. 1978-79), Ch. Women United (v.p. 1977—, chmn. adv. bd. 1980-81), Pi Gamma Mu, Delta Kappa Gamma (State Achievement award 1964, Fla. pres. 1962-63, chpt. parliamentarian 1968-73, 87, 88, 89, 90, pres., v.p., treas.). Methodist (choir mem., chmn. commn. edn. 1959-60, supt. study program 1969-70, organist 1970-77, pres. Wesley fellowship class 1972-73, chmn. adminstrv. bd. 1980, 81, 83-85 trustee 1983-88, hon. trustee 1989—, pres. bd. 1987-88, lay leader 1985, 86, fin. com., worship com., staff Parish com, 1989—, organ com., 1987—. Clubs: Pilot (charter, pres. 1954-55, 61-62), Poinsettia Garden (pres. 1984-85). Lodge: Order Eastern Star (fin. chair 1987-89), Winter Haven Woman's (edn. chmn. 1967-68, v.p. 1983-84, pres. 1984-85, parliamentarian 1986-90, dist. 9 Parliamentarian 1988-90). Home: 650 N Lake Howard Dr Apt 7B Winter Haven FL 33881

MC ARTHUR, JANET WARD, endocrinologist, educator; b. Bellingham, Wash., June 25, 1914; d. Hyland Donald and Alice Maria (Frost) McA. A.B., U. Wash., 1935, M.S., 1937; M.B., Northwestern U., 1941, M.D., 1942; Sc.D., Mt. Holyoke Coll., 1962. Diplomate: Am. Bd. Internal Medicine. Intern Cin. Gen. Hosp., 1941-42, asst. resident in medicine, 1942-43; asst. resident, rsch. fellow in medicine H.P. Walcott fellow clin. medicine Mass. Gen. Hosp., Boston, 1943-47, assoc. physician, 1959-84, assoc. children's svc., 1968-84; instr. Harvard U., 1955-57, asst. prof., 1960-64, assoc. prof., 1964-73, prof., 1973-84, prof. emeritus, 1984—; clin. prof. medicine Boston U. Sch. Medicine, 1984—; adj. prof. Sargent Coll. Allied Health Scis.

Boston U.; mem. reproductive biology study sect. NIH, 1974-78, Com. on Population Studies, 1980-84; co-dir. Vincent Meml. Rsch. Lab., 1977-79; sr. scientist U. London, 1985-86. Author: (with others) Functional Endocrinology from Birth Through Adolescence, 1952; editor: (with Theodore Colton) Statistics in Endocrinology, 1970; contbr. articles to profl. jours. Fellow A.C.P.; mem. AMA, Endocrine Soc., Am. Fertility Soc., AAAS, Boston Obstet. Soc., Phi Beta Kappa, Sigma Xi, Alpha Omega Alpha. Home: 19 Brimmer St Boston MA 02108 Office: Boston U 635 Commonwealth Ave 4th Fl Boston MA 02215

MCARTHUR, SARA DEE, psychologist; b. Atlanta, Mar. 23, 1948; d. Robert Stuart and Teena (Adams) McA.; m. Gerald P. Rudd, Dec. 24, 1972 (div. Sept. 1986); children: Samuel P., Sarita R. BA in Social Work and Psychology, Mercer U., Macon, Ga., 1970; MA in Child Devel., U. Kans., 1971, PhD in Child Psychology, 1973. Prof. N.E. Mo. State U., Kirksville, 1973-74; tchr. cons. Mary Immaculate Cath. Sch., Kirksville, 1974-76; psychologist Community Counseling Ctr., Winslow, Ariz., 1977-81, Nat. Children's Ctr. Inc., Washington, 1984-85; child psychologist Navajo Child Psychiatry Team, Navajo & Hopi Reservation, 1985-88; psychologist Albuquerque Indian Health Svc., Albuquerque, 1988—; scientist, profl. adv. com. to Surgeon Gen., Rockville, Md., 1988-91. Indian Health Svc. rep. Mental Health Bur., State N.Mex. 1989—; cons. Children's Residential Panel; Indian Health Svc. coord., rep. State N.Mex. Grant for Children and Adolescent Svc., Albuquerque, 1989—. Lt. comdr. USPHS, 1985—. Mem. Am. Psychol. Assn., N.Mex. Psychol. Assn. Office: USPHS 801 Vassar NE Albuquerque NM 87106

MCATEER, DEBORAH GRACE, travel executive; b. N.Y.C., Nov. 3, 1950; d. Edward John and Ann Marie (Cassidy) McA.; m. William A. Helms, Feb. 5, 1948; children: Elizabeth Grace, Kathleen Marie. Student, Montgomery Coll., 1969, Am. U., 1972. Sec. Polinger Co., Chevy Chase, Md., 1969-72, Loews Hotels, Washington, 1972-73; adminstr. asst. Am. Gas Assn., Arlington, Va., 1973-75; mgr. Birch Jermain Horton Bittner, Washington, 1975-77; asst. mgr. Travel Services, McLean, Va., 1977-79; founder, pres. Travel Temps, Washington, Atlanta, Phila., Miami and Ft. Lauderdale, Fla., 1979—; tchr. Montgomery Coll., Rockville, Md., 1980-84. Mem. Christ Child Soc., Washington, 1975—. Mem. Internat. Travel Soc. (pres. 1983-84), Am. Soc. Travel Agts., Pacific Area Travel Assn., Inst. Cert. Travel Cons. (cert.), Nat. Assn. Women Bus. Owners (chair membership com. 1983-84), Women Bus. Owners Atlanta (com. 1988-), Women's Commerc Club, PROST (sec. 1990). Republican. Roman Catholic. Home: 47 Delta Pl Atlanta GA 30307 Office: Travel Temps 375 Pharr Rd Ste 205 Atlanta GA 30305

MCATEER, MARY IAN, pediatrician; b. Lafayette, Ind., June 6, 1958; d. Ian Paul and Mary Lu (Dwyer) Welsh, James A. McAteer, July 24, 1982; children: Kevin James, Maureen Elizabeth, Carole Ian. BS, Purdue U., 1980; MD, Ind. U., Indpls., 1984. From intern to resident dept. pediatrics Ind. U., Indpls., 1984-87, clin. lectr. dept. pediatrics, 1987-89; pvt. practice pediatrics Castleton Pediatrics, Indpls., 1989—. Editor: You're a New Parent, 1988. Fellow Am. Acad. Pediatrics; mem. Ind. State Med. Assn. Democrat. Roman Catholic. Office: Castleton Pediatrics 7250 Clearvista Dr 205 Indianapolis IN 46256

MCAULIFFE, ROSEMARY, lawyer; b. New Rochelle, N.Y., May 24, 1927; d. William J. and Rose B. (Payne) McA. BA, Regis Coll., 1949; JD, New Eng. Sch. Law, 1954; MEd, Boston State Coll., 1971, Cert. advanced grad studies, 1981. Bar: Mass. 1956, U.S. Dist. Ct. Mass. 1957, U.S. Supreme Ct. 1961. Pvt. practice law Boston, 1956—; tchr. City of Boston, 1965—. Active World Affairs Coun., Boston, 1980-89, Smithsonian Assocs., Washington. Mem. Mass. Bar Assn., Am. Acad. Trial Lawyers, Mass. Assn. Women Lawyers (bd. dirs. 1989—). Home and Office: 61 Prince St Boston MA 02113

MCAUSLAN, MARY ELIZABETH KANE, dentist; b. Chgo., Aug. 12, 1955; d. Edward Michael and Margaret Mary (Hastings) Kane; m. David Neil McAuslan, Aug. 12, 1979; children: Eileen Jeanette, Peter David. BS, Loyola U., Chgo., 1977; DDS, U. Ill., 1981. Dentist McAuslan & McAuslan, DDS, P.C., Elgin, Ill., 1981—. Mem. ADA, Fox River Valley Dental Soc. (bd. dirs. 1989—), Elgin Dental Soc. (pres. 1988-89), Am. Assn. Women Dentists, Chgo. Dental Soc. (assoc.), Acad. Gen. Dentistry. Office: McAuslan & McAuslan DDS PC 1532 Weatherstone Ln Elgin IL 60123

MCBEE, SUSANNA BARNES, journalist; b. Santa Fe, Mar. 28, 1935; d. Jess Stephen and Sybil Elizabeth (Barnes) McBee; m. Paul H. Recer, July 2, 1983. AB, U. So. Calif., 1956; MA, U. Chgo., 1962. Staff writer Washington Post, 1957-65, 73-74, 77-79, asst. nat. editor, 1974-77; asst. sec. for public affairs HEW, 1979; articles editor Washingtonian mag., 1980-81; assoc. editor U.S. News & World Report, 1981-86; news editor Washington Bur. of Hearst Newspapers, 1987-89, asst. bur. chief, 1990—; Washington corr. Life mag., 1965-69; Washington editor McCall's mag., 1970-72. Recipient Penney-Missouri mag. award, 1969; Sigma Delta Chi Pub. Svc. award, 1969. Mem. Nat. Press Club. Home: 5190 Watson St NW Washington DC 20016 Office: 1701 Pennsylvania Ave NW Washington DC 20006

MCBRIDE, BEVERLY JEAN, lawyer; b. Greenville, Ohio, Apr. 5, 1941; d. Kenneth Birt and Glenna Louise (Ashman) Whited; m. Benjamin Gary McBride, Nov. 28, 1964; children: John David, Elizabeth Ann. BA magna cum laude, Wittenberg U., 1963; JD cum laude, U. Toledo, 1966. Bar: Ohio 1966. Intern Ohio Gov.'s Office, Columbus, 1962; asst. dean of women U. Toledo, 1963-65; assoc. Title Guarantee and Trust Co., Toledo, 1966-69; spl. counsel Ohio Atty. Gen.'s Office, Toledo, 1975; assoc. Cobourn, Smith, Rohrbacher and Gibson, Toledo, 1969-76; gen. counsel The Andersons, Maumee, Ohio, 1976—. Exec. trustee, bd. dirs. Wittenberg U., Springfield, Ohio, 1980—; trustee Anderson Found., Maumee, 1981—; chmn. Sylvania Twp. Zoning Commn., Ohio, 1970-80; candidate for judge, Sylvania Mcpl. Ct., 1975; trustee Goodwill Industries, Toledo, 1976-82, Sylvania Community Svcs. Ctr., 1976-78; founder Sylvania YWCA Program, 1973; active membership drives Toledo Mus. Art, 1977—. Recipient Toledo Women in Industry award YWCA, 1979; Outstanding Alumnus award Wittenberg U., 1981. Mem. ABA, AAUW, Ohio Bar Assn. Toledo Bar Assn. (pres., treas., chmn., sec. various coms.), Toledo Women Attys. Forum (exec. com. 1978-82), Pres. Club (U. Toledo, exec. com.). Home: 5274 Cambrian St Toledo OH 43623 Office: The Andersons 1200 Dussel Dr Maumee OH 43537

MCBRIDE, JOYCE BROWNING, accountant; b. Ga., May 28, 1927; d. Eph and Zula (Harden) Browning; grad. So. Bus. U., 1947; children—Jan Burge, Gary McBride, Kandie Lysse. Asst. controller Hampton Court Knits, Los Angeles, 1967-78; owner, mgr. McBride & Assocs. Bookkeeping Service, 1978—. Address: 2925 Tyler Ct Simi Valley CA 93063

MCBRIDE, JUDITH ELLEN, educator; b. Middletown, Ohio, Sept. 7, 1941. BA, U. Indpls., 1963; MA, Butler U., 1970. Tchr. Indpls. Pub. Schs., 1963—. Vol. Dem. Party, Marion County, 1989—. Named Outstanding Young Women Am., 1967, Tchr. of Yr. RCA, 1984; recipient Above and Beyond the Call of Duty award, 1989. Mem. AAUW (pres. 1980-82, dir. 1982-85), U. Indpls. Alumni Bd. (dir.).

MCBROOM, NANCY LEE, insurance executive; b. Tulsa, Nov. 7, 1925; d. Lee Webster and Dora Irene (Londigan) Adams; m. Robert B. McBroom, Jan. 22, 1945 (dec. Aug. 1969); children: Dacia Adams, Rene McBroom, Robert McBroom. Student, John Brown U., 1941-42, Little Rock Bus. Coll., 1941-42. Profl. horse trainer, judge, breeder N.C., Va. and Calif., 1955-75; owner Stombock's West, Inc., Del Mar, Calif., 1968-74; agt. Mut. Omaha Ins. Co., San Diego, 1978-84; owner, broker McBroom Ins. Svcs., San Diego, 1984—; dir. Dependent's Riding Program, USMC, Camp LeJeune, Va., 1963-66. Author: Handbook for Riding Instructors, 1963. Mem. com. Civitan Fund Raiser for Spl. Olympics, 1986. Mem. Nat. Assn. Securities Dealers, Rancho Bernardo C. of C. (com. 1986). Republican. Lodge: Soroptomist Internat. (mem. com. Women Helping Women 1985-86). Home: 11906-150 Paseo Lucido San Diego CA 92128 Office: McBroom Ins Svcs 16776 Bernardo Ctr Dr Suite 110B San Diego CA 92128

MCBURNEY, LINDA LEE, health facility administrator; b. Denver, June 10, 1942; d. Maurice J. and Dorothy Mae (Whitman) Mooney; m. Kenneth Robert McBurney, June 16, 1962 (div. 1980); children: Scott Robert, Laura Lynn, Brenda Sue, Valerie Kaye. BS in Bus. Adminstrn., Regis Coll., 1985. Office mgr. electrical company, Lakewood, Colo., 1980; sec. Safeco Ins. Co., Lakewood, 1980-82; office mgr. oil company, Golden, Colo., 1982; from clerical specialist to exec. sec. Cobe Labs., Lakewood, 1982-86, adminstrv. mgr., 1986-89, med. systems mfr., adminstrn. & fin. mgr. worldwide svc. orgn., 1989-90, mgr. customer engring. response ctr., 1990—; beauty cons. Mary Kay Cosmetics, Lakewood, 1986—. Mem. Golden Area Sch. Adv. Com., 1974-80, Jefferson County Sr. High Curriculum Council, 1980; room mother Kyffin Elem. Sch., Golden, numerous years; vol. Luth. Hosp. Med. Ctr., Wheatridge, Colo., 1976—; pres. Women's Assn. Arvada (Colo.) Presbyn. Ch., 1979. Mem. Assn. Field Service Mgrs., Gamma Phi Beta. Republican. Home: 5 Paramount Pkwy Lakewood CO 80215 Office: Cobe Labs Inc 1185 Oak St Lakewood CO 80215

MCCABE, JEAN MARIE, psychologist; b. Mt. Pleasant, Iowa, Mar. 28, 1952; d. James Thomas and Genevieve M. (Steffl) McC. BA, Northwest Mo. State U., 1974; MA, U. Mo., Kansas City, 1977, PhD, 1986. Lic. psychologist; cert. marriage and family therapist; cert. substance abuse specialist. Vol. VISTA, Kansas City, Mo., 1974-75; correctional treatment specialist community treatment ctr. Fed. Bur. Prisons, Kansas City, 1975-79; therapist employees asst. program St. Mary's Hosp., Kansas City, 1984-85; assoc. dir. psychol. counseling Cath. Charities, Kansas City, 1977-84; fed. probation officer U.S. Dist Cts.-Western Dist. Mo., Kansas City, 1984-86; psychol. dir. community counseling svcs. U. Mo., Kansas City, 1986—; program mgr., cons. Occupational Health Svcs., Oakland, Calif., 1988—. Founding mem. Mayor's Task Force on Alcohol and Drug Abuse, Kansas City, 1985. Recipient Outstanding Svc. award, Women's Mentor Prog., U. Mo., Kansas City, 1990. Mem. Am. Psychol. Assn. (clin.), Am. Assn. Marriage & Family Therapists (clin.), Mo. Psychol. Assn. (clin.), Greater Kansas City Psychol. Assn. (clin.), Kansas City Assn. Marriage and Family Therapists, Mo. Substance Abuse Counselors. Democrat. Roman Catholic. Home: 6329 W 75th 105 Prairie Village KS 66204 Office: U Mo Community Counseling Svcs 52nd and Holmes Ste 212 Kansas City MO 64110

MCCABE, MARY WILLIAMSON, computer systems analyst; b. Memphis, Aug. 8, 1934; d. Edwin Lacey and Mary Maxine (Maners) Williamson; m. Henry Arthur McCabe, Sept. 22, 1973; stepchildren: Patrick, Anne, Kevin, Cathleen, John. BA, Rhodes Coll., 1956. Math. tchr. Bolton (Tenn.) High Sch., 1956-57; programmer/analyst Mallory AF Sta., Memphis, 1957-61; sr. systems specialist computer dept. GE, Huntsville, Ala., 1961-66; sr. systems specialist Honeywell Info. Systems, Phoenix, 1966-78, Honeywell Bull, Mpls., 1979-88; pres. McCabe & Assocs., Inc., Minnetonka, Minn., 1990. Vol. Am. Cancer Soc., Minnetonka, 1980—. Mem. Minn. Computer Industry Coalition, Women Entrepreneur Network (affiliate). Republican. Episcopalian. Home: 4900 Winterset Dr Minnetonka MN 55343

MCCACHREN, JO RENEE, educator, pianist, musicologist; b. Eugene, Oreg., July 22, 1955; d. Hoyt McKee and Minnie Lodina (Alexander) McC. MusB magna cum laude, U. N.C., Greensboro, 1977; MusM, U. North Tex., 1979, PhD, 1989. Piano instr. Coble's Luth. Ch., Julian, N.C., 1975-77; asst. prof. Catawba Coll., Salisbury, N.C., 1984—; prin. keyboardist Salisbury Symphony, 1986—; instr. Catawba Community Music, 1985—; presenter profl. confs.; grad. teaching fellow U. North Tex., 1977-84; Am. Field Svc. exchange student, Patras, Greece, 1972; music edn. del. to Indonesia Citizen Amb. Program People to People Internat., 1990. Assoc. editor: THEORIA, 1984, 85; contbr. articles to profl. jours. Elder Presbyn. Ch., 1987—. First place winner Young Artists Competition, Salisbury Symphony Orch., 1980; Reynolds scholar U. N.C., Greensboro, 1973-77, Piano Pedagogy Inst. scholar Columbia U., 1987. Mem. Soc. for Music Theory, Salisbury Music Club (organizer, steering com. 1985-86, co-coord. 1987, performer 1986, adjudicator 1984-85), AAUW (sec. Salisbury 1985—), Pi Kappa Lambda, Mu Phi Epsilon. Democrat. Presbyterian.

MCCAFFERTY, BARBARA JEAN (B. J. MCCAFFERTY), sales executive; b. Lincoln, Nebr., Dec. 6, 1940; d. Russell Rowley and Ruth Alice (Williams) Wightman; m. Eriks Zeltins, Dec. 29, 1962 (div. Oct. 1976); 1 child, Brian K. Zeltins; m. Charles F. McCafferty Jr., Oct. 3, 1981 (div. July 1986). BS magna cum laude, Del. Valley Coll. Sci. and Agri., Doylestown, Pa., 1984; student, Drexel U., 1958-61. Dept. mgr. Strawbridge & Clothier, Neshaminy, Pa., 1968-73; asst. buyer Strawbridge & Clothier, Phila., 1973-76; office adminstr. Am. Protein Products, Croydon, Pa., 1976-78; tech. librarian Honeywell Power Sources Ctr., Horsham, Pa., 1978-85; sales dir. Colonial Life and Accident Ins., Wayne, Pa., 1985-86; adminstrn. mgr. Mobi Systems, Inc., Ft. Washington, Pa., 1986-88; spl. rep. Universal Mktg. Corp., Southampton, Pa., 1988—. Mem. NAFE, Nat. Assn. Profl. Saleswomen, Options, Inc., Franklin Mint Collectors Soc., Optomists, Shawnee-at-Highpoint Racquet Club (Chalfont, Pa.). Republican. Presbyterian. Home: 224 Hastings Ct Doylestown PA 18901

MCCAFFERY, EILEEN MARIE, financial executive; b. Lowell, Mass., Jan. 10, 1961; d. Edward L. and Marie Ann (Burke) McC. BA magna cum laude, U. N.H., 1983; student, Vanderbilt U., France, 1982. Mktg. rsch. assoc. Constitution Capital Mgmt. Inc., Boston, 1983-85, asst. v.p., 1985-89; v.p. Mass. Fin. Svcs., Boston, 1989—; portfolio asst. Bank of New Eng., N.A., Boston; admissions rep. U. N.H., Durham, 1980-83. Mem. Assn. Investment Mgmt. Sales Execs., Phi Beta Kappa. Home: 487 Washington St Brookline MA 02146

MCCAFFREY, BARBARA JEAN, buyer; b. Ridgewood, N.J., Nov. 7, 1963; d. James Frederick and Carolyn Jean (Nicholas) Koehlinger. Grad. high sch., Hingham, Mass. With Friendly's, Hingham, 1980-82; sec. Bldg. #19, Hingham, 1982-84, buyer, 1984—. Office: Bldg #19 Inc 319 Lincoln St Hingham MA 02043

MCCAIN, BETTY LANDON RAY (MRS. JOHN LEWIS MCCAIN), political party official, civic leader; b. Faison, N.C., Feb. 23, 1931; d. Horace Truman and Mary Howell (Perrett) Ray; student St. Marys Jr. Coll., 1948-50; AB in Music, U. N.C., Chapel Hill, 1952; MA, Columbia U., 1953; m. John Lewis McCain, Nov. 19, 1955; children: Paul Pressly III, Mary Eloise. Courier, European tour guide Ednl. Travel Assocs., Plainfield, N.J., 1952-54; asst. dir. YWCA, U. N.C., Chapel Hill, 1953-55; chmn. N.C. Democratic Exec. Com., 1976-79 (1st woman); mem. Dem. Nat. Com., 1971-72, 76-79, 80-85, mem. com. on Presdl. nominations (Hunt Commn.), 1981-82, mem. rules com., 1982-85; mem. Winograd Commn., 1977-78; pres. Dem. Women of N.C., 1971-72, dist. dir., 1969-72; pres. Wilson County Dem. Women, 1966-67; precinct chmn., 1972-76; del. Dem. Nat. Conv., 1972, 88; mem. Dem. Mid-term Confs., 1974, 78, mem. judicial council Dem. Nat. Com., 1984-88; dir. Carolina Tel. & Tel. Co., 1981— (1st woman). Sunday sch. tchr. First Presbyn. Ch., Wilson, 1970-71, 86-88, mem. chancel choir, 1985—, deacon, 1986—, chmn. fin. com., 1990—; treas. Wilson on the Move, 1990—; mem. Council on State Goals and Policy, 1970-72, Gov.'s Task Force on Child Advocacy, 1969-71, Wilson Human Relations Commn., 1975-78, chmn. Wilson-Greene Morehead scholarship com., 1986—; mem. career and personal counseling service adv. bd. St. Andrews Coll.; charter mem. Wilson Edn. Devel. Council; active Arts Council of Wilson, Inc., N.C. Art Soc., N.C. Lit. and Hist. Assn.; regional v.p., bd. dirs. N.C. Mental Health Assn.; pres., bd. dirs., legis. chmn. Wilson County Mental Health Assn.; bd. dirs. Friends of U. N.C.-TV, Country Doctor Mus., 1968—, Wilson United Fund; bd. govs., sec. personnel and tenure com. U. N.C., sec. budgets and fin. com. 1987—; bd. regents Barium Springs Home for Children; bd. dirs., pres. N.C. Mus. History Assocs., 1982-83, membership chair, 1987-88; co-chmn. Com. to Elect Jim Hunt Gov., 1976, 80, co-chmn. senatorial campaign, 1984; mem. N.C. Adv. Budget Com., 1981-85 (1st woman); bd. visitors Peace Coll., Wake Forest U. Sch. Law, U. N.C., Chapel Hill; co-chmn. fund drive Wilson Community Theatre; state bd. dirs. N.C., Am. Lung Assn., 1985-88. Recipient state awards N.C. Heart Assn., 1967, Easter Seal Soc., 1967, Community Service award Downtown Bus. Assocs., 1977, award N.C. Jaycettes, 1979, 85, Women in Govt. award N.C. and U.S. Jaycettes, 1985; named to Order of Old Well and Valkyries, U. N.C., 1952; named Dem. Woman of Yr., N.C., 1976. Mem. U. N.C. Chapel Hill Alumni Assn. (dir.), St. Marys Alumni Assn. (regional v.p.), AMA Aux. (dir., nat. vol. health services chmn., aux. liaison rep. Council on Mental Health, aux. rep. Council on Vol. Health Orgns.), N.C. (pres., dir., parliamentarian) med. auxs., UDC (historian John W. Dunham chpt.), DAR, N.C. Soc. Internal Medicine Aux. (pres., bd. dirs. N.C. Equity), Pi Beta Phi. The Book Club (pres.), Little Book Club , Wilson Country Club. Contbg. editor History of N.C. Med. Soc. Home: 1134 Woodland Dr Wilson NC 27893

MCCAIN, SHIRLEY JOYCE, office manager; b. Ashville, N.C., Sept. 18, 1943; d. Lee Jacob and Alta (Funk) Crist; m. Stephen D. McCain, June 26, 1965; children: David, Shari. BS, Toccoa (Ga.) Falls Coll., 1965. Office mgr., sec., treas. ABC Food Svc., Inc., Charlotte, N.C. Republican.

MCCAIRNS, RAGINA CARFAGNO, pharmaceutical executive; b. Phila., Dec. 23, 1951; d. Carmen Augustus and Regina Mary (Yost) Carfagno; m. Robert Gray McCairns Jr., Nov. 6, 1982. BS, Marymount Manhattan Coll., 1973; MS, Villanova U., 1976; cert. bus., U. Pa., 1982. Rsch. asst. Temple U. Med. Coll., Phila., 1975-77; mfg. supr. William H. Rorer, Ft. Washington, Pa., 1977-79; mgmt. trainee, tech. asst. Smith Kline & French Labs., Phila., 1979-80, shift leader antibiotics, 1980-81, validation team mem., 1984-87, validation coord., 1987; mgr. validation svcs. Smith Kline Beecham, Phila., 1987—. Mem. Parenteral Drug Assn. (bd. dis. 1985-90, chmn. spring program 1988, 90, chmn. tng. com. 1986-88), Jefferson Med. Coll. Faculty Wives Club (v.p. 1988-90, program chmn. 1988-90). Democrat. Roman Catholic. Office: 801 River Rd L-97 Conshohocken PA 19428

MCCALEB, MARY ANNE, transportation professional; b. Ponca City, Okla., Oct. 23, 1940; d. Robb Louis and Winifred Mary (Weekley) Hohstadt; m. Michael McCaleb (div. 1973); children: Alison Blair, David Keith. AA, Del Mar Jr. Coll., 1960-61; student, Tex. A&I U., 1961, Houston Community Coll., 1974. Traffic supr. DM Internat., Houston, 1976-80; project coord. Ventech Engrs., Pasadena, Tex., 1980-81; owner Instrument Specialty Co., Houston, 1981-85; mgr. customer svc. Treesweet Products Co., Houston, 1985-88; traffic mgr. Exlog, Inc., Houston, 1988-89; office mgr. PIA Mdse. Co., Houston, 1989—. Active YWCA, Houston, 1965, Tex. Dept. on Aging, 1988, Houston Food Bank, 1989, Houston Proud, 1990. Mem. Sierra Club. Home: 11311 Harwin #22 Houston TX 77072

MCCALL, DEBRA LAURETTE HANSFORD, editorial assistant; b. Phila., June 17, 1958; d. Robert Stanley and Grace Elizabeth (Garlick) Hansford; m. Milton McCall III, May 1979; 1 child: Bet'Trace Laurette McCall. Cert., LaSalle Coll., 1975, Opportunites Industrialization Ctr., Phila., 1977; student, Community Coll. Phila., 1983-85; cert. journalism/short story writing, Nat. Edn. Ctr., Scranton, Pa., 1988; cert. word perfect edn. course, Wang Labs., Inc., Phila., 1989; cert. master art, Nat. Edn. Ctr., 1988. Telemarketer Rep. State Com. Pa., Phila., 1987; editorial asst. Farm Jour. Pub., Phila., 1987—; night supr. Wadsworth Home Video, Phila., 1989—; founder, mem. M&G Enterprize. Author: (with Patrick Saucer) The Crimson Fullmoon, 1989; contbr. poems to newsletters. Patentee in field; APA Poet of Merit Am. Poetry Assn., 1989. Mem. NAFE, Am. Soc. Inventors (assoc.). Home: PO Box 53682 Philadelphia PA 19105

MCCALL, DOROTHY KAY, social worker, psychotherapist; b. Houston, July 18, 1948; d. Sherwood Pelton Jr. and Kathryn Rose (Gassen) McC. BA, Calif. State U., Fullerton, 1973; MS in Edn., U. Kans., 1978; PhD, U. Pitts., 1989. Cert. alcoholism counselor, N.Y. Counselor/intern Ctr. for Behavioral Devel., Overland Park, Kans., 1976-77; rehab. counselor Niagra Frontier Voc. Rehab. Ctr., Buffalo, 1978-79; counselor/instr. dept. motor vehicles Driving While Impaired Program N.Y. State, 1979-80; alcoholism counselor Bry Lin Hosp., Buffalo, 1979-81; instr. sch. social work U. Pitts., 1984; alcohol drug counselor The Whale's Tale, Pitts., 1984-86; sole practice drug and alcohol therapy Pitts., 1986—; faculty Chem. People Inst., Pitts., 1987-89; guest lectr. sch. social work U. Pitts., 1982-87, 89; educator, trainer Community Mental Health Ctr., W.Va., 1986-87, Tenn., 1986; tchr. Tri-Community Sch. System, Western Pa., 1984-87; cons. Battered Women's Shelter, Buffalo, 1980, Buffalo Youth and Alcoholism Abuse program, 1980; lectr. in field. Mem. Spl. Adv. Com. on Addiction, 1981-83; bd. dirs. Chem. People, Task Force Adv. Com., 1984-86; bd. dirs. Drug Connection Hot Line, 1984-86; mem. Coalition of Addictive Diseases, 1984-90; co-founder Greater Pitts. Adult Children of Alcoholics Network, 1984; mem. adv. bd. Chem. Awareness Referral and Evaluation System Duquesne U., 1988. Nat. Inst. Alcohol Abuse Tng. grantee, 1981; U. Pitts. fellow, 1983. Mem. Pa. Assn. for Children of Alcoholics (dir. 1987—, v.p. 1990), Assn. of Labor Mgmt. Adminstrs. and Cons. on Alcoholism, Nat. Assn. for Children of Alcoholics, Nat. Assn. Social Workers. Democrat. Office: 673 Washington Rd Pittsburgh PA 15228

MCCALL, LOUISE HARRUP, artist; b. Oklahoma City, July 8, 1925; d. Paul Louis and Lucile (Martin) Harrup; m. Robert Theodore McCall, July 20, 1945; children: Linda Louise, Catherine Anne. Student, Okla. State U., 1943-44, U. N.Mex., 1944-45, Art Inst., 1946; pvt. study, N.Y., 1955-65. Freelance artist Chgo., 1946-48, Tarrytown, N.Y., 1949-53, Chappaqua, N.Y., 1953-67, 68-71, London, 1967, Paradise Valley, Ariz., 1971—; owner McCall Studios, Inc., Paradise Valley, 1986—. Murals executed (with husband) Air and Space Mus., Washington, 1975-76, Johnson Space Ctr., Houston, 1978, Disney Epcot Ctr., L.A., 1983, Ariz. Indsl. Commn., Phoenix, 1986. Fundraiser Crisis Nursery, Phoenix, 1984, Ariz. Hist. Soc., Phoenix, 1986, Hospice, Phoenix, ann. 1983-88. Winner 1st Prize, State of Tex., 1943, 1st Prize, Jr. League Artists No. Westchester and N.Y., 1961. Mem. NASA Permanent Art Collection, Nat. Mus. Women in the Arts, Jr. League of Phoenix. Republican. Presbyterian. Home and Office: 4816 E Moonlight Way Paradise Valley AZ 85253

MCCALL, SUSAN ELIZABETH, small business owner; b. Ogden, Utah, Nov. 21, 1945; d. Edward George and Virginia Alene (Davis) Mester; 1 child, Melissa M. BFA, Utah State U., 1975. Office mgr. Sewing Dist., Phoenix, Ariz., 1969-70; art tchr. North Ogden City Schs., 1970-71; graphic arts Permaloy Corp., Ogden, 1972-74; regional purchasing agt. USDA Forest Service, Ogden, 1976; owner, mgr. The Flower Co., Albuquerque, 1976-89; dir. dist. 8-J Florists Transworld Delivery Assn., 1988-89; mgr. Spring Flowers, Sydney, 1990—. Recipient First Place award Utah Soc. Art, 1964. Mem. West Tex. Florist Assn., N.Mex. Floral Assn., Albuquerque Vis.' Conv. (mktg. com. 1986—), Fla. Transworld Delivery Assn. (dir. Dist. 8-J, 1988), Profl. Women in Bus. Office: The Flower Co 11004 Montgomery Blvd NE Albuquerque NM 87111

MCCALLA, SANDRA ANN, university director; b. Shreveport, La., Nov. 6, 1939; d. Earl Gray and Dorothy Edna (Adams) McC. BS, Northwestern La. State U., 1960; MS, U. No. Colo., 1968; EdD, Tex. A&M U., 1987. With Caddo Parish Sch. Bd., Shreveport, 1960-88; asst. prin. Capt. Shreve High Sch., 1977-79, prin., 1979—; dir. div. edn. Northwestern State U., Natchitoches, La., 1988—; instr. math La. State U., 1979-81. Named Educator of Yr. Shreveport Times-Caddo Tchrs. Assn., 1966, La. High Sch. Prin. of Yr., 1985, 87; recipient Excellence in Edn. award Capt. Shreve High Sch., 1982-83; Danforth fellow, 1982-83. Mem. adv. bd. Sta. KDAQ Pub. Radio, 1985—. Active Shreveport Women's Commn., 1983—. Mem. Nat. Assn. Secondary Sch. Prins., La. Assn. Prins. (Prin. of Yr. 1985), La. Assn. Sch. Execs. (Disting. Svc. award 1983), NEA, La. Educators Assn., Times-Caddo Educators Assn. (Educator of Yr. 1984), Phi Delta Kappa, Altrusa Club. Democrat.

MCCALLEY-WHITTERS, MONA K., psychologist, consultant, nurse; b. Cedar Rapids, Iowa, Jan. 29, 1956; d. Marvin Ray and Maxine Jane (Lynch) McCalley; m. Alan C. Whitters; 1 child, Aleczander Jesse. BS, Coll. of St. Teresa, Winona, Minn., 1978; PhD, U. Iowa, 1989. Lic. psychologist; RN. Residential counselor Cen. Iowa Residential Svcs., Marshalltown, Iowa, 1978-79; rsch. health specialist VA Med. Ctr., Iowa City, 1979-83; psychiat. rsch. nurse U. Iowa Hosps., Iowa City, 1983-85; psychology examiner Dept. of Corrections State of Iowa Oakdale Med. & Classification Ctr., 1985-86; intern in psychology Am. Lake VA Med. Ctr., Tacoma, 1987-88; adult psychologist Abbe Ctr. for Community Mental Health, Cedar Rapids, 1989—. Contbr. articles to profl. jours. Cons. Discovery Living for Hanicapped & Disabled Adults, Cedar Rapids, 1990—. Mem. Am. Psychol. Assn., Am. Psychol. Assn. (neuropsychology and counseling psychotherapy), Iowa Psychol. Assn., Sigma Theta Tau (Profl. Performance award 1983). Democrat. Roman Catholic. Office: Abbe Ctr Community Health 520 11th St NW Cedar Rapids IA 52405

MCCALLION, HAZEL, mayor; b. Port Daniel, Can.; m. Samuel McCallion; children—Peter, Linda, Paul. Formerly office mgr. Can. Kellogg Co.;

mayor City of Mississauga, Ont., Can., 1978—; mem. com. on transp. of dangerous goods Minister of Transport. Dep. reeve City of Streetsville, 1968, mayor, 1970-73; chmn. Mississauga Taxicab Authority, Mississauga Planning com., Mississauga Sign Com.; vice chmn. adv. com. on local govt. mgmt.; chmn. provincial mcpl. subcom. on transp. of dangerous goods; bd. dirs. Credit Valley Hosp.; 3d v.p. World Conf. of Mayors, 1989. Paul Harris fellow Rotary Internat., 1983. Mem. Streetsville C. of C. (former pres.), Assn. Municipalities Ont. (past pres.), Can. Fedn. Municipalities (bd. dirs.), Can. Jaycees (gov.); hon. mem. Polish Alliance Can., Mississauga Real Estate Bd. (hon.), Alpha Delta Kappa. Club: Mississauga Kinsmen (hon. mem.). Office: City of Mississauga, 300 City Centre Dr, Mississauga, ON Canada L5B 3C1

MCCALL-SIMPSON, MARY MUYELINDA, health service professional; b. Balsam Grove, N.C., Nov. 18, 1963; d. Lloyd and Reba (Owen) McCall; m. Jodey Marshall Simpson, June 16, 1985. RN, Presbyn. Hosp. Sch. Nursing, Charlotte, 1985. Supr., CPR instr. Brian Ctr. Care, Brevard, N.C., 1985-87; IV and medication team, relief RN charge nurse Transylvania Community Hosp., Brevard, 1987-88. James McGuire scholarship, 1982, Aux. Club scholarship Transylvonia Community Hosp. Mem. Nurses Book Soc.

MCCALLUM, GLORIA JEAN, telemarketing executive; b. Biloxi, Miss., July 26, 1954; d. Henry Lee and Jessie Mae (Calcote) McC.; 1 child, Jonathan Terrill. BS in Communications, U. Nebr., Omaha, 1980. Prodn. asst. KYNE-TV, Omaha, 1978-79, KM-TV, Omaha, 1979-80; producer/dir. Mutual of Omaha, Omaha, 1980-83; mgr. Tupperware Home Parties, Omaha, 1983-85; telemktg. asst. supr. AMRE, Inc., Irving, Tex., 1986—; owner On Line Advantage, Bedford, Tex., 1990—. Mem. Assn. Women Entrepreneurs of Dallas, NAFE.

MC CANDLESS, ANNA LOOMIS, university official; b. Aspinwall, Pa., July 21, 1897; d. George Wilberforce and Estella (Loomis) McC.; BS, Carnegie-Mellon U., 1919. Pres. Vis. Nurses Assn. of Allegheny County, 1955-57; mem. vis. com. Margaret Morrison Carnegie Coll., 1962-66; v.p. Alumni Fedn. Carnegie Inst. Tech., 1963-66. Trustee Carnegie-Mellon U., 1966—. Mem. AAUW. Clubs: Coll., Univ., Twentieth Century (pres. 1956-58) (Pitts.); Appalachian Mountain. Home: Park Plaza Apts Craig St Pittsburgh PA 15213

MCCANDLESS, BARBARA J., tax and home economics consultant; b. Cottonwood Falls, Kans., Oct. 25, 1931; d. Arch G. and Grace (Kittle) McCandless; B.S., Kans. State U., 1953; M.S., Cornell U., 1959; postgrad. U. Minn., 1962-66, U. Calif., Berkeley, 1971-72; cert. home economist. m. Allyn O. Lockner, 1969. Enrolled agt. IRS. Home demonstration agt. Kans. State U., 1953-57; teaching asst. Cornell U., 1957-58, asst. extension home economist in marketing, 1958-59; consumer mktg. specialist, asst. prof. Oreg. State U., 1959-62; instr. home econs. U. Minn., 1962-63, research asst. agrl. econs., 1963-66; asst. prof. U. R.I., 1966-67; asso. prof. family econs., mgmt., housing, equipment dept. head S.D. State U., 1967-73; asst. to sec. Dept. Commerce and Consumer Affairs, S.D., 1973-79; now cons. Mem. Nat. Council Occupational Licensing, dir., 1973-75, v.p., 1975-79. Mem. Am. Mktg. Assn., Am. Agrl. Econs. Assn., Am. Home Econs. Assn., Nat. Council on Family Relations, Am. Council Consumer Interests, LWV, Kans. State U. Alumni Assn., Pi Gamma Mu. Research on profl. and occupational licensing bds. Address: 2114 Potomac Dr Topeka KS 66611

MCCANDLESS, CAROLYN KELLER, publishing company executive; b. Patuxent River, Md., June 6, 1945; d. Stevens Henry and Betty Jane (Bethune) Keller; m. Stephen Porter McCandless, Apr. 22, 1972; children: Peter Keller, Deborah Marion. BA, Stanford U., 1967; MBA, Harvard U., 1969. Fin. analyst Time Inc., N.Y.C., 1969-72, mgr. budgets and fin. analysis, 1972-78, asst. sec., dir. internal adminstrn., 1978-85, v.p., dir. employee benefits, 1985-90; v.p human resources and adminstrn. Time Warner, Inc., N.Y.C., 1990—; voting mem. Empire Blue Cross-Blue Shield. Mem. Erisa Industry Council. Republican. Mem. Unitarian Ch. Office: Time Warner Inc 1271 Ave of the Americas New York NY 10020

MCCANN, BRIDGET ANN, assistant controller, data processing specialist; b. Mandan, N.D., Apr. 23, 1955; d. Edward Joseph McCann and Joan A. (Hartley) Anderson. AS in Acctg., Brown Inst., 1989. File clk. Marvin Oreck, Inc., Edina, Minn., 1974-75, bookkeeper, 1975-78; bookkeeper M.F. Bank & Co., Inc., Mpls., 1978-81, data processing supr., 1981-88, asst. controller, 1988—. Mem. Minn. 34/36 Users Group, Everett McClay VFW. Roman Catholic. Home: 4039-41st Avenue S Minneapolis MN 55406 Office: MF Bank & Co Inc 615 First Ave NE Minneapolis MN 55413

MCCANN, CAROL COLE, banker; b. Detroit, Dec. 7, 1945; d. John Fremont and Doris Adele (Vehmeyer) C.; m. Lee S. Friedman, June 12, 1968 (div. 1972); m. Donald Roger McCann, Nov. 19, 1980. BS, Skidmore Coll., 1968; MSW, U. Conn., 1972. Med. social worker Yale-New Haven Hosp., 1968-70; social work supr. Klingberg Family Ctrs., New Britain, Conn., 1973-75; personal banker Con.. Bank & Trust, Hartford, 1978-80; dir. tng. and devel. Barnett Bank, West Palm Beach, Fla., 1980—, br. mgr., 1981; seminar leader Atlantic High Sch., Boynton Beach., Fla., 1987, Cath. Family Svcs., Delray Beach, Fla., 1987; cons. tng. and devel. module for cert. Am. Soc. Pers. Adminstrn.; trainer local non-profit orgns. Mem. Am. Soc. Tng. and Devel. (pres. 1986-87, nat. presenter 1989), Am. Inst. Banking (v.p. edn. 1986-87, pres. 1987—). Home: 3802 Quail Ridge Dr Boynton Beach FL 33436 Office: Barnett Bank of Palm Beach 7320 S Dixie Hwy West Palm Beach FL 33405

MCCANN, DAISY S., biochemist, biochemistry educator; b. Hamburg, Fed. Republic Germany, Mar. 8, 1927; d. Robert David and Kate (Hamlet) Sheldon; m. John Joseph McCann, Aug. 5, 1950; 1 child, Robert J. BA, U. Toronto (Can.), 1950; MS, Wayne State U., 1956, PhD, 1958. Rsch. assoc. dept. chemistry Wayne State U., Detroit, 1960-67; cons. Jordan Clin. Labs., Detroit, 1966-68, assoc. dir., 1968-72; asst. prof. biol. chemistry U. Mich., Detroit, 1970-77; dir. rsch. labs. Univ. Med. Affiliates, Westland, Mich., 1970-86; assoc. prof. biol. chemistry U. Mich., Ann Arbor, 1977—; pres., dir. rsch. McCann Assocs., Inc., Wayne, Mich., 1986—; tech. dir. Newman Clin. Labs., Dearborn, Mich., 1984—; adj. assoc. prof. dept. chemistry Wayne State U., Detroit. Contbr. 74 articles to profl. jours. Mem. Clin. Ligand Assay Soc. (exec. dir. 1982—). Office: McCann Assocs Inc 3139 S Wayne Rd Wayne MI 48184

MC CANN, FRANCES VERONICA, physiologist, educator; b. Manchester, Conn., Jan. 15, 1927; d. John Joseph and Grace E. (Tuttle) Mc C.; m. Elden J. Murray, Sept. 20, 1962 (dec. Nov. 1975). AB with distinction and honors, U. Conn., 1952, PhD, 1959; MS, U. Ill., 1954; MA (hon.), Dartmouth Coll., 1973. Investigator Marine Biol. Lab., Woods Hole, Mass., 1952-62; instr. physiology Dartmouth Med. Sch., Hanover, N.H., 1959-61, asst. prof., 1961-67, assoc. prof., 1967-73, prof., 1973—; adj. prof. biol. scis. Dartmouth Coll., 1974—; mem., cons. physiology study sect. NIH, 1973-77, mem. biomed. rsch. devel. com., 1978-82, chmn, 1979; cons. Hayer Inst., 1979—; cons. staff Hitchcock Hosp., Hanover, 1980—, sr. staff rsch. Norris Catton Cancer Ctr., 1980—; mem. NRC, 1982-86; chmn. Symposium on Comparative Physiology of the Heart, 1968. Editor: Comparative Physiology of the Heart: Current Trends, 1965; contbr. numerous articles to profl. jours. Trustee Lebanon Coll., 1970-73, Montshire Mus. Sci., Hanover, 1975—, Hanover Health Coun., 1976, Lebanon Coll., 1978—; incorporator Howe Libr., 1975—. Nat. Heart Inst. fellow, 1959; NIH rsch. grantee, 1959—, Nat. Heart Inst., 1960, N.H. Heart Assn., 1964-65, Vt. Heart Assn., 1966—. Mem. AAAS, Am. Physiol. Soc., Soc. Gen. Physiologists, Biophys. Soc., Am. Heart Assn. (coun. basic sci., exec. coun. Dallas chpt. 1982-86), Soc. Neurosci., Marine Biol. Lab., LWV, Sigma Xi, Phi Kappa Phi. Office: Dartmouth Med Sch Hanover NH 03756

MCCANN, JOAN CELIA, school administrator; b. Malden, Mass., Jan. 23, 1936; d. Vincent Jacob and Helen Lorraine (Pontone) Celia; m. William J. McCann, Aug. 23, 1958; children: Susan, Peter. AB cum laude, Tufts U., 1957; MA, U. Mich., 1968; EdD, Fordham U. 1986. Tchr. 1st grade Gleason Sch., Medford, Mass., 1957-58, Hutchinson Sch., Pelham, N.Y., 1958-61; tchr. 1st grade Siwanoy Sch., Pelham, 1968-69, reading cons., 1969-71, prin., 1971-75; prin. Fox Meadow Sch., Scarsdale, N.Y., 1975—; mem. adminstrv. adv. com. internship St. John's U., 1973—; instr., mem. profl. adv. coun. Concordia Coll. Mem. Pelham Bicentennial Com., 1974—, sch. cons. Between the Lines publ., 1975; mem. adv. bd. Scarsdale Hist. Soc., 1975—; chmn. Pelham Bicentennial Ball, 1976; mem. policy bd. Westchester Prins. Ctr.; adv. com. Westchester County Office of Aging; adv. bd. Prins. Forum at Fordham U. Recipient award in appreciation for cooperation Pelham Manor Fire Dept., 1974; IDEA fellow Charles Kettering Found., 1976, 77. Mem. Internat. Reading Assn., N.Y. State Adminstrs. Assn., Nat. Assn. Elem. Sch. Prins., Nat. Congress Parents and Tchrs. (life), Am. Assn. sch. Adminstrs., Jean Piaget Soc., Jackson Coll. Alumnae Assn., U. Mich. Alumni Assn., Fordham Sch. Edn. Alumni Bd. (rec. sec.), Phi Delta Kappa, Chi Omega, Internat. Garden Club. Home: 242 Eastland Ave Pelham NY 10803 Office: Fox Meadow Sch Brewster Rd Scarsdale NY 10583

MCCANN, MARY CHERI, medical technologist, horse breeder and trainer; b. Pensacola, Fla., July 29, 1956; d. Joseph Maxwell and Cora Marie (Underwood) McC.; m. Robert Lee Spencer, July 20, 1977 (div. Nov. 1983). AA, Pensacola Jr. Coll., 1975; student, U. Md., 1977-78; BS in Biology, Troy State U., 1979; postgrad., U. Fla., 1979. Med. technologist Cape Fear Valley Med. Ctr., Fayetteville, N.C., 1981-85, Doctors Diagnostic Ctr., Fayetteville, 1985-86; sales rep. Waddell & Reed, Fayetteville, 1985-86; med. technologist Roche Biomed. Lab., Burlington, N.C., 1986-87; lab. mgr. Cumberland Hosp., Fayetteville, 1987-89, Naval Hosp., Pensacola, 1989—. With U.S. Army, 1976-77. Mem. NAFE, Am. Soc. Clin. Pathologists (registrant), Am. Quarter Horse Assn., Japan Karate Assn., Pinto Horse Assn. Am. Republican. Avocations: horses, karate, guns, oil painting. Home: 3518 N S St Pensacola FL 32505-4129 Office: Naval Hosp. Pensacola Lab Hwy 98 W Pensacola FL 32512

MCCANTS, RENEE DENISE, state official; b. N.Y.C.; d. Thomas Harold McCants and Florence Roberta (Clarke) Robinson; 1 child, Brian Kelly. BS in Labor Studies, SUNY, N.Y.C., 1986. Purchasing dir., tng. cons. Strategic Learning Systems, Queens, N.Y., 1979-86; various positions N.Y. State Dept. Labor, N.Y.C. and Albany, 1970-79; pers. adminstr. N.Y. State Dept. Labor, Albany, 1988—. Mem. Internat. Pers. Mgmt. Assn., Internat. Assn. Persons in Employment Svc., NAACP (regional v.p. N.Y. State Dept. Labor br. 1989—), Blacks in Govt. (pub. rels. officer, parliamentarian 1988-89). Office: NY State Dept Labor Rm 559 Bldg 12 State Campus Albany NY 12240

MCCANTS, ZAUDITU ESTHER, counselor; b. Chgo., Feb. 29, 1944; d. Lester and Dorothy D. Solobilings (McCants); children: Zia, Hill. BA, Calif. State U., 1966; MSW, Atlanta U., 1970; postgrad., Ill. Inst. Tech., Chgo., 1979-80, 1979-98, U. So. Miss., 1989. Cert. social worker, Md., Miss. Counselor, dist. supr. Miss. Office of Youth Svcs., Jackson; psychiatric and med. social work therapist VA Med. Ctr., Washington, L.A., Chgo.; psychiatric social work therapist St. Elizabeth's Hosp., Washington; social work therapist Family and Children's Svcs., Nashville. Mem. Nat. Assn. of Social Workers (foster care review bd. 1986, headstart policy coun. 1983-86), So. States Correctional Assn. Home: 1167 Barnes Ave Clarksdale MS 38614

MCCARTAN, LUCY, geologist; b. Miami Beach, Fla., Oct. 4, 1942; d. Arthur Austin and Edith (Newby) McC. BA, Occidental Coll., 1965; MS, Lehigh U., 1967, PhD, 1972. Rsch. geologist U.S. Geol. Survey, Reston, Va., 1973—. Author of maps, books, articles on geology of U.S. Atlantic seaboard, New Zealand, and Antarctica. Fulbright-Hays grantee, New Zealand, 1967-68; scholar AAUW, New Zealand, 1968-69; NSF Summer Teaching fellow, Fla., 1966; recipient NSF medal for Antarctic Rsch., 1980. Fellow Geol. Soc. Am.; mem. Soc. Econ. Paleontologists and Mineralogists, Clay Minerals Soc., Assn. for Women Geoscientists (bd. dirs. 1989—). Office: US Geol Survey Nat Ctr Reston VA 22092

MCCARTHY, BEVERLY FITCH, civic worker, retired educator; b. St. Louis, Aug. 10, 1933; d. Clyde and Elsie (Graf) Fitch; m. Carl M. Bosque, Sept. 13, 1958 (div. 1973); children: Charles, Elizabeth; m. John Linley McCarthy, Mar. 17, 1973. AA, L.A. City Coll., 1953; BA in Social Scis., U. Calif., Berkeley, 1955; MA in Edn., Stanford U., 1957; adminstrv. credential, U. Pacific, 1980. Mem. faculty Monterey (Calif.) Peninsula Coll., 1957-58, Santa Barbara (Calif.) City Coll., 1958-59, San Jose (Calif.) City Coll., 1959-60; tchr. Bret Harte High Sch., Angels Camp, Calif., 1960-62; instr. psychology San Joaquin Delta Coll., Stockton, Calif., 1962-85, dir. reentry program for women and men, 1974-85; mem. Stockton City Coun., Calif., 1990—. Pres. Assistance League Stockton, 1969-71, Dem. Women's Club San Joaquin County, 1987, San Joaquin chpt. Nat. Women's Polit. Caucus, 1982, Stockton Symphony Assn., 1973-77, Stockton Opera Guild, 1977-78, 87-89, Stockton Civic Theatre League, 1981-82, San Joaquin County Child Abuse Prevention Coun. Aux., 1989-90; chmn. Stockton Redevel. Commn., 1986, San Joaquin County Commn. on Status Women, 1974-82, San Joaquin Family Resource and Referral Employer-Assisted Child Care Coalition, 1986-89. Recipient Woman of Yr. award Soroptimist Club, Stockton, 1970, 74, arts recognition award Stockton Arts Commn., 1978, Women of Achievement award San Joaquin County Commn. on Status Women, 1983; Rosalie M. Stern award U. Calif.-Berkeley Alumni Assn., 1976, Alumni citation, 1985. Mem. AAUW (named gift Ednl. Found. 1977-78), Women Execs. Stockton (founder), Cal Club San Joaquin County (founder, pres. 1981-82), Stanford Women's Club San Joaquin County (founder, pres. 1974-76), Mortar Bd., Prytanean Soc., Gavel and Quill, Nu Sigma Psi, Delta Psi Omega, Pi Lambda Theta, Phi Delta Kappa. Democrat. Home: 215 W Stadium Dr Stockton CA 95204 Office: Office City Coun City Hall 425 N El Dorado St Stockton CA 95202-1997

MCCARTHY, CATHERINE FRANCES, lawyer; b. N.Y.C., Feb. 13, 1921; d. Joseph J. and Eva E. (Berger) McC.; m. Peter Donald Andreoli, Aug. 25, 1945; children—Peter, Brian, Catherine, Christine, Francine. B.S., St. John's U., 1941, LL.B., 1943; Bar.: N.Y. 1943, U.S. Dist. Ct. (so. dist.) N.Y. 1944, U.S. Supreme Ct. 1966, U.S. Ct. Appeals (2d cir.) 1975. Assoc., Spencer, Ordway & Wierum, 1942-50; sole practice, N.Y.C. and Pelham, N.Y., 1950-67; real estate atty. Gen. Foods Corp., White Plains, N.Y., 1967-68, trademark atty., 1968-73, chief trademark counsel, 1973-81, dir. legal services-trademarks, 1981-88, sole practice, Pelham, N.Y., 1988— . Recent decisions editor St. John's Law Rev., 1942-43. Mem. ABA, Assn. Bar City N.Y., N.Y. State Bar Assn., Westchester County Bar Assn., U.S. Trademark Assn. (dir. 1976-80, trademark rev. commn.). Home and Office: 134 Harmon Ave Pelham NY 10803

MCCARTHY, CHARLOTTE COLYER, sales executive; b. St. Albans, N.Y., Jan. 9, 1943; d. Ralph H. and Charlotte E. (Farrell) C. Student, SUNY, Buffalo, 1960-63; BFA, St. Thomas Aquinas, Sparkill, N.Y., 1976. Art tchr. Archdiocese of N.Y., N.Y., 1972-79; customer service mgr. MWM Dexter, W. Nyack, N.Y., 1979-81; dist. sales mgr. Avon Products, Inc., Newark, Del., 1981-83; customer service, prodn. coordinator Lorell Press, Avon, Mass., 1983-85; customer service mgr. ComWeb Graphics, Rockland, Mass., 1985-86, sales mgr., 1986-88; chmn. bd. dirs. CEI Cons., Weymouth, Mass. Mem. Nat. Assn. Female Execs. (charter), Graphic Arts Sales Found. (cert.), South Shore C. of C., Eagle Ridge Country Club. Home: 7111 Golden Eagle Ct Fort Myers FL 33912

MCCARTHY, DENISE EILEEN, psychologist; b. Syracuse, N.Y., Jan. 25, 1941; d. Raymond Dennis McCarthy and Elizabeth (Dorne) MacBrearty. BS, Cornell U., 1962; MA, Syracuse U., 1969; postgrad., SUNY, Albany, 1977-83; D in Clin. Psychology, Antioch/New Eng. Grad. Sch., Keene, N.H., 1988. Lic. psychologist, N.Y. Home econ. Monroe County Extension Svc., Rochester, N.Y., 1962-65; team leader, sr. counselor N.Y. State Dept. Labor, Albany, Syracuse, 1966-73; rehab. counselor N.Y. State Office Vocat. Rehab., Albany, 1973-80; dir. community support systems Schenectady Shared Svs., 1981-82; masters level psychologist O.D. Heck Devel. Ctr., Schenectady, 1982-83, A.I.M., Saratoga Springs, N.Y., 1983-84; staff counselor Siena Coll., Loudonville, N.Y., 1985; asst. psychologist Capital Dist. Psychiat. Ctr., Cairo, N.Y., 1985-88, assoc. psychologist, 1988—; pvt. practice, Catskill, N.Y., 1988—, Albany, 1990—. Bd. dirs. Dominion House, Schenectady, 1981-82. Mem. Am. Psychol. Assn., N.Y. State Psychol. Assn., Psychologists of Northeastern N.Y., Nat. Registry Health Svc. Providers. Home: 508 Acre Dr Schenectady NY 12303 Office: 621 Central Ave Albany NY 12206 also: 285 Main St Catskill NY 12414

MCCARTHY, DIANNE ELIZABETH, educator; b. Grand Rapids, Mich., June 6, 1957; d. Francis J. and Lorraine McCarthy. BS, Mich. State U., 1979; MS, U. N.Mex., 1982. Grad. asst. U. N.Mex., Albuquerque, 1980-82; tchr. health, track and field, cross-country coach Albuquerque Pub. Schs., 1982—; textbook reviewer Houghton Mifflin Pub. Co., 1986; strength tng. cons., Albuquerque, 1989—. Editor: International Sports Directory, 1982. Instr. CPR, ARC, Albuquerque, 1980—. Recipient Norton Kalishmen Health Promotion award, N.Mex., 1988. Mem. AAHPER and Dance, Phi Delta Kappa. Office: Valley High Sch 1505 Candelaria Albuquerque NM 87107

MCCARTHY, GRACE MARY, Canadian provincial government official; b. Vancouver, B.C., Can., Oct. 14, 1927; d. George and Allrietta (McCloy) Winterbottom; m. Raymond McCarthy, June 23, 1948; children—Mary, Calvin. Pres. Grayce Florists, Vancouver; mem. legis. assembly province of B.C., Victoria, 1966—, dep. premier, provincial sec., minister of recreation and travel industry, 1976-78, dep. premier, minister of human resources, 1978-83, minister human resources, B.C. transit, 1983-86; provincial sec. and and Minister of Govt. Services, 1986, dep. premier and minister of Econ. Devel., 1988—; commr. Bd. Parks and Pub. Recreation, 1961-66. Past pres. Vancouver Credit Women's Bus. Club, B.C. Social Credit Party; chmn. Capt. Cook Bicentennial Com., 1978, Yr. of Child, 1979; mem. nat. adv. bd. Salvation Army; bd. dirs. Can. Assn. Christians and Jews. Recipient Pres.'s award Greater Victoria Tourist Assn., Medal of Distinction Internat. Assn. Lions Clubs, H.J. Merilees award of Yr., Greater Vancouver Conv. and Visitors Assn., Marketer of Yr. award Internat. Sales and Mktg. Execs.; Silver medal Can. Govt. Fellow Coll. Fellows Royal Archtl. Inst. Can. (hon.); mem. Hastings C. of C. (1st women pres.); hon. mem. Vancouver Aquarium Assn., Florists' Transworld Delivery Service, Northwest Florist Assn., Vancouver Tourist Assn., B.C. Chefs Assn., B.C. Motels, Resorts and Trailer Parks Assn., Victoria Acadamie of Chefs de Cuisine, Van Dusen Bot. Gardens Assn. Anglican. Club: Variety Internat. (first woman mem.), Vancouver Christian Lions (first woman mem.). Lodge: Daus. of Nile. Office: Parliament Bldgs, Victoria, BC Canada

MCCARTHY, JOANNE ELIZABETH, teacher, consultant; b. Allentown, Pa., May 6, 1943; d. Robert Franklin and Sarah Elizabeth (Knauss) Schall; m. William James McCarthy, June 21, 1969. B.A., UCLA, 1968; M.Ed., U. Rochester, 1974; M.S., U. LaVerne, 1981; M.A., Mills Coll., 1983. Elem. tchr. Centralia Sch. Dist., Buena Park, Calif., 1968-70; reading specialist elem. sch. Spencerport (N.Y.) Sch. Dist., 1973-74, Wayne Central Sch. Dist., Ontario, N.Y., 1974-75; tchr. State Demonstration Project, Pittsburg (Calif.) Unified Sch. Dist., 1977-78; English and reading tchr. Vallejo (Calif.) City Unified Sch. Dist., 1978—; staff devel. cons. Profl. Devel. Ctr. Mem. NEA, Assn. Supervision and Curriculum Devel., Calif. Assn. Tchrs. English, Nat. Council Tchrs. English, Phi Delta Kappa, Pi Lambda Theta; Nat. Audubon Soc. Author publ. in field. Home: 105 Poshard St Pleasant Hill CA 94523 Office: Vallejo City Unified Sch Dist 840 Nebraska St Vallejo CA 94591

MCCARTHY, JOYCE ANN, medical technologist; b. Weirton, W.Va., July 2, 1960; d. Ray Lawrence and Edith Sophia (Zubryski) Kaczynski; m. Michael Patrick McCarthy, Sept. 22, 1984; 1 child, Laura Alyss. BS in Med. tech., Wheeling Coll., 1982. Cert. med. technologist. Med. technologist micro lab. Allegheny Gen. Hosp., Pitts., 1982; med. technologist micro lab. VA Hosp., Pitts., 1982-84; med. technologist micro lab. Misericordia Hosp., Pitts., 1984-87, supr. micro lab., 1987—; jr. varsity basketball coach, asst. varsity basketball coach Akiba Hebrew Acad., Phila., 1985-87; asst. women's basketball coach Phila. Coll. Textile & Sci., 1987-89, U. Pa., 1989-90. Mem. Am. Soc. Microbiology, Am. Soc. Clin. Pathologists. Republican. Roman Catholic. Home: 232 McGregor Dr Verona PA 15147

MC CARTHY, KATHRYN A., physicist; b. Lawrence, Mass., Aug. 7, 1924; d. Joseph Augustine and Catherine (Barrett) McCarthy. A.B., Tufts U., 1945, M.S., 1946; Ph.D., Radcliffe Coll., 1957; D.Sc. (hon.), Coll. Holy Cross, 1978; D.H.L. (hon.), Merrimack Coll., 1981. Instr. physics Tufts U., 1946-53, asst. prof., 1953-59, assoc. prof., 1959-62, prof., 1962—; dean Tufts U. (Grad. Sch.), 1969-74, provost, sr. v.p., 1973-79; research fellow in metallurgy Harvard, 1957-59, vis. scholar, 1979-80; research assoc. Baird Assocs., 1947-49, 51, Boston U. Optical Research Lab., summer 1952; assoc. research engr. U. Mich., summer 1957-58; dir. Mass. Electric Co., State Mut. Assurance Co. Trustee Southeastern Mass. U., 1972-74, Merrimack Coll., 1974-83, Coll. Holy Cross, 1980—; corporator Lawrence Meml. Hosp., 1975—, dir., 1978—, vice chmn. Fellow Optical Soc. Am., Am. Phys. Soc.; mem. Soc. Women Engrs. (sr.), Phi Beta Kappa, Sigma Xi. Roman Catholic. Home: 1580 Massachusetts Ave Cambridge MA 02138 Office: Tufts U Dept Physics Medford MA 02155

MCCARTHY, MARY MCCLOSKEY, magazine editor and publisher; b. Toledo, Nov. 27, 1923; d. Michael Earl and Helen Cecilia (Healey) McCloskey; m. John Robert McCarthy, Aug. 20, 1947 (div. 1973); children: Michael T., Sean R., Kevin J. BA in English and Journalism, Notre Dame Coll., Cleve., 1944. Reporter Toledo Times, 1944-46; assoc. editor Good Housekeeping mag., N.Y.C., 1946-47; editor Where mag., N.Y.C., 1967-75; movie reviewer Westchester mag., Mamaroneck, N.Y., 1975-77; founder, editor, pub. Quality of Life in Loisaida mag., N.Y.C., 1977—. Bd. dirs. El Bohio Cultural and Community Ctr., N.Y.C., 1980—; pres. Loisaida Craft Coop, N.Y.C., 1980-85; mem. Teenage Pregnancy Prevention Consortium, N.Y.C., 1986—, Lower East Side Anti-Drug Consortium, N.Y.C., 1989—; vice chmn. bd. dirs. 6th Street Community Ctr., N.Y.C., 1988—. Recipient Silent Hero award Charas, Inc., N.Y.C., 1986, Dedication award 6th St. Community Ctr., 1986, Viva Loisaida award Loisaida Employment Coun., 1989. Mem. AAUW (community chmn. 1977-83, N.Y. State community chmn. 1979-81), Amateur Astronomers Assn. N.Y., N.Y. Amateur Computer Club. Office: Q-L Pub Found Inc 73 Loisaida Ave C New York NY 10009

MC CARTHY, PATRICIA MARGARET, retreat house administrator, social worker; b. L.A., Mar. 2, 1943; d. Alphonsus Martin and Margaret (Kroutil) Mc C. BA, Dominican Coll., San Rafael, Calif., 1964; MSW, U. So. Calif., 1967. Lic. clin. social worker, Calif. Community organizer Holy Name Parish Archdiocese L.A., 1980-82; social worker St. Anne's Maternity Home, L.A., 1967-73, Holy Family Adoption Svc., L.A., 1973-78, Stanford Home, Sacramento, 1982-84; info. specialist Info. & Referral Svc. L.A. County, El Monte, Calif., 1984-87; exec. dir. Holy Spirit Retreat Ctr., Encino, Calif., 1987—. Mem. Jericho, L.A., 1988; inc. mem. Sisters of Social Svc. L.A., 1978—. Named Outstanding Citizen L.A. City Coun., 1982. Mem. Retreats Internat. (so. Calif. area rep.). Democrat. Roman Catholic. Office: Holy Spirit Retreat Ctr 4316 Lanai Rd Encino CA 91436

MCCARTHY, SHARON MURPHY, corporate professional; b. Syracuse, N.Y., Oct. 6, 1956; d. John Daniel and Colleen (Stapleton) Murphy. BS, LeMoyne Coll., Syracuse, 1978; MBA, Rochester Inst. Tech., N.Y., 1982. Prodn. scheduler Carrier Fin. Corp., Syracuse, 1978, buyer, 1978-79; buyer Mobil Chem. Co., Macedon, N.Y., 1979-81; buyer Gen. Electric Co., Syracuse, 1981-83, purchasing agt., 1983-85, mgr. devel. subcontracts, 1987-89, mgr. material planning and subcontracts, 1989—. Mem. Nat. Assn. Female Execs. Home: 104 Old Lyme Rd Syracuse NY 13224 Office: Gen Electric Co Electronics Park Bldg 2 Syracuse NY 13210

MCCARTNEY, CHRISTINE MAYE, psychologist, educator; b. Oakland, Calif., Mar. 14, 1949; d. Harry Hollis McCartney and Alma Ethel (Collins) McCartney York. BA in Psychology, Nursing, and Theology, U. Portland, Oreg., 1977, MEd, 1978, MS in Criminal Justice, 1980; PhD in Psychology, Purdue U., 1984. Lic. psychologist, Oreg. Nurse Sheldon A. Walker, MD, Portland, 1970-72; exec. sec. U. Portland, 1972-80; teaching asst. Purdue U., West Lafayette, Ind., 1981-82, instr., 1982-83; intern VA Med. Ctr., Portland, 1983-84; psychologist Oreg. State Hosp., Salem, 1985—; exec. sec. Oreg. Psychol. Assn., Portland, 1977-78; adj. asst. prof. U. Portland, 1989—; cons. neuropsychologist Pacific Northwest Clin. Rsch. Ctr., Portland, 1989—. Co-author: Depression and the Integrated Life, 1983. NIMH fellow, 1980-81. Mem. Am. Psychol. Assn., Alpha Tau Delta, Theta Alpha Kappa. Democrat. Roman Catholic. Office: Oreg State Hosp GT/MSP 2600 Center St NE Salem OR 97310

MCCARTY, BARBARA SMITH, county official; b. Andalusia, Ala., Sept. 7, 1940; d. Egbert L. and Gladys (Hartin) S.; m. Lucius Edard McCarty,

Apr. 21, 1961; children—Debra McCarty Slaughter, Lucius Edward, Donna McCarty Swilley. Student South Ga. Tech. Coll., 1958-60, U. Ga.-Athens, 1964—. Office mgr. to county tax commr., Americus, Ga., 1966-76; clk.-treas. Sumter County Bd. Commrs., Americus, 1976-85, chief adminstrv. officer, treas., 1985—; v.p. Assoc. Industries of Americus. Named Woman of Achievement, 1987-88. Mem. County Adminstrs. Assn. Ga., Ga. County Clks. Assn., Inst. Mcpl. Clks. Ga. Democrat. Baptist. Club: Bus. and Profl. Women's (Americus) (treas.). Lodge: Order Eastern Star (worthy matron 1979-80). Avocations: reading; walking; music. Home: PO Box 1664 Americus GA 31709 Office: County Courthouse Americus GA 31709

MCCARTY, LAURA SMITH, industrial engineer; b. Americus, Ga., Apr. 15, 1967; d. Mack Stanly and Nancy Virginia (Archdeacon) McC. B in Indsl. Engring., Ga. Inst. Tech., 1989, postgrad., 1990—. Systems engr. Computer Task Group, Atlanta, 1989-90. Allied Signal Corp. scholar Ga. Inst. Tech., 1986, 87, 88. Mem. Inst. Indsl. Engrs., NAFE, Ga. Tech. Alumni Assn. (women's com.), Alpha Pi Mu. Republican. Lutheran. Home: 1475 Mecaslin St NW #7201 Atlanta GA 30309

MCCARVER, BETTY LOUISE, nurse, educator; b. Hurley, N.Mex., Oct. 12, 1932; d. Carl Thomas and Stella Alberta (Kreamer) McLendon; m. Robert Roy McCarver Jr., Sept. 3, 1954 (div. Jan. 1975); children—Robert Roy III, Deborah Lynn McCarver Stenberg. Diploma in nursing U. Okla., 1954; B.S., Ariz. State U., 1972; MEd, No. Ariz. U., 1986. R.N. Supr. U. Okla. Childrens Hosp., Oklahoma City, 1954; instr. Research Hosp., Kansas City, Mo., 1954-55; charge nurse U.S. Army Dispensaries, Sendai, Japan, 1956-57; owner, mgr. Hallmac Foods and Camping Supplies, Scottsdale, Ariz., 1965-68; asst. exec. dir. Ariz. Nurses Assn., Phoenix, 1976-82; tng. dir. Ariz. Family Planning Council, Phoenix, 1983—. Author: Once Upon A Time: A Complete Guide to Baby Sitting, 1965, 86; Dear Gussie: The 1-2-3 of G.E.M.S., 1968. Editor Caduceus Crier, 1972-73. Chmn. various coms. Maricopa County Med. Aux., 1963-73, Ariz. Med. Aux., 1970-73; wilderness survival counselor Theodore Roosevelt council Boy Scouts Am., Scottsdale, 1971. Recipient award of honor Nat. Safety Council, 1965, 66. Mem. ANA, Maricopa County Med. Aux. (hon. life), Coun. Continuing Edn. (sec. of coun. on continuing edn.), Ariz. Nurses Assn., Ariz. Vocat. Edn. Assn., Am. Soc. Tng. and Devel., Ariz. Pub. Health Assn., Nat. Family Planning and Reproductive Health Assn. Republican. Mem. Ch. of Jesus Christ of Latter-day Saints. Avocations: hiking; backpacking; painting; sewing; travel. Home: 7124 N Via De Amigos Scottsdale AZ 85258 Office: Ariz Family Planning Council 2920 N 24th Ave Suite 26 Phoenix AZ 85015

MCCARY, DEANNA BREWER, lawyer, psychologist; b. Seymour, Ind., Feb. 9, 1943; d. James Jefferson and Maxine (Robertson) Brewer; m. Stephen Paul McCary, Jan. 23, 1988; stepchildren: Kevin Paul, Kirstin Lee. BA in English, U. Ky., 1966; MEd in Counseling, U. Houston, 1970, PhD in Psychology, 1976; JD, South Tex. Coll. Law, 1984. Bar: Tex. 1984, U.S. Dist. Ct. (so. dist.) Tex. 1985. Tchr. English U. Houston, 1969-70, teaching fellow, 1972-74, 75-76; counselor Tex. Rehab. Commn., Houston, 1970-72; clin. intern Carl V. Morrison Ctr., Portland, Oreg., 1974-75; postdoctoral fellow U. Tex. Med. Br., Galveston, 1976-78, asst. prof. pediatrics, 1978-81; law clk. to presiding justice U.S. Dist. Ct. (so. dist.) Tex., Houston, 1984-85; assoc. Brown, Sims, Wise & White, Houston, 1985—; vis. mem. faculty Driscoll Found. Children's Hosp., Corpus Christi, Tex., 1978-81; psychologist Tex. Lion's Camp for Children with Diabetes, Kerrville, 1979-81. Contbr. articles to profl. jours. Rsch. grantee U. Tex. Med. Br., 1979-80, 80-81. Mem. ABA, Tex. Bar Assn., Houston Bar Assn., Am. Psychol. Assn., Maritime Law Assn., Phi Alpha Delta. Presbyterian. Home: 7603 Westwind Houston TX 77071 Office: Brown Sims Wise & White 2000 Post Oak Blvd Houston TX 77056

MCCASKILL, PATRICIA LORENZ, cable company executive, marketing professional; b. St. Louis, Jan. 27, 1948. BA, Maryville Coll., 1970. Asst. catering mgr. Stan Musial and Biggies, St. Louis, 1970-72; coord. catering conv. Radisson Hotel, Mpls., 1972-74; mgr. sales and catering Milw. Performing Arts Ctr., 1974-75; mgr. sales Colony Hotel, St. Louis, 1975-78; dir. sales and mktg. Lennox Hotel, St. Louis, 1978-79; v.p. sales and mktg. ShowBoard, St. Louis, 1979-81; dir. sales and mktg. Warner Amex Cable Communications, St. Louis, 1981-85; advt. product mgr. Southwestern Bell Pubs., St. Louis, 1985-87; regional dir. Travel Channel, St. Louis, 1987—; chairperson St. Louis Cable TV Advt. Coop., 1983-84. Bd. dirs., com. chair Confluence, St. Louis, 1984-87; bd. dirs. cable adv. bd. Archdiocese St. Louis, 1982-85. Recipient Distinction award Cable Mktg. Mag., 1984. Mem. Women in Cable (founding pres. St. Louis chpt. 1981-84, chair Nat. Charter Recognition awards 1989-90), Cable TV Adminstrn. and Mktg. Soc. (sec. south cen. regional bd. 1990—), Mo. Cable TV Assn., Ill. Cable TV Assn. (assoc. dir.), Ohio Cable TV Assn., La. Cable TV Assn. (assoc. dir. 1989-90), Minn. Cable TV Assn., Mich. Cable TV Assn. Roman Catholic. Office: The Travel Channel 4080 Wedgeway Ct Saint Louis MO 63045

MCCASLIN, F. CATHERINE, consulting sociologist; b. Chattanooga, Feb. 21, 1947; d. John Jacob and Elizabeth Dorothy (Johnson) McC. AB, Hollins Coll., Roanoke, Va., 1969; MA, Ga. State U., 1972; PhD, UCLA, 1979. Assoc. dir. Ga. Narcotics Treatment Program, Atlanta, 1972-73; research assoc., dir. research Health Care Delivery Services, Inc., Los Angeles, 1974-76; sr. survey analyst Kaiser Found. Health Plan, Los Angeles, 1978-80; program officer The Robert Wood Johnson Found., Princeton, 1980-84; faculty U. Pa. Sch. Medicine, Phila., 1984-86; ptnr. Schuhmacher & McCaslin Assocs., Phila., 1986—; exec. dir. The H.F. Lenfest Found., Pottstown, Pa., 1988-89; mem. adv. bd. Nat. Childhood Asthma Project, NHBLI, Washington, 1982-84, adv. com. Statewide Adolescent Pregnancy, New Brunswick, 1981-84; trainee NIH, 1973-79; cons. in field. Mem. editorial bd. Jour. Health & Social Behavior, 1988—; editor Med. Sociology newsletter, 1984—; contbr. articles to profl. jours. Fellow NIMH, 1975; grantee Spl. Action Office for Drug Abuse Prevention, 1972, Robert Wood Johnson Found., 1984. Mem. Am. Sociol. Assn. (nat. council med. sociology sect. 1984—). Am. Pub. Health Assn., Sociologists for Women in Soc. Democrat. Episcopalian. Home: 130 Elfreth's Alley Philadelphia PA 19106 Office: Schuhmacher & McCaslin Assocs 24 Bank St Ste 413 Philadelphia PA 19106

MCCASLIN, TERESA EVE, management executive; b. Jersey City, Nov. 22, 1949; d. Felix F. and Ann E. (Golaszewski) Hrynkiewicz; m. Thomas W. McCaslin, Jan. 22, 1972. BA, Marymount Coll., 1971; MBA, L.I. U., 1981. Adminstrv. officer Civil Service Commn., Fed. Republic Germany, 1972-76; personnel dir. Oceanroutes, Inc., Palo Alto, Calif., 1976-78; mgr., coll. relations Continental Grain Co., N.Y.C., 1978-79, corp. personnel mgr., 1979-81, dir. productivity, internal cons., 1981-84; dir., human resources Grow Group, Inc., N.Y.C., 1984-85, v.p. human resources, 1985-86, v.p. adminstrn., 1986-89; v.p. human resources Avery Internat., Pasadena, Calif., 1989—. Career counselor Marymount Coll. Career Ctr., Tarrytown. Recipient Sustained Superior Performance award U.S. Civil Service Commn., Fed. Republic Germany. Mem. Conf. Bd., Am. Mgmt. Assn., Human Resources Coun. Roman Catholic. Office: Avery Internat 150 N Orange Grove Blvd Pasadena CA 91103

MCCAUGHEY, LORRAINE B., communications executive; b. N.Y.C., June 5, 1950; d. Carlo F. and Flora (Mongrandi) Baltera; m. Andrew G. McCaughey. BA in English and Communications, Hunter Coll., 1972. Copy editor Fairchild Publs., N.Y.C., 1971-72; journalist Advt. Age mag., N.Y.C., 1972-77; sr. v.p. The Rowland Co., N.Y.C., 1977-80; account supr. Burson-Marsteller, Toronto, Ont., Can., 1980-82, v.p., group mgr., 1982-85, sr. v.p., gen. mgr., 1985-89, pres., chief exec. officer, 1990—; Bd. dirs. BCE Mobile, Inc., Montreal, Que., Can., Exec. Cons., Ltd., Ottawa, Ont., Conf. Bd. of Can.; coun. mem. Bd. Trade of Met. Toronto, 1990—. Bd. dirs. West Park Hosp. Found., Toronto, 1988—, Jr. Achievement Met. Toronto and N.Y. region, 1985—. Mem. Can. Pub. Rels. Soc., Royal Can. Yacht Club (assoc.), RAF Club (assoc., London chpt.), Met. Club (N.Y.), Can. Club of Toronto and Montreal. Home: 87 Valecrest Dr, Islington, ON Canada M9A 4P5 Office: Burson-Marsteller Ltd, 80 Bloor St W, Toronto, ON Canada M5S 2V1

MCCAUGHRIN, WENDY BORDOFF, educator, consultant; b. Windsor, Ont., Can., Nov. 23, 1944; d. Jack and Tillie (Starker) Bordoff; B.A., Wayne State U., 1967; B.A. with honors, U. Windsor, 1974; M.A., Merrill Palmer Inst., 1977; M.S., U. Ill., 1981, PhD, 1988; m. Scott James McCaughrin, July 1, 1972. Guidance counselor, instr. high sch., Chatham, Ont., 1967-70; reading therapist, instr., Windsor, Ont., 1971-77; reading and lang. therapist The Reading Group Program, Urbana, Ill., 1980-81; researcher computer-assisted instrn. for head-injured patients, Mercy Hosp., Urbana, 1984-85; ednl. cons. Learning Abilities Program, Mercy Hosp., Urbana, 1981-87, Christie Clinic, Champaign, 1987-88; researcher transition of handicapped youth from tng. programs to competitive employment, U. Ill., 1986-87; ednl. researcher, Transition Inst. U. Ill., Urbana, 1987—. Mem. Am. Ednl. Rsch. Assoc., Am. Speech-Lang.-Hearing Assn., Orton Soc., Internat. Reading Assn., Kappa Delta Pi. Jewish. Contbr. articles to profl. jours. Home: 36 Hillside Ln Briar Cliff Mahomet IL 61853 Office: U Ill 110 Edu Bldg Urbana IL 61801

MCCAULEY, BRENDA JULIA, public relations executive; b. Boston, Aug. 22, 1929; d. John Edward and Beatrice Mary (McNally) McC. BA, U. Pitts., 1951. Pub. rels. writer Am. Standard, Pitts., 1951-57; with pub. rels. dept. Bigelow Carpet, N.Y., 1957-59; account exec. Daniel J. Edelman, Pub. Rels., N.Y., 1959-61, Alfred Auerbach, Pub. Rels., N.Y., 196-65; pub. rels. mgr. S.R. Leon Co. Adv., Pub. Rels., N.Y., 1965-71; v.p. pub. rels. Sweet & Co., Adv., N.Y., 1971-75; v.p. Harriet Schoenthal Inc., N.Y., 1975-77; pres. Brenda McCauley Assocs., N.Y., 1977—; bd. dirs. UFAC-United Furniture Action Coun., High Point; industry panel Dallas Market Ctr., 1977, Miami Home Ctr., 1983. Bd. dirs. Nat. Coun. of Women, N.Y., 1975-77, mem. exec. com., 1978-86; vol. local, congl. and nat. campaigns Rep. Party, 1960—. Recipient spl. citation award Pub. Rels. Newsletter, 1975. Mem. Internat. Furniture & Design Assn. (v.p. pub. rels. 1967, 68, 85, 86, 87, 88, nat. bd., v.p. expansion 1973, nat. pres. 1976-77, program chair 1985), Am. Soc. Internat. Designer, Casual Furniture Mfrs. Assn. (bd. judges 1976-79), South Furniture Club (High Point), Sand Bar Beach Club (bd. dirs. 1960-66, Quogue, N.Y.). Roman Catholic. Office: Brenda McCauley Assocs 141 E 44th St New York NY 10017

MCCAULEY, SHIRLEY ANN, insurance company official; b. Brookhaven, Miss., Dec. 27, 1938; d. Tillman Herring and Mary Lou (Gray) Godbold; m. John Willys McCauley, May 3l, 1958; children: Mary Margaret McCauley Knight, John Michael. BAE, U. Miss., 1966, MAE, 1975. Elem. tchr. Baton Rouge City Schs., 1967-69, Alexandria Acad., Pineville, La., 1969-7l, Oxford (Miss.) City Schs., 1971-84; rep. Nationwide Ins. Co., Oxford, 1984—. mem. adminstrv. bd. Oxford-Univ. Meth. Ch., 1989—, com. on fin., 1990. Mem. Oxford Assn. Life Underwriters (pres. 1988, plaque 1989), Oxford C. of C., Coterie Club, Kappa Delta Pi, Phi Kappa Phi, Delta Kappa Gamma (sec. 1986), Kappa Delta. Republican. Home: 212 St Andrews Circle Oxford MS 38655 Office: Nationwide Ins Co 440 N Lamar Blvd Oxford MS 38655

MC CLANAHAN, RUE (EDDI-RUE MC CLANAHAN), actress; b. Healdton, Okla.; d. William Edwin and Dreda Rheua-Nell (Medaris) McC.; m. 1st, Tom Bish, 1958; 1 child, Mark Thomas Bish; m. 2nd, Norman Hartweg; m. 3rd, Peter DeMaio; m. 4th, Gus Fisher, 1976; m. 5th, Tom Keel, 1984 (div. 1985). B.A. cum laude, U. Tulsa, 1956. Actress: Erie (Pa.) Playhouse, 1957-58; theatrical, film and TV appearances, Los Angeles, 1959-64, N.Y.C., 1964-73; mem. cast: (TV series) Maude, 1973-78, Apple Pie, 1978, Mama's Family, 1982-84, Golden Girls, 1985—; appeared on Broadway: Jimmy Shine, 1968-69, Sticks and Bones, 1972, California Suite, 1977; films include: They Might Be Giants, The People Next Door, The Pursuit of Happiness, Modern Love. Recipient Obie award for leading off-Broadway role in Who's Happy Now, 1970; Emmy award Best Actress in a comedy, 1987; named Woman of Yr., Pasadena Playhouse, 1986; Spl. scholar Pasadena (Calif.) Playhouse, 1959, Phi Beta Gamma scholar, 1955. Mem. Actors Studio, Actors Equity Assn., AFTRA, Screen Actors Guild. Office: care Witt/Thomas/Harris Prodns 846 N Cahuenga Hollywood CA 90038*

MCCLEAN, CELEITA A., consulting company executive; b. Huntington, W.Va., Dec. 14, 1956; d. Raymond Ray and Sylvia May (Kinser) Breakiron. BS in Art and Edn. cum laude, W.Va. State Coll., 1980; MS in Aviation Mgmt. cum laude, Embry-Riddle Aero. U., 1985; grad. numerous aviation and mgmt. courses, U.S. Army. Lic. comml. pilot. Counselor, tutor W.Va. State Coll., Institute, 1975-80; mgr. army program GE Aerospace, Washington, 1984-87; pres. McClean Cons. Group, Falls Church, VA., 1987—; was first woman to fly and test-fly the UH-60 "Blackhawk". Serving as co. comdr. USAR, 1987—. Recipient Sikorsky Aircraft Rescue award U.S. Army; numerous other ribbons and badges. Mem. Assn. U.S. Army, Assn. U.S. Res., Marine Corp. Aviation Assn., Army Aviation Assn. Am., Am. Defense Preparedness Assn., Naval Helicopter Soc., Am. Helicopter Soc., Nat. Assn. Female Execs., Whirly Girls, Alpha Kappa Mu. Home: 1401 Heroid Dr SE Cedar Rapids IA 52403 Office: McClean Cons Group 2179 Kings Garde Way Falls Church VA 22043 Adress: 1300 Crystal Dr #608 Arlington VA 22202-3236

MCCLEARY, BERYL NOWLIN, civic worker, travel agency executive; b. Ft. Worth, Feb. 22, 1929; d. Henry Bryant and Phyllis (Tenney) Nowlin; m. Henry Glenn McCleary, May 29, 1950; children: Laura Gail, Glenn Nowlin, Neil Ray, Paul Tenney. BS in Zoology, Tex. Tech U., 1950. Owner, mgr. Beryl McCleary Travels, Chicago, 1975-81, Denver, 1981-84. Treas. Kappa Alpha Theta Ednl. Found., Tex. Christian U., Ft. Worth, 1958-61; pres. study club Jr. Woman's Club, Ft. Worth, 1959-60; pres. Symphony League, Ft. Worth, 1961-62; v.p., dir. Ft. Worth Symphony Orch. Assn. Inc., 1961; treas. Jr. Pro-Am Tarrant County, 1961-62; corr. sec. Ft. Worth Children's Mus. Guild, 1961; sec. Tarrant County (Tex.) Democratic Exec. Com., 1956-62; pres. guild, bd. dirs. Maadi Community Ch., Cairo, 1964-66; mem. women's bd. Lincoln Park Zool. Soc., Chgo, 1976-81; mem. Episcopal Ch. Women's Diocesan Bd., Chgo., 1976-79; pres., charter mem. Rainbow Investment Club, London, 1970-71, travel dir. Over the Hill Gang Ski Team Internat., Denver, 1982-84. Mem. AAAS, DAR, Geol. Geophys. Aux., Service Club Chgo., Jr. League Denver, Denver Symphony Guild, Central City Opera Guild, Houston Symphony League, Alpha Epsilon Delta, Kappa Alpha Theta (charter mem. Gamma Phi chpt. 1953). Home: 232 Warrenton Houston TX 77024

MCCLEARY, MONICA JEAN, nurse midwife; b. St. Paul, Aug. 21, 1952; d. Robert Thomas and Lois Elizabeth (Tiling) Jackels; m. Mark Edward, Mar. 3, 1978. BA, Coll. of St. Catherine, 1974; MS, U. Minn., 1978. RN. Nurse Divine Redeemer Hosp., S. St. Paul, 1974-75, St. Joseph's Hosp., St. Paul, 1975-76; cert. nurse midwife Group Health Inc., St. Paul, 1976-87, Family Tree Clinic, St. Paul, 1987—; preterm birth instr. Group Health Inc., St. Paul, 1988—; adjunct clinical instr. U. Minn., 1978—; clinical instr. Frontier Nursing Svc., Hayden, Ky., 1985--. Mem. Maternal-Child Substance Abuse Coun., Hennepin County Cocain Abuse Task Force, Minn. Council for Chem. Abusing Women and Their Children, Minn. Perinatal Community Consortium, Group Health Inc. Formulatory Com., Minn. MG T Register. Mem. Am. Coll. Nurse Midwives (vice chmn. 1986-88), NAPARE, ILCA. Democrat. Roman Catholic. Home: 525 Staples Ave Mendota Heights MN 55118 Office: Group Health Inc 205 S Wabasha St Saint Paul MN 55107

MCCLEEREY, PATRICIA JEAN, social worker; b. Valparaiso, Ind., Feb. 26, 1950; Mem. Purdue Alumni Assn., Am. Legion Aux. (program chmn. 1986-87), Purdue Club Lincoln Hills (treas. 1982-83), Twins Found. Orgn., Beta Sigma Phi (corr. sec., 1981-82, extension officer 1983-84, Valentine Queen 1985, v.p. 1989—). BA in Sociology, Purdue U., 1972. Cert. Child Welfare Caseworker. Nursing asst. Porter Co. Meml. Hosp., Valparaiso, 1968-70; substitute tchr. Tell City (Ind.)-Troy Twp. Sch. Corp., 1974-77; social worker Perry Co. Dept. Pub. Welfare, Cannelton, Ind., 1977—; contact person Southwestern Ind. Caseworkers, Cannelton, 1987—; mem. Child Welfare Caseworker Meetings, Cannelton, 1981—. Mem. Abuse Task Force, Tell City, 1990. Mem. Purdue Alumni Assn., Am. Legion Aux. (program chmn. 1986-87), Purdue Club Lincoln Hills (treas. 1982-83), Beta Sigma Phi (corr. sec. 1981-82, extension officer 1983-84, Valentine Queen 1985, v.p. 1989—). Democrat. Roman Catholic. Home: 26 Luzern Ln Tell City IN 47586

MCCLELLAN, JOAN C., retired art educator, artist; b. Milw., Jan. 5, 1934; d. Henry and Alma (Oyaas) Osmundson; m. Robert J. McClellan, Apr. 2, 1955; children: Michael J., Linda A., Katherine M., Mary M. BS, SUNY, Buffalo, 1956; MA, Adelphi U., 1968; postgrad., SUNY, Buffalo, 1961, Hofstra U., 1966. Tchr. Harris Hill (N.Y.) Elem. Sch., 1957; art specialist Huth Rd. Sch., Grand Island, N.Y., 1958-59; art educator Prospect Ave Sch., East Meadow, N.Y., 1959-89, W.T. Clarke High Sch., East Meadow, 1959-89. Exhibited in group shows including Sarasota Art Assn., 1989, Art League of Manatee County, 1989, Federated Woman's Club, 1990, Englewood Artisan Guild, 1990 (Best of the Best award). Vol. English tchr. to Spanish immigrants, L.I., N.Y., 1987-88; vol. soup kitchen, Wyndauch, L.I., 1987-88. Mem. Englewood Artisan Guild (rec. sec. 1989-90), AAUW, Nat. Mus. Women in Arts, Venice Art League, Sarasota Art Assn., Rotonda West Federated Woman's Club (arts chmn. 1989—), K.C. Republican. Roman Catholic. Home and Studio: 16 Bunker cir Rotonda West FL 33947

MCCLELLAN, MILDRED NOLTE, music educator; b. Duluth, Minn., Aug. 19, 1922; d. Julius Mosher and Mildred (Miller) Nolte; m. Samuel Goodman McClellan, June 16, 1951; children: John Charles, Margaret. BA, U. Minn., 1943; MusB, Yale U., 1948, MusM, 1949. Instr. music dept. U. Minn., Mpls., 1949-50, Vassar Coll., Poughkeepsie, N.Y., 1950-51, South Edn Music Ctr., Boston, 1952-54, Ctr. Coll., Danville, Ky., 1976-86; pvt. tchr. Danville, 1975—. Composer: (operas) I Wouldn't Miss the Chance, 1969, Every Friday Night, 1970, Education of Henry Halifax, 1972, Tahirih, 1975, (choral) Vision, 1989; editor children's music mag., 1970—. Lt. USN, 1943-46. Recipient Charles H. Ditson, Horatio Parker awards Yale U., 1947-48. Mem. Nat. Assn. Music Tchrs., Ky. Music Tchrs. Assn. Home: 2200 Chrisman Ln Danville KY 40422

MCCLELLAND, JEAN ELIZABETH, business strategy company executive; b. Pontiac, Mich., Jan. 2, 1949; d. Edgar Wayne and Marilyn Jean (Grafton) McC.; m. Steven Douglas, 1968 (div. 1972); 1 child, Traci Lynn. Student, West Chester (Pa.) State U., 1968-78; BA in Bus., Villanova U., 1981; postgrad., Pace U., 1981, U. Tex., Dallas, 1983. Tchr. dance Louise Harrison Studios, West Chester, 1967-81; mgr., asst. contr. Rouse & Co., Malvern, Pa., 1976-79; sr. fin. analyst Exxon Office Systems, Stamford, Conn., 1978-81; project mgr. for pres. Philips Info. Systems, Dallas, 1981-84; lead strategist, asst. sec. Super Club NA, Dallas, 1988-90; exec. v.p. Praxis, Dallas, 1984-88, pres., 1990—; former real estate agt., West Chester; bd. dirs. EcoSys, Inc., Atlanta; prin., bd. dirs. Visionary, A Premier Multimedia Corp., Dallas, 1990—, Lightning Hawk Creations, Nemo, Tex., 1990—. Bd. dirs. EWM Found. for Edn., Dallas, 1988-90. Mem. World Bus. Acad., Dallas Mus. Art. Office: Praxis 18484 Preston Rd Ste Ste 102 LB 133 Dallas TX 75252

MCCLELLAND, PATRICIA G., minister; b. Warsaw, Mo., July 12, 1944; d. Gail Raymond and Martha Carolyn (Lewis) Easton; m. Lester E. McClelland, Aug. 18, 1974; 1 child, Melody. BS, U. Mo., 1968; MS, Drury Coll., 1972. Cert. tchr., Mo., Kans.; lic. counselor; ordained to ministery Unity Ch., 1986. Instr. U. Wis., Milw., 1968-78, U. Mo., Kansas City, 1968-78; tchr. Hazelwood Pub. Schs., 1974-75; author edn. materials U. Wis., 1979-80; co-minister Unity Ch., Pitts., 1985-86; sr. minister Unity Ch., Anderson, Ind., 1985-86, Warren, Ohio, 1986-87, Massillon, Ohio, 1987-89; dir. housing Southwestern Coll., Winfield, Kans., 1989—. Methodist. Mem. NAFE, Nat. Assn. of Self-Employed, Internat. New Though Alliance, Internat. Platform Assn. Home: PO Box 94 Weaubleau MO 65774 Office: Southwestern Coll 100 College St Winfield KS 67156

MCCLENDON, CHERISSE ELLA, loan company executive; b. L.A., Nov. 17, 1962; d. Jerry McClendon and Wilma (Foster) Byrd. AA, L.A. City Coll., 1984; student, Nat. U., L.A., 1984-85; diploma in Paralegal Studies, Nat. Edn. Corp., Scranton, Pa., 1989. Legal document specialist Morrison & Foerster, L.A., 1983-84; legal sec. IBM, L.A., 1984-86; word processing supr. O'Melveny & Myers, L.A., 1986—; owner TMG Financial, The McClendon Group, L.A., 1989—. Mem. NAFE. Office: TMG Financial 3325 Wilshire Blvd #700 Los Angeles CA 90010

MCCLENDON, MAXINE, artist; b. Leesville, La., Oct. 21, 1931; d. Alfred Harry and Clara (Jackson) McMillan; student Tex. U., 1948-50, Tex. Woman's U., 1950-51, Pan Am. U., 1963-64; m. Edward Edson Nichols, Mar. 28, 1967; children—Patricia Ann, Joan Terri, Christopher, Jennifer. One-man shows include: Art Mus. S. Tex., Corpus Christi, 1971, McAllen (Tex.) Internat. Mus., 1976, Amarillo (Tex.) Art Center, 1982 group shows in Wichita, Kans., 1972, Marietta, Ohio, 1975, Dallas, 1977; represented in permanent collections: Mus. Internat. Folk Art, Santa Fe, Ark. Mus. Fine Art, Little Rock, McAllen Internat. Mus., Lauren Rogers Mus., Laurel, Miss.; commns. include: Caterpillar Corp., Peoria, Ill., Union Bank Switzerland, N.Y.C., Crocker Bank, Los Angeles, Tarleton U., Tex., Hyatt Regency, Ft. Worth Forbes Inc., San Francisco, First Savs. & Loan, Shreveport, La., Continental Plaza, Ft. Worth. curator Mexican folk art McAllen Internat. s., 1974-80. Recipient judges award 4th Nat. Marietta, 1975, numerous others. Mem. World Crafts Council, Am. Crafts Council (Tex. rep. 1976-80), Tex. Designer/Craftsmen (pres. 1973-74). Christian Scientist. Home and Studio: 2018 Sharyland St Mission TX 78572

MCCLENNEN, MIRIAM J., former state official; b. Seattle, Sept. 16, 1923; d. Phillip and Frieda (Golub) Jacobs; m. Louis McClennen, Apr. 25, 1969; stepchildren: Peter Adams, James C.A., Helen, Persis, Crane, Emery. BA, U. Wash., 1945; MBA, Northwestern U., 1947. Exec. trainee Marshall Field & Co., Chgo., 1945-47; asst. buyer Frederick & Nelson (subs. of Marshall Field), Seattle, 1947-49; buyer Frederick & Nelson (subs. of Marshall Field), 1949-57; fashion coordinator, buyer Levy Bros., Burlingame/San Mateo, Calif., 1957-63; buyer Goldwaters, Phoenix, 1963-67; adminstrv. asst. to pres. Ariz. State Senate, Phoenix, 1973-76; dir. publs. Office of Sec. of State, Phoenix, 1976-87; chairwoman legis. subcom. adminstrv. procedure Ariz. State Legislature, Phoenix, 1984-85. Compiler, editor publ. Ariz. Adminstrv. Code, 1973-87, Ariz. Adminstrv. Register, 1976-87. Bd. dirs., mem. exec. com. Phoenix Art Mus. League, 1972—, Phoenix Symphony Guild, 1970-88; bd. dirs., sec. Combined Metro. Phoenix Arts & Scis., 1974-90, mem. adv. bd., 1990—; bd. dirs. Phoenix Arts Coun., Master Apprentice Programs, 1980-83; bd. dirs., mem. exec. com. Heard Mus., 1982-88, 90—, chmn. publs. com., 1982-88, chmn. program com., 1990—; mem. Ariz. State Hist. Records and Archives Bd., 1987—, Ariz. Commn. on the Arts, 1989—. Recipient Disting. Svc. award Atty. Gen. Ariz., 1987, Outstanding Svc. to People, Ariz. State Senate, 1987, Nat. Assn. Secs. of State award, 1987. Mem. English Speaking Union, Nat. Soc. Arts and Letters, Charter 100 (bd. dirs. 1981-85), Phoenix County Club, Ariz. Club. Home: 5311 LaPlaza Cir Phoenix AZ 85012

MCCLINTOCK, BARBARA, geneticist, educator; b. June 16, 1902. Ph.D. in Botany, Cornell U., 1927; D.Sc. (hon.), U. Rochester, U. Mo., Smith Coll., Williams Coll., Western Coll. for Women. Instr. botany Cornell U., Ithaca, N.Y., 1927-31, research assoc., 1934-36, former Andrew D. White prof.-at-large, from 1965; now Disting. Svc. Mem. of Carnegie Instn. of Washington Cold Spring Harbor (N.Y.) Lab.; asst. prof. U. Mo., 1936-41; mem. staff Carnegie Instn. of Washington, Cold Spring Harbor, N.Y., 1941-47, Disting. Service mem., 1967—; cons. agrl. sci. program Rockefeller Found., 1962-69. NRC fellow, 1931-33; Guggenheim Found. fellow, 1933-34; recipient Achievement award AAUW, 1947; Nat. medal of Sci., 1970; MacArthur Found. prize; Rosenstiel award, 1978; Nobel prize, 1983. Mem. Nat. Acad. Scis. (Kimber genetics award 1967), Am. Philos. Soc., Am. Acad. Arts and Scis., Genetics Soc. Am. (pres. 1945), Bot. Soc. Am. (award of merit 1957), AAAS, Am. Inst. Biol. Sci., Am. Soc. Naturalists. Office: Cold Spring Harbor Lab Bungtown Rd Cold Spring Harbor NY 11724*

MCCLINTOCK, JANET MARIE, interior designer, consultant; b. Dearborn, Mich., Dec. 7, 1947; d. Gailard and Julie (Skorina) McCarty; m. Douglas Cove McClintock, Aug. 2, 1969; children: Coleen, William, Margaret. BS in Design, U. Mich., 1969. Cert. interior designer, Mich. Asst. designer interior design svcs. U. Mich., Ann Arbor, 1968-69; interior designer KMM Assocs., Ann Arbor, 1969-70, Sperry Rand/Libr. Bur., Inc., Plymouth, Mich., 1971-76; dir. design Libr. Design Assocs., Inc., Plymouth, 1976; cons. various library projects, Mich., Ohio, Ky., Ill., 1971—. Recipient 2d Place award ASID/DuPont Corian Nat. Design, 1989. Mem. Am. Soc. Interior Designers (profl. mem., Presdl. Citation, 1983, Mich. Designer of Distinction award Mich. Chpt., 1983), Inst. Bus. Designers (profl. mem.). Roman Catholic. Office: Library Design Assocs Inc 859 S Main St Plymouth MI 48170

MCCLINTOCK, JESSICA, small busines owner, fashion designer; b. Frenchville, Maine, June 19, 1930; d. Rene Gagnon and Verna Hedrich; m. Frank Staples (dec. 1964); 1 child Scott. BA, San Jose State U., 1963.

Elem. sch. tchr. Marblehead, Mass., 1966-68, Long Island, N.Y., 1968, Sunnyvale, Calif., 1964-65, 68-69; fashion designer Jessica McClintock, Inc., San Francisco, 1969—. Active donor, AIDS and Homeless programs; scholarship sponsor Fashion Inst. Design and Merchandising. Recipient Merit award Design, 1989, Dallas Fashion award, 1988, Tommy award, 1986, Pres. Appreciation award, 1986, Best Interior Store Design, 1986, Calif. Designer award, 1985, numerous others. Mem. Coun. Fashion Designers of Am., Fashion Inst. Design & Merchandising (adv. bd. 1979—), San Francisco Fashion Industry (pres. 1976-78, bd. dirs. 1989). Office: Jessica McClintock Inc 1400 16th St San Francisco CA 94103

MCCLINTOCK, SANDRA JANISE, writer, editor; b. Connersville, Ind., July 28, 1938; d. Owen Dale and Mary Janis (Tierney) M.; m. Harvey Miles Garrison, Jr., Aug. 1, 1959 (div. 1967); children: Heidi, Katherine, H. Miles III; m. Joseph Lloyd Fagen, May 15, 1969; 1 child, Adam Joseph. BA, Drake U., 1960; postgrad., Calif. State U., Fullerton, 1966-67; cert., Am. Grad. U., 1987. Lic. gen. contractor. Coord. copy desk Time Mag., N.Y.C., 1960-62; mem. graphics prodn. staff Times-Mirror Co., L.A., 1962-64; mgr. prodn. Miller Freeman Publs., Long Beach, Calif., 1964-68; supr. Design Svc., Anaheim, Calif., 1968-73; prin. Fagen Graphics, Long Beach, 1973-77, Palomar Publs., Ranchita, Calif., 1977-84; cons. Cons. & Designers, Anaheim, 1984-87; mgr. publs. Tracor Flight Systems, Inc., Santa Ana, Calif., 1987-88; coord. publs. Rockwell Internat. Corp., Anaheim, 1988—; cons. Aerotest, Inc., Mojave, Calif., 1986, Voice Telecom Corp., Laguna Beach, Calif., 1986. Editor: Psychopharmacology, 1984, Joseph of Aramathea, 1982; guest editor Interface Age mag., 1976; contbg. editor Rockwell News in U.S. and Can., 1988. Bd. dirs. Vol. Fire Dept., Ranchita, 1979; fund raiser Dem. candidate Calif. Assembly, Orange county, 1964. Mem. NAFE, Nat. Mgmt. Assn., So. Calif. Astrological Network, Rockwell Tennis Club, Amnesty Internat. Mem. Religious Sci. Ch. Home: 442 Baywood Dr Newport Beach CA 92660

MCCLISH, C. POLLY, finance executive; b. Lubbock, Tex., May 30, 1933; d. Hershell Lee and Carrie Maude (Johnson) Ward; four children by previous marriage. AA in Bus. Psychology, Amarillo Jr. Coll., Tex., 1966; BS in Acctg., West Tex. State U., 1968, BBA, 1970. Asst. credit mgr., collection mgr. Woolco Inc., Amarillo, Tex., 1968-74; credit mgr. Sakowitz Inc., Amarillo, 1974-79; sales mgr. Med. and Profl. Mgmt. Service, Galveston, Tex., 1979-82, v.p., gen. mgr., 1982-83; pres., bd. dirs. Colelli & Assocs., Galveston, 1983-87; founder, owner MasterCheck of Galveston-Bay Area, 1988—; cons. and lectr. in field. Mem. adv. bd. Tex. Edn. Commn.; mem. aux. U. Tex. Med. Br.; mem., div. chmn. United Fund. Named Outstanding Credit Exec. of Yr., Tex., 1976, to Galveston Women's Hall of Fame for bus. and fin. category. Mem. Internat. Consumer Credit Assn. (legis. adv. council), Am. Collectors Assn. (legis. adv. com., condr. numerous seminars), Asso. Credit Bur., Retail Mchts. Assn. Tex. (pres.), Nat. Assn. Female Execs., Soc. Cert. Consumer Credit Execs., Exec. Career Women, Bus. and Profl. Women (past pres.), C. of C. (pres.'s club, honor guard, Galveston chpt.), Credit Mgmt. Assn. Tex. (past pres.), Credit Women Internat. (past pres. Lone Star council), Am. Collectors Assn. Tex. (pres.), Forgery Investigation Assn. Tex. Club: Propeller (Galveston). Address: PO Box 3189 Galveston TX 77552

MCCLISTER, DEBRA LYNN, vice president, controller; b. Trenton, N.J., Sept. 20, 1954; d. Joseph Carl and Joan Elizabeth (Pendlebury) McC. BS in Commerce, Rider Coll., 1976. Sr. auditor KPMG Peat Marwick (formerly Peat, Marwick, Mitchell & Co.), Trenton, 1976-79; chief fin. officer Advance Computer Supplies, Inc., Princeton, N.J., 1979-81; mgr. corp. acctg. Hitachi Am., Ltd., N.Y.C., 1981-84; with N.Am. Philips Corp., N.Y.C., 1984—, asst. controller, 1988, staff v.p., controller, 1988—. Mem. AICPA, Nat. Acctg. Assn., N.J. State Soc. CPAs, Mfgs. Assn. for Productivity and Innovation. Office: NAm Philips Corp 100 E 42d St New York NY 10017

MCCLOSKEY, DEBORAH HAYWOOD, healthcare administrator; b. Pitts., Dec. 29, 1952; d. Roy Everly and Amelia Lucy (Bruno) Haywood; m. Thomas William McCloskey. BS, U. Pitts., 1986. Med. asst. Samuel G. Miller, M.D., Pitts., 1972-75; lab. supr. Gastroenterology Med. Assocs., Pitts., 1975-77, Mercy Hosp. of Pitts., 1977-88; system mgr. Presbyn. U. Hosp. of Pitts., 1988—; cons. Mercy Hosp. of Pitts., 1986-88. Mem. NAFE, Am. Med. Technologist. Democrat. Roman Catholic. Home: 639 Second St Verona PA 15147 Office: Presbyn U Hosp 1400 Penn Ave Pittsburgh PA 15222

MCCLUNG, CHRISTINA JUNE, training company executive; b. Newark, N.J., Jan. 19, 1948; d. Fred and Maria (Dallinger) Palensar; m. Kenneth Austin McClung, Mar. 21, 1975. BA, Kean Coll., 1970; MA, Seton Hall U., 1973; Ed.D., U. So. Calif., 1976. Tchr. Chatham Twp. (N.J.) pub. schs., 1970-74; instructional designer Tratec Co., L.A., 1976-79; asst. prof. Lehman Coll., N.Y., 1977-79; ind. cons., 1978-80; v.p., bd. dirs. Instructional Design Group, Morristown N.J., 1980—; gen. ptnr. MGM Investments, 1985—. Author: (5 books series) Computers for Professionals, 1983. Mem. Nat. Soc. Performance Instrn., Phi Delta Kappa. Office: Instructional Design Group 144 Speedwell Ave Morristown NJ 07960

MCCLURE, ANGELINE KITCHENS, human resource management executive, consultant; b. Macon, Ga., Dec. 26, 1945; d. Benjamin Grady and Reba (Atkins) Kitchens; m. Donald Wayne McClure, Nov. 2, 1974; children by a previous marriage: Leanna Kay Oliver Linnekohl, Gregory Alan Oliver. BA in Social Sci., Hollins Coll. (Va.), 1971; postgrad. U. Va., 1972, Commonwealth U. of Va., 1972. Tchr., Ronaoke City Pub. Schs. (Va.), 1971-73, Twiggs County Pub. Schs., Jeffersonville, Ga., 1973-75; human resource specialist Charter Med. Corp., Macon, 1975-79; pers. cons. Mut. Pers. Svc., Macon, 1980-81; human resource mgr. So. Trust Ins. Co., Macon, 1981-84; mgmt. cons., owner Motivational Mgmt. Resources, Macon, 1984—; mem. employer's rel. com. Ga. Dept. Labor, 1983. Mem. Gov.'s Leadership Forum for Post-Secondary Edn., State of Ga., 1983; co-chmn. employers' rels. com. Am. Cancer Soc., Macon, 1984, 85; mem. Middle Ga. Pers. Assn. (pub. rels. dir. 1982, v.p. 1983, pres. 1984, bd. dirs. 1985), Am. Soc. Pers. Adminstrs., NAFE, Career Women's Network (bd. dirs. 1986-88, pres. elect 1989-90), Middle Ga. Employers Assn., Bus. and Industry Rels. Com., Macon C. of C., Greater Macon Women Bus. Owners (charter mem., bd. dirs. 1988, pres.-elect 1989). Baptist. Home: 3076 Tiffin Circle Macon GA 31204 Office: Motivational Mgmt Resources PO Box 6735 Macon GA 31208

MCCLURE, ANNA JO, English educator; b. Oklaunion, Tex., June 30, 1928; d. Clifford Orr and Bettie Caroline Burks; m. Robert Dale McClure, Mar. 11, 1917; children: Danny, Martha. BS in Elem. Edn., Cameron U., 1972; ME, Southwestern Okla. State U., 1975. Elem. tchr. Davidson (Okla.) Elem. Sch., 1972-73; tchr. English Davidson High Sch., 1973-76, 83—; elem. tchr. Frank Williams Elem. Sch., Davidson, 1976-83; real estate salesperson, rancer, cureal estate mgr. Frederick, Davidson, Okla., 1948—; com. mem. Four Yr. Improvement Plan, staff devel. Okla. Edn., Davidson Schs., 1987, tchr. cons. Precinct chmn. Dem. Party, Dist. 9, 1979—, co-chmn. Tillman Co., 1982-86, exec. com., 1982-86; mem. ednl. polit. action com. Zone 8, Tillman Co., 1980-86. Named Tchr. of Yr., Davidson Edn. Assn., 1979, 80, 82. Mem. NEA, Davidson Edn. Assn. (pres. elect 1988), Okla. Edn. Assn., Okla. Coun. Tchrs. English. Methodist. Home: PO Box 114 Davidson OK 73530

MCCLURE, FLORENCE HELEN, management consultant; b. Chgo., July 21, 1930; d. George and Minnie (LaBarbara) Torre; m. Richard D. McClure, Feb. 16, 1952; children: Kimbert, Brian, Douglas, Ronald. Student Ind. U., 1948-50, Kent State U., 1967-68, Lake Erie Coll., Ohio, 1969-70. Elem. sch. tchr., Geneva, Ohio, 1966-71; coordinator traffic dept. True Temper Corp., Saybrook, Ohio, 1971-72; mktg. dir. Peoples Savs. & Loan, Ashtabula, Ohio, 1973-82; pres. Chem. Seal, Inc., Grand Junction, Colo., 1982-85; mktg./personnel dir. Valley Fed. Savs. & Loan, Grand Junction, 1982-87; with customer rels. Bob Caldwell chrysler/Plymouth, Columbus, Ohio, 1988-89; v.p. sales Video Yearbook Corp., Glen Ellyn, Ill., 1989—; human resource cons., 1985—. Commr., Colo. Housing Authority, Grand Junction, 1985-87; bd. dirs. Alternative Housing Assocs., Grand Junction, 1982-87. Mem. Am. Soc. Personnel Adminstrn., Western Slope Personnel Assocs., Grand Junction C. of C. (pub. relations com. 1985-87, coll. edn. com. 1983-85). Republican. Roman Catholic. Avocations: walking, reading, traveling. Home: 117 Lakeland Pl Pickerington OH 43147

MCCLURE, JANICE LEE, state legislator, farmer, graphic designer; b. Redwood City, Calif., Jan. 1, 1941; d. D. Kelley and Roberta M. (Powell) McC.; 1 child, Keenan Kyle. BFA in Art, U. N.Mex., 1966; BFA in Design, U. Kans., 1982. Mem. Kans. State Senate, Topeka, 1989—; mem. legis. coms. Agrl. (ranking minority mem.), Confirmations, Econ. Devel.; mem. Joint Com. on Art and Cultural Resources, Fed. and State Affairs, Fin. Instns. and Ins.; mem. Agrl., Food Policy and Rural Devel. Com., State Fed. Assembly, Nat. Conf. State Legislatures. Editor, author: (with others) Haskell County, Kansas, 1989, 100 Years Beneath the Plow. Dem. precinct committeewoman, Haskell County, Kans., 1990. Mem. AAUW, Bus. and Profl. Women, Kans. Authors Club. Home: HCR 1 Box 70 Sublette KS 67877 Office: Kansas Legislature Senate Chamber Statehouse Topeka KS 66612

MCCLURE, MARY ANNE, former state legislator; b. Milbank, S.D., Apr. 21, 1939; d. Charles Cornelius and Mary Lucille (Whittom) Burges; m. D.J. McClure, Nov. 17, 1963; 1 child, Kelly Joanne. BA magna cum laude, U. S.D., 1961; postgrad., U. Manchester, Eng., 1961-62; M of Pub. Adminstrn., Syracuse (N.Y.) U., 1980. Staff asst. U.S. Senator Francis Case, Washington, 1959-61; sec. to lt. gov. State of S.D., Pierre, 1963, with budget office, 1964; exec. sec. to pres. Frontier Airlines, Denver, 1963-64; tchr. Pub. High Schs., Pierre and Redfield, S.D., 1965-66, 68-70; mem. S.D. State Senate, Pierre, 1975-89, pres. pro tem, 1979-89, vice chmn. coun. of state govts., 1987, chmn. council of state govts., 1988; spl. asst. to Pres. Bush for intergovernmental affairs, 1989—. Vice chmn. sch. bd. Redfield Ind. Sch. Dist., 1970-74. Fulbright scholar, 1961-62, Bush Leadership fellow, 1977-80. Mem. Phi Beta Kappa. Republican. Congregationalist. Home: 1630-D Beekman Pl NW Washington DC 20009

MCCLURE, POLLEY ANN, academic administrator, researcher, educator; b. Austin, Tex., Apr. 5, 1943; d. James Shelton and LaNelle (Polley) McC.; m. J.C. Randolph (div. 1980); m. John W. Smith, Apr. 2, 1983; children: John W. Jr., Brendan S. BA in Zoology, U. Tex., 1965; MA in Zoology, U. Mont., 1967, PhD in Zoology, 1970. With Ind. U., Bloomington, 1971—, dean for acad. computing, 1987—, exec. dir. univ. computing, 1989—; mem. rev. panel EPA, 1984-85. Contbr. numerous articles to profl. jours. Mem. Environ. Commn., Bloomington, 1975-76; bd. dirs. Planned Parenthood, Bloomington, 1980-82. NSF Rsch. grantee, 1973-75, NIH Rsch. grantee, 1977-83. Mem. Assn. for Computing Machinery, AAAS, Ecol. Soc. Am. (sec. physiol. ecology sect. 1983-85, chair physiol. ecology sect. 1985). Office: Ind U Franklin Hall 104 Bloomington IN 47402

MCCLURG, PATRICIA A., minister; b. Bay City, Tex., Mar. 14, 1939; d. T.H. and Margaret (Smith) McC. BA, Austin Coll., 1961; M in Christian Edn., Presbyn. Sch. of Christian Edn., 1963; BD, Austin Presbyn. Theol. Sem., 1967; postgrad., So. Meth. U., 1971-73; DD (hon.), Austin Coll., 1978. Dir. Christian edn. 2d Presbyn. Ch., Newport News, Va., 1963-65; asst. pastor Westminster Presbyn. Ch., Beaumont, Tex., 1967-71; assoc. pastor 1st Presbyn. Ch., Pasadena, Tex., 1969-71; assoc. exec. Synod of Red River, Denton, Tex., 1973-75; dir. gen. assembly mission bd. Presbyn. Ch., Atlanta, 1975-86; assoc. exec. for mission The Presbytery of Elizabeth, Plainfield, N.J., 1986—; pres. Nat. Coun. Chs. of Christ in the U.S.A., N.Y.C., 1988-89, v.p., 1985-87; del., budget com. chmn. World Coun. Chs. Assembly, Vancouver, Can., 1985; sect. leader World Coun. Chs. Mission and Evang. Confs., Melbourne, Australia, 1980. Contbr. articles to prof. jours. Mem. chs. spl. commn. on South Africa, N.Y.C., 1985—, Anti-Pollution Campaign, Pasadena, 1970. Recipient Disting. Alumni award Austin Coll., 1979. Democrat. Presbyterian. Lodge: Rotary. Office: Presbytery Elizabeth 525 E Front St Plainfield NJ 07060

MCCLURKIN, IOLA TAYLOR, biology educator, educational administrator; b. Kinston, N.C., May 22, 1930; d. Raymond Leslie and Mabel (Harris) Taylor; m. Douglas Charles McClurkin, July 23, 1958; children: Iola, Ellen, Douglas. AB, Duke U., 1952; MA, East Carolina U., 1957; PhD, U. Miss., 1965. Rsch. asst. dept. zoology Duke U., Durham, N.C., 1952-53; biology tchr. New Bern (N.C.) High Sch., 1953-57; teaching asst. dept. zoology Duke U., Durham, 1957-58; instr. biology U. Miss., University, 1958-65, asst. prof., then assoc. prof., 1965-74, prof. biology, 1975—, chmn. dept. biology, 1987-88, asst. dean Coll. Liberal Arts, 1988—, chair Commn. on Status of Women, 1985—, adminstr. minority affairs Coll. Liberal Arts, 1989—. Author: Laboratory Text for Advanced Histology, 1983, Laboratory Text for Histology, 1986. NSF fellow; named Disting. Alumna in Natural Scis., Duke U., 1987; recipient Life Svc. award Am. Cancer Soc., 1988. Mem. AAAS, AAUW, Am. Conf. Acad. Deans, Electron Microscopy Soc. Am., Histochem. Soc., Am. Inst. Biol. Scis., Am. Soc. Microbiologists, Soc. Plant Physiology, Assn. Southeastern Biologists, Miss. Acad. Sci., Miss. Assn. Women in Higher Edn., Miss. Coun. Deans and Colls. Arts and Scis., Sigma Xi. Office: Coll Liberal Arts Univ Miss University MS 38677

MCCLUSKEY, CAROLINA PACIENCIA SALAS, education educator; b. Manila, Philippines, Feb. 15, 1949; came to U.S.A., 1976; d. Conrado Antonio Peredo Salas and Josefa Felicissima Donato Paciencia. BA in Mathematics, St. Scholastica's Coll., Philippines, 1970; MS in Statistics, Ateneo de Manila U., 1976; MS in Computer Sci., Lehigh U., Bethlehem, Pa., 1978; PhD in Info. Sci., Lehigh U., 1985. Instr. Ateneo de Manila U., Philippines, 1970-76; instr. teaching asst., fellow Lehigh U., Bethlehem, Pa., 1976-84; asst. prof. Allentown campus Penn. State U., Fogelsville, 1985. Contbr. articles to profl. jours. NASA postdoctoral fellow, 1987, 88. Mem. IEEE Computer Soc., Assn. for Computing Machinery. Roman Catholic. Office: Pa State Allentown 6090 Mohr Ln Fogelsville PA 18051

MCCLYMONDS, JEAN ELLEN, marketing professional; b. Richmond, Calif., June 27, 1955; d. Rollin J. and Doris E. (Baughmann) Lepley; m. Gareth L. MCClymonds, Sept. 18, 1981. BEd, U. Calif., Berkeley, 1972; MBC, San Jose State U., 1987. Pres. Just Mktg., Scotts Valley, Calif.; dir. mktg. and nat. sales Skyway Freight Systems, Inc., Watsonville, Calif.; dir. corp. communications Madic Corp., Santa Clara, Calif.; mgr. mktg. communications Design and Test Systems div. Gould Inc., Santa Clara. Contbr. articles to profl. jours. Recipient Outstanding Achievement award Am. Trucking Assn., 1989, Sales and Mktg. Coun., 1988. Mem. Sales and Mktg. Coun., Am. Trucking Assn., Am. Mgmt. Assn., Coun. of Logistics Mgmt., Nat. Assn. for Quality Control.

MCCOLLEY, SUSANNA ANTONIA, pediatric pulmonologist; b. Glendale, Calif., July 28, 1961; d. Robert McNair and Diane Laurene (Kelsey) McColley; m. Russell Dawes Brown, June 17, 1989. BS, Northwestern U., Chgo., 1983; MD, Northwestern U., 1985. Diplomate Am. Bd. Pediatrics, Nat. Bd. Med. Examiners. Intern/resident Johns Hopkins Hosp., Balt., 1985-88; fellow in pediatric pulmonary Johns Hopkins Hosp., 1988—. Am. Lung Assn. Md. fellow, 1988—. Mem. Am. Thoracic Soc. (assoc.), Am. Acad. Pediatrics (candidate fellow). Office: Johns Hopkins Hospital 600 N Wolfe St Baltimore MD 21205

MCCOLLUM, DONNA JEWELL, lawyer; b. Youngstown, Ohio, Mar. 21, 1957; d. Charles W. and M. Joyce (Ferguson) Jewell; m. Robert Joseph McCollum, June 23, 1979; 1 child, Erin Michelle. BSAS, Youngstown State U., 1979; JD, U. Akron, Ohio, 1985. Legal advocate Battered Persons Crisis Ctr., Youngstown, 1981-83; pvt. practice law Youngstown, 1985—; asst. prosecutor Mahoning County Pros. Office, Youngstown, 1989—. Bd. dirs. Mahoning County Ct. Appointed Spl. Advs. Inc., Youngstown, 1985—, Youngstown Area Community Action Coun., 1987—. Mem. Mahoning County Bar Assn., Ohio Bar Assn., ABA, Ohio Acad. Trial Lawyers, Assn. Trial Lawyers of Am., Nat. Dist. Attys. Assn. Democrat. Presbyterian.

MCCOMMON, FAYE DI CARLA, financial broker; b. Atlanta, Nov. 26, 1955; d. Robert and Magnolia (Clemmons) McC. BBA, Ga. State U., 1985. Fin. broker McCommon Enterprises, Decatur, Ga.; mgr. Greyhound Package Express New Era Terminal Svcs., Atlanta; sales rep. Nally Chevrolet, Inc., Atlanta; property mgr. McCommon Enterprises, Decatur, Ga. Author: How to Start and Operate a Successful Home Business, 1987. Mem. NAFE, Am. Entrepreneurs Assn. C. of C. Office: 2925 Headland Dr #51 57 East Point GA 30344

MCCONNELL, BARBARA, manufacturing executive, consultant; b. Berkeley Heights, N.J., Jan. 23, 1943; d. S. Richard and Virginia (Elsum) Cherkin; m. Kevin P. McConnell, Apr. 22, 1972; children: Sarah Elizabeth, Daniel Jason. Grad. high sch., Parsippany, N.J. Exec. sec. Exxon Corp., Florham Park, N.J., 1960-64, adminstrv. asst., 1964-69; exec. adminstrv. asst. Avco Corp., LaJolla, Calif., 1970-73; exec. officer, owner McB Bears, Escondido, Calif., 1986—. Mem. NAFE. Mem. Christian Ch. Home and Office: McB Bears 380 Andreasen Escondido CA 92025

MCCONNELL, FLORENCE LEONARD, court administration professional; b. Callaway, Va., Mar. 19, 1931; d. William Marshall and Fannie Lera (Prillaman) Mullins; m. Robert W. Leonard, June 24, 1950 (div. 1983); children: Susan Gail Leonard Little, William Ralph, Molly Marie; m. Edward B. McConnell, Oct. 21, 1984; stepchildren: Annalee, Edward B. Jr., Marilyn, Barbara, William. Grad. high sch., Newport News, Va. Sec. guidance office Williamsburg (Va.)/James City County Schs., 1975-77; exec. sec. to exec. dir. Nat. Ctr. State Cts., Williamsburg, 1977-79, adminstrv. asst. to exec. dir., 1979-88, asst. to pres., 1988-90, sec., bd. dirs., 1980-90; ret., 1990. Past bd. dirs., exec. com. Newport News Operatic Soc., Wednesday Morning Music Club. Mem. Kingsmill Women's Social Club, Kingsmill Book Club. Presbyterian.

MCCONNELL, JILL ROBB, yoga and massage therapist; b. Cin., Apr. 29, 1940; d. John Leonard and Ruth Elizabeth (Miller-Boyer) Wagner; m. Richard Lee Robb, Oct. 29, 1955 (div. 1973); children: Victoria Kirby, Richard, Michelle Montague, Kirt, Craig; m. Charles Gary McConnell, Dec. 27, 1975 (div. 1984). BS in Holistic Yoga Therapy, The Union Inst., Cin., 1982. Lic. massage therapist, 1983. Buyer, mgr. Cin., 1964-66, market researcher, 1966-69, yoga therapist in pvt. practice, 1983—, non-denom. wedding minister, 1983—, massage therapist, 1984—; seminar and workshop presenter; adj. faculty Th Union Inst., Cin., 1983-87, Self-Health Inst., Lebanon, Ohio, 1988—; cons. in field, 1972—. Contbr. articles to newspapers. Leader Girl Scouts, Brownies, Cin., 1963-72, Cub Scouts, 1966-78. Recipient Outstanding Svc. Optimist Club, 1980, Multiple Sclerosis Soc., 1989. Mem. Cin. Yoga Tchrs. Assn. (program chair 1978-83), Internat. Yoga Tchrs. Assn., Am. Massage and Therapy Assn., Ohio Wellness Coalition, Internat. Assn. of Yoga Therapists. Home and Office: 5750 N Glen Rd Cincinnati OH 45248

MCCONNELL, MELISSA (MELISSA FOSTER), radio personality; b. Hays, Kans., Jan. 22, 1953; d. Henry McConnell and Lucia Maria (Ciullo) Foster; m. Hassan Reza, Aug. 8, 1979 (div. Mar. 1987); children: Christine Foster, Lucinda Foster. BA in Broadcast Communication, San Francisco State U., 1976. Lic. FCC 1st class radiotelephone operator. Midday personality, program dir. Sta. KWUN, Concord, Calif., 1976-80; nighttime personality Sta. KYA-AM-FM, San Francisco, 1980-82; evening personality, producer entertainment calendar Sta. KIOI-FM, San Francisco, 1982-87; midday personality, music dir. Sta. KEEN, San Jose, Calif., 1987—; freelance celebrity interviewer, San Francisco, 1980—; guest co-host Evening Magazine show Sta. KPIX-TV, San Francisco, 1988—. Spokesperson Concerned Citizens of the Peninsula Hosp. Dist., Burlingame, Calif., 1987. Republican. Presbyterian. Home: PO Box 5277 San Mateo CA 94402 Office: Sta KEEN PO Box 6616 San Jose CA 95150

MCCONNELL, PATRICIA ANN, health facility administrator; b. Bklyn., Feb. 28, 1935; d. Philip P. and Dagney C. (Petersen) Powers; m. Alexander McConnell, Jan . 15, 1955; children: Francis X., Robert M., Bonnie J., Douglas P. AAS in Nursing, Milw. Area Tech. Coll., Milw., 1978; student, U. Wis., 1980; BA, Nat. Coll. of Edn., 1989. RN, Ill, Iowa, Wis., Ind.; registered profl. nurse; cert. ins. rehab. specialist, cert. occupational hearing conservationist. Nursing asst., RN oncology dept. St. Luke's Hosp., Milw., 1976-79; supr. employee health dept. Harnisfeger P&H, Cudahy, Wis., 1979-82; staff nurse employee health dept. 1st Wis. Nat. Bank, Milw., 1982-83; med. svcs. cons. Crawford Risk Mgmt. Svcs., Schaumburg, Ill., 1983-86; case mgmt. specialist Nat. Rehab. Cons., Westmont, Ill., 1986-87; pres., dir. Mid-State Health and Rehab., Westmont, 1987—. Founding mem. Rape Recovery Project Hot Line, vol. support group, Chgo, 1989-90; active Ill. Coalition Against Sexual Assault, 1990; vol. literacy tutor World Relief Orgn. & Literacy Vols. of Am., 1990; den mother Cub Scouts Am., 1966-68; first aid instr. ARC, 1981—; basic life support instr. Am. Heart Assn., 1981-84; vol. religion instr. St. Helena Cath. Ch., Greendale, Wis., 1973-75. Mem. LWV, Rehab. Ins. Nurses Group (treas. 1990), Assn. Rehab. Nurses, Assn. Vocat. Rehabilitationist in Ill., Oak Brook Assn. Commerce & Industry (small bus. com. 1989-90), Dolton Regional Hosp. Aux. (charter, nominating com. and publicity chair 1965). Roman Catholic. Home: 821 Oakwood Dr Westmont IL 60559 Office: 504-A E Ogden Ave Ste 2 Westmont IL 60559

MCCONNELL, ROBIN ELLEN, human resources administrator; b. Jamaica, N.Y., Mar. 5, 1954; d. Heinz Gustav and Ruth Evelyn (Schmiedel) Korn; m. John Richard McConnell, Dec. 6, 1975; children: Janelle Allyn, Jason Alexander. AS, SUNY, Farmingdale, 1974; BS Mgmt., Communication, Adelphi U., 1989. Exec. sec. Island Leasing Corp., Westbury, N.Y., 1974-81; pers. supr. Executone, Inc., Jericho, N.Y., 1981-86; human rels. specialist Quality Care, Inc., Rockville Centre, N.Y., 1986-87; human rels. adminstr. Whitbread N.Am., Inc., Lake Success, N.Y., 1987—. Mem. NAFE, Am. Soc. Pers. Adminstrs., L.I. Diabetes Assn. Republican. Lutheran. Home: 7 Roydon Dr W North Merrick NY 11566 Office: Whitbread N Am Inc 1 Hollow Ln Lake Success NY 11042

MCCONNELL, VIOLA CARLBERG, author, editor; b. Albia, Iowa, Jan. 1, 1903; d. John Sven and Anna-Marie (Anderson) Carlberg; m. Harold Graham McConnell, Jan. 8, 1927 (wid. Feb. 1974); 1 child, Anderson Graham. BA, U. Minn., 1930, postgrad., 1957-59, 1970. Diocesan pres. Girls' Friendly (Episcopal) Soc., Minn., 1944-57; Bishop's pub. relations dir. Episcopal Diocese of Minn., 1964-79; Diocesan correspondent Living Ch. and Episc., U.S.A., Minn., 1954-86; v.p. St. Paul's Ch. Women, Mpls., 1960-64; with State Bd. Church Women United, Mpls., 1944-73; numerous positions with Episc. Ch.; State chmn. 50th anniversary State Bd. Ch. Women United, Minn., 1984-86; Episcopal rep. Minn. Coun. of Chs., Mpls., 1968-70, Radio-TV com., 1964-74; nat. missions chmn. Girl's Friendly Soc., N.Y.C., 1951-54, nat. pub. rels. chmn., 1954-57; pub. rels. dir. Internat. Ctr. of U. Minn., 1958-71; non-govt. rep. for Episcopal Exec. Bd. UN Planning Session 10th Anniversary, N.Y.C., 1954; communications cons. Minn. Episc. Diocese, 1989-90. Author: The Virgin Islands, 1952, Haiti, 1953, Focus on Liberia, 1954; editor: (mag.) Communique, Internat. Ctr. U. Minn., 1957-71; producer: (TV program) Citizens For Eisenhower in East Rm. White House, Washington, 1956; editor newsletter Episcopal Ch. Women, Diocese of Minn., communication chmn., 1982—; contbr. articles to mags., 1976-89. Pub. relations chmn. YWCA Bd., Mpls., 1946-47, 53-54, Republican Workshop, Mpls., 1947-51; rep. Police Advisory Council, Mpls., 1976-81; state radio/tv chmn., Citizens For Eisenhower, Mpls., 1956; researcher for hist. com. Friends of Inst. Mpls. Inst. Art, 1990—, vol., 1976-89; research for St. Paul's Parish Hall, Minn., 1988-90. Recipient 6 yr. svc. award ARC, Mpls., 1945, merit award Ch. Women United, 1973, Nat. Ch. Women United, N.Y.C., 1986, Valiant Woman award, WCCO Good Neighbor of N.W., 1973, Civic and Cultural Vol. award Mayor of Mpls., 1985. Mem. Religious Pub. Rels. Coun. (life, nat. bd. dirs. 1964-66, various offices Twin Cities chpt.), Ch. Periodical Club Episcopal (life), Minn. Press Club, Episcopal Communicators, Mpls. Inst. Art (guarantor), Woman's Club Mpls., Mpls. Club, Alpha Chi Omega (50 Yr. Golden Girl award Mpls. 1976, Best of Best Alumnae award Indpls. 1987). Republican. Home: 2700 W 44th St Minneapolis MN 55410

MCCONNER, ORA B., school superintendent; b. Augusta, Ga., Jan. 2, 1929; d. Landirs and Mamie (Elderidge) Williams; m. Walter R. McConner, June 27, 1953; 1 child, Susan L. BA, Paine Coll., Augusta, 1949; MA, Boston U., 1951; EdD, Nova U., Ft. Lauderdale, Fla., 1982. Instr. Paine Coll., Augusta, 1951-55; tchr. Chgo. Pub. Schs., 1956-66, adminstr., 1966-79, asst. supt., 1979-89, dist. supt., 1989—. Danforth study grantee, 1955; recipient Image award League of Black Women, 1974, Silver Beaver award Boy Scouts Am., 1985; named Educator of Yr. Chgo. Black Sch. Educators, 1984; recipient Outstanding Educator's award Beatrice Coffee's, 1989. Mem. Am. Assn. Sch. Adminstrs., Nat. Alliance of Black Sch. Educators, Council for Exceptional Children, Profl. Women's Aux. of Provident Hosp., Alpha Gamma Psi. Episcopalian. Club: Zonta (v.p., sec.). Home: 9137 S Constance Ave Chicago IL 60617 Office: Chgo Pub Schs Dist 6 4071 S Lake Park Ave Chicago IL 60653

MCCOOL, PAMELA LYNN REED, mental health services professional; b. Independence, Kans., Nov. 19, 1963; d. Billy Eugene and Mary Sue (Younger) Reed; m. Bradley Keith McCool, Nov. 2, 1985; 1 child, Tanner Keith. BS, U. Tex., Arlington, 1987. Phys. therapy asst. Dr. James Elbaor, Arlington, 1980-83; supr. cashiers Target, Arlington, 1983-84; unit sec. Mansfield (Tex.) Community Hosp., 1984-85; sec. Willow Creek Hosp., Arlington, 1986-87, ednl. tester, 1987-89, student assistance counselor, 1989-90; case mgr., counselor Oak Grove Treatment Ctr., Burleson, Tex., 1990—; coord. student assistance program Dist. Wide S.A. Program, I.S.D., Mansfield; cons. ednl. tester Carpenter & Assocs., Arlington, 1988-90, Mind Time, Arlington, 1989, Willow Creek Hosp., Arlington, 1989-90, Oak Grove Treatment Ctr., Burleson, 1990. Coach Mansfield Pee-Wee Cheerleading, 1986-90; vol. Dallas Intertribal Ctr., Dallas, 1990, Project Charlie, Kids Safe Saturday, 1990. Mem. NAFE, Nat. Orgn. Student Asst. Prevention Profls., Tex. Alcohol and Drug Abuse Consortium, Tex. State Intelligence Tng. Republican. Home: 1708 Westover Arlington TX 76015 Office: Worley Middle Sch 500 Pleasant Ridge Mansfield TX 76063

MCCORKLE, CONSTANCE MARIE, education educator; b. Kansas City, Nov. 23, 1948; d. Burford L. and Martha Marie (Hall) M.; m. Harry Robert Silver, Sept. 18, 1973 (div. 1981). BA, Rice U., 1971; MA degrees, Stanford U., 1972 and 79, PhD, 1983. Rsch. asst. U. Sci. and Technol., Kumasi, Ghana, 1973-74; rsch. affiliate Centro de Investigacion de Linguistica Aplicada, Lima, Peru, 1976-77; vis. lectr. Bridgewater (Mass.) State Coll., 1978; vis. asst. prof. Met. State Coll., Denver; adj. asst. prof. U. Denver, 1978-81; rsch. assoc. UMC and Cuzco, Peru, 1980, Am. Inst. Rsch. in the Behavioral Sci., Palo Alto, Calif., 1981-83; rsch. scientist, project anthropolist Internat. Agrl. Programs U. Wis., Madison, 1983-84; rsch. asst. prof. U. Mo., Columbia, 1985—; instr. Argentine Consulate, Houston and Lenguas Athikas, Madrid, Spain 1967-69, pvt. tour guide Mex. and Peru 1966-71. Contbr. articles to profl. jours., 1968—; editor: The Social Scis. in Internat. Agrl. Rsch., 1989—; contbr. chpts. to books. NDMFL fellow, 1977-78, NSF fellow, 1971-73; Fulbright scholar, 1987. Fellow Soc. for Applied Anthropology; mem. Am. Anthrop. Assn., AAAS, NAFE, Nat. Assn. for Practice of Anthropology, Wash. Assn. Profl. Internat. Commn. on Anthropology of Food and Food Problems, Coun. Anthropology and Nutrition, Culture and Agl. Soc., Rural Sociol. Soc., Soc. Econ. Anthropology, Am. Ethnol. Soc., Agrl. Food and Human Values Soc. Home: 220 Sunnyside Ct Columbia MO 65201

MCCORKLE, LIZA LOUISE, real estate corporation asset manager; b. Covina, Calif., Sept. 8, 1961; d. Robert Allen and Joyce Patricia (Jarzyna) Wilenken; m. Lawrence William McCorkle, Oct. 4, 1986. BA in Bus., Calif. State U., Fullerton, 1985. Lic. Calif. real estate sales, 1986. Sales rep. Lancome Cosmetics, Inc. at Bullocks, Santa Ana, Calif., 1982-85; office leasing specialist R.B. Allen Group, Office and Indsl. Brokerage, Tustin, Calif., 1986; asset mgr. The Sammis Co., Irvine, Calif., 1986—. Participant Evangelical Free Ch., Yorba Linda, Calif., 1987—. Mem. Sigma Kappa. Republican. Office: The Sammis Co 9500 Telstar Ave Ste 106 El Monte CA 91731

MCCORMACK, GRACE LYNETTE, engineering technician; b. Dallas, Nov. 2; d. Audley and Janice Meredith (Metcalf) McC. Tech. degree, Durham's Coll., 1958; grad. in civil engring., El Centro Coll., 1972; grad. in advanced surveying, Eastfield, 1975. Cert. sr. engr. technician. Contract design technician various engring firms, Dallas, 1958-70; sr. design engr. technician City of Dallas Survey Div., 1970-80, street light div., 1980—. Mem. Nat. Assn. Female Execs., Women's Forum of Am. Mem. Unity Ch. Avocations: numerology, astrology, aerobics, metaphysics, Egyptian-Arabian horses. Home: 1428 Meadowbrook Ln Irving TX 75061

MCCORMACK, KIMBERLY ROBIN, physical therapist; b. Beverly, Mass., July 25, 1960; d. Theodore Emanuel Johnson and Vizma (Aprans) Wren; m. Kevin Andrew McCormack, Oct. 4, 1987. Student, Hamilton Wenham Reg. high sch., Mass., 1978; BA in Psychology, Harvard U., Cambridge, Mass., 1982; MS in Physical Therapy, Columbia U., N.Y.C., 1984; student, Burdenko Inst., Sudbury, Mass., 1988. Lic. N.Y., Mass. Staff rehab. therapist Braintree Hosp., Mass., 1984-85, staff orthopedic therapist, 1985-86, resource clinician, 1987-88; spine specialist Middlesex Rehab. Assn., Medfield, Mass.; water therapist Burdenko Inst., Wayland, Mass., 1988--. Home: 66 Stow St Waltham MA 02154

MCCORMACK, LOWELL RAY, oil producer, document examiner, graphoanalyst, lecturer; b. Ladonia, Tex., Oct. 26, 1925; d. Lowell and Orianna (McDonnold) Coney; m. Paul H. McCormack, June 4, 1948; children: Sharron Ann, Lowell Henry. Student Rutherford Met. Coll., Dallas, 1962, U. Tex., Arlington and Dallas, Eastfield Coll., Dallas, Cooke County Coll., 1989, Gainveville, 1989—; M. Graphoanalyst, Internat. Graphoanalysis Soc. Bookkeeper, Jot-Em-Down Gin Corp., Pecan Gap, Tex., 1947, Shedd-Bartush Foods, Dallas, 1948-52; acct., credit mgr. J. P. Ashcraft Co., Inc., Dallas, 1956-65; v.p., sec.-treas. Safari Oil Corp., Dallas, 1954-88, pres. 1989—; pres. Scorpio Oil Corp., 1987—; chief fin. officer, v.p., sec.-treas. Dallas Title Co., 1965-83; instr. graphoanalysis Cooke County Coll., 1988; acctg. cons. to atty.; bd. dirs. First Nat. Bank, Cooper, Tex., 1986-87, treas. 1988-89, Butterfield Stage, Gainesville, Tex.; lectr. in field. Leader troop Girl Scouts USA, 1955-65; founder Yarn Spinners, Gainesville, 1988; mem. Newcomers Club, 1986—, pres. 1989—; mem. Bapt. Choir, Centennial Cir. Columnist Cooke County Leader, 1988. Mem. North Tex. Oil and Gas Assn., Cooke County Heritage Soc., Gainesville C. of C., Internat. Graphoanalysis Soc. (life, v.p. Tex. chpt. 1978, pres. 1979, named Graphoanalyst of Yr. 1987, keynote address speaker 1987, author weekly column Cooke County Leader 1988, Okla. seminar leader 1990), Internat. Platform Assn. Baptist. Clubs: Zonta (co-chmn. fin. com. 1982, dir., 2d v.p. 1983-84), Soroptimist, Toastmistress (pres. 1981, com. chmn. for internat. conv. 1984) (Dallas), Kiwanis (one of first women mems. Gainesville chpt., 1988, v.p. 1990—), Phi Theta Kapa (treas. Psi Iota chpt. 1990). Home: 631 S Lindsay Gainesville TX 76240

MCCORMACK, MARY BEATRICE (BEE MCCORMACK), food manufacturing executive; b. Albany, Ga., Aug. 21, 1925; d. Robert Emmet and Anna Louise (Keller) McC. BA, Ga. Coll., 1946. Dir. personnel Bobs Candies, Inc., Albany, 1946-61; v.p. Bob's Candies, Inc., Albany, 1961—. Pres. Albany Symphony, 1972-74; co-chmn. capital funds campaign Albany Mus., 1981-82, sec. 1990—; chmn. arts devel. drive Albany Arts Council, 1984; mem. Ga. Bus. Com. for the Arts, 1989—, Albany Local Devel. Commn., 1986—, Albany Clean Community Commn., 1988-90. Recipient Pro Deum et Juventatum medal Roman Cath. Diocese of Savannah, Ga., 1970, Alumni Achievement award Ga. Coll., Milledgeville, 1983; co-recipient Albany Woman of Yr. award, 1978. Mem. Nat. Confectioners Assn. (dir., v.p. 1979-84, Candy Mfr. Yr. 1981), Profit-sharing Council Am. (dir. 1975-81), Profit Sharing Research Fedn. (dir. 1978-81), Albany C. of C. (dir. 1982-85). Roman Catholic. Office: Bobs Candies Inc PO Box 3170 1505 Oakridge Dr Albany GA 31708

MCCORMICK, ALMA HEFLIN, writer, retired educator, psychologist; b. Winona, Mo., Sept. 2, 1910; d. Irvin Elgin and Nora Edith (Kelley) Heflin; m. Archie Thomas Edward McCormick, July 14, 1942; children: Thomas James, Kelly Jean. BA, Ea. Wash. Coll., 1936, EdM, 1949; PhD, Clayton U., 1977. Originator dept. severely mentally retarded Tri-City Public Schs., Richland, Wash., 1953, Parkland, Wash., 1955; co-founder, dir. Adastra Sch. for Gifted Children, Seattle, 1957-64; author profl. publs., novelscontbr. articles to various publs., 1937—. Mem. Am. Psychol. Assn., OX 5 Aviation Pioneers, Kappa Delta Pi. Republican. Roman Catholic. Editor: Cub Flyer. First Am. woman test pilot, 1942.

MCCORMICK, ELAINE ALICE, public relations executive; b. Jersey City, Nov. 19, 1943; d. Johannes and Anni (Gantenberg) Kratz; m. Thomas A. McCormick, Oct. 1, 1966; 1 child, Thomas John. Diploma in nursing, Mt. Sinai Sch. Nursing, 1964; BA summa cum laude, Georgian Ct. Coll., 1982. RN, N.Y., N.J., Fla. Staff nurse Holy Name Hosp., Teaneck, N.J., 1964-65, 69-70; office nurse Drs. Higdon, Beaugard and Fox, Teaneck, 1965-67; indsl. nurse Dun & Bradstreet, Inc., N.Y.C., 1967-69; camp nurse, ski area dir. Camp Arrowhead, Community YMCA, Marlboro, N.J., 1974-78; adminstrv. asst. DeJesse Advt., Woodbrige, N.J., 1982-83; staff writer Georgian Ct. Coll., Lakewood, N.J., 1983-84, dir. pub. rels., 1984—; cons. in field. Mem. adv. bd. Ret. Sr. Vol. Program Ocean County, Toms River, N.J., 1987—; chmn. bd. mgrs. Ocean unit Am. Cancer Soc., 1988—. Mem. Jersey Shore Pub. Rels. Assn. (2d place award 1987), Pub. Rels. Soc. Am., Toms River C. of C., Am. Mgmt. Assn. Mercy Higher Edn. Colloquium, Sigma Tau Delta. Republican. Roman Catholic. Home: 9 Pamela St Marlboro NJ 07746-1621 Office: Georgian Ct Coll Lakewood Ave Lakewood NJ 08701-9972 also: 4452 NE Ocean Blvd Jensen Beach FL 34957

MCCORMICK, JANE GRIFFEL, hospital administrator; b. Eldora, Iowa, Sept. 28, 1939; d. Raymond Richard and Ann (Janssen) Griffel; m. David R. Bradbury, June 17, 1961 (div. 1973); children: James, David, Brette; m. John Davis McCormick; stepchildren: Mark Davis, Timothy John. BA in Gen. Sci., U. Iowa, 1961; MS in Health Adminstrn., U. Mich., 1976. Asst. adminstr. Seaway Hosp., Trenton, Mich., 1976-80; adminstr. Seaway Hosp., Trenton, 1980-83, Beyer Hosp., Ypsilanti, Mich., 1984-90; v.p. planning and svc. devel. Saline Community Hosp., 1990—; bd. dirs. S.E. Mich. Hosp. Council, Southfield, Mich., 1984-88. Bd. dirs. Washtenaw United Way, Ann Arbor, Mich., 1986—, cabinet mem., 1984-86; mem. Washtenaw Community Coll. Blue Ribbon Adv. Com., 1987—; project mgr. Ypsilanti Area Indsl. Survey, 1987-88; bd. dirs. Ypsilanti Area C. of C., 1985-90, chmn., 1989; mem. Ad Hoc com. on computerized tomographic (CT) scanners Mich. Dept. Pub. Health, 1990. Mem. Am. Coll. Healthcare Execs., U. Mich. Sch. Pub. Health (lectr. 1985—), Ypsilanti Area C. of C. (bd. dirs., current chair 1989), Mich. Hosp. Assn. (consulting svcs. adv. com. 1985-88, chmn. 1988). Home: 2764 Lowell Ann Arbor MI 48103 Office: Saline Community Hosp 400 W Russell Saline MI 48176

MCCORMICK, JILL MARIE, nurse; b. Cleve., Aug. 29, 1959; d. Jerome Thomas and Lois Marie (Catalano) McC. Student, Luth. Med. Ctr. Sch. Nursing, Cleve., 1979. RN. Staff nurse Fairview Gen. Hosp., Cleve., 1979-82; charge nurse Winter Park (Fla.) Meml. Hosp., 1982--. Mem. Young Rep., Orlando, Fla., 1985. Mem. Soc. Peripheral Vascular Nurse. Roman Catholic.

MCCORMICK, LESLIE L., data processing executive; b. Angola, Ind., Apr. 9, 1961; d. Robert L. and Jacqueline (Cross) McC. BS in Mgmt., Purdue U., 1983; MBA, U. Notre Dame, Ind., 1984. Tax acct. Ernst & Whinney, South Bend, Ind., 1984-85; mgr. Tax Technology Group Arthur Andersen & Co., Chgo., 1985—. Mem. Nat. Assn. Female Execs. Episcopalian. Home: 30 E Huron Apt 3706 Chicago IL 60611 Office: Arthur Andersen & Co 69 W Washington Chicago IL 60602

MCCORMICK, MARIANN HONOR, advertising executive; b. Phila., Mar. 21, 1945; d. John A. and Honor (Cullen) McCormick; adopted dau. of Nancy Cullen Olmer. Student St. Joseph's U., 1963-67. Asst. promotion dir. Sta. WFIL-TV-FM, Phila., 1967-69; promotion dir. Rumrill-Hoyt, Phila., 1970-71, media dir., 1971-72; dir. advt. Cottman Systems, Phila., 1972-76; planning dir. Nat. Media Group, Phila., 1976-77; media/mktg. cons. Kalish & Rice, Inc., Phila., 1977-79, Mel Richman, Inc., Phila., 1979-80; v.p. media and research Blair/BBDO, Rochester, N.Y., 1980-89; dir. mktg. Jay Inc., Rochester, 1989—; guest lectr. Syracuse U., SUNY, Brockport; mem. exec. com. Rochester Communicator of Yr. Adult leader Girl Scouts Am., Phila., 1966-69; chmn. liturgy com. Mother of Sorrows Ch.; mem. exec. com. Kidney Found. Gala.; bd. dirs. Threshold. Mem. Am. Mktg. Assn., Am. Women in Radio/TV (past pres. Rochester chpt.), Rochester Advt. Council, Rochester Women's Network, Mktg. Communicators Rochester (v.p. media rels.), Media Partnership for Drug Free Am., Mensa. Democrat. Roman Catholic. Club: Poor Richard (1st v.p. 1978-79) (Phila.). Home: 1663-5 Stowell Dr Rochester NY 14616 Office: Jay Inc Sibley Tower Bldg Rochester NY 14604

MCCORMICK, MAUREEN OLIVEA, computer systems programmer; b. Toledo, Mar. 24, 1956; d. Richard Ernest and Rita Maureen (Pratt) McC. BS in Elem. Edn., Kent State U., 1978, MA Reading Specialization, 1980. Reading instr. Elyria City Schs., Elyria, Ohio, 1978-79; tchr. Wellington Village Schs., Wellington, Ohio, 1979-80; devel. edn. instr. Lorain County Community Coll., Elyria, 1980-83; computer programmer analyst Navy Fin. Ctr., Cleve., 1981-86, Naval Mil. Personnel Command, Arlington, Va., 1986; computer systems analyst Marine Corps Cen. Design & Programming Activity/MCDEC, Quantico, Va., 1986-87; computer systems programmer Navy Fin. Ctr., Cleve., 1987—. Mem. Am. Soc. Mil. Comptrollers, AAUW, TransAtlantic Brides & Parents Assn., Elyria Jr. Woman's Club. Home: 153 Burns Rd Elyria OH 44035 Office: Navy Fin Ctr 1240 E 9th St Cleveland OH 44199

MCCORMICK, NANCY JANE, counselor, consultant; b. DeLand, Fla., Nov. 28, 1935; d. John Ford and Edith Cady McCallum; m. June 15, 1956; children: Edith Jane McCormick Ufland, John Gordon, Catherine Anne. BA cum laude, U. Cen. Fla., 1977; MA, Rollins Coll., 1979. Lic. counselor, Fla. Counselor, instr. Valencia Community Coll., Orlando, Fla., 1978-81, Brevard Community Coll., Melbourne, Fla., 1981-83; pvt. practice Melbourne, 1978—; cons. Fla. Dept. Profl. Regulation, Tallahassee, 1986—. Bd. dirs. Parent Edn. Resource Ctr., Melbourne, 1985—, Brevard Achievement Ctr., Rockledge, Fla., 1989—. Mem. Am. Assn. Marriage and Family Therapy (clin.), Fla. Assn. Counseling and Devel., Fla. Mental Health Counselors Assn. (bd. dirs. 1985—, Outstanding Mental Health Svc. award 1988), AAUW, Am. Mental Health Counselors Assn. (nat. pres. 1986-89), Am. Assn. Counseling and Devel. (bd. governing coun. Washington 1986—), Soroptimist (bd. dirs. Melbourne chpt. 1984-86). Home: 1125 North A1A Apt 902 Satellite Beach FL 32937

MCCORMICK, SUSAN KONN, publishing executive; b. Cleve., Dec. 13, 1953; d. Frank Andrew and Mary Lou (Dunn) K.; m. Michael F. McCormick, May 25, 1985; 1 child, Amanda. BS, Ind. U., 1976; MBA, Stanford U., 1983. CPA, N.Y. Acct. Deloitte Haskins & Sells, Indpls., 1975-77; fin. analyst GM, N.Y.C., 1977-83; exec. Brown Bros. Harriman, N.Y.C., 1983-84; v.p. Bankers Trust Co., N.Y.C., 1984-85; treas. Scholastic, Inc., N.Y.C., 1985—. Mem. AICPA, N.Y. State Soc. CPA's, Risk Ins. Mgmt. Soc., Stanford U. Alumni Assn. Office: Scholastic Inc 730 Broadway New York NY 10003

MCCORMICK, WANDA FAY, property manager; b. Lynchburg, Va., July 7, 1948; d. Robert Lee McCormick and Marjorie A. (Coffey) Whitney; m. Robert M. Bryant, May 7, 1966 (div. 1975); 1 child, Robert Massie. Student, Danville (Va.) Community Coll., 1979, IBM Mktg. Sch., 1982, Herbert Berghof Studio, 1987-88. Mgr. Sta. WTGR, Myrtle Beach, S.C., 1982-84; account exec. Sta. WMAL, Washington, 1984-85; nat. trainer AT&T Video Teleconferencing, N.Y.C., 1985-87; mktg. dir. Manhattan Video Prodns., N.Y.C., 1987-88; pvt. practice cons. N.Y.C., 1988-89; mgr. Crown Bldg. Hdqrs. Cos., N.Y.C., 1989—. Vol. announcer In-Touch Radio, N.Y.C., 1988-89. Mem. Nat. Acad. TV, Arts and Scis., Internat. Interactive Communications Soc., NAFE. Home: 338 E 53d St Ste B New York NY 10022

MC CORMICK, WILLIE MAE WARD (MRS. WALTER WITTEN MC CORMICK), city official, retired technical specialist; b. Centerville, Tex. Oct. 17, 1908; d. William Sylvester and Lucy (Marshall) Ward; B.A., Mary Hardin Baylor Coll., 1929; M.A., Hardin Simmons U., 1931; postgrad. So. Methodist U., Tex. Woman's U.; m. Walter Witten McCormick, May 29, 1929; 1 dau., Elizabeth Ward McCormick Wilcox. Tchr. chemistry and algebra Big Spring (Tex.) High Sch., 1941-44, 45-48; weather observer for Dept. Commerce, Big Spring, 1943-44; analytical chemist Dow Chem. Co., Freeport, 1944-45; calculator Chance Vought (now Ling-Temco-Vought), Dallas, 1951-55, structural engr., 1955-63, sci. programmer, 1963-67, tech. specialist, 1967-69; sr. program analyst Univ. Computing Co., Arlington, Tex., 1970-73; adv. council 1st City Savs. of Euless (Tex.); dir. Mbank of Euless, 1985-86. Mem. Euless City Council, 1973-85, mayor pro tem, 1975-85; chmn. Trinity River Authority Central Wastewater System; mem. Water Resources Council N. Central Tex.; bd. dirs. Euless Pub. Library. Mem. AAAS, Am. Chem. Soc., Math. Assn. Am., Fedn. Am. Scientists, AAUW, Trainmen's Aux. (pres. 1940-41), Internat. Platform Assn., LWV (publicity chmn.), Metro Bus. Profl. Womens Club, Acad. Scis., Inst. Am. Chemists, Soroptimist (hon.). C. of C. (dir.). Democrat. Baptist (tchr. adult dept. Sunday sch.). Clubs: Order Eastern Star (past worthy matron), Oakcrest Woman's, Altrusa. Home: 2300 N Main Euless TX 76039

MCCORRY, MARY ELENORE, small business owner; b. Pitts., Mar. 8, 1925; d. Dana Joseph and Catherine Marie (Cummings) Fox; m. Robert Clyde McCorry, June 21, 1947 (dec. Feb. 1984); children: Diana, Mary Ann, Susan, Robert, Christopher. BA in History, Chestnut Hill Coll., 1947. Cert. tchr., Pa. Clerical worker Pitts. Nat. Bank, 1947-48; sec. Germantown Hosp., Phila., 1948-49; elem. sch. tchr. St. Paul Sch., Butler, Pa., 1954-55; owner, operator Fox Den Stitchery & Yarn Shop, Butler, 1977—; sec. bd. regents St. Fidelis Coll. & Sem., 1966-78; sec. bd. dirs. Butler Meml. Hosp., 1976-90. Vice chmn. Butler Renaissance Commn., 1983-89; chmn. Transp. Authority, Butler, 1990—. Mem. AAUW (pres. 1973), Soroptimist Internat. of Ams. (pres. Butler chpt. 1982), Downtown Butler Assn., Butler Meml. Hosp. Aux. (pres. 1974), Jr. Women's Club Butler (pres. 1956). Republican. Roman Catholic. Home: 432 N McKean St Butler PA 16001 Office: Butler Meml Hosp 911 E Brady St Butler PA 16001

MCCOWN, JUDITH PORTER, volunteer; b. Dallas, Sept. 19, 1904; d. Frederic Howard and Pauline Phillips (Gambrell) Porter; m. Henry Young McCown, Nov. 6, 1928 (Dec. 6, 1983); children: Frederic, Henry, Fairfax (dec.). BA, U. Tex., 1924. With advt. dept. A. Harris & Co., Dallas, 1926-28. Asst. editor The Daily Texas, 1923-24. Vol. Adult Day Care Ctr., Austin, 1986-88; tutor Travis County Adult Lit. Coun., Austin, 1985-89; del. Austin Met. Ministeries, 1988—; bd. mem. West Austin Care Givers, 1987—; pres. Episcopal Women, Good Shepherd, 1962. Recipient Teaching Excellence award Travis County Adult Lit., Austin, 1988. Mem. Pan Am. Round Table (dir. 1982), Austin Art League (pres. 1965-66). Republican. Episcopalian. Home: 8341 Summerwood Dr Austin TX 78759

MCCOY, ANN BRELSFORD, artist; b. Wilmington, Del., Sept. 26, 1940; d. John Willard and Ann (Wyeth) McC.; m. George Alexis Weymouth, May 13, 1961 (div. Aug. 1979); 1 child, McCoy duPont Weymouth. BA, Bennett Coll., 1960. Ptnr. Tri-County Conservancy/Brandywine River Mus., Chadds Ford, Pa., 1968-75, Kenneth Lindsey Antiques and Paintings, Chadds Ford, 1975-82; freelance artist N.Y.C., 1982—; cons. Ann B. McCoy Antiques and Interiors, Chadds Ford, 1988—. Hon. bd. dirs. Pearl S. Buck Found., Bucks County, Pa., 1989-90.

MCCOY, CAROL P., psychologist, training executive; b. Bronxville, N.Y., June 14, 1948; d. Rawley Deering and Jane (Wiske) McC.; m. Lanny Gordon Foster, Nov. 29, 1975 (div. 1985). BA, Conn. Coll., 1970; MS in Psychology, Rutgers U., 1974, PhD in Psychology, 1980. Adj. instr. psychology Rutgers U., New Brunswick, N.J., 1974-75; faculty chair dept. social sci. Misericordia Hosp. Sch. Nursing, Bronx, N.Y., 1976-79; tng. and devel. cons. Chase Manhattan Bank N.A., N.Y.C., 1980-85, tng. mgr. internat. consumer banking div., 1985-88, tng. mgr. individual banking, 1988—. Mem. Nat. Assn. Female Execs., Am. Soc. Tng. and Devel., Am. Psychol. Assn. Home: 771 West End Ave New York NY 10025 Office: Chase Manhattan Bank NA 195 Broadway New York NY 10081

MCCOY, DAWN CROWLEY, clinical nutrition specialist, food microbiologist; b. Griffin, Ga., Dec. 26, 1956; d. John Seaborn and Jackie Ann (Seymour) Crowley; m. Donald Vinson McCoy, Sept. 9, 1978. Student, Valdosta (Ga.) State Coll., 1975-76; AA in Biology, Gordon Coll., 1977; BS in Nutrition, Ga. State U., 1981. Registered/lic. dietitian. Clin. nutrition specialist Clayton Gen. Hosp., Riverdale, Ga., 1981-85; instnl. sales rep. Flav-O-Rich Dairy, Atlanta, 1985-87; quality control microbiologist Eastern Foods, Atlanta, 1987, DiGiorgio (SERV), Atlanta, 1987-89; dir. clin. nutrition dept. Tift Gen. Hosp., Tifton, Ga., 1989—; speaker Diabetes Assn., Ga., 1981-85, Heart Assn., Ga., 1981-85; cons. Tift County Hospice. Speaker numerous civic orgns., Ga., 1981—; clown CLOWNS, Ga., 1986—. Recipient Disting. Youth award Griffin Women's Club, 1975. Mem. Am. Dietetic Assn. Ga. Dietetic Assn., S.W. Ga. Dietetic Assn. (sec. 1990—, pres. elect 1990—), Inst. Food Technologists, Dietitians in Bus. and Industry, Tift County Heart Assn. (nutrition chmn. 1990—), World Clowning Assn. Republican. Lutheran. Home: Rt 7 Box 500H Tifton GA 31794 Office: Tift Gen Hosp 901 E 18th St Tifton GA 31793

MCCOY, DONNA CAROL, telecommunication supervisor; b. Carthage, Mo., Feb. 13, 1952; d. Vernon and LaVerne McCoy. BS in Biology, Mo. So. State Coll., 1976. Park ranger Dept. of Interior-Nat. Park Svc., Diamond, Mo., 1971-77; installer We. Electric, Joplin, Mo., 1977-83; field installations supr. No. Telecom, Inc., Denver, 1984—. Mem. NAFE, Women's Club, Mo. So. State Coll. Alumni Assn., Beta Sigma Phi. Home: 1633 E Lakeside Dr 180 Gilbert AZ 85234 Office: No Telecom Inc 5575 DTC Pkwy Ste 150 Englewood CO 80111

MCCOY, DOROTHY ELOISE, writer, educator; b. Houston, Sept. 4, 1916; d. Robert Major and Evie Letha (Grimes) Morgan; m. Roy McCoy, May 22, 1942; children: Roy Jr., Robert Nicholas. B., Rice U., 1938; M., Tex. A&I U., 1968; postgrad., U. Indiana, 1971, U. Calif., Berkeley, 1972, U. Calif., Santa Cruz, 1977. Cert. secondary tchr. Tchr. Corpus Christi (Tex.) Independent Schs., 1958-84, co-editor curriculum guides, 1985; freelance writer Corpus Christi, 1987—; co-owner United Iron and Machine Works, Corpus Christi, 1946-82; freelance lectr.; master tchr. Nat. Humanities Faculty, Concord, Mass., 1977-78, Nat. Coun. Tchrs. English, 1971; steering com. Edn. Summit, Corpus Christi, 1990. Author: A Teacher Talks Back, 1990; contbr. articles and columns to profl. jours. Chmn. dists. I and II Tex. Coun. English Tchrs., S.W. Tex., 1970; chmn. nominating com. Nat. Coun. Tchrs. English, steering com., 1978-80; sr. advisor to U.S. Congress, Washington, 1982-85; bd. trustees Corpus Christi Librs., 1987-90; mem. LWV, 1989—; mem. Friends Corpus Christi Librs., publicity chmn., 1988; mem. Corpus Christi Mus., Corpus Christi Arts Coun., Tex. Commn. of the Arts, 1980—; participant Walk to Emmaus Group, 1990, UPDATE, U. Tex., 1978-90. Recipient Teacher of Yr. Paul Caplan Humanitarian award, 1981, Advanced Senior Option Program award, 1968. Mem. Corpus Christi C. of C. (edn. com., program printing), AAUW, U.S. Press Club, Phi Beta Kappa. Methodist. Home and office: 612 Chamberlain Corpus Christi TX 78404

MCCOY, ELAINE JEAN, Canadian provincial official; b. Brandon, Man., Can., Mar. 7, 1946; d. John Frederick and Jean Stewart (Hope) McC.; m. Miles Hudson Patterson. BA, U. Alta., JD, Degree in Polit. Sci. Bar: Alta. 1970. Head adminstrv. advocacy bar admission program Law Soc. Alta., Edmonton, Can.; mem. pub. utilities bd. Province of Edmonton; barrister Black and Co., Calgary, Alt., Can.; minister consumer and corp. affairs Govt. of Alta., Edmonton, 1986-89, 1989—, apptd. minister labour, 1989—; also responsible for women's issues Alta. Human Rights Commn. and Personal Adminstrn. Office, 1987, 89—. Mem. Legis. Assembly Calgary West, 1986; founder, trustee Angela Cheng Mus.Found., Calgary. Mem. Canadian Bar Assn., Law Soc. Alta. Mem. United Ch. Office: Alta Legislature, 103 Legislature Bldg, Edmonton, AB Canada T5K 2B6

MCCOY, JANICE MAXINE, nurse, administrator; b. Bremerton, Wash., Oct. 11, 1945; d. C. Clark and M. Maxine (Yeakle) Kaiser; m. David L. McCoy, Aug. 27, 1966; children: Marsha Lynn, Mark David. Diploma, St. Lukes Hosp. Sch. Nursing, Cedar Rapids, Iowa, 1966; BS in Health Arts, Coll. St. Francis, Joliet, Ill., 1984; MS Health Svc. Adminstrn., Coll. St. Francis, 1986. R.N., Iowa, Ill., Fla. Office nurse to pvt. practice physician Cedar Rapids, 1966-67; staff nurse U. Iowa Hosp., Iowa City, 1969-70, St. Luke's Meth. Hosp., Cedar Rapids, 1971, Mendota (Ill.) Community Hosp., 1971-74, St. Francis Med. Ctr., Peoria, Ill., 1975-78; patient care coord. Proctor Community Hosp., Peoria, 1978-80; dir. nursing Proctor Community Hosp., 1980-82, v.p. nursing svc., 1982-89; v.p. nursing svc. Cape Canaveral Hosp., Cocoa Beach, Fla., 1989—. Author ednl. materials. Mem. Am. Orgn. Nurse Execs., Ill. Soc. Nurse Mgrs., Fla. Orgn. Nurse Execs. Methodist. Home: 3330 Spartina Ave Merritt Island FL 32953

MCCOY, JOENNE RAE, psychiatric clinic administrator; b. Detroit, Jan. 26, 1941; d. Harlan and Dorothy (Simpson) Heinmiller; children: Harlan Craig, Cathi-Jo. BA, Mich. State U., 1966; MSW, U. Mich., 1983. Tchr. pub. schs., Owosso and Garden City, Mich., 1962-73; psychotherapist, group leader Wayne County Hosp., Mich., 1981-82; psychotherapist East Point, Westland, Mich., 1982-83, Midwest, Dearborn, Mich., 1982-83; owner, dir. Personal Devel. Ctrs., Inc., Plymouth, Mich., 1981—, Co-Dependency

Specialists S.E. Mich. Ltd., Livonia, Mich., 1988—; bd. dirs. Hospice Suport Svcs., Inc., Livonia; cons. Westland (Mich.) Convalescent Ctr., 1983-89; supr. grad. students U. Mich., 1986—; cons., facilitator Women-the Emerging Entrepreneurs, Wayne State U. and Small Bus. Assn., 1985—; chmn. Substance Abuse Com., Plymouth Schs., 1982; cons. Salvation Army, Plymouth. Mem. bd. advisors (newsletter) Personal Performance, Balt., 1986—. Mem. steering com. for neighborhood programs YWCA. Soroptimist scholar, 1982. Mem. NAFE, Internat. Assn. Pediatric Social Workers, Internat. Platform Assn., Mich. Assn. Bereavement Counselors, Families in Crisis: Domestic Violence Inc., Nat. Assn. Social Workers (cert.), Am. Entrepreneurs Assn. Women's Network (pres.), Acad. Cert. Social Workers, Agora Club, Passport Club, Agora Club. Avocation: international business and finance. Home: 37644 N Laurel Park Dr Livonia MI 48152 Office: Co Dependency Specialist SE Mich Ltd PC 37677 Professional Ctr Dr Livonia MI 48154-1114

MCCOY, KATHLEEN LYNNE, writer; b. Dayton, Ohio, Apr. 25, 1945; d. James Lyons and Ethel Elizabeth (Curtis) McC.; B.S. in Journalism, Northwestern U., 1967, M.S. in Mag. Journalism, 1968; m. Robert Miles Stover, May 28, 1977. Freelance writer, 1965—; contbr. to Glamour, Mademoiselle, Ladies Home Jour., Woman's Day, Redbook, Family Circle, Cosmopolitan, TV Guide, Readers Digest, Families, Bride's, Seventeen; feature editor 'TEEN Mag., Los Angeles, 1968-77; columnist Sex and Your Body, Seventeen mag., 1983—; frequent guest various TV, radio talk shows. Mem. Screen Actors Guild, AGVA, AFTRA, NOW, Women in Communications, Soc. Profl. Journalists. Author: Discover Yourself, 1976, Discover Yourself II, 1978, The Teenage Body Book, 1979; Your Guide to Planning Your Future, 1979, The Teenage Survival Guide, 1982, Coping with Teenage Depression: A Parents Guide, 1982, The Teenage Body Book Guide to Sexuality, 1983; The Teenage Body Book Guide to Dating, 1983, The New Teenage Body Book, 1987, Growing and Changing: A Handbook for Pre-Teens, 1987, Solo Parenting: Your Essential Guide, 1987, Changes & Choices: A Junior High Survival Guide, 1989, Crisis Proof Your Teenager, 1990. Office: 1276 E Colorado Ste 208 Pasadena CA 91106

MCCOY, LINDA JANE, social work administrator; b. Cleve., Mar. 7, 1951; d. Edward and Margaret Louise (Craig) Brown; m. Albert P. McCoy, Apr. 15, 1979. Student, Oakland Community Coll., Farmington Hills, Mich., 1984-86, 88; AA, Am. Inst. For Paralegal Studies, Southfield, Mich., 1989. Cert. paralegal. Asst. payment worker Mich. Dept. Social Svcs., Detroit; video data terminal operator Detroit; data processing supr. Gross Pointe Quality Foods, Detroit, Genesco, Nashville. Home: 23015 Twining Dr Southfield MI 48075

MC COY, LOIS CLARK, county official, magazine editor; b. New Haven, Oct. 1, 1920; d. William Patrick and Lois Rosilla (Dailey) Clark; m. Herbert Irving McCoy, Oct. 17, 1943; children: Whitney, Kevin, Marianne, Tori, Debra, Sally, Daniel. BS, Skidmore Coll., 1942; student Mar. Search and Rescue Sch., 1974. Asst. buyer R.H. Macy & Co., N.Y.C., 1942-44, assoc. buyer, 1944-48; instr. Mountain Medicine & Survival, U. Calif. at San Diego, 1973-74; cons. editor Search & Rescue Mag., 1975, Rescue mag., 1988-89; coordinator San Diego Mountain Rescue Team, La Jolla, Calif., 1973-75; exec. sec. Nat. Assn. for Search and Rescue, Inc., Nashville and La Jolla, 1975-80, comptroller, 1980-82; disaster officer San Diego County, 1980-86, Santa Barbara County, 1986—; contbr. editor Rescue Mag., 1989—, editor-in-chief Response! mag., 1982-86; cons. law enforcement div.; Calif. Office Emergency Services, 1976-77; pres. San Diego Com. for Los Angeles Philharmonic Orch., 1957-58. Bd. dirs. Search and Rescue of the Californias, 1976-77, Nat. Assn. for Search and Rescue, Inc., 1980-87, pres., 1985-87, bd. trustees, 1987—; pres. Nat. Inst. For Urban Search & Rescue, 1989—; mem. Gov.'s Task Force on Earthquakes, 1981-82, Earthquake Preparedness Task Force, Seismic Safety Commn., 1982-85. Recipient Hal Foss award for outstanding service to search and rescue, 1982. Mem. AIAA, IEEE, Am. Astronautical Soc., Am. Soc. Indsl. Security, Nat. Assn. for Search & Rescue (Svc. award 1985), Coun. for Survival Edn., Mountain Rescue Assn., Nat. Jeep Search & Rescue Assn., Santa Barbara Mountain Rescue Team, San Diego Amateur Radio Club, Sierra Club. Episcopalian. Author: Search and Rescue Glossary, 1974; contbr. to profl. jours. Office: PO Box 91648 Santa Barbara CA 93190

MCCOY, MARILYN, university official; b. Providence, Mar. 18, 1948; d. James Francis and Eleanor (Regan) McC.; m. Charles R. Thomas, Jan. 28, 1983. BA in Econs., Smith Coll., 1970; M in Pub. Policy, U. Mich., 1972. Dir. Nat. Assn. for Higher Edn. Mgmt. Systems, Boulder, Colo., 1972-80; dir. planning and policy devel. U. Colo., Boulder, 1981-85; v.p. adminstrn. and planning Northwestern U., Evanston, Ill., 1985—; mem. nat. adv. panel Nat. Ctr. for Postsecondary Governance and Fin. Co-author: Financing Higher Education in the Fifty States, 1976, 3d edit., 1982. Bd. dirs. Evanston Hosp., 1988—, United Charities, Chgo., 1988—; Chgo. Met. YMCA, 1989—. Mem. Am. Assn. for Higher Edn., Soc. for Coll. and Univ. Planning (sec., pres., v.p., bd. dirs. 1980—), Assn. for Instnl. Rsch. (pres., v.p., exec. com., publs. bd. 1978-87), Chgo. Network, Chgo. Econ. Club,. Home: 1100 N Lake Shore Dr Chicago IL 60611 Office: Northwestern U 633 Clark St Evanston IL 60208

MCCOY, MARY MARGARET, bakery owner; b. Sioux City, Iowa, Feb. 2, 1948; d. Linus Clement and Cecelia Agnes (Judge) Niemeyer; 1 child, Thomas Crane. BA, St. Mary's Coll., Notre Dame, Ind., 1970; MA, Ball State U., 1973. Vice pres. State Fidelity Savs., Dayton, Ohio, 1979-82; sr. v.p. Mid-Am. Fed., Columbus, Ohio, 1982-85; pres. Fresh Bagel Factory, Centerville, Ohio, 1986—; bd. dirs. Yellow Springs (Ohio) Instruments, Co. Co-author: Curriculum Development: A Humanized Systems Approach, 1974. Bd. dirs. Greene County (Ohio) Domestic Violence Project, 1986—; chair YSI Found. Mem. Women Inc. Home: 1305 Corry St Yellow Springs OH 45387 Office: Fresh Bagel Factory 1286A N Fairfield Rd Dayton OH 45432

MCCOY, PHYLLISTINE, educational association administrator; b. Benton Harbor, Mich., Feb. 12, 1943; d. Phillip Jr. and Daisy Mae (Shaw) McC. BA, Western Mich. U., 1967, MA, 1974. Cert. tchr., Mich. High sch. reading tchr. Kalamazoo, 1967-71; reading specialist Battle Creek (Mich.) Pub. Schs., 1971-78; exec. dir. United Tchrs. of Flint, Mich., 1978-80; negotiation specialist Mich. Edn. Assn., East Lansing, 1980-83; Uniserv exec. Mich. Edn. Assn., Flint, 1983—; fin. planner A.L. Williams Assocs., Flint, 1984-89; tng. specialist Conflict Mgmt. Assocs., Flint, 1987—; cons. NEA, Washington, 1983—. Trainer United Way, Flint, 1983-84, mem. edn. and planning com., 1982-85, chair mktg. task force, 1984-85; cabinet mem. of com. resources div. United Way of Genesee and Lapeer Counties, Mich., 1989, adv. bd., 1990. Named to Western Mich. U. Minority Alumni Wall of Distinction, 1980-87. Mem. NAFE (dir. Flint chpt.), Mid-Mich. Area Exec. Assn. (exec. dir.), Mich. Profl. Staff Assn. (sec. 1979-80, v.p. 1981-83), Nat. Staff Profl. Staff Orgn., Indsl. Rels. Rsch. Assn., Christian Leadership Acad. (pres. 1990). Democrat. Mem. Church of God in Christ. Home: 1153 River Hill Dr Flint MI 48532 Office: Mich Edn Assn 5095 Exchange Dr Flint MI 48507

MCCOY, SHIRLEY TUTT, public school administrator; b. Luray, Va., May 14, 1937; d. William Roosevelt and Edity Ann (Good) Tutt; m. Melvin Rudolph McCoy, Aug. 16, 1958; children: Kimberly Lynn, Kelli Lee. BS, Va. State U., 1958; postgrad., U. Va., U. Ariz. Cert. elem. tchr. Minority achievement specialist Fairfax (Va.) County Pub. Schs., human rels. specialist, tchr.; tchr. Page County Pub. Schs., Luray, Va.; Cons. in field. Contbr. articles to profl. jours. Recipient Outstanding Svc. award PTA, Achievement award. Mem. NEA, VEA, FEA, Black Women United for Action (former founding sec., current spl. projects chair), Area III ABC-RIAC (dir., coord., founder), Phi Delta Kappa (past found. com. chair), Delta Kappa Gamma (1st v.p.).

MCCOY, SUZANNE DONAVANT, data processing executive; b. Arlington, Va., Aug. 12, 1957; d. George Philip Jr. and Mildred Frances (McDonald) Donavant; m. Michael Dale McCoy, Feb. 14, 1987; children: Melissa, Jaime. AA in Indsl. Engring., Wake Tech. Coll., 1983; student Inst. Children's Lit., Strayer Coll. Mem. prin. staff Atlantic Rsch. Co. Profl. Svcs. Group, Rockville, Md.; dir. software div. NuSkin Internat., Inc., Apex, N.C. pres. McCoy Marsh Data Cons., Apex. Mem. NAFE, North East SAS User's Group. Home: 3816 Paynes Ct Apex NC 27502

MCCRACKEN, CARON FRANCIS, communications executive, data processing consultant; b. Detroit, Jan. 12, 1951; d. WIlliam Joseph and Constance Irene (Kramer) McC. AS, Mott Community Coll., 1971; BS, Cen. Mich U., 1973; MA, U. Mich., 1978. Tchr. Elkton, Pigeon, Bayport (Mich.) High Schs., 1973-74, Davison (Mich.) Jr. High Sch., 1974-75; instr. Mott Community Coll., Flint, Mich., 1974-78; planning and research specialist Flint Police Dept., 1977-79; campus coord., programmer Systems & Computer Tech. Corp., Detroit, 1981-82, acad. specialist, 1982-83, mgr. computing systems, 1983-84, mgr. adminstrv. computing systems, 1984-85; communications analyst Fruehauf Corp., Detroit, 1985-86, sr. communications analyst, 1986-87; account cons. US Sprint Communications Co., Detroit, 1987-89; account mgr. US Sprint Communications Corp., Detroit, 1989-90; sr. mgr. Technology Specialists, Inc., Phila., 1990—; adv. bd. CONTEL Bus. Networks, Atlanta, 1987. Mem. Assn. Computing Machinery, Detroit Inst. Arts, Am. Mgmt. Assn., Bikecentennial Club (Missoula, Mont.). Club: Bikecentennial (Missoula, Mont.). Home: 3936 Digby Ct Richmond VA 23233 Office: Technology Specialists Inc Whiteland Pla Ste 160 740 E Lancaster Ave Exton PA 19341

MCCRACKEN, INA, business executive; b. Highland Park, Mich., Oct. 7, 1939; d. James Howard and Lodaskia (Smoot) Smith; children: Michalene, Colet, Paulet, Pauleta. BA, Mich. State U., 1961, MEd, 1980; EdS, Wayne State U., 1982, postgrad. Cert. tchr., adminstr., Mich. Pres. Career Mgmt. Systems, Inc., Detroit; instr. Highland Park Bd. Edn. Mem. Minoirty Bus. Inc. (corr. sec.), Phi Delta Kappa. Office: PO Box 04721 Detroit MI 48204

MCCRACKEN, LINDA, librarian, commercial artist; b. Rochester, N.Y., Apr. 13, 1948; d. Frederick Hugh Craig and Shirley Betty (Shacter) Bickford; m. Alan Cheah, June 13, 1972 (div. 1978); m. Bruce E. McCracken, Sept. 23, 1978 (div. 1985); 1 child, Karen Elizabeth. BA in History, SUNY-Geneseo, 1970, MLS, 1970. Reference libr. Northeastern U., Boston, 1971-72; asst. libr. Burlington Pub. Libr., Mass., 1972-74; rsch. asst. Data Resources, Inc., Lexington, Mass., 1974-76; comml. artist McCracken's, Wolfeboro, N.H. 1973-87; asst. libr. N.H. Vocat.-Tech. Coll., Manchester, 1985-87; libr. N.H. Hosp., Concord, 1987—. Participant paintings Horseheads Mall Art Show (3rd place award 1968); graphic artist Rare Coin Rev. mag., 1983; layout artist quar. book: Market Media Guide, 1979; author Burlington Times-Union, 1973, Pleasant News, 1987-88. Treas. Village Players, Wolfeboro, 1982-83; pub. rels. com. Gov.'s Arts Coun., Wolfeboro, 1982. Mem. State Employees Assn. N.H. Avocations: skiing, gardening, singing, acting, hiking, reading, computers. Home: Box 628 Pine Hill Rd Wolfeboro Falls NH 03896 Office: NH Hosp Profl Libr 105 Pleasant St Concord NH 03301

MCCRARY, EUGENIA LESTER (MRS. DENNIS DAUGHTRY MCCRARY), civic worker, writer; b. Annapolis, Md., Mar. 23, 1929; d. John Campbell and Eugenia (Potts) Lester; m. John Campbell Howard, July 15, 1955 (dec. Sept. 1965); m. Dennis Daughtry McCrary, June 28, 1969; 1 child, Dennis Campbell. AB cum laude, Radcliffe Coll.-Harvard U., 1950; MA, Johns Hopkins U., 1952; postgrad., Harvard U., 1953, Pa. State U., 1953-54, Drew U., 1957-58. Instr. Study of USSR, Munich, 1964. Grad. asst. dept. Romance langs. Pa. State U., 1953-54; tchr. dept. math. The Brearley Sch., N.Y.C., 1954-57; dir. Sch. Langs., Inc., Summit, N.J., 1958-69; trustee Sch. Langs., Inc., Summit, 1960-69. Co-author: Nom de Plume: Eugenia Campbell Lester, (with Allegra Branson) Frontiers Aflame, 1987. Dist. dir. Eastern Pa. and N.J. auditions Met. Opera Nat. Coun., N.Y.C., 1960-66, dist. dir. publicity, 1966-67, nat. vice chmn. publicity, 1967-71, nat. chmn. public rels., 1972-75, hon. nat. chmn. pub. rels., 1976—; bd. govs., chmn. Van Cortlandt House Mus., 1985-90. Mem. Nat. Soc. Colonial Dames Am. (bd. mgrs. N.Y. 1985-90), Met. Opera Nat. Coun., Soc. Mayflower Desc. (former bd. dirs. N.Y. soc., chmn. house com. 1986-89), Soc. Daus. of Holland Dames (bd. dirs. 1982-87, 3d directress gen. 1987—), L'Eglise du Saint-Esprit (vestry 1985-88, sr. warden 1988-90), Huguenot Soc. Am. (governing coun. 1984-90, asst. treas. 1990—), Colony Club (bd. govs., 1988—). Republican. Episcopalian. Home: 24 Central Park S New York NY 10019

MC CRAY, EVELINA WILLIAMS, librarian, researcher; b. Plaquemine, La., Sept. 1, 1932; d. Turner and Beatrice (Green) Williams II; m. John Samuel McCray, Apr. 7, 1955; 1 child, Johnetta McCray Russ. BA, So. U., Baton Rouge, 1954; MS in Library Sci., La. State U., 1962. Librarian. Iberville High Sch., Plaquemine, 1954-70, Plaquemine Jr. High, 1970-75; proofreader short stories, poems Associated Writers Guild, Atlanta, 1982-86; library cons. Evaluation Capitol High Sch., 1964, Iberville Parish Educators Workshop, 1980, Tchrs. Core/Iberville Parish, 1980-81. Contbr. poetry New Am. Poetry Anthology, 1988, The Golden Treasury of Great Poems, 1988. Vol. service Allen J. Nadler Library, Plaquemine, 1980-82; librarian Local Day Care Ctr., Plaquemine, 1978-79; appointee La. Retired Tchrs.' Com. on Info. and Protective Services, 1988—. Recipient Golden Poet award World Poetry, 1988, 89, Blue Ribbon award So. Poetry Assn., 1989. Mem. ALA, La. Library Assn., Nat. Ret. Tchrs. Assn., La Ret. Tchrs. Assn. (cons. ann. workshops 1986—, state appointee to informative and protective services com. 1988—,) Iberville Ret. Tchrs. Assn. (info. and protective services dir. 1981—). Democrat. Baptist. Home: PO Box Q Plaquemine LA 70765

MCCREA, PATRICIA ANNE, military non-commissioned officer; b. Riverside, Calif., Oct. 7, 1945; d. Clarence Edwin and Mathilda Anne (Pfarr) McC.; m. William Louis Pagels, Oct. 7, 1963 (div. June 1982); children—Susan, Theresa, Kathryn, William Patrick. Student U. Md., Evreux, France, 1962-63; BS, SUNY-Buffalo, 1983; postgrad. Genesee Community Coll., 1982-83. enlisted U.S. Army, USAR, 1974—; pers. mgmt. supr. for intelligence, security, ops. and tng. 390th Pers. and Adminstrn. Bn., Richmond, Va., 1985—; program asst. Coop. Extension, Batavia, N.Y., 1980-82; unit adminstr. U.S. Army Res., Richmond, Va., 1984-85; substitute tchr. Alexander Cen. Sch., N.Y., 1982-84; adj. faculty Genesee Community Coll., Batavia, 1982-84. Tutor, officer Lit. Vols. of Am., Batavia, 1982-84. Mem. Va. Right-to-Life Internat. Platform ASsn. Decorated Army Commendation medal, others. Mem. Assn. U.S. Army, NAFE, Am. Soc. Profl. and Exec. Women, DAV (life), Mensa, Amnesty Internat., Am. Legion, DAV Commdr.'s Club. Republican. Roman Catholic. Avocations: needlework, fencing, reading, quilting. Home: 1910 Repp St Highland Springs VA 23075 Office: 6002 Strathmore Rd Richmond VA 23237 also: 11269 E Bennett Rd Grass Valley CA 95945

MCCREA, TERRI LYN, administrative assistant; b. Abbington, Pa., Aug. 24, 1967; d. William John and Jean Carol (Stokes) McC. Student, Lake Sumter Community Coll., Leesburg, Fla., 1989-90. Sr. teller Sun Bank N.A., Leesburg, 1987-90; adminstrv. asst. System One Staffing, Maitland, Fla., 1990—. Mem. NAFE. Office: System One Staffing 2600 Lake Lucien Dr Maitland FL 32751

MCCREARY, JUDY MARIAN, insurance industry executive recruiter; b. Wichita, Kans., Feb. 6, 1946; d. Ira Jennings and Erma Opal (Wagner) Kimball; m. J. B. McCreary, Jan. 22, 1966 (div. 1987); children: Melissa, Matthew. BS in English, Emporia (Kans.) State U., 1971; MS in Curriculum, Kans. State U., 1984. Tchr. English and speech Unified Sch. Dist. 307, Brookville, Kans., 1974-81, Unified Sch. Dist. 305, Salina, Kans., 1981-87; dir. manpower and career devel. Northwestern Mut. Life Ins. Co, Kansas City, Mo., 1987-89; career cons. Northwestern Mut. Life Ins. Co, Fairway, Kans., 1990—; corp. recruiter Christopher & Long, Kansas City, 1989-90; guest lectr. Ft. Hayes State U., 1985, Kans. State U., 1986. Author: Career Path Guide, 1988. Mem. Am. Soc. Tng. and Devel. (advt. com.). Home: 4803 Broadmoor #30 Mission KS 66202

MCCREE, JEANIE COLE, nurse; b. Fostoria, Ohio, Sept. 17, 1949; d. Carlton McCree and Esther Clara (Walter) Cole; m. Danny Neil Baughman, Mar. 21, 1970 (div. 1982); children: Stephanie Ann, Shari Ann. Diploma, Med. Coll. of Ohio at Toledo, 1970. RN, Ill., Mo., Ohio. Asst. head nurse Blanchard Valley Hosp., Findlay, Ohio, 1970-72; emergency room nurse Wilson Meml. Hosp., Sidney, Ohio, 1972-76, Decatur (Ill.) Meml. Hosp., 1976-77; staff nurse The Decatur Clinic, 1977-80; loan processor The Kissell Co., Springfield, Ohio, 1983-84; pvt. practice staff relief nurse Springfield and Dayton, Ohio, 1984-85; charge nurse emergency dept. Naples (Fla.) Community Hosp., Dayton, 1985—.

MCCRIMMON, BARBARA SMITH, writer, librarian; b. Anoka, Minn., May 3, 1918; d. Webster Roy and Jessie (Sargeant) Smith; m. James McNab McCrimmon, June 10, 1939; children—Kevin Mor, John Marshall. B.A., U. Minn., 1939; M.S.L.S., U. Ill., 1961; Ph.D., Fla. State U., 1973. Asst. librarian Ill. State Nat. Hist. Survey, Champaign, Ill., 1961-62; research assoc. Bur. Community Planning, U. Ill., Champaign, 1962-63; librarian Ill. Water Survey, Champaign, 1964-65; librarian Am. Meteorol. Soc., Boston, 1965-67; editorial asst. Jour. Library History, Tallahassee, 1967-69, 73-74; adj. asst. prof. Sch. Library Sci., Fla. State U., Tallahassee, 1976-77. Author: Power, Politics and Print, 1981, Richard Garnett: The Scholar as Librarian, 1989; editor: American Library Philosophy, 1975; contbr. articles to profl. jours. Mem. ALA, Bibliog. Soc. Am., Pvt. Libraries Assn., Beta Phi Mu, Manuscript Soc. Democrat.

MCCRORY, ELLANN, radiologist; b. Butler Springs, Ala., Mar. 22, 1936; d. William Bryant and Eva Estelle (Stabler) McCrory. BS, U. Ala., 1956; MD, Med. Coll. Ala., 1960. Rotating intern Mercy Hospital Birmingham, Ala., 1960-61; resident Bapt. Meml. Hosp., Memphis, 1961-64; instr. radiology U. 1960-61; pvt. practice radiology, Fort Payne, Ala., 1975—; chief of med. staff DeKalb County Hosp., 1977; speaker in field. Trustee, pres. Landmarks Inc., 1978-79. Recipient Bausch and Lomb Sci. award, 1953. Mem. Am. Coll. Radiology, Radiol. Soc. N.A., AMA, Am. Med. Women's Assn., So. Radiol. Soc., Am. Roentgen Ray Soc., Am. Assn. Women Radiologists (treas. 1987—), Mid-South Med. Assn., Med. Assn. Ala. (v.p. 1986-87, bd. censors 1988—), Ala. Bd. Med. Examiners, Ala. State Com. Pub. Health, DeKalb County Med. Soc. (pres. 1977), So. Med. Assn., Ala. Radiol. Soc., Fort Payne C. of C. (bd. dirs. 1979-80) Ala. Hist. Soc., U. Ala. Alumni Assn. (pres. DeKalb County chpt. 1977, nat. dist. v.p.), Phi Beta Kappa, Alpha Lambda Delta. Methodist. Home: 1408 Alabama Ave SW Fort Payne AL 35967 Office: 309 Medical Center Dr PO Box 1298 Fort Payne AL 35967

MCCRORY, SHIRLEY TILL, internal bank auditor; b. Bay Minette, Ala., Apr. 1, 1935; d. Samuel Ben Sr. and P. Gertrude (Johnson) Till; m. Edward R. McCrory, Sept. 14, 1958; children: Florence Allison McCrory Myrick, Paige Loanne McCrory Tanner. Grad. high sch., Georgiana, Ala.; student. Am. Inst. Banking, Mobile and Montgomery, Ala. Teller, bookkeeper Citizens Bank, Georgiana, 1953-58; sec., bookkeeper Coastal Beauty & Barber Supply, Mobile, Ala., 1958-60; head teller Comml. Guaranty Bank, Mobile, 1965-68, Cen. Bank Mobile, 1972-74; asst. head teller Merchants Nat. Bank, Mobile, 1968-71; asst. mgr., loan officer 1st Nat. Bank Citizens Branch, Georgiana, 1975-84; auditor, compliance officer 1st Nat. Bank Greenville (Ala.), 1984—. Mem. Inst. Internal Auditing (1st v.p. 1989). Home: 560 Industry Rd Greenville AL 36037 Office: 1st Nat Bank Greenville PO Box 508 Greenville AL 36037

MCCUBBIN, SUSAN BRUBECK, real estate executive; b. Decatur, Ill., Mar. 16, 1948; d. Rodney Earl Brubeck and Marilyn Jean (McMahon) Hopkins; m. Martin Charles Resnik, May 18, 1967 (div. 1974); 1 child, Martin Charles Jr.; m. William James McCubbin, May 30, 1987. LLB, Western State U., Fullerton, Calif., 1977. Bar: Calif. 1989; lic. real estate broker, Calif. Ptnr. Blue Chip Constrn. Co., Santa Ana, Calif., 1969-73; pres. Brubeck Co., San Francisco and Newport Beach, Calif., 1973-78; sole practice San Francisco, 1978-79; sr. mktg. cons., broker Grubb & Ellis Co., San Francisco, 1979-87; pres. Greenwich Corp., San Rafael, Calif., 1987—. Columnist Automotive Age Mag., 1974-75. Chmn. U.S. Senate Primary Campaign, Orange County, Calif., 1976. Republican.

MCCUE, MIRIAM EUGENIA, retired clinical psychologist; b. Denver, Nov. 4, 1917; d. John Francis and Miriam Genevive (Keliher) Crowley; m. John Joseph Gerald McCue, Dec. 19, 1949; 1 child, Brian. BA, U. Wyo., 1939; MA, Fordham U., 1940, PhD, 1944. Prof. psychology Rosemont (Pa.) Coll., 1941-44; asst. prof. Smith Coll., Northampton, Mass., 1946-49; chief psychologist VA Clinic, Lowell, Mass., 1950-52; staff psychologist VA Med. Ctr., Bedford, Mass., 1963-84. With USN, 1944-46. Mem. Am. Psychol. Assn., Mass. Psychol. Assn., Eastern Psychol. Assn., New Eng. Soc. for Behavioral Analysis & Therapy. Republican. Roman Catholic. Home: 20 N Hancock St Lexington MA 02173

MCCUISTION, PEG OREM, hospice administrator; b. Houston, July 28, 1930; d. William Darby and Dorothy Mildred (Beckett) Orem; m. Palmer Day McCuistion, Sept. 4, 1949 (div. 1960); 1 child, Leeanne E. BBA, Southwest Tex. State, 1963; MBA, George Washington U., 1968; EdD, Wayne State U., 1989. Patient care adminstr. Holy Cross Hosp., Silver Spring, Md., 1968-79; exec. dir. Hospice of S.E. Mich., Southfield, 1979-86, Hospice Austin, Tex., 1987—; bd. dirs. Projects Transitions, Austin, 1989—, Community Home for the Elderly, Austin, 1989—. Fellow Am. Coll. Health Care Execs. (membership com.); mem. Tex. Hospice Orgn. (exec. com. standards and ethics com., edn. com., chair legis. com.). Mich. Hospice Orgn. (chair edn. com., bd. dirs.), Nat. Hospice Orgn. (chair standards and accreditation com.), Internat. Hospice Inst. (assoc.). Office: Hospice Austin 5555 N Lamar D-107 Austin TX 78751

MCCULLEY, SANDRA KAY, finance company official; b. Eccles, W.Va., Feb. 12, 1957; d. Benton H. and Nina L. (McCormick) McC. AS in Bus., Ind. U., Kokomo, 1986. Asst. mgr. Furniture City USA, Kokomo, 1978-87, Gen. Fin. Co., Kokomo, 1987-88; mgr. Am. Gen. Fin. Co., Kokomo 1988—. Mem. Kokomo C. of C., Kappa Alpha Theta. Democrat. Baptist. Home: 1103 Peace Pipe Dr Kokomo IN 46902 Office: Am Gen Fin Co 1611 E Markland Ave Kokomo IN 46901

MCCULLOCH, CATHY MARIE, sales executive; b. Ft. Benning, Ga., May 29, 1954; d. Richard and Eleanor Faye (Nusser) McC. BS in Econs. and Mgmt., Mich. State U., 1976. Sales rep. Bristol-Myers Corp., Detroit, 1977-81, Advanced Care Products div. Ortho Pharm. Corp., Columbus, Ohio, 1981-83; unit mgr. Advanced Care Products div. Ortho Pharm. Corp., Raritan, N.J., 1983-85, mgr., spl. products, 1985-87; dist. mgr. Playtex Family Products Corp., Stamford, Conn., 1987—. Mem. NAFE, Am. Mgmt. Assn. Office: PO Box 670176 Marietta GA 30066

MCCULLOUGH, BARBARA ANNE FERGUSON, facilities manager; b. Irvington, N.J., Oct. 12, 1957; d. Thomas Bernard and Barbara Louise (Davis) Downey; m. Oct. 7, 1989. BA, Kean Coll., Union, N.J., 1975-79. Cert. Tchr., N.J. Asst. office mgr. Essex Travel Service, Cranford, N.J., 1978-84, Lightolier Inc., Secaucus, N.J., 1984—; edn. planner State of N.J. Edn. Dept., (Old Bridge, N.J., 1988; facilities supr. Gen. Chem., Parsippany, N.J., 1989; facilities mgr. Electronic Data Systems, Clifton, N.J., 1989—; supr. Spl. Olympics, Cranford N.J. 1979-81; program dir. Assn. for Retarded Citizens, So. Plainfield N.J. 1980-84; organizer M.S. Found., Teaneck N.J. 1985—. Recipient Scholarship for service award Internat. Frat. Sorority Council, Union N.J., 1978, Named 1979 Who's Who in Am. Coll. and U., Kean Coll., Union N.J. 1979. Mem. Loantaka Postal Council, Mail Systems Mgmt. Assn., Am. Mgmt. Assn. Roman Catholic. Office: Electronic Data Systems 203 Main Ave Clifton NJ 07015

MCCULLOUGH, KIMBERLY ANNE, geologist, petroleum company executive, consultant; b. Winona, Minn., Feb. 17, 1956; d. Thomas O. and Barbara B. (Luker) McC. BA cum laude, Winona State U., 1977; MS, Case Western Res. U., 1978. Rsch asst. Case Western Res. U., Cleve., 1977; petrophys. field engr., prodn. unit engr., sr. geol. engr. Shell Oil Co., New Orleans, 1978-83; sr. devel. geologist, dist. exploration supr. Mark Producing, Inc., Houston, 1983-89; co-founder, pres. PetroVal, Inc., Houston, 1989—. Author: Instructional Guitar, 1974; contbr. articles to tech. jours.; song writer. Organizer Career Women's Golf Tourney, Houston, 1983-88; coach co-ednl. softball YMCA, Houston, 1984-88. Fellow HEW, 1977; Nat. Honor Soc. scholar, 1973-74. Mem. Am. Assn. Petroleum Geologists, Am. Inst. Profl. Geologists, Houston Geol. Soc. Republican. Methodist. Office: PetroVal Inc 9801 Westheimer Ste 208 Houston TX 77042

MCCULLY, RUTH ALIDA, educator; b. Port Huron, Mich., Feb. 13, 1933; d. Leon Eugene Lounsberry and Rachel Elizabeth (DeSerano) Lounsberry; m. Donald Cecil McCully, Feb. 8, 1952; children: Stephen Donald, Robert Leon, Julie Ann. BS, Ea. Mich. U., 1976, MA, 1980. Asst. children's librarian Monroe County Library, Mich., 1962-64; dir. Weekday Nursery

Sch., Youngstown, Ohio, 1964-71; dir. children's programs Lake-in-the-Woods, Ypsilanti, Mich., 1974-76; tchr. 1st grade Dundee Community Schs., Mich., 1976-88; tchr. young fives Dundee Community Schs., 1988—; tchr. young fives. Lay speaker Ann Arbor Dist., United Meth. Ch., 1979—; chmn. Dundee Community Caring and Sharing, 1982—; active Monroe County Food Bank, 1983—, Dundee Interfaith Coun., 1984—, Dundee Area Against Substance Abuse, 1984-88. Named Woman of Yr., United Meth. Women, Dundee United Meth. Ch., 1983, United Meth. Ann Arbor Dist. Caring Connection, Coun. on Ministries. Mem. NEA, Mich. Edn. Assn., Mich. Sch. Vols. Assn., Monroe County Edn. Assn., Mich. Reading Assn., Dundee Sch. Employees Club (sec. 1985-86), Nat. Assn. Edn. Young Children, Mich. Assn. Edn. Young Children. Avocations: playing piano/guitar, needlework, sketching/painting, gardening, reading. Home: 510 E Monroe St Dundee MI 48131

MCCUNE, AMY REED, evolutionary biologist; b. Cin., May 31, 1954; d. Homer Wallace and Virginia Reed (Engbers) McC.; m. David Ward Winkler, Apr. 26, 1986. BA, Brown U., 1976; PhD, Yale U., 1982. Post-doctoral fellow Miller Inst. for Basic Rsch. in Sci. U. Calif. Berkeley, Berkeley, Calif., 1982-83; asst. prof. Cornell U., Ithaca, N.Y., 1983-89; assoc. prof. Cornell U., Ithaca, 1989—; bd. govs. Am. Soc. Ichhthyologists and Herpetologists, 1989—; coun. Soc. Systematic Zoology, 1989—. Assoc. editor: Jour. of Vertebrate Paleontology, 1987-92; contbr. articles to p rofl. jours. Mem. AAAS, Soc. for the Study of Evolution, Soc. for Study of Systematic Zoology, Am. Soc. Ichthyologists and Herpetologists, Soc. Vertebrate Paleontology, Paleontological Rsch. Inst. (trustee 1985-87), Am. Assn. for Zool. Nomennature. Office: Cornell U Sect Ecology Corson Hall Ithaca NY 14853

MCCUNE, MARY JOAN HUXLEY, microbiology educator; b. Lewistown, Mont., Jan. 14, 1932; d. Thomas Leonard and Anna Dorothy (Hardie) Huxley; m. Ronald William McCune, June 7, 1965; children: Anna Orpha, Heather Jean. BS, Mont. State Coll., 1953; MS, Wash. State U., 1955; PhD, Purdue U., 1965. Rsch. technician VA Hosp., Oakland, Calif., 1956-59; bacteriologist U.S. Naval Radiol. Def. Lab., San Francisco, 1959-61; teaching assoc. Purdue U., West Lafayette, Ind., 1961-65, vis. asst. prof., 1965-66; asst. prof. Occidental Coll., L.A., 1966-69; asst. rsch. bacteriologist II U. Calif., L.A., 1969-70; affiliate asst. prof. Idaho State U., Pocatello, Idaho, 1970-80, from asst. prof. to prof. microbiology, 1980—; instr. U. Calif., Davis, 1964. Contbr. articles to profl. jours. Pres. AK chpt. PEO, Pocatello, 1988-89. David Ross fellow Purdue U., 1964; named Outstanding Alumna, Mont. State U., 1975. Mem. Am. Soc. for Microbiology (Intermountain br., v.p. 1988-89, pres. 1989-90), AAAS, N.Y. Acad. Sci., Idaho Acad. Sci. (trustee 1987—), Sigma Xi, Sigma Delta Epsilon. Presbyterian. Home: 30 Colgate Pocatello ID 83201 Office: Idaho State U Dept Biol Scis Pocatello ID 83209

MCCUNE, NANCY BENTLEY, accounting administrator; b. Eugene, Oreg., Nov. 11, 1946; d. Arleigh James and Corinne Anne (Loyd) Bentley; m. Kenneth Ray McCune, Dec. 17, 1983; children: Steven Allen Tucker, Kelly Anne Tucker. BBA, Nat. U., 1987. Supr. gen. acctg. Tarmac Calif. Inc., Indio; office mgr. Ellis Transp., Indio; staff acct. Massey Sand & Rock Co., Indio. Mem. NAFE, Data Processing Mgmt. Assn. Republican. Home: 72-970 Deer Grass Dr Palm Desert CA 92260 Office: 43-850 Monroe St Indio CA 92201

MCCURDY, MARY JACQUELINE, lawyer; b. Balt., Dec. 1, 1933; d. Robert Davis and Lillian J. (Schmidt) McC. BA, Hood Coll., 1955; JD, U. Md., 1958. Bar: Md. 1958. Asst. state's atty. County of Baltimore, 1962-63, asst. county solicitor, 1967-68; mem. Md. Ho. of Dels., 1963-66; assoc. gen. counsel Distilled Spirits Coun. U.S., 1969-76; v.p. Joseph E. Seagram & Sons, Inc., N.Y.C., 1979—. Trustee Hood Coll., Social Security Fund Distillery Wine and Allied Workers Internat. Union AFL-CIO; bd. visitors Towson State U. Mem. Md. State Bar Assn., N.Y. Bar Assn., Balt. County Bar Assn., Nat. Assn. Alcoholic Beverage Importers (bd. dirs.), Women's Assn. Allied Beverage Industries, Com. of 200. Democrat. Episcopalian. Office: Joseph E Seagram & Sons Inc 375 Park Ave New York NY 10152*

MCCURRY, VIRGINIA MARIE, funeral home executive; b. Brunswick, Mo., Aug. 13, 1928; d. Otto John and Bertha S. (Reigelsberger) Reichert; m. Laurance Elmo McCurry, Jan. 10, 1949; (dec. Dec. 1971); children—Gregory, Kenneth, Carolyn, Debra, Laurance, Richard, Kelly, Mark. Student pub. schs., Brunswick. Funeral dir. McCurry-Berry Funeral Home, Brunswick, 1965—. Active St. Mary's Alter Soc., Brunswick. Mem. Mo. Funeral Dirs. Assn., Nat. Funeral Dirs. Assn., TTT Soc. Democrat. Roman Catholic. Home: 309 Vine Brunswick MO 65236 Office: McCurry-Berry Funeral Home 511 W Broadway Brunswick MO 65236

MCCUTCHEN, AUDREY JEAN, educational counselor; b. Chgo., Mar. 23, 1942; d. Charles John and Theresa Mary (Sudlik) Walters; 1 child, Joel D. BA in Elem. Edn., Colo. State Coll., 1962; MA in Guidance and Counseling, U. Denver, 1968; MA in Mgmt., Human Rels. and Orgnl. Behavior, U. Phoenix, Denver, 1984; cert. in occupational edn., Colo. Community Colls., 1988. Cert. profl. elem. edn. tchr., Colo. Tchr. Mapleton Pub. Schs., Denver, 1962-68, ednl. counselor, 1968—, counselor, adminstrv. asst., 1976-77, counselor, spl. edn. case mgr., 1979—, counselor added dist. high risk student rsch., 1983—; chair counseling dept. Skyview High Sch., 1990—; assoc. Carlson Corp.-Performax System Internat., Denver, 1985—. Contbr. articles to profl. jours. Sch. liaison sch., hosp. and agy. com. Children's Hosp., Denver, 1986—; parenting instr. Mapleton Pub. Schs., 1987; coord. Children's Mini Sermons Unity Ch. of Denver, 1986-88, counselor, parenting coord., 1986-88; bd. dirs. Northglenn City Bd. Adjustments, 1985—, Northglenn Bond Bd., 1989-91; instr. Parks Jr. Coll., Denver, 1988—. Mem. NEA, Colo. Edn. Assn., Mapleton Edn. Assn., Am. Assn. for Counseling and Devel., Assn. for Humastic Ednl. Devel., Colo. Counseling Inst. (counselor, bd. dirs. 1985-88), Kappa Delta Pi. Home: 1283 W 103d Pl Denver CO 80221

MCCUTCHEN, EDNA ELIZABETH, counselor; b. Washington, Iowa, Sept. 6, 1914; d. Charles Sanford and Gertrude Josephine (Swift) Ragan; m. Carl Richard McC., July 3, 1938; children: Evelyn Hitchcock, Carl Richard III, Charles. BA cum laude, Calif. State U., Long Beach, 1971. Researcher State Univ. System, Iowa, 1953-62, Gallup Poll, Palos Verdes (Calif.) Estates, and Iowa, 1954-68, Palos Verdes Estates, 1960-69; counselor for family svc. Long Beach, 1971-73; social worker L.A. County, 1973-83; pvt. practice in counseling Long Beach, 1983—; vol. Gov.'s Study of Aged State of Iowa, 1960-69; lectr., substitute tchr. for Confraternity of Christian Doctrine at St. Bartholomew's, Long Beach. Insp. election bds., Los Angeles County, Long Beach, 1964—; crew leader U.S. Census, Washington County, Iowa, 1950; Eucharistic min. St. Bartholomew's Ch. Recipient Commendation Community Svc. award Family Svc., Long Beach, 1972. Mem. LWV, AAUW, Nat. Social Workers, Consumer's Union-Consumer's Rsch., DAR (sec. 1948-49), Dau. Am. Colonists, Friends of Library, Phi Kappa Phi. Home: 3435 E First St Long Beach CA 90803

MCDADE, SHARON ANN, academic administrator; b. Middletown, Ohio, Sept. 16, 1952; d. Robert James and Ferne Eileen (Hartel) McD. BS in Edn., Miami U., Oxford, Ohio, 1974; MFA in Theatre, Ohio State U., 1977; EdD, Harvard U., 1986. Asst. prof. theater Univ. Evansville, Ind., 1977-81; rsch. assoc. Consortium on Financing Higher Edn., Cambridge, Mass., 1981-82; rsch. assoc. for Dr. Ernest Lynton Univ. Mass., Boston, 1982-83; asst. sr. tutor Leverett Ho. Harvard U., Cambridge, 1981—, dir. Inst. Ednl. Mgmt., 1985—; cons. Coll. Tropical Agriculture Univ. Hawaii, Honolulu, 1988-89, Daytona Beach (Fla.) Community Coll., 1989—, Tufts Univ., Medford, Mass., 1984, Newberry Coll., Boston, 1984; presenter various profl. ednl. orgns., 1985—. Author: Higher Education Leadership Enhancing Skills Through Professional Development Programs, 1987. Harris and Eliza Kempner grad. fellow Kempner Found., Tex., 1982-83; Lehman scholar Harvard U., 1983-84. Mem. Am. Assn. Higher Edn. (bd. dirs. 1988—), Am. Coun. Edn. (mem. nat. leadership group 1985—), Am. Edn. Rsch. Assn., Nat. Assn. Student Personnel Adminstrs., Am. Coun. Edn.'s Nat. Identification Program (Mass. chpt.), Alpha Phi (pres. Boston chpt. 1982-84, Michaelanean award 1984). Presbyterian. Office: Inst Ednl Mgmt Harvard Grad Sch of Edn Gutman Libr #339 Appian Way Cambridge MA 02138

MCDAID, JANET LITWINOWICH, educational administrator; b. Kittery, Me.; d. Zenon John and Ada Margaret (Pacelt) Litwinowich; m. Edward Patrick McDaid, Aug. 28, 1969; children: Michael Fitzpatrick, Ashley Margaret. BS, Gorham State Coll., 1965; MEd, U. Wash., 1970; PhD, Claremont Grad. Sch., 1986. Cert. state adminstr., pupil pers. svcs., Calif.; lic. ednl. psychologist, Calif. Tchr. Waterville (Maine) Sch. Dist., 1967-68, Bellevue (Wash.) Sch. Dist., 1968-69; psychologist Newport New (Va.) Pub. Schs., 1970-72, Edmonds (Wash.) Sch. Dist., 1972-73; rsch. assoc. U. Wash., Seattle, 1974-76; early childhood assessment coord. Seattle Sch. Dist., 1977-81; sp. edn. program psychologist San Diego City Schs., 1981-85, program evaluator, 1986—; lectr. Hampton (Va.) Inst., 1972; cons. USIA, Washington, 1988; mem. evaluation working com. Calif. State Dept. Edn., Sacramento, 1987-89; program effectiveness Task Force, 1987-88; evaluation cons. Calif. State Dept. Justice and Edn., Sacramento, 1986—; field reader of grant proposals U.S. Dept. Edn., Washington, 1986—; adj. prof. U.S. Internat. U., Calif., 1989—. Author: Special Education in United States, 1988. Vol. U.S. Peace Corp, Kabul, Afghanistan, 1965-67; troop leader San Diego-Imperial Coun. Girl Scouts U.S., San Diego, 1984—. Grantee, Wash. State Dept. Edn., Olympia, 1979-81, Calif. State Dept. Edn., Sacramento, 1983-84. Mem. Assn. Calif. Sch. Adminstrs., Coun. Exceptional Children, Coun. Adminstrs. Spl. Edn., Am. Ednl. Rsch. Assn., Calif. Ednl. Rsch. Assn. Democrat. Roman Catholic. Office: San Diego City Schs Planning Rsch and Evaluation 4100 Normal St San Diego CA 92103

MCDANIEL, AUDREY MAY, author, radio personality, nonprofit foundation executive; b. Washington, Feb. 24, 1908; d. Dwight David and Jenette Marie (Nolan) Stansell; m. Valrie Shields McDaniel, 1941; 1 child, Val. Pres. Audrey McDaniel Faith and Hope Found., Arlington, Va., 1974—; featured personality Sta.-WFAX, Falls Church, Va., and other stas., 1963—, Abiding Love, 1974—. Featured in series Faith and Life, Sta.-WRC-TV, NBC, Washington, 1973, A Christmas Rose spl., Sta.-WTKK-TV, Manassas, Va., 1982, in series Capital Life, Sta.-WTKK-TV, 1973. Author books, including: (inspirational) The Greatest of These is Love, 1962, Forget-Me-Nots of Love, 1964, Garden of Hope, 1966, God is There, 1969, A Christmas Rose, 1971, Abiding Love, 1973, Only Believe in Him, 1977, Love's Promise, 1980, Hope for Every Heart, 1986; (autobiography) Touched by the Master, 1975; author words: Hymn Gems From Sacred Memory Time, 1967. Author, narrator audiocassette: Faith, Hope and Love, 1986. Mem. Nat. League Am. Pen Women (D.C. br.) (past nat. chaplain, Disting. Pen Woman award 1979), ASCAP, Internat. Platform Assn. Methodist. Home and Office: 5800 N 11th St Arlington VA 22205

MCDANIEL, BESSIE LEE, county government official, counselor; b. Ravenna, Ky., Aug. 8, 1937; d. Jasper and Lula Ree (Marcum) Tipton; m. Marshall Francis Gerhke, May 1, 1958 (div. Aug. 1975); children: Dawn Florence, Marshall Francis II, Michelle Robin, Hope Edwina; m. Alfred Eugene McDaniel, Nov. 11, 1986. Cert., Brook Army Med. Sch., 1956; cert. floral design, Besmar Coll., 1975; cert., Ill. Bus. Inst., 1978. Florist, co-owner Besmar Flowers, Woodstock, Ill., 1958-75; owner Besmar Kennel, Woodstock and Cary, Ill., 1963-72; mem. faculty McHenry County Coll., Crystal Lake, Ill., 1977-80; dir. Vets. Work Experience Program, McHenry County, Ill., 1977-80; state svc. officer AMVETS, Chgo., 1980-81, 84-86; nursing companion Ruth Reid Home, Hampshire, Ill., 1981-82; supt. Lake County Vets. Assistance Commn., Waukegan, Ill., 1986-90; mme. adv. coun. Vets. for Housing, Waukegan, 1986-88; mem. adv. bd. Salvation Army, Waukegan, 1987—; bd. dirs. Lake County Coalition for the Homeless, Waukegan. Charter mem. McHenry County Forum, Woodstock, 1978-80; sponsor, counselor Teenage Runaways, Woodstock, 1973-75, Troubled Teens, Woodstock, 1973-78; founder, counselor Teenage Suicide Prevention Hotline, Woodstock, 1981-83; mem. Mayor's Commn. to Keep Zion Beautiful, 1987; sponsor Prevention Child Abuse Program, 1977-78. Cpl. U.S. Army, 1955-58. Mem. AMVETS, Pearl Harbor Meml. Post 245 (life, sec. 1981), N.Chgo. VA Med. Ctr. (adv. com. 1988), Ill. Am. Vets. (life), Nat. Vets. Cemetery. Home: 445 N "C" St Poplar Bluff MO 63901

MCDANIEL, BETTY FLOWERS, social services administrator; b. Loganport, Ind., May 9, 1940; d. Mary (Smith) Moore; m. Thomas A. McDaniel (div. 1980); children: Merrijo E., Christopher A. BA, Northeastern Ill. U., 1978, Nat. Coll. Edn., Chgo., 1983. Sec. Cath. Charities, Chgo., 1967-69, office mgr., 1969-71, program dir., 1971-73, dept. dir., 1973—; aerobics dir. Hyde Park Athletic Club, Chgo., 1981-83; owner, operator Stretch-Nastics Health Fitness Studio, Chgo., 1983-85, Joyful Noise Christian Entertainment Ctr., Chgo., 1987—, adv. bd. Kaepa Aerobic Shoes, 1987—, Reebok Aerobic Shoes, 1985—, Michael Reese Health Plan, Chgo., 1985—; bd. dirs. House of Good Shephed, Chgo. Author: Health and Fitness Guide, 1987; producer, performer: Betty Mac's Free Style Workout, 1986. Bd. dirs. South Shore YMCA, Chgo., 1987—. Named one of Outstanding Women Project Image, 1985; recipient Kizzy Image award Kizzy Scholarship Fund, 1989. Mem. Cath. Charities USA, League Black Women. Mem. Pentecostal Ch. Home: 5125 S Ingleside Chicago IL 60615 Office: Cath Charities 721 N LaSalle Chicago IL 60610

MCDANIEL, LISA MAE, financial analyst; b. Winchester, Va., Nov. 7, 1964; d. Frank and Orpha (Miller) McD. BBA, Shenandoah Coll., 1988; MBA, Nova U., 1989; AAS, Lord Fairfax Coll., 1986. Budget analyst Frederick County Pub. Schs., Winchester; data processing documentation and tng. cons. BTC Enterprises Inc., Winchester; project mgr. comml. products div. Rubbermaid, Inc., Winchester, computer operator; accounts payable clk. GE, Winchester; fin. analyst Loudoun Healthcare, Inc., Leesburg, Va. Mem. First Assembly of God Campus Christian Fellowship, Lord Fairfax Leadership Orgn., Students in Free Enterprise,. Recipient Wall St. Jour. Bus. award, U.S. Achievement Acad. Scholatic All. Am. Mem. Bus. and Profl. Women, Student Govt. Assn. (sec., treas.), Phi Beta Lambda (pres.). Home: 2921 First St Winchester VA 22601

MCDANIEL, MARY GRACE COEN, dentist; b. Nashville, Oct. 22, 1958; d. Daniel Kennedy and Suzanne Elizabeth (Shea) Coen; m. Marc Warren McDaniel, Aug. 20, 1983; children: Megan Elizabeth, Melissa Grace. BS, U. Ark., 1981; DDS, Baylor Coll. Dentistry, 1985. Pvt. practice Commerce, Tex., 1985—. Mem. exec. bd. Commerce Pub. Libr., 1986-90; div. chmn. Commerce unit Am. Cancer Soc., 1986. Mem. Commerce Bus. and Profl. Women (treas. 1987, sec. 1988), Rotary Internat. (bd. dirs. 1990), Psychology Club (corr. sec. 1990), Ark. Alumni Assn., Baylor Coll. Dentistry Alumni Assn. Office: 1209 Main St Commerce TX 75428

MCDANIEL, MARY JANE, construction company executive; b. Hopkinsville, Ky., Oct. 3, 1946; d. William E. and Jane (Rowe) Porter; m. Jerry C. McDaniel, Aug. 10, 1963; children: Jerry, Michelle. Student, Gainesville (Ga.) Coll. Treas. McDaniel Grading Inc., Buford, Ga.; with data processing dept. Hess Oil Co., Atlanta; sec., bookkeeper Dixis Constrn. Co., Atlanta. Sec. Gwinnett Co. Supporters of the Gifted, 1977, v.p., 1978; sterring com. St. Edwrds Episcopal Ch., Lawrenceville, Ga., 1987. Mem. Nat. Assn. of Women in Constn. Home: 2164 Gravel Springs Rd Buford GA 30518

MCDANIEL, MYRA ATWELL, lawyer, former state official; b. Phila., Dec. 13, 1932; d. Toronto Canada, Jr. and Eva Lucinda (Yores) Atwell; m. Reuben Roosevelt McDaniel Jr., Feb. 20, 1955; children—Diane Lorraine, Reuben Roosevelt III. BA, U. Pa., 1954; JD, U. Tex., 1975; LLD, Huston-Tillotson Coll., 1984, Jarvis Christian Coll., 1986. Bar: Tex. 1975, U.S. Dist. Ct. (we. dist.) Tex. 1977, U.S. Dist. Ct. (so. and no. dists.) Tex. 1978, U.S. Ct. Appeals (5th cir.) 1978, U.S. Supreme Ct. 1978, U.S. Dist. Ct. (ea. dist.) Tex. 1979. Asst atty. gen. State of Tex., Austin, 1975-81, chief taxation div., 1979-81, gen. counsel to gov., 1983-84, sec. of state, 1984-87; asst. gen. counsel Tex. R.R. Commn., Austin, 1981-82; gen. counsel Wilson Cos., San Antonio and Midland, Tex., 1982; assoc. Bickerstaff, Heath & Smiley, Austin, 1984, ptnr., 1987—; mem. asset mgmt. adv. com. State Treasury, Austin, 1984-86; mem. legal affairs com. Criminal Justice Policy Council, Austin, 1984-86; mem. legal affairs com. Inter-State Oil Compact, Oklahoma City, 1984-86; bd. dirs. Austin Cons. Group, 1983-86; lectr. in field. Contbr. articles to profl. jours., chpts. to books. Del. Tex. Conf. on Libraries and Info. Scis., Austin, 1978, White House Conf. on Libraries and Info. Scis., Washington, 1979; mem. Library Services and Constrn. Act Adv. Council, 1980-84, chmn., 1983-84; mem. long range plan task force Brackenridge Hosp., Austin, 1981; clk. vestry bd. St. James Episcopal Ch., Austin, 1981-83, 88-90; bd. visitors U. Tex. Law Sch., 1983—, vice chmn., 1983-85; bd. dirs. Friends of Ronald McDonald House of Cen. Tex., Women's Advocacy, Inc., Capital Area Rehab. Ctr.; trustee Episcopal Found. Tex., 1986-89, St. Edward's U., Austin, 1986—, chmn. acad. com. 1988—; chmn. div. United Way/Capital area campaign, 1986; active nat. adv. bd. Leadership Am.; trustee Episcopal Sem. of SW, 1990—. Recipient Tribute to 28 Black Women award Concepts Unltd., 1983; Focus on women honoree Serwa Yetu chpt. Mt. Olive grand chpt. Order of Eastern Star, 1979, Woman of Yr. Longview Metro C. of C., 1985, Woman of Yr. Austin chpt. Internat. Tng. in Communication, 1985, Citizen of Yr. Epsilon Iona chpt. Omega Psi Phi. Mem. ABA, Am. Bar Found., Tex. Bar Found. (trustee 1986-89), Travis County Bar Assn., Travis County Women Lawyers' Assn., Austin Black Lawyers Assn., State Bar Tex. (chmn. Profl. Efficiency & Econ. Rsch. subcom. 1978-84), Golden Key Nat. Honor Soc., Longhorn Assocs. for Excellence in Women's Athletes (adv. coun. 1988—), Omicron Delta Kappa, Delta Phi Alpha, Order Coif (hon. mem.). Democrat. Home: 3910 Knollwood Dr Austin TX 78731 Office: San Jacinto Ctr 98 San Jacinto Blvd #1800 Austin TX 78701

MCDANIEL, SUSAN HOLMES, psychologist; b. Jersey City, Oct. 31, 1951; d. Grover Cleveland and Anna Lou (Toms) McD.; m. David Morton Siegel, July 22, 1984; children: Hanna, Marisa. BA, Duke U., 1973; PhD, U. N.C., 1979. Fellow in family therapy Tex. Rsch. Inst. Mental Scis., Houston, 1980; Supr., staff psychologist W. Monroe Mental Health Ctr., Rochester, N.Y., 1980-82; pvt. practice psychologist Rochester, 1980-88; assoc. prof. psychiatry and family medicine U. Rochester Sch. of Medicine, 1987—; co-dir psychosocial edn. dept. family medicine U. Rochester Sch. of Medicine, 1986—, dir. family therapy tng. program, dept. of psychiatry, 1988—. Co-author: Systems Consultation, 1986, Family-oriented Primary Care, 1990; contbr. articles to profl. jours. Recipient Nat. Patient Care award for innovation in family med. edn. Patient Care, Soc. for Tchrs. Family Medicine, 1988. Mem. Am. Family Therapy Assn., Am. Psychol. Assn. (chair legis. com. 1987—), Soc. for Tchrs. Family Medicine (task force on family medicine and family therapy). Democrat. Office: Dept Family Medicine 885 South Ave Rochester NY 14620

MCDANIEL, VIRGINIA LEE, nurse; b. Balt., Mar. 15, 1937; d. James Dabney and Mary Elizabeth (Dunn) Ferguson; m. Herbert Alton. BS in Nursing, Duke U., 1959. Nurse cons. Vocat. Placement Svsc., Richmond, Va., 1977-79; nurse Sheltering Arms Rehab. Hosp., Richmond, 1985; nurse cons. Chippenhan Hosp., Richmond, 1979—. Mem. adv. bd. Lucy Corr Nursing Home, 1988—; mem. Bon Air Hist. Soc., 1985—, membership chmn., 1987-89. Mem. Va. Assn. for Children and Adults with Learning Disabilities (corr. sec. 1980-81, dir. govt. liaison 1981-85, interagency liaison 1987-88, bd. mem. 1988—), Va. Bd. Rights of the Disabled (vice-chmn. edn. com. 1987-88), Chesterfield Assn. Children and Adults with Learning Disabilities. Home: 358 Janlar Dr Richmond VA 23235

MCDERMID, ALICE MARGUERITE CONNELL (MRS. RALPH MANEWAL MCDERMID), civic and political worker, lecturer; b. Sterling, Ill., May 25, 1910; d. William Hayes and Margaret (Durr) Connell; A.B., U. Ill., 1931; m. Ralph Manewal McDermid, Nov. 28, 1931; children—Ralph Manewal, Jane Dillon (Mrs. Anders Wiberg), Michael Metcalf, John Fairbanks. Bd. dirs. Scarsdale (N.Y.) Woman's Exchange, 1953-60; mem. social service bd. N.Y. Infirmary, 1960-76, vice chmn., 1964-76; trustees team United Hosp. Fund, 1965-75; case policy bd. Spence-Chapin Adoption Service, 1960—; fund raising Greer Sch., 1958-73, Vis. Nurse Assn., 1960-64; co-chmn. UN Program, Westchester County; founder Jane Todd Meml. Scholarship, 1966; mem. adv. council Morse Gallery of Art, Winter Park, Fla., 1974—; sec. exec. com. Morse Gallery Art Assocs., 1977-78, v.p., 1978-80, pres., 1980-82; bd. dirs. Council Arts and Scis. Central Fla., 1975-86 , v.p., 1976-78; bd. dirs. Charles Hosmer Morse Found., 1980-82. Sec., Young Republicans Ill., 1930-31; bd. dirs. Scarsdale (N.Y.) Women's Rep. Club, 1961-67, pres., 1965-67, legis. chmn., 1981—; del. Washington Conf. Nat. Fed. Rep. Women, 1965-72; mem. council Fedn. Women's Rep. Clubs N.Y. State, 1967-76; Rep. dist. leader, 1967-75; del. Rep. Jud. Conv., 1969-71; vice chmn. Rep. Town Com., 1969-75, mem. Rep. Presidents Club, Scarsdale; mem. N.Y. State Rep. Com., 1970-72; N.Y. Rep. committee woman 90th Assembly Dist., 1970-72. Recipient Rep. Woman of Yr. award, Scarsdale, 1974, other awards. Mem. Women's Rep. Federated Club of Winter Park (pres. 1978-80), Lock Haven Art Center, Friends of Winter Park Library, Winter Park Hist. Soc., English Speaking Union U.S., Town Club Winter Park, Morse Mus. Am. Art., Morse Mus. Art Assocs., Friends of Cornell Fine Arts, Loch Haven Arts Soc., Alpha Xi Delta. Episcopalian. Clubs: Scarsdale Women's, Ladies Harvard, Women's Nat. Rep. (N.Y.C.); Women's of Winter Park (dir. 1977-79), Racquet (Winter Park). Home: 1445 Granville Dr Winter Park FL 32789

MCDERMOTT, CHERYL LYNN, entertainment company executive; b. Glendale, Calif., Dec. 28, 1953; d. Henry Lawrence McDermott and Phyllis (Markel) Grisso. Student, U. Colo., 1977-78; BA, Immaculate Heart Coll., L.A., 1980; JD, Loyola U., L.A., 1983. Legal researcher MGM/UA Entertainment Co., Culver City, Calif., 1983-85; sr. contract adminstr. MGM/UA Entertainment Co., Culver City, 1985-86; dir. internat. TV distbn. Turner Entertainment Co., Culver City, 1986—; panelist, judge Emmy awards, 1987-88; judge ACE awards, 1989-90. Participant Names Project, L.A., 1988. Mem. NATAS (blue ribbon panel for Emmy awards 1987-88, 89-90), Lawyers for Human Rights, Nat. Acad. Cable Programming. Office: Turner Entertainment Co 10100 Venice Blvd Culver City CA 90232

MCDERMOTT, PATRICIA ANN, nurse; b. Bklyn., July 10, 1943; d. John J. and Lillian E. (Sweeney) Skelly; m. Joseph Kevin McDermott, Oct. 5, 1963; children—Colleen Mary, John Joseph. Diploma, Kings County Hosp. Ctr. Sch. Nursing, Bklyn., 1963; B.S. in Health Care Adminstrn., St. Francis Coll., Bklyn., 1979. Staff nurse Kings County Hosp., Bklyn., 1963-66, head nurse outpatient dept., 1966-74; evening supr. Park Nursing Home, Rockaway Park, N.Y., 1974-83; day supr. Hyde Park Nursing Home, Staatsburg, N.Y., 1984-85, dir. nursing, 1985—; propr. retail liquor bus. Active local Girl Scouts U.S.A., 1971-78, Boy Scouts Am., 1978-82, Stella Maris Parents Club, 1978-82, St. Francis de Sales Altar and Rosary Soc., 1970-83, St. Francis de Sales Little League, 1978-80, also softball coach, 1974-77. Republican. Roman Catholic. Avocations: knitting; crocheting; roller skating; bowling; oil painting. Home: 286A Shadblow Ln Clinton Corners NY 12514 Office: Hyde Park Nursing Home Rt 9 Staatsburg NY 12580

MCDERMOTT, PATRICIA LOUISE, lawyer; d. Peter A. and Emily W. McDermott;. Student, Creighton U., 1955-56; BA in Polit. Sci., Idaho State U., 1958; JD, George Washington U., 1961, LLM in Labor Law, 1964. Bar: U.S. Dist. Ct. D.C. 1961, U.S. Ct. Appeals (D.C. cir.) 1961, U.S. Supreme Ct. 1965, Idaho 1966, U.S. Dist. Ct. (ea. dist.) Idaho 1966, U.S. Ct. Appeals (9th cir.) 1966. Mem. staff U.S. senator Frank Church, 1958-61; house counsel United Planning Orgn., Washington, 1964-65; cons. office of manpower U.S. Labor Dept., 1966; ptnr. McDermott & McDermott, 1965-76; sr. ptnr. McDermott, Zollinger, Olley & Israel, Pocatello, Idaho, 1976—; instr. communications law Idaho State U., 1974-77, Rocky Mountain Labor Sch., 1975, 79; speaker various schs. and orgns. Regional v.p. Idaho Young Dems., 1966-68; mem. legis. council Idaho State Legislature, 1973—, Ho. of Reps., 1968—, house minority leader, 1975-80; mem. Idaho Bicentennial Commn., 1969-77, Idaho State Commn. on Women, 1969-72, Employment Security Adv. Council, 1983—, NAACP; mem. adv. bd. Idaho Alcohol Safety Commn., 1968-76; bd. dirs. State Legislature Leaders Found., 1978-80; bd. dirs. Idaho Spl. Olympics Inc., 1985-87; mem. Idaho Commn. on the Bicentennial of U.S. Constitution, 1985—. Recipient Cert. of Appreciation Assn. of Idaho Cities, 1974, Cert. of Appreciation Associated Students Idaho State U., 1975, Martin Luther King award NAACP, 1970. Mem. ABA, Idaho Bar Assn. (criminal law seminar 1971, corrections com., grading team 1975, 76, 78, 80, 82, 87), 6th Jud. Dist. Bar Assn. (sec., treas. 1968), Assn. Trial Lawyers Am., Idaho Trial Lawyers Assn., Eagleton Inst. of Politics, Idaho State U. Alumni Assn. (bd. dirs. 1972-77, pres. 1976), Pocatello Am. Legion, Idaho Fedn. Bus. and Profl. Women (Woman of the Yr. 1976), Pocatello C. of C. (govtl. affairs com.), Zonta, Pi Sigma Alpha, Omicron Pi. Office: McDermott Zollinger & Olley Box 3 Pocatello ID 83204 also: 218 N 10th Pocatello ID 82301

MCDEVITT, JOYCE ANN, marketing professional; b. Ridley Park, Pa., Dec. 4, 1957; d. Joseph Adolph and Louise (Colasante) Morelli; m. Michael Patrick McDevitt, Feb. 14, 1986. BS in Mktg. cum laude, U. Pa., 1982.

Internat. market analyst Franklin Mint, Franklin Center, Pa., 1982-84; asst. product mgr. Hunt Mfg., Phila., 1984-85; quality assurance analyst IMS Am., Ltd./Dun and Bradstreet, Inc., Plymouth Meeting, Pa., 1985-87, nat. field mgr., 1987—. Vol. Jr. Orange Bowl, Miami, 1986, United Cerebral Palsy Assn. Annual Benefit, Phila., 1985-88. Recipient Fundraising Vol. award United Cerebral Palsy Assn., 1986. Mem. Phila. Direct Mktg. Assn., Mktg. Rsch. Assn., Am. Mktg. Assn. Republican. Baptist. Office: IMS Am Ltd 660 W Germantown Pike Plymouth Meeting PA 19462

MCDEVITT, SHEILA MARIE, energy company executive; b. St. Petersburg, Fla., Jan. 15, 1947; d. Frank Davis and Marie (Barfield) McD. AA, St. Petersburg Jr. Coll., 1966; BA in Govt., Fla. State U., 1968, JD, 1978. Bar: Fla. 1978. Research asst. Fla. Legis. Reference Bur., Tallahassee, 1968-69; adminstr., research assoc. Constitution Revision Commn. Ga. Gen. Assembly, Atlanta, 1969-70; adminstrv. asst., analyst Fla. State Sen., Tallahassee, Tampa, 1970-79; assoc. McClain, Walkley & Stuart, P.A., Tampa, Seminole, Fla., 1979-81; govtl. affairs counsel Tampa Electric Co., 1981-82, corp. counsel, 1982-86; sr. corp. counsel Teco Energy, Inc., Tampa, 1986-89, asst. v.p., 1989—; mem. Worker's Compensation Adv. Council Fla. Dept. Labor, Tallahassee, 1984-86. Bd. dirs. Vol. Ctr. Hillsborough County, Tampa, 1984-85; vice-chmn., trustee Tampa Lowry Park Zoo Soc., 1986—, also legal advisor; mem. Fla. State Rep. Exec. Com., Tallahassee, 1974-75, Hillsborough County Reps., 1974-75, transition team Fla. Gov. Bob Martinez, 1986-87; apptd. by Senator Connie Mack to Fed. Jud. Adv. Commn., 1989. Mem. ABA, Fed. Energy Bar Assn., Fla. Bar (vice-chmn. then chmn. energy law com. 1984-87, jud. nominating procedures com. 1986—), Hillsborough County Bar Assn. (chmn. law week com. 1990—, chmn. corp. counsel com. 1986-87), Am. Corp. Counsel Assn. (bd. dirs. Cen. Fla. chpt. 1986-87), Centre Club, Tiger Bay Club, Tampa Yacht and Country Club, Tampa Club. Republican. Roman Catholic. Home: 3211 Swann Ave #201 Tampa FL 33609 Office: Teco Energy Inc 702 N Franklin St Box 111 Tampa FL 33601

MCDONAGH, JAN, pathology educator; b. Wilmington, N.C., Nov. 9, 1942; d. James B. and Mary Katherine (Elkins) McQuere; m. Richard P. McDonagh (dec. 1979); 1 child, Jonathan McDonagh; m. Eric T. Fossel, Jan. 7, 1982. BS, Wake Forest U., 1964; PhD, U. N.C., 1969. From asst. prof. to assoc. prof. pathology and biochemistry U. N.C., Chapel Hill, 1971-82; assoc. prof. pathology Harvard U. Med. Sch., Boston, 1982—. Author 14 monographs, 1 book; contbr. articles to profl. jours.; patentee in field. Grantee NIH, 1968—, Am. Heart Assn., 1977. Mem. Am. Heart Assn., Internat. Soc. on Thrombosis and Haemostasis (chair factor XIII), Am. Soc. Biol. Chemistry and Molecular Biology, Japan Haematological Soc., Am. Fed. Clin. Rsch., Phi Beta Kappa, Sigma Xi. Democrat. Episcopalian. Office: Beth Israel Hosp HMS Dept Pathology Boston MA 02150

MCDONALD, ALICE COIG, state education official; b. Chalmette, La., Sept. 26, 1940; d. Olas Casimere and Genevieve Louise (Heck) Coig; m. Glenn McDonald, July 16, 1967; 1 child, Michel. B.S., Loyola U., New Orleans, 1962; M.Ed., Loyola U., 1966; cert. rank I sch. adminstrn., Spalding Coll., 1975. Tchr. St. Bernard Pub. Schs., Chalmette, La., 1962-67; counselor, instructional coordinator Jefferson County Schs., Louisville, 1967-77; ednl. adviser Jefferson County Govt., Louisville, 1977-78; chief exec. asst. Office of Mayor, Louisville, 1978-80; dep. supt. pub. instrn. Ky. Dept. Edn., Frankfort, 1980-83, supt. pub. instrn., 1984—; bd. dirs., com. mem. Ky. Council on Higher Edn., 1984—, Ky. Juvenile Justice Com., 1984—, Ky. Ednl. TV Authority, 1984—, So. Regional Council Ednl. Improvement, 1984—. Mem. Pres.'s Adv. Com. on Women, 1978-80; active Democratic Nat. Convs., 1972, 76, 80, 84; pres. Dem. Woman's Club Ky., 1974-76 Ky. mem. Nat. Dem. Com., 1976-79, mem. exec. com. 1977—. Mem. Council Chief State Sch. Officers, Women in Sch. Adminstrn., NEA, Ky. Edn. Assn., River City Bus. and Profl. Women. Home: 6501 Gunpowder Ln Prospect KY 40059 Office: Ky Dept Edn Capital Plaza Tower 1st Floor Frankfort KY 40601

MCDONALD, ARLYS LORRAINE, librarian; b. Edison, Neb., Jan. 6, 1932; d. Leo Richard and Christine Mae (Hays) McDonald. BMus, St. Mary Plains Coll., 1963; MMus, U. Ill., 1965. Asst. prof. St. Mary Plains Coll., Dodge City, Kans., 1965-68; head, music libr. Ariz. State U., Tempe, 1968—. Author: Ned Roremi, 1989; contbg. author: Phoenix in Grove's Dictionary of American Music and Musicians, 1986. Mem. Music Libr. Assn., Music Libr. Assn. Mt. Plains Chpt., Internat. Assn.Music Librs. Ariz. State Libr. Assn. Democrat. Office: Ariz State U Music Libr Tempe AZ 85287

MC DONALD, BARBARA ANN, psychotherapist; b. Mpls., July 15, 1932; d. John and Georgia Elizabeth (Baker) Rubenzer; B.A., U. Minn., 1954; M.S.W., U. Denver, 1977; m. Lawrence R. McDonald, July 27, 1957; adopted children—John, Mary Elizabeth. Diplomate Am. Bd. Social Work; lic. psychotherapist. Day care cons. Minn. Dept. Public Welfare, St. Paul, 1954-59; social worker Community Info. Center, Mpls., 1959-60; exec. dir. Social Synergistics Co., Littleton, Colo., 1970—; cons. to community orgns., Indian tribes. Family therapist , 1979—. Bd. dirs. Vol Bur. Sun cities, Ariz., 1988, 89, 90. Named 1 of 8 Women of Yr. and featured on TV spl. Ladies Home Jour., 1974; Clairol scholar, 1974. Am. Bus. Women's Assn. scholar, 1974 Alpha Gamma Delta scholar, 1974. Mem. Minn. Pre-Sch. Edn. Assn. (hon. life), AAUW, Nat. Assn. Social Workers, Ariz. Assn. social Workers, Assn. Clin. Social Workers, Am. Bus. Women's Assn., U. Minn. Alumni Club, Alpha Gamma Delta (Disting. Citizen award 1975). Club: Altrusa (hon.). Author: Selected References on the Group Day Care of Pre-School Children, 1956; Helping Families Grow: Specialized Psychotherapy with Hearing Impaired Children and Their Families, 1984. Office: 13720 Franciscan Dr Sun City West AZ 85375

MCDONALD, BARBARA JEANNIE B., utilities analyst; d. Warren Murray and Nina Elizabeth (Ambrose) Beattie; m. James Wallace McDonald, Jan. 23, 1979; 1 child, Evan Dent McGough. BS, U. Fla., 1972, MS, 1989. Utilities analyst Gainesville Regional Utilities; owner, mgr. Creative Computer Learning Ctr., Gainesville, Fla.; math tchr., dept. chmn. Rolling Green Acad., Alachua, Fla., Trenton (Fla.) High Sch.; mktg. rep., project mgr. Geographic Systems Corp., Green Bay, Wis., 1990—. Mem. Phi Kappa Phi.

MCDONALD, BONNIE J. SHARP, publishing executive; b. Elgin, Tex., July 11, 1944; d. James Joseph and Bonnie Marie (Smith) Sharp; m. Charles Edwin McDonald Sr. Student, Austin's Coll. Bus., 1962. Pres., owner, entrepreneur The Cross Stitcher Mag. Inc., Jackson, Miss.; ops. mgr. Burnham and Co., Dallas; ptnr. McDonald Graphics, Inc., Knoxville, Tenn.; sec. Mercantile Nat. Bank, Dallas; pub. The Cross Stitcher Mag. Mem. PTA, United Meth. Women. Mem. NAFE, Assn. of Crafts and Creative Industries, Humane Soc. of the U.S., Cancer Soc., Counted Thread Soc.

MCDONALD, CAROLE ANN, design studio owner; b. Jackson, Tenn., Mar. 6, 0947; d. John Martin and Alice Geraldine Hall; m. Edward Clayton McDonald, Aug. 8, 1976; 1 child, Megan. BA, Okla. Christian Coll., 1968; MLS, George Peabody Coll., 1969; AA, Nashville Sch. Interior Design, 1990. Intern Furniture Classics, Nashville, 1989-90; sole propr. First Impressions Design Studio, Nashville, 1990—. Mem. Am. Soc. Interior Designers (assoc.). Office: 1st Impressions Design 6304 Chickering Circle Nashville TN 37215

MCDONALD, CATHERINE ALICE, sociologist, consultant; b. Middletown, Conn., Aug. 30, 1946; d. William Thomas and Rose Catherine (Romanek) Clayton; m. Kevin Lawrence McDonald, July 20, 1968. BA, U. Conn., 1969; MA, U. Hartford, Conn., 1974; PhD, U. Conn., 1986. Clin. instr. Sch. of Medicine So. Conn. State U., Farmington, 1986—; lectr. dept. sociology U. Conn., Storrs, 1980-89; cons. grant writer Hartford Primary Care Assn., 1987; project cons. Conn. Primary Care Assn., Hartford, 1988; asst. prof. pub. health So. Conn. State U., New Haven, 1989—; mem. univ. senate U. Conn., Storrs, 1980-85, mem. med. coun., Farmington, 1984-86; coord. Conn. Dept. Health Svcs., Hartford, 1988. Mem. PhD program U. Conn. Med. Sch., Farmington, 1988; gubernatorial appointee Conn. Gen. Assembly Task Force on Teenage Suicide, Hartford, 1987-89; sec. Greater Mansfield (Conn.) Coun. on the Arts, 1987. Recipient Citation, Conn. Gen. Assembly, 1989. Mem. Am. Pub. Health Assn., Internat. Sociol. Assn., New Eng. Pub. Health Assn., Conn. Pub. Health Assn. (bd. dirs. Middlefield chpt. 1986—), So. Sociology Soc., Ea. Sociol. Assn., Sociologists for Women in Soc. Home: 18 Stonemill Rd Storrs CT 06268 Office: So Conn State U Dept Pub Health New Haven CT 06515

MCDONALD, DOROTHY COLETTE, real estate broker; b. Boston, Oct. 26, 1938; d. Edward Vincent and Ethel May (Sanford) Walsh; BS, Harvard U., 1960; m. Gerald C. McDonald, May 23, 1959 (dec.); children: Gerald C., Deborah L. McDonald, Hermanson, Gregory Christopher (dec.); m. Carl H. Krauth, Jr., Dec. 15, 1980; 1 stepson, Carl H. III. Various secretarial positions, 1958-59. model, 1958-75; model, personal shopper Filene's, Chestnut Hill, Mass., 1974-78; designer program covers Boston Red Sox, 1974-76; TV facts girl for TV comml. T.V. Facts mag., 1974-75; real estate broker Channing Assocs., Inc., Wellesley, Mass., 1976-81, Boca Blossom Realty Co., Boca Raton, Fla., 1979-81, N.B. Taylor & Co., Inc., Sudbury, Mass., 1986—; fashion coord. Ava Botélle Fashions, Natick, Mass., 1988—, mgr. Newton store, 1990—. Roman Catholic. Home: 119 Oxford Rd Newton Centre MA 02159 Other: 119 Oxford Rd Newton Centre Massuchusetts and 230 N Federal Hwy Deerfield Beach FL 33441 Office: NB Taylor & Co Inc 356 Boston Post Rd Sudbury MA 01776

MCDONALD, DOROTHY MARIE, real estate broker; b. Wiley Ford, W.Va., Oct. 6, 1937; d. Quentin M. and Madeline (Branson) Rice; m. Clifton L. McDonald, June 28, 1958 (sep.); children: Clifton L. III, Theresa, Lisa. Grad. high sch., 1955. GRI. With Pitts. Plate Glass Co., Cumberland, Md., 1956-58; realtor Coldwell Banker Hopkins, Hagerstown, Md., 1979—; bd. dirs. Realtors Land Ins., 1986—, emm. nat. com., 1990. Author brochures in real estate. Mem. Citizens to Save the Md. Theatre, 1977-81, Historic Preservation Coun., Washington County, 1987—, Women's Commn., 1988-89; active League Women Voters, others in past. Named Realtor Sales Assoc. of the Yr., Greater Hagerstown Bd. Realtors, 1986, Woman on the Move, Herald Mail Newspaper, 1989, others. Mem. Realtors Inst. Md., Realtors Land Inst. (treas. 1989-90), Coldwell Banker Million Dollar Club, Nat. Assn. Real Estate Appraisers, Greater Hagerstown Bd. Realtors, Nat. Assn. Realtors, Md. Assn. Realtors, Urban Land Inst., Comml. Investment Real Estate Coun., Women's Coun. of Realtors (pres. 1989-90). Democrat. Home: 1175 Fairchild Ave Hagerstown MD 21740 Office: 1622 Dual Highway Hagerstown MD 21740

MCDONALD, GABRIELLE ANNE KIRK, federal judge; b. St. Paul, Apr. 12, 1942; d. James G. and Frances R. Kirk; m. Mark T. McDonald; children: Michael, Stacy. LLB, Howard U., 1966. Bar: Tex. 1966. Staff atty. NAACP Legal Def. and Ednl. Fund, N.Y.C., 1966-69; ptnr. McDonald & McDonald, Houston, 1969-79; judge U.S. Dist. Ct., Houston, 1979-88; now ptnr. Matthews Branscomb, Austin, Tex.; asst. prof. Tex. So. U., Houston, 1970, adj. prof., 1975-77; lectr. U. Tex., Houston, 1977-78. Bd. dirs. Community Service Option Program; bd. dirs. Alley Theatre, Houston, Nat. Coalition of 100 Black Women, ARC; trustee Howard U., from 1983; bd. vistors Thurgood Marshall Sch. Law, Houston. Mem. ABA, Nat. Bar Assn., Houston Bar Assn., Houston Lawyers Assn., Black Women Lawyers Assn. Democrat. Congregationalist. Office: Matthews & Branscomb PC 301 Congress Ave Ste 2050 Austin TX 78701*

MCDONALD, GLORIA JEANETTE, printing company executive; b. Dunn, N.C., Apr. 25, 1943; d. William Baxton and Rachel Lee (Bowden) McD.; 1 child, William D. Phillips. Student, U. N.C., 1962. Gen. mgr. The Printworks, Greensboro; sales adminstn. mgr. Standard Theatre Supply, Greensboro, N.C., rental mgr.; v.p. McDonald Printing Co., Greensboro. Mem. NAFE, Internat. Communications Industries Assn.

MCDONALD, IRENE MARY (RENE MCDONALD), editor, program coordinator; b. Nanticoke, Pa., Oct. 14, 1940; d. Nicholas Aloyisius and Irene (Zdancewicz) Negosh; m. Harry Herrand Kelejian, Feb. 23, 1963 (div.); children: David Lawrence, Douglas Mark, Melinda Kathryn; m. Frank Bethune McDonald, Nov. 7, 1987. BA in English, Hofstra U., 1962; MA in Journalism, U. Md., 1982. Sr. Fed. Emergency Mgmt. Agy. editor. Greenhorne & O'Mara, Inc., Greenbelt, Md., 1983-84; proposal writer Greenhorne & O'Mara, Inc., Greenbelt, 1984-85; faculty rsch. asst. Ctr. for Automation Rsch., U. Md., Coll. Pk., Md., 1985-89; youth program coord. Parents Without Ptnrs., Silver Spring, Md., 1989—; asst. editor The Single Parent Jour. of Parents Without Ptnrs., Silver Spring, 1989, assoc. editor, 1990—; Manuscript reviewer Parents Without Ptnrs., Inc., Silver Spring, 1989—; reporter town coverage Prince George's Jour., 1980; copy editor Ctr. for Automation Rsch., Coll. Pk., 1985-89. Editor: (newsletter) Univ. Md. Campus Club, 1977-78, Prince George's Coll. Planned Parenthood, 1981-83; Author, researcher (4-part series) Prince George's Jour., 1982; author: (rsch. report) Pub. Rels. Soc., 1982; copy editor (2 vol. text) Computer Science, 1989. Historian Univ. Pk. (Md.) Forum, 1988-89; AAUW liasion to Women's Action Coalition, Prince George's Coll., Largo, Md., 1989—; foot soldier Campaign for Claire Bigelow, House of Reps., Md.; docent (mus. tour guide) Nat. Gallery Art, Washington, 1974-76. Mem. AAUW (publs. dir. Md. div., editor jour. the Marylander 1990—, pub. info. officer Coll. Pk. br., 1987-88), membership v.p., 1988-90, membership planning strategy award Md. div., 1989), The Writer's Ctr., Women's Action Coalition. Democrat. Unitarian. Home: 4324 Woodberry St University Park MD 20782 Office: Parents Without Partners 8807 Colesville Rd Silver Spring MD 20910

MCDONALD, JANE FRANCES, insurance company executive; b. Winthrop, Mass., Dec. 19, 1940; d. William Francis and Isabelle Frances (Mythen) Moran; m. James Joseph McDonald, Aug. 21, 1965 (div. 1976); children: Maureen Lynn, Susan Jill, Kevin James. B.S. in Edn., Salem State Coll., Mass., 1962; Assoc. in Underwriting, Ins. Inst., Malvern, Pa., 1983. Tchr., East Hartford Sch. System, Conn., 1962-66; accountant Watkin Bros. Piano & Organ, Hartford, 1975-76; policy analyst Hartford Steam Boiler Insp. & Ins., 1976-80; supervising underwriter Am. Nuclear Insurers, Farmington, 1981-88, acct. exec., 1988—. Mem. Nat. Assn. Ins. Women (cert.), Am. Nuclear Soc., Nat. Assn. Female Execs., N.Y. Acad. Scis., Hartford Assn. Ins. Women (by-laws chmn. 1984-85), Amnesty Internat., Wadsworth Atheneum. Democrat. Roman Catholic. Avocations: reading, handwriting analysis, travel, crewel embroidery. Home: 675 Graham Rd South Windsor CT 06074 Office: Am Nuclear Insurers 270 Farmington Ave Farmington CT 06032

MCDONALD, JOANNE, high technology company executive; b. San Diego, June 10, 1947; d. Paul and Dolores (Paganucci) McD. B.A., U. Md., 1970. High tech. exec. ENSCO Inc., Springfield, Va., 1981—. Bd. dirs. Yorktowne Sq., Falls Church, Va., 1981; trustee Elizabeth Seton High Sch., Bladensburg, Md., 1988. Mem. Am. Soc. Tng. and Devel., Internat. Assn. Personnel Women, Am. Soc. Personnel Adminstrs., Internat. Assn. Bus. Communicaitons. Office: ENSCO Inc 5400 Port Royal Rd Springfield VA 22151

MCDONALD, KAREN DENISE, publishing company executive; b. Detroit, May 25, 1961; d. Dolzier and Larue Costello (Cooper) McD. BS in Indsl. Engring., Wayne State U., 1984; postgrad., U. Chgo., 1988—. Mfg. mgmt. trainee R.R Donnelley & Sons Co., Chgo., 1984-87, computer ops. supr., 1987—. Chmn. strategic planning comm. Metro. Bd. of Chgo. Urban League, 1987-88, co-chmn. publicity com., 1988—; guest speaker Chgo. Assn. Commerce and Industry, 1985, 87-88; vol. Adopt-A-Sch. Program, Chicago Pub. Schs.; mem. Chgo. Art Inst. Mich. Competitive Scholarship, 1984. Mem. Nat. Black MBA Assn., NAFE, U. Chgo. Women's Bus. Group. Democrat. Home: 5208 S Dorchester Chicago IL 60615 Office: RR Donnelley & Sons Co 350 E 22d St Chicago IL 60616

MCDONALD, KATHLEEN EDNA, insurance company official; b. Providence, Feb. 16, 1960; d. William Glen and Corinne Agnes (Scott) McD. AS in Acctg., Quinnipiac Coll., Hamden, Conn., 1980; BS in Communicaitons, So. Conn. State U., 1984. Claims svc. rep. Nationwide Ins. Co., Hamden, 1979-84, claims examiner, 1984-85; telephone adjuster Nationwide Ins. Co., 1985-86, sr. telephone adjuster, 1986-87; sr. claims rep. Underwriting Adjusting Co., Wethersfield, Conn., 1987-89; claim specialist Zurich Am. Ins. Co., North Haven, Conn., 1988-89, worker's compensation supr., 1989—. Mem. Nat. Ins. Assn. Women, Blue Goose. Roman Catholic. Home: 75 George St Hamden CT 06514 Office: Zurich Am Ins Co 1276 Washington Ave North Haven CT 06473

MCDONALD, KATHRYN IRENE, investment marketer; b. Grosse Pointe, Mich., Nov. 25, 1960; d. Edgar Emery and Irene Mary (Sabaugh) Lewey. BA, Mich. State U., 1982. Staff acct. Alder, Green & Hasson CPAs, Los Angeles, 1982-83; jr. acct. Honda Corp., Torrance, Calif., 1983-84; asst. v.p. Hall Fin. Group, Dallas, 1984-86; v.p. Planned Investments, Inc., San Francisco, 1986—. Mem. Internat. Assn. Fin. Planners, Sierra Club, Greepeace, World Wildlife Orgn., Cousteau Soc. Republican. Home: 120 Fernwood Dr San Rafael CA 94901 Office: Planned Investments Inc 601 California St Ste 200 San Francisco CA 94108

MCDONALD, KAY, controller; b. Mpls., May 7, 1952; d. John Clark and Inez Joan (Weber) McD.; 1 child, Marcus John. BS, St. Lawrence U., 1974; MEd, Boston U., 1975; MBA, Rivier Coll, 1984. Dir. Alcohol Rehab. Ctr., Framingham, Mass., 1975-78; personnel mgr. Prestolite Wire and Cable, Hudson, Mass., 1978-79; EEO mgr. Sanders Assocs., Nashua, N.H., 1979-81, coord. coll. recruiting, 1981-83, program adminstr., 1983-85; controller, ops. mgr. Collaborative Med. Systems, Newton, Mass., 1985-87, contr., 1987-90, dir. fin. and adminstrn., 1990—; instr. MBA program Rivier Coll., Nashua, 1984-85. Mem. Small Bus. Assn., Newton C. of C. Greater Boston Track, New Eng. Bike (Boston). Home: 1 Blaban Pl Charlestown MA 02129 Office: Collaborative Med Systems 246 Walnut St Newton MA 02160

MCDONALD, MARGUERITE FULLER, educator; b. Arlington, Mass., July 2, 1911; d. Walton Boutelle and Mary Florence (Dow) Fuller; m. Victor A. George, June 16, 1938 (dec. June 1960); children: Victor Walton, Francis Fuller; m. Harry J. McDonald, July 28, 1968. BS, Edinboro (Pa.) U., 1933. Art tchr. Aliquippa, Pa., 1933-39, Beaver (Pa.) Area Sch. Dist., 1956-73; tchr. adults Pa. State U., Beaver Falls, 1964-68; drawing tchr. pvt. sch. Sanibal, Fla., 1976-77; drawing tchr. pvt. sch. Sanibel Captiva Art League, 1976-80, ret., 1980. Bazaar chmn. Tusca-Ridge Garden Club, Beaver, 1973-86. Mem. AAUW. Home: 2293 Swedish Dr #29 Clearwater FL 34623

MCDONALD, MARIANNE, classicist; b. Chgo., Jan. 2, 1937; d. Eugene Francis and Inez (Riddle) McD.; children: Eugene, Conrad, Bryan, Bridget, Kirstie, Hiroshi. BA magna cum laude, Bryn Mawr Coll., 1958; MA, U. Chgo., 1960; PhD, U. Calif., Irvine, 1975, doctorate (hon.) Am. Coll. Greece, 1988. Teaching asst. classics U. Calif., Irvine, 1972-74, instr. Greek, Latin and English, mythology, modern cinema, 1975-79, founder, researcher Thesaurus Linguae Graecae Project, 1972; bd. dir. Centrum. Bd. dirs. Am. Coll. of Greece, 1981—, Scripps Hosp., 1981; Am. Sch. Classical Studies, 1986—; mem. bd. overseers U. Calif. San Diego, 1985—; nat. bd. advisors Am. Biog. Inst., 1982—; founder Hajime Mori Chair for Japanese Studies, U. Calif., San Diego, 1985, McDonald Ctr. for Alcohol and Substance Abuse, 1984; adj. prof. drama U. Calif., San Diego, 1990. Recipient Ellen Browning Scripps Humanitarian award, 1975; Disting. Svc. award U. Calif.-Irvine, 1982, Irvine Medal, 1987, 3rd Prize Midwest Poetry Ctr. Contest, 1987; named Philanthropist of Yr. Honorary Nat. Conf. Christians and Jews, 1986, Woman of Yr. AHEPA, 1988, San Diego Woman of Distinction, 1990. Mem. MLA, AAUP, Am. Philol. Assn., Soc. for the Preservation of the Greek Heritage (pres.), Enterprises, Am. Classical League, Philol. Assn. Pacific Coast, Am. Comparative Lit. Assn., Modern and Classical Lang. Assn. So. Calif., Hellenic Soc., Calif. Fgn. Lang. Tchrs. Assn., Internat. Platform Assn., Greek Language Found. (pres.), KPBS Producers Club, Hellenic Univ. Club (bd. dir.). Author: Terms for Happiness in Euripides, 1978, Semilemmatized Concordances to Euripides' Alcestis, 1977, Cyclops, Andromache, Medea, 1978, Heraclidae, Hippolytus, 1979, Hecuba, 1982, Hercules Furens, 1984, Electra, 1985, Ion, 1985, Trojan Women, 1988, Iphigenia in Taurus, 1988, Euripides in Cinema: The Heart Made Visible, 1983; translator: The Cost of Kindness and Other Fabulous Tales (Shinichi Hoshi), 1986; contbr. numerous articles to profl. jours. Home: Box 929 Rancho Santa Fe CA 92067 Office: U Calif Thesaurus Linguae Gracae Project Irvine CA 92717

MCDONALD, MARY ANN MELODY, investment management executive; b. Sandwich, Ill., Apr. 30, 1944; d. Theodore Harvey and Sarah Elizabeth (Itving) Larson; m. John G. McDonald, June 19, 1973. BS, No. Ill. U., 1966; MusM, New England Conservatory, 1970; studies with Nadia Boulanger, Paris, 1971; MusD, Stanford U., 1975; MBA, Harvard U., 1986. Credit analyst Wells Fargo Bank, San Francisco, 1976-77; loan officer, 1977-79, asst. v.p., 1979-80; chmn. bd. dirs. Cornwall Corp., Stanford, Calif., 1980-84; dir. client svcs. RCM Capital Mgmt., San Francisco, 1986-88, ptnr., 1989—; music lectr., guest lectr. Fontainebleau French Bus. Sch., France, 1980, Stanford U. Sloan Program, 1980, U. Chgo. Alumni Assn., 1980. Active Ill. Youth Commn., 1963-66. Recipient Rockefeller grantee Oberlin (Ohio) Coll. 1967; winner Miss Boston-Miss Am. Pageant, 1968. Mem. Stanford Alumni Assn., Harvard Alumni Assn., Sigma Alpha Iota, Kappa Delta (Telford Cup). Republican. Lutheran. Home: 1098 Vernier Pl Stanford CA 94305 Office: RCM Capital Mgmt 4 Embarcadero Ctr Ste 2900 San Francisco CA 94111

MCDONALD, MARYBETH, lawyer; b. Princeton, N.J., Aug. 10, 1955; d. F. Bennett McDonald and Mary Esther (Arvay) Carman. B Health Sci., U. Fla., 1977, JD, 1982. Bar: Fla. 1983. Assoc. Maguire, Voorhis & Wells, Orlando, Fla., 1983-86, Rissman, Weisberg, Barrett & Hurt, P.A., Orlando, 1986—. Participant Guardian Ad Litem Program, 1984—; class rep. alumni coun. U. Fla., 1986—; mem. Orlando Fire Prevention Code, 1986-87, vice chmn., 1987-88, chmn., 1988-90. Mem. ABA (del. young lawyers div. 1986), Fla. Bar (vice chmn. moot ct. com. young lawyers sect. 1984-86, sec. young lawyers sect. 1985-86, mem. ann. meeting com. 1987-90, Most Productive Young Lawyer award 1990), Orange County Bar Assn. (exec. coun. 1986-89, trustee Legal Aid Soc., 1987—, soc. pres. 1989-90, bd. dirs. ednl. trust fund 1985-89, Outstanding Exec. Coun. mem. 1987, 88, award of merit 1985), Fla. Def. Lawyers Assn., Fla. Assn. Women Lawyers, Def. Rsch. Inst., Cen. Fla. Assn. for Women Lawyers, Order of Barristers. Democrat. Presbyterian. Office: Rissman Weisberg Barrett & Hurt 201 E Pine St 15th Fl Orlando FL 32801

MCDONALD, PEGGY ANN STIMMEL, automobile company official; b. Darbyville, Ohio, Aug. 25, 1931; d. Wilbur Smith and Bernice Edna (Hott) Stimmel; missionary diploma with honor Moody Bible Inst., 1952; B.A. cum laude in Econs. (scholar), Ohio Wesleyan U., 1965; M.B.A. with distinction, Xavier U., 1977; m. George R. Stich, Mar. 7, 1953 (dec.); 1 son, Mark Stephen (dec.); m. Joseph F. McDonald, Jr., Feb. 1, 1986. . Missionary in S. Am., Evang. Alliance Mission, 1956-61; cost acct. Western Electric Co., 1965-66; acctg. mgr. Ohio Wesleyan U., 1966-73; fin. specialist NCR Corp., 1973-74, systems analyst, 1974-75, supr. inventory planning, 1975, mgr. material planning and purchasing control, 1976-78; materials mgr. U.S. Elec. Motors Co., 1978; with Gen. Motors Corp., 1978—, shift supt. materials, Lakewood, Ga., 1979-80, gen. ops. supr. material data base mgmt. Central Office, Warren, Mich., 1980, dir. material mgmt. GM Truck and Bus. div., Balt., 1980-87; vis. lectr. Inst. Internat. Trade, Jiao Tong U., Shanghai, China, 1985, Inst. Econs. and Fgn. Trade, Tianjin, China, 1986-87; part time instr. Towson (Md.) State U., 1986-87. Mem. Am. Prodn. and Inventory Control Soc., Am. Soc. Women Accts., AAUW, Balt. Exec. Women's Network, Balt. Council on Fgn. Relations, Baptist. Home: 125 Arbutus Ave Baltimore MD 21228 Office: GM Truck and Bus 2122 Broening Hwy PO Box 148 Baltimore MD 21203

MCDONALD, REBECCA ANN, natural gas company executive; b. Phoenix, June 14, 1952; d. William Robert and Regenia Lucille (Hall) Kennedy; m. John Edward McDonald Sr., May 26, 1977; 1 child, John Edward Jr. BS, Stephen F. Austin State U., 1973. Project procurement mgr., buyer Fluor Engrs. and Constructors, Houston, 1974-79; pvt. practice cons. Houston, 1979-81; devel. mgr. Panhandle Ea. Pipeline, Houston, 1981-82, mgr. customer rels., 1982-84, mgr. sales, 1984-85; mgr. gas sales Panhandle Trading Co., Houston, 1985-88, v.p., gen. mgr., 1988—; cert. power trainer Situation Mgmt. Systems, Plymouth, Mass., 1981—. Pres. bd. trustees The Chinquapin Sch., Highlands, Tex., 1986—; mem. Houston Jr. Forum, 1986—. Mem. Natural Gas Men of Houston (bd. dirs. Houston chpt.), Am. Soc. Tng. & Devel. (membership chair 1975-76, Most Valuable Mem. award 1976), Am. Bus. Women (hon. nom. bd.). Episcopalian. Office: Panhandle Trading Co 24 Greenway Pla Houston TX 77005

MCDONALD, ROSA NELL, federal research and indirect budgets manager; b. Boley, Okla., Feb. 12, 1953; d. James and Beatrice Irene (Hayes) McD. B.S., Calif. State U.-Long Beach, 1975; M.B.A., Calif. State U.-

Dominquez Hills, 1980, also postgrad. Acct., The Aerospace Corp., El Segundo, Calif., 1976-77; analytical accountant, 1977-79, budget analyst, 1979-81; sr. budget analyst, 1981-84, budget adminstr., 1984-86, mgr. indirect budgets, 1986—. Vol., Youth Motivation Task Force, El Segundo, 1980—, Holiday Project, El Segundo, 1984, 85. Recipient Adminstrn. Group Achievement award The Aerospace Corp., 1985, Robert Herndon Image award, 1988; named Woman of Yr, Aerospace Corp., 1987. Mem. Am. Bus. Woman's Assn., Nat. Assn. Female Execs., Beta Gamma Sigma. Democrat. Avocations: dancing; aerobics; reading; contests. Office: 2350 E El Segundo Blvd M3 364 El Segundo CA 90245

MCDONALD, WANDA JAMERSON, nurse; b. Chgo., Sept. 16, 1961; d. Curtis George and Wileva Delores (Gates) Jamerson; m. Steven Lamont McDonald, Sept. 22, 1984; 1 child, Steven Lamont Jr. Student, Ill. Inst. Tech., 1979-81; BSN, Rush U., 1983; MHA, Governor's State U., University Park, Ill., 1988. RN, Ill. Staff nurse Mercy Hosp and Med. Ctr., Chgo., 1983-87; coord. quality assurance Michael Reese Health Plan, Chgo., 1987—. Home: 824 N Taylor St Oak Park IL 60302 Office: Michael Reese Health Plan 2545 S King Dr Chicago IL 60615

MCDONALD, WYLENE BOOTH, pharmaceutical sales professional representative; b. Kinston, N.C., Sept. 29, 1956; d. Wiley Truett and Hilda Grey (Brinson) Booth; m. Robert H. McDonald; 2 stepchildren. BS in Nursing, Atlantic Christian Coll., 1979; MS in Nursing, East Carolina U., 1984. Pub. health nurse Sampson Co. Health Dept., Clinton, N.C., 1979-81; pub. health coordinator New Hanover Co. Health Dept., Wilmington, N.C., 1981-83; med. ctr. liaison Cape Feat Valley Med. Ctr., Fayetteville, 1984-85; profl. sales rep. Merck, Sharp & Dohme Pharm. Co., West Point, Pa., 1985-88; hosp. specialist sales rep. Merck, Sharp & Dohme, West Point, 1988-90, sr. hosp. specialist sales rep., 1990—; speaker Coastal Area Perinatal Assn., 1983, U. N.C., Wilmington, Sch. of Bus. "Career Week", 1987, 88, 89. Fund raiser March of Dimes, Fayetteville, 1987. Named one of Outstanding Young Women of Am., 1981. Mem. Am. Nurses Assn., N.C. Nurses Assn., N.C. Pub. Health Assn., AAUW, Sigma Theta Tau. Democrat. Baptist. Home and Office: 108 Seapath Estates Wrightsville Beach NC 28480

MCDONALD RASMUSSEN, MARGARET JEAN, editor; b. Burlington, Vt., Oct. 4, 1960; d. Earl George and Judith Ann (Smith) McDonald; m. Roy Parker Rasmussen III, June 12, 1987; 1 child, Cody Alexander. BA in Bus., U. Colo., 1983. Editorial asst. Omega Group Pub., Boulder, Colo., 1981-84; sr. editor Internat. Coun. for Computers in Edn., Eugene, Oreg., 1984-88; editor Ctr. for Pub. Affairs Rsch., U. Nebr., Omaha, 1988—; free-lance writer, 1989—. Tchr. prenatal water exercise Eugene Family YMCA, 1986-88. Democrat. Lutheran. Home: 4385 Mason St Omaha NE 68106 Office: UNO Ctr Pub Affairs Rsch 1313 Farnam-On-The-Mall Omaha NE 68182

MCDONNELL, CATHERINE MARIE, professional association administrator; b. Detroit, July 5, 1958; d. Ronald Jean and Betty Ann (McKaig) Grissom; m. Michael Edward McDonnell, Oct. 17, 1981. BBA, Western Mich. U., 1980. Sales Western Herald Newspaper, Kalamazoo, 1978-80, Beaumnt (Tex.) Enterprise, 1980-81; with Am. Auto. Assn., Houston, 1981—; dir. Am. Auto. Assocs., Houston, 1990—. Editor: (articles) Am. Auto. Assocs. mag., 1983-89. Chair person fundraiser Safe Kids Coalition, Houston, 1989-90. Mem. Internat. Assn. Bus. Communicators (sec. external com., dir. 1982-90), Pub. Rels. Soc. Am., Ashford Civic Assn. (recycling com. 1990), Toastmasters, Ashford Women's Club. Roman Catholic. Office: Am Auto Assn 3000 Southwest Frwy Houston TX 77098

MC DONNELL, LORETTA WADE, educator; b. San Francisco, May 31, 1940; d. John H. and Helen M. (Tinney) Wade; m. John L. McDonnell, Jr., Apr. 27, 1963 (div.); children: Elizabeth, John L. III, Thomas. BA, San Francisco Coll. for Women, 1962; MA, Stanford U., 1963; grad. Coro Pub. Affairs Tng. Program for Women, 1976; JD Golden Gate U., 1989. High sch. tchr. East Side Union High Sch. Dist., San Jose, Calif., 1962-63; project coordinator Inter Agency Collaboration Effort, Oakland, Calif., 1977—; legal asst. Pacific Gas and Electric Co., 1980—. Bd. dirs. Carden Redwood Sch., 1975-77, St. Paul's Sch., 1974-75; budget panelist United Way of Bay Area, 1975-77; community v.p. Jr. League, 1976-77, nat. conv. del., 1976; bd. dirs. Alameda County Vol. Bur., 1973-74; chmn. speakers panel Focus on Am. Women, 1973-74. Mem. Jr. League of Oakland-East Bay, Inc., Stanford Alumni. Democrat. Roman Catholic. Clubs: Stanford San Francisco Luncheon, Commonwealth. Assoc. editor The Antiphon, 1971-74.

MCDONNELL, MARY JEAN, banker; b. Wantagh, N.Y., June 26, 1960; d. Richard Kieran and Lorraine (Christ) McDonnell. BA, Pace U., 1982; postgrad., St. John's U., N.Y., 1990—. Receptionist Pace U., 1980-82; intern, pub. info. relations The Fund Modern Courts, N.Y.C., 1981-82; intern N.Y. State Dept. Probation, Mt. Kisco, N.Y., 1982; sr. teller various locations, 1987—; operational support Zone Support Centre, Uniondale, N.Y., 1982-83; platform trainee floater Various Locations, 1983-84; platform asst. Seaford, N.Y., 1984; asst. br. mgr. Carle Place, 1984-85; br. mgr. Dix Hills, 1985-87; asst. treas., br. mgr. Chase Manhattan Bank, Roslyn, 1987-88; 2d v.p. Chase Manhattan Bank, Little Neck, N.Y., 1988—. Bd. dirs. Long Island Community Program Ctr., Dix Hills, N.Y., 1986-87. Mem. NAFE, Nat. Assn. Bus. Women (dir. publicity Melville, N.Y. 1987-88, sec. 1987—). Roman Catholic.

MCDONNELL, MARY THERESA, travel service executive; b. N.Y.C., Nov. 9, 1949; d. John J. and Mary B. (Lunney) McD.; m. Robert T. Barber, Oct. 7, 1989. Mgr. Kramer Travel Agy., White Plains, N.Y., 1967-79; owner, mgr. New Trends Travel, Rye, N.Y., 1979—. Office: New Trends Travel Ltd 55 Purchase St Rye NY 10580

MCDONNELL, MARYANN MARGARET, medical marketing executive; b. Detroit, Aug. 26, 1947; d. Patrick J. and Margaret Ann (Novallo) McD.; children: Anais Kathryn Alexander, Colin Michael McDonnell. BS, Wayne State U., 1970. Consumer protection specialist FTC, Washington, 1970-73; fin. analyst Price Commn., Washington, 1972-73; co-founder Full Circle Process & Xenium, Los Gatos, Calif., 1973-77; asst. adminstr. Arts In the Image of Man, Fair Oaks, Calif., 1981-83; adminstr. Mariposa Waldorf Sch., Cedar Ridge, Calif., 1983-84; pres. Counseling Endevors, Grass Valley, Calif., 1984-86; v.p. Sr. Vision Inst., Carmichael, Calif., 1986-88; pres. Empire Health Mktg., Grass Valley, 1988—, Elder Sight Inst., Grass Valley, 1988—. Founder, chairperson Los Gatos (Calif.) Waldorf Sch. Assn., 1977; mem. Mariposa Waldorf Sch. Bd. Trustees, Cedar Ridge, 1984; founding mem. Gia Sophia, Nevada City, Calif., 1987. Mem. NAFE. Democrat. Home: 622 Alexandra Way Grass Valley CA 95949

MCDONNELL, PEGEEN ELIZABETH, accountant; b. Mineola, N.Y., Jan. 19, 1966; d. Joseph Michael and Mary Katherine (Murphy) McD. BBA, Iona Coll., 1988. Sr. acct. KPMG Peat Marwick, Jericho, N.Y., 1988—. Fellow Nat. Assn. Accts. Republican. Roman Catholic. Home: 429 Von Elm Ave East Meadow NY 11554 Office: KPMG Peat Marwick 1 Jericho Pla Jericho NY 11753

MCDONOUGH, MAMIE, public relations executive; b. Plainfield, N.J., Mar. 24, 1952; d. Peter J. and Elizabeth (Driscoll) McD. BA, Elmira Coll., 1974. Protocol asst. U.S. Dept. State, Washington, 1974-75; staff asst. Office of U.S. V.P., Washington, 1975-77; dir. info. service Rep. Nat. Com., Washington, 1977-79; pres. Festive Occasions, Inc., Washington, 1979-81; staff asst. Office of Dep. Chief of Staff The White House, Washington, 1981-82; sr. ptnr. Britt-McDonough Assocs., Washington, 1982-86; owner The McDonough Group, Washington, 1986—; Co-author, developer Student/Corp. Jr. Bd. Dirs. Program, 1984. Admissions rep. Washington area Elmira Coll., 1975-76; bd. dirs. Jr. League Washington, 1977—, Camp Fire Boys and Girls, Washington area, 1985—; mem. fin. com. various Rep. congl. campaigns, 1979—; corp. bd. Vanderbilt Mus., 1985—. Recipient Outstanding Service award Camp Fire Council, 1986. Roman Catholic. Office: 3333 K St NW Ste 210 Washington DC 20007

MCDONOUGH, MARY JOAN, lawyer, state legislator; b. Billings, Mont., May 19, 1957; d. James B. and Francis Theresa (Quilico) McD. BA in History and Polit. Sci., Rocky Mountain Coll., 1981; JD, U. Denver, 1984. Bar: Mont. 1985, U.S. Dist. Ct. Mont. 1985. With legal rsch. No. Plains Resource Coun., Billings, 1983; pvt. practice Billings, 1984—; state legislator State of Montana, Billings, 1989—; part time atty. Mont. Legal Svcs., Billings, 1985—; vice-chmn. local govt. com. Mont. Ho. Reps., Helena, Mont., 1989—. Contbr. articles to profl. jours. V.p. County Women's Dem. Club, Billings, 1986; mem. exec. com. County Dems., Billings, 1988—; alt. del. Nat. Dem. Conv., Atlanta, 1988; bd. dirs. Midland Empire Riding Acad. for the Handicapped, Billings, 1989—. Mem. ABA, Mont. Bar Assn., Yellowstone County Bar Assn., Midland Horse Show Assn. (treas., bd. dirs. Billings chpt. 1988—), Mont. Arabian Horse Assn. Roman Catholic. Home and Office: 233 Mansfield Grove Rd #305 East Haven CT 06512

MCDOUGAL, MICHELE ROGERS, healthcare administrator; d. Buddy Rogers and Mary Belle (Gaines) Gaddy; children: Daniel John. BBA summa cum laude, Nat. U., 1988. Exec. dir. Sharp Sr. Healthcare, San Diego, 1978-85, adminstr., 1985—; guest lectr. Sch. Pub. Health San Diego State U. Bd. dirs. Child Nutrition Program; vol. Am. Cancer Soc., Women's Internat. Ctr. Named Twin Honoree, YWCA, 1990. Mem. NAFE, Med. Group Mgmt. Assn. Office: 3545 4th Ave San Diego CA 92103

MCDOUGALD, DANA LOVELL, media specialist; b. Robinson, Ill., Aug. 9, 1942; d. Eugene and Martha Lefevre (Whetstone) Lovell; m. Larry Robert McDougald; children: Charles Eugene, Tracey Leigh. BA in Edn., Southeastern Okla. State U., 1964; MS, Butler U., 1980; EdD, U. Ga., 1983. Tchr. French Junction City (Kans.) Jr. High Sch., 1965-67; tchr. French and English Mt. St. Scholastica Acad., Atchinson, Kans., 1967-68; tchr. math. and reading Oconee Intermediate Sch., Watkinsville, Ga., 1970-71; tchr. English and sci. St. Michaels's Sch., Greenfield, Ind., 1973-75; media specialist Cedar Shoals High Sch., Athens, Ga., 1979—; mem. faculty ednl. media and librarianship dept. U. Ga., Athens, summer 1979, organizer and cataloger small bus. devel. library, summer 1986, asst. prof. dept. instructional tech., summer 1987, asst. prof., spring 1988. Contbr. articles to profl. jours., Sch. Library Media Ann., 1990; columnist for Library Talk. Organizer Oconee Animal Shelter, 1984, treas., 1984-88. Mem. Ga. Library Assn., Ga. Assn. Instructional Tech. (bd. dirs. 1984-86), Southeastern Library Assn., NEA, Ga. Assn. Educators, Clarke County Assn. Educators, Delta Kappa Gamma Soc. Internat. Republican. Lutheran. Home: PO Box 515 Watkinsville GA 30677 Office: Cedar Shoals High Sch 1300 Cedar Shoals Dr Athens GA 30610

MCDOUGALL, BARBARA JEAN, Canadian government minister; b. Toronto, Ont., Can., Nov. 12, 1937; d. Robert James and Margaret Jean (Dryden) Leamen; m. Peter McDougall, Sept. 6, 1963 (dec.). B.A. in Polit. Sci. and Econs. with honors, U. Toronto, 1960. Chartered Fin. Analyst. Econ. analyst Can. Imperial Bank Commerce; market research analyst Toronto Star Ltd.; mgr. portfolio investments N.W. Trust Co., Edmonton, Alta., Can., 1974-76; v.p. A.E. Ames and Co. Ltd., 1976-81, Dominion Securities Ames Ltd., 1981-82; exec. dir. Can. Council of Fin. Analysts, 1982-84, 88—; cons. govt. cabinet minister Can. Ho. of Commons, Ottawa, Ont., 1984—, minister of state for fin., 1984-86, minister of state for privatization, minister responsible for regulatory affairs, 1986-88, minister responsible for status of women, 1986-90, minister of employment and immigration, 1988—. Fin. columnist Chatelaine mag.; fin. commentator CBC Take 30; bus. columnist City Woman mag.; bus. journalist CITV Edmonton, Vancouver Sun. Chmn. City of Toronto Salvation Army 1984 Red Shield Appeal; bd. dirs. Community Occupational Therapy Assocs., chmn., 1982-84; bd. dirs. Enoch Turner Schoolhouse, Second Mile Club; counsellor Oakhalla Province Prison for Women; vice chmn. Elizabeth Fry Soc.; past pres. Rosedale Progressive Conservative Assn. Office: Ho of Commons, Parliament Bldgs, Ottawa, ON Canada K1A 0A6

MCDOUGALL, SUSAN, assistant product director; b. Pitts., Dec. 21, 1961; d. Robert James and Barbara (Hicks) McD.; m. Kirk Thomas Dackow, Sept. 24, 1988. Student, Am. Univ., 1982; BS, Carnegie Mellon U., 1983; MBA, U. Pitts., 1986. Lobbying asst. Bayh, Tabbert and Capehart, Washington, 1982; legal asst. Agent Orange plaintiffs' mgmt. com. Henderson and Goldberg, Pitts., N.Y.C., 1983-85; bus. analyst, mem. corp. staff Mobay Corp., Pitts., 1986-88, market devel. rep. Furnishings group, Specialities dept., 1988-89; asst. product dir. member svcs. The Nat. Assn. of Securities Dealers, Inc., Washington, 1990—. Office: Nat Assn of Securities Dealers 1735 K St NW Washington DC 20006

MC DOUGALL-GOODWIN, SHARON LEE, owner service business, office manager; b. Santa Monica, Calif., July 7, 1943; d. H. Deane and Dolores Virginia (Wray) Mc Cloud; m. Douglas Scott Mc Dougall, Jan. 14, 1962 (div. Mar. 1986); children: Lori Ann Mc Dougall Wilbanks, David Brian Mc Dougall; married. Student, Santa Monica Community Coll., 1961-62. Med. office mgr. D. Brachman, M.D., Fullerton, Calif., 1982-83, Stuart Kemeny, M.D., Anaheim, Calif., 1983-86, Century Clinic, Reno, 1985-86; electrocardiogram technician Cardiac Diagnostic Ctr., Reno, 1986-88; pres., owner AACRO Precision Grinding, Inc., Sparks, Nev., 1986—; cons. in bus. planning. Mem. Nev. Innovation Tech. and Entrepreneur Coun., Reno Women in Bus., Reno-Sparks C. of C. Office: AACRO Precision Grinding #4 Hardy Dr Sparks NV 89431

MCDOWD, JOAN MARIE, educator; b. Ogden, Utah, Apr. 4, 1958; d. William A. and Rosalie L. McD. BA, Wash. U., 1980; PhD, U. Toronto, 1986. Asst. prof. U. Southern Calif., 1986--; sr. research assoc. Andrus Gerontology Ctr., Los Angeles, 1986--. Contbr. articles to profl. jours. Mem. Am. Psycholo. Assn., Gerontological Soc. Am., Western Pssycholo. Roman Catholic. Office: U So Calif SGM 501 Los Angeles CA 90089

MCDOWELL, CECELIA MARIE, personnel and security administrator; b. Jacksonville, Fla., Aug. 8, 1952; d. Henry Welburn and Joyce Annette (Remion) McD. Cert., U. Ga., 1969; BS in Psychology and Spl. Edn., Armstrong State Coll., Savannah, Ga., 1972. Cert. in employee relations law. Asst. to v.p. Hilton Head (S.C) Co., 1972; land clk. Hilton Head (S.C.) Co., Hilton Head Island, 1972; asst. to account supr. Palmetto Elec. Co-op., Ridgeland, S.C., 1972-75; employment interviewer dept. labor State of Ga., Savannah, 1975-79; supr. employment adminstrn. Gulfstream Aerospace Corp., Savannah, 1979-87, supr. human resources, 1987-89; personnel/security mgr. Chrysler Techs. Airborne Systems, Savannah, 1989—; Co-owner Easy-Does-It Mobile Home Service, Savannah, 1984-86, Rayce Enterprises, Savannah, 1984-86. Mem. adv. coun. Savannah Area Vo-Tech. Sch., 1981-87, Beaufort Jasper Career Ctr., Ridgeland, 1982-89, Savannah Displaced Homemakers Program, 1981-89; sec. Chatham Savannah Humane Soc., 1982-89; instr. Ga. State Dept. Edn., 1983, Savannah Women in Mgmt. program, 1984; presenter Hodge Found., Savannah, 1984-85; trustee Savannah Tech. Found., 1987—. Mem. Am. Soc. Personnel Adminstrs., Internat. Mgmt. Coun., Gulfstream Mgmt. Assn., Savannah Symphony Assn., Savannah Shag Club. Republican. Lutheran. Home: 608 E 49th St Savannah GA 31405 Office: Chrysler Techs Airborne Sys PO Box 18408 Box 2206 D-03 Savannah GA 31418

MCDOWELL, ELIZABETH MARY, pathology educator; b. Kew Gardens, Surrey, Eng., Mar. 30, 1940; came to U.S., 1971; d. Arthur and Peggy (Bryant) McD. B Vet. Medicine, Royal Vet. Coll., London, 1963; BA, Cambridge U., 1968, PhD, 1971. Gen. practice vet. medicine, 1964-66; Nuffield Found. tng. scholar Cambridge (Eng.) U., 1966-71; instr. dept. pathology U. Md., Balt., 1971-73, asst. prof., 1973-76, assoc. prof., 1976-80, prof., 1980—. Co-author: Biopsy Pathology of the Bronchi, 1987; editor: Lung Carcinomas, 1987; contbr. numerous articles to sci. jours., chpts. to books. Rsch. grantee NIH, 1979—. Fellow Royal Coll. Vet. Surgeons; mem. Am. Assn. Pathologists, Am. Med. Writers Assn., Pathol. Soc. Gt. Britain, U.S. and Can. Acad. Pathology. Home: 602 W 37th St Baltimore MD 21211 Office: U Md 10 S Pine St Baltimore MD 21201

MCDOWELL, JANET LEE, ultrasounder, consultant; b. Spokane, Wash., June 18, 1954; d. Kenneth Lee and Dolores Jeanne (Vosahlo) McD. Cert. radiologic tech., Holy Family Hosp., 1979, cert. in diag. ultrasound, 1984; B in Health Adminstrn., Whitworth Coll., 1985, M in Health Edn., 1989. Radiologic technician Ballard Community Hosp., Seattle, 1979-81, Swedish Hosp., Seattle, 1981, Valley Medicus, Spokane, Wash., 1981; ultrasounder Holy Family Hosp., Spokane, 1981—; health promotion specialist Bond Chiropractic Health Ctr., Spokane, 1989—. Mem. Am. Registry Radiol. Technologists, Assn. Registered Diagnostic Med. Sonographers, Soc. for Pub. Health Edn., U.S. Tae-Kwon-Do Fedn., Internat. Tae-Kwon-Do Fedn. (black belt deg. 1988), Job's Daughters (Honored Queen 1972), Eagles. Home: 7523 Hughes Dr Spokane WA 99208

MCDOWELL, JENNIFER, sociologist, playwright, publisher; b. Albuquerque, May 19, 1936; d. Willard A. and Margaret Frances (Garrison) McD.; m. Milton Loventhal, July 2, 1973. BA, U. Calif., 1957, MLS, 1963; MA, San Diego State U., 1958; PhD, U. Oreg., 1973. Tchr. English Abraham Lincoln High Sch., San Jose, Calif., 1960-61; free-lance editor Soviet field, Berkeley, Calif., 1961-63; rsch. asst. sociology U. Oreg., Eugene, 1964-66; editor, pub. Merlin Papers, San Jose, 1969—, Merlin Press, San Jose, 1973—; rsch. cons. sociology San Jose, 1973—; music pub. Lipstick and Toy Balloons Pub. Co., San Jose, 1978—; composer Paramount Pictures, 1982-88; tchr. writing workshops; poetry readings, 1969-73; co-producer radio show lit. and culture Sta. KALX, Berkeley, 1971-72. Author: Black Politics: A Study and Annotated Bibliography of the Mississippi Freedom Democratic Party, 1971, Contemporary Women Poets: An Anthology of California Poets, 1977, Ronnie Goose Rhymes for Grown-ups, 1984; co-author (plays off-off Broadway) Betsy and Phyllis, 1986, Mack The Knife Your Friendly Dentist, 1986, The Estrogen Party To End War, 1986, The Oatmeal Party Comes to Order, 1986; contbr. poems, plays, essays, short stories, book revs. to lit. mags. and anthologies; researcher women's autobiog. writings, contemporary writings in poetry, Soviet studies, civil rights movement and George Orwell, 1962—; writer: (songs) Money Makes A Woman Free, 1976, Lipstick and Toy Balloons, 1990, Coffee's My Religion, 1990, She Likes Antiques and Young Men, 1990, Mack The Knife Your Friendly Dentist, 1990, In The Intergalactic Zoo, 1990, My Mother Was a Coomunist, My Father Worked for CBS, 1990, 3 songs featured in Parade of Am. Music; co-creator: musical comedy Russia's Secret Plot to Take Back Alaska, 1988. Recipient 8 awards Am. Song Festival, 1976-79, Bill Casey award in Letters, 1980; AAUW doctoral fellow, 1971-73; grantee Calif. Arts Council, 1976-77. Mem. Am. Sociol. Assn., Soc. Sci. Study of Religion, Poetry Orgn. for Women, Dramatists Guild, Phi Beta Kappa, Sigma Alpha Iota, Beta Phi Mu, Kappa Kappa Gamma. Democrat. Office: care Merlin Press PO Box 5602 San Jose CA 95150

MCDOWELL, JOSPEHINE SARGENT, education educator; b. Denver, Aug. 14, 1912; d. Wilber Hedges and Josephine (Peacock) Sargent; m. Charles Elden. AA, Colo. Women's Coll., 1932; BA, No. Colo. U., 1934. Cert. tchr.;. Tchr. local sch. dist., Colo., 1934-35; head start tchr. WPA, Grand Junction, Colo., 1936-37, Denver, 1938-40, Greeley, Colo., 1940-41; jr. high tchr. Coolidge (Ariz.) Sch. System, 1964-74; art and craft tchr. Cen. Ariz. Coll., Coolidge, 1978—. Author: (children stories) Children at Home, 1983-85. Mem. AAUW, Ariz. Edn. Assn., Desert Women's Club. Republican. Methodist. Home: 7726 E Highway 287 Lot 79 Coolidge AZ 85228

MCDOWELL, JOYCE PATRICIA, linguistics researcher; b. Worcester, Mass., Dec. 26, 1935; d. David and Rosemary Cecelia (Glodas) Dudley; m. Edward Rae Held McDowell, June 18, 1955; children: Edward R.H. Jr., James D. BA, UCLA, 1957; MA, Calif. State U., Fullerton, 1982, U. So. Calif., 1984; PhD, U. So. Calif., 1987. Lectr. Calif. State U., Fullerton, 1986, U. So. Calif., L.A., 1988; cons., linguistic researcher IBM Corp., L.A., 1987-90; v.p. Intelligent Text Processing, Inc., 1990—. Contbr. papers, articles to tech publs. Mem. Linguistic Soc. Am., Assn. Computational Linguistics, Phi Beta Kappa, Phi Kappa Phi.

MCDOWELL, KAREN ANN, lawyer; b. Ruston, La., Oct. 4, 1945; d. Paul and Opal Elizabeth (Davis) Bauer; m. Gary Lee McDowell, Dec. 22, 1979. BA, N.E. La. U., 1967; JD, U. Mich., 1971; postgrad., John Robert Powers Sch., Chgo., 1976. Bar: Ill. 1973, Colo. 1977, U.S. Dist. Ct. (so. dist.) Ill. 1973, U.S. Dist. Ct. Colo. 1977. Reference libr. assoc. Ill. State Library, Springfield, 1972-73; asst. atty. gen. State of Ill., Springfield, 1973-75; pvt. practice Boulder, Colo., 1978-79, Denver, 1979—. Mem. So. Poverty Law Ctr., Jewish Community Ctr. Mem. ABA, Colo. Bar Assn., Denver Bar Assn., Colo. Women's Bar Assn. (editor newsletter 1982-84), Toastmasters, Amnesty Internat., Colo. Trial Lawyers Assn., Colo. Soc. for Study of Multiple Personality and Dissociation, Mensa (local sec. Ann Arbor, Mich. 1968), Phi Alpha Theta, Sigma Tau Delta (pres. N.E. La. U. chpt. 1967), Alpha Lambda Delta (pres. N.E. La. U. chpt. 1964-65). Republican. Office: 1614 Gaylord St Denver CO 80206

MCDOWELL, MARY JANE, computer systems coordinator; b. Balt., Mar. 30, 1953; d. Samson and Evelyn (Stever) McD. AA with honors, Edison Community Coll., 1973; BA with high honors, Atlantic Christian U., 1976; computer cert., Edison Community Coll., 1981. Dep. clk. Clk. of Cir. Ct., Ft. Myers, Fla., 1978-88; computer systems coord. Bruce L. Scheiner Personal Injury Lawyers PA, Ft. Myers, 1988—. Mem. Barbara B. Mann Performing Arts Hall, Concerned Women for Am., Luth. Mo. Synol., Presbyn. Assn. Mem. Am. Businesswomen's Assn. (rec. sec. chpt. 1983, 87, Attending award 1984-89), AAUW (life, Eleanor Roosevelt Fund, treas. Ft. Myers Br. 1988-90), DAR, Women Aglow Fellowship Internat., Cursillo/Rd. to Emmaus, Pi Gamma Mu, Alpha Chi, Phi Theta Kappa. Republican. Presbyterian. Home: 4430 N Canal Circle NW North Fort Myers FL 33903 Office: Bruce L Scheiner Personal Injury Lawyers PA 4020 Evans Ave Fort Myers FL 33901

MCDOWELL, SUSAN GRAHAM, psychologist, service administrator; b. Evansville, Ind., Aug. 5, 1952; d. Dorwin Walter and Bettye Lisetta (Oestreicher) Graham; m. Larry Grant McDowell, Dec. 20, 1975; 1 child, Graham Scott. BS, Ind. U., 1974; MA, U. Evansville, 1977; PhD, Ball State U., 1985. Lic. psychologist, Ind. Spl. edn. tchr. Evansville-Vanderburgh Sch. Corp., 1974-80, psychologist, 1980-84, supr. psychol. svcs., 1984-89, dir. psychol. svcs., 1989—; chairperson Gov.'s Blue Ribbon Testing Adv. Panel, Indpls., 1989-90; mem. Ind. Test Adv. Coun., 1985—. V.p., bd. dirs. Southwestern Ind. Mental Health Ctr., Evansville, 1989—; bd. dirs. Evansville Assn. for Retarded Citizens, 1989—. Ball State U. fellow, 1980. Mem. Southwestern Ind. Psychol. Assn. (pres. 1989—), Ind. Psychol. Assn. (treas.), Nat. Assn. Sch. Psychologists, Am. Psychol. Assn., Ind. Ass. Sch. Psychologists, Phi Delta Kappa. Office: Evansville-Vanderburgh Sch Corp Psychol Svcs 310 SE 8th St Evansville IN 47713

MCDOWELL, VALERIE ELIZABETH, securities trader; b. Newark, July 28, 1944; d. John Santo and Anne (LaFauci) Aiello; divorced; 1 child, Allen Michael. Student, Brookdale Coll., Lincroft, N.J., 1975-77. Asst. stock-trader M.H. Meyerson, Jersey City, 1967-72; asst. to v.p. DuPont Walston, Asbury Park, N.J., 1972-74; stockbroker Smith Barney Harris Upham, Tinton Falls, N.J., 1974-78; asst. v.p., sr. trader M.H. Meyerson, Jersey City, 1978-84; sr. trader Domestic Arbitrage, Jersey City, 1984-85, Fitz, DeArman & Roberts, Mantoloking, N.J., 1985-87; pres., mng. dir. William Allen & Co., Red Bank, N.J., 1987—. Mem. Nat. Assn. Securities Dealers, Inc. (mem. arbitration panel), Securities Ind. Assn., Securities Investor Protection Corp., Red Bank C. of C. Republican. Roman Catholic. Office: William Allen & Co Inc 230 Half Mile Rd Red Bank NJ 07701

MCDUFF, JUDITH DIANE, writer, editor; b. Ft. Worth, Aug. 6, 1945; d. Alexander Geltz and Bibi Zoradell (Stone) McDade; m. Edward Smith Lindow Jr., Oct. 26, 1968 (div. Apr. 1976); m. Jack McDuff, Nov. 23, 1985. Student, SUNY, Fredonia, 1963-65; BA in Liberal Arts, Pa. State U., 1967, MA in Journalism, 1972. Teaching credential, Calif. Artists series info. specialist Pa. State U., University Pk., 1973-74; writer, editor The Holman Co., Pitts., 1975; substitute elem. tchr. Westminster (Calif.) Sch. Dist., 1978-79; cons. writing and editing various orgns., Fullerton, 1979—; publs. analyst Varco Oil Tools, Orange, 1979-80; acting publs. editor Coastline Community Coll., Fountain Valley, 1984-85, asst. publs. editor, 1980-88, community svcs. specialist, 1988-90; editor class schedule Yorba Linda Continuing Edn. Ctr., 1990—; piano tchr., Fullerton, 1988—; cons. Communications Svcs., Fullerton, 1979—; tour escort Coastline Community Coll., 1983—. Editor: Coast Communicator, 1986-88, Chinese Brush Painting, 1987. N.Y. State Bd. Regents scholar, 1963. Mem. AAUW, Master Chorale Orange County (librarian 1988-89). Republican. Home: 2720 Pine Creek Circle Fullerton CA 92635

MCELDOON, SUSAN ANN, television sales executive; b. Thief River Falls, Minn., Oct. 10, 1952; d. Lyell Chester Raymond and Eunice Virginia (Scarr) McE.; m. Nicolas Norman Smeloff, Dec. 26, 1982; children: Amy Joy, Nicholas Norman, Elizabeth Ann. BA, U. Mo., Kansas City, 1980. Broadcast producer Barickman Advt., Kansas City, Mo., 1973-80; account exec. Stuart Broadcasting/KFRM-FM, Lincoln, Nebr., 1980-81; bus. mgr. Colo. Homes and Lifestyles, Denver, 1981-82; broadcast dir. The May Co., Denver, 1982-85; mktg. mgr. KCNC-TV/NBC Broadcasting, Denver, 1985-87, local sales mgr., 1987--. Contbr. articles to Ad Marketing/Review, 1988-89. V.p. and treas. Keep the Lights Found., Denver, 1986—. Recipient Pres. of Yr. award Am. Advt. Fedn., Washington, 1989; Alex. B. Coleman shcolar U. Mo., 1979; named Advt. Profl. of Yr., Denver, 1990. Mem. Am. Advt. Fedn., Denver Advt. Fedn. (bd. dirs. 1985-88, Pres. of Yr. award 1988, Advt. Profl. of Yr. 1990). Presbyterian.

MCELENEY, BRENDA JEAN, nurse, air force officer; b. Ellendale, N.D., Nov. 1, 1956; d. Michael and Marion Verona (Merkel) Martin; m. Dennis McEleney, June 28, 1983. BS in Nursing, U. N.D., 1980; MA, Webster U., St. Louis, 1988. RN, N.D. Commd. 2d lt. USAF, 1980, advanced through grades to maj., 1990; staff nurse, Loring AFB, Maine, 1981-83; officer-in-charge inpatient unit USAF Hosp., Iraklion Air Sta., Greece, 1983-86; asst. charge nurse Wilford Hall Med. Ctr., San Antonio, 1986-87, charge nurse, 1987-88; comdr. student squadron 3790th Med. Svc. Tng. Wing, Wichita Falls, Tex., 1988—. Decorated Meritorious Svc. medal. Mem. NAFE, Am. Nurses Assn., Air Force Assn. Office: 3793d Student Squadron Sheppard AFB TX 76311

MCELHINNEY, SUSAN KAY, legal assistant; b. Greeley, Colo., May 20, 1947; d. Glenn Eugene and Maxine (Filkins) McE. Student, U. N.C., 1965-67. Adminstrv. sec. Colo. Pub. Defender, Denver, 1970-74; clk. Colo. Dist. Ct., Boulder, 1974-80; legal asst., office mgr. Law Office of Ben Echeverria, San Marcos, Calif., 1986—. Democrat. Office: Law Offices Ben Echeverria 334 Via Vera Cruz #205 San Marcos CA 92069

MCELROY, ABBY LUCILLE WOLMAN, financial consultant; b. Washington, Oct. 16, 1957; d. M. Gordon and Elaine (Mielke) Wolman; m. Peter J. McElroy, Jan. 5, 1957. BA, St. Lawrence U., 1979; MS, Ind. U., 1981. Research asst. Ctr. on Aging and Aged, Bloomington, Ind., 1980-81; technician Xerox Corp., Stamford, Conn., 1981, U.S. Fidelity and Guaranty, Balt., 1982-83; Lacrosse coach The Park Sch., Balt., 1983; mgr. The Tomlinson Craft Collection, Balt., 1983-84; account mgr. U.S. Lines, Norwalk, Conn., 1984-86; fin. cons. Shearson Lehman Hutton Inc., Westport, Conn., 1986—; guest speaker fin. segment for retirement planning course Sacred Heart U., Bridgeport, Conn., 1988. Lacrosse coach Wilton High Sch., Wilton, Conn., 1988-89. Recipient Tom & Ruth Rivers Scholarship award World Leisure & Recreation Assn., Can., 1981; London Group Study Exch. grantee Rotary Internat., 1989. Mem. Fairfield Network Exec. Women (treas. 1989—), Bridgeport Bus. Coun., Women's Lacrosse Assn. (treas. 1983-84), Am. Assn. for Fitness in Bus. and Industry (state rep. 1982-83). Office: Shearson Lehman Hutton Inc 1 Village Square Westport CT 06880

MCELROY, ANN, retired physical therapist; b. Erie, Pa., May 3, 1922; d. Herbert Louis and Jean Rebecca (Gersheimer) McElroy Hoppin. Cert. in phys. therapy, Children's Hosp., L.A., 1944; BS in Biol. Scis., Coll. William and Mary, 1950; MS in Health Sci. Edn., Case Western Res. U., 1978. Phys. therapist med. dept. U.S. Army, 1942-46; supervising phys. therapist VA Hosp., Hines, Ill., 1946-49; physical therapist Shriners Childrens Hosp., Lexington, Ky., 1950-53; physical therapist Rehab. Ctr., Kauikeolani Childrens Hosp., Honolulu, 1954-56; cons. WHO, Port-au-Prince, Haiti, 1956-57; chief phys. therapist Western Md. State Hosp., Hagerstown, 1958-60; chief phys. therapist oil intoxication program Internat. Red Cross, Méknès, Morocco, 1960-61; dir. phys. therapy Mt. Sinai Med. Ctr., Cleve., 1962-80; mgr. phys. therapy Highland View Rehab., Met. Gen. and Sunny Acres Hosps., Cleve., 1980-86; ret., 1986; mem. clin. faculty 12 midwest and ea. univs., 1963-86; advisor phys. therapy program planning Cleve. State U., 1971-75, 90—; advisor Vis. Nurse Assn., Cleve., 1978, evaluation surveyor, Akron, Ohio, 1981. Contbr. articles to profl. jours. Asst. leader Girl Scouts U.S.A., Lexington, 1950-52, leader, 1953; guest lectr. community colls., nursing schs., hosp. edn. programs and axu. meetings, Cleve., 1962-86. 2d lt. U.S. Army, 1944-46. Recipient award of honor as clin. instr. Case Western Res. U., 1971; scholar Childrens Hosp., 1943. Mem. Am. Phys. Therapy Assn. (life, former nat. chmn. membership, also local offices and com. activities, award of merit for svc. in Morocco 1962), Cleve. Photog. Soc., Cleve. Shell Club, Beta Sigma Phi (pres. Lexington City Coun. 1953). Home: 718 Park Ave N Erie PA 16502

MCELROY, CHRISTINE MARY, psychologist; b. Providence, Nov. 2, 1952; d. James Edward and Mary Louise (Young) McE.; m. Howard Charles Bauchner, Sept. 8, 1985; 1 child, Mathis Christopher. BA, Simmons Coll., 1974; MA, Boston U., 1981, PhD, 1984. Clin. intern Mass. Gen. Hosp., Boston, 1982-83; post-doctoral fellow Yale U. Med. Sch., New Haven, 1984-86; instr. Harvard Med. Sch., Boston, 1986—; clin. assoc. Mass. Gen. Hosp., Boston, 1986—; psychologist Fresh Pond Mental Health Clin., Cambridge, Mass., 1986—. Mem. Am. Psychol. Assn. Office: Fresh Pond Mental Health Clinic 650 Concord Ave Cambridge MA 02138

MCELROY, EMILIE LIN, mental health professional; b. San Francisco, Jan. 10, 1954; d. Earl Edwin and Carolyn Ardell (Brickley) McE.; m. Robert Louis Hitsman Jr., Feb. 25, 1984; children: Lynda Nicole, Devin Joseph. Student, U. Calif., Davis, 1986, U. Louisville, 1986—; BS, NYU, 1990. Artistic dir., gen. mgr. Sunshine Children's Theatre, Davis, 1977-83; counselor Progress Ranch, Inc., Davis, 1981-83; youth worker shelter house YMCA, Louisville, 1983-84, house coordinator, 1984-85; house dir. Schizophrenia Found. Ky., Louisville, 1985—; dir. Creative Cons., Lyndon, Ky., 1985—; advocate, counselor Louisville Rape Relief Ctr., 1984—. Organizer Calif. Dem. State Conv., 1982; apptd. spl. advocate Jefferson County (Ky.) Juvenile Ct. Dependency Docket. Mem. Nat. Assn. Female Execs. Roman Catholic. Home: 9110 Farham Rd Lyndon KY 40222 Office: Schizophrenia Found 1382 S 3d St Louisville KY 40208

MCELROY, JANICE HELEN, government agency executive; b. Topeka, Kans., Dec. 12, 1937; d. Rudolph Ralph and Josephine Elizabeth (Kern) Jilka; m. James Douglas McElroy, June 25, 1967; children: Helen Elizabeth, Bryan Douglas. BS, Colo. Coll., Colorado Springs, 1960; MAT, Johns Hopkins U., 1964; PhD, U.S. Internat. U., San Diego, 1970. Biology tchr. Roland Park Country Day Sch., Balt., 1962-63, Edmundston High Sch., Balt., 1964; chmn. dept. sci. Bishop's Sch., La Jolla, Calif., 1964-69; instr. Somerset County Community Coll., Somerville, N.J., 1973-75, Cedar Crest Coll., Allentown, Pa., 1976-82; dir. re-entry program Cedar Crest Coll., 1979-82; exec. dir. Resource Devel. Svcs., Allentown, 1982-86; dir. planning and devel. Montgomery County Community Coll., Blue, Pa., 1986-88; exec. dir. Pa. Commn. for Women, Harrisburg, 1988—. Research dir./editor: Our Hidden Heritage: Pennsylvania Women in History, 1983; contbr. articles to profl. jours. Mem. Women's Adv. Bd. Task Force, Lehigh County, Pa., 1981-82. Fulbright scholar, 1960; Ford Found. fellow, 1963; NSF fellow, 1965. Mem. AAUW (pres. Pa. div. 1984-88, nat. bd. dirs. 1989—), LWV, Phi Beta Kappa. Democrat. Presbyterian. Home: 2826 Crest Ave N Allentown PA 18104 Office: Pa Commn for Women PO Box 1326 Harrisburg PA 17105

MCELROY, JUNE PATRICIA, sales consultant; b. Atlantic City, Sept. 26, 1929; d. Edmund N. and Dorothy R. (McDowell) Ricchezza; m. David Waycott Carson, Apr. 8, 1947 (div. 1954); m. Ottavio Gelmi, Dec. 16, 1954 (div. 1964); 1 child, Alessandra; m. Robert Joseph McElroy, Oct. 16, 1970 (dec. May 1974). Student Temple U., 1947-48, Inst. linguistics, Georgetown U., 1951-53. Mem. staff Am. consulate gen., Milan, Italy, 1954; legis. asst. U.S. Senate, Washington, 1956; social sec. to ambassador of Finland, Washington, 1958; legis. asst. to congressman, Washington, 1960-65; sr. assoc. Gillmore M. Perry Co., Washington, 1965-76; sales exec./cons. furniture industry, Hilton Head, S.C., 1985-87; ptnr. Mfrs. Representatives Internat., 1987—. Mem. Georgetown U. Alumni Assn. Republican. Roman Catholic. Club: Army Navy (Washington). Home: 4101 Cathedral Ave NW Washington DC 20016

MCELROY, ROSEMARY, caseworker; b. Chgo., May 25, 1931; d. Paul Richard and Marie Veronica (Taft) McE. BA, Mount St. Scholastica, 1953; postgrad., Loyola U., Chgo., 1962-65. Foster caseworker Cath. Charities, Chgo., 1953-56, adoption caseworker, 1956—; agy. rep. Adoption Info. Svcs., 1963—, Child Care Assn. Adoption Coun., 1976—, State Adoption Task Force Subcom. Child Care Assn. to place Black Infants, 1988—, Cath. Charities Ill. Adoption Com., 1988—. Mem. Condominium Bd. Dirs., 1973; election judge Du Page County Election Com. Mem. Cath. Charities U.S., Child Care Assn. Ill. Roman Catholic. Office: Chicago Cath Charities 126 N Des Plaines Chicago IL 60606

MCELROY-LINDELL, LOIS ANN, economics educator; b. Portage, Wis., July 18, 1958; d. Boyd Wayne and Edith Isabella (Rye) McElroy; m. Terrence Jon Lindell, May 8, 1982. BA, U. Wis., 1980; postgrad., U. Nebr., 1980—. Grad. teaching asst. dept. econs. U. Nebr., Lincoln, 1980-84, asst. dir. Ctr. for Econ. Edn., 1983-84; instr. in econs. Wartburg Coll., Waverly, Iowa, 1984-85, asst. prof. econs., 1985—. Mem. com. on the Status of Women in the Econs. Profession. Mem. Am. Econ. Assn., Nat. Assn. Bus. Economists, AAUW (corp. rep. Waverly chpt. 1985-89), Delta Kappa Gamma. Lutheran. Office: Wartburg Coll 222 Ninth St NW Waverly IA 50677

MCELVANY, KAREN DIANE, chemistry researcher; b. Balt., Nov. 15, 1954; d. Ward Robey and Alice (Poe) McE.; m. William John Powers, Mar. 19, 1983; children: Katherine Elizabeth, Brian Ward. BA, Coll. of Wooster, 1976; MA, Washington U., St. Louis, 1977, PhD, 1980. Rsch. instr. dept. radiology Washington U. Sch. Medicine, 1979-81, rsch. asst. prof., 1981-82, asst. prof. radiation chemistry, 1982-83, dir. radiopharmacy, 1981-83; clin. rsch. assoc. Mallinckrodt, Inc., St. Louis, 1983-85, asst. dir. clin. rsch., 1985-90, assoc. dir. clin. rsch., 1990—. Contbr. articles to profl. jours., chpts. to books. Bd. dirs. Clayton (Mo.) Child Ctr., 1988—, treas., 1990—, pres. parent orgn., 1988—. Spencer T. Olin scholar, 1976-80. Mem. Soc. Nuclear Medicine (Best Contributed Presentation award Missouri Valley chpt. 1977, 78, 80, 81), Am. Chem. Soc., Phi Beta Kappa, Sigma Xi. Home: 854 Brookside Dr Saint Louis MO 63122 Office: Mallinckrodt Med Inc 675 McDonnell Blvd PO Box 5840 Saint Louis MO 63134

MCENTIRE, MALETA MAE, regional real estate manager; b. L.A., Sept. 22, 1957; d. Floyd Steven and Joan Marie (Kioskli) Odessa; m. Robert James Ornellas, Aug. 25, 1980 (div. 1982); m. Jack Walton McEntire, Jr., Oct. 25, 1986; children: Jason, Jeremy. Student, Delta Jr. Coll., Stockton, Calif., 1977. Lic. real estate ins. Personnel adminstrv. aide World Airways, Oakland, Calif., 1975-77; flight attendant World Airways, 1977-81; with sales Winner Chevrolet, Tracy, Calif., 1981-88; dir. San Joaquin County Food Bank, Tracy, 1981-85; commr. San Joaquin County, Stockton, Calif., 1981-84, Brown Bag, State of Calif., Sacramento, 1982, Food Bank, State of Calif., Sacramento, 1985; regional mgr. Sutter Office Ctr., Stockton, 1985—; bd. dirs. Downtown Devel. & Planning, Stockton; student instr. Jr. Achievement, Stockton, 1988—; mem. Na.t Assn. Notaries, State of Calif., 1988—; advisor Redevelopment Dist. IB, City of Stockton, 1987—. Author: Brown Bag Manual, 1982 (Govt. of Calif. award 1982), State of California Distribution, 1983 (Calif. Sec. of State award 1983). Advisor Stockton Rep. Com., 1976—; bd. dirs. McHenry Shelter, Tracy, 1987—; mem. Calif. Food Bank and Commodity Commn., Sacramento, 1983-385. Recipient Outstanding Sales cert. Winner Cheu, Tracy, 1984, Rescue Mission Baby Lifts cert. Govt. of Calif., 1979; named Miss Tracy-Talent, Tracy C. of C., 1975. Mem. Tracy Exchange H & S, 4-H Club Am. (advisor), Stockton C. of C. (Vol. of Yr. 1981), Lyons Club (Outstanding Citizen 1985), Jr. Achievement. Republican. Baptist. Home: 7514 Stueben Way Stockton CA 95207 Office: Sutter Office Ctr 242 N Sutter St 700 Stockton CA 95202

MCENTIRE, REBA N., entertainer; b. McAlester, Okla., Mar. 28, 1955; d. Clark Vincent and Jacqueline (Smith) McE.; m. Narvel Blackstock, 1989; 1 child, Shelby Steven McEntire Blackstock. Student elem. edn., music, Southeastern State U., Durant, Okla., 1976. Rec. artist Mercury Records, 1978-83, MCA Records, 1984—. Albums include Whoever's in New England (Gold award), 1986, What Am I Gonna Do About You (Gold award), 1987, Greatest Hits (Gold award, Platinum award, U.S., Can.), 1987, The Last One To Know (Gold award), 1988, Reba (Gold award 1988), Sweet 16 (Gold award 1989, U.S.), Reba Live (Gold award 1990) Reba compilation video (Gold award). Spokesperson Middle Tenn. United Way, 1988, Nat. and State 4-H Alumni, Bob Hope's Hope for a Drug Free Am. Recipient numerous awards in Country music including Disting. Alumni award Southeastern State U., Female vocalist award Country Music Assn., 1984, 85, 86, 87, Grammy award for Best Country Vocal Performance, 1987; named Entertainer of Yr., Country Music Assn., 1986, Female Vocalist of Yr. Acad. Country Music, 1984, 85, 86, 87, Am. Music award favorite female country singer, 1988, Am. Music award, 1989, 90. Mem. Country Music Assn., Acad. Country Music, Nat. Acad. Rec. Arts and Scis., Grand Ol' Opry, AFTRA, Nashville Songwriters Assn. Inc.

MCEVOY JOHNSTON, PAMELA, clinical psychologist; b. Forest Hills, N.Y., Mar. 8, 1937; d. Renny T. and Pamela Shipley (Sweeny) McE.; BA, U. La Verne, 1978, MS, 1980; PhD, U.S. Internat. U., 1982; m. Percy H. Johnston, Jr.; children: Michael B. Anderson, Jeffery A. Thomas, Candy L. Anderson-Smith, Kenneth L. Anderson. Data processing coordinator Ernest Righetti High Sch., Santa Maria, Calif., 1974-78; instr. psychology-sociology Allan Hancock Coll., Santa Maria, 1977-78; mental health asst. Santa Barbara City Alcoholism Dept., 1977-78; gen. mgr. Profl. Suites, San Diego, 1978-81; therapist Chula Vista (Calif.) Community Counseling Ctr., San Diego, 1978-85; research asst. U.S. Internat. U., 1979-82; research coordinator Mil. Family research Ctr., San Diego, 1981-82; assoc. dir. Acad. Assoc. Psychotherapists, 1982-86; pvt. practice, San Diego, 1982—; pres. Adv. Psychol. Health Ctr., 1987—; bd. dirs. Women's Internat. Ctr., 1984-86. Bd. dirs. San Diego County Mental Health Assn., 1978-84, Chula Vista Counseling Ctr., 1978; mem. Delinquency Prevention Commn., 1978. State fellow, 1979, 80, 81, 82, Calif. State scholar, 1976-77. Mem. Am. Psychol. Assn., Am. Assn. Marriage and Family Therapists, Calif. Assn. Marriage and Family Therapists. Republican. Roman Catholic. Home: PO Box 8946 Rancho Santa Fe CA 92067

MCEWEN, AILA ERMAN, small business owner; b. State Island, N.Y., Mar. 8, 1941; d. Theodor Diatlo and Selma Eva (Anderson) E.; m. Marvin Ross Cutson, Nov. 2, 1962 (div. Oct. 31, 1981); children: Craig Bernard, Jaana; m. Joseph McEwen, Nov. 19, 1983. BS in Mktg., Fla. State U., 1962. Asst. dept mgr. Sears Roebuck, Tampa, Fla., 1962; social worker State of Fla., Tampa, 1962-64; mgr. Aila's Decorative Hardware & Bath Gallery, St. Petersburg, Fla., 1965081; v.p., sec. So. Lock & Supply Co., Inc., St. Petersburg, 1968-81; pres. Mills Travel Svc., Inc., St. Petersburg, 1983—. Mem., benefactor Am. Stage Theater, St. Petersburg, 1988—; founding mem. Tiger Bay Club, St. Petersburg, 1984—; docent Mus. Fine Arts, St. Petersburg, 1982—. Mem. Zonta Internat., Dali Mus., Am. Soc. Travel Agents, Pacific Area Travel Agents, Suncoast Travel Industry Assn., Fla. State U. Pres.'s Club, St. Petersburg Yacht Club, Alpha Chi Omega. Republican. Jewish. Home: 1904 Kansas Ave NE Saint Petersburg FL 33703 Office: Mills Travel Svc Inc 9300 4th St N Ste B Saint Petersburg FL 33702

MCEWEN, MARY LOUISE, nurse; b. Cambridge, Mass., Apr. 10, 1960; d. James Keith and Mary Elizabeth (Arapoff) McE. BSN, Salem State Coll., 1982; MBA, U. Maine, 1987. RN, Mass., Maine; cert med.-surg. and psychiat. nurse Am. Nursing Assn. Staff nurse USAF Hosp., Beale AFB, Calif., 1982-85; staff devel. officer Maine Air NG, Bangor, Maine, 1985—; head nurse Bangor Mental Health Inst., 1987-89, asst. dir. nursing, 1989—. Recipient Presidential Achievement award, U. Maine, 1986, Maine Commendation award, Maine Air NG, 1988. Mem. NAFE, Air N.G. Nursing Assn., Air N.G. of Maine Assn., Sigma Theta Tau. Roman Catholic.

MCFADDEN, MARY, lawyer; b. Bethlehem, Pa., Nov. 7, 1950; d. Joseph B. and Catherine M. McF.; m. Lawrence T.P. Stifler, Nov. 25, 1977. BA magna cum laude, Boston U., 1972; JD cum laude, Suffolk U., 1978. Bar: Mass. 1978. Rsch. assoc. Med. Found., Inc., Boston, 1973-78; trial atty. for Child Welfare Unit, Mass. Dept. Pub. Welfare, Boston, 1978-80, Mass. Dept. Social Svcs., 1980-82; exec. sec. Mass. Commn. on Jud. Conduct, Boston, 1982-86; corp. counsel Health Mgmt. Resources Corp., 1986—. Mem. ABA, Mass. Bar Assn., Phi Beta Kappa, Psi Chi. Co-author articles on alcohol use. Office: 59 Temple Pl Ste 704 Boston MA 02111

MC FADDEN, MARY JOSEPHINE, fashion industry executive; b. N.Y.C., Oct. 1, 1938; d. Alexander Bloomfield and Mary Josephine (Cutting) McF.; m. Philip Harari; 1 child, Justine. Ed., Sorbonne, Paris, France, Traphagen Sch. Design, 1957, Columbia, 1959-62; DFA, Internat. Fine Arts Coll., 1984. Pub. relations dir. Christian Dior, N.Y.C., 1962-64; merchandising editor Vogue South Africa, 1964-65; polit. and travel columnist Rand (South Africa) Daily Mail, 1965-68; founder sculptural workshop Vukutu, Rhodesia, 1968-70; spl. projects editor Vogue U.S.A., 1970; pres. Mary McFadden, Inc., N.Y.C., 1976—; bd. dirs., advisor Sch. Design and Merchandising Kent State U., Eugene O'Neill Meml. Theatre Ctr., Nat. Am. Mus., Am. Indian Coll. Fund.; profl. com. Cooper-Hewitt Mus., Smithsonian Inst., Nat. Mus. of Design. Fashion and jewelry designer, 1973—; recipient Am. Fashion Critics award-Coty award 1976, 78, Audemars Piguet Fashion award 1976, Rex award 1977, More Coll. Art award 1977, Pa. Gov.'s award 1977, Roscoe award 1978, Pres.'s Fellows award R.I. Sch. Design 1979, Neiman Marcus award of excellence 1979, named to Fashion Hall of Fame 1979. Fellow Rhode Island Sch. Design. Mem. Fashion Group, Coun. Fashion Designers of Am. (v.p., past bd. dirs., advisor), Nat. Endowment for the Arts (bd. dirs., advisor). Office: 240 W 35th St New York NY 10001*

MCFADDEN, ROSEMARY THERESA, mercantile exchange executive; b. Scotland, Oct. 1, 1948; came to U.S. 1951, naturalized 1967; d. John and Winifred (Quinn) McFadden.; m. Brian Doherty, May 26, 1973. BA, Rutgers U., 1970, MBA, 1974; JD, Seton Hall U., 1978; hon. doctorate St. Elizabeth's Coll.-Convent Station, N.J., 1985. Bar: N.J. 1978, U.S. Dist. Ct. 1978. Spl. asst. Office of the Mayor, Jersey City, 1973-76; exec. dir. Hudson Health System, Jersey City, 1976-81; assoc. legal counsel N.Y. Merc. Exchange, N.Y.C., 1981-82, exec. v.p., 1982-84, pres., 1984-89, spl. policy advisor to bd. dirs., 1989—; of counsel Panepineto, Paolino, Doherty, Magin, Jersey City and N.Y.C., 1989—; mem. deans adv. council Rutgers U. Grad. Sch. Mgmt., Newark, 1985. Bd. dirs. Jersey City Med. Ctr., 1985-87, UNICEF, 1989—, FIA, 1989-90. Named Alumna of Yr., Rutgers U., 1985, Alumna of Yr. Seton Hall U. Mem. ABA, N.J. Bar Assn., Inst. Petroleum, Soc. Ind. Gas Mktg., Rutgers U. Alumni Assn. Roman Catholic. Avocations: travel, antique collecting. Office: Journal Square Pla Jersey City NJ 07306

MC FADDEN, SYBILL MARTIN, museum curator; b. Pitts., Mar. 22, 1918; d. Alfred Nicholas and Rachel (Church) Martin; B.A. in Journalism, Pa. State U., 1941; m. William Patrick McFadden, Aug. 19, 1942; children—Suzanne Sybill, William Patrick, Gary J. Public relations dir. advt. ARC, Eastern Area Hdqrs., Alexandria, Va., 1941-46; owner, curator Mus. Antique Dolls and Toys, Lakewood, N.Y., 1960—; artist, one-woman shows, N.Y. and Fla.; writer, photographer nat. doll and toy mags., antiques mag.; writer, columnist Hobbies Mag. Mem. United Fedn. Doll Clubs, Inc., Western N.Y. Doll Club, Fla. West Coast Doll Collectors, Doll Study Club Jamestown (founder), Doll Collectors of America. Author: Portraits in Porcelain. Home and Office: 96 W Summit Ave Lakewood NY 14750

MCFADDEN, VERONICA SANDRA, account representative; b. Wyandotte, Mich., May 14, 1967; d. Robert and Uta (Koopmann) McF. Student journalism, U. Miss., 1986-88. Asst. adminstr. Houston Golf Assn., 1986-88, tournament coord., 1988-89; account rep. Max Gruenhut Internat., Freight Forwarders, 1989—. Houston Bapt. U. scholar, 1985, U. Miss. scholar, 1986. Mem. NAFE, Women in Transp., Women's Golf Assn., Trans. Nat. Women's Golf Assn., Tex. Women's Golf Assn. Office: 2050 N Loop W Ste 200 Houston TX 77018

MCFALL, DONNA SULLIVAN, space planner; b. Long Beach, Calif., May 16, 1950; d. Don and Wanda (Trovillion) Sullivan; m. Dennis McFall, Feb. 5, 1981; children: Matthew, Jane. Student, U. Oreg., 1973. Cert. real estate broker, Oreg. Prin. McFall Assocs., Portland, Oreg.; facilities planner Tektronix, Beaverton, Oreg.; bd. dirs. Wadon Mortgage Exchange, Inc. Mem. policy bd. Religious Coalition for Abortion Rights in Oreg., 1987-90; active Congregation Beth Israel, Portland. Mem. Internat. Facilities Mgmt. Assn. (bd. dirs.), Inst. Managerial and Profl. Women.

MCFARLAND, KAY ELEANOR, state supreme court justice; b. Coffeyville, Kans., July 20, 1935; d. Kenneth W. and Margaret E. (Thrall) McF. BA magna cum laude, Washburn U., Topeka, 1957, JD, 1964. Bar: Kans. 1964. Sole practice Topeka, 1964-71; probate and juvenile judge Shawnee County, Topeka, 1971-73; dist. judge Topeka, 1973-77; justice Kans. Supreme Ct., 1977—. Mem. Kans. Bar Assn., Irish Wolfhound Clubs of Eng., Ireland and Am. Office: Kans Supreme Ct Kans Jud Ctr 301 W 10th St Topeka KS 66612*

MCFARLAND, KAY FLOWERS, medical educator; b. Daytona Beach, Fla., Jan. 27, 1942; d. Ernest Clyde and Sarah Elizabeth (Holder) Flowers; m. Dee Edward McFarland, Aug. 18, 1963; children: Grace, Joy, Eric, Sarah. BS, Wake Forest Coll., 1963; MD, Bowman Gray Sch. Medicine, 1966. Diplomate Am. Bd. Internal Medicine, Am. Bd. Endocrinology. Intern N.C. Bapt. Hosp., Winston-Salem; resident medicine Cleve. Clinic; fellow endocrinology Med. Coll. Ga., Augusta; from instr. to asst. prof. medicine Me. Coll. Ga., Augusta, 1971-77; assoc. prof. to prof. ob-gyn. Sch. Medicine U. S.C., Columbia, 1977-86, prof. medicine Sch. Medicine, 1986—, assoc. dean continuing edn. Sch. Medicine, 1986—; cons. in field. contbr. chpts. to books and articles to profl. jours. Fellow ACP; mem. Am. Diabetes Assn. (past pres. Augusta chpt., Profl. award 1975). Republican. Lutheran. Office: Univ S C Sch Medicine 2 Richland Med Park Columbia SC 29203

MCFARLAND, LYNNE VERNICE, pharmaceutical executive; b. San Antonio, Tex., June 3, 1953; d. Earle Clifford and Avis Marie (Jones) Olson; m. Marcus Joseph McFarland, July 27, 1975. BS in Microbiology, Portland State U., 1975, MS, 1980; PhD in Epidemiology, U. Wash., 1988. Pub. Health Cert. Rsch. asst. U. Oreg. Health Sci. Ctr., Portland, 1977-79, lab. supr., 1980-82; rsch intern Wash. State Pub. Health Labs, Seattle, 1981; teaching asst. Dept. Epidemiology U. Wash., Seattle, 1984, rsch. asst., 1984-88, postdoctoral researcher Dept. Med. Chemistry, 1988, lectr. Dept. Med. Chemistry, 1988, rsch. assoc. Dept. Med. Chemistry, 1988—; dir. scientific affairs Biocodex, Inc., Seattle, 1988—; reviewer McGrfaw-Hill Book Co., N.Y.C., 1982; editorial reviewer Ob-Gyn, L.A., 1989—; cons. Labs. Biocodex, 1984—. Contbr. articles to profl. jours. Lobbyist environ. issues Wash. State Biotech. Assn., Seattle, 1990; vol. Literacy Plus, Seattle, 1990. Recipient Poncin scholarshp, Seafirst Bank, Seattle, 1985-88. Mem. Am. Soc. Microbiology, Soc. for Epidemiol. Rsch., Soc. Microbiol. Ecology and Diseases, Wash. Assn. of Epidemiology. Office: Biocodex Inc 1910 Fairview Ave E #208 Seattle WA 98102

MCFARLAND, SHARON JEANNETTE, financial planner; b. Denver, July 12, 1938; d. Harmon J. and Eva I. (Miller) Bordeaux; ; children: Shannon L. Ash, Laurie S. Robledo. Student, Casper Coll., 1956-57, Olympic Coll., Bremerton, Wash., 1967-68; cert. fin. planner, Coll. for Fin. Planning, Denver, 1983-85. Exec. sec. Olympic Coll., 1969-75, instr., 1984-87; owner, mgr. Homestead Deli, Silverdale, Wash., 1981-1975-81; registered rep. IDS/Am. Express, Bremerton, 1981-83; owner, mgr. Fin. Directions, Silverdale, 1983—; specialist Gt. N.W. Fed., Bremerton, 1987—; instr. Inst. Fin. Edn., Bremerton, 1988. Mem. task force Central Kitsap Sch. Dist. 303, Silverdale, 1983-84. Recipient award C.K. Sch. Dist., 1984, cert. of appreciation AMA, Seattle, 1986. Mem. Internat. Assn. Fin. Planners, Olympic Fin. Planners Assn. (co-founder, v.p. 1986, sec.-treas. 1987), Silverdale C. of C. (exec. bd. 1983-85, centennial com. 1987-88, Mem. of Month award 1982, 83).

MCFARLAND, SUSAN LOUISE, nurse, clinical consultant; b. Reno, Aug. 10, 1958; d. William Henry and Bobbie Ann (Brown) McF. BSN, La. State U., 1981. RN, La.; registered emergency med. technician, registered emergency med. tech. instr., advanced cardiac life support instr., basic life support instr.; cert. in hyperbarics, La. Staff nurse, charge nurse, acting head nurse emergency dept. Charity Hosp. La., New Orleans; charge nurse, acting head nurse Ochsner Health Care Facility, New Orleans, 1984; head nurse emergency dept. Ochsner Found. Hosp., New Orleans, spl. relief flight nurse Ochsner flight care dept., payment systems coord., clin. cons. to bus. office; vol. examiner and preceptor emergency med. tech. students and paramedic students. Vol. ARC. Mem. La. Assn. Hosp. Admitting Mgrs., Aircraft Owners and Pilots Assn., Ninety-Nines, Alpha Delta Pi. Home: 2121 Hepburn #1209 Houston TX 77054

MCFARLAND, VEDA DIANNE, development company official; b. Nashville, Feb. 7, 1958; d. Edmond Moore and Audrey Ann (Williams) Anderson; m. Steven Wayne McFarland, May 27, 1989. Student, Mid. Tenn. State U., 1976-78; BBA, Belmont Coll., Nashville, 1982. Area supr. Opryland USA, Nashville, 1979-85; office mgr. Hawkins Devel. Co.,

Nashville, 1985—. Judge chmn. Nashville Jaycces-Miss Nashville Pageant, 1989. Scholar Jr. Achievement, Nashville, 1976. Mem. Nat. Assn. Women in Constrn. (sec. Nashville 1987-88, treas. 1988-89, forum steering com. 1988-89), Nashville Jaycees. Republican. Mem. LDS Ch. Office: Hawkins Devel Co 461 Craighead St Nashville TN 37204

MCFARLAND, VIOLET SWEET, author, educator; b. Seattle, Feb. 26, 1908; d. Judson Loring and Annie (Conners) Sweet; m. Glen W. McFarland, 1958 (div. 1965). B.A., Wash. State U., 1928; M.A., Columbia U., 1933. Tchr., Konawaena High Sch., Kealakekua, Hawaii, 1928-30, Am. Sch. in Japan, Tokyo, 1930-31; soc. editor Japan Times, Tokyo, 1930-31, Hong Kong Telegraph, 1940; edit. asst. U.S. Dept. Justice, Washington, 1934-43; real estate assoc. Long Beach Bd., Calif., 1961—. Author (as Violet Sweet Haven): Hong Kong for Weekend, 1939; Many Ports of Call, 1940; Gentlemen of Japan, 1944. Contbr. articles to profl. jours. Recipient numerous internat. lit. awards. Fellow Internat. Inst. Arts and Letters (life); mem. Nat. Press Club (life), Calif. Bd. Realtors, Delta Zeta. Avocations: travel, curator Oriental art. Address: PO Box 872 Lake Elsinore CA 92330

MCFARLANE, BETH LUCETTA TROESTER, mayor; b. Osterdock, Iowa, Mar. 9, 1918; d. Francis Charles and Ella Carrie (Moser) Troester; M. George Evert McFarlane, June 20, 1943 (dec. May 1972); children: Douglas, Steven (dec.), Susan, George. BA in Edn., U. No. Iowa, 1962, MA in Edn., 1971. Cert. tchr. Tchr. rural and elem. schs., Iowa, 1936-50, 55-56; elem. tchr. Oelwein Community Schs., Iowa, 1956-64, jr. high reading tchr., 1964-71, reading specialist, 1971-83; mayor of Oelwein, 1982—; evaluator North Cen. Accreditation Assn. for Ednl. Programs; mem. planning team for confs. for Iowa Cities, N.E. Iowa, 1985; v.p. N.E. Iowa Regional Council for Econ. Devel., 1986-89; mem. Area Econ. Devel. Com. N.E. Iowa, 1985, Legis. Interim Study Com. on Rural Econ. Devel., 1987-88; mem. policy com. Iowa League Municipalities, 1987-88; bd. dirs. Celwein Indsl. Devel. Corp., 1982—, Oelwein Betterment Corp., 1982—. V.p. Fayette County Tourism Council, 1987-88; Iowa State Steering Com. on Road Use Tax Financing, 1988-89. Named Iowa Reading Tchr. of Yr., Internat. Reading Assn. Iowa, 1978; recipient Outstanding Contbrn. to Reading Council Activities award Internat. Reading Assn. N.E. Iowa, 1978, State of Iowa's Gov.s' Leadership award, 1988. Mem. N.E. Iowa Reading Council (pres. 1975-77), MacDowell Music and Arts Orgn. (pres. 1978-80), Oelwein Bus. and Profl. Women (Woman of Yr. 1983), Oelwein Area C. of C. (bd. dirs. 1986—, Humanitarian award 1987), Delta Kappa Gamma (pres. 1980-82). Republican. Mem. Reorganized Ch. of Jesus Christ of Latter Day Saints. Avocations: bicycling, refinishing antiques, gardening. Home: 512 7th Ave NE Oelwein IA 50662 Office: City of Oelwein 20 2d Ave SW Oelwein IA 50662

MCFAUL, PATRICIA LOUISE, editor; b. Jersey City, June 28, 1947; d. James Leo and Ethel Louise (Shea) McF.; 1 child, Jennifer Jeanne. Student Nassau Community Coll., 1969-70. Pub. info. officer L.I. Cath. Newspaper, Hempstead, N.Y., 1967-68, researcher, 1968-70, staff writer, 1970-73, copy editor, 1973-78, layout and copy editor, 1978—, advt. layout editor, 1989—; readership surveyor, Rockville Centre, N.Y., 1971, 75; mem., com. chmn. Diocesan Family Life Bd., Rockville Centre, 1978-82. Researcher: Mission to Latin America, 1976. Pres. Florence A. Smith Sch. PTA, Oceanside, N.Y., 1982-84, Oceanside High Sch. Marching Band Parents Assn., 1987-89; chmn. talented and gifted com. Oceanside Council PTAs, 1984-85; elem. tchr. aide, 1985—; mem., sec.-treas. L.I. Interfaith Council, Rockville Centre, 1977-80; band dir. search com. Oceanside Sch. Dist., 1988. Recipient Citation, Diocese of Rockville Centre, 1984, 88. Mem. Cath. Press Assn. (U.S. and Can. citations 1985; mem. research com. 1975-80, mem., chmn. credentials and inspectors of elections com. 1976—, 1st place award design 1978, 86, citations 1980-85). Democrat. Roman Catholic. Avocations: flying, classical music. Home: 37 Rodney Pl Rockville Centre NY 11570 Office: The LI Catholic 115 Greenwich St Hempstead NY 11550

MCGAHA, BARBARA JOYCE, municipal administrator; b. Fairmount, Ind., Dec. 2, 1936; d. Gerald Oscar and Ruby Juanita (Ice) Earlywine; m. C.D. Merchant, Sept. 12, 1960 (div. 1974); children: Robin Lee, Steven Bradley, Kimberly Jo; m. H. Eugene McGaha, Oct. 8, 1983; stepchildren: Allison Lea, Teresa Lynn, Terra Kay and Tina Mae (twins). Student, Long Beach (Calif.) State Coll., 1961-62, Ivy Tech., 1974-75. Sec. Howard County Sheriff's Dept., Kokomo, Ind., 1975-76, IDACS coordinator, 1975-82, jail officer, 1976-82; tax assessor Ctr. Twp., City of Kokomo, 1983—; mem. Howard land com. Ctr. Twp. of Howard County, Kokomo, 1987. Vice co-chairperson Howard County Dem. Cen. Com., Kokomo, 1982, co-chairperson, 1982-83. Mem. Ind. Assessors Assn. (v.p. N.E. dist. 1989—), Howard County Womens Golf Assn. (pres. 1980-81). Office: Ctr Twp Assessor of Howard Howard County Ct House Room 204 Kokomo IN 46902

MC GANN, GERALDINE, government official; b. Bklyn., Dec. 21, 1937; d. Daniel and Geraldine (LeGrande) Essex; B.A. with honors, Hofstra U., 1974; M.Profl. Studies in Health Care Adminstrn. with honors, C.W. Post Coll., L.I. U., 1978; m. Edward J. McGann, Apr. 7, 1956; children—Daniel, Kevin, Kerrie, Jacqueline. Tchr., Hempstead and East Rockaway Schs.; coordinator sr. citizen services Town of Hempstead, N.Y., 1974-78, dep. commr. dept. services for aging, 1978-81; spl. asst. to regional adminstr. HUD, N.Y.C., 1981-83, exec. asst. to regional adminstr., 1983-87; regional dir housing, U.S. Dept. HUD Region II, 1987—. Chairperson Island Park (N.Y.) Housing Authority, 1975-81; village trustee, Island Park, N.Y., 1982-89; bd. trustees, St. Christopher Ch., Ottilie; mem. Republican Nat. Com. Mem. Am. Soc. Public Adminstrn., Assn. Pub. Adminstrn. and Health Care Profls., Women in Housing and Fin., Pi Alpha Alpha. Republican. Home: 42 Roosevelt Pl Island Park NY 11558 Office: 26 Federal Plaza New York NY 10278

MCGARR, ANITA, film company executive; b. Worthington, Minn., Nov. 21, 1951; d. James LeRoy McGarr and Dorothy Elnora (Lundbeck) Miller. Student, Am. Coll. Leysin, Switzerland, 1969-72, Inst. Advanced Edn., 1973-77, Sawyer Bus. Coll. V.p. in charge of feature film devel., chief fin. officer Windhorse Prodns., Inc., Beverly Hills, Calif.; mem. exec. mgmt. writer, producer, dir. for TV series Stingray, 1985-86, Star Trek, The Next Generation, 1988, War of the Worlds, 1988-89. Office: Windhorse Prodns Inc 157 N LaPeer Dr Beverly Hills CA 90211

MCGARR, EVELYN FRANZ, former university trustee; b. Bklyn., Apr. 5, 1910; d. Charles and Agnes Loretta (Duffy) Franz; m. John Dougherty McGarr, June 30, 1935; children: Jane McGarr Montgomery, John Dougherty Jr. AB, Adelphi Coll., 1931. Lic. secondary sch. tchr., N.Y.C. Tchr. Julia Richman High Sch., N.Y.C., 1934-35, McKee Vocat. High Sch., S.I., N.Y., 1935-58; dir. alumni rels. Adelphi U., Garden City, N.Y., 1950-54, pres. alumni assn., 1954-58, univ. trustee, 1954-63; trustee Inst. for Child Mental Health Adelphi U., Garden City, 1976-80. Mem. AAUW (v.p. br. 1962-64), Nassau Pres.'s Assn. Home: 139 Whitehall Blvd Garden City NY 11530

MCGARRY, SUSAN HALLSTEN, magazine editor; b. Mpls., June 27, 1948; d. Clarence Albert and Evelyn Mildred (Nelson) Hallsten; m. Stephen Joseph McGarry, Aug. 11, 1978. BA, U. Minn., 1973, MA, 1978. Editor-in-chief S.W. Art Mag., Houston, 1979—; freelance writer, author M. Hal Sussmann & Assocs., Houston, 1983—; bd. dirs. Ariz. Living Treasures, Sedona, 1988—. Author, editor: Taking Stock, 1986; author (with others) The Cowboy Artists of America, 1988, (catalog) Wilson Hurley, 1988. Mem. Western Writers Am. Home: 3718 Grennoch Ln Houston TX 77025 Office: SW Art Mag 5444 Westheimer Ste 1440 Houston TX 77056

MCGARVEY, ANNAMARIA JUDE, educator; b. Jersey City, N.J., Aug. 14, 1964; d. Gary Lee and Andrea Maria (Rosko) McG. BA in Art Edn., Georgian Ct. Coll., 1986, postgrad. Cert. art instr., elem. classroom tchr., N.J. Art instr. Holy Family Sch., Lakewood, N.J., 1986—, 1st grade tchr., 1986-87, art dir., 1987—; adult art instr. Jackson (N.J.) Community Sch., 1986-89; arts and crafts instr. Ocean County Dept. Parks and Recreation, Lakewood, 1987. Decorating chmn. mid-winter ball St. Mary of the Lake Ch., Lakewood, 1988—, co-chmn., 1989, centennial com., 1989—, Cath. youth orgn. asst., 1986—. Recipient Geography Awareness award State of N.J., 1989. Mem. ASCD, Nat. Cath. Educators Assn., Nat. Art Edn. Assn., Georgian Ct. Coll. Alumni Assn. Democrat. Home: 322 Central Ave Apt 1 Lakewood NJ 08701 Office: Holy Family Sch E County Line Rd Lakewood NJ 08701

MCGARY, BETTY WINSTEAD, minister, counselor, group therapist; b. Louisville, June 21, 1936; d. Philip Miller and Mary Jo (Winstead) McG.; married, 1960 (div. 1979); children: Thomas Edward, Mary Alyson, Andrew Philip Pearce. BS, Samford U., 1958; MA in Christian Edn., So. Bapt. Theol. Sem., 1961; EdD, U. Louisville, 1988. Ordained to ministry Bapt. Ch., 1986; cert. secondary tchr., Ky., Ga. Min. to youth Broadway Bapt. Ch., Louisville, 1958-60; learning disability and behavior disorders specialist Jefferson County Schs., Muscogee Schs., Cobb County Schs., Louisville, Columbus, Ga., Atlanta, 1964-88; min. to adults South Main Bapt. Ch., Houston, 1986—; marriage enrichment cons. Pastoral Inst., Columbus, 1973-76; co-founder and coord. Ctr. for Women in Ministry, Louisville, 1983-86, exec. bd. dirs. 1983—; cons. Tex. Christian Life Commn., Ft. Worth, 1989—; co-therapist pvt. practice of Elizabeth Brodie, M.D., Houston, 1989—. Author: (with others) The New Has Come, 1988; co-editor nat. newsletter Folio: A Newsletter for Southern Bapt. Women in Ministry, 1983-86. Vice-chairperson exec. bd. dirs. handicapped Boy Scouts Am., Houston, 1986—. Recipient citation for Disting. Svc. So. Bapt. Theol. Sem., 1984, Dean's citation Outstanding Achievement U. Louisville, 1988. Mem. So. Bapt. Alliance (exec. bd. dirs. 1988-90, v.p. 1990—), So. Bapt. Women in Ministry (pres. 1988-90). Democrat. Home: 2107 Bartlett Houston TX 77098 Office: South Main Bapt Ch 4100 Main St Houston TX 77002

MCGAULEY, JACQUELYNE SUE, social welfare administrator; b. L.A., Aug. 23, 1951; d. Richard Courtney and Marion Lucia (Otto) May; children: Julie Anna, Jonathan Daniel. Instr. Gen. Telephone Co., Downey, Calif.; researcher Ted Gunderson and Assocs., Santa Monica, Calif.; speaker in field. Contbr. articles to professional and popular newspapers and jours. Recognized for outstanding service to children Enough. Mem. Affirming Children's Truths (pres.), Believe the Children (exec. bd.), Childrens' Civil Rights Fund (founder), Nat. Coalition for Children's Justice, C.O.V.E.R. (founder). Office: PO Box 417 Redondo Beach CA 90277

MCGAVRAN, BRENDA JOYCE, social services administrator; b. N.Y.C., May 22, 1946; d. David William and Esther E. (Cockman) Hart; m. Dennis R. McGavran, Aug. 5, 1967 (div.); children: Christine Beth, David, Richard. BA, Drake U., 1967; MA, U. Mich., 1972. Tchr. Perry (Iowa) High Sch., 1967-68, Huron High Sch., Ann Arbor, Mich., 1968-73; instr. Post Coll., Waterbury, Conn., 1977-78; exec. dir. Group Homes of Greater Waterbury, 1978-80; regional planner N. Central Regional Support Group, Newington, Conn., 1980-82; state planning coord. Conn. Dept. Children and Youth Svcs., Hartford, 1982-84, asst. div. dir., 1984-87; regional dir. New Haven region II Conn. Dept. Children and Youth Svcs., Hamden, 1987—; chair New Haven Consortium for Substance Abusing Women and their Children, 1990—; bd. dirs. Spl. Commn. on Infant Health, New Haven, 1988—; mem. various coms. New Haven Family Alliance, 1989—. Moderator 1st Congl. Ch., Waterbury, 1980-90, chair bd. trustees, 1990—, mem. coun., 1990—; co-chair Parents' Assn. for Lamaze Method, Waterbury, 1974-75. Named to Outstanding Young Women of Am., 1980. Mem. Conn. Assn. Residential Facilities (v.p. 1979-80), Phi Beta Kappa. Democrat. Home: 27 Hewlett Waterbury CT 06710 Office: Dept Children & Youth Svcs 2105 State St New Haven CT 06511

MC GAW, JESSIE BREWER, author, educator; b. Clarksville, Tenn., Oct. 17, 1913; d. Lewis Vernon and Birdie (Basford) Brewer; A.B., Duke U., 1935; M.A., Peabody Coll., 1940; postgrad. Columbia U., 1948-50, (Fulbright scholar) Am. Acad. Rome, 1959; m. Howard Franklin McGaw, Dec. 28, 1939 (div. 1958); children—Miriam Katherine, Vernon Howard; m. Harold L. Geis, Aug. 1964 (div. 1972); m. George P. Bickford, May 24, 1986. Tchr. Latin, Ward Belmont Sch., Nashville, 1938-40; tchr. Lausanne Sch., Memphis, 1940-42; assoc. prof. English and Latin, U. Houston, 1952—. Bd. dirs. YWCA, 1957-59, Day Care Assn., 1956-61, Houston Civic Music Assn., 1958-60, Houston Council Human Relations. Recipient Cokesburg Juvenile award; Theta Sigma Phi lit. award. Fulbright grantee Am. Acad. in Rome, 1959; research grantee, 1964, 72; Delta Kappa Gamma ednl. grantee, China, 1981. Mem. Tex. Folklore Soc., South Central Modern Lang. Assn., Houston Council, Tchrs. Fgn. Lang. (treas.), League Women Voters, AAUW, Tex. Inst. Letters, U. Houston Women's Assn. (pres. 1967-68), Mus. Fine Arts (assoc.), Delta Kappa Gamma, Kappa Kappa Gamma. Democrat. Methodist. Club: University Houston Woman's (pres. 1954-55, 67-68). Author: How Medicine Man Cured Paleface Woman, 1956, History of Houston YWCA, 1957, Painted Pony Runs Away, 1958, Little Elk Hunts Buffalo, 1961, Chief Red Horse Tells About Custer, 1981, The Aztec Downfall, 1987. Translator: Heptaplus (Pico delia Mirandola), 1977. Home: 2411 Reba Houston TX 77019

MCGEADY, KATHLEEN BIRMINGHAM, program manager; b. Oceanside, N.Y., Aug. 27, 1949; d. James Joseph and Doris Martha (Fraser) Birmingham; m. Dennis J. McGeady, June 14, 1970; children: Kelly, Lauren. Student, Mercer County Community Coll., Mercer County Vocat. Tech. Sch, 1976-77. Office asst. Madison Square Garden, N.Y.C., 1967-69, PICA, N.Y.C., 1969-70; exec. sec. Pubs. Distbg. Corp., N.Y.C., 1970-74; program mgr. Princeton U.; mem. Animal Care Com. Princeton U., 1985—. Vol. libr. Plainsboro Free Pub. Libr., 1982-86; co-dir. Plainsboro Founders Day, 1982-87; co-coord. Bicycling Portion Liberty to Liberty Triathlan, Plainsboro, 1983-86; founder, dir. Bookworm Five Mile Race, Plainsboro, 1984-85; elected councilman Plainsboro Town Coun., 1986-89; acting chmn., 1987-88; vice chmn., 1986-89, chmn., 1988-89; mem. Plainsboro-Cranbury Juvenile Conf. Com., 1988—. Home: 50 Linden Ln Plainsboro NJ 08536

MCGEE, BARBARA, publishing executive; b. N.Y.C., Feb. 24, 1949; d. Adolph and Lena (Bicocchi) Marzoli; m. John McGee, June 6, 1970; 1 child, Brian. BS, Douglass Coll., New Brunswick, N.J., 1971; postgrad., Chubb Inst., Summit, N.J., 1983; cert., Small Bus. Assn., 1983. Mgr. order processing Newsweek, Inc., Mountain Lakes, N.J., 1981—. Mem. NAFE, Fulfillment Mgrs. Assn., Douglas Coll. Alumni Assn. Office: 333 Rte 46 Mountain Lakes NJ 07046

MCGEE, CARLA CREIGHTON, high school principal; b. Wichita Falls, Tex., Apr. 29, 1936; d. Frank Bryant Creighton and Loreta (Wakefield) Creighton Craig; m. Dan Franklin McGee, Sept. 18, 1958; childen: Susan McGee Crawford, Sharla McGee Sparkman, Danna McGee Manley, Bryant Craig. AA, El Centro community Coll, 1968; BA, U. North Tex., 1969, MA, 1974, MEd, 1981. Cert. secondary tchr., pub. sch. adminstr.; cert. in speech, drama, English. Tchr. Highland Park Ind. Sch. Dist., Dallas, 1969-73, Carrollton (Tex.)-Farmers Br. Ind. Sch. Dist., 1973-79, Brookhaven Community Coll., Dallas, 1978-79; jr. high sch. asst. prin. Carrollton (Tex.)-Farmers Br. Ind. Sch. Dist., 1979-81, jr. high prin., 1981-84, prin. R.L. Turner High Sch., 1984—; trainer Tex. Tchr. Appraisal System, Tex. Edn. Agy., Austin, 1985—, Edn. Svc. Ctr., Dallas, 1987—. Named Premier Prin., Tex. PTA, Austin, 1982. Mem. Tex. Assn. Secondary Prins. (chmn. curriculum com. 1984-86), North Cen. Tex. Assn. Supervision and Curriculum, Tex. Assn. Supervision and Curriculum, MetroCrest Profl. Women's Assn. 9pres. 1983-85), AAUW (pres. br. 1978-80), Exchange Club, Phi Delta Kappa (program chmn. 1987-77), Phi Lambda Theta (pres. chpt. 1989—, Delta Kappa Gamma (pres./parliamentarian 1982-84, Achievement award 1984). Republican. Baptist. Home: 2718 Selma St Dallas TX 75234 Office: Farmers Branch ISD Admin Bldg Carrollton TX 75006

MCGEE, DOROTHY HORTON, author, historian; b. West Point, N.Y., Nov. 30, 1913; d. Hugh Henry and Dorothy (Brown) McG.; ed. Sch. of St. Mary, 1920-21, Green Vale Sch., 1921-28, Brearley Sch., 1928-29, Fermata Sch., 1929-31. Asst. historian Inc. Village of Roslyn (N.Y.), 1950-58; historian Inc. Village of Matinecock, 1966—. Author: Skipper Sandra, 1950; Sally Townsend, Patriot, 1952; The Boarding School Mystery, 1953; Famous Signers of the Declaration, 1955; Alexander Hamilton-New Yorker, 1957; Herbert Hoover: Engineer, Humanitarian, Statesman, 1959, rev. edit., 1965; The Pearl Pendant Mystery, 1960; Framers of the Constitution, 1968; author booklets, articles hist. and sailing subjects. Chmn., Oyster Bay Am. Bicentennial Revolution Commn., 1971—; historian Town of Oyster Bay, 1982—; mem. Nassau County Am. Revolution Bicentennial Commn.; hon. dir. The Friends of Raynham Hall, Inc.; treas. Family Welfare Assn. Nassau County, Inc., 1956-58; dir. Family Service Assn. Nassau County, 1958-69. Recipient Cert. of award for outstanding contbn. children's lit. N.Y. State Assn. Elem. Sch. Prins., 1959; award Nat. Soc. Children of Am. Revolution, 1960; award N.Y. Assn. Supervision and Curriculum Devel., 1961; hist. award Town of Oyster Bay, 1963; Cert. Theodore Roosevelt Assn., 1976. Fellow Soc. Am. Historians; mem. Soc. Preservation L.I. Antiquities (hon. dir.), Nat. Trust Hist. Preservation, N.Y. Geneal. and Biol. Soc. (dir., trustee), Oyster Bay Hist. Soc. (pres. 1971-75, chmn. 1975-79, trustee), Theodore Roosevelt Assn. (trustee), Townsend Soc. Am. (trustee). Republican. Address: Box 142 Locust Valley NY 11560

MCGEE, EFFIE MARY, organization executive; b. Uvalda, Ga., Sept. 22, 1928; d. James Thomas and Lucinda (Tanner) Yarbrough; widow; children: Gerald D., Reginald D., Verle B. Grad., Highland Coll., 1968. Lic. cosmetologist, Ill. Psychiat. aid I Dixon (Ill.) Devel. Ctr., 1948-53; owner, operator McGee's Beauty Salon, Freeport, Ill., 1960-82; sec./receptionist Freeport Twp., 1977-80; tchr. Parenting and Pre-employment Skills Minority Tng., Freeport, 1980-85; exec. dir. Martin Luther King, Jr. Community Ctr., Freeport, 1980-88; mem. city coun. City of Freeport, 1981-85; membership specialist, field dir. Green Hills coun. Girls Scouts U.S., 1988—. Former bd. dirs. Family Life Ctr., Freeport, 1985-88, Community Action Agy., Freeport; precinct committeeman Peoples Party, Freeport, 1975-80; bd. dirs. Highland Mgmt. Inst., Freeport, 1986—, Freeport Sch. Dist., 1990—; mem., chairperson Freeport Drug Commn. 1989—. Named Prevention Person of Yr. Freeport Drug Commn., 1983; recipient Women of Excellence award Freeport YWCA, 1989. Mem. NAFE (N.Y. chpt. 1988—), LWV (bd. dirs. Freeport chpt. 1983—), Assn. Girl Scout Execs., Freeport Women's Club (v.p. from 1982, now pres.), Rotary. Democrat. Mem. Ch. of God. Home: 525 E Winneshiek St Freeport IL 61032

MCGEE, JANE MARIE, retired educator; b. Paducah, Ky., Nov. 3, 1926; d. William Penn and Mary Virginia (Martin) Roberts; m. Hugh Donald McGee, Oct. 11, 1946; children: Catherine Jane McGee Bouchard, Nancy Ann McGee Weidler. BS in Elem. Edn., Murray State U., 1948; cert. in gifted edn., Nat. Coll. Edn., 1976. Tchr. Hazel (Ky.) Pub. Schs., 1948-49, Pittsford (Mich.) Pub. Schs., 1949-50, Leal Elem. Sch., Urbana, Ill., 1950-53, Cleveland Elem. Sch., Skokie, Ill., 1953-57; pvt. tutor, pre-sch. tchr., 1953-61; tchr. Woodland Park Elem. Sch., Deerfield, Ill., 1968-83; ret., 1983; beauty and skin care cons. Mary Kay Cosmetics, Gunnison, Colo., 1984—. Soprano, Western State Coll. and Community Chorus, Gunnison, 1986—. Mem. AAUW, Top o' the World Garden Club (sec. 1984—, winner first place at numerous garden club shows). Republican. Baptist. Home: 206 N Colorado St Gunnison CO 81230

MCGEE, JOY ANN, healthcare executive; b. Pawhuska, Okla., July 22, 1946; d. Ray Garrett and Darlene Genevieve (Frazier) Lewis; m. Richard A. McGee, July 19, 1963 (div. 1988); 1 child, Tamara Lyn. AA, Westark Community Coll., 1981; BS, Coll. of Ozark, 1982; MBA summa cum laude, U. Ark., 1983, postgrad., 1985. Med. transcriptionist Holt-Krock Clinic, Ft. Smith, Ark., 1964-65, dir. occupational medicine, 1987; med. sec. Holt-Krock Orthopaedics, P.A., Ft. Smith, 1965-81, bus. mgr., 1981-83, adminstr., 1983-87; dir. clinics mgmt. and devel. Occupational Med. Clinics Am., Milw., 1987-88; exec. dir. Tex. Occupational Health Clinics, Dallas, 1988—; adj. faculty mem. Cardinal Stritch Coll., Milw., 1988—, U. Ozarks, Clarksville, Ark., 1984-87. Contbr. articles to profl. jours. Organist, Northlake Bapt. Ch., Dallas, 1989. Mem. Am. Coll. Med. Group Adminstrs., Med. Group Mgmt. Assn., NAFE, Purchasing Mgmt. Assn. Ark. (bd. dirs. 1986-87), Nat. Assn. Purchasing Mgmt. (cert.), Nat. Assn. Med. Transcription (cert.), Phi Theta Kappa. Republican. Home: 8422 Township Ln Dallas TX 75243 Office: Tex Occupational Health Cln 8226 Douglas Ave Ste 748 Dallas TX 75225

MCGEE, JOYCE FANTINO, government official, accountant; b. Chgo., July 31, 1947; d. John and Yolande Paule (MacDuff) Fantino; m. David Lee McGee, May 29, 1976; children: Erin Lillian, Richard Cody. BS, Fla. State U., 1979. CPA, Fla. Staff acct. Williams, Cox, Weidner, Cox, Tallahassee, 1979-83; tax audit specialist III Fla. Dept. Revenue, Tallahassee, 1983-85, bur. chief returns accountability, 1985-87, bur. chief of fin. and acctg., 1987-88; dir. internal audit Fla. Dept. Health and Rehabilitative Services, Tallahassee, 1988—. Fla. Inst. CPAs ednl. found. scholar., 1979; recipient Top Student award, Ernst & Ernst, 1976; Nat. Key award, Phi Chi Theta, 1978-79; Fashion Design award, 1978-79, Mildred Pepper scholar, 1968. Mem. Am. Inst. CPAs, Fla. Soc. CPAs, Phi Kappa Phi, Beta Gamma Sigma, Beta Alpha Psi. Democrat. Office: Fla Dept Health & Rehab Services 1317 Winewood Blvd Rm 412 Bldg 1 Tallahassee FL 32399-0700

MCGEE, KATHLEEN AGNES, human services executive; b. L.A., Mar. 27, 1944; d. William Raymond and Kathleen Elizabeth (Nevin) McG. BS in Pharmacy, Phila. Coll. Pharmacy and Sci., 1968. Registered pharmacist, Pa., Md., Del. Staff pharmacist Wack Apothecary, Wayne, Pa., 1968-71, Paul C. Tigue, Pharmacist, Wilmington, Del., 1970-73; dir. profl. svcs. Nat. Assn. Chain Drug Stores, Alexandria, Va., 1973-76, v.p., 1976-83; exec. dir. Retail Drug Inst., N.Y.C., 1983-84; v.p. Barr Labs., Inc., Pomona, N.Y., 1984-90, Consumer Motivation Group, Garnerville, N.Y., 1990—; co-founder Pharmacy Assocs., Inc., Wilmington, 1971. Mem. Am. Pharm. Assn., Am. Soc. Hosp. Pharmacists, Del. Pharm. Soc. (exec. dir. 1970-73), Kappa Epsilon. Republican. Roman Catholic.

MCGEE, LYNNE KALAVSKY, assistant principal; b. Jersey City, N.J., July 25, 1949; d. Michael V. and Ann (Fedowitz) K.; m. Thomas Robert, Aug. 12, 1972; children: Todd Michael, Ryan Thomas. BS, St. Francis Coll., Loretto, Pa., 1971; MEd, Seton Hall U., 1972; EDS, Fla. Atlantic U., 1978, EdD, 1986. Cert. tchr., Fla., adminstr., Fla. Asst. prin. for curriculum, math instr. Palm Beach County (Fla.) Bd. Edn., 1980-82, asst. prin. for student svcs., 1982-86, asst. prin. for adminstrn., 1986—. Mem. Assn. Supervision and Curriculum Devel., Phi Kappa Phi.

MCGEE, MARY ALICE, health science research administrator; b. Winston-Salem, N.C., Oct. 14, 1950; d. C.L. Jr. and Mary Hilda (Shelton) McG. AB, Meredith Coll., 1972. Tchr. Augusta (Ga.) Schs., 1972-73; specialist grants Med. Sch. Brown U., Providence, R.I., 1974-76; profl. basketball player, 1975-76; dir. research adminstn. Med. Sch. Brown U., Providence, 1976—; profl. basketball player, 1975-76. Bd. dirs. Sojourner House, Providence, 1983—. Mem. Soc. Research Adminstrs., Nat. Council U. Research Adminstrs. Club: Golden Retriever Am. Home: 121 Plain St Rehoboth MA 02769 Office: Brown U Med Sch Box G A322 Providence RI 02912

MCGEE, PATRICIA SABYNA, small business owner; b. Beacon Falls, Conn., June 24, 1921; d. John and Sabyna (O'Flynn) Malone; m. B. J. Bolander, Jr.,] May 7, 1977 (dec. 1988). Student, Boston U., 1971, Columbia U., 1972, U. Conn., 1973-74. Broadcaster radio and tv Hartford, Conn., 1960-64; dir. Nat. Multiple Sclerosis Soc., Hartford, 1964-73, Nat. Kidney Found., Miami, Fla., 1973-76; dir. adminstrv. svcs. Children's Psychiatric Clinics, Miami, 1976-77, Shelnut & Assocs., Augusta, Ga., 1977-81; dir. pub. rels. Telfair Inns, Augusta, 1981-83; ptnr. Bolender Holley Surveying Co., Augusta, 1984—. Bd. dirs. Women in Ga. Power, Augusta, 1982; v.p. Aux. to Augusta Shrine Club, 1983; mem. Dem. State Com. Conn., 1972-73; sec.-treas. Classic South, 1981. Mem. Pub. Rls. Soc. Am. (pres. 1974-75), Nat. Soc. Fund Raisers (pores. 1975-76), Bus. and Profl. Women's Club (pres. 1974-76), Am. Women in Radio and TV (pres. 1973, 75), Ga. Hospitality and Travel Assn. (treas. 1982-83), Women in Constrn. (dir. 198-90), SBA, Civitan Club (v.p. 1983-84). Democrat. Roman Catholic. Home: 1435 Waters Edge Dr On the Levee Augusta GA 30901

MCGEE, PATTIE LEE BIGGERS, retired principal; b. Charlotte, N.C., Jan. 5, 1906; d. John Dixon and Barbara Lee (Osborne) Biggers. AB, Randolph Macon Coll., Lynchburg, Va., 1923-27; postgrad., U. N.C., 1933. Cert. prin., N.C. Tchr. D.H. Hill Sch., Charlotte, 1927-28, Elizabeth Sch., Charlotte, 1928-35; prin. Parks Hutchison Sch., Charlotte, 1935-47, Bethune Sch., Charlotte, 1947-54, Sedgefield Elem., Charlotte, 1954-71. Producer ednl. film And Something More, 1957. Mem. AAUW, UDC, DAR, Daus. Am. Colonists, Delta Kappa Gamma. Presbyterian. Home: 5100 Sharon Rd Charlotte NC 28210

MCGERITY, MARGARET ANN, lawyer; b. Boston, Aug. 23, 1949; d. Francis Charles and Margaret Mary (Ford) McG.; m. Max Folkenflik, Apr. 3, 1971; children: Alexander, Andrew. BA, Columbia U., 1978; JD,

Benjamin N. Cardozo Sch. Law, 1981. Bar: N.Y. 1982, U.S. Dist. Ct. (so. dist.) N.Y. 1982, U.S. Dist. Ct. (ea. dist.) N.Y. 1984, U.S. Ct. Appeals (2d cir.) 1984. Artist, 1970-75; summer asst. U.S. atty. U.S. Atty.'s Office for So. Dist. N.Y., N.Y.C., 1980; asst. dist. atty. Bronx Dist. Atty.'s Office, 1981-84; assoc. Wistendahl & Folkenflik, N.Y.C., 1985—. Mem. law rev. Benjamin Cardozo Sch. Law, 1979-81. Mem. ABA, N.Y. County Bar Assn., N.Y. Woman's Bar Assn., Assn. of Bar of City of N.Y. Democrat. Roman Catholic. Home: 320 Riverside Dr New York NY 10025

MCGHEE, DONNA SUSAN, data processing executive; b. Stamford, Conn., Aug. 12, 1957; d. Richard Albert and Doris Carol (Britt) McGhee. BS in Mktg., Cen. Conn. State Coll., 1979. Sr. systems analyst Unisys Corp., Shelton, Conn., 1979—; cons. Amway Corp., Ada, Mich., 1989. Recipient Exemplary Action award, Burroughs Corp., 1986, Circle of Champions, 1985. Mem. NAFE. Baptist. Home: 54 Durant St Stamford CT 06902 Office: Unisys Corp 2 Enterprise Dr Shelton CT 06484

MCGIEHAN, DONNA ALENE, financial analyst; b. Rochester, N.Y., Nov. 30, 1957; d. Donn McGiehan and Joyce (Dominik) Balint; div. BS in Fin., George Mason U., 1988. Fin. planner Lara Millard & Assocs., Falls Church, Va., 1981-83; fin. analyst EPIC, Falls Church, 1983-85; fin. analyst, supr. Electronic Data Systems, Herndon, Va., 1985—; fin. cons., stockbroker First Potomac, Swan Securities, Falls Church, 1983—. Mem. Shearwater Sailing Club (membership chmn. 1987).

MCGILBERRY, VELMA GWEN, health care facility executive, director; b. Thomasville, Ala., Nov. 26, 1954; d. Flave and Essie Mae (Morgan) McG. BA, Livingston (Ala.) U., 1976, MA in Teaching, 1977. Instr. Camden County High Sch., St. Mary's, Ga., 1977-80; instr. Coastal Train Inst., Inc., Mobile, Ala., 1980-82, dir., mgr., 1982-85; edn. specialist U. Hosp., Augusta, Ga., 1985-88; dir. tng. and devel. S.E. Ala. Med. Ctr., Dothan, 1988—. Mem. Ala. Soc. Health, Edn. and Tng. (sec. Montgomery chpt. 1990—). Methodist. Home: 506 Mayo St Dothan AL 36301 Office: SE Ala Med Ctr Hwy 84 E Dothan AL 36302

MCGILL, EVELYN, florist; b. Yanceville, N.C., Mar. 5, 1952; d. Isaac Jr. and Rosetta (Poole) Poteat; m. LeRoy Ellis Jr., Jan. 13, 1973 (div. 1984); children: Raven Keturah, Janelle Angeline, Ginger Marie and Garrett Isaac-Lee (twins); m. David Andrew McGill, May 8, 1986; children: Le Shaun Davetta, Jerome Roland, Micah James. Cert., Maricopa City Skill Ctr., Phoenix, 1984. Cert. florist. Customer svc. clk. N.J. Bell Telephone Co., Newark, 1969-71; photographers rep. Allen Lee Page, Phoenix and East Orange, N.J., 1980-82; florist, owner Arts & Flowers Inc., Fredericksburg, Va., 1989—; dressmaker, florists to various bus. Mem. NAFE. Jehovah's Witness.

MCGILL, GRACE ANITA, corporate safety specialist, nurse; b. Lawrence, Mass., Mar. 8, 1943; d. Joseph John and Tina Mary (Sicurella) Tabacco; m. Howard L. McGill, Jr., Feb. 28, 1965; children: Cynthia, Deborah, David. RN, Mass. Gen. Hosp., 1963; BS, Lesley Coll., 1987; MS in Mgmt., Lesley Grad. Sch., 1990. Nurse Phillips Acad., Andover, Mass., 1963-65, 97th Gen. Hosp., Frankfurt, Germany, 1966, Highsmith-Rainey Hosp., Fayetteville, N.C., 1968, Lawrence (Mass.) Gen. Hosp., 1969-78, Baldpate Psychiat. Hosp., Georgetown, Mass., 1978-79; nursing staff St. Joseph's Hosp., Lowell, Mass., 1980-81; head nurse St. Joseph's Hosp., Lowell, 1981-83; occupational health nurse Wang Labs., Inc., Lowell, 1983-87, corp. safety specialist, 1987-90; health services administr. Loral Infrared and Imaging Systems, Inc., Lexington, Mass., 1990—. Bd. dirs. Family of St. Joseph's Hosp., Lowell, 1981-83. Mem. Mass. Gen. Hosp. Nurses Alumnae Assn., Am. Soc. Safety Engrs., NAFE, Lesley Coll. Allumnae, Am. Assn. Occupational Health Nurses. Episcopalian. Home: 81 Lancaster Dr Tewksbury MA 01876

MCGILLEY, SISTER MARY JANET, writer, academic administrator; b. Kansas City, Mo., Dec. 4, 1924; d. James P. and Peg (Ryan) McG. B.A., St. Mary Coll., 1945; M.A., Boston Coll., 1951; Ph.D., Fordham U., 1956; postgrad., U. Notre Dame, 1960, Columbia U., 1964. Social worker Kansas City, 1945-46; joined Sisters of Charity of Leavenworth, 1946; tchr. English Hayden High Sch., Topeka, 1948-50, Billings (Mont.) Central High Sch., 1951-53; faculty dept. English St. Mary Coll., Leavenworth, Kans., 1956-64; pres. St. Mary Coll., 1964-89, Disting. prof. English and Liberal Studies, 1990—. Contbr. articles, fiction and poetry to various jours. Bd. dirs. United Way of Leavenworth, 1966-85; mem. Mayor's Adv. Coun., 1967-72, Leavenworth Planning Coun., 1977-78; bd. dirs.Kans. Ind. Coll. Fund, 1964-89, exec. com., 1985-86, vice chmn., 1984-85, chmn., 1985-86. Recipient Alumnae award St. Mary Coll., 1969; Disting. Service award Baker U., 1981, Leavenworth Bus. Woman of Yr. Athena award, 1986. Mem. Nat. Coun. Tchrs. of English, Nat. Assn. Ind. Colls. and Univs. (bd. dirs. 1982-85), Kans. Ind. Coll. Assn. (bd. dirs. 1964-89, treas. 1982-84, v.p. 1984-85, chmn. exec. com. 1985-86), Am. Coun. Edn. (com. on women in higher edn. 1980-85), Am. Assn. Higher Edn., Kansas City Regional Coun. for Higher Edn. (bd. dirs. 1965-89, treas. 1984-85, v.p. 1986-88), Ind. Coll. Funds Am. (exec. com. 1974-77, trustee-at-large 1975-76), North Cen. Assn. Colls. and Schs. (exec. commr. Com. on Insts. Higher Edn. 1980-88, vice chair 1985-86, chair 1987-88), Leavenworth C. of C. (bd. dirs. 1964-89), Assn. Am. Colls. (commn. liberal learning 1970-73, com. on curriculum and faculty devel. 1979-82) St. Mary Alumni Assn. (hon. pres. 1964-89), Delta Epsilon Sigma. Democrat. Office: St Mary Coll 4100 S 4th St Trafficway Leavenworth KS 66048-5082

MCGILVREY, SAKURA LEE, telecommunications executive; b. South Haven, Mich., Feb. 10, 1949; d. Joseph and Mieko (Takeichi) Bowers; m. Arthur W. Williams, July 1, 1966 (div. July 1974); children: Teresa E., Bruce K.; m. Richard L. Johnson, Apr. 3, 1976 (dec. Mar. 1986); 1 child, Erin N.; m. Frank B. McGilvrey III, Aug. 21, 1987; children: Meredith M., Cara L. Student, Cameron State Coll., Lawton, Okla., 1967-69, No. Va. Community Coll., Annandale, 1975-80, 87, George Washington U., 1978-80. Supr. engring. records C&P Telephone Co. of Va., Fairfax, 1973-76, staff asst. budgeting, 1976-77; engring. clk. C&P Telephone Co. of Va., Arlington, 1969-73, supr. network adminstrn., 1977-83, supr. switching control, 1983-86; staff supr. planning new tech. C&P Telephone Co. of Md., Silver Springs, 1986-87; mgr. switching control ctr. C&P Telephone Co. of Washington, 1987—. Mem. NAFE, Telephone Pioneers Am., Am. Philatelic So., Assn. Research & Enlightenment. Office: C&P Telephone of Washington 30 E St SW Rm 508 Washington DC 20024

MCGINLEY, NANCY ELIZABETH, lawyer; b. Columbia, Mo., Feb. 29, 1952; d. Robert Joseph and Ruth Evangeline (Garnett) McG. BA with high honors, U. Tex., 1974, JD, 1977. Bar: Tex. 1977, U.S. Dist. Ct. (no. dist.) Tex. 1979. Law clk. U.S. Dist. Ct. (no. dist.) Tex., Fort Worth, 1977-79; assoc. Crumley, Murphy and Shrull, Fort Worth, 1979-81; staff atty. SEC, Fort Worth, 1981-87; br. chief SEC Los Angeles Regional Office, 1987-88, SEC Fort Worth Regional Office, 1988—. Mem. editorial staff Urban Law Rev. Mem. Tarrant County Young Lawyers Assn., Women Lawyers of Tarrant County, Fort Worth Bus. and Profl. Women's Assn., Mortar Bd., Phi Beta Kappa, Phi Kappa Phi, Alpha Lambda Delta. Methodist. Home: 201 Wilcrest #1211 Houston TX 77042 Office: 7500 San Felipe Ste 550 Houston TX 77063

MCGINN, EILEEN, public health advisor, researcher; b. Phila., Mar. 29, 1947. BA cum laude, CUNY, 1968; MPH, U. Pitts., 1974. Tchr. English Peace Corps, Dogondoutchi, Niger, 1968-70; tchr. sci. Diocese of Bklyn., 1971-72; clinic dir. Monsour Med. Ctr., Jeannette, Pa., 1974-76; grants officer Assn. for Voluntary Surg. Contraception, N.Y.C., 1976-79; program officer Planned Parenthood Fedn., N.Y.C., 1979-81; chief of party USAID/Zaire, Kinshasa, 1983-85; dep. chief of party John Snow, Inc., Nepal, Kathmandu, 1986-89; program mgr. Asia Assn. Voluntary Surg. Contraception, N.Y.C., 1989—; cons. CEDPA, Washington, 1985, Population Svcs. Internat., Washington, 1985. Author: Field Worker's Manual, 1989, Nurse's Manual, 1989; contbr. articles to profl. jours. N.Y.S. State Regents scholar, 1964-68, NYU scholar, 1982; USPHS grantee, 1972-73. Mem. Am. Pub. Health Assn., Nat. Coun. for Internat. Health. Office: 16th St Marks Pl #4C New York NY 10003

MCGINN, MARY LYN, real estate company executive; b. New Orleans, Aug. 12, 1949; d. Dan Creedon and Millicent Virginia (White) Midgett; m. Walter Lee McGinn, Mar. 14, 1985. BA, La. State U., 1970, MA, 1972; PhD, U. So. Miss., 1976; MBA, Loyola Coll., 1990. Cert. comml.-investment mem., cert. property mgr., master appraiser. Dir., prof. Dillard U., New Orleans, 1972-76, Loyola U., New Orleans, 1976-80; sr. v.p. Equity Investment Services, Inc., New Orleans, 1980-84; pres. Mgmt. Services Group, Inc., New Orleans, 1984-85, Assoc. Investment Services Inc., New Orleans, 1985-87, Northshore Property Mgmt., Inc., New Orleans, 1985-87; asst. v.p. USF&G Realty, Balt., 1987-89, v.p., 1989—; br. dirs. Children's Guild, Balt., 1988; cons. colls. and univs., 1976—. Mem. Nat. Assn. Corporate Real Estate Execs., Bldg. Owners and Mgrs. Assn., Comml.-Investment Council, Nat. Assn. Master Appraisers. Office: US Fidelity & Guaranty Co 100 Light St Baltimore MD 21202

MCGINNIS, MARCY ANN, television news executive producer; b. Long Branch, N.J., Apr. 9, 1950; d. Joseph Arthur and Ruth (Thomas) McG. AAS, Marymount U., 1970. Exec. sec. news Sta. CBS TV, N.Y.C., 1970-71, adminstrv. asst., 1971-73, asst. producer, 1973-76, assoc. producer, 1976-82, producer, 1982-85, sr. producer, 1985-89, exec. producer, 1989—. Mem. NATAS, NAFE, TV and Radio Working Press Assn. Roman Catholic. Home: 431 Lakeview Dr Oradell NJ 07649 Office: Sta CBS News 524 W 57th St New York NY 10019

MCGINNIS-SWIGER, DOROTHY KAY, real estate sales executive; b. Mechanicsburg, Pa., July 17, 1947; d. Charles Allen and Kathleen (Lauver) Nicholl; divorced; children: Shaun, Heather, Megan. Student, Allentown Hosp. Nursing Sch., 1965-67. Sales agt. Long & Foster, Realtors, Manassas, Va., 1978-85; instr. new agts. Long & Foster, Realtors, Fairfax, Va., 1985-86; sales mgr. Long & Foster, Realtors, Dale City, Va., 1985-88, Fredericksburg, Va., 1989—; sales mgr. Interstate Gen. Co., Waldorf, Md., 1988-89. Mem. Prince William Bd. Realtors (bd. dirs. 1982, chmn. awards com. 1987, chmn. community revitalization 1981, 82, Million Dollar club 1980-88, Sales Person of Yr. 1983, Top Producers club 1984), Fredericksburg Bd. Realtors (instr. new agts). Republican. Lutheran. Office: Long & Foster Realtors 1918 William St Fredericksburg VA 22401

MCGINTY, ANNE, music publishing executive; b. Findlay, Ohio, June 29, 1945; d. John E. and Elisabeth J. (Harlow) Staley; m. John Baldwin Edmondson, Dec. 31, 1977. MusB summa cum laude, Duquesne U., 1973, MusM, 1975. Flutist various orchs., chamber groups, 1964-83; prin. flutist Tucson Symphony Orch., 1967-69; editor, arranger Hansen Publs., Miami Beach, Fla., 1976-77; co-owner, pub. Edmondson & McGinty, Inc. div. Queenwood Publs., Scottsdale, Ariz., 1986—; instr. flute, Duquesne U., Carroll Coll., Trinity Coll., others, 1974-79; composer, arranger for various music pubs., 1978-86; guest conductor, U.S. and Can., 1985—. Composer works for concert band, solo, duet and trio flute, solo flute and solo clarinet with band accompaniment. Mem. ASCAP (Composer award 1986, 87, 88, 89, 90), Nat. Flute Assn. (co-editor newsletter 1974-76), Women Band Dirs. Nat. Assn. (Golden Rose award 1988). Republican. Home and Office: Queenwood Publs 11101 E Mercer Ln Scottsdale AZ 85259

MCGIRR, JACKELEN RICHARDSON, clothing designer; b. San Francisco, July 13, 1941; d. Jack Covell and Helen (York) Richardson; m. Douglas Jones, Dec. 22, 1969 (div. 1982); 1 child, Jackelen Anne; m. Wesley Neil McGirr, Feb. 7, 1987. BA, Calif. State U., Sacramento, 1963, gen. secondary credential, 1964; lic. in real estate, Fresno State Coll., 1965; MA in Clothing Design, Pacific Union Coll., 1968. Tchr. home econs. Kingsburg (Calif.) High Sch., 1963-65, Napa (Calif.) Valley Unified Sch. Dist., 1965-82; ptnr. Bottle Shop, St. Helena, Calif., 1965-71; clothing designer, Alturas, Calif., 1982-88; owner, mgr. Jackelen Custom Designed Garments, St. Helena, 1988—; cons. on cottage industry Coll. Siskeyou, Weed, Calif., 1983-85, Lassen Coll., Susanville, Calif., 1984. Exhibited designs Calif. State Fair, 1986—. Mem. Alturas Tourism Com., 1983—. Mem. AAUW, Order of Ea. Star. Republican. Presbyterian. Home and Office: 2080 Spring Mountain Rd Saint Helena CA 94574

MCGIRR, SARAH ELIZABETH, public relations and marketing executive, consultant; b. Pocatello, Idaho, Jan. 19, 1938; d. Clark Lowell Edwards and Sarah Elizabeth Pederson; m. Richard G. McGirr, Jr., Mar. 23, 1958; children: Richard G. III, Michael. Student U. Pacific, 1956-58. Clin. grants coordinator Pfizer, Inc., Groton, Conn., 1964-79; owner, operator The Quellen Group, Groton, 1980—; chmn. Women's Bus. Ownership Conf., Hartford, Conn., 1984. Mem. Rep. town mtg., Town of Groton, 1977-79, town councilor, 1979-81; chmn. Rep. City Com., 1984-85, 89—; mem. Rep. Town Com., 1977-85, emeritus, 1990—; treas. Thames East LWV, 1977-85; moderator 1st Congl. Ch. Christ, 1983-85; pres. bd. dirs. YWCA of Southeastern Conn., 1981-84; sec. Conn. Conf. on Sm. Bus., 1985; alt. U.S. Senate Com. on Sm. Bus. Adv. Council; chmn. state of Conn. U.S. Small Bus. Adv. Council; del. U.S. Conference on Small Bus., 1986; co-chair 4th Ann. Women's Congress, 1985; commr. Conn. Permanent Commn. on Status of Women, 1985—; mem. cert. panel Conn. Dept. Transp., 1987—, former chmn. Mem. Mistick River Bus. and Profl. Women (Woman of Yr. 1977, charter pres.), Conn. Fedn. Bus. Profl. Women (pres. 1983-84), Nat. Fedn. Bus. Profl. Women (leadership trainer 1984). Home: 390 Thames St Groton CT 06340 Office: The Quellen Group 349-B Mitchell St Groton CT 06340

MCGIVNEY, MARIA FRANCES, journalist, public relations professional; b. Houston, Oct. 22, 1963; d. Felix Francis and Marjory Beth (Stout) McG.; m. Jose Antonio Arrellaga, May 26, 1990. BJ, U. Tex., 1986. Media coord. Tex. Internat. Edn. Consortium, Austin, 1986-89; communications coord., writer Execucom Systems Corp., Austin, 1989—; freelance journalist, desktop pub. Austin, 1989—; editor, cons. Corridor Pub. Svcs., Austin, 1989—. Contbr. numerous articles to profl. and popular jours. Chmn. pub. rels. com., editor newsletter Tex. Ptnrs. of Ams., Austin, 1986—. Fellow Austin Writers League, Women in Communication. Roman Catholic. Home: 10610 Morado Circle #2204 Austin TX 78759 Office: Exexucom Systems Corp 108 Wild Basin/Two Wild Basin Austin TX 78746

MCGLAMERY, BARBARA COGGINS, homebuilder; b. Atlanta, Aug. 19, 1939; d. Robert Allen and Minnie (Reed) Coggins; m. Gerald G. McGlamery, Nov. 26, 1960; children: Gerald G. Jr., George L. BA, Auburn U., 1961. Sales assoc. Ronald Warren Real Estate, Florence, Ala., 1978-83, property mgr., 1984-86; v.p. So. Heritage Homes, Florence, 1985—, pres., 1987—, MLS Corp., 1989, 90. Mem. adv. bd. Kennedy-Douglass Ctr. for Arts, Florence, 1976-83; bd. dirs. Kennedy-Douglass Vols., 1976-83; mem. Salvation Army Aux. Mem. Nat. Assn. Homebuilders, Nat. Assn. Realtors, Ala. Assn. Realtors, Muscle Shoals Area Bd. Realtors, Grad. Realtors Inst. Alpha Omicron Pi (adv. bd. Alpha Kappa chpt. 1970-82). Presbyterian. Home: 157 Southland Dr Rte 9 Box 428 Florence AL 35633 Office: So Heritage Homes PO Box 674 409 N Court St Florence AL 35631

MCGLINCHEY, DIANNE WATKINS, marketing and sales executive, consultant; b. Meridian, Miss., Dec. 29, 1949; d. W. Warren and Alaine (Kynerd) Watkins; m. Bruce McGlinchey, May 27, 1979. BS summa cum laude, U. So. Miss., 1970. Supr. merchandising specialists Fla. Dept. Natural Resources, Miami, 1971-74; seafood consumer specialist mktg. div. Nat. Marine Fisheries Service, U.S. Dept. Commerce, Pascagoula, Miss., 1975-77; mgr. menu diversification and product devel. Red Lobster Inns of Am., Orlando, Fla., 1977-79; mktg. cons. McGlinchey Enterprises, Orlando, 1981-84; dir. food and beverage Kelly-Johnson, Inc., Oklahoma City, 1984-85; dir. mktg. and sales Beatrice Specialty Pet, 1985-88; cons. internat. mktg., 1988—, Gimborn Co., 1989—. Recipient citation Sec. Commerce, 1976. Mem Am. Mgmt. Assn. Republican. Methodist. Home and Office: 310 N River Oaks Rd Memphis TN 38119

MCGOUGH, JEANNNE B., police commander; b. Chgo., Nov. 15, 1948; d. James John and Margaret Jessilyn (Sullivan) McG. BA, St. Xavier Coll., Chgo., 1971; MA, U. Ill., 1975; cert. police mgmt., Northwestern U., 1982. Officer Chgo. Police Dept., 1975-78, youth officer, 1978-80, sgt., 1980-88, lt., 1988-89, comdr., 1989—; sec.-treas. Comdg. Officers and Sgts. Chgo. Police Dept. Credit Union, 1986-88; chmn. Ill. Anti Car Theft Com., Chgo., 1989—. Mem. Internat. Assn. Automobile Theft Investigators. Office: Chgo Police Dept 1121 S State St Chicago IL 60605

MCGOVERN, CATHERINE BIGLEY, educational administrator, consultant; b. N.Y., Nov. 6, 1939; d. Walter John and Catherine Bigley; m. Peter John McGovern, Dec. 6, 1938; children: Brian Peter, Sean Daniel. BA, Hunter Coll., 1961; MA, U. S.D., 1976; D in Edn., U. S. D., 1983. Asst. prof. Mt. Marty Coll., Yankton, S.D., 1977-83; dir. program and asst. prof. Valparaiso (Ind.) Univ., 1983-85; asst. prof., dir. program St. Thomas Univ., Miami, Fla., 1985-87; dir. of career svcs. Columbia Coll., Chgo., 1987-89; dir. career svcs., asst. prof.; adj. prof. Loyola U., Chgo., 1989—; co-owner Marsh McGovern Career Cons., Chgo., 1989-90. Fin. com. Old St. Mary's Ch.; established Friends of S.D. Pub. Broadcasting; mem. Joseph Jefferson awards com., Chgo. Dance Coalition Bd., Friends of Downtown Fund-Raising Com., Near North Chpt. Lyric Opera. Roman Catholic. Home: 1708 W School Chicago IL 60657

MCGOVERN, FRANCES, retired lawyer; b. Akron, Ohio, Apr. 18, 1927; d. Bernard Francis and Pauline A. (Menegay) McG. AB, U. Akron, 1948; LLB, Case Western Res. U., 1949; Bar: Ohio 1949, U.S. Dist. Ct. (no. dist.) Ohio 1951, U.S. Supreme Ct. 1963, U.S. Ct. Appeals (6th cir.) 1975. Pvt. practice, Barberton, Ohio, 1949-52; assoc. Motz, Morris, Wilson & Quine, Akron, Ohio, 1952-55; ptnr. Quine & McGovern, Akron, 1955-60, 63-65; atty. Ohio Edison Co., Akron, 1965-78, sr. atty., 1978-88, assoc. gen. counsel, 1988-89. Mem. Ohio Gen. Assembly, 1955-60, chmn. judiciary com., 1959-60; mem., chmn. Ohio Pub. Utilities Commn., 1960-63; mem. Dept. Labor Employment Security Bd., Washington, 1963-68; vice chmn. Charter Commn. Summit County, 1969-70; del., mem. platform com. Dem. Nat. Conv., 1960, del., 1964; trustee N.E. Ohio Coll. Medicine, Rootstown, 1979-81, U. Akron, 1973-82; pres. United Way, 1987-89, also bd. dirs.; sec. Employee Spl. Svcs. Commn., 1974—; bd. dirs. Med. Edn. Found. of N.E. Ohio U. Coll. Medicine, 1982—, Archbishop Haban High Sch., 1984-90. Recipient Achievement award Kappa Kappa Gamma, 1962, Akron Beacon Jour., 1968, Disting. Svc. award United Way, Akron, 1969, Disting. Alumni award U. Akron, 1989, others. Fellow Ohio State Bar Found.; mem. Ohio State Bar Assn., Akron Bar Assn., Democrat. Roman Catholic.

MCGOVERN, LAUREN MARYANNE, management consultant; b. Mpls., July 5, 1940; d. Earl James and Luverne Marion (Ramgren) McG.; m. John Joseph Feeney, June 9, 1984; stepchildren: John Patrick, William Terrance. BS, U. Minn., 1962, MS, 1968, PhD, 1974. Lic. psychologist, Minn., Pa. Sch. psychologist Mpls. Pub. Schs., 1974-75; pres. McGovern and Assocs., Mpls., 1975-78; cons. Westinghouse Electric Corp., Pitts., 1978-82, mgr., 1982-85; v.p., psychologist Drame Beam Morin, Inc., Pitts., 1985-87, sr. v.p., mgr., 1987—. Mem. Am. Psychol. Assn., Pa. Psychol. Assn., Pitts. Psychol. Assn., Pitts. Personnel Assn., Pitts. C. of C., Rivers Club Pitts. Home: 99 Parkridge Ln Pittsburgh PA 15228 Office: Drake Beam Morin Inc STe 3220 USX Tower 600 Grant St Pittsburgh PA 15219

MC GOVERN, MAUREEN THERESE, entertainer; b. Youngstown, Ohio, July 27, 1949; d. James Terrence and Mary Rita (Welsh) McG. Student pub. schs., Youngstown. Exec. sec. Youngstown Cartage Co., 1968-69; sec. Assocs. in Anesthesiology, Youngstown, 1970-71. Entertainer, 1972—; stage appearances include: The Sound of Music, 1981, The Pirates of Penzance, 1981, South Pacific, 1982, Nine, 1984, Brownstone, 1984, Guys and Dolls, 1984, Three Penny Opera, 1989; cameo appearance in movie The Towering Inferno, 1975; appeared in film Ky. Fried Theater's Airplane, 1979; albums recorded include: The Morning After, 1973 (Gold Record award), Nice To Be Around, 1974, Academy Award Performance, 1975, Maureen McGovern, 1979, Another Woman In Love, 1987, Naughty Baby, 1989; composer: Midnight Storm, 1973, If I Wrote You a Song, 1973, All I Want, 1974, Memory, 1974, Little Boys and Men, 1974, Love Knots, 1974, You Love Me Too Late, 1979, Thief in the Night, 1979, Don't Stop Now, 1979, Hello Again, 1979, Halfway Home, 1980, others. Recipient Gold Record for single The Morning After, Record Industry Assn. Am., 1973; Can. RPM Gold Leaf award, 1973; Australian gold award, 1975; resolution for bringing fame and recognition to Ohio, Ohio Senate, 1974; Grand prize Tokyo Music Festival, 1975. Mem. ASCAP, Am. Fedn. Musicians, AFTRA, Screen Actors Guild. Office: care Warner Bros Records 3300 Warner Blvd Burbank CA 91510*

MCGOVERN, PATRICIA, state senator. Mem. Mass. State Senate from Dist. 2. Mem. Mass. State Democratic Com. Office: Mass State Senate State Capitol Boston MA 02133

MCGOWAN, DIANE LYNNE, otolaryngologist; b. Elmhurst, Ill., Feb. 4, 1959; d. William O. and Frances M. (Driscoll) Webb; m. James Patrick McGowan, May 27, 1984. BA, Ill. Wesleyan U., 1980; MD, Loyola U., Maywood, Ill., 1984. Diplomate Am. Bd. Otolaryngology. Intern, then resident in otolaryngology Emory U., Atlanta, 1984-89; pvt. practice Clark-Holder Clinic, La Grange, Ga., 1989—. Mem. AMA, Am. Acad. Otolaryngology-Head & Neck Surgery, Am. Acad. Facial Plastic & Reconstructive Surgery, Med. Assn. Ga., Troup County Med. Soc., Greater Atlanta Otolaryngology-Head & Neck Surgery Soc. Methodist. Office: Clark Holder Clinic 303 Smith St La Grange GA 30240

MCGOWAN, JOANNE SUWEYN, accountant; b. Paterson, N.J., Apr. 5, 1955; d. Henry Jr. and Joan Alyce (Harrison) Suweyn; m. Jack McGowan, June 20, 1981; children: John Matthew, Joseph Anderson. BS in Journalism, U. Fla., 1976; MBA, U. Cen. Fla., 1983. CPA, Tex. Promotional writer Tupperware Home Parties, Orlando, Fla., 1976-79; pres., founder Women's Info. Network Inc., Orlando, 1979-82; documentation specialist Fla. Software Svcs., Orlando, 1982-83; v.p. fin. The Kirchman Corp., Orlando, 1983; asst. fin. mgr. Greater Orlando Aviation Authority, Orlando, 1984, mgr. of contracts, 1985; fin. planner Kingwood, Tex., 1985-87; pvt. practice Kingwood, 1988—. Contbr. articles to profl. publs. Chair Commn. on Status of Women, Orange County, Fla., 1982-84, Miriam Circle, Kingwood, Tex., 1988—; treas. Bear Br. PTA, Kingwood, Tex., 1989—. Bickel fellowship U. Fla., 1975-76. Mem. LWV, Hunters Ridge Assn. (treas. 1989), Hi-Neighbor. Republican. Presbyterian. Office: 3939 Forest Village Dr Kingwood TX 77339

MCGRADY, CORINNE YOUNG, design company executive; b. N.Y.C., May 6, 1938; d. Albert I. and Reda (Bromberg) Young; m. Michael Robinson McGrady; children: Sean, Siobhan, Liam. Student, Bard Coll., Annandale-on-Hudson, N.Y., 1960, Harvard U., 1968-69. Founder, pres. McGrady Corp. (merger with Boston Warehouse Trading Corp. 1990), East Northport, N.Y., 1970—. Acrylic works exhibited in group shows at Mus. Contemporary Crafts, N.Y.C., 1969-70, Smithsonian Instn., 1970-71, Pompidou Ctr., Paris, 1971, Mus. Sci. and Industry, 1970; sculpture exhibited at Guild Hall Show, Southampton, N.Y., 1968, Hecksher Mus., 1968. Vice pres. Woman's Internat. League for Peace and Freedom, Huntington, N.Y., 1971. Recipient Design Rev. award Indsl. Design, 1969, 70; Instant Supergraphic Indsl. Design Rev. award, 1971. Patentee cookbook stand. Home: 95 Eatons Neck Rd Northport NY 11768 Office: Corinne McGrady Designs The McGrady Corp 29 Brightside East Northport NY 11731

MCGRATH, ABIGAIL HUBBELL ROSEN, theater director, producer; b. N.Y.C., Sept. 18, 1941; d. William Warner III and Helene Virginia (Johnson) Hubbell; m. Leonard Rosen, June 10, 1960 (div. 1964); 1 child, Jason Antek; m. Anthony McGrath, May 15, 1967; 1 child, Benson Hubbell McGrath. BA, Bard Coll., 1963. Producer Off Ctr. Theatre, N.Y.C., 1968—; casting dir. The Gig, N.Y.C., 1985, Sweet Lorraine, N.Y.C., 1986; Luckiest Man in the World, N.Y.C., 1987; producer Abbie Hoffman Meml. Celebration, N.Y.C., 1989—. Producer Frankenstein, Edinburgh (Scotland) Festival; writer: (film) The Christmas Party. Office: Watson-McGrath 1501 Broadway Ste 1310 New York NY 10036

MCGRATH SANGSTON, SUSAN ELIZABETH, personnel director; b. Lansdowne, Pa., Mar. 3, 1951; d. Edward Joseph McGrath and Frances (Weaver) Theisen; m. David Ray Sangston, May 28, 1988; children: Michael, Timothy. AA, Ottumna (Iowa) Hts. Coll., 1971; BA, Northern Ill. U., 1973. Underwriter Allstate Ins. Co., Skokie, Ill., 1973; claim adj. Allstate Ins. Co., Skokie, 1973-74, human resources rep., 1974-79, human resources div. mgr., 1979-84; human resources svcs. mgr. Allstate Ins. Co., Northbrook, Ill., 1984-87; human resource mgr. Allstate Ins. Co., Skokie, 1987—; Bd. dirs. of Field Grant Com., Allstate Ins. Co. Found., Northbrook, 1987—. Adv. Ctr. for Enriched Living, Deerfield, 1988-89, Orchard Village, Skokie, 1987-89. Dir. Skokie C. of C.; mem. Northern Ill. Indsl. Assn.

(personnel com. 1987—). Roman Catholic. Home: 790 Tower Rd Winnetka IL 60093 Office: Allstate Ins Co 7770 Frontage Skokie IL 60077

MCGRAW, LAVINIA MORGAN, retail company executive; b. Detroit, Feb. 26, 1924; d. Will Curtis and Margaret Coulter (Oliphant) McG. AB, Radcliffe Coll., 1945. Sales assoc. The May Dept. Store Corp., Washington, 1977—. Mem. Phi Beta Kappa. Avocation: hiking. Home: 2501 Calvert St NW Washington DC 20008

MCGREGOR, RAYANNE, credit union administrator; b. Abilene, Tex., Sept. 5, 1962; d. Vernon Ray and Judith Ann (Beard) McG. BS, BA, U. Ky., 1987. Diamond sales assoc. Svc. Mdse. Corp., Paducah, Ky.; mgr. credit union Lourdes Hosp., Inc., Paducah. mem. NAFE, U. Ky. Alumni Assn. Home: 840 Bryant Ford Rd Paducah KY 42003

MCGREW, SUSAN MARIE, director day care facility; b. Del Rio, Tex., Apr. 6, 1962; d. Roger Henry and Monica (Shea) Herman; m. John Bradley McGrew, Apr. 30, 1988; children: Elizabeth Eileen, Roger Bradley. BA in Liberal Arts, U. Tex., 1984. Dir., owner St. Andrew's Day Care, Ft. Worth, 1981—, St. Peter's Day Care, Ft. Worth, 1982—, OLX Day Care, Ft. Worth, 1989—. Mem. NAFE, Nat. German Honor Soc., Internat. Fgn. Lang. Soc. Republican. Roman Catholic. Home and Office: 3060 Fairmeadows Lane Fort Worth TX 76123

MCGRORY, MARY KATHLEEN, academic administrator; b. N.Y.C., Mar. 22, 1933; d. Patrick Joseph and Mary Kate (Gilvary) McG. BA, Pace U., 1957; MA, U. Notre Dame, 1962; PhD, Columbia U., 1969; DHL, Albertus Magnus Coll., 1984. Prof. English Western Conn. State U., Danbury, 1969-78; dean of arts and scis. Eastern Conn. State U., Willimantic, 1978-80, v.p. for acad. affairs, 1981-85; pres. Hartford Coll. for Women, Conn., 1985—; pres. MKM Assocs., Holland, Ma., 1983—. Author: Yeats, Joyce & Beckett, 1975. Mem. bd. dirs. Hartford Hosp., 1975—; chmn. bd. of govs. Greater Hartford Consortium of Higher Edn., 1989-90. Fels Found. fellow, 1966-67, NEH summer fellow, 1975; Ludwig Vogelstein Found. travel grantee, 1973. Mem. New Eng. Jr. Community and Tech. Coll. Coun. (v.p. 1988-91), Am. Assn. Higher Edn., Med. Acad. of Am., Am. Coun. on Edn., Greater Hartford C. of C. (bd. dirs. 1989—), Hartford Club (bd. dirs. 1988—), Univ. Club Hartford. Home: 80 Elizabeth St Hartford CT 06105 Office: Hartford Coll for Women 1265 Asylum Ave Hartford CT 06105

MCGUFFIN, MARY NETA, artist, secretary; b. Granbury, Tex., Jan. 8, 1939; d. Troy Earl and Coy Clara (Jones) Everidge; m. Weldon Gene Campbell (div. Oct. 1978); children: Shelba Brady, Lynda Jackson, Rex Campbell, Alan Campbell, Billy Campbell; m. Billy Jack McGuffin; stepchildren: Jackie, John, James, Jeff. Student, Hill Jr. Coll., Cleburne, Tex., 1973, TCU Portrait, 1975, Weatherford (Tex.) Jr. Coll., 1988. Artist Neta Studio, Granbury, Tex., 1967—; sec. S.W. Bowling Svc., Granbury, 1980—; artist, bd. dirs. Running Water Draw Art Coun., Plainview, Tex., 1975-76. Artist Silent Anger & Sadness, 1976 (Blue Ribbon), Somewhere, 1980 (Plaque), Lost Dreams, 1982 (Silver award), Hondo, 1985 (Gold award). Mem. Rep. Nat. Com.; bd. dirs. Hood County Tax Payers Assn., Granbury, 1988—. Mem. Nat. Mus. Women in the Arts (chartered), Nat. Cowboy Hall of Fame, Nat. Cowgirl Hall of Fame, Nat. Trust for Hist. Preservation, Tex. Fine Arts Assn., Pecan Plantation Country Club, N.W. Art Club. Episcopalian. Home and Office: Rt 3 Box 284 Granbury TX 76048

MCGUINNESS, DEBORAH LOUISE, operations research scientist; b. Drexel Hill, Pa., Mar. 28, 1958; d. Richard Charles and Eleanor Louise (Rothermel) McG. BS in Computer Sci., Duke U., 1980; MS in Computer Sci., U. Calif., Berkely, 1981. Rsch. scientist home info. systems AT&T Bell Labs., Indpls., 1980-84; rsch. scientist Artificial Intelligence and Computing Environments AT&T Bell Labs., Murray Hill, N.J., 1984-86; rsch. scientist Artificial Intelligence Principles Rsch. AT&T Bell Labs., Murray Hill, 1986—. Mem. IEEE, Am. Assn. Artificial Intelligence, Phi Eta Sigma, Phi Beta Kappa. Office: AT&T Bell Labs 600 Mountain Ave Rm 3C 443 Murray Hill NJ 07974

MCGUINNESS, SHEILA V., human resources specialist; b. N.Y.C., Aug. 10, 1961; d. Patrick M. and Catherine F. (Farrelly) McG. BS, Pace U., 1982, MBA, 1989. Tng. support adminstr., gen. tng. specialist N.Y. Power Authority, Buchanan; human resources coord. HYPRES, Inc., Elmsford, N.Y.; coord. employee devel. and staffing Kaiser Permanente, White Plains, N.Y. Mem. NAFE, Am. Soc. Personnel Adminstrs. Home: 333 Center Dr Mahopac NY 10541

MCGUIRE, CAROL ANN, business magazine editor; b. Berea, Ohio, Nov. 13, 1950; d. Wendell Berkley and Betty Louise (Speyer) Lohr; m. Thomas Michael McGuire, Apr. 9, 1947. BS in Edn., Ohio State U., 1972. Tchr. Columbus Pub. Schs., Columbus, Ohio, 1973-85; regional mktg. dir. Soc. Bank, Columbus, 1985-87; exec. dir. Columbus Pub. Schs. Fund, 1987-88; editor Am. Fastener Jour., Powell, Ohio, 1988—. Mem. Am. Mktg. Assn., Small Mag. Pub. Assn., Advt. Fedn., Columbus Met. Club (mktg. com.). Home: 293 Hopewell Dr Powell OH 43065 Office: Am Fastener Jour 293 Hopewell Dr Powell OH 43065

MCGUIRE, DIANNE M., psychotherapist; b. Houston, Feb. 22, 1950; d. Sidney A. and Shirley Lee (Ward) Schwartz; m. Walter Fred McGuire, May 7, 1983; children: Christopher C. Broussard, Emily Nicole, Robert L. Degree in psychology, U. Houston, 1986, MS, 1988; AA, San Jacinto Community Coll., Pasadena, Tex., 1984. Cert. social worker, Tex. Psychotherapist Family Svc. Ctr., Pasadena; presenter in field. Active Multiple Sclerosis Soc. Mem. Am. Psychol. Assn., Nat. Assn. Social Workers, SWPA, WPA, Psi Chi, Phi Theta Kappa, Alpha Chi. Home: 3206 Brookhollow Deer Park TX 77536

MCGUIRE, KAREN LEE, educator; b. Washington, Dec. 21, 1946; d. Reane DeCavreal and Myra Elaine (Neitzey) Chilson; m. Thomas Francis McGuire, Feb. 7, 1946 (div. 1978); 1 child, Thomas Lee. BS, Palm Beach Atlantic Coll., 1985; MEd, Fla. Atlantic U., 1987. Editorial asst. Library of Congress, Washington, 1964-67; sec. Temple Hills (Md.) Bapt. Ch., 1970-73; legal sec. Giordano, Alexander, Hass, et al, Oxon Hill, Md., 1973-78; sec. Dept. of the Air Force, Washington, 1978-79; protocol asst. Dept. of Def., Washington, 1979-80; confidential asst. Dept. of Energy, Washington, 1980-81; adminstrv. asst. Bapt. Joint Com. Pub. Affairs, Washington, 1981-82; assoc. dean of students Palm Beach Atlantic Coll., West Palm Beach, Fla., 1982-87; staff asst. HUD, Washington, 1987; dir. hospitality and lang. missions Columbia Bapt. Ch., Falls Church, Va., 1987-90; editorial group mgr. Women's Missionary Union, SBC, Birmingham, Ala., 1990—. Dir. hospitality and lang. missions Columbia Bapt. Ch., Falls Ch., Va., 1987—. Named one of Outstanding Young Women, 1983. Mem. NAFE. Baptist. Home: 2257 Pimmit Dr 1006 Falls Church VA 22043

MCGUIRE, MARIE JOSEPHINE, high school guidance counselor; b. Jersey City, Nov. 15, 1933; d. Christopher Peter and Catherine Veronica (Ghiozzi) Marra; m. Joseph Hugh McGuire, Aug. 15, 1954 (dec. Nov. 1988). BA, Montclair State Tchrs. Coll., 1954; MA, William Paterson Coll., 1969. Tchr. elem. Bd. Edn., Secaucus, N.J., 1954-57; tchr. upper elem. Bd. Edn., Cedar Group, N.J., 1957-69, high sch. counselor, 1969—; career counselor vol. adult sch., Secaucus, 1981-83. Recipient Gov.'s Tchr. award State of N.J., 1986, Vocat. Svc. award Cedar Grove Rotary, 1987; named Outstanding Educator, Cedar Grove Jaycees, 1974, Secaucus Jaycees, 1976. Mem. Delta Kappa Gamma Soc. Internat., N.J. Delta Kappa Gamma Soc. (state chmn., communications 1982, 50th anniversary 1987, legislation 1989). Home: 12 Arn Terr Secaucus NJ 07094

MCGUIRE, NANCY L., security executive; b. New London, Conn., June 20, 1951; d. Frederick L. and Margaret (Snook) McG.; m. Paul R. Weiser, Apr. 22, 1989. BA, Whittier (Calif.) Coll., 1973; MA, Calif. State U., L.A., 1976. Rsch. asst. L.A. Dept. Mental Health; rsch. adminstr. Rand Corp., Santa Monica; sr. rsch. analyst Calif. Rsch. Corp., Santa Monica; dist. investigation mgr. Pinkerton's Inc., L.A.; corp. mgr. internal audit western zone Svc. Am. Corp., Stamford, Conn.; spokesperson and tech. advisor for film and TV prodns.; speaker in field. Mem. Am. Soc. Indsl. Security, NAFE, NOW, Alpha Kappa Delta. Office: 3201 E 59th St Long Beach CA 90801

MCGUIRE, SANDRA LYNN, nursing educator; b. Flint, Mich., Jan. 28, 1947; d. Donald Armstrong and Mary Lue (Harvey) Johnson; m. Joseph L. McGuire, Mar. 6, 1976; children: Matthew, Kelly, Kerry. BS in Nursing, U. Mich., 1969, MPH, 1973, EdD, 1988. Staff nurse Univ. Hosp., Ann Arbor, Mich., 1969; pub. health nurse Wayne County Health Dept., Eloise, Mich., 1969-72; instr. Madonna Coll., Livonia, Mich., 1973; pub. health coordinator Plymouth Ctr. for Human Devel., Northville, Mich., 1974-75; asst. prof. community health nursing U. Mich., Ann Arbor, 1975-83; asst. prof. U. Tenn., Knoxville, 1983-88; dir. Kids Are Tomorrow's Srs. Program, 1988—; resource person Gov.'s Com. Unification of Mental Health Services in Mich.; speaker profl. assns. and workshops; bd. dirs. Ctr. Understanding Aging, 1987—. Author: (with S. Clemen-Stone and D. Eigsti) Comprehensive Family and Community Health Nursing, 1981, 2d edit., 1987. Bd. dirs. Mich. chpt. ARC, 1980-83, Knoxville chpt., 1984-85; founder Knoxville Intergenerational Network, 1989. USPHS fellow, 1972-73. Mem. Nat., Mich. leagues nursing, Am., Mich. (chmn. mental health sect. 1976) pub. health assns., Nat., Mich. (dir., co-chmn. residential services com. 1976-79, chmn. health services 1979-82), Plymouth (chmn. residential services com. 1975-77) assns. retarded citizens, Sigma Theta Tau, Pi Lambda Theta, Phi Kappa Phi. Home: 11008 Crosswind Dr Knoxville TN 37922 Office: 11008 Crosswind Dr Knoxville TN 37922

MCGUIRE, SONDRA LEE, automotive executive; b. Columbus, Ohio, Nov. 9, 1941; d. Charles Richard Whitehurst and LaVerne Adele (Harlow) Battelle; m. Brandt B. Shumate, June 2, 1958 (div. Dec. 1978); children: Raymond Murl, Russell James; m. Clyde Leon McGuire, May 29, 1982. Student, U. Ariz., 1975-76, Pima Coll., 1977-81. Sales audit, payroll Levy's Dept. Store, Tucson, 1960-61; office mgr. Shumate's Custom Interiors, Tucson, 1962-78; chief exec. officer Auto Trimmer's Supply, Tucson, 1978—; cons. curriculum Sunnyside High Sch., Tucson, 1983. Contbr. articles to profl. jours. Mem. Exec. Women's Council, So. Ariz., 1980. Recipient Cert. of Appreciation award Beacon Found., 1984. Mem. Auto Service Industry Assn. (program chmn. 1985, exec. bd. dirs. Auto Trim div.1981-88, chairperson 1987, 88, cert. of appreciation award 1985, 87, Hall of Fame plaque 1987), Tucson C. of C. Republican. Baptist. Home: 8900 Bears Path Tucson AZ 85749 Office: Auto Trimmers Supply Inc 2958 E 22d St Tucson AZ 85713

MCGUIRL, MARLENE DANA CALLIS, law librarian, educator; b. Hammond, Ind., Mar. 22, 1938; d. Daniel David and Helen Elizabeth (Baludis) Callis; m. James Franklin McGuirl, Apr. 24, 1965. A.B., Ind. U., 1959; J.D., DePaul U., 1963; M.A.L.S., Rosary Coll., 1965; LL.M., George Washington U., 1978, postgrad. Harvard U., 1985. Bar: Ill. 1963, Ind. 1964, D.C. 1972. Asst., DePaul Coll. of Law Library, 1961-62, asst. law librarian, 1962-65; ref. law librarian Boston Coll. Sch. Law, 1965-66; library dir. D.C. Bar Library, 1966-70; asst. chief Am.-Brit. Law div. Law Library of Library of Congress, Washington, 1970, chief Am.-Brit. Law div., 1970—; library cons. Nat. Clearinghouse on Poverty Law, OEO, Washington, 1967-69, Northwestern U. Nat. Inst. Edn. in Law and Poverty, 1969, D.C. Office of Corp. Counsel, 1969-70; instr. law librarianship Grad. Sch. of U.S. Dept. of Agr., 1968-72; lectr. legal lit. Cath. U., 1972; adj. asst. prof., 1973—; lectr. environ. law George Washington U., 1979—; judge Nat. and Internat. Law Moot Ct. Competition, 1976-78; pres. Hamburger Heaven, Inc., Palm Beach, Fla., 1981—, L'Image de Marlene Ltd., 1986—, Clinique de Beauté Inc., 1987—, Heads & Hands Inc., 1987—, Horizon Design & Mfg. Co., Inc., 1987—; dir. Stoneridge Farm Inc., Gt. Falls, Va., 1984—. Contbr. articles to profl. jours. Mem. Georgetown Citizens Assn.; trustee D.C. Law Students in Ct.; del. Ind. Democratic Conv., 1964. Recipient Meritorious Service award Library of Congress, 1974, letter of commendation Dir. of Personnel, 1976, cert. of appreciation, 1981-84. Mem. ABA (facilities law library Congress com. 1976-89), Fed. Bar Assn. (chpt. council 1972-76), Ill. Bar Assn., Women's Bar Assn. (pres. 1972-73, exec. bd. 1973-77, Outstanding Contbn. to Human Rights award 1975), D.C. Bar Assn., Am. Bar Found., Nat. Assn. Women Lawyers, Am. Assn. Law Libraries, (exec. bd. 1973-77), Law Librarians Soc. of Washington (pres. 1971-73), Exec. Women in Govt., Nat. Lawyers Club. Home: 3416 P St NW Washington DC 20007 Office: Libr Congress Am Brit Law Div Washington DC 20540

MCGULPIN, ELIZABETH JANE, nurse; b. Toledo, Oct. 18, 1932; d. James Orville and Leah Fayne (Helton) Welden; m. Daivd Nelson Buster, Apr. 9, 1956 (div. Nov. 1960); children: David Hugh, James Ray, Mark Stephen; m. Fredrick Gordon McGulpin, Oct. 7, 1973. AA in Nursing, Pasadena City Coll., 1968. RN, Wash. Lic. nurse Las Encinas Hosp., Pasadena, Calif.; nurse Hopi Indian Reservation HEW, Keams Canyon, Ariz., 1969-70; nurse, enterostomal therapist Pasadena Vis. Nurse Assn., 1972-74; nurse Seattle King County Pub. Health, 1977-81; home care nurse Victorville, Calif., 1983-85; nurse Adult Family Home, Woodinville, Wash., 1986—; vol. nurse, counselor Child Protective Svcs., Victorville, 1984. Vol. nurse Am. Cancer Soc., Pasadena, 1973-75, United Ostomy Assn., Los Angeles, Victorville, 1973-84. Am. Cancer Soc. grantee. Mem. Vis. Nurse Assn. (Enterostomal Therpay grantee 1973). Home: 22366 Woodinville Duvall Rd Woodinville WA 98072

MCGURK, HEATHER, sales executive; b. Allentown, Pa., Apr. 5, 1966; d. James H. and Lavern M. (Kraynek) McG.; m. Robert Kremkow, Aug. 20, 1989. Degree in interior design, Mich. State U., 1987. Mgr. customer rels. Western/Pegasus Inc., Holland, Mich. Mem. Am. Soc. for Quality Control, NAFE, Delta Gamma Beta Xi Housing Corp. (pres.). Home: 1323 Steaders Pass Zeeland MI 49464 Office: 728 E 8th St Holland MI 49423

MCHENRY, DEBRA ANNE, government administrator; b. Honolulu, Aug. 24, 1953; d. Paul Hamilton and Dorothy Nell (Deen) Koogle; m. John Franklin McHenry, June 7, 1975 (div. May 1987); 1 child, Kate Deen. BS, Towson State U., 1975; MS, George Washington U., 1979. Adminstrv. officer professionalization. Mgmt. support intern Dept. Def., Ft. Meade, Md., 1975-78, personnel staffing technician, 1978-82, mgmt. analyst, 1982-84, program analyst, 1984-85, staff chief, 1985-88, mgr. software applications, 1988—. Mem. Defenders of Animal Rights Inc., Towson, Md., 1977—; mem. Chartridge Community Assn., Severna Park, Md., 1979—. Mem. NAFE, Bus. and Profl. Women (chmn. fin. com. 1988—), Women in Govt. Democrat. Roman Catholic.

MCHENRY, LOUISA BETH, special education educator; b. Malvern, Ark., Jan. 14, 1961; d. John Robert and Lou Vena (Weller) McH. BS, Henderson State U., Arkadelphia, Ark., 1983; MEd, East Tex. State U., 1987. Cert. tchr., Ark., Tex. Speech therapist Texarkana (Ark.) Pub. Sch., tchr. self-contained spl. edn. Area dir. Spl. Olympics, cert. coach; pres. Coun. for Exceptional Children, 1989. Mem. NEA, Ark. Edn. Assn., Classroom Tchrs. Assn., Alpha Sigma Alpha (rush chmn.). Republican. Presbyterian.

MCHUGH, BETSY BALDWIN, sociologist, educator, business owner; b. Concord, N.H.; d. Walter Killenbeck and Elizabeth Alice (Hunt) Slater; m. Michael Joseph McHugh, Dec. 19, 1954; children: Betsy, Michael. MusB in Vocal Music, Syracuse (N.Y.) U., 1954, postgrad., 1985—. Tchr. pub. schs. Juneau, Alaska, 1966-85; owner, founder Cashé Pub. Co., Tampa, Fla., 1985—; biologist Fish and Game Dept. State of Alaska,; owner Spin Doll Co., Saturday Shoppe. Named one of Outstanding Educators Gov. Alaska Woman's Comm., 1985. Home: 5932 Montgomery St Juneau AK 99801

MCHUGH, ERIN, creative director; b. New Bedford, Mass., July 29, 1952; d. James Francis and Dorothy Hoye (Kavanaugh) McH. Student, Bread Loaf Sch. English, Ripton, Vt.; BA, Skidmore Coll., 1974. Editorial asst. E.P. Dutton Pubs., N.Y.C., 1977-79, dir. spl. sales, 1979-80; account exec. Franklin Spier, N.Y.C., 1980-84, v.p., account exec., 1984—, v.p., assoc. creative dir., 1986—. Co-author: I Left My Fat Behind, 1982. Vol. Gay Mens Health Crisis, N.Y.C., 1988—. Mem. Pubs. Ad Club. Republican. Roman Catholic. Home: 420 E 80th St New York NY 10021 Office: Franklin Spier Inc 650 1st Ave New York NY 10016

MCHUGH, MAUREEN CARROLL, director of women's studies; b. Pitts., Sept. 2, 1952; d. Thomas F. and Alice (Carroll) McH.; m. Francis R. Barrett, June 30, 1984; children: Bridget McHugh Barrett, Maura McHugh Barrett. BA, Chatham Coll., 1974; MS in Psychology, U. Pitts., 1979, PhD in Psychology, 1983. Asst. prof. Marquette U., Milw., 1983-84; instr. Community Coll. of Allegheny County, Pitts., 1984-85; asst. prof. Duquesne U., Pitts., 1985-86; dir. women's studies Ind. U. of Pa., Indiana, Pa., 1986—; cons. in field. Author: (with others) chpt. Battered Women, 1990. State of Pa. grantee, 1988-89, 89-90. Mem. Assn. for Women in Psychology (membership chair 1990—), Am. Psychol. Assn. (chair rsch. prize com. 1986—), Nat. Women's Studies Assn., Pa. Assn. for Women's Studies (chair 1987—), NOW, Nat. Abortion Rights Action League, Ind. Coalition for Reproductive Rights and Equality, Phi Beta Kappa. Office: Ind U of Pa Women's Studies 352 Sutton Hall Indiana PA 15705

MCHUGH, TONI WALTER, sales executive; b. Milw., Nov. 25, 1946; d. Harland Anton Walter and Elizabeth (Abel) Walter Adamson; m. Harry Miller McHugh, Aug. 31, 1968; children: Meagan Elizabeth, Hilary Barbree. BBA, U. Wis., 1968; MBA, Fairleigh Dickinson U., 1985. Exec. trainee, asst. buyer B. Altman & Co., N.Y.C., 1968-69; spot TV buyer J. Walter Thompson, N.Y.C., 1969-72; founder, mgr., owner The Cheese Shop, Ridgefield, Conn., 1972-75; account rep. Sta. WSYX, Columbus, Ohio, 1986-89, nat. sales mgr., 1989—; chairperson membership com. LWV, Chester, N.J., 1976; chairperson March of Dimes Mothers March, Vernon, N.J., 1978, Adoption Fair, N.J., 1982-83, Family Services Ball, Morristown, N.J., 1985; pres. Edna Gladney N.Y. Area Aux., N.Y.C., 1980; founder, chairperson N.J. Com. for Adoption, 1980-83; bd. dirs. Nat. Com. for Adoption, Washington, 1980-86, chairperson, 1983-85; fundraiser New Vernon (N.J.) Vol. Fire Dept., 1982; fundraiser Peck Sch., Morristown, 1982-85. Named Friend of Adoption, Nat. Com. for Adoption, 1985. Mem. Jr. League of Columbus (Ohio). Republican. Avocations: tennis, golf, reading, cooking. Home: 1261 Clubview Blvd N Worthington OH 43235

MCHUGH-TURNER, KAREN LYNNE, architectural resource consultant; b. Tacoma, Wash., Feb. 21, 1960; d. Thomas Edward and Judith (Hill) McHugh; m. Brooks Courtney Turner, Apr. 9, 1988. BS, W.Va. U., 1982. Resource coordinator GN Design Assocs., N.Y.C., 1982-88; prin. Archtl. Resources, Inc., Winter Haven, Fla., 1988—. Mem. Am. Soc. Interior Designers, Inst. Bus. Designers, Assn. Resource Specialists (founding mem.). Republican. Roman Catholic. Home and Office: 1071 Medinah Way Winter Haven FL 33884

MCILWAIN, CLARA EVANS, agricultural economist, consultant; b. Jacksonville, Fla., Apr. 5, 1919; d. Waymon and Jerusha Lee (Dickson) Evans; m. Ivy McIlwain, May 15, 1942 (dec. 1987); children: Ronald E., Carol A. McIlwain Jackson, Marilyn E. McIlwain Ross, Ivy J. McIlwain Lindsay. BS, U. D.C., 1939; M Agrl. Econs., U. Fla., 1972. Notary pub., Va.; lic. life and health ins. agt., Md., Va., D.C. Statis. asst. Hist. and Statis. Analysis Div., Washington, 1962-67; statistician Econ Devel. Div. USDA, Washington, 1967-70, 72, agrl. economist, 1972-74; program analyst Office Equal Opportunity, USDA, Washington, 1974-79; staff writer Sci. Weekly, Chevy Chase, Md., 1988-89; ins. agt. A.L. Williams, Primerica, Camp Springs, Md., 1990—; workshop coord. Author: Steps to Eloquence, 1989; contbr. to profl. publs. Coord., instr. Youth Leadership and Speechcraft, Toastmasters Internat., Washington area, 1972-78; tchr., bd. dirs. Sat. Tutorial Enrichment Program, Arlington, Va., 1988-89. Rockefeller Found. scholar, 1970-72. Mem. Toastmasters Internat. (past pres. Potomac Club, Gavel award 1976, Able Toastmaster award 1978), Am. Assn. Notaries, So. Assn. Agrl. Economists, Nat. Assn. Agrl. Econs., Internat. Platform Assn. Mem. Word of Faith Ch. Office: EVans Unlimited 8350 Greensboro Dr McLean VA 22102

MCINERNEY, MARGIE LYNN, business educator; b. Frankfort, Germany, June 19, 1953; (parents Am. citizens); d. Harry M. and Marjorie (Holton) McI. BSBA, U. Akron, 1975; MBA, Marshall U., 1977; PhD, Ohio State U., 1983. Bank examiner Comptroler of the Currency, U.S. Treasury Dept., Atlanta, 1977-79; bank auditor Citizens and Southern Bank, Macon, Ga., 1979; rsch. assoc. Ohio State U., Columbus, 1980-82; asst. prof. U. N.C., Wilmington, 1982-86; assoc. prof. Marshall U., Huntington, W.Va., 1986—; adj. faculty Ohio U., South Campus, Ironton, 1987—, Cen. Mich. U., Wright Paterson AFB, 1988—. Author published mgmt. cases and academic presentations. Adminstrv. bd. dirs. First Un. Meth. Ch., Huntington, 1988-89; bd. dirs. Girls Club, Wilmington, 1983-85; advisor Sigma Nu Fraternity, Huntington, 1986. Named Outstanding Prof., Interfrat. and Panhellenic Couns., U. N.C., Wilmington, 1985; grantee AAUW, 1984, Marshall U., 1987. Mem. Acad. of Mmgt., Indsl. Rels. Rsch. Assn., Inst. Mgmt. Scis., Phi Delta Gamma, Omicron Delta Epsilon. Office: Marshall Univ College of Business Huntington WV 25701

MCINERNEY, ROSEMARIE PATRICIA, funeral director; b. Chicago, Oct. 25, 1929; d. Thomas and Margaret B. (Lally) McI.; m. William J. Barry, Dec. 3, 1977 (dec. Jan. 1985). Deg. Mortuary Adminstr., Worsham Coll., 1948; postgrad., Loyola U., Chgo. Lic. funeral director, Ill.; lic. embalmer, Ill. Sec. Mdse. Mart, Chgo., 1948-49, office mgr., 1949-51; funeral dir. Thomas McInerney's Sons, Chgo., 1951—; mgr. Thomas McInerney & Sons, Chgo., 1960—, also bd. dirs. Mem. St. Gabriel Womens Club, v.p., 1960; treas. St. Gabriel Confraternity of Christian Doctrine, 1960—; mem. Cook County Dem. Orgn. Mem. Funeral Dirs. Svcs. Associated. Roman Catholic. Office: Thomas McInerney's Sons 7901 S Komensky Ave Chicago IL 60652

MCINTOSH, CHRISTINE MARIE, plastics company executive; b. St. Louis, May 18, 1961; d. James Franklin and Catherine Anna (O'Rourke) McI. Student, U. Tex., Arlington, 1980-89. Vet. med. asst. Thornton Animal Clinic, Atlanta, 1977-80; animal med. technician Stoneridge Animal Clinic, Arlington, 1980-83; product design lab. supr. Americhem, Inc., Mansfield, Tex., 1983—. Mem. Am. Mgmt. Assn., Soc. Plastics Engrs. Mem. Unity Ch. Home: 4165 Stinwick Ln Grand Prairie TX 75052 Office: Americhem Inc 1300 Fort Worth St Mansfield TX 76063

MCINTOSH, ELAINE VIRGINIA, nutrition educator; b. Webster, S.D., Jan. 30, 1924; d. Louis James and Cora Bolita (Bakke) Nelson; m. Thomas Henry McIntosh, Aug. 28, 1955; children: James George, Ronald Thomas, Charles Nelson. BA magna cum laude, Augustana Coll., Sioux Falls, S.D., 1945; MA, U. S.D., 1949; PhD, Iowa State U., 1954. Registered dietitian. Instr., asst. prof. Sioux Falls Coll., 1945-48; instr. Iowa State U., Ames, 1949-53, rsch. assoc., 1955-62; postdoctoral rsch. assoc. U. Ill., Urbana, 1954-55; asst. prof. human biology U. Wis., Green Bay, 1968-72, assoc. prof., 1972-85, prof., 1985-90, emeritus prof., 1990—, dir. human nutrition and dietetics program, 1975—, chmn. human biology dept., 1975-80, asst. to vice chancellor, asst. to chancellor, 1974-76. Contbr. numerous articles on bacterial metabolism, meat biochemistry and nutrition edn. to profl. jours. Fellow USPHS, 1948-49; grantee U. Wis. System, 1972. Mem. Am. Dietetic Assn., Inst. Food Technologists, Wis. Dietetics Assn., Wis. Nutrition Coun. (pres. 1974-75), Sigma Xi. Republican. Office: U Wis 2420 Nicolet Dr Green Bay WI 54311-7001

MCINTOSH, KARA ANN, services executive; b. Milw., June 28, 1962; d. Danzil Jervis and Florrie Mae (Wright) M. BA, Va. Tech., 1985; postgrad., U. D.C., 1988–. Sales clk. Wild N Wooly Needle Crafts, Fairfax, Va., 1985-86; front office clk. Hampshire Hotel, Wash., 1986-87; coordinator Travel Industry Assn., Wash., 1987-88; sales mgr. Carlyle Suites Hotel, Wash., 1988–; dir. of sales Carlyle Suites Hotel, Washington, 1989—. Semi-finalist Miss DC/America Pageant, 1985. Mem. NAFE, Hotel Sales Mktg. Internat., Wash., Nat. Coalition of Black Meeting Planners, Soc. of Govt. Meeting Planners, Washington Area Tour & Travel, DC C. of C., Greater Washington Soc. Assn. Execs. Office: Carlyle Stes Hotel 1731 New Hampshire Ave Washington DC 20009

MCINTOSH, KAREN HOLT, journalist; b. Houston, June 2, 1965; d. Thomas Shirley and Audrey (Jean) McI. BA, Tex. A&M U., 1987; cert. in publ. specialization, George Washington U., 1990. Staff asst. Sec. U.S. Senate, Washington, 1987-88; fed. writer Education USA, Arlington, Va., 1988—. Mem. Edn. Writers Assn., Women in Communications, Tex. State Soc. of Washington D.C., Kappa Alpha Theta. Methodist. Home: 807 N Howard #120 Alexandria VA 22304

MCINTOSH, RHODINA COVINGTON, lawyer, international development analyst; b. Chicago Heights, Ill., May 26, 1947; d. William George and Cora Jean (Cain) Covington; m. Gerald Alfred McIntosh, Dec. 14, 1970; children: Gary Allen, Garvey Anthony, Ayana Kai. BA cum laude, Mich. State U., 1969; JD, U. Detroit, 1978. Asst. to dir. equal opportunity program Mich. State U., East Lansing, 1969-70; law clk. Bell & Hudson, P.C., Detroit, 1977-79; main rapporteur 1st All-Africa Law Conf., U. Swaziland and Botswana, 1981, lectr., 1981-83; chief info. and tech. assistance Office Pvt. and Vol. Cooperation, U.S. AID, Washington, 1983-87, chief info. and program support, 1987-88; corp. counsel Automation Rsch. Systems Ltd., Alexandria, Va., 1988—; founding bd. mem. Women's Justice Ctr., Detroit, 1975-77; coord. women's leadership conf. Wayne State U., Detroit, 1979, participant confs. and workshops. Contbr. articles and documents to profl. publs. Rep. coord. urban program, Lansing, Mich., 1979-81; chair fgn. rels. subcom. Nat. Black Women's Polit. Caucus, Washington, 1984; bd. dirs. Mayor's Com. to Keep Detroit Beautiful, 1980, Detroit Urban League, 1981, Am. Opportunity Found., Washington, 1984—. Nat. Achievement scholar Ednl. Testing Svc., Princeton, N.J., 1965, Martin Luther King Jr. Ctr. for Social Change scholar, Atlanta, 1976; recipient Detroit Edison award, 1980, New Repubs. award, Mich., 1981, Disting. Leadership award ABI, 1987. Mem. NAFE, GOP Women's Network, Delta Sigma Theta. Roman Catholic.

MCINTYRE, JUDITH WATLAND, biology educator; b. Kansas City, Mo., Aug. 19, 1930; d. Clarence and Pearl (Tyrholm) Watland; m. John Patrick McIntyre, Sept. 14, 1957; children: Perry, Richard, Anthony. BA, Carleton Coll., 1952; MA, U. Minn., 1970, PhD, 1975. Ass.t prof. biology Syracuse (N.Y.) U., 1977-80; ass.t prof. biology Utica (N.Y.) Coll., Syracuse U., 1979-81, assoc. prof., 1981-86, prof. biology, 1986—; coord./chair biology dept. Utica Coll., 1983-84, 90; sci. cons. Survival Anglia, London, 1989—. Author: Common Loon: Spirit of Northern Lakes, 1988; contbr. articles to profl. jours.; author/producer (slide/tape program) Hello, I'm a Loon!, 1985. Bd. dirs. budget panel United Way, Utica, 1982-86; pres. Kirkland Bird Club, Clinton, N.Y., 1987-89; trustee The Nature Conservancy, CNY chpt., 1983—; 1st v.p. North Am. Loon Fund, Meredith, N.H., 1988—; bd. dirs. Oikos Rsch. Found., Utica, 1976—, Wilson Ornithological Soc. (bd. dirs. Ann Arbor 1989—). Rsch. grantee NSF, 1968-71, 81-82, Nat. Geog., 1980, 89, Mercer Industries, 1986-90, Exxon, 1989-90, North Am. Loon Fund, 1981, 83, 87, 88. Mem. Am. Ornithologists' Union, Cooper Ornithol. Soc., Assn. Field Ornithologists, AAAS, Animal Behavior Soc., Minn. Ornithologists' Union, Fedn. N.Y. State Bird Clubs, Sigma Xi. Office: Utica Coll Syracuse U Burrstone Rd Utica NY 13502

MCINTYRE, KAYE, non-profit organization executive, consultant; b. Hartford, Conn., Oct. 13, 1950; d. Richard Arthur and Helen Marie (von Richter) Tillotson; m. Daniel Brian McIntyre, Feb. 21, 1969 (div. Dec. 1979). AS in Human Svcs., N.W. Conn. Community Coll., 1983; BSBA, Charter Oak Coll., 1985; MA in Liberal Studies, Wesleyan U., 1990. Counselor McCall House, Torrington, Conn., 1979-80; freelance photographer, 1980—; exec. dir. Warner Theatre, Torrington, 1982-84, Elderly Health Screening Svc., Inc., Waterbury, Conn., 1982—; cons. in field. Asst. coord. Conn. Earth Action Group, Litchfield, 1971; regional coord. Conn. Citizens Action Group, Litchfield County, Conn., 1971-72; pres. N.W. Conn. Assn. for the Arts, Inc., Torrington, 1981-84; bd. dirs. Torrington Trust for Hist. Preservation, Inc., 1981-85; 6th dist. coord. Office of Protection and Advocacy for the Handicapped and Developmentally Disabled, Litchfield County, 1982; chairperson adult programming com. YWCA of Waterbury, 1985-87; v.p. Thomaston Opera House Found., 1985-88. Recipient citation Conn. Soc. Prevention of Blindness, 1984, citation Conn. Gen. Assembly, 1984, 86, Project Health award U.S. Dept. HHS Adminstrn. Aging, 1986, Secs. Excellence award U.S. Dept. HHS Community Health Promotion Program, 1986. Mem. NAFE, AAAS, Am. League Hist. Theatres, N.Y. Acad. Scis., Community Assocs. of Conn., Inc. (bd. dirs.), Am. Pub. Health Assn., Nat. Assn. Fundraising Execs., Am. Soc. on Aging, Gerontological Soc. Am., Nat. Coun. on Aging, N.Y. Acad. Scis., Conn. Assn. Hist. Theatres (pres. 1984—), Internat. Platform Assn., Nat. Trust for Hist. Preservation, Mensa (Litchfield County coord. 1979-84). Republican. Taoist. Office: Elderly Health Screening Svc Inc 24 Central Ave Waterbury CT 06702

MCINTYRE, LORETTA MILLER, sporting goods manufacturing company executive; b. Lancaster, Pa., Nov. 18, 1944; d. Benedict and Edna (Smoker) Miller; m. Earl E. Louer, Jan. 13,1967 (div. Mar. 1971); m. Ray G. McIntyre, Sept. 15, 1977. Student pub. schs., Umatilla, Fla. Cert. tchr.; cert. dental asst. Sec. W.T. Grant Co., Mt. Dora, Fla., 1962-64; cashier Winn Dixie, Winter Park and Eustis, Fla., 1964-65; dental asst. Dr. Ray G. McIntyre, Eustis, 1966-76, Dr. Leonard Kaplan, Eustis, 1977-79; v.p., sec. Warren and Sweat Mfg. Co., Eustis, 1983—; dental assistance instr. Lake County Vocational Sch., 1970-79. Republican. Baptist. Home: PO Box 440 Grand Island FL 32735 Office: Warren and Sweat Mfg Co 38051 State Rd 19 Umatilla FL 32784

MCINTYRE, VALENE SMITH, educator; b. Spokane, Wash., Feb. 14, 1926; d. Ernst Frank and Lucy (Blachly) S.; m. Edwin Chesteen Golay, June 7, 1970 (dec. June 1980; m. Stanley George McIntyre, Nov. 26, 1983. BA in Geography, U. Calif., 1946, MA in Geography, 1950; PhD in Anthropology, U. Utah, 1966. Prof. earth sci. Los Angeles City Coll., 1947-67; prof. anthropology Calif. State U., Chico, 1967—; cons. Internat. Bank World Devel., DIAND Gov. of Canada, Ottawa, 1969, World Tourism Orgn., Madrid, 1987. Editor: Hosts & Guests: The Anthrop, 1989; producer (film). Bd. dirs. N.T. Enloe Meml. Hosp., Chico, Chico Soroptimist Club. Mem. Internat. Acad. for the Study Tourism, Anthrop. Soc. Wash., Cert. Travel Counselors, Am. Anthrop. Assn., L.A. Geog. Soc., AAUW, Butte Creek Country Club. Republican. Office: U Calif Dept Anthropology Chico CA 95929

MCINTYRE-IVY, JOAN CAROL, data processing executive; b. Portchester, N.Y., Mar. 1, 1939; d. John Henry and Molly Elizabeth (Gates) Daugherty; m. Stanley Donald McIntyre, Aug. 24, 1957 (div. Jan. 1986); children: Michael Stanley, David John, Sharon Lynne; m. James Morrow Ivy IV, June 1, 1988. Student, Northwestern U., 1956-57, U. Ill., 1957-58. Assoc. editor Writer's Digest, Cin., 1966-68; instr. creative writing U. Ala.-Huntsville, 1975; editor Strode Pubs., Huntsville, 1974-75; paralegal Smith, Huckaby & Graves (now Bradley, Arant, Rose & White), Huntsville, 1976-82; exec. v.p. Micro Craft, Inc., Huntsville, 1982-85, pres., 1985-89, chief exec. officer, chmn. bd., 1989—, also dir. and co-owner. Author numerous computer-operating mans. for law office software, 1978-88; co-author: Alabama and Federal Complaint Forms, 1979; Alabama and Federal Motion and Order Forms, 1980; also numerous articles, short stories, poems, 1955-88. Editor: Alabama Law for the Layman, 1975. Bd. dirs. Huntsville Lit. Soc., 1976-77. Hon. scholar Medill Sch. Journalism, Northwestern U., 1956. Republican. Methodist. Office: Micro Craft Inc 688 Discovery Dr Huntsville AL 35806

MCKAIN, MARY MARGARET, musician; b. Spokane, Wash., June 11, 1940; d. Neil Dunn and Elinore (Bien) McK. BA in Music and Police Sci., Calif. State U., L.A., 1968; studied trumpet with Rafael Mendez, Jane Sager, Sidney Lazar, and others. Trumpet player Peter Meremblum Jr. Symphony, 1954-59, Jack Benny at Greek Theater, 1963, Highland Park Symphony, L.A., 1955-66, Beverly Hills (Calif.) Symphony, 1960-66, South East Symphony, Downey, Calif., 1957-70, Santa Monica (Calif.) Elks Club, 1965-70, The Foresters, 1965-69, Latin Am. Symphony, L.A., 1961-63, L.A. Concert Band, Mexican Tipica Orch. Symphony, West Covina (Calif.) Symphony, 1976-79, Monterey Park (Calif.) Band, 1970-81, Calif. Concert Band, 1978-81, L.A. Police Dept. Concert Band, 1956-65, San Fernando Valley (Calif.) Opera, 1955-61, Iturbi on Tour, 1961; leader, trumpet player Pieces of 8 Polka Band, L.A., 1961—; 1st female dep. marshal, L.A., 1973; part time musician TV series Here Come The Brides, 1972, Commls., Inc. 1st Chevette, Barbary Coast (William Shatner); also recordings, 1980—. Trumpet player with Peter Meremblum Jr. Symphony, Jack Benny at Greek Theater, Highland Park Symphony, L.A., 1955-66, Beverly Hills (Calif.) Symphony, South East Symphony, Downey (Calif.) Symphony, Santa Monica (Calif.) Elks Club, The Foresters, Latin Am. Symphony, L.A., L.A. Concert Band, Mexican Tipica Orch., W. Covina (Calif.) Symphony, Calif. Concert Band, Monterey Park (Calif.) Band, L.A. Police Dept. Concert Band, San Fernando Valley (Calif.) Opera, 1955-61, Iturbi on tour, 1961; leader, trumpet player with Pieces of 8 Polka Band, L.A., 1961—. Mem. Musicians Local 47 (life), Sons and Daughters Mont. Pioneers (life), Wild Life Fedn., U.S. Humane Soc., Marshals Assn. (sec., dir.), Internat. Police Assn. Home: 43212 45th St W Quartz Hill CA 93536

MCKANDES, DOROTHY DELL, preschool director; b. Saginaw, Mich., July 5, 1937; d. William H. and Katherine (Halliday) Clark; m. Robert Henry McKandes, Jan. 8, 1928; children: Robert H. Jr., Darnell D. BA, Cen. Mich. U., 1975, MA, 1977. Co-owner Cosmopolitan Roller Rink, Saginaw, 1978-83; elem. tchr. Saginaw Pub. Schs., 1977-81, job shadow coord. student placement ctr., 1982; asst. dir. Mich. Child Care Ctr., Inc., Saginaw, 1986-89; dir. Kiddie's Kingdom Day Care, Pre-Sch. Ctr., Saginaw Township, Mich., 1990—. Mem. Mich. Adult Literacy Program, Saginaw, 1986—; bd. dirs. Bethel African Meth. Ch., Saginaw, 1987-89, Saginaw County Foster Care, 1988-89; mem. Saginaw Choral Soc., 1980. Fedn. Bus. and Profl. Women's Club scholar, 1977. Mem. Cen. Mich. U. Alumni Assn. (life), Altrusa Club, Links, Inc. (Disting. Svc. award 1990, co-founder), Alpha Kappa Alpha. Democrat. Methodist. Home: 1550 Seminole Ln Saginaw MI 48603

MCKAY, ALICE VITALICH, school system administrator; b. Seattle, Sept. 6, 1947; d. Jack S. and Phyllis (Bourne) Vitalich; m. Larry W. McKay, Aug. 14, 1973 (div. Jan. 1983). BA, Wash. State U., 1969; MEd, U. Nev., Las Vegas, 1975; EdD, U. Nev., Reno, 1986. High sch. tchr. Clark County Sch. Dist., Las Vegas, 1972-77, specialist women's sports, 1977-80, high sch. counselor, 1980-84, high sch. asst. prin., 1984—; pres. Lotus Profit, Inc., Las Vegas, 1985-86. Mem. Am. Assn. Counseling and Devel. (committee on women 1985—), Nev. State Counseling and Devel. (pres. 1985-86), Nat. Assn. Female Execs., AAUW, Phi Delta Kappa (exec. bd. 1980-82). Office: Clark County Sch Dist 2832 E Flamingo Rd Las Vegas NV 89121

MCKAY, CONSTANCE GADOW, retired hotel executive; b. Aurora, Ill., Mar. 7, 1928; d. William H. and Esther E. (Olson) Gadow. Student U. Ill., U. Wis.-Madison, U. Wis.-Milw.; widow; children: Richard A., Scott A., Mark G. Dir. catering Arlington Park (Ill.) Race Track, 1966-68, Arlington Park Hilton Hotel, Arlington Heights, Ill., 1969-85, O'Hare Kennedy Holiday Inn, 1985-89, ret. Commr., Arlington Heights Bd. Local Improvements, 1979—, Arlington Heights Relocation of Post Office Com., 1958-59, Arlington Heights Zoning Bd., 1959-60; commr. Youth Commn., 1981—. Named Outstanding Bus. Woman, Paddock Publs., Arlington Heights, 1977. Mem. Catering Execs. Club Am. Republican. Home: 1030 S Gunlock Lake Ln Minocqua WI 54548

MC KAY, EMILY GANTZ, civil rights professional; b. Columbus, Ohio, Mar. 13, 1945; d. Harry S. and Edwina (Bookwalter) Gantz; BA, Stanford U., 1966, MA, 1967; m. Jack Alexander McKay, July 3, 1965. Pub. info. specialist Community Action Pitts., 1967-68, exec. asst. to manpower dir., 1968-69, research assoc., 1969-70; free-lance cons., 1969-70; pub. relations and materials specialist Metropolitan Cleve. JOBS Council, 1971-72; research and mgmt. cons. BLK Group, Inc., Washington, 1970-73; dir. tech. products Am. Tech. Assistance Corp., McLean, Va., 1973-74; research and mgmt. cons. CONSAD Research Corp., Pitts., 1974-76, v.p., 1976-78; spl. asst. to Pres. for planning and eval. Nat. Coun. La Raza, Washington, 1978-82, v.p. research, advocacy and legislation, 1981-88, exec. v.p., 1983-88, cons. to the pres., 1988—; mem. adv. merit selection panel Superior Ct. D.C., 1987—; cons. resource devel. to SHATIL, Jerusalem, New Israel Fund, 1989—; cons. City of Cleve., Nat. Assn. Community Devel., Nat. Coun. La Raza, 1975-78, Ford Found., 1989, Nat. AIDS Networks, 1988-89; vol. cons. community based groups in Israel, 1987-89; guest faculty Union Grad. Sch. Author numerous tng. and Hispanic focused policy analysis materials. Co-chmn. Citizens Adv. Com. to D.C. Bar, 1986-87; mem. Mayor's Commn. Coop. Econ. Devel., 1981-83; non-lawyer mem. bd. govs. D.C. Bar, 1982-85; exec. com., bd. dirs. Indochina Resource Action Ctr.; co-chmn. Citizens Commn. Adminstrn. Justice, 1982-84; mem. exec. com. Coalition on Human Needs, 1981-88; mem. Washington area steering com. New Israel Fund, 1989—; co-chmn. adv. com. to Washington dist. office dir. Immigration and Naturalization Svc., 1984-88; chair Refugee Women in Devel.; mem. NAACP. Ford Found. nat. honors fellow, 1966-67; recipient I. Pat Rios award Guadalupe Ctr., 1988. Mem. Women in Communications, Phi Beta Kappa. Democrat. Home: 3200 19th St NW Washington DC 20010 Office: 810 1st St NE Ste 300 Washington DC 20002

MCKAY, KATHLEEN ANN, benefits specialist; b. Rochester, N.Y.; d. George L. and Grace E. (Monahan) McK.; m. Anthony E. Howard. AA, SUNY, Morrisville, 1968; BS, Boston State Coll., 1975; JD, Western State U., San Diego, 1979. Bar: Calif. 1980, Fed. 1980. With Community Hosp. of Chula Vista, Calif., 1978-83; v.p. human resources Santa Barbara (Calif.) Cottage Hosp., 1983-87; dir. benefit program NEA Mem. Benefits Corp., Rockville, Md., 1987—. Mem. Calif. Bar Assn., Internat. Found. Employee Benefit Plans. Office: Mem Benefits Corp NEA 51 Monroe St 200 Rockville MD 20850

MCKAY, LAURA L., banker; b. Watonga, Okla., Mar. 3, 1947; d. Frank Bradford and Elizabeth Jane (Smith) Drew; m. Cecil O. McKay, Sept. 20, 1969; 1 child, Leslie. BSBA, Oreg. State U., 1969. New br. research U.S. Bank, Portland, Oreg., 1969-80; cash mgmt. officer U.S. Bank, Portland, 1980-82, asst. v.p., 1982-87, v.p., 1987—. Vice chmn. Budget Com., North Clackamas Sch. Dist., 1982-. Mem. Nat. Corp. Cash Mgrs. Assn., Nat. Assn. Bank Women (chmn. Oreg. group 1979-80), Portland Cash Mgrs. Assn., Portland C. of C. Republican. Office: US Bank of Oreg PO Box 4412 Portland OR 97208

MCKAY, RENEE, artist; b. Montreal, Que., Can.; came to U.S., 1946, naturalized, 1954; d. Frederick Garvin and Mildred Gladys (Higgins) Smith; m. Kenneth Gardiner McKay, July 25, 1942; children: Margaret Craig, Kenneth Gardiner. BA, McGill U., 1941. Tchr. art Peck Sch., Morristown, N.J., 1955-56; one woman shows: Pen and Brush Club, N.Y.C., 1957, Cosmopolitan Club, N.Y.C., 1958; group shows include: Weyhe Gallery, N.Y.C., 1978, Newark Mus., 1955, 59, Montclair (N.J.) Mus., 1955-58, Nat. Assn. Women Artists, Nat. Acad. Galleries, 1954-78, N.Y. World's Fair, 1964-65, Audubon Artists, N.Y.C., 1955-62, 74-79, N.Y. Soc. Women Artists, 1979-80, Provincetown (Mass.) Art Assn. and Mus., 1975-79; traveling shows in France, Belgium, Italy, Scotland, Can., Japan; represented in permanent collections: Slater Meml. Mus., Norwich, Conn., Norfolk (Va.) Mus., Butler Inst. Am. Art, Youngstown, Ohio, Lydia Drake Library, Pembroke, Mass., many pvt. collections. Recipient Jane Peterson prize in oils Nat. Assn. Women Artists, 1954, Famous Artists Sch. prize in watercolor, 1959, Grumbacher Artists Watercolor award, 1970; Solo award Pen and Brush, 1957; Sadie-Max Tesser award in watercolor Audubon Artists, 1975, Peterson prize in oils, 1980; Michael Engel prize Nat. Soc. Painters in Casein and Acrylic, 1983. Mem. Nat. Assn. Women Artists (2d v.p. 1969-70, adv. bd. 1974-76), Audubon Artists (pres. 1979, dir. oils 1986-88), Artist Equity (dir. 1977-79, v.p. 1979-81), N.Y. Soc. Women Artists, Pen and Brush, Nat. Soc. Painters in Casein and Acrylic M.J. Kaplan prize 1984, Nat. Arts Club, Provincetown Art Assn. and Mus. Club: Cosmopolitan. Address: 200 E 66 St New York NY 10021

MCKEAGUE, NANCY PALMER, trade association executive; b. Detroit, Apr. 12, 1955; d. Spencer Jay and Barbara Jeanne (Murray) Palmer; m. Ronald Martin Nowak, Oct. 23, 1971 (div. 1978); children: Michael M., Melissa J.; m. David William McKeague, May 20, 1989; stepchildren: Sarah E., Laura K., Elizabeth A., Adam D. AA, Oakland Community Coll., Bloomfield Hills, Mich., 1979; BA, Spring Arbor (Mich.) Coll., 1986. Reporter The Times Newspapers, Pontiac, Mich., 1979-81; legis. aide Ho. of Reps., Lansing, Mich., 1981-84, Mich. State Senate, Lansing, 1984-85; adminstrv. aide Mich. State Senate, 1985-86; exec. v.p. Mich. Ins. Fedn., Lansing, 1986-88; pres. Mich. Ins. Fedn., 1988—; lectr. in field. Contbr. articles to profl. jours. Bd. dirs. Hwy. Safety Leaders; commr. Meridian Twp. Parks Commn., Okemos, Mich., 1984-90; state com. mem. Mich. Rep. State com., Lansing, 1987-88; exec. com. Ingham County Rep. Party, 1984-90; devel. com. Lansing Symphony Orch., 1989, bd. dirs., 1990—. Recipient Community Contbn. award, Ingham County Bd. Commrs., 1987. Mem. Mich. Soc. Assn. Execs., Coalition for Safety Belt Use (bd. dirs.). Republican. Lutheran. Home: 6364 Timber View East Lansing MI 48823 Office: Mich Ins Fedn 313 S Washington Sq Lansing MI 48933

MCKEE, BARBARA JEFFCOTT, accountant, speaker/workshop facilitator; b. Madison, Wis., Jan. 21, 1948; d. William Francis and Florence Ann (Jeffcott) McK.; m. Richard Arthur Rocha, Oct. 1, 1988. BBA, U. Wis., 1968; M in Mgmt., Northwestern U., 1982. CPA, Ill.; cert. internal auditor. Auditor Peat, Marwick, Mitchell & Co., Chgo., 1968-78; cons. Esmark, Inc., Chgo., 1978-79; audit mgr. Deloitte Haskins & Sells, Chgo., 1979-84, controller, 1984-85; v.p. Safeway Stores, Inc., Oakland, Calif., 1985-90; co-founder Success Achievers Limitless, Oakland, Calif., 1990—. Mem. AICPA, Am. Women's Soc. of CPA's, Inst. Internal Auditors. Office: Success Achievers Limitless 5255 Pinecrest Ct Oakland CA 94605

MCKEE, BARBARA JOAN, university extension agent; b. KiHanning, Pa., Mar. 9, 1942; d. Reed Clifton and Alice Marie (Cogley) Hoffman; m. William Leroy McKee, Apr. 4, 1964; children: W. Shawn, David R. BS, Pa. State U., 1964. Home economist Pa. State U. Coop. Extension, Butler, 1964-67, nutrition supr., 1975-80; extension agt. Pa. State U. Coop. Extension, KiHanning, 1980—; substitute tchr. Butler Area Sch., 1967-72; nutritionist cons. Butler, 1967-72. Elder Summit United Presbyn. Ch., Butler, 1987-88. Recipient Disting. Svc. award Nat. Assn. Extension Home Economist, Hawaii, 1989. Mem. Pa. Assn. Extension Home Economist (1st v.p. 1986-88, treas. 1988-90), AAUW, Electric Women's Round Table. Republican. Home: 409 Portman Rd Butler PA 16001 Office: Pa State U Coop Extension Rd 8 Armsdale Admn Bldg KiHanning PA 16201

MCKEE, EDITH MERRITT, geologist; b. Oak Park, Ill., Oct. 9, 1918; d. Eustis Ewart and Edith (Frame) McK.; B.S., Northwestern U., 1946. Geologist, U.S. Geol. Survey, 1943-45, Shell Oil Co., 1947-49, Arabian Am. Oil Co., 1949-54, Underground Gas Storage Co. Ill., 1956-58; ind. cons. geologist, Winnetka, Ill., 1958—; mem. environ. adv. com. Fed. Energy Adminstrn., 1974; mem. Nat. Adv. Com. Oceans and Atmosphere, 1975; speaker, cons. in field. Commr., Winnetka Park Bd., 1976-79. Fellow Marine Tech. Soc., Geol. Soc. Am.; mem. Am. Geol. Inst., Am. Inst. Profl. Geologists (cert., charter), Assn. Engring. Geologists, Ill. Geol. Soc., Am. Oceanic Orgn. Research on shore erosion, mapping of Gt. Lakes basins and deep ocean basins, global econ. devel. programs and mineral exploration, oil spill containment. Address: PO Box 3 Good Hart MI 49737

MCKEE, KAREN LYNETTE, real estate consultant; b. Scottsville, Ky., Nov. 20, 1956; d. James Monroe and Ruby Inez (Cates) Butt; m. John Belote McKee, July 16, 1954; 1 child, Jason Randolph. BS in Edn., Vanderbilt U., 1979. Instr. Sumner County Bd. Edn., Gallatin, Tenn., 1979-81; office mgr. Payne Angus Farms, Castalian Springs, Tenn., 1981-85; real estate cons. McKeeco, Inc., Nashville, 1985—; mem. Tenn. Indsl. Devel. Bd., Nashville, 1989—, So. Indsl. Devel. Bd., Nashville, 1989—. Mem. Gallatin C. of C. (Civic Vol. award 1989). Republican. Baptist. Office: MdKee Co Inc 1819 Broadway Nashville TN 37203

MCKEE, MARGARET JEAN, federal agency executive; b. New Haven, June 20, 1929; d. Waldo McCutcheon and Elizabeth (Thayer) McKee; A.B., Vassar Coll., 1951. Staff asst. United Rep. Fin. Com., N.Y.C., 1952; staff asst. N.Y. Rep. State Com., N.Y.C., 1953-55; staff asst. Crusade for Freedom (name later changed to Radio Free Europe Fund), N.Y.C., 1955-57; researcher Stricker & Henning Research Assocs., Inc., N.Y.C., 1957-59; exec. sec. New Yorkers for Nixon (name later changed to N.Y. State Ind. Citizens for Nixon Lodge), N.Y.C., 1959-60; asst. to Raymond Moley, polit. columnist, N.Y.C., 1961; asst. campaign com. Louis J. Lefkowitz for Mayor, N.Y.C., 1961; research programmer, treas. Consensus, Inc., N.Y.C., 1962-67; spl. asst. to U.S. Senator Jacob K. Javits, N.Y., 1967-73, adminstrv. asst., 1973-75; dep. adminstr. Am. Revolution Bicentennial Adminstrn., 1976, acting adminstr., 1976-77; chief of staff Perry B. Duryea (minority leader) N.Y. State Assembly, 1978; public affairs cons., 1979-80; dir. govt. relations Gen. Mills Restaurant Group, Inc., 1980-83; exec. dir. Fed. Mediation and Conciliation Service, 1983-86; mem. Fed. Labor Rels. Authority, 1986-89, chmn., 1989—; dir. Interam. Life Ins. Co., 1979-86. Mem. N.Y. State Bingo Control Commn., 1965-72 . U.S. Adv. Commn. on Public Diplomacy, 1979-82; pres. Bklyn. Heights Slope Young Rep. Club, 1955-56; co-chmn. Bklyn. Citizens for Eisenhower-Nixon, 1956; chmn. 2d Jud. Dist. Assn. N.Y. State Young Rep. Clubs, Inc., 1957-58, vice-chmn., mem. bd. govs., 1958-60, v.p., 1960-62; pres., 1962-64; mem. exec. com. Fedn. Women's Rep. Clubs N.Y. State, Inc., 1960-64, mem. council, 1964-70; mem. exec. com. N.Y. Rep. State Com. 1962-64; co-chmn. spl. assts. Rockefeller for Pres. Nat. Campaign com., N.Y.C., 1964; co-dir. N.Y. Rep. State Campaign Com., 1964; asst. campaign mgr. Kenneth B. Keating for Judge Ct. Appeals, N.Y., 1965; dir. scheduling Gov. Rockefeller campaign, 1966, Sen. Charles E. Goodell campaign, 1970; dir. scheduling and speakers' bur. N.Y. Com. to Re-elect the Pres., 1972; dir. planning, strategy and women's programs ct. Reagan-Bush campaign. Mem. bd. govs. Women's Nat. Rep. Club, N.Y.C., 1963-66. Mem. Jr. League of Bklyn. (past (dir.), Exec. Women in Govt. (chmn. 1986), Nat. Women's Edn. Fund (mem. bd.), Am. Newspaper Women's Club, Nat. Soc. Colonial Dames Am. Episcopalian. Club: Vassar (past dir.) (Bklyn.). Home: 3001 Veazey Terr NW Washington DC 20008

MCKEE, MARY ELIZABETH, producer; b. Syracuse, N.Y., Feb. 14, 1949; d. Anthony Henry and Mary (Robards) Krystosik; m. Peter S. Fama, June 27, 1970 (div. Mar. 1973); 1 child, Kiralie Fama; m. Michael R. McKee, Feb. 15, 1975 (Oct. 1978); 1 child, Quinn. BFA, Fla. Internat. U., Miami, 1974; MFA, Memphis State U., 1977. Copywriter announcer WREC/WZXR Radio, Memphis, 1978-79; creative dir. Cit Neifert & Assoc. Advt., Memphis, 1979-82; promotion dir. WGNX TV, Atlanta, 1982-86; program mgr. WVEU TV, Atlanta, 1986-90; v.p., sta. mgr. WHSP TV, Vineland, N.J., 1990—. Actor in field (Top 10 Memphis Mag. 1979). Vol. Com. to Feed the Hungry, Atlanta, 1988, Tenn. Talking Libr., Memphis, 1982; mem. Greenpeace, 1987—. Recipient Merit award Tenn. Talking Libr., 1982; named Best TV Comml. Memphis Advt. Club, 1982; Hair scholar Fla. Internat. U., 1973. Mem. AFTRA, NATAS, Am. Women Radio & TV (publicity chmn 1985-86), Nat.Assn. TV Program Execs., Platform Soc. Democrat. Roman Catholic. Home: 123 Farragut Ave Mays Landing NJ 08344 Office: WHSP-TV 4449 Delsea Dr Vineland NJ 08344

MCKEE, PATRICIA LYNN, accountant; b. Trenton, Mich., Nov. 18, 1964; d. Dianne Frances Hubble; m. Ronald McKee, May 9, 1987. BS in Acctg., Mercy Coll. Detroit, 1987. Sr. acct. R.J. Miller, PC, Highland, Mich. Roman Catholic. Home: 2760 S Hickory Ridge Rd #83 Milford MI 48380

MCKEE-HAMMAD, MARY ELLEN, educator, nurse; b. Cleve., May 27, 1950; d. William Fredric and Rita Jane (Otters) McKee; m. Wa'el David Hammad, Dec. 30, 1977; children: Ramsey David, Mark David. BS in Nursing, Case Western Res. U., 1973; grad. pediatric nurse, Cleve. Met. Gen. Hosp., 1975; MA, Emory U., 1984. Clin. nurse U. Hosps. Lakeside, Cleve., 1973-74; pediatric nurse practitioner Cleve. Met. Gen. Hosp., 1974-76, Babies and Children's Hosp., Cleve., 1976; inpatient supr. Scottish Rite Children's Hosp., Atlanta, 1976-77; cons. Clayton County Child Abuse and Neglect Program, Morrow, Ga., 1977-78; coord. child health Fulton County Health Dept., Atlanta, 1978-82, cons., 1982-85; clin. instr. Crawford Long Sch. Nursing, Atlanta, 1985-86; supply tchr. Fulton County Bd. Edn., Atlanta, 1987—; cons. Brenda P. Smith Nursing Scholarship Fund, Atlanta, 1982-88. Contbg. author tng. manuals. Com. chmn. James L. Riley Elem. Sch. PTA, 1986-87; co-pres. Heards Ferry Elem. Sch. PTA, 1987-88; founding mem. Ga. Bapt. Med. Guild, 1979-88; mem. Sandy Springs Elem. Zoning Com., 1987-88. Recipient Pres. award North Fulton Coun. PTA, 1988. Fellow Nat. Assn. Pediatric Nurses Assocs. and Practitioners; mem. Pediatric Nurse Assocs. Ohio (pres. 1975-76), Sigma Theta Tau. Home: 5590 Errol Pl NW Atlanta GA 30327

MCKEEN, LYNN MARIE, insurance company executive; b. Mars Hill, Maine, June 26, 1951; d. Theodore Frank and Lois Marie (Hubbard) Durost; m. James Elwood McKeen, Apr. 18, 1970 (div. Aug. 1980). Cert. profl. ins. woman. Legal sec. Stewart, Griffiths & Quigley, Presque Isle, Maine, 1969-71; sec., file clk. Maine Mut. Group, Presque Isle, 1971-75, policy typist, 1975-76, rating clk., 1976-77, asst. underwriter, 1977-82, staff underwriter, 1982-83, underwriting supr., 1983-85, underwriting mgr., 1986—; v.p. Maine Mut. Fire Ins. Co.; bd. dirs. Sinawik Corp. Mem. Maine Community Vol. Fire Prevention Program; mem. adv. bd. Aroostook County Action Program. Mem. Nat. Assn. Ins. Women (pres. Aroostook 1981-82, 87-88, state dir. 1983-85, Ins. Woman of Yr. 1982, state Speak-off winner 1983, regional

Speak-off winner 1984), Kiwanis. Home: 22d Strawberry Bank Presque Isle ME 04769 Office: 44 Maysville St 44 Maysville St Presque Isle ME 04769

MCKELVEY, B(ELVA) KATHLEEN, secretary, volunteer; b. Independence, Mo., July 14, 1958; d. Walter Emerson and Belva Angeline (Hughes) Baldwin; m. James Boyd McKelvey, Apr. 4, 1987. BS in Mktg., Office Adminstrn., Northwest Mo. State U., 1980. Teller, bookkeeper Sugar Creek (Mo.) Nat. Bank, 1975-80; sec. World Health Orgn. (UN), Geneva, Switzerland, 1980-84, Hallmark Cards, Inc., Kansas City, Mo., 1984—. Bell ringer Salvation Army, Independence, Mo., 1988-90; vol. Hope House, Independence, 1989—, Recycling Ctr., Independence, 1989—; mem. Ch. Women's Ministries. Mem. AAUW, Bus & Profl. Women, Profl. Secs. Internat. Republican. Reorganized Ch. of Jesus Christ of Latter Day Saints. Home: 15500 E 37th Terr Independence MO 64055 Office: Hallmark Cards Inc 2501 McGee Kansas City MO 64141

MCKENNA, FAY ANN, electrical manufacturing company executive; b. Bennington, Vt., Jan. 7, 1944; d. George Francis and Barbara Mae (Youngangel) Hoag; m. James Dennis McKenna, Sept. 3, 1963 (div. 1983); children: Russell (dec.), Laura, James, Sean, Michael. Student, Mercy Coll. Key punch operator N.Y. State Taxation and Fin. Dept., Albany, 1960-61; receptionist Trine Mfg./Square D Co., Bronx, 1972-76; clk. Square D Co., Bronx, 1976-78, exec. sec., 1978-79, personnel mgr., 1979-86; mgr. mktg. adminstrn. Trine Products Corp., 1986-89, adminstrv. mgr., 1989—. Mfg. Fund raiser YMCA, Bronx, 1979—; mem. Community Bd. #9, Bronx, 1984—. Recipient Svc. to Youth award YMCA, 1985. Mem. Adminstrv. Mgmt. Soc. Republican. Roman Catholic. Avocations: physical fitness, reading, interior decorating. Home: 4100-20 Hutchinson River Pkwy E Bronx NY 10475 Office: Trine Products Corp 1430 Ferris Pl Bronx NY 10461

MCKENNA, GWENDELINE M. (GWEN MCKENNA), retired elementary educator; b. Detroit, Apr. 28, 1920; d. Frederick and Mary Katrina (Carpenter) Cooper; m. Thomas James McKenna, Sept. 29, 1921; children: Erin Patrice Anding, Wendy Kathleen. BA, Wayne State U., Detroit, 1961; MA, U. Mich., 1969. Cert. tchr., Mich., 1966. Elem. tchr. Bloomfield Hills (Mich.) Sch. Dist., 1962-86; ret., 1986; dir. fgn. lang. program Hickory Grove Schs., Bloomfield Hills Schs., 1985-86. Presenter alcohol and drug abuse programs to local orgns. Mem. AAUW (chmn. internat. rels. 1989—), U. Mich. Alumni, Delta Kappa Gamma (pres. Birmingham chpt. 1974-76).

MCKENNA, JUDI ANN, comptroller; b. Elmhurst, Ill., Mar. 31, 1958; d. Robert L. and Shirley L. (Warnell) McK. BA, Ill. Benedictine Coll., 1978. Auditor Ill. Dept. Revenue, Chgo., 1980-81; acct. Clyde Fed. Savs., N. Riverside, Ill., 1983-85, Lippig Acctg., Lombard, Ill., 1985-86, Slupik & Assocs., Naperville, Ill., 1987-89; comptroller McKenna Tile Co. Inc., Naperville, 1989—; owner Judi McKenna Acctg., Naperville, 1979—. Cons. Ill. Benedictine Coll. Alumni Assn., Lisle, 1979—. Mem. Ill. Benedictine Coll. Alumni Assn. Republican. Roman Catholic. Office: McKenna Tile Co Inc 238 S Washington Naperville IL 60540

MCKENNA, MARGARET ANNE, college president; b. R.I., June 3, 1945; d. Joseph John and Mary (Burns) McK.; children: Michael Aaron McKenna Miller, David Christopher McKenna Miller. BA in Sociology, Emmanuel Coll., 1967; postgrad., Boston Coll. Law Sch., 1968; JD, So. Meth. U., 1971; LLD (hon.), U. Upsala, N.J., 1978, Fitchburg (Mass.) State Coll., 1979, Regis Coll., 1982; D Community Affairs, U. R.I., 1979. Bar: Tex. 1971, D.C. 1973. Atty. Dept. Justice, Washington, 1971-73; exec. dir. Internat. Assn. Ofcl. Human Rights Agys., Washington, 1973-74; mgmt. cons. Dept. Treasury, Washington, 1975-76; dep. council to Pres. White House, Washington, 1976-79; dep. undersec. Dept. Edn., Washington, 1979-81; dir. Mary Ingraham Bunting Inst., Radcliffe Coll., Cambridge, Mass., 1981-85; v.p. program planning Radcliffe Coll., Cambridge, 1982-85; pres. Lesley Coll., Cambridge, 1985—; bd. dirs. Bay Bank/Harvard Trust, Cambridge, Edn. Loan Services Inc., Braintree, Mass., Stride Rite Corp., Cambridge, Edn. Resources Inst., Boston. Bd. dirs. Mass. Higher Edn. Assistance Corp., Boston, People for Am. Way, Washington. Recipient Outstanding Contribution award Civil Rights Leadership Conf., 1978; named Woman of Yr. Women's Equity Action League, 1979, Outstanding Woman of Yr. Big Sister Assn., 1986. Democrat. Office: Lesley Coll 29 Everett St Cambridge MA 02138-2790

MCKENNA, MARY PATRICIA, educational and human resources management consultant, performance technologist; b. N.Y.C.; d. Frank and Delia (Hannon) McK. BA in Edn., Seat of Wisdom Coll., 1967; MA in Sociology, Fordham U., 1971, MS in Guidance and Counseling, 1974, PhD in Counseling and Per. Svcs., 1979. Cert. in edn. and counseling, N.Y. Grad. asst. Fordham U., N.Y.C., 1973-75; with psychol. and career counseling dept. St. Francis Coll., Bklyn.; acad. dean The Berkeley Schs., N.Y.C.; adminstr. tng. & human resource devel. Coopers and Lybrand, N.Y.C.; internal ednl. cons. Nat. Continuing Edn. div. Price Waterhouse, N.Y.C.; grad. asst. Fordham U. Author: Mid-Life Career Choices. Mem. NAFE, APA, Nat. Soc. for Performance and Instrn., Am. Soc. for Tng. and Devel., Phi Delta Kappa.

MCKENNA, SHIRLEY LEE, tile company executive; b. Chgo., Apr. 4, 1935; d. Joseph M. and Estelle N. (Blasch) Warnell; m. Robert McKenna, June 18, 1955; children: Susan, Judi, Michael. Student, U. Chgo., 1954, Art Inst. Chgo., 1955. Sec. Lisle (Ill.) High Sch., 1967-69; mgr. I.B.C. Bookstore, Lisle, 1970-78; v.p., designer McKenna Tile, Naperville, Ill., 1978—; cons. CTDI, Chgo., 1985—. Mem. NFIB, Springfield, Ill., 1987. Mem. Nat. Fedn. Ind. Bus., U.S. C. of C., Naperville Area C. of C. Roman Catholic.

MCKENNY, COLLIN GRAD, banker; b. Seattle, July 29, 1944; d. Edward Paul and Betty B. (Collins) Grad; m. Jon W. McKenny, June 15, 1975 (div. June 1982); m. Spencer Frank Ison, Dec. 31, 1985. BA, U. Wash., Seattle, 1966; MBA, Seattle U., 1969; grad., Pacific Coast Banking Sch., 1979. From mgmt. trainee to v.p. People's Nat. Bank, Seattle, 1966-85; sr. v.p. Barclays Bank of Calif., San Francisco, 1985-88, Star Banc Corp., Cin., 1988—. Treas. Salvation Army, Federal Way, Wash., 1981-83; bd. dirs. Boys & Girls Clubs, Seattle, 1982-85. Mem. Am. Bankers Assn. (bd. dirs. bancard exec. com., chmn. ann. conf. 1989—), Bankers Club, Chi Omega. Office: Star Banc Corp 425 Walnut Cincinnati OH 45202

MCKENRY, ROBYN PARADICE, state agency administrator; b. Norfolk, Va., Mar. 5, 1954; d. James Lloyd and Charlotte Jayne (Valentine) Webster; m. Walter F. Merritt, (div. Mar. 1980); m. Robert B. McKenry, Jr. AA, Seminole Community Coll., Sanford, Fla., 1973; BA in Humanities, U. West Fla., 1975, BA in Philosophy, 1975; MPA, U. Colo., 1986. Jr. fed. asst. Bur. Land Mgmt., Denver, 1977-79, computer programmer, analyst, 1979-81; computer specialist Martin Marietta Data Systems, Denver, 1981-83; sr. advanced system analyst Aramco Svcs. Corp., Houston, 1983-84; sr. software analyst Manville Svcs. Corp., Denver, 1984-85; computer technology and mktg. specialist, pvt. bus. Denver, 1985-87; adminstrv. asst. to exec. dir. E-470 Authority, Englewood, Colo., 1986-89, dir. adminstrv. svcs., 1989—. Mng. Editor (newsletter) B.L.M. Data Processing, 1980; contbg. editor (newsletter) Manville Office Automation, 1984. Vol. B.E.L.T. Com., Denver, 1988, Vote "Yes" Com., Adams County, Colo., 1988; coordinator Vols. for Outdoor Colo., Denver, 1989. Mem. Colo. Mcpl. Mgmt. Assts. Assn., Colo. Mcpl. Mgrs. (sec. 1987), Am. Soc. Pub. Adminstrs. Republican. Office: E-470 Authority 7951 E Maplewood Ave Ste 126 Englewood CO 80111

MCKENZIE, CATHERINE L., telecommunications company executive; b. Circleville, Ohio, June 25, 1941; d. Francis Joseph McKenzie and Virginia Barbara (Overley) Hall. Student, Barry U., 1987—. Mgr. corp. and community affairs So. Bell, Ft. Lauderdale, Fla., 1987—. Exec. bd. dirs. Plantation (Fla.) Gen. Hosp. Women's Adv. Bd., 1987—, Children's Cancer Caring Ctr., 1987—, Healthcare Edn. and Rsch. Found., 1987—. Mem. Broward Forum (vice chairperson 1989-90), Women's Exec. Club (pres.-elect 1990-91), Women in Communications, Inc. (bd. dirs. 1987—, co-chair 1989-91, Woman of Yr. 1989-91), Pub. Rels. Soc Am., Rotary (bd. dirs. 1987—), Greater Plantation C. of C. (exec. bd. 1987—). Office: Southern Bell 6451 N Federal Hwy Rm 1113 Fort Lauderdale FL 33308

MCKENZIE, ELIZABETH BOBO, education educator; b. Charlotte, N.C., July 30, 1928; d. George Brooks and Anna Elizabeth (Cowherd) Bobo; m. John Ward McKenzie, June 7, 1949; children: Ann M. Edwards, Emily E. BA in History, Furman U., 1948; BA in Music, Augusta Coll., 1981. Piano tchr. pvt. studio Augusta, Ga., 1960—; organist, choir master Greene St. Presbyn. Ch., Augusta, 1977—. Mem. Augusta Music Tchrs. Assn., Ga. Music Tchrs. Assn., Music Tchrs. Nat. Assn., Nat. Guild Piano Tchrs., Am. Guild of Organists. Baptist. Home: 331 Heath Dr Augusta GA 30909

MCKENZIE, SHERRIE LYNN WERNDLE, relicensing seminar coordinator; b. Lynwood, Calif., Oct. 19, 1966; d. Frank Wayne McKenzie and Sally Darlene (Mayes) Werndle. Student, Loma Linda U., 1985-87. Sec. Loma Linda U., Riverside, Calif., 1984-86; with prodn. control dept. Huntington Beach, Huntington Bch., Calif., 1988; seminar coord. Progressive Trainers, Anaheim, Calif., 1989; legal asst. Knobbe, Martens, Olson & Bear, Newport Beach, Calif., 1989—. Author: The Differences Cumpublished, 1982, Remembering Popper, 1986. Mem. Blythe Lions Club. Republican. SDA. Home: 5772 Garden Grove # 237 Westminster CA 92683

MCKENZIE, SUSAN HELEN, broadcast journalist; b. N.Y.C., Dec. 30, 1964; d. John Brewster and Ida (Hawa) Smith; m. Byron Kevin McKenzie, May 10, 1986. BA in English, Tex. A&M U., 1986; MA in Journalism, Ind. U., 1988. Broadcast journalist U.S. Army, Fort Bragg, N.C., 1988—; parachutist 1st Spl. Ops. Command, Fort Bragg, 1989—. With. U.S. Army, 1988—. Recipient South Korean Jump Wings Republic of Korea Spl. Warfare Ctr., 1989. Mem. Women in Communications, Inc., Soc. Profl. Journalists, Nat. Press Photographers Assn. Presbyterian. Home: 118 McCaskill Pl Fort Bragg NC 28307 Office: 4th Psychol Ops Group Strategic Dissemination Co Fort Bragg NC 28307

MCKENZIE-HEBERT, MARY ELIZABETH, chemical engineer; b. Port Hueneme, Calif., Apr. 1, 1955; d. Robert William and Nell (Cowart) McK.; m. Ralph Eugene Vincent, May 28, 1977 (div. Nov. 1985); children: William Joseph (dec.), Emily Rose; m. John W. Hebert, Jan. 3, 1987; 1 child, Rachel Leigh. BSChemE, La. State U., 1977. Design engr. PPG Industries, Inc., Lake Charles, La., 1977-79; environ. engr. Walk, Haydel & Assocs., Inc., New Orleans, 1984-87; environ. control engr. Ashland (Ky.) Petroleum Co., 1987-89; environ. engr. Sequa Corp., Hackensack, N.J., 1989—. Mem. NAFE, Soc. Women Engrs., Am. Inst. Chem. Engrs., Am. Electroplaters and Surface Finishers Soc., Nat. Soc. Profl. Engrs. Republican. Episcopalian. Office: Sequa Corp 3 University Pla Ste 300 Hackensack NJ 07601

MCKEON, DONNA FORILL, journalist; b. Cleve., Dec. 18, 1927; d. Paul John and Helen Ann (Winkel) Forill; m. John Vincent McKeon, Nov. 3, 1951; children: Mary Christine, Paul, Patrick. BA, St. Mary-of-the-Woods Coll., 1949; MA, Marquette U., 1951. Pub. rels. chmn. Easter Seal Soc., Madison, Wis., 1952-56, Christmas Seal Soc., Madison, 1952-56; editor Smilin'Thru, Madison, 1952-56; society asst. Madison Capital Times, Wis. State Jour., Madison, 1953-56; advt. clk. Western Auto Supply, Cleve., 1951; gen. assignment reporter West Life, Cleve., 1967-69; asst. society editor Cleve. Press, 1969-71; freelance writer Richmond (Va.) LifeStyle, 1979-82; contbg. editor Met. Woman, Richmond, 1982-86. Author: This Is Sister, 1968; contbr. articles to profl. jours., mags., newspapers. Trustee St. Mary-of-the-Woods Coll., 1971-73, mem. nat. alumnae bd., 1964-68; vol. writer Easter Seal Soc. Recipient editing and writing award Am. Newspaper Guild, 1948; service award Wis. Easter Seal Soc., 1955; hon. mention for non-fiction Pen Women Biennial award, 1982; 3d place for non-fiction Pen Women Mid-Adminstrn. Congress award, 1985. Mem. Nat. League Am. Pen Women (pres. Richmond chpt. 1982-84, state pres. Va. assn. 1985-88), Women in Communications (pres. 1953-55), Va. Press Women. Roman Catholic. Home: 1507 Regency Woods Rd Unit 304 Richmond VA 23233

MCKEOWN, ANNE WILLEMSSEN, engineering-architectural company official; b. Waterloo, Iowa, June 14, 1952; d. Raymond McKinlay and Betty Anne (McMillan) Willemssen; m. Kim I. McKeown, June 1, 1974. BA in Journalism, Iowa State U., 1974; postgrad., Creighton U., 1985-86. Cert. secondary English and journalism tchr., Iowa. Sports editor Denison (Iowa) Newspapers, Inc., 1974; circulation libr. U. Nebr. Med. Ctr., Omaha, 1975; instr. gen. and basic adult edn. Iowa Western Community Coll., Council Bluffs, 1976-79; tchr. bus. edn. Lewis Cen. Community Schs., Council Bluffs, 1979-81; mkig. coord. H. Gene McKeown & Assocs., Inc., Council Bluffs, 1981-89, benefits coord., 1989—. Actress, singer Renaissance Faire Midlands, 1987—. Bd. dirs., v.p., sec. River Cities coun. Camp Fire, 1984-88; bd. dirs., v.p., treas., sec. Bluffs Arts Coun., Council Bluffs, 1985-90; mem. steering com., speaker Local Option Tax, Council Bluffs, 1989; mem. Council Bluffs Parks, Recreation and Pub. Property Commn., 1989—; D.C. amb City of Council Bluffs, 1989, 90; supr. Sunday sch. 1st Congl. Ch., 1983-89; also numerous other civic orgns. Mem. Soc. for Mktg. Profl. Svcs., Iowa Engring. Soc. (Exceptional Svc. award 1984, mathcounts state chair 1991), Council Bluffs C. of C. (treas., bd. dirs. 1988—, D.C. amb. 1989, 90, chari-elect 1990—), Council Bluffs Svc. League (bd. dirs. 1978-85, v.p. 1984-85), AAUW (bd. dirs., v.p. 1977-78, sec. 1980), P.E.O. (v.p., sec., treas. 1978-88), Rotary. Home: 201 3d St Council Bluffs IA 51503 Office: H Gene McKeown & Assocs Inc 640 5th Ave PO Box 919 Council Bluffs IA 51502

MCKEOWN, M. MARGARET, lawyer; b. Casper, Wyo., May 11, 1951; d. Robert Mark and Evelyn Margaret (Lipsack) McK.; m. Peter Francis Cowhey, June 29, 1985; 1 child, Megan Margaret. BA in Internat. Affairs, U. Wyo., 1972; JD, Georgetown U., 1975. Bar: Wash. 1975, D.C. 1982. Assoc. Perkins Coie, Seattle, 1975-79, Washington, 1979-80; white house fellow U.S. Dept. Interior, Washington, 1980-81; ptnr., mem. exec. com. Perkins Coie, Seattle, 1981—; trustee The Pub. Defender, Seattle, 1982-85; rep. 9th Cir. Judicial Conf., San Francisco, 1985-89. Author: Girl Scout's Guide to New York, 1990; contbr. chpt. to book and articles to profl. jours. Nat. bd. dirs. Girl Scouts Am., N.Y.C., 1976-87; bd. dirs. Family Svcs., Seattle, 1982-84, Corp. coun. for the Arts, Seattle, 1988—; bd. gen. counsel Downtown Seattle Assn., 1986-89. Recipient Rising Stars of the 80's award Legal Times Washington, 1983, 100 Young Women of Promise, Good Housekeeping, 1985. Mem. ABA (ho. of dels. 1990—), Feg. Bar Assn. (trustee we. dist. 1980-90), Wash. bar Assn. (chmn. judicial recommendations 1989-90), Seattle-King County Bar ASsn. (trustee, sec. 1984-85), Am. Civil Liberties Union (chmn. legal com. 1982-85), Legal Found. Wash. (trustee, pres. 1989-90), Washington Women Lawyers (bd. dirs., pres. 1978-79), Nat. Assn. Iolta Programs (bd. dirs. 1989—), Fed. Ct. Pro Bono Civil Rights Panel. Home: 1522 40th Ave Seattle WA 98122 Office: Perkins Coie 1201 3rd Ave Seattle WA 98101

MCKEOWN, MARY ELIZABETH, educational administrator; d. Raymond Edmund and Alice (Fitzgerald) McNamara; BS, U. Chgo., 1946; MS, DePaul U., 1953; m. James Edward McKeown, Aug. 6, 1955. Supr. high sch. dept. Am. Sch., 1948-68, prin., 1968—, trustee, 1975—, v.p., 1979—. Mem. Nat. Assn. Secondary Sch. Prins., Cen. States Assn. Sci. and Math Tchrs. Nat. Coun. Tchrs. Math., Assn. for Supervision and Curriculum Devel., Adult Edn. Assn., LWV. Author study guides for algebra, geometry and calculus. Home: 1469 N Sheridan Rd Kenosha WI 53140 Office: 850 E 58th Chicago IL 60637

MCKIEL, ROBIN CAROL, art director; b. Wash., July 24, 1951; d. James Albert and Claudia Rowena (Smillie) M. BS, U. Maryland, 1980; postgrad, George Mason U. Prodn. mgr. Am. Home Econ. Assn., Wash., 1971-79; dir. promotions Pawnshop Restaurants Inc., Falls Church, Va., 1979-84; free-lance promotions RCM Graphics, Alexandria, Va., 1979-86; supr. graphic dept. ROH Inc., Arlington, Va., 1986—. Mem. coms. NOW, Alexandria, 1972-74, Nat. Women's Polit. Caucus, 1972-89, Amnesty Internat., 1988—. Mem. Washington Calligraphers Guild, Smithsonian Assocs. Democrat. Home: 19A W Chapman St Alexandria VA 22301

MCKILLIP, PATRICIA CLAIRE, operatic soloist; b. Milw., Apr. 28; d. Lester J. and Ruth J. (Lohneis) McK.; m. Mark R. Gardner, June 16, 1990. BA in English-Drama, Creative Writing, Lit., Alverno Coll., 1980; MusB in Applied Music, Alverno Coll., Milw., 1981; postgrad., Wis. Conservatory of Mus., 1981-82, U. Wis., Milw., 1982, The Juilliard Sch., 1982-84, Am. Acad. Dramatic Arts, 1983-84, Adelphi U., 1984. Soloist Amadeus Opera Co.; instr. vocal music seminars various high schs., N.Y. Performed with numerous opera cos. including The Florentine Opera Co., Music Under the Stars Prodns., Milw. Opera Co., Westchester Lyric Opera Co., Profl. Opera Workshop at Lincoln Ctr., Met. Opera Co., N.Y. Grand Opera Co., Monteverdi Opera Guild Prodns., Republic Opera Co., La Puma Opera Co., and other chamber, theater and folk groups; performed in over 50 mus. shows and prodns., 6 solo recitals, also medieval concerts, choruses, orchestras, oratorio; 42 other recitals. Music dept. scholar Alverno U. Mem. AFTRA, SAG, Nat. Assn. Music Tchrs., Music Educators Nat. Conf. (treas.), Wis. Fedn. Music Clubs, Music Clubs Am., Am. Guild Mus. Artists, Q'ahal-Liturgical Music Soc., Delta Omicron (v.p., chaplain, warden Gamma Gamma chpt., WMA State and Regional Vocal award 1978, Star of Delta Omicron award 1980, 40 music medals from state and dist. WSMA), Alpha Sigma Tau. Democrat. Roman Catholic. Home: 425 E 76th St #1C New York NY 10021

MCKILLIP (GAGE), DONNA LUANN, sales executive; b. Wabash, Ind., June 6, 1953; d. Paul Delbert and Donna Jean (Monce) Yentes; m. Jon David Gage, Mar. 17, 1972 (div. Jan. 1982); children: Jennifer, Nathaniel, Joshua. Grad. high sch., Northfield Highs Sch., Wabash, Ind., 1971. Acctg., sales sec. Wabash (Ind.) Inc., 1972-77; dealer, sales mgr. Tupperware Home Parties, Anderson, Ind., 1978-86; receptionist Vernon Manor Children's Home, Wabash, Ind., 1983-86; sales rep. ServiSoft Water Softening, Wabash, Ind., 1985—. Mem. Sigma Phi Gamma Sorority (pres. 1983-84). Methodist. Home: 1272 Stitt St Wabash IN 46992 Office: ServiSoft Water Softening 1288 Stitt St Wabash IN 46992

MCKILLOP, LUCILLE, college president; b. Chgo., Sept. 28, 1924; d. Daniel and Catherine (Hamill) McK. B.A., St. Xavier Coll., 1951; M.S., U. Notre Dame, 1959; Ph.D., U. Wis., 1965. Vis. prof. Ill. Inst. Tech., Chgo., 1969; faculty St. Xavier Coll., Chgo., 1958-59, 63-73; pres. Salve Regina Coll., Newport, R.I., 1973—; dir. Old Colony Coop. Bank, Providence, 1976-81; mem. Gov.'s Adv. Commn. Ednl. TV, 1977-82, R.I. Postsecondary Edn. Commn., 1979—, Gov.'s Commn. on Taxation, 1981-83, Gov.'s Commn. on R.I. Legis. Compensation, 1980. Trustee Newport Hosp., 1976-80; mem. corp. R.I. Blue Cross/Blue Shield, 1980—; bd. dirs. Council for Advancement Small Colls., 1978-82, Newport Music Festival, 1978—; chmn. Washington Office on Haiti, 1984—; bd. dirs. NCCJ of R.I. Inc., 1983—. Mem. Nat. Assn. Ind. Colls. and Univs. (dir. 1977-82), R.I. Ind. Higher Edn. Assn. (exec. com.), Associated Cath. Colls. and Univs. (exec. com. coll. and univ. dept. 1977-80). Office: Newport Coll Salve Regina Ochre Point Ave Newport RI 02840*

MCKINLEY, ELLEN BACON, priest; b. Milw., June 9, 1929; d. Edward Alsted and Lorraine Goodrich (Graham) Bacon; m. Richard Smallbrook McKinley, III, June 16, 1951 (div. Oct. 1977); children: Richard IV, Ellen Graham, David Todd, Edward Bacon. BA cum laude, Bryn Mawr Coll., 1951; MDiv Yale U., 1976; STM, Gen. Theol. Sem., N.Y.C., 1979; PhD, Union Theol. Sem., N.Y.C., 1988. Ordained deacon Episcopal Ch. 1980, priest, 1981. Intern St. Francis Ch., Stamford, Conn., 1976-77; pastoral asst. St. Paul's Ch., Riverside, Conn., 1979-80, curate, 1980-81; priest assoc. St. Saviour's Ch., Old Greenwich, Conn., 1982—; asst. St. Christopher's Ch., Chatham, Mass., 1987-88. Mem. Episcpal Election Com., Diocese of Conn., 1986-87, Com. on Human Sexuality, 1987—; Com. on Donations and Bequests Diocese of Conn., 1987—; sec., Greewich Com. on Drugs, 1970-71; bd. dirs. Greenwich YWCA, 1971-72. Mem. Conn. Clergy Assn. (Episcopal), Episcopal Women's Caucus, New Eng. Women Ministers Assn., Greenwich Fellowship of Clergy, Colonial Dames Am., Jr. League. Clubs: Sulgrave, Rocky Point. Avocations: theatre, concerts, swimming, sailing, reading, architecture, building and remodeling houses. Office: St Saviour's Ch 350 Sound Beach Ave Old Greenwich CT 06870

MCKINLEY, RUTH JOANN, hospice administrator, psychotherapist; b. Los Angeles, Sept. 24, 1933; d. Ward Ivan and Lilah May (Conger) Hallin; B.A., Calif. State U.-Northridge, 1966; M.S.W., U. So. Calif., 1972; Ph.D. cum laude, Am. Western U., 1981; m. John Clyde McKinley, Nov. 19, 1954 (dec. 1972); children—Terance Phillip Green, Mark Stuart. Diplomate Am. Bd. Clin. Social Work. Adminstr., Pacoima (Calif.) br. San Fernando Valley Child Guidance Clinic, 1965-68; dependency supr. placement services Los Angeles County Juvenile Ct., Van Nuys, Calif., 1968-72; psychotherapist Simi Valley and Conejo Mental Health, Ventura County Mental Health Services, Thousand Oaks, Calif., 1972-83; exec. dir. Hospice of the Conejo, 1984-86, pvt. practice psychotherapy Capper Psychiat. Med. Group, Camarillo, Calif., after 1979; exec. dir. Hospice of Conejo, 1984-86; pvt. practice Mc Kinley Assocs., 1983—; cons., tng. cons. Conejo Community Hotline. Dir., Lifeline, Westlake Village, Calif., 1972-75; mem. White Ho. Conf. on Children and Youth, 1970; mem. Ventura County Coalition Against Household Violence, 1980. Children's Bur. Fed. grantee, 1970-72. Mem. Acad. Cert. Social Workers, Soc. Clin. Social Work. Office: 199 E Thousand Oaks Blvd Thousand Oaks CA 91361

MCKINNEY, CARIE GOODMAN, environmental attorney; b. El Paso, Tex., Jan. 31, 1956; d. Jimmie Carie and Joan (Carey) Goodman; m. Daene Claude McKinney, June 16, 1984. BS in Civil Engring., Tex. Tech U., 1978; MS in Environ. Engring., Cornell U., 1984; JD, Cornell Law Sch., 1987. Bar: Calif. 1987. Engr. Region 6 EPA, Dallas, 1978-79, Nat. Enforcement Investigation Ctr., Denver, 1979-82; environ. atty. McCutchen, Doyle, Brown & Emersen, San Francisco, 1987-90. Home: 10610 Sierra Oaks Austin CA 78759

MCKINNEY, CEIL CATHERINE, military officer; b. Houston, Aug. 27, 1956; d. Barrett Travis and Dorothy Patricia (Harrington) McK.; m. Joseph P. McManus, Sept. 22, 1984. BS in Wildlife and Fishery Sciences-Ecology Option, Tex. A&M U., 1979. Commd. USN, 1979; recreational svcs. officer Naval Communications Sta., Stockton, Calif., 1979-81; officer in charge Naval Telecommunications Ctr., Naval Supply Ctr., Oakland, Calif., 1981-82; manpower and tng. analyst Naval Telecommunications Command, Washington, 1982-84; asst. officer in charge naval telecommunication ctr. Naval Air Sta., North Island, San Diego, 1984-87; enlisted programs officer Navy Recruiting Dist., Kans. City, Mo., 1987-88; mil. manpower analyst Naval Air Sta. Chase Field, Beeville, Tex., 1988—; bd. dirs. Navy Army Fed. Credit Union, 1989—; comptr., mgr. home office J.C. Enterprises. Mem. Goliad County (Tex.) Hist. Commn.; mem. Coastal Bend Coun. on Alcoholism and Drug Abuse. Mem. NAFE, Internat. Llamas Assn., Women Officers Profl. Assn., Beeville Users Group. Roman Catholic. Home: PO Box 649 107 S Commercial Goliad TX 77963

MCKINNEY, PAMELA ANNE, elementary principal; b. L.A., Sept. 25, 1947; d. Dave and Helen (Wallace) Shorter; m. Frank Alexander McKinney III, Aug. 24, 1968; children: Frank Alexander IV, Pamela Ann. AA, L.A. Harbor Coll., 1967; BA, Conn. Coll., 1973; MS, Old Dominion U., 1982; cert. in advance grad. studies, Va. Tech. U. & State Inst., 1988. Asst. buyer May Co. Dept. Stores, L.A., 1967-68, Liberty House Dept. Stores, Honolulu, 1968-70; tchr. Norfolk (Va.) Pub. Schs., 1982, Tracy (Calif.) Pub. Schs., 1975-77; tchr. Virginia Beach (Va.) Pub. Schs., 1984-80, asst. prin., 1984-89, prin., 1989—; bd. dirs. Tidewater Prin. Ctr., Norfolk. Tchr. religious edn. Holy Spirit Ch., Virginia Beach, 1986—; bd. dirs. Cath. Family and Children's Svcs., Virginia Beach, 1987—. Mem. Virginia Beach Assn. Elem. Sch. Prins., Va. assn. Elem. Sch. Prins., Nat. Assn. Elem. Sch. Prins., Am. Assn. Sch. Adminstrs., Assn. Supervision and Curriculum Devel. Home: 4705 Chalfont Dr Virginia Beach VA 23464 Office: Plaza Elem Sch 641 Carriage Hill Rd Virginia Beach VA 23452

MCKINNEY, PHYLLIS LOUISE KELLOGG HENRY, school administrator, management consultant; b. Mason City, Iowa, May 3, 1932; d. Wilbur Rhode and Dorothy Margaret (Bauer) K.; children—Curtis Dean Henry, Catherine Rose Henry Jones, David Russell Henry. A.A. in Elem. Teaching, U. No. Iowa, 1953; B.A. Calif. State U.-Los Angeles, 1963, M.A., 1968. Cert. elem. tchr., cert. reading specialist, sch. adminstrn. credential. Tchr., Arlington pub. schs., Iowa, 1951-52, St. Louis Park pub. schs., Minn., 1953-55; tchr., supr. ABC Sch. Dist., Cerritos, Calif., 1963-69; cons. in reading State Dept. of Calif., Sacramento, 1969-70; cons. in edn. Orange County Dept. Edn., Santa Ana, Calif., 1970-75; sch. adminstr. Oakwood Sch., Long Beach, Calif., 1975—; chmn. bd. dirs. New City Bank, Orange, Calif.; cons. in field. Author: Song of Sounds, 1969; (with others) Beginnings for Christian Schools, 1976. Conf. coordinator State Dept. Edn., Calif., Sacramento, Santa Barbara, 1970 (Outstanding Leadership award 1974-75). Mem. Nat. Ind. Pvt. Sch. (v.p. 1982-83, dir. seminars 1983), Pre-Sch. Assn. Calif. (legis. chair 1978-84), Reading Specialists Calif. (pres. 1970-73).

Republican. Avocations: skiing; scuba diving; painting; photography; travel. Home: 4438 Heather Rd Long Beach CA 90808 Office: Oakwood Sch 2650 Pacific Ave Long Beach CA 90806

MCKINNEY, SAN, designer, business owner; b. Ventnor, N.J., June 13, 1946; d. Gerald A. and Dorothy Eleanor Haines; m. E.C. Hollifield (div.); 1 child, Jesse Adam. BS in Comml. Design, Glassboro State U., 1970; postgrad., Temple U., Princeton U. Tchr. Somers Point (N.J.) Sch., 1972-77; art dir. Stone Mfg. Co., Greenville, S.C., 1978-81; real estate agent Beattie Huff, Greenville, 1981-83; producer, dir. Lt. Light Years Childrens TV, Greenville, S.C., 1981; founder, operator, pres. Design Know How Corp., Warwick, 1983-87; founder, operator San McKinney Assocs., The Contractors Connection, Ponns Grove, N.J., 1988—; founder Corp. Theater; speaker, cons. in field. One-woman show includes Wintergull Watercolor, Audubon Soc., 1980 (Silver award), Somers Point Library, 1972. Recipient Mini Grant State of N.J. Art Learning Ctr., 1973-74, Nat. Audubon Exhibit Silver Award Watercolor, 1980. Mem. Bus. and Profl. Womens Assn., Ind. Sq. Found. (bd. dirs.), NEA, N.J. Edn. Assn. (pres. 1979), Utility Transp. and Contractors Assn. Methodist. Home: 94 N Virginia Ave Penns Grove NJ 08069

MCKINNIE, DONNA LOUISE FONES, nurse; b. Chgo., Nov. 21, 1934; d. John McKenzie and Pauline May (Waid) Pierson; children: Denise Pletcher, Darrell, Desirée, Drew. Cert. in nursing, West Suburban Hosp., Oak Park, Ill., 1955; BS in Nursing, Ariz. State U., 1973, MS in Nursing, 1975. RN. Nurse West Suburban Hosp., Oak Park, 1955-57, asst. head nurse, 1957-60, nurse educator, 1962-65; nurse Hines (Ill.) VA Hosp., 1960-62; nurse and nurse educator Christ Community Hosp., Oak Lawn, Ill., 1965-70, Scottsdale (Ariz.) Meml. Hosp., 1970-75; obstet. nurse clin. specialist CIGNA Healthplan of Ariz., Phoenix, 1975—; instr. tng. course for prenatal educators and parenting classes ARC, Phoenix, 1970—. Author: (with others) The Harris Method of Childbirth Education, 1980, (with others) The Three Trimesters, 1983. Leader Pioneer Girls, Chgo., 1965-69; chmn. Missions Svc. Com. Bethamy Community Ch., Tempe, Ariz., 1980-85, 87—. Named Childbirth Educator of Yr. The Harris Found., 1981. Mem. Ariz. Nurses Assn., Nurses Assn. of Am. Coll. Obstetricians and Gynecologists, Sigma Theta Tau (charter mem. Beta Upsilon chpt.). Republican. Fundamentalist. Office: CIGNA Healthplan of Ariz 1920 E Baseline Rd Tempe AZ 85283

MCKINZIE, BEVERLY OMA, artist; b. Denver, Oct. 27, 1927; d. Allen Worley and Shereal (Vaagen) Chapalis; m. Raymond Clem McKinzie; children: Jeanne, Teresa, Scott, Mark. Statistician Denver Post, 1945-47; payroll clk. Firth Carpet, Firthcliffe, N.Y., 1948-49; proofreader Cornwall (N.Y.) Press, 1949-50; electronic tech. USN, Great Lakes, Ill., 1950-51; bookkeeper Foodmaker, San Diego, 1968-70; salesperson Liberty House, San Jose, 1971. Embroidered The Birth Project, 1982-83. With USN, 1950-51. Mem. Peninsula Stitchery Guild, Fiber Artisans, Handweaver's Guild Am. Home and Office: 1437 Camino Robles Way San Jose CA 95120

MCKNIGHT, BARBARA ANN FERRELL, land development company executive; b. Austin, Tex., June 28, 1938; d. Floyd E. Ferrell and Virginia Louise (Casparis) Ferrell Edwards; divorced; children: William Keith, Wendy Kay Rother, Wesleye Karen Taylor. Student Baylor U., 1956-57, Durham Bus. Coll., 1967, Houston Community Coll., 1979-80. Lic. real estate assoc., Tex. Adminstrv. asst. Ryland Group, Houston, 1973-80; project mgr. Gibraltar Savs. Assn. of Tex., Houston, 1980-84; v.p. Rheinhold Corp., Houston, 1984-85, Tex. Investment and Devel. Corp., Houston, 1985-87; adminstrv. mgr. First Southwestern Title Agy., Inc., Houston, 1987—, Am. Ch. Trust Co., 1989; owner, mgr. Barbara McKnight Cons., Houston, 1985—. Alt. del. Tex. Rep. Conv., Houston, 1976, del., Austin, 1980. Mem. NAFE. Baptist.

MCKNIGHT, ELIZABETH CONWAY, management consultant; b. Proctor, Vt., May 27, 1945; d. John Thomas and Phyllis Irene (Creaser) Conway; m. James Brian McKnight, June 6, 1964 (div. 1983). BS with honors, Northeastern U., 1975; cert., Doscher Sch. Photography, Woodstock, Vt., 1976; MA in Environ. Affairs, Clark U., 1978. Reporter AP, Boston, 1974-75; tchr. journalism and environ. sci. Lawrence Acad., Groton, Mass., 1975-78; publs. mgr. Zellars-Williams, Inc., Lakeland, Fla., 1978-79; photographer, writer E.C. McKnight, Burlington, Vt., 1979-81; communications and mktg. mgr. Dufresne-Henry, Inc., North Springfield, Vt., 1981-82; gen. mgr. Assoc. Cons., Inc., Londonderry, Vt., 1982-85; dir. ops. Group Design Architects, Rutland, Vt., 1986-90; cons., U.S. rep. Caledonian Wildlife, Inverness, Scotland, 1988—; saleswoman Vt. Real Estate Commn., 1983—; freelance photographer, writer. Chairwoman citizens adv. com. Rutland County Solid Waste Dist., 1989-90; mem. Rutland Mayor's Com. on Volvo Site Selection, 1989; cons. Rutland Partnership, 1988-90, interim dir. and mem. exec. com., 1989-90. Mem. Am. Mgmt. Assn., NAFE, Soc. Profl. Journalists. Home: PO Box 748 Boothbay Harbor ME 04538

MCKNIGHT, HARRIET MANGUS, forestry technician; b. Price, Utah, May 31, 1950; d. Harry Wayne and Rita Iona (Woody) Mangus; m. Dale Jess McKnight, Mar. 15, 1974. AA, Coll. Ea. Utah, 1970; BS, Utah State U., 1972. Cert. clin. pathologist. Microbiologist Latter-day Saints Hosp., Salt Lake City, 1973-74, Logan (Utah) Hosp., 1975-77; asst. microbiology supr. St. Mary's Hosp., Reno, 1977-79; microbiology supr. Carson-Tahoe Hosp., Carson City, Nev., 1979-82; clk. justice ct. Lander County, Austin, Nev., 1983-84; forestry technician U.S. Forest Svc., Wise River, Mont., 1985—. Home: PO Box 99 Wise River MT 59762 Office: US Forest Svc PO Box 100 Wise River MT 59762

MCKNIGHT, JOYCE SHELDON, college mentor; b. Meadville, Pa., Oct. 12, 1949; d. Seth Carlyle and Juanita Bessie (Sheets) Sheldon; m. Hugh Frank McKnight, Aug. 22, 1970; children: Frank Nathan, Joanna Michelle. BA in Psychology and Sociology, Allegheny Coll., 1971; MEd in Counseling, Gannon Coll., 1977; postgrad., Pa. State U., 1987—. Asst. met. dir. Ecumenical Inst., Chgo. and Tulsa, 1970-73; health planner East Okla. Devel. Dist., Muskogee, 1973; juvenile counselor Tulsa County Aftercare Program, 1973; program specialist psycho-social rehab. Counseling Svcs. Ctr., Corry, Pa., 1975-77; counselor Adult Diploma Program, Corry, Pa., 1974-79; dir. Anchor House Agy., Corry, Pa., 1977-78; community programs dir. Warren-Forest Counties Econ. Opportunity Coun., Warren, Pa., 1979-80; dir. Corry Ctr. Mercyhurst Coll., Warren, Pa., 1981-87; cons. Pulaski, Pa., 1987—; adj. faculty, 1981-87, program devel. cons., 1987—; adj. faculty Allegheny Coll., 1984; mentor Empire Coll. SUNY, 1989—. Contbr. rsch. papers in field. Pres., Corry Concerned for Youth, Inc., 1975-77; pres. Community Care Coun. of Agys., Corry, 1976-79, sec., 1975; mem. steering com. Vol. Action Ctr., Corry, 1977; bd. dirs. Erie County Citizens Coalition for Human Svcs., Erie, 1979-80. Horizon House for Women, 1981-87; mem. coordinating bd. Corry Reindustrialization Coun., 1983-87. Mem. Pa. Assn. Pub. Continuing Adult Edn. (dir. 1977-78), Nat. Assn. Pub. Continuing and Adult Edn., Pa. Assn. for Adult Continuing Edn. (bd. dirs. 1985—), Pa. Community Edn. Assn., Nat. Community Edn. Assn., Rural Mental Health Assn., Am. Assn. for Counseling and Devel., Corry C. of C., Corry Bus. and Profl. Women, Zonta. Methodist. Home and Office: 22 Pine St Port Allegany PA 16743

MCKNIGHT, KAREN THERESE, real estate sales executive; b. Cheyenne, Wyoming, Sept. 7, 1947; d. Delton E. and Agnes Theresa (Sahl) Bagme; m. J. Scott McKnight, Aug. 23, 1969 (div. 1987); children: Chad, Stephanie. BS, U. Puget Sound, 1969. Sales exec. The Heller Co., Bellevue, Wash., 1983-89, Windermere Real Estate, Bellevue, 1989—. Mem. Realtors Nat. Mktg. Inst. (cert. residential specialist), King County Realtors Assn. (cert. residential specialist Wash. chpt.). Republican. Ecumenical. Office: Windermere Real Estate 14504 NE 20 St Bellevue WA 98007

MCKOWEN, DOROTHY KEETON, librarian; b. Bonne Terre, Mo., Oct. 5, 1948; d. John Richard and Dorothy (Spoonhour) Keeton; m. Paul Edwin McKowen, Dec. 19, 1970; children: Richard James, Mark David. BS, Pacific Christian Coll., 1970; MLS, U. So. Calif., 1973; MA in English, Purdue U., 1985. Libr.-specialist Doheny Libr., U. So. Calif., L.A., 1973-74; asst. libr. Pacific Christian Coll., 1974-78; serials cataloger Purdue Univ. Librs., 1978-88; head children's and young adult svcs. Kokomo-Howard County Pub. Libr. (Ind.), 1988-89, coord. children's and tech. svcs., 1989—; vice chairperson Christian Edn. Com., Brady Lane Ch. of Christ, 1986-87, chairperson, 1987-88, pianist, 1978—, choir dir., 1990—; bd. dirs. Purdue Christian Campus House, 1985-90, v.p., 1986-88, pres., 1988-90. Mem. ALA, Assn. for Libr. Svc to Children, Assn. for Libr. Collections and Tech. Svcs. (bd. dirs. 1986-90, vice chairperson, chairperson elect coun. of regional groups 1986-88, chairperson 1988-90, conf. program com. 1986-88, internat. rels. com. 1986-88, micropub. com., 1986-87, subject analysis com., subcom. to rev. Dewey 621.38, 1987, membership com. 1988-90, libr. resources and tech. svcs. editorial bd. 1988-90, planning and rsch. com. 1988-90, planning com. 1990—), Libr. Adminstrn. and Mgmt. Assn., Ind. Libr. Assn. (vice chmn. tech. svcs. div. 1983-84, chmn. 1984-85), Ohio Valley Group Tech. Svcs. Librs. (vice chmn. 1984-85, chmn. 1985-86). Republican. Home: 7625 Summit Ln Lafayette IN 47905 Office: Kokomo-Howard County Pub Libr 220 N Union Kokomo IN 46901

MCKOY, ELLEN MOLLY, journalist, marketing consultant; b. Albany, N.Y., Sept. 6, 1944; d. Elias Marder and Edna (Goldman) Schwarzbart; m. Keith Constantine McKoy, Aug. 22, 1970; children: Kirk Christopher, Oral Marcel, Keith Constantine Jr. BA, Goddard Coll., Plainfield, Vt., 1965; postgrad., Bklyn. Coll., 1966-67. Tchr. Breukelen Recreation Rms., Bklyn., 1965-66; publicity asst. World Pub. Co., N.Y.C., 1966-68; publicity dir. Helmsely-Spear, Inc., N.Y.C., 1968-71; freelance fund raiser community orgns., N.Y.C., 1972-73; publicity dir. The Third Press, N.Y.C., 1973-74; gen. mgr., dir. sales and mktg. Skycoach Customizing Inc., Farmingdale, N.Y., 1975-82; contbg. editor Auto Trim News Mag., Baldwin, N.Y., 1983-88; freelance journalist, mktg. cons. EMK Mktg., Balt., 1988—; cons. Dow Chem. U.S.A., Midland, Mich., 1988, Custom Classics, Inc., Marlton, N.J., 1988—, Baycraft Fiberglass Engring., Havre de Grace, Md., 1990. Charter editor Restyling Trends & Directions mag.; editor-at-large Trucking Times Mag.; contbr. articles to profl. jours. Pres. Benjamin Franklin House Tenant Assn., Phila., 1986-88; dir. Coop City Community Sch., Brtonx, N.Y., 1974-76; co-chmn., mem. Nat. Danas Scholarship Com., 1986—. Mem. NAFE, Nat. Assn. Auto Trim Shops, Profl. Women's League. Jewish. Office: EMK Mktg 301 Warren Ave Ste 302 Baltimore MD 21230

MCLACHLAN, IVA WOLF, lawyer; b. Georgetown, Tex., June 28, 1956; d. Jay Leon and Bettie Mae (Black) Wolf; m. Donald Alan McLachlan, Mar. 14, 1981; children: Brian Alan, Amanda June. BA, Baylor U., 1978, JD, 1980. Bar: Tex. 1981, U.S. Dist. Ct. (no. dist.) Tex. 1981. Legis. asst. Tex. Legislature, Austin, summer 1974; assoc. Law Firm of Simon & Simon, Ft. Worth, 1980-82; atty. Tex. Ct. Appeals, Tyler, 1983-84, staff atty., 1988—. Sec. Tex. Lawyers' Aux., Tyler, 1986; pres. Child Nurture Club, Tyler, 1986. Mem. Tex. Bar Assn., Smith County Young Lawyers Assn., East Tex. Baylor Club (v.p. 1986-89, pres. 1989—). Republican. Baptist. Home: 2151 Santa Fe Trail Tyler TX 75703

MCLACHLIN, BEVERLEY, supreme court judge; b. Pincher Creek, Alta., Can., Sept. 7, 1943; m. Roderick McLachlin (dec.); 1 child, Angus. B.A., U. Alta., M.A. in Philosophy, LL.B. Bar: Alta. 1969, B.C. 1971. Assoc. Wood, Moir, Hyde and Ross, Edmonton, Alta., Can., 1969-71, Thomas, Herdy, Mitchell & Co., Fort St. John, B.C., Can., 1971-72, Bull, Housser and Tupper, Vancouver, B.C., 1972-75; lectr., assoc. prof., prof. with tenure U. B.C., 1974-78; appointed to County Ct., Vancouver, 1981; justice Supreme Ct. of B.C., 1981-85; justice B.C. Ct. of Appeal, 1985-88, appointed Chief Justice, 1988; justice Supreme Ct. Can., Ottawa, Ont., 1989—. Mem. editorial adv. bd. Family Law Restatement Project, 1987-88, Civil Jury Instruction, 1988; contbr. numerous articles to profl. jours. Office: Supreme Ct Bldg, Wellington St, Ottawa, ON Canada K1A 0J1*

MCLAIN, JANICE DARLENE, magazine editor and manager; b. Ottumwa, Iowa, Dec. 20, 1943; d. Arthur George and Daisy (Thompson) Sells; m. Richard L. McLain, July 4, 1964; 1 child, Christopher. BS in Journalism, Iowa State U., 1967. Asst. women's editor La Crosse (Wis.) Tribune, 1967-69, feature editor, 1969-74; with rsch. and pub. rels. depts. La Crosse Econ. Devel., 1975; pres., pub. Gazette Newspapers, La Crosse, 1976-79; with sales and pub. rels. depts. Wilson Learning, Sydney, Australia, 1980-81; news editor Minn. Suburban Newspapers, Mpls., 1986-87; rsch. asst. Custom Rsch., Mpls., 1988-89; gen. mgr., editor Format mag., Mpls., 1989—. Named Outstanding Young Alumnus, Iowa State U., 1975, Woman of Achievement, Wis. Press Woman, 1979, numerous journalism awards. Mem. Women in Communications, Minn. Newspaper Found. Home: 11300 51st Ave N Minneapolis MN 55442 Office: Format 4248 Park Glen Rd Minneapolis MN 55416

MCLAINE, ALICE JEANETTE, athletic trainer, educator; b. Caribou, Maine, July 17, 1958; d. Robert Eugene and Melba Fern (Davis) McN.; m. Lawrence West McLaine, Nov. 24, 1985. B.Edn., Ohio U., 1980; M.S., W.Va. U., 1981. Grad. asst. athletic trainer W.Va. U., 1980-81; head athletic trainer Iowa State U., Ames, 1981—. Recipient Al Hart Scholarship award, 1979-80. Mem. Nat. Athletic Trainers Assn., Iowa Athletic Trainers Assn., Am. Coll. Sportsmedicine. Methodist. Home: 505 25th St Ames IA 50010 Office: Iowa State U 111 Phys Edn Bldg Ames IA 50011

MCLANE, BOBBIE JONES, retired government official, genealogist; b. Hot Springs, Ark., Feb. 19, 1927; d. Julian Everette and Eula (Deaton) Jones; m. Gerald Bert McLane, Aug. 14, 1954. Chief clk. Army and Navy Hosp., Hot Springs, 1950-52; adminstrv. asst. Wis. Mil. Dist., Milw., 1952-54; exec. sec. to postmaster U.S. Postal Svc., Hot Springs, 1954-70, supr. employment svcs., 1970-74, dir. employee and labor rels., 1974-80; acting postmaster U.S. Postal Svc., Arkadelphia, Ark., 1978; dir. employee and labor rels. U.S. Postal Svc., Ft. Smith, Ark., 1980-86; ret., 1986; compiler, author, pub. Ark. Ancestors, 52 titles, 1962—; assoc. editor The Record, 1966—. Organizer, charter mem. Garland County Hist. Soc., Hot Springs, 1960—; bd. dirs., chmn. Ark. History Commn., 1966-80, mem., 1989—; charter mem., bd. dirs. Community Players Hot Springs, 1949-55. Recipient award for contbns. to hist. and geneal. rsch. Am. Assn. State and Local History, 1967, Bicentennial award Postmaster Gen. U.S. Postal Svc., 1976; named One of 100 Ark. Women of Achievement, Ark. Press Women, 1980; Am. Assn. State and Local History fellow Vanderbilt U., 1967. Mem. Profl. Genealogists Ark. (bd. dirs. 1988—), Ark. Geneal. Soc. (charter, bd. dirs. 1960—, past pres.). Democrat. Episcopalian. Home and Office: 222 McMahan Dr Hot Springs AR 71913-6243

MCLANE, SUSAN NEIDLINGER, state legislator; b. Boston, Sept. 28, 1929; d. Lloyd Kellock and Marion (Walker) Neidlinger; m. Malcolm McLane, 1948; children: Susan B., Donald W., Deborah, Alan, Ann Lloyd. Ed., Mt. Holyoke Coll.; LLD (hon.), New England Coll., 1983, Franklin Pierce Coll., 1988. Mem. N.H. Ho. of Reps., Concord, 1969-80; chmn. ways and means com. N.H. Ho. of Reps., 1976-80; mem. N.H. State Senate, Concord, 1980—; del. Rep. Nat. Conv., 1976; pres. N.H. Coun. Affairs, 1976-80. Office: NH State Senate State Capitol Concord NH 03301 also: 205 Mountain Rd Concord NH 03301

MCLAREN, KAREN LYNN, advertising executive; b. Flint, Mich., Feb. 14, 1955; d. Max W. and Barbara J. (Cole) Hoeffgen; m. Michael L. McLaren, June 18, 1974. AA, Mott Community Coll., Flint, 1976; BA, Mich. State U., 1978. Writer Sta. WGMZ-FM, Flint, 1979-84; writer, producer Tracy-Stephens Advt., Flint, 1984-87; pres. McLaren Advt., Troy, Mich., 1987—. Contbr. articles to profl. jours. Various pub. svc. activities include: centennial com. Wolverine region Red Cross, 1981, pub. rels. com., 1981-84. Recipient 3 Addy awards, 2 Nat. Health Care awards, Mktg. Competition award. Mem. NAFE, Womens Advt. Club Detroit (scholarship chair 1987, 88, bd. dirs. 1989, co-chair career fair 1989, 90, v.p. 1990).

MCLAREN, MARILYN PATRICIA, educator manufacturing methods, human resources specialist, aviator; b. Jamaica, N.Y., July 5, 1942; d. Raymond Lionel and Katherine Marie (Doepp) Cowan; m. Richard Edward McLaren, July 17, 1976; 1 child, Paul William Hibner. Student various aviation schs., St. Joseph's Coll., N.Y.; cert. in Leadership and Human Resources Devel. Goldratt Inst., Conn. Exec. sec. to chief design Wiedersum Assocs., architects and engrs., Valley Stream, N.Y., 1960-61; officer mgr., interior designer Keith I. Hibner, architect, Hicksville and Garden City, N.Y., 1961-73; owner, pres. Hibner Atelier, Ltd., interior design and gen. constrn., Garden City, 1968-75; office mgr. Ward Assocs./Planning Assocs., architects and engrs., Bohemia, N.Y., 1975-76; flight/ground aviation instr. Islip Aviation, Ltd. (N.Y.), 1974-77; exec. asst. to pres. Arkay Packaging Corp., Hauppauge, N.Y., 1977-86, in-house constrn. mgr., 1980-82, adminstrn. and human resources mgr., 1986-89, dir. corp. devel., 1989, dir. materials mgmt., 1989-90; owner Concepts for Constructive Change, Educators and Facilitators for Continuous Improvementm Lake Grove, N.Y., 1990—; ind. aviation flight/ground instr. airplane and instrument, 1977—; safety counselor FAA, 1974—, Eastern Region Counselor Coordinator, 1985-86; past bd. dirs., officer Aviation Council L.I.; founder Seminar on Air Travel for Everyone (S.A.F.E.), 1975, Fly-C-Cure/We Air Condition People, 1979. Author articles, seminar syllabus. Mem. nat. panel Consumer arbitrators Nat. Consumer Arbitration Program, Better Bus. Bur. Lic. comml. pilot, flight and ground instr. Mem. NAFE, Ninety-Nines (past chmn. L.I. chpt., founding internat. chmn. safety edn., Amelia Earhart Bronze medal 1975), Aircraft Owners and Pilots Assn., Nat. Assn. Flight Instrs., Soc. Human Resource Mgmt., Pers. Soc. L.I., Hauppauge Indsl. Assn., L.I. Assn., L.I. Forum For Tech., L.I. Mid-Suffolk Bus. Action, Adminstrv. Mgmt. Soc. Specialist on fear of flying, Specialist on Theory of Constraints Mgmt. Methodology. Home and Office: 3 Park St Lake Grove NY 11755

MCLAREY, SANDRA ROBERTS, medical facility administrator; b. Trenton, Fla., Dec. 3, 1940; d. Daniel Nathan and Mattie (Harllee) Roberts; m. Don C. McLarey, July 12, 1959; children: Don II, Teresa Ann. Student, Harding U., 1959-60; AA, Galveston Coll., 1972. R.N., Tex. Nurse, office mgr. to pvt. practice physician Freeport and Bryan, Tex., 1972-83; charge nurse Greenleaf Hosp., Bryan, 1983-84; hosp. supr. Greenleaf Hosp., 1984-86; nurse therapist Girlstown USA, Borger, Tex., 1986-87; adminstr. Girlstown USA, 1987—; bus. mgr. med. practice Carlsbad, N.Mex., 1989—. Adminstr., Tex. Child Care Adminstrn., 1988. Mem. ARC, Pan Am. Allergy Soc., Soc. Otological Head and Neck, AMA Aux., Bus. and Profl. Women's Assn., Phi Theta Kappa. Republican. Mem. Full Gospel Ch. Office: 2319 W Pierce St Carlsbad NM 88220

MCLAREY, TRACY ANN, marketing professional; b. Hartford, Conn., Jan. 12, 1959; d. Benoit Alfred and Gail Ann (Healy) Michaud; m. Stephen M. McLarey, Nov. 12, 1982 (div.). Grad. high sch., Bridgewater, Mass. Retail mgr. E&S Computing, Berlin, N.H., 1983-86; mktg. coord., systems analyst, exec. asst. Chisholm Washington Architects, Inc., Cambridge, Mass., 1986—. Mem. Soc. for Archtl. Adminstrs. (membership chmn. 1988-89), Nat. Assn. for Female Execs. Republican. Home: 259 Marlborough St #2 Boston MA 02115

MCLAUGHLIN, ANN, lecturer, advisor; b. Newark, Nov. 16, 1941; d. Edward Joseph and Marie (Koellhoffer) Lauenstein; m. John Joseph McLaughlin, Aug. 23, 1975. B.A., Marymount Coll. Supr. network comml. schedule ABC, N.Y.C., 1963-66; dir. alumnae relations Marymount Coll., Tarrytown, N.Y., 1966-69; account exec. Myers-Infoplan Internat. Inc., N.Y.C., 1969-71; dir. communications Presdl. Election Com., Washington, 1971-72; asst. to chmn. and press sec. Presdl. Inaugural Com., Washington, 1972-73; dir. Office of Pub. Affairs, EPA, Washington, 1973-74; govt. relations and communications exec. Union Carbide Corp., N.Y.C. and Washington, 1974-77; pub. affairs, issues mgmt. counseling McLaughlin & Co., 1977-81; asst. sec. for pub. affairs Dept. Treasury, Washington, 1981-84; under sec. Dept. of Interior, Washington, 1984-87; cons. Ctr. Strategic and Internat. Studies, Washington, 1987; sec. of labor Dept. of Labor, Washington, 1987-89; vis. fellow, trustee Urban Inst., 1989—; chmn. Pres.'s Commn. Aviation Security and Terrorism, 1989-90; mem. Am. Coun. on Capital Formation, 1976-78; mem. environ. edn. task force HEW, 1976-77; mem. Def. Adv. Com. of Women in the Svcs., 1973-74; bd. dirs. Unocal Corp., GM, Travelers Cos., Union Camp Corp., Kellogg Co., Vulcan Materials Co., Pub. Agenda Found., Nat. Alliance of Bus.; trustee Aspen Inst.; pres. Fed. City Coun., 1990—. Mem. Washington Woman's Forum, Cosmos Club, Met. Club. Republican. Roman Catholic. Office: Urban Inst 2100 M St NW Washington DC 20037

MCLAUGHLIN, AUDREY, Canadian politician; b. Dutton, Ont., Can., Nov. 7, 1936; d. W.M. and Margaret Brown; children: David, Tracy. Ed., U. Western Ont., U. Toronto, Ont. Mem. from Y.T. Ho. of Commons, 1987—; leader New Dem. Party, 1989; social scientist, cons. Office: House of Commons, Parliament Bldgs, Ottawa, ON Canada K1A 0A6*

MCLAUGHLIN, DEBORAH ANN, public relations and marketing executive; b. Hoisington, Kans., Nov. 12, 1952; d. Kenneth Theodore and Mildred Marie (Steiner) Siebert; m. Donald Raymond McLaughlin, July 17, 1976; 1 child, Kalla Dawn. AS, Barton County Coll., Great Bend, Kans., 1972; BS, Kans. State U., 1975. News editor Great Bend Tribune, 1975-76; deposition indexer Turner & Boisseau, Great Bend, 1976-77; feature editor Mid-Kans. Ruralist, Hoisington, 1977-78; copywriter, audio-editor Advt. Assocs., Great Bend, 1978-79; photographer, sales mgr. Clay Ward Color Portraits, Great Bend, 1979-80; news editor, photographer St. John (Kans.) News, 1980-83; freelance writer, photographer Great Bend, 1984-85; pres., owner McLaughlin Pub. Rels. Agy., Great Bend, 1985-87; owner Cen. Kans. Sunrise mag., Great Bend, 1987-88, Creative Mktg. Svcs., Great Bend, 1988—. Contbr. articles and photographs to various publs. Mem. Coalition for Prevention Child Abuse, Great Bend, 1986-87; mem. 75th anniversary com. Kansas State U. Coll. Journalism and Mass Communications, Manhattan, 1986. Mem. Kans. State U. Alumni Assn. Roman Catholic. Home: 1427 21st St Great Bend KS 67530 Office: 1914 12th St PO Box 1351 Great Bend KS 67530

MCLAUGHLIN, MARGUERITE P., state senator, logging company executive; b. Matchwood, Mich., Oct. 15, 1928; d. Harvey Martin and Luella Margaret (Livingston) Miller; m. George Bruce McLaughlin, 1947; children: Pamela, Bruce Jr., Cynthia. Owner, operator contract logging firm, Orofino, Idaho; mem. Idaho Ho. of Reps., 1978-80; now mem. Idaho Senate, 4th term. Trustee Joint Sch. Dist. 171, 1976-80; pres. Orofino Celebration, Inc. Democrat. Roman Catholic. Office: Idaho State Senate State Capitol Boise ID 83720*

MCLAUGHLIN, MARYELLEN, electrical engineer; b. Boston, Dec. 18, 1958; d. James Anthony and Imelda Margaret (Phelan) McL. BS in Elec. Engring., Worcester Polytechnic Inst., 1980; MS in Elec. Engring., Va. Polytechnic Inst., 1987. Mem. tech. staff Charles Stark Draper Lab., Cambridge, Mass., 1980-81; design engr. HDS, Inc., Reston, Va., 1981-85; sr. designer engr. Aiken Advanced Systems, Alexandria, Va., 1985-87; mem. tech. staff Northrop Corp., Norwood, Mass. Mem. Soc. Women Engrs., IEEE, Tau Beta Pi Engring. Honor Soc. Roman Catholic. Office: Northrop Corp 100 Morse St Norwood MA 02062

MCLAUGHLIN, MIRIAM WESTERMAN, elementary school educator; b. Adrian, Mich., Aug. 14, 1920; d. Kenneth N. and Irma Rose (Kidman) Westerman; m. Rowland H. McLaughlin, Nov. 13, 1941; children: Mary, James, Carol. BA, U. Mich., 1948, cert., 1963, MA, 1970. Cert. tchr., Mich. Kindergarten tchr. Ypsilanti (Mich) Pub. Schs., Ann Arbor (Mich.) Pub. Schs., Garden City (Mich.) Pub. Schs., South Lyon Pub. Schs., Salem, Mich. Mem. Mu Phi Epsilon (retirement award). Home: 1714 Hermitage Rd Ann Arbor MI 48104

MCLAUGHLIN, NANCY ESTHER, stockbroker, realtor, consultant; b. Yauco, P.R., May 26, 1947; d. Eli Caraballo and Catalina Antonia (Quiros) Cintron; m. Edward Charles McLaughlin, Mar. 6, 1971 (div. June 1979); children: Elisa, Eric, Matthew. Student, Old Dominion U., 1965-67; BA, U. Md., 1970; postgrad., Hartford County Community Coll., Bel Air, Md., 1974-76, 79-80. Mgr. sales Am. Foresight, Inc., Balt., 1969-70; exec. trainee Sears, Roebuck & Co., Norristown, Pa., 1970-71; asst. mgr. Lerner Shops, S. Portland, Md., 1971-74; legal sec. Lester V. Jones, Inc., Bel Air, 1980-82; realtor Russell T. Baker & Co., Bel Air, 1979-82; fin. planner Conn. Mut. Ins. Co., Norfolk, Va., 1982-83; realtor Century 21, Virginia Beach, Va., 1982—; stockbroker Dean Witter Reynolds, Inc., Virginia Beach, 1983-88, Kidder, Peabody & Co., Inc., Norfolk, Va., 1988-89; realtor Armada/Hoffler, Chesapeake, Va., 1989—; advt. account exec. Sta. WVNZ-FM, Virginia Beach, Va., 1989—; lectr. in field, Va., Md., N.C., 1969—. Contbr. articles to profl. jours. Chmn. community service Hartford County Welcome Wagon, Bel Air, 1974-76, March of Dimes Walk-A-Thon, Bel Air, 1979-80, sch. adv. com. Forest Hill (Md.) Elem. Sch., 1980-81, food and clothes dr. St. Luke's Cath. Ch., Virginia Beach, 1986—; mgr. Joseph Tydings Senatorial campaign, College Park, Md., 1969-70; pres. PTA, 1979-80; sus. mem. Repub. Nat. Com. Named Outstanding Community Citizen, City of

Balt., 1981; recipient Outstanding Performance award, March of Dimes, 1979, 80. Mem. N.Y. Stock Exchange, Nat. Assn. Securities Dealers, Tidewater and Virginia Beach Bd. Realtors, Nat. Assn. Realtors, Women's Stockbrokers Nat. Assn, Fgn. Affairs Coun. Roman Catholic. Home: 884 Stacey Pl Virginia Beach VA 23464 Office: Armada/Hoffler 5555 Greenwich Rd Virginia Beach VA 23462 also: Sta WNVZ 5555 Greenwich Rd Virginia Beach VA 23462

MCLAUGHLIN, SANDRA LEE (SANDRA LEE GIBBONS), corporate sales professional; b. Houston, May 12, 1942; d. Howard Frances Thomas and Edith Eleanor (Sachs) Gibbons; (div.); 1 child, Mary Shannon. BS, U. Mo., 1966; cert. paralegal, Ariz. State U., 1976; postgrad., Washington U., St. Louis, 1966; cert. in advanced vol. mgmt., U. Colo., 1981. Fashion promotion dir. McGreevey, Werring & Howell, N.Y.C., 1967-70; dir. spl. events Diamond Dept. Stores, Phoenix, 1970-74; social svcs. supr. Dept. Pub. Housing City of Phoenix, 1974-76; pub. info. officer State of Ariz. Dept. of Econ. security, 1976-80; dir. vol. svcs. Ariz. State Hosp., Phoenix, 1980-84; sr. sales mgr. Carefree (Ariz.) Inn, 1984-85; dir. sales, mktg. Exec. Pk. Hotel, Phoenix, 1985-87; corp. sales mgr. Scottsdale (Ariz.) Embassy Stes., 1987-89; dir. sales and mktg. Embassy Stes. Hotel, Phoenix, 1990—; owner Studio 2, Phoenix, 1970—. Writer, producer and host (TV series) The Greenwitch, Phoenix, 1977; writer and host (TV segments) Kitchen Cosmetics/PM Mag., 1982-83); writer (booklet) Kitchen Cosmetics Mag., 1983. Pres. Wesley Community Ctr., Phoenix, 1974-76; bd. dirs. YWCA, Phoenix, 1984-85; mem. Govs. Coun. Volunteerism, Phoenix, 1982-84; co-founder Compeer/Ariz., 1983, Phoenix, 1983; sec. Sojourner Ctr. for Battered Women, Phoenix, 1987-89, numerous others. Freedom Foundation Scholar, Searcy, Ark., 1958, Recipient Doc Dunham award, Maricopa County Community Coun., Phoenix, 1982. Mem. Meeting Planners Internat. (editor newsletter Sunbelt chpt. 1988-89, chmn. communications 1989—, Supplier of Yr. 1989), Dirs. of Vols. in Agys. Pres, Gamma Phi Beta. Home: 1920 E Maryland Ave Phoenix AZ 85016 Office: Embassy Stes Hotel 1515 N 44th St Phoenix AZ 85008

MCLAUGHLIN, SHARON GAIL, principal, small business owner; b. Little Rock, Jan. 2, 1946; d. William Harry and Marion Virginia (Johnson) Fowler; m. Elbert Leroy Anderson, Apr. 3, 1969 (div. 1975); 1 child, William Eric; m. James Jerry McLaughlin, Nov. 22, 1986; stepchildren: James J., Monique C. McLaughlin Hill. BA, Baker U., Baldwin City, Kans., 1968; MA, U. Mo., Kansas City, 1976; postgrad., U. Cen. Ark., Conway, 1987. Tchr. Kansas City (Mo.) Sch. Dist., 1968-77; dir. recruiting Lincoln U., Jefferson City, Mo., 1977-78; tchr., dept. chmn. Magnet Sch., Kansas City, 1978-79; asst. prin. Pulaski County Sch. Dist., Little Rock, 1979-87; prin. Little Rock Sch. Dist., 1987—; owner L Image Ltd, Little Rock, 1989—; cons. in field. Producer/dir.: Take: Teen, Bridging the Gap, 1980—; cons., writer video on minority tchrs., 1989; author prog. for women, Prisms, 1980, prog. for youth, Kaleidescope III, 1980. Named Outstanding Black Arkansan, Women in Motion, 1988, Outstanding Educator, Ark. PTA, 1988, Mrs. Ark. Am., 1990. Mem. NAACP, Nat. Assn. Black Sch. Educators, Student Adminstrs. Assn. (prog. chmn. 1986-87), Nat. Assn. Sec. Sch. Prins., Smithsonian Assocs., Urban League of Mo.-Ark., Alpha Kappa Alpha, Phi Delta Kappa. Democrat. AME Ch. Home: 2705 Chester St Little Rock AR 72206 Office: Southwest Jr High Sch PO Box 164920 Little Rock AR 72216-4920

MCLAUGHLIN, SUZANNE GILMORE, hospital administrator; b. Worcester, Mass., Oct. 8, 1945; d. Richard Fay and Ruth Myrtle (Rogers) Gilmore; m. George Bovard McLaughlin, May 18, 1985. BS in Nursing, St. Olaf Coll., Northfield, Minn., 1967; MBA, Boston U., 1977. Staff nurse Columbia Presbyn. Hosp., N.Y.C., 1967-68; asst. head nurse NYU Med. Ctr., N.Y.C., 1968-69; staff nurse, sr. staff nurse, head nurse, clin. leader Mass. Gen. Hosp., Boston, 1970-76; br. mgr. Medox, Inc., Boston, 1977-78; dir. nursing Goddard Meml. Hosp., Stoughton, Mass., 1978-85, v.p., 1985—; mem. adv. bd. Massasoit Community Coll., Brockton, Mass., 1979—, Stonehill Coll. Profl. Adv. Com., Easton, Mass., 1984-87. Editor MONE Resource Directory, 1983, 84, 85; editor Focus, 1982-84. Bd. dirs. Brockton Vis. Nurse Assn., 1986—; mem. Mass. Cultural Alliance, Boston, 1980—. Mem. Am. Orgn. Nurse Execs. (bd. dirs. 1990—), Mass. Orgn. Nurse Execs. (pres. 1989-90, past pres. 1990—, bd. dirs. 1990—), Tri-Coun. (chmn. 1989-90). Home: 10 Woodcrest Dr North Oxford MA 01537 Office: Goddard Meml Hosp 909 Sumner St Stoughton MA 02072

MCLAURIN, MARTHA REGINA, parking service company executive; b. Raleigh, N.C., Feb. 17, 1948; d. William Lentis and Martha Catherine (Hester) McL. BA, Meth. Coll., 1970. V.p., chief fin. officer McLaurin Parking Co., Inc., Raleigh, 1970—; dir. So. Nat. Bank, Cary, N.C., 1980—. Pres. bd. dirs. Raleigh Mchts. Bur., 1988-89; mem. Cary Town Coun., 1987—; chmn. Wake County Planning Bd., 1983-86. Named Outstanding Bus. Alumnus Meth. Coll., 1985, Cary's Outstanding Woman Cary Jaycettes, 1984. Mem. Nat. Parking Assn. (dir. 1979—, pres. 1989—), Parking Ind. Inst. (bd. dirs. 1987-89), Zonta (bd. dirs. 1987-89). Office: McLaurin Parking Co Inc PO Box 781 Raleigh NC 27602

MCLEAN, JANET K., marketing director; b. Atlanta, Aug. 3, 1953; d. James Hannis and Mary Owen (VanHoose) McL. BS, E. Tenn. State U., 1975. Asst. dir. mktg. West Oaks Hosp., Houston, 1983-85; dir. mktg. Belle Park Hosp., Houston, 1985-87; v.p. mktg. Northlake Regional Med. Ctr., Atlanta, 1988—; dir. devel. Hosp. Corp. Am., Nashville, 1987-88. Mem. Atlanta Ski Club. Office: Northlake Regional Med Ctr 1455 Montreal Rd Atlanta GA 30085

MCLEER, LAUREEN DOROTHY, marketing professional; b. N.Y.C., Feb. 5, 1955; d. William Myers and Una Lee (Massey) McL. BS, Columbia U., 1977; MBA, U. London, 1981. RN, N.Y.; state registered nurse Eng., Wales. Staff nurse NYU Med. Ctr., N.Y.C., 1977-78; charge nurse Scripps Clinic and Rsch. Found., La Jolla, Calif., 1979-80; clin. researcher Ayerst Labs., N.Y.C., 1982-83; sales rep. Pfizer, Inc., N.Y.C., 1983-87, Cahners Pub. Co., N.Y.C., 1988-89; dir. bus. devel. Pro Clinica, N.Y.C., 1990—. Chmn. Help Our Neighbors Eat Yr. 'Round, N.Y.C., 1987-89; trustee Murray Hill Com., N.Y.C., 1988-90; bd. dir. East Midtown Svcs. for Older People, 1987-90. Mem. AACCN, Pharm. Advt. Coun., East Midtown Svcs. for Older People (bd. dirs. 1987—). Home: 137 E 38th St New York NY 10016 Office: Pro Clinica 51 E 42d St New York NY 10017

MCLELLAN, CONNIE RAE, sales executive; b. Grand Island, Nebr., July 27, 1950; d. Bruce Gerald McLellan and Peggy Eileen (Robb) Harvatin; m. James R. Hixson, Oct. 11, 1968 (div. 1974); 1 child, Christopher James. BS, U. Nebr., 1972. Sales rep. Xerographic Supply, Denver, 1974-79; sales mgr. Communications Corp. of Am., Denver, 1979-81; regional mgr. Am. Techs., Denver, 1981-84; account exec. Bell South Communications, Dallas, 1984-89; sales exec. Centel Communications, Dallas, 1989—; v.p. Salesmen With a Purpose, Denver, 1976-80. Vol. Rep. Party, Dallas, 1984-88, 500, Inc., Dallas, 1990—; fundraiser Multiple Sclerosis Found., Denver, 1976-80; speaker Family Pl. Women's Shelter, Dallas, 1986. Mem. 500, Inc. Methodist. Home: 18749 Marsh Ln #1314 Dallas TX 75287

MCLELLAN, KRISTIN LYNN, magnetic resonance imaging technologist; b. South Weymouth, Mass., Aug. 31, 1966; d. John Bruce and Nancy Hobart (Bullard) Allen; m. Joseph G. McLellan, Jr., June 11, 1988. AS in Nuclear Med. Tech., Mass. Coll. Pharmacy, Boston, 1987. Cert. nuclear medicine technologist. Nuclear medicine technologist Mass. Gen. Hosp., Boston, 1986-88, Strong Meml. Hosp., Univ. Rochester, N.Y., 1988-89, Apollo Imaging Inc., Abington, Mass., 1989-90; magnetic resonance technologist Brockton Regional MRI, Brockton, Mass., 1989—. Active Nat. Arbor Day Assn., Nebraska City, Nebr., 1990. Recipient Achievement award, Gamma Diagnostics, 1986. Mem. Soc. Nuclear Medicine, Soc. Magnetic Resonance Imaging, Greenpeace. Home: 2 Pierce Ave Plymouth MA 02360 Office: Brockton Regional MRI 265 Westgate Dr Brockton MA 02401

MCLEMORE, TERESA SUE, accountant; b. Red Cloud, Nebr., Feb. 14, 1962; d. LeRoy Lawrence and Mary Ann (McCain) Hubl; m. James David McLemore, July 14, 1982; children: James Darrin, Amy Jean. AS (Magna Cum Laude), S.W. Okla. STate U., 1987; BA (Cum Laude), S.W. Okla. State U., 1990. Inventory crew 7-11 Convenience Stores, Okla. City, Okla., 1982-83; dept. head T G and Y, Elk City, Okla., 1983-86; clerk typist Farmers Home Adminstr., Sayre, Okla., 1986-89; guest service mgr. Holiday Inn, Elk City, Okla.; acct. Robert L. McGee, CPA, Yukon, Okla., 1989-90; comptr. Lincoln Petroleum Resources Corp., Yukon, Okla., 1990—. Mem. Women's Guild, St. Matthew's Ch., 1983--. Mem. Nat. Bus. Educator Assn., Bus. and Profl. Women's Assn., Gamma Delta Kappa, Alpha Phi Sigma. Democrat. Catholic. Home: 8102 Chukar Rd Yukon OK 73099

MCLEOD, CHERYL O'HALLORAN, artist; b. Greensburg, Pa., Nov. 12, 1944. BA in Art Edn., Ind. U., Pa., 1966; postgrad., Mass. Coll. Art, 1983-84, Boston U., 1967. Art instr. Mother Seton Regional Girls Cath. High Sch., Clark, N.J., 1990—; workship instr. Ghost Ranch Conf. Ctr., Abiquiu, N.Mex., 1988-89, Mid-West Pastel Soc., Palatine, Ill., 1989, Wilmette (Ill.) Hist. Soc., 1988, N.Mex. Art League, Albuquerque, 1987; high sch. art instr., Reading, Mass., 1981-84; elem. sch. art instr., Westford, Mass., 1966-68. Exhibited in numerous shows including Pastel Soc. Am., N.Y.C., 1988, 89, Mid-West Pastel Soc. Members Show, Libertyville, Ill., 1989, Studio-in-the-Woods, Wauconda, Ill., 1989, Talman Home Savs. Instn., Chgo., 1989, The Kemper Group, Long Grove, Ill., 1989, Art Ctr., Elk Grove, Ill., 1989, Levy Ctr., Evanston, Ill., 1989, U. Ariz., Tucson, 1988, Am. Artist Profl. League, N.Y.C., 1988, Ariz. Aqueous '88, Tubac, 1988, and others; prin. works represented in several pub. and pvt. collections. Mem. Arts Coun. Rockland, Pastel Soc. Am. (juried assoc.), Am. Artist Profl. League (juried artist), Allied Artists Am., Mid-West Pastel Soc., Chgo. Artist Coalition, Delta Phi Delta. Home: 143 Lake Nanuet Nanuet NY 10954

MCLEOD, DEBORAH JACKSON, museum official; b. Little Compton, R.I., Aug. 20, 1915; d. Eugene Bailey and Caroline Wilbour (Patten) Jackson; grad. pvt. schs.; m. Harry McIntosh McLeod, June 19, 1934 (dec.); 1 dau., Penelope McLeod Beekman; m. 2d, Wilfred A. Dunderdale, May 19, 1980. With dept. reprodns. Met. Mus., N.Y.C., 1962-63; adminstrv. asst. U.S. Com. for UNICEF, 1955-59; mem. exec. com. Bklyn. Mus., 1974-77, gov., 1975-77; mem. exec. com. council of friends Inst. Fine Arts, N.Y. U. Pierpont Morgan Library fellow, 1975-87; former mem. Friends of Asia Soc. Mem. Am. Assn. Museums (assoc.), Internat. Council Museums, Nat. Soc. Colonial Dames of Am., Clan MacLeod Soc. U.S.A., Inc. (hon.), Friend of the Frick Collection, Royal Oak Found., U.S. Assoc. of the Royal Acad. of Art London, Albert Gallatin Assocs., Colony Club, Lotos Club. Presbyterian.

MCLEOD, KATE, publishing executive; b. Boston, Dec. 16, 1944; d. David John and Alice Mary (Jones) Roach; m. John Eckner, 1970 (div. 1977); m. Jerry Meyer Flint, 1987. BA, Mt. St. Mary Coll., Hooksett, N.H., 1968; MFA, Cath. U., 1975. Promotions dir. Instl. Investor, N.Y.C., 1976-80; creative svc. mgr. Progressive Grocer, N.Y.C., 1980-81; spl. sect. mgr. Forbes Mag., N.Y.C., 1981-83; sales devel. supr. Time Mag., N.Y.C., 1984-86; pres. Delano, McLeod & Strausser, Inc., N.Y.C., 1986—. Mem. Women in Communications.

MCLEOD, LAURA LYNN, sales executive; b. Hartford, Conn., Jan. 22, 1959; d. Henry Laurence; 1 child, Candi Lynn Nickerson. Student, S. Windsor high sch., Conn.; Student, Manchester Community Coll., 1980. Cert. real estate broker, N.Y. Br. mgr. Sarah Coventry, Windsor Locks, Conn., 1976-78; area coord. Jewels by Parklane, Windsor Locks, Conn.; quality assurance United Technol., East Hartford, Conn., 1978-81; dir. sales Am. Profl. Mktg., Mass., 1981-83; sales Levitz Furniture, Garden City, N.Y., 1983-85; dir. consumer relations House of Grossman, Ltd., Farmingdale, N.Y., 1985-87; exec. v.p. Am. Networking Assocs., Farmingdale, N.Y., 1987—; cons. Nu Skin Internat., Provo, Utah, 1985, Internat. Cons. Exchange, San Diego, 1986-87; real estate sales Realty Group Cons., 1986. Author: Manual, Beginner's Guide to Network Mktg., 1985. Devel. coord. Life-Care Hospice, 1989; mem. Rte. 110 Action, Long Island N.Y. 1988—. Recipient Achievement award Am. Profl. Mktg., 1982, Levitz Furniture Corp., 1985; Outstanding Svc. award Internat. Cons. Exchange, 1986, Nat. Champions award, 1986. Mem. NAFE (network coord.). Republican. Office: Am Networking Assocs 5000 Hempstead Turnpike Farmingdale NY 11735

MCLEOD, RIMA L., physician, scientist, educator; b. Berkeley, Calif., Sept. 14, 1945; d. Ralph Waldo and Rose (Oringel) Weilerstein; m. Evan George McLeod, Sept. 9, 1967; children: Allegra Marie, Derin Bennet. AB in Zoology, U. Calif., Berkeley, 1967; MD, U. Calif., San Francisco, 1971. Diplomate Nat. Bd. Med. Examiners, Am. Bd. Internal Medicine. Resident in medicine U. Pa., Phila., 1971-73, U. Calif., San Francisco, 1973-74; fellow in infectious diseases Stanford (Calif.) U., 1975-78; attending physician Michael Reese Hosp., Chgo., 1978—; from asst. to assoc. prof. medicine U. Chgo., 1978—; cons. FDA, 1988—; mem. tropical medicine parasitol study sect. NIH-NIAID, 1989—. Contbr. articles to profl. jours., chpt. to book. Bank of Am. Giannini Found. fellow, 1977; grantee NIH, March of Dimes, FDA, 1979—. Fellow Am. Coll. Physicians, Infectious Diseases Soc. Am.; mem. AAAS, Am. Assn. immunologists, Cen. Soc. Clin. Rsch., Am. Soc. Microbiology, Chgo. Assn. Immunologists, Phi Beta Kappa. Office: Michael Reese Hosp 114 Baumgarten Lake Shore Dr at 31st St Chicago IL 60616

MCLEROY, BARBRE STRINGFELLOW, infosystems specialist; b. Atlanta, Feb. 18, 1953; d. Arthur King Jr. and Ethelyn Calloway (Lindsey) Stringfellow; m. Michael Dennis McLeroy Sr., June 28, 1975. BS, U. Ga., 1975. Data flow coord. Bd. Regents U. Ga., Athens, 1975-77, programmer, 1977-79, EDP projects analyst, 1979—. Active Focus on the Family, Calif., 1984, Precept Ministries, Tenn., 1984; supporter Intervarsity Christian Fellowship, Wis., 1984. Mem. Assn. for Computing Machinery, Concerned Women for Am., Phi Beta Kappa, Phi Kappa Phi. Office: U Ga Coll Bus Adminstrn Computer Ctr Athens GA 30602

MCLERRAN, ALICE ENDERTON, children's writer; b. West Point, N.Y., June 24, 1933; d. Herbert Bronson and Marian Irene (Doan) Enderton; m. Larry Dean McLerran, May 8, 1976. Student, Stanford U., 1950-51, 52-53; BA, U. Calif., Berkeley, 1960, PhD, 1969; MPH, Harvard U., 1974. Cert. in psychiat. epidemiology. Asst. prof. anthropology SUNY, Cortland, 1969-72; rsch. analyst Nursing Home Ombudsman Project, Boston, 1974-75; evaluator children's svcs. Mass. Mental Health Ctr., Boston, 1975-77, chief evaulation, 1978; lectr. anthropology dept. psychiatry Sch. Medicine, Harvard U., Boston, 1977-78, lectr. health svcs. Sch. Pub. Health, 1978-78. Author: The Mountain That Loved a Bird, 1985, Roxaboxen, 1990. Woodrow Wilson fellow, 1965. Mem. Soc. Children's Book Writers, Phi Beta Kappa. Home and Office: 2524 Colfax Ave E Minneapolis MN 55405

MCLOONE, JEANNE HOWE, interior designer, realtor; b. Newark, Aug. 18, 1950; d. William Benjamin and Gloria Mae (Vela) Howe; m. Mark Edward McLoone, July 8, 1975 (div. July 1982); 1 child, Angus Howe. BA, Mary Baldwin Coll., Staunton, Va., 1972. Asst. office mgr. Baker & Botts, Washington, 1973-74; asst. interior designer Jane Zivney Interiors, Phoenix, 1975-78; pres. Jeanne McLoone Designs, Inc., 1979—; interior designer, salesperson Barrow's Furniture, Phoenix, 1983—; realtor Merrill Lynch Realty, 1987—; interior designer Rosson House; customer svc. rep. Am. West Airlines, Phoenix. Mem. Phoenix Art Mus., 1978—, league bd. 1982, co-chmn. Festival of Trees, 1982, chmn. Benefactor's Trees Com., 1986; active Hospice of Valley Ann. Fall Fundraiser. Recipient cert. Assuiduité Institut de Touraine, Tours, France, 1967. Mem. Inst. Bus. Designers (affiliate). Republican. Episcopalian. Avocations: tennis, skiing, sailing, gourmet cooking, travel. Home: 6134 N 13th St Phoenix AZ 85014 Office: Barrow's Exec Furniture 2301 E Camelback Phoenix AZ 85016 also: Merrill Lynch Realty 3165 E Lincoln Dr Phoenix AZ 85016

MCMACHEN, KAY ANN, weight management center executive; b. Kalamazoo, Feb. 9, 1952; d. Walter Adelbert and Anastasia Julia (Kovarik) McM. BS, Eastern Mich. U., 1984, MS, 1986. Lic. psychologist, Mich. Adminstrv. sec. Eastern Mich. U., Ypsilanti, 1974-86; psychologist Mid Mich. Regional Med. Ctr., Midland, 1987-88, mgr., psychologist, 1988-90; mgr., psychologist HCA Coliseum Med. Ctr., Macon, Ga., 1990—; advisor Women's Health Ctr., Midland, 1988—. Facilitator Vis. Nurse Assn., Midland, 1989. Mem. NAFE, Internat. Assn. Eating Disorder Profls. Home: 143 W Ridge Circle Macon GA 31210 Office: HCA Coliseum Med Ctr 350 Coliseum Dr Macon GA 31201

MCMACKIN, LILLIAN FRANCIS, retired pediatrician; b. New Bedford, Mass., Feb. 23, 1915; d. Antone and Mary Paiva Francis; m. John F.X. McMackin; children: John, Thomas, Robert. BA, Wellesly (Mass.) Coll., 1937; MD, Boston U., 1941. Diplomate Am. Bd. Pediatrics. Gen. rotating intern Mercy Hosp., Pitts., 1941-43; gen. intern Children's Med. Ctr., Boston, 1943-44, asst. resident, 1944-45; pvt. practice Quincy, Mass., 1945-87; sch. physician Milton (Mass.) Sch., 1945-50, Quincy Sch. Physician, 1950-60, Boston U., 1960-61.

MCMAHAN, SUE EVON, travel agency executive; b. McMinnville, Oreg., Apr. 9, 1962; d. James Donald and Delores Ann (Miller) McM. BA, Linfield Coll., 1984. Jr. acct. J. Ormiston, Beaverton, Oreg., 1985; analyst Rosenbluth Travel Agy Inc, Portland, Oreg., 1985—; cons. Evergreen Internat. Aviation, McMinnville, Oreg., 1989. Fellow DAR; mem. Internat. Air Transport Assn., Airline Reporting Corp., Nat. Assn. Female Execs., Linfield Coll. Alumni Assn., Phi Sigma Sigma (shcolarship chmn. 1983-84). Republican. Roman Catholic. Office: Rosenbluth Travel Agy Inc 1991 Arch St Philadelphia PA 19103

MCMAHON, ANN MARIE, technical communicator, consultant; b. Hancock, Mich., July 11, 1950; d. John Michael and Winifred Mary (McGinty) McM. Diploma in nursing, St. Joseph Hosp. Sch. Nursing, 1971; BA in Tech. Communication, Mich. Tech. U., 1981. From sales clk. to asst. mgr. Twin City Style Shop, Hancock, 1964-71; nurse Rochester (Minn.) Meth. Hosp., 1971, Calumet Pub. Hosp., Laurium, Mich.; paramedic Mercy Ambulance, Keweenaw County, Mich., 1979; owner, mgr. Robert's Mobile Homes, Calumet, Mich., 1976-79; asst. mgr. Twin City Style Shop, Hancock, 1976-81; tech. writer Control Data Corp., Mpls., 1981-84; program mgr. Plato-Wicat Systems Co., Mpls., 1984-86; mgr. prodecures and records aviation div. Honeywell Corp., Mpls., 1986—. Author, editor: Keweenaw Tour Guide. Mem. Assn. Records Mgrs.' and Adminstrs. Internat. (pub. speaker Mpls. and New Orleans 1988-89, pub. rels. officer 1989—), Sci. and Tech. Communications Soc. Roman Catholic. Home: 9925 Russell Ave N #7 Brooklyn Park MN 55444 Office: Honeywell Comml Flight 8840 Evergreen Blvd Coon Rapids MN 55433

MCMAHON, BERNICE GEORGIA, freelance writer, retired educator; b. Davenport, Iowa, Jan. 29, 1917; d. George Henry and Bertha Anna (Jacobsen) Moore; m. Robert James McMahon, Aug. 29, 1943 (dec. 1977); children: Mary Alison, Robert Moore. Student, Augustana Coll., Rock Island, Ill., 1934-35, St. Ambrose Coll., Davenport, Iowa, 1936-38; BA cum laude, U. Iowa, 1940; postgrad., UCLA, 1953, 58, 67. Tchr. Scott County Schs., Iowa, 1935-38, 40-42, Centerville (Iowa) Sch., 1942-43; recreation dir. Chambersburg (Pa.) Recreation Dept., 1952; tchr. elem. sch., Torrance, Calif., 1954-55, Manhattan Beach, Calif., 1955-56; substitute tchr. Wiseburn Sch. Dist., Hawthorne, Calif., 1956-82; freelance writer, 1947—. Author: Everybody's Laughing, 1966, Laugh It Up, 1969; (play) Look Out for the Great Computer, 1977; contbr. articles to various publs., 1947—. Mem. Women's Fellowship of Manhattan Beach Community Ch., pres., 1988. Mem. AAUW (br. pres. 1954), AFTRA, Calif. State Tchrs. Ret., Manuscripters (sec. 1961-61), Calif. State Contesters Assn. (pres. 1978), L.A. Contesters Club (pres. 1957), Manhattan Players (sec. 1957), Windy Bayans (pres. 1962-82), Phi Beta Kappa. Democrat. Mem. United Ch. of Christ. Home and Office: 903 14th St Hermosa Beach CA 90254

MCMAHON, MARGHE MAY, sculptor; b. Palo Alto, Calif., May 7, 1954; d. Merritt Norval and Ruth Evelyn McMahon. BA in Psychobiology, U. Calif., Santa Cruz, 1975, postgrad., 1977-78. Biologist, neuropharmacology Syntex Rsch., Palo Alto, 1975-76; freelance artist Santa Cruz, Calif., 1976-81; sculptor, modelmaker Lucas Film, San Rafael, Calif., 1981—, 20th Century Fox Orion, Chris Walas Inc., L.A., 1983-88; freelance sculptor San Francisco, 1981-88. Sculptor, modelmaker GJP Prodns., Gaffney, S.C., Westport, Wash., 1988, Premavision, Sausalito, Calif., 1987, 88; painter/model maker Colossal Pictures, San Francisco, 1986, USFX, San Francisco, 1985, Indsl. Light & Magic, San Rafael, Calif., 1985; painter Rob Bottin Prodns., L.A., Dallas, Pitts., 1986, Indsl. Light & Magic, San Rafael, 1984; sculptor Indsl. Light & Magic, San Rafael, 1985; others. Home: 2382 45th Ave San Francisco CA 94116

MCMAHON, MARY FRANCES, state legislator, lawyer; b. Providence, Apr. 2, 1955; d. Paul Bernard and Mary Patrice (Schuette) McM. B.A., St. Mary's Coll., 1977; J.D., Suffolk U., Boston, 1980. Bar: R.I. 1980, Mass. 1980. Assoc. McMahon, Hendel & Mc Mahon, Pawtucket, R.I., 1980—; mem. R.I. Ho. of Reps., 1981—, chairwoman house com. on spl. legis., 1989—; lectr. R.I. Coll., Community Coll. R.I., 1986, R.I. Sch. Real Estate, 1987. Co-author: Welcome to Our House: An Introductory Guide to the Legislative Process, 1985, Welcome to Our House, 2nd edit., 1990. Chmn. Adv. Bd. Library Commrs., 1981—; mem. Nat. Conf. State Legislatures, 1981—; mem. rules com. Dem. Nat. Com., 1984; del. Dem. Nat. Conv., 1988, alt. del., 1984. Named Legislator of Yr. R.I. Libr. Assn., 1984, 85, Outstanding Young Alumna, St. Mary's Coll., 1985. Mem. R.I. Bar Assn., Mass. Bar Assn. Roman Catholic. Office: DEM Adjudication Adminstrn Bldg One Capitol Hill Providence RI 02908

MCMAHON, PATRICIA, photographer, photography educator; b. White Plains, N.Y., Feb. 6, 1959; d. Edward Joseph and Jean Mary (McLaughlin) McM. BFA, SUNY, Purchase, 1985. Black and white lab technician Cen. Color, White Plains, 1985-87; art instr. Nor-West Sch. for Handicapped, Yorktown Heights, N.Y., 1986-87; freelance photographer Hastings-on-Hudson, N.Y., 1987—; instr. photography Rye (N.Y.) Art Ctr., 1988—. Represented in juried exhbns. at The Gallery at Hastings-on-Hudson, 1986, Cabrini Gallery, Dobbs Ferry, N.Y., 1987, Neikrug Photographica, N.Y.C., 1989. Home and Studio: 21 Pleasant Ave Hastings-on-Hudson NY 10706

MCMANAMA, TRUDY E., psychologist; b. Pitts., Mar. 30, 1945; d. Francis J. and Mary Margaret (McDonough) Figura; m. Patick J. McManama, Nov. 25, 1967 (div. 1977); 1 child, Steven Patrick. B.S., Mansfield U., 1967; M.S., So. Conn. U., 1973, postgrad., 1974. Tchr. New Milford Schs., Conn., 1967-69, Shepaug Valley High Sch., Washington Depot, Conn., 1969-72; tng. cons. Danbury Area Unified Social Svcs., Conn., 1971-72; psychologist Bd. Coop. Svcs., Poughkeepsie, N.Y., 1974-75; psychologist Berrien County Ind. Sch. Dist., Berrien Springs, Mich., 1975—; cons. Stanley Clark Sch., South Bend, Ind., 1981-88; adj. prof. Ind. U., South Bend, 1979—; instr. St. Joseph Hosp., South Bend, 1985-87; elected trustee South Bend Sch. Corp., 1987, pres. 1989. Vol. Internat. Spl. Olympics, 1987; pres., Neighborhood Watch Program, South Bend, 1982-83; hospice vol., South Bend; bd. dirs. Child Abuse and Neglect Coordination Orgn., South Bend, 1986—; mem. Selective Svc. Bd., 1989; mem. Handicapped Camping Bd., 1986—; mem. Dem. Precinct Com., South Bend, 1980-82; del. Ind. Dem. State Conv., 1984. Berrien County Task Force grantee, 1979. Mem. Assn. Supervision and Curriculum Devel., NAFE, Nat. Assn. Sch. Psychologists. Democrat. Roman Catholic. Avocations: jogging, reading, cross country skiing. Home: 2725 Erskine Blvd South Bend IN 46614 Office: Berrien County Imtermediate Sch Dist 711 St Joseph Ave Berrien Springs MI 49103

MCMANIGAL, SHIRLEY ANN, college dean; b. Deering, Mo., May 4, 1938; d. Jadie C. and Willie B. (Groves) Naile. BS, Ark. State U., 1971; MS, U. Okla., 1976, PhD, 1979. Lic. med. technologist, clin. lab. dir. Med. technologist, 1958-75; chair dept. med. tech. U. So. Miss., Hattiesburg, 1979-83; chair dept. med. tech. Tex. Tech. U. Health Scis. Ctr., Lubbock, 1983-87, dean Sch. Allied Health, 1987—. Recipient Citation, State of Tex., 1988; named Woman of Yr., AAUW, Tex. div., 1990, Woman of Excellence in Edn. YWCA, Lubbock, 1990. Mem. Clin. Lab. Mgmt. Assn. (chair edn. com. 1989, 91), Am. Soc. Med. Tech., Nat. Assn. Women Deans, Adminstrs. and Counselors (mem. membership com.), So. Assn. Allied Health Deans at Acad. Health Ctrs., S.W. Assn. Clin. Microbiology, Tex. Soc. Allied Health Professions (pres. elect 1989-90), Tex. Soc. Med. Tech. (educator of yr. 1990). Home: 5402 86th St Lubbock TX 79424 Office: Tex Tech U Health Scis Ctr Sch Allied Health Lubbock TX 79430

MCMANUS, SISTER MARGARET MARY, hospital executive; b. N.Y.C., Nov. 28, 1932; d. Thomas J. and Bridget F. (McGoey) McM. BBA, St. Bonaventure U., 1968; MHA, U. Minn., 1970. Joined Franciscan Sisters, Roman Cath. Ch., 1950. Bus. mgr., controller St. Joseph's Hosp., Providence, 1951-61, adminstr., 1961-66; asst. adminstr. St. Joseph's Hosp., Tampa, Fla., 1970-72; adminstr. St. Francis Hosp., Miami Beach, Fla., 1972-83, chief exec. officer, 1983—; bd. dirs. Cath. Hospice Miami, Fla. Mem.

Miami Beach Health Adv. Com. Fellow Am. Coll. Healthcare Execs. Roman Catholic. Office: St Francis Hosp 250 W 63d St Miami Beach FL 33141

MCMANUS, MARY CHRISTINE, industrial engineer; b. Hollywood, Fla., Oct. 31, 1962; d. Walter James and Judith Ann (Weisenberger) Easterly; m. Robert McManus, July 5, 1986. BS, Va. Poly. Inst. and State U., 1985. Indsl. engr. AT&T Techs., Radford, Va.; asst. cons., asst. editor R.J. Rudden Assocs., Arlington, Va.; sr. indsl. engr. Organon Teknika Corp., Durham, N.C.; pvt. practice desktop pub., tech. writing and editing. Active Wake County Literacy Coun. Mem. NAFE, Inst. Indsl. Engrs. (sr.; past pres.-elect and chair honors and awards, now newsletter editor), Capital Area Network for Exec. Women (bd. dirs.), Soc. for Tech. Communication (chair tech. art competition, publicity chair cons. and ind. contracting profl. interest com.). Democrat. Roman Catholic. Home: 7209 Mine Shaft Rd Raleigh NC 27615

MCMASTER, JULIET SYLVIA, English language educator; b. Kisumu, Kenya, Aug. 2, 1937; emigrated to Can., 1961, naturalized, 1976; d. Sydney Herbert and Sylvia (Hook) Fazan; m. Rowland McMaster, May 10, 1968; children: Rawdon, Lindsey. B.A. with honors, Oxford U., 1959; M.A., U. Alta., 1963, Ph.D., 1965. Asst. prof. English U. Alta., Edmonton, Can., 1965-70; assoc. prof. U. Alta., 1970-76, prof. English, 1976-86, Univ. prof., 1986—. Author: Thackeray: The Major Novels, 1971, (ed.) Jane Austen's Achievement, 1976, Jane Austen on Love, 1978, Trollope's Palliser Novels, 1978, (with R.D. McMaster) The Novel from Sterne to James, 1981, Dickens the Designer, 1987; contbr. articles to profl. jours. Can. Council fellow, 1969-70; Guggenheim fellow, 1976-77; Killam fellow, 1987-89. Fellow Royal Soc. Can.; mem. Victorian Studies Assn. Western Can. (founding pres. 1972), Assn. Can. Univ. Tchrs. English (pres. 1976-78), MLA, Jane Austen Soc. N.Am. (dir. 1980—). Office: U Alta, Dept English, Edmonton, AB Canada T6G 2E5

MCMATH, ELIZABETH MOORE, graphic artist; b. Iredell, Tex., Feb. 20, 1930; d. Fred William and Elizabeth Carol (Smith) Moore; m. Charles Wallis McMath, Jan. 16, 1978; children: Charles Wallis, John Seals. BA, BS in Advt. Design, Tex. Woman's U., Denton, 1951; grad. gemologist, Gemol. Inst. Am., L.A., 1977. Layout artist Leonard's Dept. Store, Ft. Worth, Tex., 1951-52; artist/bookkeeper Bud Biggs Studio, Dallas, 1953; sec./artist Squire Haskins Studio, Dallas, 1953-54; artist/art dir. Dowdell-Merrill, Inc., Dallas, 1954-58; owner/artist Moore Co., Dallas, 1958-90. Mem. Stemmons Corridor Bus. Assn., Dallas, 1988-89. Mem. Dallas/Ft. Worth Soc. Visual Communication (founder), Tex. Woman's U. Nat. Alumnae Assn., Greater N. Tex. Orchid Soc. (treas. 1987), Big D Unit of Daylily Growers of Dallas (sec. 1989-90), Am. Plant Life Soc., Native Plant Soc. Tex. Home: PO Box 1068 Denton TX 76202

MCMATH, VIRGINIA KATHERINE See ROGERS, GINGER

MCMEEKIN, DOROTHY, botany, plant pathology educator; b. Boston, Feb. 24, 1932; d. Thomas LeRoy and Vera (Crockatt) McM. B.A., Wilson Coll., 1953; M.A., Wellesley Coll., 1955; Ph.D., Cornell U., 1959. Asst. prof. Upsala Coll., East Orange, N.J., 1959-64, Bowling Green State U., Ohio, 1964-66; prof. natural sci. Mich. State U., East Lansing, 1966-89, prof. botany, plant pathology, 1989—. Author: Diego Rivera: Science and Creativity, 1985; contbr. articles to profl. jours. Mem. Am. Phytopath. Soc., Mycol. Soc. Am., Bot. Soc. Am., Mich. Bot. Soc. (bd. dirs. 1985—), Mich. Women's Studies Assn., Sigma Xi, Phi Kappa Phi. Home: 1055 Marigold St East Lansing MI 48823 Office: Mich State U Dept Botany-Plant Pathology 335 N Kedzie East Lansing MI 48824

MCMICHAEL, KELLY LEE, customer service representative; b. Bucyrus, Ohio, Sept. 22, 1964; d. Daryle Edward and B. Marie (Jacobs) Gangluff. Student, Bowling Green State U., 1982-84. Researcher, then payroll tax technician Control Data Corp., Balt., 1986-87; sr. payroll tax technician Control Data Corp., 1987, customer svc. rep., 1988—. Vol., Balt. United Way, 1986-88, Balt. chpt. ARC, 1986-88, Spl. Olympics, Balt., 1988. Republican. Lutheran. Home: 18 S Augusta Ave Baltimore MD 21229

MCMILLAN, ADELL, educational administrator; b. Portland, Oreg., June 22, 1933; d. John and Eunice A. (Hoyt) McM. AB in Social Sci., Whitman Coll., 1955; MS in Recreation Mgmt., U. Oreg., 1963. Program dir. Erb Meml. Union, U. Oreg., Eugen, 1955-68; program cons. Willard Straight Hall, Cornell U., Ithaca, N.Y., 1966-67; assoc. dir. Erb Meml. Union, U. Oreg., Eugene, 1968-75; dir. Erb Meml. Union, U. Oreg., 1975—. Editor, co-author: College Unions: Seventy-Five Years, 1989; interviewer, editor 20 oral history interviews, 1978. Bd. dirs. United Way, Lane County, Oreg., 1976-83, 87—, pres.,1982-83, 88-90. Named Woman of Yr. Lane County Coun. Orgns., Eugene, Oreg., 1985. Mem. Assn. Coll. Unions-Internat. (v.p. 1977-80, pres. 1981-82, Butts-Whiting award 1987), Zonta Club (pres. 1984-86, dist. treas. 1990—). Democrat. Episcopalian. Office: Univ. of Oreg Erb Meml Union Eugene OR 97403

MCMILLER, ANITA WILLIAMS, army officer, transportation professional, educator; b. Chgo., Dec. 23, 1946; d. Chester Leon and Marion Claudette (Martin) Williams; m. Robert Melvin McMiller, July 29, 1967 (div. 1980). BS in Edn., No. Ill. U., 1968; MBA, Fla. Inst. Tech., 1979; M of Mil. Arts and Scis., 1990. Social worker County of Cook, Chgo., 1968-69; recruiter, dir. personnel, analyst State of Ill., Chgo., 1969-75; commd. 1st lt. U.S. Army, 1975, advanced through grades to lt. col., 1991; platoon leader, motor officer, exec. officer 155th Transp. Co., Ft. Eustis, Va. and Okinawa, Japan, 1976-78; S-1 pers. and adminstrn. officer 38th Transp. Bn., Ft. Eustis, 1978-79; installation transp. officer, fin. mgr. 3d Armor Div., Hanau, Fed. Republic Germany, 1979-82; transp. co. comdr. Hanau, 1982-83; transp. plans officer Falls Church, Va., 1983-85; tour with Sea Land Corp., Menlo Park, N.J., 1985-86; dep. comdr., ops. officer Bremerhaven (Fed. Republic Germany) Terminal, 1986-89; instr. Cen. Tex. Coll., Hanau, Fed. Republic Germany, 1981-83, Phillips Bus. Coll., Alexandria, Va., 1983-84, City Colls. Chgo., 1987-89, U.S. Army Command and Gen. Staff Coll., 1990; staff officer logistics, The Pentagon, 1990—. Contbr. articles to profl. jours. Child advocate, foster mother Army Community Service, Hanau, 1980-83; tutor Parent-Tchr. Club Hanau Schs., 1981-83; vol. Vis. Nurses Assn. No. Va., 1983-85; coordinator, English tutor Adopt-a-Sch. Project, Washington, 1983-85; treas. Bremerhaven Girl Scouts Coun., 1987-89. Mem. Nat. Def. Transp. Assn., Assn. U.S. Army, Fedn. Bus. Profl. Women, Alpha Kappa Alpha (treas. 1982-83). Home: 1935 Columbia Pike Apt 21 Arlington VA 22204

MCMORRIN, MAUREEN PETERSEN, telecommunications executive; b. Bklyn., July 17, 1955; d. Solomon B. Jr. and Mildred (Booth) Petersen; children: Nicole McMorrin, Allen McMorrin. BS in Elem. Edn., Adelphi U., 1977; postgrad., Howard County Community Coll., Columbia, Md., 1986. Cert. elem. tchr., N.Y. Elem. tchr. C.B. Jones Day Care Ctr., Amityville, N.Y., 1977-78; claims supr. Mut. of Omaha Ins. Co., Rockville, Md., 1978-82; group ins. mgr. Manor Care, Inc., Silver Spring, Md., 1982-86; sr. mgr. benefits adminstrn. MCI Communications Corp., Washington, 1986—. Participant internship program Internat. Found. Employee Benefits, 1989; mem. managed care com. Nat. Capital Area Regional Health Coalition, 1988; petitioneer Md. Citizen Action Coalition, Howard County, 1989. Mem. Am. Mgmt. Assn. (assoc.), NAFE, NBAC Black Human Resource Profls., Alpha Kappa Alpha (basilus of Kappa Epsilon 1975). Democrat. Methodist. Office: MCI Communications Corp 1133 19th St NW Washington DC 20036

MCMORRIS, GRACE ELIZABETH, banker; b. Malden, Mass., Feb. 6, 1922; d. John Edward and Selma Florence (Swanson) O'Brien; B.A., Boston U., 1944; postgrad. Ariz. State U., 1962; m. William Michael McMorris, May 14, 1944 (dec.); children—Sheila Elizabeth McMorris Christenson, Michael, James, John. Clk., Parlin Meml. Library, Everett, Mass., part-time, 1938-40; clk. student post office Boston U., 1941-42; supr. classified advt. desk The Boston Post, 1942-44; substitute tchr. public schs., Randolph, Mass., 1956-57; with Valley Nat. Bank Ariz., Phoenix, 1960-87, trust adminstr., 1969-73, trust officer, 1973-75, asst. v.p., 1975-78, v.p., 1978-87, corporate trust mgr., 1977-87, ret., 1987. cons. in field, 1988-89. Mem. Am. Soc. Corp. Secs. (pres., treas. Phoenix chpt. 1989-90, v.p.), Pi Lambda Sigma (nat. treas. 1947-48). Roman Catholic. Office: Valley Nat Bank Ariz 241 N Central Ave Phoenix AZ 85004

MCMORROW, BARBARA JEAN, educator; b. Kew Gardens, N.Y., Mar. 13, 1947; d. William and Alfreda (Weinstein) Sotnick; m. Joseph Patrick McMorrow, Mar. 17, 1978. AA, Monmouth Coll., 1969, BS, 1970, MAT, 1976; postgrad., Georgian Court Coll., Lakewood, N.J., 1985-88. Cert. secondary English tchr., prin., supr., N.J.; cert. in mgmt. Tchr. Freehold (N.J.) Regional High Sch. Dist., 1971—; workshop presenter profl. orgns., 1984—. Bd. dirs. Greater Freehold Area YMCA, 1986—; councilwoman Borough of Freehold, 1989—, police commr., mem. pers. com. , mem. property com., mem safety com., coun. rep. to Libr. Commn.; Mayor's rep. to Alliance Against Drug and Substance Abuse; mem. Youth Guidance Coun., Freehold; notary public State of N.J. Mem. Nat. Coun. Tchrs. English, NEA, Assn. for Supervision and Curriculum Devel., N.J. Edn. Assn., Monmouth County Edn. Assn., Freehold Regional High Sch. Edn. Assn., AAUW (past trustee), Nat. Mus. Women in the Arts (charter mem.), Red Headed League, Freehold Optimist Club. Democrat. Home: 26 Jerseyville Ave Freehold NJ 07728 Office: Freehold High Sch Robertsville Rd Freehold NJ 07728

MCMORROW, JULIE, clinical pharmacist; b. Perth, Australia, July 16, 1960; came to U.S., 1987; d. James and Patricia (Hart) McM. B of Pharmacy, Western Australian Inst. Tech., Perth, 1979; Graduate Diploma in Pharmacy, Curtin U., Bentley, Australia, 1983; PharmD, U. Iowa, 1989. Pharmacy intern Royal Perth Hosp., 1979-80, pharmacist, then sr. pharmacist, 1980-87; pharmacist indexer Iowa Drug Info. Svc., Iowa City, 1987-88; teaching asst., rsch. asst. U. Iowa, Iowa City, 1987-89; asst. coord. for clin. trial, dept. neurology U. Iowa Hosps., Iowa City, 1988-89; fellow in pediatric critical care drug therapy Ohio State U. and Columbus Children's Hosp., 1989—; Australian student rep. U. Iowa, 1988-89. Contbr. articles to profl. jours. Vol. resources internat. program Columbus Coun. on World Affairs, 1990—. Recipient various hosp. pharmacy awards. Fellow Pharm. Soc. Western Australia (historians com. 1984-87); mem. Soc. Hosp. Pharmacists Australia (state br. com. 1984-87, editor state newsletter), Am. Soc. Hosp. Pharmacists (Critical Care fellow 1990, founding mem. specialty group in critical care, ednl. program com. 1989—), Nat. Assn. Pharm. Students Australia (state liaison officer 1979-80, edn. v.p. 1984-85, gen. v.p. 1985-86). Office: Wexner Inst Pediatric Rsch Rm 330 700 Children's Dr Columbus OH 43205

MCMORROW, MARGARET MARY (PEG MCMORROW), retired educator; b. N.Y.C., Dec. 18, 1924; d. Patrick Joseph and Ellen Veronica (Quinn) McIntyre; m. Joseph Patrick McMorrow, Oct. 12, 1948; children: Linda Karen, Robert Michael, Patrice Ann, Jane Ellen. BS, Queens Coll., 1946; MS in Edn., Hofstra U., 1959. Space controller Am. Airlines Co., N.Y.C., 1946-48; bus. rep. N.Y. Telephone Co., N.Y.C., 1948-52; tchr. Elwood Sch. Dist, Huntington, N.Y., 1965-89, ret., 1989. Fellow Elwood Tchrs. Assn., L.I. Scribes, N.Y. State United Tchrs., Mensa; mem. Elwood Ret. Tchrs. Assn., Alpha Lambda Omicron. Roman Catholic.

MCMULLEN, BARBARA ELIZABETH, data processing company executive, writer; b. Phila., Aug. 2, 1942; d. Walter Woodrow and Nellie Elizabeth (Rojewski) Ludman; m. John F. McMullen, May 12, 1978; stepchildren: Claire Ann, Luke John. BS in Math., Pa. State U., 1963; postgrad. Pratt Inst., 1971, N.Y. Sch. Interior Design, 1973; MPA in Pub. Fin., NYU, 1976. Supr. AT&T, Mt. Kisco, N.Y., 1963-65; sr. programmer Pan Am. World Airways, N.Y.C., 1965-67; analyst N.Y. Stock Exchange, N.Y.C., 1967-69; project leader Bache Halsey Stuart, N.Y.C., 1974-76; mgr. Morgan Stanley & Co., N.Y.C., 1976-78; pres. McMullen & McMullen, Inc., Jefferson Valley, N.Y., 1978—; mem. faculty NYU, 1980-82, New Sch. for Social Research, N.Y.C., 1981—. Author: (with John F. McMullen) Microcomputer Communications, 1982; contbg. editor Computers & Electronics, 1984-85, Computer Living, 1985—, Computer Shopper, 1985—; contbg. editor PC Clones mag., 1988—; contbr. chpt. to book, articles to profl. jours. Recipient Lepesqueur award N.Y.U., 1976. Bd. dirs. Osceola Heights Assn., Jefferson Valley, 1984. Mem. Big Apple Users Group (sec. and bd. dirs. 1981-84), Boston Computer Soc., Assn. for Computing Machinery, N.Y. Personal Computer Club (sec., bd. dirs. 1982—), N.Y. Amateur Computer Club, Westchester IBM Users Group, Pa. State U. Club of N.Y. Roman Catholic. Clubs: Downtown Athletic (N.Y.C.); Jefferson Valley Racquet (N.Y.). Avocations: pvt. pilot, painting, needlework, tropical fish breeding, amateur radio. Home: Perry St Jefferson Valley NY 10535 Office: McMullen & McMullen Inc McM Plaza Jefferson Valley NY 10535

MCMULLEN, CYNTHIA DIANE, small business owner; b. El Paso, Tex., Nov. 23, 1954; d. Everett and Anna Louise (Simnacher) Bishop; m. Ralph Allison McMullen, Feb. 27, 1956; 1 child, Michael Arnett. Student, Dominican Coll., Houston, 1972-74, U. Houston, 1974-78, Delmar Coll., 1979-81. Acct. Everett Bishop, CPA, Houston, 1971-79, Don Ranley, CPA, Corpus Christi, Tex., 1979; owner Expressions in Wood, Corpus Christi, 1979—; acct. Bob Fancher, CPA, Corpus Christi, 1980. Mem. Corpus Christi Beautification Com., 1979-85; vice chmn., exec. bd. dirs. Coastal Bend Better Bus. Bur.; sec. exec. bd. dirs. Coastal Bend Furniture Mchts. Assn., also founder; active Am. Cancer Soc. Mem. S.W. Homefurnishings Assn. (bd. dirs.), Exotic Wildlife Assn., Am. Ostrich Assn., Corpus Christi C. of C., Corpus Christi 100 Club, Zonta Svc. Club. Republican. Roman Catholic. Office: Expressions in Wood 1730 S Padre Island Dr Corpus Christi TX 78416

MCMULLEN, DANA ALLYN, writer; b. New Bedford, Mass., Sept. 11, 1941; d. Albert and Evlyne (Bullen) Greenfield; m. Robert B. Reeves, Oct. 2, 1969 (div. 1977); 1 child, Jason Allyn; m. F. Wesley McMullen Jr., Sept. 12, 1987; stepchildren: Robert, William, Christopher. Student, Smith Coll., 1958-60; BA, Am. Internat. Coll., 1963. Libr. Bechtel Corp., N.Y.C., 1965-67; office mgr. Calif. Constrn. and Mgmt., Inc., Berkeley, Calif., 1972-75, Merit Tank & Body, Inc., Berkeley, 1978-81; editor-in-chief The Advocate, Fairhaven, Mass., 1984-86; mktg. coord. GHR Engring., Inc., Lakeville, Mass., 1986-87; owner WordSmith, Fairport, N.Y., 1989—. Author: (with others) Pictorial History of Fairhaven, 1986; author newspaper column Miscellany, 1985 (Best Humor Column 1985). Pres. Fairhaven Improvement Assn., 1987; town meeting mem. Town of Fairhaven, 1986. Recipient Media award Bristol County Educators, 1985, Friend of Edn., 1986. Mem. Women in Communications, Inc. (Rochester Profl. chpt.), Rochester Women's Network (assoc.), Writers & Books, Inc. Democrat. Unitarian. Home and Office: 34 Mountain Rise Fairport NY 14450

MCMULLEN, MELINDA KAE, public relations executive; b. Japan, July 20, 1957; d. Paul K. and Valerie C. McMullen. BA in Communications, U. Pacific, 1979. Account exec. Ketchum Communications, San Francisco, 1979-80, Burson-Marsteller, N.Y.C., 1980-81; mgr. pub. relations Am. Express, N.Y.C., 1981-86; dir. pub. relations Firemans Fund Ins., Novato, Calif., 1986-87; sr. v.p. Edelman Pub. Relations, San Francisco, 1987—. Recipient Silver Anvil Pub. Relations Soc. Am., 1979. Mem. Nat. Investor Relations Inst. Office: Edelman Pub Rels 456 MOntgomery St San Francisco CA 94104

MCMULLIN, JOYCE ANNE, general contractor; b. Tulsa, Jan. 6, 1952; d. Junior Lawrence Patrick and Carol Anne (Morris) McM.; m. David Lawrence Tupper, Jan. 1, 1980 (div. May 1982). BFA, Calif. Coll. Arts and Crafts, 1973. Interior designer Design Assocs., Oakland, Calif., 1974; interior designer, sales rep. Sullivan's Interiors, Berkeley, Calif., 1975; supr. bldg. maintenance Clausen House, Inc., Oakland, 1975-82; owner New Life Renovation, Lafayette, Calif., 1981—. Contbr. articles to mags., newspapers. Mem. Contra Costa Coun., Nat. Trust Historic Preservation. Mem. AAUW, NAFE, Bus. and Profl. Women, Contra Costa County Women's Network, Self-Employed Tradeswomen (sec. 1984), Leads Club.

MCMULLIN, RUTH RONEY, publishing company executive; b. N.Y.C., Feb. 9, 1942; d. Richard Thomas and Virginia (Goodwin) Roney; m. Thomas Ryan McMullin, Apr. 27, 1968; 1 child, David Patrick. BA, Conn. Coll., 1963; MS in Pub. and Pvt. Mgmt., Yale U., 1979. Market researcher Aviation Week Mag. McGraw-Hill Co., N.Y.C., 1962-64; assoc. editor, bus. mgr. Doubleday & Co., N.Y.C., 1964-66; mgr. Natural History Press, 1967-70; v.p., treas. Weston (Conn.) Woods, Inc., 1970-71; staff assoc. Gen. Electric, Fairfield, Conn., 1979-82; mng. fin. analyst GECC Transp., Stamford, Conn., 1982-84; credit analyst corp. fin. dept. GECC, Stamford, 1984-85; sr. v.p. GECC Capital Markets Group, Inc., N.Y.C., 1985-87; exec. v.p., chief operating officer John Wiley & Sons, N.Y.C., 1987-89, pres., chief exec. officer, 1989—; bd. dirs. Bausch & Lomb, Rochester, N.Y.; mem. dean's adv. bd. Sch. Mgmt. Yale U. Bd. dirs. Yale U. Alumni Fund, Yale U. Press. Mem. N.Y. Yacht Club, Stamford Yacht Club. Office: John Wiley & Sons Inc 605 3rd Ave New York NY 10158

MCMURDO, MARY-JANE, state legislator; b. Boston, Apr. 22, 1924; married; 3 children. BS, U. Tex., 1952; grad., Thai Def. Lang. Inst., 1966. Mem. Hawaii State Senate, 1985—. Democrat. Office: State Senate Rm 216 Honolulu HI 96813

MCMURRAY, BARBARA ALISA, export development director; b. Asheville, N.C., Sept. 7, 1953; d. William Dedmond and Barbara Ann (Daniels) McM. BS in Psychology, N.C. State U., 1977. Dist. sales mgr. Amerford Internat., Raleigh, N.C., 1977-81; cons. Export Fundamentals Inc., Raleigh, 1981-84; internat. account mgr. Specialized Agrl. Publs., Raleigh, 1984-86; mktg. dir. Safron Enterprises, Capetown, S. Africa, 1986-87; dir. export devel. Leather Industries Am., Washington, 1987-89; internat. mktg. dir. USA Poultry and Egg Export Coun., Tucker, Ga., 1989—. Docent N.C. Mus. Art, Raleigh, 1977-82; mem. Friendship Force, Raleigh, 1977—. Mem. Women in Internat. Trade, Delta Nu Alpha (bd. mem. 1979-81, Merit award 1980). Home: 938 Rosedale Rd NE Atlanta GA 30306

MCMURRAY, LOLLA JEAN, corporate professional; b. Sulphur, Ok., June 27, 1939; d. Clifford Orvil and Jean Francis (Webb) Kirby; m. Donald Lee King, May 1958 (div. 1959); m. Kenneth Edward McMurray, Dec. 17, 1960; children: Marlene, Julie. Student, West Valley Coll., 1983. Adminstrv. sec., office mgr. Mt. Pleasant Sch. Dist., San Jose, Calif., 1976-80; exec. sec. Micro Metallics Corp., San Jose, 1980-84; office mgr., sec. bd. dirs. G.E. Stephens & Assoc., San Jose, 1984-87; bus. office mgr. A. Hirsh & Son, San Jose, 1987—. Sec. Fred Maiten Home and Sch., San Jose, 1973. Mem. NAFE, Calif. Assn. Residential Lenders, Assn. Profl. Mortgage Women. Democrat. Lutheran. Office: A Hirsh & Son 1600 Saratoga Ave San Jose CA 95129

MCMURRIN, TRUDY ANN, publishing consultant, editor; b. Los Angeles, May 28, 1944; d. Sterling Moss and Natalie (Cotterel) McM.; m. William M. Howard, Mar. 9, 1963 (div. 1967); 1 child, Natalie Roberta Howard; m. Robert Bruce Evans, Sept. 24, 1969 (div. 1971); m. Mick McAllister, June 16, 1982. BA in History and Philosophy, U. Utah, 1981. Editor U. Utah Press, Salt Lake City, 1967-74, asst. dir., 1974-80, editor-in-chief, 1980-83; dir. So. Meth. U. Press, Dallas, 1983-86; owner Dancing Badger Enterprises, 1989—; adj. prof. dept. communication Weber State Coll., Ogden, Utah, 1986-88; mem. bus. adv. coun. Westminster Coll., Salt Lake City, 1986—, adj. prof. dept. English, 1989—; mem. bus. adv. coun. Gore Coll. of Bus.; cons. and lectr. in field. Dir. art, co-designer award-winning books, 1972—. Mem. adv. bd. Children's Mus. Utah, 1979-81; bd. dirs. Howe Bros. Pub. Co., 1979—; mem. symposium on quality in pre-coll. edn. Rowland Hall-St. Mark's Sch., 1980-81; mem. Coalition to Save Our Sch. Libraries, 1981—, Salt Lake City Ballet Guild, Utah Symphony Guild, Utah Opera Guild, Friends of Salt Lake City Library. Fellow Am. Assn. State and Local History Nat. Endowment for Humanities, 1977, Inst. Am. West, 1981-82; recipient Maud Powell Found. award, 1988. Mem. Assn. Utah Pubs. (pres. 1978-83, bd. dirs. 1987-88), Western Lit. Assn. (mem. exec. council 1987—, Weber Studies (mem. adv. bd), Soc. for Scholarly Pub., Women in Scholarly Pub., Western Writers Am., Medieval Acad. Am., Wasatch Westerners, Intermountain Booksellers Assn., Rocky Mountain Book Pubs. Assn., Com. Small Mag. Editors and Pubs. Office: Editorial and Pub Services 1260 E Stratford Ave Salt Lake City UT 84106-2727

MCNABB, DARCY LAFOUNTAIN, real estate agent; b. Middletown, N.J., Aug. 27, 1955; d. Donald Mark LaFountain and Suzanne (Gilman) LaFountain Westergard; m. Leland Monte McNabb, July 4, 1981 (div. Feb. 1989); 1 child, Leland Monte Jr. BBA in Internat. Fin. cum laude, U. Miami, 1977. Real estate agent, Grad. Realtor's Inst. Market rsch. asst. Burger King Corp., Miami, Fla., 1975-77; regional mktg. supr. Burger King Corp., Huntington Beach, Calif., 1977-78; mgr., restaurant planning Holiday Inns, Inc., Memphis, 1978-79, mgr., nat. promotions, 1979-83; dir., lodging and travel planning Holiday Corp., Memphis, 1983-86; affiliate broker The Hobson Co., Realtors, Memphis, 1986—. Mem. Friends of Pink Palace Museum, Memphis, 1987—; Family Link/Runaway Horse, Memphis, 1980-88, Foster Care Adv. Bd., Memphis, 1988—. Named Profl. Vol. of Yr., Friends of Pink Palace Mus., Memphis, 1989. Mem. Memphis Bd. Realtors (strategic planning com. mem. 1987—), Memphis Runners Track Club. Republican. Episcopalian. Home: 1948 Harbert Ave Memphis TN 38104 Office: The Hobson Co Realtors 5100 Poplar Ave #116 Memphis TN 38137

MCNABB-BEARDSLEY, SUE ELLEN, enrolled agent; b. Trenton, Mich., May 23, 1948; d. John Daniel and Barbara Jean (Benton) McNabb; m. Jerry L. Beardsley, July 3, 1982; children: Robert R. Feakes Jr., Amy Annette Feakes. BGS, U. Mich., 1979. Edn. chmn. Fla. Soc. Enrolled Agts., 1986-88; pres., prin. McNabb-Beardsley and Assocs., Inc., Sarasota, Fla., 1989—. Active Marie Selby Bot. Garden; tchr. Enrolled Agts. Study Groups. Mem. Nat. Soc. Pub. Accts., Nat. Assn. Enrolled Agts. (cert.), Nat. Assn. Tax Preparers, Accreditation Coun. for Accountancy in Fed. Taxation, Fla. Soc. Enrolled Agts., Fla. Assn. Ind. Accts., Fla. Assn. Tax Preparers, Manasota Chpt. Soc. Enrolled Agts. (tchr. study groups), Sarasota C. of C. Office: 1528 S Tuttle Ave Sarasota FL 34239

MCNAIR, PAMELA HANSEN, controller; b. Pascagoula, Miss., Dec. 27, 1963; d. John Carl and Elois (Loper) H. Student, Gulf Coast Jr. Coll., Goutier, Miss., 1980-82; BS in Acctg., U. So. Miss., 1984. Acct. Nat. Am. Cos., Goutier, 1984-85; sales rep. Contel Cellular, Mobile, Ala., 1985; co-owner, v.p. Alpha Cellular Communications, Inc., Semmes, Ala., 1985-86; asst. contoller Fla. Environ. Waste div. Waste Mgmt., Inc., Pensacola, 1986; controller Environ. Waste System div. Waste Mgmt., Inc., Ft. Walton Beach, Fla., 1986—. Mem. Nat. Assn. Female Execs., Delta Sigma Pi. Republican. Baptist. Home: 510 Sheffield Rd Fort Walton Beach FL 32561 Office: Environ Waste System PO Box 4490 Fort Walton Beach FL 32549

MCNALLEY, JANET MARILYN, trust officer; b. Denver, May 16, 1960; d. Michael Collins and Sharon Bess (Cook) McN. Student, Mt. Holyoke Coll., 1978-79; BA in Econs. with honors, Mills Coll., Oakland, Calif., 1982; MA in Social Scis., U. Calif., Irvine, 1987, elem. teaching credential, 1988. Teaching asst. U. Calif., Irvine, 1986-88; employee benefits adminstr. Western Co. N.Am., Ft. Worth, 1988-89; legal asst. Crampton, Crampton, Estrada, Wichita Falls, Tex., 1989; trust officer Ameritrust Tex. N.A., Ft. Worth, 1989—; substitute tchr. various dists., Calif., 1988. Dem. del., Ft. Worth, 1990. Mem. AAUW (membership v.p. 1990-92 charter mem. Eleanor Roosevelt Found. 1990—), Liberty Coalition, Bluebonnet Pl. Neighborhood Assn. (newsletter editor). Home: 3408 Cockrell St Fort Worth TX 76109

MCNALLY, REGINA MARIE, advertising professional; b. Phila., Oct. 8, 1965; d. John Edward and Mary Margaret (Toland) McN. BA in Journalism cum laude, Temple U., 1988. Pub. rels. asst. Nazareth Hosp., Phila., 1987-88; advt. sales asst. Phila. Mag., 1988-89, co-op. advt. sales rep., 1990—, mgr. classified advt., 1989—. Mem. Phila. Internat. Visitors Ctr., 1989-90. Mem. Golden Key Nat. Honor Soc., Phila. Club Advt. Women, Temple U. Gen. Alumni Assn., Temple U. Young Alumni (charter), Downtown Club Temple U. Office: Phila mag 1500 Walnut St Philadelphia PA 19102

MCNAMARA, ANN DOWD, medical technologist; b. Detroit, Oct. 17, 1924; d. Frank Raymond and Frances Mae (Ayling) Sullivan; m. Thomas Stephen Dowd, Apr. 23, 1949 (dec. 1980); children: Cynthia Dowd Restuccia, Kevin Thomas Dowd; m. Robert Abbott McNamara, June 15, 1985. BS Wayne State U., 1947. Med. technologist Woman's Hosp. (now Hutzel Hosp.), Detroit, 1946-52, St. James Clin. Lab., Detroit, 1960-62; supr. histo-pathology lab. Hutzel Hosp., Detroit, 1962-72, Mt. Carmel Mercy Hosp., 1972-87, ret., 1987; docent Domino's Ctr. for Architecture & Design, Ann Arbor, Mich., 1988. Mem. Am. Soc. Clin. Pathologists, Am. Soc. Med. Technology, Mich. Soc. Med. Tech., Nat. Soc. Histotechnology,

Mich. Soc. Histotechnologists, Wayne State U. Alumni Assn., Smithsonian Assocs., Detroit Inst. Arts Founders Soc. Home: 29231 Oak Point Dr Farmington Hills MI 48331

MCNAMARA, ELSA MAE BROESAMLE, sales executive; b. Pitts., June 7, 1958; d. Herman R. and Eva P. (Province) Broesamle; married May 28, 1988. Sales rep. Dardenell Publs., Pitts., 1978-80; sales rep. Advo System, Inc., Houston, 1980-82, sales mgr., 1982-83; dist. mgr. Cleve., 1983-84; regional mgr. Pitts., 1984-85; v.p. Fla. region, 1985—. Mem. Am. Mgmt. Assn., Nat. Assn. Female Execs. Office: 128 S Tryon St Ste 2200 Charlotte NC 28211

MCNAMARA, JO ANNE, nurse; b. Emmetsburg, Iowa, July 23, 1932; d. Joseph Michael and Mary Victoria (Roper) McN. BSN, Briar Cliff Coll., 1956; MA, U. Redlands, Calif., 1979. Registered nurse. Pediatric supr. St. Joseph Mercy Hosp., Sioux City, Iowa, 1955-57; staff nurse Good Samaritan Hosp., West Palm Beach, Fla., 1957-58; psychiat. supr. Glenwood Hills Hosp., Mpls., 1958-61; surg. staff nurse VA Hosp., Mpls., 1961-62; pediatric nurse Mt. Sinai Hosp., Los Angeles, 1963-64, instr. inservice, 1964-69; instr. nursing Los Angeles Unified Sch., 1970-74; edn. coordinator Century City Hosp., Los Angeles, 1975-85; coordinator quality assurance Temple Community Hosp., Los Angeles, 1986—, dir. edn., 1986—. Vol. Crisis Intervention Ctr., Los Angeles, 1984. Mem. Quality Assurance Profls., Health Edn. Council, Patient Care Assessment Council, Spina Bifida Assn., B'nai B'rith Women. Democrat. Roman Catholic. Club: Toastmasters (sec.). Home: 20130 Lorne St Canoga Park CA 91306 Office: Temple Community Hosp 235 N Hoover St Los Angeles CA 90004

MCNAMARA, JULIA M(ARY), academic administrator, foreign language educator; b. N.Y.C., Dec. 13, 1941; d. John P. and Julia (Dowd) McN. BA in History and French, Ohio Dominican Coll., 1965; MA in French, Middlebury Coll., Paris, 1972; PhD in French Lang. and Lit., Yale U., 1980; DHL (hon.), Sacred Heart U., Hamden, Conn., 1984. Mem. faculty St. William Sch., Pitts., 1963-64, Holy Spirit Sch., Columbus, Ohio, 1964-65, Newark (Ohio) Cath. High Sch., 1965-66, Northwest Cath. High Sch., West Hartford, Conn., 1966-69, St. Vincent Ferrer High Sch., N.Y.C., 1969-70, St. Mary's High Sch., New Haven, 1971-74; lectr. french Albertus Magnus Coll., New Haven, 1976-80, dean of students, 1980-82, acting pres., 1982-83, pres., 1983—; adj. prof. french Albertus Magnus Coll., 1981—; mem. Conn. Health and Edn. Facilities Authority, Hartford, 1983—; mem. exec. com. Conn. Conf. Ind. Colls., Hartford, 1982—, sec.-treas. 1986—; lectr. in field; assoc. fellow Yale U., Morse Coll. Chairperson United Way Greater New Haven, 1987; bd. dirs. St. Mary's High Sch., New Haven, 1982—, ARC; trustee Yale/New Haven Hosp., 1984—, mem. bioethics com., mem. investment com., chmn. investor responsibility com.; adv. bd. Bank of Boston-Conn., 1983-87; adv. com. Jr. League Greater New Haven, 1985; trustee Hartford Sem., 1985—. Fulbright fellow, Paris, 1977-78; Yale U. fellow, 1974-78, Am. Council on Edn. fellow, 1981; recipient Disting. Woman in Leadership award New Haven YWCA, 1984, Veritas award Providence Coll., 1987. Mem. Fulbright Alumni Assn., New Haven C. of C. (bd. dirs. 1984—), New England Assn. Schs. and Colls. Appeals Bd. Roman Catholic. Office: Albertus Magnus Coll 700 Prospect St New Haven CT 06511-1189*

MCNAMARA, KATHLEEN MICHELE, special events executive; b. Detroit, July 1, 1957; d. James Anthony and Annette Elizabeth (Rourke) McN. BBA, Wayne State U., 1981. Dir. media and visitor relations Am. Freedom Train, nationwide, 1975-76; mgr. Detroit Visitor Info. Ctr., 1978-79; pub. relations assoc. Met. Detroit Conv. Bur., 1979-82, account exec., 1982-84; mng. dir. Detroit Renaissance Found., 1984—; dir. spl. projects Detroit Grand Prix, 1984—, editor ofcl. program 1985—; mng. dir. Internat. Freedom Festival, 1984—, editor ofcl. program 1984— (Spirit of Detroit award City Council 1986); dir. Montreux Detroit Jazz Festival, 1985—. Vol. Mich.'s Thanksgiving Day Parade, 1981-86; mem. steering com. Detroit Festival of the Arts, 1987-90; del. strategic planning com. Concerned Citizens for the Arts in Mich., 1987. Recipient Creative Planning award Wayne County, 1987. Mem. Internat. Events Group (round table leader Shaping Sponsorship Soc.), Internat. Festivals Assn. (del., chair Officers of the Day), Nat. Assn. Jazz Educators (del.). Roman Catholic. Office: Detroit Renaissance 100 Renaissance Ctr Ste 1760 Detroit MI 48243

MC NAMARA, MARY ELLEN, marketing executive; b. Long Branch, N.J., May 26, 1942; d. Edward Ward and Alice Marie (Reynolds) McN.; B.A., Glassboro State U., 1965; M.B.A., N.Y.U., 1975, Advanced Prof. Cert., 1980. Tech. asst. Bell Labs., Holmdel, N.J., 1965-66, sr. tech. asst., 1966-68; programming analyst, IBM, N.Y.C., 1968-71, systems programmer, 1971-72, bus. planner, 1972-74, industry planning adminstr., Princeton, N.J., 1974-77, industry mktg. adminstr., 1977-81, product mktg. adminstr., White Plains, N.Y., 1981-83, mgr. engring. sci. programming, Boca Raton, Fla., 1983-84, mem. market research staff, White Plains, N.Y., 1984-85, mgr. market devel., Valhalla, N.Y., 1986-88, program mgr., White Plains, 1989—. Mem. Computer Soc. (chmn. 1981, v. chmn. N.J. sect. 1979-81), IEEE (sr. mem., vice chmn. Palm Beach sect. 1984), AAAS, Assn. Computing Machinery, AAUW, Assn. Women in Computing, Nat. Council Women U.S.A., Women's Econ. Roundtable, Exec. Women of Palm Beaches, N.Y. Acad. Sci., N.Y. U. Alumni Assn., Glassboro State U. Alumni Assn., Beta Gamma Sigma. Republican. Home: 310 Lake Dr Allenhurst NJ 07711 Office: 1133 Westchester Ave White Plains NY 10604

MCNAMARA, MARY ELLEN, organizational developer, clergywomen; b. Mpls., Dec. 18, 1943; d. Edward Emmanuel and Gladys Theresa (Mattson) Bjorklund; m. Peter A. McNamara II, July 26, 1969; children: Peter Alexander III, Nathaniel Paul. BA, Carleton Coll., 1965; M of Div., Harvard U., 1968. Ordained to ministry Presbyn. Ch. Program dir. St. Peter's Ch., N.Y.C., 1968-72; program dir., dep. exec. St. Peter's Ch., N.Y., 1977-80; program dir. Ctr. Ch., New Haven, Conn., 1972-74; program devel. Westminster Presbyn. Ch., Springfield, Ill., 1974-77; assoc. Gen. Assembly Mission Coun., United Presbyn. Ch., N.Y.C., 1980-83, Gen. Assembly Coun., Presbyn. Ch. USA, N.Y.C., 1983-88; dir. not-for-profit sector Mayor's Office Bus. Devel., N.Y.C., 1988—; minister mem. N.Y.C. Presbyn., 1980—. Bd. dirs. Pathways for Youth, N.Y., Christianity and Crisis, N.Y.; rsch. coun. mem. United Way, N.Y.C., 1988-89, mem. Nonprofit Coord. Com., 1988. Democrat. Home: 5411 Palisade Ave Riverdale NY 10471

MCNAMARA, SUSAN LOUISE, information systems consultant; b. Boston, May 26, 1952; d. Thomas Joseph and Louise (Downey) McN. BS, Simmons Coll., 1973; EdM, Harvard U., 1986. Tchr. Walpole (Mass.) Sch. Dept., 1973-74; programmer Savs. Mgmt. Computer Corp., Boston, 1974-76; project mgr. William Filenes & Sons, Boston, 1976-82; instr. MIS, Massasoit Community Coll., Brockton, Mass., 1982-84, 89—; v.p. Louise McNamara & Assocs., Inc., Quincy, Mass., 1982—; lectr. MIS, Northeastern U., Boston, 1978-87, sr. lectr., 1988—; instr. New Eng. Banking Inst., Boston, 1982—, mem. edn. Com., 1986-89, acad. area chmn. for MIS, 1986-89, mem. tech. adv. bd., 1988-89; team leader Peter R. Johnson & Assocs., Inc., Westwood, Mass., 1986-88. Treas. class of 1973, Simmons Coll., Boston, 1978-83, v.p., 1988—; den leader Boy Scouts Am., Milton, 1987-88, mem. troop com., 1988—. Mem. Squantum Yacht Club. Roman Catholic. Office: 41 Summit Ave Quincy MA 02170

MCNAMEE, EVELYN HAYNES, civilian military employee; b. Monticello, Miss., Dec. 10, 1947; d. Leroy and Leslie (Hammond) Haynes; m. George A. McNamee Jr., Aug. 23, 1970; children: Leonard, George Allen, Paula Elizabeth, Candace Renee. BS, Alcorn State U., Lorman, Miss., 1969; MS, Tuskegee Inst., 1971. Indsl. hygienist U.S. Army, San Diego, 1985-88; sr. indsl. hygienist USN, San Diego, 1988—. Mem. Bonita Vista Jr. High Sch. PTA, 1989-90, bd. dirs. Allen's Elem. Sch., 1989-90. Mem. Am. Conf. Govt. Indsl. Hygienists, Am. Indsl. Hygiene Assn., Navy Indsl. Hygiene Assn., NAFE, Toastmasters (past pres. local chpt.). Democrat. Roman Catholic. Home: 3124 Lynndale Ln Chula Vista CA 92010 Office: US Naval Hosp Dept Indsl Hygiene Naval Air Station North Island San Diego CA 92135

MCNAMEE, FRANCES COX, teacher; b. Tucson, Nov. 20, 1935; d. Frank G. and Mildred (Lechner) Cox; m. Milburn McNamee, Dec. 19, 1931; children: Vera McNamee Jackson, Edward M., Marianne McNamee-Staab. BA, Ft. Lewis Coll., 1964; MA, Colo. State U., 1972. Cert. tchr., N.Mex. Tchr. Farmington (N.Mex.) Pub. Schs., 1964—; head dept. Farmington High Sch., 1982-87; part time tchr. San Juan Coll., Farmington, 1972—. Leader Girl Scouts U.S.A., Farmington, 1977-85; chmn. Eagle advancement Boy Scouts Am., Farmington, 1982-85. NEH fellow, 1984; recipient Gov.'s award N.Mex. Commn. on Status of Women, 1989. Mem. AAUW (pres. San Juan br. 1971-74, 81-84, v.p. 1985-87), N.Mex. Edn. Assn. (faculty rep. 1971—). Democrat. Methodist. Home: 2305 E 17th St Farmington NM 87401 Office: Farmington High Sch 2200 Sunset Ave Farmington NM 87401

MCNAMEE, LOUISE, advertising agency executive; m. Tom M. Attended Mary Baldwin Coll., Va. With rsch. dept. Kelly Nason; exec. v.p., dir. mktg. and rsch. Della Femina, Travisano & Ptnrs., Inc. (now Della Famina McNamee, Inc.), N.Y.C., 1979-84, ptnr., 1982—, acting pres., from 1984, pres., chief operating officer, 1986—. Named Advt. Woman of Yr., Advt. Women of N.Y., 1988. Office: Della Femina McNamee Inc 350 Hudson Ave New York NY 10014*

MCNANEY, HEIDI MARIE, obstetrician-gynecologist; b. Rantoul, Ill., Jan. 26, 1956; d. Thomas W. and Judith S. (Hagues) McNancey; m. William L. Flint, Oct. 11, 1980. BA, Rollins Coll., Winter Park, Fla., 1977; MD, U. South Fla., 1980. Intern Roanoke (Va.) Meml. Hosp., 1980-81; resident in ob.-gyn. U. Va. Med. Ctr., Charlottesville, 1982-84; staff physician Dr.'s Clinic, Vero Beach, Fla., 1984-86; pvt. practice, 1986—; chmn. dept. ob/gyn Martin Meml. Hosp., Stuart, Fla., 1990—. Fellow Am. Coll. Obstetricans Gynecologists; Mem. AMA, Fla. Med. Assn., Am. Med. Womens Assn., Am. Coll. Ob.-Gyn., Am. Fertility Soc. Home and Office: 433 E Ocean Blvd Stuart FL 34994

MCNAUGHT, JUDITH, author; b. San Luis Obispo, Calif., May 10, 1944; d. Clifford Harris and Rosetta (Prince) Spath; m. J. Michael McNaught, June 1, 1974 (dec. 1983); children: Whitney, Clayton; m. Donald R. Smith. BS, Northwestern U., 1966. Pres. Pro-Temps, Inc., St. Louis, 1983-84, Eagle Syndication, Inc., Dallas, 1987—. Author Tender Triumph, 1983 (Critics Choice award 1983); Double Standards, 1984; Whitney, My Love (Best Hist. Novelist 1985), Once and Always, 1987 (Best Hist. Novel 1987), Something Wonderful 1988 (N.Y. Times Best seller, Critics Choice award Best Hist. Novel 1988), A Kingdom of Dreams, 1989 (N.Y. Times Bestseller, Award for Best Hist. Novel 1989), Almost Heaven, 1990 (N.Y. Times #1Bestseller). Mem. Romance Writers Assn., Lakewood Yacht Club. Roman Catholic. Avocations: racquetball, skiing.

MCNEAL, ANN P. WOODHULL, physiology professor; b. Orange, N.J., Oct. 20, 1942; d. James D. W. and Hazel V. Mc.; m. Albert S. Woodhull, May 1, 1965 (div. 1986); 1 child, Gordon. BA, Swarthmore Coll., 1964; PhD, U. Wash., Seattle, 1972. From asst. prof. to prof. Hampshire Coll., Amherst, Mass., 1972—. Contbr. articles to profl. jours. Mem. Peace Activists East West (sec. 1985-89), Amherst, Mass., Pelham Athletic Club (pres. 1986-89), Pelham, Mass. Mem. Am. Coll. Sports Medicine. Office: Hampshire Coll Natural Sci Amherst MA 01002

MCNEAL, AQUILLA OSBORNE, federal agency official; b. Danville, Va., May 13, 1948; d. Ellis A. and Geneva (Luck) Osborne; m. Charles L. McNeal, Aug. 18, 1973; 1 child, Christian L. BA, Beaver Coll., Glenside, Pa., 1975; MPA, Temple U., 1977. Mgmt. asst. City of Phoenix; mgmt. analyst City of San Pablo, Calif.; U.S. postal inspector U.S. Postal Inspection Svc., N.Y.C.; spl. agt. U.S. Dept. Edn., Phila. Mem. Black history com. Cherry Hill (N.J.) Minority Civic Assn., 1990, Cherry Hill PTA; mem. evangelism com. St. Andrews United Meth. Ch., 1990. Am. Polit. Sci. fellow; named one of Outstanding Young Women Am., 1983. Mem. Assn. Fed. Investigators, Fed. Law Enforcement Officer Assn. Republican. Home: 115 Saxby Terr Cherry Hill NJ 08003

MCNEAL, SHAY, advertising executive; b. Sturgis, Ky., Nov. 5, 1946; d. John H'Earl Evans and Mary Ellen Baird; 1 child, Richard McNeal (dec. 1972); 1 child, Hethur; m. Gordon K. Smith, Oct. 24, 1975 (div. 1982); 1 child, Paris. Student, DeKalb Coll. Asst. dir. Savannah St. Mission, Atlanta, 1968-70; spl. project asst. Lovable Co., Atlanta, 1970-71; assoc. buyer Montgomery Ward/Knit Div., N.Y., 1971-73; nat. fashion dir. Dan River Mills, N.Y.; mktg. dir. Macy's SE div., Atlanta, 1974-78; pres. Smith McNeal Advt., 1978-86; sr. v.p., gen. mgr. William Cook Advt., Atlanta, 1986-89; pres. Preemptive Ltd., Beverly Hills, Calif., 1989—; key cons. Jack Watson for Gov., Atlanta and Savannah; mem. faculty, jurist Portfolio Ctr., Atlanta, 1988-89. Bd. dirs. Travelers Aid, Atlanta, 1982-84; vol. ARC, Atlanta, 1978—, various advt. clubs nationwide; appointed by the gov. to Ga. Film Commn., 1989. Named one of the Top Advt. Women in the S.E. AdWeek, Atlanta, 1987. Mem. Am. Assn. Advt. Agys., Exec. Womens Assn., Atlanta Advt. Club, Ansley Golf Club Atlanta. Democrat.

MCNEAR, BARBARA BAXTER, financial executive, consultant; b. Chgo., Oct. 9, 1939; d. Carl Henden and Alice Gertrude (Parrish) Baxter; m. Robert Erskine McNear, Apr. 13, 1968 (div. 1981); 1 child, Amanda Baxter; m. Glenn Philip Eisen, June 7, 1987. B.S. in Journalism, Northwestern U., 1961. Editorial asst. Scott Foresman & Co., Chgo., 1961; pub. rels. dir. Market Facts Inc., Chgo., 1961-63; account supr. Philip Lesly Co., Chgo., 1963-68, 69; account exec. Burson-Marsteller, Chgo., 1968; dir. communications CNA Fin. Corp., Chgo., 1969-74; dir. pub. rels. Gould Inc., Chgo., 1974; v.p. Harris Bank, Chgo., 1974-80, Fireman's Fund Ins. Co., San Francisco, 1980-83; sr. v.p. First Chgo. Corp., 1983-86; v.p. communications Xerox Fin. Svcs., Inc., Norwalk, Conn., 1987—. Bd. visitors Medill Sch. Journalism Northwestern U., Evanston, Ill. Mem. Pub. Relations Soc. Am., Nat. Investor Relations Inst. (pres. Chgo. chpt. 1974-75, bd. dirs. Chgo. chpt.). Episcopalian. Club: Cliffdwellers. Home: 23 Telva Rd Wilton CT 06897 Office: Xerox Fin Svcs Inc 401 Merritt 7 Norwalk CT 06856

MCNEELY, ALMA GRETCHEN, nurse, educator, administrator; b. Detroit, Mar. 29, 1941; d. Carl Bertil and Katherine Rose (Brown) Orman; m. Joseph Francis Cavon, June 26, 1962 (div. 1981); children: Leslie Muriel Cavon Tatum, Joseph Anthony Cavon; m. Richard Irving McNeely, Dec. 18, 1981. Diploma, Harper Hosp. Sch. Nursing, 1962; BS in Nursing, Biola U., 1981; MS in Nursing, Loma Linda U., 1983; postgrad., U. San Diego, 1990. R.N., Mich., Mont., Calif. Staff nurse Harper Hosp., Detroit, 1962, Midway Hosp., St. Paul, 1963; pediatric charge nurse St. John Hosp., Detroit, 1963-64; staff nurse Mo. Bapt. Hosp., St. Louis, 1965-66; office nurse, mgr. pvt. practice plastic and reconstructive surgeon, Santa Ana, Calif., 1967-81; adj. asst. prof. nursing Mont. State U., 1983-86; doctoral fellow, rsch. asst. U. San Diego, 1986-88; adj. asst. prof. nursing Mont. State U., 1988-90, asst. to deans, 1990—. Contbg. author: Family Health Nursing, 1989, American Nursing: A Biographical Dictionary, 1988. Facilitator, Parents Anonymous, Missoula, 1984-86. Mem. Am. Nurses Assn., Mont. Nurses Assn., Am. Pub. Health Assn., Am. Assn. History of Nursing, Sigma Theta Tau. Republican. Presbyterian. Home: 1660 Amsterdam Rd Belgrade MT 59714 Office: Mont State U Coll Nursing Sherrick Hall 118 Bozeman MT 59717

MCNEELY, BEVERLY ANN, nurse; b. Abilene, Tex., Jan. 17, 1955; d. Harry David Jr. and Phyllis Mae (Rife) McN.; m. Larry Ernest Thomas, Nov. 17, 1971 (div. Apr. 1982); children: Jason John Thomas, Betsy Ann Thomas. Student, Ranger Jr. Coll., Ranger, Tex., 1980, 84, 85,87; student, Midwestern State U., Wichita Falls, Tex., 1984; writing diploma, Inst. Children's Lit., Redding Ridge, Conn., 1987. Lic. vocat. nurse; cert. emergency med. technician. Lab. aide Graham Gen. Hosp., Graham, Tex., 1971-73; 3-11 grad. nurse Graham Gen. Hosp., 1973-74; relief 3-11 nurse Garden Terrace & Burgess Manor Nursing Homes, Graham, 1975; animal technician, nurse Lake Country Vet. Clinic, Graham, 1978-82; animal technician, nurse, co-owner Dry Creek Vet. Clinic, Graham, 1982—; 3-11 charge nurse Cedar Oaks Nursing Home, Graham, 1984-85. Contbr. poetry to various publs. Sec.-treas. Humane Soc. Young County, Inc., Graham, 1988-89, also bd. dirs. Recipient award of merit World of Poetry, 1988, Golden Poet award, 1988, 89, Poet of Merit award Am. Poetry Assn., 1989. Mem. Morris Animal Found., NAFE, Amnesty Internat., Nat. Wildlife Fedn., Greenpeace. Mem. Christian Ch. (Disciples of Christ). Office: Dry Creek Vet Clinic 2401 Hwy 16 South Graham TX 76046

MCNEELY, SHARON LYNN, educational psychologist; b. Elgin, Ill., Apr. 28, 1955; d. Clyde Earl and Alice Marie (Pohland) Mc.; m. Faustino Cortes, Aug. 20, 1988. BS, U. Wis., 1976, MS, 1980, PhD, 1986. Cert. Psychology, Ill. Asst. prof. Northeastern Ill. U., Chgo., 1986—; pvt. practice psychology. Mem. Am. Psychol. Assn., Soc. Sci. Study of Sex, Am. Ednl. Rsch. Assn., Midwestern Ednl. Rsch. Assn., Midwestern Psychol. Assn., Soc. for Rsch. on Adolescence. Office: Northeastern Ill U 5500 North Saint Louis Ave Chicago IL 60625

MCNEIL, HEIDI LORETTA, lawyer; b. Preston, Iowa, Apr. 7, 1959; d. Archie Hugo and Heidi (Waltert) McN. BA in Journalism and Broadcasting with distinction, U. Iowa, 1981, JD with distinction, 1985. Bar: Ariz. 1985, U.S. Dist. Ct. Ariz. 1985, U.S. Ct. Appeals (9th cir.) 1985, U.S. Ct. Appeals (10th cir.) 1990. Sports journalist The Daily Iowan, Iowa City, 1977-81, Quad City Times, Davenport, Iowa, 1981-82; assoc. Snell & Wilmer, Phoenix, 1985—. Mem. ABA, Ariz. Bar Assn., Maricopa County Bar Assn. (bd. dirs. young lawyers div. 1987—, sec. 1989-90), Ariz. Women's Lawyers, Phoenix Assn. Def. Counsel, Phi Beta Kappa, Phi Eta Sigma. Lutheran.

MCNEIL, MONA MARGARET, clinical psychologist; b. Bklyn., Sept. 12, 1947; d. William A. and Margaret M. (Kenny) McLoughlin; m. Donald R. Takush, July 7, 1966 (div. 1981); 1 child, Melissa Takush; m. Randall Ring Kleinhesselink, Aug. 5, 1983. Student, Manhattanville Coll., 1965-66; BS in Zoology, U. Wash., 1976; MS in Clin. Psychology, Calif. State, Bakersfield, 1979; PhD in Clin. Psychology, Wash. State U., 1987. Lic. psychologist, Oreg., Wash. Psychology cons. Pioneer Community Hosp., Bakersfield, 1978-79; instr. Wash. State U., Pullman, Wash., 1983; lectr. U. Idaho, Moscow, 1984-85; psychol. asst. Lewiston, Idaho, 1981-85; intern Seattle VA Med. Ctr., 1985-86; lectr., supr. U. Idaho, Moscow, 1986-87; acting dir. alcohol studies Wash. State U., Pullman, 1988; clin. psychologist Affiliated Psychol. Assocs., Inc., Portland, Oreg., 1988—; adj. faculty Wash. State U., Pullman, 1984—. Mem. Am. Psychol. Assn., Oreg. Psychol. Assn., Nat. Register Health Svc. Providers in Psychology. Office: Affiliated Psychol Assocs 5319 SW Westgate Dr Ste 147 Portland OR 97221-2411

MCNEIL, SUE, engineering educator; b. Newcastle, Australia, June 17, 1955; d. George Peers and Norma (Avard) McGeachie; m. John Franklin McNeil, Dec. 4, 1976; children: Sarah, Emily. BS, U. Newcastle, Newcastle, Australia, 1976; B.E., U. Newcastle, 1978; MS, Carnegie Mellon U., 1981, PhD, 1983. Registered profl. engr., N.J. Asst. works engr. N.S.W. Dept. Main Rds., Singleton, Australia, 1977-79; transp. engr. Garmen Assocs., Montville, N.J., 1983-84; vis. lectr. Princeton U., Princeton, N.J., 1984-85; asst. prof. MIT, Cambridge, Mass., 1985-87; asst. prof. Carnegie Mellon U., Pitts., 1988-90, assoc. prof., 1990—. Contbr. articles to profl. jours. Doctoral dissertation fellow AAUW, 1982-83; named Presdl. Young Investigator NSF, 1987—. Mem. ASCE (chmn. facilities mgmt. task force 1988—), Inst. Transp. Engrs. (assoc.), Ops. Rsch. Soc. Am. (assoc.), Transp. Rsch. Bd. (assoc.). Office: Carnegie Mellon U Dept Civil Engring Pittsburgh PA 15213

MCNEILL, JOAN REAGIN, volunteer consultant, sales representative; b. Atlanta, July 8, 1936; d. Arthur Edward and Annie May (Busby) Reagin; m. Thomas Pinckney McNeill, Sr., Aug. 3, 1957; childen: Thomas Pinckney, Clyde Reagin. Student, U. Louisville, 1955-57; BA, U. Tenn., Chattanooga, 1976. Founding pres. Family and Childrens Svcs. Assocs., Chattanooga, 1987-88; bd. dirs. Chattanooga Symphony and Opera Assn., 1984-88, pres. 1984-87; pres. Chattanooga Ballet Assn., 1986-88; bd. dirs. U. Chattanooga Found., 1986-89; mem. vol. coun., bd. dirs. Am. Symphony Orch. League, Washington, 1986—. Recipient Outstanding Svc. award U. Tenn., Chattanooga, 1988; Colby award for volunteerism Sigma Kappa, 1990. Mem. U. Tenn. Chattanooga Alumni Assn. (pres. 1985-86). Republican. Episcopalian. Home: 7457 Preston Circle Chattanooga TN 37421 Office: Apollo Travel 5710 Brainerd Rd Chattanooga TN 37411

MCNEILLY, JEAN CRAIG See CRAIG, JEAN

MCNEILY, MARY ZORA, health facility administrator; b. Hamilton, Ont., Can., Apr. 27, 1952; came to U.S.; d. Ned and Nada Maletin; m. Curtlan McNeily, Aug., 1972; children: Shannon, Colin. BSN, Columbia Union Coll., Takoma Park, Md., 1985; MHA, Cen. Mich. U., 1987. Asst. dir. nurses, head nurse Providence Hosp., Washington; exec. dir. Prince George's Found. for Med. Care, Inc., Upper Marlboro, Md.; quality assurance mgr. Jefferson Hosp., Alexandria, Va., dir quality assurance. Capt. U.S. Army, 1978-81. Mem. Am. Hosp. Assn., Am. Med. Peer Rev. Assn., Nat. Assn. Quality Assurance Profls. Home: 6104 Kennedy Dr Chevy Chase MD 20815

MCNULTY, KRISTY LEE ANN, retired army officer; b. Woodburn, Oreg., Sept. 29, 1958; d. Donald Leo and Mildred Ann (Heisler) McN. BSN, U. Portland, 1981. Psychiatric nurse Dammasch State Hosp., Wilsonville, Oreg., 1981; clin. charge nurse U.S. Army, Ft. Sill, Okla., 1981-84; ret.; bd. dirs. Woodburn World's Berry Ctr., 1990; mem. procedure com. Reynolds Army Community Hosp., Ft. Sill, 1982-83. Contbr. articles to profl. jours; patentee in field. vol. Woodburn World's Berry Ctr., 1990—, bd. dirs.; active action alert Nat. Multiple Sclerosis Soc., N.Y.C., 1985—; participant/exhibitor Oreg. State Fair, 1985—; bd. dirs., mem. open sports com. Oreg. Games for Phys. Ltd., 1990. 1st lt. U.S. Army, 1981-84. Decorated Army Commendation medal. Mem. Oreg. Hist. Soc., Canby Swim Club, Paralyzed Vets. of Am. Republican. Roman Catholic. Home: 16280 Pudding River Rd NE Woodburn OR 97071

MCNULTY, MARY JOY, restaurant owner; b. Phila., Apr. 3, 1938; d. Sydney Bregman and Clara (Rabinowitz) Liss; m. John Joseph McNulty, Dec. 26, 1958 (div. 1975); children: Julia Ann, John Joseph, Timothy Francis, Shawn Patrick. Grad. high sch., Elkins Park, Pa. Officer N.Y. State Dept. Correction, Bedford Hills, 1960-72; owner, mgr. The Lobster Pot, Provincetown, Mass., 1973—. Formerly active youth hockey programs, town govt. coms., alcohol and drug recovery programs. Office: Lobster Pot Restaurant 321 Commercial St Provincetown MA 02657

MCNULTY, NANCY G(ILLESPIE), business writer, editor, management consultant; b. Greenville, Pa., May 1, 1919; d. Stanley A. and Bess (Anthony) Gillespie; m. Arthur P. McNulty, July 16, 1942 (dec. 1961); 1 child, Terence. BA, Thiel Coll., 1940; MA, NYU, 1948. Industry analyst Equity Corp., 1940-42; writer, researcher Time Inc., N.Y.C., 1942-45; cons., 1957-68; founder, dir. Internat. Survey of Mgmt. Edn., N.Y.C., 1968—; cons. Chase Bank World Info. Svc., Japan Soc., Am. Mgmt. Assn., Inst. for Advancement of Economy, Austria, The Conf. Bd., UN Dept. of Tech. Coop. for Devel., N.Y. State Commn. on Edn., Time Inc.; editor, writer, cons. mgmt. edn., 1968—. Editor: Training Managers-The International Guide, 1969, Management Education Programs-The World's Best, 1980, The International Directory of Executive Education, 1985; contbr. numerous articles to profl. jours. Ford Found. scholar, 1968, 78. Fellow Internat. Acad. Mgmt. (hon.); mem. N.Am. Mgmt. Coun. (v.p., editor newsletter 1990—), Internat. Cons. Found., European Found. Mgmt. Devel., Internat. Found. Action Learning, Acad. Internat. Bus., Acad. Mgt., Yale Club of N.Y.C. Episcopalian. Home and Office: 55 W 89th St New York NY 10024

MCNUTT, SUZZANNE MARIE, legal assistant; b. Walla Walla, Wash., June 3, 1962; d. John Richard and Janette Elaine (Egg) Heathman; mRobert Mark McNutt, Oct. 26, 1985. BA cum laude, Wash. State U., 1985. Fin. analyst Dean Witter Reynolds, Boise, Idaho, 1985-86, account exec., 1986-88; sr. legal asst. Boise Cascade Corp., 1988—; instr. Basic Investing for the Boise Community Ednl. System, 1986-87; bd. dirs. The Courthouse; guest lectr. Boise High Sch., 1987—. Co-chairperson United Way Fund Drive, 1988; fundraiser, vol. Discovery Ctr. of Idaho, Paint the Town, and The Hays Shelter Home, 1988—; mktg. and future planning, Jr. League of Boise, 1988—; vol. steering com. Boise Cascade Corp., 1989—; program dir. Idaho State Hugh O'Brian Youth Leadership Found., 1989—. Mem. ABA, Nat. Assn. Legal Assts., Idaho Assn. Legal Assts., Boise Area C. of C. (membership relations com. 1987—, chairperson, 1989, leadership program, 1988—). Republican. Roman Catholic. Home: 1426 Boston Dr Boise ID 83706 Office: Boise Cascade Corp One Jefferson Sq Boise ID 83728

MCOWEN, CAROL MARIE, art dealer; b. Denver, Dec. 23, 1927; d. Charles Fredrick and Hattie Eva (Richards) Coleman; m. Howard Robert McOwen; children: Robert C., Carol Lynn. M, Calif. State U., Long Beach, 1989. Ptnr., art dealer Mayoon, Long Beach, Calif., 1988—. Pres. LWV, Long Beach, 1975-76; commr. L.A. County Art Mus., 1977-84. Mem. L.A.

County Art Mus. (docent), Long Beach Art Mus., UCLA Art Gallery, L.A. Mus. Contemporary Art. Democrat. Unitarian. Home: 7326 S Marina Pacifica Long Beach CA 90803 Office: Mayoon 6475 E Pacific Coast Hwy 384 Long Beach CA 90803-4296

MCPHERSON, GAIL, advertising and real estate sales executive; b. Fort Worth; d. Garland and Daphne McP. Student U. Tex.-Austin; BA, MS, CUNY. Advt. sales exec. Harper's Bazaar mag., N.Y.C., 1974-76; sr. v.p. fashion mktg. dir. L'Officiel/Ultra mag., N.Y.C., 1976-80; fashion mgr. Town and Country mag., N.Y.C., 1980-82; v.p. advt. and mktg. Ultra mag., Tex. and N.Y.C., 1984-85; fragrance, jewelry and automotive mgr. M. Mag., N.Y.C., 1984-85; sr. real estate sales exec. Fredric M. Reed & Co., Inc., N.Y.C., 1985-88; telemktg. exec. Home-Watch Inc., Amarillo, Tex.,1989—. Sponsor Southampton Hosp. Benefit Com., N.Y.; mem. jr. com. Mannes Sch. Music, N.Y.C., Henry St. Settlement, N.Y.C. Mem. Fashion Group N.Y., Advt. Women N.Y., Real Estate Bd. N.Y., U. Tex. Alumni Assn. of N.Y. (v.p.) Republican. Presbyterian. Clubs: Corviglia (St. Moritz, Switzerland), Doubles, El Morocco (mem. jr. com. 1976-77), Le Club (N.Y.C.). Home: 3418 Rutson Dr Amarillo TX 79109

MCPHERSON, MARY PATTERSON, college president; b. Abington, Pa., May 14, 1935; d. John B. and Marjorie Hoffman (Higgins) McP. A.B., Smith Coll., 1957, LL.D. 1981; M.A., U. Del., 1960; Ph.D., Bryn Mawr Coll., 1969; LL.D. (hon.), Juniata Coll. 1975, Smith Coll., 1981, Princeton U., 1984, U. Rochester, 1984, U. Pa., 1985; Litt.D. (hon.), Haverford Coll., 1980; L.H.D. (hon.), Lafayette Coll., 1982, U. Pa., 1985; LHD (hon.), Med. Coll. Pa., 1985. Instr. philosophy U. Del., 1959-61; asst., fellow and lectr. dept. philosophy Bryn Mawr Coll., 1961-63, asst. dean, 1964-69, assoc. dean, 1969-70; dean Bryn Mawr Coll. (Undergrad. Coll.), 1970-78, assoc. prof., from 1970; acting pres. Bryn Mawr Coll., 1976-77, pres., 1978—; bd. dirs. Provident Nat. Bank of Phila., Bell Telephone Co. Pa., Dayton Hudson Corp.; mem. commn. on women in higher edn. Am. Council on Edn., bd. dirs., 1979-82. Bd. dirs. Agnes Irwin Sch., 1971—; bd. dirs. Shipley Sch., 1972—, Phillips Exeter Acad., 1973-76, Wilson Coll., 1976-79, Greater Phila. Movement, 1973-77, Internat. House of Phila., 1974-76, Josiah Macy, Jr. Found., 1977—, Carnegie Found. for Advancement Teaching, 1978-84; mem. vis. com. philosophy and religion U. Mich.; mem. adv. com. Nat. Mus., Phila., 1977-79, University City Sci. Center, 1979-85, Brookings Inst., 1984—, Phila. Contributionship, 1985—, Carnegie Corp. N.Y., 1985—. Nat. Humanities Ctr., 1986—; Amherst Coll., 1986—. Mem. Soc. for Ancient Greek Philosophy, Am. Philos. Soc. Clubs: Fullerton, Cosmopolitan. Office: Bryn Mawr Coll Merion Ave Bryn Mawr PA 19010*

MCPHERSON, MICHELLE MARIE, oil company executive; b. Artesia, N.M., Oct. 3, 1959; d. Jack O. and Lora Jane (Smith) McP. B in Acctg. N.Mex. State U., 1981. Acct. Shell Oil Co., New Orleans, 1981-83; budget and audit coord. So. Union Refining Co., Hobbs, N.M., 1983-84; crude oil acct. Navajo Refining Co., Artesia, 1984-85, supr. crude oil acctg. dept., 1985-89, mgr. crude oil svcs., 1989—. Ad writer N.Mex. State Senate Dist. Election Campaign, Artesia, 1988. Mem. NAFE, Petroleum Accts. Soc. N.Mex., Southwestern Assn. Div. Order Analysts, Artesia Writer's Guild, Pecos Diamond Toastmasters, Artesia Downtown Lions, Beta Alpha Psi (Delta Lambda cpt.), Omicron Delta Epsilon (Beta N.Mex. chpt.).

MCQUAID, PHYLLIS W., state legislator; b. Mar. 26, 1928; m. Joseph McQuaid; 8 children. Mem. Minn. State Senate, 1983—. Republican. Office: 4130 Yosemite Ave S Saint Louis Park MN 55416*

MCQUEEN, KATHRYN LYNN, special education and English language educator; b. Kansas City, Mo., Dec. 4, 1952; d. Hurtle Grover and Ruby Janet (Henderson) McQ. AA, Muskegon (Mich.) Community Coll., 1972; BA in Social Work, Mich. State U., 1974; postgrad. in counseling and guidance, U. of Consortium, 1974; cert. in elem. teaching, U. Tenn., 1978; postgrad., U. Madrid, U. Spain, 1980; MS in Edn., U. Tenn., 1981. Cert. spl. edn. and elem. tchr., Mich. Senate aide Mich. State Senate, Lansing, 1975; assistance payments worker Oceana County Dept. of Social Services, Hart, Mich., 1975-76; counselor Tenn. State Dept. of Corrections, Jackson, 1977; instr. lang. arts, reading Obion County Migrant Edn. Program, Union City, Tenn., 1979; tchr. spl. edn. Black Oak Elem. Sch., Obion County, 1979-86; tchr. English Colego Hamilton Elem. Sch., Mexico City, 1986-87; tchr. pre-first and first grade The Am. Sch. Found., Mexico City, 1987—; substitute tchr. Cen. Elem. Sch., 1978; instr. gen. ednl. devel. Obion County Sch. Participant Chimes for Charity, seven yrs.; vol. Spl. Olympics, seven yrs.; sponsor Easter Seals. Mem. NEA, Tenn. Ednl. Assn. (spl. tutor), Council for Exceptional Children. Democrat. Home: Rte 2 Box 168 Union City TN 38261

MCQUEEN, REBECCA HODGES, health care executive, consultant; b. Dothan, Ala., July 20, 1954; d. Edward Grey and Shirley Louise (Varner) Hodges; m. David Raymond McQueen, Mar. 5, 1982; children: Matthew David, Owen Grey. BS, Emory U., 1976, MPH, 1979. Research assoc. North Cen. Ga. Health Systems Agy., Inc., Atlanta, 1979-80; assoc. dir. Health Services Analysis, Inc., Atlanta, 1980-82; med. group adminstr. Southeastern Health Services, Inc./Procare, Atlanta, 1982-84; v.p. ad-minstrn., chief oper. officer SouthCare Med. Alliance, Atlanta, 1985—; cons. North Cen. Ga. Health Systems Agy., 1980-81, Region 4 HHS, Atlanta, 1980-82, instr. Applied Stats. Tng. Inst. Nat. Ctr. Health Stats., Washington, 1980-82; mem. Health Data com. and Health Cost subcom. Greater Atlanta Coalition on Health Care, 1985—. Contbr. articles to profl. jours. Mem. Morningside/Lenox Park Civic Assn. Recipient research award Nat. Conf. on High Blood Pressure Control, 1981. Mem. ACLU, NOW, Am. Pub. Health Assn. (women's caucus com., presenter 1980, 81), Am. Coll. Health-care Execs., Women Healthcare Execs., Am. Managed Care and Rev. Orgn. (presenter at nat. conf. 1989), Am. Assn. Preferred Provider Orgns., Delta Delta Delta. Democrat. Baptist. Office: SouthCare Med Alliance 3715 Northside Pkwy Bldg 400 Ste 300 Atlanta GA 30327

MCQUEEN, SANDRA MARILYN, educator, consultant; b. Greenville, S.C., Nov. 30, 1948; d. Clement Edgar and Sarah Elizabeth (Gentry) McQ. BA, Presbyn. Coll., 1970; MA, Presbyn. Sch. Christian Edn., 1972; PhD, Ga. State U., 1987. Cert. early childhood, spl. edn., gifted tchr., spl. edn. supr., Ga. Dir. christian edn. com. Rock Spring Presbyn. Ch., Atlanta, 1972-74; early childhood educator Atlanta Bd. of Edn., 1974-80, educator gifted children, 1980—; curriculum developer, in-svc. educator Atlanta Bd. Edn., 1989—. Mem. Justice for Women, Atlanta, 1980—, chair, 1985-86, co-chair, 1989-90; mem. Rock Spring Chancel Choir, Atlanta, 1978—, sec., 1987-89; mem. Rock Spring Presbyn. Ch., Atlanta, 1972—, elder, 1986-88; mem. Refugee Resettlement, Greater Atlanta Presbytery, 1989—; mem. Skyline Network, 1989—, High Mus. Young Careers, Alliance Theatre Angel, Metro Atlanta Gifted Consortium. Named Tchr. of Yr. Sutton Middle Sch., 1985; Apple Corp. grantee, 1986; recipient Fulbright Scholarship, 1990. Mem. NEA, Ga. Edn. Assn., Assn. Supervision and Curriculum Devel., Atlanta Assn. Educators, Metro Consortium Gifted Educators, Skyline Network of Foxfire, Kappa Delta Pi. Office: 4360 Powers Ferry Rd NW Atlanta GA 30327

MCQUERN, MARCIA ALICE, newspaper editor; b. Riverside, Calif., Sept. 3, 1942; d. Arthur Carlyle and Dorothy Louise (Krupke) Knopf; m. Lynn Morris McQuern, June 7, 1969. BA in Polit. Sci., U. Calif., Santa Barbara, 1964; MS in Journalism, Norhtwestern U., 1966. Reporter The Press-Enterprise, Riverside, 1966-72, city editor, 1972-74, capitol corrs., 1975-78, dep. mng. editor news, 1984-85, mng. editor news, 1985-87, exec. editor, 1988—; asst. metro editor The Sacramento Bee, 1974-75; editor state and polit. news The San Diego Union, 1978-79, city editor, 1979-84; juror Pulitzer Prize in Journalism, 1982, 83. Mem. editorial bd. Calif. Lawyer mag., San Francisco, 1983-88. Recipient Journalism award Calif. State Bar Assn., 1967, Sweep-stakes award Twin Counties Press Club, Riverside and San Bernardino, 1972. Mem. Am. Soc. Newspaper Editors, Calif. Soc. Newspaper Editors, AP Mng. Editors, Soc. Profl. Journalists, U. Calif.-Santa Barbara Alumni Assn. (bd. dirs. 1983-89). Home: 5717 Bedford Dr Riverside CA 92506 Office: Press-Enterprise Co 3512 14th St Riverside CA 92501

MCQUIDE, PAMELA ANN, nurse; b. Racine, Wis., Oct. 7, 1951; d. Arthur C. and Carol Jean (Freudenwald) Massmann; m. Lawrence J. Drexler, Apr. 1972 (div. May 1980); m. Scott Little McQuide, Sept. 4, 1982. Diploma in nursing, Columbia Hosp. Sch. of Nursing, Milw., 1977; BA in French, U. Wis., 1979; BSN, Alverno Coll., 1986. Staff nurse

Columbia Hosp., Milw., 1978-80, unit tchr., staff nurse, 1980-83, asst. head nurse, 1980-83, nurse mgr., 1985-87, patient svcs. coord., 1986-87, nurse mgr., 1987-89, spl. projects coord., 1989—; nurse intern rep., 1989—. Columnist Nursing Dimension, 1986-87, Synapse, 1987; interviewer TV show Milwaukee Observer, 1987. CPR instr., trainer Am. Heart Assn., Milw., 1978—; mem. steering com. Coalition for Recruitment and Retention of Nurses, Milw., 1987—, Sane Nuclear Energy, Washington, 1986-87; vol. kitchen coord. Gathering Food Program, job mentor Interfaith Conf. of Greater Milw. Mem. NAFE, LWV, Am. Assn. Neurosci. Nurses (legis. chair 1987—, rep. 1988—), Am. Nurses Assn., Wis. Nurses Assn. (chmn. Milw. dist. legis. com. chmn. 1987-89, pres.-elect 1988-89, pres. Milw. dist. nurses 1989—), Nat. League of Nursing, Alliance Francaise, 9 to 5. Democrat. Episcopalian. Home: 4474 N Murray Shorewood WI 53211 Office: Columbia Hosp 2025 E Newport Shorewood WI 53211

MC QUILLAN, MARGARET MARY, publishing company executive; b. N.Y.C.; d. John A. and Margaret (Higgins) McQ.; A.B., Coll. New Rochelle, 1945; M.A. Columbia U., 1948. With Harcourt Brace Jovanovich, Inc. (formerly Harcourt, Brace & World), N.Y.C., 1949-89, ret., 1989; asst. sec., 1960-70, sec., 1971-89, v.p. 1975-78, adminstrv. v.p., 1978-80, sr. v.p., 1980-89. Home: 125 Crestwood Ave Tuckahoe NY 10707 Office: Harcourt Brace Jovanovich Inc 6277 Sea Harbor Dr Orlando FL 32887

MCQUILLAN, WENDY NEWFIELD, marketing professional; b. Hartford, Conn., Apr. 3, 1939; d. Albert Hartman and Joy Frances (Bernstein) Newfield; m. Richard L. Tavrow, Aug. 30, 1964 (div.). m. Walter McQuillan, Sept. 7, 1970 (div.). BA, Skidmore Coll., 1961; MA, Columbia U., 1963, PhD, 1965. Rsch. acct. exec. Foote, cone and Belding, Young & Rubicam, N.Y.C., 1964-69; rsch. mgr. RJR Foods, N.Y.C., 1969-71; pres. Advance Data Systems, San Juan, P.R., 1971-74; v.p., assoc. rsch. dir. Grey Advt., N.Y.C., 1974-78; exec. v.p., dir. market rsch. Avis Rent-A-Car (Worldwide), Garden City, N.Y., 1979-83; acting dir. market rsch. Brit. Airways (Worldwide), London, 1983-84; pres. W.N. McQuillan/McQuillan Lists, N.Y.C., 1984-88; v.p., dir. mktg. Grey Can., Toronto, Ont., Can. 1988—; mem. rsch. authority Pacific Area Travel Assn., 1980-83; prof. psychology Am. U., San Juan, P.R., 1972-74. Math. tutor Neighborhood Assn., N.Y.C., 1984-86. Mem. Profl. Market Rsch. Soc. (Toronto), Can. Pharm. Market Rsch. Assn. (Toronto). Home: 63 St Clair W, #305, Toronto, ON Canada M4S 3C4 Office: Grey Can, 1881 Yonge St, Toronto, ON Canada M4S 3C4

MCQUIRK, ROSEMARY PUMMILL, manufacturing executive; b. Olney, Tex., Dec. 31, 1933; d. Sam Levy Pummill and Lola Myrtle (Moses) Pummill Young; m. Oliver Loving III, Nov. 11, 1950 (div. 1965); children: Robert, Stephen, Oliver IV, Gregory; m. Robert James McQuirk, Dec. 8, 1965. Diploma, Rutherford Bus. Sch., Dallas, 1966. Exec. sec. Sunshine Pecan Co., San Antonio, 1966-67; office mgr. Aircraft Maintenance Equipment Co., Dallas, 1967-68, Braewood Homes, Dallas, 1970-71, Browning & Juvenal Mfg., Garland, Tex., 1976-78; exec. sec. Core Labs., Dallas, 1974-76; co-owner, sec-treas. Time Delay Corp., Dallas, 1978—, also bd. dirs. Officer, 2nd v.p. White Rock Rep. Women's Club, 1984—. Mem. U.S. Coast Guard Aux. Methodist. Office: Time Delay Corp 10440 N Central 210 LB206 Dallas TX 75231

MCRAE, NANCY ELIZABETH, musician; b. Pinehurst, N.C., Jan. 30, 1943; d. Harris M. and Nancy T. (Thomas) McR. Student, The Citadel, 1963-64; BA, Fla. So. Coll., 1965; student, Juilliard Sch., 1966-67; MusM in Piano Pedagogy, U. S.C., 1987. Cert. piano tchr., S.C. Pvt. tchr. V. Weston Sch. of Music, Charleston, S.C., 1965-66; accompanist, coach Charleston Opera Co., 1965-66; dir. music Charleston Air Force Base, 1966; reporter, feature writer The State/Columbia (S.C.) Record, 1967-68; writer, assoc. producer S.C. Ednl. TV, Columbia, 1969-72; pvt. piano and voice tchr. Columbia, 1968-78, Georgetown, S.C., 1978-80, Litchfield Beach, S.C., 1980-87; journalist, critic The Sun News, Myrtle Beach, S.C., 1978-84; feature writer Himmelsbach Pubs., North Myrtle Beach, S.C., 1984—; sec., treas., mgr. Ellerbe (N.C.) Springs Inn & Restaurant, 1985—; sec., treas. Boone Hall Plantation, Inc., Mt. Pleasant, S.C., 1985—; bd. dirs. Wheelwright Coun. of Arts, Conway, S.C.; mem. Richmond County Tourism and Devel. Authority, Rockingham, N.C., 1989—. Mem. Music Tchr.'s Nat. Assn., S.C. Music Tchrs. Assn. (cert., chmn., editor 1976-84), Charleston County Travel Coun. (bd. dirs. 1980-84), Delta Beta, Zeta Tau Alpha (standrards chmn.). Methodist. Home: 2606 Oak Dr Pawleys Island SC 29585 Office: 126 Page St PO Box 250 Ellerbe NC 28338

MCREYNOLDS, LAURA MAGNUS, advertising executive; b. Higland Park, Ill., Nov. 12, 1959; d. Charles Alan Magnus and Nancy Stanton (Crews) Magnus; m. Anthony Joseph McReynolds, Oct. 5, 1986. BA, U. Mich., 1983. Acct. exec. Ann Arbor (Mich.) Observer, 1984-85; assoc. creative dir. Benson-Le Duc Advt., Ann Arbor, 1985-88; owner, creative dir. Reinhart, McReynolds & Magnus, Ann Arbor, 1988—. Author: (one-act play) The Unicorn, 1983 (Hopwood award 1983). Office: Reinhart McReynolds et al 285 E Liberty Ann Arbor MI 48104

MCREYNOLDS, MARY MAUREEN, municipal environmental administrator, consultant; b. Tacoma, July 15, 1940; d. Andrew Harley and Mary Leone (McGuire) Sims; m. Gerald Aaron McReynolds, Dec. 10, 1964. Student Coll. Puget Sound, 1957-59; BA, U. Oreg., 1961; PhD, U. Chgo., 1966; postgrad. San Diego State U., 1973-75. NIH postdoctoral fellow U. Tex., Austin, 1966-68, mem. adj. faculty, 1980-82, mem. bi-fellow U. Tex., Austin, 1966-68, mem. adj. faculty, 1980-82, mem. bi-ohazards com., 1981—; research assoc. Stanford U., Calif., 1968-71; chemist assoc. Syva Co., Palo Alto, Calif., 1972; environ. specialist County of San Diego, Calif., 1973-75; dept. head City of Austin, 1976-84, chief environ. officer, 1984-85, utility environ. mgr., 1985—; cons. enologist Mirassou Vineyards, San Jose, Calif., 1969-72; lectr. Wright Inst., Berkeley, Calif., 1971-72; instr. San Diego State U., 1974-75. Editor Dist. 56 newsletter, 1989—; contbr. articles to profl. pubis. U.S.-Mexico Sister Cities del., 1983-85; sponsor, chaperone Tex.-South Australia Youth Exchange, 1986; active Leadership Austin, 1987-88; mem. Austin-Adelaide Sister City Com., 1988-89, chmn., 1989—; bd. dirs. Internat. Hospitality Com., 1989—. USPHS tng. grantee U. Chgo., 1961-64; univ. fellow U. Chgo., 1961-66. Mem. Water Pollution Control Fedn. (v.p. local chpt. 1988-89, pres.-elect 1989—), Am. Planning Assn., Am. Inst. Cert. Planners (cert.), Assn. Environ. Profls., AAAS, Am. Water Resources Assn., Austin Soc. Pub. Adminstrn., Nat. Assn. Female Execs., Zeta Tau Alpha. Lodges: Soroptimists (dir. Soroptimist Manor 1978-80, 83-85, v.p. chpt. 1983-85, pres. chpt. 1985-87, chpt. dir. 1987-88, rep. youth citizenship award com. 1986-88, chmn. South Cen. region UN com. 1988—), Toastmasters (club pres. 1981, 88, area gov. 1981-82, div. lt. gov. 1983-84, Able Toastmaster award 1983, Dist. 56 Table Topics award 1986, Disting. Toastmaster award dist. 56 no. div. 1987, Outstanding Toastmaster award 1987). Avocations: gourmet food and wine. Office: City of Austin PO Box 1088 Austin TX 78767

MCROBERTS, JOYCE, state legislator; b. Salmon, Idaho, July 31, 1941; m. Darrell S. McRoberts; children: Walter, Angela, Douglas. Ed., Twin Falls Bus. Coll. Mem. Idaho State Senate. Republican. Home: 342 Monroe Pl Twin Falls ID 83301*

MCROBERTS, JUNE HATTIE, interior designer; b. Grosse Pointe, Mich., Mar. 26, 1931; d. Willard Winfield and Cleo Verna (Holloway) Bishop; m. Nelson Leon McRoberts, June 6, 1953; children: Ann McRoberts Johnson, Eric, Sara McRoberts Mascetti. AA, Coll. DuPage, 1972; postgrad., Chgo. Acad. Fine Arts, 1974-75; BA, No. Ill. U., 1981. Owner, designer June McRoberts Interiors, Batavia, Ill., 1971—; pres. Flutes & Swags Ltd., Batavia, 1988—. Contbr. pub. newsletter The Designing Eye, 1980-82. Mem. adv. com. interior design program Coll. DuPage, Glen Ellyn, Ill., 1973-80. Mem. Interior Design Soc. (copywriter newsletter 1983-85, pres. Chgo. chpt. 1985-87). Baptist. Home: 1255 Woodland Ave Batavia IL 60510

MCRORIE, ALICE RHYNE, data processing executive; b. Charlotte, N.C., Oct. 31, 1946; d. Henry Garrett and Rebecca Lee (Harrelson) Rhyne; m. Charles Winston McRorie, Nov. 1, 1969; 1 child, Karin Lindsay. BA in English, U. N.C. Greensboro, 1968. Programmer Nat. Security Agy., Ft. Meade, Md., 1968-72, Puritan Life Ins. Co., Providence, 1972-73; systems analyst Am. Railroads, Washington, 1974-79; cons. Data Base Mgmt., Inc., Springfield, Va., 1979-82; mgr., gen. application support Bur. Nat. Affairs, Inc., Washington, 1982-86, dir., info. systems devel., 1986—; sec.,

bd. dirs. Rhyne Floral Supply Mfg. Co., Dallas, N.C., 1968-72. Pres. Browne Acad. Parent-Tchr. League, Springfield, 1982-83. Mem. Data Processing Mgmt. Assn., Digital Equipment Computers Users Soc., Quality Assurance Inst. Democrat. Lutheran. Home: 4429 Willow Woods Dr Annandale VA 22003 Office: BNA Inc 1231 25th St NW Washington DC 20037

MCSHIRLEY, SUSAN RUTH, gift industry company executive, consultant; b. Glendale, Calif., July 31, 1945; d. Robert Claude and Lillian Dora (Mable) McS. B.S., U. Calif.-Berkeley, 1967. Nat. sales dir. McShirley Products, Glendale, Calif., 1967-71, Viade Products, Camarillo, Calif., 1972-80; pres. SRM Press, Inc., L.A., 1980—; nat. sales cons. Warner Bros. Records, Burbank, Calif., 1985. Author: Racquetball: Where to Play, USA, 1978. Patentee picture pen. Creator novelty trademarks including Collectable Critters, Preppy Pen, The Pig Pen, The Road Hog, The Drug Free Zone. Mem. Calif. Alumni Assn., Alpha Omicron Pi. Avocations: travel, photography, tennis, foreign languages. Home: 15947 Temecula St Pacific Palisades CA 90272 Office: SRM Press Inc 4216 1/2 Glencoe Ave Marina Del Rey CA 90292

MCSWEENEY, FRANCES KAYE, psychology educator; b. Rochester, N.Y., Feb. 6, 1948; d. Edward William and Elsie Winifred (Kingland) McS. BA, Smith Coll., 1969; MA, Harvard U., 1972, PhD, 1974. Lectr. McMaster U., Hamilton, Ont., Can., 1973-74; asst. prof. Wash. State U., Pullman, 1974-79, assoc. prof., 1979-83, prof. psychology, 1983—, chmn. dept. psychology, 1986—; cons. in field. Contbr. articles to profl. jours. Woodrow Wilson fellow, Sloan Fellow, 1968-69; NSF fellow, 1970-72; NIMH fellow, 1973. Mem. Am. Psychol. Assn., Am. Psychol. Soc., Western Psychol. Assn., Psychonomic Soc., Assn. Behavior Analysis, Phi Kappa Phi, Phi Beta Kappa, Sigma Xi. Home: SW 860 Alcora Pullman WA 99163 Office: Wash State U Dept Psychology Pullman WA 99164-4820

MCSWEENEY, JUNE ELIZABETH, printing company executive; b. Boston, June 18, 1932; d. William Earnest and Mabel Evelyn (Ricker) Mortimer; m. Charles Edward McSweeney, June 21, 1952; children: David Charles, Donna Marie, Diane June. Student Boston U., 1948-52; A.S., Northeastern U., 1970, B.S., 1974. Policywriter T.C. Curran Ins., Hyde Park, Mass. 1948-56; office mgr. Slattery Ins., Abington, Mass., 1954-70; v.p., treas. Fairmount Press, Inc., Rockland, Mass., 1967—. Chmn. edn./ bus. community Alliance Rockland pub. schs., 1982—; bd. dirs. White Island Pond Conservation Alliance, East Wareham, Mass., 1986—. Editor: MSFWC Federation Topics, 1988—. Mem. Am. Soc. Notaries, Printing Industries Am., Mass. State Fedn. Women's Clubs (Quincy, trustee endowment fund 1982-84, dir. evening div. 1986-88), Sigma Epsilon Rho, Epsilon Sigma Omicron. Home: 250 Barker Rd East Wareham MA 02538 Office: Fairmount Press Inc 496 Union St Rockland MA 02370

MCTEAGUE, LINDA BRAGDON, preservation planner, consultant; b. Rahway, N.J.; d. Lyle M. and Garnet (Gowdy) Cooper; m. John W. Bragdon; children: David A., Lucinda J. AB, Rutgers U., 1966, M of City and Regional Planning, 1984. Tchr. secondary history and Eng. Rahway High Sch. and The Vail Deane Sch., Elizabeth, N.J., 1966-84; preservation planner Union County, N.J., 1984—; adj. prof. Rutgers U., New Brunswick, 1986-88; advisor N.J. State Hist. Preservation Plan, 1987—; mem. Resource Recovery Aesthetics Rev. Com. of Union County Utilities Authority, Rahway Zoning Bd. Adjustment; cons. in field. Editor, Author: Preserving New Jersey, 1986, rev. edit., 1987; editor; designer: Rediscovery of Rahway, 1976; contbr. articles to profl. jours. State planner Washington Inaugural Bicentennial Project, 1988-89; trustee Proprietary House Assn., Perth Amboy, N.J., 1988—. Mem. Am. Planning Assn., Nat. Trust for Hist. Preservation, N.J. Hist. Soc. Home and Office: 1208 Pierpont St Rahway NJ 07065

MCVAY, DORIS ELAINE, small business owner; b. Bellaire, Ohio, Sept. 22, 1955; d. William Mansell and Eunice Juanita (Cumberledge) Hammond; m. Michael A. McVay, Dec. 17, 1977; children: Nicole Summer, Jessica Michelle. BS, W.Va. Community Coll., 1977. Mgr. Van Heusen's, Mobile, Ala.; acct. Va. Welding, Charleston; mgr. Dan Howards Maternity, Louisville; gen. mgr., owner McVay Media, Inc., Cleveland, Ohio. Leader, advisor, jr. youth group. Mem. NAFE.

MCVAY, RUTH LOUISE, retirement home administrator; b. Alexandria, S.D., Sept. 28, 1942; d. John B. and M. Lorene (Nyhouse) McV. BS, S.D. State U., 1965; MPA, Roosevelt U., Chgo., 1978. Lic. nursing home administrator administr., Wis., Ill. Statis. analyst Am. Family Ins. Co., Madison, Wis., 1965-68; recreation supr. ARC, Tex., S.C., Japan, The Philippines, 1968-72; asst. administr. Meth. Home, Chgo., 1973-77, Cen. Bapt. Home, Chgo., 1977-85; administr. Schmitt Woodland Hills, Richland Center, Wis., 1985—; bd. dirs. Hospice, Richland Center, 1985—. Mem. Ill. Assn. Homes for Aged, Wis. Assn. Homes for Aged, NAFE, United Meth. Assn. Health and Welfare Ministries, Rotary. Republican. Methodist. Home: 860 W Sunset Ln Richland Center WI 53581

MCVEY, DEVON PALMQUIST, financial company executive; b. L.A., July 15, 1961; d. Donald Harvey and Joanne (Hill) Palmquist; m. Jeffrey Scott McVey, Sept. 30, 1989. Student, U. Calif., Santa Barbara, 1979-83. Account adminstr. Pacific Investment Mgmt. Co., Newport Beach, Calif., 1983-85; mktg. assoc. Capital Guardian Trust Co., L.A., 1986-88; analyst Micronomics, L.A., 1988-89; market analyst Geneva Cos., Irvine, Calif., 1989; ops. mgr. Investors Diversified Svcs., Irvine, 1990—. Mem. Gold Club (bd. dirs. 1990). Republican. Home: 1753 Santa Ana Apt 102 Costa Mesa CA 92627 Office: IDS Fin Svcs 2 Park Plz Ste 1100 Irvine CA 92714

MCVEY, DIANE ELAINE, financial analyst; b. Wilmington, Del., Apr. 20, 1953; d. C. Granville and Margaret M. (Lindell) McV. AA in Acctg., Goldey Beacom Coll. (Del.), 1973, BS in Acctg., 1980; MBA in Mgmt., Fairleigh Dickinson U., 1985. Acct. Audio Visual Arts, Wilmington, 1973; cost acct. FMC Corp., Kennett Sq., Pa., 1973-75; asst. acct. NVF Corp., Kennett Sq., 1978-80; staff analyst GPU Nuclear, Parsippany, N.J., 1980—; owner, Demac Consulting, Dover, N.J., 1989—. Elder First Presbyn. Ch. Rockaway, N.J., 1986— session mem., 1988—. With U.S. Army, 1975-78. Mem. Assn. MBA Execs. Republican. Presbyterian.

MCVEY, MARCIA ALICE, educational administrator; b. San Jose, Calif., Aug. 31, 1934; d. Charles Thurston and Thelma (Hackett) McV.; B.A. Pomona Coll., 1955; M.A., Claremont Grad. Sch., 1959; Ed.D. (Delta Kappa Gamma Scholar), U. So. Calif., 1978. Tchr., Glendora Sch. Dist., 1955-59; tchr. Covina Valley Unified Sch. Dist., 1959-65, counselor, jr. high sch., 1965-67, asst. prin. jr. high, 1967-68, jr. high, 1968-72, 73-79; dir. curriculum and instruction Norwalk (Calif.) LaMirada Unified Sch. Dist., 1979-83; asst. supt. Centralia Sch. Dist., Buena Park (Calif.), 1983-86; deputy supt. Duarte Unified Sch. Dist., Calif., 1986—; ednl. cons.; mem. Calif. Dept. Edn. task force on conflict resolution in secondary schs., 1972-73. Community vol. Pomona Calif. Assocs.; mem. Calif. Curriculum Devel. and Supplemental Materials Commn., 1984-88. Kettering IDEA fellow, 1981. Mem. Assn. Calif. Sch. Adminstrs., Calif. Assn. Gifted, Assn. Supervision and Curriculum Devel., Calif. Inst. for Sch. Improvement (bd. dirs. 1988-89), AAUW, Phi Delta Kappa, Delta Kappa Gamma. Contbr. articles to profl. jours. Office: 1427 Buena Vista Ave Duarte CA 91010

MCVICAR, SHERRY FISHER, human resources executive; b. N.Y.C., Sept. 17, 1952; d. William Sidney and Beverly Harriet (Harris) Miller; m. Allan A. McVicar III, July 28, 1986. BA, Hofstra U., 1973; MS, Queens Coll., 1976. With Cox & Co., Inc., N.Y.C., 1973-76; mgr. tng. and labor rels. Quantor Corp., Mountain View, Calif., 1976-78; v.p. human resources Qume Corp., San Jose, Calif., 1978-87; Convergent, Inc., San Jose, 1987—; group v.p. human resources Unisys Network Computing Group, San Jose, 1989-90; v.p. human resources Unisys Computer Systems Product Group, San Jose, 1990—; cons. in field; speaker on labor rels. Mem. Am. Arbitration Assn. Office: Convergent Unisys NCG 30 E Plumeria St San Jose CA 95150

MCVICKER, MARY ELLEN HARSHBARGER, museum director, art history educator; b. Mexico, Mo., May 5, 1951; d. Don Milton and Harriet

Pauline (Mossholder) Harshbarger; m. Wiley Ray McVicker, June 2, 1973; children: Laura Elizabeth, Todd Michael. BA with honors, U. Mo., 1973, MA, 1975, PhD, Columbia, Mo., 1989. Instr. Columbia U., Mo., 1977-78, Cen. Meth. Coll., Fayette, Mo., 1978-85, mus. dir., 1980-85; project dir. Mo. Com. for Humanities, Fayette, 1981-85, Mo. Dept. Natural Resources Office Hist. Preservation, 1978-85; owner, Memories of Mo., Inc., 1986—. Author: History Book, 1984. V.p. Friends Hist. Boonville, Mo., 1982-87, pres., 1989; bd. dirs. Mus. Assocs. Mo. U., Columbia, 1981-83, Mo. Meth. Hist. Soc., Fayette, 1981-84; chmn. Bicentennial Celebration Methodism, Boonville, Mo., 1984. Mem. Mo. Alliance for Hist. Preservation (charter), AAUW (treas. 1977-79), Am. Assn. Museums, Centralia Hist. Soc. (project dir. 1978), Mus. Assocs. United Meth. Ch. (charter, bd. dir. 1981-83), Phi Beta Kappa, Mortar Bd. Democrat. Clubs: Women's (treas. 1977-79), United Meth. Women's Group (charter mem.). Avocations: collecting antiques, gardening, family farming, singing, travelling. Home: 813 Christus Dr Boonville MO 65233 Office: Memories of Mo Inc PO Box 228 Boonville MO 65233

MCWILLIAMS, CONSTANCE FLORENCE, health facility administrator; b. Pitts., Sept. 7, 1945; d. Bernard S. and Josephine (Mosakowski) Pawlowski; m. Frank X. McWilliams, Oct. 4, 1969. BSN summa cum laude, LaRoche Coll., Pitts., 1986, MSN, 1989; RN, St. Mary's Hosp. Sch. Nursing, Huntington, W.Va., 1966. RN, Pa., Ky., W.Va., Calif., Ohio, Mich., Ont., Can. Charge nurse coronary care Marquette (Mich.) Gen. Hosp., 1978; charge nurse critical care North Hills Passavant Hosp., Pitts., 1978-79; instr. Community Coll. Allegheny County, Pitts., 1980-86; nurse adminstr. Diagnostic Cardiac Lab. Assn., Pitts., 1979—. Mem. ACCN, AAANA, NAFE, Sigma Theta Tau, Theta Mu. Home: 143 Lingay Dr Glenshaw PA 15116 Office: 9104 Babcock Blvd Ste 4107 Pittsburgh PA 15237

MCWILLIAMS, MARGARET ANN, dietitian, author; b. Osage, Iowa, May 26, 1929; d. Alvin Randall and Mildred Irene (Lane) Edgar; children: Roger, Kathleen. B.S., Iowa State U., 1951, M.S., 1953; Ph.D., Oreg. State U., 1968. Registered dietitian. Asst. prof. home econs. Calif. State U., Los Angeles, 1961-66; assoc. prof. Calif. State U., 1966-68, prof., 1968—, chmn. dept., 1968-76; mem. Greater Los Angeles Nutrition Council, Calif. Liaison Council for Home Econs., Calif. Articulation for Home Econs.; mem. home econs. adv. coms. East Los Angeles Coll., Harbor Coll., Los Angeles City Coll., Pasadena City Coll., Compton Coll.; home econs. edn. and bus. adminstrs. Interdeptl. Council Food and Nutrition in Calif. Author: Food Fundamentals, 1966, 4th edit., 1985; Nutrition for the Growing Years, 1967, 4th edit., 1986, Experimental Foods Laboratory Manual, 1977, 3d edit., 1989, (with L. Kotschevar) Understanding Food, 1969, Illustrated Guide to Food Preparation, 1970, 6th edit., 1990, (with L. Davis) Food for You, 1971, 2d edit., 1976, The Meatless Cookbook, 1973, (with F. Stare) Living Nutrition, 1973, 4th edit., 1984, Nutrition for Good Health, 1974, 2d edit, 1982 (with H. Paine), Modern Food Preservation, 1977, Fundamentals of Meal Management, 1978, (with H. Heller) World of Nutrition, 1984, Parents Nutrition Book, 1986, Food: Experimental Perspectives, 1989; tech. cons., abstractor Am. Home Econs. Assn. Jour. Recipient Alumni Centennial award Iowa State U., 1971, Profl. Achievement award, 1977; Phi Upsilon Omicron Nat. Founders fellow, 1964; Home Economist in Bus. Nat. Found. fellow, 1967; Outstanding Prof. award Calif. State U., 1976. Mem. Am. Dietetic Assn., Inst. Food Technoloists, Soc. Nutrition Edn., Nat. Coun. Home Econs. Adminstrs., Phi Kappa Phi, Phi Upsilon Omicron, Omicron Nu, Iota Sigma Pi, Sigma Delta Epsilon, Sigma Alpha Iota. Home: PO Box 220 Redondo Beach CA 90277 Office: Calif State U FSCS Dept 5151 State University Dr Los Angeles CA 90277

MCWILLIAMS, SONJA LEE, transportation consultant; b. Joplin, Mo., July 29, 1947; d. Robert Lee Rogers and Dorothy Louise (Kinkade) Walton; 1 child, Tonya Lee. Grad. high sch., Kankakee, Ill. Lic. funeral dir. Broker, customer svc. rep. MCI Transporters, Joplin, 1983-85; office mgr., salesperson Greenlawn Memory Gardens, North Kingsville, Ohio, 1985-86; rate clk. Contract Freighters Inc., Joplin, 1986-87; sales agt. Transp. Mgmt. Svcs., Joplin, 1987-89; transp. cons. Beaufort Transfer Co., Joplin, 1989—. Mem. NAFE, Tri-State Traffic Club. Home: 701 Briarbrook Dr Carl Junction MO 64834

MEACHAM, HEATHER MUIR, college administrator; b. Springfield, Mass., June 25, 1941; d. Alexander Thomas and Margaret (Johnston) Muir; m. John E. Meacham, Aug. 15, 1964; children: Laurie Ann, Thomas John. BA, Chatham Coll., Pitts., 1962; MEd, Springfield Coll., 1963. Residence hall dir. SUNY, Oneonta, 1963-64; dir. student union SUNY, 1964-65; residence hall dir. Okla. State U., Stillwater, 1965-66; asst. dir. single student housing Okla. State U., 1966-68; instr. personal devel. course Alfred (N.Y.) State Coll., 1979-83, guest lectr., 1984-86, employment specialist Pub. Assistance/Comprehensive Employ., 1989—. Chmn. Ch. Coun., Union Univ. Ch., Alfred, 1985-87. Mem. AAUW (bd. dirs. 1981-87, pres. 1975-77), Assn. of Women of Alfred State Coll. (pres. 1971-72). Republican. Home: 43 Sayles St Alfred NY 14802 Office: PACE Victorian House Alfred State Coll Alfred NY 14802

MEAD, HARRIET COUNCIL, librarian, author; b. Franklin, Va., Jan. 11; d. Hutson and Ollie (Whitley) Council; m. Berne Matthews Mead, Jr., Dec. 2, 1940; children—William Whitley, Charles Council. BA, Coll. William and Mary, 1935; postgrad. Fla. State U., 1958-62, Rollins Coll., 1966, 70, 84. County libr. Carroll County, Hillsville, Va., 1935-36; city libr. Suffolk City Schs., Va., 1936-41; libr., media specialist Orange County Schs., Orlando, Fla., 1961-80. Author: The Irrepressible Saint, 1983, A Family Legacy, 1987. Contbr. article to mag. Sustaining mem. Jr. League Orlando, Winter Park, 1989, Soc. Colonial Dames in State of Fla., Orlando, 1987, Orange County Hist. Soc., 1989, LWV, Orlando, 1987. Mem. Friends of Libr., Fla. Coun. Librs., Orange County Media Specialists (pres. 1968-69), Nat. Soc. Colonial Dames, DAR, Orange County Ret. Educators. Democrat. Episcopalian. Avocation: watercolor painting. Home: 500 E Marks St Orlando FL 32803

MEAD, ROSEMARY ANTOINETTE, health service administrator; b. Ashtabula, Ohio, June 13, 1939; d. Rudolph F. and Lillian (Saverise) Venditti; m. Richard L. Mead, Oct. 25, 1958; children: Craig Richard, Christopher Lynn. Student, Kent State U., 1990—. Cert. literacy vol. Various clerical and legal secretarial positions, 1957-63; sec.-treas. Frank Nappi Found., Ashtabula, 1977-78; pub. rels. coord. Civic Recognitions Com. Ohio, Cleve., 1977-78; exec. sec. Ashtabula County Med. Ctr., Ashtabula Community Health Svcs., 1978—; co-mgr. Mead's Antique Popcorn Wagons & Talent Agy., 1970—. Bd. dirs. Salvation Army, 1985-87; vol. ARC, Ashtabula, 1968-70, Frank Nappi Found., Ashtabula, Kidney Dialysis Ctr., St. Jude Benefit, 1977-78; vol. pediatrics dept. Ashtabula County Med. Ctr.; mem. ch. choir Mt. Carmel Cath. Ch. Mem. LWV (dir. pub. rels. 1970-72, mem. com. 1972-74, treas. 1974-77, Ashtabula chpt.), Anita Girabaldi Lodge. Democrat. Roman Catholic. Home: 7429 Jefferson Rd Ashtabula OH 44004 Office: Ashtabula County Med Ctr 2420 Lake Ave Ashtabula OH 44004

MEADE, DOROTHY WINIFRED, educational administrator; b. N.Y.C., Jan. 26, 1935; d. Percival and Fraulien Franklin; m. Gerald H. Meade (div. 1987); 1 child, Myrla E. BA in Am. History, Queens Coll., Flushing, N.Y., 1970; MA in Corrective Reading, Bklyn. Coll., 1975; BA in Religious Edn., United Christian Coll., Bklyn., 1980; postgrad., Bklyn. Coll., 1984. Tchr. social studies cluster Pub. Sch. 137, Bklyn., 1979-83, curriculum coord. Follow Through Program, 1984-88, adminstrv. intern, 1983-84; staff developer social studies Cen. Sch. Dist. 23, Bklyn., 1988-89, dist. coord. Project Child, 1989—; mem. coop. bd. dis. 1053 E 13th St., Bklyn. Former mem. Ch. of the Master; participant in Crossroads Africa, 1958; nursery worker Bklyn. Tabernacle, 1986—. Mem. African Christian Tchrs., N.Y. Pub. Sch. Early Childhood Edn., N.Y. Geography Inst. Pentecostal. Home: 1053 E 13th St Brooklyn NY 11230

MEADE, MARY HENSELMAN, leasing company executive; b. Tacoma, Wash., Aug. 17, 1963; d. Roger Cambell and Donna (Rogers) Henselman; m. Vance Meade, Aug. 29, 1987. BA, Trinity U., San Antonio, 1985. Asst. mgr. Tex. Stock Exch., San Antonio; ins. supr. Enterprise Rent A Car, San Antonio; br. mgr. Enterprise Rent a Car, San Antonio. Mem. NAFE, NOW, Sigma Delta Phi. Republican. Home: 9307 Marbelhill San Antonio TX 78240 Office: 8318 Jones Maltsberger Rd Ste 103 San Antonio TX 78216

MEADE, PATRICIA SUE, marketing professional; b. Columbus, Ohio, Mar. 14, 1960; d. Harold Eugene and Glenna Rhae (Croaff) M. BS in Communications, Ohio U., 1982, M in Sports Administrn., 1984, MS in Communications, 1986. Dir. advt. The Pensacola (Fla.) Civic Ctr., 1984-85; asst. dir. mktg. Ohio Ctr. Co., Columbus, 1985-86; asst. v.p. mktg. Doctors Hosp., Columbus, 1986-88; regional mgr. mktg. Jacobs, Visconsi & Jacobs Co., Cleve., 1988-89; dir. bus. devel. and pub. affairs Deaconess Hosp., Cleve., 1989—; cons. in field, 1987—. Mem. Ohio Hosp. Assn., Am. Mktg. Assn., NAFE, New Orgn. Visual Artists. Club: Scandanavian Health Spa. Office: Deaconess Hosp 4229 Pearl Rd Cleveland OH 44109

MEADOR, ILEAN PRATER, librarian; b. Hueysville, Ky., July 14, 1934; d. Corbet and Carrie (Ratliff) Prater; m. Charley Meador, July 7, 1954. BS in Elem. Edn., Ea. Ky. State Coll., 1963, MA in Edn., MLS, 1969. Tchr. Wayland Sch., Hueysville, 1961-69; librarian Kit Carson Elem. Sch., Richmond, Ky., 1970—. Mem. Ky. Library Assn., Alpha Delta Kappa Eta. Democrat. Baptist. Home: 205 Miller Dr Richmond KY 40475

MEADOR, PATRICIA LANE, historian, educator; b. Memphis, Mar. 19, 1943; d. John Milton III and Jessie Lois (Castle) M. BS, Memphis State U., 1966; MA, U. Okla., 1970; MLS, La. State U., 1978. Cert. in archives Nat. Archives and Records Svc. Tchr. english Seinan Jo Gakuin, Kitakyushu, Japan, 1966-68; tchr. history, dean women Washington Coll. (Tenn.) Acad., 1970-71; instr. history Coll. of Emporia, Kans., 1971-73, Bapt. Christian Coll., Shreveport, La., 1973-75; archivist/assoc. libr. La. State U., Shreveport, 1975-89, asst. prof. history, 1989—. Co-author: Shreveport: A Photographic Remembrance, 1973-79, 86; contbr. articles to books. Bd. dirs. Friends of Archives of La., 1982—. Recipient Outstanding Faculty award La. State U., Shreveport, 1984. Mem. Soc. Southwest Archivists (v.p. 1978-80, pres. 1980-81, chmn. acquisitions sect. 1984-85, Disting. Svc. award 1986), La. Libr. Assn. (chmn. awards com. 1984-85), La. Hist. Assn. (chmn. archives com. 1985-86), Beta Phi Mu. Democrat. Methodist. Office: La State U Dept History One University Pl Shreveport LA 71115

MEADOR, WILMA JEAN, marketing executive; b. Gravelly, Ark., June 15, 1932; d. Ernest Cecil and Sue Frances (Poindexter) Wilson; m. John M. Meador III, Aug. 31, 1951; children: John M. IV, Matthew Warren. Student, Okla. Bapt. U., 1949-51, Okla. U., 1974-76. Exec. sec. various attys. Okla., 1953-68; adminstrv. asst. First. Am. Bank, Purcell, Okla., 1968-78; mktg. dir. Telum, Inc., Provo, Utah, 1979-86; v.p. media svcs. Am. Telemedia Network, Provo, 1986-87, v.p. pub. rels., investor rels., 1987—; sr. v.p., dir. Am. Mall Mktg., Inc., Scottsdale, Ariz., 1988—; lectr. communication seminars various cos., Utah, 1985—. Mem. Pub. Relations Soc. Am., Nat. Assn. Female Execs., Am. Mgmt. Assn. Republican. Baptist. Office: ATNN Inc 7418 E Helm Dr Scottsdale AZ 85260

MEAKIN, FAITH ANNE, librarian; b. Phila., Oct. 15, 1943; d. John Blanchard and Dorothy Aileen (Deane) M.; divorced. Student, Coe Coll., 1961-63; BA, Syracuse U., 1965, MLS, 1966. Cert. med. libr. Intern in med. libr. sci. Biomed. Libr., U. Calif., L.A., 1966-67; head, reference dept. Biomed. Libr., U. Calif. San Diego, La Jolla, 1967-78, head, pub. svcs., 1979-83; mgmt. fellow Biomed. Libr., U. Minn., Mpls., 1978-79; head reference and readers svcs. WHO, Geneva, 1983-88; exec. dir. Southeastern/Atlantic regional med. libr. svcs. U. Md. Health Scis Libr., Balt., 1989—; cons. Data-Trek, Encinitas, Calif., 1989—, Netherlands Leprosy Relief Assn., Amsterdam, 1988, Aga Khan U., Karachi, Pakistan, 1987—; project adv. Sci. Applications Internat. Corp., La Jolla, 1989—. Author: (bibliography) Spec Kit 82 Document Delivery, 1982; contbr. articles to profl. jours. USPHS intern, med. libr., L.A., 1966-67. Named to Council on Libr. Resources/Nat. Libr. Med. Health Scis. Libr. Mgmt. Intern Program, 1978-79. Mem. Med. Libr. Assn., ALA, Am. Coll. and Rsch. Libr. Assn., European Assn. Health Information and Librs., Beta Phi Mu. Home: 83 Bryan's Mill Way Catonsville MD 21228 Office: U Md Health Scis Libr 111 S Greene St Baltimore MD 21201

MEAL, LARIE, chemistry educator, consultant; b. Cin., June 15, 1939; d. George Lawrence Meal and Dorothy Louise (Heileman) Fitzpatrick. BS in Chemistry, U. Cin., 1961, PhD in Chemistry, 1966. Rsch. chemist U.S. Indsl. Chems., Cin., 1966-67; instr. chemistry U. Cin., 1968-69, asst. prof., 1969-75, assoc. prof., 1975-90, prof., 1990—, researcher, 1980—; cons. in field. Contbr. articles to sci. jours. Mem. AAAS, N.Y. Acad. Scis., Am. Chem. Soc., Internat. Assn. Arson Investigators, NOW, Planned Parenthood, Iota Sigma Pi. Democrat. Home: 2231 Slane Ave Cincinnati OH 45212 Office: U Cin 2220 Victory Pkwy Cincinnati OH 45206

MEALIA, JOANNE SCHRAM, marketing professional; b. Dearborn, Mich., Mar. 9, 1957; d. Joseph Herman and Joan Frances (Mulkeen) Schram; m. John Joseph Mealia, Oct. 23, 1982; 1 child, Alexandra Marie. BA in Bus., Mich. State U., 1979. Teaching asst. Mich. State U., East Lansing, 1977-78; computer science mktg. intern Quaker Oats Co., Chgo., 1978; mktg. rep. IBM, Indpls., 1979-81; regional specialist IBM, Toronto, Ont., Can., 1982; mktg. rep. IBM, Toronto, 1983-85, advt. mktg. rep., 1986-87; adv. instr., entry level tng. IBM, Toronto, Ont., Can., 1988; adv. mktg. rep. advanced systems mktg. IBM, Toronto, Ont., 1988—. Contbr. short story, Detroit News, (award 1968). Bd. dirs. St. Aidan Parish, Livonia, Mich., 1975; facilitator St. Gabriel Passionist Parish, Willowdale, Ont. 1983-85; fellow Jr. League, Toronto, 1986—; organizer Lunches with Leaders program, Toronto, 1974. Recipient Mich. Competitive scholars; named One of Outstanding Teenagers of Am. Fellow Women's Roundtable (sec. 1984-85); mem. Phi Beta Kappa, Kappa Delta. Republican. Roman Catholic. Club: Bayview Golf and Country (Toronto). Home: 5 Montford Dr, North York, ON Canada M1M 3H2 Office: IBM Can Ltd, IBM Tower, Toronto Dominion Ctr PO Box 15, Toronto, ON Canada M5K 1B1

MEANY, SARAH ANN, occupational therapist; b. Warren, Ohio, Feb. 20, 1928; d. Edward Anthony and Ida May (Van Cleef) M. BA, Lake Erie Coll., 1950; cert. in Occupational Therapy, Wash. U. Sch. Medicine, St. Louis, 1962. Occupational therapist Canton (Ohio) Rehab. Clinic, 1962-64, Children's Rehab. Ctr., Warren, 1964-66; dir. occupational therapy dept. Hillside Rehab. Hosp., Warren, 1966-75; owner, operator Pirate Sam, Ltd., San Salvador, The Bahamas, 1975-78; occupational therapist Wingate Oaks Ctr., Ft. Lauderdale, Fla., 1980—; owner Expertise Co., Broward County, Fla., 1987—. Author: Begin with Success - A Logical Approach to the Dressing Training of Children, 1988. Recipient Cert. Appreciation Fla. Lang. Speech and Hearing Assn., 1985. Mem. Am. Occupational Therapy Assn., Fla. Occupational Therapy Assn., Fla. Alliance of Occupational and Phys. Sch. Therapists, Council for Exceptional Children. Republican. Presbyterian. Home: 1281 NW 46th St Pompano Beach FL 33064 Office: Wingate Oaks Ctr 1211 NW 33d Terr Fort Lauderdale FL 33311

MEARA, ANNE, actress, writer; b. Bklyn., Sept. 20; d. Edward Joseph and Mary (Dempsey) M.; m. Gerald Stiller, Sept. 14, 1954; children: Amy, Benjamin. Student, Herbert Berghoff Studio, 1953-54. Apprentice in summer stock, Southold, L.I. and Woodstock, N.Y., 1950-53; off-Broadway appearances include A Month in the Country, 1954, Maedchen in Uniform, Ulysses in Uniform, 1955 (Show Bus. off-Broadway award), Ulysses in Nightown, 1958, The House of Blue Leaves, 1970, Spookhouse, 1983, Bosoms and Neglect, 1986, also with Shakespeare Co., Romeo and Juliet, Cen. Park, N.Y.C., 1957, Romeo and Juliet, 1988, Eastern Standard, 1989; film appearances include The Out-of-Towners, 1968, Lovers and Other Strangers, 1969, The Boys From Brazil, 1978, Fame, 1979, Nasty Habits (with husband Jerry Stiller), 1976; comedy act, 1963—; appearances Happy Medium and Medium Rare, Chgo., 1960-61, Village Gate, Phase Two and Blue Angel, N.Y.C., 1963, The Establishment, London, 1963; syndicated TV series Take Five With Stiller and Meara, 1977-78; numerous appearances on TV game and talk shows, also spls. and variety shows; rec. numerous comls. for TV and radio; star TV series Kate McShane, 1975; other TV appearances Archie Bunker's Place, 1979 (Co-recipient Voice of Imagery award Radio Advt. Bur. 1975); actress TV series Alf, 1986, writer, 1987; writer, actress TV movie The Other Woman, 1983 (co-recipient Writer's Guild Outstanding Achievement award 1983).

MEBANE, BARBARA MARGOT, service company executive; b. Sylacauga, Ala., July 21, 1947; d. Audrey Dixon and Mary Ellen (Yaikow) Baxley; m. James Lewis Mebane, Dec. 31, 1971; 1 child, Cieson Brooke. Grad. high sch., Albany, Ga. Line performer J. Taylor Dance Co., Miami, Fla., 1964-65; sales mgr. Dixie Readers Svc., Jackson, Miss., 1965-67; regional sales mgr. Robertson Products Co., Texarkana, Tex., 1967-75; owner, pres. Telco Sales, Svc. and Supply, Dallas, 1976—; owner The Dance Factory, ATS Svcs., Lewisville, Tex.; mem. Dance Masters, Miami, 1975—; mgmt. specialist SBA; cons. Lewisville Ballet, Gallerie Dance Ensemble, 1982; choreographer music videos for pay/cable TV, 1985; contract cons. for self-employed women; pub. speaker in field. Author: Paper on Positive Thinking, 1983. Sponsor St. Jude's Rsch. Hosp., Memphis, Cancer Rsch. Ctr., Dallas; mgr. Dance Connection; active Cancer Rsch. Found. Mem. Nat. Fedn. Ind. Businesses, Female and Minority Owned Bus. League, Assoc. Gen. Contractors (assoc.), Female Exec. Club N.Y.C. Avocations: working with children, teaching dance, writing. Home: 3701 Twin Oak Ct Flower Mound TX 75028 Office: Telco Sales Svc and Supply PO Box 29763 Dallas TX 75229

MECHERIKUNNEL, ANN POTTANAT, space scientist; b. Kerala State, India, Dec. 28, 1934; came to U.S., 1961; d. Varghese Joseph and Mariamma (Vadacherry) Pottanat; m. Thomas Paul Mecherikunnel, Sept. 23, 1961; children: Anne Rose, Paul Thomas. BS, Madras U., India, 1955; MS, Kerala U., India, 1958; PhD, George Washington U., 1970. Lectr. George Washington U., Washington, 1970-72; instr. Prince George's Community Coll., Largo, Md., 1972-74; rsch. assoc. NASA/GSFC, Greenbelt, Md., 1975-78, space scientist, 1978—; prin. investigator ERBE Sci. Team, 1980—. Contbr. articles to profl. jours. Mem. AAAS, Optical Soc. Am., Am. Geophys. Union. Home: 4110 N 16th Pl Arlington VA 22207 Office: Code 673 NASA Goddard Space Flight Greenbelt MD 22207

MECHIGIAN, NANCY LEE, word processing company executive; b. Highland Park, Mich., Feb. 8, 1941; d. John Peniamin and Arpie (Abajian) M. Student secretarial sci., Highland Park Jr. Coll., 1959-61; legal sec. studies, Florence Rose Study Course, Southfield, Mich., 1969. Sec. Mich. Employment Security Commn., Detroit, 1961-68; legal sec. Law Offices Stephen A. Crane, Southfield, Mich., 1969-71, Sheldon M. Lutz, Southfield, 1971-73, Clarence G. Carlson, Bloomfield Hills, Mich., 1975-76, Rubenstein, Allen & Isaacs, Southfield, 1976; owner, mgr. Typing By Nan, Southfield, 1977-85; account exec. 55Plus/Golden Yrs. newspaper, Southfield, 1985; sr. mcht. cons. Mich. Credit Card Svcs., Southfield, 1985; adminstrv. asst. Cliff Adams, CLU, ChFC, Troy, Mich., 1987; owner, mgr. Efficient Word Processing Svcs., Southfield, 1987—; owner Scholarships for Students, Southfield, 1989—. Data entry cons. St. John's Armenian Ch., Southfield, 1988-90, computer operator Armenia Earthquake Fund, 1988-90; nominated sec. of the day St. John's Armenian Ch. Parish Coun. Meeting, 1985. Home and Office: 19965 Butternut Ln Southfield MI 48076-1796

MEDARIS, FLORENCE ISABEL, osteopathic physician and surgeon; b. Kirksville, Mo.; d. Charles Edward and Nellie (Finley) Medaris; B.A., Coll. Wooster, 1932; D.O., Kirksville Coll. Osteopathy and Surgery, 1939; postgrad. U. Wis., Marquette U. Pvt. practice osteo. medicine and surgery, Milw., 1940—. Active Milwaukee County Mental Assn., Milw. Art Center, Friends of Art; mem. med. bd. dirs. Milw. Soc. Multiple S[illegible]erosis Soc., 1973—; mem. Mayor's Beautification Com., 1968—. Dir. [illegible]onta Manor, 1957-67, Brace Fund Bd. of Advt. Women of Milw., 1958-64, pres. bd., 1962-63, 77—; bd. mem. Bookfellows Milw.; finance com. Coll. Womens Club Found., 1971-78. Mem. Am. Osteo. Assn. (com. mental health 1964), Wis. Assn. Osteo. Physicians and Surgeons, Milw. Dist. Soc., Osteo. Physicians and Surgeons, Am. Coll. Gen. Practitioners, Applied Acad. Osteopathy, Am. Assn. U. Women, Inter-Group Council Women (pres. 1947-49, dir.), Wis. Pub. Health Assn., Council for Wis. Writers, Photog. Soc. Am., Wis. Acad. Scis., Arts and Letters, Delta Omega (nat. pres. 1952-53). Presbyn. Club: Zonta (bd. mem. Milw. 1968-69). Home: 1121 N Waverly Pl Milwaukee WI 53202 Office: 161 W Wisconsin Ave Milwaukee WI 53203

MEDCALF-DAVENPORT, NEVA ANN, school director; b. Las Cruces, N.Mex., Sept. 26, 1941; d. Morris G. May and Bernice Baxter; m. Don B. Davenport, Jan. 17, 1989; children: Morrisa, William. BS in Edn., Baldwin Wallace Coll., 1963; MA in Edn., Ariz. State U., 1969; postgrad., U. N.Mex. Cert. elem. sch. adminstr., reading specialist. Pvt. reading tutor Rochester, Mich., 1969-80; 1st grade tchr. Hope Christian Sch., Albuquerque, 1982-83, prin., 1983-90; reading supr. U. N.Mex., Albuquerque; dir. Calvary Christian Sch., Pacific Palisades, Calif., 1990—. Vol. ministry to former drug addicts and convicts Barrios for Jesus, 1988-90. Bible Study fellow City of Albuquerque, 1981-82. Mem. IRA, ASCD, Pi Lambda Theta, Phi Delta Kappa. Home: 18004 Coastline Dr #20 Malibu CA 90265 Office: Calvary Christian Sch 701 Palisades Dr Pacific Palisades CA 90272

MEDEIROS, BARBARA DENIS JEAN, retired accountant; b. Honolulu, Feb. 7, 1934; d. Anthony Sebastian and Rose (Furtado) Denis; m. Carlos Louis Medeiros, Mar. 28, 1953; children: Carlos Louis Jr., Matthew Mark, Joel Carter, Timothy Francis. Sec. The Med. Group, Kailua, Hawaii, 1956-62; preparer vital stats. Castle Med. Ctr., Kailua, 1962-77; tax preparer H&R Block Exec. Tax Service, Honolulu, 1979—, instr. income tax preparation, 1981—. Author: Eight Lines of Family Geneology, 1986. Mem. Beta Sigma Phi (pres. Honolulu chpt.). Democrat. Roman Catholic. Home: 73-4339 He'Ohe Pl Kailua-Kona HI 96740

MEDEROS, CAROLINA LUISA, transportation policy consultant; b. Rochester, Minn., July 1, 1947; d. Luis O. and Carolina (del Valle) M. BA, Vanderbilt U., 1969; MA, U. Chgo., 1971. Adminstrv. asst. Lt. Gov. of Ill., Chgo., 1972; sr. research assoc. U. Chgo., 1972; project mgr., cons. Urban Dynamics, Inner City Fund and Community Programs Inc., Chgo., 1972-73; legis. asst. to Senate pres. Ill. State Senate, Chgo. and Springfield, 1973-76; program analyst Dept Transp., Washington, 1976-79, chief, trans. assistance programs div., 1979-81, dir. programs and evaluation, 1981-88, chairwoman, sec.'s safety rev. task force, 1985-88; deputy asst. sec. for safety Dept Transp., 1988-89; cons. Patton, Boggs & Blow, Washington, 1990—. Recipient award for Meritorious Achievement, Sec. Transp. 1980, Superior Achievement award U.S. Dept. Transp., 1981, Sec.'s Gold Medal Award for Outstanding Achievement, 1986, Presdl. Rank award, 1987. Mem. Am. Assn. Budget and Program Analysis, Exec. Women in Govt., Womens Trans. Seminar, World Affairs Council of Washington, D.C. Home: 2723 O St NW Washington DC 20007 Office: Dept of Transp 400 7th St SW Washington DC 20590

MEDILL, MARY LAWSON, secretary; b. Erie, Pa.; d. John Elvin and Martha (Burdick) Lawson; m. C.W. Medill; children: John Kevin, Curtis Worthington. Freelance exec. sec.; pvt. practice River Oaks Enterprises, Houston. Author: One World of Twins: That Funny Mister You, 1989. Mem. Internat. Platform Assn. Home: PO Box 430266 Houston TX 77243

MEDINGER, ANN ELIZABETH, physician, educator; b. Phila., June 9, 1945; d. Frederick Gilbert and Jean Isabel (Marbarger) M.; m. Sean Thomas Beeny, May 30, 1977; children: Clare Margaret, Emily Ann. BA, Carleton Coll., 1967; MD, U. Pa., 1971. Diplomate Am. Bd. Internal Medicine. Assoc. prof. medicine and physiology George Washington U., Washington, 1990—; dir. pulmonary function lab. VA Med. Ctr., Washington, 1990—; mem. D.C. Pub. Health Commn. on Tobacco Abuse, Washington, 1989; community rep. NIH AIDS Ad Hoc Comm., Bethesda, Md., 1989; rep. Interagy. Task Force on Environ. Cancer, Heart and Lung Disease, Washington, 1990—. Editor: Handbook of Pulmonary Emergencies, 1986; contbr. articles to profl. jours. Fellow ACP, Am. Coll. Chest Physicians; mem. Am. Thoracic Soc., D.C. Thoracic Soc. (v.p.), Friends Med. Soc. Mem. Soc. of Friends. Office: VA Med Ctr Pulmonary Lab 50 Irving St NW Washington DC 20422

MEDLEY, MARY DEE, computer science educator; b. Milw., Aug. 17, 1943; d. John Douglass and Madeline (Otto) M.; children: Elizabeth K. Flaherty, Robert W. Flaherty, Jr. BA, Lake Forest Coll., 1982; MS, U. Ill., 1986. Asst. to actuary Washington Nat. Ins. Co., Evanston, Ill., 1965-69; teaching, rsch. asst. dept. computer sci. U. Ill., Urbana, 1982-86; asst. prof. Augusta (Ga.) Coll., 1986—; summer researcher Argonne (Ill.) Nat. Lab., 1989. Precinct chmn. Republican Party, Deerfield, Ill., 1972. Mem. Assn. Computing Machinery, IEEE, Sierra Club (mem. exec. com., chmn. outings com., 1986-89, group chmn., 1989—). Unitarian. Home: 564 Martin Ln Augusta GA 30909 Office: Augusta Coll Dept Math & Computer Sci 2500 Walton Way Augusta GA 30910

MEDLEY, SHERRILYN, auditor; b. Oneida, Ky., Sept. 7, 1946; d. Ora E. and Rheba (Allen) Rice; m. James F. Laughlin, Sept. 20, 1966 (div. Apr. 1969); m. James Silas Medley, Jan. 25, 1980. BS in Acctg., U. Ky., 1975; MBA, Xavier U., 1986. Cert. internal auditor, cert. fraud examiner. Tchr. Ky. Bus. Coll., Lexington, 1976-78; claims approver Met. Life Ins. Co., Lexington, 1967-73; staff acct. Jerrico, Inc., Lexington, 1976-77, acctg. supr., 1977-80, sr. auditor, 1980-82, internal audit supr., 1982-86; internal audit mgr., 1986-87; sr. internal. audit mgr., 1988—. Vol. Cen. Bapt. Aux., Lexington, 1984. Mem. Inst. Internal Auditors (chpt. pres. 1985-86), Nat. Assn. Accts., Bluegrass Soc. MBA's, Am. Assn. Female Execs. Beta Alpha Psi. Republican. Home: 2436 Brookshire Circle Lexington KY 40505

MEDOWAR, DEBRA BETH, utility company executive; b. Rockville Centre, N.Y., Apr. 8, 1960; d. Jerome S. and Goldie (Wenig) M. BA in French cum laude, U. Pa., 1981; MS in Mass Communications, Boston U., 1985; postgrad., NYU, 1989—. Visitor info. specialist Nat. Park Svc., Phila., 1981-82; teaching asst. Boston U., 1983; assoc. reporter Sta. WNEV-TV, Boston, 1984; reporter Sta. WBUR-FM, Boston, 1984-85; govt. rels. cons. Arts/Boston, 1985; account supr. Ruder Finn, N.Y.C., 1985-88; staff mgr. N.Y. Telephone Co., 1988—; pub. rels. cons. N.Y. Alliance for the Pub. Schs., 1989—; mktg. cons. Bel Canto Opera Co., N.Y.C., 1985—; adj. lectr. NYU Mgmt. Inst., N.Y.C., 1990—. Mem. Jr. Achievement, N.Y.C., 1988—. Mem. Pub. Rels. Soc. Am., French Inst. Office: NY Telephone Rm 4144 1095 Ave of the Americas New York NY 10036

MEDRANO, LUISA, clinical psychologist; b. Aguascalientes, Mex., Dec. 29, 1953; came to U.S., 1980; d. Maria-Luisa (Parada) M. BA in Psychology with honors, Iberoamericana U., Mexico City, 1979; D of Psychology, U. Denver, 1986. Lic. clin. psychologist, Mass., Mex. Psychotherapist Profl. Psychology Clinic, U. Denver, 1980-84; clin. fellow Mass. Mental Health Ctr., Harvard Med. Sch., Boston, 1984-85; staff psychologyst Withman (Mass.) Ctr. for Family Treatment, 1986-87; assoc. psychologist Brigham & Woman's Hosp., Boston, 1987-90; sr. staff psychologist So. Jamaica Plain Health Ctr. Brigham & Woman's Hosp. Harvard Med. Sch., Boston, 1985-90; pvt. practice Belmont, Mass., 1987—; sr. staff psychologist Trauma Clinic Mass. Mental Health Ctr. Harvard Med. Sch., Boston, 1988—; instr. psychology Dept. Psychiatry Harvard Med. Sch., 1987—; adj. faculty Mass. Sch. Profl. Psychology, Dedham, 1988—; founding mem. Boston Women's AIDS Info. Project, Boston, 1988—; v.p., bd. dirs. AIDS Action Com., Boston; bd. dirs. Latino Health Network, Boston; clin. supr. of psychology doctoral students So. Jamaica Plain Health Ctr., Brigham & Women's Hosp., 1986—, Trauma Clinic Mass. Mental Health Ctr., 1989—; staff psychologist, clin. assoc. in psychology Dept. Psychiatry Mass. Gen. Hosp. Harvard Med. Sch., 1990—. On-air family editor WBZ-TV, Boston, 1989—; contbg. editor Hispano Mass., 1990—. Scholarship Govt. Mex., 1979. Mem. APA (Hispanic Chpt.), Mass. Assn. Psychoanalytic Psychology, Boston Womans Edn. Project. Roman Catholic. Home: 16 Garrison Rd #6 Brookline MA 02146 Office: 26 Trapelo Rd Belmont MA 02178

MEDVEDOW, PHYLLIS KRONICK, service executive; b. New Haven, Feb. 18, 1931; d. Louis Barnard and Anna Helen (Skolnick) Kronick; m. Leon A. Medvedow, June 29, 1952; children: Jill Susan, Elisabeth Jane. BS, U. Conn., 1952; cert. advanced mgmt., Yale U., 1988. Exec. v.p. Congress Printers, Inc., New Haven, 1977-81; adminstrv. aide Conn. Gen. Assembly, Hartford, 1979-80; cons. community affairs Yale New Haven Hosp., 1982-83, pub. affairs specialist, 1983-85; asst. dir. community and govt. rels. Yale U., New Haven, 1985-87, assoc. dir. community and govt. rels., 1987-88, dir. community and govt. rels., 1988—; hosp. rep. Conn. Organ and Tissue Donor Coalition, New Haven, 1985—, Coalition on Financing Health Care for the Poor, New Haven, 1987—. Bd. dirs. Anti-Defamation League, New Haven, 1972-81, Shubert Performing Arts Ctr., New Haven, 1981-87; trustee, sec. chmn. door-to-door drives Metro Unit Am. Cancer Soc., Woodbridge, Conn., 1955-74; v.p. New Haven Bd. Edn., 1970-74; mem. distbn. com. New Haven Found., 1973-79; mem. distbn. com. United Way Greater New Haven, 1988—; mem. community rels. com. Greater New Haven Jewish Fedn., 1972—; mem. pub. rels. com. Vol. Action Ctr., New Haven, 1987-89, and others. Mem. Jewish Fedn. Bus. and Profl. Womens Group (bd. dirs New Haven chpt. 1986-88), Nat. Coun. Jewish Women (publicity chair 1984), Lions (1st Woman 1988—). Democrat.

MEDZERIAN, BARBARA LEWIS, psychologist; b. Pitts., Jan. 16, 1953; d. Charles William and Dorothy Ann (Kallman) Lewis; m. George J. Medzerian Jr., Aug. 18, 1979; children: Star Allyn, John Aram. PhD, U. Fla., 1979. Lic. psychologist, Fla. Drug abuse counselor Fla. Correctional Inst., Lowell, 1976-80; instr. Pensacola (Fla.) Jr. Coll., 1981-83; pvt. practice Pensacola, 1981-83; clin. dir. Avalon Ctr., Inc., Milton, Fla., 1983-87; psychologist Counseling & Psychol. Assocs., Pensacola, 1987-90; chief psychologist Fed. Bur. of Prisons, Pensacola, 1990—. Mem. Am. Psychol. Assn., N.W. Fla. Psychol. Assn., Gulf Coast Soc. Neurologists, Psychiatrists, Neuropsychiatrists and Psychologists, Am. Contact Bridge League. Office: Fed Bur of Prisons Saufley Field Pensacola FL 32509

MEE, HEIDI BAUMEISTER, educator; b. Milw., June 23, 1955; d. Hans Konrad and Shirley (Haeberle) Baumeister; m. Marlon Ray Mee, May 27, 1989. BS, U. Wis., Eau Claire, 1978; postgrad., U. Wis., La Crosse, 1988—. Cert. elem. educator, Wis. Kindergarten tchr. Tomah (Wis.) Sch. Dist., 1978—, tchr. remedial reading, math. and gifted and talented, 1979-80, co-chmn. kindergarten curriculum, 1988—, mem. sch. evaluation consortium, 1988—. Mem. Partnerships for Youth, Tomah, 1989—; bd. dirs. Area Community Theater, Tomah, 1985-87, Tomah Concert Assn., 1986—. Named Educator of Yr., Tomah Sch. Dist., 1985. Mem. Wis. Kindergarten Assn., Wis. Reading Assn., AAUW. Home: 809 McLean Ave Tomah WI 54660 Office: Tomah Sch Dist 813 Oak St Tomah WI 54660

MEE, JANICE KAY, school board executive; b. Wilimantic, Conn., July 27, 1939; d. Joseph and Katherine (Drobney) Lustig; m. Frank Thomas Mee, 1962; children: Laura Lynn, Robert Thomas, Linda Leigh. BS, U. Conn., 1962. Office mgr. Solahart of Sarasota (Fla.), 1978-80; customer svc. rep. Coast Fed. Savs. & Loan, Sarasota, 1980; mem. Sch. Bd. Sarasota County, Sarasota, 1986—. Mem. GTE Community Adv. Bd., 1987—; mem. community adv. bd. Jr. League, Sarasota, 1988—; bd. dirs., asst. to campaign chmn. United Way Sarasota County, 1989—; v.p. Consortium South Fla., 1988-89. Named Citizen of Yr., Sarasota-Manatee chpt. Phi Delta Kappa, 1981; recipient Golden Apple award Sch. Bd. Sarasota County, 1982, Community Svc. award United Way Sarasota County, 1988, Sch. Bd. Mem. of Yr. award Coun. Adminstrs. for Spl. Edn. Mem. Fla. Sch. Bds. Assn. (bd. dirs. 1988—, legis. chmn. 1989-90), Sarasota C. of C. (edn.-legis. com. 1989—), LWV, Am. Bus. Women's Assn. (citizenship award Sunrise chpt. 1989), AAUW (chmn. statewide task force on dropout prevention 1987-89). Republican. Home: 1701 Clower Creek Dr 159 Sarasota FL 34231 Office: Sch Bd Sarasota County Hatton St Sarasota FL 34231

MEEDER, DONNIS LEA, accountant, consultant; b. Stockton, Kans., May 20, 1929; d. Floyd Harold and Mabel Louise (Harsh) Kenworthy; m. Allison Woodrow Meeder, Aug. 13, 1949 (div. Mar. 1971); children: Lizbeth Louise Meeder Stone, Andrew William, Kurt Allison. Lic. contractor, Calif. Bookkeeper Pacific Laundry, San Pedro, Calif., 1946-47, San Pedro Sheet Metal Works, 1947-49; owner, mgr. Swiss Miss Goat Dairy, San Bernardino, Calif., 1951-62; bookkeeper Triangle Constrn. Co., Inc., San Bernardino, 1962-64, treas., 1964-70; treas. A-J Constrn. Co., Inc., San Bernardino, 1970-77, v.p., 1977-89; owner, mgr., cons., acct. Constrn. Bus. Svcs., Colton, Calif., 1989—. Author: (pamphlet) Consider a Career in Construction, 1976. Mem. Nat. Assn. Women in Constrn. (v.p. 1972-73, pres. 1973-74, nat. bd. dirs. 1978-79). Republican. Office: Constrn Bus Svcs 1420 E Cooley Dr Ste 200-B Colton CA 92324

MEEHAN, FANITSA FRANTZIS, interior designer; b. Tampa, Fla., June 22, 1944; d. George Theodasis and Zula (Pappas) Frantzis; m. George Francis Meehan II, July 6, 1966; 1 child, George Francis III. BA in Interior Design, Fla. State U., 1966. Interior designer Spl. Svcs. U.S. Navbal Base, Yokosuka, Japan, 1967-69, V.J. Lloyd's, San Diego, 1969-70, Sears & Roebuck, St. Petersburg, Fla., 1970; prin. Interiors by Fanitsa, Inc., St. Petersburg, 1970—; instr., interior design curriculum originator, St. Petersburg Jr. Coll., 1972-78; speaker in field. Chmn. fundraising event Pinellas Assn. Retarded Children, 1987-88, bd. dirs. black tie com., 1989—; bd. dirs. St. Petersburg sect. Am. Cancer Soc., 1988—, pres. Sword of Hope campaign, 1988-89, chmn. Love Lights a Tree, co-chmn. Sword of Hope Charity Ball, 1990; bd. dirs. Infinity Soc. for Abused Children, 1988-89; ball entertainment chmn. Am. Heart Assn., 1989—; bd. dirs., art chmn. Bayfront Med. Hosp. Aux., 1989—; bd. dirs. St. Petersburg Bar Aux., 1989—, reservations chmn., pres.-elect, 1990; chmn. spring affairs d'Art Stuart Soc. Mus. of Fine Arts, decorator Victorian Fundraiser Luncheon, 1990; active All Children's Hosp. Guild, St. Anthony's Hosp. Guild, League to Aid Retarded Children, Children's Home Soc.; mem. steering com. to elect Don Sullivan to the Fla. Senate; host Fla. Orch. Guild, 1990. Recipient Community Svc. award Am. Heart Assn., 1988, Youth Motivation award Nat. Alliance Businessmen, 1975. Mem. Am. Soc. Interior Designers (bd. dirs. Fla. chpt., v.p., past sec. Area III, newsletter editor, active state and local chpts.), Fla. Assn. Interior Designers (bd. dirs. 1989—, v.p. membership and fund raising, legis. liaison, chmn. fundraiser, chmn. designers craft market, chmn. trade show), Nat. Trust for Historic Preservation, Fla. Coalition Interior Designers, Tiger Bay Club, Delta Gamma Alumni. Republican. Greek Orthodox. Office: Interiors By Fanitsa Inc 3909 Central Ave Saint Petersburg FL 33713

MEEHAN, JOAN BARBARA, public relations professional; b. Albany, N.Y., Nov. 13, 1959; d. Francis Thomas and Mary Louise (Dinneen) M. BA, SUNY, Oswego, 1981. Sec. Am. Bankers Assn., Washington, 1981-83; adminstrv. asst. Harper Sharp & Abramson, Washington, 1983-85; assoc. account exec. Earle Palmer Brown Cos., Bethesda, Md., 1985-87; pub. rels. mgr. Manor Health Care Corp., Silver Spring, Md., 1987-89; sr. staff specialist pub. rels. ANA, Kansas City, Mo., 1989—. Mem. Pub. Rels. Soc. Am. (accredited), Internat. Orgn. Bus. Communicators. Democrat. Home: 4746 Roanoke Pkwy Apt 503 Kansas City MO 64112 Office: ANA 2420 Pershing Rd Kansas City MO 64108

MEEHAN, KANDY LEE, real estate executive; b. Alva, Okla., Mar. 17, 1951; d. Robert Leonard and Jeanette A. (Wade) Sams; m. J. Kevin Meehan, May 5, 1984; children: Caitlin Elizabeth, Carrie Kathleen. BS, Kans. State U., 1973, MS cum laude, 1974. Lic. broker Kans., Mo. Prof., head dept. Benedictine Coll., Atchison, Kans., 1974-76; sub. tchr. various sch. dists., Buffalo, 1977-78; prof. SUNY Coll., Buffalo, 1978-79; sales exec., mgr. Louis R. Trigg & Assocs., Overland Park, Kans., 1979-82; mgr., broker Coldwell Banker, Overland Park, 1983-87, Kansas City, Mo., 198-89; owner Home Rental Svcs., Inc., Overland Park, Kans., 1989—. Mem. Nat. Assn. Realtors, Kansas City Bd. Realtors, Johnson Bd. Realtors, Nat. Assn. Female Execs., Bus. and Profl. Women, Omicron Nu. Office: Home Rental Svcs Inc 10203 Metcalf Overland Park KS 66212

MEEHAN, MARJORIE MAE, health care manager and educator, nurse; b. Sanford, Mich., Oct. 20, 1935; d. Wilfred Groner and Doris (Grandy) Perrone; div. 1972; children: Jeffrey, Trent, Teresa. BSN, Adelphi U., 1965; MS, Calif. State Coll., 1972; MPA, U. Colo., 1986, doctoral studies, 1986—. Cert. graphoanalyst; cert. in nursing adminstrn., vocat. trade and tech. cert., edn. and adminstrn. cert., Calif.; RN, Mich. Charge nurse Hurley Hosp., Flint, Mich., 1956; staff nurse emergency room Jackson Meml. Hosp., Miami, Fla., 1957-58; staff nurse obstetrics U.S.N. Hosp., Quonset Point, R.I., 1960; pvt. duty nurse various cities, 1960-66; instr. med.-surgical nursing Methodist Hosp. Sch. Nursing, Memphis, 1966-68, Central Islip Psychiat. Ctr., Central Islip, N.Y., 1973-75; dir. nursing Kern Med. Ctr., Bakersfield, Calif., 1974-78; dir. nursing Denver Health & Hosps., 1978-89, oper. div. dir., 1989—; faculty nursing U. Colo., Denver, 1980—; faculty health sci. mgmt. Webster U., Aurora, Colo., 1986—; assoc. dir. Denver Nursing Project in Human Caring for AIDS Victims, 1988—; presenter hosp. assns., insts., nursing depts., 1988. Contbr. articles to Am. Jour. Nursing, 1971, Dimensions Critical Care, 1983, Nursing Adminstrn. Quar., 1988. Adv. bd. Atlantis Community, 1980-81; bd. dirs. Colo. Cancer Soc., 1979-81; orgnl. task force com. Calif. Soc. for Nursing Svc. Adminstrs., 1978-79; steering com. for hosp. design and planning Kern Med. Ctr., Bakersfield, Calif., 1976-79; adv. com. external degree nursing program and LVN-ADN program Bakersfield Coll., 1976-79; AIDS adv. coun. Dept. Health and Hosps., Denver, 1987; center assoc. dir., mem. organizing com. Denver Nursing Project in Human Caring, 1988. Fed. grant trainee Pub. Health Svc., HEW, 1963-65. Mem. Nat. League Nursing (recruitment com. 1988, resolutions com. 1988, nominating 1988), Colo. League Nursing (bd. dirs. 1984-89, scholarship chair 1986—). Office: Denver Health & Hosps 777 Bannock Denver CO 80204

MEEK, AMY GERTRUDE, retired educator; b. Frostburg, Md., Jan. 3, 1928; d. Arthur Stewart and Amy Laura (Brain) M. BS, Frostburg State U., 1950; MEd, U. Md., 1956; postgrad., Columbia U., 1964, Am. U., 1968-70. Cert. tchr., Md. Tchr. elem. sch. Prince Georges County Schs., Bradbury Heights, Md., 1950-51; tchr. elem. sch. Allegany County Schs., Cumberland, Md., 1951-60, Frostburg, 1960-84; now ret. Contbr. articles to hist. publs. Mem. Frostburg Hosp. Aux., 1987—; bd. dirs. Frostburg Hist. Mus., 1988; sec. Braddock Estates Civic Assn., Frostburg, 1988; mem. bldg. com. Frostburg Libr., 1989; tchr. Ch. Conf. Schs. of Mission, 1970; vol. tutor, 1986—; pres. Ch. Women United, 1989—. Mem. AAUW (past pres., treas. Md. div. 1974, Woman of Yr. Frostburg br. 1980), Cumberland-Hagerstown Dist. United Meth. Women (pres. 1985-89), Balt. Conf. United Meth. Women (chair fin. interpretation 1990—). Republican.

MEEK, CARRIE P., state legislator; 3 children. BS, Fla. A&M U., 1946, MS, U. Mich., 1948. Mem. Fla. Senate from Dist. 36, 1982—. Democrat. Office: 149 W Plaza Ste 236 Miami FL 33147*

MEEK, CARROLL LEE LARSON, psychologist, graphic designer; b. Whitehall, Mont., Oct. 6, 1942; d. Leland Carroll and Doris Grace (Husband) Larson; m. Saul Matthew Spiro, July 31, 1982. BA, Whitman Coll., 1964; MS, Ind. U., 1966; PhD, U. Idaho, 1972. Lic. psychologist, Wash., Idaho. Counselor U. Wis., OshKosh, 1966-68, U. Idaho Counseling Ctr., Moscow, 1968-69; psychologist Wash. State U., Pullman, 1969-82; counselor Ctr. for Personal & Family Counseling, Moscow, 1972-74; pvt. practice psychologist Pullman, 1982—; owner Graphed Charts and Kits for Miniature Needlepoint Tapestries, 1987—; mem. people/pet partnership Wash. State U., Pullman, 1979—; coord. crisis and rape intervention task force, 1980-84. Editor: Post-Traumatic Stress Disorder, 1990; contbr. articles to profl. jous. Mem. Am. Psychol. Assn., Am. Assn. Sex Educators, Counselors and Therapists, Nat. Register Health Svc. Office: SE 1205 Professional Mall Blvd, Ste 114 Pullman WA 99163

MEEK, SHELBA DIANA, accountant; b. New Martinsville, W.Va., Jan. 12, 1949; d. John Harold and Irene Marjorie (Weiss) Ferguson; m. Richard Floyd Meek, Sept. 4, 1971 (div.); children: Jennifer Christen Lea, Jessica Erin. BFA, Kent State U., 1971; postgrad., Cleve. State U. Mgr./instr. H&R Block, Cleve., 1977-84; acct. Robert Half Cleve., 1984-85; staff tax acct. Laventhol & Horwath, Cleve., 1985-90. bd. dirs. PTA, Maple Heights. Mem. Ohio Soc. CPA. Methodist. Home: 15000 James Ave Maple Heights OH 44137

MEEK, VIOLET IMHOF, chemistry educator; b. Geneva, Ill., June 12, 1939; d. John and Violet (Krepel) Imhof; m. Devon W. Meek, Aug. 21, 1965 (wid. Dec. 1988); children: Brian, Karen. BA summa cum laude, St. Olaf Coll., 1960; MS, U. Ill., 1962, PhD in Chemistry, 1964. Instr. chemistry Mount Holyoke Coll., South Hadley, Mass., 1964-65; asst. prof. to prof. Ohio Wesleyan U., Delaware, Ohio, 1965-84, dean for ednl. svcs., 1980-84; dir. annual programs Coun. Ind. Colls., Washington, 1984-86; assoc. dir. sponsored programs devel. Rsch. Found. Ohio State U., Columbus, 1986—; vis. dean U. Calif., Berkeley, 1982, Stanford U., Palo Alto, Calif., 1982; reviewer GTE Sci. and Tech. Program, Princeton, N.J., 1986-90, Goldwater Nat. Fellowships, Princeton, 1990. Co-author: Experimental General Chemistry, 1984; contbr. articles to profl. jours. Bd. dirs. Lutheran Campus Ministries, Columbus, 1988—, Lutheran Social Svcs., 1988—; chmn. synodical coms. Evangelical Lutheran Ch. in Am., Columbus, 1982—. Recipient Woodrow Wilson Fellowship, 1960. Mem. Nat. Coun. Rsch. Adminstrs. (named Outstanding New Profl. midwest region 1990), Am. Assn. Higher Edn., Phi Beta Kappa. Home: 209 W Beechwold Blvd Columbus OH 43214 Office: Ohio State Univ Rsch 1314 Kinnear Rd Columbus OH 43212-1194

MEEKISON, MARYFRAN, writer, photographer; b. Napoleon, Ohio, Apr. 9, 1919; d. Frank J. and Elizabeth (Keyes) Shaff; m. David Meekison, June 17, 1939; children: Maureen Meekison Houppert, David Francis, Beth Ann. Student, St. Mary's Coll., Notre Dame, Ind., 1936-39. Hist. writer, photographer, Napoleon, 1963—, St. Augustine Ch., 1983—. Author: (photographer) Canal Days to Modern Ways Revisited, 1984; (brochure) Canal Days to Modern Ways, 1963; mem. editorial adv. bd. Courier mag., 1989-91; contbr. articles to numerous mags. Steering com. Napoleon Susquicentennial, 1984; trustee Napoleon Pub. Lib., 1976—. Recipient Spl. citation Courier Alumnae mag., also numerous photography and writing awards. Mem. Alumnae Assn. St. Mary's Coll. (bd. dirs. 1985—), Literary Club. Democrat. Roman Catholic. Home: Box 253 318 W Washington Napoleon OH 43545

MEEKS, CAROL JEAN, educator; b. Columbus, Ohio, Mar. 9, 1946; d. Clarence Eugene and Clara Johanna (Schwartz) B.; m. Joseph Meeks, Aug. 17, 1968 (div. 1981); 1 child, Catherine Rachael. BS, Ohio State U., Mex., 1968; MS, Ohio State U., 1969, PhD, 1972. Rsch. asst., assoc. Ohio State U., Columbus, 1968-71; internship Columbus Area C. of C., Ohio, 1970; lectr. Ohio State U., Columbus, 1970, 72; asst. prof. U. Mass., Amherst, 1972-74; asst. prof. Cornell U., Ithaca, N.Y., 1974-78, assoc. prof., 1978-80; legis. fellow Senate Com. Banking, 1984; supr. economist, head housing section USDA, Washington, 1980-85; assoc. prof. housing and consumer econs. U. Ga., Athens, 1985-90; prof. U. Ga., 1990—; cons. Calif. Dept. Real Estate, 1976, Yale U., 1976-77, HUD, Cambridge, Mass., 1978, MIT Ctr. for Real Estate Devel. Ford Found. Project on Housing Policy; del. Northeast Ctr. for Rural Devel. Housing Policy Conf. Reviewer Home Econ. Rsch. Jour., 1987—, ACCI conf., 1987—; contbr. articles to profl. mags. Panel mem. Town of Amherst Landlord Tenant Bd.; bd. dirs. Am. Council Consumer Interests; adv. council HUD Nat. Mobile Home, 1978-80. Recipient Young Profl. award Ohio State U., 1979; named one of Outstanding Young Women of Am., 1979; Columbus Womens Chpt. Nat. Assn. Real Estate Bds. scholar, Gen. Foods fellow 1971-72, HEW grantee, 1978, travel grantee NSF bldg. rsch. bd. , AID grantee. Mem. Soc. Govt. Economists (bd. dirs. 1984-85, co-chmn. 1985), Am. Assn. Housing Educators (newsletter editor 1976-79, pres. 1983-84), Nat. Inst. Bldg. Sci. (bd. sec. 1984, 85, bd. dirs. 1981, 83, 85, 87—, futures commn.), Am. Real Estate and Urban Econs. Assn., Internat. Assn. Housing Sci., Com. on Status of Women in Econs., Internat. Assn. Housing Sci., Housing Mfg. Inst. Consensus Commn. on Fed. Stds., Nat. Assn. Home Bldrs. (smart house contract 1989), Epsilon Sigma Phi, Omicron Nu, others. Office: U Ga 212B Dawson Hall Athens GA 30602

MEEKS, YVONNE JOYCE, groundwater contamination engineer; b. Mpls., Nov. 11, 1955; d. Eldo Avery and Patricia Sally (Bougetz) M. BS in Geophysics, BS in Geology, U. Minn., 1983; MS in Hydrogeology, MS in Engring., Stanford U., 1986. Engr. Woodward-Clyde Cons., Oakland, Calif., 1986—. Contbr. articles to profl. jours. NSF fellow, 1983-86. Mem. Soc. Women Engrs. (chair career guidance 1988-90), ASCE, Nat. Water Well Assn. Office: Woodward-Clyde Cons 500 12th St #100 Oakland CA 94607

MEELHEIM, HELEN DIANE, nurse, nursing administrator; b. Charleston, W.Va., Mar. 25, 1952; d. Richard Young and Dolores (Frick) M. BS in Nursing, U. N.C., 1974; MS in Nursing, East Carolina U., 1982; postgrad., U. N.C. Charge nurse Pitt County Health Dept., Greenville, N.C., 1974-77; nursing adminstr. East Carolina U. Sch. of Med., Greenville, N.C., 1978—, clin. instr., 1986—; cons. Eastern Area Health Edn. Ctr., Greenville. Served to capt. Army Nurse Corps, U.S. Army Res. Mem. ANA (cert. family nurse practitioner), N.C. State Nurses Assn., N.C. Soc. Health Care Attys, The Assn. Nurse Attys., Women in Law, N.C. Assn of Women Attys., ABA (student mem.), N.C. Carolina Bar Assn., Hospice of E. Carolina, Sigma Theta Tau. Democrat. Episcopalian. Avocation: painting. Home: 32 Flemington Rd Chapel Hill NC 27514 Office: East Carolina U Sch Medicine Dept Surgery Greenville NC 27834

MEESE, ANN MARIE, property appraisal professional; b. Ord, Nebr., Feb. 28, 1959; d. Andrew B. and Genevieve J. (Boyce) Kusek; m. Darrell Dean Meese, Nov. 18, 1978; children: Jeffrey Ryan, Melissa Ann. Grad. high sch., Ord. Lic. real estate appraiser, Nebr. Cook, waitress, then asst. mgr. Ord Drive In and Restaurant, 1974-78; clk. St. Francis Hosp., Grand Island, Nebr., 1979; mgr. Parkview Motel, Ord, 1979-80; clk. Valley County Assessor, Ord, 1980-81; assessor County of Valley, Ord, 1981-88; appraisal supr. Lancaster County Assessor, Lincoln, Nebr., 1988—; speaker in field; adviser TV program on property tax, 1989. Sec.-treas. Ord/Comstock PTA, 1986-87; mem. Nebr. Ag Land Task Force, Lincoln, 1988. Mem. NAFE, Internat. Assn. Assessing Officers, Toastmasters, Ord Alumni Assn., Ord Bus. and Profl. Women. Republican. Roman Catholic. Office: Office of County Assessor County of Lancaster 555 S 10th St Lincoln NE 68508

MEESE, CELIA EDWARDS, pharmaceutical company executive; b. San Diego, May 10; d. Roy Clifford Edwards and Bessie Lucille (Lang) Hill; m. Jed D. Meese, July 6, 1963; 1 son, Scott Edwards. BA, U. Wis., 1964; BA (hon.), U. Taiwan, 1965. Office mgr. Pacific Telephone, San Jose, Calif., 1965-72; pres. Vitaline Corp., Ashland, Oreg., 1972—; v.p. RenalChem, Inc., San Jose, Calif., 1982—, Formulations Tech., Inc., Oakdale, Calif., 1982—; dir. Spectra Diagnostics, San Jose. Bd. dirs. So. Oreg. State Coll. Found.; vol. Tudor Guide. Mem. Pharm. Mfrs. Assn., Am. Soc. Bariatric Physicians, Mensa. Home: 88 Granite St Ashland OR 97520 Office: Vitaline Corp 722 Jefferson Ave Ashland OR 97520

MEFFERT, MARCELLA ANN (MARCY), freelance writer; b. Milw., June 10, 1934; d. John George and Margaret (Stankiewicz) Czarnecki; m. Roland M. Meffert, June 12, 1954; children: Jeffrey, Lisa, Sarah, Gregory, Douglas. Student, Marquette U., 1952-53, San Antonio Coll., 1983-84, U. New Orleans, 1990—. Humor columnist Citizen News, San Antonio, 1974-76; staff writer Northwest Light, San Antonio, 1976-78; staff writer, columnist San Antonio Light, 1978-81; assoc. producer Sta. WOAI Radio, San Antonio, 1981-83; with pub. rels. Sunshine Sch. for Deaf, San Antonio, 1983-84; rsch. editor Heloise, 1983—. Contbr. articles to newspapers, mags. and other publs., 1983—. Vol., bd. dirs. Sta. WRBH for the Blind, New Orleans, 1985—. Mem. Women in Communications, Inc., Tex. Press Women, Press Clubs in San Antonio, Press Clubs in New Orleans, La. Press Women, Profl. Journalism Soc. Home and Office: 6218 Argonne Blvd New Orleans LA 70124

MEFFERT-STEWART, SARAH, booking agent; b. San Antonio, May 29, 1962; d. Roland Matthew and Marcella (Czarneski) Meffert; m. John Stewart, June 16, 1984; 1 child, Matthew James Stewart. BS, Stephen F. Austin State U., 1984. 3rd class operator (for radio). Disk jockey Sta. KTFM Radio, San Antonio, 1984; disk jockey Sta. KZEP Radio, San Antonio, 1986-87; mus. instrument sales Alamo Music Co., San Antonio, 1986-87; promotions asst., audio engr. KENS II/KENS Prodns., San Antonio, 1984-85; pub. affairs dir. Sta. KRRT-TV, San Antonio, 1987-88; with advt. sales Sanren Advt., San Antonio, 1988; store mgr. Bejeweled, San Antonio, 1988-89; audio operator Sea World Tex., San Antonio, 1989; booking agt. Sturchio Entertainment, Inc., San Antonio, 1989—. Composer 3 musical arrangements, 1984. Recipient 2 Appreciation awards USAF, San Antonio, 1988, Appreciation award Voters Registration Bur., San Antonio, 1987. Mem. Women in Communications (treas. 1988-89, internship/scholarship chair 1985-88, pres. student chpt. 1983-84, founder/treas. student chpt. 1982-83). Home: 6532 Adair Dr San Antonio TX 78238 Office: Sturchio Entertainment Inc 10328 Kotzebue San Antonio TX 78217

MEGGS, MARGARET L., religious educator; b. Springfield, Tenn., Aug. 30, 1953; d. Emerson Alford and Margaret Wilkerson (Fort) M. AA with honors, Martin Meth. Coll., 1973; BA magna cum laude, Lambuth Coll., 1975; MA with highest honors, Scarritt Grad. Sch., 1986. Abstractor Vanderbilt TV News Archive, Nashville, 1976-79; coord. spl. projects Am. Cancer Soc., Nashville, 1979; coord. membership Nebr. Ednl. TV, Lincoln, 1979-81; assoc. dir. devel. Children's Hosp. Vanderbilt U., Nashville, 1981-82; devel. asst. Scarritt Grad. Sch., Nashville, 1983-84; religious edn. cons., writer United Meth. Ch. Ministry of Laity, Nashville, 1984-85; adminstrv. asst. Opportunity Devel. Ctr., Nashville, 1986-89; adminstrv. asst. Women's Studies Program Vanderbilt U., Nashville, 1989—; dir., co-founder Womanflight Ctr. for Women's Spirituality, Nashville, 1986—; cons., ritualist Unitarian Universalist Women's Fedn., nashville, 1986-89; workshop leader Women-Ch. Conf., Cin., 1987. Contbr. articles to jours. and newsletters; editor newsletters; editing team Meth. Ch. guide, 1985. Vol. domestic violence shelter YWCA, Nashville, 1986, 89; steering com. Take Back the

Night March/Rally, Nashville, 1988; co-sec. Tenn. Alliance for Choice, Nashville, 1989—. Named Vol. of Yr., Sta. WDCN-TV, 1978, Outstanding Young Woman Am., 11983, 86, Young Career Woman Yr., Music City B&PW, 1984. Mem. AAUW (life, br. pres. 1984-86, pub. info. chair 1985-87, asst. editor bulletin 1987-89, program v.p. 1988-90), Mid. Tenn. Women's Studies Assn. (charter, newsletter editor 1986-88, treas. 1988-89, convenor 1990—), NOW (cons., ritualist 1988—). Unitarian Univesalist. Office: Vanderbilt U PO Box 86 Station B Nashville TN 37235

MEGNA, DIANA TANINA, chemist; b. Bronx, N.Y., Mar. 16, 1963; d. Ignazio Salvatore and Ivette (Perez) M. BS in Chemistry, Muhlenberg Coll., 1984; M Adminstrv. Sci. and Mgmt., Johns Hopkins U., 1989. Elastomers chemist Am. Cyanamid Co., Bound Brook, N.J., 1984, sales trainee, 1984-85; composite devel. chemist Am. Cyanamid Co., Havre de Grace, Md., 1985-89, tech. svc. supr. aerospace adhesives, 1989—. Contbr. articles to profl. jours. Alumni amb. Muhlenbreg Coll., Allentown, Pa., 1984—; team capt. Am. Heart Assn., Bel Air, Md., 1990—. Mem. Soc. for Advancement Materials and Process Engring., NAFE. Office: Am Cyanamid Co 1300 Revolution St Havre de Grace MD 21078

MEGOFNA, C(HRISTINE) GAIL, correctional health and marketing professional, administrator, medical corporation manager; b. New Britain, Conn., Aug. 12, 1949; d. Edward Lucian and Mary Dorothy (Cappello) Jacynowicz; 1 child, William John, Jr. A in Bus. Adminstrn./Med. Scis., Briarwood Coll., Southington, Conn., 1969; R.N., Tunxis Sch. Nursing, Farmington, 1981; postgrad., 1981-86; A in Mktg., Tunxis Community Coll., 1984. Cert. in counseling and human services. Kinetic therapist Kinetic Concepts, San Antonio, Tex., 1981-83; mktg. cons. JM Mktg., Rocky Hill, Conn., 1983-87; area mgr. PCS div. EMPI, Fridley, Minn., 1984-85; mktg. mgr. H.L. Moore Med. Corp., New Britain, 1985-87; adminstr. Nursefinders of Hartford, Inc., 1987-88; dir. pub. relations Conn. Peer Rev. Orgn., 1988—, Mktg. Quality Care Rev., 1988—, Correctional Health Care, 1988—, Middleton, Conn.; cons., owner, pres. correctional health care. Pres. Briarwood Coll., Southington, 1967-69. Mem. Nat. Assn. Female Execs., Sales and Mktg. Execs., Conn. Bus. and Industry Assn., Am. Correctional Assn., Am. Correctional Health Services Assn. (bd. dirs.), Am. Jail Assn. (chmn. profl. adv. com.). Democrat. Roman Catholic. Club: New Britain Jr. Woman Club (health chmn. 1977, treas. 1977, sec. 1978). Avocations: golf, reading music, coaching little league. Home: 422 Clinton St New Britain CT 06053

MEHALL, MARGARET ELIZABETH, occupational therapist; b. Taunton, Mass., Sept. 8, 1940; d. Waldo Charles and Belle Louise (Hillman) Hutchinson; m. Gerald Axel Moller, June 30, 1961 (div. 1975); 1 child, Eric Axel; m. David Mehall, Mar. 1, 1985. Diploma in Nursing, Cen. Maine Gen. Hosp., 1961; AA, Dade Community Coll., Miami, Fla., 1972; BS Occupational Therapy, Fla. Internat. U., 1975. Registered occupational therapist, Fla. Cons. neuro-augmentive therapist The Pain Ctr., Miami Beach, Fla., 1975-80; adminstr. Physical Rehab. Assocs., Ft. Lauderdale, Fla., 1981-84; owner, adminstr. Creations and Alterations, Ft. Lauderdale, 1983-88, Human Resource Tech., Inc., Ft. Lauderdale, 1984—; mgr. occupational therapy Physical Rehab. Agy., Lake Worth, Fla., 1989—; rsch. assoc. The Pain Team, U. Miami Sch. Medicine, 1976-78; co-owner, adminstr. Inst. for Physical and Behavioral Medicine, Miami, 1977-80; S.E. area mgr. EMPI, Inc., 1979-81; biblical costume cons. Evang. Chs., Year Bible Com., 1976—; clin. cons. in pain mgmt., numerous hosps., clinics and schools, 1976—. Mem. Am. Occupational Therapy Assn., Fla. Occupational Therapy Assn., Internat. Assn. for Study Pain, Arthritis Found., Lupus Found., Arthritis Health Professions Assn. Republican. Presbyterian. Office: 4631 NW 31 Ave #129 Fort Lauderdale FL 33309

MEHLER, MARIANNE DORTEA SZAUER, nursing educator; b. Bethlehem, Pa., Nov. 29, 1952; d. Louis Stephen and Dortea Marg (Petrohoy) Sauer; 1 child, Mary Claire. BS in Biology and Nursing, Cedar Crest Coll., 1975; grad., Allentown Hosp. Sch. Nursing, 1973; MS in Edn., Temple U., 1979; MS in Nursing-Critical Care, Rutgers U., Newark, 1990. RN, Pa. Gen. staff and charge nurse ICU and emergency room Allentown (Pa.) Gen. Hosp., 1973-75; med. assoc., clin. specialist Lehigh Valley ENT Assocs., Allentown, 1975-77; med. dir. emergency svcs. Lehigh Valley Mall, Inc., Allentown, 1975-77; clin. instr. Lehigh Valley Hosp. Ctr., Allentown, 1977-79; clin. coord.-supr. ICU and CCU Sacred Heart Hosp., Allentown, 1979-80, asst. v.p. nursing and staff devel., 1981-82; mem. faculty St. Luke's Hosp., Bethlehem, 1982—; adj. prof. allied health and nursing, adminstrn. and bus. Northampton Coll., Bethlehem, 1982—; presenter in field. Contbr. articles to profl. publs. Mem. Am. Orgn. Nurse Execs., Am. Nurses Assn. (cert. med.-surg. nurse), Am. Assn. Critical Care Nurses, Am. Trauma Soc., Am. Med. Writers Assn., Pa. Nurses Assn. (provider bd., continuing edn. com.), ADCIS, Delphi Soc., Cath. Sokol Gymnastic Frat., Sigma Theta Tau. Home: 1740 Chester Rd Bethlehem PA 18017

MEHR, HELEN MARGULIES, psychotherapist. Assoc. in Music, U. Toronto, Ont., Can., 1933; BA in Psychology, U. Man., Winnipeg, Can., 1937; MA in Psychology, Columbia U., 1938, PhD in Psychology, 1942; student, New Sch. for Social Rsch. and William Alanson White Inst., 1941-48; attends numerous workshops and lectures in field. Instr. workshops Rorschach Inst., 1941; asst. psychology dept. Queens Coll., Flushing, N.Y., 1941-42; pvt. practice psychotherapy, 1941—; instr. CCNY, Bklyn., 1942-43; chief psychologist ednl. clinic CCNY, N.Y.C., 1942-46; psychotherapist Northside Ctr. for Child Devel., 1947-48; pvt. practice psychology, Eastfield and San Jose, Calif., 1952-55; cons. St. Christopher's Sch., Dobbs Ferry, N.Y., 1942-43, Chamberlain Children's Ctr., 1970-75; cons. child therapy Mental Health Clinic of Santa Clara County Health Dept., 1966-67; chief psychologist vis. staff Santa Clara County Hosp., cons. to pediatric residents, 1955-58. Contbr. articles to profl. jours. Chmn. for certification bill Santa Clara Valley area, 1957; bd. dirs. Hope for Retarded Children, 1957. Recipient Award of Recognition L.A. Soc. Clin. Psychologists, Outstanding Svc. to Community by Psychologist award Santa Clara County Psychol. Assn. Fellow Am. Psychol. Assn. (mem. clin. div. and Soc. for Study of Social Issues), Soc. for Projective Techniques; mem. Calif. Psychol. Assn. (mem. study group on mental retardation, chmn. com. on social issues 1982-86, Dist. Humanitarian award), Am. Assn. Humanistic Psychology, South Bay Soc. Clin. Psychologists (legis. chmn. 1967), Nat. Assn. for Gifted Children, Calif. Assn. Parents of Neurologically Handicapped Children, Am. Acad. Optometry, Am. Transpersonal Assn., LVW, Am. Assn. United Nations, Physicians for Local Responsibility, Sigma Xi.

MEHTA, EILEEN ROSE, lawyer; b. Colver, Pa., Apr. 1, 1953; d. Richard Glenn and Helen (Wahna) Ball; m. Abdul Rashid Mehta, Aug. 31, 1973. Student, Miami U., 1971-73; BA with distinction, Fla. Internat. U., 1974; JD cum laude, U. Miami, 1977. Bar: Fla. 1977, U.S. Dist. Ct. (so. dist.) Fla. 1977, U.S. Ct. Appeals (11th cir.) 1981. Law clk. to presiding judge U.S. Dist. Ct. (so. dist.) Fla., Miami, 1977-79; asst. atty. County of Dade, Miami, 1979-89; shareholder Fine Jacobson Schwartz Nash Block & England, Miami, Fla., 1989—; lectr. in field; v.p., bd. dirs. Mehtatron Enterprises, INc., Miami, Shalimar Trucking Inc., Miami. Mem. Civic Chorale of Greater Miami, 1987—. Miami U. scholar, 1971-73. Mem. ABA, Fla. Bar Assn. Office: Fine Jacobson et al 100 SE 2d St CenTrust Ctr One CenTrust Financial Ctr 100 SE 2d St Miami FL 33131

MEI, DOLORES M., research administrator; b. Ludlow, Mass., Sept. 3, 1955; d. Paul John and Pauline Lavoie M.; m. Jack Irwin, June 28, 1981 (div. Feb. 1988); 1 child, Robert Aaron. AB in Psychology cum laude, Smith Coll., 1977; MA, Columbia U., 1979, M of Philosophy, 1980, PhD, 1981. Rsch. assoc. Columbia U., Henry Krumb Sch. Mines, N.Y.C., 1981-82; mem. staff Office of Rsch. Evaluation and Assessment, Bklyn., 1982-83, evaluation mgr., 1983—; ind. cons. N.Y. Zool. Soc., Bronx, 1980-82, 86—. Recipient Nat. Rsch. Svc. award Nat. Inst. Mental Health, 1979-80. Mem. N.Y. Orgn. Devel. Network. Democrat. Roman Catholic. Home: 138 71st St #F1 Brooklyn NY 11209 Office: Office Rsch Evaltn & Assmt 110 Livingston St Rm 740 Brooklyn NY 11201

MEIER, BARBARA JANE, computer graphics professional; b. Columbus, Ohio, Aug. 13, 1961; d. Harold Carl and Betty Eileen (Ayers) M.; m. David Hales Laidlaw, Sept. 16, 1989. AB in Computer Sci., Brown U., 1983, ScM in Computer Sci., 1987; postgrad., Sch. of Mus. Fine Arts, Boston, 1988-89. Rsch. programmer dept. computer sci. Brown U., Providence, 1983-87; ind. computer graphics cons. Boston, 1987-90; visualization engr., computer animator Animated Technologies, L.A., 1990—; reviewer computer graphics and applications, IEEE, 1988. Contbr. articles to technol. publs.; artist computer images for mag. covers, various publs.; animator 16mm films: Ginger Rising, 1986, Skylight, 1989. Active Women's Polit. Action Group, Providence, 1982-83. Mem. Assn. Computing Machinery (mem. spl. interest group on computer graphcs, reviewer transactions on graphics 1989-90), Sigma Xi.

MEIER, ENGE, university administrator; b. N.Y.C., Jan. 17; d. Rudolf and Kate (Furstenow) Pietschyck; m. Alfred August Meier, Sept. 11, 1948; children: Kenneth Randolph, Philip Alan. BBA, Western States U., 1987, MBA, 1989. Tchr. nursery sch. Neu Ulm, Fed. Republic Germany, 1963-64; sec. Brewster (N.Y.) Mid. Sch., 1969-72; teaching asst. Brewster Elem. Sch., 1972-73; office asst. Bd. Coop. Edn., Yorktown Heights, N.Y., 1973-76; sec. Am. Can. Co., Greenwich, Conn., 1976-77, adminstrv. sec., 1977-79, exec. sec., 1979-84; adminstrv. asst. U. Tex., Austin, 1984-85, 88—, adminstrv. assoc., 1985-86, sr. adminstrv. assoc., 1986-88. Docent LBJ Libr. and Mus., Austin, 1984—; mem. Women's Polit. Caucus, 1988—. Mem. Women in Mgmt., Bus. and Profl. Women (pres. 1989, bd. dirs. Austin chpt. 1987—), Women's C. of C. Presbyterian. Office: U Tex 6th and Colorado Sts Austin TX 78701

MEIER, JUDY ANN, stockbroker; b. Wayne, Nebr., Aug. 4, 1943; d. Raymond Edward and Irene Evangeline (Larsen) Florine; m. Larry V. Meier, Mar. 14, 1964 (div. 1975); 1 child, Scott Gerald. Student, Wayne State Coll., Nebr., 1961-63. Sec. Midwest Land Co., Wayne, 1962-64; bookkeeper Carhart Lumber Co., Wayne, 1964-68, 70-71; sec. Sherwin Williams Co., Omaha, Nebr., 1972-80; investment exec./stockbroker Piper Jaffray & Hopwood, Omaha, 1980—. Bd. dirs. Papillion Little League Football, 1976-78. Republican. Lutheran. Home: 6122 N 100 Plaza Omaha NE 68134-1418

MEIER, KAREN LORENE, educator; b. Davenport, Iowa, Aug. 17, 1942; d. Charles Frank and Minnie Louise (Arp) Meier; BA, U. Iowa, 1963, MA, 1974. Tchr., librarian Plano (Ill.) High Sch., 1963-67; tchr. social studies Moline (Ill.) High Sch., 1967—, also secondary social studies coordinator; registered rep. 1st Investors Corp., 1987-88, Rock Island, Ill.; tchr. Davenport (Iowa) Sch. System. Bd. dirs. Quad-City World Affairs Council; active LWV. Recipient regional award Ill. State Hist. Soc. Mem. Nat. Council Social Studies, Ill. Council Social Studies (sec. 1973-74, v.p. 1974-75, 86-87, pres.-elect 1987—, bd. dirs. 1982-83, treas. 1984-86), Iowa Council Social Studies, NEA, Ill. Edn. Assn. (sec.-treas. regional council 1975-79, legis. chairperson 1980-81), Moline Edn. Assn. (pres. 1977-78), Am. Soc. Profl. and Exec. Women, Social Studies Suprs. Assn., Assn. Supervision and Curriculum Devel., AAUW, Women in Ednl. Adminstrn., (dir. 1985, pres. 1985-86, past pres. 1986-87, asst. pres. 1986-87, bd. dirs. 1987-88, bd. dirs. at large 1987-88), Iowa Women in Ednl. Leadership, Alpha Delta Kappa. Home: 1855 14th St Bettendorf IA 52722 Office: 3850 Blackhawk Rd Rock Island IL 61201

MEIER, MARY LOU, psychiatric social worker; b. St. Louis, Aug. 6, 1947; d. Zephyrin Albert and Lorraine Josephine (Kruger) Marsh; m. Kenneth Charles Meier, Feb. 3, 1968 (div. 1980); children: Scott Kenneth, Jennifer Lorraine, Kevin Reuel. BA, U. Nebr., 1976, MSW, 1977. Cert. master social worker. Psychiatric social worker Community Mental Health Ctr., Lincoln, Nebr., 1977-80; cons. New Directions, YWCA, Lincoln, 1980-83, Pioneer Mental Health Ctr., Seward, Nebr., 1981-82, 84-86; mental health counselor Nebr. Wesleyan U., Lincoln, 1980-89; psychiatric social worker Health America HMO, Lincoln, 1980-88; coordinator mental health Health America HMO, 1980—; cons./bd. pres. Grief Ctr., Lincoln, 1978-81; cons./trainer Lincoln Coun. Alcoholism & Drugs, 1988, others in past. Commr., Commn. on the Status of Women, Lincoln, 1990—. Democrat. Office: HealthAmerican HMO 220 S 17th St Lincoln NE 68508

MEIER, NANCY JO, nursing consultant; b. Sidney, Nebr., Dec. 15, 1951; d. Donald William and Clara Jo (Miller) M. BA, Midland Luth. Coll., 1974; diploma in Nursing, Immanual Hosp. Sch. Nursing, Omaha, 1974; MS in Nursing Edn., Tex. Women's U., 1978. RN, Tex. Staff nurse St. Lukes Episcopal Hosp./Tex. Heart Inst., Houston, 1974-75, Park Plaza Hosp., Houston, 1976; clin. nursing specialist Houston Thoracic and Cardiovascular Assn., 1977-78; instr. clin. nursing Cedar Sinai Med. Ctr., Los Angeles, 1978-79; dir. dept. nursing edn. Los Angeles New Hosp., 1979-80; ind. cons. nursing edn. Los Angeles, 1980-81; systems support specialist IVAC Corp., San Diego, 1981-83; med. specialist, advt. account exec. Kenneth C. Smith & Assocs., La Jolla, Calif., 1983-87; ind. nursing cons. San Diego, 1987—; cons. nursing edn. Nat. Med. Enterprises, Saudi Arabia, 1980-81, Nursing Services Internat., Los Angeles, 1980, Grossmont Hosp., San Diego, 1985; instr. cardiac life support Los Angeles chpt. Am. Heart Assn., 1978-84; lectr. in field. Organist United Meth. Ch., Sidney, 1967-69, Immanual Sch. Nursing, 1971-74, Meml. Luth. Ch., Houston, 1977-78; bd. dirs. Bluffs of Fox Run Homeowners Assn., San Diego, 1984-85, pres., 1985-86. Mem. Am. Nurses Assn., Am. Assn. Operating Room Nurses, Med. Mktg. Assn., Sigma Theta Tau. Republican. Lutheran. Home and Office: 2963 Old Bridgeport Way San Diego CA 92111

MEIKLEJOHN, (LORRAINE) MINDY JUNE, political organizer, realtor; b. Staunton, Colo., June 9, 1929; d. Edward H. and Erna E. (Schwabe) Mindrup; student Ill. Bus. Coll., 1948, Red Rocks Community Coll., 1980-81; m. Alvin J. Meiklejohn, Apr. 25, 1953; children: Pamela, Shelley, Bruce, Scott. Pvt. sec. Ill. Liquor Commn., 1948-51, David M. Wilson, Ill. Sec. of State's Office, 1951-52; flight attendant Continental Airlines, 1952-53, pvt. sec. to mgr. flight svcs. office, 1953-54; organizational dir. Colo. Rep.Party, Denver, 1981-85, mem. Cen. Com., 1987—; campaign coord. Hank Brown's Exploratory Campaign for Gov., 1985, mgr. Hank Brown for Congress, 1985-86; dep. campaign dir. Steve Schuck for Gov., 1985-86; vice chmn. 2d Congl. Cen. Com. Colo.; active campaigns; del., alt. to various, county, state, dist. and nat. assemblies and convs.; Colo. chmn. Citizens for Am., 1987—; realtor, sales assoc. Van Schaack & Co.; mem. polit. action com. Jefferson County Bd. Realtors. Mem. Jefferson County Hist. Commn., Colo., 1974-82, pres., 1979; vol. Jefferson County Legal Aid Soc., 1970-74; vice chmn. Jefferson County Rep. Party, 1977-81, exec. com., 1987; vice chmn. Colo. State Rep. Party, 1981-85; chmn. Rep. Nat. Pilot Project on Volunteerism, 1981; mem. adv. coun. U.S. Peace Corps, 1982-84; sect. chmn. Jefferson County United Way Fund Drive; mem. exec. bd. Colo. Fedn. Rep. Women; pres. Operation Shelter, Inc., 1983—; state chair Citizens for Am., 1987—; bd. dirs. Scientific and Cultural Facilities dist. 1989—, Jefferson County chpt. Am. Cancer Soc., 1987—. Lutheran. Club: Jefferson County Women's Rep. (edn. chmn. 1987—). Home: 7540 Kline Dr Arvada CO 80005

MEIL, KATE, accountant; b. N.Y.C., June 15, 1925; d. Jacob and Becky (Lichtman) Meil; 1 child, Maria Rebecca Black. BBA in Acctg., CCNY, 1949. Acct. chem., printing, garment, machine and tool, film industries, 1943-73; office mgr., acct. Barrie Imports, Inc., Upper Saddle River, N.J., 1973—. Sculptor: Mein Kind, 1976, Determined to Be, 1977, Inner Mirror, 1979, Zeyda, 1980, Meydele, 1985, Remembering, 1987, Single Parent, 1988, Survivors, 1989. Leader Hudson Ave Area Residents Assn., Edgewater, 1973; participant Can. Nat. Exhibit, 1989. Recipient Red and Blue Ribbons 3d Ann. N.J. Woodcarving and Wildlife Art Show, 1987. Mem. Salute to Women in Arts, Whittle Ones, Ethical Culture Soc., Palisades Nature Assn., Dumont Chessmates Club. Avocations: chess; theater; folk dancing. Office: Barrie Imports Inc 145 Route 17 Upper Saddle River NJ 07458

MEILACH, GERMAINE C., physical plant executive; b. Newport, Vt., Mar. 20, 1937; d. Leonce Armas and Yvonne Alice (Vezina) Desbiens; m. Robert Louis Waite, Apr. 22, 1957 (div. Oct. 1985); children: Diane M., Sandra J., Fred R., Thomas L.; m. Michael David Meilach, May 5, 1986. BS magna cum laude, Siena Coll., 1981. Registered exec. housekeeper. Night auditor Paradise Motor Inn, Bennington, Vt., 1964-66, Albany (N.Y.) Holiday Inn, 1966-69; front office mgr. Albany Hyatt Hotel, 1969-70, exec. housekeeper, 1970-72; dir. housekeeping and linen Meml. Hosp., Albany, 1972-75; custodial supr. Siena Coll., Loudonville, N.Y., 1979-86; area mgr. Facilities Resource Mgmt. Co., Madison, Conn., 1986-88, asst. dir., 1988-90; assoc. dir. Facilities Resource Mgmt. Co., 1990—. Contbr. articles to Exec. Housekeeping Today. Bd. dirs. Albany Big Bros. and Big Sisters, 1987; neighborhood chmn. Girl Scouts U.S., Bennington, 1957. Named Outstanding Returning Adult Student, Altrusa Club, Troy, N.Y., 1977. Mem. NAFE, Assn. Phys. Plant Adminstrs. (custodial standards commn. 1986—), Nat. Exec. Housekeepers Assn. (dist. gov. 1984-86, nat. bd. dirs. 1986-88, nat. treas. 1988-90). Home: 55A Charlesfield St Providence RI 02906-1157 Office: Brown U Plant Ops Dept 60 Olive St PO Box 1941 Providence RI 02912

MEINEL, MARJORIE PETTIT, optical engineer; b. Pasadena, Calif., May 13, 1922; d. Edison and Hannah (Steele) Pettit; m. Aden Baker Meinel, Sept. 5, 1944; children: Carolyn, Walter, Barbara, Elaine, Edward, Mary, David. BA, Pomona Coll., Claremont, Calif., 1943; MA, Claremont Coll., 1944. Rsch. assoc. Calif. Inst. Tech., Pasadena, 1944-45, U. Ariz., Tucson, 1974-85; mem. tech. staff Jet Propulsion Lab., Pasadena, 1985—; vis. faculty Nat. Cen. U., Chung-Li, Taiwan, 1978-80; commr. Ariz. Solar Energy Commn., Phoenix, 1975-81; mem. office tech. assessment U.S. Congress, Washington, 1974-79. Author: Applied Solar Energy, 1977, Sunsets, Twilights and Evening Skies, 1983; patentee in field. Mem. Internat. Soc. for Optical Engring., N.Y. Acad. Scis. Lutheran. Office: Jet Propulsion Lab 4800 Oak Grove Dr Pasadena CA 91109

MEINELT, ELLEN MARIE, immunologist; b. Kew Gardens, N.Y., Oct. 12, 1956; d. Kenneth Harold and Lorraine Marie (Rousseau) M. BS, U. Utah, 1978; MS, U. Minn., 1984. Clin. lab asst. I U. of Utah Med. Ctr., Salt Lake City, 1976, clin. lab asst. II, 1977-78; med. technologist Mountain Head and Neck, Layton, Ut., 1978-82; rsch. assoc. Coulter Immunology, Hialeah, Fla.; supr. Immunopath Labs., Hialeah, 1988—; cons. Davis North Internal Medicine, Layton, Utah, 1980-82. Mem. Am. Soc. for Med. Tech., Utah Soc. for Med. Tech. (student rep. 1977-88, editor-newsletter 1980-81, Spl. award 1981). Democrat. Lutheran. Home: 17034 NW 63d Pl Miami FL 33015 Office: Immunopath Labs 7300 W 20th Ave Hialeah FL 33016

MEINER, SUE ELLEN THOMPSON, nursing educator; b. Ironton, Mo., Oct. 24, 1943; d. Louis Raymond and Verna Mae (Goggin) Thompson; m. R.L. Bubb, July 18, 1964 (div. 1969); 1 child: Diane Thompson Bubb; m. Robert Edward Meiner, Mar. 5, 1971; 1 child: Suzanne Elaine. AAS, Meramec Community Coll., 1970; BS in Nursing, St. Louis U., 1978, MS in Nursing, 1982; doctoral candidate, So. Ill. U., 1986—, cert. in gerontology, 1990. RN, Med. Surg. Clinician, Mo. Staff RN St. Joseph's Hosp., St. Charles, Mo., 1976-78; nursing supr. Bethesda Gen. Hosp., St. Louis, 1975-76, 71-74; adult med. dir. Family Care Ctr.-Carondelet, St. Louis, 1978-79; program dir., lectr. Webster Coll./Bethesda Hosp., Webster Groves, Mo., 1979-82; clin. specialist sch. medicine Washington U., St. Louis, 1982; chmn. dept. nursing, asst. prof. St. Louis Community Coll., 1983-88, Barnes Hosp. Sch. Nursing, 1988-89; nat. dir. edn. Nat. Assn. Practical Nurse Edn. and Svc., Inc., St. Louis, 1984-86; mem. task force St. Louis Met. Hosp. Assn., 1987—; mem. adv. com. Bd. Edn. Sch. Nursing, St. Louis, 1986—. Contbr. articles to profl. jours. 1981-86. Chmn. bd. dirs. Creve Coeur Fire Protection Dist. Mo., 1984-89; vice chmn. Bd. Cen. St. Louis County Emergency Dispatch Svc., 1985-87; asst. leader Girl Scouts U.S., St. Louis, 1975. Mem. Creve Coeur C. of C., Am. Nurses Assn., Am. Nurses Found., Nat. League for Nursing, Sigma Theta Tau (fin. chair 1984, archivist 1985-87), Sigma Phi Omega. Republic. Lodges: Order of Ea. Star Chaplain 1970, Job's Daughter's Guardian 1979-80. Home and Office: 700 Wren Path Ct Ellisville MO 63021-4794

MEINHARDT, CAROLYN LORIS, computer consultant; b. Yankton, S.D., Dec. 23, 1949; m. Jerome F. Foecke, Nov. 11, 1982. BS, St. Cloud State U., 1974. From tchr. to bus. mgr. Pine (Minn.) City Pub. Schs., 1974-79; mgr. computer svcs. ESV Region III, St. Cloud, Minn., 1979-81; computer specialist S.D. City Schs., 1981-83; pres. Wordware, Inc., Dassel, Minn., 1983—; guest speaker several ednl. computing assn., 1982—; tech. cons. Dept of Def. Dependent Schs., Washington, 1987-88; instr. Hutchinson Tech. Inst., 1988—. Author: (textbook) Bus. Applications for the IBM-PC, 1987. Mem. Internat. Assn. Computing Edn. (pres. 1984-85), Am. Fedn. Info. Processing Soc. (bd. dirs. 1985). Home and Office: Rte 2 Box 94 Dassel MN 55325

MEINHART, ELAINE MARY KNAUB, educator; b. York, Pa., July 19, 1950; d. Richard Wilson and Patricia (Sipe) Knaub; m. Steward John Meinhart; 1 child, Judson Steward. BS in Edn., Mansfield State Coll., 1972. Cert. elem. tchr., Pa.; cert. reading specialist, Pa. Tchr. Spring Grove (Pa.) Sch. Dist., 1978-83; tchr. reading Wilson Sch. Dist., West Lawn, Pa., 1986; adult basic edn. tchr. Reading (Pa.) Area Community Coll., 1986-87; reading specialist Amity Elem. Sch., Daniel Boone Sch. Dist., Birdsboro, Pa., 1987—; seminar presenter Millersville (Pa.) U., 1986, 87. Bd. dirs. Wyomissing Hills (Pa.) Recreation Bd., 1988. Mem. AAUW, Internat. Reading Assn., Pa. State Edn. Assn., Assn. for Suprs. of Curriculum Devel., Keystone State Reading Assn., Pa. Reading Educators. Democrat. Lutheran. Home: 435 Parliament Dr Wyomissing Hills PA 19610 Office: Amity Elem Sch Daniel Boone Sch Dist Box 84 Birdsboro PA 19518

MEINHOLD, GAIL ARLENE, pharmaceutical executive; b. Ventura, Calif., Sept. 7, 1962; d. Richard Alan and Muriel Amanda (Lauritson) Mark; m. Frank Werner Meinhold, Sept. 2, 1989. BS, Calif. State U., San Luis Obispo, Calif., 1984; student, Med. Coll. Va. Hosps., 1984-85. Registered dietitian. Clin. dietitian Community Meml. Hosp., Ventura, Calif., 1985-88; pvt. practice sport nutrition counselor, 1985—; caterer Ventura, 1980—; pharm. sales rep. Mead Johnson Nutritionals, Glendale, Calif., 1988—; nutrition cons. in field. Editor: Smart Talk: Eating Healthy, 1989. Recipient Scholarship Am. Dietetic Assn. Mem. Am. Dietetic Assn., Am. Heart Assn., Team Inside Track (treas. 1988-89, newsletter editor 1987-89), Santa Barbara Athletic Assn., Phi Upsilon Omicron. Republican. Home and Office: 17 Maygreen Ct Glendale CA 91206

MEINSEN, PHYLLIS ARLENE, travel consultant; b. Bklyn., Oct. 4, 1944; d. Morris and Sarah Betty (Miller) Wahn; m. Donald Raymond Meinsen, Feb. 19, 1972; children: Stacy Bliss, Ryan Scott, Matthew Edward. Cert. travel cons. Receptionist Holiday Travel, N.Y.C., 1964-67; bookkeeper, agt. Holiday Travel, 1976-83; mgr., bookkeeper Pathway Travel, N.Y.C., 1983-86, Ctr. Travel, N.Y.C., 1987-88; agt., bookkeeper Fert & Co., N.Y.C., 1988—. Actress, stage hand N.Y.C. Firefighter Burn Ctr. Found., Randalls Island, 1987-89. Recipient Disting. Svc. Cub Scouts Am., 1985. Democrat. Jewish. Office: Fert & Co 11 Broadway New York NY 10004

MEIS, NANCY RUTH, marketing and fundraising executive; b. Iowa City, Aug. 6, 1952; d. Donald J. and Theresa (Dee) M.; m. Paul L. Wenske, Oct. 14, 1978; children: Alexis Meis Wenske, Christopher Meis Wenske. BA, Clarke Coll., 1974; MBA, U. Okla., 1981. Cultural program supr. City of Dubuque, Iowa., 1974-76; community services dir. State Arts Council of Okla., Oklahoma City, 1976-78, program dir., 1978-79; mgr. Cimarron Circuit Opera Co., Norman, Okla., 1979-82, bd. dirs., 1982-86; account exec. Bell System, Kansas City, Mo., 1982; mgr. spl. svcs. Children Internat., Kansas City, 1983-86; dir. mktg. and fund raising, 1986-87, dir. devel., 1987-88, v.p. devel., 1988-90; dir. mktg. Unimedia div. Universal Press Syndicate, Kansas City. r in field. Named Outstanding Young Woman in Am., 1977, 78. Mem. Nat. Soc. Fund Raising Exec. (Kansas City chpt. program com. 1985), Nat. Network Bus. Sch. Women (rep. 1980), Nat. Assn. Female Execs., Greater Kansas City Council on Philanthropy, Direct Mktg. Assn. Roman Catholic.

MEISNER, DEE DOLORES ANNETTE, small business owner; b. Bismarck, ND, Dec. 29, 1936; d. Richard and Annie Gertrude (Binder) Gerlach; m. James Warren Meisner, Sept. 17, 1955; children: Terry L., John Warren. BA, U. N.D., 1973; MA, Ohio U., 1974; Graduate in Modeling, John Robert Powers, Mpls., 1980. Adminstrv. Asst. to pres. and chief exec. officer William Clairmont, Inc., Bismarck, N.D., 1977; owner Orgn. Communication Ctr., Bismarck, 1976—; co-owner Meisner Co., Bismarck, 1980—; oversee and adminstrn. Dick's Potpourri, Bismarck, 1987—; rsch. cons. United Meth. Chs. Bismarck 1979; bd. dir. of cur. and devel. First United Meth. Bismarck 1976-77; communication cons. Bismarck/Mandan Bus. and Orgn. Bismarck 1976—; spokesperson/rep. Plum Tree (Bus.) Bismarck 1986—. Composer and publisher several mus. compositions including Dakota Heritage Sonata #1 (1989 Centennial Selection U. Mary), cassette tape, Christmas Love 1987; author, publisher (children's newsletters) Fun Club, Adventure Science 1984-85, (book) Christmas Tree Angel 1988. Pres. Bismarck-Mandan Community Concerts 1978, drive chmn. 1960s; bd. dirs.

and children's Edn. Com. Bismarck Art and Galleries Assn. 1987—; orgn. com. Dakota West Arts Coun., Bismarck 1978. Recipient Citizen's Award Bismarck Schs. 1950; named Hon. Soc. Bismarck Schs. 1955, Midwest Spa Spls. Featured in Spa News 1981. Mem. Nat. Spa and Swimming Pool Inst., PEO (pres. 1970, other offices), Thursday Mus. (program chmn., pres. 1989—, other offices), Bismarck Art and Gallery Assn. (bd. dirs., other offices). Office: Meisner Co 925 E Main Bismarck ND 58501

MEISTAS, MARY THERESE, endocrinologist, diabetes researcher; b. Grand Rapids, Mich., July 22, 1949; d. Frank Peter and Anne Therese (Karsokas) M. MD, U. Mich., 1975. Diplomate Am. Bd. Internal Medicine, Am. Bd. Endocrinology. Intern, then resident in internal medicine Cleve. Clinic Hosp., 1975-78, endocrinology fellow, 1978-79; fellow in pediatric endocrinology Johns Hopkins Hosp., Balt., 1979-81; diabetes researcher Joslin Diabetes Ctr., Boston, 1981-86; assoc. in medicine Brigham and Women's Hosp., Boston, 1981-86; asst. in medicine, diabetes researcher Mass. Gen. Hosp., Boston, 1986—. Contbr. articles to profl. jours. Mem. ACP, Am. Diabetes Assn., Am. Fedn. Clin. Research, Endocrine Soc. Office: Mass Gen Hosp ACC-1 Boston MA 02114

MEITIN, DEBORAH DORSKY, health care executive; b. Cleve., July 25, 1951; d. Irving and Rosalind (Lewis) D.; m. Samuel R. Meitin, Dec. 6, 1987. BS, Mich. State U., 1973; M Health Adminstrn., Ohio State U., 1981. Cert. med. technologist. Med. technologist U. Hosps., Cleve., 1974-79; adminstrv. dir. surgery and anesthesiology Cleve. Met. Gen. Hosp., 1981-86; sr. cons. Ernst & Whinney, Chgo., 1986-87; sr. v.p. Diversified Health Search, Maitland, Fla., 1988-89; pres. Health Search Cons., Altamonte Springs, Fla., 1990—; pres. Greater Fla. Devel. Co., Altamonte Springs, 1988—. Mem. bd. Jewish Fedn. Profl. Women's Group, Chgo., 1986-87; mem. coms. Jewish Community Ctr., Chgo., 1986—, Orlando, Fla., 1990—; bd. dirs. Michael Reese Hosp.-Jr. Med. Rsch. Coun., Chgo., 1986-87, Temple Israel, Orlando, 1989—. Mem. Am. Coll. Healthcare Execs., Am. Hosp. Assn., Ohio State U. Grad. Program in Health Adminstrn. Alumni Assn. (bd. dirs. 1982-84), NOW, Phi Kappa Phi, Beta Beta Beta. Democrat. Home: 268 Buttercup Circle Altamonte Springs FL 32714

MELANI, BETTY LOU, academic administrator; b. Pitts., Oct. 1, 1932; d. Cesare and Rosemary (Valdiserri) M. BS, U. Pitts., 1980. Exec. asst. Ionics Inc., Bridgeville, Pa., 1963-73; adminstrv. asst. Western Psychiat. Inst. and Clinics U. Pitts., 1973-82, asst. adminstr., 1983—, exec. adminstr. sch. medicine, 1984—; owner, prin. Country Cousins, Inc. DBA, The Enchanted Florist, 1989—; bd. dirs. Renaissance Ctr., Pitts., 1984—, v.p., 1989. Sec., bd. dirs. Foster Parents, 1968—. Mem. Exec. Women's Coun., South Park C. of C. (bd. dirs. 1989). Democrat. Roman Catholic. Office: U Pitts Sch Medicine M246 Scaife Hall Pittsburgh PA 15261

MELANSON, ANNE M., advertising agency executive. Former sr. v.p. Ted Bates Advt., N.Y.C.; sr. v.p., dir. human resources Backer Spielvogel Bates Worldwide, Inc., N.Y.C., now exec. v.p., dir. human resources. Office: Backer Spielvogel Bates Inc 405 Lexington Ave New York NY 10174*

MELARA, ANA LAURA MARTINEZ, insurance company professional; b. San Salvador, El Salvador, July 4, 1936; came to U.S., 1964; d. Miguel de Jesus and Maria Juana (Uribe) Martinez; m. Carlos Alberto Melara, Apr. 2, 1960; children: Ana Sylvia, Carolina, Carlos Eduardo. BS and Letters, Colegio La Sagrada Familia, San Salvador, 1953. With AMEX Life Assurance Co., San Rafael, Calif., 1983-85, reserve analyst, 1985-86, sr. reserve analyst, 1986-88, reinsurance acct., 1988—. Pres. Club Hispano Americano Sonoma County, Petaluma, Calif., 1983-85, v.p. 1985-86. Fellow Life Mgmt. Inst. Democrat. Roman Catholic. Home: 743 Rancho Way Petaluma CA 94952 Office: AMEX Life Assurance Co 1650 Los Gamos Dr San Rafael CA 94903-1899

MELCHER, KATHERINE JEANNETTE, public relations counsellor; b. Cedar Rapids, Iowa, Nov. 23, 1946; d. Edward Lewis and Jeanne Helen (Anderson) M.; m. Robert Marshall Read, Dec. 20, 1975 (div. 1976); m. Frank Georges Coppieters, Feb. 22, 1985. BA, Kansas U., 1968; MFA, Cornell U., 1970. Reporter Sta. WAKE-TV, Wichita, Kans., 1970-72; talk show host Sta. KMBC-TV, Kansas City, Mo., 1972-74; pub. rels. account assoc. Pat O'Neill Advt., Inc., Kansas City, 1974; dir. community svcs. U.S. Consumer Product Safety Commn., Kansas City, 1974-78; dir. pub. rels. and advt. Kansas City Philharmonic, 1979-80, Hallmark Cards, 1980-82; mktg. communications mgr. Tektronix, Inc., Redmond, Oreg., 1982-86, Photon Kinetics, Inc., Beaverton, Oreg., 1986-89; pub. relations account mgr. Karakas, VanSickle, Ouellette, Beaverton, 1989—; reporter Sta. NBC, N.Y.C., 1975-77. Mem. Am. Electronics Assn. (com. mem.), Pub. Relations Soc. Am., Govt. Info. Coun. Independent. Agnostic. Home: 5440 SW Florida Portland OR 97219 Office: Karakas VanSickle Quellette 15220 NW Greenbrier Pkwy Beaverton OR 97006

MELCHIOR, JACKLYN BUTLER, retired biochemistry educator; b. Sacramento, May 19, 1918; d. Drury DeWolf and Lalita (Jodon) Butler; m. Norten Cass Melchior, Dec. 21, 1939; children: Ernst Drury, June Ann. BS, U. Calif., Berkeley, 1941, PhD, 1946. Rsch. assoc. Northwestern U., Evanston, Ill., 1946-49; from instr. to assoc. prof. Loyola U. Med. Sch., Chgo., 1949-60; prof., chmn. dept. biochemistry Chgo. Coll. Osteo. Medicine, 1960-80. Editor Annals Ill. Acad. Sci., 1975-76; contbr. articles to profl. jours. Recipient Lederle Med. Faculty award, 1957-60. Fellow AAAS; mem. Am. Soc. Biol. Chemists. Home: 2601 College Ave Apt 212 Berkeley CA 94704

MELCONIAN, LINDA JEAN, state senator, lawyer; b. Springfield, Mass.; d. George and Virginia Elaine (Noble) Melconian. B.A., Mt. Holyoke Coll., 1970; M.A., George Washington U., 1976, J.D., 1978. Bar: Mass. Chief legis. asst. to Ho. of Reps. Speaker Thomas P. O'Neill, Jr., U.S. Congress, Washington, 1971-80; pros. atty. Hampden County Dist. Atty., Springfield, Mass., 1981-82; state senator Mass. Gen. Ct., Boston, 1983—; instr. Western New Eng. Coll., Springfield, 1978-82; Our Lady of the Elms Coll., Springfield, 1982-83. Chmn., Heart Fund Ball, Western Mass., 1983; incorporator Springfield Coll., 1982—; ex officio trustee Ella T. Grasso Found., Conn., 1982—; active Democratic State Com., Mass., 1983, Hampden County Dems. Recipient Appreciation award Vietnam Vets. of Greater Springfield, 1983; Equal Edn. for All Children award Bilingual Parents of Springfield, 1983; Appreciation award Vets.-Hampden County Council, 1984. Mem. Hampden County Bar Assn., Zonta. Club: Mt. Holyoke. Home: 257 Fort Pleasant Ave Springfield MA 01108 Office: Mass State Senate Rm 504 Boston MA 02133

MELEAR, TALLEY MURRELL, marketing professional, business owner; b. Gainesville, Tex., June 29, 1938; d. Elbert Decatur and Evelyn Murriel (Long) Prine; m. Harry Fred Melear Jr., Mar. 7, 1958 (div. Oct. 1982); 1 child, Denise Sheree. Cert. comptrometer, Bryne Comml. Sch., 1960; student, Tarrant County Jr. Coll., 1978-80; AA in Bus., Northlake Coll., 1981. File clk., rate clk. Roberts & Shea Ins., Ft. Worth, 1957-58; from file clk. to preparation clk. All State Ins., Dallas, 1958-60; rate clk. Cen. Mut. Ins., Dallas, 1968-70; mktg. and spl. order buyer NCH Corp., Irving, Tex., 1971—; co-owner The Ladies Touch, Euless, Tex., 1986—. Mem. NAFE. Baptist. Home: 800 Bell Dr Euless TX 76039 Office: NCH Corp 2727 Chemsearch Blvd Irving TX 75015

MELGAARD, MAUREEN ELIZABETH, giftware and greeting card executive; b. Hallock, Minn., June 22, 1944; d. Maurice Earl and Helen Elizabeth (Gillie) Turner; m. Larry Gene Keck, Mar. 10, 1963 (div. July 1978); 1 child, Kraig Phillip Keck. Exec. sec. Iowa Housing Devel. Corp., Des Moines, 1968-71; corp. sec. Equitable Mortgage Investment Corp., Des Moines, 1971-81; prin., owner Creative & Adminstrv. Assistance, Mpls., 1977-78; asst. to the dir. Midwest Rsch. Inst., Mpls., 1978-79; creative dir. Luverne Truck Equipment and subs., Brandon, S.D., 1980-88; mktg. dir. New Boundary Designs, Inc., Mpls., 1988-89, pres., 1989—. Author (screenplay, original score) Time of Triumph, 1987-89. Pres. Luverne (Minn.) Music Boosters, 1981-82; vol. William Janklow campaign, Brandon, 1986. Mem. Woodlake Athletic Club, Hazeltine Nat. Golf Club, Antioch Christian Fellowship, Luverne Tourist Club (sec. 1986-87). Republican. Office: New Boundary Designs Inc 1453 Park Rd Chanhassen MN 55317

MELI, MARTHA MARIA, accountant; b. Lakewood, N.J., Aug. 30, 1964; d. Francesco and Martha (Iocolano) M. BBA, U. Notre Dame, 1986. Lease analyst Kislak Co., Woodbridge, N.J. Roman Catholic.

MELIA, TAMARA MOSER, historian; b. Pasadena, Calif., Dec. 19, 1955; d. Gerald Duane and Frances Evelyn (Glover) Moser; m. Patrick Kyle Melia, May 14, 1977. BA, Sterling Coll., 1976; MA, So. Ill. U., 1979, PhD, 1987. Grad. asst. Ulysses S. Grant Assn., Carbondale, Ill., 1977-82; adj. assoc. prof. Georgetown U., Washington, 1985—; historian U.S. Navy Naval Hist. Ctr., Washington, 1982—. Author articles on Civil War subjects. Mem. Assn. for Documentary Editing, Soc. for History in Fed. Govt., Am. Hist. Assn., Orgn. Am. Historians, Civil War Round Table of D.C. (pres. 1988-89). Office: Naval Hist Ctr Washington Navy Yard Bldg 57 Washington DC 20374

MELICH, DORIS S., public service worker; b. Salt Lake City, Apr. 8, 1913; d. Edward Harrison and Marie Cushing Snyder; m. Mitchell Melich, June 3, 1935; children: Tanya Marie Melich Silverman, Michael E., Nancy Lynne, Robert Allen. BA in Western History, U. Utah, 1934. Mem. Nat. Commn. Arthritis and Related Musculoskeltal Diseases, 1974-76, Nat. Arthritis Adv. Bd., 1977-84, 86-90; Utah del. Nat. Ho. of Dels. Arthritis Found., 1982-87; pres. Arthritis Found., 1975-78, v.p., 1968-69, 73-74, Utah rep. govt. affairs com., 1983—, also bd. dirs. Active Girl Scouts U.S., Utah Ballet Guild, Utah Symphony Guild, Salt Lake Art Ctr., Utah Arts Coun., 1985—, League Rep. Women, YWCA, others. Recipient Arthritis Found. awards, Utah coun. Girl Scouts U.S. award, Merit Honor award U. Utah Emeritus Club, 1978, Minute Man award Utah N.G., 1985, Hon. Trustee Arthritis Found. award, Thanks badge Am. Phys. Therapy Assn. Mem. AAUW, Nat. Assistance League, Utah Arts Coun., Utah Women's Forum, Order Ea. Star, Alpha Delta Pi, Beta Sigma Phi (sponsor). Home: 900 Donner Way #708 Salt Lake City UT 84108

MELICK, KATHERINE, marketing executive; b. Carteret, N.J., Feb. 4, 1924; d. Stephen and Mary (Ginda) M.; m. Stanley R. Niemiec, Apr. 24, 1948 (dec. 1973). B.L., Rutgers U., 1944. Manual writer G.M. Corp., Linden, N.J., 1944-46; news asst., sec. Wall Street Jour., N.Y.C., 1946-55; exec. sec. Dow Jones & Co., Inc., N.Y.C., 1955-72, asst. to promotion mgr., 1972-74, adminstrv. mgr. mktg. services, 1975—; pres., N.J. Fedn. Women's Clubs, Carteret, 1953-55. Mem. Advt. Women N.Y., Japan Soc., AAUW, Am. Mgmt. Assn. Clubs: Rutgers (N.Y.C.), Douglass Coll. Alumnae Assn. (New Brunswick, N.J.). Office: Dow Jones & Co Inc 420 Lexington Ave New York NY 10170

MELISH, DIANE CAROL, real estate development executive; b. Bridgeport, Conn., Apr. 16, 1952; d. Leonard J. and Claire E. (Kerigan) M. BA, Wellesley Coll., 1974; M in City Planning, Harvard U., 1976. Assoc. Hammer Siler George Assocs., Washington, 1977-80; sr. analyst The Rouse Co., Columbia, Md., 1980-83; project coord., Seaport Marketplace, Inc. The Rouse Co., N.Y.C., 1983-86; prin. The Devel. Consortium, N.Y.C., 1986—. Mem. Urban Land Inst., Internat. Council Shopping Ctrs., Assn. Real Estate Women, Mcpl. Arts Soc.

MELLI, MARYGOLD SHIRE, law educator; b. Rhinelander, Wis., Feb. 8, 1926; d. Osborne and May (Bonnie) Shire; m. Joseph Alexander Melli, Apr. 8, 1950; children: Joseph, Sarah Bonnie, Sylvia Anne, James Alexander. BA, U. Wis., 1947, LLB, 1950. Dir. children's code revision Wis. Legis. Coun., Madison, 1950-53; exec. dir. Wis. Jud. Coun., Madison, 1955-59; asst. prof. to prof. U. Wis., 1959—, assoc. dean, 1970-72, Voss-Bascom prof., 1985—; mem. spl. rev. bd. State of Wis. Dept. Health and Social Svcs., Madison, 1973—; rsch. affiliate U. Wis. Inst. for Rsch. on Poverty, 1980. Author: (pamphlet) The Legal Status of Women in Wisconsin, 1977, (book) Wisconsin Juvenile Court Practice, 1978, rev. edit., 1983, (with others) Child Support & Alimony, 1988; contbr. articles to profl. jours. Bd. dirs. Am. Humane Assn., 1985—. Named one of five Outstanding Young Women in Wis., Jaycees, 1961; rsch. grantee NSF, 1983. Fellow Am. Acad. Matrimonial Lawyers (exec. editor jour. 1985—); mem. Am. Law Inst., Nat. Conf. Bar Examiners, Internat. Soc. on Family Law (chmn. bd. mgrs. 1989), State Bar Wis. (reporter family law sect.). Democrat. Roman Catholic. Home: 2904 Waunona Way Madison WI 53713 Office: U Wis Law Sch Madison WI 53706

MELLON, JOAN ANN, educator; b. Massena, N.Y., Nov. 29, 1932; d. Leo Herbert and Irene (Tyo) French; m. Donald Emmett Mellon, Aug. 24, 1963. B.A., Coll. St. Rose, 1954; M.Ed., St. Lawrence U., 1956; M.Ed., Tchrs. Coll. Columbia U. 1972, Ed.D., 1985. Tchr. math. Copenhagen Sch. Dist., N.Y., 1954-57, Massena Sch. Dist., N.Y., 1957-62; supr. student tchrs. SUNY-Albany, 1962-63; asst. prof. math SUNY-Potsdam, 1963-67; tchr. math. Long Beach Sch. Dist. (N.Y.), 1967-70; chmn. math. dept. Edgemont Sch. Dist., Scarsdale, N.Y., 1971—; instr. inservice course for elem. tchrs. SUNY-Potsdam, 1965; instr. Inst. for Jr. High Sch. Tchrs., 1966; vis. com. Middle States Assn., 1973, 76, 79. Vice grand regent Cath. Daus. Am., Norwood, N.Y., 1959, grand regent, 1960; treas. St. Lawrence Deanery of Council Cath. Women, Ogdensburg, N.Y., 1958; chmn. Jr. Cath. Daus., Norwood, 1964. Mem. Assn. Math. Tchrs. N.Y. State (exec. council 1977-78), N.Y. Assn. Math. suprs. (v.p. 1978-79), Nat. Council Tchrs. Math., Math. Assn. Am., Edgemont Tchrs. Assn. (pres.), Delta Kappa Gamma. Republican. Roman Catholic. Home: 8 Woodhaven Dr New City NY 10956 Office: Edgemont High Sch White Oak Ln Scarsdale NY 10583

MELLOR, GAIL MCGOWAN, author; b. Louisville, July 8, 1942; d. William Bringhurst and Virginia Williams (McGowan) M.; m. Jorge Alfredo Tarafa, Aug., 1963 (div. Nov. 1971); 1 child, Jorge Daniel; m. Steven Anthony Friend Weller, Feb. 13, 1988; children: William Seth, Laura Linellen. BA cum laude, Newcomb Coll., New Orleans, 1964; postgrad., Tulane U., New Orleans, 1968; teaching degree, Manhattanville Coll., Purchase, N.Y., 1971. Coordinator Paedeia Exptl. Sch., Armonk, N.Y., 1971-73; adminstr., coordinator Lakewood Community Sch., Dallas, 1973-74; prof. English Postgrad. Sch. Edn., Toluca, Mexico, 1974-75; asst. planetarium dir. John Young Planetarium, Orlando, Fla., 1976-77; med. journalist Orlando Sentinel Star and mags., 1978-79; sr. editor Louisville Today, 1980-81; contbg. editor Beaux Arts mag., Louisville, 1981-83; rsch. cons. Am. Coll. Emergency Physicians, 1985; med. writing cons. NKC Inc. and Louisville Hand Surgery, 1986—; pres. Writer's Inc., Louisville, 1980—; v.p. bd. Windsor Systems Inc., Louisville; chmn. bd. WM, Inc.; lectr. Bellarmine Coll. Author: The First Hundred Years, 1988; contbr. articles to profl. jours. and newspapers. Mem. state com. Health Care Rationing, LWV, Ky., 1985; active various civic orgns. Recipient First Pl. award Greater Orlando Press Club, 1979, Presdl. Commendation Pres. of Mexico, 1979, awards Ad. Coun., Louisville, 1982, 84, Excellence in Writing award Ky. Hosp. Assn., 1989, Internat. award for Excellence Internat. Tech. Communicators Conf., 1990. Mem. NAFE, AAAS, Soc. for Tech. Communicators (bd. dirs. local chpt., Disting. Tech. Communication award 1990), Soc. Profl. Journalists, Am Med. Writers Assn. (regional and local chpt. sec.), Am. Pub. Health Assn., Mensa.

MELLOR, ULANA, systems analyst, electrical engineer; b. Buffalo, May 23, 1952; d. Kornel and Emilia Malyna (Stawnyczyj) Dziuba; m. L. Robert Mellor III, Aug. 25, 1973. BSEE, Rochester (N.Y.) Inst. Tech., 1975, BS in Computer Sci., 1975; MS in Computer Sci., Va. Polytech. Inst., 1980. Mem. tech. staff Computer Scis. Corp., Falls Church, Va., 1975-81; sr. mem. tech. staff II Telenet Communications Corp., Reston, Va., 1981-89; mgr. network mgmt. systems devel. Sprint Internat. (formerly Telenet Communications Corp.), Reston, VA, 1989—. Mem. IEEE, NAFE, Washington Group, Oracle User's Group, Plast. Ukrainian Catholic. Office: Sprint Internat 12490 Sunrise Valley Dr Reston VA 22096

MELLOTT, KAREN ELIZABETH, systems engineer; b. Santa Monica, Calif., Apr. 3, 1956; d. Albert F. and Margaret (Owen) Mellott. MusB, Cleve. Inst. Music, 1980, MusM, 1982. Computer operator Lytkowski and Co., Cleve., 1985-86; systems engr. Electronic Data Sysems Corp., Lansing, Mich., 1986—. Home: 130 Windjammer Dr W-11 Lansing MI 48917

MELNIKOFF, SARAH ANN, gem importer, jewelry designer; b. Chgo., Feb. 12, 1936; d. Harry E. and Marie Louise (Straub) Caylor; m. Casimir Adam Jestadt, Feb. 27, 1959 (div. Sept. 1972); 1 child, Christina Marie Jestadt-Russo; m. Sol Melnikoff, July 31, 1981. Student Gemol. Inst. Am., 1968-69, Am. Acad. Art, Chgo., 1952-56, Art Inst. Chgo., 1953, Mundelein Coll., Chgo., 1953-54. Pres., Casmira Gem, Inc., Chgo., 1963—; comml. artist, Chgo., 1957-78; U.S. del. Internat. Colored Gemstone Dealers Assn., W.Ger., 1985; lectr., cons. in field. Mem. Chgo. Salesman's Alliance, MINK Inc., Women's Jewelry Assn., Am. Gem Trade Assn. (nat. sec. 1982-86, 88—, dir. 1988—), Chgo. Jewelers Assn., Women's Jewelry Assn., Inc., Am. Horse Show Assn., Am. Saddlebred Horse Show Assn., Mid-Am. Horse Show Assn. (dir. 1980-83). Republican. Roman Catholic. Avocation: horses.

MELO, DENISE MARIE, sales representative; b. Danville, Ill., Oct. 24, 1955; d. Charles Halsey Reeves and Wanda Jeanne (Chandler) Nasados; m. Steven Anthony Fontana, Sept. 9, 1978 (div. Oct. 1988); m. Mario A. Melo, Oct. 17, 1989. BS, So. Ill. U., 1977. Real estate sales Sweeney Co., Fargo, N.D., 1979-81; sales rep. Mary Kay Cosmetics, Fargo, 1980-82; owner Sip N' Dip Ice Cream Shop, Dunedin, Fla., 1982; soft goods mgr. No. Dakota State U. Book Store, Fargo; asst. mgr. The Ltd., Independence, Mo., 1985; store mgr. Shirts Illustrated, Mo., 1985-87; activities dir. La Posada Hotel, San Carlos, 1987; store mgr. Capezio Shoes, Dallas, 1987-88; sales rep. Tex., 1988--. Republican. Roman Catholic. Home and Office: 400 Red River Trail #1000 Irving TX 75063

MELONE, NANCY PAULE, management and technology educator; b. Des Moines, Dec. 17, 1948; d. Lowell Wayne and Jacqueline Lee (Richards) M.; m. John William Struchen, June 13, 1970 (div. 1976). BA, U. Iowa, 1973, MALS, 1974, MAIR, 1979; MBA, U. Minn., 1981, PhD, 1987. Media ctr. dir. Iowa City Sch. Dist., 1974-75; teaching fellow Ctr. for Labor and Mgmt., U. Iowa, Iowa City, 1975-76; rsch. assoc. Honeywell-Systems and Rsch., Mpls., 1979-80; strategy analyst First Bank Mpls., 1981-82; rsch. asst. U. Minn., Mpls., 1982-85; asst. prof. Carnegie-Mellon U., Pitts., 1987—; juror Am. Mgmt. Systems, 1988. Contbr. articles to profl. jours. Mem. Assn. Computing Machinery, Inst. Mgmt. Scis., Acad. Mgmt., Inst. Electrical & Electronic Engrs., Am. Psychological Assn., Alpha Gamma Delta. Democrat. Episcopalian. Office: Carnegie-Mellon U Grad Sch Indsl Adminstrn Pittsburgh PA 15213-3890

MELONI, LORETTA FLORENCE, educator; b. Phila., Oct. 29, 1942; d. Salvatore J. and Florence R. (De Sipio) M. BS in Edn., West Chester U., 1964, MEd, 1970; Cert. in Supervision, Villanova U., 1980; Cert. in Supervision, Curriculum and Instrn., Widener U., 1990. Elem. tchr. Chester Twp. Sch. Dist., Brookhaven, Pa., 1964-66; elem. tchr. William Penn Sch. Dist., Yeadon, Pa., 1966—, facilitator staff devel. program, innovator parallel block scheduling, 1988-89. Recipient Gift of Time Tribute Am. Family Inst., 1987. Mem. Assn. for Supervision and Curriculum Devel., Pa. Assn. for Supervision and Curriculum Devel., NEA, Pa. State Edn. Assn., William Penn Edn. Assn. Office: Park Lane Elem Sch Park Ln and Chadbourne Rd Darby PA 19023

MELOY, LINDA DIANNE, pediatrician; b. Teaneck, N.J., Sept. 2, 1955; d. Arthur Richard and Dorothea Winifred (Niehaus) M. BA, Drew U., 1977; MD, Rutgers U., 1981. Intern Med. Coll. Va., Richmond, 1982, resident, 1984; pediatrician Va. Health Dept., Petersburg, 1984—; clin. instr. Med. Coll. Va., Richmond, 1984—; physician Assn. Bapt. for World Evangelism, Philippines, 1984. Author: (booklet) God's Prescription for Life, 1985. Sunday sch. tchr. Grove Ave. Bapt. Ch., Richmond, 1984—; team mem. Multimedia Evangelism, England, 1985, 87; missionary apprentice Assn. Bapt. for World Evangelism, Peru, 1976. Fellow Am. Acad. Pediatrics. Republican. Home: 10016 C Castile Rd Richmond VA 23233 Office: Med Coll of Virginia Box 506 MCV Sta Richmond VA 23298

MELROSE, PATRICIA ANN, educator, researcher; b. Muskegon, Mich., Oct. 26, 1955; d. Donald Edward and BettiJane (Wilkinson) M. BS, Mich. State U., 1977; MS, U. Ky., 1981, PhD, 1983; postgrad., U. Rochester, 1982-84. Clin. chemist, toxicologist Internat. Clin. Labs., Lexington, Ky., 1979-82; rsch. assoc. neuroendocrine unit U. Rochester, 1982-84, asst. prof., 1984-87; assoc. prof. vet. medicine La. State U., Baton Rouge, 1987—. Contbr. articles to profl. jours. Grayson Found. fellow, 1978-82, Fed. Vet. Rsch. Fund fellow, 1978-82; NIH grantee, 1985, 87, USDA grantee, 1987-89, AVMA Found. grantee, 1989, Grayson Found. grantee, 1989; NIH scholar, 1987. Mem. AAAS, Soc. for Neurosci. (pres. local chpt. 1988—), Endocrine Soc., N.Y. Acad. Sci. Republican. Office: La State U Sch Vet Medicine Dept Anatomy Baton Rouge LA 70803

MELROY, JANE RUTH, business educator; b. Columbus, Nebr., Apr. 5, 1957; d. David Morris Sr. and Catherine Hanna (Carson) Hamilton; m. Dennis Lee Melroy, Feb. 28, 1976; children: Tobin Ray, Brent Carson, Erin Jane. BS in Edn., Kearney (Nebr.) State Coll., 1980. Cert. tchr., Nebr., Kans. Tchr. bus. York (Nebr.) High Sch., 1980-84, Broken Bow (Nebr.) High Sch., 1984-88, Skyline High Sch., Pratt, Kans., 1989—; part-time mem. adj. faculty Pratt Community Coll., 1988—. Contbr. (curriculum guide) Computers in Business Education, 1986, (handbook) Comptuer Enrichment Handbook, 1990. Rep. Broken Bow Community Edn. Bd., 1984-88; sec. vocat. adv. coun. Pratt High Sch., 1988-90; cubmaster Boy Scouts Am., Pratt, 1988-89, chmn. com., 1990—. Mem. Nat. Bus. Edn. Assn., Kans. Bus. Edn. Assn., Mountain-Plains Bus. Edn. Assn., Nebr. State Bus. Edn. Assn. (rep. Sandhill chpt. 1986-88), Skyline Edn. Assn., Kans. Nat. Edn. Assn. (bd. dirs. Ark Valley chpt. 1990—), NEA, Nebr. Future Leaders of Am. (bd. dirs. Lincoln chpt. 1986-88), AAUW, Delta Kappa Gamma International. Republican. Episcopalian.

MELTON, CATHERINE LYNN, telecommunications executive; b. St. Louis, Dec. 15, 1958; d. Lewis Ray Melton and Betty Joan (DuBois) Murphy. Student, Robertsdale Bus. Coll., 1975-77, Drake U., 1977-78, Des Moines Community Coll., 1979-82, Tampa Coll., 1988-89, Calif. Coast Coll., 1989—. Asst. ops. supr. Iowa Power and Light Co., Des Moines, 1978-83; computer operator S&L Computer Trust, Des Moines, 1983-84; sr. computer operator Pester Corp., Des Moines, 1984-86; computer operator Fotomat Corp., St. Petersburg, Fla., 1986-87; ops. tech. City of Largo, Fla., 1987-88; systems adminstr. City of Temple Terrace, Fla., 1988-89; system mgr. GTE Telecom, Tampa, 1989—. Mem. Womens Sports Found., NOW, Data Processing Mgmt. Assn., Fla. Local Govt. Data Processing, NAFE, Nat. Parks and Conservation Assn., Nat. Wildlife Fedn., Sierra Club, Cousteau Soc., Desenders Dive Club, Assn. System Mgrs. Jewish. Home: 10013 Oaklawaha Tampa FL 33617 Office: GTE Telecom PO Box 2924 Tampa FL 33601

MELTON, KAREN DALE, controller; b. Cleve., Apr. 21, 1952; d. Noel N. and Estelle L. (Midgette) M. BA, Baldwin-Wallace Coll., Berea, Ohio, 1987, MBA, 1990. Accounts payable clk. Kirkwood Industries, Cleve.; acctg. supr., controller Kaufman Container Co., Cleve., controller. Mem. NAFE. Democrat. Methodist. Office: 4700 Spring Rd Cleveland OH 44131

MELTON, LOYCE NELL, retail shop owner; b. Memphis, Jan. 27, 1938; d. Asa Edward and Ella Tramel (Mohundro) Paseur; m. Aaron V. Melton Jr., Oct. 21, 1956; children: Timothy Aaron, Kenneth Scott, Karen Denise. Grad. high sch., Memphis, 1957. Sec. Holiday Inns, Inc., Memphis, 1968-76; tax examiner IRS, Memphis, 1976-79; salesperson Joy's Fashions, Memphis, 1979-80; owner, mgr. Loyce's Boutique, Olive Branch, Miss., 1980—; writer Loyce's Fashion Focus column DeSoto County Tribune, 1988-89. Active local PTA, 1964-70; pres. Oakville Sch. PTA, 1967-68; Cub scout den leader Boy Scouts Am., 1966; tchr. children's Bible class, 1960—. Mem. Olive Branch C. of C. Mem. Ch. of Christ. Office: Loyces Boutique 9119 Pigeon Roost Ave Olive Branch MS 38654

MELTON, NANCY JEAN, educational administrator; b. Davenport, Iowa, July 31, 1943; d. William Harry Jr. and Verda Estella (Bushnell) Newhard; m. Raymond Gerald Melton, Oct. 14, 1962 (div. 1978); children: Michael Scott, David Blake, Laurel Elizabeth. BS in Edn., Southwest Mo. State U., 1965; MS in Ednl. Adminstrn., U. Mo., 1968; PhD in Edn., Fla. State U., 1976. Dir. community relations Mesa Pub. Schs., 1971-72; dir. communications and spl. projects Fla. Sch. Bds. Assn., Tallahassee, 1974-75; asst. to pres. Christopher Newport Coll., Newport News, Va., 1976-79; assoc. dir. Mariners Mus., Newport News, 1980-84; dir. mus. City of Portsmouth, Va., 1984-89; dir. info. and legis. svcs. Newport News (Va.) Pub. Schs., 1989—; cons. Fla. Dept. Edn., Tallahassee, 1973; mem. faculty Seminar for Hist.

Adminstrn., 1980-83. Bd. dirs. Cultural Alliance Greater Hampton Roads, Norfolk, 1980-89, Future Hampton Roads, Inc., Norfolk, 1989—; chmn. Newport News Cable Vision Commn., 1984. Ford Found. fellow. Mem. Nat. Identification Program for Advancement Women in Higher Edn., Rotary. Republican. Presbyterian. Office: Newport News City 12465 Warwick Blvd Newport News VA 23606

MELTON, VERA SOPHIA, interior designer; b. Oslo, Feb. 28, 1922; came to U.S., 1926; d. Karl Verner Hurtig and Olga Pauline (Frenning) Kvaas; m. Eugene E. DeLaby, Dec. 26, 1942 (div.); 1 child, Christine; m. Robert Hlavin, Dec. 11, 1971 (div.); m. Finis Melton, Nov. 19, 1989. BS summa cum laude, Woodbury U., L.A., 1975. Exec. sec. Florsheim Shoe Co., Chgo., 1946-56; sec. supr. Ralph Parsons Co., L.A., 1956-69; exec. asst. Empire Gen. Corp., L.A., 1969-72; interior designer Walter Weiss, Irvine, Calif., 1977-78, Chino Hills (Calif.) Interiors, 1988—; pvt. practice Azusa, Calif., 1984-87; mem. sales staff Walker & Lee Real Estate, Mission Viejo, Calif., 1978-83. Mem. Nat. Trust Hist. Preservation, Sons of Norway. Home: 13915 Lomitas Ave La Puente CA 91746

MELTON-SCOTT, MARY MEULI, hospital administrator, consultant; b. Dec. 4, 1943; d. August Martin and Vada Irene (Matthews) Meuli; m. James Lynn Bell, May 23, 1961 (div. 1964); 1 child, James Lynn; m. Charles David Scott, Jr., Sept. 18, 1964 (div. 1969); 1 child, Charles David III; m. Charles Tabb, Jr., June 23, 1970 (div. 1973); 1 child, Erika Elizabeth; m. Johnny Wayne Scott, 1983. BA, McMurry Coll., 1971; MS, Wright State U., 1978; PhD, Columbia Pacific U., 1983; MBA, Xavier U., Cin., 1986. Cert. alcoholism counselor, 23 states, including Ohio. High sch. tchr. Dayton pub. schs., Ohio, 1972-74; therapist Greene Hall, Greene Meml. Hosp., Xenia, Ohio, 1975-77; clin. dir. Bur. Alcoholism Svcs., Dayton, 1978-83; v.p. Dettmer Hosp./Upper Valley Med. Ctr., Troy, Ohio, 1983-86; adminstr. Valley View Hosp., Las Cruces, N.Mex., 1986-88; owner, pres. Melton-Scott Enterprises, Tipp City, Ohio, 1983-86, So. N.Mex. D.W.I. Programs, 1988—; chief fin. offier The August Corp.; cons. WORAC, Dayton, 1978-83; exec. dir. Miami County Mental Health, Ohio, 1984—; chief exec. officer Alcohol Drug Abuse Tratment Svcs., Inc., 1989—; task force chmn. Vietnam Vets. N.Mex. Mem. NAFE, Assn. Mental Health Adminstrs., Nat. Assn. Alcoholism Counselors, Nat. Coun. on Alcoholism (Ohio chpt.), Am. Coll. Health Care Adminstrs., Sigma Delta Tau. Avocations: writing, gardening, needlework, sports. Home: 4248 Mission Bell Ave Las Cruces NM 88001 Office: 1029 E Spruce Ave Las Cruces NM 88001 also: The August Corp 8000 John F Kennedy Blvd Ste 6 North Little Rock AK 72116

MELTZER, BONNIE ROSENBERG, public relations administrator, fundraiser; b. N.Y.C., June 6, 1943; d. William and Mollie (Cohen) Rosenberg; m. Jay Howard Meltzer, June 27, 1965; children: Wendy, Elizabeth, Jonathan. BA, Goucher Coll., 1965. Program assoc. N.Y. State Coun. on Arts, N.Y.C., 1967-71; asst. course writer Bus. Sch., Harvard U., Cambridge, Mass., 1965-67, 71-81; various devel. positions Wheelock Coll., Boston, 1981-87, dir. devel., 1987-89; dir. devel. Facing History & Ourselves, Brookline, Mass., 1989—. Mem. parents com. Harvard U., 1987—; mem. ann. fund com. Goucher Coll., Towson, Md., 1983—. Mem. Women in Devel. (treas., bd. dirs. 1989—). Office: Facing History & Ourselves 25 Kennard Rd Brookline MA 02146

MELTZER, DEBRA MARIE, manufacturing executive, business owner; b. Racine, Wis., Sept. 3, 1954; d. Rudolph Lawrence and Florence Marie (Nelson) M. Student, U. Wis., 1975-78. Sec. Mamco Corp., Franksville, Wis., 1979—; bd. dirs., corp. sec. Mamco Corp., Franksville; bd. dirs., corp. sec. Lexel Corp., Hutsonville, Ill., 1983—. Republican. Lutheran. Home: 5928 Belmar Ave Racine WI 53402 Office: Mamco Corp 8630 Industrial Dr Franksville WI 53126

MELTZER, E. ALYNE, teacher, social worker, volunteer; b. Jersey City, May 16, 1934; d. Abraham Samuel and Fannie Ruth (Nydick) M. BA, Mich. State U., 1956. Acctg. clerk Louis Marx Co. Inc., N.Y.C., 1957-60; social studies tchr. Haverstraw High Sch., N.Y., 1960-61; tchr. Sachem Cen. Sch. Dist., Farmingville, N.Y., 1961-63, East Paterson Sch. Dist., N.J., 1964-65; case worker Human Resource Adm. Social Service Dept., N.Y.C., 1966-89. Policy advisor Senator Roy Goodman Adv. Com., Albany N.Y. 1987—; mem. Yorkville Civic Coun., 1988—. Recipient Sabra Soc. Plaque award State of Israel New Leadership Div., N.Y.C., 1979, Prime Minister Club Plaque award State of Israel Bonds, 1986-87. Mem. Nat. Council Jewish Women (life mem. N.Y. sect. and Rockland County sect., mem. N.Y. state pub. affairs com., Nat. Citation award N.Y. sect. 1973-74, Donor award 1987-90), MSU Alumni Orgn. (life, sec. N.Y. chpt. 1959-60), Am. Jewish Com. (N.Y.C. chpt.), Hadassah (life), Womens League for Israel (life), Am. Assn. of U. Women, Am.-Israel Friendship League, Assn. of Reformed Zionists of Am. (N.Y.C. chpt.), Jewish Genealogical Soc. (N.Y.C. chpt.), Thyroid Found. of Am., Temple Shaaray Tefila.

MELVIN, MARGARET, nurse, consultant; b. Thomasville, Ga., July 13, 1927; d. Robert and Lorene Elizabeth (Barrett) M. BS in Nursing Edn., Duke U., 1953. Cert. Occupational Health Cons. Head nurse Duke U. Med. Ctr., Durham, N.C., 1947-54; charge nurse med. clinic U. Mich. Med. Ctr., Ann Arbor, 1955-59; occupational health nurse State Farm Ins. Co., Jacksonville, Fl., 1960-65; dir. ins. edn. Baptist Hosp. Med. Ctr., Jacksonville, 1965-68; various positions Wausau Ins. Co., Orlando, Fla., 1968-80; sr. cert. occupational health cons. Wausau Ins. Co., Orlando, 1980—; lectr. various hosps. and orgns. Developed, created nat. teaching program for back problems, 1976, program for emergency care industry, 1974. Am. Cancer Soc. grantee, 1968. Mem. Am. Nurses Assn., Am. Assn. Occupational Health Nurses, Fla. State Assn. Occupational Health Nruses (chmn. 1982, conf. sec. 1980-84), Am. Bd Occupational Health Nurses. Republican. Home: 244 Windmeadows Dr Altamonte Springs FL 32701

MEMBERY, JOAN HATHAWAY, plastic surgeon; b. Winterhaven, Fla., Dec. 30, 1931; d. James Garnet and Mary Ellen (Hathaway) M. AA, Stephens Coll., Columbia, Mo., 1950; BA, U. N.C., 1952; MD, U. Miami, 1962. Bd. certified gen. surgery, plastic surgery. Intern L.A. County Hosp., 1963; resident in surgery The Mayo Clinic, Rochester, Minn., 1965, Wadsworth Gen. Hosp., L.A., 1967; resident in plastic surgery UCLA, 1971; pvt. practice Miami, 1971—; staff physician So. Miami Hosp., 1972—, Bapt. Hosp., Miami, 1972—, Jackson Meml. Hosp., Miami, 1972—. Named one of Outstanding Young Women Am. Jaycees, 1966. Mem. Am. Soc. Plastic and Reconstructive Surgery, Am. Soc. Aesthetic Plastic Surgery, Greater Miami Soc. Plastic Surgery, Fla. Med. Assn., Dade County Med. Soc., The Explorer's Club, Ocean Reef Club, Royal Palm Tennis Club. Office: 7700 Red Rd Miami FL 33143

MEMMER, SANDRA KAYE, small business owner; b. Ashland, Ky., Mar. 28, 1959; d. William K. and Sandless (Cordial) McBride; m. Luis B. Boneta II, Apr. 14, 1989. AS, U. Ky., 1981. Programming mgr. Microtel, Inc., Boca Raton, Fla., 1985-87; owner, pres. Team4 Systems Support, Inc., Tampa, 1987-89, Office Dynamics, Inc., Tampa, 1989—. Mem. NAFE, Internat. Computer Cons. Assn., Internat. Tandem Users Group, Women Bus. Owners Assn. (newsletter editor Fla. chpt. 1989-90). Office: 5802 E Fowler Ave Ste B Tampa FL 33617

MEMOLO, MARY JANE, dietician; b. Niagara Falls, N.Y., Apr. 23, 1937; d. Edmund Stewart and Clara Mary (LaFrance) Milner. BS, Marywood Coll., 1959, MS, 1977. Clin. dietician Peter Bent Brigham Hosp., Boston, 1960-61, St. Louis Children's Hosp., 1961-62, Mary Hitchcock Hosp., Hanover, N.H., 1962-63; teaching dietician Pa. Hosp., Phila., 1965-67; supr. dietician Custom Mgmt. Corp., Kingston, Pa., 1970-76, Lackawanna Co. Instn. Dist., Scranton, Pa., 1976-82; dir., dietary dept. Marworth Treatment Ctr., Waverly, Pa., 1982--; cons. Hospice of Pa., Scranton, 1982--. Bd. dirs. Forest Lakes Council, Boy Scouts Am., St. Francis Assisi. Mem. AAUW, DAR. Northeast Pa. Dietetic Assn., Pa. Dietetic Assn. (pres.), Am. Dietetic Assn., Everhart Museum Assn., Lackawanna County Hist. Soc. Republican. Home: Scranton Pocono Hwy Scranton PA 18505 Office: Marworth Lily Lake Rd Waverly PA 18471

MENALDINO, SHARON ROSE, cognitive therapist, psychologist; b. Flushing, N.Y., Feb. 13, 1951; d. Edward Ermanno and Dorothy Ruth (Holmgren) M. BS, Evangel Coll., 1974; EdM, Temple U., 1976, EdD, 1981. Instr. psycholog. reading dept. Temple U., Phila., 1975-79; ednl. pscyhologist Assn. for Jewish Children, Phila., 1978-81; prof.'s asst. psychology of reading Temple U., Phila., 1978-79; reading therapist Individualized Tutorial Svc., Springfield, Pa., 1978-84; clinician reading clinic Temple U., Phila., 1979-81; cons. Cert. Pvt. Clin. for Vocat. Assessment, Phila., 1981-83; ednl. cons. ReMed Recovery Care Ctr., Jenkintown, Pa., 1986; reading/cognitive psychologist Moss Rehab. Hosp., Phila., 1981—; cognitive cons. Pvt. Ednl. Svcs., Springfield, 1983—; cognitive specialist Mainline Rehab. Assocs., Inc., Malvern, Pa., 1989—; ednl. cons. Broomhall Rehab. Assocs., Broomhall, Pa., 1988—; mem. reorganization com. Moss Rehab. Hosp., Phila., 1987-88. Coord., cons. Jacob's Ladder Tutorial Svc., Phila., 1979—; cons. Calvary Temple Christian Acad., Phila., 1977—, bd. dirs., 1981—. Named Outstanding Young American of Am., 1982. Mem. Am. Psychol. Assn. (divs. 1 and 22), Ea. Psychol. Assocs., Nat. Head Injury Found., Internat. Reading Assn.

MENCEY, HELEN V. L., educator; b. Anahuac, Tex., Oct. 19, 1960; d. Milton M. and Narvis C. (Malone) M. BFA, Sam Houston State U., 1983; tchr. certification, Lamar U., 1985; MEd, Prairie View Coll., 1989. Cert. tchr., Tex. Tchr. Rurkeville (Tex.) Ind. Sch. Dist., 1986, Port Arthur (Tex.) Sch. Dist., 1986—. Mem. NEA, Tex. State Tchrs. Assn., NAFE, Tex. Reading Assn., Internat. Reading Assn., ACLD. Home: PO Box 363 Stowell TX 77661

MENDELBERG, HAVA EVA, psychologist; b. Cordoba, Argentina, Dec. 26, 1942; came to U.S., 1975; d. Israel and Celia (Rubin) Gleser; children: Tali, Gabi. BA, Hebrew U., Jerusalem, 1969; Licenciatura, U. Madrid, 1971; MS, U. Wis., 1977, PhD, 1981. Tchr. Kibbutz, Israel, 1964-66, Inst. for Leaders From Abroad, Israel, 1966-69; psychologist Family Service, Milw., 1981-82; clin. psychologist Psychoanalytic Psychology, Milw., 1981-85; pvt. practice clin. psychology Shorewood, Wis., 1985—; clin. dir. Depression Clinic, Milw., 1989—; psychologist Municipality of Jerusalem, 1963-75, Mt. Sinai Med. Ctr., Wis., 1980-81, 81-82; prof. U. Wis., 1981-82, supr. 84-85, 1987—; asst. clin. prof. Med. Coll. Wis., 1989—; cons. Columbia Hosp., Milw., 1986—, St. Michael Hosp., Milw., 1985—, Milw. Psychiat. Hosp., 1986—; speaker in field. Contbr. articles to profl. jours. Mem. Assn. for Mental Health (chmn. 1983—) Am. Psychol. Assn., Wis. Psychol. Assn., Psychol. Assn. Israel, Psychol. Assn. Spain, World Fedn. for Mental Health, Psychologists for Social Responsiblity. Home: 1820 E Edgewood Shorewood WI 53211 Office: Depression Clinic 2577 N Downer Ave Ste 215 Milwaukee WI 53211

MENDELL, PHYLLIS, psychologist, health facility administrator, researcher, educator; b. N.Y.C., July 25, 1949; d. Morris and Esther (Spielman) Goldstein; m. André Wilson Mendell, July 4, 1979; children: D'vorah, Aliza, Mikel. BA magna cum laude, Queens Coll., 1972, MA in Physiol. Psychology, 1976; PhD in Psychology, Hofstra U., 1987. Lic. psychologist N.Y. Rsch. asst. Albert Einstein Coll. of Medicine, Bronx, 1972-74; acad. cons. Latham Pub. Co., N.Y.C., 1976-77; coord. of sci. Coll. of Discovery & Devel., N.Y.C., 1980-81; dir. rsch. NCTRH, Washington, 1983-84; therapist psychology svcs. SUNY, Farmingdale, 1986; pvt. practice clin. psychologist Huntington, N.Y., 1988—; asst. prof. psychology Adelphi U., Garden City, N.Y., 1989—; dir. psychol. svcs. Nassau Ctr. for the Developmentally Disabled, Woodbury, N.Y., 1980—; adj. prof. psychology, Nassau Community Coll., 1974-89; lectr., guest speaker Bronx Bot. Gardens, Bronx, 1983-86; guest speaker NCTRH, Ind., Phila., Washington, 1983-85, Rusk Inst., N.Y.C., 1989. Contbr. articles to profl. jours. Mem. Huntington Hist. Soc., 1989-90, Women's Sports Found., 1984—. Mem. Am. Psychol. Assn., Nassau County Regional Planning Group, ITES Spl. Edn. Task Force (chairperson behavior rev. com., 1989—, mem. rsch. rev. com. 1984—), Phi Beta Kappa. Jewish. Home: 232 Park Ave Huntington NY 11743 Office: Nassau Ctr Devel Disabled 72 Southwoods Rd Woodbury NY 11797

MENDELL, ROSALIND BREMMER, physics educator; b. N.Y.C., Oct. 20, 1920; d. Hyman and Celia (Hirschtritt) Bremmer; m. Lesley Stanley Mendell, Dec. 21, 1941; children: Laura, Henry. BS, Hunter Coll., 1940; MS, Cornell U., 1942; PhD, NYU, 1963. Instr. NYU, N.Y.C., 1942-43; physicist Columbia U. Radiation Labs., N.Y.C., 1943, Nat. Bur. Standards, Washington, 1944-45; rsch. assoc. prof. NYU, N.Y.C., 1963-73, sr. rsch. scientist, adj. assoc. prof., 1973—; vis. prof. NSF VPW, Lehman Coll., N.Y.C., 1984-85; vis. prof., chmn. physics dept. Manhattanville Coll., Purchase, N.Y., 1987-89. Contbr. articles to profl. jours. Grantee NSF, NASA, Air Force Cambridge, BNR; Pres. White fellow Cornell U.; recipient medal Soc. Pour l'Encouragement de Sci. Fellow N.Y. Acad. Scis.; mem. APS, Am. Geophysical Union, Phi Beta Kappa, Sigma Xi. Home: 89 Joyce Rd Hartsdale NY 10530 Office: NYU 4 Washington Pl New York NY 10003

MENDENHALL, WILMA ROSE, credit manager; b. Pueblo, Colo., Nov. 26, 1932; d. William Martin and Rose Dora (Lakner) Micklich; m. John Orvill Mendenhall, Sept. 20, 1952 (dec. 1985); children: Laurence, John, Cynthia, Judith, Sharon. Grad. high sch., 1950. Posting clerk GMAC, Pueblo, Colo., 1950; discount clerk GMAC, Pueblo, 1953, customer rep., 1960, credit rep.; credit supr. GMAC, Colorado Springs, 1980-85; sales supr. GMAC, 1985-88; credit mgr. GMAC, Colorado Springs, 1988--. Republican. Catholic. Home: 3161 Westcliff Dr W Colorado Springs CO 80906 Office: 1150 Academy Park Loop Ste Colorado Springs CO 80910

MENDER, MONA SIEGLER, music educator; b. Jersey City, May 24, 1926; d. George and Freda (Steierman) Siegler; m. Irving M. Mender, Aug. 25, 1946; children: Donald Matthew, Judith J. Mender. BA, Mt. Holyoke Coll., 1947. Instr. piano and music theory, Fair Lawn, N.J., 1947-75; state edn. chmn. N.J. Symphony Orch., Newark, 1980-82, state chmn. bd. regents, 1983-84, bd. dirs., 1983—. Author: Music Manuscript Preparation: A Concise Guide, 1988. Recipient Women's Network commendation Sen. Bill Bradley, 1984. Mem. Mt. Holyoke Club (South Hadley, Mass.), Mountain Ridge Country Club (West Caldwell, N.J.), Williams Coll. Faculty Club (Williamstown, Mass.), Taconic Golf Club, Plantation Golf and Country Club (Venice, Fla.).

MENDEZ, ILEANA MARIA, graphic designer, consultant; b. Washington, Mar. 14, 1952; d. Americo Jr. and Carmen Pura (Torres) M.; m. Timothy Jerome Renk, Mar. 2, 1985. BA in Design, Am. U., 1979; MFA in Graphic Design, Yale U., 1981. Freelance graphic designer N.Y.C., 1981; art dir. Sci. News, Washington, 1982-83; instr. Marymount Coll. of Va., Arlington, 1984; freelance design cons. Washington, 1983, 84, 85; designer, owner IM Design/Communication, Albuquerque, 1986—. Design dir. Women's Econ. Self-Suffiency Team, Albquerque, 1989—. Ford Found. grantee, 1980. Mem. Communication Artists of N.Mex. (v.p. 1988-89), Yale U. Alumni Assn. (bd. dirs. N.Mex. chpt. 1988-90), Toastmasters Internat. (adminstrv. v.p. 1988-89, pres. 1990). Democrat. Office: IM Design/Communication 834 Southeast Circle NW Albuquerque NM 87104-1967

MENDEZ, JANA LYNN, senator; b. Moscow, Idaho, Jan. 18, 1944; d. Earl Dean and Alverta (Dalberg) Hall; m. Richard Albert Mendez, Sept. 16, 1965; children: Amy, Jennifer, Christopher. BS in Journalism, U. Colo., 1981. Community and issue activist Boulder County Housing Authority and Citizens for the Right To Vote, Longmont, Colo., 1975-83; legis. asst. Senate Minority Leader, Denver, 1982-84; Colo. state senator, 1985—; asst. whip minority leader, 1986. Author: (with others) Chile From The Ground Up, 1982. Dem. precinct leader, area coordinator, senate dist. chmn. Boulder County, Colo., 1975-84; chair, commr. Boulder County Housing Authority, 1974-83. Regents scholar, 1963, Cervi scholar, 1980; U. Colo. Women's Ctr. grantee, 1980; named Outstanding Freshman Senator Colo. Social Legis. Com., 1985. Mem. Kappa Tau Alpha. Avocations: gardening, reading, photography, cooking. Office: State Capitol Rm 274 Denver CO 80203*

MENDEZ, OLGA A., state legislator; b. Mayaguez, P.R.. BA, U. P.R.; MEd, Columbia U., 1960; PhD in Ednl. Psychology, Yeshiva U., N.Y.C., 1975. Previously assoc. prof. SUNY-Stony Brook, research psychologist Albert Einstein Coll. Med., N.Y.C., dep. commr. N.Y.C. Agy. for Child Devel., N.Y. state senator, 1978—; del. Dem. Nat. Conv., 1980. Home: 1215 Fifth Ave Apt #15-D New York NY 10029 Office: N Y State Senate Albany NY 12224*

MENDEZ-BILLINGTON, SUSANA ELENA, addictions professional; b. Buenos Aires, Argentina, Sept. 2, 1956; d. Jose Maria and Susana (Girella) M.; m. Carlos Alberto Pena, Dec. 10, 1986 (div.); m. Gregory Michael Billington, Feb. 25, 1990. MD, Med. Sch., Buenos Aires, Argentina, 1982. Medical diplomate in Argentina; cert. addiction specialist, clin. hypnotherapist. Paramedic Gandulfo Hosp., Buenos Aires, Argentina, 1978-80; paramedic supr. Gandulfo Hosp., Buenos Aires, 1980-82, med. intern., 1982-85; psychiat. med. intern Alfaro Hosp., Buenos Aires, 1982-84; fl. supr., med. doctor Inter-Nos Pvt. Clinic, Buenos Aires, 1984-86; alcoholism counselor The Harbor, N.J., 1987-88; alcoholism supr. The Harbor, Hoboken, N.J., 1988-89; inpatient program coord. The Harbor, Hoboken, 1989—; pvt. practice; cons. Hosp. in Buenos Aires, 1988—. Mem. Argentine Soc. Sophrology, Am. Assn. for Counseling & Devel., Am. Rehab. Counseling, Mental Health Counselors Assn., Am. Soc. Addiction Medicine, Nat. Assn. Alcoholism & Drug Abuse Counselors, Nat. Guild Hypnotists. Roman Catholic. Office: Essex Allied Svcs Inc 1405 Clinton St Hoboken NJ 07030

MENDIOLA, ANNA MARIA G., mathematics educator; b. Laredo, Tex., Dec. 21, 1948; d. Alberto and Aurora (Benavides) Gonzalez; m. Alfonso Mendiola Jr., Aug. 11, 1973; children: Alfonso, Alberto. AA, Laredo Jr. Coll., Tex., 1967; BA, Tex. Woman's U., 1969, MS, 1974. Tchr. math. Laredo Ind. Sch. Dist., 1969-81; math instr. Laredo Jr. Coll., 1981—; vis. instr. St. Augustine Sch., Laredo, 1987-88; evaluator So. Assn., Corpus Christi, 1981; juror Higher Edn. Coordinating Bd. Report, San Antonio, 1989. Producer slide promo, Mathematics at LJC, 1983. V.p., bd. dirs. Our Lady of Guadalupe Sch., Laredo, 1988—; sec. Laredo Jr. Coll. Faculty Senate, 1986-87, chairperson task force on coll.-level exit competencies, 1989—; active Boy Scouts Am., 1985-86. Mem. AAUW (pres. 1979-81, v.p. 1987-89), Tex. State Tchrs. Assn., Tex. Jr. Coll. Tchrs. Assn., Am. Math. Assn. of Two Yr. Colls., Tex. Woman's U. Alumnae Assn., Blessed Sacrament Altar Soc. Democrat. Roman Catholic. Office: Laredo Junior College West End Washington St Laredo TX 78040

MENDIUS, PATRICIA DODD WINTER, editor, educator, writer; b. Davenport, Iowa, July 9, 1924; d. Otho Edward and Helen Rose (Dodd) Winter; m. John Richard Mendius, June 19, 1947; children: Richard, Catherine M. Graber, Louise, Karen M. Chooljian. BA cum laude, UCLA, 1946; MA cum laude, U. N.Mex., 1966. Cert. secondary edn. tchr., Calif., N.Mex. English teaching asst. UCLA, 1946-47; English tchr. Marlborough Sch. for Girls, L.A., 1947-50, Aztec (N.Mex.) High Sch., 1953-55, Farmington (N.Mex.) High Sch., 1955-63; chair English dept. Los Alamos (N.Mex.) High Sch., 1963-86; writer, editor Los Alamos Nat. Lab., 1987—; adj. prof. English, U. N.Mex., Los Alamos, 1970-72, Albuquerque, 1982-85; English cons. S.W. Regional Coll. Bd., Austin, Tex., 1975—; writer, editor, cons. advanced placement English test devel. com. Nat. Coll. Bd., 1982-86, reader, 1982-86, project equality cons., 1985-88; book selection cons. Scholastic mag., 1980-82. Contbr. articles to profl. jours. Chair Los Alamos Art in Pub. Pls. Bd., 1987—; chair adv. bd. trustees U. N.Mex., Los Alamos, 1987—; pres. Los Alamos Concert Assn., 1972-73. Mem. Soc. Tech. Communicators, AAUW (pres. 1961-63, state bd. dirs. 1959-63), DAR, Order of Ea. Star, Mortar Bd., Phi Beta Kappa (pres. Los Alamos chpt. 1969-72), Phi Kappa Phi, Delta Kappa Gamma, Gamma Phi Beta. Home: 124 Rover Blvd Los Alamos NM 87544 Office: Los Alamos Nat Lab Diamond Dr Los Alamos NM 87545

MENDOZA, CARMEN SIA GOMEZ, registered nurse; b. Mindanao, Philippines, Jan. 4, 1950; came to U.S., 1973; d. Pablo Sabejon and Lourdes Sia Gomez (Zayas) M. BSN, Arellano U., Manila, Philippines, 1972; postgrad., Augusta Tech. Sch., 1985. RN, Fla., Ky., Ga., N.J. Nurse Makati Med. Ctr., Manila, 1972-73, Newark (N.J.) Beth-Israel Med. Ctr., 1973-75, Louisville Gen. Hosp., 1976-79, Episc. Ch. Home, Louisville, 1979-81, Cen. State Hosp., Louisville, 1979-82, pvt. duty nursing svc., Louisville, 1981, Good Samaritan Hosp., Tampa, Fla., 1982; nurse, clin. dir. Augusta (Ga.) Correction and Med. Instn., 1983-85; lead nurse Gracewood State Sch. and Hosp., Augusta, 1985-88; nurse VA and Med. Ctr., Augusta, 1987; nurse mgr., cons. walk-in clinic, Tampa, 1981-83; nursing supr. Cen. State Hosp., 1979-82; clin. dir. ACMI, Augusta, 1983-85; lead nurse GSSH, Augusta, 1985-88; group coord., ind. distbr. Diamite Corp., 1988; pres., founder MSGM, Inc., Augusta, 1988—. Vol. Easter Seals, Augusta, 1989, Homeless and the Shut-Ins, Augusta, 1989; active YWCA, Louisville, 1976, March of Dimes, Augusta, 1990, Cancer Fund Am., Augusta, 1989. Mem. ANA, NAFE, Ga. Nurses Assn., Am. Correctional Assn., Ga. Continuing Edn. and ARP, Century Club of Am. Nurses Found., Am. Bus. Women Assn., Philippine-Am. Assn. of CSRA, Living Bank Organ Donor Assn., Am. Life League Inc. Roman Catholic. Home and Office: 911 N Willowick Dr Grovetown GA 30813

MENDOZA, JOANN AUDILET, nurse; b. Beaumont, Tex., Sept. 15, 1943; d. Jack Ernest and Ottie (Craig) Audilet; m. M.A. Mendoza, June 2, 1971; children: Danny Russell Myers, Shawna Laurene Rosco. BSN, Lamar U., Beaumont, 1989. RN, Tex. Lic. vocat. nurse Stat Care Inc., Beaumont, Jefferson County Jail Infirmary, Beaumont; lic. vocat. nurse Bapt. Hosp., Beaumont, RN staff nurse emergency room. Mem. ANA, Tex. Nurses Assn. (sec.), Lamar U. Student Nurse Assn. (sec.), Internat. Honor Soc. Nurses, Emergency Nurses Assn., Sigma Theta Tau, Phi Kappa Phi. Baptist. Home: Rte 5 Box 23 Beaumont TX 77713 Office: Bapt Hosp Dept ER PO Box 1591 Beaumont TX 77704

MENDREY, KATHLEEN LOUISE, management consultant; b. Trenton, N.J., Aug. 22, 1946; d. Francis Stephen Gregory and Kathryn May (Church-Rothermel) M.; m. Robin A. Magowan Jr., Nov. 4, 1973 (div. 1976). BFA summa cum laude, Calif. Coll. Arts and Crafts, 1970; MA (hon.), U. Pa., 1976; PhD (hon.), Harvard U., 1986. Photog. operator 3M Color Separations Packaging Fortune 500, 1963—; asst. to pres. Spring Mill Co., Phila., 1963; with Lambertville (N.J.) Nuclear Power Condenser, 1963; tchr. Valley Day Sch., Edgewood, Pa., 1965; colorist Contilla Fabrics Madison Ave., N.Y.C., 1966-67; pres., prof. Centering Sch. Arts, San Francisco and Oakland, Calif., 1970-73; dir. Restoration/French Project, Vitteaux, France, 1973-76; v.p. Island Fragrance Co., St. Thomas, V.I., 1976; pres. Presdl. Cons. Co., Boston, San Francisco, N.Y.C., and Europe, 1976—; cons. dir. Heinz Corp., Safeway Corp., Columbia Pictures, Trump Corp., U.S. Congress, Pres. of U.S., Fiat, Doubleday Co., Van Heusen Corp., Met. Mus., Baccarat, Boston Opera Co., Atomic Energy Commn., NBC, CBS, Harvard U., Dept. of Def., Boston Ballet Co., Boston Symphony, U.S. Treasury Dept., Ralph Lauren and others. Art works exhibited in group shows in Oakland and San Francisco, 1968-73. Mem. Nat. Trust for Hist. Preservation, 1985, NatTrust for a Nuclear Freeze, 1967, Mus. Fine Arts, 1987, Artists Found., 1980-87; pres. Internat. Arts Fraternity, 1964. Recipient Nobel Peace prize, 1989. Mem. Women's Ednl. Bur., Jr. League, Union for Concerned Scientists, Bucks County Geneal. Soc., Colonial Williamsburg Found., Phi Beta Kappa. Mem. Soc. Friends. Club: Trenton Country. Home and Office: Presdl Cons Co The Carriage House 30-34 E Concord St Boston MA 02118

MENEFEE, LAURA S., nurse; b. Owensboro, Ky., June 4, 1953; d. Robert Gordon and Maxine Opal (Wooten) M. BS in Nursing, Berea Coll., 1976; MS in Nursing, U. Tenn., 1986. RN, Ky., Tenn. Clinic nurse Mountain Maternal Health League, Berea, Ky., 1976-79; instr. Job Corps, Knoxville, Tenn., 1980-84; staff nurse Upjohn Health Care, Knoxville, 1985-86; leader, supr. hospice team St. Mary's Med. Ctr., Knoxville, 1985-90, gero-psychiat. nurse, 1990—; cons. in field. Instr., vol. ARC, Knoxville, 1980—. Mem. NAFE, Nat. Hospice Orgn., Am. Pub. Health Assn., Berea Coll. Alumni Country Dancers (prres. 1984—), Sigma Theta Tau. Office: Mary's Med Ctr Oak Hill Ave Knoxville TN 37917

MENES, PAULINE H., state legislator; b. N.Y.C., July 16, 1924; d. Arthur B. and Hannah H. Herskowitz; m. Melvin Menes, Sept. 1, 1946; children: Sandra Jill, Robin Joy Menes Elvord, Bambi Lynn. BA in Bus. Econs. and Geography, Hunter Coll., N.Y.C., 1945. Economist Quartermaster Gen. Office, Washington, 1945-47; geographer Army Map Service, Washington, 1949-50; chief clk. Prince George's County Election Bd., Upper Marlboro, Md., 1963; substitute tchr. Prince George's County High Schs., Md., 1965-66; mem. Md. Ho. of Dels., Annapolis, 1966—; mem. Md. Ho. Judiciary com., Annapolis, 1979—, Ho. Com. on Rules and Exec. Nominations, 1979—; chair Spl. Com. on Drug and Alcohol Abuse, Annapolis, 1986—. Active Md. State Arts Council, Balt., 1968—, Md. State Commn. on Aging,

Balt., 1975—; parlimentarian Nat. Found. for Women Legislators, Washington, 1986-87; 2d v.p. Prisoner's Aid Assn., Balt., 1971—. Recipient Internat. Task Force award Women's Yr., 1977; named to Hall of Fame Hunter Coll. Alumni Assn., 1986, Women's Hall of Fame Prince George County, 1989. Mem. Nat. Conf. State Legislators (com. on drugs and alcohol 1987), Md. NOW (Ann London Scott Meml. award for Legis. Excellence 1976), Md. Assn. Elected Women (bd. dirs. 1979—), Nat. Order Women Legislators (pres. 1979-80), Women's Polit. Caucus, LWV, Bus. and Profl. Women, B'nai B'rith. Home: 3517 Marlbrough Way College Park MD 20740 Office: Md Ho Reps 3210 Lowe State Office Bldg Rm 210 Annapolis MD 21401

MENGE, DANNETTE MARIE, petroleum engineer; b. New Orleans, Feb. 26, 1958; d. Laurence Hewitt and Gloria (Louviere) Menge. B.S. in Mech. Engring., U. New Orleans, 1981; M.S. in Petroleum Engring., Tulane U., 1987. Registerd engr.-in-tng., La. Petroleum engr. Chevron USA, Inc., New Orleans, 1981—. Mem. ASME (treas. 1980-81), La. Engring. Soc. (assoc.), Soc. Petroleum Engrs., Am. Welding Soc. (charter mem.). Democrat. Roman Catholic. Avocations: scuba diving and swimming, running, snow skiing, camping, fishing. Home: 801 Sena Dr Metairie LA 70005 Office: Chevron USA Inc PO Box 61590 New Orleans LA 70161

MENGEL, LYNN IRENE SHEETS, health facility administrator; b. Toledo, Ohio, Jan. 21, 1955; d. William Burton and Darlene Ann (Ludwikowski) Paisie; m. Marvin C. Mengel, Apr. 15, 1989; children: Christopher David, Michael Patrick. Diploma in nursing, Riverside Meth. Sch. Nursing, Columbus, Ohio, 1976. RN, Fla. Staff nurse gen. patient care Doctor's Hosp. North, Columbus, Ohio, 1976, with orthopedics, 1976-77; with isolations unit Orlando (Fla.) Regional Med. Ctr., 1977-78, head nurse med. surgical unit, 1978-80, diabetes nurse educator, 1980-81; diabetes nurse educator, head nurse, rsch. coord. Diabetes and Endocrine Ctr. Orlando, 1981-88, coord. endocrine rsch., 1988—; speaker in field; researcher. Mem. Am. Diabetes Assn., NAFE, Am. Assn. Diabetes Educators (treas. local chpt. 1983-85), Am. Mgmt. Assn. Republican. Roman Catholic. Office: 1118 S Orange Ave Ste 205 Orlando FL 32806

MENIN, LISA SARA, real estate broker, lawyer; b. N.Y.C., Jan. 12, 1958; d. Edward Bernard and Debra Naomi (Jacobson) M. BA, U. Pa., 1979; JD, NYU, 1982. Assoc. Fried, Frank, Harris, Shriver & Jacobson, N.Y.C., 1982-85; pres. Jacobson Properties, N.Y.C., 1985—. Mem. Phi Beta Kappa. Democrat. Jewish. Home and Office: 155 W 68th St New York NY 10023

MENKE, KRISTINA KAY, nurse; b. Fort Madison, Iowa, July 17, 1956; d. Cecil F. and Luella M. (Stettensmeier) M. BSN, Marycrest Coll., Davenport, Iowa, 1978. RN; cert. BLS, ACLS. Staff nurse St. Mary's Hosp., Rochester, Minn.; supr. Mayo Found., Rochester. Home: 717 Neville Ct Rochester MN 55904

MENKEN, JANE AVA, demographer, educator; b. Phila., Nov. 29, 1939; d. Isaac Nathan and Rose Ida (Sarvetnick) Golubitsky; children—Kenneth Lloyd, Kathryn Lee. A.B., U. Pa., 1960; M.S., Harvard U., 1962; Ph.D., Princeton U., 1975. Asst. in biostats. Harvard U. Sch. Pub. Health, Boston, 1962-64; math. statistician NIMH, Bethesda, Md., 1964-66; research assoc. dept. biostats., Columbia U., N.Y.C., 1966-69; mem. research staff Office of Population Research Princeton U., N.J., 1969-71, 75-87; asst. dir. Princeton U., 1978-86, assoc. dir., 1986-87; prof. sociology Princeton U., N.J., 1980-82, prof. sociology and pub. affairs, 1982-87; prof. sociology and demography U. Pa., Phila., 1987—, dir. population studies, 1989—, dir. Population Studies Ctr., 1989—; mem. social scis. and population study sect., NIH, Bethesda, Md., 1978-82, chmn., 1980-82, population adv. com. Rockefeller Found., N.Y.C., 1981—, com. on population and demography, Nat. Acad. Scis., Washington, 1978-83, com. on population, 1983-85, com. on nat. stats., 1983—, com. on AIDS research, 1987—, sci. adv. com., Demographic and Health Surveys, Columbia, Md., 1985—, sci. adv. bd., Alan Guttmacher Inst., N.Y.C., 1978—, Nat. Adv. Child Health and Human Devel. Council; cons. Internat. Centre for Diarrhoeal Disease Research, Bangladesh, Dhaka, 1984—. Author: (with Mindel C. Sheps) Mathematical Models of Conception and Birth, 1973; editor: (with Henri Leridon) Natural Fertility, 1979, (with Frank Furstenberg, Jr. and Richard Lincoln) Teenage Sexuality, Pregnancy and Childbearing, 1981, World Population and U.S. Policy: The Choices Ahead, 1986. Bd. dirs. Alan Guttmacher Inst., N.Y.C., 1981—. Nat. Merit scholar, 1957. Fellow AAAS, Am. Statis. Assn.; mem. NAS, Population Assn. Am. (Mindel Sheps award 1982, pres. 1985), Am. Pub. Health Assn. (Mortimer Spiegelman award 1975, program devel. bd. 1984-87), Am. Sociol. Assn., Soc. for Study of Social Biology, Internat. Union for Sci. Study of Population, Sociol. Research Assn., Nat. Acad. Scis. Office: U Pa Population Studies Ctr 3718 Locust Walk Philadelphia PA 19104-6298

MENKES, ALIANA BRODMANN, writer; b. Munich, Fed. Republic of Germany, Jan. 2, 1949; came to U.S., 1971; d. David and Richarda (Liebgold) Brodmann; m. Elias Judah Menkes, 1971 (dec. 1981); children: Sarah Joy, Vanessa Rachel. BA, U. Cologne, Fed. Republic of Germany, 1970. Rsch. fellow Ctr. for Judaic Studies Boston U., 1989—. Author: Und du bist ab, 1976, Damit die Welt nicht stumm bleibt, 1980, Die Geschichte von den Feigen, 1987, Ein wunderlicher Rat, 1989, Such a Noise!, 1989. Recipient grant Can. Coun., 1977. Mem. Internat. P.E.N. Soc., AAUW.

MENTZER, MERLEEN MAE, adult education educator; b. Kingsley, Iowa, July 25, 1920; d. John David and Maggie Marie (Simonsen) Moritz; m. Lee Arnold Mentzer, June 1, 1944. Student Westman Coll., 1939, Wayne State U., Nebr., 1942, Bemidji State U., 1950, Mankato Coll., 1978, U. Minn.-St. Paul, 1979. Lic. health and life ins., Minn. Tchr., Kingsley, Iowa, 1938-41; owner, mgr. Mentzer's Sundries, Hackensack, Minn., 1946-76, House of Mentzers, Pine River, Minn., 1974-77; instr. Hennepin Tech., Eden Prairie, Minn., 1978—; sales rep. in annnty and insurance investment; counselor Sr. Citizen Orgn. Ret. Execs.-Via of Mpls. C. of C. Mem. Mpls. C. of C., Hackensack C. of C., (v.p. 1970-76), Northern Lights Federated Woman's Club (pres. 1958-59). Republican. Lutheran. Avocations: dancing; bowling; reading; theatre; seminars. Home and Office: 6781 Tartan Curve Eden Prairie MN 55344

MENTZER, ROSLYN, academic administrator; b. N.Y.C., Oct. 26, 1935; d. Morris and Etta B. (Greenberg) Moskowitz; m. Alan D. Mentzer, June 21, 1953; children: Michelle, Stuart. BA, Queens Coll., 1965; MA, UCLA, 1968. Instr. L.A. Community Coll. Dist., 1968-69; v.p. United Coll. of Bus., L.A., 1969—; pres. CAPPS, Calif., 1984-87. Mem. LWV (v.p. Beverly Hills, Calif. chpt. 1969), Phi Beta Kappa. Home: 1472 Laurel Way Beverly Hills CA 90210 Office: United Coll of Bus 6690 Sunset Blvd Los Angeles CA 90028

MENTZER, TERRI LYNNE, chemical company official; b. Harrisburg, Pa., July 14, 1962; d. Edward L. and Shirley Y. (Ulsh) M. BS in Bus. Logistics, Pa. State U., 1984. Material and equipment engr. Consol. Rail Corp., Phila., 1984-88; traffic analyst Mobil Chem. Co., Canandaigua, N.Y., 1988—. Counselor Critis Hotline, Lewistown, Pa., 1986. Mem. Coun. Logistics Mgmt. (seminar com. 1988-89). Office: Mobil Chem Co 437 Ctr Rd Frankfort IL 60423

MEOLA-LIBRIZZI, ROSEMARIE M., library director; b. Newark; d. Salvatore John and Marie Jane (Consoli) Meola; (div.); children: Vincent, Steve. BA, Bloomfield (N.J.) Coll., 1965; MLS, Rutgers U., 1967; JD, Seton Hall U., 1988; postgrad., Montclair (N.J.) State Coll., 1989—. Cert. English and history tchr., N.J. Head of children svcs. Belleville (N.J.) Pub. Libr., 1965-68; asst. dir. Kearny (N.J.) Pub. Libr., 1968-69; dir. Matawan (N.J.) Joint Free Pub. Libr., 1969-71; supr. of children's svcs. Jersey City Pub. Libr., 1973-87, asst. dir., 1987-90, acting dir., 1990—; mem. adj. faculty Kean Coll., Union, N.J., 1967-73. Author: (manual) Leadership Skills Manual, 1987. Mem. ALA, N.J. Libr. Assn. (v.p., chair 100th Anniversary gala 1986-90), ALA, Hudson County Librs. Assn. (long range planning com. Essex-Hudson region). Home: 5 Squier Ct Livingston NJ 07039 Office: Jersey City Pub Libr 472 Jersey Ave Jersey City NJ 07302

MÉRAS, PHYLLIS LESLIE, journalist; b. Bklyn., May 10, 1931; d. Edmond Albert and Leslie Trousdale (Ross) M.; BA, Wellesley Coll., 1955; MS in Journalism, Columbia U., 1954; Swiss Govt. Exchange fellow, Inst. Higher Internat. Studies, Geneva, 1957; m. Thomas H. Cocroft, Nov. 3, 1968. Reporter, copy editor Providence Jour., 1954-57, 59-61; feature writer Ladies Home Jour. mag., 1957-58; editor Weekly Tribune, Geneva, Switzerland, 1961-62; copyeditor, travel sect. N.Y. Times, 1962-68; mng. editor Vineyard Gazette, Edgartown, Mass., 1970-74, contbg. editor, 1974—; asso. editor Rhode Islander, Providence, 1970-76; travel editor Providence Jour., 1976—; editor Wellesley Alumnae mag., 1979—; assoc. in journalism U. R.I., 1974-75; adj. instr. Columbia U. Sch. Journalism, 1975-76; Author: First Spring: A Martha's Vineyard Journal, 1972, A Yankee Way With Wood, 1975, Miniatures: How to Make Them, Use Them, Sell Them, 1976, Vacation Crafts, 1978, The Mermaids of Chenonceaux and 828 Other Tales: An Anecdotal Guide to Europe, 1982, Exploring Rhode Island, 1984, Castles, Keeps and Leprechauns: Tales, Myths and Legends of Historic Sites in Great Britain and Ireland, 1988; co-author: Christmas Angels, 1979, Carry-out Cuisine, 1982, New Carry Out Cuisine, 1986. Pulitzer fellow in critical writing, 1967. Mem. Soc. Am. Travel Writers. Home: Music St West Tisbury MA 02575 Office: Providence Jour Providence RI 02902

MERCANDINO, SHARON ANN, small business owner; b. Connecticut, N.J., Oct. 28, 1963; d. Joseph and Margaret (Culligan) Yiachos; m. Allen R. Mercandino, May 10, 1986. BS, Adelphi U., 1984. Pres., owner Innovative Med. Data Mgmt., Highland Lakes, N.J., 1986—; co-pres., adminstr. Shar-Al, Inc. Constrn. & Devel., Highland Lakes, 1986—; owner paperwork and office supply co. Highland Lakes, 1990—. Mem. NOW, NAFE, Kinesiotherapy Assn. (ea. chapt.), Nat. Assn. for Self-Employed, N.J. Assn. Women Bus. Owners, North Jersey Assn. Female Execs., Sussex/Warren Women Bus. Owners, Direct Mktg. Assn., Amall Bus. Assn. Office: Box 962 Neosha Rd Highland Lakes NJ 07422

MERCER, BETTY DEBORAH, electrologist, poet, writer, proofreader; b. N.Y.C., Sept. 10, 1926; d. Cecil Boyce and Martha (Romanoff) Fishbein; m. Frank Berthold Mercer, Dec. 22, 1957 (dec. Aug. 1979); children: Kenneth Arnold, Stephen Harry. BS, NYU, 1948; cert. in psychology and child guidance, Cornell U., 1951; cert. in liberal sci., Queens Coll., 1954, 55; cert., Hoffman Inst. Electrolysis, N.Y.C., 1955; cert. piano theory, Royal Conservatory Music, Toronto, 1965. Pvt. tutor English N.Y.C., 1948, proofreader, copyholder various firms, 1951-54; freelance book reviewer Viking Press, N.Y.C., 1954; clin. electrologist, 1955—; pvt. tchr. piano Muskegon, Mich., 1967—; sales rep., beauty counselor Studio Girl, Sudbury, Ont., Can., 1963-64, Blair Products, Muskegon, 1967-68, 78-80; chairperson Muskegon Writers, 1979-80, proofreader, 1988, 89. Author: (poetry book) Toward A Brighter Tomorrow. A First Collection of Twenty-Seven Published Poems, 1980; contbr. articles on sch. prayer to profl. publs. Leader Girl Guides, Sudbury,1958, local chpt. Girl Scouts U.S.A., Muskegon, 1967; libr., cart Sudbury Meml. Hosp., 1963-65; libr. Temple B'nai Israel, Muskegon,1969, 77, 78; vol. Hospice Respite Svc., Muskegon, 1989; chairperson Muskegon Hadassah, 1971-72. Recipient Silver Poet award, 5 Golden Poet awards, 10 Merit awards World of Poetry, Sacramento, 1984—, Editors Choice award Nat. Library Poetry, Owings Mills, Md., 1988, 89, Poet of Yr. award Nat. Poetry Pubs. Assn., L.I., N.Y., 1974, 76, Bronze cert. Creative Enterprises, Carson City, Nev., 1986, 87. Fellow World Lit. Assn.; mem. Clover Internat. Poetry Assn. (life, DANAE title cert. 1974-75), Am. Electrology Assn., Internat. Guild Profl. Electrologists, Electrolysis Assn. Mich., Region II Electrolysis Assn., Internat. Platform Assn., NYU Alumni Assn., AAUW (pub. com. 1967, membership com. 1985-86), NYU Club. Jewish. Home: 1422 New St Muskegon MI 49442

MERCER, JUNE GREER, retail company executive, consultant; b. Homerville, Ga., Sept. 27, 1953; d. Mack Varnedoe and Betty (English) Greer; m. Jerry L. Mercer, Dec. 11, 1981; children: Thomas Greer, Betty Dame, Lauren June. BS in Journalism and Home Econs., U. Ga., 1975, MS, 1976. Account exec. So. Bell, Griffin, Ga., 1976-78; office mgr. Jerry Mercer, Valdosta, Ga., 1981—; image cons. Beauty for All Seasons, Valdosta, 1982—; owner, buyer Big and Tall Man's Store (Unique Image, Inc.), Valdosta, 1985-87, pres. Unique Image, Inc.; sec., treas. South Ga. Emergency Physicans, Inc. Recipient Outstanding Sales Achievement award So. Bell, 1977; named one of 10 Top Cons. in S.E., 1984. Mem. Am. Council Consumer Issues, Am. Home Econs. Assn., Ga. Home Econs. Assn., DAR, Phi Kappa Phi, Phi Upsilon Omicron, Gamma Sigma Delta, Pi Kappa Alpha, Kappa Delta. Presbyterian. Clubs: Valdosta Jr. Women's (pres., Family of Yr. award, 1986), Wymodausis Woman's (3d v.p.) (Valdosta), Valdosta Jr. Svc. League. Avocations: sports, sewing, meeting people. Home: 809 Millpond Rd Valdosta GA 31602

MERCHANT, DONNA RAE, marketing professional; b. Wichita, Kans., Aug. 29, 1948; d. Raymond Houston and Edna Brooks (Waddell) Hobbs; m. Christopher Wayne, Aug. 31, 1968 (div. Aug. 1973); 1 child, Shauna Layne. Student, Wichita State U., 1966-68. Adminstrv. asst. postgrad. edn. Med. Sch. U. Kans., Wichita, 1974-80; activity coord. continuing med. edn. Wesley Med. Ctr., Wichita, 1980-84; mgr. support svcs. 9th dist. Farm Credit Svcs., Wichita, 1984-88; sales and mktg. mgr. Amb. Travel, Eugene, 1988—; cons. Jr. Leauge Wichita, 1983, Plancon, Inc., Martinsville, N.J., 1987—. Mem. Wichita Conv. & Visitors Bur., 1987, events com. Wichita Festivals, Inc., 1987; mem. Eugene Conv. & Visitors Bur., 1988—. Mem. Am. Mktg. Assn. (S.W. chpt. pres.-elect, membership chmn. bd. dirs.), Adminstrv. Mgmt. Soc., Forum for Exec. Bus. Women, Gt. Plains Bus. Adminstrn. Group, Assn. Travel Execs., Campus Life (bd. dirs.), Eugene C. of C., Eugene High Ground Assocs. (chmn.), Delta Gamma Alumni Assn. Republican. Home: 87 E 33rd St Eugene OR 97405 Office: Amb Travel 190 E 11th Eugene OR 97401

MERCIER, CHERYL GRADY, corporate communications specialist, educator; b. Decatur, Ill., Oct. 31, 1945; d. Lawrence David and Lucy Ann (Burtschi) Grady; m. Denis Mercier, Aug. 20, 1966; children: Julia Marie, Matthew Lewis, Meghan Ione. BS in Chemistry, Marian Coll., 1967; MA in Communications, Glassboro (N.J.) State Coll., 1982. Childbirth educator Turnersville, N.J., 1976—; dir. community svcs. and pub. rels. Meml. Hosp. Burlington County, Mt. Holly, N.J., 1982-86; pub. rels. dir. Newcomb Med. Ctr., Vineland, N.J., 1986-89; editorial coord. publs. U. Del., Newark, 1989-90; communications cons. MC2 Mericer & Mercier Communications Cons., Pitman, N.J., 1980—; mgr. creative communications Smith Kline Beecham, Phila., 1990—; adj. prof. Glassboro State Coll., 1987—; instr. in continuing edn. U. Del., 1989—; assoc. editor William Gladden Found., York, Pa., 1987—. Screening judge Ed Press Assn. Publs. Awards, Glassboro, 1987-90; designer Pitman Environ. Commn. Newsletter, 1989-90; chair folk festival com. Appel Farm Arts Ctr., Elmer, N.J., 1989—, Phila. Folksong Soc., 1972—. State of N.J. fellow, 1987-89. Mem. Women in Communications, Inc. (sec. 1988-89, v.p. membership com. 1989-90), Pub. Rels. Soc. Am. Roman Catholic. Home: 44 Elm Ave Pitman NJ 08071 Office: Smith Kline Beecham 1500 Spring Garden St #7929 Philadelphia PA 19101

MERCIER, JEANNETTE LORRAINE, accountant; b. Franklin, Vt., Dec. 17, 1957; d. Paul A. and Agnes (Bigras) M. AA, Champlain Coll., Burlington, Vt., 1978; student, Trinity Coll., Burlington. Acct. U. Vt., Burlington, 1978-87, payroll acctg. supr., 1987-89, dir. payroll acctg., 1989—. Trustee Haston Libr.; vol. Camp Takumta, 1978-90. Mem. Am. Payroll Assn. Home: RRi Box 1638 Franklin VT 05457

MERCOUN, DAWN DENISE, manufacturing company executive; b. Passaic, N.J., June 1, 1950; d. William S. and Irene F. (Micci) M. BS in Bus. Mgmt., Fairleigh Dickinson U., 1978. Personnel payroll coordinator Bentex Mills, Inc., East Rutherford, N.J., 1969-72; employment mgr. Inwood Knitting Mills, Clifton, N.J., 1972-75; gen. mgr. Consol. Advance, Inc., Passaic, 1975-76; v.p. human resources Gemini Industries, Inc., Clifton, 1976—. Mem. Soc. for Human Resource Mgmt., Am. Compensation Assn., Internat. Found. Employee Benefits, Earthwatch Rsch. Team (v.p. bd. dirs. contact Morris Passaic). Republican. Episcopalian. Office: 215 Entin Rd Clifton NJ 07014

MERCURIO, NANCY ANNE, education administrator; b. Detroit, Apr. 18, 1953; d. Michael M. and Helen S. (Nigohosian) Manoogian; m. Louis M. Mercurio, July 20, 1985; 1 child, Nicole. BSBA, U. Phoenix, Denver, MA in Mgmt. Human Rels. and Orgnl. Behavior; postdoctoral, Community Coll. Denver. Fin. mgr.; instr. Front Range CommunityColl., Ft. Collins, Colo.; adminstr., dir. Jack and Jill Child Devel. Ctr., Ft. Collins. Mem. NAFE. Home: 1409 Hepplewhite Ct Fort Collins CO 80526

MERDINGER, SUSAN, marketing and sales executive; b. Boston, Oct. 5, 1943; d. J. George and Bertha (Lotten) Greenfield; m. Edward Franklin Merdinger, Dec. 21, 1963; children: Mindy Beth, Matthew Joseph. AA, Green Mountain Coll., 1963. Asst. dir. pub. relations Filene's, Boston, 1963; real estate sales, Marlboro, N.J., 1970-78; nat. dir. edn. Network of Homes, Babylon, N.Y., 1978-79; v.p. homefinding Employee Transfer Co., Chgo., 1979-81; dir. mktg. Merrill Lynch Realty, Stamford, Conn., 1981-83, asst. v.p. communications and promotional svcs., 1983-84, dir. mktg. svcs., 1984-86; founder, pub. mag. Fine Homes, 1982-87; v.p. Fine Homes Internat., 1986-87; v.p. mktg. svcs., 1987-88, v.p. internat. mktg., 1988-89, v.p. internat sales and mktg., 1989-90; pres. Savoy Internat. Real Estate Ltd., 1990—; exec. v.p. and mng. ptnr. Internat. Property Councelors, Ltd., 1990—; lectr. in field. Mem. Real Estate Bd. N.Y., 1989—; bd. dirs. N.Y. coun. FIABI USA, 1988—, pres., 1990—. Mem. Fedn. Internat. des Professions Immobilieres USA (bd. dirs. N.Y. coun. 1988—). Home: 3 Horizon Rd G11 Fort Lee NJ 07024

MEREDITH, CATHERINE CIRILLO, marketing executive; b. Springfield, Mass., Dec. 5, 1942; d. Natale Vincent and Dorcas Ann (Pugh) Cirillo; children: Jennifer, Catherine, Michelle. BS, Western New Eng. Coll., Springfield, 1985. Sec. Milton Bradley Co., E. Longmeadow, Mass., 1974-78, sec. pres., 1978-84, assoc. product mgr., 1984-85, product mgr., 1985-87, sr. product mgr., 1987; sr. product mgr. Milton Bradley Co., E. Longmeadow, 1988-89; dir. mktg. Milton Bradley Co., 1989—, Coleco Industries, Conn., 1987-88. Mem. Nat. Assn. Female Exec. Office: Milton Bradley Co 443 Shaker Rd East Longmeadow MA 01028

MEREWETHER, TORKSEY ANN, construction company owner; b. Nolan, Tex., Jan. 17, 1936; d. Olan B. and Maurine L. (Finch) Ensminger; m. David Evan Merewether, July 7, 1936; children: Pamalee Merewether Prater Kimball O., David Jr. BS, U. N.Mex., 1958. Tchr. Albuquerque Pub. Sch., 1958-62; office mgr., sec./treas. Electro Magnetic Applications, Albuquerque, 1977-87; pres. Shield Rite, Inc., Albuquerque, 1987—. Past adult leader, Girl Scouts U.S., Boy Scouts Am.; past pres., Lew Wallace Sch. PTA, Albuquerque. Republican. Office: Shield Rite Inc 200 Manzano NE Albuquerque NM 87108

MERGLER, SUSAN ASHBY, broadcasting executive; b. Nassawadox, Va., Nov. 26, 1963; d. Abel Thomas Sr. and Nancy Lee (Bull) Ashby; m. Andrew Marlen Mergler, June 24, 1989. BS in Psychology and Criminal Justice, Radford U., 1986. Corp. investigator Peoples Drug Stores, Alexandria, Va., 1986-88; sr. case mgr. Community Diversion Program, Chesapeake, Va., 1988-89; account exec. Sta. WCIR-FM, Beckley, W.Va., 1989—. Republican. Methodist. Office: Sta WCIR PO Box 103 Beckley WV 25813

MERIJANIAN, JEANETTE LEWIS, nurse, health educator, consultant; b. Mason City, Iowa, June 3, 1932; d. Clifford Wilson and Ruth Evelyn Lewis; m. Aris Merijanian, Dec. 26, 1953 (div. 1978); children—Randy, Lori, Greg, John. R.N., Kahler Sch. Nursing, Rochester, Minn., 1953; B.S., U. Montevallo, 1974; M.P.H., U. Ala., 1980. R.N., Minn. Head nurse eye floor Worrell Hosp., Mayo Clinic, Rochester, 1953; float nurse Mitchell County Meml. Hosp., Osage, Iowa, part-time 1953-54; obstetric and evening supr. Riley County Hosp., Manhattan, Kans., 1954; float supr. Baptist Hosp., San Antonio, 1955-56; night supr. San Marcos (Tex.) Hosp., 1957-58; obstetric supr. St. Mary's Hosp., Bryan, Tex., part-time 1958-60; evening charge nurse Tex. A&M U. Student Health Services, College Station, 1959-61; evening nurse U. Montevallo (Ala.) Student Health Services, 1968, staff nurse 1971, 72, coordinator student health services, 1975—; nursing dir. Shelby County chpt. ARC; guest lectr. high schs. and community programs; chmn. Shelby County Teenage Pregnancy Prevention Com.; mem. Ala. Regional Prenatal Com. Mem. So. Assn. for Coll. Student affairs, Internat. Platform Assn., Soc. for Pub. Health Edn., Regional Family Planning Adv. Com., U. Montevallo Health Promotion and Wellness Task Force, Health Educators Assn. Ala. (charter, a founder), Shelby County Health Council (charter, a founder). Author: But Who Can I Ask About Growing Up, 1979; The Mysterious Body Jack Is Building, 1979. Home: 248 Highland Montevallo AL 35115 Office: U. Montevallo 6310 Student Health Services Montevallo AL 35115

MERKEL, JUDI KAY, magazine editor, educator; b. Decatur, Ind., June 4, 1946; d. Hugh David and Catherine Lucille (Fields) Mosser; m. Mark Peter Merkel, Jan. 27, 1968; 1 child, Angela. BS, Purdue U., 1968; MA, Ball State U., 1972. Cert. secondary edn. tchr., Ind. Head home econs. dept. South Adams Schs., Berne, Ind., 1972—; editor Home Cooking Mag., Berne, 1987—; bd. dirs. Ind. State Fair, Indpls., Home & Family Arts Bldg., Indpls. Editor: (cookbook) Indiana State Fair Cookbook, 1990. Bd.d irs. Dollars for Scholars, Berne, 1989-90; vice chmn. Adams County Rep., Decatur, 1990—. Recipient Ind. Lamplighter award Ind. Home Econs. Assn., 1978. Roman Catholic. Home: RR#2 Geneva IN 46740 Office: House of White Birches 306 E Parr Rd Berne IN 46711

MERKEL-HART, ANGELINE MARY, healthcare company executive; b. Ann Arbor, Mich., Jan. 24, 1960; d. Martin John and Anna Marie (Heller) Merkel; m. Scott Aubrey Hart, May 21, 1988. BBA in Mktg., Western Mich. U., 1982; postgrad., Pepperdine U., Malibu, Calif., 1988—. Mktg. rep. Xerox Corp., Lansing, Mich., 1981-83; devel. specialist Comprehensive Care Corp., Irving, Calif., 1983-85; pres. Merkel Cons., Newport Beach, Calif., 1985-87; v.p. ops. OptimumCare Corp., Laguna Niguel, Calif., 1987—. Mem. Calif. Drug and Alcohol Treatment Comm., 1989; co-chmn. mktg. Am. Cancer Soc., 1990; mem. support group Our Lady of Mt. Carmel. Mem. Am. Mktg. Assn., Newport Area Profls. (co-founder, bd. dirs. 1987-90). Republican. Home: 3912 Inlet Isle Corona del Mar CA 92625 Office: OptimumCare Corp 30011 Ivy Glenn Dr Ste 219 Laguna Niguel CA 92677

MERKLE, HELEN LOUISE, chef; b. Carrington, N.D., May 23, 1950; d. Orville F. and Lillian M. (Argue) M. BS, N.D. State U., 1972. Asst. dir. food mgmt. Stouffer's Atlanta Inn, Atlanta, 1972-74; dir. food mgmt. Stouffer's Indpls. Inn, 1974-78; adminstrv. dir. food mgmt. Stouffer's Riverfront Towers, St. Louis, 1978-80; food mgmt. cons. Fraser Mgmt., Westlake, Ohio, 1980-83; exec. chef Marriott Hotel, Cleve., 1983-89; exec. chef Snavely Mgmt. Svcs, 1989—. Recipient First Place award for soups Taste of Indpls., 1976. Mem. NAFE, Am. Culinary Fedn., Cleve. Culinary Assn. (sec. 1989), Food Svc. Execs. Assn. Democrat. Lutheran. Home: 4137 W 160th St Cleveland OH 44135 Office: Snavely Mgmt Svcs 1100 Crocker Rd Westlake OH 44145

MERKLE, SHARON ANN, laywer; b. Amsterdam, N.Y., Aug. 9, 1946; d. George William and Bernice Mary (Haig) Glenn; m. Terry L. Walton, Sept. 25, 1965 (div. July 1970); children: Todd, Tracy; m. Glenn R. Libert, Aug. 2, 1985. BS, Syracuse U., 1975; JD, Harvard Law Sch., 1978. Assoc. Stubenberg & Roney, Honolulu, 1979-82; ptnr. Case & Lynch, Honolulu, 1982-86, Anderson, Kill, Olick & Oshinsky, N.Y.C., 1987—. Mem. bd. dirs. YWCA of Oahu, Honolulu, 1983-84. Mem. Mass. Bar Assn., Hawaii Bar Assn., Am. Bar Assn. Office: Anderson Russell Kill Olick 1001 Bishop St Pacific Tower Ste 780 Honolulu HI 96813

MERMELSTEIN, ANN ADAMS, government housing officer; b. Harrisburg, Pa., July 29, 1961; d. Henry Ward and Ruby (Deiter) Adams; m. Robert Allen Mermelstein, Sept. 3, 1988. BA, Dickinson Coll., 1983; MA, Northeastern U., 1984; student, The Leadership Inst., 1984; postgrad., Elizabethtown (Pa.) Coll., 1985. Student intern Pa. Pub. Utility Comm., Harrisburg, Pa., 1982; asst. act. Pa. Housing Fin. Agy., Harrisburg, 1985—, collections coordinator, 1988, loan closing officer. Dir. 30 minute hist. firlm currently on file at Northeastern U. Strayed Away, 1984. Mem. World Wildlife Fund, Washington 1987—. Tuition Fellow Northeastern U., 1983-84. Mem. NAFE, Student Alumni Coun. Dickinson Coll., Gamma Phi Beta. Republican. Lutheran. Home: 5070 Bass Lake Dr Apt #203 Harrisburg PA 17111 Office: Pa Housing Fin Agy 2101 N Front St Harrisburg PA 17105

MERMELSTEIN, ISABEL MAE ROSENBERG, administrative financial planner; b. Houston, Aug. 20, 1934; d. Joe Hyman and Sylvia (Lincove) Rosenberg; m. Robert Jay Mermelstein, Sept. 6, 1953 (div. July 1975); children: William, Linda, Jody. Student U. Ariz., 1952, Mich. State U., 1974, Lansing (Mich.) Community Coll., 1975. Exec. dir. Shiawassee County

YWCA, Owosso, Mich., 1975-78; real estate developer F&S Devel. Corp., Lansing, Mich., 1978-79, Corum Devel. Corp., Houston, 1979-81; adminstrv. fin. planner, sr. citizen cons. Investec Asset Mgmt. Group, Inc., Houston, bd. dirs. Living Hope Care Ctr. 1981-85, Living Hope Care Paraclete Found. Author: For You! I Killed the Chicken, 1972. Mem. Older Women's League, Houston, 1st Ecumenical Council of Lansing. Recipient State of Mich. Flag, 1972, Key to City, City of Lansing, 1972-73. Mem. Internat. Women's Pilot Orgn. (The 99's), Jewish Geneal. Soc. Republican. Jewish. Lodges: Zonta, Licoma, B'nai B'rith, Hadassah, Nat. Fedn. Temple Sisterhoods. Flew All Women's Transcontinental Air Race (Powder Puff Derby), 1972, 73. Avocations: flying, gourmet cooking, needlepoint, knitting, snow skiing. Home: 4030 Newshire Houston TX 77025

MERNALYN, actress, writer, producer; b. Detroit, July 23; d. Irwin and Myldred (Kolb) Hamburger. GPA with highest honors, Northwood of Mich. Profl. model, freelance fashion cons.; creator, producer for pvt. Clubs Art Deco Fashion Shows; former fashion commentator Radio Luxembourg; nat. spokesperson Gen. Motors; internat. spokesperson Jaguar; concierge L'Ermitage Hotel Group; customer cons. Tiffany & Co., Beverly Hills; pub. rels. bunny Playboy Club Internat.; radio personality various USA stations; recurring TV roles New World TV (prime time), others; creator, pres. Pillow Talk Ltd., U.K and U.S. Author: My Book, two volumes Philosophy/Humanity, contbg. author poetry anthology to profl. journals; dir. creator, instr. of Improving Quality of Humanity classes and Personal Gratitude; Shakespearean lead actress The Globe Theatre, American debut, A Yorkshire Tragedy, Much Ado About Nothing, Twelfth Night, Taming of the Shrew, Man of La Mancha, A Streetcar Named Desire, Summer and Smoke, Who's Afraid of Virginia Woolf, Plaza Suite, See How They Run; Recurring role ABC-TV primetime sitcom New World Television, others; Appeared in motion pictures Star 80; frequent guest national talk shows, TV/Radio. Active Am. Lung Assn., Friends of Animals. Winner Miss Budweiser, Anheuser-Busch, Miss Internat. MG Brit. Leyland En.g-USA,"The Most Perfect Girl, 1990. Mem. Screen Actors Guild, Am. Film Inst., Museum of the City of New York, Los Angeles County Museum of Art, Northwood of Mich. Alumni Assn., Art Deco Soc., New York and Los Angeles, Smithsonian.

MERRIAM, MARY-LINDA SORBER, college president; b. Jeannette, Pa., May 31, 1943; d. Everett Sylvester Calvin and Madeleine (Case) Sorber; m. E. William Merriam, Dec. 14, 1969 (div. 1975). Student, Grove City Coll., 1961-63; B.A., Pa. State U., 1963-65, M.A., 1965-67, Ph.D., 1967-70. Rsch. assoc. Pa. State U., University Park, 1970-72; asst. prof. speech Emerson Coll., Boston, 1972-79, dir. continuing edn., 1974-77, spl. asst. to pres., 1977-78, v.p. adminstrn., 1978-79; asst. to pres. Boston U., 1979-81; pres. Wilson Coll., Chambersburg, Pa., 1981—; cons. Govt. E.S.E.A. Title III, Alameda County, Calif., 1968, Avon Products, Inc., N.Y.C., 1977; bd. dirs. United Telephone Systems-Ea. Group. Bd. dirs. Sta. WITF-TV, Harrisburg, Pa., 1982—, chmn., 1988-90; bd. dirs. Chambersburg Hosp., 1984-89, vice chmn., 1987-89; bd. dirs. Boston Zool. Soc., 1980-81, Arts, Boston, 1979-81, Scotland Sch. for Vets.' Children, Pa., 1984—, Chambersburg Hosp. Health Svcs., 1988—; mem. exec. com. Found. for Ind. Colls., 1989-91; mem. higher edn. com. Gen. Assembly, Presbyn. Ch., 1987-90, chmn., 1987-90; elder Falling Spring Presbyn. Ch., 1988-90; pres. Chambersburg Area Coun. for Arts, 1988-90. Recipient Athena award Chambersburg C. of C., 1988; named Disting. Alumna The Pa. State U., 1984, Disting. Daughter of Pa., 1986; fellow Am. Council Edn., 1977-78. Mem. NATAS (bd. govs. New Eng. chpt. 1980-81), Speech Communication Assn., Pa. Assn. Colls. and Univs. (exec. com. 1984-90), Assn. Presbyn. Colls. and Univs. (exec. com. 1983-88, pres. 1986-87), Am. Assn. Higher Edn., Nat. Soc. Arts and Letters, AAUW, Phi Kappa Phi, Rho Tau Sigma, Phi Delta Kappa. Office: Wilson Coll 1015 Philadelphia Ave Chambersburg PA 17201

MERRICK-MACK, JEAN ANN, research chemist; b. Charles City, Iowa, Apr. 18, 1953; d. Hollis D. and Lucile (Arthur) Merrick; m. Mark P. Mack, June 2, 1984. BS in Math. and Chemistry, Sioux Falls Coll., 1975; PhD in Phys. Chemistry, Iowa State U., 1980. Rsch. chemist Conoco, Inc., Ponca City, Okla., 1980-85; sr. rsch. chemist E.I. Du Pont de Nemours & Co., Wilmington, Del., 1985-89; rsch. assoc. Occidental Petroleum Corp., Alvin, Tex., 1989—. Contbr. articles to profl. jours. Mem. Am. Chem. Soc. (sec.-treas. 1983-84), Soc. Plastics Engrs., Soc. Rheology. Office: OxyChem Alathon Div PO Box 2917 Alvin TX 77512

MERRILL, CELIA DALE, business owner, consultant; b. Indianola, Miss., Aug. 30, 1951; d. Louis Eugene and Anna Margery (Savage) M.; m. Mark Hall, Dec. 23, 1973 (div. July 1974); m. Gary L. Benn, Apr. 20, 1984; children: Travis Owen, Carson Eugene. BA, Belhaven Coll., 1973; PhD, U. Tex., 1987. Asst. instr. U. Tex., Austin, 1975-79; sr. pers. specialist Exxon Co.-U.S.A., Houston, 1980-86; owner, cons. CM & Assocs., Albuquerque, 1987—; v.p. pub. rels. HRMA-N.Mex., Albuquerque, 1989; pres. Human Resource Mgmt. Assn. N.Mex., Albuquerque, 1990—. Contbr. articles to profl. jours. Chairperson adminstrv. coun. St. Stephen's United Meth. Ch., Albuquerque, 1989-90. Mem. Coyote Orgn. Devel. Network, Soc. for Human Resource Mgmt., Am. Soc. for Tng. and Devel., Assn. for Psychol. Type, Toastmasters Internat. Democrat. Home: 12804 Hugh Graham NE Albuquerque NM 87111 Office: CM & Assocs PO Box 13255 Albuquerque NM 87192

MERRILL, CONNIE RAE, technical writer; b. Sabetha, Kans., Oct. 2, 1947; d. Tennyson Earl and Fern Irene (Maxwell) Kelsay; m. Larry Gale Goings, Jan. 15, 1967 (div. Nov. 1977); children: Carrie Renee, Cory Gale; m. James Brian Merrill, Mar. 28, 1987. BS, Peru (Nebr.) State Coll., 1986. Stenographer Security Mut. Life Ins. Co., Lincoln, Nebr., 1965-67; deptl. sec. Nebr. Pub. Power Dist., Brownville, 1969-75, adminstrv. sec., 1975-83, regulatory compliance specialist, 1983-87, emergency preparedness specialist, 1987-89; sr. engr. tech. writer Robert J. Meyers & Assocs., Houston, 1990—. Home: 7427 Creekfield Dr Spring TX 77379 Office: Robert J Meyers & Assocs 14423 Cornerstone Village Houston TX 77014-1206

MERRILL, DALE MARIE, sales executive; b. Melrose, Mass., Feb. 21, 1954; d. Richard Paul and Rosemarie Reine (Porelle) M. BA in English, U. of Lowell, Mass., 1976; MA in Am. Studies, Boston Coll., 1983; CSS in Mgmt., Harvard U., 1989. Sales rep. A-Copy Inc., Natick, Mass., 1976-77; sales mgr. Jan Optical Co., Waltham, Mass., 1977-78; market researcher Decision Rsch. Co. div. Temple, Barker & Sloane, Lexington, Mass., 1979-81; sales rep. Henco Software Co., Waltham, 1981-82; account mgr. Univ. Computing Co., Chgo., 1982-83; regional sales mgr. CompuServe Data Techs. (formerly Software House), Cambridge, Mass., 1983-89; internat. sales mgr. Hypersoft Corp., Cambridge, 1989—; dir. sales Info. Mapping, Waltham, 1990—; bd. dirs. M.T. Corp., Woburn, Mass. Author: How to Buy Software: Avoiding the Traps Salespeople Set, 1989; author, editor: Seeds mag. (Poetry award 1972), 1971-72; contbr. poetry to mags. Organizer 18x72 project, Stoneham, Mass., 1970-71; bd. dirs. Stoneham Hist. Commn., 1976-77. Recipient Top Sales award A-Copy Inc., 1976-77, Interviewer award Decision Rsch. Co., 1981, Triple Crown Sales award, 1985, 86, 87, Million Dollar Sales Club award, 1987, 88. Mem. NAFE, NOW, Digital Equipment Co. User Soc., Boston Computer Assn. Democrat. Home: 1 Henry St Cambridge MA 02139 Office: Info Mapping 303 Wyman Waltham MA 02154

MERRILL, IRMA WADDELL, lawyer; b. Memphis, Nov. 17, 1960; d. Erich William and Irma (Waddell) M. AB, Princeton U., 1982; JD, Vanderbilt U., 1985. Bar: Tenn. 1985. Assoc. Armstrong Allen Prewitt Gentry Johnston & Holmes, Memphis, 1985-89; pvt. practice Memphis, 1989—. Assoc. editor Vanderbilt Law Rev., 1985; contbr. articles to law jours. Mem. ABA, Tenn. Bar Assn. (bd. dirs. Young Lawyers div. 1988—), Memphis Bar Assn. (bd. dirs. Young Lawyers Assn., 1987-89, pres. 1990), Assn. Trial Lawyers Am., Tenn. Trial Lawyers Assn. Home: 2038 Cowden Ave Memphis TN 38104 Office: 1075 Morgan Keegan Tower 50 N Front Memphis TN 38103

MERRILL, JUDITH ALLYN, small business owner; b. Miami, Fla., Oct. 16, 1944; d. George H. and Barbara (Cosgrove) Keyser; m. H. Taylor Merrill, Mar. 25, 1967; children: Todd Arthur, Kathryn Merver. AB, Mich. State U., 1966; MBA, La Grange (Ga.) Coll., 1989. Talk show host Sta. Cable 9, Wooster, Ohio; computer programmer analyst AT&T Long Lines, Kans. City, Mo.; owner, operator Ockfuskee Plastics, La Grange; ptnr. Dairy Queen of Troup County, La Grange; computer sci. instr. La Grange Coll. Pres. New Ventures; grad. advisor Students In Free Enterprise; advisor Jr. Achievement; pres. Parent Tchrs. Assn.; officer juvenile ct.; pres. GOP County Women. Home: 717 Camellia Dr La Grange GA 30240

MERRILL, LYNNE BARTLETT, marketing and advertising company executive; b. Southampton, N.Y., Mar. 17, 1953; d. William Stuart and Marilyn (Bake) Bartlett; m. John A. Merrill, June 1, 1974; 1 child, Michael Bartlett. BS, Boston U., 1975. Intern U.S. Congress, N.H., 1974; account exec. Creative Promotions, Dover, N.H., 1974-75; pres., owner Merrill Assocs., Inc., Kingston, N.H., 1975—; real estate salesman Kingston Real Estate, 1974—; chmn. Graniteer Awards Com., N.H., 1983—. Chmn. save-the-ch. com. Kingston Hist. Soc.; chmn. Kingston Recycling Com. Recipient numerous Laurel awards for best radio commls. Cadillac Motor Car Div., 1985, 89, best radio spot, 1985, best TV comml., 1987, Telly award for best TV comml. Ins. Div., numerous Graniteer awards. Mem. Pub. Rels. Soc. Am. (bd. dirs. Yankee chpt. 1983—, accredited), Kingston Bus. and Profl. Women's Club (past officer), Haverhill (Mass.) C. of C. (bd. dirs., v.p. 1985—, chmn. elect), Portsmouth C. of C., Seacoast Communications Network. Republican. Congregationalist. Office: Merrill Assocs Inc 11 Church St PO Box 757 Kingston NH 03848

MERRILL, TERYL TOEVS, travel agency executive; b. Wichita, Kans., Apr. 6, 1949; d. Waldo Cecil and Dorothy (Mills) Toevs; m. Richard G. Fouch, Aug. 3, 1968 (div. Dec. 1979); children: James Christopher, Jennifer Ardelle; m. Michael Curt Merrill, Nov. 14, 1987. Student, U. So. Colo., 1967-68. Travel cons. Scott Travel Svc., Pueblo, 1979-82, Cay's Travel Svc., Pueblo, 1982-84; adminstrv. asst. Freedom Homes, Pueblo, 1984; accounts payable clk. K.R. Swerdfeger Constrn., Pueblo, 1984-85; mgr. Lindberg's Internat. Tours, Pueblo, 1985-87, Let's Talk Travel, Pueblo, 1987—. Recipient Pres. scholarship U. So. Colo., 1967. Mem. Am. Soc. of Travel Agts., Cruise Line Internat. Assn., Internat. Assn. of Travel Agts. Network, Pueblo Travel Agts. Assn. (treas. 1987-89), Kiwanis (bd. dirs. elect 1989-90, 2d v.p. 1990—, charter mem. So. Colo. Prost chpt.), Gamma Delta Gamma. Home: 82 Bridle Trail Pueblo CO 81005 Office: Lets Talk Travel 332 Broadway Pueblo CO 81004

MERRILL, WENDY JANE, academic administrator; b. Waterbury, Conn., Dec. 4, 1961; d. David Kenneth and Jane Joy (Nevius) M. BA in Journalism, George Washington U., 1981. Intern in edn. HEW, Washington, summer 1978, writer, summer 1979; rsch. asst. dep. health svcs. adminstrn. George Washington U., Washington, 1979-81; sec. Nat. Assn. Beverage Importers, Washington, 1981; account exec. Staff Design, Washington, 1982; adminstrv. aide Internat. Food Policy Rsch. Inst., Washington, 1983-86; program assoc. Acad. for Ednl. Devel., Washington, 1986-87; pvt. practice cons. Washington, 1987-88; adminstrv. mgr. food and nutrition policy program Cornell U., Ithaca, 1988—; cons., editor George Washington U., 1986; cons., rapporteur Internat. Food Policy Restaurant Inst., Washington and Copenhagen, Denmark, 1987; cons., adminstr. Hansell & Post, Washington, 1987-88, Cornell U., Washington and Ithaca, 1988. Sponsor Worldvision, Tanzania, 1988—. George Washington U. scholar, 1979-81. Mem. Soc. for Internat. Devel., Assn. for Women in Devel., NAFE, Smithsonian Wilson Ctr. (chartered), Am. Mgmt. Assn. (assoc.), Sigma Delta Xi (scholar 1980). Democrat. Episcopalian. Office: Cornell U 309 Savage Hall Ithaca NY 14853

MERRIMAN, ILAH COFFEE, financial executive; b. Amarillo, Tex., Mar. 22, 1935; d. Oran and Frances Elizabeth (Rocque) Coffee; children: Pamela, Michael. BS in Math., Tex. Tech. U. Cert. secondary tchr., Tex. Pres., chief exec. officer H&R Block Inc., Houston ; pres. H&R Block Inc. Tex.; Trustee, bd. dirs. exec. bd. Tex. Tech U. ex students assn., pres., 1989; mem. steering com. Pres.'s Council, bd. dirs. Tex. Tech. Double T Connection, Tex. Tech. Found., Southwest Athletic Conf., Women's Basketball Tournament; mem. enterprize fund Dallas Chpt.; represented bd. dirs. Tex. Tech U. Cotton Bowl Assn.; Mem. Dallas Mus. Fine Art, Houston Mus. Fine Art, Dallas Shakespeare Festival, Dallas Theater Ctr., Dallas Symphony Assn., Dallas Hist. Soc., Fort Worth's Kimball Mus., AAUW, Red Raider Club of Tex. Tech U. (exec. com.). Methodist. Office: PO Box 743275 Dallas TX 75374

MERRIMAN-CLARKE, KRISTIN DEY, magazine editor; b. Urbana, Ill., Sept. 20, 1963; d. Edmund Allen and Sandra Joan (DeYoung) Merriman; m. Andrew Derrick Clarke, Oct. 14, 1989. BS, Boston U., postgrad. Reporter, sr. editor The Eye, Wilmington, Del., 1979-81; reporter The Boston Free Press, 1982-84, The Boston Tab, Allston, Mass., 1984-85; editorial asst. Art New England Mag., Brookline, Mass., 1982; reporter Lake Oswego (Oreg.) Review, 1985-86; editor, Friends of the Earth, London, 1987; asst. mag. editor, newsletter editor Izaak Walton League of Am., Arlington, Va., 1988-89, mag. editor, dir. media rels., 1989—; freelance ghostwriting, Washington, 1988—. Nat. media chair Nat. Celebration of the Outdoors, Washington, 1989-90; activist NOW, Washington, Nat. Abortion Rights Action League, Washington, Nat. Coalition Against the Misuse of Pesticides, Washington. Mem. Women in Communications, Inc., Outdoor Writers Assn. of Am., Va. Outdoor Writers. Methodist. Office: Izaak Walton League Am 1401 Wilson Blvd Level B Arlington VA 22209

MERRITT, BRENDA TRITSCHLER, dietitian, consultant; b. St. Paul, Minn., Apr. 2, 1963; d. Paul D. and Joyce E. Tritschler; m. Eric H. Merritt, Aug. 10, 1985. BS, Iowa State U., Ames, 1985. Nutritionist U.S. Army Hosp., Mons, Belgium, 1984; dietetic intern Iowa Meth. Med. Ctr., Des Moines, 1985; community nutritionist North Iowa Community Action, Mason City, 1986-88; wellness dietitian Mason City Community Sch. Dist., 1987-88; home econs. coord. North Iowa Community Coll., Mason City, 1987-89; cons. dietitian St. Joseph Mercy Hosp., Mason City, 1989—; cons. in field; coord. North Iowa Nutrition Month, Mason City, 1989; dietitian Hospice, Forest City, Iowa, 1990—. Mem. mayoral campaign coms.; nutrition cons. civic orgns. Mem. Am. Dietetic Assn., Cons. Dietitian Practice, Panhellenic Assn. (sec. 1989-90), Alpha Chi Omega. Home: 315 S Carolina Mason City IA 50401

MERRITT, JULIE ALYSON, credit administrator; b. Macon, Ga., May 21, 1963; d. John William and Latha Virginia (Rachels) M. BA, Emory U., 1985; postgrad., Ga. State U., 1989—. Contr. asst. Decatur (Ga.) Hosp., 1985-86; credit account mgr. Am. Sci. Products, div. Baxter Travenol, Stone Mountain, Ga., 1986-87; asst. area/dist. credit mgr. Sherwin Williams Co., Atlanta, 1987-89; credit adminstr. Lafarge Corp., Atlanta, 1989—. Class agt. Emory Alumni Fund Bd., Atlanta, 1987-90; del. Emory Assembly III, 1990; rep. Emory Alumni Reunion Com., 1990. Mem. NAFE, Hosp. Corp. Am., West Paces Ferry Hosp. Aux., Emory U. Young Alumni Assn., Kappa Delta. Republican. Baptist. Home: 3048 D Clairmont Rd NE Atlanta GA 30329

MERRITT, PAMELA KAY, quality assurance professional; b. Covington, Tenn., Apr. 14, 1951; d. William G. and Helen (Hanks) M. BBA, Memphis State U., 1984. Labor analyst Kimberly-Clark Corp., Memphis, 1978-80, warehouse planner, 1980-84, quality statistician, 1984-86, quality supr., 1986-87, quality engr., 1987—. Mem. Am. Soc. for Quality Control. Home: 408 Garland Ave Covington TN 38019

MERRITT, PATRICIA ANNE, data processing executive; b. Rochester, N.Y., Jan. 12, 1945; d. Richard Henry and Florence Elizabeth (Adams) M.; m. Steve Verderber, March 1981. Student Long Beach (Calif.) City Coll., 1972-74, Foothill Jr. Coll., 1974-77; grad. Bryman Paramed. Sch., San Jose, Calif., 1977; m. Steve Verderber. Data processing clk. Lincoln Rochester Trust Co., Rochester, N.Y., 1965-67; keypunch operator Eastman Kodak, Rochester, 1967-70; keypunch and verify operator Reliance Steel Co., Los Angeles, 1971; keypunch operator Automatic Data Processing, Long Beach, 1971, Fed. Civil Service, Los Alamitos, Calif., 1971-73, Varian Assos., Palo Alto, Calif., 1973-78; tech. typist, word processor lead-operator Watkins Johnson, Palo Alto, 1978-79, 79-81; supr. office systems Smith Kline Instruments, Sunnyvale, Calif., 1981-82; owner I.P.S. Info. Processing Systems, 1982-86; word processor sr. operator Palo Alto Unified Sch. Dist., 1979; independent personal beauty cons., Mary Kay Cosmetics, 1987—. Leader, Monroe County council Girl Scouts U.S.A., Rochester, 1969-70, Santa Clara County council, Mountain View, Calif., 1978-80; commr. City of Santa Clara Hist. Commn., 1983-85. Mem. Beta Sigma Phi. Home and Office: 3579 Mauricia Santa Clara CA 95051

MERRITT, SHIRLEY ANN, small business owner, interior designer; b. Abilene, Tex., June 16, 1936; d. Jesse L. and Gladys O. (Tucker) Williams; m. Allen G. Merritt, Sept. 7, 1957; children: Monte M., Mark Allen, David Matthew. BA, Tex. Wesleyan Coll., 1971; cert., Scheffield Sch. Int. Design, N.Y.C., 1988, N.Y. Sch. of Interior Design, N.Y.C., 1989. Cert. tchr., Tex. Tchr. Azle (Tex.) Ind. Sch. Dist., 1971-73, Abilene (Tex.) Ind. Sch. Dist., 1973-89; owner, designer Signatures Interiors, Abilene, 1989—; freelance designer Shirley Merritt Interiors, Abilene, 1987-89. Mem. NAFE, Tex. Assn. Interior Design, Abilene C. of C., Delta Kappa Gamma. Mem. Ch. of Christ. Office: Signatures Interiors 1633 Butternut St Abilene TX 79602

MERRITT, SUSAN MARY, computer science educator, university dean; b. New London, Conn., July 28, 1946; d. Nelson Alfred and Mary (Cory) M. BA summa cum laude, Cath. U. Am., 1968; MS, NYU, 1969, PhD, 1982. Joined Sisters of Divine Compassion, 1975; permanent cert. tchr., N.Y. Systems programmer Digital Equipment Corp., Maynard, Mass., 1969-70; tchr. Good Counsel Acad. High Sch., White Plains, N.Y., 1970-75; adj. instr. computer sci. Pace U., White Plains, 1972-78, asst. prof., 1978-82, assoc. prof., 1982-85, prof., 1985—, chmn. dept., 1981-83, dean Sch. Computer Sci., 1983—; mem. gen. coun. Sisters Divine Compassion, 1988—. Contbr. articles to profl. jours. Fellow Soc. for Values in Higher Edn.; mem. Assn. for Computing Machinery (edn. bd. 1988—), Assn. Computer Sci. and Computer Engrng. Chairmen (pres. 1989—), Phi Beta Kappa, Sigma Xi. Roman Catholic. Office: Pace U 1 Martine Ave White Plains NY 10606

MERRITT, TAMMY LYNN, healthcare professional; b. Eaton Rapids, Mich., Oct. 14, 1961; d. Clair Gerald and Joyce Louise (Freese) Whittum; m. John David Merritt, Mar. 28, 1981; children: Jessica, Kristin. AS, Davenport Bus. Coll., 1981. Receptionist Eaton Rapids Med. Clinic, 1979-84, ins. specialist, 1984-87, office mgr., 1987—. Mem. Jaycees. Republican. Home: 3471 Perkey Rd Charlotte MI 48813 Office: Eaton Rapids Med Clinic 101 Spicerville Hwy Eaton Rapids MI 48827

MERRIWEATHER-BROWN, ONDRIA, management consultant; b. Jackson, Tenn., Nov. 8, 1952; d. B.T. and France L. (Edding) Merriweather; m. Edward L. Brown, Apr. 11, 1981. BS, Tenn. State U., 1974; MS, Fla. Inst. Tech. Def. cost analyst Honeywell Avionics, Clearwater, Fla.; bus. cons. SBA, Pensacola, Fla., Tampa, Fla. Advisor Hillsborough County Sch. Bd. MBE govt. grantee; recipient award U.S. Dept. Transp. Mem. NAFE. Home: 16501 Foothill Dr Tampa FL 33601

MERRY, MARILYN DIANA HOOVER, cartographer; b. St. Louis, July 28, 1946; d. Roscoe C. S. and Elnora (Monigan) H.; m. Allan Preston Merry (div. Sept. 1978); children: Jason Kimball Ward, Meana Linette Ward. Clk., typist Army Recruit and Inductions Sta., St. Louis, 1966-67; printing control clk. U.S. Mobility Equipment Command, St. Louis, 1968-70; supply clk. U.S. Troop Support Command, St. Louis, 1970-71; clk.-typist Inst. Heraldry, Alexandria, Va., 1971-72, Med. Intelligence, Washington, 1972-73; office mgr. Yodi Enterprises, E. St. Louis, Ill., 1973-74; sec. Defense Mapping Agy., Washington, 1974-79, cartographic tech., 1979-82, cartographer, 1982—. Mem. exec. bd. Am. Cancer Soc., sec., 1985-87; mem. women's com. Coalition of Black Trade Unionists, 1989; mem. exec. bd. Washington Area Labor Com. on Cen. Am. and Caribbean, 1986-88; candidate for town coun., Capitol Heights, Md., 1986, 90; mem. community adv. com. on substance abuse County of Prince Georges, Md. Recipient Pres.'s award Am. Cancer Soc., 1985, A. Philip Randolph award SCLC, 1988, Appreciation award Coalition of Black Trade Unionists, 1989. Mem. NAACP (life), Coalition Labor Union Women (sec. D.C. chpt. 1989), Federally Employed Women (life, sec. 1979-80, 87-88, pres. Potomac Palisades chpt. 1989), A. Philip Randolph Inst., Nat. Coun. Negro Women (life), Am. Fedn. Govt. Employees (women's coord. 14th dist. 1984-88), London Woods Community Assn. (adv. com. 1984-86), Internat. Platform Assn. Baptist. Home: 5803 Falkland Pl Capitol Heights MD 20743

MERSEREAU, JOANNA HAYES, graphic artist; b. Strawn, Ill., July 12, 1928; d. Fred Elmer Hayes and Lillie May Polenz; m. John DeWitt Mersereau, June 11, 1950 (div. 1974); children: Anne Elizabeth, Juanita Louise, Guy Matthew. AA, Blackburn Coll., 1948; student, U. Ill., 1949-51. Staff artist Press-Enterprise, Riverside, Calif., 1955-64, Riverside County Schs., 1967-88; gallery owner Riverside, 1986—; v.p. Watercolor West Redlands, Calif., 1969-80; artist in residence Na Bolom Studies, Inst. of Sci., Mex., 1986-87, 89. Bd. dirs. Riverside Art Mus., 1985-86. Democrat. Home: 4290 University Ave Riverside CA 92501

MERSKEY-ZEGER, MARIE GERTRUDE FINE, retired librarian; b. Kimberley, South Africa, Oct. 10, 1914; came to U.S., 1960, naturalized, 1965; d. Herman and Annie Myra (Wigoder) Fine; m. Clarence Merskey, Oct. 8, 1939 (dec. 1982); children: Hilary Pamela Merskey Nathe, Susan Heather Merskey Sinistore, Joan Margaret Merskey Schneiderman; m. Jack I. Zeger, July 15, 1984. Grad. Underwood Bus. Sch., Cape Town, South Africa, 1934; BA, U. Cape Town, 1958, diploma librarianship, 1960. Sec. to Chief Rabbi Israel Abrahams, South Africa, 1945-49, Jewish Sheltered Employment Council, 1954-56; reference librarian New Rochelle Pub. Library, 1960-63; research librarian Consumers Union, Mt. Vernon, 1963-66; asst. readers services, head union catalog Westchester Library System, 1966-69, mem. adult services com., 1973-74, also trustee, 1989—; dir. Harrison Pub. Library and West Harrison Br., 1969-84; acting dir. Mamaroneck (N.Y.) Free Library, 1987-88, also trustee, 1988—. Pub. edn. officer USCG Aux. Flotilla 63. Author: History of the Harrison Libraries, 1980; editor: (cookbook) On Harrison's Table, 1976; Hightlights of Harrison's History, 1989, Harrison Highlights and Anecdotes, 1989. Bd. dirs. Shore Acres Point Corp., Mamaroneck, 1985-89. Recipient Brotherhood award B'nai B'rith, 1974; named Woman of Yr., Harrison, 1984. Mem. ALA, Westchester Library Assn., N.Y. Library Assn. (adult edn. com. for continuing edn. 1971-75, adult services com. 1973-75, vice chmn., 1975, exec. bd. 1981-82), Pub. Library Dirs. Assn. (tech. services com. chmn. Westchester County 1971, exec. bd. 1974-75, vice chmn. 1975), Clubs: Harrison Women's, YMCA, Harrison Hist. Soc. (bd. dirs. Charles Dawson History Ctr. (founder), Hadassah, (Harrison, N.Y.), USCG Aux. Contbr. articles to local newspapers. Home: 316 S Barry Ave Mamaroneck NY 10543

MERTENS, MARYJO ANN, academic administrator; b. Davenport, Iowa; d. Henry J. and M. Marguerite (Burns) M.; m. James Randall Judy. BA, Marycrest Coll., 1961; MA, U. Iowa, 1969. Program advisor Iowa Meml. Union U. Iowa, Iowa City, 1967-68; program dir.studentctr. U. Ky., Lexington, 1969-73, dir., 1973-80; dir.Holmes Student Ctr. No. Ill. U., DeKalb, 1980-84; coord. Ariz. State U., Tempe, 1986-87, dir. Meml. Union, 1984-87; mng. dir. Iowa State Meml. Union Iowa State U., Ames, 1987—; mgr. Cen. Ky. Concert and Lectr. Series, Lexington, 1978-80. Author: (with others) The Adminstration of College Unions and Campus. Area chmn. United Way, Lexington, 1974-75, co-chmn. DeKalb br., 1983, bd. dirs. Ames br., 1988. Mem. Nat. Assn. Campus Activities (chmn. bd. dirs. 1977-78), Found. for Edn. (chmn. bd. dirs. 1980-83). Office: Iowa State Meml Union Iowa State U Campus Ames IA 50011

MERTINS, ESTHER NICOLENE, retired university educator; b. Missouri Valley, Iowa, Apr. 16, 1904; d. Niels and Anna Pedersen; m. Albin Richard Erickson, Aug. 11, 1928 (dec. 1931); m. Louis Mertins, May 12, 1939 (dec. 1973). AB, Des Moines (Iowa) U., 1925; MA, U. Wash., 1938; postgrad., Claremont (Calif.) Grad. Sch., 1941. Registrar Ginling Coll., Nanking, China, 1926-27; sec. to pres. Grand Island (Nebr.) Coll., 1927-28; asst. sec. YWCA Iowa State Coll., Ames, 1928-29; instr. social sci. U. of Redlands (Calif.), 1935-42, registrar, 1929-69, cons., 1969-75; fgn. student adv. U. Redlands, 1950-69, registrar emeritus, 1969. Author: (book) The First Baptist Church of Redlands, California, 1887-1987; co-author: The Intervals of Robert Frost, 1947, Whose Emblem Shines Afar, 1982. Bd. dirs. YWCA, Rewdlands, 1947-53, 58-63, 83-86, pres., 1950-53, 61-63, sec., 1983; bd. dirs. Redlands Community Chest, 1951-54, v.p., 1954; sec. Redlands Fourth of July com., 1976; mem. Sister City Com., Redlands and Hino, Japan, 1963-78; pres. Friends of A.K. Smiley Pub. Libr., Redlands, 1975-79, 80-83. Named Honorary Alumni U. Redlands, 1984. Mem. AAUW (treas. local chpt. 1947-48, corp. rep. U. Redlands 1967, fellowship gift 1971, hon. life mem. 1987), AAUP (pres. area chpt. 1946-47), Pacific Coast Assn. Collegiat Registrars (treas. 1947-48, chmn. conv. 1948), Am. Assn. Collegiate Registrars (conf. news com. 1960), Zonta Internat. (pres. Redlands chpt. 1969-70,

74-75, internat. mem. com. 1970, named Woman of Achievement 1978). Democrat.

MERTZ, DOLORES MARY, farmer, legislator; b. Bancroft, Iowa, May 30, 1928; d. John Francis and Gertrude (Erickson) Shay; m. H. Peter Mertz (dec. 1983), Dec. 27, 1951; children: Peter, Mary Simpson, David, Ann Cornicelli, Helen Powell, Janice, Carol. AA, Briar Cliff Coll., 1948. Pres. Coun. Cath. Women, Sioux City, Iowa, 1986-88; first vice St. Regent Cath. Daughters of Am., Iowa, 1988—; county supr. Kossuth County, Iowa, 1983-89; legislator Iowa Ho. of Reps.(15th dist.), 1989—. Dem. precinct com. person, Kossuth County, Iowa, sec. 1975—. Recipient Womens Leadership award Iowa Lakes Community Coll., 1988; named Woman of Yr. Beta Sigma Phi Internat., West Bend, Iowa, 1989. Mem. Soroptomist Internat. (Woman of Distinction award 1987), Drama Club (pres. 1970's). Roman Catholic. Home: RR Box 128 Ottosen IA 50570 Office: Iowa State Capitol House of Representatives Des Moines IA 50319

MERTZ, JANET ELAINE, biology researcher, educator, consultant; b. N.Y.C., Aug. 9, 1949; d. Harry and Pauline (Schwartz) M.; m. Jonathan Michael Kane, Mar. 16, 1980; children: Daniel Morris Mertz Kane, Jeremy Solomon Mertz Kane. BS in Life Scis. and Elec. Engring., MIT, 1970; PhD in Biochemistry, Stanford (Calif.) U., 1975. Teaching asst. dept. biochemistry Stanford U., 1970-73; postdoctoral fellow Med. Rsch. Coun. Lab. Molecular Biology, Cambridge, Eng., 1975-76; asst. prof. oncology McArdle Lab. for Cancer Rsch. U. Wis., Madison, 1976-83, assoc. prof. oncology, 1983—; ad hoc mem. study sects. NIH, Bethesda, Md., 1981—; cons. Agrigenetics Corp., Madison, Wis., 1983-84. Mem. editorial bd. Molecular and Cellular Biology Jour., 1985—; assoc. editor: Virology Jour., 1988—; contbr. numerous articles to profl. jours. Recipient Kallman award Stanford U., 1973; Jane Coffin Childs Meml. Fund fellow, 1975-76; numerous rsch. grants. Mem. AAAS, Am. Assn. for Cancer Rsch., Am. Soc. for Biochemistry and Molecular Biology, Am. Soc. for Microbiology, Am. Soc. for Virology, Assn. for Women in Sci. Office: U Wis McArdle Lab 1400 University Ave Madison WI 53706

MESCHKE, DEBRA JOANN, polymer chemist; b. Elyria, Ohio, Oct. 22, 1952; d. Loren Willis and JoAnne Elizabeth (Meyer) M. BS, U. Cin., 1974; MS, Case Western Res. U., 1976, PhD, 1979. Sr. chemist Union Carbide Corp., South Charleston, W.Va., 1979-82, project scientist, 1982-85, chair research and devel. Exempt Women's Group, 1980-81, chair research and devel. Ctr. Safety Team, 1981-82, coordinator Polymer Methods Course, 1982-83; project scientist Union Carbide Corp., Tarrytown, N.Y., 1985-86; sr. prin. research chemist Air Products and Chems. Inc., Allentown, Pa., 1986-88, chmn. waste disposal com., 1986-88; rsch. scientist Union Carbide Corp., South Charleston, 1988—. Author chpts. in textbooks; patentee in field. Bd. dirs. Overbrook Home Owners Assn., Macungie, Pa., 1987. Case Western Res. U. grad. fellow, 1974-79. Mem. AAAS, Am. Chem. Soc. (Polymer div.), Iota Sigma Pi. Home: 2022 Parkwood Rd Charleston WV 25314

MESNEY, DOROTHY TAYLOR (HEDI MUNRO), mezzo-soprano, pianist, composer, comedienne, educator; b. Bklyn., Sept. 15, 1916; d. Franklin and Kathryn Munro Taylor; diploma Berkeley Inst., 1934; B.A., Sarah Lawrence Coll., 1938; postgrad. Columbia U., 1938-41, Juilliard Sch. of Music, 1963-71, Manhattan Sch. Music, 1971-73; m. Peter Michael Mesney, Oct. 15, 1942; children: Douglas, Kathryn, Barbara. Mezzo-soprano, operetta, mus. comedy, concert and oratorio; ch. soloist, N.Y.C., 1956—; debuts include: N.Y. Cultural Center, 1971, Carnegie Recital Hall, 1974; leading roles with local opera and Gilbert and Sullivan groups, (as Hedi Munro) comedienne, singer and songwriter various nightclubs and cabarets; appeared on Joe Franklin TV Show, Joey Adams Radio Show; dir. a-capella vocal quintet The Notebles; rec. artist Folkways Records, Musicanza Records; dir. American Experience ensemble, also An Elizabethan Encounter, Renaissance Revels; tchr. piano and singing, Douglaston, N.Y., 1958—, also tchr. introduction music classes; founder, dir. children's series Concerts for Children; founder Introduction to Music for Preschoolers; performer early Am. music for mus., hist. socs., schs., colls.; performer Renaissance music N.Y. State Renaissance Festival, 12 yrs.; 2c authority on Am. and Renaissance music. Com. chmn. PTA, Douglaston, 1952-55; den mother Greater N.Y. council Cub Scouts Am., 1953-56; Brownie leader Greater N.Y. council Girl Scouts U.S.A.; bd. dirs. Community Concerts Assn. of Great Neck, N.Y. Mem. Nat. Piano Tchrs. Guild, Nat. Fedn. Music Clubs (N.Y. chpt.), Met. Opera Guild, Tuesday Morning Music Club (pres. 1979-81). Democrat. Congregationalist. Composer hymns, songs, instrumental quartets and trios, ballades also songs for children.

MESNICK, WENDY A., public relations executive; b. East Orange, N.J., Dec. 13, 1962; d. Marvin Arthur and Joan Ailene (Schenker) M. Srudent, Internat. Inst. Madrid, Madrid, 1983; BA cum laude, SUNY, Binghamton, N.Y., 1984; postgrad., NYU, 1986-90. Mktg. sales asst. Arista Corp., N.Y., 1984-85; from asst. to asst. v.p. The Carter Orgn., N.Y., 1985—. Mem. NAFE. Home: 60 E 8th St Apt 21A New York NY 10003

MESROBIAN, ARPENA SACHAKLIAN, publisher, editor, consultant; b. Boston, Nov. ; d. Aaron Harry and Eliza (Der Melkonian) Sachaklian; m. William John Mesrobian, June 22, 1940; children: William Stephen, Marian Elizabeth (Mrs. Bruce MacCurdy). Student, Armenian Coll. of Beirut, Lebanon, 1937-38; A.A., Univ. Coll., Syracuse (N.Y.) U., 1959, B.A. magna cum laude, 1971. Editor Syracuse U. Press, 1955-58, exec. editor, 1958-61, asst. dir., 1961-65, acting dir., 1965-66, editor, 1968-85, assoc. dir., 1968-75, dir., 1975-85, 87-88, dir. emeritus, 1985; dir. workshop on univ. press. pub. U. Malaysia, Kuala Lumpur, 1985. Book rev. editor: Armenian Rev, 1967-75; mem. publs. bd. Courier, 1970—; mem. adv. bd. Armenian Rev., 1981-83; contbr. numerous articles, revs. to profl. jours. Pres. Syracuse chpt. Armenian Relief Soc., 1972-74; sponsor Armenian Assembly, Washington, 1975; mem. mktg. task force Office of Spl. Edn., Dept. Edn., 1979-84, Adminstrn. of Developmental Disabilities, HHS; mem. publs. panel Nat. Endowment for Humanities, Washington.; bd. dirs. Syracuse Girls Club, 1982-87. Named Post-Standard Woman of Achievement, 1980; recipient Chancellor's award for disting. service Syracuse U., 1985; Nat. award U.S. sect. World Edn. Fellowship, 1986; N.Y. State Humanities scholar. Mem. Women in Communications, Soc. Armenian Studies (adminstrv. council 1976-78, 85-87, sec. 1978, 85-87), Syracuse U. Library Assocs. (v.p. 1983-88), Am. Univ. Press Services (dir. 1976-77), Armenian Lit. Soc., Armenian Community Center, Assn. Am. Univ. Presses (v.p. 1976-77), UN Assn. (bd. dirs. 1983-88, v.p. 1985), Phi Kappa Phi, Alpha Sigma Lambda. Mem. Armenian Apostolic Ch. (trustee). Club: Zonta of Syracuse (pres. 1979-80, 1st v.p. 1985-86). Home: 4851 Pembridge Circle Syracuse NY 13215

MESSER, EDYTHE BARBARA, maintenance company executive; b. Bklyn., Sept. 15, 1941; d. Emanuel A. and Eva (Tartakov) Marcus; widowed, 1981; children: Heidi Sue, Stephen Dale. BS, Lesley Coll., 1963; MA, Columbia U., 1964. Tchr. Massapequa (N.Y.) Pub. Schs., 1964-65, Elmhurst (Ill.) Pub. Schs., 1965-66, Clarkstown (N.Y.) Sch., 1966-68; v.p. Accent Maintenance Corp., Ossining, N.Y., 1968-81, pres., 1981—. Vol. Am. Heart Assn., West Coun. for Arts; active Horace Greeley PTA, Chappaqua, N.Y. Mem. Bldg. Svc. Contractor's Assn., Westchester Assn. Women Bus. Owners, Ossining C. of C., Westchester C. of C. Office: Accent Maintenance Corp 109 Croton Ave Ossining NY 10562

MESSER, JANICE GRABOWSKI, management consultant; b. Wilmington, Del., July 24, 1939; d. Stanley Joseph and Helen (Pajewski) Grabowski; m. Robert Gerard Messer, Aug. 24, 1963; children: Edward C., Helen Messer Ventouris, Elizabeth S., Allison S., Robert Gerard Jr., Jonathan P., Victoria C. BA, Chestnut Hill Coll., Phila., 1961; postgrad., Inst. for Advanced Study, 1962, Adelphi U., 1961-62, Antioch-New Eng. Coll., 1989—. Owner, mgr. Ambiance, party planning, Wilmington, 1973-87; co-owner, mgr. Colonial Printing Co., Bennington, 1983-87; campaign coord. audience devel. Oldcastle Theatre Co., Bennington, Vt., 1979—; dir. Bennington Coll., 1987-88, acting dir. alumni rels., 1988-89, assoc. dir. alumni rels. and ann. giving, 1989—; grad. asst. Adelphi U., Garden City, N.Y., 1989-90; adminstr., cons. projects for Holden-Leonard Mill, 1990; cons. ARC, 1990—. Trustee Bennington Mus., 1981—; founder, vol. dir. Arts Alive!, Bennington, 1985-89; mem. nominating com. Vt. Coun. on Arts, Montpelier, 1986-87; bd. dirs., v.p. Oldcastle Theatre Co., 1988—; bd. dirs. United Way Bennington County, 1983-87; founder Bennington Aea Arts Coun., 1988; presenter, fundraiser Vt. Bicentennial Commn., Manchester, 1989. Recipient best actress award Del. Theatre, Newark, 1971; grantee Vt. Coun. on Arts, 1984-86. Mem. Coun. for Advancement and Support Edn. (grantee 1988), Nat. Assn. Fundraising Execs., AAUW, Bennington C. of C. (bd. dirs. 1981-85). Roman Catholic. Home: 125 Grandview St Bennington VT 05201

MESSER-REHAK, DABNEY LEE, physical therapist; b. Des Moines, Iowa, June 21, 1951; d. Joseph Thomas and June (Grady) Messer; m. Thomas James Rehak, June 27, 1981. BS, Chgo. Med. Sch., 1974; MS, U. Wis., 1984. Physical therapist Loyola U. Hosp., Maywood, Ill., 1974-78; faculty U. Ill. Med. Ctr., Chgo., 1978-81; physical therapist U. Wis. Hosp., Madison, 1982-84; lectr. Baxter-Travenol Labs., Deerfield, Ill., 1984—; cons. Mercy Ctr. for Health Care Services, Aurora, Ill., 1985-90, dir. physical therapy, 1986—; dir. rehab. svcs. Cen. DuPage Hosp., Winfield, Ill., 1990—; cons. Edward Hosp., Napervlle, 1984. Contbr. articles to profl. jours. Mem. NAFE, Am. Phys. Theraphy Assn. (chair dist. 1990—), Am. Coll. Sport Medicine, Bus. and Profl. Women. Presbyterian. Office: Mercy Ctr for Health Care Services 1325 Highland Ave Aurora IL 60506

MESSERSCHMITT, NORMA FLORINE, nurse; b. Long Beach, Calif., Jan. 3, 1928; d. John Homer and Bernice Mildred (Miller) Mauk; m. John Arthur Messerschmitt, Nov. 8, 1947; children—John, James, Jarrett. R.N., Long Beach City Coll., 1972. Nurse, Pioneer Hosp., Artesia, Calif., 1972-73; lab. nurse supr. Clin. Lab. St. Mary's Hosp., Long Beach, 1973—, instr. health technologies Long Beach City Coll., 1976—. Mem. Nat. Phlebotomy Assn., Internat. Platform Assn. Republican. Home: 8001 Ring St Long Beach CA 90808 Office: 1050 Linden Ave Long Beach CA 90813

MESSIN, MARLENE ANN, plastics company executive; b. St. Paul, Oct. 6, 1935; d. Edgar Leander and Luella Johanna (Rahn) Johnson; m. Eugene Carlson (div. 1972); Rick, Debora, Ronald, Lori; m. Willard Smith (dec. 1975); m. Frank Messin, Sept. 24, 1982; 5 stepchildren. Bookkeeper Jeans Implement Co., Forest Lake, Minn., 1952-53, part-time bookkeeper, 1953-57; bookkeeper Great Plains Supply, St. Paul, 1960-62; bookkeeper Plastic Products Co., Inc., Lindstrom, Minn., 1962-75, pres., 1975—; co-owner, treas. Gustaf's Fine Gifts, Lindstrom, Minn., 1985—. Bookkeeper Trinity Luth. Ch., Lindstrom, 1976-81. Mem. Nat. Assn. Women Bus. Owners, Soc. Plastic Engrs., Swedish Inst. Home: 28940 Olinda Trail Lindstrom MN 55045 Office: 30355 Akerson St Lindstrom MN 55045

MESSINA, ANTOINETTE JOSEPHINE, marketing educator, financial consultant; b. Newark, Oct. 30, 1932; d. Vincent and Catherine (D'Antoni) M.; m. Joseph A. Pagano. BA, Rutgers U., Newark, 1954; MBA, N.Y.U., 1958; PhD, U. of Rome, 1959; MA, Seton Hall U., South Orange, N.J., 1969; EdD, Rutgers U., 1979. Asst. White Weld and Co., N.Y., 1954-55; asst. trust adminstr. The Bank of N.Y., 1955-57; adminstr. Bernard Baruch Sch., CUNY, 1957-62; instr. Bernard Baruch Sch., CUNY, N.Y., Union Coll., Cranford, N.J., 1961-62; asst. prof. Kean Coll., N.J., 1962-63; asst. prof., asst. dean Seton Hall U., S. Orange, N.J., 1964-72; advisor, cons. Comprehensive Service, Gillette, N.J., 1972--; cons. Research Consultant to Asbury Park and Irvington Sch. Dist., 1977--. Author: Expanding Career Awareness, 1979. Com. sec. Essex County Prosecutor's Com. Against Narcotics and Drug Offense, 1960's, com. mem. and workshop leader Nat. Endowment for the Arts, 1970, mem. exec. council and workshop leader St. Elizabeth Inst. for the Edn. of Women., 1976-78. Mem. N.J. Fulbright Assn. (treas.), Kean Coll of Profl Women, Am. Ednl. Research Assn., Nat. Soc. for the Study of Edn., Kappa Delta Pi. Roman Catholic. Home: 26 Daugherty Ave Gillette NJ 07933

MESSING, CAROL SUE, communications educator; b. Bronx, N.Y.; d. Isidore and Esther Florence (Burtoff) Weinberg; m. Sheldon H. Messing; children: Lauren, Robyn. BA, Bklyn. Coll., 1967, MA, 1970. Tchr. N.Y.C. Bd. Edn., 1967-72; assoc. prof. Lang. arts Northwood Inst., Midland, Mich., 1973—; owner Job Match, Midland, 1983-85; cons. Mich. Credit Union League, Saginaw, 1984-87, Nat. Hotel & Restaurant, Midland, Mich., 1985-89, External Degree program, Continuing Edn. program, Northwood Inst., 1986-87, Dow Chem. Employees' Credit Union, 1988—. Author: (anthology) Symbiosis, 1985, rev. edit., 1987, Controlling Communication, 1987, rev. edit., 1989. Mem. Nat. Council Tchrs. English, LWV, Kappa Delta Pi, Delta Mu Delta. Office: Northwood Inst 3225 Cook Rd Midland MI 48640

MESSING, RITA BAILEY, pharmacology educator; b. Bklyn., July 7, 1945; d. Max and Kate (Katkin) Zimmerman; m. William Messing, June 20, 1965; children: Charles, Marion. BA, CUNY, 1966; PhD, Princeton U., 1970. Asst. prof. Rutgers U., Camden, N.J., 1969-72; rsch. assoc. MIT, Cambridge, 1973-75; asst., then assoc. rsch. psychobiologist U. Calif., Irvine, 1976-81; rsch. assoc. U. Minn. Med. Sch., Mpls., 1981-83, asst. prof. pharmacology, 1983-88, assoc. prof., 1988-90; environ. toxicologist Minn. Dept. Health, 1990—; rsch. fellow Organon Pharms., The Netherlands, 1980. Editor: Endogenous Peptides and Learning and Memory Processes, 1981. Contbr. articles to profl. jours. Patentee process for promoting analgesia. USPHS grantee, 1983-86; NSF fellow, 1966-69, Med. Found. fellow, 1974-75. Mem. AAAS, Soc. Neurosci., Am. Soc. Pharmacology and Exptl. Therapeutics, Phi Beta Kappa. Home: 735 Goodrich Ave Saint Paul MN 55105 Office: Minn Dpet of Health Div of Environ Health 925 Delaware St SE Minneapolis MN 55459-0040

MESSINGER JACKSON, SHIRLEY MAY, real estate agent; b. Somerville, N.J., Mar. 22, 1951; d. Montfort Miller and Beatrice (Harmon) Messinger; m. Robert Allan Jackson, May 24, 1975. BA, Rutgers U., 1973, postgrad.; cert., Real Estate Sch. Cen. N.J., 1984. Cert. real estate broker, 1990. Adminstrv. asst. Rutgers Coll., New Brunswick, N.J., 1973-75, asst. dir. fin. aid, 1975-79, dir. fin. aid, 1979-81; chief ops. Rutgers U., New Brunswick, N.J., 1981-87; realtor assoc. Fox and Lazo Realtors, New Brunswick, 1984—. Mem. N.J. Assn. Student Fin. Aid Adminstrs. (pres. 1984, Pres. award), Middlesex County Bd. Realtors. Home: 3 Kelly Ct Cranbury NJ 08512

MESSMER, MICHAELINE, marketing executive; b. Rochester, N.Y., Feb. 7, 1954; d. Jack and Leona Barbaras (Prebola) M. Student, So. Meth. U., Dallas, 1990—. Fin. industry cons. IBM/Hogan Systems, Dallas, 1984-86; product mktg. mgr. Computer Assocs. Internat., Dallas, 1986—. Contbg. author Nat. Assn. Bank Mgmt. and Cost Acctg. Jour., 1990—. Mem. NAFE, Nat. Corp. Cash Mgmt. Assn., Bank Adminstrn. Inst., Nat. Inst. Bus. Mgmt., Am. Mgmt. Assn. Republican.. Roman Catholic. Home: 2003 Cottonwood St Carrollton TX 75006 Office: Computer Assocs 909 Las Colinas Blvd E Irving TX 75039

MESSNER, KATHRYN HERTZOG, civic worker; b. Glendale, Calif., May 27, 1915; d. Walter Sylvester and Sadie (Dinger) Hertzog; m. Ernest Lincoln, Jan. 1, 1942; children: Ernest Lincoln, Martha Allison Messner Cloran. BA, UCLA, 1936, MA, 1951. Tchr. social studies Los Angeles schs., 1937-46; mem. Los Angeles County Grand Jury, 1961. Mem. exec. bd. Los Angeles Family Service, 1959-62; dist. atty.'s adv. com., 1965-71, dist. atty.'s adv. council, 1971-82; mem. San Marino Community Council; chmn. San Marino chpt. Am. Cancer Soc.; bd. dirs. Pasadena Rep. Women's Club, 1960-62, San Marino dist. council Girl Scouts U.S.A., 1959-68, Am. Field Service, San Marino, 1983—; pres. San Marino High Sch. PTA, 1964-65; bd. mem. Pasadena Vol. Placement Bur., 1962-68; mem. adv. bd. Univ. YWCA, 1956—; co-chmn. Dist. Atty.'s Adv. Bd. Young Citizens Council, 1968-72; mem. San Marino Red Cross Council, 1966—, chmn., 1969-71, vice chmn., 1971-74; mem. San Marino bd. Am. Field Service; mem. atty. gen.'s vol. adv. com., 1971-80; bd. dirs. Los Angeles Women's Philharm. Com., 1974—, Beverly Hills-West Los Angeles YWCA, 1974-85, Los Angeles YWCA, 1975-84, Los Angeles Law Affiliates, 1974—, Pacificulture Art Mus., 1976-80, Reachout Com., Music Center, Vol. Action Center, West Los Angeles, Calif., 1980-85, Stevens House, 1980—, Pasadena Philharm. Com., 1980-85, Friends Outside, 1983—, Internat. Christian Scholarship Found., 1984—; hon. bd. dirs. Pasadena chpt. ARC, 1978-82. Recipient spl. commendation Am. Cancer Soc., 1961; Community Service award UCLA, 1981. Contbr. articles to profl. jours. Mem. Pasadena Philharmonic, La Floristas, Huntington Meml. Clinic Aux., Nat. Charity League, Pasadena Dispensary Aux., Gold Shield (co-founder), Pi Lambda Theta (sec. 1983-89), Pi Gamma Mu, Mortar Bd., Prytanean Soc. Home: 1786 Kelton Ave Los Angeles CA 90024

MESTEL, MARIELLA, lawyer; b. Pottsville, Pa., May 28, 1948; d. Paul Albert and Ella (Deeb) Francis; m. Sanders J. Mestel, Sept. 11, 1966 (dec. Apr. 1985); children: Kimberly, Aaron. BA, U. Akron, 1974, JD, 1977. Fingerprint technician FBI, Washington, 1964-66; asst. to adminstr. Doctor's Hosp., Massillon, Ohio, 1966-68; asst. prosecutor City of Canton, Ohio, 1977-83; police and fire atty. City of Canton, 1983—; instr. law enforcement officers Ohio Peace Officers Tng. Coun. Cert., 1983—; v.p. legal office sect. Ohio Chiefs of Police, Columbus, 1989—. Bd. dirs. Family Counseling of Stark County, Canton, 1980-84, Planned Parenthood, Canton, 1987—. Mem. Ohio State Bar Assn., Stark County Bar Assn. Office: City of Canton Law Dept City Hall Canton OH 44702

METALLO, LAURA JEANNE, consultant; b. Bklyn., Apr. 1, 1946; d. George and Lena (Gubitoso) Albanese; m. Joseph N. Metallo, June 23, 1974. BA in Psychology, St. John's U., 1968; M in Profl. Studies in Human Rels., N.Y. Inst. Tech., 1980; PhD in Counselor Edn., Hofstra U., 1981; PhD in Community Psychology, Columbia U., 1982. Tchr. Nativity B.V.M., Ozone Park, N.Y., 1964-69, Immaculate Conception Sch., Fairbanks, Alaska, 1969-70, St. William The Abbot Sch., Seaford, N.Y., 1970-80; asst. prof. Five Towns Coll., Seaford, N.Y., 1980-86; cons. Regency Orgn., Port Richey, Fla., 1986—; dir. Life Mgmt. Cons., Holiday, Fla., 1986—; asst. prof. psychology Pasco Hernando Community Coll., Newport Richey, Fla., 1990—; cons. Pfizer Corp., N.Y.C., 1982-86, Charles Perry Enterprises, Baldwin, N.Y., 1984-86; bd. dirs. Hi-Hello Day Care Ctr., Freeport, N.Y., summer 1980; founder, dir. Responsible Alternatives for Therapy, Baldwin, 1980-86; substance abuse prevention specialist Pasco County Sch. Dist., 1987—. Author: The Other Side of Women, 1986, Inside An Envelope, 1986; editor: Human Sexuality, 1980; contbr. articles to profl. jours. Mem. Am. Counselors Assn., Am. Psychol. Assn. (assoc.), Nat. Orgn. of Women, Harry Benjamin Internat. Gender Dysphonia Assn., Am. Mental Health Counselors Assn., Assn. Counseling and Devel. Home: 1607 Candlewood Dr Holiday FL 33590 Office: Life Management Consultants Holiday FL 34690

METAXAS, PAMELA H., reporter; b. Lowell, Mass., Nov. 28, 1945; d. Harry Louis and Theodora George (Kanellas) M. AS, Greenfield Community Coll., 1965; BA in Journalism and French, U. Mass., 1967. Reporter Worcester(Mass.) Telegram & Gazette, 1967-68, Hartford (Conn.) Times, 1968-73, Union News, Springfield, Mass., 1973—. Former vol. Bay State Med. Ctr., Springfield. Greek Orthodox. Office: Union News Main St Springfield MA 01101

METCALF, LAURA JANE, marketing professional; b. Waynesburg, Pa., Nov. 16, 1964; d. Cecil John and Mary Jane (Pokorny) M. BS in Health Planning and Adminstrn., Pa. State U., 1987. Seminar coord. Am. Coll. Healthcare Execs., Greene County Meml. Hosp.; account rep. Am. Hosp. Assn., Chgo. Recipient Student Svc. award Pa. State Alumni, Health Planning and Adminstrn. Leadership award. Mem. NAFE, NOW, Am. Coll. Healthcare Execs., Am. Mktg. Assn., Am. Soc. Assn. Execs., Chgo. Soc. Assn. Execs., Chgo. Health Exec. Forum, Acad. for Health Svcs. Mktg. Roman Catholic. Home: 1730 S Greenwood Park Ridge IL 60068 Office: 840 N Lake Shore Dr Ste 6W Chicago IL 60611

METCALF, LINDA JO, legal assistant; b. Mpls., Mar. 23, 1948; d. William Arthur and Jane (Edgerton) Fleet; 1 stepchild, Dawn Kathleen. BA, Oglethorpe U., 1986; cert. with honors, Nat. Ctr. Paralegal Tng., 1988. Sec. Super Valu Stores, Inc., Hopkins, Minn., 1969-74, Church's Fried Chicken, Inc., Atlanta, 1974-77, Eli Lilly & Co., Atlanta, 1977-88; legal asst. Roger W. Moister, Jr., P.C., Atlanta, 1988—; grad. rep. Nat. Ctr. for Paralegal Tng. Author: Drug Testing: Public Safeguard or Corporate Headache, Products Liability with Emphasis on the Pharmaceutical Industry. Mem. Ga. Assn. Legal Assts., Profl. Legal Assts (bd. dirs.), Whale Adoption Project, Greenpeace, MADD. Republican. Episcopalian. Home: 5217 Spring Creek Ln Dunwoody GA 30350 Office: Roger Moister Jr PC 1515 3400 Peachtree Rd Atlanta GA 30326

METCALF, LYNNETTE CAROL, naval officer, journalist, educator; b. Van Nuys, Calif., June 22, 1955; d. William Edward and Carol Annette (Keith) M.; m. Scott Edward Hruska, May 16, 1987. BA in Communications and Media, Our Lady of Lake, 1978; MA in Human Rels., U. Okla., 1980; MA in Mktg. Webster U., 1986. Enlisted USAF, 1973, advanced through grades to sgt., 1975; intelligence analyst, Taiwan, Italy and Tex., 1973-76; historian, journalist, San Antonio, 1976-78; commd. officer USN, 1978, advanced through ranks to lt. comdr., 1988; pub. rels. officer, Rep. of Panama, 1979-81; mgr. system program, London, 1981-82; ops. plans/tng., McMurdo Sta., Antarctica, 1982-84; exec. officer transient personnel unit Naval Tng. Ctr., Great Lakes, Ill., 1984-86, comdg. officer transient personnel unit, 1986-87; asst. prof. naval sci. U. Notre Dame NROTC, 1987-89; nat. curriculum, 1987-89; staff communications plans U.S. Naval Forces Japan, 1989—; anchorwoman USN-TV CONTACT, 1986-87. Contbr. articles to profl. jours.; editor Naval Station Anchorline, 1979-81, WOPN Caryatides, 1985-86; author: Winter's Summer, 1983. Sec. San Vito Dei Normanni theatre group, Italy, 1975-76; coord. Magic Box Theater, Zion, Ill., 1984-86; dir. Too Bashful for Broadway variety show, Naval Tng. Ctr., 1986-87; treas. Yokosuka Little Theatre Group, 1990—. Mem. Women Officers' Prof. Network (communications chair 1985-86, programs chair 1986-87), Patron Michiana Arts and Scis. Coun., Am. Legion, JHF Theater Soc. (co-founder 1990—), McMurdo Club, Soc. of South Pole. Avocations: golf, scuba diving, traveling, reading, writing. Home: 647 Tsukui, Yokosaka Shi Houshu, Japan Office: Box 12 Comdr Naval Force Japan Code 312 FPO Seattle WA 98762-0051

METCALF, MARGARET LOUISE FABER, infosystems specialist, small business owner, consultant; b. Washington, Jan. 1, 1943; d. Marshall Lee and Martha Noreen (Mogan) Faber; m. George Taft Metcalf, June 1, 1968. BA in Math., U. Denver, 1966; JD, South Tex. Coll. of Law, 1974. Mathematician Falcon Research and Devel., Denver, 1965-67; systems analyst Chrysler Space Div., Slidell, La., 1967-68, Philco Ford, Houston, 1968-69, Lockheed Corp., Houston, 1969-70; sr. programmer Celanese Chem. Corp., Bayport, Tex., 1970-72; ch. adminstr. Epis. Ch. of the Redeemer, Houston, 1974-85; dir. Altar Guild, Houston, 1974-84; owner Celebration Designs, Houston, 1983—; cons. GTM Tech., Houston, 1986—, assoc. systems analyst, 1987—; corp. sec. Eastwood Ltd., Inc., Houston, 1982-83. Mem. Div. of World Missions, Bd. of Missions, Episcopal Diocese of Tex., 1981—. Recipient Zonta award, 1960, Amelia Earheart award. Mem. Soc. Women Engrs. (assoc.), IEEE, Assn. of Computing Machinery (local treas. 1967-72), Assn. Women Attys., South Tex. Coll. of Law Alumni Assn., U. Denver Alumni Assn. Club: Episcopal Ch. Women. Home and Office: 4609 University Oaks Blvd Houston TX 77004

METRAUX, RHODA ANNA ELIZABETH, cultural anthropoligist; b. N.Y.C., Oct. 18, 1914; d. Karl. Frederick Bubendey and Anna-Marie (Kappelmann) Epple; m. Arthur B. Proctor III, Aug. 24, 1934 (wid. 1935); m. Alfred Metraux, Feb. 5, 1941; stepchildren: Eric, Daniel Alfred. Student, Packer Collegiate Inst., Bklyn, 1927-32; BA, Vassar Coll., Poughkeepsie, 1932-34; Student, Yale U., New Haven, 1940-41; PhD, Columbia U., N.Y.C., 1946-47. Apprentice Oxford U. Press, N.Y.C, 1936-40; research asst. Nat. Research Council, Wash., 1942-43; wartime rsch. in Mexico US Dept. Agriculture, Wash., 1943; planning staff, research OSS, Wash., 1943-45; with Columbia U. Rsch. in Contemporary Cultures, 1948-53, asst. dir., 1952-53; dir. Anthropological Expedition, Montserrat, BWI, 1953-54; research fellow Studies in Human Ecology Cornell U. Med. Coll., N.Y.C., 1954-57; dir. Image of the Scientist AAAS, N.Y.C., 1959; assoc. dir. Studies in Allopsychic Orientation at Am. Mus. Nat. History, 1960-65; project dir. Cultural Structure of Perceptual Communication (NSF) Mus. Nat. History, 1965-69; field rsch. Haiti, 1941, 48, Montserrat, 1953-54, 66, Iatmul people Sepik River Papua New Guinea, 1967-68, 71-71, 72-73, 79; rsch. assoc. dept anthropology Am. Mus. Natural History. Democrat. Episcopalian. Home: Hazen Rd Sch House Greensboro VT 05826

METROS, MARY TERESA, librarian; b. Denver, Nov. 10, 1951; d. James and Wilma Frances (Hanson) Metros. BA in English, Colo. Women's Coll., 1973; MA in Librarianship, U. Denver, 1974. Adult services libr. Englewood (Colo.) Pub. Libr., 1975-81, adult services mgr., 1983-84; libr. systems cons. Dataphase Systems, Kansas City, Mo., 1981-82; circulation libr. Westminster (Colo.) Pub. Libr. 1983; pub. services supr. Tempe (Ariz.) Pub. Libr.,

1984—. Mem. ALA, Pub. Libr. Assn., Ariz. Libr. Assn, Libr. Adminstrn. and Mgmt. Assn. Democrat. Home: 1001 N Pasadena 28 Mesa AZ 85201 Office: Tempe Pub Library 3500 S Rural Rd Tempe AZ 85282

METS, LISA ANN, academic administrator; b. Lapeer, Mich., Feb. 24, 1954; d. Harald and Meeta Alexandra (Linnas) M. BA, U. Mich., 1976, cert., 1979, postgrad., 1984-87; MA, Ind. U., 1978. Asst. prof. Vincennes (Ind.) U., 1979-83, dept. chair, 1981-85, assoc. prof., 1983-85; sr. asst. to v.p. adminstrn. and planning Northwestern U., 198-90. Co-editor: Key Resources on Higher Education Governance, Management, and Leadership, 1987; co-editor: monograph Improving Teaching and Learning Through Research, 1988; editor News from SCUP, 1988—; contbr. chpt. to book and articles to profl. jours. Mem. Am. Assn. for Higher Edn., Assn. for the Study Higher Edn., Assn. for Instnl. Rsch., Soc. for Coll. and Univ. Planning, Phi Delta Kappa. Lutheran.

METTAM, NANCY ELIZABETH WIDDIS, small business owner; b. Pontiac, Mich., Nov. 12, 1935; d. Emmett Earl and Harriet Grace (O'Dea) Widdis; m. Curtis Stanley Mettam, May 31, 1954; children: Janet, Gracie, Nan, Julia. Student, Ind. U., 1953-55. Craft instr., sales assoc. Creative Corner, Danville, Ill., 1971-74; owner Mettam Safety Supply, Danville, 1974—. Pres. St. Elizabeth Hosp. Aux., 1967-68, mem. 1963-80; chmn. United Way Danville (1st woman), 1988; alderman ward 6 City of Danville Govt. (among 1st women), 1986—; bd. dirs. 1st Midwest Bank, Danville, 1985-88, Danville Area Community Coll. Found., 1986—; mem. Danville Zoning Bd. (1st woman), 1978-86. Named Woman of Yr. Bus. & Profl. Women, 1986. Mem. Danville Area C. of C. (1st woman, pres. 1985-86), Rotary, Exec. Club, Salvation Army Aux. (pres. 1979-80). Republican. Office: Mettam Safety Supply 3817 N Vermilion Danville IL 61832

METTEE-MCCUTCHON, ILA, army officer; b. Mobile, May 1, 1945; d. John Martin and Anna Ruth (Cleveland) Mettee; B.S., Auburn (Ala.) U., 1967, M.S., 1969; grad. various army schs.; m. John Robert McCutchon, Oct. 13, 1974; 1 dau., Erin Tempest. Research psychologist VA Hosp., Tuskegee, Ala., 1967-69; clin. psychologist U. Ala. Med. Center, Birmingham, 1969-71; commd. 1st lt. U.S. Army, 1971, advanced through grades to lt. col., 1987; OIC, Alcohol and Drug Abuse Rehab. Center, Presidio, San Francisco, 1971-73; strategic intelligence officer 8th Psychol. Bn., 1973-75; tactical intelligence officer, ops. officer, co. comdr. 525th MI Group CEWI (Airborne), Ft. Bragg, N.C., 1976-79; project officer Command, Control, Communications and Intelligence Directorate, Combined Arms Combat Devel. Activity, Ft. Leavenworth, Kans., 1979-82; student Command and Gen. Staff Coll., 1982-83; ops. officer Army Spl. Security Group, Washington, 1983-86; Def. Lang. Inst. Presidio of Monterey, 1986-87; chief Indication and Analysis Ctr., Republic of Panama, 1987-89; comdr. 741st M.I. Bn., Ft. Meade, Md., 1989— . Decorated Army Commendation medal (2), Meritorious Service medal (3), Army Achievement award. Mem. Assn. U.S. Army. Home: 7412 Merrimusic Circle Severn MD 21144-2241 Office: US Army 741st MI Bn Fort Meade MD 20755

METZ, MARY SEAWELL, college president; b. Rockhill, S.C., May 7, 1937; d. Columbus Jackson and Mary (Dunlap) Seawell; m. F. Eugene Metz, Dec. 21, 1957; 1 dau., Mary Eugena. B.A. summa cum laude in French and English, Furman U., 1958; postgrad., Institut Phonetique, Paris, 1962-63, Sorbonne, Paris, 1962-63; Ph.D. magna cum laude in French, La. State U., 1966; H.H.D. (hon.), Furman U., 1984; LL.D. (hon.), Chapman Coll., 1985; D.L.T. (hon.), Converse Coll., 1988. Instr. French La. State U., 1965-66, asst. prof., 1966-67, 1968-72, assoc. prof., 1972-76, dir. elem. and intermediate French programs, 1966-74, spl. asst. to chancellor, 1974-75, asst. to chancellor, 1975-76; prof. French Hood Coll., Frederick, Md., 1976-81, provost, dean acad. affairs, 1976-81; pres. Mills Coll., Oakland, Calif., 1981-90; vis. asst. prof. U. Calif.-Berkeley, 1967-68; mem. commn. on leadership devel. Am. Council on Edn., 1981—, adv. council SRI, 1985—, adv. coun. Grad. Sch. Bus. Stanford U.; assoc. Gannett Ctr. for Media Studies, 1985—; bd. dirs. PG&E, Pacific Telesis, PacTel & PacBell, Rosenberg Found., Union Bank. Author: Reflets du monde francais, 1971, 78, Cahier d'exercices: Reflets du monde francais, 1972, 78, (with Helstrom) Le Francais a decouvrir, 1972, 78, Le Francais a vivre, 1972, 78, Cahier d'exercices: Le Francais a vivre, 1972, 78; standardized tests; mem. editorial bd.: Liberal Edn., 1982—. NDEA fellow, 1960-62,, 1963-64; Fulbright fellow, 1962-63; Am. Council Edn. fellow, 1974-75. Mem. Western Coll. Assn. (v.p. 1982-84, pres. 1984-86), Assn. Ind. Calif. Colls. and Univs. (exec. com. 1982), Nat. Assn. Ind. Colls. and Univs. (govt. relations adv. council 1982-85), So. Conf. Lang. Teaching (chmn. 1976-77), World Affairs Council No. Calif. (dir. 1984—), Bus.-Higher Edn. Forum, Women's Forum West, Women's Coll. Coalition (exec. com. 1984—), Phi Kappa Phi, Phi Beta Kappa. Office: Mills Coll Office of Pres Oakland CA 94613

METZGAR, MARGARET MAXINE, psychotherapist; b. Wallace, Idaho, Jan. 29, 1953. Student, St. Patrick's Sch. Nursing, Missoula, Mont.; BA in Edn. and Human Svcs., Western Wash. U., 1982; MA in Psychology, Seattle U., 1984. Cert. paramedic, Wash. Counselor Fred Hutchinson Cancer Rsch. Ctr., Seattle; pvt. practice Seattle; adj. faculty Seattle U., Antioch U., Am. Heritage Inst. Author: Little Ears, Big Issues: Children and Loss, 1986, Crisis: Is Your School Prepared?, 1988. Active numerous community orgns. Named Silver Poet of Yr., 1982, Golden Poet of Yr., 1989. Mem. Assn. Death Edn. and Counseling, Nat. Task Force for Death Edn. in Schs. Office: 11301 5th Ave NE Seattle WA 98125

METZGER, CARINA Y. STAFFORD SMITH, education educator; b. N.J., Mar. 11, 1933; d. Edward Burke and Ottavia (Benjamin) Stafford-Smith; children: Carina, Charles Walter, Christopher, Kurt, Erik. MA, Fairleigh Dickinson, Madison, 1978; BS in Psychology, Marquette U., Milw., 1956. Kindergarten tchr. Sch. Dist. of The Chathams, N.J., 1968-89. Recipient Women of Worth award First Place Rutgers U., New Brunswick, 1988. Mem. Charlie Club (Founder & Chairperson). Democrat. Roman Catholic. Home: 26 Grove St Madison NJ 07940

METZGER, DIANE HAMILL, paralegal, poet; b. Phila., July 23, 1949; d. David Alexander Sr. and Eunice (Shelton) Hamill; m. Frank Allen Metzger, Aug. 29, 1969; 1 child, Jason Frank. AA in Bus. Adminstrn. magna cum laude, Northampton Coll., 1980; BA in Polit. Sci. magna cum laude, Bloomsburg U., 1987; paralegal cert., Pa. State U., 1988. Statistician Am. Viscose div. FMC Corp., Phila., 1967-72; research asst. Temple U., Phila., 1972-73; clk. II State Correctional Instn. at Muncy, Pa., 1977—; freelance writer and paralegal, 1989—. Author: (poems) Coralline Ornaments, 1980; lyricist: Come Now, Shepherds, 1979, Sleep Now, My Baby, 1986; poetry pub. in numerous mags., publs. including Gravida, Inside/Out, Working Parents, South Coast Poetry Jour., Pearl, Featured Poet, 1989. Recipient numerous awards for poetry including 2d place award Phila. Writers Conf., 1969, 1st prize PEN Writing Awards, 1985, 2d prize Carver Prize Essay Competition, 1986; also Citation for Outstanding Achievement Pa. Ho. of Reps., 1988, Citation for Outstanding Achievement Pa. Senate, 1988. Mem. ASCAP, Poetry Soc. Am., Mensa. Democrat. Home: 313 Barker St Ridley Park PA 19078 Office: SCIM #005634-PO Box 180-Rt 405 Muncy PA 17756

METZGER, KATHLEEN ANN, computer systems specialist; b. Orchard Park, N.Y., Aug. 4, 1949; d. Charles Milton and Anna Irene (Matwijow) Wetherby; m. Robert George Metzger, Aug. 29, 1970 (div. June 1988). BS in Edn. cum laude, SUNY Coll., Buffalo, 1970; postgrad., SUNY, Fredonia, 1975. Cert. secondary tchr. Math. tchr. Crestwood High Sch., Mantua, Ohio, 1970-71; sec., bookkeeper Maple Bay Marina, Lakewood, N.Y., 1972; math., bus. tchr. Falconer (N.Y.) High Sch., 1972-76; bookkeeper Darling Jewelers, Lakewood, 1977-78; computer operator Ethan Allen Inc., Jamestown, N.Y., 1978-79, So. Tier Bldg. Trades, Jamestown, 1979; program analyst TRW Bearings Div., Inc., Jamestown, 1980-82, Fla. Power Corp., St. Petersburg, 1982—. Campaign advisor United Way, St. Petersburg, 1985; Beachfest vol. Suncoast Children's Dream Fund, 1988-89. Mem. Data Processing Mgmt. Assn., Kappa Delta Pi. Republican. Roman Catholic. Home: 8701 Blind Pass Rd #10 Saint Petersburg FL 33706 Office: Fla Power Corp 3201 34th St S Saint Petersburg FL 33711

METZGER, MARIAN, management consultant; b. Bklyn., Mar. 19, 1931; d. William David and Marian (Kemmet) Averell; m. Lester W. Metzger, June 17, 1951 (div. Nov. 1965); children: Edward L., Leslie I. Bowden; m. Robert L. Hirsh, June 16, 1973. Grad. high sch., Bellmore, N.Y., 1948. Administrv. asst., office mgr. Profl. Mgmt. Corp., Bayshore, N.Y., 1958-65, v.p., 1965-83; exec. v.p. R.L. Hirsh Assocs., Ltd., Bayshore, N.Y., 1972-85, R.L. Hirsh Assocs., Inc., Key Largo, Fla., 1985—; co-editor, cons. Ophstart (program for eye surgeons); lectr. and instr. in field. Editorial advisor Types of Med. Practice, 1982; editorial cons. Physicians Management mag., 1974—, New Practice Planning mag., 1980—, Physicians Marketing mag., 1985-88; contbr. articles to profl. jours. Mem. Med.-Dental Hosp. Burs. Am. (pres. 1986-87), Soc. Profl. Bus. Cons. (sec., treas. 1979-82), Profl. Secs. Internat. (pres. 1966-67, Sec. of Yr. award 1969). Republican. Jewish.

METZGER, PATRICIA LOUISE, healthcare consultant; b. Steubenville, Ohio, July 17, 1950; d. Alfred Charles and Mary Josephine (Fusiek) Russell; m. Dale Henry Metzger II, Aug. 12, 1978; 1 child, Adrianne Rae. BS in Nursing, Marillac Coll., St. Louis, 1973; MSA, Cen. Mich. U., 1990. Head nurse O.L.P.H. Nursing Home, St. Louis, 1973-74, St. Francis Rehab. Hosp., Green Springs, Ohio, 1974-75, Bellevue Hosp., Ohio, 1975-77; staff nurse med./surg. St. Vincent Med. Ctr., Toledo, 1977-78; head nurse med./surg. St. Vincent Med. Ctr., 1978-81, sys. analyst, 1981-83; v.p. nursing Parkview Hosp., Toledo, 1983-86, Md. Gen. Hosp., Balt., 1986-87; asst. adminstr. Parma Community Gen. Hosp., 1987-90; mgr. healthcare consulting div. Ernst & Young, Cleve., 1990—. Counselor Jr. Achievement, Toledo, 1985. Mem. Am. Coll. Healthcare Execs., Nat. League Nurses. Home: 6151 Hickory Trail North Ridgeville OH 44039

METZGER, SHIRLEY JEAN, food industry executive; b. Estes Park, Colo., May 20, 1938; d. Wallace Newton and Ruth (Hurt) Merrick; children: Debra A., Katherine L. Pres. Sort-Rite Internat., Inc., Harlingen, Tex. Named Small Businessperson of Yr., Community Leader, Noteworthy American Nat. Fisheries Inst.; recipient Presdl. award for Excellence in Sports, 1990, Harlingen Citizen award, 1990. Mem. NAFE, Confederate Air Force, Nat. Fisheries Inst., Tex. Shrimp Assn., Lower Rio Grande Valley C. of C., La. Shrimp Assn., Nat. C. of C., Tex. Assn. Bus., Nat. Fedn. Bus. Home: PO Box 1805 Harlingen TX 78551

METZNER, BARBARA STONE, university counselor; b. St. Louis, June 9, 1940; d. Wendell Phillips and Lois Custer (Rake) Metzner. AB, Ind. U., 1962, MS, 1964, EdD, 1983; BA, Purdue U., 1979. Asst. dean students U. Ill., Urbana, 1964-68; undergrad. advisor UCLA, 1968-69; asst. dean students Ohio State U., 1969-72; student affairs officer San Diego State U., 1972-76; counselor Ind. U. - Purdue U., Indpls., 1976—; supr. Ednl. Testing Svc., Indpls., 1980—; cons., editorial bd. Nat. Acad. Advising Assn., Manhattan, Kans., 1987—; adj. prof. Ind. U., 1987—, mgr. Info Svcs., Ind. U.-Purdue U., 1989—. Contbr. articles to profl. jours. Mem. Marion County Precinct Election Bd., 1980—; exec. com. Ind. Allied Health Assn., 1983-84; VIP escort Pan Am. Games, 1987. Spencer Found. grantee, 1990. Mem. AAUW, APA, Am. Ednl. Rsch. Assn., Nat. Acad. Advising Assn., Assn. Instl. Rsch., Assn. Study Higher Edn., Kappa Alpha Theta (vol. charity benefits 1980—). Office: IUPUI 620 Union Dr UN 242 Indianapolis IN 46202

MEURICE, JULIANNE KEPLER, management consultant; b. Berkeley, Calif., May 19, 1954; d. Raymond Glen and Carol (Flint) K.; m. Gilles P. Meurice, Nov. 22, 1980; 1 child, Valerie. BA in Psychology with hons., Stanford U., 1976; MBA, Dartmouth Coll., 1978. Fin. analyst GMC, N.Y.C., 1978-79; fin. liaison Gen. Motors Espa(ñ)a, R(ü)sselsheim, Fed. Republic Germany, 1979-80; supr. planning Gen. Motors France, Gennevilliers, 1981-82; mgr. Nolan, Norton, London, 1982-83; cons. Coopers & Lybrand, Phila., 1983-85; mgr. strategic planning Libbey-Owens Ford, Toledo, 1986-87; v.p. The Carroll Group, Chgo., 1987—. Recipient Amos Tuck scholar, 1978. Office: The Carroll Group 875 N Michigan Ave Ste 3311 Chicago IL 60611

MEURY, VERONICA KMEC, medical association administrator; b. Pitts., Mar. 18, 1946; d. Andrew William and Veronica Constance (Rudzik) Kmec; m. John Nicholas Meury, Jr., Oct. 29, 1966; children: John III, Matthew, Mark. Student, U. Pitts., 1963-66. Bus. office supr. Pacific Telephone, L.A., 1969-71; asst. dir. svcs. Honolulu Club, 1981-84; nat. coord. Second Chance Hot-Line, Pitts., 1985-86; project chmn. Internat. Organ Transplant Forum, Pitts., 1985-87; exec. dir. Transplant Recipients Internat., Pitts., 1987—; bd. dirs. AIDS Task Force, Pitts., Family Resources, Pitts. Pres. Mt. Lebanon Dem. Women's Forum, Pitts., 1987—; campaign coord. June Delano for Commr., Pitts., 1989; bd. dirs. Jr. League Pitts., 1986—; pres. Symphony Guild of Honolulu, 1983-84; grad. Leadership Pitts., Class 6, 1989; assoc. vol. The Nat. Ctr., Washington, 1989; adv. mem. Mt. Lebanon Sch. Dist., Pitts., 1987; ordained elder Presbyn. Ch. Recipient Outstanding Svc. award Sta. KDKA-TV and Presbyn. U. Hosp., 1985. Mem. Am. Coun. Transplantation (bd. dirs.), Assn. of Jr. Leagues Internat. (area pub. rels. liaison), ACT Patient & Family Forum, Mt. Lebanon Garden Arts (program chair 1987-88). Office: Transplant Recipients Inter 244 N Bellefield Ave Pittsburgh PA 15213

MEUSBURGER, JOLENE ANN, accountant; b. Le Mars, Iowa, Nov. 3, 1960; d. Paul W. and Mary Rita (Buckley) Minten; m. Brad L. Meusburger, Sept. 4, 1982; children: Eric, Alex. BA, Buena Vista Coll., Storm Lake, Iowa, 1983; MBA, Wright State U., Dayton, Ohio, 1988. CPA. Acct. Frank W. Schaefer, Inc., Dayton, 1984-85; grad. asst. Wright State U., 1987-88; gen. acct. Globe Motors, Dayton, 1988-90, acctg. supr., 1990—. Home: 50 Creekview Ct Springboro OH 45066 Office: 2275 Stanley Ave Dayton OH 45404

MEUSEL, JANIS LYNN, accountant; b. St. Albans, N.Y., Feb. 2, 1956. BA, Thiel Coll., 1977; A in Applied Sci., Hudson Valley Community Coll., 1982; BBA, Siena Coll., 1985. Cert. payroll profl., 1989. Acctg. clk. N.Y. State United Tchrs., Albany, 1979-81, jr. acct., 1981-83, acct., 1983-85, spl. funds acct., 1985—; treas. Meusel Bus. Svcs., Clifton Park, N.Y., 1986—; treas. CWA Local 1141, 1987—. Treas. Christ Luth. Ch., Albany, 1982-85. Mem. Am. Payroll Assn., Clifton Park Keglers (treas. 1988-90), E&A Mixed Bowling (Albany, treas. 1986-87). Office: NY State United Tchrs 159 Wolf Rd Box 15-008 Albany NY 12212-5008

MEYER, ANDREA PEROUTKA, small business owner; b. Prague, Czechoslovakia, Nov. 29, 1963; came to U.S. 1970; d. George and Alena Peroutka; m. Dana Charles Meyer, Oct. 16, 1983. BA in Liberal Arts, U. Tex., 1985, M in Libr. of Info. Sci., 1986. Libr. IBM, Austin, Tex., 1985-86; rsch. specialist Career Track Seminars, Boulder, Colo., 1986-88; founder, pres. Working Knowledge, Boulder, 1988—; cons. The Tom Peters Group, Palo Alto, Calif., 1989—. Author: (workbooks) How to Give Presentations, 1988, Stress Management Strategies, 1987; co-author: (audio tape) How to Set Up a Corporate Library, 1989. Recipient Ray C. Janeway scholarship, Tex. Libr. Assn., 1985, Philip Morris scholarship, 1981-85. Mem. Special Libr. Assn., Toastmasters Internat., Am. Soc. Tng. and Devel., Phi Beta Kappa, Mensa. Office: Working Knowledge 515 Forest Ave Boulder CO 80304

MEYER, ANGELA, nursing educator, consultant; b. Caldwell, N.J., Sept. 25, 1933; d. Henry Joseph and Hilda (Nuzzetti) Messina; m. Clarence A. Meyer. Diploma in nursing, East Orange (N.J.) Hosp., 1954; BSN, Seton Hall U., 1958; MSN, U. Pa., 1962; postgrad., Rutgers U., 1976-79. RN, Pa., N.J., N.Y. Rep. N.Y. State Health Dept., N.Y.C., 1962-65; case finding dir. N.Y.C. Lung Assn., 1965-69; cons. Fed. Protestant Welfare Agys., N.Y.C., 1969-70; assoc. prof. nursing Bergen County Coll., Paramus, N.J., 1970-80, Ocean County Coll., Toms River, N.J., 1980—; cons. in health care. Mem. Am. Nurses Assn., East Orange Gen. Hosp. Alumni Assn., AAUW, N.J. State Nurse's Assn. (expert witness adult care), Sigma Theta Tau. Roman Catholic. Home: 1730 Rue Mirador Point Pleasant NJ 08742 Office: Ocean County Coll College Dr Toms River NJ 08742

MEYER, ANN JANE, human development educator; b. N.Y.C., Mar 11, 1942; s. Louis John and Theresa M. B.A., U. Mich., 1964; M.A., U. Calif.-Berkeley, 1967, Ph.D., 1971. Asst. prof. dept. human devel. Calif. State U.-Hayward, 1972-77, assoc. prof., 1977-84, prof., chmn. dept., 1984—. Mem. Am. Psychol. Assn., Western Psychol. Assn., Western Gerontol. Soc. Office: Dept Human Devel Calif State U Hayward CA 94542

MEYER, ANNE STRINGER, communications consultant; b. Decatur, Ala., Nov. 20, 1930; d. William Lowe Stringer and Corinne Annabelle (Stritzinger) Stringer Stanton; m. William Andrew Meyer, Sept. 9, 1949 (div. Jan. 1977); children—William Andrew, Jr., Robert Moore, Anne Elizabeth. B.A., Tulane U., 1976. Real estate agt. Stan Weber & Assocs., Metairie, La., 1971-76; owner Chateau Florist, Kenner, La., 1978-82; pub. relations dir. Goodwill Industries, New Orleans, 1982-84; community relations coordinator East Jefferson Gen. Hosp., 1984-86; prin. Anne Meyer and Assoc, Inc., Pub. Relations Cons., 1986—; free-lance artist, writer. Chmn. bus. and profl. group Goodwill Industries Vol. Services, 1984-85; chmn. thank you com. United way, 1985; mem. mayor's adv. com. City of Kenner; mem. exec. com. Pvt. Industry Council of Jefferson Parish, 1986-89. Recipient awards for drawings, 1971-72. Mem. Women in Communications (local v.p. 1983—), Pub. Relations Soc. Am., Kenner Bus. Assn. (co-founder, 1st v.p. 1979), Internat. Assn. Bus. Communicators (v.p. programs 1985), Kenner Profl. Women's Assn. (Businesswoman of Month, 1986, bd. mem. 1986-88), Kenner Bus. Assn., Jefferson Pvt. Industry Council (exec. com. 1986—), Friends of Zoo, McGehee Sch. Alumnae Assn. (sch. class rep. 1950—), Newcomb Alumnae Assn., Republican. Roman Catholic. Club: Press (New Orleans).

MEYER, BETTY JANE, former librarian; b. Indpls., July 20, 1918; d. Herbert and Gertrude (Sanders) M.; B.A., Ball State Tchrs. Coll., 1940; B.S. in L.S., Western Res. U., 1945. Student asst. Muncie Public Library (Ind.), 1936-40; library asst. Ohio State U. Library, Columbus, 1940-42, cataloger, 1945-46, asst. circulation librarian, 1946-51, acting circulation librarian, 1951-52, adminstrv. asst. to dir. libraries, 1952-57, acting asso. reference librarian, 1957-58, cataloger in charge serials, 1958-65, head serial div. catalog dept., 1965-68, head acquisition dept., 1968-71, asst. dir. libraries, tech. services, 1971-76, acting dir. libraries, 1976-77, asst. dir. libraries, tech. services, 1977-83, instr. library adminstrn., 1958-63, asst. prof., 1963-67, asso. prof., 1967-75, prof., 1975-83, prof. emeritus, 1983—; library asst. Grandview Heights Public Library, Columbus, 1942-44; student asst. Case Inst. Tech., Cleve., 1944-45; mem. Ohio Coll. Library Center Adv. Com. on Cataloging, 1971-76, mem. adv. com. on serials, 1971-76, mem. adv. com. on tech. processes, 1971-76; mem. Inter-Univ. Library Council, Tech. Services Group, 1971-83; mem. bd. trustees Columbus Area Library and Info. Council Ohio, 1980-83. Ohio State U. grantee, 1975-76. Mem. ALA, Assn. Coll. and Research Libraries, AAUP, Ohio Library Assn. (nominating com. 1978-81), Ohioana Library Assn., Ohio Valley Group Tech. Services Librarians, No. Ohio Tech. Services Librarians, Franklin County Library Assn., Acad. Library Assn. Ohio, PEO, Beta Phi Mu, Delta Kappa Gamma. Club: Ohio State U. Faculty Women's. Home: 970 High St Unit H2 Worthington OH 43085

MEYER, MRS. C. M. See DANNER, PATSY ANN

MEYER, CYNTHIA KAY, nurse; b. Wichita Falls, Tex., Mar. 6, 1952; d. Harry Lewis and Nancy Jane (Daily) Harris; m. Larry Francis Meyer, Sept. 1, 1973; children: Eric Q., Bryce J. B of Health Mgmt., U. Mo., 1987; MPH, St. Louis U., 1990. Staff nurse Meml. Community Hosp., Jefferson City, Mo., 1973-74; staff, then charge nurse St. Mary's Health Ctr., Jefferson City, 1974-77, 80-81; nurse practitioner Capitol Childrens' Clinic, Jefferson City, 1977-80; project dir., nurse practitioner Planned Parenthood Cen. Mo., Jefferson City, 1981-85; nursing cons. Mo. Dept. Health, Jefferson City, 1985-89; cons. St. Louis Dept. Community Health & Med. Care, 1989—; cons. Mo. Community Health Corp., Jefferson City, 1984, Head Start Region VII USPHS Maternal and Child Health Div., instr. pub. health courses Jefferson City. Contbr. chpts. to state govt. document Two Generations at Risk, 1987. Vol. Am. Cancer Soc., 1983, 87, Boy Scouts Am., 1985-86, United Way, 1987-89, all Jefferson City. Mem. Mo. Perinatal Assn., Mo. Family Planning Assn., Mo. Pub. Health Assn. Home: 808 LaFeil Manchester MO 63021 Office: St Louis Dept Community Medicine & Med Care Saint Louis MO 63105

MEYER, DEANNA SIPSMA, real estates sales manager; b. Kenosha, Wis., Sept. 3, 1937; d. Samuel John Sipsma and Auga Baker; m. Carl G. Meyer, June 14, 1958; children: Jerald Scott, Jill Noelle. AA, Racine-Kenosha Tchrs. Coll., Union Grove, 1956. Cert. Residential Broker. Tchr. North Bloomfield Sch., Lake Geneva, Wis., 1956-58, El Paso (Tex.) Sch., 1958-59; sales assoc. Costello Real Estate, Crystal Lake, Ill., 1977-86; tng. dir. Essex Costello Real Estate, Crystal Lake, Ill., 1986—; sales mgr. Essex Castello Real Estate, Crystal Lake, 1986-89. Com. Chairperson, Crystal Lake C. of C., Crystal Lake, Ill., 1988-89. Named: Realtor Assoc. of the Year, McHenry County Bd. of Realtors, 1984. Mem. Real Estate Brokerage Coun., McHenry County Bd. Realtors, Rotary, PEO (treas. 1988-89). United Ch. of Christ. Office: Essex Costello Real Estate 330 Virginia St Crystal Lake IL 60014

MEYER, DEBORAH LYNN, elementary school educator; b. Indpls., Sept. 15, 1948; d. Ernest Richard and Yetive Marie (Bailey) Bain; m. Roy Gene Meyer, Sept. 30, 1969; children: Tamara Marie, Tricia Jeanette. Student, U. Indpls., 1971, Ind. U., South Bend, 1983. Cert. elem. tchr., Ind. Elem. tchr. St. Anthony's Cath. Sch., Temperance, Mich., 1972-74; program coord. Internat. Inst., Flint, Mich., 1974-80; elem. tchr. La Porte (Ind.) Community Sch. Corp., 1981. Treas. Kingsbury PTA, La Porte, 1983-87; treas. Welcome Wagon Internat., 1980-84, Baha'i Faith of Scipio Twp., 1978—; mem. Kingsford Heights PTA, 1981—. BEST grantee LaPorte Community Sch. Corp., 1988. Mem. AAUW, LaPorte Fedn. of Tchrs. (bd. mem. 1985—, negotiator 1989—), Delta Kappa Gamma (treas. 1986—). Mem. Baha'i Faith. Home: 2655 S 75 W La Porte IN 46350

MEYER, DONNA MARIA, aerospace company executive; b. Washington, Mar. 14, 1950; d. Gratian Jerome and Kathryn (Sullivan) Meyer; m. James Thomas Giganti, Nov. 17, 1988; 1 child, Julia Claire Giganti. BS, U. Md., 1974. Dir. internat. fundraising Gratian Meyer & Assocs., Washington, 1970-76; legal exec. Am. Internat. Law Offices, Arlington, Va., 1976-81; exec. sales rep. Concord (N.H.) Litho Co., 1981-86; chmn., co-founder Save Sexually Abused Children, Silver Spring, Md., 1988—; pres. Youngstar Space Acad., Silver Spring, 1986—; founder The Daisy Program for the Chesapeake Inst., Nat. Resource Ctr. for Child Abuse, 1990. Author: Angela Duke Story, 1989; author, editor Children's Dictionary of Space, 1989; contbg. author Factor Ten, 1979; contbg. author: Parents Resource Book, 1990. Recipient Key to City of Guatemala, 1980. Mem. Nat. Assn. of Women Execs., Young Astronaut Coun. (chpt. leader), Jr. Engring. Tech. Soc. (chpt. leader), Ninety-Nines (Potomac). Republican. Roman Catholic. Office: 11301 Georgia Ave Ste 3 Silver Spring MD 20902

MEYER, IVAH GENE, social worker; b. Decatur, Ill., Nov. 18, 1935; d. Anthony and Nona Alice (Gamble) Viccone; A.A. with distinction, Phoenix Coll., 1964; B.S. with distinction, Ariz. State U., 1966, M.S.W., 1969; postgrad. U.S. Internat. U.; m. Richard Anthony Meyer, Feb. 7, 1954; children—Steven Anthony, Stuart Allen, Scott Arthur. Social worker Florence Crittendon Home, Phoenix, 1969-70; social worker Family Service of Phoenix, 1970-73; faculty asso. Ariz. State U., 1973; field supr. Pitzer Coll., Claremont, Calif., 1977—; social worker Family Service of Pomona Valley, Pomona, Calif., 1975—; field supr. Grad. Sch. Social Services, U. So. Calif., 1978—; pvt. practice Chino (Calif.) Counseling Center. Lic. clin. social worker, Calif. Mem. Nat. Assn. Social Workers, Acad. Cert. Social Workers. Republican. Roman Catholic. Home: 778 Via Montevideo Claremont CA 91711 Office: 12632 Central Ave Chino CA 91710

MEYER, JACKIE MERRI, publishing executive; b. Phila., Oct. 19, 1954; d. George Gilbert Meyer and Sylvia Magerman; m. W. Scot Carouge, May 23, 1982. BFA, The Cooper Union, N.Y.C., 1977. Art dir. Macmillan Pub. Co., N.Y.C., 1980-85; v.p., creative dir. Warner Books, N.Y.C., 1985—; tchr. Parsons Sch. Design, N.Y.C., 1984-85; lectr. Fashion Inst. Tech., N.Y.C., 1984-85, Am. Illustraton, N.Y.C., 1984; design cons. Adler and Adler, Bethesda, Md., 1985. Co-author: I Loathe New York, 1981. Fundraiser The Cooper Union, N.Y.C., 1977—. Recipient 170 profl. awards Alga, The Advt. Club, Desi Awards, Art Direction mag., Print mag., Graphis, Communication Arts. Mem. AFTRA, Soc. of Illustrators (bd. dirs. 1988—), Am. Inst. Graphic Arts, Art Dirs. Club (awards). Office: Warner Books Inc 666 Fifth Ave 9th Fl New York NY 10103

MEYER, JEAN, fashion consultant; b. N.Y.C., Mar. 18, 1934; d. George and Grace (Lieberman) Weingart; m. Harold Walton Meyer, Apr. 6, 1971; 1 child, Steven Michael. Student, Mayer Sch. Design, 1970. Asst. account exec. Theodore R. Sills and Co., N.Y.C., 1963-64; advt. asst. Bond Stores, Inc., N.Y.C., 1964-66; adminstrv. asst. Revlon, Inc., N.Y.C., 1966-68; asst. to pres. The Villager, N.Y.C., 1970-71; freelance fashion cons. Charlotte, N.C., 1984—; sewing tche. Mecklenburg County Home Econs., Charlotte, 1980-82, Queens Coll., Charlotte, 1988—; image seminar instr. WomanREach, Charlotte, 1986; antique textile and clothing restorer, Costume Com. Mint Mus., Charlotte, 1984—. Mem. Nat. Assn. Female Execs. Home and Office: 5805-J Sharon Rd Charlotte NC 28210

MEYER, JEANETTE MARJORIE, marketing research analyst; b. Kansas City, Mo., Apr. 15, 1961; d. Floyd W. and Marjorie L. (Vieth) M. BA, Washington U., 1983; MBA, U. Colo., 1987; postgrad., St. Peter's, Oxford, Eng., 1981. Dir. info. systems for congressman U.S. Ho. of Rep., Washington, 1983-84; market rsch. analyst Hallmark Cards, Inc., Kansas City, 1987-89; prin., owner Meyer Rsch. Svcs., Boulder, Colo., 1989—. Tutor adult literacy Boulder Pub. Libr., 1990; panel mem. Regional Review Panel for Truman Scholarship, Denver, 1990; vol. Josie Heath for Senate campaign, Colo., 1990; field coord. Dukakis Presdl. campaign, Mo., 1988. Truman scholar Harry S. Truman Found. Mo. Scholar, 1981. Mem. Am. Mktg. Assn., NOW. Office: Meyer Rsch Svcs 1877 Broadway Ste 405 Boulder CO 80302

MEYER, JUDITH LOUISE, obstetrician/gynecologist; b. East Grand Rapids, Mich., Feb. 26, 1933; d. George and Evangeline (Boerma) M. AB, Calvin Coll., Grand Rapids, 1955; postgrad., Mich. State U., 1955-56; MD, Woman's Med. Coll. Pa., 1961. Pvt. practice Grandville, Mich., 1965—; Woman's Med. Coll.; asst. clin. prof. coll. human medicine Mich. State U., Grand Rapids, 1990—. Violinist Grand Rapids Symphony, 1961, 65-74, West Shore Symphony, Muskegon, Mich., 1976-81, Kent Philharmonic, Grand Rapids, 1989—; singer Park Congl. Choir, Grand Rapids, 1987—. Fellow Am. Coll. Ob-Gyn., Am. Fertility Soc.; mem. Kent County Med. Soc. (legis. com.), Mich. State Med. soc., Woman's City Club. Republican. Mem. Reformed Ch. Am. Office: 3181 Prairie SW Grandville MI 49418

MEYER, JULIE ANN, fund-raising consultant; b. Wichita Falls, Tex., Mar. 14, 1960; d. Richard Perry and Patricia Ann (Scoville) M. BA in Communications, U. So. Calif., 1983, MA in Communications Mgmt, 1986. Coordinator event planning U. So. Calif., L.A., 1985, asst. dir. devel. Sch. Acctg., 1985-86, acting dir. devel. Sch. Acctg., 1986-87; ind. contractor apparel sales Reebok, 1987-88; event coordinator U. So. Calif., L.A., 1988-89; dir. devel. Sheriff's Youth Found., 1989—. Vol. Torrance (Calif.) Meml. Hosp., 1976-77; debutante San Pedro Peninsula Assistance League, 1976-78; mem. advance staff Reagan-Bush Campaign, 1984; mem. YES Group Little Co. of Mary Hosp. Mem. Nat. Soc. Fund Raising Execs., South Bay Young Reps., L.A. Women's Found., U. So. Calif. Assocs., Kappa Alpha Theta (historian 1979-80). Republican. Lutheran. Home and Office: 501 Herondo St Apt 30 Hermosa Beach CA 90254

MEYER, KAREN ANN GRITZAN, speech/language pathologist; b. Bronx, Nov. 7, 1947; d. Stephan and Pauline Theresa (Linkiewicz) Gritzan; m. Charles J. Meyer, Oct. 17, 1970; children: Matthew, Thomas. BA cum laude, Lehman Coll., 1969; MA (fellow), Northwestern U., 1971. Cert. speech-hearing and handicapped tchr., N.Y.; lic. speech and language pathology, N.Y. Speech and lang. pathologist Mt. St. Ursula Speech Center, Bronx, 1971; speech and lang. pathologist Westchester Assn. Retarded Children (N.Y.), 1971-72; clin. communicologist, instr. rehab. medicine Mental Retardation Inst., N.Y. Med. Coll. and Flower Fifth Ave. Hosp., N.Y.C., 1972-75; pvt. practice speech and lang. pathology for children, Brewster, N.Y., 1980—; speech language pathologist Westchester Exceptional Children's Sch., Purdys, N.Y., 1985—; adj. lectr., clin. supr. Hunter Coll. Center for Communication Disorders, 1980-85, asst. to coordinator Inst. Lang. and Learning Disabilities, 1981. Mem. Am. Speech Lang. and Hearing Assn. (cert. speech/lang. pathologist, moderator 2 sessions 1981 conf.), N.Y. State Speech Lang. and Hearing Assn. (chmn. com. career devel/student concerns and continuing edn. conv. 1984), Westchester Speech Lang. and Hearing Assn., Phi Beta Kappa. Roman Catholic. Home: 506 Village Dr Brewster NY 10509

MEYER, LINDA S., journalist; b. St. Louis, July 19, 1950; d. Charles and Betty (Hoffman) M.; m. Leonard Russ, Apr. 7, 1984. BFA, U. Cin., 1972; MA in Journalism, NYU, 1986. Editorial asst. bus. sect. St. Louis Globe-Democrat, 1970; prodn. asst. Sta. WOR-TV News, N.Y.C., 1972; news desk asst. Sta. WABC-TV News, N.Y.C., 1972-73; researcher ABC News Close-Up Documentaries, N.Y.C., 1973-75, prodn. assoc., 1975-77; press rep. ABC Inc., N.Y.C., 1977-79; radio network news writer CBS News, N.Y.C., 1979-80; segment producer, writer ABC-TV Good Morning America, N.Y.C., 1980—. Mem. Writers Guild Am. Office: ABC-TV Good Morning Am 1965 Broadway New York NY 10023

MEYER, MARILYN CLARITA, superintendent of schools; b. Cin., June 22, 1942; d. George William and Clarita (Hueil) Strassell; m. Edward Walter Meyer, May 14, 1966 (div. 1980). BS, Edgecliff Coll., 1964; M, Xavier U., Cin., 1976. Cert. supt., Ohio. Tchr. Our Lady of Lourdes Sch., Cin., 1964-66; tchr. Greenhills Forest Park City Sch., Cin., 1967-72, tchr. resource, 1972-77, instructional analyst, 1977-79; coordinator career edn. Great Oaks Joint Vocat. Sch., Cin., 1979-88; supr. Ohio HiPoint Joint Vocat. Sch., Bellefontaine, Ohio, 1988—. Treas. Birthright, Cin., 1979-80, Scholarship Fund, Cin.; trustee, treas. Imperial Oaks Condiminim, Cin.; chairperson Mayer for Ho. of Reps. campaign, Cin.; mem. state task force for career edn., 1984-86; bd. dirs. United Way, Bellefontaine, Ohio, 1989. Mem. Career Edn. Assn. (pres. 1985-86), Buckeye Assn. Sch. Adminstrs. (profl. growth com. 1984-86), Ohio Vocat. Assn. (del. 1985), Kiwanis (bd. dirs. Bellefontaine chpt. 1989-90), Soroptimist (treas. 1989-90), Longhunters Assn. (treas. 1986-87), Phi Delta Kappa. Republican. Roman Catholic. Office: Ohio Hi Point Joint Vocat Sch 2240 Rt 540 Bellefontaine OH 43311

MEYER, MARION M., editorial consultant; b. Sheboygan, Wis., July 14, 1923; d. Herman O. and Viola A. (Hoch) M. BA, Lakeland Coll., 1950; MA, NYU, 1957. Payroll clk. Am. Chair Co., Sheboygan, 1941-46; tchr. English and religion, dir. athletics Am. Sch. for Girls, Baghdad, Iraq, 1950-56; mem. edn. and publ. staff United Ch. Bd. for Homeland Ministries, United Ch. Press/Pilgrim Press, 1958-64, sr. editor, 1965-88, ret., 1988; cons. to individuals and orgns. on editorial matters and copyrights. Editor Penney Retirement Community Newsletter, 1990; writer (hymns) Look to God; Be Radiant, 1989; contbr. articles to various publs. Incorporating mem. Contact Phila., Inc., 1972, bd. dirs., 1972-75, v.p., chmn. com. to organize community adv. bd., chmn. auditing com., editor newsletter, 1972-74, pres., 1974-75, assoc. mem., 1977—; mem. ofcl. bd. Old First Reformed Ch., Phila., 1984-89; deacon United Ch. Christ, 1984—, Mid.-East Com. of Pa. SE Conf. United Ch. Christ, 1986-88. Honored as role model United Ch. of Christ, 1982, 85. Mem. AAUW. Home: PO Box 656 Penny Farms FL 32079

MEYER, MARY-BETH, child welfare administrator; b. Denton, Tex., May 10, 1950; d. Norman Carl and Elsie-Lou (Bartling) M. BA, Valparaiso U., 1972; MA, U. Chgo., 1977. Cert. Social Worker; Cert. Child Care Worker. Child care worker Pritzker Children's Ctr., Chgo., 1972-77; social worker Nachusa (Ill.) Luth. Home, 1977-78, Mary Bartelme Homes, Chgo., 1978-81; dir. child care St. Joseph's Carondelet, Chgo.; asst. dir. Interventions SMA Sch., Matteson, Ill., 1984-86; dir. Guardian Angel Home, Joliet, Ill., 1986; instr. U. Ill., Chgo., 1982. Mem. Ill. Assn. of Child Care Workers (pres. 1985-87, sec. 1987-89).

MEYER, MARY-LOUISE, art gallery executive; b. Boston, Feb. 21, 1922; d. Alonzo Jay and Louise (Whitledge) Shadman; m. Norman Meyer, Aug. 9, 1941; children—Wendy C., Bruce R., Harold Alton, Marilee, Laurel. B.A., Wellesley Coll., 1943; M.S., Wheelock Coll., 1965. Head tchr. Page Sch., Wellesley Coll., Mass., 1955-60; instr. early childhood edn. Pine Manor Coll., Brookline, Mass., 1960-65; chaplain/counselor Charles St. Jail, Boston, 1974-79; Christian Sci. practitioner, Wellesley, Mass., 1974—; owner Alpha Gallery, Boston, 1972-87 ; cons. Living & Learning Centers, Boston, 1966-69; 2d reader Christian Sci. Ch., 1979-82. Contbr. articles to profl. jours. Overseer Sturbridge Village, 1981—, trustee, 1986; visitor Am. Decorative Arts dept. Mus. Fine Arts, Boston, 1973—; chmn. Wellesley Voters Rights Com., 1983-84; state organizer Ednl. Channel 2 Group, Boston, 1960; co-founder Boston Assn. for Childbirth Edn., 1950; overseer Strawberry Banke Living Mus., 1987. Mem. Farnsworth Mus., Waldoboro Hist. Soc., Soc. for Pres. New Eng. Antiquities. Club: Wellesley Coll.

MEYER, NATALIE, state official; b. Henderson, N.C., May 20, 1930; d. Ranie Thomas and Mary Osborne (Johnson) Clayton; m. Harold Meyer, June 17, 1951; children—Mary, Becky, Amy. Student, U. No. Iowa, 1951. Tchr. pub. schs. Jefferson County, Colo., 1951-57; tchr. and prin. Ascension Luth. Ch. Midweek Sch., 1966-77; leasing mgr. for office complex, 1973; sec. of state State of Colo., Denver, 1982—. Past vice chairperson Arapahoe County Republicans, Colo.; mgr. Senator Bill Armstrong's 1974 Fifth Congl. Campaign; exec. dir. Pres. Reagan's 1976 Colo. Campaign; dir. Ted Strickland's 1978 Gubernatorial Race; mgr. Phil Winn's race for Rep. state chmn., 1980; author, adminstr. Colo. program for Rep. legis. races, 1980, other statewide campaign plans; coordinator Draft Phil Winn effort. Office: Colo State Dept 1560 Broadway Ste 200 Denver CO 80202

MEYER, PATRICIA HANES, psychiatric social worker; b. Champaign, Ill., Feb. 10, 1947; d. Walter Ernest and Mary Kathryn (Kemp) Hanes; B.A., Carroll Coll., Waukesha, Wis., 1969; M.S.W., Cath. U. Am., 1976; m. Scott Kimbrough Meyer, June 15, 1969; children—Jennifer Suzanne, Claire Catherine, John Andrew. Dir. family therapy program Fairfax County Juvenile Ct., Fairfax, Va., 1970-77; clin. instr. Georgetown U. Med. Sch., Washington, 1976-84; pvt. practice family psychiatry, 1976—. Mem. Am. Orthopsychiat. Assn., Am. Family Therapy Assn., Nat. Assn. Social Workers. Adv. editor The Family, 1977-84. Home: 3419 Tilton Valley Dr Fairfax VA 22033 Office: 10805 Parkridge Suite 230 Reston VA 22091

MEYER, SALLY CAVE, personnel director; b. Coulee Dam, Wash., Oct. 20, 1937; d. Verl Edwin and Etha Laree (Moore) Cave; m. Ronald Lee Meyer, July 27, 1957; children: John Lee, Deanna, Michael Ron, Geri Anne, Deborah Sue. BA, Wash. State U., 1959, postgrad., 1986. Cert. tchr., Wash. Tchr. English Colfax (Wash.) High Sch., 1959-60; tchr. Pasco (Wash.) High Sch., 1961-62, Chief Joseph Jr. High Sch., Richland, Wash., 1968-69; instr. Columbia Basin Community Coll., Pasco, 1962-70; mem. staff Wash. State U., Pullman, 1955-61, 71-77, dir. faculty, adminstrv., and profl. personnel, 1977—, acting dir. affirmative action program, 1986-87; coordinator Nat. Faculty Exchange Wash. State U., 1986-88; dep. chmn. Wash. State Employees Combined Fund Drive, 1987—, state steering commn., 1989—. Sec. Camp Fire Girls Am., Pullman, 1979-82; mem. Wash. State U. Pres.'s Commn. on Status of Women, 1985-88; mem. Wash. State U. Pres.'s Commn. on Status of Minorities, 1989—, Wash. State U. Pres.'s Child Care Com. Mem. NW Women's Studies Assn., Coll. and Univ. Personnel Assn., Nat. Assn. Female Execs., Lakewood Research Tng. Group, Wash. State U. Alumni Assn., Phi Delta Kappa. Office: Wash State U French Adminstrn 446 Pullman WA 99164-1049

MEYER, SANDRA W(ASSERSTEIN), financial company executive; b. N.J., Aug. 20, 1937; children—Jenifer Anne Schweitzer, Samantha Boughton Schweitzer. Student, U. Mich.; B.A. cum laude, Syracuse U., 1957; postgrad., London Sch. Econs., 1958. Advt. account exec. London Press Exchange, 1959-63; product mgr. Beecham Products Inc., Clifton, N.J., 1963-66; with Gen. Foods Co., White Plains, N.J., 1966-76; mktg. mgr. coffee div. Gen. Foods Co., 1973-74, dir. corp. mktg. planning, 1975-76; with Am. Express Co., N.Y.C., 1976-84; pres. communications div. Am. Express Co., 1980-84; mng. dir. Russell Reynolds Assocs., N.Y.C., 1985-89; sr. corp. officer corp. affairs Citicorp, N.Y.C., 1989—; bd. dirs. Munsingwear, Inc., Mpls., Horizon Internat. Foods, Boston. Trustee Met. Opera Guild, East Hampton Guild Hall; mng. dir. Met. Opera Assn. Office: Citicorp 399 Park Ave New York NY 10043

MEYER, SUELLEN JACKSON, college educator; b. Rutherford, Tenn., Apr. 12, 1944; d. David Preston and Dee (Crouse) Jackson; m. Richard C. Meyer, Oct. 23, 1941. BA in English, Emory U., 1966; MA in English, St. Louis U., 1974. Tchr. Pattonville Sch. Dist., St. Louis, 1969-72; instr. U. Mo., St. Louis, 1977-83; assoc. prof. St. Louis Community Coll., 1983-89, prof., 1989—; trainer writing group Clayton Cons. Group, St. Louis, 1986—. Contbr. articles to profl. jours. Mem. Am. Quilt Study Group, Nat. Coun. Tchrs. English, AAUW (grantee 1982). Office: Saint Louis Community Coll Meramec 11333 Big Bend Blvd Saint Louis MO 63122

MEYER, SUSAN THERESA, personnel industry executive; b. Ames, Iowa, Mar. 29, 1950; d. Robert William Keirs and Jeanne Marion (Thomas) Kaufer; m. John Allen Meyer, Dec. 18, 1972; children: Katherine Jeanne, Robert John. BS cum laude, U. Wis., 1972; MBA, Ea. Mich. U., 1982. Cert. spl. edn. tchr., Wis., Va. Spl. edn. tchr. Prince George (Va.) Pub. Schs., 1972-73; acct. DEMPUBCO Printing Co., Colorado Springs, Colo., 1973-74; adminstr., dir. EEO Dept. of Army, Frankfurt, Fed. Rep. of Germany, 1974-77; program coordinator Wake Up La., New Orleans, 1977-78; buyer Ford Motor Co., Dearborn, Mich., 1978-81; fgn. procurement specialist Ford Motor Co., Dearborn, 1981-85; pres., gen. mgr. Mgmt. Recruiters of No. Del., Wilmington, 1985—; pres. Profl. Images, 1987—; cons. Fed. Women's Program, Frankfurt, 1974-77. Bd. dirs. Milford (Mich.) Hist. Soc., 1983-85; bd. dirs. Milford Parks and Recreation Dept., 1983-85. Mem. Wilmington Women in Bus., Nat. Assn. Female Execs. Republican. Roman Catholic. Home: 16 N Cliffe Dr Wilmington DE 19809 Office: Mgmt Recruiters 501 Silverside Rd Suite 140 Wilmington DE 19809

MEYER, SYLVIA ADEY, education educator; b. Lebanon, Pa., Feb. 23, 1936; d. Stewart Rolland and Emily (Chubb) Adey; m. Lloyd Edward Meyer, Mar. 26, 1955; children: David, Allen, Evelyn Kathryn, Jane. BS in Social Studies, Millersville State Coll., 1979, MS, 1983. Sec. Milton Hershey Sch., Hershey, Pa., 1954-55; tchr. Cedar Crest High Sch., Lebanon, Pa., 1979-; cons., presenter, Nationwide Computer Svcs., Pa.,. Collector Salvation Army, Heart Fund. Mem. Am. Assn. Univ. Women. Republican. Home: 228 S Forge Rd Palmyra PA 17078 Office: Cedar Crest High Sch 115 E Evergreen Rd Lebanon PA 17042

MEYER, THERESA TUCK, secretary, treasurer; b. San Francisco, Dec. 5, 1944; d. Robert George and Jane Ellen (Kingwell) Tuck; m. John Peter Meyer; children: Peter, Jennifer, Joan, Robert. BA, U. Oreg., 1966. Sec. Pan Pacific Med. Assn., Honolulu, 1966-67, Atlas Heating & Ventilating, San Francisco, 1975—. Office: Atlas Heating & Ventilating 440 8th St San Francisco CA 94103

MEYER, WILLA DEAN, former newspaper editor; b. Farmington, Mo., Oct. 10, 1932; d. Lawrence and Clara Evalina (Williams) Thurman; m. Arthur Francis Meyer, Apr. 14, 1956; children: Cynthia Ann Meyer Butterbaugh, Larry Joe, Kevin Lee. Grad. high sch., Farmington. Sec. Mo. Dept. Revenue, Farmington, 1950-59, auditor, 1959-64; sec. Presbyn. Ch., Farmington, 1968-78; soc. editor Farmington Press, 1978-80, news editor, 1980-88. Active Farmington PTA, 1976—; bd. dirs. Mineral Area Hospice; project advisor Farmington Christian Women's Club; mem. adv. bd. Desloge Health Care Ctr.; projet dir. Downtown Farmington Orgn. Mem. Mo. Press Assn., Farmington C. of C. Democrat. Roman Catholic. Home: 1 Airline Dr Farmington MO 63640

MEYERS, ANN ELIZABETH, sports broadcaster; b. San Diego, Mar. 26, 1955; d. Robert Eugene and Patricia Ann (Burke); m. Donald Scott Drysdale, Nov. 1, 1986; children: Donald Scott Jr., Darren John. Grad., UCLA, 1978. Profl. basketball player N.J. Gems, 1979-80; profl. basketball player Ind. Pacers NBA, 1979; sports broadcaster Ind. Pacers, 1979-80; sportscaster men's basketball U. Hawaii, Honolulu, 1981-82; sportscaster men's and women's basketball UCLA, 1982-84; sportscaster volleyball, basketball, softball, tennis ESPN, 1981-89; sportscaster Olympic Games ABC, L.A., 1984; sportscaster volleyball, softball, tennis, basketball, soccer Sportsvision, 1985-87; sportscaster volleyball, basketball, softball Prime Ticket, 1985—; sportscaster Goodwill Games, WTBS, 1986, 90. Winner Silver medal Montreal Olympics, 1976; All-Am. UCLA, 1975, 76, 77, 78; 1st woman named to Hall of Fame UCLA, 1987; named to Women's Sports Hall of Fame, 1987, Orange County Sports Hall of Fame, 1987. Office: c/o Lampros and Roberts 16615 Lark Ave #101 Los Gatos CA 95030

MEYERS, BEVERLY JEAN, health care executive; b. Quincy, Ill., Feb. 10, 1949; d. Fred C. Sr. and Ann Catherine (Heaton) M. Med. record technician's degree, Sch. Med. Record Technician, Kansas City, Mo., 1968. Accredited record technician. Pers. asst. St. Joseph Hosp., Kansas City, 1967; co-asst. med. record St. Mary's Hosp., Kansas City, 1968-72; mgr. med. record Blessing Hosp., Quincy, Ill., 1972-74; health record analyst Boone Hosp. Ctr., Columbia, Mo., 1975, med. audit coord., 1975, asst. dir. med. records, 1975-80, mgr. health info. svcs., 1980-83, health data supr., 1983-87, dir. med. record, 1987—; cons. Hermann (Mo.) Area Dist. Hosp., 1989—. Mem. panel of practitioners Med. Records Briefing publ., 1989—. Mem. NAFE, Am. Med. Record Assn., Mo. Med. Record Assn. (legis. com. 1981, edn. com. 1989), Mid-Mo. Med. Record Assn. (numerous offices), Columbia C. of C. (Women's Network). Home: 1005 Pheasant Run Dr Columbia MO 65201 Office: Boone Hosp Ctr 1600 E Broadway Columbia MO 65201

MEYERS, CHRISTINE LAINE, publishing and media executive, consultant; b. Detroit, Mar. 7, 1949; d. Ernest Robert and Eva Elizabeth (Laine) M.; 1 child, Kathryn Laine; m. Oliver S. Moore III, May 12, 1990. BA, U. Mich., 1968. Editor, indsl. relations Diesel div. Gen. Motors Corp., Detroit, 1968; nat. advt. mgr. J.L. Hudson Co., Detroit, 1969-76, mgr. internal sales promotion, 1972-73, dir. pub., 1973-76; nat. advt. mgr. Pontiac Motor div., Mich., 1976-78; pres., owner Laine Meyers Assocs., Troy, Mich., 1978—; dir. Internat. Inst. Met. Detroit, Inc. Contbr. articles to profl. publs. Mem. bus. adv. council Cen. Mich. U., 1977-79; mem. pub. adv. com. on jud. candidates Oakland County Bar Assn. Named Mich. Ad Woman of Yr., 1976, one of Top 10 Working Women Glamour mag., 1978, one of 100 Best and Brightest Advt. Age, 1987; recipient Vanguard award Women in Communications, 1986. Mem. Internat. Assn. Bus. Communicators, Adcraft Club, Women's Advt. Club (1st v.p. 1975), Women's Econ. Club (pres. 1976-77), Internat. Women's Forum Mich. (pres. 1986—), Internat. Inst. of Detroit (bd. dirs. 1986-89), Detroit C. of C., Mortar Board, Quill and Scroll, Pub. Relations Com. Women for United Found., Founders Soc. Detroit Inst. Arts, Fashion Group, Pub. Relations Soc. Am., First Soc. Detroit (exec. com. 1970-71), Kappa Tau Alpha. Home: 1780 Kensington Bloomfield Hills MI 48013 Office: Laine Meyers Inc 3645 Crooks Rd Troy MI 48084

MEYERS, DOROTHY, educator, writer; b. Chgo., Jan. 9, 1927; d. Gilbert and Harriet (Levitt) King; m. William J. Meyers, Oct. 9, 1947; children: Lynn, Jeanne. BA, U. Chgo., 1945, MA, 1961, postgrad.; postgrad. Columbia U., New Sch. Social Research, Northwestern U. Instr. sr. adults, Chgo. Bd. and/City Colls. Chgo., 1961-78; coord. pub. affairs forum and health maintenance program City Colls. Chgo.-Jewish Community Ctrs., Chgo., 1975-78; lectr. adult program City Colls. Chgo., 1984; tchr. Dade County Adult Edn. Program, Miami, Fla., 1983-85; discussion leader Brandeis U. Adult Edn., 1985-86; cons., lectr. in field. Contbr. articles to profl. jours. Chmn. legis. PTA; discussion leader Great Decisions, 1984-86; chmn. civic assembly Citizens Sch. Com.; v.p. community rels. Womens Fedn. and Jewish United Fund; discussion leader LWV, Gt. Decisions, Fgn. Policy Assn.; program chmn. Jewish Community Ctrs., 1966-67, mem. sr. adult com.; bd. dirs. coun. Jewish Elderly, Open U.; mem. art and edn. com. Chgo. Mayor's Com. for Sr. Citizens and Handicapped; mem. com. on media Met. Coun. on Aging. Mem. Am. Sociol. Assn., Gerontol. Assn., Nat. Coun. Aging, Chgo. Met. Sr. Forum (media com.), Coun. Women Chgo. Real Estate Bd., Women in Communications, Chgo. Real Estate Bd., Nat. Assn. Real Estate Bds., Art Inst. Chgo., Mus. Contemporary Art, Soc. Contemporary Art. Office: 77 W Washington St Chicago IL 60602

MEYERS, JAN, congresswoman; b. Lincoln, Nebr.; m. Louis Meyers; children—Valerie, Philip. A.A. in Fine Arts, William Woods Coll., 1948; B.A. in Communications (hon.), U. Nebr.-Lincoln, 1951; LittD, William Woods Coll., 1986. Mem. Overland Park City Council, Kans., 1967-72; also pres.; mem. Kans. Senate, 1972-84, chmn. pub. health and welfare com., local govt. com.; mem. 99th-102nd Congresses from 3d Kans. Dist., mem. com. foreign affairs, small bus. com., select com. on aging, others; mem., former house vice chmn. Environ. and Energy Study Conf. 3d dist. co-chmn. Bob Dole for U.S. Senate, 1968; chmn. Johnson County Bob Bennett for Gov., 1974; mem. Johnson County Community Coll. Found.; bd. dirs. Johnson County Mental Health Assn. Recipient Outstanding Elected Ofcl. of Yr. award Assn. Community Mental Health Ctrs. Kans., Woman of Achievement Matrix award Women in Communications, Disting. Service award Bus. and Profl. Women Kansas City, Community Service award Jr. League Kansas City, 1st Disting. Legislator award Kans. Assn. Community Colls., Outstanding Service award Kans. Library Assn., United Community Services, Kans. Pub. Health Assn., award Gov.'s Conf. Child Abuse and Neglect, Outstanding Legislator award Kans. Action for Children, Friend award Nat. Assn. County Park and Recreation Ofcls., 1987, numerous others. Mem. LWV (past pres. Shawnee Mission). Methodist. Office: US Ho of Reps 1507 Longworth House Bldg Washington DC 20515

MEYERS, JANE KINNEY, library consultant; b. Ligonier, Pa., Oct. 30, 1953; d. Harold Jennings and Mary (Seamon) Kinney; m. Kenneth Kerry Meyers, Jan. 23, 1988; 1 child, Penelope Frances. Student, Chatham Coll., 1971-72; BA in English Lit. summa cum laude, U. Ariz., 1976; MLS, U. Md., 1978. Reference asst. Ligonier Pub. Libr., 1976; libr. Nat. Tech. Inst., Md., 1978; reference libr. Nat. Agrl. Libr., Beltsville, Md., 1978; libr. Costabile Assocs., Washington, 1978-82; libr. agr. and rural devel. dept. World Bank, Washington, 1982-84; cons. Logical Tech. Svcs. Corp., 1984-85, King Rsch., Inc., 1985; libr. Ministry of Agr., Lilongwe, Malawi, 1986-89; libr. cons. Washington, 1989—; cons. U.S. AID, Washington, 1983-85; nat. system rep. documentation symposium Consultative Group on Internat. Agrl. Rsch., Patancheru, India, 1989; lectr. Malawi Libr. Assn., Lilongwe, 1987-88; coord. course on agrl. librs. Commn. of EEC, Lilongwe, 1987; presenter Seminar on nat. Policy on Libr. and Info. Svcs., Lilongwe, 1987. Contbr. articles and conf. papers to profl. jours.; author: A Training Plan for Use of A.I.D.'s Development Information System, 1985; assoc. editor: Health Organizations of the U.S., Canada and Internationally, 4th edit., 1977; compiler of thesaurus for Vols. in Tech. Assistance, 1978. Scholar U. Ariz., 1975. Mem. Spl. Librs. Assn., Internat. Assn. Agrl. Librs. and Documentalists, U.S. Agrl. Info. Network, Internat. Fedn. Libr. Assns. and Insts., Phi Beta Kappa, Phi Kappa Phi. Democrat. Roman Catholic. Home and office: 508 7th St SE Washington DC 20003

MEYERS, JODIE ANN, consultant, writer; b. Chgo., July 23, 1954; d. Gerald Edwin and Linda Rae (Elder) M.; m. Frederick J. Morrison III, June 29, 1985; 1 child, Ann Marie. Student, Coll. of Du Page (Ill.), 1974-75. Estimator Clark & Barlow Hardware, Chgo., 1977; estimator, detailer Colo. Springs (Colo.) Supply, 1978, Circle Hardware, Chgo., 1979-84; warehouse mgr. DITTCO Products, Inc., Atlanta, 1984-87; purchasing agt., warehouse mgr. Piedmont Hardware, Atlanta, 1987-89; field sales mgr. DITTCO Products, Inc., Atlanta, 1989; cons., specification writer Waller Davis Assocs., Atlanta, 1989—. Speaker Nat. Abortion Rights Action League, Chgo., 1982-84. Mem. Door and Hardware Inst. (v.p. Ga. chpt. 1989—, sec. 1987-89, Paul Kelley scholarship 1988, Wm. A. Healy award 1986). Democrat. Roman Catholic. Home: 5903 Button Gwinnett Pl Norcross GA 30093

MEYERS, JOYCE SELBER, lawyer; b. Phila., Aug. 23, 1942; d. Samuel and Reba (Lampert) Selber; children: Jonathan R., Karen E.; m. Gerald F. Adams. BA summa cum laude, U. Pa., 1964, JD cum laude, 1980; MA, Syracuse (N.Y.) U., 1969. Bar: Pa. 1980, U.S. Dist. Ct. (ea. dist.) Pa. 1981, U.S. Ct. Appeals (3d cir.) 1981, U.S. Supreme Ct. 1986, U.S. Dist. Ct. (mid. dist.) Pa. 1989, U.S. Ct. Appeals (fed. cir.) 1989. Tchr. English East Syracuse-Manoa High Sch., 1964-68; instr. English Onondaga Community Coll., Syracuse, 1968-70; various part-time teaching positions Miami, Fla., 1970-73; advising coord. Minn. Higher Edn. Coordinating Commn., Rochester, 1974-76; assoc. Schnader, Harrison, Segal & Lewis, Phila., 1980-89, Cozen and O'Connor, Phila., 1989—; vol. atty. Women Against Abuse, Phila., 1982-89; bd. dirs. Support Ctr. for Child Advs., Phila. County conv. del. Dem. Party, Rochester, 1974-76. Mem. ABA, Pa. Bar Assn., Phila. Bar Assn., Phila. Assn. Def. Counsel, NOW, ACLU, Phi Beta Kappa. Office: Cozen and O'Connor 1900 Market St 3d Fl Philadelphia PA 19103

MEYERS, KAREN DIANE, lawyer, educator, insurance officer; b. Cin., July 8, 1950; d. Willard Paul and Camille Jeannette (Schutte) M.; m. William J. Jones, Mar. 27, 1977. BA summa cum laude, Thomas More Coll., 1971;

MBA, MEd, Xavier U., 1978; JD, U. Ky., Covington, 1978. Bar: Ohio 1978, Ky. 1981; CLU; CPCU 1987. Clk. to mgr. Baldwin Co., Cin., 1966-78; prof. instr. bus. Thomas More Coll., Crestview Hill, Ky., 1978—; asst. sec., asst. v.p., sr. counsel The Ohio Life Ins. Co., Hamilton, 1978—. Bd. dirs. ARC, Hamilton, 1978-83, vol. 1978—; bd. dirs. YWCA, Hamilton, 1985—. Gardner Found. fellow, 1968-71, CLU Am. Coll., 1981. Fellow Life Mgmt. Inst. Atlanta; mem. ABA, Soc. Property Casualty Underwriters, Cin. Bar Assn., Butler County Bar Assn. Roman Catholic. Home: 7903 Hickory Hill Ln Cincinnati OH 45241

MEYERS, KAREN LORAYNE DONNELL, rehabilition counselor; b. Augusta, Ga., Aug. 11, 1952; d. James Moncie and Ruby Lorayne (Bartlett) Donnell; m. Joseph Arthur Meyers, July 2, 1982. BA in Psychology, Augusta Coll., 1974. Instr. YWCA, Augusta, 1971, asst. dir. summer camp, 1971; recreation leader II, Gracewood State Sch. and Hosp., Ga., 1972-74, work therapist, 1974-84, med. librarian, 1984, work therapist, 1984-87, rehab. counselor, 1987—; investigator EEO devel. team, 1979-84; mem. women's guild Doctors Hosp., Augusta, 1982. Jr. bd. dirs. USO, Augusta, 1971; bd. dirs. Augusta Tng. Shop for Handicapped, 1979-80. Mem. Zeta Tau Alpha (Eta Mu chpt.). Republican. Episcopalian. Avocations: reading, sewing, gardening. Home: Rte 4 Box 262 Hephzibah GA 30815 Office: 1727 Wrightsboro Rd PO Box 12007 Augusta GA 30914-2007

MEYERS, LYNN BETTY, architect; b. Chgo., Dec. 2, 1952; d. William J. and Dorothy (King) M.; m. Dana Terp, May 17, 1975; children: Sophia, Rachel. Student, Royal Acad. Architecture, Copenhagen, Denmark, 1971; BArch, Washington U., St. Louis, 1974, MArch, 1977. Registered architect, Ill. Architect Holabird & Root Architects, Chgo., 1973, 76, Hist. Pullman Found., Chgo., 1975, Jay Alpert Architects, Woodbridge, Conn., 1976, City of Chgo. Bur. Architects, 1978-80; sole practice architecture Chgo., 1980-82; prin., architect Terp Meyers Architects, Chgo., 1982—. Exhbns. include: Centre George Pompidou, Paris, 1978, Fifth Internat. Congress Union Internat. Des Femmes Architects, Seattle, 1979, Frumkin Struve Gallery, Chgo., 1981, Art. Inst. Chgo., 1983, Inst. Francais d'Architecture, Paris, 1983, Mus. Sci. and Industry, Chgo., 1985; pub. in profl. jours. including Progressive Architecture, Modo Design, Inland Architect, 1984, Chgo. Archtl. Jour., 1983, L.A. Architect; work featured in various archtl. books; exhibited 150 Yrs. of Chgo. Architecture, Mus. Sci. and Industry, Chgo., 1985, Chgo. Women in Architecture - Progress and Evolution, Chgo. Hist. Soc., 1974-84. Recipient Progressive Architecture mag. award, 1980, citation Archtl. Design, 1980. Mem. AIA (task force com. for 1992 World's Fair, 1st place award L.A. Real Problems Competition 1986, Art By Architects award 1989, Art award 1990), Union Internat. Des Femmes Architects, Chgo. Women in Architecture (v.p. 1980-81, Allied Arts award 1974), Young Chgo. Architects. Office: Terp Meyers Architects 919 N Michigan Ave Chicago IL 60611

MEYERS, MAY LOU, associate psychologist, educational consultant; b. Austin, Tex., May 21, 1930; d. Ira William and Gertrude (Tebbs) Wilke; m. Carol Hansford Meyers, Mar. 22, 1951; children: Donna Michelle Spillers, Duane Randall. BA, U. Tex., 1951, MS, 1979. Lic. assoc. psychologist, Tex. Psychol. assoc. Charles T. Fries, Tyler, Tex., 1979-88; assoc. sch. psychologist Whitehouse (Tex.) Ind. Sch. Dist., 1980—. Mem. Am. Psychol. Assn., East Tex. Psychol. Assn., Phi Beta Kappa, Pi Lambda Theta. Presbyterian. Home: Rt 7 Box 176 Jacksonville TX 75766 Office: 615 S Broadway Tyler TX 75701

MEYERS, SHARON DEAN, lawyer; b. Munich, Germany, Oct. 27, 1953; d. A.M. Robert Dean and Jeanine (Marshall) Ablett; m. Andrew L. Meyers, Aug. 17, 1974; children: Andrew C.M., Jeffrey P.M. BS, U. Maryland, 1974; JD, Vermont Law Sch., 1979. Bar: Mass. 1979, U.S. Dist. Ct. 1979, U.S. Ct. Appeals (1st cir.) 1980, U.S. Ct. Appeals (4th cir.) 1989. Special edn. tchr. William Penn Sch. Dist., Lansdowne, Pa., 1974-76; asst. dist. attorney Suffolk County Dist. Attorney, Boston, 1979-81, Essex County Dist. Attorney, Salem, Mass., 1981-83; attorney Law Office of Richard D. Glovsky, Boston, 1983-86, Smith, McNulty & Kearney, Lynn, Mass., 1986–; delegate Am. Bar Assn., 1978-79; treas. Neighborhood Legal Services, Lynn, 1985–; lectr. Boston U., 1986-87. Co-author: Vermont Water Law & Rights, 1979. Clk. Lynn Youth Found., Mass., 1986-87, bd. mem. Family and Children's Svc. of Greater Lynn, Inc., 1989; trustee Atlanticare Med. Ctr., 1990—. Mem. Mass. Bar Assn., Women's Bar Assn. (dir. pub. relations 1984-86), Nat. Ski Patrol System, Kappa Delta Pi, Phi Delta Phi, Delta Gamma. Office: Smith McNulty and Kearney 150 Market St Lynn MA 01901

MEYERS, SHARON MAY, sales executive; b. Whittier, Calif., Feb. 8, 1946; d. Hubert Miller and Garnet May (Prater) Jones; m. Gary Lee Klink, June 18, 1966 (div.); children: Robert Douglas, Jeffrey Loren; m. Carl Eugene Meyers, Dec. 16, 1989. Student Pasadena Coll. (scholar), 1963-65; AA, Rio Hondo Coll., 1978; student Calif. State U.-Fullerton, 1978; BSBA, U. Redlands, 1982. Sec. Armorlite Lens Co., Pasadena, 1963-64, James, Pond & Clark, Pasadena, 1964-65; sales sec. Fiberboard Paper, Commerce, Calif., 1965-67; instr. aide East Whittier Sch. Dist., Calif., 1974-78; sales rep. Gen. Can Co., Montebello, Calif., 1978-86, Brouse-Whited Creative Packaging, Marina del Rey, Calif., 1986; br. mgr. Gen. Can Inc., Hayward, Calif., 1986-88; bus. banking mgr. Wells Fargo Bank, N.A., San Jose, Calif., 1988-89. Sec. ch. bd. Ch. of the Nazarene, 1973-76, children's dir., 1965-69; youth dir. Women's Christian Temperance Union, 1965-69; treas. P.T.A., 1977-79; bd. dirs. Bay Area Crisis Nursery, Concord, Calif.; vol. Valley Meml. Hosp. Emergency Room, Livermore, Calif. Mem. NAFE. Republican. Avocations: writing, golfing, snorkling, cooking. Office: Moore Bus Products 6050 Erin Park Dr Colorado Springs CO 80918

MEYERS, SUSAN MORAND, publishing executive, researcher; b. Harrisburg, Pa., June 10, 1957; d. Martin J. and Jean S. Morand; m. Frederic A. Meyers, Oct. 13, 1984. BA, Cornell U., 1979. Asst. v.p. Nat. WS Connect, Washington, 1982-83, Mercer-Meidinger, Inc., Pitts., 1984-85, Hay/Huggins Co., Inc., Phila., 1986—.

MEYERS-DAY, LINDA LEE, fund raising consultant; b. Covington, Ky., July 10, 1939; d. Ralph and Hester Elizabeth (McEndre) York; m. William Fay Walker, Aug. 16, 1959 (div. 1971; 1 child, William F.; m. Alan G. Meyers, May 1971. BS in Social Sci., 1970. Adminstrv. asst. Children's Home of Cin., 1973-76; modernization coordiantor State of La., New Orleans, 1978-87; devel. officer St. Michaels' Farm for Boys, Picayune, Miss., 1988-90; owner Leealan Enterprises, New Orleans, 1989—; preds. Les Petites Ecoles de la Novelle Orleans, New Orleans, 1977-88. Author: Study of the Homosexual Subculture, 1973; author poetry. Capt. U.S. Army, 1957-63. Recipient Freedom award, Freedom Found., 1958, Award of Merit, Internat. Assn. Rights of Children, 1960, Poets award, Nat. Poetry Assn., 1988. Democrat.

MEYER TRACY, CATHERINE MARIE, hospital planner; b. Green Bay, Wis., July 16, 1952; d. Edward Louis and Ursula Lorraine (Lauerman) Meyer; married, Dec. 1989. Student, U. Wis., Green Bay, 1973, U. Wis., 1979, 82-83; BA in Psychology, Newton and Boston Coll., 1975; MHA, Xavier U., 1985. Travel cons. Hemispheric Travel, Madison, Wis., 1976-76; pvt. practice real estate Madison, 1976-78; staff trainer United Cerebral Palsy, Madison, 1978; out-patient clinic coord. U. Wis. Hosps. and Clinics, Madison, 1979-82; adminstrv. resident The Jewish Hosp., Cin., 1985; dir. planning St. John's Hosp., Springfield, Ill., 1986—. Contbr. articles to profl. jours. Mem. Symphony Orch. Guild, Springfield, 1988—, Jr. League of Springfield, 1987—; vol. United Way of Sangamon County, Springfield, 1986—, cons. and planning coms., 1986—; bd. dirs. Land of Lincoln Girl Scout coun., Springfield, 1988—. Fedn. Am. Hosps. Found. scholar, 1984; recipient Vol. award United Way, 1985, 86, 87, 88, 89, Long Range Planning Assistance award Lincoln Land Epilepsy Assn., 1987. Mem. Am. Hosp. Assn.'s Soc. Healthcare Planning and Mktg. Roman Catholic.

MEYST, AMELIA SUE, public relations executive; b. Dallas, Nov. 15, 1946; d. Billy Bryan and Marilyn Lane (Hargis) Thorn; divorced; 1 child, Stuart Gardner Meyst. Founder, co-pub., editor Richmond (Va.) Lifestyle mag., 1974-79; dir. pub. relations Stuart Ford, Inc., Richmond, 1979-83, MRM Advt., Richmond, 1983-85; pres. A.S. Meyst & Co. Advt., Richmond, 1985-86; sr. account exec. The Martin Agy., Richmond, 1986—. Founder/editor The Richmond Guidebook, 1978, 79. Recipient Addy award for copywriting Advt. Club Richmond, 1985. Mem. Pub. Relations Soc. Am. (v.p., program chmn. Old Dominion chpt. 1980-81). Office: The Martin Agy 500 N Allen Richmond VA 23220

MICELI, MOTHER IGNATIUS, missionary sister; b. N.Y.C., Mar. 14, 1918; d. Joseph and Cecelia (Torre) M. BS, Regis Coll.; MEd, Loyola U., New Orleans; M Religious Edn., Seattle U.; postgrad., U. Denver, 1968-69. Coordinator religious programs All Souls Ch., Englewood, Colo., 1968-71, dir. home instr. for adults, 1971-72, dir. adult edn., 1972—; dir. religious edn. Assumption, Welby, Colo., 1973-77, Holy Cross, Thornton, Colo., 1971-73; instr. religion various missions, 1968—. Author: (poems) Leaves Of Thought, 1980, Random Thoughts and Meditations, 1968, Colorado and St. Francis Xavier Cabrini, M.S.C., poetry and photography book Life's Seasons; VCR The Life of Mother Cabrini, The History and Meditations on the Rosary. Mem. Internat. Bibl. Assn., Religious Edn. Assn. U.S., Religious Edn. Assn. Can., Kappa Delta Pi. Home: Cabrini Shrine Golden CO 80401 Office: All Souls Ch Religious Edn Office 435 Pennwood Circle Englewood CO 80110

MICHAEL, CONNIE ELIZABETH TREXLER, account executive; b. Charlotte, N.C., Nov. 26, 1945; d. Jack P. and Patricia (Doolan) Trexler; m. William Michael, July 23, 1966 (sep. Mar. 1989); children: Brent P., Christopher Paul. Student, U. N.C., Greensboro, 1963-65. Retail store owner The Casual Closet, Falls Church, Va., 1967-70; advt. dir. Roscoe Griffin Shoes, Raleigh, N.C., 1977-80; account exec. The Rockport Co., Marlboro, Mass., 1980-89, Deer Stags Inc., N.Y.C., 1990—. Mem. Nat. Shoe Travelers Assn., Southeastern Shoe Travelers Assn. Office: 4212 Wingate Dr Raleigh NC 27609

MICHAEL, DOROTHY ANN, nurse, naval officer; b. Lancaster, Pa., Sept. 20, 1950; d. Richard Linus and Mary Ruth (Hahn) Michael. Diploma, R.N., Montgomery Hosp. Sch. Nursing, Norristown, Pa., 1971; BS in Nursing, George Mason U., 1980; MS in Nursing U. Tex. Health Sci. Ctr., 1985. Commd. ensign U.S. Navy, 1970, advanced through grades to comdr. Nurse Corps, 1989; staff nurse Nat. Naval Med. Ctr., Bethesda, Md., 1971-73; charge nurse Naval Hosp., Guantanamo Bay, Cuba, 1973-74, Naval Regional Med. Ctr., Phila., 1974-76, Naval Hosp., Keflavik, Iceland, 1977, Naval Hosp., Bethesda, 1980-84, sr. nurse, asst. officer-in-charge Br. Med. Clinic, Naval Weapons Ctr., China Lake, Calif., 1986-89; coord. quality assurance Naval Hosp., Oakland, Calif., 1989—; splty. advisor to dir. Navy Nurse Corp., Navy Med. Command, Washington, 1983-84. V.p. Deepwood Homeowners Assn., Reston, Va., 1978-82; advisor, com. mem. Reston Found., 1979. Recipient R.W. Bjorklund Mgmt. Innovator award Kern County, Calif., 1988, Comdr.'s Award for Outstanding Professionalism in Pub. Health Support, 1988. Mem. NAFE, Calif. Soc. for Nursing Service Adminstrs., Am. Public Health Assn., Vietnam Vets Am., Nat. Assn. Quality Assurance Profls., Am. Nurses Assn. (cert. nursing adminstrn.), Sigma Theta Tau. Roman Catholic. Home: 2510 Lynn Ave Concord CA 94520

MICHAEL, MARY AMELIA, headmaster; m. Eugene G. Michael; children: David, Douglas, Gregory. BA, Albertus Magnus Coll.; MS, U. Bridgeport, 1975; CAS, Fairfield U., 1982. Cert. secondary sch. sci. tchr., ednl. adminstr. Housemaster, sci. tchr. Fairfield (Conn.) Pub. Schs., adminstrv. housemaster. Contbr. articles to profl. jours. Mem. AAUW, LWV, Conn. Assn. Suprs. and Curriculum, Fairfield Sch. Adminstrs. Assn. Home: 942 Valley Rd Fairfield CT 06432 Office: 760 Stilson Rd Fairfield CT 06430

MICHAEL, PHYLLIS CALLENDER, composer; b. nr. Berwick, Pa., Dec. 24, 1908; d. Bruce Miles and Emma (Harvey) Callender; grad. Bloomsburg Coll., 1928; B. Mus., U. Extension Conservatory, Chgo., 1953; m. Arthur L. Michael, Aug. 21, 1933; children: Robert Bruce, Keith Winton. Elem. tchr. Berwick Schs., 1928-33; substitute tchr. Shickshinny and Northwest Area, Pa., 1954-66; tchr. Northwest Area High Sch., 1966-71; gen. tchr. piano, organ, theory and voice, 1943—; hymnwriter, poet, author, composer, 1943—. Recipient first place in Nat. Favorite Hymns contest for Take Thou My Hand, 1953, Cert. of Merit for disting. service to composition outstanding hymns, 1967, and others. Adv. mem. MBLS. Mem. Nat. Ret. Tchrs. Assn., Internat. Platform Assn., Nat. Soc. Lit. and the Arts, Hymn Soc. Am. Author: Poems for Mothers, 1963, Poems From My Heart, 1964, Beside Still Waters, 1970, Fun to Do Showers, 1971, Bridal Shower Ideas, 1972, Is my Head on Straight, 1976, This Is Christmas, 1985, Quotes, 1986, Surely Goodness and Mercy, 1986, Hi, Lord!, 1987, Bright Tomorrows, 1989; contbr. songs, articles, poems to books, hymn-books, booklets, mags. Address: Oak Haven RFD 3 Shickshinny PA 18655

MICHAEL, SANDRA DALE, professor of reproductive endocrinology; b. Sacramento, Calif., Jan. 23, 1945; d. Gordon G. and Ruby F. (Johnson) M.; m. Dennis P. Murr, Aug. 12, 1967 (div. 1974). BA, Calif. State Coll., Sonoma, 1967; PhD, U. Calif., Davis, 1970. NIH postdoctoral fellow U. Calif., Davis, 1970-73, asst. rsch. geneticist, 1973-74; asst. prof. SUNY, Binghamton, 1974-81, assoc. prof., 1981-88, prof. reproductive endocrinology, 1988—; cons. in field; grant reviewer NIH, NSF, USDA and others; presenter in field. Contbr. articles to profl. jours. Vice chair Tri Cities Opera Guild, Binghamton, 1987-90, chair 1990—; mem. Harpur Forum, Binghamton, 1987—, SUNY Found., Binghamton, 1990—. Grantee NIMH, 1976-79, Nat. Cancer Inst., 1977-80, 83-87, Nat. Inst. Environ. Health Scis., 1979-80, NSF, 1981-83, NIH, 1987—. Mem. Endocrine Soc., Soc. for the Study of Reproduction, Soc. for the Study of Fertility, Am. Soc. for the Immunology of Reproduction, Soc. for Exptl. Biology and Medicine, N.Y. Acad. Sci., Sigma Xi. Office: Dept Biol Scis SUNY Binghamton NY 13901

MICHAEL, SUZANNE, state agency administrator, sociologist; b. Ft. Bragg, N.C., Feb. 21, 1951; d. Walter Otto and Carola (Nussbaum) M. BA, SUNY, Binghampton, 1973; MS, Columbia U., 1976; postgrad., CUNY, 1982—. With Downstate Med. Ctr., Bkyn., 1976-84, dir. treatment, 1981-83, chief social worker, 1981-84; dir. interagy. affairs Bur. Sch. Children & Adolescent N.Y.C. Dept. Health, 1984-89, dir. program devel. and community affairs subdiv. Child &, 1989—; co-founder, co-chair N.Y.C. Social Workers Coop., 1976-82; cons. People Against Sexual Abuse, Bklyn., 1985-87; N.Y.C. Bd. Edn., 1988-89; mem. N.Y.C. HIV Rev. Panel, 1985—; coord. N.Y.C. Pediatric HIV Adv. Unit, 1987—. Mem. social svc. bd. N.Y. Soc. for Ethnical Culture, N.Y.C., 1982-88; v.p. for programs N.Y. Soc. for Ethical Culture, N.Y.C., 1984-88. NIMH grantee, 1977. Mem. Am. Pub. Health Assn., Phi Beta Kappa. Home: 160 W 71st St New York NY 10023 Office: NYC Dept Health 125 Worth St Box 25 New York NY 10013

MICHAEL, (MARIE) TONI (ANTONIETTE), technical writer; b. Torrance, Calif., May 24, 1941; d. Charles Philip and Ethel Lucille (Raley) M.; m. Donald Allen Griffin, Nov. 16, 1962 (div. July 1977); children: Donald Kristin, Eric Blair, Patrick Michael; m. Willard Earl Myers, May 5, 1978 (div. June 1981). BA, San Diego State U., 1975. Adminstrv. asst. Nat. Semicondr., Santa Clara, Calif., 1976-77; tech. writer Computer Scis. Corp., San Diego, 1977-80; cons. on tech. and bus. writing, San Diego, 1980-85, 87-89; tech. writer Siltronix, San Diego, 1985-87, Systems Engrng. & Mgmt. Co., San Diego, 1989—; workshop leader Writers Bookstore and Haven, San Diego, 1987-88. Co-author: Algorithms for Personal Computing, 1986, Parents' Guide to Educational Software and Computers, 1989; contbr. articles to newspapers and mags. Mem. Mid-City Community Orch., San Diego, 1982—. Mem. Writers Haven, Rosicrucian Order. Democrat. Office: SEMCO 8525 Gibbs Dr Ste 304 San Diego CA 92123

MICHAELIS, MARGARET HELMLY, sales executive; b. Savannah, Ga., Aug. 20, 1961; d. Hugh Lee III and Margaret (Westberry) Helmly; m. Scott Lee Michaelis, May 28, 1988. BA, U. Ga., 1983; MBA, Breneau U., Gainesville, Ga., 1987. In sales Marshall Industries, Norcross, Ga., 1984-85, Tools Systems Inc., Tucker, Ga., 1985-87; dist. sales mgr. Knotts Co., Berkeley Hts., N.J., 1987—. Contbr. articles to newsletters. Mem. Nat. Orgn. for Female Execs. Presbyterian.

MICHAELSON, RUTH LENORE, magazine publishing company executive; b. Arlington Hts., Ill., Jan. 22, 1961; d. Robert Thomas and Lenore Lucille (Simons) M. BA in Communications, Colligiate Inst., London, 1985. Sec. ACBI Architects, Rolling Meadows, Ill., 1985-86; data entry asst. CTi, Carol Stream, Ill., 1986-87, data entry supr., 1987-88, subscription svcs. supr., 1988-89, circulation mgr., 1989—; circulation mgr. North Shore Mag., Winnetka, Ill., 1989—. Mem. NAFE. Office: North Shore Magazine 874 Green Bay Rd Winnetka IL 60193

MICHAK, HELEN BARBARA, educator, nurse; b. Cleve., July 31; d. Andrew and Mary (Patrick) M. Diploma Cleve. City Hosp. Sch. Nursing, 1947; BA, Miami U., Oxford, Ohio, 1951; MA, Case Western Res. U., 1960. Staff nurse Cleve. City Hosp., 1947-48; pub. health nurse Cleve. Div. Health, 1951-52; instr. Cleve. City Hosp. Sch. Nursing, 1952-56; supr. nursing Cuyahoga County Hosp., Cleve., 1956-58; pub. information dir. N.E. Ohio Am. Heart Assn., Cleve., 1960-64; dir. spl. events Higbee Co., Cleve., 1964-66; exec. dir. Cleve. Area League for Nursing, 1966-72; dir. continuing edn. nurses, adj. assoc. prof. Cleve. State U., 1972-86. Trustee N.E. Ohio Regional Med. Program, 1970-73; mem. adv. com. Dept. Nursing Cuyahoga Community Coll., 1967-87; mem. long term care com. Met. Health Planning Corp., 1974-76, plan devel. com. 1977—; mem. policy bd. Ctr. Health Data N.E. Ohio, 1972-73; mem. Rep. Assembly and Health Planning and Devel. Commn., Welfare Fedn. Cleve., 1967-72, Cleve. Community Health Network, 1972-73, United Appeal Films and Speakers Bur., 1967-73; mem. adv. com. Ohio Fedn. Lic. Practical Nurses, 1970-73; mem. tech. adv. com. TB and Respiratory Disease Assn. Cuyahoga County, 1967-74; mem. Ohio Commn. on Nursing, 1971-74; mem. citizens com. nursing homes Fedn. Community Planning, 1973-77; mem. com. on home health services Met. Health Planning Corp., 1973-75; mem. profl. adv. com. on home care Fairview Gen. Hosp., 1987, 88, 89. Mem. Nat. League Nursing (mem. com. 1970-72), Am. Nurses Assn. (accreditation visitor 1977-78, 83-88) Ohio Nurses Assn., (com. continuing edn. 1974-79, 82-84, 89—, chmn. 1984-85), Greater Cleve. (joint practice com. 1973-74, trustee 1975-76) Nurses Assn., Cleve. Area Citizens League for Nursing (trustee 1976-79, v.p. 1988-90), Zeta Tau Alpha. Home and Office: 4686 Oakridge Dr North Royalton OH 44133

MICHALS, LEE MARIE, travel agency executive; b. Chgo., June 6, 1939; d. Harry Joseph and Anna Marie (Monaco) Perzan; children: Debora Ann, Dana Lee, Jami. BA, Wright Coll., 1959. Internat. travel sec. E.F. MacDonald Travel, Palo Alto, Calif., 1963-69; pres. Travel Experience, Santa Clara, Calif., 1973-87, ret., 1987; ptnr. Cruise Connection, Mountain View, Calif., 1983-85 . Mem. Am. Soc. Travel Agts., Inst. Cert. Travel Agts., Bay Area Travel Assn., Pacific Area Travel Agts., San Jose Women in Travel (1st v.p. 1989). Office: Travel Experience 2975 Bowers Ave #102 Santa Clara CA 85051 also: 1622 El Camino Real Mountain View CA 94040

MICHALSKI, CELESTE C., manufacturing executive; b. 1942. BS, Amherst Coll., 1964; MBA, U. Pa., 1966. With Arthur Andersen, 1966-75, Hueblein, Inc., 1975-79; dir. acctg. controls of packaging group Am. Can Co., 1979-82, corp. dir. budgets & analysis, 1982-83, asst. corp. contr., 1983-85, v.p., asst. corp. contr., 1985-88; v.p., contr. Gencorp, Inc., Akron, Ohio, 1988—. Office: Gencorp Inc 175 Ghent Rd Akron OH 44313*

MICHALSKI, KAREN MARIE, veterinarian; b. Detroit, Oct. 14, 1960; d. Lawrence and Jeanette Mary (Kiwicz) M. BS in Biochemistry, Oakland U., 1982; DVM, Mich. State U., 1987. Staff veterinarian Humane Soc. Animal Clinic, Utica, Mich., 1987-88, North Suburban Vet. Hosp., Sterling Heights, Mich., 1988, Profl. Vet. Hosps., Madison Heights, Mich., 1988-89; owner, veterinarian St. Francis Animal Hosp., Utica, 1989—. Musician St. Edmund's Cath. Ch., Warren, Mich., 1987-89; folk music dir. St. Athanasius Cath. Ch., Fraser, Mich., 1989. Mem. AVMA, Mich. Vet. Med. Assn. Office: St Francis Animal Hosp 16611 21 Mile Rd Utica MI 48087

MICHAM, NANCY SUE, information systems executive; b. Toledo, May 15, 1956; d. Charles Edward and Dorothy Ruth (Bittner) Linker; m. Donald Thomas Kerner, June 20, 1975 (div. June 1980); m. Ray David Micham, III, May 19, 1984; 1 child, Brittni Mae. AS with high honors, U. Toledo, 1980; BSM cum laude, Pepperdine U., 1983. Cert. systems profl.; cert. aerobics instr. Programmer, Owens-Ill., Toledo, 1973-80; programmer analyst Smith Tool Co., Irvine, Calif., 1980-82; systems analyst Denny's, Inc., La Mirada, Calif., 1982-83; sr. corp. systems analyst, mgr. corp. systems group Libbey-Owens-Ford Co., Toledo, 1983-86, pres. Seagate Systems Cons., 1986—. Participant ToledoScape. Mem. Nat. Mgmt. Assn., Assn. Systems Mgmt., Inst. for Cert. of Systems Profls., NAFE. Republican. Roman Catholic. Avocations: travel, backpacking, bicycling.

MICHAUD, NORMA ALICE, real estate renovator; b. Concord, N.H., May 6, 1946; d. Leon Charles and Goldie May (Maxfield) Palmer; m. Bob Michaud, July 21, 1973; 1 child, Derrick Charles. Grad., Concord Sr. High Sch. With adminstrn. ins. industry United Life & Accident Ins. Co., Concord, N.H., 1965-68, 71-74; data processor ins. industry Blue Cross/Blue Shield, Concord, 1968-71; adminstr. fed. agy. U.S. Govt., Ger., 1976—; house renovator, 1988—. Nominee Pub. Svc. award GEICO, 1989. Mem. NAFE, Nat. Wildlife Assn., PACE Lit. Soc., Nat. Geographic Soc., Non-Commd. Officers Club. Methodist.

MICHEL, BARBARA RULE, sales executive; b. Wilmington, Del., Mar. 22, 1957; d. Joseph McBath and Jean Elizabeth (Tuckerman) R. BS in Biology, Emory U., 1979; MBA in Mktg., Ga. State U., 1982. Research analyst Majers Corp., Atlanta, 1982-83; mgr. market research Stone Mfg. Co., Greenville, S.C., 1983-85; asst. mgr. sales research L'eggs Products, Inc., Winston-Salem, N.C., 1985-88, mgr. sales forecasting, 1988—; cons. Edwards Baking Co., Atlanta, 1982. Vol. Big Sister Program. Mem. Am. Mktg. Assn., Alpha Mu Alpha, Chi Omega (pres. chpt. 1978-79, sec. 1977-78). Club: Symphony Chorale (Winston-Salem). Avocations: singing, ice skating, swimming, sports. Office: L'eggs Products Inc 5660 University Pkwy Winston-Salem NC 27105

MICHEL, HARDING BOEHME, marine biology educator; b. Louisville, Aug. 17, 1924; d. Henry Oscar and Mary Cornell (Inman) Boehme; m. Oscar Theodore Owre, Aug. 4, 1948 (div. 1967); 1 child, Caroline Harding Owre; m. John Field Michel, Nov. 24, 1970. BS, Duke U., 1946; MS, U. Miami, Coral Gables, Fla., 1949; PhD, U. Mich., 1957. Instr. U. Miami, Coral Gables, Fla., 1952-56, asst. prof., 1957-67, assoc. prof., 1967-70, prof., 1970-84, prof. emeritus, 1984—; cons. com. on the effects of herbicides in Vietnam NAS, Washington, 1972-74, Batelle Meml. Inst., Seattle, 1977-78, Fla. Inst. for Oceanography, St. Petersburg, 1980-81, Lawrence Berkeley lab. U. Calif., Berkeley, 1980-81; scientist Kuwait Inst. for Sci. Rsch., 1979-82. Author: Copepods of the Florida Current, 1967, The Free-Living Lower Invertebrates, 1968, Caribbean Zooplankton, 1976; contbr. articles to profl. jours. Rsch. grantee NSF, NIH, Office of Naval Rsch., 1964-76. Mem. Marine Biol. Assn. of the UK, Internat. Oceanographic Found., Key Biscayne Yacht Club, Kappa Kappa Gamma, Phi Beta Kappa, Sigma Xi. Republican. Home: 5000 Hammock Lake Dr Miami FL 33156 Office: U Miami Rosenstiel Sch Marine and Atmospheric Sci 4600 Rickenbacker Causeway Miami FL 33149

MICHEL, MABLE SOUDELIER, health facility nurse administrator; b. Houma, La., Nov. 17, 1951; d. Alton Paul and Mable (Falgout) Soudelier; m. Michael S. Russell, Aug. 11, 1970 (div. 1982); m. Hilton J. Michel, Dec. 6, 1986. AS in Nursing, Nicholls State U., 1975, BSN, 1989; postgrad., Tulane U. Cert. nurse adminstr. Staff RN ICU Terrebonne Gen. Med. Ctr., Houma, 1975-79, head nurse ICU, 1979-82, unit coord., 1982-84, asst. dir. nursing, 1984-86, dir. nursing, 1986—; bd. dirs. South La. Vocat. Tech. Sch. for Lic. Practical Nurses. Mem. Am. Nursing Assn., Thibodeaux Dist. Nurses Assn. (bd. dirs.), La. Hosp. Assn. of Nurse Execs. Democrat. Roman Catholic.

MICHEL, MARY LYNN, financial analyst; b. Pitts., June 13, 1962; d. Robert Earl and Elaine Regina (Mielcarek) M.; m. Brian Joseph Conboy, May 9, 1988. BSBA, Duquesne U., 1984; MBA, Carnegie-Mellon U., 1986; doctoral student, Columbia U., 1990—. Asst. mgr. Chem. Bank, N.Y.C., 1986-87; asst. v.p. Scudder Stevens & Clark, N.Y.C., 1988-90; student curriculum reviewer Carnegie-Mellon U., Pitts., 1986. Vol., Epiphany Ch. Elderly Assistance, N.Y.C., 1989-90. Recipient Fin. Exec.'s Inst. award, 1984; Arthur Carter scholar Am. Acctg. Assn., 1985, Herb Finney scholar Delta Sigma Pi, U. Pitts., 1984. Mem. Nat. Assn. Accts., NAFE, Mensa. Home: 558 W 113th St Apt 1B New York NY 10025 Office: Columbia U Grad Sch of Bus New York NY 10027

MICHEL, SHARON LEE, systems and programming executive; b. Waterloo, Wis., Dec. 23, 1946; d. Charles Raymond and Harriet Agatha (Sheridan) M. BS, U. Wis., Stevens Point, 1969. Systems analyst Employee Trust Funds State of Wis., Madison, 1976-79, dir. systems mgmt. bur., 1979-84, chief applications devel. Natural Resources, 1984—. Vice chmn. orgn. Dem. Party Dane County, Madison, 1986, co-chmn., 1987-88; mem. Dem. Party Wis. Elections Commn., 1988-90; elected ward com. women Dem. Party, 1989-90; mem. Nat. Women's Polit. Caucus-Dane County; co-chmn. Polit. Action Com., 1989—. Mem. NAFE, Data Processing Mgmt. Assn. (v.p., sec. so. Wis. chpt. 1983, v.p. 1984, Individual Performance award 1985, exec. v.p. 1989, pres. 1990), NOW. Democrat. Roman Catholic. Home: 4849 Sheboygan Ave #319 Madison WI 53705 Office: Resources State Wis PO Box 7921 Madison WI 53707

MICHELINI, SYLVIA HAMILTON, auditor; b. Decatur, Ala., May 16, 1946; d. George Borum and Dorothy Rose (Swatzell) Hamilton; m. H. Stewart Michelini, June 4, 1964; children: Stewart Anthony, Cynthia Leigh. BSBA summa cum laude, U. Ala., Huntsville, 1987. Acct. Ray McCay, CPA, Huntsville, 1987-88; auditor Def. Contract Audit Agy., Huntsville, 1989—. Mem. Exec. Bd. Decatur City PTA, 1976-78; pres., v.p. Elem. Sch. PTA, Decatur, 1977-79; leader Girl Scouts Am. and Cub Scouts, Decatur, 1972-77; active in local ARC, 1973-77, Decatur Civic Band, 1989—. Mem. Nat. Assn. Accts. (dir. commmunity svc. 1987-88, v.p. adminstrn. and fin. 1988-89, pres. 1989-90), Am. Soc. Women Accts. (chpt. treas. 1989-90, dir. chpt. devel. 1989-90), Assn. Govt. Accts., AAUW (chpt. treas. 1988-90), Inst. Internat. Auditors, Phi Kappa Phi. Baptist. Home: 2801 Sylvia Dr SE Decatur AL 35603 Office: Def Contract Audit Agy 107 Jefferson St Huntsville AL 35801

MICHELMAN, PEGGY CRYSTAL, financial planner, consultant; b. N.Y.C., Dec. 27, 1932; d. Clement S. and Beatrice F. (Moss) Crystal; m. Charles D. Michelman (dec. Aug. 1981); children: David, Beth Gross, Jill Pappas, Amy. BA in History, Wheaton Coll., 1954. With personnel dept., asst. buyer R.H. Macy & Co., N.Y.C., 1954-56; dist. adminstr. Congressman Ogden R. Reid, White Plains, N.Y., 1962-74; ptnr. Reid, Michelman & Assocs., White Plains, 1974-85; sr. adminstr. Circle Cons. Group, Inc., N.Y.C., 1985—. Bd. dirs., mem. govt. rels. com. Blythedale Children's Hosp., Valhalla, N.Y., 1988—; bd. dirs., treas. North Castle Pub. Library, Armonk, N.Y., 1987—; bd. dirs., chmn. New Orch. of Westchester, Valhalla, 1987—, chmn., 1990—; bd. dirs. United Way of Westchester, White Plains, 1979-85. Mem. Fin. Women's Assn. of N.Y. Democrat. Jewish. Home: 29 N Lake Rd Armonk NY 10504 Office: Circle Cons Group Inc 600 Third Ave New York NY 10016-1903

MICHELS, CAROLL CHESY, artist career consultant, writer; b. Washington, Mar. 3, 1943; d. Max M. and Billie (Gordon) Chesy. Student, Richmond Profl. Inst., 1961. Co-founder, dir., artist Haus-Rucker, Inc., N.Y.C., 1969-78; artist career cons. N.Y.C., 1978—; dir. 4th Internat. Festival Films on Architecture and Planning, N.Y.C., 1982-84; lectr. New Sch. for Social Rsch., N.Y.C., 1987-88. Author: How To Survive and Prosper as an Artist, 1983, rev. edit., 1988; contbg. editor Art Calendar, , 1989—; exhibited in group shows Walker Art Ctr., Mpls., 1971, Georges Pompidou Ctr., Paris, 1977, Inst. for Art and Urban Resources, N.Y.C., 1988. N.Y. Coun. for Humanities grantee, 1983, Internat. Fund for Promotion Culture-UNESCO grantee, 1983, Nat. Endowment for Arts grantee, 1973, 82, N.Y. State Coun. for Arts grantee, 1976, 83; fellow Alden B. Dow Creativity Ctr., Northwood Inst., Midland, Mich., 1990. Home and Office: 491 Broadway 11th Fl New York NY 10012

MICHELSON, PAMULA KAY, clinical psychologist; b. Ft. Dodge, Iowa, July 4, 1953; d. Loren Eugene Lumsden and Janis Lee (Nylander) Enfield; m. Richard Albert Michelson, Mar. 30, 1984; children: Stacy Pamela, Dawn Marie. BA summa cum laude, U. Minn., 1979; MA, Kent State U., 1983, PhD, 1987. Lic. clin. psychologist, Ohio. Intern VA Hosp., Cleve., 1986-87; dir. Kevin Coleman Mental Health Ctr., Kent, Ohio, 1988—; adj. prof. Kent State U., 1989—; trustee Akron (Ohio) Child Guidance Ctr., 1986—, Summit County Mental Health Assn., Cuyahoga Falls, Ohio, 1988-89; orgn. founder ADD Family Support Group, Akron, 1987—; bd. dirs. Child Sexual Abuse Com., Kent, 1988—; presenter at profl. confs. Dir. circle Akron Art Mus., 1990. NIMH fellow, 1981-82. Mem. Am. Psychol. Assn., Ohio Psychol. Assn., Akron Area Profl. Psychologists, Summit County Mental Health Assn., Akron Jr. League. Home: 705 Merriman Rd Akron OH 44303 also: Res Psychol Cons 421 Graham Rd Cuyahoga Falls OH 44221

MICHETTI, SUSAN JANE, print media specialist; b. Kenosha, Wis., Dec. 20, 1948. BA cum laude, U. Wis., 1981; Cert. A, B, C for real estate law, appraisal and mktg., Gateway Tech. Inst., Kenosha, 1979; postgrad., Carthage Coll., Kenosha, 1984. Lic. real estate appraiser, Wis. Project dir. Big Bros./Big Sisters of Kenosha County, Wis., 1978-79; tchr. Kenosha Unified Sch. Dist., 1979-84; newspaper editor U. Wis., Parkside, 1980-81; news reporter Milw. Sentinel, 1982-83; news reporter, newscaster Sta. WRJN Radio, Racine, Wis., 1982-84; quar. report writer, editor, designer Kenosha Unified Sch. Dist., 1983-84; book editorial and prodn. coord. McDougal, Littel Co., Skokie, Ill., 1985, Scott, Foresman and Co., Glenview, Ill., 1985-88; proprietor Michetti Multi-Media Assocs., Kenosha, 1971—; instr. profl. devel. U. Wis., Parkside, 1988-89; fin. svcs. editor Phillips Pub., 1986-87, 90—; mng. editor Nat. News Syndicate, Washington, 1982-89; cons. in field. Contbr. articles to profl. jours. Media coord. Tony Earl Gov. campaign, Kenosha, 1982; media cons. Friends of Peter Barca for State Legis., Kenosha, 1985—; art fair asst. Friends of Kenosha Pub. Mus., 1986—; prog. devel. com. Racine Hist. Soc. and Pub. Mus., 1984-85. Scholar, Kenosha Found., 1979-81, Kenneth L. Greenquist, 1980, Vilas, 1968-71, Ida D. Altemus, 1969-70. Mem. NAFE, Am. Soc. Profl. and Exec. Women, Nat. Writers Union, Internat. Soc. Unified Sci., Nat. Audubon Soc., Sierra Club (BiNat. Gt. Lakes com. 1990—, vice chair S.E. Gateway Group 1990—, conservation chmn. 1983-86, chmn. water toxics 1988-89, chmn. air toxics 1988-89). Home and Office: Michetti Multi-Media Assocs PO Box 54 Kenosha WI 53141

MICHIE, MARY, sculptor; b. Ripon, Wis., Aug. 8, 1922; d. Don and Frances Miller; m. Norman D. Michie, Dec. 23, 1943; children: Peter, Christopher, Sarah, Adam. BA cum laude, Ripon Coll., 1943; studied sculpture, Cen. Sch. Art, London, 1949-52; MA in Art Edn., U. Wis., 1962. narrator Music Lady Sta. WHA, 1953-60; project asst. U. Wis. extension, 1963-67, art specialist, 1973-77, instr. Rhinelander Sch. Arts, 1978, 79, 80; art researcher, Kenya, East Africa, 1967-71; cons. and lectr. in field. One-woman shows include Wright Warehouse Mus., 1978; exhibited in group shows at Fanny Garver Gallery, 1981, Pillsbury Midwest Juried Exhibition, 1981, Seuferer-Chosy Gallery, 1983, Artspirit Sings, 1989-91; represented in permanent collections Milw. Art Mus., Rahr-West Mus., Madison Art Ctr.; prin. works include bronze sculpture for Marshfield Health Clin., Pub. Libr. Tomah, Wis. Sch. Visually Handicapped; contbr. articles to profl. jours. Home: 212 Bordner Dr Madison WI 53705

MICHLIN, ROSE ANN, banker; b. Wilmington, Del., Jan. 1, 1952; d. Jesse J. and Hedwig R. (Babicki) Karpinski; m. Stephen H. Michlin, Feb. 2, 1973; children: Nathan, Sarah. Student, U. Del., 1980-85. Account svcs. rep. to intermediate return items clk. Del. Trust Co., Wilmington, 1969-74; supr. account svcs. to mgr., asst. v.p. demand deposits Wilmington Savs. Fund Soc., Wilmington, 1974-85; customer svc. supr. M Bank U.S.A., Wilmington, 1985-86; instr. Del. Tech. Community Coll., Wilmington, 1987-88; asst. v.p. Barclays Bank of Del., Wilmington, 1988—. Democrat. Jewish. Office: Barclays Bank of Del 1405 Foulk Rd Wilmington DE 19803

MICHUDA, NANCY MARIE, child developmental psychologist; b. Chgo., Aug. 17, 1956; d. Anton George and Lorraine Josephine (King) M. BA, U. Notre Dame, 1978; postgrad., U. Fla., 1980; MS, U. Miami, Fla., 1986, PhD, 1986. Asst. tchr., family counselor St. Vincent De Paul Children's Ctr., Chgo., 1978-79; rsch. assoc. Shands Teaching Hosp./U. Fla., Gainesville, 1980-81, Mailman Ctr. Child Devel./Jackson Meml. Hosp., Miami, 1981-82; dir. in-hosp. devel. svcs. U. Miami Med. Ctr./Mailman Ctr./Jackson Meml. Hosp., Miami, 1982-84; project dir. U. Miami Med. Sch./Jackson Meml. Hosp., 1984-85; rsch. cons., mgmt. rev. specialist State of Fla., Tallahassee, 1986-87; psychol. resident Psychol. Specialists, P.A., Miami, 1987—; program dir. cons. child evaluation program North Shore Med. Ctr., Miami, 1987—; exec. bd. Fla. Consortium of Newborn Intervention Programs, Orlando, 1982—; instr. dept. psychology U. Miami, 1984; co-author Fla. Statutes Bill Amendment, Sect. 2, Sec. H11.1071, 1987; design monitor team mem. State of Fla. Competency Rsch. Project, Tallahassee, 1989-90. Notre Dame Meml. scholar, 1989-90. Mem. Am. Psychol. Assn., Fla. Perinatal Assn., Assn. for Children with Learning Disabilities, U. Notre Dame Alumni Assn., Notre Dame Club Palm Beach, Perinatal Network South Fla., Assn. for Care of Children in Hosps., Phi Kappa Phi. Roman Catholic.

MICK, DIANE JOAN, nurse; b. Pottsville, Pa., June 21, 1955; d. Stanley Philip and Helen Josephine (Padrazas) M. BA, West Chester (Pa.) U., 1977; AS in Nursing, Gwynedd-Mercy Coll., 1983, MS in Nursing, 1991. Critical Care RN, Pa. Instr. music Braun Sch. Music, Pottsville, 1978-79; nurse Sacred Heart Hosp., Norristown, Pa., 1983; critical care nurse Grand View Hosp., Sellersville, Pa., 1983-84, Montgomery Hosp., Norristown, Pa., 1984—. Mem. Am. Assn. Critical Care Nurses, Gamma Theta Upsilon. Democrat. Roman Catholic. Home: 28 Bittersweet Ct Norristown PA 19403-2904 Office: Montgomery Hosp Powell and Fornance Sts Norristown PA 19401

MICK, MARGARET ANNE, communication executive; b. Phila., Apr. 24, 1947; d. Charles Philip and Helen Margaret (Amig) Maurer; m. Donald Kenneth Mick, Sept. 8, 1979. BS with honors, Pa. State U., 1969; MA, NYU, 1972. Assoc. producer Visual Edn. Corp., Princeton, N.J., 1972-73; program devel. specialist AEtna Life & Casualty, Hartford, Conn., 1973-78; sr. program devel. specialist AEtna Life & Casualty, Hartford, 1978-81, mgr. audiovisual communications, 1981-82, dir. audiovisual and mktg. communications, 1982-84, dir. mktg. communications, 1984-86, dir. bus. devel., 1986-88, dir. customized communications, customer consulting svcs., 1988—; juror EFLA Am. Film Festival, Hartford, 1977-79. Writer, dir., producer TV films including (edn.) PAC-Man in the Money Works. Mem. Info. Film Producers Am. (chmn. 1981, treas. 1982, Conn. Valley Chpt.), Internat. TV Assn. (chmn. 1983), Hartford Women's Network, Mature Market Inst., Bus. and Profl. Advt. Assn. Republican. Home: 23 Fawnbrook Ln Simsbury CT 06070

MICKA, SALOMEA SOPHIE (SALLY MICKA), information systems executive; b. Milford, Conn., May 9, 1940; d. Stanley John and Sophie Frances (Ignatowski) Kamykowski; m. Edward John Micka, June 16, 1962; children—Edward John, Sally. B.A. in Physics, Cath. U. Am., 1962. Data base cons., various orgns., 1968-76; br. chief Energy Research and Devel. Agy., Germantown, Md., 1976-77; mgr. Internat. Atomic Energy Agy., UN, Vienna, 1977-81; asst. to dir. Dept. Energy, Germantown, 1981-83; group mgr., v.p. Technassociates, Inc., Rockville, Md., 1983—; pres. SEMCOM Assocs., Inc., Gaithersburg, Md., 1984-87; v.p. Maxima Data Systems Corp., 1986-88; regional mgr. Oracle Corp., Bethesda, Md., 1988—; Mem. AimS-2K Data Base Mgmt. Users Group (pres. 1976-770, Nat. Assn. Female Execs., Assn. Women in Computing, Nat. Assn. Women Bus. Owners, Montgomery County C. of C. Democrat. Roman Catholic. Club: Women's Golf Montgomery County. Avocations: golf, reading, hiking. Home: 6566 N Military Tr PO Box 66 West Palm Beach FL 33407

MICKLE, KATHRYN ALMA, security company executive; b. Pittsfield, Mass., May 17, 1946; d. Frederick Louis and Bertha Laura (Webster) Wick; m. William Joseph Mickle III, May 11, 1968; children: William J. IV, Deborah Sharon. cert. in nursing Cooley Dickinson Hosp., Northampton, Mass., 1967. Charge nurse Berkshire Med. Ctr., Pittsfield, 1967-75; intensive and coronary care nurse, 1975-81; nursing cons. Springside Nursing Home, Pittsfield, 1974-76; owner New Eng. Security, Pittsfield, 1978—. Stage mgr. Doo Wah Days Variety Show, 1989-90. Active Western Mass. coun. Girl Scouts U.S., 1975—; bd. dirs. Citizen's Against Child Abuse, 1989—; dir., tchr. Dalton Bible Sch., Mass., 1979-83; vice chmn. bd. Berkshire County Christian Sch., 1984-86, bd. chmn., 1986-88, sec. bd. dirs., 1982-84; chmn. pub. rels. exec. com. Billy Graham Crusade, Pittsfield area, 1982; Dalton coord. Silvio O. Conte Re-election Campaign, 1984. Recipient numerous sales awards Dynamark Inc., 1980—; Appreciation award Dalton Vacation Bible Sch., 1983. Fellow Cen. Berkshire C. of C., Cooley Dickinson Alumni Assn. Congregationalist. Avocations: arts and crafts, swimming, reading, gardening, camping. Home: 72 Braeburn Rd Dalton MA 01226 Office: New England Security 316 Merrill Rd Pittsfield MA 01201

MICKLOS-MAISEY, JANET M., human services director; b. Jacksonville, Fla., July 24, 1947; d. Thomas Anthony and Yolanda Mae (Murphy) Micklos; married; children: Shawn E. Satterthwaite, Ryan W. Satterthwaite; m. Terry Mercer Maisey, May 28, 1988. BA, U. No. Colo., 1969; MA disting. grad., Webster U., 1985. Phys. edn. tchr. Terrell Wells Middle Sch., San Antonio, 1969-70; fitness instr./gymnastic coach Victor Valley Community Coll., Apple Valley, Calif., 1977-79; dir. phys. dept. Victor Valley YMCA, Victorville, Calif., 1978-79; secretarial support, joint mil. mission aid to Turkey, Ankara U.S. Logistics Group, Ankara, Turkey, 1981-82; secretarial support, logistic group Ankara, Turkey Joint U.S. Mil. Mission Aid to Turkey, Ankara, 1982-83; pub. edn. dir. Alamo Area Rape Crisis Ctr., San Antonio, 1986-88; admissions coord. Horizon Hosp., San Antonio, 1988; psychiat. counselor Portsmouth Pavilion, Portsmouth, N.H., 1988-89; dir. human svcs. Rockingham County (N.H.) Dept. of Corrections, Brentwood, 1989—. Mem. gov's. coun. on volunteerism, Seacoast. Mem. Am. Correctional Assn., Am. Jail Assn., AAUW. Republican. Methodist. Office: Rockingham County Dept Corrections PO Box 339 Epping NH 03042

MICUCCI, PATRICIA, primary educator; b. Chgo., Mar. 30, 1934; d. Charles Pasquale and Mildred (Damato) M. BEd, Nat. Coll. Edn., 1955; MEd, U. Ill., 1963. Cert. tchr., Ill. Tchr. kindergarten School Dist. #74, Lincolnwood, Ill., 1955-74, tchr. pre-kindergarten, 1974—, chmn. dept. early childhood, 1982—; mem. kindergarten curriculum com. Lincolnwood, 1986—. Author kindergarten curriculum handbooks; contbr. articles to profl. jours. Named Outstanding Tchr., Grade Tchr. mag., 1968, one of Outstanding Young Women of Am., 1970. Mem. PTA, Instr. Pre-school Book Club, Delta Kappa Gamma. Republican. Roman Catholic. Office: School Dist #74 6950 N East Prarie Rd Lincolnwood IL 60645

MIDDLETON, CAROLE FOSTER, insurance broker, consultant; b. Weymouth, Mass., Dec. 24, 1946; d. David Warren and Hazel Margaret (McRae) Foster; m. Finley N. Middleton, II, Mar. 23, 1974. BA, Coll. St. Catherine, 1968; BS, Rutgers U., 1974; MA, Webster U., 1987. Claims supr. Allstate Ins. Co., 1969-74; asst. account exec. Johnson & Higgins, Brazil, 1974-76; new bus. prodn. mgr. Edward Lumley & Sons, South Africa, 1976-77; asst. v.p. Johnson & Higgins, N.Y.C., 1977-81; asst. v.p. Alexander & Alexander, N.Y.C., 1981-83; pres. Lynmar Internat., Yonkers, N.Y., 1983—, Foxberry Press, Gourmet Internat., Shopping & Mailing Internat., Assn. for Living Abroad (all subs.); adj. faculty mem. Webster U., Leiden campus; speaker on sales techniques, internat. ins., fgn. investment in the U.S., women in ins., women's networking, multinat. corps., expatriates columnist Wall St. Woman, 1979-80. Editor Chronicle mag., 1984-86; author: Managing Multinational Risk, 1990. Bd. dirs. Bklyn. YWCA, 1980-83, chmn. fin. com., treas., 1982; chair Reps. Abroad-Netherlands, 1987-88. Mem. Nat. Assn. Ins. Women, Am. Mgmt. Assn., Nat. Fedn. Bus. and Profl. Women, Assn. Profl. Ins. Women (adv. bd. 1982-83), Women's Econ. Round Table, Internat. Women's Club Phila. (founder, 2d v.p. 1989-90, program chmn. 1989-90, membership chmn. 1990—, 1st v.p. 1990—), Am. Women's Club Denmark (pres. 1986-87), Wall St. Bus. and Profl. Women's (past pres.) Club, Women's Nat. Rep. Club. Presbyterian.

MIDDLETON, DIRONDA LYNN (DIRONDA LYNN PEMBERTON), accountant, tax consultant; b. Clovis, N.Mex., Oct. 29, 1950; d. Robert James and Ruby Joyce (Pond) Pemberton; m. Michael H. Williams, Aug. 30, 1968 (div. Apr. 1978); children: Diedra Michelle, Robert Michael, Matthew Aaron; m. David Owen Middleton, Oct. 26, 1980; 1 adopted child, Chadlee Donald Michael. Grad. high sch., Clovis. Tax cons. H & R Block, Topeka, 1973-74; saleswoman Stanley Home Products, Topeka, 1974-75, Sara Coventry, Topeka, 1977-78; owner, mgr., acct., tax cons. Facts 'n' Figures, Topeka, 1974-81, Small Bus. Bookkeeping and Tax Services, Topeka, 1981—; asst. Mize, Houser, Mehlinger, Kimes, CPA's, Topeka, 1978; acct. Hwy. Oil Co., Topeka, 1978-79, Cobler and Cummings, CPA's, Topeka, 1979-81. Baptist. Office: Small Bus Bookkeeping and Tax Services PO Box 2603 Topeka KS 66601

MIDDLETON, LEE, artist, sculptor; b. Springfield, Ohio, Aug. 2, 1940; d. James Clifton and Alberta Deen (Bennington) Taylor; m. William Edwin Rader, Mar. 30, 1963 (div. Oct. 1972); children: Michael David Rader, Brynn Erynn Rader Riordan; m. Lloyd Michael Middleton, Apr. 25, 1976 (div. May 1990). Chief designer, sculptor Middleton Doll Co., Belpre, Ohio, 1978—; chief exec. officer Middleton Doll Corp., Belpre, Ohio, 1980—. Editor, pub. (poetry quar. under name of R. Lee Rader) Reach Out, 1970-73; author Soft Touch books, 1973-76; author (short story) Christian Life Mag., 1978; contbr. dollmaking articles to various trade publs. Mem. Marietta (Ohio) C. of C., 1989, Belpre C. of C., 1989, Parkersburg (W.Va.) Bur. Tourism, 1989. Named Small Bus. Person of Yr., SBA, Ohio, 1989, nominee Artist Doll of Yr., Doll Reader mag., 1985, nominee Dolls Award of Excellence, Dolls mag., 1989, 90. Mem. United Fedn. Doll Collectors (Chmn.'s award), Doll Artisan Guild, Internat. Dollmakers Assn., Assn. Rotational Molders, Toy Mfgrs. Am. Republican. Office: Middleton Doll Co 1301 Washington Blvd Belpre OH 45714

MIDDLETON, MARILYN WAGNER, physician; b. New Orleans, May 21, 1925; d. Reginald Conrad and Bernice (Noble) Wagner; m. Stanton Levi Middleton, Nov. 24, 1949; children: Diana Lynn Middleton Cook, Stanton Levi III. BA, Tulane U., 1946, MD, 1950. Anesthesiologist Ear, Eye, Nose and Throat Hosp., New Orleans; staff physician Charity Hosp., New Orleans, 1977—; mem. staff La. State U. Med. Sch., New Orleans, 1977—. Mem. AMA, La. Med. Soc., Orleans Med. Soc. Home: 1507 Robert E Lee Blvd New Orleans LA 70122

MIDLARSKY, ELIZABETH, psychologist educator; b. Brooklyn; d. Abraham Allan and Frances Lucille Rae (Wiener) Steckel; m. Manus Issachar Midlarsky, June 25, 1961; children: Susan Rachel, Miriam Joyce, Michael George. BA, CUNY, 1961; MA, Northwestern U., 1966, PhD, 1968. Lic. psychologist, Colo., Mich. Asst. prof. psychology U. Denver, 1968-73; dir. research and evaluation Park East Mental Health Ctr., Denver, 1973-75; assoc. prof., dir. psychology training prog. Met. State Coll., Denver, 1975-77; chmn. dept. psychology U. Detroit, 1978-81, dir. ctr. for study devel. aging, 1981-90, assoc. prof., 1977-83, prof. psychology, 1983-90; prof. psychology Tchr.'s Coll. Columbia U., N.Y., 1990—; initial rev. group mem. NIMH, Bethesda, Md., 1976-82; mem. site rev. groups Nat. Heart, Lung and Blood Inst., Bethesda, 1985-86, study sect. NIH, Bethesda, 1986—. Editor: Acad. Psychology Bull., 1982-86; co-editor: Humboldt Jour. of Social Relations, 1987; contbr. articles to profl. jours. 1980, Nat. Inst. Aging, 1982-85, AARP Andrus Found., 1982-83; AAUW fellow, 1974-75. Fellow Am. Psychol. Assn.; mem. Gerontol. Soc. Am. (exec. com. of prog. com. 1983-84), Soc. Psychol. Study Social Issues, Am. Orthopsychiatric Assn., Mich. Psychol. Assn. (exec. council mem). Jewish. Avocations: singing; playing piano; writing poetry; walking; riding horses. Home: 3 Falcon Rd East Brunswick NJ 08816

MIDLER, BETTE, singer, entertainer, actress; b. Honolulu, 1945; m. Martin von Haselberg, 1984; 1 child, Sophie. Student, U. Hawaii, 1 year. Debut as actress film Hawaii, 1965; mem. cast Fiddler on the Roof, N.Y.C., 1966-69, Salvation, N.Y.C., 1970, Tommy, Seattle Opera Co., 1971; nightclub concert performer on tour, U.S., from 1972; appearance Palace Theatre, N.Y.C., 1973; TV appearances include Tonight Show; appeared Clams on The Half-Shell Revue, N.Y.C., 1975; recs. include The Divine Miss M, 1973, Bette Midler, 1973, Broken Blossom, 1977, Live at Last, 1977, Thighs and Whispers, 1979, New Depression, 1979, Divine Madness, 1980, No Frills, 1984; motion picture appearances include The Rose, 1979, Jinxed, 1982, Down and Out in Beverly Hills, 1986, Ruthless People, 1986, Outrageous Fortune, 1987, Big Business, 1988, Beaches, 1988, Stella, 1990; appeared in cable TV (HBO) prodn. Bette Midler's Mondo Beyondo, 1988; author: The Saga of Baby Divine, 1983. Recipient After Dark Ruby award, 1973; Grammy awards, 1973, 1990; spl. Tony award, 1973; Emmy award for NBC Spl., Ol' Red Hair is Back, 1978. Office: care Atlantic Records 75 Rockefeller Pla New York NY 10019*

MIEL, VICKY ANN, municipal government executive; b. South Bend, Ind., June 20, 1951; d. Lawrence Paul Miel and Virginia Ann (Yeagley) Hernandez. BS, Ariz. State U., 1985. Word processing coordinator City of Phoenix, 1977-78, word processing adminstr., 1978-83, chief dep. city clk., 1983-88, city clk. dir., 1988—; assoc. prof. Phoenix Community Coll., 1982-83, Mesa (Ariz.) Community Coll., 1983; speaker in field, Boston, Santa Fe, Los Angeles, N.Y.C. and St. Paul, 1980—. Author: Phoenix Document Request Form, 1985, Developing Successful Systems Users, 1986. Judge Future Bus. Leaders Am. at Ariz. State U., Tempe, 1984; bd. dirs. Fire and Life Safety League, Phoenix, 1984. Recipient Gold Plaque, Word Processing Systems Mag., Mpls., 1980, Green Light Productivity award City of Phoenix, 1981, Honor Soc. Achievement award Internat. Word Processing Assn., Willow Grove, Pa., 1981. Mem. Assn. Info. Systems Profls. (internat. dir. 1982-84), Internat. Inst. Mcpl. Clks. (cert.), Am. Records Mgrs. Assn., Assn. Image Mgmt., Am. Soc. Pub. Adminstrs., Am. Mgmt. Assn. Lodge: Soroptimists. Office: City of Phoenix 251 W Washington Phoenix AZ 85003

MIELE, HAZEL DONNELLY, educational administrator; b. Somerville, Mass., Apr. 27, 1936; d. William J. and Lillian (Graham) Donnelly; m. Benedetto A. Miele, Oct. 10, 1954; children: Brenda, Benedetto A. Jr., Judith, Eric W. BA, Framingham (Mass.) State Coll., 1986. Social and edn. reporter Marlboro City Post newspaper, 1971-72; staff asst. Heller Grad. Sch., Brandeis U., Waltham, Mass., 1981-85, registrar, dir. admissions, 1985-89, asst. dean adminstrn. and edn., 1989—. Elected to Sch. Com., Marlborough, Mass., 1973-77; mayoral appointee to Marlborough High Sch. Bldg. Project, 1975-78; del. Mass. Dem. Conv., 1982, 86, 88, 90; bd. dirs. Marlborough Hosp., Marlborough, 1987—; chair Marlborough Commn. Bicentennial of U.S. Constn., 1987—; past bd. dirs. Friends of Marlborough Pub. Libr.; affirmative action officer Marlborough Dem. Com., 1989—. Roman Catholic. Home: 595 Hosmer St Marlborough MA 01752

MIELKE, MARY MARGARET, librarian; b. Glencoe, Minn., Jan. 14, 1947; d. Howard Ferdinand and Eileen Frieda (Krecklau) Mielke; div.; children: Michael, Nicole. BS in English, Libr. Sci., St. Cloud State U., 1969, postgrad., 1982-84. Librarian Brooten Pub Schs., Brooten, Minn., 1972-81; instructional designer Wilson Learning Corp., Eden Prairie, Minn., 1984-85; trainer U.S. West, Mpls., 1986; librarian Mpls. Pub. Schs., 1986-87, Coopers and Lybrand, 1988—. Office: Coopers and Lybrand 1000 TCF Tower Minneapolis MN 55402

MIER, PHYLLIS JEAN, program analyst; b. Muncie, Ind., Aug. 9, 1949; d. Philip Wilber and Helen Elizabeth (Moore) M. BA, Ball State U., 1971; postgrad., U. Md. LicensedMd., Va., D.C., Ind. Tchr. Montgomery County Pub. Schs., Rockville, 1971-74; tchr., mgr. Sears, Roebuck and Co., Arlington, Va., 1974-77; cons. Greenhorne and O'Mara, Inc., Riverdale, Md., 1977-78; program analyst Fed. Emergency Mgmt. Agy., Washington, 1978—, sr. program analyst, 1988—; asst. coordinator, driver Sunderland (Md.) Vanpools, 1980—; transportation, tour cons. Calvert Transportation Systems, Sunderland, 1980—; prin. Mier Computer Services, Huntingtown, Md., 1987; co-owner Vanpools Plus, Inc., Huntingtown, Mo., 1988—. Mem. Nat. Assn. Female Execs. (Who's Who in Female Execs. 1987), Beta Sigma Phi (pres. 1977, 81, 84, 85, council pres. 1977, 84). Home: 1847 Cliff Dr Huntingtown MD 20639 Office: Fed Emergency Mgmt Agy 500 C St SW Washington DC 20472

MIESEL, ROCHELLE KRISTAL, construction executive; b. Chgo., Mar. 26, 1941; d. Allen Joseph and Edith (Lipsey) Kristal; m. Victor C. Miesel, Dec. 28, 1979. BA in English Edn., McNeese State U., Lake Charles, La., 1963, MEd in Counseling and Guidance, 1967. English tchr. Calcasieu Parish Sch. Bd., Lake Charles, 1963-67, counselor, 1967-80; dir. of placement Median Sch. of Allied Health Careers, Pitts., 1981-83; counselor McGuffey Sch. Dist., Claysville, Pa., 1983-84; field rep. Henry F. Teichmann, Inc., Pitts., 1984-89; asst. mgr. ea. oper. LILJA Constrn. Corp., Pitts., 1989—. Mem. AAUW, NAFE, Am. Bus. Women's Assn. (pres. 1970), McNeese State U. Alumni (bd. dirs. 1975-79), So. Assn. Sec. Schs. and Colls. Evaluation Team, Delta Kappa Gamma.

MIESNER, TERRY ANN, software engineer; b. Washington, Mo., Oct. 23, 1961; d. Norbert James and Delores Alvina (Altholz) M. BS in Info. Systems Mgmt., SW Mo. State U., 1984. Assoc. programmer McDonnell Douglas Corp., St. Louis, 1984-86, software engr., 1986-90, sr. programmer/

analyst, 1990—; fitness instr. YMCA, St. Louis, 1987-88. Mem. Internat. Dance and Exercise Assn. (cert.). Roman Catholic. Home: 958 Barcroft Woods Ct Manchester MO 63021 Office: MC3062363 PO Box 516 Saint Louis MO 63166-0516

MIESSE, MARY ELIZABETH (BETH MIESSE), educator; b. Amarillo, Tex.; M.Ed. in Guidance and Counseling, M.A., W. Tex. State U., Canyon, 1952, M.B.A., 1960; M.Personnel Service, U. Colo., Boulder, 1954. With various bus. firms and radio stas., 1940-47; prof. Amarillo (Tex.) Coll., 1947-63; tchr. pvt. and pub. schs., also TV work, 1963-78; spl. edn. cons., writer, 1978—. Mem. NEA, ASCAP, Nat Fed. State Poetry Socs., Poetry Soc. Tex., Tex. State Tchrs. Assn., Bus. Profl. Womens Club, Am. Bus. Women's Club, Toastmistress Internat., Am. Psychol. Assn., North Plains Assn. for Children with Learning Disabilities, Panhandle Profl. Writers, AAUP, AAUW. Pioneered in ednl. TV in West Tex.; recipient awards in typewriting and ednl. TV; elected to Top Ten Women of Yr., Am. Bus. Women's Assn. Cert. in spl. edn. supr., spl. edn. counselor, ednl. diagnostician, spl. edn. (lang. and/or learning disabled, mentally retarded) tchr., profl. counselor, profl. tchr., supt., prin., Tex. Editor, Tex. Jr. Coll. Tchrs. Assn. publ., 7 yrs. Producer radio poetry show. Mem. Panhandle Profl. Writers, ASCA Writers. Home and Office: PO Box 3133 Valle de Oro TX 79010

MIGALA, LUCYNA JOZEFA, broadcaster, arts administrator, radio station executive; b. Krakow, Poland, May 22, 1944; d. Joseph and Estelle (Suwala) M.; came to U.S., 1947, naturalized, 1955; student Loyola U., Chgo., 1962-63, Chicago Conservatory of Music, 1963-70; BS in Journalism, Northwestern U., 1966. Radio announcer, producer sta. WOPA, Oak Park, Ill., 1963-66; writer, reporter, producer NBC news, Chgo., 1966-69, 1969-71, producer NBC local news, Washington, 1969; producer, coord. NBC network news, Cleve., 1971-78, field producer, Chgo., 1978-79; v.p. Migala Communications Corp., 1979—; program dir., on-air personality Sta. WCEV, Cicero, Ill., 1979—; lectr. City Colls. Chgo., 1981, Morton Coll., 1988. Columnist Free Press, Chgo., 1984-87. Founder, soloist, artistic dir., gen. mgr. Lira Singers, Chgo., 1965—; mem., chmn. various cultural coms. Polish Am. Congress, 1970—; bd. dirs. Nationalities Svcs. Ctr., Cleve., 1973-78; bd. dirs., v.p. Cicero-Berwyn Fine Arts Coun., Cicero, Ill.; mem. City Arts I and II panels Chgo. Office of Fine Arts, 1986-89; v.p. Chgo. chpt. Kosciuszko Found., 1983-86; bd. dirs. Polish Women's Alliance Am., 1983-87, Ill. Humanities Coun., 1983-89, mem. exec. com., 1986-87; bd. dirs. Ill. Arts Alliance, 1989—; founder, gen. chmn. Midwest Chopin Piano Competition (now Chgo. Chopin Competition), 1984-86; founding mem. ethnic and folk arts panel Ill. Arts Coun., 1984-87. Recipient AP Broadcasters award, 1973, Emmy award NATAS, 1974; Washington Journalism Ctr. fellow, spring 1969. Mem. Soc. Profl. Journalists. Office: Sta WCEV 5356 W Belmont Ave Chicago IL 60641 also: The Lira Singers 3750 W Peterson Chicago IL 60659

MIHALIK, PHYLLIS ANN, consulting executive, educator, public speaker; b. Cleve., Mar. 11, 1952; d. Henry Arvon and Dorothy (Markovich) Trepal; m. John P. Mihalik, Aug. 5, 1972. AA, Lakeland Coll., 1982; BS in Computer Sci., Lake Erie Coll., 1986; MBA, Case Western Res. U. Acct. Picker Internat., Highland Heights, Ohio, 1977-80, programmer, analyst, 1980-82, fin. systems analyst, 1982-83; sr. systems analyst Harris, Solon, Ohio, 1983-84, mgr. systems and programming, 1984-86, dir. internal audit, 1986-88; pres., owner Productivity & Mgmt. Cons., Chardon, Ohio, 1988—; faculty mem. Lakeland Coll., Mentor, Ohio, 1987—. Author: Introduction to PC's, 1989, Managing the PC Work Environment, 1989. Mem. Data Processing Mgmt. Assn., Assn. for Systems Mgmt., Women Bus. Owners. Republican. Office: Productivity and Mgmt Cons 11457 Fowlers Mill Chardon OH 44024

MIHALKO, PATRICIA JOYCE, educator; b. Detroit, Dec. 19, 1940; d. Joseph and Helen Christine (Mohnach) M. BS, SUNY, Cortland, 1963; MS, Ind. U., 1969. Permanent cert. in phys. edn., N.Y. Tchr. Cooperstown (N.Y.) High Sch., 1963-89. Founder Cooperstown Internat. Field Hockey Trips, 1975—; state chmn. Empire State Games, Field Hockey, 1978; coach "C" Camp Olympic Devel. Program, Smith Coll., Mass., 1982. Named to Hall of Fame Inductee SUNY, 1985, Amateur Sports Hall of Fame, Johnstown, Pa., 1985. Mem. N.Y. Pub. Sch. Athletic Assn. (sports chmn., Service Honor 1980), N.Y. State Coaches Assn., Nat. Fedn. Interscholastic Coaches (Outstanding Coach 1984), N.Y. State Tchrs. Assn., Nat. Edn. Assn. Democrat. Roman Catholic. Clubs: Adirondack Mountain (Lake Placid, N.Y.), Mohawk Bicycle (Utica, N.Y.). Home: Cary Park Rd Box 275 Richfield Springs NY 13439 Office: Hamilton Coll Clinton NY 13323-9989

MIHELICH, JEANETTE AMELIA, retired educator; b. Chgo., June 20, 1921; d. Wesley Leo and Esther Lucille (Maxson) VanOsdol; m. John William Mihelich, Dec. 22, 1946; children: John William Jr., Kathryn Lee, Margaret Lucille. BA with honors, Hanover (Ind.) Coll., 1944; postgrad., U. Ill., 1945-46. Cert. secondary tchr., Ind. Secondary sch. South Bend (Ind.) City Schs., 1966-74; adj. prof. edn. Ind. U., South Bend, 1977-81; ret., 1981; secondary tchr. C.O.G. program YWCA, South Bend, 1971-74; program dir., interviewer TV program Status of Women, 1978-79. Editor newsletter UN Assn. U.S.A. St. Joseph County, 1984—. Pres. South Bend Mayor's Commn. on Status of Women, 1978-79; precinct committeeman South Bend Rep. Com., 1979-87, 90—; scholarship chmn. South Bend Area Panhellenic, 1971-72; pres. Presbyn. Women, South Bend, 1975-79, 83-85, chmn. nominations synod bd., 1990-93; mem. Women's Assn. South Bend Symphony Orch. Mem. AAUW (pres. 1966-68, 75-77, state bd. dirs. 1970-79, named fellowship award 1980), Am. Assn. Ret. Persons (tax counselor South Bend 1977—, coord. IRS tax aide program 1983—), Ladies of Notre Dame (pres. 1986-87), Delta Epsilon, Alpha Delta Pi (pres. 1958-60, 80-82).

MIHNAK, DEBORAH ANN, nurse; b. Steubenville, Ohio, Apr. 16, 1959; d. John Sebastian and Mary Ann (Duska) M. BSN, Wheeling (W.Va.) Coll., 1981; MSN, LaRoche Coll., 1990. RN, Pa., Ohio, W.Va. Nurse Allegheny Gen. Hosp., Pitts., 1981-87, West Penn Hosp., Pitts., 1987—. Mme. Am. Soc. Personnel Adminstrs. (sec. 1989—), Am. Assn. Critical Care Nurses. Roman Catholic. Home: 201 Benita Dr Mingo Junction OH 43938

MIHOOVER, JANIS DARLENE, respiratory therapy technician; b. Trinidad, Colo., Sept. 20, 1951; d. Fred Relfred and Evelyn Marie (Harper) Wright; m. Randall Dean Mihoover, July 25, 1970; children: Jack Justin, Nicholas Dugan. Student, Trinidad State Jr. Coll., 1969-71. Cert. respiratory therapy technician. Equipment technician St. Anthony Hosp. Systems, Denver, 1972-73, mem. staff, ICU technician, 1973-76, supr. therapy, 1976-86; mem. staff, ICU technician Swedish Med. Ctr., Englewood, Colo., 1986-88, St. Luke's Hosp., Bethlehem, Pa., 1988—. Home: 949 E 6th St Bethlehem PA 18015 Office: St Luke's Hosp 801 Ostrum St Bethlehem PA 18015

MIJALIS, ELAINE JEAN, public relations and communications executive; b. Miami, Fla., Sept. 2, 1955; d. Charles James and Jean S. (Sohara) Cavalaris; divorced; children: Marie Kristen Mijalis and Jeanne Virginia Mijalis (twins). BS in Journalism, U. Colo., 1977. Intern Sta. WPLG, Miami, 1973; intern Sta. WTVJ, Miami, 1975; pub. rels. dir. Farmers Seafood Co., Inc., Shreveport, La., 1978-81; mktg. analyst Ryan and Co., Shreveport, 1986; programming cons. NASA, Huntsville, Ala., 1986-87; communications cons. NASA, Washington, 1987; mktg. cons. Classroom Earth, Shreveport, 1986-88; dir. pub. rels. Southfield Sch., Shreveport, 1987-88; communications/pub. rels. coord. Miami Country Day Sch., 1988-90; dir. admissions Ransom Everglades Sch., Miami, 1990—. Bd. dirs. Ransom Everglades Sch. Alumni Assn., Miami, 1989—, Deaf Action Ctr. N.W. La., Shreveport, 1987-89; commr. La. Gov.'s Mansion Commn., 1983-88; mem. Jr. League Miami, 1989—, communications com., 1990—; bd. dirs. Shreveport Regional Arts Coun., 1987-89; regional recruiter U. Colo., 1987—; founding bd. mem. Pub. Radio Sta. KGNU, 1979-82; exec. bd. Shreveport Symphony Women's Guild, 1986-88, Shreveport Opera Guild, 1987-88. Recipient Spl. Merit most improved publs. Coun. for Advancement and Support of Edn., Dist. III, 1990. Mem. Women in Communications (chmn. fund raising Miami chpt. 1990), EDNL Network (Miami), Nat. Sch. Pub. Rels. Assn., Fla. Motion Picture and TV Assn., Pi Beta Phi. Greek Orthodox. Home: 600 NE 36 St No 2018 Miami FL 33137 Office: Ransom Everglades Sch Dir Admissions 3575 Main Hwy Miami FL 33133

MIKALCHUS, ELEANOR SMOLKIS, business owner; b. Waterbury, Conn., Apr. 10, 1939; d. John Anthony and Anna Mary (Kudzma) Smolkis; m. John H. Mikalchus; children: Laura, John R. BS, Central Conn. State U., 1961; MA, Fairfield U., 1965; postgrad., Cen. Conn. State U., 1981. Instr., coordinator Mattatuck Community Coll., Waterbury, Conn., 1976-77; instr. Tunxis Community Coll., Farmington, Conn., 1977-78, Post Coll., Waterbury, 1978; acct. asst. Chase Nuclear, Waterbury, 1978; program coordinator Lark Industries, Torrington, Conn., 1978-79; tchr., coordinator Regional Dist. 10, Burlington, Conn., 1979-84; adminstr. Clifford Cooper Architects, Litchfield, Conn., 1984-85; tchr., cons. Bus. Careers Inst., Waterbury, 1985-86; owner One-Stop Bus. Svcs., Litchfield, Conn., 1986—. Pres., Litchfield Parish coun., 1984; com. mem. United Way, Torrington, 1989; vol. Warner Theater, Torrington, 1989. Mem. New Milford Arts Coun., Am. Indian Archtl. Inst., Friends Plumb Library (sec. 1974-75), NAFE, Litchfield County Women's Network, N.W. Conn. C. of C. (co-chmn. Expo 88, 89), Nat. Assn. Secretarial Svcs.

MIKE, MARJOREE D., college student activities director; b. Alexandria, La., Dec. 28, 1963; d. Jim G. and Marquerite (Davis) M. BS in Bus. Adminstrn./Mktg., Northwestern State U., Natchitoches, La., 1985, MA in Student Personnel Svcs., 1988. Prodn. sec. Steel Magnolias, Tri-Star Prodn., Natchitoches, 1988; admissions counselor, recruiter Northwestern State U., Natchitoches, 1988-89; dir. student activities Centenary Coll., Shreveport, La., 1989—; advisor student activities bd. Centenary Coll., Shreveport, 1989—. Mem. Sigma Kappa (advisor Northwestern State U. chpt. 1988—). Roman Catholic. Office: Centenary Coll 2911 Centenary Blvd Shreveport LA 71134-1188

MIKEL, CHARLENE ANN, social worker, consultant, lecturer, editor; b. Oswego, Kans., Sept. 30, 1938; d. Warren Fowler and Gladys Maude (Hoke) Hardwick; m. Robert Andrew Mikel, Oct. 22, 1960 (div. July 1979); children: Cassandra, Mark. B.S. in Edn., Kans. State Coll., 1960; M.S.S.W., U. Mo., 1968. Social worker State of Kans., Topeka, 1964-66, 67-69, med. social worker 1976-82; social worker S.E. Kans. Mental Health, Humboldt, 1970-74; cons. Charlene Mikel Cons., Oswego, 1982—, editor, 1984— ; lectr. Labette Community Coll., Parsons, Kans., 1983—, Barton County Community Coll., Great Bend, Kans., 1982—. Active 4-H. Mem. Nat. Assn. Social Workers, Kans. Soc. Clin. Social Workers, Am. Legion Aux. (past pres. local chpt.). Republican. Methodist. Avocations: sewing; reading; travel. Home and Office: PO Box 204 Oswego KS 67356

MIKEL, MARY EBERLEIN, sales executive; b. Albany, N.Y., Oct. 3, 1959; d. James J. and Rosemary A. (Connell) Eberlein; m. Daniel J. Mikel, Aug. 13, 1983; children: James, Caitlin. BS in Mgmt., St. John Fisher Coll., Rochester, N.Y., 1981; postgrad., Am. Coll. With sales dept. 3M Bus. Methods Inc., Rochester; dir. brokerage-mktg. Nat. Life Vt., Rochester; account exec. Essex Investment Group, Inc., Rochester. Mem. NAFE, Rochester Womens Network, Rochester Life Underwriters (pres.). Home: 581 Pinegrove Ave Rochester NY 14617

MIKE-NARD, BEVERLY JEAN, nurse; b. Youngstown, Ohio, Nov. 3, 1957; d. Michael Ablen and Marion Charlotte (Saba) Mike; children: Stacy Nicole, Kenneth Robert Jr. Nursing diploma, St. Elizabeth Hosp. Med. Ctr., 1978; student, Youngstown State U., 1988-89, Pa. State U., 1989—. Nurse asst. St. Elizabeth Hosp. Med. Ctr., 1977-78, nurse orthopaedic dept., 1978-81, RN Neonatal ICU, 1982—. Active PTA, Austintown, Ohio, 1985-89, Poland, Ohio, 1989—. Mem. Nat. Assn. Neonatal Nurses, Nurses Assn. Am. Coll. Ob-Gyn (cert.), Nat. Apostolate of Maronites. Democrat. Roman Catholic. Home: 3330 Partridge Park Dr Poland OH 44514-2807 Office: St Elizabeth Hosp Med Ctr 1040 Belmont Ave Youngstown OH 44504

MIKIEWICZ, ANNA DANIELLA, marketing and sales representative; b. Chgo., Dec. 22, 1960; d. Zdislaw and Lucy (Magnusewska) K. BS in Mktg., Elmhurst Coll., 1982; postgrad. Triton Coll. Asst. to Midwestern regional mgr. Meister Pub. Co., Chgo., 1983; sales rep. First Impression, Elk Grove, Ill., 1984; mktg. and customer svcs. rep. Airco Ind. Gases, Broadview and Carol Stream, Ill., 1985, Yamazen USA, Inc., Schaumburg, Ill., 1985-88; mktg. and sales coord. Kitamura Machinery U.S.A, Inc., 1988—. Named Chgo. Polish Queen Polish Am. Culture Club, 1983-84. Mem. NAFE. Republican. Roman Catholic.

MIKULSKI, BARBARA ANN, senator; b. Balt., July 20, 1936; d. William and Christina Eleanor (Kutz) M. B.A., Mt. St. Agnes Coll., 1958; M.S.W., U. Md., 1965; LL.D. (hon.), Goucher Coll., 1973, Hood Coll., 1978. Tchr. Mt. St. Agnes Coll., 1969; tchr. Community Coll. Balt., 1970-71, VISTA Tng. Ctr., 1965-70; with Balt. Dept. Social Services, 1961-63, 66-70, York Family Agy., 1964, Assoc. Catholic Charities, 1958-61; mem. Balt. City Council, 1971-76; mem. 96th-99th Congresses from 3d Md. Dist., 1979-87, mem. interstate, fgn. commerce, mcht. marine coms.; U.S. senator from Md., 1987—, mem. appropriations, environment, pub. works, labor, human relations, small bus. coms.; mem. Congl. Steel Caucus, Congresswomen's Caucus, Democratic Study Group, Environ. Study Conf., Mems. Congress for Peace Through Law; cons. Nat. Ctr. Urban Ethnic Affairs, others. Contbr. articles to mags. and newspapers. Bd. dirs. Valley House; nat. bd. dirs. Urban Coalition; mem. Polish Women's Alliance, Polish Am. Congress, Citizens Planning and Housing Assn., S.E. Community Orgn.; chmn. com. community devel. Archdiocesan Urban Commn.; mem. nat. com. Muskie for Pres., 1971-72; chmn. com. del. selection and party structure Dem. Nat. Com.; Dem. nominee U.S. Senate, 1974, Ho. of Reps., 1976; mem. Dem. Nat. Strategy Council. Named Woman of Yr. MS. mag., 1987; first woman apptd. to U.S. Ho. Reps. energy and commerce com.; elected to represent Dem. Party in both houses of Congress; first Dem. woman elected to U.S. Senate in her own right. Mem. Nat. Women's Polit. Caucus, Nat. Bus. and Profl. Women's Assn., Am. Fedn. Tchrs., Nat. Assn. Social Workers, LWV. Office: US Senate 320 Hart Office Bldg Washington DC 20510-2003*

MILANES, LILA DU-BREUIL, resource teacher; b. Havana, Cuba, Jan. 18, 1925; came to U.S., 1970; d. Jesu's and Ursilina (Costa) Du-Breuil; m. Jose' N. Milanes, Jan. 6, 1956 (dec. 1979); 1 child Cory Jo Zornizer. Tchr. Cert., Normal Sch. of Havana, Cuba, 1943; DEd, U. Havana, 1949; continuing edn., in Cuba, 1949-55, in U.S., 1972-80. Cert. (life) elementary tchr., Calif., secondary (1991), specialist. Tchr. Cuban Elem. Schs., Havana, 1943-56; prin. Cuban Elem. Sch., Havana, 1956-57; sch. insp. Dist. 3 Cuban Elem. Schs., Havana, 1957-59; Spanish tchr. Geo. Washington Sch., Cartegena, Colombia, 1961-70, Berlitz Schs., Beverly Hills, Calif., 1971-72; sustitute tchr. L.A. Unified Sch. Dist., 1973-75, ESL tchr., 1975-76, Spanish tchr., 1976-88, resource bilingual tchr., 1988—; leader in-svc. tng. Cuban schs. staff, 1952-53; instr. U. Pepperdine, 1975-76; translator for Spanish speaking parents conferences, L.A., 1975-78. Contbr. articles to profl. jours., newspapers, Havana, 1950s. Vol. Cuban Refugee Com. Enrique Serrano, Torrance, Calif. 1973; sec. Parents Adv. Coun., Wilmington, Calif., 1974-75; sec. PTA Trinity St. Sch., L.A., 1988—. Many academic awards in Cuba and the U.S. Republican.

MILANI, DIVA, interior designer; b. N.Y.C., Feb. 14, 1958; d. Egidio and Albina (Mazza) M. BA, Queens Coll., 1982; cert., Parsons Sch. Design, N.Y.C., 1984. Graphic artist, advt. designer, layout-mech. artist N.Y.C.; design cons., mktg. dir. Custom Interior Decorating Svc., N.Y.C., Trans-Designs, N.Y.C., Design Pavilion, Pelham, N.Y.; interior designer Astoria, N.Y., Maurice Villenay/Roche Bobois, Scarsdale, N.Y.; lectr. and seminar leader in field. Recipient Most Profl. award N.Y. Apt. and Home Show, 1988, Best of Show award Schlott Design and Remodeling Show, also various awards for design and leadership. Mem. NAFE. Home: 31-44 43d St Astoria NY 11103 Office: Maurice Villency/Roche Bobois 678 White Plains Rd Scarsdale NY 10583

MILANO, CAROL ELLEN, marketing executive, business owner; b. Bklyn., Aug. 12, 1946; d. Harry I. and Ann Blanche (Kogut) Fingerroth; m. Albert C. Milano, July 23, 1967 (div. 1970); m. Leonard A. Mednick, Sept. 6, 1987; stepchildren: Risa, Robert. BA in English, Bklyn. Coll., 1967; MA in Counseling, NYU, 1977. Project dir. Neighborhood Youth Corps, Washington, 1967-69; rsch. asst. Barbara Seaman: Free & Female, N.Y.C., 1971; counselor N.Y.C. Methadone Maintenance Program, N.Y.C., 1972-74, DC 37, N.Y.C., 1976-78; pres. Milano Assocs., N.Y.C., 1977—; publicist New Line Cinema, N.Y.C., 1970; adj. prof. NYU, 1978—, Sch. Visual Arts, N.Y.C., 1983—; co-founder Brownstone Bus. Group, Bklyn., 1987—; lectr. Can. Ctr. for Philanthropy, Toronto, 1988, Fund Raising Day in N.Y.C., 1985, 87, 88, Rice U. Pub. Inst., Houston, 1987. Author: (with others) Prentice-Hall Directory of Executive Search, 1986, Profitable Careers in Non-Profit, 1987, Secretarial Practice Made Simple, 1990; columnist Oriental Rug mag., 1989—, Bklyn. Bus. Seminar leader Small Bus. Devel. Ctr., 1988, 89; advisor Red Hook Arts Ctr., Bklyn., 1987; guest speaker Bklyn Pub. Library, 1987-89; co-chairperson Bklyn Mktg. Expo, 1989-90. Mem. Bklyn. Communication Arts Profls. (v.p. 1988-90), Nat. Writers Union, Am. Women's Econ. Devel. Corp., Editorial Freelancers Assn. Office: Milano Assocs 652 Carroll St Brooklyn NY 11215

MILBERG, SUSAN BODNER, public relations executive; b. N.Y.C., Apr. 20, 1949; d. Milton Meyer and Muriel Ruby (Walash) Swersky; m. Lawrence Bodner, Oct. 25, 1970 (div. June 1975); children: Jennifer Lynn Bodner, Jason Ross Bodner; m. Barry A. Milberg, Apr. 14, 1983. BA in Edn., U. Md., 1970; BA in English, 1971; paralegal cert., Barry Coll., 1980; MBA, Ga. State U., 1980. Tchr. devel. curriculum Solomon Shecter Hillel Community Day Sch., North Miami Beach, Fla., 1974-77; English tchr. Hebrew Acad. Atlanta, 1977-78; life underwriter, estate planner Life Va. Ins., Atlanta, 1978-79; paralegal, probate and estate mgmt. Abrams, Anton Robbins, Resnick, Schneider & Mager, Hollywood, Fla., 1980-81; svc. cons. mktg. dept. Southern Bell, Ft. Lauderdale, Fla., 1981-83; dir. community rels. The Jewish Home, Atlanta, 1984-87; dir. pub. info. The United Jewish Fedn. Metrowest, East Orange, N.J., 1988—; pubs. rep., adminstr. The Metrowest Jewish News, East Orange, 1988—; cons. pub. rels. for philanthropic orgn. and 16 beneficiary agys., East Orange, 1988—. Pub. (community resource book) Metrosource, 1990. Life mem. Nat. Coun. Jewish Women, Millburn-Shorthills, 1984—. Mem. N.J. Press Women (state and nat. communications awards 1990), NAFE, N.J. Exec. Women. Office: United Jewish Fedn Metrowest 60 Glenwood Ave East Orange NJ 07017

MILBRATH, MARY MERRILL LEMKE, quality assurance professional; b. Evanston, Ill., Aug. 13, 1940; d. William Frederick and Martha Merrill (Slagel) Lemke; m. Gene McCoy Milbrath, Aug. 22, 1964; children: Elizabeth Ann, Sarah Toril Jeanne. BA in Biology, Albion Coll., 1962; MS in Plant Pathology, U. Ariz., 1966. Microbiologist Abbott Labs., North Chicago, Ill., 1962; toxicologist U. Ariz., Tucson, 1965-67; toxicologist U. Ill., Urbana, 1976-77, entomologist, 1978; plant pathologist State of Oreg., Salem, 1979, chemist, 1980-82; sr. quality supr. Siltec Corp., Salem, 1983—; Active Ill. Emergency Svcs.toxic sub task force U. Ill., Urbana, 1978; mem. Responsible Corp. Citizens Com., Salem, 1989—. Mem. citizens adv. com. Sch. Bd., Urbana, 1975-76; campaigner Oreg. 5th Dist. race, Salem, 1984, Oreg. Nat. Abortion Rights Assn. League, Salem, 1986. NDEA fellow U.S. Dept. Def., 1962. Mem. Am. Soc. for Quality Control, AAUW (interest group chmn.), Willamette U. House Corp. (treas. 1982-85), Delta Gamma (pres. Salem Alumnae chpt. 1987-89, treas. Salem Alumnae chpt. 1981-85, scholarship advisor Willamette U. chpt. 1986-90). Office: Siltec Corp 1351 Tandem Ave Salem OR 97303

MILCH, PAMELA H., television producer; b. Bronx, N.Y., Feb. 9, 1960; d. Edward and Sylvia (Nessman) M. BS cum laude, Syracuse U., 1982. Prodn. technician Cablevision, Woodbury, N.Y., 1983-85, dir., editor, 1985-86; producer News 12 L.I., Woodbury, 1986-88; sr. producer Fin. News Network, N.Y.C., 1988—. Youth dir. United Synagogue Youth, Babylon and Queens, N.Y., 1983-88. Office: Fin News Network 1251 6th Ave Concourse Level I New York NY 10020

MILDON, MARIE ROBERTA, association executive; b. Pittsburg, Calif., Apr. 18, 1935; d. Samuel Ward and Roberta Alice (Trumpower) Wilson; m. James Lee Mildon, Sept. 17, 1958; 1 dau., Laura Marie. B.S., U. Nev.-Reno, 1983. News editor Seaside News Sentinel (Calif.), 1956-58; adminstrv. asst. for corp. devel. Crown Zellerbach, San Francisco, 1959-64; assoc. dir. Nat. Council Juvenile and Family Ct. Judges, Reno, Nev., 1969—; tng. dir. Nat. Coll. Juvenile Justice, Reno, 1971-72; apptd. cons. to task force on abused and neglected children Mo. Supreme Ct. Alt. trustee John Shaw Field Found., Reno, 1979-85; trustee Cystems, Inc., Juris/Amicus, Inc. Co-author: Model Statute for Termination of Parental Rights, 1976; Model Statute on Juvenile and Family Court Records, 1981; My World To Share, 1982. Editor: Judicial Concern for Children in Trouble, 1974; Juvenile and Family Law Jour., 1985—; prodn. editor Juvenile and Family Law Digest, 1986-88. Office: U Nev Campus Jud Coll Bldg Reno NV 89557

MILDVAN, DONNA, infectious diseases physician; b. Phila., June 20, 1942; d. Carl David and Gertrude (Tebet) M.; m. Rolf Dirk Hamann; 1 child, Gabriella Kay. AB magna cum laude, Bryn Mawr Coll., 1963; MD, Johns Hopkins U., 1967. Diplomate Am. Bd. Internal Medicine and Infectious Diseases. Intern, resident Mt. Sinai Hosp., N.Y.C., 1967-70, fellow, infectious diseases, 1970-72; asst., assoc. prof. clin. medicine Mt. Sinai Sch. Medicine, N.Y.C., 1972-87; prof. clinical medicine Dept. Medicine, Mt. Sinai Sch. Medicine, N.Y.C., 1987-88, prof. medicine, 1988—; physician-in-charge infectious diseases Beth Israel Med. Ctr., N.Y.C., 1972-79; chief, div. infectious diseases Beth Israel Med. Ctr., 1980—; mem. AIDS charter rev. com., NIH/Nat. Inst. Allergy and Infectious Diseases, Bethesda, 1987—; cons. FDA, Rockville, 1987—, Ctrs. for Disease Control, Atlanta, 1985-86; among first to describe AIDS, first to describe "Pre-AIDS" and AIDS Dementia, 1982, among first to study AZT, 1986; Keynote speaker, II Internat. Conf. on AIDS, Paris, 1986 and other achievements in field; Sophie Jones Meml. lectr. in infectious diseases U. Mich. Hosps., 1984. Contbr. numerous articles to profl. jours; co-editor two books, several book chpts. and abstracts on infectious diseases and AIDS. Recipient Woman of Achievement award AAUW, 1987; contract for antiviral therapy in AIDS, NCI/Nat. Inst.Allergy and Infectious Diseases, 1985-86, grant, N.Y. State AIDS Inst., 1986-87, subcontract, Nat. Inst. Allergy and Infectious Diseases, 1987-91; Henry Strong Denison scholar, Johns Hopkins U. Sch. Medicine, 1967. Fellow Infectious Diseases Soc. Am.; mem. Am. Soc. Microbiology, AAAS, Harvey Soc., Internat. AIDS Soc. Democrat. Jewish. Office: Beth Israel Med Ctr First Ave at 16th St New York NY 10003

MILES, BARBARA ANN, health care facility administrator, nurse; b. Huron, S.D., July 4, 1940; d. Marvin Christian and Lucy Johanna (DeYoung) Roesch; m. Frederick Dean Miles Jr., May 6, 1967; 1 child, Frederick Dean III. R.N., Presbyn.-St. Luke's Hosp. Sch. of Nursing, Chgo., 1961; student U. Ill.-Chgo., 1965, Case Western Res. U., 1963-65. R.N., Ill., Ohio, Ariz. Asst. head nurse Tucson Med. Ctr., 1971-72; supr. Desert Samaritan Hosp., Mesa, Ariz., 1972-74; nurse mgr. McDowell facility Cigna Health Plan of Ariz., Phoenix, 1974-83, assoc. adminstr., 1983-85, adminstr., 1985—; nat. vice adv. bd. Health Occupations, 1989—; state chairperson nursing contest Vocat. Indsl. Clubs of Am., Phoenix, 1984—, nat. chairperson nursing contest, 1985—. Mem. Am. Acad. Ambulatory Nursing Adminstrs., Chandler C. of C. Methodist. Avocations: playing piano; reading; crafts. Home: 1019 E Vinedo Ln Tempe AZ 85284 Office: Cigna Health Plan Ariz 1349 W Chandler Blvd Chandler AZ 85224

MILES, CHARLENE, small business owner; b. Pine City, Ark., Dec. 4, 1928; d. Albert and Katherine (Coakes) Banks; m. James Dixon Jr., Jan. 5, 1947 (div. 1955); children: James Walter II, Shirley; m. Joe Miles, Apr. 21, 1955 (dec.); 1child, Donell. AA, Shorter Coll., Little Rock, Ark., 1946; cert., Buffalo (N.Y.) Beauty Coll., 1960. Lic. cosmetologist. Technician Posner Beauty Products, N.Y.C., 1960-63; instr. Peter Piccolo Beauty Sch., Buffalo, 1974-75; founder, pres. Charlene's Unisex Salon of N.Y., Detroit, 1975—; judge Student Cosmetology Assn., Buffalo, 1980—. Pres. Profls. Against Drugs, Detroit, 1988—; corp. dir. Op. Push, Chgo., 1987—. Named Pres. of Yr. CUS Bd. Dirs., 1984. Mem. Nat. Hairdressers Assn., Pacesetters (outstanding service award 1984), Mary B. Tolbert Assn., Beverly Area Planning Assn. Democrat. Home: 36026 Castlemeadow Dr Farmington Hills MI 48024 Office: Charlenes Unisex Salon NY 433 5th Ave New York NY 10016

MILES, CHRISTINE MARIE, museum director; b. Madison, Ind., Mar. 2, 1951; d. Leland Weber and Mary Virginia (Geyer) M.; B.A., Boston U., 1973; M.A., George Washington U., 1982; postgrad. Mus. Mgmt. Inst., 1985. Curatorial asst. Mus. of the City of N.Y., 1973-75; art gallery dir. South Street Seaport Mus., N.Y.C., 1975-77; researcher AIA Found., Washington, 1978-80; dir. Fraunces Tavern Mus., N.Y.C., 1980-86, Albany (N.Y.) Inst. History and Art, 1986—; bd. dirs. Gallery Assn. of N.Y. State, Lower Manhattan Cultural Council, Hist. Albany Found., Fedn. Hist. Services; council mem. N.Y. State Assn. Museums; mus. aid panel N.Y. State Council on Arts, 1985-88. Author, writer/coordinator, compiler of catalogs in field. Mem. Am. Assn. Mus. Office: Albany Inst History & Art 125 Washington Ave New York NY 12210

MILES, DONNA JEAN, pharmacy executive; b. Seattle, Aug. 11, 1944; d. David Harrison and Mary Lou (Dressen-Sasser) Palmer; m. Donald Lewis Miles, Dec. 27, 1966; children: Kristin Amy, Scott Braden. BS in Pharmacy, U. Washington, 1967. Registered pharmacist, Wash. Staff pharmacist Woods Lakeshore Pharmacy, Kirkland, Wash., 1967-76, Pay'n Save Drugs, Inc., Seattle, 1976-86; pharmacist, mgr. Evergreen Pharmacy, Kirkland, 1986-87; pres., owner PharmaStaff, Inc., Bellevue, Wash., 1987—. Mem. Wash. State Pharmacists Assn. (bd. mgrs. 1987-90, chmn. mem. 1988-90, vice speaker of senate, 1989-90), East King County Pharmacists Assn. (v.p. 1987-89), Nat. Assn. Temporary Svcs., Wash. Assn. Temporary Svcs., Univ. Wash. Alumni Assn., Sammamish High Sch. Booster Club, Lambda Kappa Sigma. Office: PharmaStaff Inc 10900 NE 8th #900 Bellevue WA 98004

MILES, JANICE ANN, news reporter; b. Abilene, Tex., July 22, 1949; d. Theodore Winston and Clarice (Bule) M.; m. Martin Jerome Wiesenthal, Feb. 24, 1973; children: Alexis Ann Wiesenthal, Alison Claire Wiesenthal. BFA, U. Tex., 1971; postgrad., Trinity U., 1980. Social worker Tex. Dept. Human Svcs., San Antonio, 1971-79; TV news reporter Sta. KENS-TV, San Antonio, 1981—. Bd. dirs. Sunshine Cottage Sch. for Deaf Children, 1982-89, San Antonio Botanical Ctr., 1984-90, Univ. Presbyn. Children's Ctr., San Antonio, 1986-90, San Antonio Day Hosp., 1990; deacon Univ. Presbyn. Ch.; mem. adv. bd. 24th St. Experiment Theatre, San Antonio. Recipient Guardian Angel award Boysville, Inc., 1987, Barbara Jordan award Gov.'s Com. for Disabled Persons, 1988, 90, Pat Weaver award Nat. Muscular Dystrophy Assn., 1989, Recognition award Lighthouse for the Blind, 1990. Mem. Women in Communications Inc., San Antonio 100, San Antonio Forum. Presbyterian. Office: KENS-TV Eyewitness News 5400 Fredricksburg Rd San Antonio TX 78229

MILES, JOANNA, actress; b. Nice, France, Mar. 6, 1940; came to U.S., 1941, naturalized, 1941; d. Johannes Schiefer and Jeanne Miles; m. William Burns, May 23, 1970 (div. 1977); m. Michael Brandman, Apr. 29, 1978; 1 child, Miles. Grad., Putney (Vt.) Sch., 1958. Mem. Actors Studio, N.Y.C., 1966, Los Angeles Classic Theatre, 1986. Appeared in: motion pictures The Way We Live Now, 1969, Bug, 1975, The Ultimate Warrior, 1975, Golden Girl, 1978, Cross Creek, 1983, As Is, 1986, Blackout, 1988, Rosencrants and Guildenstern Are Dead, 1990; numerous television films, including In What America, 1965, My Mothers House, 1968, Glass Menagerie, 1974 (2 Emmy awards), Born Innocent, 1974, Aloha Means Goodbye, 1974, The Trial of Chaplain Jensen, 1975, Harvest Home, 1977, Fire in the Sky, 1978, Sophisticated Gents, 1979, Promise of Love, 1982, Sound of Murder, 1983, All My Sons (PBS), 1986, 87, The Right To Die, 1987; episodes in numerous TV series including Barney Miller, Dallas, St. Elsewhere, The Hulk, Trapper John, Kaz, Cagney and Lacey, Studio 5B, 1989, Star Trek The Next Generation, 1990; stage plays Walk-Up, 1962, Once in a Life Time, 1963, Cave Dwellers, 1964, Drums in the Night, 1968, Dracula, 1968, Home Free, 1964, One Night Stands of A Noisy Passenger, 1972, Dylan, 1973, Dancing for the Kaiser, 1976, Debutante Ball, 1985, One Flew Over The Cuckoo's Nest, 1989, Growing Gracefully, 1989; performed in radio shows Sta. KCRW Once in a Lifetime, 1987, Babbit, 1987, Sta. KPFK, Grapes of Wrath, 1989; playwright, v.p. Brandman Productions. Pres. Children Giving Children. Recipient Am. Women in Radio and TV award, 1974, Actors Studio Achievement award, 1980. Mem. Acad. Motion Picture Arts and Scis., Acad. TV Arts and Scis., Dramatists Guild. Office: 250 W 57th St New York NY 10019 also: Bauman Hiller & Assocs 5750 Wilshire Blvd #54 Los Angeles CA 90036

MILES, LAVEDA ANN, advertising executive; b. Greenville, S.C. Nov. 21, 1945; d. Grady Lewis and Edna Sylvia (Mahaffey) Bruce; m. Charles Thomas Miles, Nov. 10, 1974; 1 son, Joshua Bruce. A. in Bus. Adminstrn., North Greenville Jr. Coll. Traffic mgr. WFBC-TV, Greenville, S.C., 1968-74; pub. service dir., traffic mgr. WTCG-TV, Atlanta, 1974-75; traffic mgr. Henderson Advt. Co., Greenville, 1975-77, broadcast coordinator, 1977-79, dir. broadcast bus., 1979-82, dir. broadcast bus., v.p., 1982-89, bus. mgr. creative dept., 1989—. Named one of 100 Best and Brightest Women for 1988 Ad Age and Advt. Women of N.Y. Mem. Advt. Fedn. of Greenville (sec. 1979-81). Democrat. Baptist. Office: Henderson Advt Co 60 Pelham Pointe Greenville SC 29602

MILES, MARGARET, librarian; b. San Francisco, May 6, 1963; d. Robert Donald and Norma Ann (Crawford) Hughes; m. Thomas Alan Miles, May 14, 1988. BA in English, U. Calif., Davis, 1985; M Libr. and Info. Studies, U. Calif., Berkeley, 1987. Children's libr. Tracy (Calif.) br. Stockton-San Joaquin County Pub. Libr., 1987-89; chmn. children's film com. Stockton-San Joaquin County Pub. Libr., Stockton, 1987-89; supervising children's librarian Downtown br. Sacramento Pub. Library, 1990—. Amy Wood Nyholm scholar, 1987. Mem. ALA, Calif. Libr. Assn. (children's svcs. chpt. film com. 1989), AAUW, Phi Kappa Phi. Office: Sacramento Pub Library 1010 8th St Sacramento CA 95814

MILES, SONIA ROSEMARIE, psychiatrist; b. Kingston, Jamaica, Mar. 6, 1944; came to U.S.A., 1963; d. Harry Charles and Doris Lee (Shackleford) Anderson; m. Joseph J. Miles, July 1969; children: Shawn, David. BSc, St. Bonaventure U., 1968; MD, U. Medicine & Dentistry N.J., Piscataway, 1981. Residency, fellowship St. Vincent's Hosp., N.Y.C., 1981-85; fellowship U. Medicine & Dentistry N.J. Robert Wood Johnson Med. Sch., 1985-86; clin. asst., prof. U. Medicine & Dentistry N.J. RWJ Med. Sch., 1986; prof., unit chief adolescent extended treatment Unit Community Mental Health Ctr. at Piscataway; teaching assoc., coordinator, research AUTISM, 1986-88. Mem. American Psychiatric Assn. Office: U Medicine & Dentistry NJ RWJ Med Sch Community Mental Health Ctr 671 Hoes Ln Piscataway NJ 08854

MILES, TONI L., data processing executive; b. Orange, Tex., Mar. 6, 1953; d. Richard T. and Donie L. (Creel) Miles; m. Mitchell H. Francis, May 29, 1976. AAS in Data Processing, Tarrant County Jr. Coll., Ft. Worth, Tex., 1973; BBA, U. Tex., 1975. Sr. program estimator Gen. Dynamics Corp., Ft. Worth, 1976-81; MIS dir. Arlington (Tex.) Meml. Hosp., 1981—. Mem. Star Products User Group, Tex. Hosp. Info. Systems Soc., Healthcare Info. Mgmt. Systems Soc. Office: Arlington Meml Hosp 800 W Randol Mill Rd Arlington TX 76012

MILES-LAGRANGE, VICKI, state legislator; b. Oklahoma City, Sept. 30, 1953; d. Charles and Mary (Greenard) Miles; m. Jacques Lagrange. BA, Vassar Coll., 1974; LLB, Howard U., 1977. Formerly trial atty. U.S. Dept. Justice; congl. aide Speaker of the Ho., Rep. Carl Albert; mem. Okla. Senate from Dist. 48, 1987—. Democrat. Baptist. Home: 4020 N Lincoln #204 Oklahoma City OK 73105*

MILEY, DEBORAH KARLENE, social worker; b. Sweetwater, Tex., Dec. 16, 1949; d. Jackson Emilius Burns and Odell L. (Casbeer) Leeder; m. Robert Francis Miley, June 6, 1970 (div. Nov. 1980); children: Rene Louise, Gina Christine. AA, Sinclair Community Coll., 1986; BA, U. Dayton, 1988; aircraft elec. systems specialist, Community Coll. AFB, Chanute AFB, Ill., 1979. Licensed social worker. Clk. typist Div. Tex. State Govt., Austin, Tex., 1968-70; reader Tex. Press Assn., Austin, 1980-81; staff sgt. USAFR, 1978-83; tutor Sinclair Community Coll., Dayton, Ohio, 1984; therapist asst. Eastway Corp., Dayton, 1988—; initiator Advocacy Program for Mentally Retarded, Biloxi, Miss., 1974-75. Libr. organizer Sacred Heart Ch., Austin, 1976-78; asst. den leader Cub Scout Troop 99, Dayton, 1984-85; vol. tchr. aide for sch. for retarded citizens, Biloxi, 1974-75; musician for prayer group for Our Lady of Mary Ch., Dayton, 1981-83. Roman Catholic. Office: Eastway Corp 600 Wayne Ave Dayton OH 45410-1199

MILFORD, PATRICIA POLINO, drapery company executive, interior designer; b. Detroit, June 2, 1940; d. John and Madeline Rose (Graham) Polino; m. Laurence Milford, Apr. 18, 1959 (div. Nov. 1983); children: Laurence, Sherri Lynne, Jeffrey Shane. With James Renfrew & Snook & Assocs., Royal Oak, Mich., 1956-58; legal sec. Renfrew & Assocs., Royal Oak, Mich., 1958-60; v.p. Spring Crest Draperies, Naples, Fla., 1975-83, pres., 1983—; pres. Patricia Polino Milford Interior Designer Inc., Naples. Inventor solarium shade. Mem. adv. council Spring Crest County Internat. Mem. Am. Soc. Interior Designers, Naples C. of C., Nat. Fed. Ind. Bus., Collier County Builders and Contractors Assn. (advt. bd., regional adv. mem. to Spring Crest Co.), Kiwanis. Office: Spring Crest Draperies 7600 Trail Blvd N Naples FL 33963

MILIONE, JEANETTE MARGARET, state official; b. Bklyn., May 12, 1947; d. James Vincent and Rose Marie (DeSarlo) Calvacca; divorced; 1 child, Jamie Michelle. Student, Cornell U., 1971, SUNY, 1986, L.I. U., 1986. Sec. to adminstrv. asst. Office N.Y. State Compt., N.Y.C., 1965-67, adminstrv. and secretarial asst. to state comptr., 1967-84, adminstr., audit mgr., 1985—. Contbr. articles to mgmt. newsletter. Fundraiser March of Dimes, 1986; sec. Cicero Civic Assn.; mem. Am. Com. on Italian Migration, Citizens for Better Govt.; chmn. youth svc. planning com. Community Bd. 3, S.I., N.Y.; coord. N.Y. State Savs. Bond Campaign, 1986-90; campaign coord. N.Y. State Employees Federated Appeal, 1987, 88, 89; active numerous local, state and nat. polit. campaigns; campaign leader Nat. Fedn. Rep. Women; corr. sec. Richmond County Women's Rep. Club; mem. Richmond County Rep. Com.; also others. Named One of Outstanding Women in Govt., 1988, 90. Mem. Am. Soc. Profl. and Exec. Women, Orgn. N.Y. State Mgmt. and Confidential Employees (v.p. N.Y.C. chpt.), Orgn. N.Y. State Profl., Sci. and Tech. Employees. Roman Catholic. Office: Office NY State Compt 270 Broadway 19th Fl New York NY 10007

MILK, LESLIE BERG, editor; b. N.Y.C., Feb. 20, 1943; d. Sydney S. and Shirley (Balmuth) Berg; m. Benjamin L. Milk, Mar. 24, 1968; children: Jeremy Lechtman, Meredith Balmuth. BA, Syracuse U., 1963. Writer Soap & Detergent Assn., N.Y.C., 1963-65; asst. pub. rels. dir. Nat. Coun. Jewish Women, N.Y.C., 1965-69; writer Barton-Gillet Co., N.Y.C., 1969; exec. dir. Mainstream, Inc., Washington, 1976-80; dir. info. employment standards adminstrn. U.S. Dept. Labor, 1980-81; dir. pub. affairs Ctr. for Strategic and Internat. Studies, 1982-86; columnist The Washington Post, 1982; assoc. editor The Washingtonian mag., Washington, 1986—; columnist The Jour. newspapers, 1983—. Vice chair Montgomery County Commn. for Handicapped Individuals, suburban Md., 1979-80; bd. dirs. Leonard Cheshire Found., Washington, 1978-80; pres. Jewish Found. for Group Homes, 1984-86 (S. Robert Cohen award 1990). Recipient Capital Press Women award, 1976, Mass Media award AAUW, Washington, 1988, 90. Office: The Washingtonian 1828 L St NW Washington DC 20036

MILKS, SALLY ANN, food service manager, dietitian; b. Bradford, Pa., Nov. 29, 1949; d. John David and Pearl Marie (Meier) Morrison; m. Frank Elmer Milks, Aug. 18, 1973 (div. 1978); 1 child, Jason Michael. B.S. in Edn., Mansfield State Coll., 1971; student Indiana U. of Pa., 1969-71. Registered dietitian. Clin. dietitian St. Vincent Med. Ctr., Erie, Pa., 1971-72, 73-74; dietetic intern Shadyside Hosp., Pitts., 1972-73; cons. dietitian Sheridan Manor Nursing Home, Buffalo, 1975-77; nutrition instr. E.J. Meyer Sch. Nursing, Buffalo, 1975-77, chief clin. dietitian, 1977-78; asst. dir. food services ARA Services, Erie County Med. Ctr., 1978-79, dir. food services, 1979-82, dist. mgr., Phila., 1982—; mem. adv. council Buffalo State U., 1985—; guest lectr. food and nutrition dept., 1980—. Ho. of dels. United Way of Buffalo and Erie County, 1983-85. Mem. Am. Dietetic Assn., Erie County Assn. for Retarded Children (2d v.p. 1983-85, chmn. residential services com. 1981-87). Home: 17 Apollo Dr Amherst NY 14120 Office: ARA Services 11103 Pepper Rd Hunt Valley MD 21031

MILLANE, LYNN, town official; b. Buffalo, N.Y. Oct. 14, 1928; d. Robert P. Schermerhorn and Justine A. (Ross) m. J. Vaughan Millane, Jr.; Aug. 16, 1952 children: Maureen, Michele, John, Mark, Kathleen. EdB, U. Buffalo, 1949, EdM, in Health Education 1951. Mem. Amherst Town Bd., 1982—, dep. town supr., 1990—; pres., E. J. Meyer Hosp. Jr. Bd., 1962-64; pres. Aux. to Erie County Bar Assn., 1966-68; pres. Women's Com. of Buffalo Philharm. Orch., 1976-78, v.p. adminstrn., 1975-76, v.p. pub. affairs, 1974-75, chmn. adv. bd., 1979-82; v.p. Buffalo Philharm. Orch. Soc., Inc., 1976-78, mem. coun., trustee, 1979-87, bd. overseers, 1987—; dir. 8th judicial dist. N.Y. State Assn. of Large Towns, 1989-90, 90-91; 1st v.p. Fans for 17, 1980-82; 1st. v.p. Friends of Baird Hall, SUNY-Buffalo, 1980-82; exec. bd. mem. Longview Protestant Home for Children, 1979-85, 2d v.p., 1982-85; bd. dirs. ARC, Town of Amherst br., 1982—, by-laws com., 1981, 84, chmn. sr. concerns com., 1982—, liaison code of ethics com., 1987-89; bd. dirs. Amherst Symphony Orch. Assn., 1981-87, roster chmn., 1982-84, nominating chmn., 1985-86; nat. music com. Women's Assn. for Symphony Orchs. in Am. and Can., 1977-79; coun. mem. Am. Symphony Orch. League; sec. Amherst Sr. Citizen's Adv. Bd., 1980-81, liaison from Amherst Town Bd., 1982—; mem. 1st adult day svcs. adv. bd., 1st records mgmt. adv. bd.; dir.-at-large community adv. coun. SUNY-Buffalo, 1981—; co-assoc. chmn. maj. gift div. capital campaign Daemen Coll., 1983-84; co-chmn. Women United Against Drugs Campaign, 1970-72; founding mem. Lunch and Issues, Amherst, 1981—; mem. edn. com. Network in Aging of Western N.Y., Inc., 1982-89, bd. dirs., 1982-89, housing com., 1987-89; bd. dirs. Amherst Elderly Transp. Corp., 1982-89; liaison to and established 1st adult day svcs. adv. bd. in Amherst, 1988; committeeman dist. Town of Amherst Republican Com.; treas. Town and Country Rep. Club, 1980-81; mem. nominating com. Fedn. Rep. Women's Clubs Erie County, 1980; exec. bd. mem. Women's Exec. Coun. of Erie County Rep. Com., 1969-71; dir. Amherst Rep. Women's Club, 1963-65. Pi Lambda Theta National Honorary-1950. Named Homemaker of Yr., Family Circle Mag., 1969; Woman of Substance, 20th Century Rep. Women, 1983; Woman of Yr., Buffalo Philharm. Orch. Soc., Inc., 1982; Outstanding Woman in Community Svc., SUNY-Buffalo, 1985; recipient Good Neighbor award Courier Express, 1978; Merit award Buffalo Philharm. Orch., 1978; award Fedn. Rep. Women's Clubs Erie County, 1982; Disting. Service award Town of Amherst Sr. Ctr., 1985. Mem. Amherst C. of C. (VIP dinner com. 1984), LWV, SUNY-Buffalo Alumni Assn. (life, presdl. advisor 1977-79). Lodge: Zonta (pres. Amherst chpt. 1986-88). Office: 5583 Main St Amherst NY 14221

MILLAR, LAURIE SUE, university administrator; b. Saginaw, Mich., May 12, 1961; d. Robert Lynwood and Virginia Lee (Clark) Rusch; m. Todd Wesley Millar, Dec. 1, 1984; children: Caitlin Sue, Jacob Christian. BSBA, Cen. Mich. U., 1984. Acct. Saginaw div. GM, 1982-85; bus. systems analyst Oldsmobile div. GM, Lansing, Mich., 1986-88; asst. payroll mgr. Mich. State U., East Lansing, 1985-86; bus. adminstr. Purdue U., West Lafayette, Ind., 1988-89, systems support adminstr., 1989-90, systems/accounts payable adminstr., 1990—. Mem. NAFE. Presbyterian. Home: RR 3 Box 2 State Rd 43 S Brookston IN 47923 Office: Purdue U Acctg Dept Freehafer West Lafayette IN 47907

MILLAR, MARGARET ELLIS, author; b. Kitchener, Ont., Can., Feb. 5, 1915; d. Henry William and Lavinia (Ferrier) Sturm; m. Kenneth Millar (pseudonym Ross Macdonald), June 2, 1938 (dec.); 1 dau., Linda Jane (dec.). Student, U. Toronto, 1933-36. Author: The Invisible Worm, 1941, The Weak-Eyed Bat, 1942, The Devil Loves Me, 1942, Wall of Eyes, 1943, Fire Will Freeze, 1944, The Iron Gates, 1945, Experiment in Springtime, 1947, It's All in the Family, 1948, The Cannibal Heart, 1949, Do Evil in Return, 1950, Vanish in an Instant, 1952, Rose's Last Summer, 1952, Wives and Lovers, 1954, Beast in View, 1955, An Air That Kills, 1957, The Listening Walls, 1959, A Stranger in My Grave, 1960, How Like an Angel, 1962, The Fiend, 1964, The Birds and the Beasts Were There, 1968, Beyond This Point Are Monsters, 1970, Ask for Me Tomorrow, 1976, The Murder of Miranda, 1980, Mermaid, 1982, Banshee, 1983, Spider Webs, 1986; also writer short stories and TV plays. Recipient Edgar award for Beast in View Mystery Writers Am., 1956, Woman of Yr. award L.A. Times, 1965, Grandmaster award Mystery Writers Am., 1982. Mem. Mystery Writers Am. (pres. 1957). Home: 87 Seaview Dr Santa Barbara CA 93108

MILLAR, MARIAN M., library supervisor; b. Ripley, Ohio, Sept. 3, 1926; d. Kenneth N. and Anna Lucy (Emery) McVey; m. Ronald C. Millar, Aug. 20, 1950 (dec. 1974); 1 child, Mark K. BS in Edn., Wilmington (Ohio) Coll., 1949; MLS, Kent (Ohio) State U., 1977. Tchr. Fairfield Schs., Leesburg, Ohio, 1949-52, Richville Elem. Sch., Perry Twp., Ohio, 1953-57, Dellroy (Ohio) Elem. Sch., 1957-59; libr. Hoover High Sch., North Canton, Ohio, 1965-67; elem. libr. supr. Massillon (Ohio) City Schs., 1967-85, ret., 1985. Martha Holden Jennings Found. scholar, 1978-79. Mem. AAUW (program v.p.). Mem. Soc. of Friends. Home: 8236 Willowdale Lake Ave NW North Canton OH 44720

MILLARD, LAVERGNE HARRIET, free-lance artist; b. Chgo., July 8, 1925; d. Lewis and Julia (Smolk) Bassmire; student Chgo. Art Inst., 1937-39; m. Samuel Costales, 1943 (div. 1957); m. Bailey Millard, Mar. 9, 1958 (div.); children—Bryan Lewis Costales, Julianne, Juanita Crump, Candace Lynn Millard. Cocktail waitress Verdis, Grant Street, Concord, Calif., 1955-61; mgr. used book shop Joyce Book Shop, Concord, 1964-79, seller art works, own prints; freelance artist, 1979—. Recipient ribbons local fairs, art shows. Republican. Copyright holder for pastel art work. Home and Office: 1890 Farm Bureau Rd Apt 11 Concord CA 94519

MILLENDER-MCDONALD, JUANITA, school system administrator; b. Birmingham, Ala., Sept. 7, 1938; d. Shelly and Everlina (Dortch) M.; m. James McDonald III, July 26, 1955; children: Valeria, Angela, Sherryll, Michael, Roderick. BS, U. Redlands, Calif., 1980; MS in Edn., Calif. State U., L.A., 1986; postgrad., U. So. Calif. Manuscript editor Calif. State Dept. Edn., Sacramento; dir. gender equity programs L.A. Unified Sch. Dist. City councilwoman, Carson; bd. dirs. S.C.L.C. Pvt. Industry Coun. Policy Bd., West Basin Mcpl. Water Dist., Cities Legis. League (vice chmn.; mem. Nat. Women's Polit. Caucus; mem. adv. bd. Comparative Ethnic Tng. U. So. Calif.; founder, exec. dir. Young Advocates So. Calif. Mem. NEA, Nat. Assn. Minority Polit. Women, NAFE, Nat. Fedn. Bus. and Profl. Women, Assn. Calif. Sch. Adminstrs., Am. Mgmt. Assn., Nat. Coun. Jewish Women, Carson C. of C., Phi Delta Kappa. Office: LA Unified Sch Dist 1320 W Third St Ste 101 Los Angeles CA 90017

MILLENSON, DEBRA ANN, lawyer; b. Cleve., July 24, 1947; d. Morton B. and Judith Leah (Rehmar) M. BA, Mich. State U., 1967; JD, U. Mich., 1970. Bar: La. 1970, U.S. Dist. Ct. (mid. dist.) La. 1970, U.S. Ct. Appeals (5th cir.) 1970, U.S. Supreme Ct. 1974, U.S. Dist. Ct. D.C. 1974, D.C. 1976, U.S. Dist. Ct. (we. dist.) Tex. 1978. Staff atty. Lawyers Constn. Def. Com., New Orleans, 1970-72; pvt. practice law New Orleans, 1972-73; trial atty. EEOC, Washington, 1973-82; sr. trial atty. U.S. Dept. Labor, Washington, 1982—. Author: (with others) Employment Discrimination Law, 1981—. Chair ACLU, Va., 1976-78. Mem. ABA (subcom. chair labor and EEO com. 1985—). Office: US Dept Labor Office of Solicitor 200 Constitution Ave NW Washington DC 20210

MILLER, ADELE ENGELBRECHT, educational administrator; b. Jersey City, July 31, 1946; d. John Fred and Dorathea Kathryn (Kamm) Engelbrecht; m. William A. Miller, Jr., Dec. 21, 1981. BS in Bus. Edn., Fairleigh Dickinson U., 1968, MBA magna cum laude, 1974; cert. in pub. sch. adminstrn. and supervision, Jersey City State Coll., 1976. Bus. tchr. Jersey City Bd. Edn., 1967—, coord. coop. office edn. programs, 1973—, acting v.p., 1985-86, prin. of summer sch., 1986; adj. instr. St. Peter's Coll., 1974-75; curriculum cons. Cittone Bus. Sch., 1981-82; mem. adv. coun. Dickinson High Sch., 1973—, chmn., 1978-80; organizer, bd. dirs. Frances Nadel and Cooke-Connolly-Coffey-Witt Faculty Meml. Scholarships, 1978—; trustee Dickinson High Sch. Parents Coun., 1985—. Co-author: New Jersey Cooperative Office Education Coordinators Resource Manual, 1984; author coop. office edn. study course Jersey City Public Schs., 1980, 84. Mem. Citizens Adv. Coun. to Mayor of Jersey City, 1968-71; organizer, dir. Jersey City Youth Week, 1970-72; mem. juvenile conf. com. Hudson County Juvenile Ct., 1978—; v.p., sec., trustee, chmn. dinner-musicale Jersey City Coll.-Community Orch., 1979—; Explorer Scouting adv. bd. Hudson-Hamilton coun. Boy Scouts Am., 1985—; trustee Jersey City YWCA, 1988—. Recipient Dickinson High Sch. Key Club Tchr. of the Yr. award, 1971; named Educator of the Yr. Dickinson High Sch. Parents Coun., 1987, 88. Mem. NEA, N.J. Edn. Assn., Jersey City Edn. Assn. (bldg. dir.), N.J. Coop. Office Edn. Coords. Assn. (pres., v.p., sec. treas.), N.J. Fedn. Women's Clubs, Jersey City Women's Club (scholarship chmn., adviser Jr. Woman's Club), AAUW (edn. chmn., sec. N.J. div., del. to White House briefing on edn., women's issues, arms control), AAUW Coll. Clubs Jersey City. Home: 91 Sherman Pl Jersey City NJ 07307 Office: Dickinson High Sch 2 Palisade Ave Jersey City NJ 07306

MILLER, ADRIENNE NYMAN, health care consultant; b. Kearney, N.J., Feb. 8, 1954; d. David and Betty Pearl (Kinsler) Nyman; m. Ira Jay Miller, Aug. 31, 1989. BA, U. Pa., 1975; MBA, Cornell U., 1981. Regional fin. asst. Hosp. Corp. of Am. Mgmt. Co., Nashville, 1981-82; specialist Hosp. Corp. of Am., Nashville, 1982-86, cons., 1984-86; sr. cons. Hosp. Corp. of Am., Dallas, 1986—. Mem. Am. Mktg. Assn. (founding mem. health care spl. interest group), Am. Hosp. Assn. (mem. issues and policy com., health care planning and mktg. society 1988), Acad. Health Svcs. Mktg. (awards judge 1989). Home: 3310 Leahy Dr Dallas TX 75229 Office: Quorum Health Resources 15851 Dallas Pkwy Ste 500 Dallas TX 75248

MILLER, AILEEN ETTA MARTHA, medical association administrator, consultant; b. Sullivan, Ind., Oct. 4, 1924; d. Arthur Henry and Alice Marie (Michael) Dettmer; m. Robert Charles Miller, Sept. 1, 1945; children: Robert Conrad, Debra Carol, Theresa Marie. D of Chiropractic, Palmer Coll. Chiropractic, 1945. Sec. Soroptimist Internat., East Detroit, Mich., 1951-52, Mich. State Chiropractic Assn. Dist. 1, East Detroit, 1957-58, Macomb County Chiropractic Assn., East Detroit, 1982-86; pres. Macomb County Chiropractic Assn., Warren, Mich., 1986-87; cons. Chiropractic Physicians, Warren, 1986—. Mem. Internat. Chiropractic Assn., Mich. State Chiropractic Assn., Nat. Upper Cervical Chiropractic Assn., Roy Sweat Rsch. and Edn. Found., Mich. Chiropractic Coun., Am. Chiropractic Assn., Found. Chiropractic Edn. and Rsch., Palmer Coll. Alumni Assn., Atlas Orthogonal Assn. Republican. Office: Chiropractic Physicians 30020 Schoenherr Warren MI 48093

MILLER, ANNE SMALL, educator; b. Calhan, Colo., Sept. 15, 1907; d. Richard Webster and Florence (Blower) Small; m. Purviance Miller, Aug. 14, 1932; 1 child, Judith Anne. BA with honors, Colo. Coll., 1926; MA, Smith Coll., 1928. Tchr. tng., 1928; tchr. language and edn. Clarke Sch. for Oral-Aural Deaf, Northampton, Mass., various positions; tchr. Clarke Sch. Summer Inst., Northampton, ret., 1974; lectr. Internat. Congress for Deaf, Manchester, England, 1958, Northampton, 1967, Stockholm, Sweden, 1970; panel mem. and lectr. various profl. confs.; TV appearances; conducted workshops on language, speech, curriculum, sex edn. at various profl. functions in U.S.; summer camp work with hearing children; speech-reading classes for adults and children, demonstrations at Rockport, Mass. Art Assn. Contbr. articles to profl. jours. Smith Coll. Trustee fellow, 1927-28. Mem. Teachers Union, Phi Beta Kappa. Unitarian. Home: 4 Cathedral Ave Rockport MA 01966

MILLER, BARBARA JEAN, healthcare executive; b. Maracaibo, Venezuela, Feb. 27, 1952; came to U.S. 1969; d. Charles Knower and Joyce (Sampson) M. MBA, U. Dallas, 1979. CPA, Tex. Asst. to dean adminstrn. U. Dallas, Irving, 1974-80; staff acct. Sedco Oil, Dallas, 1980-81; v.p. fin. Dallas-Ft. Worth Hosp. Coun., Irving, 1982-87; dir. fin. Arlington (Tex.) Meml. Hosp. Found., 1987—; bd. dirs. Lone Star chpt. Healthcare Fin. Mgmt. Assn., Dallas; tchr. Basic Healthcae Fin. course So. Meth. U., 1988. Pres. Homeowner's Assn. Mem. AICPA, Tex. Soc. CPA, Dallas Chpt. Tex. Soc. CPA, Sigma Iota Epsilon, Las Colinas Sports Club. Republican. Office: Arlington Meml Hosp 800 W Randol Mill Rd Arlington TX 76012

MILLER, BARBARA STALLCUP, medical foundation administrator; b. Montague, Calif., Sept. 4, 1919; d. Joseph Nathaniel and Maybelle (Needham) Stallcup; m. Leland F. Miller, May 16, 1946; children—Paula Kay, Susan Lee, Daniel Joseph, Alison Jean. B.A., U. Oreg., 1942. Women's editor Eugene (Oreg.) Daily News, 1941-43; law clk. to J. Everett Barr, Yreka, Calif., 1943-45; mgr. Yreka C. of C., 1945-46; Northwest supr. Louis Harris and Assocs., Portland, Oreg., 1959-62; dir. pub. relations and fund raising Columbia River council Girl Scouts U.S.A., 1962-67; pvt. practice pub. relations cons., Portland, 1967-72; adviser of student publs., asst. prof. communications U. Portland, 1967-72, dir. pub. relations and info., asst. prof. communications, 1972-78, dir. devel., 1978-79, exec. dir. devel., 1979-83; assoc. dir. St. Vincent Med. Found., 1983-88; dir. planned giving Good Samaritan Found., 1988—. Pres. bd. dirs. Vols. of Am. of Oreg., Inc., 1980-84, pres. regional adv. bd., 1982-84; chmn. bd. dirs. S.E. Mental Health Network, 1984-88; nat. bd. dirs. Vols. of Am., Inc., 1984—. Recipient Presdl. Citation, Oreg. Communicators Assn., 1973, Matrix award, 1976, 80, Miltner award U. Portland, 1977. Mem. Nat. Assn. Hosp. Devel., Nat. Soc. Fundraising Execs., Women in Communications (NW regional v.p. 1973-75, Offbeat award 1988), Nat. Fedn. Press Women, Oreg. Press Women (dist.

dir.), Pub. Rels. Soc. Am. (dir. local chpt., Marsh award 1989), Oreg. Fedn. Womens Clubs (communications chmn. 1978-80), Alpha Xi Delta (found. trustee, editor 1988—). Unitarian. Clubs: Portland Zenith (pres. 1975-76, 81-82), City Club of Portland. Contbr. articles to profl. jours. Home: 1706 SW Boca Ratan Dr Lake Oswego OR 97034 Office: 1015 NW 22d Ave Portland OR 97210

MILLER, BARBARA STEPHENSON, real estate executive; b. L.A., Apr. 7, 1950; d. Joseph Flaum and Morgan (Malinow) Miller. AA in History, Orange Coast Coll., 1970; BA in History, San Jose State U., 1973; MA, UCLA, 1980. Tchr. English as 2d lang. various colls., San Jose, Calif., 1980-87; realtor Coldwell Banker, Campbell, Calif., 1987-89, Century Medallion, Cupertino, Calif., 1989—; bd. dirs. Community Housing Developers. Chmn. polit. affairs com. Grassroots Polit. Workshop, San Jose, 1989; bd. dirs. Community Housing Developers; liaison to WATCH. Mem. Nat. Assn. Realtors, Calif. Assn. Realtors, San Jose Dept. Realtors (polit. affairs com. 1987—), Women's Coun., NAFE, 99 Club. Office: Century Medallion 10370 S De Anza Blvd Cupertino CA 95014

MILLER, BETH, Spanish and Portugese educator; b. Chgo., Jan. 13, 1941; d. Bert and Anita (Lome) Kurti; 1 child, Samantha. Postgrad., U. Madrid, 1960-61; BA summa cum laude, Northwestern U., 1962; MA, U. Calif., Berkeley, 1965, U. Calif., Berkeley, 1973. Asst. prof. Spanish and French SUNY, New Paltz, 1968-69; instr., asst. prof. Rutgers U., New Brunswick, N.J., 1969-76; assoc. prof. U. So. Calif., Los Angeles, 1976—, chmn. dept. Spanish and Portugese, 1977-78; cons. Guggenheim Found., Nat. Endowment for Humanities, U. Calif. Press. Author: La Poesia Constructiva de Jaime Torres Bodet, 1974, Mujeres en la Literatura, 1978, Rosario Castellanos: Una Conciencia Feminista en Mexico, 1983, 26 Autoras del Mexico de Hoy, 1978, Uma Consciencia Feminista: Rosario Castellanos, 1987, A la Sombra del volcan: La Narrativa mexicana actual, 1990: editor: Women in Hispanic Literature: Icons and Fallen Idols, 1982; translator: Siete poetas norteamericanas, 1977; assoc. editor Melus, 1977; mem. editorial bd. Caribe, Latin Am. Lit. Rev. Mem. Venice Town Council, Calif., 1987-88. Grantee Rutgers U., 1972-75, U. So. Calif., 1974-75, Del Amo Found., 1976-77, Am. Council Learned Socs., 1979, Colo. Endowment for Humanities, 1985; grantee in aid Am. Council Learned Socs., 1987; Nat. Women's Assn. fellow; Fulbright-Hays Commn. sr. fellow, 1985, 86. Mem. Latin Am. Studies, AAUW (awards 1986, 87), Inst. Internat. Lit. Iberoamericana, Am. Tchrs. Spanish and Portugese, Pacific Coast Council Latin Am. Studies. Home: 36 Navy St Apt 7 Venice CA 90291 Office: U So Calif Dept Spanish and Portuguese Los Angeles CA 90089-0358

MILLER, BETTY BROWN, free-lance writer; b. Altus, Ark., Dec. 21, 1926; d. Carlos William and Arlie Gertrude (Sublett) Brown; m. Robert Wiley Miller, Nov. 15, 1953; children: Janet Ruth, Stephen Wiley. BS Okla. State U., 1949; MS, U. Tulsa, 1953; postgrad., Am. U., 1966-68. Tchr. LeFlore (Okla.) High Sch., 1947-48, Osage Indian Reservation High Sch., Hominy, Okla., 1948-50, Jenks (Okla.) High Sch., 1950-51; instr. Sch. Bus., U. Tulsa, 1950-51; tchr. Tulsa public schs., 1951-54; instr. Burdette Coll., Boston, 1954-55; reporter Bethesda-Chevy Chase Tribune, Montgomery County, Md., 1970-73; freelance writer, contbr. newspapers and mags., 1973—. V.p. Kenwood Park (Md.) Citizens Assn., 1960; mem. Ft. Sumner Citizens Assn., editor newsletter, 1969; mem. Md. State PTA, editorial coord. leadership conf., 1973-74; chmn. Montgomery County Forum for Edn., 1970-75. Mem. Nat. Soc. Arts and Letters (past editor mag., bd. dir. pub. rels., past nat. corr. sec.), Nat. League Am. Pen Women (budget chmn., past nat. treas.) PEO, Montgomery County Press Assn., Internat. Platform Assn., Capital Speakers Club of Washington (past pres.), Adventures Unltd., U.D.C., Soc. Descs. of Washington's Army at Valley Forge (nat. comdr. in chief, past insp. gen.), DAR, Huguenot Soc. (v.p. 1989—, past bd. dirs.), Washington Club, Sedgeley Club (pres. 1985-88, Phila.) Republican. Address: PO Box 573 Valley Forge PA 19481

MILLER, BETTY CAROL, school system administrator; b. Mercer, Pa., Mar. 30, 1945; d. John Dyer and Mary Elizabeth (Shuler) Little; 1 child, Christopher Carl John. Student, Strayer Coll., Washington. Planner I, II, III, sec. Fairfax County (Va.) Pub. Schs. Mem. NAFE. Home: PO Box 182 Aldie VA 22001

MILLER, BETTY JEAN, feature film distribution company executive; b. Cleve., Nov. 13, 1958; d. Lester Theodore and Edith Frances (Dressel) M.; m. Paulo Carlos de Oliveira, July 14, 1984. AB magna cum laude, Brown U., 1980. Pres., owner Gingham Girls & Guys, Cleve., 1972-77; music parlegal Mitchell, Silberberg & Krupp, L.A., 1981; asst. Sotheby Parke Bernet, L.A., 1982; dir. music contracts adminstrn. Columbia Pictures, L.A., 1982-84; dir. adminstrn. Kodiak Films, L.A., 1985-87; v.p. corp. projects Skouras Pictures, Inc., L.A., 1987—. Mem. Women in Film Internat. (steering com., festival liaison 1985-87), Am. Film Mktg. Assn. (outreach com. 1986-87), NAFE. Office: Skouras Pictures Inc 1040 N Las Palmas Ave Hollywood CA 90038

MILLER, BETTY JO, machine manufacturing company executive; b. Pitts., July 27, 1924; d. Paul Haines and Ella Irene (Berkey) Young; m. Clifford Miller, Feb. 16, 1946; 1 child, Paul David. B.S. in Bus., Burdett Coll., 1950; postgrad. MIT, 1960. With engring. dept. Armstrong Cork, Braintree, Mass., 1942-44; pvt. sec. F.S. Webster Co., Boston, 1944-46; acct., treas. Braintree Tool Co., Inc., 1952-75, pres., 1975-89; acct. Blackburn Sheetmetal, Braintree, 1954-78, Micro Hydraulic Valves, Braintree, 1955-80, Mandel E. Cohen, M.D., Boston, 1964—, Howie and Cramond, Inc., Quincy, Mass., 1974-88, Smith Harrison Co., Inc., 1969—; pvt. practice, Braintree, 1989—; notary pub. Mass., 1970—; IRS rep. Holtsville, N.Y., 1984. Patentee electric undercutter and armature turning tools. Clk. of the polls, Braintree, 1964—; sec. Hampshire Shores Assn., 1967—; acct., tax specialist Braintree gardners guild, 1983—. Mem. Braintree Bd. Trade, Nat. Fedn. Ind. Bus., South Shore C. of C., U.S. SBA, Nat. Bus. Assn., Braintree Women's Club (pres. 1982-83) treas., auditor 1968—), Gen. Fedn. Women's Clubs, State Fedn. Womens Clubs. Republican. Avocations: golf; bowling; bridge. Office: 31 Waldron Rd Braintree MA 02184

MILLER, BEVERLY B., professor; b. Champaign, Ill., Feb. 8, 1933; d. Delbert Ray and Alice May (Mears) Hershbarger; 1 child, Lori Andrea. BS, Eastern Ill. U., 1955; MLS, U. Ill., 1967. Head librarian Rantoul (Ill.) High Sch., 1965-67; prof. Eastern Ill. U., Charleston, 1967—. Author: Literary Reflections, 1978; contbr. articles to profl. jours. Mem. AAUW (program v.p.). Home: 1129 Woodlawn Dr Charleston IL 61920 Office: Eastern Ill U Charleston IL 61920

MILLER, BEVERLY M., treasurer; b. Memphis, Oct. 2, 1949; d. Enos Park and Ruth (Kempel) Moomau; m. Dennis Reed Miller, Nov. 21, 1950 (div. 1985); children: Heather, Holly. Student, Memphis State U., 1967-70, U. Ark., 1972; BSBA, U. Phoenix, 1984. Lic. real estate agt., Calif. Mktg. adminstr. Condor Systems, Inc., San Jose, Calif., 1981-83; info. security specialist Stanford Telecommunications, Inc., Santa Clara, Calif., 1983-84; supr. security svcs. adminstrn. SRI, Internat., Menlo Park, Calif., 1984-85; mgr. bus. ops. Deskin Rsch. Group, Inc., Santa Clara, 1985-88, asst. treas., 1988-90, treas., v.p. fin., 1990—; treas. Nat. Contract Mgmt. Assn., San Francisco, 1989; cons. Small Govt. Contractors, San Jose, 1988—, various non-profit orgns., San Jose, 1987—; speaker in field. Pres. bd. dirs. Next Door Solutions to Domestic Violence, San Jose, 1988—, treas., 1987. Recipient Resolution for Outstanding Community Svc. Sen. Dan McCorquadale, 1990. Mem. Nat. Classification Mgmt. Assn. (chmn. membership 1983-85), Am. Soc. Indsl. Security. Lutheran. Office: Deskin Rsch Group Inc 2270 Agnew Rd Santa Clara CA 95054

MILLER, BEVERLY WHITE, college president; b. Willoughby, Ohio; d. Joseph Martin and Marguerite Sarah (Storer) White; m. Lynn Martin Miller, Oct. 11, 1945 (dec. 1986); children: Michaela Ann, Craig Martin, Todd Daniel, Cass Timothy, Simone Marguerite. AB, Western Res. U., 1945; MA, Mich. State U., 1957; PhD, U. Toledo, 1967; LHD (hon.), Coll. St. Benedict, St. Joseph, Minn., 1979; LLD (hon.), U. Toledo, 1988. Chem. and biol. researcher, 1945-57; tchr. schs. in Mich., also Mercy Sch. Nursing, St. Lawrence Hosp., Lansing, Mich., 1957-58; mem. chemistry and biology faculty Mary Manse Coll., Toledo, 1958-71; dean grad. div. Mary Manse Coll., 1968-71, exec. v.p., 1968-71; acad. dean Salve Regina Coll., Newport, R.I., 1971-74; pres. Coll. St. Benedict, St. Joseph, Minn., 1974-79, Western New Eng. Coll., Springfield, Mass., 1980—; cons. U.S. Office Edn., 1980; cons. in field.; mem. Pvt. Industry Council, exec. com., 1984—, Springfield. Author papers in field. Corporator Mercy Hosp., Springfield, Mass. Recipient President's citation St. John's U., 1979; also various service awards. Mem. Am. Assn. Higher Edn., AAAS, Assn. Cath. Colls. and Univs. (exec. bd.), Internat. Assn. Sci. Edn., Nat. Assn. Ind. Colls. and Univs. (govt. rels. adv. com., bd. dirs. 1990—), Nat. Assn. Biology Tchrs., Assn. Ind. Colls. and Univs. of Mass. (exec. com. 1981—, vice chmn. 1985-86, chmn. 1986-87), Nat. Assn. Rsch. Sci. Teaching, Springfield C. of C. (bd. dirs.), Am. Assn. Univ. Adminstrs. (bd. dirs. 1989—), Delta Kappa Gamma, Sigma Delta Epsilon. Office: Western New Eng Coll 1215 Wilbraham Rd Springfield MA 01119-2684

MILLER, BILLIE RUTH, guidance counselor; b. Abilene, Tex., July 9, 1924; d. George Bruce and Cordelia (Chaffin) Darnell; m. Lloyd Nathaniel Hawkins, Sept. 6, 1942 (dec. June 1962); children—Billy Loyd, Garry Lynn, Bruce Russell; m. J. Robert Miller, Mar. 27, 1969. BA, McMurry Coll., 1966; M.Ed., Hardin Simmons U., 1971; postgrad. U. Tex.-Arlington, 1972, No. Ariz. U., 1973, Abilene Christian U., 1977. Cert. counselor, Tex.; nat. cert. counselor. Cons. Cogdell News Co., Abilene, 1945-47, sec., acct., 1942-45; tchr., counselor Kayenta Boarding Sch., Ariz., 1966-67; head guidance dept. Crownpoint Boarding Sch., N.Mex., 1967-71; edn. service officer 96 CSG/DPE, Dyess AFB, Tex., 1973-75, guidance counselor, 1971-73, 75—, edn. lectr., 1971—, edn. service officer, 1986—; pvt. practice counseling, Abilene, 1971—, guest appearances TV stas., Abilene. Vice pres. Abilene Art Forum, 1954; pres., historian N.A.T.I.O.N.S Club, Abilene, 1960, 61. Recipient Superior Performance award Civilian Personnel Dyess AFB, Tex., 1984, achievement award Dir. Personnel Dyess AFB, 1983, Notable Achievement, 1987, Cert. Appreciation, 1987, Superior award 1988, 89; Ora Negra Am. Bus. Women Assn. ednl. scholar, 1967. Mem. Am. Assn. Counselor Devel. (nat. cert. 1983), Nat. Vocat. Counselor Devel., Tex. Assn. Counseling Devel. (cert. 1983), Mil. Edn. Counselor Assn. (treas. 1981-82), Western Horizon Am. Bus. Women Edn. Assn. (chmn. 1983, Woman of Yr. 1979), Mensa (sec. Abilene chpt. 1963-64), United Daus. Confederacy (sec. 1947-48). Republican. Baptist. Lodge: Order of Ea. Star (worthy matron 1957-58, dep. grand matron 1960), Dau. of Nile (Princess Badoura 1989). Avocations: amateur archaeology; astronomy; camping and rafting; painting; knitting. Home: 1857 Sycamore Abilene TX 79602 Office: 96 CSG/DPE Dyess AFB Abilene TX 79607

MILLER, BONNIE SEWELL, marketing professional; b. Junction City, Ky., July 24, 1932; d. William Andrew and Lillian Irene (McCowan) Sewell; m. William Gustave Tournade Jr., Nov. 5., 1950 (div. 1974); children: Bonnie Sue Tournade Zaner, William Gustave III, Sharon Irene Tournade Harris; m. Bruce George Miller, Nov. 15, 1981. BA, U. South Fla., 1968, MA, 1973. Cert. tchr., Fla. Chair dept. English Tampa (Fla.) Cath. High Sch., 1972-78; tchr. Clearwater (Fla.) High Sch., 1978-80; mgr. prodn. svcs. Paradyne Corp., Largo, Fla., 1980-83; freelance writer, cons. Tampa, 1983-84; mgr. product documentation PPS, Inc., Largo, 1984-86; mgr. mktg. communications PPS, Inc., 1986-87; writer Nixdorf Computer Corp., Tampa, 1988-89; mktg. dir. Suncoast Schs. Fed. Credit Union, Tampa, 1989—; instr. English, Hillsborough Community Coll., Tampa, 1975-87; cons. bus. writing, Coronet Instrnl. Media Writing Project, Tampa, 1976, Nat. Mgmt. Assn., Tampa, 1981-87. Contbr. tech. articles to various publs. Vol. SERVE, Tampa; legis. chair Tampa PTA, 1965; judge speech contest Am. Legion, Tampa, 1976; vol. North Tampa Vol. Libr., 1988. NEH fellow, 1975. Mem. Internat. Assn. Bus. Communicators, Soc. Tech. Communicators, Nat. Assn. of Exec. Women, Am. Assn. Bus. Women, Toastmasters Internat., Kappa Delta Pi. Democrat. Baptist. Home: 4014 Hudson Terr Tampa FL 33624 Office: 6801 E Hillsborough Ave Tampa FL 33610

MILLER, CAROL A., medical group administrator; b. Handcock, Ind., Dec. 3, 1939; d. Hubert C. and Dorothy B. (Wallace) Graham; m. David R. Miller, Feb. 15, 1974. BSBA, Ind. U. Bus. mgr. Ga. Vascular Clinic, P.C., Atlanta, 1976-78, Nephrology and Internal Medicine, Inc., Indpls., 1979-83; administr. Ind. Ctr. for Surgery and Rehab. of Hand, Indpls., 1983—. Mem. Am. Coll. Med. Group Adminstrs., Med. Group Mgmt. Assn., Ind. Med. Group Mgmt. Assn., Ind. Fedn. Ambulatory Surg. Ctrs. Office: Ind Ctr for Surgery & Rehab of the Hand 8501 Harcourt Rd PO Box 80434 Indianapolis IN 46280

MILLER, CAROL ELAINE, accountant; b. Chgo., Mar. 21, 1961; d. Charles Herbert Moore Jr. and Betty (Jordan) Owens; m. Steven Royce Miller, Oct. 25, 1986. BS in Accountancy, U. Ill., 1983. CPA, Ill. Internal auditor J.C. Penney Co., Schaumburg, Ill., 1983-85; staff acct. Odell Hicks and Co., CPAs, Chgo., 1985-86; corp. acct. Budget Rent A Car, Chgo., 1986-87; pvt. practice Markham, Ill., 1987—. Mem. AICPA, Ill. Soc. CPAs, Nat. Assn. Tax Practitioners, Chgo. Computer Soc. Office: 16601 S Kedzie Ste 101 Markham IL 60426

MILLER, CHERYL DENISE, graphics design company executive; b. Washington, Dec. 16, 1952; d. Horace Riley and Norma (Sabino) Holmes Weston; m. Phillip M. Miller, June 16, 1973. BFA in Graphic Design, Md. Inst. Coll. Art, 1974; MS Communications Design, Pratt Inst., 1985. Freelance designer Washington, 1976-78; graphic designer Sta. WTOP-TV, Washington, 1974-76; Sta. WRC-TV, NBC, Washington, 1978-80; art dir. Sta. WHMM-TV, Howard U., Washington, 1980-82; pres. Cheryl D. Miller Design, Inc., N.Y.C., 1982—. Recipient award of excellence Broadcast Design Assn., 1982, Desi, 1983, Ceba Awards, 1985, N.Y. Art Dirs. Club, 1987. Mem. Am. Inst. Graphic Art. Office: 353 Lexington Ave New York NY 10016

MILLER, CHERYL LEA, administrative assistant; b. Washington, Pa., Apr. 26, 1964; d. Ralph Herbert and Betty Jane (Phillips) M.; 1 child, Amber Megan. Secretarial cert., Bradford Sch., Pitts., 1983. Sec. First Nat. Bank & Trust Co., Washington, 1984-85; with payroll dept. Songer Corp., Washington, 1986-88, adminstrv. asst., 1988—. Mem. NAFE, Pa. Assn. Notaries, Profl. Secs. Internat. Office: Songer Corp 455 Racetrack Rd Washington PA 15301

MILLER, CHERYL WAAGE, school administrator; b. Independence, Mo., Mar. 25, 1949; d. Cecil Eldridge and Hazel Lorraine (Schnakenberg) Waage; m. Gregory Lawrence Miller, Nov. 21, 1970; children: Kimberly Lynn Miller, Melissa Susanne Miller. BA in Edn., Mo. U., 1971; postgrad., Lee Coll., 1973; MS in Edn., Kans. U., 1983; postgrad., Ottawa (Kans.) U., 1987-89. Cert. tchr., Kans., Mo., reading specialist, Kans. Sub-tchr., reading cons. Shawnee Mission (Kans.) Dist., 1980-83; tchr. Cairo (Arab Republic Egypt) Am. Coll., 1983-86; vice-prin. Holy Cross Sch., Overland Park, Kans., 1987—; goodwill ambassador to USSR, Cairo Am. Coll., 1984, to Kenya, 1985, to India, People's Republic China, and Japan, 1986. Bd. dirs. Temp. Lodging for Children, Inc., Olathe, Kans., 1982-83, Shawnee Mission Area Coun. PTA, 1980-81, Kansas City (Mo.) Jr. Women Philharmonic Assn., 1980-83. Make the Grade grantee Southwestern Bell Found. and Kans. Ednl. Excellence Program, 1989. Mem. Internat. Reading Assn., Nat. Cath. Edn. Assn., Assn. for Supervision & Curriculum Devel., Johnson County Young Matrons, Alpha Delta Pi. Republican. Roman Catholic. Home: 12300 W 102nd St Lenexa KS 66215 Office: Holy Cross School 8101 W 95th St Overland KS 66212

MILLER, CHRISTINE MARIE, automotive company executive; b. Williamsport, Pa., Dec. 7, 1950; d. Frederick James and Mary (Wurster) M.; m. Robert M. Ancell, Mar. 30, 1985. BA, U. Kans., 1972; MA, Northwestern U., 1978, PhD, 1982. Pub. rels. asst. Bedford County Commr., Bedford, Pa., 1972-73; teaching asst. Northwestern U., Evanston, Ill., 1977-80; asst. prof. U. Ala., Tuscaloosa, 1980-82, Loyola U., New Orleans, 1982-85; vis. prof. Ind. U. Sch. Journalism, Bloomington, 1985-86; mktg. dir. Nat. Inst. Fitness & Sport, Indpls., 1986-88; program dir. Nat. Entrepreneurship Acad., Bloomington, 1986-88; mgmt. assoc. community and media rels. Subaru-Isuzu Automotive, Inc., Lafayette, Ind., 1988—. Contbr. articles to profl. jours. Bd. dirs. Indpls. Entrepreneurship Acad., 1988—, Area IV Agy., Greater Lafayette Mus. of Art, 1989—. Mem. Naval Res. Assn., U.S. Navy League, Pub. Rels. Soc. Am., Popular Culture Am., Internat. Motor Press Assn., Indpls. Press Club. Presbyterian. Home: 4403 Sugar Maple Dr Lafayette IN 47905 Office: Subaru Isuzu Automotive 5500 State Rd 38 E Lafayette IN 47905

MILLER, CHRISTY LYNN, personnel management consultant; b. Seattle, Oct. 6, 1955; d. Harold Russell and Beverly (Lanier) M. BA in Health, Phys. Edn., Seattle U., 1977, BA in Edn., 1980. CErt. tchr., Wash. Tchr., coach Highline Swim Club/Seattle Sch. Dist., 1977-81; counselor div. juvenile rehab. Dept. Social and Health Svcs., Snoqualmie, Wash., 1980-85; clin. dir. div. juvenile rehab. Dept. Social and Health Svcs., Ellensburg, Wash., 1985-88; trainer Dept. Social and Health Svcs. and Dept. Corrections, Seattle, 1985—; cons. Koss Personnel Consulting, Bellevue, Wash., 1988—; speaker in field; adv. bd. human resources program U. Wash. Mem. Inst. Reality Therapy (cert., scholarship com. chair Northwest region 1988-91), Soc. Human Resource Mgmt., Pacific Northwest Personnel Mgrs. Assn., Wash. Software Assn., Bothell C. of C., Seattle U. Alumni Assn. (Century Club 1983—). Office: Koss Personnel Consulting 10602 38th Pl Ste 101 Kirkland WA 98033

MILLER, CONNIE RASCHKE, christian educator; b. San Antonio, Aug. 7, 1943; d. Elbert Franklin and Genevieve (Aaron) Raschke; m. Charles Wallace Miller Jr., Dec. 23, 1972; children: David Riedel, Geoffrey Wallace. BS, Tex. Woman's U., Denton, 1961-65; Student, Moody Bible Inst., Chgo., 1981-83. Tex. Tchrs. Cert. (home econ.). Dir. tng. Hecht Co. Stores, Falls Ch., Va., 1968; asst. supr. Group Hospitalization Inc., Wash., 1969-71; interviewer Tex. Employment Commission, San Antonio, 1971-73; dir., organizer Moab Christian Acad., Moab, Ut.; teaching Precepts Ministries Tucson, 1988-90. Sec. Phi Upsilon Omicron, Denton, Tex., 1965; Historian Delphi Soc. Denton, 1965; Tchr. Leader Pioneer Girls Am. Conserned Women Am. Tucson, 1988-89. Republican. Christian. Home: 4551 W Joshua Ln Tucson AZ 85714

MILLER, CYNTHIA LYNNE, professor; b. Milton, Mass., June 19, 1952; d. Donald Ross and Constance Helen (Higgins) M. BA, Skidmore Coll., 1974; MA, U. Wis., 1975, PhD, 1978. Postdoctoral fellow U. Kans., Lawrence, 1978-80; asst. professor U. Western Ontario, London, Ontario, Can., 1980-84; assoc. prof., dir. women's studies U. Houston-Clear Lake, Houston, Tex., 1984--; regional coordinator South Central Women's Studies Assn., 1988--. Contbr. articles to jours. bd. dirs. Tex. Abortion Rights Action League, Houston, 1987--. Recipient: Grant, Nat. Scis. and Engring. Research Council, 1980-84; Grant, Social Scis. and Humanities, Can., 1982-84; Grant, Health and Welfare Can., 1984-88. mem. Assn. for Women in Psychology, Soc. for Research in Child Devel., Nat. Women's Studies Assn., Nat. Orgn. for Women. Democrat. Office: Univ of Houston Clear Lake 2700 Bay Area Blvd Houston TX 77058

MILLER, D(ALE) MERRILY, educational consultant; b. Yonkers, N.Y., Mar. 3, 1943; d. Stanley and Pearl Sylvia (Colin) Dulman; children: Logan, Sloan, Dane. A.B. cum laude, Vassar Coll., 1965; M.A., Memphis State U., 1968; Ed.M., Columbia U., 1972, Ed.D., 1974. Tchr., Yonkers (N.Y.) Bd. Edn., 1968-72; mem. faculty Fairleigh Dickinson U., Teaneck, N.J., 1972-73; coordinator ednl. services Massive Econ. Neighborhood Devel. Corp., N.Y.C., 1973-74; dir. ednl. research The Door, N.Y.C., 1974-75; asst. prof. dept. psychology, edn., and services Grad. Sch. Edn., Fordham U., Tarrytown, N.Y., and Lincoln Center, N.Y.C., 1976-83, assoc. prof. 1986-88; pvt. practice ednl. cons., ednl. therapy, Katonah, N.Y., 1981—; faculty Coll. New Rochelle, 1984-86; adj. assoc. prof. Fordham U. Grad. Sch. Edn., 1986-88; assoc. prof. Mt. St. Mary Coll., 1988—; cons. in field specializing in curriculum based assessment and ednl. consultation, collaborative consultation, behavior mgmt., instructional adaptations for main streaming; cons. N.Y. State Dept. Edn., Office for Educating Children with Handicapping Conditions. Mem. Council for Exceptional Children, Am. Psychol. Assn., Assn. for Children with Learning Disabilities, N.Y. Educators of Emotionally Disturbed, Assn. Women Adminstrs. of Westchester County, Assn. for Psychol. and Ednl. Cons., Conn. Ednl. Cons. Network. Home and Office: 26 Cherry St Katonah NY 10536

MILLER, DAWN MARIE, systems analyst; b. Mpls., Aug. 19, 1964; d. Marvin Chester and Carol Ann (Killeen) M. BS, Tex. A&M U., 1986. Systems analyst Exxon Chem. Co., Baytown, Tex., 1986-90; systems coord. Exxon Chem. Co., Houston, 1990—. Big Sister Big Bros. & Sisters, Baytown, 1988-89; cons. Jr. Achievement Project Bus., Houston, 1988—. Mem. NAFE, Baytown Profl. Forum (membership chair 1987-88, sec. 1988-89, facilities chair 1989—), Exxon Employees Baytown. Democrat. Roman Catholic.

MILLER, DAWN MARIE, media marketing specialist, meteorologist; b. Hartford, Conn., Sept. 17, 1963; d. Eugene E. Miller and Audrey E. (Flagg) Laurel; m. Dennis James Miller, Sept. 9, 1989. BS, SUNY, Oneonta, 1985. Customer support specialist WSI Corp., Bedford, Mass., 1985-87; in media (TV) mktg. WSI Corp., Billerica, Mass., 1987—. Mem. Am. Meteorol. Soc., Oneonta Alumni Assn. Republican. Episcopalian. Home: 10 Hartford Ln Forest Ridge Nashua NH 03063 Office: WSI Corp 4 Federal St Billerica MA 01821

MILLER, DEANE GUYNES, shop owner; b. El Paso, Tex., Jan. 12, 1927; d. James Tillman and Margaret (Brady) Guynes; degree in bus. adminstrn. U. Tex., El Paso, 1949; m. Richard George Miller, Apr. 12, 1947; children: J. Michael, Marcia Deane. Owner four Merle Norman Cosmetic Studios, El Paso, 1967—; pres. The Velvet Door, Inc., El Paso, 1967—; dir. Mountain Bell Telephone Co. Pres. bd. dirs. YWCA, 1967; v.p. Sun Bowl Assn., 1970; bd. dirs. El Paso Symphony Assn.; bd. dirs., treas. El Paso Mus. Art, pres., trustee, 1990; chmn. bd. El Paso Internat. Airport; bd. dirs., sec. Armed Services YMCA, 1987, 1st v.p., 1990. Named Outstanding Woman field of civic endeavor, El Paso Herald Post. Mem. Women's C. of C. (pres. 1969), Pan Am. Round Table (dir., pres. 1987). Home: 1 Silent Crest St El Paso TX 79902 Office: 122 Thunderbird St El Paso TX 79912

MILLER, DEBORAH ANN, corporate controller; b. Nashville, Tenn., Sept. 20, 1949; d. Melvin Keith and Elnora Ann (Smith) Fields; Dennis Edward Miller, Feb. 12, 1977. Assoc. in acctg., Chesterfield Marlboro Tech., Cheraw, S.C., 1984; BBA, U. Mary Hardin-Baylor, Belton, Tex., 1986. Regional acct. Universal Mobile Services Corp., Nashville, 1975-77; acct. Truckstops of Am., Nashville, 1977-79; acct., adminstrn. asst. Continental Companies, Hudson, Fla., 1979-81; personal, comml. Lindsay Ins. Agy., Bennettsville, S.C.; sr. internal auditor Health Trust, Nashville, 1987-88; corp. controller Lincoln Cross Inc., 1988--. Key coordinator United Way, Nashville, 1988, 89. Mem. Nat. Assn. of Female Execs., MENSA. Home: 2214 Oak Leaf Dr Franklin TN 37064 Office: Lincoln Cross Inc 1900 Church St Ste 301 Nashville TN 37203

MILLER, DEBORAH JEAN, training and document consultant; b. Elmhurst, Ill., Oct. 2, 1951; d. Thomas Francis and Ruthe Conn (Johnston) M. BFA, Ill. Wesleyan U., 1973; MA, Northwestern U., 1974. Pres. Miller & Assocs., Evanston, Ill., 1980—. Mem. Soc. Tech. Communication, Ind. Writers Chgo. (bd. dirs. 1985-86), Chgo. Coun. Fgn. Rels., Nat. Soc. Performance and Instrn. (Chgo. chpt.), Nat. Orgn. Women, Northwestern U. Alumni Assn. Office: 814 Mulford St Evanston IL 60202

MILLER, DEBRA ANN, reading specialist; b. Frostburg, M.D., Nov. 21, 1955; d. Robert Wayne and Martha Ann (Staup) M. BS (elem. edn.), Frostburg State U., 1977, MEd (reading edn), 1980; PhD (reading edn.), U. M.D., College Park, 1986. PhD- Cert. Reading Specialist. Reading specialist Salisbury Pub. Sch. Title I, Salisbury, Pa., 1977-81; fed. prog. coordinator Salisbury Pub. Sch. Title I, Salisbury, 1978-81; classroom reading tchr. Hammond Middle Sch., Laurel, M.D., 1981-86; clin. coordinator U. M.D. Reading Ctr., College Park, M.D.; reading specialist Running Brook Elem., Columbia, M.D., 1986-89; reading researcher collaborative rsch.-action based, College Park, Md., 1984-89; clin. supr. U. Md. Reading Ctr., College Park, 1985-89; tchr. rep. Parent Adv. Coun.-Chpt. 1, Columbia, 1986-89. Author: Internat. Reading Assoc., World Congress, Brisbane, Australia, 1988, St. of M.D. Reading Yearbook, 1987, Sch. Library Media Jour., 1986. Coord. Baby's Fist Book Program Tech. Sch., Columbia, Md. Mem. Howard County Internat. Reading Assn. (sec. 1987-89), Internat. Reading Assn., Nat. Edn. Assn., M.D. State Tchrs. Assn. Republican. Methodist. Home: 8611 Falls Run Rd Ellicott City MD 21043 Office: Howard County Sch 10918 Rt 108 Columbia MD 21043

MILLER, DEMETRA FAY PELAT, educator, city councilman; b. Painesville, Ohio, June 15, 1933; d. William Anthony and Helen (Mimo) Pelat. Grad., Monticello Jr. Coll., Alton, Ill., 1953; BS in Edn., Kent State U., 1955, postgrad., 1957-63; postgrad., John Carroll U., 1957-63. Tchr. Grant Elem. Sch., Cuyahoga Falls, Ohio, 1955-57, Benjamin Franklin Elem. Sch., Euclid, Ohio, 1957-58, Meml. Park Elem. Sch., Euclid, 1958-87, Lincoln Elem. Sch., Euclid, 1987—. Mem. Euclid City Coun., 1983—; sec. Citizens' Pet Responsibility Com., 1978—; trustee Shore Civic Cultural Ctr., 1988—; treas. Euclid Women's Caucus, 1978-79, v.p., 1981-83, pres., 1983; bd. dirs. YwCA-YMCA, Euclid, 1985—; mem. women's jr. bd., vol. Euclid Gen. Hosp., 1967—; mem. Euclid Devel. Corp., Euclid Recreation Commn., 1985—; former mem. citizens adv. bd. Regional Transit Authority; past mem. Euclid Charter Rev. Commn.; chmn. Euclid City Growth, Devel. and Zoning Commn., 1989—. Named Woman of Yr., Euclid Women's Caucus, 1985, Euclid Citizen of Yr., Am. Legion Post 343, 1986, cert. of appreciation YWCA-YMCA, 1989, One of Most Interesting People award Cleve. Mag., 1990. Mem. NEA (nat. del. 1978-89), Ohio Edn. Assn. (del. 1977—), Euclid Tchrs. Assn. (pres. 1978-79, 83-84, Outstanding Educator award 1979), Ednl. Coun. Cuyahoga County (pres. 1981-82), Coalition Major Ednl. Orgns., Delta Kappa Gamma. Greek Orthodox. Home: 25601 Zeman Ave Euclid OH 44132 Office: Euclid Bd Edn 651 E 222d St Euclid OH 44132

MILLER, DENISE MARY, clinical nurse specialist; b. East Orange, N.J., June 29, 1959; d. Edward Joseph and Barbara Frances (Green) M. BS in Nursing, Trenton State Coll., 1981, BA in Psychology, 1981; MS in Adult Psychiatric Nursing, Rutgers U., 1988. RN, cert. psychiat. and mental health. Cert. psychiat. and mental health nurse Miami Children's Hosp., 1982-84; asst. patient care coord. Newark Beth Israel Med. Ctr., 1984-88; psychiat. clin. nurse specialist St. Michael's Med. Ctr., Newark, 1988—; clin. instr., Rutger's U., 1989—. Sec. Grad. Nurse Alliance, Rutgers U., Newark, 1988; judge Nat. Client Counseling Competition law student div. ABA, 1988. Recipient Fellowship Fed. Govt. Tng. Grant, Rutgers U., 1988. Mem. Am. Psychiat. Nurses Assn., Sigma Theta Tau. Republican. Roman Catholic. Home: 315 New Market Rd Dunellen NJ 08812 Office: St Michael's Med Ctr Dr Martin Luther King Blvd Newark NJ 08812

MILLER, DIANE DORIS, executive search consultant; b. Sacramento, Calif., Jan. 18, 1954; d. George Campbell and Doris Lucille (Benninger) M. B.A., U. Pacific, 1976; BA, Golden Gate U., 1985, MBA, 1987. Mgr., A.G. Spanos, Sacramento, 1977-81, Lee Sammis, Sacramento, 1981-83; v.p. Consolidated Capital, San Francisco, 1983-86; ptnr. McCracken, Wilcox & Bertoux, Sacramento, 1986—. Bd. dirs. Sacramento Symphony En Corps, 1982-84, Sacramento Ballet, 1983-84, 86—, Sacramento Symphony Assn., 1988—, Oakland Ballet, Calif., 1984-85. Named Vol. of Yr., Junior League, 1983, Bus. Vol. in the Arts, Sacramento C. of C., 1989. Mem. U. Pacific Alumni Assn. (bd. dirs. 1978-85). Republican. Avocations: ballet, water sports.

MILLER, DIANE DROPSEY, hospital administrator; b. Gary, Ind., Apr. 29, 1929; d. Lawrence Alton and Tirzah Catherine (Butler) Dorsey Dropsey; children: Michael, Phillip, William, David. RN, Gary Meth. Hosp. Sch. Nursing, 1952. Staff nurse Gary Meth. Hosp., Ind., 1952-53, asst. head nurse, 1960, night supr., 1961-62; office nurse Dr. H.M. English, Gary, 1953-54; pvt. duty nursing, Gary, 1954-60; nursing svcs. administr. Harrison County Hosp., Corydon, Ind., 1962-70, assoc. exec. dir., 1970—; cons. Accreditation Standards for Hosps., Ind. and Ky., 1978-85. Mem. adv. com. Ind. U. Sch. Nursing, 1981-83; mem. Fed. Rels. Com., Ind., 1984; chairperson adminstrv. bd. Corydon Meth. Ch., 1987, 88, 89; bd. dirs. Harrison County Hosp. Found., 1985—, vol. Hospice, 1988; mem. steering com. Town of Corydon, 1987-88, Main Street Corydon Inc., 1987—. Mem. Am. Soc. Nursing Svc. Administrs. (membership com. 1981-82), Am. Nurses Assn., Bus. and Profl. Women's Assn. (v.p. 1976; Outstanding Woman of Yr. 1985), Nursing Administrn. Coun., Meth. Hosp. Sch. Nursing Alumni (past pres.), Ind. Soc. Nursing Svc. Adminstrs. (past pres., bd. dirs. 1976-77, 79, 80, 81, 83), Ind. State Bd. Nursing (registration and edn. com.), Ind. State Nurses Assn. (commn. on practice 1983), Ind. Hosp. Assn.(council on manpower and edn., 1984—, task force on nursing 1988, 89), Southeastern Ind. Soc. Hosp. Nursing Svc. Adminstrs. (past pres.); Ind. and Harrison Counties C. of C. (victim assistance task force 1988, substance abuse prevention coalition 1989—). Democrat. Home: 425 Williar Ave Corydon IN 47112 Office: Harrsion County Hosp 245 Atwood St Corydon IN 47112

MILLER, DOLORES ANN, municipal government official; b. Gary, Ind., Jan. 12, 1929; d. Frederic Clarence and Ida Bertha (Schoenrock) Herron; m. James D. Miller, Aug. 22, 1953 (div. 1978); children: Valerie, Lucia, Harry. BS in Edn., Ind. U., 1952; BS in Library Sci., Washington U., St. Louis, 1975. Cert. mcpl. clk. 1989. Tchr. Gary Sch. Dist., 1952-53, Martinsville (Ind.) Sch. Dist., 1953-56; librarian St. Louis Pub. Library, 1975-78; city clk. City of University City, Mo., 1978—. Bd. dirs., West End Players Guild, St. Louis, 1984-87. Mem. Internat. Inst. Mcpl. Clks., Mo. City Clks. and Fin. Officers (bd. dirs. ea. div. 1988—). Unitarian. Office: City of University City 6801 Delmar Blvd University City MO 63130

MILLER, DONNA JEAN, physical education teacher; b. Gunnison, Colo., Feb. 10, 1948; d. Harry Edwin and Rebha Edwina (Baker) M. BA, Western State Coll., 1970; postgrad., U. No. Colo., 1975-76; student, Pueblo, 1990—. Cert. physical edn. and math. tchr., Colo. Physical edn. tchr. Holly (Colo.) Sch. Dist., 1970-75, Las Animas (Colo.) Sch. Dist., 1976-89; program presenter Colo. Dept. of Edn. Showcase, Denver, 1987, Ark. Valley Bd. of Coop. Ednl. Svcs., La Junta, Colo., 1988 (cons. 1988-89). Coord. Voluntary Recreational Programs for Children and Adults, Las Animas, 1976-89; instr. Am. Red Cross, Las Animas, 1984-89; fund raiser Am. Heart Assn., Las Animas, 1984-89. Mem. AAUW (pres., sec. 1980-89, edn. found. chair), Colo. Assn. Health, Physical Edn., Recreation and Dance (tchr. of yr. 1988), Am. Assn. Health, Phyiscal Edn. and Recreation, Delta Kappa Gamma (sec. 1988-89). Republican. Methodist.

MILLER, DOROTHY ANNE SMITH, cytogenetics educator; b. N.Y.C., Oct. 20, 1931; d. John Philip and Anna Elizabeth (Hellberg) Smith; m. Orlando Jack Miller, July 10, 1954; children: Richard L., Cynthia K., Karen A. BA in Chemistry magna cum laude, Wilson Coll., Chambersburg, Pa., 1952; PhD in Biochemistry, Yale U., 1957. Rsch. assoc. dept. ob-gyn Columbia U., N.Y.C., 1964-72, from rsch. assoc. to asst. prof. dept. human genetics-devel., 1973-85; prof. depts. molecular biology and genetics and pathology Wayne State U., Detroit, 1985—; vis. scientist clin. and population cytogenetics unit Med. Rsch. Coun., Edinburgh, Scotland, 1983-84; vis. prof. dept. genetics and molecular biology U. degli Studi Rome, 1988. Contbr. numerous articles to sci. jours. Grantee March of Dimes Birth Defects Found., 1974—, NSF, 1983-84. Mem. Am. Soc. Human Genetics, Genetics Soc. Am., Phi Beta Kappa. Presbyterian. Home: 1915 Stonycroft Bloomfield Hills MI 48304 Office: Wayne State U 540 E Canfield Detroit MI 48201

MILLER, EDNA RAE ATKINS, educator; b. Clarksville, Ark., Dec. 28, 1915; d. Sammie Lawrence and Dora May (Turner) Atkins; m. Oscar E. Miller, Feb. 27, 1936; children: Myrna Sue Miller Hanses, William Samuel. BE, Sacramento State Coll., 1966. Tchr. one rm. sch. Johnson County, Ark., 1933-35; tchr. elem. Placerville, Calif., 1953-61; tchr. spl. edn. and mentally retarded County of El Dorado, Placerville, Calif., 1961-74; ret. El Dorado (Calif.) County, 1974. Mem. Friends of the Libr. of El Dorado County, Placerville, 1974—; historian People-to-People Internat., 1975-90, Sister City Program, 1975-90. Recipient Cert. of Appreciation, Lung Assn. Sacramento and Emmagrant Trails, 1978, Cert. of Appreciation, Ret. Tchrs. of El Dorado County, 1984, 86, 88. Mem. El Dorado County Hist. Soc., Children's Home Soc. (assoc.), AAUW, Epsilon Chi chpt. Delta Kappa Gamma (pres. Placerville chpt. 1966-68). Democrat. Baptist. Home: 3222 Gerle Ave Placerville CA 95667

MILLER, ELIZABETH ANN, accountant; b. Salt Lake City, June 19, 1962; d. Stephen Paul and Elinor Marguerite (Heffernan) Gent; m. Robert Anthony Miller, July 16, 1983; children: Stephanie Lynn, Michael Anthony. Student, U. Mo., 1983—. Sec. Am. Cancer Soc., St. Louis, 1981-83; acctg. clk. Mercantile Bank, N.A., St. Louis, 1983-86; fin. analyst coop. Monsanto Agrl. Co., St. Louis, 1989, fin. reporting coop., 1990, internat. gen. ledger acct., 1990—. Co-leader Girl Scouts U.S., Florissant, Mo., 1989. Louise Anthes scholar Alpha Sigma Lambda, 1988, 89, U. Mo. scholar, 1986—, Ednl. Found. Mo. Soc. CPAs scholar, 1989. Office: Monsanto Agrl Co 800 N Lindbergh Saint Louis MO

MILLER, ELIZABETH JANE, historian; b. Pitts., Sept. 21, 1953; d. Albert and Phyllis (Lewandowski) M. BA in Am. Studies and History, Am. U., 1975; MA in Am. Studies, George Washington U., 1977. Curator Columbia Hist. Soc., Washington, 1977-84, dir., 1984-85; dir. Maine Hist. Soc., Portland, 1985—; adj. prof. New Eng. Studies Program, U. So. Maine; cons. curator NAS, Washington, 1983-84. Co-author exhbn. pamphlet: Lighthouse of the Sky, 1983; contbr. articles to profl. jours. Mem. Am. Assn. Mus., Orgn. Am. Historians, Am. Assn. for State and Local History (grantee 1983), New England Mus. Assn. Office: Maine Hist Soc 485 Congress St Portland ME 04101

MILLER, ELOUISE DARLENE, educator; b. Alton, Kans., Nov. 24, 1930; d. Clarence Sylvester and Laura Areta (Sparks) M. B.S., Ft. Hays State U., 1956, M.S., 1961, Ed.S., 1970; postgrad. Temple U., 1966. Tchrs. cert., Kans. Tchr. Liberty Sch., Alton, Kans., 1948-49, Mt. Hope Sch., Osborne, Kans., 1949-50, Woodston Grade Sch., Kans., 1950-55; 1st grade tchr. United Sch. Dist. 489, Hays, Kans., 1956-65, tchr. kindergarten, 1965—, kindergarten chmn., 1983—; tchr. remedial reading, fed. program, Hays, summers, 1970—. Primary supt. Meth. Sunday Sch., Hays, 1976—. Named to Kans. Tchrs.' Hall of Fame Inc., 1989. Mem. Internat. Reading Assn. (charter pres. 1965-67, NEA (pres. Hays 1962-63, del. Kans. 1980—), AAUW, Meth. Ch. Women, Kans. Hist. Soc., Hays Arts Council, Delta Tau (pres. Hays 1959-61), Delta Kappa Gamma, Phi Delta Kappa (Cunningham award 1989), Phi Kappa Phi. Avocations: traveling; reading; jogging; bicycling. Home: 2729 Hickory St Hays KS 67601 Office: Lincoln Sch 1906 Ash St Hays KS 67601

MILLER, ELVA RUBY CONNES (MRS. JOHN R. MILLER), civic worker; b. Joplin, Mo.; d. Edward and Ada (Martin) Connes; student Pomona Coll., part-time, 1936-56; m. John R. Miller, Jan. 17, 1934 (dec. Nov. 1968). Entertainer various night clubs, supper clubs, also Hollywood Bowl, 1967; TV appearances; rec. artist Capitol Records, 1966—, Amaret Records, 1969—; appeared in motion pictures. Active Girl Scouts U.S.A., 1933-58; hon. mem. Mayor's Com. for Sr. Citizens, L.A., 1966; mem. Music Ctr. L.A. County. Recipient awards including Thanks badge Girl Scouts U.S.A., 1956, Key to City, Mayor San Diego, 1967, plaque Dept. of Def. for trip to Vietnam, 1967. Mem. Gen. Alumni Assn. U. So. Calif. (life). Republican. Presbyterian. Home: 9585 Reseda Blvd Northridge CA 91324

MILLER, EMILIE F., state legislator; b. Chgo., Aug. 11, 1936; d. Bruno C. and Etta M. (Senese) Feiza; m. Dean E. Miller; children: Desireé M., Edward C. BS in Bus. Adminstrn., Drake U., 1958. Asst. buyer Jordan Marsh Co., Boston, 1958-60, Carson, Pirie, Scott & Co., Chgo., 1960-62; dept. mgr., asst. buyer Woodward & Lothrop, Washington, 1962-64; polit. cons. various cos., Va., 1980-87; legis. aide Senator Adelard Brandt, Va., 1980-83; legis. cons. Va. Fedn. Bus. Profl. Women, 1986-87; senator Va. Gen. Assembly, Richmond, 1988—; mem. Edn. and Health com., Gen. Laws com., Local Gov. com. Guest editorial writer No. Va. Sun, 1981; host, producer weekly TV program, Channel 61. Mem. State Cen. Com. Dem. Party Va., Richmond, 1974—; chmn. Va. Assoc. Dem. County and City Chmn., 1980, Fairfax County Dem. Com., 1976-80; past v.p. Women's Nat. Dem. Club.; bd. dirs. Mental Health Assn. No. Va., 1980—, State Mental Health and Mental Retardation Bd., 1982-88; fin. dir. Saslaw for Congress, 1984; state labor coord. Robb-Davis-Baliles Joint Campaign; bd. dirs. Stop Child Abuse Now, 1988; chmn. Va. Assn. Community Svcs. Bd., 1980-82; v.p. Fairfax County Coun. of Arts, exec. com., internat. childrens festival; mem. exec. bd. Mantua Citizens' Assn., 1985-87, nat. alumni bd. J.A. Achievement, BRAVO adv. com. for the first Gov.'s Awards for the Arts in Va., 1979-80; lay tchr. St. Ambrose Cath. Ch., 1963-80; del. to White House Conf. on Children, 1970. Recipient Woman of Achievement award Fairfax (Va.) Bd. Suprs., 1982, Community Svc. award Friends of Victims Assistance Network, Fairfax, 1988, Disting. Grad. award Jr. Achievement, 1973. Mem. Fairfax County Coun. Arts (v.p. 1988—), Fairfax County C. of C., Cen. Fairfax C. of C., Bus. and Profl. Women's Fedn. Va., Tower Club (Fairfax), Downtown Club (Richmond). Home: 8701 Duvall St Fairfax VA 22031

MILLER, ERICA T(ILLINGHAST), aesthetician, skincare and cosmetics company executive, writer; b. Laramie, Wyo., Oct. 17, 1950; d. Walter McNab and Martha (Brown) M. Student Sophia U., Tokyo, 1969-72, U. Md., Tokyo, 1969-72, Simultaneous Interpreting Acad. Tokyo, 1974; cert. Christian Shaw Sch. Beauty, London, 1973, Kanebo Total Beauty Acad., 1974; internat. diploma CIDESCO, 1977. Instr., Nakano Am. English Ctr., Tokyo, 1969-72; instr., researcher Kanebo Cosmetics Inc., Tokyo, 1973-76, internat. cons., 1976—; dir. edn. Aestheticians Internat., Dallas, 1976-79; pres. Correlations Inc., Dallas, 1979—; dir. skin care sect. Esthetics Am., 1986-88; instr. Purdue U., 1989; cons. Nieman Marcus Greenhouse, Arlington, Tex., 1981—. Mem. adv. bd. San Jacinto Coll., Houston, 1989—, Skyline High Sch., Dallas, 1989—. Assoc. pub., editor Aesthetics World Mag., 1980-85; contbr. articles to various publs.; translator tech. film. Mem. Aestheticians Internat. (dir. edn. 1976-79), Am. Inst. Esthetics (lectr.), Nat. Hairdressers and Cosmetology Assn. (dir. skin care sect. aesthetics com.), Dallas C. of C., North Dallas C. of C. Republican. Episcopalian. Avocations: tennis, English riding, swimming, care and training of animals. Office: Correlations Inc 4803 W Lovers Ln Dallas TX 75209

MILLER, ESTELLE LEE, lawyer, political consultant; b. N.Y.C., Nov. 30, 1929; d. Jacob and Theresa (Smith) Lieberman; m. T.E. Miller; children: Robert M., Lindajean Duff. AB, Bklyn Coll., 1949; postgrad., U. Miami, 1952-53; LLB, U. Wis., 1954. Bar: Wis. 1954. Trial lawyer FTC, Washington, 1956-58, FPC, Washington, 1958, CAB Gen. Counsel Office, Washington, 1958-61; exec. dir. mktg. FMG Telecomputer Ltd., 1984-85; pres., chief exec. officer MillerMedia, 1986-89; pres. Miller Cons. Group Ltd., Pompano Beach, Fla., 1989—; guest lectr. various univs. Author: Dinner at Bedingfield Inn, 1975, Women in the White House, 1976; lectr. seminars Faculty, Campaigns and Elections Mag., 1986—; contbr. articles to profl. jours. Spl. cons. Rep. Nat. Com., Washington; guest participant White House Conf. Internat. Coop., 1962, Gov.'s Pre White House Conf. Librs., 1977; instr. campaigns La., Va., Tex., Okla., Ga., Fla.; regional coord. Pres.' Environ. Merit Awards Program; chmn. Nat. Bicentennial Commn., Lumpkin, Ga.; co-chmn. So. Rep. Leadership Conf., 1984; del. Rep. Nat. Conv., Dallas, 1984, Reagan-Bush commn., 1984, Bush-Quayle Commn., 1988; cons. Solidarity Citizens Com., Poland, 1990. Recipient Ga. Vol. Svc. award, 1976, Meritorious Svc. award Am. Revolution Bicentennial Adminstrn., 1976. Mem. Am. and Internat. Assn. Polit. Cons., Columbus Country Club, Capitol Hill Club. Home: Longview Farms Lumpkin GA 31815 Office: Miller Cons Group Ltd 1280 S Powerline Ste 708 Pompano Beach FL 33069

MILLER, ESTHER JEAN, hotel executive; b. Elmira, N.Y., Nov. 6, 1947; d. Robert Malcolm and Mildred Mary (Mazzella) Johnson; m. Robert Daniel Miller, Feb. 14, 1970; 1 child, Amy Jean. BA, Nazareth Coll., Rochester, N.Y., 1969; postgrad., Holiday Inn U., Olive Branch, Miss., 1983, 84. Cert. hotel adminstr. Tchr. Bishop Kearney High Sch., Rochester, 1970; mgr. dining rm. Howard Johnson's, Oswego, N.Y., 1972-75; dir. sales Holiday Inn, Oneonta, N.Y., 1975-79, asst. innkeeper, 1980-81, food and beverage dir., 1982-84, gen. mgr., 1984—; asst. mgr. Abigail's Restaurant, Redmond, Wash., 1981; catering mgr. Bellvue (Wash.) Hilton, 1982; treas., RPM Assocs. Oneonta, 1989—. Treas., dir. Otsego County Tourism acct. Bur., Cooperstown, N.Y., 1984—; bd. mem. econ. adv. bd. SUNY Oneonta, 1989—; sec. I-88 Com.,Oneonta, 1988-89. Mem. United Restaurant, Hotel and Tavern Assn., Del.-Otsego Mgmt. Assn., Oneonta Profl. Women's Network, Otsego County C. of C., Leatherstocking, N.Y. Roman Catholic. Office: Holiday Inn PO Box 634 Rt 23 E Oneonta NY 13820

MILLER, GENEVIEVE, medical historian; b. Butler, Pa., Oct. 15, 1914; d. Charles Russell and Genevieve (Wolford) M. A.B., Goucher Coll., 1935; M.A., Johns Hopkins U., 1939; Ph.D., Cornell U., 1955. Asst. in history of medicine Johns Hopkins Inst. of History of Medicine, Balt., 1943-44, instr., 1945-48, research assoc., 1979—; asst. prof. history of medicine Sch. Medicine, Case Western Res. U., Cleve., 1953-67, assoc. prof., 1967-79, assoc. prof. emeritus, 1979—; research assoc. in med. history Cleve. Med. Library Assn., 1953-62, curator Howard Dittrick Mus. of Hist. Medicine, 1962-67, dir. Howard Dittrick Mus. Hist. Medicine, 1967-79. Author: William Beaumont's Formative Years: Two Early Notebooks 1811-1821, 1946; The Adoption of Inoculation for Smallpox in England and France (William H. Welch medal Am. Assn. for History of Medicine 1962), 1957; Bibliography of the History of Medicine of the U.S. and Canada, 1939-1960, 1964; Bibliography of the Writings of Henry E. Sigerist, 1966; Letters of Edward Jenner and Other Documents Concerning the Early History of Vaccination, 1983; assoc. editor Bull. of History of Medicine, 1944-48, acting editor, 1948, mem. adv. editorial bd. 1960-90; mem. bd. editors Jour. of History of Medicine and Allied Scis., 1948-65; editor Bull. of Cleve. Med. Library, 1954-72; editor newsletter Am. Assn. for History of Medicine, 1986—; contbr. articles in field to profl. jours. Am. Council Learned Socs. fellow, 1948-50; Dean Van Meter fellow, 1953-54. Alumna trustee Goucher Coll., Balt., 1966-69. Hon. fellow Cleve. Med. Library Assn.; mem. Am. Assn. for History of Medicine (pres. 1978-80, mem. council 1960-63), Am. Hist. Assn., Internat. Soc. for History of Medicine, Soc. Archtl. Historians, Phi Beta Kappa; corr. mem. fgn. socs. for history of medicine. Democrat. Home and Office: Judson Manor 1890 E 107 St Apt 816 Cleveland OH 44106

MILLER, HARRIET SANDERS, art center director; b. N.Y.C., Apr. 18, 1926; d. Herman and Dorothy (Silbert) S.; m. Milton H. Miller, June 27, 1948; children—Bruce, Jeffrey, Marcie. B.A., Ind. U., 1947; M.A., Columbia U., 1949; M.S., U. Wis., 1962, M.F.A., 1967. Dir. art sch. Madison Art Ctr., Wis., 1963-72; acting dir. Center for Continuing Edn., Vancouver, B.C., 1975-76; mem. fine arts faculty Douglas Coll., Vancouver, 1972-78; exec. dir. Palos Verdes Art Center, Calif., 1978-84; dir. Junior Arts Center, Los Angeles, 1984—; one woman exhibits at Gallery 7, Vancouver, 1978, Gallery 1, Toronto, Ont., 1977, Linda Farris Gallery, Seattle, 1975, Galerie Allen, Vancouver, 1973. Mem. Calif. Art Edn. Assn., Calif. Confedn. of Arts, Museum Educators of So. Calif., Arts and Humanities Symposium. Office: Junior Arts Ctr 4814 Hollywood Blvd Los Angeles CA 90027

MILLER, HELEN MARIE DILLEN (MRS. J. CARTER MILLER), bus. exec.; b. Sedalia, Mo.; d. John Barney and Lulu (Blume) Dillen; student Central Coll., 1936-37; m. J. Carter Miller, Dec. 3, 1941; 1 son, J. Carter. Sec.-treas. Midwest Supply Co., Lansing, Ill., 1946—, Midwest Supply Co. of Can., 1946—; sec.-treas. Carter Controls, Inc., Lansing, also Livonia, Mich., 1952—, v.p., 1956—; v.p. Carter Controls Internat., Windsor, Can., Antwerp, Belgium, 1960—; sec.-treas. Carter Controls U.K. Ltd., Sheffield, Eng., Carter Controls, GmbH, Busingen, Germany, Carter Controls., A.G., Schaffhausen, Switzerland. Social worker ARC, Hammond, Ind., 1942-44. Mem. Principia Patrons No. Ind. (pres. 1963-65), Chgo. Symphony, Sarah Siddons Soc., Chgo. Art Inst. Christian Scientist. Clubs: Principia Mothers (dir. Chgo. 1962-64); Fortnightly, Woman's Athletic (Chgo.); Woodmar Country (Hammond); Everglades (Palm Beach, Fla.). Home: 1731 Wilson Ave Munster IN 46321 also: Ibis Isle Rd Palm Beach FL Office: 2800 Bernice Rd Lansing IL 60438

MILLER, IRIS ANN, architectural consultant, urban designer, educator; b. Pitts., Jan. 6, 1938; d. Bernard and Sadye (Topel) Ress; m. Lawrence Alan Miller, Jan. 24, 1959; children: Bradley Stuart, Richard Lyle, Stefan Ress. BS cum laude, U. Pitts., 1959, MEd in Secondary Edn., 1961; postgrad. in psychology and counseling, U. Md., 1962-68; MArch, Cath. U. Am., 1979. Tchr. various pub. and pvt. schs., Pitts., Monroeville, Pa., Montgomery County, Md., 1959-61, 63-64; free lance landscape design Washington, 1965-81; architecture design and research O'Neil and Manion Architects, Bethesda, Md., 1979, 81; architecture design and drawing Frank Schlesinger Architects/Planners, Washington, 1979-80; cons. architecture, landscape and urban design Washington, 1982—; vis. asst. prof., vis. lectr. Cath. U. Am., Washington, 1986-89, dir. landscape and architecture studies, 1986-89; urban design cons. Techworld, Washington, 1984-86; devel. dir. Tech 2000 Mus., 1985-86; developer, presenter lectr. series resident assoc. program Smithsonian Instn., Washington, 1982, 83, 85, 87, 89; dir., founder 8th St. Mall Assn. project, Washington, 1986—, Charrette urban design seminar, Washington, Dallas, Alexandria, Va., St. Louis and Cleve., 1982-89; initiator, participant Sarasota (Fla.) Regional Urban Design Assistance team, 1983, seminar Nat. Gallery Art, Washington, 1984, Nat. Arboretum, 1988, symposium Cath. U. of Am., 1990. Curator, author exhbn. and catalogue Sumner Sch. Mus., 1987; co-curator, author exhbn. and catalogue Octagon Mus., 1987; project dir., curator 1991 Bicentennial Paris-Washington Exhbn., 1987—. Co-chmn. stamp com. Bicentennial Washington, 1987—; founding mem. Washington Network, 1986—; mem. adv. panel L'Enfant Forum, Washington, 1987—, Hist. Georgetown Found., 1989—; trustee John J. Sexton Fund for Local Govt. Studies, Sch. Pub. Affairs, U. Md., College Park, 1983—; dir., founder Pub.-Pvt. Partnership and Univ. Program, Cath. U. Am., Washington Pub. Schs., 1985—. Recipient Travel Study award Cath. U. Am., 1979, Program Devel. award Cath. U. Am., 1978; research grantee Govt. France, 1985; grantee Nat. Endowment for Arts, 1982. Mem. U.S.-Internat. Coun. on Monuments and Sites (program speaker 1987), Friends Vieilles Maison Francaise (program speaker 1987), AIA, (regional urban design com., chmn. edn. subcom 1987—, chmn. edn. conf. 1983, edn. com. D.C. chpt. 1981-83, Charrette co-chmn., program devel. award 1982), Assn. Collegiate Schs. Architecture (speaker N.E. region conf. 1989, chmn. panel 1989, 90, chair collegiate exhbn. for excellence in urban design, 1990), Am. Soc. Landscape Architects, Alpha Epsilon Phi (pres. D.C. alumni 1965-67). Home: 3820 52d St NW Washington DC 20016 Office: 914 11th St NW Washington DC 20001

MILLER, JANE ANDREWS, accountant; b. Nashville, Aug. 14, 1952; d. Joseph Raymond Andrews and Allison (Bartlett) Fang; m. Thomas C. Heselton, June 22, 1970 (div. 1978); 1 child, Elizabeth Lyn; m. Keith Evan Miller, Apr. 14, 1984. Degree in Bus. Typing and Computers, Fairfax Bus. Sch., Va., 1974. Adminstrv. asst. T.J. Fannon & Sons, Alexandria, Va., 1973-79; distbn. clk., adminstrv. asst. U.S. Post Office, Merrifield, Va., 1980-83; acct., sec., treas. Aux. Electric Power Co., Fairfax, Va., 1983—; pvt. practice, investment counselor, Fairfax; sec., treas. AEPCO, Inc., K & J, Inc., 1990—. Mem. Friends of Calypso; assoc. mem. Smithsonian Inst.; notary pub., 1990—. Mem. Hist. Preservation Soc. Republican. Avocations: gardening, music, interior design, drama.

MILLER, JANEL HOWELL, psychologist; b. Boone, N.C., May 18, 1947; d. John Estle and Grace Louise (Hemberger) Howell; B.A., DePauw U., 1969; postgrad. Rice U., 1969; M.A., U. Houston, 1972; Ph.D., Tex. A&M U., 1979; m. C. Rick Miller, Nov. 24, 1968; children—Kimberly, Brian, Audrey, Rachel. Asso. sch. psychologist Houston Ind. Sch. Dist., 1971-74; research psychologist VA Hosp., Houston, 1972; asso. sch. psychologist Clear Creek Ind. Sch. Dist., Tex., 1974-76; instr. psychology, counseling psychology intern Tex. A. and M. U., 1976-77; clin. psychology intern VA Hosp., Houston, 1977-78; coordinator psychol. services Clear Creek Ind. Sch. Dist., 1978-81, assoc. dir. psychol. services, 1981-82; pvt. practice, Houston, 1982—; faculty U. Houston-Clear Lake, 1984—; adolescent suicide cons., 1984—. DePauw U. Alumni scholar, 1965-69; NIMH fellow U. Houston, 1970-71; lic. clin. psychologist, sch. psychologist, Tex. Mem. Am. Psychol. Assn., Tex. Psychol. Assn., Houston Psychol. Assn. (media rep. 1984-85), Am. Assn. Marriage and Family Therapists, Tex. Assn. Marriage and Family Therapists, Houston Assn. Marriage and Family Therapists. Home: 806 Walbrook Dr Houston TX 77062 Office: Southpoint Psychol Svcs 11550 Fugua St Ste 450 Houston TX 77034

MILLER, JANET RUTH, management consultant, educator,; b. Phila., Jan. 1, 1946; children: Robert, Debra. BA in Liberal Arts, Antioch U. West, San Francisco, 1982; MS in Human Resource Mgmt. and Devel., Chapman Coll., Orange, Calif., 1984; currently postgrad., U.S. Internat. U., San Diego. Cert. lifetime instr., Calif. Systems analyst Xerox Corp., So. Calif., 1975-80; mgr. Xerox Corp., Calif., 1980-89; pres. J. Miller & Assocs., Huntington Beach, Calif., 1989—; adj. instr. U. Phoenix, So. Calif. div. 1989—, Chapman Coll., 1986-88. Co-author: Organizational and Human Resources Sourcebook, 1989; contbr. articles and newsletters to profl. publs. Mem. Am. Soc. Tng. and Devel., NAFE, Huntington Beach C. of C. Home and Office: 612 Amber Dr Huntington Beach CA 92648

MILLER, JANICE, interior designer; b. Jacksonville, Fla., Oct. 5, 1925; d. Paul Jerome and Tola (Sherman) Walker; m. John Edwin Miller, June 7, 1949; children: Rebecca Ann M., Patricia Blair. BFA cum laude, Wesleyan Coll., Macon, Ga., 1947; MFA, Boston U., 1966. Pvt. art tchr. Weston, Mass., 1962-63; tchr. Brookline (Mass.) pub. schs., 1963-66; faculty mem.

State Coll. Mass., Bridgeport, 1966-67; designer Ruth Batchelder, 1967-71; dir. Janice Miller Assocs., Brookline, 1971—, Art for Industry, 1972—. Mem. Am. Archives of Art New Eng., Am. Soc. Interior Designers, Boston U. Visual Arts Alumni Assn., Boston C. of C. (mem. exec. club), Brookline Arts Ctr., Friends of Boston Art, Boston Cir. for Charity, Nat. Art Dealers Assn., Internat. Furnishing & Design Assn. (pres. 1980, nat. dir. 1982-83), New Eng. Sculptures Assn., Inst. Contemporary Art. Episcopalian. Home: 19 Winchester St #907 PO Box 38 Brookline MA 02146

MILLER, JANICE ANN, nurse; b. Blue Island, Ill., Oct. 18, 1949; d. Charles Howard and Arlene Grace (Froehlich) M. BS in Nursing, U. Ill., Chgo., 1971. Staff nurse Christ Hosp., Oak Lawn, Ill., 1971-75, asst. head nurse, 1975-79; office nurse Fausto Ciulini, MD, Chgo., 1979-81, Carvallo & Cupic, Chgo., 1981-89, S.W. Cardiology, Orland Park, Ill., 1989—. Chairperson risk factor com. Am. Heart Assn., South Cook County Div., Chgo. Mem. Am. Pub. Health Assn., Nurses Environ. Health Watch, Internat. Polio Network, NAFE, Midwest Alliance in Nursing, Ill. Nurses Assn. (bd. mem. dist. 20, chmn. pub. rels. com., past editor newsletter), U. Ill. Alumni Assn., Sigma Theta Tau.

MILLER, JEANNE-MARIE ANDERSON (MRS. NATHAN J. MILLER), English educator, academic administrator; b. Washington, Feb. 18, 1937; d. William and Agnes Catherine (Johns) Anderson m. Nathan John Miller, Oct. 2, 1960. BA, Howard U., 1959, MA, 1963, PhD, 1976. Instr. dept. English Howard U., Washington, 1963-76, asst. prof., 1976-79, assoc. prof., 1979—, also asst. dir. Inst. Arts and Humanities, 1973-75, asst. acad. planning office, v.p. for acad. affairs, 1976-90; cons. Am. Studies Assn., 1972-75, Silver Burdett Pub. Co., Nat. Endowment for Humanities, 1978—; adv. bd. D.C. Libr. for Arts, 1973—, John Oliver Killens Writers Guild, 1975—, Afro-Am. Theatre, Balt., 1975—. Editor, Black Theatre Bull., 1977—; Realism to Ritual: Form and Style in Black Theatre, 1983; assoc. editor Theatre Jour., 1980-81; contbr. articles to profl. jours. Mem. Washington Performing Arts Soc., 1971—, Friends of Sta. WETA-TV, 1971—, Mus. African Art, 1971—, Arena Stage Assos., 1972—, Washington Opera Guild, 1982—, Wolf Trap Assocs., 1982—. Ford Found. fellow, 1970-72; So. Fellowships Fund fellow, 1972-74; Howard U. research grantee, 1975-76; Am. Coun. Learned Socs. grantee, 1978-79; Nat. Endowment Humanities grantee, 1981-84. Mem. Nat. Coun. Tchrs. of English, Coll. English Assn., Am. Studies Assn., Am. Theatre Assn., AAUP, AAUW, D.C. LWV, Common Cause, ACLU, Am. Acad. Polit. and Social Sci., Coll. Lang. Assn., MLA, Am. Assn. Higher Edn., Nat. Assn. Women Deans, Adminstrs. and Counselors, Friends Kennedy Ctr. for Performing Arts, Pi Lambda Theta. Democrat. Episcopalian. Home: 504 24th St NE Washington DC 20024

MILLER, JEANNETTE LEAH, dietitian; b. Bismarck, N.D., Mar. 16, 1941; d. Marie Schultz; m. Bruce L. Miller, May 23, 1965; children: Allen, Geoffrey, Kendall, Karla. Student, Bismarck Jr. Coll., 1959-60; BS, N.D. State U., 1963. Registered dietitian. Dietetic intern Peter Bent Brigham Hosp., Boston, 1964; therapeutic dietitian Buffalo Gen. Hosp., 1965-66; clin. dietitian Children's Hosp., Buffalo, 1966-68; cons. dietitian Our Lady of Victory Hosp., Lackawanna, N.Y., 1969-71, Bristol Nursing Home, Attleboro, Mass., 1972-73; nutrition instr. Iowa Cen. Community Coll., Ft. Dodge, 1979; pvt. practice Ft. Dodge, 1983-89; vice chmn. Bd. Dietetic Examiners, Iowa, 1986-89. Author: (with others) Healthy Holiday Cookbook, 1984, Fresh Start weight control prog. Chmn. fin. com., bd. dirs. Lakota Coun. Girl Scouts, Ft. Dodge, 1985-89. Mem. AAUW (grantee 1987), Am. Dietetic Assn., Iowa Dietetic Assn., No. Cen. Iowa Dist. Dietetic Assn. (pres., sec., treas.), Women's Profl. Netwrok (treas. 1986-88). Democrat. Presbyterian. Home and Office: Heritage Hills #19 Carbondale IL 62901

MILLER, JO CAROLYN, family and marriage counselor, educator; b. Gorman, Tex., Sept. 16, 1942; d. Leonard Lee and Vera Vertie (Robison) Dendy; m. Douglas Terry Barnes, June 1, 1963 (div. June 1975); children—Douglas Alan, Bradley Jason; m. Walton Sansom Miller, Sept. 19, 1982. B.A., Tarleton State U., 1964; M.Ed., U. North State, 1977. Tchr., Mineral Wells (Tex.) High Sch., 1964-65, Weatherford (Tex.) Middle Sch., 1969-74; counselor, instr. psychology Tarrant County Jr. Coll., Hurst, Tex., 1977-82; pvt. practice family and marriage counseling, Dallas, 1982—. Author: (with Velma Walker, Jeannene Ward) Becoming: A Human Relations Workbook, 1981. Mem. womens' com. Dallas Ballet; vol. Am. Heart Assn. in Tex., Dallas chpt., 1983-84. Mem. Tex. State Bd. Examiners Profl. Counselors, Tex. Assn. Counseling and Devel., Am. Assn. Counseling and Devel., Am. Mental Health Counselors Assn., North Central Tex. Assn. for Counseling and Devel., Tex. Mental Health Counselors Assn. Methodist. Home: 3556 Binkley Ave Dallas TX 75205

MILLER, JOAN MARIE NONNENMOCHER, church secretary; b. Lancaster, Pa., Apr. 20, 1935; d. Jason Kurtz and Lillie Serena (Fisher) Nonnemocher; m. Richard Horace Miller, July 21, 1956; children: Carol L. Hendershot, Ann M. Wolf, Susan D. Fegley. AA, Harrisburg Inst. Med. Arts, 1955. Med. asst. E.M. Solomon, M.D., Lancaster, 1955-56; sec. G.W. Davis Oil Co., Lancaster, 1956-59; office mgr. Progressive Design and Machine Co., Lancaster, 1973-81; sec., office mgr. Covenant United Meth. Ch., Lancaster, 1981—. Mem. Profl. Assn. of United Meth. Ch. Secs. (cert. sec. 1988). Republican. Home: 20 Strasburg Pike Lancaster PA 17602-4120

MILLER, JUDITH ANN, financial executive; b. Chgo., Sept. 8, 1941; d. Frank G. and Kathryn M. (Stocklin) Bell; m. William J. Shrum, Aug. 3, 1958 (div. 1976); children: Steven W., Vickie L. White, Lisa A. Rhodes, Mark A., Brian D.; m. William L. Miller Jr., Nov. 28, 1976. Student, Ind. Cen. Coll., 1959-60, DePaw U., 1964-65. Office cashier, mgr. G.C. Murphy Co., Indpls., 1967-70; asst. treas., office mgr. Missions Blvd. Fed. Credit Union, Indpls., 1970-72; treas., office mgr. Bd. Higher Edn., Christian Ch. (Disciples of Christ), Indpls. and St. Louis, 1972-77; dir. fin. Mt. Olive United Meth. Ch., Arlington, Va., 1978-79; exec. dir. Interfaith Forum on Religion, Art and Architecture, Washington, 1979-82; devel. assoc. Nat. Benevolent Assn., Des Moines, Iowa, 1982-85; adminstrv. asst. Davis, Hockenberg, Wine, Brown, Koehn & Shors, Des Moines, 1985-88; fin. officer Episcopal Diocese of Iowa, Des Moines, 1988—. Mem. citizen adv. coun. Parkway Schs., St. Louis, 1976-77; county rep., mem. Fairfax County Sch. Bd. adv. coun., Springfield, Va., 1979-81; treas. congl. campaign Des Moines, 1983-85; mem. exec. St. Louis Children's Home, 1976-78; v.p., treas. Emmaus Fellowship Project on Aging, Washington, 1980-82; bd. dirs. Urban Mission Coun., Des Moines, 1983-86, Pre-Trial Release Prog., Des Moines, 1984-87; mem. steering com. Iowa Interfaith Network on AIDS, Des Moines, 1989—. Named Vol. of Yr., Iowa Victorian Soc., 1985, Our Community Kitchen, 1986. Mem. Nat. Soc. Fund Raising Execs. (chpt. sec. 1985-87), Nat. Assn. Ch. Bus. Adminstrs., NAFE. Democrat. Mem. Christian Ch. (Disciples of Christ). Home: 1207 21st St West Des Moines IA 50265 Office: Episcopal Diocese of Iowa 225 37th St Des Moines IA 50312

MILLER, JUDITH MARIE, sanitation professional; b. Lebanon, Mo., Aug. 3, 1942; d. Francis Lawrence and Neva Frances (LeFever) Charbonneau; m. Dean H. Miller; 1 child, Dana Merrill. Grad. high sch., Springfield, Mo. Sec. Allstate Insurance, Northbrook, Ill., 1969-76; office mgr. Kobiske Industries, Inc., Loyal, Wis., 1976-79; exec. asst., sec. Marshfield (Wis.) Med. Found., 1979-89; v.p., sec., treas. Lien Infection Control Systems, San Mateo, Calif., 1989—. Cubmaster, Boy Scouts Am., Loyal, 1988—. Mem. Loyal C. of C. (sec. 1977-78), Grafton Jaycettes (pres. 1965-66). Home: 305 N Thomas St Loyal WI 54446 Office: Lien Infection Control Sys 100 S Ellsworth Ave 9th Fl San Mateo CA 94401

MILLER, JUDY STATMAN, advertising agency executive; b. Dallas, June 1, 1938; m. Paul P. Miller, Dec. 20, 1970; 1 child, Jennifer. Student, U. Tex. Buying supr. Tracy-Locke, Dallas, 1971-75, assoc. media dir., 1975-79, media group head, 1979-84, v.p., 1979-86, broadcast dir., 1984-86, sr. v.p., dir. media buying, 1986—. Office: Tracy-Locke PO Box 50129 Dallas TX 75250*

MILLER, JULIE ANN, training consultant, writer; b. El Paso, Tex., Dec. 20, 1955; d. Eugene Russell and Ramona Marie (Barney) Schaafsma; m. Christopher John Miller, June 18, 1983; children: Karin Elizabeth, Sarah Anne. BS in Child Devel., Purdue U., 1978, MS in Instructional Systems, 1982. Tchr., adminstr. Finnish-Am. Soc. Kindergarten, Lahti, Finland, 1978-79; developer computer-based learning games Data Command, Kankakee, Ill., 1980; author, researcher Growing Child, Lafayette, Ind., 1981; editor, author indsl. engring. dept. Purdue U., West Lafayette, Ind., 1981-83; tech. writer Lincoln Inst. of Land Policy, Cambridge, Mass., 1984-85; tng. cons. Motorola, Sherwin-Williams, Ernst & Whinney Nat. Offices, Glidden Paints, 1986-89; pres. Miller Tng. Devel., Inc., Rocky River, Ohio, 1988—. Author: (book) Guidelines for Teachers, 1979; contbr. articles to profl. jours. Vol. Headstart Program, Tippecanoe County, Ind., 1977. Recipient Marek Journalism Scholarship, Gamma Phi Beta, 1977; Best Language Arts Software, LEARNING mag., 1983. Mem. Am. Soc. Tng. and Devel., Am. Assn. Artificial Intelligence, Nat. Soc. Performance and Instrn. (pres. N.E. Ohio chpt. 1989-90). Home: 2727 Hampton Rd Rocky River OH 44116 Office: Miller Training Devel PO Box 16512 Rocky River OH 44116

MILLER, KAREN JEAN, occupational therapist, activity therapy administrator; b. Massillon, Ohio, Jan. 6, 1951; d. Clyde Albert and Jean Evelyn (Baker) M. B of Music Edn., Capital U., 1973; B of Music Therapy, Mich. State U., 1974; M of Occupational Therapy, Western Mich. U., 1979. Youth counselor, supr. ops. Roush Treatment and Rehab. Ctr., Lima, Ohio, 1975-77; occupational therapist Riverside Hosp., Toledo, 1979-80, St. Charles Hosp., Toledo, 1980-82; dir. dept occupational therapy Kings Daughter's Hosp., Ashland, Ky., 1982-85; supr. dept. occupational therapy Cen. State Hosp., Louisville, 1985-87; cons. KMI Med. Ctr. (name now Ten Broeck), Louisville, 1986-87, dir. therapeutic activities, 1987—; cons. Jefferson Hosp., Jeffersonville, Ind., 1986-89, Louisville Luth. Home, 1987-89. Author: Treatment with Music, 1979. Mem. Am. Occupational Therapy Assn., Ky Occupational Therapy Assn. (sec. 1986-89, pres. 1989—), Nat. Assn. for Music Therapy, NAFE, Nat. Assn. Activity Therapy and Rehab. Programs. Home: 10709 Colonial Woods Way Louisville KY 40223 Office: Ten Broeck Hosp 8521 LaGrange Rd Louisville KY 40242

MILLER, KAREN LEWIS, music educator; b. Rahway, N.J., Nov. 9, 1942; d. Ralph Edward and Carol Georgiana (Peterson) Lewis; m. Myron Marcus Miller, Aug. 11, 1973 (div. Feb. 1980); children: William T. Meglaughlin, David B. Meglaughlin. AB, Vassar Coll., 1964; postgrad., Union Theol. Sem. Sch. Music, 1964-65. Organist Presbyn. Ch., Springfield, N.J., 1964-67, 1st Meth. Ch., Westfield, N.J., 1967-68, United Presbyn. Ch., Plainfield, N.J., 1973; choir dir. Wesleyan Community Ch., San Juan, P.R., 1974-75; minister of music Fanwood (N.J.) Presbyn. Ch., 1975-82; clinician, sales agt. Schulmerich Carillons, Sellersville, Pa., 1982-85; organist, handbell dir. Liberty (N.J.) Corner Presbyn. Ch., 1982-86; organist, choir dir. Adirondack Community Ch., Lake Placid, N.Y., 1986—; tchr. music St. Agnes Cath. Sch., Lake Placid, 1987—; pvt. practice piano instr., 1966—. Composer in field. Guest recitalist Westfield Men's Glee Club, Fanwood, 1977, 79; guest dir. Jr. Choristers Festival, Crescent Ave. Presbyn. Ch., Plainfield, 1980, 81, Somerset Hills Area Jr. Choristers Festival, Millington, N.J., 1984; mus. dir. Community Theatre Players, Lake Placid, 1987. Mem. Am. Guild English Handbell Ringers (rep. Ea. area 1985-86), Am. Guild Organists (sub-dean Valcour chpt. 1990—), N.Am. Guild of Change Ringers, Kiwanis (bd. dirs. Lake Placid chpt. 1988—). Republican. Roman Catholic. Home: 37 Evans Rd Lake Placid NY 12946

MILLER, KAREN-ANN, military career officer, consultant; b. Washington, Aug. 31, 1949; d. Clair Leon and Dorothy Genevieve (Fink) M.; m. David Manuel Gonzalez, Apr. 11, 1970 (div. June 1979); 1 child, Kevin Manuel. AA, St. Petersburg Jr. Coll., 1969; BA, Northeastern Ill. U., 1977. Enlisted USN, 1972, commd. ensign, 1978, advanced through grades to lt. comdr.; aviation electronics Naval Air Sta., Glenview, Ill., 1974-77, with ground tng. programs, 1978-79; with maintenance material div. Helicopter Tng. Squadron 8, Milton, Fla., 1980-82; with maintenance material and quality assurance Patrol Squadron 44, Brunswick, Maine, 1982-85; asst. maintenance officer Naval Sta. Rota Spain, 1985-88; fleet support equipment mgr. Naval Air Force Atlantic Fleet, Norfolk, Va., 1988—; workshop facilitator Good Samaritan Episcopal Ch., Virginia Beach, Va., 1990—. Lay reader, chalicer Good Samaritan Episcopal Ch., Virginia Beach, 1988-90, sr. warden, 1990—. Mem. Mil. Order World Wars (life), Dunedin Hist. Soc. (life), Assn. Psychol. Types, NAFE, Electronic Networking Assn., Nat. Writers Club. Republican. Office: CNAL Code 5324 Naval Air Sta Norfolk VA 23511

MILLER, KIM ELIZABETH, educational services company executive; b. Bridgeport, Conn., July 7, 1956; d. Robert Joseph and Mary Barbara (Monahan) Loch; m. David R. Miller, Aug. 31, 1979 (div. Nov. 1988). Student, Trinity Coll., Burlingtn, Vt., 1974-75; BA in English, Regis Coll., 1978; MA in English, Goergetown U., 1984. Cert. secondary tchr., Conn. Tchr. Dept. Def. Dependent Schs., Okinawa, Japan, 1979-82; sales rep. Sta. KHFM, Albuquerque, 1982-84; asst. prof. English Strayer Coll., Washington, 1984-86; writer 1985 Armed Forces Inaugural Com., Washington, 1984-85, chief plans div. for 1989, 1986—; mgr. emergency mgmt. tng. program U.S. Army Corps of Engrs., Washington, 1985-86; pres., owner Essential Edn. Services, Annapolis, Md., 1986—; cons. Ketron, Inc., Carlisle, Pa., 1987—; asst. prof. English Prince Georges Community Coll., Largo, Md., 1989-90. Yearbook advisor Kubasaki High Sch., Okinawa, 1979-82; pres. Am.-Japanese Welcome Club, 1980-81; pres. South River Manor Civic Assn., 1989-90. Recipient Comdr.'s award Dept. Army, 1985, commendation, 1986, Superior Civilian Svc. award Dept. Def. Armed Forces Inaugural Com., 1989. Mem. Am. Soc. for Tng. and Devel., Am. Def. Preparedness Assn., Nat. Assn. Female Execs., Soc. Am. Mil. Engrs. Republican.

MILLER, LILLIAN A., health science association administrator; b. N.Y.C., Aug. 14, 1936; d. James B.D. and Easter M. (Miller) Varner; children: Lauri R. Michel, Robin L., Karen L. Gamble, Mark E. Student, Temple U., Phila., Julia Richman high sch., N.Y.C., 1954; MA, Goddard Coll., Plainfield, Vt., 1984. Coordinator Del. Valley Fair House, Phila., 1965-68; co-ordinator Wellsprings Ecumenical Ctr., Germantown, Pa., 1968-71; unit coordinator Eagleville Hosp. & Rehab. Ctr., Pa., 1971-73; coordinator Albert Einstein RMH - MRC, Phila.; unit dir. WAA Emergency Shelter, Germantown, Pa., 1979-82; region prevention coord. Northwestern Community Service Bd., Va., 1979-82; clinical services adminstr. Dept. Health, Territory of V.I., 1982--; pres. Lam Inc., St. Thomas, V.I., 1982—; assoc. mem. V.I. Med. and Counseling Svcs., 1989—. Vol. United Way, St. Thomas, 1988. Mem. Caribbean Women's Network, Nat. Assn. Female Execs., Human Systems Council, Nat. Black Alcoholism Council. Office: Knud Hansen Complex Saint Thomas VI 00801

MILLER, LINDA LAEL, writer; b. Spokane, Wash., June 10, 1949; d. Grady Eugene and Hazel Loraine (Bleecker) Lael; m. Rick Martin Miller, Oct. 12, 1968 (div. July 1987); child, Wendy Diane. Author: Fletcher's Woman, 1983, Desire and Destiny, 1983, Banner O'Brien, 1984, Willow, 1984, Snowflakes on the Sea, 1984, Part of the Bargain, 1985, State Secrets, 1985, Corbin's Fancy, 1985, Memory's Embrace, 1986, Lauralee, 1986, Ragged Rainbows, 1986, Wanton Angel, 1987, Moonfire, 1988, Used-To-Be Lovers, 1988, Only Forever, 1989, Angelfire, 1989, My Darling Melissa, 1990. Recipient Most Sensual Historicals award Romantic Times mag., 1985. Mem. Romance Writers Am. Methodist.

MILLER, LINDA LOU, association executive, communications specialist; b. Pottsville, Pa., Feb. 5, 1955; d. Cletus Isaac and Erma Ruth (Brown) M.; m. William Joseph Murray Jr., July 23, 1989; 1 stepchild, Nathan Andrew. BA, Shippensburg (Pa.) U., 1977. Copywriter, media buyer Williams & Assocs., Harrisburg, Pa., 1977-78; dir. communications Pa. Newspaper Pub.'s Assn., Harrisburg, 1978-82; dir. alumni affairs Shippensburg U., Pa., 1982-85; exec. v.p. Pa. Soc. Assn. Execs., Harrisburg, 1985-90; dir. communications The Milton Hershey (Pa.) Sch., 1990—. Sec. Kimberley Meadows Civic Assn., Mechanicsburg, Pa., 1990; adv. coun. Shippensburg U., 1990. Mem. Pa. Pub. Rels. Soc., Internat. Assn. Bus. Communicators, Am. Soc. Assn. Execs. (past bd. dirs. 1989, cert.), Conf. Assn. Soc. Execs. (pres. 1988-89), Allied Socs. Coun. (chmn. 1988-89). Home: 27 Conway Dr Mechanicsburg PA 17055 Office: The Milton Hershey Sch Founders Hall Hershey PA 17033

MILLER, LOIS KATHRYN, virology educator; b. Lebanon, Pa., Oct. 8, 1945; d. Clarence Elmer and Naomi Alice (Gibson) M.; m. Karl Edward Espelie, June 13, 1974; 1 child, Erin Marie. BS, Upsala Coll., 1967; PhD, U. Wis., 1972. Postdoctoral fellow Calif. Inst. Tech., Pasadena, 1972-74, Imperial Cancer Rsch. Fund, London, 1974-76; prof. U. Idaho, Moscow, 1976-86, U. Ga., Athens, 1986—; cons. Syntex Corp., Palo Alto, Calif., 1989—. Contbr. numerous articles to profl. jours. Recipient Merit award NIH, 1986. Mem. AAAS (coun. 1987-89), Am. Soc. Virology (coun. 1989—). Office: U Ga Dept Entomology Athens GA 30602

MILLER, LOIS LEA, artist; b. Texarkana, Tex., Sept. 16, 1929; d. George Newton and Daisy Rena (Alford) Gage; m. Jack Curtis Miller, Sept. 1, 1950 (div. 1963); 1 child, Jackie Lee. B.F.A., U. Houston, 1977, M.A., 1983. Ind. Artist, instr., lectr., writer NASA, Johnson Space Ctr., Houston, 1989, ret.; judge art scholarship com. Houston Livestock Show and Rodeo, 1983—. Chmn. bd. dirs. Krishen Found. for Arts and Scis., 1981—; mem. Houston chpt. Tex. Head Injury Found. Mem. NOW (state rep. Bay area chpt.), AAUW, Am. Fedn. Govt. Employees (1st v.p. legis. coord. 1980-89, 1st v.p. emeritus 1989—), Soc. for Tech. Communications, Nat. Tech. Assn. (Houston chpt.), Am. Bus. Women's Assn., Houston Fedn. Profl. Women, U. Houston Alumni Assn., U.S.A.F. Aerobatic Team Alumni Assn. Democrat. Roman Catholic. Clubs: Toastmasters, Mensa. Home: 9702 Palmfield St Houston TX 77034 Office: PO Box 34642 Houston TX 77034

MILLER, LOUISE ANNE, financial analyst; b. West Rockhill Twp., Pa., Mar. 23, 1963; d. Harold Eugene and Eleanor Jane (Perrin) M. BS in Acctg., AS in Computer Infosystems, Quinnipiac Coll., 1984. CPA, Conn. Staff acct. Deloitte, Haskins & Sells, New Haven, 1984-85, in-charge acct., 1985-86, sr. acct., 1986-87; sr. acct. Uniroyal Chem. Co., Inc., Middlebury, Conn., 1987-89, sr. treasury analyst, 1989-90, sr. acctg. analyst, 1990—. Republican. Presbyterian. Office: Uniroyal Chem Co Inc World Hdqrs Benson Rd Middlebury CT 06749

MILLER, LYNN MARIE, secretarial and word processing service executive; b. Cleve., June 25, 1958; d. Richard Robert and Frances Marie (Hoskin) M.; m. Michael Gerald Berendsen, Nov. 1977 (div. May 1979); 1 child, Marie Diane Miller. Student pub. schs., Cleve. Asst. sec. to pres. R.O. Hull Co., Cleve., 1976; coordinator customer service Lott & Geckler, Cleve., 1978-81; sec., coordinator customer service Brown Derby, Inc., Walton Hills, Ohio, 1981-83, Midwestern Land Devel. Corp., Cleve., 1983-85; sec. Johnston, Leach, McDonough & Eddy, A.C., Parkersburg, W.Va., 1985-87 ; mgr. office Richard Thomas, Atty., 1987; dir. Noble County Child Support Enforcement Agy. (formerly Noble County Bur. of Support), Caldwell, Ohio, 1987—; ptnr., v.p. F & L Enterprises, Caldwell, 1985—. Co-producer Noble County Performing Arts, 1986, producer, 1987. Chmn. publicity Community Christmas, Noble County Jr. Women's League, Caldwell, 1985, sec., 1986; treas.-elect Lit. Club, Caldwell; youth leader Meth. Youth Fellowship; organist Caldwell United Meth. Ch., 1989—. Mem. Noble County Bus. and Profl. Women (Young Careerist chmn. 1986, pub. rels. chmn. 1987-88, parliamentarian 1989, Young Careerist award 1985-86), Nat. Assn. Female Execs., Farmingdale C. of C., Caldwell Mchts. Assn., Ohio Office Edn. Assn. (historian and voting del. 1974-75), Ohio Geneal. Soc. (v.p. Noble County chpt. 1986), Lit. Club (treas. Caldwell chpt. 1987), Order Ea. Star (assoc. conductress 1986, assoc. matron 1987, worth matron 1988-89). Avocations: amateur and semi-professional theatre, cross-stitch. Home: RD 4 Caldwell OH 43724 Office: Noble County Child Support Enforcement Agy PO Box 185 Caldwell OH 43724

MILLER, LYNNE MARIE, environmental company executive; b. N.Y.C., Aug. 4, 1951; d. David Jr. and Evelyn (Gulbransen) M. AB, Wellesley Coll., 1973; MS, Rutgers U., 1976. Analyst Franklin Inst., Phila., 1976-78; dir. hazardous waste div. Clement Assocs., Washington, 1978-81; pres. Risk Sci. Internat., Washington, 1981-86, Environ. Strategies Corp., Vienna, Va., 1986—, Environ. Strategies Ltd., London, 1986—. Editor: Insurance Claims for Environmental Damages, 1989, editor-in-chief Environ. Claims Jour.; contbr. chpts. to books. Named Ins. Woman of Yr. Assn. Profl. Ins. Women, 1983. Mem. Am. Cons. Engrs. Coun., AAAS, N.Y. Acad. Sci., Washington Wellesley Club. Office: Environ Strategies Corp 8521 Leesburg Pike Ste 650 Vienna VA 22182

MILLER, MADELYN SUE, advertising executive; b. Chgo., Mar. 4, 1947; d. Seymour and Estelle (Klotwogg) Jensky. Student, NYU, 1966-67; B.A. in Journalism, U. Mich., 1968; m. Howard Brian Miller, May 26, 1968; children: Mallorie Ann, Gregory Scott. Copywriter Young & Rubicam, Detroit, 1968-69, Yaffe Stone August, Huntington Woods, Mich., 1969-70, Dancer Fitzgerald Sample, N.Y.C., 1970-71, Neiman-Marcus, Dallas, 1975-76; sr. copywriter Tracy, Dallas, 1976-81; pres. Madelyn Miller, Inc., Dallas, 1982—. Adv. bd. Dallas Art Inst.; mem. Leadership Dallas; chmn. counselor's program PRSSA. Recipient Clio award, 1981; Matrix award Outstanding Dallas Woman in Advt., 1981, Effie award, 1980, Addy award (2), 1980, Bravo award (4) Detroit Art Dirs. Club, 1981, numerous others. Mem. S.W. Assn. Advt. Agys. (bd. dirs.), Dallas Soc. Visual Communications (Bronze medal, Bronze award 1979, cert. of merit 1979), Women in Communications (student pres. 1968), Dallas Advt. League (cert. of merit 1979), Internat. Assn. Bus. Communicators, Pub. Rels. Soc. Am., Bus. and Profl. Advt. Assn., Am. Inst. Graphic Artists, Northwood Inst. Am. Women in Radio and TV, Dallas C. of C. (pub. rels. chmn., small bus. coun.), Mensa, CEO Club, Hadassah Nat. Fedn. Jewish Women's Club, Leadership Dallas. Home: 9619 Rocky Branch Dallas TX 75243 Office: 8140 Walnut Hill Ln Ste 411 Dallas TX 75231

MILLER, MARCY JENNIFER, police officer, artist, writer; b. Phoenix, May 20, 1963; d. Robert Leonard and Elizabeth May (Walker) M. AA, Scottsdale Community Coll., 1984; BA, U. Ariz., 1986. Cert. law enforcement officer, Ariz.; cert. substitute tchr., Ariz. Dir. Bob Parks Gallery, Scottsdale, Ariz., 1986-87; vet. technician Sahuaro Vet. Clinic, Scottsdale, 1987; police officer Scottsdale Police Dept., 1987—; mem. mounted div., 1990—. Contbr. fiction and poetry to popular publs. Advisor Explorer Scouts of Boy Scouts Am., Scottsdale, 1988—; mem. Scottsdale Police Issues Task Force, 1989—. Recipient lifesaving award City of Scottsdale, 1988. Mem. Faternal Order Police, Sierra Club, Phi Beta Kappa (mentor Phoenix 1989—). Home: 5202 E Cactus Rd Scottsdale AZ 85254 Office: Scottsdale Police Dept 9065 E Via Linda Scottsdale AZ 85260

MILLER, MARGARET JEAN, career counselor, educator; b. Spokane, Wash., Aug. 14, 1943; d. James Wellington and Mildred Grace (Ryan) Bowlby; m. William Dale Miller, Aug. 4, 1988; children: Jeanine Grace Yaezenko, Juliet Marie Peters, James Lee Hoskins. BA, BS, Boise State Coll., 1970; MEd, U. Idaho, 1986, PhD, 1989. Cert. counselor kindergarten-12, social studies tchr. 7-12. Social studies tchr. Boise (Idaho) Ind. Sch. Dist., 1970-77; legal sec. James L. Schoenhut, Atty. at Law, McCall, Idaho, 1980-84; social studies tchr. Shoshone County Sch. Dist., Kellogg, Idaho, 1984-86, high sch. counselor, 1986-87; mid. sch. counselor Pullman (Wash.) Sch. Dist., 1987-88; instr. U. Idaho, Moscow, 1986-88; student svcs. counselor Coll. Great Falls, Mont., 1988-89, adj. grad. faculty mem., 1988—; career counselor Great Falls Pub. Schs., 1989—; trainer Wash. Substance Abuse Abatement Program 1987-89; bd. dirs. Cascade County Mental Health Assn., Great Falls; sch. liaison YWCA Expanding Your Horizons, Great Falls, 1989—. Co-author: (curriculums) Career Infusion, 1973, Geography, 1974, Humanities, 1986, Career Education, 1990. Trustee McCall-Donnelly Sch. Bd., 1982-84. Mem. Am. Assn. Counseling and Devel., Assn. Counselor Edn. and Supervision (govt. rels. com. 1989—, standard revisions com. 1990—), Nat. Career Devel. Assn. (ethics com. 1989—), Idaho Career Devel. Assn. (chairperson Rocky Mountain region standard revisions com.), Montana Assn. for Counseling and Devel., P.E.O. Quaker. Office: Coll Great Falls 1301 20th St S Great Falls MT 59405 also: Great Falls High Sch 1900 2d Ave S Great Falls MT 59405

MILLER, MARGERY SILBERMAN, psychologist, speech and language pathologist, higher education adminstrator; b. Roslyn, N.Y., May 7, 1951; d. Bernard and Charlotte (Schatzberg) Silberman; m. Mark Howard Miller, Sept. 5, 1971; children—Kip Lee, Tige Justice. Lic. speech pathologist, N.Y., Md.; cert. tchr. nursery-6th grades, spl. edn., N.Y., advanced profl. tchr. speech and hearing, Md.; cert. sch. psychologist, Md. B.A., Elmira Coll., 1971; M.A., NYU, 1972; Ed.S., M.S., SUNY-Albany, 1975; postgrad. in psychology Georgetown U., 1984—; MA Towson State U., 1987. Speech and lang. pathologist Mental Retardation Inst., Flower and Fifth Ave. Hosp., N.Y.C., 1971-72; community speech/lang. pathologist N.Y. State Dept. Mental Hygiene, Troy, dir. speech and hearing services, 1972-74; instr. communication disorders dept. Coll. of St. Rose, Albany, N.Y., 1975-77;

clin. supr. U. Md., College Park, 1978; speech/lang. pathologist Md. Sch. for Deaf, Frederick, 1978-84; auditory devel. specialist Montgomery County Pub. Schs., Rockville, Md., 1984-87; coordinator Family Life program Nat. Acad. Gallaudet U., Washington, 1987-88, interim dir., 1988-89, dir. Counseling & Devel. Ctr. N.W. Campus, 1989—; part-time assoc. prof. psychology Gallaudet U.; instr. sign lang. program Frederick Community Coll.; dance instr. for deaf adolescents; diagnostic cons. on speech pathology; mem. editorial rev. com. Gov.'s Devel. Disabilities Council of Md., 1984; presenter at confs. Author: It's O.K. To Be Angry, 1976; contbr. chpt. to Cognition, Education, and Deafness: Directions for Research and Instruction, 1985; contbr. articles to profl. jours. Vol. Emergency Interpreting for Deaf; choreographer Miss Deaf Am. Pageant, 1984. Office of Edn. Children's Bur. fellow, 1971. Mem. Am. Speech, Lang. and Hearing Assn. (cert. clin. competence in speech/lang. pathology), Md. Speech, Lang. and Hearing Assn., D.C. Speech, Lang. and Hearing Assn., Nat. Assn. of Deaf, Nat. Assn. Sch. Psychologists, Am. Psychol. Assn. Jewish. Home: 12316 Triple Crown Rd North Potomac MD 20878 Office: Gallaudet U 1640 Kalmia Rd NW Washington DC 20012

MILLER, MARIAN KATHRYN, data processing executive; b. Washington, Dec. 28, 1942; d. Gantt William Jr. and Marian (Behm) M.; m. Jordan Allyn Zeidwig, June 21, 1971, (div. Aug. 1977); 1 child, Daniel Alan. BA, U. Del., 1966. Math., sci. tchr. Manpower Devel. and Tng., Wilmington, Del., 1964-65; programmer Atlantic Aviation, Wilmington, 1965-66; programmer, NASA - Apollo orbit prediction IBM, Washington, 1966-70; systems analyst - FAA install IBM, Indpls., 1970-73; programmer - FAA collision avoidance IBM, Atlantic City, N.J., 1973-75; systems analyst IBM, Atlanta, 1975-82; customer support IBM, Irving, Tex., 1982—. Vol. tchr. Irving Ind. Sch. Dist., 1982-84; hosp. vol. St. Paul Med. Ctr., Dallas, 1988-89, Parkland Meml. Hosp., Dallas, 1989; crisis minister Episcopal Ch. of Transfiguration, Dallas, 1987-89, youth sponsor, 1986-88; flood disaster vol. ARC, Dallas, 1989. Mem. Isthmus Inst. (mem. devel. chmn. 1988-89), Am. Assn. Univ. Women (publicity chmn. Irving chpt. 1988). Republican. Home: 809 W Northgate Dr Irving TX 75062

MILLER, MARY ELIZABETH See JACOBS, LIBBY

MILLER, SISTER MARY STEPHANIE, nun, health care administrator; b. Morrilton, Ark., Aug. 27, 1940; d. Simon John and Elizabeth Josephine (Pfeifer) M. BS, St. Louis U., 1964, Maryville Coll., St. Louis, 1973. Fiscal svcs. dir. St. Edward Mercy Hosp., Ft. Smith, Ark., 1964-68, asst. adminstr., 1969-71; asst. treas. Sisters of Mercy-Province St. Louis, 1973-74, treas., 1974-80; adminstrv. asst. St. John's Regional Health Ctr., Springfield, Mo., 1981-82, v.p., 1982—, also chair bd. dirs.; treas. St. Joseph's Regional Health Ctr., Hot Springs, Ark., 1982—; chair bd. dirs. Mercy Hosp., Mansfield, Mo. Home: 1260 E Sunshine Springfield MO 65804 Office: St John's Regional Health Ctr 1235 E Cherokee Springfield MO 65804

MILLER, MELANIE LEE, marketing consultant; b. Denver, Aug. 14, 1952; d. Neal Clark and Jacqueline Jean (Westbrook) Yorker; m. M. Russell Waln, Feb. 23, 1974 (div. Apr. 1981); m. Samuel M. Miller, Sept. 21, 1981; 1 child, Jacqueline Alicia . BS, U. Wyo., 1975, MS, 1977. Cert. home economist. Trainee Albany County, U. Wyo., Laramie, 1970-74; home economist, 4-H agt., county chmn. Fort Hall Indian Reservation and U. Idaho, Fort Hall, 1977-81; 4-H agt. Umatilla County and U. Oreg., Pendleton, 1981; mng. editor Fed. Bar Assn., Washington, 1981-82; dir. industry svcs. Nat. Peanut Coun., Alexandria, Va., 1982-88; pres. Commodity Cons., Arlington, Va., 1988-89; sr. account exec. Hill and Knowlton Pub. Affairs Worldwide, 1990—; cons. Nat. 4-H Ctr., Washington, 1982-83. Leader 4-H, Laramie, Wyo., 1970-72, Girl Scouts U.S., Arlington, Va., 1986-87; vol. presdl. campaign, Washington, 1988. Mem. Am. Home Econs. Assn., Home Economists in Bus. (pub. rels. 1986-87), Nat. Assn. Female Execs. Republican. Methodist. Home: 2629B S Walter Reed Dr Arlington VA 22206 Office: Hill and Knowston Pub Affairs Worldwide 901 31st St NW Washington DC 20007

MILLER, NANCY SMITH, teacher; b. Hammond, Ind., Jan. 27, 1951; d. George Henry and Henrietta May (Griese) Smith; m. Robert Thomas Miller, June 6, 1981; 1 child, Amanda Louise. BS in Edn., Ind. U., 1973, MS in Edn., 1976. Sci. and math. tchr. Monroe County Schs., Bloomington, Ind., 1974-75; kindergarten tchr. Monroe County Schs., Bloomington, 1975—, 1975—. Vice pres. Monroe County Humane Assn., Bloomington; pres. Girls Club Aux., Bloomington; v.p. bd. dirs. Monroe County Girls Club; mem. Monroe County Coord. Community Child Care Assn., BloomingtonMonroe County Dem. Com.; bd. dirs. Monroe County Dem. Women's Club; troop leader Girl Scouts U.S. Mem. NEA, Ind. State Tchrs. Assn., Pi Lambda Theta, Chi Omega (advisor, pledges & social), Chi Omega Alumni, Ind. U. Alumni. Office: Univ Elem Sch 930 E State Rd 46 By-Pass Bloomington IN 47401

MILLER, PAMELA, fund raising executive; b. Indpls., June 14, 1958; d. Russell Paul and Bettie LaVona (Moore) M. BA, Rockhurst Coll., Kansas City, Mo., 1980; MBA, Rockhurst Coll., 1988. With Ernst & Whinney, Kansas City, Mo., 1980-81; claims rep. Cigna Companies, INA, Aetna, Bloomington, Minn., 1981-83; dir. corp. rels. Rockhurst Coll., Kansas City, 1983-86; assoc. kaleidoscope adminstr. Hallmark Cards, Inc., Kansas City; assoc. dir. devel. Camp Fire, Inc. (Nat.), Kansas City, 1987-90; mktg. rep. Boatmen's Trust Co., Kansas City, 1990—. Bd. dirs. Ernest Shepherd Meml. Youth Ctr., Liberty, Mo., 1973-77; counselor Heart of Am. Citizenship Forum, 1974-76; vol. North Kansas City Meml. Hosp., 1975-76; intern Office of U.S. Senator John Danforth, 1978; co-founder Harry S. Truman Libr. Inst., 1978—; co-founder Harry S. Truman Scholarship Nat. Alumni Assn., 1979—; mem., zoo parent Friends of Zoo, Kansas City, 1984—; bd. dirs. North Kansas City Pub. Libr., 1988—. Fellow Harry S. Truman Library Inst., 1978—. Mem. Centurions C. of C. (chmn. pub. rels.). Office: Boatmen's Trust Co PO Box 419038 Kansas City MO 64183

MILLER, PATRICIA L. G., computer systems designer; b. Akron, Ohio, May 24, 1940; d. Ralph F. and Esta M. (Tremain) Gallogly; m. James R. Miller, Dec. 24, 1966. BA, U. Pa., Phila., 1963. Cons. GE Info. Svcs. Co., Phila., 1983-86; sr. systems cons. Trigon Group, Inc., Phila., 1986-87; sr. cons. Keane, Inc., Wayne, Pa., 1987—. Republican.

MILLER, PATRICIA LOUISE, state legislator, nurse; b. Bellefontaine, Ohio, July 4, 1936; d. Richard William and Rachel Orpha (Williams) Miller; m. Kenneth Orlan Miller, July 3, 1960; children: Tamara Sue, Matthew Ivan. RN, Meth. Hosp. Sch. Nursing-Indpls., 1957; BS, Ind. U., 1960. Office nurse A.D. Dennison, MD, 1960-61; staff nurse Meth. Hosp., Indpls., 1959, Community Hosp., Indpls., 1958; representative, State of Ind., Dist. 50, Indpls., 1982-83, senator, State of Ind., Dist. 32, Indpls., 1983—, mem. edn., health welfare and aging, labor and pension, legis. apportionment and elections coms., chmn. interim study com. pub. health and mental health Ind. Gen. Assembly, 1986. Mem. Bd. Edn., Met. Sch. Dist. Warren Twp., 1974-82, pres., 1979-80, 80-81; mem. Warren Twp. Citizens Screening Com. for Sch. Bd. Candidates, 1972-74, 84, Met. Zoning Bd. Appeals, Div. I, City-County Council, 1972-76; bd. dirs. Central Ind. Council on Aging, Indpls., 1977-80; mem. State Bd. of Voc. and Tech. Edn., 1978-82, sec., 1980-82; mem. Gov.'s Select Adv. Commn. for Primary and Secondary Edn., 1983; precinct committeeman Republican Party, 1968-74, ward vice chmn., 1975-78, ward chmn., 1978-85, twp. chmn., 1985—; del. Rep. State Conv., 1968, 74, 76, 1980, sgt. at arms, 1982, mem. platform com., 1984; del. Rep. Nat. Conv., 1984; active various polit. campaigns; bd. dirs. PTA, 1967-81; pres. Grassy Creek PTA, 1971-72; state del. Ind. PTA, 1978; mem. child care adv. com. Walker Career Center, 1976-80, others; bd. dirs. Ch. Fedn. Greater Indpls., 1979-82, Christian Justice Center, Inc., 1983-85, Gideon Internat. Aux., 1977—; mem. United Meth. Bd. Missions Aux. of Indpls., 1974-80, v.p., 1974-76; bd. dirs. Lucille Raines Residence, Inc., 1977-80; exec. com. S. Ind. Conf. United Meth. Women, 1977-80, lay del. S. Ind. Conf. United Meth. Ch., 1977—, fin. and adminstrn. com., 1979—, planning and research com., 1980—co-chmn. law adv. com., chmn. health and welfare, conf. council ministries, also mem. task force, bd. ordained ministry, also panel, chmn. com. on dist. superintendency, dist. council on ministries; sec. Indpls. S.E. Dist. Council on Ministries, 1977-78, pres., 1982; chmn. council on ministries Cumberland United Meth. Ch., 1969-76; chmn. stewardship com. Old Bethel United Meth. Ch., 1982-85, fin. com., 1982-85, adminstrv. bd., mem. council on ministries, 1981-85. Recipient Phi Lambda Theta Honor for outstanding contbr. in field of edn., 1976; Woman of the Year, Cumberland Bus. and Profl. Women, 1979; Ind. Voc. Assn. citation award, 1984, others. Mem. Indpls. Dist. Dental Soc. Women's Aux., Ind. Dental Assn. Women's Aux., Am. Dental Assn. Women's Aux., Council State Govt. (intergovtl. affairs com.), Nat. Conf. State Legislatures (health com.), others. Clubs: Warren Twp. Rep. Franklin Rep., Lawrence Rep., Center Twp. Rep., Fall Creek Valley Rep., Marion County Council Rep. Women, Ind. Women's Rep., Indpls. Women's Rep., Ind. Fedn. Rep. Women, Nat. Fedn. Rep. Women, Beech Grove Rep., Perry Twp. Rep. Home: 1041 S Muesing Rd Indianapolis IN 46239*

MILLER, PAULA BELINDA, college administrator; b. Portsmouth, Va., Jan. 12, 1957; d. Dupont Preston Smith and Patricia Ann Fisher; m. Julian Lovelle Miller, Jr., Oct. 3, 1984; 1 child, Joshua Preston Miller. BA, Flagler Coll., St. Augustine, Fla., 1979; MEd, U. North Fla., 1986. Placement specialist Goodwill Ind. of N. Fla., Jacksonville, 1980-82, evaluation specialist, 1982-83; evaluator/placement specialist Meml. Reg. Rehab. Ctr., Jacksonville, 1983-84; evaluator/placement specialist Fla. Community Coll., Jacksonville, 1984-86, disabled student svcs. officer, 1986-87, disabled student svcs. dir., 1987-89, asst. dean of student affairs, 1989—; trainer Bell South "Return to Learn," Jacksonville, 1988-89, editor (one of four), 1988-89. Editor Jobnet newsletter, 1987-89. Mem. Jacksonville Community Council, Inc., 1988—, Gov.'s Alliance for Employment of Handicapped Persons, Tallahassee, 1986-87; elected trustee Goodwill Industries Inc., N.E., Fla., 1990—; apptd. to nat. bd. Nat. Assn. Adults With Spl. Learning Needs, 1990—; bd. dirs. Goodwill Industries of N.E. Fla., 1990-91. Mem. Flagler Coll. Alumni Assn. (bd. dirs. 1983-89), Nat. Rehab. Assn., Gov.'s Employment Alliance, Am. Assn. Women in Community and Jr. Colls., Fla. Alliance for the Employment of the Handicapped (v.p. 1986), Fla. Rehab. Assn. (chpt. pres. 1986, bd. dirs. 1982—, state bd. mem. 1989-90), Fla. Assn. Postsec. Profls. for Disabled Students (sec. 1987-88), Fla. Assn. Community Colls. (Equity Commn. rep. Dist. II, 1989—, north campus rep.), N.E. Fla. Consortium for Deaf and Hard of Hearing (sec. 1986-87, pres. 1989-90), Leadership Jacksonville, Nat. Assn. Adults with Spl. Learning Needs (bd. dirs. 1990-91). Democrat. Office: Fla Community Coll 4501 Capper Rd A-122 Jacksonville FL 32218

MILLER, PAULETTE MARIE, enterostomal therapist; b. McKeesport, Pa., Aug. 24, 1948; d. Paul and Elizabeth Ann (Mihal) Magoch; m. David Lee Miller, Feb. 26, 1968 (div. 1980); 1 child, Kelly Renee. Degree in nursing, McKeesport Hosp., 1969; cert., Emory U., 1976; postgrad., Coll. of Charleston (S.C.). Cert. enterostomal therapist, S.C., RN, Tex., S.C., Fla. Emergency room staff nurse Good Samaritan Hosp., West Palm Beach, Fla., 1972; head nurse burn trauma unit Med. U. S.C. Hosp., Charleston, 1972-74; oncology specialty nurse Drs. Paul Underwood and Myron Lutz, Charleston, 1974-77; asst. dir. nursing Dialysis Clinic, Inc., Charleston, 1977-78; edn. coordinator Lowcountry Regional Emergency Med. Svc., Summerville, S.C., 1978-80; clin. supr. ICU Trident Regional Med. Ctr., Charleston, 1980-81, asst. dir. nursing specialty areas, 1981-83; dir. nursing Tidelands Gen. Hosp., Channelview, Tex., 1983; mgr. corp. svcs. Support Systems Internat., Inc., Charleston, 1987-89; nat. accounts mgr. long term care div. Support Systems Internat., Inc., 1990—. Contbr. articles to profl. jours. Recipient Young Careerist Bus. and Women's Fedn., 1976. Mem. Internat. Assn. Enterstomal Therapists. Home: 2274 Ashley River Rd 414 Charleston SC 29414 Office: Support Systems Internat 4349 Corporate Rd Charleston SC 29405

MILLER, PHYLLIS YVONNE, actuarial associate; b. Quincy, Fla., Oct. 11, 1951; d. Chester Wayne and Ruth L. (McCoy) M.; m. Steven Paul Kopp, Jan. 13, 1973 (div. Apr. 1976); 1 child, Steven Wayne. BS, Ariz. State U., 1983, MS, 1985. Svc. rep. Aetna Ins. Co., Phoenix, 1982-86; actuarial assoc. A.A.S., Phoenix, 1986—. Fellow Life Mgmt. Inst.; mem. NAFE, Mensa, Phoenix Bulldog Club, Greenpeace, Phi Beta Kappa, Phi Rho Pi. Republican. Home: 3621 N 68th St Scottsdale AZ 85251 Office: Actuarial & Adminstrv Svcs 4500 N 32d St Phoenix AZ 85018

MILLER, REBECCA HARVEY, health organization executive, nurse; b. Syracuse, N.Y., Mar. 29, 1952; d. Robert Calvin and Betty Lee (Davidson) Harvey; m. Thomas Joseph John Miller, May 30, 1976; children: Gretchen Rebecca, Shannon Marilee, Lucas Harvey. BS in Nursing, U. Rochester, 1974. Staff nurse pediatrics Strong Meml. Hosp., Rochester, N.Y., 1974-76; comml. fisher Marine Vessel George W, Kodiak, Alaska, 1976-77; staff nurse Kodiak Island Hosp., 1977; clinic nurse Island Med., Kodiak, 1978-80, Kodiak Area Native Assn., 1980-82; sch. nurse Kodiak Island Borough Sch. Dist., 1982-87; comml. fisher Marine Vessel Echo, Kodiak, 1978; hospice nurse Rochester Hospice Inc., Rochester, N.Y., 1987-88; chief exec. officer Miller Corp., Richmond, Va., 1988-89, Pitts., 1989—; health fair coord. Health Fair Alaska, Kodiak, 1983-87; CPR instr. Am. Heart Assn., Kodiak, 1980-87; med-evac nurse Kodiak Island Hosp., 1980-87. Nurse coord. ARC, Kodiak, 1982-83, CPR instr., 1982-87, pres., 1985-87; synchronized swim instr-show creator, 1976-77. Energy grantee State of Alaska, Kodiak, 1981. Mem. AAUW (membership v.p. 1980-81, pres. 1981-82). Home: 2461 Bellwood Dr Pittsburgh PA 15237

MILLER, ROSEMARY MARGARET, accountant; b. Jersey City, Jan. 3, 1935; d. Joseph John and Marguerite (Delatush) Corbin; m. James Noyes Orton, 1956 (div. 1977); m. Julian Allen Miller, Oct. 14, 1978; children: Alexandria Lynn Hayes, Jennifer Ann Orton Cole. Student Barnard Coll., 1953-54, Rutgers U., Newark, 1954-56, Howard U., 1962-63, No. Va. Community Coll., 1976-83; AA, Thomas A. Edison State Coll., 1981; BS in Acctg., U. Md., 1987; cert. H & R Block, 1981. Bookkeeper Gen. Electronics, Inc., Washington, 1970-73; cost acct. Radiation Systems, Inc., Sterling, Va., 1973-80; acct. Bilsom Internat., Inc., Reston, Va., 1980-83; sales mgr. Bay Country Homes, Inc., Fruitland, Md., 1984; sr. staff acct. Snow, Powell & Meade, Salisbury, Md., 1985-86; acct. Meadows Hydraulics, Inc., Fruitland, Md., 1987-88; acct. Porter & Powell CPAs, Salisbury, 1988—; owner, prin. RCOM Cons., acctg., bookeeping, taxes, Princess Anne, Md. Mem. Accreditation Council for Accountancy (accredited 1981), Nat. Soc. Public Accts., Nat. Acct. Assn., Nat. Student Bus. League, Alpha Kappa Mu. Democrat. Lutheran. Home: Rte 2 Box 255 E 33 Princess Anne MD 21853-9655 Office: 107 High St PO Box 153 Salisbury MD 21803

MILLER, SHARYL KAY, insurance company executive; b. Worthington, Minn., Feb. 27, 1945; d. Harold Joseph and Evelyn Marie (Skyberg) Erickson; children: Dennis Dean, Shari Lee; m. John Miller, Dec. 3, 1988. Grad. high sch., Waseca, Minn. Registered psychiat. tech., Minn.; lic. ins. Psychiat. tech. St. Minn., Fairbault, 1966-67; counselor special schs. St. Minn., Owatonna, 1967-72; office mgr. Pepsi-Cola, Taylorville, Ill., 1975-79; sales assoc. Am. Family Life Assurance Co., Columbus, Ga., 1979-80, mgr. dist., 1980-82, mgr. regional, 1982-85, mgr. St. Ill., 1985—; speaker Women's Expo '87, Ea. Ill. U., 1987. Treas. Sr. Baseball League, Taylorville, 1980-82; pres. PTA, Taylorville, 1981-82. Named Bus. Assoc. of Yr. ABWA, 1986-87. Mem. NAFE, Rsch. Inst. Am. Inc. Personal Report, Nat. Women's Econs. Alliance, Jaycees (Named one of Outstanding Young Women in Am. 1975), Owatonna Club. Republican. Methodist. Office: Am Family Life Assurance Co PO Box 1327 Effingham IL 62401

MILLER, SHERRY L., public relations executive; b. Crawfordsville, Ind., June 15, 1962; d. William G. and Violet F. (Reynolds) Newell; 1 child, Nicholas. Lic. ins. agt. Owner, pres. Indy Ionics, Inc., Indpls.; regional mgr. Am. Income Life, Louisville, Ky.; mgr. Am. Income Life, Dayton, Ohio.

MILLER, SHIRLEY MARIE, computer programmer; b. Monroe, Wis., Jan. 25, 1957; d. Lawrence Leslie and Catherine Marie (Lawver) Gissing; m. Shane Michael Miller, June 1, 1984. AS in Bus. Adminstrn., Highland Community Coll., Freeport, Ill., 1983; BS in Bus. Mgmt., Cardinal Stritch Coll., Milw., 1989, postgrad., 1989—. Receptionist H&R Block, Brodhead, Wis., 1974-75; clk. typist Swiss Colony Data Ctr., Monroe, 1975-76, data entry operator, 1977; data entry operator Economy Fire & Casualty Co., Freeport, Ill., 1977-78, computer operator, 1978-80; computer operator Burgess, Inc., Freeport, 1981; programmer trainee Advance Transformer Co., Monroe, 1981-82, programmer, operator, 1982-84, computer programmer, 1984—. Musician Freeport Concert Band, 1981—; vol. Freeport Pk. Dist., 1988, Freeport Jaycees, 1988. Recipient scholarship Ill. State, Freeport, 1980, Found. scholarship, State Bank, Freeport, 1980. Mem. Am. Fedn. Musicians. Methodist. Office: Advance Transformer Co 350-21 St Monroe WI 53566

MILLER, SIEGLINDE F., Small business owner; b. Boeblingen, Baden-Wurh, Fed. Republic of Germany, Feb. 20, 1941; Arrived in US 1971.; m. Garland A. Miller. Privat Handelsschule, Privat Handelsschule Tech Coll, West Germany, 1958-59. Office clerk Mercedes Benz, Sindelfingen, Germany, West Germany, 1960-65; registrar, translator US Dependent Sch., Boblingen, Germany, 1965-70; adminstr. asst. Hdqrs. VII COSCOM, Boblingen, Germany, 1970-71; sec. Pub. Schs. of Pemberton Twp., Brownsmills, N.J.; sec., translator Hdqrs. European Command, Stuttgart, Germany, 1974-75; gas & oil producer G.A. & S. Miller, Ohio, 1986--. Mem. Assoc. Photographer Internat. Protestant.

MILLER, STEPHANIE ANN, public relations executive; b. Perkasie, Pa., Oct. 8, 1964; d. Leon Mason and Marie Ann (Teti) M. BA in Journalism, Temple U., 1986, postgrad. in bus. adminstrn., 1986—. Publicity coordinator WCAV-TV, Phila., 1986-87; communications mgr. Greater Phila. C. of C., 1987-88; sr. account exec. Lewis Gilman/Golin Harris, Phila., 1988-89; acct. supr. Tierney Group, Phila., 1989—; cons. Benjamin Franklin Bridge Lighting Corp., Phila., 1987—. Disc jockey Assoc. Svcs. for Blind, Phila., 1985—; tutor Phila. Mayor's Commn. on Literacy, 1986—. Mem. Pub. Relations Soc. Am., Phila. Pub. Relations Assn., Sigma Delta Rho (v.p. 1985-86). Home: 219 Bypass Rd Perkasie PA 18944 Office: Tierney Group 260 S Broad St Philadelphia PA 19102

MILLER, SUSAN LEIGH, assistant principal; b. Wayne, Nebr., Apr. 27, 1961; d. Elton Emil and Jolene Mae (Micanek) M. BS, Concordia Tchrs. Coll., 1983; MA in Ednl. Psychology, Wichita State U., 1987. 7th grade lang. arts tchr. Alliance (Nebr.) Pub. Schs., 1983-85; gifted edn. coord. South Cen. Kans. Spl. Edn. Coop., Iuka, 1985-86; gifted edn. cons. N.W. Kans. Ednl. Svc. Ctr., Colby, 1986-89; sr. high sch. asst. prin. Piper Sch. Dist., Kansas City, 1989—; sec. Kaw Valley League Middle Sch., Kansas City, 1989—; athletic dir. Prins. Assn. Piper Sr. High Sch., Kansas City, 1989—. Mem. N.W. Kans. Community Orch., Colby, 1987, Western Plains Arts Assn., Colby, 1987. Kans. Rural Spl. Educator's Project grantee Kans. State U., 1989, Kans. Com. for the Humanities grantee, 1988. Mem. AAUW, Greater Kansas City Assn. for Supervision and Curriculum Devel., Nat. Assn. of Secondary Prins., Kanas Coaches Assn., Nat. High Sch. Athletic Coaches Assn., Nat./State Leadership Tng. Instn. on Gifted and Talented, Nat. Assn. for Gifted/Talented/Creative Children, Kans. Assn. for Gifted Children (exec. bd.), Profl. Advs. for Gifted Edn., Am. Legion Aux. (Anton Bokemper Post 81 1987—), Am. Assn. Supersision and Curriculum Devel., Philanthropic Edn. Assn. (chpt. CZ), Phi Delta Kappa. Republican. Lutheran. Home: RR 2 Wakefield NE 68784 Office: Piper Sr High Sch 4400 N 107th St Kansas City KS 66109

MILLER, TERESA WELCH, writer; b. Dayton, Ohio, Sept. 4, 1963; d. Harold Dixon and Pauline (Randolph) Welch; m. Richard Thomas Miller, Oct. 1, 1988. BA in English and Writing, Maryville (Tenn.) Coll., 1985. Editorial asst. dept. conservation State of Tenn., Nashville, 1984; writer, prodn. mgr. W.D. Stone and Assocs. Advt., Cookeville, Tenn., 1985-87; corp. communications leader Averitt Express, Inc., Cookeville, 1987-88; writer, editor Designs By Norvell, Inc., Alexandria, Tenn., 1989—. Contbr. articles to profl. jours. Presdl. scholar Maryville Coll., 1981. Mem. NAFE. Office: Designs By Norvell Inc PO Box 37 115 Edgewood St Alexandria TN 37012

MILLER, TERRY LYNN, microbiologist; b. Fulton, Ky., July 9, 1945; d. John Gilbert and Dorothy (McClain) M. BS, U. Ky., 1967; MS, N.C. State U., 1969; PhD, U. Ill., 1973. Rsch. assoc. Dept. Dairy Sci. U. Ill., Urbana, 1973-74; rsch. scientist I Wadsworth Ctr. for Labs. and Rsch. N.Y. State Dept. Health, Albany, 1974-76, rsch. scientist II, 1976-82, rsch. scientist III, 1982-83, rsch. scientist IV, 1983—; assoc. prof. Dept. Environ. Health and Toxicology Sch. Pub. Health Svcs. SUNY, N.Y. Dept. Health, Albany, 1986—. Editorial bd. Applied and Environ. Microbiology, 1980-85; contbr. articles to profl. jours. Fellowship Deutscher Akademischer Austauschdienst, Phillips U., 1977. Mem. AAAS, N.Y. Acad. Scis., Am. Soc. Microbiology, Internat. Union of Microbiol. Socs. (mem. taxonomic subcom. on methonogenic archaeobacteria 1985—). Office: NY State Dept Health Wadsworth Ctr Labs & Rsch Albany NY 12201-0509

MILLER, THERESA ANN WENDLING, video production company executive; b. Detroit, Jan. 23, 1965; d. Clair and Lucille Wendling; m. Keith O. Miller, Sept. 16, 1988. AAS, Ferris State U., Big Rapids, Mich., 1985, BS in TV Prodn., 1987. Pres. Mktg. with Media, Berkley, Mich., 1987—. Mem. Internat. TV Assn., Detroit Producers Assn. Roman Catholic.

MILLER, TRACEY LEE, record company executive; b. Atlantic, N.J., July 29, 1959; d. Frederick George Miller and Ellen Elaine (Maxwell) Stewart. BA in Polit. Sci., Fairleigh Dickinson U., 1982. Asst. to mgr. Twp. of Weehawken, N.J., 1982-83; mgr. Mason's Island (Conn.) Yacht Club, 1983-84; prin. Fake Doom Records, Inc., Bloomfield, N.J., 1982-86, Miller Inc. Promotions, Clifton, N.J., 1986-88; publicity dir. KSA, N.Y.C., 1989; publicity mgr. Profile Records, Inc., N.Y.C., 1988-89, nat. media dir., 1989—. Pres. Atlantic High Sch. Reunion Com., Mays Landing, N.J., 1982—. Mem. Am. Film Inst., Ind. Label Assn., ASCAP, Phi Beta Kappa. Democrat. Home: PO Box 165 Clifton NJ 07011 Office: Profile Records Inc 740 Broadway New York NY 10003

MILLER, TRUDY JOYCE, retail executive, publisher; b. Chgo.; d. Leonard John and Evelyn Grace (Winter) Clarke; m. William Robert Miller, Oct. 8, 1960; children: William, James, Brian, Catherine. Student, Marycrest Coll., 1959; student in Interior Design, Art, Prairie State Coll., 1975; student in Publishing, Northwestern U., 1983. Reporter, feature writer Hammond (Ind.) Times, 1967-73, Village Press, South Holland, Ill., 1973-75; owner The Emporium, Glenwood, Ill., 1975-76, Second Thoughts, Chicago Heights, Ill., 1976—; pres. retail outlet Second Thoughts Inc., Chicago Heights, 1984—; editor Second Thoughts Publishing, Chicago Heights, 1982—; bd. dir. Fashion Consortium, Chgo., 1984-86; speaker in field. Author: 1983 Guide to Suburban Resale and Thrift Shops, Where to Find Everything For Practically Nothing in Chicagoland, 1984, 86. Bd. dirs. econ. devel. Thornton Coll., South Holland, 1983-85; mem. small bus. adv. bd. Prairie State Coll., Chicago Heights, 1984-85; fashion show coordinator Operation ABLE Past 50 Job Fair, Chicago Heights, 1985. Mem. Nat. Assn. Resale and Thrift Shops (founder, bd. dirs., sec. 1984-86, pres. 1986—, editor newsletter 1987—, coord. 1st, 2d, 3d annual confs. 1988-90), Internat. Assn. Ind. Pubs., Chgo. Women in Pub., Nat. Assn. Women Bus. Owners, South Suburban Assn. Commerce and Industry, Women in Mgmt., So. Suburban Network (bd. dirs., editor newsletter 1984-85), Toastmasters (v.p. 1984-85). Roman Catholic. Office: Second Thoughts Inc 153 Halsted Chicago Heights IL 60411

MILLER, YVONNE BOND, state legislator, educator; b. Edenton, N.C.; d. John and Pency Bond. BS, Va. State Coll., Petersburg, 1956; postgrad., Va. State Coll., Norfolk, 1966; MA, Columbia U., 1962; PhD, U. Pitts., 1973; postgrad., CCNY, 1976. Tchr. Norfolk Pub. Schs., 1956-68; asst. prof. Norfolk State U., 1968-71, assoc. prof., 1971-74, prof., 1974—, head Dept. Early Childhood/Elem. Edn., 1980-87; mem. Va. Ho. Dels., Richmond, 1983-87, mem. edn. com., health, welfare and instns. com., militia and police com., 1983-87; mem. Va. Senate, Richmond, 1987—, mem. commerce and labor com., local govt. com., rehab. and social svcs. com., 1987—; cons. to chs., parent orgns. and community groups. Commr. Ea. Va. Med. Authority; adv. bd. Va. Div. Children; active C.H. Mason Meml. Ch. of God in Christ. 1st black woman to be elected to Va. Legislature, 1983, 1st black woman to be elected to Va. Senate, 1987. Mem. Nat. Alliance Black Sch. Educators (bd. dirs.), Va. Assn. for Early Childhood Edn., Zeta Phi Beta (past officer). Office: 2816 Gate House Rd Norfolk VA 23504 Office: Norfolk State U 2401 Corprew Ave Norfolk VA 23504 also: Va Senate Gen Assembly Bldg Rm 386 Richmond VA 23219

MILLER, ZESTA FAYEDENE, physical fitness facility administrator; b. High Point, N.C., June 30, 1938; d. Claude Elihue Overby and Margaret Caroline (Jones) Mandel; m. Warren Gary Miller, Apr. 6, 1968; 1 child, Diane Cheryl. Diploma in nursing, Union Meml. Hosp., Balt., 1959. RN,

Balt. Operating room supr. Union Meml. Hosp., 1959-70; adminstr. Fitness Corp. Am., Balt., 1970—. Democrat. Lutheran. Office: Fitness Corp Am 6701 Moravia Park Dr Baltimore MD 21237

MILLER, ZOYA DICKINS (MRS. HILLIARD EVE MILLER, JR.), civic worker; b. Washington, July 15, 1923; d. Randolph and Zoya Pavlovna (Klementinovska) Dickins; grad. Stuart Sch. Costume Design, Washington, 1942; student Sophie Newcomb Coll., 1944, New Eng. Conservatory Music, 1946; grad. Internat. Sch. Reading, 1969; m. Hilliard Eve Miller, Jr., Dec. 6, 1943; children: Jeffrey Arnot, Hilliard Eve III. Fashion coordinator, cons. Mademoiselle mag., 1942-44; instr. Stuart Summer Sch. Costume Design, Washington, 1942; fashion coordinator Julius Garfinckel, Washington, 1942-43; star TV show Cowbelle Kitchen, 1957-58, Flair for Living, 1958-59; model mags. and comml. films, also nat. comml. recs., 1956—; dir. program devel. Webb-Waring Lung Inst., Denver, 1973—. Mem. exec. com., bd. dirs. El Paso County chpt. Am. Lung Assn., 1954-63; mem. exec. com. Am. Lung Assn. Colo., 1965-84, bd. dirs. 1965-87, chmn. radio and TV council, 1963-70, mem. med. affairs com., 1965-70, pres., 1965-66, procurer found. funds, 1965-70; developer nat. radio ednl. prodns. for internat. use Nat. Tb and Respiratory Disease Assn., Am. Lung Assn., 1963-70, coord. statewide screening programs Colo., other states, 1965-72; chmn. benefit fund raising El Paso County Cancer Soc., 1963; founder, coordinator Colorado Springs Debutante Ball, 1967—; coordinator Nat. Gov.'s Conf. Ball, 1969; mem. exec. com. Colo. Gov.'s Comprehensive Health Planning Council, 1967-74, chmn., 1972-73; chmn. Colo. Chronic Care Com., 1971-72, chmn. fund raising, 1970-72, chmn. spl. com. congressional studies on nat. health bills, 1971-73; mem. Colo.-Wyo. Regional Med. Program Adv. Council, 1969-73; mem. Colo. Med. Found. Consumers Adv. Council, 1972-78; mem. decorative arts com. Colorado Springs Fine Arts Ctr., 1972-75; founder, state coordinator Nov. Noel Pediatrics Benefit Am. Lung Assn., 1973-87; founder, state pres. Newborn Hope, Inc., 1987—. Recipient James J. Waring award Colo. Conf. on Respiratory Disease Workers, 1963; Zoya Dickins Miller Vol. of Yr. award established Am. Lung Assn. of Colo., 1979; Nat. Pub. Relations award Am. Lung Assn., 1979, Gold Double Bar Cross award, 1980, 83; named Humanitarian of Yr., Am. Lung Assn. of Colo., 1987. Lic. pvt. pilot. Mem. Nat. (chmn. nat. father of year contest 1956-57), Colo., El Paso County (pres. 1954, TV chmn. 1954-59) cowbelle assns., Colo. Assn. Fund Raisers. Club: Broadmoor Garden (ways and means chmn. 1967-69, civic chmn. 1970-71, publicity chmn. 1972, awards chmn. 1987—, spl. events chmn. 1988) (Colorado Springs, Colo.). Contbr. articles, lectures on health care systems and fund raising. Home: 74 W Cheyenne Mountain Blvd Colorado Springs CO 80906

MILLER-BLAZAK, KRISTINE ANN, human resources administrator, postmaster; b. Rochester, N.Y., Aug. 25, 1949; d. Walter W. and Catherine E. (Voellinger) Miller; m. Stephen A. Blazak, Aug. 3, 1980; children: Julia, Margot. BS, SUNY, Brockport, 1971. Mgr. EEO U.S. Postal Svc., Rochester, N.Y., 1982-83, mgr. tng., 1985-87; postmaster U.S. Postal Svc., Wayland, N.Y., 1988-89, Holcomb, N.Y., 1990—; EEO counselor, investigator U.S. Postal Svc., Rochester, N.Y., 1980-88; motivational counselor, cons., 1990—; editor Rochester Postal Times, 1986-88. Mem. NAFE, Rochester Postal Womens Network (recorder 1986-88), Nat. Assn. Postmasters, Adam Walsh Child Resource Ctr. Home: 830 Blossom Rd Rochester NY 14610-1915 Office: US Postal Svc 3 W Main St Holcomb NY 14469-9998

MILLERS, EDIE (EDIE BAZZANO), children's clothing designer; b. Riga, Latvia, Feb. 15, 1938; came to U.S., 1951; d. Roberts and Sofija (Svite) M.; m. Rudolf Valdmanis, Oct. 3, 1964 (div. 1970); 1 child, Marita; m. Pat Bazzano, Nov. 21, 1976. BA, Fashion Inst. Tech., 1960. Designer Little Fashion, N.Y.C., 1961-63, Pemay, N.Y.C., 1963-70, Doe Spun, N.Y.C., 1970-72, Thomas Textile, N.Y.C., 1972-75; pres. Play Pen Set, Hastings-on-Hudson, N.Y., 1975—. Bd. dirs. Gallery at Hastings, Hastings-on-Hudson, 1987, Am. Field Svc. Hastings-on-Hudson, 1984—. Mem. Fashion Group, Westchester Assn. Women Bus. Owners, Nat. Assn. Female Execs. Lutheran. Office: Play Pen Set 40 Amherst Dr Hastings-on-Hudson NY 10706

MILLETT, KATHERINE MURRAY (KATE MILLETT), political activist, sculptor, artist, writer; b. St. Paul, Sept. 14, 1934; m. Fumio Yoshimura, 1965. B.A. magna cum laude, U. Minn., 1956; postgrad. with 1st class honors, St. Hilda's Coll. Oxford, Eng., 1956-58; Ph.D., Columbia U., 1970. Instr. English U. N.C. at Greensboro, 1958; file clk. N.Y.C., kindergarten tchr., 1960-61; tchr. Barnard Coll., 1964-68; formerly tchr. English Bryn Mawr (Pa.) Coll.; disting. vis. prof. Sacramento (Calif.) State Coll., from 1973; founder Women's Art Colony Farm, Poughkeepsie, N.Y. Sculptor, Tokyo, 1961-63; co-producer, co-dir. film Three Lives, 1970; one-woman shows Minami Gallery, Tokyo, Judson Gallery, Greenwich Village, 1967, Soho Gallery, N.Y.C., 1976, 78, 80, 82, 84, 86, Women's Bldg., L.A., 1977; one-woman drawings Andre Wanters Gallery, N.Y.C., 1977, Chuck Levitan Gallery, N.Y.C., deVille Galerie, New Orleans, Emma Gallery, Berlin, 1980; author: Sexual Politics, 1970, The Prostitution Papers, 1973, Flying, 1974, Sita, 1977, The Basement, 1979, Going to Iran, 1982, The Loony Bin Trip, 1990. Mem. Congress of Racial Equality, from 1965; chmn. edn. com. NOW, 1966, active supporter women's liberation groups. Mem. Phi Beta Kappa. Office: care Georges Borchardt Inc 136 E 57th St New York NY 10022

MILLEY, JANE ELIZABETH, academic administrator; b. Everett, Mass., May 20, 1940; d. Walter R. and Florence (Leach) M. MusB, Boston U., 1961; MA in Music, Columbia U., 1966; PhD in Higher/Post Sec. Edn.-Adminstrn., Syracuse (N.Y.) U., 1977; piano study with Claude Frank, Martin Canin and Maria Clodes, 1963-75. Coord., founder, pianist Elmira (N.Y.) Coll. Fine Arts Trio, 1967-75; instr. music Elmira Coll., 1967-70, asst. prof. music, 1970-75, dir. arts and scis. program, 1974-75; rsch. assoc. Syracuse U., 1975-76, adminstrv. asst. to dean Coll. Arts and Scis., 1976-77; div. dean humanities and fine arts Sacramento City Coll., 1977-80; assoc. dean sch. fine arts, prof. music Calif. State U., Long Beach, 1980-81, interim dean, sch. fine arts, prof. music, 1981-82, dean, sch. fine arts, prof. music, 1982-84; arts advisor to chancellor Calif. State Univ. System, 1983-84; chancellor N.C. Sch. Arts U. N.C., Winston-Salem, 1984-89; sr. fellow Am. Assn. State Colls. and Univs., Santa Rosa, Calif., 1989—; speaker, cons. in field. Contbr. articles to profl. jours. Ex officio bd. dirs. Regional Arts Found., 1982-84, N.C. Scenic Studios, 1984—, N.C. Dance Theatre, 1984—, N.C. Shakespeare Festival, 1984—; bd. dirs. Sacramento Film Festival, 1979-80, Long Beach Grand Opera, 1980; charter mem., founder Sacramento Exptl. Theatre, 1978-84. Commendation for outstanding svc. Los Rios Community Coll. Bd. Trustees, 1980, Sacramento City Coll., 1980. Mem. AAUW (found. adv. com. 1987—), Am. Assn. State Colls. and Univs. (chmn. arts com. 1986—), Nat. Assn. State Univs. and Land Grant Colls. (U. N.C. rep. commn. on arts 1986—), Internat. Coun. Fine Arts Deans, N.C. Women's Forum, N.C. Assn. Women Deans Adminstrs. Counselors, Winston-Salem Leadership Group, Kappa Delta Pi, Pi Kappa Lambda.

MILLIGAN, NONA V., retired elementary educator, pianist; b. Triadelphia, Ohio, Apr. 13, 1916; d. Harry Milton Nelson and Goldie Edna (Loughman) Nelson-Lipp; m. Dana Clifton Milligan, May 27, 1951. BS in Edn., Ohio U., 1941. Cert. elem., history, English and music tchr., Ohio. Tchr., prin. Muskingum County, Ohio, 1936-39, tchr. grades 5 and 6, 1939-43; tchr. grade 5 Zanesville (Ohio) Pub. Schs., 1943-51; pvt. tchr. music Zanesville, 1939-53, Takoma Park, Md., 1959-70; ret., 1970; pianist accompanying chorus Lewisdale Sch., Md., 1976-81. Chief judge at voting Takoma Park Bd. Elections, 1968-74; substitute ch. organist, Zanesville, Columbus, Ohio, Silver Spring, Md., 1952-70. Mem. Takoma Park Women's Club (1st v.p. 1974-76, pres. 1976-78), D.C. Fedn. Women's Club (2d v.p. 1978-80, 1st v.p. 1980-82, pres. 1982-84), Conf. 7 States (chmn. S.E. region 1986, v.p. 1990—), Sligo Creek Club (program chmn. 1960—, sec. 1970).

MILLIGAN, SHIRLEY ANN, education educator; b. Bklyn., Sept. 27, 1957; d. Eddie and Louise (Everett) M.; 1 child, Bryan. BA, Bklyn. Coll., 1982, MS, 1986. Tchr. Bklyn. Bd. Edn., 1982—, ednl. dir., 1989—; edn. dir. Kiddie Christian Nursery, 1983-87; exec. dir. Tiny Town Pre-Sch., Bklyn., 1986—. Mem. NAFE. Democrat. Baptist. Home: 724 E 27th St Brooklyn NY 11210 Office: Clara Barton High Sch 901 Classon Ave Brooklyn NY 11225

MILLIKEN, SUSAN JOHNSTONE, mathematician, educator, government official; b. Woodstock, Conn., 1922; d. Francis U. and Violet Floyd (Ward) Johnstone; m. Peter H. Milliken, Dec. 15, 1950; children: Peter H. III, Frances U. Johnstone Balsam. AB, Vassar Coll.; MA, Columbia U. Chief statistician, research analyst E. W. Axe & Co., investment counsel, N.Y.C., 1940-42, 48-52; economist War Prodn. Bd., Washington, 1943-44; chief economist for sugar and allied products OPA, Washington, 1945-46; head sugar price control USDA, 1947-52; profl. genealogist Washington, 1953—; tutor in stats., math., French, econs. Columbia U., 1962-66, N.Y. Bd. Edn., 1966-83. Author articles in field. Life mem. Gov. William Bradford Compact, editor bull., 1963-69. Mem. Colonial Dames Am. (docent, co-chmn., house com. mus., hospitality com.), Soc. Daus. Holland Dames, N.Y. Geneal. and Biog. Soc. Episcopalian. Home: 423 W 120th St New York NY 10027

MILLS, ANN, educator; b. Newberry, S.C., July 12, 1935; d. Hubert Roy and Ruby (Bedenbaugh) M. BS in Elem. Edn., Newberry Coll., 1957; postgrad., U. S.C. and Clemson U. Tchr. Alice Drive Elem. Sch., Sumter, S.C., 1957-87; ret., 1987—. Mem. AAUW, PTA (life), Ret. Educators of Newberry County, Delta Kappa Gamma. Republican. Lutheran. Home: Rt 2 Box 134 Newberry SC 29108

MILLS, ARLENE EDNA, retired naval nurse; b. Poynette, Wis., Aug. 5, 1932; d. Kenneth Lyle and Mathilda Anna (Bartmann) M. Diploma in Nursing, Ancker Hosp., St. Paul, Minn., 1953; BSN, U. Wash., Seattle, 1968; MS in Mgmt., Naval Postgrad. Sch., Monterey, Calif., 1975. RN. Staff nurse VA, Mpls., 1953-56; staff nurse, lab. tech., bookkeeper Poynette Hosp., 1956-62; staff nurse USN St. Albans (N.Y.) Naval Hosp., 1962-64; staff nurse U.S. naval ship Gen. Hugh Gaffey-Mil. Sea Transp. Svc., 1964-66; staff nurse USN, evening supr. Bremerton (Wash.) Naval Hosp., 1966, 1978-81; staff nurse USN U.S. Naval Hosp., Camp Lejeune, N.C., 1968-70, USS Sanctuary, Vietnam, 1970-71, U.S. Naval Hosp., Camp Pendleton, Calif., 1971-73; nursing edn. coord. Oak Knoll Naval Hosp., Oakland, Calif., 1975-78; dir. med. edn. and reserve liaison officer U.S. Naval Hosp., Bremerton, Wash., 1973-78; coord. internal medicine Balboa Naval Hosp., San Diego, 1981-83. Bd. dirs. Congregational Counseling Network Luth. Social Ministry S.W., Phoenix, 1989—. Mem. Ret. Officers Assn., Am. Legion, U.S. Naval Inst. Republican. Lutheran.

MILLS, CAROL MARGARET, business consultant, public relations consultant; b. Salt Lake City, Aug. 31, 1943; d. Samuel Lawrence and Beth (Neilson) M.; BS magna cum laude, U. Utah, 1965. With W.S. Hatch Co., Woods Cross, Utah, 1965-87, corp. sec., 1970-87, traffic mgr., 1969-87, dir. publicity, 1974-87; cons. various orgns., 1988—; dir. Hatch Service Corp., 1972-87, Nat. Tank Truck Carriers, Inc., Washington, 1977-88; bd. dirs. Intermountain Tariff Bur. Inc., 1978-88, chmn., 1981-82, 1986-87; bd. dirs. Mountainwest Venture Group. Fund raiser March of Dimes, Am. Cancer Soc., Am. Heart Assn.; active senatorial campaign, 1976, gubernatorial campaign, 1984, 88, congl. campaign, 1990, vice chair voting dist., 1988-90, chmn. 1990—; witness transp. com. Utah State Legislature, 1984, 85; apptd. by gov. to bd. trustees Utah Tech. Fin. Corp., 1986—, corp. sec., mem. exec. com., 1988—. Recipient service awards W. S. Hatch Co., 1971, 80; mem. Pioneer Theatre Guild, 1985—; V.I.P. capt. Easter Seal Telethon, 1989, 90, recipient Outstanding Vol. Svc. award Easter Seal Soc. Utah, 1989, 90. Mem. Nat. Tank Truck Carriers, Transp. Club Salt Lake City, Am. Trucking Assn. (public relations council), Utah Motor Transport Assn. (dir. 1982-88), Internat. Platform Assn., Beta Gamma Sigma, Phi Kappa Phi, Phi Chi Theta. Home and Office: 77 Edgecombe Dr Salt Lake City UT 84103

MILLS, CHRISTINE ANNE, finance company executive; b. Hartford, Conn., May 16, 1954; d. Eugene E. and Margaret J. (Sliney) Apruzese; m. Peter E. Mills, Apr. 16, 1955. Bs in Music Edn., Western Conn. State U., 1977. Cert. music tchr. Music specialist Wolcott (Conn.) Bd. Edn., 1977-79; asst. v.p., dist. mgr. Household Fin. Corp., Canton, Mass., 1979—. Recipient Disting. Performance award Yamaha Music Corp., Calif., 1987, 89, 90. Mem. NAFE, Credit Women Assn. (v.p. 1989, 90—), U.S. C. of C., West Hartford C. of C. Roman Catholic. Office: Household Fin Corp 7 S Main St West Hartford CT 06107

MILLS, FRANCES DEBRA, computer educator, consultant; b. Bainbridge, Md., May 10, 1954; d. Merl Eugene and Frances J. (Smith) Clark; m. Donald Joe Mills, Jan. 22, 1976; 1 child, Frances Maria. BS, Ea. Ill. U., 1984; student, Danville (Ill.) Acad. Coll., 1981-84. Cert. tchr., Ill. Ptnr. Clark's Insulation Svc., Danville, 1977-80; tchr. computers Oakwood High Sch., Fithian, Ill., 1984—; computer cons. Mills Computer Cons. & Svcs., Indianola, Ill., 1989—; intern Vocat. Instruction Practium, Ill., 1987, 90; part-time instr. in computers Danville Area Community Coll., 1986. Mem. com. Georgetown (Ill.) High Sch. 75th Homecoming, 1990. Mem. Cen. Ill. Bus. Edn. Assn. (v.p. 1986, pres. 1987), Info. Processing Adv. Com. (coord. 1990—). Mem. Soc. of Friends. Home: RR#1 Box 153 Indianola IL 61850 Office: Oakwood High Sch RR#2 Fithian IL 61844

MILLS, GAIL FENLEY, publisher; b. Lufkin, Tex., Feb. 9, 1948; d. James Lewis and Lillee May (Hobbs) Fenley; m. Robert Leslie Mills, Jr., Dec. 25, 1944; 1 child, Maria Elyse. BFA cum laude in Art, Memphis State U., 1970. With TV foster childrens program Sta. WJTV, Jackson, Miss., 1970-74; party cons. United Rental, Justin, Costa Mesa, Fountain Valley, Calif., 1974-77; civic worker Jr. League, Buffalo, 1975-76; model Cain Slocum, Nashville, 1977-78; saleswoman, account exec. Channel 24, 1979-80; saleswomen, slaes mgr., gen. mgr., pub. Germantown (Tenn.) News, 1980—. Mem. city bd. 200; hon. mem. Brooks Art Gallery. Mem. Nat. Alumni Assn. (bd. dirs.), Germantown C. of C. Baptist. Home: 8451 Briarbirch Cove Germantown TN 38138 Office: Germantown News 7545 North St Germantown TN 38138

MILLS, JOYCE REYNOLDS, psychological examiner; b. Jackson, Ms., July 31, 1947; d. George Marshall and Eleanor (Paschall) Reynolds; m. Harry Lee Mills, Jr., Sept. 17, 1944; children: Candice Michelle, Courtney Sullivan. Student, Millsaps Coll., Jackson, 1965-66; BA, Miss. State U., Starkville, 1969, MS, 1970; MEd., U. of S. Ala., Mobile, 1976. Research assoc. Dept. of Psychiatry and Human Behaviour, Jackson, Ms., 1970-73; family counselor Harrison County Family Court, Gulfport, Miss., 1973-74; grad. asst. Dept. of Special Edn. U., Ala., Mobile, Ala., 1974-75; social worker Huntsville Madison County Sr. Ctr., Huntsville, Ala., 1976-78; tchr. Montessori Ctr., Nashville, Tenn., 1981-86; psychological examiner Barbara Gregg and Assoc., 1986-88, Mills and Assoc., Nashville, 1988--. Contr. articles to profl. jours. Mem. adminstrv. bd. Crievewood United Meth. Ch., Nashville, 1987-89; room mother Franklin Rd. Acad., Nashville, 1988-89; sec. Wesley Class Crievewood United Meth., 1988-89; grade level rep. Franklin Rd. Acad. Parent Networking Programme, 1989. Recipient Pi Delta Phi Miss. State U., Starkville, Miss., 1967, Scholastic scholar Millsaps Coll., Jackson, 1965-66, Scholastic scholar Phi Kappa Phi Miss. State U., Starkville, 1968; NSF fellowship, 1969-70; named One of Outstanding Young Women in Am., 1983. Assoc. Mem., Am. Psychological Assn., Assn. for Advancement of Behavior Therapy; Mem., Tenn. Assn. of Psychological Examiners, Phi Kappa Phi. Methodist.

MILLS, LINDA S., public relations executive; b. San Antonio, June 26, 1951; d. Frank M. and Betty A. (Young) M. BA, St. Mary's U., 1971. Asst. dir. Paseo Del Rio Assn., San Antonio, 1971-74; mktg. officer Frost Nat. Bank, San Antonio, 1974-79; account exec. Fleishman Hillard Inc., St. Louis, 1979-81, v.p., sr. ptnr., 1981-85, exec. v.p., sr. ptnr., 1985—, dir. corp. planning, 1986—; bd. dirs. Fleishman Hillard U.K. Ltd., London, FH et Associes, Paris. Mem. Pub. Relations Soc. Am. Club: Noonday (St. Louis) (bd. dirs.). Office: Fleishman Hillard Inc 200 N Broadway Saint Louis MO 63102*

MILLS, LYNNE MARIA, investment officer; b. Minden, Nebr., Dec. 16, 1954; d. Lee Howard and LeVada Mae (Casper) M. BS, Nebr. Wesleyan U., Lincoln, 1977; MBA, U. Denver, 1978. Chartered fin. analyst6. Security analyst MIMLIC Asset Mgmt. Co., St. Paul, 1978-80; sr. security analyst MIMLIC Asset Mgmt. Co., 1980-82, investment officer, 1982-86, sr investment officer, 1988—; mng. dir. RRY Holdings, L.P., Pineville, Pa., 1986-88. Mem. Twin Cities Soc. Security Analysts. Office: MIMLIC Asset Mgmt Co 400 N Robert St Saint Paul MN 55101

MILLS, MARGARET, retired association executive; b. Levenshulme, Eng., Dec. 16, 1921; came to U.S., 1953, naturalized, 1973; d. Leonard and Katharine (Howard) M. Student, U. London, 1939-42, Colegio Superior de Vicosa, Minas Gerais, Brazil, 1943-45. Translator, writer O Observador Economico, Rio de Janeiro, 1945-47; researcher Brazilian Embassy, London, 1948-53; asst. dir. purchasing commn. Brazilian Treasury Del., N.Y.C., 1954-64; asst. Cheryl Crawford Prodns., 1965-67; asst. to dir. AAAL, N.Y.C., 1968-73, exec. dir., 1973-90. Democrat. Office: Am Acad Inst Arts & Letters 633 W 155th St New York NY 10032*

MILLS, MARTHA ALICE, lawyer; b. Lansing, Mich., May 11, 1941; d. Edward Lucien and Muriel (Eastman) M.; m. A. Patrick Papas, Mar. 17, 1940. BA cum laude, Maclester Coll., St. Paul, 1964; JD cum laude, U. Minn., 1965. Bar: U.S. Ct. Appeals (5th cir.) 1967, U.S. Ct. Appeals (7th cir.) 1970, (6th cir.) 1987, U.S. Supreme Ct., 1970. City atty. Fayette, Miss., 1969; chief counsel Lawyer's Com. for Civil Rights Under Law, Cairo, Ill., 1969-71, Lawndale Legal Svcs. Office, Chgo. Legal Svcs., 1971; assoc. Schiff, Hardin and Waite, Chgo., 1971-75; instr. IIT Chgo. Kent Coll. of Law, 1976-82; owner Martha A. Mills, Ltd., 1976-79; ptnr. Cotton, Watt, Jones and King, Chgo., 1980-86, Foss, Schuman, Drake and Barnard, Chgo., 1986-88, Gottlieb and Schwartz, Chgo., 1989-90; of counsel Schaefer, Rosenwein & Fleming, Chgo., 1990—; fed. defender panel, U.S. Dist. Ct. for the No. Dist. Ill., Ea. Div., 1974—; bd. dirs. Legal Assistance Found., 1989—. Contbr. articles to legal publs. Advisor to youth group St. Andrews Greek Orthodox Ch., Chgo., 1986—. Fellow Am. Coll. Trial Lawyers; mem. ABA (governing coun. litigation sect. 1979-84, Chgo. Bar Assn., 7th Cir. Bar Assn. Home: 1021 W Bryn Mawr Chicago IL 60660

MILLS, MARY ETTA CARROLL, nursing administration educator; b. Balt.; d. Gordon Atkinson and Mary Jennings Carroll (Weiss) M. BS in Nursing, U. Md., Balt., 1971, MS, 1973; ScD, Johns Hopkins U., 1979; cert. in bus., U. Pa., 1988. Staff nurse Mercy Hosp., Balt., 1967-72; clin. specialist, quality assurance project dir. U. Md. Hosp., Balt., 1973-78, dir. quality assurance, rsch. and edn., 1978-81; v.p. nursing U. Md. Med. System, Balt., 1981-88; assoc. prof. nursing adminstrn. Sch. Nursing U. Md., Balt., 1988—; vice chmn. adv. bd. Hosp. Licensing and Certification, Balt., 1987—; mem. gov.'s task force to study crisis in nursing, Md., 1987-88, Md. Health Resources Planning Commn., Balt., 1985—. Contbr. articles to profl. jours., 1982-89. Active awards, grants and scholarship com. Am. Lung Assn. of Md., Balt., 1981—. Mem. Am. Nurses Assn., Am. Orgn. Nurse Execs., Am. Pub. Health Assn., Am. Assn. Critical Care Nurses, Md. Orgn. Nurse Execs. (bd. dirs. dist. 2 1988—), Nat. Hon. Pub. Health Soc. (active membership induction 1988), Sigma Theta Tau, Phi Kappa Phi. Roman Catholic. Office: Univ Md Sch Nursing 655 W Lombard St Baltimore MD 21201

MILLS, MIRIAM NAOMI, theater director, academic administrator; b. Newark, Oct. 2, 1949; d. Edgar and Gerda (Kreitler) M.; m. Tharyle J. Prather, Dec. 21, 1975; 1 child, Daniel Jason. Cert., Am. Acad. Drama Arts, 1969; student, Seton Hall U., 1971; BA, Rutger U., 1973; MFA, Rutgers U.-Mason Gross, 1977. Cert. tchr., N.J. Asst. bus. mgr. McCarter Theater, Princeton, N.J., 1981-83; head of drama H.S. of Performing Arts, Trenton, 1983-86; asst. prof. Mercer County Coll., Trenton, 1986—; instr. Trenton State Coll., Ewing, N.J., 1986—; cons. Rider Coll., Lawrenceville, 1979—, Notre Dame Performing Arts Program, Lawrenceville, 1985—. Contbr. articles to profl. jours. Worker Crisis Intervention Ctr., Adrian, 1978-79; organizer NOW, Hightstown, 1981-84. Named Best Dir. Rutgers U., 1973. Democrat. Jewish. Home: 11 Colonial Lake Dr Lawrenceville NJ 08348 Office: Trenton State Coll Trenton NJ 08650

MILLS, NANCY STEWART, chemistry educator; b. Osceola, Nebr., Mar. 31, 1950; d. Robert Lees and Margaret Eva (Stewart) M.; m. Mark Alan Hurd, Aug. 20, 1977; children: Caroline Margaret Mills Hurd, William Clark Mills Hurd. BA, Grinnell Coll., 1972; PhD, U. Ariz., 1976. Asst. prof. Carleton Coll., Northfield, Minn., 1977-79; asst. prof. Trinity U., San Antonio, 1979-83, assoc. prof., 1983-89, prof., chmn. chemistry dept., 1979—; mem. dept. rev. team Macalester Coll., St. Paul, 1989, Bowdoin Coll., Brunswick, Maine, 1986. Contbr. articles to profl. jours. Grantee NSF, Welch Found., Petroleum Rsch. Fund., Rsch. Corp., 1977—; recipient Outstanding Teaching and Campus Leadership award Sears Roebuck Found., 1990. Mem. AAUP, Sigma Xi. Home: 137 Alta San Antonio TX 78209 Office: Trinity U 715 Stadium Dr San Antonio TX 78284

MILLS, SUSAN BETH, student; b. Waynesville, N.C., Sept. 4, 1965; d. Harold Wayne and Jennie Mae (Huskey) M. BS in Home Econs., Lamar U., 1986. Crewperson McDonald's, Orange, Tex., 1984-85; salesperson White House, Port Arthur, Tex., 1985-86, Dillard's, Beaumont, Tex., 1986-87, Sunni's Fashions, Beaumont, 1987-89. Allied Health scholarship Orange Meml. Hosp. Corp., 1989-91; recipient U.S. scholastic All-Am. award, 1990. Mem. Student Dietetic Assn. (v.p. 1989-90), South Tex. Dietetic Assn. Republican. Southern Baptist. Home: 8282 Cambridge #1307 Houston TX 77054

MILLS, VELMA LOUISE, video store owner; b. Baytown, Tex., Jan. 25, 1956; d. Calvin Andrew Mills and Laura Louise (Singletary) Mills-Waldrum; m. Kenneth James Arnold, Feb. 14, 1976 (div. 1981); m. George Storm Walmsley, Jan. 21, 1989 (div. 1990). Student, Lee Coll., Baytown, 1984. File clk. Tex. Commerce Bank, Houston, 1973-75; proof dept. operator teller First Am. Bank, Baytown, 1975-77; receiving equipment warehouse-clerical Brown and Root Inc., Channelview, Tex., 1977-78; interior decorator Montgomery Wards, Pasadena, Tex., 1978-81, numerous orgns. in Tex., 1981-84; owner, pres. The Video Place of Am., Inc., Baytown, 1984—. Historian, library vol. Baytown Jr. Forum, 1989-90; bd. mem. Grace United Meth. Ch., 1988—, fin. com. 1990. Mem. Baytown C. of C. (membership com. 1984—), East Harris County Med. Aux. (social com. 1989-90). Democrat. Methodist. Home: Greenfield Condominium 2105 Cedar Bayou Rd #210 Baytown TX 77520 Office: The Video Place of Am Inc 2101 Bay Plaza Baytown TX 77520

MILLS-NOVOA, BEVERLY ANN, psychologist; b. Indpls., Apr. 23, 1954; d. P. Gerald and Arzella (Thompson) Mills; m. Avelino Mills-Novoa, Aug. 27, 1977; children: Nicole, Megan. BA, Earlham Coll., 1976; MA, U. Minn., 1978, PhD, 1980. Lic. cons. psychologist; lic. career counselor. Cons. Control Data Corp., Mpls., 1980-83, sr. cons., 1983-87; cons. McLagan Internat., St. Paul, 1987-88; asst. prof. Coll. of St. Thomas, St. Paul, 1988-89; pvt. practice Flagstaff, Ariz., 1989—. Author: (play) Last Laugh, 1972. Named one of Outstanding Young Women of Am., 1978. Mem. Am. Soc. Tng. and Devel., Am. Psychol. Assn., Minn. Career Devel. Assn. (bd. dirs. 1983-86), Phi Beta Kappa. Mem. Am. Soc. Friends Ch. Home and Office: 3923 N General Cir Flagstaff AZ 86004

MILMAN, DORIS HOPE, pediatrics educator, psychiatrist; b. N.Y.C., Nov. 17, 1917; d. Barnet S. and Rose (Smoleroff) Milman; m. Nathan Kreeger, June 15, 1941; 1 child, Elizabeth Kreeger Goldman. BA, Barnard Coll., 1934; MD, NYU, 1942. Intern Jewish Hosp., Bklyn., 1942-43, resident, 1944-46, fellow in pediatrics, 1946-47; postgrad. extern in psychiatry Bellevue Hosp., N.Y.C., 1947-49; pediatric psychiatry attending Jewish Hosp., Bklyn., 1950-56; asst. prof. pediatrics Health Sci. Ctr. at Bklyn. SUNY, 1956-67, assoc. prof. pediatrics, 1967-73, prof. pediatrics, 1973—, acting chmn. dept. pediatrics, 1973-75, 82; pvt. practice child and adolescent psychiatry, Bklyn., 1950-90; vis. prof. Ben Gurion U. of the Negev, Bearsheva, Israel, 1977. Mem. adv. bd. N.Y. Assn. for the Learning Disabled, N.Y.C., 1975-80. Grace Potter Rice fellow Barnard Coll., 1938-39; recipient Disting. Alumni award Barnard Coll., 1986. Fellow Am. Acad. Pediatrics (emeritus), Am. Psychiat. Assn. (life); mem. Am. Orthopsychiat. Assn. (life), Am. Pediatric Soc. (emeritus), N.Y. Pediatric Soc. (emeritus), AAAS. Home: 126 Westminster Rd Brooklyn NY 11218 Office: SUNY Health Sci. Ctr at Bklyn Box 49 450 Lenox Rd Brooklyn NY 11203

MILMAN, PATRICIA ELLEN, professional society administrator, consultant; b. N.Y.C., Mar. 17, 1950; m. Irving M. Milman; children: John H. Haman, Lori B. Haman. BA cum laude, CUNY, 1983. Chief statis. div. Nat. Assn. Mut. Savs. Banks, N.Y.C., 1976-84; dir. adminstrn. Am. Med. Women's Assn., Inc., N.Y.C., 1985-88, acting exec. dir., 1986; mgr. governance ops. ASME, N.Y.C., 1989-90, dir. bd. ops., 1990—; mktg. and sales cons. Lightning Up, Inc., N.Y.C., 1988—. Mem. Am. Soc. Assn. Execs., N.Y. Soc. Assn. Execs., Chinese Shar-Pei Club Am., Shar-Pei Club

N.E. (com. mem. Rescue League 1987—). Office: ASME 345 E 47th St New York NY 10017

MILNAR, ROSA FAY, international management consultant; b. New Orleans, July 16, 1947; d. Grover Cleveland and Agnes (Ehrhardt) Walk; m. Lawrence Milnar, Aug. 12, 1971 (div. Sept. 1975); 1 child, Christopher Ray. BA in English, U. New Orleans, 1969, MA in English, 1971; MS in Human Resource Mgmt., Nova U., 1981. English lang. instr. Nicholls State U., Thibodaux, La., 1971-72; real estate mgr. Bond, Inc., New Orleans, 1972-74; mgr. tng. Ochsner Hosp., New Orleans, 1978-79, GM, George Engine Co., New Orleans, 1979-81; supr. Coopers & Lybrand, Houston, 1982-86; prin. Mercer-Meidinger, Houston, 1986; assoc. King, Chapman & Broussard, Inc., Houston, 1986-89; ptnr. Ramsey-Sellers Assocs., Inc., Houston, 1989—; chair learning resources div. Delgado Coll., New Orleans, 1974-76, adj. faculty, 1974-81, North Harris County Coll., Houston, 1982—; cons. in field, New Orleans, 1976-81, Orgnl. Mgmt. Assn., New Orleans, 1981-82; adj. mgmt. Ind. U., 1978-81; author, presenter seminars in field, 1976—. Contbr. articles on mgmt. to profl. jours., horse tng. to Horse Sheet Mag. Leader Girl Scouts U.S., New Orleans, 1971-73, Boy Scouts Am., New Orleans, Houston, 1981-85; mem. Pres. Council Basic Edn., Washington, 1977-81. Recipient Cert. Appreciation Mayor of Houston, 1985, Mayor of Austin, 1985; named Outstanding Leader Boy Scouts Am., 1983-85. Mem. Am. Bus. Women's Assn., Nat. Female Exec. Assn., Am. Soc. Tng. and Devel. (Nat. com. 1979-80, bd. dirs. New Orleans 1979-81, Outstanding Trainer 1980, bd. dirs. Houston, 1982-84), U.S. Dressage Found., Houston Dressage Soc. (Houston Livestock show and rodeo officer, speakers com. 1986, Big Mouth award 1986, 87, 88, 89, 90), Nat. Bus. Women's Bus. Owners Assn. Democrat. Roman Catholic. Club: Appaloosa Horse. Home: 9038 Colleen St Houston TX 77080 Office: Ramsey-Sellers Asscs Inc 11000 Richmond Ave Houston TX 77042

MILNE, DENIA BETH, personnel manager; b. Peoria, Ill., Jan. 12, 1954; d. Louis Bernard and Helen Louise (Janzen) Spinder; m. Jeff Milne, Apr. 26, 1986; children: Brian, Steven. BS, Eastern Ill. U., 1988. Mgr. personnel Schumacher Electric Corp., Hoopeston, Ill.; personnel asst. Quaker Oats Co., Danville, Ill. Mem. Am. Soc. Personnel Asminstrs., C. of C., Personnel Roundtable, Mgmt. Club Danville, Exec. Club Danville, Nat. Honor Soc.

MILNE, FLORENCE EMILY, civic volunteer; b. Phoenix, Sept. 17, 1926; d. Riley White and Clara Luretta (Lavender) Geary; m. John Francis Milne, July 15, 1948; children: Margaret, Kathleen, Eileen, Michael, Lorraine, Patrick, Morgan-Anne. BA, U. Ariz., 1948. Mem. AAUW (pres. 1990—), A Woman's Place of Sarasota Inc. (treas. 1986—), Sr. Friendship Ctrs., Inc. (2nd v.p. 1987), Mortar Bd., Phi Beta Kappa. Roman Catholic. Home: 2707 Webber St Sarasota FL 34239

MILNE, MARGERY JOAN, natural history educator, consultant, author; b. N.Y.C., Jan. 18, 1922; d. Samuel and Rebecca Greene; m. Lorus Johnson Milne, 1944. BA, Hunter Coll., 1941; MA, Columbia U., 1942, Radcliffe Coll., 1943; PhD, Radcliffe Coll., 1945. Prof. biology U. Vt., Burlington, 1948-49; prof. zoology U. N.H., Durham, 1950-52, lectr., 1952-65, lectr. in writing sci., 1965-75; instr. sci. U. N.H. System, 1975—, instr. nonfiction writing, instr. Elderhostel, 1980—, instr. Sch. for Lifelong Learning, 1985—; cons. on ecology and zoology Reader's Digest, 1988—; semester at sea lectr. U. Pitts., 1985. Author: (with Lorus J. Milne) The World of Night, 1960, The Senses of Animals and Men, 1962, Water and Life, 1964, North American Birds, 1969, The Nature of Plants, 1971, Invertebrates of North America, 1972, Ecology Out of Joint, 1977, Audubon Society Field Guide to North American Insects and Spiders, 1980, Animal Babies: Behavior and Learning, 1989, also numerous others; co-author numerous books for juveniles, including Nature's Clean-up Crew (Jr. Lit. Guild award 1982), A Shovelful of Earth, 1987, Understanding Radioactivity, 1989; contbr. over 100 articles to popular mags. Keeper of swans Town of Durham, 1969—. Recipient sci. writing award AAAS, 1949, Eugene Saxton Lit. award Harper & Row Pubs., 1950; grantee Nat. Geog. Soc., 1966; South Africa Leader-Exchange fellow, UN ednl. fellow, N.Z. Fellow Explorers Club; mem. Soc. Women Geographers, Phi Beta Kappa, Sigma Xi, Phi Sigma, Phi Kappa Phi. Republican. Unitarian. Home: One Garden Ln Durham NH 03824 Office: U NH System Durham NH 03824

MILNER, BRENDA ATKINSON LANGFORD, neuropsychologist; b. Manchester, Eng., July 15, 1918; emigrated to Can., 1944; d. Samuel and Leslie (Doig) Langford. B.A., Cambridge (Eng.) U., 1939, M.A., 1949, Sc.D., 1972; Ph.D., McGill U., 1952; LL.D. (hon.), Queen's U.; ScD (hon.) U. Manitoba, U. Lethbridge, Mt. Holyoke Coll., U. Laval, U. Toronto; LHD (hon.), Mt. St. Vincent U., 1988; Hon. D. U. de Montréal, 1988. Exptl. officer U.K. Ministry of Supply, 1941-44; prof. agrégé Institut de Psychologie, Université de Montréal, 1944-52; rsch. assoc. psychology dept. McGill U., Montreal, 1952-53, lectr. dept. neurology and neurosurgery, 1953-60, asst. prof., 1960-64, assoc. prof., 1964-70, prof. psychology, 1970—; head neuropsychology rsch. unit Montreal Neurol. Inst., 1953—; Clothworkers fellow Girton Coll., Cambridge, 1972-73. Mem. editorial bd. Neuropsychologia, 1973—, Behavioral Brain Rsch., 1980, Hippocampus, 1990. Career investigator Med. Rsch. Coun. Can., 1964—; recipient Disting. Sci. Contbn. award Am. Psychol. Assn., 1973; Karl Spencer Lashley award Am. Philos. Soc., 1979; Izaak Walton Killam Meml. prize Can. Coun., 1983; Hermann Von Helmholtz prize Cognitive Neuroscience Inst., 1984; Officier de l'Ordre nat. du Que., 1985; Ralph W. Gerard prize Soc. for Neuroscience USA, 1987; named Officer Order of Can., 1984; William James fellow Am. Psychol. Soc., 1989. Fellow Royal Soc. London, Royal Soc. Can., Am. Psychol. Assn., AAAS, Can. Psychol. Assn.; mem. Am. Epilepsy Soc., Am. Neurol. Assn., Association de Psychologie Scientifique de Langue Française, Brit. Soc. Exptl. Psychology, Exptl. Psychol. Soc., Psychonomic Soc., Eastern Psychol. Assn., Internat. Neuropsychology Symposium, Soc. Neurosci. (Ralph W. Gerard prize 1987), NAS (fgn. assoc.), Am. Acad. Neurology (assoc.), Assn. Rsch. in Nervous and Mental Diseases (assoc.), Royal Soc. Medicine (affiliate), Sigma Xi. Office: Montreal Neurol Inst, 3801 University St, Montreal, PQ Canada H3A 2B4

MILSAP, REBECCA LYNN, pharmacist; b. Pitts., June 2, 1952; d. Walter Alan and Stella Mae (Hermes) M. BS, U. Mich., 1975, PharmD, 1977. Registered pharmacist, N.Y., Mich. Pharmacy resident Univ. Hosp.-U. Mich. Med. Ctr., Ann Arbor, Mich., 1975-77; instr. Coll. of Pharmacy, U. Mich., Ann Arbor, 1976-77; clin. coord. Cornell Med. Ctr.-N.Y. Hosp., N.Y.C., 1977-80; rsch. fellow pharmaceutics dept. SUNY, Buffalo, 1980-82, asst. prof. Sch. Pharmacy, 1983-85; rsch. assoc. Inserm Sch. Pharmacy, Marseille, France, 1982-83; grad. tchr. Roswell Park Meml. Inst., Buffalo, 1985-87; clin. assoc. dir. pharmacy dept. Sisters of Charity Hosp., Buffalo, 1987-90; lectr. pharmacology Sch. Nursing, Cornell U., N.Y.C., 1978-79; med./profl. advisor McAluley-Seton Home Care, Buffalo, 1988—. Contbr. chpt. to Pediatric Pharmacokinetics, 1986. Active Albright Knox Art Gallery, Buffalo, 1983—. R.A. Deno scholar U. Mich., 1975; rsch. study grantee Children's Hosp., Buffalo, 1983-85. Mem. AAAS, Am. Soc. Hosp. Pharmacists, Am. Soc. Clin. Pharmacology Therapeutics, Sierra Club, Rho Chi (Alpha chpt.). Home: PO Box 64 Hertel Sta Buffalo NY 14216

MILSTEAD, KATHRYN FUNDERBURK, data processing manager; b. Washington, Dec. 21, 1962; d. William Seaborn and Wilma Kathryn (Tracy) Funderburk; m. Richard Wayne Milstead, Feb. 14, 1986; children: Laura Kathryn, Brian Richard. BBA, Northeast Louisana U., 1984. Programmer N-Sure Systems, Monroe, L.A., 1985; sr. programmer, analyst Ouachita Computer Systems, Monroe, 1985-87; asst. EDP mgr. Electronic Management Systems, Monroe, 1987—. Dir. Twin City Volleyball League, Monroe, 1987—. Mem. Pi Sigma Epsilon (treas. 1981-83, corr. sec. 1983-84). Republican. Mem. Christian Ch. Home: 204 Brownlee Rd #6 Calhoun LA 71225 Office: Electronic Mgmt System 2813 Desiard St Monroe LA 71201

MILTON, JOYCE LYNNE, author; b. McKeesport, Pa., Jan. 12, 1946; d. Joseph Kent and Elsie Matilda (Wilson) M.; m. Jerrold B. Alpern, Jan. 4, 1969 (div. 1975). BA, Swarthmore (Pa.) Coll., 1967; MLS, Pratt Inst. Tech., 1969. Librarian trainee N.Y. Pub. Library, N.Y.C., 1967-69; librarian Walden Sch., N.Y.C., 1969-71; assoc. editor Kirkus Revs., N.Y.C., 1971-77; author, researcher, and freelance direct mail copywriter HBJ Press, Boston and N.Y.C., 1978-81; freelance writer Bklyn., 1981—. Author: (with Ronald Radosh) The Rosenberg File, 1983 (named one of best books of 1983, N.Y. Times), Vicki, 1985; The Yellow Kids: Foreign Correspondents in the Heyday of Yellow Journalism, 1989, Whales: The Gentle Giants, 1989. Recipient Oppy award Internat. Spy Soc., 1983. Mem. Author's Guild, Mystery Writers AM. Democrat. Home: 60 Plaza St Brooklyn NY 11238

MILTON, NANCY MELISSA, geobotanist, siscence policy analyst; b. Salem, Oreg., July 17, 1942; d. Claude Ellis and Angeletta (Skidmore) Milton; div.; 1 child, Megan. BS, Howard U., 1973; PhD, Johns Hopkins U., 1981. Geobotanist U.S. Geol. Survey, Reston, Va., 1975-89; sci. policy analyst Exec. Office of Pres.-Office of Mgmt. and Budget, Washington, 1989—; vis. prof. Mackay Sch. Mines, U. Nev., Reno, 1988-89; invited speaker, symposia chmn. in field. Contbr. articles to profl. jours. Mem. AAAS, Va. Acad. Sci., Am. Geophys. Union, Am. Soc. Photogrammetry and Remote Sensing, Geosci. of Remote Sensing Soc.-IEEE, So. Appalachian Bot. Club, Assn. for Women Geoscientists. Office: Office of Mgmt and Budget 725 17th St NW Washington DC 20503

MIMS, INKA FREDOTOVICH, business owner; b. Split, Croatia, Yugoslavia, Jan. 2, 1937; came to U.S., 1947; d. Vinko Krist and Srecka Dobrila (Grancaric) Fredotovich; m. Sam Stewart Mims, Aug. 25, 1956; children: Tania Aarhus, Sam, Inka P., Ben. BA, La. State U., Baton Rouge, 1975. With Young Fashions, Baton Rouge, 1977—, v.p., 1983—, co-owner, 1986—. Republican. Home: 2144 Monaco Baton Rouge LA 70815 Office: Young Fashions Inc 5758 Essen Ln Baton Rouge LA 70810

MIMS, JUDY F., insurance agent; b. Raleigh, N.C., Dec. 10, 1950; d. Marvin C. and Lara (Faulkner) Frazier; m. Bobby C. Mims, Aug. 11, 1974; children: Billy, Belinda. Student, St. Joseph's Coll.; AAS, Wake Tech. Coll., 1987. Lic. real estate broker, N.C. Agt. Mut. of N.Y., Raleigh; supr. adminstrv. support systems Exide Electronics, Raleigh; statistician recruiting bn. U.S. Army, Raleigh; controller accounts maintenance IRS, Raleigh. Recipient DAR Good Citizen award; scholar FTA, Women's Club, Pilot Club. Mem. NAFE, IEEE, Raleigh Bus. and Profl. Womens Assn., Raleigh Assn. Life Underwriters, Am. Mgmt. Assn., Wake Forest C. of C. (4th July exec. bd.), Kiwanis, Optimists.

MINA-MORA, MRS. PAUL J. See OLSON, DORISE EVELYN

MINARIK, ELSE HOLMELUND (BIGART MINARIK), author; b. Aarhus, Denmark, Sept. 13, 1920; d. Kaj Marius and Helga Holmelund; m. Walter Minarik, July 14, 1940 (dec.); 1 child, Brooke Ellen; m. Homer Bigart, Oct. 3, 1970. BA, Queens Coll., 1940. Tchr. 1st grade, art, pub. schs., Commack, N.Y., 1950-54; author children's books: Little Bear, 1957; Father Bear Comes Home, 1959; Little Bear's Friend, 1960; Little Bear's Visit, 1961; No Fighting, No Biting, 1958; Cat and Dog, 1960; The Winds That Come From Far Away, 1960; The Little Giant Girl and the Elf Boy, 1963; A Kiss for Little Bear, 1968; What If, 1987; Percy and the Five Houses, 1988. Mem. PEN Club. Home: Rural Delivery Barrington NH 03825

MINCHENER, VICKI PAULSON, educator; b. Miami, Fla., Dec. 25, 1946; d. Harry Vernon and Mary Elizabeth (Cooper) Paulson; m. Scott H. Minchener, Oct. 28, 1975 (div. Sept. 1980); children: Sarah MaryBeth, Katherine Hope. BA, Barry U., 1968; MA, U. Dayton, 1970. Instr. U. Dayton, 1968-70; tchr. St. Bartholomew Sch., Miramar, Fla., 1971-73, St. Thomas Aquinas High Sch., Ft. Lauderdale, Fla., 1973-74; dir. Children's Ctr. North Shore Med. Ctr., Miami, 1974—; cons. Edn. Assocs., Miramar, 1987—. Dep. registrar Child Care Com. LWV, Miami, 1989—; mem. Child Care Com. Greater Miami C. of C., 1989—. Recipient grad. fellowship U. Dayton, 1968-70. Mem. Nat. Assn. for the Edn. of Young Children, NAFE, South Fla. Assn. on Children Under Six, Nat. Assn. Hosp. Affiliated Child Care Programs. Home: 9300 Dunhill Dr Miramar FL 33025

MINDELL, SARA MARIE, product development technologist; b. Storm Lake, Iowa, Jan. 27, 1958; d. Olaf Elmer Langland and Carolyn Jean (Anderson) Ludwig; m: Mark Gregory Mindell, Oct 18, 1986; 1 stepchild, Ryan Joel. AS in Culinary Arts, Grand Rapids (Mich.) Jr. Coll., 1987. Charley's Crab Restaurant Charley's Gala Restaurant, Grand Rapids, 1982-86; chef tech. Bil-Mar Foods, Inc., Zeeland, Mich., 1987-88, Sara Lee, Inc., Zeeland, 1988-90; asst. chef Steelcase Inc., 1990—; nutrition cons. Omnitrition Internat., Dallas, 1989—. Vol. Humane Soc. of Mich., Grand Rapids, 1988-89. Mem. NAFE. Republican. Office: Sara Lee Corp 8300 96th Ave Zeeland MI 49464

MINDES, GAYLE DEAN, educator; b. Kansas City, Mo., Feb. 11, 1942; d. Elton Burnett and Juanita Maxine (Mangold) Taylor; BS, U. Kans., 1964; MS, U. Wis., 1965; EdD, Loyola U., Chgo., 1979; m. Marvin William Mindes, June 20, 1969 (dec.); 1 son, Jonathan Seth. Tchr. pub. schs., Newburgh, N.Y., 1965-67; spl. educator Ill. Dept. Mental Health, Chgo., 1967-69; spl. edn. supr. Evanston (Ill.) Dist. 65 Schs., 1969-74; lectr. Northeastern Ill. U., Chgo., 1974, Loyola U., Chgo., 1974-76, Coll. St. Francis, Joliet, Ill., 1976-79, North Park Coll., Chgo., 1978; cons. Chgo. Head Start, 1978-79; asst. prof. edn. Oklahoma City U., 1979-80; vis. asst. prof., rsch. assoc. Roosevelt U. Coll. Edn., Chgo., 1983-87, assoc. prof., dir. R&D, dir. tchr. edn., dir. early childhood, chair Roosevelt U. Senate, 1989—; cons. Arts Coun. Oklahoma City, Indian Affairs Commn., 1979-80, Lincolnwood (Ill.) Pub. Schs., Chgo. Pub. Schs., Atwood Sch. Dist, Chgo. Assn. Reatrded Citizens, Nat. Assn. Tech. Tng. Schs., Ill. State Bd. Edn., Itasca Pub. Schs., Decatur Pub. Schs., Robin Scholarship Found., 1982—, ednl. orgns. Assoc. editor Ill. Sch. R & D; editor Ill. Div. Early Childhood Edn. Adv. Com. to Ill. Bd. Edn.; contbr. articles to profl. jours. Bd. dirs. North Side Family Day Care, 1981, bd. northside affiliates Mus. Contemporary Art; trustee Roosevelt U., 1987—; mem. edn. adv. com. Okla. Dept. Edn., 1979-80; mem. adv. bd. bilingual early childhood program Oakton Community Coll.; mem. adv. bd. early childhood tech. assistance project Chgo. Pub. Schs., Lake View Mental Health, 1986—; mem. planning com. Lake View Citizens Coun. Day Care Ctr., 1978-79, local planning coun. Ill. Dept. Child and Family Svcs.; chmn. teen com. Florence G. Heller JCC, membership com.; mem. adv. bd. Harold Washington Coll. Child Devel., regional tech. assistance grant LICA. Cerebral Palsy Assn. scholar, 1965; U. Wis. fellow in mental retardation, 1964-65; U. Kans. scholar, 1960. Fellow Am. Orthopsychiat. Assn.; mem. AAUP, Assn. Supervision and Curriculum Devel., Assn. Children with Learning Disabilities, Nat. Assn. Edn. Young Children, Am. Ednl. Rsch. Assn., Coun. for Exceptional Children, Ill. Coun. for Exceptional Children, Coun. for Adminstrs. Spl. Edn., Coun. on Children with Behavioral Disorders, Soc. for Rsch. in Child Devel., Alpha Sigma Nu, Phi Delta Kappa, Pi Lambda Theta. Office: Roosevelt U Coll Edn Chicago IL 60605

MINDT LONG, W. KAYE, clinical social worker; b. St. Paul, Feb. 22, 1953; d. Erwin Etmor and Wanda (Goodwin) Mindt; m. Craig Freeland Long, Dec. 23, 1979; l child, Jennifer Nicole. BS, BSW, Nebr. Wesleyan U., 1980; MSW, U. Nebr., Omaha, 1988. Cert. social worker, Nebr. Protective svcs. worker Nebr. Dept. Social Svcs., Grand Island, 1980-85, permanency reviewer, 1985-88; pvt. clin. social worker, Grand Island, 1988—; tng. cons. Dept. Social Svcs., Lincoln, 1981-88; cons. Hall County Children's Village, Grand Island, 1986—. Mem. Com. Against Sexual Child assault, Grand Island, 1984-87; mem. Nat. Coalition Against Sexual Assault, 1990—; AIDS educator Train the Trainer Prog., 1990—; critical incident stress debriefer team Region 3, State Nebr., 1989—. Scholar P.E.O., 1989. Mem. Nat. Assn. Social Workers. Democrat. Methodist. Office: 1811 W 2d St Ste 330 Grand Island NE 68803

MINER, DORIS P., state legislator; married; 4 children. Rancher; former mem. S.D. Ho. of Reps.; now mem. S.D. Senate; del. Dem. Nat. Party Conf., 1978, Dem. Nat. Conv., 1980. Roman Catholic. Office: RR 2 Box 132 Gregory SD 57533*

MINER, JACQUELINE, political consultant; b. Mt. Vernon, N.Y., Dec. 10, 1936; d. Ralph E. and Agnes (McGee) Mariani; B.A., Coll. St. Rose, 1971, M.A., 1974; m. Roger J. Miner, Aug. 11, 1975; children—Laurence, Ronald Carmichael, Ralph Carmichael, Mark. Ind. polit. cons., Hudson, N.Y.; instr. history and polit. sci. SUNY, Hudson, 1974-79. Republican county committeewoman, 1958-76; vice chmn. N.Y. State Ronald Reagan campaign, 1980; candidate for Rep. nomination for U.S. Senate, 1982; co-chair N.Y. state steering com. George Bush for Pres. campaign, 1986-88; chmn. Coll. Consortium for Internat. Studies; mem. White House Outreach Working Group on Central Am.; co-chmn. N.Y. State Reagan Roundup Campaign, 1984—; mem. nat. steering com. Fund for Am.'s Future. Mem. U.S. Supreme Ct. Hist. Soc., P.E.O. Address: RD 2 Box 110E Hudson NY 12534

MINGOIA, MICHELE ANN, software engineer, consultant; b. Buffalo, July 26, 1954; d. Michael Anthony and Beatrice Grace (Short) Mingoia. BS in Engnrg., Rensselaer Poly. Inst., 1975, M in Engring., 1976; MBA, Duquesne U., 1980. Asst. systems programming officer Mellon Bank N.A., Pitts., 1976-80; systems programming officer SunBank Svc. Corp., Orlando, Fla., 1981-84; cons., owner Sabco Svc. Co., Orlando, 1985-87; cons. Cap Gemini Am., Maitland, Fla., 1988—. Bd. dirs. Citrus Chase Homeowners Assn., Orlando, 1985-86. Mem. Soc. Women Engrs. (pres. cen. Fla. sect. 1988—, author, editor newsletter 1988-90), Mensa, Cen. Fla. Pleasure Divers, Rensselaer Alumni Assn. Democrat.

MINGOUS, LOUADA FRANCES, hospital supervisor; b. Indpls., Oct. 27, 1947; d. Francis Olandon Mingous and Clara Katherine (Lucas) Fuel. AS, Purdue U., 1981, BS, 1983; MSW, Ind. U., 1990. Various sec. positions Meth. Hosp., Indpls., 1969-82, office mgr. fiscal services, 1982-83, sec. med. technology, 1984, adminstrv. sec. quality assurance, 1984-85, supr. clin. lab. office, 1986-88. Bd. dirs. Christian Youth Crusaders, Indpls., 1970-71, Young Teens Free Meth. Ch., Indpls., 1972. Ind. U. fellow, 1989-90. Mem. Nat. Assn. Social Workers. Avocations: music, profl. cake decorating, bowling, reading. Office: Meth Hosp Inc 1701 N Senate Blvd Indianapolis IN 46202

MINISTER, KRISTINA, speech communication educator; b. Dayton, Ohio, Aug. 27, 1934; d. Roy J. and Margaret (Chatterton) Arndt; m. Edward Minister, Mar. 1959 (div. 1972); children: Matthew, Margaret; m. Hal W. Howard, Sept. 10, 1977. BFA, Ohio U., 1958; MA, Columbia U., 1962; PhD, Northwestern U., 1977. Instr. speech St. John's U., Bklyn., 1962-65, Bowdoin Coll., Brunswick, Maine, 1969-71; asst. prof. speech communication U. Ariz., Tucson, 1974-77, Calif. State U., Northridge, 1978-79; vis. asst. prof. communication Ariz. State U., Tempe, 1979-82; oral historian Oral History Ctr., Inc., Phoenix, 1982-89; prof. speech and communication, dir. women's studies Midway (Ky.) Coll., 1989—; cons. oral history to bus., civic orgns., mus. and schs., 1982-89. Author: Oral History: The Privilege You Inherit, 1985; contbr. scholarly essays to various publs. Mem. NOW, Women in Communication, Speech Communication Assn., Oral History Assn., Am. Folklore Soc., Western States Communication Assn. Democrat. Unitarian Universalist. Office: Midway Coll 512 E Stephens St Midway KY 40347-1120

MINK, MAXINE MOCK, real estate executive; b. Lakeland, Fla., Jan. 17, 1938; d. Idus Frank and Elizabeth (Warren) Mock; student Fla. So. Coll.; children: Lance Granger, Justin Chandler. With Union Fin. Co., Lakeland, Fla., 1956-62; partner/owner S & S Ent. & Arrow Lake Mobile Home Pk., Lakeland, Fla., 1957-66; head bookkeeper Seaboard Fin., Lakeland, 1964-68; partner Custom Chem., Inc., Lakeland, 1968-75; partner Don Emilio Perfumers, Newport Beach, Calif., 1978-79; owner Maxine Mink Public Relations, Newport Beach, 1978-83; fine homes and relocation specialist Merrill Lynch Realty, Newport Beach, 1985—. Bd. dirs. Guild of Lakeland Symphony Orch., 1972-75; mem. Lakeland Gen. Hosp. Aux., 1974-76, Mus. Modern Art. Mem. Newport Beach C. of C., Hoag Hosp. Aux., Nat. Assn. Female Execs., Orange County Music Center Guild. Republican. Clubs: Balboa Bay, Sherman Library and Gardens, The 552. Office: PO Box 1262 Newport Beach CA 92663

MINK, PATSY TAKEMOTO, congresswoman; b. Paia, Maui, Hawaii, Dec. 6, 1927; d. Suematsu and Mitama (Tateyama) Takemoto; m. John Francis Mink, Jan. 27, 1951; 1 child, Gwendolyn. Student, Wilson Coll., 1946, U. Nebr., 1947; BA, U. Hawaii, 1948; LLD, U. Chgo., 1951; DHL (hon.), Chaminade Coll., 1975, Syracuse U., 1976, Whitman Coll., 1981. Bar: Hawaii. Pvt. practice Honolulu, 1953-65; lectr. U. Hawaii, 1952-56, 59-62, 79-80; atty. Territorial Ho. of Reps., 1955; mem. Ter. Hawaii Ho. of Reps., 1956-58, Ter. Hawaii Senate, 1958-59, State Hawaii Senate, 1962-64, 89-92d Congresses from Hawaii, 93-94th Congresses from 2d dist. Hawaii; appointed to fill vacancy 101st Congress; elected to 102d Congress, 1990; mem. U.S. del. to UN law of Sea, 1975-76, Internat. Woman's Yr., 1975, UN Environment Program, 1977, Internat. Whaling Commn., 1977. Charter pres. Young Dem. Club Oahu, 1954-56, Ter. Hawaii Young Dems., 1956-58; del. Dem. Nat. Conv., 1960, 72, 80; nat. v.p. Young Dem. Clubs Am., 1957-59; v.p. Ams. for Dem. Action, 1974-76, nat. pres. 1978-81; mem. nat. adv. com. White House Conf. on Families, 1979-80; mem. nat. adv. coun. Federally Employed Women, Adv. Com. for Campaign for UN Reform. Recipient Leadership for Freedom award Roosevelt Coll., Chgo., 1968, Alii award 4-H Clubs Hawaii, 1969, Nisei of Biennium award, Freedom award Honolulu chpt. NAACP, 1971, Disting. Humanitarian award YWCA, St. Louis, 1972, Creative Leadership in Women's Rights award NEA, 1977, Human Rights award Am. Fedn. Tchrs., 1975. Office: US House of Reps Offices of House Members Washington DC 20515*

MINKIN, JEAN ALBERT, research physicist; b. Phila., Nov. 17, 1925; d. Nathan and Fanny Ruth (Toll) Albert; m. Max Minkin, June 22, 1947; children: Brian Steven, Andrew Bennett. BA, Bryn Mawr Coll., 1947. Rsch. engr. Franklin Inst. Labs., Phila., 1947-51; physicist Nat. Bur. Standards, Washington, 1951-52; rsch. assoc. Inst. Cancer Rsch., Phila., 1960-68; rsch. physicist U.S. Geol. Survey, Reston, Va., 1968—. Contbr. articles to sci. jours. Mem. Am. Assn. Petroleum Geologists, Mineralogical Soc. Am. Office: US Geological Survey National Center MS954 Reston VA 22092

MINKOFF, ANDREA EHRLICH, real estate corporation officer; b. Chgo., Oct. 19, 1941; d. Joe Charles and Corinne (Freed) Ehrlich; m. Sherman Martin Minkoff, Feb. 12, 1966; children: Erica, Anthony. Student, U. Calif., Berkeley, 1959-60; BA, Ariz. State U., 1963; MA, UCLA, 1964. Cert. real estate profl., Ariz. Tchr. Alhambra High Sch., Phoenix, 1964-66, 66-67; unit supr. Office Econ. Opportunity, Chgo., 1966; owner, ptnr. FM Equities, Phoenix, 1985—; member, spokesperson Magnet Sch. Task Force, Phoenix Union High Sch. Dist., 1983-84. Bd. dirs. Jewish Fedn. Greater Phoenix, 1977—, sec. 1985-86, v.p., 1986-89, pres., 1989—; bd. dirs. United Jewish Appeal, Women's Div., N.Y.C., 1985—, exec. com. western region, L.A., 1983—; chmn. United Jewish Campaign, Phoenix, 1988-89; bd. dirs. Coun. of Jewish Fedn., N.Y.C., 1989—. Recipient Young Leadership award, Jewish Fedn. of Greater Phoenix, 1977, Gold Meir award, 1988, Community Rels. award, Am. Jewish Com., Phoenix, 1988; Woodrow Wilson Fellow, 1963-64. Mem. Phi Kappa Phi. Democrat. Home: 6522 N 2nd St Phoenix AZ 85012 Office: FM Equities 6522 N 2nd St Phoenix AZ 85012

MINKOFF, SANDRA RITA, education educator; b. Chgo., May 21, 1936; d. Edward and Rachel (Bernstein) Cohen; m. Robert Minkoff, June 17, 1956; children: Michael, Eileen. Assocs., Wright Coll., Chgo., 1954-56; BE, Chgo. Tchrs. Coll., 1956-57; postgrad., Inst. Psychoanalysis, 1971-72; MA in Guidance and Counseling, Northeastern Ill. U., 1984. Tel. operator Ill. Bell. Tele., Chgo., 1953-54; group leader Jewish Community Ctr., Chgo., 1954-56; receptionist Dr. Arnold Black, Chgo., 1955-56; kindergarten tchr. Bright and Bradwell Schs., Chgo.; tchr. Beal Sch., Chgo., 1957-58, Kitty Coll., 1966-67, Stone Sch., Chgo., 1967-82; tchr. reading resource Stone Scholastic Acad., Chgo., 1982-88, counselor, 1988-. Mem. PTA, Sch. Counselor Assn. Office: Stone Scholastic Acad 6239 N Leavitt Chicago IL 60659

MINKS, PAMELA ALSWORTH, secondary educator; b. Texas City, Tex., Aug. 14, 1944; d. Calvin Derrick and Alena Pauline (Thompson) Alsworth; m. Jack Elton Johnson, May 27, 1966 (div. Nov. 1985); children: Derrick Scot, Karl Edward; m. David Arthur Minks, Feb. 21, 1987. BS, Sam Houston State Coll., 1966. Cert. secondary educator, La., Tex. Secondary educator Bryan (Tex.) Pub. Schs., 1966-69, Arden Cahill Acad., New Orleans, 1972-73, Cypress-Fairbanks Ind. Sch. Dist., Houston, 1989—. Co-author: G.P.A. Healy, 1976. Author: Karl Fights Leukemia, 1982. Bd. dirs. Ronald MacDonald House, New Orleans, 1981; pres. Tall Timbers Owners Assn., New Orleans, 1981-83; pres. La. Chpt. Nat. Sudden Infant Death Syndrome Found., New Orleans, 1975-77. Republican. Methodist.

MINNELLI, LIZA, singer, actress; b. Los Angeles, Mar. 12, 1946; d. Vincente and Judy (Garland) M.; m. Peter Allen, 1967 (div. 1972); m. Jack Haley, Sept. 15, 1974 (div.); m. Mark Gero, Dec. 4, 1979. Appeared in Off-Broadway revival of Best Foot Forward, 1963; recorded You Are For Loving, 1963, Tropical Nights, 1977, Liza Minelli at Carnegie Hall, 1987; appeared with mother at London Palladium, 1964; appeared in Flora, the Red Menace, 1965 (Tony award), The Act, 1977 (Tony award), The Rink, 1984; nightclub debut at Shoreham Hotel, Washington, 1965; films include Charlie Bubbles, 1967, The Sterile Cuckoo, 1969, Tell Me That You Love Me, Junie Moon, 1970, Cabaret, 1972 (Oscar award), That's Entertainment, 1974, Lucky Lady, 1975, A Matter of Time, 1976, Silent Movie, 1976, New York, New York, 1977, Arthur, 1981, Rent A Cop, Arthur on the Rocks, 1988, Sam Found Out, 1988; albums include: Results, 1989; appeared on TV in own spl. Liza With a Z, 1972 (Recipient Emmy award); other TV appearances include Goldie and Liza Together, 1980, Baryshnikov on Broadway, 1980, The Princess and the Pea, Showtime, 1983, A Time to Live, 1985. Also awarded the Brit. equivalent of the Oscar for Best Actress, 1972, Italy's David di Donatello award (twice), the Valentino award. Office: care PMK Pub Rels 1776 Broadway New York NY 10019

MINNER, RUTH ANN, state senator; b. Milford, Del., Jan. 17, 1935; m. Roger Minner. Student Del. Tech. and Community Coll. Office receptionist Gov. of Del., 1972-74; mem. Del. Ho. of Reps., 1974-82; mem. Del. Senate, 1982—; mem. Dem. Nat. Com., 1988. Home: RD 3 Box 694 Milford DE 19963 Office: Del State Senate Legislative Bldg Dover DE 19901*

MINNETTE, RHONDA WILLIAMS, sales marketing representative; b. Evansville, Ind., Oct. 10, 1952; d. Raymond Howard and Bonnie (Huebner) Williams; m. Timothy Lee Minnette, July 11, 1982; children: Erin Ashly, Taylor Lauren. BS in Edn., Ind. State U., 1974; MA in Curriculum and Instrns., Fla. Atlantic, Boca Raton, 1978-79. Tchr. Broward County Sch. System, Ft. Lauderdale, Fla., 1974-81; sales rep. Breon Labs., Ft. Lauderdale, 1981-82, Glaxo, Inc., Ft. Lauderdale, Fla., 1982—. Co-writer Ft. Lauderdale Emergency Sch. Aid Act, 1981. Mem. Women in Sales, Classroom Tchrs. Assn.-NEA (del. 1975-76). Republican. Office: Glaxo Inc 5 Moore Dr Research Triangle Park NC 27709

MINNICE, KAREN ANN, association executive; b. Chgo., Jan. 15, 1947; d. Carl F. and Lillian (Rottinger) Egerer; m. Dennis M. Minnice, Oct. 4, 1969; 1 child, Paul Augustine. BA, DePaul U., 1968. Tchr. St. Teresa Sch., Chgo., 1968-74; program dir. World Without War Coun., Chgo., 1974-77, co-dir., 1977-80; program dir. Mid-Am. Com. Internat. Bus. and Govt. Cooperation, Chgo., 1981-83; coord. internat. programs U. Ill., Chgo., 984-88; program cons. John D. and Catherine T. MacArthur Found., Chgo., 1988-89; founder, dir. Heartland Internat., Chgo., 1989—; dir. World Without War Coun., Chgo., 1987—, Jane Addams Conf., Chgo., 1989—. Editor: Salt II: Facts, Values, Choices, 1977. Co-founder Alliance Cath. Laity, Chgo., 1976-80, Chgo. Call to Action, 1977-80. Recipient community svc. award Assn. Chgo. Priests, Chgo., 1979. Mem. Third Tuesday Club. Home: 2430 N Spaulding St Chicago IL 60647 Office: Heartland Internat 2d Fl 421 S Wabash St Chicago IL 60605

MINNIE, MARY VIRGINIA, social worker, educator; b. Eau Claire, Wis., Feb. 16, 1922; d. Herman Joseph and Virginia Martha (Strong) M. BA, U. Wis., 1944; MA, U. Chgo., 1949, Case Western Reserve U., 1956. Lic. clin. social worker, Calif. Supr. day care Wis. Children Youth, Madison, 1949-57; coordinator child study project Child Guidance Clinic, Grand Rapids, Mich., 1957-60; faculty, community services Pacific Oaks Coll., Pasadena, Calif., 1960-70; pvt. practice specializing in social work various cities, Calif., 1970-78; cons., educator So. Calif. Health Care, North Hollywood, Calif., 1978—; med. social worker Kaiser Permanente Home Health, Downey, Calif., 1985-87; assoc. Baby Sitters Guild, Inc., 1987—; cons. Home Health, 1987—; pres. Midwest Assn. Nursery Edn., Grand Rapids, 1958-60; bd. dirs., sec. So. Calif. Health Care, North Hollywood; bd. dirs., v.p. Baby Sitters Guild Inc., South Pasadena; cons. project Head Start Office Econ. Opportunity, Washington, 1965-70. Mem. Soc. Clin. Social Workers, Nat. Assn. Social Workers, Nat. Assn. Edn. Young Children (1960-62). Democrat. Club: Altrusa (Laguna Beach, Calif.) (pres. 1984-87). Home and Office: 1622 Bank St S Pasadena CA 91030

MINOR, LINDA BARSOM, special education educator, writer; b. Biloxi, Miss., Oct. 29, 1950; d. George Kasper and Judith Buel (Reed) Barsom; m. John Edward Dean, June 15, 1974; children: Justin Ryan, Jeffrey Taylor; m. Wade L. Minor, Jr.; 1 child, Stephanie-Nicole. BS, Fla. State U., 1972; postgrad. Valdosta State Coll., 1973-74; MEd, U. New Orleans, 1976; student Inst. Children's Lit., 1982-83. Cert. spl. edn. tchr., Ala. Tchr. for multi-handicapped Ochlocknee Children's Ctr., 1972-73; tchr. for emotionally disturbed North Andrews Gardens Elem. Sch., Ft. Lauderdale, Fla., 1973-75; dir. program for devel. delayed DePaul Hosp., New Orleans, 1975-76; treas., bd. dirs. Minor & Gillions Masonry; free-lance writer children's stories and books, Mobile, Ala., 1983—; flight instr., Suburban Airservice, Laurel, Md., 1987-88; mem. core staff First Chance Project, Ochlocknee Children's Ctr., 1972-74, mem. curriculum devel. staff, 1973-74, coordinator Climax Children's Ctr., 1973-74; del. Internat. Council for Exceptional Children Conv. from Fla. State U., 1972, S.W. Ga., 1973. Sec., bd. dirs. Mobile area LWV, 1984-86, chmn. War Vets. Study, 1985—; accident prevention counselor FAA, Balt., 1987—; v.p., co-founder Mobilians for Better Nutrition, 1982; mem. exec. bd., chairperson after sch. activities Thunder Hill PTA, 1987-88; active LaLeche League, 1977-81; tchr. confraternity on Christian doctrine St. Clements Ch., Ft. Lauderdale, 1974-75, St. Joan of Arc Ch., Mobile, 1981—; tutor learning disabled children Rotary Rehab. Ctr., 1984-85, Old Dauphin Way Sch., 1985-86; mem. exec. bd. PTA, Columbia, Md. Named Tchr. of Yr. of Exceptional Children for Southwest Ga., Ga. Fedn. Council for Exceptional Children 1974. Mem. Nat. Trust for Hist. Preservation, Hist. Mobile Preservation Soc., Aircraft Owners and Pilots Assn., Oakleigh Garden Soc., Spring Hill Food Coop., Zeta Tau Alpha. Republican. Roman Catholic. Club: Port City Pacers Road Runners (Mobile). Home: 7101 Long View Rd Columbia MD 21044

MINTER, JIMMIE RUTH, accounant; b. Greenville, S.C., Sept. 28, 1941; d. James C. and Lois (Williams) Jannino; B.S. Acctg., U. S.C., 1962; m. Charles H. Minter, Nov. 3, 1972; 1 child, Regina M.; stepchildren: Rhonda, Julie, Gregg. Asst. controller Package Supply & Equipment Co., Greenville, 1964-70, Olympia Knitting Mills, Spartanburg, S.C., 1970-72; controller Diacou Knitting Mills, Spartanburg, 1972-74; adminstr. Atlanta Med. Specialists, P.C., Riverdale, Ga., 1974-79; adminstr., corp. sec. David L. Cooper, M.D. P.C., Riverdale, 1979-89; acct. Ted L. Griffin Enterprises, Jonesboro, Ga., 1988—. Program chmn. 4th of July Celebration and Beauty Pageant, City of Riverdale; mem. exec. com. Clayton County Dem. Party, 1987—; active local and state election campaign fund raising. Mem. Am. Bus. Women's Assn. (chpt. Bus. Woman of Yr. 1969), Nat. Assn. Female Execs. Home: 1244 Branchfield Ct Riverdale GA 30296 Office: 10159 Tara Blvd Ste C Jonesboro GA 30236

MINTURN, DARBY, dietitian; b. Vancouver, Wash., Sept. 9, 1947; d. Howard Brigham and June Margaret (Keyes) M. BS in Zoology, Ohio U., 1969; MBA, Baldwin-Wallace Coll., 1989. Registered and lic. dietitian, Ohio. Dietitian I, Fairview Hosp. and Tng. Ctr., Salem, Oreg., 1977-79; renal rsch. dietitian U. Oreg. Health Scis. Ctr., Portland, 1979-81; staff clin. dietitian St. Luke's Regional Med. Ctr., Sioux City, Iowa, 1981-84; clin. nutrition coord. St. Joseph Hosp. and Health Ctr., Lorain, Ohio, 1984—. Mem. Am. Dietetic Assn., Ohio Dietetic Assn., Lorain County Dietetic Assn., Cleve. Dietetic Assn., Res. Officers Assn. U.S. (life), Assn. Mil. Surgeons U.S. Republican. Episcopalian. Home: 2844 Collins Dr Lorain OH 44053-1146 Office: St Joseph Hosp & Health Ctr 205 W 20th St Lorain OH 44052

MINTZ, CAROL SUE, program development specialist; b. Grand Rapids, Aug. 20, 1940; d. Wallace Henry and Bernice (Boynton) Jackson; m. Leigh Wayne, June 14, 1939; children: Kevin Randall, Susan Carol. BA, U. Mich., 1962, postgrad., 1962; MS, Calif. State U., Hayward, 1982. Tchr. Oakland (Calif.) Unified Sch. Dist., Oakland, Calif., 1962-66, Hayward Unified Sch. Dist., 1966-69, Castro Valley (Calif.) Unified Sch. Dist., 1975-80, San Leandro (Calif.) Unified Sch. Dist.; ednl. adminstr. Calif. State U., Hayward, 1982—. Vol. Am. Heart Assn., Hayward, ARC, Hayward; cub scout leader Boy Scouts Am., Hayward; youth leader YMCA; active Dem. Nat. Party, Hayward. Recipient Vol. award Boy Scouts Am., 1981. Mem. AAUW, NEA, Calif. Tchrs. Assn., Nat. Assn. Female Execs., Sierra Club, Nature Conservancy. Home: 5940 Highwood Rd Castro Valley CA 94552 Office: Calif State U Hayward CA 94542

MINTZ, LENORE CHAICE (LEA MINTZ), personnel company executive; b. N.Y.C., Aug. 6, 1925; d. Abraham and Eva (Kornblith) Chaice; m. Lewis R. Mintz, July 4, 1944; children: Richard Lewis, Alan Lee, Douglas Chaice. Student, U. Mich., 1942-44; BA magna cum laude, U. Bridgeport, 1976. Cert. personnel cons. Office mgr., personnel cons. Golden Door, Inc., Norwalk, Conn., 1970-78; v.p. permanent div. Aubrey Thomas, Inc., Stamford and Norwalk, 1978-84; sr. v.p. Aubrey Thomas Temps., N.Y., N.J., Conn., Pa., 1984-88; area v.p. Mid-Atlantic div. Talent Tree Personnel Svcs., 1988-89; v.p. bus. devel. Human Resources, Inc., Norwalk, Stamford, Statford and North Haven, 1989-90; prin. Lea Mintz & Assocs.c., Norwalk, 1989—; speaker, panel mem., condr. workshop and seminars; justice of peace Fairfield County, Conn., 1954—; bd. corporators Norwalk Savs. Soc. Mem., chmn. Norwalk Bd. Edn., 1966-72; mem. Norwalk Planning and Zoning Commn., 1971-73, Conn. Edn. Coun., 1979-83, Conn. Small Bus. Adv. Coun., 1984-86; mem. regional adv. coun. Norwalk State Tech. Coll., 1988—; pres. Norwalk Community Coll. Found.; 1988-90, bd. dirs. 1964—; del. numerous Dem. state and county convs.; mem. adv. coun. displaced homemakers Bridgeport YWCA; v.p. Greater Norwalk Community Coun., 1973-75; life mem. Women's Aux. Jewish Home for Aged in Conn.; active numerous other orgns. Recipient numerous awards including Woman of Yr. award Norwalk Bus. and Profl. Womens Club, 1984, Outstanding Women of Decade award UN Assn. Conn., 1987. Mem. Women in Mgmt. (Ann. Recognition award Conn. and Met. N.Y. area 1988), Internat. Assn. Personnel Women, Greater Norwalk C. of C. (bd. dirs. 1980-84, Athena award 1986), Nat. Coun. Jewish Women (life), LWV, Midday Club Stamford, B'nai B'rith (life), Alpha Sigma Lambda. Home and Office: 4 May Dr Silvermine Norwalk CT 06850 Office: Human Resources Inc 607 Main Ave Norwalk CT 06851

MINUTILLA, ROSEMARIE JOAN, nursing educator; b. Bayonne, N.J., Sept. 28, 1943; d. Joseph and Mary Angela (Martorano) M. BS in Nursing, Georgetown U., 1966; MA in Nursing, NYU, 1973; PhD, U. Nebr., 1983. RN, N.J. Instr., dept. head, psychiat. nurse Muhlenberg Hosp. Sch. Nursing, Plainfield, N.J., 1967-72; asst. prof. U. Nebr. Coll. Nursing, Omaha, 1973-74, chmn. dept., 1974-78, master tchr. cons., 1978-79; assoc. prof. U. Evansville, Ind., 1980-88, asst. dean, 1980-88; prof. nursing, chmn. dept., co-chmn. health sci. Coll. of St. Scholastica, Duluth, Minn., 1988—; peer reviewer HHS, Washington, 1989. Recipient recognition award Ind. Nurses Assn., 1988. Mem. Nat. League for Nursing, Midwest Alliance in Nursing, Minn. Nurses Assn., Sigma Theta Tau. Office: Coll of St Scholastica 1200 Kenwood Ave Duluth MN 55811

MIRABELLA, GRACE, magazine publishing executive; b. Maplewood, N.J., June 10, 1930; d. Anthony and Florence (Bellofatto) M.; m. William G. Cahan, Nov. 24, 1974. BA, Skidmore Coll., 1950. Mem. exec. tng. program Macy's, N.Y.C., 1950-51; mem. fashion dept. Saks Fifth Ave., N.Y.C., 1951-52; with Vogue mag., N.Y.C., 1952-54, 56-88; assoc. editor Vogue mag., 1965-71, editor-in-chief, 1971-88; publ. dir. Mirabella mag., 1988—; mem. pub. relations staff Simonetta & Fabiani, Rome, Italy, 1954-56; hon. bd. dirs. Catalyst; lectr. New Sch. Social Research. Adv. bd. Columbia U. Sch. Journalism. Decorated cavalier Order of Merit Republic of Italy; recipient Outstanding Grad. Achievement award Skidmore Coll., 1972; Fashion Critics award Parsons Sch. Design, 1985; Woman of Distinction award Birmingham-So. Coll., 1985, Girl Scouts Am. Leadership award, 1987, Excellence in Media award Susan G. Komen Found., 1987, Equal Opportunity award NOW, 1987; officer Order of Merit, Republic of Italy, 1987; Mary Ann Magnin award, 1988; Achievement award Am. Assn. Plastic and Reconstructive Surgery, 1988; Spl. Merit award Coun. Fashion Designers Am., 1989. Mem. Women's Forum N.Y. Office: Mirabella Mag 10 E 53d St New York NY 10022

MIRAGLIA, JANET, sales professional; b. Newark, N.J., June 7, 1956; d. Joseph and Grace (Nitti) M. BA, Averett Coll., 1978. Mgr. area sales Quality Temps, Union City, N.J.; mgr. Jonathan Royce, Union, N.J. Mem. NAFE.

MIRAGLIO, ANGELA MARIA, dietitian; b. Chgo., Sept. 12, 1944; d. Charles A. and Rose C. (Moles) M.; m. Robert S. Schwartz, Oct. 22, 1983. BS, Mundelein Coll., 1966; MS, U. Chgo., 1975. Registered dietitian. Clin. nutrition dir. West Suburban Kidney Ctr., Oak Park, Ill., 1974-78; clin. nutritionist Pediatric Outpatient Clinics U. Chgo., 1978-83; owner AMM Nutrition Services, Hinsdale, Ill. and Chgo., 1984—; part-time instr. Chgo. City-Wide Coll., 1979-81; lectr. DePaul U. Sch. Nursing, Chgo., 1978-80. Author: Food Composition Tables for Renal Diets, 1978; contbr. articles to profl. jours. Bd. dirs. Dorridge Condominium Assn., Chgo. Mem. Am. Dietetic Assn. (bd. dirs. Chgo. chpt.), Am. Diabetes Assn., Am. Assn. Diabetes Educators, Soc. for Nutrition Edn., Chgo. Dietetic Assn. (sec. 1969-71), Chgo. Nutrition Assn. Roman Catholic. Home: 5402 S Dorchester #2 Chicago IL 60615 Office: AMM Nutrition Services 120 E Ogden Ave Suite 13 Hinsdale IL 60521

MIRANDA, BONNY LOUISE, accountant; b. Yakima, Wash., Mar. 24, 1941; d. Roi Thomas and Elinor Marie (Hegge) Leadon; m. James Russell Miranda, June 22, 1966 (div.); children: Molly Ann, Gregory James, Michael Anthony. BBA in Profl. Acctg., Gonzaga U., 1963. Treasury clk. Gen. Telephone Co. N.W., Spokane, Wash., 1963-64; jr. acct. Roger Frucci & Assocs., Spokane, 1965-66; acct. I City of Spokane, 1977-78, acct. II, 1978—; bd. dirs. Spokane City Credit Union, vice chmn. bd. dirs., 1985, chmn. bd. dirs., 1986-87. Tabulation supr. March of Dimes Telethon, Spokane, 1984-85. Mem. Wash. Fin. Officers Assn. (Profl. Fin. Officer award 1984, 90), Govt. Fin. Officers Assn., Nat. Mgmt. Assn. (bd. dirs. 1987-89, Supporter of Yr. 1987), Toastmasters Internat. (dist. treas. 1988-89, Competent Toastmaster award 1988, Able Toastmaster award 1990). Roman Catholic. Home: 5707 N Forest Blvd Spokane WA 99205 Office: City of Spokane Finance Dept 808 W Spokane Falls Blvd Spokane WA 99201

MIRELES, SANDRA, civilian air force employee; b. San Antonio, Dec. 19, 1964; d. Homero and Consuelo (Silva) M. BBA, U. Tex., San Antonio, 1988. Gen. supply specialist San Antonio Air Logistics Ctr. USAF, San Antonio, 1988—. Mem. Kelly Mgmt. Assn., NAFE. Home: 6104 Jeff Loop San Antonio TX 78238 Office: San Antonio Air Logistics Ctr SA-ALC/SFRM Kelly AFB TX 78241-5000

MIRIPOL, JERILYN ELISE, poet, writing and art therapist; b. Chgo., Jan. 22; d. Albert and Janice (Tuchin) M.; m. Richard Palmer Van Duyne, Dec. 30, 1986. BA in English Lit., Northeastern Ill. U., 1974. Writing therapist Northshore Retirement Hotel, Evanston, Ill., 1983; creative writing tchr. Oakton Community Coll., Evanston, 1985—; writing therapist St. Francis Hosp., Evanston, 1989—; attended numerous writing workshops; writing facilitator for individual students, Chgo. 1987—; tchr. writing therapy to mental health profls. and caregivers, U. Wis., Milw., 1989. Author: Discovering Self-Awareness Through Poetry, 1987, The Sounds Were Distilled (poetry), 1977; author numerous poems. Vol. Ridgeview Nursing Home, Evanston, 1982-83. Artist-in-residence Evanston Twp. High Sch., 1988; grantee Dawes Sch., Evanston, 1987; recipient scholarship Squaw Valley Community of Writers, Olympic Valley, Calif., 1980, Ragdale Found., 1985. Mem. NOW, PEN, UNICEF, ACLU, Women's Internat. League for Peace, Humanitas Internat. (human rights com.), Amnesty Internat., Am. Acad. Poets, Ill. Alliance of Arts, Greenpeace. Home: 1520 Washington Ave Wilmette IL 60091

MIRK, JUDY ANN, elementary educator; b. Victorville, Calif., June 10, 1944; d. Richard Nesbit and Corrine (Berghoefer) M. BA in Social Sci., San Jose (Calif.) State U., 1966, cert. in teaching, 1967; MA in Edn., Calif. State U., Chico, 1980. Cert. elem. edn. tchr., Calif. Tchr. Cupertino (Calif.) Union Sch. Dist., 1967—; lead tchr. lang. arts Dilworth Sch., San Jose, 1988-90, mem. supt.'s adv. team, 1986—, mem. student study team, 1987—. Mem. Calif. Tomorrow. Mem. Assn. for Supervision and Curriculum Devel., Daytime Drama Guild (charter), Calif. Assn. for Counseling and Devel., Mary Beth Evans Fan Club, Matthew Ashford Fan Club, Phi Mu. Republican. Home: 4132 Valerie Dr Campbell CA 95008 Office: Cupertino Union Sch Dist 10301 Vista Dr Cupertino CA 95014

MIRKIN, SHERRIL ANN, elementary school educator; b. Indpls., May 25, 1932; d. Marcus and Inda Zabet (Wohlfeld) Katz; m. Sam Mirkin, Sept. 6, 1953; children: David, Kathy. BA in English magna cum laude, Ind. U., 1957; MA in Edn., St. Marys Coll., 1967. Elem. tchr. South Bend (Ind.) Community Sch. Corp., 1961—. Mem. Internat. Reading Assn., Questers (pres. 1987-88), Phi Beta Kappa. Democrat. Jewish. Home: 15635 Springmill Dr Mishawaka IN 46545

MIRSKY, SONYA WOHL, librarian, curator; b. N.Y.C., Nov. 12, 1925; d. Louis and Anna (Steiger) Wohl; m. Alfred Ezra Mirsky, Aug. 24, 1967 (dec. June 1974). B.S. in Edn., CCNY, 1948; M.S.L.S., Columbia U., 1950. Asst. libr. Rockefeller U., N.Y.C., 1949-60, assoc. libr., 1960-77, univ. libr., 1977—; trustee Med. Libr. Ctr. N.Y., 1965—, v.p., 1980-88; cons. libr. mgmt. Mem. Bibliog. Soc. Am., Bibliog. Soc. Can., Bibliog. Soc. Gt. Britain, Soc. Bibliography of Natural History. Home: 450 E 63rd St Apt 8I New York NY 10021 Office: Rockefeller U Libr 1230 York Ave New York NY 10021-6399

MIRSKY, SUSAN, personnel director; b. N.Y.C., Nov. 5, 1939; d. Ira Albert and Ethel Maxine (Goldstein) Schur; m. Stanley Mirsky, Jan. 24, 1963; children: Jennifer L., Jonathan S. BA, Smith Coll., 1961; postgrad., NYU, 1961-62. Employment interviewer Met. Life Ins. Co., N.Y.C., 1962-63, supr. employment, 1963-66; personnel adminstr. J. Walter Thompson Co., N.Y.C., 1981-82, personnel mgr., 1982-84, v.p., dir. U.S. personnel, 1985-86, sr. v.p., worldwide personnel dir., 1986—. Adv. mem. Boys Harbor, N.Y.C., 1963—; mem. dr.'s com. Mt. Sinai Med. Ctr., N.Y.C., 1985—. Mem. N.Y. Persnnel Mgmt. Assn., N.Y. Human Resource Planners. Office: J Walter Thompson Co 466 Lexington Ave New York NY 10017*

MIRZA, LEONA LOUSIN, educator; b. Chgo., July 1, 1944; d. Max B. and Opal Lousin; B.A. in Math., North Park Coll., Chgo., 1965; M.A. in Edn., Western Mich. U., Kalamazoo, 1967, Ed.D. in Edn., 1972; m. David B. Mirza; children—Sara Anush, Elizabeth Ann. Tchr. Kalamazoo Pub. Schs., 1965-69; asso. prof. edn. North Park Coll., 1969—. Chmn. adv. com. on edn. in Ill., 1975-77. Mem. Nat., Ill. assns. supervision and curriculum devel., Ill. Assn. Colls. of Tchr. Edn., Ill. Assn. Tchrs. Edn. in Pvt. Colls. (officer 1974-86). Contbr. articles to profl. jours. Specialist in elem. curriculum and adminstrn. Home: 795 Lincoln Ave Winnetka IL 60093 Office: 3225 W Foster Ave Chicago IL 60625

MISHOE, RAINELLE DIXON, educator; b. Burlington, N.C., Feb. 18, 1950; d. James Milo and Nellie (Rainey) Dixon; m. Harmon W. Mishoe Jr., Apr. 23, 1988; 1 child from previous marriage, Jessica Rainelle Tinsley. BA in English, N.C. State U., 1972. Cert. tchr., real estate broker. Tchr. Richard B. Harrison Jr. High Sch., Selma, N.C., 1972-73, Flat Rock (N.C.) Jr. High Sch., 1973-79; owner, designer The Finishing Touch, Carolina Beach, N.C., 1981-87; tchr. lang. arts Lake Forest Jr. High Sch., Carolina Beach, N.C., 1987-88; tchr. English Hoggard High Sch., Wilmington, N.C., 1988—; chmn. curriculum com. Henderson County Bd. Edn., Hendersonville, N.C., 1978-79; mem. archtl. rev. bd. Old Chimney Homeowners Assn., 1985-86. Feature writer Hendersonville Times News, 1976-77. Pres. Hendersonville Jaycettes, 1975, treas., 1976, chmn. bd. dirs., 1977; mem. family life com. First United Meth. Ch., Hendersonville, N.C. Recipient Dist. Spoke award Hendersonville Jaycettes, 1977; named Outstanding Jaycette, Hendersonville Jaycettes, 1976. Mem. Nat. Home Furnishings Assn., So. Home Furnishings Assn., Cape Fear Sales and Mktg. Assn. (social chmn. 1986), Kappa Kappa Iota (historian 1977, v.p. 1978, pres. 1979, chmn. bd. dirs. 1980-81). Democrat. Methodist. Club: Jr. Woman's (Hendersonville). Home: 214 Chimney Ln Wilmington NC 28403

MISHRA, KAREN ELIZABETH, marketing executive; b. Lansing, Mich., July 4, 1963; d. Thomas William and Martha Lynne (Isbell) Repaskey; m. Aneil Kumar Mishra, June 22, 1985. BA, Albion Coll., 1985; MBA, U. Mich., 1988. Coop. edn. Buick Olds Cadillac Group, Lansing, Mich., 1982-85; promotions intern N.Y. Arts program, 1983; coll. grad. in tng. Buick Olds Cadillac, Gen. Motors, Lansing, Mich., 1985-86; coord. Buick Old Cadillac, Gen. Motors, Lansing, Mich.; promotions coord. Jacobson Stores, Jackson, Mich., 1987; mkt. analyst Johnson Controls, Inc., Manchester, Mich., 1988-89; sales analyst Johnson Controls, Inc., Manchester, 1989-90, price adminstrn./promotions mgr., 1990—; pres. U. Mich. Bus. Sch. Student Council., Ann Arbor, 1987-88. Composer Born Today, 1981, Let Your Light So Shine, 1981. Vol. William Lucas for Gov. Campaign, Lansing, Mich., 1985; mem. Lange Early Music Ensemble, Lansing, 1985; adv. Mortar Bd. Nat. Honor Soc., Ann Arbor, Mich., 1986-88; com. mem. Episcopal Ch. Planned Giving, Detroit, 1989; chorister St. Clares Ch. Choir, Ann Arbor, 1988—. Mem. Am. Mktg. Assn. Republican. Episcopalian. Home: 2966 Birch Hollow Dr Apt 1B Ann Arbor MI 48108 Office: Johnson Controls Inc 912 City Rd Manchester MI 48158

MISNER, LORRAINE, laboratory technologist; b. Fitchburg, Mass., June 24, 1948; d. Cedric Winfield and Pearl Erma (Hallisey) M. BA in Biology, Fitchburg State Coll., 1971; MS in Med. Technology, Anna Maria Coll., 1983. Lab. technologist Leominster (Mass.) Hosp., 1971-87; research asst. U. Lowell (Mass.) Research Found., 1987—. Piccolo Townsend (Mass.) Military Band, 1964—; mem. choir United Ch. of Christ. Mem. Am. Soc. of Clin. Pathologists (assoc., registrant), Am. Soc. for Med. Technology, Mass. Soc. for Med. Technology.

MISSANA, LINDA MARIE, fraternal organization administrator; b. Port Huron, Mich., Feb. 17, 1948; d. Frank Harold and Hazel Marie (Elsholz) Carrier; m. Gilbert Missana, Apr. 3, 1971. BA, Siena Heights Coll., 1988. Nat. frat. dir. N.Am. Benefit Assn., Port Huron, Mich., 1981—. Contbr. articles to profl. mags. Mem. Blue Water Women's League, Port Huron, 1986-90; com. mem. Mich. Rep. Party, Port Huron, 1971. Mem. Mich. Frat. Congress (pres. 1984-85, 85-86, Fraternalist of the Yr. 1986). Republican. Methodist. Home: 1996 Michigan Ave Marysville MI 48040

MISSAVAGE, ANNE EVELYN, surgeon; b. La Rochelle, France, Feb. 2, 1955; (parents Am. citizens); d. Edward Jr. and Freda A. (Dunnam) M.; m. Thomas Clark, Nov. 1, 1986. BS in Chemistry, U. Mich., 1976; MD, Wayne State U., Detroit, 1980. Resident in gen. surgery Wayne State U., 1980-85; chief burn study br. Inst. Surg. Rsch. U.S. Army, Ft. Sam Houston, Tex., 1985-87; dir. burn unit U. Calif., Davis, 1988—, asst. prof. surgery, 1988—; cons. Calif. Dept. Forestry & Fire Protection, Sacramento, 1988-89. Author: (with others) Current Therapy in Vascular Surgery, 1987, Surgical Care of the Elderly, 1987. Mem. AMA, Am. Med. Women's Assn., Assn. Acad. Surgery, Am. Burn Assn., Alpha Omega Alpha. Office: Dept Surgery 4301 X St Sacramento CA 95817

MISSELDINE, CAROL KAY, university administrator; b. Milw., May 16, 1959; d. Albert and Amanda Christine (Mertens) M.; m. Edward Lee Groves, Aug. 22, 1987. BS, Mich. State U., 1981; MS in Resource Devel., Coll. of Agriculture and Natural Resources. Soil conservationist USDA Soil Conservation Svc., Ann Arbor and Bad Axe, Mich., 1980-84; regional dir. midwestfield office Am. Farmland Trust, East Lansing, 1984-87; mgr. groundwater edn. Mich. program Mich. State U., East Lansing, 1988—. Co-author: Planning and Zoning for Farmland Protection: A Community Based Approach, 1987; author: Michigan Land and Soil Resources: A Status Report, 1985. Founder, coord. Mich. Pro-Choice Network, 1989; mem. steering com. Lansing area Advocates for Choice, 1989—, v.p. polit. action com., 1990—; bd. dirs. Mich. Environ. Coun., 1989—. Mem. League Women Voters (off-bd. chair Mich. chpt.), Tri-County Recyclers (chair fundraising com. 1988), Soil and Water Conservation Soc. Am. (former chair Mich. land use com.), NAFE, Clean Water Incentives Program Com. (adv. com. 1986). Office: Mich State U Inst Water Rsch 334 Natural Resources Bldg East Lansing MI 48824

MISTER, COLEEN WARREN, school principal; b. North Wilkesboro, N.C., July 16, 1934; d. Granville and Ruby (Colvard) Warren; m. James M. Mister, July 31, 1954; children: David James, Steven Michael. BS in Elem. Edn., Towson State U., 1962; MEd, Salisbury State U., 1975. Cert. tchr., reading specialist, supr., and adminstr., Md. Trademark rep. Reubin H. Donnelly Corp., Balt., 1953-57; tchr. Balt. County Pub. Schs., Towson, Md., 1957-62, Worcester County Pub. Schs., Newark, Md., 1969-76; curriculum planner Pocomoke Middle Sch., Pocomoke City, Md., 1976-84, prin., 1987—; asst. prin. Snow Hill (Md.) Middle Sch., 1984-87. Chair numerous coms., sec. Delmarva Campers, 1973-90; bd. dirs. Maple Shade Boys Home, 1975-77. Mem. ASCD, NEA, Nat. Middle Sch. Assn., Md. Middle Sch. Assn., Soroptimists (sec. local chpt. 1987-90), Delta Kappa Gamma, Phi Delta Kappa. Office: 800 8th St Pocomoke City MD 21857

MITCHELL, ADA MAE BOYD, advertising executive; b. Nov. 23, 1927; d. Allen T. Boyd and Marjorie (Bigger) Boyd Mills; 1 child, Joseph W. Student, NYU, 1972-73. Supr. Faberge, Inc., Mahwah, N.J.; mgr. Demostration Svcs. and Promotional Monies; mgr. accounts receivables, credit mgr. Faberge, Inc., Mahwah, N.J. Pres. Urban League Guild, Bergen County, N.J., 1982—, bd. dirs., 1982-83; treas. Bethany Presbyn. Ch., Englewood, N.J., 1975, fin. sect., 1966-67, chairperson bldg. and renovation com., 1978-81, choir mem., elder, 1979—; 1st Black woman moderator Presbytery of Palisades-Presbyn. Ch., 1986. Mem. NAFE, NAACP, Order Eastern Star (Queen of Sheba chpt. #4, worthy matron 1982-83).

MITCHELL, ANDREA, journalist; b. N.Y.C., Oct. 30, 1946; d. Sydney and Cecile Mitchell. B.A., U. Pa., 1967. Polit. reporter KYW Newsradio, Phila., 1967-76; polit. corr. Sta. KYW-TV, Phila., 1972-76; corr. Sta. WTOP-TV, Washington, 1977-78; gen. assignment and energy corr. NBC News, Washington, 1978-81; White House corr. NBC News, 1981-88, chief congl. corr., 1989—; instr. Gt. Lakes Colls. Assn., 1974-76; co-anchor Summer Sunday, USA, NBC-TV News, 1984, substitute anchor Meet the Press, 1988—. Overseer Coll. Arts and Scis. U. Pa., 1989—. Recipient award for public affairs reporting Am. Polit. Sci. Assn., 1969, Public Affairs Reporting award AP, 1976; AP Broadcast award, 1977; named Communicator of the Yr., Phila. chpt. Women in Communications, 1976, Woman of the Yr., Phila. chpt. Am. Women in Radio and TV, 1989. Mem. Sigma Delta Chi (award for broadcast reporting Phila. chpt. 1975). Club: Nat. Press, White House Corrs. Assn. Office: 4001 Nebraska Ave NW Washington DC 20016

MITCHELL, ANN BUFORD, health service executive, consultant; b. Sycamore, Ill., Mar. 22, 1925; d. Morgan and Anna Corinne (Leathers) Buford; m. George E. Mitchell, Aug. 27, 1949 (div. 1966); children: Jennifer Ann, Lane Buford, Nancy Katherine. BA, U. Cin., 1947. Rsch. asst. Children's Hosp., Cin., 1947-49; dir. family planning OEO, Napa, Calif., 1966-68; exec. dir. Planned Parenthood Assn. Cin., 1968-90; chmn. Ohio Planned Parenthood Affiliates Com., 1972-74, Gt. Lakes Exec. Dirs. Coun., 1974-76; cons. Gov.'s Task Force, Columbus, Ohio, 1975, Ohio Dept. Pub. Health, 1983-84; v.p., bd. dirs. Zero Population Growth, 1977-82; rep. U.S.A. Maternal and Child Health Orgns. in trip to Republic of China; mem. Mayor's Task Force on Teen Pregnancy, 1985. Founder, bd. dirs. Vasectomy Svcs., Inc., 1970-83; organized Freedom of Choice Coalition, Ohio, 1976; mem. Christ Hosp. Instl. Rsch. Rev. com., 1982-89, steering com. to study future financing of reproductive health care, 1984; mem. Nat. Abortion Rights League. Recipient Best Feminist award Cin. Magazine, 1987, Outstanding Women's Achievement award Cin. Women's Polit. Caucus, 1988, ACLU award, 1989, Career Woman of Achievement award YWCA, 1989, Disting. Alumnae award, U. Cin. Women's Studies, 1990. Mem. NOW, NARAL, Am. Pub. Health Assn., Feminist Congress Bd., Network Health Mgrs., Met. Exec. Dirs. Coun. Planned Parenthood/World Population (sec. 1972-74, 80-82, steering com. 1972—), Cin. Women's City Club. Home: 1303 Shakerdale Rd Cincinnati OH 45242

MITCHELL, BETTY JO, writer, publisher; b. Coin, Iowa, May 2, 1931; d. Edith Darrah McWilliams; B.A., S.W. Mo. State U., Springfield; M.S.L.S., U. So. Calif. Asst. acquisitions librarian Calif. State U., Northridge, 1967-69, librarian for personnel and fin., 1969-71, acting asso. library dir., 1971-72, asso. dir. univ. libraries, 1972-81; owner Viewpoint Press, Tehachapi, Calif.; cons. Western Interstate Commn. for Higher Edn. USOE Inst. for Tng. in Staff Devel. Problem Solving; participant workshops in field. Bd. dirs. San Fernando Valley council Girl Scouts U.S.A., 1974-77, employed personnel com., 1979-81; bd. dirs. Bear Valley Springs Condominium Owners Assn., 1978, Empyrean Found., 1978-81. Mem. Assn. Women in Computing (bd. dirs. 1987-89), ALA (mem., chmn. various coms.), Nat. Library Assn., Calif. Library Assn., Assn. Calif. State U. Profs. (sec., exec. com., 1971-72), AAUP, Pi Beta Chi, Alpha Mu Gamma. Co-author: Cost Analysis of Library Functions: A Total System Approach, 1978; author: ALMS: A Budget Based Library Management System, 1982; co-author: How to See the U.S. on $12 a Day; speaker profl. confs.; contbr. writings to profl. publs.; editor Staff Development column in Special Libraries, 1975-76. Home: Star Route 3 Box 4600-7 Tehachapi CA 93561 Office: PO Box P Tehachapi CA 93561

MITCHELL, CAROLANN, nursing educator; b. Portsmouth, Va., Aug. 31, 1942; d. William Howell and Eleanor Bertha (Wesarg) M.; m. David Alan Friedman, June 17, 1971 (div. 1988). Diploma, NYU, 1963; BS, Columbia U., 1968, MA, 1971, EdM, 1974, EdD, 1980. Charge nurse Nassau County Med. Ctr., East Meadow, N.Y., 1963-65; staff nurse Meml. Hosp., N.Y.C., 1965-68; head nurse, supr. Community Hosp. at Glen Cove (N.Y.), 1969-71; assoc. prof. dept. nursing Queensborough Community Coll. CUNY, Bayside, 1971-80; assoc. prof. Marion A. Buckley Sch. Nursing Adelphi U., Garden City, N.Y., 1981-88; ednl. cons. Nat. League for Nursing, N.Y.C., 1980-81; prof. sch. nursing SUNY, Stony Brook, 1988—, chmn. adult nursing, 1988—; mem. faculty Regents Coll. degrees in nursing program SUNY, Albany, 1978—, cons., 1978—. Editor Scholarly Inquiry in Nursing Practice jour., 1983—; contbr. articles to profl. jours. Robert Wood Johnson clin. nurse scholar postdoctoral fellow U. Rochester (N.Y.), 1983-85. Mem. Am. Nurses Assn., Nat. League for Nursing, Gerontol. Soc. Am., N.Am. Nursing Diagnosis Assn., Soc. for Research in Nursing Edn.

MITCHELL, CASSANDRA WALTON, restauranteur; b. San Francisco, Dec. 25, 1946; d. Clayton Edward and Mari-Jane (Walton) M. Student, U. Calif., Berkeley, 1964-65; BFA, San Francisco Art Inst., 1969; postgrad., Dominican Coll., 1989-90. Food service mgr. San Francisco Art Inst., 1969-71; organic farmer Napa, Calif., 1970-76; grapevine nursery mgr. Cal-Vine Nursery, St. Helena, Calif., 1972-75; restaurant proprietor The Diner, Yountville, Calif., 1975—. Coun. mem. Yountville Town Coun., 1986—; mem. Nature Conservancy, San Francisco, 1979—, Greenpeace, San Francisco, 1985—, Sierra Club, San Francisco, 1980—, Napa Valley Land Trust, St. Helena, 1986—; dir. Napa Valley Women's Network. Recipient Silver medal, Best Breakfast in No. Calif., Sta. KQED-Focus Mag., San Francisco, 1986, Best Breakfast in Bay Area, Cooks Mag., N.Y.C., 1989; named Spécialtiés De La Maisons Gourmet mag. 1988. Mem. Soup and Bread Soc. (coord. 1986—), NOW, No. Calif. Restaurant Owner's Guild. Democrat. Home: PO Box G Yountville CA 94599 Office: The Diner 6476 Washington St Yountville CA 94599

MITCHELL, CATHERINE SUE, principal; b. Memphis, Dec. 13, 1941; d. Robert Louis Sr. and Sarah Evelyn (Cole) Rawls; 1 child, Shawn Fitzgerald. BA, Lemoyne Coll., Memphis, 1967; cert., U. S.C., 1978; MEd, Memphis State U., 1978, postgrad., 1979-80. Cert. tchr., Tenn. Tchr. Memphis City Schs., 1967-80, asst. prin., 1980-84, prin., 1984—; Owner C&S Enterprises, Memphis. Active on State Career Ladder Sounding Bd.; mem. Tenn. 3d Grade Adv. Bd., 1990—. Fellow GE Corp., 1978, Nat. Assn. Elem. Sch. Prins., 1986. Mem. Memphis Pub. Sch. Prin. Assn. (parliamentarian 1987-88, treas. 1988-90, pres. 1990—), Women in Edn. (sec. 1987—), Prin.'s Study Coun. (sec. 1987-90, del. 1987—, v.p. 1990—), Black Bus. Assn., Memphis Area C. of C. Democrat. Baptist. Home: 2199 Cambridge Dr Memphis TN 38106 Office: Coro Lake Elem Sch 1560 Drew Rd Memphis TN 38109

MITCHELL, CHERRY ANNE, financial planner; b. Glendale, Calif., Nov. 14, 1950; d. John R. and Mabel B. (Stevenson) M. AA in Nursing, Los Angeles Valley Coll., 1971. Cert. Fin. Planner; RN, Calif. Registered rep. and agt. Prin. Fin. Group, Visalia, Calif., 1984-87; agt. Prin. Fin. Group, Visalia, 1984—; registered rep. Foothill Securities, Inc., Visalia, 1987-88, SunAm. Securities, Inc., Visalia, Calif., 1988—. Vol. Hospice of Tulare County Guild, Visalia, 1986-87, pres. 1989-90. Mem. Inst. Cert. Fin. Planners, Networking for Women (bd. dirs. Visalia chpt. 1986-90, treas. 1989), Kaweah Bus. and Profl. Women (pres. 1989-91), Tulare-Kings Assn. Life Underwriters (sec., treas. 1985-89, v.p. 1989-90, pres.-elect 1990-91), Estate Planning Coun. of Tulare County, Visalia C. of C. Republican. Baptist. Home: 5621 W Elowin Dr Visalia CA 93291 Office: Prosperity Planning Services 350 W Caldwell Ave Visalia CA 93277

MITCHELL, CHERYL ELAINE, marketing executive; b. Oceanside, N.Y., Dec. 27, 1951; d. Harold Bertram and Doris Meredith (Hose) M. BA in History, Polit. Sci., Hartwick Coll., 1973; postgrad., Syracuse U., 1973-75. Campaign staffer Udall for Pres., N.Y., 1975-76; sr. writer Syracuse (N.Y.) Record, 1976-78; assoc. nat. dir. pub. relations Cushman & Wakefield, Inc., N.Y.C., 1978-81; sr. account exec. JP Lohman Orgn., N.Y.C., 1981-84; v.p. SPGA Group, N.Y.C., 1984-86; pres. Mitchell & Assocs., N.Y.C., 1986—; lectr. in field; press agt. to internat. real estate developers, architects and filmmakers. Contbr. articles to profl. jours; prin. works include numerous corp. and product brochures, advt. and publicity. Recipient ANDY award Art Dirs. N.Y., 1983, Champion award of excellence Graphic Arts Exhbn., 1985, Award of Merit Design and Mktg. Communications, 1986. Mem. Assn. Real Estate Women, Comml. Real Estate Women, NAFE, Alliance of the Bldg. Community (bd. dirs.). Democrat. Lutheran. Office: Mitchell & Assocs 36 W 20th St New York NY 10011

MITCHELL, CONSTANCE AYER, design analyst; b. Painesville, Ohio, Oct. 9, 1952; d. Russell Ayer and Jean Ann (Hanna) Poxon; m. Leslie Olan Mitchell, Feb. 5, 1972; children—Bryan, Brandon. A.A., Lakeland Coll., Ohio, 1973. Programmer, analyst Curtis Industries Inc. div. Congoleum, Eastlake, Ohio, 1973-79; asst. to sr. v.p. Lake Nat. Bank, Painesville, 1979-81; sr. programmer analyst Picker Internat., Highland Heights, Ohio, 1981-83; sr. analyst George Worthington Co., Mentor, Ohio, 1983-86; with application devel. The Lubrizol Corp., Wickliffe, Ohio, 1986—; cons. and lectr. in field. Co-author: data processing systems. Mem. Nat. Assn. Female Execs. Episcopalian. Avocations: reading; photography. Home: 8715 Maple Glen Dr Chardon OH 44024 Office: The Lubrizol Corp 29400 Lakeland Blvd Wickliffe OH 44092

MITCHELL, DEE A., information processing executive; b. Jim, W.Va., Dec. 17, 1946; d. George Edgar and Nina Maude (Collins) Shirley; m. Kermit H. Mitchell, June 26, 1964 (div. 1980); children: Jeffery H., Eric J. Student, DePaul U., Chgo., Coll. of DuPage, Glen Ellyn, Ill. Bookkeeper TV Jay Co., Chgo., 1965-67; sec. to pres. Blue Shield Assoc., Chgo., 1968-71; dir. word processing Blue Cross/Blue Shield, Chgo., 1971-87; office automation devel. mgr. Interim Sys. Corp., Northbrook, Ill., 1987—; lectr. in field. Advisor to bd. Malcolm X Coll., Chgo., 1981-84, Triton Community Coll., 1981-84, Whitney Young Bus. Inst., Chgo., 1981-84, Benito Juarez High Sch., Chgo., 1984-87. Named Outsanding Mem. of the Yr., Assn. Info. Sys. Profls., 1982. Fellow Assn. Info. Sys. Profls., Chgo. Computer Soc., NAFE, Am. Soc. Tng. and Devel., Rothkamp Matchbook Soc., Word Processing Mgmt. Assn. Chgo. (past pres.). Republican. Home: 711 Wauconda Rd Wauconda IL 60084 Office: Interim Systems Corp 500 Skokie Blvd #300 Northbrook IL 60062

MITCHELL, ELIZABETH IRWIN, interior designer; b. Buffalo, May 20, 1957; d. Robert James Armstrong Irwin and Barbara Butler (Baird) Palladino; m. William Avery Mitchell, May 14, 1988; 1 child, Henry Butler. BFA, Ringling Sch. of Art and Design, 1985. Interior designer Gasparilla Interiors, Boca Grande, Fla., 1985-87; co-owner Interarc Assocs., Sarasota, Fla., 1987-88; pres. Designs on East Inc., Sarasota, 1988—. Mem. Am. Soc. Interior Designers. Republican. Episcopalian. Home: 637 Corwood Dr Sarasota FL 34234 Office: Design on East Inc PO Box 49064 Sarasota FL 34230

MITCHELL, GWENDOLYN VAN DERBUR, lawyer; b. Denver, Aug. 29, 1931; d. Francis Stacy and Gwendolyn (Olinger) Van D.; m. Robert L. Falkenberg, Jr., Feb. 6, 1954 (div. Aug. 1971); children: Robert L. III, Nancy Elaine; m. Ernest Albert Mitchell, May 14, 1972. BA, U. Colo., Boulder, 1953; JD, U. Mo., 1957. Bar: Kans. 1957, Calif. 1974, U.S. Dist. Ct. (no. dist.) Calif. 1978. Assoc. Henry, Shankel, Gilman, Falkenberg & Rainey, Overland Park, Kans., 1957-72; asst. to exec. dir. San Francisco Neighborhood Legal Asst. Found., 1973-75; assoc. Lawrence Stotter Law Offices, San Francisco, 1975-82, Carr, McClellan, Ingersoll, Thompson & Horn, Burlingame, Calif., 1982-85; v.p., sec., corp. counsel European Asiatic Mktg., San Mateo, Calif., 1986-88; pvt. practice, San Mateo, Calif., 1986—. Bd. dirs. Mills-Peninsula Hosps. Mem. ABA, Calif. State Bar Assn., Bar Assn. San Francisco, San Mateo County Bar Assn. Republican. Presbyterian. Office: 2000 Alameda de las Pulgas Ste #160 San Mateo CA 94403

MITCHELL, HELEN BUSS, associate dean continuing education; b. N.Y.C., July 17, 1941; d. Joseph William and Helen Ruth (Fitz) Buss; m. Joseph Rocco Mitchell, June 20, 1964; 1 child, Jason Christopher. AB, Hood Coll., Frederick, 1963; MEd, Loyola Coll., Balt., 1974, MMS, 1978; PhD, U. Md., Balt., 1990. Tchr. Howard County Pub. Sch., Ellicott City, Md., 1963-67; freelance writer Balt. News Am., Balt., 1972-75; columnist Cen. Md. News, Ellicott City, 1972-77; coord. adult basic edn. Howard Community Coll., Columbia, Md., asst. dir. continuing edn., 1977-79, dir., 1979-83, exec. dir., 1983-86, assoc. dean, continuing edn., 1986—, chmn. instrnl. self study, 1987-89. Author: History of the Orton Society, 1974, The Physics Teacher, 1976; editor Hood Coll. Alumni Mag., 1973-75; contbr. articles to Catalyst. Mem. Howard County Study Commn. on Status of Women, 1972, Leadership Howard County, 1987-88; bd. dirs. Howard County Hist. Soc., 1989. Mem. Nat. Coun. Instrnl. Adminstrs., Nat. Community Edn. Assn., Md. Deans Continuing Edn. (pres. 1983-84), Alpha Sigma Nu, Delta Kappa Gamma, Phi Kappa Phi. Democrat. Roman Catholic. Office: Howard Community Coll 10650 Hickory Ridge Rd Columbia MD 21044

MITCHELL, JANE THERESA, banker; b. Barberton, Ohio, Apr. 16, 1957; d. Aldo Roosevelt and Mary Josephine (Platner) Paolano; m. John S. Mitchell, Aug. 11, 1979. BSBA, U. Akron, 1979, MBA, 1983. Vice pres. mktg. Society Bank, Canton, Ohio, 1982-88; adminstrv. officer, mgr. advt. and communications Banc One, Columbus, Ohio, 1988—. Mem. Advt. Fedn. Home: 1932 Stratshire Hall Ln Powell OH 43065 Office: Banc One 841 Greencrest Dr Columbus OH 43271-1022

MITCHELL, JANET ALDRICH, fund raising executive, reference materials publisher; b. Providence, Jan. 12, 1928; d. Norman Ackley and Janet (Gordon) Aldrich; m. Raymond Warren Mitchell, Jan. 9, 1954 (div. 1967); children—Lydia Aldrich, Polly Burbank. A.B., Smith Coll., 1949; M.Ed., Rutgers U., 1975. Engaged in devel. various non-profit orgns., 1954-72; dir. devel. Wilson Fellowship Found., Princeton, N.J., 1972-74; dir. spl. projects N.J. Dept. Higher Edn., Trenton, 1974-76; pub., editor-in-chief Mitchell Guide, Princeton, 1976-87; pres., chmn. Mitchell Guide, 1987—; cons. to numerous non-profit orgns., 1976-86; lectr. Adult Sch., Princeton, 1983-84. Editor: Directory of Woodrow Wilson Fellows, 1968; Guide to Federal Aid to Higher Education, 1975; Higher Education Exchange, 1978; A Community of Scholars, 1980. Exec. officer Princeton Community Democratic Orgn., 1984-86; elected mem. Princeton Twp. Com., 1987-89; mem. NAACP Legal Def. Fund, 1980—; trustee N.J. Hist. Soc., 1984-86. Episcopalian. Clubs: Smith Coll. (pres. 1968-70), Princeton Dog (bd. dirs. 1962-68). Avocation: breeding and showing standard poodles. Home: 731 Princeton-Kingston Rd Princeton NJ 08540 Office: Mitchell Guide PO Box 413 Princeton NJ 08542

MITCHELL, JEANNE OLSON, mining and minerals company executive; b. Orlando, Fla., Oct. 10, 1959; d. Carl Howard and Mary Jane (Jattuso) Olson; m. Douglas Keith Mitchell, Feb. 16, 1985. AA, Lake-Sumter Community Coll., Leesburg, Fla., 1978; BS, U. Fla., 1980, MS, 1981. Grad. asst., U. Fla., Gainesville, 1981, interium dir. instr. materials, 1982; info./press rels. staff mem. Future Farmers Am., Alexandria, Va., 1982-83; dir. pub. rels. Fla. Sugar Cane League, Clewiston, Fla., 1983-86; pub. rels. advisor Mobil Mining & Minerals Co., Nichols, Fla., 1986-89; community rels. advisor Mobil U.S. Mktg. & Refining-Beaumont, Tex., Refinery. Bd. dirs. Polk County Econ. Devel. Coun., mem. Lakeland Chamber Host Task Force; mem. Leadership Fla. Author and editor curriculum guides. Mem. Nat. Assn. Female Execs., Pub. Rels. Soc. Am., Fla. Pub. Rels. Assn. (bd. dirs. 1985, 86, 87, 88, Golden Image award 1983, 84, 85, 87, Member of Yr. 1990), Mulberry C. of C. (1st v.p., bd. dirs., v.p. spl. events 1989, pres. elect 1990), Fort Meade C. of C. (bd. dirs.), Mulberry Svc. Ctr. (pres.), Leadership Lakeland Alumni. Baptist. Office: Mobil Mining & Minerals Co PO Box 311 Nichols FL 33863

MITCHELL, JO ANN, newspaper feature editor; b. Hale County, Tex., Feb. 16, 1935; d. Phillip Thomas and Lillie Adele (Henderson) Huffine; m. James Clayton Mitchell, Oct. 30, 1954; children: Jerry Michael, James Lawrence, Jana Lynn Mitchell Hill. Student, Tex. Women's U., 1952-54; BS in English, West Tex. State U., 1964, MS in English, 1975. Cert. elem. and secondary tchr., Tex. Tchr. English and journalism White Deer (Tex.) Sch. Dist., 1964-65; tchr. English Pringle Sch. Dist., Stinnett, Tex., 1966-73; radio news dir. Sta. KQTY, Borger, Tex., 1976-84; reporter Borger News-Herald, 1984-85, Lifestyle editor, 1985—; corr. Sta. KAMR-TV, Amarillo, Tex., 1986—. Recipient Mark Twain award AP, Dallas, 1980, Column writing award Tex. Mng. Editors Assn., Dallas, 1983, 88, Sch. Bell award Ret. Tchrs. Assn. Tex., 1988. Mem. Tex. Press Women (writing awards 1988), Panhandle Press Assn. (writing awards 1985, 86, 87), Nat. Fedn. Press Women, Borger C. of C. (editor newsletter 1980-84, publicity com. Women's Div. 1980-88). Republican. Methodist. Home: 300 Mesquite St Borger TX 79007 Office: Borger News-Herald 209 N Main St Borger TX 79008-5130

MITCHELL, JO KATHRYN, hospital technical supervisor; b. Clarksville, Ark., Dec. 1, 1934; d. Vintris Franklin and Melissa Lucile (Edwards) Clark; m. James M. Mitchell, June 4, 1955 (dec. Feb. 1973); children: James, Karen Ann, Leslie Kay, Vicki Lynn. Student, U. Ark., Fayetteville, 1952-53; student, Coll. Ozarks, 1953-54, U. Ark., 1954-55, Little Rock U., 1958. Technologist clin. chemistry U. Hosp., Little Rock, 1956-57, asst. supr., 1957-59, rsch. technologist, 1960-62, asst. supr. clin. chemistry, 1979-82, supr. clin. chemistry, 1982—; technologist Conway County Hosp., Morrilton, Ark., 1959; office mgr., co-owner Medic Pharmacy, Little Rock, 1962-71; owner The Cheese Shop, Little Rock, 1977-80. Adult advisor Order Rainbow Girls local, Little Rock, 1970-84, state, Ark., 1977-84. Mem. Pharmacy Aux. (pres. 1967-69), Order Eastern Star. Methodist. Office: U Hosp Ark 4301 W Markham SLOT 502 Little Rock AR 72205

MITCHELL, JONI (ROBERTA JOAN ANDERSON), singer, songwriter; b. Ft. Macleod, Alta., Can., Nov. 7, 1943; d. William A. and Myrtle M. (McKee) Anderson; m. Chuck Mitchell (div.); m. Larry Klein, Nov. 21, 1982. Student, Alta. Coll. Albums include Song to a Seagull, Clouds, Ladies of the Canyon, Blue, For the Roses, Court and Spark, 1974, Miles of Aisles, Hissing of Summer Lawns, 1975, Hejira, 1976, Don Juan's Reckless Daughter, Mingus (Jazz Album of Year and Rock-Blues Album of Year, Downbeat mag. 1979), Shadows and Light, 1980, Wild Things Run Fast, 1982, Dog Eat Dog, 1986, Chalk Mark in a Rainstorm, 1988. Address: care Peter Asher Mgmt 644 N Doheny Dr Los Angeles CA 90069

MITCHELL, JUDITH MARIE, psychologist, research psychologist, counselor; b. Los Angeles, Oct. 1, 1950; d. Glen H. and Carla Jane (Bilderback) Taylor; m. Paul Francis Mitchell, Dec. 29, 1969 (div.); 1 child, Jennifer Ann. BA, Calif. State U., Northridge, 1976, MA, 1980; PhD, UCLA, 1987. Research and data mgmt. asst. County Office Alcohol Abuse, Los Angeles, 1977-78; vocat. youth counselor, statis. reporter Seventh Step Found., Los Angeles, 1978-79; rehab. counselor San Fernando (Calif.) Valley Assn. for Retarded, 1979-80; vocat. counselor, VA Hosp., Sepulveda, Calif., 1980-81; staff research assoc. Neuropsychiat. Inst. UCLA, 1981-85; postgrad. research assoc. Sch. Pub. Health UCLA, 1986-88; research psychologist U. So. Calif. Rehab. and Tng. Ctr. on Aging, 1988—. Contbr. articles to profl. jours. Fellow Mabel W. Richards Assn., 1974-77, Calif. State U., Northridge, 1974-76, U. Women's Club, 1978, UCLA, 1981-84, 85-86. Mem. Am. Psychol. Assn.

MITCHELL, MARGARET ANNE, Canadian legislator; b. Brockville, Ont., Can., July 17, 1925; d. Clarence W. and Earnestine (Dutton) Learoyd; m. Claude Frederick Mitchell, May 6, 1956. Ed., McMaster U., Hamilton, Ont., U. Toronto, Ont. Mem. Can. Ho. of Commons, 1979—; community devel. worker. Mem. B.C. Assn. Social Workers. Mem. New Democratic Party. Address: 1176 Skeena St, Vancouver, BC Canada V5K 4V5*

MITCHELL, MOZELLA GORDON, educator, minister; b. Starkville, Miss., Aug. 14, 1936; d. John Thomas and Odena Mae (Graham) Gordon; m. Edrick R. Woodson, Mar. 20, 1951 (div. 1974); children: Cynthia LaVern, Marcia Delores Woodson Miller. AB, LeMoyne Coll., 1959; MA in English, U. Mich., 1963; MA in Religious Studies, Colgate-Rochester Divinity Sch., 1973; PhD, Emory U., 1980. Instr. in English and Speech Alcorn A&M Coll., Lorman, Miss., 1960-61; instr. English, chmn. dept. Owen Jr. Coll., Memphis, 1961-65; asst. prof. English and religion Norfolk State Coll., U. Norfolk, Va., 1965-81; asst., then assoc. prof. U. South Fla., Tampa, 1981—; pastor Mount Sinai AME Zion Ch., Tampa, 1982-89; presiding elder Tampa dist. AME Zion Ch., 1988—; co-dir. Ghent VISTA Project, Norfolk, 1969-71; vis. asst. lectr. U. Rochester, N.Y., 1972-73; vis. assoc. prof. Hood Theol. Sem., Salisbury, N.C., 1979-80; cons. Black Women and Ministry, Interdenominational Theol. Ctr. Author: Spiritual Dynamics of Howard Thurman's Theology, 1985; staff writer AMEZION Sunday sch. lit., 1981-; editor Martin Luther King Meml. Series in Religion, Culture and Social Devel., 1987-; contbr. articles to profl. jours., essays to books; mem. editorial bd. Cornucopia Reprint Series Wyndham Hall Press. Bd. dirs. Nat. Farmworkers Ministry, Tampa, 1987—, AME Zion Ch. Connectional Coun., Charlotte, 1984—; mem. Tampa-Hillsborough County Human Rels. Coun., 1987—; pres. Fla. Coun. Chs., Orlando, 1988-90, recipient ecumenical leadership citation, 1990; selected as at-large accredited visitor 7th Assy. of World Coun. Chs., Canberra, Australia, 1991. Nat. Doctoral Fund fellow, 1978-80; NEH grantee, 1981, Fla. Endowment Humanities grantee, 1990—, USF Rsch. Coun. grantee, 1990—. Mem. Coll. Theology Soc., Am. Acad. Religion, Soc. for the Study of Black Religion, Joint Ctr. for Polit. Studies, Black Women in Ch. and Soc., Alpha Kappa Alpha. Democrat. Methodist. Office: U South Fla 310 CPR 4202 Fowler Ave Tampa FL 33620

MITCHELL, NANCY STACK HANLON, social worker; b. Boston, May 31, 1931; d. William A. and Frances W. (Sheehan) Hanlon; m. William T. Mitchell, Apr. 19, 1968; 1 child, Ellen Maeve. BA, Elmira Coll., 1953; MSW, Boston Coll., 1955. Social worker Boston Floating Hosp., 1955-57; social worker, supr. dept. psychiatry U. Colo. Med. Ctr., Denver, 1957-62; social work supr. Denver Gen. Hosp., 1962-63; chief of social work Tufts-New Eng. Med. Ctr., Boston, 1963-67; social worker Sanborn Jr. High Sch., Concord, Mass., 1967-68; sr. social worker Mass. Soc. for the Prevention of Cruelty to Children, Boston, 1978-81; social worker J.P. Day Care Ctr., Boston, 1982-83; social worker, supr. failure to thrive team Boston City Hosp., 1984—; mem. adv. com. Office for Children of Inner City, Boston Dept. Social Svcs., 1986-88, 89—. Mem. Dem. Ward Com., Ward 4, Boston, 1971—, chair, 1974-78, 90—. Mem. Nat. Assn. Social Workers. Office: Boston City Hosp 818 Harrison Ave Boston MA 02118

MITCHELL, PAULA RAE, nursing educator; b. Independence, Mo., Jan. 10, 1951; d. Millard Henry and E. Lorene (Denton) Gates; m. Ralph William Mitchell, May 24, 1975. BS in Nursing, Graceland Coll., 1973; MS in Nursing, U. Tex., 1976; postgrad. N.Mex. State U. RN, Tex., Mo.; cert. childbirth educator. Commd. capt. U.S. Army, 1972; ob-gyn nurse practitioner U.S. Army, Seoul, Korea, 1977-78; resigned, 1978; instr. nursing El Paso Community Coll. (Tex.), 1979-85, dir. nursing, 1985—, acting div. chmn. health occupations, 1985-86, div. chmn., 1986—, curriculum facilitator, 1984-86; ob-gyn nurse practitioner Planned Parenthood, El Paso, 1981-86, mem. med. com., 1986-89. Author: (with Grippardo) Nursing Perspectives and Issues, 1989; contbr. articles to profl. jours. Founder, bd. dirs. Health-C.R.E.S.T., El Paso, 1981-85; mem. pub. edn. com. Am. Cancer Soc., El Paso, 1983-84; mem. El Paso City-County Bd. Health, 1989—; mem. Govt. Applications Rev. Com., Rio Grande Coun. Govts., 1989—. Decorated Army Commendation medal, Meritorious Service medal. Mem. Nat. League Nursing (mem. resolutions com. Assocs. Degree coun. 1987-89), Am. Soc. Psychoprophylaxis Obstetrics, Nurses Assn. Am. Coll. Obstetricians & Gynecologists (cert. in ambulatory women's health care; chpt. coord. 1979-83, nat. program rev. com. 1984-86, corr. 1987-89), Advanced Nurse Practitioner Group El Paso (coord. 1980-83 legis. committee 1984), Orgn. Advancement Assoc. Degree Nursing (Tex. membership chmn. 1985-89, chmn. long range goals com. 1989—), Am. Vocat. Assn., Am. Assn. Women Community & Jr. Colls., Nat. Coun. Occupational Edn. (mem. articulation task force), Nat. Coun. Instructional Adminstrs., Sigma Theta Tau, Phi Kappa Phi. Mem. Christian Ch. (Disciples of Christ). Home: 4616

Cupid Dr El Paso TX 79924 Office: El Paso Community College PO Box 20500 El Paso TX 79998

MITCHELL, RUTH ELLEN (BUNNY MITCHELL), advertising executive; b. Mpls., Jan 2, 1940; d. Burt and Helen (Bolnick) Horwitz; div.; children: Cathy Ann, Thomas Charles, Andrew Robert. Student UCLA, 1957, U. Minn., 1960. Substitute tchr. Holy Innocents' Sch., Atlanta, 1972-76; mem. staff Issues Dept., Carter-Mondale, Atlanta, 1976; office mgr. Atlanta Area Family Psychiatry Clinic, 1976-79; account exec. Am. Advt. Distributors, Atlanta, 1979-81, Brown's Guide Ltd., Atlanta, 1981-82; account mgr. Billian Pub., Atlanta, 1983-85; regional sales dir. Am. Hosp. Pub., Inc., Chgo., 1985—; cons. G.C.C., Inc., Atlanta, 1982-83. Bd. dirs. Nat. Council Jewish Women, Mpls., 1963-70, Temple Israel Sch., Mpls., 1964-68, Minn. Symphony Assn., Mpls., 1963-71; The Temple Sisterhood, Atlanta, 1972-77, Holy Innocents' Sch., Atlanta, 1973-77; vol. fundraiser KTCA-TV Pub. Broadcasting Svc., Mpls., 1968-71, WETV-TV, Atlanta, 1976-80; vol. Northside Hosp., Atlanta, 1971-77, Arts Festival of Atlanta, 1971-80, Holy Innocents' ch. summer program, 1974-76, Buckhead Mental Health Clinic, Atlanta, 1975-77. Mem. Nat. Assn. Profl. Saleswomen, Bus./Profl. Advt. Assn., Am. Advt. Fedn., Atlanta Advt. Club, Mag. Advt. Reps. of the South (sec. 1982-83, v.p. 1983-84, 88-89), High Mus. Art., Atlanta Symphony Orch., Found. for Hosp. Art Assn. (spl. events coord. 1987-88, bd. trustees 1988—), Atlanta Ballet, Southeastern Hosp. Conf. (mem. exhibits com. 1988, 89, 90), Ravinia Club. Home: 7155 Roswell Rd #57 Atlanta GA 30328 Office: 1117 Perimeter Ctr W 5 Fl E Atlanta GA 30338

MITCHELL, SALLY JEAN, college dean; b. Ft. Dodge, Iowa, Dec. 7, 1934; d. Damian Anthony and Mary Genevieve (Fitzgerald) M. BA in History and Edn., Briar Cliff Coll., 1965; MA in Theatre Arts, U. Iowa, 1971; EdS in Devel. Edn., Appalachian State, 1986. Cert. tchr. Tchr. St. Michael's Sch., Sioux City, Iowa, 1955-57; Tchr. St. Joseph Sch., Ashton, Iowa, 1957-61; tchr. St. John's Sch., Bancroft, Iowa, 1961-63, St. Mary Sch., Waterloor, Iowa, 1963-65; dean women Heelan Cath. High Sch., Sioux City, 1965-71; asst. prof. Briar Cliff Coll., Sioux City, 1971-78, assoc. dir. admissions, 1978-81, dir. retention, 1981-86; dir. admissions Incarnate Word Coll., San Antonio, 1986-89, dean enrollment, 1989—. Contbr. articles to newspaper and profl. jours. Mem. AAUW, San Antonio, 1989, Archdiocesan Vocation Com., San Antonio, 1987—; liturgical asst.; deaconate program tchr. Mem. Nat. Assn. Coll. Admissions Counselors, Tex. Assn. Coll. Admissions Counselors, Tex. Assn. Coll. Registrars and Admissions Officers, Nat. Assn. Devel. Educators, Sisters of St. Francis. Democrat. Roman Catholic. Office: Incarnate Word Coll 4301 Broadway San Antonio TX 78209

MITCHELL, SERETTE ELIZABETH, law enforcement official; b. Chgo., July 24, 1953; d. Otis Joseph and Luna Mae (Lucas) M. AA, Compton Community Coll., 1976; BA in Sociology, Calif. State U., L.A., 1980. Cert. motorcycle mechanic. Profl. roller skater Nat. Skating Derby, Hollywood, Calif., 1970-77; mail carrer, clk. U.S. Postal Service, L.A., 1977-78; tutor Compton (Calif.) Community Coll., 1979-80; recreation leader Lynwood (Calif.) Parks & Recreation, 1980-81; sub. tchr. Compton (Calif.) Sch. Dist., 1981-82; police officer Compton Police Dept., 1982—. Boxing coach Sheriff's Amateur Athletic League, Lynwood, 1988—; rape/crisis intervention counselor YWCA, Compton, 1989—; guest speaker annual career awareness day, Lynwood Unified Sch. Dist., 1982; speaker career day, L.A. Unified Sch. Dis.t, 1983, Compton Unified Sch. Dist., 1979; social change accessor, Calif. State Coll. Dominguez Hills., City of Lynwood, 1977. Mem. Compton Police Officers Assn., Peace Officers Rsch. Assn. Calif., Internat. Union Police Assn., Alpha Gamma Sigma Tau (membership chmn. 1975-76), Calif. State U. Giving Club. Democrat. Office: PO Box 180 West Covina CA 91793

MITCHELL, SHIRLEY ANN, business owner, travel agent; b. Wilber, Nebr., Nov. 25, 1939; d. Emil and Mamie (Javorsky) Duba; m. Mac L. Mitchell, Feb. 28, 1959; 1 child, Kim Leann Mitchell Hajek. Grad. high sch., Crete, Nebr. Asst. to tourism dir. and sec. Nebr. Game & Parks Commn., Lincoln, 1957-69; transp. law sec. Crete (Nebr.) Carrier Corp., 1969-72; tour escort, sales N.Am. Tours, Lincoln, 1972-81; travel agt. Via Van Bloom Travel, Lincoln, 1981-82; owner, mgr. Happy Vagabond Travel and Tours, Crete, 1982—. Mem. Nat. Geog. Soc. Nat. Arbor Day Found., Nat. Wildlife Soc., Nat. Audobon Soc., Airlines Reporting Corp., Internat. Airlines Travel Agt. Network, Cruise Lines Internat. Assn., Amtrak.

MITCHELL, SHIRLEY MARIE, auditor; b. L.A., Nov. 11, 1953; d. William Ward and Dorothy Lillian (Hull) Smith; m. Robert Maurice Mitchell, Oct. 6, 1973; children: Robert William, Teresa Marie. Student, Compton (Calif.) Jr. Coll., 1972-73; cert. in programming, Control Data Inst., L.A., 1972. Inventory clk. Robert Hall Clothes, Lynwood, Calif., 1969-71; distbn. clk. Collins Radio, Newport Beach, Calif., 1972; payroll clk. Automated Data Processing, Long Beach, Calif., 1972; computer operator Compton Hosp., 1972, Collins Radio, Newport Beach, 1972-73; payroll clk. Network Data Processing, Cedar Rapids, Iowa, 1973-75; auditor Aegon USA, Cedar Rapids, 1981—; carrier Penny Saver, Marion, Iowa, 1985—. Mem. choir Meth. Ch., Marion, 1984-88; com. mem. Boy Scouts Am., Marion, 1982—, den leader Cub Scouts Am., 1985; troop leader, resource person Girl Scouts U.S.A., Marion, 1982—. Scholar Control Data Inst., 1971, Future Tchrs. Club, Lynwood, 1971. Democrat. Home: 1540 A Ave Marion IA 52302 Office: Aegon USA 4333 Edgewood Rd NE Cedar Rapids IA 52499

MITCHELL, STEPHANIE J., lawyer, government official; b. Lytham St. Annes, Lancashire, Eng., May 20, 1957; came to U.S., 1962; d. Frank and Jeanne (Booth) M. Student, Chinese U., Hong Kong, 1976-77; AB with distinction, Cornell U., 1978, JD, 1980. Bar: D.C. 1980, U.S. Ct. Appeals (fed. cir.) 1988, U.S. Ct. Internat. Trade, 1988. Assoc. Akin, Gump, Strauss, Hauer & Feld, Washington, 1980-83; internat. trade specialist Office Peoples Republic of China and Hong Kong, Washington, 1983-84; assoc. Kaye, Scholer, Fierman, Hays & Handler, Washington and Beijing, 1984-87; atty.-advisor office chief counsel for import adminstrn. U.S. Dept. Commerce, Washington, 1987-90, with spl. projects on Cen. and Ea. European Law, Office of Gen. Counsel, 1990—; isntr. Intenrat. Law Inst., Washington, 1986; adj. prof. Cornell U. Law Sch., 1990; mem. adv. bd. East Asia program Cornell U., Ithaca, N.Y., 1986—; fluent in Chinese, French, Spanish, Russian langs. Mng. editor China Law Reporter, 1987—; contbr. articles to legal books and jours. Mem. ABA, Women's Bar Assn. D.C., Women's in Internat. Trade, D.C. Bar Assn. Jewish. Office: US Dept Commerce 14th and Pennsylvania Ave Washington DC 20230

MITCHELL, SUSAN EVELYN, computer marketing executive; b. Patterson, Calif., Oct. 20, 1953; d. Carl William and Luanna (Scott) M.; m. Michael Stankovic, Sept. 17, 1950; children: Brandi L., Daniel R. BA, Skadron Bus. Coll., 1972; postgrad., U. Calif., Irvine, 1974; MNA, San Francisco State U., 1979. Exec. Tymshare, Inc., Newport Beach, Calif., 1974-75, applications cons., 1975-77, sales rep., 1977-80; br. mgr. The Computer Co., Richmond, Va., 1980-83; v.p. sales Bankmatic Systems, Portland, Oreg., 1983-85; pres., founder Mydas Mktg., Boulder City, Nev., 1985—; cons. Palo Alto (Calif.) Research Group, 1985-87; assoc. Western Ind. Bankers, Oakland, Calif., 1985—. Editor: Micro-Computer Software, 1986. Mem. PTA, Boulder City, 1985—, Girl Scouts U.S., Las Vegas, 1986—. Mem. NAFE, Calif. Bankers Assn., Credit Union Nat. Assn., Fin. Instn. Mktg. Assn., Boulder C. of C. Republican. Episcopalian. Office: Mydas Mktg 557 California St Ste 56 Boulder City NV 89005

MITCHELL, TANDIE VERA, wilderness expedition/all-terrain vehicle administrator; b. Carlisle, Pa., Nov. 12, 1942; d. Charles Howard and Vera Oleta (Gadberry) M.; m. Donald Jerry Bain (div. May 1978); Robert Kugler, David, Dean; m. Robert Anthony Astenius, Jan. 1, 1981. AA, Long Beach City Coll., 1974; BA, Calif. State U., Long Beach, 1978; postgrad., The Union Inst., 1990—. Cert. community clin. psychology, Calif. Originator, producer, concert fundraiser, ops. dir. Snow Summit Jr. Race Team, Big Bear Lake, Calif., 1981; press dir. Snow Summit Women's Pro Ski Racing Tour, Big Bear Lake, 1981; co-founder, cons. S.M.A.R.T. Assocs., Long Beach, Calif., 1978—; pres. Adventure Expeditions of the Wilderness, Inc., Big Bear Lake, 1983-88, All Terrain Vehicle Riding Acad., Big Bear Lake, 1985—; Hot Air Balloon Race producer at Cal 500, Ontario Motor Speedway, Calif., 1979-80; writer USDA grant for tree conservation, 1989-90. Editor: Guide to High Country Life, 1982; contbr. articles to newspaper and mags. Co-chmn. publicity com. City Council Candidate, Long Beach, 1977; planning com. coordinator Long Beach Commn. Status Women, 1975; adminstr. youth employment program Voter Edn. Project, Long Beach, 1975; yoga instr. Parks and Recreation Dept., Big Bear Lake, 1981. Mem. Am. Diabetes Assn. (support group facilitator 1988), Specialty Vehicle Inst. Am. (ATV instr. 1985—). Native American, Assiniboine Tribe. Republican. Office: All Terrain Vehicle Riding Acad PO Box 447 Ramona CA 92065

MITCHELL, VELDA JEAN, filter manufacturing company personnel executive; b. Alton, Ill., July 27, 1937; d. Glenn Kessinger and Eunice Ruth (Jarvis) Saxton; m. Spencer L. Middlecoff, Oct. 20, 1957 (div. 1980); children: Laura A. Middlecoff Decker, Mark S. m. Robert E. Mitchell, May 31, 1986. Student in bus. mgmt. Sinclair Coll., Dayton, Ohio, 1986—. Exec. sec. Sinclair Refining, Hartford, Ill., 1955-58, Laclede Steel Co., Alton, Ill., 1958-71; personnel specialist Fram Corp., Greenville, Ohio, 1974-80, supr. employee rels., 1980-83, supr. human resources Automotive Aftermarket div. Allied-Signal Corp., 1983—; mem. audit com. Fram Credit Union. Mem. adv. bd. Ansonia Schs. Bus. Edn., 1980—, Greenville Schs. Bus. Edn., 1982—; adv. com. individualized study, Sinclair Coll., Dayton, Ohio; mem. local and regional Pvt. Industry Coun., 1988—; mem. edn. com., adv. bd. Edison State Coll. Darke County Ctr., 1988—; chair edn. com. Darke County C. of C. Indsl. Mgt. Assn., 1988—; trustee Hospice, 1988—. Recipient Nat. award NACo, 1989. Mem. Personnel Assn. SW Ohio, NAFE, Indsl. Mgmt. Assn., Sertoma. Office: Fram Allied Aftermarket Martz & Jackson St Greenville OH 45331

MITCHELL, VERNICE VIRGINIA, nurse, poet, author; b. Scott, Miss., Mar. 11, 1921; d. Isaiah and Martha Magdalene (Edwards) Smith; m. Willis Mitchell, Aug. 17, 1940; children: Elaine, Kenneth, Liethia, John, Ransom, Paul. Diploma, Princeton Continuation Coll., 1955. Nurse Cook County Sch. Nursing, Chgo., 1951-59, U. Ill. Hosp., Chgo., 1959-67, Grant Hosp., Chgo., 1967-78, Northwestern Meml. Hosp., Chgo., 1979-84; with U. Ill. Hosp. Aetna Nurse's Registry, Chgo., 1984—. Author: The Book Success Through Spiritual Truths, 1987, (poems) A Women, Chicago, The 12 Months; also numerous poetry and musical lyrics; guest poet on Dial-A-Poem, Chgo., 1988-89. Chmn. cookbook project 1988-89. Recipient merit cert. Am. Poetry Assn., 1982, merit cert. World of Poetry, 1983, 85, Golden Poet award, 1986, 87, 88, Silver Poet award, 1989, 90. Club: 6700 Emerald Ave. Block (pres. 1971—).

MITCHELSON, BONNIE ELIZABETH, politician, nurse; b. Winnipeg, Man., Can., Nov. 28, 1947; d. Henry Alfred and Millie Christine (Leslie) Bester; m. Donald Mitchelson, Aug. 30, 1969; children: Michele, Scott. Diploma in nursing, Winnipeg Sch. Nursing, 1968, ICU course, 1969. Nurse various hosps., Winnipeg, 1968-86; legis. dep. health critic Urban Affairs Critic, 1986-87; minister Ministry of Culture, Heritage and Recreation, Winnipeg, 1988—. Mem. adminstrn. Man. Lotteries Found. Act., 1988—.

MITELMAN, BONNIE COSSMAN, advertising executive, writer, lecturer; b. Flint, Mich., Feb. 15, 1941; d. Maurice B. and Frieda H. (Ragir) Cossman; student U. Mich., 1958-61; B.A., Northwestern U., 1969; M.A., Manhattanville Coll., 1977; m. Stanley D. Lelewer, Mar. 12, 1961 (div. 1969); children—Joanne, Stephen; m. 2d, Alan N. Mitelman, July 23, 1972; 1 son, Geoffrey. Copywriter trainee Dancer-Fitzgerald-Sample, Inc., Chgo., 1956-60; advt. copywriter Spiegel, Inc., Chgo., 1961-63; freelance advt. and public relations writer, Chgo., N.Y., 1963—; co-founder Mitelman & Assocs., Briarcliff Manor, N.Y., 1972—; adj. lectr. dept. history Mercy Coll., Dobbs Ferry, N.Y., 1979—; contbr. articles to N.Y. Times, Reform Judaism, 1977—. Mem. Am. Hist. Assn., Women in Communications, Authors Guild. Author: Mothers Who Work: Strategies for Coping; mem. editorial bd. Reform Judaism, 1977—. Home: 639 Pleasantville Rd Briarcliff Manor NY 10510

MITRANY, DEVORA LANG, marketing consultant, writer; b. Oak Park, Ill., Mar. 20, 1947; d. John Joseph and Frances Elizabeth (Kirke) Lang; m. Douglas Allen Braun, Sept. 16, 1967 (div. Sept. 1976); m. Stanton Mitrany, Feb. 7, 1988. BA cum laude, Beloit Coll., 1969; postgrad., Boston U., 1971-72. Tchr. First Baptist Presch., Oak Park, 1966, 67-68, St. Brigid Sch., Boston, 1969-72; regional adminstr. TRW Fin. Systems, Wellesley, Mass., 1972-76; mgr. mktg. communications Computer Sharing Svcs., Denver, 1976-82; dir. corp. communications Corp. Mgmt. Systems, Denver, 1982-85; sr. copywriter On-Line Software Internat., Fort Lee, N.J., 1985-86; mgr. corp. communications Health Mgmt. Systems, N.Y.C., 1986-89; dir. pub. rels. Am. Sephardi Fedn., 1989—. Pub. rels. dir., mem. bd. dirs. Internat. Coalition for the Revival for the Jews for Yemen, 1989—; warden, vestry mem. Trinity Ch., Wrentham, Mass., 1974-76; mem. vestry St. Philip and St. James Episcopal Ch., Denver, 1983; vol. Hospice of Holy Spirit, Lakewood, Colo., 1980-83; bd. dirs. Talia Hadassah, 1986—; dir. pub. rels. Bus. Roundtable on Nat. Security, Colo., 1983-84. Mem. Denver Advt. Fedn. (bd. dirs. 1981-83, Alfie award 1984), Colo. Conf. Communicators (Denver Advt. Fedn. liasion 1981-84), Bus. Execs. for Nat. Security, Am. Sephardi Fedn. (edn. com. 1987-89). Jewish. Democrat.

MITTLER, DIANA, music educator and administrator, pianist; b. N.Y.C., Oct. 19, 1941; d. Franz and Regina (Schilling) Mittler; m. Victor Battipaglia, Sept. 5, 1965 (div. 1982). B.S., Juilliard Sch., 1962, M.S., 1963; D.M.A., Eastman Sch. Music, 1974. Choral dir. William Cowper Jr. High Sch. and Springfield Gardens Jr. High Sch., Queens, N.Y., 1963-68, coordinator of music Flushing High Sch., Queens, 1968-79; asst. prin. music Bayside High Sch., Queens, 1979-86; assoc. prof. music Lehman Col. CUNY, 1986-87, prof., 1987—, choral dir., 1986—; dir. ednl. projects New World Records, 1987—; cons. Sta. WNET; assoc. condr. Queens Borough-Wide Chorus, 1964-70; pianist, founder Con Brio Chamber Ensemble, 1978; faculty So. Vt. Music Festival, 1979-83; soloist with N.Y. Philharmonic, 1956; solo and chamber music appearances; examiner N.Y.C. Bd. Edn. Bd. Exams., 1985—. Author: 57 Lessons for the High School Music Class, 1983. Choral dir. and accompanist various charitable, religious, mil., civic holiday functions. N.Y. State Regents scholar, 1958-62; scholarships, Juilliard Sch. and Eastman Sch. Music. Contbr. articles to music publs. Mem. Golden Key Soc., Music Tchrs. Nat. Assn., Am. Choral Dirs. Assn., Music Edn. Nat. Conf., Sonnech Streelty Club, Delta Kappa Gamma. Democrat. Home: 108-57 66th Ave Forest Hills NY 11375 Office: Lehman Coll Music Dept Bedford Pk Blvd W Bronx NY 10468

MITTMAN, ILENE LOIS, museum manager; b. Chgo., Sept. 4, 1935; m. Charles Mittman, June 23, 1957; children: Scott Harvey, Brian Sheldon, Jeffrey Alan, David Saul. BA in Sociology, U. Mich., 1957; MBA in Bus., Pepperdine U., 1983. Dir. personnel Hart Schaffner & Marx, Chgo., 1957-58; program coord. Emperor Sch., Temple City, Calif., 1976-81; with utility mgmt. dept. L.A. Dept. Water & Power, 1985-87; ops. mgr. Fresno (Calif.) Art Mus., 1987—. Bd. dirs. Coleman Chamber Music Assn., Pasadena, Calif., 1984-86, Pasadena com. L.A. Philharm., 1985-86, Fresno Philharm. Women's League, 1988-89. Mem. AAUW, Fresno Women's Network, Leadership Fresno. Home: 2310 W Robinwood Ln Fresno CA 93711 Office: Fresno Art Mus 2233 N First St Fresno CA 93703

MITZMAN, SHARON LEE, business owner; b. Paterson, N.J., Apr. 19, 1953; d. Barnett and Muriel (Saks) M. BA, Ohio State U., 1975; MBA, U. Miami, 1979. Office adminstr. Cowen & Co., N.Y.C., 1983-86; pres., owner Forget Me Knot Worldwide Gift Svc., Inc., N.Y.C., 1986—. Office: Forget Me Knot Worldwide Gift Svc Inc 632 Broadway 6th Fl New York NY 10012 also: 9465 Wilshire Blvd Ste 859 Beverly Hills CA 90212

MIYASAKI, NOLA NOBUYO, athlete manager, lawyer; b. Honolulu, Jan. 1, 1958; d. Robert Masakazu and Margaret (Hirano) M. BA, Stanford U., 1980; JD, U. Calif., San Francisco, 1984. Law clk. to presiding justice Supreme Ct. State of Hawaii, Honolulu, 1984-86; assoc. Rush, Moore, Craven & Stricklin, Honolulu, 1986-88; account exec., agent for golfers Internat. Mgmt. Group, Cleve., 1988—. Active on Jr. Com. Great Lakes Theatre Festival, Cleve., 1989. Mem. ABA, Calif. Bar Assn., Hawaii State Bar Assn., Jr. League of Cleve. Office: Internat Mgmt Group 1 Erieview Pla Ste 1300 Cleveland OH 44114

MIZER, KAREN MARY, rehabilitation specialist, business executive; b. Bklyn., Sept. 13, 1954; d. Joseph Peter and Lois (Swenson) McCafferty; m. Jay McGowan, Dec. 19, 1976 (div. 1978); m. Orville Charles Mizer, Jan. 20, 1979; children: Thomas Aquinas, Kathryn Ann Marie, Elizabeth Ann. BBA summa cum laude, U. Md.-Okinawa, 1982. Cert. ins. rehab. specialist Mgr. Em-R's Jewelers, Rockaway Beach, N.Y., 1974-79; naval hosp. corpsman USN, San Diego, 1974-79; adminstrv. officer U.S. Marine Corps, Okinawa, Japan, 1979-82; mgr., counselor AAA Employment, Gainesville, Fla., 1982-84; rehab. specialist Orlando Cons., Gainesville, 1983-84, rehab. specialist, owner TMS Assocs., Gainesville, 1984-90, Karen Mizer & Assocs., 1990; realtor assoc. O'Brien Real Estate, Gainesville, 1990—; rehab. specialist Orlando Cons., Gainesville, 1983-84. Author, photographer mag. articles. Vol. United Way, Gainesville, 1985. Served with USN, 1976-79. Mem. Fla. Assn. Rehab. Providers, Nat. Assn. Female Execs., Gainesville C. of C. (ambassador 1985—), Phi Kappa Phi. Republican. Roman Catholic. Club: Navy Wives (pres., pub. relations officer Okinawa 1979-82, Navy Wife of Yr. 1981). Avocations: Reading, swimming, boating. Home: 717-106 SW 75th St Gainesville FL 32607 Office: Karen Mizer & Assocs PO Box 1702 Gainesville FL 32602

MIZEREK, DIANE MARIE, engineer; b. Belleville, N.J., Jan. 11, 1963; d. Francis Joseph and Margaret Mary (Stack) M. BSEE, General Motors Inst., 1986. Co-operative GM Cadillac Div., Grand Blanc, Mich., 1981-86, manufacturing engr., 1986-87; maintenance planner Miller Brewing Co., Albany, Ga., 1987-89, staff engr. Author Thesis, The Design of Computer Assisted Maintenance Management at BOC Grand Blanc, 1986. Mem. Inst. of Electrical and Electronic Engrs., Eta Kappa Nu. Roman Catholic. Home: 4000 Gillionville Rd # 123 Albany GA 31707

MIZUTANI, DIANE LISA, nuclear medicine technologist; b. Berkeley, Calif., Feb. 19, 1963; d. Henry Yoshio and Hisako (Yoshii) M. BA in Biophysics, U. Calif., Berkeley, 1984; Cert. in Nuclear Medicine Technology, U. Calif., San Francisco, 1986. Licensed in nuclear medicine technology, Calif. Nuclear medicine technologist Seton Med. Ctr., Daly City, Calif., 1987-90, John Muir Med. Ctr., Walnut Creek, Calif., 1990—. Named Student of the Year U. Calif. San Francisco, 1987. Mem. Soc. Nuclear Medicine.

MMAHAT, ARLENE CECILE, steel company executive, insurance company executive, civic activist; b. New Orleans, Oct. 5, 1943; d. John Alden and Margaret Therese (Nuccio) Montgomery; divorced; children—Arlene, Amy, John Anthony, Jr. B.A., La. State U., 1965. Clk., Shell Oil Co., New Orleans, 1965; claims rep. Social Security, New Orleans, 1966-67; chmn. bd. New Era Tubulars, New Orleans, 1979-84; chief exec. officer Olympia Tubular Corp., New Orleans, 1984-88; ins. broker Frank B. Hall of La., New Orleans, 1988—. Bd. dirs. New Orleans Symphony, 1983-86 , chmn. musicians adv. com., 1984, 85, membership chmn., 1985, oil and gas chmn. devel. com., 1983, devel. chmn. pub. sector, 1984; mem. Houston Bus. Council, 1980—, Dallas Regional Bus. Council, 1987—, New Orleans Mus. Art Odyssey, 1987; Ind. Women's Orgn., 1968—steering com. Internat. Gastroenteroly Research Fellowship Fund, Tulane U. Med. Ctr.; mem. adv. bd. Kennedy Ctr. for Performing Arts, 1980, Loyola U. Sch. Music, 1982—, New Orleans Mus. Art, 1986— ; fin. advisor New Orleans Symphony Soc. Jr. Com., 1977-79, fin. chmn., 1976; bd. dirs. Young Audiences, Inc., 1985—; mem. nat. adv. bd. on tech. and the disabled U.S. Dept. HHS; bd. dirs. Leukemia Soc. Am., Inc., 1978, corp. del., 1979; founder Ladies Leukemia League, Nat. Assn. Women Bus. Owners chpt. 1980; Odyssey Weekend chmn. New Orleans Mus. Art, 1985, fellows, 1983; mem. adv. com. St. Michael's Sch. for Spl. Students, 1978—, fin. chmn., 1977, mem. fin. com., 1973-76; fin. chmn. La. Landmarks Soc., 1973-75; bd. dirs. Preservation Resource Ctr., 1980, ways and means com., 1979, Christmas Benefit advisor, 1975, 76, mem. Women in Bus./ Women in Politics, Acad. Sacred Heart Adv. Study Com. Assoc. producer Film Am., Inc. Gottschalk, A Musical Portrait, 1986. Named One of 10 Outstanding Persons, New Orleans Inst. Human Understanding, 1977; One of 83 People to Watch in 1983, New Orleans Mag.; recipient Vol. Activist award Germain Monteil and D.H. Holmes Co., Ltd., 1977. Democrat. Roman Catholic. Home: 2434 St Charles Ave Apt 501 New Orleans LA 70130 Office: Frank B Hall La NSN 3045 New Orleans LA 70113

MOBLEY, KAREN RUTH, art gallery director; b. Cheyenne, Wyo., Aug. 26, 1961; d. David G. and Marlene G. (Franz) M. BFA, U. Wyo., 1983; MFA, U. Oka., 1987. Sales assoc. Morgan Gallery, Kansas City, Mo., 1984-85; grad. asst. U. Okla. Mus. Art, Norman, 1985-87; dir. Univ. Art Gallery N.Mex. State U., Las Cruces, 1988—; guest artist Okla. City Community Coll., 1986. Paintings exhibited in numerous exhibitions including Phoenix Triennial, 1990. Named Outstanding Young Women Am. Mem. Am. Assn. Mus., Mountain Plains Mus. Assn., N.Mex. Mus Assn., Coll. Art Assn., Phi Beta Kappa, Phi Kappa Phi. Home: PO Box 3817 UPB Las Cruces NM 88003 Office: U Art Gallery NMex State U Box 30001 Las Cruces NM 88003

MOBLEY, MONA LEJEUNE, writer, lecturer, Bible educator; b. Lucedale, Miss., Aug. 29, 1933; d. Cecil and Birdie Lee (Adams) McLeod; m. Harold Dean Mobley, Dec. 19, 1952; children—Stephen, Tamara, Twayne, Timothy. Student Freed-Hardeman Coll., 1952; French lang. cert. Grenoble Inst., Florence, Italy, 1970. Legal sec. for various attys., Wichita Falls, Tex., 1975-79; missionary Ch. of Christ, Florence, Italy, 1961-71, Montreal, Can., 1971-75; lectr., writer, 1961—; tchr. Ch. of Christ, Channelview, Tex., 1979-89, counselor, Tex., Italy, Can., 1961—; lectr. various religious functions, Europe and U.S., 1961—. Author: Joyful Hospitality, 1983; Because I'm a Woman ... Please Understand, 1983; From Mom With Love, 1985, also articles. Sec. Forest River Estates Civic Club, Channelview, 1980. Democrat. Avocations: painting, various crafts, homemaking, volunteer work.

MOBLEY, NORMA MASON GARLAND, real estate corporation officer; b. Rocky Mount, N.C., Sept. 6, 1923; d. Roscoe Gibbs and Elizabeth Estelle (James) Garland; m. Joseph Kinsey Murrill, Jr., Dec. 29, 1942 (div. Oct. 1983); children: Joseph K. III, James B.; m. Leon Jay Mobley; m. May 18, 1984. Student, Va. Intermont Jr. Coll., 1942, Mary Washington U., 1942, Edgecombe Community Coll., 1979, U. N.C., 1980. Lic. real estate broker, N.C.; cert. real estate appraiser. Assoc. broker Charter Assocs., Rocky Mount, 1980-83, Wayne Ferrell Real Estate, Rocky Mount, 1983-84, Gary Mortan and Assocs., Jacksonville, N.C., 1984-85; pres., broker-in-charge Wright Properties, Inc., Jacksonville, 1985—. Officer, bd. dirs. Rocky Mount Jr. Guild, 1953-84; bd. dirs. YWCA, 1961-65. Mem. Jacksonville Bd. Realtors, N.C. Assn. Realtors, Nat. Assn. Realtors, Nat. Assn. Real Estate Appraisers, Nat. Trust Historic Preservation, Nat. Assn. Female Execs. Republican. Methodist. Home: RR 02 Box 109 Beulaville NC 28518 Office: Wright Properties Inc 405 Johnson Blvd Jacksonville NC 28540

MOCARSKI, CARA SCHMID, hospital executive; b. Bridgeport, Conn., Mar. 9, 1958; d. Carl Edwin and Donna Jean (DiPronio) Schmid; m. Ronald Zenon Mocarski, Oct. 17, 1981. BA in History, Syracuse U., 1980, BS in Mag. Writing, 1980; MA Corp. Communications, Fairfield U., 1985. Editorial asst. Main Hurdman, Stamford, Conn., 1981; mag. coord. History Book Club, Stamford, 1981-84; asst. dir. pub. affairs Park City Hosp., Bridgeport, Conn., 1984—, sec. credit union, 1987-89. Mem. steering com. United Way, Bridgeport, 1987-88, mem. pub. rels. com., 1989-90; communications chmn., v.p., bd. dirs. Am. Heart Assn., Bridgeport, 1987-89; communications chmn. Am. Cancer Soc., Bridgeport, 1988-89; com. mem. Southend Partnership, Bridgeport, 1989-90. Recipient advt. award Healthcare Mktg. Report, 1986, spl. recognition Fairfield County div. Am. Heart Assn., 1988. Mem. Bus. Mgmt. Assn. (mem., chmn. communications com. 1987-90), AAUW (pub. info. officer Bridgeport br. and Conn. chpt. 1986-88), Park City Hosp. Employee Recreation Club (pres. 1988-90). Republican. Roman Catholic. Home: 36 Mulberry Ln Huntington CT 06484 Office: Park City Hosp 695 Park Ave Bridgeport CT 06604

MOCH, MARY INEZ, nun, teacher, librarian; b. Chgo., Aug. 13, 1943; d. Charles Michael and Mary Anna (Howanic) M. AA, Felician Coll., Chgo., 1964; BA, Mundelein Coll., 1968; MA, No. Ill. U., 1976. Joined Felician Sisters, Roman Catholic Ch., 1961. Tchr. St. Turibius Sch., Chgo., 1964-65, St. Damian Sch., Oak Forest, Ill., 1966-67, 75-80; tchr., librarian St. Florian Sch., Hatley, Wis., 1968-72, Christ the King Sch., Lombard, Ill., 1972-75; librarian Providence High Sch., New Lenox, Ill., 1980-82, Montay Coll.,

Chgo., 1982—. Mem. ALA, Cath. Libr. Assn., Pvt. Acad. Librs. Ill. (sec.-treas. 1987-90), Felician Libr. Svc. (co-author audio visual processing manual 1980, sec. 1979-80). Office: Montay Coll 3750 W Peterson Ave Chicago IL 60659

MOCHARY, MARY VERONICA, lawyer; b. Budapest, Hungary, Sept. 7, 1942; d. Alexander and Elizabeth (Aranyi) Kasser; m. Stephen E. Mochary, Sept. 25, 1965; children: Alexandra, Veronica, Matthew, Neal. BA, Wellesley Coll., 1963; JD, U. Chgo., 1967. Bar: Ark. 1968, N.J. 1970. Ptnr. Fayetteville, Ark., 1968-70, Mochary & Mochary, Montclair, N.J., 1970-85, Cerny & Mochary, Montclair, 1970-85, Lane & Mittendorf, Woodbridge, N.J., 1984—; pres. Technopulp, Inc., Montclair, 1982—, Iamco, Inc., Montclair, 1982—; ptnr. Kand M Co., Montclair, 1982—, Atlantic Highlands Real Estate, Montclair, 1982-89; dep. legal advisor U.S. Dept. State, 1985-89, dep. spl. negotiator for property issues, 1989—. Mayor Twp. of Montclair, 1980-84; mgr. Kasser Art Found., Montclair, 1982—; Rep. candidate U.S. Senate, State of N.J., 1984; co-chmn. re-election campaign Tom Kean for Gov., N.J., 1985; treas. Com. N.J. Rep. Women in 1985; mem. regional adv. bd. Anti-Defamation League of B'nai B'rith, Montclair Library Bd., 1980—, Montclair Twp. Council, 1980—, regional adv. bd. Raoul Wallenberg Com. of U.S., 1985—; chmn. Rep. Task Force Women's Polit. Caucus N.J., Overseas Neighbors Internat., 1985; bd. dirs. Am. Hungarian Found., 1970—, Found. Ednl. Alternatives, Urban League, 1985—. Recipient Disting. Service award Am. Hungarian Found., 1984. Mem. ABA, N.J. Bar Assn., Ark. Bar Assn., N.J. Conf. Mayors, N.J. Elected Women Ofcls., Suburban Essex Bus. and Profl. Women (named Women of Yr. 1985). Clubs: Wellesley (N.J.) (pres. 1983-84); Essex Falls Country; Ocean Reef. Other: US Dept State Lagal Advisor 2201 C St NW Washington DC 20520

MOCK, BETTE MARIE, computer executive; b. Pontiac, Mich., July 2, 1937; d. John Phillips and Rosalie (Custer) Coder; m. Charles Robert Mock, June 18, 1960; children: Steven, Douglas, Katherine. BS, U. Md., 1959. Instr. zoology U. MD., College Park, 1958-60; supr. tchr. Dept. Edn. U. Md., College Park, 1963; sci. tchr. Prince George's County Schs., Hyattsville, Md., 1960-63; trainer, tester Gallaudet U., Washington, 1973-81; owner Mock's Computer Svcs., Bowie, Md., 1983—; researcher USDA, Washington, 1958, 59, 61; ednl. specialist U.S. Weather Bur., Washington, 1962; cons. Incoming Calls Mgmt. Inst., Annapolis, Md., 1984—, v.p. 1986—; v.p., sec., treas., editor Service Level Newsletter, Inc., Bowie, 1986—. Treas. St. Matthews United Meth. Ch., Bowie, 1984—, Gloria Ringers Handbell Choir, Bowie, 1984—. Named one of Outstanding Young Women Am., 1965; recipient Vol. award Bowie Recreation Council, 1979. Mem. Internat. Customer Service Assn., Newsletter Assn., Nat. Assn. Female Execs., Washington Apple Pi. Democrat. Home and Office: Mock's Computer Svcs 3516 Moylan Dr Bowie MD 20715

MOCK, LINDA COLANGELO, adhesives manufacturing company executive; b. N.Y.C., Mar. 22, 1948; d. Daniel John and Frances (Avena) Colangelo; m. Paul John Mock, Aug. 2, 1969; children: Caroline, Bradley. Student, Clarkson U., 1966-68; BSME, Columbia U., 1970; MBA in Econs. and Fin., Fairleigh Dickinson U., 1982. Plant engr. Western Electric Co., N.Y.C., 1970-72, Buffalo, 1972-74; lectr. Fairleigh Dickinson U., Teaneck, N.J., 1980-85; pres., owner Marks Adhesive Co. Inc., Wyckoff, N.J., 1985—. Treas. Jr. Woman's Club Bergenfield (N.J.), 1983-85, pres., 1985-87. Mem. Omicron Delta Epsilon. Roman Catholic. Office: Marks Adhesive Co Inc 430 W Main St Wyckoff NJ 07481

MOCK, SANDRA FORD, lawyer; b. Edgewood, Md., Jan. 12, 1944; d. William V. and Lydia (Schmitz) Ford; children from previous marriage: Robert L., Traci L.; m. Darryl L. Mock. BS, Sacramento State U., 1965; JD, J.F. Kennedy U., 1986. Fingerprint agt. Dept. Justice, Sacramento, 1965-70; legal officer Calif. Beer Wholesalers Assn., Sacramento, 1975-80; with sales dept. Joseph Schlitz Brewing Co., San Francisco, 1980-82; nat. account mgr. Pabst Brewing, San Rafael, Calif., 1982-83; mktg. dir. Bracco Distbn. Co., San Francisco, 1983-84; with Office Dist. Atty., Martinez, Calif., 1985-87; assoc. Sellar, Hazard, Snyder, Kelly & Fitzgerald, Walnut Creek, Calif., 1988—. Republican. Seventh Day Adventist. Office: Sellar Hazard Snyder Kelly & Fitzgerald 1111 Civic Dr Ste 300 Walnut Creek CA 94553

MODARRESSI, MRS. TAGHI M. See TYLER, ANNE

MOE, VIDA DELORES, civic worker; b. Ryder, N.D., Feb. 29, 1928; d. John Nelson and Inga Marie (Lewis) Ahlgran; m. Placido Ferdinand, July 28, 1950 (div.); children: Terrence Paul, Star Marie; m. Edgar Louis Moe, May 24, 1970 (dec. 1983). Student, Minot State U., 1964-66; diploma interior decorating, LaSalle Extension U., 1976. Clk.-typist Base Supply, Minot AFB, N.D., 1960-61, clk.-stenographer Base Housing, 1961-62, 74, sec. MIADS Direction Ctr., 1962-63, with QC Br., 1963-64, with dept. acctg. and fin., 1964-65, with USAF Regional Hosp., 1965-66, with Minuteman AFSC, 1966-67, 74-75, with 5th Bomb Wing, 1967-70, with 1st Missile Wing, 1973-74, with dept. mil. personnel, 1975-76, sec. disaster preparedness, 1987—; sec., salesperson Allen Realty, Minot, 1980-85. Pres. City Art League, 1977-79, 86-87; chmn. Carnegie Restoration and Art Ctr. Project, 1980-87; bd. dirs. Patrons of Libr., Minot, 1978-87, sec., 1979-80, v.p., 1981, pres., 1982-83; v.p. 40/50 Rep. Women Minot, 1982, chair decorations com., 1983; historian Minot Rep. Women, 1984-86. Recipient Superior Performance award 5th Bomb Wing, Minot AFB, 1968, Devotion to Vol. Duty award USAF Regional Hosp., Minot, 1983, 86, Superior Performance Cash award Dept. of Air Force 857 Combat Support Group, 1988, 89.. Mem. N.D. Bus. and Profl. Women's Club (rec. sec. 1978-79, 81-82), Minot Bus. and Profl. Women's Club (pres. 1981-82), Am. Legion Aux. (judge jr. art posters contest 1980-82, pres. 1982-84), Minot Shrine Hosp. Aux. (v.p. 1984, 85, pres. 1986, 87), Beta Sigma Phi (v.p. Laureate Epsilon chpt. 1981-82, pres. 1983-85, Valentine Queen 1985, Girl of Yr. 1985, preceptor Eta chpt., Girl of Yr., 1980, life), MidState Porcelain Artists Guild (v.p. 1983 89, pres. 1984) Club, Order Eastern Star (North Dakota Grand chpt., grand rep. 1979-81, dist. dep. 1982-83, chair credentials com. 1983-84, Grand Martha 1984-85, Grand Electra 1985-86, chmn. registration com. 1986-87, assoc. Grace Conductress 1987-88, Grand Conductress 1989-90, Worthy Matron Minot chpt. 1976, 87, 88-89). Lutheran. Avocations: china painting, oil painting, sewing, tennis, embroidery. Home: 705 25th St NW Minot ND 58701

MOE-FISHBACK, BARBARA ANN, counselor, educator; b. Grand Forks, N.D., June 24, 1955; d. Robert Alan and Ruth Ann (Wang) Moe; m. William Martin Fishback. BS in Psychology, U. N.D., 1977, MA in Counseling and Guidance, 1979, BS in Elem. Edn., 1984. Cert. elem. counselor, Ill. Tchr. United Day Nursery, Grand Forks, 1977-78; social worker Cavalier County Social Services, Langdon, N.D., 1979-83; elem. sch. counselor Douglas Sch. System, Ellsworth AFB, S.D., 1984-87, Jacksonville (Ill.) Sch. System, 1987—. Vol. Big Sister Program, Grand Forks, 1978-84; leader Pine to Prairie Girl Scout council, Langdon, N.D., 1980-82; tchrs. asst. Head Start Program, Grand Forks, 1979. Mem. Am. Assn. Counseling and Devel., NEA, Ill. Assn. Counseling and Devel., Ill. Sch. Counselor Assn., AAUW (local br. newsletter editor 1980-81, br. sec. 1981-83), Ill. Edn. Assn., Am. Sch. Counselor Assn., Kappa Alpha Theta (newsletter, magazine article editor 1976-77). Club: Jaycettes (Langdon) (dir. 1982-83). Avocations: cooking, camping, curling, ceramics, creative writing. Home: 1712 Nita Ln Jacksonville IL 62650 Office: Jacksonville Sch Dist Jacksonville IL 62650

MOELLER, HELEN HERGENRODER, ceramic engineer; b. Buffalo, Apr. 30, 1954; d. Ralph Joseph and Barbara C. (Anetzberger) Hergenroder; m. Robert Emil Moeller, May 29, 1976; 1 child, Robert E. Jr. BS in Ceramic Engring., Alfred U., 1976; MS in Engring. Adminstrn., George Washington U., 1980. Rsch. engr. Babcock & Wilcox Co., Lynchburg, Va., 1976-84; group supr. Babcock & Wilcox Co., 1984—. Patentee in field; contbr. to profl. publs. Master gardener Va. Extension Svc., Lynchburg, 1987—. Mem. ASTM (sec. 1984-90), Am. Ceramic Soc., Soc. for Advancement of Material and Process Engring. Office: Babcock & Wilcox Lynchburg Rsch Ctr PO Box 11165 Lynchburg VA 24506

MOELLER, LAURA LEE, retail executive, library consultant; b. St. Louis, Feb. 20, 1927; d. Edwin Charles and Henrietta Maude (Schelp) Luedde; m. Gerald Herbert Moeller, June 25, 1949; children: Dereck John, Dori Lee, Merry Cay. AB, Harris Tchrs. Coll., St. Louis, 1948; sch. libr. cert., Washington U., St. Louis, 1965. Elem. tchr. Howard Sch., St. Louis, 1948-50, Bay View Sch., Norfolk, Va., 1951; libr. East Ladue Jr. High Sch., St. Louis, 1965-77; mgr., buyer Wornall House Mus. Shop, Kansas City, Mo., 1978-79; owner, mgr. Crabtree & Evelyn London on Plaza, Kansas City, 1979—. Vice pres. Women's Coun. U. Mo., Kansas City, 1984-85. Mem. Mo. Assn. Sch. Librs. (pres. 1976-77), Plaza Mchts. Assn. (nominating com. 1981), AAUW, DAR, Wives of Rotarians (v.p. 1983-84), Rockhill Tennis Club. Presbyterian. Home: 420 W 50th St Kansas City MO 64112 Office: Crabtree & Evelyn 505 Nichols Rd Kansas City MO 64112

MOELLER, MARY ELLA, home economist, educator, radio commentator; b. Southampton, N.Y., Mar. 11, 1938; d. Harry Eugene and Edith Leone (Reester) Parsons; m. James Myron Moeller, Aug. 5, 1961; 1 child, Mary Beth. B.S. in Home Econs., U. Nebr., 1960; M.L.S., SUNY-Stony Brook, 1977. Tchr. home econs. Port Jefferson Schs., N.Y., 1960-70; home econs. program asst. Suffolk County Coop. Extension of Cornell U., Riverhead, N.Y., 1972-82; tchr. home econs. Eastport High Sch., Riverhead, 1982-85, South County Schs., Bellport Middle Sch., N.Y., 1985—; host Ask Your Neighbor, Sta. WRIV, Riverhead, 1982-87; trainer Home Econs. Entrepreneurship N.Y. State Edn. Dept., 1986—; mem. home and career skills regional team N.Y. State Edn. Dept., 1984-86; mem. consumer homemaking adv. bd. Bd. Coop. Edn. Contbr. monthly articles to consumer publs. Mem. N.Y. State Home Econs. Assn., Am. Home Econs. Assn. (cert. home economist), Suffolk County Home Econs. Assn., DAR (historian 1985), Eastern Star (matron 1970). Home: PO Box 377 Miller Place NY 11764 Office: Bellport Middle Sch Kreamer St Bellport NY 11713

MOELY, BARBARA E., psychology researcher, educator; b. Prairie du Sac, Wis., July 17, 1940; d. John Arthur and Loretta Ruth (Giese) M.; children: John Jacob Moely Wiener, David Andrew Moely Wiener. Student Carroll Coll., 1958-60; BA, U. Wis., 1962, MA, 1964; PhD, U. Minn., 1968. Asst. prof. U. Hawaii, Honolulu, 1967-71; research psychologist UCLA, 1971-72; asst. prof. Tulane U., New Orleans, 1972-75, assoc. prof. psychology, 1975-85, prof., 1985—; Contbr. articles to profl. jours. Grantee La. Commn. Extension and Continuing Edn., 1973-74, U.S. Office Edn., Handicapped Personnel Preparation, 1977-80, Tulane U., 1973, 75, 77, 78, 83-84, Inst. for Mental Hygiene, City of New Orleans, 1983-84, Nat. Inst. Edn., 1983-84. Mem. Soc. Research in Child Devel., Am. Psychol. Assn., Am. Ednl. Research Assn., Southwestern Soc. for Research in Human Devel. (pres. 1986-88), Phi Beta Kappa (pres. Alpha chapter La. 1981-82). Office: Dept Psychology Tulane Univ New Orleans LA 70118

MOENCH, PRISCILLA WATERS, banker; b. Charleston, S.C., May 4, 1957; d. William Swain and Roberta (Searle) Waters; m. Darrell Wayne Moench, Mar. 7, 1981; 1 child, Katerine Lynne. BA, Furman U., 1979. Asst. NBE (nat. bank examiner) U.S. Treasury Dept., Jacksonville, Fla., 1979-81; loan rev. specialist Fla. Nat. Bank, Jacksonville, 1981-83; loan rev. officer Sun Bank of Fla., Inc., Orlando, 1983-85; real estate loan officer, asst. v.p. Sun Bank of Jacksonville, N.A., 1985-86; credit rev. officer, asst. v.p. First Union Nat. Bank of Fla., Jacksonville, 1986-87, sr. credit rev. officer, asst. v.p., 1987-89, sr. credit rev. officer, v.p., 1989—. Sunday sch. tchr. Southside Bapt. Ch., Jacksonville, 1989—, mem. handbell choir, 1989—. Mem. AAUW (auditor, bd. dirs. Jacksonville chpt. 1987-89, corr. sec., bd. dirs. 1989-90). Republican. Office: First Union Nat Bank of Fla PO Box 2080 Jacksonville FL 32231-0525

MOENTMANN, MELANIE RUTH, food service executive; b. Norborne, Mo., May 7, 1960; d. Earl Kenneth and Virginia Lee (Mueller) M. BS in Home Econs., U. Mo., 1982. Dir. food svc. ARA Svcs., Chgo., 1982-84; dir. client ops. CH Health Techs., St. Louis, 1984-86; food svc. mgr. Jefferson Arms, St. Louis, 1986-87, Beverly Enterprises, Cahokia, Ill., 1987; dir. food svc. University City (Mo.) Pub. Schs., 1987-90, Wentzville (Mo.) Pub. Schs., 1990—. Mem. Greater St. Louis Sch. Food Svc. Dirs. Assn. (sec. 1988-89, v.p. 1990), Mo. Sch. Food Svc. Assn., St. Louis Dietetic Assn., Mo. Dietetic Assn. Republican. Lutheran. Office: Wentzville PUb Schs #1 Campus Dr Wentzville MO 63385

MOFENSON, LYNNE MERYL, pediatrician; b. Phila., Oct. 24, 1950; d. Howard Charles and Lois (Stugart) M.; m. Bruce Leslie Katz, Aug. 28, 1972; 1 child, Jessica Ann Mofenson Katz. BA magna cum laude, SUNY at Stony Brook, 1971; MD, Albert Einstein Coll. Medicine, 1977. Diplomate Nat. Bd. Med. Examiners. Intern, residency Pediatric Childrens Hosp., Boston, 1977-79; instr. pediatrics Harvard Med. Sch., Children's Hosp., Boston, 1977-79; chief resident pediatrics U. Mass. Med. Sch., Worcester, 1979-80, fellow infectious disease, 1981-83, assoc. internal medicine & pediatrics, 1982-89; hosp. epidemiologist Marlboro (Mass.) Hosp., 1983-85; pvt. med. practice Northboro, Mass., 1983-85; asst. commr. Communicable Disease Control, Mass. Dept. Pub. Health, Boston, 1985-89; assoc. br. chief for clin. rsch. NIH, Pediatric Adolescent & Maternal AIDS Br., Bethesda, Md., 1989—; Mem. Cen. AIDS Rev. Bd., Mass. Dept. Social Svcs., 1988-89, Sub-com. on Clin. Trials & Rsch., Gov.'s Task Force on AIDS, Mass. Dept. Pub. Health, 1988-89, Pediatric Core Com., AIDS Clin. Trials Group, NIH, 1989—; reviewer Year 2000 Nat. Health Objs.; co-chair workshop HIV Infection in Women Childbearing Age, 1989; manuscript rev. bd. Am. Jour. Pub. Health. Contbr. numerous articles to profl. jours. Recipient Commr. Family Resource Program award Dept. Social Svcs., 1989, Teaching award City Boston Sch. System, 1989, Gov.'s Proclamation award, 1989, Citation for Scholastic Achievement Am. Med. Women's Assn., 1977, Neurobiology award Albert Einstein Coll. Medicine, 1974, Regents Scholarship N.Y. State, 1968, Nat. Merit Scholarship Finalist, 1968. Fellow Alpha Omega Alpha, Am. Acad. Pediatrics; mem. Mass. Med. Soc., AMA, Am. Pub. Health Assn., Am. Soc. for Microbiology. Democrat. Jewish. Office: Nat Inst Child Health 6120 Executive Blvd Ste 700 Bethesda MD 20892

MOFFAT, MARYBETH, automotive company executive; b. Pitts., July 25, 1951; d. Herbert Franklin and Florence Grafe (Knerem) M.; m. Brian Francis Soulier, Nov. 30, 1974 (div.). BA, Carroll Coll., 1973. Indsl. engring. technician Wis. Centrifugal Co., Waukesha, Wis., 1976-77; indsl. engr. Utility Products, Inc., Milw., 1977-79; spl. projects mgr. Bear Automotive (div. SPX Corp.), Bangor, Pa., 1980—. Group home house parent Headwaters Regional Achievement Ctr., Lake Tomahawk, Wis., 1974. Mem. Am. Inst. Indsl. Engrs., MTM Assn. for Standards Rsch., Indsl. Mgmt. Soc., Alpha Gamma Delta (standards chmn. 1971-72). Republican. Methodist. Avocations: skiing, horseback riding, swimming, reading. Home: Spring Ridge Apts #P-23 Whitehall PA 18052 Office: Bear Automotive Svc Equipment Co S Main and Werner Sts Bangor PA 18013

MOFFATT, MINDY ANN, teacher, educational and research consultant; b. Mpls., Aug. 3, 1951; d. Ralph Theron and La Vone Muriel (Bergstrom) M. Student, UCLA, 1972-73; BA, Calif. State U., Fullerton, 1975, MS in Adminstrv. Svcs., 1990. Cert. elem. tchr., Calif. Tchr. early childhood edn. program Meadows Elem. Sch., Valencia, Calif., 1977-78; tchr. United Parents Against Forced Busing, Chatsworth, Calif., 1978-80; founding tchr. Gazebo Two Sch. for Young Gifted and Creative Children, Summerville, S.C., 1980-81; tchr. Anaheim Union High Sch. Dist., Anaheim, Calif., 1981-89, mentor, tchr., 1985-88; with Greentree Elem. Sch., Irvine, Calif., 1989—; cons. writing project U. Calif., Irvine, 1982—; textbook cons. McDougal, Littell & Co., Evanston, Ill., 1984-86; facilitator Summer Tech. Tng. Inst., Irvine, 1987. Co-author: Practical Ideas for Teaching Writing as a Process, 1986, 87. Mem. Friends of the River, San Francisco, Handgun Control, Inc., Washington; active The Nature Conservancy, Arlington, Va.; sponsor English Council Orange County. Mem. NEA, Calif. Assn. Tchrs. of English, NOW, Nat. Coun. Tchrs. English, Nat. Writing Project, Sierra Club, Friends of the River, Handgun Control Inc., Computer Using Educators. Democrat. Unity Ch. of Truth. Club: Our Ultimate Recreation (Orange County, Calif.) (social com. chairperson 1983, backpacking chairperson 1983).

MOFFETT, DAWN SCHULTEN, elementary educator; b. Phila., Nov. 22, 1946; d. Emil Ferdinand and Helen Marie (McPhee) Schulten; m. Thomas Lee Moffett, July 25, 1970; children: Carolyn Dawn, Deborah Leanne, William Lee. BS, Bloomsburg U., 1968; postgrad., Temple U., 1969-71. Cert. tchr., Pa. Tchr. 4th grade Hatboro-Horsham Sch. Dist., Horsham, Pa., 1968-69, tchr. 1st grade, 1969-72; kindergarten tchr.'s aide Quantico (Va.) Sch. Dist., 1972-73; kindergarten tchr. U-Gro Learning Centres, Palmyra, Pa., 1986-87; subs. tchr. Cen. Dauphin Sch. Dist., Harrisburg, Pa., 1988-90, Lower Dauphin Sch. Dist., Hummelstown, Pa., 1988-90, Milton Hershey Sch., Hershey, Pa., 1987-90; tchr. 2d grade Lebanon (Pa.) Sch. Dist., 1990—. Sch. dir. Derry Twp. Sch. Dist., Hershey, 1983-87, Dauphin County Vo-Tech Sch., Harrisburg, 1984-87; trustee First United Meth. Ch., 1988—, mem. council of ministries, 1988—; sec. Derry Twp. Library Bd., 1988—; trustee, sec. Dauphin County Library Bd., 1988—; mem. Hershey Library Endowment Bd., 1986-88; pres. Friends of Hershey Pub. Library, 1986-88; active PTO. Recipient Svc. award Pa. Sch. Bds. Assn., 1987, Dauphin County Tech. Sch., 1987, Derry Twp. Sch. Dist., 1987. Mem. AAUW (pres. Hershey 1978-80, Outstanding Woman of Yr. 1982), Pa. Libr. Assn. Republican. Home: 357 Laurie Ave RD 1 Hummelstown PA 17036

MOFFETT, PAMELA AMY, hospital executive; b. Ephrata, Wash., June 4, 1954; d. George Edward and Amy Elizabeth (Bailey) M. Student, Everett (Wash.) Community Coll., 1973, USN Hosp. Corps Sch., Great Lakes, Ill., 1974. Psychiat. nursing asst. Ingleside Hosp., Rosemead, Calif., 1980-82, adminstrv. coordinator, 1982-85, dir. materials mgmt., 1985—. Vol. Nixon re-election campaign, Everett, 1972. Served with USN, 1974-76. Mem. Calif. Assn. Hosp. Purchasing and Materials Mgrs. (sec. Los Angeles, Orange, San Bernadino and Riverside Counties, 1986—), Rainbow Girls. Methodist. Office: Ingleside Hosp 7500 E Hellman Ave Rosemead CA 91770

MOFFO, DOREEN ANN, nurse; b. Waterbury, Conn., Dec. 27, 1962; d. John Thomas Moffo and Nanc Ann (Brewer) CarAngelo. AA, Palm Beach Jr. Coll., Lake Worth, Fla., 1986, AS in Nursing, 1987. Unit sec. Martin Meml. Hosp., Stuart, Fla., 1982-86; RN Coastal Health Care Corp., Stuart, 1986-89, Conn. Health Agy., 1989—. Leader, svc. team mem. Girl Scouts U.S., Palm Glades Girl Scout Coun., 1987-89; leader, svc. team mem., trainer Girl Scouts U.S., Conn. Trails Coun., 1989—; sch. vol. J.D. Parker Elem. Sch., Stuart, 1988-89; active environmental svc.groups. Home: 139 Wesley St Waterbury CT 06708

MOFFORD, ROSE, governor of Arizona; b. Globe, Ariz., June 10, 1922; m. T.R. Mofford (div.). Attended pub. schs. Sec. to Joe Hunt, Ariz. State Treas., 1941-43, Ariz. State Tax Commr., 1943-54, Wesley Bolin, Ariz. Sec. of State, 1954-55; asst. sec. of state State of Ariz., Phoenix, 1955-75; asst. dir. of revenue State of Ariz., 1975-77, sec. of state, 1977-88, governor, 1988—. Democrat. Office: Office of Gov 1700 W Washington St Phoenix AZ 85007*

MOGERMAN, VERONICA LINDA, organizational administrator; b. Vaughn, N.Mex., Jan. 5, 1954; d. Isidro Joseph and Stella Miriam (Gallegos) Romero; m. Michael Scott Mogerman, Sept. 24, 1978. BA, U. Rochester, 1976, St. Joseph Coll., 1985. Physician, nurses asst. Linwood-Bryant Hosp., Buffalo, 1976-77; acctg. coordinator U. N.Mex., Albuquerque, 1977-78; scientific editor, typist The Sackler Sch. of Medicine, Tel Aviv, Israel, 1978-79; adminstrv. asst. Albany Travel Ltd., Tel Aviv, 1979-81; office mgr. Ketchum Distributors, Inc., Newington, Conn., 1981-84; exec. asst. Greater Hartford Bd. Realtors, Inc., West Hartford, Conn., 1984-85, Coopers & Lybrand, Hartford, Conn., 1985-89, Orthopedic Assocs. of Hartford, P.C., 1989—. Editor (newsletter) The Workpaper, 1986; contbr. articles to synagogue pub. Organizer, fund raiser Hartford Easter Seals Rehab. Ctr., 1986-88, Newington Children's Hosp., 1986-87; active Women's Orgn. for Conservative Judaism, 1981-88; mem. Greater Hartford Jewish Fedn., Conn. Opera. Recipient Congressman's Medal of Merit U.S. Congress, 1972. Fellow John F. Kennedy Meml. Libr. Found.; mem. AAAS, NAFE, Am. Mgmt. Assn., Nat. Audubon Soc., Aux. of AMA, Smithsonian Assocs., The Wilderness Soc., Am. Assn. Individual Investors, Conn. Opera Assn., Mystic Seaport Mus. Assn., Wadsworth Atheneum, Math. Assn. Am., Nat. Mus. Women in the Arts, Bus. and Profl. Women's Orgn., Cousteau Soc., U. Rochester Alumni Assn. (treas. Aura, Conn. chpt.). Democrat.

MOGFORD, SHARON MARIE, state official; b. Kerrville, Tex., Mar. 4, 1959; d. Harold Lamar, Sr., and Mary Elizabeth (Phipps) M. B.B.A., S.W. Tex. State U., 1981. CPA, Tex. With State Auditor's Office, Austin, Tex., 1981-88 , asst. state auditor, 1981-83, in-charge asst. state auditor, 1983-85, supervising asst. state auditor, 1985-88, asst. dir. acctg., 1988, dir. internal audit, 1988—. Mem. AICPA. Republican. Baptist. Avocations: scuba diving, softball, snow skiing. Home: 2724 Cross Bend Rd Plano TX 75023

MOGGE, HARRIET MORGAN, educational association executive; b. Cleve.; d. Russell VanDyke and Grace (Wells) Morgan; m. Robert Arthur Mogge, Aug. 17, 1948 (div. 1977); 1 child, Linda Jean. BME, Northwestern U., 1959; postgrad., Ill. State U., 1969. Instr. piano, Evanston, Ill., 1954-58; instr. elem. music pub. schs., Evanston, 1959; editorial asst. archivist Summy-Birchard Co., Evanston, 1964-66, asst. to editor-in-chief, 1966-67, cons., 1968-69, ednl. dir., 1969-74, also historian, 1973-74; supr. vocal music jr. high sch., Watseka, Ill., 1967-68; asst. dir. profl. programs Music Educators Nat. Conf., Reston, Va., 1974-84, dir. meetings and convs., 1984—, mgr. direct mktg. svc., 1981-89. Mng. editor Am. Suzuki jour., 1972-74, Gen. Music Today, 1987—; mgr. diplay advt. Model T Times, 1971—. Active various community drives. Mem. Music Educators Nat. Conf., Am. Choral Dirs. Assn., In and About Chgo., Music Educators Assn. (bd. dirs.), Suzuki Assn. Ams. (exec. sec. 1972-74), Nat. Assn. Expn. Mgrs. (cert.; mem. edn. com. 1979-88, chmn. edn. com. 1985-87, bd. liaison edn. com. 1987-88, bd. dirs. Washington chpt. 1983-85, nat. bd. dirs. 1986—, del. to conv. liaison coun. 1989-90, nat. v.p. 1989, nat. pres. 1990), Mu Phi Epsilon, Kappa Delta (province pres. 1960-66, 72-76, regional chpts. dir. 1976-78, nat. dir. scholarship 1981-84). Republican. Presbyterian. Clubs: Bus. and Profl. Women's (Watseka) (bd. dirs. 1968-70); Antique Automobile (registrar ann. meeting 1961-86), Model T Ford Internat. (v.p. 1971-72, 76-77, pres. 1981, treas. 1983-87, bd. dirs. 1971-87). Home: 1919A VillaRidge Dr Reston VA 22091 Office: 1902 Association Dr Reston VA 22091

MOHEL, SELMA ZIPPERT, retired educator, book reviewer; b. N.Y.C., July 25, 1911; d. Bernard and Bessie (Meyer) Zippert; m. Hyman L. Mohel, Mar. 31, 1931; children: Judith D., Beth D. BA, NYU, 1931. Tchr. New Bedford (Mass.) Pub. Schs., 1958-80; corporator New Bedford Instn. for Savs., 1976-86; lectr. Southeastern Mass. U. Continuing Edn., 1979-82. Bd. dirs. Old Dartmouth Hist. Soc. Whaling Mus., 1981-85; mem. nat. women's com. Brandeis U., 1960-62, pres. New Bedford chpt., 1960-62; past program dir. Hadassah, Jewish Women's Profl. Club, Sisterhood of Tiferish Israel. Mem. AAUW (past study group leader, cert. of achievement, 1987), Coll. Club New Bedford (spokeswoman Women's Month 1989). Home: 243 Hawthorn St New Bedford MA 02740

MOHLER, LINDA S., teacher; b. Carlisle, Pa., June 26, 1949; d. John William and Betty Louise (Gelsinger) Cline; m. Richard McClellan, Dec. 1, 1973; children: RAchel Elizabeth, Sarah Christine. AB in English, Music, Dickinson Coll., Carlisle, Pa., 1971; postgrad., Temple U., Phila., 1971; MEd in Reading, Shippensburg U., 1974; postdoctoral, Pa. State U., 1989—. Tchr., Reading Specialist. Tchr. of English, dir. of Children's Theater Cumberland Valley Sch. Dist., Mechanicsburg, Pa., 1970-72; tchr. of English, dir. of Children's Theatre Carlisle Area Sch. Dist., Pa., 1972-73; tchr. of English Mifflin County Sch. Dist., Lewistown, Pa., 1982, reading specialist; reading com. Mifflin County Sch. Dist., Lewistown, 1988. Mem. AAUW (pres. Mifflin County chpt. 1976-78), Internat. Reading Assn., Nat. Edn. Assn., Pa. State Edn. Assn., Assn. of Mifflin County Educators, Mifflin Juniata Legal Spouses (pres. 1980-82), Mifflin County Music Club. Democrat. Home: 12 Fairview Pl Lewistown PA 17044

MOHN, ELAINE LOUISE, nursing educator; b. Canton, Ohio, July 8, 1948; d. Harold Joseph and Marjorie Evelyn (Altemus) M. Diploma in Nursing, Akron (Ohio) Gen. Med. Ctr.; BA in Health Edn., U.No. Colo., 1972, MA in Health Edn., 1979; BS in Nursing, Met. State Coll., Denver, 1978; EdD in Ednl. Adminstrn., Brigham Young U., 1987. RN, Ohio, Colo., Oreg. Staff nurse Akron (Ohio) Gen. Hosp., 1969; charge nurse Barberton (Ohio) Citizens Hosp., 1969-70, Weld County Gen. Hosp., Greeley, 1970-73; instr. nursing Larimer County Vocat.-Tech. Ctr., Ft. Collins, Colo., 1973-77; staff and charge nurse Presbyn. Med. Ctr., Denver, 1977-79; instr. nursing, coord. ADN program Chemeketa Community Coll., Salem, Oreg., 1979-89; coll. researcher, grant writer Chemeketa Community Coll., 1989-90; instr, nursing, 1990—; staff nurse Poudre Valley Hosp., Ft. Collins, part-time 1975-76; instr. Arapahoe Community Coll., Littleton, Colo., part-time, 1978; presenter in field. Mem. Nat. League for Nursing, Am. Vocat. Assn., Oreg. Coun. ADN Programs (pres. 1982-83), Oreg. Vocat. Assn., Oreg. Soc. Health Occupation Educators (pres. 1983-86). Office: Chemeketa Community Coll 4000 Lancaster DR Salem OR 97309

MOHNEY, SHARON EILEEN, marketing management executive; b. Bremerton, Wash., Dec. 7, 1944; d. Forest N. and Jane Ellen (Patnoe) Erlandsen; m. Gayle Alexander Mohney Jr., Dec. 14, 1968. BA, U. Wash., 1971. Mktg. rep. BASF, Williamsburg, Va., 1974-84; mktg. specialist Allied Corp., Petersburg, Va., 1984-85; mktg. mgr. Allied-Signal Corp., Petersburg, 1985-90; mgr. bus. planning Allied-Signal Corp., 1990—; speaker Nat. Conv. of Assn. Sch. Bus. Ofcls., San Antonio, 1987, ann. conv. Am. Floorcovering Assn., 1989. Contbr. articles to profl. jours. Tutor literacy program, 1990—. Mem. Am. Mktg. Assn., Inst. Bus. Designers, Internat. Facility Mgmt. Assn. (speaker 1987 conv.), Calligraphy Guild. Office: Allied-Signal Inc PO Box 31 Petersburg VA 23804

MOHR, BARBARA JEANNE, educator; b. Santa Monica, Calif., Jan. 26, 1953; d. Edgar Kirchner and Beatrice Jeanne (Anderson) M. BA, Calif. State U., 1976, MS, 1982. Multiple Subject Teaching Credential, 1977, Single Subject Tchr. Credential, 1977. Substitute tchr. Fullerton (Calif.) Sch. Dist., 1977-78, tchr., 1978—; mentor Fullerton Sch. Dist., 1984—; calligraphy tchr., Laguna Rd. Sch. Arts Program, 1985—. Advisor Just Say No Club, Fullerton, 1986—, student coun. advisor Laguna Rd. Sch., 1988—. Recipient Hon. Svc. award Laguna Rd. Sch. PTA, 1989, named Tchr. of Yr., 1989. Mem. NEA, ASCD, Computer Using Educators, Calif. State U. Alumni Assn., Fullerton Elem. Tchrs Assn., Calif. Tchrs. Assn., Phi Kappa Phi.

MOHRDICK, EUNICE MARIE, nurse, health educator; b. Alameda, Calif.; d. Walter William and Eunice Marie (Connors) M. BS in Nursing Edn., U. San Francisco, 1955; MA in Edn. spl interest, San Francisco State Coll., 1967; Pub. Health Cert., U. Calif., San Francisco, 1968; EdD, Western Colo. U., 1977. RN, Calif. Nurse, supr. St. Mary's Hosp., San Francisco, 1943-45, supr., instr., 1955-60, 62-65; asst. dir. nursing, tchr. nursing history St Mary's Coll. of Nursing, San Francisco, 1953-55; tchr. home nursing Mercy High Sch., San Francisco, 1960-61; tchr. Health, Family Life San Francisco Unified Schs., 1968-83; tchr. Holistic Health Contra Costa Coll., 1981-86; cons. pvt. practice Albany, Calif., 1986—; tchr. El Cerrito (Calif.) Senior Ctr., 1986-88. Author: Elementary Teacher Handbook, How to Teach Sex Education, Grades, 4,5,6, 1977. Mem. Madonna Guild, San Francisco, 1986—, v.p., 1989—, Half Notes' Singing Club to Sick and Spl. Needy, 1970—. Recipient Title 1 Grant U. Calif. San Francisco, 1968, Workshop Grant for Culture Inter-relationship Study, Singapore, UNESCO, Washington U., St. Louis, 1973. Mem. AAUW, San Francisco State U. Alumna, U. San Francisco Nursing Alumni (charter mem., bd. dirs. 1974-88), Mensa. Republican. Roman Catholic. Home & Office: 555 Pierce St #129 Albany CA 94706

MOHRMANN, SUE ROSS, education educator; b. Liberty Hill, Tex., Oct. 7, 1940; d. Vaden Bennett and Nelwyn Belle (Callaway) Ross; m. Leonard E. Mohrmann, Jr., June 18, 1966; children: Leonard E. III, Vaden, Nelwyn. BS, U. Tex., 1966; MEd, Tex. A&M U., 1981, PhD, 1987. Tchr. Leon County Bd. Pub. Instrn., Tallahassee, 1966-72, Bryan (Tex.) Ind. Sch. Dist., 1972-73, 77-81; rsch. assoc. Tex. A&M U., College Station, 1981-87; reading specialist Leander (Tex.) Ind. Sch. Dist., 1987-88; asst. prof. edn. Tex. A&I U., Kingsville, 1988—, dir. reading, 1988—. Contbr. articles to profl. jours. Mem. Nat. Reading Conf., Nat. Coun. Tchrs. English, Internat. Reading Assn., SW Ednl. Rsch. Assn., Tex. Reading Assn., Phi Kappa Phi. Mem. Ch. of Christ. Office: Tex A&I U Dept Edn Kingsville TX 78363

MOISAN, ANNE SHERMAN, food products executive; b. Westport, N.Y., Feb. 20, 1936; d. Richard Gough and Patti (Medary) Sherman; m. Craig Mitchell Johnson, Sept. 1, 1956 (div. Apr. 1974); children: Craig Mitchell Jr., Anne Elisabeth, Scott Cunningham; m. Charles Moisan, Feb. 20, 1990. Student, Skidmore Coll., 1954-55. Asst. sec., treas. Champlain Valley Seed Growers, Westport, N.Y., 1974-81, asst. mgr., 1981-85; mem., treas. bd., bus. mgr. Champlain Valley Milling Corp., Westport, 1985—; owner Champ Enterprises, Westport, 1984—. Mem. Adirondack North County Assn. (bd. dirs. 1988—). Republican. Episcopalian. Office: Champlain Valley Milling 110 Pleasant St PO Box 454 Westport NY 12993

MOISE, REBECCA ZERBY, social worker; b. Iowa City, Nov. 24, 1944; d. Lewis Kenneth and Margaret Ellen (Schiller) Zerby; m. Ronald Joseph Byrne, Apr. 9, 1962 (div. 1966); 1 child, Tonia-Marie Byrne Wander; m. Edwin Evariste Moise, Aug. 21, 1976; 1 child, Andrew Philip. BA, Mich. State U., 1967; PhD, U. Chgo., 1974; MSW, U. Mich., 1977. Lectr. U. Chgo., 1973; rsch. assoc. Ill. Drug Abuse Program, Chgo., 1973-74; cons. Pub. Service Inst., Chgo., 1972-73, Inst. for Pub. Policy Studies, Ann Arbor, Mich., 1975; cons., rsch. assoc., Women's Drug Rsch. U. Mich., Ann Arbor, 1977-83; pvt. practice Clemson, S.C., Anderson, S.C., 1984—; vis. asst. prof. Clemson (S.C.) U., 1984; instr. Tri-County Tech. Coll., Pendleton, S.C., 1986—. Contbr. articles to profl. publs.; editorial asst., tech. reviewer: Treatment Services for Drug Dependent Women, Nat. Inst. Drug Abuse, 1981-82. Mem. Clemson Area Arts Coun., 1986-89. Postdoctoral fellow, Ctr. for Chinese Studies, U. Mich., Ann Arbor, 1974-75, dissertation fellowship, NIMH, Chgo., 1972-73. Mem. AAUW (program v.p. 1986-88, womens worth chmn. 1988-89, named gift honoree 1988), Nat. Assn. Social Workers, Popular Culture Assn., Am. Sociol. Assn. Democrat. Unitarian. Home: 107 Karen Dr Clemson SC 29631 Home: 1208 Ella St Anderson SC 29621 Office: Tri-County Tech Coll PO Box 587 Pendleton SC 29670

MOJICA, AURORA, association executive; b. Mayaguez, P.R., Feb. 19, 1939; d. Luis Martinez and Anna Celida (Montalvo) Perez; m. Aristides Mojica, Jan. 19, 1957 (div. July 1967); children: Ty, Marc Anthony, Raymond Francis, Sharai, Angeles. BS in Mgmt. and Labor Rel., Cornell U., 1979; postgrad., PACE Univ. Asst. dir. Attica Commn., N.Y.C., 1974, South Bklyn. Health Ctr., N.Y.C., 1975-79; sec. to the dept., dir. community rels. (1st woman apptd.) Fire Dept. N.Y.C., 1979-81; dir. pub. community rels. WYC Koff Heights Hosp., N.Y.C., 1981-84, Interfaith Adopt-A-Bldg., N.Y.C., 1984-86; dir. women health svcs. Woodhull Med. and Mental Health Ctr., N.Y.C., 1986-87; dir. individual and family grants program Fed. Emergency Mgmt. Agy., P.R., 1987-88; exec. dir. Nat. Image, Inc., Washington, 1988—; cons. Agy. for Internat. Devel., Mex., Costa Rica and Peru, 1981—; trainer Venezuela and P.R., Cornell U. P.R. Studies, N.Y., 1971—; trainer and bd. dirs. Neighborhood Reinvestment, N.Y.C., 1984-86. Selected participant Nat. Hispana Leadership Inst., 1990. Recipient Susan B. Anthony award for Pub. Svc., NOW, N.Y.C., 1981, Cert. of Recognition Sesame Street CTW, N.Y.C. 1983, Public Svc. award U.S. Dept. Labor, 1985; Named Hispanic Woman of the Yr. in Health award Hispanic Woman's Network, Bklyn., 1987. Republican. Roman Catholic. Office: Nat Image Inc 810 First St NE Washington DC 20002

MOKE, ANNE MARIE, hospital radiology manager; b. Bowdle, S.D., Apr. 6, 1955; d. Frank Sigfred and Mary Marie (Kappenman) Imberi; m. Arlen James Moke, Oct. 3, 1975. Student radiologic tech., St. Joseph Hosp.Tech., Mitchell, S.D., 1973-75. Radiologic technologist staff St. Joseph Hosp., Mitchell, S.D., 1975-80; sonographer St. Joseph Hosp., 1980-82, asst. chief, 1982-85, radiology mgr., 1985—. Mem. S.D. Soc. Radiologic Technologists (treas. 1981-87, pres.-elect 1988-89, pres. 1989-90), Am. Soc. Radiologic Technologists (region IV sonography del. 1986-88, chmn. sonography com. 1988-90), Soc. Diagnostic Sonographers (state rep. 1985-86), Minn. Soc. Diagnostic Sonographers. Home: 1032 E 2nd Mitchell SD 57301

MOKULIS, PAULA, graphic arts analyst; b. Hartford, Conn., Apr. 2, 1947; d. John George and Stephanie (Kyc) M. BA, U. Conn., 1969; AAS summa cum laude, North Va. Community Coll., Alexandria, 1984. Writer, editor Hartford Ins. Group, 1969-71; mgmt. analyst Travelers Ins. Co., Hartford, 1971-72; asst. editor TV Guide mag., Atlanta, 1972; clk. typist Bur. Medicine and Surgery USN, Washington, 1973, writer U.S. Navy Medicine mag., editor, 1973-74; sec. sec. of Def., Washington, 1974-78; exec. sec. Def. Resource Mgmt. Study, Washington, 1978-79; sec. Joint Chiefs of Staff, Washington, 1979; mgmt. asst. U.S. Sec. Def., Washington, 1979-80; graphic arts analyst U.S. Army Visual Info. Ctr., Washington, 1980-86, system adminstr. computer network, 1986—; copywriter Sta. WETA, pub. radio. Designer exhibit panels Gen. Floyd Parks Meml. Corridor, The Pentagon, 1988; contbg. designer bicentennial medallion Dept. Def., 1988; poetry pub. in anthology. Recipient Comdr.'s award for civilian svc., 1988. Democrat. Roman Catholic. Office: US Army Visual Info Ctr Pentagon Washington DC 20310

MOLER, ELIZABETH ANNE, lawyer; b. Salt Lake City, Jan. 24, 1949; d. Murray McClure and Eleanor Lorraine (Barry) M.; m. Thomas Blake Williams, Oct. 19, 1979; 1 child, Blake Martin Williams. BA, Am. U., 1971; postgrad., Johns Hopkins U., 1973; JD, George Wash. U., 1977. Bar: D.C. 1978. Law clk. Sharon, Pierson, Semmes, Crolius & Finley, Washington, 1975-76; chief legis. asst. Senator Floyd Haskell, Washington, 1973-75; counsel com. on energy and natural resources U.S. Senate, Washington, 1976-77, counsel, 1977-81, minority counsel, 1981-87, sr. counsel, 1987-88; mem. FERC, Washington, 1988—. Mem. ABA. Democrat. Home: 1537 Forest Ln McLean VA 22101 Office: FERC 825 N Capitol St NE Rm 9006 Washington DC 20426

MOLINARI, SUSAN K., congresswoman; b. S.I., N.Y., Mar. 27, 1958; d. Guy V. and Marguerite (Wing) M.; m. John Lucchesi. BA, SUNY, Albany, 1980, MA, 1982. Former intern for State Senator Christopher Mega; former rsch. analyst N.Y. State Senate Fin. Com.; former fin. asst. Nat. Rep. Gov.'s Assn.; ethnic community liaison Rep. Nat. Com., 1983-84; councilwoman N.Y.C., 1986-90; mem. 101st, 102nd Congresses from N.Y. 14th Dist., 1990—. Roman Catholic. Office: 1723 Longsworth Washington DC 20515-3214*

MOLINARO, VALERIE ANN, lawyer; b. N.Y.C, Oct. 21, 1956; d. Albert Anthony and Rosemary Rita (Zito) M.; m. Howard Robert Birnbach. BA with honors, SUNY, 1978; JD, Syracuse U., 1980, MPA, 1980. Asst. counsel. New York State Housing Finance Agy., N.Y.C., 1980-82; assoc. counsel, asst. secy. N.Y. State Urban Devel. Corp., N.Y.C., 1982-85; assoc. Mudge Rose Guthrie Alexander & Ferdon, N.Y.C., 1985-87, Bower & Gardner, N.Y.C., 1988, Hawkins, Delafield & Wood, N.Y.C., 1988—. Author: Am. Bar Assn. Jour., 1981. Mem. N.Y. State Bar Assn. (tax exempt finance com.), Assn. of Bar of City of N.Y., Nat. Assn. Bond Lawyers. Office: Hawkins Delafield & Wood 67 Wall St New York NY 10005

MOLITOR, DORIS JEAN, management executive; b. St. Cloud, Minn., July 15, 1957; d. Andrew Leo and Eunice (Brown) M.; m. Todd Vern Waters, Aug. 22, 1981. BS, U. Minn., 1984. Legal asst. U.S. Ho. Rep., Washington, 1977-80; asst. campaign mgr. to congressman U.S. Ho. Rep., St. Cloud, 1978; pres., owner Expressive Interiors, Mpls., 1982-83; consumer promotion planner Gen. Mills, Inc., Mpls., 1984-88; pres. promotion group WatersMolitor, Inc., Mpls., 1988—. Vol. miscellaneous polit. campaigns, Minn., 1989—. Mem. Promotion Mktg. Assn. Am. Office: WatersMolitor Inc 11900 Wayzata Blvd Ste 206 Minneapolis MN 55434

MOLLINGER, JUDITH ELLEN, lawyer, industrial and labor relations specialist; b. Phila., Nov. 20, 1943; d. Owen Samuel and Florence (Devinski) M. BA, U. Conn., 1965; JD, Temple U., 1980. Bar: Pa. 1980, N.J. 1981, U.S. Dist. Ct. (ea dist.) Pa. 1981. Social worker Pa. Dept. Welfare, 1965-70; rep. AFSCME, AFL-CIO, Phila., 1970-80; staff atty. Pub. Employment Rels. Commn., Trenton, N.J., 1980-85; indsl. rels. rep. Beverly Enterprises, Rockville, Md., 1986-87; dir. employee and labor rels. food and svcs. mgmt. div. Marriott Corp., Washington, 1988—; adj. prof. Widener U., Chester, Pa., 1985-86. Mem. ABA, NAFE, Pa. Bar Assn., Phila. Bar Assn., Am. Mgmt. Assn., Indsl. Rels. Rsch. Assn., Coalition of Labor Union Women, Temple U. Law Sch. Women's Caucus, Phi Kappa Phi. Office: Marriott Corp Internat Hdqr Food and Svcs Mgmt Div 1 Marriott Dr Washington DC 20058

MOLLOY, ELIZABETH ANN, banker; b. Red Bank, N.J., Nov. 3, 1964; d. Peter Edward Molloy and Elizabeth Ann (Mullen) Purvis. BS, Cornell U., 1985. Mgr. Citicorp Credit Svc., Inc., N.Y.C., 1986—. Mem. Nat. Assn. Young Profl. Women, Am. Mgmt. Assn., Cornell Alumni. Office: Citicorp Credit Svc Inc 3940 Olympic Blvd Erlanger KY 41018

MOLNAR, HARRIET L., training executive; b. Armstrong County, Pa., Apr. 22, 1938; d. Robert Lincoln and Margaret Elizabeth (Brothers) Held; 1 child, Terry Lee. AA, Harrisburg Community Coll., 1972. Allowance specialist, team leader Navy Ship's Parts Control Ctr., Mechanicsburg, Pa.; cons. Mechanicsburg, Pa. Mem. NAFE, USN Inst. Federally Employed Women (Naval Supply Systems Command Leadership award 1988), Am. Soc. Tng. Devel.

MOLNAR, LAURIE DENNERY, reading specialist; b. New Orleans, Jan. 6, 1958; d. Theodore Dennery and Joyce (Joseph) Sabatier; m. Stephen Alexander Molnar, July 1, 1989. BS in Edn., Spl. Edn., Louisiana State U., 1980; M in Ed Cons., Lesley Coll., 1986. Resource room tchr. Sebastian Roy Sch., Yscloskey, La., 1980-81; classroom tchr. Carrollton Sch., New Orleans, 1981-84; reading clinician Kennedy Meml. Hosp., Brighton, Mass., 1986-88; reading tchr. Boston Community Schs., Jamaica Plain, Mass., 1988—; writing program cons. Kennedy Hosp. Inpatient Program, Brighton, 1988; asst. dir. children's programs Arnold Arboretum Harvard U. Author: (Book) Maria Returns Home, 1989. Rep. Agassiz Sch. Reading Program, Boston, 1989. Mem. Assn. for Supervision and Curriculum Devel., New Eng. Reading Assn., Greater Boston Reading Council, Internat. Reading Assn., Mass. Reading Assn. Democrat.

MOLT, CYNTHIA MARYLEE, author, publisher; b. Sierra Madre, Calif., Nov. 1, 1957; d. Lawrence Edward and Evelyn Mary (Novak) Molt. BA in English Lit., Calif. State U., Long Beach, 1980. Mng. editor Assoc. Graphics, Arts and Letters, Monrovia, Calif., 1981-87, pub., sr. and mng. editor, 1987—, authenticator, 1981—; author McFarland and Co., Inc., Pubs., Jefferson, N.C., 1988-90, Greenwood Press, Inc., Westport, Conn., 1989—; Author: (film) Gone with the Wind; A Complete Reference, 1990, (a bio-bibliography) Vivien Leigh, 1989—; author, editor mag. The Wind, 1981-89, Calif. Film, 1987-89; spl. corr. Monrovia News-Post, 1985; corr. G.W.T.W. Collector's Club Newsletter, 1979-82, Monrovia Rev., 1975. Author: (film) Gone with the Wind: A Complete Reference, 1990, (a bio-bibliography) Vivien Leigh, 1989—; author, editor mag. The Wind, 1981-89, Calif. Film, 1987-89; spl. corr. Monrovia News-Post, 1985; corr. G.W.T.W. Collector's Club Newsletter, 1979-82, Monrovia Rev., 1975. Vol. adminstrv. asst. student activities Monrovia High Sch., 1976. Mem. Gone with the Wind Soc. (pres. 1985-89), Am. Biog. Inst. (mem. rsch. bd. advisors 1989—), Vivien Leigh Fan Club (pres. 1987-89), Clark Gable Fan Club (pres. 1987-89), Grace Kelly Fan Club (pres. 1987-89). Republican. Roman Catholic. Home and Office: 364 N May Ave Monrovia CA 91016

MONACO, LENORA MAE, design consultant; b. Phila., Dec. 11, 1942; d. Leonard Anthony and Laura Louise (Gagnon) M.; m. Thomas E. Inks, July 19, 1968 (div. 1976); children: Shawn Anthony, Michael Thomas E. BA, U. Calif., Berkeley, 1964; diploma, Savannah Sch. Interior Design, 1969. Lic. real estate assoc., Calif. Packaging designer Mobil Chem. Corp., Woodland, Calif., 1960-64; interior decorator Brewer's, Sacramento, 1964-65, Cannell & Chaffin, L.A., 1965-66; flight attendant Continental Airlines, L.A., 1966-68; owner, gen. mgr. Country Charisma Gifts, Sacramento, Woodland, Calif., 1971-78; real estate agt. George Willis & Assocs., Woodland, 1978-80; exec. sec. to pres. PFA Fin. Svcs., Davis, Calif., 1980-82; sr. corp. officer, asst. sec. of corp. Bank of Woodland, 1982-87; co-mgr., design cons. The Ltd., Woodland, 1988—. Bd. dirs., officer, Woodland Opera House, Inc., 1983—, chmn. restoration project, 1985-89; bd. dirs., past chmn. Woodland City Parking/Circulation Commn. Mem. U. Calif. Alumni Assn. (pres.), Nat. Bd. Realtors, Calif. Bd. Realtors, LWV, Yolo County Hist. Soc. (bd. dirs., past officer). Republican. Roman Catholic. Home: 550 Walnut St Woodland CA 95695

MONAGAN, MARILEE, state agency administrator; b. Stockton, Calif., Sept. 9, 1947; d. Robert Timothy JR. AND Margaret Ione (Angwin) M. AA, Am. River Coll., Sacramento, 1981; BA, Nat. U., Sacramento, 1986. Legis. sec. Calif. State Senate, Sacramento, 1968-73; info. service dir. Calif. Research, Sacramento, 1973-74; cons. Calif. State Assembly, Sacramento, 1974-81; spl. asst. U.S. Dept. Health and Human Services, Washington, 1981-83; exec. officer Calif. Dept. Social Services, Sacramento, 1983—; mem. State Maternal, Child and Adolescent Health Bd., Sacramento, 1985—, Child Devel. Programs adv. com., Sacramento, 1986—. Mem. Sacramento Pub. TV, 1975—, Sacramento Pub. Radio, 1986—, Sacramento Symphony Support Group, 1983—, Citizens for a Better Sacramento, 1988—; co-founder Gov.'s Women Appointees Council State of Calif., 1984—; chair Rep. task force Nat. Women's Polit. Caucus of Calif., 1980-81; bd. dirs. Calif. Rep. League, 1975—. Mem. Child Welfare League of Am., Sacramento Women's Network, Friends of 6. Club: Comstock (Sacramento). Home: 2912 Pasatiempo Pl Sacramento CA 95833

MONAGHAN, NANCY C., journalist; b. Olean, N.Y., May 13, 1945; d. Stephen Francis Cipot and June (Butler) Cipot Duffey; m. G. Patrick Monaghan Jr., June 24, 1967 (div. 1973). Student U. Rochester, 1974-75. Mng. editor City Newspapers, Rochester, N.Y., 1973-75; pres. Mill Sq. Communications, Rochester, 1975-77; reporter, day metro editor Democrat and Chronicle, Rochester, 1977-82, metro editor, 1982; nat. editor, day nat. editor USA Today, Washington, 1982-84, mng. editor, news, 1984-89; pres., pub. Pub. Opinion Newspaper, Chambersburg, Pa., 1989—. Chmn. Nat. Communications Council, Va. Tech., Blacksburg, 1986-89; mem. Wilson Coll. and Pa. State U./Mt. Alto Pres.' Adv. Couns., 1989—. Recipient Matrix award Women in Communications, 1982, Spot News Reporting award N.Y. State AP, 1979, 82, Legal Reporting award N.Y. State Bar Assn., 1981, Govt. Reporting, award N.Y. State Pubs. Assn., 1973, 74, Polit. Reporting award N.Y. State Pubs. Assn., 1975. Mem. Am. Newspsaper Pubs., AP Mng. Editors (gen. news com.), Nat. Soc. Profl. Journalists (nat. membership chmn. 1984-85, Rochester chpt. pres. 1980-81, Washington chpt. treas. 1988-89). Office: Pub Opinion Newspaper 77 N 3d St Chambersburg PA 17201

MONAHAN, KATHLEEN MARIE, management executive; b. Wash., July 25, 1947; d. Patrick H. and Gertrude (Pennell) M.; m. Edward H. Barker III, Oct. 15, 1966 (div. 1978); children: Edward H. IV, Christian M.; m. R. Frank Busby, Dec. 31, 1979 (dec. 1990). Student, Ohio U., Athens, 1965-66, Nova Community Coll., Alex, Va., 1977; BBA in Acctg., George Wash. U., 1979; MBA in Fin., Am. U., Wash., 1986. Pub. auditor Touche Ross, Wash., 1979; gen. mgr. Busby Assocs., Inc., Arlington, Va., 1979-81; negotiator Dept. Navy, Naval Sea System Command, Wash., 1981—; principle contracting officer Dept. Navy Naval Sea System Command, Wash., 1986—; br. head Dept. Navy, Naval Sea System Command, Wash., 1988—. Recipient Fellowship award Sec. Navy Graduate Sch., 1985-86. Mem. Finl. Mgmt. Assn. Office: CDR Naval Sea Systems Comm Dept Navy Code 0262 Washington DC 20362

MONAHAN, KATHLEEN MARY, retired investment company executive; b. Long Beach, N.Y., Mar. 30, 1938; d. Henry Christian and Daphne Elizabeth (Mulligan) Schlaich; m. Charles Joseph Monahan, Sept. 10, 1960; children: Bryan Charles, Daniel John, Mary Kathleen. BA, Dunbarton Coll., 1959; MS in Edn., St. John's U., 1960. Cert. permanent tchr., N.Y. Grad. asst. St. John's U., Jamaica, N.Y., 1959, adminstrv. asst., 1959-60; tchr. Abbey Lane Sch., Levittown, N.Y., 1960-61; corp. treas. Bus. Investment Group Montgomery County, Inc., Rockville, Md., 1985-90; ret., 1990—. Block capt. Old Farm Civic Assn., Rockville, 1973; mem. Parents Exec. Coun., Loyola Coll., Md. Mem. Nat. Capital Law League, AAUW (chairperson cultural interests Bethesda and Chevy Chase brs.), Nat. Mus. for Women in the Arts (charter mem.). Avocations: travel, theater, yoga, aerobic dance. Home: 7018 Old Cabin Ln Rockville MD 20852

MONAHAN, MARIE TERRY, lawyer; b. Milford, Mass., June 26, 1927; d. Francis V. and Marie I. (Casey) Terry; m. John Henry Monahan, Aug. 25, 1951; children: Thomas F., Kathleen J., Patricia M., John Terry, Moira M., Deirdre M. AB, Radcliffe Coll., 1949; JD, New Eng. Sch. Law, 1975. Bar: Mass. 1977, U.S. Dist. Ct. Mass. 1978, U.S. Supreme Ct. 1982. Tchr. French and Spanish Holliston (Mass.) High Sch., 1949-52; pvt. practice Newton, Mass., 1977—. Mem. Mass. Bar Assn., Mass. Assn. Women Lawyers (pres. 1986). Home and Office: 34 Foster St Newtonville MA 02160

MONAHAN, MARILYN GRACE, educational administrator; b. Holyoke, Mass., Feb. 11, 1948; d. Michael and Grace (Ramondetta) M. BEd, Westfield State Coll., 1970; MEd, U. N.H., 1975. Tchr. Elem. Sch., Alton, N.H., 1970-72, Goffstown, N.H., 1972-83; pres. Nat. Edn. Assn., N.H., 1983—. Mem. Gov.'s Adv. Com. Educational Block Grants 1981, N.H. Constitutional convention, 1984. Mem. Nat. Edn. Assn. (st. exec. bd. 1977—, v.p. 1981-83), Nat. Council St. Edn. Assns., N.H. Educators Polit. Action Com., St. Council Tchr. Edn. Roman Catholic. Home: 962 Goffstown Rd Manchester NH 03102 Office: NEA 103 N State St Concord NH 03301

MONAT-HALLER, ROSALYN KRAMER, service executive; b. Charleston, S.C., Apr. 25, 1945; d. Isadore and Irma Kramer; m. Raphael M. Haller, July 24, 1983; children: David Kramer, Adam Jeffrey. BS, Emerson Coll., 1966; MEd, Boston U., 1967. Lic. profl. counselor; lic. independent social worker, speech pathologist, S.C. Dir. therapeutic svc. SCDMR Coastal Ctr., Ladson, S.C., 1967—; coord. Carolina Cleft Lip & Palate ctr., Charleston, 1967—; profl. counselor, social worker, speech pathologist Allied Therapeutic Svcs., Summerville, S.C., 1986—. Author: (book, video tape) Sexuality and the Mentally Retarded; presenter workshops on Sexuality and the Mentally Retarded; appeared on the Phil Donahue Show. Chmn. state-wide bd. Very Spl. Arts S.C., Ladson; bd. mem. Sexual Abuse Task Force, Charleston, The Children's Ctr., Charleston. Mem. Am. Assn. of Sex Educators, Counselors and Therapists, Am. Assn. for Counseling and Devel., Am. Speech, Lang. and Hearing Assn. Home: 104 Martin Ln Summerville SC 29485

MONCHEK, LANA TERI, university administrator; b. Bronx, N.Y., Sept. 17; d. Sydney and Pearl (Ungar) M. EdB, SUNY, Buffalo, 1968; MEd, U. Miami, 1969; EdS, U. Fla., 1974; JD, U. Miami, 1981; PhD, U. Fla., 1982. Bar: Fla., 1981. Tchr. Broward County Pub. Schs., Hollywood, Fla., 1969-81, Dade County Pub. Schs., Miami, Fla., 1982-83; asst. dir. devel. research U. Miami, Coral Gables, Fla., 1983-85, dir. devel. research, 1985—. Bd. dirs. Goldstein Hebrew Acad., Miami, 1985-87; vol. Miami Youth Mus., 1985-86; mem. Ctr. for Fine Arts, Miami, Dade County Planned Giving Council, 1985—, Council Advancement and Support of Edn., 1983—; mem. bench and bar unit B'nai B'rith, Dade County, Fla.; vol. guide Vizcaya, Dade County, 1986. Office: U Miami Dept Devel Rsch 5807 Ponce de-Leon Blvd Miami FL 33124 also: PO Box 248073 Miami FL 33124

MONCYS, MARIA TERESA, teacher; b. Kraslava, Daugaupils, Latvia, June 6, 1931; d. Benedikt and Marija (Gaidelils) Milass; m. Kazimieras Mocys, May 29, 1954; 1 child, Linda Maria. BA, Lake Forest Coll., 1966; M in Edn., U. Lavern, 1977. Tchr. Mundelein Elem. Sch., 1966-76; cons. The Fourth-R-Responsbility, Mundelein, Ill., 1977-80, Mundelein Elem. Sch. Dist. 75, 1977-80, Responsibility Edn., Mundelein, Career Edn., Mundelein, 1977-80; tchr. Mundelein Elem. Sch. Dist. 75, 1981—. Mem. Am. Assn. U. Women, Mundelein Elem. Edn. Assn., Ill. Edn. Assn., Nat. Edn. Assn., United Lithuanian Relief Orgn. Republican. Roman Catholic. Home: 700 Liberty Bell Ln Libertyville IL 60048

MONDECAR, MERCEDES CONSUELO, biology educator; b. Jamaica, N.Y., July 6, 1951; d. Ernest Elias and Marjorie Louise (Inwood) M. BS, Ga. State U., 1972; MS, U. Ga., 1974; PhD, U. Ark., 1982. Vis. asst. prof. U. Dallas, Irving, Tex., 1983; rsch. assoc. Bishop Coll., Dallas, 1983-84; instr. Dallas County Community Coll. System, Dallas, 1983-85; rsch. assoc. So. Meth. U., Dallas, 1984-85; asst. prof. Spelman Coll., Atlanta, 1985-87, Morehouse Coll., Atlanta, 1987-88; asst. prof. biology Xavier U. La., New Orleans, 1988—; faculty participant EG&G Idaho, Inc., Idaho Falls, 1986, 87, 88; summer faculty rsch. participant Argonne (Ill.) Nat. Lab., 1989. Vol. registrar Dallas Mus. Natural History, 1983-85; vol. Bachman Therapeutic Recreation Ctr., Dallas, 1984-85, DeKalb Recreation, Parks and Cultural Affairs, Decatur, 1986-88. Ga. Bd. Regents scholar, 1968-69. Mem. AAAS, Am. Soc. Microbiology, Sigma Xi, Alpha Lambda Delta, Beta Beta Beta. Office: Xavier U La Palmetto and Pine Sts New Orleans LA 70125

MONEK, DONNA MARIE, pharmacist; b. New Brunswick, N.J., Aug. 9, 1947; d. James Frank and Angeline Eleanor (Marzella) M. BS, Phila. Coll. of Pharmacy, 1970; MBA, Fairleigh Dickinson U., East Rutherford, N.J., 1976. Reg. pharmacist, N.J. Staff pharmacist Freehold (N.J.) Area Hosp., 1971-72, dir. pharmacy, 1972-76; pharmacy adminstr. Rahway (N.J.) Hosp., 1976—; cons. home health care intravenous therapy, Rahway, N.J., 1985. Rep. committeewoman Middlesex County, 1972-86; Bd. of Health, Metuchen, N.J., 1987—. Mem. Am. Soc. Hosp. Pharmacists, N.J. Hosp. Assn.

(group purchasing 1980-88, chairperson profl. standards 1989-90, vice chairperson state pharmacy com. 1990—), Am. Pharm. Assn., N.J. Soc. Hosp. Pharmacists, N.J. Pharm. Assn., Metuchen Rep. Club., Cranford Dramatic Club, Kappa Epsilon. Roman Catholic. Office: Rahway Hosp 865 Stone St Rahway NJ 07065

MONFERRATO, ANGELA MARIA POOLE, entrepreneur, investor, writer; b. Wissembourg, Alsace-Loraine, France, July 19, 1948; came to U.S., 1950; d. Albert Carmen and Anna Maria (Vieri) M.; m. James William Joseph Poole. Diplomate, Pensionnat Florissant, Lausanne, Switzerland, 1966-67; BS in Consumer Related Studies, Pa. State U., 1971, postgrad., 1971-72; postgrad., Mitchel-Giurgola Architects, 1974-75. Simultaneous translator Inst. for Achievement of Human Potential, Phila., 1976-78; art dir. The Artworks, Sumneytown, Pa., 1975-76; asst. productionist Film Space, State College, Pa., 1976; real property mgr. Pla. 15 Condominium, Ft. Lauderdale, Fla., 1979-80; legal asst. Ft. Lauderdale, Fla., 1981-85; saleswoman Rising Sun the Real Estate Corp. South Fla., Ft. Lauderdale, 1986—; pres. Kideos Video Prodns., 1985—, photographer, designer. Filmmaker Red Cross Canoe and Kayak Safety Film, 1976; patentee reflective vest. Home and Office: Box 333 Cascade CO 80809

MONGARELLA, GEORGENE HUGHES, interior designer; b. Yonkers, N.Y., May 28, 1951; d. George Victor Hughes and Joan Alicia (Smith) Dobransky; m. Joseph Andrew Mongarella, Nov. 18, 1973. A in Interior Design, N.Y. Sch. Design, 1978; BA in Bus. Adminstrn., Mercy Coll., Dobbs Ferry, N.Y., 1986. Hostess, bookkeeper Red Coach Grill, Yonkers, 1967-69; mgr. customer svc. Consol. Edison Co., White Plains, N.Y., 1969-86; chief exec. officer The Color Schemer Ltd., Scarsdale, N.Y., 1983—. Advisor Jr. Achievement, Elmsford, 1981-83; cons. Yonkers Pub. Schs., 1986, Masked Ball, Am. Leukemia Soc., Elmsford, 1987; fundraiser Westchester Leukemia Soc., Elmsford, N.Y., 1987-88; fundraiser, tchr. design Yonkers Bd. Edn., 1988—; designer Gala Gourmet, March of Dimes, Rye, N.Y., 1989. Mem. Profl. Women in Constrn. (bd. dirs. 1986-87), Am. Soc. Interior Designers, Am. Womens Econ. Devel., Yonkers C. of C., Interior Design Soc., Illuminating Engring. Soc., Scarsdale Antiques Club. Republican. Roman Catholic. Home and Office: The Color Schemer Ltd 18 Coralyn Rd Scarsdale NY 10583

MONGOLD, SANDRA K., corporate executive; b. Springfield, Ohio, Aug. 14, 1947; d. Robert Harold and Norma Jean (Fennessy) Rine; m. Alan Darrell Mabry, Aug. 18, 1968 (div. 1977); m. Danny Willard Mongold, Nov. 16, 1979; children: Brian Alan Mabry, Krista Marie Mabry. Student, Wright State U., Urbana Coll., So. State Coll., Ohio. Acctg. clk. Irwin Co., Wilmington, Ohio, 1968-80, asst. treas., 1980-85, treas., 1985—, new product com., 1985—. Mem. adv. bd. So. State Coll. Mem. Nat. Assn. Accts., Nat. Assn. Female Execs., Am. Mgmt. Assn., Nat. Corp. Cash Mgmt. Assn., Wilmington C. of C. (dir., bd. dirs., treas. 1990). Republican. Presbyterian. Avocations: golf, bowling. Home: 330 Washington Ave Wilmington OH 45177 Office: Irwin Co 92 Grant Wilmington OH 45177

MONICAL, MARY CHRISTINE, biotechnology marketing executive; b. Cin., Apr. 6, 1950; d. Robert Duane and Carol Arnetha (Dean) M. B.S., U. Miami, 1972, postgrad., 1973; postgrad. Butler U., 1980. Tech. specialist Am. Dade div. Am. Hosp. Supply Corp., Miami, Fla., 1976-79; sales rep. Gen. Diagnostics Co., Morris Plains, N.J., 1980-81, microbiology specialist, 1981-83; sales rep. Coulter Immunology, Hialeah, Fla., 1983-85, regional sales mgr., 1985-86, mktg. dir. FAST Systems, Inc., Gaithersburg, Md., 1986—. Recipient best sales tng. performance award Gen. Diagnostics, 1980; named to Pres.'s Club, Outstanding Sales Rep., Coulter Electronics, 1984-85, 85-86. Home: 20415 Sunbright Ln Germantown MD 20874

MONK, DARILYN ANITA, pharmaceutical company executive; b. Gary, Ind., Sept. 13, 1951; d. James Williams Jr. and Jean Anita (Johnson) Campos; m. Amos J. Monk, May 8, 1984; children: Lance, Juadrena, Tawana. BA in Journalism, Ind. U., 1974. With Abbott Labs., Abbott Park, Ill., 1986—, supr., 1986—. Founder, editor newsletter CCS Express, 1988. Vice pres. Dist. 6 Sch. Bd., Zion, Ill., 1987—; mem. Lake County Bus. Edn. Consortium, 1989—. Mem. NAFE, Ind. U. Alumni Assn. Baptist. Home: 1913 Gideon Zion IL 60099 Office: Abbott Labs One Abbott Pkwy D36MAP304W Abbott Park IL 60064

MONK, JANICE JONES, women's studies researcher, university program administrator; b. Sydney, Australia, Mar. 13, 1937; came to U.S., 1961; d. Harold Frederick and Edith Emily (Collins) J.; m. David Monk, July 31, 1964. BA with honors, U. Sydney, 1958; MA, U. Ill., 1963, PhD, 1972. Instr. geography U. Ill., Urbana, 1967-72, asst. prof., 1972-80; assoc. dir. women's studies U. Ariz., Tucson, 1980-83, exec. dir., 1983—; cons. Nat. Geog. Soc., 1979-81, 86, 87; mem. U.S. Nat. Com. Internat. Geog. Union, Washington, 1980-88, vice chairperson gender study group, 1988—; bd. dirs. Ctr. for Geography in Higher Edn., Oxford, Eng. Co-editor: Women and the Arizona Economy, 1987, The Desert is No Lady, 1987, Western Women: Their Land, Their Lives, 1988; contbr. articles to various publs. Mem. rsch. com. nat. bd. YWCA, N.Y.C.; bd. dirs. Prescott Coll., 1990—. Mem. Assn. Am. Geographers (councilor 1978-81, meritorious svc. award perspectives on women group 1988), Nat. Coun. Geog. Edn. (sec. 1984-86, bd. dirs. 1980-83), Nat. Women's Studies Assn., Soc. Woman Geographers (Washington, nat. counselor). Office: U Ariz SW Inst Rsch Women 102 Douglass Tucson AZ 85721

MONNOT, GAIL ECHOLS, university program director; b. L.A., Nov. 29, 1941; d. James Jack and Paschal (Morris) Echols; m. LeRoy Dean Severe, Nov. 21, 1962 (dec. 1970); children: Christopher, Ammie, Steve, Tom; m. Michael Roger Monnot, Sept. 30, 1972; 1 child: Tim. BA in English, Okla. State U., 1963, MS in Mass Communications, 1986. Donor rsch. specialist, proposal writer Okla. State U. Found., Stillwater, 1986-88; communications coord. Okla. State U. Alumni Assn., Stillwater, 1988—; pub. info. officer Okla. State U., Stillwater, 1988—. Group leader annual fund drive Boy Scouts Am., Stillwater, 1990. Mem. NAFE, Coun. Advancement and Support Edn. Democrat. Roman Catholic. Home: 516 Harned Stillwater OK 74075 Office: Okla State U 217 Public Information Stillwater OK 74078

MONRO, FRANCES BERNIECE, secondary educator; b. Winnipeg, Manitoba, Canada, Sept. 6, 1922; d. Angela Helen (Ester) DacKey; m. Robert Lewis Monro. BS, Mo. U., Columbia, Mo., 1960; MA in Edn., Mo. U., 1961. Cert. secondary educator, Calif., Mo. Tchr. Adams Jr. High Sch., Los Angeles, 1962-63, Excelsior High Sch., Norwalk, Calif., 1963-81, John Glenn High Sch., Norwalk, 1981—. Editor: Collection of Mystery Stories by Students, 1986-89, Collection of Poems, 1989, Creative Writing Jour. (John Glenn High Sch.). Mem. AAUW, Calif. Assn. Tchrs. of English, Pi Lambda Theta. Republican. Home: 1710 Longfellow Rd Orange TX 77630 Office: John Glenn High Sch 13520 Shoemaker St Norwalk CA 90650

MONROE, JULIA KATHRYN, program analyst; b. Sacramento, Nov. 21, 1961; d. William K. and Jackelean D. (Burton) M. BA in English, U. Calif., Davis, 1984, postgrad., 1985. With Army C.E., Sacramento, 1986-88, program analyst, 1988—; instr. video about computer software Army C.E. Author: (with others) Safety Pals Tackle Peer Pressure and Babysitting, 1988. Mem. Jr. League of Sacramento, Inc., Kappa Kappa Gamma (corr. sec. Davis chpt. 1983). Republican. Home: 3241 Clairidge Way Sacramento CA 95821 Office: Army C E 650 Capitol Mall Sacramento CA 95814-4794

MONROE, KAREN MARIE, newspaper reporter; b. Santa Monica, Calif., Feb. 28, 1962; d. Lewis Bell and Norma (Romaine) Barnes; m. Michael James Monroe, Apr. 15, 1989. Student, Humboldt State U., 1980-82; BA in Journalism, Calif. State U., Long Beach, 1985; postgrad., UCLA, 1987-89. Reporter Grunion Gazette, Long Beach, 1984-86; svc. coord. Adia Pers. Svcs., L.A., 1986; account exec. Good Life Ind. Jour., Santa Monica, 1986-87; editor Long Beach News & Entertainment, 1988; reporter Wave Newspapers, L.A., 1988, features editor, 1988-89; freelance writer L.A. and Santa Monica, 1989—; reporter L.A. Ind. Newspapers, 1989—; freelance writer Intersound Inc., West Hollywood, Calif., 1990—. Republican. Presbyterian. Home: 417 Tamarack Ave Unit 46 Apt 46 Inglewood CA 90301

MONROE, MARGARET ELLEN, retired library educator; b. N.Y.C., May 21, 1914; d. Ralph Brigham and Ruth (Cleaveland) M. BA, N.Y. State Coll. for Tchrs., 1935, BS in Libr. Sci., 1936; MA in English, Columbia U., 1939, D. Libr. Sci., 1962. Cert. pub. libr., N.Y. Br. libr., readers adviser, discussion program supr. N.Y. Pub. Libr., N.Y.C., 1939-51; materials specialist, dir. Am. Heritage Project, ALA, Chgo., 1951-53; from asst. prof. to assoc. prof. grad. sch. libr. svc. Rutgers U., New Brunswick, N.J., 1953-63, prof. grad. sch. libr. svc., 1963-81, dir. grad. sch. libr. svc., 1963-70, dir. program on libr. svc. to aging, 1975-77; del to IFLA conf., Moscow, Leningrad, USSR, 1970; pres. Assn. Libr./Info. Student Edn., 1971-72. Author: Library Adult Education, 1963; sr. author: The Challenge of Aging, 1983; editor, author: Reading Guidance & Bibliotherapy, 1971 (pub. issue report) The Challenge of an Aging Society, 1985. Bd. dirs. Madison (Wis.) Sr. Ctr., 1983-87, pres., 1985-86, organizer "Challenge of an Aging Soc., 1986-87; chmn. study com. on long-term care LWV of Dane County, 1988. Fellow for doctoral study Fund for Adult Edn., 1954-55; recipient Disting. Contbn. Edn. for Librarianship award Beta Phi Mu, 1972, Profl. Contbn. to Library and Info. Sci. Edn. award, 1987, Disting. Alumni award Columbia U. Sch. Library Svc. Alumni Assn., 1990; named in recognition in hon. book Festscrift: Reader Services in Libraries (Gail Schlachter, editor). Mem. ALA (pres. adult svcs. div. 1953-83, former chmn. com. on accreditation, Margaret E. Monroe Library Svcs. award named in honor), AAUW, Nat. Coun. Aging. Democrat. Mem. United Ch. of Christ.

MONROY, GLADYS H., lawyer; b. N.Y., Aug. 29, 1937; d. Henry B. and Leanora E. (Low) Chu; m. Jaime L. G. Monroy (div.); m. C. Lawrence Marks, Nov. 29, 1980. BA, Hunter Coll., N.Y., 1957; MS, NYU, 1968, PhD, 1973; JD, U. San Francisco, 1986. Bar: Calif. Lab. technician Sloan-Kettering Institute, N.Y., 1957-60; lab. technician Pub. Health Research Inst., N.Y., 1960-63, research asst., 1963-68; post doctoral fellow Albert Einstein Coll. of Med., Bronx, N.Y., 1973-77; asst. prof. N.Y. Med. Coll., Valhalla, 1977-79; acquisitions editor Acad. Press, Inc., 1979-81; reseach assoc. U. Calif., San Francisco, 1981-83; atty. Irell & Manella, Menlo Park, Calif., 1986-90, ptnr., 1990—. Contbr. articles to profl. jours. Mem. bd. dirs. Project Hogar De Los Ninos, Menlo Park, Calif., 1987, mem. Profl. Women's Network, San Francisco, 1988-. Mem. ABA, Am. Intellectual Property Law Assn., Am. Soc. Human Genetics, Am. Chem. Soc., Calif. Bar Assn., San Francisco Intellectual Property Law Assn., Peninsula Patent Law Assn., Am. Soc. Microbiology, Phi Alpha Delta. Office: Irell & Manella 545 Middlefield Rd Menlo Park CA 94025

MONSON, ANN MARIE, dentist; b. Salem, Mass., Oct. 30, 1951; d. Donald E. and Millie (Allen) M.; m. Donald R. Cain; May 5, 1984. BA, U. Conn., 1974, DMD, 1978. Pvt. practice Spokane, Wash., 1981—; dental dir. Interlake Sch., Medical Lake, 1983—; chmn. Dental Disciplinary Bd. of State of Wash. Pres., bd. dirs. Spokane (Wash.) Ballet Co., 1988. Capt. USAF, 1978-81. Mem. Wash. State Dental Assn., ADA, Spokane Dist. Dental Soc. Roman Catholic. Office: S 3009 Mt Vernon St Spokane WA 99223

MONSON, CAROL LYNN, osteopathic physician, psychotherapist; b. Blue Island, Ill., Nov. 3, 1946; d. Marcus Edward and Margaret Bertha (Andres) M.; m. Frank E. Warden, Feb. 28, 1981. B.S., No. Ill. U., 1968, M.S., 1969; D.O., Mich State Coll. Osteo. Medicine, 1979. Lic. physician, Mich., diplomate Am. Bd. Osteo. Gen. Practitioners, Am. Bd. Osteo. Gen. Practice. Expeditor-psychotherapist H. Douglas Singer Zone Ctr., Rockford, Ill., 1969-71; psychotherapist Tri-County Mental Health, St. Johns, Mich., 1971-76; pvt. practice psychotherapy, East Lansing, Mich., 1976-80; intern Lansing Gen. Hosp., Mich., 1979-80, residency dir. family practice, 1988—; pvt. practice osteo. medicine, Lansing, 1980—; mem. staff Ingham Med. Hosp., Lansing Gen. Hosp., chmn. gen practice, 1987-89; field instr. Sch. Social Work, U. Mich., 1973-76; clin. instr. Central Mich. Dept. Psychology, 1974-75; clin. prof. Mich. State U., 1980-88, asst. prof., 1988—, tng. supr. family medicine residency, 1988—; mem. adv. bd. Substance Abuse Clearinghouse, Lansing, 1983-85, Kelly Health Care, Lansing, 1983-85, Americor Health Svcs., Lansing, 1984—. Mem. Am. Osteo Assn., Am. Assn. Family Practice, Internat. Transactional Analysis Assn., Mich. Assn. Physicians and Surgeons, Ingham County Osteo. Assn., Nat. Assn. Career Women (conv. com. 1984—), Lansing Assn. Career Women. Lodge: Zonta (chmn. service com. Mid Mich. Capital Area chpt.). Avocations: gardening; orchid growing; antique collecting. Office: 7201 W Saginaw St Ste 305 Lansing MI 48917

MONSON, DIANNE LYNN, educator; b. Minot, N.D., Nov. 24, 1934; d. Albert Rachie and Iona Cordelia (Kirk) M. B.S., U. Minn., 1956, M.A., 1962, Ph.D., 1966. Tchr., Rochester Pub. Schs. (Minn.), 1966-59, U.S. Dept. Def., Schweinfurt, W.Ger., 1959-61, St. Louis Park Schs. (Minn.), 1961-62; instr. U. Minn., Mpls., 1962-66; prof. U. Wash., Seattle, 1966-82; prof. English edn. U. Minn., Mpls., 1982—, chmn. Curriculum and Instrn., 1986-89. Co-author: New Horizons in the Language Arts, 1972; Children and Books, 6th edit., 1981; Experiencing Children's Literature, 1984; (monograph) Research in Children's Literature, 1976; Language Arts Teaching and Learning Effective Use of Language, 1988. Recipient Outstanding Educator award U. Minn. Alumni Assn., 1983. Fellow Nat. Conf. Rsch. in English (pres. 1990—); mem. Nat. Coun. Tchrs. of English (exec. com. 1979-81), Internat. Reading Assn. (dir. 1980-83), ALA, U.S. Bd. Books for Young People (pres. 1988-90). Lutheran. Home: 740 River Dr Saint Paul MN 55116 Office: U Minn 350 Peik Hall Minneapolis MN 55455

MONSON, NANCY ELEANOR, association executive, consultant; b. Upper Darby, Pa., Aug. 1, 1942; d. Albert Wesley and Dorothy Eleanor (Fretz) Eckenroth; m. Jeffrey Stewart Monson, Dec. 30, 1961; children: Patricia Eleanor, David William. AA, Moorpark Coll., 1978; B Gen. Studies in Communications, Mgmt., U. Tex., Dallas, 1985; M Liberal Arts, So. Meth. U., 1986. Lic. real estate broker, Calif. Real estate assoc. Century 21, Thousand Oaks, Calif., 1976-81; v.p. mktg. and communications The exec. Connection, Richardson, Tex., 1981-83; exec. dir. Cultural Arts Coun. Plano, Tex., 1984; intern Dallas Dept. Pub. Affairs, 1985; exec. dir. Freedom of Info. Found. of Tex., Dallas, 1987—; cons. in field. Columnist Tex. Women's News, 1987-89. Chair communications, adminstrv. bd. Lovers Lane Meth. Ch., 1989. Mem. LWV, Women in Communications, Tex. Media Coalition, Am. Soc. Assn. Execs., Nat. Soc. Fundraising Exec., Tex. Soc. Assn. Execs., Dallas-Ft. Worth Assn. Execs., Press Club Dallas, Dallas Womens Found., Leadership Plano, Leadership Dallas. Republican. Home: 3301 Henri Ct Plano TX 75023 Office: Freedom of Info Found Tex 400 S Record St 6th Fl Dallas TX 75202

MONSON, NANCY PECKEL, writer, editor; b. N.Y.C., Mar. 11, 1959; m. John C. Monson, June 18, 1988. BS magna cum laude, Boston U., 1979. Actress, 1979-86; adminstrv. asst. MIT, Cambridge, 1981; assoc. editor Profl. Postgrad. Svcs., Secaucus, N.J., 1984-87; writer, contbg. editor Cardiology Product News, East Orange, N.J., 1985-86; assoc. editor, reporter The Convention Reporter Group, Secaucus, 1985-88, editor, 1988-90; freelance health writer and editor Pomona, N.Y., 1984—; freelance entertainment writer Pomona, 1988—. Mem. AFTRA, SAG, NAFE. Office: 425 Country Club Ln Pomona NY 10970

MONT, HALLIE BUCHANAN, pediatrician; b. L.A., May 9, 1922; d. Alfred Gordon and Edith Ellen (Hamilton) Buchanan; m. Charles Hansen Mont, June 26, 1944; children: Diane Patrice, Charmain Suzanne. BA, UCLA, 1944; MD, SUNY, 1947. Diplomate Am. Bd. Pediatrics. Intern Calif. Hosp., L.A., 1947-48; resident in pediatrics L.A. Children's Hosp., L.A., 1948-50; pvt. practice L.A. County, 1950—; mem. staff L.A. Children's Hosp., St. Joseph Med. Ctr., Burbank, Calif.; courtesy staff Valley Pres Hosp., Van Nuys, Calif., Verdigo Hills Hosp., Glendale, Calif. Mem. L.A. County Med. Assn., Calif. Med. Assn., Southwestern Pediatric Soc., Am. Acad. Pediatrics. Office: 303 S Glenoaks Blvd Ste 1 Burbank CA 91502

MONTAGUE, BARBARA ANN, chemist; b. Hagerstown, Md., Aug. 29, 1929; d. Daniel Junkin and Alma Hazel (Lehman) Montague. AB, Randolph-Macon Woman's Coll., 1951. Chemist plastics dept. rsch. div. E.I. DuPont Co., Wilmington, Del., 1951-60, info. chemist, 1960, head plastics dept. Info. Ctr., 1961-64, devel. coordinator DuPont Cen. Report Index, 1964-67, supr. Cen. Report Index, 1967-74, mgr. adminstrv. svcs. photo products dept., internat. div., 1974-76, mgr. info. systems devel., 1976-77, personnel asst., 1977-79, compensation mgr., 1979-80, cons. corp. employee relations dept., 1980—. Deacon Presbyn. Ch., Wilmington, 1983—. Mem. Am. Chem. Soc., DAR, Alpha Delta Pi. Republican. Home: 668 Meeting House Rd Hockessin DE 19707 Office: EI DuPont Co Employee Relations Dept Wilmington DE 19898

MONTAGUE, RENE ANN, pharmacist; b. Ashtabula, Ohio, Oct. 19, 1960; d. Donald Emanuel Lucha and May Belle (Hines) VandenAkker; m. Jon Jerome Montague, Nov. 21, 1981; children: Clinton Rostov, Natasha Ann. AS, Grand Rapids Jr. Coll., 1980; BS in Pharmacy, Ferris State Coll., 1982. Registered Pharmicist, Mich., Alaska, No. Ter. Australia. Intern Ingham Med. Ctr., East Lansing, Mich., 1981-82; intern Casuarina Pharmacies, Darwin, No.Ter., Australia, 1983, pharmacist, 1983; pharmacist Hewitt's Drug Store, Anchorage, 1983, Med. Arts Pharmacy, Anchorage, 1983-85, Carr's Quality Ctrs., Anchorage, 1985-89, Fred Meyer Pharmacy, Anchorage, 1989—. Mem. Am. Pharm. Assn., Alaska Pharm. Assn. Home: 2440 Eagle River Rd Eagle River AK 99577 Office: Fred Meyer Pharmacy 1000 E Northern Lights Blvd Anchorage AK 99508

MONTANARO-MCMULLEN, LINDA, educator; b. Painesville, Ohio, Feb. 15, 1945; d. Lunda and Mary Ann (Tabone) Brafford; m. Robert D. McMullen, Aug. 19, 1988; children: Melinda, Joseph, Melissa, Jason. BS, Kent State U., 1968; M, Ariz. State U., 1983. Tchr. Phoenix Union High Sch. Dist., Met. Tech. Vocat. Inst. Phoenix, Geneva (Ohio) High Sch.; bookkeeper/credit investigator Sears Roebuck, Ashtabula, Ohio. Mem. Nat. Bus. Edn. Assn. (speaker/presenter 1989—), Ariz. Bus. Edn. Assn., Western Bus. Edn. Assn., Internat. Soc. Supr. and Curriculum Devel., NEA, Ariz. Edn. Assn., Am. Vocat. Edn. Assn., Ariz. Vocat. Edn. Assn., NAFE, NOW, Disabled Am. Vets. (aux.).

MONTEFERRANTE, JUDITH CATHERINE, cardiologist; b. N.Y., Jan. 27, 1949; d. Stanley and Monica (Vinckus) Sosaris; m. Ronald J. (div. 1983); 1 child, Jason Paul; m. Roger E. Salisbury, Mar. 3, 1990. BS, Adelphi U., Garden City, 1970; MS, SUNY, Buffalo, 1973; MD, Mt. Sinai, N.Y.C., 1978. Attending N.Y. Med. Coll., Valhalla, N.Y., 1983-84; pvt. practice White Plains, N.Y., 1984--; bd. dirs. Am. Heart Assn., Westchester, N.Y., 1987--. Contbr. articles to profl. jours. fellow Am. Colls. of Cardiology, Am. Coll. of Physicians. Fellow Council on Clinical Cardiology of AHA, N.Y. Cardiological Soc.; mem. Political Action Com. of Westchester County Med. Soc., FACC, FACP, Soc. of Critical Care Medicine, AMA. Office: Ste 403 White Plains NY 10605

MONTEITH, DIANNE SOUTHER, education educator, educational administrator; b. Union Center, Wis., Nov. 4, 1935; d. John Patrick and Genevieve (Hahn) Souther; m. John J. Monteith, May 30, 1960 (div. Apr., 1989); children: J. Jay, Bruce S. BS, Marquette U., 1957; MEd, U. Delaware, 1977, PhD, 1983. Psychometrist Racine (Wis.) Vocat. and Adult Sch., 1957-61; tchr. Stone Bank (Wis.) Sch. Dist., 1961, Colt's Neck (N.J.) Sch. Dist., 1964-69, Mt. Pleasant Sch. Dist., Wilmington, Del., 1969-76; pres., dir. Monteith Schs., Inc., Wilmington, 1978-84; exec. v.p. Sharon, Inc., Wilmington, 1984-85; prof. S.C. State Coll., Orangeburg, 1986—; cons. PeeDee Tchrs. Incentive Program, Sumter, S.C., 1988—, Marion-Dillon Tchrs. Incentive Program, 1990—, Westinghouse, Inc., Fayetville, S.C., 1988. Editor jour. Explorations in Education, 1990; contbr. articles to profl. jours. Participant Leadership Orangeburg County, 1990. Mem. AAUW (treas. 1988-90), Nat. Coun. Prof. Edn. Adminstrs., Ea. Edn. Rsch. Assn., Am. Ednl. Rsch., So. Regional Edn. Assn., Phi Delta Kappa (v.p. programs, 1988-90). Republican. Office: SC State Coll Box 2015 Orangeburg SC 29117

MONTEL, JANET MARIE, financial administrator; b. Fort Morgan, Colo., Aug. 28, 1954; d. Heinz Nicholas and Thea Mae (Groves) Silz; m. Jeffrey Lynn Montel, Jan. 4, 1976; 1 child, Ian Norvell. BS, Colo. State U., 1976; MBA, U. Colo., 1989. Bookkeeper Ft. Morgan (Colo.) Community Hosp., 1978-79, data processing mgr., 1979-81, mgr. bus. office, 1981-85, v.p. fin., 1985-86; dir. fin. Brim Hosp. Inc. dba Ft. Morgan Community Hosp., 1986—; fin. cons. Mem. Festival in the Park, Ft. Morgan, 1983—; participant Wirth Washington Seminar, 1989; bd. dirs. Future Bus. Leaders of Am., Ft. Morgan, 1989. Mem. Hosp. Fin. Mgmt. Assn., Omicron Nu. Home: 921 Delores Fort Morgan CO 80701 Office: Fort Morgan Community Hosp 1000 Lincoln St Fort Morgan CO 80701

MONTGOMERY, BETTY D., state legislator. BA, Bowling Green State U.; JD, U. Toledo, 1976. Former criminal clk. Lucas County Common Pleas Ct.; asst. pros. atty. County of Wood, Ohio, pros. atty., 1980-88; asst. pros. atty. City of Perrysburg, Ohio; mem. Ohio Senate, 1989—. Mem. Nat. Dist. Atty. Assn., Ohio Bar Assn., Toledo Bar Assn., Wood County Bar Assn. Address: 11145 Riverbend W Ct Perrysburg OH 43551*

MONTGOMERY, BILLIE LEE, rehabilitation executive; b. Marion, Ky., July 13, 1953; d. Arland and Eva Lee (Gilland) Ramage. AA in Nursing, Paducah Community Coll., 1973. RN, Ky.; cert. ins. rehab. specialist.; qualified rehab. coord., Ky. Staff nurse Crittenden County Hosp., Marion, Ky., 1973-75; commd. 2d lt. USAF, 1975, advanced through grades to capt., 1978; staff nurse, Moody AFB USAF, Valdosta, Ga., 1975-79; nursery supr. U.S. Air Force Acad. Hosp., Colorado Springs, Colo., 1979-82; resigned USAF, 1982; indsl. nurse Ohio River Steel Co., Calvert City, Ky., 1983-85; rehab. specialist Intracorp, Louisville, 1985-87; rehab. supr. Eckman/Freeman, Louisville, 1987-90, mgr. supervision, devel. and tng., 1990—. Mem. NAFE, Nat. Assn. Rehap. Profls. in Pvt. Sector, Assn. Rehab. Nurses, Ky. Assn. Rehab. Nurses, U.S. Humane Soc. Democrat. Baptist. Office: Eckman Freeman Embassey Sq Louisville KY 40224

MONTGOMERY, CHARLOTTE A., cultural organization administrator; b. Taylorville, Ill.; d. Merle P. and Mary L. (Pile) Vancil; m. David E. Montgomery; children: Jason, Daphne, Benjamin. Student, Lincoln Land Community Coll., Sagamon State U. Chief fiscal officer Ill. State Mus. Soc., Springfield. Mem. NAFE, AMA, Women in Mgmt., Soc. Non-Profit Orgns., Ill. Arts Alliance, Ill. Mus. Soc., Smithsonian Inst. (assoc.), Phi Theta Kappa.

MONTGOMERY, DENISE KAREN, nurse; b. N.Y.C., Dec. 23, 1951; d. Thomas Cornell and Dorothy Marie (Castine) Simons; m. Timothy Bruce Montgomery, July 19, 1974 (div. Feb. 1981); m. Joseph Samuel Montgomery, Aug. 20, 1983. A.D.N., San Jacinto Coll., 1971. RN, Tex. Charge nurse Aaron's Women's Clinic, Houston, 1977; rsch. asst. dept. obgyn Baylor Coll. Medicine, Houston, 1977-81, nursing supr., 1979-81, program coord. population control program, 1979-81; nurse Dr. Eric J. Haufrect, Houston, 1982-83; office mgr., supr. Dr. J.S. Montgomery III, 1987—, Dr. Samuel Law, Houston, 1983-84. Contbr. articles to med. jours. Recipient Disting. Pub. Svc. award Am. Heart Assn., 1976; recipient several grants. Mem. Nat. Assn. Coll. Ob-Gyn. Democrat. Roman Catholic. Home: 8202 N Tahoe Houston TX 77040

MONTGOMERY, GLADYS (GLADYS MONTGOMERY SINGER), writer; b. Natick, Mass.; d. Charles Norton and Myrtle (Cates) Taylor; B.A., Wellesley Coll.; m. Alexander John Montgomery (dec. 1955); m. 2d, Russell E. Singer, 1975 (dec. 1975). Sci. and semi-tech. writer McGraw-Hill mags. in Washington office, 1942-61, Washington reporter editor Textile World, 1943-46, Washington reporter Electronics, 1943-44, Washington editor, 1944-57, Washington rep., Nucleonics, 1947-48, co-editor, 1949-52; Washington reporter Bus. Week, 1952-61; feature writer Sci. Illustrated, 1957-61; then freelance, now ret. Mem. Pres.'s Adv. Com. on Arts, Kennedy Center, 1970-76; bd. dirs. D.C. League Republican Women 1983-85; adv. com. Former Senator Margaret Chase Smith Library, 1984—. Interviewee Washington Press Club Found. Oral History Project, 1990. Recipient citation Armed Forces Communications and Electronics Assn., 1970. Mem. AAAS, Nat. Assn. Sci. Writers, Women's Nat. Press Club (pres. 1957-58), Nat. Press Club, Am. News Women's Club. Clubs: Sulgrave, Chevy Chase, Wellesley College (Washington). Home: 2725 29th St NW Apt 605 Washington DC 20008

MONTGOMERY, JANET ANN, publisher; b. Elma, Wash., Nov. 12, 1946; d. Leslie E. and Marian E. (Bullock) Hicks; divorced; children: Stacy Lynn, Michele Lee. Salesperson Century 21 Real Estate, Madison, Wis., 1977-81; founder/mgr. Housework Anonymous, Madison, 1983-86; founder, chief exec. officer Sr. News and Views, Rohnert Park, Calif., 1986—. Leader Girl Scouts U.S., Madison, 1980-82; tchr. personal growth seminars, Madison, 1984; core leader Caring Community, Madison, 1984-85. Mem. NAFE, Santa Rosa C. of C. Office: Senior News and Views 2 Padre Pkwy Rohnert Park CA 94928

MONTGOMERY, JUDY G(LASS), child care center executive; b. Jacksonville, Fla., July 19, 1945; d. Paul H. and Pearle V. (Greene) Glass; m. Jack T. Montgomery, Jan. 4, 1970; 1 child, Sean Christopher. BS in Math., La. State U., 1967. Group chief operator South Central Bell Telephone Co., Baton Rouge, 1967-69; systems analyst Sperry Univac, Baton Rouge, 1969-70; pres. M & M Playland Inc., Baton Rouge, 1973-87, L'Ecole, Inc., Baton Rouge, 1976-87, Child Care Info., Baton Rouge, 1984—; cons. in field. Author: Door To Learning, 1983; contbg. author and mem. adv. bd. for tng. manuals Day Care Directions, 1984. Chairperson La. Women's Conf. on Day Care, Baton Rouge, 1977; day care rep. Senator Thomas Hudson, Baton Rouge, 1977; mem. Gov.'s Council on Children, La., 1980; lobbyist children's services Baton Rouge, 1976—; bd. dirs. Baton Rouge Vocat. Tech. Sch., 1980—. Mem. La. Fedn. Child Devel. Ctrs. (lobbyist 1976-81, pres. 1978-81), Baton Rouge C. of C. (edn. com. 1980). Avocations: reading, sewing. Office: Child Care Info Inc PO Box 45212 Dept 223 Baton Rouge LA 70895

MONTGOMERY, LOLA JUNE, retired psychology educator; b. Larkinburg, Kans., June 16, 1917; d. Charles LeRoy and Katie (Sauer) M. AB, U. Kans., 1941; MA, U. No. Colo., 1944; EdD, Columbia U., 1958; postgrad., Chgo. U., U. Minn., 1953, 56. Tchr. Rural Dist. 63, Atchison County, Kans., 1935-37, Cheyenne County Community High Sch., St. Francis, Kans., 1941-43; instr. social and biol. scis. Pueblo (Colo.) Jr. Coll., 1944-46; dean of women Mayville (N.D.) State Tchrs. Coll., 1946-47; dir. student personnel Phillips U., Enid, Okla., 1948-63; prof. developmental and counseling psychology U. No. Colo., Greeley, 1962-83, now prof. emeritus; cons. in field. Author: Young Adults: A Call to Dialogue, 1980. Vol. tchr. Orange Peel Clinic alternative sch., Greeley, 1987—. Danforth scholar, 1956. Mem. Am. Psychol. Assn. Democrat. Home: 2043 22d Ave Apt 205 Greeley CO 80631

MONTGOMERY, RUTH C., state legislator; m. Robert H. Montgomery. Former mem. Tenn. State Ho. of Reps.; now mem. Tenn. State Senate. Republican. Home: 3433 Parkcliffe Dr Kingsport TN 37664*

MONTGOMERY, SUSAN RENEE, medical group administrator; b. Gary, Ind., July 10, 1954; d. Dewitt and Vinie Estelle (Winchester) Eskridge; divorced; children: Thomas Andrew, Nathan Dewitt Harris. Student, Purdue U., 1984—. Adminstrv. asst. Continental Bank, Chgo., 1972-74; acctg. clk. U.S. Steel Corp., Gary, 1974-80, metall. technician, 1980-83; registrar Meth. Hosp., Gary, 1983-86, personnel coord., 1986-88; sec., treas. Words Unltd., Inc., Gary, 1988, bus. mgr., 1988—; adminstr. Chiola Med. Assocs., P.C., Gary, 1988—. Mem. NAFE, Am. Coll. Med. Group Adminstrs., Med. Group Mgmt. Assn., Inst. Indsl. Engrs. Democrat. Baptist. Office: Chiola Med Assocs PC 3535 Broadway Gary IN 46409

MONTGOMERY, SUZANNE HOWARD, psychologist; b. Atlanta, Apr. 19, 1949; d. Douglas Legate and Patricia Jean (Younkins) Howard; m. William McKinley Copley III, June 14, 1985. BA, U. Fla., 1971, PhD, 1982; MSW, Mich. State U., 1973. Lic. psychologist, Fla. Dir. aftercare svcs. Mental Health ctr. Univ. Hosp., Jacksonville, Fla., 1976-77, dir. mental health cons. and edn. Mental Health ctr., 1977-80, dir. tng. and devel., 1981-85; owner, cons. psychologist Montgomery, Copley & Assocs., Inc., Jacksonville, 1985—. Mem. allocation panel United Way Fund, 1988; chairperson panel United Way Fund, 1988; chairperson Fla. Community Coll. of Jacksonville, Open Campus Adv. Com., 1982—; bd. dirs. Mental Health Resource Ctr., Jacksonville, 1985—, pres., 1989—; mem. Jacksonville Women's Network, 1983—; bd. dirs., tng. chmn. Jacksonville Jr. League, 1985-87. Mem. Am. Psychol. Assn., Am. Soc. Personnel Adminstrs., Fla. Psychol. Assn., Phi Kappa Phi, Phi Alpha. Home: 925 Alhambra Dr N Jacksonville FL 32207 Office: Montgomery Copley & Assocs 1812 Atlantic Blvd Jacksonville FL 32207

MONTGOMERY, VELMANETTE, state senator; b. Tex. M.Ed., NYU; student U. Ghana. Mem. N.Y.C. Dist. 13 Sch. Bd., 1977-80, pres., from 1977; former co-dir. advocacy group Child Care Inc.; mem. N.Y. Senate, 1984—, mem. child care, consumer protection, health, social services, commerce and mental hygiene coms. Fellow Inst. Ednl. Leadership, 1981, Revson Found., 1984. Democrat. Office: 70 Lafayette Ave Brooklyn NY 11217 Other: N Y State Senate Albany NY 12224*

MONTGOMERY, YOLONDA DENESE, engineer, computer systems analyst, software executive; b. Columbus, Ohio, June 14, 1958; d. Harry Ulysses and Willie Nell (Haley) Murph; m. Willie Lewis Montgomery, Mar. 22, 1980; children: Tonisha Rochelle, Candice Sherese. Student, Nat. Cryptologic Sch., 1984-86; BSBA, Ohio State U., 1980; postgrad., Cen. Mich. U., 1988. Systems analyst and test mgr. Joint Interoperability for Tactical Command/Control Systems, Langley AFB, Va., 1981-82; joint systems analyst USAF, 1982; computer systems analyst, programmer Ft. Meade, Md., 1983-87; software installation test engr., integration sect. mgr. Geodynamics Corp., Gaithersburg, Md., 1987-90, software installation and integration sect. mgr., 1990—. Mem. Provinces Civic Assn., Jessup, 1984—. Capt. USAF, 1981-87. Named one of Outstanding Young Women Am., 1988. Mem. NAFE, Am. Mgmt. Assn., Armed Forces Communications and Electronics Assn., Sigma Iota Epsilon. Democrat. Home: 1820 Lasalle Pl Severn MD 21144-1612 Office: Geodynamics Corp 18500 Office Park Dr Gaithersburg MD 20879

MONTI, LAURA ANNE, psychology educator; b. Evanston, Ill., Feb. 28, 1959; d. LeRoy John and Mary Alice (Foley) M. BA in Psychology, U. Ariz., 1981; MA in Cognitive Psychology, Loyola U., Chgo., 1986, PhD, 1987; postgrad., Menninger Found., 1988. Mem. bd. dirs., co-owner Monti & Assocs. Inc., Arlington Heights, Ill., 1976—; v.p., co-owner MAM Imports and Creative Gifts, Kildeer, Ill., 1986-89; lectr. psychology Loyola U., Chgo., 1986-89; asst. prof. North Park Coll., Chgo., 1989—; vis. rsch. specialist U. Ill.-Ill. Inst. Devel. Disabilities, 1989-90; cons. Walter H. Sobel FAIA & Assocs., Chgo., 1986—, Yate and Auberle, Oakbrook, Ill., 1987-88. Contbr. articles to profl. jours.; co-author tech. reports to various orgns. Tuition scholar Loyola U., Chgo., 1983-84; recipient Grad. Assistantship, Loyola U., Chgo., 1986. Mem. Am. Psychol. Assn. (div. psychology of women, 1989—, gen. psychology, media psychology, exptl. psychology 1989—), Psi Chi (faculty rep. for North Park Coll. 1989—), Sigma Alpha Iota. Roman Catholic. Home: 632 Happfield Arlington Heights IL 60004

MONTIEL, SUE, healthcare facility administrator; b. Pitts., Kans., Dec. 5, 1960; d. Raymond Matthew Herbat and Judith Kay (Mills) Vincent; m. Uziel Montiel, Oct. 1, 1989. BS in Behavioral Sci. summa cum laude, Westminster Coll. of SLC, 1983; AA in Nursing magna cum laude, Weber State Coll., 1984; BS in Edn. cum laude, Calif. State U., Fresno, 1987. Dir. nursing svcs. Avenal (Calif.) Dist. Hosp., 1987-88; asst. adminstr. patient care svcs. Coalinga (Calif.) Dist. Hosp., 1989.

MONTLE, JANICE E., food company executive; b. Winchester, Mass., Jan. 15, 1951. BA, Mt. Holyoke Coll., 1972; MBA, Harvard U., 1974. Sr. v.p., chief fin. officer Pepsi-Cola Co., Somers, N.Y., v.p., chief fin. officer Bottling Group; v.p., controller PepsiCo Internat., Purchase, N.Y.; dir. corp. planning Pepsi-Co., Inc., Purchase, N.Y.; sr. investment officer Citibank, N.A., N.Y.C.; bd. dirs. Pepsi-Cola Bottling No. Calif., 1988—. Mem. Harvard Bus. Sch. Club (Westchester/Fairfield) (bd. dirs. 1986-87), Delta Beverages Inc. (bd. dirs. 1988—). Office: Rtes 35 and 100 Somers NY 10589

MONTOOTH, SHEILA CHRISTINE, state agency administrator; b. Pasadena, Calif., Mar. 12, 1952; d. Gerald Frank and Janet Laura (Ebert) M. BS, Calif. State U., L.A., 1974; MPA, Calif. State U., 1985. CPA, Calif. From auditor 1 to tax auditor IV State Bd. of Equalivation, Pasadena, 1974-81; supr. tax auditor 1 State Bd. of Equalivation, West Los Angeles, Calif., 1981-83; bus. taxes adminstr. III State Bd. of Equalivation, Lakewood, Calif., 1984-87; bus. taxes adminstr. IV State Bd. of Equalivation, Downey, Calif., 1987—. Recipient Bronze award United Way, Los Angeles, 1984, Gold award, 1985. Republican. Roman Catholic. Home: 3507 Wildwood St El Monte CA 91732 Office: State Bd of Equalivation 11229 Woodruff Ave Downey CA 90241

MONTY, GLORIA, television producer; b. Union City, N.J.; d. Joseph and Concetta M. (Mango) Montemuro; m. Robert Thomas O'Byrne, Jan. 8, 1952. B.A., NYU; M.A., Columbia U. Dir. New Sch. of Research, N.Y.C., 1952-53; dir. Old Towne Theatres, Smithtown, N.Y., 1952-56, Abbey Theatre Workshop, N.Y.C., 1952-56; cons. ABC. Dir. numerous TV shows including Secret Storm, 1956-72, Bright Promise, numerous episodes ABC Wide World Entertainment; exec. producer General Hospital, 1977-86, The Hamptons, 1983-85, made-for-TV movies including Confessions of a Married Man, 1982, The Imposter, 1984; exec. producer in devel. for primetime TV 20th Century Fox, 1987-90. Recipient Emmy awards, 1982, 84, award Am. Soc. Lighting Dirs., 1979, Most Successful TV Show in History of TV award ABC, 1982, Spl. Editors award Soap Opera Digest, numerous others; named Woman Yr., Paulist Choristers So. Calif., 1986. Mem. Women in Film, Dirs. Guild Am. (exec. com.), Stuntman's Assn. (hon.). Clubs: Thunderbird Country (Rancho Mirage, Calif.); Bel Air Country (Calif.).

MONYEK, MARCIA EDITH, marketing executive; b. Chgo., Oct. 30, 1959; d. Robert H. and Harice (Kinsler) M. BA, Wake Forest U., 1980; JD, DePaul U., 1983; postgrad. cert. in mgmt. devel., Harvard U., 1988. Bar: Ill. 1984. Staff mktg. promotions Crain Communications, Chgo., 1980-81; account exec. Hill and Knowlton, Inc., Chgo., 1981-83, account. supr., 1983-84, v.p., 1984-87; v.p. mktg. World Book Inc., Chgo., 1987—; asst. adj. prof. Ill. Inst. Tech. Sch. Bus., Chgo., 1984-89. Bd. dirs. Lyric Opera Guild of Chgo., Gilbert and Sullivan, Chgo., 1985-86; mem. Jr. League of Chgo., 1981-88. Named One of Outstanding Young Women of Am., 1988. Mem. ABA (task force on outreach to pub.), Direct Mktg. Assn., Nat. Investor Rels. Inst. (sec. 1985-86, v.p. programs 1986-87), Young Execs. Club (v.p. communications 1986-87), Ptnrships in Edn. (adv. bd.), Standard Club (lt. mem. com. 1986-89), Internat. Club. Home: 2800 Lake Shore Dr Chicago IL 60657 Office: Marcy Monyek and Assocs Inc 333 N Michigan Ave Chicago IL 60601

MONZINGO, AGNES YVONNE, veterinary technician; b. Mangum, Okla., July 16, 1942; d. Ira Lee and Opal Alice (McAlexander) Mayfield; m. Monty Brent Monzingo, Dec. 14, 1959; children: Tara, Dawn, Michael, Kermit. AS, San Antonio Coll., 1969. Mgr. Tupperware Corp., Wichita Falls, Tex., 1966-69; with La Louisiane, San Antonio, 1974-79; counselor Diet Ctr., Duncanville, Tex., 1984-87; vet. technician DeSoto (Tex.) Animal Hosp., 1985—. Author: (weekly column) Happy Tracks, 1981. Pres. Dallas Stake Primary, 1983-88; commr. Boy Scouts Am., 1988—. Recipient Wood Badge, Boy Scouts Am., 1987. Mem. Tex. Assn. Animal Technicians (pres. 1988, com. chair 1990—), Am. Boxer Club, Dallas Boxers Club (sec. 1982—). Mormon.

MOODY, JUDITH BARBARA, independent consultant; b. Detroit, Oct. 14, 1942; d. Philip Earl and Barbara Marie (Wheeler) M.; m. Alexander C. Brown, 1964 (div. Dec. 1973); m. Thomas Raymond Worsley, Jan. 2, 1979; children: Cynthia Ann, Stephen James (stepchildren). BS, U. Mich., 1964, MS, 1967; PhD, McGill U., Montreal, 1974. Cert. Profl. Geologist #566, Ind. Rsch. asst. U. Mich., Ann Arbor, 1965; vis. scientist U. Liege, Belgium, 1968-70; asst. prof. U. N.C., Chapel Hill, 1974-80; project mgr. Battelle Meml. Inst., Columbus, Ohio, 1981-88; ind. cons., pres. J. B. Moody and Assocs., Columbus, 1988—; lectr. in geology. Mem. editorial bd. Geology, 1984-89; contbr. articles to profl. jours. Named one of Outstanding Young Women of Yr. Columbus YWCA, 1987. Mem. AAUW (life), Am. Geol. Inst. (com. women geosci. 1973-77), Geol. Assn. Can. (com. status women in earth scis. 1972-76), Assn. Women Geoscientists Found. (advisor 1983-85, 88—), Assn. for Women Sci. (Cen. Ohio chpt. 1984-85, v.p., pres., Outstanding Scientist of Yr. Cen. Ohio chpt. 1989), Geol. Soc. Am., Am. Geophys. Union, Geochem. Soc., Mineral. Soc. Can. (Hawley award 1986), Am. Men and Women of Sci. Office: 1989 W 5th Ave Ste 11 Columbus OH 43212

MOODY, LINDA A., college chaplain; b. Garden City, Mich., Oct. 19, 1954; d. Dean A. Moody and Barbara (E.) Caton. BA, U. Mich., 1975, EdM, 1976; MDiv, So. Seminary, Louisville, Calif., 1980; postgrad., Grad. Tech. Union, Berkeley, Calif. Instr. Mich. Lang. Sch., Anaco, Venezuela, 1975, Escuela Anaco, Anaco, Venezuela, 1976, English Lang. Inst. U. Mich., Ann Arbor, 1976; tchr. Concord (Mich.) High Sch., 1976-78; chaplain Brookville Lake Ministry, Iowa, 1979-80; minister Beechmont United Meth. Ch., Louisville, 1979-80; assoc. dir., instr. English Ctr. for Internat. Women Mills Coll., Oakland, Calif., 1981—, chaplain, 1985—; coord. UN Decade Women Regional Meeting, 1985, Nat. Steering Com., Women Ministry Conf. Am. Bap. Ch., 1986-88, Com. Ministry Am. Bapt. Ch. West, 1987-89, adv. bd. Refugee Project, Am. Bapt. Ch. of West, 1985—. Editor: Journal of Women and Religion, 1976; contbr. articles to profl. jours. Bd. dirs. Lakeshore Ave Bapt. Ch., 1985-88; chmn. Women in Theology Task Force, 1979-80, Am. Bapt. Campus Found., 1975-76. Stephen Bufton scholar, 1987, Margaret Frost trust scholar, 1979, project re-new grant, AAUW, 1987. Mem. Am. Acad. Religion, Nat. Assn. Coll. U. Chaplains, Nat. Campus Ministry Assn. Office: Mills Coll Office of Chaplain 500 MacArthur Blvd Oakland CA 94613

MOODY, RHEA PHENON, banking executive; b. Portland, Ind., Oct. 6, 1930; d. George D.C. and Mollie (Evans) M.; m. Phillip L. Bond, Sept. 5, 1974 (div. Dec. 1979). BS in Acctg., Ind. U., 1959. Mgr., teller First Nat. Bank, East Chgo., 1959-66; credit officer Lasalle Nat. Bank, Chgo., 1966-73; asst. v.p. State Nat. Bank, Evanston, Ill., 1973-77; v.p. Lakeview Bank, Chgo., 1977-81, W.N. Lane Interfinancial, Northbrook, Ill., 1981-83, Uni Banc Trust, Chgo., 1983-85, Republic Bank, Lubbock, Tex., 1985-86, Sunbelt Savings, Dallas, 1986—. Cpl. WAC, 1952-55. Home: 6006 Jereme Trail Dallas TX 75252 Office: Sunbelt Savs FSB 300 E Carpenter Frwy Irving TX 75016-0969

MOOK, SARAH, chemist; b. Bklyn., Oct. 29, 1929; d. Wong and Lie Won (Woo) M.; B.A., Hunter Coll., 1952; postgrad. Columbia U., 1954-57, 62-65, U. Hartford, 1958-59. Cartographic aide U.S. Geol. Survey, Dept. of Interior, Washington, 1952-54; research asst. Mineral Beneficiation Lab., Columbia U., N.Y.C., 1954-57; analytical chemist nuclear div. Combustion Engring., Inc., Windsor, Conn., 1957-59; research scientist Radiation Applications Inc., Long Island City, N.Y., 1959-62; chemist Marks Polarized Corp., Whitestone, N.Y., 1962-64; sr. chemist NRA Ins. subs. Nuclear Research Assos., Inc., New Hyde Park, N.Y., 1964-75; clin. chemist Coney Island Hosp., Bklyn., 1974-84, mem. community bd., 1978-84; chemist Bellevue Hosp. Ctr., N.Y.C., 1984-89, prin. chemist, 1989—; mem. adv. com. to state assemblyman, State of N.Y., 1970-72. Trustee Park Avenue Christian Ch., 1973—, sec., 1973-80, vice chmn., 1980-81, chmn. bd. trustees, 1981-82, mem. ofcl. bd., 1962—, vice chmn., 1974-76, pres. Christian Women's Fellowship, 1962-65, elder Park Ave. Christ. Ch., 1982. Mem. Am. Assn. Clin. Chemistry, AAAS. Republican. Contbr. articles on inorganic chemistry to profl. publs. Home: 2042 E 14th St Brooklyn NY 11229 Office: 462 1st Ave New York NY 10016

MOON, MARCIA A., education administrator; b. Tempe, Ariz., May 1, 1945; d. Howard Gilbert and Emlyn R. (Griggs) Smith; m. Oris Berton Moon, Mar. 25, 1967; children: Rnee Suzanne, Jeffrey Oris. BS, U. Oregon, 1967; MEd, Central Wash. U., 1972. program administrator certified, Washington. Speech therapist Yakima County Coop., Yakima, Wash., 1967-69; head start tchr. Ephrata Sch. Dist., Ephrata, Wash., 1970; speech therapist Ephrata Sch. Dist., Ephrata, 1972-75, remedial reading tchr., 1977-79, speech therapist, 1979-89, fed. program dir., 1989—; workshop presenter Community Coll. Edn. Svc. Dists.; chmn. curriculum guide Spl. Edn., 1989. Mem. Community Concert Assn., Ephrata, Wash., 1970—; vol. election campaign com.Ephrata, 1978. Mem. AAUW (pres. local chpt. 1978-80), Bus. and Profl. Women (Woman of Achievment Wash., 1979), Washington Edn. Assn. (local rep.), Northwest Women in Edn. Admstrn., Assn. Supervision and Curriculum Devel., Beta Sigma Phi (Girl of Year 1975, pres. 1976-77, valentine queen, 1979, pres. coord. coun.). Democrat. Methodist. Office: Ephrata Sch Dist #165 PO Box #788 Ephrata WA 98823

MOON, MARJORIE RUTH, former state treasurer; b. Pocatello, Idaho, June 16, 1926; d. Clark Blakeley and Ruth Eleanor (Gerhart) M. Student, Pacific U., 1944-46; A.B. in Journalism cum laude, U. Wash., 1948. Reporter Pocatello Tribune, 1944, Caldwell (Idaho) News-Tribune, 1948-50; Salt Lake City bur. chief Deseret News, Boise, Idaho, 1950-52; owner, operator Idaho Pioneer Statewide (weekly newspaper), Boise, 1952-55; founder, pub. Garden City (Idaho) Gazette, 1954-68; partner Sawtooth Lodge, Grandjean, Idaho, 1958-60; ptnr. Modern Press, Boise, 1958-61; treas. State of Idaho, Boise, 1963-86; owner, pub. Kuna-Melba News, 1987—, Valley News, Meridian, Idaho, 1988—. Chmn. Idaho Commn. on Women's Programs, 1971-74; del. Dem. Nat. Nominating Conv., 1972, 76, 80, 84; Dem. candidate Lt. Gov., Idaho, 1986; mem. Idaho Commn. for the Blind, 1987-90, chmn., 1989-90. Named Idaho Statesman of Yr. Pi Sigma Alpha of Idaho State U., 1989. Mem. Nat. Assn. State Treas. (sec.-treas. 1976-78, regional v.p. 1978-79, 84-85), Nat. Fedn. Press Women, Idaho Press Women (past pres.), Kuna C. of C. (sec. treas. 1987-88-89), Soroptimists (pres. club 1971-73). Congregationalist. Office: PO Box 207 Boise ID 83701

MOON, MARLA LYNN, optometrist; b. Connellsville, Pa., July 31, 1956; d. George Donnelly and Pauline Harriet (Hough) M. BS, Pa. State U., 1978, Pa. Coll. of Optometry, Phila., 1980; OD, Pa. Coll. of Optometry, Phila., 1982. Cert. Nat. Bd. Examiners, Pa., N.J. Bds. of Optometric Examiners. Intern Gesell Inst. for Human Devel., New Haven, Conn., 1981, U.S. Military Acad., West Point, N.Y., 1981, Dr. William Moskowitz, Somerville, N.J., 1981-82, Elwyn Ins., Feinbloom Ctr., Phila., 1982; resident The Eye Inst. Pediatrics Unit, Phila., 1982-83; ptnr. Drs. Carlin and Moon, State Coll., Pa., 1983—; vis. lectr. Dominican Coll. Orangeburg, N.Y., 1985, Pa. State U., University Pk., Pa., 1985-89; faculty Pa. Coun. Horseback Riding for Handicapped., State Coll. Pa., 1988-90; cons. JMS Mobility Assocs., Inc., Paoli, Pa., 1983—, Univ. Hosp. & Rehab. Ctr., Elizabethtown, Pa., 1988—, John Heinz Rehab. and Med. Ctr., Wilkes-Barre, Pa., 1990—. V.p., adv. bd. Learning Disabilities Assn., State Coll., 1983—; com. chmn. Local Children's Team, State Coll., 1985—; pres., bd. dirs. Cen.-Clear Child Svcs., Phila., 1984—; mem. Task Force Project Self Sufficiency, Bellefonte, Pa., 1988—; bd. dirs. Pa.-Del. Assn. for Educators and Rehab. of Blind and Visually Impaired, Harrisburg, Pa., 1988—. Recipient Phila. County Optometric Soc. award, 1982, Knight-Henry Meml. award, Optometric Extension Program, Phila., 1982. Mem. Am. Optometric Assn. (optometric recognition 1985-90), Pa. Optometric Assn. (chmn. 1989-90), Mid-Counties Optometric Soc. (v.p. 1990-91), Pa. State Alumni Assn. (life mem.), Altrusa Club (v.p., sec. 1987-91), Omega Epsilon Phi. Office: Drs Carlin and Moon 423 S Pugh St State College PA 16801

MOON, MONA MCTAGGART (FAY), educator; b. Buffalo, N.Y., Oct. 4, 1934; d. William Daniel and Helen Violet (Dubin) McTaggart; m. James McCallum Moon, July 14, 1957; children: Douglas, Melisa, Bruce. BA, UCLA, 1955; MA, San Diego State U., 1985. Lic. tchr., Calif., cert. adminstrn., supervision, Calif. Tchr. high sch. Acalanes High Sch., Lafayette, Calif., 1956-61, San Diego Unified Sch. Dist., 1967-82; pres. Motivation Dynamics, San Diego, 1982—. Contbr. articles to profl. jours. Dir. LWV San Diego, 1967-72. Recipient Outstanding Contbn. award Calif. Assn. Dirs. of Activities. Mem. Am. Soc. for Tng. and Devel., Nat. Speakers Assn., Phi Beta Kappa. Republican. Presbyterian.

MOONEY, DONNA HANCOCK, nurse; b. Salisbury, N.C., Sept. 4, 1951; d. Richard Evely and Hazel (Martin) Hancock. BS in Nursing, Western Carolina U., 1973. Staff nurse neurosurg. ICU Duke U. Med. Ctr., Durham, N.C., 1973-75; staff nurse ICU/CCU Transylvania Community Hosp., Brevard, N.C., 1975-78, head nurse med./surg., 1980-83; inspector N.C. Drug Commn., Dept. Human Resources, Raleigh, 1983-86; discipline cons. N.C. Bd. Nursing, Raleigh, 1987—; mem. faculty Continuing Edn. Resources, FAyetteville, N.C., 1989—. Mem. vestry St. Ambrose Episcopal Ch, Raleigh, 1988—. Mem. Am. Nurses Assn., N.C. Nurses Assn. Democrat. Episcopalian. Home: 1037 High Lake Ct Raleigh NC 27606 Office: NC Bd Nursing 3724 National Dr Raleigh NC 27602

MOONEY, NANCY, design-typography studio owner; b. Teaneck, N.J., Mar. 13, 1959; d. Edmund John and Eleanor Elsie (Szehi) M. BFA, Western Mich. U., 1982. Jeweler Detroit, 1978-80; stained glass artist Franklin, Mich., 1981; sales/jeweler Sher Designs/Renaissance Faire's, Kenosha, Wis., 1982; neon signmaker W. Bloomfield, Mich., 1983; with export sales Osterholz, Fed. Republic Germany, 1984-85; keyliner/designer Multicraft Graphics, Madison Heights, Mich., 1985; art dir. EMC Graphics, W. Bloomfield, 1986; owner Graphic Prodns., Farmington Hills, Mich., 1986—. Ford Found. grantee Western Mich. U., 1981. Mem. Typographers Internat. Assn., Women's Advt. Club Detroit, Am. Inst. Graphic Arts. Office: Graphic Prodns 28000 Middlebelt Ste 50 Farmington Hills MI 48323

MOONEY, PATRICIA ANNE, marketing professional; b. Bronx, N.Y., June 6, 1948; d. Peter Joseph and Helen (Houlihan) M.; m. Anthony John Grasso, Nov. 21, 1970 (div. 1977); 1 child, A. Benjamin. BA, Coll. New Rochelle, N.Y., 1970, MS, 1975. Tchr. Archdiocese of N.Y., Harrison, 1970-78; salesperson N.Y. Telephone, N.Y.C., 1978-82; instr. AT&T, Aurora, Colo., 1983; sales mgr. AT&T, N.Y.C., 1984, mgr. sales support dept., 1985; mgr. pricing and contract support dept. AT&T, Morristown, N.J., 1986; mgr. new bus. support dept. AT&T, Bridgewater, N.J., 1987; dir. mktg. AT&T, Englewood, Colo., 1988—. Active Colo. Forum, Denver, 1989—, Douglas County (Colo.) Econ. Devel., 1988—, South Metro Econ. Devel., Englewood, 1990—. Mem. Phi Kappa Gamma. Roman Catholic. Home: 9729 E Pinewood Ave Englewood CO 80111 Office: AT&T 6200 S Syracuse Ave Englewood CO 80111

MOONEY, VITA MARIA ELENA, social studies educator, tax examiner; b. Riverdale, N.Y., Aug. 29, 1941; d. Giovanni Carman and Carmela Helen (Salvatore) Mariella; m. James Vincent Mooney, Aug. 18, 1962 (div. Aug. 1972); children: Lisa C., Paul F., Timothy J. BA Social Scis., BA Psychology, Nazareth Coll., 1977; postgrad., SUNY, Stony Brook, 1986—. Caseworker Dept. Social Svcs., Rochester, 1979-80; substitute tchr. 6 sch. dists., Rochester and L.I., N.Y., 1980—; tax examiner IRS, Holtsville, N.Y., 1988—. Insp. Bd. Elections, Suffolk County, 1986—; vol. geriatric unit Brookhaven Meml. Hosp., 1979, consumer com. U. Rochester Community Outreach, 1973-79. Mem. Nat. Treasury Employees Union., N.Y. State Tchr.'s Union. Home: 6 Sugarbush Ln Coram NY 11727 Office: IRS Holtsville NY 11742

MOON-MEIER, DELIA ANN, business manager, marketing professional; b. Kansas City, Mo., Apr. 19, 1965; d. William Isham and Carolyn Blance (Cusac) Moon; m. David H. Meier, Sept. 5, 1987. BBA in Mgmt., U. Iowa, 1987. Asst. to pres. Iowa 80 Truckstop, Inc., Walcott, Iowa, 1986-88; bus. mgr. Iowa 80 Truckstop, Inc., 1988—; v.p. mktg., sec. CAT Scale Co., Walcott, 1988—; corp. sec. Truckstop Distibutors, Inc., Walcott, 1988—; corp. asst. sec. I-80 Investments Co., 1988—. Com. chmn. Quad Cities Truckers Jamboree, Walcott, 1984—; project bus. cons. Jr. Achievement, Davenport, 1989-90. Mem. Nat. Assn. Truckstop Operators (polit. action com. 1988—), Jaycees (dir. Davenport chpt. 1989), U. Iowa Alumni Assn., Delta Zeta. Methodist. Office: Iowa 80 Truckstop Inc I 80 and Exit 284 Walcott IA 52773

MOONS, KARLA R., investment broker; b. Lewiston, Maine, Aug. 6, 1946; d. Charles Frederick and Alice Eliza (Bishop) Ranger; m. Larry Lee Moons, Sept. 26, 1964; children: Lorie Anne Moons Wacaster, Frederick Lee. BA, U. South Ala., 1969; MS, Troy State U., 1977. Tchr. Cottage Hill Bapt. Ch., Mobile, Ala., 1969-72, Coving County Sch. Bd., Collins, Miss., 1972-76, Mobile County Sch. Bd., 1976-83; investment broker A.G. Edwards & Sons, Inc., Daphne, Ala., 1983—; speaker in field. Bd. dirs. local chpt. Nat. Kidney Found.; bd. dirs. Carver State Tech. Coll. Found., Drug Edn. Coun., Inc.; deacon local Bapt. ch. Mem. AAUW, Internat. Assn. Fin. Planning, Bay Area Security Dealers, Leadership Mobile Alumni Assn., Mobile Opera Guild (governing bd.), Kiwanis, Delta Kappa Gamma (chpt. pres., mem. state exec. bd.). Republican. Home: 6607 Chimney Top Dr N Mobile AL 36695

MOOR, DINA MAVIS, advertising agency executive; b. Phoenix, Aug. 23, 1943; d. Isaac Lowery and Anna Mavis (Stinson) M.; student State U. Iowa, 1961-62; B.A., So. Meth. U., 1967; M.B.A., U. Dallas, 1976; 1 child, Aaron Michael. Freelance model, 1965-71; sec. to academic dean U. Dallas, 1971-72, asst. to dean, 1972-74, dir. affiliated programs, 1974-76; dir. Mgmt. Labs. Am., Exec. Edn. Inst., Ctr. for Publishing, 1974-76; owner Moor and Assocs., Inc., Dallas, 1976—; pres. The Mktg. Corps., Inc., 1988—, mktg., advt., pub. rels., 1988—; bd. dirs. Peninsula MarCom Exchange; owner Standby Club, Highlands Trading Co.; dir. Lynn Weiss & Assos.; bd. dirs. Screen Actors Guild and AFTRA, 1967-70. Pres. Am. Parenting Assn. Recipient Wall St. Jour. award, 1976. Mem. Savs. Instns. Mktg. Soc. Am., Sales and Mktg. Execs. Dallas, Women in Communications, Inc., Peninsula

Mktg. Assn., North Dallas C. of C., Grad. Sch. Mgmt. Alumni Assn. (past pres.), IABC, PRSA, Sigma Iota Epsilon. Episcopalian. Clubs: Slipper, 500 Inc. (past dir.). Office: The Mktg Corps Inc 3080 Olcott Ste 202 B Santa Clara CA 95054

MOORE, ALDERINE BERNICE JENNINGS (MRS. JAMES F. MOORE), association and organization associate; Sacramento, Apr. 17, 1915; d. James Joseph and Elise (Thomas) Jennings; BA, U. Wash., 1941; m. James Francis Moore, Aug. 14, 1945. Sec. to div. Plant supr. Pacific Tel. & Tel. Co., Sacramento, 1937-39; exec. sec. Sacramento Community Chest Fund Raising Dr., 1941; sec. USAAF, Mather Field, Sacramento, 1942; statistician Calif. Western States Life Ins. Co., 1943; treas. Women's Aux. Stranger's Hosp., Rio de Janeiro, Brazil, 1964-65. Vice pres. Douglaston (N.Y.) Women's Club, 1955; mem. Douglaston Garden Club, 1951-55; pres. Nina Opland chpt. Women's Cancer Assn. U. Miami, 1960-61; corr. sec. Coral Gables (Fla.) Garden Club, 1960-62; pres. Miami Alumnae Club of Pi Beta Phi, 1961-62; mem. Putnam Hill chpt. D.A.R., Greenwich Conn., 1967-75, Palm Beach chpt., 1978—; mem. Woman's Club, Greenwich, Conn., 1967-75; mem. Women's Panhellenic Assn., Miami, 1961-62; internat. treas. Ikebana Internat., Tokyo, Japan, 1966-67, parliamentarian Tokyo chpt., 1966-67, N.Y. chpt., 1968-69; mem. Coll. Women Assn. Japan, 1965-66; mem. Tchrs. Assn. Sogetsu Sch. Japanese Flower Arranging, 1966—. Served to lt. WAVES, 1943-45. Mem. Internat. Platform Assn., AAUW, Pi Beta Phi (local v.p. alumnae club 1969-71). Baptist. Club: Steamboat Investment (pres. 1972-73). Home: 316 Fairway Ct Atlantis FL 33462

MOORE, ALEDA MAJOR, insurance company executive, real estate executive; b. Greenville, S.C., May 18, 1927; d. Carl Shaw and Amelia Marie (Kellett) Major; m. Curtis Odell Moore, Mar. 17, 1951; 1 child, Brian Stanley. Grad., Draughn's Bus. Coll., Greenville, 1950, Ins. Inst. Am., 1975, S.C. Assn. Realtors, 1980. Cert. pub. ins. woman. Sec. J.P. Stevens & Co., Greenville, 1945-55; legal sec. Bailey & Dority, Attys., Greenville, 1961-73; with ins. dept. Curtis Moore Co., Mauldin, S.C., 1973—, with real estate dept., 1980—. Mem. Nat. Assn. Realtors, Greenville Bd. Realtors, S.C. Assn. of Realtors, Nat. Assn. of Ins. Women, S.C. Ind. Ins. Agts., Greenville Assn. Ins. Women, Inc. Mem. Ch. of Christ. Home: 216 Vesper Circle Mauldin SC 29662 Office: 611 N Main St PO Box 675 Mauldin SC 29662

MOORE, ALISON TETENMAN, public relations executive; b. Los Angeles, Sept. 19, 1964; d. Henry Aaron and Arlene Sylvia (Hoffberg); m. Robert Lee, Jan. 10, 1987. BA in Journalism, Humboldt State U., Arcata, 1987. Communications specialist Nat. Environ. Tng. Assn., Scottsdale, Ariz., 1987-88; mktg., publs. asst. Internat. Assn. Mgrs. Inc., Scottsdale, Ariz., 1988-89; promotions coordinator ARC, L.A., 1990—. Mem. NAFE, So. Calif. Ventura Publishers Users Group. Home: 301 N 85th Pl Mesa AZ 85207

MOORE, BARBARA DEMONT, administrative law judge; b. Jacksonville, Fla., May 1, 1944; d. Clifton Frank Mitchell and Voncile (Deal) DeMont; m. Wesley Rice Moore, Jr., Sept. 17, 1966 (dec. 1968). Student, U. Wis., 1962-63; BA, U. Md., 1966, postgrad., 1969-70; JD, UCLA, 1972. Legis. fellow Calif. State Assembly, Sacramento, 1972-73, legis. cons. to majority leader, 1973-79; mem. Calif. Pub. Employment Rels. Bd., Sacramento, 1979-82; adminstrv. law judge Calif. Agrl. Labor Rels. Bd., Sacramento, 1982—. Founding mem. Women in Politics, Sacramento, 1974-79, Nat. Mus. of Women in Arts, Washington, 1988—; mem. Sacramento Old City Assn., Sacramento, 1974-78. Calif. Legis. fellow Calif. State Assembly Rules Commn., 1972. Mem. Calif. State Bar (co-chair labor rels. com. 1982-84, human rights com. 1976-80), Nat. Assn. of Women Judges, Calif. Women Lawyers, Phi Beta Kappa, Phi Alpha Theta. Office: Calif Agrl Labor Rels Bd 915 Capitol Mall Sacramento CA 95814

MOORE, CANDACE RAE, registered nurse; b. Indpls., Sept. 21, 1952; d. Lowell Emerson and Ruby Everlyn (Fessler) M. RN, Orange Meml. Sch. Nursing, 1973; student, U. Tampa, 1983—. RN Fla., N.Y. Nursing asst. to operating room staff nurse Orlando (Fla.) Regional Med. Ctr., 1973-81; operating room staff nurse Gateway Community Hosp., St. Petersburg, Fla., 1981-83; operating room educator Tampa (Fla.) Gen. Hosp., 1983-87; clin. specialist Laserscope, San Jose, Calif., 1987-90; customer support specialist Laserscope, San Jose, 1990—; RN-Operating Room Skills Course Instr., Tampa Bay Evening Vocat. Sch., 1985, 86, (asst. 1984). Contbr. articles to profl. jours. Recipient Julia Flom scholarship U. Tampa, 1989. Mem. Assn. Operating Room Nurses (various positions), Nurse Cons. Assn., Am. Soc. for Laser Medicine and Surgery, Inc. Office: Laserscope 3052 Orchard Dr San Jose CA 95134

MOORE, CAROL ANN, engineering manager; b. Rochester, N.Y., Feb. 24, 1947; d. Duane G. Lent and Dorothy Sackett (Crump) Derr; m. Paul Allan Moore, May 10, 1969; 1 child, Meredith Joy. BS, Grove City Coll., 1968. Mathematician Gen. Dynamics, Rochester, 1968-73; mgr. programming George D.B. Bonbright & Co., Rochester, 1971-73; programmer, analyst Xerox Corp., Rochester, 1973-74; sr. system analyst Info. Assocs., Rochester, 1981-84; mgr. Computer Consoles, Inc., Rochester, 1984—. Home: 354 Shadowbrook Dr Webster NY 14580

MOORE, CAROL LYNN, association executive; b. Daytona Beach, Fla., Jan. 27, 1960; d. Albert M. Moore and Elaine (Thomas) Kershaw. BA in English, Emory U., 1982. Sales rep. Terrace Garden Inn Hotel, Atlanta, 1982-84; program mgr. Internat. Bus. Coun., Atlanta, 1984—; exec. dir. Soc. Internat. Bus. Fellows, Atlanta, 1988—. Bd. dirs. Camp High Harbor, YMCA, 1989—. Mem. Nat. Soc. Internat. Bus. Fellows (asst. sec.-treas. S.E. chpt. 1985—, nat. asst. sec.-treas. 1988—), Am. Soc. Assn. Execs., Ga. Soc. Assn. Execs., Japan Am. Soc. Ga., Atlanta Com. on Fgn. Rels., Am. Canoe Assn. (1st place Southeastern whitewater championship 1987, 88), Atlanta Whitewater Club (v.p. 1987, pres. 1988), Toastmasters, The Golfe. Home: 3009 Hilltop Dr Atlanta GA 30341 Office: Soc Internat Bus Fellows One Park Place S Ste 1001 Atlanta GA 30303

MOORE, CAROL MILLINGHAUSEN, corporate executive; b. Phila., Mar. 21, 1953; d. Harry Paul and Mary Isabelle (Evans) Millinghausen; m. Albert W. Moore, June 9, 1973 (div. Nov. 1983); children: Kristina Carol, Albert W. IV. BA, Ursinius Coll., 1974. With Maxima Magnetics, Inc., Hatboro, Pa., 1983—, v.p. sales div., 1986-88, gen. mgr., 1989—. Mem. Soc. Motion Picture and TV Engrs., Internat. TV Assn., Women's Group (leader Abington, Pa. chpt. 1989—). Republican. Lutheran. Home: 1867 Cleveland Ave Abington PA 19001 Office: Maxima Magnetics Inc 18 300 Bonair Ave Hatboro PA 19040

MOORE, CAROLYN CALISTA, computer consultant; b. Ft. Worth, July 2, 1953; d. Melville Locke Moore and Henrietta Robin (Eliot) Garstka. Computer programmer Jefferson County Cts., Golden, Colo., 1973-79; database adminstr. Guaranty Nat. Ins., Englewood, Colo., 1979-84, State of Colo., Denver, 1984-86, KN Energy, Inc., Lakewood, Colo., 1986-87; systems cons. Wang Labs., Inc., Englewood, 1988; pvt. practice Denver, 1989—. Vol. Sta. KCFR-Nat. PUb. Radio, Denver, 1981—; newsletter vol. Vols. for Outdoor Colo., Denver, 1987-89; v.p. Mile Hi Aux.-Nat. Asthma Hosp., Denver, 1989—. Mem. Software AG Users Group (program coord. Denver chpt. 1987).

MOORE, CELESTA ROSE, elementary educator; b. Kansas City, Mo., Dec. 20, 1944; d. Kenneth Lee and Ruth (Powell) M. BA, William Jewell Coll., Liberty, Mo., 1967; MA in Edn., U. Mo., 1972. Elem. tchr. North Kansas City Sch. Dist., Gladstone, Mo., 1967—; bd. dirs. youth camp leader Christian Ch. Disciples Christ, Trenton 1965, vacation bible sch., 1974-75. Co-author: Our Heritage Will Light Our Path, 1987. Asst. leader Girl Scouts, Liberty 1978-79; chmn. bd. Liberty Christian Ch., 1983-84. Mem. AAUW (pres. 1975-77), Mo. State Tchrs. Assn. (treas. 1986-88), North Kansas City Community Tchrs. Assn., Delta Kappa Gamma (pres. 1988—). Democrat. Office: Linden West Sch 7400 N Main Gladstone MO 64118

MOORE, CHARLOTTE ELEANOR, nutritional counselor; b. Denver, Nov. 15, 1923; d. Charles Mayo and Sylvia (Barnett) Witt; m. William P. Moore, Mar. 28, 1987; children: Julie Ann Gilliam, Mary Lisa Zuchegno. Student, U. Northern Colo., 1940-42; BA, Rockmont Coll., 1981. Cert. live cell technician. Tchr. Englewood (Colo.) Schs., 1943-45; sec. to supr. of schs. and sch. bd. Town of Truth or Consequences, N.Mex., 1945-47; office mgr. Crusader Oil Corp., Denver, 1947-49; ind. nutritional counselor Englewood, Colo., 1983—. Sec. libr. bd. Colo. Women's Coll., Denver, 1963-65; deacon Wellshire Presbyn. Ch., Denver, 1984-87; mem. various coms. Salvation Army, United Way, Planned Parenthood. Republican. Home and Office: 4060 S Bellaire Englewood CO 80110

MOORE, DANA L., health facility administrator, psychologist; b. Clinton, Okla., June 11, 1933; d. J. Strother and Jessie L. (Harris) M.; m. Calvin R. Watson, Jan. 19, 1976. BA, Austin Coll., 1966; MA, W.Va. U., 1971, PhD, 1976. Lice. clin. psychologist, D.C., Tenn. Intern Dede Wallace Ctr., Nashville, 1972, jr. clin. psychologist, 1972-75; clin. psychologist VA Med. Ctr., Nashville, 1976-77; edn. specialist Dept. Veterans Affairs, Washington, 1978-85, exec. dir. leadership, 1985—; clin. psychologist The MenCtr., Washington, 1988—. Contbr. chpt. to book. Treas., Old North Port Community Assn., Alexandria, Va., 1979-85; adv. bd. Nat. Found. for Study and Treatment of Pathol. Gambling, Washington, 1982-84. Mem. Am. Psychol. Assn. (Disting. Svc. award 1990, coun. rep. 1987-90), Nat. Register Health Svc. Providers Psychology (chair appeal bd. 1982-84), Assembly Scientist-Practitioner Psychologists (mem.-at-large), D.C. Psychol. Assn., Leadership Va. Alumni Assn. Office: Dept Veterans Affairs 810 Vermont Ave NW 053C Washington DC 20420

MOORE, DORA VIOLA, manager early childhood education program; b. Kwiguk, AK, July 13, 1948; d. Willie and Catherine (Andrews) M. Student, AK Meth. U., 1973-74; AA in Early Childhood Edn., Kuskokwim Community Coll., Bethel, AK, 1980; BA in Edn., Pacific Oak Coll., 1982, AK Pacific U., 1984. Store/pool hall mgr. M.B. Moore & Co., Emmonak, AK, 1966-70; tchr.'s aide Headstart Rural Community Action Program, Emmonak, AK, 1971-72, tchr. dir., 1972-79; field trainer Headstart Rural Community Action Program, Anchorage, 1979-84, community specialist, 1979-84, regional mgr., 1989—; Yupik lang. translator Historic Sites, Ceremonial Sites, Emmonak, 1984-85; dancing com. folklore, Georgetown U., Washington, 1984, others. Roman Catholic. Home: 1461 W 26th Ave Anchorage AK 99503 Office: Rural Community Action Prog 731 East 8th Anchorage AK 99520

MOORE, EDWINA VESTA, educator, violinist; b. Detroit, Feb. 2; d. Edwin Allen and Vesta Rae (Ellison) Pierse; m. H. Chester Moore, June 23, 1973 (div. 1982). BMus, U. So. Calif., 1950, postgrad., 1960. Cert. elem. and secondary tchr., Calif. Tchr. instrumental music Long Beach (Calif.) Unified Schs., 1950—; concertmaster Long Beach Symphony, 1965-73, 1st violinist, 1973—; violinist Pacific Symphony, Orange, Calif., 1982-84, Southcoast Symphony, Costa Mesa, Calif., 1986—, Irvine (Calif.) Symphony, 1986—; 1st violinist Heritage String Quartet, Long Beach, 1987—; master tchr. Orange County High Sch. Performing Arts, 1989—. U. So. Calif. scholar, 1948-50. Mem. Music Educators Nat. Conf., Musicians Union (life mem. Long Beach local). Republican. Home: 3933 Virginia Rd Apt 204 Long Beach CA 90807

MOORE, (MARGARET) ELEANOR MARCHMAN, ret. librarian; b. Pinckard, Ala., Nov. 6, 1913; d. Robert Lee and Eleanor Rowena (Paris) Marchman; A.B., Fla. State Coll. for Women, 1936; B.S. in L.S., George Peabody Coll. for Tchrs., 1947, M.A. in Library Sci., 1962; m. James William Moore, Feb. 22, 1934 (div. 1940); 1 son, John Robert. Tchr. Alva (Fla.) High Sch., 1938-40, Wacissa (Fla.) Jr. High Sch., 1940-43; librarian Bartow (Fla.) Sr. High Sch., 1943-45, 48-67, Bartow Pub. Library, 1945-48; cataloger Roux Library, Fla. So. Coll., Lakeland, 1967-70, reference librarian, 1970-75; co-sponsor Polk County Student Library Assn., 1957-59; intern tchr. Fla. State U.; former mem. evaluating team So. Assn. Secondary Schs. and Colls. Recipient Polk County Career Increment award, 1961. Mem. NEA, Beta Phi Mu, Delta Kappa Gamma. Democrat. Baptist. Address: 251 Marilyn Dr Lafayette LA 70503

MOORE, ELIZABETH DOREEN, state government administrator; b. N.Y.C., July 29, 1954; d. William A. and M. Doreen Moore; m. Jimmy Lee Miller, Dec. 21, 1984. BS, Cornell U., 1975; JD, St. John's U., Jamaica, N.Y., 1978; DCL (hon.), St. John's U., N.Y.C., 1989. Bar: N.Y. 1979. Atty. Consolidated Edison, N.Y.C., 1978-79; atty. Am. Express Co., N.Y.C., 1979-80; mgr. Equitable Life Assurance Soc. of U.S., N.Y.C., 1981; asst. counsel Gov.'s Counsel's Office, Albany, N.Y., 1981-83; first asst. counsel, 1983-87; dir. Gov.'s Office Employee Relations, Albany, 1987—; chair N.Y. State Ethics Commn., Albany, 1988—; mem. adv. coun. N.Y. State Vol. Svcs. Corp., Albany, 1989—, Task Force on Work & Family, Albany, Spl. Prosecutor Screening Com., Albany. Recipient Legis. Assistance award N.Y. State NAACP, 1986; Henry F. Toll fellow Coun. State Govts., Lexington, Ky., 1987. mem. Women Execs. in State Govt. Democrat. Episcopalian. Office: Govs Office Employee Relations Agency Bldg 2 12th Fl Albany NY 12223

MOORE, ELIZABETH ELKINS, hospital administrator; b. Jersey City, N.J., Sept. 1, 1946; d. Philip Gerald and Francine (Cohen) Elkins; children: Amanda Michele, Gregory Alexander. BS, Ithaca Coll., 1968; MA, Columbia U., 1980; MBA, Baruch Coll., 1990. Registered phys. therapist; lic. nursing home adminstr. Phys. therapist Bronx (N.Y.) Mcpl. Hosp. Ctr., 1969-79; chief phys. therapist Bergen Pines County Hosp., Paramus, N.J., 1979-81; cons. Calder & Moore, Teaneck, N.J., 1981-83; asst. exec. dir., long term care Bergen Pines County Hosp., Paramus, N.J., 1983-86, asst. exec. dir. long term care, psychiatry, 1986—; mem. adv. com. Mental Health Bd., Bergen County, 1987—, Alcohol and Drug Abuse Bd., 1988—; mem. Youth Svcs. Commn., Bergen County, 1988—, Human Svcs. Adv. Coun., Bergen County, 1984—. Bd. dirs. Shelter Our Sisters, Teaneck, 1989—. Mem. Assn. Mental Health Adminstrs., Am. Coll. Health Care Adminstrs., Am. Coll. Health Care Execs. Office: Bergen Pines County Hosp E Ridgewood Ave Paramus NJ 07652

MOORE, ELLEN ANN, medical technologist; b. Colorado City, Tex., Jan. 31, 1936; d. J. Verner and Lila Elvis (McCurry) Glover; m. Bennie Glyn Steel, Dec. 21, 1957; children: Elizabeth Ann, Sharon Lee, Carolyn Elaine; (div. 1978); m. William Fowler Moore Sr., Feb. 14, 1982. Student, Shannon Meml. Hosp. Sch. Med. Tech., San Angelo, Tex., 1956; BS cum laude, Southwestern U., Georgetown, Tex., 1958. Chief technologist St. Johns Hosp., San Angelo, 1957; technologist Commanche County Meml. Hosp., Lawton, Okla., 1958; rsch. technologist Tex. A&M U., College Station, 1963-66, 69-71; chief technologist Kowierschke Pathology Lab., Bryan, Tex.; rsch. technologist USDA, College Station, 1971-; founding pres. Bryan/College Station Soc. Med. Tech., 1964; area mgr. Fed. Women's program USDA, College Station, 1987-89. Contbr. articles to profl. jours., 1974—. Treas. Women's Civic League, Bryan, 1987—. Named one of Outstanding Young Women of Am., 1970. Mem. Am. Soc. Clin. Pathologists (assoc.), Federally Employed Women, Electron Microscopy Soc. Am., Tex. Soc. Electron Microscopy, Alpha Chi. Home: 509 E North Ave Bryan TX 77801 Office: USDA Rte 5 Box 810 College Station TX 77840

MOORE, EMMA SIMS, executive secretary; b. Branford, Fla., Oct. 27, 1937; d. Lawton Edward and Annie Ruth (Hewitt) Sims; m. H. Dean Moore, Sr., Sept. 30, 1961; 1 child, H. Dean Jr. Secretarial sci., Jones Coll., 1955; B., Butler U., 1984; M., Ind. Wesleyan U., 1989. Cert. profl. sec. Sec. to svc. mgr. Buick Motor div. GM, Jacksonville, Fla., 1956-72, Charlotte, N.C., 1972-74; sec. to br. mgr. Motors Holding div. GM, Washington, 1974-78, Phila., 1978-82; exec. sec. to dir. product support Allison Gas Turbine div. GM, Indpls., 1982—. Mem. exec. com. Boy Scouts Am., West Chester, Pa., 1981-82. Mem. Profl. Secs. Internat. (v.p. 1986-87, pres. 1987-89 500 chpt., Sec. of Yr. 1986, 89 500 chpt., 1989 Ind. div.), CPS Acad., CPS Soc. Indpls., Secretarial Adv. Coun. Internat. Tel. & Tel. Inst., Nat. Assn. Exec. Secs., Nat. Assn. Female Execs. (profl. secs. internat. goodwill people to people del. to People's Republic of China, Singapore, Thailand, Indpnesia, and Hong Kong). Baptist. Home: 645 Sugarbush Dr Zionsville IN 46077

MOORE, EVIE B., president and owner; b. Nashville, Nov. 24, 1945; d. Arron Charlton and Myriam (Jones) B.; m. Stanley Vance Overstreet, May 4, 1963 (div. May 1979); children: Tracey Lynn Lawhon, Tammy Jean Pearson; m. Jack Donnis Moore, Apr. 3, 1990. Student, U. Tenn., 1967-74, Voluntee State Coll., 1978-81. Acct., office mgr. Myers Truck & Caster Sales Co., Nashville, 1963-81, outside sales, 1981-82; dist. sales mgr. Tenn. Wheel & Rubber, Nashville, 1982-84; pres., owner Georgia Material Handling, Lithonia, Ga. Mem. Order Eastern Star. Baptist. Home: 1511 Stoneleigh Cir Stone Mountain GA 30088 Office: Georgia Material Handling 6440 Hillandale Rd Lithonia GA 30058

MOORE, FAY LINDA, computer programmer; b. Houston, Apr. 7, 1942; d. Charlie Louis and Esther Mable (Banks) Moore; m. Noel Patrick Walker, Jan. 5, 1963 (div. 1967); 1 child, Trina Nicole Moore. Student, Prairie View Agrl. and Mech. Coll., 1960-61, Tex. So. U., 1961. Instr. Internat. Bus. Coll., Houston, 1965; keypunch operator IBM Corp., Houston, 1965-67, sr. keypunch operator, 1967-70, programmer technician, 1970-72, asst. programmer, 1972-73, assoc. programmer, 1973-84; sr. assoc. programmer, 1984-87, staff programmer, 1987—. Recipient Apollo Achievement award Nat. Aeronautics & Space Adminstrn., 1969. Mem. NAFE, Internat. Platform Assn., Booker T. Washington Alumni Assn., Ms. Found. for Women, Inc., Data Processing Mgmt. Assn. Democrat. Roman Catholic. Avocations: personal computing, board games. Office: IBM Corp 3700 Bay Area Blvd MC 6402A Houston TX 77058-1199

MOORE, FAYE HALFORD, jewelry manufacturer; b. Granville, Tenn., Oct. 16, 1941; d. Benton Mack and Dora Mai (Carter) Halfacre; m. Travis Edward Halford, Jan. 2, 1965 (div. 1989); children: Kristi Faye, Trent Edward; m. Charles Harold Moore, Jan. 23, 1989. BSBA, Tenn. Technol. U., 1963. Exec. sec. E.I. du Pont de Nemours, Old Hickory, Tenn., 1963-65, Amoco, New Orleans, 1965-66; adminstrv. asst. Thompson & Moss, Atlanta, 1967-72; founder, owner Strictly Natural, Ltd., Atlanta, 1975—, Elegant Accessories, Internat., Atlanta, 1980—. Pres. Sandy Springs Arts and Heritage Soc., Atlanta, 1986; founding dir. Leadership Sandy Springs, 1987; bd. dirs. Lexington Philharmonic, Lexington, 1989, Lindsey-Wilson Coll., Columbia, Ky., 1989; bd. dirs. Cardinal Hill Hosp., Lexington, 1989. Named Citizen of Yr. Sandy Springs Jr. Women's Club, 1976. Mem. Women Bus. Owners, Assn. Women Entrepreneurs (founder), Women's Commerce Club, Kiwanis. Democrat. Methodist. Home: 5900 Russell Cave Rd Lexington KY 40511 Office: Strictly Natural Ltd 1845 The Exchange Atlanta GA 30339

MOORE, HAZEL GOODALL, small business owner; b. Memphis, June 19, 1939; d. Eddie Lee Goodall and Robbie (Aldridge) Johnson; married Nov. 1955; children: Jacqueline Davis Mayo, Chiquita Davis, Debra Denise Davis Rich, Robbie Nell Davis; m. Jayne Delaine Moore, Jan. 16, 1975. Grad., Molar's Beauty Sch., 1970. Hair stylist Goldsmith's Dept. Store, Memphis; owner Hazel's Hair Fashion II, Memphis, 1985-88, Hazel's Hair Fashion I, Memphis, 1974—; gov. appointee Bd. of Cosmetology, Tenn.,1987, chmn., 1990—. Adv. com. Booker T. Washington Vocat. Sch., 1980; coord. curlathon Le Moyne-Owen Coll. United Negro Coll. Fund, 1982; chmn. Memphis Entertaining com., 1982-88; bd. dirs. State Bd. Cosmetology, 1987, Miss and Mr. Black Teenage Tenn. Pageant, 1988. White House guest, Washington, 1980; named one of Ten Best Dressed Women Nat. Coun. Negro Women, 1981; recipient Svcs. Rendered and Dedication award Memphis Regional Sickle Cell Anemia Coun., 1982, Outstanding Accomplishments in Bus. award, 1984, cert. Recognition City Coun., Memphis, 1985, Outstanding Bus. award (Benny) Black Mchts. Assn., Memphis, 1985, (Omni) 1988, col. a.d.c. Gov. Tenn., 1989. Mem. Nat. Cosmetology Assn., Tenn. Beauticians Assn. (trade show chmn. 1981, 3d v.p. 1984-86), Shop Owner League Number I (v.p. 1980-84), Tenn. Top Ten Hairdressers (past v.p.), Sigma Chi Zeta (v.p. 1982-85). Democrat. Baptist. Home: 1799 Westmore St Memphis TN 38106 Office: 4105 Elvis Presley Blvd Memphis TN 38116

MOORE, HELEN ELIZABETH, reporter; b. Rush County, Ind., Dec. 19, 1920; d. John Brackenridge and Mary Amelia (Custer) Johnson; m. John William Sheridan, July 6, 1942 (dec. Jan. 1944); m. Harry Evan Moore, May 15, 1954; 1 child, William Randolph. BS, Ind. U., 1972, MS, 1973. Ofcl. ct. reporter 37th Jud. Cir., Brookville, Ind., 1950-60; freelance reporter Rushvile, Ind., 1960—; conv. reporter various assns. With USMC, 1943. Recipient Sagamore of the Wabash award Gov. Ind., 1984. Mem. Women Marines Assn. (charter, nat. pres. 1966-68), Am. Legion Aux. (various offices 1950—, pres. Ind. dept. 1966-67, conv. reporter), Bus. and Profl. Women (dist. dir., various offices 1967—), Nat. Shorthand Reporters Assn. (registered profl. reporter), Ind. Shorthand Reporters Assn. (state treas., edit. Hoosier Reporter, chmn. legal directory), German Geneal Soc. Am., Ind. German Heritage Soc. (state dir. 1984—, pres. 1990-91), Ind. U. Alumni Assn., Hist. Soc., Internat. Platform Assn., Eight and Forty (subs. Am. Legion Aux., nat. sec.-treas.). Democrat. Methodist. Home and Office: PO Box 206 Rushville IN 46173

MOORE, JACQUELINE, professional speaker, author; b. Chgo., June 13, 1937; d. Clyde Charles and Elizabeth (Lynk) Knudson; m. James Harold Moore, Aug. 5, 1978; children: Jill Louise, Jeffrey James Richards. Postgrad., U. Wisc.; AA, N. Hennipin St. Coll., Mpls.; BA, Met. St. U., St. Paul; PhD, Nat. Christian U. Mo., 1983. Ordained minister Light of Christ Sem. Surgical technician No. Meml. Hosp., Golden Valley, Mn., 1973-74; reg. nurse U. Minn., 1974-75, Sacred Heart Med. Ctr., Spokane, Wa., 1975-76, St. Mary's Hosp., Mpls.; internat. speaker Wakinyan Inst., Mpls., 1977—, Personal Growth Found., 1978-82; RN Golden Valley (Minn.) Health Ctr., 1980-85. Author: Patterns for Change, 1982, Inner Space, 1986, Color Sense, 1986, Wakankana of the Sun, 1989. Mem. Nat. Speakers Assn., Spiritual Frontiers Fellowship, Nat. Assn. Female Execs., Nat. Orgn. Women. Office: 4245 46th Ave N Minneapolis MN 55422

MOORE, JANET MARIE, state official; b. Butler, Pa., Mar. 13, 1947; d. Jesse Robert and Katherine Mae (Pisor) Moore; Asso. in Specialized Bus., New Castle Bus. Coll., 1972. Cost accountant Package Products Inc., Pitts., 1967-68; audit clk. Liberty Mut. Ins. Co., New Castle, Pa., 1968-71; acct. S.R. Snodgrass & Co., C.P.A.s, New Castle, 1971-74; clerical supr. Pa. vital records Pa. Dept. Health, New Castle, 1974—; pvt. practice acctg., Volant, Pa., 1974—. Mem. Owner Handler Assn., Nat. Rifle Assn. (life), Am. Numismatic Assn. Democrat. Presbyterian. Club: New Castle Kennel (sec. 1978, dir. 1977-81, v.p. 1979-81). Home: RD 3 Box 101 Volant PA 16156 Office: PO Box 1528 New Castle PA 16103

MOORE, JANET RUTH, nurse, educator; b. Bridgeport, Conn., Sept. 19, 1949; d. Robert Hartland and Florence (Merritt) Bessom; m. William James Moore, Sept. 5, 1971; children: Jeffrey, Gregory. AA, Green Mountain Coll., 1969; diploma, Mass. Gen. Hosp., 1974; BS in Nursing, Am. Internat. Coll., 1980. RN, Mass. Nurse's aide Lynn (Mass.) Hosp., 1967-69, staff nurse, 1972-73; nursing asst. U.S. Army Hosp., Ft. Polk, La., 1971-72; staff nurse Ludlow (Mass.) Hosp., 1980-85; staff edn. instr. Springfield (Mass.) Mcpl. Hosp., 1985-88; dir. staff edn. Jewish Nursing Home, Longmeadow, Mass., 1988—; nurse Camp Wilder, Springfield, 1981-84; clin. instr. Holyoke (Mass.) Community Coll., 1990—. Mem. Jr. League of Springfield, 1981-88, Community Health Edn. Council for Children and Adolescents; bd. dirs. Mass. Soc. for Prevention of Cruelty to Children, Springfield, 1985—, Coun. of Chs., chairperson, Div. on Aging, 1989—. Mem. Am. Nurses' Assn. (cert. gerontol. nurse), Wilbraham (Mass.) Jr. Women's Club, Alpha Chi. Home: 104 Burleigh Rd Wilbraham MA 01095 Office: Jewish Nursing Home 770 Converse St Longmeadow MA 01109

MOORE, JEAN SUTHERLAND, English educator; b. London, Jan. 17, 1924; came to U.S., 1946; d. Edwin George and Gwendolyn (Thomas) Sutherland; m. Garland V. Moore, Sept. 9, 1944 (div. 1970); children: Lois Moore Wyche, Sandra, Jack. AB, Belmont (N.C.) Abbey Coll., 1963; MEd in English, U. N.C., Greensboro, 1964; postgrad., U. N.C., Chapel Hill, 1965. Prof. of English Belmont Abbey Coll., 1964—. Author short stories, articles; editor: Shop Boy, 1982. Mem. group homes bd. Cerebral Palsy. Lilly Found. fellow, 1977, NEH seminar mem., 1977. Mem. AAUW (bd. dirs. 1988—), 19th Century Studies in South, Victorian Inst., James Joyce Found., James Joyce Soc., Toastmasters (award 1985), Delta Epsilon Sigma. Roman Catholic. Office: Belmont Abbey Coll Belmont NC 28012

MOORE, JERI, advertising executive; b. L.A., May 28, 1953; d. John C. and Virginia (Titus) M.; m. Timothy W. Radder, Sept. 1979 (div. 1984); m. Miles Ross Kuhn, Sept. 30, 1984; children: Christopher Ross, Kacy Lynn. Rsch. supr. Haug Assocs., L.A., 1972-74; dir. advt. rsch. Communicus, Inc., L.A., 1974-78; rsch. cons. various cos. L.A., 1978-79; sr. v.p., dir. strategic planning and rsch. DDB Needham, L.A., 1979-87, sr. v.p., dir. acctg. mgmt., 1987-88; sr. v.p., dir. mktg. decision systems DDB Needham,

Chgo., 1988—. Mem. Am. Mktg. Assn., Ad Club of Chgo., Am. Assn. Pub. Opinion Rsch. Office: DDB Needham 303 E Wacker Dr Chicago IL 60601

MOORE, JOAN ELIZABETH, human resources executive, lawyer; b. Valleyfield, Que., Can., Apr. 29, 1951. BS in Social Scis., Mich. State U., 1973; JD, Case Western Res. U., 1976. Bar: Ohio 1977; cert. systems profl. Pers. exec. Ford Motor Co., Dearborn, Mich., 1976-80; cons. James Lash & Co., Southfield, Mich., 1980-83; pres., owner The Arbor Cons. Group, Inc., Plymouth, Mich., 1983—; owner Integrated Pers. Systems Inc., Plymouth, 1986—. V.p., bd. dirs. Pvt. Industry Coun., Wayne County, Mich., 1985-87; grad. Leadership Detroit VII, 1986, active alumni bd.; mem. computer subcom. Mich. Tech. Coun., 1986—; bd. dirs. Am. Cancer Soc. Mem. ABA, Ohio Bar Assn., Pvt. Industry Coun. (v.p. 1985-87), Mich. Tech. Coun., Leadership Detroit Alumni, Am. Soc. Pers. Adminstrs. Home: 1703 E Stadium Ann Arbor MI 48104 Office: The Arbor Cons Group 711 W Ann Arbor Trail Plymouth MI 48170

MOORE, JOANNE IWEITA, pharmacologist, educator; b. Greenville, Ohio, July 23, 1928; d. Clarence Jacob and Mary Edna (Klepinger) M. A.B., U. Cin., 1950; Ph.D., U. Mich., 1959. Rsch. asst. Christ Hosp. Inst. Med. Rsch., Cin., 1950-55; rsch. asst. U. Mich., Ann Arbor, 1955-57, teaching fellow, 1957-59; postdoctoral fellow in pharmacology Emory U., Atlanta, 1959-61; asst. prof. pharmacology U. Okla. Coll. Medicine, Oklahoma City, 1961-66, assoc. prof., 1966-71, prof., interim chmn., 1971-73, prof., chmn. dept., 1973—, acting chmn., 1969-71; mem. gen. research support rev. com. NIH, 1975-79, biomed. scis. study sect., 1986-90. Contbr. articles to profl. jours. USPHS grantee, 1963-69, 72-74, 79-87. Mem. Am. Soc. Pharmacology and Exptl. Therapeutics, Assn. Med. Sch. Pharmacology, Am. Heart Assn. (bd. dirs. Okla affiliate 1973-88, pres. 1979-80, chmn. bd. 1983-85, bd. Okla. Metro div. 1988—, pres. 1989-90), N.Y. Acad. Scis., Soc. for Exptl. Biology and Medicine, AAAS, Sigma Xi. Office: U Okla Coll Medicine Dept Pharmacology 753 BMSB OUHSC Oklahoma City OK 73190

MOORE, JOSEPHINE CARROLL, neuroanatomy educator, occupational therapist; b. Ann Arbor, Mich., Sept. 20, 1925; d. Arthur Dearth and M. Josephine (Shaffer) Moore. BA, U. Mich., 1943; BS, Eastern Mich. U., 2954; MS, U. Mich., 1959, PhD, 1964. Instr. Eastern Mich. U., Ypsilanti, 1955-58; instr. U.Mich., Ann Arbor, 60-64, asst. prof., 1964-66; asst. prof. U. S.D., Vermillion, 1966-70, assoc. prof., 1970-74, prof. anatomy (neuroanatomy), 1974—; lectr. rehab. confs. in U.S., Can., Mex., Switzerland, Australia, N.Z., 1958—. Contbr. chpts. to books, articles to profl. jours. Mem. vestry St. Paul's Episcopal Ch., Vermillion, 1966—. Fellow Am. Occupational Therapy Assn. (Eleanor Clark Slagel award 1975); mem. Am. Occupational Therapy Found., AAAS, Am. Assn. Anatomists. Republican. Office: U SD Med Sch 414 E Clark St Vermillion SD 57069

MOORE, JOYCE KRISTINA, financial director; b. Phila., June 19, 1955; d. Oscar Herbert Hariu and Virginia Wilson (Guss) Leas ; m. William Burns Moore, June 20, 1980 (div. 1990); children: William Patrick, Kristofer Sean. Student, Beloit Coll., 1973-74, U. Pa., 1974-75, Lafayette Coll., 1984-88. With photographic sales staff MacCallum Stores, Ardmore, Pa., 1974-77; photographer Clair Pruett Studios, Drexel Hill, Pa., 1977-80; photographic cons. Dan's Camera City, Allentown, Pa., 1980-81; contr., co-founder BioService, Inc., Bethlehem, Pa., 1985-89; contr. Mega Video Inc., Easton, Pa., 1989-90; dir. of fin. Community Action Com. of Lehigh Valley, 1990—. Former mem. Warren County Dem. Com., Phillipsburg, N.J., 1981-83; overseer Religious Soc. Friends, 1986—; bd. dirs. Spring Garden Children's Sch., Easton, Pa. Mem. LWV (bd. dirs. Easton area 1987—, pres. 1989—), Balloon Fedn. Am., Gt. Ea. Balloon Assn. Office: Community Action Com of Lehigh Valley 520 Broad St Bethlehem PA 18018

MOORE, KAREN LINDSAY, marketing professional, philosopher, aesthetician; b. Lewiston, Idaho, Nov. 24, 1946; d. Gene Dale and Wilma Marie (Shore) Moore; children: Ashley Michelle, Shawn Michael. BA, U. Colo., 1971, MA, 1979, PhD, 1982. Dir. rsch. and devel. Celestial Seasonings, Inc., Boulder, Colo., 1974-77; dir. mktg. svcs. Celestial Seasonings, Inc., Boulder, 1978—; instr. philosophy U. Colo., Boulder, 1982-83; pres. Living Found., Boulder, 1971-75, Philosophy, Inc., Boulder, 1983-87. Creator, dir. Celestial Seasonings corp. aesthetic and identity packaging, advt., 1974—. Recipient Excellence awards for Art Illustration/Dir., Communication Arts Mag., Palo Alto, Calif., 1984, 87. Mem. Am. Philos. Assn. Office: Celestial Seasonings Inc 1780 55th St Boulder CO 80301

MOORE, KATHERINE B., delivery service executive; b. Norfolk, Va., Oct. 30, 1941; d. William Grant Bell and Katherine (Scott) Bell Weller; children: Ira, Katherine L. BA, U. N.C., Wilmington, 1972; student, East Carolina U., 1975, Webster U., 1984. Pres., chief exec. officer Eastern Delivery Svc., Inc., Wilmington, N.C.; tchr. Ft. Hunt High Sch., Alexandria, Va., Cape Fear Community Coll., Wilmington, McClintock Jr. High Sch., Charlotte; instr. Central Piedmont Community Coll., Charlotte. Chmn., New Hanover County Human Rels. Commn. Mem. Greater Wilmington C. of C., Lower Cape Fear Coun. Arts, YWCA (Achievement award 1985, Avon Women of Enterprise award 1990, adv. bd.), Econ. Growth Women's Form N.C., Com. of 100 (bd. dirs.).

MOORE, LIBBIE ANN, lawyer; b. Great Bend, Kans., Oct. 17, 1960; d. Luther William and Erma Virginia (Willard) M. BA, Kans. State U., 1983; JD, Washburn U., 1986. Bar: Kans. 1986, U.S. Dist. Ct. Kans. 1986. Asst. county atty. Barton County Attys. Office, Great Bend, 1986-90, county atty., 1990—; mem. adv. bd. Cen. Kans. Casa, Inc., Great Bend, 1987-90. Mem. Coalition for Prevention of Child Abuse, Great Bend, 1988-90, CASA, 1987-90. Coalition, 1988-90; bd. dirs. Big Bros./Big Sisters, Great Bend, 1990—. Mem. ABA, Kans. Bar Assn., Kans. County and Dist. Attys. Assn., Barton County Bar Assn., Great Bend C. of C., Soroptimist Internat., Phi Alpha Delta. Republican. Mem. Christian Ch. Office: Barton County Atty's Office Barton County Courthouse PO Box 881 Great Bend KS 67530

MOORE, LINDA ELY, personnel coordinator; b. Chambersburg, Pa., Sept. 28, 1942; d. Richard G. and Janet B. (Kraiss) Ely; m. Brooke Noel Moore, Mar. 21, 1971; children: Sherry Lynne, William James. AA, Md. Med. Secretarial Sch., 1962. Sec. U. Pitts Falk Clinic, 1962-63, Children's Hosp. Orthopedics, Pitts., 1963-64, Shriners Burn Inst., Cin., 1970; adminstrv. asst. Paradise Bd. Realtors; exec. sec. Nat. Med. Enterprises, Inc., Chico, Calif., 1978-81; bus. mgr. Sports Medicine & Fitness Ctr., 1981-83; personnel coordinator Chico Community Hosp., 1982--. Mem. Calif. Hosp. Personnel Mgrs. Assn. Office: Chico Community Hosp 560 Cohasset Rd Chico CA 95926

MOORE, LINDA JEAN, army officer; b. Neenah, Wis., Nov. 4, 1954; d. Glen Carl and Virginia Agnes (Coppens) Bruss. BA cum laude, U. Md., 1986. Stenographer Home Mut. Ins. Co., Appleton, Wis., 1973-74; adminstrv. asst. mcpl. office Town of Menasha, Wis., 1974; enlisted U.S. Army, 1975; personnel staffing specialist, adminstrv. officer SHAPE U.S. Army, Belgium, 1978-83; instr. Inst. Personnel and Resource Mgmt. U.S. Army, Ft. Benjamin Harrison, Ind., 1983-84; adminstrv. supr. Mil. Personnel Ctr. U.S. Army, Alexandria, Va., 1984-87; adminstrv. supr., Pentagon U.S. Army, Washington, 1987—. Mem. Nat. Mus. Women in Arts, Alpha Sigma Lambda, Phi Kappa Phi. Home: 5719 Lawsons Hill Ct Alexandria VA 22310

MOORE, LINDA KATHLEEN, personnel agency executive; b. San Antonio, Tex., Feb. 18, 1944; d. Frank Edward and Louise Marie (Powell) Horton; m. Mack B. Taplin, May 25, 1963 (div. Feb. 1967); 1 child, Mack B.; m. William J. Moore, Mar. 8, 1967 (div. Nov. 1973). Student, Tex. A&I Coll., 1962-63. Co-owner S.R.O. Internat., Dallas, 1967-70; mgr. Exec. Girls Pers. & Modeling Svcs., Dallas, 1970-72, Gen. Employment Enterprises, Atlanta, 1972-88; owner, mgr. More Pers. Svcs., Atlanta, 1988—; Contbr. short story to Writer's Digest. Mem. NAFE, Women Bus. Owners, Nat. Fedn. Bus. and Profl. Women's Clubs, Nat. Assn. Women Cons., Am. Soc. Profl. and Exec. Women, C. of C. (speaker's bur.), Better Bus. Bur. Office: More Pers Svcs 230 Peachtree St Ste 900 Atlanta GA 30303

MOORE, LINDA MARIE ZAJICEK, travel company owner; b. Binghamton, N.Y., Feb. 2, 1943; d. Louis Paul and Mary (Opryshka) Zajicek; m. Charles Edward Moore, Feb. 2, 1963; children: Kimberly Anne, Robert Charles. BSBA, Bryant Coll., 1963; postgrad., Eastern Coll., St. Davids, Pa., 1970. Cert. cruise counselor. Adminstrn. asst. ALCOA, Hartford, Conn., 1963-65; pers. adminstr. Volkswagen Northeastern, Waltham, Mass., 1965-67; adminstrv. specialist GCA Corp., Burlington, Mass., 1967-69; sales mgr. Avon Products, Inc., Newark, Del., 1973-78; account exec. Encore Travel, Naperville, Ill., 1984-86; owner The Traveler's Connection, Naperville, 1986-87; owner, pres. Travel Mktg. Assocs., Wilmington, N.C., 1987—; speaker community orgns., 1975—. Author leisure travel guidebook and mktg. book. Leader Girl Scouts Am., Wayne, Pa., 1970-72; asst. leader Boy Scouts Am., 1987-88; vol. Am. Heart Assn., Wayne, 1969-79; bd. dirs. YWCA, 1989—; chair fin. devel. Women of Achievement, 1989-90, co-chair mktg. com., 1990—; sec. Rowland PTA, 1973-74; mem. funding com. Mill St. Sch., Naperville, Ill., 1983-84; chairperson door prizes Red Cross Ball, 1989-90; chairperson vacation raffle Hospice Festival of Trees, 1988; v.p. Jr. Saturday Club, 1973-74, Naperville Welcome Wagon, 1983-84; class parent Alderman Sch., 1987, Cape Fear Acad., Wilmington, 1989; pres. Main Line Welcome Wagon, 1972-73, Main Line Newcomers Club, 1972-73; tchr. St. Timothy's Luth. Ch., Naperville. Named Woman of Achievement Town of Wilmington, N.C., 1988. Mem. NAFE (bd. dirs. 1987—, chpt. founder 1989), Nat. Network Women in Sales (local pres. 1986, nat. pres. 1987, bd. dirs. 1987-91, Kievman Leadership award 1986), Women in Mgmt., Am. Soc. Assn. Execs., Assn. Execs. N.C., Am. Soc. Tng. & Devel., Upper Main Line Women's Investment Assn., Bus. and Profl. Women (v.p. 1974-75, conv. del. 1975), Travel Coun. N.C., Wilmington C. of C., Inst. Cert. Travel Agts. (coord. study group 1988-90), Chgo. Women in Travel, Execs. Breakfast Club Oakbrook, Naperville Jr. Women's Club.

MOORE, LINDA PERIGO, writer; b. Evansville, Ind., Nov. 25, 1946; d. John Myrl and Loraine Jeannette (Hudson) Perigo; m. Stephen Howard Moore, Aug. 12, 1967; 1 child, Jackson Stuart Moore. BS, Miami U., Oxford, Ohio, 1968; MS, MEd, U. Louisville, 1973. Instr., St. Joseph Infirmary, Louisville, 1969-71; tng. dir. Park-DuValle Neighborhood Health Ctr., Louisville, 1971-74; counselor Charlestown High Sch. (Ind.), 1974-75; tng. dir. Midtown Mental Health Ctr., Indpls., 1977-79; freelance writer, 1980—; cons. Kelly & Assocs., Indpls., 1977-81; instr. Ind. U., Indpls., 1979-81, instr., U. So. Ind., 1986. Bd. dirs. Jr. League Evansville, 1982-84, Mothers Assn. Evansville Day Sch., 1985-87, Evansville Mus. Arts and Sci. Guild, 1982-88; pres. Parent, Tchr., Student Assn., Cen. High Sch., 1989-91. Author: Does This Mean My Kid's a Genius?, 1981; (with Mary Kay Ash) On People Management, 1984, 2nd. ed., 1986, Mary Kay; You're Smarter Than You Think, 1985, Japanese and Swedish edits., 1986; (with Bart Conner) Winning the Gold, 1985; (with Richard Simmons) Reach for Fitness, 1986; (with Walter M. Bortz) One Million Hours, 1990; (with Robert Eliot A Change of Heart, 1990; (TV script for PBS) Tootie Tittlemousie and the Lights of Christmas, 1988 (Ohio State award 1989); contbr. articles in mags. and trade jours; tv appearances include: Oprah Winfrey Show, Today, Sonya Live, Larry King.

MOORE, LINDA PICARELLI, insurance executive; b. Bklyn., Jan. 13, 1943; d. Anthony Joseph and Alma Patricia (D'Angio) Picarelli; m. William H. Moore, Nov. 11, 1962 (div. 1974); 1 child, David A.; m. Spiro D. Demetriou, Dec. 9, 1977. Student, Wagner Coll., 1976, Coll. Ins., 1977-80. Licensed ins. broker. Ins. clk. Tchrs. Ins. and Annuity Assn., N.Y.C., 1959-61; claim examiner Aetna Life and Casualty Co., N.Y.C., 1961-63; claim supr. Northeastern Life Ins. Co., N.Y.C., 1963-66; corr. collector Dun and Bradstreet, S.I., N.Y., 1972-73; asst. underwriter Duncanson and Holt, Inc., N.Y.C., 1973-85; underwriting mgr. CNA Ins. Cos., N.Y.C., 1985-87; account mgr. Marsh and McLennan Group Assn., N.Y.C., 1987-89; asst. mgr. Home Ins. Co., N.Y.C., 1989—; asst. dir. spl. benefits div. Cigna Ins. Co., Phila., 1989—. Mem. Am. Spl. Risk Assn., Amnesty Internat. Democrat. Roman Catholic.

MOORE, LISBETH A., medical technologist; b. Green Bay, Wis., Dec. 17, 1960; d. Robert B. and Jean Claire (Moutrie) M. BS in Biology, Med. Technology, George Mason U., 1984. Rsch. technician NSF-George Mason U., Fairfax, Va., 1980-82; med. technologist Fairfax Hosp. Assn., Falls Church, Va., 1985-86, Mary Washington Hosp., Fredericksburg, Va., 1986-89; med. technologist transfusion svc., clin. pediatrics Duke U. Med. Ctr., Durham, N.C., 1989—. Mem. Am. Soc. Clin. Pathologists (cert.), Alpha Sigma Chi, Tau Kappa Epsilon. Home: 910 Constitution Dr Apt 813 Durham NC 27705

MOORE, LORI LYNN, magazine official; b. Harbor City, Calif., June 25, 1967; d. Jerry O'Dell Moore and Ann Marie (Wilson) Huggins. BA, U. Calif., San Diego, 1988. Promotions mgr. 'Teen Mag., L.A., 1988—. Writer screenplay A Dog's Tale, 1989. Mem. Lomita (Calif.) Sister City Assn., 1988. Scholar women's div. Lomita C. of C., 1984. Mem. U. Calif.-San Diego Alumni Assn. Republican. Office: 'Teen Mag 8490 Sunset Blvd Los Angeles CA 90069

MOORE, LUCILE, retired teacher, volunteer librarian; b. Lauderdale, Miss., Jan. 21, 1910; d. John W. and Mary Evelyn (McCay) Ramsey; m. Paul H. Moore, July 12, 1934; children: Beverly, Richard, Virginia, James. BS, Miss. So. U., 1930; postgrad., U. Ill., 1932-33, Chico (Calif.) State Coll., 1962-64. Tchr. English and Latin, 1930-34; libr. Orinda, Calif., 1951-53; tchr. Stamford, Conn., 1954-59; high sch. tchr. English and Latin Chico, 1959-68; elem. libr. Chico (Calif.) Unified Dist., 1968-75; vol. libr. Butte County Libr., Chico, 1975—. Recipient Neal Dow PTA hon. svc. award Calif. Congress of Parents and Tchrs., 1971, Outstanding Contbn. to the Field of Edn. award Beta Tau chpt. of Alpha Delta Kappa. Mem. Butte County Ret. Tchrs., Alpha Delta Kappa (pres. Fidelis chpt. 1986-87). Republican. Home: 708 Earl Ave Chico CA 95978

MOORE, MAGGIE L., mental health program coordinator; b. Atlanta, June 12, 1965; m. Lawrence E. Sr. Moore; children: Lawrence Jr., Eric. BA, Clark Coll., 1965; student, Brigham Young U., 1966; cert., Ga. State U., 1967. Coord. Ctr. Multicultural Resource Mental Health Assn. Atlanta; tchr. Atlanta Bd. Edn., Ogden (Utah) City Sch. System. Mem. Mental Health Assn. (staff coun.), Atlanta Coun. Intern Orgns., Assn. Counseling and Devel., Ga. Assn. Multicutltural Counseling and Devel., League Women Voters, YWCA, Alpha Kappa Alpha.

MOORE, MARCIA WILLIAMS, corporate professional; b. Welch, Okla., June 19, 1939; d. Oren Earnest Moore and Bernadine (Highsmith) Lawson; children: Tom, LeAnn, John Williams. BS, Fresno State Coll., 1969. Bus. mgr. Pathol. & Clin. Svcs., Fresno, Calif., 1967-88, T.C. Nelson, MD, Fresno, 1967—; corp. sec., half owner Golden Valley Transport Inc., Fresno, 1987. Mem. Clin. Lab. Mgmt. Assn., Female Execs., Calif. Med. Assts. Assn. (dir.-at-large 1984, chmn. membership com. 1987, Med. Asst. of Yr. award 1985), Fresno Women's Network. Democrat. Baptist. Office: Golden Valley Frozen Food Transport Inc Fresno CA 93729

MOORE, MARGARET ANNE FORT, rental property executive; b. Charlotte, N.C., Aug. 26, 1933; d. Risden Sherrill and Margaret Elizabeth (Hodges) F.; m. Ralph Eugene Moore, June 19,1954 (div. 1973); children: Ralph Eugene Moore Jr., Melanie Margaret McNutt. BA, Erskine Coll., Due West, S.C., 1955; student, U. South Fla., 1965, 70-71, 74, 86, Furman U., 1975, Fla. So. Coll., 1976, Manatee Community Coll., Bradenton, Fla., 1987. Social worker Dept. Pub. Welfare, Abbeville, S.C., 1955-56; teacher Pub. Schs. Polk, Osceola, Hall counties., Fla. Ga., 1957-74; sales rep. Ency. Britannica Ednl. Corp., Chgo., 1974-76; teacher Sarasota County Pub. Schs., Sarasota, Fla., 1976-82; office mgr. Atlantic So. Prodns. Inc., Sarasota, Fla., 1982-84; teacher Sarasota County Pub. Schs., Sarasota, Fla., 1984-85; v.p. Atlantic So. Prodns. Inc., Sarasota, Fla., 1985-87; mgr. rental property Sarasota, Fla., 1979—; bd. dirs. Village Brooke Condominium Assoc., Sarasota, 1980-82; county del. Fla. Ed. Assoc. Conf., Tampa, 1980; dir student intern teachers, Fla. Pub. Schs., 1971,74,76. Mem. Sarasota Classified Teacher Assoc. (sch. rep. 1980-82). Republican. Home and Office: 4574 W Robin Hood Trail Sarasota FL 34232

MOORE, MARGARET PERLIN (PEG MOORE), financial services company executive, business consultant; b. Chgo., June 15, 1935; d. Clarence Arthur Perlin and Helen Ilene (Gragg) Alltop; m. Jimmy Nelson Moore, Oct. 29, 1955; 1 child, Marcia Moore King. Student, U. Ill., 1953-56; BS, U. Balt., 1973; M of Adminstrv. Sci., Johns Hopkins U., 1977. Audit supr. First Nat. Bank Md., Balt., 1973-76; sr. auditor Comml. Credit Co., Balt., 1976-78; divisional adminstr. Monumental Life Ins. Co., Balt., 1978-83; dir. programs MBR Internat., Inc., Tustin, Calif., 1983-85; v.p., bd. dirs. Topmast, Inc., Temecula, Calif., 1985—; treas., bd. dirs. Calmoc Enterprises, Inc., Temecula; founder Speedy Tax, Temecula. Creator Sommelier's Choice varietal wine jelly. Sec. City Incorp. Com., Temecula, Calif., 1988, coun. mem. City of Temecula, 1989; bd. dirs. Sam Hicks Monument Pk. Found., Temecula, 1988—. Named Spouse of Yr. Rancho Temecula Murrieta Kiwanis Club, 1987. Mem. DAR, Inland Soc. Tax Cons., So. Calif. Culinary Guild, Temecula Valley C. of C., Rancho Temecula Exch. Club (sec., treas. 1987-89, bd. dirs. 1989-90), Temecula Valley Wine Soc., Internat. Wine and Food Soc., Alpha Delta Pi (chpt. advisor). Republican. Home: 41747 Borealis Dr Temecula CA 92390 Office: Topmast Inc 27740 Jefferson Ave #220 Temecula CA 92390

MOORE, MARJORIE SILCOX, dietitian; b. Mpls., Aug. 27, 1935; d. Walter Bruce and Ruth May (Davis) Silcox; m. Howard Warner Moore, June 29, 1957; children—Michael Howard, Meri Beth. B.S., Iowa State U., 1957. Therapeutic dietitian Luth. Hosp., Balt., 1957-61; pvt. practice as cons. dietitian, Nashville, 1972-75; clin. dietitian Bapt. Hosp., Nashville, 1975-83, chief clin. dietitian, 1983—; mem. adv. bd. Health Promotions and Fitness Ctr., Nashville, 1984—. Advisor, Care Line Social Action Group on Aging, Nashville, 1982—; bd. dirs., pres. Head's Up Child Devel. Ctr., Nashville, 1984—. Mem. Tenn. Dietetic Assn. (chmn. long range fund raising com. 1988-89), Nashville Dist. Dietetic Assn. (diet manual com.). Democrat. Methodist. Avocations: needlework, knitting, music, reading, weight lifting. Home: 836 Clematis Dr Nashville TN 37205 Office: Baptist Hosp 2000 Church St Nashville TN 37236

MOORE, MARY, advertising agency executive. Formerly sr. v.p. Humphrey Browning MacDougall Inc. (now HBM/Creamer), Boston, exec. v.p., creative dir., then pres. creative dir.; vice-chmn., chief creative officer Wells Rich Greene Worldwide, 1988—. Office: Wells Rich Greene Inc 9 W 57th St New York NY 10019

MOORE, MARY NEEDHAM, faculty member; b. Cambridge, Mass., Feb. 28, 1934; d. Horace Richmond and Elizabeth (Burk) Needham; children: John, Jennifer, David, Bradford. AB, Bates Coll., 1957; MEd, St. Joseph's U., 1973; MSN, U. Pa., 1979, PhD, 1986. RN, Pa., Va. Asst. prof. Widener U., Chester, Pa., 1974-80; teaching fellow U. Pa., Phila., 1980-81, instr., 1981-85; asst. prof. U. Va., Charlottesville, 1985-90; assoc. prof. Coll. of New Rochelle, N.Y., 1990—; manuscript cons. F.A. Davis Co., Phila., 1982, Addison-Wesley Pub. Co., Menlo Park, Calif., 1983; mem. rev. panel Jour. Nursing Rsch.; cons. in field. Contbr. articles to profl. jours. Mem. Am. Nurses Assn., AAUP, Nat. Assn. Orthopaedic Nurses (chairperson rsch. 1983-85), AM. Nephrotology Nurses Assn. (rev. panel), Nurses in Washington Roundtable, So. Nursing Rsch. Soc., Sigma Theta Tau. Republican. Presbyterian. Home: 2305 Glenn Ct Charlottesville VA 22903

MOORE, MARY SUSAN, psychologist; b. Denver, Mar. 2, 1945; d. George Crosby and Jessica Frances (Barnard) Moore; m. Richard Hideki Okada June 1969 (div. 1974); m. James Donald Meiss, Jan. 8, 1980. BA in English Lit., Pomona Coll., Claremont, Calif., 1967; Cert. Edn., San Francisco State U., 1968; MS in Ednl. Psychology, Calif. State U., Hayward, 1978; PhD in Clin. Psychology, Calif. Sch. Profl. Psychology, Berkeley, 1981. Tchr. San Francisco Unified Sch. Dist., 1968-71; sch. psychologist Raskob Clinic, Holy Names Coll., Oakland, Calif., 1977-79; adj. asst. prof. Coll. Edn., U. Tex., Austin, 1981-84; staff psychologist Mental Health Unit, Student Hosp., U. Tex., Austin, 1984-85; lectr. Dept. Psychology U. Tex., 1985-86; rsch. assoc. Brunel U., London, 1987; cons., lectr. in psychology Boulder, Colo., 1988—; cons. in field; clin. dir. Child and Family Therapy Clinic, U. Tex., Austin, 1985-86. Contbr. articles to profl. jours. Soroptomist pre-docotral fellow, 1980; Hogg Found. for Mental Health grantee, 1985; Fulbright rsch. grantee, 1985-86. Mem. Am. Psychol. Assn., Tex. Psychol. Assn., Colo. Psychol. Assn., World Assn. Infant Psychiatry and Allied Disciplines.

MOORE, MARY TYLER, actress; b. Bklyn., Dec. 29, 1936; d. George and Marjorie Moore; m. Richard Meeker; 1 child, Richard (dec.); m. Grant Tinker, 1963 (div. 1981); m. Robert Levine, 1983. Chmn. bd. MTM Enterprises, Inc., Studio City, Calif. Appeared in TV series Richard Diamond, Private Eye, 1957-59, Dick Van Dyke Show, 1961-66, Mary Tyler Moore Show, 1970-77, Mary, 1978, Mary Tyler Moore Hour, 1979, Mary, 1985, miniseries Gore Vidal's Lincoln, 1988; in TV movies Love American Style, 1969, Run a Crooked Mile, 1969, First You Cry, 1978, Heartsounds, 1984, Finnegan Begin Again, 1984, numerous others; in films X-15, 1961, Thoroughly Modern Millie, 1967, Don't Just Stand There, 1968, What's So Bad About Feeling Good?, 1968, Change of Habit, 1969, Ordinary People, 1980 (Acad. Award nominee for best actress 1981), Six Weeks, 1982, Just Between Friends, 1986; appeared on Broadway in Whose Life Is It Anyway?, 1980, Sweet Sue, 1987; in TV spl. How to Survive the Seventies, 1978, How To Raise a Drug Free Child. Recipient Emmy award Nat. Acad. TV Arts and Scis. 1964-65, 73-74, 76, Golden Globe award 1965, 81; named to TV Hall of Fame, 1985. Office: care Agy Performing Arts Inc 9000 Sunset Blvd Ste 1200 Los Angeles CA 90069*

MOORE, MELANIE ETHEL, sales executive; b. Swainsboro, Ga., Mar. 19, 1952; d. William Walker and Elizabeth (DuPree) M. Student, Ga. State U., 1975, 78-80; BA, Agnes Scott Coll., 1974. Research assoc. Emory U., Atlanta, 1974-77; customer service rep. VWR Sci., Atlanta, 1978-80, interactive purchasing, 1980-81, sales rep., 1981-83; regional mgr. Precision Sci., Chgo., 1983-84; regional sales mgr. Ohaus Scale Corp., Florham Park, N.J., 1984-88; tech. sales rep. EM Sci., Gibbstown, N.J., 1989—. Contbr. articles to profl. jours. Grantee NSF, 1973. Mem. AAUW, NAFE, DAR. Baptist.

MOORE, MOLLIE, bank executive; b. Key West, Fla., Jan. 14, 1950; d. Richard LeRoy and Annabell (Hart) Moore; m. Clarance Montgomery Northington, June 22, 1972 (div. May 1974); m. Marvin Woodrow, May 12, 1975; children: Hollie Lynn, Marvin Thomas. Postgrad., Old Donioion U., Norfolk, 1969, Tidewater Community Coll., Va. Beach, 1972, U. Richmond, 1978; Cert., U. Va., Charlottesville, 1984. Cashier Bruce Flournoy Ford, Norfolk, Va., 1969-70; adminstrv. sec. Nansemond Correctional Unit, Franklin, Va., 1973-74; various positions money transfer Nancy Transfer, United Va. Bank, Richmond, 1974-76; bank accts. clerk United Va. Bank, Richmond, investment officer, 1979-80; asst. v.p. United Va. Bank, 1980-86, Crestar Investment Bank, Richmond, 1986-. sec. Broadmeadows Civic Assn., Richmond, 1975. Mem. Real Time User Group (chmn.), Nat. Coun. for Uniform Interest Compensation, Nat. Coun. for Uniform Interest Compensation-Communication Com., Am. Bankers Assn., Va. Bankers Assn. Office: Crestar Investment Bank 919 E Main St Richmond VA 23219

MOORE, PATRICIA A., real estate company officer; b. N.Y.C., Nov. 16, 1944; d. Pat and Patrina (Travali) Ciardullo. BA, Alfred U., 1966; MA, U. Miami, 1968. Lic. real estate broker, Calif; cert. tchr., Fla., Calif.; lic. ins. agt. Pres. Cert. Brokers Am., Inc., Concord, Calif.; broker, owner Cert. Brokers Concord, Cert. Brokers Antioch, Calif.; v.p. Gen. Home Loans, Concord; v.p. Network Real Estate of No. Calif., Inc., also bd. dirs. Treas. ERA North Bay Coun., 1985—; sec. Nat. Corp. Relocation Coun., 1986-87, v.p., 1988—. Mem. Nat. Assn. Real Estate Appraisers, U.S. and local C. of C., NAFE, Eta Mu Alpha.

MOORE, PATRICIA ANN, marketing and sales executive; b. Huntington, NY, July 16, 1954; d. Joseph Nicholas and Dorothy Patricia (Olszewski) Mamola; m. William Martin Moore, Feb. 15, 1986. Grad., U. Santa Clara, 1976. Ops. mgr. Laguna Fed. Savs. & Loan, Orange, Calif., 1977-79; customer svc. rep. Bentley Labs., Irvine, Calif., 1979-80, mgr. custom products, 1980-82, internat. custom product specialist, 1981-82; dist. sales mgr. Am. Bentley Labs., San Francisco, 1982-83, Nellcor, Inc., San Francisco, 1983-84; product mgr. Nellcor, Inc., Hayward, Calif., 1984-85, nat. accounts mgr., 1986-88, internat. distbn. mgr., 1985-88; dir. internat. mktg. and sales NATUS Med., Inc., Foster City, Calif., 1989—. Mem. Nat. Account Mktg. Assn. Republican. Roman Catholic. Home: 926 Aruba Ln Foster City CA 94404-3802 Office: NATUS Medical Inc 324 Lakeside Dr Foster City CA 94404

MOORE, PATRICIA KAY, market research administrator; b. Peoria, Ill., Jan. 20, 1947; d. David Harold and Mary Jane (Gregoryk) Jenkins; m. James Christopher Moore, Jan. 11, 1980. BS in Bus. Adminstrn., U. Mo., 1978, MBA, 1981. Planning analyst Emerson Electric Corp., St. Louis, 1972-79; mgr. mktg. adminstrn. Emerson Electric WED, Houston, 1979; dir. mktg. adminstrn. HBE Corp., St. Louis, 1979-82; mgr. market research Emerson Electric ESD, St. Louis, 1982—; instr. U. Mo.; cons. project bus. Advisor Jr. Achievement. Recipient Woman Leader award YWCA. Mem. Am. Mktg. Assn., U. Mo. Alumni Assn. Home: 6 Geyer Wood Ln Frontenac MO 63131 Office: Emerson Electric ESD 8100 W Florissant St MS 3216 Saint Louis MO 63136

MOORE, PEGGY SUE, corporation financial executive; b. Wichita, Kans., June 16, 1942; d. George Alvin and Marie Aileene (Hoskinson) M. Student, Wichita State U., 1961-63, Wichita Bus. Coll., 1963-64. Contr. Mears Electric Co., Wichita, 1965-69; exec. v.p., sec., treas., chief fin. officer CPI Corp., Wichita, 1969—, also bd. dirs.; Trustee Fringe Benefits Co., Kansas City, Mo., 1984-85. Active Rep. Nat. Com., Washington, 1985-86, task force, 1986—; treas., bd. dirs. Good Shepherd Luth. Ch., Wichita, 1980-85, mem., 1977—; active Wichita Commn. on Status of Women, 1988. Mem. NAFE, DAR, Nat. Assn. of Women Bus. Owners, Wichita C. of C., Women's Nat. Bowling Assn. (bd. dirs., pub. com. 1969-76), Internat. Platform Assn., Kans. Purveyors Assn. (bd. dirs. 1988-89), Women's Speakers Bur. Office: CPI Corp 816 E Funston Wichita KS 67211

MOORE, SALLY JANE, writer; b. Buffalo, Feb. 12, 1936; d. Harold E. and Ruth E. (Hertzel) Choate; m. Richard E. Moore, Dec. 10, 1960; children: Sara-Lynn Slusher, Karen Penrose, Thomas C. Student, Mount Holyoke Coll., 1954-56. Ski editor, columnist Journal Inquirer, Manchester, Conn., 1970-76; dir. pub. info. Am. Heart Assn. Greater Hartford, Conn., 1976-77; ski columnist Phila. Inquirer, 1977-79; chief of media and pub. rels. Pa. Bur. Travel Devel., Harrisburg; freelance writer/photographer, 1985—. Mem. Soc. Am. Travel Writers, U.S. Ski Writers Assn. Democrat. Home: 1226 Blossom Terr Boiling Springs PA 17007

MOORE, SALLY JOY DONDROE, administrative assistant; b. Mt. Vernon, N.Y., Mar. 31, 1943; d. Richard Anthony and Mildred Ruth (Dawley) Donohue. Sec. Rystan Co., Mt. Vernon, 1961-63; personnel clk. sec. Babcock & Wilcox Co., N.Y.C., 1963-70; administrv. asst. Consumers Union, Mt. Vernon, 1970—. Mem. New Rochelle Bus. & Profl. Women (sec. 1977-79), New Rochelle N.Y.C (sec. 1980-83), N.Y. Zool. Soc. The Delta Soc., The Cousteau Soc. Protestant. Office: Consumers Union 256 Washington St Mount Vernon NY 10553

MOORE, SANDRA KAY, small business owner; b. Balt., Sept. 20, 1957; d. George Leru and Catherine Emily (Albright) Moore; 1 child from previous marriage, Catherine Earlene. Grad., No. High Sch., Balt., 1975. Word processor Balt., 1975-79; joint ptnr. Ultimate Dating Svcs., Balt., 1979-81; pres., owner Exquisite Dating Experiences, Mechanicsville, Md., 1981-83; adminstrv. asst. Office of Personnel Mgmt., Washington, 1983-85; computer cons. Bensalem, Pa., 1985-87; pres., owner S & L Ent., Bensalem, 1987—; pres. Infinity Artists and Entertainment, Inc., N.Y.C., 1990—. Mem. NAFE, Tower-Bucks County C. of C. Office: 2321 Street Rd #306 Bensalem PA 19020

MOORE, SARAH COPELAND, cafeteria manager; b. Ensley, Ala., Sept. 24, 1939; d. Susie Florence (Denson) Bradford; m. John Harris Moore, June 18, 1958; children: Valerie M. Cottingham, Alesia R., Derrick F. Student, Clark Coll., Atlanta, 1957-58; BS, Miles Coll., 1963; postgrad., U. Montevallo, 1971-72; MEd, Ala. State U., 1976. With U.S. Dept. Agr. Stablzn. & Conservation Svc., Birmingham, Ala., 1965-71; food svc. supr. Jefferson County Commn., Birmingham, 1972-74, sr. food svc. supr., 1974-83, mgr. cafeteria, 1983—. Trustee Greater Temple Bapt. Ch., 1976—, tchr. Sunday sch., 1972—. Recipient Hermon H. Long Community Svc. award The Greater Birmingham Inter-Alumni Community, 1990, Cert. of Appreciation, Miles Coll. Alumni, 1979, Nat. Voluntary Health Agys. of Ala., 1984-90, Blood Drive award ARC, Birmingham, 1989; named for Outstanding and Dedicated Svc., Greater Temple Bapt. Ch., Birmingham, 1976, 70-80, 86, 87. Mem. AAUW, Top Ladies of Distinction (corr. sec. Birmingham Met. chpt. 1988), Birmingham Restaurant Assn., Jefferson County Restaurant Assn., Nat. Coun. Negro Women, Gamma Phi Delta (Alpha Xi chpt., scholarship com. 1988—, Alpha Xi 25th Anniversary plaque 1987). Democrat. Home: 2736 Parklawn Ave SW Birmingham AL 35211

MOORE, SHIRLEY BEAHAM, real estate professional, civic worker; b. Tucson, July 28, 1934; d. Thomas Graham and Virginia (Ruthrauff) Beaham; m. Jack K. Moore, Jr., June 30, 1956 (div. June 1969); children: Catherine Lee Puccetti, Alan Graham. BA, Scripps Coll., 1956. Exec. dir. Pima chpt. Ariz. Kidney Found., Tucson, 1977-81; realtor assoc. Roy H. Long Realty, Tucson, 1982—; organizer, participant Southwestern Sch. Behavioral Health Studies, Tucson, 1977-78. Civic worker, Tucson, 1958—; bd. dirs. Planned Parenthood So. Ariz., 1959-65, v.p., 1962, pres., 1963-64; bd. dirs. Jr. League Tucson, 1962-73, Alcoholism Council Tucson, 1977-87; bd. dirs. St. Luke's in Desert, Inc., 1975-86, 1990—; mem. planning com., 1984—; area chmn. ARC, 1964; bd. dirs. St. Luke's Bd. Visitors, 1968-78, v.p., 1974, pres., 1975; bd. dirs. Tohono Chul Park, 1990; co-chmn. U.S. Senatorial Campaign, Pima County, 1972; invitations and gen. arrangements chmn. Tucson Symphony Cotillion, 1973, 74; participant Ariz. Town Hall, Grand Canyon, 1975; mem. Ariz. Acad., 1975-84; rep. alumnae admissions Scripps Coll., 1979-84. Mem. Tucson Bd. Realtors, U. Ariz. Pres.'s Club, P.E.O. Republican. Episcopalian. Office: Roy H Long Realty 6424 E Tanque Verde Tucson AZ 85715

MOORE, SHIRLEY THROCKMORTON (MRS. ELMER LEE MOORE), accountant; b. Des Moines, July 4, 1918; d. John Carder and Jessie (Wright) Throckmorton; student Iowa State Tchrs. Coll., summers 1937-38, Madison Coll., 1939-41; M.C.S., Benjamin Franklin U., 1944; CPA, Mc.; m. Elmer Lee Moore, Dec. 19, 1946; children: Fay, Lynn Dallas. Asst. bookkeeper Sibley Hosp., Washington, 1941-42, Alvord & Alvord, 1942-46, bookkeeper, 1946-49, chief accountant, 1950-64, fin. adviser to sr. ptnr., 1957-64; dir. Allen Oil Co., 1958-74; pvt. practice acctg., 1964—. Mem. sch. bd. Takoma Acad., Takoma Park, Md., 1970—; mem. hosp. bd. Washington Adventist Hosp., 1974-85; chmn. worthy student fund Takoma Park Seven Day Adventist Ch., 1987—; trustee Benson Found., 1963—; vol. Am. Women's Voluntary Svc., 1942-45. Recipient Disting. Grad. award Benjamin Franklin U., 1961. Mem. Am., D.C. (pub. rels. com. 1976—) insts. CPAs, Am. Women's Soc. CPAs, Am. Soc. Women Accts. (legislation chmn. 1960-62, nat. dir. 1952-53, nat. treas. 1953-54), Bus. and Profl. Women's Club (treas. D.C. 1967-68), Benjamin Franklin U. Alumni Assn. (Disting. Alumni award 1964, charter, past dir.), D.A.R., Md. Assn. CPAs (charter chmn. membership com. Montgomery Prince George County 1963-64, chmn. student rels. com. 1964-67, pres. 1968-69, mem. fed. tax com. 1971-73). Mem. Seventh Day Adventist Ch. Contbr. articles to profl. jours. Home and Office: 1007 Elm Ave Takoma Park MD 20912

MOORE, SUSAN EVELYN, chemist, biologist; b. Mobile, Ala., July 20, 1954; d. Thurston Theodore and Evelyn (Patty) M. BS magna cum laude, Mobile Coll., 1976; postgrad. U. South Ala. Tech. dir. Ala. Lions Eye Bank, Birmingham, 1979-81; chem. cons. Merck & Co., Inc., Birmingham, 1981-84; indsl. chemist Ashland Co., Huntsville, Ala., 1984-85; electron microscopist U. Ala., Birmingham, 1986-88; supr. Immune Cytopenia Lab., 1988—. Mem. choir Shades Mountain Baptist Ch., 1980—. U. South Ala. research grantee, 1977-79. Mem. Nat. Assn. Female Execs. (charter), Electron Microscopy Soc. Am., Ala. Soc. Electron Microscopists, Nat. Assn. Sports Ofcls. (charter), Nat. Fedn. Interscholastic Ofcls. Assn. (charter), Ala. High Sch. Athletic Assn. (basketball and football approved), Amateur Softball Assn. (umpire). Republican. Baptist. Avocations: tennis, antique refinishing, softball, basketball. Home: 1219-I Beacon Pkwy E Birmingham AL 35209 Office: U Ala Comprehensive Cancer Ctr 1824 6th Ave S WTI 210 Birmingham AL 35294

MOORE, SUSAN LYNN, marketing executive; b. Freeport, N.Y., Mar. 21, 1949; d. Robert Emmett Moore and Margaret Ann (Moline) Reich; m. Frank Badalucco (div. Dec. 1974); 1 child, Lisa; m. Gary Wayne Sitton, May 22, 1981. A. in Gen. Studies, Pima Community Coll.; BSBA, U. Phoenix, 1989; postgrad. U. Ariz. Lic. real estate salesperson, Ariz.; commd. peace officer, Ariz. Pvt. investigator, L.I., N.Y., 1969-73; investigator Office of Spl. Investigations, N.Y. Dept. Social Services, Bayshore, 1973-74; sgt. USAF, Davis Monthan AFB, Tucson, Ariz., 1974-77; sr. investigator criminal div., Pima County Atty.'s Office, Tucson, 1977-80, 88-crime program dir. (CrimeStoppers), 1980-87; exec. v.p. Southern Ariz. Home Builders Assn., 1988; v.p. new bus. devel. Lockard Constrn., Inc., Tucson, 1988—; founding mem., dir. CrimeStoppers USA, 1980-82. Mem. Gov. Bruce Babbitt's Crime Commn., Phoenix, 1984; dir. Tucson Community Found., 1985—; founder, chmn. Missing Children's Task Force, Tucson, 1985—. Named to Teaching Individuals Positive Solutions/Protective Strategies Adv. Council Ariz. Supreme Ct., 1985—; adv. bd. O'Reilly Care Ctr.; co-chmn. adv. bd. Tucson Internat. Film Festival; chmn. exec. coun. Boys and Girls Clubs of Tucson. Mem. Tucson Met. C. of C. (Outstanding Community Service award 1984, prevention com. 1983—), Rotary. Avocations: aerobics, free weights, running, bicycling. Home: 1871 S Skyview Pl Tucson AZ 85748 Office: Lockard Constrn Inc 1900 W Grant Rd Tucson AZ 85745

MOORE, TANNA LYNN, real estate consulting company executive; b. Columbus, Ohio, Oct. 19, 1954; d. Richard Owen and Marianne Ruth (Daries) M.; m. Craig Thomas Swaggert, Aug. 31, 1986; stepchildren: Mitchell, Nickolas. BA in Econs., Kenyon Coll., 1976; MBA, Dartmouth Coll., 1978. With project mgmt. Gen. Mills Inc., 1978-82; account exec., v.p., sr. v.p. U.S. Communications Corp., Mpls., 1982-90; sr. v.p. Keewaydin Group, Inc., Mpls., 1990—; lectr. St. Thomas Coll., St. Paul, prof., 1987; lectr. U. Minn., St. Paul; lectr. promotional mktg., client relationships and career planning to ednl. instns.; bd. dirs. Sta. KTCA-TV, Mpls. Bd. dirs. Illusion Theater, Mpls., 1979-86, chairperson Crystal Ball, 1987; bd. dirs. Downtown YMCA, Mpls.; mktg. cons. Am. Cancer Soc., Walker Art Ctr., Mpls. Presbyterian. Home: 4705 Fremont Ave Minneapolis MN 55409 Office: Keewaydin Group Inc 80 S 8th St Minneapolis MN 55402

MOORE, VIRGINIA BRADLEY, librarian, educator; b. Laurens, S.C., May 13, 1932; d. Robert Otis Brown and Queen Esther (Smith) Bradley; m. David Lee Moore, Dec. 27, 1957 (div. 1973). B.S., Winston-Salem State U., 1954; M.L.S., U. Md., 1970. Cert. in libr. sci. edn. Tchr. John R. Hawkins High Sch., Warrenton, N.C., 1954-55, Happy Plains High Sch., Taylorsville, N.C., 1955-58, Young and Carver elem. schs., Washington, 1958-65; libr. Davis and Minor elem. schs., Washington, 1965-72, Ballou Sr. High Sch., Kramer Jr. High Sch., Washington, 1972-75, 78-80, Anacostia Sr. High Sch., Washington, 1975-77, 80—; class, club sponsor, 1975— chmn. competency-based curriculum D.C. Pub. Schs., 1978—; speaker, presenter Ch. and Synagogue Libr. Assn., 1975, 80, 83; dir. ch. libr. workshops Asbury United Methodist Ch., Washington, 1972-74, 76; mem. 1st libr. and info. sci. del. to People's Republic China, 1985. Author: (bibliography) The Negro in American History, 1619-1968, 1968; TV script for vacation reading program, 1971, sound/slide presentation D.C. Church Librs.' Bicentennial Celebration, 1976; video script and tchr.'s guide for Nat. Libr. Week Balloon Launch Day, 1983; bibliography Black Literature/Materials, 1987; contbr. articles to profl. jours. Rec. sec. Washington Pan-Hellenic Coun., 1975; libr. Mt. Carmel Baptist Ch., Washington, 1984. Recipient certs. of award D.C. Pub. Libr., 1980, D.C. Pub. Schs., 1983; NDEA scholar Central State Coll., Edmond, Okla., 1969, U. Ky., 1969; scholar Ball State U., 1969; grad. fellow U. Md., 1969. Mem. NEA (life), ALA (councilor-at-large 1983-91), LWV, Internat. Assn. Sch. Librs., Am. Assn. Sch. Librs. (coms. 1973-83), D.C. Assn. Sch. Librs. (pres. 1971-73, citation 1973, newsletter editor 1971-75, 83, Soc. Sch. Librs. Internat., Internat. Assn. Sch. Librs., Freedom to Read Found., Intellectual Freedom Roundtable (bd. dirs., exec. com. 1989—), D.C. Libr. Assn., Md. Ednl. Media Orgn., Internat. Platform Assn., Prince Georges County LWV, S.E. Neighbors Club, Zeta Phi Beta (v.p. chpt. 1972-74), Delta Kappa Gamma (v.p. 1990—). Democrat. Home: 2100 Brooks Dr Apt 721 Forestville MD 20747 Office: Anacostia Sr High Sch 16th and R Sts SE Washington DC 20020

MOORE, YVONNE L.H.R., retail manager; b. Newark, N.J., July 24, 1943; d. Marion and Ola D. (Johnson) Laughlin; m. Jesse Moore, Sept. 23, 1984; children: Durand, Anthony, Yvette. Student, Essex County Coll., 1978. Store mgmt. A&E Corp., Ridgefield, N.J.; store mgr. Lerner Ltd., N.Y.C. Mem. NAFE, NAACP, DAV (life aux.).

MOORE-CARROLL, PATRICIA SUSAN, hairdresser, make-up artist; b. Toledo, Ohio, June 14, 1957; d. Wilford Henderson and Beatrice Ann (Otting) Moore; married, Oct. 10., 1986. Lic. cosmetologist. Hairdesigner Country Charm Beauty Salon, Swanton, Ohio, 1975; mgr. Tory's Services, Inc., Swanton, 1975-80; owner Patty and Co. Hairdesigners, Swanton, 1980—; owner Jhirmack Lyceum, Redding, Calif., 1979; advisor Penta County Cosmetology Dept; adv. com., Penta County Vocat. High Sch., 1979—. Mem. Nat. Hairdresser and Cosmetology Assn. Democrat. Roman Catholic. Office: Patty and Co 137 Airport Hwy Swanton OH 43558

MOORE-DAY, BONNIE LOU, corporate professional; b. East Orange, N.J., July 10, 1956; d. Clinton Hoyt and Hannabel (Borst) Moore; m. Garrison Glenn Day, Dec. 12, 1987. AA, East Los Angeles Jr. Coll., 1977; BA in Early Childhood Edn., Calif. State U., Los Angeles, 1985. Tchr. Gerber's Child Ctr., Los Angeles, 1977-78; options prin. Bateman Eichler, Los Angeles, 1978-84; compliance dir. Cantor Fitzgerald & Co., Inc., Los Angeles, 1984—; sec. Cantor Fitzgerald Fin. Corp., Los Angeles, 1989—. Mem. Nat. Assn. Securities Dealers (bd. arbitrators), Nat. Soc. Compliance Profls. Republican. Presbyterian. Lodge: Order Ea. Star (matron 1986-87). Home: 4633 Ocean View Blvd La Canada CA 91011 Office: Cantor Fitzgerald & Co Inc 1840 Century Park East 9th Floor Los Angeles CA 90067

MOOREHEAD, VICTORIA ROSE, sales executive; b. Cleve., Aug. 24, 1951; d. Walter George and Stella (Petrella) Tuleta; m. Richard Manford Moorehead, Sept. 11, 1971 (div. 1982). BA, Cleve. State U., 1974. Cert. secondary edn. tchr., Ohio, W.Va., Pa. Dist. mgr. Revco Drug Stores, Inc., Cleve., 1969-78; sales mgr. Revlon Beauty Care div., N.Y.C., 1978-79; sales mgr. spl. commodity div. Carolina Freight Carriers Corp., Weirton, W.Va., 1979-82; sales rep. gen. commodity div. Carolina Freight Carriers Corp., Cherryville, N.C., 1982; mgr. nat. accts. svc. Transport, Inc., Nashville, 1982—. Mem. Future Bus. Leaders Am. (pres. 1968-69), Traffic Club Cleve., Akron Club, Quill & Scroll Writing Soc., Delta Nu Alpha. Democrat. Roman Catholic. Home: 9640 E River Rd PO Box 38207 Olmsted Falls OH 44138 Office: Svc Transport Inc 668 Euclid Ave Ste 535 Atrium Office Pla Cleveland OH 44114

MOORHOUSE, LINDA VIRGINIA, symphony orchestra administrator; b. Lancaster, Pa., June 26, 1945; d. William James and Mary Virginia (Wild) M. BA, Pa. State U., 1967. Sec. San Antonio Symphony, Tex., 1970-71, adminstrv. asst., 1971-75, asst. mgr., 1975-76; gen. mgr. Canton (Ohio) Symphony, 1977—. Mem. Ohio Arts Coun. Music Panel, 1980-82, 87-89, Mich. Arts Coun. Music Panel, 1986; bd. dirs. Stark County unit Arthritis Fedn., 1986—, treas., 1989—. Mem. Met. Orch. Mgrs. Assn. (pres. 1983-85), Orgn. Ohio Orchs. (pres. 1985-86), Am. Symphony Orch. League (bd. dirs. 1983-85). Office: Canton Symphony Orch 1001 Market Ave N North Canton OH 44702

MOOSBRUGGER, MARY COULTRIP, marketing research company executive; b. Urbana, Ill., Sept. 1, 1947; d. Donald Lyle and Charlotte Carole (Barkes) Coultrip; m. John Robert Moosbrugger, Apr. 24, 1971; children: Peter John, Kathryn Rose. BA in English, U. Ill., 1969; MBA in Mktg., U. Chgo., 1982. Study mgr. Booz, Allen & Hamilton, Chgo., 1972-73; rsch. supr. Quaker Oats Co., Chgo., 1974-75; mgr. mktg. rsch. Sara Lee Co., Deerfield, Ill., 1976-77; pres., chief exec. officer Moosbrugger Mktg. Rsch., La Grange, Ill., 1977—. Mem. Am. Mktg. Assn. Office: 901 W Hillgrove La Grange IL 60525

MOOSE, LYNNE SUZANNE, insurance agent; b. Hickory, N.C., Aug. 2, 1966; d. Raymond Richard and Lynne Paula (Wilson) M. BS in Econs., N.C. State U., 1988. Food show coord. Merchants Distbrs. Inc., Hickory, N.C., 1980-84; rec. staff Town of Maiden (N.C.), 1981-84; computer analyst MDI, Hickory, 1985; officer mgr. Formbar, Inc., Raleigh, N.C., 1986-88; dist. agt. Prudential Ins. Co., Greensboro, N.C., 1888-89; sales agt. State Farm Ins. Co., Lexington, N.C., 1989-90; assoc. agt. Nationwide Ins. Co., Lexington, N.C., 1990—. Mem. Lexington Assn. Life Underwriters (treas., membership chmn.), NAFE, N.C. State U. Alumni Assn. Methodist. Office: Nationwide Ins PO Box U Lexington NC 27292

MORAGNÉ E SILVA, MICHÈLE LOWE, educator; b. White Plains, N.Y., May 23, 1955; d. John Hutchins and Catherine Theresa (Kelley) M.; m. Amandio. BA, Bucknell U., 1977; MEd, Rhode Island Coll., 1981; postgrad., U. Tex., 1983. Instr. Am. Language Inst., Porto, Portugal, 1978-79; instr., cons. Rhode Island Coll., Providence, Rhode Isla. 1980-83; asst. instr. U. Tex., Austin, 1984-85; asst. prof., dir. English for internat. students St. Edward's U., Austin, 1985—. Pub. (composition textbook) Authentic Writing; contbr. articles to profl. jours. Mem. Tchrs. English to Speakers of Others Langs. (conv. presentor 1981-88), Nat. Coun. Tchrs. English, Fgn. Lang. Edn. Ctr. Student Assn. (sec., v.p.). Democrat. Roman Catholic. Home: 804 Emerald Wood Dr Austin TX 78745 Office: St Edwards U 3001 S Congress Ave Austin TX 78704

MORAHAN, PAGE SMITH, microbiology and immunology educator; b. Newport News, Va., Jan. 7, 1940; d. Robert Bruce and Margaret (Coleman) Smith; m. Neil Morahan, Nov. 9, 1963 (div. 1977); m. John Acton, Jan. 4, 1986. BA, Agnes Scott Coll., Decatur, Ga., 1961; MA, Hunter Coll., 1964; PhD, Marquette U., 1969. Asst. prof. Med. Coll. Va., Richmond, 1971-74, assoc. prof., 1974-81, prof., 1981-82; prof., chmn. dept. microbiology and immunology Med. Coll. Pa., Phila., 1982—; mem. adv. com. manpower rev. com. Nat. Cancer Inst., Washington, 1976-81, rev. com., 1986-90; mem. external adv. bd. Allegheny Singer Rsch. Inst., Pitts., 1990—; course dir. W. Alton Jones Cell Sci. Ctr., Lake Placid, N.Y., 1980-81. Contbr. over 100 articles and revs. to profl. jours., chpts. to books. Bd. dirs. Spring Garden Hist. Dist. Civic Assn., Phila., 1985-86; mem. adv. bd. 1st United Meth. Ch. Germantown, Phila., 1990. Recipient rsch. career devel. award NIH, 1974-79, Lindback award for teaching excellence in basic sci. Lindback Found., 1988; named Outstanding Woman in Sci., 1982; grantee Nat. Inst. Arthritis and Infectious Disease, 1987-92, NIMH, 1989-94, Nat. Cancer Inst., 1989-92. Mem. AAAS, Am. Acad. Microbiology, Am. Assn. Immunologists, Am. Assn. for Cancer Rsch., Soc. Toxicology, Am. Soc. Mirology, Soc. Immunopharmacology, Soc. for Exptl. Biology and Medicine, Soc. Virus Rsch., Reticuloendothelial Soc., Am. Soc. for Microbiology (med. microbiology and immunology com. 1989-92), Assn. Med. Microbiology Chairmen (councilor 1986-88, pres. 1989), Phi Beta Kappa, Sigma Xi. Office: Med Coll Pa 3300 Henry Ave Philadelphia PA 19129

MORAITIS, KAREN KARL, real estate broker; b. Orange, Tex., Sept. 28, 1943; d. Richard Louis and Betty (Crandall) Karl; m. George Reynold Moraitis, Aug. 14, 1965; children: George Reynold Jr., Alexandra. BS in Advt., U. Fla., 1965; MEd, Fla. Atlantic U., 1968, EdS, 1974. Cert. real estate broker. Welfare worker State of Fla., Ft. Lauderdale, 1967; guidance counselor Broward County Pub. Schs., Ft. Lauderdale, 1968-70; adj. faculty Fla. Atlantic U., Boca Raton, 1971-74; real estate assoc. Blackwell Realty, Ft. Lauderdale, 1976-77; real estate broker Karen Moraitis Realty, Inc., Ft. Lauderdale, 1978—. Editor: Official Florida Publications, 1966. Mem. Pres.'s Council U. Fla., 1980—, scholarship ptnr. Gator Boosters, 1983—; pres. Harborside at Hillsboro Beach (Fla.) Condominium Assn., 1982, Parent Tchr. Student Orgn. Ft. Lauderdale High Sch., 1985—, Parent Tchr. Student Assn. Sunrise Middle Sch., Ft. Lauderdale, 1986; v.p. PTA Bayview Elem. Sch., Ft. Lauderdale, 1980; chmn. Winter Cotillion, Ft. Lauderdale, 1986-88; bd. dirs. Sunrise Intracoastal Homeowners Assn., 1977, Broward County Zoning Bd., 1980-81, Imperial Village Condominium Assn., Ft. Lauderdale, 1983; ambassador edn. City of Ft. Lauderdale, 1986-88. Served with USN, 1965. Mem. Ft. Lauderdale Bd. Realtors, Nat. Assn. Realtors, Fla. Assn. Realtors, Ft. Lauderdale High Sch. Boosters (pres. 1984-85, 87-88). Democrat. Office: Karen Moraitis Realty Inc 915 Middle River Dr Ste 502 Fort Lauderdale FL 33304

MORALES, ADELA, controller; b. Colonia Dublan, Chihuqhua, Mex., Oct. 15, 1942; came to U.S., 1958; d. Rodolfo M. and Rosa (Tafoya) Salais; m. Frank A. Morales, May 15, 1965. BBA, U. Albuquerque, 1984. Bookkeeper Stauffer Chem. Co., Los Angeles, 1967-71; acct. Amerdyne Industry, Pico Rivera, Calif., 1971-76, Century Carpet Mill, Inc., City of Industry, Calif., 1976-78, Reserve Oil and Minerals, Inc., Albuquerque, 1980-84; controller Sandia Mfg. Corp., Albuquerque, 1978-80, S.W. Community Health Svcs., Albuquerque, 1984—. Mem. Am. Soc. Women Accts., Nat. Assn. Female Execs. Republican. Home: 6105 Buenos Aires Pl NW Albuquerque NM 87120 Office: SW Community Health Svcs 4775 Indian School Rd NE Albuquerque NM 87125

MORALES, HORTENSIA MARIA, health facilities administrator; b. Matanzas, Cuba, Sept. 30, 1944; came to U.S., 1961; d. Eliodoro Andres Hernandez and Hortensia (Gonzalez Acevedo) Naranjo; m. Jose Rodobaldo Morales, July 28, 1971; children: Jose Andre, Cristina Hortensia. AA, Miami Dade Jr. Coll., 1968; BS, U. Miami, 1971; postgrad., Fla. Internat. U., 1989—. Cert. med. technologist. Lab. evening clk. Variety Children's Hosp., Miami, 1968-69; med. technologist John Elliot Blood Bank, Miami, 1969, Mt. Sinai Hosp., Miami Beach, 1969; med. technologist Cedars of Lebanon Hosp., Miami, 1970-73, sect. head radioimmunoassay, 1973-74; microbiologist Coral Gables (Fla.) Hosp., 1974-75, lab. dept. head, 1975—; guest lectr. Fla. Internat. U., Miami, 1977; inspector Coll. Am. Pathologists, Skokie, Ill., 1978—; cons. Charter Cir. Hosp., Richmond, Va., 1987. Mem. Am. Soc. Med. Technologists, Am. Soc. Clin. Pathologists. Republican. Roman Catholic. Home: 6047 SW 25 St Miami FL 33155

MORALES, NAOMI M., training director; b. Riverside, Calif., May 10, 1954; 1 child, David. BA, Scripps Coll., 1976; MA, Claremont Grad. Coll., 1977; student, UCLA, 1984—. Div. mgr., coord. employee involvement, cons. in mgmt. devel. and culture change Gen. Dynamics, Pomona, Calif., 1984-89; corp. dir. tng. and orgn. devel. Gen. Dynamics, St. Louis, 1989—. Author: Managing Employee Involvement, 1985, Survey of Employees: Manager Guide, 1986, Survey Manager Manual, 1988. Mem. ASTD, NAFE. Office: Gen Dynamics Pierre Laclede Ctr Saint Louis MO 63105

MORALEZ, JOSELYN HOPE, special education educator; b. Lordsburg, N.Mex., July 7, 1966; d. Mary Lou Chavez. BS, N.Mex. State U., 1988. Instr. elem. spl. edn. Animas (N.Mex.) Pub. Schs., 1989-90, Lordsburg (N.Mex.) Pub. Schs., 1990—. Mem. Coun. for Exceptional Children, Phi Kappa Delta. Office: Cen Grade Sch 207 High Lordsburg NM 88045

MORAN, BARBARA BURNS, librarian, educator; b. Columbus, Miss., July 8, 1944; d. Robert Theron and Joan (Brown) Burns; m. Joseph J. Moran, Sept. 4, 1965; children: Joseph Michael, Brian Matthew. AB, Mount Holyoke Coll., S. Hadley, Mass., 1966; M.Librarianship, Emory U., Atlanta, 1973; PhD, SUNY, Buffalo, 1982. Head libr. The Park Sch. of Buffalo, Snyder, N.Y., 1974-78; assoc. prof. Sch. Info. and Libr. Sci., U. N.C., Chapel Hill, 1981—, asst. dean, 1987-90, dean, 1990—; participant various seminars; evaluator various edn. progs.; cons. in field. Author: Academic Libraries, 1984; co-author: (with Robert D. Stueart) Library Management, 3rd edit. 1987; contbr. articles to profl. jours, chpts. to books; reviewer Jour. Acad. Librarianship, 1988—. Coun. Libr. Resources grantee, 1985, Univ. Rsch. Coun. grantee, 1983, 89, others. Mem. ALA, AAUP, Assn. for Library and Info. Sci. Edn., Popular Culture Assn., N.C. Library Assn., Assn. for Study of Higher Edn., Beta Phi Mu. Home: 1307 LeClair St Chapel Hill NC 27514 Office: U NC Sch Info & Libr Sci Chapel Hill NC 27599-3360

MORAN, JULIETTE M., management consultant; b. N.Y.C., June 12, 1917; d. James Joseph and Louise M. B.S., Columbia U., 1938; M.S., NYU, 1948. Research asst. Columbia U., 1941; jr. engr. Signal Corps Lab., U.S. Army, 1942-43; with GAF Corp. (formerly Gen. Aniline & Film Corp.), 1943-82; successively jr. chemist process devel. dept., tech. asst. to N.Y. process devel. dept., tech. asst. to dir. Central Research Lab., tech. asst. to dir GAF Corp., 1953-55, supr. tech. service comml. devel. dept., 1955-59, sr. devel. specialist, 1959-60, mgr. planning, 1961, asst. to the pres., 1962-67, v.p., 1967-71, sr. v.p., 1971-74, exec. v.p., 1974-80, dir., 1974-83, vice chmn., 1980-82, cons., 1982—. Bd. dirs. N.Y. State Sci. and Tech. Found. Recipient Greater N.Y. Advt. award for excellence in communications N.Y. chpt. Assn. Indsl. Advertisers, 1972, Alumni Achievement award N.Y. U. Grad. Sch. Arts and Scis., 1977. Fellow AAAS, Am. Inst. Chemists; mem. Am. Chem. Soc., Comml. Devel. Assn. Home: 10 W 66th St New York NY 10023

MORAN, KATHERINE JEAN, accountant; b. Bridgeport, Conn., Apr. 19, 1958; d. Walter William Yodis and Patricia Ann (Hogan); m. Lyle Patrick, Oct. 19, 1980; (div. Feb. 7, 1985); 1 child, Joshua Adam. Acctg., Butler Bus. Sch., Bridgeport, 1987. Misc. prodn. salesperson Misc. Retailers, 1975-77; toolsetter, packer Remington Arms Co., Inc., Bridgeport, 1978-85; various positions Remgrit Corp., Bridgeport, 1986--. Active Conn. Pub. TV, Little League. Mem. MADD, Mystic Marine Life Aquarium. Home: 112 Gray St Huntington CT 06484 Office: Remgrit Corp 939 Barnum Ave Bridgeport CT 06608

MORAN, MARY CHAPAR, mayor, business executive; m. Stephen Moran; 3 children. Formerly with pub. rels. dept. Avco; former office mgr. Toth and Formato Realtors; former mem. mayor's commn. on sr. citizens, mem. schs. desegregation task force City of Bridgeport, Conn., mayor, 1989—; various bus. offices. Co-founder New Rep. Voice; state chair Reps. for Ella Grassa, 1978; active neighborhood assns., other civic assns. Mem. Bridgeport Bd. Realtors (creator; polit. affairs chair 1989). Office: City of Bridgeport 45 Lyon Terr Bridgeport CT 06604*

MORAN, PATRICIA ROSE, management consultant; b. Lake Forest, Ill., Aug. 17, 1930; d. Frank Laurence and Rose Cecelia (Walczak) M. BA in Mgmt., Carthage Coll., 1975. Sec. to dir. guidance Lake Forest (Ill.) High Sch., 1947-54; adminstrv. asst. dietetic svc. VA Med. Ctr, North Chicago, Ill., 1954-55, various fiscal svcs. positions, 1955-75; quality assurance coord. VA Med. Ctr., North Chicago, Ill., 1975-89, risk mgr., 1989—. Mem. Internat. Mgmt. Coun. (pres. local chpt. 1970-71, 1st v.p. div. 4, 1971-72, coun. v.p. 1972-74, exec. v.p. 1974-75, pres. 1975-76, chmn. numerous coms.), Inst. Cert. Profl. Mgrs. (cert. mgr., bd. regents 1984—, vice chmn., 1986-87, chmn. 1987-89), Am. Soc. Quality Control. Republican. Roman Catholic. Home: 243 Lincoln Ave Waukegan IL 60085 Office: Vet Affairs Med Ctr North Chicago IL 60064

MORANDA, NANCY LEIGH, retail executive; b. Canandaigua, N.Y., Sept. 17, 1957; d. Wilfred Thurston and Mary Elizabeth (Cotton) M.; m. Leslie Edward Sacani, Sept. 20, 1986. BS, Rochester (N.Y.) Inst. Tech., 1979. Asst. buyer Sibley, Lindsay & Curr, Co., Rochester, 1979; from asst. market rep. to market rep. Assoc. Dry Goods Corp., N.Y.C., 1979-83; market rep. May Merchandising Corp., N.Y.C., 1983-89; buyer gifts, candy, gourmet, SFA Logo Shop, Saks Fifth Ave., N.Y.C., 1989—.

MORAVEC, LISA KAY, nurse; b. Ft. Wayne, Ind., May 2, 1962; d. Todd Leinginger and Phillis Elaine (Bott) M. AS, Ball State U., 1983; cert., Ind. Vocat. Coll., 1985; BS, Hawaii Loa Coll., Kaneohe, 1988. RN, Ind. Nursing asst. Parkview Meml. Hosp., Ft. Wayne, 1976-77, Parnell Park Nursing Ctr., Ft. Wayne, 1977-78; nurse Riverview Care Ctr., Ft. Wayne, 1985-86, U. Park Nursing Ctr., Ft. Wayne, 1985-86, Castle Med. Ctr., Kailua, HI, 1987; registered nurse Castle Med. Ctr., Kailua, 1989; mgr. Stat Care North, Ft. Wayne, 1990—; cons., Castle Med. Ctr., Kailua, 1988-89. Photographer, Portraits plumeria, 1986 Finalist, 1987, Temple Reflections 1987 Finalist 1988. Vol. Young People's Support Ctr., Honolulu, 1988. National Collegiate Achievement Acad. scholar, 1988. Mem., Nat'l Dean's List, 1988, Sigma Theta Tau, 1988. Dem. Catholic. Home: 2803 Garden Park Dr Fort Wayne IN 46825 Office: Stat Care North 2510 DuPont Rd Fort Wayne IN 46825

MORAY, SHERRY, prima ballerina; b. Highland, Ill., Sept. 20, 1963; d. Richard Dean and Mary Maxine (Rupe) Murray. Studied with Keith Allison, Ellis DuBoulay, Maria Tallchief, Paul Mejia, Daniel Duell and Larry Long. Dancer Stuttgart (Fed. Republic Germany) Ballet Co., 1977-79; ballerina Chgo. City Ballet, 1980-87; prin. ballerina Ballet Chgo., 1988—. Guest artist various ballet cos., ballet festivals, Jacobs Pillow and including the famed Edinburgh Arts Festival in Scotland; ballerina in numerous prodns. including Cinderella, Romeo & Juliet, Swan Lake, The Nutcracker, Hamlet, Die Fledermaus, Don Quixote, Divertimento No. 15, Concerto Barocco, Apollo, Le Corsaire, Rubies, Agon, Four Temperaments, Allegro Brillante, Valse Fantasie, Raymonda, Who Cares?, Sylvia Variations, Evening Perfumes, Brahms Waltzes, Bizet Suite, The Seasons, Joie De Vivre, Stars and Stripes, Love Songs, Brandenburg II, A Little Mozart, Unanswered Question, Ave Maria, Seven Poetic Waltzes, Glazounov's Violin Concerto, River Suite, Capriccio Per Domani, Five Movements Opus 5, Tango Classico, Rodin, Ballo Imperiale, The Sirens, Chicago, By-Django. Office: 1939 Berry Ln Des Plaines IL 60018

MOREHEAD, MILDRED ADA, physician, social medicine educator, researcher; b. Norristown, Pa., May 11, 1919; d. Turner Gustavus and Sara Mildred (Bachenheim) M. Student Duke U., 1937-40; M.D., COlumbia U., 1943; M.P.H., Harvard U., 1948. Resident, Bellevue Hosp., N.Y.C., 1943-44; epidemiologist Inst. Inter Am. Affairs, Brazil, 1948-53; assoc. dir. Health Ins. Plan of N.Y.C., 1953-60; asst. prof. Columbia Sch. Public Health, N.Y.C. 1961-69; prof. epidemiology and social medicine Albert Einstein Med. Coll., N.Y.C., 1969—; cons. HIP, 1982—; bd. dirs. Bronx PSRO, 1976-85; med. bd., Mcpl. Hosp. Ctr., 1985—. Contbr. articles to profl. jurs. Served to capt. USPHS, 1945-47. Fellow Am. Pub. Health Assn.; N.Y. Acad. Medicine; mem. N.Y.C. Pub. Health Assn. (Haven Emerson award 1980), N.Y. State Pub. Health Assn. Avocation: gardening. Office: Albert Einstein Med Coll 1300 Morris Park Bronx NY 10461

MOREHEAD-MORRIS, PATRICIA S., state senator; b. Falls City, Nebr., July 21, 1936; d. Leo L. and Luella (Dowell) Stalder; m. Richard S. Morris, 1988. Student MacMurray Coll., 1954-55; B.S., U. Nebr., 1958. Mem. Nebr. State Senate, 1983-88. Mem. Gage County Democratic Women. Mem. PEO, Blue Valley Home Economists, Am. Trap Shooting Assn., Phi Upsilon Omicron, Chi Omega. Democrat. Office: 2317 Elk St PO Box 369 Beatrice NE 68310 also: 739 Calle del Resplandor Santa Fe NM 87501

MOREHOUSE, SHERRI K., small business owner; b. Lynwood, Calif., July 2, 1955; d. David E. and Hazel M. (Harter) M. AA, Fullerton Coll., 1976; BS, Fullerton State U., 1978. Lic. pvt. investigator. Owner, pres. Morehouse and Assocs., Orange, Calif.; asst. v.p. Calif. City Bank, Orange; lenging officer Eldorado Bank, Tustin, Calif.; investigator ICA, Costa Mesa, Calif. Mem. NAFE, SCCCG.

MORELAND, SUZANNE, physiologist; b. Honolulu, Nov. 23, 1951; d. William Weidel and Dorothy (Maskell) Mras; m. Robert Scott Moreland, May 11, 1985. BA, U. South Fla., 1973, PhD, 1979. Postdoctoral fellow U. Va., Charlottesville, 1979-82; rsch. investigator The Squibb Inst. for Med. Rsch., Princeton, N.J., 1982-86; sr. rsch. investigator The Squibb Inst. for Med. Rsch. (named changed to The Bristol-Myers Squibb Pharm. Rsch. Inst.), Princeton, N.J., 1986—. Mem. AAAS, Am. Physiol. Soc., Biophys. Soc., Physiol. Soc. Phila., N.Y. Acad. Scis., Am. Heart Assn. Office: Bristol-Myers Squibb Pharm Rsch Inst PO Box 4000 Princeton NJ 08543

MORELLA, CONSTANCE ALBANESE, congresswoman; b. Somerville, Mass., Feb. 12, 1931; d. Salvatore and Mary Christine (Fallette) Albanese; m. Anthony C. Morella, Aug. 21, 1954; children: Paul, Mark, Laura; guardians of: Christine, Catherine, Louise, Rachel, Paul, Ursula. AA, Boston U., 1950, AB, 1954; MA, Am. U., 1967, D of Pub. Svc. (hon.), 1988; D of Pub. Svc. (hon.), Norwich U. and Dickinson Coll., 1989. Tchr. Montgomery County (Md.) Pub. Schs., 1956-60; instr. Am. U., 1968-70; prof. Montgomery Coll., Rockville, Md., 1970—; mem. Md. Ho. Dels., Annapolis, 1979-86, 100th-102nd Congresses from 8th Md. dist., 1987—. Trustee Capitol Coll., Laurel, Md., 1977—, Trinity Coll., Washington, 1984—; mem. found. bd. Shady Grove Hosp., Rockville, 1986—; pres. Montgomery County Commn. for Women, Rockville, 1973-74; vice chair adv. com. C & O Canal Nat. Hist. Park, 1976-78. Recipient Disting. Alumna award Am. U., 1980, 82, Disting. Legislator award Md. Victims Advocacy Network, Annapolis, 1985, Health Care award Found. for Nursing of Md. Inc., 1988; named to Collegium of Disting. Alumni, Boston U., 1987; named Woman of Commitment, ADL, 1987, Woman of Yr. Nat. Assn. Women Judges Dist. 4, 1987, An Outstanding Mother, Nat. Mother's Day Com., 1988. Mem. AAUW, Women's Inst., League of Women Voters, Bus. and Profl. Women at Large, Montgomery County Hospice Soc. Republican. Roman Catholic. Lodge: Zonta (hon., Woman of Yr. 1984). Office: US Ho of Reps 1024 Longworth Office Bldg Washington DC 20515

MORELLO, CAROL JEAN, veterinarian, marketing executive; b. Worcester, Mass., Dec. 12, 1957; d. Louis Alfred and Rose (Calce) M.; m. Kelly Brian Moran, Sept. 26, 1987. BA, Assumption Coll., Worcester, Mass.; 1979; MA, Smith Coll., 1981; VMD, U. Pa., 1987. Staff veterinarian Fanwood (N.J.) Animal Hosp., 1987-88, Whitehouse Vet. Hosp., Whitehouse Station, N.J., 1988—; sales rep., v.p. mtkg. CeramOptec Inc., Bonn, Fed. Republic Germany, 1989—. Mem. AVMA, Am. Animal Hosp. Soc., N.J. Vet. Medicine Assn., N.J. Vet. Acad. Medicine and Surgery, Sigma Xi, Phi Zeta, Alpha Psi.

MORENO, MICHELLE ADRIENNE, banker; b. Chgo., Nov. 25, 1959; d. Nicholas and Estelle Catherine Raimondi; m. German Gustavo Moreno, Aug. 11, 1984. Diplome superieur, Chamber Commerce and Industry, Paris, 1980; BA in Econs. and French, U. Ill., 1981; MBA, Calif. State U., Fullerton, 1986. Chartered fin. analyst. Sec., file clk., head rsch. dept. Nat. Survey Svc., Inc., Chgo., 1972-81; personnel asst. CF Industries, Inc., Long Grove, Ill., 1981; sec. Wiliam Dodd Law Offices, Champaign, Ill., 1981-82, Union Bank Switzerland, Chgo., 1982-83; head credit adminstrn. Union Bank Switzerland, L.A., 1983-87; head credit adminstrn. Union Bank Switzerland, Chgo., 1987-88, account mgr., asst. v.p., 1988—. ORT scholar, 1977. Mem. Fin. Mgmt. Assn., Investment Analysts Soc. Chgo., Internat. Assn. Students Econs. and Commerce, Pi Delta Phi, Sigma Kappa. Office: Union Bank Switzerland 30 S Wacker Dr Chicago IL 60606

MORENO, SUSAN INGALLS, physician; b. Camden, N.J., Apr. 16, 1959; d. Vito Nicholas and Judith Ann (Wilson) M.; m. Jens Christian Schoening, June 17, 1989. AB, Bryn Mawr Coll., 1981; MD, Med. Coll. Pa., 1986. Med. Diplomate. Med. intern Crozer Chester Med. Ctr., 1986-87; resident U. Pa. Hosp., 1987-90; staff physician rehab. medicine svc. Phila. VA Med. Ctr., 1990—. Recipient Thomas J. Watson Fellowship, Thomas J. Watson Found. Providence 1981-82. Mem. AMA, Am. Congress Phys. Medicine and Rehab., Am. Acad. Phys. Medicine and Rehab. Democrat. Roman Catholic. Home: 336 Manton St Philadelphia PA 19147

MORENZI, VANESSA ANN, orthodontist, educator; b. Pitts., Jan. 28, 1958; d. Vincent A. and Mary M. (Curran) M.; m. Mark A. Ruggerio, June 25, 1983. BA, Bucknell U., 1979; DMD, U. Pa., 1983, orthodontic cert., 1989. Pvt. practice Haddonfield, N.J., 1983-87, 89—; clin. prof. orthodontics U. Pa., Phila., 1983—. Pres. class of 1979, Bucknell U., Lewisburg, Pa., 1979—. Recipient excellence in clin. teaching award U. Pa., 1986. Mem. ADA, Am. Assn. Orthodontists, So. Dental Soc., N.J. Dental Assn., Jr. Women's Club Haddon Fortnightly. Office: 265 Kings Hwy E Haddonfield NJ 08033

MORETZ, CHERYL ANN, educational administrator; b. Bound Brook, N.J., May 27, 1950; d. Joseph Gerard and Claire Mae (Blume) Neach; 1 child, Christin Ann Moretz. BS in Secondary Edn., Bucknell U., 1972; EdM in Elem. Edn., Rutgers U., 1980. Cert. supr., elem. tchr., N.J. Tchr. Monmouth Junction (N.J.) Elem. Sch., 1980-87, asst. prin., 1987—; ednl. cons. N.L. Assocs., Inc., Hightstown, N.J., 1985—. Author: (simulation game) Stock Market, 1988, Who Am I? series, 1990. Mem. Assn. Supervision and Curriculum Devel. Office: Monmouth Junction Elem Sch Ridge Rd Box 184 Monmouth Junction NJ 08824

MORETZ, LORI SUSAN, librarian; b. Pa.; d. David Eckert and Barbara (Knecht) Mest; m. Brian David Moretz, June 19, 1982. BS, Millersville U., 1981. Librarian Stanley-Vidmar Inc., Allentown, Pa., 1981--. Office: Stanley-Vidmar Inc 11 Grammes Rd Allentown PA 18103

MOREY, HELEN JEAN, controller; b. St. Paul, Sept. 23, 1940; d. Robert Warren and Dorothy Loraine (Ernst) Torgersen; m. Larry Leroy Anners, Sept. 8, 1962 (div. 1985); children: Joyce, Laura, Steven; m. Charles Edward Morey, July 4, 1987; step child, Michal. BS, L.A. State Coll., 1963. Cert. cash mgr., Calif. Contr. Adams Rite Products, Inc., Glendale, Calif., 1977—. Vol. Kaiser Hosp., Panorama City, Calif., 1989—, Republican Party, various cities in So. Calif., 1967—; deacon Presbyn. Ch., Granada Hills, Calif., 1970's. Mem. Nat. Acctg. Assn., Contrs. Coun., Nat. Corp. Cash Mgrs. Assn., Internat. Soc. Retirement Planners. Home: 4859 Matilija Ave Sherman Oaks CA 91423 Office: Adams Rite Products Inc 540 W Chevy Chase Dr Glendale CA 91204

MOREY, MARION LOUISE, former quality control chemist; b. Chgo., May 2, 1926; d. Oscar Gilbert and Esther Naomi (Carlson) Engstrom; m. Howard Elmer Morey, Mar. 2, 1957; children: Richard, David. BS summa cum laude, Elmhurst Coll., 1947; postgrad., Northwestern U., Chgo., 1952-54, Loyola U., Chgo., 1955-56. Quality control chemist Wander Co., Villa Park, Ill., 1947-57. Master gardener vol. U. Ill. Coop. Extension Svc., Amboy, Ill., Dixon, Ill., 1988-90; vol. tchr. English as a second lang. Sauk Valley Community Coll., Dixon, 1980; mem. Dixon Family YMCA, sec. 1969-79, pres., 1982-84, bd. dirs.; mem. YMCA of the USA-Midwest Field, 1983-84 (Lowell Linnes Leadership award 1984). Mem. AAUW (pres. Dixon br. 1980-82), P.E.O. (treas. Ill. chpt. 1989-90). Presbyterian. Home: 1127 N Dement Ave Dixon IL 61021-1237

MOREY, MELINDA LOUISE, educator; b. Seattle, Apr. 21, 1955; d. Victor Edward Shaver and Loretta Lorraine (Healy) Morgan; m. Dale Franklin Morey, Aug. 26, 1978 (div. Nov. 1984); children: Ryan Franklin, Derek Emerson. AA in Edn., Centralia Community Coll., Wash., 1976; BA in Edn., Western Wash. U., 1978; cert. in edn., Cen. Wash. U., 1985. Elem. tchr. North Thurston Sch. Dist., Lacey, Wash., 1979—. Mem. NEA, Wash. Edn. Assn., North Thurston Edn. Assn. Roman Catholic. Home: 4314 30th Ave SE Lacey WA 98503 Office: North Thurston Sch Dist 305 College St NE Lacey WA 98503

MORGA BELLIZZI, CELESTE, editor; b. N.Y.C., Mar. 8, 1921; d. Louis and Emma (Macari) Morga; m. John J. Bellizzi, Sept. 1, 1942; children: John J., Robert F. Student, Columbia U., 1940-41, SUNY, Albany, 1970. Cert. med. lab. technician. Medical lab. technician USMC Hosp., N.Y.C., 1942, Woman's Hosp., N.Y.C., 1942-52; spl. investigator N.Y. State Atty. Gen.'s Office, Albany, 1958-65; editor Internat. Drug Report publ., The Narc Officer publ. Internat. Narcotic Enforcement Officers Assn., Albany, 1965—. Dir. Albany Inst. History and Art, 1988-90, N.Y. State Press Women, Albany, 1987; advisor UN NGO Drug Com., N.Y.C., 1980-90, White House Conf. Drug Free Am., Washington, 1987; mem. com. Bethlehem Drug Prevention Program, Delmar, N.Y., 1987-90, Action Commn. Narc Edn., Delmar, 1984-90; v.p. Women's Rep. Party Albany, 1972. Recipient Pres.'s award INEOA, 1982, Disting. Svc. award Houston Police Dept., 1981. Mem. Nat. Fedn. Press Women, Nat. Press Club, Univ. Club, Albany Country Club, Aberdeen Country Club. Office: Internat Narcotic Enforcement Officers Assn 112 State St Albany NY 12207

MORGAN, BARBARA JOAN, real estate broker; b. Mattoon, Ill., July 5, 1940; d. Wendel Lewis and Helen Irene (Adkins) Huddlestun; m. David A. Morgan, Aug. 22, 1958; children—Wendy A., Eric W., D. Gregory. B.S. in Edn., Ea. Ill. U., 1962. Tchr. Lincoln Sch., Mattoon, Ill., 1962-66; real estate broker, Paris, Ill. 1974—; real estate broker, owner Paris Realty, 1978—; real estate tchr. Lakeland Jr. Coll., Mattoon, 1980—; appointed to Region 23 Pvt. Industry Council, 1987. Pres. Paris Newcomers club, 1974-75; chair United Way of Edgar County, 1988. Named Paris Woman of Yr., 1985-86. Mem. Ill. Assn. Realtors (inst. grad. 1977, cert. residential specialist 1979), East Central Ill. Bd. Realtors (pres. 1978-79, 88—), Bus. and Profl. Women Paris (pres. 1983-84), Paris C. of C. (v.p. 1984-86). Republican. Clubs: Altrusa, Prairies Edge Toastmaster's (charter mem.). Lodge: Order Eastern Star. Office: Paris Realty 207 N Central St Paris IL 61944

MORGAN, BETTY LOU, sales executive; b. St. Louis, Dec. 28, 1931; d. Grant L. and Selma G. (Stelter) Fults.; 1 child, Alan. Student, Ind. U., 1954. Sec. Ralston Purina Co., St. Louis, 1954-61; media buyer William Douglas McAdams, N.Y., 1961-63; media dir. Ridgway Adv. Agy., St. Louis, 1963-72; account exec. The Katz Agy., St. Louis, 1972-80; sales mgr. Christal Radio, St. Louis, 1980-84, v.p., 1984—. Mem. Nat. Agri-Mktg. Assn., Nat. Assn. Farm Broadcasters, St. Louis. Office: Christal Radio 10 Broadway Saint Louis MO 63102

MORGAN, CATHY LYNN, athletic trainer; b. Topeka, Aug. 5, 1959; d. Francis Leroy and Sheila Nadine (Eidman) M. BS in Physicial Edn., Kans. State U., 1984; MS in Exercise Physiology, Ariz. State U., 1990. Nat. cert. athletic trainer. Trainer athletic Ariz. State U., Tempe, 1984-86, Ather Sports Injury Clinic, Castro Valley, Calif., 1990; credit asst. Lesher Communications, Inc., Walnut Creek, Calif., 1988; cash mgmt. asst. The Pacific Bank, N.A., San Francisco, 1988-90; legal asst. Pillsbury Madison and Sutro, San Francisco, 1990—; examiner Nat. Athletic Trainers Assn., Calif., 1986-88. Mem. Nat. Athletic Trainers Assn., Am. Coll. Sports Med., Alpha Sigma Tau. Republican. Methodist.

MORGAN, CONSTANCE LOUISE, real estate executive; b. Denver, July 24, 1941; d. Willis Stephen and Evelyn (Rutar) Claus; m. Robert M. Morgan, Jan. 3, 1963; children: Stephen, Melayne. BS, U. N. Mex., 1963. Lic. real estate broker. Realtor, assoc. Investors Realty, Tallahassee, 1980-82, br. mgr., 1982-83; pres., broker Connie Morgan Realty, Inc., Tallahassee, 1983—; founder Network for Ind. Brokers, 1989—. Chmn. Docents-Fla. Gov. Mansion, Tallahassee, 1979-80; pres. Newcomers-Univ. Women, Tallahassee, 1968; bd. dirs. Tallahassee Symphony Orch., 1990—. Mem. Nat. Assn. Realtors, Fla. Assn. Realtors, Tallahassee Bd. Realtors (chmn. Multiple Listing Svc. 1984), Tallahassee Community Realty Group, Tallahassee C. of C. (bd. dirs. 1984-86, 89—), Chi Omega (treas. 1962), Phi Gamma Nu (pres. 1962). Home: 835 Lakeshore Dr Tallahassee FL 32312 Office: Connie Morgan Realty Inc 2810 Remington Green Circle Tallahassee FL 32308

MORGAN, DELORIS JACKSON, real estate; b. Lumberton, N.C., Oct. 11, 1947; d. James Graham and Bessie Edna (Byrd) J.; m. Ted G. Morgan, June 17, 1967 (div. 1978); children: Donna Nicole Morgan. Grad., Realtors Inst., 1987. Lic. realtor; lic. broker. Retail sales mgr. Montgomery Wards, Newport News, Va., 1978-82; residential resale agt. Mulder Realty, Newport News, 1982-84, Roberson & Assoc., Newport News, 1984-85, Rose & Kenneth Realty, Virginia Beach, Va., 1985—; mem. Am. Home Week Com. 1985-88, Indoctrination Course for Bd. of Realtors, 1986-87. Founder Site Agts. Anonomous of the Peninsula, a support group of Peninsula Home Bldrs. Sales and Mktg. Coun., exec. and nominating coms., 1989—. Named Member Gallery of Stars, Homes & Land Mag., Newport News, 1983, named Site Mgr. for Carleton Falls of Newport News, 1989. Mem. NAFE, Nat. Assn. Realtors, Newport News-Hampton Bd. Realtors (Outstanding Salesmanship Club 1983, 84, 86, 87), Peninsula Home Builders Sales and Mktg. Coun. (Sales award 1985, 86, 87, 88, 89, 90), Peninsula Sales and Mktg. Execs. Ltd. Republican. Baptist. Office: Rose & Krueth Realty 703 Thimble Shoals Blvd Newport News VA 23606

MORGAN, DIANE M., manufacturing executive; d. Robert And Lorraine (Murdock) St. George; 1 child, Kari Anne. Owner, pres. B & L Rubber Stamps, Manchester, N.H.; typesetter, mgr. B and L Rubber Stamps, Manchester, N.H. Mem. NAFE, Women Owner's Network. Office: B & L Rubber Stamps 817 Perimeter Rd Box 4735 Manchester Airport Manchester NH 03108

MORGAN, DIANE POPE, sales professional; b. Macon, Ga., Mar. 17, 1949; d. Bruce G. Jr. and Anna Virginia (Brown) Pope; m. Jim Marion Jr. Morgan, July 27, 1969; children: Jim III, Sara. Student, Macon Coll.; diploma in textiles, Ga. Tech., 1980; cert., H & R Block, 1978. Coord. cost and waste, adminstrv. mgr., mgr. dept. Glen Raven Mills, Inc., Macon, 1970-89; dir. purchasing Am. Office, Macon, 1989; with sales, customer svc. and tech. svcs. depts. Bearings & Drives, Inc., Macon, 1989—; co-owner Happy Balloons-N-Such, 1984—. Mem. key vol. staff Muscular Dystrophy Assn., 1985—; leader Boy Scouts Am., 1986—, com. mem. Cherry Blossom Festival. Recipient Trail Blazer II award Boy Scouts Am., 1990. Mem. NAFE, Ga. Jaycees (past region dir., mem. congress #134 1985—), Ga. Jaycettes (internal dir., internal v.p. and pres. local chpt. 1980-85, dir., treas., mgr. state store program), Macon Jaycettes (regional treas., Outstanding Mem. 1980-85), Women of the Moose (ritual dir. 1970—, Hope award 1989-90, Faith award 1987-88, named Co-Worker of Month 85, 86, 87, 88, 89, 90, Co-Worker of Yr. 1990). Baptist. Home: 4151 W Hickory Ct Macon GA 31210 Office: Bearings & Drives Inc 585 Lower Poplar St PO Box 4325 Macon GA 31213

MORGAN, DONNA J., psychotherapist; b. Edgerton, Wis., Nov. 16, 1955; d. Donald Edward and Pearl Elizabeth (Robinson) Garey. BA, U. Wis., Whitewater, 1983, MS, 1985. Cert. psychotherapist, Wis., mental health, alcohol and drug counselor. Pvt. practice Janesville, Wis.; clin. supr. Stoughton (Wis.) Hosp. Mem. underaged drinking violation alternative program County of Rock, 1986—, mem. task force on child sexual abuse, 1989—. Mem. Am. Assn. Counseling and Devel., Am. Psychol. Assn., Am. Assn. Marriage and Family Therapy, Wis. Mental Health Counselor Assn., Wis. Assn. Counseling and Devel., Am. Mental Health Counselor Assn., Alpha Kappa Delta, Psi Chi. Office: Bridgeway Psychol Assocs 20 E Milwaukee Ste 310 Janesville WI 53545

MORGAN, ELIZABETH ANNE, small business owner; b. Mpls., Mar. 30, 1947; d. Reymond Fauche and Sara Catherine (Foorman) Kirkman; m. R. Hugh Morgan, Dec. 28, 1968 (div. 1975); 1 child, Kirk Bennett; m. Michael Ross Boyer, Dec. 31, 1982. BS in Speech, Northwestern U., 1969. Copywriter Kay Jewelers, Inc., Washington, 1969-72; decorator J.C. Penney, St. Paul, 1973-75; field sales rep. Pitney Bowes, Mpls., 1975-77, field sales mgr., 1977-80; area sales mgr. Pitney Bowes, St. Louis, 1980-81; field sales rep. Pitney Bowes, San Diego, 1982; owner, operator Listeninc, San Diego, 1983, Golden Triangle Leasing, San Diego, 1984—; treas. Le Tip, San Diego, 1984-87. Fundraising chmn. San Diego Women's Opportunities Week, 1986, calendar editor, 1987-88; tutor adult literacy San Diego Community Coll., 1987—. Mem. AAUW (v.p. program 1988—), Western Assn. Equipment Lessors. Office: Golden Triangle Leasing 3604 4th Ave Ste 8 San Diego CA 92103

MORGAN, ELLEN NANNIE, insurance agent; b. Battle Creek, Mich., Oct. 18, 1935; d. Rex Hyder and Merle Beatrice (Christmas) Copeland; m. George E. Morgan, July 15, 1954; children: Catherine Morgan Hornaday, Cheryl L. Turner. Cert. ins. counselor, profl. ins. woman. Sec. Solko Ins. Agy., Battle Creek, 1952-63; office mgr. Combined Ins. Agys. and Shay Ins. Agy., Battle Creek, 1963-84; owner Morgan-Shay Ins. Agy., Battle Creek, 1984—. Named Ky. Col., 1973; recipient Woman of Yr. award Am. Bus. Women's Assn., 1985, Mich. Ins. Woman of Yr. award, 1989. Mem. Ind. Ins. Agts. Am. (bd. dirs. 1983—), Ind. Ins. Agts. Mich. (com. mem. 1985—), Profl. Ins. Agts. Am. and Mich. (chmn. cert. ins. counselor com. 1988), Nat. Assn. Ins. Women (Woman of Yr. award 1974), So. Mich. Ins. Womens Assn. (numerous offices), Ind. Ins. Agts. Battle Creek (pres.). Office: Morgan-Shay Ins Agy 157 E Columbia Ave Battle Creek MI 49015

MORGAN, EVELYN BUCK, nursing educator; b. Phila., Nov. 3, 1931; d. Kenneth Edward and Evelyn Louise (Rhineberg) Buck; m. John Allen McGeary, Aug. 15, 1958 (div. 1964); children—John Andrew, Jacquelyn Ann McGeary Keplinger; m. Kenneth Dean Morgan, June 26, 1965 (dec. 1975). R.N., Muhlenberg Hosp. Sch. Nursing, 1955; B.S. in Nursing summa cum laude, Ohio State U., 1972, M.S., 1973; Ed.D., Nova. U., 1978. R.N., N.J., Ohio, Fla., Calif.; cert. specialist Am. Nurses Assn. Psychiat.-Mental Health Clin. Specialists; advanced R.N. practitioner Fla. Bd. Nursing. Staff nurse Muhlenberg Hosp., Plainfield, N.J., 1955-57; indsl. nurse Western Electric Co., Columbus, Ohio, 1957-59; supr. Mt. Carmel Hosp., Columbus, 1960-65; instr. Grant Hosp. Sch. Nursing, 1965-72; cons. Ohio Dept. Health, 1972-74; prof. nursing Miami (Fla.)-Dade Community Coll., 1974—; family therapist Hollywood Pavilion Hosp., 1977-82; pvt. practice family therapy, Ft. Lauderdale, Fla., 1982—. Sustaining mem. Democratic Nat. Com., 1975—. Mem. Am. Nurses Assn., Fla. Council Psychiat.-Mental Health Clin. Specialists, Am. Nurses Found., Am. Holistic Nurses Assn., Sigma Theta Tau. Democrat. Roman Catholic.

MORGAN, GEORGIA BAZACOS, freelance writer; b. Richmond, Va., Jan. 17, 1926; d. John George and Photini (Derdevanis) Bazacos; m. Joel L. Morgan, May 22, 1965. Student, U. Md., 1945, Va. Commonwealth U., 1959-60; creative writing, Old Dominion U., 1988. Sec. A.H. Robins Co. Inc., Richmond, Va., 1949-62, librarian, 1959-62; bd. dirs. Willowood Corp., Norfolk, Va., 1986-88; pres. Va. (Bapt.) Ministers' Wives, 1980-81; pres., sec. Willowood Corp., 1986-88. Contbr. articles to prof. jours., Chmn. Book, Pharm. Lib. Directory, 1962. Sec. Internat. Christian Leadership Natl. Presidential Prayer Breakfast, Wash. 1963-64, volunteer aid, Norfolk Gen.

Hosp., 1977-78; bus. mgr., mktg. dir. Heritage Oaks Retirement Ctr., Richmond. Mem. Tidewater Tennis Ctr. Republican. Baptist.

MORGAN, GRETNA FAYE, automotive executive; b. Galveston, Ind., Aug. 24, 1927; d. Fred Monroe and Vera Arnetha (Oakley) Goodier; m. Marvin L. Morgan, Mar. 30, 1946; children: Gary Lynn, Vonna Annette, Marvin Richard, Darla Sue, Janice Arnetha. Diploma in cosmetology, Approved U., Indpls., 1946. Sales distributor Kirby Co., Ft. Wayne, Ind., 1955-62; with Dana Corp., Churubusco, Ind., 1962—; plant mgr. Dana Corp., Athens, Ga., 1978-81, Churubusco, Ind., 1981—; bd. dirs. Passages, Inc., Whitley County. Chmn. mayor's com. Employment Handicapped, Athens, Ga., 1980-81; mem. interview bd. selection com. Congressman Dan Coats Mil. Acad., Ft. Wayne, 1985-88, bus. adv. bd. Whitley County Opportunity Ctr., Columbia City, Ind., 1986—, Chem. Dependency Task Force Whitley County, Ind. Gov.'s Task Force on Drunk Driving, budget com. Whitley County United Way; bd. regents Dana U., Toledo, 1978-82; bd. dirs., pres. Whitley County Jr. Achievement, 1977-78; bd. dirs. Passages, Inc., Columbia City, Ind., 1989—, Whitley County Meml. Hosp. Found., Columbia City, 1989—. Mem. Calvary Temple Worship Ctr. Home: RR 1 Box 96 Albion IN 46701 Office: Dana Corp US 33 PO Box 245 Churubusco IN 46723

MORGAN, HOLLY ANN HERRICK, anesthesiologist, pediatrician; b. Washington, Aug. 18, 1958; d. Arthur Bertram and Genett Louise (Herrick) Jebens; m. Bruce Kendal Morgan, Aug. 6, 1988. AB, Harvard U., 1980; MD, U. Calif., San Francisco, 1985. Diplomate am. Bd. pediatrics, Nat. Bd. Med. Examiners. Resident in pediatrics Children's Hosp. Med. Ctr., Oakland, Calif., 1985-86; resident in pediatrics Mass. Gen. Hosp., Boston, 1986-88, resident in anesthesiology, 1988-89, 90—; resident in anesthesiology Plymouth (Eng.) Gen. Hosp., 1989-90. Contbr. articles to profl. publs. Fellow Am. Acad. Pediatrics; mem. Phi Beta Kappa, Alpha Omega Alpha. Home: 4 Brimmer St Boston MA 02108

MORGAN, INGA BORGSTROM, educator, pianist; b. Amarillo, Tex.; d. August and Charlotte (Jonsson) Borgstrom; m. Edwin Phillip Morgan, Aug. 23, 1942; 1 child, Kent August. Grad. Amarillo Jr. Coll., 1938; Mus.B., Eastman Sch. Music, 1940, Mus.M., 1944, performer cert., 1942; postgrad. Sommer Akademie, Mozarteum, Salzburg, Austria, 1969, 71; student Friederich Wuhrer, Max Landow, Lilly Larsen, Esther Jonsson, Radie Britain. Mem. faculty, dept. music Coll. Fine Arts, U. Tex., Austin, 1942-43, N. Tex. State U., Denton, 1944-45; prof. music and piano Sch. Music, U. N.C., Greensboro, 1946-89, emeritus, 1989—; cons.; concert pianist, harpsichordist, lecture-recitalist, accompanist. Mem. Am. Liszt Soc., Coll. Music Soc., Music Tchrs. Nat. Assn., N.C. Music Tchrs. Assn., Southeastern Hist. Keyboard Soc. (life, charter mem.), Greensboro Music Tchrs. Assn., Am.-Scandanavian Found., Vasa Order (officer), Pi Kappa Lambda, (past officer), Mu Phi Epsilon. Presbyterian. Club: Euterpe Music. Home: 1005 Guilford Ave Greensboro NC 27401

MORGAN, KIMBERLY ANN, medical society official; b. Flint, Mich., Sept. 28, 1963; d. Michael Robert and Louise Ann (Olsick) Bushell; m. Troy Ray Morgan, Aug. 20, 1983; 1 child, Jamie Marie. AS in Bus. Adminstrn., Ill. Cen. Coll., 1984; BA in Mgmt., Sangamon State U., 1987. Receptionist Peoria (Ill.) Med. Soc., 1980-81, sec., 1981-84, adminstrv. asst., 1985-88, asst. to exec. v.p., 1989—. Mem. Am. Assn. Med. Soc. Execs., Am. Assn. Med. Assts., Ill. Med. Assts. Assn. (chmn. pub. rels. com. Peoria chpt. 1989—), Ill. Notary Pub. Assn., NAFE. Republican. Home: 7521 Sagewood Dr Peoria IL 61604 Office: Peoria Med Soc 434 1st Nat Bank Bldg Peoria IL 61602

MORGAN, LEE ANNE, advertising agency executive; b. Cleve., Aug. 27, 1943; d. Victor and Helene (Sieracki) DeCapite; m. Arthur Allan Anderson, Oct. 29, 1983. Student Adelphi U., 1977-78. Account supr. Ogilvy & Mather, N.Y.C., 1969-77, Doyle Dane Bernbach, N.Y.C., 1978-81, Lord Geller Frederico, Einstein, N.Y.C., 1981-82; dir. new bus. devel. Dancer Fitzgerald Sample, N.Y.C., 1982-84; sr. v.p., mktg. dir. Ketchum Advt./USA, N.Y.C., 1984-85; pounding prin. Morgan Anderson & Co., 1985—; dir. Mountain Lifesprings Ltd. Mem. Advt. Club N.Y. (chmn. 1985 and 1986 Andy awards). Clubs: Nat. Arts, Maltby Valley Falls. Office: Morgan Anderson & Co 136 W 24th St New York NY 10011

MORGAN, LINDA C., industrial engineer; b. Plainfield, N.J., Mar. 7, 1958; d. Luther William and Dolores Odessa (Minor) Hammond; m. Bruce A. Morgan, July 3, 1982; children: William, Eric. BS in Indsl. Engring., N.J. Inst. Tech., 1982. Mgr. sect., corp. indsl. engr. Ethicon, Inc., Somerville, N.J., indsl. engr.; assoc. project coord. Johnson & Johnson Internat., New Bruinswick, N.J.; assoc. indsl. engr. Ortho Diagnostics, Inc., Raritan, N.J. Editor co. newsletter. Recipient N.J. Black Achievers award, 1988. Mem. Am. Inst. Indsl. Engrs., NAFE.

MORGAN, LINDA ROGERS, reporter; b. Seattle, Jan. 18, 1950; d. Fred and Frances (Teitelbaum) Rogers; m. Michael Edward Morgan, Aug. 8, 1971; children: Melissa, Todd. BA with great distinction, U. Calif., Berkeley, 1971; M in Journalism, UCLA, 1972. Editorial asst. Teen mag., L.A., 1972-73; advt. copywriter Big S Sporting Goods, L.A., 1973; instr. journalism and communications Bellevue (Wash.) Community Coll., 1975—; feature editor Via mag., Seattle, 1983-84; freelance writer, 1980—; humor columnist Mercer Island (Wash.) Reporter, 1989—, reporter, 1990—; nat. conf. speaker Journalism Edn. Assn., 1990. Bd. dirs. Herzl-Ner Tamid, Mercer Island, 1985-87, Mercer Island Youth Theater, 1987-88, Jewish Transcript, Seattle, 1989-90. Recipient writing awards Pacific N.W. Writers Conf., 1984, Washington Newspaper Pubs. Assn., 1987, 89. Mem. Women in Communications Inc., Washington Press Assn. (judge student contest 1989, writing awards 1989, 90), Nat. Edn. Assn., Phi Beta Kappa, Sigma Delta Chi (writing award 1988).

MORGAN, M. JANE, computer systems consultant; b. Washington, July 21, 1945; d. Edmond John and Roberta (Livingstone) Dolphin; 1 child, Sheena Anne. Student U. Md., 1963-66, Montgomery Coll., 1966-70; BA in Applied Behavioral Sci. with honors, Nat.-Louis Univ., 1987, MS in Mgmt., 1990. With HUD, Washington, 1965-84, computer specialist, 1978-84; pres., chief exec. officer Systems and Mgmt. Assocs., 1983-87; dir. systems engring. Advanced Technology Systems, Inc., Vienna, Va., 1984-86; chief tech. staff Tech. and Mgmt. Services, Inc., 1986-89; sr. cons. Advanced Tech. Systems Inc., Vienna, 1989; sr. computer scientist Integrated Systems div. Computer Scies. Corp., 1989—; mgmt. cons. Mem. Am. Mgmt. Assns. Episcopalian. Club: Order Eastern Star.

MORGAN, MADEL JACOBS, retired archives and library administrator; b. Rosedale, Miss., Apr. 26, 1918; d. Charles Clark and Vera (Joest) Jacobs; m. Adlia Morgan, June 11, 1940 (dec. Dec. 1984); 1 child, Susan Miller Griffith; m. Murray Davis Stringer, Apr. 26, 1988. B.A., Miss. U. for Women, Columbus, 1939; library cert., Miss. Coll., 1960. Libr. St. Andrews Sch., Jackson, 1955-68; spl. programs cons. Miss. Libr. Commn., Jackson, 1968-79; dir. archives and libr. div. Miss. Dept. Archives and History, Jackson, 1979-88, ret., 1988; mem. Miss. Hist. Records Adv. Bd., 1981—. Geneal. editor Jour. Miss. History, 1953—. Mem. ALA (council 1971-75), Miss. Libr. Assn. (pres. 1979), Soc. Am. Archivists, Nat. Assn. Govt. Archives and Records Adminstrs. (bd. dirs. 1985-86), Libr. Svcs. and Constrn. Act (adv. council), Nat. Soc. Colonial Dames Am., Order of the First Families of Miss. Democrat. Episcopalian. Home: 644 Rice Rd Ridgeland MS 39157

MORGAN, MARITZA LESKOVAR, painter; b. Zagreb, Yugoslavia, Nov. 20, 1920; came to U.S., 1929, naturalized, 1930; d. Josef and Paula Mihailovic (Yunkovic) Leskovar; m. Norman Charles Morgan, May 10, 1941; children: Vincent, Penelope, Jonathan, Christopher, Catherine. M.A., Cornell U., 1944; DFA, Westminster Coll., 1989. Music editor Chautauguan Dailey, Chautaugua, N.Y., 1969—. One woman shows: Central Cathedral, N.Y.C., 1982, Downtown Cathedral, Rochester, N.Y., 1982, Bryn Mawr (Pa.) Presbyn. Ch., 1982, 86, Univ. Christian Ch., Austin, Tex., 1986, Old Scots' and Pine St. Ch., 1987 (pres.), Princeton Theol. Sem. (in conjunction with 175th anniversary of its founding), N.J., 1988, represented in permanent collections Hurlbut Ch., Chautaugua, All Souls Unitarian Ch., Tulsa, Downtown Presbyn. Ch., Rochester, Presbyn. Ch., Warren, Pa., St. Joseph Ch., Erie, Pa.; ofcl. artist Presbyn. Ch.'s 200 Anniversary of First Synod, St. Louis and Phila., 1988—; executed mural Mellon Cathedral, Pitts. Transl.: The Cunning Little Vixen (Rudolf Tesnohildek), 1984. Home: 10 Forest Ave Chautaugua NY 14722

MORGAN, MARY LOUISE FITZSIMMONS, fund raising executive; b. N.Y.C., July 22, 1941; d. Robert John and Mary Louise (Gordon) Fitzsimmons; m. David William Morgan, Aug. 7, 1971; children: Mallory Siobhan, David William. BA, Marquette U., 1964; MA, Catholic U., Wash., 1966. Asst. prof. Monmouth Coll., West Long Branch, N.J., 1966-69; campaign dir. United Way - N.Y.C., 1969-80; pres. Morgan Communications, N.Y.C., 1980-82; capital campaign dir. YMCA of Greater N.Y., 1982-85; dir. devel. N.Y. Med. Coll, Valhalla, 1985-88; counsel Challenger Ctr., Va., 1988—; v.p. Ctr. Molecular Medicine & Immunology, Newark, 1989—; dir. Casita Maria Inc., N.Y.C. 1975—; pres., founding dir. Achievement Rewards for Coll. Scientists Inc., N.Y.C. 1978-80. Author: Thesis, The directorial Influence of Joan Littlewood on Contemporary Theatre 1966. Sec. Darien Democratic Town Com., Conn. 1984--; Vice Chmn. Darien Nominating Com., Conn. 1986--. Recipient 50th Anniversary Award Casita Maria Inc., N.Y.C. 1984. Mem. Nat. Soc. Fund Raising Execs., Nat. Soc. Hosp. Adminstrn., Spring Lake (N.J.) Bath and Tennis Club. Democrat. Roman Catholic. Home: 14 Anthony Ln Darien CT 06820 Office: Ctr for Molecular Medicine One Bruce St Newark NJ 07103

MORGAN, MYFANWY IRENE, registered nurse; b. Pitts., Nov. 27, 1951; d. Thomas George II and Irene (Koproski) M. BA, Duquesne U., 1973, BSN, 1980; M. in Nursing, Emory U., 1987. RN. Staff nurse Allegheny Gen. Hosp., Pitts., 1981-83; staff nurse Doctors Meml. Hosp., Atlanta, 1984-85; staff nurse Wesley Woods Hosp., Atlanta, 1987-89, head nurse, 1989; staff nurse Northside Hosp., Atlanta, 1985—; clin. instr. Brenau Coll. Nursing, Gainesville, Ga., 1990. Recipient Fed. Clin. traineeship VA Hosp., Decatur, Ga., 1986. Mem. Am. Heart Assn., Met. Atlanta Advanced Psychiat. Practice in Nursing Group, Ga. Nurses Assn., Sigma Theta Tau. Democrat. Roman Catholic. Home: 1414 K Post Oak Dr Clarkston GA 30021

MORGAN, REBECCA QUINN, state senator; b. Hanover, N.H., Dec. 4, 1938; d. Forrest Arthur and Rachel (Lewis) Quinn; m. James C. Morgan, June 10, 1960; children: J. Jeffrey, Mary Frances. BS, Cornell U., 1960; MBA, Stanford U., 1978. Trustee Palo Alto (Calif.) Bd. of Edn., 1973-78; asst. v.p. Bank of Am., Sunnyvale, Calif., 1978-80; county supr. County of Santa Clara, San Jose, Calif., 1980-84; senator State of Calif., Sacramento, 1984—; bd. dirs. Calif. Leadership, Sacramento, 1987—. Mem. adv. bd. YWCA, Palo Alto, 1983—, Palo Alto Adolescent Svcs., 1975—, Pub. Svc. Ctr., Stanford, Calif., 1985—. Named Calif. Legislator of Yr, Sch. Bd. Assn. of Sacramento, 1987, Calif. Probation Parole and Correctional Assn., 1987-88, Calif. Sch. Age Consortium, 1989, Calif. NOW, 1990, Woman of Achievement Santa Clara County, 1983. Mem. Calif. Elected Women's Assn. Republican. Office: State Capitol Rm 4090 Sacramento CA 95814

MORGAN, RHEA VOLK, veterinarian; b. Peoria, Ill., Mar. 23, 1952; d. Louis Francis and M. Joyce (Whitacre) Volk. BS in Vet. Medicine, U. Ill., 1974, DVM, 1976. Diplomate Am. Coll. Vet. Internal Medicine. Intern South Shore Vet. Assn., South Weymouth, Mass., 1976-77; resident internal medicine Angell Meml. Animal Hosp., Boston, 1977-80, staff internal medicine, ophthalmology, 1980-87; resident ophthalmology coll. vet. medicine U. Tenn., Knoxville, 1987-88; staff ophthalmology, internal medicine Angell Meml. Animal Hosp., Boston, 1988—; dir. nursing and ICW, Angell Meml. Hosp., Boston, 1978-84; guest lectr. sch. medicine Boston U., 1983—; clin. asst. prof. Tufts Sch. Vet. Medicine, Grafton, Mass., 1983—. Editor: Handbook of Small Practice, 1988; author: Manual of Small Emergencies, 1985; editor Advances in Small Animal Medicine and Surgery, 1988—; contbr. 25 sci. papers to profl. jours. Mem. Am. Vet. Medicine Assn., Am. Animal Hosp. Assn. (Disting. Svc. award 1990, Outstanding Svc. award Region I, 1988), Mass. Vet. Medicine Assn., Am. Assn. Vet. Clinicians, Am. Soc. Vet. Ophthalmology, Vet. Laser Interest Group. Office: Angell Meml Animal Hosp MSPCA 350 S Huntington Ave Boston MA 02130

MORGAN, ROBIN EVONNE, magazine editor, author, journalist; b. Lake Worth, Fla., Jan. 29, 1941; 1 child, Blake Ariel. Grad. with honors, The Wetter Sch., 1956; student, pvt. tutors, 1956-59, Columbia U. Free-lance book editor, 1961-69; editor Grove Press, 1967-70; editor, columnist "World" Ms. Mag., N.Y.C., 1974-87, editor-in-chief, 1990—; vis. chair and guest prof. women's studies New Coll., Sarasota, Fla., 1973; disting. vis. scholar, lectr. Ctr. Critical Analysis of Contemporary Culture, Rutgers U., 1987; invited spl. cons. UN com. UN Conv. to End All Forms Discrimination Against Women, Sao Paulo and Brasilia, Brazil, 1987; mem. adv. bd. ISIS (internat. network women's internat. cross-cultural exch.); spl. advisor gen. assembly conf. on Gender UN Internat. Sch., 1985-86; free-lance journalist, lectr. cons., editor, 1969—; invited speaker numerous confs., orgns., acad. meetings, U.S. and abroad. Author, compiler, editor: Sisterhood Is Powerful: An Anthology of Writings From the Women's Liberation Movement, 1970, Swedish edit. 1972, Sisterhood Is Global: The International Women's Movement Anthology, 1984, U.K., 1985; author: (nonfiction) Going Too Far: The Personal Chronicle of a Feminist, 1978, German edit. 1978, The Anatomy of Freedom: Feminism, Physics and Global Politics, 1982, fgn. edits. U.K. 1984, Germany, 1985, Argentina, 1986, The Netherlands, 1988, The Demon Lover: On the Sexuality of Terrorism, 1989, fgn. edits. U.K. 1989, Japan 1990, (fiction) Dry Your Smile: A Novel, 1987, U.K. edit. 1988, The Mer-Child: A New Legend, 1990, (poetry) Monster: Poems, 1972, Lady of the Beasts: Poems, 1976, Death Benefits: Poems, 1981, Depth Perception: New Poems and a Masque, 1982, Upstairs in the Garden: Selected and New Poems, 1968-88, 1990, (plays) In Another Country, 1960, The Duel, 1979; co-editor: (with Bunch and Weeks) The New Woman: Anthology, 1969; contbr. numerous articles, essays, book revs., poems to various publs.; presenter poetry readings univs., poetry ctrs., radio, TV, others, 1970—. Mem. first women's liberation caucus CORE, 1965, Student Nonviolent Coordinating Com., 1966; organizer first feminist demonstration against Miss Am. Pageant, 1968; founder, pres. The Sisterhood Fund, 1970; founder, pres. N.Y. Women's Law Ctr., 1970; founder N.Y. Women's Ctr., 1969; co-founder, bd. dirs. Feminist Women's Health Network, Nat. Battered Women's Refuge Network, Nat. Network Rape Crisis Ctrs.; bd. dirs. Women's Fgn. Policy Coun.; adv. trustee Nat. Women's Inst. for Freedom of Press; founding mem. Nat. Mus. Women in Arts; co-founder, mem. steering com. Sisterhood is Global Inst. (think-tank), 1984, sec., 1989, co-organizer, U.S. mem. official visit Coalition of Phillipines Women's Movement, 1988; chair N.Y. state com. Hands Across Am. Com. for Justice and Empowerment, 1988. Recipient Front Page award for disting. journalism, Wonder Woman award for internat. peace and understainding, 1982; writer-in-residence grantee Yaddo, 1980; grantee Nat. Endowment for Arts, 1979-80, Ford Found., 1982, 83, 84. Mem. Feminist Writers' Guild, Media Women, Women's Action Alliance, N.Am. Feminist Coalition, Pan Arab Feminist Solidarity Assn. (hon.), Israeli Feminists Against Occupation (hon.). Office: Ms Mag 1 Times Sq New York NY 10036

MORGAN, SHARON DENISE, research company executive; b. Arab, Ala., July 13, 1964; d. Ralph Junior King and Erma Dean (Smith) Norris; m. Timothy Dee Morgan, June 4, 1988. AS in Bus. Adminstrn., Snead State Jr. Coll., Boaz, Ala., 1984; BSBA in MIS, U. Ala., Huntsville, 1986. Patient svcs. rep. Arab Hosp., 1981-84, coord. patient accounts, 1984; customer svc. rep. DeltaCom, Arab, 1984-86; exec. asst. v.p.'s Brindlee Mountain Telephone Co., Arab, 1986-87; mktg. mgr. DeltaCom, Birmingham, Ala., 1987-88; MIS mgr. DeltaCom, Huntsville, 1988-90; pres., chmn. bd. dirs. Morgan Rsch. Corp., Huntsville, 1990—. Baptist. Home: 106 Millstone Ln Madison AL 35758 Office: 3311 Bob Wallace Ave Huntsville AL 35805

MORGAN, WANDA BUSBY, health care executive, educator; b. Cromwell, Okla., Aug. 27, 1930; d. Charles C. and Gladys J. (Beaty) Busby; m. James O. Morgan, Oct. 23, 1954; children: Terri, Kathleen, Martha. BA, Lincoln (Ill.) Christian Coll., 1954; MA, Kans. State U., 1973; postgrad., Cen. State U., Edmond, Okla., 1977-79, U. Okla., 1980-84, Purdue U., 1983. Prof. Manhattan (Kans.) Christian Coll., Manhattan, 1970-74, Bethany (Okla.) Nazarene Coll., 1981-84; instr. Moravian Coll., Bethlehem, Pa., 1984-85, Allentown Coll., Center Valley, Pa., 1985-88; edn. coordinator Sacred Heart HealthCare System, Allentown, Pa., 1985-87; v.p. Sacred Heart Health Care System, Allentown, Pa., 1987—; cons. Communication Arts, Ltd., Allentown, 1978—; advisor Okla. Dept. Edn., Oklahoma City, 1981; tchr., cons. U. Okla. Dept. Edn., Norman, 1980—, Okla. Writing Project, 1980—. Author: Bridging the English Gap, 1983; co-author: Grammar, Ltd., 1983. Mem. adv. bd. Lehigh County (Pa.) Human Svcs. Dept., 1986-89, chmn., 1988-89. Fellow U. Okla., 1980. Mem. Am. Soc. Healthcare Mktg. and Pub. Rels., Hosp. Assn. Pa. (mem. pub. rels. and mktg. div.), Okla. Coun. Tchrs. of English (vice chair coll. sect. 1983-84). Democrat. Presbyterian. Office: Sacred Heart Hosp 421 Chew St Allentown PA 18102

MORGANFIELD, MERCY DELLA, pharmaceutical representative; b. Chgo., Nov. 11, 1960; d. Muddy Waters McKinley and Lois (Anderson) M. BA in Liberal Arts, Jackson (Miss.) State U., 1982. Retail mgr. Lerner Retail Outlet Store, Vicksburg, Miss., 1982-83; retail mgr., trainer Lerner Retail Outlet Store, New Orleans, 1983-84; med. sales rep. Roeing/Pfizer Pharms., New Orleans, 1984-86, sr. med. svc. cons., 1986-88; corp. career and devel. assoc. Roeing/Pfizer Pharms., N.Y.C., 1988—. Vol. health drives New Orleans Med. Assn., 1985; vol. Children's Hosp., New Orleans, 1987—; mem. Nat. Soc. Young Dems., 1987—. Mem. Nat. Soc. Pharm. Sales Trainers, New Orleans Chgp. Black Women in Bus., NAACP. Democrat. Baptist. Home: 150 Joralemen Brooklyn NY 10112 Office: 235 E 42d St New York NY 10017

MORGANJONES, KAREN IRENE, computer consultant; b. Orange, Calif., June 15, 1956; d. Donald William and Jean (Simion) Snyder; m. Jesse Owen MorganJones, Sept. 14, 1985. BA in Psychology, UCLA, 1982. Mgr. data processing Rogerson Aircraft Corp., Irvine, Calif., 1980-86; cons. mfg. CSC Compufact, Inc., Garden Grove, Calif., 1986-89; computer and bus. cons. KMJ Cons., Fullerton, Calif., 1989—. Republican. Roman Catholic.

MORGAN-POND, CAROLINE GAIL, physics educator; b. Morristown, N.J.; d. Samuel Pope and Caroline (Annin) Morgan. BA, Swarthmore Coll., 1973; PhD, Princeton U., 1980. Rsch. assoc. NYU, N.Y.C., 1980-83; mem. tech. staff Riverside Rsch. Inst., N.Y.C., 1983-84; asst. prof. Wayne State U., Detroit, 1984-89; assoc. prof. physics Wayne State U., 1989—; cons. in field. Contbr. articles to profl. jours. Vol., Contact Lifeline, Detroit, 1985—. Nat. Merit scholar, 1969-70; fellow NSF, 1973-76; grantee various govt. orgns. Mem. Am. Phys. Soc., Phi Beta Kappa, Sigma Xi. Methodist. Office: Wayne State Univ Physics Dept Detroit MI 48202

MORGART, MICHELE, psychologist, consultant; b. Phila., July 2, 1947; d. Robert Paul and Elizabeth (Byrne) M.; divorced; 1 child, Michael Paul. BA in Psychology and English, U. Akron, Ohio, 1981, MA in Psychology, 1984. Dir. Teenage Parents, Akron, 1984-85; counselor and edn. specialist Timken Mercy Med. Ctr., Canton, Ohio, 1985—; cons. Summit County Adolescent Task Force Svcs. Network, Akron, 1988—; cons. C.A.R.E. Community Drug Edn., Cuy Falls, Ohio, 1984. Vol. Summit County Drug Bd., Akron, 1978-81. Mem. Am. Psychol. Assn. (cert.), Employee Asst. Profl. Assn., Psi Chi, Phi Sigma Alpha. Office: Timken Mercy Med Ctr 1320 Timken Mercy Dr Canton OH 44708

MORGENTHAL, BECKY HOLZ, computer service company owner; b. Altadena, Calif., Aug. 5, 1947; d. E. William and Elizabeth (DeLong) Holz; m. Roger Mark Morgenthal, Aug. 12, 1972. AA, Goldey Beacom Coll., 1967; grad., Wilson Coll., 1990. Clk. Hercules, Inc., Wilmington, Del., 1969-71; acct. Beth Products, Lebanon, Pa., 1971-72; adminstrv. asst. Legal Services, Inc., Carlisle, Pa., 1973-76; office mgr. CEMI Corp., Carlisle, 1976-77; acct. Tressler Luth. Services, Camp Hill, Pa., 1978-79, Benatec Assocs., Inc., Camp Hill, 1979-82; fin. analyst Electronic Data Systems, Camp Hill, 1983-87; owner B.H. Morgenthal Computer Services, Carlisle, 1982—; pres. Legal Eye Aerial Photography. Pres. Carlisle Jr. Civic Club, 1979-80, v.p., 1978-79; active Diocese of Harrisburg, Pa., 1985-89, chmn. pro-life com., 1988-89; mem. Council of Cath. Women, Carlisle, 1986—. Republican. Home: 1311 Windsor Ct Carlisle PA 17013-3562

MORGNER, EVELYN, investment consultant, senior manager; b. Arlington, Va., Apr. 28, 1955; d. Richard Johann and Eleonore (Holz) Morgner. AB, Bryn Mawr Coll., 1977; MSc in Econs., London Sch. Econs., 1980. Fin. analyst Hornblower Weeks Noyes & Trask, N.Y.C., 1977; fin. planner Merrill Lynch, N.Y.C., 1978-79; investment cons. KPMG Peat Marwick, N.Y.C., 1981—; bd. dirs., treas. Rebecca Kelly Dance Co.'Appleby Found., N.Y.C., 1989—. Contbr. articles to profl. jours. Vice chmn. Mgmt. Coun. 1989-90. Home: 305 W 98th St Apt 5FNOR New York NY 10025 Office: KPMG Peat Marwick 345 Park Ave New York NY 10154

MORI, HANAE, fashion designer; b. Muikaichi, Shimane, Japan, 1926; m. Ken Mori, May 1947; children: Akira, Kei. BA in Lit., Tokyo Women's Christian Coll., 1947. Pres., founder, designer Hanae Mori Group, N.Y.C., 1951—; uniform designer Japan Airlines, Tokyo, 1967, 70, 73; costume designer Monaco Ballet, 1976, Paris Opera Ballet, 1986, (opera) Madame Butterfly at La Scala, Milan, 1985. Author: Designing for Tomorrow, 1978, A Glass Butterfly, 1984, Hanae Mori 1960-1989, 1989. Adviser Ministry of Cultural Affairs, Tokyo; mem. overseas bd. Boston Symphony Orch.; mem. various cultural coms., Tokyo. Recipient Neiman Marcus award, 1973, Purple Ribbon, Govt. of Japan, 1988, La Croix Chevalier des Arts et Lettres, Govt. of France, 1984, Legion of Honor, 1989. Mem. Chambre Syndicale de Haute Couture Parisienne. Office: Hanae Mori USA Inc 550 7th Ave 21st Fl New York NY 10018

MORIARTY, ANNA MARIE, secondary school educator; b. Goshen, Ind., May 28, 1945; d. Frank B. Moriarty and LaVon Edith (Rohrer) Moriarty Troup. BA, Siena Hts. Coll., 1967; postgrad., Goshen Coll., 1969-70; MA, Bradley U., 1975. Children's librarian Plymouth (Ind.) Pub. Library, 1967-68; tchr. Latin and English Peoria (Ill.) High Sch., 1971—. Mem. Peoria Fedn. Tchrs., Hansons of John Clayton. Roman Catholic. Home: 505 W Albany Peoria IL 61604 Office: Peoria High Sch 1615 N North St Peoria IL 61604

MORICH, JOYCE PIGEON, alcohol/drug abuse services professional, consultant; b. Charleroi, Pa., Dec. 1, 1954; d. Joseph Jr. and Alma Louise (McGavitt) Pigeon; m. Randolph Paul Morich, May 15, 1976; children: Chad Vincent, Dana Elizabeth. BS in Social Work, Calif. State Coll., Pa., 1975; MS in Community Agy. Counseling, Calif. U. Pa., 1989. Case worker to acting supr. Adult Svcs. Washington (Pa.) County, 1976-80; office site mgr. Redevel. Authority Washington County, California, 1980-83; church sec. and supt. Bentleyville (Pa.) Wesleyan Ch., 1983-86; mental health specialist I Partial Hospitalization, Monessen, Pa., 1986-87; treatment specialist Mon Valley Drug & Alcohol, 1987-89, clin. supr., 1989—; cons. Women's Resource Ctr., Uniontown, Pa., 1983. Cons., counselor Bentleyville Wesleyan Ch., 1987—. Named Outstanding Young Woman of Am., Outstanding Young Women of Am. Bd., 1983, 86, 87. Mem. AAUW (interbr. coun. rep. 1981-83, br. pres. 1981-85, Pa. div. Most Valuable Person 1985-87, Outstanding Woman award 1983, 2nd pl. in newsletter competition 1984), Am. Assn. Counseling Devel., Zeta Tau Alpha. Democrat. Home: RD #1 Box 214A Daisytown PA 15427 Office: Mon Valley Drug & Alcohol Eastgate 8 Monessen PA 15062

MORIMOTO, AKIKO CHARLENE, educator; b. Los Angeles, May 2, 1948; d. Satosu Don and Midori Jean (Ohira) M. B, Calif. State U., Los Angeles, 1971. Cert. secondary tchr., Calif., adult edn. tchr., Calif. Tchr. Los Angeles City Schs., 1972-77; instr. U. Calif., San Diego, summers 1983-85; tchr. Vista (Calif.) Unified Sch. Dist., 1977—; cons. San Diego Area Writing Project, La Jolla, Calif., 1981—; bd. dirs. Greater San Diego Council Tchrs. of English; table leader Calif. Assessment Program-Writing, San Diego, 1987—, Calif. Lit. Project, 1988—. Co-author: (with others) Foundations of Art Education, 1973; editor (dist. lit. mag.) Visions of Our Youth, 1986, 87. Mem. Old Globe Theatre, San Diego, 1985—. Named Vista Mentor Tchr. Vista Unified Sch. dist., 1986-89. Mem. Calif. Assn. Tchrs. of English (Excellence in Classroom award 1988), Assn. San Diego Educators of Gifted, Calif. Assn. of Gifted, Nat. Council Tchrs. of English, Whole Lang. Coun., Nat. Writing Project, Greater San Diego Council Tchrs. English (Excellence in Classroom award 1988), Calif. Reading Assn., Greater San Diego Reading Assn. Democrat. Home: 704 C-6 Regal Rd Encinitas CA 92024 Office: 740 Olive Ave Vista CA 92083

MORIN, NANCY RUTH, botanist; b. Albuquerque, N.Mex., Feb. 16, 1948; d. Seale E. Fuller and Nan (Dunford) Rearick; m. Jerome Morin, 1969 (div. 1971). AA, City Coll. of San Francisco, 1973; AB, U. Calif., Berkeley, 1975; PhD, U. Calif., 1980. Research/teaching asst. U. Calif., Berkeley, 1975-80; postdoctoral fellow Smithsonian Instn., Washington, 1980-81; editor Annals of the Mo. Bot. Garden, St. Louis, 1981-86; curator of herbarium Mo. Bot. Garden, St. Louis, 1981-88, head dept. botany, 1981-88; co-founder, editor Herbarium News, St. Louis, 1981—; convening editor Flora of North Am. Project, St. Louis, 1983—, head dept. botanical info. mgmt., 1989—; adj. prof. U. Mo., St. Louis, 1983—. NSF grantee, 1977-79, 82—. Mem. AAAS, Am. Inst. Biol. Scis., Am. Soc. Plant Taxonomists, Bot. Soc. Am., Internat. Assn. Plant Taxonomy, Mo. Native Plant Soc. (editor Missouriensis 1983-86), Phi Beta Kappa. Democrat. Home: 6035 Eitman Saint Louis MO 63139

MORISATO, SUSAN CAY, actuary; b. Chgo., Feb. 11, 1955; d. George and Jessie (Fujita) M.; m. Thomas Michael Remec, Mar. 6, 1981. BS, U. Ill., 1975, MS, 1977. Actuarial student Aetna Life & Casualty, Hartford, Conn., 1977-79; actuarial asst. Bankers Life & Casualty, Chgo., 1979-80, asst. actuary, 1980-83, assoc. actuary, 1983-85, health product actuary, 1985-86, v.p., 1986—; participant individual forum Health Ins. Assn. Am., 1983. Mem. adv. panel on long term care financing Brookings' Inst. Fellow Soc. Actuaries (conv. speaker 1988, workshop leader 1990, news editor health sect. news 1988-1990, conf. speaker ann. pvt. long term care ins. 1990); mem. Am. Acad. Actuaries, Health Ins. Assn. Am. Long Term Care Task Force, Chgo. Actuarial Assn. (sec. 1983-85, program com. 1987-89), Phi Beta Kappa, Kappa Delta Pi, Phi Kappa Phi. Office: Bankers Life & Casualty Co 4444 W Lawrence Ave Chicago IL 60630

MORITZ, JANE ANDREWS, health science association administrator; b. Storm Lake, Iowa, Jan. 4, 0454; d. Wayne Henry and Bernice (Niehaus) Andrews; m. Timothy Leo Moritz, Sept. 2, 1972; children: Erica Marie, Sarah Ann. BA, Buena Vista Coll., 1986; MS, Iowa State U., 1990. Swim instr. YMCA, Storm Lake, 1970-74, gymnastics instr., 1971-74, aquatic dir., 1974-81; aerobics dir. Fitness & Health Ctr., Storm Lake; owner, operator Storm Lake, 1982-84; aquatic dir. Buena Vista Coll., 1981-84; wellness dir. Buena Vista Coll., Storm Lake, 1984-88, faculty lectr., 1986-88; owner, exec. cons. The Wellness Works, Storm Lake, 1988-; dir. Well Life Ctr. Trinity Reg. Hosp., Fort Dodge, 1989—. Active ARC, Am. Heart Assn. Mem. Nat. Wellness Assn., IDEA Club. Roman Catholic. Home: 208 West 2nd Storm Lake IA 50588

MORLOCK, JILL ELIZABETH, telecommunications industry professional; b. Flint, Mich., Jan. 15, 1963; d. John Edward and Barbara Ann (Meir) M. BS in Math., Sch. Ozarks, 1985. Analyst Southwestern Bell Telephone, St. Louis, 1985-87, program analyst, 1987-89; systems analyst Southwestern Bell Tel., St. Louis, 1989-90, mgr. cost studies, 1990—. Mem. Bus. and Profl. Women (Young Careerist 1987), Profl. Women of Southwestern Bell, St. Louis Jaycees. Roman Catholic.

MORONEY, LINDA L. S. (MUFFIE MORONEY), lawyer, educator; b. Washington, May 27, 1943; d. Robert Emmet and Jessie (Robinson) M.; m. Clarence Renshaw II, Mar. 28, 1967 (div. 1977); children: Robert Milnor, Justin W.R. BA, Randolph-Macon Woman's Coll., 1965; JD cum laude, U. Houston, 1982. Bar: Tex. 1982, U.S. Ct. Appeals (5th cir.) 1982, U.S. Dist. Ct. (so. dist.) Tex. 1982, U.S. Supreme Ct. 1988. Law clk. to assoc. justice 14th Ct. Appeals, Houston, 1982-83; assoc. Pannill and Reynolds, Houston, 1983-85, Gilpin, Pohl & Bennett, Houston, 1985-88, Vinson & Elkins, Houston, 1989—; adj. prof. law U. Houston, 1986—. Mem. ABA, State Bar of Tex., Houston Bar Assn., Order of the Barons, Phi Delta Phi. Episcopalian. Home: 3730 Overbrook Ln Houston TX 77027 Office: Vinson & Elkins 1001 Fannin St Houston TX 77002

MORPHEW, DOROTHY RICHARDS-BASSETT, artist, real estate broker; b. Cambridge, Mass., Aug. 4, 1918; d. George and Evangeline Booth (Richards) Richards; grad. Boston Art Inst., 1949; children—Jon Eric, Marc Alan, Dana Kimball. Draftsman, United Shoe Machinery Co., 1937-42; blueprinter, advt. artist A.C. Lawrence Leather Co., Peabody, Mass., 1949-51; propr. Studio Shop and Studio Potters, Beverly, Mass., 1951-53; tchr. ceramics and art, Kingston, N.H., 1953—; real estate broker, pres. 1965-81; two-man exhbn. Topsfield (Mass.) Library, 1960; owner, operator Ceramic Shop, West Stewartstown, N.H. Served with USNR, 1942-44. Recipient Profl. award New Eng. Ceramic Show, 1975; also numerous certificates in ceramics. Home: 557 Palomino Trail Englewood FL 34223 Studio: Algonac Ave Cliffs ME 03910

MORR, DARLENE CARTER, chemist; b. Ft. Gaines, Ga., Sept. 17, 1957; d. Oscar Merlyn and Connie Janice (Fleming) Carter; m. David Wayne Morr, June 28, 1980. BS in Biology-Chemistry, Troy State U., 1980; post-grad., Fla. Inst., 1987—. Technician SCI Systems, Inc., Huntsville, Ala., 1981-83, assoc. engr., 1983-85; customer rep. Mary Kay Cosmetics, Dallas, 1985-86; assoc. chemist Thiokol Co., Huntsville, 1986—. Mem. Am. Bus. Women's Assn. (sec. 1987-88), Nat. Mgmt. Club, Huntsville Young Profls., Thiokol Mgmt. Club (Christmas chmn. 1987-89, dir. 1990, awards dir. 1990). Republican. Baptist. Home: 12024 Runningmeade Trail Huntsville AL 35803

MORR, HELEN YVONNE, small business owner; b. Middletown, Ohio, Sept. 4, 1938; d. Volnia Alexander and Dora Katherine (Gilbert) Gentry; m. Jack L. Phillips, Sept. 8, 1961 (div. Sept. 1972); 1 child, Karla Renae Spitzlei; m. Fred E. Morr, Nov. 20, 1973. Student, Middletown Bus. Coll., 1965-67, Mt. St. Joseph Coll., 1979. Office mgr. Congl. Office 24th Dist., Middletown, 1967-71, Ohio River Basin Commn., Cin., 1971-78; sec., treas. Continental Farm and Land Mgmt. Co., Cin., 1974—; co-owner F.E. & H.Y. Morr Ins. Co., Cin., 1978-85; dir. Molitor Loan and Bldg. Co., Cin., 1978-85; pres., record producer MoPro Records, Inc., Cin., 1981—; talent booker MoPro Midwest Booking Agy., Cin., 1987—. Producer numerous jazz albums. Field coordinator Lukens for Gov. campaign State of Ohio, 1970; hosp. vol. Womens Aux. St. Francis Hosp., Cin., 1980-81; campaign coordinator Morr for Congress, 1st Congl. Dist., 1986. Mem. Nat. Acad. Recording Arts and Sci., Internat. Assn. Jazz Record Collectors, Nat. Assn. Jazz Educators, Cin. Jazz Forum, Cin. Jazz Soc. Republican. Episcopalian. Clubs: Bankers, Western Hills Country (Cin.); Capital Hill (Washington). Home: 375 Compton Rd Cincinnati OH 45215 Office: MoPro Records Inc 2959 Kling Ave Cincinnati OH 45211

MORR, THERESA HELEN, aircraft industrial program specialist; b. Balt, June 3, 1939; d. Bernard Francis and Sonia Veronica (Borden) Greene; (divorced). AA, Charles County Community Coll., 1984. Adminstrv. asst. Naval Aviation Logistics Ctr., Patuxent River, Md., 1977-81; equipment specialist Naval Aviation Logistics Ctr., Patuxent River, 1981-85, configuration mgmt. specialist, 1985-86, program analyst, 1986-87, aircraft indsl. program specialist, 1987-; editor Clarke Engrng. Assoc. Cons. Firm, Lexington Park, Md., 1986-88. Contbr. articles to nat. mags. Mem. Laubach Lit. Internat., Nat. Writer's Club, Toastmasters. Democrat. Roman Catholic. Home: 318 Esperanza Dr Lexington Park MD 20653

MORRIN, VIRGINIA WHITE, educator; b. Escondido, Calif., May 16, 1913; d. Harry Parmalee and Ethel Norine (Nutting) Rising; B.S., Oreg. State Coll., 1952; M.Ed., Oreg. State U., 1957; m. Raymond Bennett White, 1933 (dec. 1953); children: Katherine Anne, Marjorie Virginia, William Raymond; m. 2d, Laurence Morrin, 1959 (dec. 1972). Social caseworker Los Angeles County, Los Angeles, 1934-40, 61-64; acctg. clk. War Dept., Ft. MacArthur, Calif., 1940-42; prin. clk. USAAF, Las Vegas, Nev., 1942-44; high sch. tchr., North Bend-Coos Bay, Oreg., 1952-56, Mojave, Calif., 1957-60; instr. Antelope Valley Coll., Lancaster, Calif., 1961-73; ret., 1974. Treas., Humane Soc. Antelope Valley, Inc., 1968—. Mem. Nat. Aero. Assn., Calif. State Sheriffs' Assn. (charter assoc.), Oreg. State U. Alumni Assn. (life). Mailing: 3153 Milton Dr Mojave CA 93501

MORRIS, ARLENE MYERS, marketing professional; b. Washington, Pa., Dec. 29, 1951; d. Frank Hayes Myers and Lula Irene (Slusser) Kolcan; m. John L. Sullivan, Feb. 17, 1971 (div. July 1982); m. David Wellons Morris, July 27, 1984. BA, Carlow Coll., 1974; postgrad., Western New England Coll., 1981-82. Sales rep. Syntex Labs., Inc., Palo Alto, Calif., 1974-77; profl. sales rep. McNeil Pharm., Spring House, Pa., 1977-78, mental health rep., 1978-80, asst. product dir., 1981-82, dist. mgr., 1982-85, new product dir., 1985-87, exec. dir. new bus. devel., 1987-89, v.p. bus. devel., 1989—. Mem. Found. of Ind. Colls., Phila., 1989. Home: 374 Stormfield Dr Harleysville PA 19438 Office: McNeil Pharm Spring House PA 19438

MORRIS, BARBARA ALBERS, freelance writer; b. Bklyn., Mar. 28, 1956; d. Henry Frederick and Dorothy (Johnson) Albers; m. Gilbert Harold Morris, May 19, 1984; children: Sarah Anne, Allison Leah. BA in English, SUNY, Stony Brook, 1977; MA in Journalism, NYU, 1981. Staff writer Continental Corp., N.Y.C., 1977-78, editor, 1978-80; asst. pub. rels. dir. Ind. Ins. Agts. of Am., N.Y.C., 1982-85; dir. pub. rels. Ins. Agts. Am., N.Y.C., 1985-87; freelance writer, editor Ind. Ins. Agts. Am. Oakland, N.J., 1987—; managing editor Atlantic States Ins.; assoc. editor Forum mag. Democrat. Home and Office: 39 Oneida Ave Oakland NJ 07436

MORRIS, BARBARA-ALLEN WILKEY, educator; b. Raleigh, Oct. 14, 1945; d. John Wesley and Ruby (Allen) Wilkey; m. Charles Edward Kearney Morris, Jr., Dec. 16, 1967; 1 child, John David. BA, Christopher Newport Coll., Newport News, 1984; student, Princeton U., 1972; Wives' Support MA (hon.), Princeton U. Grad. Coll. Cert. collegiate profl., Va. With Newport News Shipyard, 1967-68, City of Hampton (Va.), 1968-72; cons. researcher Princeton U. Grad. Cool. Coop Playsch., 1971, coordinator, researcher, fundraiser, 1972; staff chaperone/hostess Miss World-USA Beauty Pageant, Hampton, 1972; coordinator youth, lectr. Hilton Presbyn. Ch., Newport News, 1972—; fundraiser, educator Am. Cancer Soc., Peninsula Unit, Newport News, 1972—; coordinator internship Va. Living Mus., Newport News, 1981-83; civic coordinator, lectr., writer City of Newport News, 1972—; dir., actor TV Channel 29, Hampton City Schs., 1982; lectr. in field; cons. in field. Contbr. to profl. jours., ednl. TV progrs. Del. Va. Women's Conf., Richmond, 1988, 89. Mem. Nat. Geographic Soc., Calligraphers Guild of the Peninsula (exec. bd. pub. rels. 1984-86), NAFE, Christopher Newport Coll. Alumni Assn., Parents of Hampden-Sydney Coll., Garden of Va., Va. Peninsula Rose Soc., Am. Rose Soc., No. Va. Woman 90's (del.), Capitol Women's Network, Princeton Club of Washington, Skyline Clubs of Crustal City. Presbyterian. Home: 1505 Crystal Dr #609 Arlington VA 22202 Office: L'Enfant Pla PO Box 23773 Washington DC 20026-3773

MORRIS, CAROL J., financial services specialist; b. Miami, Fla., May 12, 1953; d. R.L. and Norene (Bennett) M. BA, U. South Fla., 1979. Internal auditor Pillsbury Co., Miami, 1982-83; acct. Ind. Pension Svcs. Inc., Miami, 1983-84; asst. to adminstr. pension plan DWG Corp., Miami Beach, Fla., 1984—. Mem. NAFE. Republican. Baptist.

MORRIS, CAROLINE JANE MCMASTERS STEWART (MRS. FRANCIS J. MORRIS), librarian; b. Ridley Park, Pa., Sept. 14, 1923; d. James Sterrett and Mildred M. (McCloskey) Stewart; BS in Commerce, Drexel U., 1950, MLS, 1964; m. Francis Joseph Morris, Feb. 3, 1951; 1 son, Edward James. Adminstrv. trainee John Wanamaker, Phila., 1946-50; serials librarian Penn Morton Colls., Chester, Pa., 1964-65; dir. libraries and archives Pa. Hosp., Phila., 1965—; cons., 1970—; instr., leader several library workshops Am. Hosp. Assn., Cath. Hosp. Assn., Med. Library Assn. Mem. Emergency Aid Pa., 1960—. Served with WAVES, 1943-45. Mem. ALA, AAUP, AAUW, Nat. Med. Library Assn. (sect. chmn. 1970 pres. local chpt. 1978—), Spl. Libraries Assn., Med. (local chpt. pres. 1969-70), Prospect Park library assns., D. of R. (pres. Pa. 1947—), Victorian Soc. Am., Soc. Am. Archivists, Manuscript Soc., Delaware County Hist. Soc., Hist. Delaware County, Soc. Preservation Landmarks, Hist. Soc. Pa., Oral Hist. Soc., Geneol. Soc. Pa., Hort. Soc. Pa., Dames Loyal Legion (state pres. 1966-68), Phila. Mus. Art, Am. Assn. Records Mgrs., Am. Soc. Profl. and Exec. Women, Drexel U. Alumni Assn. (pres. 1969-71). Club: Art Alliance (Phila). Home: 1553 Schiavello Dr Swarthmore PA 19081 Office: Pa Hosp 8th and Spruce Sts Philadelphia PA 19107

MORRIS, CHRISTINE COALSON, financial services executive; b. Orange, Calif., Dec. 24, 1952; d. Coalson Clyde and Jessie Jean (Crawford) M. BS, U. Utah, 1975; postgrad., Loma Linda (Calif.) U., 1975-77. Corp. sec. Jefcol, Laguna Beach, Calif., 1977-79, N. Laguna Fin., Laguna Beach, 1979-81, Perry Morris Corp., Newport Beach, Calif., 1981-82; v.p. Perry Morris Corp., Newport Beach, 1982-83, exec. v.p., 1983—; with U. So. Calif. Assocs., Los Angeles, 1988—. Mem. Found. Christian Living, Pauling, N.Y., 1984—; mem. bus. coun. Fine Arts Mus., San Francisco, 1988—; sponsor Spl. Olympics, Orange County, Calif., 1988. Mem. Am. Assn. Equipment Lessors, Western Assn. Equipment Lessors, San Francisco C. of C., Prime-time Athletic Club (Burlingame, Calif.), Delta Gamma. Republican. Presbyterian. Office: Perry Morris Corp 2755 Campus Dr Ste 190 San Mateo CA 94403

MORRIS, DIANA ETHELREDA, infosystems specialist; b. Newark, Apr. 10, 1940; d. Joseph Martin and Elsie (Ondejka) Galik; m. Allan Harvey Morris, Apr. 24, 1964 (div. 1973); m. Craig Allan Manister, July 10, 1985. BA, CUNY, 1974, MA, 1976. Prodn. supr. Crowell, Collier & MacMillan, N.Y.C., 1968-71; asst. to creative dir. Helena Rubenstein, Inc., N.Y.C., 1971-73; assoc. editor Women Artists News, N.Y.C., 1978-81; sec. to pres. Protestant Episcopal Ch. Am., N.Y.C., 1981-83, bus. systems analyst, 1983-85; info. systems mgr. Gen. Convention of the Episcopal Ch., N.Y.C., 1985—; systems task force mem. Episcopal Ch., N.Y.C.; vice chmn. Coun. for Info. Systems, N.Y.C., 1988—. Assoc. editor: (newspaper) Women Artists News, 1978-81. Mem. NAFE, Artists Fedn. (pres. 1978-79). Democrat. Byzantine Catholic. Office: Episc Ch Ctr 815 Second Ave New York NY 10017

MORRIS, DIANE CAROL, information management specialist; b. Springfield, Ill., Nov. 20, 1964; d. Donald J. and Linda L. (Lane) M. BBA, Western Ill. U., 1986; postgrad., U. Mich., 1989—. Sr. cons. Peterson & Co. Consulting, Chgo., 1986-88; document mgmt. supr. Hinshaw, Culbertson, Moelmann, Hoban & Fuller, Chgo., 1988-89. Office: Hinshaw Culbertson et al 222 N LaSalle St Chicago IL 60601

MORRIS, DOROTHY EDITH, real estate executive; b. College Point, N.Y., Sept. 22, 1931; d. Conrad Vincent and Frances Sarah (Aiken) Kohler; m. Kenneth Baker Morris, Sept. 3, 1960; children: Laura Susan, Sandra Lee. AAS, Manhattan Coll., 1986; student, Hofstra U., 1952-54, Westchester Community Coll., Valhalla, N.Y., 1971-72. Lic. real estate broker. Bus. woman mgr. Beneficial Fin. Corp., N.Y.C., 1949-63; salesperson Peggy Carnegie Real Estate, N.Y.C., 1971-73; owner/operator Morris Real Estate, N.Y.C., 1973—; arbitrator Am. Arbitration Assn., N.Y.C. and N.Y.C. Real Estate Bd., 1980—, guest lectr. Pace Univ., Manhattan Coll. and IBM Corp. Hdqtrs. Mem. Downtown Community Council, N.Y.C., 1981—. Mem. N.Y.C. Real Estate Bd., N.Y. State Soc. Realtors, Nat. Assn. Realtors, N.Y. State Soc. Real Estate Appraisers, Nat. Soc. Rev. Appraisers, East Side C. of C. (N.Y.). Home: 388 Cedar Dr West Briarcliff Manor NY 10510 Office: Morris Real Estate 280 Madison Ave New York NY 10016

MORRIS, ELIZABETH TREAT, physical therapist; b. Hartford, Conn., Feb. 20, 1936; d. Charles Wells and Marion Louise (Case) Treat; BS in Phys. Therapy, U. Conn., 1960; m. David Breck Morris, July 10, 1961; children: Russell Charles, Jeffrey David. Phys. therapist Crippled Children's Clinic No. Va., Arlington, 1960-62, Shriners Hosp. Crippled Children, Salt Lake City, 1967-69, Holy Cross Hosp., Salt Lake City, 1970-74; pvt. practice phys. therapy, Salt Lake City, 1975—. Mem. Am. Phys. Therapy Assn., Am. Congress Rehab. Medicine, Salt Lake Area C. of C., Friendship Force Utah, U.S. Figure Skating Assn. Home: 4177 Mathews Way Salt Lake City UT 84124 Office: 2178 So 900 East Ste 3 Salt Lake City UT 84106

MORRIS, GRETCHEN SUZANNE, transportation executive, consultant; b. Detroit, May 8, 1963; d. Richard Frederic and Betty Jean (McNaughton) M. BA, U. Mich., 1985; postgrad., Ctr. for Creative Studies, 1987. Account exec. JL Communications, St. Clair Shores, Mich., 1985-87, sr. account exec., 1987-88; pres. Metro Messenger, Grosse Pointe Woods, Mich., 1988—; owner M Graphics, Grosse Pointe Woods, 1988—; real estate agt. R.G. Edgar & Assocs., Grosse Pointe Farms, 1981-88, cons., 1988—; cons. Mack Ave USA, Grosse Pointe, 1988—. Mem. Hill Assn., Grosse Pointe, 1989—; bd. dirs. Mack Ave USA, 1988-89. Mem. Metro E. C. of C., Grosse Pointe Theatre. Republican. Lutheran. Home: 1016 Lakepointe Grosse Pointe Park MI 48230 Office: Metro Messenger Inc 19650 Harper Ave Grosse Pointe Woods MI 48236

MORRIS, HILDRED ANN, billing coordinator; b. Columbus, Miss., Jan. 28, 1955; d. Jesse James and Lizzie Mae (Short) Morris. AS in Med. Assisting, Akron U., 1977; AA in Arts, Cuyahoga Community Coll., 1990. Air cleaner insp. Fort Motor Co., Sandusky, Ohio, 1977; secretarial asst. Cmmunity and Tech. Coll., Akron U., 1977; billing coordinator dept. family medicine Univ. Hosps., Cleve., 1978—. Mem. Nat. Assn. Exec. Females, Zeta Phi Beta. Democrat. Baptist. Home: 11328 Euclid ave Apt 503 Cleveland OH 44106

MORRIS, JANINE INEZ, marketing executive; b. Hampton, Va., June 1, 1956; d. Owen Glenn and Moree (Glover) M.; m. Kerry James Comeaux; children: Kyle Jarrett, Kayla Janine. BS, Tex. A&M U., 1978. Programmer, analyst St. Luke's Episcopal Hosp., Houston, 1978-79; systems analyst Exxon Chemical, Houston, 1979-81; advanced systems specialist United Gas Pipeline, Houston, 1981-84, supr. human resource info., 1984-86, supr. compensation and human resource info., 1986-87, supr. benefits, 1987-88; supr. contract adminstrn. LASER Mktg. Co., Houston, 1988—. Capt. United Way campaign, Houston, 1985, 86; com. mem. St. Giles Presbyn. Ch., Houston, 1987; sec. Oaks of Inwood Civic Assn., Houston, 1987. Named Outstanding Woman of Yr. Houston YWCA's, 1986. Mem. Am. Mgmt. Assn., Am. Compensation Assn., Human Resource Systems Profls. Office: LASER Mktg Co PO Box 3327 Houston TX 77253-3327

MORRIS, JOYCE DARLENE, travel consultant; b. Normal, Ill., Nov. 2, 1937; d. Richard Edison and Margaret Amelia (Scholl) Rigg; m. Robert Alan Morris, Dec. 5, 1959; children: Linda, Laura, Rob. BS in Journalism, Northwestern U., 1959. Pub. relations asst. Curtiss Candy Co., Chgo., 1959; acct. asst. Daniel Edelman Agy., Chgo., 1959-61; travel cons. West Travel, Manchester, Mo. Mem. AAUW (1st v.p. 1989), New Neighbors (1st v.p. 1988).

MORRIS, KATHLEEN ELIZABETH, entertainment executive; b. Norfolk, Va., Jan. 27, 1949; d. Olive Pearce and Dorothea Sivila (Long) Morris. AA, Glendale Jr. Coll., 1970. Broadcast coordinator Chiat/Day Advt., L.A., 1971-72; producer's asst. Whitson & Assocs., Hollywood, Calif., 1972-74; adminstr. Image West, Hollywood, 1974-75; prodn. coordinator Sunlight Pictures, Hollywood, 1975-76; producer Perks Plus, Hollywood, 1976-77; prodn. adminstr. Sandy Howard Prodns., L.A., 1977-79, Film Fin. Group, Ltd., L.A., 1979-82; v.p., sec. PSO Delphi Corp., L.A., 1982-86; v.p., ptnr. Cinecorp, North Hollywood, 1986—. Republican. Episcopalian. Home: Fairlea Ranch Badger CA 93603 Office: Cinecorp 4000 Warner Blvd Burbank CA 91522

MORRIS, LOIS LAWSON, education educator; b. Antoine, Ark., Nov. 27, 1914; d. Oscar Moran and Dona Alice (Ward) Lawson; m. William D. Morris, July 2, 1932 (dec.); 1 child, Lavonne Morris Howell. B.A., Henderson U., 1948; M.S., U. Ark., 1951, M.A., 1966; postgrad. U. Colo., 1954, Am. U., 1958, U. N.C., 1968. History tchr. Delight High Sch., Ark., 1942-47; counselor Huntsville Vocat. Sch., 1947-48; guidance dir. Russellville Pub. Sch. System, Ark., 1948-55; asst. prof. edn. U. Ark., Fayetteville, 1955-82, prof. emeritus, 1982—; ednl. cons. Ark. Pub. Schs., 1965-78. Mem. Commn. on Needs for Women, 1976-78, Hist. Preservation Alliance Ark.; pres. Washington County Hist. Soc., 1983-84; v.p. Pope County Hist. Assn.; bd. dirs. Potts Inn Mus. Found. Named Ark. Coll. Tchr. of Year, 1972; recipient Plaque for outstanding svcs. to Washington County Hist. Soc., 1984. Mem. Ark. Coun. Social Studies (sec.-treas.), Washington County Hist. Soc. (exec. bd. 1977-80), NEA, Nat. Coun. Social Studies, Ark. Edn. Assn., Ark. Hist. Assn., AAUW, U. Ark. Alumni Assn., LWV, Phi Delta Kappa, Kappa Delta Pi, Phi Alpha Theta. Democrat. Episcopalian. Address: 1601 W 3d St Russellville AR 72801

MORRIS, LYNNE LOUISE, psychotherapist; b. Youngstown, Ohio, Nov. 5, 1946; d. Richard Davies and Elsie Margaret Raymond) B.A., Westminster Coll., Pa., 1969; MSW, NYU, 1971. Cert. clin. social worker. Social worker Community Service Soc., N.Y.C., 1971-74, Altro Health and Rehab. Services, Inc., N.Y.C., 1974-79; field instr. Hunter Coll. Sch. Social Work, NYU Grad Sch. Social Work, 1974-79; clin. coordinator Montefiore Hosp. and Med. Center, Bronx, N.Y., 1979-81; asst. dir. II, social service dept. Montefiore Hosp., Bronx, 1981-83; pvt. practice psychotherapy, N.Y.C., 1976—; sr. staff therapist Counseling and Human Devel. Center, N.Y.C., 1979—. Contbr. articles of profl. jours. including Jour. Geriatric Psychiatry, 1975; abstractor Abstracts for Social Workers, 1975. Fellow N.Y. State Soc. Clin. Social Work Psychotherapists; mem. Nat. Assn. Social Workers (clin. diplomate), Acad. Cert. Social Workers, Am. Assn. Pastoral Counselors (profl. affiliate). Mem. profl. adv. com. Cary Addis Meml. Found. Home and office: 161 W 75th St 2C New York NY 10023

MORRIS, MARGARET ELIZABETH, marketing professional; b. N.Y.C., Nov. 1, 1962; d. John Daniel and Jean Bingham (MacCollom) M. BA in English, Georgetown U., 1984. Mem. staff mktg. programs AT&T Nat. Fed. Mktg., Arlington, Va., 1985; mktg. tech. cons. AT&T Nat. Fed. Systems, Washington, 1985-87; tech. cons. computer mktg. Cin. Bell Tel. Co., 1987—. Editor: (newsletter) District Action Project RAP, 1981-82. Intern Citizen's Complaint Ctr., Washington, 1981-82. Mem. NAFE, Nat. Network of Women in Sales (pres. Cin. chpt., bd. dirs.), Data Processing Mgmt. Assn. (bd. dirs., v.p. publs., student chpt. liaison), Cin. Updowntowners, Soroptimist Internat. Office: Cin Bell Tel Co 201 E 4th St Rm 102-1115 Cincinnati OH 45202

MORRIS, MARY ANN, bookkeeper; b. Great Falls, Mont., Feb. 16, 1946; d. Francis Leonard and Dorothy Irene (Howe) De Lacey; m. Donald Edward Wermuth, June 29, 1968 (div. Jan. 1974); 1 child, Deborah Ann; m. Larry Dallas Morris, Apr. 23, 1977; stepchildren: Serena Jo, Bradley Dwayne, Brian Dale, Bruce Dean. Student, North Idaho Coll., 1985. Sales clk. Dundas Office Supply, Great Falls, 1964-68, Stationer's Office Supply, Tacoma, 1969-70; bookkeeper Miller's Office Supply, Puyallup, Wash., 1971-72, Judge Moving & Storage (Allied), Great Falls, 1973-74; bookkeeper, credit mgr. Meadow Gold Dairy, Great Falls, 1974; pro-rate clk. Builders Transport, Great Falls, 1975-77; bookkeeper C&S Glass, Coeur d'Alene, Idaho, 1978-81, Morris Trucking, Coeur d'Alene, 1977-82, LDM Transport, Hayden Lake, Idaho, 1982—. Mem. Women's Retail Credit Mgrs. Assn. Republican. Home and Office: N 10371 Hillview Dr Hayden Lake ID 83835

MORRIS, M(ARY) ROSALIND, cytogeneticist, educator; b. Ruthin, Wales, May 8, 1920; came to U.S., 1942, naturalized, 1954; d. Aneurin Edmund and Celia Charles (Evans) M. BS in Horticulture, Ont. Agrl. Coll., Guelph, Can., 1942; PhD in Plant Breeding and Genetics, Cornell U., 1947. Mem. faculty U. Nebr., Lincoln, 1947—, prof. agronomy, 1958-90, prof. emeritus, 1990—. Contbr. chpts. to textbooks, articles to sci. jours. U. Nebr. Johnson Faculty fellow, Calif. Inst. Tech., Pasadena, 1949-50; John Simon Guggenheim Found. fellow, Sweden and Eng., 1956-57. Fellow Am. Soc. Agronomy, Crop Sci. Soc. Am., AAAS; mem. Genetics Soc. Am., Genetics Soc. Can., AAUW, Audubon Naturalists' Club, Lincoln Camera Club, Sigma Xi, Gamma Sigma Delta. Office: U Nebr Dept Agronomy Lincoln NE 68583-0915

MORRIS, PATRICIA ALPHA, civil engineer; b. Vicksburg, Miss., Nov. 20, 1962; d. Jesse Anderson and Alpha (Lockhart) M. BS in Civil Engring., Tulane U., 1984; postgrad., Miss. State U., 1985—. Civil engr. U.S. Army Engr. Waterways Experiment Sta., Vicksburg, 1984—. Mem. Soc. Am. Mil. Engrs., ASCE, Soc. Tulane Engrs., Blacks in Govt. (treas. 1986-87, bd. dirs. 1988-89), Nat. Coun. Negro Women, Internat. Soc. for Terrain-Vehicle Systems, Vicksburg-Warren County C. of C. (leadership coun.), Delta Sigma Theta (v.p. 1990—, sec. 1984-88). Democrat. Baptist. Office: Waterways Experiment Sta 3909 Halls Ferry Rd Vicksburg MS 39180-6199

MORRIS, PATRICIA ARMSTRONG, publications director; b. Jacksonville, Fla., Sept. 27, 1957; d. Howard Davis and Gloria Lynn (Tharpe) Armstrong; m. Ralph Stephenson Morris, Apr. 2, 1977; children: Brian Stephenson, Kelley Lynn, Kimberly Raye. BS in Journalism, U. Fla., 1978. Accredited pub. rels. profl. Para-profl. Alachua County Sch. Bd., Gainesville, Fla., 1976; pub. rels. asst. Shands Teaching Hosp., Gainesville, 1978-79; sec. U. Fla. Found., Gainesville, 1981-83; info. specialist, editor Coll. Engring. U. Fla., Gainesville, 1983-88, coord. info. and publs. Coll. Medicine, 1988—; cons. Gainesville Dept. Civil Engring., 1987-88. Editor: Fla. Engr., 1984-88, U. Fla. Physician, 1988—. Mem. Fla. Pub. Rels. Assn. (pres. Gainesville chpt. 189-90, state v.p. accreditation 1990-91, Golden Image award 1989, award of distinction 1986, Grand-all Golden Image award 1990), Assn. Am. Med. Colls. (group on pub. affairs). Democrat. Baptist. Office: Univ Fla Coll Medicine Box J 253 Health Sci Ctr Gainesville FL 32610

MORRIS, RUTH ANN, nurse executive; b. Hammond, Ind., Feb. 12, 1947; d. Harold August and Lorraine (Blount) Hopp; m. Wayne Thomas Morris, Aug. 26, 1978. BS in Nursing, Ind. U. Sch. of Nursing, 1969; MS in Nursing, Ind. U., 1976. Nurse intern St. Catherine Hosp., East Chgo., Ind., 1969-70, Vets. Adminstrn. Hosp., Indpls., 1970-71; psychiatric clin. nurse specialist Community Hosp., Indpls., 1972, nurse mgr., 1973-80, dir. nursing, 1980-87, v.p., 1987--; clin. asst. prof. Ind. Univ., 1976-80; lect. Marion Coll. Indpls.,. Chmn. Vol. Hosps. Am., 1987--. Fellow, Wharton Progam for Nurse Exec., mem. Am. Orgn. Nurse Exec., Nat. Office: Community Hosp 1500 N Ritter Ave Indianapolis IN 46219

MORRIS, SANDRA CHASS, gifted educator, reading specialist; b. Pitts., Mar. 7, 1936; d. Benjamin P. and Rose (Knapp) Chass; m. Leslie R. Morris, Dec. 23, 1956; children: Hallie J., Lee J. BS in Edn., U. Pitts., 1957; MS in Edn., SUNY, Fredonia, 1976; MS, U. New Orleans, 1984, postgrad., 1984—. Cert. gifted and reading specialist, elem. edn. tchr., Pa., Tex., La., N.Y. Tchr. Moon Union Schs., Coraopolis, Pa., 1957-59, El Paso (Tex.) Pub. Schs., 1959-60; tchr. Falk Lab. Sch. U. Pitts., 1960-61; tchr. Stroud Union Schs., Stroudsburg, Pa., 1969-70; instr. reading Delgado Community Coll., New Orleans, 1976-77; tech. asst. La. State Right to Read, Baton Rouge, 1977; reading specialist Jefferson Pub. Sch. System, Harvey, La., 1977-84, gifted educator, 1984—; presenter to confs. in field. Co-editor: Choosing a Bibliographic Utility, Interlibrary Loan Policies Directory, 4th edit. Pres. Internat. Reading Jefferson Coun., 1983-84, mem. dir., 1984-86; pres. New Orleans Hadassish B'not Shalom, 1981-83, 88-89; bd. dirs. So. region Hadassah, 1982-83, 88-89, chairperson speakers bur., 1989—; liaison Reading for Gifted and Creative Students, 1988—. Mem. La. Reading Assn. (bd. dirs. 1983—), Internat. Reading Assn. (membership dir. 1988—), Nat. Assn. for Gifted Children. Home: 4709 Senac Dr Metairie LA 70003 Home: 2247 Center Terr #3 Grand Island NY 14072

MORRIS, SHARON LOUISE, marketing professional; b. Washington, Feb. 9, 1956; d. George Arthur Jr. and Shirley Ann (Dickinson) S.; m. Brian Stanley Morris, Feb. 9, 1979; children: Jessica Kristin, Krystle Maria. BS, Atlantic Christian Coll., Wilson, N.C., 1978. Cert. Elem. Edn. and Math. Cashier Safeway Finance, Wilson, N.C., 1980-81; cashier Proident Finance, Wilson, 1981-85; mktg. svc. mgr. Beneficial of N.C. Inc., Wilson, 1985—; ins. agt., Cen. Nat. Life Ins., Wilson, 1988—. Notary Pub., State of N.C., 1986—. Democrat. Methodist. Home: 1201 Herring Ave Wilson NC 27893 Office: Beneficial of NC Inc 2405 W Nash St Wilson NC 27893

MORRIS, STEPHANIE ANNE, archivist; b. Phila., June 28, 1950; d. Royal Ferdinand Jr. and Betty (Wells) M. BS in Biology with honors, Stonehill Coll., 1972; MA in History of Sci. and Tech., U. Pa., 1975; PhD in History, Temple U., 1988. Archival assoc. Franklin Inst., Phila., 1972-77; archivist Coll. of Physicians of Phila., 1977-78; data mgr. Ctr. for Immigration Rsch., 1978-86; project archivist Union League of Phila., 1988; asst. dir. documentation strategy Nat. Found. for History of Chemistry, 1989—; archival cons. St. Christopher's Ch., Phila., 1989-90. Author, editor: The Franklin Institute and the Making of Industrial America, 1987. Instr. USCG Aux. Flotilla 2-76, Phila., 1975-77. Mem. Acad. Cert. Archivists, Mid-Atlantic Regional Archives Conf., Soc. for History of Tech. Office: Nat Found History Chemistry 3401 Walnut St #460B Philadelphia PA 19104-6228

MORRIS, SUSAN ELIZABETH, computer company administrator; b. Louisville, Jan. 10, 1952; d. Adam and Agnes Bertha (Huber) M.; B.S. in Commerce, U. Louisville, 1978. Paralegal law firm Wyatt, Grafton & Sloss, Louisville, 1973-79; systems installer HBO & Co., Inc., San Mateo, Calif., 1979-81; systems specialist Whittaker Medicus, Evanston, Ill., 1981-83; product installation mgr. Computer Synergy, Inc., Oakland, Calif., 1983; adv. analyst, mgr. Shared Med. Systems, Oakland, 1983-88, mgr. mktg. support, 1988—. Active Third Century, Louisville, 1978-79. Mem. Bus. and Profl. Women's Assn., NOW, Ky. Hist. Soc., U. Louisville Alumni Assn., U.S. Capital Hist. Soc., Greenpeace, Internat. Platform Assn., Calif. Hist. Soc., Sierra Club; Louisville Preservation Alliance. Democrat. Roman Catholic. Club: Filson. Home: 317 Maden St Fredericksburg VA 22401

MORRIS, SUSAN MARIE, librarian; b. Marshalltown, Iowa, Oct. 28, 1955; d. Donald Leroy and Lorena Pearl (Mitchell) M. BME, Wartburg Coll., 1977; MALS, U. Iowa, 1983. Tchr. vocal music Ayrshire (Iowa) Consol. Sch., 1978-80, Fayette (Iowa) Community Sch., 1980-81; libr. I Quincy (Ill.) Coll., 1983-85; cons. Great River Libr. System, Quincy, 1985-87; cataloging libr. Wartburg Coll., Waverly, 1987—. Contbr. articles to profl. jours. Mem. cen. com. Bremer County Dems., Waverly, 1988—; pres. Wartburg Symphony Assn., 1990—; treas. Friends of the Waverly Pub. Libr., 1989—. State of Iowa scholar, 1977. Mem. Iowa Libr. Assn. (v.p., pres.-elect tech. svcs. sect. 1990—, chair pub. rels. com. 1990—), ALA, AAUW (issues chair 1989-90). Home: 421 8th St NW Waverly IA 50677 Office: Wartburg Coll Libr 222-9th St NW Waverly IA 50677

MORRIS, SUSAN MCDONALD, financial company executive; b. Orange, Calif., Mar. 1, 1946; d. Coalson Clyde and Jesse Jean (Crawford) Morris; B.A., U. So. Calif., 1968. Press sec. Orozco for Congress, 1968; coordinator field services U. So. Calif., Los Angeles, 1969; dir. donor relations U. So. Calif., 1971, dir. event planning from 1976; pres., owner McDonald Morris & Assocs., Inc., Los Angeles, 1981-85; v.p. Perry Morris Corp., Irvine, Calif., 1985—. Mem. Los Angeles World Affairs Council, Town Hall Calif. Republican. Presbyterian. Club: Los Angeles Athletic. Home: 59 Sea Pine Newport Beach CA 92660

MORRIS, SYLVIA MARIE, administrative manager; b. Laurel, Miss., May 6, 1952; d. Earlene Virginia (Cameron) Stewart; m. James D. Morris, Jan. 29, 1972; children: Cedric James, Taedra Janae. Student, U. Utah, 1970-71. From adminstrv. sec. to adminstrv. mgr. mech. engring. U. Utah, Salt Lake City, 1972—. Mem. Community Devel. Adv. Bd., Salt Lake City, Utah, 1984—; nom. chmn. and del. to Dem. Mass Meeting, 1988. Mem. NAACP, NAFE, Consortium Utah Women in Higher Edn. Baptist. Home: 964 No 1500 W Salt Lake City UT 84116 Office: Univ Utah 3209 MEB Mech Engr Dept Salt Lake City UT 84112

MORRIS, TAMMY MYNETTA, aerospace company executive; b. Arcadia, Calif., Feb. 25, 1959; d. Harold Johnston and O. Ruth (Hatton) M. BA in Tech. Writing, Calif. State U., Long Beach, 1981, MA in Computer Documentation, 1983. Hardware tech. writer Beckman Instruments Inc., Fullerton, Calif., 1983-84; tng. instr., writer TRW, Redondo Beach, Calif., 1984-85, hardware tech. writer, 1985-87, mgr. tech. documentation, sect. head tech. documentation, 1987—; instr. Golden West Coll., Huntington Beach, Calif., 1987—. Musician Pacific Wind Ensemble, Long Beach, Calif., 1987—. Named Charter mem. Nat. English Honor Soc. Mem. Soc. for Tech. Communications (lectr. 1986), IEEE Computer Soc., Assn. for Computing Machinery, Calif. Assn. Faculty in Tech. and Profl. Writing (lectr. 1984-87, bd. dirs. 1986), Jaycees, Sigma Alpha Iota. Lodge: Job's Daughters. Home: PO Box 1091 Palos Verdes Estates CA 90274 Office: TRW One Space Park 04/1699 Redondo Beach CA 90278

MORRIS, TERESA ANN, nurse; b. Bklyn., Oct. 19, 1960; d. Robert Joseph and Rose Marie Louise (Cavallo) M. BSN, Duquesne U., 1983. From staff nurse I to staff nurse II Presbyn. Univ. Hosp., Pitts., 1983-88, adminstr. on duty, 1988-90; clin. coord. liver transplant unit, Pitts., 1990—. Mem. Hawthorne Village Homeowners Assn., Pitts., 1989—; vol. Pitts. Marathon, 1989—. Mem. Sigma Theta Tau. Roman Catholic.

MORRIS, THELMA LOVETTE, speech/language specialist; b. Pitts., Oct. 17, 1948; d. William James and Thelma (Williams) Lovette; m. Gregory Alden Morris, July 27, 1978. BS, Carlow Coll., Pitts., 1970; MA, U. Pitts., 1976. Lic. speech/lang. pathologist, Pa. Interviewer Housing Authority City of Pitts., 1970; tchr. for hearing impaired Pitts. pub. schs., 1970-71; speech/lang. specialist, 1971—; coordinator AT&T/Milliones Partnership, Pitts., 1988-89. Pres. Jr. League Pitts., 1989—; v.p., bd. dirs. Big Bros. and Sisters Greater Pitts., 1986—; mem. alumnae bd. dirs. Carlow Coll., Pitts., 1988-89, Family Resources, Pitts., 1988—, Horizon Homes, Inc., Pitts., 1986—; bd. dirs. Friends of the Carnegie Libr. Pitts., 1989—. Recipient Alumnae award for community svc. Carlow Coll., 1985. Mem. Am. Speech-Lang.-Hearing Assn., Pa. Speech-Lang.-Hearing Assn., Southwestern Pa. Speech, Lang., Hearing Assn., Pitts. Fedn. Tchrs., Nat. Assn. Negro Bus. and Profl. Women's Clubs (pres. 1979-81), Pierians, Inc. (corres. sec. 1988-89), Alpha Kappa Alpha, Delta Epsilon Sigma. Democrat. Presbyterian. Home: 920 Clarissa St Pittsburgh PA 15219 Office: Pittsburgh Public Schs Pittsburgh PA 15219

MORRISON, BETTY LEE YARBOROUGH, office manager; b. Pinehurst, N.C., Mar. 12, 1946; d. Charlie D. and Jessie Lee (Wallace) Yarborough; m. Arthur Dale Morrison, Feb. 1, 1964; children: Lindale Maire, Melanie Anne. Student, Sandhills Community Coll., 1977. Office mgr. Pinehurst (N.C.), Inc., 1973-77; controller Morrison, Inc., West End, N.C., 1977-79; controller, sec., treas. Stuart-Fitchett, Southern Pines, N.C., 1979-89; adminstrv. asst., office mgr. Allied Wood Industries, Inc., Southern Pines, 1989—. Chmn. Miss Noel Pageant, Pinehurst, 1985-87; mem. campaign com. United Way, So. Pines, 1986. Mem. Bus. and Profl. Women's Club (Woman of Yr. 1986, v.p. local chpt.), League Women Voters, So. Pines Jaycees, Sanhills Bus. & Profl. Women's Orgn. (pres.). Republican. Baptist. Lodge: Does. Home: Rt 1 Box 333 West End NC 27376 Office: Allied Wood Industries Inc PO Box 1823 Southern Pines NC 28387

MORRISON, CARBERTA ANN, banker; b. Wilmington, Del., Apr. 26, 1957; d. Harry Andrew and Frances (Kesler) M. BA, Rutgers U., 1978; MBA, Temple U., 1983. Staff acct. Price Waterhouse & Co., Phila., 1978-79; acctg. control specialist Girard Bank (now Mellon East), Phila., N.J., 1979-81; ind. cons. Girard Bank (Now Mellon East), Cherry Hill, N.J., 1981-83; sr. cons. Arthur Andersen, Phila., 1983-85, Deloitte, Haskins & Sells, Princeton, N.J., 1985-86; mgr. fin. svcs. and cons. Arthur, Young, Phila., 1986-88; v.p. Core Status Fin. Corp., Phila., 1988—; mem. exec. bd. Phila. Fin. Assn.; dinner chair Stephen Girard Award Dinner. Chmn. Cherry Hill Twp. Rent Review Bd., 1986—; bd. dirs. Hollybush Festival, Glassboro, N.J., 1988—, Painted Bridge Art Ctr., Phila., 1987—.

MORRISON, CAROL WEISS, guidance counselor; b. Phila.; d. Isadore and Helen (Murzin) Weiss; divorced; l child, Glenn Scott. BA, Wilkes Coll., 1949; MEd, Temple U., 1966, Beaver Coll., 1979. Lic. guidance counselor, Pa. Caseworker Dept. Pub. Assistance, Phila., 1950-53; social worker Phila. Dept. Welfare, 1953-59; counselor Phila. Sch. Dist., 1963—, spl. edn. tchr., 1987, 88, 89, leader human rels. workshop, 1974-77; counselor Biomed. Sci. Program Temple U., Phila., 1980-86; speaker Pa. State U., Phila., 1989. Sch. Dist. Phila. grantee, 1966. Mem. Am. Assn. for Counseling and Devel. (panel mem. 1989), Phila. Personnel and Guidance Assn. (co-chmn. membership 1965-68), Temple U. Alumni Assn. (life), Woodmere Art Gallery, Phila. Mus. Art., Wilkes Coll. Alumni Assn., Beaver Alumni Assn. Home: Wyncote House Apt 507 25 Washington Ln Wyncote PA 19095-1409

MORRISON, CHERYL LYNN, oil company executive; b. Galveston, Tex., Mar. 12, 1953; d. James Harry and Dorothy Eloise (Weed) M. BS in Biology, U. Ala., Tuscaloosa, 1975, BS in Petroleum Engring., 1979. Assoc. ops. engr. Getty Oil Co., Mobile, Ala., 1979-82; prodn. engr. Getty Oil Co., Kilgore, Tex., 1982-85; drilling engr. Mobil Oil Co., Lafayette, La., 1985-87; drilling engr. Mobil Oil Co., Houston, drilling supr., 1987-89; drilling rep. Chevron USA, Lafayette, 1989—. Vol. Reps. Mobile, 1980. Mem. Soc. Petroleum Engrs. (sec., treas., bd. dirs. 1980-89), Tex. State Profl. Engrs., Desk & Derrick Soc. Republican. Methodist. Home: PO Box 670094 Houston TX 77267

MORRISON, CONNIE FAITH, state legislator, realtor; b. Washington; d. Graham Edward and Cora E. (Smith) Wilson; m. George H. Morrison, May 14, 1955; 4 children. AA, Mpls. Community Coll., 1980. Photojournalist Dakota County Tribune, 1970-76; pub. affairs writer, pub. info. coord. Ind. Sch. Dist. 191, 1976-80; ind. realtor, 1980—; mem. I-R caucus Minn. Ho. of Reps., 1981-81, mem., 1986—; adv. bd. Norwest Bank, Bloomington, Minn. Mem. exec. bd. Mpls. United Way, 1988—; co-chairwoman Com. to Elect Rep. Women, St. Paul, 1987—; mem. Burnsville (Minn.) City Coun., 1977-82; mayor City of Burnsville, 1982-86, chairwoman chem. health com., 1987—; chairwoman adv. bd. Grace United Meth. Ch., Burnsville, 1986-90; bd. dirs. Minn. League of Cities, 1983-86. Mem. Rotary (hon.). Home: 909 W 155th St Burnsville MN 55337

MORRISON, DEBRA LYNN, financial planner; b. Mercer, Pa., Mar. 26, 1956; d. Norman Lewis and Mary Boneta (Zahniser) M. BSBA, Messiah Coll., 1978; cert. fin. planner, Coll. for Fin. Planning, Denver, 1987. Cert. fin. planner. Claims adjuster Nationwide Ins., Harrisburg, Pa., 1978; spl. rep. John Hancock Life Ins., Camp Hill, Pa., 1978-79; ins. and investment cons. John Hancock Cos., Camp Hill, 1979-80; dir. tax-advantaged Manzi and Assocs., Ridgewood, N.J., 1980-86; cert. fin. planner The Fin. Network, Clifton, N.J., 1986-88; cert. fin. planner, stockbroker, gen. securities prin. Fin. Roadmaps, Inc., Fairfield, N.J., 1988—. Contbr. articles to profl. jours. Vol., donor Make-A-Wish Found., N.J., Spl. Olympics of N.J., Piscataway; donor Habitat for Humanity, Americus, Ga. Mem. NAFE, Internat. Assn. for Fin. Planning, Inc., The Registry of Fin. Planning Practitioners, Nat. Assn. Life Underwriters, N.J. Assn. Women Bus. Owners. Democrat. Home: 11 Yearling Trail Hewitt NJ 07421 Office: Fin Roadmaps Inc 710 Rt 46E Ste 103 Fairfield NJ 07004

MORRISON, DELCY SCHRAM, psychodramatist; b. Chgo., Apr. 15, 1935; d. Harry Samuel and Gertrude (Hackman) Schram; children: John, Christopher. BA, Columbia Pacific U., 1982, MA, 1984. Asst. to dir. psychodrama dept. Camelback Hosp., Phoenix, 1974-78; co-dir. Western Inst. for Psychodrama, Phoenix, 1978—; supr. psychodrama dept. Scottsdale (Ariz.) Camelback Hosp., 1980—; cons. Northern Ariz. Univ. Counseling Dept., Flagstaff, 1978—, Holocaust Remembrance Conf., West Lafayette, Ind., 1984, 88, United Hosp., Grand Forks, N.D., 1985, St. Joseph Hosp., Wichita, 1986. Author: (with Elaine Eller Goldman) Psychodrama: Experience and Process, 1984; video tape: (with Elaine Eller Goldman, Mark S. Goldman) Psychodrama, 1990; contbr. articles to psychol. jours. Fellow Am. Soc. Group Psychotherapy and Psychodrama; mem. Am. Group Psychotherapy Assn., Ariz. Group Psychotherapy Soc., Fedn. Trainers and Tng. Programs in Psychodrama.

MORRISON, (GRACE) DORIS, painter, lecturer; b. Alameda, Calif., Apr. 21, 1906; d. Edward Alexander and Emma Doris (Harris) Cochran; m. Robert Rixford Morrison, Feb. 19, 1927 (dec. May 1982). Grad., Cleve. Inst. Art, 1948, BFA, 1949; student in printmaking, Coll. Marin, 1961-62; student in copper jewelry enamelling, Santa Barbara Coll., 1980-82. curator, exhibitor various works Cabrillo Art Ctr., Santa Barbara, 1980-85, The Santa Barbara Scene, 1989; one-woman show Astra Gallery El Paseo Santa Barbara, 1988. Mem. Mayor's Bicentennial Cultural Arts Com. fund raising for library, Santa Barbara 1976; co-dir. gallery Santa Barbara Arts Council, 1986-89. Mem. Marin Soc. Artists (life pres. 1965-66), Santa Barbara Art Assn. (pres. 1977-78) Artists Equity, (bd. dirs. Santa Barbara chpt. 1986-87). Home: 4280 Calle Real #7 Santa Barbara CA 93110

MORRISON, GLORIA JEAN, film producer; b. Alhambra, Calif., Apr. 12, 1948; d. Dominick Vincent Gabriel and Thelma Adeline (Phillips) Bartholomeo; m. Michael Joseph Morrison; children: Sean Joseph, Jason Bartholomew. AA, Fullerton (Calif.) Jr. Coll., 1968; BA, Calif. State U., Fullerton, 1970. Freelance actress Los Angeles, N.Y.C., 1968-88; dir. Spa Formula, Los Angeles, 1978-80; A.I.P. Movie Prodn. Co., Los Angeles, 1986-87; pres., chief exec. officer Unistar Internat. Pictures & Releasing Corp., Hollywood, Calif., 1987—; speaker Orange County (Calif.) Schs., 1988-89; mem. Women In Films, Hollywood, 1987-89, Women In Cable, Hollywood, 1986-89; tchr. Actor's Gym, Hollywood, 1989; mem. bodybuilding coord. com., 1986-89; with Miss Winters-liquor filled Chocolates, 1986. Mem. DAR, 1965. Named Miss Congeniality, Placentia (Calif.) Beauty Contest, 1965; first runner up Miss Los Angeles Contest, 1972; Miss Tall Universe, 1971. Mem. SAG, AGVA. Am. Fedn. TV Arts, Equity. Office: Unistar Internat Pictures & Releasing Corp 1119 N McCadden Pl Hollywood CA 90038

MORRISON, GRACE BLANCH SIMPSON, auditor, accountant, government official; b. Waterloo, Iowa, Dec. 18, 1933; d. Lyle Meredith and Grace Luella Blanch Simpson; B.S., So. Meth. U., 1956; M.Ed., U. Houston, 1973; C.P.A., Tex.; m. Glenn Harry Murphree, July 2, 1955 (dec.); children: Gregory Alan, Gina Grace; m. Henry Joseph Morrison, Jr., July 23, 1974. Tchr. math., Mesquite (Tex.) Ind. Sch. Dist., 1957-58, Clear Creek Ind. Sch. Dist., Seabrook, Tex., 1967-73, Richardson (Tex.) Ind. Sch. Dist., 1973-74; equal opportunity asst. Office for Civil Rights, HEW, Dallas, 1974-75; govt. relations specialist, consumer affairs officer Region VI, Dept. Energy, Dallas, 1975-81; audit acctg. aide IRS, Dallas, 1981-82, revenue agt., 1982-85; sr. auditor Def. Contract Audit Agy., Dallas, 1985—. Mem. AICPA, Tex. Soc. CPA's, Dallas Soc. CPA's, Mensa, White Rock Bus. & Profl. Women's Club, Nat. Assn. Parliamentarians, Puppeteers Am., Assn. Govt. Accts. Unitarian. Home: 4116 Amy Dr Mesquite TX 75150 Office: Def Contract Audit Agy 1100 Commerce St Rm 3B17 Dallas TX 75242-0397

MORRISON, GWENDOLYNN SUE SLOVER, chamber of commerce administrator; b. Armstrong, Mo., Feb. 21, 1945; d. Leon A. and Dorothy R. (Robinson) Slover; m. Donald Joe Morrison, Sept. 13, 1963; children: Tracy, Kent. Program dir. Econ. Devel. Program, Georgetown, Tex., 1982-84; bus. devel. officer First Nat. Bank, Georgetown, 1984-88; adminstr. Georgetown C. of C., 1988—; bd. dirs. Economic Devel. Program, Georgetown. Mem. Women's Polit. Caucus; bd. dirs. Goergetown Pub. Library, 1985—, Handcrafts Unltd., Georgetown, 1987—, Downtown Georgetown Assn.; chmn. Tourism Devl. Bd., Georgetown. Mem. Am. Bus. Women, Nat. Assn. Bank Women, Nat. Assn. Female Execs., So. Indsl. Devel. Council, Tex. Indsl. Devel. Council, Georgetown C. of C. (exec. dir. 1988—). Home: 219 Serenada Dr Georgetown TX 78628 Office: Georgetown C of C 100 Stadium Dr Georgetown TX 78627

MORRISON, HELEN, human resources specialist; b. Dearborn, Mich., Jan. 18, 1928; d. Eli and Latinka (Chickara) Wercely; m. Donald Clifford Morrison, Mar. 22, 1947; children: Jack Clifford, Gary Lee, Timothy Alan. BA, U. Mich., 1978, postgrad. Owner, operator Career Life Planners, Grosse Ile, Mich.; interim assoc. exec. Presbytery Detroit; interim pastoral assoc. Fort Street Presbyn. Ch., Detroit; interim dir. for Christian edn. First Presbyn. Ch., Dearborn, Mich., 1990—; intern pub. adminstrn. City of Southfield, Mich., 1977-78. Mem. adv. Coun. PSCE Ctr. Aging; bd. dirs. Info. Ctr. Inc., Presbyn. Village, Inc.; mem. Grosse Ile Twp. Elected Officials Salary Com. Mem. ASTD, AAUW. Address: PO Box 328 Grosse Ile MI 48138

MORRISON, JOAN, writer; b. Hinsdale, Ill., Dec. 20, 1922; d. Werner Lars and Neva (Lewis) Wehlen; m. Robert Thornton Morrison, June 19, 1943; children: Robert Kirby, James Vaughan, Susan Signe. BA, U. Chgo., 1944. Adj. prof. Morris County Coll., Dover, N.J., 1974-88, New Sch. for Social Research, N.Y.C., 1988-89; writer Morristown, N.J., 1970—. Author: From Camelot to Kent State, 1987, American Mosaic, 1980; contbr. articles, poems to popular and profl. jours. Mem. Am. Studies Assn., Oral History Assn., Nat. Soc. Arts & Letters, Authors' Guild, AAUW. Democrat. Home: 64 Spring Brook Rd Morristown NJ 07960

MORRISON, KAY ELLEN, business owner, photographer; b. Bedford, Ind., June 12, 1961; d. Patricia Sue (Kindred) Morrison. Student, Ivey Tech. Coll., 1983-85. Owner Morrison Photography, Bedford, 1979—, Morrison Crafts, Bedford, 1980—, Morrison Dog Tng., Bedford, 1983—; freelance writer, 1981—; freelance photographer, 1979—. Author: (play) Lost in the Shuffle, 1987. Mem. Little Theatre, Bedford. Mem. Humane Soc., Nat. Wildlife Soc., World Wildlife Soc. Home and Office: 836 Lincoln Ave Bedford IN 47421

MORRISON, NAN JODY, management consultant; b. Patchogue, N.Y., Jan. 31, 1962; d. Herbert and Lila (Rosen) M. BS in Applied Math., Yale U., 1983; MBA, Harvard U., 1987. Tech. analyst Morgan Stanley, N.Y.C., 1983-85; assoc. Temple, Barker & Sloane, Lexington, Mass., 1987—. Office: Temple Barker & Sloane 33 Hayden Ave Lexington MA 02173

MORRISON, SUSAN M., bishop; d. D. David and Katherine Morrison. Student, Drew U., Boston U. Ordained to ministry United Meth. Ch., 1974. Short-term missionary to Brazil; assoc. pastor Silver Spring, Md.; pastor Greenbelt, Md.; former mem. nat. jud. coun., dist. supt. Balt. conf. United Meth. Ch., 1980-86, dir. Balt. conf. coun., 1986—; bishop Eastern Pa. and P.R. confs. United Meth. Ch., Valley Forge, Pa., 1988—. Office: United Meth Ch PO Box 820 Valley Forge PA 19482*

MORRISON, TAMARA KYLE, scenic artist, set designer, small business owner; b. White Plains, N.Y., Aug. 4, 1949; d. Dana E. Jr. and Margaret D. (Davis) M. AA, Briarcliff Coll. for Women, 1969; BS, Ind. U., 1971, MEd in Filmmaking, 1979. Gallery painter Fla., 1971-77; set dresser, scenic artist Sunn Classic Motion Pictures, Salt Lake City, 1978-79; scenic artist Sta. WBBM-TV, CBS, Chgo., 1980-84; owner, operator Tamara Inc. Backdrops, Chgo., 1985—. Mem. Women in Film (mem. various coms. 1986—), United Scenic Artists Union Local 350, Pi Beta Phi. Republican. Presbyterian. Office: Tamara Inc Backdrops 1225 W Morse Ave Chicago IL 60626

MORRISON, TONI (CHLOE ANTHONY MORRISON), novelist; b. Lorain, Ohio, Feb. 18, 1931; d. George and Ella Ramah (Willis) Wofford; children—Harold Ford, Slade Kevin. B.A., Howard U., 1953; M.A., Cornell U., 1955. Tchr. English and humanities Tex. So. U., 1955-57, Howard U., 1957-64; editor Random House, N.Y.C., 1965—. Author: The Bluest Eye, 1970, Sula, 1974, Song of Solomon, 1977, Tar Baby, 1983, Beloved, 1987 (Pulitzer prize, Robert F. Kennedy Book award, Melcher Book Award, Unitarian Universalist Assn., 1988). Mem. Author's Guild (council). Office: care Random House 201 E 50th St New York NY 10022*

MORRISON, WINIFRED ELAINE HAAS, social services administrator, educator; b. Buffalo, Aug. 31; d. Edward Albert and Elaine Magdalene (McNamara) Haas; m. Robert Charles Morrison; children: Robert Edward, James Richard. BS in Edn., SUNY, Buffalo, MS in Edn. magna cum laude, 1964, PhD, 1984, postgrad.; MLS, SUNY, Geneseo, 1969; postgrad., Harvard U., UCLA. Instr., Genesee Community Coll., 1972-78, 80, also asst. prof. State U. Coll., Buffalo, 1973-77; instr. corr. course Empire State Coll., Saratoga Springs, N.Y., 1975-78; dir. early edn. div. Park Sch., Buffalo, 1960-74, dir. lower sch., 1974-78; mem. faculty ednl. studies, lectr., SUNY, Buffalo, also coordinator child care adv. service Early Childhood Research Ctr., Amherst campus, 1978-80; dir. children's services Erie County Assn. for Retarded Children, 1980-83, exec. dir., 1983—; chmn. early childhood com. Nat. Office Gifted and Talented, HEW, 1976; panelist symposium Chautauqua Inst., 1974. Author: This Book is About Your School, Early Education Unit, 1976, Primary Unit, 1977, You Are Your Child's First Teacher, 1974, (with Carol Woodard) You Can Help Your Baby Learn, 1979, (with Betty Jenkins) (screening materials) Kiddy Kards, 1982. Pres. bd. dirs. Day Care Council Western N.Y., 1971-72; adv. com. parenthood edn. project Buffalo and Erie County council Girl Scouts U.S., 1972-76; child adv. com. child/adult edn. project Western N.Y. div. Salvation Army, 1977-82; TV and reading com. WNED-TV Public Broadcasting, 1977-79; chmn. community com. Erie Community Coll., 1971-72; hon. chmn. Week of the Young Child; pres. Erie County Adv. Council on Disabled, 1986-88. Recipient Outstanding Service award Villa Maria Coll. Child Devel. Adv. Council, 1979, 84, Outstanding Achievement award YWCA of Buffalo and Erie County, 1985. Mem. AAUW, Nat. Assn. Edn. of Young Children, Council Exceptional Children, World Orgn. Presch. Edn., Ctr. Women in Mgmt. (bd. dirs. 1983-88, Mgr. of Yr. award 1987), Am. Mgmt. Assn., ALA, Nat. Assn. Supervision and Curriculum Devel., N.Y. State Council for Children, Zonta (pres.), Rotary, Pi Lambda Theta (pres. Alpha Nu chpt. 1985-87, sec. N.E. region 1990—, Outstanding Pi Lambda Thetan award 1987, Lillian and Henry Barry award 1989), Phi Delta Kappa (v.p. Alpha Psi chpt.). Home: 13 Karen Dr Tonawanda NY 14150 Office: 101 Oak St Buffalo NY 14203

MORRISS, MARY RACHEL, art educator, painter; b. Memphis; d. William Dale and Lizzie Henrie (Woodward) M. BS, Memphis State U., 1927; postgrad., U. Colo., 1931, 34, 37, 40; various art workshops Maxine Masterfield, 1983, 84. Cert. high sch. tchr., Tenn. Tchr., Bellevue Sch., Memphis, 1936-66; ret.; pvt. art classes, Memphis, 1966—; represented by Paul Edelstein Gallery, Memphis. Exhibited in group juried shows Cen. South Parthenon, Nashville, Hunter Ann. Show, Delta Annual, Little Rock, Mid-Am., Owensboro, Ky., 1979, Mid-South Memphis Brooks Gallery, So. Watercolor Soc., 1983, 86, 89, 90, Patrons' Watercolor Gala, Oklahoma City, 1983, 84, Tenn. Watercolor Soc. Annual Traveling Show, 1980-82, 84, 88, 90, Ga. Watercolor Soc., 1986, So. Watercolor, 1989 (Merit award), J.J. White Meml. Watercolor, 1989, and many others; represented in numerous pub. and pvt. collections; one woman shows include Parthenon Galleries, Nashville, Comml. Appeal, Memphis, 1989, numerous others. Recipient Best Cotton Design award Memphis Brooks Mus.; Purchase prize Mid-South Fair, 1971, Best in Show and 1st in watercolors, 1985, 86; 2d prize J.J. White 1988, 89, 90. Meml. Watercolor juried exhbn.; Doochin of Madison award Central South, 1984, and many other awards. Mem. Tenn. Watercolor Soc. (David Wade Meml. award 1988, artist mem.), So. Watercolor Soc.(signature mem., merit award 1989), Friends of Dixon Gallery, Memphis Watercolor Soc., Ga. Watercolor Soc. Presbyterian. Home: 4819 Parkside Ave Memphis TN 38117

MORRISSEY, ANDREA, elementary school educator; b. Kingston, Pa., June 29, 1962; d. Andrew Frances and JoAnne (Schwab) Korshalla; m. Kenneth Scott Morrissey, Nov. 25, 1989. BA in Sociology and Psychology, Glassboro (N.J.) State Coll., 1984; elem. teaching cert., Rutgers U., 1986. Cert. elem. sch. tchr., N.J. Tchr. East Brunswick (N.J.) Pub. Schs., 1986—, home instr., 1986-90; tchr. Ridgewood (N.J.) pub. schs., 1990—; pvt. tutor, Asbury Park, N.J.; mem. Earth Day com. Chittick Sch., East Brunswick, 1990. Active Lincoln Ctr. for Arts in Edn., N.Y.C., 1988—. Roman Catholic. Home: 34 Taplin Ave Maywood NJ 07607

MORROS, LUCY SCHMITZ, academic administrator. Dean of coll. Westbrook Coll., Portland, Maine, until 1985; pres. Barat Coll., Lake Forest, Ill., 1988—. Office: Barat Coll Office of Pres Lake Forest IL 60045*

MORROW, CHERYLLE ANN, accountant, bankruptcy, consultant; b. Sydney, Australia, July 3, 1950; came to U.S., 1973; d. Norman H. and Esther A. E. (Jarrett) Wilson. Student, U. Hawaii, 1975; diploma Granville Tech. Coll., Sydney, 1967. Acct., asst. treas. Bus. Investment, Ltd., Honolulu, 1975-77; owner Lanikai Musical Instruments, Honolulu, 1980-86, Cherylle A. Morrow Profl. Svcs., Honolulu, 1981—; fin. managerial cons. E.A. Buck Co., Inc., Honolulu, 1981-84; contr., asst. trustee THC Fin. Corp., Honolulu, 1977-84, bankruptcy trustee, 1984—; v.p., sec., treas. Innervation, Inc., 1989—; panel mem. Chpt. 7 Trustees dist. Hawaii U.S. Depart. Justice, 1988—. Mem. Small Bus. Hawaii PAC, Lanikai Community Assn., Arts Coun. Hawaii, vol., mem. Therapeutic Horsemanship for Handicapped, Small Bus. Adminstrn. (women in bus. com. 1987—). Mem. Australian-Am. C. of C. (bd. dir. 1985—, corp. sec. 1986—, v.p. 1988-90), NAFE, Pacific Islands Assn. Women (corp. sec./treas. 1988—), Pacific Islands Assn. (asst. treas. 1988—). Avocations: reading, music, dancing, sailing, gardening.

MORROW, ELIZABETH, sculptress, educator, museum association administrator, business owner; b. Sibley, Mo., Feb. 28, 1947; d. Elman A. and Lorine (Hostetter) M.; married, 1970 (div. 1979); children: Jan Pawel, Lorentz Arthur. Student, U. Okla., 1960-62; BFA, U. Kans., 1964, MFA, 1967, postgrad., 1971; postgrad., U. Minn., 1965. Pres. E. Morrow Co., Kansas City, Mo., 1966-67; head dept. art U. Hawaii, Honolulu, 1968-69, Tarkio (Mo.) Coll., 1973-74; exec. dir. Pensacola (Fla.) Mus. Art, 1974-76; pres., owner Blair-Murrah Exhibitions, Sibley, Mo., 1980—. Del. White House Conf. on Small Bus., 1986. Lew Wentz scholar U. Okla., 1961-62. Mem. Internat. Coun. of Mus., Internat. Coun. Exhbn. Exch., Internat. Soc. Appraisers, Am. Assn. Mus., Nat. Orgn. of Women Bus. Owners, AAUW, Ft. Osage Hist. Soc., Friends Art, Delta Phi Delta. Republican. Home: Vintage Hill Orchard Sibley MO 64088 Office: Blair-Murrah Hostetter Rd Sibley MO 64088 also: 7 rue Muzy, PO Box Nr 554, 1211 Geneva 6 Switzerland

MORROW, EMILY RUBENSTEIN, lawyer, estate planner; b. Poughkeepsie, N.Y., Sept. 14, 1952; d. Lewis W. and Erica (Beckh) Rubenstein; m. Paul L. Morrow; 1 child, Lillian. BA summa cum laude, Oberlin Coll., 1974; JD, U. Buffalo, 1977. Bar: N.Y. 1978, Ill. 1979, Vt. 1982. Law clk. to presiding justice N.Y. State Supreme Ct., Syracuse, N.Y., 1977-78; assoc. Altheimer & Gray, Chgo., 1978-80; sr. tax counsel Cen. Carolina Bank, Durham, N.C., 1980-82; assoc. Pierson, Attolter & Wadhams, Burlington, Vt., 1982-86; ptnr. Dinse, Erdmann & Clapp, Burlington, 1986—; adj. prof. bus. law Trinity Coll., Burlington, 1983-84; adj. prof. comml. law St. Michaels Coll., Burlington, 1984-85; bd. dirs. Shelburne Farms, 1987—, Howard Bank, Burlington, Vt. Mem. editorial adv. bd. Vt. Woman Pubs., Burlington, 1986-89. Bd. govs. Med. Ctr., Hosp. of Vt., Burlington, 1985—; bd. dirs. Chittenden County United Way, Burlington, 1985-88; chmn. Vt. Whey Pollution Abatement Authority, Cabot, 1985-86. Mem. ABA (real property com., probate and trust law com., taxation com.), Vt. Bar Assn., Chittenden County Bar Assn., Internat. Assn. Fin. Planners, Am. Coll. Trust and Estate Counsel, Rotary, Phi Beta Kappa, Zonta. Office: Dinse Erdmann & Clapp 209 Battery St Burlington VT 05401

MORROW, JENNIFER LEE, psychologist, management consultant; b. Chgo., Oct. 7, 1955; d. Charles J. Kristufek and Marguerite Anne (Morrow) Baumgardner; m. Fred A. Mauck, Oct. 17, 1984. BA, U. Ill., Chgo., 1978, MA, 1982, PhD, 1984; postgrad. in clin. psychology, Northestern U., Chgo., 1978-79. Lic. psychologist, Ill. Market researcher, orgn. cons. Chgo., 1979-85; assoc. Hay Mgmt. Cons., Chgo., 1985-86; mgr. orgn. effectiveness practice mgmt. cons. div. Peat Marwick Main & Co., Chgo., 1986—; pro bono cons. Old St. Patrick's Ch., Chgo., 1988, Nat. Ctr. for Laity, Chgo., 1989; manuscript reviewer Ctr. for Creative Leadership, Greensboro, N.C., 1988-89; presenter in field, 1981—. Contbr. articles to profl. publs. Bd. dirs. Contact Chgo.-Community Connection, 1989—; mem. Christian Laity Chgo. Mem. Am. Psychol. Assn., Greater Chgo. Assn. Indsl. and Orgnl. Psychologists, Human Resource Mgmt. Assn. Chgo., Genesis II, Phi Beta Kappa, Phi Kappa Phi, Alpha Lambda Delta. Republican. Roman Catholic. Office: Peat Marwick Main & Co 303 E Wacker Dr Chicago IL 60601

MORROW, JOYCE L., pharmaceutical chemist; b. Camden, N.J., Apr. 15, 1964; d. John Lane and Emma Bernice (Redenius) M. BSc., Cabrini Coll., Radnor, Pa., 1986. Cert. Chemist, N.J., Pa. Asst. student chemist Cabrini Coll., Radnor, Pa., 1983-86; chemist Concord Chem., Camden, N.J., 1986, William H. Rorer, Ft. Wash., Pa., 1986--. Vol. Environ. Commn., Runnemede N.J., 1986--, Vineland State Sch. For Girls, N.J., 1986--, Phila. Sch. System to Promote Sci., 1989. Mem. Am. Chem. Soc., Am. Inst. Chemists, Am. Assn. for Adv. Sci., Assn. MBA Execs., Am. Legion Aux. Lodge. Republican. Lutheran. Home: 920 Eagle Rd Wayne PA 19087

MORROW, LAURA ANNETTE, marketing professional; b. Tulsa, Okla., Nov. 14, 1958; d. William Lane and Betty (Whaley) Storey; m. James A. Morrow, May 5, 1984; children: Patrick, Anna, Katherine. BFA, U. Tulsa, 1980; MA, U. Okla., 1983. Comml. designer Ad 2, Inc., Tulsa, Okla., 1980-81; grad. rsch. asst. U. Okla., Norman, Okla., 1981-82; v.p. Profl. Systems Svcs., Tulsa, 1982-83; dir. of mktg. Commn. & Research MCC Ctr. Line, Tulsa, 1983-84; coll. instr. Tulsa Jr. Coll., 1982-88; reg. mktg. dir. Century HealthCare Corp., Tulsa, 1984-88; corp. mktg. dir. Cent. HealthCare Corp., Tulsa, 1988-89; regional mktg. dir. Psychiatric Insts. Am., Washington, 1989-90; asst. v.p. mktg. and devel. Children's Med. Ctr., Tulsa, 1990—. Author: presentation, Effective Advt. Strategies 1987-88. Author: (presentation) Effective Advt. Strategies, 1987-88; recipient audio projects award Nat. Assn. Pvt. Psychiat. Hosps., 1986, 88, internat. newsletters award, feature articles award, spl. purpose pub. award, 1987, gold medal award 1987-88, internat. newsletters award, pub. rels. campaign, 4-color brochures award, 1986, Pub. Rels. Soc. Am., Silver Link merit awards, 1987, Gold Ring merit awards Bus. and Profl. Advt. Assn., 1986, 88, Addy and citations Tulsa Advt. Fedn., 1989, gold award. Mem. Am. Mktg. Assn. (competition judge 1986; Health Svcs. Mktg. Award 1987-88). Home: 1239 E 29th St Tulsa OK 74114 Office: Childrens Med Ctr 5300 E Skelly Dr Tulsa OK 74135

MORROW, MARY KATHERINE, transportation executive, fashion executive; b. Cleve., Jan. 17, 1957; d. Ben and Scottie (Herndon) M.; children: Jatera Quashonda, Lloyaal Jha Queleon. Student, L.A. Airport Coll. Ctr., 1979-81. Customer svc. rep. Mileage Plus program United Airlines, L.A., 1983-87; owner The Remembered Woman Inc., L.A., 1981—; bus operator So. Calif. Rapid Transit Dist., L.A., 1983—; ind. personal shopper, buyer, fashion cons. Mem. Nat. Assn. Female Execs., Young Black Profls., Ladies and Knights. Home and Office: The Remembered Woman Inc 2300 Victoria Ave #203 Los Angeles CA 90016

MORROW, MARY LOUISE STIREWALT, guidance counselor; b. Hickory, N.C., June 4, 1935; d. Walter Lee and Alberta Louise (Boliek) S.; m. James Mack Jr. Morrow, June 24, 1958; children: Mary Jane Morrow Crossno, Thomas Lee. BA, U. N.C., 1956, MEd, 1957. Guidance counselor Mooresville (N.C.) Graded Sch. Dist., 1957-58, 66—, tchr., 1959-60. Chmn. Mooresville Human Rels. Commn., 1986-89; chmn. bd. South Iredell Am. Cancer Soc., Mooresville, 1989-90, pres., crusade co-chmn., 1988-89. Named Youhg Educator of Yr., Jaycees, Mooresville, 1970-71; Disting. Citizen award, Town of Mooresville, 1989. Mem. AAUW (pres. Mooresville br. 1989-90), Big Bros./Big Sisters Iredell County (founder, chmn. 1983-84, bd. dirs. 1979-86, Disting. Svc. award 1987), Southern Assn. Colls. and Schs. (mem. vis. evaluation team 1979—), N.C. Personnel and Counseling Assn. (chmn. human rights and opportunities com. 1974-75), DAR (Mary Slocumb chpt.), Delta Kappa Gamma (v.p. Alpha Xi chpt. 1990-92). Home: 718 S Magnolia St Mooresville NC 28115 Office: Mooresville Jr High Sch 160 S Magnolia St Mooresville NC 28115

MORROW, NANCY ANN, marketing executive; b. Atlanta, Feb. 12, 1958; d. Donald Paul and Patricia Ann (McNellis) Halsey; m. Gregory Charles Morrow, Apr. 29, 1989. BS, Ball State U., 1979, MBA, 1988. Pub. relations asst. Reid Meml. Hosp., Richmond, Ind., 1979-81; dir. community rels. Reid Meml. Hosp., 1981-87; dir. mktg. Hendricks Community Hosp., Danville, Ind., 1987-89, Ind. U. Credit Union, Bloomington, 1989—. Chmn. All-Am. City Com., Richmond, 1985-87; pres. Whitewater Opera Co., Richmond, 1986-87; bd. dirs. Girls' Club of Richmond, 1983-87, United Way Wayne County, Richmond, 1985-87. Recipient All-Am. City award Nat. Civic League, 1987. Mem. Ind. Soc. for Healthcare Pub. Rels. and Mktg. (sec.-treas. 1988-89, conf. speaker 1988-89), Am. Soc. for Hosp. Mktg. & Pub. Rels., Am. Mktg. Assn., Ind. Soc. for Hosp. Planning & Mktg., Leadership Bloomington. Office: Indiana Univ Credit Union PO Box 368 Bloomington IN 47402

MORROW, PATRICIA ANN, public relations executive; b. Kinston, Pa., Sept. 20, 1959; d. John Jerome and Patricia Ann (Rutkoski) S. BA, Wilkes Coll., Wilkes-Barre, Pa., 1981. Dir. communications Penn's Woods Girl Scouts, Wilkes-Barre, 1981-84; sr. media specialist Girl Scouts USA, N.Y.C., 1984-86; sr. acct. exec. Ruder Finn & Rotman, N.Y.C., 1986-87, Creamer Dickson Basford, N.Y.C., 1987-88; acct. supr. Ketchum Communications, N.Y.C., 1988-89, v.p., 1989-90; mgr., product pub. rels. Boehringer Ingelheim Pharms., Inc., Danbury, Conn., 1990—. Mem. Women in Communications, Am. Soc. Hosp. Pharmacists, Am. Med. Writers Assn., Nat. Assn. Sci. Writers. Home: 828 Bronx River Rd Bronxville NY 10708

MORROW, SUSAN DAGMAR, psychic, educator, writer, consultant; b. Harrisburg, Pa., July 10, 1932; d. William Lime and Margaret Louise (Deckard) Brubaker; m. Henry Taylor Morrow, June 9, 1952 (div. Mar. 1984); children: Quenby Anne Morrow Smith, Christopher Brian. Student Carnegie Inst. Tech., 1950-52, U. Ariz., 1952-54, U. Calif., Berkeley Ext., 1960-72, Foothill Coll., 1980-81. Self-employed psychic, psychic tchr., Palo Alto, Calif., 1976-80, Mountain View, Calif., 1980—; psychic, tchr. Seekers Quest Profl. Ctr., San Jose, Calif., 1983-87; tchr. Sunnyvale Community Ctr., 1977-87; tchr. San Andreas Health Council, Palo Alto, 1981-83; lectr. U. Calif., Berkeley, 1978-87, Foothill Coll., Los Altos, Calif., 1980; lectr. in field; medium, cons. in cases of mental disorientation to psychologists, Palo Alto and Mountain View, 1978-84. Contbr. articles on psychic awareness to various publs. Mem. Assn. Psychic Practitioners (co-founder, v.p. 1982-83, editor and writer newsletter 1982-83), Assn. Research and Enlightenment, Inst. Roetic Sci., Friends of the Animals. Democrat. Methodist. Avocations: mediumship, painting, swimming, sailing, skiing.

MORROW, SUSAN H., interior designer; b. Bklyn., Aug. 27, 1943; d. Murray and Roslyn (Benjamin-Polsky) Chalkin; m. Robert Morrow (div.); children: Christopher, Andrew. BFA, Syracuse U., 1964; MA, NYU, 1965; cert. Post Coll. With Bagatelle Assocs., Roslyn, N.Y., 1972-74, The Wallpaper Place, Roslyn, 1974-75, Trio Designs, Huntington, N.Y., 1975-80, SHS Designs, Inc., North Hills, N.Y., 1980—; designer Designs For ..., Manhasset, N.Y., 1981—, ptnr., 1982—; pres. Wallpapers and ..., 1985—; designer Cinderella Project, Bklyn. Union Gas Urban Renewal, 1979, Human Resources, Ind. Living Project, 1982—; designer Designs For..., Roslyn, N.Y.; designer and converter Class Reunion, 1987. Designer Showcase Mansions; contbr. articles to mags. Co-chairperson budget adv. com. Roslyn Schs.; v.p. Norgate Civic Assn., Roslyn. Named Woman of Yr., Hadassah, 1974. Mem. Am. Soc. Interior Designers, 110 Assn. Profl. Women, Assn. Environ. Designers, Mensa, Internat. Platform Assn., LWV (v.p.). Home: PO Box H Sea Cliff NY 11579 Office: Designs For 24 Skillman St Roslyn NY 11576

MORROW-JONES, HAZEL ANN, city and regional planning educator; b. New Brighton, Pa., June 1, 1952; d. Delbert Leroy and Doris Dean (Clark) M.; m. Charles Ralph Morrow-Jones, May 19, 1974. BA, Macalester Coll., St. Paul, 1974; MA, Ohio State U., 1976, PhD, 1980. Asst. prof. city and regional planning U. Colo., Boulder, 1980-88, Ohio State U., Columbus, 1988—; faculty fellow Office of Geriatrics/Gerontology, Ohio State U., 1988—; panel mem. Ohio Housing Rsch. Network, Cleve., 1989—; cons. Rural Homelessness - Ohio State Social Wk. project, Columbus, 1989—; profl. staff Inst. Behavioral Sci., Boulder, 1984-88. Contbr. articles to profl. jours., chpts. to books. Recipient Huntington award, Ohio State U., 1980; rsch. grantee, NSF, 1986-88, Assn. Am. Geographers, 1986, HUD, 1985. Mem. Nat. Coun. Geog. Edn., Population Assn. Am., Am. Real Estate and Urban Econs. Assn., Assoc. Collegiate Schs. Planning, Am. Planning Assn., Population Geography Specialty Group (bd. dirs. 1984-87), Urban Geography Specialty Group (past chmn. bd.). Office: Ohio State Univ 190 W 17th Ave Columbus OH 43210-1320

MORSCHING, GERMAINE ANN, public relations executive; b. Kilkenny, Minn., Jan. 3, 1934; d. Anthony William and Regina Edith (Hager) Weaver; m. Jarvis Harold, June 16, 1956 (dec. Dec. 1984); children: Gene Arden, Deanna Lynn Long, Kevin William. Prin. sec. U. Minn., St. Paul, 1951-56; sec. to br. mgrs. GM Acceptance Corp., Huron, S.D., 1964-82, credit rep., 1982-84, credit supr.; custom rels. supr. GM Acceptance Corp., South Sioux City, Nebr., 1985-86, 88—, credit supr., 1986-87, sales supr., 1987-88; office pres. Credit Women Internat., Huron, 1983-84. Vol. United Way, Sioux City, 1987-89. Democrat. Roman Catholic. Home: 3700 28th St #483 Sioux City IA 51105 Office: General Motors Accp Corp 200 E 39th St South Sioux City NE 68776

MORSE, EMILY BOMBERGER (SWOPE), educator; b. Tulpehocken Twp., Pa., May 10, 1899; d. Daniel and Mary Jane (Baumberger/Bomberger) Swope; m. Wilbert Morse, Aug. 22, 1923; children: Winifred Morse McLachlan, Mary Ellen Morse Branin. Tchr.'s cert., Keystone State Normal Sch., Kutztown, Pa., 1919; BS in Elem. Edn., Newark State Tchr.'s Coll., 1958. Tchr. elem. sch. Northampton, Pa., 1919-23, Verona, N.J., 1951-64. Author (all with Winifred McLachlan): The Swope Family Book of Remembrance, 1972, The Baumberger/Bomberger Family Book of Remembrance, 1982, The Morse Family Book of Remembrance, 1978. Chairperson Needlers, United Hosps. Med. Ctr., Newark. Mem. AAUP, AAUW, DAR, Ladies Aux. of VFW, Jost Schwab & Kakob Schwob Family Assn. (founder, award for Swope book 1973, award for perpetuating Swope reunion for 21 yrs. 1989). Home: 680 E First South Parklane Apt 221 Salt Lake City UT 84102

MORSE, HAZEL RED, investment services specialist; b. Bar Harbor, Maine, June 19, 1937; d. Forrest L. and Beulah (Ramsdell) Hamblen; divorced; children: Raymond Lee, Cheryl Barg, Lowell Lee. Student, Broward Community Coll., 1969; cert. in real estate, U. Conn., 1979; BS, Nova U., 1986. Cert. real estate assoc.; registered rep. in mut. funds. Office mgr. Ramada Inn, Ft. Lauderdale, Fla., 1969-70; receptionist Le Club Internat., Ft. Lauderdale, 1970-71; acct. City of Ft. Lauderdale, 1971-75; supr. admissions Nova U., Ft. Lauderdale, 1975-79; billing registrar North Cen. Conn. Health Maintenance Orgn., East Hartford, 1979-80; auditor Beach Club Hotel, Ft. Lauderdale, 1980-82; payroll coord. North Broward Med. Ctr., Pompano Beach, Fla., 1982-87; rep. 1st Investors, Ft. Lauderdale, 1987—; chairperson edn. com. North Broward Med. Ctr., 1986-87, bd. dirs. credit union, 1985-87; bus. cons. Appeared in several movies, TV. commls., model print-ads. Mem. fin. com. Rep. party, Ft. Lauderdale, 1985; re. United Way, Ft. Lauderdale, 1982-86. Mem. Nova U. Alumni Assn. (bd. dirs.), Notary Pub. Assn., NAFE, Fla. Govtl. Secs. Assn. (bd. dirs. 1972-75), Mensa. Home: 1111 NE 30th Dr Fort Lauderdale FL 33334

MORSS, ESTHER PROCTOR, graduate student; b. Boston, Jan. 10, 1964; d. Everett and Mary Abagail (Shiverick) M. BS, Calif. Inst. Tech., 1986; MSAA, U. Wash., 1990. Lab. asst. Calif. Inst. Tech. Dept. Mech. Engr., Pasadena, Calif., 1985-86; research asst. U. Wash. Dept. Aeros. and Astron., Seattle, 1986-89; with space systems div. Gen. Dynamics, San Diego, Calif., 1990—.

MORTENSEN, ELLEN L., mathematics educator; b. Passaic, N.J., Aug. 31, 1943; d. Nathan Walter and Louise (Salerno) McDavitt; m. Eugene Phillips Mortensen, Aug. 8, 1964; children: Jeffrey Phillips, Jennifer-Kristen. BS in Edn., U. Hawaii, 1966; MEd, Seton Hall U., 1970. Cert. tchr. K-12, art, 7-12 math. Math. tchr. Hawaii Dept. Edn., Honolulu, 1966-67, Ridgewood (N.J.) Schs., 1968-69, Northeast Ind. Sch., San Antonio, Tex., 1967-68, Montgomery County (Md.) Schs., 1969-76, Fairlawn (N.J.) Bd. Edn., 1976—; class advisor Fairlawn Bd. Edn., 1980—; lectr. Nat. Coun. Tchrs. Math., 1975. Leader Brownies, Girls Scouts U.S., Upper Saddle River, N.J., 1989-90; v.p. League of St. Joseph's Hosp., Paterson, N.J., 1980-88. Recipient grants NSF, Incarnate Word Coll., Am. U. of Md., 1967-73. Mem. PTA, Women's Club. Roman Catholic. Home: 8 Iron Latch Ct Upper Saddle River NJ 07458

MORTENSEN, SUSAN MARIE, manufacturing company executive; b. Portland, Oreg., Jan. 24, 1950; d. Leslie Dean Mortensen and Kathryn Merdell Huff; m. José Garcia Ruiz, Oct. 25, 1986. BA, U. Portland, 1972. Advt. dir. B.A.C. Inc., Portland, 1972-76, v.p., 1976-81; exec. dir. Econ. Devel. Assn. Skagit County, Inc., Mt. Vernon, Wash., 1982-86; mgr. Sugiyo U.S.A., Inc., Anacortes, Wash., 1986-87, exec. dir., 1987—. Active Skagit County Tourism Task Force., Washington, 1984; rep. Team Wash. Asian Mission, Japan, 1986; ambassador Wash. Partnership for Econ. Devel., 1984—; mem. Project '90's, 1989; bd. dirs. TAste of Skagit, 1990; mem. adv. bd. Skagit Valley Coll., 1990. Mem. Japan-Am. Soc., Econ. Devel. Execs. Wash. (bd. dirs. 1985—), Anacortes C. of C. Jansen Found. grantee, 1985, Team Wash. Dept. Trade, 1985, Local Devel. Fund Matching Dept. Com. Devel., Washington, 1986.

MORTERA, MARIANNE HIDALGO, occupational therapist; b. Manila, Sept. 6, 1961; d. Antonio Narciso and Gloria (Hidalgo) M. BA in Biology, Capital U., 1983; MA in Occupational Therapy, NYU, 1987. Registered occupational therapist. Occupational therapist Mt. Sinai Hosp., N.Y.C., 1987-88, Rusk Inst. Rehab. Medicine/NYU Med. Ctr., N.Y.C., 1988—; neurology teaching asst. NYU, 1990—. Mem. Am. Occupational Therapy Assn. Roman Catholic.

MORTHAM, SANDRA BARRINGER, state legislator; b. Erie, Pa., Jan. 4, 1951; d. Norman Lyell and Ruth (Harer) Barringer; m. Allen Mortham, Aug. 21, 1950; children: Allen Jr., Jeffrey. AS, St. Petersburg Jr. Coll., 1971; BA, Eckerd Coll. Personnel dir. Capital Formation Counselors, Inc., Bellair Bluffs, Fla., 1972—; commr. City of Largo, Fla., 1982-86, vice mayor, 1985-86; mem. Fla. Ho. of Reps., 1986—. Bd. dirs. Performing Arts Ctr. & Theatre, Clearwater, Fla.; exec. com. Pinellas County Rep. Com., Rep. Nat. Com. Named Citizen of Yr., 1990; recipient numerous outstanding legislator awards, achievement among women awards from civic and profl. orgns. Mem. Am. Legis. Exch. Coun., Nat. Rep. Legislators Assn., Largo C. of C. (bd. dirs. 1987—, v.p.). Presbyterian. Clubs: Largo Jr. Woman's (pres., Woman of Yr. award 1979), Suncoast Community Woman's (pres., Outstanding Service award 1981, Woman of Yr. award 1986), Suncoast Tiger Bay, Greater Largo Rep., Belleair Rep. Woman's, Clearwater Rep. Woman's. Home: 2860 Vernon Terr Largo FL 34640 Office: 152 8th Ave SW Largo FL 34640

MORTHLAND, CONSTANCE AMELIA GRANT (MRS. ANDREW NORTHLAND), civic worker; b. Eng., Mar. 31, 1915 (came to U.S. 1919, naturalized 1940); d. Douglas Gordon and Maud (Smith) Grant; ; A.B. summa cum laude, Stanford, 1936; m. Andrew Morthland, Aug. 8, 1937; children—Joan (Mrs. Warren C. Hutchins), Patricia (Mrs. James F. Draper). Research asst. RKO Studios, 1936-39; story dept. analyst Paramount Studios, 1941-46; free lance writer, 1955-60; cons. overseas program Stanford U. Pres. Friends of Claremont Colls., 1976-78; mem. Friends of Radcliffe Coll., 1962-70; chmn. fin. com. Episcopal Ch. Women, 1959-60; mem. exec. bd. Assistance League, 1968-69; staff mem. Laguna-Moulton Community Playhouse, 1961—, editor Callboard, 1955-—; community adviser Jr. League, 1973-75. Trustee Pitzer Coll., Claremont, Calif.; bd. overseers Claremont Coll., 1965-73; bd. dirs. Lyric Opera Assn. Orange County, 1973-84, Continuing Edn. at Claremont Coll., 1973-77; trustee South Coast Med. Center; exec. bd. Assocs. of House Ear Inst.; bd. dirs. Research Assocs. U. Calif.-Irvine Coll. Medicine, 1983—, mem. brain mng. com., 1989—. Recipient Journalism award Sigma Delta Chi, 1936, Calif. Internat. Woman award 1971. Mem. Soc. Preservation Rural Eng. (hon.), Daus. Brit. Empire (regent 1980—), Aircraft Owners and Pilots Assn., Ninety-Nines. Clubs: Stanford (Orange County sec.); Stanford Profl. Women's; Women's University (London); Newport Harbor Yacht; El Miguel Country; N.Y. Yacht. Home: 165 Moss Point Laguna Beach CA 92651

MORTIMER, ANITA LOUISE, lawyer, consultant, educator; b. Jefferson City, Mo., July 2, 1950; d. Ross Maitland Snell and Viola Alice (Leigh) M. BA, Graceland Coll., 1973; JD, Washburn U., 1976. Bar: Kans. 1976, U.S. Dist. Ct. Kans. 1976, Mo. 1980, U.S. Dist. Ct. (we. dist.) Mo. 1980, U.S. Ct. Appeals (8th cir.) 1980, U.S. Supreme Ct. 1980. Tng. cons. Orgn. to Counter Sexual Assault, Mo., Iowa, Kans., Ill., 1979-80; asst. dist. atty. Wyandotte County, Kansas City, Kans., 1976-80; asst. U.S. atty. U.S. Dept. Justice, Kansas City, Mo., 1980—; appointee Organized Crime and Drug Enforcement Task Force, 1988; cons. Govs. Task Force on Rape Prevention, Mo., 1979-80; instr. Nat. Coll. Dist. Attys., 1980, various camps and retreats, family-related topics, various seminars for fed. agts.; bd. dirs. SHARE, Inc. Contbr. articles to profl. jours. Bd. dirs. Met. Orgn. to Counter Sexual Assault, Kansas City, 1976-80; apptd. to Presdl. Com. on Status of Women, 1979-80; trustee Independence (Mo.) Regional Health Ctr., 1990—; mem. Ctr. Stake Strategic Planning Commn. RLDS, 1989-90; apptd. chair World Ch. Task Force on Singles' Ministry RLDS, 1990—. Named to Honorable Order of Ky. Cols., Gov., 1980. Mem. ABA, Mo. Bar Assn., Assn. Women Lawyers, Kansas City Met. Bar Assn.; Alumni Assn. Graceland Coll. (bd. dirs. 1987, pres. 1988), John Whitmer Hist. Soc. Mem. Reorganized Ch. of Jesus Christ of Latter Day Saints. Clubs: MOCSA (Kansas City), Friends of Art. Office: US Dept Justice US Courthouse 811 Grand Rm 549 Kansas City MO 64106

MORTON, BERNICE FINLEY, nurse; b. Detroit, Aug. 29, 1923; d. Virgil and Minnie Alice (Batchelor) Finley; B.S.N., Wayne State U., 1954, M.S.N., 1961; Ph.D., U. Mich., 1980; m. Donald Allen Morton, Oct. 1, 1949; children: Donna Jean, Mildred Ellen. Staff nurse Grace Hosp., Detroit, 1948; pub. health nurse Detroit Dept. Health, 1948-58; instr. Deaconess Sch. Nurses, Detroit, 1960-62; instr. med. terminology Highland Park (Mich.) Community Coll., 1962; asst. dir. Met. Hosp., Detroit, 1962-63; mem. faculty Wayne State U., 1963—, assoc. prof. nursing, chmn. community health nursing, 1973—, minority affairs officer, 1977—, also mem. speakers' bur. vis. prof. Howard U., 1983-84; dir. nursing svc. Model Neighborhood Comprehensive Health Care Ctr., 1969-72; mem. Mayor Detroit Adv. Com. Health, 1970-72; cons., reviewer in field. Horace Rachkam fellow, 1975;

grantee USPHS, 1959; Martin L. King/Rosa Parks scholar, Oakland U., Rochester, MI, 1988; recipient Nightingale award finalist Oakland U., 1989. Mem. AAUP, Am. Nurses Assn., Nat. League Nursing, Am. Pub. Health Assn., Detroit Dist. Nurses Assn., Mich. Nurses Assn. (bd. dirs. pub. health nursing Detroit dist. 1987—), Am. Assn. History Nursing, Mus. African-Am. History, Wayne State U. Wayne State U. Alumni Assn., U. Mich Alumni Assn., Smithsonian Assocs., Societas Docta, Sigma Theta Tau, Delta Sigma Theta, Chi Eta Phi. Author papers in field. Address: 3790 Sturtevant Ave Detroit MI 48206

MORTON, CAROLINE JULIA, marketing executive; b. N.Y.C.; BS in Edn., U. Pa.; MBA, N.Y. U.; grad. cert. in profl. writing and effective communication, CCNY. Vice pres. mktg. mgmt. V-TEC Corp., Hopewell, Va.; pres. CMR Co., Hopewell; past cons. Advt. Women of N.Y. Mem. Am. Mktg. Assn. (past dir.), Advt. Women of N.Y., Fedn. Profl. Bus. Women, Am. Mgmt. Assn., AAUW. Contbr. articles to profl. jours. Address: PO Box 841 Hopewell VA 23860

MORTON, JOANNE MCKEAN, computer educator, consultant; b. New London, Conn., Dec. 3, 1953; d. Newton Hubbard and Lucille (Paganetti) McK.; m. Michael McNally Morton, Sept. 16, 1978. BA, Conn. Coll., 1976; MBA, Rensselaer Poly. Inst., 1985. Dept. mgr. Great Atlantic & Pacific Tea Co., Inc., Springfield, Mass., 1976-84; research asst. Hartford Grad. Ctr., Conn., 1985, adj. lectr. Sch. Mgmt., 1986—; lectr. courses in mktg. and computer applications; founder, pres. Morton & Assocs. Tax and Accounting Svcs., 1986—; enrolled agent Dept. Treasury, 1990. Mem. Nat. Assn. Enrolled Agents, Conn. Soc. of Enrolled Agts. Office: Hartford Grad Ctr 8 Clifton St Waterford CT 06385-1307

MORTON, MARGARET E., state legislator; b. Pocahontas, Va., June 23, 1924; m. James F. Morton. Formerly mem. Conn. Ho. of Reps.; now mem. from dist. 23 Conn. Senate; vice-chair Conn. Legis. Black and Hispanic Caucus. Del. Dem. Nat. Conv., 1980, 84. Mem. Nat. Council Negro Women (life), NAACP, NOW, Nat. Black Caucus State Legislators. Episcopalian. Home: 25 Currier St Bridgeport CT 06607 Office: Conn State Senate Hartford CT 06106*

MORTON, MARILYN MILLER, educational administrator, genealogy and history educator; b. Water Valley, Miss., Dec. 2, 1929; d. Julius Brunner and Irma Faye (Magee) Miller; m. Perry Wilkes Morton Jr., July 2, 1958; children: Dent Miller Morton, Nancy Marilyn Morton Driggers, E. Perian Morton Ethridge. BA in English, Miss. U. for Women, 1952; MS in History, Miss. State U., 1955. Cert. secondary tchr. Tchr. English Starkville (Miss.) High Sch., 1952-58; part-time instr. Miss. State U., 1953-58; mem. Spl. Collection staff Samford U., Birmingham, Ala., 1984—; lectr. genealogy and history, instr. genealogy Inst. Genealogy & Hist. Rsch., Samford U., Birmingham, 1985—, assoc. dir., 1985-88, exec. dir., 1988—; founding dir. SU British Inst. Genealogy & Hist. Rsch. Samford U., Birmingham and British Isles, 1986—; lectr. in field. Contbr. articles and book revs. to profl. jours. Active Birmingham chpt. Salvation Army Aux., 1982—. Fellow Irish Geneal. Rsch. Soc., London; mem. Internat. Soc. British Genealogy and Family History, Nat. Geneal. Soc. (mem. nat. program com. 1988—, lectr. nat. meetings), Soc. Genealogists London, Irish Geneal. Rsch. Soc. (London), Antiquarian Soc. Birmingham (sec. 2d v.p. 1982-84), DAR (regent Cheaha chpt. 1977-78), DAR Am. Colonists (regent Edward Waters chpt. 1978-79), Phi Kappa Phi (charter mem. Samford U. chpt. 1972). Baptist.

MORTON, TAMARA TURNER, educator; b. Macon, Ga., Oct. 25, 1960; d. Donald Lawrence and Sara Catherine (Hatcher) Turner; m. William Joseph Morton, Jr., Nov. 20, 1982. BS in Edn., U. Ga., 1982; MEd, Valdosta State Coll., 1987. Cert. tchr., Ga. Lead tchr. Southside Elementary Sch., Cairo, Ga., 1982-84, 86—, lead tchr., math resource tchr., 1985-86; lead tchr., math resource tchr. Washington Middle Sch., Cairo, 1984-85; media com. Southside Elementary Sch., 1983-84, elementary math. coun., 1984-87, publicity person, 1985-86. Pres. Grady County Kidney Found., Cairo, 1984-85, Grady County ARCH Com., Cairo, 1985-87. Named Alumnus of Yr., Grady County U. Ga. ARCH Group, 1987. Mem. U. Ga. Alumni Soc. (bd. mgrs., 2d dist. v.p. 1986-88), Cairo Jr. Woman's Club (pres. 1984-85), Phi Kappa Phi, Kappa Delta Pi. Home: 420 Twelth Ave NW Cairo GA 31728 Office: Southside Elementary Sch 491 3d St SE Cairo GA 31728

MORTZ, BETTY JANE, school nurse; b. Mansfield, Ohio, June 21, 1924; d. Albert Bryan and Lestia Faye (Young) Hamman; m. Howard Leroy Mortz, Dec. 21, 1954; children: Steven Howard, Lestia Ann. RN, Mansfield Gen. Hosp., 1945; BS, Ohio State U., 1951. Health credential Calif. State U., L.A. Office nurse Dr. Karl Langacher, Mansfield, 1946-48; staff nurse Ohio State U. Hosp., Columbus, 1948-49, St. Francis Hosp., Columbus, 1949-51; instr. St. Francis Hosp. Sch. Nursing, Columbus, 1951-53, L.A. County Gen. Hosp. Sch. Nursing, 1953-56; sch. nurse Paramount (Calif.) Unified Sch. Dist., 1980—. Mem. AAUW (pres. 1983), NEA, Nat. Soc. DAR (chaplain 1987-89), Nat. Assn. Sch. Nurses, Calif. Sch. Nurses Orgn., L.A. County Sch. Nurses Assn., Calif. Tchrs. Assn., Calif. State Congress of Parents and Tchrs., Nat. Mus. Women in the Arts (charter), Long Beach Civic Light Opera, Ohio Order Eastern Star (Ruth chpt. #17), Delta Kappa Gamma. Methodist. Home: 8520-B Century Blvd Paramount CA 90723 Office: Paramount Unified Sch Dist 15110 California Ave Paramount CA 90723

MOSAK, BARBARA MARCIA, television station designer; b. Chgo., Nov. 14, 1950; d. Joseph and Anna (Rabinovitz) M. BA in Design with honors, U. Ill., Chgo., 1976. Tchr. art Temple Emanuel, Chgo., 1973-74; graphic designer Belham & Assocs., Inc., 1974-76, Sta. WFLD-TV, Field Communications, Chgo., 1976-77; graphic artist Sta. WBBM-TV, CBS, Chgo., 1977-87, art dir., 1987-88, design dir., 1988—; freelance designer, Chgo. Contbg. author: TV Guide Tune-In Advertising, 1988 (Judge's Choice award 1988). Vol. video artist Communication for Social Change, Chgo., 1974; vol. designer Kidney Found. Ill., 1974-76, NOW, Chgo., 1975; vol. designer, tutor Jewish Vocat. Svc., Chgo., 1981-82. Recipient Desi award Graphics Design: USA, 1981, cert. of leadership YWCA, Chgo., 1983. Mem. Broadcast Designers Assn., NATAS (judge Emmy nominations Chgo. 1978-79), Soc. Typog. Arts. Office: Sta WBBM-TV 630 N McClurg Ct Chicago IL 60611

MOSCATI, MAREE, financial planner; b. N.Y.C., Aug. 28, 1952; d. Anthony and Theresa (Costanzo) M.; m. Joel Azrikan, Jan. 14, 1988; stepdaughters: Melissa, Sara. A in Merchandising, Lab. Inst. Merchandising, N.Y.C., 1975; B in Bus. and Fin., NYU, N.Y.C., 1979. NASD series 7 lic., NASD series 63 lic.; CLU; chartered fin. cons. Co-founder Fin. Awareness Programs, Hollywood, Fla.; co-founder For Women Only, Hollywood. Bd. dirs. City of Hollywood Econ. Rev. Named Supercharger, First Union Bank, as part of Winner's Circle, Winners News Network. Mem. Broward South Life Underwriters (bd. dirs.), Nat. Assn. Women Bus. Owners, Zonta Internat. (membership com.), Coral Gables C. of C., Weston C. of C. (com. for women in bus., network com.), Nat. Assn. Life Underwriters. Homee: 14721 N Beckley Sq Davie FL 33325 Office: Fin Awareness 4651 Sheridan St Ste 400 Hollywood FL 33021

MOSELEY, VIRGINIA DOUGLAS, retired English educator; b. Gainesville, Tex., Jan. 31, 1917; d. Edward Hilary and Leslie (Jones) M. BA, U. Okla., 1938, MA, 1948; PhD, Columbia U., 1958. Cert. tchr., Tex., Okla. Tchr. Gainesville High Sch. and Jr. Coll., 1938-44; asst. prof. English Southeastern State U., Durant, Okla., 1947-55, No. Ill. U., DeKalb, 1955-65; prof. Tex. Woman's U., Denton, 1966-69, U. Ottawa (Ont., Can.), 1969-82; retired, 1982. Co-translator (from Russian): Those Americans, 1964; author: James Joyce and the Bible, 1967; contbr. articles to profl. pubs. Mem. San Mateo Hist. Soc., 1986—; elder Westminster Presbyn. Ch., DeKalb, 1964-65, Knox Presbyn. Ch., Ottawa, 1973-82. Mem. James Joyce Found., AAUW, Newcomers Club, Alpha Chi Omega.

MOSER, JEANETTE BARBER, paralegal nurse, utilization review analyst; b. Kerrville, Tex., July 23, 1952; d. Travis Joel and Julia Evelyn (Enid) Barber; m. Francis G. Davis Jr., Nov. 6, 1971 (div. Aug. 1983); children: Francis G. III, Joshua E., Patrick B. Assoc. degree, Del Mar Coll., 1980; student, Pan Am. U., 1986-88, Corpus Christi State U., 1986—. RN, Tex.; cert. Am. Bd. Quality Assurance and Utilization Rev. Staff, relief charge nurse labor and delivery Meml. Med. Ctr., Corpus Christi, Tex., 1980-85; utilization rev. coord. Tex. Med. Found., Austin, 1985-86, Hosp. Corp. Am. Rio Grande Regional Hosp., McAllen, Tex., 1986-88; utilization rev. analyst, dept. head Rehab. Hosp South Tex., Corpus Christi, 1988-89; cons. Brin & Brin, Corpus Christi, 1985, paralegal nurse, 1989—. Researcher, co-editor paper on J.H. Sparks Civil War Diary, 1989. Den leader Corpus Christi Cub Scouts Am., 1979; CPR instr. ARC, 1987; mem. Am. Cancer Soc., 1987. Mem. Mystery Readers. Democrat. Baptist. Homw: 2209 Dorchester Corpus Christi TX 78418 Office: Brin & Brin PC 1202 3d St Corpus Christi TX 78404

MOSER, SARAH GUNNING, manufacturing engineer, small business owner; b. Seattle, Sept. 17, 1953; d. Harvey Dade and Grace Wills (Bell) Gunning; m. Lawrence Herman Moser, May 18, 1985; 1 child, Grace Elizabeth. BA in Archtl. Planning, The Evergreen State Coll., Olympia, Wash., 1975; mfg. engrng. cert., Boeing Mfg. Engrng. Sch., Everett, Wash., 1980. Asst. variety dept. mgr. The Safeway Corp., Seattle, 1977-79; mfg. engr. Boeing Co., 747/767 div., Everett, 1980-82; sr. mfg. engr. McDonnell Douglas Helicopter Co., Mesa, Ariz., 1982-87; co-owner Moser Design Assocs., Vashon, Wash., 1988—, Moser Design Svcs., Vashon, Wash., 1989-90; bus. mgr. for opera singer Patricia S. Lott, Vashon, 1989-90; engrng. trainer McDonnell Douglas Helicopter Co., Mesa, 1986-87, procedure writer, 1986-87; procedure writer The Boeing Co., Everett, 1981. Community outreach speaker Alcohol Pub. Info. Com., Wash., 1976-80, 88-89; coord. Women's Ctr. Evergreen State Coll., Olympia, 1973-74; trainer, bd. dirs. Sta. KAOS-FM, Olympia, 1972-74; soloist Unity Ch. of Truth, Seattle, Everett, 1978-82; guest soloist various chs.; co-chair Vashon-Maury Island Babysitting Coop., 1988-89, chair 1989. Recipient Cost Savs. awards Boeing Co., 1980-82. Mem. AIAA, NAFE, Soc. Mfg. Engrs., Internat. Exec. Devel. Inc. Mem. Unity Ch. of Truth. Office: Moser Design Assocs PO Box 1406 Vashon WA 98070

MOSES, DEBORAH WATSON, investment counsellor; b. Concord, Mass., June 25, 1951; d. William Bryan and Jean (Watson) M.; m. Maurice Pierre Tonissi II, June 25, 1988. BA, Goucher Coll., 1973; MBA, Babson Coll., 1976. Chartered fin. analyst. Rsch. analyst Sun Life of Can., Wellesley, Mass., 1976-81; v.p. Scudder Stevens & Clark, Boston, 1981—. Mem. Mass. Audubon Soc. (dir. 1988—), Goucher Coll. Alumni Assn. (pres. Boston). Republican. Episcopalian. Home: 35 Beacon St Boston MA 02108 Office: Scudder Stevens & Clark 175 Federal St Boston MA 02110

MOSES, JANET ESTELLE, data processing programmer/analyst; b. Balt., Apr. 27, 1946; d. Kayton Gutman and Estelle Willner (Kahn) M. Student, U. Grenoble, France, 1967; BA in English and French, Baldwin-Wallace Coll., 1968; BA in Acctg., Loyola Coll., Balt., 1980; M of Liberal Arts with honors, Johns Hopkins U., 1985. Exec. trainee Hutzler's, Balt., 1968-69, asst. buyer, 1969-71, buyer, 1971-76; mgr. Millison's Clothing for Children, Balt., 1976-77; bank examiner Md. Div. Bldg., Savs. and Loan Assns., Balt., 1979-80; data processing programmer/analyst Md. Dept. Pub. Safety and Correctional Svcs., Pikesville, 1980—. Mem. Johns Hopkins Alumni Assn., Balt. Mus. Art, Md. Pub. TV. Office: Md Dept Pub Safety and CS PO Box 5743 Pikesville MD 21208

MOSES, KATHY SUE, registered nurse; b. Cin., Nov. 22, 1948; d. Ausben and Martha Jane (Gephart) M. Diploma in nursing, Jewish Hosp. Sch. Nursing, Cin., 1969; BA, Xavier U., 1990. RN, Ohio; cert. critical care nurse. RN, staff and charge nurse Jewish Hosp., Cin., 1969-79; RN, staff nurse Am. Nursing Care, Cin., 1979-83; RN staff nurse, open heart ICU Jewish Hosp., Cin., 1983-89, RN, asst. dir. open heart ICU, 1989—. Vol. Bethany House Shelter, Cin., 1987—. Mem. Am. Assn. Critical Care Nurses, Sierra Club, Audubon Soc., Greenspeace.

MOSES, MARY JANE, personnel director; b. Long Beach, Calif., July 2, 1928; d. Benjamin Harrison and Joy (Denison) Heim; m. Joseph H. Shireman, Aug. 5, 1947 (div. 1958); children: Terrance B., Lewis J.; m. J. Neil Moses, Nov. 25, 1961. AA, Cuesta Coll., San Luis Obispo, Calif., 1978; BS, U. San Francisco, 1980, MPA, 1982. Classified pers., payroll specialist Calif. Poly. State U., San Luis Obispo, 1960-61; co-owner Sun Newspaper, Morro Bay, Calif., 1961-68; owner, prin. Hearth and Home Shop, Morro Bay, 1968-70; cert. payroll exec. San Luis Coastal Unified Sch. Dist., 1972-76; coordinator, pers. and affirmative action Cuesta Coll., 1976-79; dir. pers. San Luis Obispo County Office Edn., 1979—; tchr., presenter Calif. Poly. State U., 1983—. Contbr. articles to profl. publs. Mem. Central Coast Dem. Club, Morro Bay, 1965—. Mem. Pers. Adminstr. County Offices Edn., Cen. Coast Pers. Assn., Tri-Counties Sch. Pers. Assn., Quota Internat. (pres. 1966-67), Morro Bay Club (dist. gov. 1971-72). Office: S Luis Obispo Ctr Office Ed Hwy 1 Rancho El Chorro San Luis Obispo CA 93403

MOSES, SUSAN COLLEEN, interior designer; b. Long Beach, Apr. 1, 1953; d. David Ray and Donna May (Millner) Wertz; m. Michael Meyer Moses, July 15, 1978 (div. Sept. 26, 1986). BArch, Orange Coast Coll., 1984. Owner Susan Moses, Beverly Hills, Calif., 1978—. Home: 9666 Yoakum Dr Beverly Hills CA 90210

MOSHER, SALLY EKENBERG, lawyer; b. N.Y.C., July 26, 1934; d. Leslie Joseph and Frances Josephine (McArdle) Ekenberg; m. James Kimberly Mosher, Aug. 13, 1960 (dec. Aug. 1982). MusB, Manhattanville Coll., 1956; postgrad., Hofstra U., 1958-60, U. So. Calif., 1971-73; JD, U. So. Calif., 1981. Bar: Calif., 1982. Musician, pianist, tchr., 1957-74; music critic Pasadena Star-News, 1967-72; mgr. Contrasts Concerts, Pasadena Art Mus., 1971-72; rep. Occidental Life Ins. Co., Pasadena, 1975-78; v.p. James K. Mosher Co., Pasadena, 1961-82, pres., 1982—; pres. Oakhill Enterprises, Pasadena, 1984—; assoc. White-Howell, Inc., Pasadena, 1984—. Contbr. articles to various publs. Bd. dirs. Jr. League Pasadena, 1966-67, Encounters Concerts, Pasadena, 1966-72, U. So. Calif. Friends of Music, Los Angeles, 1973-76, Pasadena Arts Council, 1986—, pres., 1989—; v.p., bd. dirs. Pasadena Chamber Orch., 1986-88, pres., 1987-88; mem. Calif. 200 Council for Bicentennial of U.S. Constn., 1987-90; commr. Endowment Adv. Commn., Pasadena, 1988—; bd. dirs. Calif. Music Theatre, 1988-90, Pasadena Hist. Soc., 1989—, I Cantori, 1989—, Foothill Area Community Svcs., 1990—. Manhattanville Coll. hon. scholar, 1952-56. Fellow Fellows of Contemporary Art (Los Angeles); mem. ABA, Calif. Bar Assn., Nat. Assn. Realtors, Calif. Assn. Realtors, Pasadena Bd. Realtors, Assocs. of Calif. Inst. Tech., Kappa Gamma Pi, Mu Phi Epsilon, Phi Alpha Delta. Republican. Club: Athenaeum. Home: 1260 Rancheros Rd Pasadena CA 91103 Office: 711 E Walnut St Ste 407 Pasadena CA 91101

MOSHY, DIANA BOUTROSS, executive assistant, real estate broker; b. Bklyn., Nov. 3, 1953; d. Edward Nagib and Ann Rita Boutross; m. Frederick Charles Moshy, Oct. 7, 1954. Student, Pace U., 1976—. Asst. convention coordinator Independent Ins. Agts. Am., N.Y.C., 1973-76; real estate broker N.Y.C., 1976—; exec. asst. 1st Boston Corp., N.Y.C., 1980, Citibank NA, N.Y.C., 1980-81, Kissinger Assoc., N.Y.C., 1981-84, Home Group, N.Y.C., 1984-86, Backer Spielvogel Bates, N.Y.C., 1986-89; lic. real estate broker Nasco Cons., Inc., N.Y.C., 1990—. Repubican. Roman Catholic Maronite. Home: 8701 Shore Rd #428 Brooklyn NY 11209 Office: Nasco Cons Inc 17 Battery Pl New York NY 10174

MOSIER, JOAN MARIE, social services administrator; b. Nanticoke, Pa., July 7, 1953; d. John Peter and Eleanor Natalie (Brezinski) Bogdan; m. Bradley Gerald Mosier, (div.). BA, Bloomsburg State Coll., 1974; MPA, Marywood Coll., 1986. Psychiat. aide Danville (Pa.) State Hosp., 1974-76; caseworker Columbia County Children & Youth Svcs., Bloomsburg, Pa., 1976-81, casework supr., 1981-84, adminstr., 1984—; bd. sec. Columbia County Human Svcs. Coalition, Bloomsburg, 1988—; pres., charter mem. Big Bros./Big Sisters of Columbia County, Bloomsburg, 1987—; mem. adv. bd. Columbia/Montour/Snyder/Union Mental Health/Mental Retardation Program, Danville, 1987—, Press-Enterprise Brighter Christmas Fund com., Bloomsburg, 1987—; pres. Bloomsburg U. Social Welfare Program Advisors, 1989—. Treas., trustee Columbia Day Care, Inc., Bloomsburg, 1987—; bd. sec. Vol. Recycling, Inc., Bloomsburg, 1980—; founder, registar, fin. chair Columbia/Montour Women's Conf., Bloomsburg, 1979—. Recipient Outstanding Woman award Columbia-Montour Women's Conf., 1988, Domestic Violence Awareness Month recognition Women's Ctr., 1987. Mem. AAUW (cert. achievement 1987, outstanding woman 1982), Am. Soc. for Pub. Adminstrn., Pa. Children and Youth Adminstrs. Assn., Pi Alpha Alpha. Democrat. Roman Catholic. Home: 564 E Third St Bloomsburg PA 17815-1913 Office: Columbia County Children and Youth Svcs 26 W First St Bloomsburg PA 17815-1105

MOSIER, VIRGINIA LOU, educator; b. Clinton, Okla., Dec. 2, 1951; d. Bert Eugene and Martha Virginia (Fike) M. BE, Abilene Christian U., 1973; MS, East Tex. State U., 1980; PhD, U. North Tex., Denton, 1989. Cert. tchr. Bus. tchr. Christian Schs., Inc., Dallas, 1973-77; sec. Underwood, Neuhaus Co., Inc., Houston, 1977-78; bus. tchr. Magnet High Sch., Dallas, 1978-79; vocat. tchr. Mesquite (Tex.) High Sch., 1979-81; curriculum writer East Tex. State U., Commerce, 1980; vocat. tchr. J.J. Pearce High Sch., Richardson, Tex., 1981-89; tchr. office adminstrn. Richardson High Sch., 1989—; presenter T & I Summer Workshop, Houston, 1983-87; mem. Coordinated Vocat. Acad. Edn. Co-op Organizing Com., 1983-88; adj. prof. rural schs., Tex., 1984-86, U. North Tex., Denton, 1984-85, East Tex. State U., Commerce, 1986, S.W. Tex. State U., San Marcos, 1990. Author: Coordinated Vocational Academic Education Curriculum Guide, 1980, Vocational Opportunities Clubs of Texas Competitive Guide, 1985, Vocational Opportunities Clubs of Texas Advisor's Tool Kit, 1986. Sec. Christian Schs. PTA, Dallas, 1976-77. Recipient Outstanding Tchr. award Richardson Assn. for Children with Learning Disabilities, 1985. Mem. Tex. Bus. Edn. Assn. (pres., v.p., sec. 1982-85, state legis. com. 1986, Tchr. of Yr. award Dist. 10 1984), Assn. Tex. Profl. Educators, Am. Vocat. Assn., Tex. Indsl. Vocat. Assn., Tex. Vocat Tech. Assn., Assn. Supervision and Curriculum Devel., Phi Delta Kappa, Iota Lambda Sigma (state and area outstanding tchr. awards 1985). Republican. Mem. Ch. of Christ. Home: 2805 St George Garland TX 75044

MOSKAL, JANINA, high technology manufacturing executive; b. Czerna, Poland, June 6, 1944; came to U.S., 1963; d. Stanislaw and Agata (Kleczek) Kot; m. Tadeusz J. Moskal, Dec. 29, 1960 (div. 1981); children: Robert R., Thomas L. Student, L.I. U., 1976-78; AAS, Nassau Community Coll., 1980. Machine operator Photocircuits Corp., Glen Cove, N.Y., 1966-70, programmer, 1970-72, supr., 1972-81, engr. process support, 1981-83, systems mgr. laser graphics, 1984-86; gen. mgr., ptnr. NC Design Corp., Williston Park, N.Y., 1983-84; systems mgr. Parlex Corp., Methuen, Mass., 1984-87; mfg. specialist Rothtec Engraving Corp., New Bedford, Mass., 1987—; owner, prin. JM Cons., Glen Cove, 1987—; organizer, instr. tech. courses and seminars, 1980-81, 1986-87. Officer Polish Nat. Home, Glen Cove, 1975-79, Polonia, Glen Cove, 1978. Republican. Roman Catholic. Office: JM Cons Co 109 Shore Rd Glen Cove NY 11542

MOSKOWITZ, MIRIAM SHERRI, nurse, legal nurse consultant; b. N.Y.C., Apr. 25, 1953; d. Irving and Lillian E. (Horodner) M. BS in Nursing, SUNY, Binghamton, 1976; MS in Nursing, Hunter Coll., 1981. RN, N.Y. Med.-surg. and psychiat. nurse Mt. Sinai Hosp., N.Y.C., 1976-79; psychiat. nurse Bellevue Hosp., N.Y.C., 1979-81; head psychiat. nurse Queens (N.Y.) Hosp. Ctr., 1981; clin. nurse specialist Met. Hosp., N.Y.C., 1981-85; asst. dir. CASES, Inc. and Compumed Rsch., N.Y.C., 1985—; clin. rsch. assoc. Ayest Labs., N.Y.C., 1987-88. Mem. N.Y.C. Dem. Com. Recipient svc. award Mt. Sinai Hosp., 1977; grantee NIMH, 1979. Mem. Am. Nurses Assn., Am. Assn. Legal Nurse Cons., N.Y. State Nurses Assn., Sigma Theta Tau. Jewish. Office: CASES Inc 301 E 50th St New York NY 10022

MOSKOWITZ, RANDI ZUCKER, nurse; b. N.Y.C., Oct. 19, 1948; d. Seymour and Gertrude (Levy) Zucker; R.N., Jewish Hosp. & Med. Center Sch. Nursing, 1969; BA, Marymount Manhattan Coll., 1975; MS, Hunter Coll., 1979; MBA, Columbia U., 1990; m. Marc N. Moskowitz, July 11, 1976. Gen. staff nurse neurosurgery unit, N.Y. Hosp., N.Y.C., 1969-71, sr. staff nurse Recovery Room, 1971-76, nurse coordinator utilization rev., 1976-79; health educator Office of Cancer Communications, Meml. Sloan-Kettering Cancer Center, 1979-81; adminstrv. nurse oncologist Bklyn. Community Hosp. Oncology Program, Meth. Hosp., 1981-83, grants coordinator radiotherapy dept., 1983-86; adminstr. Ambulatory Oncology Ctr., Columbia-Presbyn. Med. Ctr., N.Y.C., 1986-89; adminstr. Surg. Day Hosp., Meml. Sloan-Kettering Cancer Ctr., 1990—; Masters prof. oncology Columbia U. Sch. Nursing. Co-editor Oncology Nursing: Advances, Treatments and Trends into the Twenty-first Century; contbr. articles to profl. jours. Mem. Am. Public Health Assn., Oncology Nursing Soc. (sec. N.Y.C. chpt. 1983-87, pres. 1988-89). Home: 222 E 80th St New York NY 10021 Office: Meml Sloan-Kettering Cancer Ctr 1275 York Ave New York NY 10021

MOSS, ALISON LESLIE, retail executive; b. Miami Beach, Fla., Mar. 13, 1959; d. Stanton Roy and Honey Cynthia (Benjamin) Moss; m. William James Shay, Jr., Nov. 27, 1981 (div. 1983). Student, U. Kans., 1976-77, Travel Coll., Beverly Hills, Calif., 1978. With Chanin's, L.A., 1977, L'Tonary, L.A., 1977-78; sales mgr. Jean St. Germain, L.A., 1978-79; travel agt./mgr. Viajes Gemini Express, L.A., 1979-81, Trindle Travel, Mechanicsburg, Pa., 1981-82; merchandiser/mgr. Ron Boutwell Ent./Dugan, North Hollywood, Calif., 1982-84; travel agt. Beverly Wilshire Travel, Beverly Hills, 1982-85; dir. Class Act Mgmt., Inc., Studio City, Calif., 1983-86; merchandiser Sunshine Country Co., Kowloon, Hong Kong, 1985—; with computer dept. No!Jeans/Tarrant Co., Inc., Kowbon, Hong Kong, 1988; agt. MDR Travel, Marina Del Rey, Calif., 1988—. Mem. Am. Soc. Travel Agts., Nat. Parrot Assn. Democrat. Jewish. Office: Sunshine Country Co, 401-2 World Fin Centre, Harbor City Hong Kong

MOSS, ANDREA, volunteer; b. Balt., Feb. 19, 1943; d. Manuel and Sylvia (Fox) Schwartz; m. Paul Moss, Oct. 23, 1966; Danielle Lea, Kevin Scott, Shara Alyse. BS, U. Md., 1965. Restaurant critic and writer: Gastronome, 1987; bd. advisors Insider's Guide to Florida Restaurants. Pres. Svc. League, Monmouth Med. Ctr., Long Branch, N.J., 1971-73; corr. sec., ball chmn. Ruth Newman Shapiro Cancer & Heart Fund, Atlantic City, N.J., 1977—, bd. dirs, fine arts com. Congregation Beth Israel, Northfield, N.J., 1977—; mem. Atlantic City Med. Ctr. Aux.; co-chmn. Shore Chpt. World Affairs Coun. Phila., Atlantic City, 1985—; nat. bd., founder, chmn. Atlantic County Chpt. Am. Assocs. Ben Gurion U. of the Negev, 1986—; co-chmn. Pro-Am LPGA Atlantic City Classic Golf Tournament, 1985—; Nat. Hostess Com. The Miss America Pageant, Atlantic City, 1989—; mem. nat. gastronome advt. com. Chaine des Rotisseurs, 1990—. Named Showstopper of the Year, The Sun Newspaper, Atlantic City, 1985. Mem. AAUW, Confrere de la Chaine des Rotisseurs (Dame de la Chaine). Republican. Home: 204 Arbor Ct E Linwood NJ 08221

MOSS, DEBRA ANN, trade association executive; b. Madison, Wis., Nov. 10, 1953; d. Simon and Joyce Gwynth (Ruppel) Moss. BA in Journalism, U. Wis., 1977. Meeting coordinator Am. Soc. for Indsl. Security, Arlington, Va., 1977-83; dir. meetings Assn. Gen. Mdse. Chains, Washington, 1983-84; conv. dir. United Fresh Fruit and Vegetable Assn., Alexandria, Va., 1984-89, v.p., 1989—. Mem. Bicentennial Commn., Madison, 1975-76. Mem. Meeting Planners Internat., Nat. Assn. Exposition Mgrs., Am. Soc. Assn. Execs., Greater Washington Soc. Assn. Execs. Home: 6100 Scotch Dr Alexandria VA 22310 Office: United Fresh Fruit and Vegetable Assn 727 N Washington St Alexandria VA 22314

MOSS, ELIZABETH LUCILLE (BETTY MOSS), transportation company executive; b. Ironton, Mo., Feb. 13, 1939; d. James Leon and Dorothy Lucille (Russell) Rollen; m. Elliott Theodore Moss, Nov. 10, 1963 (div. Jan. 1984); children: Robert Belmont, Wendy Rollen. BA in Econs. and Bus. Adminstrn., Drury Coll., 1960. Registrar, transp. mgr. Cheley Colo. Camps, Inc., Denver and Estes Park, 1960-61; office mgr. Washington Nat. Ins. Co., Denver, 1960-61; sec. White House Decorating, Denver, 1961-62; adminstrv. asst. Ringsby Truck Lines, Denver, Oakland, Calif., and Los Angeles, 1962-67, System 99 Freight Lines, L.A., 1967-69; terminal mgr. System 99 Freight Lines, Stockton, Calif., 1981-84; adminstrv. asst. Yellow Freight System, Los Angeles, 1969-74, Hayward, Calif., 1974-77; ops. mgr. Yellow Freight System, Urbana, Ill., 1977-80; sales rep. Calif. Motor Express, San Jose, 1981; regional sales mgr. Schneider Nat. Carriers, Inc., No. Calif., 1984-86; account exec. TNT-Can., Nev. and Cen. Calif., 1986-88; mgr. Interstate-Intermodal Divs. HVH Transp., Denver, 1988-89; regional sales mgr. MNX, Inc., Northern Calif., 1989—; chmn. op. council for San Joaquin and Stanislaus Counties Calif. Trucking Assn., 1983-84; planning adv. com. Truck Accident Reduction Projects, San Joaquin County, 1987-88. Mem. Econ. Devel. Council Stockton C. of C., 1985-86; active Edison High Sch. Boosters,

1982-88. Mem. Nat. Def. Transp. Assn. (bd. dirs. 1986-87), Stockton Traffic Club (bd. dirs. 1982-84, Trucker of Yr.), Cen. Valley Traffic Club, Oakland Traffic Club, Delta Nu Alpha (bd. dirs. Region 1 1982-84, v.p. Chpt. 103 1984-85, pres. 1985-86, chmn. bd. 1985-87, regional sec. 1987-88, Outstanding Achievement award 1986, 88). Methodist. Home: 900 Cambridge Dr #174 Benicia CA 94510

MOSS, GAYLA LOUISE, lawyer; b. Abilene, Tex., Aug. 7, 1960; d. Arlo Duane and Merlene Joy (Cole) M. BS in Acctg., Brigham Young U., 1982, JD, 1985. Bar: Ariz. 1985. Assoc. Lewis and Roca, Phoenix, 1985-89; in-house counsel Motorola, Inc., Phoenix, 1989—. Bd. dirs. Valley Big Bros.-Big Sisters, Mesa, Ariz., 1987—. Mem.ABA, Maricopa County Bar Assn., Ariz. Mountaineering Club. Republican. Mormon. Office: Motorola Inc 3102 N 56th St Phoenix AZ 85072

MOSS, JAIME RUTH, accountant; b. Sacramento, Oct. 27, 1948; d. Richard Levick and Margaret Elise (Schweitzer) M.; m. David Robison, Dec. 18, 1981 (div. June 1986). BA in Psychology, U. Calif., Sacramento, 1972. Advt. asst. Cost Plus Imports, San Francisco, 1972-74; casino croupier Harvey's Wagon Wheel, Lake Tahoe, Nev., 1974-81; bursar asst. U. San Francisco, 1982; acct. Greenpeace merchandising, San Francisco, 1982-83; tax cons. David M. Stone Assocs., San Francisco, 1982-84; fin. mgr. Vista Neighborhood Housing Svcs., Boise, Idaho, 1984-86, Boise Neighborhood Housing Svcs., 1986-87; fiscal officer Mountain States Health Corp., Boise, 1987—. Mem. AAUW (treas. Lake Tahoe chpt. 1979, conv. planner San Francisco chpt. 1982, treas. Boise chpt. 1984-85), Ctr. of Peace (treas. 1987-90), Aikido Club of Boise. Democrat. Office: Mountain States Health Corp 1303 W Fort Boise ID 83702

MOSS, JEAN, photographer; married; 1 child, Sarah. Student, U. Wis.; studied with Ansel Adams, Yosemite National Park, Calif. Formerly with Sedelmaier Film Prodns., Inc., Chgo.; photographer Esquire mag.; comml. photographer Chgo. Office: Jean Moss Photography Inc 1255 S Michigan Ave Chicago IL 60607*

MOSS, LESLIE OTHA, corrections officer; b. Detroit, Mar. 8, 1952; d. Lonnie and Emma (Robinson) M. Bachelors, U. Mich., 1982; student, Wayne State U., 1986—. Technician oper. rm. Sinai Hosp., Detroit, 1972-75; nurses' technician Detroit Osteopathic Hosp., 1976-83; supr. Southfield (Mich.) Placement Ctr., 1983-85; rsch. asst. Wayne County Commr.'s Office, Detroit, 1985-86; fin. aid counselor Wayne State U., 1986-87; probation officer State of Mich. Dept. Corrections, 1988—; sgt. of arms Detroit Police Res., 1987—. Advisor Congressman George Crokette, Detroit, 1989; rsch. asst. Commr. George Cushingberry, Detroit, 1987-88. Mem. NAFE, Assn. Pre-Med Students (cons. 1988—), NAACP (advisor 1989), Assn. Psychologists, Golden Key Soc. (life). Home: 1579 Kendall Detroit MI 48238

MOSS, LYNDA BOURQUE, museum director; b. Torrington, Wyo., Mar. 15, 1950; d. Leroy Alfred and Mary (Halley) Bourque; m. Thomas Charles Moss, Jan. 31, 1970; children: Heather, Christopher Eric. BFA, U. Nebr., Omaha, 1977; MA, U. No. Iowa, 1979; MFA, Mont. State U., 1984. Guest lectr. U. Nebr., Omaha, 1977-78; program developer Children's Mus., Omaha, 1977-78; gallery asst. U. No. Iowa, Cedar Falls, 1978-79; curator edn. Western Heritage Ctr., Billings, Mont., 1979-83, dir., 1986—; adj. prof. Ea. Mont. Coll., Billings, 1985-87; curator Mont. Art Gallery Dirs., Kalispell, 1986-87. Represented in pub. and pvt. collections, Am. Northwest. Art scholar Washington U., St. Louis, 1968-70. Mem. Internat. Coun. Mus., Am. Assn. Mus., Coll. Art Assn. Democrat. Home: 2540 Hoover Billings MT 59102 Office: Western Heritage Ctr 2822 Montana Ave Billings MT 59101

MOSS, MONIKA, entertainment manager; b. Washington, Mar. 24, 1961; d. Donald T. Moss and May Kathryn (Hill) Haugstad; m. Rodney K. Robinson, Dec. 16, 1989. BFA, Howard U., 1983; MFA, Columbia U., 1987. Pres. MKM Mgmt. Inc., N.Y.C., 1988—. Recipient the Rothberg fellowship, N.Y.C., 1984, 85. Mem. AUDELCO, Alliance Resident Theatres N.Y.

MOSS, PATRICIA DIANE, bank examiner; b. Richwood, W.Va., Aug. 22, 1960; d. James Russell and Sandra June (Hamric) M. BBA, Fairmont State Coll., 1982. Nat. bank examiner Office of the Comptr. of the Currency, Washington, 1981—. Mem. Moral Majority. Mem. Nat. Assn. Female Execs. Republican. Mem. Assemblies of God. Office: Comptr of the Currency 6100 Fairview Rd Charlotte NC 28210

MOSSAIDES, PAULA XENIS, software professional; b. Bronx, N.Y., Aug. 12, 1954; d. Paul and Melika (Antoniades) M.; m. Michael Stephen Miller, May 29, 1976; 1 child, Neil Paul. BS iin Math., MIT, 1976; MS in Computer Sci., Oreg. State U., 1985. Rsch. asst. MIT Architecture Machine Group, Cambridge, 1973-76; engr., then mgr. Tektronix, Wilsonville, Oreg., 1976-89; software mgr. NCR, Atlanta, 1989—. Patentee in field. Office: NCR 500 Tech Pkwy NW Atlanta GA 30313

MOSSBLAD, SANDRA ANN, designer, artist; b. Omaha, Apr. 18, 1957; d. Karl Gunnar and Doris May (Anderson) M. BFA, U. Mich., 1979. Designer Jack Lenor Larsen, Inc., N.Y.C., 1979-85; designer, owner S.A. Mossblad, N.Y.C., 1979—. Fulbright scholar Sweden, 1985-86. Mem. Kappa Alpha Theta. Republican. Lutheran. Office: 265 W 37th St Ste 2102 New York NY 10018

MOSSER, AMY ALETHA, systems engineer; b. Decatur, Ill., July 7, 1963; d. John Darwin and Helen Edith (Deane) M. BA, Northwestern U., Evanston, Ill., 1985. Systems engr. IBM, Gaithersburg, Md., 1985—; tutor Montgomery Coll., Rockville, Md., 1987-90. Vol. Montgomery Hospice Soc., Chevy Chase, Md., 1987-90, Jr. Achievement, 1990. Recipient IBM Formal award IBM, 1987, Fund for Community Svc. award IBM, 1989. Mem. Northwestern U. Alumni, Chi Omega Alumnae. Democrat. Home: 20400 Ambassador Terr Germantown MD 20874

MOSSMAN, DEBORAH JEAN, civil engineer, educator, researcher; b. Nuremberg, Fed. Republic Germany, Dec. 4, 1956; d. William James and Emily Wilheimina (Mead) McKechnie; m. Craig James Mossman, July 16, 1988. BSCE, MIT, 1979; MSME, Manhattan Coll., 1983; PhD, U. Iowa, 1988. Registered profl. engr. Jr. sanitary engr. Mass. Dept. Environ. Quality Engring., Westborough, 1979-82, sr. sanitary engr., 1982-83, prin. sanitary engr., 1983-84; post-doctoral assoc. Iowa Inst. Hydraulic Rsch., Iowa City, 1988; asst. prof. U. Mo.-Columbia, Independence, 1989—. Contbr. articles to profl. jours. Recipient Environ. Chemistry Grad. Student award Am. Chem. Soc., 1985; fellow U.S. EPA, 1982. Mem. AAUW (Am. fellowship 1987), ASCE (control mem. 1990—), Soc. Women Engrs. (faculty advisor), Assn. Environ. Engring. Profs., Internat. Assn. Water Pollution Rsch. & Control. Office: Univ Mo 600 W Mechanic St Independence MO 64050

MOSSO, CLAUDIA GRUENWALD, journalist, translator; b. Frankfurt, West Germany, Sept. 26, 1952; came to U.S., 1955.; d. Geza and Marianne (Pabst) Gruenwald; m. Craig W. Mosso, May 28, 1976 (div. 1984); 1 child, Brent. BA in Journalism, Pa. State U., State Coll., 1974. Dir. pub. rels. United Way of Erie County, Pa., 1975-76; pres. Translation & Interpreter Svc., North East, Pa., 1976--; reporter North East Breeze, 1986--; cons. fgn. langs. and customs usage. Translator, abstracter numerous articles, 1976—. Mem. AAUW (fin. sec. 1982-84), Am. Translators Assn., Assn. Profl. Translators, N.E. Ohio Translators Assn. Office: Translation & Interpreter 10134 Ashton Rd North East PA 16428

MOSTEHY, RANDA, account executive; b. Cairo, June 30, 1962; d. Mahmoud Ragai and Aida (Chohayeb) M. AA, Alexandria U., 1982. Cert. personnel cons. Bookkeeper Hunterlab, Reston, Va., 1982-85; acct. Health Ins. Assn. Am., Washington, 1985-86; account exec. US Sprint Telecommunications, Reston, 1986-87; mgr., account exec. Forbes Assocs., North Bethesda, Md., 1987—. Mem. UN Assn., Washington, 1987-89, NOW, Washington, 1988-89. Mem. NAFE (charter). Democrat. Moslem. Home: 337 Missouri Ave NW Washington DC 20011

MOSTI, ELLEN LOUISE, clinical pharmacist; b. Steubenville, Ohio, Nov. 29, 1961; d. Myron Eugene and Anne Mary (Krnich) M. BS in Pharmacy, Duquesne U., 1985, D Pharmacy, 1987. Lic. pharmacist, Ohio, Pa., W.Va. Pharmacy intern St. John's Hosp., Steubenville, 1981-83; pharmacist Rite Aide Pharmacy, Steubenville, 1985-86; resident in pharmacy Mercy Hosp., Pitts., 1986—; asst. dir. pharmacy Ruby Meml. Hosp., W.Va. U. Hosp., Morgantown, W.Va., 1987—. Mem. Am. Soc. Hosp. Pharmacists, W.Va. Soc. Hosp. Pharmacists (sec. 1988-90), Am. Pharm. Assn., Rho Chi, Phi Lambda Sigma (pres. 1984-85). Democrat. Presbyterian. Home: 1224 Van Voorhis Rd Unit H7 Morgantown WV 26505 Office: Ruby Meml Hosp WVa U Hosps West Va U Hosps Morgantown WV 26506-8045

MOSZKOWSKI, LENA IGGERS, teacher; b. Hamburg, Mar. 8, 1930; d. Alfred G. and Lizzie (Minden) M.; m. Steven Alexander, Aug. 29, 1952 (div. 1977); children: Benjamin Charles, Richard David, Ronald Bertram. BS, U. Richmond, 1948; MS, U. Chgo., 1953; PhD candidate, UCLA, 1958. Tchr. Lab. asst. U. Chgo. Ben May Cancer Research Lab., Chgo., 1951-53; biology, sci. tchrs. Bishop Conaty High Sch., Los Angeles, 1967-68; chemistry, sci. tchr. St. Paul High Sch., Santa Fe Springs, Calif., 1968-69; chemistry, human ecology tchr. Marlborough Sch., Los Angeles, 1969-71; biology, sci. ecology tchr. Los Angeles Unified Sch. Dist., 1971—. Author: Termite Taxonomy Cryptotermes Haviland and C. Krbyi, Madagscar, 1955, Ecology and Man, Parallels in Human and Biological Ecology, 1977. Founder, adminstr., com. mem. UCLA Student (and Practical Assistance Cooperative Furniture), Los Angeles, 1963-67; active participant UCLA Earth Day Program, Los Angeles, 1970. Recipient Va. Sci. Talent Search Winner Va. Acad. of Sci., 1946; Push Vol. Tchr. award John C. Fremont High Sch., Los Angeles, 1978. Mem. Nat. Assn. of Biology Tchrs., Nat. Sci. Tchrs. Assn., Nat. Edn. Assn., United Tchrs. of Los Angeles, Sierra Club, Sigma Xi. Democrat. Jewish. Home: 2567 S Barrington Ave Los Angeles CA 90064

MOTHERAL, M. SUSAN, management consultant; b. Ft. Worth, July 1, 1952; d. Carl Paxton and Sally (Skelton) M. AB, Grinnell (Iowa) Coll., 1974; PhD, Duke U., 1982; MBA, So. Meth. U., 1990. Lab. coord. Duke U., Durham, N.C., 1974-80; rsch. assoc. Tex. A&M U., College Station, Tex., 1981-82; sales assoc. Donaldson, Lufkin and Jenrette, Dallas, 1983-84; real estate rsch. and mktg. Harvey and Assocs., Ft. Worth, 1985-87; cons. Safety and Productivity, Ft. Worth, 1987-88; pres. Motheral and Assoc., Ft. Worth, 1988—. Contbr. articles to profl. jours. Mem. Leadership, Ft. Worth, 1985-86. Fellow NIH, 1981. Mem. Forum Ft. Worth (bd. dirs. 1986-89), Grinnell Coll. Alumni Assn. (bd. dirs. 1984-90), Ft. Worth Garden Club, Am. Soc. Safety Engrs. (assoc.), Ft. Worth Club, Sigma Xi (assoc.). Republican.

MOTLEY, ANDREA YVETTE, non-commissioned army officer; b. Westchester, N.Y., Feb. 25, 1958; d. Henry Tase Motler Jr. and Lillian Ruth (Keaton) Hampton. Grad. high sch., Mt. Vernon, N.Y. Enlisted U.S. Army, 1977, advanced through grades to staff sgt., 1983; electronics technician 513th Maintenance Co., 3d Armored Cav. Regt., Ft. Bliss, Tex., 1978-79; race rels. equal opportunity liaison 71st Maintenance Bn. VII Army, Fed. Republic Germany, 1979-80; phys. fitness supr. 107 Maintenance Bn., 7th Inf. Div., Ft. Ord, Calif., 1980-81; deep sea diver 86th Engr. Bn., Ft. Belvoir, 1981, 84, 85, U.S. Army Petroleum Distbn. Terminal, Pohang, Republic of Korea, 1983-84; non-commd. officer in charge comdrs. total fitness course Office Asst. Chief Staff, Ft. Hood, Tex., 1985-87; field recruiter U.S. Army Recruiting Command, West Point, N.Y., 1987-88; instr. electronics U.S. Army Electronic Tech. Div., Ft. Gordon, Ga., 1988-89; drill sgt. C Co. 360th Sig Bn. 15th BdE, Ft. Gordon, Ga., 1990—; EEO counselor U.S. Army, 1979-89. Vol. Shilow Community Ctr., Augusta, Ga., 1989. Mem. Signal Corps Regtl. Assn., Armed Forces Communications and Electronics Assn., Nat. Trust for Hist. Preservation, Earthwatch, Smithsonian Assocs., NRA, Profl. Assn. Diving Instrs., Nat. Assn. Diving Schs. Roman Catholic. Home: PO Box 7007 Fort Gordon GA 30905 Office: C Co 360th Sig Bn 15 Sig BdE Fort Gordon GA 30905

MOTOLA, NANCY CARMEN, chemist; b. Hartford, Conn., Apr. 21, 1952; d. Joseph V. and Rose T. (Botto) M. BA in Chemistry, Cen. Conn. State U., 1974; MS in Medicinal Chemistry, U. R.I., 1979, PhD in Pharm. Sci., 1983. Rsch. investigator E.R. Squibb & Sons, Inc., New Brunswick, N.J., 1983-87, tech. supr., 1987-88, sr. regulatory mgr., 1988-89; sr. regulatory adminstr. Abbott Labs., Abbott Park, Ill., 1989—. Troop leader Del-Raritan Valley coun. Girl Scouts U.S., 1988-89. Mem. Am. Chem. Soc., Drug Info. Assn., Regulatory Profl. Affairs Assn., Princeton Ski Club (adminstr. sec. 1989). Democrat. Home: 911 Vose Dr Gurnee IL 60031 Office: Abbott Labs Pharm Products Div Abbott Park IL 60064

MOTT, ALYCE EVELYN, theatrical stage director; b. Adrian, Mich., Sept. 2, 1946; d. Harold R. and Inez Evelyn (Walker) M. BS in Edn., Bowling Green State U., 1968; MA in Edn., U. Mich., 1973, Siena Heights Coll., 1976. Instr. physical edn. and health Adrian (Mich.) Pub. Sch., 1968-74; resident character actress Barn Theatre-AEA Theatre, Augusta, Mich., 1974-78; instr. English and Humanities Adrian (Mich.) Pub. Sch., Adrian, 1976-81; freelance stage actress N.Y.C., 1981-83; resident character actress Mountain Playhouse, Jennerstown, Pa., 1982, 84; resident dir. Lighthouse of Manhattan, N.Y.C., 1988-89, directing mem. Play Market, N.Y.C., 1986—, dir., reader Theatre of Open Eye, N.Y.C. 1987—; judge Daytime Emmies Academy of TV Arts and Scis., N.Y.C. 1989-90. Dir. Amahl and Night Vis. Lincoln Ctr., N.Y.C., 1985-86. Vol. Riverside Ch. Mens Shelter, N.Y.C., 1986-88; mem. Riverside Ch., N.Y.C., 1981—, Adrian Community Chorus, 1970-81, Met. Singers, N.Y.C., 1981—. Mem. Soc. Stage Dirs and Choreographers, Actor's Equity Assn., Screen Actor's Guild, Am. Dirs. Inst. Democrat.

MOTT, KAREN RAE, manager; b. Orchard, Nebr., Nov. 26, 1942; d. Ranold Archie and Margaret (Mader) Wehenkel; m. Dennis Lee Mott, Feb. 21, 1944; children: Nicole Renee, Bryan Ranold. BS, Okla. State U., 1987. Coordinator transfer credit evaluation Okla. State U., 1987. Mem. Okla. Assn. Collegiate Registrars and Admissions Officers. Republican. Lutheran.

MOTT, MARY ELIZABETH, educator; b. West Hartford, Conn., July 10, 1931; d. Marshall Amos and Mary Salome (Herman) M. B.A., Conn. Coll. Women, 1953; M.A., Western Res. U., 1963. Cert. tchr., Ohio; cert. computer tchr., Ohio. Mgr. sales promotion Cleve. Electric Illuminating Co., 1953-60; tchr. Newbury Bd. Edn., Ohio, 1960-67, West Geauga Bd. Edn., Chesterland, Ohio, 1967—; chmn. state certification com. in computers ECCO, Mayfield, Ohio, 1983—, exec. bd., 1980—. Asst. dir. West Geauga Day Camp, Chesterland, 1968. Mem. Ednl. Computer Consortium Ohio, Delta Kappa Gamma. Republican. Clubs: MAC Users Group, NEO Apple Corps, Nat. Assn. Playing Card Collectors. Avocations: golf, travel, reading, gardening, computers. Office: Westwood Sch 13738 Caves Rd Chesterland OH 44026

MOTT, WANDA LAURIE THORNTON, physician; b. San Antonio, Oct. 20, 1952; d. Tull and Evelyn Evangeline (Wilson) Thornton; children: Manning Marshall Mott, III and Malek Mpinduzi Mott. BA, Smith Coll., N. Hampton, 1973; Student, U. Penn. Med. Sch., Phila., 1973-74; MD, Bayor Coll. Medicine, Houston, 1977. Physician Houston Women's OB/GYN Assoc., Houston, 1981--; clin. instr. Baylor Coll. Medicine Houston, 1981--; med. dir. Planneed Parenthood Houston, 1982-87; mem. hosp. com. St. Luke's Episcopal Hosp. Houston, 1981--, Woman's Hosp. Tex. Houston, 1981--. Researcher: Grant Baylor Coll. Med. & Mead Johnson, 1986--. Vol. Resident Jeff Davis Teen Clinic Houston, 1979-81; Consulting & Referring Physician Shape Community Ctr. Houston, 1979--; Pub. Speaker Profl. & Religious Orgns. Houston, 1981--; Sponsor The Ensemble Theatre Houston,S 1983--. Recipient Magna Cum Laude Smith Coll. N. Hampton, 1973, Phi Beta Kappa Smith Coll. N. Hampton, 1973, Women on the Move Houston Post & Tex. Exec. Women Houston, 1988, Outstanding Community Leader Weekend Outlook Channel 11 (CBS) Houston, 1987, Outstanding Community Leader Evening News Channel 13 (ABC) Houston, 1989. Office: Houston Women's Ob-Gyn Assn 7580 Fannin Ste 240 Houston TX 77054

MOTZENBECKER, HELEN KENNY, real esate broker, developer; b. Orange, N.J., June 9, 1929; d. Thomas F. and Mary I. (Gilhooly) Kenny; m. Paul D. Motzenbecker, Feb. 24, 1957; children: Paul D., Douglas E., Susan M., Elizabeth K. BS in Econs., Chestnut Hill Coll., 1950; tchr. cert., Seton Hall U. Lic. real estate broker. Ptnr. The Kenny Press, Newark, 1950-66; broker Degnan Realty, West Orange, N.J., 1966-76; owner, pres., broker Pelmot Realty Corp., Summit, N.J., 1976—. Civil activist Fair Housing Coun., Trenton, 1985-89; vice chmn. Dem. Com., Millburn, 1990. Recipient 1st Builders Remedy award Fair Housing Coun., 1989. Mem. The Racquets Club (trustee, bldg. com. 1978-80, asst. treas. 1988-90). Roman Catholic.

MOTZKIN, EVELYN HERSZKORN, psychiatrist; b. Warsaw, Poland, Jan. 12, 1933; d. Joseph and Eda (Itzkowitz) Herszkorn; m. Donald Motzkin, 1955; children: Patricia, Linda, Neil, Nancy, Richard, Lisa. M.D., SUNY, 1958; Ph.D. in Psychoanalysis, So. Calif. Inst. Psychoanalysis, 1978. Intern Vassar Bros. Hosp., 1958-59; fellow in endocrinology Baylor U., Houston, 1960-62, resident in psychiatry, 1962-64; resident in psychiatry VA Hosp., Sepulveda, Calif., 1965-67; pvt. practice psychiatry and psychoanalysis, Encino, Calif., 1967—; cons. Sepulveda VA Hosp., 1967-68, Jewish Home for Aged, 1968-71; clin. instr. UCLA Neuropsychiat. Inst., 1969-71; instr. So. Calif. Psychoanalytic Inst., 1980—; coord. U. Judaism Extension Div. and So. Calif. Psychoanalytic Inst., 1983; mem. staff Woodview Calabasas Hosp., Med. Ctr. Tarzana, Calif., Encino Hosp., Calif., Rancho Encino Hosp. Initiator, chmn. psychiat. div. San Fernando Valley United Jewish Welfare Fund, 1977, 78; major gifts co-chmn. United Jewish Appeal, San Fernando, 1979; mem. community rels. coun. United Jewish Fedn., 1982-86, bd. dirs. 1986-88; bd. dirs. Assn. Mental Health Affiliation with Israel; pres. Calif. chpt. Women's Pro-Israel Nat. Polit. Action Com., 1986-88; founding pres. Women's Alliance for Israel Polit. Action Com., 1988-89; chmn. psychiat. div. San Fernando Valley United Jewish Welfare Fund, 1988-89. Recipient Ben Gurion award San Fernando Valley State of Israel Bonds Med. Div., 1977. Mem. So. Calif. Psychoanalytic Soc. (exec. com. 1980-81, sec. treas. 1981-83, chmn. membership com. 1983), Am. Psychiat. Assn., So. Calif. Psychiat. Assn., Internat. Psychoanalytic Assn., Am. Psychoanalytic Assn., Israeli Med. Assn., Physicians for Israel. Office: Motzkin Med Corp 5353 Balboa Blvd Encino CA 91316

MOUCHLY-WEISS, HARRIET, business executive; b. N.Y.C., Aug. 12, 1942; d. Robert and Anita (Hearshen) Berg; m. Charles Weiss, Sept. 13, 1975; children; Noa, Yoav. BA, Muhlenberg Coll., 1960; MA in Clin. Psychology, Hebrew U., 1964. Clin. psychologist Hadassah Hosp., Israel, 1962-65; chmn. Ruder Finn & Rotman, Internat. Ptnrs., N.Y.C. and Washington, 1968-86; sr. v.p. Ruder Finn & Rotman, N.Y.C., 1980-86; pres. GCI Internat., N.Y.C., 1986—; bd. dirs., Dialogic, Belgium, GCI Sterling, U.K., Delaitte et Associes, France, Greco, France, GCI Chiappe Bellodi, Italy, GCI Ringpress, Germany, GCI Boetes, Holland, GCI Alonso y Asociados, Mex., GCI Indo-Pr, Indonesia. Bd. dirs. N.Y. State Gov.'s World Trade Coun., Com. for Econ. Growth Israel, U. Haifa, Indo-PR, Indonesia; trustee Internat. Ctr. for Peace in the Mid. East. Recipient cert. of appreciation, HUD. Fellow Am. Survey Inst.; mem. Women in Communications, Women's Forum, Pub. Rels. Soc. Am., Com. of 200 (internat. chair). Office: GCI Internat 777 3rd Ave 23rd Fl New York NY 10017

MOUCHY, DUCHESSE DE, vineyard executive; b. N.Y.C., Jan. 31, 1935; arrived in Luxembourg, 1967; d. Clarence Douglas and Phyllis Chess (Ellsworth) Dillon; m. James Brady Mosely (annuled 1963); 1 child, Joan Dillon Moseley Bryan; m. His Royal Highness Prince Charles of Luxembourg (dec. 1977); children: Princess Charlotte, Prince Robert; m. Philippe de Noailles Duc de Mouchy, Aug. 3, 1978. Diploma, Foxcroft Coll., Middleburg, Va., 1952; student, Vassar, 1952. Asst. Paris editor The Paris Rev., 1958-65; pres. Domaine Clarence Dillon S.A., Paris, 1975—, Infirmes des Moteurs Cérébraux-Kräzbierg, Dudelange, Luxembourg, 1977—; pres. Union Banques Suisses, Luxembourg, 1977-82. Mem. Am.-Luxembourg Soc. (pres. 1967-78). Club: Inner-Wheel (Luxembourg) (pres. 1968-78). Office: Domaine Clarence Dillon SA, Chateau Haut Brion, 26 Rue de la Pepiniere, 75008 Paris France

MOULDING, MARY BAKER, civic worker; b. Peoria, Ill., Aug. 15, 1907; d. Murray Morrison and Mary (Lyman) Baker; m. Arthur Tilt Moulding, Apr. 9, 1932 (dec. 1977); children—Patricia Moulding Hibben, Murray. Student Marot Jr. Coll., Thompson, Conn., 1925-26, Bradley U., 1928. Mem. founders' council Field Mus. Natural History, Chgo.; mem. women's bd. Field Mus.; mem. Winnetka aux. Rush-Presbyn. St. Luke's Hosp., Chgo.; mem. orch. assn. Chgo. Symphony Orch. Antiquarian Soc., Art Inst., Chgo.; mem. governing bd. Art Inst., Chgo. Hort. Soc.; mem. Chgo. Hist. Soc., Ill. State Hist. Soc., Audubon Soc., Hawaiian Mission Children's Soc., Jr. League of Evanston, Bahamas Nat. Trust, Nature Conservancy, Nat. Soc. Colonial Dames of Am. in Ill., Lyman Mission House and Mus. Assn., vestry Ch. of St. Christopher, Lyford Cay, Nassau, Bahamas; Bishop's Assocs., Diocese of Chgo. Author: (with Arthur T. Moulding) Shells at Our Feet, 1967. Dedications: Two species of shells Field Mus. Natural History, Chgo., 1985. Republican. Episcopalian. Clubs: Chgo. Shell, Woman's Athletic, Fortnightly (Chgo.); Winnetka Garden; Nassau Garden (Bahamas); Lyford Cay; Indian Hill. Avocations: conchology; horticulture; conservation; music.

MOULDS, JOANN MARY, immunogeneticist; b. Youngstown, Ohio, June 24, 1949; d. Emil Joseph and Theresa Frances (Gonda) Vukovich; m. Jay Hawkins Edwards, Sept. 5, 1971 (div.); m. John James Moulds, Sept. 10, 1983. BS, Ariz. State U., 1971; MS, U. Houston, 1986; PhD, U. Tex. Health Sci. Ctr., 1989. Med. technologist St. Luke's Hosp., Phoenix, 1971-74, Meml. Hosp., Redding, Calif., 1974-75; blood bank supr. Mt. Diablo Hosp., Concord, Calif., 1976-79; edn. coordinator U. Tex. Med. Br., Galveston, 1979-85; grad. rsch. asst. U. Tex. Health Sci. Ctr., Houston, 1986-89; rsch. assoc. U. Tex. Health Sci. Ctr., 1989-90; rsch. fellow Sch. of Medicine Washington U., St. Louis, 1990—. Co-editor: Scientific and Technical Aspects of the MHL, 1989, Monoclonal Antibodies, 1989; contbr. articles to profl. jours. Am. Assn. Blood Banks grantee, 1988; recipient Transfusion Med. Academic award, Nat. Heart, Lung Blood Inst., 1987, Sci. Excellence award, Sigma Xi, Larry Trow Edn. award, S. Cen. Assn. Blood Banks, 1986. Mem. South Cen. Assn. Blood Banks (bd. dirs. 1986-87), Am. Assn. Blood Banks (adv. bd. 1982-85), Am. Soc. Med. Tech. (sci. sect. rep. 1983-85), AAAS, Assn. for Women in Sci., Internat. Soc. Blood Transfusions, Invitational Conf. of Investigative Immunohematologists, Sigma Xi. Office: Washington U Sch Medicine Box 8045 Saint Louis MO 63110

MOULTON, GRACE CHARBONNET, physics educator; b. New Orleans, Nov. 1, 1923; d. Wilfred J. and Louise A. (Hellmers) Charbonnet; m. William Gates Moulton, June 1, 1947; children: Paul Charbonnet Moulton, Nancy Gates Moulton. BA, Tulane U., 1944; MS, U. Ill., 1948; PhD, U. Ala., 1962. Asst. prof. physics U. Ala., Tuscaloosa, 1962-65; asst. prof. physics Fla. State U., Tallahassee, 1965-74, assoc. prof. physics, 1974-80, prof. physics, 1980—; cons. State Bd. Regents, Fla., 1984-85, Fla. Univ. System, 1989-90. Referee jour. articles Jour. Chem. Physics, Radiation Rsch.; contbr. many sci. rsch. articles to profl. jours. Four Yr. Undergrad. scholar Tulane U., scholar U. Ill.; rsch. grantee NIH. Mem. Am. Phys. Soc., (mem. coun. southeastern sect. 1988—). Office: Fla State U Dept Physics Tallahassee FL 32304

MOULTON, JOY WADE, genealogist, writer; b. Oxnard, Calif., Nov. 30, 1928; d. Merle E. and Elouise (Morgan) Wade; m. Edward Quentin Moulton, Jan. 2, 1954; children: Jennifer Moulton Fairchild, Charles, David Frederick II, Alison Joy. AB, U. Calif., Berkeley, 1950; MS, Wellesley Coll., 1953. Cert. genealogist. Instr. Ohio State U., Columbus, 1954-66, 73-83; spl. writer Columbus Dispatch, 1975—; genealogist Columbus, 1973—. Author: Genealogical Resources in English Repositories, 1988; columnist Find Your Ancestors, Columbus Dispatch, 1975—, Western Res. Family Tree, Western Res. mag., 1977-79. Pres. women's bd. Columbus Mus. Art, 1982-83; mem. Upper Arlington (Ohio) Arts Commn., 1976-81; chmn. Greater Columbus Arts Festival, 1974. Mem. Women in Communications, Nat. League Am. Pen Women, Soc. Genealogists (London), Internat. Soc. Brit. Genealogy and Family History (pres. 1989—, editor newsletter 1986—), Coun. Genealogy Columnists (pres. 1989—), Nat. Geneal. Soc., Ohio Geneal. Soc., Ohio Hist. Soc. (trustee 1976-79), New Eng. Hist. Geneal. Soc. (trustee 1979-81), Assn. Profl. Genealogists (trustee 1985-87). Home: 1303 London Dr Columbus OH 43221

MOULTON, KATHERINE KLAUBER, hotel executive; b. Buffalo, Nov. 28, 1956; d. Murray Joseph and Joanna (Brown) Klauber; m. Michael Arthur Moulton, July, 10, 1982. BS, Cornell U., 1978. Hotel and restaurant designer Cini-Grissom Assoc., Potomac, Md., 1978-82; gen. mgr.

Colony Beach & Tennis Resort, Longboat Key, Fla., 1982—; owner Le Tennique, Longboat Key, 1982—; exec. v.p., cons., designer Total Environments, Longboat Key, 1982—; exec. v.p. The Reserve Devel., Longboat Key, 1985—. Contbr. articles to restaurant and hotel design mags. Mem. Coquille, Sarasota, Fla., 1982—; organizer, fund raiser St. Jude's Children's Research Hosp., 1982—. Mem. Cornell Soc. of Hotelmen. Office: Colony Beach & Tennis Resort 1620 Gulf of Mexico Dr Longboat Key FL 34228

MOULTON, PATRICIA JEAN, nurse; b. Montpelier, Vt., Aug. 21, 1948; d. Harry Barrows and Laura Mae (Allen) M. BSN, U. Vt., 1970; MSN, Seton Hall U., 1979. Staff nurse VNA of Boston, 1970-71, Community Nursing Svc. of Montclair, N.J., 1972-79; nurse practitioner VA Med. Ctr., E. Orange, N.J., 1980-83; adminstr. long term home care div. W. Essex Community Health Svcs., Fairfield, N.J., 1983-87; nursing supr. VNA of Bayonne, N.J., 1987-88; assoc. dir. nursing Vis. Health Svcs. of N.J., Totowa, 1988—. Contbr. articles to profl. jours. Instr., trainer nursing and health svcs. Montclair chpt. ARC, 1985—; mem. Montclair Health & Human Svcs. Com., 1987—. Recipient Samuel Eshborn Svc. award NYU, 1988, Rudin Family Student award NYU, 1988. Mem. N.J. State Nurses Assn. (bd. dirs. dist. 1 1985-89), Am. Nurses Assn., AAUW, Am. Nurses Found., Sigma Theta Tau. Episcopalian. Home: 364 Orange Rd Apt C-2 Montclair NJ 07042 Office: Vis Health Svcs of NJ 783 Riverview Dr PO Box 70 Totowa NJ 07511

MOULTON, SARA JONENE, management consultant; b. Rapid City, S.D., Dec. 11, 1958; d. Harold William and Ora Mae (Hoffman) Moulton. BBA, Colo. State U., 1981; MBA, U. North Colo., 1987. Cert. mgmt. acct. Intern Solar Energy Rsch. Inst., Golden, Colo., 1980; retail acct. Western Grocers, Inc., Denver, 1981-82, acctg. mgr., 1982; office mgr. Trivest Corp., Denver, 1982-83; contract adminstr. Storage Tech. Corp., Louisville, 1984-85, sr. fin. analyst, 1985-86, fin. mgr., 1986-88; mgmt. cons. Deloitte & Touche, Denver, 1988-90; mgmt. cons., mgr. Ernst & Young, Denver, 1990—; presenter in field. Contbr. articles to profl. pubs. Cellist Arapahoe Philharmonic Denver, 1982—, Golden Symphony. Mem. Applewood Investment Club, Beta Gamma Sigma (v.p. 1980-81), Phi Kappa Phi. Republican. Office: Ernst & Young 4300 Republic Pla Denver CO 80202

MOULTON-PATTERSON, LINDA, television executive; b. L.A., June 29, 1943; d. William George and Ethel (Page) Baker; m. Jerry M. Patterson; children: Wendy, Julie. BA, U. Calif., Berkeley, 1965; MPA, Calif. State U., Long Beach, 1982. Cert. tchr., cert. sch. adminstr., Calif. Tchr., asst. prin. Savanna Sch. Dist., Anaheim, Calif., 1966-83; aide Congressman Jerry Patterson, Santa Ana, Calif., 1983-85; v.p. programming and govt. affairs Rogers Cable TV, Garden Grove, Calif., 1985—. Pres. bd. trustees Huntington Beach (Calif.) Union High Sch. Dist., 1983—; bd. dirs. United Way, No On Drugs In Schs., Coalition Concerned with Adolescent Pregnancy, Hunting Beach Youth Shelter; trustee Coastline Regional Occupational Program, v.p., 1983-86. Democrat. Methodist. Office: Rogers Cable TV 7441 Chapman Garden Grove CA 92641

MOUNDS, LEONA MAE REED, teacher; b. Crosby, Tex., Sept. 9, 1945; d. Elton Phillip and Ora Lee (Jones) Reed; m. Aaron B. Mounds Jr., Aug. 21, 1965 (div.); 1 dau., Lisa Nichelle. BS in Elem. Edn., Bridgewater State Coll., 1973; MA in Mental Retardation, U. Alaska, 1980. Cert. tchr. Alaska, Colo., Tex., Mass., cert. adminstrv. prin. Tchr., Sch. Dist.# 11, Colorado Springs, Colo., 1973-75; tchr. Anchorage Sch. Dist., 1976-78, 80—, mem. maths. curriculum com., reading contact tchr., mem. talent bank. Tchr. Del Valle (Tex.) Sch. Dist., 1979-80; adminstrv. prin. intern Anchorage Sch. Dist., 1989—; elem. prin. intern. Bd. dirs. Urban League, 1974; 1st v.p. PTA, Crosby, Tex.; del. Tex. Dem. Conv., 1980; chmn. dist. 13 Dem. Party; mem. Alaska Women Polit. Caucus; bd. dirs. C.R.I.S.I.S. Inc.; tchr. religious edn., lay Eucharist minister St. Martin De Pores Roman Cath. Ch., St. Patrick's Ch.; pres. Black Educators of Pike Peak Region, 1974; mem. NAACP, Coun. for Exception Children. With USAF, 1964-66. Alaska State Tchr. Incentive grantee, 1981, Ivy Lutz scholar, 1972. Mem. NEA (human rels. coord. Alaska chpt., region 6 bd. dirs., bd. dirs Alaska chpt., vice-chmn. women's caucus), LWV, Anchorage Edn. Assn. (minority chmn. 1982—, mem. black caucus polit. action com., v.p. programs 1986-88), Anchorage Edn. Assn. (v.p. programs com. 1986-87, women's caucus), Assn. Supervision and Curriculum Devel., Alaska Women in Adminstrn., Prins. Assn.

MOUNT, KAREN, municipal government official; b. Long Branch, N.J., June 3, 1953; d. John Washington and Josephine Marion (Monahan) M.; m. Frank G. Siciliano, May 31, 1980 (div. Nov. 1985). Grad. high sch., Highlands, N.J. Registered mcpl. clk., N.J. Prin. tax clk., dep. borough clk. Borough of Highlands, 1971-77, borough clk., 1985-87; sec. Perkin-Elmer Corp., Oceanport, N.J., 1977-80, Rudolf, Cinnamon & Calafato, Ocean Township, N.J., 1981-82; exec. sec. Intravest, Inc., Ocean Township, 1983-85; borough clk. Borough of Tinton Falls, N.J., 1987—. Recipient Resolution Honor award State Senate of N.J., 1985. Mem. Mcpl. Clks'. Assn. of N.J., Internat. Inst. of Mcpl. Clks., Mcpl. Clks'. Assn. of Monmouth County. Methodist. Home: Southbrook Dr Bldg 12 Apt 40B Eatontown NJ 07724

MOUNT, WARD (PAULINE WARD), artist; b. Batavia, N.Y., Jan. 8, 1898; d. Fred Kendall and Nellie L. (Dowsey) Ward; m. Elmer Marshall Mount; 1 son, Marshall. Grad., Flushing High Sch.; student, New York Univ., Art Students League; pupil of, Gertrude Gardner, Kenneth Hayes Miller, Albert P. Lucas, Joseph P. Pollia. Former head of dept., oil painting and sculpture N.J. State Tchrs. Coll.; founder, former dir. of art classes at the Jersey City Med. Center, N.J.; dir., instr. Ward Mount Art Classes. Represented by paintings and sculptures in permanent collections pvt. colls., art museums, U.S. and fgn., including, N.A.D., Library of Congress, Nat. Sculpture Soc., Archtl. League N.Y., Allied Artists Am., Allied Arts Mus., N.Y.C., Acad. Allied Arts, N.Y.C., Am. Brit. Art Center, Kearny Mus., Mont Clair Art Mus., Audubon Artists, Pa. Acad., Westchester Art Assn., Mus. Modern Art, N.Y.C., Macy Galleries, Smithsonian Inst., The Carlebach Galleries, N.Y.C., Worlds Fair N.Y., Medallic Art, Lever House, N.Y. Hist. Soc., Columbia U. Library, Marquis Biog. Library, Chgo., Riverside Mus., Nat. Arts Club, Am. Heart Assn., Trenton State Mus., Audubon Artists, Hudson River Mus., Delgado Mus., Jersey City Mus., Provincetown Art Gallery, Bergen County (N.J.) Mus.; Designed: bronze Medal of Honor for, Painters and Sculptors Soc. N.J., 1947; Christmas card for, Am. Heart Assn., 1971. Hon. fellow J.F. Kennedy Found. With U.S. Army, World War I. Recipient numerous awards and prizes for sculpture and painting, including Gold medal Woman of Achievement, Jersey Jour., 1971; Plaque of Honor, Jersey City Mus., 1980, citation Jersey City Hist. Assn., 1987; named Artist of Yr., Hudson Artists, 1984; honoree at Statue of Liberty Gala, 1986. Fellow Royal Soc. of Arts (Eng.), Internat. Inst. Arts and Letters; mem. Painters and Sculptors Soc. N.J., Inc. (founder, hon. pres.), Artists Equity, Internat. Platform Assn., DAR, Women of the Arts Mus. (charter), Acad. of Italy (gold medal mem.), Vets. of World War 1, several other artists and sculptors assns. Republican.

MOUNT, WENDY ELIZABETH, marketing professional; b. Morristown, N.J., July 19, 1954; d. Wadsworth Walter and Doris (Ogden) M. Assoc. in Nursing, Somerset Cnty Coll., 1979; BS, Bloomfield Coll., 1988. RN, N.J. Staff nurse Fair Oaks Hosp., Summit, N.J., 1979-85, nursing care coordinator, 1985-87; retail sales rep. Bell Atlantic Mobile Systems, Basking Ridge, N.J., 1988; mktg. assoc. New Medico Healthcare Systems, Lynn, Mass. Mem. Maine Hist. Soc. (direct descendant of Peleg Wadsworth Sr., gen. in Revolutionary War; Peleg Wadsworth Jr., gen. in War of 1812; and Henry Wadsworth Longfellow). Republican.

MOUNTAIN, EVELYN MARIE, osteopathic physician; b. Brownsville, Pa., Dec. 4, 1917; d. Frank Lloyd Mountain and Katharyn Hensel. Postgrad., Allegheny Gen. Hosp., Pitts., 1938; BS, U. Pitts., 1950; DO, Des Moines Still Coll., 1955. Staff nurse Allegheny Gen. Hosp., 1939-44; head nurse, instr. medicine and urol. nursing Sch. Nursing Perry Twp., Fayette, Pa., 1944-51; intern Community Hosp. Lancaster (Pa.), 1955-56, mem. staff, 1956—; pvt. practice Marietta, Pa., 1956—. Mem. Am. Osteo. Assn., Pa. Osteo. Med. Assn., Lancaster Soc. Osteo. Phys. Surgery. Republican. Home: 274 W Market St Marietta PA 17547 Office: Community Hosp Lancaster 1100 E Orange Lancaster PA 17604

MOUNTZ, LOUISE CARSON SMITH, librarian; b. Fond Du Lac, Wis., Oct. 20, 1911; d. Roy Carson and Charlotte Louise (Scheurs) Smith; m. George Edward Mountz, May 4, 1935 (dec. Oct. 3 1951); children: Peter Carson, Pamela Teeters Mountz McDonald. Student, Western Coll., 1929-31; AB, The Ohio State U., 1933; MA, Ball State U., 1962; postgrad., Manchester Coll., 1954, Ind. U., 1960-61. Cert. tchr., Ind. Tchr. Monroeville (Ind.) High Sch., 1953-54, Riverdale High Sch., St. Joe, Ind., 1954-55; libr. High Sch., Avilla, Ind., 1955-58; head libr. Penn High Sch., Mishawaka, Ind., 1958-67, Northwood Jr. High Sch., Ft. Wayne, Ind., 1967-69, McIntosh Jr. High Sch., Auburn, Ind., 1969-74; dir. Media Ctr. DeKalb Jr. High Sch., Auburn, Ind., 1974-78; ret., 1978; cons. media ctr. planning Penn-Harris-Madison Sch. Corp., Mishawaka, 1966-67. Author: Biographies of Junior High Schools; contbr. articles to profl. jours. Bd. dirs. DeKalb County chpt. ARC, 1938-42, 51-53, DeKalb County Heart Assn., 1946-52, DeKalb County Community Concert Assn., 1946-58, Am. Field Service Mishawaka chpt., 1960-67. Mem. AAUW, ALA, NEA, World Confedn. Orgns. Teaching Professions, Nat. Council Tchrs. English, NEA, Ind. Sch. Librarians Assn. (dir. 1963-67), Internat. Assn. Sch. Librarianship, Ft. Wayne Philharmonic Orch. Assn., Ft. Wayne Art Mus., Ind. Assn. Ednl. Communication and Tech., Assn. Ind. Media Educators, Ind. Tchrs. Assn., Ind. Garrett, DeKalb County, Allen County, Ft. Wayne Hist. Socs., DeKalb County, Ind., Nat. Ret. Tchrs. Assns., Nat. Trust Hist. Preservation, Delta Kappa Gamma (charter mem., v.p. Beta Beta chpt. 1960-62), Kappa Kappa Kappa (st. officer 1941-45, pres. Alpha Chi chpt. 1938-40, Garrett Assoc. chpt. 1971-73), Delta Delta Delta (house pres.), DeKalb Meml. Hosp. Women's Guild (life). Methodist. Lodge: Order Ea. Star. Clubs: Greenhurst Country, Ft. Wayne Women's, Athena Lit. (hon. mem.), Ladies Lit. of Auburn.

MOUSHEY, LOIS ANN, nurse; b. Pensacola, Fla., Oct. 3, 1953; d. Michael Clarence Moushey and Sally Moushey (Keller) Groote; m. John Patrick Ryan, May 8, 1980; children: James Moushey Ryan, Anna Moushey Ryan. BSE, U. Kans., 1975; BSN, 1977, MA, 1983. RN, Kans. Emergency room nurse U. Kans, Kansas City, Kans., 1976-78; instr. nursing Area Vocat. Tech. Sch., Kansas City, 1979-80; health educator Cath. Social Svc., Kansas City, 1981-83; staff RN Nova Home Health, Kansas City, 1984-90, Olsten Home Health, Kansas City, Mo., 1990—, Am. Nursing Resources, Kansas City, Mo., 1983—; nurse researcher U. Kans. Mem. Adv. Bd. Kans. City Tech. Sch., 1981—, Friends Art, Kans. City, Mo., 1975—, Friends Libr., Kans. City, Mo. Mem. Am. Holistic Nurses Assn., Women's Health Network, Sigma Theta Tau. Home: 612 Tenny St Kansas City KS 66101

MOUSSEAU, DORIS NAOMI BARTON, elementary school principal; b. Alpena, Mich., May 6, 1934; d. Merritt Benjamin and Naomi Dora Josephine (Pieper) Barton; m. Bernard Joseph Mousseau, July 31, 1954. AA, Alpena Community Coll., 1954; BS, Wayne State U., 1959; MA, U. Mich., 1961, postgrad., 1972-75. Profl. cert. ednl. adminstr., tchr. Elem. tchr. Clarkston (Mich.) Community Schs., 1954-66; elem. sch. prin. Andersonville Sch., Clarkston, 1966—, Bailey Lake Sch., Clarkston, 1979—. Cons., rsch. com. Youth Assistance Oakland County Ct. Svcs., 1968-88; leader Clarkston PTA, 1967—; chair Clarkston Sch. Dist. campaign, United Way, 1985, 86; mem. allocations com. Oakland County United Way, 1987-88. Recipient Outstanding Svc. award Davisburg Jaycees, Springfield Twp., 1977, Vol. Recognition award Oakland County (Mich.) Cts., 1984. Fellow Assn. Supervision and Curriculum Devel., MACUL (State Assn. Ednl. Computer Users); mem. NEA (del. 1964), Mich. Assn. Elem. and Middle Sch. Prins. (treas., regional del. 1982—, pres.-elect region 7 1988-89, program planner), Mich. Edn. Assn. (pres. 1960-66, del. 1966), Clarkston Edn. Assn. (author, editor 1st directory 1963), Mich. Elem. and Middle Sch. Prins. Assn. (pres. 1989-90, sr. advisor 1990-91), Women's Bowling Assn., Elks, Spring Meadows Golf Club, Phi Delta Kappa, Delta Kappa Gamma (pres. 1972-74, past state and nat. chmn., Woman of Distinction 1982). Republican. Home: 6825 Rattalee Lake Rd Clarkston MI 48016 Office: Clarkston Community Schs Bailey Lake Sch 8051 Pine Knob Rd Clarkston MI 48016

MOUTON, SYLVIA CRAIG, treasurer; b. Yantley, Ala., Nov. 23, 1951; d. Lewis E. and Monzellar (Gordon) Craig; m. Kenneth J. Mouton, June 26, 1976; children: Jarek Ahmad, Justin Craig. BA, So. U., New Orleans, 1972; MBA, U. Southwestern La., 1981. Lic. real estate salesperson, La. Acct. So. Supermarket Svcs., Lafayette, La.; tax. mgr. Stone Petroleum Corp., Lafayette; treas. So. Coop. Devel. Fund Ind., Lafayette; bd. dirs. Lafayette Ctr. Cert. Devel. Corp. Past mem. Mayor's Commn. Needs of Women, Lafayette; mem. regional adv. coun. for vocat. tech. schs. Recipient Teens Softball Coach award. Mem. NAFE, Nat. Assn. Realtors, Acadiana Onyx Women Soc. (past pres.).

MOUZAKES-SILER, HELEN HARRIET (ELENA MOUZAKES-SILER), retired secretary, professional lyric soloist; b. Detroit, Nov. 16, 1929; d. Constantine Demetrius and Alexandra (Poulos) Mouzakes; m. John Floren Siler, Oct. 12, 1980 (dec. Oct. 1988). Student, Detroit Conservatory Music, 1944-47; student, Wayne U., 1950-52, Detroit Bus. Inst., 1948-49. Choir dir., soloist Greek Orthodox Annunciation Cathedral, 1948-52; Exec. sec. Ford Motor Co., Dearborn, Mich., 1949-82; profl. lyric soprano Elena the Singing Sec'y, Livonia, Mich., 1978—. Mem. Founder's Soc. Detroit Inst. Arts, Daus. of Penelope (pres.). Greek Orthodox.

MOUZON, MARGARET WALKER, information services executive; b. Durham, N.C., Aug. 22, 1940; d. James Carlisle and Elizabeth (Walker) M.; m. Wayne T. VanWagoner, 1959 (div. 1971); children: William Thomas VanWagoner, Margaret Michelle Hallgren. BA, U. Mich., 1975, MA in Libr. Sci., 1982. Asst. mgr. Van Ness Book Shoppe, Washington, 1971-73; tchr. Monroe County Sch., Key West, Fla., 1975-79, Grace Luth., Key West, Fla., 1979-80; tchr. math. Ann Arbor (Mich.) Adult Edn., 1984-88; pres. Mouzon Info. Svcs., Ann Arbor, 1983—; editor in chief Am. Disability Evaluation Rsch. Inst., Ann Arbor, 1989—. Author: (bibliography) Child Passenger Restraint System, 1982, Medical Legal Aspects Of DCE's, 1989, Stress and Disability, 1989. Bd. dirs. LWV, mem. Nat. Safety Coun. Mem. Mich. Data Base Users Group, Nat. Safety Coun., Beta Phi Mu, Phi Kappi Phi, Pi Lambda Theta. Home: 2687 Apple Way Ann Arbor MI 48104 Office: Mouzon Info Svcs PO Box 670 Ann Arbor MI 48105

MOWATT, MARY LUCINDA, infosystems specialist; b. Parsons, W.Va., Oct. 4, 1961; d. Deloris Ann (McCrum) Lowther; m. John R. Mowatt III, Dec. 6, 1980; children: John, Christopher. Student, Md. U., 1988—. Computer programmer Md. Dept. Health and Human Svcs., Rockville, 1978-85, clk. typist, 1979-82; computer specialist Md. Dept. Agriculture, Hyattsville, 1985-86, supervisory computer specialist, 1986—. Treas. Mt. Ranier (Md.) Civic Assn., 1986-87; sec. Mt. Ranier Vol. Fire Dept., 1987—. Mem. Nat. Assn. Female Execs., Federally Employed Women, Capital Personal Computer Users Group. Republican. Pentacostal. Home: 3106 Upshur St Mount Ranier MD 20712 Office: Md Dept Agriculture 6505 Belcrest Rd Rm 218 Hyattsville MD 20782

MOY, AUDREY, retail buyer; b. Bronx, N.Y., May 6, 1942; d. Ferdinand Walter Melkert and Stella (Factorow) Schroff; m. Edward Moy, Aug. 16, 1974. B.A. in Biology, Hunter Coll., 1964, M.A. in Biology, 1966. Asst. buyer Bonwit Teller, N.Y.C., 1961-68; dept. mgr. Franklin Simon, N.Y.C., 1968; asst. buyer Saks Fifth Ave., N.Y.C., 1968-73; buyer Martins, Bklyn., 1973, Belk Store Svcs., N.Y.C., 1974—. Mem. NAFE. Avocations: cooking, bird watching, fishing, gardening.

MOY, CARA L., chemical engineer; b. Chgo., Aug. 31, 1964; d. Yin Poy and Mee Lan (Chin) M. BS, Northwestern U., 1987. Coop. engr. USG Corp., Libertyville, Ill., 1984-86; process coord. petrochemicals isomerization process and systems devel. UOP, Riverside, Ill., 1987—; engr.-in-tng. State of Ill. Dept. Registration, Springfield, Ill., 1987—. Asst. leader Girl Scouts U.S., Wilmette, Ill., 1988. Mem. Am. Inst. Chem. Engrs., Soc. Women Engrs., Nat. Assn. Asian-Am. Profls., MENSA, Delta Zeta. Office: UOP 25 E Algonquin Des Plaines IL 60017-5017

MOYA, SARA DREIER, municipal government official; b. N.Y.C., June 9, 1945; d. Stuart Samuel and Hortense (Brill) Dreier; m. P. Robert Moya, May 30, 1966; children: J. Brill, Joshua D. BA, Wheaton Coll., Norton, Mass., 1967; postgrad., Mills Coll., Oakland, Calif., 1967-68. Mem. Paradise Valley (Ariz.) Town Coun., 1986—, vice mayor, 1990—; pres. Ctr. for Acad. Precosity, Ariz. State U., Tempe, 1987—; dir. Valley Leadership, Inc., Phoenix, 1988—; bd. dirs. Data Network for Human Svcs.; participant 3d session Leadership America. Mem. Citizens Adv. Bd. Paradise Valley Police Dept., 1984-86, Valley Citizens League Task Force on Edn.; chair Maricopa Assn. Govts. Task Force on Homeless, 1989—; mem. FEMA bd. MAricopa County, 1989—. Mem. Ariz. Women in Mcpl. Govt. (sec. 1988—, bd. dirs. 1986—, pres. 1989-90), Maricopa Assn. Govts. (regional coun. 1988—), Ariz. Acad., Paradise Valley Country Club. Republican. Home: 5119 E Desert Park Ln Paradise Valley AZ 85253 Office: Town Paradise Valley 6401 E Lincoln Dr Paradise Valley AZ 85253

MOYARS-JOHNSON, MARY A., university administrator; b. Lafayette, Ind., July 19, 1938; d. Edward Raymond and Veronica Marie (Quigg) Moyars; m. Raymond Leon Molter, Aug. 1, 1959 (div. 1970); children: Marilyn Eileen Molter Davis, William Raymond, Ann Marie. BS, Purdue U., West Lafayette, Ind., 1960, postgrad., 1985—. Grader great issues Purdue U., West Lafayette, 1960-63, writer ednl. films, 1962-65, publicity dir. convocations and lectures, 1969-74, devel. officer Sch. Humanities, 1979-88, asst. to dir. Optoelectronics Rsch. Ctr., 1989—; tchr. English and math. Benton Community Schs., Fowler, Ind., 1966-69; pub. rels. dir. Sycamore Girl Scout Coun., Lafayette, Ind., 1974-78; dir. pub. info. Ind. Senate, Majority Caucus, Indpls., 1977-78; sr. script writer Walters & Steinberg, Lafayette, 1988-89. Author: Colonial Potpourri, 1975; co-author: Historic Colonial French Dress, 1982; contbr. articles to profl. jours. Bd. govs. Tippecanoe County Hist. Assn., Lafayette, 1981—. Mem. Women in Communications, Inc. (v.p. program, Pres. award 1983), Ctr. for French Colonial Rsch. (dir. 1986-89, editor 1988-89), Am. Hist. Assn., Germanna Found., Palatines to Am., Ind. History Assn., Ind. Hist. Soc. Roman Catholic. Home: 924 Elm Dr West Lafayette IN 47906 Office: Sch Elec Engring Purdue U West Lafayette IN 47907

MOYER, GERALYN MARIE, nurse; b. Phila., Feb. 6, 1959; d. Francis Aloyuisous and Regina Agnes (Haney) M. BSN, Temple U., 1986; student, Hahnemann U., 1980-83; MSN, U. Pa., 1990. RN, Pa.; lic. advanced med.-surg. nurse, Pa. Chief staff GCC Cinema, Phila., 1975-83; staff and charge nurse Temple Hosp., Phila., 1986-87; staff nurse U. Pa. Hosp., Phila., 1988-89, Presbyn. Hosp., Phila., 1987-89; charge nurse Frankford Hosp., Phila., 1988—; traveling nurse Holy Cross Hosp., Fla., summer 1987; seminar speaker various hospss., Phila., 1987—; cons. Jeannes Hosp., Phila., 1989-90. Contbr. articles to profl. jours. Mem. ANA (com. mem. 1986—), Nat. League Nursing (com. mem. 1986—), Pa. Nurses Assn., Nurses Connection, NAFE, Cath. Youth Orgn. Democrat. Home: 10931 Modena Dr Philadelphia PA 19154 Office: St Agnes Med Ctr 1900 S Broad St Philadelphia PA 19145

MOYER, KERRI SALLS, documentation consultant; b. Framingham, Mass., May 3, 1954; d. Frederick Hedderman and Therese Jane (Healy) S.; m. Alan James Moyer, Feb. 11, 1984; 2 children. BA, Bates Coll., 1976; MBA, Boston U., 1984. Tchr. Peace Corps., Dassa-Zoumé, Benin, West. Africa, 1976-78; tech. aide Mitre Corp., Bedford, Mass., 1979-80; tech. writer Data Gen., Westboro, Mass., 1980-81; sr. tech. writer Atex Inc. (subs. Kodak), Bedford, 1982-83, supr. tech. documentation, 1984, mgr. tech. documentation, 1985, sr. mgr. product mktg., 1986-88; pres. DocTech, Westford, Mass., 1988—. Mem. Natural Resource Council Maine, Augusta, 1976—, Westford Conservation Commn., Mass. 1985—; coordinator Baha'i area Mass. Mem. NAFE, Soc. Tech. Communicators (sr.), Soc. for Documentation Profls., Mgmt. Women's Assn., Freelance Editorial Assn., Boston Computer Soc., Boston U. Alumni Assn. (admissions com.), Phi Sigma Iota (chpt. pres. 1975-76). Office: PO Box 1065 Westford MA 01886

MOYER, LYNNE DENISE, insurance executive; b. San Gabriel, Calif., Aug. 24, 1963; d. James Allen and Barbara Joyce Moyer. BS, U. Calif., Davis, 1985. Property/package underwriter The Hartford Ins. Group, Brea, Calif., 1985-87; comml. prodn. underwriter The Hartford Ins. Group, Diamond Bar, Calif., 1987-88; account exec. Am. Internat. Group Risk Mgmt., L.A., 1988-90, regional underwriting mgr., 1990—. Mem. Soc. Chartered Property & Casualty Underwriters, So. Calif. Underwriters Assn. Republican. Home: 201 Sea View Manhattan Beach CA 90266

MOYER, MARLENE CYNTHIA, finance director; b. Rome, N.Y., Jan. 3, 1949; d. Stanley and Norma Draper Zbiegen; m. Gordon Lee Moyer; children: Joanne Marie, Robert John. AA with honors, Southeastern Community Coll., 1979; BS in Acctg., U. N.C., Wilmington, 1985. Licensed real estate broker, N.C. Libr. aide Jervis Libr., Rome, N.Y., 1965-67; transit clk. First Citizens Bank & Trust Co., Charlotte, N.C., 1967-68; accounts receivable bookkeeper Reeves Telecom Corp., Boiling Spring Lakes, N.C., 1972-73; dep. clk. Brunswick County Register of Deeds, Bolivia, N.C., 1976-79; asst. comptroller Greene & Companies, Wilmington, N.C., 1979-80; office mgr. Miller-Motte Bus. Coll., Wilmington, 1980-83; acctg. technician New Hanover County Fin. Dept., Wilmington, 1983-86; acct., fiscal monitor Care Fear Coun. of Govts., Wilmington, 1986—. Vol. supr. Hospice Festival of Trees, Wilmington, 1985—; vol. United Cerebral Palsy Telethon, Wilmington, 1985—; mem. CAP, New Hanover Commn. For Women, pres. 1989—; bd. dirs. Family Svcs., Wilmington, 1989—. Mem. Am. Bus. Women's Assn. (past pres. Scotch Bonnet chpt. 1986-87, star award 1987, pres. Greater Wilmington chpt. 1989—), Nat. Assn. Accts. Downtown Bus. and Profl. Women's Group, Laney Parent Tchr. Sch. Orgn. Home: 3 Ballard Dr Castle Hayne NC 28429 Office: Cape Fear Coun Govts Ste 2 313 N Front St Wilmington NC 28402

MOYER, SANDRA JEAN, youth organization administrator; b. Allentown, Pa., Oct. 24, 1943; d. Arnold Wesley and Edith Arlene (Swartz) M. AB, Thiel Coll., 1965; MA, Cornell U., 1966. Tchr. math. Easton (Pa.) Area High Sch., 1966-71; camp adminstr., field dir., bookkeeper, registrar Green Meadows coun. Girl Scouts U.S., Champaign, Ill., 1971-77; camp adminstr., pub. rels. dir. Irish Hills coun. Girl Scouts U.S., Jackson, Mich., 1977-80; exec. dir. Treaty Line coun. Girl Scouts U.S., Richmond, Ind., 1980-87; dir. fin. and adminstrn. Girl Scouts of Greater Phila., 1987—. Mem., treas. Altrusa, Richmond, 1981-87; sec. YWCA, Richmond, 1984-87; mem., pres. United Way Agy. Execs., Richmond, 1980-87; treas. Friends Com. on Scouting, 1989-90. Mem. AAUW (treas. Richmond br. 1985-86), Assn. Girl Scout Exec. Staff (membership chair 1981-84), Appalachian Mountain Club. Mem. Soc. of Friends. Home: 219 Rena St Philadelphia PA 19111 Office: Girl Scouts Greater Phila 7 Benjamin Franklin Pkwy Philadelphia PA 19103

MOYLAN, SUSAN NELIS, director; b. Evergreen Pk., Ill., Nov. 23, 1941; d. William M. Jr. and Rosemary (Luken) Nelis; m. William D. Moylan Jr., July 10, 1965; children: Elizabeth, Catherine, Rosemary, Martha. BS, Loyola U., Chgo., 1964. Dir. bus. and industry ctr. Elgin (Ill.) Community Coll., 1979—. Mem. ethics com. St. Joseph Hosp., Elgin, 1988—; mem. exec. com. Dukane Coun., Geneva, Ill., 1983, 89—; mem. com. Nat. League of Cities, Washington, 1988—; councilwoman City of Elgin, 1985—; bd. dirs. St. Edward High Sch. Found., Elgin, 1986—; pres. elect United Way of Elgin, 1982-88, 90—; 1st v.p. Big Bros./Big Sisters, Elgin, 1984—. Named Polit. Leader of the Yr., Assn. for Ind. Devel., 1988. Mem. Elgin C. of C. (chair women's coun. 1984-85), Rotary. Republican. Roman Catholic. Office: Elgin Community Coll 1700 Spartan Dr Elgin IL 60123

MOZER, DORIS ANN, writer; b. July 10, 1929; d. Charles Ross and Mary Margaret (Redmiles) Werner; children from previous marriage: Stephen, Judith, Mary Catherine, Laura, John. BA, N.Mex. State U., 1963, MA in English, 1970; postgrad. in English, U. Md., 1982. Grad. asst. N.Mex. State U., 1963-65, instr., 1969-75; free-lance editor, 1969—; editor Sibyl-Child, women's arts and cultural jour., 1976—; grad. asst. U. Md., College Park, 1976-78, dir. Writing Center, 1978-80, acad. adviser, internship coordinator, 1980-82; tech. writer Environ. Satellite Data, Inc., Suitland, Md., 1982-84, RCA, Moorestown, N.J., 1984-88; communication specialist Scicon, Inc., New Castle, Del., 1988-90; cons. ARCO Chem., Newtown Square, Pa. V.p., publicity chmn. Las Cruces (N.Mex.) Children's Theatre, 1968; pres., publicity chmn. Las Cruces Theater Guild, 1969. Folger Shakespearean Inst. fellow, 1979. Mem. Phi Kappa Phi. Democrat. Roman Catholic. Author: (poetry) The Quickest Promise Home. Home: 219 Chestnut St New Castle DE 19720 Office: Scicon Inc New Castle DE 19720

MOZO, ANN ELIZABETH, respiratory therapist; b. Denville, N.J., Jan. 4, 1958; d. Don C. (stepfather) and Naomi Ruth (Berry) Gottlob. B of Health Scis., U. Mo., 1980; MS in Pub. Health, U. N.C., 1986. Registered respiratory therapist. Respiratory therapist Duke U. Med. Ctr., Durham, N.C., 1980-87; clin. rsch. assoc. Clin. Rsch. Internat., Reseach Triangle Park, N.C., 1987—. Mem. Am. Assn. Respiratory Therapy, 1978-87, Durham Jaycees, 1990. Mem. Assn. Clin. Pharmacology. Methodist. Home: 10 Hearthwood Circle Durham NC 27713

MOZZER, ALANNA, educator; b. Cumberland, Md., Mar. 17, 1752; d. Alexander John and Anna May (Kuczynski) M. BA, U. Hartford, W. Hartford, Conn., 1974; MA, George Wash. U., Wash. D.C., 1978; student, Westfield State Coll., Mass., 1979-82. Cert. Tchr., Mass. Tchr. Valleyhead Sch., Lenox, Mass., 1975-76; edn. specialist Wethersfield Historical Soc., Conn., 1978; tchr. Cape Cod Outdoor Edn. Ctr., Yarmouth, Mass., 1979; counselor, tchr. Eagle Hill Sch., Hardwick, Mass.; resource room aide Hadley Pub. Schs., Mass., 1982; planetarium lectr., tchr. astronomy Springfield (Mass.) Sci. Mus., 1982—; spl. edn. tchr. Easthampton (Mass.) Pub. Schs., 1982—; thcr. Mass. Migrant Edn. Program, Springfield Holyoke Mass., 1983-86; civics tchr. Westfield Summer Sch., Mass. 1988; field reviewer Council for Exceptional Children. Editor: John Proctor and Some of His Descendants, 1985. Mem. Planetary Soc., Westfield Hist. Soc., Springfield Libr. and Mus. Assn., AAUW (sec. Springfield 1988—), Easthampton Edn. Assn., Springfield Stars Club. Roman Catholic. Home: 144 White St Springfield MA 01108 Office: White Brooke Mid Sch Easthampton MA

MROZEK, COLETTE ANN, healthcare recruiter; b. Milw., Feb. 19, 1950; d. Peter F. and Doris (Boucher) Mrozek; m. Richard Glodek, May 27, 1978 (div. 1983); 1 child, Heather Noel. AS, Solano Community Coll., Suisun City, Calif., 1983, student, 1990—; student, U. Calif., Davis, 1990—. Air traffic controller USAF, Hamilton AFB, Calif., 1968-72; sales asst. ITT Worldcomm Inc., San Francisco, 1972-73; command and control specialist USAFR, March AFB, Calif., 1974-76; command and control specialist USAFR, Milw., 1976-77, air frt. specialist, 1977-82; unit on-the-job tng. mgr. USAFR, Travis AFB, Calif., 1982-83; parts clk. NCR Corp., San Francisco, 1982-83; recruiter USAFR, Travis AFB, 1983-87; health professions recruiter USAFR, McClellan AFB, Calif., 1987-89; with Tng. & Field Svc. Legalstaff, Sacramento, 1989-90. With USAFR, 1972-74, 89—. Named Top Nurse Recruiter 1st and 3rd quar. 1989, Top Nurse Recruiter 1988, others. Mem. Nat. Assn. Health Care Recruiters, Bay Area Assn. Health Care Recruiters, Sacramento/Sierra Assn. Health Care Recruiters, Sacramento Womens Network, Bus. and Profl. Women, Polish Legion of Am. Vets., Cath. War Vets., Air Force Sgts. Assn. Democrat. Roman Catholic. Home: 722 Christie Ct Davis CA 95616

MUCCI, CATHERINE LEOLA, film company executive; b. Tillsonburg, Ont., Can., Nov. 21, 1957; came to U.S., 1986; d. Adolf Erhard and Inez Victoria (Brinn) Kunkel; m. Richard Joseph Mucci, Dec. 22, 1984. BA, U. Western Ont., 1984. Paralegal Siskind, Cromarty, London, Ont., 1978-80, Cockburn, Foster, London, 1980-82; dir. creative affairs VM Am.-Westwood Personalities, L.A., 1986-87; pres. On-Core Prodns., Burbank and Rancho Mirage, Calif., 1987—; bd. dirs. Desert Films, Las Vegas, Nev.; owner The Zebra's Mane, Family hair salon, Palm Desert, Calif., 1989—; owner Expeditions Travel, Rancho Mirage, 1990—. Author screenplays. Conservator Ctr. for Reprodn. Endangered Species. Mem. NAFE, Writers Guild Am., World Wildlife Fund, Nature Conservancy, Women's Network, Coachella Valley Club, Leads Club, City Palm Desert Club (conservation com.), PETA. Office: On-Core Prodns 42446 Bob Hope Dr #228 Rancho Mirage CA 92270

MUCH, KATHLEEN, editor; b. Houston, Apr. 30, 1942; d. C. Frederick and Ortrud V. (Lefevre) M.; m. W. Robert Murfin, Aug. 17, 1963 (div. 1981); children—Brian C., Glen M.; m. Paul Stanley Peters Jr., Jan. 1, 1988. B.A., Rice U., 1963, M.A., 1971, postgrad., 1978. Clk., Tex. State Library, Austin, 1963-64; tchr. Kinkaid High Sch., Houston, 1964-66; editorial asst. Rice U., 1969-71, assoc. editor, 1972-81; freelance writer Houston and Palo Alto, Calif., 1971—; dir. info. Meth. Hosp., Houston, 1981-84; sr. editor Addison-Wesley Pub. Co., Menlo Park, Calif., 1984-86; editor Ctr. for Advanced Study in Behavioral Scis., Stanford, Calif., 1986—. dir. Tex. Wordworks, Inc. Active Houston Ballet Guild, Rice U. Fund Council, Friends of Stanford String Quartet, Stanford Music Guild, Bus. Vols. for Arts. Mem. Internat. Assn. Bus. Communicators, Soc. Tech. Communication, Phi Beta Kappa. Editor, contbr. profl. jours. Office: Ctr for Advanced Study 202 Junipero Serra Blvd Stanford CA 94305

MUCHMORE, CAROLIN M., real estate corporation officer; b. Aug. 18, 1944; d. Alfred G. and Mary K. (Lang) Columbo; m. Robert W. Muchmore, Mar. 17, 1962; children: Kim A. Wimmer, Dana A., Robert Jr. Cert. real estate broker. Mgr. guest rels. Great Adventure, Jackson, N.J., 1974-79; sales rep. Mut. of Omaha, Ins., Freehold, N.J., 1980-81; sales assoc. Sterling Thompson Realtors, Howell, N.J., 1979-82, Weichert Realtors, Manalapan, N.J., 1982-84; br. mgr. Weichert Realtors, Howell, 1984—; hosting dir. Sister Cities, Howell, 1988—; instr. Cuyahoga Anti-Discrimination, Aberdeen, N.J. 1989, Weichert-Orientation Sch., Aberdeen, 1984—. Com. Muscular Dystrophy, Ocean Twp., 1979-85, Spl. Olympics, Monmouth County, 1983-86; chmn. Toys for Tots, Monmouth and Ocean County, 1988-89. Recipient N.J. State Million Dollar Club, N.J. Assn. Realtors, 1981-88, N.J. State Pres. Club, 1985-86. Mem. Grad. Realtors Inst., Womens Council Realtors (pub. rels. officer), Howell C. of C., Jackson C. of C., BPOE (hon. mem.), Real Estate Brokerage Coun., Nat. Assn. Real Estate Appraisers, Nat. Assn. Real Estate Owned Brokers. Home: 2 Cuomo Ct Millstone NJ 07726

MUCHOWSKI, PATRICE MAUREEN, psychologist; b. Boston, June 17, 1951; d. William Stanley and Maureen V. (Harrold) M. BA, Newton Coll. Sacred Heart, 1973; MS, Boston U., 1974, ScD, 1980. Cert. alcohol counselor. Exec. dir. Alcoholism Counselor Ctr., Taunton, Mass., 1974-77; staff psychologist Mt. Pleasant Hosp., Lynn, Mass., 1977-81; dir. psychol. svc. Doctors Hosp., Worcester, Mass., 1982-85, treatment dir., 1986-88; v.p. clin. svcs. AdCare Hosp., Worcester, 1988—. Contbr. articles to profl. jours. Fellow Am. Coll. Addiction Treatment Adminstrn. (v.p.); mem. Alcohol and Drug Problems Assn. (bd. dirs.), Nat. Com. on Cert. of Alcohol Adminstrn. (sec.), Worcester C. of C. Office: AdCare Hosp 107 Lincoln St Worcester MA 01605

MUDD, ANNE CHESTNEY, mathematics educator, real estate agent; b. Macon, Ga., June 30, 1944; d. Bard Sherman Chestney and Betty (Bartow) Houston; m. Charles Lee Mudd, Dec. 28, 1963; children: Charles Jr., Richard, Robert Jason. BA, U. Louisville, 1966, MA, 1976. Math statistican U.S. Bur. Census, Jeffersonville, Ind., 1966-70; instr. math. U. Louisville, 1975-77, Coll. DuPage, Glen Ellyn, Ill., 1978-85; tchr. math., substitute tchr. Lyons Twp. High Sch., La Grange, Ill., 1986—; realtor First United Realtors, Western Springs, Ill., 1989—; math tutor Louisville 1969-77, Western Springs, Ill. 1977—. Mem. steering com. Village Western Springs, 1986-87. Mem. Children's Theater Western Springs (bd. dirs. 1987—), LWV (pres. 1983-85, bd. dirs. 1981-86), Lyons Twp. High Sch. Com. Student Discipline, Western Springs Hist. Soc., Nat. Council Tchrs. Math., Nat. Platform Assn., Nat. Assn. Realtors, (LaGrange Bd. Realtors, DuPage Bd. Realtors. Club: Met. Math. of Chgo. Home: 3958 Hampton Ave Western Springs IL 60558

MUDD, SUSAN ELIZABETH, publishing executive; b. Balt., Md., Dec. 30, 1955; d. John Edward and Alice Maureen (O'Toole) M. AA, Essex Community Coll., 1976; BA, Mt. Saint Mary's Coll., 1978. Traffic coordinator Sta. WBAL, WIYY, Balt., 1970-83; copy writer Top Club Line, Balt., 1983-86; freelance copywriter Words At Work, Balt., 1983-86; columnist Md. Musician, Lineboro, Md.; ptnr. Md. Musician Mag., Balt., 1986-87; owner Md. Musician Mag. Inc., 1987-. Contbr. articles to profl. jours. Home: 517 W Joppa Rd Towson MD 21204 Office: Md Musician Mag Inc 7510 Horford Rd Baltimore MD 21234

MUDGET, VICKY ELAINE, controller; b. Fremont, Mich., Oct. 21, 1955; d. Jerry Alan and Susanne Barbara (Kowatch) Mudget; m. Daniel George Sovinski, Aug. 11, 1979 (div. 1984); children: Jason Daniel, Sally Susanne. BBA, We. Mich. U., 1977. Assoc. acct. Internat. Paper Co., Clinton, Iowa, 1978-80; asst. controller Internat. Paper Co., Cin., 1980-82; controller Gilliland Transfer Co., Fremont, Mich., 1983-87; — Guardsman Products, Inc., —, 1987—. Bus. ldr. Jr. Achievement, Clinton, 1979-80; com. chmn. C. of C. of Fremont, 1987-88.

MUEHLBAUER, RENICE ANN, public relations consultant, writer; b. Milw., Jan. 2, 1947; d. Fredrick and Lucia (Stewart) Fregin; m. Thomas George Muehlbauer, July 5, 1968; children: Jennifer Jean, Whitney Susan. BA, U. San Diego, 1988, postgrad., 1989—. Pres. Chubby Bumpkins, Inc., Houston, 1980-82; contracts adminstr. Gulf States Computer Svcs., Houston, 1980-82; pres. RAM Prodns., Houston, 1981-82, Pizza Internat., Inc., Houston, 1982-84; contracts adminstr. First Alliance Corp., Houston, 1982-85; freelance pub. rels. cons. San Diego, 1985—. Tutor U. San Diego Writing Ctr., 1987-89; founder, dir. pub. rels.-tng. Montgomery County (Tex.) Crisis Action Line, Houston, 1979-84; founder, v.p., bd. dirs. Montgomery County Rape Crisis Coalition, 1982-84, speaker, 1982-84; speaker Rape Trauma Coalition, 1982-84; mem. prodn. com. Community Women Together, Montgomery County, 1980-82; pres. Living Arts Coun., Houston, 1980-81. Named Woman of Yr. YWCA, 1981, 82. Mem. Am. Assn. Bus. Women (dir. activities Houston chpt. 1983-84), Bus. Women's Forum (bd. dir. community awareness Houston chpt. 1982-83), Assn. Women Bus. Owners, Lions (hon.), Phi Alpha Delta.

MUEHRCKE, JULIANA OBRIGHT (JILL MUEHRCKE), publisher, editor; b. Aurora, Ill., Sept. 3, 1945; d. Russell B. and Constance (Rennels) Obright; m. John Evans, Sept. 24, 1965 (div. 1968); 1 child, Andrea Marit; m. Phillip C. Muehrcke, July 22, 1969. Student, U. Colo., 1963-67; BA, U. Wash., 1971. Author textbooks Prentice Hall Textbooks, Englewood Cliffs, N.J., 1967-80, Macmillan Co., N.Y.C., 1973-74, Denoyer-Geppert, Chgo., 1980-82, Harcourt Brace, N.Y.C., 1981-82, Scott Foresman, Glenview, Ill., 1982-83; owner JP Publs., Madison, Wis., 1978—; mng. editor Sunshine Newspaper, Madison, 1981-83, Nonprofit World Jour., Madison, 1983—. Mem. Friends of the Madison Pub. Libr., 1987—, Madison Literacy Coun., 1988—. Mem. Women in Communications Inc. (v.p., membership chair 1987—), Am. Assn. Suicidology (bd. sec. Wis. chpt. 1988—), Alliance for the Mentally Ill, Dane County Mental Health, Univ. League (events chair 1972—). Office: Soc for Nonprofit Orgns 6314 Odana Rd Ste 1 Madison WI 53719

MUELLER, ANNE, legislator; b. Atlanta, Oct. 5, 1929; d. Howard Raymond O'Quin and Bessie Kate (Bell) Brace; m. Hans Kurt Mueller; children: Yvonne Marie Key, Heidi Spivey, Mark Jennings. BS in Zoology, U. Ga., 1951. Registered med. technologist. Med. technologist Grady Hosp., Atlanta, 1953—, St. Joseph Hosp., Atlanta, 1957, Meml. Hosp., Waycross, Ga., 1958-59; legislator Ga. Ho. of Reps., 1983—. Mem. Savannah (Ga.) area Rep. Women, sec., 1980-81, v.p., 1981-82, Ga. Fedn. of Rep. Women, Savannah, dist. dir., 1986—. Republican. Baptist. Home: 13013 Hermitage Rd Savannah GA 31419 Office: #404 LOB 18 Capitol Sq Atlanta GA 30334

MUELLER, BARBARA RUTH, journalist; b. Milw., Sept. 10, 1925; d. Edward Philip and Winifred Rose (Moffott) Mueller. Student, U. Wis., 1943-46, U. Minn., 1956. Freelance writer Jefferson, Wis., 1956—; freelance editor Jefferson, 1961—. Editor: Anthology - American Philatelic Congress Book, 1960-61, 86—; editor Essay Proof Jour., 1963—, U.S. Specialist, 1972-78, Paper Money, 1963-84; author: Common Sense Philately, 1956, United States Postage Stamps, 1958, Postage Stamps and Christianity, 1964; contbr. entries to encys. including Colliers, Funk and Wagnalls. Recipient Lichtenstein medal, Collectors Club of N.Y., 1981, Luff award, Am. Philatelic Soc., 1956, Writers Unit Hall of Fame, 1978, McCoy and Fawcett awards, 1955, 87, Cryer award Am. Philatelic Rsch. Libr. Am. Philatelic Soc. Fellow Royal Philatelic Soc. London; mem. Am. Philatelic Soc., Am. Numismatic Soc., Philatelic Found. Republican. Lutheran.

MUELLER, BETTY JEANNE, social work educator; b. Wichita, Kans., July 7, 1925; d. Bert C. and Clara A. (Pelton) Judkins; children—Michael J., Madelynn J. M.S.S.W., U. Wis., Madison, 1964, Ph.D. (E.B. Fred fellow, Nat. Inst. Child Health and Human Devel. fellow), 1969. Asst. prof. U. Wis., Madison, 1969-71; vis. asso. prof. Bryn Mawr (Pa.) Coll., 1971-72; asso. prof., dir. social work Cornell U., Ithaca, N.Y., 1972-78, prof. human services studies, 1978—; nat. cons. Head Start, Follow Through, Appalachian Regional Commn., N.Y. State Office Planning Services, N.Y. State Dept. Social Services, N.Y. State Div. Mental Hygiene, Nat. Congress PTA, ILO. Author: (with H. Morgan) Social Services in Early Education, 1974, (with R. Reinoehl) Computers in Human Service Education, 1989; contbr. articles to profl. jours. Grantee HEW, 1974-76, 79-80, State of N.Y., 1975—, Israeli Jewish Agy., 1985-87, Israeli Nat. Council for Research, 1986-87; Fulbright Research award, 1990—. Mem. Am. Sociol. Assn., Internat. Conf. Social Welfare, Nat. Assn. Social Workers, Council Social Work Edn., Chi Omega. Democrat. Unitarian. Home: 11 Forest Ln Ithaca NY 14850 Office: Cornell U Human Services Studies N139MVR Hall Ithaca NY 14853

MUELLER, MARGARET REID, social worker; b. Cleve., Aug. 20, 1929; d. James Sims and Felice (Crowl) Reid; B.A., Smith Coll., 1951; M.A., Case Western Res. U., 1969, M.S.W., 1973; m. Werner D. Mueller, Sept. 6, 1952; children—Fred, John, Lydia, Felice, Omar. Social worker Cleve. Soc. for the Blind, 1969-71; social worker Childrens Services, Cleve., 1973-75; social worker Cuyahoga County Juvenile Ct., Cleve., 1975-86, supr. probation dept., 1975-86. Candidate for U.S. Ho. of Reps. Editor newsletter SPEAKOUT, 1989—. Mem. Acad. Certified Social Workers, Nat. Assn. Social Workers. Republican. Presbyterian. Clubs: Kirtland Country, Womenspace, Jr. League. Home: 8848 Music St Novelty OH 44072

MUELLER, MARILYN JEAN, insurance company executive; b. Shawano, Wis., Mar. 19, 1946; d. Raymond Walter and Kathryn Ruth (Arveson) M. BA in English, U. Wis., Oshkosh, 1968, BA in Spanish, 1968. CLU; chartered fin. cons. Group rep. Wash. Nat. Ins. Co., Columbus, Ohio, 1968-73, asst. mgr., 1973-79; asst. mgr. Wash. Nat. Ins. Co., Phila., 1979-82, group mgr., 1982—; regional rep. Field Mgmt. Coun., Evanston, Ill., 1982-83, sec., 1988. Tutor Literacy Vols. of Am., Voorhees, N.J., 1986—. Mem. CLU/Chartered Fin. Cons. South Jersey. Repubican. Lutheran. Office: Wash Nat Ins Co One Greentree Centre Ste 313 Marlton NJ 08053

MUELLER, MARY KATHRYN, counselor; b. Cedar Rapids, Iowa, Feb. 11, 1961; d. Edsel and Maren (Strand) Grams; m. Kenneth Robert Mueller, Nov. 5, 1988; 1 child, Berit Andrah. BA in Psychology, U. Wis., 1984; postgrad., U. Minn., 1988—. Counselor St. Joseph's Home for Children, Mpls., 1987-88, Booth Brown House, St. Paul, 1988. Vol. Big Bros./Big Sisters, Mpls., 1987—; election judge voter registration drive City of Mpls., 1988—. With USAF, 1984-87. Named one of Outstanding Young Women in Am., 1982. Mem. NOW, Minn. Chem. Dependency Assn., Am. Assn. for Counseling and Devel., Assn. for Humanistic Edn. and Devel., Alpha Xi Delta Alumni Assn. Home: 5101 14th Ave S Minneapolis MN 55417

MUELLER, NANCY SCHNEIDER, biology educator; b. Wooster, Ohio, Mar. 8, 1933; d. Gilbert Daniel and Winifred (Porter) Schneider; m. Helmut Charles Mueller, Jan. 27, 1959; 1 child, Karl Gilbert. AB in Biology, Coll. of Wooster, 1955; MS in Zoology, U. Wis., 1957, PhD in Zoology, 1962. Instr. zoology U. Wis., Madison, 1966; asst. prof. poultry sci. and zoology N.C. State U., Raleigh, 1968-71; vis. prof. biology N.C. Cen. U., Durham, 1971-73, assoc. prof., 1973-79, prof., 1979—; vis. scientist Universitat Wien, Vienna, Austria, 1975. Contbr. articles, abstracts to profl. publs. Mem. Am. Soc. Zoologists, Am. Ornithologists Union, Cooper Ornithol. Soc., Wilson Ornithol. Soc., Wis. Acad. Sci., Arts and Letters, N.C. Acad. Sci., LWV (bd. dirs. 1988—, natural resources com. 1988—), Sigma Xi. Home: 409 Moonridge Rd Chapel Hill NC 27516 Office: NC Cen U Dept Biology Durham NC 27707

MUELLER, PEGGY JEAN, dance educator, choreographer, rancher; b. Austin, Tex., June 14, 1952; d. Rudolph George Jr. and Margaret Jean (Locke) M.; m. John Yerby Tarlton, June 24, 1972 (div. June 1983). BS in Home Econs., Child Devel., U. Tex., 1974. Dance tchr. Shirley McPhail Sch. Dance, Austin, 1972-75; dance tchr. Jean Tarlton Sch. Dance, Alpine, Tex., 1975-77, College Station, Tex., 1977-80; dance tchr. Sul Ross State U., Alpine, 1975-77, Tex. A&M U., College Station, 1977-80, A&M Consol. Community Edn., Coll. Station, 1977-78, Jean Mueller Sch. Dance, Austin, 1980—, U. Tex., Austin, 1980—; dancer, contest judge Great Tex. Dance-Off, Austin, 1985-86; equestrian com. mem. Austin-Travis County Livestock Show and Rodeo, 1980—, trail ride chmn., 1986—; trail boss, pres. Austin Founders Trail Ride, 1986—; choreographer, head cheerleader Austin Texans Pro Football Team, 1981. Dancer Oklahoma, Austin, 1969, Kiss Me Kate, Austin, 1970; choreographer, lead role Cabaret, Alpine, 1976. Active Women's Symphony League Austin, 1972—, Settlement Club, Austin, 1987—; mem., recreation chmn. St. Martin's Evang. Luth. Ch., Austin, 1972—. Recipient Outstanding Trail Rider of Yr. award Wild Horse Trail Ride, Okla., 1984; named Tex. First Lady Trail Boss, Gov. Mark White, Mayor Frank Cooksey, Austin City Coun., 1986, Judge Bill Aleshire, Travis County Commrs., 1989, Outstanding Intramural Sports Team Mgr.-Player, Tex. A&M U., 1979. Mem. Tex Assn. Tchrs. of Dancing, Inc., U.S. Twirling and Gymnastics Assn., Univ. Tex. Ex-Students Assn., Tex. Execs. in Home Econs., Am. Vet. Med. Assn. Aux. (v.p. 1978-79, pres. 1979-80), Am. Horse Shows Assn., Internat. Arabian Horse Assn., Austin Women's Tennis Assn. (v.p. 1985-86, pres. 1986-90, spl. events chmn. 1990—), Houston Salt Grass Trail Ride Assn., San Antonio Alamo Trail Ride Assn., Ft. Worth Chisholm Trail Ride Assn., U. Tex. Longhorn Alumni Band, Austin C. of C., Am. Bus. Women's Assn., Zeta Tau Alpha (alumnae photographer, social advisor, 1982-87, treas. 1987-89, publicity chmn. 1989 Easter Seals fundraiser), Austin Alumnae Panhellenic Assn. (1st v.p. 1989-90, fush forum chmn. 1990, pres. 1990—), Omicron Nu (v.p. 1973-74), Jr. Austin Woman's Club (historian 1990—), Austin Country Club, Zeta Tau Alpha (alumnae photographer, social advisor 1982-87, treas. 1987-89, publicity chmn. 1989, Easter Seals fundraiser). Republican. Clubs: Cen. Tex. Arabian Horse, Capitol Area Quarter Horse Assn., Jr. Austin Woman's, Austin Country. Home: 1506 Hardouin Ave Austin TX 78703 Office: Jean Mueller Sch Dance PO Box 14762 Austin TX 78761

MUELLER, SANDRA RENEE, perfume company official; b. St. Louis, June 12, 1962; d. Francis Edward and Karen Marie (Klein) M. BA magna cum laude, St. Louis U., 1984; M Internat. Bus., U. S.C., 1986. Jr. cons., intern F.M.S., Inc., Paris, 1985-86; prodn. and import mgr. Georges Gotlib, Inc., N.Y.C., 1986-88; promotional purchasing agt. Parfums Stern, Inc., N.Y.C., 1988, mgr. prodn. planning and inventory control, 1988—. Democrat. Roman Catholic. Home: 1352 1st Ave Apt 3B New York NY 10021 Office: Parfums Stern Inc 9 West 57th St 34th Flr New York NY 10019

MUELLER, SHANNON MARIE, infosystems specialist; b. Aberdeen, Wash., Apr. 26, 1963; d. Edward Maurice and Janice Dee (Lilly Bridge) Knodle; m. Gary Edward Mueller, Aug. 13, 1983; children: Christopher Jordon, Kaly Alyse. AA in Gen. Bus. and Computer Sci., Belleville (Wash.) Community Coll., 1986; cert. fire sci. studies, North Seattle Community Coll., 1982; student, Roosevelt U., 1989—. Cert. EMT, Wash. Staffing coord. Virginia Mason Hosp., Seattle, 1983-87; systems specialist Bob Hope Heart Inst., Seattle, 1985-87, Am. Hardware Mfg. Assn., Schaumburg, Ill., 1987—; coord. patient classification, nursing utilization Va. Mason Hosp., Seattle, 1984-87. Recipient scholarship Wash. State Fire Chiefs and Firefighters Assn., 1981. Mem. NAFE, Digital Equipment Corp. Users Soc. Office: Am Hardware Mfg Assn 931 N Plum Grove Rd Schaumburg IL 60175-4796

MUENSTER, KAREN, state legislator; m. Ted Muenster, 1965; children: Ted, Mary, Thomas. Student, Sacred Heart Women's Coll., Wichita, Kans., U. Nebr. Councilperson City of Vermillion, S.D., 1975-77; mem. S.D. State Senate, 1985—; mem. Dem. Forum, Nat. Dem. Policy Commn. Mem. LWV, Questers, Nat. Dem. Women's Club (elected minority whip senate 1988, exec. bd. 1986), Alpha Xi Delta. Office: 117 N Duluth Ave Sioux Falls SD 57104*

MUENSTERMAN, VIVIAN DARLENE, dental instructor; b. Glendale, Calif., Dec. 29, 1942; d. Wilton D. and Beatrice (Earl); m. John Paul, Mar. 26, 1982. Postgrad., UCLA, 1978; student, Calif. State U., 1978, Calif. State U., 1989. Registered Dental Asst. Dental asst. Dr. J.W. Symonds Jr., Upland, Calif., 1968-76, Dr. Robert Lawson, Upland, Calif., 1961-64, Riverside Regional Occupational Program, 1974-83; coordinator Region II State Dept. of Edn., San Bernardino, Calif.; coord. Registered Dental Assocs. Program, Claremont, Calif., 1982-89; affiliate faculty Am. Heart Assn., Riverside, 1975—; coord. Calif. Indsl. Tech. Edn., Calif., 1982-89; tchr. Calif. U. Consortium, 1982-87. Author: Dental Assisting, 1989, State Dental Assisting Curriculum Frameworks State Dept. of Edn. Past pres. Calif. Assn. Health Careers; coord. Riverside Community Dental Health Program, Riverside, 1978-82. Recipient Nat. Edn. award U.S. Office of Edn., Riverside, 1982, Distinctive Service award State Dept. of Edn., Sacramento, 1987, Nominated Twice for Tchr. of the Year, 1985-86. Mem. Cousteau Soc., Sierra Club, Calif Assn. of Health Careers Educators, Vocat. Indsl. Clubs of Am., Calif Indsl. Tech. Consortium Coord., Am. Dental Assts. Assn., Wrightwood Art Assn., Am. Vocat. Assn. Democrat. Home: 5858 Monte Vista Unit 33 West Cajon Valley CA 92371 Office: Baldyview Regional Occupati 8880 Benson Montclair CA 91763

MUETH, JANE ELLEN, educator; b. Bellville, Ill., Feb. 19, 1946; d. Charles John and Marjorie Jane (Hempen) M. BA, So. Ill. U., Edwardsville, 1969, MA, 1976. Cert. secondary tchr. in speech and theater. Tchr. speech, drama, film Dist. 201 West Pub. Schs., Belleville, 1970—; facilitator Transformational Fantasy, Belleville, 1987—. Reader for blind Our Lady of Snows Ch., Belleville, 1980-84; founder Comet Prodns., Belleville, 1982, sec.-treas., 1982-84. Mem. Internat. Listening Assn., Nat. Coun. on Self Esteem, Internat. Platform Assn., Assn. for Supervision and Curriculum Devel. Home: 8 Dale Allen Dr Belleville IL 62223 Office: Dist 201 BTHS West 2600 W Main St Belleville IL 62223

MUFFOLETTO, MARY LU, school program coordinator, consultant; b. Chgo., May 25, 1932; d. Anthony Joseph and Lucile (Di Giacomo) M. B in Philosophy, DePaul U., 1959; ME, U. Ill., 1967. Tchr. secondary edn. Community Cons., Palatine, Ill., 1959-65; tchr. gifted children Sch. Dist. 15, Palatine, 1965-67, curriculum supr., 1967-75, dir. gifed edn. program, 1972—, coord. state and fed. programs, 1975—; assoc. prof. Nat. Coll. Edn., Evanston, Ill., 1979—; chairperson State Bd. of Edn. Adv. Com. on Gifted Edn., Springfield, Ill., 1977-85. Mem. Nat. Coun. for Social Studies, Assn. for Curriculum and Supervision, U. Ill. Alumni Assn. (pres. Champaign chpt. 1982-85), Phi Delta Kappa (sec. 1985-87). Home: 21302 Brandon Rd Kildeer IL 60047 Office: Community Cons Sch Dist 15 505 S Quentin Rd Palatine IL 60067

MUGGIA, JUDITH PALMER, selectman; b. Boston, Jan. 2, 1938; d. Robert Sterling and Edith (Morse) Palmer; m. Albert L. Muggia, Oct. 10, 1959; children: Robert A., William A., Frank C. RN, Mass. Gen. Hosp., Boston, 1959. Obstet. nurse Hartford (Conn.) Hosp., 1959-60, Grace-New Haven (Conn.) Hosp., 1960-62, Winchester (Mass.) Hosp., 1962-64, St. Mary's Hosp., Gallup, N.Mex., 1968-70; clin. supr. Planned Parenthood Clinics, Albuquerque, 1970-72; selectman Winchester, 1985—, chmn. selectmen, 1987-88; care worker Hospice, Winchester-Arlington, Mass., 1983-85. Mem. Winchester Town Meeting, 1979—, mem. fin. com., 1981-83. Recipient Svc. Recognition awards Mystic Valley Mental Health Assn., Arlington, Mass., 1970-78. Mem. Women Elected Mcpl. Officers, Womens Statewide Legis. Network, Mass. Selectmen's Assn., Middlesex County Selectmens Assn. (pres. 1988—), LWV (state budget rev. com. 1980, pres. Winchester chpt. 1983-85), Winchester C. of C. (founding dir. 1981, 83-85, Svc. Recognition award 1980). Quaker. Home: 14 Dartmouth St Winchester MA 01890

MUGGLI, CLARA BARBARA, civic worker; b. Hebron, N.D., Nov. 10, 1927; d. Matt and Mary (Schneider) Maershbecker; student Dickinson State Coll.; m. Ewald Muggli, Sept. 27, 1948; children: Allen, Linda, Joyce, Carol, Gary, Holly. Tchr. rural schs., 1945-48; county chmn. establishment Bookmobile, 1960, bd. dirs., 1960—; bd. dirs., librarian Glen Ullin (N.D.) Public Library, 1956—; social services home health aide, 1972-76; co-owner, mgr. Rock Mus., Glen Ullin, 1970—, also instr. rocks and minerals, 1970—; sec. Glen Ullin Hist. Soc., 1978—; tchr. Sacred Heart Ch., 1969-89, dir. religious edn., 1982-89; weekly columnist Glen Ullin Times, 1977-84. Recipient State Homemakers award for Cultural Arts, 1975; K. C. Religious Edn. award, 1979-89; Best of Show award Dakota Gem and Mineral Show, 1979, 84, Women Centennial award N.D. Commn. on Status of Women, 1989. Mem.

Morton County Hist. Soc. (centennial com. 1989), Central Dakota Gem and Mineral Assn., Badlands and Knife River Rock Clubs, Art Assn., Am. Legion Aux. Club: Homemakers. Co-author: Glen Ullin Yesteryears, 1983, A Century of Catholicism, 1984. Home: 701 Oak Ave E Glen Ullin ND 58631 Office: Sacred Heart Ch Glen Ullin ND 58631

MUHAMMAD, ALBERTA, nurse; b. Norristown, Pa., Apr. 20, 1937; m. Jace and Mattie Anna (Culbreath) Henley; m. Ellsworth Hadley, Sept. 3, 1962 (div. Oct. 1965). Diploma in nursing, Temple U., Phila., 1960; BS in Nursing, Moravian Coll., Bethlehem, Pa., 1961. Cert. mental health and psychiat. nurse. Psychiat. head nurse Norristown State Hosp., 1960-63, 78-87, Commonwealth of Pa., Phila. and Embreeville, 1963-67; pvt. duty nurse to Hon. Elijah Muhammad, leader of Nation of Islam Chgo., 1967-75; staff nurse Chgo. Osteo. Med. Ctr., 1975-78; nursing instr. Nation of Islam, 1970-78; psychiatric nurse instr. Norristown State Hosp. and Embreeville State Hosp., 1961-62, 65-67. Mem. Pa. Nurses Assn., Prog. Women's League, Inc. (pres. 1986-87). Democrat. Muslim. Home: 21 E Freedley St Norristown PA 19401

MUHAMMAD, FAREEDA SAAHIR, business owner; b. Mobile, Ala., Dec. 27, 1936; d. Peter Nelson and Helen Elizabeth (Wilson) Foster; m. Na'eem I. Muhammad, Sept. 13, 1980; children: Doris, Bekkah, Madinah, Mustaafa. Student, Portland Community Coll., Portland, Oreg., 1955. Lic. tax. cons., ins. profl. Dir. Ednl. Testing Svc., Portland, Oreg.; dir. Muhammad's Mosque 2, Chgo., 1973-77; owner Ameen Exec. Svcs., Portland, 1977—. Editor: Nature's Little Fables, 1983. Exec. com. United Way Oreg., Portland, 1988; bd. dirs. N.E. Community Devel. Corp., Portland, 1985-88, N.E. Coalition of Neighborhoods, Portland, 1986. Mem. Ins. Women Oreg., Independent Ins. Agts. Oreg., Oreg. State Tax Preparer & Consultants, Am. United Fund. Muslim. Home: 5529 NE 25th Portland OR 97211 Office: Ameen Exec Svcs PO Box 11156 Portland OR 97211

MUHLEMAN, JANET CHRISTIE, design, advertising firm executive, designer; b. Dayton, Ohio, July 23, 1951; d. John Louis and Mary Griffith (Hallenbeck) M.; m. Robert John Cotman, Apr. 1982 (div. Oct. 1986); 1 son. BS in Indsl. Design, Ohio State U., 1973, MA in Design Planning, 1975. Grad. teaching assoc. Ohio State U., Columbus, 1973-75; exec. v.p. Group 243 Design, Columbus, 1974-75, Ann Arbor, Mich., 1975-81, pres., 1981—; pres., dir. Image Masters, Ann Arbor, 1981-88, chmn. 1988—; chmn. Portfolio Contract Furniture, Ann Arbor, 1983-89, sec./treas., 1989—; chmn. Group 243, Atlanta, 1984—, Ashlar Devel., Ann Arbor, 1985—; pres., chief exec. officer Group 243, Inc., Ann Arbor, 1981—; bd. dirs. Ross Roy Group, Inc. Chmn. adv. com. Washtenaw Community Coll., Ann Arbor, 1984—; mktg. com. chmn., mem. exec. com., bd. dirs. Ann Arbor Summer Festival; dept. chmn. Washtenaw United Way, 1988. Recipient various awards for creative work. Mem. Soc. Typographic Arts, Am. Inst. Graphic Arts (adv. com.), Am. Mgmt. Assn., Com. of 200, Young Pres.' Orgn., Pres.'s Forum, Mich. State C. of C. (bd. dirs. 1987-89), Am. Assn. Advt. Agys. (bd. regents 1987), Greater Detroit C. of C. (chairperson 1987), Ann Arbor C. of C. (bd. dirs. 1985-88, vice chmn. 1987), Assn. Profl. Design Firms (dir.). Republican. Clubs: Adcrafters, Economic (Detroit); The List (Ann Arbor). Avocations: motherhood, cooking, dance. Office: Group 243 Inc 1410 Woodridge Ave Ann Arbor MI 48105

MUHLERT, JAN KEENE, art museum director; b. Oak Park, Ill., Oct. 4, 1942; d. William Henry and Isabel Janette (Cole) Keene; m. Christopher Layton Muhlert, Jan. 1, 1966; 1 son, Michael Keene. B.A. in Art and French, Albion (Mich.) Coll., 1964; M.A. in Art History, Oberlin (Ohio) Coll., 1967; student, Neuchatel (Switzerland) U., Inst. European Studies, Paris, Inst. de Phonetique, Acad. Grande Chaumiere. Asst. curator Allen Meml. Art Mus., Oberlin, 1967-68; asst. curator 20th Century painting and sculpture Nat. Collection Fine Arts, Smithsonian Instn., Washington, 1968-73; assoc. curator Nat. Collection Fine Arts, Smithsonian Instn., 1974-75; dir. U. Iowa Mus. Art, 1975-79, Amon Carter Mus., Ft. Worth, 1980—. Author museum brochures, catalogues. Mem. Nat. Mus. Act Adv. Council, 1980-83, vis. com. Allen Meml. Art Mus. of Oberlin (Ohio) Coll., 1977—. Grantee Nat. Endowment Arts-Donner Found., 1979. Mem. Assn. Art Mus. Dirs. (trustee 1981-82, 84-86, chmn. govt. and art com. 1982-84), Western Assn. Art Mus. (regional rep. 1978-79), Am. Assn. Mus. (commn. for new century 1981-84), Am. Arts Alliance (dir. 1980-86, vice-chmn. 1982-84). Office: Amon Carter Mus 3501 Camp Bowie Blvd PO Box 2365 Fort Worth TX 76113

MUIR, HELEN, journalist, author; b. Yonkers, N.Y., Feb. 9, 1911; d. Emmet A. and Helen T. (Flaherty) Lennehan; student public schs.; m. William Whalley Muir, Jan. 23, 1936; children: Mary Muir Burrell, William Torbert. With Yonkers Herald Statesman, 1929-30, 31-33, N.Y. Evening Post, 1930-31, N.Y. Evening Jour., 1933-34, Carl Byoir & Assos., N.Y.C., and Miami, Fla., 1934-35; syndicated columnist Universal Svc., Miami, 1935-38; columnist Miami Herald, 1941-42; children's book editor, 1949-56; women's editor Miami Daily News, 1943-44; freelance mag. writer, numerous nat. mags., 1944—; drama critic Miami News, 1960-65. Trustee Coconut Grove Libr. Assn., Friends U. Miami Libr., Friends Miami-Dade Pub. Libr.; vis. com. U. Miami Librs.; bd. dirs. Miami-Dade County Pub. Libr. System; mem. State Libr. Adv. Coun., 1979—, past chmn. Recipient award Delta Kappa Gamma, 1960; Fla. Libr. Assn. Trustees and Friends award, 1973; trustee citation ALA, 1984; named to Fla. Women's Hall of Fame, 1984. Mem. Women in Communications (Community Headliner award 1973), Soc. Women Geographers. Clubs: Florida Women's Press (award 1963); Cosmopolitan (N.Y.C.); Biscayne Bay Yacht. Author: Miami, U.S.A., 1953, 2d rev. edit., 1990, Biltmore: Beacon for Miami, 1987. Home: 3855 Stewart Ave Miami FL 33133

MUIR, SANDRA MAY, school system administrator; b. Bowling Green, Ohio, Aug. 28, 1956; d. Winfield Scott and Norma Marie (Ernsthausen) M. BS in Edn., Bowling Green State U., 1978; MEd, U. Toledo, 1981. Cert. in spl. edn., elem. edn., supervision, principalship, guidance & counseling. Remedial math. instr. Penta County Vocat. Schs., Perrysburg, Ohio, 1978-81; job placement coord. Penta County Vocat. Schs., 1981-86, career devel. coord., 1986-87; supr. career edn. and attendance Lucas County Office Edn., Toledo, Ohio, 1987—; adminstrv. coun. Lucas County Office Edn., Toledo, 1987—, G.E.D. chief adminstr., 1987—. Participant Nat. Alliance of Businesses. Mem. Am. Assn. Counseling and Devel., Am. Vocat. Assn., Ohio County Supts. Assn., Children's Miracle Network, Shadow Valley Tennis Club, Phi Delta Kappa. Republican. Presbyterian. Home: 521 W Harrison Ave Maumee OH 43537-2025 Office: Lucas County Office Edn 1 Government Ctr Ste 400 Toledo OH 43604-2244

MUIR-BROADDUS, JACQUELINE ELIZABETH, psychology educator; b. Brantford, Ontario, Canada, Dec. 14, 1961; came to U.S., 1986; d. Jack Edward and Ellen Joann (MacKinnon) M. BA, U. Guelph, Can., 1984, MA, 1986; PhD, Fla. Atlantic U., 1990. Teaching asst. U. Guelph, Guelph, Ontario, Canada, 1984-86; rsch. asst. Fla. Atlantic U., Boca Raton, 1986-90, instr., 1987, 89; asst. prof. Southwestern U., Georgetown, Tex., 1990—; temporary psychometrist Bd. of Edn. City of Hamilton, Ontario, Canada, 1985; intern psychometrist Hosp. for Sick Children, Toronto, 1985, Wellington County Sch. Bd., 1985; adj. instr. Broward Community Coll., Coconut Creek, Fla., 1987. Author: (with others) Annals of Child Development, 1988, Interactions Among Strategies, Knowledge, and Aptitude in Cognitive Performance, 1990, Children's Strategies: Contemporary Views of Cognitive Development, 1990. Sr. leader START program, U. Guelph, Ontario, Canada, 1985; mem. dean's adv. com. Fla. Atlantic U., Boca Raton, 1988-89. Recipient Alma Mater scholarship, Entrance scholarship, U. Guelph, 1980, Daniel Brown Meml. scholarship , Fla. Atlantic U., 1988; finalist Thesis Contest Ontario Psychol. Assn., 1986. Mem. (student) Soc. for Rsch. in Child Devel., Am. Psychol Assn. Home: 3524 Greystone Dr #200 Austin TX 78731 Office: Southwestern U Dept Edn Georgetown TX 78626

MUKHERJEE, BHARATI (MRS. CLARK BLAISE), author, English educator; b. Calcutta, India, July 27, 1940; d. Sudhir Lal and Bina (Banerjee) M.; m. Clark L. Blaise, Sept. 19, 1963; children: Bart Anand, Bernard Sudhir. BA, U. Calcutta, 1959; MA, U. Baroda, India, 1961; MFA, U. Iowa, 1963, PhD, 1969. Asst. prof. English McGill U., Montreal, Can., 1969-73, assoc. prof., 1973-78, prof., 1978-80; assoc. prof. Montclair (N.J.) State College, 1984-87; prof. CUNY, 1987-89, U. Calif., Berkeley; vis. prof. of writing U. Iowa, Iowa City, 1979, 82; vis. prof. English, Skidmore Coll., Saratoga Springs, N.Y., 1979-70, 81-82, Emory U., Atlanta, 1983. Author: (fiction) Jasmine, 1989, The Middleman, 1988 (Nat. Book Critics Circle award 1989), Darkness, 1985, Wife, 1975, The Tiger's Daughter, 1972; co-author: (non-fiction) The Sorrow and the Terror, 1988, Days and Nights in Calcutta, 1977, film script, 1989; contbr. short stories, essays and book revs. to several jours. Recipient awards Nat. Endowment for the Arts, 1986, Can. Coun. of India, 1976; Guggenheim fellow, 1978. Mem. PEN. Hindu. Mailing Address: care Elaine Markson 44 Greenwich Ave New York NY 10011

MUKOYAMA, HELEN KIYOKO, social worker; b. Paia, Maui, Hawaii, Nov. 13, 1914; d. Ginichi and Shio (Takahashi) Takehara; m. Teruo Mukoyama, June 11, 1936 (div. 1956); children: Marshall H., Howard T., Wesley K. BA, Simpson Coll., 1937; postgrad., U. Denver, 1936; MA, U. Chgo., 1943. Caseworker Chgo. Welfare Adminstrn., 1938-41; Caseworker Cook County Dept. Welfare, Chgo., 1945-46, cons. to Japanese Ams. relocating to Chgo., 1945-46; cons. to Japanese Ams. relocating to Chgo. Ill. Public Aid Commn., Chgo., 1945-46, welfare adminstrv. aide supr., 1949-69; caseworker Travelers Aid Soc.-Immigrants Service, Chgo., 1951-65; intake worker Homemaker Service, Chgo., 1951-65, Salvation Army Family Service, Chgo., 1957-65; social work supr. intake Ill. Dept. Children and Family Services, Chgo., 1965-67; caseworker III Salvation Army Family Service, Chgo., 1967-72; casework supr. Jewish Family and Community Services, Chgo., 1972-73; supr. intake Council for Jewish Elderly, Chgo., 1973-77, supr. community aides and welfare adminstrv. coordinator, 1977-79; coordinator elderly housing Japanese Am. Service Com., Chgo., 1977-79; mgr. Heiwa Ter. Japanese Am. Elderly Housing, Chgo, 1980—; mem. Japanese Am. Housing Bd. Contbr. articles to profl. jours. Mem. Council of Ministries, Welfare Div. United Meth. Ch., 1963-69. Recipient Cert. Merit award Japanese Am. Service Com., 1963, 82, Plaque Japanese Housing Corp. Heiwa Terr., 1984, Spl. award Japanese Am. Redress Com., 1983. Mem. Acad. Cert. Social Workers, Nat. Assn. Social Workers, Ill. Cert. Social Workers, Chgo. Human Relations Commn., Japanese-Am. Citizens League, Japanese-Am. Soc., Art Inst. Chgo., Epsilon Sigma, Pi Gamma Mu. Methodist. Home: 912 S Mason Ave Chicago IL 60644 Office: 920 W Lawrence St Chicago IL 60640

MULARI, MARY ELIZABETH, retail store owner, author, publisher; b. Biwabik, Minn., Oct. 6, 1947; d. Arvid John and Helmi Viola (Peramaki) Koski; m. Barry A. Mulari, Aug. 12, 1972. BS, U. Minn., Duluth, 1970. Jr. high tchr. Benson (Minn.) Secondary Sch., 1970-71; jr. high tchr. Forest Lake (Minn.) Pub. Schs., 1971-73, Aurora (Minn.)-Hoyt Lakes Pub. Schs., 1974-76; retail store owner Aurora Surplus Store, 1973—; author, self pub. Mary's Prodns., Aurora, 1982—; freelance sewing tchr. Mary's Prodns., Aurora, 1982—. Author: Designer Sweatshirts, 1983, Applique Design Collection, 1984, MORE Designer Sweatshirts, 1986, Country Style Appliques, 1987, Adventure in Applique, 1989, Accents for Your Style, 1990. Trustee Aurora Pub. Libr. Bd., 1983—; com. mem.. Arts Bd.-Community Edn., Aurora, 1979—; com. mem. Minn. Gov.'s Pre-White House Conf. on Libr. and Info. Svcs., 1989-91. Lutheran. Home: 731 Maple Dr Aurora MN 55705 Office: Marys Prodns 217 N Main Box 87 Aurora MN 55705

MULARSKI, VICTORIA A., consultant flavor analyses; b. Adams, Mass.; d. Walter F. Sr. and Frances (Meczywor) M. BA, Syracuse U., postgrad. Research asst. N.Y. Hosp., Cornell Med. Ctr., N.Y.C.; biochemist Lahey Clinic, Boston; mem. staff Arthur D. Little, Inc., Cambridge, Mass., 1954-70, asst. dir. flavor profile panel tng., 1956-67, dir. flavor profile panel tng., 1967-70; cons. flavor profile Adams, Mass., 1970—. Profl. mem. Inst. Food Technologists. Roman Catholic. Home and Office: 68 Orchard St Adams MA 01220

MULDAUR, DIANA CHARLTON, actress; b. N.Y.C., Aug. 19, 1938; d. Charles Edward Arrowsmith and Alice Patricia (Jones) M.; m. James Mitchell Vickery, July 26, 1969 (dec. 1979); m. Robert J. Dozier, Oct. 11, 1981. B.A., Sweet Briar Coll., 1960. Actress appearing in: Off-Broadway theatrical prodns., summer stock, Broadway plays including A Very Rich Woman, 1963-68; guest appearances on TV in maj. dramatic shows; appeared on: TV series Survivors, 1970-71, McCloud, 1971-73, Tony Randall Show, 1976, Black Beauty, 1978; star: TV series Born Free, 1974, Hizzoner, 1979, Fitz & Bones, 1980, Star Trek, The Next Generation, 1988-89; NBC miniseries A Year in the Life, 1986; Star-Trak: The Next Generation, 1988-89; TV movie Murder in Three Acts, The Return of Sam McCloud, 1989; TV series L.A. Law, 1989-90; motion picture credits include McQ. Bd. dirs. Los Angeles chpt. Asthma and Allergy Found. Am.; bd. advisors Nat. Ctr. Film and Video Preservation, John F. Kennedy Ctr. Performing Arts, 1986. Recipient 13th Ann. Commendation award Am. Women in Radio and TV, 1988, Disting. Alumnae award Sweet Briar Coll., 1988. Mem. Acad. Motion Picture Arts and Scis., Screen Actors Guild (dir. 1978), Acad. TV Arts and Scis. (exec. bd., dir., pres. 1983-85), Conservation Soc. Martha's Vineyard Island. Office: Care Clarke Lilly 333 Apolina Ave Newport Beach CA 92662

MULDROW, TRESSIE WRIGHT, psychologist; b. Marietta, Ga., Feb. 1, 1941; d. Festus Blanton and Louise Williams Wright Summers; BA, Bennett Coll., 1962; MS, Howard U., 1965, PhD, 1976; 1 child, DeJuan Denise. Research asst. W.C. Allen Corp., Washington, 1966-68; personnel research psychologist Dept. Navy, Washington, 1968-73, Office Personnel Mgmt., CSC, 1973-79; chief, adv. council on alternative selection procedures Office Personnel Mgmt., Washington, 1979-86, chief consultative services, 1986—; lectr. Howard U., 1979. Mem. Washington Inter-Alumni council United Negro Coll. Fund, 1970—, pres., 1988—; trustee Bennett Coll., vice chmn., 1985—; v.p. Family Life Ctr. Br., Boys and Girls Clubs of Washington, 1984—. Named Alumnae of Yr., United Negro Coll. Fund, 1971, recipient Individual Achievement award, 1985; Outstanding Alumnae Morehouse Coll., 1978. Mem. Bennett Coll. Alumnae Assn. (nat. pres. 1978-85, Alumnae of Yr. award 1987), Am. Psychol. Assn., Nat. Assn. Black Psychologists Delta Sigma Theta. Presbyterian. Contbr. articles to profl. publs. Office: 1900 E St NW Washington DC 20415

MULFORD, PHILIPPA GREENE, writer; b. N.Y.C., May 29, 1948; d. Philip Murray and Constance (Clarke) Greene; m. R. Edward Mulford, Sept. 29, 1978; stepchildren: Nicholas, Leslie. BA, Skidmore Coll., Saratoga Springs, N.Y., 1970. Feature writer/reporter Clinton (N.Y.) Courier, 1971-73; exec. dir. Cen. N.Y. Community Arts Coun., Inc., Utica, N.Y., 1971-78; arts mgmt. cons. Clinton, 1978-79. Author: If It's Not Funny, Why Am I Laughing?, 1982, The World is My Eggshell, 1986 (Best Book for Yr. U. Iowa 1987), Everything I Hoped for, 1990; contbr. articles to profl. jours. Pres. Town of Kirkland United Way, Clinton, 1989—. Home: RR 1 Box 14 Clinton NY 13323

MULLANEY, DORA AILEEN, school psychologist; b. Norfolk, Va., Aug. 29, 1943; d. Luther Austin and Ethel Aileen (Hall) Arrant; m. James F. Chase, June 13, 1964 (div. 1976); children: Pamela Lynn, Brian James; m. Gerard Joseph Mullaney, Mar. 29, 1980. BA in Edn., Kent (Ohio) State U., 1966, MEd, 1976. Cert. sch. psychologist, Ohio. Ednl. cons. Child Guidance Ctr., Akron, Ohio, 1976-77; sch. psychologist Akron Pub. Schs., 1977—; pvt. practice psychol. counselor, Akron, 1988-89. Mem. Nat. Assn. Sch. Psychologists (recognition of Best Practice 1988), Ohio Sch. Psychologists Assn., Kent/Akron Area Sch. Psychologist Assn., Akron Edn. Assn. (union rep. 1988—), Delta Kappa Gamma. Democrat. Presbyterian. Home: 808 Forestview Dr Tallmadge OH 44278 Office: Akron Pub Schs 70 N Broadway Akron OH 44308

MULLARKEY, MARY J., state supreme court justice; b. New London, Wis., Sept. 28, 1943; d. John Clifford and Isabelle A. (Steffes) M.; m. Thomas E. Korson, July 24, 1971; 1 child, Andrew Steffes Korson. BA, St. Norbert Coll., 1965; LLB, Harvard U., 1968; LLD (hon.), St. Norbert Coll., 1989, St. Norbert Coll., 1989. Bar: Wis. 1968, Colo. 1974. Atty.-advisor U.S. Dept. Interior, Washington, 1968-73; asst. regional atty. EEOC, Denver, 1973-75; 1st atty. gen. Colo. Dept. Law, Denver, 1975-79, solicitor gen., 1979-82; legal advisor to Gov. Lamm State of Colo., Denver, 1982-85; ptnr. Mullarkey & Seymour, Denver, 1985-87; justice Colo. Supreme Ct., Denver, 1987—. Recipient Alumni award St. Norbert Coll., De Pere, Wis., 1980. Fellow Colo. Bar Found., ABA Found.; mem. ABA, Colo. Bar Assn., Colo. Women's Bar Assn. (recognition award 1986), Denver Bar Assn. Office: Colo Supreme Ct 2 E 14th Ave Denver CO 80203

MULLEEDY, JOYCE ELAINE, nursing service administrator, educator; b. Paterson, N.J., Aug. 30, 1948; d. Edward and Jane (Van De Weert) Schuurman; m. Philip Anthony Mulleedy, May 14, 1982. BS, Paterson State Coll., 1970. RN, cert. emergency nurse, emergency med. technician, paramedic. Pub. health nurse Vis. Nurse Assn. of No. Bergen County, Ramsey, N.J., 1970-72; health dir. Camp Fowler Assn., Speculator, N.Y., 1973-76; exec. dir. Am. Cancer Soc., Speculator, 1976-77; pub. health nurse Hamilton County Nursing Service, Lake Pleasant, N.Y., 1977-80, supervising pub. health nurse, 1980-82, dir. patient services, 1982-86; quality assurance specialist Susquehanna-Adirondack Regional Emergency Med. Services Program, 1986—; cons. dir. Home Health Care of Hamilton County, Inc., Indian Lake, N.Y., 1979-84. Author instructional booklet: Assessing Your Patients, 1983, (pamphlet) A Note to Parents, 1985. Bd. dirs. Am. Cancer Soc.-Hamilton County Unit, Speculator, 1972-76, Speculator Vol. Ambulance Corps, Inc., 1974-81, ARC-Hamilton County chpt., Lake Pleasant, N.Y., 1981-88; mem. adminstrv. bd. dirs. Grace United Meth. Ch., Speculator, 1982—. Martha Hazen Scholar Am. Legion, 1966; recipient Service award Am. Legion, 1977. Mem. N.Y. State Assn. County Health Ofcls., Adirondack-Appalachian Regional Emergency Med. Services Council (chmn. 1982-87, chmn. tng. com. 1982—), Emergency Nurses Assn., Hamilton County Emergency Med. Services Council (sec.-treas. 1974—, instr. 1974—), Dirs. of Northeastern N.Y. Home Health Agys. Republican. Home: PO Box 203 Elm Lake Rd Speculator NY 12164 Office: Susquehanna Adirondack Regional Emergency Med Services Program PO Box 212 Speculator NY 12164

MULLEN, DOROTHY MAE HUFFMAN, small business owner; b. Norphlet, Ark., Jan. 27, 1936; d. Harry Jones and Maebelle Pauline (Meinelt) Huffman; m. Billy Wayne Mullen, Dec. 23, 1955; 1 child, Harry Benjamin. Student, U. So. Miss., 1987-88, Miss. GulfCoast Community Coll, 1988-89. Lic. real estate broker. Ins. clerk Southeastern Life Ins. Co., Hattiesburg, Miss., 1956-58; sec. Vickers Homes, Inc., Pascagoula, Miss., 1959-66; prin. Mullen Secretarial, Pascagoula, Miss., 1988 --. Mem. exec. com. Eastlawn Elem. PTA, Pascagoula, 1973-77; pres. Pascagoula High Sch. Soccer Boosters Club, 1983-84, Pascagoula Garden Club, 1989-90; mem. missions com. First United Meth. Ch., Pascagoula, 1988-90; dir. Am. Cancer Soc., Pascagoula, 1989-90. Mem. Homebuilders Assn. Jackson County (exec. officer 1973--), Jackson County Bd. Realtors (exec. officer 1974--), Miss. Assn. Realtors (mem. exec. officers adv. coun. 1985 --). Home: 2303 Fernwood St Pascagoula MS 39567

MULLEN, JULIA ELIZABETH, investment advisor; b. N.Y.C., Feb. 24, 1930; d. Donald Arney and Julia Rives (Broadbent) M. BA, Wellesley Coll., 1951; postgrad., NYU, 1961-64. Sec. Upsala Coll., E. Orange, N.J., 1952-54; sec., trainee J. Walter Thompson, N.Y.C., 1954-56; sec. Reeves Bros., N.Y.C., 1956-61; sec. to asst. v.p. investments counseling dept. Chem. Bank, N.Y.C., 1961-84; v.p. The Portfolio Group, N.Y.C., 1984—; membership com. Office Execs. Assn., N.Y.C., 1958-61; participant exec. mgmt. seminars Harvard Bus. Sch., 1975. Mem. Arts Coun. Essex County N.J., Wellesley Club N.J. Republican. Presbyterian. Home: 112 Connett Pl South Orange NJ 07079 Office: The Portfolio Group 30 Rockefeller Plaza New York NY 10112

MULLEN, REGINA MARIE, lawyer; b. Cambridge, Mass., Apr. 22, 1948; d. Robert G. and Elizabeth R. (McHugh) M. BA, Newton Coll. Sacred Heart, 1970; JD, U. Va., 1973. Bar: Pa., Del., U.S. Dist. Ct. Del., U.S. Ct. Appeals (3d cir.), U.S. Supreme Ct. Dep. atty. gen. State Del. Dept. Justice, Wilmington, 1973-79, state solicitor, 1979-83, chief fin. unit, 1983-88; v.p., dep. gen. counsel MBNA Am. Bank, N.A., Newark, Del., 1988—; Mem. Bd. Bar Examiners, State Del., Wilmington, 1979-89. Mem. fin. com. Chesapeake Bay Girl Scout Coun., Wilmington, 1985—, bd. dirs., 1988—, v.p., 1990—. Mem. ABA, Del. State Bar Assn. (chair adminstrv. law sect. 1983-85). Democrat. Roman Catholic. Office: 400 Christiana Rd Newark DE 19713

MULLENIX, MARTHA BODE, publisher, editor, printing company executive; b. Bandera, Tex., Mar. 2, 1940; d. Walter O. and Mathilda (Illhardt) Bode; m. J.C. Mullenix, Feb. 18, 1961; children: David, Darryl, Dale, Sandra. Grad. pub. schs., Seguin, Tex. Underwriter, exec. sec. Schuessler Ins. Agy., Seguin, 1958-68; bookkeeper, office mgr. Seguin Agri-Bus., Inc., 1968-70; office mgr., area acct. Nat. Farmers Orgn., Seguin, 1972-79; editor Goliad (Tex.) Advance Guard, 1982-83; editor, pub., founder Texan Express, Goliad, 1983—; owner, mgr. Regal Printers, Goliad, 1983—. Treas., sec. Goliad County Hist. Commn., 1984-88; dist. treas. adult leaders 4-H Club, 1984-88; v.p. Goliad Athletic Booster Club, 1989. Recipient Outstanding Adult Leader award dist. 14, State of Tex., 4-H Club, 1987. Mem. Tex. Press Assn., Goliad County C. of C. (bd. dirs. 1983-88, pres. 1988, Anne Kohler Citizen of Yr. award 1988), Herman Sons Dance (v.p. 1988). Methodist. Office: Texan Express PO Box 1 Goliad TX 77963

MULLER, BRIGITTE DENISE, French educator; b. Rouen, Seine Maritime, France, July 25, 1921; came to U.S., 1950; d. René Charles Robert and Denise Volpert; m. George Henry Muller, Aug. 24, 1940; children: Frank, Christine, Philip. BA, Eastern Mich. U., 1964; MA, U. Mich., Ann Arbor, 1966; doctorate, U. Aix-Marseille, France, 1970. Teaching fellow U. Mich., Ann Arbor, 1965-67; instr. Eastern Mich. U., Ypsilanti, 1965-67, asst. prof., 1967-72, assoc. prof., 1972-78, prof. in french, 1978-88, prof. emerita, 1989—. Author numerous book revs. and articles. V.p. The Advanced Ideas Rsch. and All in Recreation Found., Shell Lake Camp Maple City, Mich., 1967—. Named "Chevalier" of the Palmes Académiques The French Govt., Paris, 1984, Disting. Prof. Mich. Assn. of Governing Bds. of Colls. & Univs., Lansing, Mich. Mem. AAUW, Am. Assn. Tchrs. French, Am. Coun. Teaching of Fgn. Langs., Phi Kappa Phi. Office: AIR Found 1605 Main St Sarasota FL 33577

MULLER, ELSIE FERRAR, psychotherapist, psychiatric social worker; b. Worcester, Mass., Apr. 7, 1913; d. Frederic and Anne (Binns) Bonnet; B.S., Alfred U., 1934; M.S.W., U. Mo., Columbia, 1969; postgrad. U. Mo., Kansas City, 1962-63; m. Frederick Wentworth Muller, Oct. 10, 1936 (div. 1961); 1 dau., Jean Ferrar Muller Mackimmie. Lic. clin. social worker. Art. instr. Alfred U., 1935-36; art therapist Gillis Home, Kansas City, Mo., 1958-70; psychotherapist Ozanam Home, Kansas City, Mo., 1970—; art therapy cons. Jackson County, Kansas City, Mo., 1975-78, Wyandotte County Sch. Social Workers, Kansas City, Kans., 1978—. Mem. Nat. Assn. Social Workers, Acad. Social Workers, Am. Art Therapy Assn. (hon. life), Am. Soc. Psychopath. Expression (editorial adv.), Nat. Register Clin. Social Workers. Episcopalian. Home: 1420 Upper Dr NE Pullman WA 99163-4305

MULLER, LINDA LEE, sales executive; b. Texas City, Tex., Dec. 12, 1939; d. Leon Troxlar and Loretta Eugenia (Dugat) M. BS in Chemistry cum laude, Lamar U., 1961; MS in Organic Chemistry, Tulane U., 1965. Tchr. gen. sci. Blocker Jr. High Sch., Texas City, 1961-62; asst. prof. St. Mary's Dominican Coll., New Orleans, 1965-69; rsch. chemist USDA, So. Rsch. Ctr., New Orleans, 1969-82; med. sales rep. Stuart Pharm., Lake Charles, La., 1982-84; regional ops. supr. Stuart Pharm., Dallas, 1984-85, dist. sales mgr., 1985-87; dist. sales mgr. ICI Pharma, Wilmington, Del., 1987—; mem. adv. com. Nat. Inst. Health Pub., New Orleans, 1981. Contbr. articles to jours. Mem. Fed. Bus. Assn., New Orleans, 1970-82, Zonta Internat., New Orleans. Rockefellow grantee, Tulane U., 1966. Mem. NAFE, Am. Bus. Women's Assn. Republican. Episcopalian. Home: 7312 Elizabeth Pl Plano TX 75025 Office: ICI Pharma Wilmington DE 19000

MULLER, MARGIE H., state bank commissioner; b. Los Angeles, Nov. 30, 1927; d. S. Jack and Marjorie (Ullman) Hellman; m. Steven Muller, June 19, 1951; children: Julie, Elizabeth. BA, UCLA, 1949. Sales promotion asst. Joyce (Calif.) Ltd., London, 1950-51; copywriter Hamrick Advt., Ithaca, N.Y., 1951-54; sr. assoc. Conant and Co., N.Y.C., 1954-57; mgr. advt. and pub. relations Theodore Presser Co., Bryn Mawr, Pa., 1957-58; acct. exec. Laux Advt., Ithaca, 1959-60; asst. v.p. mktg. Tompkins County Trust Co., Ithaca, 1960-71; v.p. Md. Nat. Bank, Balt., 1971-77; sr. v.p. Union Trust Bancorp., Balt., 1977-83; state bank commr. Balt., 1983—. Contbr. articles to profl. jours. Bd. dirs. The Leadership, Balt., 1985-87; pres. Balt. Promotion Coun., 1974-75, Health and Welfare Coun. Cen. Md.,

1982-85; mem. adv. commn. Md. Dept. Econ. and Community Devel., 1975-83; trustee McDonough Sch., 1980-85. Mem. Bank Mktg. Assn. (bd. dirs. 1974-78, mem. exec. com. 1977-78, nat. conv. chmn. 1977), Nat. Assn. State Credit Union Suprs. (bd. dirs. 1984-88), Conf. State Bank Suprs. (bd. dirs. 1988—, vice chmn. 1990—). Office: State Bank Commr The Brokerage 34 Market Pl Ste 800 Baltimore MD 21202

MULLER, PATRICIA ANN, nursing administrator and educator; b. N.Y.C., July 22, 1943; d. Joseph H. and Rosanne (Bautz) Felter; m. David G. Smith, Mar. 19, 1987; children: Frank M. Muller III, Kimberly M. Muller. BSN, Georgetown U., 1965; MA, U. Tulsa, 1978, EdD, 1983. RN. Staff devel. coord. St. Francis Hosp., Tulsa, 1978-79, asst. dir. for nursing svc., nursing edn., 1979-82, dir. dept. edn., 1982—; presenter various confs. and convs., 1978—. Contbr. articles to profl. jours. Mem. ANA, NLN, Am. Soc. for Nursing Svc. Adminstrs., Am. Soc. for Health Manpower Edn. and Tng., Okla. Nurses Assn., Okla. Soc. for Nursing Svc. Adminstrs., Sigma Theta Tau. Office: St Francis Hosp 6161 S Yale Ave Tulsa OK 74136

MULLETTE, JULIENNE PATRICIA, health center administrator, television personality and producer, author; b. Sydney, Australia, Nov. 19, 1940; came to U.S., 1953; d. Ronald Stanley Lewis and Sheila Rosalind Blunden (Phillips) M.; m. Fred Gillette Sturm, Nov. 24, 1964 (div. Dec. 1969); m. Kenneth Walter Gillman, Dec. 27, 1971 (div. Dec. 1978); children: Noah Khristoff Mullette-Gillman, O'Dhaniel Alexander Mullette-Gillman. B.A., Western Coll. for Women, Oxford, Ohio, 1961; postgrad., Harvard U., 1964, U. Sao Paulo, Brazil, 1965, Inst. do Filosofia, Sao Paulo, 1965, Miami U., Oxford, 1967-69. Tchr. English, High Mowing Sch., Wilton, N.H., 1962-64, Stoneleigh-Prospect Hill Sch., Greenfield, Mass., 1964; seminar dir. Western Coll., Oxford, Ohio, 1967-69; pres. Family Tree, The Home Univ., Montclair, N.J., 1978-80; dir. Pleroma Holistic Health Ctr., Montclair, 1980—; dir. Astrological Rsch. Ctr., Sydney, Australia, 1983; hostess (radio talk show) You and the Cosmos Sta. WFMU, East Orange, N.J., 1985, The Juliette Mullette Show, Connections TV, Newark, 1985—, The Juliette Mullette Show Sta. WFDU, Fairleigh Dickinson U., N.J., 1986—; founder Spiritual Devel. Rsch. Group 1986—; pvt. astrology counselor, 1962—; lectr., speaker worldwide, 1968—; guest on radio and TV shows, U.S. and Can., 1962—; host syndicated radio talk show The Juliette Mullette Show, N.Y., N.J., 1987—; owner, pres. Moonlight Pond, Woodbourne, N.Y., 1988—; founder The Spiritual Devel. Ctr., 1986—, Pleroma Found. for Astrological Rsch. and Studies, 1990; breeder, trainer llamas, alpacas and other exotic animals. Author: The Moon-Understanding the Subconscious, 1973; also articles, 1968—; founding editor KOSMOS mag., 1968-78, The Jour. of Astrological Studies, 1970; contbg. columnist I Love Cats, 1988—. Founder local chpt. La Leche League, Montclair, 1974. Mem. AAUW (chair cultural affairs Montclair chpt.), Spiritual Devel. Group (founder 1987), Internat. Soc. Astrological Research (founding pres. 1968-78), Am. Fedn. Astrologers (cert.), Société Belge d'Astrologie, Am. Assn. Humanistic Psychology, AAUW (dir. cultural affairs 1987—), NAFE, Internat. Llamas Assn. Avocations: competitive tennis, local theatre, singing.al theatre, singing. Home: 89 A Star Rt Woodbourne NY 12788

MULLIN, CONSTANCE, management; b. Annapolis, Md., May 31, 1939; d. Jacques Redway and Louise Hopkins (Kemp) Hammond; m. Michael Mullin. BA, Radcliffe Coll., 1961; MA, San Diego State U., 1966. Tchr. Dana Hall Sch., Wellesley, Mass., 1962-64; lect. San Diego State Univ., 1966-68; editorial asst. John Wiley & Sons, La Jolla, Calif., 1971-81; writer Sea World, San Diego, 1984-85; founder, dir. Classical Performing Artists Mgmt., La Jolla, 1985--. Chmn. Early Childhood Edn., La Jolla Elem., 1974-76; pres. Friends, La Jolla Chamber Music Soc., 1978-80. Mem. Western Alliance Arts Adminstr., Assn. Calif. Symphony Orchestras,. Democrat. Office: Classical Performing Artists Mgmt 7758 Ludington Pl La Jolla CA 92037-3806

MULLIN, CYNTHIA MARIE, speech pathologist; b. Phila., Sept. 4, 1956. BE, Ind. U. of Pa., 1978; MA, Memphis State U., 1980. Cert. clin. competence in speech-language pathology. Speech pathologist Joplin (Mo.) Regional Ctr. for Devel. Disabled, 1980-82, Nevada (Mo.) State Sch. and Hosp., 1982-83; speech pathologist, dir. psychoeducation HSA Heartland Hosp., Nevada, 1982-86; speech pathologist, psychometrist Nevada Mental Health Svcs., 1984-85; area coord. Mo. Spl. Olympics, Nevada, 1984-86; speech pathologist Midwest Rehab. Ctr., Kansas City, Mo., 1985, Bur. of Spl. Health Care Needs, Jefferson City, Mo., 1984—, Joplin R-8 Sch. Dist., 1986-87; speech pathologist, owner Cynthia M. Mullin & Assoc., Joplin, 1983—.

MULLIN, DELCIE ANN, radio news director; b. Norristown, Pa., Apr. 2, 1955; d. David Daniel and MaryGrace (Serpico) M. BA in Liberal Arts, Pa. State U., 1977. News anchor, reporter Stas. WAEB and WXKW, Allentown, Pa., 1978-82; reporter, anchor Sta. WPOP-Newsradio, Hartford, Conn., 1982-86, news dir., 1986—. Vol. AIDS edn. com. ARC, Farmington, Conn., 1988—. Recipient awards for coverage Hurricane Gloria AP and UPI, Hartford and Boston, 1986, for radio features Conn. Minute, NHL Allstar Game AP Broadcasters, 1986. Mem. Women in Communications (speaker), AP (scholarship com. 1988-89). Office: Sta WPOP 345 E Cedar St Newington CT 06111

MULLINEAUX, JEWEL E., retired educator; b. N.Y.C., June 14, 1917; d. Aubrey Vibbert and Bertye (Winterling) Brooks; m. Donald Hammond Mullineaux, Sept. 15, 1948. BA with hons. in Spanish, Goucher Coll., 1938; postgrad., Temple U., 1938, U. Pa., 1940; MA, U. Md., 1954. Counselor, tchr., interviewer City of Balt., 1938-42; supr., counselor War Man Power Commn., Balt., 1942-48; chief exams. and recruitment Civil Svc. Commn. Balt., 1948-67; assoc. prof. career selection, career counselor Community Coll. Balt., 1967-74; cons. police patrolmen selection, various U.S. cities. Editor Macca Media jour., 1970-73; contbr. articles to profl. jours.; co-author: (novel) Shadow and Shield, 1981; author short stories and poetry. Sec.-treas. Am. Soc. Pub. Adminstrs., Balt., 1950-52; mem. Mid.-Atlantic Assn. Jr. Colls., 1967-74, Mid-Atlantic Career Counseling Assn., 1967-74, Senator John Marshall Butler's Com. Disting. Women Leaders, 1954; pres. city coun. Beta Sigma Phi, Balt., 1947; all offices local chpt. Beta Sigma Phi, Balt., 1938-50; mentor teenagers Nu Phi Mu, Balt., 1948-50; mem. Halifax Humane Soc., Daytona Beach, Fla., 1980—, Nat. Wildlife Fedn., 1985—. Recipient Cert. Appreciation personnel dept. City of Phila., 1966, Cert. of Award, Ga. State Writing Competition, 1989, Goldkey, Phi Kappa Phi, 1954. Mem. AAUW (mentor creative writers' group, Book award), Republican Club (Daytona Beach), Halifax River Yacht Club. Christian Scientist. Home: The Landmark 404 S Beach St Apt 202 Daytona Beach FL 32114

MULLINS, ANNA CRABTREE, cosmetologist; b. Clintwood, Va., July 3, 1946; d. John B. and Nancy Maxine (Fleming) Crabtree; m. Danny Sylvan Mullins; children: Shelley Denise, Sheri Rebecca Epling. Cert. in cosmetology, Va. Ferrell-Del Mar Coll., 1966. Stylist Hair Fashions by Eric, Detroit, 1966-68, Curls ala Mode, Detroit, 1968-69; owner, stylist Ann's Styling Salon, Haysi, Va., 1970-72, Ann's Beauty Salon, Vamsant, Va., 1972-76; stylist Flair Beauty Salon, Bristol, Va., 1976-78; owner, mgr., stylist Hair Concept 2000, Bristol, 1978—; mem. adv. com. Va. High Cosmetology, Bristol, 1978-89; advisor Future Cosmetologist of Am., Richmond, 1987-89. Mem. Keep Bristol Beautiful Com., 1985-89. Mem. Nat. Cosmetologists Assn., Quad City Affiliate, Bristol C. of C. Baptist. Home: 406 Huron Rd Bristol VA 24201 Office: Hair Concept 2000 1061 Old Abingdon Pike Bristol VA 24201

MULLINS, ELIZABETH IONE, sociology educator; b. Colemaine, Minn., Sept. 6, 1928; d. Edgar R. and Bess (Redhed) M. BA, Miami U., Oxford, Ohio, 1950; MA, U. Ill., 1954; PhD, Ind. U., 1975. Tchr., Blue Ash High Sch., Ohio, 1950-53; student personnel rep. Ind. U., Bloomington, 1954-57; coordinator activities ctr. Sch. of So. Ill. U., Carbondale, 1957-65; vis. lectr. Ind. U., 1972-73; asst. prof. sociology Kent State U., Ohio, 1973—. Co-editor Sociol. Focus, 1980-88, Regimal SWS Newsletter, 1988— . Mem. ACLU, Common Cause, North Central Sociol. Assn. (exec. council 1980—), Am. Sociol. Assn. (com. 1972-75), NOW, Women Studies Assn., AAUP, Alpha Kappa Delta (v.p. 1974-78). Office: Kent State U Lowery Hall Kent OH 44242

MULLINS, OBERA, microbiologist; b. Egypt, Miss., Feb. 15, 1927; d. Willie Ree and Maggie Sue (Orr) Gunn; B.S., Chgo. State U., 1974; M.S. in Health Sci. Edn., Governors State U., 1981; m. Charles Leroy Mullins, Nov. 2, 1952; children—Mary Artavia, Arthur Curtis, Charles Leroy, Charlester Teresa, William Hellman. Med. technician, microbiologist Chgo. Health Dept., Chgo., 1976—. Mem. AAUW, Am. Soc. Clin. Pathologists (cert. med. lab. technician). Roman Catholic. Home: 9325 S Marquette St Chicago IL 60617 Office: 3026 S California Ave Chicago IL 60623

MULLINS, ROBIN HASSLER, health services professional; b. Pitts., Nov. 30, 1953. BSFR, W.Va. U., 1976. Environ. health specialist Allegheny County, Pitts., 1977-79; supr. food svc. W.Va. U. Med. Ctr., Morgantown, 1979-80; sanitarian Brooke County Health Dept., Wellsburg, W.Va., 1980-83; sanitarian health div. State of W.Va., Charleston, 1983—; W.Va. pesticide applicator, HCFA cert. life safety code surveyor, HCFA cert. health surveyor.

MULRENNAN, SHEILA, insurance consulting firm executive; b. Irvington, N.J., Apr. 15, 1950; d. William Joseph and Mary Louise (Dolan) M. BA, Memphis State U., 1972, MA, 1975. Claims adjustor Safeco Ins. Co., Springfield, N.J., 1975-76; claims supr. Employers Ins. Wausau, W. Orange, N.J., 1976-80; casualty analyst Corroon & Black N.Y., N.Y.C., 1980-82; cons. N.Y.C., 1982-85; pres. IAG Ltd., N.Y.C., 1985—; speaker Exec. Enterprises, N.Y.C., 1986—, Risk & Ins. Mgmt. Soc., N.Y.C., 1988—, Northwest Ctr. for Profl. Devel., Seattle, 1988. Co-author: Insurance Claims for Environmental Damages, 1989; editor Ins. Archaeology; Risk Management mag., 1989. Fundraiser Cerebral Palsy, N.Y.C., 1984—, Anchor House, Trenton, N.J., 1986—; founding mem. Nat. Mus. Women in the Arts, Washington, 1987—; mem. NOW, Washington, 1986—. Mem. Assn. Profl. Ins. Women, Nat. Assn. for Female Execs., Am. Women for Econ. Devel. Office: IAG Ltd 240 Madison Ave New York NY 10016

MULRONEY, MILA, wife of Canadian prime minister; b. Sarajevo, Yugoslavia, July 13, 1953; d. Dmitrije and Bogdanka Pivnicki; m. (Martin) Brian Mulroney, May 26, 1973; children—Caroline Anne, Benedict Martin, Robert Mark, Daniel Nicolas Dimitri. Faculty of Engring, 1973-76, Concordia U., Montreal, Que., Can. Hon. chairperson Can. Cystic Fibrosis Found., U. Ottawa Heart Inst.; nat. patron Read Can.; patron Genesis Rsch. Found., Can. Rhett Syndrome Assn.; hon. bd. mem. Women and the Arts Man., Inc. Home: 24 Sussex Dr, Ottawa, ON Canada K1M 1M4 Office: care Office of Prime Minister, Langevin Block, 80 Wellington St Ste 129, Ottawa, ON Canada K1A 0A2

MULROONEY, JACQUELINE DOWNING, computer consulting company executive; b. Buffalo, Oct. 3, 1957; d. John Gilbert and Betty (Rycroft) Downing; m. Galen Edward Mulrooney, Oct. 24, 1987. BA, Colgate U., 1979. Sr. analyst Advanced Tech. Systems, Vienna, Va., 1979-81; project leader Microtemps, Greenbelt, Md., 1981-82; prin. J.P. Systems, Springfield, Va., 1982—; Author: (software package) TimeTrak. Del. Mt. Vernon Dist. Rep. Cen. Com., 1986. Mem. Washington Ind. Computer Cons. Assn. (bd. dirs. 1986—, chmn. govt. rels. com. 1986, pres. 1988-89). Home: 8162 Willowdale Ct Springfield VA 22153-3624

MULROONEY, VIRGINIA FRANCES, history educator; b. Rochester, N.Y., Sept. 27, 1939; d. Francis Patrick and Viola Vivian (Cody) M. AA, Santa Monica Coll., 1959; BA, UCLA, 1961, MA, 1963, PhD, 1975. Prof. history L.A. Valley Coll., Van Nuys, 1964-83, West L.A. Coll., Culver City, 1988—; vice chancellor personnel L.A. Community Coll., 1983-88. Mem. Orgn. Am. Historians, Am. Fedn. Tchrs. (pres. 1971-83). Democratic. Roman Catholic. Office: West Los Angeles Coll 4800 Freshman Dr Culver City CA 90230

MULVANEY, MARY FREDERICA, systems analyst; b. N.Y., Nov. 27, 1945; d. Michael Joseph and Mary Catherine (Clapper) M. BA, Marymount Coll., 1967; MA, U. Va., 1968. Cert. data processor Inst. Certification of Computer Profls., Ill. Computer systems analyst Dept. of Def., Ft. Meade, Md., 1968-74; sr. programmer analyst Planning Rsch. Corp., McLean, Va., 1974-83; mem. tech. staff Fed. Systems Group TRW Inc., Fairfax, Va., 1983—. Mem. Data Processing Mgmt. Assn., Computer Measurement Group, Digital Equipment Corp. Users Soc. Roman Catholic. Office: TRW Fed Systems Group PO Box 10400 Fairfax VA 22031

MULVANEY, MAUREEN GAIL, lecturer, counselor, educator; b. Norfolk, Va., Oct. 2, 1950; d. Paul Leo and Mary Patricia (Landry) M.; m. James Matthew Keith, July 10, 1976 (div. Nov. 1985). B.A., Troy State U., 1972; Ed.M., Boston U., 1980. Social services asst. U.S. Govt., Augsburg, W.Ger., 1980; clin. psychologist William Beaumont Army Med. Ctr., El Paso, Tex., 1984; counselor Adlerian Family Counseling Ctr., Litchfield Park, Ariz., 1984—; instr. Grand Canyon Coll., Phoenix, 1984—; profl. speaker, Phoenix, 1985—; cons. stress mgmt. corp. orgns., Phoenix, 1985-86; cons. Carl Hayden High Sch., Phoenix, 1986, Maryvale High Sch., Phoenix, 1986. Author: The Stress Strategists, 1986. Active Mothers Against Drunk Drivers, El Paso, 1985. Recipient Certs. of Achievement, Dept. of Army, 1981. Mem. Am. Personnel and Guidance Assn., Nat. Speakers Assn., Am. Assn. Female Execs., NOW, Phoenix C. of C. Democrat. Roman Catholic. Avocation: cons. to women's athletic teams. Home: 8118 N 38th Ave Phoenix AZ 85051

MULVEY, MARGARET ELLEN, zoologist, researcher; b. Waterbury, Conn., Apr. 12, 1952; d. Donald James and Ellen Ann (Murphy) M.; m. Michael Charles Newman, May 24, 1980; children: Benjamin, Ian. BA, U. Conn., 1974, MS, 1976; PhD, Rutgers U., 1981. USPHS postdoctoral fellow U. Calif.-San Diego, La Jolla, 1982-83; vis. scientist Savannah River Ecology Lab., Aiken, S.C., 1983—; part-time faculty mem. U. S.C., Aiken, 1984—; adj. asst. prof. Wake Forest U., Winston-Salem, N.C., 1986—. Contbr. articles to profl. jours. Mem. Soc. for the Study of Evolution, Malacological Union, Am. Genetic Assn. Office: Savannah River Ecology Lab PO Drawer E Aiken SC 29802

MUMMA, KAROLYN, hospital administrator; b. Evanston, Ill.; d. George Edwin and Leonora (Kimball) M.; children: John Gorter, Douglas Gorter, Louise Kimball Hammer. BSW, Cornell U., 1978; MSW, Va. Commonwealth U., 1982. Lic. clin. social worker; cert. addictions counselor. Clin. social worker Savannah, Ga., 1982—; mgr. Clark Ctr., Meml. Med. Ctr., Savannah, 1985—. Mem. Nat. Assn. Social Workers, Clin. Social Work Assn.(pres.), Mental Health Assn. (v.p.), Am. Hosp. Assn., Omicron Nu, Phi Kappa Phi. Address: 416 E 61st St Savannah GA 31405 Office: Clark Ctr 5002 Waters Ave Savannah GA 31405

MUNCEY, BARBARA DEANE, company execuitve; b. Welch, W.Va., July 12, 1952; d. Juan Irvin and June Henryetta (Dowse) M. AB, Marshall U., Huntington, W.Va., 1974; postgrad., U. Ill., 1980; postgrad, U. Mich, 1984-85; postgrad., U. Oklahoma, 1987. Cons. Heartside Neighborhood Assn., Grand Rapids, Mich., 1979-80; asst. dir. Muncey Devel. Corp., Grand Rapids, Mich., 1979-80; coord. Northeast Mich. Econ. Devel. Assn., Gayland, Mich., 1980-81; dir. of econ. devel. Grand Rapids Internat Tribal Council, Mich.; dir. Sterling Indsl. Devel. Com., Ill., 1986--; v.p. Sauk Valley Area Econ. Devel. Assn., 1989--, mem. Whiteside Co. Regional Planning Comm., 1987--. Mem. Rep. Women's Club. Mem. NAFE, Am. Econ. Devel., Ill. Devel. Coun., Mich. Indsl. Devel., Mid-Am. Econ. Devel. Coun. Baptist. Office: Sterling Ind Devel Com 1741 Industrial Dr Sterling IL 61081

MUNCH, JEAN, accountant; b. Tampa, Fla., June 19, 1932; d. Mitchell Lefler and Theresa (Thiele) M.; m. Axel Munch; children: Deborah, Veronica, Donald Patterson. Student, Hillsborough Community Coll., 1983. Lic. real estate. Corp. officer mgr. Colony Shops, Tampa; regional office mgr. Hertz Corp., Tampa; dist. office mgr. Ryder Truck Rental, Tampa. Mem. NAFE. Home: 116 Morrow Cir Brandon FL 33510

MUNCIE, ALETHA MCCROSKEY, elementary school educator; b. Mar. 31, 1920; d. David Earl and Georgia Edna (Hughbanks) McCroskey; m. Richard George Muncie, Nov. 26, 1942; children: Shirley, Doris Muncie Smith, Kay Muncie Norvell. BA in Edn., East Cen. State U., Ada, Okla., 1942. Cert. libr. Tchr. grades 1-8 Tecumseh, Okla., 1943; owner pvt. kindergarten Mangum, Okla., 1955; tchr. Putman Schs., Oklahoma City, 1958-61; tchr., vice prin. Manhattan (Kans.) Pub. Schs., 1962-72; tchr. Park Ridge (Ill.) Pub. Schs., 1975-83; ret. Mem. mayor com. on noise level of O'Hara Airport, 1978; mgr. county Rep. office, Manhattan, 1971; edn. dir. Meth. Ch., Park Ridge, 1975. Mem. AAUW (recording sec. 1988-90). Home: 19606 130 Ave Sun City West AZ 85375

MUNCY, MARTHA ELIZABETH, retired newspaper publisher; b. Dodge City, Kans., Nov. 5, 1919; d. Jess C. and Juliet Mildred (Pettijohn) Denious.; m. Howard E. Muncy, June 5, 1943 (div. 1969); children: Martha Juliet, Suzanne M. Kerr, Howard E. Jr. Student, Lindenwood Coll. for Women, 1937-38; BA, U. Kans., 1941. Advt. mgr. Dodge City Broadcasting Co., 1942-43, copywriter, 1944-46, pres., 1973-88; saleswoman Boot Hill Mus., Inc., Dodge City, 1963; pub., pres. Dodge City Daily Globe, 1973-88. Mem. Kans. Cavalry, Topeka, 1976—; bd. dirs. Arrowhead West, Inc., Dodge City, 1976—, Dodge City Roundup, Inc., 1976—, Dodge City Crimestoppers, 1985—; bd. dirs., sec. Ford county Hist. R.R. Preservation and Found., Dodge City, 1984—; trustee William Allen White Found., Lawrence, Kans., 1984—. Recipient Outstanding Service award Dodge City Lions, 1981; named Kans. Outstanding Rehab. vol. Kans. Rehab. Assn., 1985. Mem. Kans. Press Women (Woman of Achievement award 1984), S.W. Kans. Press Women, S.W. Kans. Edit. Assn. (Outstanding Journalism award 1982), Dodge City Media Pros, Am. Assn. Univ. Women, Dodge City Women's C. of C., Dodge City C. of C., The Philomaths, DAR, P.E.O., Sigma Delta Chi. Republican. Presbyterian. Home: 511 Annette Dodge City KS 67801

MUND, GERALDINE, federal judge; b. L.A., July 7, 1943; d. Charles J. and Pearl (London) M. BA, Brandeis U., 1965; MS, Smith Coll., 1967; JD, Loyola U., 1977. Bar: Calif. 1977. Bankruptcy judge U.S. Cen. Dist. Calif., 1984—. Past pres. Temple Israel, Hollywood, Calif. Mem. ABA, L.A. County Bar Assn. Office: US Dist Ct 312 N Spring St Los Angeles CA 90012*

MUNDER, TERRIE HOLLOWED, personal and family counselor; b. Berwyn, Ill., Aug. 7, 1930; d. James Aloysius and Marie (Nohava) Hollowed; m. John E. Birch, Nov. 4, 1950 (div. Apr. 1969); children—John Edward, Christopher James, Terrie Johnice Birch Kallal, Laurence Patrick; m. 2d, Lee Munder, May 11, 1983. B.A. cum laude in Psychology, Rosary Coll., 1974; M.S. in Counseling Psychology, George Williams Coll., 1976. Sec.-treas. John Birch & Co., Lombard, Ill., 1953-66, prin. Terrie Birch & Co., Lombard, 1953-66, Alert Carpentry, Lombard, 1953-66, Durable Masonry, Inc., Lombard, 1953-66, Cherrywood Homes, Lombard, 1953-66; travel counselor, 1969-71; vocat. testing and counselor Women's Inc., Hinsdale, Ill., 1975-78, Office Manpower Planning, DuPage County (Ill.) Ctr., Wheaton, 1975-78; dir. vol. services Holy Family Hosp., Des Plaines, Ill., 1978-83, mem. aux.; mem. adv. com. Bensenville Home Soc. Ret. Sr. Vol. Program. Meml. and honor chmn., dir. Infant Welfare Soc., Chgo., 1963-65, pres. Western Springs Ctr., 1967; mem. career adv. council Wheeling (Ill.) High Sch. Mem. Ill. Soc. for Dirs. Vol. Services, Am. Soc. Dirs. Vol. Services, Chgo. Council Dirs. Vol. Services (edn. chmn.), U. Ill. Alumni Assn., AAUW, Drama League, Mensa, Pi Gamma Mu. Club: Oak Brook Women's. Home: 3406 Adams Rd Oak Brook IL 60521-2708

MUNDORFF SHRESTHA, SHEILA ANN, cariologist; b. Rochester, N.Y., Dec. 14, 1945; d. Karl Mundorff and Elizabeth Mary (Braun) Ross; m. Buddhi Man Shrestha, June 18, 1988. BS in Biology, Nazareth Coll., Rochester, 1967; MS in Microbiology, U. Rochester, 1984. Lab. technician Eastman Dental Ctr., Rochester, 1967-69, rsch. asst., 1969-71, rsch. assoc., 1971-90, small animal expt. coord., 1984-90, sect. head animal rsch., 1987-90, chmn. Instl. Animal Care and Use Com., 1990—; Mem. animal resource group Am. Dental Assn. Health Found., Chgo., 1981-83; cons. working group Sci. Consensus Conf.-Assessment of Cariogenic Potential of Foods, San Antonio, 1985. Patentee in field. CPR instr. ARC, Rochester, 1978-90. NIH, Nat. Inst. Dental Rsch. grantee, 1986, 87, 88. Mem. Am. Assn. Dental Rsch. (sec.-treas. Rochester sect. 1977-90), Am. Chem. Soc. Roman Catholic. Office: Eastman Dental Ctr 625 Elmwood Ave Rochester NY 14620

MUNFORD, JOAN HARDIE, member House of Delegates, corporate executive; b. Blacksburgh, Va., Oct. 25, 1933; d. John Dewey and Hester Robate (Price) Hardie; m. William Thomas Munford, 1951; 1 child, Mary Ellen. Student, Radford Coll., 1952. Adminstr. Heritage Hall Nursing Home, Blacksburg, 1975-80; v.p. HCMF Corp., Blacksburg, 1980—; mem. Ho. of Dels. State of Va., 1981; mem. bd. advisors Nat. Bank of Blacksburg; mem. occupation adv. com. Montgomery County Health; bd. dirs. Radford Community Hosp. Named Woman of Yr. News Messenger, 1978-79; recipient Community Leader Citation KPEX/Holiday Inn, 1983. Democrat. Baptist. Home: 205 E Eakin St Blacksburg VA 24060 Office: HCMF Corp 1480 S Main St Blacksburg VA 24060

MUNGER, SHARON, market research firm executive; M. Robert Munger; 3 children: Shawn, Shane, Blair. Grad. Vanderbilt U. Sec., data processor, acct. exec. M/A/R/C, Inc., Irving, Tex., from 1973; now pres., chief operating officer Irving, Tex. Office: M-A-R-C Inc 7850 N Belt Line Rd Irving TX 75063*

MUNN, KELLY ANN, computer company executive; b. San Francisco, Nov. 25, 1956; d. Albert Joseph and Barbara Ann (Hansson) M.; m. Steve Dunlap Thues, Sept. 20, 1987. BA, San Francisco State U., 1980. Trainer Computer Expressions, San Francisco, 1981-82, System Star, San Francisco, 1982-83; dir. tng. Applied Computer Cons., Oakland, Calif., 1983-89; mgr. product sales tng. Microsoft Corp., Redmond, Wash., 1989—; cons. Marin (Calif.) Computer Ctr., 1982-83, Heald Bus. Sch., San Francisco, 1982-83, San Francisco Jewish Community Ctr., 1983-84, Meals on Wheels, San Francisco, 1987-89. Mem. ASTD. Home: 21007 SE 28th Pl Issaquah WA 98027 Office: Microsoft One Microsoft Way Redmond WA 98052-6399

MUNN, SUSAN ANN, accountant; b. Luton, Eng., May 28, 1961; came to U.S., 1973; d. Robert Victor and Joan (Beattie) M. AA, Lorain Community Coll., 1984; BA, Baldwin Wallace Coll., 1986, MBA, 1988. Bookkeeper G.C. Murphy Co., North Ridgeville, Ohio, 1979-80; dept. mgr. Zayre, North Olmsted, Ohio, 1980-82; contr. B.M. Rebuilders, Inc., Elyria, Ohio, 1981—; treas. B.M. Rebuilders, Inc., sec. 1983. Mem. Rocky River Presbyn. Ch., 1986. Mem. Am. Mgmt. Assn., Internat. Platform Assn., Internat. Pers. Mgmt. Assn., Slender You, Fun in the Sun, Baldwin Wallace Alumni Assn., J. Sorensen's Aerobic Club, B-W Women's Club. Home: 4860 Mills Creek Ln North Ridgeville OH 44039 Office: BM Rebuilders Inc 940 Cleveland St Elyria OH 44035

MUNNELL, ALICIA HAYDOCK, economist; b. N.Y.C., Dec. 6, 1942; d. Walter Howe Haydock and Alicia (Wildman) Haydock Roux; m. Thomas Clark Munnell (div.); children: Thomas Clark Jr., Hamilton Haydock; m. Henry Scanlon Healy, Feb. 2, 1980. BA in Econs., Wellesley, 1964; MA in Econs., Boston U., 1966; PhD in Econs., Harvard U., 1973. Staff asst. bus. rsch. div. New Eng. Tel. Co., Boston, 1964-65; teaching fellow econs. dept. Boston U., 1965-66; rsch. asst. for dir. econ. studies program Brookings Instn., Washington, 1966-68; teaching fellow Harvard U., Cambridge, Mass., 1971-73; asst. prof. econs. Wellesley Coll., Mass., 1974; economist Fed. Res. Bank Boston, 1973-76, asst. v.p., economist, 1976-78, v.p., economist, 1979-84, sr. v.p., dir. rsch., 1984—; mem. Gov.'s Task Force on Unemployment Compensation, Mass., 1975; mem. spl. funding adv. com. for Mass. pensions, 1976; mem. Mass. Retirement Law Commn., 1976-82; staff dir. joint com. on pub. pensions Nat. Planning Assn., 1978; mem. adv. com. for urban inst. HUD grant on state-local pensions, 1978-81; mem. pension rsch. council Wharton Sch. Fin. and Commerce, U. Pa., 1979—; mem. adv. group Nat. Commn. for Employment Policy, 1980-81; mem. adv. bd. Nat. Aging Policy Ctr. in Income Maintenance, Brandeis U., 1980-84; participant pvt. sector retirement security and U.S. tax policy roundtable discussions Govt. Rsch. Corp., 1984; mem. supervisory panel Forum Inst. of Villers Found., 1984; mem. Medicare working group, div. of health policy rsch. and edn. Harvard U., 1984-87; mem. Commn. on Coll. Retirement, 1984-86; mem. com. to plan major study of nat. long term care policies Inst. Medicine, Nat. Acad. Scis., 1984-87; mem. steering com. Am. Assn. Ret. Persons, 1987—; mem. adv. council Am. Enterprise Inst., 1987—; com. mem. Inst. Medicine, Nat. Acad. Scis. Human Rights Com., 1987—; co-founder, pres. Nat. Acad. Social Ins., 1986—; bd. dirs. Pension Rights Ctr.; mem. program rev. com. Brigham and Women's Hosp., 1988—; mem. Commn. to Rev. Mass. Anti-Takeover Laws, 1988-89, econs. vis. com. MIT, 1989—. Author: The Impact of Social Security on Personal Saving, 1974, Future of Social Security (various awards), 1977, Pensions for Public Employees, 1979, The Economics of Private Pensions, 1982; editor: Lessons from the Income Maintenance Experiments, 1987; (with others) Options for Fiscal Reform in Massachusetts, 1975; contbr. chpts. and articles to profl. jours. Mem. Inst. Med. Nat. Acad. Scis., Nat. Acad. Pub. Adminstrn. Office: Fed Res Bank Boston 600 Atlantic Ave Boston MA 02106

MUNRO, ALICE, author; b. Wingham, Ont., Can., July 10, 1931; d. Robert Eric and Anne Clarke (Chamney) Laidlaw; m. James Armstrong Munro, 1951 (div. 1976); children: Sheila, Jenny, Andrea; m. Gerald Fremlin, 1976. Student, U. Western Ont., 1949-51. Author: (short stories) Dance of the Happy Shades (Gov.-Gen.'s Lit. award 1969), 1968, A Place for Everything, 1970, Lives of Girls and Women (Can. Booksellers award), 1971, (short stories) Something I've Been Meaning To Tell You, 1974, Who Do You Think You Are?, 1978, Stories of Flo and Rose (Gov.-Gen.'s Lit. award 1979), 1979, The Moons of Jupiter, 1982, (short stories) The Progress of Love (Gov.-Gen.'s Lit. award 1987), 1987, (short stories) Friend of My Youth, 1990. Recipient Can.-Australia Lit. Prize, Marian Engel award, 1986. Office: care Alfred A Knopf Inc 201 E 50th St New York NY 10022*

MUNRO, C. LYNN, communications consultant; b. Oak Park, Ill., June 15, 1949; d. Paul H. Munro and Ruth H. (Fauteck) Meyer. BA, U. Iowa, 1970, MA, 1973, PhD, 1975. Cert. prodn. and inventory control mgr. Rsch. asst. U. Iowa, Iowa City, 1971-73, instr., 1973-75; asst. prof. Kendall Coll., Evanston, Ill., 1977-81; assoc. prof. U. Mo., Kansas City, Mo., 1981-85; communications cons. Blair Murrah, Sibley, Mo., 1985—; pres. Qualiwrite, Belton, Mo., 1985—; tech. cons. Longview Coll./AT&T, Lee's Summit, Mo., 1985—; mfrs. rep. EZ Touring, San Diego, 1987—; sr. tech. writer Applied Communications, Overland Park, Kans., 1989—; cons. PanHandle Eastern, Kansas City, 1982-83. Author: The Galbraithian Vision, 1977, A Man Before His Time, 1988; contbr. articles to profl. jours. Bd. dirs. BMW Motorcycle Owners Am., St. Louis, 1983-88; reviewer Nat. Endowment for the Humanities, Washington, 1980-87; coord. Afro-Am. Summer Inst., Iowa City, 1971-73. Home and Office: 16603 Kentucky Belton MO 64012

MUNRO, CRISTINA STIRLING, artistic director; b. London, May 22, 1940; m. Richard Munro (div. 1986); children: Alexandra, Nicholas. Attended various artistic schs., London. Mem. ballet corps Sadlers Wells Opera Ballet, London, 1960-62, Het Nederlands Ballet, The Netherlands, 1962-63; soloist London Festival Ballet, 1963-72; prin. soloist Eliot Feld Ballet, N.Y.C., 1972-75; prin. dancer, artistic dir. Old Dominion U., Norfolk, Va., 1975; artistic dir. Louisville Ballet Co., 1975-79; ballet mistress Houston Ballet, 1979-85; dir. Munro Ballet Schs., Corpus Christi, Tex., 1985—; artistic dir. Corpus Christi Ballet, 1985—; guest artist and choreographer numerous cos. in U.S. Recipient Giovanni Martini award. Mem. Imperial Soc. Tchrs. of Dance, Royal Acad. Dancing, Brit. Actors Equity Assn., Am. Guild Mus. Artists. Office: Munro Ballet Studios/ Corpus Christi Ballet 5610 Everhart Rd Corpus Christi TX 78411

MUNRO, HEDI See MESNEY, DOROTHY TAYLOR

MUNROE, DONNA SCOTT, information systems and management consultant; b. Cleve., Nov. 28, 1945; d. Glenn Everett and Louise Lenox (Parkhill) Scott; m. Melvin James Ricketts, Dec. 23, 1968 (div. Aug. 1979); 1 child, Suzanne Michelle; m. Peter Carlton Munroe, Feb. 14, 1981. BS in Sociology, Portland (Oreg.) State U., 1976, BS in Philosophy, 1978, MS in Sociology, 1983. Lectr. Portland State U., 1977-79; writing, editorial cons. Worth Pubs., N.Y.C., 1978-79; statis. cons. Health Scis. U., Morrison Ctr. Youth Svcs. U. Oreg., Portland, 1979-82; tech. writer Equitable Savs & Loan, Portland, 1981-82; mgr. acct. and projects. Electronic Data Systems, Portland, 1982-87; sr. mgmt. cons. to corp. exec. mgmt for strategic planning Computer Mgmt. Systems, Inc., Portland, 1987—. Mem. Am. Mgmt. Assn., Am. Soc. for Quality Control, City Club of Portland, Sigma Xi. Democrat. Episcopalian. Home: 536 SW Cheltenham St Portland OR 97201 Office: Computer Mgmt Systems Inc 0234 SW Bancroft Portland OR 97201

MUNROE, MARIA LYN, rehabilitation educator; b. Gadsden, Ala., Oct. 4, 1946; d. Cecil Hutto and Frances Evelyn (Teague) M.; 1 child, Eve Shanna Wade. BS, Auburn U., Auburn, 1964-67; MA, U. of Alabama, Birmingham, 1978-79; postgrad., U. Alabama, Birmingham, 1989—; cert. fellow, Am. Acad. Pain Mgmt. Dir. Alabama State Dept. of Edn, Birmingham, Ala., 1977-79; exec. v.p Learning Ctr. of Am., Inc., Birmingham, 1979-81; branch mgr./dir. of rehabilitation Crawford and Co., Crawford Health & Rehabilitation Services, Birmingham, 1981-84; exec. v.p Lakeshore Rehabilitation Hosp. & Complex, Birmingham; ptnr. and vocational counselor Rehabilitation Mgmt. Services (RMS), Birmingham, 1988--; owner and rehabilitation cons. Munroe and Assoc., 1986--; bd. dir., Workshops for the Blind and Disabled, Birmingham, Ala., 1986--, Phoenix Rising, (cognitive retraining for brain injured persons), Birmingham, 1986--; program dir., Am. Acad. of Physical Medicine and rehabilitation 1988 annual conf., Seattle, 1987-88. mem. adv. coun. (rehab.) Auburn Univ. Grad. Sch. Methodist. Home: 163 Condominium B Birmingham AL 35216 Office: Munroe and Assoc 2302 Tenth Court South Birmingham AL 35216

MUNROE, MARY LOU SCHWARZ (MRS. ROBERT E. MUNROE), educational administrator; b. Denver, Nov. 18, 1927; d. John Anthony and Lutie A. (Benefiel) Schwarz; m. Robert E. Munroe; children: Robert M., Carol E., John E. Dir. Jr. and Collegiate Great Books Program, Archdiocese of Denver, 1961-71, leader tng. staff, 1963-71, archdiocesan dir. grade and high sch., 1966-71; undergrad. counselor Sch. Edn. U. Denver, 1971-74; adminstrv. dir., ednl. coord. child and adolescent prog. Mt. Airy Psychiat. Ctr., Denver, 1975—; feature writer Register, Denver, 1963-71; lectr., workshop dir. Loretto Heights Coll., 1966, regional tng. ctrs. for religion tchrs., 1967—. Author: Counseling the Parishoner, 1967. Mem. steering com. Cinema Critique Series of Denver, 1967; mem.-at-large Bd. Cath. Edn. of Denver Met. Area, 1969—, pres., 1974-75; mem. Denver Met. Adv. Com. Cath. Edn., 1968-69, Juvenile Ct. Task Force, 1969. Named Woman of Yr., Archdiocese of Denver Edn. Assn., 1971; named to Denver Post Gallery of Fame, 1975; recipient papal medal Pro Ecclesia et Pontifice, 1975; Dr. Mary Lou Munroe Learning Ctr. dedicated in her honor, 1985. Mem. Cath. Edn. Guild, Mortar Bd., Ednl. Forum Colo. (charter), Phi Beta Kappa, Kappa Delta Pi, Delta Kappa Gamma, Phi Delta Kappa, Delta Gamma. Home: 3131 E Alameda Ave Apt 1301 Denver CO 80209

MUNROE, SHIRLEY ANN, hospital association executive, health care consultant; b. Mpls., Mar. 31, 1924; d. Laurence John and Esther (Tuttle) M.; pre-nursing cert. La Sierra Coll., Arlington, Calif., 1943; R.N., Glendale Sanitarium and Hosp. Sch. Nursing, 1946; postgrad. UCLA Extension, 1953-55, Los Angeles City Coll., 1948-51; cert. U. Calif. at Santa Cruz extension, 1971; m. Stanley G. Fjelstrom, Dec. 26, 1954 (div. June 1957). Chief nurse, office mgr. for pvt. practice physicians, Los Angeles, 1946-51; bus. mgr. Bolander Clinic and Emergency Hosp., Van Nuys, Calif., 1951-56, Mendocino Med. Ctr., Ukiah, Calif., 1956; adminstr. Hillside Community Hosp., Ukiah, 1956-78, sec., 1956-78; dir. Ctr. for Small or Rural Hosps., Am. Hosp. Assn., Chgo., 1978-79, dir. constituency programs, 1979-83, exec. dir. constituency sects., 1984-85, v.p., 1985-88; mem. adv. and eval. com. Ukiah Dist. Sch. Vocat. Nursing, 1965-78; faculty U. Calif. extension at Berkeley, Basic Adminstrn. Hosp. Adminstrs. Program, 1966-70; dir., sec. Obs. Investment Co., Ukiah, 1957-67. Asst. dir. pub. relations alumni postgrad. assembly Loma Linda U., Los Angeles, 1949-55; dir. pub. relations world meeting Aerospace Med. Assn., Los Angeles, 1953; chmn. re-edn. nursing com. Calif. Dept. Employment, 1962; cons. lectr. nurse aide edn., adult edn. Willits, Ukiah high schs., 1962; chmn. Career Project for Sr. High Sch. Girls, 1962-64; mem. Mendocino-Lake adv. com. Regional Med. Program, 1969-73; mem. vocat. edn. adv. com. Ukiah Unified Sch. Dist., 1970-73. Soloist, Presbyn. Ch., Ukiah, 1956-69, Ukiah Oratorio Soc., 1958-65; supt. children's edn. Seventh-day Adventist Ch., 1961-64, dir. pub. relations, 1967-78, chmn. fin. com., 1967-78, mem. ch. bd., 1967-78, mem. exec. com. Ill. conf., 1983-89, soloist, 1958-78; mem. ch. bd. Seventh-day Adventist Ch., Elmhurst, 1979-89, dir. music, mem. ch. bd., Roswell, N.Mex., 1989—, dir. ch. ministries, 1990—; co-chmn. edn. com. Mendocino County br. Am. Cancer Soc., 1961-62, bd. dirs., 1961-76, pres., 1963-65; mem. steering com. Am. Heart Assn., Mendocino County br. Calif. Heart Assn.; chmn. trustees Tri-County Pre-Payment Medi-Cal Pilot Project, State of Calif., 1969-71; trustee Nor Coa Health, 1967-76, 1st v.p. 1969-71, pres., 1971-72, chmn. South Planning council, 1972-74; mem. Mendocino-Lake counties council, 1966-76; bd. dirs. Mendocino County chpt. ARC, 1968-70; bd. dirs. Blue Cross No. Calif., 1971-78, exec. bd., 1973-78, hosp. provider rep., 1970-78; leader del. People to People Internat. U.S. Citizen Ambassador Program, 1981; mem. bd. Adventist Health System/North, 1981-87, chmn. strategic planning com., 1983-87; mem. bd. Hinsdale Hosp., 1979—, mem. joint conf. com., 1980-89, chmn. strategic planning com., 1983-88; bd. dirs. Broadview Acad., Lafox, Ill., 1983-86, Roswell Symphony Orch., 1990—. Recipient Civic Participation award, Outstanding Women in Professions award Calif. Fedn. Bus. and Profl. Women's Clubs, 1965; Outstanding Service award Mendocino-Lake br. Am. Cancer Soc., 1963, 64, 65, Notable Service award, 1968; Walker fellow, 1973. Mem. Am. Hosp. Assn. (ho. of dels. 1974-78, regional adv. bd. 1974-78, rural resource com. 1976-78, v.p.), Calif. Hosp. Assn. (membership com. 1960-61; legis. liaison 1960, panel hosp. peer rev. adminstrs. 1968-78; mem. ins. com. 1971-78), Redwood Empire Hosp. Conf. (ins. com. 1957-59, exec. com. 1968-71, 1st v.p. 1968, pres. 1969), Hosp. Council No. Calif. (bd. dirs. 1968-77, pres. 1975-76, chmn. com. on program and edn. 1968-70), Assn. Western Hosps. (edn. research found. council 1963-65), Glendale Sanitarium and Hosp. Sch. Nursing Alumni Assn. (pres. Glendale 1947-48), Bus. and Profl. Women's Club (exec. bd. 1957-61, pres. 1959-60, 3d v.p. 1960-61, career advancement com. 1961-62, chmn. personal devel. com. 1962-64, mem. bd. 1962-65, music chmn. Redwood Empire dist. 1960-61), Republican. Club: Soroptimist (pres. Ukiah 1971-72, music chmn. 1962-63, service com. 1961-78, editor bull. 1965-66, Woman of Achivement award 1965, dir. 1970-73). Home: 707 W Mescalero Rd Roswell NM 88201

MUNSELL, SUSAN GRIMES, state legislator, accountant; b. Highland Park, Mich., June 21, 1951; d. Chauncey Gale and Shirley Mabel (Rick) Grimes; m. Frank Edward Munsell, Dec. 5, 1980. BA, Mich. State U., 1973; MBA, U. Mich., 1979. CPA, Mich. Cons. Harris, Kerr, Forster & Co., CPAs, Los Angeles, 1973-76; mgr. Lucky Duck Nursery & Day Care Ctr., Brighton, Mich., 1976-77; tax intern Coopers & Lybrand, CPAs, Detroit, 1978; mem. tax staff Arthur Andersen & Co., CPAs, Detroit, 1979-83; prin. Susan Grimes Munsell, CPA, Fowlerville, Mich., 1983—; mem. Mich. Ho. of Reps., Lansing, 1987—. Dep. treas. Livingston County (Mich.) Reps., 1985-86; active local Girl Scouts U.S. Named One of 10 Outstanding Young People in Mich. Mich. Jaycees, 1986. Mem. LWV (various offices 1976—), NOW (various offices 1977—), Am. Inst. CPA's, Am. Women's Soc. CPA's, Am. Bus. Women's Assn., Mich. Assn. CPA's. Methodist. Home: 209 W Sibley St Howell MI 48843 Office: Mich Ho of Reps State Capitol Bldg Lansing MI 48913

MUNSHAW, NANCY CLARE, urban planner; b. Maryville, Mo., Sept. 24, 1947; d. Waldo C. and Mary Jane (Butcher) Thompson; 1 child, Peter. BA, U. Mo., 1970; M in Urban Planning, U. Ill., 1979. Planner City of Lafayette (La.), 1979-81; planning and community devel. dir. City of Rolla (Mo.), 1981-85; housing and community devel. dir. City of Webster Groves (Mo.), 1985-87; exec. dir. Old Webster Redevelopment Corp.; pres. Pub. Interest Planning, St. Louis, 1988-89; planning adminstr. St. Lucie County, Fort Pierce, Fla., 1989. Co-author: Policy Studies Personnel Directory, 1979; contbr. articles to profl. jours. bd. dirs. LWV, 1972-81; vacancy com. chmn. Adequate Housing for Missourians, 1987-88. Recipient Econ. Devel. Inst. Thesis award So. Indsl. Devel. Council, 1986. Mem. Am. Planning Assn. (sec. St. Louis sect. 1985-86), Am. Inst. Cert. Planners, Nat. Assn. Housing and Redevelopment Officials. Democrat. Mem. United Church of Christ. Office: 2300 Virginia Ave Fort Pierce FL 34982

MUNSON, JANIS ELIZABETH TREMBLAY, engineering company executive; b. Beverly, Mass., Dec. 17, 1948; d. Louis Story Tremblay and Doroth Ellen (Burnham) Tonkin; divorced. BS in Geology summa cum laude, Boston U., 1976, M in Urban Planning, 1982. Libr. United Engrs. & Constructors, Boston, 1971-73, land use planner, 1973-76, lead land use planner, 1976-80, supervising lic. engr., 1980-87, mgr. planning group, 1989, head mktg. analysis svcs. group power div., 1987-89, environ. cons., 1987—. Bd. dirs. Ctr. City Residents Assn., Phila., 1986; mem. Multiple Sclerosis Soc.; vol. for disabled. Mem. Am. Planning Assn., Am. Inst. Cert. Planners (assoc.), World Affairs Council. Republican. Congregationalist. Home: 2401 Pennsylvania Ave 3C-50 Philadelphia PA 19130 Office: United Engrs and Constructors 300 S 17th St Philadelphia PA 19101

MUNSON, JULIE ANN, insurance company executive; b. Warsaw, Ind., Dec. 18, 1950; d. Ben L. and Lois L. (McDaniel) Detterman; m. Herbert A. Munson, June 3, 1983. Student, Ball State U., 1971. Lic. land title agt.;. Abstracter Warsaw (Ind.) Abstract & Title Corp., 1971-74; owner Warsaw Abstract& Title Corp., 1975--. Bd. dirs. Big Brothers, Big Sisters, Warsaw, 1988--. Mem. NAFE, Am. Land Title Assn., Nat. Home Builders Assn., Kosciusko Home Builders Assn., Ind. C. of C., YMCA, Greater Warsaw Area C. of C., Ind. Republican. Office: Warsaw Abstract & Title Corp 104 E Ft Wayne St Warsaw IN 46580

MUNSON, LUCILLE MARGUERITE (MRS. ARTHUR E. MUNSON), real estate broker; b. Norwood, Ohio, Mar. 26, 1914; d. Frank and Fairy (Wicks) Wirick; R.N., Lafayette (Ind.) Home Hosp., 1937; A.B., San Diego State U., 1963, student Purdue U., Kans. Wesleyan U.; m. Arthur E. Munson, Dec. 24, 1937; children—Barbara Munson Papke, Judith Munson Andrews, Edmund Arthur. Staff and pvt. nurse Lafayette Home Hosp., 1937-41; indsl. nurse Lakey Foundry & Machine Co., Muskegon, Mich., 1950-51, Continental Motors Corp., Muskegon, 1951-52; nurse Girl Scout Camp, Grand Haven, Mich., 1948-49; owner Munson Realty, San Diego, 1964—. Mem. San Diego County Grand Jury, 1975-76, 80-81, Calif. Grand Jurors Assn. (charter). Home: 5765 Friars Rd Apt 200 San Diego CA 92108 Office: 2999 Mission Blvd # 102 San Diego CA 92109

MUNSON, NANCY KAY, lawyer; b. Huntington, N.Y., June 22, 1936; d. Howard H. and Edna M. (Keenan) Munson. Student, Hofstra U., 1959-62; JD, Bklyn. Law Sch., 1965. Bar: N.Y. 1966, U.S. Supreme Ct. 1970, U.S. Ct. Appeals (2d cir.) 1971, U.S. Dist. Ct. (ea. and so. dists.) N.Y. 1968. Law clk. to E. Merritt Weidner Huntington, 1959-66, sole practice, 1966—; mem. legal adv. bd. Chgo. Title Ins. Co., Riverhead, N.Y., 1981—; bd. dirs., legal officer Thomas Munson Found. Trustee Huntington Fire Dept. Death Benefit Fund; pres., trustee, chmn. bd. Bklyn. Home Aged Men Found. Mem. ABA, N.Y. State Bar Assn., Suffolk County Bar Assn., Bklyn. Bar Assn., NRA, DAR, Soroptimists (past pres.). Republican. Christian Scientist. Office: 197 New York Ave Huntington NY 11743

MUNZER, ELEANOR ROE, sales executive; b. Canisteo, N.Y., Aug. 13, 1921; d. Glenn Shattuck and Myra (Petty) Roe; m. Robert Leslie Munzer, Nov. 26, 1947 (div. 1963); children: Catherine Munzer Ackert, Joyce Ann Munzer Cole. Student, Hills Bus. Coll., 1942, Midwestern Broadcasting Coll., Chgo., 1964. Owner, mgr. Part-Time Personnel, Chgo., 1977-78; ins. broker Tampa, 1984-90; sales assoc. 1st Fla. Realty, Tampa, 1988-89; mgr. telemktg. Fred Astaire Dance Studio, Tampa, 1990—; internat. negotiator various countries, 1969-77. Author: A President's Honor, 1970; writer; recording artist: (albums) American Trees and Silver Trees, 1970, Great Grandmother and Musical Bells, 1972, Nations and Christmas Lights, 1979. Mem. Tampa Woman's Club. Republican. Home and Office: 112 W Stanley St Tampa FL 33604

MUORIE, IDA ROSEMARY, finance executive; b. Detroit, Jan. 2, 1950; d. Garbe and Ethel (Jones) Davis; m. Issmaiel Ali Muorie, Dec. 1, 1950. BS, Ga. State U., 1977; JD, Howard U., 1980. Dir. employee rels. Federated Dept. Stores, Inc., Cin., 1980-85; adjunct prof. U. Cin., 1982-84; chief exec. officer, entertainment lawyer Spl. Talent Mgmt. Entertainment Group, Cin., 1985-87; option specialist Internat. Trading Group, Miami, Fla., 1987-89, Cargill Investor Svcs., Coral Gables, Fla., 1989—; energy trading specialist in field; cons. American Mgmt. Assn. Operation Enterprises, N.Y., 1980-84, American Law Libr. Assn., Cin., 1983. Author: poem anthology, Love's Greatest Treasures, Poetic Voices of Am., On the Threshold of a Dream, 1988. Contbr. Camillus House, Miami, 1987—. Internat. Coun. Middle-East Affairs fellow, Syria, Lattikia, 1988. Mem. ABA, Nat. Futures Assn., Writer Guild of Am., Fla. Writer's Assn. Roman Catholic. Home: 1805 Sans Souci Blvd Miami FL 33181 Office: Cargill Investor Svcs 100 Miracle Mile Coral Gables FL 33134

MURAD, TARRUNUMN, management and hotel chain executive; b. Sialkot, Pakistan, Dec. 18, 1951; came to U.S., 1982; d. Jalil-Ur Rhaman and Ashraf (Rahman) Khan; m. Tajjammal Murad, Nov. 23, 1974; children: Rehan, Zeeshaan. Grad., Punjab U., Lahore, Pakistan, 1972. Articled clk. A.F. Ferguson & Co., Lahore, 1968-73; mgr., gen. mgr. various govt. and pvt. orgns., various cities, Pakistan, 1974-80; dir. Tramz Mgmt. Inc., 1981—; chief exec. officer Tramz Hotels Inc., Dewitt, N.Y., 1987—; pres. Tramz Mgmt. Inc., Dewitt. Mem. Rep. Congl. Leadership Coun., Washington, 1989—. Fellow Inst. Chartered Accts. Pakistan. Islam. Office: Tramz Mgmt Inc 5788 Wide Waters Pkwy Dewitt NY 13214

MURASHIMA, KUMIKO, artist, educator; came to U.S., 1967; d. Minoru and Michiko (Nagashima) M. BFA in Fiber Arts, Women's Coll. Fine Arts, 1962; MFA in Fiber Arts, Ind. U., 1970. Craftsman apprentice Serizawa Dyed Paper Inst., Tokyo, 1963-65; freelance textile designer Izumi Archtl. Design Co., Tokyo, 1965-67, Saphier, Lerner, Schindler Environetics, Inc., Chgo., 1970-71; asst. prof. art dept. Glassboro (N.J.) State Coll., 1971—, assoc. prof. art dept., 1974—; artistic dir. Trio Creations, Inc., Glassboro, 1987—. Recipient Malcolm Koch Mus. Purchase, Evansville (Ind.) Mus. Art, 1969, Wilber D. Peat Meml. award, 1970, Mr. and Mrs. Paul Arnold Merit award Herron Mus. Art, 1971; Craftsman's fellow N.J. State Coun. on Arts, 1985. Mem. Am. Crafts Coun., Artists Equity Assn. (Dorothy Grafly Meml. award 1981), Coll. Art Assn. Am., N.J. Designer and Craftsmen, Inc. (chairperson 1985-87), Am. Fedn. Tchrs. Home: PO Box 515 Williamstown NJ 08094 Office: Glassboro State Coll US Rte 322 and Heston Rd Glassboro NJ 08028

MURCHISON, LAURA EDWARDS, retail executive; b. Hartford, Ala., Nov. 13, 1954; d. Beverly Eugene and Laura (Ward) Edwards; m. Carl Wesley Nobles II, June 26, 1976 (div. Feb. 1982); m. Jimmy H. Murchison, Apr. 4, 1989. Cert. in fashion merchandise, Bauber Fashion Coll., 1974. Asst. mgr. Leon's, Montgomery, Ala., 1974-75; mgr. dept. Pizitz, Montgomery, 1975-76; mgr. store, tng. Brooks, Montgomery, 1976-79; owner, mgr. Rag House, Wetompka, Ala., 1979-81; mgr. store Added Dimensions, Montgomery, Ala., 1981-82; mgr. area Added Dimensions, Jacksonville, Fla., 1982-83; mgr. dist. Added Dimensions, Miss., Fla., 1983-90, regional mgr. southern region, 1990—. Mem. Nat. Assn. Female Execs. Methodist. Home: 409 Green St Wetumpka AL 36092 Office: Added Dimensions 2981 E S Blvd Montgomery AL 36116

MURCHISON, NOLA FAYE, librarian; b. Galva, Ill., Mar. 1, 1929; d. John Harold and Eva Mildred (Kling) M.; m. Albert Raisbeck, Aug. 25, 1951 (div. 1955); 1 child, Rory John; m. Richard Lutz, Oct. 8, 1960 (div. 1972); children: Eve Lutz-Smith, Elizabeth Lutz Roush, Lewis. AA, Stephens Coll., 1948; BS in Journalism, U. Ill., 1951; MLS, U. Wis., Milw., 1970; postgrad., U. Wis., Madison, 1976. Library dir. Harvard (Ill.) Pub. Library, 1970-73; librarian Broward County Library, Ft. Lauderdale, Fla., 1974-79, Sheridan (Wyo.) County Library, 1980, Ariz. Dept. Corrections, Tucson, 1981-83; sr. librarian Calif. Dept. Corrections, Chino, 1983-84; librarian, br. head Desert Hot Springs (Calif.) Br. Library, 1984-85, Indio (Calif.) Regional Br. Library, 1985—. Author papers in field. 1st lt. USAF, 1958-59. Recipient John Cotton Dana award ALA, 1980. Mem. Calif. Library Assn., Indio Women's Club, DAV, Phi Mu. Democrat. Unitarian. Office: Indio Resource Br Libr 200 Civic Center Mall Indio CA 92201

MURDOCK, BETSY BOLAND, hospital administrator; b. Hempsted, N.Y., Aug. 12, 1949; d. Robert Charles and Helen Margaret (O'Connell) Boland; m. James A. Murdock, Feb. 25, 1977; children: Josiah Bartlett, Meghan Boland. BA in Pub. Adminstrn., U. Pitts., 1987, MBA, 1989. Exec. sec. Chesapeake & Ohio Rwy., Cleve., 1969-73, Cleve. Clinic Found., 1973-77; adminstrv. asst. to pres. AHERC/Allegheny Gen. Hosp., Pitts., 1977-83; asst. sec. to bds. Allegheny Health Svcs., Inc., Pitts., 1983-87, asst. to pres., 1983-86, asst. v.p., 1986-87; asst. v.p. Allegheny Gen. Hosp., Pitts., 1987—; mem. faculty Allegheny Gen. Mgmt. Devel. Program, Pitts., 1988—. Contbg. author: The Whole Manager, 1989. Mem. steering com. United Way campaign, Allegheny Gen. Hosp., Pitts., 1984—; mem. Allegheny Pres. award Selection Com., 1988—; chmn. Central Blood Bank 1989 Drive, Pitts., 1989. Methodist. Home: 287 Rockdale Rd Butler PA 16001 Office: Allegheny Gen Hosp 320 E North Ave Pittsburgh PA 15212

MURDOCK, JOYCE MARILYN, education specialist; b. L.A., Dec. 7, 1929; d. Lyle James and Mildred Elizabeth (Fleere) Schneider; m. Stanley Allen Murdock, June 14, 1952 (dec. Jan. 1966); children: Dale, Gary, Lynn, Mark. BS, Wash. State U., 1951; edn. credential, U. Calif., Berkeley, 1973, Calif. State U., Hayward, 1973. Comptometer operator Pacific Telephone, San Francisco, 1947, Macy's Dept. Store, San Francisco, 1948; comml. clk. Villa Chartier Restaurant, San Mateo, Calif., 1951; tchr. Sunnyside (Wash.) Sch. Dist., 1951-52, Midland (Mich.) Pub. Schs., 1952-53; substitute tchr. Mt. Diablo Unified Sch. Dist., Concord, Calif., 1973-76, noon supr., 1972—; coord. Mt. Diablo Unified Sch. Dist., Concord, 1978—, Clayton (Calif.) Community Sch., 1978—; supr. Clayton Community Sch. Stay, Play and Learn Childcare, 1982—, Clayton Community Sch. Transitions Preschool, 1988—. Bd. dirs. Clayton Hist. Soc., 1980, docent (Svc. award); mem. election bd. Contra Costa County, Clayton; mem. bd. Clayton Community Sch., 1979-90 (10th Anniversary award 1989); mem. Save Mt. Diablo Environ. Group. Mem. AAUW (hospitality chair 1976-78, edn. chair Clayton chpt. 1984, Named scholar 1986), Sierra Club, Keep Afloat Investment Club (v.p. 1989-90), Phi Beta Kappa, Phi Kappa Phi, Pi Lambda Theta. Republican. Home: 5858 Pine Hollow Rd Clayton CA 94517-1130 Office: Clayton Community Sch 5880 Mount Zion Dr Clayton CA 94517-1130

MURDOCK, MICHELE, communications company executive; b. New Haven, Conn., Sept. 9, 1942; d. Charles Lewis and May B. (Roy) M.; m. Peter J. Stein, June 7, 1981; 1 child, Michael Victor Murdock. AB, Trinity Coll., Washington, 1964; MA, Anenberg Sch. Communications U. Pa., Phila., 1965. Prodn. asst. The Mike Douglas Show, Phila., 1965-67; on camera moderator WACU-TV, Phila., 1966; producer, writer Guidance Assocs., Harcourt, Brace Jovonovich, Inc., N.Y.C., 1967-74; editor, producer Joshua Tree Prodns., N.Y.C., 1974; producer Children's TV Workshop, N.Y.C., 1974; pres., producer edn. and corp. tng., gender, race and mgmt. devel. Murdock Communications, Inc., N.Y.C., 1975—; media cons. Task Force on Minor Head Injury, NYU, N.Y.C., 1988-89. Producer sound filmstrip: Nuclear Profliferation: Race to Extinction, 1981 (Gold Cindy award 1981); producer sound slide presentation: The Corning Children's Center Story, 1981 (Silver Cindy award 1981); co-dir. N.Y. Women in Bus. Week Merrill Lynch Data Ctr. Del. White House Conf. on Small Bus., Washington, 1980. Recipient Bronze medals Internat. Film and TV Awards, 1981, 82. Mem. Info. Film Producers Assn., Assn. Ind. Video and Rilmmaker, Am. Soc. Tng. and Devel., N.Y. Women in Film., Princeton Club. Democrat. Roman Catholic. Home and Office: 205 W 89th St New York NY 10024 Office: Murdock Communications Inc 225 W 57th St New York NY 10019

MURDOCK, MICHELLE MARIE, marketing executive; b. Columbus, Ohio, Nov. 18, 1959; d. Louis Joseph and Barbara Jean (Stites) M. BA in Econs., U. Conn., Stamford, 1982. Membership rep. CUC Internat., Inc., Stamford, 1984-85, membership coord., 1985-86, asst. mgr. account mgmt., 1986-87, asst. mgr. mktg. svcs., 1987, mgr. mktg. svcs., 1987-89, dir. mktg. ops., 1989—; cons. on young careerists Bus. and Profl. Women's Club, Inc., Stamford, 1990. Recipient cert. of appreciation Bus. and Profl. Women's Club, Inc., 1990. Mem. NAFE. Office: CUC Internat Inc 707 Summer St Stamford CT 06901

MURDOCK, MONI (MARY MARGARET MURDOCK), marriage and family therapist; b. Mishawaka, Ind., Jan. 19, 1938; d. Joseph Weldon and Evelyn Mary (Diroll) Hennessy; m. Charles William Murdock, May 25, 1963; children: Kathleen Tracy, Michael Hennessy, Kevin Charles, Sean Joseph. BS cum laude, Marquette U., 1959; MSW, Loyola U., Chgo., 1961; postgrad., The Family Inst., Ill., 1975-77. Caseworker Ill. Children's Home and Aid Soc., Chgo., 1961-64; clin. social worker Logan Ctr., South Bend, Ind., 1973, St. Joseph County Mental Health Ctr., South Bend, 1974-75; clin. social worker Doyle Ctr. Loyola U., Chgo., 1975-77, clin. supr., 1977-87; pvt. practice psychotherapy The Family Ctr., Evanston, 1979—; mem. adv. bd. Ctr. for Family Studies inst. psychiatry Northwestern Meml. Hosp., 1978-89, pres. alumni bd., 1980-83, part time faculty mem., 1983—; chair gov. bd. Family Inst., 1987-89, mem. gov. bd., 1978—; mem. adj. faculty Loyola U. Sch. Social Work, 1984—; chmn. Chgo. family therapy conf. Ctr. for Family Studies, 1980. Bd. dirs., co-founder Little Flower Montessori

Sch., South Bend, 1969-74; chmn. adult edn. Little Flower Parish, South Bend, 1971-73, St. Athanasius Parish, Evanston, 1976-79; del. Nat. Assembly Cath. Laity, Notre Dame, Ind., 1981; invited as child and family mental health del. to People's Republic of China, 1987. Grantee HEW, 1959-60; stipentee VA, 1960-61. Mem. Am. Family Therapy Assn. (charter), Am. Assn. Marriage and Family Therapy (clin., approved supr.), Nat. Assn. Social Workers (cert., clin.), Register Clin. Social Workers (clin. diplomat). Democrat. Home: 2527 Marcy Ave Evanston IL 60201 Office: The Family Ctr 1830 Sherman Ave Evanston IL 60201

MURDOCK, PAMELA ERVILLA, wholesale travel company executive, retail travel company executive; b. Los Angeles, Dec. 3, 1940; d. John James and Chloe Conger (Keefe) M.; children—Cheryl, Kim. BS, U. Colo., 1962. Pres., Dolphin Travel, Denver, 1972-87; owner, pres. Mile Hi Tours, Denver, 1974—, MH Internat., 1987—, Mile-Hi Advt. Agy., 1986— . Named Wholesaler of Yr., Las Vegas Conv. and Visitors Authority, 1984. Mem. Am. Soc. Travel Agts., Colo. Assn. Commerce and Industry, Nat. Fedn. Independent Businessmen, NAFE, Internat. Platform Assn. Republican. Home: 5565 E Vassar Ave Denver CO 80222 Office: Mile Hi Tours Inc 2120 S Birch Denver CO 80222

MURLIN-GARDNER, MICHELLE, actress; b. Harrisburg, Pa., Jan. 3, 1964; d. William and Dolores (Murlin) Gardner. Student, Carnegie-Mellon U., 1981-82; BFA in Dance, Point Park Coll., Pitts., 1984. Singer, dancer Walt Disney World, Orlando, Fla., 1984-85, Tokyo Disneyland, 1985; actress, singer, dancer Pitts. Civic Light Opera, 1986, various musical prodns., various cities, 1987—. Performed in numerous musical prodns. including CATS, 1987-89, Les Miserables, 1989—. Active numerous AIDS benefits, 1987—. Fellow Actors Equity Assn., SAG. Roman Catholic.

MURNIN, BETTE F., retired government executive; b. Omaha, Mar. 10, 1918; m. Joseph Albert Murnin, Mar. 9, 1971; children—Robert Manning, Christopher Hill Maxwell. BS, Baker U. 1940; MS in Edn., Ind. U.-Bloomington, 1960; postgrad. various schs. 1961-85. Field supr. Ind. Dept. Pub. Instruction; dir. guidance Merrillville, Ind.; tchr. Jr. high sch., Elkhart, Ind.; program officer Office Edn. Dept. Edn., 1968-84; pres. U.S. Dept. Edn. Region VIII Am. Fed. Govt. Employees Local Union #3898, 1977-82; nat. exec. bd. Am. Fed. Govt. Employees Nat. Council #252 U.S. Dept. Edn., 1982-84; mem. Sixth Congl. Dist. Edn. Com., 1984—. Bd. dirs. Gary Players, 1961-64, Lake County chpt. Am. Cancer Soc., 1960-72, sec. 1962, 64, state bd. dirs. 1965, 72; pres. PTA, Merrillville, 1965; program chmn. 1964; nat. committeewoman Colo. Young Democrats, 1950; capt. Jefferson County Democrats, 1949-52; program chmn. Jefferson County Jane Jeffersons; bd. dirs. Jefferson County Community Chest 1949-55; chmn. Roosevelt Jr. High Sch. faculty. Baker U. scholar; U.S. Govt. grantee. Mem. Ind. Personnel and Guidance Assn. (founder), Alpha Chi Omega.

MURO-GARCIA, LINDA CHRISTINE, organization/behavior consultant, social worker; b. San Bernadino, Calif., Dec. 29, 1951; d. Paul and Mary Esther (Garcia) Muro; children: Gina Marie, Steven Michael. AA, San Bernadino Valley Coll., 1978; BS, U. San Francisco, 1987; MSW, U. So. Calif., 1990. Supr. San Bernadino County Health Dept., San Bernadino, 1972-77; program coordinator Human Studies Ctr., Santa Ana, Calif., 1978-86; dir. seminars and consultation services London Assocs. Internat., Santa Ana, 1986—; clin. and cons. tng. Clinica Neuva Esperanza, Santa Ana, 1988-89, Orange Child Guidance, 1989-90; exec. dir. Am. Bd. Clin. Hypnosis in Social Work, 1988—. Mng. editor ABCD Reports, 1988; assoc. editor Internat. Bull. Medicine and Psychology. Mem. Crisis Intervention Team ARC, 1989—. Honorary Fellow, Milton H. Erickson Advanced Inst., Sydney, Australia, 1984. Fellow Internat. Acad. Medicnie and Psychology; mem. Soc. Clin. and Experimental Hypnosis (conf. co-chmn., 1987), Nat. Assn. Social Workers, Soc. Clin. Social Work. Office: London Assocs Internat 1125 E 17th St Suite E-209 Santa Ana CA 92701

MURPHREE, SHARON ANN, lawyer; b. Maryville, Tenn., June 14, 1949; d. R.L. and Alice (Pierick) M. BS, U. Tenn., 1970; JD, South Tex. Coll. Law, 1987. Bar: Tex. 1988. Pvt. practice law Houston, 1988—; trainee Harvard Negotiation Project, 1990; with Harvard Negotion Project, 1990. Conbtr. articles to profl. jours. Mem. Foley's Women's Adv. Bd., Houston, 1988. Mem. ABA, Tex. Bar Assn., Assn. Trial Lawyers Am., Assn. Women Attys. Houston, Tex. Trial Lawyers Assn., Houston Bar Assn., Inst. For Injury Reduction (life), Women in Law, Phi Delta Phi. Democrat. Roman Catholic. Office: 5757 Westheimer Ste 3-109 Houston TX 77057

MURPHY, ANNE G., marketing executive; b. Terre Haute, Ind., Nov. 27, 1950; d. George Henry and Julia Anne (Neimeyer) Gurchick; m. Thomas N. Murphy Jr. B., Ind. State U., 1972; M., Nova U., 1989. With comml. sales Selkirk Communications, Ft. Lauderdale, Fla., 1980-81; mgr. customer relations Selkirk Communications, 1981-83, mktg. mgr., 1983-87, mktg. dir., 1987—. Recipient Mktg. award Cable Mktg., N.Y., 1984, WIL Industry award, 1987, CTAM award (mktg.), 1985, 86, 87, Addy award Ft. Lauderdale Advt. Assn., 1986, 87. Mem. Women in Cable (pres. S. Fla. chpt. 1984-89), Cable Coop. S. Fla. (pres. 1985-88).

MURPHY, ANNE ST. GERMAINE, educator; b. Norwich, Conn., Dec. 14, 1951; d. Henry William and Evelyn Alice (La Croix) S.; m. Stephen Joseph Murphy, June 15, 1974; children: Alison Jeanne, Brian Stephen. BA, Merrimack Coll., 1973; M in Maths., Worcester Poly. Inst., 1990. Cert. tchr., Mass., Conn. Tchr. maths. Norwich (Conn.) Free Acad., Conn., 1973-74; new bus. adminstr. Home Life Ins., Wellesley, Mass., 1974-77; tchr. maths. Walnut Hill Sch., Natick, Mass., 1978—, head dept. maths.; tutor Natick High Sch., 1978—. Vol. PTO Bennett Hemenway Sch. Mass., 1982-89; tchr. St. Zepherins Parish, Wayland, Mass., 1985-87; mem. Mass. Fair Share. Mem. Acad. Women Allied for Rights and Equality. Democratic. Roman Catholic. Home: 4 Mark St Natick MA 01760

MURPHY, CAROL ANN, employment executive; b. Bklyn., Jan. 6, 1942; d. Jacob Phillip and Florence (Newto) Christman; m. Richard Murphy, Apr 8, 1961 (div. June 1984); children: Richard Michael, John Matthew. Student, SCC, Selden N.Y., 1989. Mgr. sect. chief IRS, Holtsville, N.Y., 1972-88, EEO officer, 1988--; Speaker on EEO IRS. 1988--. Mem. Fed. Employed Women. Roman Catholic. Office: IRS Box 53 444 Greenbelt Pkwy Holtsville NY 00501

MURPHY, COLLEEN FRANCES, public relations executive; b. Litchfield, Ill., Mar. 17, 1960; d. Carl Maurice and Margaret Evelyn (McAnarney) M.; m. James Arnold Buck, Jan. 10, 1987. BS, So. Ill. U., 1982. Pub. relations rep. Ill. Consol., Mattoon, 1982-84; mktg. mgr. Mercy Hosp., Urbana, Ill., 1984-86; account exec. Cohn & Wolfe/Burson-Marstellar, Atlanta, 1987; sr. account exec. DKB Pub. Relations, Atlanta, 1987-88; ind. pub. relations cons. Decatur, Ill., 1988-89; dir. clin. mktg. SIU Sch. Medicine, Springfield, Ill., 1989—; cons. pub. relations Families First, Atlanta, 1987—. Bd. dirs. YWCA. Mem. Pub. Rels. Soc. Am. (bd. dirs. Cen. Ill. chpt. 1986, v.p. 1987), YMCA (bd. dirs. Decatur Area 1989—). Home: 9 Powers Lane Pl Decatur IL 62522 Office: PO Box 19230 Springfield IL 62794-9230

MURPHY, COLLEEN PATRICIA, data processing executive; b. St. Louis, Jan. 8, 1943; d. Raymond Edward and Ellen Sophia (Munthe) M.; m. Marvin A. Brueckner, May 16, 1959, (div. Apr. 1963); children: Michelle Quentin, Raymond Edward, Brigdid Ellen, Jerry John. AAS Clin. Lab. Tech., St. Louis Community Coll., 1979, AAS Data Processing, 1985, Cert. Proficiency, 1988. Clin. lab. technician Compton Hill Hosp., St. Louis, 1979-80; computer cons. M.E. Mullen, Dr. Medicene, Profl. Corp., Mexioc, Mo., 1984; supr., campus computing ctr., ednl. asst. St. Louis Community Coll. at Forest Park, St. Louis, 1985—; cons. Lake St. Louis Fire Dept., 1986-89, Midwest Rehab. Ctr., Lake St. Louis, 1987-89, P. Rexroat, Pacific, Mo., 1987-89, Mary Mullen, Dr. of Medicine Profl. Corp., Mexico, 1984-89. Mem. Data Processing Mgrs.' Assn. Office: St Louis Community Coll 5600 Oakland Ave Saint Louis MO 63110

MURPHY, DEBORAH JUNE, lawyer; b. Clinton, Tenn., Dec. 19, 1955; d. Robert Carlton and Mary Ruth (Melton) M.; m. Charles L. Beach, Dec. 9, 1987. BS, U. Tenn., 1977; postgrad. Vanderbilt U., 1983; JD, Nashville YMCA Law Sch., 1987. Bar: Tenn. 1987. Bank officer C&C Bank, Oak Ridge, 1975-76; tax auditor State of Tenn., Knoxville, 1977-82, Nashville, 1983-85, legal advisor, 1985-86; with office legal services Tenn. Gen. Assembly, Nashville, 1986-87; atty. U.S. Dept. Treasury, 1987—; instr. Draughons Coll., Knoxville, 1978-81. Mem. Tenn. Homecoming 1986 Com. Mem. ABA, Tenn. Bar Assn., Assn. Trial Lawyers Am., Tenn. Trial Lawyers Assn., Anderson County Bar Assn., Lawyers Assn. for Women, The Young Lawyers Conf., Sigma Delta Kappa. Democrat. Methodist. Avocation: travel. Home: 512 S Oakwood Ave Clinton TN 37716 Office: IRS 710 Locust Ave 4th Fl Knoxville TN 37901

MURPHY, DENISE ANN, sales executive; b. Washington, Oct. 11, 1957; d. George Edward and Marian Lucille (Sliney) M. BS, U. Colo., 1984. Bus. med. data analyst Hadley Meml. Hosp., Washington, 1973-76, various med. support positions, 1976-85; sales rep. Nabisco Brands, Inc., Denver, 1985-87; regional sales mgr. Dr. Pepper/7-UP Co., Dallas, 1987—. Mem. UN Assn. (Colo. div.), Denver Jaycees. Democrat. Roman Catholic. Home: 141 S Joliet Circle #14-304 Aurora CO 80012

MURPHY, DIANA E., federal judge; b. Faribault, Minn., Jan. 4, 1934; d. Albert W. and Adleyne (Heiker) Kuske; m. Joseph E. Murphy, Jr., July 24, 1958; children: Michael, John E. BA magna cum laude, U. Minn., 1954, JD magna cum laude, 1974; postgrad., Johannes Gutenberg U., Mainz, Germany, 1954-55, U. Minn., 1955-58. Bar: Minn. 1974. Assoc. Lindquist & Vennum, 1974-76; mcpl. judge Hemmepin County, 1976-78; dist. judge State of Minn., 1978-80; U.S. dist. judge Dist. of Minn., Mpls., 1980—; instr. law sch. U. Minn., Atty. Gen.'s Advocacy Inst.;. Bd. editors: Minn. Law Rev., Georgetown U. Jour. on Cts., Health Scis. and the Law, 1989—. Bd. dirs. Spring Hill Conf. Ctr., 1978-84, Mpls. United Way, 1985—, treas. 1990—, Bush Found., 1982—, chmn. bd., 1986—; bd. dirs. Amicus, 1976-80, also organizer, 1st chmn. adv. coun.; mem. Mpls. Charter Commn., 1973-76, chmn., 1974-76; bd. dirs. Ops. De Novo, 1971-76, chmn., 1974-75; mem. Minn. Constl. Study Commn., chmn. bill of rights com., 1971-73; regent St. Johns U., 1978-87, 88—, vice chmn. bd., 1985-87; mem. Minn. Bicentennial Commn., 1987-88; trustee Twin Cities Pub. TV, 1985—; bd. dirs. Sci. Mus. Minn., 1988—. Fulbright scholar; recipient Amicus Founders' award, Outstanding Achievement award YMCA. Fellow Am. Bar Found.; mem. ABA (Ethics and Profl. Responsibility Judges Adv. Com. 1981-88), Minn. Bar Assn. (bd. govs. 1977-81), Hennepin County Bar Assn. (gov. coun. 1976-81), Am. Law Inst., Am. Judicature Soc. (bd. dirs. 1982—, v.p. 1985-88, treas. 1988-89, chmn. bd. 1989—), Nat. Assn. Women Judges, Minn. Women Lawyers, U. Minn. Alumni Assn. (bd. dirs. 1975-83, pres. 1981-82), Fed. Judges Assn. (bd. dirs. 1982—, v.p. 1984-89, pres. 1989—), Hist. Soc. for Eighth Cir. (bd. dirs. 1988—), Fed. Jud. Ctr. (bd. dirs. 1990—), Order of Coif, Phi Beta Kappa. Office: US Dist Ct 670 US Courthouse 110 S 4th St Minneapolis MN 55401

MURPHY, EDRIE LEE, hospital laboratory administrator; b. Redwood Falls, Minn., Dec. 4, 1953; d. Melvin Arthur and Betty Lou (Wenholz) Timm; m. David Joseph Murphy, July 28, 1984. B.S. in Med. Tech. summa cum laude, Mankato State U., 1976; M.B.A., Coll. of St. Thomas, 1984. Registered med. technologist. Med. technologist Children's Hosp., St. Paul, 1976-81, chemistry supr., 1981-85, lab. mgr., 1985—. Contbr. articles to profl. jours. Charles H. Cooper scholar, 1975. Mem. Am. Soc. Med. Tech., Minn. Soc. Med. Tech., Am. Assn. Clin. Chemists, Clin. Lab. Mgmt. Assn., Phi Kappa Phi. Club: Elan Vital Ski (v.p. membership 1981-82) (Mpls.). Avocations: photography, sailing, skiing, tennis, travel. Office: Children's Hosp 345 N Smith Saint Paul MN 55102

MURPHY, EILEEN MARGARET, obstetrics and gynecology educator; b. N.Y.C., Feb. 24, 1956; d. Leo Joseph and Josephine (Licardi) M.; m. Charles Joseph Ryan III, Sept. 18, 1987; children: Katherine Elizabeth, Kristen Cory. BA, Wells Coll., 1978; MD, SUNY, Syracuse, 1982. Diplomate Am. Bd. Ob-Gyn. Resident in ob-gyn Med. Coll. Pa., Phila., 1982-86; pvt. practice, Phila., 1986-87; clin. instr. U. Mich. Med. Ctr., Ann Arbor, 1987-89; asst. prof. ob-gyn SUNY Health Sci. Ctr., Syracuse, 1989—, coord. urodynamic testing unit, 1989—; med. dir. U. Mich. Health Ctr., Northville, 1987-89. Fellow Am. Coll. Ob-Gyn (jr.); mem. Am. Uro-Gynecology Soc., Norman Miller Soc., Phi Beta Kappa. Office: SUNY Health Sci Ctr Dept Ob-Gyn 750 E Adams St Syracuse NY 13120

MURPHY, EVELYN FRANCIS, state official; b. Panama Canal Zone, May 14, 1940; d. Clement Bernard and Dorothy Eloise (Jackson) M. AB, Duke U., 1961, PhD, 1965; MA, Columbia U., 1963; hon. degrees, Regis Coll., 1978, Curry Coll., Northeastern U., Simmons Coll., Wheaton Coll., Anna Maria Coll., Bridgewater State Coll., Salem State Coll., Emmanuel Coll.; hon. degree, Suffolk U. Pres. Ancon Assocs., Boston, 1971-72; ptnr. Llewelyn-Davies Assocs., N.Y.C., 1973-74; sec. environ. affairs Commonwealth of Mass., Boston, 1975-79, sec. econ. affairs, 1983-86, lt. gov., 1987—. Recipient Disting. Svc. award Nat. Sierra Club, 1978, Nat. Govs. Assn. 1978, Outstanding Citizen award Mass. Audubon Soc., 1978; Harvard U. fellow, 1979-80. Mem. Women Execs. in State Govt. (chair 1987). Democrat. Office: Lt Govs Office State House Boston MA 02110

MURPHY, FRANCES LOUISE, II, journalism educator, newspaper publisher; b. Balt.; d. Carl James and L. Vashti (Turley) M.; m. James E. Wood (div.); children: Frances Murphy Wood Draper, James E. Jr., Susan Wood Barnes. BA, U. Wis., 1944; BS, Coppin State Coll., Balt., 1958; MEd, Johns Hopkins U., 1963. City editor Balt. Afro-Am., 1956-57; dir. News Bur., Morgan State Coll., Balt., 1964-71; chmn. bd. dirs. Afro-Am. Newspapers, Balt., 1971-74; assoc. prof. journalism SUNY, Buffalo, 1975-85, Howard U., Washington, 1985—; editor Washington Afro-Am., 1951-56, pub., 1987—; bd. dirs. Afro-Am. Newspapers, Balt., 1985-87; mem. adv. bd. Partnership Inst., Washington, 1985—. Trustee State Colls. Md., 1971-76; nat. bd. dirs. NACCP, 1971-76. Named One of 100 Most Influential Black Ams., Ebony mag., 1973, 74, Disting. Marylander, Gov. State of Md., 1975; recipient Ida B. Wells award Congl. Black Caucus, 1989. Mem. Nat. Newspaper Pubs. Assn. (editorial com. 1987—, merit award 1987, 89), Soc. Profl. Journalists, Links, Capital Press Club (exec. bd. 1987—), Delta Sigma Theta. Democrat. Episcopalian. Home: 5709 1st St NW Washington DC 20011 Office: Washington Afro-Am 2002 11th St NW Washington DC 20001

MURPHY, FRANCINE, chemist; b. Chester, Pa., Dec. 9, 1940; d. William P. and Rita N. (Shields) Cranny; m. James J. Murphy, Aug. 26, 1961; children: Ellen M., James J., Daniel L. AAS magna cum laude, Bergen Community Coll., 1979; BS magna cum laude, Iona Coll., 1986. Sr. lab. technician Lehn & Fink Products, Montvale, N.J., 1979-85, jr. chemist, 1985-88; chemist Airwick Industries, Wayne, N.J., 1988—. Mem. Handgun Control, Washington, 1989—, Common Cause, Washington, 1989—. Mem. Soc. Cosmetic Chemists, Alpha Sigma Lambda. Roman Catholic. Office: Airwick Industries 1655 Valley Rd Wayne NJ 07474

MURPHY, GRACE ELIZABETH, health care financial specialist, nun; b. Lansing, Mich., May 6, 1949; d. Earl A. and Jane F. (Walker) M. BS in Secondary Edn., U. Albuquerque, 1972; MBA, U. Notre Dame, 1981. Joined Sisters of Charity, Roman Cath. Ch., 1967. Tchr., asst. prin. San Felipe Sch., Albuquerque, 1972-73; tchr. Carroll High Sch., Dayton, Ohio, 1973-79; fiscal project specialist Good Samaritan Hosp., Cin., 1981-87, dir. fiscal planning, 1987—; fin. com. St. Joseph Health Network, Mt. Clemens, Mich., 1984—. Trustee Seton High Sch., Cin., 19083-89, Eldermount, Cin., 1985—, Archdiocesan Consultation Svcs., Cin., 1987—; vol. Cin. Bicentennial Commn., 1988. Mem. NAFE, Healthcare Fin. Mgrs. Assn. Office: Good Samaritan Hosp 3217 Clifton Ave Cincinnati OH 45220

MURPHY, IRENE HELEN, publishing executive; b. Boston; d. Charles Leo and Irene Muriel (Finney) M. BA, Regis Coll., 1958; MA, Boston Coll., 1963, Northeastern U., Boston, 1968, Manhattanville Coll., 1969. Tchr. elem. sch. Boston, high sch. dir. guidance, ednl. adminstr., prof. master tchr. program, 1969—; prof. N.Y.C.; dir. sch. services Glencoe Pub. Co., Mission Hills, Calif., 1969—, v.p.; vis. lectr. univs., Australia, Can. Author series ednl. games for children. Recipient Gold Seal Recognition award Today's Cath. Tchr., 1987. Mem. Nat. Cath. Edn. Assn., Nat. Assn. Female Execs., AAUW, Jordan Hosp. Club, St. Peter Cath. Women's Club, Adminstrs. Club, Passport Club. Roman Catholic. also: 2677 SW Thunderbird Trail Stuart FL 33497

MURPHY, JANET GORMAN, college president; b. Holyoke, Mass., Jan. 10, 1937; d. Edwin Daniel and Catherine Gertrude (Hennessey) Gorman. B.A., U. Mass., 1958, postgrad. 1960-61, Ed.D., 1974, LL.D. (hon.) 1984; M.Ed., Boston U., 1961. Tchr. English and history John J. Lynch Jr. High Sch., Holyoke, 1958-60; tchr. English, Chestnut Jr. High Sch., Springfield, Mass., 1961-63; instr. English and journalism Our Lady of Elms Coll., Chicopee, 1963-64; mem. staff Mass. State Coll., Lyndonville, Vt., 1977-83; pres. Mo. Western State Coll., St. Joseph, 1983—. Mem. campaign staff Robert F Kennedy Presdl. Campaign, 1967. Recipient John Gunther Tchr. award NEA, 1961, award Women's Opportunity Com., Boston Fed. Exec. Bd., 1963; named one of 10 Outstanding Young Leaders of Greater Boston Area, Boston Jr. C. of C., 1973. Office: Mo Western State Coll 4525 Downs Dr Saint Joseph MO 64507-2294*

MURPHY, JEANETTE CAROL, education educator; b. Hot Springs, S.D., June 6, 1931; d. George W. and Jessie S. (Whetstone) M.; A.B., U. S.D., 1960; M.S. in Edn. Adminstrn., Chadron State Coll., 1978, Ed.S. Ednl. Adminstrn., 1979, Ph.D in Ednl. Adminstrn., U. Mo., 1987. Mgr. central supply and operating rooms Luth. Hosp., Hot Springs, 1957-58, 60-61; tchr. Spanish and French, Sidney (Nebr.) High Sch., 1962-64; registered clk. Peninsula Hosp., Burlingame, Calif., 1964-65; tchr. San Lorenzo Valley Unified Schs., Felton, Calif., 1965-67; propr. Masters Career Inst., Salinas, Calif., 1969-70; tchr. Oglala Community High Sch., Pine Ridge, S.D., 1970-72, Hot Springs High Sch., 1971-73; clk. Fall River County (S.D.) Treas.'s Office, 1973-74; Title I adminstr. Loneman Day Sch., Ogala, S.D., 1974-75, adminstr., 1975-77; contract dir. and exec. officer bd. Unified Sch. Bd. Found., Inc., Pine Ridge, 1977-78; grad. asst. div. edn. and psychology Chadron (Nebr.) State Coll., 1978-79; supt. schs. Lyman (Nebr.) Pub. Schs., 1979-80, Kadoka (S.D.) Sch. Dist., 1981-83; registered rep. for IDS/Am. Express, 1983-84; grad. teaching asst. doctoral program in edn. adminstrn. with spl. emphasis in polit. sci. U. Mo., 1984-86 ; asst. state dir. for Mo. North Central Assn., 1984-86; asst. prof. edn. Kearney (Nebr.) State Coll., 1987—; rsch. assoc. joint effort U. Mo.-Columbia and Mo. House of Reps., 1985-86. Contbr. to profl. publs. Chairperson Heart Fund Drive, Hot Springs, 1974-76; Bible sch. tchr. United Presbyn. Women, 1976-77; mem. choir Presbyn. Ch., 1970-76. Served with WAC, 1954-57. Mem. Am. Assn. Sch. Adminstrs., Mizzou Alumni Assn., Assn. Supervision and Curriculum Devel., Nebr. Assn. Supervision and Curriculum Devel., Daus. of Nile, Internat. Order Job's Daus. of S.D. (past. grand guardian, grand sec.), Order Ea. Star (past matron), Delta Kappa Gamma, Phi Delta Kappa. Democrat.

MURPHY, JO ANNE, data processing administrator; b. Chgo.; d. Joseph Francis and Elizabeth M. (Nowak) M. BS, Coll. St. Francis, 1970; MEd in Adminstrn. and Supervision, U. Ill., 1977. Cert. adminstr. and supr., Ill.; joined Sisters of St. Francis, Roman Cath. Ch., 1965. Tchr. St. Jude Sch., Joliet, Ill., 1969-70; math tchr. St. Raymond Sch., Joliet, 1970-75; prin. St. Matthew Day Sch., Champaign, Ill., 1976-78, St. John Sch., Joliet, 1978-82; math instr. Coll. St. Francis, Joliet, 1983-85; computer specialist Our Lady of Angels Retirement Home, Joliet, 1983-85; programmer/analyst Household Internat., Northbrook, Ill., 1985-88; ops. mgr. Coll. of St. Francis, Joliet, 1988-90; coord. Peoria Diocesan Prins., Champaign, 1976-78, Joliet Diocesan Prins., 1978-82; cons. Sisters of St. Francis, Joliet, 1972-90, Vicar for Religious, Joliet, 1990—. Mem. NAFE, Digital Equipment Users Group. Home: 1114 Loral Ave Joliet IL 60435 Office: College of St Francis 500 Wilcox St Joliet IL 60435

MURPHY, JOANNE BECKER, writer; b. Detroit; d. Louis Norman and Gertrude Margaret (Kornmeier) Becker; m. Joseph A. Murphy, Jr., June 24, 1961; children: Michael Ellis, Joseph A. III. BA in Journalism, Mich. State U., 1958; MA in Humanities, Wayne State U., 1975. Communications WBZ TV, Boston, 1958-60, The Jam Handy Orgn., Detroit, 1960-62, Detroit Symphony Orch., 1969-70; freelance writer, editor Detroit, 1980-90, Washington, 1990—. Contbg. writer: Glass: State of the Art, 1989, Affecting Change, 1986; editor: As Parents We Will, 1985 (1st Place award Pub. Svc. Nat. Found. for Alcoholism Communications); writer, editor publs. for arts and human svcs. orgns. Mem. program bd. Grosse Pointe (Mich.) War Meml. Program Bd., 1987-90; bd. dirs. Detroit Artists Market, 1982-90, Mich. Metro Girl Scout Coun., 1972-78, Family Svcs. Detroit and Wayne County, 1970-76; bd. of canvassers Grosse Pointe Sch. System, 1986-90. Named one of 50 Outstanding Women Mich. State U., 1958. Mem. Women in Communications, Inc., Washington Ind. Writers, Women's Econ. Club Detroit (co-chair scholarship com. 1987-88), Kappa Alpha Theta. Home and Office: 2717 O St NW Washington DC 20007

MURPHY, JOANNE M., marketing executive; b. Holyoke, Mass., Dec. 31, 1957; d. LeRoy Paul and Rose Marie (Danehey) Miller; m. Dennis Francis Murphy III, June 2, 1979; 1 child, Dennis Francis IV. AS in Bus. Studies, Holyoke Community Coll., 1979; BA in Mktg., U. Mass., 1980. Account rep. Xerox Corp., Hartford, Conn., 1980-82; sr. account exec. Exxon Office Systems, Stamford, Conn., 1983-85; area sales cons. ShareTech, Hartford, 1985-86; sr. mktg. rep. Honeywell Info. Systems, Glastonbury, Conn., 1986-87; account mgr. CompTech, Inc. div. Computer Horizons, Inc., 1987—. Editor shared tenant newsletter, 1985. Mem. Data Processing Mgmt. Assn., Orgn. for Profls. in Telecommunication. Republican. Roman Catholic. Avocations: skiing, tennis, golf, personal computers. Home: 195 Firetown Rd Simsbury CT 06070 Office: CompTech Inc 500 Winding Brook Dr Glastonbury CT 06033

MURPHY, JOANNE MCCORMICK, small business owner; b. Buffalo, N.Y., Aug. 23, 1932; d. John Milton and Mildred Dorothy (Maher) McC.; m. John Joseph Murphy, May 24, 1952; children: James, Kathleen Carroll, Paul, Thomas. Student, Oglethorpe, Atlanta, 1967-69; AS, Tempe U., Phila., 1980. Cert. Landscape Designer, Pa. Landscape designer Whitemarsh Nursery, Plymouth, Pa., 1980-81; owner Down to Earth Landscape Design & Contracting, N. Wales, Pa., 1981--. Designer Christmas Caravan of Homes, North Pa. Hosp. Aux., 1983-89; bd. mem. N. Pa. Symphony Orch., Lansdale, 1989; exec. bd. Temple U. Horticultural Alumni Assn., Ambler, Pa., 1983-85. Founding mem. Landscape Design Network (pres. 1985-87), Assn. Profl. Landscape Designers (recording sec. 1989). Republican.

MURPHY, JUDITH CHISHOLM, trust company executive; b. Chippewa Falls, Wis., Jan. 26, 1942; d. John David and Bernice A. (Hartman) Chisholm. BA, Manhattanville Coll., 1964; postgrad., New Sch. for Social Research, 1965-68, Nat. Grad. Trust Sch., 1975. Asst. portfolio mgr. Chase Manhattan Bank, N.A., N.Y.C., 1964-68; trust investment officer Marshall & Ilsley Bank, Milw., 1968-72; asst. v.p. Marshall & Ilsley Bank, 1972-74, v.p., 1974-75; v.p., treas. M&I Investment Mgmt. Corp., Milw., 1975—; v.p. M&I Marshall & Ilsley Trust Co. Ariz., Phoenix, 1982—, Marshall & Ilsley Trust Co. Fla., Naples, 1985—; coun. mem. Am. Bankers Assn., Washington, 1984-86; govt. relations com. Wis. Bankers Assn., Madison, 1982-88. Contbr. articles to Trusts & Estates Mag., 1980, ABA Banking Jour., 1981, Maricopa Lawyer, 1983. Chmn. Milw. City Plan Commn., 1986—; commr. Milw. County Commn. on Handicapped, 1988—; bd. dirs. Cardinal Stritch Coll., Milw., 1980-89, Children's Hosp. Wis., Milw., 1989—. Recipient Outstanding Achievement award YWCA Greater Milw., 1985, Sacajawea award Profl. Dimensions, Milw., 1988, Pro Urbe award Mt. Mary Coll., 1988; named Disting. Woman in Banking, Comml. West Mag., 1988. Mem. Milw. Analysts Soc. (sec. 1974-77, bd. dirs. 1977-80), Nat. Assn. Bank Women (bd. dirs., v.p. 1976-80), Am. Inst. Banking (instr. 1975-78), TEMPO (charter), Profl. Dimensions (hon.), University Club, Woman's Club Wis., Rotary. Democrat. Roman Catholic. Home: 1139 N Edison St Milwaukee WI 53202 Office: M&I Investment Mgmt Corp 770 N Water St Milwaukee WI 53202

MURPHY, JUNEANN, microbiologist, educator; b. Chickasha, Okla., Mar. 13, 1937; d. Evard William and Ann (Adwan) Wadsworth; m. George W. Murphy, Sept. 2, 1967; children: Cynthia Ann Murphy-Erdosh, Sally E. BS, U. Okla., 1959, MS, 1961, 65, PhD, 1969. Asst. prof. microbiology U. Okla., Norman, 1970-81, dir. med. tech., 1978-82, assoc. prof. microbiology, 1981-86, prof. microbiology, 1986-88, GLC prof. microbiology, 1988-89, GLC prof. microbiology Health Sci. Ctr., 1989—; study section mem. NIH-Div. Rsch. Grants, Bethesda, Md., 1983-87; vis. asst. prof. U. Okla., Norman, 1969-70; vis. asst. prof. of clin. immunology U. Colo. Health Sci. Ctr., Denver, 1979. Mem. Am. Soc. Microbiology, Am. Assn. Immunologist, Med. Mycology Soc. of Ams., Internat. Soc. Human and Animal

Mycology. Democrat. Methodist. Home: 2328 Ashwood Norman OK 73071 Office: Univ Okla Health Sci Ctr PO Box 26901 Oklahoma City OK 73190

MURPHY, KATHLEEN MARY, law firm manager; b. Bklyn., Dec. 16, 1945; d. Raymond Joseph and Catherine Elizabeth (Kearney) M. BA in Edn., Molloy Coll., 1971; MS in Edn., Bklyn. Coll., 1975. Cert. elem. sch. tchr., N.Y. Elem. sch. tchr. various parochial schs. L.I., Bklyn., Queens, N.Y., 1969-80; from asst. prin. to prin. parochial sch. Queens, 1980-82; supr.-trainer Davis, Polk, Wardwell law firm, N.Y.C., 1982-88; mgr. Schulte Roth & Zabel, N.Y.C., 1988—; trainer program for new employees, 1984; speaker edn. topics, Bklyn., Queens, 1979-81. Mem. NAFE. Democrat. Roman Catholic.

MURPHY, KATHRYN MARGUERITE, archivist; b. Brockton, Mass.; d. Thomas Francis and Helena (Fortier) M. A.B. in History, George Washington U., 1935, M.A., 1939; M.L.S., Cath. U., 1950; postgrad. Am. U., 1961. With Nat. Archives and Records Service, Washington, 1940-89, ret., supervisory archivist Central Research br., 1958-62, archivist, 1962—, mem. fed. women's com. Nat. Archives, 1974, rep. to fed. women's com. GSA, 1975; docent, 1989—; lectr. colls., socs. in U.S., 1950—; lectr. Am. ethnic history, 1978-79. Founder, pres. Nat. Archives lodge Am. Fedn. Govt. Employees, 1965—, del. conv., 1976, 78, 80, recipient award for outstanding achievement in archives, 1980. Recipient commendation Okla. Civil War Centennial Commn., 1965; named hon. citizen Oklahoma City, Mayor, 1963. Mem. ALA, Soc. Am. Archivists (joint com. hosp. libraries 1965-70), Nat. League Am. Pen Women (corr. sec. Washington 1975-78, pres. chpt. 1978-80), Bus. and Profl. Womens' Club Washington, Phi Alpha Theta (hon.). Contbr. articles on Am. ethnic history to profl. publs. Home: 1500 Massachusetts Ave NW Washington DC 20005 Office: Nat Archives and Records Service 7th and Pennsylvania Aves NW Washington DC 20408

MURPHY, LINDA SUE, city official; b. Lynchburg, Va., June 7, 1948; d. Carter P. and Dorothy L. (Clark) Tucker; m. Daniel K. Murphy, Mar. 25, 1972; 1 child, Krystal Grace. Student, Longwood Coll., 1966-68. Exec. sec. First Nat. Bank of Anchorage, Seward, Alaska, 1976-80; clk. of ct., asst. magistrate Alaska Ct. System, Seward, 1980-81; city clk., personnel officer City of Seward, 1981—. Sec., Seward Concert Assn., 1982; chmn. Seward Sch. Adv. Bd., 1983; v.p. bd. dirs. Seward Life Action Council, 1983-84, pres. bd. dirs., 1984-86; chmn. Seward-Obihiro Sister City Com., 1984. Mem. Internat. Inst. Mcpl. Clks., Alaska Assn. Mcpl. Clerks (sec. 1984-85, v.p. 1985-86, pres. 1986-87), Alaska Women in Govt. (v.p. 1985-87), Bus. and Profl. Women's Club (v.p. 1988-89, pres. 1989-90), Rotary (bd. dirs. 1989—). Democrat. Home: NHN Salmon Creek Rd Seward AK 99664 Office: Seward City Hall PO Box 167 Seward AK 99664

MURPHY, MARGARET H., federal judge; b. 1948. BA, Queen's Coll., Charlotte, N.C.; JD, U. N.C. Admitted to bar, 1973. Bankruptcy judge U.S. Dist. Ct. (no. dist.) Ga. Office: US Dist Ct 1755 US Courthouse Atlanta GA 30303*

MURPHY, MARGARETTE CELESTINE EVANS, educator, writer; b. Chgo., June 25, 1926; d. Crawford and Ethel Hazel (Cartman) Evans. Ph.B., U. Chgo., 1945, M.A., 1949, postgrad., 1950-79, Ph.D., Colo. Christian Coll., 1972; m. Robert H. Murphy, Sept. 25, 1949; children: Linda, Michelle. Tchr. English, Spanish and French Willard Elem. Sch., 1950-52, McKinley High Sch., 1952-60, chmn. fgn. langs. dept. Crane High Sch., 1960-64, Harlan High Sch., Chgo., 1967—; tchr. TESL, Chgo. City Jr. Colls., 1976—. Mem. Women's Share in Pub. Svc., Brazilian Soc. Chgo., Am. Security Council (nat. adv. bd.), U. Chgo. Alumni Assn., AAUW, Esperanto Soc. Chgo., Alpha Kappa Alpha. Republican. Roman Catholic. Club: 1200 of Chgo. Author: Note on Martínez Zuviría, Argentinian Novelist, 1949. Home: 8742 S Colfax Ave Chicago IL 60617 Office: care Mrs Eva C Martin and Linda M Murphy 907 Polk Ave Memphis TN 38104

MURPHY, MARY ANN BURNETT, health facility administrator; b. Sentinel, Okla., Sept. 11, 1954; d. Bill J. Burnett and Melvena Lou (Hartson) M.; m. Larry E. Murphy, Aug. 6, 1977. BSN, Cen. State U., Edmond, Okla., 1976. Cert. advanced cardiac life support, provider and instr. Staff RN, critical care Coral Reef Gen. Hosp., Miami, Fla., 1978; charge nurse, staff RN North Trident Regional Hosp., Charleston Heights, S.C., 1979-80; critical care float team, staff RN Medical U. S.C. Hosp., Charleston, S.C., 1980-81; GN, RN Jackson County Meml. Hosp., Altus, Okla., 1976-77, critical care staff RN, 1981-82, staff devel. dir., 1982-83, critical care staff RN, 1983-85, critical care clin. coord., 1985-87, house supr. Mem. AACN. Address: 709 Hayes Altus OK 73521 Office: Jackson County Meml Hosp 1200 E Pecan Altus OK 73521

MURPHY, MARY C., state legislator. B.A., Coll. St. Scholastica; postgrad. U. Minn., Macalester Coll., U. Wis.-Superior, Am. U. High sch. tchr.; mem. Minn. Ho. of Reps., 1976—, mem. appropriations, commerce, econ. devel./ housing, labor-mgmt. relations coms. Trustee St. Mary's Hosp., Duluth, Minn.; bd. dirs. Minn. Alliance for Sci. and Tech.; mem. adv. com. Home Econs. Vocat. program Hermantown Community Schs.; active del. Duluth Central Labor Body AFL-CIO; mem., lector St. Raphael's Parish; dir. State Democratic Farmer-Labor Party, 1972-74, chmn. 8th Dist. credentials com., 1974—, chmn. St. Louis County Legis. Delegation, 1985-86. Mem. Duluth Fedn. Tchrs. (1st v.p. 1976-77, various coms.), Minn. Fedn. Tchrs. (legis. com. 1972-75), Am. Fedn. Tchrs. (del. nat. convs.), Coalition Labor Union Women, Minn. Hist. Soc., Alpha Delta Kappa. Office: State Office Bldg Saint Paul MN 55155

MURPHY, MARY KATHLEEN CONNORS, college administrator, writer; b. Pueblo, Colo.; d. Joseph Charles and Eileen E. (McDermott) Connors; m. Michael C. Murphy, June 6, 1959; children: Holly Ann, Emily Louise, Patricia Marie. AB, Loretto Heights Coll., 1960; MEd, Emory U., 1968; PhD, Ga. State U., 1980. Tchr. English pub. schs., Moultrie, Ga., 1959, Sacramento, 1960, Marietta, Ga., 1960-65, DeKalb County, Ga., 1966; tech. writer Ga. Dept. Edn., 1966-69; editorial asst. So. Regional Edn. Bd., Atlanta, 1969-71; dir. alumni affairs The Lovett Sch., Atlanta, 1972-75, dir. publs. and info. svc., 1975-77; coord. summer series in aging Ga. State U., 1979; dir. devel. found. rels. Ga. Inst. Tech., 1980-87, dir. devel., 1987-89; asst. dir. devel. for spl. gifts U Ga., 1989—; state coord. for Ga., Am. Coun. on Edn. nat. identification program for women in higher edn. administrn., 1983-85; presenter profl. confs.; freelance edn. writer, 1968—; co-author: Fitting in as a New Service Wife, 1966; contbr. and contbg. editor numerous articles on teaching, secondary edn., higher edn., and fund raising to profl. publs.; columnist Daily Jour., Marietta, 1963-67, The Atlanta Constn., 1963-68; editor: Cultivating Found. Support for Edn., 1989. Bd. advisors Bridge Family Counseling Ctr., 1981-86, Northside Sch. Arts, 1981-83; bd. dirs. Atlanta Women's Network, 1982-84, v.p., 1983-84; prin., bd. dirs. Sch. Religion, Cathedral of Christ the King, 1979-84; publicity chmn. Phoenix Soc. Atlanta, 1981—, adv. bd., 1988—; mem. allocations com., exec. com. United Way Met. Atlanta, 1983; bd. counseling Fulton Svc. Ctr., Met. Atlanta chpt. ARC, 1982-83; mem. Leadership Atlanta, class of 1983-84; group facilitator, 1984-85, co-chmn. edn. program, 1987. NDEA fellow, 1965-66; Adminstrn. of Aging fellow, 1977-79; recipient Image Maker award Atlanta Profl. Women's Directory, Inc. 1984. Mem. Coun. for Advancement and Support of Edn. (publs. com., alumni adv. com., dist. III bd., 1981—, chmn. corp. and found. support conf., N.Y.C., 1985, maj. donor rsch. conf. N.Y.C. 1985, matching gift conf., Tampa, 1989, dist. III conf. chmn. 1986, chair-elect dist. III bd. case nat., 1989-91, chair, 1991—, case membership svcs. com. 1989—) Nat. Assn. Ind. Schs. (publs. com.), Edn. Writers Assn., Am. Vocat. Assn., Nat. Soc. Fund Raising Execs. (v.p. Ga. chpt. 1985, pres. 1986-87, mem.-at-large nat. bd. 1985-89, chmn. pub. rels. com. 1985-87, asst. treas., chair audit com., mem. exec. com. 1988-90), Kiwanis (co-chair membership com. Atlanta club 1990—), Phi Delta Kappa, Kappa Delta Pi (pres. 1980-81). Home: 2903 Rivermeade Dr NW Atlanta GA 30327

MURPHY, MARY KATHRYN, industrial hygienist; b. Kansas City, Mo., Apr. 16, 1941; d. Arthur Charles and Mary Agnes (Fitzgerald) Wahlstedt; m. Thomas E. Murphy Jr., Aug. 26, 1963; children: Thomas E. III, David W. BA, Avila Coll., Kansas City, 1962; MS, Cen. Mo. State U., 1975. Cert. in comprehensive practice of indsl. hygiene. Indsl. hygienist Kansas City area office Occupational Safety and Health Adminstrn., 1975-78, regional indsl. hygienist, 1979-86; dir. indsl. hygiene Chart Svcs., Shawnee, Kans., 1986-87; dir. indsl. hygiene and hazardous substance control Hall-Kimbrell Environ. Mgmt. and Pollution COntrol, Lawrence, Kans., 1987-88, mgr. dept. indsl. hygiene div. environ. mgmt. and pollution control, 1988-89; dir. indsl. hygiene Hazardous Waste Div. Burns & McDonnell, Engrs., Architects, Kansas City, Mo., 1989—; asst. dir. safety office U. Kans. Med. Ctr., 1978-79. Summer talent fellow Kaw Valley Heart Assn., 1961. Mem. Am. Indsl. Hygiene Assn. (sec.-treas. Mid-Am. sect. 1978-79, bd. dirs. 1981, mem. auditcom.), Am. Chem. Soc., Am. Conf. Govt. Indsl. Hygienists (mem. chem. agts. threshold limit value com.), Am. Acad. Indsl. Hygiene, N.Y. Acad. Scis., AAAS, Internat. Soc. Environ. Toxicology and Cancer, Am. Coll. Toxicology, Am. Conf. on Chem. Labeling. Home: 10616 W 123d St Overland Park KS 66213 Office: Burns & McDonnell Engrs Architects & Cons 4800 E 63d Kansas City MO 64130

MURPHY, MARYNELL, business owner; b. Waco, Tex., Apr. 21, 1954; d. James Austin and Betty (Thaxton) M. BS, So. Meth. U., 1976, MBA, 1977. Owner Four Leaf Clover, Dallas, 1978-85, In the Pub. Eye, Dallas, 1985—. Mem. Jr. League Dallas, Wadley Guild, Dallas, Susan Komen Found., Dallas, Art Reach Aux., Dallas. Recipient So. Meth. U. scholarship, 1975. Mem. So. Meth. U. Alumni Assn., So. Meth. U. MBA Assn. Democrat. Episcopalian. Clubs: Cotillion (pres. 1982-83), Slipper (Dallas) (treas. 1983-84). Home: 4333 Druid Ln Dallas TX 75205 Office: In the Pub Eye 5526 Dyer Suite 1113 Dallas TX 75206-5021

MURPHY, MAUREEN ANN, political consultant; b. Southampton, N.Y., May 27, 1935; d. Sylvester and Mary (Anderson) Willmott; m. Gregory Murphy, Feb. 11, 1961; children: David, Tereasa. Grad. high sch., Riverhead, N.Y. Legis. tracking staff Legislex, Phoenix, 1979-81; campaign coor., then vol. coord. fundraising Maricopa Women's Polit. Caucus, Phoenix, 1981-82; campaign schedular Goddard for Mayor campaign, Phoenix, 1983; sales rep. P.V. Voice Newspaper, Phoenix, 1984-87; campaign mgr. Parks for City Coun. campaign, Phoenix, 1987; membership dir. Paradise Valley C. of C., Phoenix, 1988-89; cons., prin. Maureen Murphy & Assocs., Phoenix, 1985—. Mem. Paradise Valley Community Coun., Phoenix, 1977—, Paradise Valley Community Coll. Task Force, 1981-82, Paradise Valley Town Hall, Phoenix, 1988-90; co-chair Paradise Valley Awarness Festival, Phoenix, 1987—. Mem. LWV (Equal Rights Amendment chair 1975-82), Ariz. Women's Polit. Caucus (state chair 1979-82), Nat. Women's Polit. Caucus (del.-at-large 1989-91), Noon Lions. Republican. Roman Catholic. Home and Office: Maureen Murphy & Assocs 10850 N 37th Way Phoenix AZ 85028

MURPHY, MELINDA LYNN, hospital executive, nurse; b. Evansville, Ind., May 1, 1944; d. Lewis Oliver and Marion Maxine (Wilson) Lynn; m. James Benton Murphy, Aug. 13, 1977; children: Cari Lynn Webb, Warren Leland Sizemore. AD, U. Ky., 1972; BS, U. Evansville, 1974; MS, U. Okla., 1984. RN. Staff nurse intensive care unit Community Meth. Hosp., Henderson, Ky., 1972-74; nurse instr. Bacone Coll., Muskogee, Okla., 1974-76; nurse supr. Muskogee VA Med. Ctr., 1976-79, Tulsa VA Outpatient Clinic, 1979-85; asst. chief nursing Muskogee VA Med. Ctr., 1985-86, assoc. chief nursing, 1986-88, adminstrv. asst. to chief staff, 1988-90; staff profl. affairs VA Cen. Office, Washington, 1990—. Contbr. articles to profl. jours. Mem. Sigma Theta Tau. Office: Muskogee VA Med Ctr Honor Heights Dr Muskogee OK 74401

MURPHY, NANCY ANN, code enforcement officer; b. Columbus, Nebr., May 15, 1936; d. Chester Thomas and Louise Frances (Byrnes) Isgrig; m. James Gordon Reisner, Aug. 22, 1957 (div. Aug. 1971); children: Christopher A., Frances L., Thomas W., Andrew P.; m. John Michael Murphy, July 8, 1978; stepchildren: Linda K., Timothy C. Student, U. Nebr., 1954-57, Lower Columbia Coll., 1969-79. Pvt. practice residential design Omaha, 1958-66; engring. technician Trojan nuclear project Wismer & Becker, Rainier, Oreg., 1975-76; engring. technician Weyerhaeuser Co., Longview, Wash., 1976-80; field engr. Weyerhaeuser Co., Columbus, Miss., 1980-82; zoning and housing officer bldg. dept. City of Columbus, 1983—. Mem. exec. bd. Cowlitz County Health Systems Agy., Longview, 1978-79; chmn. citizens rev. com. United Way of Lowndes County, Columbus, 1985—. Mem. Nat. Assn. Women in Constrn. (charter, bd. dirs. 1978-79), Nat. Assn. Home Builders, Miss. Women in Mcpl. Govt., Bus. and Profl. Women's Club (treas. 1986-87, 89-90, pres. 1988-89), DAR (chpt. regent 1989-93), Habitat for Humanities (bd. dirs. Columbus-Lowndes County chpt., co-chair bldg. com.). Republican. Episcopalian. Club: Scuba (Columbus). Home: 207 Jones Circle Columbus MS 39701 Office: City of Columbus Bldg Dept 513 Main St PO Box 1408 Columbus MS 39703

MURPHY, NANCY L., state legislator; b. Dec. 31, 1929; divorced; children: Michael, Julea, Mark. Mem. Md. Ho. of Dels., from 1982; state senator Md. Senate; mem. Dem. State Cen. Com., 1978-82. Mem. adv. bd. Greater Balt. Med. Ctr. Named Woman of Yr., Bus. and Profl. Women's Club, 1984. Mem. LWV, Md. Assn. Elected Women, Ind. Women's Dem. Club. Methodist. Office: 5443 Valley Rd Baltimore MD 21228-5217*

MURPHY, PATRICIA, academic administrator, learning disabilities specialist; b. Oceanside, N.Y., July 18, 1959; d. Leo and Carmella (Croce) M. BS, Adelphi U., 1981, MS, 1982; cert. advanced study, Hofstra U., 1988. Cert. elem. and spl. edn. tchr., ednl. adminstr. Spl. edn. tchr. presch. devel. program North Shore U. Hosp., Westbury, N.Y., 1982-86, ednl. coord., 1986-89; pvt. practice Oceanside, N.Y., 1983—; asst. prin. bd. coop. edn. svcs. Nassau County Early Childhood Intervention Ctr., 1989—; presentor conf. sessions Presch. Pragmatics, 1988-89. Ralph McNeil Meml. scholar Adelphi U., 1981. Mem. L.I. Assn. Spl. Edn. Adminstrs., Nassau Suffolk Adminstrv. Women in Edn., Kappa Delta Pi.

MURPHY, PATRICIA A, speech and language pathologist, learning specialist; d. Michael and Nora (Dennehy) M. BA in Speech Pathology and Audiology, NYU, 1968, MA in Communication Scis., 1970, MA in Learning Disabilities and Reading, 1977; postgrad. in Ednl. Psychology, Columbia U., 1986—; MSW, NYU, 1989. Lic. speech lang. pathologist; cert. social worker. Speech-lang. pathologist Goldwater Meml. Hosp./NYU Med. Ctr., N.Y.C., 1970-78; lang. learning specialist in child and adolescent psychiatry Met. Hosp., N.Y.C., 1980-85, 86-90; cons. speech-lang. pathologist Mary Manning Walsh Nursing Home, N.Y.C., 1974—. Social worker St. Luke's Comprehensive Alcohol Treatment Program, 1990—. Mem. Nat. Assns. Social Workers, Am. Speech-Lang. and Hearing Assn., Orton-Dyslexia Soc., NYU Alumni Assn., Hunter Coll. Alumni Assn., Applachian Mountain Club. Home: 1619 3d Ave Apt 3CE New York NY 10128

MURPHY, PATRICIA SUE, hospital administrator; b. Cedar Rapids, Iowa, Jan. 13, 1961; d. James Frank and Rosemary Catherine (Maiers) Neuses; m. Timothy P. Murphy, Feb. 7, 1987. BS in Econs., U. Iowa, 1984; M Health Adminstrn., St. Louis U., 1986. Facility planner, contracts administr. St. Charles Hosp., Oregon, Ohio, 1986-88; v.p. St. Michael Hosp., Milw., 1988—; bd. dirs. St. Michael Doctor's Assn., 1989-90. Vol. ARC, St. Louis, 1984-86; participant Toledoscape, 1988, Oreg. Growth Corp., 1988. Mem. Am. Hosp. Assn., Am. Coll. Healthcare Execs. Home: 5026 N Idlewild Whitefish Bay WI 53217 Office: St Michael Hosp 2400 Villard Ave Milwaukee WI 53201

MURPHY, RHONDA FOSTER, small business owner; b. Fayetteville, N.C., Dec. 7, 1962; d. William Martin and Lena Mae (Williams) Foster.; m. Alvin Dexter Murphy, May 16, 1987; children: Tiffany Renee, Joseph Michael, Dexter Jr. Student, Shaw U., 1989. Sales mgr. Miller & Rhoads, Fayetteville, 1980-82; asst. mgr. Lerner Shops Inc., Fayetteville, 1982-84; area mgr. Worldbook Inc., Chgo., 1984-87; dir. Cameo Lingerie, Dallas, 1987; pres., owner A.R. Murphy & Assocs., Fayetteville, 1987—; founder, bd. dirs. Ms. Black Sophisticate Internat., Fayetteville, 1988; coord. Internat. Edn. Forum, Albany, Ga., 1989; beauty cons. Mary Kay Cosmetics, 1989—. Vol. ARC, Girl Scouts U.S., 1989. Mem. NAFE (bd. dirs. network), Friends Lupus Found. Program Adminstr., Bus. Profl. Women, Nat. Assn. Black Women Entrepeneurs, Nat. Coalition of Black Women Meeting Planners. Democrat. Baptist. Home: 524 Ijams St Fayetteville NC 28301

MURPHY, SANDRA JEAN, freight transportation administrator; b. St. Louis, Sept. 2, 1950; d. Joseph Richard and Loretta Mae (Mack) M. AAS in Retail Mgmt., Jefferson Jr. Coll., Hillsboro, Mo., 1970. Salesperson May Co., St. Louis, 1970-72; exec. asst. Cavato Inc., St. Louis, 1972-78; dept. mgr., buyer J.C. Penney, Inc., St. Louis, 1978-80; coord. Roadway Express, Inc., St. Louis, 1980—. Mem. NAFE, NOW (treas. St. Louis chpt. 1989—, sec. 1986, chair task forces women and AIDS, mammography 1989, fundraising chair 1990). Home: 3014 Keokuk St Saint Louis MO 63118

MURPHY, SHEILA ELLEN, university program director; b. Mishawaka, Ind., Apr. 5, 1951; d. Thomas Timothy and Bernadean Rita (Flynn) M. AB, Nazareth Coll., 1973; MA, U. Mich., 1974; PhD, Ariz. State U., 1980. Cert. community coll. tchr., Ariz. Asst. prof. English, Bay de Noc Coll., Escanaba, Mich., 1974-76; research asst. Ariz. State U., Tempe, 1977-78; mgmt. trainer Ramada Inns, Phoenix, 1980-82, mgmt. devel. specialist, 1982-84, mgr. ops. tng., 1984-85, dir. Ramada Mgmt. Inst., 1985-87, v.p. reservations, 1987-90; exec. dir. bus. and mgmt. programs U. Phoenix, 1990—. Author: Virtuoso Bird, 1981; Late Summer, 1984, With House Silence, 1986, Practical Motivation Handbook, 1986, Obeli: 21 Contemplations, 1990. Contbr. poems to mags. Mem. Am. Soc. for Tng. and Devel., Phi Delta Kappa. Democrat. Roman Catholic. Office: U Phoenix 4615 E Elwood St Phoenix AZ 85040

MURPHY, S(USAN) (JANE MURPHY), small business owner; b. Williamsport, Pa., Dec. 26, 1950; d. Jack W. and Edythe J. (Grier) M.; m. Michael J. Sanchez, Dec. 30, 1979. BBA, Pa. State U., 1978. Gen. mgr. Murphy Swift Homes, Hummelstown, Pa., 1970-75; owner, operator Murphy's Home Ctr., Hummelstown, 1975-79, 1985—; mgr. Builder's Emporium, San Diego, 1979-80; entrepreneur Castle in the Sand, San Diego, 1980-83; adminstr. Sohio Constrn., Prudhoe Bay, Alaska, 1983-85; cons. in field; dealer Servistar Home Ctrs. Photographs displayed at San Diego Art Inst. Vol. Hershey (Pa.) Free Ch. Donald MacIntyre scholar, 1979, Class of 1920 scholar, 1979, Congressman Kunkel scholar, 1979. Mem. Pa. Hardware Assn., Hummelstown C. of C., Better Bus. Bur. Evangelical Christian.

MURPHY, TERESA HODES, nursing service executive; b. Kansas City, Mo., Nov. 28, 1955; d. Richard Erb and Barbara Marie (Altman) Hodes; m. Rick S. Murphy. Apr. 23, 1988. BS in Biology magna cum laude, Regis Coll., 1978; BS in Nursing, U. Colo., 1980; MBA, U. Phoenix, 1987. RN. Nurse Denver Gen. Hosp., 1980-82, asst. head nurse, 1982-86; head nurse Rose Med. Ctr., Denver, 1986-87; br. dir. Favorite Nurses, Denver, 1987-90; nat. dir. traveling nurses div. Favorite Nurses, Kans., 1990—. Contbr. papers to nursing jours. Mem. Nat. Orgn. Female Execs., Network for Profl. Devel., Colo. Assn. Healthcare Staffing and Svcs. (bd. dirs.). Roman Catholic. Home: 11527 Rosehill Overland Park KS 66210 Office: Favorite Nurses 7255 W 98th Terr Overland Park KS 66210

MURPHY, VANISSA DAWN, music educator; b. Smithville, Tenn., Aug. 8, 1953; d. Clarence E. and Mary Lucille (Groom) Braswell; m. Gordon Chittenden Murphy, May 29, 1976; 1 child, Briana Elizabeth. MusB, Middle Tenn. State U., 1975; MusM, U. Ky., 1977; Student, U. North Tex., 1985—. Systems programmer Amdahl Corp., Sunnyvale, Calif., 1978-81, Bapt. Med. Systems, Little Rock, 1983-84; teaching fellow music dept. U. North Tex., Denton, 1985-88; asst. prof. music dept. U. Wis., Eau Claire, 1989—; instr. U. Ark., Little Rock, 1981-84, U. North Tex., 1985-87, East Central U., Ada, Okla., 1989. U.S. Achievement Acad. scholar, 1988. Mem. Denton Music Tchrs. Assn. (festival chair 1988), Piano Repertoire Group (pres. 1982-84), AAUW (cultural affairs chair 1988, recording sec. 1989), Tex. Music Educators Assn., Tex. Group Piano Assn., Pi Kappa Lambda. Democrat. Baptist. Home: 3602 White Birch Ct Eau Claire WI 54701 Office: Univ Wis Eau Claire WI 54701

MURRAY, ANGIE ANNA ALICE, government official; b. Thibodaux, La., July 6, 1949; d. Edward Justin Paul and Anna Angelina (Himmler) Hebert; m. Walter Thomas Murray, Mar. 21, 1970; children: Thomas Joseph, Anthony Michael. Speedwriting Cert., Sawyer Secretarial Sch., 1974. Mem. customer service staff European Exchange System, Ramstein, Ger., 1967-68; buyer, expeditor Thurow Electronics, Tampa, Fla., 1968-70; quotation clk. Thomas & Betts Co., Elizabeth, N.J., 1970-75; cost acct., girl Friday, Fulton Shirt Co., Elizabeth, 1975-76; office sec. Rapides Parish Police Jury, Alexandria, La., 1977-81, parish sec., 1981—; sec. Rapides Parish Stormwater Mgmt. and Drainage Dist., 1983—. Recipient Journalism award Noncommd. Officers Wives Club, 1967. Mem. Am. Soc. Notaries, Sec.-Treas. Orgn. of La. (v.p.), VFW Aux. Democrat. Roman Catholic. Avocations: reading, handicrafts. Home: PO Box 187 Elmer LA 71424 Office: Rapides Parish Police Jury PO Box 1150 Alexandria LA 71309

MURRAY, ANITA JEAN, data processing executive, consultant; b. Pitts., May 22, 1943; d. Julius and Nancy (Betza) Czujko; m. Christopher H. Murray, Apr. 6, 1968 (div. 1976), m. 2d, May 1, 1989. BS in Psychology, U. Pitts., 1964; MS in Stats., Stanford U., 1967. Cert. data processor. Systems analyst Pan Am. World Airways, N.Y.C., 1967-69; asst. contr. Bunge Corp., N.Y.C., 1969-79; prin. nat. office Arthur Young & Co., N.Y.C., 1979-82; v.p. mgmt. info. systems Murjani Internat. Ltd., Saddle Brook, N.J., 1982-85; pres. Amston Mgmt., Inc., N.Y.C., 1985—; seminar leader Am. Mgmt. Assn., N.Y.C., 1979-82. Author: Minicomputer Bus. Solutions, 1981. Pres. Married Ams. for Tax Equality, N.Y.C., 1973-76; chmn. office mgmt. com. Community Bd. 1, N.Y.C., 1983. Mem. Data Processing Mgmt. Assn. (speaker 1981-82), Internat. Platform Assn., Am. Women Entrepreneurs, Skating Club of N.Y., Collier Athletic Club (Naples, Fla.). Office: Amston Mgmt Inc 52 Laight St New York NY 10013

MURRAY, ANNE, singer; b. Springhill, N.S., Can., June 20, 1945; d. Carson and Marion (Burke) M.; m. William M. Langstroth, June 20, 1975; children: William Stewart, Dawn Joanne. B.Phys. Edn., U. N.B., 1966, D.Litt. (hon.), 1978; D.Litt. (hon.), St. Mary's U., 1982. Rec. artist for, Arc Records, Can., 1968, Capitol Records, 1969—; appeared on series of TV spls., CBC, 1970-81, 88-89; star CBS spls., 1981-85; toured N. Am., Japan, England, Germany, Holland, Ireland, Sweden, Australia and New Zealand, 1977-82; albums include A Little Good News, As I Am, 1988, Greatest Hits, vols. I and II, 1989, Harmony, 1987, I Will, 1990, others. Hon. chmn. Can. Save the Children Fund, 1978-80. Recipient Juno awards as Can.'s top female vocalist, 1970-81; Can.'s Top Country Female Vocalist, 1970-86; Grammy award as top female vocalist-country, 1974; Grammy award as top female vocalist-pop, 1978; Grammy award as top female vocalist-country, 1980, 83; Country Music Assn. awards, 1983-84; named Female Rec. Artist of Decade, Can. Rec. Industry Assn., 1980, Top Female Vocalist 1970-86; star inserted in Hollywood Walkway of Stars, 1980; Country Music Hall of Fame Nashville; Decorated companion Order of Can. Mem. AFTRA, Assn. Canadian TV and Radio Artists, Am. Fedn. Musicians. Office: Balmur Ltd, 4881 Yonge St Ste 412, Toronto, ON Canada M2N 5X3

MURRAY, BETTY JEAN KAFKA, plant physiologist, researcher; b. Council Bluffs, Iowa, June 6, 1935; d. Adolph Joseph and Loretto Audrey (Hobel) Kafka; m. Brownson Murray, June, 14, 1958; 1 child, Michael Maxwell. BBA, U. Mich., 1957, PDD in Biology, 1979, MS in Biology, 1983, PhD in Botany, 1987. Exec. trainee Jordan Marsh, Boston, 1957-58; founder, owner, mgr. Marigold Marsh Tree Farm, Manchester, Mich., 1980—; rsch. fellow U. Mich., Ann Arbor, 1987—. Contbr. articles to profl. publs. Mem. AAAS, Am. Soc. Plant Physiologists, Am. Assn. Nurserymen, Scroll, Kappa Kappa Gamma, Sigma Xi. Republican. Roman Catholic. Office: Marigold Marsh Tree Farm 15490 Buss Rd Manchester MI 48158

MURRAY, CHERRY ANN, physicist, researcher; b. Ft. Riley, Kans., Feb. 6, 1952; d. John Lewis and Cherry Mary (Roberts) M.; m. Dirk Joachim Muehlner, Feb. 18, 1977; 1 child, James Joachim. BS in Physics, MIT, 1973, PhD in Physics, 1978. Rsch. asst. physics dept. MIT, Cambridge, 1969-78; rsch. assoc. Bell Labs., Murray Hill, N.J., 1976-77; mem. tech. staff AT&T Bell Labs., Murray Hill, 1978-85, disting. mem. tech. staff, 1985-87, dept. head low-temperature and solid-state physics rsch., 1987—; co-chair Gordon Rsch., Wolfeboro, N.H., 1982, chair, 1984. Contbr. numerous articles to profl. jours. and chpts. to books. NSF fellow, 1969; IBM fellow MIT, 1974-76. Fellow Am. Phys. Soc. (Maria Goeppart-Mayer award 1989), Sigma Xi. Office: AT&T Bell Labs 600 Mountain Ave Murray Hill NJ 07974

MURRAY, CHERRY ROBERTS, artist, fine arts educator; b. Colfax, La., Jan. 3, 1921; d. John Bunyon and Mary (Procter) Roberts; student U.

N.Mex., 1940-41; B.F.A., U. Tex., 1942; student Nagayama Studio, Tokyo, 1955; studied under numerous profl. artists, including Ward Lockwood, Best-Mougourd, Maynard Dixon, Millard Sheets, Peter Hurd, Georgia O'Keefe, Vincent Farrell; m. John Lewis Murray, May 2, 1942; children—John Roberts, James Procter (dec.), Cherry Ann, Nancy Lee. Tchr. painting, U.S., 1939-54, 70—, Japan, 1954-56, 60-64, Pakistan, 1957-60, Korea, 1965-68, Indonesia, 1968-70; instr. fine arts Pima Coll. East, Tucson, 1979—; exhbns. include: Baluche Regiment, Cherat, West Pakistan, 1965-68, Am. Embassy Residence, Seoul, Korea, 1965-68, Djarkarta, Indonesia, 1968-70, Abba Gallery, 1978-80, Kay Bonfoey Gallery, 1980, Rentschler Gallery, 1980, Casa Grande Art Gallery, Tucson, 1980; represented in permanent and pvt. collections: U. Tex., U. N.Mex., Nagayama Studio, Tokyo, Ayub Kahn, Baluche Regiment, West Pakistan, Mitha Collection, Lahore, Pakistan, Sir Ian McKensie, Brit. Isles, H. Allen Loomes, Australia, Ambassador Yehuda Horam, Israel, Chote-Kholgvista, Thailand, Kopper, Indonesia, Galbraith, Washington, USIS, Indonesia, Am. Embassy, Djarkarta, Am. Embassy, Seoul, Lathrum, Hicks, Woods, Elliott collections (all Washington), Valley Nat. Bank, City of Douglas, Old Adobe Patio Gallery, Pima Community Coll. East,others. Recipient 56 awards, 1975-86, including: Creative Artist of Yr. award, 1976; 1st pl. award So. Ariz. Watercolor Guild, 1978; Merit award Watercolor Southwest III, Houston, 1978; Best of Show award Nat. League Am. Pen Women, 1978; Tchr. of Yr. award Pima Coll. East, 1983. Mem. AAUW, U. Tex. Art Assn. (1st pres.), So. Ariz. Watercolor Guild (hon.), Tubac Center of the Arts, Santa Cruz Valley Art Assn., Sierra Vista Art Assn., Ariz. Watercolor Soc., Archeol. and Hist. Soc., Nat. Soc. Arts and Letters, Southwestern League Fine Arts, Gem and Mineral Soc., Nat. League Am. Pen Women, Pilot Internat. Democrat. Presbyterian. Home: 12420 Calle del Gorrion Tucson AZ 85748 Office: Pima Community College 8202 E Poinciana Dr Tucson AZ 85730 Office: Pima Coll E Tucson AZ 85710

MURRAY, CYNTHIA ANN, lumber executive, real estate agent; b. Marlin, Tex., Dec. 27, 1956; d. Johnny Hilton Sr. and Wilta June (Johnson) Stewart; m. Lawrence James Murray, May 22, 1976; 1 child, Jason Ray. Cert. in real estate, Temple (Tex.) Jr. Coll., 1979. Lic. real estate broker, Tex. Exec. asst. Oasis Water Co., Waco, Tex., 1975-76, Air Systems, Inc., Temple, 1976-77; exec. asst., property mgr. Reagan Investments, Temple, 1977-79; sales and administrn. mgr. Tumac Lumber Co., Inc., Irving, Tex., 1979—; cons. Reagan Investments, Temple, 1979-82. Recipient Sales award Willamette Industries Surelam Div., 1985. Mem. Nat. Assn. for Female Execs. Republican. Baptist. Club: Los Colinas Sports (Irving). Office: Tumac Lumber Co Inc 9901 E Valley Ranch Pkwy #2800 Irving TX 75063

MURRAY, CYNTHIA JO, federal official; b. Vanderhoof, B.C., Canada, Aug. 12, 1959; d. Donald Eugene and Gale Ellen (Lunger) M. BS in Elem. Edn., U. Mont./Western Mont. Coll., 1988. Cert. tchr., Mont. Owner, mgr. The Attic Antiques and Art, Dillon, Mont., 1979-84; exec. dir. Beaverhead C. of C., Dillon, 1984-86; substitute tchr. Sheridan (Mont.) Pub. Schs., 1988-89; project coord., govt. liaison Anderson/Schellack Consulting Engrs., Dillon, 1989—; cons. Jack Creek Rd. Task Force, Ennis, Mont., 1989—; advisor Basin Planning for Water Use, Mont., 1990; lobbyist govt. affairs East Bench Irrigation Dist.-Phase III. Vice-chmn. Beaverhead County Dem. Cen. Com., 1986-89, chmn., 1989—; adviser People's Choice on Sales Tax, Helena, Mont., 1990; Congl. liaison Operation Grassroots-Cedit Union Systems campaign, 1990—; mem. Dem. State Cen. Com., Mont. Dem. Party, Helena, 1989—; del. Mont. Dem. Platform Conv.; mem. Montana County Chairs Assn., Western Polit. Sci. Assn., Mont. Dem. State Cen. Com. Mem. NAFE, Mont. Tourism/Recreation Coun., We. Polit. Sci. Assn., Mont. County Charis Assn. Home: 202 E Dillon St Dillon MT 59725 Office: Anderson/Schellack Consulting Engrs 30 S Montana St Dillon MT 59725

MURRAY, ELEANOR F., educator, freelance writer; b. Omaha, Nov. 30, 1916; d. Fred Blatchford and Calista June (Reynolds) Greusel; m. Jack Earl Buckley, June 15, 1970 (dec. Nov. 1977); m. Hubert Larkin Murray; children: Thomas M.B. Hicks, Mary E. Sharp, Barbara L. Wilke. BS in Edn., U. Nebr., 1939. Cert. tchr. of English. Newswriter Etowah Observer, Alabama City, Ala., 1939-40; feature writer Stars 'n Stripes, Tokyo, 1947-51; columnist Japan Times, Tokyo, 1949-51; in pub. relations Am. Internat. Underwriters, Tokyo, 1948-51; writer news and features Paterson (N.J.) Evening News, 1952-54; tchr. Riverdale (N.J.) Sch., 1954-55, Panama Canal Zone Schs., 1955-60, Skokie (Ill.) Schs., 1961-66; freelance writer Sebring, Fla., 1980—. Author: (non-fiction) Bend Like the Bamboo, 1982, Growing Up In Aunt Molly's Omaha, 1990; (poetry) Cherokee County Summer, 1981, God's Green Valley, 1983; author articles. Democrat. Presbyterian. Home: 3816 Sunbird Circle Sebring FL 33872

MURRAY, FLORENCE KERINS, state supreme court justice; b. Newport, R.I., Oct. 21, 1916; d. John X. and Florence (MacDonald) Kerins; m. Paul F. Murray, Oct. 21, 1943; 1 child, Paul F. A.B., Syracuse U., 1938; LL.B., Boston U., 1942; student, R.I. Coll. Edn., 1942, Ed.D. (hon.), 1956; grad., Nat. Coll. State Trial Judges, 1966; LL.D. (hon.), Bryant Coll., 1956; LL.D., R.I. U., 1963, Mt. St. Joseph Coll., 1972, Providence Coll., 1974, Roger Williams Coll., 1976, Salve Regina Coll., 1977, Johnson and Wales Coll., 1977. Bar: Mass., R.I., U.S. Supreme Ct. Sole practice Newport, 1947-52; mem. firm Murray & Murray, Newport, 1952-56; assoc. judge R.I. Superior Ct., 1956-78; presiding justice Superior Ct. R.I., 1978-79; assoc. justice R.I. Supreme Ct., 1979—; staff, faculty adv. Nat. Jud. Coll., Reno, Nev., 1971-72, dir., 1975-80, chmn., 1979-87, chair emeritus, 1990—; legal adv. R.I. Girl Scouts; sec. Commn. Jud. Tenure and Discipline, 1975-79; participant, leader various legal seminars. Mem. R.I. Senate, 1948-56; chmn. spl. legis. com.; mem. Newport Sch. Com., 1948-57, chmn., 1951-57; mem. Gov.'s Jud. Coun., 1950-60, White House Conf. Youth and Children, 1950, Ann. Essay Commn., 1952, Nat. Def. Adv. Com. on Women in Service, 1952-58, Gov.'s Adv. Com. Mental Health, 1954, R.I. Alcoholic Adv. Com., 1955-58, R.I. Com. Youth and Children, Gov.'s Adv. Com. on Revision Election Laws, Gov.'s Adv. Com. Social Welfare, Army Adv. Com. for 1st Army Area; mem. civil and polit. rights com. Pres.'s Commn. on Status of Women, 1960-63; mem. R.I. Com. Humanities, 1972—, chmn., 1972-77; mem. Family Ct. Study Com., R.I. com. Nat. Endowment Humanities; bd. dirs. Newport YMCA; sec. Bd. Physicians Service; bd. visitors Law Sch., Boston U.; bd. dirs. NCCJ; mem. edn. policy and devel. com. Roger Williams Jr. Coll.; trustee Syracuse U.; pres. Newport Girls Club, 1974-75, R.I. Supreme Ct. Hist. Soc. Served to lt. col. WAC, World War II. Decorated Legion of Merit, Army Commendation ribbon; recipient Arents Alumni award Syracuse U., 1956, Carroll award R.I. Inst. Instn., 1956, Brotherhood award NCCJ, 1983, Judge of Yr., Nat. Assn. Women Judges, 1984, Herbert Harley, Am. Judicature Soc., 1988, Outstanding Woman, Bus. and Profl. Women, 1972. Mem. Am. Arbitration Assn., Nat. Trial Judges Conf. (state chmn. membershiup com., sec. exec. com.), New Eng. Trial Judges Conf. (com. chmn. 1967), ABA (chmn. credentials com. nat. conf. state trial judges 1971-73), Boston U. Alumni Coun., Am. Legion (judge adv. post 7, mem. nat. exec. com.), AAUW (chmn. state edn. com. 1954-56), Bus. and Profl. Women's Club (past state v.p., past pres. Newport chpt., past pres. Nat. legis. com.), Alpha Omega, Kappa Beta Pi. Club: Auota (past gov. internat., past pres. Newport chpt.). Home: 2 Kay St Newport RI 02840 Office: Supreme Ct 250 Benefit St Providence RI 02903

MURRAY, GERI D., travel consultant; b. Chgo., Oct. 7, 1927; d. Frances Edward and Geraldine (Luce) Dunlap; m. Donald James Murray, Oct. 9, 1948; children: Cheryl, Lynda, Donald D., Patrick, Michael, Joyce, Janyce. Student, DePaul U., 1948, Triton Coll.; BS, U. Mo., 1975. Asst. supr. bidding and contract div. Hauserman Co., Hillside, Chgo., 1967-72; asst. to pres. First Fed. Savs. and Loan Proviso Twp., Hillside, Ill., 1972-74; asst. mgr. product sales R.W. Mitchell & Co., Bellwood, Ill., 1974-75; agt. purchasing Reynolds Electric, Maywood, Ill., 1975-77; exec. dir. West Suburban Neighborhood Preservation Agy., Bellwood, 1978-83; comml. salesperson real estate Remax, Elmhurst, Ill., 1983-88; cons. Banque Travel, Oakbrook, Ill., 1988-89; acct. exec. Alpha Travel, Inc., Addison, Ill., 1989—; cons., tchr. Network Rehab.-Cook County, Bellwood, 1976-83, pres. 1984. Pres. PTA West Proviso High Sch., 1954-75; dir. Hillside Planning Commn., 1972-84; mem. adv. council Suburban Cook County Area Agy. Aging, 1984. Mem. Nat. Assn. Housing Rehab. Ofcls., Am. Planning Assn. (past state Ill. membership chmn.), Met. Planning Assn., Bellwood C. of C. (dir. 1984). Republican. Roman Catholic. Lodge: Women Moose. Home: 1 S 278th Stratofrd Ln Villa Park IL 60181

MURRAY, SISTER JEAN CAROLYN, college president; b. Broadview, Ill., May 30, 1927. B.A., Rosary Coll., River Forest, Ill., 1949; Ph.D. in French Lang. and Lit., Fribourg, 1961. Instr. French Rosary Coll., 1961-66, asst. prof., 1966-68, assoc. prof., 1968—; pres. Rosary Coll., River Forest, Ill., 1981—; bd. dirs. Fenwick Prep. High Sch. Editor: La genese Dialogues des Carmelites, 1963; editor, translator: Correspondance, choisie et presentee, Vol. I, Combat pour la verite Vol. II, Comban pour la liberte, 1971. Mem. West Cook County Heart Assn., Leadership Greater Chgo. Assocs. Mem. MLA, Am. Assn. Tchrs. French, Ill. Fgn. Lang. Tchrs. Assn., Associated Colls. Ill., Univ. Club Chgo., Chgo. Network, Econ. Club, Fedn. Ind. Colls. and Univs. (bd. dirs.). Office: Rosary Coll 7900 W Division St River Forest IL 60305

MURRAY, JEANNE See STAPLETON, JEAN

MURRAY, JEANNE EVELYN, insurance executive; b. Phoenix, Dec. 20, 1932; d. Thomas Lott and Bernice O. (Lockhart) Pettus; m. Richard C. Murray, May 2, 1952; children: Donn R., Susan Murray Hopkins. Student, Lamson Bus. Coll., Phoenix, 1950-52, Phoenix Jr. Coll., 1953-54, Scottsdale Community Coll., Ri, Phoenix, 1954. Sec. E. R. Livermore Adjustment Co., Phoenix, 1952-54, Allstate Ins. Co., Phoenix, 1954-56, State Farm Ins., Phoenix, 1956-60; claim adjuster, investigator, pvt. investigator Panarello Adjustment Co., Scottsdale. Fund raiser Am. Cancer Soc., Phoenix, 1975—, Am. Heart Assn., 1975—. Mem. Ariz. Ins. Claims Assn., Ariz. Pvt. Investigation Assn., U.S. Tennis Assn., Amateur Athletic Assn., Scottsdale Racquet Club. Republican. Methodist. Home: 8407 E Monterey Way Scottsdale AZ 85251 Office: Panarello Adjustment Co 7540 First St Scottsdale AZ 85251

MURRAY, JELENA JOVANOVIC, communications executive; b. Belgrade, Yugoslavia, Oct. 22, 1955; came to U.S., 1972; naturalized, 1984; d. Vitomir and Milica (Stajic) Jovanovic. Grade Superieure, Conservatoire de Musique D'Alexandrie, 1972; BS, U. Tex., Dallas, 1977; grad., Comml. Coll. Inc., Real Estate Inst., Dallas, 1986. Ind. cons. Dallas, 1980—; successively dir. mktg. rsch., dir. sales and mktg., dir. planning and analysis U.S. Telecom, Dallas, 1982-85; asst. v.p. New Bus. Devel. Internat. Telecharge, Inc., Dallas, 1986-89; co-founder, gen. ptnr. Tex. Enterprises, Dallas, 1986—. Fgn. Student grantee, music grantee; Rotary Internat. scholar. Mem. NAFE, AT&T Cons. Network, The Internat. Craniofacial Found. (founding mem.), Phi Theta Kappa. Republican. Serbian Orthodox. Address: 4151 Glenwick Ave #2 Dallas TX 75205

MURRAY, JULIA KAORU (MRS. JOSEPH MURRAY), occupational therapist; b. Wahiawa, Oahu, Hawaii, 1934; d. Gijun and Edna Tsuruko (Taba) Funakoshi; m. Joseph Edward Murray, 1961; children: Michael, Susan, Leslie. BA, U. Hawaii, 1956; cert. occupational therapy U. Puget Sound, 1958. Therapist, Inst. Logopedics, Wichita, Kans., 1958; sr. therapist Hawaii State Hosp., Kaneohe, 1959; part-time therapist Centre County Ctr. for Crippled Children and Adults, State College, Pa., 1963; vice chmn. adv. bd. Hosp. Improvement Program, East Oreg. State Hosp., Pendleton, 1974; v.p. Ind. Living, Inc., 1976-79; job search instr.; mem. adv. com. Oreg. Ednl. Coordinating Commn., 1979-82; mem. Oreg. Bd. Engring. Examiners, 1979-87; supr., occupational therapist Fairview Tng. Ctr., Salem, Oreg. Rep. from Umatilla County Commrs. to Blue Mountain Econ. Devel. Council, 1976-78; mem. Ashland Park and Recreation Bd., 1972-73; vice chmn. adv. bd. LINC, 1978; mem. exec. bd. Liberty-Boone Neighborhood Assn., 1979-83. Mem. Am. Occupational Therapy Assn., Oreg. Occupational Therapy Assn., Hawaii Occupational Therapy Assn. (sec. 1960) Occupational Therapy Assn., LWV (bd. dirs. Pendleton 1974, 77-78, pres. 1975-77; bd. dirs. Oreg. 1979-81, Ashland 1967-71, v.p. 1970). Office: Fairview Tng Ctr 2250 Strong Rd SE Salem OR 97310

MURRAY, LILLIAN ANDERSON, developer/fundraiser; b. Liberal, Kans., Oct. 13, 1943; d. Hudson Lycurgus and Lillian Cecilia (Yates) A.; m. Michael Robert, July 10, 1965 (div. Jan. 1988); children: Robert Michael and Anne Cecilia. BS in Elem. Edn., U. Tex., Austin, 1965; BS, Tex. A&I, Kingsville, 1971. Spl. Edn. and Elem. Edn. Teaching Cert. Tchr. Pa. Ind. Schs., 1965-66, Houston Ind. Schs., 1966-67, Nueces County MH/MR-Opportunity Hse., Corpus Christi, Tex., 1968-73; community vol. Jr. League; Art Mus. S. Tex.; C.C. Aquarium Assn.; Palmer Dr, Corpus Christi, Tex.; ins. agent Sid Murray Co., Corpus Christi, Tex., 1973—; devel. dir. Tex. State Aquarium, 1987-90; dir. Art Mus. S. Tex., Corpus Christi, 1990—; sec. Del Mar Coll. Found. Corpus Christi, 1984—; adv. bd. Ctr. for Profl. Edn. Corpus Christi, 1986—; profl. adv. Funding and Devel. Jr. League Corpus Christi, 1988—; bd. visitors McDonalds Obs., U. Tex., 1986—. Co-Author Curriculum Guide "Nueces County MH/MR-Curriculum Guide for the Trainable." Co-chmn. Tourism: The Future of a Region Conf. Corpus Christi, 1987; sec. State Bar of Tex. Dist. Griedvance Com., 1987—. Named Outstanding Leadership Corpus Christi Alumnae 1988. Mem. Leadership Tex. II, Leadership Am. III, Leadership Corpus Christi, C. of C. (Leadership award). Democrat. Roman Catholic. Home: 13513 King Philip Ct Corpus Christi TX 78418

MURRAY, LOIS A. HEIL, lawyer; b. Marshfield, Wis., June 3, 1953; d. Frank N. and Bertha J. (Hafenbreadl) Heil; B.A., B.S. in Acctg., U. Wis., River Falls, 1974; J.D. cum laude, U. Minn., 1978; m. Alan E. Murray, Aug. 18, 1973. Tax examiner Minn. Dept. Revenue, 1974-75; admitted to Wis. bar, 1978, Minn. bar, 1978, U.S. Dist. Ct. bar, 1978; law clk. firm Ralph Senn, River Falls, 1976; research asst. to prof. law and asso. dean Sch. Law, U. Minn., Mpls., 1976-78; law clk. Honeywell, Inc., Mpls., 1977; assoc. firm Heywood, Cari & Murray and predecessor, Hudson, Wis., 1978-80, partner, 1980—; mem. faculty Wis. Indianhead Tech. Inst., Hudson Community Edn. Bd. dirs. West Central Wis. Action Agy., 1984-85. Mem. State Bar Assn. Wis., State Bar Assn. Minn., Am. Bar Assn., St. Croix Valley Bar Assn., AAUW, LWV, Hudson Area C. of C. Roman Catholic. Home: 600 7th St Hudson WI 54016 Office: Micklesen Bldg 204 Locust St Hudson WI 54016

MURRAY, MARILYN C., quality assurance professional; b. Syracuse, N.Y., Apr. 15, 1946; d. James Barstow and Evelyn (Burg) M. BA, Elmira Coll., 1967. Div. mgr. quality assurance, quality control Coulter Immunology div. Coulter Corp., Hialeah, Fla.; dir. quality control Technicon, Middletown, Va.; supr. quality control Becton Dickinson, Broken Bow, Nebr. Mem. Broken Bow Sch. Bd., 1980-81; leader Broken Bow 4-H. Mem. AACC, ACS, ASQC, NAFE, U.S. Dressage Assn., Am. Horse Show Assn., Gold Coast Dressage Assn. (sec. horse show 1988—). Republican. Methodist. Home: 15131 Leeds Ln Davie FL 33331 Office: Coulter Immunology 560 W 20th St Hialeah FL 33010

MURRAY, MARY MCFARLANE, genealogist; b. Tulsa, Dec. 28, 1947; d. John Robert Kincaid and Letha Nadine (Robertson) Hansen; m. Richard Walter Berge, Feb. 21, 1965 (div. 1972); children: Renae Marie Gerhardstein, Rachelle Ann Dunne; m. Timothy Winslow Murray, Feb. 14, 1987. Student, Grossmont Coll., 1977, U. Md., Berlin, 1983; AA, Fresno City Coll., 1988; BS, Fresno State U., 1990. Various positions Dept. Motor Vehicles, Sacramento, Calif., 1971-74; various positions acctg. Calif. Bd. Equalization, Sacramento, 1975-79; asst. tax collector, treas. County of Madera, Calif., 1986—. Served as sgt. U.S. Army, 1980-86. Mem. Madera County Genealogy Soc. (treas. 1990), Taxpayers Assn. of Madera County (pres. 1990), Rebekah Madera Lodge. Republican. Unitarian. Lodge: Soroptimists. Home: 19420 Panoramic Dr Madera CA 93638 Office: Madera County Govt Ctr 209 W Yosemite Madera CA 93637

MURRAY, MARY RAYMOND, public relations executive; b. Gardner, Mass., Sept. 22, 1947; d. Paul Henry and Mary Raymond (Proctor) M. BA in English with honors, LeMoyne Coll., 1969. Asst. pub. info. Bus. Sch. Harvard U., Boston, 1969-71; mng. editor Bus. Atlanta Mag., 1972-75, editor, 1975-77; market analyst Land Data Corp., Atlanta, 1974-77; account exec. Daniel J. Edelman Inc., Chgo., 1977-79, account supr., 1979-81, v.p., 1982-83, sr. v.p., 1983-84; exec. v.p., gen. mgr. Daniel J. Edelman Inc., St. Louis, 1984—. Contbr. articles to Bus. Atlanta Mag. Mem. V.P. Fair Found. Pub. Relations Com., St. Louis, 1985—; chmn. recruitment/devel. com. vol. action ctr. United Way, St. Louis, 1986—, vice chmn., 1988—; bd. dirs. St. Louis Charitable Found., St. Louis, 1986—; instr. Jr. Achievement Project Bus., St. Louis, 1987—. Recipient Golden Trumpet-Mktg. award Publicity Club Chgo., 1981, Merit Mktg. award Publicity Club Chgo., 1983, Merit Communications award Internat. Assn. Bus. Communicators, 1986, Silver Quill award Internat. Assn. Bus. Communicators, 1987. Mem. Pub. Relations soc. Am. (Silver Anvil Mktg. award 1984). Office: Edelman Pub Rels 100 N Broadway Saint Louis MO 63102*

MURRAY, MAUREEN T(HERESA), nursing home administrator; b. Newton, Mass., May 17, 1947; d. James Henry and Rosaleen Rita (Lopas) M. AA with highest honors, Cape Cod Community Coll., West Barnstable, Mass., 1985; BS magna cum laude, Stonehill Coll., 1987. Licensed nursing home adminstr., Mass. Adminstr. The Leland Home, Waltham, Mass., 1987-89, The Med-Vale Nursing Home, Medfield, Mass., 1989—; notary pub., Waltham, Mass., 1988—. Assoc. mem. bd. dirs. Big Brothers and Sisters of Cape Cod and the Islands, Hyannis, Mass., 1983—. Mem. The Mass. Long Term Care Found. Inc. (coun. of staff devel. , insvc. dirs.), Am. Coll. of Health Care Adminstrs., New England Gerontol. Assn., Assoc. Grantmakers of Mass., Inc., The Nat. Coun. on the Aging, Inc., Assn. of Mass. Homes for the Aging. Roman Catholic. Office: The Leland Home 21 Newton St Waltham MA 02154

MURRAY, MELITA FRANCES, sales executive; b. Mt. Vernon, Tex., Sept. 9, 1931; d. Luther Henry J. and Nora Ethel (King) Johnson; 1 child, Lanora Reneé Rivers. Grad., Mt. Pleasant High Sch. With Stanley Home Products, Mt. Pleasant, Houston, Springfield, Mo., 1960—, div. mgr., 1960-67, area mgr., 1967-74, regional mgr., 1975-84; v.p. sales Stanley Home Products, Westfield, Mass., 1985—. Mem. Ch. of Christ. Home: 608 Raton Pass Irving TX 75063 Office: Stanley Home Products 333 Western Ave Westfield MA 01085

MURRAY, PATTY, state senator; b. Seattle, Oct. 11, 1950; d. David L. and Beverly A. (McLaughlin) Johns; m. Robert R. Murray, June 2, 1972; children: Randy P., Sara A. BA, Wash. State U., 1972. Sec. various cos., Seattle, 1972-76; citizen lobbyist various ednl. groups, Seattle, 1983-88; legis. lobbyist Orgn. for Parent Edn., Seattle, 1977-84; instr. Shoreline Community Coll., Seattle, 1984—; mem. Wash. State Senate, Seattle, 1989—. Mem. bd. Shoreline Sch., Seattle, 1985-89; mem. steering com. Demonstration for Edn., Seattle, 1987; founder, chmn. Orgn. for Parent Edn., Wash., 1981-85; lst Congl. rep. Wash. Women United, 1983-85. Recipient Recognition of Svc. to Children award Shoreline PTA Coun., 1986, Golden Acorn Svc. award, 1989; Outstanding Svc. award Wash. Women United, 1986, Outstanding Svc. to Pub. Edn. award Citizens Ednl. Ctr. NW, Seattle, 1987. Democrat. Home: 528 NW 203rd Pl Seattle WA 98177 Office: Senate Office 17544 Midvale Ave N Seattle WA 98133

MURRAY, ROCHELLE ANN, librarian; b. Davenport, Iowa, Dec. 14, 1936; d. Walter Raymond Conrad and Lila Bernice (Kroeger) M. BA, Marycrest Coll., Davenport, Iowa, 1959; MA, U. Wis., 1968. Art, film and music librarian Davenport Pub. Library, 1959-65, young people's librarian, 1960-65, head adult svcs., 1964-65, mgr. children's svcs., 1965—; cons. Davenport Mcpl. Art Gallery, 1959-65; asst. counselor Ann Emery Hall, Madison, Wis., 1964-67; hostess weekly radio program WOC-Radio, Davenport, 1963-81; chmn. Childrens Lit. Festival, Moline, Ill., 1983—, Salute to Authors, Davenport, 1985—. Com. mem., local library reading chmn. Nat. Coun. Christians and Jews, Davenport, 1966-70, Operation Clean Davenport, 1983—. Named Outstanding Friend of Writers, Writers Studio, Moline, 1987. Fellow ALA (mag. com. 1965-70), AAUW, Iowa Library Assn., Kappa Gamma Pi (pres. 1959-60), Beta Phi Mu, Alpha Delta Kappa. Republican. Lutheran. Home: 3120 Jefferson Ave Davenport IA 52803 Office: Davenport Pub Library 321 Main St Davenport IA 52801

MURRAY, SARAH SHOWALTER, banker; b. Boulder, Colo., Jan. 28, 1959; d. Emmet M. and Beverly Joan (Reeves) Showalter; m. Morgan Joseph Murray Jr., May 23, 1987. BA in Econs., Spanish, St. Lawrence U., 1981. Lic. stockbroker. Cons. communications Exec., Inc., Dallas, 1982; asst. sales Smith Barney Upham Harris, Inc., Dallas, 1983-85, Prudential-Bache, N.Y.C., 1985-86; sr. securities officer The Depository Trust Co., N.Y.C., 1986—. Active in choir St. Teresa's Ch., Summit, N.J., 1988-89. Mem. Jr. League of Summit (active mem.). Republican. Roman Catholic. Home: 390 Morris Ave Summit NJ 07901

MURRAY, SUZANNE HELEN, medical librarian; b. Syracuse, N.Y., Feb. 19, 1932; d. James Patrick and Helen Elizabeth (Wait) M. BS, Le Moyne Coll., Syracuse, N.Y., 1954; MS, Syracuse U., 1960. Reference, circulation libr. Upstate Med. Center Libr., Syracuse, N.Y., 1960-62; collection, devel. libr. Upstate Med. Center Libr., Syracuse, N.Y., 1963-67; libr. cons. Regional Med. Program, Syracuse, N.Y., 1969-73; assoc. dir. Upstate Med. Center Libr., Syracuse, 1973-75; interim dir. SUNY Health Sci. Center Libr., Syracuse, 1985-87; dir. librs. SUNY Health Sci. Center Libr., 1987. Author: Contb. Articles to Profl. Jours. 1973-85. Vol. Religion Frat., Nat. Bd. Govs. LeMoyne Coll., Syracuse, N.Y., 1980; del. People to People's Med. Libr. Delegation to People's Republic China, 1989. Recipient grant Cen. N.Y. Libr. Resource Coun., Syracuse, 1989. Mem. Med. Libr. Assn., Spl. Librs. Assn., Upstate NY and Ont. Chap. Med. Libr. Assn., Theta Chi Beta, Beta Phi Mu, Zonta (dir. 1987). Roman Catholic. Home: The Orchard #8 Fayetteville NY 13066

MURRAY, VERNA HAZARD, educator; b. Brownstown, Ind., Oct. 26, 1909; d. Milton and Grace (Waldorf) Hazard; m. Edmund Allen Murray, Jan. 4, 1934 (dec. May 1983); children: Thomas Edmund, James Hazard. AS, Ball State U., Muncie, Ind., 1929; student, Ohio State U., Columbus, 1932; BS, Butler U., 1949. Tchr. Seymour (Ind.) Pub. Sch., 1929-34; child visitor Jackson County (Ind.) Welfare Dept., 1942-45; tchr. Seymour Community Sch., 1948-71, ret., 1971. active local vol. lit. program. Mem. AAUW (v.p., sec., tredas. Seymour chpt.), Friday Mag. Club (pres. 1990—), Delta Kappa Gamma (v.p. Seymour chpt. 1964—). Mem. Christian Ch. Home: 1012 Ewing St Seymour IN 47274

MURRAY-KEETZ, MADELYN PATRICIA, educator, artist; b. Schenectady, N.Y., Nov. 17, 1959; d. John Herbert and Marie Jane (Marchigiani) Murray; m. Edward John Keetz, Oct. 11, 1987. BS, Cornell U., 1981; MS in Edn., Coll. St. Rose, 1985. Asst. to sr. fashion editor Harpers Bazaar, N.Y.C., 1981-83; asst. fashion editor Self Mag., N.Y.C., 1983; art tchr. Schenectady City Schs., 1985-88; art tchr., specialist Creative Arts in Edn. Sch., Schenectady, 1988—; owner M.P. Murray Handpainted Silks. Mem. Schenectady Mus.; designer Crafts Coun. Mem. N.Y. State Art Tchrs. Assn. Democrat. Roman Catholic.

MURREL, KATHLEEN RICE, computer services company executive; b. Ann Arbor, Mich., Mar. 4, 1953; d. Thomas Russell and Thelma Joyce (Mullreed) Rice; m. Richard Lee Murrel, Sept. 18, 1982. A.B.A., Cleary Coll., Ypsilanti, Mich., 1973, A.B.A. in Data Processing, 1983; B.B.A. in Data Processing, 1986. Sec., Midwest Microwave, Ann Arbor, 1973-75; office asst. Kurkjian-Samborn, Ann Arbor, 1975-76; legal asst. Dever Profl., Ann Arbor, 1977-78; computer installation expeditor Mfg. Data Systems, Ann Arbor, 1979-83; mgr. office adminstrn. Anvil Corp., Ann Arbor, 1984—; owner, pres. Murrel's Word Processing Services, Ann Arbor, 1976—. Mem. Nat. Assn. Female Execs. Avocations: reading; sports, gardening. Home: PO Box 220 Dexter MI 48130-0220 Office: Anvil Corp PO Box 1088 Ann Arbor MI 48106

MURRELL, CASTELLA BURNLEY, biology educator, consultant; b. Nashville, Jan. 26, 1926; d. Stephen Alexander and Maynie (Young) Burnley; m. Irvin Maurcie Murrell (dec. 1975); children—Janis, Irvin, Bertrand, Audrey. B.S., U. Louisville, 1948; M.S., U. Ill., Urbana, 1950; postgrad. U. Chgo., summers 1960-65. Microbiologist Provident Hosp., Chgo., 1950-52; research asst. U. Ill.-Chgo., 1952-54; microbiologist U. Chgo., 1954-58; research asst. Armour Research, Chgo., 1959-60; tchr. biology Chgo. Bd. Edn., 1960—, biology cons., 1969-72. Contbr. articles to profl. jours. Recipient Sci. Fair awards Chgo. Area Sci. Tchrs. Assn., 1964, 65, 67, Ill. Outstanding Tchr. award Chgo. Bd. Edn., 1966, Fellowship Honor award, 1967, citation Chgo. Heart Assn., 1967, 68. Mem. Nat. Sci. Tchrs. Assn., Nat. Assn. Female Execs., Ill. Soc. Microbiologists, Ill. Sci. Tchrs. Assn., Chgo. Biology Roundtable, Christian Educators Assn., Alpha Kappa Alpha. Methodist. Avocations: photography; tennis. Home: 9730 S Green St Chicago IL 60643

MURRELL, JANICE MARIE, mezzo-contralto; b. St. Louis, Nov. 29, 1937; d. Carnal A. Propps and Edna (Hogan) Murrell-Propps. DMus., Kroeger Music Inst., St. Louis, 1971; D in Vocal Arts Culture, Juilliard Sch. Music, 1979. Singer-actress Mcpl. Opera Assn., St. Louis, 1970-86, Bardstown (Ky.) Theatre, 1978; vocal instr. St. Louis Pub. Schs., 1970—. Appeared in concerts wordlwide, including Washington, 1978, London, 1989; writer poetry and song lyrics. Decorated dame dr. Knights of Jerusalem. Mem. Confedn. of Chivalry, World Concern, Friends of Placido Domingo, Met. Opera Assn., St. Louis Symphony Women's Assn., Nat. Platform Assn., Nat. Assn. Women Execs. Lutheran. Home: 5556 Riverview Blvd Saint Louis MO 63120

MURRILLO, KATHLEEN MARIE, construction company official; b. Elizabeth, N.J., Mar. 21, 1958; d. Gerald Anthony and Beverly Ann (Dearstyne) M. Grad. high sch., Middlesex, N.J. Helper Dumar, Inc., Bound Brook, N.J., 1979-80; journeyman roofer Dumar, Inc., Bound Brook, 1980-81, formeman, 1981-83, supr., 1983-84, project coordinator, 1984-87; project coordinator Dumar Constrn. Svcs., Middlesex, 1987-90, v.p. tech. svcs., 1990—. Home: 1511-B W Camplain Rd Manville NJ 08835 Office: Dumar Constrn Services 5 Ivanhoe St Bridgewater NJ 08807

MURTHA, GERILYNN QUATAMA, environmental specialist; b. New York, Aug. 25, 1956; d. James E. and Eileen V. (Riess) M. BS in Biology/Geology, SUNY, Purchase, 1978. Cert. safety executive. Mgr. quality assurance United Abrasives, Mt. Vernon, N.Y., 1977-78; environ. specialist Dames & Moore, Cranford, N.J., 1978-82; environ. specialist Storch Engrs., Florham Park, N.J., 1982-84, assoc., 1984-87, ptnr., 1987—, dir. environtl., 1986—. tchr., counselor Spl. Children Assn., N.Y., 1978. Mem. Nat. Water Well Assn., Hazardous Waste Control Research Inst., World Safety Execs. (cert.), N.J. Engring. Assn. (cons. 1986). Office: Storch Engrs 220 Ridgedale Ave Florham Park NJ 07932

MURTHA, PATRICIA ANN, data processing consultant; b. White Plains, N.Y., Oct. 22, 1947; d. John Joseph and Mabel Lee (McGlothlin) M. BS Edn., SUNY, Buffalo, 1969; MA, NYU, 1974; Associate, Rockland Community Coll., Rockland, N.Y., 1980; MBA, Iona Coll., 1980. CLU. Tchr. Stamford Pub. Schs., Stamford, Conn., 1969-79; programmer Texaco, Harrison, N.Y., 1979-81; program analyst Clairol, Stamford, 1981-82; systems analys Met. Life Ins. Co., N.Y.C., 1982-87; systems cons. Met. Life Ins. Co., 1987—; tchr. Westchester Community Coll., Westchester Valhalla, N.Y., 1981-82. Vice pres. Tappan Ct. Tenant Assn., Tarrytown, N.Y., 1988—. Regents scholar N.Y. State, 1965-69.

MUSACCHIO, MARILYN JEAN, nurse-midwife, educator; b. Louisville, Dec. 7, 1938; d. Robert William and Loretta C. (Liebert) Poulter; m. David Edward Musacchio, May 13, 1961; children: Richard Peter, Michelle Marie. BSN cum laude, Spalding Coll., 1968; MSN summa cum laude, U. Ky., 1972, degree in Nurse-Midwifery, 1976; postgrad., Case Western Res U., 1988—. RN; cert. nurse-midwife; advanced registered nurse practitioner; registered nurse-midwife. Staff nurse gynecol. unit St. Joseph Infirmary, Louisville, 1959-60, staff nurse male gen. surgery unit, 1960; instr. St. Joseph Infirmary Sch. Nursing, Louisville, 1960-71; from asst. prof. to assoc. prof., dir. dept. nursing edn. Ky. State U., Frankfort, 1972-75; asst. prof. U. Ky. Coll. Nursing, Lexington, 1976-79, assoc. prof., coord., 1979—, acting coordinator nurse-midwifery, 1982-84, coordinator for nurse-midwifery, 1987—; cons. in field. Mem. editorial bd. Jour. Obstet., Gynecol. and Neonatal Nursing, 1976-82; author pamphlet; contbr. articles to profl. jours. Active St. James Parish Coun., chmn., 1980-81; mem. Louisville Fire Prevention Coun., 1973-80, Louisville Safety Coun., 1973-80. Col. Army Nurse Corps, USAR. Recipient Disting. Citizen award City of Louisville, 1977; recipient scholarships and fellowships, other awards. Mem. Am. Nurses Assn. (nurse researcher council 1985—), Nat. League for Nursing, Nurse Assn. of Am. Coll. Obstetricians and Gynecologists (charter; nat. sec. 1970-72, chmn. Dist. V 1969), Am. Coll. Nurse-Midwives, Internat. Childbirth Edn. Assn., Am. Soc. Psychoprophylaxis in Obstetrics, Nat. Assn. Parents and Profls. for Safe Alternatives in Childbirth, Ky. Acad. Sci., Res. Officers Assn., Assn. Mil. Surgeons U.S., Nat. Assn. Female Execs., Kappa Gamma Pi, Sigma Theta Tau. Roman Catholic. Home: 1502 Cherokee Rd Louisville KY 40205-1122

MUSE, HELEN ROSE, special education supervisor; b. Bay City, Tex., May 2, 1937; d. Edwin Henry and Helen H. (Dudlifiski) Coble; m. Ralph P. Muse Jr., Feb. 23, 1957; children: Ralph J. (dec.), Rosemarie Sheets, Angela McClanahan. Student, N. Tex. U., 1955-56, Tex. Christian U., 1956; BS, Pan Am. U., 1974, MEd, 1979. Cert. elem. tchr., Tex. Tchr. Harlingen (Tex.) Schs., 1974-80, diagnostician, 1980-89. Mem. St. Francis Ch. Altar Soc., La Feria, Tex., 1979—, Assn. for Retarded Citizens, 1987—. Mem. Tex. Ednl. Diagnosticians Assn. (pres. elect 1988—, v.p. 1987-88, parliamentarian 1986-87), Harlingen Consol. Ind. Sch. Dist. (spl. edn. adv. com. 1987—), Tex. Profl. Ednl. Diagnosticians, Kappa Delta Pi. Democrat. Roman Catholic. Home: PO Box 877 La Feria TX 78559 Office: Harlingen Consol Ind Sch 1409 E Harrison St Harlingen TX 78550

MUSE, PATRICIA ALICE, writer, educator; b. South Bend, Ind., Nov. 27, 1923; d. Walter L. and Enid (Cockerham) Ashdown; student Columbia U., 1946; B.A., Principia Coll., 1947; postgrad. Seminole Community Coll., 1977, U. Central Fla., 1978, 79, 80, 81, 82; m. Kenneth F. Muse, Dec. 2, 1950; children—Patience Eleanor, Walter Scott. Substitute tchr. public schs., Key West, Fla., also Brunswick, Ga., 1962-68; free lance writer, Casselberry, Fla., 1968—; novels: Sound of Rain, 1971, The Belle Claudine, 1971, paperback, 1973, Eight Candles Glowing, 1976; creative writing instr., Valencia Community Coll., 1974-75; instr. various writers confs. Community resource vol. Orange County (Fla.) Sch. Bd. (cert. of appreciation 1975, 76, 77); tutor Adult Literacy League, 1983—.

MUSE, RAQUEL, insurance investigator; b. Wichita, Kans., Feb. 22, 1962; d. Antonio Jr. and Janet Lois (Stowell) Garza; m. F. Scott Muse, Jan. 2, 1988. BBA in Mktg., Ea. N.Mex. U., 1984. Ins. investigator Equifax Svcs., Inc., Clovis, N.Mex., 1984—. Mem. AAUW (v.p. 1988-90). Republican. Lutheran. Home: 133 Westerfield Place Clovis NM 88101 Office: Equifax Svcs Inc 400 Pile Clovis NM 88101

MUSETTI, MYRTLE JANE HOLT, clinical nurse specialist, community health nurse; b. Phila.; d. Herbert Spencer and Janet Muir (Bald) Holt; m. Carl Francis Musetti, Sept. 17, 1960 (div. Oct. 1980); children: Mary C. Musetti Cave, Carl T., Andrew R., Janet, Rachel. BSN, Thomas Jefferson U., 1981; MSN, U. Pa., 1987. Cert. in oncology; cert. clin. specialist med. surg. nursing. Staff nurse Hosp. of U. Pa., Phila., 1981-84; pub. health nurse Community Nursing Svc. Delaware County, Lansdowne, Pa., 1984-86; staff nurse U. Pa.-Presbyn. Med. Ctr., Phila., 1986-89; community health nurse Community Health Affiliates, Ardmore, Pa., 1989—; clin. nurse specialist West Jersey Hosp., Camden, N.J., 1987—. Bd. dirs. Camden County unit Am. Cancer Soc., 1989—, chmn. svc. and rehab., 1989—; bd. dirs. Upper Merion unit Am. Cancer Soc., 1989—, chmn. pub. edn., 1989—; pres. bd. dirs. Uppermerion Park and Hist. Found., King of Prussia, Pa., 1988—. Mem. Oncology Nursing Soc., Wayne Woods Garden Club (silver award 1977, staging award 1985). Republican. Episcopalian. Home: 379 Heritage Ln King of Prussia PA 19406

MUSGRAVE, THEA, composer, conductor; b. Edinburgh, Scotland; m. Peter Mark, 1971. Ed., Edinburgh U., Paris Conservatory; Mus.D. (hon.). Composer: opera A Christmas Carol (first performed Va. Opera Assn., 1979), Harriet, the Woman Called Moses (1st performed Va. Opera 1985); ballet Beauty and the Beast, 1969; The Phoenix and the Turtle and The Five Ages of Man for choir and orch, Triptych for tenor and orch; opera Mary Queen of Scots; clarinet, horn and viola concertos Night Music for chamber orch; chamber concertos 1, 2 and 3, other vocal, chamber and orchestral works. Address: care Theodore Presser Co Presser Pl Bryn Mawr PA 19010

MUSGROVE, JUDY AUTRY, advertising company executive; b. San Antonio, Tex., Aug. 5, 1946; d. Monte L. and Mary E. (Hohner) Autry; divorced. Student U. Tex., 1964-68. Bus. mgr. Emergency Med. Services, P.A., Houston, 1974-81; mgr. bus. affairs Eisaman Johns & Laws Advt., Houston, 1981-83, v.p. bus. affairs, 1983—; guest lectr. women's profl. orgn., U. Houston. Mem. adv. bd., retired sr. vol. program Tex. Exec. Women, chmn., 1989—; vol. Bellaire Hosp. Cardiac Care Program, 1979-80; chmn. com. Greater Hartford Open Golf Tournament, 1970-71; mem. Nashville Symphony Women's Guild, 1972-73; bd. dirs. Houston Met. Ministries, 1989—. Mem. Am. Bus. Women's Assn. (dir. 1980-87, v.p. 1981, Woman of Yr. 1984), Fedn. Houston Profl. Women (organizing chmn. 1981, pres. 1982, exec. bd. 1983, 86-87, com. chmn. 1989-90) NAFE. Home: 7022 Jetty Ln Houston TX 77072 Office: 2121 Sage Rd Ste 200 Houston TX 77056

MUSHIK, CORLISS, state legislator; b. Hillsboro, N.D.; d. Kenneth M. and Edith (McDonald) Dodge; m. William Mushik, 1950; 1 child, Ross Dodge. Student, Coll. of St. Benedict's, 1941-42. Realtor; mem. N.D. State Ho. of Reps., 1971-84; now senator from dist. 34 N.D. State Senate. Chmn. N.D. Am. Revolution Bicentennial Com. Mem. LWV, PEO. Democrat. Office: 608 3rd St NW Mandan ND 58554 Other: PO Box 188 Mandan ND 58554*

MUSOLINO-ALBER, ELLA MARIE, professional tennis executive; b. N.Y.C., Apr. 22, 1942; d. Frank and Eva Patricia (Yarusevich) Grassi; m. Ronald J. Musolino, Oct. 14, 1962 (div. 1978); 1 child, Dennis Alexander; m. Robert E. Alber, Jan. 31, 1988. Sec. U.S. AEC, N.Y.C., 1959-61; sales asst. De La Rue Banknote Co., N.Y.C., 1961-66; sales and service rep. U.S. Banknote Corp., N.Y.C., 1966-67; gen. mgr. N.Y. Apples Team Tennis, N.Y.C., 1976-78; pres., founder Sports Etcetera, Inc., N.Y.C., 1978—; tournament mgr. U.S. Open Tennis Championships, 1969-75; tournament dir. Avon Championships, Madison Sq. Garden, 1979-82, Va. Slims Championships, 1983—. Mem. Women's Profl. Tennis Assn. Republican. Roman Catholic. Office: Sports Etcetera Inc 4 Penn Plaza New York NY 10001

MUSSELMAN, DEBORAH MYERS, pharmacist; b. Urbana, Ohio, June 2, 1964; d. Jerry Page and Nancy Jane (Miller) Myers; m. Gale Clinton Musselman, Jr., Oct. 10, 1987. BS in Pharmacy and Biology, Ohio No. U., 1987. Registered pharmacist, Ohio. Clk. Groveport (Ohio) Pharmacy, 1981-84, pharmacy intern, 1984-85; pharmacy intern Lancaster (Ohio) Fairfield Community Hosp., 1986; staff pharmacist Mt. Carmel East Hosp., Columbus, Ohio, 1987-88; pharmacist, asst. mgr. Super X OH 277, Lancaster, Ohio, 1988—; refief pharmacist Extended Care Pharmacy, Columbus, 1987—, Groveport Pharmacy, 1987-88. Mem. DAR, Urbana, 1983, Groveport United Meth. Ch., 1977. Mem. Ohio State Pharm. Assn. Republican. Office: Super X Ohio 277 1635 Rivervalley Circle Lancaster OH 43130

MUSSELMAN, KATHLEEN J., hospital administrator; b. Roaring Spring, Pa., Jan. 7, 1957; d. David Martin and Irene Mae (Mickel) M. BSBA, Ithaca Coll., 1987; MA in Bus. Adminstrn., U. Pitts., 1990. Pers. asst. Nason Hosp., Roaring Spring, 1973-83; mgr. bus. office Rehab. Hosp. Altoona, Pa., 1985-87, dir. human resources, 1987—. Mem. Christian Women's Fellowship, Blair County, Pa., 1989-90. Mem. Healthcare Human Resource, Blair County Human Resource Mgmt. Assn. (program dir. 1989-90), Bus. and Profl. Women. Democrat.

MUSSELMAN, LOIS, manufacturing executive. Grad., U. Ky., 1968. Asst. mgr. advt. Begley Drug, 1969-70; staff writer Commonwealth of Ky., 1970-72; dir. pub. rels. Ky. Dem. Party, 1973-75; exec. dir. Hist. Events Celebration Commn., 1976; free-lance writer, 1977-79; press sec., various other adminstrv. positions Gov. John Y. Brown of Ky., 1979-82; sr. v.p. corp. communications Brown-Forman Corp., Louisville, 1982—. Office: Brown-Forman Corp 850 Dixie Hwy Louisville KY 40201*

MUSTARDE, BONNIE JEAN, finance company executive; b. Ft. Worth, Tex., Apr. 23, 1959; d. Robert Gow and Ruth Leonore (Kline) M. BA cum laude, Tex. Luth. Coll., 1981; postgrad., Am. Coll., Bryn Mawr, Pa. Mgr. monthly payment plan Farmers Inc. Group, Austin, Tex.; claims svcs. mgr., claims staff specialist Farmers Ins. Group, Austin. Recipient Academic honors in finance Fin. Exec. Inst., 1981. Mem. NAFE, Nat. Assn. Ins. Women, Tex. Luth. Coll. Alumni Assn., Toastmasters Internat. (past pres., Outstanding Svc. award, 1986, 87), Austin Jaycees (past mgmt. devel. v.p., past pub. affairs v.p., past pers. mgmt. v.p., Officer of Quarter, 1986), Tex. Jaycees (past dir. pub. rels.). Lutheran.

MUSTIFUL, JUNE CAROLYN LEWIS, insurance company administrator; b. Brookhaven, Miss.; d. James Calvin Lewis and Melba Ruth (Knight) Cain; m. George Ellis Mustiful, June 18, 1958 (div. 1972); 1 child, Denise Mustiful-Martin. BA, Fisk U., 1974; MPA with honors, Roosevelt U., 1976. Instr., dental assting supr. dental clinic Martin Luther King Neighborhood Health Ctr., Chgo., 1968-72; mgr. govt. health, market rsch. CNA Ins. Co., Chgo., 1976-77, mgr. spl. projects, personnel, 1978-79, mgr., group ins. publs., 1980-85, mgr. group benefits communications and tng., 1986-90; account mgr. group long term care ins. CNA Ins. Co., 1990—; commr. governing bd. Chgo. Health Systems Agy., Chgo., 1983-88. Editor, writer: (newsletter) CNA Group Perspectives, 1980—. Fundraising com. Women for Washington, Chgo., 1982-85; rally com. Women for Pincham, Chgo., 1990; friend of bd. Ghana Cultural Inst., Chgo., 1990; chpt. mem. Africare, Chgo., 1990. Recipient Scientific Clinician's award Nat. Dental Assn., 1970, Jamaican Dental Assn., 1971. Mem. Women in Communications, Inc., Edn. Advancement Found., AKArama Found. (v.p. 1990-91), Chgo. Urban League, Chgo.-Fisk U. Alumni Assn., Roosevelt Alumni Assn., Alpha Kappa Alpha (reporter to nat. jour. 1982-83, ann. fundraising chmn. 1986, founder's day chmn. 1987, historian 1988-89, v.p. 1990-91, Women of Yr. 1987). Home: 8735 S Calumet Ave Chicago IL 60619 Office: CNA Ins Cos CNA Plaza Chicago IL 60685

MUSTONE, AMELIA P., state legislator; b. Salem, Mass., July 16, 1928; d. Udo A. and Alberta (Durand) Poppey; m. John J. Mustone, 1950; children: John, Lisa, Mary Ellen, Paul, Anastasia, Jessica. B.A., Goddard Coll., Vt. Pres., Meriden Bd. Edn., Conn., 1974-78; mem. Conn. State Senate from 13th Dist., 1979—, dep. majority leader, 1987—. Mem. Nat. Conf. State Legislators, Council on State Govts., Caucus New Eng. State Legislators, Conn. Women's Polit. Caucus, Conn. Student Loan Found.; mem. Martin Luther King Jr. Commn.; active YMCA. Recipient Citizen of Yr. award Civitan Club, 1978, 1st Eleanor Roosevelt award NOW. Mem. AAUW, Meridan LWV, Latin Am. Soc. (hon.), Am. Assn. Retail Persons, NAACP. Roman Catholic. Lodge: Soroptimist Internat. Home: 34 Tunxis Circle Meriden CT 06450

MUZZARELLI, LISA MARY, social services administrator; b. Chgo., Sept. 8, 1961; d. John Adrian and Nancy Jo (Moran) Muzzarelli; divorced; m. Mark Hardy. AA, Ill. Valley Community Coll., 1981; B in Social Work, Ill. State U., 1983. Lic. foster care rep. Outreach coord., acting dir. Against Domestic Violence, La Salle County, Ill., 1983, clin. specialist, 1983-85, acting dir., 1985, clin. dir., 1985-87; counselor Covenant Children's Home, Princeton, Ill., 1988-89; mktg. mgr. Galerie'd' Art, Peru, Ill., 1984-89; foster care worker Vietnamese youth Cath. Social Svc., La Salle, 1989—; foster care caseworker, licensing rep. Vol. United Way, La Salle County Youth Svc. Bur., Ottawa, Ill., 1980-82; adv. bd. mem. Prairie State Legal Svcs., Ottawa, 1983—; legis. chair Ill. Valley Nat. Orgn. for Women, 1985-87. Scholar LaSalle County Community 708 Mental Health Bd., 1981. Mem. Nat. Assn. of Social Workers, Social Work Club. Democrat. Home: 2627 W 2d St Peru IL 61354 Office: Cath Social Svc 542 Crosat St La Salle IL 61301

MUZZY, DIANA LEE, bicycle clothing manufacturing company executive; b. Hanover, Pa., Oct. 28, 1949; d. Leo Esiah and Alice Wilkinson (Rudolph) M. B.S., U. Calif.-Berkeley, 1972. Lic. animal health technician, Calif. Asst., Orinda Vet. Clinic, Calif., 1971-74; animal health technician Wilson Animal Hosp., Concord, Calif., 1974-78; co-owner, co-operator Vigorelli, Oakland, 1979—. Cons. Battered Women's Alternatives, Concord, Calif., 1981-84. Mem. Women's Sports Found. Democrat. Avocation: running. Office: Vigorelli 2200 Adeline St Suite 250 Oakland CA 94607

MYATT, SUE HENSHAW, gerontological activity therapy consultant; b. Little Rock, Aug. 16, 1956; d. Bobby Eugene and Janett Lanell (Ahart) Henshaw; m. Tommy Wayne Myatt; children: James Andrew, Thomas Ryan. BS in Psychology, Old Dominion U., 1978, MS in Ednl. Counseling, 1982. Cert. activity cons. Nat. Cert. Council of Activity Profls. and Cons. Dir. activity Manning Convalescent, Portsmouth, Va., 1983-84, Camelot Hall, Norfolk, Va., 1984-86; coord. activities Beverly Manor, Portsmouth, 1986-87, Gerogian Manor Assisted Living Facility, 1989-90; dir. activities Huntington Convalescent Ctr., Newsport News, Va., 1990—; instr. Tidewater Community Coll., 1990. Mem. Nat. Assn. Activity Profl. (cert. legis. com.), Va. Assn. Activity Profl. (v.p. 1986-87, creator logo), Va. Recreation and Park Soc. (sr. sect.), Hampton Roads Activity Profls. Assn. (sec. 1985-86, pres. 1986-87, v.p. 1987-88). Home: 705 Gladesdale Dr Chesapeake VA 23322

MYER, CAROLE WENDY, veterinary radiologist; b. N.Y.C., Mar. 14, 1944; d. John Paul and Lydia Estelle (Quinones) Myer; m. Charles Edward Bynner, Oct. 30, 1971. DVM, Cornell U., 1967; MS, Ohio State U., 1974. Diplomate Am. Coll. Vet. Radiology. Assoc. veterinarian Dueland Vet. Clinic, S.I., N.Y., 1967-70; radiology resident Ohio State U., Columbus, 1970-74; clin. instr. Ohio State U., 1974-75, asst. prof., 1975-81, assoc. prof. vet. radiology, 1981—; sec. chief Ohio Sate U. Vet. Radiology Sect., 1986—. Editorial bd. Am. Animal Hosp. Assn. jours., 1985—; contbr. numerous articles to profl. jours., chpts. to books. Mem. Ohio State U. Alumni Assn., Vet. Ultrasound Soc., Internat. Vet. Radiology Soc., Am. Vet. Med. Assn. Republican. Methodist. Office: Ohio State Univ Vet Hosp 1935 Coffey Rd Columbus OH 43210

MYER, MARI LYNN, lawyer; b. Gainesville, Fla., Apr. 22, 1961; d. Marshall Everett Jr. and Virginia Dell (McCalvin) M. BA, Wellesley Coll., 1983; JD, Boston U., 1986. Bar: Tex. 1986, Ga. 1988, U.S. Ct. Appeals (9th cir.) 1986. Jud. law clk., staff atty. Superior Ct. Guam, Agana, 1986-87; jud. law clk. Supreme Ct. Republic of Palau, Koror, 1987; assoc. Drew Eckl & Farnham, Atlanta, 1988—. Mem. ABA, State Bar Ga., State Bar Tex., Atlanta Bar Assn., Atlanta Wellesley Coll. Club. Democrat. Methodist. Office: Drew Eckl & Farnham 880 W Peachtree St Atlanta GA 30309

MYERS, CAROLE ANN, health transportation service executive; b. Henderson, Ky., June 14, 1938; d. James Newton and Rosalene Alberta (Eakins) Wade; m. Lawrence William Myers, Dec. 28, 1957 (dec. Feb. 1980); children: Patti Myers Crisler, Nancy Myers Allen, Sandra Myers Kowalski, Mark William. Cert. EMT, St. Francis Hosp., 1971; student, Butler U., 1979. Cert. emergency med. tech., paramedic. Pres., chief exec. officer Myers Ambulance Svc., Greenwood, Ind., 1966—. Mem. adv. bd. USA Congl. Fire Svcs. Inst., 1989—. Named Disting. Hoosier by Gov. of Ind., 1984. Mem. Rep. Sen. Innner Circle (life), Ind. Ambulance Assn. (pres. 1983-85, treas. 1986—), Ind. Emergency Med. Svcs. Commn. (commr., Disting. Svc. award 1988), Am. Ambulance Assn. (sec. 1983-84, treas. 1985-86, v.p. 1987-88, pres. 1989-90, Woman of Yr. 1983), Greater Greenwood C. of C. (bd. dirs., sec. 1988, Outstanding Bus. award 1989). Home: 150 N Madison Ave Greenwood IN 46142 Office: Myers Ambulance Svc Inc 1416 E Epler Ave Indianapolis IN 46227

MYERS, DARLENE MARIE, dance studio owner, choreographer; b. Schenectady, N.Y., July 25, 1950; d. Raymond Charles and Marie (Walsh) M. Grad. high sch., Schenectady, N.Y. Dancer Pa. Ballet Co., Phila., 1968-70; tchr., choreographer Schenectady Civic Ballet, 1970-76, Electronic Body Arts, Albany, N.Y., 1978-79; dir. dance Schenectady Arts Council, 1978-79; ballet mistress, choreographer Saratoga Ballet Co., Saratoga Springs, N.Y., 1980-81; artistic dir. Guilderland (N.Y.) Ballet Workshop, 1980-84; head dance program SUNY, Albany, 1981-85; founder, dir. Myers Studio and Art Gallery, Schenectady, 1985—; adj. prof. arts Union Coll., Schenectady, 1980-84; cons. Proctors Theater, Schenectady, 1985—; dir. Myers Dance Co., Schenectady, 1985—, annual summer dance camp hiring guest tchrs. from N.Y.C. Ballet; artistic dir. Myers Ballet Co.; choreographer, producer annual full length Nutcracker, Schenectady. Contbr. (jour. collection) Ariadne's Thread, 1982; choreographer ann. full-length Nutcrackers and a spring concert of new repetoire. Grantee CETA, 1978, 80, Adirondack Jr. Ballet, 1982, 83. Mem. Albany Leagu of Arts. Office: 1020 Barrett St Schenectady NY 12305

MYERS, HELEN LORETTA, property manager; b. Hammond, Ind., Sept. 22, 1934; d. Leslie Gilbert and Bessie Vickers (Pollard) Coapstick; m. Ivan Oteen Myers, Dec. 2, 1961 (dec. 1978). Student, St. Joseph's Coll., East Chicago, Ind., 1957-59. Sec., State Farm Ins., Griffith, Ind., 1969; owner, operator Myers' Restaurant, Hartford, Ky., 1969-77, Highland Body Shop, Ind., 1977-84; supr. Kelly Services, Merrillville, Ind., 1984-86, resident br. mgr., Chgo., 1985-87; property mgr. Cypress Trace Shipping Ctr., Ft. Myers, Fla., 1987—; mem. adv. com. Daley Coll., Chgo.; mem. Hyde Park C. of C., Automotive Service Councils (sec.-treas. 1977-86). Republican. Club: Scherwood Golf (Schererville, Ind.). Lodge: Eastern Star (matron 1967-68, state appts., Grand rep. to Ala. 1974-78). Avocations: golf, reading, hand crafts, walking, bicycling. Home: 13300 S Cleveland Ave Fort Myers FL 33907 Office: Kelly Services 7601 S Kostner Chicago IL 60652

MYERS, ILA MAY, rancher, social worker; b. Miami, Okla., May 10, 1921; d. Emmett Clarence and Nora Belle (Chitwood) M. AA, Northea. Okla. A&M Coll., 1941; BS, Kans. State Coll., 1968. Cert. social worker, Okla. Elem. tchr. Quapaw (Okla.) City Schs., 1941-46; social worker Okla. Dept. Human Svcs., Miami, 1946-51, case work supt., 1951-63, county adminstr., 1963-73, supr. day care licensing for 11 counties, 1973-80; rancher Miami, 1977—. Bd. dirs. Okla. Lung Assn., 1979—; elder lst Presbyn. Ch., Miami, 1984—, past deacon, 1981-84; sec. bd. dirs. Friendship House, 1976-89; del. Citizen Amb. Program to Russia, 1989; mem. Miami Dem. Women's Orgn., Miami, 1989—, Okla. Dem. Com., 1989—; chair Okla. Christmas Seal, Ottawa County, 1989-90. Mem. Miami Bus. and Profl. Women's Orgn. (v.p., state pres. 1978-79), AAUW (treas. Miami 1985-86, v.p. 1987-88), Miami Community Concert Assn., Miami Travel Club (treas.), Okla. Bus. and Profl. Women's Club (coord. Nat. Conv. San Antonio 1981, state conv. chair 1972, mem. nat. bd. dirs. 1978-79), Phi Theta Kappa. Home: Box 776 1206 D St NE Miami OK 74355

MYERS, INA VETRA, paralegal, management consultant; b. North Wilkesboro, N.C., Jan. 2, 1916; d. Cager Guy and Dora Ethel (Whittington) M. Grad., N Wilkesboro High Sch., 1933. Legal sec. Kyle Hayes, Atty. at Law, North Wilkesboro, N.C., 1935-42; reporter, sec. Morris Field Army Air Base, Charlotte, 1943-45; paralegal Hayes and Hayes, Attys., North Wilkesboro, 1945—; cons. N.B. Smithey Stores, Inc., North Wilkesboro, 1983—. Mem. North Wilkesboro Woman's Club, Garden Path Garden Club, Nat. Trust for Historic Preservation, Smithsonian Nat. Assocs., N.C. Mus. Hist. Assocs., Colonial Williamsburg, Rebekah's (Affiliate of Odd Fellows sec. 1961-62), Kiwanis. Republican. Baptist. Home: 1005 Trogdon Ave North Wilkesboro NC 28659

MYERS, JENNIFER LYNN, program consultant, academic program advisor; b. South Bend, Ind., Jan. 27, 1953; d. Franklin Joseph and Patricia Jean (Megan) Wild; m. Steven Paul Schook, June 14, 1975 (div. June 1979); m. Duane Hopper Myers, June 14, 1983. BA with honors, Mich. State U., 1975; MA with honors, Boston U., 1986; postgrad., The George Washington U., 1988—. Tchr. Elgin (Okla.) Pub. Schs., 1976-79; vol. coord. Marie Detty Youth Svc. Ctr., Lawton, Okla., 1976-79; cosmetic trainer, Cosmetic Splty. Labs. Marshall Field, Lawton, Chgo., 1979-82; tchr., dept. of def. dependent schs. Heidelberg (Germany) Am. High Sch., 1983-88, SHAPE Am. High Sch., Mons, Belgium, 1983-88; program advisor The George Washington U., Washington, 1988—; program cons. Acad. for Ednl. Devel., Nat. Inst. for Work and Learning, Washington, 1989—; cons. Gen. Motors, Detroit, 1988, Nat. C. of C., Washington, 1989, Dept. of Army, Ft. Belvoir, Va., 1988—; com. mem. Human Resource Devel. Network (editor 1989-90), The George Washington U., Washington, 1989-90. Author: Media Resource Guide, 1990. Mem. Am. Soc. Tng. and Devel. (rsch. com. staff mem. 1989—), Am. Assn. for Adult and Continuing Edn. (com. mem. 1988-89). Home: 1230 23rd St NW Apt 607 Washington DC 20037 Office: Nat Inst Work and Learning Acad Ednl Devel 1255 23rd St NW Washington DC 20037

MYERS, JO ANN, insurance agency executive; b. Allentown, Pa., Aug. 16, 1946; d. Charles Henry and Isabelle Lillian (Haggerty) Breyer; m. Richard Earl Myers, Dec. 4, 1965 (div. July 1977). Grad. high sch., East Greenville, Pa. Underwriter Harleysville (Pa.) Ins. Co., 1964-70, Edward G. Murphy, Inc., Ambler, Pa., 1970-81; kmgr., ptnr., officer E.G. Murphy III, Inc., Colmar, Pa., 1981-89; part owner, officer George H. Sterner Agy. Inc., Pennsburg, Pa., 1990—; cons. E.G. Murphy III, Inc., Colmar, Pa., 1990; gen. ptnr. Jo Ann Myers Real Estate Partnership, Pennsburg, 1985-87, Meljo Enterprises, Pennsburg, 1987—. Mem. reunion planning com. class of 1964,

Upper Perkiomen High Sch., East Greenville, 1968—; mem. East Greenville Centennial Com., 1978. Mem. NAFE, Profl. Ins. Agts. Assn., VFW Ladies Aux., Rolls Royce Owners Club. Democrat. Home and Office: 332 Geryville Pike RD 1 Pennsburg PA 18073

MYERS, KIM LORRAINE, state official; b. Perth Amboy, N.J., Jan. 26, 1957; d. Edward Miles and Elizabeth Maude (Peffer) M. AAS, Middlesex County Coll., Edison, N.J., 1990. Crew chief, liaison officer, 2d lt. Colonia (N.J.) First Aid Squad, 1978-84; asst. to owner Gloria Wagner Antiques, 1984—; driver lic. examiner N.J. Div. Motor Vehicles, various locations, 1983-88; safety specialist N.J. Div. Motor Vehicles, Rahway, 1988—; driver improvement analyst N.J. Div. of Motor Vehicles, Wayne, 1989—; trustee, recording sec., cadet advisor Colonia First Aid Squad, 1978-84. Mem. DECA, Delta Epsilon Chi. Republican. Baptist. Home: 80 McKinley Ave colonia NJ 07067 Office: NJ Dept Law & Pub Safety 25 S Montgomery Trenton NJ 07067

MYERS, LAURA ANN, journalist; b. Las Vegas, Aug. 26, 1961; d. William Herbert and Monte Jean (Madden) M. BA in Journalism, U. Nev., 1985. Govt. reporter Reno (Nev.) Gazette-Journal, 1985-87; newswoman AP, Reno, 1987-90, San Francisco, 1990—. Author: (newspaper articles) Execution of Eddie Cole 1985 (2d place Nev./Calif. AP hard news story), Gambler's Special Bus Crash, 1986 (2d place Nev./Calif. AP hard news story). Named Best Hard News Reporter, Best Feature Writer, Best Newspaper Writer, U. Nev., Reno Sch. of Journalism, 1985. Democrat. Office: Associated Press Fox Plaza Market St San Francisco CA 94109

MYERS, LILY ELIZABETH, communications executive; b. Niscayuna, N.Y., Dec. 17, 1948; d. Robert Howard and Sophie (Yurek) M.; m. Robert Reeve Rue, Aug. 27, 1985; stepchildren: Anna, Christian. BA, Northeastern U., Boston, 1970. Tng. cons. Mitterling Method, Winchester, Mass., 1982-85; human resource devel. officer Bank New Eng., Boston, 1985-88; prin., co-founder Rue Communications Systems, Peterborough, N.H., 1988—; mem. adj. faculty Bryant Coll., Smithfield, R.I., 1982—; mem. faculty Boston Ctr. for Adult Edn., 1978-82, Actors Circle Theater, 1988—, Monadnock Community Edn., Peterborough, 1989; intern U. Mass. Med. Ctr. Stress Reduction Clinic, Worcester, 1989. Active Peterborough Community Theatre, 1988-89. Mem. Am. Soc. Tng. and Devel., Peterborough C. of C. Democrat. Home: 13 Casalis Rd Peterborough NH 03458 Office: Rue Communications Systems PO Box 774 Peterborough NH 03458

MYERS, LORA BELLE, hospital administrator; b. Rome, N.Y., Dec. 19, 1954; d. Cecil Harold and Alice Mae (Berbaum) M. BA, SUNY, Oswego, 1976; MA, New Sch. for Social Research, 1981. Sr. investigator Bur. Performance Analysis N.Y. City Comptroller Office, 1980-81; budget analyst Health & Hosps. Corp., N.Y.C., 1981-83; budget dir. Coney Island Hosp., Bklyn., 1983-87, dir. planning and budget, 1987-89; deputy budget dir. Health and Hosps. Corp., N.Y.C., 1989—. Named Mgmt. Fellow Nat. Assn. Pub. Hosps., 1989, Fellow of Hunter, Brookdale Sch. Aging, 1989. Democrat.

MYERS, MARCIA K., teacher; b. Terre Haute, Ind., July 24, 1938; d. Darrel Franklin and Margaret (Brake) Marvel; m. James Richard Myers, July 10,1966; children: Margaret, Bert, Paul. BS, Indiana State U., 1959, MS, 1963. Cert. elementary teacher, reading specialist. Tchr. Vigo County Community Schs., Terre Haute, Ind., 1959-66; supervising tchr. Vigo County Community Schs., Terre Haute, Ind., 1962-66; tchr. Huntington (Ind.) County Community Schs., 1965-66; reading specialist United Sch. Dist. #214, Ulysses, Kans., 1978-84; tchr. United Sch. Dist. #214, Ulysses, 1984—. Leader, coun. mem. 4-H Clubs Grant County, Kans., 1980-82; supt. Grant County 4-H Fair, 1981-84. Recipient 1st place award, Econ. Edn. Coun. Dist. 3, 1982. Mem. AAUW (v.p. local chpt. 1988-90), NEA, Kans. Edn. Assn., Grant County Tchrs. Assn. (nominee Master Tchr. award 1986), Western Trails to Reading (pres. 1984-85), Internat. Reading Assn, Kans. Reading Assn., Phi Delta Kappa. Republican. Methodist. Home: 1001 Arapahoe Ulysses KS 67880 Office: United Sch Dist 214 600 W Nebraska Ulysses KS 67880

MYERS, MELANIE JEAN, banker; b. Detroit, Aug. 3, 1955; d. Eugene A. and Marjorie (Johnson) Myers. BA in Bus. Adminstrn., Ea. Mich. U., Ypsilanti, 1977. Asst. v.p. Nat. Bank of Detroit, 1978—. Leader Girl Scouts U.S.A., Detroit,1986-89; big sister Big Bro./Big Sisters, Detroit, 1988-89. Mem. Ea. Mich. U. Alumni Assn., Phi Gamma Nu. Home: 2372 Highland Detroit MI 48206

MYERS, NATALIE LAPKIN, social worker; b. San Francisco, July 30, 1916; d. Henry Edward and Annette Marian (Willinger) Lapkin; m. Robert Myers, Sept. 8, 1940 (div. Sept. 1959); 1 child, Susan Anne Myers Teixeira. AB, U. Calif., Berkeley, 1937, U. Calif., Riverside, 1968. Social worker I Santa Clara Co. Dept. Social Svcs., San Jose, Calif., 1964-65; social worker II San Bernardino (Calif.) Dept Social Svcs., 1965-76; social worker III State of Calif. Dept Social Svcs., Community Care Licensing, San Bernardino, 1976-81; Commr. Riverside County Commn. for Women, Palm Springs, Calif., 1983—; docent Palm Springs Desert Mus., Palm Springs, 1984—. Pres. Angleview Crippled Childrens Found., Palm Springs, 1961, Nat. Coun. Jewish Women, Fresno, 1947-48; chairperson Women for Kennedy, Riverside County, 1960; found, bd. dirs. Coachella Valley Women's Network, 1985—. Democrat. Jewish. Home: 6293 Niblick Palm Springs CA 92264

MYERS-MAY, YVETTE, psychologist, health science association administrator. PhD in Human Devel., U. Md., 1982. Prof. Towson (Md.) State U., 1971-85; founder, pres. The Ctr. for Human Devel., Inc., Balt., 1976—; mem. adj. faculty early childhood edn. dept. Community Coll. Balt., 1974-76, mem. adj. faculty psychology dept., 1971-77, mem. adj. faculty, 1973-74. Contbr. articles to profl. jours. Rep. to bd. for Village of Hickory Reed, Md., Columbia (Md.) Early Childhood Edn. Bd., 1977-79; mem. migrant-early childhood edn. bd. Md. State Dept. Edn., 1978-79; mem. bd. trustees Children's Guild, Balt., 1983-85; bd. dirs. Magic Me, Balt., 1988—; mem. minority mental and phys. health enhancement task force City of Balt. Dept. of Health, 1988—; mem. filming com. for children's adv. bd. Abell Found., Balt., 1988—. Mem. Am. Acad. Sci., Am. Psychol. Assn.

MYERS MEDEIROS, PATRICIA JO, entrepreneur; b. Cairo, Ill., July 24, 1942; d. Leon Lester and Thelma Elizabeth (Frey) Jones; m. Zan Albert Myers, Mar. 30, 1967 (div. Jan. 1983); 1 child, Zan Robert; m. Gene Alexander Medeiros, Dec. 31, 1988. Student, Sawyer Sch. Computer Sci., North Hollywood, Calif., 1961, Living Waters Bible Coll., Pasadena, Calif., 1975, Narramore Found. Psychology, Rosemead, Calif., 1980, Richards Hairmasters U., Ontario, Calif., 1988. Computer scientist C. F. Braun Internat., Alhambra, Calif., 1965-67, Fluor Corp., Irvine, Calif., 1967-70; psychol. counselor Living Waters, Pasadena, 1973-76, Christian Ctr., Arcadia, Calif., 1977-86; real estate investor Upland, Calif., 1983-88; tchr. personal enrichment clubs and classes Narramore Christian Found., Rosemead, 1979-85; investor Valencia, Valencia and Upland, Calif., 1983—; tchr. counselor tng. seminars Narramore Found., Rosemead, 1980-89, fin. freedom seminars various locations, 1983-89, Richards Hairmasters U., Ontario, Calif., 1988. Mem. Rep. Senatorial Inner Circle, Upland, 1985-88; mem. Dare Program-Dare to Keep Kids Off Drugs, Upland, Valencia, 1985; supporter Handicap Children Through Upland, Valencia, Ontario and San Bernardino (Calif.) Police, 1985-88; active ARC. Mem. NAFE.

MYERS-TURNER, DARAUGH ANNE, architect; b. Lock Haven, Pa., July 16, 1956; d. Marceau Chevalier and Judity May (Kleine) M.; m. William Reynolds Turner, Aug. 8, 1981; 1 child, Ashley Anne. BA, Bucknell U., 1978; MArch, Rice U., 1983. Designer Marks & Salley, Inc., Houston, 1979-81, Thompson-Frater Assocs., Houston, 1985-87, L. Barry Davidson Architects, Houston, 1987-88; owner Design Svcs., Houston, 1988—. Chair cultural arts Harvard Elem. PTA, Houston, 1989-90; vol. Channel 8 Pub. TV. Mem. Proctor Plaza Civic Club.

MYLANDER, LISA ANNE, retail executive; b. Columbus, Ohio, Sept. 25, 1962; d. David Charles and Sandra Jean (Ailes) M. BS, Ohio State U., 1984. Asst. buyer jr. sportswear Lazarus div. Federated, Columbus, Ohio, 1984-86; asst. buyer missy activewear Lazarus div. Federated, Cin., Ohio, 1986-87, assoc. buyer jr. wovens, 1987-88; buyer plus sizes Target div. Dayton Hudson Corp., Mpls., Ohio, 1988-90; buyer Target div. Dayton Hudson Corp., Mpls., Minn., 1988-90; buyer, Lane Bryant div. Limited, Inc., Columbus, 1990—. Chairperson Target Ready-to-Wear, United Way campaign, Mpls., 1988, 89. Mem. Tau Beta Sigma (v.p. 1984-85), Zeta Tau Alpha (standard Chair, 1983-84). Republican. Lutheran. Office: Lane Bryant 2800 Corporate Exchange Dr Columbus OH 43231

MYRDAL, ROSEMARIE CARYLE, state legislator; b. Minot, N.D., May 20, 1929; d. Harry Dirk and Olga Jean (Dragge) Lohse; m. B. John Myrdal, June 21, 1952; children: Jan, Mark, Harold, Paul, Amy. BS, N.D. State U., 1951. Registered profl. first grade tchr., N.D. Tchr. various sch. dists., Park River, Gardar and Edinburg, N.D., 1951-71; bus. mgr. Edinburg Sch. Dist., 1974-81; mem. N.D. Ho. of Reps., Bismarck, 1985—; sch. evaluator Walsh County Sch. Bds. Assn., Grafton, N.D., 1983-84; evaluator, work presenter N.D. Sch. Bds. Assn., Bismarck, 1983-84; mem. sch. bd. Edinburg Sch. Dist., 1981-90; adv. com. Red River Trade Corridor, 1989-90. Co-editor: Heritage '76, 1976. Precinct committeewoman Gardar Twp. Rep. Com., 1980-86; leader Hummingbirds 4-H Club, Edinburg, 1980-83; bd. dirs. Camp Sioux Diabetic Children, Grand Fors, N.D., 1980-90, N.D. affiliate Am. Diabetes Assn., 1989-91, Families First-Child Welfare Reform Initiative, Region IV, 1989-90; chmn. N.D. Ednl. Telecommunications Coun., 1989-90; vice chmn. N.D. Legis. Interim Jobs Devel. Commn., 1989-90. Mem. AAUW (pres. 1982-84 Pembina County area), Pembina County Hist. Soc. (historian 1976-84), Northeastern N.D. Heritage Assn. (pres. 1986—), Red River Valley Heritage Soc. (bd. dirs. 1985—). Lutheran. Club: Agassiz Garden (Park River) (pres. 1968-69). Home and Office: Rte 1 Box 151 Edinburg ND 58227

MYRICK, IRMA S. KITCHEN, early childhood educator; b. Scottsbluff, Nebr., Sept. 21, 1915; d. Harry Albert and Vera Johanna (Haefflin) Stackhouse; m. Harold Gordon Kitchen, Aug. 29, 1944 (wid. Jan. 1973); 1 child, Judith Helen Kitchen Candow; m. George Myrick, Sept. 27, 1975. BA, U. Denver, 1937; MEd, Johns Hopkins U., 1967. Cert. kindergarten, primary tchr. 1st grade tchr. various schs., 1937-43; employee rels. counselor Marana (Ariz.) Army Air Base, 1943-45; dir. kindergarten Greenwood Nursery Sch., Balt., 1948-51; dir. day sch. Ch. of the Redeemer, Balt., 1951-67; asst. chief Health Dept., Div. Child Day Care, Balt., 1967-76; exec. dir. Balt. County 4C Council, Towson, Md., 1976-78; cons., early childhood edn. Balt., 1967—; reading lab asst. Stoneleigh Pub. Schs., Balt., 1975-76; instr. Towson State U., 1976-77; co-organizer Child Study Ctr. for Infant Study, Balt., 1986-89, John F. Kennedy Inst. for Mentally and Physically Handicapped Children, Balt., 1982-89, Human Resources Devel. Agy, Dundalk, Md., 1973. Author newsletter for children and parent ctrs., 1950-70. Registrar League of Women Voters, Balt., 1984-88; developer Long Term Balt. County Steering Com., 1977-78; petitioner Common Cause in Md., 1960-89, Sierra Club of Md., 1989; organizer Community Coodinated Child Care, 1973, Assn. for Pre-Sch. Leaders and Staff, 1957-58 and others. Mortar Bd., U. Denver, 1936. Mem. AAUW (reporter, bd. dirs. 1987—), OMOEP, Balt. Assn. Pre-Sch. Edn. (pres. 1957), Children's Guild for Emotionally Disturbed Children, Md. Council on Family Rels. (treas. 1976), Women's Club of Roland Park, Balt. Symphony Assocs., Balt. Opera Guild, Kappa Delta Pi, Pi Gamma Mu, Psi Chi and others.

MYRICK, KIMBERLY MARIE, corporate controller; b. Daytona Beach, Fla., Dec. 10, 1960; d. Ralph Marvin and Barbara (McDermott) M. BS in Acctg., U. Cen. Fla., Orlando, 1989, postgrad., 1989—. Asst. mgr. D.H. Svc. Co., Orlando, 1979-84; corp. contr. Lifetron, Inc., Orlando, 1984—. Mem. NAFE. Republican. Baptist. Home: 5990-104 Scotchwood Glen Orlando FL 32822 Office: 390 N Orange Ave Orlando FL 32801

MYRICK, MARILOU RIGHTLEY, management consultant; b. Salt Lake City, Sept. 18, 1947; d. Richard Paul Carpenter and Edythe Louise (Schoppe) Bowlin; m. Timothy W. Rightley, Apr. 8, 1967 (div. 1981); children: Kristen, Kevin, Keith; m. Timothy Myrick, July 30, 1988. BA, Ind. U., 1974; AAS, Ivy Tech. Inst., 1978. Dir. design Tami Products, Inc., Ft. Myers, Fla., 1978-80; tng. dir. Hunter Douglas, Inc., Maywood, N.J., 1980-85; gen. mgr. Accountemps, Cleve., 1985-89; pres. Pro Resource, Inc., Cleve., 1989—. Mem. Am. Mgmt. Assn., Sales and Mktg. Execs., Nat. Assn. Personnel Cons., Employment Mgmt. Assn. Roman Catholic. Office: Pro Resource Inc 20600 Chagrin #430 Cleveland OH 44122

MYRICK, SUE, advertising agency executive, mayor; b. Tiffin, Ohio, Aug. 1, 1941; d. William Henry and Margaret Ellen (Roby) Wilkins; m. Jim Forest (div.); children: Greg, Dan; m. Wilbur Edward Myrick Jr., Sept. 11, 1977; children: Mia, Miesa, Alex. Student, Heidelberg Coll., 1959-60. Exec. sec. to mayor and city mgr. City of Alliance, Ohio, 1962-63; dir. br. office Stark County Ct. of Juvenile and Domestic Rels., Alliance, 1963-65; pres. Myrick Agy., Charlotte, N.C., 1971—; mayor of Charlotte, 1987—; Active Heart Fund, Multiple Sclerosis, March of Dimes, Arts and Scis. Coun. Fund Dr.; mem. adv. bd. Uptown Shelter, Uptown Homeless Task Force, bd. dirs. N.C. Inst. Politics, Sister Cities Internat.; pres. Nat. Conf. Rep. Elected Ofcls., Pres. Bush's Affordable Housing Commn.; founder, coord. Charlotte vol. tornado relief effort; pres. bd. dirs. Handicapped Organized Women; mem. adv. bd. U.S. Conf. Mayors; mem.-at-large Charlotte City Coun., 1983-85, Sister Cities Internat.; lay leader, Sunday sch. tchr. 1st United Meth. Ch.; treas. Mecklenburg Ministries; trustee U.S. Conf. of Mayors. Recipient Woman of Yr. award Harrisonburg, Va., 1968; named one of Outstanding Young Women of Am., 1968. Mem. NAFE, LWV, Women's Polit. Caucus, Charlotte C. of C., Beta Sigma Phi. Republican. Club: Tower. Home: 310 W 8th St Charlotte NC 28202 Office: Myrick Advt 505 N Poplar St Charlotte NC 28202 also: City of Charlotte 600 E 4th St Charlotte NC 28202

MYRICK, VERA MAE, hospital executive; b. Shawnee, Okla., Dec. 11, 1952; d. Ray Edward and Elsie Mae (Dennison) Whitecotton; m. John Christopher Myrick, Jan. 2, 1983. Grad. high sch., Shawnee. Circulation sec. Shawnee News Star, 1970-73; bus. office mgr. Shawnee Med. Ctr. Hosp., 1973—. Mem. Bus. and Profl. Women, Shawnee. Democrat. Baptist. Home: 621 Pennsylvania St Shawnee OK 74801 Office: Shawnee Med Ctr Hosp 1102 W MacArthur PO Box 909 Shawnee OK 74801

MYSLIWIEC, CHRISTINE ROSE, educator; b. Rochester, N.Y., Mar. 19, 1950; d. Casmer J. and Virginia M. (Siwicki) M. AA, AS, St. Petersburg (Fla.) Jr. Coll, 1981; BA, U. South Fla., Tampa, 1984. Cert. elem. tchr. Math tchr. Diocese St. Petersburg, 1984-86, Pinellas County Sch. Bd., St. Petersburg, 1986-88, Hillsborough County Sch. Bd., Tampa, 1988—. Mem. Suncoast Assn. Tchr. Tng., Kappa Delta Pi (sec. 1983-86).

NABER, CYNTHIA SHERIDAN, communications specialist, educator; b. Fremont, Nebr., Nov. 16, 1949; d. Harvey William and Eunice Cynthia (Ball) N. AA, Am. River Coll., 1969; BA, Calif. State U., Sacramento, 1974, MA, 1989. Dispatcher Sacramento Police Dept., 1974—, tchr., 1985—; clergy, co-pastor Universal Fellowship of Met. Community Ch., Modesto, Calif., 1986—; founder, dir. N.W. dist. UFMCC, Sacramento, 1986-89, asst. clergy rep., 1988. Sec. Sacramento Police Athletic League, 1983, bd. dirs., 1984. 010Mem. Ministerial Assn. of Modesto, Calif. State U.-Sacramento Alumni Assn., NAFE, Sigma Kappa (sec. 1971-74). Democrat. Home: 1488 33d St Sacramento CA 95816 Office: MCC Modesto PO Box 3092 Modesto CA 95353

NACHAMIE, SUSAN SCHIFFRES, psychologist; b. N.Y.C., May 8, 1942; d. Stanley Saul and Sarah (Horowitz) Schiffres; m. Benjamin Abraham Nachamie, June 16, 1963; children: Stanley, Allison, Stephen, Karen. AB magna cum laude, Vassar Coll., Poughkeepsie, N.Y., 1963; PhD, Columbia U., 1969; postgrad., Tchrs. Coll., N.Y.C., 1990—. Cert. early childhood tchr., N.Y. Early childhood tchr. N.Y.C., 1963-81, ind. researcher, 1971-77; guest lectr. Hunter Coll. Ctr. for Tchrs. of Gifted and Talented, N.Y.C., 1980-82; cons. psychologist Ednl. Records Bur., N.Y.C., 1983—. Mem. N.Y. County Dem. Com., N.Y.C., 1977—. N.Y. State Regents and Vassar scholar, 1959-63, Klingenstein fellow Columbia U., 1963-66, NSF summer fellow, 1965, N.Y. State Regents Coll. teaching fellow, 1963-66. Mem. Am. Psychol. Assn., N.Y. Vassar Club (alumni admissions com. 1977—, nominating com. 1988—), Phi Beta Kappa. Home: 1175 York Ave New York NY 10021

NACHBAR, RANDA ROEN, editor; b. Chickasaw, Okla., July 7, 1956; d. Sheldon and Selma (Pollets) Roen; m. Daniel Walter Nachbar, Mar. 29, 1986. BA in Child Devel., Kirkland-Hamilton Coll., Clinton, N.Y., 1978; MS in Early Childhood Edn., Bank Street Coll., N.Y.C., 1984. Substitute tchr. N.Y.C. Pub. Schs., 1978-79, kindergarten and elem. tchr., 1979-82, 84-88; tchr. Rodeph Sholom Nursery Sch., N.Y.C., 1982-84; editor Day Care and Early Edn., N.Y.C., 1981—; staff developer Resolving Conflict Creatively Program, N.Y.C., 1988—, feature editor, 1989-90; reviewer Young Children jour., Washington, 1989-90; workshop leader Agy. for Child Devel., N.Y.C., 1990. Author: (handbook) Writing for Publication, 1986. Mem. project bd. Nat. Urban League. Mem. Early Childhood Edn. Coun. (bd. dirs. 1988—, chmn. pub. policy com. 1988—). Office: Day Care and Early Edn 233 Spring St New York NY 10013

NACHBAR HAPAI, MARLENE M., research center administrator, entomologist; b. Honokaa, Hawaii, July 11, 1949; d. Myron Alexander and Mary Mae (Andrade) Nachbar; m. Archie Hapai III; children: Alicia Mae Laulaniuluokaniu, Archie Ai Moikeha IV. BA in Biology, Gonzaga U., 1970; MS in Entomology, U. Hawaii, 1977, PhD in Entomology, 1981. Cert. basic and profl. tchr., Hawaii. Tchr. sci. and math. Kohala High and Elem. Sch., Honomakau, Hawaii, 1970-76; grad. rsch. and teaching asst. U. Hawaii at Manoa, Honolulu, 1976-78, ednl. assoc., 1980-82, instr. biology, 1981-86; tchr. biology and chemistry Hilo (Hawaii) High Sch., 1978-79; asst. prof. biology and ci. edn. U. Hawaii, Hilo and Manoa, 1987-89; asst. dir. Ctr. for Gifted-Talented Native Hawaiian Children U. Hawaii, Hilo, 1989—; trainer Pacific region Hawaii Nature Study Program, Honolulu, 1980—; sci. resource person Hawaii Dept. Edn., 1982—; originator, coord. Adopt-A-Scientist Program, State of Hawaii, 1983-85; Hawaii coord. Focus on Excellence in Genetic Engring., 1984-85; chief judge Hawaii Dist. Sci. Fair, Hilo, 1987—. Author: Insects, 1980, Interacting with your Environment, 1985 (Francis David Meml. award 1985), Bug Play, 1990. Mem. planning com. Richardson Ocean Ctr., Hilo, 1982—; trainer Waikiki Aquarium Docent Program, Hilo, 1984-88; reviewer, mistress ceremonies Marine Sci. Symposium, Hilo, 1986—. Mem. Entomol. Soc. Am., Nat. Sci. Tchrs. Assn., Hawaiian Entomol. Soc., Hawaiian Acad. Sci., NAEYC, Hawaiian Sci. Tchrs. Assn. (past pres., bd. dirs.), Sigma Xi (rec. sec., past pres. Hilo). Home: PO Box 707 Kurtistown HI 96760 Office: U. Hawaii 523 W Lanikaula Hilo HI 96720-4091

NACOL, MAE, lawyer; b. Beaumont, Tex., June 15, 1944; d. William Samuel and Ethel (Bowman) N.; children: Shawn Alexander Nacol, Catherine Regina Nacol. BA, Rice U., 1965; postgrad., S. Tex. Coll. Law, 1966-68. Bar: Tex. 1969, U.S. Dist. Ct. (so. dist.) Tex. 1969. Diamond buyer/appraiser Nacol's Jewelry, Houston, 1961—; pvt. practice law, Houston, 1969—. Author, editor ednl. materials on multiple sclerosis, 1981-85. Nat. dir. A.R.M.S. of Am. Ltd., Houston, 1984-85. Recipient Mayor's Recognition award City of Houston, 1972; Ford Found. fellow So. Tex. Coll. Law, Houston, 1964. Mem. Houston Bar Assn. (chmn. candidate com. 1970, chmn. membership com. 1971, chmn. lawyers referral com. 1972), Assn. Trial Lawyers Am., Tex. Trial Lawyers Assn., Am. Judicature Soc. (sustaining), Houston Fin. Coun. Women. Presbyterian. Office: 600 Jefferson Ste 690 Houston TX 77002

NADDAFI, NANCY LEE, legislative writer, lobbyist, accountant; b. South Bend, Ind., Apr. 16, 1947; d. Charles Thomas Vice and Eva Marie (Williams) Reynolds; m. Abbas Manochr Naddafi, Oct. 1, 1966 (div. May 1983); children: Stuart N., Michael M. Student, Chriss Bus. Coll., Anaheim, Calif., 1965-66, Riverside Community Coll., Calif., 1981-83. Receptionist Occidental Life Ins., L.A., 1965-66; mgr., contr. Eidelman Constrn. Co., Westminster, Calif., 1967-71; full charge bookkeeper, mgr. G.D. Masonry, Yorba Linda, Calif., 1972-74; contr., office mgr. Elam's Huntington Beach, Inc., Fullerton, Calif., 1974-78; ptnr. at large Porter & Wagner CPA, Riverside, 1978; office mgr., fin. statements acct. Del-Casa Corp., Corona, Calif., 1983; contr. Telepro Proplus Systems, Inc. A MacDonnel Douglas subs., Corona, 1984; acct. City of Perris, Calif., 1987—. Author and copyright holder immigration reform legis., 1983-86, silver and gold bullion coins legis., U.S. fed. lottery, unanimous draft of USA born, vidoecassette recorder collectors items, VCR home librs., coll. on tape, 1983—. Republican. Home: 15065 Lake Mathews Dr B Gavilan Hills Perris CA 92370-0561 Office: Busy Bee Investments & Cos 15065 Lake Mathews Dr B Perris CA 92370-0561

NADER, JULIANNA CHAPMAN (JULIE NADER), computer company administrator; b. Pitts., Sept. 14, 1935; d. Robert James and Hazel Taylor (Snyder) Chapman; m. Philip Robert Nader, June 29, 1959 (div. Dec. 1982); children: Richard Harrison, Stephanie Taylor. B Music Edn., Coll. of Wooster, Ohio, 1957; postgrad., San Jose State U., 1989—. Cert. elem., secondary and jr. coll. tchr. Music tchr. Pitts.-Crescent Pub. Sch., 1957-59; vocal music tchr. elem. and jr. high West Irondequoit (N.Y.) Pub. Schs., 1959-61; tutor and substitute tchr. Rochester (N.Y.) Pub. Schs., 1961-63; voice instr. Galveston Coll. and La Marque High Sch., Tex., 1974-84; administr. ASK Computer Systems, Inc., Los Altos, Calif., 1984-89, adminstr. resource ctr., 1989—; vocal music judge Atlanta and Tex., 1965-80; profl. singer, Pitts., Rochester, San Francisco, Atlanta, Galveston, Tex.; soloist Lyric Theatre San Francisco, 1963-65, Scola Cantorum, 1989; chair music com. Aeseuplapians, 1959-62. Contbr. articles to Galveston Daily News; alto soloist Pitts., Rochester, San Franciso lyric theaters, 1959-85; soloist Seola Cantorum, 1989. Com. mem. Citizens for Quality, Integrated Edn., Rochester, 1959-63; com. chairperson Rochester Area Women for Peace, 1966-69; weekly vol. ednl. TV sta., Rochester, 1966-73; edn. com. Ch. Women United, Rochester, 1968-72; founder Galveston Chamber Music Soc., 1976, Galveston County Lupus Support Group, 1978; co-founder Mid-Peninsula Lupus Support Group, 1980; founding mem. Clean Galveston Com., 1981, Kick Illegal Drugs, Galveston, 1982; organizer Health Project Olympics, U. Tex. Med. Sch., 1982; bd. dirs. Youth Shelter of Galveston, 1976-79.; coord. Vols. for 1st Pre-Kindergarden Screening, 1978; mem. planning commn. com., Galveston City Coun., 1978; active Planned Parenthood. Recipient Citizenship award Am. Legion, 1949, Outstanding Svc. citation Youth Shelter of Galveston, 1979. Mem. Calif. Assn. Profl. Music Tchrs., Music Tchrs. Nat. Assn., Nat. Assn. Tchrs. Singing, LWV (bd. dirs. Galveston chpt. 1974-78, co-moderator radio program 1982-83), Stanford Art Mus., San Francisco Mus. Soc., Sierra Club, MADD, Stanford Singles Club (past membership com.), Sierra Club, Toastmasters Internat. (pres., toastman). Democrat. Methodist. Home: 457 Sierra Vista #8 Mountain View CA 94043-2981 Office: ASK Computer Systems Inc 2440 El Camino Real W PO Box 7640 Mountain View CA 94039-7640

NADERI, JAMIE BENEDICT, hazardous waste services brokerage executive; b. New Castle, Pa., Aug. 6, 1951; d. Harold James and June Marilyn (Sipe) Benedict; children: Robert Brian, Eric James. Student, New Castle Bus. Coll., 1967-69, Truckee Meadows Community Coll., 1979-82. Lic. practical nurse, Pa. Treas. Reno Little Theatre, 1979-80, 80-81. Mem. Women in Constrn., Nat. Assn. Female Execs., Physicians Nurses Assn., Nat. Found. of Lic. Practical Nurses. Presbyterian. Office: Moheat Inc 15915 Katy Frwy Ste 170 Houston TX 77094

NADZICK, JUDITH ANN, accountant; b. Paterson, N.J., Mar. 6, 1948; d. John and Ethel (McDonald) N.; B.B.A. in Acctg., U. Miami (Fla.), 1971. Staff accountant, mgr. Ernst & Whinney, C.P.A.s, N.Y.C., 1971-78; asst. treas. Gulf & Western Industries, Inc., N.Y.C., 1979-83, asst. v.p., 1980-82, v.p., 1982-83; v.p., corp. controller United Mchts. and Mfrs. Inc., N.Y.C., 1983-85, sr. v.p., 1985-86, exec. v.p., chief fin. officer, 1986—, also bd. dirs. 1987—. C.P.A., N.J. Mem. Am. Inst. C.P.A.s, Nat. Assn. Accts., N.Y. State Soc. C.P.A.s, U. Miami Alumni Assn., Delta Delta Delta. Roman Catholic. Home: 2 Lincoln Sq Apt 15G New York NY 10023

NAESER, NANCY DEARIEN, geologist, researcher; b. Morgantown, W.Va., Apr. 15, 1944; d. William Harold and Katherine Elizabeth (Dearien) Cozad; m. Charles Wilbur Naeser, Feb. 6, 1982. BS, U. Ariz., 1966; PhD, Victoria U., Wellington, New Zealand, 1973. Geol. field asst. U.S. Geol. Survey, Flagstaff, Ariz., 1966, postdoctoral research assoc., Denver, 1979-81, geologist, 1981—; sci. editor, Jour. Geology and Geophsyics, New Zealand Dept Sci. and Indsl. Research, Wellington, 1974-76; postdoctoral rsch. assoc., U. Toronto, Ont., Can., 1976-79; postdoctoral rsch. assoc. U.S. Geol. Survey, Denver, 1979-81, geologist, 1981—; adj. prof. Dartmouth Coll., Hanover, N.H., 1985—, U. Wyo., Laramie, 1984—. Editor: Thermal History of Sedimentary Basins - Methods and Case Histories, 1989; contbr.

articles on fission-track dating to profl. jours., 1977—. Fulbright fellow New Zealand, 1967-68. Fellow Geol. Soc. Am.; mem. Am. Assn. Petroleum Geologists, Soc. Econ. Paleontologists and Mineralogists, Geol. Soc. New Zealand, Mortar Bd., Rotary, Phi Kappa Phi. Republican. Methodist. Office: US Geol Survey Mail Stop 424 Federal Ctr Denver CO 80225

NAGEL, MADELINE, advertising executive; b. Bklyn., Nov. 6, 1939; d. Ira and Dorothy (Lichter) N. BA, U. Calif., Berkeley, 1961. Media dir. Foote, Cone & Belding, Los Angeles, 1961-79; sr. v.p., media dir. Foote, Cone & Belding, N.Y.C., 1979-82; v.p., mktg. ABC-TV, N.Y.C., 1982—. Office: Capital Cities/ABC Inc 77 W 66th St New York NY 10023

NAGEL, TRACY LYNN, marketing professional; b. Berea, Ohio, Mar. 13, 1967; d. David Carl Nagel and Mariland Grace (Stanclift) Morsfield. BBA, Baldwin Wallace Coll., 1989. Mktg. intern Soc. Corp., Cleve., 1988-89, market rsch. specialist, 1989—. Mem. NAFE. Democrat. Home: 26623 Bruce Rd Bay Village OH 44140

NAGY, CHRISTA FIEDLER, biochemist; b. Marienbad, Bohemia, Czechoslovakia, July 8, 1943; d. Herbert A. Fiedler and Anna C. (Gluth) Rathmann; m. Bela Imre Nagy, Aug. 22, 1969; 1 child, Byron. BS in Biology, Fairleigh Dickinson U., 1967, MS in Biochemistry, 1974; PhD in Biochemistry, Rutgers U., 1981. Assoc. scientist Hoffmann-La Roche Inc., Nutley, N.J., 1975-80, sr. scientist, 1981-88, assoc. rsch. investigator, 1988—. Mem. AAAS, N.Y. Acad. Scis., Am. Soc. Biol. Chemists, Soc. for Investigative Dermatology, Inflammation Rsch. Assn. Roman Catholic. Office: Hoffmann LaRoche Inc 340 Kingsland St Nutley NJ 07110

NAGY, DREW POLLANDER, human resources manager; b. Winston-Salem, N.C., Nov. 7, 1961; d. Peter Martin and Geraldine Drew (Dixon) Pollander; m. Paul Dennis Nagy, Sept. 10, 1988. BA, U. N.C., Greensboro, 1984; MS, U. N.C., Chapel Hill, 1986. Wellness dir. Brown-Wooten Mills, Inc., Burlington, N.C., 1986-89; program mgr. Burke/Taylor Assocs., Research Triangle Park, N.C., 1989—. mem. bus. and industry adv. com. to N.C. Gov.'s Coun. on Phys. Fitness and Health, 1988-89. Recipient Wellness in Bus. Week proclamation Gov. James G. Martin, N.C., 1987. Mem. Wellness Coun. Piedmont (bd. dirs. 1988-89, outstanding del. of yr. 1987), Am. Assn. Counseling and Devel. (cert. rehab. counselor, nat. cert. counselor), DAR. Democrat.

NAHIGIAN, ALMA LOUISE, technical documentation manager; b. Peabody, Mass., Sept. 17, 1936; d. Walter Daniel and Alma Edith (Knowles) Higgins; m. Franklin Roosevelt Nahigian, April 30, 1961; children: Ellen Elise, Dana Leigh, Catherine Elizabeth. AA, Boston U., 1956, BS, 1958, MS in Journalism, 1963. Editor nat. and spl. projects Boston U. News Bur., 1959-61; writer, editor Nutrition Found., N.Y.C., 1961-63; writer, editor, cons. Cambridge (Mass.) Communicators, Tech. Edn. Research Ctr., Harvard U., Cambridge, Smart Software, Inc., Belmont, Mass., 1970-82; tech. editor Digital Equipment Corp., Bedford, Mass., 1979-84; prin. tech. writer, editor Wang Labs, Inc., Lowell, Mass., 1984-89, documentation sect. mgr., 1989—; instr. Harvard U., Cambridge, 1988, Northeastern U., Boston, 1989; guest lectr. Northeastern U., Boston, 1979, 88, 89—, Radcliffe Coll., Cambridge, 1979. Contbr. numerous articles to profl. pubs. Active, LWV, Arlington, Mass., 1963-73. Mem. Soc. for Tech. Communication (bd. dirs. Boston chpt.). Democrat. Roman Catholic. Home: 30 Venner Rd Arlington MA 02174 Office: Wang Labs Inc One Industrial Ave Lowell MA 01851

NAIL, ELIZABETH JOANA, developer, fundraiser, consultant; b. Dinuba, Calif., Mar. 17, 1937; d. Arthur Andrew Whitaker and Mildred Louise (Kennedy) Barker; m. Fred David Bethel, Mar. 20, 1954 (div. 1961); children: Fred David Jr., Arthur Wayne; m. Russell James Nail, Sept. 3, 1964; 1 child, Timothy Russell. Grad. high sch., Selma, Calif.; grad., Am. Inst. Banking. Sec. utilities div. Crocker-Anglo Bank, Selma, 1956-61; adminstrv. sec. 1st Western Bank, Fresno, Calif., 1961; utility clk., sec. United Calif. Bank, Fresno, Visalia, Hanford, Calif., 1963-71; with Wells-Fargo Bank, Hanford, 1971-72; sec., office mgr. Kings County Econ. Devel., Hanford, 1972-75; adminstrv. sec. Growers & Mchts. State Bank, Selma, 1977-78; v.p., mgr. Imperial Savs. Assn., Hanford, 1978-86; devel. coord. Hanford Community Med. Ctr., Hanford, 1987—; mem., bd. dirs. Profl. Bus. Women, 1957-63; mem. Am. Inst. Banking, 1957-72, bd. dirs. Madera-Fresno chpt., chmn. women in banking, 1959, bd. dirs. Sequoia chpt., 1962-64; cons. Mary Kay Cosmetics, Hanford, 1975—. Bd. dirs. Hanford Improvement Assn., 1980—, pres., 1985-87; bus. leadership lector, speaker Hanford Union High Sch., Kings Regional Occupational Program; hospitality min., eucaristic min., instr. catechism, mem. parish fin. com. Roman Cath. Ch. Mem. Nat. Assn. for Hosp. Devel., Nat. Soc. Fundraising Execs., Hanford C. of C. (amb. 1979—, bd. dirs. 1980-86), Soroptimists (bd. dirs. 1980—, pres. 1987—). Republican. Home: 2423 Oakes Ln Hanford CA 93230 Office: Hanford Community Med Ctr 450 Greenfield Hanford CA 93230

NAIL, SHARON ALEXIS, company official, resume writer; b. Detroit, Nov. 5, 1949; d. Alexander and Smelia (Vucelich) Savitsky; m. James E. Nail, Dec. 3, 1969 (div. June 1972). AS, Macomb Community Coll., Warren, Mich., 1979. Office clk. Household Fin. Corp., Mt. Clemens and Hamtramck, Mich., 1966-67; sec.-stenographer U.S. Army Tank-Automotive Command, Warren, Mich., 1967-76; adminstrv. sec. to scout exec. Detroit Area coun. Boy Scouts Am., 1976-89; exec. asst. to pres. Intraco Corp., Troy, 1989—; prodn. interviewer Maritz Mktg. Rsch., Warren, 1987; interviewer, recruiter Product Consumer Evaluations, Farmington Hills, Mich., 1987-89; owner, mgr. Sunrise Resume Writing Svcs., East Detroit, Mich., 1988—. Mem. Profl. Secs. Internat. (com. chmn. 1980—), NAFE, Wolverine Postcard Club (life, editor hobby newsletter-bull. 1974-87). Republican. Office: Intraco Corp 1410 Allen Dr Troy MI 48083

NAIRN, PENNY SUE, day care center operator; b. San Diego, Sept. 25, 1949; d. Tyrus Demoval and Mary Helen (Lindsey) Daniel; div.; children: Peggy Sue, William Joseph, Tammy Elaine, Thomas Miton, Danielle Nadine, Connie Michelle. Grad. high sch., Van Nuys, Calif. Owner, operator P&P Family Day Care, Sepulveda, Calif. Home: 15300 Dearborn Sepulveda CA 92343 Office: P&P Family Day Care 15300 Dearborn Sepulveda CA 91343

NAKAI, TERESA, reclamation specialist; b. Shiprock, N.Mex., Dec. 17, 1960; d. Gabriel and Virginia (Joe) N. BS in Crop and Soil Sci., N.Mex. State U., 1983. Environ. technician Utah Internat., Fruitland, N.Mex., 1982; water resource technician engrs. office State of N.Mex., Roswell, 1984-86; reclamation specialist mining and minerals div. State of N.Mex., Santa Fe, 1986—. Office: State of NMex Mining & Minerals Div 525 Camino de los Marquez Santa Fe NM 87501

NAKAJIMA, YASUKO, medical educator; b. Osaka, Japan, Jan. 8, 1932; came to U.S., 1969; d. Isao and Taeko Nakagawa; m. Shigehiro Nakajima; children: Hikedo H., Gene A. MD, U. Tokyo, 1955, PhD, 1962. Intern U. Tokyo Sch. Medicine, 1955-56, resident, 1956-57, instr., 1962-67; assoc. prof. Purdue U., West Lafayette, Ind., 1969-76, prof., 1976-88; prof. anatomy and cell biology U. Ill. Coll. Medicine, Chgo., 1988—; vis. rsch. fellow Coll. Physicians and Surgeons, Columbia U., N.Y.C., 1962-64; asst. rsch. anatomist UCLA Sch. Medicine, 1964-65; vis. rsch. fellow Cambridge U., 1967-69. Contbr. articles to sci. jours. Fulbright travel grantee, 1962-65. Mem. AAAS, Soc. Neurosci., Am. Soc. Cell Biology, Am. Assn. Anatomists, Biophys. Soc., Marine Biol. Lab. Corp. Office: U Ill Coll Medicine 808 S Wood St Dept Anatomy-Cell Biology Chicago IL 60612

NAKASHIAN, MARY ROSE, human services executive; b. Hoboken, N.J., Nov. 20, 1947; d. Harry and Loretta Frances (Speer) N.; m. Christopher Brown, Aug. 26, 1972 (div. Mar. 1987). AA, Edward Williams Coll., 1967; BA, Fairleigh Dickinson U., 1969, U. New Haven, 1983; MA, U. New Haven, 1985; cert., Harvard U., 1985. Adminstrv. asst. CBS Labs. and ICI Americas, Inc., Stamford, Conn., 1969-72; social worker Travelers Aid Soc., Hartford, Conn., 1972-73, Wilmington, Del., 1972-73; cons. Klingberg Child and Family Ctr., Inc., New Britain, Conn., 1973-74; eligibility supr. Dept. Income Maintenance, State of Conn., Hartford, 1974-78; tng. supr. Dept. Income Maintenance, State of Conn., 1978-81, legis. commr., 1981-83, dep. commr., 1983-88; assoc. dir. state and local policy div. Nat. Ctr. for Children in Poverty, Columbia U., N.Y.C., 1989-90; 1st dep. commr. Human Resources Adminstrn. N.Y.C., 1990—; summer faculty U. Calif., Davis, 1988; participant steering com. for welfare reform Am. Pub. Welfare Assn., Washington, 1986-88; guest lectr. grad. sch. social work U. Conn., West Hartford, 1983-88. Officer, bd. dirs. YWCA Greater Hartford, 1988; mem., bd. dirs. Inst. for Community Research, Hartford, 1988; former mem. Steering Com. for Nat. Welfare Reform, Task Force for Case Mgmt. to Implement Welfare Reform; mem. Riverside Park Fund. Named one of Women in Leadership YWCA, Hartford, 1984. Mem. Am. Soc. Pub. Adminstrs., Sierra Club. Democrat. Home: 410 Riverside Dr Apt 22A New York NY 10025 Office: Human Resources Adminstrn 250 Church St Rm 1416 New York NY 10013

NAKER, MARY LESLIE, export transportation company executive; b. Elgin, Ill., July 6, 1954; d. Robert George and Marilyn Jane (Swain). BS in Edn., No. Ill. U., 1976, MS in Edn., 1978, postgrad., 1980; postgrad., Coll. Fin. Planning, 1990. Cert. tchr., Ill., fin. paraplanner. Retail sales clk. Fin'n Feather Farm, Dundee, Ill., 1972-75; self-employed tchr., South Elgin, Ill., 1974-78; teaching asst. Sch. Dist #13, Bloomingdale, Ill., 1976-78, substitute tchr.; office mgr. Tempo 21, Carol Stream, Ill., 1978-82, LaGrange, Ill., 1982-85; sales coord. K&R Delivery, Hinsdale, Ill., 1986-89; fin. planner coord. Elite Adv. Svcs., Inc., Schaumburg, Ill., 1989-90; adminstrv. coord. Export Transports, Inc., Elk Grove Village, Ill., 1990—. Leader Girl Scouts U.S.A., 1972-77, camp counselor, 1972-79. Recipient Music Scholarship PTA, U. Wis., 1967, PTA, U. Iowa, 1968-69. Mem. Nat. Geographic Soc., Smithsonian Assn. Lutheran. Home: 1782A Gloucester Ct Wheaton IL 60187 Office: Export Transports Inc 1650 Carmen Dr Elk Grove Village IL 60007

NALEWAJA, DONNA, state legislator; m. John Nalewaja; 4 children. BA, U. Minn. Realtor; mem. N.D. Ho. of Reps., 1983-85; now state senator N.D. Senate. Mem. N.D. Coalition Adult Literacy. Mem. N.D. State Union Women's Club. Home: 1121 11th St N Fargo ND 58102*

NALL, LAWANDA CAROL, organization executive, research manager; b. Monroeville, Ala., July 19, 1964; d. Charles Edward and Willie Earline (Brantley) N. AA, Pensacola Jr. Coll., 1983, AS, 1984; BS, MS, Columbia Pacific U., 1986. Nursing asst. W.D. McMillan Hosp., Brewton, Ala., 1982; nursing asst. Sacred Heart Hosp., Pensacola, Fla., 1982-83, unit sec., 1984; nursing supr. Columbia Regional Med. Ctr., Andalusia, Ala., 1984-85, dir. edn., 1984-85; dir. nursing Perry Community Hosp., Marion, Ala., 1985; nursing instr. S.W. Va. Community Coll., Logan, 1986; clin. dir. nursing Med. Ctr. Baton Rouge, 1987-88; dir. nursing Terrell (Tex.) Community Hosp., 1988, clin. rsch. assoc. Drug Rsch. and Analysis, 1988-90; pres. Com Corp., 1986—. Author: Manual of Inservice Education, 1985, Manual of Effective Communication, 1986, others. Mem. Am. Nurses Assn. (cert. advanced nursing adminstr. 1988), Am. Assn. Critical Care Nurses, Emergency Nurses Assn., NAFE, Am. Heart Assn. (cert. basic cardiac life support system, advanced cardiac life support system 1984—). Avocations: oil painting, interior decorating, singing, piano and guitar. Home: Rte 2 Box 123 Castleberry AL 36432

NALLEY, BLANCHE ALMEDIA (MEDA NALLEY), real estate development executive, property management director; b. Rocky Mount, N.C., June 26, 1939; d. Walter McDonald, Jr., and Ella Blanche (Phelps) Peacock; m. Richard Kingsman Nalley, Jr., Jan. 16, 1960 (div. 1967); children—Michelle, Karen, Natalie. A.A., U. Fla., 1960. Controller, sta. WPGC, Washington, 1965-68, Trans Continental Industries, Washington, 1968-71, Atlantic Elec. and Bldrs. Hardware, Washington, 1971-74, LBG Distrbrs., Washington, 1974-79; dir. property mgmt., devel. and constrn. Ingersoll & Bloch Chartered, Washington, 1979-89; owner, operator pastry shop, Waynesboro, Pa., 1989—; renovation cons. Nunnery Assocs., Washington, 1983-85, J.C. Assocs., Washington, 1984-89; constrn. cons. P St Assn., Washington, 1985-86; owners rep. 801 Pa. Ave. Assn., Washington, 1985-86; ptnr. Bldg. Services and Maintenance, Inc., Washington, 1986-89. Active design and constrn. hist. structures into office space, 1985-86, renovation hist. landmark bldg., 1985-86. Vol. Alexandria Hosp., Va., 1984; v.p. Elem. Sch. PTA, Hyattsville, Md., 1975, sec. Middle Sch. PTA, 1975. Mem. Property Mgmt. Assn., Apt. Office Bldg. Assn., Multi Housing Assn. Republican. Avocations: running, aerobics, swimming, crocheting, cooking. Home: 15B S Oller Ave Waynesboro PA 17268 Office: 27 E Main St Waynesboro PA 17268

NAMENY, GRACE WESTBERG, retired educational administrator; b. Chgo., July 28, 1921; d. Karl Emil and Amanda (Carlson) Westberg; m. William Francis Nameny, Feb. 1, 1946; children: Kim, James, Phillip. BS, Chgo. Tchrs. Coll., 1941; MA, Northwestern U., 1946; postgrad., Stanford U., 1948-49, 57-59. Cert. elem. tchr., Calif., spl. edn., secondary tchr., Jr. coll. tchr., gen. adminstrn. Tchr. spl. edn. Chgo. Pub. Schs., 1943-47; prin., cons. San Mateo County (Calif.) Pub. Schs., 1948-49; tchr. adult edn. Santa Clara County Pub. Schs., Santa Clara, Calif., 1955-59; prin. St. Andrew's Sch., Saratoga, Calif., 1960-61. Vol. Bechtel Internat. Ctr., Stanford U., Palo Alto, Calif. Mem. AAUW, Saratoga Foothill Club. Episcopalian.

NANASY, CONNIE SMITH, educator; b. Longview, Tex., Oct. 7, 1932; d. Marshall Neal and Mattie Jean (Koonce) Smith; children: Mary Jean Smith, James Alfred Smith; m. Frank P. Sainburg, Aug. 5, 1954 (div. June 1970); children: Frank Sainburg Jr., Scott Sainburg, Robert Sainburg; m. Emery Nanasy, July 5, 1990. AA, Long Beach City Coll., 1971; BA cum laude, Calif. State U., Long Beach, 1972; MA, U.S. Internat. U., 1984. Instrumental and vocal music instr. Ocean View Sch. Dist., Huntington Beach, Calif., 1973-90, tchr., 1987—. Painter 200 oil paintings. Flutist Bellflower (Calif.) Symphony, 1972-74; pianist Long Beach City Coll. Stage Band, 1965-75, Connie Colburn Combo, Lakewood, Calif., 1976-80; percussionist Long Beach City Coll. Concert Band, 1973-74. Mem. Ocean View Tchrs. Assn., Calif. Tchrs. Assn. Democrat. Home: 5116 Elderhall Ave Lakewood CA 90712 Office: Ocean View Sch Dist 17200 Pinehurst Ln Huntington Beach CA 92647

NÁNAY, JULIA, oil and gas consulting company executive; b. Budapest, Hungary, Mar. 15, 1951; came to U.S., 1957; d. Endre and Marta (Medvegy) N.; 1 child, Ilona Clara. BA, UCLA, 1973; MA in Law and Diplomacy, Tufts U., 1976. Asst. v.p. NE Petroleum Co., Boston, 1976-83; v.p. Charter Oil Co., Washington, 1983-85; dir. Petroleum Fin. Co., Washington, 1985—. Author: Transylvania: The Hungarian Minority in Rumania, 1974; contbr. chpt. to book. Mem. Phi Beta Kappa. Lutheran. Home: 1233 29th St NW Washington DC 20007 Office: Petroleum Fin Co 1140 Connecticut Ave NW Washington DC 20036

NANCE, BETTY LOVE, librarian; b. Nashville, Oct. 29, 1923; d. Granville Scott and Clara (Mills) Nance. BA in English magna cum laude, Trinity U., 1957; AM in Library Sci., U. Mich., 1958. Head dept. acquisitions Stephen F. Austin U. Library, Nacogdoches, Tex., 1958-59; librarian 1st Nat. Bank, Fort Worth, 1959-61; head catalog dept. Trinity U., San Antonio, 1961-63; head tech. processes U. Tex. Law Library, Austin, 1963-66; head catalog dept. Tex. A&M U. Library, College Station, 1966-69; chief bibliographic services Washington U. Library, St. Louis, 1970; head dept. acquisitions Va. Commonwealth U. Library, Richmond, 1971-73; head tech. processes Howard Payne U. Library, Brownwood, Tex., 1974-79; library dir. Edinburg (Tex.) Pub. Library, 1980—; pres. Edinburg Com. for Salvation Army. Mem. ALA, Pub. Library Assn., Tex. Library Assn., Hidalgo County Library Assn. (v.p. 1980-81, pres. 1981-82), Pan Am. Round Table of Edinburg (corr. sec. 1986-88, assoc. dir. 1989-90), Edinburg Bus. and Profl. Womens Club (founding bd. dirs., pres. 1986-87, bd. dirs. 1987-88), Alpha Lambda Delta, Alpha Chi. Methodist. Club: Zonta (bd. dirs. West Hidalgo club 1986-88). Home: 1602 John St Apt 4 Edinburg TX 78539 Office: Edinburg Pub Libr 401 E Cano St Edinburg TX 78539

NANCE, JEAN CLAIRE, educator; b. Henrietta, Okla., Oct. 4, 1924; d. Roy Elmer and Mabel Clair (Bailey) Everett; m. C. Frank Nance, Aug. 28, 1943; children: John Franklin, Kenneth Neil, David Alan. BA in English, U. Tex., El Paso, 1968. Certified secondary sch. tchr. in English and Speech, Tex. Tchr. El Paso (Tex.) Schs., 1968-82; mem. curriculum com., El Paso, Tex., 1970-72. Author: (course of study) Southwest Literature, 1971, Bible as Literature, 1971, Creative Writing, 1972. Pres. City-Coun. PTA, El Paso, 1963-64. Named Tchr. of Year, El Paso High School, 1976. Mem. AAUW, Nat. Retired Tchrs. Assn., Tex. Retired Tchrs. Assn., El Paso Retired Tchrs Assn. Methodist. Home: 2700 Pierce El Paso TX 79930

NANCE, MARY JOE, educator; b. Carthage, Tex., Aug. 7, 1921; d. F. F. and Mary Elizabeth (Knight) Born; B.B.A., North Tex. State U., 1953; postgrad. Northwestern State U. La., 1974; M.E., Antioch U., 1978; m. Earl C. Nance, July 12, 1946; 1 child, David Earl. Tchr., Port Isabel (Tex.) Integrated Sch. Dist., 1953-79; tchr. English, Tex., 1965, Splendora (Tex.) High Sch., 1979-80, McLeod, Tex., 1980-81, Bremond, Tex., 1981-84. Vol. tchr. for Indian students, 1964-65, 79. Served with WAAC, 1942-43, WAC 1945. Recipient Image Maker award Carthage C. of C., 1984; cert. bus. educator. Mem. Nat. Bus. Edn. Assn., NEA, Tex. Tchrs. Assn., Tex. Bus. Tchrs. Assn. (cert. of appreciation 1978), Nat. Women's Army Corps Vets. Assn., Air Force Assn. (life), Assn. Supervision and Curriculum Devel., Council for Basic Edn., Nat. Hist. Soc., Tex. Council English Tchrs. Baptist.

NANCE, MARY JUDENE, consultant; b. Pittsburg Kans., Mar. 31, 1961; d. Paul Edward and Mary Louise (Crosetto) Bresnick; m. David Ray Nance, Aug. 3, 1985. BBA in Mktg., Pittsburg State U., Kans., 1983; postgrad., Pittsburg State U., 1988—. Mkt. rsch. analyst McNally Pittsburg, (Kans.) Inc., 1983-86; pres. Rsch. Svcs., Pittsburg, 1986—; small bus. counselor The Inst. for Econ. Devel., Pittsburg, 1987—. Mem. Pittsburg Now, 1986—, Revolving Loan Fund, 1988-89, steering com. PittsburgMain St. Inc., 1988—; commnr. Pittsburg Bd. of City Commnrs., 1987-89; bd. dirs. Friends of Leonard Axe Libr., Pittsburg, 1988—. Named Young Careerist Bus. & Profl. Women, Dist. #3, Kans., 1986; recipient Elizabeth Bird Small award, Alpha Sigma Alpha, 1983. Mem. Pittsburg Area C. of C., Pittsburg State U. Alumni Assn. (bd. dirs. 1986—), Alpha Kappa Psi (pres. 1982-83), Phi Kappa Phi, Rotary Club. Republican. Roman Catholic.

NANK, LOIS RAE, financial executive; b. Racine, Wis., Jan. 6; d. Walter William August and Lanora Elizabeth (Freymuth) N. BS in Econs., U. Wis., 1962; postgrad. in profl. mgmt., Fla. Inst. Tech., 1977. Contract specialist U.S. Naval Ordnance Sta., Forest Park, Ill., 1963-66, U.S. Army Munitions Command, Joliet, Ill., 1966-72; plans/program specialist U.S. Army Munitions Command, Joliet, 1972-73, U.S. Army Armament Command, Rock Island, Ill., 1973-77; chief budget office U.S. Army Auto Log Mgmt. System Act, St. Louis, 1977-81; sr. budget analyst U.S. Army Materiel Command, Alexandria, Va., 1981-87; fin. mgr. Def. Mapping Agy., Reston, Va., 1987—. Council mem. Bread of Life Luth. Ch., Springfield, Va., 1986—, chair person; bd. dirs. Cedar Wood Homeowners' Assn., 1975-77, Oak Homeowners' Assn. 1980-81. Mem. NAFE, Am. Soc. Mil. Comptrollers, Va. Assn. Female Execs., Order of Ea. Star. Home: 7812 O'Dell St Springfield VA 22153 Office: Def Mapping Agy Reston VA 22102

NANSON, DEBORAH FAYE, sales executive; b. Oklahoma City, Feb. 19, 1953; d. Billy Gene Hale and Margery Faye (Cave) Adams; m. Rickey Lynn Nanson, Dec. 24, 1971 (div. Feb. 1987); children: Rhett Thomas Lynn, Krystal Lynn, Jeffrey Lynn. Registered vet. technician, Tex. Vet. technician Rutherford Vet. Hosp., Dallas, 1975-78; relief vet. technician San Antonio, 1978-79; vet. office mgr. Turtle Creek Animal Hosp., San Antonio, 1980-85; vet. technician, surgery/lab Vet Care Ctr., Spring, Tex., 1985-86; health technologist U. Tex. Health Sci. Ctr., Dallas, 1986-87; sales rep. Hills Pet Products, Topeka, 1987—. Mem. Tex. Assn. Animal Technicians (bd. dirs., treas., editor newsletter), North Am. Vet. Technician Assn., Inc. Home: 8926 San Fernando Way Dallas TX 75218

NAPIER, LOIS CHRISTINE, teacher; b. Cheshire, Ohio, June 28, 1942; d. Walter W. and Pauline (Athey) Rife; m. Lark Napier, Mar. 23, 1963 (div. 1979); children: Lark Jr., Kevin T. BS, Ohio U., 1974. Elem. cert. learning disabilities, educable mentally retarded. Trainable tchr. Guiding Hand Sch., Cheshire, 1972-74; elem. tchr. Kyger Creek Local Sch., Cheshire, 1974; devel. handicapped tchr. Gallia County Sch., Gallipolis, Ohio, 1974; treas. Gallia County Local Edn. Assn., 1981-83, pres. 1984-87; vice chmn. So. Tri-County Uniserv Coun., Waverly, Ohio, 1986-90, chmn. 1990—. Twp. chmn. Gallia County Rep. Club, 1985-86, Flora Pomona Grange, Pomeroy, Ohio, 1985-87, Cires #778 Star Grange, Dexter, Ohio, 1989—. Mem. AAUW (pres. 1986-88), Southeastern Ohio Edn. Assn., Ohio Edn. Assn., Gallia County Local Edn. Assn. (pres. 1984-87). Methodist. Home: 2036 Jessie Creek Rd Bidwell OH 45614 Office: Cheshire-Kyger Elem Sch Rt 1 Cheshire OH 45620

NAPIERSKI, GERALDINE E., dentist, educator; b. Buffalo, Apr. 12, 1949; d. Walter A. and Josephine M. (Kokoszka) N.; m. Andrew L. Jakubowski, Oct. 7, 1978. BS cum laude, St. Bonadventure U., 1970; DDS, Georgetown U., 1974. Resident in gen. practice VA Med. Ctr., Buffalo, 1974-75, staff dentist, 1975—; clin. instr. SUNY, Buffalo, 1976—; dir. geriatric and long term care program VA Med. Ctr., Buffalo; mem. adv. bd. Erie Community Coll. Sch. Dental Hygiene, Buffalo, 1978-83. Contbr. articles to profl. jours. Mem. Am. Assn. Women Dentists (editor 1986-88, sec. 1989-90, Svc. award 1988), ADA, Dental Soc. of State of N.Y., Acad. Dentistry for the Handicapped, Am. Soc. for Geriatric Dentistry. Office: VA Med Ctr 3495 Bailey Ave Buffalo NY 14215

NAPOLITANO, ROSALBA GINA, data processing executive; b. Chgo., Nov. 3, 1961; d. Joseph Anthony and Maria (Rende) N. Cert. early childhood edn, Triton Coll., 1985. Dispatch, adminstrn. mgr. ADP/BISG, Trevose, Pa., 1983-89; dispatcher, adminstrv. mgr. Brokerage Info. Svcs. Group, ADP; asst. tech. ops. IBM, Chgo., 1989—. Mem. sch. bd. com., Sacred Heart Cath. Sch., Melrose Park, Ill., 1984-87; youth group leader, Sacred Heart Ch., Melrose Park, 1986-87; vol. ARC; mem. Starlight Found. Roman Catholic. Home: 120 N Oltendorf Streamwood IL 60107

NAPPER, JEAN ANN, college administrator; b. Bayonne, N.J., July 17, 1930; d. John Joseph and Anna (Hewitt) Monahan; m. David Emrys Napper (div. 1980); children: Janet Lynn, Keith Emrys. BS in Edn. cum laude, Montclair State Coll., 1951; MA in Edn. with honors, CUNY, 1978; postgrad., SUNY, Albany, 1980. Cert. secondary English and social studies tchr., sch. adminstr. and supr., N.Y. Tchr. Milburn (N.J.) High Sch., 1951-55; dir. continuing edn. Chappaqua (N.Y.) Sch. Dist., 1973-78; dir. Career Counseling Ctr. Putnam-North Westchester Bd. Coop. Ednl. Svcs., Yorktown, N.Y., 1978-79; assoc. supr. div. continuing edn. N.Y. State Edn. Dept., Albany, 1979-86; dir. ednl. svcs. Port Washington (N.Y.) Pub. Sch. Dist., 1986-88; dir. continuing and community edn. svcs. Bronx (N.Y.) Community Coll., 1988—; conf. presenter in field; dir. Regional Tng. Network for Career Counseling and N.Y. State CASSET/ACCESS Tech. Assistance, 1988—; adj. instr. CUNY, 1990; appointed by N.Y. State Commn. of Edn. as mem. N.Y. State Adult Learning Svcs. Coun., 1990—. Contbr. articles to profl. publs. Founding mem. bd. dirs. Scituate (Mass.) Arts Coun., 1964; bd. dirs. LWV, New Castle, N.Y., 1968-73, pres., 1973; vol. Chappaqua Sch. Dist., 1972-78; mem. New Castle Zoning Bd. Appeals, 1971-75, chmn., 1975; bd. dirs. Chappaqua Orchl. Assn., 1986-87. Grantee N.Y. State Gov.'s Office Employee Rels., 1989-91, N.Y. State Edn. Dept., 1986-90. Mem. N.Y. State Assn. for Continuing and Community Edn. (bd. dirs. 1975-78, v.p. 1979, conf. com. 1983, 85-87), Westchester Assn. for Continuing Edn. (founding bd. dirs. 1974-79), Vocat. Edn. Assn. N.Y. Office: Bronx Community Coll GRH417 181st and University Ave Bronx NY 10453

NAPPO, ELIZABETH HUBBELL, industrial engineer; b. Chgo., May 3, 1959; d. Daniel Vincent and Elizabeth Ann (Damyan) Hubbell; m. Philip George Nappo III, May 25, 1986. BSIE, Northwestern U. Tech. Inst., 1981; MSIE, Columbia U., 1988. Mfg. mgmt. trainee Gen. Elec. Co., Brockport, N.Y., 1981-82, Salem, Va., 1982-83; analytical cons. Gen. Elec., Bridgeport, Conn., 1983-86; supr. advanced mfg. engring. Pitney Bowes, Stamford, Conn., 1986-87; mgr. process technology Pitney Bowes, Stamford, 1987-89; dir. mfg. Branson Ultrasonics div. Emerson Electric Co., 1989—. Mem. Computer and Automated Systems Assn., Am. Prodn. and Inventory Control Soc., Inst. Indsl. Engrs. (sr. mem.), Kappa Alpha Theta. Home: 35 Clocks Ln Darien CT 06820

NARA, BONNIE ANN, psychologist; b. Connellsville, Pa., Jan. 29, 1949; d. Edward G. and Edith R. (Fasson) N.; m. James V. Morley, Oct. 28, 1989. BA with honors, Seton Hill Coll., 1970; MEd, Calif. U. Pa., 1971, MS with highest honors, 1980; PhD, U. W.Va., 1981. Cert. sch. psychologist,

Pa. Counselor Uniontown (Pa.) Area Sch. Dist., 1974-86; psychologist Ctr. for Motivation and Achievement, Pitts., 1986—. Chair personnel com. Twin Trees, Inc., Connellsville, 1979-85, chairperson, 1982-83; mem. Westmoreland County Prevention of Child Abuse, Greensburg, Pa., 1983-86. Mem. NEA, AAUW, Am. Counseling and Psychol. Assn., Pa. Edn. Assn., Pa. Psychol. Assn. Republican. Roman Catholic. Club: Our Lady of Mt. Carmel (Connellsville). Lodge: Lioness.

NARASIMHAN, PADMA MANDYAM, physician; b. Bangalore, India, Mar. 19, 1947; came to U.S., 1976; d. Alasingracher Mandyam and Alamela Mandyam Narasimhan; m. Mandyam N. Venkatesh, Mar. 28, 1981 (div.) 1 child, Ravi. Student, Delhi U., New Delhi, 1964, MBBS, 1969; MD, Maulana Azad Med. Coll., New Delhi, 1970. Diplomate Am. Bd. Internal Medicine. Intern in internal medicine Flushing Hosp., N.Y.C., 1976-77; resident in internal medicine Luth. Med. Ctr., N.Y.C., 1977-79; fellow hematology, oncology Beth-Israel Med. Ctr., N.Y.C., 1979-81; asst. prof. King Drew Med. Ctr., L.A., 1983-87, Harbor UCLA, Torrance, 1987—. Mem. editorial bd. Jour. Internal Medicine, 1986—. Mem. ACP, Am. Soc. Clin. Oncology, So. Calif. Acad. Clin. Oncology. Hindu. Home: 6604 Madeline Cove Dr Rancho Palos Verdes CA 90274 Office: Harbor UCLA 100 W Carson St Torrance CA 90509

NARDI-RIDDLE, CLARINE, state attorney general; b. Clinton, Ind., Apr. 23, 1949; d. Frank Jr. and Alice (Mattioda) Nardi; m. Mark Alan Riddle, Aug. 15, 1971; children: Carl Nardi, Julia Nardi. AB, Ind. U., 1971, JD, 1974. Cert. tchr., Ind. Staff atty. Ind. Legis. Svc. Agy., Indpls., 1974-78, legal counsel, 1978-79; dep. corp. counsel City of New Haven, 1980-83; counsel to atty. gen. State of Conn., Hartford, 1983-86, dep. atty. gen., 1986-89, acting atty. gen., 1989, atty. gen., 1989—; asst. counsel state majority Conn. Gen. Assembly, Hartford, 1979, legal rsch. asst. to prof. Yale U., New Haven, 1979; legal counsel com. on law revision Indpls. State Bar Assn., 1979; mem. Chief Justice's Task Force on Gender Bias, Hartford, 1988-90; mem. ethics and values com. Ind. Sector, Washington, 1989-90. Bd. visitors Ind. U., Bloomington, 1974—; mem. Gov.'s Missing Children Com., Hartford, Conn. Child Support Guidelines Com., Gov.'s Task Force on Justice for Abused Children, Hartford, 1988-90. Named Conn. History Maker Women's Bur. & Permanent Commn. on Status of Women, U.S. Dept. Labor, 1989. Mem. ABA, Conn. Bar Assn. (Citation of Merit women and law sect. 1989), Nat. Assn. Attys. Gen. (chair charitable trusts and solicitation 1989-90), New Haven Neighborhood Music Sch. Club. Democrat. Presbyterian. Office: Office of Atty Gen 55 Elm St Hartford CT 06106

NARDONE, COLLEEN BURKE, school psychologist; b. Grand Rapids, Minn., Feb. 22, 1940; d. Edmund and Pearl (Persons) Burke; m. James Nardone, June 9, 1962; children: Ann Nardone-Jensen, Edward. BS, U. Minn., Mpls., 1962; MA, U. Minn., Duluth, 1975; postgrad., U. Wis., Superior, 1982-84, U. N.D., Grand Forks, 1989—. Diplomate Am. Bd. Sch. Psychologists. Tchr. Sch. Dist. 1, Mpls., 1962-64, Sch. Dist. 381, Two Harbors, Minn., 1964-66, Sch. Dist. 317, Deer River, Minn., 1968-69, Sch. Dist. 316, Pengilly, Minn., 1969-70, Sch. Dist. 002, Hill City, Minn., 1971-86; sch. psychologist International Falls, Minn., 1986-88; asst. prof. Bemidji (Minn.) State U., 1988-89. Bd. dirs. Arrowhead Regional Devel. Commn., Duluth, Minn., 1981—, chmn., 1990—; vice chair Housing and Redevel. Authority, Grand Rapids, 1986—; pres. Northspan Group, Duluth, 1989-90. Mem. AAUW, League Women Voters, Bus. and Profl. Women, No. Minn. Citizens League (pres. 1988-90). Democrat. Episcopalian. Home: 2606 Audrey Ln Grand Rapids MN 55744

NARDUZZI, JOANN VIRGINIA, physician; b. Pittsburgh, July 24, 1937; d. Anthony and Lucy Rose (Connochiari) N.; m. James D. Hockenberry, July 4, 1969; children: James D. Jr., Andrea J. BS, U. Pitts., 1958, MD, 1962. Intern Mercy Hosp., Pittsburgh, 1962-63, med. resident, 1963-65; endocrinologist U. Pittsburgh, 1965-67; dir. med. edn. Mercy Hosp., Pittsburgh, 1971—, chief Div. of Endocrinology, 1971-88; med. dir. clin. rev. progs. Mercy Hosp., 1988—; lectr. on diabetes Roerig Co., Upjohn cos., 1980—. Contbr. articles to profl. jours. Lantern Com. U. Pittsburgh, 1988; Hosp. Auxillary Mercy Hospital, 1970. fellowship Am. Coll. of Physician, 1972. Mem. Am. Diabetes Assn. (pres.) AMA, Pa. Med. Soc., Endocrine Soc., Am. Coll. Utilization Review Physicians, AOA, Phi Beta Kappa. Republican. Roman Catholic. Office: Mercy Hosp 1400 Locust St Pittsburgh PA 15219

NARHI, SALLY ANN, principal; b. Hancock, Mich., July 15, 1948; d. Arvi Matius and Gladys Bell (Campbell) N.; m. Raymond John Clark, June 14, 1975; 1 child, Arvid John Narhi Clark. BS, Mich. State U., 1969, MA, 1972, PhD, 1981. Cert. tchr., Mich. Substitute tchr. Lansing (Mich.) Sch. Dist., 1970-71; high sch. tchr. Portland (Mich.) Pub. Schs, 1971-82, tchr. cen. office adminstr., 1982-83; high school prin. Baraga (Mich.) Area Schs., 1983-89, L'Anse (Mich.) Area Schs., 1989—. Co-Editor: Michigan 4-H International Cookbook, 1972, editor: (book) Together Again; contbr. articles to mags. Active VFW Aux. Post 7646, Alston, Mich., 1965—, Mich. 4-H Internat. Mich.State U., 1970—, Nat. Internat. Farm Youth Exchange Assn., Washington, 1970—. Recipient 4-H Alumni award Mich. 4-H Program, 1985; named Tchr. of Yr. City of Portland, 1981-82. Mem. Prin's. Round Table, Mich. Assn. Secondary Sch. Prin., Natl. Assn. of Secondary Sch. Prin., AAUW, Delta Kappa Gamma, Alpha Delta Kappa, Omicron Nu, Phi Delta Kappa. Office: L'Anse Area Schs 210 N 4th St L'Anse MI 49946

NARODICK, SALLY G., financial executive; b. Clinton, Mass., June 26, 1945; d. Morris and Dorothy Gould; m. Kit G. Narodick, Apr. 11, 1970; children—Lisa, Philip. BA, Boston U., 1962; MA in Teaching, Columbia U., 1969; MBA, N.Y. U., 1973. Security analyst Paine Webber Jackson & Curtis, N.Y.C., 1971-73; security analyst Seattle-First Nat. Bank, 1973-75, mgr. asset-liability, 1975-79, mgr. loan rev. and exams., 1979-80, sr. v.p., controller, 1980-84, sr. v.p., dist. mgr., 1984-87; pres. Narodick, Ross & Assocs., Seattle, 1987-89; chief exec. officer Edmark Corp., Bellevue, Wash., 1989—, also bd. dirs.; bd. dirs. Pacific Northwest Bank, Harbor Properties Inc., Wash. Energy Corp. Trustee Lakeside Sch., Virginia Mason Hosp., Seattle Found. Mem. Inst. Mgmt. Cons., Wash. State Soc. CPAs, Seattle C. of C. (treas. 1982-83, bd. dirs., chmn.), Rainier Club (trustee, treas.), Columbia Tower Club. Office: Edmark Corp PO Box 3903 Bellevue WA 98009-3903

NARRIN, ROBERTA PETRONELLA, financial consultant; b. Providence, Oct. 11, 1939; d. Anthony and Maria G. (Barra) Petronella; m. Sidney Narrin, April 22, 1961 (div. Nov. 1971); children: Christine E. De Pari, Anthony F. Student, Bryant Coll., 1959; cert., Nat. Assn. Securities Dealers, 1978. CLU, Pa. Exec. sec., adminstrv. asst. Allied Adjustment Svcs., Providence, 1967-71; account exec. Advertisers Workshop, East Providence, R.I., 1971-75; pres. Roberta Narrin Assocs., Providence, 1975-77, A Chris Corp., Providence, 1980—; fin. cons. Phoenix Mut. Life Ins., One-120 Assocs. MBF, Inc., Providence, 1977—. Pres. PTA, No. Providence, 1969; v.p. R.I. Assn. Brain Injured, No. Providence, 1968; sec. The Learning Ctr., Providence, 1977-79, R.I. Assn. Retarded Children, 1970—; mem. West Bay Residential Human Rights Commn., Cranston Chpt. Retarded Citizens March of Dimes, R.I. Estate Planning Coun. Mem. NAFE, R.I. Assn. Life Underwriters (bd. dirs., Nat. Quality award 1981—, pub. rels., editor Life Notes), R.I. Chpt. CLU's (R.I. chpt. pub. rels.), Million Dollar Round Table. Office: MBF Inc 300 Centerville Rd Warwick RI 02886

NARUSIS, REGINA GYTÉ FIRANT, lawyer; b. Kaunas, Lithuania, Oct. 12, 1936; came to U.S., 1949, naturalized, 1955; d. Victor and Eugenia S. (Cesnavicius) Firant; m. Bernard V. Narusis, June 19, 1959; children: Victor John, Ellen Marie, Susan Marie. BA, U. Ill., 1957, JD, 1959. Bar: Ill. 1960. Ptnr. Narusis & Narusis, Cary, Ill., 1961—; atty. City of McHenry (Ill.), 1973—; village atty. Fox River Grove, Ill., 1967-73; asst. state's atty., McHenry County, Ill., 1968-75, head juvenile div., 1968-75. Mem. McHenry County Bd. Health, Woodstock, Ill., 1964-75, McHenry County Welfare Services Com., 1968-75; mem., pres. Dist. 46 Sch. Bd., McHenry County, 1964-79; mem. adminstrv. council, mem. exec. bd. Marian Cen. Cath. High Sch., 1981—; bd. dirs. Cath. Found. for People of Diocese of Rockford, Ill., 1988—; chpt. pres. Lithuanian Am. Community, Inc., 1989-90 (mem. Coordinating Comm. of Nat. Exec. Comm. 1990—); Mem. Ill. Bar Assn., McHenry County Bar Assn., Women's Bar Assn., Am. Judicature Soc., Nat. Dist. Attys. Assn., Kappa Beta Pi. Address: 213 W Lake Shore Dr Cary IL 60013

NASALROAD, KENNIETH JEAN, import executive; b. Oak Harbor, Wash., Dec. 10, 1950; d. Edward Clifton and Norma Jean (Kent) Bickmore; m. Ralph Floyd Nasalroad, June 15, 1974; children: Raymond Douglas, Ralph Eric. AA in Math., Reedley (Calif) Jr. Coll., 1972. Adminstrv. asst. Kings Canyon Unified Sch. Dist., Reedley, 1970-72; computer operator Sequoia Forest Industries div. Wickes Co., Dinuba, Calif., 1972-74; office mgr. Therm'x Corp. div. Buchmin Glass Corp., Reedley, 1974-78, gen. mgr., 1978—. Treas. Monday Mixed 4-Some Bowling League, Dinuba, 1973-76, Noah's Ark Child Care Ctr., Reedley, 1981-83, Reedley Youth Soccer League, 1989—, Grant PTC, 1989—; pres. Reedley Kings Canyon Youth Soccer League, 1990—, 86-87, sec., 1983-84, spl. events. chmn., 1987-89. Mem. Warehouse Distbrs. Assn., NAFE, Orange Cove Women's Club (mem. chmn. 1984-85). Republican. Home: 110 Sixth St Orange Cove CA 93646 Office: Therm'x Corp 835 S Frankwood Ave Reedley CA 93654

NASH, ALANNA KAY, critic, writer; b. Louisville, Aug. 16, 1950; d. Allan and Emily Kay (Derrick) N. BA, Stephens Coll., 1972; MS, Columbia U., 1974. Music critic Louisville Courier Jour., 1977; writer, producer Sta. WHAS, Louisville, 1980; pres. Alandale Prodns., Louisville, 1981—; freelance writer specializing in the arts Stereo Review, Esquire, N.Y. Times, Entertainment Weekly, Ms., Glamour, Working Woman, Sat. Evening Post, Video Review, 1964—. Author: Dolly, 1978, Behind Closed Doors: Talking with the Legends of Country Music, 1988, Golden Girl: The Story of Jessica Savitch, 1988; co-producer TV documentary The Deaners: Cause Without a Rebel; writer, producer network and syndicated radio spls. Recipient Nat. Prodn. awards Alpha Epsilon Rho, 1971. Mem. Soc. Profl. Journalists (bd. dirs. Louisville chpt. 1987—), Authors Guild, Country Music Assn. Republican. Methodist. Home and Office: 703 Alta Vista Rd Louisville KY 40206

NASH, CLARA MAE, shop owner, genealogist; b. Hempstead, Tex., July 7, 1935; d. Albert Marvin Massey and Ida Mae (Dobbins) Ritter; m. George Phillip Nash, Jan. 5, 1952; children: Patricia Elaine Nash Weger, Kenneth Eric, Alicia Kae. Student, Bakers Bus. Coll., 1954, La Salle Extension Coll., 1960-61, Cleveland Community Coll. Acct., tax expert various cos. and individuals, 1963-76; mgr. Savings and Loan, Denton, Tex., 1975-76; profl. geneal. researcher, 1976-87; clk. Corner Kitchen, 1987-89; jewelry merchandiser A.A.I., 1987-89; owner Campus Cubbard, Boiling Springs, N.C., 1989 --. Author, pub.: Old Red River Ancestor Charts and Family Sheets, 1985; (with Lynda Massey) Marriages Southern District Okla. Indian Territory, 1980, Index to N. Founder Denison (Tex.) Libr. Geneal. Soc., 1979; founding mem. pub. staff The Grayson Gateway, 1979; pres. Bryan County Heritage Soc., Durant, Okla., 1982-84; foundingpres., organizer Heritage Libr., Calera, Okla., 1983-84. Mem. Daughters of the Confederacy (Julia Child's chpt.), various geneal. and hist. socs. Democrat. Baptist. Home: 833 Earl Rd Shelby NC 28150 Office: Campus Cubbard PO Box 941 Boiling Springs NC 28017

NASH, JULIE WATTS, librarian; b. Wichita, Kans., June 28, 1956; d. William Eugene and Patsie Lee (Monson) Watts; m. Larry J. Nash, Feb. 14, 1981. B.G.S., Emporia State U., 1978; M.L.S., Emporia State U., 1982. Head br. librarian Kansas City (Mo.) Pub. Library, 1980-81; acquisitions librarian Park Coll. Library, Parkville, Mo., 1981-82; pub. services librarian Monessen (Pa.) Pub. Library, 1983-84; head br. librarian Lane Rd. Library, Columbus, Ohio, 1984—; research cons. Compucare, Inc., Pitts., 1983. Mem. ALA, Kappa Delta Pi. Republican. Presbyterian. Home: 7687 Foxboro Ct Columbus OH 43085 Office: 1945 Lane Rd Columbus OH 43220

NASH, JUNE CAPRICE, anthropology professor; b. Salem, Mass., May 30, 1927; d. Joseph Bausley and M. Josephine (Salloway) Bousley; m. Manning Nash, Sept. 1952 (div. 1967); children: Eric, Laura; m. Herbert Menzel, July 1, 1972. BA, CUNY, 1948; MA, U. Chgo., 1953, PhD, 1960. Asst. prof. Chgo. Tchrs. Coll., Chgo., Ill., 1960-63, Yale U. New Haven, Conn., 1963-68; assoc. prof. NYU, 1968-72; prof. CUNY, 1972—; disting. vis. prof. Am. U., Cairo, 1978, U. Colo., Boulder, 1988—; vis. prof. SUNY, Albany, 1988-89; disting. prof. CUNY, N.Y.C., 1990. Author: In The Eyes of the Ancester, 1970, We Eat the Mines and The Mines Eat Us, 1979, Dependency and Exploitation in Bolivian Mining Communities, 1989, From Tank Town to High Tech: The Clash of Community and Industrial Cycles, 1989. Mem. Soc. for the Anthropology of Work (pres., 1988—), Assn. Polit. and Legal Activities (pres. 1983), Am. Anthropology Assn., Am. Ethnographic Soc. Home: Prospect St Box 711 Planfield MA 01070 Office: CUNY 137th Convene New York NY 10031

NASH, LILLIAN DOROTHY, gynecologist; b. Lyndhurst, N.J., Jan. 27, 1931; d. Wilfrid Joseph and Lillian Bernadette (Rogers) N. BS, Chestnut Hill Coll., Phila., 1953; MD, Med. Coll. Pa., Phila., 1957. Diplomate Am. Bd. Ob-Gyn. Rotating intern Orange Mem. Hosp., Orange, N.J., 1957-58; asst. resident St. Clare's Hosp., N.Y.C., 1958-60, chief resident, 1960-61; asst. resident Sloane Hosp., N.Y.C.; asst. physician The Roosevelt Hosp., N.Y.C., 1965-71, Community Mem. Hosp., N.J., 1971-73; gynecologist Fertility Rsch., N.Y.C., 1977-89; assoc. attending physician St. Barnabas Med. Ctr., 1983—; asst. attending physician St. Lukes Roosevelt Hosp., 1984—; asst. prof. SUNY, Stonybrook, 1973-76; clin. instr. Ob-gyn. Coll. P and S Columbia, N.Y.C., 1984—. Barnes Foster fellow Sloane Hosp. Women, N.Y.C., 1962-65, NIH Trainee grantee, 1962-65, Ford Found. fellow, 1962-65. Fellow Am. Coll. Ob-gyn.; mem. Am. Fertility Soc., Am. Assn. Gyn Laparoscopists, Women's Med. Assn. N.Y., N.Y. Gynecol. Soc. Roman Catholic. Home: 425 E 72d St New York NY 10021 Office: 15 James St Florham Park NJ 07932 also: 601 Madison Ave New York NY 10011

NASH, MARJORIE ANN MOSS, philosophy educator; b. Houston, May 28, 1948; d. Cary Bennett and Ellen Marguerite (Covington) Moss; m. Robert Webster Nash Jr., Sept. 3, 1966. BA, U. Houston, 1979, MA, 1982; postgrad., Rice U., 1983—. Asst. corp. sec. 1st Am. Title Co. Houston, 1971-74; instr. philosophy U. Houston, 1979-82, acting coordinator honors program, 1985, acad. advisor honors program, 1986-87; instr. philosophy Houston Community Coll., 1987—. Mem. child support enforcement adv. coun. Tex. Atty. Gen.'s Office, 1988—; mem. adv. coun. Houston YWCA, 1988. AAUW grantee, 1986. Mem. Philosophy Sci. Assn., Community Colls. Humanities Assn., AAUW (dir. women's issues Tex. div. 1988—), Peace Links. Democrat. Methodist. Home: 1238 Almond Grove Dr Houston TX 77077

NASH, MYRTLE CORLISS, psychologist; b. N.Y.C., Mar. 7, 1915; d. Augustin Pride and Hazel Bonney (Keene) Corliss; m. Thomas Nash, July 17, 1943 (dec. 1944); 1 child, Patrick. AB, Swarthmore (Pa.) Coll., 1937; MA, Bryn Mawr (Pa.) Coll., 1938, PhD, 1950. Asst. prof. psychology Drake U., Des Moines, 1952-54; assoc. prof. psychology Southwestern at Memphis, 1954-62, Converse Coll., Spartanburg, S.C., 1962-67; prof. Keuka Coll., Keuka Park, N.Y., 1967-70; clin. psychologist Spartanburg Area Mental Health Ctr., 1971-84, ret., 1984. Mem. Am. Psychol. Assn. Democrat. Mem. Soc. of Friends. Home: 1020 W Peace St Apt H-1 Raleigh NC 27605

NASH, PAIGE EILEEN, public relations executive; b. Dallas, Apr. 18, 1961; d. Michaux Jr. and Eileen (Ruebel) N. Student, So. Meth. U., 1979-81, U. Tex., 1981-83. Mktg. exec., new accounts Bent Tree Nat. Bank, 1984-85; soc. editor, columnist Park Cities People Newspaper, 1986-87; pub. rels. exec., mktg. prof. Carter-Nash, Inc., Dallas, 1987—; Bd. dirs. Jr. League of Dallas, Cattle Baron's Ball for Am. Cancer Soc., pub. rels. chmn. 1989-90; bd. dirs. Leukemia Luncheon/Fashion Show, pub. rels. chmn. 1988; bd. dis. Debutantes Charity Ball, 1985-87; women's adv. bd. Dallas Bapt. U., 1985-87; vol. Parkland Meml. Hosp. Adv. bd. Ultra Mag. Black Book. Mem. Dallas Zool. Soc., Pi Beta Phi Alumnae. Home: 3924 Fairfax Ave Dallas TX 75209

NASH, RUTH COWAN (MRS. BRADLEY D. NASH), journalist; b. Salt Lake City, Utah; d. William Henry and Ida (Baldwin) Cowan; A.B., U. Tex., 1923; m. Bradley D. Nash, June 30, 1956. Tchr. pub. high sch., San Antonio, 1924-27; reporter San Antonio Evening News, 1928, United Press, 1929; corr. AP, Chgo., 1929-40, Washington, 1940-43, 45-56, war corr., North Africa, Gt. Britain, Europe, 1943-45, retired, 1956; free-lance journalist, 1956—; asst. to undersec. of health edn. and welfare, 1958-61; pub. relations dir. women's div. Rep. Nat. Com., Washington; mem. Def. Adv. Com. on Women in the Services, 1958-61. Clubs: Nat. Press, Washington Press (pres. 1947-48), Overseas Press, Am. Newswomen's; Writer and Press (London). Home: High Acres Farm Rte 3 Box 122 Harpers Ferry WV 25425

NASH, SONJA HUDDLESTON, teacher; b. Albuquerque, Jan. 25, 1947; d. Leo Neal Huddleston and Beatrice Lucille (Bell) Biers; m. James Allen Nash, Dec. 27, 1969 (div. 1989); 1 child, Cressinda. BS, Tarleton Coll., Stephenville, Tex., 1969. Cert. tchr., Tex. Tchr. Amarillo (Tex.) Pub. Schs., 1969-73, Lubbock (Tex.) Ind. Sch. Dist., 1973-74, 75—. Mem. Delta Kappa Gamma (pres. 1988-90, conv. co-chair Alpha State Conv. 1990). Episcopalian. Home: 2616 74th Pl Lubbock TX 79423

NASH, VERONICA, advertising agency executive. Sr. v.p., assoc. creative dir. Ogilvy & Mather Advt., N.Y.C., until 1990; sr. v.p., sr. group creative dir. Grey Advt., Inc., N.Y.C., 1990—. Office: Grey Advt Inc 777 3d Ave New York NY 10017*

NASHAN, JOY ORTIZ, corporation professional; b. Santa Fe, N.M., Mar. 18, 1948; d. Willie Velarde and Edith June (Ellis) Ortiz; m. CharlesL. Nashan Jr., June 20, 1970; children: Kevin M., Dawn M., Christopher D. Grad. high sch., Santa Fe, N.Mex., 1966. Bd. dirs. Sunwest Bank, Santa Fe; chmn. Hist. Design Review, 1986, chmn. St. Vincent Hosp. bd. trustees, 1988—. Chmn. Cuisines Santa Fe Am., Cancer Soc., 1986. Republican. Roman Catholic. Home: 345 Delgado Santa Fe NM 87501 Office: La Tertulia Restaurant 416 Agua Fria Santa Fe NM 87501

NASI, CYNTHIA WILBERG, sales executive; b. Price, Utah, Sept. 11, 1960; d. LaGrand and Charlotte (Van Buren) Wilberg; m. Robert A. Nasi, Sept. 28, 1985; 1 child, Shalyn Amanda. BS magna cum laude, U. Utah, 1982. Mgr. L.A. unit Procter & Gamble, Orange, Calif., 1982-85; mgr. N.Y. dist. Boise Cascade, Manhattan, N.Y., 1985-86; nat. account mgr. Lever Bros., Englewood Cliff, N.J., 1986-87; sales mgr., dir. nat. sales A.C. Nielsen, Hackensack, N.J., 1987-88; account dir. Actmedia, Darien, Conn., 1988—.

NASON, DOLORES IRENE, computer company executive, eucharistic minister; b. Seattle, Jan. 24, 1934; d. William Joseph Lockinger and Ruby Irene (Church) Gilstrap; m. George Malcolm Nason Jr., Oct. 7, 1951; children: George Malcolm III, Scott James, Lance William, Natalie Joan. Student, Long Beach (Calif.) City Coll., 1956-59; cert. in elem. teaching, Immaculate Heart Coll., 1961, cert. teaching, 1962, cert. secondary teaching, 1967; attended, Salesian Sem., 1983-85. Cert. religious edn. for elem. teaching. Buyer J. C. Penney Co., Barstow, Calif., 1957; prin. St. Cyprian Confraternity of Christian Doctrine Elem. Sch., Long Beach, 1964-67; prin. summer sch. St. Cyprian County Community Dist. Elem. Sch., Long Beach, 1965-67; pres. St. Cyprian Confraternity Orgn., Long Beach, 1967-69; dist. co-chmn. L.A. Diocese, 1968-70; v.p. Nason & Assocs., Inc., Long Beach, 1978—; pres. L.A. County Commn. on Obscenity & Pornography, 1984—; eucharistic minister St. Cyprian Ch., Long Beach, 1985—; bd. dirs. L.A. County Children's Svcs., 1988—; vol. Meml. Children's Hosp., Long Beach, 1977—; mem. scholarship com. Long Beach City Coll., 1984-90, Calif. State U., Long Beach, 1984-90. Mem. Sunland-Tujuna (Calif.) Citizens-Police Coun., 1987—; mem. adv. bd. Pro-Wilson 90 Gov., Calif., 1990; mem. devel. bd. St. Joseph High Sch., 1987—; pres. St. Cyprian's Parish Coun., 1962—; mem. Long Beach Civic Light Opera, 1973—, Assistance League of Long Beach, 1976—. Mem. L.A. Fitness Club, U. of the Pacific Club, K.C. (Family of the Month 1988). Republican. Roman Catholic.

NASON, HEATHER ELIZABETH, oil industry executive; b. Caribou, Maine, Sept. 13, 1959; d. Howard Earl and Murna Inez (Hemphill) N. BBA, U. Tex., San Antonio, 1981. Asst. mgr. Best Products, Inc., San Antonio, 1981; safety dir. Rio Grande Drilling Co., San Antonio, 1981-83; exec. adminstr. Arctic Red Resources Corp., San Antonio, 1983—. Mem. NAFE, U. Tex. San Antonio Alumni Assn., Young Leaders Club. Republican. Presbyterian. Home: 13746 Fairway Hedge San Antonio TX 78217 Office: Arctic Red Resources Corp 1250 NE Loop 410 Ste 71 San Antonio TX 78209

NASON, THELMA STEIN (TEMA NASON), writer, teacher; b. N.Y.C.; d. Gerson and Bella (Czernitzski) Stein; m. Alvin Nason, Oct. 18, 1944 (dec. Jan., 1978); children: Deborah R., Steffi R., Jean L., Gerson S., Benjamin M. BA, Bklyn. Coll., 1941; postgrad. U. Chgo., 1941-42; MA, Johns Hopkins U., 1968. Instr. econs. Williams Coll., Williamstown, Mass., 1942-43; wage and disputes analyst War Labor Bd., Chgo., N.Y.C., 1943-44; labor rep. CIO, N.Y.C., Washington, San Francisco, 1944-47; cons. Md. Planning Commn., 1952-53; instr. writing Johns Hopkins U., Balt., 1969-78; freelance writer, Balt., 1958—; sr. research assoc. sociology Brandeis U., Waltham, Mass., 1980—. Author: A Stranger Here, Myself, 1977, Ethel: A Novel About Ethel Rosenberg, 1990, various short stories. Contbr. articles to jours., newspapers. Vis. scholar Bunting Inst., Radcliffe Coll., Cambridge, Mass., 1979-80. Fellow MacDowell Colony, Peterborough, N.H., Va. Ctr. for Creative Arts, Sweetbriar. Mem. PEN, Yaddo, Poets and Writers Assn., Nat. Writers Union. Avocations: theatre, reading, music, swimming, walking.

NASS, DEANNA ROSE, counselor, professor; b. N.Y.C., June 30, 1939; d. Nat. and Jean (Mark) Spitzer. BFA, U. Chgo., 1961, MFA, 1964; MA, NYU, 1969; MPhil, PhD, Columbia U., 1979. Art tchr. N.Y.C. Bd. Edn., 1964-68; assoc. prof., counselor Dept. Student Svcs., CUNY, 1968—. Editor: The Rape Victim, 1977; contbr. articles to profl. jours. Recipient Full Tuition Scholarship U. Chgo., 1964; Grantee Drug Edn. Program, 1970-71; recipient Cert. Recognition U.S. Dept. Labor, 1976. Mem. Am. Assn. U. Profs., Phi Delta Kappa, CUNY Acad. for Humanities & Scis. Home: 225 E 73rd St New York NY 10021

NASSAU, ELIZABETH SUSSMAN, university adminstrator; b. Binghamton, N.Y., Mar. 16, 1956; d. Robert and Louise (Azersky) Sussman; m. Richard Nathan Nassau, July 19, 1986; 1 stepchild, William Dean. BA in English, SUNY, Binghamton, 1977; MA in English, U. Ill., 1981. Mktg. communications coordinator Link Flight Simulation-The Singer Co., Binghamton, 1981-82; dir. external programs SUNY Sch. Mgmt., Binghamton, 1982-86; dir. Ctr. Bus., Industry and Govt. West Chester (Pa.) U., 1986—, asst. dean Univ. Coll., 1989—. Pres. and co-founder Delaware Valley Stepfamilies, West Chester, 1987—. Mem. Am. Soc. for Tng. and Devel., Council on Adult and Exptl. Learning, Nat. Soc. for Performance Improvement, West Chester C. of C. (edn. com. 1987—). Democrat. Jewish. Office: West Chester U Ctr for Bus Industry and Govt 140 Bull Ctr West Chester PA 19383

NASSIF, MERPH (CAROLYN O. NASSIF), freelance artist, art educator; b. Schenectady, N.Y., Jan. 26, 1928; d. Charles Sanders and Claira B. (Williams) Oliver; m. Paul T. Schwabe, Jan. 26, 1946 (div. 1964); children: Susan L., Paula L. Kot, Jan M. Bowen, Keith C., Kim A. Arpy, Tami Fisher, Darcy Mascardini; m. David J. Nassif, 1964 (dec. Oct. 1985). With acctg. dept. various cos., 1950-75; artist N.E. U.S. and, Fla., 1976—; watercolor instr. Sarasota, Fla., 1978—; scenery designer Church St. Actors, Montrose, Pa., 1977-78; art dir. Hill Country Gallery, Montrose, 1977-80; graphic artist Nutmeg Ballet, Torrington, Conn., 1985; art cons. N.E. C. of C., Torrington, 1982-85; pictorial map artist Ind. graphic Supplies, N.E. Conn., 1984-85. Artist, contbg. poet: The Poetry of Art, 1983; watercolor, pastel and pen and ink works include Abandoned Academics (best of show award 1976; recipient numerous other awards, 1977—); represented in many pvt. and pub. collection throughout U.S.A. Mem. Internat. Soc. Artists (juried), Am. Watercolor Soc. (juried), Sarasota Art Assn., Hill Country Artists (founder), Women in the Arts, Federated Women of Am., The Gourmands of Sarasota, Loners of Am. Home and Studio: 7125 Fruitville Rd #445 Sarasota FL 34240 Home (summer): 3 Helen Ct Scotia NY 12302

NASTIUK, VIRGINIA, sewing pattern development company executive; b. Seattle, Jan. 28, 1923; d. Otto Carl and Sylvia Blanche (Raffel) Vieweg; children: Linda Kaye, Gary Michael. Mfr., designer Jinni, Inc., Seattle; dir. sewing sch. Frederick & Nelson, Seattle; pres. Personal Pattern Devel., Bothell, Wash. Author tech. books for patternmaking; contbr. articles to profl. publs.; subject of recent PBS-TV series; developer exclusive system of computer patternmaking for the human form.

NATAF, HELENE MICHELE, accounting services company executive; b. Tunis, Tunisia, Mar. 13, 1939; came to U.S., 1986; m. Nataf Jean Pierre; children: Patrick, Isabelle, Marc-Andre. PhD Money, Banking, Fin., U. Aix-Marseille III, 1983, PhD, 1985. Mgr. of family-owned properties Avignon, France, 1960-73; pres. gift shop Brignoles, France, 1969-79; acct. import-export fimr Marseilles, 1979-82, mgmt. and fin. cons., 1982-86; mgr. acctg. firm N.Y.C., 1986-87; pres., owner S.O.S. Mgmt. Inc., N.Y.C., 1988—. Trea. Europe-USA 2000, N.Y.C., 1987. Mem. Fin. Women Assn. N.Y. Office: SOS Mgmt Inc 60 E 42nd St 1544 New York NY 10165

NATALE, LYNDA LEE, life insurance company executive; b. Washington, Pa., Nov. 22, 1959; d. Michael Richard and Helen Jeanne (Bodmer) Hordies; m. Ronald D. Natale, Oct. 12, 1985. BA, California (Pa.) U., 1981; postgrad., Santa Clara U., 1988-89. Word processor Aetna Life Ins. Co., Pitts., 1981-85; dist. office coord. Guardian Life Ins. Co., San Jose, Calif., 1985-89; mktg. coord. CPS Bus. Systems, Inc., Dallas, 1989—. Mem. NAFE, Am. Mgmt. Assn. Democrat. Presbyterian.

NATALICIO, DIANA S., university president; b. St. Louis, Aug. 25, 1939; d. William and Eleanor J. (Biermann) Siedhoff. BS in Spanish summa cum laude, St. Louis U., 1961; MA in Portuguese lang., U. Tex., 1964, PhD in Linguistics, 1969. Chmn. dept. modern langs. U. Tex., El Paso, 1973-77, assoc. dean liberal arts, 1977-79, acting dean liberal arts, 1979-80, dean Coll. Liberal Arts, 1980-84, v.p. acad. affairs, 1984-88, pres., 1988—; mem., chair Fed. Res. Br. Bank Bd., El Paso. Co-author: book Sounds of Children, 1977; contbr. articles to profl. jours. Mem. exec. com. Cultural Planning Project, El Paso, 1984-86; bd. dirs. Pub. TV, El Paso 1975-84; participant Leadership El Paso, 1980-81. Named Woman of the Yr. in Edn., El Paso Women's Polit. Caucus, 1982; Fulbright fellow, 1961-62; Woodrow Wilson fellow, 1961-62; NDEA fellow, 1966-69. Mem. Linguistic Soc. Am., Tchrs. English to Speakers Other Langs. (pres. local chpt.), Am. Assn. Tchrs. Spanish and Portuguese, Phi Kappa Phi (pres. local chpt.). Home: 711 Cincinnati El Paso TX 79902 Office: U Tex University Ave El Paso TX 79968-0500

NATHANSON, A. LYNN, broadcasting executive; b. Sydney, N.S., Can., Dec. 4, 1955; came to U.S., 1970, permanent resident, 1978; d. Norris Lionel and Reva (Brook) N.; m. Mark Joseph Pandiscio, Oct. 8, 1978; 1 child, Jennifer Cara. AB in Music and French, Brown U., 1977. Program mgr., announcer Sta. CJCB-FM, Sydney, 1978; floor dir., asst. dir. Sta. WJAR-TV, Providence, R.I., 1979-80; devel. officer Boston Biomed. Research Inst., 1980-81; concert mgr. Mus. Fine Arts, Boston, 1980-81, mgr. Remis Auditorium, 1982-84; sr. v.p. Sta. WCRB, Charles River Broadcasting, Waltham, Mass., 1984-87; sr. v.p., gen. mgr., 1987—; cons. Stas. CJCB-AM, CKPE-FM, Sydney. Chmn. Flights of Fancy Gala fundraiser Dana Farber Cancer Inst., Boston, 1986; bd. dirs. Friends of Dana Farber Cancer Inst., 1985—; mem. benefit com. Pro Arte Chamber Orch., 1986; adv. bd. ART-SMART, 1989. Mem. New Eng. Broadcasting Assn., Classic Music Broadcasters Assn., Concert Music Broadcasters Assn. (bd. dirs. 1987—, v.p. 1988—), Assn. for Classical Music, Advt. Club of Boston, Boston Symphony Assn. Vols. Jewish. Avocations: piano, singing, swimming, skiing. Home: 241 Perkins St J-202 Boston MA 02130 Office: Sta WCRB Charles River Broadcasting 750 South St Waltham MA 02254

NATHANSON, LINDA SUE, technical writer, software training specialist, systems analyst; b. Washington, Aug. 11, 1946; d. Nat and Edith (Weinstein) N.; m. James F. Barrett. BS, U. Md., 1969; MA, UCLA, 1970, PhD, 1975. Tng. dir. Rockland Research Inst., Orangeburg, N.Y., 1975-77; asst. prof. psychology SUNY, 1978-79; pres. Cabri Prodns., Inc., Ft. Lee, N.J., 1979-81; research supr. Darcy, McManus & Masius, St. Louis, 1981-83; mgr. software tng., documentation On-Line Software Internat., Ft. Lee, 1983-85; pvt. practice cons. Ft. Lee, 1985-87; founder, exec. dir. The Edin. Group, Inc., Gillette, N.J., 1987—. Author: (with others) Psychological Testing: An Introduction to Tests and Measurement, 1988; contbr. articles to mags. and profl. jours. Recipient Research Service award 1978; Albert Einstein Coll. Medicine Research fellow, 1978-79. Jewish. Home and Office: 102 Sunrise Dr Gillette NJ 07933

NATORI, JOSIE CRUZ, apparel executive; b. Manila, May 9, 1947; came to U.S., 1964; d. Felipe F. and Angelita A. (Almeda) Cruz; m. Kenneth R. Natori, May 20, 1972; 1 child, Kenneth E.F. BA in Econs., Manhattanville Coll., 1968. V.p. Merrill-Lynch Co., N.Y.C., 1971-77; pres. The Natori Co., N.Y.C., 1977—; bd. dirs. Fashion Group Internat., N.Y.C. Bd. dirs. Philippine Am. Found., Internat. Women Forum; trustee Manhattanville Coll. Recipient Human Relations award Am. Jewish Com., N.Y.C., 1986, Harriet Alger award Working Woman, N.Y., 1987, Castle award Manhattanville Coll., Purchase, 1988. Mem. Com. of 200. Home: 45 E 62nd St New York NY 10021 Office: Natori Co 40 E 34th St 18th Fl New York NY 10016

NATZKE, GAIL LOUISE, music educator; b. Ackley, Iowa, Mar. 31, 1932; d. Fred Max and Fannie Winifred (Dreyer) Schoeneman; m. Daryl Maurice Thompson, June 22, 1951 (div. Jan. 1982); children: Kent Fred, Todd Jeffrey; m. William August Natzke, Oct. 29, 1988. Student, U. Colo., 1951, 52-54, U. No. Iowa, 1970, La Verne Coll., 1976, Wartburg Coll., 1978. Pvt. practice piano teaching various locations, 1951-88; organist Meth. Ch., Shefield, Iowa, 1975-77. Author, pub.: Grandma's Remedies and Recipes, 1980; creator adult music course, 1981; speaker Suzuki method various orgs., 1980-86. Bd. dirs. sole mem. research com. Multiple Sclerosis League, Waterloo, 1969-72 (Cert. Appreciation 1974); charter mem. Mediation and Justice in Divorce, Waverly, Iowa, 1984-85. Mem. Nat. Music Tchr.'s Assn. (feature writer 1982-85), East Valley Suzuki Assn., Treble Cleff, Sweet Adelines, Easter Star (pianist, sec. 1962-69). Republican. Lutheran-Baptist. Home and Office: 1401 N Miller Mesa AZ 85203

NATZKE, PAULETTE ANN, manufacturing executive; b. Wausau, Wis., Oct. 23, 1943; d. Milton L. and Geraldine J. (Henrichs) Marth; m. Kenneth A. Natzke, June 29, 1963; children: Jerome E., Julie J. Sec. Marth Wood Shavings Supply, Marathon, Wis., 1973-85; pres. Marth Wood Shavings Supply, Marathon, 1985—; v.p. Marth Transp. Inc., Marathon, 1984—; bd. dirs. Marth Found., Marathon. Mem. Cen. Wis. Ceramic Assn. (cert. tchr., Best Show award 1981, Best Booth Show award 1982). Republican. Lutheran. Home: 6752 St Hwy 107N Marathon WI 54448 Office: Marth Wood Shavings Supply Inc Rt 2 Marathon WI 54448

NAUDZIUS, RUTH WINTERS, image consultant, home economist; b. Georgetown, Ill., May 5, 1929; d. Ernest Bruce and Melba Meryl (Shepler) Winters; m. Donald Anthony Naudzius, July 1, 1949; children: Laura Kay Naudzius Miller, Lonn Colin. BS with honors, U. Ill., 1951, MEd, 1956. Cert. home econs. tchr., Ill. Home econs. asst. broadcaster Sta. WILL, Urbana, Ill., 1949; home econs. extension specialist U. Ill., 1951; tchr. home econs. Sch. Dist. of Matoon, Ill., 1951-52, Deland-Weldon, Ill., 1952-54, Sch. Dist. 64, Park Ridge, Ill., 1963-79; image cons. Color 1 Assoc., Park Ridge, 1983—; assoc., 1987—; guest lectr. Oakton Coll., 1986—. Contbr. articles to profl. jours. Morava scholar U. Ill., 1948-51. Mem. Women in Mgmt. (chmn. fundraising Chgo. chpt. 1988—), AAUW (membership com.), 20th Century Club, Antique Rovers, Omicron Nu. Republican. Mem. Soc. of Friends. Office: Color 1 Assoc 414 S Lincoln Park Ridge IL 60068

NAUGHTON, ANN ELSIE, educator; b. N.Y.C., Apr. 27, 1942; d. George and Wilma (Lubitz) Bruning; m. Gerald Richard Naughton, Dec. 26, 1965 (dec. Apr. 1983); 1 child, Jonathan. BA, CUNY, 1963; MA, Columbia U., 1965; postgrad., Greenburgh Inst. Tchrs. Social worker div. child and family welfare Westchester County, Yonkers, N.Y., 1963-64; tchr. Hastings-on-Hudson (N.Y.) Pub. Schs., 1965—; tchr. Lincoln Ctr. Inst., N.Y.C., 1986—. Mem. Hastings Tchrs. Union (mem.-at-large exec. com. 1982—, state facilitator and trainer N.Y. parent tchr. confs. 1988—, exec. com. 1982-88, corresponding sec. 1989—). Republican. Home: 31 Walbrook Rd Scarsdale NY 10583 Office: Hastings-on-Hudson Pub Schs Hastings-on-Hudson NY 10706

NAUGHTON, MARIE ANN, corporate executive; b. Boston, Feb. 19, 1954; d. Robert J. and Beatrice T. (McDonald) N.; B.S. in Speech magna cum laude, Emerson Coll., 1976; M.A., Ind. U., 1977; Cert. spl. studies bus. and adminstrn. Harvard U., 1989. speech-lang. pathologist Dedham (Mass.) pub. schs., 1977-79; speech-lang. pathologist Mass. Gen. Hosp., Boston, 1979-81; speech pathologist Mt. Auburn Hosp., Cambridge, Mass., 1982-84; mgr. Curtis-Newton Corp., Spltys. Div., 1984—. Fellow Soc. for Ear, Nose and Throat Advances in Children; mem. Am. Speech, Lang. and Hearing Assn. (cert. clin. competence), Mass. Speech and Hearing Assn., Zeta Phi Eta. Club: Northeastern Young Lumber Execs. Author: A Coarticulation Manuel for the Remediation of /S/, 1979. Home: 77 Circuit Rd Dedham MA 02026 Office: 963 Watertown St West Newton MA 02165

NAUSCH, MELISSA BETH, registered nurse; b. Bronx, N.Y., Aug. 17, 1961; d. Frank Robert and Harriet Ann (Jelinek) N. AA, Farmingdale (N.Y.) U., 1981; BSN, Coll. Tech., Utica, N.Y., 1983. LPN, RN, N.Y. Staff nurse Cen. Suffolk Hosp., Riverhead, N.Y., 1983-84; charge nurse Smithtown (N.Y.) Gen. Hosp., 1984; charge nurse Community Hosp. West Suffolk, Smithtown, 1984-88, RN endoscopy unit, 1988-89, staff nurse, 1989-90, RN cardiac care unit, 1990—. Mem. N.Y. State Nurses Assn., Sigma Theta Tau. Home: 47 Maple Glen Ln Nesconset NY 11767 Office: Community Hosp West Suffolk Rt 111 and Rt 347 Smithtown NY 11780

NAVARRO, JANYTE JANEEN, environmental educator; b. LaJara, Colo., Apr. 14, 1935; d. John Charles Blissard and Mary Margaret (Mathias) Tedesco; m. Daniel David Myers (div. 1968); children: Kelli, Keith, Kim; m. Rafael Fowler Navarro; children: Eric, Marshall, Laura Lynne, Mitchell. Student, Colo. U., 1954-55, U. N.Mex. Owner Poodle Breeding Bus., Albuquerque, 1964-67, Jan-Knits, Albuquerque, 1973-74, Sharing is Caring, Albuquerque, 1980—; bd. dirs. Fiesta de Shaklee, Albuquerque, 1981—. Producer: (video) The Sponsoring Process, 1981; articles, newsletters in field. Mem. Rio Grande Sales Leaders Assn. (pres. 1984, 86). Home: 1505 Gretta NE Albuquerque NM 87112 Office: Sharing Is Caring 1505 Gretta NE Albuquerque NM 87112

NAVARRO, KARYL KAY, educator; b. Detroit, Dec. 6, 1956; d. Richard Charles and Vera Clair (Gemeinhardt) Carlson; m. Andrew J. Navarro, June 24, 1986. MusB, U. Mich., 1979; MS in Music Edn., U. Ill., 1982. Cert. tchr., Fla. Tchr. elem. music Community Sch. Dist. 5, Franklin Sch., Sterling, Ill., 1979-81; tchr. Hialeah-Miami Lakes High Sch. Dade County Pub. Schs., Hialeah, 1982-89, supervising tchr., 1984-88; tchr. Miami Lakes Jr. High Sch. Dade County Pub. Schs., 1984-87; dir. vocal music New World Sch. of the Arts, Miami, Fla., 1989—; pvt. instr. piano and voice, 1979—; adjudicator solo-ensemble Dist. 5, Moline, 1980; choreographer HML Singers, Hialeah, 1982-89; condr. Honors Music Festival Dade County Pub. Schs., Miami, Fla., 1985; accompanist Civic Chorale U. Miami, Coral Gables, Fla., 1987; clinician U. Miami Honor Choir Festival. Arranger marching band and choral music, 1979—; dir., producer: (musicals) L'il Abner, 1982, Aria da Capo, 1982. Mem. Miami Zool. Soc., 1985, gallon donor club ARC, Miami, 1986; dir. HML Singers, Young Ams. Nat. Invitational Performance Choir Festival, Hollywood, Calif., Festival Internat. de Musique, Quebec, Can.; peer tchr., Dade County Pub. Schs. Recipient Fla. Master Tchr. award State of Fla., 1986, Clin. Supervising Tchr. award U. Miami, 1989-90. Mem. Nat. Assn. Tchrs. of Singing, Am. Choral Dirs. Assn., Music Educators Nat. Conf., Fla. Music Educators Assn., Dade County Music Educators Assn. (treas. 1986-87), Fla. Vocal Assn. (dist. chair 1987—, adjudicator 1989, 90), United Tchrs. Dade, U. Mich. Alumni Assn. Republican. Home: 1078 Laguna Springs Dr Fort Lauderdale FL 33326 Office: New World Sch of Arts 401 NE 2d Ave Miami FL 33132

NAVARRO, SALLY MARIE, entrepreneur; b. Chgo., Sept. 29, 1954; d. Vincent James and Vera Ann LoBurgio; m. Michael A. Navarro, Aug. 29, 1948; 1 child, Miki Lynn. Adminstrv. supr. JMB Realty Corp., Chgo., 1978-88; pres. North Mich. Office Supplies, Inc., Chgo., 1988—, North Mich. Office Svcs., Inc., Chgo., 1988—; chief exec. officer Fingers In Motion, Inc.; v.p. Computer Supplies, Inc. Mem. ACLU, Nat. Assn. Women Bus. Owners. Democrat. Roman Catholic. Home: 17 W 126 Elm St Hinsdale IL 60521 Office: North Mich Office Svcs 211 E Ontario Ste 200 Chicago IL 60611

NAVIN, MARYANN ELIZABETH, securities trader; b. Boston, Feb. 12, 1951; d. John Ambrose and Margaret Elizabeth Hann; m. John Joseph Navin, June 2, 1973. Student, Simmons Coll., Boston. With John Hancock Mut. Life Ins. Co., Boston, 1969—, sec., 1969-73, trading clk., 1973-76, trading asst., 1976-81, asst. trader, 1981-83, bond trader, 1983—. Democrat. Roman Catholic. Office: John Hancock Mut Life Ins Co 200 Clarendon St Boston MA 02117

NAVRATILOVA, MARTINA, professional tennis player; b. Prague, Czechoslovakia, Oct. 18, 1956; came to U.S., 1975, naturalized, 1981; d. Miroslav Navratil and Jana Navratilova. Student, schs. in Czechoslovakia. Profl. tennis player, 1975—. Author: (with George Vecsey) Martina, 1985. Winner Czechoslovak Nat. singles, 1972-74, U.S. Open singles, 1983, 84, 86, 87, U.S. Open doubles, 1977, 78, 80, 83, 84, 87, U.S. Open mixed doubles, 1987, Va. Slims Tournament, 1978, 83, 84, 85, 86, Wimbledon singles, 1978, 79, 82, 83, 84, 85, 86, 87, 90, Wimbledon women's doubles, 1976, 79, 81, 82, 83, 84, 86, Wimbledon mixed doubles, 1985, French Open singles, 1982, 84, Australian Open singles, 1981, 83, 85, Australian Doubles (with Nagelsen), 1980, (with Shriver), 1982, 84, 84, 85, 87, 88, 89, Grand Slam of Women's Tennis, 1984; named Hon. Citizen of Dallas, AP Female Athlete of Yr., 1983. Mem. Women's Tennis Assn. (dir., exec. com.). Office: care Sargent Hill 525 Bailey Fort Worth TX 76107 also: US Profl Tennis Assn 6701 Hwy 58 Harrison TN 37341*

NAYLOR, MARY, nurse; b. Salt Lake City, Mar. 25, 1955; d. Hyrum Dean and Mary Rae (Featherstone) N. AA, Ricks Coll., Rexburg, Idaho, 1975; BS, Brigham Young U., 1976; cert. practical nursing, Idaho State U., 1980; AD in Nursing, SUNY, Albany, 1987. RN, Idaho, Utah. Staff nurse Ea. Idaho Regional Med. Ctr., Idaho Falls, 1980-90, Holy Cross Hosp., Salt Lake City, 1990—; counselor Community Health Fair, Idaho Falls, 1983. Active Young Reps., Idaho Falls, 1973-74; judge Idaho Vocat. Indsl. Clubs of Am., 1982. Recipient Leah D. Wistoe award Bigham Young U., 1976, Silver medal in practical nursing Idaho Vocat. Indsl. Clubs Am. Skills Olympics, 1980. Mem. ANA, Phi Kappa Phi. Mem. Mormon Ch. Home: 1340 E 4750 S #D-10 Salt Lake City UT 84117 Office: Holy Cross Hosp 1050 E S Temple Salt Lake City UT 84117

NAZARETH, ANNETTE LAPORTE, lawyer; b. Providence, Jan. 27, 1956; d. George Robert and Dolores (LaPorte) N.; m. Roger Walton Ferguson Jr., May 3, 1986. AB in History and Econs., Brown U., 1978; JD, Columbia U., 1981. Assoc. Davis Polk & Wardwell, N.Y.C., 1981-86; gen. ptnr., gen. counsel Mabon, Nugent & Co., N.Y.C., 1986—. Mem. Securities Industry Assn., Phi Beta Kappa. Home: 160 Overlook Rd New Rochelle NY 10804 Office: Mabon Nugent & Co 1 Liberty Pla 165 Broadway New York NY 10006

NEAL, BONNIE JEAN, real estate professional; b. Kansas City, Mo., Apr. 24, 1930; d. David Ira and Juanita Mae (Duncan) Johnson; m. Howard Stranton Neal, July 24, 1948 (div. Oct. 1972); children: Randall Stranton, William Scott, Douglas Kelly. Student, U. Omaha, 1980-86, Londay Sch. Real Estate, Omaha, 1987. Data processing supr. Enron Corp., Omaha, 1980-85, adminstrv. support analyst, 1985-86; real estate sales agt. Allen, Young Assocs., Omaha, 1987-88, Home Real Estate (merger Allen Young Assocs. and Wurdeman & Maenner), Omaha, 1988—; Active PTA, Council Bluffs, Iowa, 1957-59; vol. March of Dimes, Council Bluffs, 1963—; mem. com. Realtors Polit. Action. Fellow Omaha Bd. Realtors; mem. Women's Bowling Assn. Democrat. Baptist. Lodge: Order Eastern Star (25-yr. award 1980). Home: 3303 6th Ave Council Bluffs IA 51501 Office: Coldwell Banker Action Real Estate 1301 Gold Coast Rd Papillion NE 68046

NEAL, BRENDA JOYCE CHAPLIN, educator, consultant; b. Beaufort, S.C., Mar. 29, 1946; d. Benjamin and Grayce (Horry) Chaplin; m. Danny Phillip Neal, Dec. 21, 1968; children: Keya Danielle, Ryan David. BS, N.C. Cen. U., 1969; postgrad., Cen. Mich. U., Andrews AFB, 1976, Washington Montessori Inst., 1980, Prince George Community Coll., 1987, 88, 89. Tchr. Bonds-Wilson High Sch., North Charleston, S.C., 1968, Am. Learning Ctr., Washington, 1969-73, Project BUILD, Washington, 1972-73, D.C. Skills Ctr., Washington, 1973-77; adminstrv. asst. Capitol Hill Montessori Sch., Washington, 1977-79, dir., 1979-89; program dir. Prince George (Md.) Pub. Schs., 1989; cons. Modern Tech., Prince George County, 1989. Mem. Royal Oak Civic Assn., Landover, Md., 1975, Camp Springs Civic Assn., 1987, Oxon High Sch. PTA, Oxon Hill, 1990, Middleton Valley Home-Sch. Assn., Camp Springs, 1987, PTA-Lord Baltimore Camp Springs; named to mayor's task force Office of Early Childhood Edn., Washington, 1986. Recipient Outstanding Svc. award Ch. of St. Timothy, 1985; named to Supr.'s Hall of Fame Gallaudet U., 1987; named Women In Leadership fellow Jr. League Washington and Coro Found., 1989. Mem. NAFE, Assn. Montessori Internat. U.S.A., N.Am. Montessori Tchrs. Assn., Montessori Adminstrs. Coun., Episcopal Ch. Women (pres. St. Timothy chpt. 1978-80), Daughters of King (v.p. St. Timothy chpt. 1989—), Alpha Kappa Alpha. Democrat. Home: 6306 Shopton Pl Temple Hills MD 20748

NEAL, CONSTANCE, insurance sales representative, underwriter; b. Evansville, Ind., Nov. 20, 1942; d. William Sr. and Marie (Osborne) Ricketts; m. Elijah Neal Sr., Mar. 28, 1959 (div. June 1979); children: Eleanor Marie, Karen Lynn, Elijah Neal Jr. Student, Sawyer Bus. Coll., Hammond, Ind., 1981. Unit sales mgr. Bankers Life & Casualty Co., Merrillville, Ind., 1987-88, sales rep., 1982-87, 89—; instr. Bankers Life & Casualty Co., Northbrook, Ill., 1984. Mem. Nat. Assn. Life Underwriters (Health Ins. Quality award 1990, Nat. Sales Achievement award 1990), Polit. Action Com. of Nat. Assn. Life Underwriters. Office: Bankers Life & Casualty Co 1000 E 80th Pl Ste 316N Merrillville IN 46410

NEAL, JOYCE OLIVIA, utility company executive; b. Jamaica, N.Y., Aug. 11, 1943; d. Nathaniel Grant and Ernestine (Wilson) Thomas; m. Robert Lee Neal Jr., Dec. 16, 1959 (div. Dec. 1972). AAS, SUNY, Farmingdale, 1979; BBA, Hofstra U., 1983. Keypunch operator E.B.S. Data Processing, Amityville, N.Y., 1968-71, asst. supr., 1971-72; keypunch operator Long Island Lighting Co., Hicksville, N.Y., 1972-78, asst. systems designer, 1978-79, assoc. systems designer, 1979-81, systems designer, 1981-84, systems analyst, 1984-85, project leader, 1985-89, sect. supr., 1989—. Tutor Literacy Vols. Am., Nassau County, N.Y., 1988—; vol. United Negro Coll. Fund, Nassau County, 1985—; bd. dirs. Suffolk County Housing Authority, Hauppauge, N.Y., 1985. Walter A. Lynch scholar SUNY, Farmingdale, 1979; recipient Cert. Appreciation, U.S. Assn. Evening Students, 1978-82, nat. sec. 1982. Mem. NAFE, NAACP, Coll. Scholarship Svc. (Cert. Appreciation, Talent Roster 1979), Black Women's Alliance Inc. (co-founder, pres. 1979-81, 84-85, 90—, treas. 1986-89, Appreciation award 1989), Take Off Pounds Sensibly (founder Amityville chpt., leader 1974-78, 81-84, 86-87), Phi Theta Kappa, Alpha Beta Gamma, Alpha Sigma Lambda. Baptist. Office: Long Island Lighting Co 175 Old Country Rd Hicksville NY 11801

NEAL, LEORA LOUISE HASKETT, social services administrator; b. N.Y.C., Feb. 23, 1943; d. Melvin Elias and Miriam Emily (Johnson) Haskett; m. Robert A. Neal, Apr. 23, 1966; children: Marla Patrice, Johnathan Robert. BA in Psychology and Sociology, City Coll. N.Y., 1965; MS in Social Work, Columbia U., 1970, cert. adoption specialist, 1977; IBM cert. community exec. tng. program, N.Y., 1982. Cert. social worker N.Y. state. Caseworker N.Y.C. Dept. Social Service, 1965-67, Windham Child Care, N.Y.C., 1967-73; exec. dir. Assn. Black Social Workers Child Adoption Counseling and Referral Service, N.Y.C., 1975—; cons. adoption, adoption tng. N.Y. State Dept. Social Service, Columbia U. Sch. Social Work, N.Y.C. Human Resources Adminstrn., U. La. New Orleans. Child Welfare League Am. fellow, 1976; recipient cert. No Time to Lose Award N.Y.S. Dept. Social Svcs., 1989. Mem. NAFE, Columbia U. Alumni Assn., City Coll. N.Y. Alumni Assn., Missionary Com. Revival Team (outreach chairperson 1982-88). Democrat. Office: Assn Black Social Workers Adoption Service 271 W 125th St Room 414 New York NY 10027

NEAL, MARGARET RUTH, librarian; b. Murray, Ky., Jan. 29, 1944; d. Thomas Harrison and Ruth (Overbey) Crider; m. Roger Alan Neal, Aug. 7, 1966; children: Roger Thomas, Alana Rene, Brian Wolfe. BSc., Murray State U., Ky., 1966; MSc., U. Ill., Urbana, 1970. Libr. skills tchr. Danville (Ill.) Community Consol. Sch. Dist. #118, 1966-68; libr. East Park Jr. High, Danville, Ill., 1968-71; part-time ref. libr. Danville Pub. Library, Ill., 1972-75; libr. North Ridge Jr. High Sch., Ill., 1972-76; eng. tchr. East Park Middle Sch., Danville, Ill., 1976-87; head lib. Danville High Sch., Ill., 1987--; sch. dist. rep. Instrl. TV., Urbana Ill. 1987; workshop presenter Sch. Reviewer for Sch. Library Journal Book Review, How a Horse Grew Course. Co-pres. Booster Club, Catlin, Ill, 1986—. Recipient Computer Circulation System award Chap. II, 1986-89, Ill. Area IV Grant, 1989. Mem. Am. Library Assn., Nat. Edn. Assn., Ill. Edn. Assn., Danville Edn. Republican. Baptist. Office: Danville High Sch Libr 202 East Fairchild Danville IL 61832

NEAL, MARGARET SHERRILL, writer; b. Memphis, Apr. 13, 1950; d. Wilburn Franklin and Merle Aileen (Willis) N. BA, Memphis State U., 1972, postgrad., 1973; MS, Columbia Pacific U., 1984. Air traffic controller FAA, Memphis, 1974-76, New Bern, N.C., 1976-81, Vero Beach, Fla., 1981-83; detection systems specialist U.S. Customs Service, Miami, 1983-87, intelligence rsch. specialist, 1987-89; ret.; ret., 1989. Mem. Smithsonian Inst., Internat. Oceanographic Found., Mensa, Nat. Trust for Hist. Preservation, Assn. for Rsch. and Enlightenment, Greenpeace, Soc. for the Prevention of Cruelty to Animals, English Speaking Union, Scottish Soc. of Mobile, Clan Macneil Soc. Republican. Presbyterian.

NEAL, MICHELLE LEE, bailbond woman; b. Ft. Wayne, Ind., July 7, 1968; d. Daniel Lynn and Marsha Ann (Beber) Neal; children: Nicholas Khanseng Neal. Grad., Northside High Sch., Ft. Wayne, Ind., 1987. With U.S. R.R. Retirement, Ft. Wayne, Ind., 1987; bailbonding/sec. Jacklee & Assocs., Ft. Wayne, 1988—; notary pub. State of Ind. Mem. Ind. Surety Agts. (adv. bd. 1988—), Taxpayers for Justice. Republican. Home: 2417 E State Blvd Fort Wayne IN 46805

NEAL, TERESA SCHREIBEIS, educator; b. Wheatland, Wyo., Mar. 19, 1956; d. Gene L. and Bonnie Marie (Reed) S.; m. Michael R. Neal, Apr. 7, 1990. BA in Am. Studies, U. Wyo., 1978, BA in English Edn., 1978; MA in History, U. So. Calif., 1989, postgrad., 1989—, Cert. Studies of Women and Men in Soc. Cert. secondary edn. tchr., Wyo. Tchr. lang. arts and social studies, asst. coach Carbon County Sch. Dist. 1, Rawlins, Wyo., 1978-86; asst. lectr. freshmen writing program U. So. Calif., L.A., 1986-90; participant critical thinking and humanities secondary edn. project NEH, Wyo., 1985-86. Mem., chair Reading Is Fundamental Program, Rawlins, 1983-85. Mem. AAUW, Western Assn. Women Historians, G. Autrey Mus. Western Art. Office: U So Calif History Dept University Pk Los Angeles CA 90089-0034

NEDD, PRISCILLA ANNE, motion picture film editor; b. Indpls., Apr. 6, 1955; d. Jerome Hoard and Betty Anne (Dorn) N. AA, Pierce Jr. Coll., Woodland Hills, Calif., 1975. Assoc. film editor An Officer and a Gentleman, Paramount Pictures, Hollywood, Calif., 1981-82; film editor Eddie and the Cruisers Aurora Prodns., Berverly Hills, Calif., 1982-83; The Flamingo Kid ABC Motion Pictures, Century City, Calif., 1984; No Small Affair Columbia Pictures, Burbank, Calif., 1984; Lucas 20th Century Fox Films, Century City, 1985; Street Smart Canon Pictures, Beverly Hills, 1986; Tucker: The Man and His Dream Lucas Films, Nicasio, Calif., 1987-88; Dead Poet's Society Disney Studio, Burbank, Calif., 1989; Pretty Woman, 1989-90, Guilty by Suspicions, Warner Bros., Burbank, 1990. Mem. Motion Picture Editors Guild, Am. Cinema Editors, Acad. Motion Picture Arts and Scis. Office: Harris & Goldberg Agy 2121 Ave of Stars Ste 950 Los Angeles CA 90067

NEDERLANDER, MARJORIE SMITH, interior designer and decorator; b. Springfield, Mo., Nov. 10, 1922; d. Laurence Jabe and Harriet George S.; m. William Howard Breech, Mar. 16, 1945 (div. Sept. 1971); children: William Kimball Breech, Kathryn Breech Raft; m. Harry Jay Nederlander, July 2, 1976. Student, Sullins Coll., 1938-40, U. Mo., 1940-41, Am. Acad. of Dramatic Art, 1941-42. Prin. Marjorie Breech Interiors, Bloomfield Hills, Mich., 1970—; bd. dirs. S.E. region Mich. Nat. Bank of Detroit. Bd. govs. Cransbook Acad. Art, 1987—; trustee, asst. sec. Mich. br. Leukemia Soc. of

Am. 1987—; trustee, exec. com. Detroit Hist. Soc., 1988—. Mem. Village Club. Episcopal.

NEDERVELD, RUTH ELIZABETH, real estate executive; b. Hudsonville, Mich., Oct. 29, 1933; d. Ralph and Hattie (Ploeg) Schut; m. Terrill Lee Nederveld, June 6, 1952; children: Courtland Lee, Valerie Lynn Nederveld Heisey, Darwin Frederic. Degree in Real Estate, U. Mich., 1979; student, Pa. State U., Centre Hall, 1973, Aquinas Coll., Grand Rapids, Mich., 1974; degree, Grad. Realtors Inst., 1979. Cert. residential specialist; registered securities agt. With sales dept. Field Enterprises, Lancaster, Pa., 1962-72; sales assoc. E. James Hogan, Lancaster, 1972-74, C-21 Packard, Grand Rapids, Mich., 1974-80; assoc. broker comml. div. Markland Devel., Inc., Grand Rapids, 1980-86, Am. Acquest Realty, Inc., Grand Rapids, 1986-89; broker, owner R.E. Nederveld Realtors, Ada, Mich., 1989—. Pres. Civic Nucomers of Grand Rapids, 1978; trustee, elder Forest Hills Presbyn. Ch., Cascade, Mich., 1983-86. Mem. Nat. Assn. Realtors (mem. comml. dept. 1973—), Mich. Assn. Realtors, Grand Rapids Real Estate Bd., Woman's Council Realtors (corr. sec. 1986-87), Nat. Assn. Female Execs., Assn. Sales and Mktg. Execs. (exec. dir. internat. chpt. 1977-84, pres. Grand Rapids chpt. 1986-87). Republican. Lodge: Order of Eastern Star. Office: RE Nederveld Realtors 8815 Vergennes NE Ada MI 49301

NEDZA, SANDRA LOUISE, manufacturing executive; b. Chgo., Aug. 20, 1951; d. Thomas and Ina Louise (Wilson) Ingle; m. James Owen Earnest, May 5, 1973 (div. Nov. 1984); m. Ronald Edward Nedza, Nov. 22, 1986; 1 child, Thomas Edward. Student acctg., Met. Sch. Bus., Chgo., 1970. Accounting clk. Gane Bros. & Lane, Inc., Chgo., 1967-72; advanced from expediter to buyer Hammond Organ Co., Chgo., 1972-84; buyer Indsl. Rsch. Products, Inc., Elk Grove Village, Ill., 1984—. Mem. Jobs Daughters, 1967—. Mem. Alpha Iota (scholarship key 1970). Lutheran. Clubs: Juke Box Sno-Riders (sec. 1986-87) (Fox Lake, Ill.), Lakeview Sno-Riders. Lodge: Lioness (v.p. 1985-88, pres. 1988-89) (Chgo.). Home: 1418 S Robert Dr Mount Prospect IL 60056 Office: Indsl Research Products Inc 409-415 Busse Rd Elk Grove Village IL 60007

NEEB, JUDY ANN, school psychologist; b. Elmore, Ohio, Apr. 15, 1937; d. Glen A. and Tavvy C. (Sprought) Druckenmiller; m. Paul E. Neeb, Aug. 10, 1957; children: Derek, Dean, Holli. BS in Edn. cum laude, Bowling Green State U., 1959, MEd, 1964; specialist in arts in pscyhology, Ea. Mich. U., 1981. Cert. tchr., Ohio; cert. sch. psychologist, Mich., Ill. Tchr. Woodville (Ohio) Pub. Schs., 1957-61, sub. tchr., 1961-63, elem. prin., 1963-66; sub. tchr. Woodville Local Schs. and Eastwood Local Schs., 1966-69; ednl. cons. Sandusky County Schs., Fremont, Ohio, 1969-72; elem. prin. Woodmore Local Schs., Woodville, 1979-80; sch. psychologist Saline Sch. Dist., Livonia Pub. Schs., Mich., 1981-83, Wayne-Westland Community Schs., Westland, Mich., 1983-85; sch. psychologist Allendale Resdl. Treatment Ctr., Lake Villa, Ill., 1985-90, ednl. coord., sch. psychologist, 1990—; cons. Allied Pscyhol. Svcs., Vernon Hills, Ill., 1986—. Bd. advisor, writer Kidding Around Mag., Royal Oak, Mich., 1983-85. Bd. dirs. Maumee Valley Girl Scout Council, Toledo, 1957-72, Huron Valley Girl Scout Council, Ypsilanti, Mich., 1972-85; v.p. Ann Arbor Area Assn. for Gifted and Talented, 1981-85; bd. dirs. Washtenow Assn. for Retarded Citizens, Ann Arbor, 1984-85. Named one of Outstanding Young Women In Am., 1970. Mem. APA, Nat. Assn. Sch. Psychologists, Ill. Assn. Sch. Psychologists, Coun. for Exceptional Children, Ill. Assn. Behavior Disorders, AAUW (publicity and membership chair, membership chair Wheeling-Buffalo Grove chpt. 1986—), Beta Sigma Phi, Phi Kappa Phi. Home: 253 Armstrong Dr Buffalo Grove IL 60089 Office: Allendale Treatment Ctr Offield Dr Lake Villa IL 60046

NEECE, OLIVIA HELENE, interior designer; b. L.A., Jan. 3, 1948; d. Robert and Beatrice Pearl Ernst; m. Huntley Lee Bluestein, 1967 (div. 1974); children: Melissa Dawn, Brendon Wade; m. Anthony Ray Neece, Mar. 20, 1977. Cert. interior design, UCLA, 1972-75; BSBA, U. So. Calif., 1990. Cert. Nat. Council Interior Design Qualification; lic. gen. contractor Calif. Staff designer Frances Lux Designs, L.A., 1974; project designer Yates Silverman Inc., L.A., 1974-77; owner Olivia Neece Planning & Design, Tarzana, Calif., 1977-86; v.p. project devel. Design Services/Aircoa, Englewood, Colo., 1986-87; v.p. project adminstrn. Hirsch-Bedner Assoc., Santa Monica, Calif., 1987-88; treas./sec. Eon Corp/Ernst, Luce, Neece Assocs., L.A., 1980—; owner Olivia Neece Planning & Design, Tarzana, 1988—; speaker in field; instr. UCLA Extension Program, 1981-83. Coauthor: A Step by Step Approach to Hotel Development, 1988; conbtr. articles to profl. jours. Vol. restoration San Diego RR Mus., 1985-88. Recipient Holiday Inn Devel. award, Foster City, Calif., 1986, Warwick, R.I., 1988, 1st and 2d place awards Lodging Hospitality Designers Circle, 1987, Gold Key award Russell St. Inn, 1986. Mem. Inst. Bus. Designers (v.p., bd. dirs.), Am. Soc. Interior Designers (1st place award portfolio competition 1974), Illumination Engring. Soc. (1st place residential design 1982), Am. Hotel and Motel Assn., L.A. County Mus. Art (charter mem.), Decorative Arts Coun., Nat. Coun. Interior Design Qualifications. Office: Olivia Neece Planning & Design 18200 Rosita St Tarzana CA 91356

NEECE-BALTARO, LAURA ELIZABETH, marketing executive; b. Washington, Dec. 5, 1951; d. Talmadge Macon and Edith Glenn (Shepherd) Neece; m. Richard Juan Baltaro, Sept. 9, 1972; 1 child, Elizabeth Beatrice. Student, Earlham Coll., 1969-72; BA in Anthropology, Ohio State U., 1974; MBA in Mktg., U. R.I., 1986. Adminstrv. UN Food and Agrl. Orgn., Rome, 1975-83; internship coord. U. R.I., Kingston, R.I., 1984-86; mktg. cons. R.I. Hosp. Trust Nat. Bank, Providence, 1986-87; mgmt. analyst Med. Claims Rev. Svcs., Bethesda, Md., 1988-89; mktg. mgr. and dir. litigation support svcs. Med. Claims Rev. Svcs., Bethesda, 1989—. Liason Jr. Achievement of R.I., Providence, 1985-86. Mem. NAFE, Phi Kappa Phi, Beta Gamma Sigma. Mem. Soc. of Friends. Office: Med Claims Rev Svcs 7910 Woodmont Ave Ste 700 Bethesda MD 20814

NEEDELL, ELISE LOUISE, health agency executive; b. Summit, N.J., Jan. 8, 1957; d. Bernard and Barbara (Pintof) N. BA, Fla. Atlantic U., 1980. Vol. oncology unit John Runnels Hosp. (N.J.), 1978-79; vol. Ctr. for Group Counseling/Cancer Groups, Boca Raton, Fla., 1979-80; counselor Big Bros./Big Sisters, Ft. Lauderdale, Fla., 1980, Sexual Assault Treatment Ctr., Ft. Lauderdale, 1981; pres., chmn. bd. Cancer Counseling Inc., Houston, 1982—; cons. M.D. Anderson Hosp., Hermann Hosp., Am. Cancer Soc., Baylor Coll. Medicine Grand Rounds, Houston Group Psychotherapy Assn., Occupational Nurse Assn. and others. Mem. children's com. Mental Health Orgn., Houston, 1986-89, mem. children's consortium, 1987. Recipient numerous grants Union Pacific Found., Ray C. Fish Found., Meridian Oil, Shell Oil, Fondren Found., Cullen Trust for Health Care, William Stamps Farish Fund, Arthur Anderson & Co., Price Waterhouse Burlington Resources, Vinson & Elkins. Office: Cancer Counseling Inc 2211 N Norfolk Houston TX 77098

NEELD, VAUGHN DELEATH, technical publications editor; b. Denison, Tex., June 15, 1943; d. Ernest Woodrow and Jewel Frances (Thomas) N.; m. David LeRoy Davis, Aug. 19, 1961 (div. Jan. 1974); children: Kerry Dawn, York David, Shan Michelle, Ryan Neeld. Student, Okla. Coll. for Women, 1961-62, Grand Rapids Jr. Coll., 1968-70, Colo. State U., 1971-82, U. Tex., El Paso, 1985-86. Phototypesetter The Estes Park (Colo.) Trail-Gazette, 1973, The Type House, Ft. Collins, Colo., 1973-75, The Triangle Rev., Ft. Collins, 1975-78; editorial asst. U.S. Geol. Survey, Golden, Colo., 1978-79, U.S. Forest Svc., Ft. Collins, 1979-83; editorial asst. U.S. Army, Ft. Bliss, Tex., 1983-84, tech. publ. editor, 1984-86; tech. publ. editor U.S. Army, Ft. Leavenworth, Kans., 1986—; cons. Eng., tutor Colo. State U., Fort Collins, 1978-79, editorial asst., 1980-82. Author numerous poetry; artist: drawing, paintings appeared in The Arts Mag., 1969, exhibited at Christian Art Show, 1966, Luth. Art Show, 1967, Grand Rapids, Larimer County Fair (Best Show, First place), Stone Lion Book Store, 1982 (Third place), Ft. Collins Gallmeyer and Livingston Mfg. Co. Logo Contest, 1968 (Second place); photographer one woman show Rocky Mountain Forest and Range Experiment Sta., 1981, exhibited at Larimer County Fair, 1982 (Second place), Western Camera Photography Contest, 1983 (First place); singer: Okla. Coll. for Women Chorus, 1961-62, Ft. Collins Lyric Opera "Carmen" 1982, Parkville, Mo. Philharm., 1988; make up artist River City Community Players, Leavenworth, Kans., 1988. Instr. water safety ARC, Grand Rapids, Mich., 1967-70, Estes Park, 1971-73, Boy Scouts Am., Ft. Collins, 1973-76; vol. instr. water therapy for the physically impaired, Ft. Leavenworth, 1986-88; photographer, artist, archivist, vol. Hueco Tanks State Park, El Paso, 1983-84; vol. dirt mover Coe Lake Pueblo Archeological Dig., Ft. Bliss, 1985; mem. Human Rels. Commn., 1989-90. Mem. Smithsonian Assocs., Officers Club Ft. Leavenworth, Ancient Mystical Order Rosae Crucis. Mem. Ch. of Christ. Home: 622 Pawnee Leavenworth KS 66048 Office: Doctrinal Lit Mgmt Office US Command and Gen Staff Coll Rm 207 Bell Hall Fort Leavenworth KS 66017

NEELY, KAREN S., computer programmer; b. Landsdowne, Pa., Oct. 18, 1962; d. William Merguard and Alice Martha (Foster) N. Student, Delaware County Community Coll., Media, Pa., 1982-84; cert. in computer programming, Computer Learning Ctr., Phila., 1990. Interviewer, clk., telemarket rep. Chilton Rsch. Svcs., Radnor, Pa., 1983-86; secondary market specialist Main Line Fed. Savs. Bank, Villanova, Pa., 1987-88; mortgage loan post closer Norwest Mortgage, King of Prussia, Pa., 1988-89; computer programmer Conrail Corp., Phila., 1990—; SIG leader King of Prussia mini-bd. BBS, 1990—. Contbr. poetry to anthology and lit. mag. Mem. Data Processing Mgmt. Assn., Assn. for Women in Computing, Women in Info. Processing. Home: 132-A Conestoga Rd Wayne PA 19087 Office: Conrail Corp 32d and Market Sts Philadelphia PA 19104-2849

NEELY, KIMBERLY DORRISTENE, marketing professional; b. Chgo., Sept. 15, 1964; d. Samuel Morse and Dorristene (Hillard) N.; m. Alex Duval du Buclet, Aug. 12, 1989. BS in Mktg., U. Ill., 1987; MBA in Mktg., U. Chgo., 1989. Advt. intern Gen. Motors Corp., Detroit, 1988; mktg. analyst AT&T, Oak Brook, Ill., 1989—. Gen. Motors Corp. fellow, 1987-89. Mem. NAFE, Inroads Alumni, Alpha Kappa Psi. Home: 360 E Randolph St #1404 Chicago IL 60601 Office: AT&T 1111 W 22d St Oak Brook IL 60521

NEESON, MARGARET GRAHAM, writer; b. Toronto, Ontario, Canadian, Dec. 27, 1918; Arrived in US 1943; d. Francis Ronald and Helen Marguerite (Phelan) G.; m. Jack McHenry, July 31, 1918; 1 child, John David. BA, McGill U., Montreal, 1936-40; BS, Columbia Sch. of Journalism, N.Y.C., 1942-43. Proof reporter Standard Times, Sherbrooke, Quebec, 1940-41; reporter New Bedford Standard Times, 1943-44; pub. relations Cleve. Health Museum, 1946-48; instr. Henry W. Grady Sch., Athens; movie researcher Dixie Mag., Athens, Ga., 1948-49; pub. relations Carolina Art Assn., S.C., 1949-50; feature writer News & Courier, Charleston, 1950-52; assoc. editor The Skipper Mag., Annapolis, Md., 1954-71; Freelance writer 1971--. Author: On Solid Granite, 1974, Marguerite's Story, 1990; contbr. articles to profl. jours. Episcopalian. Address: Box 143 Spruce Head ME 04859

NEFF, ARLENE MERLE, investment business owner; b. Pitts., Dec. 11, 1946; d. Arthur Merle and Agnes May (Mapes) Neff; m. Raymond Louis Clark, Oct. 19, 1968 (div. 1976). BS, U. Pitts., 1975, MBA, 1981. Ops. rsch. analyst steel div. USX Corp., Pitts., 1969-73, market rsch. analyst, 1973-79, sr. staff analyst planning, 1979-81, mktg. specialist, 1981-82; registered rep. Parker/Hunter Inc., Pitts., 1983-87; prin. A. Neff Assocs., Pitts., 1987—; bd. dirs. Pitts. Countywide Corp., chmn. loan rev. com., 1989—. Mem. loan rev. com. Urban Redevel., Pitts., 1985-88; chmn. Women-In-Touch, Pitts., 1988; planning chair Women-In-Touch Invitational, 1986-87, mem. steering com., 1985-90; fin. chair Career Network Day, Pitts., 1986. Mem. Nat. Assn. Women Bus. Owners (bd. dirs. Pitts. chpt. 1985-88), Internat. Assn. for Fin. Planning, Pitts. Assn. for Fin. Planning (bd. dirs., pub. awareness chmn. 1990—), Downtown Neighborhood Assn., Zonta Internat. (fin. chmn. Pitts. chpt. 1985-87, 89—, bd. dirs. Pitts. chpt. 1987-88), River's Club. Office: A Neff Assocs Washington Pla Pittsburgh PA 15219

NEFF, BARBARA ESTELLA, engineer; b. Cumberland, Md., Feb. 20, 1950; d. Jesse Wilson and Marianna (Brant) N. BSME, U. Ariz., 1972; MS in Engring., U. Mich., 1977; Student, Chrysler Inst., 1974. Mechanical engr. Chrysler Corp., Highland Park, Mich., 1972-74; assembly engr. Hughes Aircraft Co., Tucson, 1974-75; materials engr. Chrysler Corp., Highland Park, 1975-77; product planner Ford Motor Co., Dearborn, Mich., 1977-82; sr. staff engr. Mack Trucks, Inc., Allentown, Pa., 1987--; instr. U. N.C., Charlotte, 1983-87. Pres. Sharon Hills Heighborhood Assn., Charlotte, 1985-87. Mem. Soc. Automotive Engrs. (chmn. 1989, disting. younger mem. 1986). Office: Mack Truck Inc 2100 Mack Blvd Allentown PA 18105

NEHLSEN, KERRI SAVAGE, speech-language pathologist; b. Bklyn., Sept. 19, 1961; d. Patrick Francis Savage and Joanne Rose (Cartisano) Gonnella; m. Michael James Nehlsen, Apr. 25, 1986. BA, St. John's U., Jamaica, N.Y., 1983; MS, Bklyn. Coll., N.Y., 1985. Speech pathologist, cons. Guild for Exceptional Children, Bklyn., 1984-90; classroom speech therapist League Sch., Bklyn., 1984-86, clinical speech pathologist, 1985-89; dept. coordinator of clinical speech services High Road Sch., East Brunswick, N.J., 1989—; supr. High Rd. Sch., East Brunswick, N.J., 1989—; therapy coord. Pace Clin. Svcs., 1989—. Recipient Mayor's Vol. Youth Coun. award Mayor's Office of N.Y.C., 1983. Mem. Am. Speech Lang. Hearing Assn., N.J. Speech Lang. Hearing Assn. Republican. Roman Catholic. Home: 136 Wilcox Ct Matawan NJ 07747 Office: High Rd Sch 11 Lexington Ave East Brunswick NJ 08816

NEIBAUER, BONNIE VIRGINIA, cardiac surgery nurse; b. Takoma Park, Md., Feb. 4, 1951; d. Robert Alfred and Alice Maree (Crews) Deutsch; m. Ray Neibauer, June 20, 1972; 1 child, Bonny Brooke. BS in Nursing, Columbia Union Coll., 1973; MS in Nursing, Cath. U. of Am., 1982. Critical care nurse II, III Washington Adventist Hosp., Takoma Park, 1972-73, critical care nurse I, asst. head nurse, 1974-78, clin. instr. open heart, 1978-81, head nurse cardiac surgery, 1981—; adj. faculty sch. nursing Columbia Union Coll., Takoma Park, 1978—; cons. Makati (Philippines) Med. Ctr. Cardiac Surgery Team, 1989—; instr. Am. Lung Assn., Washington, 1981. V.p. Greencastle Lakes Homeowners Assn., Burtonsville, Md., 1986, 87. Mem. NAFE, Am. Assn. Critical Care Nurses (pres. Greater Washington area chpt. 1983-84, program chairperson 1982-83), Am. Heart Assn., Mended Hearts. Republican. Home: 3668 Turbridge Dr Burtonsville MD 20866 Office: Washington Adventist Hosp 7600 Carroll Ave Takoma Park MD 20912

NEIDHART, CAROL LYNN, medical oncology representative; b. Mt. Vernon, OH, Sept. 18, 1953; d. Clair Edwin and Merry Evelyn (Burke) Neidhart. BA, Miami U., Oxford, Ohio, 1975. Sr. med. rep. CIBA-Geigy Co., Summit, N.J., 1976—; clin. conf. moderator, 1980—; speaker Pharm. Mfrs. Assn. Mem. Nat. Assn. Female Execs. Republican. Methodist. Home: 90 Blenheim Rd Columbus OH 43214

NEIL, JESSIE PRUITT, business executive, civic worker; b. Pasadena, Calif., Oct. 20, 1927; d. Cecil D. and Jessie (Parsons) Pruitt; BA, U. So. Calif., 1950; m. Edmund R. Neil, Mar. 24, 1956; children: Edmund R. II, Jessica R., Richard William. Dir. design Leland Gardens Bldg. Corp., 1950-56; sales dir. Washington Sq. Bldg. Corp., 1950-52; pres. Barrett Devel. Corp., 1951-70; sec. Reliance Bldg. Corp., 1951-68; self-employed home designer, 1953; sec. So. Counties Escrow, 1956-77; pres. Futuramic Homes, Inc., 1956-68, Desert and Delta Safaris, Inc., Desert and Delta Safaris Pty. Ltd., Botswana, Africa, Desert and Delta Air Svcs., Mokoro Holdings Ltd., Maun Properties. Founder Cardiac League, Guild of Huntington Meml. Hosp., 1963; pres. Cardiac League, 1966-68, pres. Women's Council, 1967; v.p. San Marino League, 1968-73; pres. docent council Pasadena Art Mus., 1971-72; mem. Costume Council L.A. County Mus.; assoc. U. So. Calif.; patron, mem. membership council Pasadena Art Mus.; mem. Founders L.A. Music Ctr.; hon. life mem. Arcadia Meth. Hosp.; Blue Ribbon 400 of L.A. Music Ctr. Recipient graphics award Pasadena Arts Council, 1968; Eve award. Mem. World Affairs Council, Internat. Platform Assn., Fellows Pasadena Art Mus., Assistance League So. Calif., Nine O'Clock Players, Delta Zeta. Home: 500 E Del Mar Apt 34 Pasadena CA 91101 Office: Pvt Bag 10, Maun Botswana

NEIMAN, TANYA MARIE, lawyer; b. Pitts., June 28, 1949; d. Max and Helen (Lamaga) N. AB, Mills Coll., 1970; JD, U. Calif. Hastings Coll. of Law, San Francisco, 1974. Bar: Calif. 1975. Law assoc. Boalt Hall U. Calif., Berkeley, 1974-76; pub. defender State of Calif., San Francisco, 1976-81; assoc. gen. counsel, dir. vol. legal services Bar Assn. San Francisco, 1982—. Mem. ABA (speaker 1985—, Harrison Tweed award 1985), Calif. Bar Assn. (exec. com. 1984—, legal svcs. sect.), Golden Gate Bus. Assn. Found. (v.p. grant making 1985—), Nat. Conf. Women and Law (speaker 1975—), Nat. Lawyers Guild, Socorro Soc. (sec. 1989—). Office: Bar Assn San Francisco 685 Market St San Francisco CA 94105

NEIMARK, TANYA LEE, broadcast executive; b. Chgo., June 18, 1960; d. Philip John Neimark and Eileen Penny (Bank) Dolnick. BA in Communications, Columbia Coll., 1983; postgrad., Colo. Coll., 1977-78. Dir. on-air promotion WGN-TV, Chgo., 1979-83; mgr. creative svcs. Twentieth Century Fox, L.A., 1977; dir. creative svcs. Tribune Entertainment, Chgo., 1988—. editor newsletter That's Entertainment, 1988—. Bd. dirs. Cinema/Chgo. Mem. NAFE, Nat. Assn. Broadcast Mktg. Execs. (program distributors adv. bd. 1988—, Gold Medallion award 1986, 88, 89). Office: Tribune Entertainment 435 N Michigan Ave Chicago IL 60611

NEIMARK, VASSA, interior architect; b. Miami, Fla., Dec. 9, 1954; d. William Rolla and Bettijean (Davison) Meyer; m. Philip John Neimark, Oct. 29, 1982. Student, Art Inst. Ft. Lauderdale, 1974, Art Inst. Chgo., 1980. Owner, prin. The Vassa Group, Ltd. (formerly Vassa Internat. Ltd.), Chgo., 1979—. Contbr. articles to local mag. Bd. dirs. Mric Michael Med. Found., Chgo., Expressways Mus., Chgo., Orchard Village Home for Retarded Adults, Park Ridge Youth Campus, Des Plaines, Ill. Recipient Star on Horizon award Chgo. Mdse. Mart-Chgo. Design Sources, 1985, Spl. Recognition in Design award, 1987. Mem. Internat. Soc. Interior Designer (bd. dirs. 1985-86), Women in Design Industry, IFA Found. North Am. (v.p.), Carlton Club, Club Internat. Office: The Vassa Group Ltd 224 E Ontario Chicago IL 60611

NEJELSKI, MARILYN M., civil rights advocate; b. Horton, Kans., July 12, 1934; d. Ray Leonard Mills and Bonnie Marie (Davis) Westberg; m. Paul Arthur Nejelski, Oct. 2, 1965; children: Nicole Rena, Stephen Downing. BA, George Wash. U., 1957; MA, NYU, 1974. Libr. asst. Washington Post, Washington, 1957-58; adminstrv. asst. White House Congl. Rels., Washington, 1961-64; intelligence rsch. analyst Dept. State, Washington, 1964-68; rsch. analyst Fed. Trade Commn., Washington, 1979-80; appointments sec. Nat. Women's Polit. Caucus, Washington, 1980-85; rsch. and project devel. Ind. Cons., Bethesda, Md., 1985-87; exec. dir. Women Judges' Fund for Justice, Washington, 1987—. Contbr. articles to profl. jours. Mem. Washington Bar Study Com. on Gender Bias in Cts., 1987-89. Recipient awd. Women's Action Orgn., State/ICA/AID, 1981, Superior Hon. awd. Dept. State, 1966. Mem. Asia Soc. Roman Catholic. Office: Women Judges' Fund Justice 733 15th St NW 700 Washington DC 20816

NELIPOVICH, SANDRA GRASSI, artist; b. Oak Park, Ill., Nov. 22, 1939; d. Alessandro and Lena Mary (Ascareggi) Grassi; m. John Nelipovich Jr., Aug. 19, 1973. BFA in Art Edn., U. Ill., 1961; postgrad., Northwestern U., 1963, Gonzaga U., Florence, Italy, 1966, Art Inst. Chgo., 1968; diploma, Accademia Universale Alessandro Magno, Prato, Italy, 1983. Tchr. art Edgewood Jr. High Sch., Highland Park, Ill., 1961-62, Emerson Sch. Jr. High Sch., Oak Park, 1962-77; batik artist Calif., 1977—; illustrator Jolly Robin Publ. Co., Anaheim, Calif., 1988—; supr. student tchrs., Oak Park, 1970-75; adult edn. tchr. ESL, ceramics, Medinah, Ill., 1974; mem. curriculum action group on Human Dignity, EEO workshop demonstrator, Oak Park, 1975-76; guest lectr. Muckenthaler Ctr., Fullerton, Calif., 1980, Niguel Art Group, Dana Point, Calif., 1989, Anaheim Hills Women's Club, 1990; fabric designer for fashion designer Barbara Jax, 1987. One-woman shows include Lawry's Calif. Ctr., Los Angeles, 1981-83, Whittier (Calif.) Mus., 1985-86, Anaheim (Calif.) Cultural Ctr., 1986-88, Ill. Inst. Tech., Chgo., 1989, Muckenthaler Cultural Ctr., Fullerton, 1990; also gallery exhibits in Oak Brook, Ill., 1982, La Habra, Calif., 1983; represented in permanent collections McDonald's Corp., Oak Brook, Ill., Glenkirk Sch., Deerfield, Ill., Emerson Sch., Oak Park, Ill., and in galleries in Laguna Beach, Calif., Maui, Hawaii, Mich., N.J.; illustrator for Jolly Robin Pub. Co., Anaheim, 1988—; poster designer Saratoga Fine Arts Show, 1989. Recipient numerous awards, purchase prizes, 1979—. Mem. AAUW (hospitality chmn. 1984-85), Oak Park Art League, Orange Art Assn. (jury chairperson 1980), Anaheim Art Assn., Muckenthaler Ctr. Circle. Roman Catholic. Club: Anaheim Hills Women's. Home and Office: 5922 Calle Cedro Anaheim CA 92807

NELLESSEN, ROBYN CELESTE, environmental laboratory official; b. Paterson, N.J., Sept. 24, 1956; d. John Paul and Carmella A. (Padula) N. BA in Biology, William Paterson Coll., 1978. Lic. sewerage treatment plant operator. Lab. technician Edward R. Grich Inc., Pequannock, N.J., 1981-85; lab. mgr., supr. Two Bridges Sewerage Authority, Lincoln Park, N.J., 1985—. Mem. Am. Chem. Soc., Water Pollution Control Fedn. (aux.). Home: 3 Ackerson Ave Pequannock NJ 07440 Office: Two Bridges Sewerage Lincoln Blvd Lincoln Park NJ 07035

NELLIGAN, KATHERINE ROSALIE, nurse, educator; b. Balt., Nov. 23, 1938; d. Joseph Ross and Katherien Marie (Kennedy) Prevost; m. Maurice John Nelligan, Sept. 22, 1962; children: Margaret Rosalie, Joseph Maurice, Elizabeth Marie. BS, Upsala Coll., E. Orange, N.J., 1988; postgrad., Kean Coll., Union, N.J., 1988-90; Dipl. in Nursing, Mercy Hosp., Balt., 1959. RN, N.J. Neonatal staff Mercy Hosp., Balt., 1959-60; pediatric head Children's Hosp., Balt., 1960-61; staff STewart & Co., Balt., 1961-62; pediatric office nurse Drs. Bauerschaub & Besson, Catonsville, Md., 1962-63; sch. nurse The Center Sch., Warren, N.J., 1978-79, 86-87; nurse/substitute tchr. Warren Twp. Sch., 1983-89; athletic office mgr. The Pingry Sch., Warren, 1989—. Author poetry. Lector, mem. choir Our Lady of the Mt. Parish, Warren, 1975—; library aide Warren Twp. Libr., 1983-87; active N.J. Right to Life; vice chmn. Friends of the Warren Libr., 1984-85. Recipient John Fetting award for excellence in bedside nursing Mercy Hosp., 1959. Mem.AAUW (telephone chmn. 1989—, Mature Woman's scholar, 1987), League for Ednl. Advancement of RN's (bd. dirs., librarian). Republican. Roman Catholic. Home: 154 Mountainview Rd Warren NJ 07060 Office: The Pingry School Martinsville Rd Martinsville NJ 08836

NELSON, AGNES MIRIAM, chemicals executive; b. Timisoara, Romania, Jan. 16, 1951; came to U.S., 1978.; d. Emery Gustav and Lillian (Roth) Weisz; m. Clinton D. Nelson, Apr. 26, 1975. Student, U. Timisoara, 1973-76, Loyola U., Chgo., 1979-84, Roosevelt U., Chgo., 1984-85. Lab asst. Detergent Co., Timisoara, 1970-71; assembly line worker Electromotor Co., Timisoara, 1971-73; color matcher Ferro Corp., Chgo., 1979-81; offset print researcher A.B. Dick Co., Niles, Ill., 1981-83; coatings researcher Desoto Co., Des Plaines, Ill., 1983-85; office mgr. CD Nelson Mfg. Co., Chgo., 1985-86; pres. Jewelers Equipment & Tools, Chgo., 1986—; translator Cosmopolitan Bur., Chgo., 1982—, Interlingua, Ltd., Chgo., 1982—; psychic cons. Pvt. and Groups, Skokie, 1981-87; tchr. Hebrew Beginners and Advanced, 1973. Contbr. articles to profl. jours. Leader Girl Scouts U.S., Timisoara, 1962-68, Youth Orgn., Timisoara, 1968-70. Mem. Am. Bus. Women (award of honor 1981), Nat. Assn. Female Execs., Nat. Assn. Future Women. Republican. Jewish. Office: Jewelers Equipment & Tools 5 N Wabash Suite 818 Chicago IL 60602

NELSON, ALICE ELIZABETH HILL, museum docent; b. Oakland, Calif., Jan. 19, 1921; d. George Clayton Hill and Netha Alice (Hall) Hill-Kinkead; m. James Walter Nelson, Jr., June 13, 1942; children: James W. III, Georgeanne Cusic, Susan Brewster, Karen McCormick, Marjorie Moon. BA, U. Calif., Berkeley, 1942; BFA, Cardinal Stritch Coll., 1968. Pres. Literary League, Meadville, Pa., 1972-74; docent Milw. Art Mus., 1978—, lectr. Art History, 1984—; artist in residence Herb Soc. Am., Milw., 1975-85. One woman show, paintings, sculptures Studio San Damiano, Milw., 1968; two women show, paintings, sculptures Meadville, Pa., 1973. Bd. dirs. Milw. Symphony Women's League, 1960-69. Named Docent of Year Milw. Art Mus., 1984. Mem. League of Milw. Artists, AAUW (bd. dirs., sec. Wis. chpt. 1963-66), Women's Club of Wis. (Art Com. 1987-89), Alpha Omicron Pi, Prytanean (pres. 1941-42). Republican. Episcopalian. Home: 3366 N Lake Dr Milwaukee WI 53211 Studio: N67 W32426 Wildwood Pt Rd Hartland WI 53029

NELSON, AMERICA ELIZABETH, pediatrician; b. Chgo., Apr. 9, 1932; d. Lorenzo Raymond and Blanche Juanita (Crawford) Nelson; A.B. in English, U. Mich., Ann Arbor, 1952, M.S. in Zoology, 1954; postgrad. Tenn. State U., 1952-53, U. Chgo., 1955-56; M.D., Howard U., 1961; M.P.H., U. Ill., 1973. Intern, Hahnemann Med. Sch. and Hosps., Phila., 1961-62; resident pediatrics Michael Reese Hosp., Chgo., 1962-63, U. Mich., Ann Arbor, 1964; practice medicine specializing in pediatric cardiology, Detroit, 1963; with father, practice medicine specializing in pediatrics, Baldwin,

Mich., 1964-71, 75—; pediatrician Tice Clinic, U. Ill., Cook County Hosp., 1965, 66; pediatrician Mile's Sq. Health Center, Chgo., 1967; pediatrician Infant Welfare Soc., Chgo., 1968; cons. pediatrician, child devel. Kalamazoo Child Guidance Clinic, 1969-70, coordinator drug abuse program, 1969-70; med. dir. Chgo. Residential Manpower Center, 1971-72; pediatrician, child devel. Dyslexia Meml. Inst., Chgo., 1972—; founder, project dir., med. dir. Deerwood Developmental Center, Inc., Cherry Valley Twp., Lake County, Mich.; lectr. U. Ill. at Chgo. Circle, 1972-73; clin. instr. U. Ill.-Presbyn.-St. Luke's Hosp.; asst. prof. Mental Retardation Inst., N.Y. Med. Coll., 1974; cons. in field. Mem. AAAS, Pi Lambda Theta. Contbr. articles to profl. jours. Home: PO Box 760 Baldwin MI 49304

NELSON, ANGELA ROBINSON, corporate adminstrative coordinator; b. Macon, Ga., Oct. 8, 1956; d. James and Addie (Zellner) Robinson; m. Hardrick Nelson, Aug. 12, 1979. BS, Ga. Southwestern Coll., 1978. Corp. operator Macon (Ga.) Coll., 1978-79; sec. Med. Ctr. Cen. Ga., Macon, 1979-80, exec. sec., 1980-90; owner Your Bus. Specialist, Macon, 1983—; corp. adminstrv. coord. Hemlock Anesthesia Assocs., Macon, 1983—. V.p. Delta Sigma Theta, Ga. Southwestern Coll., Americus, 1977; song leader, mem. New St. James Lodge #340, Macon, 1980—; asst. tchr. Greater Turner Tabernacle AME Ch. Sun. Sch., Macon, 1973-81. Recipient Outstanding Young Women Am. award, 1985, Cert. of Recognition Bethel AME Ch., 1984-89, Pres.'s Fitness award Southwest High Sch., 1972, Profl. Performance award, 1990; named 2000 Notable Am. Women, 1990. Mem. Am. Soc. Profl. & Exec. Women, Nat. Notary Assn., NAFE, Bethel Gospel Choir, Greater Turner Tabernacle A.M.E. Ch., W.R. Wilkes Club, M.A.D.D. (program chairwoman 1985—). Democrat. Methodist. Home: 15C Chatfield Dr Stone Mountain GA 30083

NELSON, APRIL LYNN, librarian; b. Plainfield, N.J., May 17, 1960; d. Ralston J. and Eileen M. (Creed) N. BA in Econs., Kean Coll. N.J., 1983; MPA, Calif. State U., 1986; MLS, Rutgers U., 1988. Substitute tchr. Long Beach Island Consolidated Sch. Dist., Surf City, N.J., 1986—, Barnegat (N.J.) Unified Sch. Dist., 1987—; substitute media specialist Pinelands Regional High Sch., Tuckerton, N.J., 1987; collection devel. asst. Georgian Court Coll., Lakewood, N.J.; library page Ocean County Library, Ship Bottom, N.J., 1988; reference libr. County of L.A. Pub. Libr. Manhattan Beach Br. Libr., 1989—. Author: pub. awareness media slogans, Crime, 1986. Life mem. Long Beach Hist. Soc., Beach Haven, N.J., 1987, dir. pub. service announcements, WKNJ AM Radio Sta., Union, 1982-83. Mem. AAUW, N.J. Library Assn., Am. Soc. Pub. Adminstrn., Am. Library Assn., Western Govtl. Research Assn., Calif. State U. Sailing Assn. Republican. Episcopalian. Home: 5241 E The Toledo Long Beach CA 90803

NELSON, ARLENE B., state legislator; b. Doniphan, Nebr., July 15, 1925; m. Milford R. Nelson, 1946; children: Donna, Dennis. Student, U. Nebr. Sales mgr. Morton Aircraft, Omaha, 1942-46; bookkeeper Twin Rivers Co., Grand Island, Nebr., 1946-53; farmer, 1953-82; program asst. Agrl. Stabilization Conservation Service, 1983-84; mem. Nebr. State Legislature, 1984—. Mem. LWV. Democrat. Methodist. Office: 3127 Woodridge Blvd Grand Island NE 68801*

NELSON, ARLENE CASSELL, disability analyst; b. Port Chester, N.Y., May 27, 1952; d. Curtis Emmett and Rose (Lucente) Cassell; m. Alan S. Nelson, May 13, 1989. BA, SUNY, Cortland, 1974, MA, 1975; cert. labor studies, George Meany Ctr., 1987; cert. fin. studies, Fairfield U., 1980. Tchr. jr. high sch. English Homer Cen. Sch., N.Y., 1975-76; parent effectiveness trainer Cortland County, N.Y., 1976-77; tchr. sr. high sch. English DeRuyter Cen. Sch., N.Y., 1977-79; internal auditor Village Savs. Bank, Port Chester, N.Y., 1979-81; instr. Am. Inst. Banking, White Plains, N.Y., 1980-81; disability analyst N.Y. State Social Svcs., Albany, N.Y., 1981—. Editor: (newsletter) Shop Talk, 1985-87. March of Dimes, bd. dirs., 1987-88, vol. trainer, 1986; Am. Heart Assn., vol. 1985; mem. N.Y. Pub. Int. Rsch. Group, 1986-89. Mem. Nat. Assn. Disability Examiners, Internat. Found. Employee Benefits, Svc. Employees Internat. Union, Pub. Employees Fedn. (exec. bd. 1984—, contract negotiatior 1987-88, adminstr. 1985—, shop steward 1981—). Democrat. Roman Catholic. Home: 9 Abbott Dr Poestenkill NY 12140

NELSON, BARBARA ANNE, lawyer; b. Mineola, N.Y., Jan. 16, 1951; d. Richard William and Dorothee Helen (Thorne) N. BA, Inter Am. U. P.R., 1972; JD, New Eng. Sch. Law, 1975. Legal editor Prentice Hall Pub. Co., Englewood Cliffs, N.J., 1976-77; assoc. Antonio C. Martinez Law Firm, N.Y.C., 1977-79, Pollack & Kramer, N.Y.C., 1979-83; pvt. practice N.Y.C., 1983-90; sr. ptnr. Nelson & Turkhud, N.Y.C., 1990—. Author, speaker tng. film. Mem. ACLU, Am. Immigration Lawyers Assn., Legal Aid Soc. N.Y., Amnesty Internat., Asia Soc. Home: 324 W 14th St Apt 5-A New York NY 10014 Office: Nelson & Turkhurd 132 Nassau St Ste 219 New York NY 10038

NELSON, BARBARA KAY, insurance agent, financial services consultant; b. Dayton, Ohio, May 20, 1947; d. Orville James and Catherine Ann (Pentenburg) Weber; m. Theodore Joseph Nelson II, Nov. 8, 1969; children—Theodore Joseph III, Jason Michael. B.A., U. Dayton, 1969; M.A., Webster U., 1985. TV co-host Sta. WHIO-TV, Dayton, 1969; dept. mgr. Elder-Beerman, Dayton, 1969-70; customer service rep. Ohio Bell Telephone, Dayton, 1970; adminstrv. coordinator AmeriSource, San Antonio, 1984-86; agt. N.Y. Life Ins., 1986-89; sales mgr. John Hancock Fin. Svcs., 1989—. chair bd. San Antonio Women's C. of C. Tex., 1988—; sec. bd. dirs. Network Power Tex., 1987—. Mem. exec. bd. Oak Grove Elementary Sch. PTA, San Antonio, 1981-83; mem. San Antonio Assn. Life Underwriters, San Antonio C. of C., religious edn. com. St. Mark's Ch., San Antonio, 1983-84; mem. North San Antonio Chamber/Pub. Art, 1984-85. Mem. Nat. Assn. Female Execs. Club: FLW Officers Wives (pres. 1980-81). Avocations: art; jogging; bicycling; racquetball; reading.

NELSON, BONNIE KAY, educator; b. Paso Robles, Calif., Aug. 3, 1950; d. Vernon Carroll and Hilda Marie (Engelke) N. Degree in standard elem. edn., Calif. Poly. State U., San Luis Obispo, 1973, cert. early childhood edn., 1976. Tchr. kindergarten Paso Robles Union Elem. Sch. Dist., 1973—; sch. improvement project coordinator Paso Robles Union Elem. Sch. Dist., 1980-83, sch. site council chmn., 1981-82. Recipient Svc. award, Paso Robles PTA, 1983; named Outstanding Young Educator for Paso Robles, 1985, Outstanding Young Educator for State Calif., 1986. Mem. Paso Robles Tchrs. Assn. (pres. 1980-82), Computer Using Educators, Cen. Coast Math. Coun., North County Athletic Assn. (exec. bd. 1987—), San Luis Obispo Antique Bottle Soc. (communications officer 1980—), Phi Delta Kappa, Delta Kappa Gamma (communications officer 1988-90, K-1 mentor tchr. 1988—). Republican. Baptist. Home: 124 21st St Paso Robles CA 93446

NELSON, CANDACE THERASE, accountant; b. N.Y.C., Mar. 23, 1961; d. Bernard John and Joan Theresa (Dannic) N. BBA, Pace U., 1983. CPA, N.Y. Sr. acct. Ernst & Whinney, N.Y.C., 1983-85, Gencorp/RKO Gen., N.Y.C., 1985-87; sr. auditor Times Mirror Co., Hackensack, N.J., 1987-89; operational acctg. mgr. Univision, Inc., Secaucus, N.J., 1989—. Office: Univision Inc 24 Meadowland Pkwy Secaucus NJ 07094

NELSON, CAROL ANN, systems analyst; b. Long Branch, N.J., Oct. 21, 1952; d. Robert Morse Sr. and Helen (Jeter) Leonard; children: Anthony Kenneth, Brandy Nicole. BA magna cum laude, St. Mary's U., San Antonio, 1979. Configuration mgmt. specialist Analytics, Inc., Tinton Falls, N.J., 1984-86; computer systems analyst Dept. of Defense, 1986-88; systems requirements analyst Unisys Corp., Eatontown, N.J., 1988-89; computer systems analyst U.S. Army, 1989—. Lt. USN, 1980-84. Xerox scholar. Mem. NAFE, Armed Forces Communications Electronics Assn. Democrat. Methodist. Office: Commander CECOM Amsel Rd SE AIN TP Fort Monmouth NJ 07703

NELSON, CAROLE ANN, merchandise manager; b. Detroit, Dec. 27, 1941; d. Harold R. and Kathleen M. (McCauley) N. BS, Wayne State U., Detroit, 1965. Owner, operator Tour Today, Detroit, 1969-71; salesperson Mt. Vernon Mills Inc.; mdse. advisor GSUSA, N.Y.C., 1971-78; mdse. mgr. infants products Riegel Consumer Products Div. Mt. Vernon Mills Inc., Johnston, S.C., 1978—. Mem. NAFE, Network Augusta, Univ. Hosp. Women's Vol. Bd. Office: PO Box E Johnston SC 29832

NELSON, CLARA SINGLETON, aerospace company executive; b. Union Ridge, Tenn., Apr. 10, 1935; d. Ernest Caldwell and Willie Emma (Hord) Singleton; m. Joe Edward Nelson, July 26, 1953; children: Drexel Edward, Dorissia Lynett. Student Tenn. State U., 1961-62, Middle Tenn. State U., 1974; AS, Motlow Coll., 1978. Cert. personnel specialist. Sec., adminstrv. asst. Bedford County Sch., Shelbyville, Tenn., 1957-64; sec., personnel asst. Aro, Inc., Arnold Air Force Sta., Tenn., 1964-71; mem. pub. relations staff, job interviewer Employment Security, Shelbyville, 1971-81; personnel rep. Calspan Corp., Arnold Air Force Sta., 1981—; mem. adv. bd. Tenn. Area Vocat. Sch., Shelbyville, 1979—, Bedford Moore Vocat. Ctr., Shelbyville, 1979—; cons., dir. Career Devel. Workshops, Shelbyville. Chmn. adv. commn. Equal Employment Opportunity, 1983—, improvement com. Tullahoma Job Service, Tenn., 1985—; mem. Tenn. Gov.'s Better Schs. Com., 1985—; mem. Patrons Council Argie Cooper Library, Shelbyville; Bus. Adv. Group Motlow State Coll., Tullahoma; trustee Motlow Coll. Found. Recipient cert. of appreciation ARC, 1985. Mem. Highland Rim Personnel Assn. (treas. 1983-84, 87, sec. 1988, chair program com. 1989), Nat. Assn. Female Execs. (network dir. 1985), Tenn. State U. Cluster (chmn. com. 1984—), Tenn. Placement Assn. Club: Better Homes and Gardens (v.p. Shelbyville). Methodist. Avocations: reading, gardening. Home: 118 Scotland Heights Shelbyville TN 37160 Office: Calspan Corp Mail Stop 430 Arnold Air Force Station TN 37389

NELSON, CYNTHIA KAYE, training professional; b. Kearney, Nebr., May 8, 1949; d. LeRoy J. and W. Eileen (Schmidt) Wacker; m. James C. Nelson (div. 1987); children: Alexis Ann, Whitney Eileen. BA, U. No. Iowa, 1971; postgrad., No. Ill. U., 1973. Cert. tchr., Ill., Mo. Tchr. Dixon (Ill.) Pub. Schs., 1972-74, Maplewood (Mo.)-Richmond Heights Sch. Dist., 1974-75; counselor Mo. Bus. Men's Clearing House, St. Louis, 1975-76; dir. edn. Deltex Co., Naperville, Ill., 1982-84; trainer Electronic Data Systems Co., LaGrange, Ill., 1985-86; learning technologist Bellcore Tng. and Edn. Ctr., Lisle, Ill., 1988-90; tng. instr. Fujitsu Network Switching, Raleigh, N.C., 1990—. Mem. Am. Soc. Tng. and Devel., Alpha Chi Omega, Beta Sigma Phi. Republican. Lutheran. Office: Fujitsu Network Switching 4403 Bland Rd Raleigh NC 27609

NELSON, DEBORAH JEANNE, costume designer; b. Rush City, Minn., May 19, 1952; d. Harley William and Carol Jeanne (Loop) N.; m. Samy Hassan Ahmed, May 14, 1977 (div. Aug. 1988); m. Peter Charles Rech, Oct. 7, 1990. BFA, Mpls. Coll. Art and Design, 1974. Libr. asst. Mpls. Coll. Art and Design, 1970-74, head patternmaker extension div., 1978-81; with alterations dept. J.C. Penney, Inc., Mpls., 1973-76; asst. designer Sanford, Inc., Mpls., 1974-75; head patternmaker/asst. designer Daj Inc, Mpls., 1975-78; owner, designer Satin Stitches, Coon Rapids, Minn., 1978—. Mem. Women's Entrepeneaur Network, Fashion Group, Anoka C. of C., Twin City Bridal Assn. Methodist. Office: Satin Stitches 11894 Reisling Blvd NW Coon Rapids MN 55433

NELSON, DOROTHY WRIGHT (MRS. JAMES F. NELSON), federal judge; b. San Pedro, Calif., Sept. 30, 1928; d. Harry Earl and Lorna Amy Wright; m. James Frank Nelson, Dec. 27, 1950; children: Franklin Wright, Lorna Jean. B.A., UCLA, 1950, J.D., 1953; LL.M., U. So. Calif., 1956. Bar: Calif. 1954. Research assoc. fellow U. So. Calif., 1953-56; instr., 1957, asst. prof., 1958-61, assoc. prof., 1961-67, prof., 1967, assoc. dean., 1965-67, dean., 1967-80; judge U.S. Ct. Appeals for 9th Circuit, 1980—; cons. Project STAR, Law Enforcement Assistance Adminstrn.; mem. select com. on internal procedures of Calif. Supreme Ct., 1987—. Author: Judicial Administration and The Administration of Justice, 1973; Contbr. articles to profl. jours. Co-chmn. Confronting Myths in Edn. for Pres. Nixon's White House Conf. on Children, Pres. Carter's Commn. for Pension Policy, 1974-80; bd. visitors U.S. Air Force Acad., 1978; bd. dirs. Council on Legal Edn. for Profl. Responsibility, 1971-80, Constnl. Right Found., Am. Nat. Inst. for Social Advancement; adv. bd. Nat. Center for State Cts., 1971-73. Named Law Alumnus of Yr. UCLA, 1967; recipient Profl. Achievement award, 1969; named Times Woman of Yr., 1968; recipient U. Judaism Humanitarian award, 1973; AWARE Internat. award, 1970; Ernestine Stalhut Outstanding Woman Lawyer award, 1972; Coro award for edn., 1978. Fellow Am. Bar Found., Davenport Coll., Yale U.; mem. Bar Calif. (bd. dirs. continuing edn. bar commn. 1967-74), Am. Judicature Soc. (dir.), Assn. Am. Law Schs. (chmn. com. edn. in jud. adminstrn.), Am. Bar Assn. (sect. on jud. adminstrn., chmn. com. on edn. in jud. adminstrn. 1973—), Phi Beta Kappa, Order of Coif (nat. v.p. 1974-76), Jud. Conf. U.S. (com. to consider standards for admission to practice in fed. cts. 1976-79). Office: US Ct Appeals Cir PO Box 91510 Pasadena CA 91109*

NELSON, ELAINE MARIE, public relations official; b. Brigham City, Utah, Jan. 9, 1939; d. Ernest Leland and Louise (Philpott) N.; m. Richard T. Barck, June 23, 1962 (div. July 1975); children: Russell Alan, Leah Marie. BA in History and Govt. cum laude, Mills Coll., 1961. Secondary teaching credential, Calif. Tchr. English, San Jose (Calif.) Unified Sch. Dist., 1962-63; supr. tech. publs. Electroglas, Santa Clara, Calif., 1977-80, mgr. mktg. communications, 1980-81, mgr. mktg. and sales support svcs., 1981-84; mgr. corp. communications Gen. Signal-Xynetics, Santa Clara, 1984-86; prin., owner, mgr. MarCom Mgmt., Palo Alto, Calif., 1986-88; mgr. pub. rels. Genelabs Inc., Redwood City, Calif., 1989—. Mem. exec. bd. Los Altos (Calif.) Dem. Club, 1968. Mem. Internat. Assn. Bus. Communicators. Home: 550 Shannon Way Apt 6208 Redwood Shores CA 94065 Office: Genelabs Inc 505 Penobscot Dr Redwood City CA 94063

NELSON, ELIZABETH ALICE, health facility administrator; b. San Francisco, Nov. 29, 1948; d. Carroll D. and Martina P. (Van Gerve) Funk; m. James A. Nelson, Apr. 1, 1967 (div. 1979); children: James C., Lori A. BBA, Am. Internat. Coll., Springfield, Mass., 1988. Emergency room receptionist William W. Backus Hosp., Norwich, Conn., 1977-78, welfare accounts analyst, 1978-79, EDP coord., 1979-81, budget and reimbursement mgr., 1981-83; v.p., chief fin. officer Johnson Meml. Hosp., Stafford Springs, Conn., 1983—, sr. v.p. fin., 1984—; bd. dirs., sec.-treas. North Cen. Ct. Physicians Assn., Enfield, Conn., Johnson Med. Office Assn., Enfield, Evergreen Health Corp., Wellcare, Inc., Stafford Springs, Johnson Healthcare Inc., JMH Devel. Fund, Inc., Somers Place Assn., Inc., Somers, Conn. Editor, creator monthly newsletter Cub Scouts, 1975. Commr. Gov.'s Blue Ribbon Commn. on State Health Ins., Hartford, Conn., 1989-90; speaker spl. meeting with HCFA ins. reps. U.S. Congress, Washington, 1986, 89, 90, Older Adults Svc. and Info. System, Enfield, 1989; vol. ARC, Cleve., Mare Island, Calif., Norwich Pub. Schs., 1962-79; active JMH Women's Aux., 1986. Named Valedictorian Am. Internat. Coll., 1988; recipient Cert. of Appreciation Western New Eng. Coll., 1986, Citation Gen. Assembly Conn., 1990, Excellence in English Medal Bd. Edn., Cleve., 1967; recognized for outstanding svc. to boys Boy Scouts Am., 1977. Mem. Healthcare Fin. Mgmt. Assn. (sec. 1986-88), Chief Fin. Officers Forum (chmn. 1989), Com. on Fin., NAFE, Alpha Sigma Lambda. Home: 199 Kozley Rd Tolland CT 06084

NELSON, ETHELYN BARNETT, civic worker; b. Bessemer, Ala., Jan. 16, 1925; d. Laurence McBride and Ethel Victoria Fortesque (King) Barnett; student Huntingdon Coll., 1943, U. Ala., 1948, George Washington U., 1948-49, 74; m. Stuart David Nelson, May 6, 1949; children—Terryl Lynn, Cynthia Dianne, Jacqueline Margo. Sec., U.S. Air Force, Montgomery, Ala. and Panama Canal Zone, 1944-49; sec. to dep. undersec. U.S. Dept. State, Washington, 1951-53, U.S. Ho. of Reps. and U.S. Senate, 1959-60; adminstrv. asst. editorial div. Nat. Geog. Soc., Washington, 1962-65; rec. sec. Dist. IV, Nat. Capital Area Fedn. Garden Clubs, Inc., Washington, 1981-83. Mem. Women's Com. Nat. Symphony Orch., The English-Speaking Union, Vols. for Washington Ballet, Washington Opera Guild. Mem. Salvation Army Aux., Suburban Hosp. Assn. Republican. Clubs: Landon Woods Garden (pres. 1978-80), Congressional Country; Capital Speakers (Washington). Patentee. Home: 6410 Maiden Ln Bethesda MD 20817

NELSON, FRANCES ROBERSON, registered nurse; b. Savannah, Ga., Apr. 13, 1945; d. Johnnie Roberson and Christine (Madison) Roberson Taylor; m. Robert Lee Suggs, June 3, 1966 (div. Oct. 1968); 1 child, Anthony Avery; m. Bobby Nelson, Mar. 3, 1980; children: Nanette Frazier, Robert. AA, Armstrong State Coll., Savannah, 1974. Shift supr. Ga. Rehab. Hosp.-State of Ga., Savannah, 1975-82; charge nurse Charter Hosp. of Savannah, 1988—; staff nurse Meml. Med. Ctr., Savannah, 1974-75, charge Nurse, 1982—. Mem. Nat. Assn. for Female Execs., Savannah Black Nurses Assn., Active Registered Nurses Innovators. Office: Meml Med Ctr 4700 Waters Ave Savannah GA 31405

NELSON, GENEVA E., museum administrator; b. Louisville, Oct. 4, 1942; d. James Huston and Minnie (Mucker) N. BSBA, U. Louisville, 1984; AA, Jefferson Community Coll., Louisville, 1982; postgrad., U. Louisville. Adminstrv. mgr., membership coord. Mus. History and Sci., Louisville, v.p. adminstrn. and employee rels., chmn. minority affairs; sr. arbitrator Better Bus. Bur.; mentor bus. program Urban League. Noted speaker ch. engagements. Selected to study mus. mgmt. Smithsonian Instn. Mem. NAACP, Adminstrn. Mgmt. Soc., NAFE, Soc. Human Resources. Office: 727 W Main St Louisville KY 40202

NELSON, GENEVIEVE MURIEL, principal; b. Lafayette, Minn., Nov. 7, 1921; d. Hugo E. and Anna Elizabeth (Lund) Swenson; m. Lennart Vincent Nelson, June 11, 1944. BS, Macalester Coll., 1954, MS, 1958; Specialist, St. Thomas Coll., St. Paul, 1979; DEdn, Clayton (Mo.) U., 1982. Tchr. Lafayette (Minn.) Pub. Schs., 1942-50, Lafayette Sch. and Homecroft Sch., St. Paul, 1950-58; TV tchr. sci. KTCA, St. Paul, 1958-61; supr. elem. curriculum St. Paul, 1961-65; prin. St. Anthony Park Sch., St. Paul, 1965-77, Prosperity Heights Sch., Frost Lake Sch., St. Paul, 1978-81; ednl. cons. St. Paul Pub. Schs., 1981—. Recipient Outstanding Svc. to Health Edn. award Minn. TB and Health Assn., 1958, Community Friendship award Langford Park Recreation Ctr., St. Paul, 1976, Profl. Svc. award St. Paul Community Edn. Adv. Coun., 1981, Community Svc. award Minn. Community Edn. Assn., 1981. Mem. AAUW, Nat. Elem. Prins. Assn. (life), St. Paul Retired Tchrs. Assn. (co-chmn. telephone 1984—), PTA (life), Alpha Delta Kappa (state recording sec. 1988-90, v.p. 1990—), Kappa Delta Pi. Home: 1145 W County Rd B2 Roseville MN 55113

NELSON, GRACE RAND, nurse; b. Tacoma, May 10, 1950; d. William T. and Grace K. (Scull) Rand; m. George Kopf. BA in German, Hood Coll., 1972; MA in ESL and Linguistics, U. Minn., 1974; postgrad., U. Ariz., 1984-85; BSN cum laude, Am. U., 1985. RN, Md., D.C., Jamaica. Mem. curatorial staff, sec. Nat. Gallery Art, Washington, 1980-82; instr. English, U. Minn., Mpls., 1974-77; vol., tchr. English, Peace Corps, Tunis, Tunisia, 1978-80; vol. Peace Corps, Sanaa, Yemen Arab Republic, 1985-87; nurse George Washington U. Hosp., Washington, 1987-88, Univ. Hosp. W.I., Kingston, Jamaica, 1988—; cons. Nursing Coun. Jamaica, Kingston, 1989—. Author: Nuclear Energy, 1981. Recipient spl. recognition Peace Corps, 1986; Fulbright grantee, Yugoslavia, 1974. Mem. Assn. Oper. Room Nurses, Jamaica Oper. Theatre Nurses League, Jamaica-Am. Soc., Liguanea Club, Sigma Theta Tau. Home: 24812 Via San Felipe Mission Viejo CA 92692 Office: Dept. State Kingston Washington DC 20521-3210

NELSON, GWENDOLYN DIANE, property management specialist; b. Little Rock, Nov. 13, 1950; d. Milton Donaghey and Dora Elizabeth (Gillespie) N. BBA, U. Ark., 1972; MBA, Calif. State U., Dominguez Hills, 1979, postgrad. in voice/piano, 1980-81; postgrad. in acctg., UCLA, 1973-84. Adminstrv. asst. Ark. Plan, Inc., Little Rock, 1969-73; acct. Hughes Aircraft Co., L.A., 1973-80, ops. auditor, 1986-90, property mgmt. specialist, 1990—; dir. music dept. Baldwin Hills Baptist Ch., L.A., 1979—; auditor Baldwin Hills Baptist Ch., 1983—; cons. Air Force Procurement, Contractor Ops. Revs., L.A., 1984-88. Author music: (Christian mus. drama) Wings Like Eagles, 1988, mus. dir., L.A., 1988-89. Mem. Heritage Music Found., Mu Phi Epsilon, Alpha Kappa Alpha (grad. advisor 1978-79, del. 1980-81), Nat. Property Mgmt. Assn. Home: 227 East Plymouth St Inglewood CA 90302

NELSON, HEDWIG POTOK, financial executive; b. Detroit, Oct. 6, 1954; m. Richard Alan Nelson. BA with honors, U. Mich., 1976; MBA, Am. U., 1980. Fin. asst. antitrust div. U.S. Dept. Justice, Washington, 1979-80; fin. analyst corp. treasury Martin Marietta Corp., Bethesda, Md., 1980-81, fin. adminstr. aggregates div., 1981-83, sr. fin. adminstr. bus. devel. data systems div., 1983, mgr. fin. planning and analysis, 1983-85; mgr. mergers and acquistions M/A-COM Devel. Corp., Rockville, Md., 1985-87; fin. and investment advisor, small bus. cons. Fulton, Lauroesch and Assocs., Bethesda, 1987-88; sr. analyst group fin. Marriott Corp., Bethesda, 1988-89, mgr. bus. planning, hotel div., 1989-90; mgr. planning and analysis, geon vinyl div. BF Goodrich, Cleve., 1990—. Mem. NAFE (treas. Montgomery County chpt. 1987-88), Nat. Women's Econ. Alliance. Home: 88 Mackinaw Ave Fairlawn OH 44333 Office: B F Goodrich Geon Vinyl Div 6100 Oak Tree Blvd Cleveland OH 44131

NELSON, JANE ELEANOR, seminar coordinator; b. Akron, Ohio, Feb. 9, 1959; d. Roger Hilding and Martha Jane (Dixon) N. BS, Purdue U., 1981; M in Advt., Mich. State U., 1983. With advt. sales dept. Titsch & Assocs., Denver, 1984-85; N.E. mgr. Am. Ski Assn., Denver, 1985-86; with advt. sales dept. Sentinel Newspapers, Denver, 1986-87, Gen. Communications, Denver, 1987-88, Nat. Conf. State Legislators, Denver, 1988—. Mem. Denver Advt. Fedns., Purdue Club of Denver (treas. 1985-87, v.p. 1987-88, pres. 1988—). Office: Nat Conf State Legislators 1050 17th St Ste 2100 Denver CO 80265

NELSON, JANET KATHRYN, broadcast engineer; b. Indpls., Jan. 15, 1954; d. Robert Eddinger and Carol Jean (Nelson) N.; m. Phillip Edward Callighan, Sept. 6, 1975; 1 child, Elliot Nelson. BA, North Cen. Coll., Naperville, Ill., 1975; tech. cert. DeVry Inst. Broadcast personality Sta. WGSB, Geneva, Ill., 1975-79, Sta. WYEN-FM, Des Plaines, Ill., 1977-79; sales rep. MCI Telecommunications, Chgo., 1979-80; asst. engr.-charge WGN-TV, Chgo., 1981—; v.p. Ctr. Communications, Inc., Lombard, Ill., 1985—. Mem. Nat. Acad. TV Arts and Scis., Alumni Bd. North Cen. Coll. (pres. 1989). Avocations: music, sports. Home: 1531 S Lloyd Ave Lombard IL 60148 Office: Ctr for Communications Inc 945 Springer Dr Lombard IL 60148

NELSON, JANICE EILEEN, paralegal; b. Worcester, Mass., Oct. 1, 1943; d. Joseph and Sally (Kosakowski) Rubler; m. Henry T. Knittel, Jr., Oct. 16, 1965 (div. 1979); children: Christie, Robin, Marcelle, Gary; m. David Nelson, Apr. 11, 1980 (div.). Grad., North High Sch., Worcester, Mass., 1961. Respiratory therapist St. Vincent Hosp., Worcester, 1963-65, Nassau Community Hosp., Mineola, N.Y., 1966-67, Good Samaritan Hosp., West Islip, N.Y., 1968-69; campaign mgr. Former Selectman Thomas Collimore, Fairfield, Conn., 1975, Former State Senator Myron Ballen, Fairfield, 1976; respiratory therapist VA Med. Ctr., West Haven, Conn., 1980-82; med. asst. Reproductive Med. Assocs., New London, Conn., 1983-86; paralegal O'Brien & Shafner, Groton, Conn., 1986—. Author poetry in Am. Poetry Anthology, 1986, 87; artist of pastels, oils, charcoal and watercolor; photographer of landscapes. Mem. Rep. Town Mtg., Dems., Groton, 1987-89, Dem. Town Com., 1987-89, Ctr. for Study of the Presidency, Rep. Presdl. Task Force, 1989—, Acad. Polit. Sci., 1988-89; founding sponsor Challenger Ctr., 1990; mem. Environ. Def. Fund; mem. Ox-Fam Am., 1989; founding mem. Am. Air Mus. in Britain; hospitality hostess Rep. Women's Club; elected mem. Rep. Town Com., 1986, dist. leader. John F. Kennedy Libr. hon. fellow, 1989. Mem. Nat. Mus. of Women in the Arts, Natural Resources Def. Council, Nat. Assn. Female Execs., Am. Acad. Polit. and Social Sci., Wilderness Soc., Internat. Sculpture Ctr., Sotheby's (charter), Nat. Trust, Folio Soc. Roman Catholic. Home: 103 Branford Ave Groton CT 06340 Office: OBrien Shafner 475 Bridge St Groton CT 06340

NELSON, JANICE MARIAN, pathologist, educator; b. Jamestown, N.Y., Nov. 1, 1951; d. Donald Lawrence and Marian Gertrude (McDonnell) N. BS in Biology, Syracuse U., 1973; MD, SUNY, Syracuse, 1976. Diplomate Am. Bd. Pathology, Am. Bd. Blood Banking. Resident in anatomic pathology U. Fla. Med. Ctr., Gainesville, 1976-78; resident and fellow in clin. pathology Los Angeles County-U. So. Calif. Med. Ctr., L.A., 1978-81, assoc. med. dir. blood bank, 1981—; asst. prof. pathology U. So. Calif. Sch. Medicine, L.A., 1982-88, assoc. prof. pathology, 1988—. Fellow Am. Soc. Clin. Pathologists (dep. commr. commn. on continuing edn. 1984—, mem. rsch., devel. and strategic planning com. 1986-89, bd. dirs. 1989—), Coll. Am. Pathologists; mem. Acad. Clin. Lab. Physicians and Scientists, Am. Assn., Blood Banks, Internat. Soc. Blood Transfusion. Democrat. Office: LA Co-U So Calif Med Ctr 1200 N State St Box 771 Los Angeles CA 90033-1084

NELSON, JANIE RISH, hospital executive; b. Gloster, Miss., Mar. 1, 1941; d. William Hubert and Essie Dell (Davis) Rish; m. John Preston Nelson, Jr., Aug. 19, 1984. Student S.W. Miss. Jr. Coll., 1959-61, Stephens Coll., 1981—. Accredited record technician. Admissions clk. Field Hosp., Centreville, Miss., 1963-68, asst. dir. med. records, 1968-73; dir. med. records West Feliciana Parish Hosp., St. Francisville, La., 1976—. Med. records cons. Beverly Enterprises & Centreville Health Care, 1983-84. Mem. nat. adv. bd. Am. Security Council, 1984-85; mem. U.S. Congl. Adv. Bd. for La., 1985; fund raiser Republican Com., 1984. Mem. Am. Med. Records Assn., La. Med. Records Assn., Nat. Assn. Female Execs., Tumor Registration Assn. La., Miss. Sheriffs Assn. (hon.). Republican. Presbyterian. Club: Civic. Avocations: Reading; public speaking; gardening. Home: PO Box 374 Centreville MS 39631

NELSON, JUDY, computer programer, systems analyst; b. Jersey City, June 16, 1954; d. Charles and Edwina (Fimbel) N. AAS, Bergen Community Coll., Paramus, N.J., 1989; RMA, Lyons Ednl. Ctr., Hackensack, N.J., 1973. Programmer, analyst Simon and Schuster, Englewood Cliffs, N.J. Mem. Phi Theta Kappa (pres. Alpha Epsilon Phi chpt., co-recipient Tuchman merit award 1988).

NELSON, KARIN BECKER, child neurologist; b. Chgo., Aug. 14, 1933; d. George and Sylvia (Demansly) Becker; m. Phillip G. Nelson, Mar. 20, 1955; children: Sarah Hammack, Rebecca, Jenny Walker, Peter. MD, U. Chgo., 1957; Student, U. Minn., 1950-53. Cert. child neurology Am. Bd. Psychiatry and Neurology. Intern rotating Phila. Gen. Hosp., 1957-58; asst. resident neurology U. Md. Sch. Medicine, Balt., 1958-59; resident neurology George Washington U. Sch. Medicine, Washington, 1959-62; cons. in med. neurology St. Elizabeth's Hosp., Washington, 1960-62; registrar to outpatients Nat. Hosp., Queen Sq., London, 1963; med. officer perinatal rsch. br. Nat. Inst. of Neurol. Disorders and Blindness, NIH, 1964-67; asst. prof. neurology George Washington U., Washington, 1970-72; assoc. neurologist Children's Hosp. of D.C., Washington, 1967-71; instr. neurology George Washington U., Washington, 1967-70; attending neurologist Children's Hosp., Washington, 1971-73, 78—; assoc. clin. prof. neurology George Washington U., Washington, 1972—; cons. Nat. Inst. Child Health and Human Devel., 1975-80, orphan products devel. initial rev. group FDA, 1983-86, Boston Collaborative Drug Surveillance Group, 1985-86, vaccine Am. Acad. Pediatrics, 1985, 87, Dept. Health, State of Calif. Birth Monitoring Group, 1986—, Ctr. for Disease Control Birth Defects Monitoring Com., 1987; med. officer Nat. Inst. Neurol. Disorders and Blindness, NIH, Bethesda, 1972—; med. staff Children Hosp., Washington, 1962—; mem. adv. bd. Internat. Sch. Neuroscis., Venice, Italy, rev. bd. Nat. Inst. Aging. Editor: Workshop on the Neurobiological Basis of Autism, 1979, (with J.H. Ellenberg) Febrile Seizures, 1981; editorial bd. Pediatric Neurology, 1984-90, Brain and Development, 1984—, Neurology, 1985-88, Paediatric and Perinatal Epidemiology, 1987—, Developmental Medicine and Child Neurology, 1988; field editor Epilepsy Advances; contbr. papers to profl. jours. Recipient Spl. Recognition award USPHS, 1977, Spl. Achievement award USPHS, 1981, United Cerebral Palsy Weinstein-Goldenson Rsch. award 1990. Fellow Am. Acad. Neurology (exec. bd. 1989—, councillor); mem. Child Neurology Soc. (program chmn. 1973, liaison to Nat. Inst. of Neurol. and Communicative Disorders andBlindness, 1975-80, ethics com. 1985-87, by-laws com. 1990—, ad hoc com. for consensus statement of DPT immunizations and the cen. nervous system 1990—), Am. Acad. for Cerebral Palsy and Devel. Medicine (program chmn. 1985), Am. Epilepsy Soc., Am. Neurol. Assn., Alpha Omega Alpha. Democrat. Jewish. Office: NIH 7550 Wisconsin Ave Rm 700 Bethesda MD 20892

NELSON, KATHLEEN ETHEL, educator; b. Burlington, Iowa, Jan. 12, 1947; d. William Leo and Ethel Irene (Horn) Scully; m. Arthur Oren Nelson, Aug. 22, 1970; 1 child, Sara Louise. Student U. No. Iowa, 1967-68; BS in Edn., N.E. Mo. State U., 1971; student, Marycrest Coll, Davenport, Iowa, 1973-76, 84, 86. Cert. tchr., Iowa, Mo. Tchr. Cen. Lee Community Sch. Dist., Donnellson, Iowa, 1971—, coach, 1971-88, mentor for at risk students, 1989-90. Mem. care rev. com. Ft. Madison (Iowa) Care Ctr., 1986—; mem. program planning com. YMCA, Ft. Madison, 1989—; lector Sacred Heart Cath. Ch., Ft. Madison, 1987—. Mem. AAUW (v.p. 1986-88), NEA, Iowa State Edn. Assn., Cen. Lee Edn. Assn., AAHPER, Delta Kappa Gamma. Democrat. Office: Cen Lee Community Sch Dist Donnellson IA 52625

NELSON, KAY LOUISE, money management company executive; b. Lafayette, La., Aug. 28, 1956; d. Joseph Madison and Peggy Louise (McIntire) N. BA in Econs., U. Del., 1976; MBA in Fin., Tulane U., 1978. Security analyst SunTrust Banks, Atlanta, 1978-81; v.p. instnl. equities Howard, Weil, Labouisse, Friedrichs, Inc., New Orleans, 1981-86; owner, dir. Nelson Capital Corp., New Orleans, 1986—; fin. cons. Scharff & Jones, Inc., New Orleans, 1986-87. Bd. dirs. Tulane U., New Orleans, 1987—; mem. La. Com. for Fiscal Reform, 1987-88; coord. Rep. Nat. Conv., New Orleans, 1988. Mem. Fin. Analysts Fedn., Fin. Analysts New Orleans. Roman Catholic. Home: 4605 St Charles Ave New Orleans LA 70115 Office: 939 LaFayette St Ste 325 New Orleans LA 70113

NELSON, LAURA KAY, editor; b. Larned, Kans., May 12, 1962; d. Keith Charles and Thelma Wandalee (Wright) N.; m. Scott Cormack. A.A., Dodge City Community Coll., 1982; B.S., U. Kans., 1984. Reporter Tiller & Toiler, Larned, Kans., 1984; area reporter Tribune, Great Bend, Kans., 1984-85; assoc. editor High Plains Jour., Dodge City, Kans., 1985-89. Bd. dirs. Great Salt Plains Recreational Devel. Assn. Mem. U. Kans. Alumni Assn. and Journalism Soc., Red Carpet Country (bd. dirs.). Democrat. Avocations: archeology, travel, photography. Home: RR 1 Byron OK 73723

NELSON, LAYNE MEREDITH, association executive; b. Cleve., Oct. 18, 1952; d. Merlyn Eugene and Joyce (Wilson) Meredith; m. Jonathan Clare Nelson, Aug. 24, 1985; children: Bradley Clare, Cassidy Joyce. BS, Miami U., Oxford, Ohio, 1974; MBA, U. So. Calif., 1984. Asst. mgr. Foxmoor Casuals, Cin., 1974-75; asst. buyer The Broadway, L.A., 1976-78; buyer The Broadway, 1978-81, Shelly's Tall Girl Shops, L.A., 1981-83; owner, mgr. Powder Prodns., Inc., Crested Butte, Colo., 1983-85; asst. exec. dir. Gunnison (Colo.) Country C. of C., 1985-86, exec. dir., 1986—; guest lectr. Western State Coll. Gunnison, 1988-89. Inst. for Leadership Devel. scholar, 1987, 90. Mem. AAUW, Colo. C. of C. Execs. (bd. dirs. 1987).

NELSON, LINDA CAROL, corporate chief executive officer, president; b. Knoxville, Tenn., Feb. 18, 1954; d. Solon Morris and Dorothy Thelma (Randles) Woods. Diploma, Looking Glass Modeling Sch., Knoxville, 1969; BA in Polit. Sci. and Psychology magna cum laude, U. Tenn., 1975; BBA in Acctg. summa cum laude, Ga. State U., 1978. Cert. of mgmt. acctg. Pvt. investigator Hanover Security Systems, Knoxville, 1968-74; instr. profl. devel. series, course instr. Dale Carnegie Inst., Atlanta, 1980-89; office mgr. Dale Carnegie Inst., Knoxville, 1969-75; legal asst. office of regional atty. HEW, Atlanta, 1975-76; tech. support staff dist. conf. U.S. Treasury Dept., Atlanta, 1976, instr., tng. analyst continuing profl. edn., 1976-88, internal revenue agt., tax technician of exam. div., 1976-79, recruiter, 1979-86, fed. racketeering investigator strike force program, 1986, coord. Joint Com. Taxation in Congress, 1986-87, resident lead instr. S.E. Region, 1987-88; consolidations tax dept. staff mgr. Bellsouth, Atlanta, 1985-86; ind. mgmt. cons. Peachtree City, Ga., 1986; pres., chief exec. officer Exec. Svcs. Inc., Atlanta, 1988—; team coord. large case exam. U.S. Treasury Dept., Atlanta, 1980-85. Hospitality com. mem. Atlanta Women's Network, 1990—; vol. worker Eagles Boy's Ranch, Atlanta, 1986—; vol. counselor Atlanta Home for Abused Children, 1980—; Sunday sch. tchr., greeter Northside Community Ch., 1989; fundraiser Atlanta Symphony Orch., 1985-86; cons. adopt-a-student program, 1985-86; vol. missions program 1st Bapt. Ch., Atlanta, 1986; key person United Way Atlanta Combined Fed. Campaign, 1978-84; calling com. Norcross (Ga.) United Meth. Ch., 1983-84; coord. blood drive ARC, Atlanta, 1984; vol. nursery worker Rock of Ages Ch., Atlanta, 1975; choir mem. Rehoboth Bapt. Ch., Atlanta, 1987—; vol. counselor Helen Ross McNabb Ctr., Knoxville, 1970-72. Recipient citation U.S. Sec. Labor Brennan; named one of Outstanding Young Women of Am., 1984. Mem. NAFE, Nat. Assn. Accts. (program speaker Atlanta chpt. 1980—), High Mus. Art Young Career Mems.' Guild, Young Women of the Arts, Am. Soc. for Tng. and Devel. (vol. placement com. 1988—), Atlanta Skylarks, Ga. State U. Alumni Assn., U. Tenn. Alumni Assn., Golden Key Nat. Honor Soc., Mortar Bd., Atlanta Lawn Tennis Assn., So. Athletic Club, Atlanta Ski Club, So. Bicycle League, Phi Beta Kappa, Delta Gamma, Beta Alpha Psi, Pi Sigma Alpha, Pi Kappa Phi, Alpha Lambda Delta. Home: 6001 Meadowbrook Dr Norcross GA 30093 Office: Exec Svcs Inc PO Box 450822 Atlanta GA 30345-0822

NELSON, LINDA JANE, loan officer; b. Daytona Beach, Fla., Jan. 24, 1957; d. William and Ann Juliet (Sherman) N. Degree in Internat. Bus., The Netherlands Sch. Bus., Breukelen, Holland, 1978; BS cum laude, U. Fla., 1979; MA, U. Pa., 1983; MBA, NYU, 1984. Intern Dept. External Econ. Rels. N.V. Philips, Eindhoven, Holland, 1978; assoc. internat. mgmt. Drexel Burnham Lambert, Inc., N.Y.C., 1980; rsch. analyst U. Pa., Phila., 1983; second v.p. N.Am. corp. fin. The Chase Manhattan Bank, N.A., N.Y.C., 1984—. Vol. Sloan Kettering Hosp., N.Y.C., 1984-85, Bush Campaign, N.Y.C., 1988; mem. United Jewish Appeal. Grad. fellow Rotary Internat., 1981-82; recipient Fla. Banker's Found. scholarship U. Fla., 1979. Mem. Fgn. Policy Assn. Young Profls., N.Y. Assn. Bus. Economists. Jewish. Home: 430 E 86th St #2D New York NY 10028

NELSON, MARTHA JANE, magazine editor; b. Pierre, S.D., Aug. 13, 1952; d. Bernard Anton and Pauline Isabel (Noren) N. BA, Barnard Coll., 1976. Mng. editor Signs: Jour. of Women in Culture, N.Y.C., 1976-80; editor Ms. Mag., N.Y.C., 1980-85; editor-in-chief Women's Sports and Fitness Mag., Palo Alto, Calif., 1985-87; exec. editor Savvy, N.Y.C., 1988-89, editor-in-chief, 1989—. Editor: Women in the American City, 1980; contbr. articles to profl. jours. Bd. dirs. Painting Space 122, N.Y.C., 1982-85, Urban Athletic Assn. Mem. Am. Soc. Mag. Editors. Office: Savvy mag 3 Park Ave New York NY 10016

NELSON, MARY CARROLL, artist, author; b. Bryan, Tex., Apr. 24, 1929; d. James Vincent and Mary Elizabeth (Langton) Carroll; m. Edwin Blakely Nelson, June 27, 1950; children: Patricia Ann, Edwin Blakely. BA in Fine Arts, Barnard Coll., 1950; MA, U. N.Mex., 1963. Juror Am. Artist Golden Anniversary Nat. Art Competition, 1987, Don Ruffin Meml. Art Exhbn., Ariz., 1989, N.Mex. Arts and Crafts Fair, 1989; moderator Harwood Found. Art History Conf., 1987; curator Shrines, 1988. Group shows include N.Mex. Mus. Fine Arts Biennial, 1987, N.Mex. Lightworks, 1990, Level to Level, Ohio Layering, 1990, Artist as Shaman, Ohio, 1990, The Box Show, Tex., 1990; represented in pvt. collections in: U.S., Fed. Republic of Germany, Eng. and Australia; author: American Indian Biography Series, 1971-76, (with Robert E. Wood) Watercolor Workshop, 1974, (with Ramon Kelley) Ramon Kelley Paints Portraits and Figures, 1977, The Legendary Artists of Taos, 1980, (catalog) American Art in Peking, 1981, Masters of Western Art, 1982, Connecting, The Art of Beth Ames Swartz, 1984, (catalog) Layering, An Art of Time and Space, 1985, (catalog) Layering/Connecting, 1987; contbg. editor Am. Artist, 1976—, Southwest Art, 1987—; editor (video) Layering, 1990. Mem. Albuquerque Arts Bd., 1984-88. Mem. Soc. Layerists in Multi-Media (founder 1982), Nat. Fedn. Press Women, N.Mex. Press Women. Home: 1408 Georgia St NE Albuquerque NM 87110

NELSON, MARY ELLEN DICKSON, actuary; b. Mpls., Mar. 24, 1933; d. William Alexander and Laura Winona (Baxter) Dickson; m. David Aldrich Nelson, Aug. 25, 1956; children: Frederick Dickson, Claudia Baxter, Caleb Edward. BA, Vassar Coll., 1954; postgrad., Cambridge (Eng.) U., 1954-55. Rsch. assoc. N.Am. Life & Casualty Co., Mpls., 1955-56; actuarial asst. John Hancock Mut. Life Ins. Co., Boston, 1956-58; actuary David R. Kass & Assocs., Cleve., 1973-74; pres. Nelson & Co., Cleve., 1975, Conrad, Nelson & Co., Cleve., 1975-81, Nelson & Co., Cleve. and Cin., 1981—; bd. dirs., Blount, Inc., Montgomery, Ala.; enrolled actuary, Joint Bd., Dept. Labor/Dept. Treasury, 1976—. Fulbright scholar, 1954-55. Fellow Soc. Actuaries, Phi Beta Kappa; mem. Am. Acad. Actuaries, Cin. Actuaries Club, Midwest Pension Conf. (vice chairperson Ohio Valley chpt. 1990—), Bankers Club. Republican. Office: Nelson & Co Ste 1120 105 W 4th St Cincinnati OH 45202-2735

NELSON, MARY PENNELL, political worker; b. Seattle, May 3, 1943; d. Maynard Lyman and Ellen (Rowland) Pennell; m. Kenneth Miles Nelson, Nov. 25, 1967; children: Caleb, Joshua Matthew, Matthew Benjamin. BA, Smith Coll., 1965; MA ion Pub. Policy and Mgmt., U. So. Maine, 1988. Adminstrv. asst. MIT, Cambridge, 1965-70; councillor, chmn. Falmouth (Maine) Town Coun., 1983-89. Mem., chmn. Brookline (Mass.) Conservation Commn., 1971-80; vice chmn. Maine Devel. Found., Augusta, 1987-89; treas. Portland (Maine) Symphony Orch., 1988—; chmn. bd. trustees Portland Sch. Art, 1989—; trustee Smith Coll., 1980-83. Mem. Maine Mcpl. Assn. (pres. 1987-88, exec. com. 1986-89), Smith Coll. Alumnae Assn. (pres. 1980-83), Phi Kappa Phi. Democrat. Unitarian. Home: 213 Foreside Rd Falmouth Foreside ME 04105

NELSON, MARY S., state legislator; b. Boston, May 3, 1943; children: John, Michael, Jamie. Tchr. Perkins Sch. Blind, 1967-77; lectr. River Coll., 1977-78; selectman Nashua, N.H., 1983-85; mem. N.H. Ho. of Reps., 1983-85, N.H. State Senate, 1986—; del. Dem. State Conv., 1982, 84; cons. on employment and tng. of handicapped, 1977—. Mem. N.H. Order of Women Legislators (pres. 1986—), Phi Delta Kappa. Democrat. Roman Catholic. Home: 18 Stanley Ln Nashua NH 03062 Office: N H State Senate Concord NH 03301

NELSON, MARY VIRGINIA BOLES, educator; b. Clearco, W.Va., Apr. 28, 1938; d. John Ford and Martha Jayne (Burdiss) Boles; m. Orville Ramsey Nelson, Jr., July 1, 1959; children: Orville III, Scott Anthony. BS in Edn., James Madison U., 1961, MS in Edn., 1967; postgrad., Frostburg State U., 1982-85. Cert. elem.-middle sch. prin., supr., elem.-middle sci. tchr., sec. sci. tchr. Tchr. Columbia St. Elem., Cumberland, Md., 1961-62; tchr. Cresaptown Elem., Cresaptown, Md., 1962-84, Braddock Middle Sch., Cumberland, 1984-89; vice prin., team leader tchr. Mt. Savage (Md.) Sch., 1989—. Editor (newsletters) FACT, 1978-83, Assn. News, 1986—. Exec. officer Western Md. Cen. Labor Coun., Cumberland, 1978-83, Polit. Action Club Tchrs., LaVale, Md., 1986-89, Women's 4th Dist. Dem. Club., Cumberland, 1988-90, pres., 1990—, Allegany County Dem. Club, Cumberland, 1987-89. Mem. Nat. Assn. Elem. Sch. Prins., Allegany County Tchrs. Assn. (pres. 1987—), Md. State Tchrs. Assn. (women's com. 1985-90, leadership trainer 1989—, del., named Most Valuable Person 1988), NEA (del.), AAUW (pres. 1971-75, treas. 1975-76, Name grantee Md. div. 1975), Women of Elks (pres. 1972-73), Alleghany County Elem. Sch. Adminstrs., Phi Delta Kappa. Presbyterian. Home: Maple Ln Rawlings MD 21557-0142 Office: Mt Savage Sch RR 1 Box 112-A Mount Savage MD 21545

NELSON, MAUREEN DANETTE, public relations specialist; b. Oakland, Calif., May 5, 1960; d. Irwin Reed and Edith Irene (Floersch) N. BA in Journalism, Calif. State U., Chico, 1982. Prodn. asst. North Lake Tahoe Bonanza Newspaper, Incline Village, Nev., 1982-83; entertainment reporter The Sentinel, Santa Cruz, Calif., 1983-84; pub. rels. asst. Community Hosp., Santa Cruz, 1983-84; editorial asst., copy editor Circle Track mag., L.A., 1984-85; asst. mng. editor 4-Wheel and Off Rd. mag., L.A., 1985-87; editorial prodn. mgr. Hot Rod mag., L.A., 1987-89; account exec. Manning, Selvage & Lee, Universal City, Calif., 1989-90; sr. account exec. Hill and Knowlton, L.A., 1990—. Mem. Motor Press Guild, Internat. Motor Press Assn., Mus. Contemporary Art Contemporaries. Democrat. Roman Catholic.

NELSON, MAUREEN ELIZABETH, food service manager; b. Fargo, N.D., May 30, 1939; d. Walter Raub and Inez Miriam (Moffitt) Bartholomew; m. Donald Paige Nelson, Apr. 14, 1962 (div. July 1989); children: Kyle Owen, Kerry Evan. BS, U. Minn., Minneapolis, 1961. Home econs. tchr. Hancock (Minn.) High Sch., 1961-62; nurse aide Fair Oaks Nursing Home, Mpls., 1963-64; home econs. tchr. Paynesville (Minn.) High Sch., 1964-68, Rocori High Sch., Cold Spring, Minn., 1968-81; owner, mgr. Garden of Eden Greenhouse, Gentryville, Ind., 1981-87; food svc. mgr. Profit Care Nursing Ctr., Dale, Ind., 1982-86, Huntingburg (Ind.) Convalscent Ctr., 1986—; pres. Cold Spring Edn. Assn., 1972-73; govtl. relations council Minn. Edn. Assoc. St. Paul, 1974-77; mem. advisory bd. Minn. State Assoc. Future Homemakers St. Paul, 1975-76. Coord., program chair Women in Networking, Evansville, Ind., 1986—; presiding ptnr. Win Investment Club, Evansville, 1987—; bd. mem. Recorder Women's Resource Ctr., Evansville, 1988—; bd. mem., sec., pres., newsletter editor Hoosierette chpt. Sweet Adelines, Inc., Evansville, 1986—; campaign mgr. State Legis. Campaign Dist. 16B, Paynesville, 1978-80; treas. Legis. Dist. Rep. party, St. Cloud, 1977-81; co-coordinator Internat. Women's Day Coalition, 1989—. Republican. Methodist. Home: 4994 Fairmont Dr Evansville IN 47715

NELSON, MAXINE MARIE, newspaper columnist, researcher, reporter; b. Harlan County, Nebr., Nov. 4, 1932; d. Carl Olaf and Mora Katherine (Stark) Zimmerman; m. June 2, 1952; children: Paula Boyd, Carl, Bob, Johanna Vandenburg, Eric. BSc, U. Nebr., 1956. Cert. English and speech tchr. Lectr. Weight Watchers of Greater Wichita, Kans., 1973-85; columnist, reporter Colby (Kans.) Free Press, 1983—. Mem. Thomas County Coun. on Aging, Colby, 1984—; leader Girl Scouts U.S., Hays, Kans. and Scottsbluff, Nebr., 1965-73, Boy Scouts Am., Hays and Scottsbluff, 1966-75, mem. dist. com., Colby, 1978—; sec. Extension Homemakers Coun., Colby, 1987—. Mem. Colby Bus. and Profl. Women (pres. 1989-90, bd. dirs. dist. 8, 1990—), Colby Press Women (pres. 1989-90), Domestic Engr. Extension Unit (pres. 1984-87), AAUW (sec., treas. 1984-85), Rebecca Winters Geneal. Soc. (pres. Scottsbluff chpt. 1970-71). Mormon. Home: 760 S Garfield Colby KS 67701 Office: Colby Free Press Colby KS 67701

NELSON, MERLE CHANDLER, real estate executive; b. Nicholson, Ga., June 30, 1908; d. Berry G. and Addie Lavina (Harris) Chandler; m. Ealton Louis Nelson, Dec. 2, 1938; children: Joan Harris Nelson Mulholland, Jean Nelson Amann. Student, Am. U., 1938-41, George Washington U., 1937-38. Exec. sec. Civil Aeros. Bd., Washington, 1938-41; real estate broker No. Va. Bd. Realtors, Fairfax, 1957-87; pres. Nelson Realty, Inc., Arlington, Va., 1957-87, also chmn. bd. dirs. Mem. Arlington County Dem. com., Arlington, 1955-56. Mem. Lake Barcroft Civic Assn. Democrat. Home: 3816 Lakeview Terr Falls Church VA 22041 Office: Nelson Realty Inc 5537 Lee Hwy Arlington VA 22207

NELSON, NANCY JANE, mortgage comny executive, commercial loan specialist; b. Greenwood, S.C., Apr. 11, 1956; d. George Dewey and Mary Helen (Capps) N.; m. Terry Alan Evans, Aug. 23, 1975 (div. 1979); 1 child, Brandon Gregory. Grad., Nova U., Ft. Lauderdale, Fla., 1983. Cert. tchr.; lic. mortgage broker. Emergency room clk. Self Meml. Hosp., Greenwood, 1974-78; gen. mgr. First Fla. Sanitation, Ft. Lauderdale, Fla., 1979-82; export mgr. Carvel Corp., Ft. Lauderdale, Fla., 1983-86; account exec. Guardian Savs. and Loan, Ft. Lauderdale, Fla., 1987-89; v.p. residential lending Nat. Mortgage Ctr. Inc., Ft. Lauderdale, 1989—. Contbr. short stories, poems to mags. Mem. Ft. Lauderdale C. of C. Republican. Baptist. Office: Nat Mortgage Ctr Inc 500 W Cypress Creek Rd Ste 380 Fort Lauderdale FL 33309

NELSON, NATALIE ANN, marketing professional, bartender; b. Austin, Tex., May 31, 1962; d. Robert Henry Nelson and Annette Beatrice (Berger) Gilbert. BBA, James Madison U., 1984. Lic. health and life ins. broker. Salesperson Nat. Bus. Systems, Rockville, Md., 1984-85; crew mem. Hornblower Yacht's, Inc., Coronado, Calif., 1986-87; mem. bar staff Coconut's of Shelter Island, Calif., 1986-87, Chgo. Bar & Grill, Washington, 1987-88, Paul Mall of Georgetown, D.C., 1988-89, Sign of Whale-Geca, Inc., Falls Church, Va., 1987—; ind. contractor Matol Botanical Am.-Nat. Assn. Pvt. Enterprise, Alexandria, Va., 1989—; trainer Geca, Inc., Falls Church, 1987—; cons. and trainer Matol Botanical Am., Alexandria, 1989—. Sponsor Kids, Heroes Md. Assn. D.C. Met. Police, 1987—; fund-raiser Multiple Sclerosis Soc., Washington, 1988. Named Ms. Drink of Month Bartender Mag., Sept.-Dec., 1989. Mem. Multi Level Mktg. Internat. Assn., Am. Mktg. Assn. Republican. Roman Catholic. Home and Office: 6007-B Curtier Dr Alexandria VA 22310

NELSON, NETTE ADALINE, finance company executive; b. Hood River, Oreg., June 23, 1939; d. Burt Cheney and Ethel Gertrude (Taylor) Nelson; m. Charles Luther Blaylock, July 1961 (div. 1968); children: Charles Wayne, Dennis Ray, Meri Jo. Student, Oreg. State U., 1957-59; BA, U. Nebr., 1983; MPA, Harvard U., 1984. With Lockheed, Sunnyvale, Calif., 1959-62; asst. to mgr. Fairchild Semiconductor, Mountain View, Calif., 1962-68; asst. to state planner Office of Gov., Salem, Oreg., 1968-69; assoc. planner Daniel, Mann, Johnson & Mendenhall, Portland, 1969-74; exec. asst. to dir. Dept. Land Conservation & Devel., Portland/Salem, Oreg., 1974-75; dir. statewide progs. Exec. Dept., State of Oreg., Salem, 1975-80; dir./cons. Nebr. Telecom & Info. Ctr., Lincoln, 1984-87; v.p. Nebr. R&D Authority, Lincoln, 1987-89, pres., 1989-90; lobbyist various orgns. Contbr. articles to profl. jours. V.p., bd. dirs. Heartland Ctr. for Leadership Devel., Lincoln, 1988—; bd. dirs. Nebr. Venture Group, Prairie Fire; advisor to legis. New Horizons for Nebr. project, Lincoln, 1987—; chmn. Nebr. Edn. Tech. Consortium, Lincoln, 1984—; mem. New Seeds for Nebr. project, Lincoln, 1988—. Mem. Community Devel. Soc., Newcomer Soc., Planning Forum, Sertoma, Torch Club, Women's Inst. for Theology, Univ. Club. Office: Nebr Rsch/Devel Auth NBC Ctr #646 Lincoln NE 68508

NELSON, NEVIN MARY, interior designer; b. Cleve., Nov. 5, 1941; d. Arthur George Reinker and Barbara Phyllis (Gunn) Parks; m. Wayne Nelson (div. 1969); children: Doug, Brian. BA in Interior Design, U. Colo., 1964. Prin. Nevin Nelson Design, Boulder, Colo., 1966-70, Vail, Colo., 1970—; program chmn. Questers Antique Study Group, Boulder, 1969. Coord. Bob Kirscht for Gov. campaign, Eagle County, Colo., 1986; state del. Rep. Nat. Conv., 1986, 88; county coord. George Bush for U.S. Pres. campaign, 1988; chmn. Eagle County Reps., 1989—. Mem. Am. Soc. Interior Designers, Pro Denver Club. Episcopalian. Home: Box 1212 Vail CO 81658 Office: 2271 N Frontage Rd W Vail CO 81657

NELSON, PAMELA, state legislator; m. Vic Nelson; 2 children. Former mem. S.D. State Ho. of Reps.; now senator S.D. State Senate; Democrat. Roman Catholic. Home: 2505 S Marion Rd Sioux Falls SD 57106*

NELSON, PATRICIA SWEAZEY, international management consultant; b. Seattle, Mar. 5, 1927; d. Manley Earl and F. Pauline (Pickard) S.; m. Russell Paul Nelson; children—Cynthia, Andrea, Barry. BA magna cum laude, U. Wash., 1971; postgrad. Whitworth Coll., 1985. Interpreter Italian prisoners of war U.S. Army, Seattle, 1944-45; interpreter, adminstr. troubleshooter Pomona Valley Community Hosp., 1951-53; lead tchr. of Kindergarten, program developer, co-dir. Alpental Kinderschule, Seattle Day Nursery, 1956-69; export/import mgr. Warn Internat., Seattle, 1971-72; trainer computer transition and corp. hdqrs. mgmt. devel. team Unigard Ins., Seattle, 1972-74; dir. Nelson Internat. Assocs., Seattle, 1974—; researcher/cons. Swissair Transport, 1982—, field counselor expatriate families abroad, 1980—. Author: Guide to Girl Scout Backpacking, 1965. Coun. cons. in Alpine travel Girl Scouts U.S.A., Seattle, 1960-67, also trainer, leader, explorer advisor; designer, dir. commissary program, bd. dirs. King County Search and Rescue Assn., 1967-74; dir. sites, program developer, Lichtenfeld Backpacking Encampment, 1964-67; adj. faculty City Univ. Seattle, 1975-79, Cen. Washington U., 1978—. Mem. Assn. for Tng. and Devel., Soc. for Internat. Edn., Tng. and Rsch.

NELSON, PAULA MORRISON BRONSON, educator; b. Memphis, Mar. 26, 1944; d. Fred Ford and Julia (Morrison) Bronson; m. Jack Marvin Nelson, July 13, 1968; children: Eric Allen, Kelly Susan. BS, U. N. Mex., 1967; MA, U. Colo., Denver, 1985. Physical edn. tchr. Grant Union Sch. Dist., Sacramento, Calif., 1967-68; physical edn. tchr. Denver Pub. Schs., 1968-74, with program for pupil assistance, 1974-80, chpt. 1 reading specialist, 1983—; tchr. ESL Douglas County Pub. Schs., Parker, Colo., 1982-83; demonstration tchr. Colo. Edn. Assn., 1970-72; curriculum com. mem. Denver Pub. Schs., 1970-72, Douglas County Accountability Com., Castle Rock, Colo., 1986-89. Co-author: Gymnastics Teacher's Guide Elementary Physical Education, 1973, Applauding Our Constitution, 1989; producer slide shows Brotherhood, 1986, We the People...Our Dream Lives On, 1987, Celebration of Cultures, 1988. Pub. Edn. Coalition grantee, Denver, 1987, 88, grantee Rocky Mountain Global Edn. Project, 1987, Wake Forest Law Sch., Winston-Salem, N.C., 1988, 89. Mem. Windstar Found., Colo. Coun. Internat. Reading, Internat. Reading Assn., Nat. Soc. for Study of Edn., Colo. Coun. for the Social Studies, Am. Fedn. Tchrs., Denver Fedn. Tchrs. Republican. Methodist. Home: 10488 E Meadow Run Parker CO 80134

NELSON, ROBBIN NEWEL, university program director; b. Oak Park, Ill., May 5, 1948; d. William Royal and Marilyn Dana (Habich) Olson; m. Michael Edward Nelson, July 17, 1971; children: Dana Michelle, Tracey

Caroline. BS in Med. Technology, No. Ill. U., 1970, MSEd in Profl. Edn., 1977. Med. technologist ASCP. Staff technologist Swedish Am. Hosp., Rockford, Ill., 1970-71, Crestwood Hosp., Huntsville, Ala., 1971-72; staff technologist Swedish Am. Hosp., Rockford, Ill., 1972-73, instr. microbiology Sch. Med. Technology, 1972-78, supr. microbiolgy, 1973-78; staff asst. U. Ill. Chgo. Office of Continuing Edn., Rockford, 1978-80, sr. program coord., 1980-84, asst. dir., 1984-87; regional program dir. U. Ill. Office of Statewide Programming, Rockford, 1987—; advisor Coun. on Continuing Edn. for Profl. Nurses, Rockford, 1978—, UICOM-R Continuing Med. Edn. Com., Rockford, 1978—; institutional rep. Regional Consultative Coun., northern Ill., 1987—; steering com. Human Svcs. Tng. Coordination Coun., northern Ill., 1989—. Bd. dirs. Am. Cancer Soc.-Winnebago County, Rockford, 1981-87; dist. coord. Girl Scouts U.S., Rockford, 1982-83. Mem. Am. Soc. Clin. Pathologists (assoc), Nat. Univ. Continuing Edn. Assn., Ill. Coun. on Continuing Higher Edn., AAUW. Office: U Ill 1601 Parkview Ave Rockford IL 61107

NELSON, SALLY IRENE, insurance agency executive; b. Rockland, Maine, Mar. 15, 1941; d. Edward Michael and Anne Laura (Taylor) Gluse; divorced; children: Erik O., Gayle Anne. Grad. high sch., S. Portland, Maine. Sales rep. Blue Cross/Blue Shield, Portland, Maine, 1975-80, Turner Barker, Portland, Maine, 1980-85; pres. Nelson, Desmond and Payne, Inc., Falmouth, Maine, 1984—. Legis. chairperson State of Maine, 1987-89; mem. fin. com. Martin's Point Health Care Ctr., 1987—; bd. dirs. United Way, 1984—. Mem. Maine Assn. Life Underwriters (bd. dirs. 1983—, legis. chmn. 1983—), Nat. Assn. Life Underwriters (subcom. 1986—, recognition of quality and achievement com. 1988-89, fed. law and legis. subcom. on health 1989—), Am. Bus. Women's Assn. (gen. chmn. 1991 N.E. regional spring conf., Woman of Yr. award 1984), NAFE. Democrat. Home: 368 Westbrook St The Hedges #8 South Portland ME 04106 Office: Nelson Desmond and Payne Inc 366 US Rt 1 Falmouth ME 04105

NELSON, SARAH MILLEDGE, archaeology educator; b. Miami, Fla., Nov. 29, 1931; d. Stanley and Sarah Woodman (Franklin) M.; m. Harold Stanley Nelson, July 25, 1953; children: Erik Harold, Mark Milledge, Stanley Franklin. BA, Wellesley Coll., 1953; MA, U. Mich., 1969, PhD, 1973. Instr. archaeology U. Md. extension, Seoul, Republic Korea, 1970-71; asst. prof. U. Denver, 1974-79, assoc. prof., 1979-85, prof. archaeology, 1985—, chair dept. anthropology, dir. women's studies program, 1985-87; vis. asst. prof. U. Colo., Boulder, 1974. Active Earthwatch, 1989—. Southwestern Inst. Rsch. on Women grantee, 1981, Acad. Korean Studies grantee, Seoul, 1983, Internat. Cultural Soc. Korea grantee, 1986, Scholarly Communication award People's Republic of China, NAS, 1988; recipient Outstanding Scholar award U. Denver, 1989. Fellow Am. Anthrop. Assn.; mem. Soc. Am. Archaeology, Assn. Asian Studies, Royal Asiatic Soc., Sigma Xi (sec.-treas. 1978-79), Phi Beta Kappa. Democrat. Home: 4970 S Fulton St Englewood CO 80111 Office: U Denver Dept Anthropology Denver CO 80208

NELSON, SARAH SUZANNE, insurance executive; b. July 22, 1942. CLU, Chartered Fin. Con., CPCU. Ins. profl. U.S. Life Ins., DAllas, 1987—. Mem. Am. Soc. CLU, Chartered Fin. Con. Assn., Soc. CPCU. Home: 4404 Wind River Ln Garland TX 75042

NELSON, SHANNON, purchasing manager, sales consultant; b. Salt Lake City, Sept. 17, 1961; d. Alan Ray and Gwendolyn Loy (Sparrow) N. Student, Stanford (Calif.) U., 1981; BA in Chemistry, U. Utah, 1984. Purchasing agt. Henricks Techs., Inc., Chamblee, Ga., 1985-87; purchasing mgr. Accu-Tech. Cable, Inc., Roswell, Ga., 1987-90; sales cons. network products group Accu-Tech. Cable, Inc., Atlanta, 1990—. U. Utah scholar, 1981-83. Mem. Nat. Assn. Purchasing Mgmt., Ga. Assn. Purchasing Mgmt., NAFE. Office: Accu Tech Cable Inc 250 William St Ste 2110 INFORUM Atlanta GA 30303

NELSON, SUSAN, travel company executive; b. Elgin, Ill., July 12, 1936; d. Paul Jackson and Dorothy (Nelson) Trautt; m. Barton R. Nelson, Dec. 29, 1955; children: Betsy, Eric, Matthew. Leisure agt. Wilson World Travel, St. Charles, Ill., 1973-77, mgr., 1977-78; sr. agt. Travel & Transport, Inc., St. Charles, 1979-83, mgr., 1983-87; mgr. Travel & Transport, Inc., Lisle, Ill., 1987—. Mem. Women in Mgmt., Inst. Cert. Travel Agts. (Chgo. regional coord., Travel and Transport study group). Office: Travel & Transport 4343 Commerce Ct Lisle IL 60532

NELSON, SUSAN MARGARET, marketing professional; b. Burbank, Calif., Feb. 3, 1960; d. Ray and Marlys Corene (Rue) Aldana; m. Anthony Allen Nelson, Sept. 8, 1988. BA in Exptl. Psychology, U. Calif., Santa Barbara, 1982; MBA in Mktg., U. Calif., Irvine, 1985. Rsch. devel. asst. Allergan Pharms., Irvine, 1983-84; mktg. cons. The Irvine Co., Irvine, 1984-85; mktg. and media analyst Taco Bell Corp., Irvine, 1985-87; market analyst Geneva Corp., Irvine, 1987-89; dir. mktg. Abigail Abbott Personnel Co., Tustin, Calif., 1989—. Contbr. articles to various publs. Mem. Direct Mktg. Club So. Calif., Grad. Sch. Mgmt. Alumni Assn., Kappa Alpha Theta. Republican. Lutheran. Home: 216 Corona St Long Beach CA 90803 Office: Abigail Abbott Personnel Co 660 W 1st St Tustin CA 92680

NELSON, TERRY ELLAN ELISABETH, minister; b. Chgo., Nov. 17, 1954; d. Julius Paul Kastens and Janice Joy (Johnson) and Mary Ann (Reisner); m. Lee Alan Nelson, May 28, 1983. Student, Ea. Ill. U., 1976-78; BA, Valparaiso U., 1981; MDiv, Christ Sem., 1985. Ordained 1985. Clk., typist R. Cooper, Jr., Des Plaines, Ill., 1972-73; statis. typist A.B. Dick Co., Niles, Ill., 1973-76; nurse aide Hilltop Nursing Home, Charleston, Ill., 1977-78; crew trainer McDonald's Corp., Valparaiso, Ind., 1978-81; fieldwork pastor Luth. Ch. of the Living Christ, Florissant, Mo., 1981-83; intern pastor Wiley Luth. Ch., Ellisville, Ill., 1983-84; fieldwork pastor Immanuel Luth. Ch., Park Ridge, Ill., 1984-85; owner, operator Nelson Catering, St. Louis and Chgo., 1982-85; vacancy pastor Zion Luth. Ch., International Falls, Minn., 1985-86; exec. sec. Boise Cascade Corp., 1987; chaplain USN, Phila., 1987—. Contbr. articles to profl. jours. Mem. Canton (Ill.) Ministerial Assn., 1983-84, International Falls Ministerial Assn., 1985-86. Lt. USN, 1988. Mem. AAUW.

NELSON, THERESA DECKER, small business owner; b. Struthers, Ohio, June 7, 1926; d. John Juros and Pauline (Irek) Plummer; m. Robert Leo Decker (div. 1963), John Robert Nelson, Mar. 31, 1968 (div. 1979); children: Jonathan Lee Decker, Nancy Marie Decker Wiggles North. Student, Reynolds Electronic Acctg. Sch, Dayton, 1967, Davenport Coll., Kalamazoo, Mich., 1984; student architecture and art, Chgo., 1988; BS in Mktg., U. Ill., Chgo., 1988. Co-owner Frosty Knoll Fruit Farms, South Haven, Mich., 1944-63; exec. adminstr. Rest Haven Nursing Home, Chgo., 1963-66; bus. mgr. Wigglesworth Imports Inc., Glenview, Ill., 1966-69, Bell Lincoln Mercury, Inc., Highland Park, Ill., 1970-73, Glenview Mktg. Corp., 1974-76; pres. Nelson Mktg. Corp., Mich., 1980-84; owner and pres. Recharge Technol. Mich., Inc., Bangor, 1988—; judge Allegan County Fair Assn., Mich. 1958-59; presentation coach Future Farmers of Am., South Haven, 1962; mktg. cons. Chgo., 1988—; speaker in field, Chgo., 1988—; organizer reg. symposiums numerous colls. and univs., Chgo. and no. Ill. Exhibit designer Mich. State Fair 1958-62; writer ednl. children's TV shows Your World and Mine, 1978-79; author tng. manuals and articles to profl. jours. Staff asst. Jaws of Life telethon, South Haven, 1978; producer community ednl. TV, South Haven, 1978-79. Recipient Outstanding Achievement award AMA, Chgo., 1988, Outstanding Mktg. Student award AMA, Chgo., 1988, Communication in Media award, City of Bangor, 1989. Mem. Golden Key Nat. Honor Soc. (pres. Ill. chpt.), Beta Gamma Sigma Honor Soc., Phi Kappa Phi Honor Soc. Republican. Anglican Catholic. Home: 8 Oliver St Bangor MI 49013 Office: 11 W Cass St Bangor MI 49013

NELSON, TONI COOKE, real estate broker; b. Houston, Sept. 9, 1949; d. Alan Theodore Jr. and Lydia (Parker) Cooke; m. William Crayton Nelson Jr., Nov. 27, 1970; children: Tricia Leigh, William Crayton III. Student, Tex. Tech U., 1967-70; BBA in Mktg., U. Houston, 1971; grad., Realtors Inst., 1984. Field supr. market research Higginbotham Assocs., Houston, 1971-76; agt. Laguardia, Gavrel and Kirk Real Estate, Houston, 1982-83; mgr., broker Gary Greene Realtors/Better Homes and Gardens, Missouri City, Tex., 1983—, also bd. dirs.; instr. Mktg. Specialist Sch., 1987. Author Real Estate Data Market Report, 1985. Chmn. Community Revitalization Com., auction Ft. Bend chpt. Texans War on Drugs, 1988 ; sponsor Tex. War on Drugs, Sugar Land, 1987, auction chmn., 1988, Women's Refuge Ctr./Ft. Bend, Sugar Land, 1987; sequincentennial life mem. Tex. Real Estate Polit. Action Com., Sugarland, 1984—. Mem. Tex. Assn. Realtors (bd. dirs.), Ft. Bend County Bd. Realtors (bd. dirs. 1984-86, pres. 1988—), Grad. Realtors Inst., Ft. Bend C. of C. (leadership 2000, president's coun., bd. dirs. 1989-92, v.p. edn. and arts div. 1990), Women's Coun. Realtors (liaison 1987), Realtors Nat. Mktg. Inst. (cert. residential specialist, residential broker). Republican. Episcopalian. Home: 1418 Sugar Creek Blvd Sugar Land TX 77478 Office: Gary Greene Realtors 3536 Hwy 6 Sugar Land TX 77479

NELSON, VICTORIA C., utilities executive; b. Detroit, June 20, 1958; d. William Lee and Naomi Wahneeta (Walden) N. BA, Oakland U., Rochester, Mich., 1981. Cert. test adminstr., energy cons., Mich., N.C. Sales clk. Detroit Audio Systems, 1975-77; assembly clk. Ford Motor Co., Dearborn, Mich., 1977; dispatcher Oakland U., 1977-78; probation officer Oakland County, Royal Oak, Mich., 1978-79; customer svcs. rep. Consumers Power Co., Royal Oak, Mich., 1979-80, customer field rep., 1980-81, energy cons., 1981-85, human resource adminstrn., 1985—. Mem. founders soc. Detroit Inst. Arts, 1988. Mem. NAFE. Democrat. Presbyterian. Home: 19431 Archer Detroit MI 48219 Office: Consumers Power Co 4600 Coolidge Hwy Royal Oak MI 48068

NELSON, VIOLET M., nursing educator; b. Camden, N.J., Jan. 19, 1935; d. Cecil W. and Helen (Landenberger) Rotzell; m. Glenn A. Nelson, Aug. 30, 1958; children: Faith, Paul, JoyAnne, Hope. BA with honors, San Jose State U., 1975, MA, 1977. RN; cert. in gerontology. Dir. staff devel. Our Lady of Fatima Villa, Saratoga, Calif., Mission SNF, Santa Clara, Calif.; instr. Mission Coll., Santa Clara, DeAnza Coll., Cupertino, Calif.; lectr. San Francisco Bay Area Hosps.; bd. dirs. RN State of Calif. C.E. for Nurses. Vol. instr. ARC. Mem. Peninsula Skilled Nurses Assn., CAHF Long Term Care Nurses. Republican. Baptist. Home: 1295 S Cawston Ave 78 Hemet CA 92343

NELSON CRESKEY, MARGUERITE, educator; b. S.I., N.Y., June 23, 1947; d. Arthur Clayton and Marguerite Mary (Hansen) Nelson; m. John Joseph Creskey, May 16, 1970. AB magna cum laude, Boston Coll., 1969; MS in Edn., SUNY, Plattsburgh, 1973; post master's cert. in gerontology, Yeshiva U., 1982; postgrad., Fordham U., N.Y.C. Cert. elem. and spl. edn. tchr., N.Y. Pre-primary tchr. Pub. Sch. 22R, N.Y.C. Bd. Edn., S.I., 1969-70; primary tchr. Oak Street Sch., Plattsburgh, 1971-73, Laurel Plains Sch., Clarkstown Cen. Schs., New City, N.Y., 1973-78, Resource Rm. Lakewood Sch., Congers, N.Y., 1978—; mem. adj. faculty St. Thomas Aquinas Coll., Sparkill, N.Y., 1985-89, Fordham U., Lincoln Ctr., N.Y.C., 1990—; presenter in field., 1984—. Contbr. articles to profl. jours. Mem. West Br. Conservation Assn., N.Y.C. Recipient Impact II Tchrs. Recognition award, Impact of Rockland and Westchester, 1984; grantee Chpt. II, 1983-84, Clarkstown Cen. Schs., 1986-90; nominee Outstanding Educator of Yr. Nat. PTA. Mem. Am. Ednl. Rsch. Assn., Assn. for Children with Learning Disabilities, Coun. for Exceptional Children, Nat. Assn. for Poetry Therapy, Assn. for Retarded Citizens, AAUW, Rockland County Hist. Soc. Home: 667 S Mountain Rd New City NY 10956 Office: Lakewood Elem Sch 77 Lakeland Ave Congers NY 10920

NEMARA, VANESSA ANNE, federal official; b. Middle Village, N.Y., Aug. 24, 1953; d. Frank Joseph and Ann Margaret (O'Mara) Nemara; 1 child, Sophia Marie. BS in Police Sci., John Jay Coll., 1975, MA in Criminal Justice, 1980. Salesperson Lane Bryant Dept. Store, N.Y.C., 1973-74; from procurement clk. to supervisory contract specialist Gen. Svcs. Adminstrn., N.Y.C., 1974-85, procurement analyst, 1986-88; supr. contract specialist U.S. Dept. Agr., Orient Point, N.Y., 1985-86, USCG, Governor's Island, N.Y., 1988—. Roman Catholic. Home: 56 Flower Rd Valley Stream NY 11581-1610 Office: USCG Bldg 400 M Rm 207M VPL-1 Governor's Island NY 10004-5085

NEMEROFF, CAROL JILL, psychology educator; b. Montreal, Que., Can., Aug. 17, 1960; d. Moe Coleman and Sybil Lynn (Moidel) N. BA in Psychology summa cum laude, McGill U., Montreal, 1981; MA in Psychology, U. Pa., Phila., 1982, PhD, 1988. Cert. psychologist, Ariz. Instr. psychology dept. psychology U. Pa., Phila., 1983-87; grad. trainee McArthur Found., Phila., 1987-88; asst. prof. dept. psychology Ariz. State U., Tempe, 1988—; intern psychology Temple U. Health Scis. Ctr., Phila., 1986-87; group therapist Temple Group Med. Practices, 1987-88; occasional reviewer Child Devel., Tempe, 1989-90. Contbr. articles to profl. jours., chpts. to books. Active Earth Trust, Phila., 1987—. Social Scis./Humanities Rsch. Coun. Can. doctoral fellow, 1982-85, NIH biomed. sub award, 1988-89. Mem. Am. Psychol. Assn., Am. Psychol. Soc., Western Psychol. Assn. Office: Dept Psychology Ariz State U Tempe AZ 85287-1104

NEMIR, ROSALEE, pediatrician; b. Waco, Tex., July 16, 1905; d. David and Emma (Shakir) N.; m. Elias J. Audi, July 1934 (dec. 1968); children: Elaine, Alfred, Robert. BA, U. Tex., Austin, 1926; MD, Johns Hopkins U., 1930; ScD (hon.), Colgate U., 1974. Instr. Med. Coll. NYU, N.Y.C., 1933-39, asst. prof., 1939-50, prof., 1959—; vis. prof. microbiology Columbia U. Coll. Physicians and Surgeons, N.Y.C., 1958-59; dir. pediatric rsch. and edn. N.Y. Infirmary, N.Y.C., 1966-73; mem. expert panel on tuberculosis Dept. Health City of N.Y., 1988-89. Contbr. rsch. articles to med. jours. Bd. mgrs. Intercollegiate Br. YMCA, 1954-64, Bklyn. Arthritis and Rheumatism Found., 1954-56, Bklyn. chpt. ARC Greater N.Y., 1973-74; bd. dirs. Bklyn. Kindergarten Soc., 1954—, Willoughby House Settlement, Bklyn., 1955-68, Am. Middle East Rehab., 1971-76, Am. Near East Refugee Aid, 1976-89; trustee Judson Health Ctr., 1963-75; mem. women's com. Boston Symphony Orch., Bklyn., 1950-68, 73; treas. Charles H. Malik Edn. and Loan Fund, 1968-89; rep. Nat. Bicentennial Svc. Alliance, 1975. Decorated medal of Cedars of Lebanon, Republic of Lebanon, 1968; recipient recognition award Bklyn. Kindergarten Soc., 1987, Emily Dunning Barringer award Gouveneur Hosp., 1989, numerous others. Mem. Am. Acad. Pediatrics, Soc. Pediatric Rsch., Am. Pediatric Soc., N.Y. Acad. Medicine, Am. Coll. Chest Physicians, Am. Thoracic Soc., N.Y. Acad. Scis. (hon.)AMA (Physician's Recognitian award 1978), Am. Med. Women's Assn. (Elizabeth Blackwell award 1970), Women's Med. Soc. N.Y. State (Woman of Yr. 1973), Med. Women's Internat. Assn. (hon.), N.Y. County Med. Soc., Soc. Adolescent Medicine, Soc. Alumni Bellevue Hosp., Cosmopolitan Club, Phi Beta Kappa. Home: 7 Monroe Pl Brooklyn NY 11201

NEMIRO, BEVERLY MIRIUM ANDERSON, writer, educator; b. St. Paul, May 29, 1925; d. Martin and Anna Mae (Oshanyk) Anderson; m. Jerome Morton Nemiro, Feb. 10, 1951 (div. May 1975); children: Guy Samuel, Lee Anna, Dee Martin. Student Reed Coll., 1943-44; BA, U. Colo., 1947; postgrad., U. Denver. Tchr., Seattle Pub. Schs., 1945-46; fashion coordinator, dir. Denver Dry Goods Co., 1948-51; fashion model, Denver, 1951-58, 78—; fashion dir. Denver Market Week Assn., 1952-53; free-lance writer, Denver, 1958—; moderator TV program Your Preschool Child, Denver, 1955-56; instr. writing and communications U. Colo. Denver Ctr., 1970—, U. Calif., San Diego, 1976-78, Met. State Coll., 1985—; dir. pub. relations Fairmont Hotel, Denver, 1979-80; free lance fashion and TV model; author: The Complete Book of High Altitude Baking, 1961, Colorado a la Carte, 1963, Colorado a la Carte, Series II, 1966, (with Donna Hamilton) The High Altitude Cookbook, 1969, The Busy People's Cookbook, 1971 (Better Homes and Gardens Book Club selection 1971), Where to Eat in Colorado, 1967, Lunch Box Cookbook, 1965, Complete Book of High Altitude Baking, 1961, (under name Beverly Anderson) Single After 50, 1978, The New High Altitude Cookbook, 1980. Co-founder, pres. Jr. Symphony Guild, Denver, 1959-60; active Denver Art Mus., Denver Symphony Group. Recipient Achievement Rewards for Coll. Scientists, Sante Fe Opera, Denver Ear Inst., Top Hand award Colo. Authors' League, 1969, 72, 79-82, 100 Best Best Books of Yr. award N.Y. Times, 1969, 71; named one of Colo.'s Women of Yr., Denver Post, 1964. Mem. Pub. Relations Soc. Am., Am. Soc. Journalists and Authors, Nat. Writers Club, Colo. Authors League (dir. 1969—), Authors Guild, Authors League Am., Friends Denver Library, Rotary, Sigma Delta Chi, Kappa Alpha Theta. Address: 420 S Marion Pkwy Apt 1003 Denver CO 80209

NEMKO, BARBARA GAIL, academic coordinator, educational planner; b. Bronx, N.Y., Jan. 24, 1945; d. Herbert and Leona (Beder) Padrid; m. Martin Nathan Nemko, Dec. 26, 1976; 1 child, Amy Helene. BA, Queens Coll., 1964, MS, 1972; PhD, U. Calif.-Berkeley, 1981. Dir. of evaluation (partnership) U. Calif.-Berkeley, 1978-80; project dir. Calif. State Dept. Edn., U. Calif.-Davis, 1979—; cons. Berkeley Unified Sch. Dist., 1974-75, Sonoma State U., Rohnert Park, Calif., 1983—, Calif. State U.-Sacramento, 1983—, Calif. State U.-Los Angeles, 1985—, Calif. Poly. U., Pomona, 1986—; mem. regional action team State Dept. Edn., Sacramento, 1984—; co-host Schooltak program Sta. KALW, San Francisco. Author: Resources, Strategies, and Directions to Better Serve Disadvantaged Students in Career-Vocational Programs, 1983; (with M. Nemko) How to Get Your Child a Private School Education in a Public School. Mem. Calif. Assn. Vocat. Educators, Am. Vocat. Assn. Jewish. Avocations: tennis, theatre, music, reading. Home: 5936 Chabolyn Terr Oakland CA 94618 Office: U Calif Dept Applied Behavioral Scis AOB 4 Davis CA 95616

NEMMERS, SHERRY J., advertising agency executive; b. Blue Mountain Lake, N.Y., Aug. 11, 1954; d. Michael John and M. Jane (Santoro) Jacobs; m. Barry H. Nemmers, May 6, 1978. Student, Dartmouth Coll., 1974-75, U. Strasbourg, France, 1975; AB, Vassar Coll., 1976. Writer Grey Advt., N.Y.C., 1976-77; writer Dancer Fitzgerald Sample, Inc., N.Y.C., 1977-82, v.p., head creative group, 1982-83, sr. v.p., assoc. creative dir., 1983-84; sr. v.p., creative dir. DFS/Dorland Worldwide, N.Y.C., 1984-87, Saatchi & Saatchi DFS Compton, N.Y.C., 1987—; judge CLIO Awards, N.Y.C., 1980-82, The Hatch Awards, Boston, 1982; cons. Chandelle Farms, Holcomb, N.Y., 1986-87; cons., bd. dirs. Profl. Media Services, Boston, 1985-87. Creator: (animated character) McGruff, the Crime Dog (Pub. Service award 1987); founder, editor Out of the Blue, 1975, The Vassar Quar., 1979; contbr. articles to Dan's Papers, 1974-77. Writer Ad Council, Nat. Crime Coalition, N.Y.C., 1977-87, Fresh Air Fund, N.Y.C., 1980-87, Breast Exam. Ctr. Harlem, N.Y., 1982-85; mem. Blue Mountain Lake Performing Art Ctr., 1980-87. Recipient CLIO awards, N.Y.C., 1980-84, Effie awards, N.Y.C., 1983-85, The One Show award, N.Y.C., 1984, 85, 86, Internat. Radio and TV award Cannes (France) Film Festival, 1985. Mem. Advt. Women of Am. Roman Catholic. Club: Yale. Office: Saatchi & Saatchi Advt 375 Hudson St New York NY 10014*

NEMSER, LYNN SEAVEY, human resources consultant; b. Taunton, Mass., Sept. 2, 1949; d. Robert Warren and Dorothy Irene (MacLeod) Seavey; m. Michael Frederick Nemser; 1 child, Stephanie Robin. BA in Am. Studies, William Smith Coll., Geneva, N.Y., 1971. Job placement counselor U. Pa., Phila., 1972-74, 75-76; recruiting cons. E.I Du Pont de Nemours & Co., Inc., Wilmington, Del., 1974-75; compensation analyst Colonial Penn Group, Phila., 1977-78; exec. recruiter The Borton-Wallace Co., Chadds Ford, Pa., 1978-79; project mgr. recruiting The Vanguard Group, Inc., Valley Forge, Pa., 1985-87; human resources cons. Data Gen. Corp., Pitts., 1988—; ptnr. Burkholder & Nemser, Inc., Pitts., 1987—. Mem. Soc. for Human Resource Mgmt. (cert.), Pitts. Personnel Assn., Employment Mgmt. Assn. (profl. devel. com. 1988—). Office: Data General Corp 200 Fleet St #5005 Pittsburgh PA 15220

NENSTIEL, SUSAN KISTHART, insurance professional office adminstrator; b. Hazleton, Pa., Aug. 21, 1951; d. Frank W. and Mary A. (Price) Kisthart; m. David W. Nenstiel, June 4, 1977. BS, Pa. State U., 1973; MBA, Wilkes (Pa.) Coll., 1982. Control mgr. Barrett, Haentjens & Co., Hazleton, 1973-79, export mgr., 1979-86; exec. dir. Leadership Hazleton, 1986-87; devel. officer Planned Parenthood of NE Pa., Wilkes-Barre, 1986-87; ins. agt., office mgr. Nenstiel & Nenstiel, West Hazleton, Pa., 1988—. Pres. YWCA, Hazleton, 1983-85, Womens Coalition of Greater Hazleton, 1987—; sec. Govt. Study Commn., Hazleton, 1984-85; bd. dirs. United Way Greater Hazleton, 1986; trustee, sec. Hazleton Area Pub. Library, 1987—; chair Luzerne County Commn. for Women, 1988—; mem., chair Hazleton City Zoning Bd., 1988—; treas. Pa. Women's Campaign Fund, 1987—. Named one of Outstanding Women Penns Woods Coun. Girl Scouts U.S.A., 1977, Outstanding Young Women in Am., 1985, Woman of Yr. Soroptomist Internat., 1984; recipient Luzerne County Pathfinder's award, 1990. Mem. AAUW (br. pres. 1977-79, state sec. 1981-83, state treas. 1983-85, Br. Outstanding Woman of the Yr. 1980, assn. women's issue com. 1989—), LWV, Internat. Platform Assn., NAFE, Nat. Assn. Ins. Women. Republican. Home: 537 W Diamond Ave Hazleton PA 18201

NEOFES, MELISSA PATTERSON, account executive; b. Pitts., Sept. 21, 1958; d. William George and Agnes (Smith) N. BA, Duquesne U., 1980; MPIA, U. of Pitts., 1982. Lic. health and life ins. rep. Intern Internat. div. Westinghouse Electric, Pitts., 1982; sales rep. Internat. Bus. Assocs., Pitts., 1983-84; telemktg. rep. Blue Cross and Blue Shield of the Nat. Capital Area, Washington, 1984-85, acct. exec., 1985-86, sr. acct. exec., 1986—; guest mem. Diplomatic Corps of Washington, 1987—. Vol. Dem. Nat. Com., Washington, 1988, sr. high youth advisor Immanuel Ch. on the Hill, Alexandria, 1987—. Mem. NAFE, Nat. Assn. for Fgn. Student Affairs, Internat. Found. of Employee Benefits, Nat. Cathedral, Smithsonian Instn. Democrat. Episcopalian. Office: BCBSNCA 550 12th St S W Washington DC 20065

NERNESS, REBECCA J., sales executive; b. Des Moines, Aug. 4, 1955; d. Harlan D. and Jane P. (Hutson) Nerness. BS, Iowa State U., 1977. Cert. leadership and supervisory skills Nat. Seminar, Karrass Negotiating Seminar. Reg. mgr., filter specialist Honeywell, Inc., Mpls.; field sales mgr. MicroS-witch-Honeywell, Freeport, Ill.; area sales mgr. Gelman Scis., Inc., Ann Arbor, Mich. State of Iowa scholar. Mem. Nat. Restaurant Assn., Am. Welding Soc., Am. Filtration Soc. Home: 2440 Salem B2 Woodridge IL 60517

NESBITT, LENORE CARRERO, federal judge; m. Joseph Nesbitt; 2 children: Sarah, Thomas. A.A., Stephens Coll., 1952; B.S., Northwestern U., 1954; student U. Fla. Law Sch., 1954-55; LL.B., U. Miami, 1957. Private practice, Nesbitt & Nesbitt, 1960-63; spl. asst. attorney gen., 1961-63; research asst., Dade County Circuit Ct., 1963-65; with Law Offices of John Robert Terry, 1969-73; counsel, Fla. State Bd. Med. Examiners, 1970-71; with Petersen, McGowan & Feder, 1973-75; judge, Fla. state courts, 1975-82; judge, U.S. Dist. Ct. (so. dist.) Fla., Miami, 1983—. Mem. Am., Fla. Bar Assns., U.S. Jud. Conf. Com. on Criminal Law and Probation Adminstrn. Office: US Dist Ct 301 N Miami Ave Miami FL 33128-7784

NESBITT, MARGOT LORD (MRS. CHARLES R. NESBITT), fine arts appraiser; b. Tonbridge, Kent, Eng., Feb. 13, 1927; d. Douglas G.R. and Octave (Waghorne) Lord; came to U.S., 1930, naturalized, 1937; BA in English Lit., U. Okla., 1950, BFA in Art History, 1970, MA, 1975, PhD, 1988; m. Charles R. Nesbitt, June 6, 1948; children—Nancy Margot, Douglas Charles, Carolyn Jane. Ordained deacon Episcopal Ch., 1988. Appraiser fine arts, Oklahoma City, 1968—; treas. Apollo Oil Corp., 1974—. Mem. Okla. Arts and Humanities Council, 1971-76; mem. women's com. Oklahoma City Symphony, 1964-89; life mem. Okla. Art Center, women's bd., 1962-63; chmn. art collection State of Okla., 1975-76; bd. dirs. Okla. Found. for Disabled, 1972-75; bd. advisers Nat. Trust Historic Preservation, 1976-81. Mem. English Speaking Union, Okla. Hist. Soc. (dir. 1975-85), Hist. Preservation Oklahoma City (treas. 1977-80), Am. Soc. Appraisers (sr. mem.; pres. Okla. chpt. 1978-79), Appraisers' Assn. Am., Kappa Alpha Theta (pres. alumni chpt. 1962-64, Okla. chmn. Theta Link 1965-66, treas. corp. bd. 1976-77). Democrat. Episcopalian (treas. assemblies 1971-72, mem. women's bd. 1971-72, treas. altar guild 1972-73, treas. St. Paul's Cathedral 1976-78, mem. vestry 1978-85, jr. warden 1978-82, 84-85), deacon, 1988—. Clubs: Connoisseur (pres. 1956-57); Early American Glass (treas. 1973-75). Address: 1703 N Hudson St Oklahoma City OK 73103

NESBITT, RADIAN BETH, owner, school director; b. Portland, Oreg., June 2, 1945; d. Rader Berg and Cecylle Fern (Keller) Pedersen; m. John Marshall Nesbitt, July 3, 1965; children: Tamara Jean, Susan Marie. BS in Edn., Portland State U., 1975. Day care coordinator Lower Columbia Coll., Longview, Wash., 1973-74; presch. tchr. Lower Columbia Coll., Longview, 1975-76; presch. tchr. Bates Tech. Inst., Tacoma, 1978-79, instr. children, 1979-80; arts council coordinator Washington County Schs., Plymouth, N.C., 1981-82; owner, instr. Art Sch., Plymouth, 1983; adult instr. Beaufort Community Coll., Washington, N.C., 1982-89; owner, dir. Funworks Presch., Plymouth, 1984—. Contbg. author (book) Working With Your Child, 1987. Pres. Washington County Arts Coun., Inc., Plymouth, 1989-91, v.p. Dramatic Arts, 1986-89; mem. Washington County Hist. Soc., Plymouth, 1989—, Hosp. Auxiliary, Plymouth, 1989—; bd. dirs. United Way, Plymouth, 1981-83. Recipient Best-In-Show-Art Work award Washington County Arts Council, 1981, Vol. award Washington County Schs.,

1989. Mem. AAUW (pres. 1983-89, v.p. state div. 1988-90), N.C. Assn. for the Edn. Young Children, N.C. Day Care Assn. Presbyterian. Home: 314 Hampton Dr Plymouth NC 27962 Office: Funworks Preschool 406 E 3rd St Plymouth NC 27962

NESHIEM, ROBERTA MARY, marriage, family and child therapist; b. Pitts., May 10, 1934; d. Frank J. Grundler and Marion Bertrum; children: Michael, Scott, Kim. BA, Mansfield (Pa.) State Coll., 1956; MA, San Diego State U., 1959; PhD, Newport U., 1979. Counselor Hemet (Calif.) High Sch., 1967, Fullerton (Calif.) High Sch., 1968-73, Lowell High Sch., Fullerton, 1973-78; dir., psychotherapist Ctr. for Creative Growth, Fullerton, 1979—. Author: column Dear Dr. Bobbi, 1983, Vitality mag., 1984, Fullerton Calendar, 1984. Mem. YWCA, Fullerton. Mem. Calif. Assn. for Counseling and Devel. (bd. dirs. 1987—), Calif. Assn. Marriage and Family Therapists, Calif. Mental Health Counselors Assn. (pres. 1987), Calif. Soc. for Hynosis in Family Therapy. Office: Ctr for Creative Growth 2555 E Chapman Ave 300-37 Fullerton CA 92631

NESMITH, FRANCES JANE, education consultant; b. Tulsa, Nov. 6, 1926; d. George W. and Frances Pearl (Hendrix) N. BA, U. Houston, 1947; MA in Polit. Sci., Columbia U., 1951; postgrad., U. Tex., 1957, 58, 61-64; EdD, Columbia U., 1968. Cert. edn1. adminstr. Tchr. Houston Ind. Sch. Dist., 1947-58; lectr. U. Houston, 1956-58; tchr. Austin (Tex.) Ind. Sch. Dist., 1958-69; instr. Columbia U., N.Y.C., 1964-66, Austin Community Coll., 1973-74; coord. secondary social studies Austin Ind. Sch. Dist., 1969-86; adj. assoc. prof. Coll. Edn., U. Tex., Austin, 1986—; edn. cons. Austin, 1986—; cons. Addison-Wesley Pub. Co., Menlo Park, Calif., 1987—, State Bar Tex., Austin, 1989—, Learned & Tested, Inc., Orlando, Fla., 1986. Author: Texas Teacher Appraisal Systems - Economics, 1987, World History, 1988; guest editor Southwestern Jour. Social Education, 1981; co-author: The Story of Texas, 1963. Mem. Travis County Hist. Commn., Austin, 1978—; pub. mem. Citizens and Law Focused Edn. Com. State Bar Tex., Austin, 1983-86; mem. adv. coun. Lifetime Learning Inst., Austin, 1989—. Heft scholar Columbia U., N.Y.C., 1966; recipient Leon Jaworski award Tex. Young Lawyers, State Bar Tex., Austin, 1986, George Washington medal Freedoms Found., Valley Forge, Pa., 1986. Mem. Nat. Coun. Social Studies, Tex. Coun. Social Studies (mem. exec. bd.), Austin Coun. Social Studies (exec. sec. 1969-86), Tex. State Tchrs. Assn. (life), Tex. State Hist. Assn., Delta Kappa Gamma (internat. fellow 1965), Phi Delta Kappa. Democrat. Methodist. Home and Office: 2605 Salado Austin TX 78705

NESMITH, LINDA CAROL, computer software professional; b. Abilene, Tex., June 22, 1950; d. C.W. and Margie Ann (Truitt) N. BS with highest honors, U. Tex., 1972. From software architect to programs mgr. Asia/Pacific Group IBM, Austin, Tex., 1978-88, programs mgr. world trade support, 1989—; guest speaker Coll. Bus. Adminstrn. U. Tex., Austin, 1984-86. Active in Adopt-A-Sch., Austin, 1985-86. Mem. Toastmasters Internat., Sierra Club. Mem. Unity Ch.

NESSON, MARLENE, information systems executive; b. Elizabeth, N.J., Mar. 6, 1956; d. Theodore Aaron and Mary (Monticello) N. BA, Kean Coll., Union, N.J., 1978. Programmer analyst N.Y. Life Ins., 1978-83; product cons. Dun & Bradstreet, 1983-86; mgr., customer support svcs. Dun & Bradstreet Computing Svcs., Wilton, Conn., 1986-89; internat. tech. mgr., prosuct line mgr. Info. Builders, Inc., N.Y.C., 1989—; speaker Focus Users Group, London, 1987, Madrid, 1987-88. Vol. Mothers Against Drunk Drivers, Conn., 1989. Roman Catholic. Home: 28 Davenport Ave Westport CT 06880

NESTOR CASTELLANO, BRENDA DIANA, real estate executive; b. Palm Beach, Fla., Nov. 10, 1955; d. John Joseph and Marion O'Connor Nestor; m. Robert Castellano. Student, U. Miami, Fla., 1978. Lic. real estate broker, Fla. Salesman Oscar E Dooley, Inc., Miami, Fla., 1978-80; prin. Brenda Nestor Assocs, Inc., Miami Beach, Fla., 1980—; sr. v.p., bd. dirs. D.W.G. Corp., N.V.F. Corp., Salem Corp., Southeastern Pub. Svc., Graniteville Corp., Essex Ins., Chespeak Ins.; exec. v.p. Security Mgmt. Named Ms. Charity City of Miami, 1985. Mem. Miami Beach Bd. of Realtors (bd. dirs. 1984—), Real Estate Securities & Exch. Com. Roman Catholic. Clubs: Le Club (N.Y.C.); La Gorce Country (Miami Beach), Surf (Miami Beach). Home and Office: 6917 Collins Ave Miami Beach FL 33141

NETHERTON, JANET L., social worker; b. Blackwell, Okla., Aug. 20, 1952; d. George Max and Mary Louise (Steichen) Klein; children: Ginnie, Carrie. Student, Northeastern A & M Coll., 1983. Social worker II Noble County Dept. Human Svcs., Perry, Okla., 1986—. Mem. Nat. Assn. Am. Bus. Clubs (treas. 1990—), Okla. Health and Welfare Assn., Am. Health and Welfare Assn., Okla. Pub. Employees Assn., Band Boosters Club, Tip-In Club, Takedown Club, Okla. State U. Posse Club, Kappa Delta Alumni Assn. Democrat. Roman Catholic. Home: 1904 Ridgecrest Dr Perry OK 73077

NETSCH, DAWN CLARK, state official; b. Cin., Sept. 16, 1926; BA with distinction, Northwestern U., 1948, JD magna cum laude, 1952; m. Walter A. Netsch. Bar: Ill, D.C. Law clk. U.S. Dist. Ct. Chgo.; adminstrv. and legal aide Ill. Gov. Otto Kerner, 1961-65; prof. law Northwestern U., 1965—; pvt. practice, Washington and Chgo.; mem. Ill. Senate; elected Ill. comptroller, 1990. Del. Ill. Constl. Conv. Author: (with Daniel Mandelker and Peter Salsich) State and Local Government in a Federal System; contbr. articles to legal jours. Mem. ABA, LWV, ACLU (bd. dirs. Ill. div. leadership coun.), Chgo. Bar Assn., Econ. Club. Office: Office of Comptr 201 State House Springfield IL 62706 also: 761 W Diversey Ste 211 Chicago IL 60614

NETTER, CORNELIA ANN, real estate broker; b. N.Y.C., July 11, 1933; d. Frank H. and Mary (MacFadyen) N.; divorced; 1 child, Cornelia Jr. Student, U. Denver, 1951-53, C.W. Post Coll., 1958-60; BS, N.Y. State Regents, 1972. Sec. Newsday Bus. Office, Garden City, N.Y., 1959-61; adminstrv. asst. to U.S. Senator J.K. Javits N.Y., 1961-66; spl. asst. to Gov. Nelson A. Rockefeller Office of Gov., N.Y.C., 1966-69; pub. affairs dir. N.Y. State Health Planning Commn., 1969-72; dir. human resource planning and programs N.Y. State Office Planning Svcs., Albany and N.Y.C., 1972-76; pres. Netter Communications, N.Y.C., 1976-83, Netter Real Estate, N.Y.C., 1983—, Independent Brokers Network, 1988—. Founding mem. N.Y. State Women's Polit. Caucus, Albany, 1971; mem. Rep. Family Com., 1986—; mem. steering com. Breakthru Found., N.Y.C., 1983-85; bd. dirs. N.Y. Citiworks, 1987-90; dep campaign mgr. Rockefeller Gubernatorial Campaign, N.Y.C., 1966, dir. spl. groups, 1970; co-campaign mgr. for N.Y., Nixon Presdl. Campaign, 1968, dir. ethnic and spl. groups, 1972; candidate for N.Y. State Assembly, 1974; mem. Rep. County Com. Mem. Nat. Assn. Realtors, Real Estate Bd. N.Y. (legis. com.), Downtown Brokers Assn. (chmn. polit. action com.), Greenwich Village C. of C. (bd. dirs. 1988—). Office: Netter Real Estate 853 Broadway #1020 New York NY 10003

NETTER, VIRGINIA THOMPSON, produce company owner; b. Hardyville, Ky., Nov. 2, 1931; d. Duluth Sydnor and Vera (Asbury) Thompson; m. S. Mitchell Netter, Oct. 4, 1947; children: Ronald Lee, Candace Netter Harrison. BA, U. Louisville, 1982; MA in Counseling/Clin. Psychology, Spalding U., 1989. Owner, Netter Produce Co., Louisville, 1954—, Big Four Farms, Belmont, Ky., 1959—. Named to Hon. Order Ky. Cols., 1982. Mem. Woodcock Soc., Psi Chi, Phi Kappa Phi. Avocations: ballroom dancing, horseback riding, travel. Home: 1029 Alta Vista Rd Louisville KY 40205 Office: Netter Produce Co 331-335 Produce Plaza Louisville KY 40202

NETTESHEIM, CHRISTINE COOK, federal judge; b. Oakland, Calif., Aug. 25, 1944; d. Leo Marshall and Carolyn Grant (Odell) Cook; m. Paul Henry Nettesheim, Feb. 18, 1978. BA, Stanford U., 1966; JD, U. Utah, 1969. Bar: Utah 1969, D.C. 1972, Calif. 1982. Clk. to chief judge U.S. Ct. Appeals (10th cir.), 1969-70; trial atty. U.S. Dept. Justice, Washington, 1970-72, Fed. Trade Commn., Washington, 1972-74; litigation Hogan & Hartson, Washington, 1974-76; spl. counsel Pension Benefit Guaranty Corp., Washington, 1976-78; asst. gen. counsel U.S. Ry. Assn., Washington, 1978-80; litigation Shack & Kimball P.C., Washington, 1980-83; judge U.S. Claims Ct., Washington, 1983—. Mem. State Bar Assn. Calif., D.C. Bar Assn., Order of Coif. Republican. Presbyterian. Office: US Claims Ct 717 Madison Pl NW Washington DC 20005

NETTLESHIP, LOIS E., history educator; b. Bklyn., June 14, 1942; d. Charles and Ethel (Bernstein) Shankman; m. William. A. Nettleship, Aug. 14, 1966; children: Elizabeth, Anna. BA, Sarah Lawrence Coll., 1964; MA, Columbia U., 1966; DPhil., U. Sussex, Eng., 1976. Mem. faculty Johnson County Community Coll., Overland Park, Kans., 1975—; dir. Johnson County Ctr. for Local History, Overland Park, Kans., 1983—. Author numerous books on local Kans. history, 1986—; contbr. articles to profl. jours. Mem. Johnson County Bicentennial Commn., 1987-88. Woodrow Wilson Found. fellow 1964, NEH fellow 1980, 82; named Innovator of Yr. League for Innovation, 1984. Mem. Kans. Com. for the Humanities (bd. dirs. 1987—), Kans. Hist. Tchrs. Assn. (pres. 1987-88), Kans. State Hist. Soc. (editorial com. 1988—). Home: 4607 W 63d St Shawnee Mission KS 66208

NEUBAUER, CARLYLE E., communications specialist; b. Clinton, Iowa, May 2, 1921; d. Carl Fred and Emma Marie (Meyer) N.; children: Celia June, Laurance William, Jan Marie, Philip Carl. BS, U. Ill., 1949. City editor Arcola (Ill.) Record-Herald, 1949-54; editor Shelbyville (Ill.) Dem., 1954-56; editorial writer Decatur (Ill.) Herald Review, 1956-60; mng. editor Lakeland (Fla.) Ledger, 1960-63, Sarasota (Fla.) Herald-Tribune, 1963-68; exec. editor Palm Beach Post & Times, West Palm Beach, Fla., 1968-85; products coord. City of West Palm Beach, 1985-87; newsletter editor C. of C., West Palm Beach, 1988-89; communications specialist C. of C., Palm Beach Gardens, Fla., 1990—; market rep. Kopper Popper, Jupiter, Fla., 1989—. Mem. Kiwanis. Presbyterian. Home: 5402 Canyon Trail West Palm Beach FL 33405 Office: C of C 1983 PGA Blvd Palm Beach Gardens FL 33408

NEUFELD, ELIZABETH FONDAL, biochemist, educator; b. Paris, Sept. 27, 1928; U.S. citizen; m. 1951. Ph.D., U. Calif., Berkeley, 1956; D.H.C. (hon.), U. Rene Descartes, Paris, 1978; D.Sc. (hon.), Russell Sage Coll., Troy, N.Y., 1981, Hahnemann U. Sch. Medicine, 1984. Asst. research biochemist U. Calif., Berkeley, 1957-63; with Nat. Inst. Arthritis, Metabolism and Digestive Diseases, Bethesda, Md., 1963-84, research biochemist, 1963-73, chief sect. human biochem. genetics, 1973-79, chief genetics and biochem. br., 1979-84; prof., chmn. dept. biol. chemistry UCLA Sch. Medicine, 1984—; USPHS fellow U. Calif., Berkeley, 1956-57. Named Passano Found. sr. laureate, 1982; recipient Dickson prize U. Pitts., 1974, Hillebrand award, 1975, Gairdner Found. award, 1981, Albert Lasker Clin. Med. Rsch. award, 1982, William Allan award, 1982, Elliott Cresson medal, 1984, Wolf Found. prize, 1988. Fellow AAAS; mem. NAS, Am. Acad. Arts and Sci., Am. Soc. Human Genetics, Am. Chem. Soc., Am. Soc. Biol. Chemists, Am. Soc. Cell Biology, Am. Soc. Clin. Investigation. Office: UCLA Sch Medicine Dept Biol Chemistry Los Angeles CA 90024-1737

NEUGARTEN, BERNICE LEVIN, social scientist; b. Norfolk, Nebr., Feb. 11, 1916; d. David L. and Sadie (Segall) Levin; m. Fritz Neugarten, July 1, 1940; children: Dail Ann, Jerrold. B.A., U. Chgo., 1936, Ph.D., 1943; D.Sc. (hon.), U. So. Calif., 1980, Cath. U., Nijmegen, 1988. Research assoc. Com. on Human Devel., U. Chgo., 1948-50, asst. prof., 1951-60, asso. prof., 1960-64, prof., 1964-80, chmn., 1969-73; prof. social service adminstrn. U. Chgo., 1978-80, mem. com. on policy studies, 1979-80; prof. human devel. and social policy Northwestern U., 1980-88; Rothschild disting. scholar, prof. emeritus U. Chgo., 1988—; mem. council U. Chgo. Senate, 1968-71, 72-75, 78-80, chmn. council com. on univ. women, 1969-70; nat. adv. council Nat. Inst. on Aging, 1975-76, 78-81, Fed. Council on Aging, 1978-81; dep. chmn. White House Conf. on Aging, 1980-81. Author: (with R.J. Havighurst) American Indian and White Children: A Social-Psychological Investigation, 1955, reprint, 1969, (with R.J. Havighurst) Society and Education, 1957, rev., 1962, 67, 75, (with Assocs.) Personality in Middle and Late Life, 1964, reprint, 1980, (with J.M.A. Munnichs et al) Adjustment to Retirement, 1969, (with R.P. Coleman) Social Status in the City, 1971, Middle Age and Aging, 1968; co-editor: (with H. Eglit) Age Discrimination, 1981, Age or Need? Public Policies for Older People, 1982; assoc. editor Jour. Gerontology, 1958-61, Human Devel., 1962-68; adv. or cons. editor other profl. jours., 1959—; author monographs, research papers and reports. mem. various adv. bodies. Recipient Am. Psychol. Found. Disting. Teaching award, 1975, Disting. Psychologist award Ill. Psychol. Assn., 1979, Sandoz Internat. Prize for Gerontol. Research, 1987. Fellow AAAS, Am. Psychol. Assn. (coun. rep. 1967-69, 73-76, Disting. Sci. Contbn. award for div. 20, 1980), Am. Sociol. Assn., Gerontol. Soc. Am. (pres. 1968-69, Kleemeier award for rsch. in aging 1971, Brookdale award for disting. contbn. 1982, Disting. Mentor award 1988), Am. Acad. Arts and Scis., Internat. Assn. Gerontology (governing coun. 1975-78, chmn. N. Am. exec. com. 1983-85); sr. mem. Inst. Medicine of NAS (com. on aging soc. 1982-87). Home: 5801 Dorchester Ave Chicago IL 60637

NEUHOFF, KATHLEEN TOEPP, veterinarian; b. South Bend, Ind., Nov. 2, 1953; d. Frank Conrad and Rosemary (Williams) Toepp; m. Kenneth Leo Neuhoff, June 27, 1953; children: Carolyn, Patricia, Michael. BS in Agr., Purdue U., 1976, DVM, 1979. Diplomate Am. Bd. Veterinary Practitioners, 1989. Assoc. Magrane Animal Hosp., Mishawaka, Ind., 1979-83; dir. Magrane Animal Hosp., South Bend, Ind., 1983—; pres. bd. dirs. Animal Emergency Clinic, South Bend, 1988—, St. Michael's Elem. Sch., 1989—; cons. on animal control South Bend City Coun., 1987. Contbr. articles to profl. jours and book revs. to popular mags. Bd. dirs. St. Michael's Elem. Sch., Plymouth, Ind., 1989—. Recipient Humanitarian Svc. award Humane Soc. St. Joseph County, 1985. Mem. AVMA, Am. Animal Hosp. Assn. (area dir. 1988—), Am. Assn. Avian Veterinarians, Ind. Vet. Med. Assn. (pub. rels., ethics and animal welfare coms. 1984—), Michiana Vet. Med. Assn. (sec. 1986-87, treas. 1987-88, v.p. 1988-89, pres.-elect 1989-90), Am. Horse Show Assn., Lake Michigan Hunter-Humper Assn., Michawaka C. of C. (Svc. award 1990). Republican. Roman Catholic. Office: Magrane Animal Hosp 2324 Grape Rd Mishawaka IN 46545

NEUMAN, CYNTHIA JEAN, psychologist; b. Bronx, N.Y., June 3, 1943; d. Raymond Edward and Carmen Grace (Kingsley) N.; m. Richard Ansel Rawson, Apr. 20, 1986. BBA, Tulane U., 1964; MS, U. New Orleans, 1976; PhD, U. Miami, 1981. Lic. psychologist, Calif. Rsch. supr. So. Cen. Bell Telephone and Telegraph, New Orleans, 1964-67; mktg. staff asst. Pacific Telephone, San Francisco, 1967-70, staff statistician, 1970-72; med. rsch. asst. La. State U. Med. Ctr., New Orleans, 1974-76; actuarial rsch. analyst Blue Cross of No. Calif., Oakland, Calif., 1976-77; intern, staff psychologist Patton (Calif.) State Hosp., 1979-84; staff psychologist Calif. Med. Facility, Vacaville, Calif., 1984-86, Sutter Meml. Hosp., Sacramento, 1986-87; pvt. practice Sacramento (Calif.) Psychol. Svcs., 1986—. Mem. Am. Psychol. Assn., Calif. Assn. Psychol. Providers (pres. 1988-90), Nat. Register Health Svc. Providers in Psychology, Calif. Psychol. Assn., Sacramento Valley Psychol. Assn., Am. Coll. Forensic Psychology, Assn. for the Advancement Psychology, Forensic Mental Health Assn. Calif., Omicron Delta Epsilon, Beta Gamma Sigma, Phi Chi Theta, Psi Chi, Phi Kappa Phi. Office: Sacramento Psychol Svcs 1409 28th St Ste 202 Sacramento CA 95816

NEUMAN, LINDA KINNEY, state supreme court justice; b. Chgo.. BA, U. Colo., 1970, JD, 1973. Judge 7th Jud. Dist., Iowa, 1982-86; justice Iowa Supreme Ct., Des Moines, 1986—. Office: Iowa Supreme Ct State Capitol Bldg Des Moines IA 50319

NEUMAN, NANCY ADAMS MOSSHAMMER, civic leader; b. Greenwich, Conn., July 24, 1936; d. Alden Smith and Margaret (Mevis) Mosshammer; B.A., Pomona Coll., 1957, LL.D., 1983; M.A., U. Calif. at Berkeley, 1961; D of Humanities (hon.), Westminster Coll., 1987; m. Mark Donald Neuman, Dec. 23, 1958; children: Deborah Neuman Metzler, Jennifer Fuller, Jeffrey Abbott. William A. Johnson Disting. lectr. Am. govt. Pomona Coll., 1990. Pres., Lewisburg (Pa.) area League Women Voters, 1967-70; bd. dirs. LWV Pa., 1970-77, pres., 1975-77; bd. dirs. LWV U.S., 1977-90, 2d v.p., 1978-80, 1st v.p., 1982-84, pres., 1986-90; mem. Pa. Gov.'s Commn. on Mortgage and Interest Rates, 1973, Pa. Commonwealth Child Devel. Com., 1974-75, Nat. Commn. on Pub. Svc., 1987-90; bd. dirs. Housing Assistance Council, Inc., Washington, 1974—, pres., 1978-80; bd. dirs. Nat. Council on Agrl. Life and Labor, 1974-79, Nat. Rural Housing Coalition, 1975—, Pa. Housing Fin. Agy., 1975-80, Jud. Inquiry and Rev. Bd. Pa., 1989—; Disciplinary Bd. Supreme Ct. Pa., 1980-85; mem. Pa. Gov.'s Task Force on Voter Registration, 1975-76, Nat. Task Force for Implementation Equal Rights Amendment, 1975-77; mem. adv. com. Pa. Gov.'s Interdepartmental Council on Seasonal Farmworkers, 1975-77; mem. Appellate Ct. Nominating Commn. Pa., 1976-79; mem. Fed. Jud. Nominating Commn. Pa., 1977-85, chmn., 1978-81, 82-83; mem. Pa. Gov.'s Study Commn. on Pub. Employee Relations, 1976-78; del. Internat. Women's Yr. Conf., 1977; bd. dirs. ERAmerica, Inc., 1st v.p., 1977-79, Nat. Low Income Housing Coalition, 1979-82; Rural Am., 1979-81, Fed. Home Loan Bank Pitts., 1979-82; mem. Nat. Adv. Com. for Women, 1978-79; mem. nat. adv. com. Pa. Neighborhood Preservation Support System, 1976-77; bd. dirs. Pa. Women's Campaign Fund, 1984-86, Rural Coalition, Washington, 1984-90, Com. on the Constitutional System, 1988—, Am. Judicature Soc., 1989—; trustee Citizen's Rsch. Found., 1989—; Virginia Travis lectureship Bucknell U., 1982. Recipient Disting. Alumna award MacDuffie Sch. for Girls, 1979, Liberty Bell award Pa. Bar Assn., 1983, Barrows Alumni award Pomona Coll., 1987, Thomas P. O'Neill Jr. award for exemplary pub. svc., 1989; named Disting. Daughter of Pa., 1987. Mem. ABA (accreditation com. 1990—), Am. Arbitration Assn. (bd. dirs. 1986—). Home: 132 Verna Rd Lewisburg PA 17837

NEUMANN, MAY ALTHEA, retired special education educator; b. Balt., Mar. 23, 1924; d. Henry Neumann and Dorothea Augusta Clas. BS, Capital U., Columbus, 1946; MEd, U. Pitts., 1953. Elem. tchr. Geneva, Ohio, Bridgeport, Ohio, 1948-50; tchr. USAF Oversea Sch., Landsberg, Germany, 1950-51; spl. edn. tchr. Martins Ferry, Ohio, 1951-68, Middlesex Elem. Sch., Balt., 1968-89; ret., 1989. Pres. Luth. Ch., 1986-89, Women of Luth. Ch., 1986-89. Mem. Nat'l Edn. Assoc., St. Lutheran Ch. (pres. 1986-89), Women Lutheran Ch. (pres. 1968-89). Republican.

NEUMANN, NANCY RUTH, studio teacher; b. L.A., Feb. 1, 1948; d. Robert Thomas and Frances Andersen; m. Bernd Fritz Dietmar Neumann, June 26, 1971; children: Peter, Christina, Linda, Christoph, Karin. BA, U. Calif., Riverside, 1969; MA, Sorbonne U., Paris, 1971; credentials, Calif. State U., San Bernardino, 1985. Cert. community coll. tchr., various subjects, Calif., studio tchr., Calif. Missionary, reading instr. Maroua, Cameroon, Africa, 1971-73; instr. Pasadena (Calif.) City Coll., 1974-75; secondary tchr. Riverside (Calif.) Christian Sch., 1985-86; studio tchr. Vista Films, Culver City, 1986, Hollywood (Calif.) Studios, 1986-88, Paramount Studios, Hollywood, Calif., 1986-90, MGM - Lorimar Prodns., Culver City, Calif., 1986-90, Universal Studios, Universal City, Calif., 1986-90, R.J. Louis Prodns., Burbank, Calif., 1987, Michael Landon Prodns., Culver City, 1987-88, Carsey-Werner Prodns., L.A., 1988; instr. Riverside Community Coll., 1988; studio tchr. Bob Booker Prodns., Hollywood, 1988—; exec. producer Am. Pictures, Riverside, 1989—; studio tchr. NBC Prodns., Burbank, 1990; pvt. tutor, Riverside, L.A., 1987—; drama coach Grace Ch., Riverside, 1981-82, Magnolia Ave. Bapt. Ch., Riverside, 1988-89; studio tchr. with NBC. Author: several plays, 1981-89; writer 70 songs, 1968—. Coach for mock trial Riverside Christian High Sch., 1985-86; choir dir. Riverside Christian Sch., 1985-86; Sunday sch. tchr. Grace Bapt. Ch., Harvest Christian Fellowship, Riverside, Vineyard Christian Fellowship, Riverside, Magnolia Ave. Bapt. Ch., Riverside, 1968-89; children's ch. dir. Grace Bapt. Ch., 1981-82. Mem. Nat. Assn. Christian Educators, Internat. Alliance of Theatre and Stage Employees, Internat. Platform Assn., Greater L.A. World Trade Ctr. Assn., Sons of Norway (study scholar 1967), Delta Phi Alpha. Republican. Home: 1787 Prince Albert Dr Riverside CA 92507 Office: Bob Booker Prodns 6605 Eleanor Los Angeles CA 90038

NEUMARK, GERTRUDE FANNY, materials science educator; b. Nuremberg, Germany, Apr. 29, 1927; came to U.S., 1939; d. Siegmund and Bertha (Forchheimer) N.; m. Henry Rothschilld, Mar. 18, 1950. BA, Barnard Coll., 1948; MA, Radcliffe Coll., 1949; PhD, Columbia U., 1951. Advanced rsch. physicist Sylvania Rsch. Labs., Bayside, N.Y., 1952-60; sr. mem. tech. staff Philips Labs., Briarcliff Manor, N.Y., 1960-85; prof. materials sci. Columbia U., N.Y.C., 1985—; cons. Am. Inst. Physics, N.Y.C., 1968-69; NSF vis. prof., 1982. Contbr. numerous articles to sci. jours., chpt. to book; patentee in field. Rice fellow, 1948, Dana fellow, 1948, AAUW Anderson fellow, 1951. Fellow Am. Phys. Soc. (Goeppert-Meyer award com. 1987-89); mem. Materials Rsch. Soc., Electrochem. Soc. (sr.), Soc. Women Engrs. (sr.), Am. Chem. Soc. Office: Columbia U 1137 SW Mudd Bldg New York NY 10027

NEUMEISTER, SUSAN MARY, librarian; b. Buffalo, May 23, 1958; d. Edward John and Regina Mary (Winnicki) N. BA in Geography, SUNY, Buffalo, 1980, MLS, 1982. Clk. Health Scis. Library SUNY, Buffalo, 1978-81, grad. asst., 1981-82, library aide, 1982, cataloger cen. tech. services, 1982—. Librarian Buffalo chpt. ARC, 1983—. Grantee, 1987-88. Mem. ALA, N.Y. Library Assn., SUNY Librarians Assn., Online Audiovisual Catalogers, Western N.Y./Ont. Assn. Coll. and Research Libraries. Democrat. Roman Catholic. Home: 16 Block St Buffalo NY 14211 Office: SUNY Cen Tech Services Lockwood Library Bldg Buffalo NY 14260

NEUMILLER, CATHERINE ANNE, marketing director; b. Galesburg, Ill., Feb. 27, 1964; d. Harry Jacob and Joan Christine (Dilts) N. Student, Macalester Coll., 1982-83; BA, The Coll. of Wooster, 1986. Lifeguard, water safety instr. City of Galesburg (Ill.) Recreation Dept., 1980-86; data processing Admissions, Coll. of Wooster, 1983-86; camp counselor Camp Kamaji for Girls, Cass Lake, Minn., 1984; dark rm. technician News. Svcs., Coll. of Wooster, 1984-86; bicycle mechanic Dave's Schwinn, Inc., Galesburg, 1986-87; freelance photographer The Register mail, Galesburg, 1987; copywriter Sears, Roebuck & Co., Chgo., 1987-89, mktg. dir., 1989—; freelance photographer and videographer, 1988—. Recipient Mktg. Excellence award Sears, Roebuck & Co., 1988, Nat. Presbyn. Scholarship Wooster & Macalester Colls., 1982-86. Republican. Presbyterian. Home: 1040 W Granville Ave #1007 Chicago IL 60660

NEUTZLING, VIRGINIA RUTH, healthcare coalition executive director; b. Canton, Ohio, Dec. 10, 1942; d. James F. and Ruth E. (Swank) Roush; m. Homer S. Neutzling, Sept. 26, 1964 (dec. July 1976); children: Melanie L., Kimberly L., H. Lee. Grad., Mercy Profl. Sch. Nursing, 1963; BS, Walsh Coll., 1982; MEd, Kent State U., 1985. RN, Ohio. From staff nurse to head nurse Timken Mercy Med. Ctr., Canton, Ohio, 1963-77; staff nurse UpJohn Healthcare Svcs., Canton, 1979-83; health educator Stark County Health Dept., Canton, 1983-87; exec. dir. Stark County Health Care Coalition, Inc., Canton, 1987—; mem. refinement adv. com. of Ohio Dept. Health Diagnosis Related Groups; trustee Drs. Hosp. Inc. of Stark County. Mem. adv. com. YMCA Big Bros.-Big Sisters Greater Canton, 1986—, ARC, Canton, 1986—, Rotary, 1989; chmn. Health Care for Uninsured, Canton, 1988—. Mem. Nat. Wellness Assn., Nat. Assn. for Female Execs., Ohio Pub. Health Assn., Northeastern Ohio Wellness Com. (chair 1987—). Democrat. Roman Catholic. Home: 2223 45th St NE Canton OH 44705 Office: Stark County Health Care Coalition Inc 2878 Whipple Ave NW Canton OH 44708

NEUWIRTH, BEBE, dancer, actress; b. Newark, Dec. 31; d. Lee Paul and Sydney Anne Neuwirth; m. Paul Dorman. Student, Juilliard Sch., 1976-77. Appeared on Broadway and internationally as Sheila in A Chorus Line, 1978-81; other Broadway appearances include West Side Story, 1981, Little Me, 1981, Sweet Charity, 1985-87 (Tony award for Best Supporting Actress in a Musical, 1985-86); prin. dancer Dancin', 1982; appeared with Pa. Stage Co. in Just So, 1984; choregrapher, leading dance role Kicks, 1984; appeared with N.Y.C. Comedy Cabaret in Upstairs at O'Neal's, 1982-83; TV appearances include series Cheers (Emmy award for Best Supporting Actress in a Comedy Series 1990). Vol. performances for March of Dimes Telethon, 1986, Cystic Fibrosis Benefit Children's Ball, 1986, Ensemble Studio Theater Benefit, 1986, Circle Repertory Co. Benefit, 1986, all in N.Y.C. Democrat. Address: care The Gage Group Inc 9229 Sunset Blvd Ste 306 Los Angeles CA 90069*

NEUWIRTH, SHERRI GAY, marketing research company executive; b. Bklyn., Dec. 25, 1953; d. David Israel and Minnie Neuwirth. BA, SUNY-Stony Brook, 1974; M.Mgmt., Northwestern U., 1980. Tchr., Kings Park Sch. Dist., N.Y., 1975-77; office mgr. Regal Packaging Co., Roslyn, N.Y., 1977-78; rsch. assoc. Quaker Oats Co., Chgo., 1979-80; project mgr. Elrick & Lavidge, Chgo., 1980-85, v.p., 1985-87, v.p., gen. mgr., Paramus N.J., 1987-89, sr. v.p., gen. mgr., 1989—. Treas. 2658 N. Orchard Condo Assn., Chgo., 1983-86, pres. 1986; vol. tutor Fourth Presbyn. Ch., Chgo., 1984-87. Mem. Am. Mktg. Assn., Northwestern U. Profl. Women's Assn. (program dir. 1985-87), Sierra Club (chair Rockland County com. 1990—). Democrat. Jewish. Avocations: bicycling, swimming, hiking. Office: Elrick & Lavidge Inc One Mack Ctr Dr Paramus NJ 07652

NEVES, STELLA BOUDRIAS, temporary services executive; b. Boston, Mar. 3, 1949; d. Albert Joseph and Stella Ann (Shimkus) Boudrias; m. Alfred F. Neves, June 14, 1969 (div. 1978); children: Alexandria Lee, Jennifer Lynn. BA, U. Hartford, 1970. Pres. Home Nursing Svc., Hartford, 1973-80; pres. Womyn Inc. doing bus. as Koenig's Art Supply, Old Saybrook, Conn., 1980-83; pres. The Freelance Exchange, Inc., Farmington, Conn., 1983—. Chmn. bd. dirs. ARC, Hartford, 1984-85, Art Guild Farmington, chmn. membership. Mem. Women in Communications, Advt. Club Greater Hartford, Farmington C. of C. Democrat. Avocations: Skiing, gourmet cooking. Office: Freelance Exchange Inc 309 Farmington Ave Farmington CT 06032

NEVILLE, MARGARET COBB, physiologist, educator; b. Greenville, S.C., Nov. 4, 1934; d. Henry Van Zandt and Florence Ruth (Crozier) Cobb; m. Hans E. Neville, Dec. 27, 1957; children: Michel Paul, Brian Douglas. BA, Pomona Coll., 1956; PhD, U. Pa., 1962. Asst. prof. physiology U. Colo. Sch. Medicine, Denver, 1968-75, assoc. prof., 1975-82, prof., 1982—, dir. MD/PhD program Health Sci. Ctr., 1985—. Editor: Lactation: Physiology, Nutrition, Breast Feeding, 1983 (Am. Pubs. award 1984), Human Lactation I, 1985, The Mammary Gland, 1987; contbr. numerous articles to profl. jours. Recipient Rsch. Career Devel. award NIH, 1975. Mem. AAAS, Am. Physiol. Assn., Am. Soc. Cell Biology, Internat. Soc. Rsch. in Human Milk and Lactation, Phi Beta Kappa. Office: U Colo Dept Physiology Box C240 Denver CO 80262

NEVILLE, SUSAN DIANE, health services coordinator; b. Punxsutawney, Pa., May 23, 1960; d. William Harmon and Patricia Ann (Sprankle) Neville. BA in Sociology/Social Work, Indiana U. of Pa., 1983. Caseworker Jefferson County Children and Youth, Brookville, Pa., 1983-88; health, mental health and nutrition coordinator Jefferson-Clarion Head Start, Brookville, 1988—; dir. adult recreation program Jefferson County Assn. for Retarded Citizens, Punxsutawney, 1986—; mem. core team Jefferson County Social Services, Brookville, 1987—. Bd. dirs. Child Find, Punxsutawney, 1986-88; mem. com. Run for Someone Spl., Sykesville, Pa., 1985—, Help the Children, Punxsutawney, 1990—. Republican. Methodist. Home: RD 4 Box 440 Punxsutawney PA 15767 Office: Jefferson-Clarion HeadStart Days Inn RD 5 Box 156-C Brookville PA 15825

NEVIN, JEAN SHAW, knitwear designer; b. Bklyn., Dec. 21, 1934; d. Marshall Robert and Dorothy Frances (Brown) Shaw; m. Robert Stephen Nevin, Dec. 9, 1955. BA in English, SUNY, Albany, 1956. Textbook and freelance editor, 1959-74; printmaker, papermaker Jean Nevin Gaphics, Indpls., 1969-84; owner, mgr., knitwear designer Chameleon, Indpls., 1985-88; pres., knitwear designer Knitting Machine Shop, Inc., Indpls., 1988—; Instr. print and paper making Indpls. Art League, 1974-83, exhibits coord., 1969, 73, edn. coord., 1979-80, editor Artifacts, 1968-69, 72-73; editor, pub. Swatchnotes, 1987—. Exhibited prints and handmade paper to nat. group shows and galleries, 1970-84; designer wearable art kits. Mem. Women's Bus. Initiative. Office: Knitting Machine Shop Inc 6350 W 37th St Indianapolis IN 46224

NEVINS, SHEILA, television director and producer; b. N.Y.C.; d. Benjamin and Stella N.; B.A., Barnard Coll., 1960; M.F.A. (Three Arts fellow), Yale U., 1963; m. Sidney Koch; 1 son, David Andrew. TV producer Great Am. Dream Machine, NET, 1970-72, The Reasoner Report, ABC, 1973, Feeling Good, Children's TV Workshop, 1975-76, Who's Who, CBS, 1977-78; dir. documentary programming Home Box Office, N.Y.C., 1978-86, v.p. family programming and documentaries, 1986—; pres. Spinning Reels, Inc., 1982-86. Bd. dirs. Women's Action Alliance. Recipient Peabody award, 1986. Mem. Writers Guild Am., Women in Film.

NEW, ANNE LATROBE, public relations, fund raising executive; b. Evanston, Ill., May 10, 1910; d. Charles Edward and Agnes (Bateman) N.; m. John C. Timmerman, Sept. 30, 1933; 1 child, Jan LaTrobe. AB, U. S.C., 1930; postgrad., Hunter Coll., 1930-31, NYU, 1932-33. APR (Accredited Pub. Relatons Practitioner). Editorial asst. Pictorial Review Mag., N.Y.C., 1930-32; copy asst. J. Walter Thompson Co., N.Y.C., 1932-33; sub editor Cosmopolitan Mag., N.Y.C., 1933-37; with Girl Scouts of the U.S., N.Y.C., 1937-57, chief pub. rels. officer, 1945-57; dir. pub. info. edn. Nat. Recreation and Park Assn., 1957-66; special asst. gen. dir. Internat. Social Svc. Am. Branch, N.Y.C., 1966-68; dir. devel. Nat. Accreditation Coun. for Agys. Serving Blind and Visual Handicapped, N.Y.C., 1969-78; pres. Timmerman & New Inc., Mamaroneck, N.Y., 1980—; founding cons. Opengate, Somers, N.Y., 1968, cons. White Plains Council of Community Svcs., 1969, mgmt. cons. Paralyzed Vets. of Am., Washington, 1980. Contbr. articles to profl. jours. Mem. Westchester Dem. Com. Westchester County, 1963-67, 89—; bd. dirs. Mamaroneck N.Y. United Fund, 1963-64; chmn. nominating com. LWV, Mamaroneck, 1988, chmn. by-law com., 1989; warden emerita St. Thomas' Episc. Ch., Mamaroneck. Mem. Pub. Rels. Soc. Am. (bd. dirs. N.Y. chpt. 1958-72), Women Execs. Pub. Rels. (sec. 1962-63), Nat. Soc. Fund Raising Execs. (bd. dirs. greater N.Y. chpt. 1978-84), Phi Beta Kappa (Alpha chpt.). Democrat. Office: Timmerman & New Inc 235 S Barry Ave Mamaroneck NY 10543

NEW, KARYN MARIE, communications executive; b. Berkeley, Calif., Mar. 9, 1945; d. Kermit Magnus and Gladys Miriam Paulson; m. Farrell Jordan Pollnow, May 29, 1989; 1 child, Elanor May New. BS in Journalism and Advt., U. Colo., 1967. Advt. asst. Denver, 1968-69; word processor/typesetter various orgns., San Francisco, 1970-72; adminstrv. asst. Chevron Oil, San Francisco, 1973-78; freelance writer Walnut Creek, Calif., 1978-83; assoc. editor Fancy Publs., San Clemente, Calif., 1983-85; mng. editor Fancy Publs., San Juan Capistrano, Calif., 1985-86; editor Fancy Publs., Irvine, Calif., 1986-88, editorial dir., 1988—. Office: Fancy Publs PO Box 6050 Mission Viejo CA 92690

NEWANDEE, KIMBERLY ANN, pharmacist; b. Saigon, Vietnam, Oct. 30, 1963; came to U.S., 1975; d. Andrew Alan and Pamela Ann (Pham) N. BS in Pharmacy, U. Conn., 1985; MS in Pharmacy, St. John's U., Jamaica, N.Y., 1988; MBA, Rutgers U., 1990. Lic. pharmacist, N.J., Conn., N.Y. Pharmacy intern Manchester (Conn.) Meml. Hosp., 1982-85; pharmacy extern Kaiser Health Orgn., East Hartford, Conn., 1983-85; pharmacist Rite Aid Pharmacy, Lake Hopatcong, N.J., 1986-89; teaching fellow St. John's U., Jamaica, 1986-88; pharmacist Morristown (N.J.) Meml. Hosp., 1988—; mgmt. cons. Rutgers U., Newark, 1989; drug safety surveillance specialist Worldwide Regulatory Affairs Schering-Plough Rsch., Kenilworth, N.J., 1990—. Advisor Vietnamese Student Assn. at Rutgers U., New Brunswick, 1988-89. U. Conn. scholar, 1982, State of Conn. scholar, 1982-85. Mem. Nat. Assn. Hosp. Pharmacists, Nat. Assn. Retail Druggists, NAFE, Rho Chi. Democrat. Buddhist. Home: 17 Gloucester Rd Parsippany NJ 07054

NEWBERG, DOROTHY BECK (MRS. WILLIAM C. NEWBERG), portrait artist; b. Detroit, May 30, 1919; d. Charles William and Mary (Labedz) Beck; student Detroit Conservatory Music, 1938; m. William C. Newberg, Nov. 3, 1939; children: Judith N. Bookwalter, Robert Charles, James William, William Charles. Trustee Detroit Adventure, 1967-71, originator A Drop in Bucket Program for talented inner-city children. Bd. dirs. Bloomfield Art Assn., 1960-62, trustee 1965-67; bd. dirs. Your Heritage House, 1972-75, Franklin Wright Settlement, 1972-75, Meadowbrook Art Gallery, Oakland U., 1973-75; bd. dirs. Sierra Nevada Mus. Art, 1978-80; mem. Nev. Mus. Art; mem. chief's adv. group Reno Police Dept. Recipient Heart of Gold award, 1969; Mich. vol. leadership award, 1969, Outstanding Vol. award City of Reno, 1989-90. Mem. No. Nev. Black Cultural Awareness Soc., Sierra Art Found., Birmingham Soc. Women Painters. Roman Catholic. Home: 2000 Dant Blvd Reno NV 89509

NEWBERRY, ELIZABETH CARTER, owner greenhouse and floral company; b. Blackwell, Tex., Nov. 25, 1921; m. Weldon Omar Newberry, Sept. 24, 1950 (dec. Nov. 1984); 1 child. Student Hardin Simmons U., 1938-39. Office mgr. F. W. Woolworth, Abilene, Tex., 1939-50; acct. Western Devel. & Investment Corp., Englewood, Colo., 1968-72; owner, operator Newberry Bros. Greenhouse and Florist, Denver, 1972—; bd. dirs. Western Devel. and Investment Corp. Englewood, Colo., 1979-87. Pres. Ellsworth Elem. Sch. PTA, Denver, 1961-62; v.p. Hill Jr. High Sch. PTA, Denver. Home: 201 Monroe Denver CO 80206 Office: Newberry Bros Greenhouse 201 Garfield Denver CO 80206

NEWBILL, SALLIE PULLER, state senator; b. Roanoke Rapids, N.C., June 23, 1940; d. Timberlake Meredith and Mary Gillam (Williams) Puller; m. Thomas Carroll Newbill, July 2, 1966; children: Sallie Gillam, Thomas Carroll III. MA, U. Va., 1961; MEd, Ga. State U., 1972. Tchr. San Diego Unified Sch. System, 1961-63, Tauranga Girls Coll., New Zealand, 1963-64, Bangkok Internat. Sch., Thailand, 1964-65; journalist Richmond (Va.) Times Dispatch, 1965-66; tchr. Fulton County, Atlanta, 1966-68; research writer Ga. State Dept. Edn., Atlanta, 1968-70; state senator Ga. Gen. Assembly, 1986—; v.p. S&N Enterprises, Atlanta, 1984-86; state news dir. Rep. House Caucus, Atlanta, 1983-86. First woman Rep. elected to Ga. Senate, 1986; v.p. Rep. Women, Atlanta, 1985-86, Fulton County Reps., Atlanta, 1985-86. Mem. Sandy Springs C. of C. Methodist. Clubs: Greater Marietta Rep. Womens; Rep. Women of Northside. Office: State Senate Atlanta GA 30334*

NEWBURG, BETTY A., teacher; b. Garretson, S.D., Nov. 10, 1931; d. Edwin O. and Minnie M. (Falk) Thompson; m. Warren E. Newburg, Apr. 9, 1951; children: Terri, Traci, Toni. BS, Sioux Falls Coll., S.D.; MA, Augustana Coll., Sioux Falls; postgrad., U. S.D. Tchr. Verdi, Minn., 1951-52, Luverne, Minn., 1952-53, Iowa City, 1953-54, Lake Lillion, Minn., Sioux Falls, 1954-55, S.D., 1964—. Mem. accredition team for State of S.D., Pierre 1988. Mem. AAUW Sioux Falls S.D., S.D. Social Studies Assn., Delta Kappa Gamma. Home: 608 Annway Dr Sioux Falls SD 57103

NEWCORN, CLAUDIA DANA, consumer products company executive, helicopter pilot; b. N.Y.C., Aug. 9, 1958; d. Andrew Robert and Ruth Ann (Duplain) N. BA, Wellesley Coll., 1981; MBA, Northeastern U., 1986. Research asst. Harvard Bus. Sch., Boston, 1981-82; dir. mktg. research Gen. Computer Co., Cambridge, Mass., 1982-84; asst. mgr. internat. mktg. services Polaroid Corp., Cambridge, 1985; asst. editor Nolan, Norton & Co., Lexington, Mass., 1985-86; asst. product mgr. Silkience Brand, Gillette Corp., Boston, 1986-87, assoc. product mgr. Toni Homewaves Brand, 1987-88; product mgr. Toni Homewaves and Epic Waves Brands, 1988-89; mktg. mgr. Bartles & Jaymes E&J Gallo Winery, 1989—. Author (poems): Tent: Napkin Poems, 1988; co-author: Tentatively: Bit Parts, 1986; author numerous pub. poems. Named golden Poet 1985-88, Silver Poet, 1989; Wellesley Coll. scholar, 1981. Mem. Smithsonian Instn., Cousteau Soc., Sigma Xi (assoc.), Beta Gamma Sigma, Phi Kappa Phi. Avocations: scuba diving, helicopter flying, mountain climbing, chess, costume design. Home: 1225 Marilyn St Modesto CA 95350

NEWELL, ALMA (LISA NEWELL), company executive, consultant; b. Beaver Falls, Pa., Oct. 21, 1936; d. Charles Edward and Mary Alma (Novak) Kralic; m. Everett William Newell, June 9, 1956 (div. Mar. 1971); children: Lawrence Dean, Debora Lynn, Everett William II. Grad. high sch., Beaver Falls. Lic. real estate agt., Calif. Adminstr. asst. to dir. sales U.S. Stoneware, Tallmade, Ohio, 1969-71; exec. sec. B.F. Goodrich Co., Akron, Ohio, 1971-76; real estate agt. Licensee, L.A., 1977-78, Four Seasons Real Estate, 1978, Am. Calif. Devel., 1978; v.p. E.A.C. Constrn. Corp., L.A., 1978-80; corp. sec., v.p. Bedford Group, Inglewood, Calif., 1980—; cons. Pacific Architronics, Pacific Palisades, Calif. Hosp. vol., Ohio, 1972-76; vol. fund raiser for afflicted children, L.A. County, 1977—. Mem. Nat. Notary Assn. Democrat. Roman Catholic. Office: The Bedford Group 9920 S La Cienega Blvd 700 Inglewood CA 90301

NEWELL, CHARLDEAN, academic administrator; b. Ft. Worth, Oct. 14, 1939; d. Charles Thurlow and Mildren Dean (Looney) N. BA, U. North Tex., 1960, MA, 1962; PhD, U. Tex., 1968; cert., Harvard U., 1988. Instr. U. North Tex., Denton, 1965-68, asst. prof., 1968-72; assoc. prof., dir. Fedn. North Tex. Area Univs., Denton, Dallas, 1972-74; assoc. prof., assoc. v.p. acad. affairs U. North Tex., Denton, Dallas, 1974-76, assoc. prof., chair dept. polit. sci., 1976-80, prof. polit. sci., 1980—, assoc. v.p., spl. asst. to chancellor, 1982—; cons. Miss. Bd. Trustees State Instns. Higher Learning, Jackson, 1983-84, Ednl. Testing Svc., Princeton, N.J., 1980-82, 85; bd. dirs. Mcpl. Clks. Ednl. Found., Pasadena, Calif. Author: (with others) Texas Politics, 1990, City Executives: Leadership Roles, Work Characteristics and Time Management, 1989; contbr. articles to profl. jours. Chair charter rev. com. City of Denton, 1978-79; mem. adv. com. Ann's Haven Hospice, Denton, 1981-85; mem. exec. coun. Episc. Diocese Dallas, 1985-88; mem. Civil Svc. Commn., City of Denton, 1989—. Mem. Am. Soc. for Pub. Adminstrn. (sect. chmn. 1982-83, mem. editorial bd. 1985-88), Internat. Personnel Mgmt. Assn. (regional program com. 1982-83), Am. Polit. Sci. Assn., Policy Studies Orgn., Southwestern Polit. Sci. Assn. (sec., treas. 1975-79), Denton C. of C., Denton Tennis Assn., Pi Sigma Alpha (exec. coun.). Democrat. Home: 709 Mimosa Dr Denton TX 76201 Office: U North Tex PO Box 5367 Denton TX 76203-5367

NEWELL, ELIZABETH JEANIE BROOME, brokerage company executive; b. Washington, Dec. 8, 1956; d. Eugene Macon Broome Sr. and Margie Elizabeth (Hodge) Goodyear; m. Clifford Anthony Newell, Aug. 16, 1975; 1 child, Lauren Elizabeth. BA, U. S.C., 1976, BS, 1979, MBA, 1981; real estate diploma, Columbia (S.C.) Real Estate, 1980. Lic. real estate broker, S.C. First v.p. Gene Broome Systems, Columbia, S.C., 1976-81; fin. cons. Merrill Lynch, Columbia, 1981-87; resident v.p., mgr. Prudential-Bache Securities, Columbia, 1987—; bd. dirs. Gene Broome Systems, Inc., Columbia, 1979—, BT's Sportswear, Columbia, 1986—; cons. Electronic Realty Inc., Columbia, 1982—; instr. Dale Carnegie, Columbia, 1984. Author: Policies and Procedures, 1981; editor: Super Stocks, 1986. Speaker United Way of Midlands, Columbia, 1983, 84; liaison Adopt-a-Sch. Progam, Columbia, 1983-85; mem. Ednl. TV Endowment, Columbia, 1987—; project bus. coord. Jr. Achievement, 1988-89. Mem. Columbia C. of C. (charter), Columbia Zool. Assn., MENSA (bd. dirs. memberships 1986-87, pres. 1990—), Carolina Bus. and Profl. Women (1st v.p. 1983-84, 87—, pres. 1984-850, Columbia Sales and Mktg. Execs. (bd. dirs. memberships 1984), McKissick Mus., Gibbes Planetarium, Columbia Mus. Art. Club: Landmark Sertoma. Home: 141 Kerryton Rd Columbia SC 29223 Office: Prudential Bache Securities 1330 Lady St Suite 205 Columbia SC 29201

NEWELL, GLADYS ELIZABETH, former educator, civic worker; b. Ticonderoga, N.Y., Aug. 31, 1908; d. Charles R. and Elizabeth (Ives) N.; A.B., SUNY, Albany, 1930, M.A., 1935. Tchr., Corinth (N.Y.) High Sch., 1930-33, Bethlehem Central High Sch., Delmar, N.Y., 1933-45; supr. social studies Bethlehem Central Schs., Delmar, 1946-71; mem. N.Y. State Regents Com. on Exams., 1950-53, N.Y. Social Studies Council Curriculum Com., 1961-63, N.Y. State Mental Health Planning Commn., 1963-64. Bd. dirs., v.p. SUNY, Albany Benevolent Assn.; adv. com. N.Y. delegation White House Conf., 1955; mem. local bd. Literacy Vols., bd. dirs. Ticonderoga area. Recipient Bus. and Profl. Women Outstanding Citizen award Tri-Village area, 1953; State Coll. Alumni Bertha E. Brimmer award for outstanding teaching, 1955; Citizenship Conf. Outstanding Tchr. award Syracuse U., 1962; Distinguished Alumnus award State U. at Albany, 1969. Mem. N.Y. State Tchrs. Assn. (dir. 1950-69, pres. 1966-67), Eastern Zone Bethlehem Central (a founder, past pres.), Albany Supervisory Dist. (past pres.) tchrs. assns., NEA (life mem., rep. of N.Y. State Tchrs. Assn. at tchr. edn. and profl. standards meetings), N.Y. State (past pres.), Capital Dist. (past pres.), Nat. councils social studies, LWV (past pres. Albany County), UN Assn. U.S.A. (past chpt. dir.), World Affairs Council (past dir. Albany), AAUW (1st v.p. Essex County br.), Fort Carillon Bus. and Profl. Women's Club, N.Y. State Ret. Tchrs. Assn. (del. to Gov.'s Conf. Librs. 1978), N.Y. Ret. Tchrs. Assn., New Horizons Club (pres. local chpt.), Delta Kappa Gamma, Pi Gamma Mu. Methodist. Contbr. articles to profl. jours. Home: 17 John St Ticonderoga NY 12883

NEWELL, JEANNE ANN, child care executive; b. Oakland, Calif., May 31, 1947; d. Eugene Fletcher and Frances Elaine (Storey) N.; children: Lisa, Kira, Brenna. Cert. in day care, U. Minn., Competency Based Tng. and Assessment, 1984. Cert. child care provider. Owner Jeanne's Kid's Korner, Ill., Minn., 1967—; cons. in field, 1977—. Mem. Minn. Assn. for Edn. of Young Children, Nat. Alliance Homebased Bus. Women, Greater Mpls. Day Care Assn. (trainer 1987—), Hennepin County Family Day Care Assn. (trainer 1986—, editor Bootline News 1986-87), Minn. Licensed Family Child Care Assn., Women's Entrpreneur Network, Bklyn. Pk. Ptnrs. in Child Care. Roman Catholic. Home and Office: 7421 74th Way Brooklyn Park MN 55428

NEWELL, KATHERINE ANN, lawyer; b. Phila., May 5, 1947; m. Francis P. Newell, Aug. 16, 1975. AB magna cum laude, Temple U., 1969; JD cum laude, Villanova U., 1975; LLM, Georgetown U., 1979. Bar: Pa. 1975, D.C. 1980. Atty.-advisor Office of Chief Counsel, Dept. Treasury, Washington, 1975-78; assoc. firm Schnader, Harrison, Segal & Lewis, Phila., 1978-86; ptnr. Baskin, Flaherty, Elliott & Mannino, P.C., Phila., 1986—; mem. adj. faculty grad. tax program Villanova U. Law Sch., 1983—. Mem. ABA (tax-exempt fin. com. sect. taxation 1982—), Pa. Bar Assn., D.C. Bar Assn., Phila. Bar Assn., Phila. Fin. Assn. (bd. dirs.), Phila. Fin. Assn. (bd. dirs.), Preservation Techniques (bd. dirs.). Office: Baskin Flaherty Elliott & Mannino P C 3 Mellon Bank Ctr Suite 1800 Philadelphia PA 19102

NEWELL, MARY ETNA (KEY), contract specialist, psychologist; b. New Smyrna, Fla., Nov. 28, 1944; d. Edward D. and Jackie (Futch)ú Key; m. Stanley A. Newell Jr., Aug. 28, 1965 (div. 1976); children: Kimberly, Stanley III, Derek, Paige. AA in Psychology, Baylor U., 1965; BA in Psychology, Rider Coll., 1985, MA in Psychology, 1987, D of Psychology, 1989; postgrad., Princeton U. Tchr. elem. sch. Lake Wales, Fla., 1965-66; with nursing profession County Hosp., Mt. Holly, 1968-73; pvt. practice legal sec. Mt. Holly, 1974-79; pvt. practice chiropractic asst. Riverton, N.J., 1974-78; paralegal EPA, Phila., 1979-81; personnel asst. U.S. Fed. Govt., Phila., 1981-82; engring. sec. Def. Indsl. Supply Ctr., Phila., 1982-83; dental hygiene author Dr. Robert Thomas Bosco, Rome, Italy, 1983-85; contract specialist def. pers. support ctr. U.S. Dept. Def., Phila., 1985—; mem. emergency med. procurement team U.S. Dept. Def., Phila., 1985-87, mem. U.S. Fed. Govt. task force, 1989—. Author: Classics of Muscular Exercise, 1966, Dental Hygiene in Europe, 1983, Sociology of Architecture, 1984. Mem. Phila. Zoo, 1977—, Phila. Art Mus., 1981—, Mus. of Fine Arts, Boston, 1989—. Recipient Ladies' Single Tennis Champion award, State of Fla., 1963, Seascape Artist award, 1963, Beauty Contestant award, 1963, Excellence award Pres. James Carter, 1980, Disting. Sr. award, Rider Coll., 1985, Bi-Lingual Coll. award Princeton; Charlotte Newcombe Found. fellow, 1986-89. Mem. Burlington County (N.J.) Police Wive's Assn. (originator, pres. 1974, award 1976), Rider Coll. Alumni Assn. Republican. Methodist. Home: Camelot Ct E15 532 Brookhaven Rd Brookhaven PA 19015 Office: PO Box 4 Oaklyn NJ 08107

NEWELL, REBECCA G., psychiatric nurse; b. Savannah, Ga., July 4, 1953; d. Henry Morgan and Julia (Rogers) Grimes; AA, Armstrong State Coll., 1973, BS in Nursing, 1980; postgrad. Sch. Grad. Nursing, Med. Coll. Ga., 1980-81; m. E. Andrew Newell, June 14, 1980. With Charter Hosp. of Savannah (Ga.), staff nurse, 1973-74, head nurse, 1974-75, coordinator utilization rev. and staff devel., 1975-80, asst. dir. nursing, 1980-82, nursing adminstr., 1982-89, dir. nursing and adminstr. Adult Psychiat. Svcs., 1989—; adj. faculty Armstrong Coll. Sch. Nursing. cons. Council Recruitment and Retention of Nurses, 1978—; profl. staff exchange cons. Named one of Outstanding Young Women Am.; recipient Leadership award Vocat. Indsl. Clubs Am., 1971. Mem. Am. Nurses Assn., Ga. Nurses Assn., Ga. Orgn. Nurse Execs., Ga. Hosp. Assn., Armstrong State Coll. Hon. Soc. for Nursing, Ga. So. Coll. Hon. Soc. for Nursing, Savannah Women's Network, Sigma Theta Tau. Baptist. Home: 11 Ramsgate Rd Savannah GA 31419 Office: 1150 Cornell Ave Savannah GA 31406

NEWHOUSE, MRS. EDWARD See DELAY, DOROTHY

NEWKERK, DEBORAH, advertising agency executive. Former sr. v.p. DFS Direct (now Saatchi & Saatchi Direct), N.Y.C., exec. v.p., pres. for N.Am., 1990—. Office: Saatchi & Saatchi Direct 375 Hudson St New York NY 10014*

NEWLAND, RUTH LAURA, small business owner; b. Ellensburg, Wash., June 4, 1949; d. George J. and Ruth Marjorie (Porter) N.; m. Thomas Arnold, Oct. 18, 1979 (div. Nov. 1986). BA, Cen. Wash. State Coll., 1970, MEd, 1972; EdS, Vanderbilt U., 1973; PhD, Columbia Pacific U., 1981. Tchr. Union Gap (Wash.) Sch., 1970-71; ptnr. Newland Ranch Gravel Co. (div. Beazers of London), Yakima, Wash., 1970—, Arnold Artificial Limb, Yakima, 1981-86; owner, pres. Arnold Artificial Limb, Yakima and Richland, Wash., 1986—; ptnr. Newland Ranch, Yakima, 1969—. Mem. Yakima Greenway Found.; contbg. mem. Dem. Nat. Com. George Washington scholar Masons, Yakima, 1967. Mem. NOW, Am. Orthotic and Prosthetic Assn., Vanderbilt U. Alumni Assn., George Peabody Coll. Alumni Assn., Columbia Pacific U. Alumni Assn., Internat. Platform Assn., Nat. Antivivisection Soc. (life), World Wildlife Fund., Nat. Audubon Soc., Greenpeace, Mus. Fine Arts (Boston), ACLU, Humane Soc. of U.S., Wilderness Soc., Coun. Econ. Priorities, Emily's List, Sierra Club (life). Democrat. Seventh-Day Adventist. Home: 2004 Riverside Rd Yakima WA 98901-9539 Office: Arnold Artificial Limb 9 S 12th Ave Yakima WA 98901

NEWLANDS, SHEILA ANN, financial director; b. Worcester, Mass., Mar. 8, 1953; d. Joseph and Doris Edna (Bachand) N; m. Domenic Victor Testa Jr., Oct. 2, 1976 (div. 1983). BA summa cum laude, Worcester State Coll., 1975; cert. interior design, Bunkerhill Community Coll., 1976; MS, Simmons Coll., 1976; MBA, Suffolk U., 1983. Cert. real estate broker, Mass. Dir. health scis. library Lynn Hosp., Mass., 1976-78, Mt. Auburn Hosp., Cambridge, 1978-81; assoc. fin. analyst Data Gen., Westboro, Mass., 1981-82, fin. analyst, 1982-84, sr. fin. analyst, 1984; fin. analyst Chateau Sainte Michelle Winery, Woodinville, Wash., 1985-86, dir. fin., 1986—; guest lectr. Simmons Coll. Sch. Library Sci., Boston, 1980-81. Mem. Burlington (Mass.) Conservation Commn., 1978-84. Mem. Fin. Mgmt. Honor Soc., Phi Alpha Theta. Club: Mountaineers (Seattle). Home: PO Box 514 Issaquah WA 98027 Office: Chateau Sainte Michelle Winery One Stimson Ln Woodinville WA 98072

NEWLIN, BEVERLY AGNEW, nurse; b. Greenwood, S.C., June 16, 1947; d. Caroll Erskine Agnew and Belle A. Finley; m. Kimrey Dayton Newlin, Sr., Mar. 9, 1968; children: Kim Jr., Stephanie, Laurie. Diploma in nursing, Greenville Hosp. Sch. of Nursing, 1965-68. RN. Nurse Wadley Hosp., Texarkana, Tex., 1968-69, Kenner Army Hosp., Ft. Lee, Va., 1970-78; staff nurse Miami Childrens Hosp., Coral Gables, Fla., 1979—. Mem. campaign staff to elect Bruce Hoffman for Ho. of Reps., dist. 114, Coral Gables, 1986, 89; active PTA. Republican. Presbyterian. Home: 755 Allendale Rd Key Biscayne FL 33149 Office: Miami Childrens Hosp Coral Gables FL 33134

NEWMAN, ANNETTE GOERLICH, shopping center manager; b. Fresno, Calif., Jan. 19, 1940; d. David August and Mary Eloise (Simpson) Goerlich; Pharm.D., U. Calif., San Francisco, 1963; children—Anne Kristen, Mark David, Gregory Hartley. Pharmacist, Village Drug, 1963-69; relief pharmacist, 1969-72; store mgr. The Drug Store of Fig Garden Village, 1972-77; mgr. Fig Garden Village Shopping Center, Fresno, 1977—; dir. Fig Garden Mcht. Assn.; sec., treas. bd. dirs. Fig Garden Village, Inc. Active Fresno Community Analysis Citizens Com., Littlest Angel chpt. Children's Home Soc., Ladies Aid to Retarded Children, Women's Symphony League; bd. dirs. St. Agnes Med. Found., St. Agnes Endowment Com.; mem. adv. bd. Exceptional Parents Unltd.; mem. adv. bd. Sch. Arts and Humanities Adv. Bd. Calif. State U., Fresno, 1988—; mem. council of 100, Fresno Art Ctr. Women's Yr. Nominee, Rosalie M. Stern award, 1971, 72; registered pharmacist, Calif. Mem. Fresno-Madera Pharm. Assn., Pharm. Alumni Assn. U. Calif., Nat. Assn. Female Execs., Jr. League of Fresno, AAUW, Alpha Phi. Home: 3909 W Fir Ave Fresno CA 93711 Office: 5082 N Palm Ave Suite A Fresno CA 93704

NEWMAN, BARBARA POLLOCK, journalist and author TV and print; b. N.Y.C., June 15, 1939; d. Irving G. and Jeanne (Ginsberg) Pollock; div.; 1 child, Penelope. BA, Mount Holyoke Coll., 1960; MA, Columbia U., 1962. Legis. asst. Rep. James Scheuer, Washington, 1964-65, Mayor John Lindsay, N.Y.C., 1965-67; mem. President's Nat. Adv. Commn. on Civil Disorders, Washington, 1967-79; reporter, interviewer Nat. Pub. Radio, N.Y.C., 1971-78; investigative reporter, producer "20/20" ABC News, Washington, 1978-81; exec. producer Jack Anderson Confidential, Washington, 1982-83; pres. Praetorian Productions, Inc., Washington, 1984—; moderator Nat. Town Meetings, Pub. TV, 1975-78; Hostess McNeill Lehrer Report, Aug. 1977; mem. adv. bd. Washington Journalism Review, 1977-80. Author: The Covenant: Love and Death in Bierut, 1989; contbr. news and editorial articles to newspapers, popular jours. Recipient Peabody award thorugh Nat. Pub. Radio, 1972, Ohio State award, 1973, 74, 76, Silver Gavel award, ABA,

1974, Cadmus award, Am. Lebanese League, 1981; Emmy nominee, 1981 for investigative reporting. Home: 5336 29th St NW Washington DC 20015

NEWMAN, CLAIRE POE, corporate executive; b. Jacksonville, Fla., Dec. 12, 1926; d. Leslie Ralph and Gertrude (Criswell) Poe; student Fla. State Coll. for Women, 1944-45, Tulane U., 1971-73; m. Robert Jacob Newman, July 3, 1948; children—Leslie Claire, Robert, Christopher David. Co-owner Vineyards in Burgundy, France. Mem. various coms. New Orleans Mus. Art. Mem. Women's com. New Orleans Philharmonic Symphony Assn., 1961—, chmn. orch. rels. com., 1961-63; chmn. New Orleans Easter Seal Drive, 1963; La. trustee Nat. Soc. Crippled Children and Adults, 1963-65. Mem. Women's Aux. C. of C., New Orleans Soc. Archeol. Inst. Am. (v.p. 1972-74), Confrérie des Chevaliers du Tastevin, Sigma Kappa. Club: Metairie Country, Kitzbuehel (Austria) Golf, Golden Skibook (Kitzbuehel), Pass Christian (Miss.) Yacht; Ski (Arlberg). Home: 1111 Falcon Rd Metairie LA 70005 : Tiemberg Kitzbuehel, Austria

NEWMAN, DELLA, ambassador; married Wells B. McCurdy. Pres., owner Village Real Estate, Inc., Seattle; treas. Pacific Factors Ltd.; propr. Braemar Assocs.; amb. to New Zealand and Western Samoa, Wellington, 1989—. Bd. dirs. Wash. Inst. for Policy Studies; del. Rep. Nat. Conv., 1980, 88; spl. events dir. Wash. Reagan-Bush Campaign, 1980; co-chmn. Reagan-Bush Fin. Com., 1984; chmn. Wash. George Bush for Pres. Campaign, 1987-88. Office: Am Embassy, 29 Fitzherbert Ter, Thorndon, Wellington New Zealand also: Comml Sec Am Embassy Wellington FPO San Francisco CA 96690*

NEWMAN, DOROTHY ANNE, educator; b. Minden, La., Jan. 25, 1947; d. George Malcolm and Neva Estelle (Reeder) Temple. AA, Kilgore Coll., 1967; BA summa cum laude, East Tex. Bapt. Coll., 1972; MA, Stephen F. Austin State U., 1979. Cert. tchr., Tex. Tchr. social studies Marshall (Tex.) Ind. Sch. Dist., 1974—, sponsor student council, 1975—; bd. dirs. Tex. Energy Edn. Day Project, Austin, 1982—. Mem. regional planning com. Youth Alcohol and Treatment Conf., Austin, 1983. Recipient awards for energy edn. day project, nat. student safety program, alcohol edn. project, Excellence award for U. Tex., Austin, 1988; named Outstanding High Sch. Tchr., So. Meth. U., 1988; Tex. Edn. Agy. Energy and Environ. Edn. award, Tex. Humanities Outstanding Tchr. award, 1990. Mem. Tex. Classroom Tchrs. Assn. (membership chmn. 1981-82), Nat. Coun. for Social Studies, Tex. Coun. for Social Studies (curriculum coun. 1990—), East Tex. Coun. on Social Studies, Nat. Assn. Workshop Dirs., Tex. Assn. Student Couns. (state sec. 1981-82, 88-89, parliamentarian 1983-84), Phi Alpha Theta, Alpha Chi. Republican. Methodist. Office: Marshall High Sch 1900 Maverick Dr Marshall TX 75670

NEWMAN, EDITH SQUIRE, educator; b. Cleve., Aug. 16, 1938; d. Nelson Elbert and Edith Eveline (Swaysland) Squire; m. Robert Beauchamp Newman III, June 26, 1980; children: Thomas David, John Daniel. BS, U. Minn., 1961; MA in Liberal Learning, Marietta (Ohio) Coll., 1988. Permanent teaching cert., Ohio, N.Y. Tchr. Mpls. Pub. Schs., 1961-63, Waterloo (Iowa) Community Schs., 1963-4, Anoka-Hennepin Ind. Sch. Dist. 11, Coon Rapids, Minn., 1964-65, Seneca Falls (N.Y.) Pub. Schs., 1965-66; elem. tchr. Belpre (Ohio) City Schs., 1971—; cons. Tchr.'s Workshop, Sta. WOUB-TV, Athens, Ohio, 1981. Jennings scholar Belpre City Schs., 1976-77. Mem. Internat. Reading Assn. (pres. heritage coun. 1981-83), Belpre Edn. Assn. (v.p. 1978-79, rep. 1988-89), SE Ohio Reps. Coun., AAUW (pres. Marietta br. 1981-83, chmn. pub. policy 1989—). Unitarian. Home: 304 Lawton Rd Marietta OH 45750

NEWMAN, EILEEN MERYL, computer executive; b. Queens, N.Y., June 6, 1961; d. Lorraine (Siegel) N. BS in Engring., U. Pa., 1982, MS in Engring., 1983; MBA, Hofstra U., 1985. Assoc. engr. Sperry Corp., Great Neck, N.Y., 1983-85, computer instr., 1984-85; product mgr., sr. engr. Gen. Instrument, Hicksville, N.Y., 1985—. Mem. IEEE, Assn. of Old Crows, U. Pa. Alumni Club. Home: 6 Holiday Park Dr Williston Park NY 11596 Office: Gen Instrument Corp 600 W John St Hicksville NY 11802-0709

NEWMAN, ESTELLE RUTH, rehabilitation counselor, occupational therapist; b. N.Y.C., Apr. 25, 1935; d. Nathan and Clara (Wattman) Glotzer; m. Malcolm Newman, June 11, 1955; children: Roberta, Leonard, Alisa. BS in Occupational Therapy, Columbia U., 1956; MEd in Rehab. Counseling, Hofstra U., 1978. Occupational therapist L.I. Devel. Ctr., Melville, N.Y., 1969-71; sr. occupational therapist L.I. Devel. Ctr., Melville, 1979; vocat. rehab. counselor VESID, Hauppauge, 1979-82, sr. vocat. rehab. counselor, 1982—; sr. vocat. rehab. counselor, 1982—; cons. in home modifications and adapted equipment VESID, N.Y. Edn. Dept., 1979. Bd. dirs. Kehillath Shalom Synagogue, Cold Spring Harbor, N.Y., 1986-89, pres., 1989—; mem. Witness for Peace, Washington and N.C., 1986—. Mem. Nat. Rehab. Assn., Am. Occupational Therapy Assn., L.I. Rehab. Assn., L.I. Dist. Occupational Therapy Assn., Rehab. Engring. Soc. N.Am., NOW (bd. dirs. 1986—), Mensa. Democrat. Jewish. Home: 12 Beal Ct Huntington NY 11743 Office: VESID NYSED NYSOB Veteran's Hwy Hauppauge NY 11788

NEWMAN, JACQUELINE M., home economics educator, researcher; b. N.Y.C., July 6, 1932; d. Morris and Yetta (Goodman) Muller; m. Leonard Newman, June 14, 1953; children: Michael Jay, Beverly Ellen Newman Wolcott. BS in Edn., SUNY, New Paltz, 1953; MA in Home Econs., NYU, 1975, PhD in Home Econs., 1980. Tchr. 3d grade Newton (Mass.) Pub. Schs., 1953-54; substitute tchr. Smithtown (N.Y.) Cen. Sch. Dist., 1958-74, instr. in ethnic food and food habits, 1968-76; adj. instr. in Chinese food and food habits NYU, N.Y.C., 1975-77; adj. instr. in nutrtion N.Y. Inst. Tech., Commack, 1978-79; adj. instr. in food svc. mgmt. N.Y. Cooking Ctr. New Sch. for Social Rsch., N.Y.C., 1980-81; prof. home econs. dept., grad. program coord. Queens Coll. CUNY, Flushing, 1980—; presenter, lectr. in field. Author: Melting Pot: An Annotated Bibliography and Guide to Food and Nutrition Information for Ethnic Groups in America, 1986, Chinese Cookbooks: An Annotated Bibliography of English Language Volumes Worldwide, 1987; contbr. numerous articles to profl. jours. Mellon Found., CUNY, 1982-84; Ctr. for Intercultural Communication Rsch. scholar, 1983. Fellow Am. Coll. Nutrition; mem. Am. Home Econs. Assn., Am. Edn. Rsch. Assn., Am. Dietetic Assn., Am. Anthropol. Assn., Am. Inst. Wine and Food, Am. Assn. for Asian Studies, Culinary Historians of N.Y. (co-founder, treas. steering com. 1985-87, pres. 1989-91), Food Nutrition Coun. Greater N.Y. (bd. dirs. 1980-83), Food Svcs. Mgmt. Edn. Coun., Inst. Food Technologists, Internat. Assn. for the Study of Traditional Asian Medicine, Soc. for Nutrition Edn., Spl. Libr. Assn. Office: CUNY-Queens Coll Home Econs Dept Flushing NY 11367-0904

NEWMAN, JANE, advertising agency executive; b. Woking, Surrey, Eng., Oct. 22, 1947; came to U.S., 1978; d. Ronald William and Victoria (Brady) N.; m. Tom Carroll, Aug. 2, 1989; 1 child from previous marriage, Matthew. BA, Sussex U., Eng., 1969; MA, Lancaster U., Eng., 1970. Account planner Boase Massimi & Pollett, London, Eng., 1970-78; account mgr. Needham Harper & Steers, Chgo., 1978-79, Ammurati & Puris, N.Y.C., 1979-81; vice chmn., dir. strategic planning Chiat/Day/Mojo Advt., N.Y.C., 1981—. Office: Chiat/Day/Mojo 79 Fifth Ave New York NY 10003

NEWMAN, JANICE MARIE, business owner, lawyer; b. N.Y.C., Aug. 11, 1951; d. Robert (dec.) and Clara (White) Swindler; m. Roger Kevin Newman, Jan. 20, 1972 (div. July 1980); 1 child, Germaine M. Swindler-Newman (dec.). BA, Smith Coll., 1973; JD, Rutgers U., 1980. Bar: N.J. 1983, U.S. Supreme Ct. 1987. Adminstrv. asst. Corp. Ann. Reports, N.Y.C., 1972-73; pub. rels. asst. Lippincott & Margulies, N.Y.C., 1973; journalist Essex Forum Newspaper, East Orange, N.J., 1973; pub. info. officer City of Newark, 1974-82; producer, host Newark and Reality TV show, Newark, 1974-85; asst. communications dir. Mayor's Office, Newark, 1982-86; legis. liaison, publ. info. officer N.J. Div. on Women, Trenton, 1988—, acting dir., 1990, women svcs. coord., 1990—; pres., owner J.M. Newman & Assocs.; appt. to N.J. Supreme Ct. Com. on Women in the Cts., 1990—. Mem. editorial bd. N.J. Lawyer mag., 1987—; contbr. articles to mags. Trustee Interest on Lawyers Trust Accounts, 1988—; bd. dirs. Instrns., Exposures, Experiences, 1983-87, Greater Newark Conservancy; state sec. Women's Polit. Caucus N.J. Recipient Pub. Svc. award N.J. Voice Newspaper, 1977, Achievement award Minority Contractors and Craftsmen Trade Assn., 1982, award Nat. Council Negro Bus. and Profl. Women Legal Achievement, 1987, award N.J. Unit Nat. Assn. Negro Bus. and Profl. Women's Clubs, 1987; named to Outstanding Young Women Am. U.S. Jaycees, 1984. Mem. Nat. Assn. Media Women (rec. sec. 1985-87, Media Woman of Yr. award 1985, pres. N.J. cpt. 1986-88), N.J. State Bar Assn. (Young Lawyers Div. Community Svc. award 1989, mem. pub. rels. com. 1987—, 2d vice-chair women's rights sect., 1990-91, 1st vice chair, 1991—; mem. minorities in the profession sect.), N.J. Women Lawyers Assn. pres. 1986-88, chair pub. rels. com., mem. women's rights sect.), Nat. Coun. Negro Women, Garden State Bar Assn., Women's Polit. Caucus (N.J. state sec. 1989—). Episcopalian. Home: 115 Sunset Ave PO Box 6070 Newark NJ 07106

NEWMAN, JEANNE LOUISE, association executive; b. Boston, June 29, 1946; d. William Collyer and Barbara (Bailey) Smith; m. Harry Stephen Newman, June 9, 1968 (div. 1977); children: Michael Stephen, Catherine Louise. BSBA, Am. U., 1968. Bookkeeper Am. Pharm. Assn., Washington, 1968-69; bus. mgr. Soc. Photog. Scientists and Engrs., Washington, 1969-73; controller Nat. Ctr. for Vol. Action, Washington, 1973-75; fin. officer Bur. Rehab., Washington, 1975-79; acting dir. bus. affairs Assn. Am. Med. Colls., Washington, 1979-88, dir. fin. services, 1988—. Treas. Potomac Valley Civic Assn., 1975-77; pres. Franconia Commons Homeowners Assn., Alexandria, Va., 1982—. Mem. Nat. Assn. Female Execs., Am. Soc. of Assn. Execs. Office: Assn Am Med Colls 1 DuPont Cir NW Washington DC 20036

NEWMAN, KAREN BETH, electrical engineer; b. Ann Arbor, Mich., May 16, 1960; d. John Henry Jr. and Sylvia June (Butts) N. BSEE, Mich. State U., 1982. Assoc. application design engr. Kellogg Co., Battle Creek, Mich., 1982-84, application design engr., 1984-86; systems engr. Electronic Data Systems, Auburn Hills, Mich., 1986-88; process control mgr. Electronic Data Systems, Ypsilanti, Mich., 1988—. Troop leader Explorer Computer Post, Boy Scouts Am., Ypsilanti, 1988—. Mem. IEEE, Tau Beta Pi. Home: 1014 Traver Ct Ann Arbor MI 48105 Office: Electronic Data Systems 2625 Tyler Rd Ann Arbor MI 48198

NEWMAN, KIM DIANE, government official; b. Springfield, Mass., Feb. 13, 1954; d. Joseph Milton and Shirley Eleanor (Allen) Landry; m. George Alan Newman Jr., May 10, 1975 (div. Feb. 1981). Assoc. Bus., Bay Path Coll., 1974; postgrad., Eastern Conn. State U., 1987—. Adminstrv. contracting officer Dept. Def., East Hartford, Conn., 1974—. Author: Guide to Federal Employment, 1984, Industrial Resource Management Equipment Utilization, 1983. Mem. ABA (govtl. bus. assoc. 1990, pub. contract law sect. 1990), Nat. Contract Mgmt. Assn., Conn. Fed. Women's Assn. (founder fed. exec. bd. 1985—), Fed. Women's Program (mgr. 1983-87), Mensa. Roman Catholic. Office: DCMAO Hartford 130 Darlin St East Hartford CT 06108

NEWMAN, LINDA, construction company executive; b. Bklyn., July 10, 1937; d. Max and Mae (Goldlust) Lukin; m. Morton Newman, Dec. 29, 1956; children: Jeffrey H., Karen M., Susan L. Student, Hunter Coll., 1955-57. Adminstrv. asst. Princeton Park, Shoreham, N.Y., 1971-73; asst. to pres. Imperial Gardens, South Setauket, N.Y., 1973-76; ops. mgr. Princeton Park, Dix Hills, N.Y., 1976-80, v.p. ops., 1980-83; dir. sales, mktg. and advt. DiCanio, Smithtown, N.Y., 1983-89; v.p. Cons., Inc., Dix Hills, N.Y., 1990—. Recipient Best Newspaper Advertisement award Profl. Builder Mag., 1987. Mem. Nat. Assn. Home Builders, Women's Am. Orgn. for Rehab. and Tng. (charter, Imperial Woods chpt. pres. 1981-82), L.I. Builders Inst. (cert.). Office: Cons Inc 42 Cedar Ridge Ln Dix Hills NY 11746

NEWMAN, MARGARET ANN, nurse; b. Memphis, Oct. 10, 1933; d. Ivo Mathias and Mamie Love (Donald) N.; B.S.H.E., Baylor U., 1954; B.S.N., U. Tenn., Memphis, 1962; M.S., U. Calif., San Francisco, 1964; Ph.D., N.Y.U., 1971. Dir. nursing, asst. prof. nursing Clin. Research Center, U. Tenn., 1964-67; asst. prof. N.Y.U., 1971-75, asso. prof., 1975-77; prof. in charge grad. program and research dept. nursing Pa. State U., 1977-80, prof. nursing, 1977-84; prof. nursing U. Minn., 1984—. Travelling fellow New Zealand Nursing Ednl. & Rsch. Fund, 1985. Recipient Outstanding Alumnus award U. Tenn. Coll. Nursing, 1975; Disting. Alumnus award NYU Div. Nursing, 1984; Am. Jour. Nursing Scholar, 1979-80. Fellow Am. Acad. Nursing. Author: Theory Development in Nursing, 1979; Health as Expanding Consciousness, 1986; editor: (with others) Source Book of Nursing Research, 1973, 2d edit., 1977. Research on patterns of person-environment interaction as indices of health as expanding consciousness; also models of profl. practice. Office: 6-101 Health Scis Unit F 308 Harvard St Minneapolis MN 55455

NEWMAN, MAXINE PLACKER, insurance consultant; b. Haslem, Tex., Nov. 21, 1922; d. L. H. and Beatrice Rosetta (Stuart) Placker: B.S., Stephen F. Austin State U., 1943; m. Robert Wayne Newman, May 23, 1975; 1 son, Stephen Randall Hillin (by previous marriage). Acct., Lamar U., Beaumont, Tex., 1956-58; office mgr. Williamson Ins. Agy., Beaumont, 1958-72; v.p. Alexander & Alexander, Dallas, 1972-79; cons. Bellefonte Ins. Co., Cin., 1979—; v.p. Ralph K. Kemp & Assocs., Inc. office mgr., treas. Ralph K. Kemp & Assocs., Inc., Dallas, 1979—. . Mem. Am. Bus. Women Assn. (Woman of Yr. 1979), Nat. Assn. Ins. Women, Dallas Assn. Ins. Women, Beta Sigma Phi (Woman of Yr. 1966). Republican. Baptist. Clubs: Trophy, Women's, Trophy Ladies Golf Assn. Address: 114 Carnoustie Dr Trophy Club TX 76262

NEWMAN, NANCY JEAN, physician, educator; b. Glen Cove, N.Y., June 24, 1956; d. Abraham Barry and Edna (Blueweiss) N. AB, Princeton (N.J.) U., 1978; MA, U. London, 1980; MD, Harvard U., 1984. Intern in medicine Mass. Gen. Hosp., Boston, 1984-85, resident in neurology, 1985-88; fellow in neuro-ophthalmology Mass. Eye and Ear Infirmary, Boston, 1988-89; dir. neuro-ophthalmology Emory U. and Clinic, Atlanta, 1989—. Contbr. articles to profl. jours. Marshall scholar U.K. Parliament, 1978-80; recipient Moses Taylor Pyne prize Princeton U., 1978. Mem. AMA, Am. Acad. Neurology, Frank Walsh Soc., N.Am. Neuro-Ophthalmology Soc., Med. Assn. Ga., Med. Assn. Atlanta, Southeastern Neuro-Ophthalmology Soc. Avocations: travel, theatre, golf. Office: Emory Clinic/Eye Ctr 1327 Clifton Rd NE Atlanta GA 30322

NEWMAN, PAULINE, federal judge; b. N.Y.C., June 20, 1927; d. Maxwell Henry and Rosella N. B.A., Vassar Coll., 1947; M.A., Columbia U., 1948; Ph.D., Yale U., 1952; LL.B., NYU, 1958. Bar: N.Y. 1958, U.S. Supreme Ct. 1972, U.S. Ct. Customs and Patent Appeals 1978, Pa. 1979, U.S. Ct. Appeals (3d cir.) 1981, U.S. Ct. Appeals (fed. cir.) 1982. Research chemist Am. Cyanamid Co., Bound Brook, N.J., 1951-54; mem. patent staff FMC Corp., N.Y.C., 1954-75; mem. patent staff FMC Corp., Phila., 1975-84, dir. dept. patent and licensing, 1969-84; judge U.S. Ct. Appeals (fed. cir.), Washington, 1984—; bd. dir. Research Corp., 1982-84; program specialist Dept. Natural Scis. UNESCO, Paris, 1961-62; mem. State Dept. Adv. Com. on Internat. Indsl. Property, 1974-84; lectr. in field. Contbr. articles to profl. jours. Bd. dirs. Med. Coll. Pa., 1975-84, Midgard Found., 1973-84; trustee Phila. Coll. Pharmacy and Sci., 1983-84. Mem. ABA (council sect. patent trademark and copyright 1983-84), Am. Patent Law Assn. (bd. dirs. 1981-84), U.S. Trademark Assn. (bd. dirs. 1975-79, v.p. 1978-79), Am. Chem. Soc. (bd. dirs. 1972-81), Am. Inst. Chemists (bd. dirs. 1960-66, 70-76), Pacific Indsl. Property Assn. (pres. 1979-80). Clubs: Vassar, Yale. Office: US Ct Appeals 717 Madison Pl NW Washington DC 20439*

NEWMAN, PEGGY JO, physician; b. Hollis, Okla., Feb. 8, 1926; d. Jess Alan and Eula B (Jackson) Newman. BA, Stephen F. Austin Coll., 1944; postgrad., Southwestern Med. Found., 1948. Intern in surgery Albany (N.Y.) Gen. Hosp., 1948-49; research fellow in pharmacology Tufts Coll. Med. Sch., Boston, 1949-50, asst. prof. pharmcology, 1950-51; resident gen. practice St. Mary's Infirmary, Galveston, Tex., 1951-53; staff physician Shepperd Mem. Hosp., Burnet, Tex., 1953--; med. dir. coronary care unit, 1969-81, 83—; med. dir. Emergency Med. Svcs., 1987—. Mem. AMA, Rodeo and Fair Assn., Tex. Med. Assn., Tex. and Am. Acad. of Family Physicians. Republican. Baptist. Home: 511 Hamilton Creek Dr Burnet TX 78611 Office: Sheppard Med Surg Clinic Highway 29-W Burnet TX 28611

NEWMAN, PHYLLIS, counselor, therapist, hypnotist; b. N.Y.C., Aug. 20, 1933; d. Max and Frieda Yetta (Pechter) Hershkowitz; B.S., Mercy Coll., 1977; M.S., L.I.U., 1979; m. Milton Newman, Dec. 28, 1952; children—Renee Holly, Eileen Sharon, Jeffrey Mark. Pvt. practice hypnosis and therapy, Peekskill, N.Y., 1977—; lectr. in field; lectr. Pepsico Fitness Ctr., Purchase, N.Y., 1984, Purdue U., 1986, 88, Girl Scouts' Council, local radio; dir. counseling Hypnosis Group, 1979—. Mem. parents exec. bd. Purdue U., 1978-83, mem. pres.' council, 1983—; mem. Hand to Mouth Players, Garrison, N.Y.; bd. dirs. Yorktown (N.Y.) Community Players, 1989—. Mem. Am. Assn. Counseling and Devel., Am. Mental Health Counselors Assn., N.Y. Soc. Ericksonian Hypnosis, Am. Assn. Profl. Hypnotherapists. Contbr. articles to profl. jours. Club. Deans. Address: 2 Gallows Hill Rd RFD Box 2 Peekskill NY 10566

NEWMAN, SERAINE DIANNE, trance medium, psychic, parapsychologist, teacher and researcher; b. Cleve., Mar. 8, 1942; d. Herman and Helen Newman; div.; children: Bret Jordan, Todd Jason Bluffestone. Student, Ohio U., 1960-61; bus./secretarial degree, Spencerian Bus. Coll., 1960; student, Cuyahoga Community Coll., 1976, Internat. Coll. Spiritual Scis., Montreal, Can., 1986. Cert. Hospice including bereavement counseling. TV model Cleve., 1962; designer Interior and Exterior Speculation Homes, Cleve., 1974-75; innovator parapsychology/metaphys. discussion group, medium Ft. Lauderdale, Miami, Fla., 1981—; producer, radio talk show hostess (Deene Newman) New Insights, Sta. WDNA Community Radio, Miami, 1988-89; founder, exec. dir. Meta Fellowship, Inc., Miami, 1988; co-founder Mysticons, Cleve., 1974; internat. bus. and personal cons.; lectr. at leading south Fla. univs.; developer, leader monthly in-house ednl. programs, seminars, spl. events, south Fla., 1980-85; documented communication of the deceased soul via trance mediumship, 1974—; documented sci. experiment proved objective evidence of life after death via trance mediumship, 1983. Editor Women's Am. ORT, Cleve., 1970s, Cleve. Jr. C. of C. publ., 1963; columnist monthly mag. South Fla., 1984. Chmn. bd. dirs. The Roundtable of the Light Ctrs., Miami, 1981-85. Mem. Fla. Soc. Psychical Rsch., Spiritual Adv. Coun. (Orlando, Fla., assoc., minister). Home and office: The Meta Fellowship Inc The Moors Atriums 6628 NW 178 Terr Hialeah Post Office FL 33015

NEWMAN, SUZANNE DINKES, advertising agency executive; b. Bklyn., Apr. 28, 1949; d. Philip and Natalie (Hollander) Dinkes; m. Ralph Michael Newman, Mar. 9, 1975. Student, Cooper Union, 1967-71, Sch. Visual Arts, N.Y.C., 1971-72. Asst. art dir. Lincoln Ctr. Programs, N.Y.C., 1973-74; art dir. BimBamBoom Mag., Yonkers, N.Y., 1974, Fairfax Advt., N.Y.C., 1974-75; dir. ops. TBE Advt., Yonkers, 1975-87, chief exec. officer, 1987—; art dir. Time Barrier Express, Yonkers, 1975-80; concert coordinator Classic Harmony Prodns., N.Y.C., 1975; spl. event planner The Left Bank, Mount Vernon, N.Y., 1980-81; spl. event cons. Glen Island Casino, New Rochelle, N.Y., 1984-85; event coordinator, Top Brass, Yonkers, 1986-87; art dir., cons. various music publs., 1974-80. Editor: Rockin' in the Fourth Estate, 1979-80. Art dir.: White and Still All Right!, 1977, Sun Records, 1980, The Buddy Holly Story, 1979. Recipient Disting. Leadership and Service award Westchester County C. of C., 1985. Mem. Westchester Small Bus. Council (communications chmn. 1984-85), Westchester Assn. Women Bus. Owners, Am. Women Entrepreneurs, Yonkers C. of C., Council for Arts Westchester. Democrat. Jewish. Avocations: reading; antiques; gardening. Office: TBE Advt 999 Central Ave Yonkers NY 10704

NEWSOM, DOUGLAS ANN JOHNSON, author, journalism educator; b. Dallas, Jan. 16, 1934; d. J. Douglas and R. Grace (Dickson) Johnson; BJ cum laude, U. Tex., 1954, BFA summa cum laude, 1955, M in Journalism 1956, PhD, 1978; m. L. Mack Newsom, Jr., Oct. 27, 1956 (dec.); children: Michael Douglas, Kevin Jackson, Nancy Elizabeth, William Macklemore. Gen. publicity State Fair Tex., 1955; advt. and promotion Newsom's Women's Wear, 1956-57; publicity Auto Market Show, 1961; lab. instr. radio-tv news-writing course U. Tex., 1961-62; local publicist Tex. Boys Choir, 1964-69, nat. publicist, 1967-69; pub. relations dir. Gt. S.W. Boat Show Dallas, 1966-72, Family Fun Show, 1970-71, Horace Ainsworth Co., Dallas, 1966-76; pres. Profl. Devel. Cons., Inc., 1976-89; faculty Tex. Christian U., Ft. Worth, 1969—, prof. dept. journalism, chmn. dept., 1979-86, adviser yearbook and mag., 1969-79; dir. ONEOK Inc., diversified energy co., 1980—; Fulbright lectr. in India, 1988. Sec.-treas. Public Relations Found. Tex., 1979-80, also trustee; public relations chmn. local Am. Heart Assn., 1973-76, state public relations com. 1974-82, chmn., 1980-82; trustee Inst. for Pub. Rels. Research and Edn., 1985—; mem. Gas Research Adv. Council, 1981—. Fellow Pub. Rels. Soc. Am. (nat. edn. com. 1975, chmn. 1978, nat. faculty adviser, chmn. edn. sect.); mem. Assn. Edn. in Journalism (pres. public relations div. 1974-75, nat. pres. 1984-85), Women in Communications (nat. conv. treas. 1967, nat. public relations chmn. 1969-71), Tex. Public Relations Assn. (dir. 1976-84, v.p. 1980-82, pres. 1982-83), Am. Women in Radio and TV, Mortar Bd. Alumnae (adviser Tex. Christian U. 1974-75), Phi Kappa Phi, Kappa Tau Alpha, Delta Delta Delta. Episcopalian. Author: (with Alan Scott) This is PR, 1976, 3d edit., 1984, (with Judy Van Slyke Turk) 4th edit., 1989, (with Bob Carrell) Writing for Public Relations Practice, 1989, 2d edit., 1986, (with Jim Wollert) Media Writing, 1984, 2d edit., 1988; editorial bd. Public Relations Rev., 1978—. Home: 4237 Shannon Dr Fort Worth TX 76116 Office: Tex Christian U Dept Journalism PO Box 32930 Fort Worth TX 76129

NEWTON, DOROTHY RUTH ARMSTRONG, retired principal; b. Dallas, Sept. 8, 1923; d. Albert Frederick and Mayme B. (Miller) Armstrong; B.A., U. Tex., Arlington, 1967, M.A., 1973; adminstr.'s cert. North Tex. State U., 1980; m. James L. Newton, Mar. 27, 1942; children—Diana Jay, Rena Kathleen, Carole Ruth. Sec., Reconstrn. Fin. Corp., CSC, Washington, 1941-42; tchr. Jefferson Middle Sch., Grand Prairie, Tex., 1968-69; tchr. Grand Prairie High Sch., 1969-81, asst. prin., 1981-85, prin. alternative edn. ctr. Grand Prairie Ind. Sch. Dist., 1985-88, ret., 1988; bd. dirs. Children First Ctr. Served with Women's Res., USMC, 1943-45. Cert. tchr. for life, cert. sch. adminstr., Tex. Mem. Assn. Supervision and Curriculum Devel., Nat. Assn. Secondary Prins., Tex. Assn. Secondary Schs. Prins., Grand Prairie Prins. Assn., Assn. Tex. Profl. Educators (local treas. 1980-81), AAUW, Rejabian Club, Federated Woman's Club, Phi Delta Kappa. Republican. Mem. Christian Ch. (Disciples of Christ).

NEWTON, GALE JOANN, financial consultant; b. Mich., Nov. 23, 1954; d. Gilbert Allen Sr. and Marjorie J. (Lockard) N. Student, Grand Valley State U., Allendale, Mich., 1978; cert., Life Underwriter Tng. Coun., 1983, 85, 87, 88, 89. Registered rep. Investors Diversified Svcs., Grand Rapids, Mich., 1980-83; acct. exec. Primus Fin. Svcs. Inc., Grand Rapids, 1983-87; cons. Stifel, Nicolaus & Co., Grand Rapids, 1987—; v.p. bd. Attitudinal Healing Ctr. Grand Rapids. Pres. Midwest Mich. Herb Assn., 1989-90; bd. dirs. Attitudinal Healing Ctr. of Grand Gapids. Grant Taggart scholar Am. Coll., 1985. Mem. Nat. Assn. Profl. Sales Women, Mich. Profl. Sales Women, NAFE, Nat. Assn. Life Underwriters, Mich. and Grand Rapids Life Underwriters, Midwest Mich. Herb Assn. (pres.). Office: Stifel Nicolaus Inc 4450 Cascade Rd SE Grand Rapids MI 49546

NEWTON, KAREN CANTEY, teacher; b. Florence, S.C., July 23, 1959; d. Emory Davis and Margaret Nell (Duke) Cantey; m. Donald Michael Newton, July 20, 1985. BS, Francis Marion Coll., Florence, S.C., 1981, MS, 1985. Admissions clk. Bruce Hosp., Florence, 1978-81; tchr. Florence Pub. Schs., 1981—. Sec. Assn. Parents and Tchrs., Florence, 1987-88. Mem. Bapt. Young Women Florence, Zeta Tau Alpha. Republican. Home: 1323 Edgewood Ave Florence SC 29501 Office: Briggs Elem Sch 1012 Congaree Dr Florence SC 29501

NEWTON, RHONWEN LEONARD, microcomputer consultant; b. Lexington, N.C., Nov. 13, 1940; d. Jacob Calvin and Mary Louise (Moffitt) Leonard; m. Willoughby Newton III, Aug. 7, 1965; children: Blair Armistead, Allison Page, William Brockenbrough III. AB, Duke U., 1962; MS in Edn., Old Dominion U., 1968. French tchr. Hampton (Va.) Pub. Schs., 1962-65, Va. Beach (Va.) Pub. Schs., 1965-66; instr. foreign lang. various colls. and univs., 1967-75; foreign lang. cons. Portsmouth (Va.) Pub. Schs., 1973-75; dir. The Computer Inst., Inc., Columbia, S.C., 1983; pres., founder The Computer Experience, Inc., Columbia, 1983-88; computer cons. Columbia, 1988—. Author: WordPerfect, 1988, All About Computers, 1989, Microsoft Excel for the Mac, 1989, Introduction to the Mac, 1989, Introduction to DOS, 1989, Introduction to Lotus 1-2-3, 1989, Advanced Lotus 1-2-3, 1989, Introduction to WordPerfect, 1989, Advanced WordPerfect, 1989, Introduction to DisplayWrite 4, 1989, WordPerfect for the Mac, 1989, Introduction to Microsoft Works for the Mac, 1990. Mem. Columbia Planning Commn., 1980-87; bd. dirs. United Way Midlands, Columbia, 1983-86; bd. dirs. Assn. Jr. Leagues, N.Y.C., 1980-82; trustee

Heathwood Hall Episcopal Sch., Columbia, 1979-85. Republican. Episcopalian. Home and Office: 1635 Kathwood Dr Columbia SC 29206

NEWTON-CERKAS, PAULA SUE, technical institute administrator; b. Neenah, Wis., May 3, 1951; d. Paul John and Helen Ethel Ann (VanEnkVoort) Newton; m. Stephen L. Cerkas, Jan. 10, 1971; children: Gretchen, Rebecca. BS, U. Wis., 1973; MS, U. So. Ill., 1978. Manpower specialist S.C. Employment Security Commn., Charleston, 1974-76, training counselor, 1976-78; area program mgr. So. Research and Devel. Commn., Laurens, S.C., 1978-80; cons., adminstr. CORBIA, Greenville, S.C., T.R. McConnell & Co., Charleston, 1981-82; owner, cons. Procurement Specialists of Charleston, 1982-83; evaluator Lanier Area Tech. Sch., Oakwood, Ga., 1985; dir. spl. programs, pub. relations, mktg. Lanier Tech. Inst., Oakwood, Ga., 1985--. Contbr. articles to profl. jours. Vol. Gainesville, 1986-88; pres. League of Women Voters, Gainesville, Ga., 1987—; grants chair Adolescent Pregnancy Coalition, Gainesville, 1988—; exec. coun. Rape Response, Inc., Gainesville, 1989. Mem. Mtn. Energy Consortium, Ga. Sch. Pub. Relations Assn., Nat. Assn. Female Execs., Nat. & Ga. Vocat. Assns., Nat. & Ga. Displaced Homemakers Networks. Roman Catholic. Home: 3502 Thompson Bend Gainesville GA 30506

NEZWORSKI, M. TERESA, psychologist; b. Ft. Worth, Oct. 13, 1954; d. Leo R. and Grace Alee (Lamm) N.; m. Michael J. Mahoney, Apr. 23, 1984; 1 child, Maureen Elizabeth Mahoney. BA, Wash. U., 1977; PhD, U. Minn., 1983. Tchr. Ctr. for New Ways in Edn., Human Devel., St. Louis, 1976-77; from research asst. to teaching asst. Inst. for Child Devel., Mpls., 1977-80; from residence advisor to sr. residence advisor U. Minn., 1978-79; research asst. Dept. Psychiatry St. Paul Ramsey Hosp.; psychology intern Mpls. Children's Hosp., 1982-83; asst. prof. Dept. Psychology The Penn. State U., Pa., 1983-85; clin. dir. Counseling Psychology Clin., U. Calif., Santa Barbara, 1986—; dir. tng. Counseling Psychology Program, U. Calif., Santa Barbara, 1989—. Editor Clinical Implications of Attachment, 1988. V.p. Bd. dirs. West Campus Pt. Homeowners Assn., Santa Barbara, 1986--, bd. mem. St. Marks Parish, Isla Vista, Calif., 1989--. Danforth fellow. Mem. Soc. for Rsch. in Child Devel., Am. Psychol. Assn., Assn. for the Advancement of Behavior Therapy, Soc. for Values in Higher Edn., Phi Beta Kappa. Democrat. Roman Catholic. Office: U Calif Dept Edn Counseling Psychology Clin Santa Barbara CA 93106

NGUYEN, ANN CAC KHUE, pharmaceutical and bioorganic chemist; b. Sontay, Vietnam; came to U.S., 1975; naturalized citizen; d. Nguyen Van Soan and Luu Thi Hieu. BS, U. Saigon, 1973; MS, San Francisco State U., 1978; PhD, U. Calif., San Francisco, 1983. Teaching and research asst. U. Calif., San Francisco, 1978-83, postdoctoral fellow, 1983-86; research scientist U. Calif., 1987—. Contbr. articles to profl. jours. Recipient Nat. Research Service award, NIH, 1981-83; Regents fellow U. Calif., San Francisco, 1978-81. Mem. AAAS, Am. Chem. Soc., Bay Area Enzyme Mechanism Group, Nat. Coop. Drug Discovery Group, Am. Assn. of Pharm. Scientists. Roman Catholic. Home: 1488 Portola Dr San Francisco CA 94127 Office: U Calif Dept Pharm Chemistry San Francisco CA 94143

NGUYEN, XUAN-BA THI, engineer; b. Mytho, Vietnam, Feb. 17, 1959; came to U.S., 1975; d. Nhac Dinh and Bich-Du Thi (Ho) N.; m. Kiet Tuan Huynh, Apr. 21, 1984. BSEE magna cum laude, U. Portland, 1982. Intern Hewlett Packard, Vancouver, Wash., 1981-82; design engr. Floating Pt. Systems Inc., Beaverton, Oreg., 1982-84; devel. engr. Honeywell, Inc., Seattle, 1984-87, sr. devel. engr., 1987—; project leader, Honeywell, Inc., Seattle, 1989—; speaker Honeywell Micro-Electronics Conf., Mpls., 1988. Contbr. articles to profl. jours. Mem. IEEE, NSPE (treas. Portland chpt. 1981-82), Toastmasters Internat. Buddhism. Home: 2321 218th Pl SW Brier WA 98036 Office: Honeywell Marine Systems 6500 Harbour Hgts Pkwy Everett WA 98036

NICCOLINI, DIANORA, photographer; b. Florence, Italy, Oct. 3, 1936; came to U.S., 1946, naturalized, 1960; d. George and Elaine (Augsbury) N. Student Hunter Coll., 1955-62, Art Students League, 1960, Germain Sch. Photography, 1962. Med. photographer Manhattan Eye, Ear and Throat Hosp., 1963-65; organizer med. photography dept., 1st chief med. photographer Lenox Hill Hosp., 1965-67; organizer, head dept. med. and audio visual edn. St. Clare's Hosp., N.Y.C., 1967-76; mem. Third Eye Gallery, N.Y.C., 1974-76; owner Dianora Niccolini Creations, 1976—; instr. photography Camera Club N.Y., 1978-79, Germaine Sch. Photography, 1978-79, N.Y. Inst. Photography, 1981-83; one woman shows 209 Photo Gallery, Top of the Stairs Gallery, Third Eye Gallery, 1974, 75, 77, West Broadway Gallery, N.Y.C., 1981, Camera Club N.Y., 1982, Photographics Unltd. Gallery, N.Y.C., 1981; project dir. Photography over 65, N.Y.C., 1978; pub. portfolios; author: Women of Vision, 1982, Men in Focus, 1983; editor: P.W.P. Times, 1981-82; contbr. to photog. books, 1979, 80; contbg. editor Functional Photography, 1979-80, N.Y. Photo Dist. News, 1980. Mem. Women Photographers N.Y. (founder 1974), Biol. Photog. Assn., Assn. Ind. Video and Filmmakers, Internat. Ctr. Photography, Am. Soc. Mag. Photographers, Am. Soc. Picture Profls., Profl. Women Photographers (coord. 1980-84), Unity Ctr. Practical Christianity. 1982; Men in Focus, 1983; editor: P.W.P. Times, 1981-82; contbr. to photog. books, 1979, 80; contbg. editor Functional Photography, 1979-80, N.Y. Photo Dist. News, 1980. Home: 356 E 78th St New York NY 10021

NICHOLAS, CECILE TERESA, office manager; b. Fall River, Mass., Aug. 4, 1958; d. Leo M. and Mary (Regan) N.; children: Keith E. Nicholas, Christine E. Chamberlain. Student, Bunker Hill Community Coll., 1978. Adminstrv. asst. traffic dept. Clark Franklin Press, Westwood, Mass., 1980-83; computer specialist 25th Century Mktg., Newton, Mass., 1983-84; office mgr. AmPrint, Natick, Mass., 1984—. Mem. U.S. Jaycees of Norwood. Mem. NAFE, Printing Inst. of New Eng.

NICHOLAS, CINDY, Canadian provincial official; b. Toronto, Ont., Can., Aug. 20, 1957; d. James Paul and Victoria (Dube) N.; m. Raymond Leslie LeGrow, Mar. 28, 1987; 1 child, Leahanne Nichole. BS, U. Toronto, 1979; LLB, U. Windsor, 1982. Bar: Ont. 1984. Assoc. R. Alan Eagleson Q.C., Toronto, 1982-83; lawyer, program officer Donner Canadian Found., Toronto, 1984-87; M.P. Ho. of Commons Riding of Scarborough Centre, Ont., 1987. Swam English Channel 19 times. Mem. Law Soc. Upper Can., ACTRA, Order of Can. Office: Ont Parliament, Legis Assembly, Toronto, ON Canada M7A 1A2

NICHOLAS, NICKIE LEE, industrial hygienist; b. Lake Charles, La., Jan. 19, 1938; d. Clyde Lee and Jessie Mae (Lyons) N.; B.S., U. Houston, 1960, M.S., 1966. Tchr. sci. Pasadena (Tex.) Ind. Sch. Dist., 1960-61; chemist FDA, Dallas, 1961-62, VA Hosp., Houston, 1962-66; chief biochemist Baylor U. Coll. Medicine, 1966-68; chemist NASA, Johnson Spacecraft Center, 1968-73; analytical chemist TVA, Muscle Shoals, Ala., 1973-75; indsl. hygienist, compliance officer Occupational Safety and Health Adminstrn., Dept. Labor, Houston, 1975-79, area dir., Tulsa, 1979-82, mgr., Austin, 1982—; mem. faculty VA Sch. Med. Tech., Houston, 1963-66. Recipient award for outstanding achievement German embassy, 1958, Suggestion award VA, 1963, Group Achievement award Skylab Med. Team, NASA, 1974, Personal Achievement award Dept. Labor Fed. Women's Program, 1984, Career Achievement award Federally Employed Women, Inc., 1988. Mem. Am. Chem. Soc. (dir. analytical group Southeastern Tex. and Brazosport sects. 1971, chmn. elect 1973), Am. Assn. Clin. Chemists, Am. Harp Soc., Fed. Exec. Assn. (pres. 1984-85), Kappa Epsilon. Home: 1305 Shannon Oaks Austin TX 78746 Office: 611 E 6th St Suite 303 Austin TX 78701

NICHOLLS, SANDRA ANNE, corporate communications specialist, teacher; b. Ottawa, Ont., Can., Aug. 20, 1944; d. Elias John and Pauline Sophia (Ross) Karam; m. Peter Franics Nicholls, Oct. 25, 1965 (div. Apr. 1989); children: Catherine Dianne, Peter Jeffrey. AS in Commerce, Henry Ford Community Coll., Dearborn, Mich., 1983; BS in Bus. Mugmt., Detroit Coll. of Bus., Dearborn, 1990. Tchr. Ottawa Separate Schs., 1964-66; legal sec. Messner, LaBine & Vairo, Houghton, Mich., 1967-70; sec. adminstrn., budget coord. Ford Motor Co., Dearborn, Mich., 1978-85, adminstrv. coord., budget coord. corp. advt. div., 1985—. Bd. dirs. Dearborn Pastoral Counseling Ctr., 1986—; pres. Am. Bapt. Chs. Mich., East Lansing, 1987-88, Am. Bapt. Chs. S.E. Mich., 1985-86; co-founder, chmn. Dearborn Ecumenical Orgn., 1978-81. Mem. Colony Club Dearborn (pres. 1976-77). Office: Ford Motor Co PO Box 1899 Rm 737 Dearborn MI 48121-1899

NICHOLS, ALLIE JO, retired telecommunications executive; b. Wickes, Ark., Nov. 5, 1932; d. Luther Sebrin Nichols and Ruth May (Ross) Ford; m. Clarence Lee Cook, Jan. 29, 1960 (div. 1965). Student, Coll. of the Ozarks, 1951-52; A in Bus., St. Joseph Coll., 1957; AS, North Am. Inst., 1959; student, Ariz. State U., 1963-65. Mgr. communications exec. offices Ramada Inns, Phoenix, 1965-67; mgr. traffic Mountain Bell, Phoenix, 1967-73; facilities planner Mountain Bell, Denver, 1973-78, intra-lata planner, 1980-83, product specialist, 1983-85; toll switch planner AT&T, Denver, 1973-80; mgr. product selection, evaluation U.S. West, Denver, 1983-89. Mem. N. Mex. Grassroot Dems., Santa Fe, 1955—; officer Sloan's Lake Citizen Group, Denver, 1977—; mem. NW Denver Dems., 1980—; adv. bd. Denver Ch. Assn., 1981—; mem. Our Lady of the Bell, Denver. Mem. Soc. of Women Engrs., U.S. West Women, Alliance of Profl. Women, Pioneers of Am. Roman Catholic. Home: PO Box 1246 Moriarty NM 87035

NICHOLS, BARBARA ANN, social worker; b. Chgo., May 20, 1947; d. John and Helen (Rak) Suczulak; children: Jason, Jay. AAS, Coll. of DuPage, 1978; BGS, Roosevelt U., 1980; MSW, George Williams Coll., 1982, MBA, 1984. Program planner Elmhurst (Ill.) Coll., 1979-80; social worker Lyons Twp., LaGrange, Ill., 1982-85; caseworker State of Ill. Dept. Children and Family Svcs., Chgo., 1985-86; placement counselor Coll. of DuPage, Glen Ellyn, Ill., 1986-88; community social worker Lisle Twp. Youth Com., Naperville, Ill., 1988—. Bd. dirs. People's Resource Ctr., Wheaton, Ill., 1984—. Mem. Acad. Cert. Social Workers. Home: 5700 Hillcrest #2H Lisle IL 60532

NICHOLS, EDIE DIANE, executive recruiter; b. Grahamstown, Eastern Cape Province, Republic of South Africa, Mar. 28, 1939; came to U.S., 1963; d. Cyril Doughtry and Dorothy Ethel (Nottingham) Tyson; m. John F. Nichols, Dec. 16, 1962; 1 child, Ian Tyson. Adminstrv. asst. Am. Acad. Medicine, N.Y.C., 1963-64, Jack Lenor Larsen, Inc., N.Y.C., 1964-70; v.p. John Scott Fones, Inc., N.Y.C., 1971-76, Howard J. Rubenstein Assocs. Inc., N.Y.C., 1976-80; dir. communications Carl Byoir & Assocs., N.Y.C., 1981-83; account supr. Hill and Knowlton, N.Y.C., 1983-85; broker Cross & Brown Co., N.Y.C., 1986-88; exec. recruiter Marc Nichols Assocs., Inc., N.Y.C., 1989—. Trustee Cen. Park Hist. Soc., N.Y.C., 1978-80. Mem. NOW, N.Y. Women in Communications (pub. rels. chair 1980-81, v.p., programs bd. dirs 1985-87), Fin. Women's Assn. of N.Y. Republican. Episcopalian. Club: City of N.Y. (trustee, v.p., fin. and devel. 1987-89). Home: 16 Stuyvesant Oval New York NY 10009 Office: Marc Nichols Assocs Inc 271 Madison Ave New York NY 10016

NICHOLS, ELAINE C., adminstrative assistant; b. Blue Ridge, Ga., Jan. 12, 1947; d. Carlos J. and Artie L. (Ross) Chambers; m. Johnny L. Nichols, Mar. 12, 1971; children: Shannon, Jerry. Student, North Ga. Tech. and Vocat., Clarkesville, 1966, Tri-County Community Coll., Murphy, N.C. Cert. CPS. Adminstrv. asst. Arbor Acres Farm, Inc., Blairsville, Ga. Mem. NAFE, PSI, Clay County C. of C. Avocations: sewing, reading, gardening.

NICHOLS, ELIZABETH CHRISTIE, auditor; b. Rolla, Mo., Feb. 26, 1963; d. Chester Encell II and Carolyn Louise (Gregg) N. BBA, Mesa State Coll., 1986. Promotions specialist, sales dir. Peppermill's Western Village, Sparks, Nev., 1985-87; internal auditor Harrah's Resort Hotels & Casinos, Reno, Nev., 1987-89; asst. gen. mgr. Prospect Reef Resort, Brit. V.I., 1989-90. Vol. Spl. Olympics. Mem. NAFE, Nat. Assn. Accts., Inst. Internal Auditors (IIA com.). Republican. Home: 1192 LaVia Way Sparks NV 89434

NICHOLS, IRENE DELORES, real estate professional; b. Kansas City, Mo., Mar. 7, 1938; d. Verne Keith Covell and Louise Lena (Janeski) Covell Jackson; children: Todd Martin Hesher, Tedd Matthew Hesher. BS, U. Fla., 1980; AA in Tech. Arts, Johnson County Coll., 1986. Cert. paralegal; lic. securities, ins. dealer, Mo. and Kans. Legal sec. Lathrop, Koontz, Righter, Clagett, Parker and Norquist, Kansas City, 1972-75; fashion model Patricia Stevens Agy., Kansas City, 1975-76; with legal dept. U.S. Dept. Treasury, Kansas City, 1981-84; fin. planner, rep. IDS Am. Express, Overland Park, Kans., 1984-85; with real estate dept. Gage and Tucker, Kansas City, 1985—. Mem. Kansas City Ballet Guild, 1970, Clay County Task Force for Juvenile Detention, Liberty, Mo., 1970; life mem. Nat. PTA, 1970—; sch. dist. lobbyist to Mo. Ho. Reps., Senate, Jefferson City, 1971; v.p. North Kansas City Dem. Club, 1976. Mem. Kansas City Assn. Legal Assts., Internat. Assn. Fin. Planners, The Crossings (pres., bd. dirs.), Diplomats (bd. dirs.), Brookridge Country Club (Overland Park). Club: Brookridge Country (Overland Park). Office: Gage and Tucker 2345 Grand Ave Kansas City MO 64108

NICHOLS, MARTHA JEAN, retail executive; b. Marceline, Mo., Dec. 1, 1941; d. Rodney William and Bertie (Dick) Belt; m. Harvey Lee Nichols, Jan. 21, 1961; children: Kathaleen Kay, Christopher Harvey, Tamara Diane. Diploma, Buchanan High Sch., Troy, Mo., 1959. File clk. Del-Mar Med. Ctr., St. Louis, 1959-60; data key punch operator Hussman Refrigeration Co., St. Louis, 1960-63, Vicker Oil Co., St. Louis, 1963-64; cashier Nichols' Auto Parts and Svc. Ctr., Arvada, Colo., 1977-81; owner, mgr. Penguins Ballet and Ice Skate Boutique, Arvada, 1982—. Republican. Mem. Christian Ch. (Disciples of Christ). Home: 6687 Zang Ct Arvada CO 80004 Office: Penguins Ballet & Ice Bout 9222 W 58th Ave Arvada CO 80002

NICHOLS, MARY IVANCEVIC, controller; b. Norwalk, Conn., Mar. 10, 1951; d. Walter Charles and Erna Jane (Michel) Ivancevic; m. James Cortlandt Nichols, Apr. 10, 1976; 1 child, Kimberly Michel. BA, Syracuse U., 1973; postgrad., U. Bridgeport, 1988—. From sec. to svc. supr. Wilks Sci. Corp., S Norwalk, Conn., 1973-76; order entry, customer service supr. Wilks Sci./Foxboro Analytical, S Norwalk, Conn., 1976-80; sales adminstrn. dept mgr. Foxboro Analytical, S Norwalk, Conn., 1980-84; acctg., office mgr. Gen. Analysis Corp., S. Norwalk, Conn., 1985-87; controller, asst. corp. sec. Gen. Analysis Corp., Conn., 1987--. Fellow mem. Nat. Assn. Female Execs. Roman Catholic. Office: Gen Analysis Corp 140 Water St South Norwalk CT 06854

NICHOLS, NANCY, business executive, financial consultant; b. Monroe, Mich., Dec. 1, 1939; d. Joseph William and Eva Arlene (Smith) Smith; m. Raymond Arlyn Nichols, Jan. 17, 1959; children: Anita Marie Nichols Baran, Amy Beth Nichols Forrest. Student U. Mich., 1972, Siena Heights Coll., 1983. Sales staff Glover Real Estate, Adrian, Mich., 1972-75; mgr. Bennett Ambulance, Tecumseh, Mich., 1972-75; acting dir. Lenawee Health Dept., Adrian, 1975-78; owner, capt. Anywhere Sports Fishing, Monroe, 1978—; assoc., cons. Stauder, Barch & Assoc., Inc., Ann Arbor, Mich., 1985-89, corp. v.p., 1989—; speaker seminars concerning fin., pub. health laws and regulations, unification of health systems, county govt., women in decision making roles. Bd. dirs. U. Mich. Sch. Pub. Health, 1980-85, Community Mental Health Bd. Lewanee County, 1975-84; mem. exec. bd. Tecumseh Housing Commn., 1975—; chmn. exec. com. South Cen. Substance Abuse Commn., 1976-84; chairperson Human Svc. Bd., 1976-78, Lewanee County Dem. Party, Adrian, 1972—, chmn. 1985-88, Lewanee County Health Bd., 1976-78, Lewanee County Energy Task Force, 1980-81; candidate for state rep. Lewanee County, 1984; county commr. Lewanee County, 1974-84; mem. Industry/Edn. Coordinating Council (3 counties), 1983-85, State Health Coordinating Coun., 1980-84, Selection com. for State Dir. Pub. Health, 1981, State Mich. com. for Unification of Pub. Mental Health System, 1979, State Mich. Substance Abuse Consolidation Task Force, 1975-76, Mich. Assn. Bds. Health, 1976-84, pres. 1983; bd. dirs. Mich. Mid-South Health Systems Agy., 1976-83, pres. 1981; mem. adv. com. Great Lakes Fishery, 1986—. Named Democrat of Yr. Lenawee Dem. Party, 1985; recipient Mich. Legis. Cert. Tribute for Outstanding Svc. in Health field, 1983, 85, Mich. Minuteman Citation Honor for Promoting Mich. and community, 1979; Namesake of the Nancy Nichols Award for Outstanding contribution to the Substance Abuse field by the Substance Abuse Program Directors in Calhouns, Hillsdale, Jackson and Lenawee Counties, 1983. Mem. Bus. and Profl. Women, Mich. Assn. of Counties, Mcpl. Fin. Officers Assn., Mich. Mcpl. League, Detroit Bond Club, Safari Club, Order Eastern Star (past matron). Democrat. Methodist. Home: 216 N Oneida St Tecumseh MI 49286 Office: Stauder Barch & Assocs Inc 3989 Research Park Ann Arbor MI 48108

NICHOLS, VERONA SCHMIDT, university administrator; b. Fond du Lac, Wis., Mar. 9, 1942; d. Wallace Edgar and Clara Helena (Koepp) Schmidt; m. David C. Nichols, Aug. 26, 1962; 1 child, Cynthia Nichols Harmelink. Student, U. Wis., River Falls, 1960-62; BE summa cum laude, Northeast Mo. State U., 1970, MA, 1971. Adminstrv. sec. Lilly Rare Book Library, Bloomington, Ind., 1962-66; tchr. Kirksville (Mo.) Jr. High Sch., 1972; psychometrist Northeast Mo. State U., Kirksville, 1973-76; dir. student activities Northeast Mo. State U., 1976-88, asst. dean of colls., 1988—. Publicity chair, Kirksville Com. to Retain City Mgr. Govt., 1982; mem. adv. com., Kirksville Sr. High Sch., 1983-86. Mem. Mo. Coll. Personnel Assn. (program presenter 1987), Northeast Mo. Guidance Assn., Nat. Assn. Student Personnel Adminstrs. (program presenter 1988), Sojourners, Univ. Women, Faculty Wives , Kirksville Regional Arts Coun., Kirksville C. of C. (edn. com. 1983-85), Phi Delta Kappa. Republican. Office: Northeast Mo State U McClain Hall 204 Kirksville MO 63501

NICHOLS, VICKI ANNE, financial consultant, librarian; b. Denver, June 10, 1949; d. Glenn Warner and Loretta Irene (Chalender) Adams; B.A., Colo. Coll., 1972; postgrad. U. Denver, 1976-77; m. Robert H. Nichols, Oct. 28, 1972 (div.); children—Christopher Travis, Lindsay Meredith. Treas., controller, dir. Polaris Resources, Inc., Denver, 1972-86; controller InterCap Devel. Corp, 1986-87; treas., controller, dir. Transnat. Cons., Ltd., 1986—; librarian Jefferson County (Colo.) Pub. Library, 1986—; dir., owner Nichols Bus. Services. Home: 4305 Brentwood St Wheat Ridge CO 80033 Office: 1825 Lawrence St Suite 333 Denver CO 80202

NICHOLS, VIRGINIA V., insurance agent, accountant; b. Monroe County, Mo., Oct. 26, 1928; d. Elmer W. and Frances L. (McKinney) N.; student Belleville (Ill.) Jr. Coll., 1959-60, Rockhurst Coll., 1964-65, Avila Coll., Kansas City, Mo., 1981-84. Sec., Panhandle Eastern Pipeline Co., Kansas City, Mo., 1964-65, St. Louis County Dept. Revenue, 1965-69, Forest Park Community Coll., 1969-71, Nooney Co., St. Louis, 1971-77, J. A. Baer Enterprises, St. Louis, 1979; acct. Panhandle Eastern Pipe Line Co., Kansas City, Mo., 1979-85. Vol., ARC, 1965—. Mem. Am. Soc. Women Accts., Profl. Secs. Internat. (Sec. of Year 1969, sec. Mo. div. 1975-76), Jr. Women's C. of C. (Girl of Year 1975, pres. 1974-75), Soroptimist Internat. (treas. Kansas City chpt. 1990—). Republican. Catholic. Home: PO Box 5832 Kansas City MO 64111

NICHOLSON, EDNA ELIZABETH, retired public health official; b. Redwood Falls, Minn., Dec. 23, 1907; d. Ernest Crawford and Alma (Bordeaux) N.; A.B., U. Mich., 1930, M.S. in Pub. Health, 1931, cert. social work, 1931. Nat. Tb Assn. fellow in social research, 1930-31; med. social work ARC, U.S. Naval Hosp., Great Lakes, Ill., 1931-33; asst. dir. med. relief service Cook County Bur. Public Welfare, Chgo., 1933-35; instr. social aspects of nursing Cook County Sch. Nursing and asst. dir. social service Cook County Hosp., Chgo., 1935-37; dir. med. relief service Chgo. Relief Adminstrn., 1938-42; vis. lectr. Sch. Hygiene and Pub. Health, U. Mich., 1939; cons. on med. assistance, bur. pub. assistance Fed. Security Agency, 1942-44; dir. Central Service for Chronically Ill, Inst. Medicine, Chgo., 1944-54; exec. dir. Inst. Medicine of Chgo., 1955-64; sr. specialist program ops. and standards Med. Services Adminstrn., HEW, 1964-71; spl. lectr. program in hosp. adminstrn. Northwestern U., 1945-60; tech. adviser Commn. on Chronic Illness, 1949-56. Recipient Cancer Care award Nat. Cancer Found., 1955. Mem. Am. Public Health Assn., Phi Beta Kappa, Delta Omega, Sigma Kappa. Author: Terminal Care for Cancer Patients, 1950; Surveying Community Needs and Resources for Care of the Chronically Ill, 1950; The Nurse and Chronic Illness, 1953; Planning New Institutional Facilities for Longterm Care, 1956; A Comprehensive Community Plan for Meeting the Problems of Chronic Illness, 1959. Contbr. to profl. jours. Home: 315 N La Grange Rd La Grange Park IL 60525

NICHOLSON, FREDA HYAMS, museum executive, medical educator; b. Asheville, N.C., Sept. 10, 1934; d. John Fred and Thelma (Lewis) Hyams; m. Henry Hale Nicholson, Jr. M.D., Sept. 24, 1956; children: Henry Hale III, Miller, J. Christie, Michael, Amanda, Stuart. R.N., St. Joseph's Hosp., 1955; BS in Nursing and Biology, Queens Coll., 1959, LHD (hon.), 1982; MEd, U. N.C.-Charlotte, 1976. Surg. nurse Ochsner Clinic, New Orleans, 1955-56; nursing adminstr. Presbyn. Hosp., Charlotte, N.C., 1956-59; instr. biology and nursing Cen. Piedmont Coll., Charlotte, part-time 1965-71; instr. nursing U. N.C., Charlotte, part-time 1976-81; health educator, edn. curator Charlotte Nature Mus., 1971-80, now exec. dir.; acting dir. Discovery Place, Charlotte, 1981; exec. dir., chief exec. officer Sci. Mus. (Discovery Place-Nature Mus.), 1981—; cons. health Health Adventure, Asheville, 1968; mem. mus. planning com. Sci. Mus. Project, Little Rock, 1984; in internat. partnership NEA, Washington, 1983; mem. U.S. Cultural Commn./India, participant in seminar in India, 1984; mem. adv. panel NSF, 1988—; bd. dirs. First Union Nat. Bank N.C. Bd. dirs. United Way, Charlotte, 1983, March of Dimes, Charlotte, 1978-83, Jr. Achievement, 1983—, Mission Air, 1984—; cons. Gov.'s Com. for Econ. Growth through Edn., 1984; mem. exec. bd. N.C. Sch. of Math. and Sci., 1986—; active mem. local, state and nat. med. auxs., 1956—; mem. bd. visitors J.C. Smith U., Charlotte, 1983—; mem. adv. panel Nat. Sci. Found., 1988—. Named Woman of Yr., City of Charlotte, 1982, Nat. Outstanding Alumna Alpha Chi Omega, 1983, Outstanding Alumna Queens Coll., 1982. Mem. Women Execs., Assoc. Sci./Tech. Ctrs. (sec. 1984-90, pres. 1990), Internat. Coun. Mus. (commr. Semocet-Sci. 1988—), Am. Assn. Mus. (commr. for accreditatiomn, at-large coun. mem. 1989—), S.E. Mus. Coun., Greater Charlotte C. of C. (advt. com.), Jr. Women, Guild of Nature Mus., AAUW. Office: Nature Mus 301 N Tryon St Charlotte NC 28202

NICHOLSON, LINDA BARTON, accountant; b. Phila., Feb. 18, 1949; d. A. Daniel Jr. and Evelyn (Ketcham) Barton; m. Bruce Allen Nicholson, Apr. 22, 1972; children: Jessica, J. Barton. BA, Skidmore Coll., 1971; postgrad., Temple U., 1976-78. Dir. student fin. aid dept. Moore Coll. of Arts, Phila., 1971-72; mgr. Tax-Man, Inc., Cambridge, Mass., 1972-75; systems analyst Safeguard Bus. Systems, Inc., Ft. Washington, Pa., 1976-81; owner Linda B. Nicholson Tax and Acctg. Svcs., Huntingdon Valley, Pa., 1981—. Ch. sch. tchr. Ch. of the Advent, Hatboro, Pa., 1984—, vestry mem., 1984-87; co-leader Brownie Troop, Hatboro, 1987-88; bd. dirs., pres. bd. Union Library Co. Hatboro, 1985—. Mem. Nat. Soc. Tax Profls., Yacht Club Stone Harbor. Republican. Episcopalian. Home and Office: 2350 Fairway Rd Huntingdon Valley PA 19006

NICHOLSON, MARILYN DIETZ, public relations executive; b. Syracuse, N.Y., Apr. 16, 1926; d. Robert Henry and Irene Jessica (Wakelee) D.; m. Robert J. Nicholson, Dec. 21, 1984; stepchildren: Gail, Margaret, William, John. Student, Syracuse U., 1962-66. Community relations assoc. Unite Way C.N.Y., Syracuse, 1956-66; community relations assoc. Sta. WCNY-TV (PBS), Liverpool, N.Y., 1966-69; communications dir. Merchants Bank, Syracuse, 1969-71; pub. relations dir. St. Camillus Health and Rehab., Syracuse, 1971—; exec. dir. St. Camillus Found., Syracuse, 1982—. Newspaper columnist Syracuse Post Standard, 1962—. Mem. C.N.Y. chpt. Nat. Soc. Fund-Raising Exec.; past corp. mem. United Way C.N.Y., 1985 allocations rev. task force, past pub. rels. com.; past adv. coun. for the elderly and handicapped Onondaga County Pub. Library; pub. relations adminstrs. officer C.N.Y. Hosp. Assn.; mem., past com. person N.Y.S. Home Care Assn., profl. adv. com. St. Camillus Home Health Care Agy., mem. C.N.Y. chpt., past officer Women in Communications Inc.; C.N.Y. chpt. adv. com., nat. patient svcs. adv. com., past pres. Arthritis Found. Recipient Golden Age award Syracuse Salvation Army, Community Better Life award Am. Nursing Home Assn., 1975, Vol. Leadership award Nat. Arthritis Found., 1978, Pres.'s Citation, Pub. Relations Soc. Am., 1981, Appreciation cert. Am. Assn. Retired Persons, 1985; named Woman of Achievement in Communications, Syracuse Post Standard, 1969. Mem. Met. Commn. on Aging for Syracuse and Onondaga County (commr. 1971-79), Nat. Coun. on Aging (sr. ctrs. and long-term care sect.), Am. Women Radio/TV (past pres.), C.N.Y. Bus./Indsl. Communicators (former officer), Syracuse Press Club (assoc.). Office: St Camillus Health and Rehab 813 Fay Rd Syracuse NY 13219

NICHOLSON, MICHELLE RENEE, early childhood specialist; b. Hillsdale, Mich., Sept. 18, 1960; d. Jean and Vivian Marie (Carpenter) Helmick; m. Clement Lynn Nicholson, Aug. 22, 1987. BS in Spl. Edn., Ea. Mich. U.,

1982; MEd in Early Childhood, U. Colo., Denver, 1986. Cert. spl. edn. and early childhood spl. edn. tchr., Colo. Primary spl. edn. tchr. Houston Ind. Sch. Dist., 1982-83; presch. spl. edn. tchr. Devel. Pathways, Aurora, Colo., 1983-86; spl. edn. cons. Elizabeth (Colo.) Consol. Schs., 1983-84; parent-child coord., infant specialist Laradon, Denver, 1987—; presenter, speaker family focus project U. Colo., Denver, 1988-89; case mgr. Mile High Down's Assn. Project, Denver, 1989; mem. Parent Adv. Com. to Kid Found./Devel. Techs., 1989; participant outreach tng. Carl Dunst Family Enablement Project, 1990; coord. for family-focused tng. of grad. early childhood spl. edn. program U. Colo., Denver, 1990; bd. dirs. Colo. Div. Early Childhood, 1990; adv. to Children's Campaign Grant Project, 1989 and others. Office: Laradon 5100 Lincoln Denver CO 80216

NICHOLSON, MYREEN MOORE, artist, researcher; b. Norfolk, Va., June 2, 1940; d. William Chester and Illeen (Fox) Moore; m. Roland Quarles Nicholson, Jan. 9, 1964 (dec. 1986); children: Andrea Joy, Ross (dec. 1965); m. Harold Wellington McKinney II, Jan. 18, 1981; 1 child, Cara Isadora. BA, William and Mary Coll., 1962; MLS, U. N.C., 1971; postgrad. Old Dominion U. 1962—64, 64-67, 75-85, 86—, The Citadel, 1968-69, Hastie Sch. Art, 1968, Chrysler Mus. Art Sch., 1964. English tchr., Chesapeake, Va., 1962-63; dept. head, Portsmouth (Va.) Bus. Coll., 1963-64; tech. writer City Planning/Art Commn., Norfolk, 1964-65; art tchr. Norfolk pub. schs., 1965-67; prof. lit., art Palmer Jr. Coll., Charleston, S.C., 1968; librarian Charleston Schs., 1968-69; asst. to asst. dir. City Library Norfolk, 1970-72, art and audio-visual librarian, 1972-75, rsch. librarian, 1975-83, librarian dept. fiction, 1983—; dir. W. Ghent Arts Alliance, Norfolk, 1978—. Poet-in-schs., Virginia Beach, Va., 1987. Book reviewer Art Book Revs., Library Jour., 1973-76; editor, illustrator Acquisitions Bibliographies, 1970—; juried exhibits various cities including Grand Hyatt, Washington, 1987, by Joan Mondale; curator of Freer Gallery; contbr. art and poetry to various publs. Mem. Virginia Beach Arts Ctr., 1978—, bd. dirs. W. Ghent Art/Lit. Festival, 1979; poetry reading Poetry Soc. Va., Va. Ctr. for Creative Arts, Sweetbriar, 1989; graphics of hundreds of celebrities from life. Recipient various art and poetry contests; Coll. William and Mary art scholar, 1958; Nat. Endowment Arts grantwriter, 1975; bd. dirs. Tidewater Literacy Coun., 1971-72; co-chair Tidewater Artists Grantwriting, 1989-90; adminstr. Tidewater Artists Grants, 1990—; reader poetry Va. Ctr. for Creative Arts, Sweetbriar., 1989. Mem. ALA (poster sessions rev. com. 1985-87, pub. relations judge, subcom. communications 1988-90), Pub. Library Assn. (com. bylaws and orgns 1988-90), Va. Library Assn. (pub. relations com. 1984-86, grievance and pay equity com. 1986-88, Logo award 1985), Southeastern Library Assn. (Rothrock award com. 1986-88), Poetry Soc. Va. (ea. pres. 1986-89, nominating com. 1989-90, state corr. sec., editor newsletter 1990—), Art Libraries Soc. N.Am., Tidewater Artists Assn. (bd. dirs. 1989—, co-chmn. grantwriting com. 1989-90, chair grantwriting com. 1990—), Southeastern Coll. Art Assn., Acad. Am. Poets, Internat. Platform Assn. (artists assn., selected judge speaking ladder 1988—), Old Dominion U. Alumni Assn. (artistic dir. Silver Reunion), Southeastern Soc. Archtl. Historians, Ikara (pres. 1989—), Va. Writers Club. Home and Office: 1404 Gates Ave Norfolk VA 23507

NICHOLSON, SHELIA ELAINE, production manager, sales executive; b. Bklyn., Jan. 20, 1963; d. Emmett Sr. and Louise (Ashford) Caldwell; m. Gerard Nicholson, Aug. 2, 1986. BS, Hampton U., 1985. Adminstrv. asst. Lazar Mgmt. Techs. Inc., N.Y.C., 1985-86; mgr. print prodn. The Wessel Co./Horah Graphics, N.Y.C., 1986-87, 88—; acctg. clk. The Howard Marlboro Group, N.Y.C., 1987-88. Mem. NAACP, CORE, NAFE, Women's Direct Response Group. Democrat. Baptist. Home: 743 Greene Ave Brooklyn NY 11221 Office: The Wessel Co/Horah Graphics 370 Lexington Ave New York NY 10017

NICKEL, ROSALIE JEAN, reading specialist; b. Hooker, Okla., Oct. 10, 1939; d. Edwin Charles and Esther Elizabeth (Wiens) Ollenburger; m. Ted W. Nickel, June 3, 1960; 1 child, Sandra Jean. BA, Tabor Coll., 1961; MA, Calif. State U., Fresno, 1970. Cert. tchr., Calif. Elem. tchr. Visalia (Calif.) Pub. Schs., 1961-62; overseas tchr. Kodaikanal Internat. Sch., Madras State, India, 1963-65; tchr. Mendota (Calif.) Jr. High Sch., 1966; elem. tchr. Fresno Pub. Schs., 1966-68, reading specialist, reading resource tchr., 1987—; elem. tchr. Inglewood (Calif.) Pub. Schs., 1968-73; spl. reading tchr. Tulsa Pub. Schs., 1974-81; salesperson, mgr. Compaq, Marion, Kans., 1981-85; gifted student tchr. Wichita (Kans.) Pub. Schs., 1986; evaluator State Textbook Com., Tulsa, 1976, 78. Newsletter editor Marion County Arts Council, 1981-82. Co-dir. Am. Field Service, Tulsa, 1980-81; v.p. Women's Federated Clubs Am., Marion, 1985-86; pres. Butler Mennonite Brethern Women's Fellowship, 1989—. Mem. Internat. Reading Assn., Tulsa Reading Assn., Fresno Area Reading Council. Home: 2821 W Compton Ct Fresno CA 93711 Office: Fresno Unified Schs Tulare and M Sts Fresno CA 93701

NICKEL, SUSAN EARLENE, physical education educator, financial analyst; b. Fort Madison, Iowa, June 27, 1951; d. Earl Dean and Irma Ellen (Ivins) N. BE, Northeast Mo. State U., 1973. Phys. edn. tchr. Ft. Madison (Iowa) Sr. High. Sch., 1974-79; phys. edn. specialist L.A. Unified Sch. Dist., 1979—; fin. planner, then mgr. Martin Fin. Svcs., Marina Del Rey, Calif., 1986-89; owner Fin. Assocs., Marina del Rey, Calif., 1989—. Bd. dirs. Connexxus Womens' Ctr., Los Angeles, 1985-87, profl. women's facilitator, 1984—; vol. facilitator Los Angeles Womens' Ctr., 1981-84; vol. Spl. Olympics, U.S. Assn. for Blind Athletes, Exceptional Games, Women's Wheelchair Basketball Assn., all Los Angeles. Mem. Los Angeles Adapted Phys. Edn. Assn. (bd. dirs.), Calif. Assn. Health, Phys. Edn., Recreation and Dance, Bus. and Profl. Alliance, Nat. Assn. Female Execs. Office: Fin Assocs 14020 D Marquesas Way Marina del Rey CA 90292

NICKELL, KATHERINE MARY, professional association executive; b. Binghamton, N.Y., Sept. 12, 1960; d. Frederick Thomas and Helen Margaret (Rakauskas) Guley; m. Daniel Boone Nickell, Sept. 10, 1988. BS in Mgmt., U. Scranton, Pa., 1982; MBA in Mktg., U. Scranton, 1984. Programmer IBM, Poughkeepsie, N.Y., 1982-83; bus. counselor Small Bus. Devel. Ctr. U. Scranton, Pa., 1983-85; mktg. mgr. Penn Cen. Tech. Security Co., Marlton, N.J., 1985-89; sr. bus. analyst Vitro Corp., Silver Spring, Md., 1987-89; dir. mktg. and sales div. Am. Speech-Lang.-Hearing Assn., Rockville, Md., 1989—. Mem. Am. Mktg. Assn., Am. Mgmt. Assn., Omicron Delta Epsilon. Roman Catholic. Home: 8522 Betterton Ct Vienna VA 22182 Office: Am Speech-Lang-Hearing Assn 10801 Rockville Pike Rockville MD 20852

NICKELSON, KIM RENÉ, internist; b. Chgo., Feb. 13, 1956; d. Robert William and Carolynn Lucille (Marts) N.; m. Louis Peter Sguros. BS in Chemistry, U. Ill., 1978; MD, Loyola U., Maywood, Ill., 1981. Diplomate Am. Bd. Internal Medicine. Intern and resident in internal medicine Luth. Gen. Hosp., Park Ridge, Ill., 1981-84; pvt. practice Oakbrook, Ill., 1984-87, Plantation, Fla., 1987—; adj. attending staff Rush-Presbyn. St Luke's Med. Ctr., Chgo., 1984-87; assoc. attending staff Hinsdale (Ill.) Hosp., 1984-87, Humana Bennett Hosp., Plantation, Plantation Gen. Hosp., Universal Med. Ctr., Plantation. Musician Elk Grove (Ill.) Community Band, 1978-87, Hollywood (Fla.) Symphony Orch., 1987—, Sunrise (Fla.) Pops Symphony, 1987—, Deerfield (Fla.) Community Band, 1987—. Mem. ACP, Internat. Horn Soc. Office: Humana Health Am 5701 Sunrise Blvd Plantation FL 33313

NICKLES, CONNIE SUE, auditor, accountant; b. Orville, Ohio, July 5, 1960; d. James Leroy and Nellie Marie (Berg) N. BSBA, Ohio No. U., 1982. CPA, Ohio. Staff auditor Arthur Andersen, Cleve., 1982-84; internal auditor Russell, Burdsall & Word Corp., Mentor, Ohio, 1984; audit mgr. Touche Ross & Co., Cleve., 1984-89; controller, bus. mgr. Cen. Cadillac Co., 1989—. Trustee, co-chmn. fin. com. Women's Community Fund. Mem. AICPA, Ohio Soc. CPAs, Comml. Real Estate Women, East 13th St Racquetball Club. Home: 2202 Acacia Pk Blvd #2516B Lyndhurst OH 44124

NICKLES-MURRAY, ELIZABETH, advertising executive, writer; b. Miami Beach, Fla., May 29, 1948; d. Arnold C. and Audrey (Reid) Nelson. B.S., Northwestern U., 1968; M.A., DePaul U., 1970. Creative supr. Esquire Inc., Chgo., 1975-76; copy supr. Marsteller Inc., Chgo., 1976-77; assoc. creative dir. J. Walter Thompson, Chgo., 1977-80; sr. v.p. D'Arcy MacManus Masius, Chgo., from 1980; then exec. v.p., creative dir., Warwick Advertising, N.Y.C.; exec. v.p., exec. creative dir., Ketchum Advt./N.Y. until 1990; cons. ptnr. Nickles & Ashcraft, Chgo., from 1978; founder & dir. Update: Women, research survey, from 1980. Author: The Coming Matriarchy, 1982, Girls in High Places, 1986, Hype, 1989. Contbr. articles to popular mags. Named Outstanding Young Woman Achiever Nat. Council Women U.S., 1982, All Time Top 10 Working Women Glamour Mag., 1984. Named Chgo. Advt. Woman of Yr., 1982. Office: Ketchum Advt NY 220 E 42nd St New York NY 10017

NICKOLICH, BARBARA ELLEN, controller; b. Reno, Nev., Feb. 26, 1937; d. John Henry and Helen Alta (Smith) Heward; m. Ted. R. Nickolich, June 20, 1964 (div. Oct. 1980); children: Tanya Renee, Theresa Ellen, Todd Stephen. BA in Political Sci., U. Nev., 1960; MA in Geography, Ariz. State U., 1965. Tchr. Cen. High Sch., Phoenix, 1961-64, Sparks (Nev.) High Sch., 1964-66; co-owner La Pinta Restaurant (Mex. Food Restaurant), Reno, Nev., 1976-80; acctg. liaison Coldspring Instrument Co., Scottsdale, Ariz.; acct. Roth and Co., Phoenix, 1981-82, Plaza Three (Modeling Agy.), 1982; adminstr. SurgiSite (Outpatient Surg. Fac.), Phoenix, 1982-85; gen. mgr. rest Vincent Guerithault on Camelback, Phoenix, 1985-88; controller Citadel Devel. Corp., Scottsdale, Ariz., 1988--. Senator at large Student Body Govt., U. Nev., 1959-60, Las Guis chmn. Heard Museum, 1968-69, Brownie troop leader Girl Scouts Am., Phoenix, 1972-75. Grantee U.S. Govt., Fulbright Scholarship, U. Philippines, 1960-61. Mem. Soroptimist Internat. Camelback (asst. treas. 1957-58), Kappa Alpha Theta (pres. Phoenix alumnae chpt. 1974-75), Order of Rainbow for Girls, Masons (grand worthy advisor Nev. chpt. 1957-58). Republican. Presbyterian.

NICKOLS, LOUISE M., municipal official; b. Norfolk, Nebr., Jan. 4, 1935; d. Otis Samuel and Ida Matilda (Christian) Eason; m. Lewis W. Nichols, Nov. 15, 1984 (dec. July 1986). Cert. notary public. Report clk. Travelers Ins., Oklahoma City, 1961-62; from sec. III to adminstrv. asst. III Pub. Works, City of Salem (Oreg.), 1962-88, mgmt. analyst, 1988—. Mem. NAFE, Am. Soc. Pub. Adminstrs., Bus. Women's Inst. (charter). Office: 555 Liberty St SE Rm 325 Salem OR 97301

NICKUM, MARY JOSEPHINE, librarian; b. Richmond, Ind., Nov. 6, 1945; d. Joseph and Mary Margaret (McGaffney) Stumreiter; m. Richard Erle Lewis (div. Apr. 1985); children: Darrel Jay, Ryan Alois; m. John Gerald Nickum. BA, Northland Coll., Ashland, Wis., 1967; M. Lib., U. Wash., Seattle, 1968; MAIS, Oreg. State U., Corvallis, 1983. Librarian U.S. Environ. Protection Agy., Duluth, Minn., 1968-74; zool. oceanog. In Oreg. State U., Corvallis, Oreg., 1974-82; editor Am. Fisheries Soc., Bethesda, Md., 1982-85; project mgr. Fish & Wildlife Reference Service, Bethesda, Md.; pres. Nickum & Nickum, Inc., Rockville, 1987--. Den leader Boy Scouts of Am.; dist. tng. coord. Cub Scouts, Corvallis, 1978-82. Mem. Outdoor Writers Assn. of Am., Am. Fisheries Soc. Home: 12174 Island View Circle Germantown MD 20874 Office: Fish & Wildlife Reference Svc 5430 Grosvenor Ln Ste 110 Bethesda MD 20814

NICOL, MARJORIE CARMICHAEL, research psychologist; b. Orange, N.J., Jan. 6, 1926; d. Norman Carmichael and Ethel Sarah (Siviter) N. BA, Upsala Coll., MS, 1978; MPh, PhD, CUNY, 1988. Art dir. Finneran Advt. Co., N.Y.C., 1944-47; mgr. advt. prodn. RCA, Harrison, N.J., 1948-58; advt. mgr., writer NPS Advt., East Orange, N.J., 1960-67; pres. measurement and eval., chief exec. officer, psychol. evaluator Nicol Evaluation Svc., Millburn, N.J., 1967—; chief exec. officer., dir. Rafiki, Essex County, N.J., 1965—. Author: Nicol Index. Officer Montclair Rehab. Orgn., 1981—; founder Met. Opera at Lincoln Ctr. Republican. Presbyterian. Home: 89 Linden St Millburn NJ 07041 Office: PO Box 111 Millburn NJ 07041

NICOLAÏ, JUDITHE, import-export company executive; b. Lawrence, Mass., Dec. 15, 1945; d. Victor and Evelyn (Otash) Abisalih; m. Munir Tawfiq Said, Mar. 23, 1990. Student in photography, L.A. City Coll., 1967, UCLA, 1971; AA in Fgn. Langs., Coll. of Marin, 1983; hon. degree, Culinary Inst., San Francisco, 1981. Photographer Scott Paper Co., N.Y.C., 1975; owner, operator restaurant The Raincheck Room, West Hollywood, Calif., 1976; prin., pres., chief exec. officer, photographer fashion Photographie sub. Nicolaï Internat. Svcs., Nice, France, 1977—; prin., pres., chief exec. officer, instr. catering and cooking Back to Basics sub. Nicolaï Internat. Svcs., San Francisco, 1980—; chief photographer exhibit and trade show, chief of staff food div. Agri-Bus. U.S.A., Moscow and Washington, 1983; head transp. U.S. Summer Olympics, L.A., 1984, interpreter for Spanish, French, Portuguese, and Italian, 1985; prin., pres., chief exec. officer, interpreter Intertrans subs. (Nicolaï Internat. Svcs.), San Francisco, 1985—; founder, pres. Nicolaï Internat. Svcs., San Francisco, 1985—. Contbr. column on food and nutrition to jour., 1983-84. Mem. Alpha Gamma Sigma. Office: Niconor Internat Corp & Nicolaï Internat Svcs 2269 Chestnut St Ste 237 San Francisco CA 94123

NICOLETTI, MYRA DIANE, freelance writer; b. Phila., Nov. 17, 1950; d. John Joseph and Palmyra Amelia (Martin) Kamar; m. Eugene Alfonso Nicoletti, Jr., Mar. 30, 1974; children: Diane, Christopher. BS, Syracuse U., 1972. Copywriter Sta. WFLN, Phila., 1972-74; ops. dir. Sta. WCMB, Wormleysburg, Pa., 1974-75; prodn. dir. Sta. WHP-TV, Harrisburg, Pa., 1975-82; freelance writer Hummelstown, Pa., 1982—. Editor: Hershey Rotary Cookbook, 1985. Vol. Hershey (Pa.) Pub. Libr., 1988—. Mem. AAUW (editor newsletter Hershey br. 1986-88, scholarship dir. 1988—). Republican. Roman Catholic. Home: 1431 Jill Dr Hummelstown PA 17036

NICOLL, ANNE LOUISE, hospital association director; b. New Haven, Conn., July 22, 1962; d. Charles Fredrick and Anne Catherine (Scannell) N. BS in Polit. Sci., Drew U., 1984. Legis. asst. to congressman U.S. Ho. of Reps., Washington, 1985-88; assoc. dir. legis. affairs-policy Am. Hosp. Assn., Washington, 1988—; Congl. adv. Washington Workshops Found., 1984—. Democrat. Roman Catholic. Office: Am Hosp Assn 50 F St NW 1100 Washington DC 20001

NICOLLE, LORI ANNE, lawyer; b. Oyster Bay, N.Y., Dec. 8, 1961; d. Jean-Loup Roger and Joanne Juliet (Dellaquilla) N.; m. David Alan Good. BA, Rutgers Coll, 1983; JD, N.Y. Law Sch., 1986. Bar: Md., 1986. Assoc. Frank, Beinstein, Conaway & Goldman, Balt., 1986—. Mem. Natl. Assn. of Bond Lawyers, ABA, Maryland State Bar Assn., Baltimore City Bar Assn. Office: Frank Beinstein et al 300 E Lombard St Baltimore MD 21202

NICOLOSI, DOROTHY EMILY, fundraising executive; b. N.Y.C., July 15, 1931; d. Thomas and Aurora (Scoppa) Nicolosi. BS in Edn., Fordham U., 1963, cert. Introductory Mgmt. Devel., 1967, cert. Advanced Mgmt. Devel., 1968; M. in Public Adminstrn., NYU, 1979. Exec. sec. Arabol Mfg. Co., N.Y.C., 1950-55; rsch. asst. Smith Richardson Found., N.Y.C., 1955-60; cons. Robert A. Taft Meml. Found., Washington, 1960-61; asst. sec., office mgr. United Student Aid Fund, Inc., N.Y.C., 1961-63; sec., treas., exec. adminstr. Nat. Strategy Info. Ctr., Inc., N.Y.C., 1963-84, v.p., treas., 1984-88, dir., 1978—; bd. dir. spl. fundraising projects, grants coord. Coll. Mount St. Vincent, Riverdale, N.Y., 1988—. Mem. Am. Acad. Polit. and Social Sci., Am. Soc. Pub. Adminstrn., Acad. Polit. Sci. Republican. Roman Catholic. Home: 3103 Fairfield Ave Riverdale NY 10463

NIDIFFER, JANA, coordinator college program; b. Indpls., Aug. 2, 1957; d. Thomas Edward and Ethel Cloene (Shipp) N. BEd, Ind. U., 1979, MEd, 1982; postgrad., Harvard U., 1990—. Tchr., dir. community affairs William Smith High Sch., Aurora, Colo., 1979-80; asst. to dean Honors div. Ind. U., Bloomington, 1980-82; asst. dean of coll. Brandeis U., Waltham, Mass., 1982-88; chair, editor Undergrad. Rsch. Program, Waltham, 1982-88; chair Prizes and Awards Com., Waltham, 1985-88; chair of governance Consortium for Edn. of Non-Traditional Students, 1985-87; founder, coord. Brandeis Adult Scholar Program, Waltham, 1986-88; presentor Nat. Conf. Student Devel., Storrs, Conn., 1987. Editor: Jour. of Undergraduate Research, 1982-88; author: Faculty Advising Handbook, 1985, 86, 87. Com. chair NOW, Bloomington, 1981-82. Mem. Am. Edn. Rsch. Assn., History of Edn. Soc., Mass. Assn. Women Deans, Adminstrs., and Counselors (gender in curriculum com. Harvard U. 1988—). Democrat. Home: 28 Irving St Apt 21 Cambridge MA 02138

NIECE, JULIE COLE, pharmaceutical executive; b. Monett, Mo., Sept. 23, 1945; d Russell Allen and Julia Agnes (Gimbel) Cole; m. George S. Devins, Sept. 1990. Grad., St. John's Mercy Sch. Nursing, Springfield, Mo., 1968. RN. Critical care nursing St. Luke's Hosp., Kansas City, Mo., 1968-71; staff devel. instr. Shawnee Mission Med. Ctr., Merriam, Kansas, 1971-76; dir. edn. & training Olathe Community Hosp., Kansas, 1976-79; cont. edn. editor Greater Kansas City Nursing Journal, Mo., 1979-81; dir. nursing & allied health cont. edn. Johnson County Community Coll., Overland Park, Kansas, 1981-83; pharmaceutical sales rep. Fisons Corp., Boston, 1983-88; product rep. Hoffman-La Roche, Kansas City, Mo., 1988-90; pharmaceutical study coord. Devins Clinic, Kansas City, Mo., 1990—; bd. mem. Kansas City Allergy & Asthma Found. Am., Kansas City 1983-; mktg. mgr. Internat. Med. Tech. Cons. Inc., Prairie Village Kansas 1988. Co-author: R.N. Mag., I.V. Antibiotic Therapy 1974, Nursing Procedure. Nursing procedure instr. Am. Heart Assn., Olathe & Merriam, Kansas, 1973-81. Mem. Dimensions Unlimited, Inc., NAFE, Kansas City Consensus. Home: 9223 Slater Overland Park KS 66212

NIED, HARRIET THERESE, landscaping company executive; b. Elyria, Ohio, Apr. 3. 1923; d. Henry Andrew and Kataryn Patricia (Siekierska) Zaremba; m. Michael Ernest Nied, Aug. 22, 1942; children: Kathryn Marie, Judith Boynton, Michaeline Wideman, Ellan Murphy, Gregory Michael. With Censorship Office, El Paso, 1942-43; promotional salesperson Aluminum Co. Am., 1945-51; store mgr. Nied Garden Ctr. Co., Northfield, Ohio, 1960-78, sec., treas., 1978—. Consumer advocate. Recipient Commendation plaque Nordonia Hills C. of C., 1986. Mem. Women in Bus. (mem. scholarship com.), Nordonia PTA. Democrat. Roman Catholic.

NIEDERMEIER, MARY B., retired nutrition educator; b. Webster Groves, Mo., Oct. 20, 1914; d. Albertus and Daisey May (Christman) Wickersham; m. Walter H. Niedermeier, Sept. 9, 1939; children: Gail Santarelli, Bart Niedermeier. BS, Mich. State U., 1937; MA, Columbia U., 1957, profl. diploma, 1959. Cert. in dietetics, Miami Valley Hosp., Dayton, Ohio, 1938. Dist. nutritionist N.J. State Dept. of Health, Newark; instr. nutrition edn. Sch. of Dentistry Fairleigh Dickinson U., Teaneck, N.J.; instr. nutrition edn. Sch. of Nursing St. Louis U. Bd. deacons Rancho Bernardo Presbyt. Ch., 1975-77; treas. PEO-TV chpt., Rancho Bernardo, 1990; bd. dirs. Rancho Bernardo Oaks North Community Ctr., 1974-76. Grace McCloud fellow. Mem. AAUW, AAUP, Am. Dietetic Assn., Calif. Deitetic Assn., N.J. Dietetic Assn., Alpha Omicron Pi. Republican. Home: 17411 Plaza dela Rosa San Diego CA 92128

NIEDZIELSKI, MARGARET MARY, nurse; b. King of Prussia, Pa., Sept. 2, 1961; d. Bronislaw and Maria (Hartl) N. Student, Coll. Misericordia, Dallas, Pa., 1979-81, Immaculata Coll., Malvern, Pa., 1981-82; diploma, Brandywine Sch. Nursing, Coatesville, Pa., 1986; BSN, U. Md., Balt., 1990. RN, Pa; cert. in critical care. Staff nurse The Bryn Mawr (Pa.) Hosp., 1986—, Grad. Hosp., Phila., 1988—. Fellow AACCN. Democrat. Roman Catholic. Home: 1051 Penn Circle G108 King of Prussia PA 19406

NIEHAUS, CHLOE MAE, teacher; b. Tompkinsville, Ky., Dec. 7, 1929; d. Herbert J. and Hallie (Wheat) Turner; m. Charles L. Niehaus, June 29, 1957 (dec. 1973). Student, Western U., Bowling Green, Ky., 1948-49, Lindsey Wilson Coll., Columbia, Ky., 1950, 51; BS, Butler U., Indpls., 1960; MS, Ind. U., 1971. Cert. elem. tchr., Ky., Ind. Elem. tchr. Monroe County Schs., Tompkinsville, 1949-52, Hancock County Schs., Mt. Comfort, Ind., 1953-55, Marion County Sch. Ctr. Twp., Margaret McFarland Sch., Indpls., 1955-62; elem. tchr. Indpls. Pub. Schs., Margaret McFarland Sch., 1962-89, ret., 1989. Named to Outstanding Elem. Tchrs. Am., 1972. Mem. Ind. Ret. Tchrs. Orgn., Marion County Ret. Tchrs. Assn., Butler U. Alumni Assn., Ind. U. Alumni Assn., Sigma Delta Pi. Democrat. Roman Catholic.

NIEHAUS, LORENE MATHEWSON, health care executive; b. Chgo., June 27, 1959; d. Joseph Deyo and Mary Lorene (Ingalls) Mathewson; m. Christopher James Niehaus, July 6, 1985; 1 child, Scott Andrew. AB, Smith Coll., 1981; M. in Mgmt., Northwestern U., 1986. Mgmt. trainee, rep., leading officer Mfrs. Hanover Trust Co., N.Y.C., 1981-84; assoc. planning and mktg. Evang. Health Systems, Oak Brook, Ill., 1986-88; mgr. of health car rsch. Heidrick and Struggles, Chgo., 1988—; bd. dirs. Mid-Am. Nat. Bank Chgo. Mem. Am. Soc. Healthcare Human Resources Adminstrn., Women Health Execs. Network Chgo., Chgo. Health Execs. Forum, Am. Coll. of Health Execs. Presbyterian. Office: Heidrick and Struggles 125 S Wacker Dr Chicago IL 60606

NIEHAUS, NANCY RUTH, social worker; b. St. Louis, Sept. 2, 1945; d. Eldon Louis and Ruth Katherine (Baumberger) DeCosted; m. Frederick Morris Niehaus, May 19, 1973; 1 child, Katherine. BA, DePauw U., 1967; MA in Teaching, Ind. U., 1970; MSW, Okla. U., 1988. Cert. tchr., Ind. Tchr. Vincennes (Ind.) U., 1967-74, N.E. Okla. A&M Coll., Miami, Okla., 1976-89; dir. Norse Campus Ministry, Miami, 1980-82; outreach worker Ottawa County Nutrition Program, Miami, 1983-87; social worker Bapt. Regional Health Ctr., Miami, 1987-88; pvt. practice Community Svcs. Cons., Miami, 1988—; cons. Ottawa County Health Dept., Miami, 1988. Treas. Ottawa County Teen Ctr., Inc., Miami, 1989; state committeewoman Ottawa County Rep. Party, Miami, 1984; progra, dir. Students for Ottawa Svcs., 1989—. Recipient Pres.' Children's Safety Partnership award Rep. Women, 1987. Mem. Kiwanis. Presbyterian. Home and Office: Community Svcs Cons 114 D NW Miami OK 74354

NIELSEN, GAIL ANN, radiologic technologist; b. Waterloo, Iowa, Mar. 30, 1947; d. Raymond Zack and Marlys Leota (Timmerman) Eikenberry; m. David Harry Nielsen, June 8, 1968; children: Jennifer Lyn, Kristen Michelle. BS Health Care Adminstrn., St. Joseph's Coll., Windham, Maine, 1989. Staff technologist Allen Meml. Hosp., Waterloo, 1967-69, 72-75, supr. vascular imaging, 1973-80, asst. dir. radiology, 1975-84, adminstrv. dir. radiology svcs., 1984—; vol. technologist U.S. Army Hosp., Bremerhaven, Fed. Republic Germany, 1970-71; instr. radiologic tech. edn., Waterloo, 1975—. Vol. ARC, Waterloo, 1986-88, United Way Black Hawk County, 1987-89, Cedar Valley Breast Cancer Awareness Task Force, Waterloo, 1988—. Recipient letter of commendation U.S. Army, 1971. Mem. Am. Soc. Radiologic Technologists (registered AART 1967, Matt Keilley Meml. award 1990), Am. Healthcare Radiology Adminstrs. (sec. 1988-90, lectr. 1989, nat. stats. chmn. 1989—, apptd. to summit on manpower 1990—), Iowa Soc. Radiologic Technologists (sec., lectr. 1985, pres. N.E. dist. 1976-77, 81-82), Toastmasters (edn. com. Waterloo 1987-88). Lutheran. Office: Allen Meml Hosp 1825 Logan Ave Waterloo IA 50703

NIELSEN, LAURA CHRISTINE, investment company executive; b. Fairbanks, Alaska, Nov. 2, 1960; d. Raymond Elzworth Nielsen and Jacqueline Ann Marie (Harmon) Butler. Diploma in sci. and bus., Coll. of Marin, 1983; student, U. Calif., Berkeley, 1984. Office mgr. Suzanne Sammis Personal Mgmt. Co., Corte Madera, Calif., 1981-83; mktg. asst. pub. rels. dept. Investment Mortgage Internat., San Francisco, 1983-84; loan funder/closer 1st Calif. Mortgage Co., San Rafael; regional mgr. Desert Bay Investment Corp., Corte Madera, 1987—; office mgr. Smith-Thomas Investment Svcs., Inc., Corte Madera, 1987—; cons. real-corp. mortgage banking, San Francisco, 1985-87, Dan Dominguez Hi-Tech Leasing Co., Sausalito, Calif., 1987-89. Vol. pub. rels. com. Just Say No, 1987—, March of Dimes, 1988—, Just Say No to Drugs, Cystic Fibrosis Found., Oakland Athletics. Recipient telecommunications award Stanford U. Med. Ctr. Mem. Mensa. Republican. Roman Catholic. Home: PO Box 754 Tiburon CA 94920 Office: Smith-Thomas Investment Svcs Inc 770 Tamalpais Dr Ste #206 Corte Madera CA 94925

NIELSEN, SUSAN EILEEN, educator; b. North Platte, Nebr., Dec. 27, 1949; d. Verling Eugene and Clovis Claudia (Claussen) Homan; m. Kirk J. Nielsen, Aug. 19, 1972; children: Michelle, Mindi, Timothy. BS, U. Nebr., 1972, postgrad., 1973; postgrad., Wayne State U., 1984; M., Kans. State U., 1988. Cert. edn. Reading instr. Cedar Bluffs (Nebr.) Pub. Schs., 1975-77; gifted facilitator Unified Sch. Dist., Colby, Kans., 1985—. Southwestern Bell grantee, 1989, Kans. Edn. grantee Kans. Dept. Edn., 1989; recipient NEA A award, 1989-90. Mem. AAUW (pres.-elect Colby chpt. 1990-91), Kans. Gifted & Talented (area rep. 1990-91), Colby Tchrs. Assn. (c. of c. rep. 1989-90), Xi Zeta Upsilon (corresponding sec. 1989-90), Delta Kappa Gamma.

NIELSON, NORMA LEE, business educator; b. Augusta, Ga., Dec. 26, 1953; d. Norman Lyle and Betty Lou (Buckner) Parrott; m. Mark G. Nielson, Nov. 20, 1985 (div. 1988); 1 child, Eric Gordon. BS, Northwest

Mo. State U., 1974; MA, U. Pa., 1976, PhD, 1979. CLU. Asst. prof. Iowa State U., Ames, 1977-79, U. So. Calif., L.A., 1979-84; cons. profl. Mercer-Meidinger, L.A., 1984-85; assoc. prof. Oreg. State U., Corvallis, 1985-90; prof. Oreg. State U., 1990—. Developer software; contbg. author: Handbook for Corporate Directors, 1985; contbr. articles to profl. publs. Vol. Linn-Benton Food Share, Corvallis; bd. dirs. Corvallis Community Day Care, Inc., 1988—. Andrus Found. rsch. grantee, 1989—. Mem. Am. Risk and Ins. Assn. (bd. dirs. 1990—), Western Risk and Ins. Assn. (officer 1981-84), Risk and Ins. Mgmt. Soc. Office: Oreg State U Coll Bus Bexell Hall 200 Corvallis OR 97331-2603

NIEMANN, CHRISTI CAY, paralegal; b. Valparaiso, Ind., Oct. 5, 1956; d. Harold Wilson Jr. and Alice Eileen (Wild) Williams; m. Richard Roy Niemann, Nov. 1, 1980; children: Jeffrey Patrick, Julia Cay. BA, Bethany Bible Coll., 1978. Lic. ins. adjuster, Alaska; cert. tchr. Calif. Tchr. Foothill Christian Sch., Milpitas, Calif., 1978-79; account exec. Murray, Bradley & Peterson Pub. Rels., Anchorage, Alaska, 1979-81; claims adjuster Providence Washington Ins., Anchorage, 1981-82; workers compensation claims supr. Am. Internat. Adjustment Co., Anchorage, 1982-83; paralegal Staley, De-Lisio, Cook & Sherry, Anchorage, 1983-84; paralegal workers compensation specialist Mason & Griffin, Anchorage, 1985—. Co-editor: Lighter Than Air Cookbook, 1980. Bd. dirs. Abbott Loop Community Council, Anchorage, 1982-84. Mem. Alaska Pub. Interest Research Group, Alaska Assn. Legal Assts., Pub. Relations Soc. Am., Advt. Fedn. Alaska, Alaska Adjusters Assn. Republican. Office: Mason & Griffin 1600 A St Suite 101 Anchorage AK 99501

NIEMI, JANICE, state legislator, lawyer; b. Flint, Mich., Sept. 18, 1928; d. Richard Jesse and Norma (Bell) Bailey; m. Preston Niemi, Feb. 4, 1953 (divorced 1987); children—Ries, Patricia. B.A., U. Wash., 1950, LL.B., 1967; postgrad. U. Mich., 1950-52; cert. Hague Acad. Internat. Law, Netherlands, 1954. Bar: Wash. 1968. Assoc. firm Powell, Livengood, Dunlap & Silverdale, Kirkland, Wash., 1968; staff atty. Legal Service Ctr., Seattle, 1968-70; judge Seattle Dist. Ct., 1971-72, King County Superior Ct., Seattle, 1973-78; acting gen. counsel, dep. gen. counsel SBA, Washington, 1979-81; mem. Wash. State Ho. of Reps., Olympia, 1983-87, chmn. com. on state govt., 1984; State Ho. of Reps., Olympia, 1983-87; sole practice, Seattle, 1981—; mem. White House Fellows Regional Selection Panel, Seattle, 1974-77, chmn., 1976, 77; incorporator Sound Savs. & Loan, Seattle, 1975. Bd. dirs. Allied Arts, Seattle, 1971—; Ctr. Contemporary Art, Seattle, 1981-83, Women's Network, Seattle, 1981-84 & Pub. Defender Assn., Seattle, 1982-84; bd. visitors dept. psychology U. Wash., Seattle, 1983-87, bd. visitors dept sociology, 1988—. Named Woman of Yr. in Law, Past Pres.'s Assn., Seattle, 1971; Woman of Yr., Matrix Table, Seattle, 1973, Capitol Hill Bus. and Profl. Women, 1975. Mem. Wash. State Bar Assn., Wash. Women Lawyers. Democrat. Home: 226 Summit Ave E Seattle WA 98102

NIERENBERG, IVEY LOIS, funding consultant; b. Stockton, Calif., Jan. 28, 1925; d. Jesse Vertner and Nelda Marie (Prairie) Mendenhall; m. Paul Curtis Phillips, Jan. 19, 1952 (div. 1954); 1 child, Teresa Gale Phillips; m. Edwin Harold Nierenberg, Aug. 24, 1967; children: Jess David, Miriam Molly, Rachel Hanah. BA, San Jose U., 1947; postgrad., UCLA, 1956-57, U. Hawaii, 1964, Stanford U., 1965. Cert. elem. tchr., Calif. Tchr. Hubbard Sch., L.A., 1956-58; tchr. Santa Rita Sch., Los Altos, Calif., 1958-64; Egan Intermediate Sch., Los Altos, 1964-67; vol. exec. dir. Art-Rise, Inc., San Mateo County, Calif., 1975-85; energy agt. North Peninsula Neighborhood Svcs. Ctr., South San Francisco, Calif., 1984-86; substitute tchr. San Bruno (Calif.) Park Sch. Dist., 1986-88; exec. dir. Landlord-Tenant Hotline, San Mateo County, Calif., 1987-89; funding cons. Paintbrush Diplomacy, San Bruno, 1989, Suicide Prevention & Crisis Ctr., Burlingame, Calif., 1990—; vol. tutor Tongan immigrants, San Bruno, 1970, Project Read, South San Francisco, 1985-87; peer counseling vol. Peer Counseling Program, San Mateo County, 1989-90. Author: (lit. guide) Benjamin West, 1964, (curriculum guide) Summer School, 1965; co-author: (lit. guide) Charlotte's Web, 1966 (award of excellence State of Calif. 1967), (curriculum guide) Crestmoor High School Guide, 1969. Chair San Bruno Art Assn., 1973-79; founder Art-Rise Inc., San Mateo County, 1975-86, San Bruno St. Festival, 1977-80. Recipient Award of Excellence Art Editor, State of Calif. Bd. Edn., 1970, Pub. Svc. award North County B.d Realtors, San Bruno, 1979, Proclamation of Community Svc., City of San Bruno Coun., 1985, Congl. Cert. of Appreciation, U.S. Congress, 1985; named OUtstanding vol., Vol. Bur. San Mateo County, 1981. Mem. AAUW, Am. Assn. Retired Persons, Phi Kappa Pi (alumni mem.). Home: 2510 Crestmoor Dr San Bruno CA 94066

NIERENBERG, SONDRA, realtor; b. Chgo., Feb. 26, 1936; d. Isidore Carnow and Emily (Penzick) Padnos; m. Ronald Nierenberg, Dec. 14, 1958; children: Iris, Caryn, Laura. BS, U. Ill., 1957; grad., Real Estate Inst., 1985. Lic. realtor. Speech therapist Chgo., 1957-80; geriatric occupational therapist Glen Oaks, Northbrook, Ill., 1957-80; real estate agt. Kahn Realty, Highland Park, Ill., 1981—. Mem. Nat. Assn. Realtors (cert. residential specialist residential sales coun. Realtors Nat. Mktg. Inst. 1988), Womens Coun. Realtors, North Shore Bd. Realtors. Office: Kahn Realty 1893 Sheridan Highland Park IL 60035

NIERENBERG, SUSAN, nurse-midwife; b. Englewood, N.J., Aug. 10, 1955; d. Theodore Nierenberg and Roslyn Holtzman. BA, Rutgers U., 1977; BS, Cornell U., 1979; MS, Georgetown U., 1984. Staff RN Roosevelt Hosp., N.Y.C., 1979-83; nurse-midwife preceptor U. of Medicine & Dentistry of N.J., Newark, 1985-85; staff nurse-midwife Albert Einstein Coll. Medicine Jacobi Hosp., Bronx, 1985-89, Albert Einstein Coll. Medicine Montefiore Med. Group, Bronx, 1989—. Author: Jour. Nurse Midwifery, 1988. Mem. Nat. Women's Health Network, 1979, Nat. Women Polit. Caucus, 1979, Nat. Abortion Rights Action League, 1977. Named Teaneck Jr. Citizen of the Month Teaneck City Club, N.J., 1970; saluted by Greater N.Y. March of Dimes Campaign for Healthier Babies, 1990. Mem. Am. Coll. Nurse Midwives, Coun. of Childbirth Edn. Specialists, Internat. Childbirth Edn. Assn., Nat. Perinatal Assn., N.Y. Perinatal Assn., N.Y. Chpt. Am. Coll. Nurse Midwives. Democrat. Jewish. Office: Midwifery Group OB/Gyn Acad Assn 2330 Eastchester Rd Bronx NY 10461

NIES, HELEN WILSON, federal judge; b. Birmingham, Ala.; d. George Earl and Lida Blanche (Erckert) Wilson; m. John Dirk Nies ; children: Dirk, Nancy, Eric. BA, U. Mich., 1946, JD, 1948. Bar: D.C. 1961, U.S. Supreme Ct. 1962. Atty. Dept. Justice, Washington, 1948-51, Office Price Stblzn., Washington, 1951-52; assoc. Pattishall, McAuliffe and Hofstetter, Washington, 1960-66, resident ptnr., 1966-77; ptnr. Howrey & Simon, Washington, 1978-80; cir. judge U.S. Ct. Customs and Patent Appeals, 1980-82; judge U.S. Ct. Appeals Fed. Cir., 1982-90, chief judge, 1990—; mem. jud. conf. U.S. Com. on Bicentennial of Constitution; mem. public adv. com. trademark affairs Dept. Commerce, 1976-80; mem. adv. bd. BNA's Patent Trademark and Copyright Jour., 1976-78; bd. visitors U. Mich. Law Sch., 1975-78; adv. for restatement of law of unfair competition Am. Law Isnt., 1986—; speaker World Intellectual Property Forum, Forum of Judges, Calcutta, 1987. Recipient Athena Outstanding Alumna award U. Mich., 1987. Mem. ABA (chmn. com. 203, 1972-74, com. 504, 1975-76), Bar Assn. D.C. (chmn. patent trademark copyright sect. 1975-76, dir. 1976-78), U.S. Trademark Assn. (chmn. lawyers adv. com. 1974-76, bd. dir. 1976-78), Am. Patent Law Assn., Fed. Bar Assn., Nat. Assn. Women Lawyers (Woman Lawyer of Yr. 1980), Order of Coif, Phi Beta Kappa, Phi Kappa Phi. Office: US Ct Appeals 717 Madison Pl NW Washington DC 20439

NIGHTINGALE, ELENA OTTOLENGHI, physician, geneticist, administrator; b. Livorno, Italy, Nov. 1, 1932; (came to U.S., 1939) d. Mario Lazzaro and Elisa Vittoria (Levi) Ottolenghi; m. Stuart L. Nightingale, July 1, 1965; children—Elizabeth, Marisa. A.B. summa cum laude, Barnard Coll., 1954; Ph.D., Rockefeller U., 1961; M.D., NYU, 1964. Asst. prof. Cornell U. Med. Coll., N.Y.C., 1965-70; asst. prof. Johns Hopkins U., Balt., 1970-73; fellow in clin. genetics and pediatrics Georgetown U. Hosp., Washington, 1973-74; sr. staff officer Nat. Acad. Scis., Washington, 1975-79; sr. program officer Inst. Medicine, Nat. Acad. Scis., Washington, 1979-82, sr. scholar in residence, 1982-83; spl. advisor to pres. Carnegie Corp. of N.Y., N.Y.C., 1983—; vis. assoc. prof. Harvard U. Med. Sch., Boston, 1980-84, vis. lectr., 1984—; mem. recombinant DNA adv. com. NIH, Bethesda, Md., 1979-83. Editor: The Breaking of Bodies and Minds: Torture, Psychiatric Abuse and the Health Professions, 1985, Prenatal Screening, Policies and Values: The Example of Neural Tube Defects, 1987, Before Birth: Prenatal Screening for

Genetic Disease, 1990; contbr. numerous sci. articles to profl. publs. Bd. dirs. Ctr. for Youth Svcs., Washington, 1980-84, Sci. Svc. Inc., Washington, 1985—, Amnesty Internat., U.S.A. Sloan Found. fellow, 1974-75. Fellow AAAS (chmn. com. on sci. freedom and responsibility 1985-83), N.Y. Acad. Scis.; mem. Harvey Soc., Am. Soc. Microbiology, Am. Soc. Human Genetics (social issues com. 1982-85), Genetics Soc. Am., Inst. Medicine of NAS (chmn. com. on health and human rights 1987—), Phi Beta Kappa, Sigma Xi. Office: Carnegie Corp NY 437 Madison Ave New York NY 10022

NIHART, RUTH LUCILLE, accountant; b. St. Johns, Mich.; d. Herman L. and Dorothy R. (Luecht) Pasch; m. Wayne D. Britten; m. Charles E. Nihart; children: Bonnie L. Britten, Gregory, Rachel R. Student, Cen. Mich. U., 1962-63, Lansing Community Community Coll., 1969. CPA. Staff acct. Harris, Reames & Ambrose, CPA's, Lansing, Mich., 1964-70, Resource Control, Inc., Lansing, 1971-72, Charles E. Nihart & Co., P.C., Lansing, 1972-75; pvt. practice St. Johns, Mich., 1975-85; prin. Ruth L. Nihart, P.C., St. Johns, 1985—; v.p. Aaro Rentals, Inc., Lansing, 1979-90, Aaro Energy, Inc., Lansing, 1986-90; tchr. enrollment exam rev. course IRS, 1979-81. Bd. dirs. Clinton Area New Devel. Orgn., 1986-89, St. Johns, Small Bus. Assn. Mich., Kalamazoo, 1971-87; del. Mich. Conf. on Small Bus., Lansing, 1981; mem. pastoral bd. 1st Congl., St. Johns, 1986-89, also bd. trustees, 1990—; mem. pastoral bd. Clinton County Arts Coun., St. Johns, 1988—; active Accreditation Coun., 1987—. Mem. Am. Inst. CPA's (mem. tax div.), Mich. Assn. CPA's, Nat. Soc. Pub. Accts. (fed. tax com.), Ind. Accts. Assn. Mich. (1st woman pres. 1984-85, Acct. of Yr. 1986, chair state affairs com. 1979-84). Office: 218 N Clinton Ave Saint Johns MI 48879

NILES, AMY, advertising executive, actress; b. N.Y.C., Nov. 20, 1959; d. Gerald T. and Edith (Nathanson) N. BS, NYU, 1979. Actress Fantasticks, N.Y.C., 1977-78; actress CBS Love of Life, N.Y.C., 1977-79; casting asst. TNI Casting, N.Y.C., 1979-80; actress Evita, N.Y.C., 1980-83; producer Conroy Prodns., Inc., N.Y.C., 1983-85; pres Broadway Knitworks Inc., N.Y.C., 1983-85; owner Yarns & Bonds, Inc., N.Y.C., 1985—; dir. advt. sales Key Plate News, N.Y. and Stockton, N.J., 1989—; tchr. Yarns & Bonds, Inc., 1985—. Contbr. articles to profl. jours. Mem. Nat. Needlework Assn., SAG, AFTRA, Actors Equity Assn., Bklyn. C. of C., Knitting Guild, Silon Family Circle. Office: Yarns & Bonds Inc 297 7th Ave Brooklyn NY 11215

NILES, BARBARA ELLIOTT, psyanalyst; b. Boston, Jan. 31, 1939; d. Byron Kauffman and Helen Alice (Heissler) Elliott; m. John Denison, June 25, 1960 (div. 1981); children: Catherine, Andrew. AA, Briarcliff Coll., 1958; BA, SUNY, 1984; MSW, Hunter Coll., 1986. Cert. social worker. Exec. com. Legal Aid Soc. Women's Aux., 1965-67; sec. Water Quality Task Force Scientists' Com. for Pub. Info., 1973-74; founding dir., sec. Consumer Action Now Inc., 1970-77; dir. devel. Consumer Action Now's Council Environ., 1976-77; dir. 170 Tenants Corp., 1979-81; mem. pub. interest com. Cosmopolitan Club, 1979-82; dir. INFORM Inc., 1978-84; pvt. practice psychotherapy and psychoanalysis, 1986—. Editor: biography: Off the Beaten Track, 1984. Mem. Nat. Assn. Social Workers. Clubs: Cosmopolitan (N.Y.C.), The Vincent (Boston). Home: 170 E 79th New York NY 10021 Office: 230 Central Park W New York NY 10024

NILL, HEATHER ANNE, finance executive; b. Dayton, Ohio, Jan. 29, 1963; d. Donald and Anne (Steele) N. BBA, U. Cin., 1986. Lic. ins. agt.; Ind. Arbitrage account asst. GEM Savs., Dayton, Ohio, 1983-85; mgr. Beneficial, Inc., Richmond, Ind., 1986—. Advisor Jr. Achievement, 1986. Mem. Am. Bus. Women's Assn. (publicity com.), Richmond Area Credit Assn., Richmond Area C. of C. Home: 3516 N A #1D Richmond IN 47374 Office: Beneficial 708 Promenade Richmond IN 47374

NILON, LAURA ANN, movie studio executive; b. Bronx, N.Y., Feb. 21, 1960; d. Edward and Joan (Amabile) N. Student, Hunter Coll., 1977-79, Marymount Coll., N.Y.C., 1981-83. Mgr. traffic NBC Radio, N.Y.C., 1977-81; sr. evaluator MTV Network, N.Y.C., 1981-82; mgr. audio-visuals sales, Bus. Images, N.Y.C., 1982-83; audio-visual dir. Ter & Co./Paper prodn. Faces, N.Y.C., 1983-84; bus. mgr. Katz Sports, N.Y.C., 1984-85, Katz TV, N.Y.C., 1985-88; estimator prodn. Disney-MGM Studio, Orlando, Fla., N.Y.C., 1989-90; mgr. client svcs. Disney-MGM Studio, 1990—. Tutor Vol. Svcs. Children, N.Y.C., 1986-88; vol. soup kitchen St. John Divine Cathedral, Children, N.Y.C., 1988. Home: 6810 Tanglewood Bay Dr #313 Orlando FL 32821 Office: Disney MGM Studio PO Box 10200 Orlando FL 32830

NIM, NAOMI BARBARA, educator, political organizer; b. Lynn, Mass., Jan. 13, 1948; d. David Jonas and Rebecca (Singerman) Gordon; m. Carlos Da Cruz Sao Pedro, July 19, 1969 (div. 1978); 1 child, Lara Sao Pedro; m. Jerome Michael Segal, Mar. 5, 1989. Student, L'Institut d'Etudes Politques, Paris, 1967-68; BA in French, Elmira Coll., 1969; MEd., Lesley Coll., 1978; EdD in Multicultural Edn., U. San Francisco. Cert. bilingual tchr. Bilingual tchr. Salem Pub. Schs., Salem, Mass., 1973-81; arts administr. Salem Pub. Schs., 1978-81; dance tchr. San Francisco Ballet Pub. Sch. Program, 1981-82; dir. St. John's Tutoring Ctr., San Francisco, 1983-88; cross-cultural trainer Community Bds. San Francisco, 1988; polit. organizer San Franciscans for Peace & Justice in the Middle East, 1988; polit. organizer Jewish Peace Lobby, College Park, Md., 1989—, nat. administrv. dir., 1989—; vis. scholar Ctr. for Comparative Edn., Sch. of Edn. U. Md., 1989-90; cons. Friends of Yesh G'vul, San Francisco, 1988. Conflict mediator Community Bds. San Francisco, 1982-88; nat. bd. mem. Am. Friends Neve Shalom/Wahat Al-Salam, 1985—; nat. coun. New Jewish Agenda, 1988-89; campaign co-chair Proposition W Campaign-for Peace and Justice in the Middle East, San Francisco, 1988. Harney fellow U. San Francisco, 1985. Mem. Consortium for Peace Rsch. and Edn., Israel Studies Assn. Democrat. Jewish.

NIMKIN, MARGARET LEE, photographer; b. N.Y.C., June 4, 1955; d. Bernard William and Jean (Horowitz) N. BA, U. Pa., 1977. Photographer Sotheby's, N.Y.C., 1978-85; owner, photographer Maggie Nimkin Photography, N.Y.C., 1985—. One woman show, Chinese Cultural Ctr., N.Y.C., 1987; contbr. photographs to art books. Democrat. Jewish. Home and Studio: 333 E 79th St Apt 2T New York NY 10021

NIPERT, DONNA ANN See BARRETT, JESSICA

NISHIO, KAREN T., health science educator; b. Honolulu, May 11; d. Hideki and Shigeme (Fujimoto) Tanaka; m. Frank Yoshiharu Nishio; children: Joseph Michael, David Mark. BS, U. Dayton, 1952; MS, UCLA, 1957; EdD, U. Pacific, 1984. RN. Staff nurse St. Francis Hosp., Honolulu, 1949-50; asst. instr. St. Francis Hosp. Sch. of Nursing, Honolulu, 1950-51, asst. dir., 1952-55; instr. Providence Coll. of Nursing, Oakland, Calif., 1955-56; asst. prof. San Jose (Calif.) State Coll., 1957-59, Fresno (Calif.) State Coll., 1959-60; assoc. prof. Calif. State U., Fresno, 1966-70, prof., 1970-88, chair, 1984-88; prof., chair U. Hawaii at Manoa, Honolulu, 1988—. Contbr. articles to numerous jours. Pres. Nurses Assn. Hawaii, Honolulu, 1951; v.p. Hawaii League for Nursing, Honolulu, 1951; bd. dirs. Calif. League for Nursing, San Francisco, 1958, pres. Fresno chpt. 1960. Mem. Am. Assn. U. Profs., Nat. League for Nursing, Nursing Honor Soc., Nursing Administrs. Coun. Democrat. Roman Catholic. Home: 1119 W Escalon Fresno CA 93711

NISSEN, JUDY KAY, college administrator; b. George, Iowa, Mar. 24, 1942; d. Theodore and Marie Myrtle (Ackerman) Harms; m. Gordon Lee Elzenga, June 13, 1964 (dec.); m. James Gould Kerr, Aug. 15, 1973 (div. Jan. 1982); children: Jodi (dec.), Jana (dec.); m. Robert Eugene Nissen, Sept. 4, 1983; stepchildren: Melinda Duffy, Kathy Howell, Matt, Mary Riley, Jennifer Sagar. BA in Vocat. Home Econs. Edn., U. No. Iowa, 1963; MA in Higher Edn., Northeast Mo. State U., 1987; ABD, PhD, Iowa State U., 1988—. Tchr. vocat. home econs. Tyler (Minn.) Community Sch., 1963-66, Le Mars (Iowa) Community Schs., 1968-78; tchr. home econs. Ft. Dodge (Iowa) Community Sch., 1966-67, Sioux City (Iowa) Cen. Sch., 1967-68; substitute tchr. U.S. Dept. Def. Sch., Seoul, Republic of Korea, 1978-80; trainer, retail salesperson Stretch & Sew Fabrics, Colorado Springs, Colo., 1980-81; coord. bus. and home econs. adult edn Iowa Valley Community Coll., Marshalltown, 1981-86; dir. small bus. devel. Iowa Valley Community Coll., Marshalltown, 1986—, cons., 1986-88; trainer Fisher Controls, Marshalltown, 1987-88; presenter workshops Iowa Community Coll., 1986-90. Vol. ACE/SCORE, Marshalltown, 1984—. Named Woman

of the Yr., Marshalltown chpt. Am. Bus. Women's Assn., 1985; nominated to Women of Achievement YMCA, 1985, Leadership for a New Century Inst., 1989-90. Mem. Am. Soc. Tng. and Devel., Iowa Assn. Lifelong Learning (treas. 1987-89, Disting. Svc. award 1984), Am. Home Econs. Assn., Am. Vocat. Assn., Mo. Valley Edn. Assn., Marshalltown C. of C., Grinnell (Iowa) C. of C., Iowa Falls (Iowa) C. of C., TTT (chpt. pres. 1985-86), Phi Kappa Phi, Alpha Delta Kappa (corr. sec. 1986-88). Home: 1914 S 5th Ave Marshalltown IA 50158 Office: Iowa Valley Community Coll 3700 S Ctr St Marshalltown IA 50158

NISWONGER, JEANNE DU CHATEAU, biologist, writer; b. Indpls.; d. Simon Nicholas and Portia (Reeves) Du Chateau; m. Joseph Niswonger; children: Kenneth Arnold, Laura Elaine, Nancy Jo. AB, Miami U., Oxford, Ohio; postgrad., Washington Sch. Psychiatry; MA, PhD, Calif. Western U. Rsch. assoc. HEW and W.Va. Dept. Health, Charleston; rsch. biologist Bio-Rsch. Inst., Fla. So. Coll., Lakeland, 1958-61; writer Tampa (Fla.) Tribune, 1960-70. Assoc. editor Fla. Medaux, 1963-65; editor Lake Region Naturalist, 1959-69, asst. editor Fla. Naturalist, 1964-70; editor Fla. Wilderness Calendar, 1964-67; author: That Doll Ginny; Troll Dolls. Mem. bd. dirs. Polk Pub. Mus.; dir. pub. rels. Polk County Coun. Parents and Tchrs.; pres. Fla. chpt. Nature Conservancy. Mem. Fla. Audubon Soc. (mem. adv. bd. 1960-72), Lake Region Audubon Soc. (pres. 1960-65), AAUW (br. sec. 1962-64), Wildlife Soc., Wilderness Soc., Am. Soc. Mammalogists, Am. Assn. Zool. Parks and Aquariums, Izaak Walton League, Fla. Wildlife Fedn. (dir. 1974—), Nat. Wildlife Fedn., Am. Mus. Natural History, Fla. Zool. Soc., Defenders of Wildlife, Nat. Parks and Conservation Assn., Nat. League Am. Pen Women (treas., pres. 1987—), United Fedn. Doll Clubs (bd. mgmt.), Ginny Doll Club (pres.). Home: 305 W Beacon Rd Lakeland FL 33803

NITTISKIE, LESLIE COLLIN, managing editor; b. Dover, Del., Dec. 7, 1957; d. Richard E. and Natalie E. (Wible) Collin; m. Edward J. Nittiskie Jr. BA in English, Northland Coll., 1980. Editor Reuben H. Donnelly Corp., Cin., 1980; contbg. editor Bldg. Cin., Cin., 1980-81; contract negotiator Hill AFB, Ogden, Utah, 1981-84; reporter New Bern (N.C.) Sun Jour., 1985, community editor, 1985-86; speakers bureau adminstr. Corp. for Open Systems, McLean, Va., 1986-88; mng. editor Corp. for Open Systems, McLean, 1988—. Author/editor: (newsletter) The Cos Network, 1988-89; contbr. articles to jours. Mem. Am. Soc. Assn. Execs., Nat. Assn. Corp. Speakers Activities, Washington Women in P.R., Hill AFB Restoration Club (pub. rels. officer 1982-84). Republican. Mem. United Ch. of Christ. Office: Corp for Open Systems 1750 Old Meadow Rd Ste 400 McLean VA 22102

NIX, ALICE PEARL, retired college professor; b. Choestoe, Ga., Dec. 12, 1912; d. Columbus H. and Lillie Irene (Henson) N. AB, Piedmont Coll., 1940; M in Edn., U. Ga., 1946, D in Ednl. Psychology, 1959. Elem. sch. tchr. White County Schs., 1930-31, 32-34, Hall County Schs., Gainesville, Ga., 1935-36; elem. sch. tchr. White County Schs., Cleveland, Ga., 1936-40, secondary English tchr., 1940-45, curriculum cons., 1945-47; dir. guidance tchr. edn. Truett-McConnell Coll., Cleveland, 1947-57; cons. tchr. edn. North Ga. Coll., Dahlonega, summers 1951-54; counselor, instr. U. Ga., Athens, Ga., 1958-59; prof. psychology, dir. psychoednl. svcs. West Ga. Coll., Carrollton, Ga., 1959-78; pres. Am. Assn. Retired Persons, Carrollton, 1984-86, Retired Tchrs. Assn., Carrollton, 1986-90. Author: (Book) Reflections of the Mind of Christ from the Gospels, 1985; contbr. articles to profl. jours. Mem., past pres. League of Women Voters of Carrollton, 1960-89; mem., chmn. Mental Health Assn. Adv. Council, Carrollton, 1976-88. Mem. Am. Psychol. Assn., Ga. Psychol. Assn., Southeastern Psychol. Assn., BPW Club (pres. 1972-74), Civic Woman's Club (dept. chmn.), Delta Kappa Gamma (state officer, dist. dir., local pres. 1964-66, 82-84), Kappa Delta Pi. Democrat. Baptist. Home: 229 Griffin Dr Carrollton GA 30117

NIX, BARBARA LOIS, real estate broker; b. Yakima, Wash., Sept. 25, 1929; d. Martin Clayton and Norma (Gunter) Westfield; m. A.A. Sierra Coll. 1978; m. B.H. Nix, July 12, 1968; children—William Martin Dahl, Theresa Irene Dahl; step-children—Denise Leon, Denise Lynn. Bookkeeper, office mgr. Lakeport (Calif.) Tire Service, 1966-69, Dr. K.J. Absher, Grass Valley, Calif., 1972-75; real estate sales and office mgr. Rough and Ready Land Co., Penn Valley, Calif., 1976-77, co-owner, v.p., sec., 1978—, also of Wildwood West Real Estate and Lake of the Pines Sales. Youth and welfare chmn. Yakima Federated Jr. Women's Club, 1957; den mother Cub Scouts, 1959-60; leader Girl Scouts, 1961-62; mem. Friends of Hospice; exec. bd. dirs. Sierra, Nev. Meml. Hosp. Found. Recipient Pres.'s award Sierra Coll., 1973; others. Mem. Penn Valley C. of C., Nat. Assn. Female Execs., Antique Soc. Penn Valley (founder, pres. 1978), St. Mary's Coll. Aux., Sierra Nevada Meml. Hosp. Aux., Nevada County Arts Council. Democrat. Roman Catholic. Clubs: Job's Daus. (life), Lady Elks. Home: 19365 Wildflower Dr Penn Valley CA 95946 Office: PO Box 191 Rough and Ready CA 95975

NIX, BEVERLY ANN, broadcast executive; b. Hobbs, N.M., Apr. 1, 1951; d. Vance I. and Betty Lea (Hunsinger) N. BA, Calif. State U., L.A., 1974; JD, Southwestern U. Sch. Law, 1978. Staff atty. legal dept. Warner Bros. TV, Burbank, Calif., 1979-80, assoc. dir. legal and adminstrv. affairs, 1980-82, dir. bus. affairs, 1982-83, v.p. bus. affairs, 1983-90; sr. v.p. bus. affairs Warner Bros. TV, 1990—. Mem. Acad. TV Arts and Scis., Nat. Captioning Inst. Corp. Adv. Coun., Calif. Arboretum Found. Office: Warner Bros TV 4000 Warner Blvd Burbank CA 91522

NIX, PAMELA DIANNE, insurance underwriter advisor; b. Franklin, N.C., July 2, 1964; d. Jimmy Allen and Eunice Virginia (Bryson) N. BS, Tift Coll., 1986. Ins. underwriter advisor Frank B. Hall, Atlanta. Mem. NAFE. Home: 632 Briar Hill Ln C Riverdale GA 30274

NIXDORF, BRENDA BRAUER, legal administrator, paralegal; b. Storm Lake, Iowa, Sept. 1, 1957; d. William Rolland Brauer and Sandra Ellen (Bihrer) Brown; m. Dennis Charles Nixdorf, Oct. 10, 1981. BA in Criminal Justice, U. Nev., Las Vegas, 1980, MA in Sociology, 1982; AA, Edmonds Community Coll., 1985. Legal sec. Wickwire, Lewis, Goldmark & Schorr, Seattle, 1983-86; paralegal, legal administr. Hendricks & Lewis, Seattle, 1986—. Mem. Wash. Legal Assts. Assn., Phi Kappa Phi. Office: Hendricks & Lewis 2675 1st Interstate Ctr 999 Third Ave Seattle WA 98104

NIXON, AGNES ECKHARDT, television writer, producer; m. Robert Nixon; 4 children. Student, Sch. Speech, Northwestern U. Writer for radio and TV; freelance writer for: TV programs Hallmark Hall of Fame, Robert Montgomery Presents, Studio One; creator, packager, head writer: daytime TV series All My Children; creator nightime mini-series The Manions of America; creator, packager daytime TV series One Life to Live; creator, packager: daytime TV series Loving; co-creator: daytime TV series As The World Turns; formerly head writer, The Guiding Light, daytime TV series Another World. Recipient Trustees award Nat. Acad. TV Arts and Scis., 1981; Super Achiever award Jr. Diabetes Found.; Wilmer Eye Inst. award. Mem. Internat. Radio and TV Soc., Nat. Acad. TV Arts and Scis. Address: 774 Conestoga Rd Rosemont PA 19010

NIXON, BARBARA ELIZABETH, clergy person; b. Detroit, Aug. 3, 1954; d. Glenn Curry and Irma Mary (Nisbet) N. BA, Kirkland Coll., Clinton, N.Y., 1976; MA, Columbia U., 1981; Dip.C.S., Regent Coll., Vancouver, B.C., 1983; MDiv, Yale U., 1987. Minister, dir. edn. A Christian Ministry in the Nat. Pks., Kings Canyon Nat. Park, Calif., 1975; dance instr. Kirkland and Hamilton Colls., Clinton, N.Y., 1976-77; adminstrv. asst. Christian Counseling & Psychtherapy Ctr., N.Y.C., 1978-80; ednl. and cultural programmer Columbia U., N.Y.C., 1980-81; ministry intern Christ Episcopal Ch., Wesleyan U. Greenwich and Middletown, Conn., 1984-85; seminarian asst. The Episcopal Ch. at Yale, New Haven, 1986-87; asst. chaplain and tchr. St. Paul's Sch., Concord, N.H., 1987-88; residence dir. Gordon Coll., Wenham, Mass., 1989—; asst. rector Calvary Episcopal Ch., Danvers, Mass., 1989, St. John's Episcopal Ch., Vernon, Conn., 1990—; cons. in field; dancer Boston Liturgical Dance Ensemble, 1988-90, Cambridge Ct. Dancers, Boston, 1988—. Dancer, choreographer Boston U. Sch. Theology, Women and the Word Conf., 1989. Panel mem. bicentennial conf. Christians for Bibl. Equality, Mpls., 1989; mem. Conn. diocesan commn. on higher edn. Mem. Christians for Bibl. Equality, Appalachian Mt. Club, Hamilton Coll. Alumni Assn., Yale U. Alumni Assn. Office: St Johns Episcopal Ch PO Box 2237 Vernon CT 06066-1637

NIXON, JOYCE ELAINE, chiropractor, educator, consultant; b. Corning, N.Y., Feb. 17, 1925; d. Douglas Lewis and Mina Phiolana (Barnes) Williams; m. Lewis Earl Nixon, June 21, 1946 (div. Nov. 1958); 1 child, Deborah Joy. BA, Webster U., 1945; postgrad., SUNY, Geneseo, 1952-53; student, PBTS Bible Inst., 1946. Adminstr., chiropractic technician Dr. DeLue, Nunda, N.Y., 1958-85, cons., 1986—; instr. Sacro Occipital Research Soc. Internat., Inc., Omaha, 1966-79. Active Genessee Valley Council on Arts, Geneseo, 1967—; pres., bd. dirs. Nunda Community Home, Inc., 1983—. Mem. Internat. Platform Assn., N.Y. State Chiropractic Women's Aux., Nat. Assn. for Female Execs. (N.Y. State chpt.), Sacro Occipital Research Soc. (internat. sec. 1965-70, officer 1976, Disting. Profl. Service Founder's award 1976, Pres.' award 1980), N.Y. State Bus. and Profl. Women's Assn. (bd. dirs. 1963-71), Internat. Fedn. Bus. and Profl. Women, Geneva Bus. and Profl. Womens Clubs Inc. Republican. Home: 3 Meadowbrook Terr Dansville NY 14437

NIXON, MARNI, singer; b. Altadena, Calif., Feb. 22, 1930; d. Charles and Margaret (Wittke) McEathron; m. Ernest Gold, May 22, 1950 (div. 1969); children: Andrew Maurice, Martha Alice, Melani Christine; m. Lajos Frederick Fenster, July 23, 1971 (div. July 1975); m. Albert David Block, Apr. 11, 1983. Student opera workshop, Los Angeles City Coll., UCLA, U. So. Calif., Tanglewood, Mass. Dir. vocal faculty Calif. Inst. Arts, Valencia, 1970-72; pvt. tchr., 1970—, pvt. voice tchr., coach, condr. master classes, 1970—; head apprentice div. Santa Barbara Music Acad. of West, 1980; formerly dir. opera workshop Cornish Inst. Arts, Seattle.; tchr. in field; judge Met. Opera, Internat. Am. Music Awards, Nat. Inst. Music Theatre, 1984, 85-86, 87; panelist New Music, Nat. Assn. Tchrs. Singing. Child actress Pasadena (Calif.) Playhouse, 1940-45, soloist Roger Wagner chorale, 1947-53, appeared with New Eng. Opera Co., Los Angeles Opera Co., also Ford Found. TV Opera, 1948-63, San Francisco Spring Opera, 1966, Seattle Opera, 1971, 72, 73; classical recitals and appearances with symphony orchs. throughout U.S., Can., also Eng., Israel, Ireland; appeared on Broadway as Eliza Doolittle in My Fair Lady, 1964; in motion picture as Sister Sophia in Sound of Music, 1964; also in numerous TV shows and night clubs; star children's ednl. TV show Boomerang, ABC-TV, from 1975; off-Broadway show Taking My Turn, from 1983; taped for Great Performances PBS-TV Role of Edna; voice dubbed in for musical motion pictures; rec. artist for Columbia, Mus. Heritage Records, Capital, RCA Victor, Ednl.Records, Reference Recs., Varese-Sarabande, Nonesuch; played violin at age 4; studied in youth orch., 10 yrs; studied voice at age 10. Bd. dirs. Naumburg Symphony Orch. Recipient 4 Emmy awards for best actress, 2 Action for Childrens TV awards, 1977; nominee Drama Desk award; recipient Chgo. Film Festival award, 1977, Gold Record for Songs from Mary Poppins, 2 time Grammy award nominee Nat. Acad. Rec. Arts and Scis. (1st rec. Cabaret Songs and Early Songs by Arnold Schoenberg, RCA, 1977 and 1st rec. Emily Dickinson Songs by Aaron Copland, Reference Recs., 1988.

NIXON, PATRICIA RYAN (THELMA CATHERINE NIXON), wife of former President of U.S.; b. Ely, Nev., Mar. 16, 1912; m. Richard Milhous Nixon, June 21, 1940; children: Patricia (Mrs. Edward Finch Cox), Julie (Mrs. Dwight David Eisenhower II). Grad. cum laude, U. So. Calif., 1937, L.H.D., 1961. X-ray technician N.Y.C., 1931-33; tchr. high schs. Cal., 1937-41; govt. economist, 1942-45. Promoter of world wide humanitarian service, volunteerism in U.S. Decorated grand cross Order of Sun for relief work at time of massive earthquake, 1971; Peru; grand cordon Most Venerable Order Knighthood Pioneers Liberia, 1972; named among most admired women George Gallup polls, 1957, 68, 69, 70, 71. *

NIXON, SHIRNETTE MARILYN, chemical company administrator; b. N.Y.C., Apr. 14, 1947; d. Clifford Bernard and Edna Lucille (Anglin) N. BA in English, Bklyn. Coll., 1969. Pers. asst. Mut. N.Y., N.Y.C., 1969-73; editorial asst. Franklin Watts Inc., N.Y.C., 1973-76; adminstrv. sec. for pers. Pfizer Inc., N.Y.C., 1976-82, adminstrv. sec. for tax, 1982—, oral communication specialist, 1988-90. Turstee Day Star Bapt. Ch., Bronx, N.Y., 1980—; mem. YWCA Helpline. Recipient Spl. Recognition Letter Mayor David Dinkins. Mem. AAUW, Internat. Tng. in Communication (com. chmn. 1973—, editor Adventures 1975, Town Crier 1976, del. 1990-91, speaking awards 1973), Bklyn. Coll. Alumni Assn. Democrat. Office: Pfizer Inc 235 E 42d St New York NY 10017

NIXON, SUZI, small business owner; b. Tucson, Apr. 24, 1950; d. Hugh Pryor and Mary-Pauline (Hurst) C.; m. Bruce Lee Batterson, Aug. 1970 (div. 1975); 1 child, Stephani Cole Batterson; m. R. Peter Nixon, Mar., 1990. AA, San Diego Mesa Coll., 1976; BA, San Diego State U., 1978; postgrad., U. Calif., Santa Barbara, 1978-79. Peer counselor San Diego Mesa Coll., 1974-76; adminstrv. asst. San Diego State U., 1976-78; owner Suzi's Spa Svcs., Pleasant Hill, Calif., 1978—. Mem. Friends of the Tucson Pub. Libr. Mem. Psi Chi. Republican. Pentecostal. Home and Office: 510 Cooper Dr Benicia CA 94510

NIXON, TAMARA FRIEDMAN, banker; b. Cleve., June 3, 1938; d. Victor and Eva J. (Osteryoung) Friedman; m. Daniel D. Nixon, June 14, 1959; children: Asa Joel, Naomi Devorah, Victoria Eve. BA with honors in econs. (Wellesley scholar), Wellesley Coll., 1959; MBA, U. Pitts., 1961. Asst. economist Fed. Res. Bank, N.Y.C., 1959-60, 61-62; economist R.P. Wolff Econ. Rsch., Miami, Fla., 1972-75; econ. cons., Miami, 1975-79; sr. v.p. Washington Savs. & Loan Assn., Miami Beach, Fla., 1979-81; pres. T.F. Nixon Econ. Cons. Inc., 1982—; sr. v.p. CenTrust Savs. Bank, 1984-89 ; real estate feasibility cons.; investment adminstr. U. Pitts. fellow, 1961. Land use chmn. Dade County chpt. LWV, 1975-76. Mem. Econ. Soc. S. Fla. (v.p. programs, dir.), Am. Econ. Assn. Office: 4646 N Bay Rd Miami Beach FL 33140

NIZNIK, MONICA LYNNE, history professor; b. Detroit, Dec. 3, 1953; d. Valentine Joseph and Helen (Banayk) N.; m. David Lee Salvaterra, Aug. 3, 1981; children: Andrew Joseph, Emily Elizabeth. BS, Eastern Mich. U., 1976; MA, U. Notre Dame, 1977, PhD, 1981. Cert. in Archives Mgmt. Archivist Corcoran, Youngman, Rowe, Washington, 1979-80; instr. in history Loras Coll., Dubuque, Iowa, 1981-82, U. Dubuque, 1982; archives asst. Loras Coll., Dubuque, 1981-82; asst. editor W.C. Brown Pubs., Dubuque, 1982-84; dir. of devel. Wahlert High Sch., Dubuque, 1984-86; freshmen registration counselor Loras Coll., Dubuque, 1988-90, asst. prof., 1986—; mentor Loras Coll., Dubuque, Iowa, 1988-90; mem. editorial bd. Delta Sigma Epsilon, Loras Coll., 1989—. Religion tchr. St. Columbkille Parish, Dubuque, 1988-89; ballet tchr. YWCA, Dubuque. Recipient Bd. of Regents scholarship Eastern Mich. U., Ypsilanti, 1972-76, Hearst fellowship U. Notre Dame, 1979-80, Rsch. fellowship FDR Presidential Libr., Hyde Park, N.Y., 1979, Dissertation Rsch. fellowship, U. Notre Dame, 1980-81. Mem. AAUW, Orgn. Am. Historians, League of Women Voters, YWCA. Roman Catholic. Home: 5315 Saratoga Rd Dubuque IA 52001 Office: Loras Coll PO Box 822 Dubuque IA 52001

NJAKA, SHIRLEY, real estate executive; b. Auburn, Ala., Jan. 3, 1954; d. Percy and Lou Emma (Crenshaw) Cook; m. Chinyere Ike Njaka, June 19, 1976; children: Chinelo Lataucha, Nkechi Deanna, Ijeoma Nicole. BS, Tuskegee U., 1976; student, U. Minn. Property mgr. Shirlike Apts., Hopkins, Minn.; reinsurance broker A.E. Strudwick Co., Edina, Minn.; owner Njaka Pilgrim Cleaners, Hopkins; v.p. Shirlike, Inc., Hopkins. Notary public, Hennepin County. Mem. NAFE, Better Bus. Bur., Multi-Housing Assn., Midtown Owners Assn., Internat. Fabricare Inst., Minn. Fabricare Inst., Twin West C. of C. Home: PO Box 595 Hopkins MN 55343

NOAH, HOPE ELLEN, editor, speech educator, broadcaster, writer; b. N.Y.C., Sept. 17, 1943; d. Mortimer and Anne (Forscher) Shaff; m. Lester Noah, Oct. 30, 1969 (div. July, 1985); children: Meredith Ayn, Allison Jane. BS in Speech, Emerson Coll., 1965. Cert. tchr. speech, English, drama, N.Y., N.J. Film producer Rossmore Prodns. and Selling Methods, Inc., N.Y.C., 1965-66; high sch. English tchr. New City, and Mt. Vernon, N.Y., Fair Lawn, N.J., 1966-73; pvt. teaching practice, profl. speech writer and cons. various locations, 1972—; sales rep. Wordex Corp., Fair Lawn, 1978-80; spl. assignment, summer sch. tchr. Fair Lawn Bd. Edn., 1980-81; writer weekly column A Single Look and spl. feature articles Bergen News, Palisades Park, N.J., 1982-89; producer, programmer, host weekly program "Hope with Singles" Sta. WMCA-Radio, N.Y.C., 1983-84; columnist, cons. Single Times, N.Y.C., 1984-86; editor-in-chief N.J. Singles Mag., Totowa, 1985-86, Single People mag., Dynasty Media Pubs., Englewood Cliff, N.J., 1985-86, Pizzazz, N.Y.C. tri-state entertainment mag., U.S. Pub. Inc., Rutherford, N.J., 1986-87; owner Noah Communications, 1986—; pvt. practice advt. and pub. relations, small bus. cons., 1982—; dir. creative advt., creator of "Hope" columns, TODAY newspapers, Wayne, N.J., 1982-84; pub. speaker, guest radio and TV shows including The David Letterman program; cons. to industry, hosps.; performer comml. voice-overs; lectr. in field. Columnist News Pub. Co., 1986—, Spotlight mag., 1987—; entertainment writer Cross Over the Bridge column, N.Y.C.; regular contbr. travel writings, book revs., articles and columns to various mags., bus. jours. and other publs. V.p., then pres. Ridgewood, N.J. B'Nai B'rith Women, 1976-78; mem. adv. bd. Barnett Temple, 1989-90. Named one of Eighty-Five N.J. Residents to Watch N.J. Monthly Mag., 1985. Mem. AFTRA, Emerson Coll. Alumni Assn., Glen Rock (N.J.) C. of C., Rotary. Jewish. Home: 26 Leone Ct Glen Rock NJ 07452

NOAH, JULIA JEANINE, librarian; b. Craig, Mo., July 14, 1932; d. Hiram Curtis and Eloise Julia (Puckett) True; m. Raymond Laverne Noah, Sept. 5, 1954; children: David Scott, Danny Ray, Deborah Jill, Douglas True. BS, U. Ill., 1953; MA in Library Sci., U. South Fla., 1983. Asst. rsch. librarian Parke, Davis & Co., Detroit, 1953-55; cataloging librarian U. Mo., Columbia, 1955-57; sch. librarian High Point Elem. Sch., Clearwater, Fla., 1968; library aide Clearwater High Sch., 1973-78; reference asst. Dunedin (Fla.) Pub. Library, 1978-84, dir. info. svcs., 1984-88, library dir., 1988—. Mem. ALA, Fla. Library Assn., Pub. Library Assn., Southeastern Library Assn., Fla. Pub. Library Assn., DAR, AAUW, Questers, Rotary, Phi Kappa Phi, Beta Phi Mu. Republican. Presbyterian. Office: Dunedin Pub Library 223 Douglas Ave Dunedin FL 34698

NOALL, NANCY ANN, lawyer; b. Cleve., May 5, 1957; d. John Bennett and Constance Marie (Vachon) N. BA, John Carroll U., 1977; JD, Case Western Res. U., 1981. Bar: Ohio 1981. Mgr., asst. mgr. Mr. Chicken, Willoughby, Ohio, 1973-81; assoc. Chattman Garfield Friedlander & Paul, Cleve., 1981-84; assoc. Walter, Haverfield, Buescher & Chockley, Cleve., 1984-88, ptnr., 1989—. Mem. Cleve. Bar Assn. (labor sect.). Roman Catholic. Office: Walter Haverfield et al 1215 Terminal Tower Cleveland OH 44113

NOBILE, KARIN ANN, publications manager; b. New Haven, Feb. 17, 1960; d. Martin and Linde Nobile. B, Albertus Magnus Coll., 1989. Asst. distbn. mgr. Saab-Scania Am. Inc., Orange, Conn., 1980-81; consumer relations asst. Saab-Scania Am. Inc., Orange, 1981-82, consumer relations coordinator, 1982-85, consumer relations mgr., pubs. mgr., 1986--; asst. coordinator WTNH Channel-8 Prodn High Sch. Bowl, New Haven, 1987-88; freelance writer New Haven County Woman, 1988, Sachem Publ. Assocs., Guilford, Conn. Editor: Saab Prospects, Saab Soundings, 1988--. Fund raiser Am. Heart Assn, Madison, Conn., 1985, Cystic Fibrosis Found., Guilford, 1986; planning com. New Haven Bed Race Benefitting Fresh Air Fund, 1987-88. Mem. Women in Communications, Alpha Sigma Lambda. Home: 75 S Main-D Branford CT 06405

NOBLE, MARION ELLEN, home economist; b. Blanchardville, Wis., Feb. 18, 1914; d. Dwight Eldridge and Doris Edna (Parkinson) Baker; m. B. Frank Smyth (dec. 1979); children: William, Ann Marris, Robert, Larry, Margaret Decker; m. George C. Noble. BS, U. Wis., Madison, 1936. V.p. Smyth Bus Systems, Canton, Ohio, 1950; womens editor Radio Station WFAH, Alliance, Ohio, 1952-58; home economist Extension Service Ohio State U., Columbus, 1961-69. Contbr. articles to profl. jours. Named Woman of the Year Urban League, Canton, 1964. Mem. AAUW, Nat. Assn. Extension Home Economists, Pacific Pioneer Broadcasters, Home Econs. Club, Thimble Collectors Internat., Ladies Oriental Shrine of North Am., Phi Upsilon Omicron, Epsilon Sigma Phi. Republican. Methodist. Home: 3240 A San Amadeo Laguna Hills CA 92653

NOBLE, SUNNY A., business owner; b. Moorhead, Minn., May 22, 1940; d. Albert Ferdinand and Annette Edina (Wyman) Meyer; m. Eric Scott Noble, Apr. 11, 1980; children: Chris Koshiol, Kelly Ann Brinar. MBA, U. Calif., Berkeley, 1960. Qualified parapsychologist, Minn. Mgr. Spear & Hill Attys., N.Y.C., 1969-70; mgr. exec. property mgmt. May Co. Dept. Stores, La Jolla, Calif., 1981-82; owner, pres. Country Computer Stores, Bakersfield, Calif., L.A, and others, 1984—. Author: (newspaper column) That Computes, 1984-88, The Storyteller, 1987—. Mem. Toastmasters Internat. (ednl. v.p. 1988), Mensa, Beta Sigma Phi. Home and Office: 3159 Lemonwood Dr Lancaster CA 93536

NOBLIT, BETTY JEAN, publishing technician; b. St. Elmo, Ill., June 12, 1948; d. Clyde W. and Lucille M. (Haggard) N. Grad. in restaurant and club food mgmt., LaSalle U., 1973; grad., Am. Sch. Travel, 1975. Teletype puncher Sarsota (Fla.) Herald-Tribune, 1968-70, Pueblo Chieftain, 1970—; unified composer; pagination operator Star Jour. Pub. Co., Pueblo, Colo.; personal corr. Prime Min. Indira Gandhi. Mem. NAFE, Pueblo Hist. Soc., Nat. Geog. Soc. Home: 109 Idaho 2W Pueblo CO 81004

NOBLITT, NANCY ANNE, aerospace engineer; b. Roanoke, Va., Aug. 14, 1959; d. Jerry Spencer and Mary Louise (Jerrell) N. BA, Mills Coll., Oakland, Calif., 1982; M.S. in Indsl. Engring., Northeastern U., 1990. Data red specialist, Universal Energy Systems, Beaver Creek, Ohio, 1981; aerospace engr. turbine engine div. components br. turbine group aero-propulsion lab. Wright-Patterson AFB, Ohio, 1982-84, engine assessment br. spl. engines group, 1984-87; lead analyst cycle methods computer aided engr. Gen. Electric Co., Lynn Mass., 1987-90, Lynn PACES project coord., 1990—. Math and sci. tutor Centerville Sch. Bd., Ohio, 1982-86, math. and physics tutor Marblehead Sch. Bd., Mass., 1988—; rep. alumnae admissions Mills Coll., Boston area, 1987—; house staff mem. Me and Thee Coffeehouse, Marblehead. Recipient Notable Achievement award U.S. Air Force, 1984; recipient Special award Fed. Lab. Consortium, 1987. Avocation: book collecting. Home: 35 State St Marblehead MA 01945 Office: Gen Electric Co AEBG Lynn MA 01910

NOBOA-STANTON, PATRICIA LYNN, commercial real estate executive; b. Cin., Sept. 6, 1947; d. William Emile and Marie Virginia (Ballbach) Hakes; m. Donald R. Stanton, Nov. 10, 1987; children from previous marriage: Aric Israel, Rene Carlos. Diploma Presbyn.-St. Luke's Sch. Nursing, Chgo., 1967, Nat. Inst. Real Estate, 1989, No. Va. Community Coll., 1990. Supr. patient care Alexandria Hosp., Va., 1976-78; pres. Renaissance Reprographics, Inc., Reston, Va., 1985-89; pres. Va. Leasing & Copying Inc., Reston, 1978-89; realtor Wellborn Comml., 1989—; publ. and health cons. Atlantic Resources Corp., 1990—. Pres. Reston Bd. Commerce, 1985, founding bd. dirs. 1982-85, v.p. 1984, sec. 1983; v.p. Planned Community Archives, Inc., 1985-88; mem. regional com. United Way, 1985-87; Dulles Area Regional Council steering com., 1985-88; bd. dirs. N. Va. Local Devel. Corp., 1987—; bd. dirs. Fairfax Symphony, Reston Bd. Commerce, 1989. Named Reston Citizen of Yr., 1985; named Small Bus. Person of Yr. Fairfax County Commn. for Women, 1985-87. Mem. Northern Va. Assn. Realtors, Nat. Assn. Realtors, Va. Assn. Realtors, Nat. Assn. Quick Printers (bd. dirs. Capital chpt. 1984—, vice chair 1987—), Internat. Platform Assn., Fairfax County C. of C. (bd. dirs. 1985-86, 87—), Herndon C. of C., Washington-Dulles Task Force. Episcopalian. Lodge: Rotary. Avocations: computers, music, flying. Office: Wellborn Comml 1801 Reston Pkwy Reston VA 22090 also: Renaissance Reprographics 13873 Park Center Rd Suite 137 Herndon VA 22071

NOCHMAN, LOIS WOOD KIVI (MRS. MARVIN NOCHMAN), educator; b. Detroit, Nov. 5, 1924; d. Peter K. and Annetta Lois (Wood) Kivi; A.B., U. Mich., 1946, A.M., 1949; m. Harold I. Pitchford, Sept. 6, 1944 (div. May 1949); children: Jean Pitchford Horiszny, Joyce Lynn Pitchford Undiano; m. 2d, Marvin A. Nochman, Aug. 15, 1953; 1 son, Joseph Asa. Tchr. adult edn., Honolulu, 1947, Ypsilanti (Mich.) High Sch., 1951-52; spl. instr. English, Wayne State U., Detroit, 1953, 54; tchr. Highland Park (Mich.) Coll., 1950-51, instr. English, 1954-83. Mem. exec. bd. Highland Park Fedn. Tchrs., 1963, 64, 65, 66, 71, 72, mem. 1st bargaining team, 1965-66, 73, del. to Nat. Conv., 1964, 71, 72, 73, 74, rep. higher edn. to Mich. Fedn. Tchrs. Exec. Com., 1972, 73, 74, 75, 76; mem. faculty adv. com. Gov.'s Commn. on Higher Edn., 1973—. Tchr. Baha'i schs., Davison, Mich., 1954, 55, 58, 59, 63, 64, 65, 66, Beaulac, Que., Can., 1960, Greenacre, Maine, 1965; sec. local spiritual assembly Baha'is, Ann Arbor, 1953, sec., Detroit, 1954, chmn., 1955; mem. nat. com. Baha'is U.S., 1955-68; sec. Davison Bahai Sch. Com. and Council, 1956, 58, 63, 64, 65, 66, 67, 68; Baha'i lectr. Mem. Modern Lang. Assn., Nat. Council Tchrs. English, Mich. Coll. English Assn., Am. Fedn. Tchrs., Nat. Soc. Lit. and Arts, Women's Equity and Action League (sec. Mich. chpt. 1975-79), Alpha Lambda Delta, Alpha Gamma Delta. Contbr. poems to mags. Avocation: U.S. Swimming Master Champion. Home: 25227 Parkwood Huntington Woods MI 48070

NODDINGS, NEL, education educator, writer; b. Irvington, N.J., Jan. 19, 1929; d. Edward A. Rieth and Nellie A. (Connors) Walter; m. James A. Noddings, Aug. 20, 1949; children: Chris, Howard, Laurie, James, Nancy, William, Sharon, Edward, Vicky, Timothy. BA in Math., Montclair State Coll., 1949; MA in Math., Rutgers U., 1964; PhD in Edn., Stanford U., 1973. Cert. tchr., Calif., N.J. Tchr. Woodbury (N.J.) Publ Schs., 1949-52; tchr. math. dept. Matawan (N.J.) High Sch., 1958-62, chair, asst. prin., 1964-69; curriculum supr. Montgomery Twp. Pub. Schs., Skillman, N.J., 1970-72; dir. precollegiate edn. U. Chgo., 1975-76; asst. prof. Pa. State U., State College, 1973; from asst. prof. to assoc. prof. Stanford (Calif.) U., 1977-86, prof., 1986—; bd. dirs. Ctr. for Human Caring Sch. Nursing, Denver, 1986—; cons. NIE, NSF and various sch. dists. Author: Caring: A Feminine Approach to Ethics and Moral Education, 1984, Women and Evil, 1989, (with W. Paul Shore) Awakening the Inner Eye: Intuition in Education, 1984; mem. adv. bd. Am. Jour. of Edn., Nat. Women's Studies Assoc. Jour., 1988—; contbr. articles to profl. jours. Mem. disting. women's adv. bd. Coll. St. Catherine. NSF fellow Rutgers U., 1962-64. Fellow Philosophy of Edn. Soc. (pres. elect 1990-91); mem. Am. Ednl. Rsch. Assn., Am. Philos. Assn., Phi Beta Kappa (vis. scholar). Office: Stanford U Sch Edn Stanford CA 94305

NOE, ELNORA (ELLIE NOE), chemical company executive; b. Evansville, Ind., Aug. 23, 1928; d. Thomas Noe and Evelyn (West) Dieter; student Ind. U.-Purdue U., Indpls. Sec., Pitman Moore Co., Indpls., 1946; with Dow Chem. Co., Indpls., 1960—, public rels. asst. then mgr. employee communications, 1970-87, mgr. community rels., 1987—, DowBrands Inc., 1986—; vice chmn. corp. affairs discussion group, 1989—, chmn., 1989-90; mem. steering com. Learn About Bus. Recipient 2d place award as Businesswoman of Yr., Indpls. Bus. and Profl. Women's Assn., 1980, Indpls. Profl. Woman of Yr. award Zonta, Altrusa, Sorptomist & Pilot Svc. Clubs, 1985. Mem. Am. Bus. Women Assn. (Woman of Yr. award 1965; past pres.), Ind. Assn. Bus. Communicators (communicator of yr. 1977), Women in Communications (Louise Eleanor Kleinhenz award 1984), Nat. Fedn. Press Women, Women's Press Club Ind. (past v.p.), Zonta (dist. public rels. chmn. 1978-80, area dir. 1980-82, pres. Indpls. 1977-79). Office: PO Box 68511 Indianapolis IN 46268

NOE, JUANITA LOUISE, science administrator, nurse; b. Maryville, Tenn., July 6, 1947; d. Geter Plato and Lucy Jane (Williams) Jenkins; m. John Edward Noe Jr., July 13, 1969; children: Chris Randal, Jonathan Daniel. Diploma in nursing, U. Tenn., 1968. RN, Tenn. With U. Tenn. Hosp., Knoxville, 1968-81, mgr. psychiat. unit, 1972-76, with quality assurance utilization rev., 1976-81; dir. quality assurance Ft. Sanders Regional Med. Ctr., Knoxville, 1981-84; planner Ft. Sanders Alliance, Knoxville, 1984-86; exec. dir. Thompson Cancer Survival Ctr., Knoxville, 1986—; bd. dirs., sec. Ft. Sanders Credit Union, Knoxville, 1984—; bd. dirs. Preferred Health Partnership, Knoxville, 1986—; bd. dirs. adv. bd. Am. Lung Assn., Knoxville, 1988—. Mem. Soc. for Ambulatory Care Profls., Intravenuous Nurse's Soc., Am. Mktg. Assn., Nat. Coalition for Cancer Surviorship. Republican. Baptist. Home: 3417 Peppermint Hills Dr Maryville TN 37804 Office: Thompson Cancer Ctr 1915 White Ave Knoxville TN 37916

NOE, JUDITH ANN, data processing executive, management consultant; b. Grosse Pointe, Mich., Apr. 9, 1945; d. George Emil and Henrietta Frances (Kerbrat) N. BS in English, Loyola U., Chgo., 1967. Employment interviewer Ill. State Employment Svcs., Chgo., 1967-69; programmer Kemper Ins., Chgo., 1969-70; programmer, analyst City Colls. of Chgo., 1970-71; systems analyst Oakton Community Coll., Morton Grove, Ill., 1971-76; project mgr. SEI Computer Svcs., Chgo., 1976-79; mng. cons. Automation Design, Inc., Chgo., 1979-83; pvt. practice cons. Chgo., 1982-87; pres., owner Strategic Advantage, Niles, Ill., 1987—. Mem. Data Processing Mgmt. Assn. Democrat. Roman Catholic. Office: Strategic Advantage 7065 W Seward St Niles IL 60648

NOEL, BARBARA HUGHES MCMURTRY, music educator; b. Mt. Vernon, Wash., Feb. 27, 1929; d. Lowell Robinson and Mary Evelyn (Hayton) Hughes; children: Sarah Kathleen, Martha Elizabeth. BM, U. Ky., 1951, MM, 1952; PhD, U. Ill., 1972; student, Oberlin Conservatory, 1947-49. Instr. music Union Coll., Barbourville, Ky., 1952-54; instr. music and fine arts Annie Wright Sem., Tacoma, Wash., 1957-63; organist, choirmaster Episc. churches, Calif., Wash., 1954-66; chmn. music dept. U. Richmond (Va.), 1971-76, Mankato (Minn.) State U., 1976-78; dean coll. humanities and fine arts Tex. Woman's U., Denton, 1978-81; dean coll. visual and performing arts Southeastern Mass. U., North Dartmouth, 1981-89, prof. music, 1990—; cons. for various music orgns. and univs., 1976—, textbook pubs., 1980—; reviewer Nat. Endowment for the Humanities. Book reviewer Providence Sunday Jour., 1984—; contbr. articles to music jours.; contbr. New Grove Dictionary of Music, 1974. Bd. dirs. Community Symphony Orchs., Mankato, 1976-78, New Bedford, Mass., 1981-87. Grad. fellow Danforth Found., U. Ill., 1966-71. Mem. Coll. Music Soc. (treas. 1983-87, v.p. 1979-83, coun. mem.), Nat. Assn. Schs. Music (undergrad. commr. 1978-81). Episcopalian. Home: 73 Tucker Ln North Dartmouth MA 02747 Office: Southeastern Mass U North Dartmouth MA 02747

NOEL, JEANNE KAY, consultant to biotechnology companies; b. Grosse Pointe, Mich., June 26, 1946; d. Wade Stephen and Katharine Adair (Jahimiak) Fuller; m. James Morris Noel, Dec. 19, 1970. BS, U. Mich., 1967, PhD, 1970. NIH rsch. fellow UCLA, 1971-74; dir. R & D, sci. products div. Abbott Labs., L.A., 1974-78; dir. mktg. Alpha Therapeutic Corp., L.A., 1978-81; mgr. healthcare devel. Cetus Corp., Emeryville, Calif., 1981-83, dir. diagnostics bus., 1983-86; pres., cons. J. Kay Noel & Assocs., Inc., El Cerrito, Calif., 1986—; sci. adviser, Digene, Inc., Silver Spring, Md., 1988—; bd. dir. Internat. Biotech. Labs., Inc. Mem. AAAS, Am. Assn. Clin. Chemistry, Sigma Xi.

NOEL, TALLULAH ANN, health science association executive; b. Detroit, Oct. 21, 1945; d. Harry Carababas and Ruby Dimple (Gentry) Caruso; m. Vernon E. Noel (div. 1965); children: Cynthia L. Robbins, Kimberly J. Wise. AA in Nursing, Morton Coll., Cicero, Ill., 1976; BS, Coll. St. Francis, Joliet, Ill., 1983; MSc in Mgmt., Nat.-Louis U., Evanston, Ill., 1990. RN. Staff nurse Mt. Sinai Hosp., Chgo., 1976-78, head nurse, 1978-79, critical care nurse, 1979-80, oncology clinician, 1980-82; head nurse McNeal Hosp., Berwyn, Ill., 1982-84; dir. nursing Nursefinders of Elmwood Park (Ill.), 1984-86; dir. profl. svcs. Nursefinders of Chgo., Elmwood Park, 1986-87, v.p. profl. svcs., 1987-88, v.p. ops., chief oper. officer, 1988—. Bd. dirs. Morton Coll. Found., 1987-88, Chgo. Heart Assn., 1985—, Grant Works Children's Ctr., Cicero, 1982-85. Mem. Women's Health Exec. Network, Nat. League Nursing, Oncology Nursing Soc., Am. Fedn. Home Health Agys., Assn. Critical Care Nurses, others. Democrat. Roman Catholic. Office: Nursefinders 593 N York Rd Elmhurst IL 60126

NOEL, TREVIA GRIFFIN, educator; b. Martinsville, Va., Jan. 23, 1949; d. James Lee and Naomi G. (Millner) Randolph; m. Elijah H. Griffin, Aug. 22, 1968 (div. 1985); children: Tonya Vona, Elijah Herbert III; m. Wilbert E. Noel, Nov. 21, 1987. BS, N.C. A&T State U., Greensboro, 1971. Tchr. D.C. Pub. Schs., Washington, 1973-89, Prince Georges County Schs., Suitland, Md., 1989—; cons. Athena Data Systems, Washington, 1986-87, Fin. Svcs., Inc., Ft. Washington, Md., 1987-89. Historian Ft. Lincoln Sch. PTA, Washington, 1979; sponsor Children's Internat. Summer Villages, Washington, 1985-88. Mem. Nat. Coun. Tchrs. Math. Home: 11916 Autumnwood Ln Fort Washington MD 20744

NOELL, IVANA MAE, environmental scientist; b. Laramie, Wyo., Sept. 15, 1936; d. Ivan Henry and Verna Louise (Korinek) Thompson; m. Leonard Clay Gardner; m. Frederick Ross Roland; 1 child, Terence Craig. AA, Stockton Jr. Coll., 1955; student, St. John's Coll., Annapolis, Md., 1960-61; BA in Zoology, U. Calif., Santa Barbara, 1964, MA in Zoology, 1969, postgrad., 1989—. Cert. jr. coll. tchr., Calif. Teaching assoc. dept. biol. scis. U. Calif., Santa Barbara, 1969-71; environ. scientist Henningson, Durham &

Richardson, Santa Barbara, 1974-75; instr. life sci. div. Santa Barbara City Coll., 1973-84, lectr. environ. studies program, 1977; instr. Santa Rosa (Calif.) Jr. Coll., 1977-78; botanist Bur. Land Mgmt., Ukiah, Calif., 1979-82; inspector, air quality planning asst. Air Pollution Control Dist., Santa Barbara, 1985-87; staff biologist Tetra Tech, Inc., San Bernadino, Calif., 1988—; vis. instr. Yosemite Inst., Yosemite Nat. Park, 1972. Contbr. papers to profl. publs., poems to literary publs. Vol. El Miraso Urban Polyculture Farm, Santa Barbara, 1972. Campbell fellow, 1964-65; Orgn. Tropical Studies grantee, 1964. Mem. Ctr. for Postmodern World, Soc. Ethnobiology, Am. Inst. Biol. Scis., Santa Barbara Botanic Garden, Calif. Native Plant Soc. (rare plant coordinator 1981). Home: PO Box 40108 Santa Barbara CA 93140

NOETH, CAROLYN FRANCES, speech and language pathologist; b. Cleve., July 21, 1924; d. Sam Falco and Barbara Serafina (Loparo) Armaro; m. Lawrence Andrew Noeth Sr., June 29, 1946; children: Lawrence Andrew Jr. (dec.), Barbara Marie Heaney. AB magna cum laude, Case Western Res. U., 1963; MEd, U. Ill., 1972; postgrad., Nat. Coll. Edn., 1975—. Lic. speech and lang. pathologist, Ill. Speech therapist Chgo. Pub. Schs., 1965; speech, lang. and hearing clinician J. Sterling Morton High Schs., Cicero and Berwyn, Ill., 1965-82, tchr. learning disabilities/behavior disorders, 1982, dist. ednl. diagnostician, 1982-84; Title I Project tchr., summers 1966-67, lang. disabilities cons., summers 1968-69, in-service tng. cons., summer 1970, dir. Title I Project, summers 1973-74, learning disabilities tchr. W. Campus of Morton, 1971-75, chmn. Educable-Mentally Handicapped-Opportunities Tchrs. Com., 1967-68, spl. edn. area and in-sch. tchrs. workshops, 1967—. Precinct elections judge, 1953-55; block capt. Mothers March of Dimes and Heart Fund, 1949-60; St. Agatha's rep. Nat. Catholic Women's League, 1952-53; collector for charities, 1967; mem. exec. bd. Morton Scholarship League, 1981-84, corr. sec., 1981-83; vol. Am. Cancer Soc., 1985—; vol. judge Ill. Acad. Decathlon, 1988—. First recipient Virda L. Stewart award for Speech, Western Res. U., 1963, recipient Outstanding Sr. award, 1963. Mem. Am. (certified), Ill. speech, language, and hearing assns., Council Exceptional Children (div. for learning disabilities, chpt. spl. projects chmn., exec. bd. 1976-81, chpt. pres. 1979-80), Council for Learning Disabilities, Profls. in Learning Disabilities, Internat. Platform Assn., Kappa Delta Pi, Delta Kappa Gamma (chmn., co-chmn. chpt. music com. 1979—, mem. state program com. 1981-83, chpt. music rep. to state 1982—). Roman Catholic. Clubs: St. Norbert's Women's (Northbrook, Ill.), Case-Western Res. U. Ill. Alumni Assns., Lions (vol. Northbrook, 1966—). Chmn. in compiling and publishing Student Handbook, Cleve. Coll., 1962; contbr. lyric parodies and musical programs J. Sterling Morton High Sch. West Retirement Teas, 1972-83. Home and Office: 1849 Walnut Circle Northbrook IL 60062

NOGALES, PATTI DIANE, author; b. Caracas, Bolivar, Venezuela, Feb. 8, 1961; came to U.S., 1978; d. Antonio and Patti Bernice (McDaniel) N. BA in Philosophy, St. John's Coll., Annapolis, Md., 1982; MA in English, No. Ariz. U., 1988. Instr. The Orme Sch., Mayer, Ariz., 1982-84; counselor No. Ariz. U., Flagstaff, 1985-86, instructional specialist, 1986-88. Author: (textbooks) Apple Works for Teachers, 1986, Apple Works for Students, 1989, Works for Students, 1990. Mem. NAFE, Ariz. Civil Liberties Union (bd. mem. 1987-88), Mensa, Phi Kappa Phi.

NOLAN, DENISE SUSAN, psychologist; b. Lawton, Okla., July 2, 1952; d. Conway Garlington and Doris Vernelle (Smart) N. BS, Cameron U., 1979; MEd, Okla. U., 1986. With New Directions, Inc., Lawton, 1982—; profl. counselor New Directions, Inc., 1988—; substitute tchr. Lawton Pub. Schs., 1985-88; psychologist, technologist Army Rsch. Inst., Ft. Sill, Okla., 1988—. Vol. counselor Rape Crisis Team Comanche County, 1982—, Dr. Robert Schuller Crystal Cathedral, Garden Grove, Calif., 1983-84. Named Most Outstanding Young Woman of Am., 1985. Fellow Okla. Assn. Counseling and Devel., Nat. Women's Coalition Against Domestic Violence and Sexual Assault, Comanche County Mental Health Assn.; mem. Hospice. Democrat. Office: New Directions Inc 903 F Ave Lawton OK 73501

NOLAN, DIANE AGNES, art director; b. Orange, N.J., Oct. 21, 1939; d. John Dominick and Fannie (Covino) Frisoli; m. Norman Samuel Nolan, Sept. 29, 1962. BFA, Pratt Inst., Bklyn., 1961. Staff artist Gitten Studios, West Orange, N.J., 1961-62; package designer Owens-Ill., Holmdel, N.J., 1962-73; pres. Diane Nolan Design Studio, Middletown, N.J., 1973-80; designer and art dir. Lanmark Group, Tinton Falls, N.J., 1980-85; art dir. Oldhands, Inc., West End, N.J., 1985—, Sci. Models, Inc., Berkeley Heights, N.J., 1986—, MicroMark, Berkeley Heights, N.J., 1986—; research asst. Otto Penzler, author, N.Y.C., 1976; design cons. Automated Data Assocs., Rahway, N.J., 1966-82. One-man shows: United Counties Trust Co., Berkley Heights, N.J., 1982, Guild of Creative Art, Shrewsbury, 1966; group shows include: Arthritis Found., Rumson, 1969, Old Mill Gallery, Tinton Falls, 1967, Newark Mus., N.J., 1962, IBM Gallery, N.Y.C., 1961. Recipient First Place award Middletown (N.J.) Twp. state wide art exhibit, state juried exhibit, 1968; Hon. Mention award, Guild Creative Art, Shrewsbury, N.J., 1973; 2d Pl. award Monmouth County, Middletown, N.J., 1976; named Woman of Yr., Baker St. Irregulars, N.Y.C., 1978. Mem. Internat. Soc. Netsuke Collectors, AAUW, AMA Aux., Mus. Natural History, Jersey Shore Pub. Relations and Advt. Assn. Member of National Association For Female Executives. Republican. Roman Catholic. Club: Mini Tonga Soc. Home: 68 Crest Rd Middletown NJ 07748 Office: Scientific Models Inc 340 Snyder Ave Berkeley Heights NJ 07729

NOLAN, DORIS JOHNSON, investment properties owner/manager; b. Angier, N.C., Mar. 30, 1933; d. Joseph Marion and Mamie (Weeks) Johnson; m. Perry S. SAmuels, Jan. 6, 1954 (div. Jan. 1985); children: Les, Ellen, Brad, Elizabeth; m. John F. Nolan. BBA, U. N.C., Greensboro, N.C., 1952. With CIA, Washington, 1952-54; newspaper advt. exec. Suburban Life, Cin., 1973-84; mgr. bus. & indsl. review Cin. Post, 1984-89; owner, manager Nolan Properties, 1989—. Pres. Riverside Civic Assn., Covington, Ky., 1988-89; trustee Riverwalk Bicentennial Trust Fund, Cin., 1989; bd. dirs. Friends of Covington, 1989; host Internat. Visitors Ctr., Cin., 1989. Named Outstanding Member Women's Crisis Ctr., 1985; recipient Beautification of Blighted Places award City of Covington, 1985. Episcopalian. Home: 322 E 2d St Covington KY 41011 Office: Cincinnati Post 309 Garrard St Covington KY 41011

NOLAN, IRENE CLARE, newspaper editor; b. Bklyn., Oct. 2, 1946; d. Raymond Jerome and Jean Cross (Rodriguez) Clare; divorced; children: Kathleen Ann, James Christopher. BA in Journalism, Ind. U., 1971. News clk., writer The Courier-Journal, Louisville, 1969-71, reporter, 1971-77, asst. features editor, 1977-78, features editor, 1978-79, asst. mng. editor features, 1979-84, asst. mng. editor news, 1985, dep. mng. editor features, 1985-86, dep. mng. editor news, 1986-87, mng. editor, 1987—. Mem. Am. Soc. Newspaper Editors (chair ethics com. 1988, Pulitzer Prize juror 1988-89, vice-chair bulls. com. 1989, chair, 1990-91), AP Mng. Editors Assn. Office: Courier-Jour Co 525 W Broadway Louisville KY 40202

NOLAN, LORENE SUSAN, nurse; b. San Pedro, Calif., Mar. 8, 1958; d. Robert Forrest and Rita (Telesco) N. AA, Harbor Coll., 1978. RN, Calif. Staff nurse, then staff rsch. assoc. Harbor/UCLA Med. Ctr., Torrance, 1978-82; spl. projects nurse Cedars Sinai Med. Ctr., L.A., 1982-86; critical care staff nurse San Pedro (Calif.) Peninsula Hosp., 1980—; clin. cons., EMTEK Health Care Systems, Inc., Tempe, Ariz., 1985-86, clin. applications specialist, 1986—; clin. cons., Oximetrix, Inc., L.A., 1985-86; instr. CPR, L.A. chpt. Am. Heart Assn., 1988—. Contbr. to profl. publs. Mem. IEEE, Soc. Clin. Data Mgmt., Am. Assn. Critical Care Nurses, Soc. Critical Care Medicine, Am. Nurses Assn. Republican. Home: 934 W 13th St #5 San Pedro CA 90731 Office: EMTEK Health Care Systems 2929 S Fair Ln Tempe AZ 85282

NOLAN, LOUISE MARY, school system administrator, author; b. Boston, Sept. 28, 1947; d. John Joseph and Helen (Spiers) N. BA, Regis Coll., 1969; MEd, Boston U., 1971 postgrad., 1981-82; postgrad Fitchburg State Coll., 1972-74, Salem State Coll., 1977-79; Ph.D., Boston Coll., 1986. Counselor Camp Thoreau, Inc., Concord, Mass., 1964-68; tchr., chmn. sci. dept. John F. Kennedy Meml. Jr. High Sch., Woburn, Mass., 1969-86; asst. supt. schs. for curriculum and instrn. Woburn Pub. Schs., 1986—; initiator Woburn-Sci. Specialist Program; co-owner Ruth and Louise Silkscreening, Lexington, Mass., Fancypants, Carlisle, Mass.; bd. dir. ecology program Curry Coll., Milton, Mass., 1977, Mass. Mid. Sch. Sci. Fair Olympics. Author: Y.E.S.-A Comprehensive Guide to Students Educationg Youth in Environmental Sciences; Bioluminescence-An Experimental Guide; Marine Plankton; Heath Physical Science, 1983, 87. Active New Eng. League Mid. Schs., Nat. League Mid. Schs. Vice chmn. Mass. Sci. Fair Com. NSF grantee, 1972-73, 77-79, 81-82; chemistry fellow Boston U., 1983-84; For a Cleaner Environ. grantee, 1984-86. Mem. NEA, AAAS, Mass. Tchrs. Assn., Nat. Assn. Sci. Tchrs., Mass. Assn. Sci. Tchrs., Nat. Assn. Biology Tchrs., Nat. Assn. Rsch. in Sci. Teaching, Middlesex County Tchrs. Assn., Biology Roundtable, Woburn Tchrs. Assn., Mass. Supts. Assn., Beta Beta Beta, Pi Lambda Theta, Mus. Fine Arts Club, Lit. Guild Club, Concord Art Assn. Club, Mus. of Sci. Theatre Guild Club. Democrat. Roman Cathlic. Home: 9 Stevens Rd Lexington MA 02173 Office: Joyce Jr High Sch Adminstrn Offices Locust St Woburn MA 01801

NOLAN, VICTORIA HOLMES, theater director; b. Portland, Maine, June 15, 1952; d. Herbert Wallace and Diane Katharine (Kremm) N.; m. Clarkson Newell Crolius, Aug. 30, 1980; children: Covey Emmeline, Wilhelmina Adams. BA magna cum laude, U. Maine, 1976. Publicity asst. Loeb Drama Ctr. Harvard U., Cambridge, Mass., 1975; pub. rels. asst. to dir. Sch. for Arts Boston U., 1975-76; mgmt. asst. TAG Found., N.Y.C., 1976-77; mng. dir. Ram Island Dance Co., Portland, 1977-78; dir. devel. Ctr. Stage, Balt., 1979-81, assoc. mng. dir., 1981-87; mng. dir. Ind. Repertory Theatre, Indpls., 1988—; cons. Fedn. for Extension and Devel. Am. Profl. Theatre, N.Y.C., 1979-87; program evaluator NEA, Washington, 1988-89. Nat. Performing Arts Mgmt. fellow Exxon, Doner Fedn. and NEA, 1978. Home: 421 Blue Ridge Rd Indianapolis IN 46208 Office: Ind Repertory Theatre 140 W Washington St Indianapolis IN 46208

NOLAND, ANNGINETTE ROBERTS, national sorority executive; b. Stillwater, Okla., Sept. 30, 1930; d. Cecil Andrew and Gladys Leah (Woods) Roberts; m. Thomas Vaughan Noland, June 11, 1949; children: Nanette Noland Crocker, Thomas Vaughan Noland, Bruce Andrew Noland. Student, Okla. State U., 1948-49; cert. in planning, U. Wis. Chpt. advisor Kappa Delta Sorority, Stillwater, 1953-54, Baton Rouge, 1956-59; province pres. Kappa Delta Sorority, Miss., 1970-77; chpt. dir. II Kappa Delta Sorority, 1977-84, nat. dir. scholarship program, 1984-87, past mem. evaluation com., chmn. conv. scholarship banquet com., 1985, chmn. fellowships evaluation com., 1984-87; accounts receivables clk. Sta. WLOX-TV, Biloxi, Miss., 1973-76, sales asst., 1976-82, nat. sales asst. and polit. sales, 1982-84, nat. sales supr., 1984—. Recipient Outstanding Svc. award Sta. WLOX-TV, 1976, Order of the Emerald Kappa Delta Sorority, 1988. Mem. NAFE, DAR (treas. Biloxi chpt. 1983-89, corr. sec. 1989—), S.C. Geneal. Soc. (Old Edgefield chpt.), Okla. Geneal. Soc. (Going Snake dist. chpt.), Colonial Dames XVII Century (corr. sec. local chpt. 1985-87, pres. 1987-89, 2d v.p. 1989—, state chmn. Colonial Heritage Week 1989—), UDC (1st v.p. local chpt. 1990—), Gulf Coast Community Concert Assn., Hibernia Soc., Sons and Daus. Pilgrims, Daus. Am. Colonists, Biloxi Yacht Club (aux. corr. sec. 1986-88, sec. 1989-90). Republican. Episcopalian. Home: 2441 Old Bay Rd Biloxi MS 39531 Office: Sta WLOX-TV PO Box 4596 Biloxi MS 39535-4596

NOLAND, CARA HOLLY, information management consultant, information system design company owner; b. Marietta, Ohio, Dec. 16, 1958; d. Lloyd Henry and Ethel May (Beare) N.; m. Patrick P. Truex, Oct. 22, 1988. Grad., U. Mich., 1981. Programmer, analyst Tenn. Gas Transmissions div. TENNECO, Houston, 1982; analyst CACI, Mechanicsburg, Pa., 1983-86; systems analyst Tidewater Cons., Inc., Arlington, Va., 1986-87; sr. cons. Performance Resources, Inc., Falls Church, Va., 1987-89; owner ICON Info. Concepts in Mgmt., Alexandria, Va., 1989—. Office: 516 Tennessee Ave Alexandria VA 22305

NOLAND, COOKIE KATHERINE, real estate professional; b. San Antonio, Nov. 18, 1944; d. Alfred Gus and Katherine (Banspach) Gaulé; m. Harold Eugene Noland, Apr. 20, 1963; children: Michelle Katherine, Katrina Ann. Student, Tex. Tech. U., 1988. Prin. Cookie K. Noland, Realtor, Lubbock, 1973—. Mem. Friends of Libr., Ballet Lubbock, Lubbock Bd. Realtors, Tex. Assn. Realtors, Nat. Assn. Realtors, Villas Home Assn. Republican. Lutheran. Home: 4918 92d St Lubbock TX 79424 Office: PO Box 53562 Lubbock TX 79453

NOLAND, MARIAM CHARL, foundation executive; b. Parkersburg, W.Va., Mar. 29, 1947; d. Lloyd Henry and Ethel May (Beare) N.; m. James Arthur Kelly, June 13, 1981. BS, Case Western Res. U., 1969; M in Edn., Harvard U., 1975. Asst. dir admissions, fin. aid Baldwin-Wallace Coll., Berea, Ohio, 1969-72; asst. dir. admissions Davidson (N.C.) Coll., 1972-74; case writer Inst. Edn. Mgmt., Cambridge, Mass., 1975; sec., treas., program officer The Cleve. Found., 1975-81; v.p. The St. Paul Found., 1981-85; pres. Community Found. for S.E. Mich., 1985—; vice chair, bd. trustees Coun. of Mich. Founds., Grand Haven, Mich., 1988—. Mem. steering com. Leadership Detroit, 1988—, Metro Detroit Gives, 1988—. Mem. Detroit Com. Fgn. Rels., Detroit Econ. Club. Office: Community Found Southeastern Mich 333 W Fort St Ste 2010 Detroit MI 48226

NOLAND, PATRICIA ANN, state legislator; b. Seattle, Dec. 30, 1945; d. Gordon F. Watson and Ruth A. (Young) Kalbach; m. C. Glenn Noland, Feb. 3, 1973 (div. 1978); m. John S. Bogers, Jan. 23, 1988. Studeht, Ft. Steilacoom Community Coll., 1968-70. Clk., sec. State Wash., Olympia, 1964-67; sec., computer programmer Weyerhaeuser Corp., Tacoma, 1967-70; computer programmer City Tucson, 1970-72; adminstrv. asst. ITT Canon Electric, Santa Ana, Calif., 1972-73; city clk. City Casa Grande, Ariz., 1973-76; town mgr. Town Oro (Ariz.) Valley, 1979-83; v.p. HDC, Inc., Tucson, 1983-86; owner Patricia Noland Cons., Tucson, 1983—; state legislator Ariz. Ho. of Reps., Phoenix, 1989—. Pres. Tucson Classics, Inc., 1981-84, Pima County Rep. Club, 1977-78; pres., bd. dirs. Tucson Resident Found., 1978-86; chmn., mem. gov.'s coun. Devel. Disabilities, Phoenix, 1982-85; mem. Pima County Bond Adv. Coun., Tucson, 1978-85. Mem. So. Ariz. Homebuilders (bd. dirs. 1987-89, Assoc. of Yr. 1987), Ariz. Planning Assn., Ariz. Order Women Legislators, Nat. Order Women Legislators. Home: PO Box 30042 Tucson AZ 85751 Office: Ariz Ho of Reps 1700 W Washington Phoenix AZ 85007

NOLDER, SHARLENE J., engineering technician; b. Olean, N.Y., Nov. 21, 1949; d. Arthur J. and Una M. (Mitchell) N. AAS, Monroe Community Coll., 1976; postgrad. in indsl. tech., SUNY, Binghamton, 1982—. Asst. to the office engr. Greenman-Pedersen Assocs. PC, Dansville, N.Y., 1977; engring. technician N.Y. State Dept. Transp., Rochester, N.Y., 1977-78; hwy. constrn. inspector SSV and K, Rochester, 1978-79; engring. technician Columbia Gas of N.Y., Inc., Binghamton, 1980—. Co-chair spl. events and projects Sta. WSKG Pub. TV, 1989. Mem. IMC (v.p.), NAFE. Home: PO Box 1720 267 Court St Binghamton NY 13902

NOLES, SHARON REBECCA, salon owner, hairstylist, consultant, speaker; b. San Diego, Apr. 3, 1946; d. Ernest H. and Maye (Eversole) Martin; 1 child, Steven Scott. Prin. Noles Hair Co., Duncanville, Tex., 1979—; owner, cons. New Image Concepts, Duncanville, 1988—; presenter seminars. Mem. Nat. Speakers Assn., North Tex. Speakers Assn., Am. Hairdressers Assn. Office: 223 N Cedar Ridge St Dencanville TX 75116

NOLES, TAMMY GAYE, writer; b. Fairfield, Calif., Oct. 11, 1965; d. Ellen LaVon (Aldridge) N. AS, Northlake Coll., Irving, Tex., 1986; BA, U. North Tex., Denton, 1989. Intern Las Colinas Weekly, Irving, 1988; freelance reporter Irving Community TV Network, 1987—; staff writer, news editor Las Colinas People newspaper, Irving. Mem. NAFE, Alpha Epsilon Rho. Baptist.

NOLL, MARY LOU, instructor, consultant, nurse; b. Martins Ferry, Ohio, Sept. 29, 1954; d. Edward Noll and Margaret Regina (Falkenstein) Ferda. Diploma in nursing, Ohio VAlley Gen. Hosp., 1975; BSN, Ohio U., 1977; MSN, Ohio State U., 1979; PhD, U. Tex., 1987. Staff nurse Ohio Valley Med. Ctr., Wheeling, W.Va., 1975-77; instr. Sch. Nursing Ohio Valley Gen. Hosp., Wheeling, 1977-80, chmn. sr. level Sch. Nursing, 1980-83; clin. specialist Santa Rosa Med. Ctr., San Antonio, 1983-88; instr. Sch. Nursing U. Tex. Health Sci. Ctr., San Antonio, 1986—. Mem. editorial bd.: Clin. Issues in Critical Care Jour., 1989—; contbr. articles to profl. jours. Mem. Am. Assn. Critical Care Nurses, Am. Nurses Assn., Nat. League Nursing, Phi Kappa Phi, Sigma Theta Tau. Office: U Tex Health Sci Ctr 7703 Floyd Curl Dr San Antonio TX 78284

NOLT, SALLY KULP, educator, educational consultant; b. Lancaster, Pa., Apr. 11, 1946; d. Harold E. and Dorothy (Newcomer) Kulp; m. Christian B. Nolt, June 1, 1968 (div. Feb. 1983); children: Kelly, Kristi. BS in Elem. Edn., West Chester U., 1968; MS in Elem. Edn., Millersville U., 1971, reading cert., 1974; postgrad. in edn., Temple U., 1984—. Cert. elem., spl. edn. for physically handicapped tchr., reading specialist, Pa. Tchr. Manheim (Pa.) Cen. Sch. Dist., 1968—, mem. parent adv. com., 1975—, mem. curriculum coun., 1986-89; clk.-typist Three Mile Island, Middletown, Pa., summers 1979-81; ednl. cons. Sec. Elizabethtown (Pa.) Bd. Health, 1980—; bd. dirs. Lancaster County Coun. on Alcohol and Drug Abuse, 1982-85; charter sec. Greater Elizabethtown Dem. Club, 1970-74; sec., v.p., pres. Elizabethtown Jayceettes, 1972-78; sec., bd. dirs. Eliabethtown Fair, 1985—. Mem. NEA, Assn. for Supervision and Curriculum Devel., Pa. State Edn. Assn., Manheim City Edn. Assn., Lancaster-Lebanon Reading Assn., Keystone Reading Assn., Elizabethtown Area Grange (v.p. 1988-90). Home: 25 Iris Circle Elizabethtown PA 17022

NOONAN, JACQUELINE ANNE, pediatrics educator; b. Burlington, Vt., Oct. 28, 1928. BA, Albertus Magnus Coll., 1950; MD, U. Vt., 1954, DSc (hon.), 1980. Diplomate Am. Bd. Pediatrics, Am. Bd. Pediatric Cardiology. Intern N.C. Meml. Hosp., Chapel Hill, 1954-55; resident in pediatrics Children's Hosp., Cin., 1955-57; rsch. fellow Children's Med. Ctr., Boston, 1957-59; asst. prof. pediatrics State U. Iowa Sch. Medicine, 1959-61; asst. prof. pediatrics cardiology U. Ky. Coll. Medicine, Lexington, 1961-64, assoc. prof., 1964-69, prof., 1969—, chmn. dept. pediatrics, 1974—; mem. embryology and human devel. study sect. NIH, 1973-78; mem. U.S.-USSR Symposium on Congenital Heart Disease, 1975; mem. sub-bd. pediatric cardiology Am. Bd. Pediatrics, 1977-82; examiner Nat. Bd. Med. Examiners, 1982—; participant various confs. in field; vis. prof. Vanderbilt U., Nashville, 1987; speaker in field. Contbr. articles, revs. to med. publs.; mem. editorial Am. Jour. Diseases Children, 1970-80, Am. Jour. Med. Edn., 1975-78, Pediatric Cardiology, 1978—. Recipient Helen B. Fraser award, 1975. Mem. Am. Acad. Pediatrics (cardiology sect. chmn. 1972-74), Am. Coll. Cardiology (gov. Ky. 1989—), Am. Fedn. Clin. Rsch., AMA, Assn. Med. Sch. Pediatric Dept. Chmn. (exec. com. 1978-81), Fayette County Med. Soc., Irish-Am. Pediatric Soc., Ky. State Med. Assn., NIH Alumni Assn., Soc. Pediatric Rsch., So. Soc. Pediatric Rsch. (pres. 1972). Office: U Ky Med Ctr Pediatrics 800 Rose St Lexington KY 40536

NOONAN, MELINDA DUNHAM, nurse, educator; b. Peoria, Ill., Feb. 19, 1954; d. Emmett Maxwell Dunham and Dixie Maurine (DeCounter) Widner; m. Robert Joseph Noonan; children: Alissa, Meris. Diploma, Ravenswood Hosp. Sch. Nursing, 1977; BSN cum laude, U. Ill., Chgo., 1989. Med. asst. James J. Hines, M.D., S.C., Chgo., 1973-76; staff nurse Northwestern Meml. Hosp., Chgo., 1978-79, asst. head nurse, 1979-80, staff nurse, 1980-83, parent educator, 1983—; founder, bd. dirs. Mothers Organized for Mutual Support, Chgo, 1981-89; creator, coordinator Beyond The Birth Experience Program, Chgo., 1983—; coord. Health Learning Ctr. Northwestern Meml. Hosp., 1989—. Contbg. author: Drugs, Alcohol, Pregnancy and Parenting, 1988. Bd. dirs. Mothers Organized for Mut. Support, 1981-88. Mem. Family Resource Coalition, Nurses Assn. of Am. Coll. Ob-Gyn, Internat. Childbirth Edn. Assn. Democrat. Roman Catholic. Lodge: Rebekah (v. grand 1981-82, noble grand 1982-83). Home: 3414 W Glenlake Chicago IL 60659 Office: Northwestern Meml Hosp Health Learning Ctr Ste 467 Prentice Chicago IL 60611

NORA, AUDREY HART, physician; b. Picayune, Miss., Dec. 5, 1936; d. Allen Joshua and Vera Lee (Ballard) H.; m. James Jackson Nora, Apr. 9, 1966; children: James Jackson Jr., Elizabeth Hart. BS, U. Miss., 1958, MD, 1961; MPH, U. Calif., 1978. Diplomate Am. Bd. Pediatrics, Am. Bd. Hematology and Oncology. Resident in pediatrics U. Wis. Hosp., Madison, 1961-64; fellow in hematology/oncology Baylor U., Tex. Childrens Hosp., Houston, 1964-66, asst. prof. pediatrics, 1966-70; assoc. clin. prof. pediatrics U. Colo. Sch. Medicine, Denver, 1970—; dir. genetics Denver Childrens Hosp., 1970-78; cons. maternal and child health USPHS, Denver, 1978-83, asst. surgeon gen. regional health adminstr., 1983—; commd. med. officer USPHS, 1978, advanced through grades to asst. surgeon gen., 1983; adv. com. NIH, Bethesda, 1975-77; adv. bd. Metronet Health, Inc., Denver, 1986—, Colo. Assn. Commerce and Industry, Denver, 1985—. Author: (with J.J. Nora) Genetics and Counseling in Cardiovascular Diseases, 1978, (with others) Blakiston's Medical Dictionary, 1980, Birth Defects Encyclopedia, 1990; contbr. articles to profl. jours. Recipient Virginia Apgar award Nat. Found., 1976. Fellow Am. Acad. Pediatrics; mem. Am. Pub. Health Assn. (governing coun. 1990—, coun. mem. maternal and child health 1990—), Commd. Officers Assn., Am. Soc. Human Genetics, Teratology Soc., Western Soc. Pediatric Rsch. Presbyterian. Office: USPHS 1961 Stout St Denver CO 80294

NORA, HOPE, health facility administrator; b. Laredo, Tex., June 4, 1949; d. Felix C. and Esperanza (Coronado) Rocha; m. Amaury Nora, June 19, 1971; children: Amaury E., Araceli E. BS, U. Houston, 1971; MS, Tex. A&I U., 1972; PhD, U. Houston, 1986. Staff psychologist, counselor Tex. Commn. for Vocat. Rehabv., Laredo, Tex., 1973-78; dir. programs Laredo State Ctr. for Human Devel., 1978-82; dir. clin. programming Los Encinas Hosp., Pasadena, Calif., 1987-89; dir. clin./support svcs. Woodland Hosp., Hoffman Estates, Ill., 1989—. Mem. Am. Psychol. Assn. (cert.). Democrat. Home: 2841 Farmington Rd Northbrook IL 60062 Office: Woodland Hosp 1650 Moonlake Blvd Hoffman Estates IL 60194

NORBERG, ANN DEE HODAK, educator; b. L.A., Sept. 19, 1944; d. Bart Nicholas and Anna Rose (Derigo) Hodak; m. Gary William Norberg; 1 child, Monet Annique. Student, Long Beach City Coll., 1964; BA, Calif. State Coll., Long Beach, 1968; postgrad., Chapman Coll., Orange, Calif., 1974-76; postgrad. in English/Comparative Lit., U. Calif., Irvine. Cert. tchr., Calif. TV actress Honolulu, 1968-70; model Vogue Modeling Agy., Long Beach, 1969-72; master tchr., art rep. Anaheim (Calif.) Elem. Sch. Dist., 1972-79; tchr., art curriculum design coord. Big Pine (Calif.) Sch. Dist., 1980-82; tchr., personnel interviewer Bishop (Calif.) Union Sch. Dist., 1982—; master tchr., Chapman Coll., U. Calif.-Irvine, Calif. State Coll., Fullerton and Long Beach, 1973-76; mem. adminstrv. law panel for incompetent tchrs. Santa Ana Sch. Dist., 1973-76. Profl. vocalist Madrigal Choral Group, 1962-64, New Troubador Singers, 1962-65. Mem. NEA, Calif. Tchrs. Assn., Bishop Edn. Assn., Calif. Elem. Edn. Assn. Republican. Presbyterian. Office: Bishop Union Sch Dist 800 W Pine St Bishop CA 93514

NORCEL, JACQUELINE JOYCE CASALE, educational administrator; b. Bklyn., Nov. 19, 1940; d. Frederick and Josephine Jeanette (Bestafka) Casale; m. Edward John Norcel, Feb. 24, 1962. BS, Fordham U., 1961; MS, Bklyn. Coll., 1966; 6th yr. cert. So. Conn. State U., 1980; postgrad. Bridgeport U. Elem. tchr., pub. schs., N.Y.C., 1961-80; prin. Coventry Schs., Conn., 1980-84, Trumbull Schs., Conn., 1984—; guest lectr. So. Conn. State U., 1980—; cons. Monson Schs., Mass., 1984; mem. adj. faculty Sacred Heart U., Fairfield, Conn., 1985—. Editor: Best of the Decade, 1980. Contbr. articles to profl. jours. Chmn. bldg. com. Trumbull Bd. Edn., 1978-80; chmn. Sch. Benefit Com., Trumbull, 1985-86; catechist Bridgeport Diocese, Roman Cath. Ch., Conn., 1975-85, youth minister, 1979—, coordinator, evaluator leadership tng. workshops for teens and adults, 1979-84. Recipient Town of Trumbull Service award, 1982, Nat. Disting. Prin. award, 1988. Mem. N.E. Regional Elem. Prins. Assn. (rep. 1984-86, sec. 1986-87), Elem. Middle Sch. Prins. Assn. (pres. 1985-86, Pres.'s award 1981-85), Adminstrn. and Supervision Assn. (sec. 1980-81, pres. 1981-82, exec. bd. 1982-83), Hartford Area Prins. and Suprs. Assn. (local pres. 1981-82), Nat. Assn. Elem. Sch. Prins. (zone I dir. 1987-90, Conn. State Prin. Acad. Adv. Bd. 1986-88, del. to gen. assemblies 1984-88, bd. dirs. 1987—), Assn. Supervision and Curriculum Devel., Conn. Assn. Supervision and Curriculum Devel., Trumbull Adminstrs. Assn. (pres.-elect 1989—), Eastern Conn. Council of Internat. Reading Assn., New Eng. Coalition Ednl. Leaders, Associated Tchrs. of Math. in Conn., Phi Delta Kappa, Pi Lambda Theta (Beta Sigma chpt.), Delta Kappa Gamma. Republican. Home: 5240 Madison Ave Trumbull CT 06611 Office: Tashua Sch 401 Stonehouse Rd Trumbull CT 06611

NORDHAGEN, HALLIE HUERTH, nursing home administrator; b. Sarona, Wis., Apr. 2, 1914; d. Mathias James and Ethel Elizabeth (Fann) Huerth; B.Ed., U. Wis., Superior, 1938, M.A., 1949; m. Carl E. Nordhagen, May 24, 1947; children—Bruce Carl, Brian Keith. Prin., tchr. Wis. Public Schs., 1932-46; supervising tchr. Wis. Community Coll., 1946-48; psychiat. adminstr. Trempealeau County Health Care Center, psychiat. nursing home, Whitehall, Wis., 1959—; mem. Wis. Nursing Home Adminstrs. Examining Bd.; fellow Menninger Clinic, Topeka, 1979-81. Chairperson BRAD Assn./Acohol & Drug Abuse, mem. Trempealeau County Alliance Drug Free Youth. Recipient Disting. Service award in edn. and hosp. adminstrn., London, 1967, award for services to human services programs Wis. Assn. Human Services, 1972, award for outstanding services to exceptional children Assn. Retarded Children, 1978, award for accomplishments in human resources Trempealeau County Conservation Service, 1981; Wis. State Senate citation, 1983; citatioin Wis. Gov., 1984. Mem. Wis. Assn. County Homes, Wis. Edn. Assn., Wis. Assn. Human Services Programs, Internat. Platform Assn., Am. Lutheran Ch. Women. Clubs: Whitehall Country, Women's. Author: Wisconsin Indians, 1966. Home: 2220 Claire St Whitehall WI 54773

NORDIN, PHYLLIS ECK, sculptor, designer, consultant; b. Chgo. Student Beloit Coll., Wayne State U.; B.S., U. Toledo, 1963, B.A. cum laude, 1972; postgrad. Sch. Design, Toledo Mus. Art. Design and art cons. various builders, chs., businesses and individuals, 1972—; instr. Lourdes Coll. Sylvania, Ohio, 1986—, U. Toledo, 1986—. Prin. works include large bronze sculptures Lucas County Main Library, Toledo, Christ figure St. Joan of Arc Ch., Maumee, Ohio, Ronald McDonald House, Toledo, First English Evangel. Luth. Ch., Grosse Pointe Woods, Mich., Christ Presbyn. Ch., Covenant Presbyn. Ch., Toledo, Toledo Hosp., Reynolds Br. Library, Toledo, stone wall mural Epworth United Methodist Ch., Toledo, Beloit Coll., Wis., bronze fountain U. Toledo, bronze life-size children Treasure Coast Mall, Stuart, Fla., welded steel sculpture Town Ctr. Mall, Port Charlotte, Fla., Carey (Ohio) Bank, Toledo Bank, Bi-Centennial Park, Toledo, wood wall carvings 1st Meth. Ch., LaGrange, Ill., ferro-cement abstract Flower Hosp., Sylvania, Ohio; numerous others; exhibited Allied Artists Am., Salmagundi Club, Audubon artists, N.Am. Sculpture exhibit; numerous others. Represented by Collectors Corner Toledo Mus. Art, 1970—. Recipient Alpha award Foothills Art Ctr., 1983, 1st prize Ann. Nat. Art Exhbn., 1978, also numerous others. Mem. Arts Commn. Greater Toledo, Toledo Design Rev. Bd., Nat. Assn. Women Artists, Interfaith Forum Religion Art Architecture, Ohio Designer Craftsmen, Ohio Liturgical Art Guild, Toledo Modern Art Group (trustee 1982-87), Catharine Lorillard Wolfe Art Club, Phi Kappa Phi (hon.). Home and Studio: 4035 Tantara Rd Toledo OH 43623

NORDMANN, NANCY OLIVIA, educational services administrator; b. Atlanta, June 5, 1945; d. Robert Foster Jr. and Leila (Howard) House; m. Gary Arnold Nordmann, June 9, 1966 (div. 1982); 1 child Leila Olivia. BS in Edn. cum laude, U. Ga., 1966; MA, U. Chgo., 1974. Instr. U. Chgo., 1974-75, Roosevelt U., Chgo., 1975; extraordinary services provider children psychiat. unit Michael Reese Hosp., Chgo., 1978-80; therapeutic interventional specialist Children's Day Hosp., Rush-Presbyn. St. Luke's Med. Ctr., Chgo., 1980-81; ednl. dir. Children and Family Services Shelter, Chgo., 1981-83; diagnostic resource specialist Chgo. Bd. Edn., 1983-89, resource specialist, 1989—; rec. sec. Bur. Spl. Needs, Chgo., 1985-86; bd. dirs. Spl. Needs Adv. Council, 1985-86, sec. 1986-87. Active local arrangements com. Council for Exceptional Children, Spl. Arts Festival com., Jr. League Chgo.; vice-chmn. mgmt. assistance to nonprofit orgns. Support Ctr., 1985-86; sec. bd. dirs. Lincoln Park Plaza Assn., 1985-88, pres. bd. dirs., 1989—; program chmn. Shakespeare Repertory, 1990—; mem. parents coun. Latin Sch. Chgo., Jr. League of Chgo. USPHS fellow, 1972-73, 1973-74, U. Chgo. fellow, 1981-82; Ill. Dept. Mental Health and Devel. Disabilities grantee, 1981. Mem. NAFE, PEN. Clubs: Women's Athletic, Mill Creek Hunt (Lake Forest, Ill.), Racquet of Chgo. Home: 1926 N Mohawk St Chicago IL 60614

NORDMEYER, MARY BETSY, educator; b. New Haven, May 19, 1939; d. George and Barbara Stedman (Thompson) N. ABPhil, Wheaton Coll., Norton, Mass., 1960; MA, San Jose State U., 1968; AS in Computer Sci., West Valley Coll., 1985. Cert. tchr. spl. edn., Calif.; cert. secondary tchr., Calif. Instr. English Santa Clara (Calif.) Unified Sch. Dist., 1965-77, vocat. specialist, 1977—, dir. project work ability, 1984—, also mem. community adv. com.; facilitator Project Work-Ability, Region 5, 1985-86, sec., 1988-90. Author poetry, 1960, Career and Vocat. Edn. for Students With Spl. Needs, 1986; author/designer Career English, 1974, Career Information, 1975. Recipient Outstanding Secondary Educator award, 1975, Award of Excellence, Nat. Assn. Vocat. Edn., 1984; named Tchr. of Yr. in Spl. Edn., Santa Clara Unified Sch. Dist., 1984-85. Mem. Calif. Assn. Work Experience Educators, Sierra Club, Epsilon Eta Sigma. Democrat. Home: 14920 Sobey Rd Saratoga CA 95070 Office: Santa Clara Unified Sch Dist 1889 Lawrence Rd Santa Clara CA 95052

NORDSTROM, MARY SUSAN, secondary and adult educator; b. Grand Rapids, Mich., July 5, 1952; d. Fredrik Gustaf and June Maxine (Upton) N.; m. June 24, 1978 (div. Jan. 1983). BA, U. Mich., 1972-74, postgrad., 1979. Cert. secondary educator. Community aide Grand Rapids (Mich.) Pub. Schs. Continuing Edn., 1975, tchr., 1975-84, acad. advisor, 1984—. Editor Homebound Adult Student newspaper, 1983-84. Vol. Grand Rapids Pub. Schs. Millage Campaigns, Career Expo, Grand Rapids, 1988, Greater Grand Rapids Charity Golf Classic, 1983-89; mem. Blodgett Hosp. Ronald Yaw Guild, E. Grand Rapids, 1986-87. Mem. NEA, Mich. Ednl. Assn., Mich. Assn. Acad. Advisors for Community Edn. (chairperson membership 1987—. Home: 1108 Paradise Lake Dr SE Grand Rapids MI 49546 Office: Ottawa Community Edn 2055 Rosewood SE Grand Rapids MI 49506

NORDYKE, CHARLOTTA FINCHER, business development consultant; b. Shreveport, La., June 24, 1953; d. Amzie Evans and Doris Eva (Wilson) Fincher. BA, N.E. La. U., 1975, MBA, 1979. Speech therapist Bossier Parish Sch. Bd., Benton, La., 1975-77; admissions counselor N.E. La. U., Monroe, 1977-78, grad. asst., 1978-79; material planner AT&T Consumer Products (formerly Western Electric), Shreveport, 1980-81; mktg. rep IBM Corp., Shreveport, 1982-85; dir. Small Bus. Devel. Ctr. La. State U., Shreveport, 1985—. Chmn. Tng. and Edn. Needs Taskforce of Greater Shreveport Econ. Devel. Found., 1988, Govt. Procurement Initiative of Econ. Devel. Taskforce, 1989; mem. adminstrv. bd. First United Meth. Ch., 1988-90, La. Indsl. Devel. Execs. Assn., So. Indsl. Devel. Coun. Mem. River Cities Network Club (pres. 1990), Rotary. Republican. Home: 119 Fountainbleu Shreveport LA 71115 Office: La State U Small Bus Devel Ctr 1 University Pl Shreveport LA 71115

NORDYKE, ELEANOR COLE, population researcher, public health nurse; b. Los Angeles, June 15, 1927; d. Ralph G. and Louise Noble (Carter) Cole; m. Robert Allan Nordyke, June 18, 1950; children: Mary Ellen Nordyke-Grace, Carolyn Nordyke Cozzette, Thomas A., Susan E., Gretchen C. BS, Stanford U., 1950; P.H.N. accreditation, U. Calif.-Berkeley, 1952; MPH, U. Hawaii, 1969. RN. Pub. health nurse San Francisco Dept. Health, 1950-52; nurse-tchr. Punahou Sch., Honolulu, 1966-67; clinic coordinator East-West Population Inst., East-West Ctr., Honolulu, 1969-75, population researcher, 1975-82, research fellow, 1982—; cons. Hawaii Commn. on Population, Honolulu, 1970-83; mem. Hawaii Policy Action Group for Family Planning, Honolulu, 1971-89, chmn., 1976-77. Author: The Peopling of Hawaii, 1977, 2d rev. edit., 1989, A Profile of Hawaii's Elderly Population, 1984, (with Robert Gardner) The Demographic Situation in Hawaii, 1974, mem. editorial bd. Hawaiian Jour. History, 1980—; contbr. articles to profl. jours. Bd. dirs. YMCA Central, Honolulu, 1970—; vice chmn. bd., 1978-79, chmn. Camp Erdman, 1989—; bd. dirs. Hawaii Planned Parenthood, Honolulu, 1974-78, Friends of Library of Hawaii, 1985-87, Hawaii Pacific U., 1988—, mem. adv. coun.; trustee Hawaiian Hist. Soc., 1978-82; trustee Arcadia Retirement Residence, Honolulu, 1978-87. Mem. Population Assn. Am., Population Reference Bur., Hawaii Pub. Health Assn., Am. Statis. Assn., Hawaii Econ. Assn., Hawaiian Hist. Soc., Stanford Nurses Alumni Assn., Phi Beta Kappa. Democrat. Congregationalist. Clubs: Stanford of Hawaii, Gen. Fed. Women's History (Honolulu). Home: 2013 Kakela Dr Honolulu HI 96822 Office: Population Inst East-West Ctr 1777 East-West Rd Honolulu HI 96848

NOREIKA, SOFIA, real estate broker, owner; b. Naples, Italy, Aug. 20, 1945; d. Antonio and Anna (Gambardella) DeFelice; m. Peter Charles Noreika, Apr. 29, 1972; children: Timothy J., Steven P. Student, Greater Hartford Community Coll., 1970-71; real estate sales lic., U. Conn., 1980, diploma in real estate appraisal, 1985; diploma in real estate finance, 1988. Hostess Holiday Season Restaurant, Waterbury, Conn., 1974-79; owner Sofia Tops Plus, Woodbury, Conn., 1979-84; realtor RE/MAX Properties Unltd., Southbury, Conn., 1984—; owner Re/MAX Action Realty, Watertown, Conn., 1988—; land developer, Watertown, 1987. Den mother Boy Scouts Am., Bethlehem, Conn., 1980-83; vol. Bethlehem Elem. Sch., 1980-85; fund raiser Little League Baseball, Bethlehem, 1983-85, United Way, 1989; sponsor Greater Watertown 1989. Mem. Waterbury Bd. Realtors, Nat. Assn. Realtors, Conn. Assn. Realtors, Multiple Listing Svc., RE/MAX Hundred Percent Club, RE/MAX Internat. Referral Network. Republican. Roman Catholic. Home: 132 Carriage Dr Middlebury CT 06762 Office: RE/MAX Action Realty 1044 Main St Watertown CT 06795

NOREK, FRANCES THERESE, lawyer; b. Chgo., Mar. 9, 1947; d. Michael S. and Viola C. (Harbecke) N.; m. John E. Flavin, Aug. 31, 1968 (div.); 1 child, John Michael. B.A., Loyola U., Chgo., 1969, J.D., 1973. Bar: Ill. 1973, U.S. Dist. Ct. (no. dist.) Ill. 1973, U.S. Ct. Appeals (7th cir.) 1974. Assoc. Alter, Weiss, Whitesel & Laff, Chgo., 1973-74; asst. states atty. Cook County, Chgo., 1974-86; assoc. Clausen, Miller, Gorman, Caffrey & Witous P.C., 1986—; mem. trial practice faculty Loyola U. Sch. Law, Chgo., 1980—; judge, evaluator mock trial competitions, Chgo., 1978—; lectr. in field. Recipient Emil Gumpert award Am. Coll. Trial Lawyers, 1982. Mem. Chgo. Bar Assn. (instr. fed. trial bar adv. program young lawyer's sect. 1983-84). Office: Clausen Miller Gorman Caffrey & Witous PC 10 S LaSalle St Chicago IL 60603

NORELLI, PATRICIA ANN, educator; b. McKeesport, Pa., July 13, 1941; d. Patrick and Lillian (Colaizzi) N. B.A., Clark U., 1963, M.A., 1964. Tchr. English, asst. program supr. Stoneham High Sch., Mass., 1966—. Named Horace Mann Tchr. of the Yr., 1986-88. Mem. Stoneham Tchrs. Assn., Mass. Tchrs. Assn., NEA, Nat. Coun.Tchrs. English, Mensa. Roman Catholic. Avocations: gardening, running. Home: 3 Harrison St Stoneham MA 02180

NOREM, BONNIE LOU, electronics executive; b. Columbus, Ohio, July 4, 1936; d. William Paul Atwood and Lena Bell (Coey) Wolford; m. David Marlowe Norem, Mar. 20, 1965; children: Kimberlie, Mark, Chris, Jon. Student, Capital U., 1954-55, Ohio State U., 1955-58, Am. U., 1963-64; BS in Psychology, George Mason U., 1978. Sr. systems programmer Gen. Electric, Bethesda, Md., 1961-65, Arlington, Va., 1975-79; project leader Inco., Inc., McLean, Va., 1979-81; prin. engr. H.R.B. Singer Inc., Lanham, Md., 1981-83; sr. systems analyst Ultra Systems, Inc., Hanover, Md., 1983-86; pres. MAI Enterprises, Inc., Annandale, Va., 1986—. Pres. Bethlehem Women's Orgn., Fairfax, Va.; treas. Bethlehem Luth. Ch., Fairfax; capt. For Intermediate Sympathetic Help, Fairfax Organization Christian Jewish United in Svc. Mem. IEEE, Assn. Study of Dreams (mem. chmn. 1986-87), ACM, No. Va. Minority Bus. and Profl. Assn. (bd. dirs. 1990), Mem. D.C. Dream Community, Washington Dream Group (co-chmn. 1986). Republican. Home: 6612 Spring Valley Dr Alexandria VA 22312

NORFLEET, BARBARA CHAPMAN, educator; b. San Francisco, Sept. 27, 1943; d. Thomas Jefferson and Ann (Troya) Chapman; m. Nat M. Norfleet, June 25, 1962 (div. Apr. 1976); children: Tracie, N. Mark. BA, U. Hawaii, 1969, MA, 1971. Lectr. U. Hawaii, Honolulu, 1979—; seminar leader various Japanese Univ.'s, Honolulu, 1986—; instr. Kapiolani Community Coll., Leeward Community Coll., Coll. Continuing Edn. and Community Svc. Performer, storyteller folklore, creative and comtemporary. Pres. Jr. League of Honolulu, 1975. Mem. Storytelling Assn. of Hawaii (bd. dirs.), U. Hawaii Profl. Assembly, Outrigger Canoe Club. Home: 1612 Wilhelmina Rise Honolulu HI 96816 Office: Dept Speech U Hawaii Manoa George Hall 318 Honolulu HI 96822

NORFLEET, FRANCESCA MARIA, water heater manufacturing company official; b. Patuxent River, Md., Feb. 19, 1953; d. William Francis and Olive June (Holiman) King; m. Rickey Alan Norfleet, July 24, 1975; children: Randall Alan, Robyn Leigh. BS in Chemistry, U. Colo., 1975. Lab. technician Quaker Oats Co., Pascagoula, Miss., 1973, 74, Ralston-Purina Co., Denver, 1973-75; asst. quality mgr. Napko Paint Co., Houston, 1976-78; lab. technician State Industries, Inc., Ashland City, Tenn., 1982-85, customer svc. rep., 1985-87, asst. to v.p. sales Apollo Hydroheat and Cooling div., 1987—. Pres. Rosary Guild, Nashville, 1986-87; v.p. Parish Coun., Ashland City, 1987-88. Mem. NAFE, DAR, Al-Anon. Democrat. Office: Apollo Hydroheat & Cooling Cumberland St Ashland City TN 37015

NORKIN, CYNTHIA CLAIR, physical therapist; b. Boston, May 6, 1932; d. Miles Nelson and Carolyn (Green) Clair; m. Stanislav A. Norkin, Feb. 19, 1955 (dec. 1970); 1 child, Alexandra. BS in Edn., Tufts U., 1954; cert. phys. therapy Bouve Boston Coll., 1954; MS, Boston U., 1973, EdD, 1984. Instr. Bouve-Boston Coll., 1954-55; staff phys. therapist New Eng. Med. Center, Boston, 1954-55; staff phys. therapist Abington Meml. Hosp., Abington, Pa., 1965-70, Eastern Montgomery County Vis. Nurse Assn., 1970-72; asst. prof. phys. therapy Sargent Coll., Boston U., 1973-84; assoc. prof. phys. therapy, dir. Sch. Phys. Therapy, Ohio U., Athens, 1984—; cons. Boston Center Ind. Living, Cambridge Vis. Nurse Assn., Mass. Medicaid Cost Effectiveness Project, 1978; sec. Health Planning Council Greater Boston, 1976-78; book, manuscript reviewer F.A. Davis Co., 1986—. Trustee Brimmer and May Sch., 1980. Mem. AAAS, Am. Phys. Therapy Assn. (on site evaluator commn. on accreditation 1986—), Mass. Phys. Therapy Assn. (chmn. Mass. quality assurance com. 1980-83), Am. Public Health Assn., Mass. Assn. Mental Health, Athens County Vi. Nurse Assn. (sec. adv. council 1984—). Episcopalian. Author: (with others) Joint Structure and Function: A Comprehensive Analysis, 1983; (with D.J. White) Joint Measurement: A Guide to Goniometry, 1985.

NORLAND, CHERYL M., management consultant; b. Freeport, N.Y., Aug. 22, 1950; d. Stuart A. and Lora J. (Wilken) Maclachlan; m. Eric A. Norland, Nov. 21, 1971; children: Edward, Martin. BS, Ill. Inst. Tech., 1972. Project dir. J. Ross Assocs., Cranbury, N.J., 1976-78; office mgr. Michael Burns AIA, Princeton, N.J., 1985-87; prin. CMN Assocs., Cranbury, 1987—. Bd. dirs. Cranbury Housing Assocs., 1984—, treas., 1985—. Mem. SAA, NAFE, Am. Mgmt. Assn. Home: 55 S Main St Cranbury NJ 08512 Office: PO Box 50 Cranbury NJ 08512

NORMAN, JESSYE, soprano; b. Augusta, Ga., Sept. 15, 1945; d. Silas Sr. and Janie (King) N. B.M. cum laude, Howard U., 1967; postgrad., Peabody Conservatory, 1967; M.Mus., U. Mich., 1968; MusD (hon.), U. South, 1984, Boston Conservatory, 1984, U. Mich., 1987, U. Edinburgh, 1989, Cambridge U., 1989. Debut, Deutsche Oper, Berlin, 1969, Italy, 1970; appeared: in operas Die Walküre, Idomeneo, L'Africaine, Marriage of Figaro, Aida, Don Giovanni, Tannhauser, Gotterdammerung, Ariadne auf Naxos, Les Troyens, Dido and Aeneas, Oedipus Rex, Hérodiade, Les Contes d'Hoffmann; debut in operas, La Scala, Milan, Italy, 1972, Salzburg Festival, 1977, U.S. debut, Hollywood Bowl, 1972, appeared with, Tanglewood Festival, Mass., also Edinburgh (Scotland) Festival, debut, Covent Garden, 1972; appeared in 1st Great Performers recital, Lincoln Center, N.Y.C., 1973—; other guest performances include, Los Angeles Philharm. Orch., Boston Symphony Orch., Am. Symphony Orch., Chgo. Symphony Orch., San Francisco Symphony Orch., Cleve. Orch., Detroit Symphony, N.Y. Philharm. Orch., London Symphony Orch., London Philharm. Orch., BBC Orch., Israel Philharm. Orch., Orchestre de Paris, Nat. Symphony Orch., English Chamber Orch., Royal Philharm., London Phila. Orch., Milw. Symphony Orch., Stockholm Philharm. Orch., Vienna Philharm. Orch., Berlin Philharm. Orch.; tours, Europe, S. Am., Australia, numerous recs., Columbia, EMI, Philips Records. Recipient 1st prize Bavarian Radio Corp. Internat. Music Competition, 1968, Grand Prix du Disque, Acad. du Disque Francais, 1973, 76, 77, 82, 84, Deutsche Schallplatten, Preis, 1975, 81, Alumni award U. Mich., 1982, Outstanding Musician of Yr. award Musical Am., 1982, Grand Prix du Disque Academie Charles Cros, 1983, Commandeur de l'Ordre des Arts et des Lettres, France, 1984, Grammy awards, 1980, 82, 85, numerous other awards; named hon. life mem. Girl Scouts U.S., 1987. Mem. Royal Acad. Music (hon.), Alpha Kappa Alpha, Gamma Sigma Sigma, Sigma Alpha Iota, Pi Kappa Lambda. Club: Friday Morning Music (Washington). Office: care Shaw Concerts Inc 1995 Broadway New York NY 10023*

NORMAN, JULIE ANNE, social worker; b. Burlington, Iowa, Nov. 4, 1943; d. Clarence E. Norman and Dorothy (Jankowski) Dickson; m. John J. Peterson, July 10, 1970; 1 child, David. BA, Northeast Mo. State U., 1967; JD, DePaul U., 1984. Caseworker Lee County Dept. Social Svcs., Ft. Madison, Iowa, 1967-68, Ill. Dept. Pub. Aid, Chgo., 1968-72; social worker, supr., child protection investigator Ill. Dept. Children and Family Svcs., Chgo., 1972-88; therapist, ptnr. Profl. Counseling Svcs., South Elgin, Ill., 1985-86; therapist HELP (Human Effective Living Program), Chgo., 1988-89; social worker juvenile div. Cook County Pub. Defender's Office, Chgo., 1990—; mem. Cook County State's Atty.'s Juvenile Task Force, Chgo., 1988-89. Contbr. articles to profl. pubis. Chmn. social responsibility com. Unitarian-Universalist Ch., Oak Park, 1990—, vice chmn. svc. com., Chgo., 1990, regional coord., 1990. Mem. NOW, Am. Fedn. State, County, Mcpl. Employees (editor newspaper 1974-78, steward). Democrat. Home: 1164 S Elmwood Oak Park IL 60304 Office: Cook County Pub Defender's Office 1100 S Hamilton Chicago IL 60621

NORMAN, MARSHA, playwright; b. Louisville, Sept. 21, 1947; d. Billie Lee and Bertha Mae (Conley) Williams. B.A., Agnes Scott Coll., 1969; M.A.T., U. Louisville, 1971. Tchr. in Ky.; work with disturbed children Ky. Central State Hosp.; book editor, reviewer for Louisville Times; author (plays) Getting Out (John Gassner New Playwrights Medallion, Outer Critics Circle) 1977; other plays include Third and Oak, 1978, Circus Valentine, 1979, The Holdup, 1980, 'Night, Mother, 1982, Traveler in the Dark, 1984; author (novel) The Fortune Teller, 1987; author (collection) Four Plays by Marsha Norman, 1988. Recipient Susan Smith Blackburn prize for 'Night, Mother, 1982; Pulitzer prize for drama for 'Night, Mother, 1983; Nat. Endowment for Arts grantee, 1978-79; Rockefeller playwright-in-residence grantee, 1979-80; Am. Acad. and Inst. for Arts and Letters grantee. Office: Jack Tantleff 375 Greenwich St Ste 700 New York NY 10013

NORMAN, MARY MARSHALL, college president; b. Auburn, N.Y., Jan. 10, 1937; d. Anthony John and Zita Norman; B.S. cum laude, LeMoyne Coll., 1958; M.A., Marquette, U., 1960; Ed.D., Pa. State U., 1971. Tchr., St. Cecilia's Elem. Sch., Theinsville, Wis., 1959-60; vocat. counselor Marquette U., Milw., 1959-60; dir. testing and counseling U. Rochester (N.Y.), 1960-62; dir. testing and counseling, dean women, asso. dean coll., asst. dean students, dir. student activities, asst. prof. psychology Corning (N.Y.) Community Coll., 1962-68; research asst. Center for Study Higher Edn., Pa. State U., University Park, 1969-71; dean faculty South Campus, Community Coll. Allegheny County, West Mifflin, Pa., 1971-72, exec. dean, coll. v.p., 1972-82; pres. Orange County Community Coll., 1982—; cons. Boricua Coll., N.Y.C., 1976-77; reader NSF, 1977-78; mem. govtl. commn. com. Am. Assn. Community and Jr. Colls., 1976-79, bd. dirs., 1982—; mem. and chmn. various middle state accreditation teams. Bd. dirs. Orange County United Way. Mem. Am. Assn. Higher Edn., Nat. Assn. Women Deans Counselors, Am. Assn. Women in Community and Jr. Colls. (charter, Woman of Yr. 1981), Pa. Assn. Two-Yr. Colls., Pa. Assn. Acad. Deans, Pitts. Council Women Execs. (charter), Am. Council on Edn. (Pa. rep. identification women for adminstrn. 1978—), Pa. Council on Higher Edn., Orange County C. of C., Gamma Pi Epsilon. Contbr. articles to profl. jours. Home: 8 Crabapple Ln Middletown NY 10940 Office: 115 South St Middletown NY 10940

NORMAN, SHARON ANNE, printing company executive, consultant; b. Ft. Worth, June 27, 1939; d. William M. and Donna M. Young; m. Dick Crawford Norman, Aug. 31, 1957; children: Richard Alan, William Russell, Randal Crawford. BS in Human Rels., U. San Francisco, 1985. Sec., treas. DD Assocs., Santa Clara, Calif., 1964-80, 84—, pres., 1980-84; pres. Comml. Press (N&N Enterprise), Sand City, Calif., 1985—; cons. in field; bd. dirs. Monterey (Calif.) Fed. Credit Union. Treas. YWCA, Monterey, 1989—; pres. Vol. Ctr., Monterey, 1990—. Printing Industry of No. Calif. scholar, 1982. Mem. Soroptimists (pres. 1989-90). Republican. Presbyterian. Office: N&N Enterprise/Comml Press 465 Reservation Rd Marina CA 93933

NORMAN, SHIRLEY ANN, health care products company executive; b. Trenton, N.J., May 31, 1940; d. Samuel Oscar and Josephine (Williams) N.; divorced; children: Belinda Rainer, Robert Edward Rainer Jr. BS, Coppin State Tchrs. Coll., Balt., 1974. Statis. clk. Trenton High Sch., 1958, N.J. State Dept. Labor, Trenton, 1959-60; cataloger Library of Congress, Washington, 1961-64; tchr. Florence Crittington Svc., Balt., 1974-76; asst. city planner City of Seaside, Calif., 1977-81; health rep. Am. Home Health Care, Oakland, Calif., 1981-85; pres., owner Am. Health Care Products, Monterey, Calif., 1987—. Mem. NAACP, U.S. C. of C., Carch. Monterey C. of C., Better Bus. Bur., New Monterey Bus. Assn., Soroptimists (alt. del. 1989-90), Lions Internat., Delta Sigma Theta. Democrat. Office: Am Health Care Products 740 Lighthouse Ave Monterey CA 93940

NORMILE, BARBARA, systems manager, consultant; b. Trenton, N.J., Jan. 4, 1951; d. William Donald and Beatrice Marie (Noon) N. BS in Edn., St. Francis Coll., Loretto, Pa., 1972; postgrad., Pa. State U., State College, Pa., 1976; student, Mercer County Community Coll., Trenton, N.J., 1983, 85-86. Cert. elem. and secondary math. tchr., N.J., Pa. Tchr. math. and sci. St. Anthony Sch., Trenton, 1972-77; tchr. math Cumberland Regional High Sch., Seabrook, N.J., 1977-82; programmer N.J. Dept. Human Services, Trenton, 1982-84; programmer/analyst Computer Services Group, Trenton, 1984; sr. computer systems designer Martin Marietta Data Systems, Princeton, N.J., 1984-86; sr. systems mgr. Storey/Ross/Barker, Inc., Lambertville, N.J., 1987—; union rep. Cumberland Regional Edn. Assn., Seabrook, mem. negotiating team, 1980-81; computer tchr. West Windsor/Plainsboro (N.J.) Adult Edn., 1983-86. Dem. committeewoman, Bridgeton, N.J., 1980. Memm. N.J. Novell Users Group, MDBS Users Group, ORACLE Users Group, NAFE, Gamma Sigma Sigma. Home: 249 Hobart Ave Trenton NJ 08629 Office: Storey/Ross/Barker Inc 17A Church St Lambertville NJ 08530

NORMINGTON, NORMA SHOTWELL, secretary; b. Lakewood, Ohio, Apr. 7, 1924; d. Phillip Bassett and Alice Mae (Teed) Shotwell; m. Joshua James Normington, July 18, 1944; children: Peter Jay, Patricia Jean Normington Zieher. BS in English, U. Wis., 1948. Cert. tchr., Wis. Tchr. Madison (Wis.) East High Sch., 1948-50, Belmont (Calif.) Primary Grades, 1951; sec.-treas. Saddle Mound Cranberry Co., City Point, Wis., 1975—, also bd. dirs. Bd. dirs. U. Wis. Found., Madison, 1985—. Mem. AAUW (sec. 1953, pres. 1954), Marshfield Women's Club, Wood County Rep. Women's Club, Sigma Alpha Iota. Home and Office: 3203 Hwy 54 W City Point WI 54466

NORQUIST, ELLEN JOHNSON, sales executive; b. Sacramento, Mar. 8, 1951; d. Richard Lloyd and Muriel (Cannon) Johnson; m. Roger William Norquist, Mar. 20, 1982. BA, U. Calif., San Diego, 1973. Rsch. assoc. Scripps Inst., La Jolla, Calif., 1974-76, U. Calif., San Diego, 1976-78; sales rep. Amicon Corp., Boston, 1978-81, Mallinckrodt, Inc., St. Louis, 1981-84; nat. sales mgr. Nichols Inst. Diagnostics, San Juan Capistrano, Calif., 1984—. Office: Nichols Inst Diagnostics 26441 Via De Anza San Juan Capistrano CA 92675

NORRELL, J. ELIZABETH, psychology and sociology educator; b. Louisville, Apr. 25, 1958; d. John Alvin and Eloise (Goodin) Miller; m. Thomas H. Norrell, Aug. 16, 1980. BA, Furman U., Greenville, S.C., 1979; MS, Winthrop Coll., Rock Hill, S.C., 1980; PhD, U. Ga., Athens, 1984. Assoc. prof. psychology and sociology Erskine Coll., Due West, S.C., 1985—; adj. prof. family studies Erskine Theol Sem., Due West, 1986—; dir. Seminar for Tomorrow's Leaders, Rotary Internat. Program, Erskine Coll., 1986—; dir. social svcs. for swing-bed program Abbeville (S.C.) County Hosp., 1986—. spl. editor Family Sci. Rev. Jour., 1989. Mem. Augusta Symphony Orch., 1974-76, Amnesty Internat., People for Ethical Treatment Animals, Greenpeace, World Wildlife Fund. Recipient Appreciation award Rotary Internat., 1987, 88, 89. Mem. Nat. Coun. Family Rels., Soc. Sci. Study Religion, AAUW, Am. Sociol. Assn., Southeastern Coun. on Family Rels. (rsch. chmn. 1987—, program chair 1990). Democrat. Methodist. Office: Erskine Coll Due West SC 29639

NORRELL, SUSAN T., manufacturing engineer; b. Montgomery County, Ky., Dec. 12, 1959; d. Paul Taylor and Zula Ann (Detherage) Sorrell; 1 child, Valerie Lynn. BS in Indsl. Edn. and Tech., Ea. Ky. U., 1981; postgrad., U. Colo., Denver, 1984. Cert. just-in-time mfg. techniques, statis. process control, material requirements planning. Mfg. engring. supr. Mfg. Med. Equipment, Littleton, 1983-88; mfg. engr. Bd. Electro Med. Systems, Englewood, Colo., 1989-90; cons. Mfg. Tech. Network, Littleton, Colo., 1989—. Mem. NAFE, Inst. Indsl. Engrs., Kappa Alpha Theta. Home and Office: 11724 Elk Head Range Rd Littleton CO 80127

NORRGARD, KRISTIN ANN, magazine publisher; b. London, June 19, 1957; came to U.S., 1959; d. John Thomas and Barbara Ann (Erikson) N. BA, William Smith Coll., 1979. Account mgr. The Media Book, N.Y.C., 1979-80; dir. advt. Ad Forum mag., N.Y.C., 1980-83; nat. account mgr. Ladies' Home Jour., N.Y.C., 1983-85; dir. advt. Savvy Woman mag., N.Y.C., 1985-86, pub., 1986-90, v.p., 1988-90; assoc. pub. Inc. mag., N.Y.C., 1990—. Active Jr. League of Greenwich (Conn.), 1979-80, Jr. League of N.Y.C., 1980-87, Fountain House, N.Y.C., The Manhattan Soc., N.Y.C. Mem. Advt. Women N.Y.C., Ad Club N.Y. Republican. Congregationalist. Office: Inc Mag 488 Madison Ave New York NY 10021

NORRIS, ANNETTE CROCKETT, customer relations manager; b. Dermott, Ark., Oct. 21, 1940; d. Robert R. and Frances (Hooks) Crockett; children: Cynthia, Susan. Student, U. Ark., Monticello, 1958-60. Exec. sec. Kast Metals Corp., Shreveport, La., 1971-74, prodn. mgr., 1975-86, upgrade-x-ray mgr., 1986-88, customer rels. mgr., 1988—. Pres. East Kings Homeowners Assn. Mem. American Foundry Soc. Home: 1820 E Kings Hwy Shreveport LA 71105

NORRIS, CAROL ANN, assistant to hospital executive; b. Pana, Ill., Sept. 2, 1961; d. Patrick Edward and Barbara Caroline (Cerven) N. B., U. Ill., 1983; M. Healthcare Adminstrn., Washington U., 1986. Research asst. Warner Health Svcs., St. Louis, 1985-86; adminstrv. resident St. Joseph's Hosp., Savannah, Ga., 1986-87; asst. to the pres. St. Joseph's Hosp., 1987—; bd. dirs. Mercy Fed. Credit Union. Mem. pub. edn. com. Am. Cancer Soc., Savannah, 1987—; company chmn. United Way Campaign, Savannah, 1987—. Mem. Ga. Hosp. Assn. (sec.-treas. Southeast dist. 1988—), Savannah Area Coun. Healthcare Execs. (pres. 1990—), Healthcare Info. and Systems Mgmt. Soc., U. Ill. Alumni Assn., Washington U.'s Health Adminstrn. Program Alumni Asn., Savannah C. of C. (health and safety com. 1987—), Beta Sigma Phi (pres. Savannah city coun., 1990—, treas. 1988-89). Roman Catholic. Office: St Joseph's Hosp 11705 Mercy Blvd Savannah GA 31420

NORRIS, CATHERINE BOWDEN, educator; b. Gastonia, N.C., Mar. 10, 1930; d. George Stewart and Laura Heilig (Lentz) Bowden; m. Jeff Lawrence Norris, Sept. 8, 1929; children: Jeff Lawrence, Laura Catherine, Norris Frock. BA in Elem. Edn., Lenoir-Rhyne Coll., Hickory, N.C., 1952. Cert. tchr., N.C. Tchr. Hickory City Schs., 1952-55; tchr., dir. Corinth United Ch. of Christ Kindergarten, Hickory, 1962—. Chmn. task force Catawba County Day Care, Newton, N.C.,; mem. edn. com. Catawba County Tech. Coll., Hickory; mem. exec. bd. N.C. Luth. Synod, Salisbury; pres. Hickory Community Concert Assn., 1983-85. Mem. Nat. Assn. Edn. of Young Children, AAUW (pres. Hickory chpt.), N.C. Kindergarten Assn. (sec.). Democrat. Home: 356 7th Ave NE Hickory NC 28601 Office: Corinth United Ch of Christ 150 16th Ave NW Hickory NC 28601

NORRIS, CHARLENE MARIE, software engineer, business owner; b. Havre de Grace, Md., Mar. 19, 1958; d. Charles Edward and Ruth Lucille (Parks) N.; m. Steven Wayne Cockerham, 1979 (div. 1981); m. John Arthur Davenport III, Apr. 3, 1982; 1 child, John Arthur IV. BS in Computer Sci., Loyola Coll., 1986, postgrad., 1986-87, 89—. Sr. programmer AMTOTE Systems, Hunt Valley, Md., 1978-82; sr. systems engr. E.M.C. Controls, Hunt Valley, 1982-83; mgr. software engring. div. Catalyst Rsch., Owings Mills, Md., 1983-90; mgr. software devel. GeneSys Data Techs., Hunt Valley, Md., 1990—; cons., owner SoftSide Computer Svcs., Reisterstown, Md., 1983—. Personnel officer CAP, Carroll County, Md., 1986-89. Mem. IEEE, Computer Users Group, NOW, Digital Equipment Computer Users Soc. Republican. Lutheran. Office: SoftSide Computer Svcs PO Box 300 Owings Mills MD 21117

NORRIS, ELIZABETH DOWNE, librarian; b. White Plains, N.Y., Apr. 25, 1914; d. Albro Farwell and Alice Elizabeth (Morse) Downe; B.A., Smith Coll., 1936; M.Div., Yale U., 1939; M.L.S., Columbia U., 1955; 1 son, Donald E. Norris. Asst. residence dir. New Haven YWCA, 1940-42; religious edn. librarian Union Theol. Sem., N.Y.C., 1953-57; librarian NCCJ, N.Y.C., 1957-63; head librarian Nat. Bd. YWCA, N.Y.C., 1963—, dir. Nat. Bd. Archives Project, 1976—, YWCA historian, 1980—. Recipient Henry Foote Lewis prize in religion, 1934. Mem. Spl. Libraries Assn., Soc. Am. Archivists. Mem. United Ch. Christ. Editor: Feminine Figures: Selected Facts about American Women and Girls, 1968-72; Subject Headings on Women, 1973; Recent Trends in Professionalism, 1973; The YWCA Advances Women's Rights, 1855-1989, 1989; Dairy of a Volunteer, 1983; Women and Children First; a Century of YWCA Services to Children, 1984, The YWCA Secretary Searches for Professionalism 1889-1955, 1989; contbg. librarian Mental Health Book Rev. Index, 1961-72; editor, mem. adv. com. Books for Brotherhood, ann. 1957-76; contbr. articles to jours. Home: 505 La Guardia Pl New York City NY 10012 Office: 726 Broadway New York NY 10003

NORRIS, FRANCES MCMURTRAY, government official; b. Jackson, Miss., Mar. 27, 1946; d. William and Helen Frances (Dutton) McMurtray; m. Stephen Leslie Norris, Oct. 8, 1981. B.S., U. Miss., 1968, postgrad. in law, 1973; M.S.L.S., U. Ky., 1970; postgrad. program for med. librarians, U. Tenn., 1970-71. Legis. asst. to G. V. Montgomery, U.S. Ho. of Reps., Washington, 1974-78; staff asst. to Trent Lott rules com. U.S. Ho. of Reps., Washington, 1979-80; asst. to Republican whip U.S. Ho. of Reps., Washington, 1981-82; dir. legis. liaison Dept. Edn., Washington, 1983; dep. asst. sec. for legis. Dept. Edn., 1984-85, asst. sec. for legislation, 1986-88; dir. Congl. rels. Office of Nat. Drug Control Policy, Washington, 1988-90; spl. asst. to Pres. for legis. affairs The White House, Washington, 1990—. Pres. Miss. Soc. of Washington, 1983-84. U.S. Govt. fellow U. Ky., Lexington, 1969-70. Republican. Presbyterian. Home: 8015 Greenwich Woods Dr McLean VA 22102 Office: The White House Washington DC 20500

NORRIS, MARGARET SWANN, psychiatrist; b. Tampa, Fla., Aug. 8, 1925; d. Thomas Burnett and Margaret (Gaines) Swann; m. John Langdon Norris; children: John, Thomas, Charles, Edith. AB, Sweet Briar (Va.) Coll., 1945; MD, Cornell U., 1949. Intern Fitkin Hosp., Neptune, N.J., 1952-53; pvt. practice Spring Lake Heights, N.J., 1956-57; staff physician Davidson County Health Dept., Nashville, 1958-60; staff physician student health svc. Vanderbilt U., Nashville, 1960-81; resident in psychiatry Vanderbilt Hosp., Nashville, 1981-84; pvt. practice Nashville, 1984—; clin. asst. prof. psychiatry Vanderbilt Med. Sch., Nashville, 1986—. Bd. dirs. St. Augustine's Episcopal Chapel, Nashville, 1979—. Mem. Am. Psychiat. Assn., Tenn. Psychiat. Assn., Nashville Acad. Medicine, Tenn. Med. Assn. Democrat. Home: 2407 Fairfax Ave Nashville TN 37212 Office: 300 25th Ave N Ste 6 Nashville TN 37203

NORSMAN, ANNETTE SONJA, health association administrator, educator; b. Council Bluffs, Iowa, May 5, 1941; d. George Waldemar and Martha Desideria (Olson) Wahlin; m. Jerry Lynn Norsman, June 15, 1963 (div. 1988); children: Brian Jerome, Brent Andrew, Caroline Louise. AA, Riverside Coll., 1961; BA, Augustana Coll., 1963; MS, U. Wis., 1987. Cert. tchr., Ill., Conn., Calif., Wis. Tchr. Hartford (Conn.) Pub. Schs., 1963-64, Berkeley (Calif.) Pub. Schs., 1964-65, Milw. Pub. Schs., 1965-66, Madison (Wis.) Pub. Schs., 1966-68; coordinator grants project Assn. Retarded Citizens, Madison, 1975-77, dir. tng. outreach, 1977-80; exec. dir. Wis. Assn. Devel. Disabilities, Madison, 1980-87, Wis. Ret. Tchrs. Assn., Madison, 1987—; mem. nat. adu. bd. Accreditation Standards Commn. on Accreditation Rehab. Facilities, Tucson, 1985; mem. nat. consortium community health service Adminstrn. Devel. Disabilities, Washington, 1987. Co-producer (video tape) Commit to the Community 1986, Are We Ready to Listen? 1985; author/editor: (instructional series) Patterns for Participation, 1984. Chmn., pres. Wis. Coalition Arts and Human Needs, Milw., 1984-86; bd. dirs. Madison Art Ctr., 1976-78; v.p., pres. Madison Art Ctr. League, 1974-78; mem. Symphony League, Madison. Mem. Assn. Retarded Citizens (nat. adv. self advocacy 1984-86, nat. conv. program com. 1984-86), Am. Assn. Mental Deficiency, Coun. Advancement Citizenship, Ind. Sector, New Concepts Found. (treas., bd. dirs.). Lutheran. Home: 5405 Hammersley Rd Madison WI 53711 Office: Wis Ret Tchrs Assn 2564 Branch St Middleton WI 53562

NORTH, CAROL SUE, psychiatrist; b. Keokuk, Iowa, May 6, 1954; d. Ray Stemen and Doris Evelyn (Wood) N. BS in Gen. Sci., U. Iowa, 1976; MD, Washington U., St. Louis, 1983. Resident in psychiatry Barnes Hosp., Washington U. Med. Sch., St. Louis, 1983-87; rsch. fellow Washington U. Dept. Psychiatry, St. Louis, 1987-90, instr., 1987-89, asst. prof., 1989—; staff psychiatrist Grace Hill Neighborhood Health Ctr., St. Louis, 1987—. Author: Welcome, Silence, 1987; contbr. articles to profl. jours. Nat. Inst. Alcoholism and Alcohol Abuse grantee, 1988—, Nat. Hazards Rsch. Applications Info. Ctr. grantee, 1987-88. Mem. AMA, Am. Med. Women's Assn., Am. Psychiatric Assn., Life History Rsch. Soc., Ea. Mo. Psychiat. Soc. (exec. coun.), St. Louis Track Club, St. Louis Alliance for the Mentally Ill, Nat. Alliance for Mentally Ill. Presbyterian. Office: Dept Psychiatry Washington U Sch Medicine 4940 Audubon Ave Saint Louis MO 63110

NORTH, KATHRYN E. KEESEY (MRS. EUGENE C. NORTH), retired educator; b. Columbia, Pa., Jan. 25, 1916; d. Issac and Elizabeth (French) Keesey; B.S., Ithaca Coll., 1938; M.A., N.Y. U., 1950; m. Eugene C. North, Aug. 18, 1938. Dir. music Cairo (N.Y.) Central Sch. Dist., 1938; music edn. cons. Argyle (N.Y.) Central Sch. Dist., 1939; dir. gen. music curriculum Hartford (N.Y.) Central Sch. Dist., 1939; mem. staff Del. Dept. Pub. Instrn., Dover, 1943; dir. music edn. Herricks (N.Y.) Pub. Schs., 1944-71; ret., 1971. Vis. lectr. Ithaca Coll., summers 1959, 60, 62-65, Fairleigh-Dickinson U., Rutherford, N.J., summer 1966, Albertus Magnus Coll., New Haven, summer 1968; instr. Adelphi Coll., 1954-55, Sch.. Edn., N.Y.U., 1964-65. Mem. Music Educators Nat. Conf., N.E.A., N.Y. State Sch. Music Assn., N.Y. State Tchrs. Assn., Nassau Music Educators Assn. (exec. bd. 1947-58), N.Y. State Council Adminstrs. Music Edn. (chpt. v.p. 1967-68), Herricks Tchrs. Assn. (pres. 1948), Sigma Alpha Iota. Mem. Order Eastern Star. Home: 1645 Calle Camille La Jolla CA 92037

NORTHAGE GLICK, JENNIFER ISABELLA, sales executive; b. South Bend, Ind., Mar. 30, 1953; d. John Robert Phillips and Genevieve (Troyer) Northage; m. Stephen Merle Glick, May 11, 1986; 1 child, Jayne Christina; stepchild, Stephanie Nicole Benton. BA, Goshen Coll., 1976; MBA, Ind. U., South Bend, 1988. Graphic layout copywriter The Mail Journal, Milford, Ind., 1977-79; illustrator, graphic artist Ganshorn Plummer, Syracuse, Ind., 1979-80; sales rep., graphic artist Goshen News, 1980-84; dir. of mktg. sales and prodn. for cooperative recruitment Nat. Rsch. Ctr. for Coll. and Univ. Admissions, Kans. City, 1984-88; mktg. coord. Fourth Freedom Forum, Goshen, Ind., 1989—; student adviser Ind. U. South Bend, 1985--. Vice Committee Person Citizens for Puro Mayor, Goshen, 1985-87, Goshen City Plan Commn., 1987—. Recipient Acrylics Third Place No. Ind. Biennial Art Show, South Bend, 1974, Best Acrylics Niles Art Show, Mich., 1974. Mem. AAUW, Sigma Iota Epsilon. Democrat. Mennonite. Office: Fourth Freedom Forum 803 N Main St Goshen IN 46526

NORTHCROSS, LYDIA ANN, probation officer, social worker; b. Detroit, Oct. 15, 1955. BS in Social Work, Eastern Mich. U., 1978; MSW, Wayne State U., 1984. Cert. social worker, Mich. Youth counselor Comprehensive Youth Services, Detroit, 1979-80; case mgr. Wayne Ctr. for Retarded, Detroit, 1980-82; social work therapist Devel. Ctrs., Inc., Detroit, 1982-83; juvenile probation officer Wayne County Probate Ct., Detroit, 1984—; prin. Met. Residential Care Systems, Detroit, 1987—; prodn. asst. Mental Health Performing Arts Assn., Detroit, 1983. Mem. Nat. Assn. Social Workers, Mich. Residential Care Assn., Nat. Assn. Female Execs., Nat. Assn. Residential Care Facilities, Mich. Soc. Clin. Social Work, NAACP, Ea. Mich. U. Alumni Assn., Wayne State U. Alumni Assn., Fraternal Order of Police. Democrat. Office: Wayne County Juvenile Ct 1025 E Forest Ave Detroit MI 48207

NORTHCROSS, WENDY GERADINE, chamber of commerce administrator; b. Royal Oak, Mich., Mar. 31, 1954; d. Howard Benson Gerad Kittredge and Dorothy Judith (Mercer) Rockwell; m. Walter VanTrees Northcross, July 14, 1984. AA, Cape Cod Community Coll., 1974. Adminstrv. asst. ITT Grinnell, Providence, 1974-75; admistrv. asst. Travelers Ins., Hartford, Conn., 1975, Puritan Clothing Co. of C.C., Hyannis, Mass., 1976-81; bus. mgr. Sta. WOCB-WSOX Radio, West Yarmouth, Mass., 1981-84; office mgr. McAllister Assn., Hyannis, Mass., 1984-85; mortgage banker Bank of New Eng., Hyannis, 1985-88; exec. dir. Hyannis Area C. of C., Hyannis, 1988—; bd. dirs. Main St. Hyannis Inc., Barnstable Heritable Group, Hyannis; adv. bd. Child Care Resource Exchange, Hyannis, 1988—. Author: (travelogue) Travelers Trip through Historic Route 6A, 1990. Treas. Tom Lynch Com., Centerville, Mass., 1980—; notary pub. Commonwealth of Mass., 1982-92; adv. bd. Salvation Army, Hyannis, 1989—. Named for vol. effort Barnstable Selectmen, 1990. Mem. U.S. C. of C., Mass. Assn. C. of C. Execs. (scholar 1989), New Eng. Assn. C. of C. Execs., Am. C. of C. Execs., NAFE. Democrat. Congregationist. Office: Hyannis Area C of C 319 Barnstable Rd Hyannis MA 02601

NORTHCUTT, MARIE ROSE, educator; b. White Plains, N.Y., Feb. 2, 1950; d. Carlo and Marcelline Marie Rose (Benoit) DeMarco; m. Kenneth Walter Northcutt, Mar. 17, 1984; children: James Lee, Thomas Joseph. BA, Lynchburg Coll., 1972; MA, Columbia U., 1977. Cert. elem. and secondary tchr., N.Y. Tchr. Petersburg (Va.) Pub. Schs., 1972-74; asst. relocation mgr. Ticor Co., White Plains, 1974-75; 3d grade tchr. Resurrection Sch., Rye, N.Y., 1975-76; 6th grade tchr. Harrison (N.Y.) Cen. Sch. Dist., 1976-78, learning disabilities specialist, 1981—; tchr. of emotionally handicapped N.Y.C. Schs., 1978-80; learning evaluator Empire State Coll., White Plains, 1981-82; ind. evaluation cons., White Plains, 1981—. Mem. Harrison High Sch. PTA, 1980—. Mem. Assn. for Children with Learning Disabilities, Westchester County Assn. for Children with Learning Disabilities, Orton Soc., Phi Delta Kappa. Roman Catholic. Home: 81 Griffin Pl White Plains NY 10603 Office: Harrison Cen Sch Dist Union Ave Harrison NY 10528

NORTHCUTT, MARY SUE, neurobiology researcher; b. Decatur, Ill., Apr. 6, 1943; d. Hugh Jubb and Helen Ruth (Bernard) Caudle; m. R. Glenn Northcutt, June 26, 1965. BA, Millikin U., Decatur, Ill., 1966; MA in Anthropology, Case Western Res. U., 1972; MA in Am. Culture, U. Mich., 1976. Social worker Ill. Dept. Pub. Aid, Champaign, 1966-68; rsch. asst. U. Mich., Ann Arbor, 1972-86; rsch. and adminstrv. assoc neurobiology unit U. Calif., La Jolla, 1986—. Mem. J.B. Johnston Club (founding, sec.-treas. 1982—). Home: 8144 Paseo del Ocaso La Jolla CA 92037 Office: U Calif San Diego Scripps Instn Oceanography Dept Neurosci A-001 La Jolla CA 92093-0201

NORTHRUP, JOAN COOKE, healthcare executive, consultant; b. Phila., Sept. 2, 1953; d. Joseph Thomas and Lillian Josephine (Tjarks) Cooke. AS, Columbus (Ohio) State U., 1973; BS, Franklin U., 1980. With HealthAm. Corp., 1982-86; reg. mktg. dir. HealthAm. Corp., Columbus, Ohio, 1984-85; v.p. ops. Health Am. Corp., Columbus, Ohio, 1985-86; sr. v.p. Vol. Health Plan, Nashville, 1986-87; exec. v.p. Managed Care Products, Inc., Columbus, 1987-89; regional strategic planner Humana, Inc., Miami, Fla., 1989-90; assoc. exec. dir. Humana, Inc., 1990—. Mem. Group Health Assn. Am., NAFE. Office: Humana Med Plan 1505 NW 167th St Miami FL 33169

NORTHUP, ANNE MEAGHER, state legislator; b. Louisville, Jan. 22, 1948; d. James L. and Floy Gates (Terstegge) Meagher; m. Robert Wood Northup, Apr. 12, 1969; children: David, Katherine, Joshua, Kevin, Erin, Mark. BA in Econs., St. Mary's Coll. Notre Dame, South Bend, Ind., 1970. Mem. Ky. Ho. of Reps., Frankfort, 1987—; mem. fin. adv. bd. EPA, 1989—. Mem. Louisville Jr. Circle, 1980—, Lexington Rd. Preservation Area, 1987—, v.p., 1987—; mem. Jefferson County Rep. Exec. Com., Louisville, 1987—. Mem. Nat. Order Women Legislators, Louisville Younger Women's Club, 1982—. Roman Catholic. Home: 3340 Lexington Rd Louisville KY 40206 Office: Ky Ho of Reps Legis Offices Capitol Annex Frankfort KY 40601

NORTHWAY, WANDA L., realty company executive; b. Columbia, Mo., July 11, 1942; d. Herman W. and Goldie M. (Wood) Proctor; m. Donald H. Northway, June 12, 1965; 1 child, Michelle D. Student U. Mo., 1966. Lic. real estate agt., Mo.; grad. Realtors Inst. Realtor, assoc. Gentry Real Estate Co., Columbia, 1969-80; realtor Griffin Real Estate Co., 1980-81; pres., realtor, ptnr. House of Brokers Realty, Inc., Columbia, 1981—; pres., organizer Realtor-Assoc. Sales Club, Columbia, 1975; pres. Columbia Bd. Realtors, 1982. Contbr. articles to realty mags. Sunday sch. tchr., girls' aux. leader Baptist Ch.; vol. ARS, local hosp; campaign worker for Columbia legislators; mem. allocation com. United Way; active vol. Am. Cancer Soc. and Heart Assn. Named Realtor Assoc. of Yr., Columbia Bd. Realtors, 1974, Realtor of Yr., 1980. Mem. Mo. Assn. Realtors (state dir. 1974-77, Realtor Assoc. of Yr. award 1977), Realtors Nat. Mktg. Inst. (cert. residential specialist 1978), Nat. Assn. Realtors, (nat. dir. 1977), Epsilon Sigma Alpha (state corr. sec., local pres.). Republican. Baptist. Clubs: Million Dollar; Federation of Women's (pres. Mo. 1980). Office: House of Brokers Realty Inc 1316 Parkade Blvd Columbia MO 65203

NORTON, ANDRE ALICE, author; b. Cleve.; d. Adalbert and Bertha Stemm N. Librarian Cleve. Public Library, until 1951. Author 112 books. Mem. PEN Women, Sci. Fiction Writers Am.

NORTON, BILLIE FOSTINA, social services administrator; b. Topeka, Sept. 10, 1927; d. Verlette Floyd Williams and Ann Leona (Foster) Card; m. Ralph G. Norton (div.); children: Michael, Audré Marie, Anthony. BA in Behavioral Sci., Ursuline Coll., 1976; MSW, Smith Coll., 1983. Cert. alcoholism counselor. Lab. technician Blood Bank of ARC, Cleve., 1951-70; alcoholism social worker Hough-Norwood Health Ctr., Cleve., 1972-77; treatment specialist Alcoholism Services of Cleve., 1977-79; staff counselor employee assistance program Cuyahoga County Commrs., Cleve., 1980-81; alcoholism and chem. dependency treatment coordinator Ctr. for Human Services, Cleve., 1981—; mem. exec. com. Regional Coun. on Alcoholism, Cleve., 1981-88; pvt. practice, 1979—. Mem. Nat. Assn. Female Execs., Nat. Black Alcoholism Assn., Cleve. Chpt. Alcoholism Counselors Ohio. Club: Toastmistress. Office: West Ctr for Human Services 3929 Rocky River Dr Cleveland OH 44111

NORTON, DIANA MAE, data communications executive; b. Kansas City, Kans., Oct. 11, 1945; d. William Kenneth and Dora Mae Welch; m. Herbert Oliver Norton, July 12, 1969; children: Heather Alice, Claire Elizabeth. AB in Math. and Physics, Park Coll., 1967; MS in Physics, NYU, 1969; M in Engring. Mgmt., Northwestern U., 1989. Mem. tech. staff AT&T Bell Labs, Naperville, Ill., 1978-85, 86-88; supr. AT&T Bell Labs., Naperville, Ill., 1988—; mem. tech. staff AT&T Info. Systems, Naperville, 1985-86. Mem. vestry St. Barnabas Episcopal Ch., Glen Ellyn, Ill., 1986-88, past pres. Episcopal Ch. Women at St. Barnabas. Recipient numerous Exceptional Contribution awards AT&T Bell Labs. Club: Toastmasters (Indian Hill, Ill.) (pres. 1979). Home: 3 S 164 Cypress Dr Glen Ellyn IL 60137 Office: AT&T Bell Labs 2000 N Warrenville Rd Naperville IL 60566

NORTON, ELEANOR HOLMES, lawyer, educator; b. Washington, June 13, 1937; d. Coleman and Vela (Lynch) Holmes; m. Edward W. Norton, 1965; children: Katherine, John H. BA, Antioch Coll., 1960, MA in Am. Studies, 1963; LLB, Yale U., 1964; LLD (hon.), Cedar Crest Coll., 1969, Bard Coll., 1971, Princeton U., 1973, Marymount Coll., 1974, CCNY, 1975, NYU, 1978, Howard U., 1978, Brown U., 1978, Wilberforce U., 1978, Wayne State U., 1980, Syracuse U., 1981, Yeshiva U., 1981, Lawrence U., 1981, Emanuel Coll., 1981, Spelman Coll., 1982, U. Mass., 1983, Smith Coll., 1983, Med. Coll. Pa., 1983, Tufts U., 1984, Bowdoin U., 1985. Bar: Pa., 1965, U.S. Supreme Ct., 1968. Law clk. presiding justice Fed. Dist. Ct., 1964-65; asst. legal dir. ACLU, 1965-70; exec. asst. to mayor N.Y.C., 1971-74, chmn. commn. humanities, 1970-77; chmn. commn. humanities EEOC, 1977-81; sr. fellow Urban Inst., 1981-82; prof. law Georgetown U., 1982—; chmn. nat. adv. coun. ACLU; elected del. from D.C. to U.S. Congress, 1990. Author: (with others) Sex Discrimination and the Law: Causes and Remedies, 1975; contbr. articles to profl. jours. Trustee Community Found. Greater Washington, Rockefeller Found., Yale Corp.; bd. dirs. A. Philip Randolph Inst., Bethune Mus. and Archives Nat. Historic Site; catalyst Ctr. Nat. Policy, Manpower Demonstration Research Corp., Martin Luther King, Jr. Ctr. Social Change, Nat. Black Leadership Roundtable, Nat. Polit. Congress Black Women, Nat. Urban Coalition, Pitney Bowes Corp., So. Christian Leadership Conf.; adv. bd. Nat. Women's Polit. Caucus, Women's Law and Policy Fellowship, Workplace Health Fund; chmn. Commn. Future of Women in Workplace, Nat. Adv. Council ACLU; mem. Am. Council Edn., Council Minority Edn., Council Fgn. Relations, U.S. Citizens Com. Monitor Helsinki Accords, exec. panel Ford Found. Project Future of Welfare State, Nat. Acad. Scis. Com. Effects Tech. Change Employment and Working Environment. Recipient Young Woman of Year award Jr. C. of C., 1965; One of 25 Most Influential Women in Am. award Newspaper Enterprise Assn., 1977; Louise Waterman Wise award Am. Jewish Congress, 1971; Harper fellow Yale Law Sch., 1976; vis. Phi Beta Kappa scholar, 1985. Mem. Nat. Acad. Scis. (numerous coms.). Office: Citizens for Eleanor Holmes Norton 513 C St NE Washington DC 20002 also: Georgetown U Law Ctr 600 New Jersey Ave NW Washington DC 20001*

NORTON, ELIZABETH WYCHGEL, lawyer; b. Cleve., Mar. 25, 1933; d. James Nicolas and Ruth Elizabeth (Cannell) Wychgel; m. Henry Wacks Norton, July 16, 1954 (div. 1971); children: James, Henry, Peter, Fred; m. James Cory Ferguson, Dec. 14, 1985 (div. Apr. 1988). BA in Math., Wellesley Coll., 1954; JD cum laude, U. Minn., 1974. Bar: Minn. 1974. Summer intern Atty. Gen.'s Office, St. Paul, 1972; with U.S. Dept. Treasury, St. Paul, 1973; assoc. Gray, Plant, Mooty, Mooty & Bennett, P.A., Mpls., 1974-79, prin., 1980—. Trustee YWCA, Mpls., 1979-84, 89—, co-chmn. deferred giving com., 1980-81, chmn. by-laws com., bd. dirs., 1976-77, lectr.; treas. Minn. Women's Campaign Fund, 1985, guarantor, 1982-83, budget and fin. com. bd. dirs., 1984-87; trustee Ripley Meml. Found., 1980-84; treas. Johnes-Hairston Home, 1967, bd. dirs., 1962-69, 2d v.p., chmn. fin., 1968-69; mem. sen. David Durenberger's Women's Network, 1983-88. Durant scholar. Mem. ABA (family law sect. mediation task force 1983-84), Minn. Bar Assn. (family law sect., human rights com. mem., lectr., task force on uniform marital property act 1984-85), Hennepin County Bar Assn. (pres. 1987-88, pres. elect 1986-87, treas. 1985-86, sec. 1984-85, chmn. task force pub. edn. 1985, chmn. fam. law sect. 1979—, exec. com. family law sect. 1979—, lectr.), Minn. Inst. Legal Edn. (lectr.), Minn. Women's Lawyers Inc. (co-chmn. appointments com. 1980-81, exec. com.), U. Minn. Law Sch. Alumni Assn. (bd. dirs. 1975-81, exec. com. alumnae 1981-83, Phi Beta Kappa, Mpls. Club, Wellesley Club. Home: 1399 Orono Ln Wayzata MN 55391 Office: Gray Plant Mooty Mooty & Bennett 33 S 6th St 3400 City Ctr Minneapolis MN 55402

NORTON, GALE, state attorney general; b. 1954. BA, U. Denver, JD. Bar: Colo. 1978. Elected atty. gen. of Colo., 1990. Office: Law Dept State of Colo Office of Atty Gen 1525 Sherman St Rm 518 Denver CO 80203*

NORTON, JEANNA, systems professional; b. Gadsden, Ala., Dec. 24, 1952; d. Eugene Woodrow and Lillian Nora (Street) N. Student, U. Ala., Huntsville. Freelance automation specialist N.Y.C.; office mgr. James Booker & Assoc. P.C., Atlanta; dir. info. systems Long, Aldridge & Norman Attys. at Law, Atlanta; sr. mktg. support analyst Docutronics, Inc., Atlanta; computer svcs. technician King and Spalding Attys. at Law, Atlanta. Mem. AISP (sec.), NAFE. Home: 4701 Flat Shook Rd 39F Union City GA 30291

NORTON, KAREN ANN, accountant; b. Paynesville, Minn., Nov. 1, 1950; d. Dale Francis and Ruby Grace (Gehlhar) N. BA, U. Minn., 1972; postgrad. U. Md., 1978; cert. acctg. U.S. Dept. Agr. Grad. Sch., 1978; postgrad. Calif. State Poly. U.-Pomona, 1984—. CPA, Md. Securities transactions analyst Bur. of Pub. Debt., Washington, 1972-79, internal auditor, 1979-81; internal auditor IRS, Washington, 1981; sr. acct. World Vision Internat., Monrovia, Calif., 1981-83, acctg. supr., 1983-87; sr. systems liaison specialist, Home Savs. Am., 1987—; cons. (vol.) info. systems John M. Perkins Found., Pasadena, Calif., 1985-86. Author (poetry): Ode to Joyce, 1985 (Golden Poet award 1985). Second v.p. chpt. Nat. Treasury Employees Union, Washington, 1978, editor chpt. newsletter; mem. M-2 Prisoners Sponsorship Program, Chino, Calif., 1984-86. Recipient Spl. Achievement award Dept. Treasury, 1976, Superior Performance award, 1977-78; Charles and Ellora

Alliss scholar, 1968. Mem. Covenant Ch. Avocations: chess, racquetball, whitewater rafting.

NORTON, LOUISE CHARNETTE, nutritionist; b. Plattsburg, Mo., Nov. 17, 1941; d. Robert Rea and Helen Louise (Ditmars) N. BS, U. Mo., 1963, MS, 1976. Product mgr. Am. Hosp. Supply Co., McGaw Park, Ill., 1974-76; dir. dietetics Bethany Med. Ctr., Kansas City, 1976-82; dir. food and nutrition svcs. U. Chgo. Med. Ctr., 1982-86; dir. nutrition and food svcs. U. Tex. M.D. Anderson Cancer Ctr., Houston, 1986-88; owner The Norton Group, Houston, 1989—; mem. industry adv. team Am. Dietetic Assn. Found., Chgo., 1987-88. Lt. Col. U.S. Army, 1981-88. Allied health grantee HEW, 1974. Mem. Am. Dietetic Assn. (mgmt. practice group), Tex. Dietetic Assn., South Tex. Dietetic Assn., Am. Soc. Hosp. Food Svc. Adminstrs., Soc. Food Svc. Mgrs., PEO (Chgo.). Mem. Ch. of the Brethren. Home: 919 Fox Borough Ln Missouri City TX 77489 Office: The Norton Group 5818 Beverly Hill Ln Houston TX 77489

NORTON, ROBYN LYNN, nurse; b. Phoenix, May 19, 1963; d. Kenneth Arthur and Marjorie (Egan) N. ADN, Glendale Community Coll., 1990. RN, Ariz. Group facilitator St. Luke's Behavioral Health Ctr., Phoenix, 1987, milieu technician, 1987, counselor I, 1987—; staff nurse Westbridge Residential Treatment Ctr., Phoenix, 1990—. Recipient award Sun City Rotary, 1989; Betty Gerhardt scholar, 1988. Mem. Glendale Assn. of Student Nurses. Democrat. Office: St Lukes Behavioral Health 1800 E Van Buren Phoenix AZ 85006

NORTON, SHARON SUE, educational administrator; b. Marquand, Mo., Jan. 27, 1942; d. William Alexander and Stella Evelyn (Gibbs) Lux; m. Jake Norton, Jr., Dec. 26, 1959; children: Julie Leigh, Heather Lynn. BS in Edn., S.E. Mo. U., 1966; MEd, Drury Coll., 1971. Cert. prin., Mo. Tchr. Mehlville Sch. Dist., St. Louis, 1966-71, office coord. work study program, 1973-85, asst. prin., 1986—; guest lectr. So. Ill. U., Edwardsville. Co-producer, co-writer (video) Interview Do's and Dont's, 1983; author: Messenger: A Day in the Life of and Assistant Principal. Asst. troop leaderr Girl Scouts U.S.A., St. Louis County, 1980—; mem. steering com. project graduation Mehlville Mother's Club, 1988—. Mem. Nat. Assn. Secondary Sch. Prins. (presentor 1990), Assn. for Supervision and Curriculum Devel., Mo. Assn. Secondary Sch. Prins., St. Louis Area Secondary Prins. (treas. 1989-90), Assn. Univ. Women, Optimists, Delta Kappa Gamma, Phi Delta Kappa. Baptist. Home: 5156 Bryncastle Pl Saint Louis MO 63128 Office: Oakville Sr High Sch 5557 Milburn Rd Saint Louis MO 63129

NORTON, SUSAN JEAN, nurse; b. Portland, Maine, Feb. 10, 1958; d. William Louis and Maybelle Ella (Haley) N. BS in Nursing, St. Anselm Coll., 1980. RN. Nurse St. Joseph's Hosp., Lowell, Mass., 1980-81, John I Kennedy Hosp., Stratford, N.J., 1981-83, Yale New Haven Hosp., 1983-86, The Children's Hosp., Boston, 1986—. Mem. Nat. Assn. Neonatal Nurses. Democrat. Roman Catholic. Home: 60 Pleasant St #317 Arlington MA 02174 Office: The Childrens Hosp 300 Longwood Ave Boston MA 02115

NORTON, VIRGINIA SKEEN (MRS. JOHN H. NORTON, JR.), civic worker; b. Atlanta, June 1, 1907; d. Lola Percy and Rebecca (Baldwin) Skeen; A.B., Agnes Scott Coll., 1928; student Columbia U., 1934-35; m. John Hughes Norton, Jr., Dec. 16, 1938; children—Virginia Skeen Norton Kraft, John Hughes III. With personnel dept. Retail Credit Co., Atlanta, 1929-31, sec. to v.p., gen. mgr. Davison-Paxon, Co., Atlanta, 1931-34; with Aluminium Ltd., N.Y.C., 1935-41, sec. to pres., 1937-41; sec. to pres. Colonial Williamsburg, Inc., N.Y.C., 1943-44. Bd. dirs. North Shore Assos. Chgo. Commons, 1951-54, Infant Welfare Soc. Chgo., 1953-54, Catherine Morrill Day Nursery, Portland, Maine, 1956-59. Mem. Central Fla. Civic Theater Guild, Loch Haven Arts Soc., Winter Park Meml. Hosp. Aux., Morse Art Gallery Assocs. (dir. 1982-84), Nat. Soc. Colonial Dames Am. Episcopalian. Address: 1620 Mayflower Ct Apt A-606 Winter Park FL 32792

NORVELL, NANCY KATHLEEN, psychologist, educator; b. Atlanta, Aug. 17, 1957; d. Lauren and Lois (Dozier) N.; m. Timothy Lee Boaz, May 20, 1989. BA, U. Va., 1979; MS, Va. Commonwealth U., 1981, PhD, 1984. Lic. psychologist, Fla. Intern in psychology Brown U., Providence, 1983-84; asst. prof. dept. clin. and health psychology U. Fla., Gainesville, 1984-89; vst. asst. prof. dept. law and mental health U. South Fla., Tampa, 1989—, clin. asst. prof. dept. medicine, div. cardiology, 1989—; pvt. practice Tampa, 1989—; cons. div. cardiology U. Fla., 1989—. Co-author: Facilitating Stress Management, 1990, Stress Management for Law Enforcement, 1990; contbr. numerous articles to profl. jours. Vol. Ctr. for Women, Tampa, 1990—; mem. membership com. Mental Health Assn. Hillsborough County, Tampa, 1990—. Mem. Am. Psychol. Assn. (Excellence in Cons. Rsch. award 1986), Soc. Behavioral Medicine, Assn. Advancement Behavior Therapy (program com. 1988-90), Fla. Psychol. Assn. (steering com., women's issues com. 1989—, columnist monthly newsletter), Phi Kappa Phi. Democrat. Office: 3450 E Fletcher Ave #100 Tampa FL 33613

NORWOOD, ALICE LYNN, accountant, city official; b. Oklahoma City, May 19, 1962; d. Bobby J. and Dorothy F. (Jenkins) Perry; m. Steven P. Norwood, June 18, 1988. BBA, Tex. A&M U., 1984. Acct. City of Euless, Tex., 1984-89, asst. fin. dir., 1989—. Mem. Govtl. Fin. Officers Assn., Govtl. Fin. Officers Assn. Tex., NAFE, Tex. Mcpl. League. Home: 1203 Trenton Euless TX 76040

NORWOOD, BARBARA MANN, uniform company official; b. Ft. McPherson, Ga., Sept. 2, 1946; d. John Robert and Marion Evelyn (Miller) Mann; m. Robert Jordan Gravley, Oct. 8, 1961 (div. 1972); children: Robert Jordan Jr., John Robert, Tria Sheree; m. Donald Weyman Norwood, Mar. 11, 1982. Student, Kennesaw Coll. Vocat.-Tech., Marietta, Ga., 1972. Sales rep., mgr. Mann's Uniforms, Smyrna, Ga., 1959-76; sales rep. Martin's Uniforms, Atlanta, 1976-79; account exec. Banner Uniforms, Atlanta, 1979—. Lt. col., a.d.c. Staff of Gov. of Ga., 1972—; advisor congl. reelection com., 1979. Mem. Sales and Mktg. Execs., Ga. Motor Trucking Assn., Women of the Moose. Republican. Presbyterian. Home: 919 Woodward Circle Mableton GA 30059 Office: Banner Uniforms 437 Armour Circle Atlanta GA 30324

NORWOOD, JANET LIPPE, government official; b. Newark, Dec. 11, 1923; d. M. Turner and Thelma (Levinson) Lippe; m. Bernard Norwood, June 25, 1943; children—Stephen Harlan, Peter Carlton. BA, Douglass Coll., 1945; MA, Tufts U., 1946; PhD, Fletcher Sch. Law and Diplomacy, 1949; LLD (hon.), Fla. Internat. U., 1979; LL.D. (hon.), Carnegie Mellon U., 1984. Instr. Wellesley Coll., 1948-49; economist William L. Clayton Ctr. Tuft U., 1953-58; with bur. labor stats. Dept. Labor, Washington, 1963—; dep. commr., then acting commr. bur. labor stats. Dept. Labor, 1975-79, commr. labor stats. bur. labor stats., 1979—. Author papers, reports in field. Recipient Disting. Achievement award Dept. Labor, 1972, Spl. Commendation award, 1977, Philip Arnow award, 1979, Elmer Staats award, 1982, Pub. Svc. award, 1984; named to Alumni Hall of Fame, Rutgers U., 1987; recipient Presdl. Disting. Exec. rank, 1988, Profile in Excellence citation Office of Pers. Mgmt., 1989. Fellow AAAS, Am. Statis. Assn. (past pres.), Royal Statis. Soc., Nat. Assn. Bus. Economists; mem. Am. Econ. Assn., Indsl. Rels. Rsch. Assn., Women's Caucus in Stats., Com. Status Women Econs. Profession, Internat. Statis. Inst., Internat. Assn. Ofcls. Stats., Nat. Acad. Pub. Adminstrn., Douglass Coll. Soc. Disting. Achievement, Am. Statis. Assn. (pres. 1989). Home: 6409 Marjory Ln Bethesda MD 20817 Office: Labor Dept Labor Stats Bur 441 G St NW Washington DC 20212

NORWOOD, JOY JANELL, real estate executive; b. Barnes, Kans., Aug. 25, 1936; d. Howard Clayton and Gladys Melveno (Wells) Cook; divorced; 1 child, Rebecca. Student, U. Colo., 1958-63; grad., Realtors Inst. Ohio State U., 1977. Lic. real estate broker, Ohio. Registered rep. First Investors Corp., Boston, 1966-68; area supr. Wohl Shoe Co., Boston, 1968-70; residential real estate broker Coldwell Banker, Cin., 1970-78, comml. real estate broker, 1978-80; comml. real estate broker Rubloff, Cin., 1980-82; real estate rep. Ky. Fried Chicken/Zantigo, Louisville, 1982-86; v.p. Otto Realty Corp., Cin., 1987-89; pres. Joy Norwood & Assocs., Westchester, Ohio, 1989—. Jr. high sch. tchr. Mason (Ohio) Ch. Christ, 1986—, mem. choir., 1986—. Served with U.S. Army, 1955-58. Mem. Nat. Assn. Corp. Real Estate Execs., Internat. Council Shopping Ctrs., Cin. Bd. Realtors (polit. affairs com. 1974, Million Dollar Club award, 1972-79), Cin. Hist. Soc. Republican. Club: Flying Neutrons (Cin.). Office: Joy Norwood & Assocs 8547 Ashwood Dr Westchester OH 45069

NOTERMAN, SISTER MARJORIE L., academic administrator; b. Adams, Minn., Oct. 3, 1946; d. Matthias Hubert and Anna Helen (Boegeman) N. BA, Marillac Coll., St. Louis, 1969; MEd, U. Ariz., 1979; PhD, Loyola U., Chgo., 1988. Tchr. St. Alphonsus Sch., Prospect Heights, Ill., 1969-73; tchr., asst. prin. St. Raphael Sch., Chgo., 1973-75; prin. St. Theresa Sch., Palatine, Ill., 1975-84; pres. Mallinckrodt Coll. of the North Shore, Wilmette, Ill., 1986-90; adminstr. Loyola U., Chgo., 1990—; trustee Mallinckrodt Coll. of the North Shore, 1980-90; cons. Jospehinum High Sch., Chgo., 1976, St. Viator High Sch., Arlington Heights, Ill., 1986. Mem. History of Women Religious, Fedn. Ind. Ill. Colls. and Univs. (exec. com. 1989), Wilmette C. of C., Sisters of Christian Charity (councilor 1980-88). Rotary. Roman Catholic. Office: Mallinckrodt Campus of Loyola U Wilmette IL 60091

NOTH, NANCY CLAIRE, university official; b. Indpls., Mar. 24, 1950; d. John F. and Mary Jane (Heinen) N.; m. Allen R. Heryford. B.A., Purdue U., 1972; M.A., U. Mont., 1975; Ph.D., Wash. State U., Pullman, 1983. Sch. psychologist pub. schs., Mont., 1975-78; asst. dir. career svcs. Wash. State U., Pullman, 1981-83; dir. career planning and placement U. Ark., Fayetteville, 1983-86; dir. bus. & liberal arts U. Iowa, Iowa City, 1986-89, asst. dean, dir. external programs, 1989—; cons. in field. Mem. M.W. Coll. Placement Assn., Rocky Mountain Coll. Placement Assn. Office: U Iowa 24 Phillips Hall Iowa City IA 52242

NOURSE, JENNIFER JON WILLIAMS, anthropology educator; b. Knoxville, Tenn., Feb. 5, 1953; d. John Sanders Gilbert Williams and Sue Elizabeth (Anderson) Male; m. James Cummings Nourse, June 10, 1972 (div. Nov. 1980); m. Edward Eric Gable, Apr. 30, 1983. BA, U. Tenn., 1975; MA, U. Va., 1981, PhD, 1989. Instr. anthropology U. Richmond, Va., 1987-89, vis. asst. prof., 1989-90, asst. prof., 1990—; instr. Mary Washington Coll., Fredericksburg, Va., 1988. Fulbright-Hayes fellow, 1984, fellow Wenner-Gren Found., 1984, Gov.'s fellow State of Va., 1987. Mem. Am. Assn. Anthropology. Democrat. Unitarian. Office: U Richmond Dept Sociology and Anthropology Richmond VA 23173

NOVAK, ANN-NADINE, software engineer; b. Cleve., Sept. 14, 1951; d. Joseph Paul and Evelyn Johanna (Suchina) N. BS in Math., Cleve. State U., 1972, BS in Computer Info. Scis., 1974, MS in Indsl. Engring., 1978. Programmer/analyst Standard Oil Co., Cleve., 1973-75, systems analyst/programmer, 1975-78, systems analyst, 1978-81; sr. systems analyst Ernst & Whinney, Cleve., 1981-84, supr., 1985, mgr., 1985-88; software engr. Cutler/Williams, Independence, Ohio, 1989—. Mem. Cleve. Chpt. Am. Inst. Indsl. Engrs. (numerous com. positions, acting treas. 1985-86, immediate past pres. 1986-87, bd. dirs. 1987-90, Excellence award 1982, 85), Data Processing Mgmt. Assn., Am. Assn. Individual Investors.

NOVAK, DARIA IRENE, import-export company executive; b. Norwalk, Conn., Feb. 1, 1957; d. Joseph and Irene Novak. Cert., Georgetown U., 1975; postgrad., George Washington U., 1979-81; BA, U. Wyo., 1978; cert., Taiwan Nat. Normal U., Taipei, 1980. With U.S. Dept. of State, Washington, 1979-89, officer Asian and pub. affairs, 1985-86, spl. asst. to asst. sec. of state for East, 1986-89; dir. internat. div. Thomas Wilck Assocs., Irvine, Calif., 1989-90; pres. Trinity West, San Clemente, Calif., 1990—; instr. No. Va. Community Coll., Arlington, 1989. Author, researcher: China: The Rise to World Power, 1983; contbg. editor U.S.-Asia mag., 1989—. Chair pub. affairs and ways and means com. Great Falls (Va.) Fire Dept., 1983-87. Mem. Women in World Trade (bd. dirs. pub. rels. com. 1990—), Calif.-Taiwan Trade and Investment Coun. (corp. com. L.A. chpt. 1990—), Orange County World Trade Ctr. Assn., NAFE, Irvine C. of C. (internat. affairs com. 1990—). Republican. Roman Catholic. Office: Trinity West 260 Avenida Montalvo Ste C San Clemente CA 92672

NOVAK, JO-ANN STOUT, chemical engineer; b. Glen Ridge, N.J., June 25, 1956; d. Herbert Austin and Anna (Messina) Stout; m. John Robert Novak Jr., Oct. 30, 1976; B. in Chem. Engring., Ga. Inst. Tech., 1977; M.B.A., Oakland U., 1984. Cert. engr.-in-tng., Ga.; registered profl. engr., Mich. Trainee AC Spark Plug div. GM, Flint, Mich., 1977-78, chemist, 1978-79, exptl. chemist, 1979-81, mfg. engr., 1981-84, sr. mfg. engr., 1984-87; sr. mfg. project engr., 1987-89, mgr. bus. and engring. processes, 1989—. Mem. Am. Electroplaters Soc. (dir. Saginaw Valley br. 1981-83, ednl. chmn. 1984-85, sec.-treas. 1985-86, 2d v.p. 1986-87, 1st v.p. 1987-88, pres. 1988-89), Am. Inst. Chem. Engrs., Soc. Mfg. Engrs. Office: AC Rochester div GMC 1300 N Dort Hwy Flint MI 48556

NOVAK, LINDA MOSES, editor; b. Louisville, Nov. 23, 1949; d. James Nicholson and Doris Marie (Younker) Moses; m. John Howard Novak, May 10, 1986. BA in English magna cum laude, Ind. U., 1971, MA in Journalism, 1977. Traffic coord. Ind. U. Instructional TV, Bloomington, 1973-77; writer, dir. Allied Internat. Films, Washington, Ind., 1978-79; writer, editor United Dairy Industry Assn., Am. Dairy Assn., Rosemont, Ill., 1979-86; editor internal communications USG Corp., Chgo., 1986—. Editor (employee publ.) Looking Ahead, 1986—. Fundraiser LifeSpan, Des Plaines, Ill., 1981—; mem. His. Soc. Arlington Heights (Ill.), 1986—. Fellow sch. journalism Ind. U., 1972. Mem. Internat. Assn. Bus. Communicators, Am. Fedn. State, County and Mcpl. Employees (local pres. 1974-76), Des Plains-Park Ridge NOW (treas. 1981), Phi Beta Kappa. Democrat.

NOVAK, MARIAN JOYCE, data processing specialist, programmer; b. McKeesport, Pa., July 2, 1954; d. Andrew Michael and Agnes Marie (Andrews) Rusnock; m. John Andrew Novak, June 19, 1982. Cert. in programming, Computer Systems Inst., 1975; student, Community Coll. Allegheny County, 1976-81, 89—, Clarion (Pa.) U., 1983-85. With Equibank, Pitts., 1973-75, tape libr., 1975-76, computer operator, 1976-77; computer operator Blue Cross of Western Pa., Pitts., 1977-79; shift supr. County of Allegheny, Pitts., 1979-82; data processing supr. Charles Tool & Supply, Shippenville, Pa., 1984-86; data processing mgr., programme West Elizabeth Lumber Co., Elizabeth, Pa., 1988—. Mem. Data Processing Mgmt. Assn., NAFE. Office: West Elizabeth Lumber Co 1 Chicago Ave Elizabeth PA 15037

NOVAK, SANDRA BERNADEAN, science specialist; b. New Prague, Minn., Aug. 6, 1953; d. Lando Andrew and Angeline (Vohnoutka) Busch; m. David L. Novak, Aug. 7, 1976; children: Drew, Lindy, Dylan. BS, St. Cloud U., 1975; MEd, U. Minn., 1986; postgrad., Coll. St. Thomas, 1988—. Elem. tchr. Mazeppa Sch. Dist., 1975-76, Ind. Sch. Dist., Burnsville, Minn., 1977-88; elem. sci. specialist Ind. Sch. Dist., Burnsville, Minn., 1988—; chairperson Sci. Curriculum Evaluation Com., Burnsville, 1988—. Com. bd. Park Recreation Com., 1979-81. Mem. Nat. Sci. Tchr. Assn., Minn. Sci. Tchr. Assn., Minn. Edn. Assn. Office: Ind Sch Dist 13109 City Rd 5 Burnsville MN 55337

NOVELLO, ANTONIA COELLO, U.S. surgeon general; b. Fajardo, P.R., Aug. 23, 1944; d. Antonio and Ana D. (Flores) Coello; m. Joseph R. Novello, May 30, 1970. BS, U. P.R., Rio Piedras, 1965; MD, U. P.R., San Juan, 1970; MPH, Johns Hopkins Sch. Hygiene, 1982. Diplomate Am. Bd. Pediatrics. Intern in pediatrics U. Mich. Med. Ctr., Ann Arbor, 1970-71, resident in pediatrics, 1971-73, pediatric nephrology fellow, 1973-74; pediatric nephrology fellow Georgetown U. Hosp., Washington, 1974-75; project officer Nat. Inst. Arthritis, Metabolism and Digestive Diseases NIH, Bethesda, Md., 1978-79, staff physician, 1979-80; exec. sec. gen. medicine B study sect., div. of rsch. grants NIH, Bethesda, 1981-86; dep. dir. Nat. Inst. Child Health & Human Devel., NIH, Bethesda, 1986-90; surgeon gen. HHS, Washington, 1990—; clin. prof. pediatrics Georgetown U. Hosp., Washington, 1986, 89, Uniformed Svcs. U. of Health Scis., 1989; mem. Georgetown Med. Ctr. Interdepartmental Rsch. Group, 1984—; legis. fellow U.S. Senate Com. on Labor and Human Resources, Washington, 1982-83; mem. Com. on Rsch. in Pediatric Nephrology, Washington, 1981—; participant grants assoc. program seminars Nat. Inst. Arthritis, Diabetes and Digestive and Kidney Diseases, NIH, Bethesda, 1980-81; pediatric cons. Adolescent Medicine Svc., Psychiat. Inst., Washington, 1979-83; nephrology cons. Met. Washington Renal Dialysis Ctr. affiliate Georgetown U. Hosp., Washington, 1975-78; phys. diagnosis class instr. U. Mich. Med. Ctr., Ann Arbor, 1973-74; chair Sec.'s Work Group on Pediatric HIV Infection and Disease, DHHS, 1988; cons. World Health Orgn., Geneva, 1989. Contbr. numerous articles to profl. jours. and chpts. to books in field; mem. editorial bd. Internat. Jour Artificial Organs, Jour. Mexican Nephrology. Served to capt. USPHS, 1978—. Recipient Intern of Yr. award U. Mich. Dept. Pediatrics, 1971, Woman of Yr. award Disting. Grads. Pub. Sch. Systems, San Juan, 1980, PHS Commendation medal HHS, 1983, PHS Citation award HHS, 1984, Cert. of Recognition, Div. Research Grants NIH, 1985, PHS Outstanding medal HHS, 1988, PHS Unit Commendation, 1988, PHS Surgeon Gen.'s Exemplary Svc. medal, 1989, PHS Outstanding Unit citation, 1989, DHHS Asst. Sec. for Health Cert. of commendation, 1989. Fellow Am. Acad. Pediatrics; mem. AMA, Internat. Soc. Nephrology, Am. Soc. Nephrology, Latin Am. Soc. Nephrology, Soc. for Pediatric Rsch., Am. Pediatric Soc., Assn. Mil. Surgeons U.S., Am. Soc. Pediatric Nephrology, Pan Am. Med. and Dental Soc. (pres.-elect, sec. 1984), D.C. Med. Soc. (assoc.), Alpha Omega Alpha. Home: 1315 31st St NW Washington DC 20007 Office: Office of Surgeon Gen 200 Independence Ave SW Washington DC 20201

NOVETZKE, SALLY J., ambassador; b. Stillwater, Minn., Jan. 12, 1932; married; 4 children. Student, Carlton Coll., 1950-52. Amb. to Malta, Valletta, 1989—. Mem., legis. rep. Nat. Coun. on Vocat. Edn.; mem. adv. coun. for career edn., mem. planning coun. Kirkwood Community Coll.; bd. dirs. Cedar Rapids (Iowa) Symphony; trustee Hoover Presdl. Libr.; precinct chmn. Iowa Rep. Com., 1976-88, state chmn., 1985-87; chmn. Linn County Rep. Com., 1980-83; mem. adv. bd. Iowa Fedn. Rep. Women, 1987-89; vice chmn. campaign adv. bd. Nat. Fedn. Rep. Women, 1987-89; mem. Iowa Rep. Cen. Com., 1982-85; Iowa co-chmn. George Bush for Pres., 1988. Office: Am Embassy, St Anne St, 2d Fl, Development House, Valletta Malta*

NOVEY, LINDA SIMMONS, management and service consultant; b. Dyersburg, Tenn., Oct. 18, 1940; d. L. Doyle and Mary Jane (Alsup) Moore; m. George Thomas Novey, Apr. 1, 1981; children: Lori, Jane, Paula; stepchildren: George, Clifford. BA, U. Calif., Berkeley, 1962; postgrad., U. Tenn., 1964-74, U. So. Calif., 1964-74. Pres. Simmons Conventions Inc., Columbia, S.C., 1975-79; mng. ptnr. Abbott Simmons Mktg. Assocs., Memphis, 1979-81; exec. v.p. Cohen & Henry, Virginia Beach, 1981-84, Hospitality Standards Ltd., Skokie, Ill., 1981-82; pres. Novey Enterprises, Atlanta, 1984—; mem. adv. bd. Discovery Learning Inc., Atlanta, Atlanta Concierge Assocs., Ga. State U., Atlanta; guest lectr. Ohio State U., U. Ark., Western Ill. U., Queen Margaret Coll., Scotland; graduation speaker Brighton (Eng.) Poly. Coll.; keynote speaker UPIGH, Budapest, Hungary, 1988, Internat. Symposium for Entrepreneurs, Edinburgh, Scotland, 1988. Author: The Smile Parade, 1980. Mem. The Algonquin Round Table Forum, N.Y.C. Recipient Spl. Person of Yr. award S.C. C. of C., 1972; named Woman of Yr. Fla. Jr. Woman's Club, 1975. Mem. Ga. Hospitality and Tourism Assn., NAFE, Ga. Exec. Women's Network, Nat. Assn. Profl. and Bus. Women, Atlanta Consultants Soc. (founding bd.), Women's Commerce Club, Internat. Com. for Atlanta C. of C., Forward Atlanta Com., Internat. Alliance Bus. Women. Republican. Office: Novey Enterprises Box 97 Norcross GA 30091

NOVGOROD, NANCY, editor-in-chief. B in Art History, Mt. Holyoke Coll. With New Yorker mag., 1976-81; from asst. editor to exec. editor Clarkson N. Potter, Inc., 1981-87; sr. editor House & Garden mag., N.Y.C., 1987-88, editor-in-chief, 1988—. Office: House & Garden Conde Nast Bldg 350 Madison Ave New York NY 10017*

NOVICK, WILMA JOYCE, nurse; b. Umatilla, Fla., Feb. 14, 1938; d. Jesse Boyington and Mary Welva (Bobo) Lyle; m. Jerome Novick, Feb. 1, 1969 (div. Jan. 1975); 1 child, Elizabeth Ellen Higginbotham. Lic. practical nurse, Orange County Vocat. Sch., Orlando, Fla., 1971; diploma in nursing, Valencia Community Coll., Orlando, 1975. RN, Fla. Mem. critical care sr. staff Orlando Regional Med. Ctr., 1975-86, acting head nurse, asst. head nurse, 1986-89, patient care coord., 1988, sr. staff nurse, 1989—. Scholar Sertoma Club, Orlando, 1970. Republican. Home: 10377 Ocoee-Clarcona Rd Apopka FL 32703

NOVIKOFF, PHYLLIS MARIE, medical researcher, educator, consultant; b. N.Y.C., Dec. 3, 1936; d. Michael and Dora (Paglia) Iaciofano; m. Alex Benjamin Novikoff, Dec. 1, 1968 (dec. Jan. 1987). BA, Hunter Coll., 1958; MS, NYU, 1971, PhD, 1976. Rsch. asst. Meml. Sloan-Kettering Inst., N.Y.C., 1958-69; rsch. fellow assoc. Hopital St. Antoine, Paris, 1969-70; rsch. asst, cell biology Albert Einstein Coll. Medicine, N.Y.C., 1958-69, assoc., 1970-76, asst. prof., 1976-82, assoc. prof., 1982—; vis. asst. prof. U. Fla., Gainesville, 1975-76; mem. NIH, Washington, 1983-87. Contbr. articles to profl. jours. Grantee NIH, Nat. Cancer Inst., 1989-91. Mem. Am. Assn. Cancer Rsch., Am. Soc. Pathologists, Am. Soc. Cell Biology, Histochem. Soc. (counselor 1988—), Fedn. Am. Socs. Exptl. Biology. Office: Albert Einstein Coll Med 1300 Morris Park Ave Ullmann 423 New York NY 10461

NOVINA, TRUDI (MRS. CHARLES E. COAKLEY), public relations executive, writer; b. N.Y.C.; d. Isidor and Lillian (Greenberg) N.; m. Leo H Papazian, June 24, 1956; (dec. 1964); children: Lyssa D. Papazian, Gregory M. Papazian; m. Charles E. Coakley, Apr. 27, 1968. BA in English, Bklyn. Coll., 1950; MBA in Mktg., Fordham U., 1981. Reporter, asst. women's editor N.Y. World Telegram & Sun, 1950-54, home furnishings editor, 1957-60; freelance writer N.Y.C., 1960-64; dir. home furnishings publicity Donald Degnan Assoc., N.Y.C., 1964-69; publicity mgr. Fibers Div. Allied-Signal, Inc., N.Y.C., 1969—. Editor: House and Garden mag., 1965; contbr. to various mags. Mem. Internat. Furnishings and Design Assn., Fashion Group (v.p. local chpt.), Overseas Press Club. Office: Allied Fibers 1411 Broadway New York NY 10018

NOVITSKI, LOIS CONRAD, county agency administrator; b. Scranton, Pa., Jan. 24, 1937; d. Lewis Charles and Mary (Szurkos) Conrad; m. Victor A. Novitski (dec.), June 2, 1956; children: Mary Lou E. Jordan, Nancy V. Runta. Student, Wilkes-Barre Bus. Coll., 1956, Wilkes Coll., 1979. With credit dept. People's Outfitting Co., Wilkes-Barre, Pa., 1954-56; adminstrv. asst. U.S. Dept. HUD, Wilkes-Barre, 1972, fin. dist. agt., 1972-74; bookkeeper Luzerne County Employees Retirement System, Wilkes-Barre, 1974-82, retirement coordinator, 1982—. Mem. Ladies Aux. (recording and fin. sec. Kingston, Pa. chpt. 1958-78). Democrat. Roman Catholic. Office: Luzerne County Retirement New Courthouse Annex Wilkes-Barre PA 18711

NOVITT, RITA AMELIA, sales manager; b. Elizabeth, N.J., July 12; d. Adam and Victoria (Cieslak) N. BA in Econs. and Sociology, Douglass Coll. Lic. real estate sales person, N.J. With Johnson & Johnson, New Brunswick, N.J., 1972—; mgr. sales rels. Johnson & Johnson, New Brunswick, 1978—; Pres., bd. dirs. Raritan Credit Union. Bd. dirs., exec. com. United Way, George Washington coun. Boy Scouts Am.; chmn. Douglass Coll. 50th Anniversary Celebration; trustee Thomas A. Edison State Coll., N.J., fin. and adminstrn. com.; rev. team and advisor nat. fellowship program W.K. Kellogg Found.; trustee Fielding Inst., Santa Barbara, Calif., 1985, vice-chmn. bd. trustees, 1986, chmn. devel. com. and instl. advancement, 1988—. Mem. N.J. Credit Union League, Queenston Common Condominium Assn. (pres.), Middlesex County Alumnae Assn. (pres.), Douglass Coll. Alumnae Assn. (v.p.). Home and Office: 5 Gordon Way Princeton NJ 08540

NOVORRO, JANE, graphic design executive; b. Long Beach, N.Y., Apr. 13, 1961; d. David and Barbara (Smook) N. BFA in Graphic Design, Carnegie-Mellon U., 1982. Jr. graphic designer Lamplight Group, N.Y.C., 1982-83; sr. graphic designer Notovitz & Perrault Design, N.Y.C., 1983-86; freelance graphic designer Jane Novorro Graphic Design, N.Y.C., 1986-87; owner, pres. Ocean Graphic Design, Inc., Long Beach, 1987—. Mem. Advancement for Commerce and Industry, Long Beach Humane Soc. (v.p. 1989—). Democrat.

NOVOTNY, DEBORAH ANN, financial executive; b. Oak Lawn, Ill., Sept. 23, 1964; d. Russell Anthony and Barbara J. (Doran) N. BA in Econs.,

Northwestern U., 1986; postgrad., U. Minn., 1988—. Lic. mutual fund mktg. analyst. Mgr. lab., cons. Northwestern U., Evanston, Ill., 1983-86; asst. mgr. microcomputer services Sara Lee Corp., Chgo., 1986; sr. cons. Lante Corp., Chgo., 1987-88; fin. exec. IDS Fin. Svcs., Inc., Mpls., 1988—. Active teen retreat team St. Michael's Ch., Orland Park, Ill., 1978-84. Ill. State scholar. Mem. Macintosh Users Group, Chi Omega Rho (charter, chmn. housing assn. 1986—). Office: IDS Fin Svcs Inc IDS Tower 10 Minneapolis MN 55440

NOWAK, CAROL A., city official; b. Buffalo, Mar. 5, 1950; d. Walter S. and Stella M. (Gurowski) N. AAS in Bus. Adminstrn., Erie Community Coll., Buffalo, 1986; student, SUNY, Buffalo, 1986—. With Liberty Nat. Bank/Norstar, Buffalo, 1968-70; with City of Buffalo, 1970-74, asst. adminstrn. and fin., 1974-82, pension clk., adminstr. city police and fire pension fund, city clk., 1982-90, sr. coun. clk., city clk., 1990—. Artist, designer holiday greeting cards, 1984—. Mem. NAFE, Golden Key Nat. Honor Soc., Alpha Sigma Lambda Nat. Honor Soc. Home: 422 Dingens St Buffalo NY 14206 Office: City of Buffalo City Clerk's Office 1308 City Hall Buffalo NY 14202

NOWAK, JACQUELYN LOUISE, consultant, realtor; b. Harrisburg, Pa., Sept. 2, 1937; d. John Henry and Irene Louise (Clark) Snyder; children: Andrew Alfred, IV, Deirdre Anne. Student, Pa. State U., 1973-74; BA, Lycoming Coll., 1975. Editorial writer Patriot News Co., Harrisburg, Pa., 1957-58; dir. West Shore Sr. Citizens Ctr., New Cumberland, Pa., 1969-72; exec. dir. Cumberland County Office Aging, Carlisle, Pa., 1972-80; bur. dir. Bur. Advocacy, Pa. Dept. Aging, Harrisburg, 1980-88; exec. asst. to Pa. Senator Jonh D. Hopper, Senate Com. on Aging and Youth, 1989; owner D&J Prodns., Art and Handcrafted Teddy Bears 1986, Ted E. Bear's Emporium, Harrisburg, 1988; assoc. Century 21 Piscioneri Realty, Inc., Camp Hill, Pa.; cons. in aging; recorder Pa. Gov's. Coun. Aging Cen. Region, 1972-74; chmn. pub. rels., 1973-74; mem. state planning com. Pa. State Conf. Aging, 1974, panelist, 1975-78; mem. state bd. Pa. Coun. Homemakers-Home Health Aide Svcs., 1972-80, v.p., 1975, chmn. ann. meeting, 1973-75; sr. citizens subcom. chmn. Pa. Atty. Gens. Commn. to Prevent Shoplifting, 1983; mem. adv. com. Tri-County Ret. Sr. Vol. Program, 1972-74; bd. dirs. Coun. Human Svcs. Cumberland, Dauphin, and Perry Counties, 1973-74; mem. svc. com. Family and Children's Svc. Harrisburg, 1970-74, mem. policy com., 1973-74, bd. dirs. Cumberland County unit Am. Cancer Soc., 1964-76, state del., 1964-66, chmn. county pub. rels., 1965-66, cancer crusade chmn., 1964. Recipient Herman Melitzer award, Pa. Conf. Aging, 1978; named Woman of the Yr. Sta. WIOO Radio, Carlisle, Pa., 1979. Mem. Nat. Assn. Area Ags. on Aging (bd. dir. 1975-80, pres. 1976-77; sec. 1978-79), Pa. Watercolor Soc., Harrisburg Art Assn., Mechanicsburg Art Ctr. (pres. 1987-90, bd. dirs. 1984—), Gerontol Soc. Am., Am. Trauma Soc. (Pa. div. state bd. 1985-88), Older Women's League (founder chpt.), Lycoming Coll. Alumni Assn. (exec. bd. 1987-89), Pa. Fedn. of Women's Club (div. chmn. 1972-76), Torch Club (pres. 1987-88, 2d v.p. 1985-86), Zonta Internat. (sec. 1986-89). Home and Office: 1809 English Dr Mechanicsburg PA 17055

NOWELL, ELIZABETH CAMERON CLEMONS, author; b. Berkeley, Calif.; d. Alfred George and Edith (Catton) Cameron; AB San Jose State Coll., 1928; MA, Stanford U., 1937; m. Wood Clemons, Dec. 22, 1946 (div. Dec. 1958); m. Arthur G. Robinson, May 27, 1961 (dec. Jan. 1967); m. Nelson T. Nowell, Feb. 15, 1969 (dec. Sept. 1973). With edn. dept. San Jose State Coll., 1928-39, in service tng. U. Calif. Extension Div., 1939-42; elem. editor The John C. Winston Co., 1942-43, Silver Burdett Co., 1943-44, D.C. Heath, 1944-46; instr. English dept. U. Minn., 1947; writing, editing publs. services Gen. Mills, 1947-50; freelance writer, 1950—; mem. faculty Monterey Peninsula Coll., Monterey, Calif., 1978-83; reading cons. Monterey City Sch., 1959-62, assoc. editor Calif. edit. Am. Home Mag., 1965-70; mem. seminar faculty Embroiderers Guild, 1980; judge needle-work Good Samaritan Hosp., L.A.s, 1977, 79, 83, 87, Montalvo Center for Arts, Saratoga, Calif., 1980, 82, Status Needle Art Show, Burlingame, Calif., 1982, Altrusa Needlework Exhbn., Santa Maria, Calif., 1982, Scripps Meml. Hosp., La Jolla, Calif., 1980, 86, others. Bd. dirs. Community Hosp. Aux.; bd. dirs. Harrison Meml. Library, 1971-76, Monterey Symphony Assn., 1974-75; vestryman St. Dunstan's Episcopal Ch., 1974-77. Mem. Nat. League Am. Pen Women, Authors Guild, LWV, Nat. Embroidery Tchrs. Assn. (nat. dir. 1978-81), Embroiderers Guild Am. (nat. dir. 1978-81, nat. fin. com. 1984-87; nat. fin. guidelines chmn. 1986-87; nat. judges cert. com. 1984—, chmn. 1987; pres. chpt. 1977-78; judge needlework exhbns. 1977—, historian 1988-89), Kappa Alpha Theta, Pi Lambda Theta, Delta Phi Upsilon, Kappa Delta Pi, Delta Kappa Gamma. Republican. Episcopalian. Clubs: Casa Abrego (historian 1979-83), Monterey Peninsula Country, Soroptimist. Author: The Pixie Dictionary, 1953; the Catholic Child's First Dictionary, 1954; The Winston Dictionary for Canadian School Children, 1955; Away I Go, 1956; All About Baby, 1956; I Live on A Farm, 1956; A Wish for Billy, 1956; Wings, Wheels, and Motors, 1957; The Big Book of Real Fire Engines, 1958; The Big Book of Real Trains, 1958; The Big Book of Real Trucks, 1958; Rodeo Days, 1960; Shells Are Where You Find Them, 1960; Rocks and The World Around You, 1960; Big and Little, 1961; Tide Pools and Beaches, 1964; Waves, Tides, and Currents, 1967; Here and There Stories; Now and Then Stories; Near and Far Stories; A Source Book for the Teaching of Literature for Children (all 1967); The Seven Seas, 1971; The Friendly Frog, 1971; What I Like, 1971; Guidelines for Treasurers, 1987; also feature articles in nat. mags. Address: PO Box 686 Carmel CA 93921

NOWELL, LINDA G., sales professional; b. Ft. Worth, Apr. 24, 1949; d. Jesse Wayne and Bennie Dale (Flint) Stallings; m. W. Don Nowell, Nov. 4, 1983. BA, North Tex. State U., 1970. Cert. secondary tchr.; lic. real estate salesperson, Tex. Former edn. coord. Tex. Farm Bur., Waco; owner Parallels in Design, Cranfills Gap, Tex.; v.p. Nowell Equipment Co. (co. sold 1989), Cranfills Gap; ind. sales rep. Jostens Printing and Pub. div., Owatona, Minn.; former edn. coord. Tex. Farm Bur., Waco. Recipient South Cen. Regional Pacer award, 1982, Sales Commitment Achiever award, 1982, 83, 84. Mem. NAFE. Home and Office: PO Box 137 Cranfills Gap TX 76637

NOWICKI, ALICIA LEIGH, music therapist; b. Santa Monica, Calif., Aug. 31, 1947; d. Henry T. and Mary Eleanor (Buck) N. MusB in Music Therapy, U. of the Pacific, 1969; MPA, U. San Francisco, 1987. Registered music therapist; cert. neurolinguistic programming practioner. Music therapy intern Milw. County Mental Health Ctr., 1969; music therapist Kedren Mental Health Ctr., L.A., 1970, Camarillo (Calif.) State Hosp., 1970-76; music therapist Porterville (Calif.) Devel. Ctr., 1977, 78-83, rehab. cons., office quality assurance, 1983—; music therapist Agnew's Devel. Ctr., San Jose, Calif., 1977-78. Co-author: Beyond The Sound: A Technical and Philosophical Approach to Music Therapy, 1977. Mem. Nat. Assn. Music Therapy, Mu Phi Epsilon. Home: 480 Randy St Porterville CA 93257 Office: Porterville Devel Ctr PO Box 2000 Porterville CA 93258

NOWIK, DOROTHY ADAM, medical equipment company executive; b. Chgo., July 25, 1944; d. Adam Harry and Helen (Kichkaylo) Wanaski; m. Eugene Nicholas Nowik, Aug. 9, 1978; children—George Eugene, Helen Eugene. A.A., Columbia Coll., 1980. Sec., adminstrv. asst. to pres. Zenco Engring Corp., Chgo., 1970-71; sales rep. Medizenco USA Ltd., Chgo., 1971-73; ptnr. Pacific Med. Systems, Inc., Bellevue, Wash., 1973-76, pres., 1976—. Mem. Nat. Assn. Female Execs. Mem. Orthodox Ch. Am. Home: 10249 SE 7th St Bellevue WA 98004 Office: 15055 NE Bel-Red Rd Bellevue WA 98007

NOXON, MARGARET WALTERS, community volunteer; b. Detroit, Dec. 16, 1903; d. George Alexander and Ethelwyn (Taylor) Walters; grad., Liggett Sch. for Girls, Det., 1922; life teaching certificate Wayne State U., 1925; student Columbia Tchrs. Coll., 1939-40; m. Herbert Richards Noxon, July 15, 1926 (dec. Aug. 4, 1971). Bd. dirs. Coll. Club, Detroit, 1925-30; mem. Salvation Army Aux., Detroit, 1926—; mem. Coll. Club, Summit N.J., 1941—; historian D.A.R., N.Y.C., 1943-46, vice regent, 1946-49; dir. New Eng., Women, 1961-64; dir. Woodycrest-Five Points Child Care, 1961-77; bd. dirs. ARC, Summit, N.J., service com. chmn. uniforms and insignias, 1943-45; v.p. N.Y. Infirmary Aux., N.Y.C., 1948-58, bd. dirs., 1959-80. Recipient award for meritorious personal service ARC, 1945. Mem. Nat. Inst. Social Scis., Grand Jury Assn. N.Y. County, D.A.R. (dir. 1950-70), St. David's Soc. State N.Y., English-Speaking Union, Daus. Am. Colonists, AAUW, Southampton Colonial Soc., Nat. Woman's Farm and Garden Assn. (dir. met. br. 1975—, dir. N.Y. State div. 1978-80, mem. nat. council 1978-80), Ch. Women's League for Patriotic Service, Women's Bible Soc. N.Y., Alpha Sigma Tau. Republican. Presbyterian. Clubs: Southampton (N.Y.) Bath and Tennis, City Gardens (dir. 1963-68, mem. adv. com. 1968-74, dir. 1974-80, adv. bd. 1980-83), York (bd. govs. 1965-66, 73-77), Barnard (trustee 1979-81), Sorosis (v.p. 1979-81), Regency (N.Y.C.). Home: 1100 Madison Ave Apt 10C Box 86 New York NY 10028

NOYES, ELISABETH J., university system administrator; b. Hilversum, The Netherlands, Oct. 15, 1940; came to U.S., 1951, naturalized, 1966; d. Louis Jan and Wilhelmina Louise (Bollee) van Epen; m. Arnold Eugene Noyes, Sept. 2, 1961; children: James Louis, Edwin Willard. Postgrad., Middlebury Coll., 1961; MA, U. Mass., 1962; MEd, Salem (Mass.) State Coll., 1966; EdD, Nova U., 1976. Instr. German and English North Shore Community Coll., Beverly, Mass., 1965-68, assoc. prof., 1970-76, div. chairperson, 1972-74; dept. chairperson White Pines Coll., Chester, N.H., 1968-70; prof. Mt. Wachusett Community Coll., Gardner, Mass., 1974-75; div. chairperson Bunker Hill Community Coll., Boston, 1976-78, asst. dean, 1978-83; acad. program officer Mass. Bd. Regents of Higher Edn., Boston, 1983-87; dir. acad. planning and program devel. Univ. System N.H., Durham, 1987—; mem. N.H. Post Secondary Edn. Commn., 1987—; cons. N.J. Dept. Higher, Trenton, 1986-89. Trustee White Pines Coll., Chester, 1974-85, Notre Dame Prep. Sch., Fitchburg, Mass., 1980-85, Nashoba Community Hosp., Ayer, Mass., 1983—, chmn. nursing home com., 1985—; chairperson Shirley (Mass.) Sch. Com., 1974-80; moderator Town of Shirley, 1983—; bd. dirs. Mass. Moderators' Assn., 1988—. Grantee Internat. Edn. Consortium, 1978, Am. Assn. Women Community & Jr. Colls., 1981—; recipient N.H. Phi Delta Kappa award, 1989. Mem. Nat. Coun. Tchrs. English, Conf. on Coll. Composition and Communication, Mass. Women in Pub. Higher Edn. (exec. com. 1982-86, treas. 1983-86), N.H. Women in Higher Edn. Assn., N.E. Regional Conf. on English in two-yr. colls. (exec. com. 1981-84, treas. 1982-84), Greater Boston Regional Edn. Coun. (vice chmn., chair 1978-86), Nat. Coun. State Dirs. Community and Jr. Colls. (system rep.), Modern Lang. Assn., N.E. Regional Conf. on Teaching Fgn. Langs., Chi Omega, Altrurian. Unitarian. Home: 45 Lancaster Rd Shirley MA 01464 also: 1090 S Collier Blvd 312 Marco Island FL 33937 Office: Univ System New Hampshire Dunlap Ctr Durham NH 03824

NOYES, NANCY POPE, public relations executive; b. Salem, Mass., Mar. 6, 1964; d. John David and Virginia Lee (Starr) Pope; 1 child, Beckett Pope Noyes. BA, Dartmouth Coll., 1986. Owner, operator Blueberry Puffin, Marblehead, Mass., 1986-89; asst. buyer Filene's Dept. Store, Boston, 1986-87; mgr. Carroll Reed Shop, Boston, 1987; asst. dir. devel. The Pingree Sch., South Hamilton, Mass., 1987-89; mgr., owner Rockmore Restaurant, Salem, Mass., 1989—; ednl. dir. Charles River Boat Co. Inc., Marblehead, Mass., 1989—; liaison, interviewer Dartmouth Coll., Hanover, 1982—; bd. dirs. Dartmouth Bowl Program of the Northshore Club of Mass. Contbr. articles to mag. Chmn. Winter Carnival Coun., Hanover, N.H., 1984-86; devel. officer Internat. Olympic Sailing Devel. Fund, Marblehead, 1987—; mem. Student Life Com. Mem. Pingree Sch. Alumni Assn. (v.p.), Jr. League Boston, Ea. Yacht Club. Republican. Home: 423 Ocean Ave Marblehead MA 01945

NOZIGLIA, CARLA MILLER, director forensic services, forensic scientist; b. Erie, Pa., Oct. 11, 1941; d. Earnest Carl and Eileen (Murphy) Miller; m. Keith William Noziglia, Nov. 21, 1969; children: Pama Noziglia Cook, Kathryn J. BS, Villa Maria Coll., 1963; MS, Lindenwood Coll., 1984. Med. technologist Monmouth (N.J.) Gen. Hosp., 1963-64; spl. chem. medicine technologist Hamot Hosp. Med. Ctr., Erie, Pa., 1965-69; pathologist's assoc. Galion (Ohio) Comm. Hosp., 1969-75; dir. crime lab. Mansfield (Ohio) Police Dept., Richland County Crime Lab., 1978-81; crime lab. supr. St. Louis County Police, Clayton, Mo., 1981-84; dir. crime lab. Las Vegas (Nev.) Met. Police, 1984-88, dir. lab. svcs., 1988—. Tech. abstracts editor Jour. Police Sci. and Adminstrn., 1983—; editorial bd. Jour. of Identification, 1988—; contbr. to (book) Journal of Police Science, 1989, Encyclopedia of Police Science, 1989—. Recruiter United Blood Svcs., Las Vegas, 1986—; bd. dirs., v.p. Community Action Against Rape, Las Vegas, 1987—. Recipient Ohio award Ohio House of Reps., 1981, Alumni of Yr. award Villa Maria Coll., 1981; named Woman of Yr. Am. Bus. Women's Assn., 1988, Outstanding Cath. Erie Diocese N.W. Pa., 1988, Woman of Achievement Las Vegas C. of C., 1989. Fellow Am. Acad. Forensic Sci. and Criminalistics (sect. sec. 1986—, sect. chmn. 1987, bd. dirs. 1988—); mem. Am. Soc. Crime Lab. Dirs. (bd. dirs. 1980-87, treas. 1981-82, 88—, pres. 1986-87), Clin. Lab. Scientists Nev. (cert.), Nat. Assn. Female Execs., Internat. Assn. Identification, S.W. Assn. Forensic Scientists, Calif. Assn. Crime Lab. Dirs., Midwest Assn. Forensic Scientists, Am. Bus. Women's Assn., Soroptimists. Republican. Roman Catholic. Office: Las Vegas Metro Police Forensic Lab 6765 W Charleston Blvd Las Vegas NV 89102-9003

NUDELMAN, SHIRLEY SOBLE, freelance writer, public relations specialist; b. Portland, Oreg., Jan. 21, 1933; d. Samuel and Ida Esther (Director) Soble; m. Jerome Robert Nudelman, Aug. 15, 1954; children: Sheila Nudelman Casimo, Sharon Nudelman Morell, Jeffrey. BS in Art Edn., U. Oreg., 1954. In sales, design and pub. rels. Carpet Designers, Portland, 1975-76; in sales and window decoration Jeri's, Portland, 1976-79; devel. dir. Sta. KBOO, Portland, 1980-81; with pub. rels. and promotions Samuels & Nudelman Promotions, Portland, 1983-88; freelance writer and editor Nudelman Promotions, Portland, 1988—. Editor: The Best Tennis Lesson You Ever Had; contbr. monthly newspaper column, 1971-88. Docent, Portland Art Mus., 1970s; bd. dirs. Oreg. Sch. Arts and Crafts, 1980, Oreg. Speech an dHearing League, 1980s, Young Audiences, 1980, Mittleman Jewish Community Ctr., 1979-83; bd. dirs., chair beautification com. Nevah Shalom Synagogue, 1987—. Recipient Beautification Com. award Solomon Schecter Conservative Synagogues Am., 1989. Mem. Women in Communications. Democrat. Home: 4023 SW Jerald Ct Portland OR 97221 Office: Nudelman Promotions 4023 SW Jerald Ct Portland OR 97221

NUGENT, BARBARA ANN, medical facilty administrator; b. Bklyn., Nov. 25, 1941; d. Joseph William and Catherine Theresa (Bykowska) Vanderbosch; (div.); children: Mary Ann, Joseph. Student, Molloy Coll., Rockville Centre, N.Y., 1959-61; BS in Nursing, D'Youville Coll., 1963; MPA, Pa. State U., 1988. RN; cert. nursing adminstrn. Nursing supr. USNR, St. Albans, N.Y., 1963-65, Sasebo, Japan, 1965-66; staff nurse VA, East Meadow, S.C., 1970-71; instr. NASSAR Sch., Charleston, 1971-75; dir., home health agy. Tempo Svcs., Fresh Meadow, N.Y., 1976; instr. Gloria K. Sch., Great Neck, N.Y., 1976; staff nurse, ICU Harrisburg (Pa.) Hosp., 1977; staff nurse, head nurse supr. VA Med. Ctr., Lebanon, Pa., 1977-85, resource allocation, DRG and UR coord., 1985-87, staff asst. to med. ctr. dir., 1987-89; staff asst., dir. VA Med. Ctr., Balt., 1989—; cons. Pa. State U., Harrisburg, 1988-89, Regional Dir., VA Region 2, Durham, N.C., 1985-89; bd. advisors Susquehanna Health Care, Harrisburg, Pa., 1976-82. Author: The Effect of Utilization Review on the VA's Resource Allocation Methodology, 1988. Parish coun. St. Mary's Ch., Lebanon, Pa., 1985-87; multimedia instr. ARC, Lebanon, 1985-86; cons., facilitator Open Encounter, Ephrata, Pa., Canadaigua, N.Y., 1982-84; program devel. Pa. Right to Life, Lebanon, 1982-84; active Friendship Fire Co., Lebanon. Lt. USNR, 1963-66. Recipient Spl. Contribution award, Regional Dir. VA, Durham, 1988, Recognition award Mil. Order of Purple Hearts, Lebanon, 1984. Mem. VA Employees Assn., Am. Legion Aux. Roman Catholic. Office: VA Med Ctr 3900 Loch Raven Blvd Baltimore MD 21218

NUGENT, CATHERINE MARIE, producer, director; b. Flushing, N.Y., Sept. 22, 1966; d. David and Margaret Mary Nugent. BA in Bus. Adminstrn., Molloy Coll., Rockville Centre, N.Y., 1987. Prodn. technician Cablevision Systems Corp., Woodbury, N.Y., 1987-89, producer, dir., 1989—. Producer dir. local programming and pub. svc. announcements. Winner Folio award, 1990. Republican. Roman Catholic. Office: Cablevision Systems Corp 338 Ocean Ave Lynbrook NY 11797

NUGENT, LORI S., lawyer; b. Peoria, Ill., Apr. 24, 1962; d. Walter Leonard and Margery (Frost) Meyer; m. Shane Vincent Nugent, June 14, 1986. BA, Knox Coll., 1984; JD, Northwestern U., Chgo., 1987. Bar: Ill. 1987, U.S. Dist. Ct. (no. dist.) Ill. 1988. Assoc. Peterson, Ross, Schloerb & Seidel, Chgo., 1987—. Co-author: Punitive Damages: A Guide to the Insurability of Punitive Damages in the United States and Its Territories, 1988. Mem. ABA, Ill. Bar Assn., Chgo. Bar Assn. Office: Peterson Ross Schloerb & Seidel 200 E Randolph Dr Ste 7300 Chicago IL 60601

NUGENT, NELLE, theater, film and television producer; b. Jersey City, May 24, 1939; d. John Patrick and Evelyn Adelaide (Stern) N.; m. Donald G. Baker, June 6, 1960 (div. 1962); m. Benjamin Janney, June 22, 1969 (div. Apr., 1980); m. Jolyon Fox Stern, Apr. 7, 1982; 1 child, Alexandra Fox Stern. B.S., Skidmore Coll., 1960, D.H.L. (hon.), 1981. Chmn. bd. McCann & Nugent, Prodns. Inc. (mgmt. and prodn. co.), N.Y.C., 1976-86; pres. Foxboro Prodns., Inc., N.Y.C., 1985—; pres., chief exec. officer Foxboro Entertainment, 1990—. Stage mgr. various off-Broadway shows, 1960-64; prodn. asst.: Broadways plays Any Wednesday, 1963-64, Dylan, 1964, Ben Franklin in Paris, 1964-65; stage mgr. Broadway shows, 1964-68; prodn. supr., then gen. mgr., 1969-70, asso. mng. dir. Nederlander Corp., operating theaters and producing plays in, N.Y.C. and on tour, 1970-76; producer: Dracula, 1977 (Tony award), The Elephant Man, 1978 (Tony award, Drama Critics award), Morning's at Seven, 1980 (Tony award), Home, 1980 (Tony nomination), Amadeus, 1981 (Tony award); also produced: Rose and Piaf, 1980, The Life and Adventures of Nicholas Nickleby, 1981 (Tony award, Drama Critics award), The Dresser (Tony award nominee), 1981, Mass Appeal, 1981; The Lady & The Clarinet, 1982; The Glass Menagerie (revival), 1983; Painting Churches (Obie award), 1983; Total Abandon, 1983; All's Well That End's Well, 1983 (Tony nominee); Pilobolus Dance Company, 1983; Pacific Overtures (revival), 1984; Much Ado about Nothing/Cyrano de Bergerac (repertory) (Tony award nominees), 1984; Leader of the Pack (Tony award nominee), 1985, The Life and Adventures of Nicholas Nickleby (revival) (Tony award nominee), 1986; producer: TV spls.; Morning's At Seven, Piaf; Pilobolus; producer A Fighting Choice, Walt Disney Prodns., 1986, Phoenix Entertainment Group, 1986-88, A Conspiracy of Love, New World TV, 1987, The Final Verdict, TNT, 1990; exec. producer CBS TV pilot Morning Maggie, 1987, Dick Clark Prodns., 1988—. Bd. dirs. A.W.E.D. Office: Foxboro Prodns 313 E 61st St Ste 1B Ste 1B New York NY 10021

NUGENT-CROCITTO, MARGARET MARY, jewelry designer; b. Bronx, N.Y., Aug. 15, 1966; d. James and Margaret (Malagrino) N.; m. Joseph Michael Crocitto, Aug. 19, 1989. AS in Fashion Buying and Merchandising, Fashion Inst. Tech., N.Y.C., 1986, AS in Jewelry Design, 1988. Jewelry designer Honey Gamboge, N.Y.C., 1987-88, B. Stienberg Kaslo, N.Y.C., 1988-89, Van Mosman Merchandising, N.Y.C., 1989-90; design dir. Discovery Jewelry, N.Y.C., 1990—. N.Y. State Regents scholar, 1980. Mem. NAFE. Office: Discovery Jewelry 15 W 36th St New York NY 10018

NUMBERS, JUDY M., association manager; b. El Paso, Tex., Oct. 29, 1949; d. Wayne H. and Marie (Lindsey) N. BS, U. Ariz., Tucson, 1971; MBA, Ariz. State U., Tempe, 1985. Bus. Interior Design. Interior designer W.R. Schulz & Assocs., Phoenix, 1972-73, Doug Frank Devel., Phoenix, 1973-74, Cavalier Homes, Phoenix; v.p., finance Clark-Wayland, Inc., Phoenix, 1976-88; owner Logistics Unlimited, 1988--; adv. bd. Biltmore Nat. Bank, Phoenix, 1987—; sec. Leaders & Exec. Associating for Devel. Phoenix, 1988—; dir. mem. Impact for Enterprising Women, Phoenix, 1988—. Bd. sec., treas. YWCA Maricopa County, Phoenix, 1988-89, exec. dir., 1990—; bd. pres. Youth Evaluation & Treatment Ctrs., Phoenix, 1987-91; bd. sec. Ariz Women's Initiative, Phoenix, 1989; task force mem. Valley Citizen's League, Phoenix, 1988-89. Class VIII Participant Valley Leadership, Inc., Phoenix, 1986-87; Delegate Ariz. Women's Town Hall, Phoenix, 1987-88. Mem. Ariz. Fed. Bus. & Profl. Women, Inc. (pres. 1986-87), Econ. Club of Phoenix, Ariz. Masterworks Chorale Phoenix, Soroptimist Internat. of Phoenix. Republican.

NUNGESSER, MARTHA KATE, environmental scientist, researcher; b. Chapel Hill, N.C., July 8, 1953; d. William Charles and Thelma June (Barton) N.; children: Brian Daniel Esserlieu, Sarah Lindsey Esserlieu. BA, Austin Coll., Sherman, Tex., 1975; MS in Environ. Scis., U. Tex., Dallas, 1978. Demographer North Cen. Tex. Coun. Govts., Arlington, Tex., 1975-76; rsch. asst. U. Tex., Dallas, 1976-78; rsch. technician Savannah River Ecology Lab., Aiken, S.C., 1978-79; regional ecologist Oak Ridge (Tenn.) Nat. Lab., 1979-83; environ. cons. Esserlieu Assocs., Palo Alto, Calif., 1983-84; sr. assoc. Environ. Sci. Assocs., San Francisco, 1984; database mgr., tech. writer Pacific Gas & Electric Co., San Francisco, 1984-88; environ. rsch. assoc. Lawrence Berkeley (Calif.) Lab., 1988-89; rsch. asst. dept. environ. scis. U. Va., Charlottesville, 1989—; cons. Citizens Com. to Complete the Refuge, Palo Alto, Calif., 1985-87, co-chmn., 1985-89; rep. Wetlands Adv. Task Force, San Francisco Bay Estuary Project, 1988-89. Founder, pres. Citizens for Open Space in Alvarado, Union City, Calif., 1986-89; bd. dirs., 2d v.p. Santa Clara Valley Audubon Soc., Palo Alto, 1986-89; mem. Nat. Leadership Environ. Coun., 1989—. Mem. Sigma Xi (assoc.), Alpha Chi. Home: 140 Guilford Ln Charlottesville VA 22901 Office: U Va Dept Environ Scis Clark Hall Charlottesville VA 22903

NUNN, MARGARET BAKER, owner boutique; b. Blue Creek, W.Va., Dec. 24, 1912; d. Arthur and Ethel (Reynolds) Baker; m. William L. Nagy, Aug. 27, 1932 (dec. July 1971); children: William L., Beverly N. Nicklaus; m. Harold Denton Nunn, Nov. 21, 1972. Student, W.Va. Sch. Bus., Fairmont, 1931, Evening Vocat. Sch., Tampa, Fla., 1967. Salesperson S. S. Klein Agy., Pitts., 1936-46; owner, broker Beverly Realty Co., Pitts., 1946-59; owner Christmas Shoppe, St. Pete Beach, Fla., 1961-64, Barefoot Browser, St. Pete Beach, 1964-80, Peg Nunn's Pla. 100, St. Petersburg, Fla., 1979—. founder Boys Club of St. Petersburg, 1972, Abilities Rehabilitation Ctr. Guild, Clearwater, Fla., 1977; pres. Women's C. of C., Treasure Island, Fla., 1966-67, Soroptimist Internat., Treasure Island, 1972; dir. corp. bd. Boys Clubs of Pinellas County, Pinellas Park, Fla., 1972-89, Pinellas County Anti-Crime Com., St. Pete Beach, 1972; elected mem. Castle Shannon Sch. Bd., Pitts., 1959. Named Queen of Hearts, Am. Heart Assn., St. Petersburg, 1977, Woman of the Yr., Beta Sigma Phi, St. Petersburg, 1981, to Hall of Fame, Women's Svc. League, St. Petersburg, 1988. Mem. The Pla. Shoppes Mchts. (pres. 1987-89), Beach Mchts. Assn. (v.p. 1986-89), NAFE. Republican. Lutheran. Home: One Beach Dr Ste 2205 St Petersburg FL 33701 Office: 111 2d Ave NE Ste 100 Saint Petersburg FL 33701

NUNNALLY, SUE ANN, educator; b. Seattle, Feb. 6, 1959; d. Bruce W. and Betty Jane (Porter) N. BA, U. So. Calif., 1981; postgrad., Pepperdine U. Cert. master tchr. multi-subjects, social sci., gifted and talented edn. Mentor tchr. Oceanside (Calif.) Unified Sch. Dist., sch.-based coord. South Oceanside Elem. Sch. CTIP grantee, Nat. Geog. grantee. Mem. ASDEG, CAG, CMA, NEA, NSTA, OTA, Compuser User Edn., Internat. Reading Assn.

NUNNERLEY, SANDRA T., interior design executive; b. Wellington, New Zealand, Jan. 11, 1953; came to U.S., 1979; d. Thomas L. Nunnerley and Lorraine Mary (Sadler) Warren. BFA in Architecture, U. Sydney, Australia, 1974. Asst. to curator Bonython Gallery, Sydney, 1974-76; asst. to prin. Nancy Hoffman Gallery, N.Y.C., 1979-80; ptnr. L.S.K. Designs, N.Y.C., 1980-81; prin., pres. Sandra Nunnerley Inc., N.Y.C., 1981—. Contbr. articles to profl. jours. Mem. N.Y. Hist. Soc. (com. mem.), Cathedral St. John the Divine (com. mem.), DIA Art Found. (com. mem.), Kips Bay Designers (com. mem.), Allied Bd. Trade.

NUOTIO-ANTAR, VAPPU SINIKKA, physicist; b. Helsinki, May 17, 1940; came to U.S., 1976, naturalized, 1984; d. Martti Johannes and Aune Aili (Paavola) Nuotio; m. Basil Niman Antar, Dec. 20, 1974; children: Allie, Annie. BS, U. Helsinki, 1965, MS in Theoretical Physics, 1968, MS in Applied Math., 1969, PhD Theoretical Physics, 1970. Rsch. and teaching asst. U. Helsinki and Acad. Finland, 1966-76; asst. prof., physics U. Tenn. Space Inst., Tullahoma, 1976-88; sr. physicist USBI div. United Techs., Huntsville, Ala., 1988—; Brown found. fellow U. South, Sewanee, Tenn., 1977-78; tchr. math. and French, Moore County High Sch., Lynchburg, Tenn., spring 1980; physicist space scis. lab. NASA Marshall Space Flight Ctr., Huntsville, 1985.; scientist Phys. Rsch., Inc., Huntsville, 1986-87. Contbr. articles to sci. jours. Choir soloist Trinity Luth. Ch., Tullahoma, 1976-84, Grace Luth. Ch., Huntsville, 1985—. ASLA-Fulbright fellow, 1970-71, Zonta Amelia Earhart fellow, 1971-72; Govt. of Denmark exchange scholar, 1972-73, Govt. of Fed. Republic Germany postdoctoral scholar, 1973, NATO scholar, 1984. Mem. Internat. Soc. for Optical Engring., Soc. Mfg. Engrs., Machine Vision Assn., AAUW, Sigma Xi. Home: 12021 Comanche Trail Huntsville AL 35803

NUSBAUM, MARLENE ACKERMAN, marketing professional; b. Portsmouth, Va., June 13, 1949; d. Martin and Betsy Freda (Katz) Ackerman; m. Robert Collier Nusbaum Jr., June 27, 1971; 1 child, Jessica Lynn. AA, U. Sorbonne, 1969; student, Université d"Orléans Tours, 1970; BA magna cum laude, Rutgers U., 1971; MA, Brown U., 1973, PhD with distinction, 1980. Tchr. French Dana Hall Sch., Wellesley, Mass., 1974-75; master French and German Groton (Mass.) Sch., 1975-80; French instr. dept. humanities MIT, Cambridge, 1981; assoc., product mgr. Digital Equipment Corp., Maynard, Mass., 1981-83; mktg. mgr. interactive video Digital Equipment Corp., Bedford, Mass., 1983-85; pvt. practice mktg. cons. Newton, Mass., 1985—; mem. mktg. adv. com. GlobalSports Ltd., Boston, 1989—; cons., editor Heinle & Heinle Pub., Boston, 1981. Co-author (with Verdier) Parlez Sans Peur!, Holt, Rinehart and Winston, 1983. Campaign worker Dukakis for pres., Boston, 1987-88; organizer Class Size PTA Com., Newton, 1986-88; chairperson roundtable, exec. com. Newton PTA Coun., 1987-88. Mem. N.E. Conf. Tchrs. of Fgn. Langs., Am. Coun. Tchrs. Fng. Langs., Mass. Fgn. Lang. Assn. Jewish.

NUSE, THELMA PAULINE, educator; b. Caldwell, Kans., Jan. 16, 1934; d. Edwin Clarence and Edna Dorothy (Lungren) Johnson; m. LaVern Lee Nuse, Dec. 28, 1958 (dec. 1981); children: Dale Alan, Derald Leroy, Danita Rae. BA, Southwestern Coll., Winfield, Kans., 1957; MA, Northwestern Coll., Alva, Okla., 1974. Tchr. pub. schs., Goddard, Kans., 1951-61, Caldwell pub. schs., Kans., 1970—; conductor workshops/seminars in field. Community and project leader 4-H Club; weekend cook at nursing home. Mem. Internat. Reading Assn., Caldwell Tchrs. Assn., Kans. Edn. Assn., Kans. State Coll. Assn. Republican. Methodist. Home: 121 S Osage St Caldwell KS 67022-1644

NUSIM, ROBERTA, publisher; b. N.Y.C., Dec. 1, 1943; d. Seymour and Ranna (Weiner) N.; m. Stephen Jablonsky, Aug. 29, 1965. B.A. in English, CCNY, 1964; M.A., CUNY, 1966. Tchr. N.Y.C. Bd. Edn., 1964-73; v.p. program devel. Mind, Inc., Westport, Conn., 1973-76; pres. Mind Media, 1976-78; founder, pres. Lifetime Learning Systems, Fairfield, Conn., 1978—; founder dir. The Film Study Guild, 1979—. Editor: Let's Talk About Health, 1980. Mem. NAFE, Am. Film Inst., Women in Communications, Ednl. Press Assn. Am., Assn. Supervision and Curriculum Devel. Avocations: reading, painting. Office: Lifetime Learning Systems Inc Box 305 Easton CT 06612

NUSSBAUM, MARTHA CRAVEN, philosophy and classics educator; b. N.Y.C., May 6, 1947; d. George and Betty (Warren) Craven; m. Alan Jeffrey Nussbaum, Aug., 1969 (div. 1987); 1 child, Rachel Emily. BA, NYU, 1969; MA, Harvard U., 1971, PhD, 1975; LHD (hon.), Kalamazoo Coll., 1988. Asst. prof. philosophy and classics Harvard U., Cambridge, 1975-80, assoc. prof., 1980-83; vis. prof. philosophy, Greek and Latin Wellesley (Mass.) Coll., 1983-84; assoc. prof. philosophy and classics Brown U., Providence, R.I., 1984-85, prof. philosophy, classics and comparative lit., 1985-87, David Benedict prof. philosophy, classics and comparative lit., 1987-89, univ. prof., 1989—; rsch. advisor World Inst. Devel. Econs. Rsch., Helsinki, Finland, 1986—. Author: Aristole's De Motu Animalium, 1978, The Fragility of Goodness, 1986, Love's Knowledge, 1990; editor: Language and Logos, 1982. Soc. Fellows Harvard U. jr. fellow, 1972-75, Humanities fellow Princeton U., 1977-78, Guggenheim Found. fellow, 1983, NEH fellow, vis. fellow All Souls Coll., Oxford, Eng., 1986-87. Fellow Am. Acad. Arts and Scis.; mem. Am. Philos. Assn. (exec. com. Ea. div. 1985-87, chair com. internat. cooperation, ex-officio mem. nat. bd. 1989—), Am. Philol. Assn. Office: Brown U Depts Philosophy and Classics Box 1918 Providence RI 02912

NUSSMAN, DONNA SUE, nurse; b. Birmingham, Ala., Sept. 14, 1957; d. Vernon Slade Jr. and Norma Sue (Kesterson) Bumgarner. BSN, U. N.C., 1979, MSN, 1990. RN, N.C. Nurse extern Charlotte (N.C.) Orthopaedic Hosp., 1975-79; pvt. scrub nurse Miller Orthopaedic Clinic, Charlotte, 1979-84, rsch. analyst, 1984—; dir. operating room Univ. Meml. Hosp., Charlotte, 1985-88; orthopaedic clin. coordinator Charlotte Meml. Hosp., 1988-90; orthopaedic CNS Carolinas Med. Ctr., Charlotte, N.C., 1987-90; med. illustrator PBS TV, Charlotte, 1990—. Exec. com. Providence United Meth. Ch., Charlotte, 1984—. L.P. Whitehead scholar U. N.C., 1979, AMA scholar, 1979. Mem. Assn. Operating Rm. Nurses (exec. com. 1979—), Am. Heart Assn. (instr. 1976—, advanced cardiac life support provider 1980—), Am. Nurses Assn., Ski Bees, Sigma Theta Tau (exec. com. 1979—, pres. 1980), Phi Kappa Phi. Republican.

NUTT, NAN, church administrator; b. Pasadena, Calif., Dec. 25, 1925; d. Paul Geltmacher and Estelle Boggs (Love) White; m. David Ballard Norris, Jan. 8, 1944 (div. 1966); children: Teresa, Anita, Carol, Steven; m. Evan Burchall Nutt, July 12, 1969. AA, Chaffee Jr. Coll., Calif., 1967; BA, Pomona Coll., 1969. Adminstrv. asst to dept. head sch. elec. engring. U. Tenn., Knoxville, 1952-53; adminstrv. asst. to minister of ch. edn. United Congl. Ch., Claremont, 1955-62; adminstrv. asst. to personnel dir. Pomona Coll., Claremont, 1962-63; bus. mgr. 1st Congl. Ch., Long Beach, Calif., 1982-86, ch. adminstr., 1986—. Chmn. Nat. Women's Polit. Caucus, Tucson, 1972, nat. rep. Ariz., 1973-79, chmn. greater Long Beach, 1981, vice chmn., Calif., 1986-88; pres. Coalition for ERA, Ariz., 1973-79; commr. Cultural Heritage Commn., Long Beach, 1985-87, chair, 1987—; mem. adv. bd. Plymouth West Older Adult Svc. and Info. System, 1989—. Democrat.

NUTTER, JUNE ANN KNIGHT, exercise physiologist, educator; b. Des Moines, Jan. 22, 1947; d. Joseph Willard and Jean Roena (Eyestone) Knight; m. Lester Albert Nutter, Aug. 25, 1968; children: Melissa Ann, Jacqueline Christine. BS in Phys. Edn. with distinction, U. Okla., 1969; MA in Exercise Sci., U. Nebr., 1982, PhD in Exercise Physiology, 1987. Exercise test technologist. Thcr. phys. edn. Douglas Sch. System, Ellsworth AFB, S.D., 1979-80; grad. teaching asst. U. Nebr., Omaha and Lincoln, 1980-82, 83-85; intern St. Joseph's Hosp., Omaha, 1985; instr. Denver Tech. Coll., Colorado Springs, Colo., 1988, Chapman Coll., Colorado Springs, 1987-88; asst. prof., coord. exercise program Wake Forest U., Winston-Salem, N.C., 1988-89; asst. prof. R.I. Coll., Providence, 1989—; cons. R.I. Dept. Edn., Providence, 1990, Measurement, Inc., Durham, N.C., 1990. Contbr. articles to profl. jours. Com. chmn. Family Svcs., Ellsworth AFB, 1978-79. Grantee U. Nebr., 1982, 86, NIH, 1986. Mem. Am. Coll. Sports Medicine, AAHPER, R.I. Assn. for Health, Phys. Edn., Recreation and Dance, New Eng. Ednl. Rsch. Orgn.

NWOSU, CAROLINE CHINWE, financial planner; b. Igbo-ukwu, Anambra, Nigeria, Nov. 15, 1960; came to U.S., 1983; d. Livinus Umeodiche and Josephine (Omambala) Ezeanyaeche; m. Sunday Chikwado Nwosu, Oct. 2, 1945; children: Nnabugwu I., Nnanyelugo Chukwudi. BBA in Acctg., Howard U., Washington, 1987; postgrad., Howard U., Cath. U. of Am. Cert. gerontologist; lic. ins. rep, Md., D.C., Va.; lic. home health aide/CPR. Acctg. clk. Gov.'s Office, Enugu, Nigeria, 1980-83; asst. supr. K-Mart, Marshall, Tex., 1983-84; office mgr. Health First Med. Ctr., Rockville, Md., 1984-87; fin. planner, ins. rep. Equitable Life Assurance Soc., Rockville, 1987-89; pres. NICCO Enterprises, Ltd., Adelphi, Md., 1989; long-term health care adminstr. Emy & Assocs., Hyattsville, Md., 1989—; nursing asst. Greater S.W. Hosp., Washington, 1986-89; dir. sales Fossil Fuel Co., Washington, 1989, Kid's First Day Care; pres. People's Affordable Ins. Founder, pres. United African Network, Washington, 1987—; treas. African Community Episcopal Ch., choir pres. and organizer. Recipient Manpower award 1988, DSF award 1989. Mem. NAFE (bd. dirs.), Minority Women in Bus. Enterprises, Nat. Assn. Accts., Nat. Assn. Black Accts., Nat. Assn. Life Underwriters, D.C. Life Underwriters Tng. Coun., Women Life Underwriters Confederation, Nigerian Women in Health-Related Professions, Langley Pk. Community Club. Home: 8006 18th Ave Hyattsville MD 20783 Office: NICCO Enterprises Ltd PO Box 7962 Adelphi MD 20783

NYDAM, DARLENE, sales professional; b. Paterson, N.J., Nov. 17, 1961; d. Frank Nydam and Wilma Margie (Kuiken) Redner; m. Lawrence Louis Mazzarini, Mar. 23, 1990. BA in Communications, Pa. State U., 1986. Sales asst. Fox Television Channel 5, Manhattan, N.Y., 1985-86; sales coord. Wold Satellite Communication, Manhattan, 1986-87; sales rep. Russ Berrie Co., Oakland, N.J., 1987—. Home: 254 Glen Ave Midland Park NJ 07432

NYE, MIRIAM MAURINE BAKER, writer; b. Castana, Iowa, June 14, 1918; d. Horace Boies and Hazel Dean (Waples) Hawthorn; B.A., Morningside Coll., 1939, postgrad., 1957-58; postgrad. U. Ariz., 1973, U. S.D., 1975-77, New Coll., U. Edinburgh (Scotland), 1974; m. Carl E. Baker, June 21, 1941 (dec. 1970); children—Kent Alfred, Dale Hawthorn; m. 2d, John Arthur Nye, Dec. 25, 1973. Tchr. jr. high sch., Rock Falls, Ill., 1939-41, Moville (Iowa) Community Sch., 1957-62, Woodbury Central Community Sch., Climbing Hill, Iowa, 1962-64; homemaking columnist Sioux City (Iowa) Jour.'s Farm Weekly, 1953-81; author: Recipes and Ideas From the Kitchen Window, 1973; But I Never Thought He'd Die: Practical Help for Widows, 1978; speaker, Iowa, Nebr., Minn., S.D. Counselor, Iowa State U., 1972—; county adv. Iowa Children's and Family Services, 1980-84; mem. public relations com. Farm Bur., Woodbury County, 1980-82; advisor nat. orgn. for help to widows THEOS, Sioux City chpt., 1981-90; lay del. Iowa United Meth. Conf., 1981-83. Recipient Alumni award Morningside Coll., 1969, Service award Woodbury County Fair, 1969, Friend of Extension award Iowa State U., 1981. Mem. AAUW, Iowa Fedn. Women's Clubs (dist. creative writing chmn. 1978-80), Common Cause, Alpha Kappa Delta, Sigma Tau Delta. Methodist. Home and Office: Box 419 Moville IA 51039

NYE DEHAAN, SUSAN JANET, psychiatric social worker; b. Chgo., Mar. 12, 1945; d. John Lawrence and Rose Emelia (Koller) Shanske; m. Jay Michael Nye, Sept. 20, 1969 (div. 1974); m. Harry Clifford DeHaan, Jan. 14, 1984; children: Jennifer, Katherine. BA in Sociology, Calif. State U., Fresno, 1968; BA in Psychology, Calif. State U., Hawyard, 1973; MSW, Calif. State U., Fresno, 1977. Lic. clin. social worker, Idaho, Calif. Social worker various county agencies, Calif., 1968-75; clin. social worker Porterville (Calif.) Community Counseling Ctr., 1975-76; adminstrv. and teaching intern Calif. State U., Fresno, 1976-77; dir. social svcs. Comprehensive Youth Svcs., Inc., Fresno, 1978-81; instr. social work Calif. State U., Fresno, 1977-82; behavior cons. Edwin M. Hamlin Jr., M.D., Inc., Fredsno, 1980-84; pvt. practice social work Fresno, 1981-84; behavioral sci. faculty U. Calif., San Francisco, 1982-84; clin. social worker Idaho Region V Mental Health Svcs., Jerome, 1984-86; pvt. practice social work Twin Falls, Idaho, 1985—. Contbr. articles to profl. jours. Mem. Nat. Assn. Social Workers, Soc. Clin. Social Workers, Twin Falls County Mental Health Assn., Nat. Ichthyosis Found. (pres. 1986-87), Phi Gamma Mu7. Office: 162-6th Ave North Twin Falls ID 83301

NYGREN, LINDA LAVERNE, interior designer; b. Bismarck, N.D., May 14, 1947; d. Helge Eugene and Laverne (Klusmann) N. AA, Russell Sage Coll., 1989. Asst. to dir. community rels. Scripps Meml. Hosp., LaJolla, Calif., 1974-81; adminstrv. asst. N.Y. State Bar Assn., Albany, 1982-83; exec./personal sec. to state senator Martin M. Solomon State of N.Y., Albany, 1983-88; interior designer, lighting cons. The Lamplighter, Albany, 1988-90. Mem. ASID (allied), Nat. Mus. for Women in the Arts. Democrat.

NYHLEN, KAREN ELIZABETH, TV, music, video and film producer; b. Kalamazoo, Mich., Oct. 6, 1960; d. Roger Henry and Marie Anne Jeannette (Moison) N. BA in Polit. Sci.English magna cum laude, SUNY, Albany, 1982; MS in TV/Radio/Film magna cum laude, Syracuse (N.Y.) U., 1986. Acctg. clk. Home & City Savs. Bank, Albany, N.Y., 1981-82; adminstrv. asst. Goldome Commercial Realty, Buffalo, 1983; pub. rels. asst. Allentown Assn., Nat. Register Historic Dists., Buffalo, 1983-85; teaching asst. Syracuse (N.Y.) U.-Newhouse, 1985-86; acquisitions asst. CBS/Fox Video, N.Y.C., 1987—; reporter-byline Real Estate Weekly-Trade Mag., N.Y.C., 1987-88; producer Young Gited & Broke, N.Y.C., 1987-88; staff writer Plaza Mag., Albany, N.Y., 1982; teaching asst. Syracuse U., 1985. Producer music video: Fun With Bad Boys, 1988, Electric Dance Hop, 1990; video script writer music video: Planet E, 1989. Syracuse U. fellow, 1986. Republican. Home: 632 E 11th St Apt 11 New York NY 10009

NYLANDER, SUZANNE HILMA, sales and marketing executive; b. San Francisco, Oct. 1, 1956; d. Earl Robert and Constance Upton (Arnold) Martin. AA, City Coll. of San Francisco, 1976; BS, U. Calif., Berkeley, 1982. Lic. optometrist, Calif. Pvt. practice optometry Santa Monica, Calif.; tech. advisor Coburn Optical Industries, Tulsa, sales cons., regional sales mgr.; dir. profl. rels. Am. Optical, Southbridge, Mass.; lectr. in field. Recipient honor Am. Optometric Found., Irvin M. Borish Clin. Rsch. award. Home: 150 Vernon Ave 395 Vernon CT 06066

NYY, LINDA KATHLEEN, travel educator; b. Detroit, June 12, 1950; d. Edwin Eugene and Bernice Rose (Berner) N. BS in Edn., Ga. So. Coll., 1972. Corp. travel agt. PCA Travel, Charlotte, N.C., 1974-75; vacation travel agt. Rich's Travel, Atlanta, 1975-77; fgn. travel specialist Travelanes, Inc., Dunwoody, Ga., 1977-81; mgr. travel agy. Travelanes, Inc., 1981-83; owner, dir. Acad. Travel Arts, Atlanta, 1983-86, prin., 1986—; travel instr. Oglethorpe U., Atlanta, 1986—, Phillips Coll., 1989—; speaker in field; bd. dirs. Bahamas Tourism Inst., Nassau. Author: Vacation CounSelling, 1989. Mem. Travel Industry Assn. Ga. Office: 4000 Eula Circle Atlanta GA 30360

OAKAR, MARY ROSE, congresswoman; b. Cleve., Mar. 5, 1940; d. Joseph M. and Margaret Mary (Ellison) O. BA in English, Speech and Drama, Ursuline Coll., Cleve., 1962, LHD (hon.); MA in Fine Arts, John Carroll U., Cleve., 1966; LLD (hon.), Ashland (Ohio) Coll. Instr. English and drama Lourdes Acad., Cleve., 1963-70; asst. prof. English, speech and drama Cuyahoga Community Coll., Cleve., 1968-75; mem. Cleve. City Council from 8th Ward, 1973-76; mem. 95th-102nd Congresses from 20th Dist. Ohio, mem. Pepper Commn. on Long Term Health Care; chair subcom. on econ. stabilization; chair task force on social security, elderly, women, chair subcom. on personnel and police, mem. banking, fin. and urban affairs com., select com. on aging, post office and civil service com., com. on house adminstrn., also numerous subcoms. Founder, vol.-dir. Near West Side Civic Arts Center, Cleve., 1970; ward leader Cuyahoga County Democratic Party, 1972-76; mem. Ohio Dem. Central Com. from 20th Dist., 1974; trustee Fedn. Community Planning, Cleve., Health and Planning Commn. Cleve., Community Info. Service Cleve., Cleve. Soc. Crippled Children, Public Services Occupational Group Adv. Com., Cuyahoga Community Coll., Cleve. Ballet, Cleve. YWCA. Recipient Outstanding Service awards OEO, 1973-78, Community Service award Am. Indian Center, Cleve., 1973, Community Service award Nationalities Service Center, 1974, Community Service award Club San Lorenzo, Cleve., 1976, Cuyahoga County Dem. Woman of Yr., 1977, Ursuline Coll. Alumna of Yr. award, 1977, awards Irish Nat. Caucus, awards West Side Community Mental Health Center, awards Am. Lebanese League, awards Spanish Christian Orgn., awards Cleve. Fedn. Am.-Syrian Lebanese Clubs; cert. appreciation City of Cleve.; Woman of Yr. award Cuyahoga County Women's Polit. Caucus, 1983; decorated Knight of Order of St. Ladislaus of Hungary. Office: US House of Reps 2231 Rayburn Washington DC 20515 also: 523 Federal Courthouse 215 Superior Ave Cleveland OH 44114*

OAKES, ELLEN RUTH, psychotherapist, health institute administrator; b. Bartlesville, Okla., Aug. 19, 1919; d. John Isaac and Eva Ruth (Engle) Harboldt; m. Paul Otis Oakes Sr., June 12, 1937 (div. April 1974); children: Paul Otis Jr., Deborah Ellen, Nancy Elaine Masters; m. Siegmar Johann Knopp, Nov. 24, 1975. BA in Sociology, Psychology summa cum laude, Oklahoma City U., 1961; MS in Clin. Psychology, U. Okla., 1963, PhD, 1967. Lic. clin. psychologist, Okla. Chief psychometrist Okla. U. Guidance Ctr., Norman, 1962; psychology trainee VA Hosp., Oklahoma City, 1962-64, Cerebral Palsy Ctr., Norman, Okla., 1964-65; psychology intern Guidance Service, Norman, 1965-66, staff psychologist, 1966-67; asst. prof. psychology Okla. U. Med. Sch., Oklahoma City, 1967-70; supr. psychology interns Okla. Univ. Health Scis. Ctr., 1967-80; founder, dir. Timberridge Inst., Oklahoma City, 1970-90, pres., 1980-90; pvt. practice clin. psychologist Oklahoma City, 1970—; instr. Okla. U. extension course, Tinker AFB, Oklahoma City, 1963, U. Okla., 1965-66; discussion leader Inst. for Tchrs. of Disadvantaged Child Oklahoma City Sch. System, 1966; leader group therapy sessions Asbury Meth. and Westminster Presbyn. Chs., Oklahoma City, 1966; mem. psychology team confs. for hearing disorders, Okla. U. Med. Sch., 1967-70; cons. Oklahoma City Pub. Schs., 1970-72; cons., group leader halfway house, 1972; lectr. chs., PTAs, hosps.; reviewer Am. Psychol. Assn. Civilian Health and Med. Program of the Uniformed Svcs., 1978-89. Contbr. articles to profl. jours. Speaker Okla. County Mental Health Assn. Ann. Worry Clinic, St. Luke's Ch., Oklahoma City, 1968—; speaker psychology dept. Sorosis Club, St. Luke's Ch. Mem. Am. Psychol. Assn. (mem. peer rev. project with CHAMPUS 1978-89), Okla. Psychol. Assn. (pres. 1975-76), Okla. State Psychologist Licensing Bd. Office: Timberridge Inst 2000 SE 15th Bldg 400 Ste E Edmond OK 73013

OAKLAND, VELMA LEANE, educator; b. Moorhead, Minn., Dec. 29, 1939; d. Alfred J. and Annie (Klusman) Kuvaas; m. Aug. 17, 1959 (div. 1986); 1 child, Terry Lee. BS in Edn., Mayville State U., 1966; MS in Edn., N.D. State U., 1969. Cert. elem. tchr., Minn. Tchr. Granville (N.D.) Pub. Schs., 1960-62, Tappen (N.D.) Pub. Schs., 1962-64, Hughes Elem. Sch., Red Lake Falls, Minn., 1964—. Head start dir. Inter County Community council, Red Lake Falls, Minn., 1970-73; comr. HUD, 1988; mem. Red Lake County Fair Bd., 1988—; mem. exec. com. 7th Congrl. Dist., 1988. Mem. Minn. Edn. Assn. (sec. 1979—, treas. 1983—, exec. com. 1983—), Pine to Prairie Coop. Ctr. (adv. com.), Delta Kappa Gama. Home: 118 Main Ave Red Lake Falls MN 56750 Office: Hughes Elem Sch Red Lake Falls MN 56750

OAKLEY, CAROLYN LE, state legislator, small business owner; b. Portland, Oreg., June 28, 1942; d. George Thomas and Ruth Alveta Victoria (Engberg) Penketh; m. Donald Keith Oakley, June 27, 1965; children: Christine, Michelle. BS in Edn., Oreg. State U., 1965. Educator Linn County (Oreg.) Schs., 1965-76; owner Linn County Tractor, 1965—; mem. Oreg. Legis. Assembly, Salem, 1989—; mem. exec. bd. Oreg. Retail Coun., 1987—. Chmn. Linn County Rep. Cen. Com., 1982-84; chmn. bd. dirs. North Albany Svc. Dist., 1988—, Salvation Army, Linn and Benton Counties, 1987—; vice-chmn. bd. trustees Linn-Benton Community Coll. Found., 1987—; pres. Women for Agr., Linn and Benton Counties, 1984-86. Named Woman of Yr. Albany chpt. Beta Sigma Phi, 1970. Mem. Albany C. of C. (bd. dirs. 1986—), Linn County Rep. Women (legis. chmn. 1982—). Republican. Methodist. Home: 3197 Crest Loop NW Albany OR 97321 Office: Oreg Legis Assembly State Capitol Salem OR 97310

OAKLEY, DEBORAH JANE, researcher, educator; b. Detroit, Jan. 31, 1937; d. George F. and Kathryn (Willson) Hacker; m. Bruce Oakley, June 16, 1958; children: Ingrid Andrea, Brian Benjamin. BA, Swarthmore Coll., 1958; MA, Brown U., 1960; MPH, U. Mich., 1969, PhD, 1977. Dir. teenage and adult programs YWCA, Providence, 1959-63; editorial asst. Stockholm U., 1963-64; rsch. investigator, lectr. dept. population planning U. Mich., 1971-77; asst. prof. community health programs U. Mich., Ann Arbor, 1977-79, asst. prof. nursing rsch., 1979-81, assoc. prof., 1981-89, prof., 1989—, interim dir. Ctr. Nursing Rsch., 1988—. Author: (with Leslie Corsa) Population Planning, 1979; contbr. articles to profl. jours. Recipient Margaret Sanger award Washtenaw County Planned Parenthood, 1975; Outstanding Young Woman of Ann Arbor award Jaycees, 1970. Mem. Am. Pub. Health Assn. (chmn. population sect. council), Internat. Union Sci. Study Population, Midwest Nursing Rsch. Soc., Population Assn. Am., Delta Omega. Democrat. Home: 5200 S Lake Rd Chelsea MI 48118 Office: U Mich Sch Nursing Ann Arbor MI 48109

OAKLEY, MARGARET MARY, nurse; b. Glennonville, Mo., May 27, 1929; d. Elmer George and Amna Mary (Fuemmeler) Smith; m. Gene Elroy Oakley,. BSc., U. Nev., 1971. Community health nurse Washoe County Dist. Health Dept., Reno, Nev., 1972—; chmn. adv. bd. Sparks After Sch. Child Care, Nev. 1975-76. Com. Mem. Washoe County Child Care Adv. Bd., Reno Nev. 1975, mem. sr. legal adv. bd. Mem. Nev. Pub. Health Assn. (sec. 1976-77), AAUW. Democratic. Home: 4210 Hackamore Reno NV 89509

OAKLEY, MARY ANN BRYANT, lawyer; b. Buckhannon, W.Va., June 22, 1940; d. Hubert Herndon and Mary F. (Deeds) Bryant; m. Godfrey P. Oakley, Jr., Sept. 2, 1961; children—Martha, Susan, Robert. A.B., Duke U., 1962; M.A., Emory U., 1970, J.D., 1974. Tchr., Winston-Salem/Forsyth County Schs., N.C., 1961-65; assoc. Margie Pitts Hames, Atlanta, 1974-80; ptnr. Stagg Hoy & Oakley, Atlanta, 1980-83, Oakley & Bonner, Atlanta, 1984—; adj. prof. trial practice Ga. State U., 1986—; bd. dirs. Plaintiff Employment Lawyers Assn.; coodr. PELA, Ga. Contbr. articles to law jours. Notes and Comments editor Emory Law Jour., 1973-74. Author: Elizabeth Cady Stanton, 1972; Bd. dirs. Atlanta Met. YWCA, 1975-79, lst v.p., 1978-79, Leadership Atlanta, 1979; bd. dirs. Ga. chpt. ACLU, 1981-83; trustee Unitarian Universalist Congregation Atlanta, 1977-80, pres., 1979-80, mem. Unitarian Universalist Commn. Appraisal, 1980-85; bd. dirs. Unitarian Universalist Service Com., 1984—, v.p., 1986-88, pres. 1988—. Nat. Merit scholar, 1958. Mem. ABA, Am. Judicature Soc., State Bar Ga. (chmn. individual rights sect. 1979-81, chmn. bench and bar com. 1984-87), Atlanta Bar Assn., Lawyers Club Atlanta, No. Dist. Bar Council, 1982-86, Ga. Assn. Women Lawyers, Ga. State Bar Disciplinary Bd. (investigative panel 1985-88, chmn., 1987-88), Gate City Bar Assn., Ga. Bd. Bar Examiners, Assn. Trial Lawyers of Am., Ga. Women's Polit. Caucus, LWV, Phi Beta Kappa, Order of Coif. Home: 897 Barton Woods Rd NE Atlanta GA 30307 Office: 133 Carnegie Way Ste 508 Atlanta GA 30303

OAKLEY, WANDA FAYE, management consultant, educator; b. Durham, N.C., June 27, 1950; d. Joseph Napolian and Doris Gray (Thomas) O. BSBA, U. N.C., 1971, postgrd., 1972-73. CPA, N.C. Acct. Oakley Motors, Durham, 1965-73; controller Airheart Ins. Agy., Inc., Durham, 1973-75; controller, owner Quality Car Wash, Durham, 1974-83; acct. computer svcs. dept. William H. Mitchell, P.A. and CPAs, Durham, 1983-84; mgr. John Anderson & Assocs., Inc., Durham, 1984-85; v.p. CMS Svcs., Inc., York, S.C., 1985-86; adminstr. N.C. State U., Raleigh, 1986-89; pvt. practice bus. cons. Raleigh, 1989—; instr. Wake Tech. Community Coll., Raleigh, 1985—, Small Bus. Ctr., Johnston Community Coll, Smithfield, N.C., 1990—; proctor N.C. State Bd. CPA Examiners, Raleigh, 1986—; bus. cons. in field. Fellow N.C. Assn. CPAs, AICPA, ASWA; mem. NAFE, Exersafety Internat. (master's cert. 1984), U. N.C. Alumni Assn. (life). Home: PO Box 3257 Durham NC 27715-3257 Office: 453 Westcliffe Ct Raleigh NC 27606-2227

OAKS, M(ARGARET) MARLENE, minister; b. Grove City, Pa., Mar. 30, 1940; d. Allen Roy and Alberta Bell (Pinner) Eakin; m. Lowell B. Chaney, July 30, 1963 (dec. Jan. 1977); 1 child, Christopher Allen; m. Harold G. Younger, Aug. 1978 (div. 1986); children: Linda Michelle, Lowell B. Chaney; m. Gilbert E. Oaks, Aug. 3, 1987. BA, Calif. State U., L.A., 1972; religious sci. studies with several instrs. Ordained to ministry Ch. Religious Sci., 1986. Educator Whittier (Calif.) Sch. Dists., 1972-74, Fullerton (Calif.) Coll., 1974-75, Garden Grove (Calif.) Sch. Dist., 1974-78; minister, founder Community Ch. of the Islands now Ch. of Religious Sci., Honolulu, 1978-80; minister Ch. of Divine Sci., Pueblo, Colo., 1980-83; minister, founder Ch. Religious Sci., Palo Alto, Calif., 1983-86; minister First Ch. Religious Sci., Fullerton, 1986—; workshop leader Religious Sci. Dist. Conv., San Jose, Calif., 1985, 88, 89, Golden Valley Unity Women's Advance, Mpls., 1986, 87, Qume Corp., San Jose, 1985; guest presenter convs. numerous civic and religious sci. orgns., 1979—. Author: Old Time Religion is a Cult, 1985, Beyond forgiveness, 1985, The Christmas in You, 1985, The Worthiness Issue, 1985, Ki Aikido, The Inner Martial Art, 1986, Service, The Sure Path to Enlightenment, 1986, Stretch Marks on My Aura, 1987, Beyond Addiction, 1989; contbr. articles to profl. publs. and mags.; host weekly radio or cable TV programs, Honolulu, 1978-80, Pueblo, Colo., 1981-82; guest various radio programs, San Francisco. Del. 1st Soviet/Am. Citizens Summit Conf., 1988, 89; mem. Coun. of 100, Ctr. for Soviet/Am. Dialogue. Named Outstanding Businesswoman, Am. Businesswomen's Assn., 1989. Mem. Fullerton Interfaith Ministerial Assn. (sec., treas. 1987-89), United Clergy of Religious Sci., Internat. New Thought Alliance (pres. Orange County chpt. 1987-90, pres. for Bay Area 1984-85, co-chairperson 1990 Congress, mem. Asilomar com. 1989—), Kappa Delta Pi. Republican. Office: First Ch Religious Sci 117 N Pomona Ave Fullerton CA 92632

OATES, JOYCE CAROL, author; b. Lockport, N.Y., 1938; d. Frederic James and Caroline (Bush) O.; m. Raymond Joseph Smith, Jan. 23, 1961. BA, Syracuse U., 1960; MA, U. Wis., 1961. Prof. English U. Detroit, 1961-67, U. Windsor, Ont., Can., 1967-87; writer-in-residence Princeton (N.J.) U., 1978-81, prof., 1987—. Author: (short story collections) By the North Gate, 1963, Upon the Sweeping Flood, 1966, The Wheel of Love, 1970, Marriages and Infidelities, 1972, The Hungry Ghosts, 1974, The Goddess and Other Women, 1974, Where Have You Been, 1974, The Poisoned Kiss and Other Portuguese Stories, 1975, The Seduction and Other Stories, 1975, Crossing the Border, 1976, Night-Side, 1977, Last Days, Raven's Wing, The Assignation, 1988; (novels) With Shuddering Fall, 1965,

A Garden of Earthly Delights, 1967, Them, 1969 (Nat. Book award 1970), Wonderland, 1971, Do With Me What You Will, 1973, The Assassins, 1975, Childwold, 1976, The Triumph of the Spider Monkey, 1977, Son of the Morning, 1978, Unholy Loves, 1979, Cybele, 1979, Bellefleur, 1980, A Sentimental Education, 1981, Angel of Light, 1981, A Bloodsmoor Romance, 1982, Mysteries of Winterthorn, 1984, Solstice, 1985, Wild Nights, 1985, Marya, 1986, You Must Remember This, 1987, (as Rosamond Smith) The Lives of the Twins, 1987, American Appetites, 1989, (as Rosamond Smith) Soul-Mate, 1989, Because It Is Bitter, and Because It Is My Heart, 1990, Nemesis, 1990, I Lock My Door Upon Myself, 1990; (poetry collections) Women in Love, 1968, Expensive People, 1968, Anonymous Sins, 1969, Love and Its Derangements, 1970, Angel Fire, 1973, Dreaming America, 1973, Men Whose Lives Are Money, 1978, The Time Traveler, 1990; (plays) The Sweet Enemy, 1965, Sunday Dinner (produced at Am. Place Theatre), 1970, Miracle Play, 1974, Daisy (produced at Cubiculo Theatre), N.Y.C., 1980, In Darkest America (produced at Louisville Festival), 1990, I Stand Before You Naked (Am. Place Theatre), 1990; (essays) The Edge of Impossibility, 1971, The Poetry of D.H. Lawrence, 1973, New Heaven, New Earth, 1974; (criticism) The Profane Art, 1984, On Boxing, 1987, (Woman) Writer, 1988; editor: Ont. Rev., The Best American Short Stories, 1979, also fiction in nat. mags. Recipient O. Henry Prize Story award, 1967-68, Nat. Book award, 1970, Rea award for the Short Story, 1990, Alan Swallow award for fiction, 1990; Guggenheim fellow, 1967-68. Mem. Am. Acad. and Inst. Arts and Letters. Office: Princeton U Dept English Princeton NJ 08544*

OATNEY, CECILIA KAY, military officer; b. McCall, Idaho, May 18, 1956; d. Cecil Edward and Ruby Ilene (Wine) O. BBA in Acctg., Idaho State U., 1978; MS in Econs. and Ops. Research, Colo. Sch. Mines, 1987. Commd. 2d lt. U.S. Army, 1978, advanced through grades to maj., 1990; platoon leader A, B & C Cos. 8th signal bn. U.S. Army, Bad Kreuznach, Fed. Republic of Germany, 1978-81, bn. logistics officer 8th signal bn., 1981; div. radio officer 142d signal bn. U.S. Army, Ft. Hood, Tex., 1982-83, co. comdr. C Co. 142d signal bn., 1983-85, asst. ops. officer 142d signal bn., 1985; chief market analysis 6th recruiting brigade U.S. Army, Ft. Baker, Calif., 1987-89; command and gen. staff coll. U.S. Army, Leavenworth, Kans., 1989-90; chief strategic systems plans br. 5th signal command U.S. Army, Fed. Repubic of Germany, 1990—. Pres. 4-H Club, Valley County, Idaho, 1973-74. Mem. Armed Forces Communication-Electronics Assn., Assn. U.S. Army. Home: PO Box 92 Donnelly ID 83615 Office: HHC 5th Signal Command Box 514 APO NY 09056

O'BANNION, MINDY MARTHA MARTIN, registered nurse; b. Cushing, Okla., Aug. 19, 1953; d. John William and Martha Florence (Vineyard) Martin; student Okla. State U., 1971-73, Oscar Rose Jr. Coll., 1973; grad. St. Anthony Sch. Nursing, 1975; m. William Neal O'Bannion, Oct. 9, 1976; children: Mindi Martha Mae, William Neale Aaron. Nursing asst. Cushing Mcpl. Hosp., 1973-75, head nurse surg. fl., 1975-76, charge nurse med. unit, 1978-79, 82-83; staff nurse Met. Hosp., Dallas, 1985; staff nurse med. unit Mesquite (Tex.) Community Hosp., 1985-87; nurse post partum unit Trinity Med. Ctr., Carrollton, Tex., 1987—. Mem. social com. Royal Haven Bapt. Ch. Women's Missionary Union, Dallas, 1977-78; mem. extension dept. nursery First Bapt. Ch., Cushing, 1979-82, extension dept. presch., 1982-84; mem. extension dept presch. Royal Haven Bapt. Ch., Dallas, 1986-87; treas., mem. nominating com. Joyce Harms group Women's Missionary Union; ckerk, charter mem. Brookhaven Bapt. Ch., Framers Branch, Tex., 1989—. Mem. Am., Tex., Okla. State nurses assns., St. Anthony Hosp. Sch. Nursing Alumnae, Bluebonnet Shelties (founder Farmers Br. chpt.), Tau Beta Sigma, Alpha Xi Delta (corr. sec. 1973). Baptist. Home: 2939 Oxfordshire Ln Farmers Branch TX 75234

O'BANNION, TAMI HELÈNE, museum curator, director; b. Beaumont, Tex., Feb. 14, 1963; d. James Bruce and Lorena Helène (Hodge) O'B. BS in Wildlife & Fisheries Sci., Tex. A&M U., 1985. Full-time intern Star of Republic Mus., Washington, Tex., 1985; conservation technician Tex. Conservation Ctr. McFaddin Ward House Mus., Canyon, Tex., 1986; curator, dir. Confederate Air Force Mus., Harlingen, Tex., 1986—. Contbg. writer, photographer bi-monthly mag. Mem. NAFE, Am. Assn. State and Local History, Am. Assn. Mus., Nature Conservancy, Sierra Club, Tex. Assn. Mus., Century Club Tex. A&M U. Office: Confederate Air Force Mus 1 Heritage Way Harlingen TX 78551

OBERHAUSEN, JOYCE ANN WYNN, aircraft company executive, artist; b. Plain Dealing, La., Nov. 12, 1941; d. George Dewey and Jettie Cleo (Farrington) Wynn; m. James J. Oberhausen, Oct. 15, 1966; 1 child, Georgann; children by previous marriage: Darla Renee Estein Oberhausen Minor, Dale Henry Estein Oberhausen. Student Ayers Bus. Sch., Shreveport, 1962-63, U. Ala., 1964-65. Stenographer, sec. Lincoln Nat. Life Co., Shreveport, 1965-66; sec. Baifield Industries, Shreveport, 1975-86; internat. art tchr., Huntsville, Ala., 1974—; v.p., co-owner Precision Splty. Co., Huntsville, 1966—, Mil. Aircraft, Huntsville, 1979—; pres., owner Wynnson Enterprises, Huntsville, 1983—; owner, artist, designer Wynnson Galleries Pvt. Collections, Florist, Meridianville, 1987; owner North Ala. Wholesale Flowers, 1988—, Wynnson Enterprises Mil. Packaging Co., 1988—. Co-founder Nat. Mus. Women in Arts; active Nat. Mus. Women in Arts. Mem. NAFE, Internat. Porcelain Guild, People to People, Porcelain Portrait Soc., United Artists Assn., Am. Soc. of Profl. and Executive Women Hist. Soc., Nat. Trust Hist. Preservation, Internat. Platform Assn., Met. Mus. Art., Smithsonian Assn., Assn. Community Artists, Rep. Senatorial Inner Circle, Ala. Sheriffs Assn., C. of C., Better Bus. Bur., Huntsville Art League and Mus. Assocs.. Avocations: oil painting, antiques, handicrafts, gourmet cooking, horseback riding. Home: 156 Spencer Dr Meridianville AL 35759 Office: Precision Splty Corp 150 Wells Rd Meridianville AL 35759

OBERMEYER, THERESA NANGLE, educator; b. St. Louis, July 25, 1945; d. James Francis and Harriet Clare (Shafer) Nangle; m. Thomas S. Obermeyer, Dec. 23, 1977; children: Thomas Jr., James, Margaret and Matthew (twins). BA, Maryville Coll., St. Louis, 1967; MEd, St. Louis U., 1970, PhD, 1975. Lic. real estate broker. Dir. student activities Lindenwood Colls., St. Charles, Mo., 1969-70; asst. dean of students Loyola Coll., Balt., 1972-73; asst. dir. student activities St. Louis Community Coll., St. Louis, 1973-78; dir. student activities U. Alaska, Anchorage, 1978-79; instr. sociology Chapman Coll., Anchorage, 1980—; secondary tchr. McLaughlin Youth Ctr. for Juvenile Delinquents, 1984—; mem. Anchorage Sch. Bd., 1990—. Contbr. articles to profl. jours. Commr. Mcpl. Health Commn. Anchorage, 1980-81, exec. board; vol. Rogers Park PTA, Anchorage. Recipient NDEA scholarship, 1970-72, Title I Grant U. Md. and Loyola Coll., 1972-73, Fed. Women's Equity Act U.S. Dept. Edn. U. Alaska, 1978-79; named Fulbright fellow Project India, 1974, Project Jordan, 1977. Mem. DAR (bd. dirs. Anchorage chpt. 1979—, state of Alaska sec. 1989—), AAUW (bd. dirs. Anchorage br. 1980-81), Am. Soc. Pub. Adminstrn. (pres. and bd. dirs. southcentral chpt. 1981). Home: 3000 Dartmouth Dr Anchorage AK 99508 Office: McLaughlin Youth Ctr 2600 Providence Dr Anchorage AK 99508

OBERNDORF, MEYERA E., mayor; m. Roger L. Oberndorf; children: Marcie, Heide. BS in Elem. Edn., Old Dominion U., 1964. Broadcaster Sta. WNIS, Norfolk, Va.; mem. city coun. City of Virginia Beach, Va., 1976—, vice-mayor, 1986, mayor, 1988—. Mem. exec. bd. Tidewater coun. Boys Scouts Am.; bd. dirs. Virginia Beach Pub. Libr., 1966-76, chmn. bd., 1967-76. Mem. AAUW, U.S. Conf. Mayors, Va. Mcpl. League (exec. bd.), Nat. League Cities (vice-chmn.), Princess Anne Women's Club. Jewish. Home: 5404 Challedon Dr Virginia Beach VA 23462 Office: Mcpl Ctr Virginia Beach VA 23456-9002*

OBERSTAR, HELEN ELIZABETH, cosmetics company executive; b. Ottawa, Ill.; d. Milton Edward and Helen (Herrick) Weiss; m. Edward Charles Oberstar, Feb. 3, 1945 (dec. 1984). BS in Chemistry, Monmouth (Ill.) Coll., 1943; postgrad., Northwestern U., Chgo., 1947-49; LLD (hon.), Monmouth Coll., 1987. Asst. food technologist Standard Brands, Inc., Bklyn., 1943-45; chemist Miner Labs., Midwest div., Arthur D. Little, Chgo., 1946-50; rsch. chemist/rsch. supr. Toni Co., div. Gillette Co., Chgo., 1951-65; group leader rsch. and devel. Shulton, Inc., Clifton, N.J., 1965-72; sect. leader rsch. and devel. Am. Cyanamid, Clifton, 1972-75; mgr. rsch. and devel. Clairol Bristol Myers Internat., Stamford, Conn., 1975-82; dir. tech. Clairol Bristol Myers Squibb Consumer Products Group Internat., Stamford, 1982—. Patentee in field. Recipient Disting. Alumni award Monmouth Coll., 1986. Mem. Soc. Cosmetic Chemists (house chmn. 1963-64), Cosmetic Toiletries Fragrance Assn. Episcopalian. Home: 512 Belden Hill Rd Wilton CT 06897 Office: Bristol-Myers Squibb 2 Blachley Rd Stamford CT 06922

OBERSTEIN, MARYDALE, geriatric specialist; b. Red Wing, Minn., Dec. 30, 1942; d. Dale Robert and jean Ebba-Marie (Holmquist) Johnson; children from previous marriage: Kirk Robert, Mark Paul; m. William Bruce Oberstein, June 19, 1972; children: MaryJean, Brennon. Student, U. Oreg., 1961-62, Portland State U., 1962-64, Long Beach State U., 1974-76. Cert. geriatric specialist, Calif. Florist, owner Sunshine Flowers, Santa Ana, Calif., 1982—; pvt. duty nursing aide Aides in Action, Costa Mesa, Calif., 1985-87; owner, adminstr. Lovelight Christian Home for the Elderly, Santa Ana, 1987—; activity dir. Bristol Care Nursing Home, Santa Ana, 1985-88; nursing home activist to reform laws to force bad homes out, 1984-86; founder, tchr. hugging classes/healing therapy, 1987—; bd. dir. Orange County Coun. on Aging., 1984—. Chairperson Helping Hands, 1985—, Woman Aglow Orange County, 1985—, Pat Robertson Com. 1988, Orange County Bush for Pres. campaign, 1988. Recipient Carnation Silver Bowl Carnation Svc. Co., 1984-85; named Woman of Yr. Kiwanis, 1985; honored AM L.A. by Calif. Lt. Gov. McCarthy, 1984. Mem. Calif. Assn. Residential Care Homes, Orange County Epilepsy Soc. (bd. dirs. 1986—), Calif. Assn. Long Term Facilities. Home: 2722 S Diamond Santa Ana CA 92704

OBERT, JESSIE CRAIG, nutritionist, consultant; b. Port Byron, Ill., Mar. 26, 1911; d. Walter Thomas and Clara D.C. Craig; m. Carl B. Obert, Dec. 7, 1935 (dec. 1943). BA, Park Coll., Parkville, Mo., 1931; SM, U. Chgo., 1943; PhD, Ohio State U., 1951. Nutritionist Chgo. Welfare Dept., 1937-42; dir. nutrition ARC, Phoenix, 1943-47; instr. Ohio State U., Columbus, 1947-51, UCLA, 1952-53; chief div. nutrition L.A. County Health Dept., L.A., 1953-76; ind. nutrition cons. L.A., 1976—. Author college textbook: Community Nutrition, 1986. Named Disting. Alumna, Ohio State U., 1976, Park Coll., 1978; recipient recognition for svc. Am. Home Econs. Assn., 1970. Mem. AAUW, Women's City Club Pasadena, Pasadena Athletic Club, Am. Dietetic Assn. (del. 1965-71), Calif. Dietetic Assn. (outstanding mem. award 1977, Dolores Nyhus award 1989), Soc. Nutrition Edn., Am. Pub. Health Assn. Home: 5122 Bomer Dr Los Angeles CA 90042

OBLINGER, JOSEPHINE KNEIDL HARRINGTON (MRS. WALTER L. OBLINGER), state agency administrator; b. Chgo., Feb. 14, 1913; d. Thomas William and Margaret (Kneidl) Harrington; B.S., U. Ill., 1933; J.D., U. Detroit, 1968; L.H.D., Sioux Empire Coll., 1966; m. Walter L. Oblinger, Apr. 27, 1940; 1 son, Carl D. Tchr. Lanphier High Sch., Springfield, Ill., 1951-62; clk. Sangamon County, assessor Capital Twp., Springfield, 1962-69; asst. dir. Ill. Dept. Registration and Edn., Springfield, from 1970; exec. dir. Gov.'s Com. on Voluntary Action, 1970-73; asst. to pres. Lincoln Land Community Coll., 1973-77; dir. Ill. Dept. on Aging, 1977-78; mem. Ill. Ho. Reps., 1978-85; dir. Gov.'s Office Sr. Involvement, 1985—. Sec. Springfield and Sangamon County Community Action, 1965-70 pres., 1970-74; mem. finance com. Child and Family Service, Springfield, 1965-70; mem. Nat. Com. for Day Care of Children, from 1960; mem. I-SEARCH: Task Force on Alzheimer's Disease of So. Ill. U.; pres. Springfield Fedn. Tchrs. AFL-CIO, 1957-59, Ill. Fedn. Tchrs. AFL-CIO, 1959-63; mem. adv. com. to Gov.'s ACTION Office; mem. Planning Consortium for Services to Children in Ill., pres., 1978-79; chmn. mothers' march Sangamon County March of Dimes, 1980; bd. dirs., sec. Villa Vianney Retirement Ctr., Ill. Humanities Council, YWCA, Fed. Council on Aging, officer, Republican Women's Luncheon Club, 1959, pres., 1963-67; chmn. Sangamon County Rep. com., from 1965; past pres. Ill. Fedn. Rep. Women. Del. to White House Conf. on Children, 1960; chairperson Com. Women's Affairs White House Conf. Aging, 1981. Bd. dirs., pres. Sangamon-Menard County Council on Alcoholism and Drugs, 1964-89, Nat. Center Vol. Action; mem. bd. Sangamon County Salvation Army, Ret. Sr. Vol. Program, Edn. Alumnae Assn., Sangamon County Lit. Council. Recipient Golden Anniversary Salute to Older Illinoisans award Blue Cross/Blue Shield, 1987, Nat. Coun. Aging Vol. award, 1989. Mem. Ill. Assn. County Clks. and Recorders (past pres.), Am. Bus. Women's Assn., ABA, Ill. Bar Assn., Sangamon County Bar Assn., Am. Assn. Vol. Services Coordinators (dir., chmn. pub. policy com.), NAACP (exec. bd.), Urban League, Am. Arbitration Assn., U. Ill. Alumni Assn., Nat. Assn. Recorders and Clks., Sangamon County Hist. Soc., Ill. Gerontology Consortium (v.p. cen. region), Ill. Council Continuing Edn. (exec. com.), P.E.O., Springfield Women's Club, Kappa Delta Pi, Sigma Delta Pi, Delta Delta Delta. Clubs: Springfield Women's; Altrusa (pres. 1968-70) (Springfield). Home: RR 1 Williamsville IL 62693 Office: Gov's Office Sr Involvement Stratton Bldg Room 107 Springfield IL 62706

OBOYSKI-BATTELENE, JOANNE MARIE, television and film producer; b. Newark, Mar. 27, 1956; d. Raymond Adolf Oboyski and Bertha Marie Webber; Russell Allen Battelene, June 25, 1952. Student, Bergen Community Coll., Paramus, 1981. FCC Gen. Radio/Telephone Operators License. Mgr. post duplication Panavideo Prodn, N.Y.C., 1983-84; assoc. producer, prodn. sec. PM Mag. Sta. WNYW-TV Fox, N.Y.C., 1979-85, producer, 1979-85; booth pa/prod. sec. Life's Most Embarrassing Moment Reeves Entertainment, Los Angeles; asst. to supervising producer MacGyver Paramount Pictures, Hollywood, 1985-88; prodn. mgr. Creative License, 1988; asst. assoc. prod. Quantum Leap Universal Studios, Universal City, Calif., 1988—. Recipient Iris Award N.A.T.P.E. (Nat'l assn. of TV prog. exec.), 1985, Comm. Arts Award Bergen Community Coll, 1981, Community Arts Scholarship, Bergen Community Coll. 1981, Merit Scholarship Bergen Community Coll. 1981. Felow Phi Theta Kappa Chpt. V.P. 1979-81. Roman Catholic. Office: Universal Studios 100 Universal City Pla Universal City CA 91608

O'BRIANT, JANNIS LYNN, librarian; b. Amarillo, Tex., Apr. 9, 1950; d. Dennis Woodson and Carrie Jane (Wade) O'B. BA, West Tex. State U., 1972, MEd, 1984. Tchr. Shamrock (Tex.) Ind. Sch. Dist., 1972-73; tchr. Amarillo Ind. Sch. Dist., 1973-84, tchr., librarian, 1984—. Mem. Tex. Classroom Tchrs. Assn., Tex. Tchrs. Assn., Amarillo Classroom Tchrs. Assn., Aircraft Owners and Pilots Assn., Tex. Assn. Gifted and Talented, Tex. Libr. Assn., CAP, Alpha Delta Pi, Alpha Delta Kappa, Kappa Kappa Iota. Democrat. Methodist. Home: 3611 Cline Amarillo TX 79110

O'BRIEN, ANNA BELLE CLEMENT, state senator; b. Scottsville, Ky.; d. Robert S. Clement; m. Charles H. O'Brien; 3 stepchildren. Student McMurry Coll., Abilene, Tex. Former mem. Tenn. Ho. of Reps.; mem. Tenn. State Senate, 1976—. Active Am. Legion Aux., Cumberland County Mental Health Assn., DAR, Cumberland County Beautiful Assn., Hosp. Aux.; adv. council Maccasin Bend Psychiat. Hosp., Chattanooga; bd. dirs. Plateau Mental Health Ctr., Cookeville, Tenn.; bd. dirs. Wharton Nursing Home, Cumberland County, Crossville C. of C. Mem. Bus. and Profl. Women's Club, Democratic Women's Club. Clubs: Top Town Garden, Marie Ervin Home Demonstration, Lake Tansi Village Women's. Baptist. Office: Tenn Senate State Capitol Nashville TN 37219*

O'BRIEN, ANNE PACE, medical center administrator, real estate salesperson; b. Pittston, Pa., Feb. 2, 1930; d. Leo Aloyious Pace and Catherine (Ceceal) O'Rourke; m. Vincent Anderson O'Brien, Nov. 15, 1952; children: Lou Anne, Catherine, Vincent II (dec.), Sean, Jeremy, Daniel, Megan. Student, St. Joseph's Coll., 1969-70; RN, St. Mary's Hosp. Sch. Nursing, Hoboken, N.J., 1952. Pres., adminstr., owner Community Med. Ctr., Northport, N.Y., 1961—; assoc. Olita Real Estate, Kings Park, N.Y., 1966—; owner, pres., mgr. Mallow Marsh Farm Stables, Northport, N.Y., 1979—. Dir., pres. St. Charles Aux. (Northport chpt.), 1964-65; dir. St. Charles Aux. Coordinating Coun., Port Jefferson, N.Y., 1966-78; Womens Aux. to Med. Soc., L.I., N.Y., 1972-82; pres. Cystic Fibrosis Found., 1974-75, dir., 1968-70; mem. Nassau-Suffolk Dist. II Councilar Women's Aux., 1976-77. Mem. State N.Y. Med. Soc. Roman Catholic. Home: 115 Sunken Meadow Rd Northport NY 11768 Office: Community Med Ctr 1014 Fort Salonga Rd Northport NY 11768-2525

O'BRIEN, CAROL JEAN, municipal government parks administrator; b. Chgo., June 18, 1939; d. Charles August and Frances Carolyn (Reese) Boeck; m. Thomas Joseph McEvoy, Oct. 18, 1958 (div. Mar. 1982); 1 child, Corrine Marie McEvoy; John Patrick O'Brien, July 18, 1985 (div. Mar. 1988). Grad. high sch., Maywood, Ill., 1957. Mfrs. rep. Midwest Cen., Chgo., 1969-71; supt. recreation Wood Dale (Ill.) Park Dist., 1977-87, bus. mgr., 1988-89, exec. dir. parks and recreation, 1989—. Mem. Nat. Parks and Recreation Assn., Suburban Parks and Recreation Assn. (chairperson 1983-85, sec. 1985-86, spl. projects com. 1986—), Ill. Parks and Recreation Assn., Wood Dale C. of C. (dir. and sec. 1989—). Lutheran. Office: Wood Dale Park Dist 533 N Wood Dale Rd Wood Dale IL 60191

O'BRIEN, CATHERINE LOUISE, museum administrator; b. N.Y.C., July 21; d. Edward Denmark and Catherine Louise (Browne) O'B.; m. Philip R. James (div.); m. Sterling Noel (div.). B.A., Finch Coll., N.Y.C.; postgrad. Williams Coll., Williamstown, Mass., Sarah Lawrence Coll. Reprodn. mgr. Met. Mus. Art, N.Y.C., 1975—. Exhibited in group shows at Parrish Art Mus., Southampton, N.Y., 1965-70, Met. Mus. Art, N.Y.C., 1975-85, Guild Hall Exhibit, East Hampton, N.Y., 1965-85. Mem. aux. Southampton Hosp., 1970-85; founder East Hampton Horse Show, Ladies Village Improvement Soc., East Hampton, 1970—; mem. fair coms. St. James Ch., N.Y.C., St. Luke's Ch., East Hampton, 1970-85; mem. alumnae adv. bd. Marymount Coll., N.Y.C., 1984-86, Women's Nat. Rep. Club, N.Y.C. Mem. DAR (vice regent East Hampton chpt. 1974-85), Colonial Dames Am. (archives com. 1980-85), Daus. Brit. Empire (historian 1978-85), United Daus. Confederacy (state historian 1970-85), Daus. Colonial Wars (corr. sec. 1983-85), Sons and Daus. of the Pilgrims (corr. sec. 1983-85), Victorian Soc., Soc. Mayflower Descs. (life), English Speaking Union, New Eng. Soc. (mem. ball com. 1983-86), Daus. of Cin. (historian 1979-85), Squadron "A". Republican. Episcopalian. Clubs: Devon Yacht, Maidstone (East Hampton, N.Y.); Southampton Yacht (N.Y.); Metropolitan (N.Y.C.) (women's com., chmn. debutante ball 1980-84); Reciprocal/India House, St. Anthony Union League (N.Y.C.). Avocations: show horses; dogs. Home: 605 Park Ave New York NY 10021 Office: Met Mus Art Fifth Ave New York NY 10028

O'BRIEN, ERIN KATHLEEN, personnel specialist; b. Northampton, Mass., Mar. 23, 1952; d. Roger Stephen and Mary Figgie O'B. BS, North Adams State Coll., 1976; AA, Greenfield Community Coll., 1974. Personnel adminstr. supr. Shawnut Worcester Co. Bank, Worcester, Mass.; staff coord. Personnel Pool of Springfield, West Springfield, Mass.; sr. employment counselor Bank of New Eng. West, Springfield, Mass.; pers. mgr. E&J Distbrs., Inc./Trico Svcs., Northampton, Mass. Mem. Easthampton Rep. Town Com., del. state conv., 1990. Home: 22 Lyman Ave Easthampton MA 01027 Office: E&J Disbrs Inc/Trico Svcs 99 Industrial Dr Northampton MA 01027

O'BRIEN, JOAN KAREN, addictions counselor, consultant; b. Hagerstown, Md., Nov. 13, 1952; d. Harold Paul and Geraldine Ann (Goldsworthy) O'B. BS in Sociology, Frostburg U., 1983. Affiliate mem. Sch. Sisters Notre Dame, Balt., 1975-79; asst. dept. mgr. K-Mart Corp., Frederick, Md., 1980-85; addictions counselor Frederick County Health Dept., Frederick, 1984-85, Carroll County Health Dept., Westminster, Md., 1985; asst. dir. pub. rels. Mountain Manor Treatment Ctr., Emmitsburg, Md., 1985-88; addictions counselor Baltimore County Office Substance Abuse, Randallstown, Md., 1988—; info. specialist Nat. Inst. on Drug Abuse Substance, Rockville, Md., 1988—. Mem. Frederick Dem. Com., 1971—; tchr. Cath. Deaf Balt., 1970-76. Fellow Nat. Assn. Alcoholism and Drug Abuse Counselors, Cert. Alcoholism Counselors Md., AAUW. Office: Office Substance Abuse 8737-B Liberty Rd Randallstown MD 21133

O'BRIEN, LORETTA SULLIVAN, lawyer; b. Boston, June 13, 1930; d. Franklin James and Frances Gertrude (Sullivan) O.; m. William P. Shields, Aug. 27, 1949 (div. 1971); children: Candice P., Leslie A. BA, U. Mass., 1969; postgrad. cert. in social work, Simmons Coll., Boston, 1973; JD, New Eng. Sch. Law., 1977. Bar: Mass. 1977. Founder, owner Norwood Legal Ctr., Norwood, Mass., 1978—. Mem. Norwood Bar Assn., Western Norfolk Bar Assn., Norfolk County Bar Assn., Mass. Bar Assn., Appalachian Mountain Club. (bd. dirs.). Office: Norwood Legal Ctr 1 Walpole St Ste 1 Norwood MA 02062

O'BRIEN, LUCREZIA FLORENCE, cosmetics company executive; b. Albany, N.Y., Jan. 28, 1940; d. Joseph John and Christina E. (Pustorino) Toste; children: Thomas, Jr., Stephanie. Lic. cosmetologist, Ill. Mgr. Face & Figure Salon, Hinsdale, Ill., 1960-70; founder, pres. LaFinesse, Inc., Lisle, Ill., 1970—. Chmn. benefit dance local Am. Cancer Soc., Riverwalk Naperville; co-developer Child Protection Program; active YMCA, Naperville Heritage Soc., Naperville Humane Soc.; vol. Good Samaritan Hosp. Mem. Nat. Cosmetologist Assn., Ill. Cosmetologist Assn., Chgo. Cosmetologist Assn. (chmn. various coms. 1984—, co-chmn. edn. com. 1986—, bd. dirs., treas. 1984—), Women in Mgmt. (program com. 1985—, spl. events com., speakers arrangement com. 1986—, Woman of Achievement award, Charlotte Danstrom award 1987), Naperville C. of C. (relations com. 1984—, chmn. ann. golf tournament, bd. dirs. 1985—, v.p. 1988—). Office: LaFinesse Inc 501 Ogden Ave Lisle IL 60532

O'BRIEN, MARY DEVON, communications executive, consultant; b. Buenos Aires, Argentina, Feb. 13, 1944; came to U.S., 1949, naturalized, 1962; d. George Earle and Margaret Frances (Richards) Owen; m. Gordon Covert O'Brien, Feb. 16, 1962 (div. Aug. 1982); children: Christopher Covert, Devon Elizabeth; m. Christopher Gerard Smith, May 28, 1983. BS, Rutgers U., 1975, MBA, 1976. Controller manpower Def. Communications div. ITT, Nutley, N.J., 1977-80, adminstr. program, 1977-78, mgr. cost, schedule control, 1978-79, voice processing project, 1979-80; mgr. project Avionics div. ITT, Nutley, 1980-81, sr. mgr. projects, 1981—; cons. strategic planning, N.J., 1983—; bd. trustees South Mountain Counseling Ctr., 1987—; lectr. in field. Author: Pace: System Manual, 1979, Voices, 1982; contbr. articles to profl. jours. Chmn. Citizens Budget Adv. Com., Maplewood, N.J., 1984-87, chmn. recreation, libr., pub. svcs., 1982-83, chmn. pub. safety, emergency svcs., 1983-84, chmn. schs. and edn., 1984-85; bd. dirs., officer Civic Assn., Maplewood, 1984—; bd. trustees United Way Essex and West Hudson Community Svc. Coun., 1988—; first v.p. Maplewood Civic Assn., 1987-89, pres., 1989—; chmn. Maple Leaf Svc. award Com., 1987-89, Community Svc. Coun. of Oranges and Maplewood Homelessness, Affordable Housing, Shelter Com., 1988—; co-chmn. speaker's bur. United Way, 1989—; v.p. mktg. United Way Community Svc. Coun. of Orange and Maplewood, 1990—; nat. chmn. Project Mgmt. Jour. Survey; mem. Maplewood Zoning Bd., 1983—; officer, mem. exec. bd. N.J. Project Mgmt. Inst., 1985—, pres., 1987-88; bd. dirs. Performance Mgmt. Assn.; chmn. Charter Com.; chmn. Internat. Project Mgmt. Inst. Jour. and Membership survey, 1986-87, mktg. com., 1986—, long range planning and steering com., 1987—; bd. dirs., vice chmn. Coun. Chpt. Pres. Interaction Com., 1986—, Internat. Project Mgmt. Inst.; v.p. Internat. Project Mgmt. Inst. Region II, 1989-90; adv. bd. Project Mgmt. Jour., 1987—, N.J. PMI Ednl., 1987—; liaison officer Internat. Project Mgmt. Inst. and Performance Mgmt. Assocs.; mem. MCA/N.J. Blood Bank Drive; trustee community svc. coun. and edn. program United Way Essex and West Hudson, 1988—. Recipient spl. commendation for community svc. Twp. Maplewood, 1987; First Place award Anti-Shoplifting Program for Distributive Edn. Club Am., 1981, N.J. Fedn. of Women's Clubs, 1981, 82, Retail Mchts. Assn., 1981, 82; Commendation and Merit awards Air Force Inst. Tech., 1981; Pres.'s Safety award ITT, 1983; State award N.J. Fedn. of Women's Clubs Garden Show, 1982, Outstanding Pres. award Internat. Project Mgmt. Inst., 1988, Outstanding Svc. and Contbrn. award 1986-87; Cert. Spl. Merit award N.J. Fedn. of Women's Clubs, 1982, Disting. Contbn. award United Way, 1990. Mem. Internat. Platform Speakers Assn., Grand Jury Assn., Telecommunications Group and Aerospace Industries Assn., Women's Career Network Assn., Nat. Security Indsl. Assn., Assn. for Info. and Image Mgmt., Internat. Project Mgmt. Inst. (liaison officer), Performance Mgmt. Assn, ITT Mgmt. Assn., NAFE, Rutger's Grad. Sch. Bus. Mgmt. Alumni Assn., LWV, Maplewood Women's Evening Membership Div. (pres. 1980-82). Home: 594 Valley St Maplewood NJ 07040 Office: ITT Avionics 100 Kingsland Rd Clifton NJ 07014

O'BRIEN, MARY KAYE, researcher; b. Freeport, Ill., June 16, 1960; d. Joseph Emmett O'Brien and Beverly Ann (Swarts) Lewis; m. Donald James Bushelle, June 5, 1982. BS, U. Iowa, 1982; MA, Drake U., Des Moines, 1984. Rsch. analyst Communication Devel. Co., West Des Moines, Iowa, 1984-85, project mgr., 1985-86; sr. rsch. assoc. Market Decision Assocs., Seattle, 1986; rsch. coord. KCTS TV, Seattle, 1986-88, rsch. mgr., 1988-90; mkt. rsch. analyst U. Wash. Med. Ctr., Seattle, 1990—; dir. Mktg. and Communications Assoc., Seattle, 1989—. Grad. Student rsch. grantee Drake U., Des Moines, 1984. Mem. Midwestern Psychol. Assn., Puget Sound Rsch. Forum. Home: 1402 SW Webster St Seattle WA 98106 Office: U

Wash Med Ctr Rm BB318 1959 NE Pacific St RC-35 Rm BB367 Seattle WA 98195

OBRIEN, PATRICIA MARY, education educator; b. Fall River, Mass., Jan. 12, 1951; d. William Joseph and Constance Loyola (Morgan) O. AA, Dean Jr. Coll., Franklin, Mass., 1970; BA, Salve Regina Coll., Newport, R.I., 1972. Tchr. Mt. St. Joseph, Fall River, 1972-73, Fall River Pub. Sch., 1973-80; edn. specialist Commonwealth Mass. Dept. Edn., Lakeville, 1980—; chairperson basic skills plus com. S.E. Regional Edn. Ctr., Middleboro, Mass., 1988—, chairperson dropout prevention com. Joint Fall River Dept. of Edn., Lakeville, 1983—. Fellow Inst. Ednl. Leadership, New Eng. Assn. Sch. & Colls. Democrat. Roman Catholic. Office: SE Regional Edn Ctr 33 Main St Ste 2 Lakeville MA 02347

O'BRIEN, PATRICIA NEVIN, computer scientist; b. Hanover, Pa., June 13, 1957; d. Malcolm Hugh and Lida Mae (Smith) Nevin; m. Thomas Gerard O'Brien, May 2, 1981; 1 child, Thomas Joseph. BS in Psychology, Towson State U., 1978, MA, 1980. Rsch. asst. Johns Hopkins U., Balt., 1980-82; programmer-analyst Johns Hopkins U., Towson, Md., 1982; ops. rsch. analyst U.S. Army, Aberdeen, Md., 1983-84, 86-87; officer BDM Corp., Albuquerque, 1984-85; pres. Maverick, Inc., Albuquerque, 1985-86; chief analysis div. Def. Test and Evaluation Support Agy., Albuquerque, 1987-89; ops. rsch. analyst Operational Test and Evaluation Ctr. USAF, Albuquerque, 1989—. Mem. Armed Forces Communications and Electronics Assn. Office: HQAFOTEC/OASC Kirtland AFB NM 87117

O'BRIEN, ROMAINE M., nursing educator; b. Chgo., Aug. 8, 1936; d. John Matthew and Alvina Ann (Schmautz) O'B. Diploma, Oak Park Sch. Nursing, 1967; BA in Psychology, De Paul U., Chgo., 1974; BHS, Governors State U., 1977, MSN, 1980. RN. Coord. practical nurse program Thornton Community Coll., South Holland, Ill.; instr. nursing St. Xavier Coll., Chgo.; staff devel. coord. Americana Health Care Ctr., Westmont, Ill.; instr. Oak Forest (Ill.) Hosp.; speaker in field. Eucharistic min. local Roman Catholic Ch., 1985-88, instr. CCD, 1983-85, mem. ministry of care com.; mem. Slovenian Women's Union, 1978-89. Mem. ANA, NLN, Ill. Nurses Assn. (sec. 1981-83, bd. dirs. 1983-85, numerous positions), Am. Diabetic Assn., Bus. and Prof. Women's Club (del. 1981, 83, 85, 86 , scholarship chmn. 1985-86, treas. local dist. 1985-86, recording sec. 1986-87, chmn. pub. rels. 1987-88, numerous positions, Woman of Yr. 1982, Woman of Achievement 1988, Sigma Theta Tau, Psi Chi. Home: 16712 Elm South Holland IL 60473

O'BRIEN, SUE, journalist; b. Waukon, Iowa, Mar. 6, 1939; d. John Gordon and Jean (Schadel) O'B.; children—Peter, Sarah, Andrew. B.A., Grinnell Coll., 1959; M.P.A., JFK Sch. Govt., Harvard U., 1985. Reporter, KTLN/KTLK Radio, Denver, 1968-70; anchor, reporter KBTR-AM, Denver, 1970-73; anchor, reporter, commentator KOA-AM/TV, Denver, 1973-75; corr. NBC Radio, N.Y.C., 1975-76; news dir., exec. editor KOA AM/FM/TV, Denver, 1976-80; press sec. Gov. Colo., Denver, 1980-85; campaign mgr. Roy Romer 1985-86; asst. city editor The Denver Post, 1987-88; assoc. prof. journalism Sch. Journalism & Mass Communication, U. Colo., Boulder, 1988—; adj. assoc. prof. U. Colo. Grad. Sch. Pub. Adminstrn., 1986—. Chmn., Christian Social Relations div. Episcopal Diocese Colo., 1964-68; chmn., editor Colo. Journalism Rev., 1974-75; press sec. Coloradans for Lamm/Dick, 1982. Recipient Headliner award Women in Communications Colo., 1972, Big Hat award U. Colo. Soc. Profl. Journalists, 1973, Alumni award Grinnell Coll., 1974. Mem. Soc. Profl. Journalists (v.p. 1977-78), Radio and TV News Dirs. Assn., Mortar Bd., Phi Beta Kappa. Democrat. Episcopalian. Club: Denver Press. Home: 17 Ogden St Denver CO 80218 Office: U Colo Sch Journalism and Mass Communication Box 287 Boulder CO 80309

O'BRIEN, SUSAN THERESA, service representative; b. Winthrop, Mass., Aug. 18, 1965; d. Paul Thomas and Diane Theresa (Larkin) O'B. BS, Suffolk U., 1987. Front end supr. Liberty Market, Winthrop, 1983-85; supr. Lease It Corp., Boston, 1985-87; svc. rep. New England Telephone, Boston, 1987—. Roman Catholic.

O'BRIEN-PENNISI, MARY EVELYN, color consultant; b. Long Beach, N.Y., Aug. 12, 1946; d. William Maddox and Agnes Elizabeth (Sweeney) O'Brien; m. Peter Pennisi, Feb. 3, 1968 (div. Nov. 1987); 1 child, Mark Edward. Student Fashion Inst. Tech., N.Y.C., 1964-65, student Brown's Bus. Sch., Rockville Center, N.Y., 1965-66, Parsons Sch. Design, White Plains, N.Y., 1975. Rep., Color Me Beautiful, Tex., 1979-83; owner, operator The Color Studio, Richardson, Tex., 1983—; prin. Communicative Seminars, Inc., Richardson, 1984—, The Color Studio Eyewear, Richardson, 1983—; realtor assoc. Henry S. Miller Residential Real Estate Services Corp., Richardson, 1987—. Author tng. manual. Mem. Am. Bus. Women's Assn., Richardson C. of C., Dallas C. of C., Dallas Better Bus. Bur. Avocations: skiing, walking, designing clothing. Home: 1202 Eton Dr Richardson TX 75080 Office: Henry S Miller Residential Real Estate Service Corp 1535 Promenade Ctr Richardson TX 75080

O'BRYAN, MARY JOSEPHINE, sales and marketing official; b. Louisville, Sept. 6, 1952; d. Charles Marion and Mary Ramona (Sims) O.'B; m. Jonathan Edgar Peara, May 19, 1989. BA, Western Ky. U., 1974; M Internat. Adminstrn., Sch. for Internat. Tng., Brattleboro, Vt.; 1983. Dir. social svcs. Vols. Edn. and Social Svcs., Dallas, 1978-81; legal rep. Counseling Svcs. for Immigrants, San Antonio, 1982-85; lang. specialist dept. civilian personnel U.S. Govt., Torejon de Ardoz, Spain, 1986-87; fgn. admissions officer Internat. Fine Arts Coll., Miami, Fla., 1987-88; sales and mktg. rep. Midland Svcs., Miami, 1988—. Mem. Profl. Women's Sales and Mktg. Assn., NAFE, NOW, Sierra Club. Democrat. Home: 1414 Milan Ave Coral Gables FL 33134 Office: Midland Svcs 2545 NW 7th Ave Miami FL 33122

O'BRYON, LINDA ELIZABETH, television executive, anchor; b. Washington, Sept. 1, 1949; d. Walter Mason Ormes and Iva Genevieve (Batrus) Ranney; m. Dennis Michael O'Bryon, Sept. 8, 1973; 1 child, Jennifer Elizabeth. BA in Journalism cum laude, U. Miami, Coral Gables, Fla. News reporter Sta. KTVX, Salt Lake City, 1971-73; documentary and pub. affairs producer Sta. WPLG-TV, Miami, Fla., 1974-76; producer, reporter, news dir. then v.p. for news and pub. affairs, exec. editor and co-anchor The Nightly Business Report Sta. WPBT-TV (PBS), Miami, 1976—. Recipient award Fla. Bar, Tallahasse, 1977, 2 awards Ohio State U., 1976, 79, local Emmy award So. Fla. chpt. Nat. Acad. TV Arts and Scis., 1978, award Corp. for Pub. Broadcasting, 1978, Econ. Understanding award Amos Tuck Sch. Bus. Dartmouth Coll., Hanover, N.H., 1980, award Fla. AP, 1981, 1st prize Nat. Assn. Rea Hors, 1986, Bus. News Luminary award Bus. journalism Rev., 1990. Mem. Nat. Acad. TV Arts and Scis. (former bd. dirs.), Radio-TV News Dirs. Assn., Sigma Delta Chi. Republican. Roman Catholic. Office: Sta WPBT-Channel 2 14901 NE 20th Ave Miami FL 33181

OCCELLI DE SALINAS DE GORTARI, YOLANDA CECILIA, wife of president of Mexico; m. Carlos Salinas de Gortari; children: Cecilia, Emiliano, Juan Cristobal. Address: Palacio Nacional, 06220 Mexico City Mexico*

OCCHIUZZO, LUCIA RAJSZEL, restaurant executive; b. Casablanca, Morocco, Nov. 5, 1951; came to U.S., 1958, naturalized, 1973; d. Tadeusz Joseph and Irmina Elizabeth (Wacholska) Rajszel; m. Joel Occhiuzzo, Dec. 9, 1976. BA, Montclair U., 1974. Owner, pres. Mr. O's, Dallas, 1977-83, L n J's Restaurant & Club, Richardson, Tex., 1984—. Guest star Sta. Telecable TV, 1985; L n J's Restaurant subject of TV program, 1986; contbr. articles to newspapers. Recipient Restaurant of Month award Dallas Times Herald, 1978. Mem. Richardson C. of C., ASCAP. Republican. Roman Catholic. Avocations: music, photography, writing. Home: 156 Hidden Cir Richardson TX 75080 Office: L 'n J's Restaurant & Club 2475 Promenade Ctr Richardson TX 75080

OCHENKOWSKI, JANICE, real estate services company executive; b. Chgo., June 7, 1948; d. Frank and Julia (Ochol) O. BA in English, Cardinal Stritch Coll., 1970; Assoc. in Risk Mgmt., Ins. Sch. Chgo., 1982. Tchr. English and French St. Joseph High Sch., Chgo., 1970-80; v.p. risk mgmt. LaSalle Ptnrs. Ltd., Chgo., 1980—; instr. Bldg. Owners & Mgrs. Inst., Chgo., 1985; speaker Ins. Distaff Execs. Assn., Chgo., 1985. Essay contest judge Rhine Post 2729 VFW, Chgo., 1972-79; vol. Polish Welfare Assn., Chgo., 1980—, St. Pancratius Roman Catholic Ch., Chgo., 1982—, Mercy Boys Home. Mem. Risk Ins. Mgmt. Soc. (bd. dirs. 1984-86, sec. 1986-87, 1st v.p. 1987-88, pres. 1988-89, instr. 1986— Chgo. chpt., speaker local and nat. 1984—), Industry Group-Real Estate Mgmt. & Devel. (chairperson 1984-85), Alumni Assn. Cardinal Stritch (fundraiser chairperson 1975, 78, 80), Nat. Council of Real Estate Investment Fiduciaries (risk mgmt. com. 1989—). Office: LaSalle Ptnrs Ltd 11 S LaSalle St Chicago IL 60603

OCHS, JENNIFER ANN, electrical engineer; b. Englewood, N.J., May 16, 1965; d. Henry P. and Joan (McCloskey) Ochs. BS in Elec. Engring., Fairleigh Dickinson, 1986, MSEE, 1988. Elec. engr. Lorch Electronics Corp., Englewood, N.J., 1985-87; teaching fellow Fairleigh Dickinson U., Teaneck, N.J., 1986-87; tech. staff Bell Communications Rsch., 1987—; mem. affirmative action com. Bell Communications Rsch., Piscataway, N.J., 1988-89. Vol. Englewood (N.J.) Hosp., 1981-83; mem. Sierra Club, 1987-90, Natural Resources Defense Coun., 1989-90; corp. fundraising coord., United Way, Bell Communications Rsch., Piscataway, N.J. Recipient Honors Rsch. Fellowship, Farleigh Dickinson U., Teaneck, N.J., 1986-88. Mem. IEEE, AAUW, Soc. of Women Engrs., Sigma Xi, Phi Omega Epsilon, Eta Kappa Nu, Pi Mu Epsilon.

O'CONNELL, AGNES ANNE NAHMIE, psychology educator; b. Bklyn.; d. Nahmie Sheehan and Mary (Saqqal) Nahmie; m. Thomas Donald O'Connell; children: Mary Anne, Brian Thomas. BA, Douglass Coll., Rutgers Univ., 1971; MS, Rutgers U., 1972, PhD, 1974. Lic. psychologist, N.J. Tchg. asst. Rutgers U., New Brunswick, N.J., 1973, instr., 1974; asst. prof. CUNY, Staten Island, N.Y., 1974-75; asst. prof. Montclair (N.J.) State Coll., 1975-84, mem. staff, psych. svcs., 1975—, assoc. prof., 1984—; dir. Community Psychology Programs, Montclair State Coll., 1977—; cons. editor various jours., 1975—. Sr. author/editor: Eminent Women in Psychology, 1980 (Disting. Publ. award 1981), Models of Achievement, Vol. 1, 1983, Vol. 2, 1988, Women in Psychology, 1990; key developer The Academic Game, 1980; contbr. articles to profl. jours. Burns-Marvin fellow Rutgers U., 1971-72; Russell scholar Rutgers U., 1972-73; rsch. grantee Montclair State Coll., 1979-80, 81-82, 84-88, 89-90; Am. Coun. on Edn. Cert. Recognition, 1986. Fellow APA (div. 35 chmn. various coms. and task forces, mem. exec. com. 1976-78, 79-81, 88—, div. 27 mem. Coun. of Community Psychology Program Dirs., program rev. com. 1981, 86-89), Am. Psychol. Soc., Psi Chi (cert. recognition 1979-89). Office: Montclair State Coll Upper Montclair NJ 07043

O'CONNELL, ANN, state legislator; b. Albuquerque, Aug. 3, 1934; d. James Aubrey and Dorothy Nell (Batsel) Gray; m. Robert Emmett O'Connell, Feb. 21, 1977; children: Ervin Jeffery, Aubrey Gray. Student, U. N.Mex. Exec. dir. Blvd. Shopping Ctr., Las Vegas, Nev., 1968-76, Citizen Private Enterprise, Las Vegas, 1976; media supr. S.W. Advt., Las Vegas, 1977—; mem. Nev. Senate, 1984—; owner Comfort Inn, Las Vegas; owner, mgr. 2 Christian supply ctrs. Chmn. govt. affairs, vice chmn. commerce and labor, mem. taxation com. Rep. Nat. Conf. State Legislators Edn. Commn. of the States; pres. explorer div. Boulder Dam Area coun. Boy Scouts Am., Las Vegas, 1979-80; pres. Citizens Pvt. Enterprise, Las Vegas, 1982-84, Secret Witness, Las Vegas, 1981-82; vice chmn. Gov.'s Mental Health Mental Retardation, 1983—, mem. adv. bd. State Mental Hygiene and Mental Retardation Adv. Bd. Recipient Outstanding Citizen award City of Las Vegas, Silver Beaver award Boy Scouts Am., 1980, Women of Achievement award, 1988, Free Enterprise award, 1988. Home: 7225 Montecito Circle Las Vegas NV 89120 Office: 2550 S Rainbow Blvd Las Vegas NV 89102

O'CONNELL, CATHERINE ANN, library director; b. Balt., Apr. 8, 1946; d. Timothy Edward and Claire Cecilia (Mewshaw) O'C.; m. C. Michael Helmer, May 28, 1977 (div. June 1980). BA, U. Md., 1968; MS in LS, U. Ill., 1971. Cert. permanent profl. libr., Mich. Reference asst. Pub. Libr. Annapolis (Md.) and Anne Arundel County, 1968-70, br. libr., 1971-72; head adult svcs. Washington County Free Libr., Hagerstown, Md., 1972-76, asst. dir., 1976-84; dir. Pub. Librs. Saginaw (Mich.), 1984—; cons. Hagerstown Bus. Coll., 1973-76. Bd dirs. Pride, Inc., Saginaw, 1987—. Recipient Sam Shapiro award U. Ill. Libr. Sch., 1972; Md. Libr. Assn. scholar, 1971. Mem. ALA, Pub. Libr. Assn. (bd. dirs. 1988—), Mich. Libr. Assn., White Pine Libr. Coop. (bd. dirs. 1984—), Valley Libr. Consortium (bd. dirs. 1984—), Mgmt. and Adminstrv. Caucus (bd. dirs. 1988—), Zonta, Rotary, Beta Phi Mu. Office: Pub Librs Saginaw 505 Janes St Saginaw MI 48605

O'CONNELL, SISTER COLMAN, nun, college administrator, consultant. BA in English, Speech, Coll. St. Benedict, St. Joseph, Minn., 1950; MFA in Theater, English, Cath. U., 1954; PhD in Higher Edn. Adminstrn., U. Mich., 1979; student, Northwestern U., Birmingham U., Stratford, Eng., Denver U., Stanford U., Sophia U., Tokyo. Entered Order of St. Benedict. Tchr. English Pierz (Minn.) Meml. High Sch., 1950-53, Cathedral High Sch., St. Cloud, Minn., 1950-53; chairperson theater and dance dept. then prof. theater Coll. of St. Benedict, St. Joseph, 1954-74, dir. alumnae, parent relations, ann. fund, 1974-77, dir. planning, 1979-84, exec. v.p., 1984-86, pres., 1986—; cons. Augsburg Coll., Mpls., 1983-85, Assn. Cath. Coll. and Univs., 1982, Minn. Pvt. Coll. Council, 1982, SW (Minn.) State U., Marshall, 1980-82, Wilmar (Minn.) Community Coll., 1980-82, Worthington (Minn.) Community Coll., 1980-82, U. Minn., Morris, 1980-82; bd. dirs. Security Fin., St. Cloud, 1987—. Mem. St. Cloud Area C. of C. (bd. dirs. 1987-90). Office: Coll of St Benedict 37 College Ave Saint Joseph MN 56374-2099

O'CONNELL, ERIN MAUREEN, telecommunications executive; b. Balt.; d. Christopher James and Beverly Ann (Quinn) O'C. BA, Western Md. Coll., 1983; postgrad., U. Balt., 1989—. Crisis counselor Grassroots, Inc., Columbia, Md., 1983-84; housing supr. Vantage Pl., Inc., Columbia, 1983-84; customer svc. rep. Baxter Healthcare, Columbia, 1984-88; sales rep. J & H Berge, Inc., South Plainfield, N.J., 1988; account exec. MCI Telecommunications, Inc., Rockville, Md., 1988—. Mem. AAUW, Tech. Sales Assn. Republican. Office: MCI Telecommunications 1901 Research Blvd Ste 400 Rockville MD 20850

O'CONNELL, JANE S., retired education educator; b. Mineola, N.Y., Nov. 22, 1930; d. William Richard and Ruey Wilcox (Skinner) Stahley; m. William Valentine O'Reilly, Aug. 15, 1953 (dec. Sept. 1973); 1 child, Christine Ellen O'Reilly; m. James D. O'Connell, June 12, 1982; 1 stepchild, James D. Jr. BS in Edn., SUNY, Fredonia, 1952; MA in Curriculum Devel., Hofstra U., 1968. Cert. sch. dist. adminstr., sch. adminstr. and supervision, reading specialist, spl. edn., tchr. Tchr. Hicksville (N.Y.) Pub. Schs., 1952-53, Pennsbury Pub. Schs., Yardley, Pa., 1953-57, Plainview (N.Y.) Pub. Schs., 1958-61; tchr., adminstr. Commack (N.Y.) Pub. Schs., 1961-86; instr. Hofstra U., Hempstead, 1967; adj. asst. prof. Dowling Coll., Oakdale, N.Y., 1968-81; pres. Nassau/Suffolk Coun. of Adminstrv. Women in Edn., Nassau/Suffolk Counties, N.Y., 1984-86; cons. Three Village Sch. Dist., Stony Brook, N.Y., 1985; conf. planner Long Island Educators Coun. of Gifted/Talented, Commack, N.Y., 1984. Contbr. L'Overture Newsletter, 1987-90. Pres. Milw. Florentine Opera Club (guild), 1990-92; docent Milw. Symphony Orch. League, 1986-91; bd. dirs. Florentine Opera Co., 1990-92; mem. exec. com., 1990-92; com. mem. Ea. Wis. Met. Opera Auditions, 1986-91; mem. Opera Guild Met. Opera, Opera Guild Lyric Opera Chgo., Opera Guild N.Y.C. Opera Co.; mem. Friends of Milw. Ballet. Experienced Tchr. fellow HofstraU., 1967-68; recipient Life-time Ednl. Achievement award Nassau/Suffolk Coun. of Adminstrv. Women in Edn., 1986, Vol. award First Stage, Milw., 1986-90. Mem. PEO (pres. reciprocity Waukesha County 1990-91), The MacDowell Club, Elm Grove Woman's Club. Home: 13400 Wrayburn Rd Elm Grove WI 53122

O'CONNELL, KATHLEEN ANN, real estate sales and leasing agent; b. Washington, May 19, 1956; d. Thomas Joseph and Gwendolyn Grace (Evans) O'C. BS in Sociology, Coe Coll., 1978; postgrad., U. Okla., 1981. Lic. real estate, Md. Asst. libr. Tulsa City-County Library, Tulsa; owner Blue Sky Tanks, Tulsa; adminstrv. asst. Jeffery L. Smith, CLU, ChFC, Tulsa; comml. sales and leasing agt. Land and Comml., Inc., Clinton, Md. Editorial bd. Washington Area Realtor Mag., 1988. Named Top Pub. Speaker Md. Fedn. of Bus. and Profl. Women. Mem. South Prince George's County Bd. of Trade (rec. sec.), South Prince George's Bus. and Profl. Women (pres.-elect, Outstanding Young Careerist), Women in Land Devel., Prince George's County Assn. of Realtors (comml., indsl., land com.), Suburban Md. Comml. Real Estate Women, Mortar Bd., Phi Beta Kappa, Phi Kappa Phi, Alpha Lambda Delta. Home: 11666 Cosca Park Dr Clinton MD 20735 Office: Land & Commercial Inc 7901 Branch Ave Clinton MD 20735

O'CONNELL, MARY ITA, psychotherapist; b. Balt., July 3, 1929; d. Richard Charles and Ona (Buchness) O'C.; m. Leon Jack Greenbaum, Dec. 28, 1962 (div. Jan. 1986); children: Jessie A., Elizabeth K. BA, U. Md., 1956; postgrad., Am. U., 1960—; M in Creative Arts and Therapy, Hahnemann Med. Coll., 1978. Registered Acad. Dance Therapists. Tchr. Robert Cohan Sch. Dance, Boston, 1958-61; instr., choreographer Wheaton Coll., Norton, Mass., 1959-60, Harvard/Radcliffe Colls., Boston, 1960-62; tchr., performer, choreographer Profl. Studios, Washington, 1962-69; asst. prof., adminstr. Fed. City Coll., Washington, 1969-74; movement psychotherapist Woodburn Ctr. for Community Mental Health, Fairfax, Va., 1975-76, Gundry Hosp., Balt., 1976-77, Prince Georges' Community Mental Health Dept., Capitol Heights, Md., 1978-80; lectr. George Washington U., D.C., 1981-85; pvt. practice psychotherapy Silver Spring, Md., 1977—; sr. movement psychotherapy Regional Inst. for Children and Adults, Balt., 1983-87; movement cons. Ctr. for Youth Services, Washington, 1981-83; movement psychotherapist Wickersty and Assocs., Washington, 1985-87, Community for Creative Non-Violence Women's Shelter, Washington, 1986, LICSW, Washington, 1989. Choreographer, soloist (dance performance) The Artist: A Theatre Happening, 1963; choreographer, co-dir. (outdoor dance event) Tree Sculpting, 1974; choreographer (dance performance) Excitations, 1967, A Dance Event, 1974; soloist, New England Opera, 1961; performer, choreographer WGBM TV/Laboratory Concert Series, 1961; performer, CBS-TV/Erika Thimey Dance Theatre, 1965; guest artist, Harford Coll. Art Festival, 1967. U. Md. scholar, 1955-56. Mem. Dance Circle of Boston (life, pres. 1959-61), Modern Dance Council of Washington (exec. bd dirs., editor 1965-69), Am. Dance Therapy Assn. (treas. metro chpt. 1977-81), Assn. Humanistic Psychology, Family Therapy Network, Am. Dance Guild, NIH (movement specialist 1978-79). Democrat. Home and Office: 16 Sussex Rd Silver Spring MD 20910

O'CONNELL, ROSANN JOY, retail antique pocket billiard table executive; b. Bridgeport, Conn., July 15, 1946; d. Julius and Minnie (Polokoff) Grossman; m. Edward Michael O'Connell, Oct. 10, 1942. Lic. practical nurse, Bullard Havens Tech. Inst., 1973; AS, U. New Haven, 1988; LPN, Bullard Haven Tech. Inst. Charge nurse Jewish Home for the Elderly, Fairfield, Conn., 1973-77; owner, chief exec. officer Side Door Lounge, Greensboro, N.C., 1978-80; owner, co. exec. Time After Time, Danbury, Conn., 1983—; appraiser pocket billiard tables; instr. pocket billiards. Mem. Amnesty Internat., 1989, Greenpeace, 1989, World Wildlife, 1989, Nat. Humane Soc, 1989. Mem. Billiard Congress Am. Jewish. Office: 5 Padanaran Rd Danbury CT 06811

O'CONNOR, BARBARA BLOUGH, education educator; b. Avon, Feb. 14, 1932; d. Leo Alvin and Philomena (Whitman) Blough; m. Stan Edward O'Connor, Aug. 7, 1954; children: Amy M. Domanico, Christian, Kevin, Todd. BSEd, Kent State U., 1954. Cert. elem. tchr., Ohio. Elem. tchr. S. Euclid-Lyndhurst, Ohio, 1954-55, Green Local Schs., Greensburg, Ohio, 1966—; mem. Sci. Graded of Study, Greensburg, 1986—, Communication Arts, Greensburg, 1987—; med. editorial bd. Touch of Green, 1986—. Mem. Akron (Ohio) Civic Theater, 1980—, Weathervane Theater Women's Bd., Akron, 1980—. Mem. Internat. Reading Assn., Jefferson Grange, Kappa Kappa Iota. Democrat. Roman Catholic. Home: 3047 Lomae Rd Akron OH 44312 Office: Green Schs Kleckner Elem 1900 Greensburg Rd Greensburg OH 44232

O'CONNOR, BETTY LOU, service executive; b. Phoenix, Oct. 29, 1927; d. Georg Eliot and Tillie Edith (Miller) Miller; m. William Spoeri O'Connor, Oct. 10, 1948; children: Thomas W., William K., Kelli Anne. Student, U. So. Calif., 1946-48, Calif. State U., Los Angeles, 1949-50. V.p., treas. O'Connor Food Svcs., Inc., Jack in the Box Restaurants, Granada Hills, Calif., 1983—; pres. Western Restaurant Mgmt. Co., Granada Hills, 1986—. Recipient Frannie award Foodmaker, Inc., Northridge, Calif., 1984. Mem. Jack in the Box Franchisee Assn., Spurs Hon. (sec. U. So. Calif. 1947-48), Associated Women Students (sec. U. So. Calif. 1946-47); Gamma Alpha Chi (v.p. 1947-48), Chi Omega. Republican. Roman Catholic. Office: Western Restaurant Mgmt Co 10727 White Oak Ave Suite 204 Granada Hills CA 91344

O'CONNOR, BRIDGET MARIE, utilities executive; b. N.Y.C., Aug. 14, 1948; d. James Patrick and Eileen Bernadette (Wallace) Rafferty; m. Steven Charles O'Connor, Oct. 2, 1971; children: Charles, Stephanie, Josephine, Patrick. BA in Biology, Georgian Ct. Coll., Lakewood, N.J., 1970; MA in Molecular Biology, CUNY, 1972. Rsch. asst. to Prof. Ruth Sager Hunter Coll., N.Y.C., 1971-73; adjunct lectr. Bronx Community Coll., 1972; lectr. Camden County Coll., Blackwood, N.J., 1973-74; examiner (GED) Cape May County (N.J.) Vocat. Edn., Cape May Court House, 1985-86; recycling edn. specialist Cape May County Mcpl. Utilities Authority, Cape May Court House, 1986—; adj. lectr. Stockton State Coll., Pomona, N.J., 1989—. Mem. Middle Twp. Solid Waste Adv. Coun., Middle Twp. Environ. Commn. Mem. AAUW, LWV (fouding mem., sec. 1988—), Assn. N.J. Recyclers. Home: 24 Rita Dr Cape May Court House NJ 08210 Office: Mcpl Utilities Authority PO Box 610 Cape May Court House NJ 08210

O'CONNOR, CAROL ANN, psychologist; b. N.Y.C., Apr. 4, 1958; d. James Joseph and Margaret Delores (Rodgers) O'C.; m. James Robert Jacobs, Oct. 15, 1988. BA summa cum laude, St. Lawrence U., 1980; PhD, U. Health Scis., 1988. Lic. psychologist, Ill. Permanent substitute tchr. Ogdensburg (N.Y.) Free Acad., 1980-81; group therapist Ctr. for Med. Psychology, Des Plaines, 1985-86; psychol. cons. Focus Med. Treatment Ctr., Deerfield, Ill., 1984-86; group therapist Teenage Med. Svcs., Mpls., 1986-87; intern in clin. psychology U. Minn., Mpls., 1986-87; rehab. psychologist Ravenswood Hosp., Chgo., 1988-89, psychol. cons., 1989-90; psychotherapist Chgo. Stress Ctr., 1984-86, 87—; pvt. practice Skokie, Ill., 1990—. Mem. Anti-Cruelty Soc., Humane Soc., Greenpeace, Amnesty Internat., People for the Ethical Treatment Animals, Animal Rights Mobilization, World Wildlife Fund, African Wildlife Fund, Animal Legal Def. Fund; vol. Evanston (Ill.) Animal Shelter, 1990—; supporter local AIDS orgns. Recipient U. Health Scis. fellowship, 1981. Mem. Am. Psychol. Assn., Ill. Psychol. Assn., Phi Beta Kappa, Omicron Delta Kappa. Democrat. Roman Catholic. Office: 9933 Lawler Ste 535 Skokie IL 60077

O'CONNOR, CAROLYN RIESTER, rheumatologist; b. Phila., July 9, 1952; d. Hubert A. and Clara (Schaefer) Riester; m. William H. O'Connor, June 6, 1981; children: Erica C., William R. BS, Yale U., 1974; MD, Columbia U., 1978. Diplomate Am. Bd. Internal Medicine and Rheumatology. Intern and resident N.Y. Hosp./Cornell Med. Ctr., N.Y.C., 1978-81; fellow in rheumatology Boston U. Arthritis Ctr., 1981-83; pvt. practice acad. medicine/specialist in rheumatology Camden, N.J., 1983—; asst. prof. medicine U. Medicine and Dentistry N.J. Robert Wood Johnson Med. Sch., Camden, 1981-89, assoc. prof. clin. medicine, 1989—. Fellow Am. Coll. Rheumatology; mem. ACP. Office: Dept Medicine Cooper Hosp 3 Cooper Plaza Camden NJ 08103

O'CONNOR, COLLEEN MARY, hospital financial executive; b. Kansas City, Mo., Aug. 29, 1956; d. Thomas Joseph and LaVern Minnie (Schneemann) O'C. AA in Bus. Adminstrn., St. Louis Community Coll., Kirkwood, Mo., 1976; BSBA cum laude, St. Louis U., 1977, MBA, 1982. Registered fin. advisor. Payroll cost analyst Edison Bros. Stores, Inc., St. Louis, 1977-78; bank examiner Fed. Res. Bank St. Louis, 1978-85; fin. analyst, treas. Spl. Sch. Dist. St. Louis County, St. Louis, 1985-87; mgr. acctg. Daus. Charity Nat. Health System, Inc., St. Louis, 1987-90; chief fin. officer HCA Mgmt. Co., Inc. at Calais (Maine) Regional Hosp., 1990—; treas. Daus. Charity Nat. Purchasing Svcs., Inc., St. Louis, 1987-88; tax preparer, 1978—; portfolio mgr., 1985—. Mem. Hosp. Fin. Mgmt. Assn., Nat. Assn. Accts., NAFE, Calais Rotary, Calais Lions. Republican. Roman Catholic. Home: St Croix Dr RFD 1 Box 149 Calais ME 04619 Office: Calais Regional Hosp 50 Franklin St Calais ME 04619

O'CONNOR, DENISE LYNN, marketing communications executive; b. West Palm Beach, Fla., Oct. 29, 1958; d. Joseph John and Ada Colleen (Doyle) Fields; m. William York O'Connor, May 31, 1985. BS in Bus., Fla.

State U., 1979; MBA, Fla. Inst. Tech., 1983, postgrad. in elec. engring., 1984-86. Cons. Small Bus. Inst., Tallahassee, 1979; mgr. select accts. Burroughs, West Palm Beach, 1980-81; mgr. mktg. communications Harris-Satellite Communications, Melbourne, Fla., 1981-84; sect. mgr. mktg. communications Gen. Electric Info. Svcs., Rockville, Md., 1984-86; mgr. pub. rels. Mgmt. Sci. Am., Atlanta, 1986-88; pres., owner Mktg. Communications Cons., Atlanta, 1988—; cons. Sci.-Atlanta (Ga.), Inc., 1988—. Author (brochure) Genie, 1986 (Disting. award Soc. for Tech. Communications); editor (brochure) Electronic Data Interchange, 1986 (Excellence Soc. for Tech. Communications). Vol. Atlanta (Ga.) Humane Soc., 1988, (mem. auxiliary, 1989—). Mem. AAUW, Soc. for Tech. Communications, PEO (v.p. reciprocity 1990-91, chmn. Internat. Peace scholarship 1990), Atlanta Lawn & Tennis Assn. (pres. B-5 team 1989), Country Club South, Delta Zeta Sorority Alumnae. Republican. Methodist. Home: 1696 Heritage Ln Stone Mountain GA 30087 Office: Marketing Communications 1696 Heritage Ln Stone Mountain GA 30087

O'CONNOR, DORIS JULIA, oil company foundation executive; b. N.Y.C. Apr. 30, 1930; d. Joseph D. and Mary (Longinotti) Bisagni; m. Gerard T. O'Connor, Oct. 8, 1950 (div. Dec. 1972); 1 dau., Kim C. BA cum laude in Econs., U. Houston, 1975. Adminstrv. asst. Shell Cos. Found., Inc., N.Y.C., 1966-71, asst. sec., Houston, 1971-73, sec., 1973-76, sr. v.p., dir., mem. exec. com., 1976—. Corp. assoc. United Way of Am., Washington, 1976—; corp. advisor Bus. Com. of Arts, N.Y.C., 1976—; del. Bus. Com. of Arts, Houston, 1982-87; dir. Ind. Sector, Washington, 1981-89, vice chmn., 1983-87; mem. contbns. coun. Conf. Bd., N.Y.C., 1976—; advisor Coun. of Better Bus. Burs., Washington, 1975—, vice chmn., 1983-87. Mem. Omicron Delta Epsilon. Club: Pla. (bd. govs. 1987-89).

O'CONNOR, FRANCINE MARIE, magazine editor; b. Springfield, Mass., Apr. 8, 1930; d. Wallace Harold and Celestine Margaret (Morrison) Provost; m. John Francis O'Connor, Dec. 27, 1951; children—Margaret Anne McGlynn, Kathryn Mary Boswell, Timothy John. Grad. high sch., Springfield. Editorial asst. Liguori Publs., Mo., 1975-76, assoc. editor, 1976-79, mng. editor, 1979—, also author children's bulls. and books. Author ABC's of Faith series including The Stories of Jesus, 1982, The ABC's of the Rosary, 1984, Special Friends of Jesus, 1986, The ABC's of the Mass, 1989, The ABC's of the Sacraments, 1989, The ABC's of the Old Testament, 1989, The ABC's of Prayer, 1989. Den mother Boy Scouts Am., Webster Groves, Mo., 1963; religious edn. tchr. Our Lady Queen of Peace Roman Catholic Ch., House Springs, Mo., 1976-77. Mem. Cath. Press Assn., Secular Franciscans St. Louis. Home: 158 Crest Manor Park House Springs MO 63051 Office: Liguorian 1 Liguori Dr Liguori MO 63057

O'CONNOR, SISTER GEORGE AQUIN (MARGARET M. O'CONNOR), college president, sociology educator; b. Astoria, N.Y., Mar. 5, 1921; d. George M. and Joana T. (Loughlin) O'C. B.A., Hunter Coll., 1943; M.A., Catholic U. Am., 1947; Ph.D. (NIMH fellow), NYU, 1964; LL.D. Manhattan Coll., 1983. Tchr., St. Joseph's High Sch., Bklyn., 1944-45; mem. faculty St. Joseph's Coll., Bklyn., 1946—; prof. sociology and anthropology St. Joseph's Coll., 1966—, chmn. social sci. dept., 1966-69, pres., 1969—; trustee L.I. Regional Adv. Council Higher Edn. Author: The Status and Role of West African Women: A Study in Cultural Change, 1964. Fellow African Studies Assn., Am. Anthrop. Assn.; mem. Bklyn. Ednl. and Cultural Alliance (trustee 1972—), Bklyn. C. of C. (dir. 1973—), Alpha Kappa Delta, Delta Epsilon Sigma. Office: St Joseph's Coll Br Campus 155 Roe Blvd Patchogue NY 11772*

O'CONNOR, JULIA ELIZABETH, cytotechnologist; b. Wichita, Kans., Aug. 15, 1962; d. Billy Beryl and Cecelia Ann (Lumpkin) Bentley; m. Kevin Michael O'Connor, May 21, 1988. B of Gen. Studies, Wichita State U., 1986; student cytotech. sch., St. Francis Hosp., Wichita, Kans., 1985; AA, Neosho Community Coll., Chanute, Kans., 1982. Registered cytotechnologist, Conn. Sr. cytotechnologist Clin. Pathology Lab. Med. Assn., Austin, Tex., 1988—. Mem. Internat. Acad. Cytology, Tex. Soc. Cytoloty, Am. Soc. Clin. Pathologists, Young Republicans, Wichita State U. Alumni Assn. Roman Catholic. Home: 8309 Rockwood Ln Austin TX 78758

O'CONNOR, JUNE ELIZABETH, religious studies educator; b. Chgo., June 3, 1941; d. Philip Kevin and Eva Marie (Ennis) O'C.; m. Harry Hood, Aug. 11, 1973; 1 child, Meagan Hood. BA in English Lit., Mundelein Coll., 1964; MA, Marquette U., 1966, Temple U., 1972; PhD, Temple U., 1973. Instr. theology Mundelein Coll., Chgo., 1965-69, Temple U., Phila., 1970-73; asst. prof. religion U. Calif., Riverside, 1973-79, assoc. prof., 1979—, chmn. program in religious studies, 1985—; instr. theology Rosary Coll., River Forest, Ill., 1971; cons. William H. Sadlier Pubs., N.Y., 1971-81. Author: The Quest for Political and Spiritual Liberation: A Study in the Thought of Sri Aurobindo Ghose, 1977; assoc. editor Jour. Religious Ethics, 1978-82, mem. editorial bd. 1982-85; contbr. articles to profl. jours. Grantee U. Calif., Riverside, 1975—. Mem. Am. Acad. Religion (pres. Western region 1984-85, v.p., program chmn. 1983-84, mem. nat. com. on edn. study of religion), Soc. Christian Ethics (bd. dirs. 1979-83, 90-94, chmn. Pacific sect. 1977-78, vice chmn., program chmn. 1976-77), Coll. Theology Soc., Danforth Found. (assoc.), Pacific Coast Theol. Soc., Soc. Values in Higher Edn. Office: U Calif Program Religious Studies Riverside CA 92521

O'CONNOR, KATHLEEN LUCILLE, health care executive; b. Long Beach, Calif., Nov. 30, 1944; d. Remi Charles and Lucille (Stockwell) O'Connor; m. Ernst O. Kaemke, July 5, 1969 (div. 1983); 1 child, Remi Miles. BA, U. Wash., 1966, MA, 1970, postgrad., 1972-78. Spl. asst. to v.p. for acad. affairs U. Wash., Seattle, 1979-81; spl. asst. Office of V.P., Health Scis. U. Wash., 1979-81; adminstr. Pacific N.W. Long-term Care Ctr., Inst. of Aging, Seattle, 1981-85; prin. O'Connor Communications, Seattle, 1985—; dir. Medicare mktg. Network Health Plan, Mercer Island, Wash., 1988-89. Editor: Alzheimer Caregiver, 1986; author poetry various pubs.; author spl. edit.: Health Care, 1987 and You, 1987. Pres. Voice for Choice Polit. Action Com., Seattle, 1990—; panel mem. Vol. Mil. Retiree Healthcare, 1987—; bd. dirs. Boys/Girls Club, Seattle, 1990—. Mem. Pub. Rels. Soc. Am., Leadership Tomorrow Alumni Assn. (governing com. 1987-90, newsletter editor 1987-90), Rotary Internat. Home: 1418 N 48th St Seattle WA 98103 Office: O'Connor Communications 1418 N 48th St Seattle WA 98103

O'CONNOR, MARTHA SUSAN, educator; b. Manitowoc, Wis., Dec. 16, 1941; d. Kenneth Meredith and Lillian Margaret (Schneider) O'C.; m. Richard Lawrence Allen, Oct. 9, 1961 (div. 1977); children: Richard Phillip, Gregory Scott; m. Stephen Michael Serebin, May 21, 1988. BS, U. Wis., 1973, MS, 1981; PhD, George State U., 1990. Cons., coord. Health Svc. Mgmt., Milw., 1975-76; sr. therapist Mt. Sinai Med. Ctr., Milw., 1976-82; instr. Milw. Area Tech. Coll., 1982-83; assoc. prof. Med. Coll. of Ga., Augusta, 1983—; cons. Friendship Community Ctr., 1983—, Edgefield Mental Health Ctr., 1988, Alexander's Corner, 1984-85, Augusta Correctional Inst., 1984-85, N.Y. State Bd. of Edn., 1990. Bd. dirs. Viacom Pub. Access, Shorewood, 1980-83, LWV, 1984-88, Mental Health Assn. of Greater Augusta, 1983-89, pres.-elect, 1989-90. Mem. Am. Occupational Therapy Assn. (sec. 1985), Ga. Occupational Therapy Assn. (Job Placement chair 1990). Home: 310 McCormick Rd Martinez GA 30907 Office: Med Coll of Ga EF 102 Dept Occupational Therapy Augusta GA 30912

O'CONNOR, MARY B., not-for-profit consultant; b. Leominster, Mass., Apr. 7, 1940; d. T. Frank and Carolyn Elizabeth (Hannigan) Bagley; m. Daniel J. O'Connor Jr., June 9, 1962; children: Daniel J., Mark T., Maureen, Carolyn O'Connor Fulton. AB, Trinity Coll., Washington, 1961. V.p. Sci. and Tech. Mus. Atlanta; pres. Mary B. O'Connor & Assocs., Atlanta. Named 1989 Woman of the Yr., Women's Commerce Club, YWCA Woman of Achievement award. Bd. dirs. St. Joseph's Hosp. Found. Mem. Nat Soc. Fundraising Execs. (bd. dirs.), Atlanta Conv. and Visitors Bur. (bd. dirs.), Leadership Atlanta Alumni Assn. Home: 24 Northwood Ave Atlanta GA 30309

O'CONNOR, MAUREEN, mayor; b. San Diego, July 14, 1946; d. Jerome and Frances O'Connor; m. Robert O. Peterson, 1977. B in Psychology and Sociology, San Diego State U., 1970. Tchr., counselor Rosary High Sch., 1970-71; council mem. City of San Diego, 1971-79, dep. mayor, 1976, mayor, 1986—; with Calif. Housing Fin. Agy., 1977-79; mem. Met. Transit Devel. Bd., 1976-81; port commr. San Diego, 1980-85; mem. Rules, Legis., and Intergovtl. Relations com.; chmn. pub. services and safety com. 1974-75; mem. League Calif. Cities' Com. on Human Resources Devel., Natl League Cities' Manpower and Income Support com.; chmn. mayor's crime commn. Roman Catholic. Office: City of San Diego Office of Mayor 202 C St San Diego CA 92129*

O'CONNOR, PATRICIA WEEKS, nursing home adminstrator; b. Buffalo, N.Y., Oct. 18, 1961; d. Edward Charles and Margaret Mary (Reddington) Weeks; m. Gerard Edward O'Connor, May 27, 1989. BA, SUNY, Buffalo, 1983, Masters in Social Work, 1985. Lic. nursing home adminstr., N.Y. Adminstrv. asst. Buffalo (N.Y.) Gen. Hosp., 1985-1988, asst. adminstr., 1988-1989; adminstr. Downtown Nursing Home, Buffalo, N.Y., 1989—; dir./secy. Western N.Y. Assn. of Homes and Services for the Aging, Buffalo, 1990—; adv. Episcopal- Gen. Homecare, Buffalo, 1988—, Longterm Home Healthcare Program, Buffalo, 1988—. founding mem. and dir., Niagra Gateway Assn., Buffalo, N.Y., 1989. Mem. Western N.Y. Assn. of Homes and Services for the Aging, Network in Aging, SUNY, Buffalo, Alumni Assn., Deaconness Found., Inc. (secy./treas. 1985—). Democrat. Roman Catholic.

O'CONNOR, PEGGY LEE, computer company manager; b. Chgo., Apr. 20, 1953; d. William Stanley and Eleanor Sopie (Levandowski) Czaska; m. Charles B. O'Connor, III, Feb. 14, 1978. BS in Biology, Northeastern Ill. U., 1982; MBA, No. Ill. U., 1985. Emergency med. technologist, 1976-82; instr. Chgo. City Wide Colls., 1976-81; program dir. U. Ill. Hosp. 1979-81; program dir. Fermilab, Roselle, 1978-82; dist. adminstrv. mgr. Decision Data Svc., Schaumburg, Ill., 1981-89; mgr. sales svc. Putman Pub., 1989— Recipient award Summit Club 1987, 88, 89. Mem. NAFE, NWAAR, Women in Info. Processing, Women in Bus., Pres's. Club (chairperson bd. dirs. Avocation: computers. Office: Putman Pub 301 E Erie Chicago IL 60611

O'CONNOR, RUTH ELKINTON, real estate executive, consultant; b. Oakland, Calif., May 19, 1927; d. Alfred Cope and Anna (Lydia) Elkinton; m. Roger Edward O'Connor, Oct. 12, 1950; children: Bruce E., Colleen, Lynn, Michael E., John E. AA, U. Calif., 1949. Salesman Ruth Hendrickson, Realtor, Honolulu, 1966-68; salesman, broker John D. McCurry, Realtor, Honolulu, 1968-76; prin. broker O'Connor Realty, Honolulu, 1976-80; owner, pres. R.E.O. Inc., Honolulu, 1980—; owner Ga. Manor Nursing Home, Amarillo, Tex., 1981—; pres. Farm and Land Brokers, Honolulu, 1972; mem. profl. standards com. Grievance Honor Bd., Honolulu, 1983-85. Editor: Friends of Samoa, 1979. Recipient Exchangor of the Yr. award The Investment Group, Realtors, 1968, Councelor of the Yr. award The Investment Group, Realtors, 1969, Arts Council award Govt. of Am. Samoa, 1980. Mem. Honolulu Bd. Realtors (dir. 1970-72), Hawaii Bd. Realtors, Nat. Assn. of Realtors (real estate aviation chpt.), Internat. Real Estate Fedn., Nat. Assn. Female Execs., Pan Pacific S.E. Asian Women (life), Arts Council (dir. 1976-79), The Ninety-Nines (Hawaii del. 1985, Silver Wings), Profl. Assn. Diving Instrs., Tex. Nursing Home Assn., Am. Nursing Home Assn., Am. Health Care Assn., Outrigger Canoe Club, Berkeley City Club, Alpha Omicron Pi. Mem. Soc. of Friends. Office: REO Inc 417 Kanekapolei St Ste 103 Honolulu HI 96815

O'CONNOR, SANDRA DAY, U.S. Supreme Court justice; b. El Paso, Tex., Mar. 26, 1930; d. Harry A. and Ada Mae (Wilkey) Day; m. John Jay O'Connor, III, Dec. 1952; children: Scott, Brian, Jay. AB in Econs. with great distinction, Stanford U., 1950, LLB, 1952. Bar: Calif. Dep. county atty. San Mateo, Calif., 1952-53; civil atty. Q.M. Market Ctr., Frankfurt am Main, Fed. Republic of Germany, 1954-57; sole practice Phoenix, 1959-65; asst. atty. gen. State of Ariz., 1965-69; Ariz. state senator, 1969-75, chmn. com. on state, county and mcpl. affairs, 1972-73, majority leader, 1973-74; judge Maricopa County Superior Ct., 1975-79, Ariz. Ct. Appeals, 1979-81; assoc. justice Supreme Ct. U.S., 1981—; referee juvenile ct., 1962-64; chmn. vis. bd. Maricopa County Juvenile Detention Home, 1963-64; mem. Maricopa County Bd. Adjustments and Appeals, 1963-64, Anglo-Am. Legal Exchange, 1980, Maricopa County Superior Ct. Judges Tng. and Edn. Com., Maricopa Ct. Study Com.; chmn. com. to reorganize lower cts. Ariz. Supreme Ct., 1974-75; faculty Robert A. Taft Inst. Govt.; vice chmn. Select Law Enforcement Rev. Commn., 1979-80. Mem. bd. editors Stanford (Calif.) U. Law Rev. Mem. Ariz. Personnel Commn., 1968-69, Nat. Def. Adv. Com. on Women in Services, 1974-76; trustee Heard Mus., Phoenix, 1968-74, 76-81, pres., 1980-81; mem. adv. bd. Phoenix Salvation Army, 1975-81; trustee Stanford U., 1976-80, Phoenix County Day Sch.; mem. citizens adv. bd. Blood Services, 1975-77; nat. bd. dirs. Smithsonian Assocs., 1981—; past Rep. dist. chmn.; bd. dirs. Phoenix Community Council, Ariz. Acad., 1970-75, Jr. Achievement Ariz., 1975-79, Blue Cross/Blue Shield Ariz., 1975-79, Channel 8, 1975-79, Phoenix Hist. Soc., 1974-77, Maricopa County YMCA, 1978-81, Golden Gate Settlement. Recipient Ann. award NCCJ, 1975, Disting. Achievement award Ariz. State U., 1980; named Woman of Yr., Phoenix Advt. Club, 1972. Lodge: Soroptimists. Address: US Supreme Ct 1 First St NE Washington DC 20543*

O'CONNOR, SARA ANDREWS, theater director; b. Syracuse, N.Y., Apr. 5, 1932; d. Harlan Francis and Ethel (Hoyt) Andrews; m. Boardman O'Connor, Aug. 23, 1955 (div. 1969); children: Ian, Douglas. BA with high honors, Swarthmore Coll., 1954; MA, Tufts U., 1955. Assoc. producer Theatre Co. of Boston, 1965-68, producer, 1969-71; pub. relations dir. Repertory Theatre of New Orleans, 1968-69; mng. dir. Cin. Playhouse, 1971-74, Milw. Repertory Theater, 1974—; cons. Found. for Extension and Devel. Am. Profl. Theatre, N.Y.C., 1973-83. Translator; (plays) The Workroom, 1979, At Fifty, She Discovered The Sea, 1982, Them, 1985, A Flea In Her Ear, 1986, The Puppetmaster of Lodz; The Mizer, 1988, Gone Hunting, 1989. Mem. Schlitz Audubon Ctr., Milw., 1980—, Amnesty Internat., N.Y.C., 1981—, ACLU, 1981—, Milw. Art Mus.; bd. dirs. Woodland Pattern, Milw., 1985—. Recipient Sacajawea award Profl. Dimensions, 1985. Mem. Internat. Theatre Inst. (bd. dirs. 1980-83), Am. Arts Alliance (bd. dirs. 1981-87), Dramatists Guild, League Resident Theatres (pres. 1984-87, v.p. 1972-79), Theatre Communications Group (bd. dirs. 1978-82, pres. 1982-84), Wis. Citizens for the Arts, Theater Jocks (founder). Zen Buddhist. Office: Milw Repertory Theater 108 E Wells St Milwaukee WI 53202

O'CONNOR, TRACY ALLEN, paralegal; b. Almont, Mich., July 10, 1964; d. James Franklin O'Connor and Robin (Bishop) Manning. BS, Western Mich. U., 1986. Cert. paralegal, S.C. Mortgage processing specialist Banc-Plus Mortgage Corp., Kalamazoo, 1987-88; foreclosure specialist Fleet Real Estate Funding, Florence, S.C., 1988-89; paralegal Hutchen's Co., Inc., Aiken, S.C., 1989—. Mem. Nat. Paralegal Assn., Nat. Criminal Justice Assn., Nat. Fedn. Paralegal Assns., NAFE, Sigma Sigma Sigma. Home: 212 Limerick Dr Aiken SC 29801 Office: Hutchen's Co Inc 951 Millbrook Ave Aiken SC 29801

O'CONNOR-BROKAW, CHRISTINE, editor; b. Indpls., Apr. 8, 1962; d. James Daniel and Anna Louise (Colvin) O'Connor; m. David Scott Brokaw, May 31, 1986. BA in Journalism, Ind. U., 1984. Reporter ad sales dept. Ind. Racquet Sports Newspaper, Indpls., 1984-85; publs. coord. nat. hdqrs. Am. Coll. of Sports Medicine, Indpls., 1985-89; mng. editor camping mag. nat. hdqrs. Am. Camping Assn., Martinsville, Ind., 1989—. Editor (newsletter) Scrubmates, 1990—. Mem. Women in Communications, Inc., Ind. U. Alumni Assn., Phi Eta Sigma, Alpha Lambda Delta. Office: Am Camping Assn/Camping Mag Bradford Woods SR 67 N Martinsville IN 46151-7902

O'DAY, SHARON, marketing professional; b. Morristown, N.J., May 23, 1948; d. William Raymond and Jean Scott (Donaldson) O'D. Student, U. So. Calif., 1967-69, Fairfield (Conn.) U., 1977-79; MBA, U. Pa., 1981. Asst. mgr. pub. relations Carajás Iron Project Amazon, Rio de Janeiro, 1974-76; asst. to pres. Polycast Tech. Corp., Stamford, Conn., 1977-79; dir. mktg. Godiva Chocolatier S.A., Brussels, 1981-83; dir. internat. sales and mktg. Godiva Chocolatier Inc., N.Y.C., 1983; dir. mktg. Cognac Louis Royer, Jarnac, France, 1984-86; pres. Images de Marque, Inc., Miami, Fla., 1986—; cons. internat. mktg. various European corps. in Belgium, France and Italy, 1986—. Republican. Home and Office: 1925 Brickell Ave Apt #D813 Miami FL 33129

ODDI, PHYLLIS MARIE, computer systems administrator; b. Boston, July 14, 1931; d. Philip Meadows and Gladys Eleanor (Wood) Mays; m. John Joseph Stock, Aug. 17, 1957 (dec. 1977); children: Mary, Joann, Margaret, John, Teresa, Philip, Christine, Elizabeth; m. Donato A. Oddi, June 27, 1981. BA in Econs., Albertus Magnus Coll., 1953. Internat. rep. Internat. Ladies Garment Workers Union, AFL, N.Y.C., 1954-58; reporter, writer, editor Wellesley (Mass.) Townsman, 1972-80; mgr. research and records Babson Coll., Babson Park, Mass., 1980-86; computer systems adminstr. Gen. Cinema Theatres, Chestnut Hill, Mass., 1987—. Town meeting mem. Wellesley Town Meeting, 1973-85; study com. sec. Morses Pond, Wellesley, 1987-88. Mem. Boston Computer Soc. Democrat. Roman Catholic. Home: 14 Avon Rd Wellesley MA 02181 Office: Gen Cinema Theatres 27 Boylston St Chestnut Hill MA 02167

O'DELL, KAROL JOANNE, experimental prototype company executive; b. Lafayette, Colo., Jan. 4, 1936; d. Clarence Willis and Thelma (Stoner) O'D. Student Wayne State U., 1953-56, U. Detroit, 1956-57. Sec. IBM, Detroit, 1957-59; from bookkeeper to office mgr. Jo-Ad Industries, Inc., 1959-84, v.p., 1984—. Treas. Detroit Puppeteers Guild, 1983—; active Salvation Army. Mem. Nat. Assn. Female Execs., Fellowship Christian Magicians, Puppeteers Am., Fellowship Christian Puppeteers, Unima U.S.A., Commerce Alumni Assn. Avocations: puppetry; religious education; reading.

O'DELL, LYNN MARIE LUEGGE (MRS. NORMAN D. O'DELL), librarian; b. Berwyn, Ill., Feb. 24, 1938; d. George Emil and Helen Marie (Pesek) Luegge; student Lyons Twp. Jr. Coll., La Grange, Ill., 1957; student No. Ill. U., Elgin Community Coll., U. Ill., Coll. of DuPage; m. Norman D. O'Dell, Dec. 14, 1957; children—Jeffrey, Jerry. Sec., Martin Co., Chgo., 1957-59; dir. Carol Stream (Ill.) Pub. Library, 1964—; chmn. automation governing com. DuPage Library System, v.p., 1982-85, pres. exec. com. adminstrv. librarians, 1985-86. Named Woman of Year, Wheaton Bus. and Profl. Woman's Club, 1968. Mem. ALA, Ill. Library Assn., Library Adminstrs. Conf. No. Ill. Lutheran. Home: 182 Yuma Ln Carol Stream IL 60188 Office: 616 Hiawatha Dr Carol Stream IL 60188

ODELL, MARY JANE, former state official; b. Algona, Iowa, July 28, 1923; d. Eugene and Madge (Lewis) Neville; m. John Odell, Mar. 3, 1967 (dec.); children: Brad Chinn, Chris Odell; m. Ralph Sigler, Nov. 22, 1987. B.A., U. Iowa, 1945; hon. doctorate, Simpson Coll., 1982. Host public affairs TV programs Des Moines and Chgo., 1953-79; with Iowa Public Broadcasting Network, 1975-79, host Assignment Iowa, 1975-78, host Mary Jane Odell Program, 1975-79; sec. of state State of Iowa, 1980-87; tchr. grad. classes in communications Roosevelt U., Chgo., Drake U., Des Moines. Chmn. Iowa Easter Seals campaign, 1979-83; mem. Midwest Com. Future Options; bd. dirs. Iowa Shares. Recipient Emmy award, 1972, 75; George Washington Carver award, 1978; named to Iowa Women's Hall of Fame, 1979. Republican. Mailing Address: 725 Hickman Rd Des Moines IA 50314*

ODEN, CHANDRA RENEE, school supervisor, researcher; b. Detroit, Jan. 8, 1968; d. Rumor Lawerence and Geraldine (Gaddis) O. BA in Mktg. and Psychology, Mich. State U., East Lansing, 1990. Sales assoc. Ltd. Express, Harper Woods, Mich., 1985-86; asst. to dir. youth corp Mich. Dept. of Labor, Detroit, 1986; staff asst. DuPont, Mt. Clemens, Mich., 1987, 88; minority aide Office of Minority Student Mich. State U., 1987-89; sales assoc. Polo/Ralph Lauren, Stamford, Conn., 1989; bus. analyst GE Capital, Stamford, 1989. Mem. programming bd. Mich. State Leadership Conf., East Lansing, 1987; lobbyist Mich. Collegiate Coalition, East Lansing, 1989-90. Shriners scholar, 1981, Dow Chem. scholar, 1990. Mem. Mich. State U. Student Coun. (vice chairperson 1988-89), Green Club (pres. 1989-90). Home: 12333 E Outer Dr Detroit MI 48224 Office: 275 Snyder Hall East Lansing MI 48224

ODEN, JEAN PHIFER, special education teacher; b. Chgo., May 2, 1936; d. Dillard James and Lena (Conner) Phifer; m. James Edward Oden, Apr. 26, 1959; 1 child, Eric James. BE, Chgo. Tchrs. Coll., 1958; MEd in Learning Disabilities, Chgo. State U., 1973; postgrad., Nat. Coll. Edn., Evanston, Ill., 1986—, cert. advance studies, 1987. Tchr. elem. schs. Chgo., 1958-73, tchr. learning disabilities elem. schs., 1973-81, cons. spl. edn., ind. edn. program facilitator, 1981; learning disability specialist Phillips High Sch., Chgo., 1982-87, Englewood High Sch., Chgo., 1987—; mem. Ill. Guidelines for Learning Disabilities Devel. Com., Springfield, Ill., 1981—, Com. to Devel. State Test for Learning Disabilities Tchrs., Springfield, 1986; chair subcom. on research Ill. Dept. Rehab. Svcs., Chgo, 1985—, State Test for Learning Disabilities Tchrs., Springfield, 1986—. Speaker for fair housing Nat. Urban League, N.Y.C. Conf., 1980; mem. Congl. Victory Fund, Chgo., 1984, So. Christian Leadership Conf., Met. Chgo., 1979-81, Harold Washington Mayoral Summit Parent/Community Council on Chgo.'s Ednl. Reform, 1987—, Mayor Sawyer's Edn. Summit on Sch. Reform, 1988; charter mem. Rep. Presdl. Advisory Task Force, 1989; mem. NAACP. U.S. Dept. Edn. grantee, 1986; recipient Citizenship award Chgo. Mayor, 1984, Cert. of Merit NAACP Southside Br. 1978; named State Advisor U.S. Congl. Adv. Bd., 1985. Mem. United Neighborhoods Intertwined for Total Equality (founder, exec. dir., researcher), Assn. for Citizens with Learning Disabilities, Council for Exceptional Children (liaison to state bd. Ill. div. for citizens with learning disabilities 1980), LWV, Spl. Edn. Tchrs. Assn. (1st pres., founder, rsch. and program dir. Chgo. Met. Sch.), Black Parents United for Edn. and Related Svcs. (founder), Assn. for Supervision and Curriculum Devel. Mem. Carter C.M.E. Ch. Clubs: Lehigh Country (Fla.); Thousand Trails (Ottawa, Ill.).

O'DESS, MARY ABIGAIL, lawyer; b. Detroit, May 21, 1954; d. Laurence G. and Naomi V. (Michau) O'D.; m. William J. Hein, Nov. 19, 1983. BS, No. Mich. U., 1975; JD, U. Mich., 1977. Bar: Wis. 1978, U.S. Dist. Ct. (ea. dist.) Wis. 1978. Assoc. Jacobson & Hupy, S.C., Milw., 1978—. Mem. Jr. League Milw., 1983-85; sec. Wis. Coalition for Adv., Madison, 1982-83; bd. dirs. Milw. Women's Ctr., 1981-83, pres., 1983. Mem. Wis. Bar Assn., Wis. Mortgage Bankers Assn. (affiliate), Young Lawyers Assn., Phi Kappa Phi, Omicron Delta Nu, Phi Alpha Theta. Office: Jacobson & Hupy SC 152 W Wisconsin Ave #316 Milwaukee WI 53203

ODOM, BETH HELEN, educator; b. Orlando, Fla., Nov. 25, 1960; d. John Elliott and Barbara Ann (Craig) Mercer; m. Jeffrey Lanier Odom, May 7, 1988. BA cum laude, Fla. State U., 1981; MFA, U. Calif., Davis, 1985. Actress The Acad. Theatre, Atlanta, 1985-88, educator, 1987; educator Evenings at Emory, Atlanta, 1985-86, DeKalb Coll., Atlanta, 1987—, Literacy Action, Atlanta, 1989-90; state TV satellite coord., 1990—; speech cons. Peg Avery and Assoc., Roswell, Ga., 1989—, Buckhead Toastmasters, Atlanta, 1989, speech coach DeKalb Coll.-North, Dunwoody, Ga., 1989—. Appeared in plays Headlines, Pull, 1986, The Canterbury Tales, 1987, In Memory of Trees, 1988; dir. off-Broadway play The Best Christmas Pageant Ever, 1989. Judge Gwinnett Govs. Honors Program., Atlanta, 1987. Recipient Irene Ryan award Am. Coll. Theatre Festival, 1984. Mem. Atlanta Whitewater Assn., Delta Zeta. Republican. Protestant. Home: 5893 Four Winds Dr Lilburn GA 30247 Office: Literacy Action 42 Spring St SW Atlanta GA 30303

ODOM, LINDA ANN, clinical psychologist; b. Macon, Ga., Apr. 30, 1945; d. Edwin Jacobs and Ann Louise (Bashinski) O.; m. David Williams McMillan, june 22, 1975 (div. 1983); m. Murray Wilton Smith, Mar. 6, 1988. BA, U. N.C., 1967; MA, George Peabody Coll., 1969; PhD, Vanderbilt U., 1979. Program cons. Child and Youth Devel. Inst., Tenn. Dept. Mental Health, Nashville, 1971-72; rsch. assoc. project on classification of exceptional children Vanderbilt U., Nashville, 1972-74; rsch. asst. conceptual project on emotional disturbance U. Mich., Nashville, 1974-75; staff mem. human devel. liaison tng. program George Peabody Coll., Nashville, 1975-76; rsch. asst. Ctr. for Study of Families and Children, Vanderbilt U., Nashville, 1976; project coord. Ctr. Community Studies George Peabody Coll., Nashville, 1977-79; pvt. practice Nashville, 1979—. Contbg. author: The Futures of Children, 1975, A Study of Child Variance: Exercise Book, 1975. Mem. Am. Psychol. Assn., Tenn. Psychol. Assn.

ODOM, LINDA LOVE, nurse, pharmaceutical sales specialist; b. Oxford, Jan. 2, 1962; d. Joseph Rufus and Ann Louise (Warner) O. BS in Nursing, U. Mississippi, Jackson. Intensive care nurse St. Dominic Hosp., Jackson, 1985-86; henrice doctor's hosp. ICM, Richmond, 1986; coronary care nurse Latter-day Saints Hosp., Salt Lake City, 1986; telemetry nurse U. Utah, Salt Lake City; emergency room nurse Meridian Regional Hosp., 1987;

pharmaceutical sales Merck Sharp & Dohme, 1987—. Mem. Mississippi Nursing Assn. Home: 2973 Lakerun Circle Memphis TN 38119

ODOM, SUSAN ANN, program analyst; b. Jacksonville, Ill., May 10, 1957; d. Richard Arlington Jr. and Virginia Lea (Quinlan) Osborne; m. David Lee Odom, Aug. 29, 1979; 1 child, Hope Leigh. Student, U. Ill., 1976-80, Trinity Coll., Washington, 1984-87. Prin. investigator U.S. Army Corps of Engrs., Champaign, Ill., 1979-84; mgmt. analyst U.S. Army Corps of Engrs., Washington, 1984-87, with Office of Strategic Initiatives, 1988-89, strategic mgmt. analyst Resource Mgmt. Directorate, 1989—; army staff program analyst Mil. Constrn. Appropriation, Alexandria, Va., 1987-88; v.p. DSH Enterprises, Springfield, Va., 1986—; Army Corps of Engrs. rep. Tri-services Com., Washington, 1986—; program mgr. Leadership Conf., 1989, 90; project mgr. Focus 89, 90 U.S. Army Corps Engrs. mgmt. emphasis program. Mem. Automated Data Processing Profls., Nat. Assn. Female Execs. Roman Catholic.

O'DONNELL, LINDA FLEMING, accountant; b. Newark, Dec. 26, 1953; d. Haydn Joseph and Helena Marie (Cawley) Fleming; m. Mark P. O'Donnell, Sept. 28, 1974; children: Cheryl, Christine. BS, Rider Coll., Lawrenceville, N.J., 1974. CPA, N.J. Prin. Mortension and Assoc., P.C., Cranford, N.J. Mem. Assn. Acctg. Firms Internat. (chairwoman pers. com.), N.J. Soc. CPAs, AICPAs. Address: 340 North Ave Cranford NJ 07016

O'DONNELL, THERESE M., university director; b. Chgo., May 24, 1966; d. Charles J. and Mary Helen O'Donnell. BS in Communications and Mktg., DePaul U., 1988, postgrad., 1988—. Grad. asst. DePaul U., Chgo.; asst. dir. student activities Roosevelt U., Chgo.; law clk. Teller, Levit & Silvertrust, Chgo. Schmidt Leadership scholar. Mem. NAFE, Women in Communications.

O'DONNELL, V. RUTH HENSLEY, educational administrator, retired; b. Mt. Selman, Tex., Aug. 23, 1920; d. Tom Morris and Velma Elvada (Warren) Hensley; m. Edward Baxter O'Donnell, June 16, 1945; 1 child, Edward Baxter Jr. BA, Stephen F. Austin U., 1941; MA, Memphis State U., 1959; postgrad., U. Tenn., 1979, Am. Mgmt. Assn. Leadership Tng, 1981. Cert. tchr., Tenn. Tchr. elem. Kilgore, Tex., 1941-45, Alameda (Calif.) City Schs., 1945, East High Sch., Memphis, 1951-58; supr. of instruction Memphis City Schs., 1958-79, coord. of instruction, 1979-82; ret., 1982; cons. Am. Sch., Guatemala City, 1966, 88; coord. Tchr. Exch. with Am. Sch. Guatemala and Memphis, 1966-79. Key woman for Germantown Meth. Ch. to Meth. Hosp. Aux., Memphis, 1984-86, United Meth. Ch. to Ch. Women United, Memphis, 1987—. Recipient Spl. Mission Recognition award Germantown United Meth. Women, 1985. Mem. Tenn. Ret. Tchrs. Assn., Memphis and Shelby County Ret. Tchrs. Assn., DAR (historian 1986—), Colonial Dames (nat. def. chmn. 1983—), AAUW. Republican. Home: 1816 Hunters Creek Dr Germantown TN 38138

O'DONOHUE, CYNTHIA HELMINTOLLER, scientist; b. Washington, Oct. 3, 1936; d. Peter Constant Jr and Mary Lucile (McLearen) Helmintoller; m. Walter J. O'Donohue, Aug. 8, 1957 (div. 1976); 1 child, Diane L.; m. William A. Farone, Jan. 1, 1983. AB, Randolph-Macon Woman's Coll., 1957; MS, U. Richmond, 1967, MBA, 1979. Rsch. asst. rsch. and devel. Am. Tobacco Co., Richmond, Va., 1957-61; lab. supr. Med. Coll. Va., Richmond, 1961-63; with Philip Morris, Richmond, 1965-84, mgr. rsch. and devel., 1979-81, sr. staff analyst, 1981-83, asst. plant mgr., 1983-84; cons. Advanced Sci. Applications Inc., Wilton, Calif., 1985-86; chem. specifications, quality control Kendall McGaw, Irvine, Calif., 1986-88, mgr. rsch. and devel., 1988—. Mem. adv. bd. ChemTech, 1978-81; mem. editorial adv. bd. Jour. Chem. Info. and Computer Sci., 1976-81; contbr. articles to profl. jours. Mem. Am. Chem. Soc. (chmn. div. chem. info. 1980), N.Y. Acad. Sci., AAAS, Phi Beta Kappa. Home: 14112 Picasso Ct Irvine CA 92714-1824 Office: Kendall McGaw Labs Inc 2525 McGaw Ave Irvine CA 92714-5895

O'DOWD-JANA, PATRICIA MARGARET, educator, author; b. Easkey, Ireland, Mar. 23, 1949; came to U.S., 1968; d. James and Margaret Theresa (Keogh) O'Dowd; m. Denis I. Jana, June 2, 1978; 1 child, Jennifer Erin. BA, U. San Diego, 1975; MS, Pepperdine U., 1977. Cert. tchr., reading specialist, community coll. instr., Calif. Tchr., reading specialist pub. and pvt. schs. Calif., 1968-74, curriculum writer, 1974—; prof. Calif. Community Colls., 1976-83; adj. prof. Nat. U., San Diego, 1978-83; lectr. U. Calif., San Diego, 1978—, U. Hawaii, Honolulu, 1983—; prin. Pat O'Dowd Test Preparation Seminars, Del Mar, Calif, 1979—; cons. San Diego City Schs., 1982—, Hawaii and Maui City Schs., 1986—, Calif. Council for Humanities, 1986; cons. test-taking skills, 1979—. Author: Preparation for the CLEP, 1982, 2d edit., 1988, How to Prepare for the GRE, 1984, How to Prepare for the GMAT, 1984, Preparation for the RN Test, 1985; contbr. articles to ednl. jours. Bd. dirs. San Diego chpt. Multiple Sclerosis Soc., 1983—. Mem. Nat. Assn. Female Execs. Republican. Roman Catholic. Home: 13261 Denara Rd San Diego CA 92130 Office: Pat O'Dowd Test Prep Seminars PO Box 2074 Del Mar CA 92014

ODVARKO, JAROSLAVA, chiropractor, educator; b. Jablonec nad Nisou, Czechoslovakia, Oct. 28, 1950; came to U.S., 1969; d. Lubomir and Marie (Plachá) O. BS, Marycrest Coll., 1973; postgrad., Ill. State U., 1973; DC cum laude, Palmer Coll. of Chiropractic, 1976. Lic. chiropractor, Iowa, Fla., Ill., Okla.; cert. Sacro-Occipital Technique instr. Pvt. practice Lakeland, Fla., 1977, Bettendorf, Iowa, 1977—; instr. in clinic chemistry, Palmer Coll. of Chiropractic, 1977-78, in sacro-occipital technique, 1978-80; asst. prof. in clin. scis., 1979-85; lectr. on nutrition, 1982-87. Recipient Dr. Agnes Mae High Palmer award, 1976, Chiropractor of Yr. award Dr. A.H. Palmer, 1986; named to Honorable Order of Ky. Colonels, 1977. Mem. Craniopathic Soc. Internat., Sacro-Occipital Rsch. Orgn. Internat. (treas. 1980-87, bd. dirs., Chiropractor of Yr. 1982), Am. Chiropractic Orgn., Sigma Phi Chi (bd. dirs., Chiropractor of Yr. 1986). Office: 1618 Grant St Bettendorf IA 52722

OEHRLEIN, MARY LOU, architect; b. Clinton, Iowa, Dec. 7, 1950; d. Gilbert Joseph and Virginia Marie (Thrun) O.; m. David Evans Heacock, Jan. 16, 1979. BArch, Iowa State U., 1973. Registered architect, D.C., Md., Va. Staff architect Hist. Am. Bldgs. Survey U.S. Nat. Parks Service, Washington, 1972-74; archtl. conservator Universal Restoration, Inc., Washington, 1975; v.p. Bldg. Conservation Tech., Washington, 1975-83; sr. assoc., dir. Washington office The Ehrenkrantz Group, 1978-83; prin. Oehrlein & Associates, Washington, 1984—; reviewer State of Va. Div. Hist. Landmarks, Richmond, 1985—; bd. dirs. Cosmos Club Hist. Preservation Found., Washington, 1987—. Author handbooks on hist. property and maintenance. Bd. dirs. D.C. Preservation League, 1987—, Cosmos Club Hist. Preservation Found., Washington, 1987—. Recipient Cert. Appreciation Town of Leesburg, Va., 1987. Mem. AIA (v.p. Washington chpt. 1987, pres. 1988—, numerous awards 1983-86), Assn. Preservation Tech., Constrn. Specifications Inst. (bd. dirs. Washington chpt. 1983-85), Soc. Archtl. Historians (sec. Latrobe Chpt. 1983-84), Preservation Round Table. Club: Washington. Home: 4354 Westover Pl NW Washington DC 20016 Office: Oehrlein & Assocs 1702 Connecticut Ave NW Washington DC 20009

OERKFITZ, ROBIN LEIGH, secretarial service owner; b. Elgin, Ill., Sept. 25, 1963; d. Delwin James Oerkfitz and Loretta I. (Gabrielsen) Oerkfitz Wright; m. Vincent D. Belletini, Nov. 26, 1983 (div. 1988). Cert. legal sec., Robert Morris Sch., Chgo., 1983. With sales Temporary Employee Svcs., Inc., New Bern, N.C., 1984-85; gen. mgr., part-owner Midwest Temps & Secretarial Svc., Crystal Lake, Ill., 1986—. Sub-chair heart throb auction Am. Heart Assn., Crystal Lake, 1988-89, chairperson, 1991; co-chair parade Crystal Lake Gala week, 1989, 90. Recipient Disting. Svc. award Crystal Lake Jaycees, 1990. Mem. NAFE, Nat. Assn. Secretarial Svcs., Bus. and Profl. Women Assn. (pres. 1989-90), Crystal Lake C. of C. (expo chair person 1989-90, dir. 1990-93), Dundee C. of C. (pres. 1988), Kiwanis (sec. Crystal Lake chpt. 1989-90). Home: 404 A St Johns Rd Woodstock IL 60098 Office: Midwest Temps & Sec Svc 405 Virginia St Crystal Lake IL 60014

OERTLEY, KAREN OBERLAENDER, publishing company executive; b. Newark, Sept. 4, 1952; d. Ernest Joseph Jr. and Kathryn (Weber) Oberlaender; m. Charles Robert Oertley, Sept. 5, 1976; 1 child, Jennifer Leigh. Student, Colo. Coll., 1972; BA, Knox Coll., 1974. Copywriter, layout artist Sears, Roebuck & Co., Nashville, 1975-78; promotion mgr. Amusement Bus., Billboard Publs., Nashville, 1978-83, promotion dir., 1983-85, dir. mtkg., 1985-87, gen. mgr., 1987—; pub. Amusement Bus./BPI, Inc., Nashville, 1989—. Lincoln-Douglas grantee, 1970-74. Mem. Acad. Country Music, Country Music Assn. (talent buyers subcom. 1989—), Nashville Figure Skating Club (bd. dirs. 1989—). Office: BPI Communications Inc 49 Music Sq W Nashville TN 37203

OESTERLING, WENDY LEE, training company executive; b. Circleville, Ohio, Oct. 11, 1949; d. Victor K. and Mary R. (Young) O.; m. James S. Greene, July 7, 1979; children: Jennifer, Julie, Matthew. Student, Conn. Coll., 1967-68; MusB, Wittenberg U., 1972. Systems instr. Info. Control Systems, Ann Arbor, Mich., 1974-76; mktg. rep. Alphatext Ltd., Ottawa, Ontario, Can., 1976-78; edn. specialist Advanced Systems, Inc., Toronto, Ontario, Can., 1978-79; mktg. rep. Advanced Systems, Inc., 1979-81, mgr. eastern Can., 1981-83, mgr. major accounts, 1983-84; dir. corp. communications Advanced Systems, Inc., Arlington Heights, Ill., 1984-85; v.p. sales ops. Advanced Systems, Inc., 1985-86; v.p. fed. systems div. Applied Learning, Arlington, Va., 1986-89; v.p. certification and testing Roach Orgn., Alexandria, Va., 1989—; bd. dirs. Nat. Tng. Systems Assn., McLean, Va.; chmn. Can. Community Computer Educators Nat. Conf., Toronto, 1983. Mem. Am. Soc. for Tng. & Devel., Women in Govt. Relations, Coalition for Open Markets & Expanded Trade. Episcopalian. Office: Roach Orgn 1201 E Abingdon Dr Alexandria VA

OESTREICHER, ANETTE MURIEL, publishing company and healthcare public relations executive; b. N.Y.C., Nov. 14, 1943; d. William and Ruth (Blanshaft) O.; m. John Diamante, Sept. 5, 1969 (div. Dec. 1977). BS in Biology, City Coll. N.Y., 1965; MS in Biology, NYU, 1969. Bur. chief Internat. Med. News Group, Rockville, Md., 1973-79; asst. mng. editor Med. Tribune, N.Y.C., 1979-81; mng. dir. Ctr. for Med. Communications (div. J. Walter Thompson Healthcare), N.Y.C., 1981-83; editor, publisher Med. World News HEI Publishing, Houston, 1983-87; exec. v.p., dir. healthcare communications Cohn & Wolfe, N.Y.C., 1987-89; bd. dirs., editorial adv. bd. Hippocrates mag., 1987—. Fellow NIH, 1968-69. Mem. N.Y. Acad. Scis., Nat. Assn. Sci. Writers, Am. Med. Writers Assn., Pharm. Advt. Coun.

OETJENS, REBECCA ELIZABETH, psychologist, consultant; b. Detroit, Oct. 13, 1951; d. Peter and Nancy Joanne (Drummond) Spurck; m. John Robert Oetjens, June 26, 1971; 1 child, Elizabeth Genevieve. BA, Oakland U., Rochester, Mich., 1973, MA, 1976; PhD, U. Detroit, 1982. Lic. psychologist, Mich. Instr. Oakland Community Coll., Southfield, Mich., 1980-81; therapist Family Counseling Ctr., Sterling Heights, Mich., 1981-85; psychologist cons. Meth. Children's Home, Detroit, 1985-86; clin. psychologist Eastwood Community Clinics, Troy, Mich., 1985—; cons., supr. Macomb County Youth Svcs., Mt. Clemens, Mich., 1988—; cons. plus program Rochester (Mich.) Youth Svcs., 1989—. Bd. dirs. Fairview Farms Homeowners Assn., Rochester, 1988—; mem. Dinosaur Hill Nature Preserve, Rochester, 1988—. Mem. APA, Mich. Psychol. Assn., Mich. Women Psychologists, Mich. Soc. for Psychoanalytic Psychology, Oakland U. Alumni Assn. Home: 1348 E Fairview Rochester Hills MI 48306 Office: Eastwood Community Clinics 1771 W Big Beaver Rd Troy MI 48084

OETTIG, MILDRED KATHERINE See SQUAZZO, MILDRED KATHERINE

OFFERLE, JOAN MELINDA, psychologist; b. Geneseo, Ill., Oct. 8, 1945; d. Laurel E. and Roseann (Lough) O. BA, George Mason U., Fairfax, Va., 1978; PhD, Va. Commonwealth U., 1985. Lic. psychologist, Tex. Sec. various cos., 1965-71; ticket agt. Japan Air Lines, Washington, 1971-76; psychotherapist in pvt. practice Austin, Tex., 1985—; group facilitator Women's Counseling & Resource Ctr., Austin, 1986—; contract therapist Waterloo Counseling Ctr., Austin, 1987—. Mem. Am. Psychol. Assn., Tex. Psychol. Assn., Capital Area Psychol. Assn. (pres. 1990). Office: 7320 N Mopac #402 Austin TX 78731

OFFERMAN, CHRISTIANE TOENNE, marketing consultant; b. Hannover, Germany, Apr. 30, 1947; came to U.S., 1977; d. Adolf and Eva (Kretzschmar) Toenne; m. Louis Offerman, May 15, 1983; children: Anna, Elena. MBA, U. Hamburg, Fed. Republic Germany, 1972; postgrad. Clark U., 1977-78. Project dir. GFM, Hamburg, 1973-74, Makrotest, Dusseldorf, Fed. Republic Germany, 1974-75, Delphi Marktforschung, Dusseldorf, 1975-80; ptnr. Delphi Sales Cons., Inc., Lexington, Mass. and Chatham, N.J., 1980-84, Oasis Consulting, Inc., N.Y.C., 1984—. Pub. rels. coord. Amnesty Internat., Dusseldorf, 1975-77, group leader, Worcester, Mass., 1977-78. Mem. Smaller Bus. Assn., NAFE. Lutheran. Office: Oasis Cons Inc 230 W 13th St New York NY 10011

OFFET, BETTY VIE, municipal official; b. Decatur, Ala., Sept. 22, 1934; d. Ira Edward and Ethel Novella (Vest) Cheatham; m. Harold L. Offet, June 5, 1959 (div. 1971); children: Gary A., Kimberli S., Kristan K., Konne J. B of Social Work, Nazareth Coll., 1978; MPA, Sangamon State U., 1983. Coord. pub. affairs Kalamazoo Community Action Program, 1971-73; program dir. Retired Sr. Vol. Program, Kalamazoo, 1973-75; program coord. Human Svcs. Commn. Kalamazoo County, Kalamazoo, 1975-78; project dir. Tri-County Anti-Crime Project, Peoria, Ill., 1978-81; exec. dir. Peoria Neighbor Housing Svcs., 1981-85; dir., social svcs. dept. aging, disability City of Chgo., 1985-89, regional dir. dept. aging, disability, 1989—. Contbr. articles to newspapers, Scope dept. newsletter, 1986—. Fin. officer Ill. Women's Agenda, Chgo., 1990; bd. dirs. Ind. Voters of Ill., 1985-90, Planned Parenthood of Peoria, 1979-84. Recipient certs. appreciation Family Health Ctr., Kalamazoo, 1976, Planned Parenthood, Peoria, 1984, Suburban Kiwanis, Peoria, 1979, Nat. CAA Exec. Dirs. Assn., Washington, 1976. Mem. NOW (pres. Chgo. chpt. 1986-88). Democrat. Unitarian. Home: 5053 S Ellis #2 Chicago IL 60615 Office: Southwest Multipurpose Ctr 6117 South Kedzie Ave Chicago IL 60629

OFTE-GIBSON, NANCY CAROLYN, lawyer; b. Norfolk, Va., Dec. 10, 1957; d. Donald and Margaret Mae (McKenny) Ofte; m. Thomas Coulter Gibson, Aug. 8, 1981. BA, Furman U., 1980; postgrad., Emory U. Sch. Law, 1981-82; JD, George Washington U., 1985. Bar: D.C. 1985, U.S. Ct. Appeals (D.C. cir.) 1988. Info. analyst Raytheon Svc. Co., Arlington, Va., 1980-81, 82-83; assoc. cons. Booz Allen & Hamilton Inc., Arlington, 1983-85; corp. counsel Booz Allen & Hamilton Inc., Bethesda, Md., 1985-89, assoc. gen. counsel, 1989-90; dep. gen. counsel Systems Ctr. Inc., Reston, Va., 1990—. Vol. mediator Multi Door Dispute Resolution Program, Washington, 1988-89; vol. Lawyers for Bush/Quayle, Washington, 1989. Mem. D.C. Vol. Bar Assn., Wshington Met. Area Corp. Counsel Assn. (bd. dirs. 1989—, treas. 1990—). Republican. Home: 621 Springvale Rd Great Falls VA 22066 Office: Systems Ctr Inc 1800 Alexander Bell Dr Reston VA 22091

O'GARA, BARBARA ANN, soap company executive; b. Newark, Aug. 8, 1953; d. Frank Percy and Rose (Giordano) Stevens. AA, Keystone Jr. Coll., 1973; BS, U. Ariz., 1976. Media buyer Wells, Rich, Green/Townsend, Irvine, Calif., 1977-80; dist. sales mgr. Armour-Dial, Phoenix, 1980-82; regional sales mgr. Guest Supply, Inc., North Brunswick, N.J., 1982-85; dir. hotel sales Neutrogena Corp., Los Angeles, 1985—. Keystone Jr. Coll. scholar, 1972, Morris County scholar, 1971; recipient Outstanding Sales Accomplishment award Armour-Dial, 1981. Mem. Am. Mgmt. Assn., Am. Hotel & Motel Assn., Nat. Assn. Female Execs. Republican. Roman Catholic. Avocations: tennis, jogging, aerobics. Home: 219 33rd St Manhattan Beach CA 90266 Office: Neutrogena Corp 5760 W 96th St Los Angeles CA 90045

OGDEN, JOANNE, real estate executive; b. Cumming, Ga., Apr. 9, 1941; d. Crafton Kemp Sr. and Mary Evelyn (Willis) Brooks; m. William Rush Williams, Jan. 3, 1961 (div. 1966); 1 child, Paul Rush Williams; m. Cecil Leavern Ogden, Sr.; stepchildren: Cecil Laverne Jr., Michael Vann. Grad. high sch., Cumming. Prin. Ogden & Ogden, Milledgeville, Ga., 1966—. Candidate Baldwin County Commnr., Milledgeville, 1984. Mem. Nat. Geog. Soc., Better World Soc., Cousteau Soc., Audubon Soc., Smithsonian Inst., U.S. C. of C., 700 Club (Virginia Beach). Republican. Methodist. Home: 402 Allen Memorial Dr SW Milledgeville GA 31061 Office: Ogden & Ogden 2600 Irwinton Rd Milledgeville GA 31061

OGDEN, VALERIA JUAN, management consultant; b. Okanogan, Wash., Feb. 11, 1924; d. Ivan Bodwell and Pearle (Wilson) Munson; m. Daniel Miller Ogden Jr., Dec. 28, 1946; children: Janeth Lee Ogeden Martin, Patricia Jo Ogden Hunter, Daniel Munson Ogden. BA magna cum laude, Wash. State U., 1946. Exec. dir. Potomac Coun. Camp Fire, Washington, 1964-68, Ft. Collins (Colo.) United Way, 1969-73, Designing Tomorrow Today, Ft. Collins, 1973-74, Poudre Valley Community Edn. Assn., Ft. Collins, 1977-78; pres. Valeria M. Odgen, Inc., Kensington, Md., 1978-81; exec. dir. Nat. Capital Area YWCA, Washington, 1981-84; nat. field cons. Camp Fire, Inc., Kansas City, Mo., 1984-85; exec. dir. Clark County YWCA, Vancouver, Wash., 1985-89; pvt. practice mgmt. cons. Vancouver, 1989—; lectr. in field.; adj. faculty pub. adminstrn. program Lewis and Clark Coll. Portland (Oreg.) State U., 1979—; v.p. Pvt. Industry Coun., Vancouver, 1986. Author: Camp Fire Membership, 1980. County V chair Larimer County Dems., Ft. Collins, 1974-75; mem. precinct com. Clark County Democrats, Vancouver, 1986—; mem. Wash. State Coun. Vol. Action, Olympia, 1986—; treas. Mortar Bd. Nat. Found., Vancouver, 1987—; mem. Clark County Coun. Homeless, Vancouver, 1989—. Named Citizen of Yr. Ft. Collins Bd. of Realtors, 1975; recipient Gulick award Camp Fire Inc., 1956, Alumna Achievement award Wash. State U. Alumni Assn., 1988. Mem. Nat. Assn. YWCAED (nat. bd., nominating com. 1988-90), Women in Action, Internat. Assn. Vol. Adminstr. (pres. Boulder 1989—), Philanthropic and Ednl. Orgn., Phi Beta Kappa. Unitarian. Home and Office: 3118 Royal Oaks Dr Vancouver WA 98662

OGG, MARY ANN, animal health technologist; b. Richman, Ind., Oct. 20, 1948; d. Cecil C. and Doris (Randall) O. BS, Morehead State U., 1977. Farm helper Luther Ogg Farm, Eaton, Ohio, 1958-72; with dairy improvement dept. Ohio Agrl. Svcs., Columbus, Ohio, 1972-75; meat grader USDA, Amarillo, Tex., 1979-80; animal health technician USDA, Oklahoma City, 1981—. Advisor 4-H. Recipient Avian Influenza Helper award USDA, 1984. Mem. Nat. Poultry Improvement Assn. Home: 15300 Harrell Dr Moore OK 73160

OGILVIE, MARGARET PRUETT, counselor; b. McKinney, Tex., Jan. 8, 1922; d. William Walter and Ida Mae (Houk) Pruett; B.A., Baylor U., 1943; M.Ed., Hardin Simmons U., 1968; m. Frederick Henry Ogilvie, May 13, 1943; children: Ida Margaret, James William. Tchr. pub. and pvt. schs., Tex., Calif., Alaska, W.Ger., 1944, 53-65; guidance counselor Dentsville High Sch., Columbia, S.C., 1968-69, Northwest H.S., Clarksville, Tenn., 1970-72; personal and marital counselor, Fairfield Glade, Tenn., 1972—; co-owner F & M Gems & Jewelry. Treas. Officers' Wives Club, Ft. Irwin, Calif.; chmn. vols. ARC, Ft. Irwin, 1965; pres. Women's Golf Assn., Ft. Irwin, 1965-66; v.p. Ch. Women United, Crossville, Tenn., 1972-74; bd. dirs. Cumberland County Mental Health Assn., 1975-87; mem. legis. com. and pub. affairs com. Tenn. Mental Health Assn., 1976-81, mem. exec. bd., 1977-86; vol. Christian Svc. Corps, 1985—, Home Mission Bd. of So. Bapt. Conv., 1985-87; mem. Middle Tenn. com. Internat. Women's Yr., 1975; bd. dirs. Battered Women, Inc., Crossville, 1984-85. Mem. Am. Personnel and Guidance Assn., Nat. Ret. Tchrs. Assn., Bus. and Profl. Women's Club (chmn. 1973-75), DAR (parliamentarian Crab Orchard chpt. 1981), Pi Gamma Mu. Democrat. Baptist (choir dir., organist 1972—). Clubs: Fairfield Glade Women's (parliamentarian 1974-77), Fairfield Glade Ladies (chmn. scholarship com. 1989-90), Fairfield Glade Women's Golf Assn. (pres. 1973, 2d v.p. 1986), Fairfield Glade Sq. Dance; Order Eastern Star (Amanda chpt. IV). Home: 240 Snead Dr PO Box 1522 Fairfield Glade TN 38557

OGLE, MARY ELLEN, vice president nursig & surgical services; b. Waterbury, Conn., Oct. 11, 1944; d. William Joseph and Louise Jean (Brinche) Roach; m. William Henry Ogle, July 12, 1974; children: Patricia, Tracy. BSN, Syracuse U., 1969; MSN, Calif. State U., 1981. Staff nurse St. Joseph's Hosp., Syracuse, 1967-69; nursing supr. Meriden Wallingford Hosp., Meriden, Conn., 1969-71; nursing supr. ob-gyn clinic U.S. Army Hosp., Berlin, W. Germany, 1971-73; dir. home health, hosp. St. Agnes Med. Ctr., Fresno; unit dir. St. Agnes Med. Ctr., Fresno, 1979-81; asst. v.p. nursing St. Agnes Med. Ctr., 1981-83; v.p. nursing St. Agnes Med. Hosp., Fresno, 1983--; sec. Calif. Soc. Nsg. Administrn., Sacramento, 1988--; bd. mem. Calif. Soc. Nsg. Administrn., Sacramento, 1986-88. Author: Oncology Nsg Forum, 1982. Mem. Am. Orgn. Nurse Exec., Calif. Soc. Nursing (bd. mem. 1986-88), Service Administr. (sec. 1988--), Sigma Theta Tau Nursing, Alumni Assoc. Democrat. Roman Catholic. Office: St Agnes Med Ctr 1303 E Herndon Ave Fresno CA 93710

OGLE, PEGGY ANN, human services consultant; b. Washington, Feb. 3, 1950; d. William Paul and Lurlene (Lazenby) Ogle. A.A., Miami Dade Coll., 1969; B.S., Fla. State U., 1972, M.S., 1976. Cert. tchr., Fla. Spl. educator Jackson County Schs., Marianna, Fla., 1972-73; edn. dir. Sunland-Tallahassee, Fla., 1974-76; program supr. BARA, Tallahassee, 1976-77; program examiner Dept. of H.R.S., Tallahassee, 1977-79; program adminstr. Dept. of H.R.S.-V., St. Petersburg, Fla., 1979; dir. client services PARC Ctr., St. Petersburg, 1979-82; pres. Program Design Inc., St. Petersburg, 1982—, Personal Fitenss by Program Design Inc.; strategic planning cons. Ann Storck Ctr., Ft. Lauderdale, Fla., 1982-86; cons. State of Fla., Tallahassee, 1982-86; staff trainer, cons. ARA DevCon, Tallahassee, 1984-86; researcher, cons. L.R. O'Neall & Assocs., Tallahassee, 1984-86; mgr. quality assurance contract Healthcare and Retirement Corp. Am. Author: Being Human, 1983, Mirador: An Assessment Guide for Persons with Profound Functional Defecits and Complex Health Care Needs; editor: Developmental Nursing, 1985; contbr. articles to profl. jours. Chmn. Pinellas County Housing Coalition, St. Petersburg, 1982-83. State of Fla. grad. fellow, 1975; recipient Citizenship award, DAR, 1972. Mem. Am. Assn. Mental Deficiencies (gen. div. chmn. S.E. affiliate), Assn. for Severly Handicapped, Life Concepts, Inc. Avocations: tennis; swimming; skiing. Office: Program Design Inc 224 Cordova Blvd NE Saint Petersburg FL 33704

O'GRADY, ELINOR M., secretarial service owner; b. Chgo.; d. Arthur O. and Anna L. (Miller) Atkins; m. Norman Hohnstock, Oct. 12, 1940 (div. 1945); 1 child, Judith A.; m. Michael A. O'Grady, Jr., Dec. 16, 1950; 1 child, Michael A. Office mgr. N. Soifer, M.D. & Assocs., Dayton, Ohio, 1950-79; pres. Park Ave. Secretarial Service, Dayton, 1980—. Mem. Tri-City Bus. and Profl. Women (sec. 1983-84, pres. 1987-89), Profl. Secs. Internat., Am. Bus. Women Assn. (pres. 1986-88, Woman of Yr. 1987), Assn. Female Execs., Nat. Assn. Secretarial Services. Club: Pilot (pres. 1984-85) (Kettering, Ohio). Avocations: golf, landscape gardening, boating, sailing, crocheting. Home: 2513 Hackney Dr Kettering OH 45420 Office: Park Ave Secretarial Service 53 Park Ave Dayton OH 45419

O'GRADY, JEAN PATRICIA, lawyer; b. Bronx, N.Y., July 18, 1951; d. Martin F. and Joan Terese (Gore) O'G. BA, Fordham U., 1972, JD, 1986; MLS, St. John's U., Jamaica, N.Y., 1980. Bar: N.Y. 1987. Researcher Vera Inst. Justice, N.Y.C., 1972-74; rackets investigator Dist. Atty.'s Office, Kings County, Bklyn., 1974-75; social work asst. N.Y. Foundling Hosp., N.Y.C., 1976-77; reference libr. Sch. Law Pace U., White Plains, N.Y., 1978-82; asst. libr. Proskauer Rose Goetz and Mendelsohn, N.Y.C., 1982-84; dir. legal info. services, assoc. Shea and Gould, N.Y.C., 1984—; mem. adv. bd. Westlaw-West Svcs. Inc., St. Paul, 1987—, Legal Star Communications, L.A.; adj. prof. Palmer Sch. Libr. and Info. Sci., L.I. U., Brookville, N.Y. Adv. bd. ARC in Greater N.Y. Disaster Svcs., 1988—, bd. dirs., 1990—; mem. Mead Data Cen.'s Coun. for conf. on teaching legal rsch. in pvt. practice. Mem. ABA, N.Y. State Bar Assn., Am. Assn. Law Libr., Law Libr. Assn. Greater N.Y. (pres. 1990). Democrat. Roman Catholic. Home: 254 Martine Ave White Plains NY 10601 Office: Shea & Gould 1251 Ave of the Americas New York NY 10020

OHANESIAN, SUSAN MARIE, social services administrator; b. Bridgeport, Conn., Nov. 18, 1949; d. Nicholas Anthony and Jeanette Mary (Aniolowski) Yanosy; m. George Vaughn Ohanesian, Apr. 28, 1973. BA, U. Conn., 1971; MSSW, Columbia U., 1979; Cert. in Social Work Adminstrv., Hunter Coll., 1985. Employment interviewer Conn. Unemployment Dept., Bridgeport, 1971-73; legal asst. Mendes & Mount, N.Y.C., 1973-74; milieu therapist The Bridge, N.Y.C., 1976-77; asst. editor Matthew Bender & Co., N.Y.C., 1974-77; asst dir. mental health Palisades Gen. Hosp., North Bergan, N.J., 1981-85; clinic dir. C.S.S. BRC Human Svcs. Corp., N.Y.C., 1985-86; dir. Social Svc. Project Return Found., Inc., N.Y.C., 1986-88, Artemis/Women's Spl. Svcs. Project Return Found., Inc., N.Y.C., 1988; coord. clin. support svcs. Project Return Found., Inc., Bronx, 1988—; pres.

HPAE, AFT/AFL-CIO, North Bergen, N.J., 1980-81; regional coord. E.M.H.S.P. Assn. N.J., North Bergen, 1985. Contbr. articles to profl. jours. Panlist N.Y. State Conf. on Substance Abuse-Relapse Prevention, 1987-88. Mem. Acad. Cert. Social Workers, Nat. Assn. Social Workers, N.Y. Assn. Social Workers, N.Y. Assn. Substance Abuse Program, N.Y. State Coun. on Alcoholism.

O'HANLON, DOROTHY ETTA, controller; b. Greensboro, N.C., Sept. 23, 1932; d. Claude Parrill and Eunice Gertrude (Grantham) Smith; m. William David O'Hanlon, Apr. 25, 1957; children: Liza, Seaneen, Margaret, Charles and James (twins), Grace. BA, Greensboro Coll., 1954; Cert. book-keeping, Intersboro Inst., N.Y.C., 1955. Sec. L.J. Phillips-Wood, Dolson, Real Estate, N.Y.C., 1955-58; housing asst. N.Y.C. Housing Authority, 1978-79; office mgr., controller Empire Realty Mgmt. Co., Inc., N.Y.C., 1980—. Pres. West Side Community Nursery Parent's Assn., N.Y.C., 1971-72; pres. De Hostos Apartments Tenant's Assn., 1977-79, treas., 1989—. Mem. Nat. Trust for Hist. Preservation, NOW, Amnesty Internat., Smithsonian Assocs., Nat. Mus. Women in the Arts. Democratic. Methodist. Home: 201 W 93rd St 20C New York NY 10025

O'HARA, MARGARET, lawyer; b. St. Louis, May 11, 1951; d. James Doris and Ida May (Hillemeyer) O'H.; m. Robert Alan Bush, Nov. 28, 1976; children: G. Daniel, Jessica May. BA magna cum laude, U. Calif., Irvine, 1973; JD, UCLA, 1976. Bar: Calif. 1978. Atty. Gray Law Legal Svcs., L.A., 1980-81; ptnr. Jacoby & Meyers, Glendale, Calif., 1981-89; pvt. practice Glendale, 1989—; mediator Superior Ct. North Cen. Dist., Glendale, 1989. Mem. State Bar of Calif. (family law sect.), L.A. County Bar Assn. (family law sect.), San Fernando Valley Bar Assn. Democrat. Office: 144 N Glendale Ave Ste 300 Glendale CA 91206-4903

O'HARA, MAUREEN, professor of finance; b. Phila., June 13, 1953; d. Redmond J. and Leonore (O'Connor) O'H.; m. David Easley.; 2 children. BS, U. Ill., 1975; PhD, Northwestern U., 1979. Prof. fin. Cornell U., Ithaca, N.Y., 1979—. Office: Cornell U Johnson Grad Sch of Mgmt Ithaca NY 14853

O'HARE, CARRIE JANE, audio engineer, musician; b. N.Y.C., May 17, 1959; d. Alan Joseph and Phyllis Marie (Hannett) O'H.; m. Thomas K. Hogan, May 6, 1990. MusB in Audio Rec., Guitar Performance, Berklee Coll. Music, 1981. Audio engr. Saturday Night Live Saturday Night Live, NBC, N.Y.C., 1982—; audio cons. Easton Union Ch., Hainesport, N.J., 1985—. Composer: Spare Change, 1978, Never Got Away From Love, 1980. Acitve Greenpeace, Amnesty Internat., Earthwatch. Mem. Audio Engrng. Soc., NARAS, Soc. Motion Picture TV Engrs., Nat. Acad. TV Arts and Scis. Democrat. Office: NBC 30 Rockefeller Pla New York NY 10112

OHLHAUSEN, BEVERLY J., company executive; b. Grand Island, Nebr., May 24, 1931; d. Paul Antone and Lillian Elvera (Hansen) Bartunek; m. Howard Gary Ohlhausen, Sept. 6, 1953; children: David, Steven, Michael, Julie. BA, U. Iowa, 1953; postgrad., Prairie State Coll., Olympia Hills, Ill., Drake U., Des Moines, 1949. Exec. v.p., sec., dir. Unelko Corp., Scottsdale, Ariz. Sponsor Scottsdale Arts Ctr., 1990. Mem. Kappa Kappa Gamma. Republican. Presbyterian. Home: 7458 E Northern Ave Scottsdale AZ 85258 Office: Unelko Corp 7428 E Karen Dr Scottsdale AZ 85260

OHLSON, SARA FAYE, real estate executive; b. Paris, Ark., Dec. 29, 1944; d. Clifford Andrew Odom and Nellie Beatrice (Love) Riedl; m. Glyn Dean Albertson, July 15, 1962 (div. 1977); children: Candace, Julia, Jeffrey, Jennifer; m. Bradley Kent Ohlson, June 14, 1980. Grad., Real Estate Inst., Wichita, 1989. Realtor Coldwell Banker Dinning Beard, Wichita, 1984-86; assoc. broker Plaza Del Sol Realtors, Inc., Wichita, 1986—. Mem. Realtors Polit. Action Com., Wichita, 1986—. Mem. Wichita Area Bd. Realtors, Kans. Assn. Realtors (mem. Honor Soc.), Nat. Assn. Realtors (mem. residential sales coun., mem. various coms.). Lutheran. Home: 3220 Elmwood Wichita KS 67218 Office: Plaza Del Sol Realtors 6100 E Central 215 Wichita KS 67208

OHM, HOLLY VAN VALKENBURGH, educator, librarian; b. N.Y.C., Nov. 22, 1936; d. Horace Bulle and Viola Frieda (Gerfe) Van Valkenburgh; children: Leland V. Lammert, Jeni L. Moradi, Gary F. Ohm. BA, U. Colo., Boulder, 1957; MA, U. Denver, 1965; MEd, Lesley Coll., Cambridge, Mass., 1988. Cert. tchr., Wyo. Tchr. Davidson County Schs., Antioch, Tenn., 1958-60; tchr. Boulder Valley Schs., Boulder and Canfield, Colo., 1960-61, sch. libr., 1961-66; libr. Sheridan (Wyo.) Coll., 1966-74; franchise holder Western Welcome Svc., Sheridan, 1974-80; project adminstr. U.S. Dept. Energy Weatherization, Sheridan, 1979-84; sch. libr. Wind River Indian Schs., Ethete, Wyo., 1984-88; systems coord. Baker & Taylor, Reno, 1988-89; libr. Reno Bus. Coll., 1989—. Treas. Sheridan County Recreation Bd., 1975-79, Sheridan Alternate Energy Coun., 1977-84. Mem. ALA, AAUW (br. pres. 1975-76), Nev. Libr. Assn., Wyo. Ednl. Media Assn., Nat. Bus. Edn. Assn., Mountain Plains Libr. Assn. Home: 157 Greenridge Dr Reno NV 89509 Office: Reno Bus Coll 140 Washington St Reno NV 89509

OJAKLI, SUMYA, promotion director; b. Oklahoma City, May 10, 1961; d. Sadeddin Said and Mary Josephine (King) O. BA in Communications cum laude, L.I. U., 1984. Orientation coordinator, leadership trainer C.W. Post, Greenvale, N.Y., 1982-83, TV prodn. teaching asst., 1983-84; account exec., art dir. Nat. Imagemakers, N.Y.C., 1984-85; producer, designer Sumai Prodns., Bklyn., 1984-87; mktg. mgr. corp. communications Graphic Media Inc., N.Y.C., 1985-88; ptnr., designer Melted Ice Prodns., N.Y.C., 1988—. Published in 24 mags. Arts career adviser to coll. students, N.Y.C., 1986—; mem. Starlight Found. Recipient 2 DESI awards, 1986; named Outstanding Trade Ad Campaign Art Dir. Mag., Trade Advt. award Art Direction Mag. Mem. Am. Mktg. Assn., Am. Film Inst., N.Y. Acad. TV Arts and Scis., Nat. Assn. Female Execs., Ad Club of N.Y., Pub.'s Ad Club. Republican. Home: 351 Marine Ave Brooklyn NY 11209 Office: Billboard Mag 1515 Broadway New York NY 10036

OKAMOTO, KAREN SACHIKO, accountant; b. Torrance, Calif., Sept. 14, 1961; d. Ben Goro and Joanne O. BA cum laude, U. of the Pacific, 1983. Acctg. asst. Hughes Aircraft Co., El Segundo, Calif., 1983-85, acct. I, 1985-87, fin. analyst, 1987-88; acct. sr. Henry Co., Huntington Park, Calif., 1988—. Active World Wildlife Fund, Washington, 1987—, Greenpeace, Washington, 1989—. Recipient scholarship, Mabel Wilson Richards, L.A., 1981, 82, Japan Studies Inst., San Francisco, 1981. Mem. Long Beach (Calif.) Computer Club, Asian Alliance (Stockton, Calif.) (v.p. 1981-82). Methodist. Home: 5847 Fanwood Ave Lakewood CA 90713 Office: Henry Co 2911 E Slauson Ave Huntington Park CA 90255

O'KEEFE, BEVERLY DISBROW, state official; b. Wilton, Conn., Sept. 1, 1946; d. Harry Harbs and Jane Corrine (Young) Disbrow; children: Marcia Corrine, Jennifer Lynn; m. John Patrick O'Keefe, Aug. 1981 (div. 1985). AA, Berkshire Community Coll., 1973; BA in Psychology, U. Mass., 1975; MPA, U. S.C., 1979. Lic. social worker, S.C. Statis. clk. U. S.C., Columbia, 1976-78; pub. adminstr. employment and tng. Office of Gov., State of S.C., Columbia, 1976-78, 88—; project coord. Trident Tech. Coll., Charleston, S.C., 1981-82; office mgr. Med. U. S.C., Charleston, 1983-85; coord. bus. svcs. AMI East Cooper Community Hosp., Mt. Pleasant, S.C., 1985-87; mktg. rep. R.L. Bryan Co., Columbia, 1987; pub. adminstr. S.C. Dept. Social Svcs., Columbia, 1988; pub. adminstr., employment and tng. Office Gov. State S.C., Columbia, 1988-89; mem. employment and tng. staff City of Norfolk (Va.) Div. Soc. Svcs., 1990—. Editor newsletter Friends of Library, 1982-84. Sec. Friends Charleston County Library, 1981-82, pres. 1982-84; bd. dirs. Wando High Sch. Local Adv. Coun., Mt. Pleasant, 1981-84; pres. Wando High Sch. PTA, 1982-83, editor newsletter, 1982-85. Mem. Am. Soc. Pub. Adminstrs., Am. Psychol. Assn., Am. Pub. Welfare Assn., Southeastern Employment and Tng. Assn., Phi Theta Kappa. Democrat. Roman Catholic. Home: 3317 Rosebriar Ct Virginia Beach VA 23452 Office: Div Soc Svcs 220 W Brambleton Norfolk VA 23510

O'KEEFE, CHRISTINE MARIE, matchmaking company executive; b. Chgo., Nov. 25, 1951; d. James Lloyd and Doris Ruth (Lindgren) O'K. Grad., Coll. of DuPage, Glen Ellyn, Ill., 1971. Pres. Christine Okeefe Ltd., Beverly Hills, Calif., 1986—; v.p. Gt. Expectations, L.A., 1986-88. Fund raiser L.A. Mission, 1986; active fund raising Big Sisters L.A., 1989.

O'KEEFE, KATHLEEN MARY, state government official; b. Butte, Mont., Mar. 25, 1933; d. Hugh I. and Kathleen Mary (Harris) O'Keefe; B.A. in Communications, St. Mary Coll., Xavier, Kans., 1954; m. Nick B. Baker, Sept. 18, 1954 (div. 1970); children—Patrick, Susan, Michael, Cynthia, Hugh, Mardeen. Profl. singer, mem. Kathie Baker Quartet, 1962-72; research cons. Wash. Ho. of Reps., Olympia, 1972-73; info. officer Wash. Employment Security Commn., Seattle, 1973-81, dir. public affairs, 1981—; freelance writer, composer, producer, 1973—. Founder, pres. bd. Eden, Inc., visual and performing arts, 1975—; public relations chmn. Nat. Women's Democratic Conv., Seattle, 1979, Wash. Dem. Women, 1976—; bd. dirs., public relations chmn. Eastside Mental Health Center, Bellevue, Wash., 1979-81; Dem. candidate Wash. State Senate, 1968. Recipient Black Community award for composition The Beaufort County Jail, Seattle, 1975, Silver medal Seattle Creative Awards Show for composing, directing and producing Rent A Kid, TV public service spot, 1979. Mem. Wash. Press Women. Democrat. Roman Catholic. Author handbook on TV prodn., guide to coping with unemployment; composer numerous songs, also producer Job Service spots. Home: 4426 147th Pl NE A-12 Bellevue WA 98007 Office: 212 Maple Park Olympia WA 98504

O'KEEFE, NANCY JEAN, real estate company executive; b. Mpls., Jan. 26, 1926; d. Dana Charles and Bonnie Theresa (Lane) Eckenbeck; m. John Robert O'Keefe, Sept. 11, 1946 (div. June 1977); children: Teresa O'Keefe Ankeny, J. Patrick, Leslie O'Keefe Kelly, Bridget O'Keefe Gidley, Elizabeth O'Keefe Skrivseth, Peter C. BS in Social Welfare, U. Minn., 1973. Cert. real estate specialist, Minn., real estate appraiser, Minn.; grad. Real Estate Inst. Sales agt. Harvey Hansen Realty, Edina, Minn., 1976-87; pres., mgr., agt. 1st Mpls. Realty, Edina, 1987—. Mem. 5th Dist. Rep. Com., Mpls., 1951-52, Minn. Rep. Cen. Com., 1951-52; dist. chmn. fund drive ARC, Mpls., 1956; city chmn. fund drive March of Dimes, Mpls., 1957, 58; bd. dirs. St. Barnabas Hosp., Mpls., 1960-61; pres. Mpls. League Cath. Women, 1974-75. Mem. Minn. Assn. Realtors (bd. dirs. 1990-92), Greater Mpls. Assn. Realtors (bd. dirs. 1986-89, chmn. arbitration bd. 1988, Super Sales Agt. award 1982), Profl. Women's Appraisal Assn., Am. Arbitration Assn. (panel), Pi Beta Phi. Roman Catholic. Home: 5208 W 56th St Edina MN 55436 Office: Mpls Realty 3918 Sunnyside Rd Edina MN 55424

O'KEEFE, PATRICIA RIGG, public relations professional; b. Gary, Ind., Sept. 6, 1926; d. Harry and Beulah May (Reynolds) Rigg; m. Raymond Charles O'Keefe, Apr. 26, 1952 (div. 1962); children: Kathleen O'Keefe Reed, Ann Elizabeth. BS, Ind. U., 1948. Copywriter Young & Rubicam, Chgo., 1948-53; writer Smith, Bucklin & Assocs., Chgo., 1963-70, dir. pub. rels., 1970-80; dir. communications Am. Assn. Affirmative Action, Chgo., 1985—; dir. communications Nat. Assn. Perinatal Addiction Rsch. and Edn., Chgo., 1987—, sec., newsletter editor, 1988—. Mng. editor Kennedy's Career Strategist, 1985—; contbr. articles to various publs. Dir. vols. The Birth Project, Houston, 1980-83. Mem. Women in Communications, Chgo. Soc. Assn. Execs. Office: Burnison Martello & Assocs 11 E Hubbard St Chicago IL 60611

OKELL, JOBYNA LOUISE, public health administrator, accountant; b. Miami, Fla., Nov. 21, 1937; d. George Shaffer and Evelyn Maude (Pottmyer) O. B.B.A., U. Miami-Fla., 1961; postgrad. U. Miami, 1962, Nova U., 1976—. Acct. Crippled Children's Soc., Miami, 1964-65, Am. Coll. Found., Miami, 1965-66; owner Jobyna's Miniatures, Coral Gables, Fla., 1978—; exec. dir., adminstr., corp. dir. Fla. Health Profl. Svcs., Inc., Coral Gables, 1967—. Dist. chmn. Young Dems. Dade County and Fla., 1956-68; regent DAR, Coral Gables chpt., 1968-91, active Irish Georgian Soc., English Speaking Union; treas., bd. dir. Merrick Manor Found., 1974-75; active Friends of Libr., U. Miami, 1982-90. Recipient Outstanding County Young Democrat award Young Dems. Fla., 1964, Truman award Outstanding Young Dem. Young Dems. Dade County, 1965, Outstanding Jr. DAR, 1972. Mem. Dade/Monroe Assn. Home Health Agys. (pres., bd. dir. 1974-76), Health Planning Coun. South Fla., Health Systems Agy. South Fla., Fla. Assn. Home Health Agys., South Fla. In-Home Svcs. (pres. 1985-90), Red-Sunset Mchts. Assn., Nat. Assn. Miniature Enthusiasts, Internat. Guild Miniature Artisans, Ocean Waves Guild, Am. Philatelic Soc., Miami Pioneers, Inc., Hawaiian Philatelic Soc., Nat. Quilting Assn., Am. Quilter's Soc., Geneal. Soc. Greater Miami, Gamma Alpha Chi, Alpha Delta Pi. Republican. Episcopalian. Home: 715 Palermo Ave Coral Gables FL 33134 Office: Fla Health Profl Svcs Inc 1510 Venera Ave Coral Gables FL 33146

OKOSHI, SUMIYE, artist; b. Seattle; d. Masanari and Riyoko (Fukuda) Ushiyama; student Rikkyo Jogakuin U. and Seattle U., 1954-57, Henry Fry Mus. Modern Art, Seattle, 1957-59; m. George Mukai, Mar. 21, 1976. One-woman shows include Gallery Internat., N.Y.C., 1970, Miami Mus. Modern Art, 1970, Westbeth Courtyard Gallery, N.Y.C., 1972, Galerie Salson, Tokyo, 1982, St. Peter's Ch. Living Room Gallery, N.Y.C., 1987, Viridian Gallery, N.Y.C., 1987, Port Washington Pub. Libr., 1989; exhibited in group shows Met. Mus. Art, N.Y.C., 1977, World Trade Center, N.Y.C., 1979, Tokyo Nat. Mus., 1979, Pace U. Gallery, Briarcliff, N.Y., 1981, Joslyn Center Arts, Torrance, Calif., Newark Mus., 1983, Bergen Mus. Art and Scis., 1983, Am. Acad. Arts and Scis., 1984, Nassau Community Coll., 1985-86, Port Washington Pub. Library, L.I., N.Y., 1985, Hudson River Mus., 1985, NAWA Ann. Javits Fed. Bldg., 1986, Sao Paulo and N.Y. Culture Exchange, 1988, Hyndai Gallery, Pusan, Korea, 1988; represented in permanent collectiosn at Miami Mus. Modern Art, Low Gallery, U. Miami, Port Washington Pub. Libr., Nat. Women's Edn. Center, Japan. Mem. Japanese Artists Assn. N.Y., Nat. Women Artists Assn. Recipient Belle Crimer award. Episcopalian. Office: 55 Bethune St G226 New York NY 10014

OKUN, GAIL SHEILA, academic administrator; b. Bklyn., Apr. 6, 1943; d. Edward and Anne (Stenzler) Jasowitz; m. Clark N. Okun, Nov. 9, 1963; children: Scott Andrew, Peter Heath. BS, LIU, 1966; MEd, William Paterson Coll., 1985. Instr. high sch. N.Y.C. Pub. Schs., 1966-67, Pompton Lakes (N.J.) High Sch., 1967-69; adminstr., dir. Ft. Lee (N.J.) Montessori Sch., 1976-79; instr. The Berkeley Sch., Little Falls, N.J., 1980—; chairperson secretarial sci. and info. processing dept. Berkeley Coll. Bus., Little Falls, N.J., 1986-87; cons. N.Y., N.J., Conn., 1981—. Dem. com. person, Wayne, N.J., 1985—. Mem. Am. Soc. Tng. and Devel., Internat. Reading. Assn., Assn. Info. System Profls., Ea. Bus. Edn. Assn., N.J. Bus. Edn. Assn., N.J. Edn. Assn., Delta Pi Epsilon. Jewish. Home: 45 Princeton Pl Wayne NJ 07470 Office: The Berkeley Coll Bus 44 Rifle Camp Rd West Paterson NJ 07424

OLAETA, JULIA O'KEEFFE, retired elementary school principal; b. Silver Lake, Oreg., Jan. 26, 1923; d. Cornelius Michael and Myrtle Alice (McKune) O'Keeffe; m. Franklin Paul McCurry, Dec. 30, 1944 (div. 1959, dec. 1976); children: Mary Alice Barber, Ann Kathaline Lang, Patricia Louise Williams, Paul Michael McCurry; m. Thomas Olaeta, June 24, 1978. BA, Oreg. State Coll., 1944; MA, Fresno State U., 1960. Tchr. home econs. Portland (Oreg.) Sch. Dist., 1944-45; demonstration tchr. Oreg. State U., Corvallis, 1945-46; elem. sch. tchr. Atwater (Calif.) Elem. Sch., 1956-66, elem. sch. prin., 1966-84. Editor sch. curriculum, 1968. Mem. bd. Kingsview Wk. Experience Ctr., Atwater, 1984—. Mem. AAUW, Assn. Calif. Sch. Adminstrs., Calif. Ret. Tchrs. (treas. 1988—), Atwater Women's Club, Delta Kappa Gamma (chartering pres. 1981-84), Beta Sigma Phi (chpt. pres. 1988-89). Republican. Roman Catholic. Home: 2115 3d St Atwater CA 95301

OLANICH, CATHERINE CECILIA, lawyer; b. Pottstown, Pa., Apr. 16, 1959; d. John Olanich and Mary (Gacek) Elms. BA in Econs., Villanova U., 1981; JD, St. John's U., Jamaica, N.Y., 1984. Bar: N.Y. 1985, Pa. 1985, U.S. Dist. Ct. (ea. dist.) Pa. 1986. Law clk. Superior Ct. Pa., Erie, 1984-85; assoc. Hoyle, Morris & Kerr, Phila., 1985—. Vol. Support Ctr. for Child Advocates, Phila., 1986—, Phila VIP Program, 1987—, Phila. Vol. Lawyers for the Arts, 1990. Nat. Merit scholar, 1977-81, St. Thomas More scholar, 1981-84. Mem. ABA, Pa. Bar Assn., N.Y. State Bar Assn., Phila. Bar Assn. Republican. Office: Hoyle Morris & Kerr 1 Liberty Pl 1650 Market St Philadelphia PA 19103

OLANSKY, ILENE ROSEN, educator, civic leader; b. L.A., Sept. 10, 1930; d. Sam and Ruth (Wersbe) Rosen; m. Howard Olansky, June 21, 1953; children: Ellen Sue, Dale Judith. BS, UCLA, 1952; postgrad., U. Md., 1967, Vanderbilt U., 1973, Sarah Lawrence Coll., 1979. Tchr. Sweetwater Union High Sch. Dist., Nat. City, 1953-54; tchr., dept. chair L.A. Unified Sch. Dist., 1954-65; instr. CSU Northridge, 1978-79; apptd. Presdl. del. White House Conf. on Children and Youth, Washington, 1970; bd. of zoning appeals City of L.A., 1984—; mem. MOU working group U.S. Health & Human Svcs. Dept., 1985—. Bd. dirs. United Way; bd. dirs. Jewish Fedn. Coun. L.A., 1986-89, v.p., 1983-85, 86—. Recipient Community Concern award AAUW, 1978, Volunteer Service award L.A. City Human Rels. Com., 1976, Leadership, Gold Key and Mendenhall award United Way, 1983, 88. Home: 12523 Rye St Studio City CA 91604

O'LAUGHLIN, SISTER JEANNE, university administrator. Pres. Barry U., Miami. Office: Barry U 11300 NE 2d Ave Miami FL 33161

O'LAUGHLIN, MARJORIE HARTLEY, state official. Ed. at Ind. Univ., Bloomington. Formerly city clerk Indpls., clerk Ind. Supreme Ct., Ct. Appeals, treas. of Ind., 1987—; formerly vice-chmn. Marion County Rep. Cen. Com., exec. dir. Greater Indpls. Rep. Fin. Com., treas. Hoosiers for Bob Orr coms., 1980, 84. Mem. Nat. Assn. State Treas., Nat. Fed. Rep. Women, Kiwanis of Indpls., Kappa Alpha Theta. Office: Treasury Dept 242 State House Indianapolis IN 46204*

OLBERDING, ELAINE JOHNSON, computing company executive, educator; b. Jacksonville, Fla., Dec. 24, 1955; d. Paul Eleftereous and Rose (George) Johnson; m. Gary Lee Olberding, Mar. 19, 1988; 1 child, Michael Paul. BA in Mgmt., U. South Fla., 1979; MBA, U. North Fla., 1982. Cert. sr. prof. in human resources. Adminstrv. coord. Blue Cross-Blue Shield, Jacksonville, 1973-77; tng. coord. 1st Nat. Bank Fla., Tampa, 1980; dir. pers. Suddath Van Lines, Inc., Jacksonville, 1982-88; v.p. human resources Barnett Computing Co., Jacksonville, 1988—; adj. prof. U. North Fla., Jacksonville, 1987—. Recipient Tribute to Women in Industry award YWCA, Jacksonville, 1988. Mem. Soc. Human Resource Mgmt. (sec. 1987-88, treas. 1988-89, Human Resource Profl. of Yr. 1990), U. North Fla. Alumni Assn., Phi Kappa Phi, Beta Gamma Sigma. Republican. Presbyterian.

OLBUM, CAROLYN, artist, sculptor; b. Pitts., May 10, 1937; d. Harry and Fay (Sigal) Gurrentz; m. Glen Olbum, Mar. 25, 1956; children: Jon, Jennifer, David-Aaron. Student, Carnegie Mellon U., 1965-68; BA, Chatham Coll., 1971. One-woman shows include Charleston (W.Va.) Mus. Art, Images Gallery Contemporary Art, Ketchum, Idaho, 1982, Francine Seders Gallery, Seattle, 1984, Slippery Rock (Pa.) U., 1986, Neville Mus. Art, Green Bay, Wis., 1986, Blue Sky Gallery, Pitts., 1987; exhibited in numerous group shows, 1971—, including Carnegie Mus. Art, Pitts., 1977, 80-83, 87, 88, Smithsonian Instn., Washington, 1986, So. Alleghenies Mus. Art, 1988; represented in corp. and pvt. collections. Bd. dirs. Sun Valley (Idaho) Ctr. for Arts, 1983-84, nat. bd., 1989—; mem. arts com. Jewish Community Ctr., Pitts., 1988—; mem. adv. coun. Elkhorn Music Festival, Sun Valley. Recipient juror's award Jewish Fedn. N.J., 1981. Mem. Internat. Sculpture Soc. (assoc.), Assoc. Artists Pitts. Republican. Home and Studio: 5251 Fair Oaks St Pittsburgh PA 15217

OLDENBURG, KIMBERLE MARIE, hospital administrator; b. Cheyenne, Wyo., Aug. 17, 1957; d. Robert Lee and Eileen Ida (Schubbe) O. BS in Acctg., U. Wyo., 1979. Pub. staff acct. McKee, Marburger & Co., PC, Lander, Wyo., 1979-83; corp. acct. V&P Enterprises, Lander, 1983-84; acctg. mgr. Campbell County Meml. Hosp., Gillette, Wyo, 1984-87, contr., 1987-88, v.p. fin., 1988—. Mem. Hosp. Fin. Mgmt. Assn. (sec.-treas. Wyo. chpt. 1988-89, v.p. 1989—), Credit Women Internat., Bus. Women's Orgn., Toastmasters, Rotary Internat., Mortar Bd., Pi Beta Phi (Bernice Applery McWhinney scholar 1978), Phi Gamma Nu, Omicron Delta Kappa, Beta Alpha Psi. Republican. Lutheran. Home: 608 Frontier Dr Gillette WY 82716 Office: Campbell County Meml Hosp 501 S Burma Ave Gillette WY 82716

OLDHAM, JEAN KAE, public relations executive; b. Mpls., Feb. 13, 1952; d. Donald Allen and Blanche Barbara (Stumm) Tnuftedal; m. Terry Matthew Larson, Dec. 20, 1973 (div. 1979); m. James D. Oldham III, July 28, 1979; stepchildren: Melissa Anne Oldham, James D. Oldham IV. B. magna cum laude, Memphis State U., 1987, postgrad., 1988—. Dir. pub. rels. Oldham Crane & Rigging, Memphis, 1986-89; freelance pub. rels. specialist Walker & Assocs., Memphis, 1986, The Comml. Appeal, Memphis, 1985-87; dir. pub. rels. United Way Greater Memphis, 1989—. Author: Drums Beyond the Mountains, 1989; contbr. articles to profl. jours. Vol. LeBonheur Children's Med. Ctr., Memphis, 1988-90, Memphis In May Festival, 1990, Sta. WKNO TV, Memphis, 1990, Zool. Soc., Memphis, 1990; pub. rels. dir. Good Shepherd Luth. Ch., Memphis, 1986-89; publicity dir. Luth. Women's Missionary League, Memphis, 1983-87; bd. dirs. Heart at Work, Am. Heart Assn., Memphis, 1989-90; dir. spl. events 1990 United Way, 1989 (Second Century award 1990). Recipient Gold Key award Pub. Rels. Student Soc. Am., L.A., 1987. Mem. Pub. Rels. Soc. Am. (edn. liaison 1988-90, Outstanding Advisor 1989), Women in Communications Inc. (sec. 1990), Soc. Profl. Journalists. Republican. Office: United Way Greater Memphis 400 Union Ave Memphis TN 38103

OLDHAM, MARYLYN TYRA, landscape contractor; b. Cin., Jan. 8, 1964; d. Robert Todd and Bettye Jean (Torrey) O.; m. Carlos Luigi Dominick, Sept. 17, 1988. BS in Bus. Mgmt., Fisk U. Pres., owner Oldham Tree Farm, Inc., Cin., 1978-82; data entry operator Gen. Electric Corp., Cin., 1985; mgr. Marriot Corp., Washington, 1987; mgr., estimator Urban Landscape, Washington, 1987-89; pres., chief exec. officer Oldham Tree Farm, Inc., Suitland, Md., 1987—. Author poems. Mem. Young Reps., Silver Spring, Md., 1988. Mem. Am. Assn. Nurserymen, Landscape Contractors Asssn., Nat. Landscape Assn., Black Caucus. Office: Oldham Tree Farm Inc 3816 Old Silver Hill Rd Suitland MD 20746

OLDHAM, MAXINE JERNIGAN, real estate broker; b. Whittier, Calif., Oct. 13, 1923; d. John K. and Lela Hessie (Mears) Jernigan; m. Laurance Montgomery Oldham, Oct. 28, 1941; 1 child, John Laurence. AA, San Diego City Coll., 1973; student Western State U. Law, San Diego, 1976-77, LaSalle U., 1977-78; grad. Realtors Inst., Sacramento, 1978. Mgr. Edin Harig Realty, LaMesa, Calif., 1966-70; tchr. Bd. Edn., San Diego, 1959-66; mgr. Julia Cave Real Estate, San Diego, 1970-73; salesman Computer Realty, San Diego, 1973-74; owner Shelter Island Realty, San Diego, 1974—. Author: Jernigan History, 1982, Mears Geneology, 1985, Fustons of Colonial America, 1988, Sissoms. Mem. Civil Svc. Commn., San Diego, 1957-58. Recipient Outstanding Speaker award Dale Carnegie. Mem. Nat. Assn. Realtors, Calif. Assn. Realtors, San Diego Bd. Realtors, San Diego Apt. Assn., Internationale des Professions Immobilieres (internat. platform speaker), DAR (vice regent Linares chpt.), Colonial Dames 17th Century, Internat. Fedn. Univ. Women. Republican. Roman Catholic. Avocations: music, theater, painting, geneology, continuing edn. Home: 3348 Lowell St San Diego CA 92106 Office: Shelter Island Realty 2810 Lytton St San Diego CA 92110

OLDHAM, PHYLLIS VIRGINIA KIDD, librarian; b. Lafayette, Ind., Mar. 19, 1926; d. Hulbert Haven and Grace Ellene (Doup) Kidd; BS, Purdue U., 1948, MS, Butler U., 1966; 1 child, Stephen Kidd. Tchr. English, Jefferson High Sch., Lafayette, 1950; tchr., librarian Tudor Hall Sch., Indpls., 1954-70; librarian Park Tudor Sch., 1970—; mem. exec. bd. Central Ind. Area Library Svcs. Authority, sec., 1983-85. Mem. People-to-People Internat., dist. dir. Student Ambassador Program, 1970-80; chmn. bd. Cen. Christian Ch., Indpls., 1979-81, 89—; mem. vol. council Indpls. Zool. Soc. Mem. ALA, Marion County Librarians Assn. (pres. 1969-72), Ind. Media Educators, Kappa Delta Pi, Delta Kappa Gamma (treas. Alpha Eta chpt. 1974-80), Pi Beta Phi. Home: 7015 Warwick Rd Indianapolis IN 46220 Office: Park Tudor Sch Libr 7200 N College Ave Indianapolis IN 46240

OLDS, SHARON, poet; b. San Francisco, Sept. 19, 1942. BA, Stanford U., 1964; PhD, Columbia U., 1972. Lectr.-in-residence on poetry Theodor Herzl Inst., 1976-80; vis. tchr. poetry NYU, 1983, 85, Sarah Lawrence Coll., 1984, Columbia U., 1986, others. Author: Satan Says, 1980 (San Francisco Poetry Ctr. award 1981), The Dead and Living, 1984 (Lamont Poetry Selection, Am. Acad. Poets 1984, Nat. Book Critics Circle award 1985), The Gold Cell, 1987; contbr. poetry to numerous anthologies. Fanny Hurst chair Brandeis U., 1986. Guggenheim fellow, 1981-82; Nat. Endowment for Arts grantee, 1982-83. Home: 250 Riverside Dr New York NY 10025*

OLDS, SHARRON LEE, leasing company executive; b. Highland Park, Mich., Nov. 3, 1939; d. Emil and Sally (DiBlasi) O. Departmental sec. Wayne State U. Libraries, Detroit, 1958-76; mng. coordinator Jack Barnes Dance Ctrs., West Bloomfield, Mich., 1976-80; br. office mgr. Corp. Funding, Inc., Birmingham, Mich., 1980-84; v.p. Corp. Resources, Inc., Birmingham, 1984-89; owner Annie's Book Stop, 1989—; pres. Shoestring Enterprises, Ltd. Mem. NAFE, Am. Booksellers Assn., Mich. Booksellers Assn., West Bloomfield C. of C. Republican. Avocations: dancing, flying, table tennis. Office: Annie's Book Stop Simsbury Pla West Bloomfield MI 48322

O'LEARY, ALICE, advertising agency executive; b. Medford, Mass., Jan. 24, 1932; d. Arthur J. O'Leary and Alice T. (Dyer) O'Leary O'Brien. Studied voice and piano, pvt. music schs., Boston and N.Y.C., 1950-54. Profl. singer, 1950-54; v.p. Joseph Mack Assocs., N.Y.C., 1960-70; pres. Syndicated Airtime, N.Y.C., 1970-75; sr. v.p. Hartel, Cataland & Gornick, N.Y.C., 1975-76, Altschiller, Reitzfeld & Jackson, N.Y.C., 1976-78; founder Feron/O'Leary (now Kaprielian/O'Leary), N.Y.C., 1980; now pres., chief exec. officer Kaprielian/O'Leary. Co-developer, producer cassettes Cook Along with James Beard, 1974. Mem. Am. Assn. Advt. Agys. (bd. dirs. N.Y. council 1984), Advt. Women N.Y., Advt. Agy. Found. Avocations: tennis, skiing. Office: Kaprielian O'Leary 99 Madison Ave New York NY 10016*

O'LEARY, FLORENCE ANN, civil engineer; b. Chester, Pa., Jan. 11, 1954; d. James Daniel O'Leary and Patricia Ruth (McCleary) Ross. BS in Indsl. Edn., Southwest Mo. State U., 1975; MS in Indsl. Edn., Northwest Mo. State U., 1976; BS in Civil Engring., U. Mo., Rolla, 1983; postgrad., Portland (Oreg.) State U., 1988—. Draftsman Mo. State Hwy. Dept., Joplin, 1973; jr. high indsl. arts instr. Sudlow Jr. High, Davenport (Iowa) Community Schs., 1976-77; draftsman, civil engring. technician cen. div. Martin Marietta Aggregates, Cedar Rapids, Iowa, 1977-78; design draftsman REA Magnet Wire Co., Inc., Ft. Wayne, Ind., 1979; electronics draftsman Cen. Security and Electric, Rolla, 1981-83; technician U.S. Forest Svc., Mark Twain Nat. Forest, Rolla, 1980-83, civil engr., 1984; civil engr. geotechnical U.S. Forest Svc., Mt. Hood Nat. Forest, Gresham, Oreg., 1984-88, U.S. Forest Svc., Gifford Pinchot Nat. Forest, Cook, Wash., 1989—. Sunday sch. tchr. St. Anne's Cath. Ch., Portland, Oreg., 1987—. Future Tchrs. Am. scholar, 1971, Minority Engring. scholar U. Mo., Rolla, 1981, Regents scholar Southwest Mo. State U., 1973. Mem. ASCE, AAUW (Edn. Found. grantee 1989-90), Phi Theta Kappa, Epsilon Pi Tau. Roman Catholic. Home: 2755 NE Hogan Dr 12 Gresham OR 97030

O'LEARY, GERTRUDE EILEEN, social services administrator, public leadership trainer; b. Monticello, Iowa, Dec. 28, 1941; d. Thomas Clarke and Rose (Littlefield) Brokaw; m. Lawrence Robert O'Leary, Oct. 6, 1962; children: Elizabeth Jane, Julia Anne, Bridgette Suzanne. RN, St. Louis City Hosp., 1962; cert., Coro Found., St. Louis, 1983. Clin. instr. St. Louis State Hosp., 1962-63; RN various hosps., St. Louis, 1964-72; cons., trng. Monsanto Fund, St. Louis, 1982-83, 88—; exec. dir., founder Interfaith Partnership, St. Louis, 1983-88, pres., 1989-90; pres. O'Leary, Brokaw & Assocs., St. Louis, 1973—; dir. fellow program Coro Found., St. Louis, 1989—; chmn. Youth 2000, 1988—; bd. dirs. Youth Svcs. Network, 1988-90. Bd. dirs. Operation Child Save, 1988—, St. Louis Hunger Coalition; facilitator various charitable, health care orgns. Recipient Malacchi award Temple Israel, 1988, Regional citation U.S. Dept. Health & Human Svcs., 1985; named to Nat. Honor Soc., 1959, Nursing Sch. Honor Soc. Fellow Coro Alumni Assn. Roman Catholic. Office: O'Leary Brokaw & Assocs 43 Aberdeen Pl Saint Louis MO 63105

O'LEARY, HAZEL R., power company executive; b. Newport News, Va., May 17, 1937; d. Russell E. and Hazel (Palleman) Reid; m. John F. O'Leary, Apr. 24, 1980; 1 child, Carl G. Rollins. BA, Fisk U., Nashville, 1959; JD, Rutgers U., Newark, 1966. Cert. fin. planner; bar: N.J., D.C. V.p., gen. counsel O'Leary Assocs., Inc., Washington; exec. v.p. No. State Power Co., Washington. Mem. Phi Beta Kappa. Home: 414 Nicollet Mall Minneapolis MN 55403

O'LEARY, ROBERTA ANN, advertising executive, desktop publisher; b. Houston, Aug. 23, 1962; d. Richard Robert and Daphne Gloria (Nielson) O'Leary. BA in Communications, U. Calif., Santa Barbara, 1984. Program writer/producer KGOV Channel 19, Santa Barbara, 1984-85; mgr., asst. buyer Expressions, Santa Barbara, 1985; exec. asst. El Encanto Motel and Villas, Santa Barbara, 1986; spl. projects coordinator Kinko's Svc. Corp., Ventura, Calif., 1987-88; owner Inside News, Santa Barbara, 1988—; advt.account coordinator Slade Creative Mktg., Santa Barbara, 1989—. Panhellenic scholar, 1984. Mem. Women in Communications Inc. (bd. dirs. 1988-89), Santa Barbara Ad Club, Kappa Alpha Theta. Home: 3458 Richland Dr Apt 30 Santa Barbara CA 93105 Office: Slade Creative Mktg PO Box 484 Santa Barbara CA 93105

O'LEARY MOORE, DONNA MARIE, radiation therapy technologist; b. Buffalo, Sept. 15, 1964; d. John Joseph and Ruth Marie (Mackey) O'L.; m. William Paul Moore, Sept. 26, 1987. AAS in Radiotherapy Option, Erie Community Coll., 1986. Radiation therapist Finger Lakes Radiation Oncology, Clifton Springs, N.Y., 1986-87, Four County Radiation Oncology, Utica, N.Y., 1987—, Erie County Med. Ctr., Buffalo, 1987—. Author pamphlet: Radiation Therapy for Benign Bone Disorder, 1988.

OLEEN, LANA, state legislator; b. Kirksville, Mo., Apr. 26, 1949; d. Robert James and Frances (Primm) Scrimsher; m. Kent E. Oleen; children: Brooke, Bentson, Juan Carlos. BS in Edn., Emporia State U., 1972. Tchr. Council Grove, Kans., 1972-74, St. George, Kans., from 1978; communications coord. Woodward-Clyde Cons., San Francisco, 1974-75; mem. Kans. State Senate; mem. Rep. Precinct Com., 1978—. Active Kans. Rep. Women, Riley County Rep. Women. Mem. NEA, Nat. Coun. Tchrs. of English. Lutheran. Home: 1631 Fairchild Manhattan KS 66502*

OLEEN-BURKEY, MERRIKAY ADELLE, research epidemiologist, educator, pharmacist; b. Princeton, Minn., Oct. 30, 1949; d. Walter Burdette and Virginia Emelia (Carlson) Oleen; m. Jeff Ray Burkey, July 7, 1990. BS in Pharmacy, N.D. State U., 1972, MS in Pharmacy, 1975; PhD in Social and Adminstrv. Pharmacy, U. Minn., 1985. Registered pharmacist, N.D., Minn. Pharmacist intern Mora (Minn.) Drug Co., 1972-73; pharmacy resident VA Med. Ctr., Fargo, N.D., 1973-75; asst. dir. clin. pharmacy svcs. Brokaw Hosp., Normal, Ill., 1976-79; dir. drug info. Wash. State U., Pullman, 1979-81; Kellogg Found. fellow U. Minn., Mpls., 1981-84; research epidemiologist Upjohn Co., Kalamazoo, 1985—; adj. prof. epidemiology Western Mich. U., Kalamazoo, 1988—. Contbr. articles to profl. jours. Vol. CROP Walk, 1987-90, Planned Parenthood, 1986-90; recorder/bookkeeper organ fundraising com. Prince of Peace Luth. Ch., Portage, Mich., 1987-89. Named Hosp. Pharmacist of Yr., Ill. Coun. Hosp. Pharmacists, 1979; Kellogg Found. fellow U. Minn., 1981-84. Mem. Am. Pub. Health Assn., Soc. Epidemiologic Rsch., Am. Pharm. Assn., Am. Soc. Hosp. Pharmacists, Internat. Soc. Pharmacolpidemiology, Drug Info. Assn., Indsl. Epidemiologists Forum, LWV (sch. bd. observer Portage chpt. 1986-88). Lodge: Vasa. Home: 3762 Tartan Circle Portage MI 49002 Office: Upjohn Co 7000 Portage Rd Kalamazoo MI 49001

OLEKSEY, VICKY JOYCE, banker; b. Glasgow, Mont., Dec. 12, 1952; d. Frank Smith Jr. and Mary Helen (Smith) McIntyre; m. John Peter Oleksey, Jr., Aug. 7, 1976 (div. May 1984); 1 child, Kathryn Elizabeth. Student, U. Colo., 1973-76, U. Md., Fed. Republic Germany, 1977-81; BSBA, U. Phoenix, 1984; MBA, Boise State U., 1988. Keytape operator 1st Security Bank, Glasgow, 1968-71; programmer analyst Baldwin Data Svcs., Denver, 1973-76; acctg. technician dept. non-appropriated funds U.S. Govt., Ramstein, Fed. Republic Germany, 1977-79, systems operator dept. non-appropriated funds, 1979-80; programmer analyst II, United Banks Colo., Denver, 1982-85; programmer analyst Moore Fin. Group, Boise, Idaho, 1985-87, career developer, 1987-89; mgr. quality assurance West One Bancorp, Boise, 1989—. Mem. personnel com., leader single parents group 1st Presbyn. Ch., Boise, 1988-89. Recipient outstanding project chmn. award, Jaycee of Month award U.S. Jaycees-Idaho, 1989. Mem. Am. Bus. Womens Assn. (v.p. Boise 1987-88, Woman of Yr. award 1987), Boise Jaycees (v.p. for mgmt. devel. 1989). Republican. Episcopalian. Home: 11895 Musket Dr Boise ID 83704 Office: West One Bancorp Box 7648 Boise ID 83707

OLIAN, JOANNE CONSTANCE, curator, art historian; b. N.Y.C., d. Richard Edward and Dorothy (Singer) Wahrman; m. Howard Olian; children: Jane Wendy, Patricia Ann. Student, Syracuse U.; BA, Hofstra U., 1969; MA, NYU/Inst. Fine Arts, 1972. Grad. internship Met. Mus., N.Y.C., 1973; asst. curator Mus. of City of N.Y., 1974, curator costume collection, 1975—; lectr. Parsons Sch. Design; vis. lectr. Musée des Arts Decoratifs, Paris, summer 1983, 84, 85. Author: The House of Worth: The Gilded Age, 1860-1918, 1982; editor: Authentic French Fashions of the Twenties, 1990; contbr. articles to profl. jours., chpts. to books. Mem. Internat. Council Mus. (costume com.), Costume Soc. Am. (dir. 1976-79, 83-86), Fashion Group (bd. dirs. 1985-86), Centre Internat. d'Etude des Textiles Anciens. Club: Cosmopolitan (N.Y.C.). Home: Shepherds Ln Sands Point NY 11050 Office: Mus City NY 1220 Fifth Ave New York NY 10029

OLIN, JACQUELINE S., museum administrator; b. Lansford, Pa., Nov. 27, 1932; d. Walter F. and Anna C. (Strickler) Smith; m. Charles H. Olin, Dec. 26, 1955; children: Deborah Olin Norris, David Lind. BS, Dickinson Coll., 1954; MA, Harvard U., 1955. From rsch. chemist to asst. dir. archaeometric rsch. Smithsonian Instn., Washington, 1963—. Editor: Search for Ancient Tin, 1979, Archaeological Ceramics, 1982, Proceedings 24th Internat. Archaeometry Symposium, 1986. Recipient fellowship Nat. Endowment for Humanities, 1970, Rsch. awd. U.S.-Spain Commn. Edn. and Culture. Fellow Am. Inst. Conservation of Hist. Artistic Works (sec. 1980-81), Internat. Inst. Conservation of Hist. Artistic Works. Home: 9506 Watts Rd Great Falls VA 22066

OLIN, JANET L., government official; b. Birmingham, Mich., Nov. 7, 1955; d. Rolland Gustav and Jeanne Brooks (Kiefer) Olin. Grad., Western Mich.U., 1974; horsemaster, Potomac Horse Ctr., Gaithersburg, Md., 1976; postgrad., Palm Beach Jr. Coll., 1979—. Front office mgr. Holiday Inn, Petoskey, Mich., 1977-79; sales assoc. Advt. Svcs. Am., Boca Raton, Fla., 1079; comml. loan specialist Gulfstream Bank N.Am., Boca Raton, 1979-81; v.p., mgr. 1st Am. Bank & Trust, Boynton Beach, Fla., 1981-83; legis. aide State Rep. Messersmith, Tallahassee, 1983-90; asst. to commr. Fla. Pub. Svc. Commn., Tallahassee, 1990—. Contbr. articles to profl. jours. Mem. Boynton Beach Rds. Task Force; bd. advisors Women's Ctr. of Excellence. Named one of Outstanding Young Women Am., 1985. Mem. Northwood Inst. Enterprisers (bd. dirs., membership chmn.), Boynton Beach C. of C. (chmn. bus. svcs. com. 1982-84), Am. Bus. Women's Assn. (Golden Sands treas. 1983, programs com. chmn. 1982), Loggerhead Club (pres. 1989-90), Gulfstream Rep. Club (bd. dirs.), Fla. Hist. Preservation Soc., Nat. Wildlife Fedn., Fla. Farm Bur. Office: Commr Messersmith 101 E Gaines St Rm 118 Tallahassee FL 32399-0853

OLIPHANT, BETTY, ballet school director; b. London, Eng., Aug. 5, 1918. Studied classical ballet under Tamara Karsavina and Laurent Novikoff; student, Queen's and St. Mary's Colls.; LLD (hon.), Queen's U., 1978, Brock U., 1978, U. Toronto., 1980. Prin. dancer and arranger Prince & Emile Littler Prodns., London, 1936-46; dance arranger Howard & Wyndham, London, 1936-46; tchr. ballet London, 1936-40; dancer, dance arranger and ballet mistress Blue Pencils Concert Party, Eng., 1944-46; tchr. ballet Oliphant Sch., Toronto, Can., 1948-59; ballet mistress Nat. Ballet of Can., Toronto, 1951-62; prin. and dir. Nat. Ballet Sch., 1959; asso. artistic dir. Nat. Ballet of Can., 1969-75; artistic dir. Nat. Ballet Sch., 1975-89, founder and artistic advisor, 1989—; reorganized Ballet Sch. of Royal Swedish Opera, 1967, of Royal Danish Theatre, 1978; mem. jury Internat. Ballet Competition, Moscow, 1977-81, III Internat. Ballet Competition, Jackson, Miss., 1986. Contbr. articles on dance and teaching to profl. publs. Decorated officer Order of Can., 1972, Companion Order of Can., 1985; Order of Napolean (France), 1990; recipient Centennial medal, 1967, Molson prize, 1978, Diplome d'Honneur Can. Conf. Arts, 1982, Lifetime Achievement award, Toronto Arts Awards Found., 1989. Fellow Imperial Soc. Tchrs. of Dancing (examiner), Ont. Inst. Studies in Edn., 1985; mem. Can. Dance Tchrs. Assn. (founder, past pres.), Internat. Soc. of Tchrs. of Dancing, Can. Assn. Profl. Dance Orgns. (founding mem.). Office: Nat Ballet Sch, 105 Maitland St, Toronto, ON Canada M4Y 1E4

OLIPHANT, ERNIE L., safety educator, public relations executive, consultant; b. Richmond, Ind., Oct. 25, 1934; d. Ernest E. and Beulah A. (Jones) Reid; m. George B. Oliphant, Sept. 25, 1955; children—David, Wendell, Rebecca. Student, Earlham Coll., 1953-55, Ariz. State U., 1974, Phoenix Coll., 1974-78. Planner, organizer, moderator confs., programs for various women's clubs, safety assns., 1971-86; nat. field coordinator Operation Lifesaver, Inc., 1986—; assoc. dir. Operation Lifesaver Nat. Safety Council, Phoenix, 1978-86; cons. Fed. R.R. Adminstrn.; lectr. in field.; adviser Am. Ry. Engring. Assn., Calif. Assn. Women Hwy. Safety Leaders, numerous others. Mem. R.R./Hwy. grade crossing com. Ariz. Corp. Commn.; mem. transp. and system com. Ariz. Gov.'s Commn. on Environment; mem. Ariz. Gov.'s Council Women for Hwy. Safety; mem. motor vehicle traffic safety at hwy.-r.r. grade crossings com., roadway environment com., women's div. com. Nat. Safety Council; mem. Phoenix Traffic Accident Reduction Program; task force mem. U.S. Dept. Transp. on Grade Crossing Safety. Recipient Safety award SW Safety Congress, 1973; citation of Merit Adv. Commn. on Ariz. Environment, 1974; Gov.'s award for hwy. safety, 1978; Gov.'s Merit of Recognition Outstanding Service in Hwy. Safety, 1980. Mem. Assn. R.R. Editors, NAFE, Inc., Pub. Relations Soc. Am., R.R. Pub. Relations Assn., committees Nat. Acad. Scis. (dir. transp. research, planning, adminstrn. of transp. safety com., r.r.-hwy. grade crossing safety com.), Women's Transp. Seminar, Ariz. Fedn. Women's Clubs (named pres. of yr. 1968), Ariz. Safety Assn. (safety recognition award 1975), Gen. Fedn. Women's Clubs (internat. bd. dirs.), Nat. Assn. Women Hwy. Safety Leaders, Soc. Govt. Planners, Inc., Phi Theta Kappa. Republican. Quaker. Author of tech. publs.

OLIVARIUS-IMLAH, MARYPAT, sales, advertising and marketing executive; b. Bklyn., Oct. 25, 1957; d. Kenneth William Joseph and Ann Marie (Beckley) Olivarius; m. Craig Alexander Olivarius-Imlah, Sept. 18, 1982; children: Christopher Edward, Jamison Robert. BS in Mktg. and Communications, Ramapo State Coll. N.J., 1979; MBA in Mktg. and Mgmt., Fairleigh Dickinson U., 1985. Researcher, pub. rels. MacNeil/Lehrer Report, WNET-TV, N.Y.C., 1977; salesperson Terrace Realty, Montvale, N.J., 1977-79; direct mail advt. copywriter Prentice-Hall, Inc., Englewood Cliffs, N.J., 1979-81; editor, promotional designer Beauty & Barber Supply Inst., Englewood, N.J., 1981-83; nat. dir. advt. and pub. rels. Emerson Radio Corp., North Bergen, N.J., 1983-85; founder, pres. Imagery Print & Advt., Print Brokerage, Hinesburg, Vt., 1985—; bd. dirs. Chittenden County Ct. Diversion Program. Mem. Lake Champlain Regional C. of C. Democrat. Roman Catholic. Office: Beecher Hill Rd Hinesburg VT 05461

OLIVARRI, LEAH PAGAN, management consultant; b. Houston, June 13, 1951; d. John Shaw and Shirley (Andrew) Pagan; m. George Placido Olivarri, Nov. 28, 1975. BA magna cum laude, Mt. Holyoke Coll., 1973; MA, U. Tex., 1976, postgrad., 1977-79. Project mgr., research asst. RPC, Inc., Austin, Tex., 1976-79; analyst City of Corpus Christi, Tex., 1980-81, asst. to city mgr., 1981-84, dir. adminstrv. services, 1984-86; prin. Wolfe and Assocs., Albuquerque, 1986; owner, operator Olivarri and Assocs., Corpus Christi, 1987—; v.p. Money Mgmt., Inc., Corpus Christi, 1983-86. Contbr. articles to profl. jours. Pres. Nueces County Child Welfare Bd., Corpus Christi, 1981-85; co-chair City of Corpus Christi United Way Campaign, 1982; mem. Leadership Corpus Christi, 1983, Tex. Productivity Com., Austin, 1984-86. Mem. Mt. Holyoke Alumni (rep. Tex. alumni 1982-87). Club: Am. Contract Bridge League. Home: 4934 High Meadow Corpus Christi TX 78413 Office: Olivarri and Assocs Inc PO Box 271096 Corpus Christi TX 78427

OLIVER, ADELA, management consultant; b. N.Y.C.; d. Irving and Lilyan Lipton. BA, Bklyn. Coll., 1959; MS, CCNY, 1966; PhD, Yeshiva U., 1973; married; children: Meryl Fern, Julia Susan. Asst. prof. psychology and counseling John Jay Coll. CUNY, 1971-76; internal human resource cons. Met. Life Ins. Co., 1976-79; v.p. Lee Hecht & Assos., N.Y.C., 1979-82; dir. human resource planning and devel. Coopers & Lybrand, 1983-84; pres., chief exec. officer Oliver Human Resource Cons., Inc., 1984—; cons. Ford Found., U.S. Army, Stamford Research Inst., Am. Inst. Banking. NDEA fellow, 1968-69. Mem. Met. N.Y. Assn. Applied Psychology (exec. bd. dirs. 1977—; pres. 1980-81), Am. Psychol. Assn., Human Resource Planning Soc., Soc. for Indsl. and Orgnl. Psychology. Home: 120 W 97th St Apt #11I New York NY 10025 Office: Oliver Human Resource Cons Inc 250 W 57th St New York NY 10107

OLIVER, BONNIE BONDURANT, educational telecommunications company executive, consultant; b. St. Louis, Jan. 25, 1933; d. Benjamin Burns and Florence Mary (Spencer) Bondurant; m. Donald Edgar Wiese, June 19, 1954 (div. 1972); children: Kurt Rowland, Martha Jill Wiese Reid; m. Raymond Elliott Oliver, Dec. 8, 1972. BA, Monmouth Coll., Ill., 1954; MA, U. Mo., 1957; postgrad. U. Calif., Irvine, 1963-65. Lic. tchr., Calif.; lic. in ednl. adminstrn. Sci. TV tchr. Santa Ana Schs., Calif., 1966-70; dir. dist. media Santa Ana Unified Schs., 1970-72; adminstr. Regional Ednl. TV, Downey, Calif., 1973-78; mgr. edn. tech. unit Calif. Dept. Edn., Sacramento, 1978-81; dep. dir. Calif. Pub. Broadcasting Commn., Sacramento, 1981-83; pres. Oliver and Co., Los Angeles, 1983-89; pres. Bonnie Oliver Prodns., Inc., 1989—; project dir. Sta. KCET-TV, L.A.; dir. L.A. Project Literacy Us (Plus) Task Force; cons. Calif. Dept. Edn., Sacramento, Ky. Ednl. TV, Lexington, Merrill Communications, Phoenix, Ency. Brit., Chgo. Recipient Achievement Commendation City of Los Angeles, 1987. Contbr. articles to popular mags. Mem. friends com. Orange Commn. on Status of Women, Santa Ana, 1976, L.A. Reading Project (LARP) City Libr., Friends com. Coro Found.; chmn. adv. com. Internat. Childrens TV, Washington, 1979; bd. dirs. Internat. Childrens TV, 1979-81, Pub. Svc. Satellite Consortium; trustee Stanford Home for Children, Sacramento, 1980-84. C-Span Cable Network fellow, Washington, 1980; recipient Susan B. Anthony Communications award Hollywood chpt. Bus. and Profl. Women, 1987. Mem. Acad. TV Arts and Sci., Am. Assn. For Adult Continuing Edn., Internat. Correctional Edn. Assn., Assn. for Edn. Communications and Tech., Am. Mgmt. Assn., Calif. State Dept. Edn. Adult Learning Task Force, Kappa Kappa Gamma Alumnae Assn. Republican. Home: 3805 Karen Lynn Dr Glendale CA 91206

OLIVER, BONNIE KLISCZ, mortgage company executive; b. West Bend, Wis., June 24, 1944; d. Edwin Leslie and Helen Louise (Schuppel) Ahlers; m. Anthony W. Kliscz, July 17, 1962 (div. Dec. 1982); children: Todd Anthony, Terry John; m. Wayne Darrell, Feb. 28, 1985. Grad., Realtors Inst. Cert. realtor, Wis., Minn. Reporter, writer Fremont (Nebr.) Tribune, 1970; real estate salesperson Gerrard Realty, La Crosse, Wis., 1971-74; loan officer No. Fed. Savs. & Loan, St. Paul, 1974-75; real estate salesperson Gerrard Realty & The Wheeler Co., La Crosse, 1975-82; regional loan originator Norwest Mortgage Corp., Madison, Wis., 1983; mortgage loan specialist Mortgage Options, La Crosse, 1983-85, pres., 1985—; company rep. Greater La Crosse C. of C., 1983-87. Mem. Greater La Crosse Bd. Realtors, Nat. Assn. Realtors, Wis. Realtors, Assn., La Crosse Area Home Builders Assn. Democrat. Lutheran. Home: 522 S 23d St La Crosse WI 54601 Office: Mortgage Options La Crosse 505 King St La Crosse WI 54601

OLIVER, CARLA RAE, educator; b. Canyon, Tex., July 26, 1947; d. Willis Truit and Evelyn Joye (Waltman) Hedges; m. Elton Leroy Boyd, Jan. 2, 1971 (div. 1978); m. Forrest Dee Oliver, Apr. 5, 1980; children: Brandi Anne, Christopher Ryan. BFA, West Tex. State U., 1971; elementary tchr. cert., Sul Ross Coll., 1978. Tchr. Eagle Pass (Tex.) Ind. Sch. Dist., 1978-80, Ector County Ind. Sch. Dist., Odessa, Tex., 1984—; workshop instr. Ector County Ind. Sch. Dist., Odessa, Tex., 1986. Mem. Odessa Symphony Guild. Mem. AAUW (v.p. programs local chpt.), Tex. State Tchrs. Assn. Republican. Methodist. Home: 4444 Haner Dr Odessa TX 79762

OLIVER, DENISE A, social worker. B, U. Toledo, 1976. Dist. super. Mo. Bur. for the Blind, Kansas City, social worker; counselor, handicapped specialist Ohio Bur. Employment Svcs., Findlay. Adv. bd. Program for the Blind Rehab. Inst. Recipient Disting. Svc. award Nat. Libr. Congress. Mem. NAFE, Nat. Rehab. Assn., Assn. and Edn. of Visually Imparied, Adminstrn. Mgmt. Soc. Home: 11306 Oak #6 Kansas City MO 64114 Office: 615 E 13th St Rm 409 Kansas City MO 64106

OLIVER, DIANN, telephone company official; b. Lake Charles, La., Oct. 21, 1951; d. Kermit and Edna (Carlock) O. Grad. high sch., Westlake, La. With South Cen. Bell, Lake Charles, La., 1969-74; switch person South Cen. Bell, New Orleans, 1974-75; supr. electronic switching system South Cen. Bell, Alexandria, La., 1975-88; supr. power systems South Cen. Bell, Shreveport, La., 1988—. Troop leader Cen. La. coun. Girl Scouts U.S.A., 1983-88; bd. dirs., event dir. Alexandria Spl. Olympics, 1981-88; bd. dirs. March of Dimes, Alexandria, 1985-87; rape crisis vol. and trainer Family Counselling Agy., Alexandria, 1985-88; vol., trainer Boys Club, Alexandria, 1986-87; bd. dirs., sports dir. Shreveport Shreveport Spl. Olympics, 1988—; v.p. Alexandria Jaycees, 1984-88; clown Internat. Spl. Olympics, Baton Rouge, 1983. Recipient cert. of appreciation La. Spl. Olympics, 1981-88, La. Spl. Edn. Ctr., 1983, 84; Outstanding Young Woman award Alexandria Jaycees, 1984, Dist. Dir. award, 1985, Presdl. award of honor, 1986, Outstanding Svc. award Alexandria Telephone Pioneers, 1984, 86, recognition award Alexandria Jaycee Women, 1984, 85, Outstanding Community Svc. award Sta. KRRV, 1986, proclamation for outstanding community svc. Alexandria Mayor's Office, 1986. Mem. Shreveport Jaycees. Democrat. Baptist. Home: Little River Rd Birmingham AL 35213 Office: Bell South Svcs 65 Bagby Dr Rm 224 Birmingham AL 35209

OLIVER, ELIZABETH KIMBALL, writer, historian; b. Saginaw, Mich., May 21, 1918; d. Chester Benjamin and Margaret Eva (Allison) Kimball; m. James Arthur Oliver, May 3, 1941 (div. July 1967); children: Patricia Allison Karambay, Dexter Kimball. BA, U. Mich., 1940. Tchr. Dexter (Mich.) High Sch., 1940-41; libr. Sherman (Conn.) Libr. Assn., 1966-75; pres. Sherman (Conn.) Libr. Assn., 1983-84; writer, historian, 1976—; reporter Sherman Sentinel, 1965-70; editor newsletter Sherman Hist. Soc., 1977-78; columnist Citizen News, Fairfield County, Conn., 1981-83. Author: History of Staff Wives-AMNH, 1961, Background and History of the Palisades Nature Association, 1964, History and Architecture of Grace United Methodist Church, 1990. Vol. N.Y. Hist. Soc., N.Y.C., 1961-65; treas. Coburn Cemetery Assn., Sherman, 1976-82; historian Greenbrook-Palisades Nature Assn., Tenafly, N.J., 1962-64. Mem. AAUW, Friends of the Libr. (life mem.), St. Augustine Hist. Soc., Emil Maestre Music Assn., St. Augustine Woman's Club (Cert. of Appreciation 1990). Republican. Congregationalist. Home: 22 Park Terrace Dr Saint Augustine FL 32084

OLIVER, HELEN THERESA, humanities educator; b. Montserrat, British West Indies, June 20, 1949; came to U.S.; d. Winford Andrew and Margaret Eliza Ann (Francis) Green; m. Sylvester Walker Oliver, Dec. 29, 1979; 1 child, Jabari Ayinde. B in Edn., U. Nottingham, England, 1975; diploma in Edn., U. London, 1978; MEd, U. Miss., 1983. Cert. guidance counselor. Tchr. Newington Green Jr. Sch., London, 1975-76, Starcross Girls' Sch., London, 1976-80; dist. mgr. Avon Products, Inc., Atlanta, 1982-84; prof. Rust Coll., Holly Springs, Miss., 1983—; adj. prof. Hackney F.E. Coll., London, 1977-78; pres. Positive Attitudes, Holly Springs, 1984—; advisor literary club Rust Coll., 1987—; coord., resource person Marshall County Spelling Bee, Holly Springs, 1987—. Columnist: The South Reporter, 1987—; author: Romancing Existence, 1988; editor: Infopro, 1990. Ford Found. fellow, 1987-88; named one of Outstanding Young Women Am., 1986. Mem. Phi Delta Kappa, Delta Sigma Theta (program chair 1989—), Kappa Delta Pi. Roman Catholic. Office: Rust Coll 150 Rust Ave Holly Springs MI 38635

OLIVER, JOYCE ANNE, journalist, editorial consultant, columnist; b. Coral Gables, Fla., Sept. 19, 1958; d. John Joseph and Rosalie Cecile (Mack) O. BA in Communications, Calif. State U., Fullerton, 1980, MBA, 1990. Corp. editor Norris Industries Inc., Huntington Beach, Calif., 1979-82; pres. J.A. Oliver Assocs., La Habra Heights, Calif., 1982—; corp. editorial cons. Norris Industries, 1982, Better Methods Cons., Huntington Harbour, Calif., 1982-83, Summit Group, Orange, Calif., 1982-83, UDS, Encinitas, Calif., 1983-84, MacroMarketing, Costa Mesa, Calif., 1985-86, PM Software, Huntington Beach, Calif., 1985-86, CompuQuote, Canoga Park, Calif., 1985-86, Nat. Semicondr. Can. Ltd., Mississauga, Ont., Can., 1986, Maclean Hunter Ltd., Toronto, Ont., 1986-90; Frame Inc., Fullerton, Calif., 1987-88, The Johnson-Layton Co., L.A., 1988-89, Corp. Rsch. Inc., Chgo., 1988; mem. Rsch. Coun. of Scripps Clinic and Rsch. Found., 1987-90; bus. columnist Mktg. News, 1990—. Contbg. editor Computer Resell., monthly, 1982-85; spl. feature editor Cleve. Inst. Electronics publ. The Electron, 1986-89; contbg. editor Reseller Mgmt. mag., 1987-89, Can. Electronics Engring. mag., 1986-90, west coast editor, 1990—; contbr. PC Week, The NOMDA

Spokesman, Entrepreneur, Adminstrv. Mgmt., High-Tech Selling, Video Systems, Tech. Photography, Computing Canada, Stores, Bus., Leadership & Orgn. Devel. Jour., HR Mag. Mem. IEEE, Am. Mktg. Assn., Internat. Platform Assn., Soc. Photo-Optical Instrumentation Engrs., Inst. Mgmt. Scis., Nat. Writers Club (profl.), Internat. Mktg. Assn., Soc. Profl. Journalists. Republican. Roman Catholic. Office: JA Oliver Assocs 2045 Fullerton Rd La Habra Heights CA 90631

OLIVER, MARGUERITE BERTONI, food service executive; b. Ann Arbor, Mich., June 5, 1929; d. Ralph Angelo and Margaret Amelia (Rovegno) Bertoni; m. William John Oliver, May 28, 1949; children: R. Scott, Catherine Oliver Allen, Susan M. Mgr. complaint dept. Sears Roebuck Co., Ann Arbor, 1949-50; dir. meals-on-wheels program U. Mich. Hosp., Ann Arbor, 1974-76; fund raiser U. Mich. Art Sch., Ann Arbor, 1976-80; founder Pastabilities (named outstanding pasta shop in U.S. by CNN TV), Ann Arbor, 1980—; participant, speaker Midwest Assn. State Depts. Agr., 1987; mem. adv. com. Gov.'s Conf. on Future of Mich. Agr., 1988; co-chmn. Gov.'s Conf. on Agr., 1989. Mem. com. on aging Ann Arbor Council, 1970-74; bd. dirs. Hands-On-Mus., Ann Arbor, 1980-82; mem. mkt. commn. Ann Arbor, 1982—; founded Internat. Neighbors; mem., adv. com. Mich. Future 2020 Team; trustee Washtenaw Community Coll., 1989—; mem. Mich. Dept. Agr. Industry Task Force, 1990. Recipient Washtenaw Community Service award Washtenaw Community Coll., 1985. Democrat. Roman Catholic. Club: Women's City. Home: 2892 Bay Ridge Dr Ann Arbor MI 48103 Office: Pastabilities 212 E Kingsley St Ann Arbor MI 48104

OLIVER, PATRICIA LEANENE, public relations executive; b. Jasper County, Mo., Oct. 10, 1938; d. Alonzo Lee and Gladys Valeria (Wood) LeMasters; m. William E. Estes, June 25, 1960 (div. Aug. 1974); 1 child, Phillip Mason; m. David William Oliver, July 20, 1984. AA in Pub. Rels. and Advt., St. Louis Community Coll., 1983. Sec. several local cos., Carthage, Mo., 1955-60; with pub. rels. McDonnell Douglas, St. Louis, 1960-73, spl. events adminstr., 1973-82; pub. rels. mgr. McDonnell Douglas, Kennedy Space Center, Fla., 1982—; chmn. Joint Industry Press Ctr., Kennedy Space Center, 1989-90; mem. planning com. Leadership Brevard, Brevard County, Fla., 1988-90, bd. dirs., 1988-90. Mem. grants com. Brevard Cultural Alliance, Brevard County, Fla., 1989; sec. Am. Cancer Soc., Merritt Island, Fla., 1989-90, mem. adv. coun. cen. east coast dist., Orlando, Fla., 1989-90, field service com. Fla. unit, Tampa, 1987-89. Recipient 2d pl. award advt. Nat. Fend. Press Women, 1981, 1st pl. award advt. Mo. Press Women Assn., 1981; named Vol. of Yr., Am. Cancer Soc., Merritt Island, Fla., 1989. Mem. Fla. Pub. Rels. Assn. (pres. 1987-88), Canaveral Press Club. Republican. Methodist. Home: 2355 Lake Front Ct Merritt Island FL 32953 Office: McDonnell Douglas PO Box 21233 Kennedy Space Center FL 32815

OLIVER, ROSE WARSHAW, psychologist, psychotherapist; b. Poland, Mar. 9, 1910; d. Nathan and Celia (Cohn) Warshaw; came to U.S., 1914, naturalized, 1926; B.A., Barnard Coll., 1931; M.A., Queens Coll., City U. N.Y., 1967, Ph.D., Grad. Center, 1973; postgrad. fellow Inst. Rational Emotive Therapy, 1975; m. Juan Oliver, Sept. 1937; children: Teressa, John. Adj. asst. prof. psychology City U. N.Y., 1969-75; staff psychotherapist, mem. supervisory faculty Inst. Rational Emotive Therapy, N.Y.C., 1975; pvt. practice psychology and psychotherapy, Queens, N.Y.C., 1975—; workshop leader; lectr. in field; bd. profl. advisors Inst. Rational Emotive Therapy. Cert. psychologist, N.Y. Co-author: (with Frances Bock) Coping with Alzheimer's: A Caregiver's Emotional Survival Guide, 1987; contbr. articles to profl. jours. Mem. Am. Psychol. Assn., N.Y. State Psychol. Assn., Nassau County Psychol. Assn., N.Y. Soc. Clin. Psychologists. Home: 161 W 61st St New York NY 10023

OLIVER, SHARLYN CHYREL, librarian; b. Ft. Smith, Ark., June 1, 1948; d. William H. and Evelyn Clark (Wilson) O. BS in Elem. Edn., David Lipscomb U., 1968; MA in Elem. Edn., Murray State U., 1973; postgrad., U. Louisville, 1978. Cert. elem. tchr., libr. prin., secondary libr., in curriculum supervision, Ky. Tchr. Met. Nashville-Davidson County, Nashville, 1969-70, Ballard County Schs., Wickliffe, Ky., 1970-71, Caldwell County Schs., Princeton, Ky., 1971-72; libr. Marshall County Schs., Benton, Ky., 1972-73, Jefferson County Schs., Louisville, 1973—; coach Chess Jefferson Town High Sch., Louisville, 1983-88, Debate, 1986—, Academics, 1987—; coord. Homework Hotline, Jefferson Town High Sch., Louisville, 1983—. Named Ky. Colonel, State of Ky., 1988. Mem. NEA, Ky. Edn. Assn., Jefferson County Tchrs. Assn., Ky. Libr. Assn., Mensa, Atari Exchange Louisville (libr. 1987—). Democrat. Mem. Ch. of Christ. Office: Jeffersontown High Sch 9600 Old Six Mile Ln Jeffersontown KY 40299-2399

OLIVERIO, ANTOINETTE FRANCES, secondary school educator; b. Cleve., Jan. 27, 1948; d. John L. and Katherine M. (Grassi) O. BS in Edn., Kent State U., 1976; MEd, U. Houston, 1983. Cert. English, speech, history, reading tchr., Ohio, Calif., Tex. Tchr. Nordonia High Sch., Northfield, Ohio, 1976-79, Patrick Henry Jr. High Sch., Houston, 1979-84, James Ford Rhodes High Sch., Cleve., 1984—; instr. Cuyahoga Community Coll., Warrensville, Ohio, 1988—, Mayfield (Ohio) Schs., 1988-89. Cleve. Found. grantee, 1986. Mem. Greater Cleve. Tchrs. English, Nat. Coun. Tchrs. English. Democrat. Roman Catholic. Office: Cleveland City Schs 1360 E 6th St Cleveland OH 44114

OLIVIER, NANCY, painter; b. Bklyn., Dec. 13, 1954; d. Lino Louis and Ann (Sbrigato) O.; m. Carl A. Giliberto, May 21, 1988. BA in Fine ARts, Painting, Hofstra U., 1976. artist-in-residence Altos de Chavron Art Colony, Dominican Republic, 1985. One woman shows include Works on Paper, 55 Mercer Gallery, N.Y.C., 1989, 90; exhibited in group shows at Color Xerox Art Show, Club 57, N.Y.C., 1980, 80 Washington Sq. East Galleries, N.Y.C., 1983, Pub. Image Gallery, N.Y.C., 1983, Inroads Gallery, N.Y.C., 1985, Principal Gallery, Altos de Chavon, 1985, On The Wall Gallery, N.Y.C., 1986, Everson Mus. Fine Art, Syracuse, N.Y., 1986, Emerging ARtist Prog., A.I.R. Gallery, 1989, Randall Gallery, St. Louis, 1989, The Topical Rainforest Show, N.Y.C.,1989. Artistspace grantee, 1989. Mem. ACLU, 55 Mercer Artist Gallery. Democrat.

OLKKOLA, JUDITH A., management executive; b. Worcester, Mass., Mar. 3, 1948; d. Edward N. LaVigne and Margaret (Mombourquette) O. AB in Art, Anna Maria Coll., 1970. Pres., ind. practice Ocean Spray Irrigation, Inc, West Yarmouth, Mass.; art supr. Town of Yarmouth. Mem. Rotary. Address: PO Box 1333 South Yarmouth MA 02664

OLLIS, LINDA NEU, hospital administrator, consultant; b. Pitts., Oct. 2, 1952; d. Kenneth Edward and Rose (Rush) Neu; m. John Wilson Ollis, June 11, 1983. BS in Phys. Therapy, U. Pitts., 1974, MPH with honors, 1977; postgrad., U. Calif., L.A., 1984-85. Phys. therapist Allegheny Valley Hosp., Natrona Heights, Pa., 1974-75; asst. adminstr. Montefiore Hosp., Pitts., 1977-82; assoc. cons. Hamilton/KSA, Dallas, 1982-84; dir. mktg. and new bus. St. Vincent Med. Ctr., L.A., 1984-85; asst. adminstr. Pacific Presbyn. Med. Ctr., San Francisco, 1985-87; v.p. U. Hosps. of Cleve., 1987-89; sr. assoc. adminstr. Grossmont Hosp., La Mesa, Calif., 1989—. Mem. editorial bd.: Jour. of Consumer Mktg. mag., 1984; founder, editor: newsletter HENC, 1986-87 (Founder's award 1987); contbr. articles to profl. jours. Mem. United Way/CHAD steering com. HEW grantee, 1977. Mem. Am. Coll. Healthcare Execs., Healthcare Exec.'s N.E. Ohio (com. chair 1988-89), Healthcare Exec.'s No. Calif. (chair communications com. 1986-87), Healthcare Execs. San Diego, S.D. Women in Health Care. Office: Grossmont Hosp 5555 Grossmont Ctr Dr La Mesa CA 92041

OLMAN, MARYELLEN, human resources administrator; b. Grand Rapids, Mich., Dec. 24, 1946; d. Norman Adolph and Mary Irene (McCarthy) Olman; m. Richard Isaac Fine, Nov. 25, 1982; 1 child, Victoria Elizabeth. BA in Community Svc., Mich. State U., 1968. Legis. researcher Hon. Gerald R. Ford, U.S. Ho. of Reps., 1969-71; spl. asst. Hon. Jack F. Kemp, U.S. Ho. of Reps., 1971-74; personnel analyst Los Angeles City Housing Authority, 1975-78; profl. placement rep. Gen. Telephone of Calif., Santa Monica, 1978-81, mgmt. staffing adminstr., 1981-84; human resource adminstr. Law Offices Richard I. Fine & Assocs., 1985—. Mem. Los Angeles Internat. Visitors Assn., 1982—; mem. founders circle Los Angeles Music Ctr. Mem. Am. Soc. Personnel Adminstrs., Coll. Placement Coun., Western Coll. Placement Assn., Personnel and Indsl. Rels. Assn., The Seedlings. Republican. Home: 5331 Horizon Dr Malibu CA 90265

OLMEDO, KIM ELLEN, social worker; b. Orlando, Fla., Dec. 10, 1959; d. Lorenzo and Mildred Maxine (Morris) O. BA, U. Tex., 1982, MSW, 1990. Cert. social worker, Tex. Psychiatric nursing asst. The Oaks Treatment Ctr., Austin, Tex., 1981-85; referral coord. Learning Abilities Ctr., Austin, 1986; social worker child protective svcs. div. Tex. Dept. Human Svcs., Arlington, 1986. Mem. NASW. NAFE. Office: Tex Dept Human Svcs 410 W Sanford Ste 2400 Arlington TX 76011

OLMEDO-BORECKY, STEPHANIE KATHRYN, air force officer; b. Denver, Jan. 16, 1950; d. Juanita (Morales) Putnam; m. Steven John Borecky, Sept. 23, 1978; children: Kittrick John, Kyle Stephen, Kurt Adair. MA, U. No. Colo., 1979. Tchr. of deaf Amoskeege Sc. Dist., Claremont, N.H., 1973, Gov. Baxter Sch. for Deaf, Falmouth, Maine, 1973-74, Pueblo Sch. Dist., Colo., 1975-77; commd. 2d lt. U.S. Air Force, 1981, advanced through grades to capt., 1985; exec. support officer Ellsworth AFB, S.D., 1981-85, Dyess AFB, Tex., 1985—. Mem. Air Force Assn., Nat. Assn. Female Execs. Roman Catholic. Home: 2957 Stonecrest Dr Abilene TX 79606 Office: 96 Combat Support Group Dyess AFB TX 79607

OLMSTED, JOANNA BELLE, cell biology educator; b. Chgo., Mar. 8, 1947; d. Charles Edward and Hazel (Wiggers) O.; m. Douglas Hugh Turner, Aug. 27, 1977; 1 child, Richard. BA, Earlham Coll., 1967; PhD, Yale U., 1971; postgrad., U. Wis., 1971-74. Asst. prof. cell biology U. Rochester, N.Y., 1975-81, assoc. prof., 1981-87, prof., 1987—; mem. molecular cytology study sect. NIH, Bethesda, Md., 1987-90. Fellow NIH, 1968-74. Mem. Am. Soc. for Cell Biology (councillor 1980-82, publs. com. 1983-85, edn. com. 1989—). Office: U Rochester Dept Biology Rochester NY 14627

O'LOONEY, PATRICIA ANNE, medical program administrator; b. Bridgeport, Conn., Dec. 2, 1954; d. John Joseph and Marjorie Ellen (Curran) O'L. BA in Molecular Biology, Regis Coll., 1976; MS in Biochemistry, George Washington U., 1978, PhD in Biochemistry, 1982. Rsch. asst. biochemistry dept. George Washington Med. Sch., Washington, 1976-82, teaching asst., 1978-81, rsch. assoc., 1982-84, sr. rsch. scientist, 1984-86, asst. prof. medicine and biochemistry, 1986-88; asst. dir. The Nat. Multiple Sclerosis Soc., N.Y.C., 1988-90, assoc. dir. rsch. and med. programs, 1990—; vis. lectr. George Washington Med. Sch., 1988—. Author: Lipoprotein Lipase, 1987; contbr. articles to profl. jours. Recipient New Investigator Rsch. award NIH, 1985. Mem. Am. Soc. for Biochemistry and Molecular Biology, N.Y. Acad. Scis., Assn. for Women in Sci., The Mid-Atlantic Lipid Soc., Sigma Xi, Beta Beta Beta. Republican. Roman Catholic. Office: Nat Multiple Sclerosis Soc 205 E 42nd St New York NY 10017

OLSEN, INGER ANNA, psychologist; b. Copper Mountain, B.C, Can., Dec. 25, 1926; d. Dagmar O.; B.S., Wash. State U., 1954, M.S., 1956, Ph.D., 1962. Psychiat. nurse Provincial Mental Health Services B.C., 1947-51, psychologist, 1956-58; psychologist Vancouver (B.C.) City Met. Health Services, 1958-60, Wash. State U. Student Counseling Center, Pullman, 1960-62; sr. psychologist Met. Health Services, Vancouver, 1962-66; instr. psychology Vancouver Community Coll., 1966-87; docent Vancouver Aquarium Assn. Bd. dirs. Second Mile Soc., 1975-89. Mem. Assn. Childhood Edn. Internat., Am. Psychol. Assn., B.C. Psychol. Assn., Gerontol. Soc., Can. Assn. Gerontology, B.C. Assn. Gerontology, Phi Beta Kappa, Sigma Xi, Alpha Kappa Delta. Contbr. articles to profl. jours. Home: 1255 Bidwell St, Apt 1910, Vancouver, BC Canada V6G 2K8

OLSEN, MIRIAM GLADYS, nursing educator, consultant; b. Poston, Ohio, Sept. 9, 1923; d. Isaac Albert and Saima Suzanne (Rhoenbek) Nurmi; m. James Karge Olsen, July 27, 1946; children: Karge (dec.), Karen Ballard, Erik. Diploma in nursing, Luth. Hosp. Sch. Nursing, 1944; BSN in Edn., Loyola U., Chgo., 1949; postgrad., Case Western Res. U., 1947; cert. in health edn., William Paterson Coll., 1972. RN, Ariz. Dir. Cuyahoga Falls (Ohio) Sch. Practical Nursing, 1968-69; instr. William Paterson Coll., Wayne, N.J., 1971-72, Rutgers U., Newark, 1972-73; dir. staff devel. Bethesda Hosp., Zanesville, Ohio, 1973-75; asst. prof. Muskingum Area Tech. Coll., Zanesville, 1975-77; instr. nurse edn. Ohio U., Zanesville, 1977-79; nurse health educator Ill. State U., Normal, 1979-86; part-time cons. Scottsdale (Ariz.) Unified Sch. Dist., 1989—. Author, editor: (monthly column) Vital Signs, 1983-86. Mem. Phoenix Art Mus., 1987-90; bd. dirs. State Lung Assn., Newark, 1970-71. 2d lt. U.S. Army, 1945-46. Democrat. Presbyterian. Home: 7813 E Northland Dr Scottsdale AZ 85251

OLSEN, SUZANNE, elementary teacher; b. LaCrosse, Wis., Jan. 2, 1944; d. Leo Edward and Eleanor Marie (Hasselbusch) Miltner; m. Glenn Warren Olsen, Aug. 27, 1966; children: Teresa, Catherine, Gregory, John. BA, Seattle U., 1966; MA, U. Utah, 1983. Tchr. Weber State U., Ogden, Utah, 1982-83, St. Mark's Sch.-Rowland Hall, Salt Lake City, 1983—. Mem. Birthright Utah(steering com., 1979), Salt Lake City. active Demo.(voting del., 1980-82), Salt Lake City, City Creek Canyon Project(steering com.), Salt Lake City. Named Teacher of the Yr., Kiwanis Club, Salt Lake City, 1988. Mem. Nat. Jr. Classical League(state chmn.), Region 7 Conf. Nat. Assn. Student Couns.(co-chmn., 1987), Utah Classical Assn.(sec. treas., 1985-90), Phi Kappa Phi. Roman Catholic. Office: St Mark s Sch Rowland Hall 843 Lincoln St Salt Lake City UT 84102

OLSEN-FULERO, LYNDA LAVERNE, psychology educator; b. McMinnville, Oreg., Nov. 16, 1947; d. Vernon Hilmar and Eunice Audrey (Evans) Olsen; m. Michael Alex McDonald, Dec. 19, 1969 (div. 1979); 1 child, Ariel Claire; m. Solomon M. Fulero, Jan. 1, 1982; 1 child, David Nathan. BA, Mills Coll., Oakland, Calif., 1970; MA, Portland (Oreg.) State U., 1973; PhD, U. Oreg., 1979. Lic. psychologist, Ohio. Vis. asst. prof. Wright State U., Dayton, Ohio, 1979-82; asst. prof. Antioch Coll., Yellow Springs, Ohio, 1982-84; asst. prof. Miami U., Hamilton, Ohio, 1984-88, assoc. prof., 1988—. Contbr. articles to profl. jours. Mem. Am. Psychol. Assn., Midwestern Psychol. Assn., Soc. for Rsch. in Child Devel., Phi Beta Kappa. Democrat. Home: 517 Winding Way Kettering OH 45429 Office: Miami U 1601 Peck Blvd Hamilton OH 45011

OLSEN-STENGLEIN, KAREN MARIE, sales executive; b. Highland Park, Mich., June 21, 1953; d. Henry Olaf and Harriet H. (Caruana) Olsen; m. Harold John Stenglein III, Apr. 11, 1987. BA in English and Psychology, Wayne State U., 1971-75. Mktg. support specialist Xerox Corp., Southfield, Mich., 1976-79, office systems cons., 1979-81, Gen. Motors nat. account rep., 1982-83, major account mktg. exec., 1981-89; sr. account mgr. Ungermann-Bass, Southfield, 1989—. Mem. NAFE, Soc. Mfg. Engrs., Computer Graphics Assn., Antique and Classic Boat Assn. Presbyterian. Home: 909 Columbia Berkeley MI 48072-1918 Office: Ungermann-Bass 27700 Northwestern Hwy Ste 121 Southfield MI 48034

OLSHAN, KAREN, advertising agency executive. Former v.p., then sr. v.p. Batten Barton Durstine & Osborn (now BBDO), N.Y.C.; exec. v.p., dir. rsch. svcs. BBDO N.Y., N.Y.C., 1989—. Office: BBDO NY 1285 Ave of the Americas New York NY 10019*

OLSON, BARBARA MARTHA, educator; b. Chgo., Dec. 12, 1943; d. Joseph Martin and Clara Gertrude (Dryjanski) Zbylski; m. William Kevin, Feb. 5, 1966; children: Kirsten Claire, Julie Ann, David Channing. BA, Mundelein Coll., Chgo., 1965. Cert. elem. tchr., Ill. 1st grade tchr. Sch. Dist 111, Burbank, Ill., 1965-68, kindergarten tchr., 1968-69; substitute tchr. Sch. Dists. 113, 92C & 33C, Lemont & Lockport, Ill., 1975-81; tchr. Lemont Sch. Dist. #113, 1981-84; adminstr. Phoenix Builders, Lockport, 1984-87; pres. Parent Power, Lemont, 1987-90; cons. Design for Chance, Chgo., 1988-89, Network, Tinley Park, 1988-89. Parish chmn. SPRED, St. Alphonsus, 1987-89; St. Michaels, Orland Park, 1982-85, Archdiocese of Chgo., Chgo., 1979; Vol. Special Recreation Assn., Romeoville, 1977-89. Mem. St. Alphonsus Women's Club, Homer Twp. BPW Historian, Homer Twp Reb. Women's, Homer Women Network. Republican. Roman Catholic. Home: 15112 W Orchard Ln Lockport IL 60441

OLSON, BONNIE BRETERNITZ-WAGGONER (MRS. O. DONALD OLSON), civic worker; b. North Platte, Nebr.; d. Floyd Emil and Edith (Waggoner) Breternitz; AB, U. Chgo., 1947; m. O. Donald Olson, May 17, 1944; children: Pamela Lynne, Douglas Donald. Dep. clk. Dist. Ct., Lincoln County, Nebr., 1940-42; advt. researcher Burke & Assoc., Chgo., 1942; contbg. newspaper columnist Chgo. Herald-Am., 1943; social worker A.R.C., Chgo., 1942-44, Sacramento, Calif., 1944, Amarillo, Tex., 1945; exec. sec. Econometrica, Cowles Commn. for Rsch. in Econs., Chgo., 1945-47; interior designer, antique dealer. Col.; participant Chgo. Maternity Ctr. Fund Drive, 1953, Chgo. Coun. on Fgn. Rels., 1948-54; mem. Colo. Springs Community Council, 1956-58, chmn. children's div., 1956-58, mem. exec. bd., 1956-58, mem. budget com., 1957-58; mem. Colorado Springs Charter Assn., 1956-60, mem. exec. bd., 1957-59, sec., 1958; chmn. El Paso County PTA, Protective Svcs. for Children, 1959-61; chmn. women's div. fund drive ARC, 1961; mem. League Women Voters, 1957—, mem. state children's law com., 1961-63; chmn. ad hoc com. El Paso County Citizens' Com. for Nat. Probation and Parole Survey, Juvenile Ct. Procedures and Detention, 1957-61; mem. children's adv. com. Colo. Child Welfare Dept., 1959-63, chmn., 1961; del. White House Conf. on Children and Youth, 1960, 70; sec. Citizens Ad Hoc Com. for Comprehensive Mental Health Clinic for Pikes Peak Region, 1966—; mem. Colorado Springs Human Rels. Commn., 1968-71; sustaining mem. Symphony Guild, 1970-72, Fine Arts Ctr., 1957—; mem. Pikes Peak Mental Health Ctr., 1964-67 (bd. dirs.); Colo. observer White House Conf. on Aging, Colo. Gov.'s Conf. on Aging, 1981, Dist. Atty.'s Child Abuse Task Force, 1986; participant Career Planning Documentary Film Radcliffe Coll. Career Svcs., 1990. Recipient Lane Bryant Ann. Nat. Awards citation, 1971; alumni citation for pub. service U. Chgo., 1961. Mem. Am. Acad. Polit. and Social Sci., Nat. Trust Historic Preservation, Women's Ednl. Soc. Colo. Coll. (life), Council on Religion and Internat. Affairs. Episcopalian. Clubs: Quadranglar, University (Chgo.). Home: 169 Linden Dr Cohasset MA 02025-1525

OLSON, DIANA CRAFT, image and etiquette consultant; b. Langley, Va., May 5, 1941; d. Winfred O. and Joyce (Clark) Craft; m. Robert J. Olson, May 30, 1976; children: Stacey Ann, Kirsten Lowry. BA, U. Tex., 1963; MA, San Francisco State U., 1970; cert. color cons., Fashion Acad., Costa Mesa, Calif., 1979. Tchr. USAF, P.R., 1963-64, Long Beach (Calif.) Unified Sch. Dist., 1964-68, South San Francisco (Calif.) Unified Sch. Dist., 1968-79; pres. Diana's Color Collage & Color Collage Inst., Pasadena, Calif., 1979—; etiquette affiliates Dorthea Johnson and Marjabelle Stewart, Washington, 1988—; cons. Weight Watchers Internat., L.A., Ventura, Calif., 1987—, 1st Interstate Bank, L.A., 1990, Marriott Hotels, Long Beach, 1989. Contbr. articles to mags. Speaker Women in Action, Pasadena, Calif. 1989. Mem. NAFE, Assn. Image Cons. Internat. (sec. 1989-90), Exec. Women Am. Republican. Presbyterian. Office: Diana's Color Collage 123 S Los Robles Ave Pasadena CA 91101

OLSON, DONNA RAE, clinical chemistry technologist; b. St. Louis, Oct. 20, 1947; d. Roy William and Ann Elizabeth (O'Donnell) O. B.A. in Biology, Cath. U. Am., 1964, B.S. in Med. Tech., 1966, M.A. in Ednl. Tech., 1973, Ed.D. in Ednl. Tech., 1985; M.A. in Health Care Mgmt. and Supervision, Central Mich. U., 1981. Cert. Clin. Lab. Scientist, Nat. Cert. Agy. for Med. Lab. Personnel, 1989. Clin. chemistry supr. Washington Hosp. Center, 1965-69, teaching coordinator Sch. Med. Tech., 1969-72; clin. chemistry technologist NIH, Bethesda, Md., 1972—. Recipient various govt. awards. Mem. Am. Soc. Clin. Pathologists (affiliate), Am. Soc. Med. Technologists, Am. Mgmt. Assn., Clin. Lab. Mgmt. Assn., D.C. Soc. Med. Tech. (ednl. coordinator 1979-81), Md. Soc. Med. Tech. Home: 6001 Landon Ln Bethesda MD 20817 Office: Clin Chem Service NIH Bethesda MD 20814

OLSON, DORISE EVELYN (MRS. PAUL J. MINA-MORA), artist; b. N.Y.C., June 8, 1932; d. Athur C. and Anna (Carlson) O.; student Art Student's League, L.I. Art League, Woodstock, N.Y., Traphagen Sch. Design, N.Y.; m. Raul J. Mina-Mora, Oct. 27, 1967. One-man shows at Caravan House Galleries, Lord & Taylor's Galleries, Different Drummer Gallery, 1976, Nat. Art League, Wickford Art Gallery, W. Ris Galleries, N.J., Rosequist Gallery, Ariz.; exhibited in group shows at Bklyn. Mus., Nat. Arts Club, Nat. Acad., Nat. Acad. Fine Arts, Met. Mus. Arts, Community Gallery with Burr Artists, 1977, Goldsboro (N.C.) Art Mus., 1977, Parrish Art Mus., 1970, 72, Springfield (Mass.) Art Mus., Stony Brook U., Cork Gallery, Avery Fisher Hall, Lincoln Center, 1980, others; represented in pvt. collections; tchr. painting Islip Art Mus. Demonstrator watercolor for various schs. and pvt. clubs. Recipient award Bus. and Profl. Women's Club, N.Y.C., 1967; gold medal Knickerbocker Artists, 1968; Hydenryk award Catherine Lorillard Wolfe Art Club, 1969; 1st place award in watercolor Bklyn. Mus. competition, 1966, 67, 69, Windsor and Newton award, Nat. Arts League Gold medal, 70, Grumbacher award 1971, 1st prize for watercolor Malverne Artists, 1973, best watercolor award Burr Artists, 1974, Forbes award, 1981, Newman award Nat. Soc. Painters in Casein and Acrylic, 1981, others. Mem. Am. Artists Profl. League (award 1979), Allied Artists Am., Nat. Soc. Painters in Casein and Acrylic, Knickerbocker Artists (award 1979), Nat. Arts Club, Audubon Artists. Address: 87 Central Blvd Box 256 Oakdale NY 11769

OLSON, DOROTHY MAY, buyer; b. Woburn, Mass., May 6, 1938; d. George Burton Sr. and Gladys Beatrice (Jones) Perkins; m. Kenneth Morris Olson Jr., June 4, 1951. BS, Northeastern U., 1980. From clk. to stenographer RCA Corp., Burlington, Mass., 1963-67, sec., 1967-80, buyer, 1980-88; buyer GE Aerospace, Burlington, 1988—.

OLSON, ELIZABETH JEANETTE, county official; b. Ogden, Utah, June 21, 1951; d. Jennings Grandee and Annette Lucille (Driver) O.; 1 child, Katelin Elizabeth Olson. BS in Child Devel./Family Rels., Weber State Coll., 1973; postgrad., U. Utah, 1988—. Tchr. Community Coop. Nursery Sch., Ogden, Utah, 1973-74; instr. child and family studies Weber State Coll., Ogden, 1975-77, dir. infant edn. project, 1974-77; trainer Head Start program Westminster Coll., Salt Lake City, 1977-78; coord. single parent program YWCA of Ogden, 1978-79; adminstr. pvt. sector initiative program Weber County Corp., Ogden, 1979-84, adminstr. retired sr. vol. program, 1984-85, social svcs. planner, 1985-86, human svcs. planner, 1986—; chairperson planning com. Weber Human Svcs. Planning, Ogden, 1989—; researcher Mission 2000 Elderfocus Task Force, Ogden, 1987—. Editor: (pamplets) Parent Infant Education, 1977; co-author: Parent Infant Education Project, 1972. Bd. dirs. Ogden Mcpl. Employees Credit Union, 1984-88, pres. bd. dirs., 1986-87; mem. Ogden Symphony-Ballet Assn., 1984-89, sec. bd. dirs., 1986-87; mem. St. Paul Parent Tchr. League, 1988—, fall fundraiser chair 1989, head rm. mother, 1989-90. Recipient Svc. to the Elderly award Eagles, Ogden Aerie 2472, 1984. Fellow MPA Student Assn. (pres.). Lutheran. Office: Weber County Corp 2650 Lincoln Ave Rm 204 Ogden UT 84401

OLSON, GEN, state legislator; b. May 20, 1938. BS, U. Minn. Mayor Minnetrista, Minn., 1981-82; mem. Minn. State Senate, 1983—. Former mem. Park and Recreation Commn., Planning and Zoning Commn., Police Commn., City Council. Republican. Office: 6750 Country Rd 110 W Mound MN 55364*

OLSON, JANICE LYNN, real estate executive; b. Washington, Feb. 13, 1946; d. Charles Arthur and Jean Elizabeth (Mudd) O.; divorced; 1 child, Robert. Dir. mktg. Homart Devel. Co., San Bernardino, Calif., 1974-76; property mgr. Homart Devel. Co., Brea, Calif., 1976-82; dir. pub. affairs. Homart Devel. Co., Chgo., 1982-85; gen mgr. Homart Devel. Co., Mesa, Ariz., 1985—. Contbr. articles to profl. jours. Active Mesa Growth Com., 1988—; chmn. of the bd. Mesa unit, bd. dirs. Am. Cancer Soc., 1987—. Recipient Jake award Am. Cancer Soc., 1987, Vol. of Yr. award Am. Cancer Soc., 1989. Mem. Internat. Coun. Shopping Ctrs., Mesa Southwest Mus. Guild, Southwest Archeol. Team. Office: Homart Devel Co 2104 Fiesta Mall Mesa AZ 85202

OLSON, JEANNINE EVELYN, history educator; b. Caledonia, Minn.; d. Aloysius and Evelyn Hazel (Ellingson) Fahsl; children: Karen, Daniel, Rebecca. BA, St. Olaf Coll., Northfield, Minn., 1961; MA, Stanford U., 1962, PhD, 1981; postgrad., U. Minn. Teaching asst. U. Minn., Mpls., 1972-76; asst. prof. San Francisco Theol. Sem., San Anselmo, Calif., 1979-86; mem. doctoral faculty Grad. Theol. Union, Berkeley, Calif., 1979-86; asst. prof. history R.I. Coll., Providence, 1986-90, assoc. prof., 1990—; mem. Internat. Congress for Luther Resch., Erfurt, Ger. and Oslo, Norway, 1983, 88; mem. Task Force on the Confessional Nature of the Ch., Presbyn. Ch., 1983-86. Author: Histoire de L'Eglise, 1972, Calvin and Social Welfare,

1989; contbr. articles to profl. jours. Danforth Found. fellow, 1976-81, Govt. of France rsch. grantee, 1978-79, Am. Coun. Learned Socs. grantee, 1982, Nat. Endowment for Humanities grantee, Geneva, 1985. Mem. Renaissance Soc. Am., 16th Century Studies Soc., Calvin Studies Soc., Am. Soc. Reformatin Rsch., Am. Soc. Ch. History, AAUW, Bus. and Profl. Women, R.I. Hist. Assn., New Eng. Master Swim Club, Rinconada Master Swim Club, Phi Beta Kappa. Home: 48 Lauriston St Providence RI 94306 Office: RI Coll Dept History Providence RI 02908

OLSON, JUDITH MARY REEDY, public information officer, senator; b. Mitchell, S.D., June 24, 1939; d. John Marvin and Camille (Murphy) Reedy; m. Robert George Olson, Aug. 5, 1961; children: Jeffrey, Jennifer, Jon, Jaime, Jason, Jeremy. EdB, U. Tucson, 1961; MEd, S.D. State U., 1984; postgrad., U. S.D., 1985—. Cert. secondary tchr., edn. adminstrn. Tchr. jr. high sch. Mpls. Pub. Schs., 1961-63; mem. State Bd. Edn., S.D., 1972-83, pres., 1975-78; dir. S.D. Edn. Policy Seminar, 1975-79; substitute tchr. Rapid City (S.D.) Schs., 1979-81, tchr. adult basic edn., 1979-81, supr. community relations, 1981-88, supr. community edn., pub. info., 1988—; senator S.D. Legis. (dist. 33), Pierre, S.D., 1989—; speaker, cons. sch. bds., adminstrs., tchrs., sch. dists., pub. relations, various states, 1972—. Bd. dirs. Black Hills Symphony, 1987—. Mem. AAUW (Women of Worth award), Rotary, PEO, Delta Kappa Gamma. Democrat. Roman Catholic. Home: 4603 Ridgewood St Rapid City SD 57702 Office: Rapid City Area Schs 300 6th St Rapid City SD 57702*

OLSON, JULIE ANN, systems consultant, educator; b. Oklahoma City, May 14, 1957; d. Willard Alton and Ruth Harriet (Ehlers) O.; m. Kevin Peter McAuliffe, Oct. 12, 1985. BA in History, Augustana Coll., 1979; MBA, Keller Grad. Sch. Mgmt., Chgo., 1989. Systems analyst Continental Bank, Chgo., 1979-82; sr. systems cons., adminstrv. mgr. Computer Ptnrs., Oakbrook, Ill., 1982—; instr. data processing Oakton Community Coll., Des Plaines, 1983—, faculty coord. accelerated data processing cert. program. Exec. dir., chmn. scholarship Miss N.W. Communities Inc., Des Plaines, 1984-88. Mem. Data Processing Mgmt. Assn. (asst. faculty coord. Student chpt. 1985-87), NAFE. Lutheran. Avocations: classical pianist, reading, flamenco dancing, snow skiing, cross stitch. Home: 401 S Pine Mount Prospect IL 60056-3723 Office: Computer Ptnrs 2021 Spring Rd Ste 200 Oak Brook IL 60521-1854

OLSON, JULIE ANN, architectural firm official; b. Lebanon, Oreg., Oct. 25, 1958; d. Royal Dean and Betty Jane (Gunson) LeClerc; m. Clinton Douglas Olson, June 8, 1985. AS, Judson Bapt. Coll., Portland, Oreg., 1978; BS in Edn., Oreg. State U., 1981. Legis. aide Oreg. Ho. of Reps., Halsey and Salem, 1981-82, Salem, 1982-83, 85; campaign coord. Donna Zajonc for Sec. State, Salem and Portland, 1983-84; office mgr. Architects Barrentine.Bates.Lee, Lake Oswego, Oreg., 1985-88, assoc. ptnr., 1990—; owner, mgr. LeClerc Exec. Shopping Svc., Lake Oswego, 1987—. Mem. Soc. for Mktg. Profl. Svcs. (bd. dirs. Portland 1989-91, v.p. edn. 1989-91). Republican. Office: Architects Barrentine Bates Lee 200 N State St Lake Oswego OR 97034

OLSON, JULIE EILEEN, software engineer; b. Providence, R.I., June 2, 1959; d. Roy Edward and Helen Marie (Wallin) O. BA, North Pk. Coll., 1980; MS in Indsl. Relations, Loyola U., 1985. Asst. supr. outpatient lab. Swedish Covenant Hosp., Chgo., 1977-80; data processing mgr. Pelam Health Systems, Chgo., 1980-85, mgr. customer svcs., 1985-88, dir. operations, 1988-89, dir. software products, 1989—. Mem. North Bus. Indsl. Coun., Chgo. Mem. Great Lakes Orgn., Mass. Gen. Hosp. Utility Multi-Programming Sys. Users Group (pres. 1990). Office: Pelam Health Systems 2810 W Foster Ave Chicago IL 60625

OLSON, KATHY RAE, educator; b. Bismarck, N.D., Oct. 24, 1950; d. Raymond Charles and Virginia Ann (Mason) Lynch; m. Barth Eugene Olson, Aug. 11, 1973; 1 child, William Raymond. B.S., U. N.D., 1972; MS in Spl. Edn., U. N.D., 1987. Cert. elem. tchr. with spl. edn. credential, N.D. Instr., Grafton State Sch., N.D., 1972-74; tchr. spl. edn. Grand Forks Sch. Dist., N.D., 1974—; dir. Agassiz Enterprises. Bd. dirs. Assn. Retarded Citizens; dir. spl. needs recreation program Grand Forks Park Bd., 1973-76; mem. Spl. Olympics Area Mgmt. Team, 1984—. Named N.D. Tchr. of Yr., Coun. of Chief State Sch. Officers, 1981. Mem. AAUW, Delta Kappa Gamma (sec. 1984-86), Alpha Phi (alumni pres. 1984-86), Pi Lambda Theta, Phi Delta Kappa. Republican. Roman Catholic. Avocations: sporting events, civic work, cross stitch, outdoor activity. Home: 3208 Walnut St Grand Forks ND 58201

OLSON, MARIAN EDNA, nurse, social psychologist; b. Newman Grove, Nebr., July 20, 1923; d. Edwrd and Ethel Thelma (Hougland) Olson; diploma U. Nebr., 1944, BS in Nursing, 1953; MA, State U. Iowa, 1961, MA in Psychology, 1962; PhD in Psychology, UCLA, 1966. Staff nurse, supr. U. Tex. Med. Br., Galveston, 1944-49; with U. Iowa, Iowa City, 1949-59, supr. 1953-55, asst. dir. 1955-59; asst. prof. nursing UCLA, 1965-67; prof. nursing U. Hawaii, 1967-70, 78-82; dir. nursing Wilcox Hosp. and Health Center, Lihue, 1970-77; chmn. Hawaii Bd. Nursing, 1974-80; prof. nursing No. Mich. U., 1984-88. Mem. Am. Nurses Assn. (mem. nat. accreditation bd. continuing edn. 1975-78), Nat. League Nursing, Am. Hosp. Assn., Am. Public Health Assn., LWV. Democrat. Roman Catholic. Home and Office: 6223 County 513T Rd Rapid River MI 49878

OLSON, MARIAN KATHERINE, federal agency administrator, publisher, information broker; b. Tulsa, Oct. 15, 1933; d. Sherwood Joseph and Katherine M. (Miller) Lahman; BA in Polit. Sci., U. Colo., 1954, MA in Elem. Edn., 1962; EdD in Ednl. Adminstrn., U. Tulsa, 1969; m. Ronald Keith Olson, Oct. 27, 1956. Tchr. public schs., Wyo., Colo., Mont., 1958-67; teaching fellow, adj. instr. edn. U. Tulsa, 1968-69; asst. prof. edn. Eastern Mont. State Coll., 1970; program assoc. research adminstrn. Mont. State U., 1970-75; on leave with Energy Policy Office of White House, then with Fed. Energy Adminstrn., 1973-74; with Dept. Energy, and predecessor, 1975—, program analyst, 1975-79, chief planning and environ. compliance br., 1979-83; regional dir. Region VIII Fed. Emergency Mgmt. Agy., 1987—; pres. Solar Sense of Colo., Lawyers' Rsch., Bannack Pub. Co. Contbr. articles in field. Grantee Okla. Consortium Higher Edn., 1969, NIMH, 1974. Mem. Am. Soc. for Info. Sci., Am. Assn. Budget and Program Analysis, Women in Energy, Internat. Assn. Ind. Pubs., Mont. Assn. Disaster and Emergency Coords., Colo. Emergency Mgmt. Assn., Kappa Delta Pi, Phi Alpha Theta, Kappa Alpha Theta. Republican. Home: 707 Poppy Dr Brighton CO 80601 Office: FEMA Denver Fed Ctr Bldg 710 PO Box 25267 Denver CO 80225-0267

OLSON, RUE EILEEN, librarian; b. Chgo., Nov. 1, 1928; d. Paul H. and Martha M. (Fick) Meyers; m. Richard L. Olson, July 18, 1964; children: Catherine, Karen. Student Herzl Coll., 1946-48, Northwestern U., 1948-50, Ill. State U., 1960-64, Middle Mgmt. Inst. Spl. Librs. Assn., 1985-87. Acct. Ill. Farm Supply Co., Chgo., 1948-59; asst. libr. Ill. Agrl. Assn., Bloomington, 1960-66, libr., 1966-86, dir. libr. svcs., 1986—; bd. dirs. Corn Belt Libr. System, 1989—. Mem. area Com. Nat. Libr. Week, 1971, area steering com., 1972; mem. steering com. Illinet/OCLC, 1985-87; mem. adv. council of librs. Grad. Sch. Libr. Sci. U. Ill., 1976-79; mem. Ill. State Libr. Adv. Com. for Interlibr. Cooperation, 1979-80; del. Ill. White House Conf. on Libr. and Info. Svcs., 1978; coordinator Vita Income Tax Assistance, Bloomington, Ill., 1986-89, preparer 1978—. Mem. Am., Ill., McLean County (pres. 1970-71) Libr. Assns., Spl. Librs. Assn. (pres. Ill. chpt. 1977-78, first to be named Disting. Mem. food, agr. and nutrition div. 1989), Ill. OCLC Users Group (treas. 1988-90), Internat. Assn. Agrl. Librs. and Documentalists, Am. Soc. Info. Sci., Am. Mgmt. Assn., Zonta (pres. 1987-89), Bloomington Club. Office: Ill Agrl Assn 1701 Towanda Ave Bloomington IL 61701

OLSZEWSKI, DEBORAH D., lawyer; b. Grove City, Pa., Jan. 14, 1950; d. Rudolph Harry and Yolanda DeAugustino (Ottolini) D.; m. Edmund Lucien Olszewski, Oct. 10, 1982; children: Eleanore Lee, Stephanie Louise, Jane Elizabeth, Anne Deborah. BA, U. Pitts., Pa., 1970; MA, Edinboro State Coll., Pa., 1976; JD, U. Pitts., 1979. Reporter Allied Newspaper, Mercer, Pa., 1971-72; pub. rels. Boston Store, Erie, Pa., 1972; social worker Hamot Med. Center, Erie, Pa., 1973, Children's Services of Erie Co., 1973-75; law clerk Allegheny County Legal Dept., Pa., 1977-78; law clerk, atty. Fine, Perlow and Stone, Pitts., Pa., 1978-80; assoc. Egler & Reinstadtler, Pitts., 1980-82, Trushel, Klym & Olszewski, Pitts., 1982—. Mem. Allegheny County Bar Assn. (health law sect., civil litigation sect., former mem. judiciary com.), Def. Rsch. Inst., Pa. Bar Assn. (civil litigation sect., profl. liability sect.), Acad. Trial Lawyers Allegheny County. Office: Trushel Klyn & Olszewski 1207 5th Ave Pittsburgh PA 15219

OLTMAN, ELIZABETH ANN, agricultural products analyst; b. Sycamore, Ill., Sept. 10, 1963; d. William Henry Perkins and Mary Virginia (Jones) Ballenger; m. Troy John Oltman, Oct. 3, 1981. Student, Kishwaukee Community Coll., Malta, Ill., 1989—. Sec., computer operator De Kalb (Ill.) Agr. Rsch., 1981-84; coop. advt. coord. De Kalb-Pfizer Genetics, 1984-87, mktg. promotions coord., 1987-89, corn product analyst, 1989—. Home: 611 De Kalb Ave Sycamore IL 60178 Office: De Kalb Genetics Plant 3100 Sycamore Rd De Kalb IL 60115

OLZENDAM, HARRIETT STEELE, retired lawyer; b. Dover, N.H., Aug. 5, 1914; d. Enoch Ned and Lena Marion (Steele) O.; B.A., Wellesley Coll., 1936; M.A., Trinity Coll., 1942; J.D. with distinction, U. Conn., 1946. Admitted to Conn. bar, 1946, Fed. Dist. bar, 1948; with The Travelers Ins. Co., Hartford, Conn., 1937-79, chief contract underwriter, 1951-61, asst. sec., 1961-69, sec., 1969-79. Mem. residence com. YWCA, Hartford, Conn., 1964-79, dir., 1971-77, sec., 1972-74, v.p., 1974-75, pres., 1975-77, mem. fin. com., 1975-79, personnel com., 1979-82. Mem. ABA, Conn. Bar Assn., Hartford County Bar Assn., Am. Judicature Soc., Mental Health Assn. Conn. (nominating com. 1976-78, trustee 1979-81), Conn. Ins. Assn. (group com.), Conn. Health Reins. Assn. (chmn. forms com.), Soc. Group Contract Analysts, Wellesley Coll. Alumnae Assn., U. Conn. Sch. Law, Trinity Coll. alumni assns., Mark Twain Meml., Wadsworth Atheneum, Antiquarian and Landmarks Soc. Conn., Conn. Hist. Soc., Hartford Architecture Conservancy, Nat. Audubon Soc., Nat. Wildlife Fedn., Smithsonian Assos., Hartford Easter Seal Rehab. Ctr. Republican. Congregationalist. Clubs: Wellesley (fin. chmn. 1975-77, 1st v.p. 1977-79), Quota (corr. sec. Hartford 1970-78, 1st v.p. 1978-81, 2d v.p. 1981-87), Town and County (gov. 1978-82, rec. sec. 1979-80, 83-85, personnel com. 1978-82, chmn. personnel com. 1980-82, fin. com. 1979-82, 85—, exec. com. 1979-84). Address: 2012 Blvd West Hartford CT 06107

OM, WENDY, critical care nurse; b. Ogden, Utah, Jan. 15, 1956; d. Floyd Lavern and June (Henderson) Naylor; m. Robert G. Hruska (div.); children: Ti, Elijah I., Ananda Moya, Yukimi. BS in Nursing, Weber State Coll., 1989. RN, Utah. Operating room nurse IHC McKay-Dee Hosp., Ogden, Utah, 1987—. Mem. AORN, Nightingale Soc. Home: PO Box 1722 Ogden UT 84402-1722

O'MALLEY, ALICE THERESA, biology educator; b. Clinton, Mass., Apr. 1, 1929; d. Gerald Francis and Elizabeth Irene (Fury) O'M. BA, Anna Maria Coll., Paxton, Mass., 1958; MA, Clark U., 1961, PhD, 1965. Asst. prof. State Coll., Fitchburg, Mass., 1965-66, assoc. prof. biology, 1966—. Roman Catholic. Office: State Coll Pearl St Fitchburg MA 01420

O'MALLEY, HONOR, hearing educator; b. N.Y.C., Oct. 11; d. Thomas and Josephine (Navoni) O'M.; m. Roger N. Anderson; children: Roger, Jon, Forrest. BA, Marymount Manhattan Coll., 1971; MS, Purdue U., 1973, PhD, 1977. NSF postdoctoral research fellow Northwestern U., Evanston, Ill., 1978; assoc. prof., coord. audiology programs and hearing rsch. lab. Tchrs. Coll., Columbia U., N.Y.C., 1978—. Contbr. articles to profl. jours. Postdoctoral Research fellow NIH, 1977. Mem. Acoustical Soc. Am. (tech. com. 1985-88), Am. Speech, Lang. and Hearing Assn. (audiologic standards com. 1988—), Assn. for Research on Otolaryngology, Am. Geophys. Union. Home: 106 Morningside Dr Apt 51 New York NY 10027 Office: Tchrs Coll Columbia U 525 W 120th St New York NY 10027

O'MALLEY, KATHLEEN ANN, assistant U.S. attorney; b. Nanticoke, Pa., Oct. 2, 1955; d. Thomas Joseph and Regina Frances (Leyman) O'M. BA with honors, Wilkes Coll., 1976; JD, Dickinson Sch. of Law, 1979. Bar: Pa. 1979, U.S. Ct. Appeals (3d cir.) 1979, Fla. 1986, U.S. Supreme Ct. 1986, U.S. Ct. Appeals (11th cir.) 1984. Assoc. Ball & Skelly, Harrisburg, Pa., 1979-83; asst. U.S. atty. U.S. Dept. Justice, Jacksonville, Fla., 1983—. Recipient Cert. Appreciation, Palatka (Fla.) Police Dept., 1986, U.S. Secret Svc., 1986. Mem. Fed. Bar Assn. (treas. Jacksonville chpt. 1988—), Cath. Lawyers Guild. Republican. Roman Catholic. Office: Office of US Atty 311 W Monroe St Rm 409 Jacksonville FL 32202

O'MALLEY, MARJORIE GLAUBACH, financial executive; b. Orange, N.J., Apr. 28, 1950; d. Robert M. and Joanne (Weil) Glaubach; m. Charles A. O'Malley III, Dec. 27, 1969; children: Gregory, Ashley. BA in Econs., U. Pa., 1969. With Old Stone Bank, Providence, 1970-75, v.p., 1975-76; sr. v.p., treas. Old Stone Bank and Old Stone Corp., Providence, 1976-80; dir. corp. fin. Conn. Gen. Corp., Hartford, 1980-81; 2d v.p., dept. head mktg. pensions Cigna Corp., Hartford, 1981-85, v.p. fin. employee benefit group, 1985-89; v.p. corp. acctg. and planning Cigna Corp., 1989—. Mem. health Planning Coun. R.I., 1976-79, Statewide Planning Coun. R.I., 1978; mem. bd. Health Sys. Agy.-North Cen. Conn., Hartford, 1980. Mem. Life Ins. Mktg. and Rsch. Assn. (chmn. group and pension com. 1989), New Eng. Econ. Project (bd. mem. 1976-79, treas. 1978-79). Home: 23 Henley Way Avon CT 06001 Office: Cigna Corp Hartford CT 06152

OMAN, DEBORAH SUE, health science facility administrator; b. North Platte, Nebr., Aug. 26, 1948; d. Rex Ardell and Opale Louise (Smith) O. BS, Kearney State Coll., 1970; postgrad., U. Nebr., 1987—. Med. technologist Physicians Pathology Labs., Lincoln, Nebr., 1970-71; med. technologist student health Colo. State U., Ft. Collins, 1971-72; supr. hematology lab. Bryan Meml. Hosp., Lincoln, 1972-76; sect. supr. hematology/coagulation Clin. Labs. of Lincoln div. Nichols Inst. Labs., 1976—; adj. prof. sch. of med. technology Nebr. Weslyan U., Lincoln, 1979-85; courtesy instr. Med. Tech. div. U. Nebrs., Omaha, 1990—. Contbr. articles to profl. jours. Mem. Am. Soc. Clin. Pathologists (cert., affiliate, recognition award 1986), Lancaster Soc. Med. Technologists. Republican. Mem. Christian Ch. Club: Cornhusker Ski (pres. 1982-83). Office: Clin Labs of Lincoln Plaza Mall South 1919 S 40th St Suite 333 Lincoln NE 68506

OMAN, WANDA ARLINE MCCAMEY, controller; b. Grove City, Pa., July 1, 1926; d. Judson Russell and Ellen Carlie (Bassett) Hulbert; m. Nial McCamey, June 12, 1948 (dec. Mar. 1986); children: Julee Ann Snow, Amy Cay; m. Dale N. Oman, May 21, 1990. Student, Am. Inst. of Banking, 1970's. Bookkeeper, teller 1st Nat. Bank, Grove City, Pa., 1944-48; banker Mellon Nat. Bank, Harrisville, Pa., 1948-53, 56-57; teller, auditing & acctg. 1st Nat. Bank, Slippery Rock, Pa., 1972-85; contr. Mercer County, Pa., 1986—; Sec. Mercer County Retirement Bd., 1986—. Mem. Grove City Adv. Com., 1981-85, Mercer City Selective Svc. Bd. (1st woman), 1972-74, Humane Soc., Mercer County, 1980-85; former Area chmn., Grove City; bd. dirs. Grove City Area Schs., 1983-85; past pres. Grove City Rep. Women; former vice chmn. Mercer County Rep. Com. Mem. Bus. and Profl. Women, Pa. State Assn. County Contrs., Nat. Assn. City Treas. and Fin. Officers, Hist. Soc. (life), DAR (Gen. Hugh Mercer chpt.), DAC (charter James Steele chpt.), VFW Aux. (past treas., pres. 1960-61, pres. Mercer County Coun. 1972-73, pres. Dist. 28 1971-72), Grove City Vets. Coun. (life), Odd Fellows. Mem. Christian Missionary and Alliance Ch. Home: 130 Todd Ave Hermitage PA 16148 Office: Mercer County Courthouse Diamond St Mercer PA 16137

O'MARA, CATHERINE ANNE, newspaper editor; b. Athens, Greece, Aug. 21, 1964; came to U.S., 1965; d. John William and Elaine (Gramis) O'M. BA, U. Calif., Santa Barbara, 1986; MA, Syracuse U., 1989. Graphic artist Dulco Printing, Inc., Fresno, Calif., 1988, Syracuse (N.Y.) Newspapers Group, 1989; mng. editor The Independent, Montrose, Pa., 1989—. Fundraiser coord. Dems. and Calif. Farmers for Fair Legis., Fresno, 1988. Fellow Poynter Inst. for Media Studies, 1989. Mem. Soc. Profl. Journalists, Soc. Newspaper Design (participant, staff 10th ann. nat. competition 1989). Greek Orthodox. Home: 3179 W Los Altos Fresno CA 93711

O'MARA, PEGGY NOREEN, editor, publisher; b. Kenosha, Wis., May 14, 1947; d. Oliver Edward and Ruth Helen (Slater) O'M.; m. John William McMahon, May 27, 1973 (div. Aug. 1989); children—Lally, Finnie, Bram, Nora. B.S., U. Wis.-Milw., 1970. Tchr. high sch. Alamogordo High Sch., N.Mex., 1971-72; tchr. spl. edn. Zia Sch., Alamogordo, 1972-73; M.B.A. coord. U. Utah, Holloman AFB, N.Mex., 1973; free-lance writer, 1973-77; assoc. editor Mothering Mag., Albuquerque, 1978-80, editor, pub., Santa Fe, 1980—; leader La Leche League, Franklin Park, Ill., 1975-82. Editor: Mother Poet, 1983, Schooling at Home: Parents, Kids, and Learning, 1990, Being a Father: Family, Work, and Self, 1990. Bd. dirs. Midwifery Tng. Inst., Albuquerque, 1983-86 , N.Mex. State Midwifery Adv. Bd., Santa Fe, 1984-89. Mem. Midwives Alliance N.Am., Internat. Childbirth Edn. Assn., Nat. Fedn. Press Women (1st pl. award 1984), Nat. Assn. Safe Alternatives in Birth, N.Mex. Press Women (1st pl. awards 1984), N.Mex. Press Assn. Avocations: herb gardening, ornithology, alternative health. Home: Rte 7 Box 124K Santa Fe NM 87505 Office: Mothering Publs PO Box 1690 Santa Fe NM 87504

O'MEALLIE, KITTY, artist; b. Bennettsville, S.C., Oct. 24, 1916; d. Earle and Rosa Estelle (Bethea) Chamness; m. John Ryan O'Meallie, June 27, 1939 (dec. Apr. 26, 1974); children—Sue Ryan, Kathryn Bethea; m. Lee Harnie Johnson, Aug. 21, 1976. BFA Tulane U., 1937; postgrad., 1954-59. One-woman shows include Masur Mus., Monroe, La., 1979, Marlboro County Mus. of S.C., 1975, Meridian Mus. Art, Miss., 1981, 85; exhibited in group shows at New Orleans Mus. Art, Contemporary Art Ctr., Meadows Mus., Cushing Gallery, SE Ctr. of Contemporary Art, Art 80, Art Expo West, Art Expo 81. Represented in permanent collections New Orleans Mus. Art, Tulane U. Pan-Am. Life Ctr., Masur Mus. Art, Meridian Mus. Art. Nat. officer Newcomb Coll. Alumnae Assn., 1964-66; lectr. exhibitor for many charitable orgns. Recipient award WYES-TV, 1979, Hon. Invitational New Orleans Women's Caucus, 1986, numerous awards and prizes in competitive exhibitions. Mem. Womens Caucus for Art, New Orleans Womens Caucus for Art, Chi Omega Alumnae Assn. (pres. mothers' club 1964), Town and Country Garden Guild (pres. 1970, 1986). Avocations: birdwatching; bridge. Home and Office: 211 Fairway Dr New Orleans LA 70124

O'MORCHOE, PATRICIA JEAN, pathologist, educator; b. Halifax, Eng., Sept. 15, 1930; came to U.S., 1968; d. Alfred Eric and Florence Patricia (Pearson) Richardson; m. Charles Christopher C. O'Morchoe, Sept. 15, 1955; children: Charles E.C., David J.C. BA, Dublin U., Ireland, 1953, MB, Bch., BAO, 1955, MA, MD, 1966, MD. Intern Halifax (Yorkshire) Gen. Hosp., Eng., 1955-57; instr., lectr. physiology Dublin U., 1958-59, 59-63; instr. pathology Johns Hopkins U., Balt., 1961-62, 68-72, asst. prof. pathology, 1972-74; rsch. assoc. surgery, pathology Harvard U., Boston, 1962-63; asst. prof. anatomy U. Md., 1970-74; assoc.prof., prof. pathology, anatomy Loyola U. Chgo., 1974-84; prof. pathology, cell and structural biology U. Ill, Urbana, 1984—; staff pathologist VA Hosp., Danville, Ill., 1989—; courtesy staff pathologist Covenant Hosp, Urbana, 1984—. Contbr. numerous articles to profl. jours. Mem. Internat. Acad. Cytology, Internat. Soc. Lymphology (auditor 1989—), N.Am. Soc. Lymphology (sec. 1988-90, treas. 1990—), Am. Soc. Cytology, Am. Assn. Anatomists, Ill. Soc. Cytology. Home: 2709 Holcomb Dr Urbana IL 61801 Office: U Ill Coll Med 506 S Mathews Urbana IL 61801

ONAGA, CORINNE YURIE, human resources specialist; b. Puuene, Hawaii, Sept. 28, 1952; d. Daniel T. Onaga and Miyoko Higa; 1 child, Brandon. Benefits coord. The Westin Maui, Lahaina, Hawaii, 1987-89, employment mgr., 1989, human resources mgr., 1989—; employment rep. Sheraton Maui, Lahaina, Hawaii. Mem. NAFE, Soc. for Human Resource Mgmt. Home: 80 Makomako St Haliimaile HI 96768

ONA-SARINO, MILAGROS FELIX, physician, pathologist; b. Manila, May 8, 1940; came to U.S., 1965, naturalized, 1983; d. Venancio Vale Ona and Fidela Torres Felix; m. Edgardo Formantes Sarino, June 11, 1966; children: Edith Melanie, Edgar Michael, Edenn Michele. AA, U. Santo Tomas, Manila, 1959, MD cum laude 1964. Diplomate Am. Bd. Pathology. Rotating intern N.Y. Infirmary, 1965-66; resident in anatomic and clin. pathology Lenox Hill Hosp., N.Y.C., 1966-71; asst. adj. pathologist, 1972-74; assoc. pathologist St. Francis Med. Ctr., Trenton, N.J., 1974-84, Hamilton Hosp., N.J., 1974-84; pathologist, chief lab. svc. Louis A. Johnson VA Med. Ctr., Clarksburg, W.Va., 1984—; clin. instr. pathology Columbia U. Coll. Physicians and Surgeons, N.Y.C., 1973-85; clin. asst. prof. pathology, W.Va. U. Sch. Medicine. Fellow Am. Soc. Clin. Pathologists, Coll. of Am. Pathologists; mem. Internat. Acad. Pathology, N.Y. Acad. Scis. (life). Office: Louis A Johnson VA Med Ctr Clarksburg WV 26301

ONASSIS, JACQUELINE BOUVIER KENNEDY, editor, widow of 35th president of U.S.; b. Southampton, N.Y., 1929; d. John Vernou III and Janet (Lee) Bouvier; m. John Fitzgerald Kennedy, 35th pres. of U.S., Sept. 12, 1953 (dec. Nov. 22, 1963); children: Caroline Bouvier, John Fitzgerald, Patrick Bouvier (dec.); m. Aristotle Onassis, Oct. 20, 1968 (dec. Mar. 1975). Grad., Miss Porter's Sch., Farmington, Conn., 1947; student, Vassar Coll., 1947-48, The Sorbonne, Paris, 1949; BA, George Washington U., 1951. Inquiring photographer Washington Times-Herald (now Washington Post and Times Herald), 1952; planned and conducted restoration of decor The White House, 1961-63; cons. editor Viking Press, 1975-77; assoc. editor Doubleday & Co., N.Y.C., 1978-82, editor, 1982—, now sr. editor. Trustee Whitney Mus. Am. Art. Recipient Prix de Paris Vogue mag., 1951, Emmy award for pub. service, 1962. Address: 1041 Fifth Ave New York NY 10028 Office: Doubleday 666 Fifth Ave 20th fl New York NY 10103*

O'NEAL, CAROLE KELLEY, health sciences administrator; b. Lawrenceville, Ga., June 20, 1933; d. Daniel Claude Jr. and Connie Fay (Moore) Kelley; m. Donald E. O'Neal, Jan. 24, 1953; children: Sharon Lee O'Neal Altenbach, Terrence P. Student, U. Ga., 1950-52, Massey Bus. Coll., 1952-54, Oglethorpe U., 1981-82. Office mgr. Photostat Corp., Atlanta, 1954-56; from sec. to office mgr. pvt. physician Atlanta, 1970; pres., owner Profl. Practice Services Inc., Atlanta, 1980—; mng. dir. Found. for Edn. Aesthetic Plastic Surgery, Atlanta, 1974—; cons. plastic surgery office mgmt., 1983—. Contbr. articles to profl. jours. Mem. Alliance Theater Guild. Mem. Plastic Surgery Adminstrv. Assn. (pres. 1983-84), Pi Beta Phi Alumnae. Republican. Office: Profl Practice Services Inc 4200 Northside Pkwy Bldg 10 Atlanta GA 30327

O'NEAL, DOROTHY DECKER, fabric sales company executive; b. Akron, Ohio, Dec. 8, 1923; d. Clyde Earl and Mary Iva (King) Decker; m. Robert Frank O'Neal, Dec. 4, 1943; 1 child, Aileen Adele. Purchasing agt. Firestone Tire and Rubber Co., Akron, 1941-43; free lance fashion model, Little Rock, 1944-46; freelance fashion cons., Akron, 1947-52; owner, mgr. Canal Shop, Peninsula, Ohio, 1953-60, Fashion With Fabrics, Sierra Vista, Ariz., 1979-89, The Fabric Connection, Sierra Vista, 1989—. Editor: Bi-Centennial Cook Book, 1976; Yule in the Mules Cook Book, 1977. Chmn. Goldwater for Pres. Com., Battle Creek, Mich., 1963-64. Mem. Greater Fedn. Women's Clubs, Am. Assn. Hosp. Auxs. Republican. Unitarian. Club: The Internat. Fashion Group (N.Y.C.). Avocations: sewing, cooking, fashion shows, travel, career seminars. Home: 4391 Plaza Oro Loma Sierra Vista AZ 85635 Office: The Fabric Connection 4391 Plaza Oro Loma Sierra Vista AZ 95635

O'NEAL, HARRIET ROBERTS, psychologist, psycholegal consultant; b. Covington, Ky., Dec. 28, 1952; d. Nelson E. and Georgia H. (Roberts) O'N. Student, U. Paris Sorbonne, 1972; BA in Psychology, Hollins Coll., 1974; JD, U. Nebr., 1978, MA in Psychology, 1980, PhD in Psychology, 1982. Program dir., therapist Richmond Maxi Ctr., San Francisco, 1979-81; clin. coord., therapist Pacifica (Calif.) Youth Svc. Bur., 1981-83; staff psychologist Kaiser-Permanente Med. Ctr., Walnut Creek, Calif., 1983—; psycholegal cons., Nebr., 1975-79, Calif., 1979—; oral exam commr. Calif. Bd. Behavioral Sci. Examiners, Sacramento, 1982—; pvt. practice psychotherapy, Pleasant Hill, Calif., 1985—, Lafayette, Calif., 1987—; psycholegal cons., presenter San Francisco State U., 1980, U. Calif., San Francisco, 1980, VA Med. Ctr., San Francisco, 1983. Cons. Nebr. Gov.'s Commn. on Status of Women, 1975, 78. NIMH fellow, 1974-79. Mem. Am. Psychol. Assn., Calif. Psychol. Assn., Phi Beta Kappa, Psi Chi. Club: Commonwealth (San Francisco). Home: 645 Preakness Dr Walnut Creek CA 94596 Office: Kaiser-Permanente Med Ctr Mental Health Dept 1425 S Main St Walnut Creek CA 94596

O'NEAL, KELLE SNYDER, real estate company official; b. Ft. Worth, May 29, 1948; d. David Connell and Marianne (Blocker) Snyder; m. John Franklin O'Neal, July 22, 1977. BJ, U. Tex., 1970. Press sec. Senator and Mrs. Lloyd Bentsen, Houston, 1970; staff mem. Senator Lloyd Bentsen

Washington, 1971-77; realtor Merrill Lynch Realty, Arlington, Va., 1985—. House chmn. Jr. League, Washington, 1978-82; vol. staff Joan Mondale, Washington, 1979. Mem. No. Va. Bd. Realtors (Million Dollar Club).

O'NEAL, MARGARET FUNDERBURK, consulting and purchasing firm owner; b. LaGrange, Ga., Jan. 12, 1949; d. George William and Margaret Cleaveland (Dodd) Funderburk; m. William Ennis O'Neal, Aug. 30, 1969. B.A., Agnes Scott Coll., 1971. Mgr. The Frog Pond, Inc., Atlanta, 1976-79; project mgr. ADM Assocs. Inc., Atlanta, 1979-82; pres., owner Focus Interior Contracting, Inc., Atlanta, 1982—. Methodist. Club: Women Bus. Owners (Atlanta). Avocation: reading. Office: Focus Interior Contracting 1900 Emery St Ste 430 Atlanta GA 30318

O'NEAL, RUTH, pediatrician, educator; b. Dunn, N.C., June 7, 1915; d. Joseph Bryan and Jane (Wilson) O'N. AB, Transylvania U., 1939; MD, Med. Coll. Va., 1943; MS in Pediatrics, U. Minn., 1948; DSc (hon.), Atlantic Christian Coll., 1983. Diplomate Am. Bd. Pediatrics. Intern Med. Coll. Va., Richmond, 1943-44; Mayo Found. fellow Mayo Clinic Rochester, Minn., 1944-48; practice medicine specializing in pediatrics, Winston-Salem, N.C., 1948-69; asst. in clin. pediatrics Bowman Gray Sch. Medicine, Wake Forest U., Winston-Salem, 1948-51, instr., 1951-59, asst. prof., 1969-72, assoc. prof., 1972—; assoc. dir. pediatrics Reynolds Meml. Hosp., Winston-Salem, 1969-72, dir., 1972-77; mem. staff N.C. Bapt. Hosp., Forsyth Meml. Hosp.; lectr. in field. Contbr. articles to med. jours. Co-leader Triad coun. Girl Scouts U.S.A., 1954-56, bd. dirs., 1957-60, 61-64, active various coms., 1957—; mem. numerous coms. 1st Christian Ch., Winston-Salem, 1985—, elder, 1974-79; chmn. camp com. local YWCA, 1967-69, bd. dirs., 1967-69; mem. Citizens Planning Com., Winston-Salem, 1963-64; bd. dirs. Forsyth Heart Assn., 1957-80, Polio Found., 1962-65, Day Care Assn. Task Group, 1970, Urban Coalition Day Care Assn., 1970, Forsyth unit Am. Cancer Soc., 1970-80, March of Dimes, 1972—, N.W. Childhood Devel. Bd., Planned Parenthood, 1978-85, Santree Retirement Home, 1978-84, Disciples Christ Nat. Benevolent Bd., 1980-86, Battered Women's Svcs., Inc., 1982-85, Childrens Ctr. for Physically Handicapped, 1982—. Mem. AMA, Mayo Found. Alumni Assn., Minn. U. Alumni Assn., Med. Coll. Va. Alumni Assn., Transylvania U. Alumni Assn., Atlantic Christian Coll. Alumni Assn., Soc. for Rsch. in Child Devel., Forsyth County Med. Soc. (sch. com. rep. 1976-80), Forsyth County Cystic Fibrosis Assn., Med. Soc. N.C., N.C. Pediatric Soc., N.C. Mental Hygiene Soc., So. Med. Assn., Am. Acad. Pediatrics, Ambulatory Pediatric Assn., So. Soc. for Pediatric Research, Internat. Coll. Pediatrics, Am. Womens Med. Assn., Nat. Assn. Child Abuse and/or Neglect, Internat. Soc. for Prevention of Child Abuse and Neglect, So. Med. Soc., Bus. and Profl. Women's Club, N.C. Art Soc., N.C. Soc. for Preservation Antiquities, Photog. Soc. Am., Piedmont Craftsmen, Soroptimist (life), Order of Eastern Star. Democrat. Home: 445 Springdale Ave Winston-Salem NC 27104 Office: Wake Forest U Sch Medicine 300 S Hawthorne Rd Dept Pediatrics Winston-Salem NC 27103

O'NEAL, SUSAN A., personnel executive; b. Fontana, Calif., Jan. 28, 1962; d. Stanley and Clara May (George) Stain; m. Gary O'Neal, May 18, 1988. BA, UCLA, 1984. Asst. dir. legal svcs. ATV Music Pub., L.A.; legal sec. Oak Media, L.A.; billing asst. Cox, Castle & Nicholson, L.A.; personnle mgr. Berger, Kahn et al, Marina de Rey, Calif. Office: 4215 Glencoe Ave Marina del Rey CA 90292

O'NEAL, TOSHA DIERDRE, audio visual specialist; b. Granit City, Ill., Sept. 13, 1961; d. Ronald Edward and Margaret Amelia (Strauther) O'N. BA, Clark Coll., 1983. Photojournalist Urban Coalition of Mpls., 1984; pub. info. coord. City Coun., St. Paul, Minn., 1984; radio announcer CBLS, Mpls., 1984; customer svc. specialist Group W Cable TV, Roseville, Minn., 1984-86; pub. access coord. Mpls. TV Network, 1986-87; audio visual prodn. specialist Potomac Electric Power Co., Washington, 1988—; exec. producer Entre Amis A/V Prodns., Lanham, Md., 1989—; mentor Langley Jr. High Sch., Washington, 1989; instr. Advanced Career Tng., Washington, 1989-90. Producer/assoc. producer video programs (Best Children's Program award 1986, Best Music video award 1986, Satban music video - first place award 1987) United Way programs (first place 1989-90). Vol. tchr. of English, Spanish Ednl. Devel. Ctr., Washington, 1988-90; vol. Project Harvest Food Drive, Washington, 1988-89, Earth Day 1990, Washington. Named to Outstanding Young Women of Am., 1988, Outstanding Female in Media, Alpha Kappa Alpha, 1987. Mem. Internat. TV Assn., Women in Communications, Inc., D.C. TV Assn., Nat. Fedn. Local Cable Programs, Zeta Phi Beta (chpt. pres. 1981-82). Republican. Office: Entre Amis 5445 85th Ave Ste 101 Lanham MD 20706

O'NEALE, ROSALYN TAYLOR, management consultant; b. Louisville, Ky., June 21, 1950; d. Charles Edward Smith and Katherine (Taylor) O'N. Grad., Ind. U., 1973; M in Social Work, U. Louisville, 1980; postgrad., Fielding Inst., Santa Barbara, Calif., Harvard U. Mgr. corporate recruiting Lincoln Nat. Life Ins. Co., Ft. Wayne, Ind., 1975-78; sr. ptnr. Smith - Hires Assocs., Wilmington, Del., 1978-80; mgmt. devel. and employment cons. Control Data Corp., Phila., 1979-80; pres. R. Taylor O'Neale Assocs., Acton, Mass., 1981—; affirmative action cons. Digital Equipment Corp., Maynard, Mass., 1981-82, employment mgr., 1982-83, orgn. devel. cons., 1983-85, valuing differences mgr., 1985—. Named Woman of Achievement in Bus. and Industry, Young Woman's Christian Assn., Boston, 1985. Mem. Urban Leauge Black Execs. Exchange Prog., Nat. Orgn. Devel. Network, Am. Soc. Tng. and Devel., Internat. Soc. for Intercultural Edn., Tng. and Research, Alpha Kappa Alpha. Democrat. Episcopalian. Home: 3301 Benton St Santa Clara CA 95051

O'NEAL-SMITH, MELBA MARGO, health care executive; b. Marietta, Ohio, Mar. 20, 1951; d. Vaughn Everett and Velma May (Prine) O'Neal; m. Jay Pierce Smith, June 21, 1976 (div. Aug. 1983). BS in Nutrition, Ohio State U., 1978; postgrad., U. Phoenix, Orange County, Calif., 1984, 85. With Riverside Meth. Hosp., Columbus, Ohio, 1970-78; clinic adminstr. Ohio State U., Columbus, 1978-81; cons., mktg. rep. Control Data Corp., Cleve., 1981-83; mktg. mgr. Nat. Med. Computers, San Diego, 1983-84; ind. cons. Orange County, 1984-86; dir. mgmt. info. systems FHP, Inc., Fountain Valley, Calif., 1986-87, assoc. v.p. mgmt. info. systems, 1987-90, assoc. v.p. ops., 1990—; cons., speaker in field, 1985—. Author several poetry books. Counselor Big Bros./Big Sisters Am., Cleve., 1981; counselor, sponsor Post Adoption Ctr. Research, San Francisco, 1983. Mem. Med. Group Mgmt. Assn., Nat. Assn. Female Execs., Group Health Assn. Am., Am. Hosp. Assn. Home: 31434 Flying Cloud Dr Laguna Niguel CA 92677

O'NEIL, MARY AGNES, health science facility administrator; b. Bridgeport, Conn., Sept. 26, 1926. Diploma in nursing, St. Vincent's Hosp., Bridgeport, 1947; BS, St. Joseph's Coll., Emmitsburg, Md., 1952; MS in Nursing Services Adminstrn., Boston Coll., 1960; LLD (hon.), Sacred Heart U., Bridgeport, 1974. Nurse St. Vincent's Hosp., 1947-48, dir. nursing, 1961-63, assoc. adminstr., 1969, adminstr., 1969-74, chmn. bd. dirs., 1969-76, coordinator constrn., in-residence chmn. bd. dirs., 1973—; 3d directress Sisters of Charity Sem., Emmitsburg, 1949-54; supr. nursing services Carney Hosp., Boston, 1954-57, dir. nursing svcs., 1957-60, adminstrv. asst. patient care svcs., 1960-61, asst. to pres., 1981-83; assoc. adminstr. St. Mary's Hosp., Troy, N.Y., 1963, adminstr., 1963-69, pres., chief exec. officer, chmn. bd. dirs., ex-officio lay adv. bd., 1976—; sr. v.p., chmn. bd. dirs. Good Samaritan Hosp., Pottsville, Pa., 1983-86, chmn. bd. dirs., v.p. corp. affairs, 1986, chmn. corp. reorgn., chmn. bd. dirs., bd. liaison, 1986—; mem. Upper Hudson sub-area council, mem. project rev. com. Health Systems Agy. of Northeastern N.Y.; mem. regional bd. Nat. Comml. Bank and Trust Co., N.Y., 1979; bishop's rep., mem. legis. com. N.Y. State Council Cath. Hosps., 1980; rep. governing bd. Iroquois Hosp. Consortium, Inc., N.Y., 1980; mem. Green Island Bridge Task Force Com., Troy, 1981. V.p. Greater Bridgeport C. of C., 1975; mem. mayor's human rights commn. City of Troy, 1976; bd. dirs. Northeastern/Southeastern Shared Services of Daus. of Charity, 1977, treas. Eastern Coop. Services, 1980, chmn. investment com., 1981, mem. health adv. commn. N.E. Province, 1986; v.p. govtl. relations City of Troy, 1978; hon. chmn. Upper Hudson area chpt. Am. Diabetes Assn., Inc., 1978-79; bd. dirs. Blue Cross of Northeastern N.Y., 1977; bd. dirs. Lourdes Hosp., Binghamton, N.Y., 1985, chmn. evaluation com., 1987; mem. adv. bd. Jr. League, Troy, 1979; mem. St. Mary's Hosp. Found. Bd., 1981. Recipient Community Services award City of Troy, 1968, Leadership and Service cert. Conn. Hosp. Assn., 1973, Community Service and Accomplishment award Sta. WICC-FM, 1974, Community Service award Sta. WNAB-FM, 1975, Key to City Mayor of Brideport, 1975; named one of Outstanding Women of State of Conn., Gov. Ella Grasso, 1976; Sister Mary Agnes Day proclaimed by City of Bridgeport, 1976, Sister Mary Agnes Day proclaimed by City of Troy, 1981. Fellow Am. Coll. Hosp. Adminstrs.; mem. Hosp. Assn. Northeastern N.Y. (mem. program com. 1978, chmn. bylaws com. 1979). Democrat. Office: DePaul Provincial House 96 Menands Rd Albany NY 12204

ONEIL, SUSAN JEAN, media specialist; b. Decatur, Ill., Nov. 19, 1952; d. Richard Greer and Patricia Jane (Miller) Schenk; m. Kevin E. Oneil, Feb. 10, 1952; children: Erin and Patrick. BA, Ill. Wesleyan U., Bloomington, 1974; MSEd, Northern Ill. U., Dekalb, 1978, Northern Ill. U., Dekalb, 1989. K-9 Teaching 6-12 Teaching, Standard Special as Media Specialist. Tchr. Waldo Jr. High, Aurora, Ill., 1975-76; commercial loan cons. Control Data, Naperville, Ill., 1978-79; tchr. Braidwood Jr. High, Braidwood, Ill., 1979-80; librarian Forrestville Sch. Dir., Forreston, Ill.; media specialist Byron Middle Sch., Byran, Ill., 1982—; pres. Byron Fedn. Tchrs. Byron, 1984-86. Recipient Electronic Reference Grant Franklin Computers Byron, 1989. Mem. Ill. Libr. Assn., Ill. Sch. Libr. Media Assn., Northwestern Consortium of Media Dir. Democrat. Methodist. Office: Byron Middle Sch Library Tower Rd Byron IL 61010

O'NEILL, BEVERLY LEWIS, college president; b. Long Beach, Calif., Sept. 8, 1930; d. Clarence John and Flossie Rachel (Nicholson) Lewis; m. William F. O'Neill, Dec. 21, 1952. AA, Long Beach City Coll., 1950; BA, Calif. State U., Long Beach, 1952, MA, 1956; EdD, U. So. Calif., 1977. Elem. tchr. Long Beach Unified Sch. Dist., 1952-57; instr., counsellor Compton (Calif.) Coll., 1957-60; curriculum supr. Little Lake Sch. Dist., Santa Fe Springs, Calif., 1960-62; women's advisor, campus dean Long Beach City Coll., 1962-71, dir. Continuing Edn. Ctr. for Women, 1969-75, dean student affairs, 1971-77, v.p. student svcs., 1977-88, supt.-pres., 1988—, exec. dir. Found., 1983—. Advisor Jr. League, Long Beach, 1976—, Nat. Coun. on Alcoholism, Long Beach, 1979—, Assistance League, Long Beach, 1982—; bd. dirs. NCCJ, Long Beach, 1976—, Meml. Hosp. Found., Long Beach, 1984—, Met. YMCA, Long Beach, 1986—, United Way, Long Beach, 1986—. Named Woman of Yr., Long Beach Human Rels. Commn., 1976, Disting. Alumni of Yr.,Calif. State U., Long Beach, 1985, Long Beach Woman of Yr., Assistance League Aux., 1987; recipient Hana Solomon award Nat. Coun. Jewish Women, 1984, Outstanding Colleague award Long Beach City Coll., 1985. Mem. Assn. Calif. Community Coll. Adminstrs. (pres. 1988—), Calif. Community Colls. Chief Exec. Officers Assn., Rotary, Soroptomists (Women Helping Women award 1981, Hall of Fame award 1984). Democrat. Office: Long Beach Community Coll 4901 E Carson St Long Beach CA 90808

O'NEILL, JUNE ELLENOFF, economics educator; b. N.Y.C., June 14, 1934; d. Louis and Matilda (Liebstein) Ellenoff; m. Sam Cohn, 1955 (div. 1961); 1 child, Peter; m. David Michael O'Neill, Dec. 24, 1964; 1 child, Amy. BA, Sarah Lawrence Coll., Bronxville, N.Y., 1955; PhD, Columbia U., 1970. Econs. instr. Temple U., Phila., 1965-68; rsch. assoc. Brookings Instn., Washington, 1968-71; sr. economist Pres.'s Coun. Econ. Advisors, Washington, 1971-76; chief human resources budget Congl. Budget Office, Washington, 1976-79; sr. rsch. assoc. The Urban Inst., Washington, 1979-86; dir. Office Policy and Rsch. U.S. Commn. Civil Rights, Washington, 1986-87; prof. econs. and dir. Ctr. for Study of Bus. and Govt. Baruch Coll., CUNY, 1987—; mem. Nat. Adv. Com., The Poverty Inst., U. Wis., 1988—. Contbr. articles to profl. jours. Rsch. grantee, U.S. Dept. Labor, NICHD, Dept. Health & Human Svcs., others. Mem. Am. Econs. Assn. (bd. dirs. com. on status of women). Republican. Jewish. Home: 420 Riverside Dr New York NY 10025 Office: Baruch College CUNY 17 Lexington Ave Box 348A New York NY 10010

O'NEILL, KATHERINE TEMPLETON, university administrator, journalist; b. Moline, Ill., Jan. 13, 1949; d. Morris John and Patricia (Collins) Templeton; 1 child by previous marriage, Carolyn Patricia Coquillette; m. William James O'Neill Jr., July 18, 1987; children: Alec, Sara, Jessie, Laura O'Neill. BS in Nursing, U. Mich., 1971; postgrad., St. Clare's Hall, Oxford, Eng., 1971-72; MS in Nursing, Boston U., 1974. RN, Ohio, Mass. Instr. Mass. Gen. Hosp., Boston, 1974-76; assoc. prof. Ursuline Coll., Cleve., 1976-81; dir. devel. Ohio Coll. Podiatric Medicine, Cleve., 1985-86, dir. devel., pub. rels., 1986-87; dir. Chisholm Halle Costume Wing We. Res. Hist. Soc., Cleve., 1988-90; fashion editor Chagrin Valley Times, 1989—; v.p., bd. dirs. Cleve. Health Edn. Mus., 1983—; v.p., bd. dirs. Cleve. Music Sch. Settlement, Cleve., 1983—. Corp. bd. dirs. Hathaway Brown Sch., 1981—, pres. alumnae bd. dirs., 1984-86; bd. dirs. Cleve. Ballet, 1987—. Office: We Res Hist Soc 10825 East Blvd Cleveland OH 44106

O'NEILL, MARGARET, psychological counselor; b. Youngstown, Ohio, Jan. 23, 1935; d. Julius and Anna (Zakel) Huegel; m. Thomas B. O'Neill, Oct. 21, 1971 (div. 1979); children by previous marriage—Paul McCann, Kathleen McCann, Kevin McCann. B.S. in Nursing, UCLA, 1961, M.S. in Nursing, 1963; M.A. in Counseling, Calif. Luth. Coll., Thousand Oaks, 1974; Ph.D. in Psychology, U.S. Internat. U., San Diego, 1986. Cert. hypnotherapist, Calif. Instr. Ventura Coll., Calif., 1965-69, dept. chair, 1969-74, coordinator Women's Ctr., 1974-79, counselor, 1979—; marriage, family and child therapist, cons., Ventura, 1981—; trainer, cons. County of Ventura, 1984—. Bd. dirs. Ventura County chpt. ARC. Mem. Am. Assn. Holistic Health, Nat. Assn. Female Execs., Ventura County Psychol. Assn., Calif. Assn. Marriage Family Therapists. Republican. Unitarian Universalist. Avocations: reading; dancing; hiking; walking. Office: 2590 E Main St Suite 202 Ventura CA 93003

O'NEILL, MARY JANE, health agency executive; b. Detroit, Feb. 24, 1923; d. Frank Roger and Kathryn (Rice) Kilcoyne; Ph.B. summa cum laude, U. Detroit, 1944; postgrad. U. Wis., 1949-50; m. Michael James O'Neill, May 31, 1948; children: Michael, Maureen, Kevin, John (dec.), Kathryn. Editor, East Side Shopper, Detroit, 1939-45; club editor Detroit Free Press, 1945-48; reporter UP, Milw. and Madison, Wis., 1949; dir. public relations Fairfax-Falls Church (Va.) Community Chest, 1955-60; copy editor Falls Ch. Sun-Echo, 1958-60; free-lance writer, Washington, 1960-63; assoc. editor Med. World News, Washington, 1963-66; dir. public relations Westchester Lighthouse, N.Y. Assn. for Blind, 1967-71; dir. public edn. The Lighthouse, N.Y.C., 1971-73, dir. public relations, 1973-80; exec. dir. Eye-Bank for Sight Restoration, Inc., 1980—. Bd. dirs. N.Y. Regional Transplant Program, 1987—. Mem. Women in Communications (pres. N.Y. chpt. 1980-81), Eye-Bank Assn. Am. (lay adv. bd. 1981-83, dir. 1983-86), Public Relations Soc. Am., Women Execs. in Pub. Relations (dir. 1982-88, pres. 1986-87), N.Y. Acad. Scis., Cosmopolitan Club. Office: 210 E 64 St New York NY 10021

O'NEILL, MAUREEN ANNE, arts administrator, city administrator; b. Seattle, Nov. 11, 1948; d. Robert P. and Barbara F. (Pettinger) O. B.A. in Sociology cum laude, Wash. State U., 1971; M.A., Bowling Green State U., 1972. Grad. asst. dept. coll. student personnel Bowling Green (Ohio) State U., 1971-72; asst. coordinator coll. activities SUNY-Geneseo, 1972-75, acting coordinator coll. activities, 1975-76; regional mgr. northeast Kazuko Hillyer Internat. Agy., N.Y.C., 1976-77; mgr. pub. performing arts U. Wash., Seattle, 1977-81; mgr. performing and visual arts Parks and Recreation, City of Seattle, 1981-83, recreation dist. mgr., 1983—; cons.Nat. Endowment for Arts: Site Evaluator, 1980; interarts panel 1981; multi-music panel 1988, 89; workshop presenter Washington Parks and Recreation, 1989, Washington Recreation and Parks to Washington State Arts Commn., 1988, 89, 90, bd. dirs. liaison; mem. program and edn. com. Seattle Art Mus., 1981—; workshop presenter Nat. Recreation and Parks Assn. Regional Confs., 1985-86; mem. conf. com. Internat. NW Parks and Recreation Assn. Conf., 1986. Bd. dirs. Bumbershoot-Seattle Arts Festival, 1979, 80; bd. dirs. Northwest Folklife Festival, 1982—, treas., 1985, 86, pres. 1986-89; cantor Sacred Heart Ch., Seattle, 1982—; mem. Seattle Art Mus. Mem. Nat. Entertainment and Campus Activities Assn. (bd. dirs., dir. 1969-72, Cert. of Appreciation 1975), Western Alliance Arts Adminstrs. (v.p. 1978-80), Wash. State Folklife Coun., Allied Arts Seattle, Seattle Folklore Soc., Wash. Recreation and Parks Assn., Nat. Recretation & Pks. Assn., Phi Beta Kappa, Mu Phi Epsilon, Alpha Delta Pi. Roman Catholic. Home: PO Box 19278 Seattle WA 98109 Office: 100 Dexter Ave N Seattle WA 98109

O'NEILL, PATRICIA MARGARET, nursing educator; b. Bayshore, N.Y., Apr. 25, 1948; d. Joseph William and Margaret (Campion) Tmay; m. Edward R. O'Neill, Apr. 20, 1970 (div. May 1974); 1 child, Brian E. BS in Nursing, D'Youville Coll., 1970; MA in Liberal Studies, SUNY, Stony Brook, 1980. RN, cert. sch. nurse/tchr. Supr. of nurses Buffalo (N.Y.) Columbus Hosp., 1970-73; emergency room nurse Brookhaven Hosp., Patchogue, N.Y., 1973-74; sch. nurse, tchr. Sachem Sch. Dist., Holbrook, N.Y., 1974—; part-time nurse in med. unit Suffolk County Correctional Facility, Riverhead, N.Y., 1982-87; nurse/supr. Racquette Lake (N.Y.) Camps, summers 1975-77, Sachem Day Camp, summers 1977-79, Suffolk Day Camp, Bayport, N.Y., summers 1979-81; summer sch. nurse, Sachem Sch. Dist., 1985-90. Pres. Spl. Edn. Parent Tchr. Assn., Patchogue, 1980-82, legis. chmn., 1978-80; mem. Epilepsy Assn. of Suffolk County, Inc., 1976-80; mem. Tamarac Sch. PTA, 1976—. Mem. N.Y. State Assn. Sch. Nurses. Roman Catholic. Home: 10 Redwood Ct Selden NY 11784 Office: Sachem Sch Dist 245 Union Ave Holbrook NY 11741

ONKEN, LISA SIMON, psychologist, researcher; b. Butler, Pa., June 26, 1954; d. Ralph and Charlotte (Tulchin) Simon; m. James Byron Onken, Nov. 9, 1985; children: Laura Cielle, Allison Michelle. BS magna cum laude, Tufts U., Medford, Mass., 1976; MA, Northwestern U., Evanston, Ill., 1980, PhD, 1981. Lic. psychologist, Md. Lectr. Northwestern U., 1981, 84; intern in psychology Cook County Hosp., Chgo., 1982-83; vis. staff psychologist U. Ill., Chgo., 1984-85; rsch. psychologist Walter Reed Army Inst. Rsch., Washington, 1985-87, Nat. Inst. on Drug Abuse, Rockville, Md., 1987—. Contbr. articles to profl. jours. Walter Dill Scott Rsch. fellow Northwestern U., 1978. Mem. Am. Psychol. Assn., Soc. Psychotherapy Rsch., Phi Beta Kappa, Psi Chi. Office: Nat Inst Drug Abuse 5600 Fishers Ln Rockville MD 20857

ONLEY, SISTER FRANCESCA, college president; b. Phila., Mar. 4, 1933; d. Edward Patrick and Marie (Rice) O. B.A., Holy Family Coll., 1959; M.S., Marywood Coll., 1966; Ph.D., So. Ill. U., 1986. Cert. secondary counselor, Penn. Tchr. Nazareth Acad. Grade Sch., Phila., 1952-64; tchr. Nazareth Acad., Phila., 1964-67, vice prin., counselor, 1967-72, prin., 1972-80; asst. to pres. Holy Family Coll., Phila., 1980-81, pres., 1981—; bd. dirs. Comcast, Phila., 1983—. Bd. officer, sec. N.E. br. ARC, Phila., 1984—, bd. dirs., 1983—. Recipient Alumni award Holy Family Coll. Alumni 1982. Mem. Mid. State Assn. Schs. and Colls., Assn. Governing Bds., Coun. Ind. Colls., N.E. C. of C. (bd. dirs. 1983—). Roman Catholic. Office: Holy Family Coll Grant and Frankford Aves Philadelphia PA 19114

ONO, YOKO, conceptual artist, singer, recording artist; b. Tokyo, Feb. 18, 1933; U.S. citizen; m. John Ono Lennon, Mar. 20, 1969 (dec. 1980); children: Kyoko, Sean; Student Peers' Sch., Gakushuin U., Tokyo, Sarah Lawrence Coll., Harvard U. One-woman shows include Alchemical Wedding, Albert Hall, London, 1967, Evening with Yoko Ono, Birmingham, 1968, Event, U. Wales, 1969, Everson Mus., Syracuse, N.Y., 1971, others; exhibited Fluxshoe, Sch. Art, Falmouth, Cornwall, Eng., 1972; recorded albums: (with John Ono Lennon) Two Virgins, 1968, Life With Lions, 1969, Wedding Album, 1970, Live Peace In Toronto (1969), 1970, Some Time in New York City, 1972, Double Fantasy, 1980 (Grammy award Album of Yr. 1981), Milk and Honey, 1984; solo albums include Yoko Ono/Plastic Ono Band, Fly, Approximately Infinite Universe, Feeling the Space, Season of Glass, Starpeace, 1985; composer numerous songs including Don't Worry Kyoko, Mummy's Only Looking For Her Hand in the Snow, Walking on Thin Ice (Grammy award nomination Best Female Rock Performance on Single 1981), Don't Be Sad. Author six film scripts, Tokyo, 1964, thirteen film score scores, London, 1967, John & Yoko Calendar, 1970, (book) Grapefruit, 1964, London, 1970, A Hole to See the Sky Through, N.Y., 1971. Office: Studio 1 1 W 72nd St New York NY 10023*

ONOFRIO, JANIS LYNN, chemist; b. Grosse Point, Mich., June 22, 1963; d. Francis Joseph and Anne Margaret (Rezak) S. Student, Kalamazoo Coll., 1981-82; BS in Chemistry and German, Lake Forest Coll., 1985. Research chemist Domino Amjet, Inc., Waukegan, Ill., 1985-87; research asst. Baxter Healthcare Corp., Round Lake, Ill., 1987—. Scholar Ruth Boot Found., 1981, Am. Legion, 1981. Mem. Am. Chem. Soc., Phi Sigma Iota. Roman Catholic. Office: Baxter Healthcare Corp Wilson Rd and Rt 120 Round Lake IL 60073

ONORATO, SUSAN DOBBS, accountant; b. Camden, N.J., July 20, 1964; d. Robert Kenneth and Dorothy (Garwood) Dobbs; m. Kenneth James Onorato, Sept. 20, 1986. BSBA, Bloomsburg U. Pa., 1986. Inventory control analyst Barry Chocolate, Inc., Pennsauken, N.J., 1986-88; acctg. mgr. Credit Lenders Svc. Agy., Gibbsboro, N.J., 1988-89; asst. contr. MJL Corp., Berlin, N.J., 1989—. Auditor Ashland (N.J.) Evangelical Presbyn. Ch., 1988-89, chmn. auditing com., 1990. Mem. NAFE. Presbyterian.

OOSTERHOF, DARLENE KOBES, computer scientist; b. Holland, Mich., Apr. 22, 1945; d. John Fred and Irene (Elzinga) Kobes; m. Albert Carlyle Oosterhof, June 24, 1967. BS in Chemistry, Hope Coll., 1967. Chemist Fla. State U., Tallahassee, 1973-84, computer scientist, 1984—. Presbyterian. Home: Rte 2 Box 4442 Crawfordville FL 32327 Office: Fla State Univ Dept Meteorology Tallahassee FL 32306

OPELT, RILLA ANNE, seniors program coordinator; b. Duluth, Minn., Aug. 7, 1939; d. Frank Louis and Mabel Hester (Chapman) DeBot; m. Alexander Lambi Stolis, May 6, 1961 (div. 1969); children: Alexander Jr., Roxanne Kathryn, Pauline Madeline, Rilla Marie; m. Bud T. Opelt, Nov. 8, 1969; children: Buddy Jr., Theanne Lenore. BA in Social Work, St. Scholastica, 1961, BA in Elem. Edn., 1969, MA in Psychology, 1988. Owner, operator Mother's Helper's Inc., Duluth, 1965-79; elem. tchr. Duluth Sch. Dist., 1969-75; sec. Minn. Power, Duluth, 1978, info. specialist, 1978-90, seniors' program coord., 1990—; cons. Personalized Cons., Duluth, 1988—. Dir. Prolife Info. Network, Duluth, 1983—; dist. chmn. 7th Senate Dist. Reps., 1983-90; candidate State Ho. of Reps., 1988. Mem. Rep. Women. Roman Catholic. Club: Community.

OPENDEN, LORI, television talent and casting executive; b. L.A.; d. Morris and Gladys (Schwartz) Linder; m. Jeff Openden, June 18, 1972; children: Danny, Jamie. BA, Calif. State U., Northridge, 1973. Casting dir. Four D Prodns., Hollywood, Calif., 1975-77, MTM Prodns., Studio City, Calif., 1977-84; pvt. practice Lori Openden Casting, L.A., 1984-85; v.p. casting NBC, Burbank, Calif., 1985-88, v.p talent, 1989—. Mem. Casting Soc. Am. (Artios award-dramatic casting for Hill Steet Blues, 1985, Cheers, 1985). Office: NBC Entertainment 30 Rockefeller Pla New York NY 10112

OPHEIM, ROBERTA CLAIRE, consulting company executive; b. Virginia, Minn., Sept. 20, 1948; d. Harden Robert and Romelle Claire (Sandberg) Bloomquist; m. Gary Warren Opheim, July 26, 1969; children: Justin Robert, Scott Warren. BA, Gustavus Adolphus Coll., 1970; cert. in small bus. mgmt., 916 Voc-Tech, 1983. Customer svc. rep. Northwestern Bell Telephone, St. Paul, 1971-75; owner Hickory Dickory Dock, Stillwater, Minn., 1977-86; pres. Objectives Inc., Stillwater, 1986—. Mem. small bus. adv. coun. Congressman Arlan Erdahl, 1980, small bus. adv. bd. 916 Voc-Tech, White Bear, 1981-83; del. Minn. Conf. Small Bus., 1981, 87; pres. Downtown Coun., Stillwater, 1984; mem. Stillwater City Coun., 1986—, Stillwater Parks and Recreation Commn., 1986—, Stillwater Downtown Planning Com., 1987—; mem. Mpls.-St. Paul Airport Adequacy Study Task Force, Airport Sight Search Com., Met. Coun. Twin Cities, 1989—; bd. dirs. Stillwater Area Schs. Partnership Plan, 1987—. Named Outstanding Community Bus. Leader Jaycees, 1984. Mem. NAFE, Nat. Assn. Women Bus. Owners, Jaycee Women (v.p. 1979, treas. 1980), Stillwater C. of C. (pres. 1986, 87). Office: Objectives Inc PO Box 518 Stillwater MN 55082

OPLINGER, KATHRYN RUTH, computer specialist; b. Wadsworth, Ohio, Apr. 18, 1951; d. Herman Carl and Blanche Ruth (White) Simshauser; m. Douglas E. Oplinger, July 26, 1986; children: Raymond, Karla, Kathleen. Student, Washington Coll., 1969-71, Kennesaw (Ga.) State Coll., 1988-89. Pres., chief exec. officer Disc, Ltd., Atlanta, 1981—; cons. mgmt. info. systems Procter & Gamble, Atlanta, 1989—; spokesperson, designer Saks Fifth Ave, nationwide, 1981-86. Firestone Found. scholar, 1969. Mem. NAFE, Am. Bus. Women's Assn., Lions Internat. (pres. Woodstock, Ga. chpt. 1986-87). Republican. Methodist. Office: Disc Ltd 1000 Parkwood Cir Ste 950 Atlanta GA 30339

OPPEDISANO, SUZANNE MARIE, marketing professional, dentist; b. Boston; d. Rocco Louis and Ruth Margaret (Webb) O. BS, Tufts U., 1976; DMD, U. Pa., 1980; MBA, Wharton, 1986. Adj. faculty U. Pa. Sch. Dental Medicine, Phila., 1984-86; nat. sales analyst E.R. Squibb & Sons, Princeton, N.J., 1986-87; cons. Prudential Life Ins. Co, Princeton, 1987-88; asst. product dir. Johnson & Johnson Dental Care Co., New Brunswick, N.J., 1988; asst. prof. U. of The Pacific, San Francisco, 1989—; Intern prodn. mgmt. Pharm. div. CIBA-Geigy, Summit, N.J., 1985; student cons. Albert Einstein Hosp., Phila., 1985. Contbr. articles to profl. jours. Served to capt. U.S. Army, 1980-84. Armed Forces Health Professions scholar U.S. Army Dental Corps. Mem. ADA, Wharton Alumni Assn.

OPPENHEIM, JUDITH R., orthopedic surgeon; b. Detroit, July 2, 1946; d. Louis and Evelyn (Kurlander) Oppenheim. BS with honors, U.Mich., 1968, MS with honors, 1973; MD, U. Ill., 1979. Diplomate Am. Bd. Orthopedic Surgery. Tchr. New Trier Twp. High Sch. West, Northfield, Ill., 1968-72, 73-75; resident in orthopedic surgery U. Okla., Oklahoma City, 1979-82, U. Mo., Kansas City, 1982-84; orthopedic surgeon Cigna Health Plans, L.A., 1984-87; clin. fellow in orthopedic surgery U. Toronto-Sunnybrook Hosp., 1987-88; fellow in orthopedic surgery Pee Dee Orthopedics, Florence, S.C., 1988; orthopedic surgeon Permanente Med. Assn. of Dallas, 1988—. Recipient William F. Branstrom award U. Mich., 1965; Student Leadership award U. Ill., 1979. Mem. Am. Acad. Orthopedic Surgeons (candidate), Sunnybrook Orthopedic Soc., Ruth Jackson Soc., Am. Med. Women's Assn., Am. Coll. Sports Medicine. Jewish. Office: Permanente Med Assn Tex 7777 Forest Ln Bldg C Dallas TX 75230

OPPENHEIM, MARTHA KUNKEL, pianist, educator; b. Port Arthur, Tex., June 25, 1935; d. Samuel Adam and Grace (Moncure) Kunkel; m. Russell Edward Oppenheim, June 18, 1960; children—Lauren Susan, Kristin Lee Oppenheim Mortenson. MusB with honors, U. Tex., 1957; MusM, U. Tex., 1959; diploma in piano Juilliard Sch. Music, 1960; student Am. Conservatory, Fontainebleau, France, 1956, 58. soloist, Amarillo (Tex.) Symphony, Austin (Tex.) Symphony, U. Tex. Orch., San Antonio Symphony, Dallas Symphony, Heilbronner Kammer Orch., Heilbron, Germany; solo and chamber music recitals in Tex., N.Y., France; mem. Halcyon Trio, 1974-77; teaching asst. U. Tex., 1957-59, 68-69; pvt. piano tchr., San Antonio, 1962—. Recipient 1st Place award Internat. Piano Recording Festival, Nat. Guild Piano Tchrs., 1956, 57, 1st Place award Tuesday Mus. Club Young Artist Competition, 1956, 1st Place award Young Artist Competition, Amarillo Symphony, 1959; 1st Place award G. B. Dealey Competition, Dallas Symphony and Dallas Morning News, 1959; Scholar U. Tex., Juilliard Sch. Music. Mem. Music Tchrs. Nat. Assn., Tex. Music Tchrs. Assn., San Antonio Music Tchrs. Assn., Sigma Alpha Iota, Pi Kappa Lambda. Presbyterian. Club: Tuesday Musical (San Antonio) (bd. dirs.). Home and Office: 9118 E Valley View Ln San Antonio TX 78217

OPPENHEIMER, HEATHER LEIGH, computer scientist; b. Oneida, N.Y., Aug. 26, 1949; d. Bruce James and Mary Janice (Smith) Partridge; m. Martin Lee Oppenheimer, May 23, 1971; children: Jesse Craig, Corey Deborah, Katherine Yael. BA, Oberlin Coll., 1970; MEd., U. Oreg., 1971; M in Computer Sci., U. Ill., 1984. Elem. tchr. Coos Bay (Oreg.) Sch. Dist., 1970-71; spl. edn. tchr. Terra Nova Integrated Sch. Bd., Gander, Nfld., Can., 1971-72; prin., tchr. Browndale Schs., Vancouver, B.C., Can., 1972-74; kindergarten tchr. Rimbey (Alta., Can.) Sch. Dist., 1975-77; tchr. insvc. cons. Ill., 1979-82; tchr. gifted Champaign (Ill.) Sch. Dist., 1981-82; mem. tech. staff software R & D AT&T Bell Labs., Columbus, Ohio, 1985—. Mem. White House Coun. on Children and Youth, 1980; bd. dirs. Sinai Temple Sisterhood, Champaign, Ill., 1980-83. Mem. Assn. for Computing Machinery, NAFE. Democrat. Jewish. Home: 230 N Merkle Rd Bexley OH 43209 Office: AT&T Bell Labs 6200 E Broad St Columbus OH 43213

OPPENHEIMER, SUZI, state senator; m. Martin J. Oppenheimer; children: Marcy, Evan, Josh, Alexandra. BA in Econs., Conn. Coll. for Women; MBA, Columbia U. Former security analyst L.F. Rothschild Co., N.Y.C.; mayor Village of Mamaroneck, N.Y., 1977-84; mem. N.Y. State Senate, 1985—; ranking mem. commerce, econ. devel. and small bus., mem. edn., child care, consumer protection, transp., drugs coms., chmn. Senate Minority Task Force on Women's Issues. Former pres. Mamaroneck LWV, Westchester County Village Ofcls. Assn., Westchester Mcpl. Planning Fedn. Democrat. Office: 515 Legislative Office Bldg Albany NY 12247 Other: NY State Senate Albany NY 12224

OPPERMAN, AMELIA, food products executive; b. Mexico City, Feb. 26, 1939; d. Rudolpho and Amelia (Blythe) Cardenas; m. Gilbert L. Opperman, Dec. 29, 1962; children: Gilbert III, Eric M., Karl A. Student, Purdue U., 1977, Ind. U., 1977-81. Co. pres. Gilmol Corp., Champaign, Ill., 1982--. Office: Gilmol Corp Box 6419 Champaign IL 61821

O'QUINN, RUTH GRANGER, English educator; b. Pollock, La., May 12, 1925; d. James Andrew and Ruth Margaret (Clinton) Granger; m. Hansel Benson O'Quinn, Sept. 25, 1943 (dec. July 1967); children: Hansel Benson Jr. (dec.), Carol Anne. BA, La. Coll., 1959; MEd, Northwestern La. State U., Natchitoches, 1962. Tchr. English Tioga (La.) High Sch., 1960-65; libr. Grenada (Miss.) County Schs., 1965-67; tchr. English Bolton High Sch., Alexandria, La., 1967-69; tchr. English, chmn. dept. Alexandria Sr. High Sch., 1969-85; sch. bd. dirs. Rapides Parish, Alexandria, 1986—; edn. lobbyist Legis. Sessions, Baton Rouge, 1967-85; mem. English curriculum com. State Dept. Edn., Baton Rouge, 1974-75; mem. adv. com. La. Tchr. Evaluation Program, 1988—. Sustaining mem. Rep. Nat. Com., Washington; mem. Nat. Fedn. Rep. Women, Washington. Mem. Nat. Sch. Bds. Assn., La. Sch. Bds. Assn., La. Assn. Classroom Tchrs. (state pres. 1983-84), AAUW, Delta Kappa Gamma, Alpha Chi. Office: Rapides Parish Sch Bd Sixth and Beauregard Alexandria LA 71303

ORAN, ELAINE SURICK, computational physicist, engineer, chemist; b. Rome, Ga., Apr. 16, 1946; d. Herman E. and Bessye R. (Kolker) Surick; m. Daniel Hirsh Oran, Feb. 1, 1969. A.B., Bryn Mawr Coll., 1966; M.Ph., Yale U., 1968, Ph.D., 1972. Research physicist Naval Research Lab., Washington, 1972-76, supervisory research physicist, 1976-82, sr. scientist reactive flow physics, 1982—; head Ctr. for Reactive Flow and Dynamical Systems; mem. adv. bd. NSF; cons. to U.S. govt., agys., NATO. Author: Numerical Simulation of Reactive Flow, 1987. Editorial bd. Prog. Ener. Comb. Sci. Contbr. numerous articles to profl. jours., chpts. to books. Recipient Arthur S. Flemming award, 1979, Women in Sci. and Engring. award, 1988; publs. award Naval Research Lab., 1979, 80, 83, 85; grantee USN, NASA, USAF, Defense Advanced Rsch. Projects Agy. Fellow AIAA (pubs. com. 1986—); mem. AAAS, Am. Geophys. Union (publs. com. 1982-86), Am. Phys. Soc. (exec. com. fluid dynamics div. 1986, 88, exec. com. computer physics 1989—), Combustion Inst. (bd. dirs. 1990—), Internat. Colloquium Dynamic Energy Systems (bd. dirs. 1989—), Sigma Xi. Office: Naval Rsch Lab Code 4404/4004 Washington DC 20375

ORAN, GERALDINE ANN, teacher; b. Burleson, Tex., June 27, 1938; d. Clyde Lloyd and Ruth (Baxley) Renfro; m. Francis Larry Oran, Dec. 18, 1960; children: Angelique Michelle, Jeremy Lloyd. AS summa cum laude, Roane State Community Coll., Harriman, Tenn., 1976; BS summa cum laude, U. Tenn., 1978, MS summa cum laude, 1990. IBM instr., office mgr. Kelsey-Jenney Bus. Coll., San Diego, 1958-61; exec. sec. Bendix Corp., San Diego, 1961-62; ednl. adminstr. South Harriman Bapt. Ch., 1964-74; tchr. Midtown Elem., Harriman, 1979-87; adminstrv. intern Danforth Found. Leadership 21, 1989; asst. prin. Cherokee Mid. Sch., Kingston, Tenn., 1990—; adminstrv. intern Danforth Found. Leadership 21. Mem., sec., treas., pres. PTA and PTO, Harriman, 1967-81; active Cancer, Heart Fund and March of Dimes, Harriman, 1979—; dir. vacation Bible sch. South Harriman Bapt. Ch., 1983-86, tchr. women's Bible sch., 1965—; club sponsor Tenn. Just Say No to Drugs Team, Roane County, 1985-87; mem. Task Force on Middle Schs., Tenn. Dept. Edn., 1990. Named Tchr. of Yr., Roane County, 1987; selected Danforth Found. admintrv. intern, 1989. Mem. ASCD, Tenn. Assn. Supervision and Curriculum Devel., Tenn. Assn. Mid. Schs., Nat. Assn. Secondary Sch. Prins., Nat. Assn. Elem. Sch. Prins., NEA (del. rep. 1985-86), Tenn. Edn. Assn. (del. rep. 1984-86, Outstanding Service award 1985-86), Roane County Edn. Assn. (membership chairperson 1984-85, pres. 1985-86), Gamma Phi Beta, Kappa Delta Pi, Phi Kappa Phi. Baptist. Home: PO Box 917 Harriman TN 37748-0917 Office: Cherokee Mid Sch Paint Rock Ferry Rd Kingston TN 37763

ORAV, HELLE REISSAR, retired dentist; b. Tartu, Estonia, July 10, 1925; came to U.S., 1949, naturalized, 1954; d. Johan and Adele Johanna (Minski) Reissar; m. Arnold Orav, May 30, 1952; children: Ilmar Erik, Hillar Thomas. Student Friedrich Alexander U., Erlangen, West Germany, 1946-49; DDS, NYU, 1952. Practice dentistry, N.Y.C., 1952, 60, 62, 68, Valencia, Venezuela, 1953-68. Counselor, Red Cross, Valencia, 1954-55; past mem. Rotary Ladies Republican. Lutheran. Clubs: Country of Maracaibo (Venezuela); Palm Beach Polo and Country (Fla.); Korp Filiae Patriae (N.Y.C.). Avocations: Pre-Colombian art, bridge, travel, swimming, reading. Home: 860 Fifth Ave New York NY 10021 also: 44 Cocoanut Row Palm Beach FL 33480

ORAZIO, JOAN POLITI, financial planning company executive; b. N.Y.C., Mar. 24, 1930; d. Joseph and Anna B. Politi; B.S., Mercy Coll., 1975; cert. fin. planner Coll. Fin. Planning, 1979; m. Dr. Louis D. Orazio, Aug. 24, 1952; children—Louise Orazio Mason, Joanne Orazio Tonkin, Paul, Phyllis Orazio Kearsing. Exec. v.p. Gary Goldberg & Co., Suffern, N.Y., 1977—; instr. Rockland Community Coll., 1977-84 ; workshop leader, seminar speaker various colls., corps. community orgns., 1970—. Trustee Rockland Community Coll. Mem. Internat. Assn. Fin. Planners, Inst. Cert. Fin. Planners, Nat. Orgn. Italian Am. Women, Nat. Assn. Female Execs., Rockland County Bus. and Profl. Women. Roman Catholic. Lodge: Kiwanis. Home: 17 Wilder Rd Suffern NY 10901 Office: Gary Goldberg & Co Inc 75 Montebello Rd Suffern NY 10901

ORCHARD, DONNA LEE, box company executive; b. Kansas City, Mo., Dec. 27, 1931; d. Max Edward and Ruth Louise (Kerst) Arenson; m. Edgar L. Orchard, Feb. 5, 1957; children—Laura Ellen Orchard Massie DiCamp, Barri Louise Orchard Sapp, Caroline Courtney Orchard Cahill. Student Washington U., St. Louis, 1950, U. Mo.-Kansas City, 1952. Office mgr. Gentry & Voskamp Architects, Kansas City, 1953-57; sec., synopsis editor for publ. release Sovereign TV Prodn. (Gen. Electric, Dupont Theaters), Hollywood, Calif., 1951-52; pres., owner Orchard Box Co., St. Louis, 1979—; v.p. Orco Sales Co. Patentee in field. Pres., Washington U. Women's Soc., St. Louis, 1982-84; bd. mem. Temple Israel, St. Louis, 1982-87; sec. Gateway Theater, St. Louis; life mem., v.p. Primitive Arts Soc., St. Louis Art Mus., 1980-81; bd. dirs. St. Louis Opera Guild, founder womens com. 1960-63; bd. dirs., life mem. Jewish Hosp. Aux., Brandeis U.; bd. dirs. St. Louis Symphony Womens Soc., St. Louis Zoo Assn., League of Women Voters, 1958-59; life mem. Hilton Theater, Webster Coll. Mem. Nat. Assn. Women Bus. Owners, Kansas City C. of C. (wage and hour com. 1955-57). Republican. Club: Whittemore House. Avocations: collector of art, gardening, raising of Koi, research of art and oriental porcelains. Home: One Robindale Dr Saint Louis MO 63124 Office: Orchard Box Co 1326 Baur Blvd Saint Louis MO 63132

ORCUTT, BEN AVIS, social work educator; b. Falco, Ala., Oct. 17, 1914; d. Benjamin A. and Emily Olive Adams; A.B., U. Ala., 1936; M.A., Tulane U., 1939, M.S.W., 1942; D.S.W., Columbia U., 1962. Social worker, acting field dir. ARC, LaGarde Gen. Hosp., New Orleans, Fort Benning (Ga.) Regional Hosp., 1942-46; chief social work svc. VA regional office, Phoenix, 1946-51, chief social work svc. unit outpatient office, Birmingham, Ala., 1954-57, 58; rsch. asst. Rsch. Ctr. Sch. Social Work, Columbia U., N.Y.C., 1960-62, field adv. social work, 1962, assoc. prof. social work, 1965-76; assoc. prof. social work La. State U., Baton Rouge, 1962-65; prof. social work, dir. doctoral program U. Ala., University, 1976-84; rsch. cons. Tavistock Centre, London, 1972. Author: Science and Inquiry in Social Work Practice, 1990, (with Harry P. Orcutt) America's Riding Horses, 1958, (with Elizabeth R. Prichard, Jean Collard, Austin H. Kutscher, Irene Seeland, Nathan Lefkowitz) Social Work with the Dying Patient and the Family, 1977, (with others) Social Work and Thanatology, 1980; editor: Poverty and Social Casework Svcs., 1974; editorial bd. Jour. Social Work, 1982-84; contbr. articles to profl. books and jours. Mem. alumni bd. Sch. Social Work, Columbia U., 1985-88. NIMH fellow, 1957-60. Mem. Council Social Work Edn., Nat. Assn. Social Workers, Found. Thanatology, N.Y. Acad. Scis., Ala. Conf. Social Welfare, Group for Advancement Doctoral Edn. (steering com., editor newsletter 1980-83). Episcopalian. Club: Zonta. Home: 222 Fox Run Tuscaloosa AL 35406 Office: PO Box 1935 University AL 35486

ORDOWER, MYRNA E., insurance broker; b. Chgo., Oct. 8; d. Abe Herman and Gussie (Rubinsky) Berliner; m. Sidney L. Ordower, Mar. 4, 1961; children: Cheryl, Karyn, Steven. Student U. Ill., Northwestern U. Underwriter Bergman & Lefkow Ins., Chgo.; unit mgr. Near North Ins., Chgo., 1974-82; owner, pres. Myrna Ordower Enterprises, Chgo., 1982—; v.p., stockholder Rockwood Co., 1982—, also bd. dirs. Founder, Women's Exec. Network, Chgo., 1983—; co-founder Corp. Connections, Chgo., 1985. Bd. dirs. Little City Found. for Mentally Retarded Children, Women's bd. Chgo. Urban League; fund raiser Muscular Dystrophy, Chgo.; del. White House Conf. Small Bus., 1986; active Ill. Ins. Task Force, 1986. Recipient Outstanding Leadership proclamation Mayor of Chgo. Eugene Sawyer, 1988. Mem. Nat. Assn. Women Bus. Owners (bd. dirs.), Nat. Assn. Ins. Women. Home: 5502 S Harper Ave Chicago IL 60637 Office: Myrna Ordower Enterprises 20 N Wacker Dr Chicago IL 60606

ORDUNA-MUSLIMANI, MARIA, insurance sales executive; b. La Paz, Colombia, Feb. 11, 1959; came to U.S., 1967; d. Segismundo Orduna and Ana Lucrecia Traslavina; m. Nazeir Muslimani, July 27, 1985. BS in Lang. Arts, Georgetown U., 1982. Supr. Deak-Perera, Washington, 1983-84; ins. agt. Mut. of Omaha Cos., Washington, 1984-87, sales mgr., 1987-90, income protection specialist, 1990—. Chairperson Sacred Heart Trilingual Parish Coun., Washington, 1987-90, Sacred Heart Hispanic Coun., 1988-90. Mem. NAFE, Nat. Assn. Health Underwriters (registered, health ins. quality award 1985, 86), Nat. Coun. Hispanic Women, U.S. Hispanic C. of C., Ibero-Am. C. of C. Roman Catholic. Home: 9515 Tippett Ln Gaithersburg MD 20879 Office: Mut of Omaha 1666 Connecticut Ave NW 2d Fl Washington DC 20009

ORDWAY, ELLEN, biology educator, entomology researcher; b. N.Y.C., Nov. 8, 1927; d. Samuel Hanson and Anna (Wheatland) O. B.A., Wheaton Coll., Mass., 1950; M.S., Cornell U., 1955; Ph.D., U. Kans., 1965. Field asst. N.Y. Zool. Soc., N.Y.C., 1950-52; research asst. Am. Mus. Natural History, N.Y.C., 1955-57; teaching asst. U. Kans., Lawrence, 1957-61, research asst., 1959-65; asst. prof. U. Minn., Morris, 1965-70, assoc. prof. biology, 1970-85, prof., 1986—; cooperator and cons. U.S. Dept. Agr. Bee Research Lab., Tucson, Ariz., 1971, 1983. Contbr. articles to sci. jours. Mgr. preserves Nature Conservancy, Mpls., 1975—; lectr. Morris area service clubs, 1972—. Mem. Ecol. Soc. Am., Entomol. Soc. Am., Soc. Systematic Zoology, Soc. Study Evolution, Kans. Entomol. Soc., Internat. Bee Research Assn., AAAS, AAUP (v.p. 1975-76, sec.-treas. 1971-73 Morris chpt.), Sigma Xi, Sigma Delta Epsilon. Episcopalian. Avocations: travel, photography, raquetball, exploring natural environments, wilderness, areas, etc. Office: U Minn Div Sci and Math Morris MN 56267

O'REILLY, LOUISE, electric company executive; b. Melrose, Mass., Sept. 11, 1948; d. Whitney and Shirley (Moore) Gerrish; m. Richard Wayne Halle, May 10, 1969 (div. 1985); m. William R. O'Reilly, May 20, 1988. Student, U. Mich., 1966-69; BS in Chem. Edn., U. Mass., 1971, MEd, 1974; MS in Indsl. Adminstrn., Union Coll., 1984. Tchr. chemistry R.C. Mahar Regional Sch., Orange, Mass., 1971-74, Portland (Conn.) High Sch., 1974-76; self employed, 1976-78; fuel chemist Encotech Inc., Schenectady, N.Y., 1978-80; tng. specialist Gen. Electric Co., Schenectady, 1980-84, mgr. entry level tng., 1984-86, mgr. power gen. tech. tng., 1986-90, mgr. human resource programs, 1990—. Mem. Elfun Soc., Schenectady, 1987. Mem. Am. Soc. Tng. and Devel. Office: Gen Electric Co 1 River Rd Bldg 273-150 Schenectady NY 12345

O'REILLY-KEDDY, EVE MARIE, retail executive; b. Lawrence, Mass., Mar. 10, 1957; d. William and Jacqueline (Desprez) O'R.; m. James L. Keddy, May 6, 1984; 1 child, Colleen; 2 stepchildren: Philip, Pamela. BA in Econs., Harvard U., 1979; student, Boston Coll. Sch. of Mgmt., 1988—. Asst. buyer Filenes Dept. Store, Boston, 1979-80; acct. exec. Wamsutta Mills, N.Y.C., 1980-82; mgmt. auditor State Auditor of Mass., Boston, 1982-84; store owner, mgr. Littlefield and O'Reilly Ltd., Foxboro, Mass., 1984—. Dancer Boston Ballet Co., 1970-75. Mem. AAUW, Tri-town C. of C. Home: 5 Allens Way Foxboro MA 02035

OREM, SANDRA ELIZABETH, health systems administrator; b. Balt., Sept. 26, 1940; d. Ira Julius and Mabel Ruth (Peeples) O. Diploma, Ch. Home and Hosp. Sch. Nursing, 1962; BS with honors, The Johns Hopkins U., 1968; MS, U. Md., 1972. Staff, charge nurse Ch. Home and Hosp., Balt., 1962-63; asst. instr. Ch. Home and Hosp. Sch. Nursing, Balt., 1963-64, instr., 1964-70; clin. nurse specialist Johns Hopkins Hosp., Balt., 1972-77, asst. dir. nursing, 1977-79, dir. nursing, 1979-87; clin. assoc. faculty The Johns Hopkins U. Sch. of Nursing, 1984-87; program dir., instr. intermediate massage course Balt. Holistic Health Cr., 1987—; pres. Nursing Edn. and Cons. Service, Inc., Balt., 1976-78, Oasis Health Systems, Inc., Balt., 1987—. Contbr. articles to profl. publs. Vol. Office on Aging, Balt., 1982-83, Boy Scouts Am., Balt., 1984-85. Mem. Am. Holistic Nurses Assn., Ch. Home and Hosp. Sch. Nursing Alumni Assn. (treas. 1970-72, pres.-elect 1975-76), Nat. Assn. Female Execs., NOW, Balt.-Am. Massage Therapy Assn., Md. Assn. Massage Practitioners, Johns Hopkins U. Alumnae Assn., Sigma Theta Tau. Democrat. Episcopalian.

ORENSTEIN, MYRA GOLDSTEIN, advertising company executive; b. Malden, Mass., Feb. 18, 1952; d. Maurice and Ruth Blume G.; m. Louis Jay, Aug. 23, 1981; children: Daniel Jacob, Rebecca Nicole. BA in English, Case Western Res. U., 1973. Proofreader, copywriter Glidden Paint Co., Cleve., 1973-74; copywriter Griswold Eshleman, Cleve., 1974-75; pub. rels. profl. Mid-Continent Tel. Co. (now Alltel), Hudson, Ohio, 1975-76; v.p., creative dir. Ross Salupo Advtg., Cleve., 1976-80; copy, contact Richard Desberg & Assoc., Beachwood, Ohio, 1980-81; pres. MDG&O Advt. Inc., Cleve., 1981—; v.p. CATV, Inc., Cleve. Writer: Cleveland Mag., 1974-75, Crains Cleve. Bus., 1980. Recipient Award of Distinction, Cable Mktg., 1983, Awards of Excellence, Cleve. Soc. Communcations Arts, 1983, Art Dirs. N.Y., 1984, Ohio Hosp. Assn., Bronze Quill award Internat. Assn. Bus. Communicators, 1987. Mem. Coun. Small Bus. Enterprises, Cleve. Growth Assn., Heights C. of C. Democrat. Jewish. Home and Office: 2533 Euclid Heights Blvd Cleveland OH 44106

O'RISKY, DOROTHY SANDRA, educator; b. Evansville, Ind., July 26, 1939; d. Richard Henry and Bonita Frances (Hahne) O'R. BA, Carson Newman Coll., 1961; MA, Northwestern U., Evanston, Ill., 1967. Tchr. French and Spanish Mt. Vernon (Ind.) Sr. High Sch., 1963—. Mem. Ohio Valley Hospice, Evansville, 1987—; bd. trustees Salem Cemetery, Evansville, 1989—. Mem. NEA, Am. Assn. Tchrs. of French, AAUW (state editor 1985-86, br. pres. 1986-88), Delta Kappa Gamma (chpt. pres. 1978-80, state 2d v.p. 1987-89, state 1st v.p. 1989—). Baptist. Home: 6724 Briar Ct Evansville IN 47711-1608 Office: Mt Vernon Sr High Sch 700 Harriet St Mount Vernon IN 47620

ORKWIS, ROSE ANN ELENA, administrative assistant; b. Kew Gardens, N.Y., Apr. 6, 1946; d. Archie and Lucy (Placente) Traini; m. Richard Chester Orkwis, Feb. 25, 1968; children: Eric, Douglas, Vanessa. Student, Suffolk Community Coll., Bayshore, N.Y., 1986. Custom house broker Elco Shipping, N.Y.C., 1968-70; vol. with learning disabled children, 1970-86; paraprofl. for learning disabled, emotionally disturbed, speech impaired children BOCES III, Lindenhurst, N.Y., 1986—; founder All That Glitters is Not Gold. Editor (newsletter) The Who's News, 1980-84. Treas., pres. PTA, P.S. 64, Ozone Park, N.Y., 1978-84; tutor Vols. of Am., Ozone Park, 1976-85. Mem. NAFE, Spl. Edn. PTA. Roman Catholic. Home: 502 10th St West Babylon NY 11704

ORLANDO, ANDREA LEE, financial planner; b. N.Y.C., Sept. 19, 1953; d. Julius Jean and Margaret Jane (Leichter) Matto; m. Dino Fontana, Aug. 4, 1974 (div. 1980); m. Gary William Orlando, June 19, 1983. BS in Acctg., Fairleigh Dickinson U., 1975, MBA in Fin., 1982. Cert. fin. planner. Owner, mgr. Dean Andre Inc., Englewood, N.J., 1974-79; asst. mgr. sales T.J. Lipton Inc., Moonachi, N.J., 1978-80; mgr. sales audit Petrie Corp., Secaucus, N.J., 1980-82; controller Data Mgmt. Services, N.Y.C., 1982-85; planner fin. Madison Fin. Group, Green Village, N.J., 1985-87; fin. planner Summit Fin. Resources, Livingston, N.J., 1987—; adviser fin. Am. Stage Corp., Teaneck, N.J., 1985—, Summit Fin. Resources, Livingston, N.J. Sec. Concerned Citizens Assn., Denville, N.J., 1985; fund raiser Am. Lung Assn., Elizabeth, N.J., 1982;. Mem. Nat. Assn. Accts., NAFE, Internat. Assn. Fin. Planners, Internat. Conf. Fin. Planners, N.J. Assn. Women Bus. Owners, Hunterdon County C. of C., Carpe Diem Club. Republican. Presbyterian. Club: Rockaway River Country (Denville).

ORLANDO, FRANCES, office manager, paralegal; b. Bklyn., Nov. 9, 1954; d. Gaspar and Rose (Errera) O. BA magna cum laude, Marymount Manhattan Coll., 1976; cert. paralegal, Paralegal Inst., 1989. Claims examiner Underwriters Adjusting Co., N.Y.C., 1976-79; claims rep. Atlantic Mut. Ins. Co., N.Y.C., 1979-83; office mgr. Johnson, Tannen, Brecher, Fishman, Feit & Heller, P.C., N.Y.C., 1983—. Mem. Manhattan Paralegal Assn., Alpha Chi. Democrat. Roman Catholic.

ORLANDO, JOY ANN, educator; b. New London, Conn., Mar. 12, 1965; d. Christian Joseph and Kathleen Teresa (Foss) O. AS in Mktg. and Mgmt., Johnson & Wales U., Providence, 1986; BS in Bus. Edn., Mgmt., Johnson & Wales U., 1988. Tchr. Adminstrv. asst. Naval Underwater Systems Ctr., New London, Conn., 1983-85; computer asst. Naval Underwriter Systems Ctr., New London, Conn., 1986-87; tchr. aide, tutor Johnson & Wales U., Providence, 1985-87; analyst Aquidneck Mgmt. Assn., New London, Conn.; legal asst. Conn., 1988--; instr. adult and evening bus. program Towns of Old Lyme, Montville, East Lyme and New London. Contributing Mem. Planned Parenthood Fedn. of Am., Nat. Orgn. of Women. Mem. Nat. Assn. of Female Execs., Nat. Bus. Edn. Assn., Am. Entrepreneurial Assn., MADD. Democrat. Roman Catholic. Home: 11 Palmer Dr Gales Ferry CT 06335

ORLANDO, KATHY REBER, human resource manager; b. Reading, Pa., Nov. 17, 1942; d. Clarence I. and Mildred M. (Mildenberger) Reber; m. Frank P. Orlando, Aug. 23, 1942; children: Jeffrey M., Christopher R. Grad., Quality Coll., Winter Park, Fla., 1988; Student, Pa. State U., 1990—. Book keeper, sec. Albert Tire Svc., Reading, 1960-67; legal sec. Ehrlich & Ehrlich, Reading, 1967-74, Edward D. Trexler, Jr., Reading, 1974-79, Wright, Manning & Sagendorph, Norristown, Pa., 1980-83; pers. asst. Videotek, Inc., Pottstown, Pa., 1983-86; notary pub., 1974—; human resources mgr. Videotek, Inc., Pottstown, 1986—. Contbr. articles to profl. jours. Vol. Babe Ruth Baseball, 1986—; sunday sch. aid St. Basil the Gt. Roman Cath. Ch., 1981. Mem. Kimberton Youth Athletic League (treas., vol.), Phoenix-Marion Youth Club (team mother 1979-86, vol.), Soc. For Human Resource Mgmt. Greater Pottstown Chpt. (chmn. publicity), Nat. Assn. Female Execs., Nat. Assn. Legal Secretaries, Pa. Assn. Legal Secretaries (treas., historian, publ. editor, 1970-86), Berks County Legal Secretaries Assn. (pres., v.p., treas., historian, publ. editor, 1970-86). Democrat. Home: 1209 S Rapps Dam Rd Phoenixville PA 19460 Office: Videotek Inc 243 Shoemaker Rd Pottstown PA 19464

ORLANS, F(LORA) BARBARA, bioethics associate; b. Birmingham, Eng., Jan. 14, 1928; came to U.S., 1956; d. Christopher and Flora Christine (Brookes) Hughes; m. Herbert C. Morton, June 19, 1982; children: Andrew Brookes Orlans, Nicholas Motcomb Orlans. BSc in Physiology/Anatomy, Birmingham (Eng.) U., 1949; MS in Physiology, London U., 1954, PhD in Physiology, 1956. Physiology instr. dept. medicine Johns Hopkins Hosp., Balt., 1956; rsch. pharmacologist Nat. Heart Inst., NIH, Bethesda, Md., 1956-60; freelance writer, 1967-73; sr. staff scientist Med. Ctr. George Washington U., Washington, 1973-74; health scientist adminstr. Nat. Heart, Lung & Blood Inst. NIH, Bethesda, 1974-77; exec. dir., adv. coun. Heart Inst. NIH, Bethesda, 1977-70; staff scientist cardiac diseases NIH, Bethesda, 1979-84; dir. Scientists Ctr. Animal Welfare, Bethesda, 1984-88; rsch. assoc. Kennedy Inst. Ethics Georgetown U., Washington, 1989—; founding pres. Scientists Ctr. Animal Welfare, Bethesda, 1978-84; chair Parks Found. for Animal Welfare, Portland, Maine, 1987-90. Author: Animal Care: From Protozoa to Small Mammals, 1977; editor: Scientific Perspectives on Animal Welfare, 1982, Effective Animal Care & Use Committees, 1987; contbr. articles to refereed jours. Grantee Geraldine R. Dodge Found., Morristown, N.J., 1980—, ethical values program NSF, 1987-88. Mem. Am. Soc. Pharmacology, Nat. Sci. Tchrs. Assn., N.Y. Acad. Scis., Nat. Assn. Biology Tchrs. Office: Kennedy Inst Ethics Georgetown U 37th and P St NW Washington DC 20057

ORLY, ELVIRA JOLAN, lawyer; b. Berkeley, Calif., Nov. 22, 1948; d. Cyrill Vladimir and Elvira Maria (Erni) O.; m. Joseph A. Jeffrey, Aug. 17, 1979 (dec. June 1990). BS, U. Calif., Berkeley, 1970; MBA, JD, U. Calif., 1975. Bar: Calif. 1976, D.C. 1878. Tax atty. Pettit & Martin, San Francisco, 1975-76; legis. dir. for Senator S.I. Hayakawa, Washington, 1976-80; dir. legis. and regulatory affairs Edison Electric Inst., Washington, 1980-82, Getty (Texaco), Washington, 1982-85, Allied Signal, Washington, 1985-88; Washington counsel Browning-Ferris Industries, 1988-89; v.p. market devel. Browning-Ferris Industries, The Netherlands, 1989-90; v.p. European community affairs Browning-Ferris Industries. Bd. dirs., Codornices coun Camp Fire Girls, 1973-75. Mem. world champion U.S. Fencing Team, 1974, 75, U.S. Olympic fencing squad, 1976. Mem. ABA, Calif. Bar Assn., D.C. Bar Assn., U.S. Fencing Assn. (treas. 1987—), Tax Coalition (bd. dirs. 1983-86), Behind the Tree Tax Group (chmn. 1985), Nat. Women's Econ. Alliance (bd. govs. 1983—), Women in Govt. Rels., Assn. Former Senate Employees, Prytanean Club, Jr. League, Beta Gamma Sigma, Alpha Xi Delta. Office: Browning Ferris Industries, PO Box 2449, 3500 GK Utrecht The Netherlands

ORMES, MARY ANN, social service director; b. Crawfordsville, Ind., June 10, 1925; d. Frederick Keegan Otto and Gladys (Roach) Otto Peck; m. Robert Verner Ormes, Sept. 2, 1950 (dec. 1984); children: Julia C., Carolyn V., Margaret F. BA, Miami U., Oxford, Ohio, 1947. Exec. dir. Sr. Citizens Employment & Svcs. of Alexandria (Va.) Inc., 1974—. Bd. dirs. LWV, Alexandria, 1955-58, United Way, 1963-69, pres., 1967-69. Home: 2810 Central Ave Alexandria VA 22302

ORMSBY, DEBRA HOBIN, educator; b. Buffalo, Aug. 23, 1952; d. James Floyd and Margaret Ann (Farrell) Hobin; m. Wayne Keith Ormsby, July 14, 1978. AA, Hilbert Coll., 1972; BA, SUNY, Fredonia, 1974, MA, 1977; cert. advanced study ednl. adminstrn., SUNY, Fredoia, 1990. Cert. tchr., N.Y. Instr. Pine Valley Cen. Sch., South Dayton, N.Y., 1974—, chair English dept., 1978—; asst. prin. Pine Valley Cen. Sch., South Dayton, 1987—; student tchr. coord., advanced placement program coord. Fredonia State Univ. Coll., 1987—. Contbr. to local newspaper. Named Tchr. of Excellence award N.Y. State Engring. Coun., 1987-88, U.S. Nat. Collegiate award U.S. Achievement Acad., 1989. Mem. AAUW (v.p. 1988-90, edn. found. chair 1986-88), Lakeshore Women's Coalition. Office: Pine Valley Cen Sch Rte 83 South Dayton NY 14138

ORNBURN, KRISTEE JEAN, accountant; b. Moberly, Mo., Feb. 24, 1956; d. Lloyd Edward and Ruth Maxine (Major) O. AA, Moberly Jr. Coll., 1976; BSBA magna cum laude, U. Mo., Columbia, 1978. CPA, Mo. Teller City Bank & Trust, Moberly, 1974-78; supr. gen. ledger Orscheln Farm & Home Supply, Moberly, 1978-80, supr. accounts payable, 1980, supr. sr. acctg., 1981-82, mgr. acctg., 1982-86; controller Orscheln Consumer Products Div., Moberly, 1986—. Youth worker Carpenter St. Bapt. Ch., Moberly. Recipient Youth Leadership award Moberly C. of C., 1974. Mem. Am. Inst. CPAs, Mo. Soc. CPAs, AAUW (v.p.), Am. Bus. Women's Assn., U. Mo. Alumni Assn. Democrat. Club: Bapt. Young Women (Moberly). Office: Orscheln Farm & Home Supply 339 N Williams Moberly MO 65270

ORNDOFF, BETTY KATHERINE MADAGAN, educator; b. Winchester, Va., Nov. 17, 1934; d. Harold Fred Sr. and Mildred Catherine (Anderson) Madagan; m. Edwin Pifer Orndoff, Dec. 21, 1958; 1 child, Edwina Katherine. BS, James Madison U., 1958. Cert. tchr. Va. Tchr. Robinson Meml. Sch., Winchester, Va., 1958-59; sales assoc. Bell's Ladies, Winchester, 1970-80; tchr. Va. Ave Sch., Winchester, 1959-61, Kline Sch., Winchester, 1961-63; owner, mgr. Orndoff's Appraisal & Auction Svc., Winchester, 1973—, appraiser, 1987—; substitute tchr. Frederick County Pub. Sch., Winchester, 1963-86. Libr. chairwomen The Women's Civic League of Winchester, fashion show com., 1964-89, bd. dirs. 1973-88; vol. Preservation of Hist. Winchester, Winchester-Frederick County Hist. Soc.; v.p. Blue Ridge Dem. Women, charter mem., 1970, publicity chairwoman 1985-86; active Shenandoah Valley Music Festival, 1986—, Shenandoah Arts Coun., 1989—, Friends of Handley Libr., 1980—, Dem. Nat. Com., 1988—, Dem. Party of Va., 1983—, Winchester Dem. Com.; asst. to audio-visual chair Blue Ridge Fine Arts League, Inc., 1981-88; auction chair Winchester-Frederick County C. of C., 1983-89. Mem. AAUW (treas. 1982-85, membership v.p. 1985-88, 90—, bd. dirs. Winchester br. 1982—, life mem. 1959—), The Club Continental (charter mem. 1959). Home and Office: 621 S Stewart Winchester VA 22601

ORNSTEIN, ETHEL RAE COHODAS, civic worker, retired educator; b. Marinette, Wis., Feb. 12, 1905; d. Aaron Modecai and Geraldine Helen (Mansfield) Cohodas; m. Harold Abraham Ornstein, June 30, 1934 (dec.); children: Gerri, Lee, Frye. Student, Sorbonne, France, 1924; BA, U. Mich., 1925, MA, 1928. Asst. prin. St. Mary's Coll., St. Mary's City, Md., 1925-28; dept. head East Sr. High Sch., Green Bay, Wis., 1929-34. Author: I Believe. Pres. Outagamie County United Way, Appleton, Wis., 1954-56, Vis. Nurse Assn., Appleton, 1957-61, Outagamie County Mental Health Assn., 1961-65; mem. Appleton Parks and Recreation Commn., 1950-62, Govs. Commn. on Human Rights, 1960-68, Wis. Arts Coun.; founder, pres. Fox Valley Symphony Orch. Assn.; liaison officer Outagamie County; chair Peabody Manore Retirement Home; chmn. Salvation Army, Appleton, 1964-68; past edn. dir. YMCA, Appleton; edn. chmn. Sisterhood Temple Emanuel, Sarasota, Fla., Selby Libr. Bd., Sarasota; mem. social planning com. Hadassah, Sarasota; Appleton urban rep. to Outagamie County Bd. for Rural Problems. Named Woman of Yr., Appleton C. of C., 1963, Orchid Lady, Appleton Post Crescent,1964, Woman of Decade, City of Appleton, 1970. Mem. AAUW (past pres. 1940), John and Mable North Ringling Mus., Sarasota Opera Assn., Nat. Coun. Jewish Women, Am. Assn. for Rehab., Asolo Ctr. for Performing Arts, Century Club of Sarasota Meml. Hosp. (life), Sarasota Rotary Anns (life). Republican. Home: 770 S Palm Ave Embassy House Sarasota FL 34236

OROSZ, JULIA ELIZABETH, nurse, educator, consultant; b. Alliance, Ohio, Nov. 5, 1948; d. William and Rachel (Dosa) O. Nursing diploma Luth. Hosp. Sch. Nursing, Cleve., 1970; BS in Nursing, U. Cin., 1973; MS in Nursing, U. Ala.-Birmingham, 1975. RN, Ohio, Tex. Staff nurse Children's Hosp. Akron, Ohio, 1970-71, 75-77; health clinic nurse U. Cin., 1972-73; asst. prof. Maryville Coll. St. Louis, 1977-80, U. Tex. Health Sci. Ctr., San Antonio, 1980-84; clin. specialist Barberton Citizen's Hosp., Ohio, 1984-85; regional perinatal edn. coordinator Children's Med. Ctr., Akron, 1985—; health care assoc. Sch. Medicine, Washington U., St. Louis, 1978-79; mem. adolescent pregnancy task force on community awareness Summit County Adolescent Services Network, 1985—; grad. asst. prof. Kent State U. Sch. Nursing, 1987-89; chmn. health care services Luth. Ch. Mo. Synod: Internat. Youth Gathering, 1983. Editor NeoGram, 1985-87; contbg. mng. editor Northeast Ohio Perinatal Newsletter, 1985—. Vol. ARC, San Antonio, Akron, 1970—; speaker San Antonio Coalition for Children, Youth and Families, 1980-84, Children's Med. Ctr., Akron, 1985—; vol. Carter Presdl. Campaign, Akron, 1976; pres. employee found. Children's Hosp. Med. Ctr., Akron, 1990; mem. child find subcom. Ohio Dept. Health, 1987. Named to Outstanding Young Women Am., U.S. Jaycees, 1981, 83; Klaus Meml. scholar Luth. Hosp. Sch. Nursing, 1970; grad. fellow U. Ala.-Birmingham, 1973. Mem. LWV, Nurses Assn. of the Am. Coll. of Ob-gyn. (ednl. coordinator Ohio sect. 1987-89), Nat. Assn. Neonatal Nurses (charter), Nat. Perinatal Assn. (coun. 1986—), Ohio Perinatal Assn. (bd. dirs. 1985—, pres. elect 1989), U. Cin. Alumni Assn. (life), Nat. Mus. Women in the Arts (charter), Sigma Theta Tau. Avocations: counted cross stitch, piano, pipe organ, cooking, painting, race walking. Home: 2436 Chatham Rd Akron OH 44313 Office: Children's Med Ctr of Akron Div Neonatology 281 Locust St Akron OH 44308

O'ROURKE, MARGUERITE PATRICIA, insurance company official; b. N.Y.C., May 10, 1950; d. William Lawrence and Olive Rose (Ponte) O'R.; B.A. in Polit. Sci. (Ednl. Opportunity grantee, N.J. State scholar), Am. U., 1972. Adminstrn. asst. Asso. Merchandising Corp., Washington, 1972-73; various positions Savage/Fogarty Co., Inc., Alexandria, Va., 1973-79; property mgr. Community Mgmt. Corp., Reston, Va., 1979-80; property mgr. Braedon Cos., Washington, 1980-81, dir. property mgmt., 1981-82; v.p. bldgs. adminstrn. Smithy Braedon Property Co., Washington, 1982-83; sr. real estate officer-asset mgmt. Northwestern Mut. Life Real Estate Div., 1983—; corp. sec. Savage/Fogarty Co., Inc., 1978-79. Intern Senator Claiborne Pell, R.I., 1971. Mem. Inst. Real Estate Mgrs., Internat. Council Shopping Ctrs., Nat. Assn. Female Execs., Washington Bd. Realtors, Save The Bay, Environ. Def. Fund, Union Concerned Scientists, Cousteau Soc., Nat. Trust for Historic Preservation, Smithsonian Instn., Am. Film Inst. Office: 1133 20th St Washington DC 20036

ORPHANIDES, NORA CHARLOTTE, ballet educator; b. Bklyn., June 4, 1951; d. M.T. and Mary Elsie (Tilly) Feffer; m. James Mark Orphanides, July 1, 1972; children: Mark, Elaine, Jennine. BA, CUNY, 1973; postgrad., Joffrey Sch., N.Y.C., 1970-75, Sch. Princeton Ballet, 1976-86. Cert. speech and hearing handicapped tchr. Sr. sales assoc. Met. Mus. Art, N.Y.C., 1970-86; membership asst. Patrons Lounge, M.M.A., N.Y.C., 1987—; mem. faculty Princeton (N.J.) Ballet Soc., 1983—. Mem. cast Princeton Ballet ann. Nutcracker, 1985—. Fundraising gala chmn. Princeton Ballet, 1985, 86, chmn. spl. events, 1987—, trustee, 1986—; vol. libr. Plainsboro (N.J.) Free Libr., 1985; program solicitation chmn. to benefit Princeton Med. Ctr., 1988, T-shirt chmn. benefit, 1990; mem. worship and arts commn. Nassau Presbyn. Ch., 1989, 90; dinner chmn. Bach Music Festival, Nasau Ch., 1989, Music Festival Nassau Ch., Cambridge Singers, 1990. Mem. Princeton Med. Ctr. Aux. Democrat. Home: 35 Brearly Rd Princeton NJ 08540 Office: Princeton Ballet Soc 262 Alexander St Princeton NJ 08540

ORPHANOS, MARY JOAN, communications executive; b. Chgo., Apr. 23, 1960; d. George James and Mary Elizabeth (Quinn) O. AAS, Coll. Dupage, Ill., 1980. Tester Rockwell Communications, Downers Grove, Ill., 1977-81, electronic technician, 1981-85, tech. support engr., 1985—. Recipient Voice of Democracy award VFW, 1976. Democrat. Roman Catholic. Home: 214 Porter Ln Bolingbrook IL 60439 Office: Rockwell Communications 8245 S Lemont Rd Downers Grove IL 60516

ORR, AMY, art educator; b. Washington, July 15, 1954; d. Harold and Sara (Bloomfield) Taubin; m. Ami Orr, Aug. 8, 1974 (div. Aug. 1984); m. John Robert Woodin, May 7, 1989. BFA, Bezalel Acad., Jerusalem, 1972-77; MA, U. of the Arts, Phila., 1981; MFA, Tyler Sch. Art, 1989. Art program dir. Bucks County Community Coll., Newtown, Pa., 1981-85; asst. prof. art Rosemont (Pa.) Coll., 1985—. Editor, author: Artists Guide to Philadelphia, 1981, 2nd edit., 1982, 3rd edit., 1984, 4th edit., 1987, 5th edit., 1990; one woman and group shows include Design Arts Gallery, Drexel U., Phila., 1990, Nexus Found. for Today's Art, Phila., 1989, Temple Gallery, Phila., 1989, Perkins Ctr. for the Arts, Moorestown, N.J., 1989. Home: 4834 Walton Ave Philadelphia PA 19143 Office: Rosemont Coll Montgomery Ave Philadelphia PA 19010

ORR, KAY A., governor of Nebraska; b. Burlington, Iowa, Jan. 2, 1939; d. Ralph Robert and Sadie Lucille (Skoglund) Stark; m. William Dayton Orr, Sept. 26, 1957; children: John William, Suzanne. Student, U. Iowa, 1956-57. Exec. asst. to Gov. Charles Thone, Lincoln, Nebr., 1979-81; treas. State of Nebr., Lincoln, 1981-86, gov., 1987—. Del., mem. platform com. Rep. Nat. Conv., 1976, 80, 84, co-chmn. 1984, chmn. 1988; trustee Hastings (Nebr.) Coll., 1985—; mem. Commn. on Presdl. Debates; chmn. Nat. Gov.'s Assn. Transportation, Commerce and Communications; mem. Nat. Gov.'s Assn. Task Force on Fgn. Markets; mem. Nat. Adv. Coun. on Rural Devel., 1988. Named Outstanding Young Rep. Woman in Nebr., 1969, Nebr. Wildlife Fedn. Conservationist of Yr., 1989. *

ORR, LILLIAN JENELL BROWN, publishing executive; b. Atlanta, Feb. 17, 1952; d. Sanford O'Neal and Clara Lillian (Simmons) Brown; m. David Paul Orr, Apr. 28, 1972; children: Deborah Cheryl, Stephanie Michelle. G-rad. high sch., Conyers, Ga. Gen. mgr. Citizen Pub. Co., Inc., Conyers, 1969—. Sec.-treas. New Life Praise Ctr. Mem. NAFE, Am. Bus. Women's Assn (pres., chair publicity com., treas. New Roc charter chpt., Woman of Yr. 1988), Am. Inst. Profl. Bookkeepers (chmn. Strut com.). Office: Citizen Pub Co Inc 969 S Main St Conyers GA 30207

ORR, MARCIA, child development researcher; b. Anamosa, Iowa, Mar. 2, 1949; d. Harold Edward Eiben and Clara Elizabeth (Hubbard) E.; m. Robert J. Orr, Sept. 6, 1969; 1 child, Jennifer. Student, U. Iowa, 1977; student, St. Xavier Coll., Chgo., 1981. Edn. Bookkeeper Monticello State Bank, 1967-69; exec. sec. Davenport Bank and Trust, 1969-73; asst. educator Elisabeth Ludeman Devel. Ctr., Park Forest, Ill., 1979; tchr. Flossmoor Hills (Ill.) Elem. Sch., 1980-1984; exec. dir. Co-Care, Inc., Park Forest, 1984-89; child development researcher Flossmoor, Ill., 1989—; officer Boleo Childcare Ctr., Iowa City, 1975-77. Religion Tchr. Infant Jesus of Prague Flossmoor Ill. 1982--; Chorus Flossmoor Ill. 1987-89. Mem. Nat. Sec. Assn., Womens Club, PTO. Democratic. Catholic. Home and Office: 2250 Marston Ln Flossmoor IL 60422

ORR, MARJORIE ANN, sales/marketing training executive; b. Houston, Nov. 13, 1961; d. John H. and Ann Salome (McLaughlin) O. BBA, Tex. Tech U., 1984. Sales rep. Dun Bradstreet, Dallas; mktg. mgr. Chgo. region Am. Learning Corp., Chgo., eastern div. mktg. mgr., dir. of Britannica, learning ctr.; ind. sales rep. Rocky Mountain Bankcard System. With Tex. State Guard, 1980-82. Recipient Nat. Golden Attitude award, Nat. Outstanding Mgmt. award, 4 nat. sales awards, 3 regional mktg. awards. Home: 1461 Creekside Dr Wheaton IL 60187

ORR, SANDRA JANE, pharmacist, civic worker; b. Marion, Ohio, June 27, 1930; d. Lawrence Edward and Wanita Izell (Noyes) Schneider; m. Ross Moore Orr, Jr., Aug. 12, 1951; children: Sandra K. Orr Whiston, Sara L. Orr Cochrane. BS in Pharmacy, Med. Coll. Va., 1952. Pharmacist Atkiinson & Howard, Richmond, Va., 1952-54, Schneider's Walgreen Agy., Kenton, Ohio, 1954-73; part-time pharmacist Drug Svc., Bethlehem, Pa., 1954-57, Fastchnacts' Drug, Bethlehem, 1954-57. One-woman shows in oils, pastels and watercolors. Ball chmn. St. Luke's Hosp., Bethlehem, 1987; bd. dirs. Hist. Bethlehem, 1988—; liturgical dance dir. 1st Presbyn. Ch., 1968, 78; needlework instr. YMCA, 1980-81; movement instr. Orff tchrs., ballet instr. Lehigh U. football team, 1966; docent Allentown Art Mus., 1956-68, Art Goes to Sch., 1960-62. Mem. Jr. League Lehigh Valley. Republican. Presbyterian. Home: 405 High St Bethlehem PA 18018

ORR, THERESA J. CASTELLANA, academic official; b. Waltham, Mass., Dec. 5, 1941; d. Angelo and Josephine (Vaccarello) C.; divorced; children: Lisa M., Allison J. BA, Brandeis U., 1963; MEd, Northeastern U., 1976. Tchr. Waltham Pub. Schs., 1963-71; asst. dir. fin. aid Brandeis U., Waltham, 1971-77; dir. fin. aid Sch. Medicine Tufts U. Sch. Medicine, Boston, 1977-80; dir. fin. aid Sch. Medicine Harvard Med. Sch., Boston, 1980-90, asst. dean student affairs, 1990—; chmn. Loan Counseling Task Force Mass., 1983-88; rec. sec. 13 Med. Sch. Consortium, 1984-87; mem. faculty Nat. Assn. Coll. and Univ. Bus. Officers, 1986—; cons. U. Iowa Med. Sch., 1987; lectr., conf. presenter. Contbr. articles to profl. publs. Chmn. parent's council Merrimack Coll., North Andover, Mass., 1985-88; faculty coordinator Harvard U. Program for Persons with Disabilities, 1988—. Recipient spl. ann. award Mass. Higher Edn. Assistance Corp., 1988. Mem. Am. Assn. Med. Colls. (fin. aid com. northeast group student affairs 1982-86), Nat. Assn. Student Fin. Aid Adminstrs., Mass. Assn. Student Fin. Aid ADminstrs., Harvard Fin. Aid Officers Council (chmn. 1984-85), Cath. Alumni Club (Boston). Office: Harvard U Med Sch 25 Shattuck St Boston MA 02115

ORR-CAHALL, CHRISTINA, art gallery director, art historian; b. Wilkes-Barre, Pa., Apr. 12, 1947; d. William R.A. and Anona (Snyder) Boben; m. Richard Cahall; children: Fitz, Walker. BA magna cum laude, Mt. Holyoke Coll., 1969; MA, Yale U., 1974, M in Philosophy, 1975, PhD, 1979. Curator of collections Norton Gallery Art, West Palm Beach, Fla., 1975-77; asst. prof. Calif. Poly. State U., San Luis Obispo, 1978-81, Disting. prof., 1981; dir. art div., chief curator Oakland (Calif.) Mus., 1981-88; chief exec. officer Corcoran Gallery Art, Washington, 1988-89, dir.; dir. Norton Gallery and Sch. of Arts, West Palm Beach, 1990—. Author: Addison Mizner: Architect of Dreams and Realities, 1974, Gordon Cook, 1987; editor: The Art of California, 1984. Office: Norton Gallery and Sch Art 1451 S Olive Ave West Palm Beach FL 33401*

ORRIS, MICHELE MARIE, public relations, marketing and advertising consultant; b. Norwalk, Conn., Feb. 23, 1958; d. Stephen Joseph and Arcenia (Rodriguez) O. Student, U. N.Mex., 1976-78; BA with honors, U. Bridgeport, 1980, postgrad., 1981-83. Tchr. Norwalk Pub. Schs., 1981-83; head tchr. presch. Norwalk YMCA, 1983-84; exec. dir. Norwalk Seaport Assn., 1984-86; cons., 1986-87, Barnum Festival, Bridgeport, Conn., 1987-88, P.T. Barnum Found., Bridgeport, 1987; mgr. communications Human Resources Inc., Stamford, Conn., 1987; owner, mgr. Michele Orris, Norwalk, Conn., 1988—; dir. pub. rels. YWCA of Stamford, 1989—; dir. pub. rels. YWCA of Stamford (Conn.), 1989—. Past sec., pres. Marvin Beach Assn., East Norwalk; asst. dir. pub. rels. Conn. Women's Celebration, 1986; chmn. subcom. auditorium com. New City Hall, Norwalk; active numerous other civic orgns.; bd. dirs. Southwestern Conn. coun. Girl Scouts U.S., 1987—; bd. dirs. pub. rels. and devel. Stamford (Conn.) YWCA, 1989. Recipient award City of Norwalk, 1987. Mem. Greens Farms Acad. Alumni Assn. (pres., class sec.), Phi Sigma Iota (life). Democrat. Roman Catholic. Home and Office: 108 Gregory Blvd Norwalk CT 06855

ORTBERG, NATALIE ANN JARAMILLO, aerospace engineer; b. Albuquerque, June 29, 1957; d. John Gilbert and Anita (Blackwood) Jaramillo; m. Kenneth Lynn Ortberg, Dec. 18, 1976; children: Adam Jaramillo, Katherine Lynn. BS in Bus. Mgmt., U. LaVerne, Calif., 1980. Assoc. planning analyst ITT Fed. Electric, Vandenberg AFB, Calif., 1977-80; info. systems mgr. Mountain Bell, Mesa, Ariz., 1980-82; field engr. Martin Marietta Aerospace, Vandenberg AFB, 1982-85; sr. test engr. Martin Marietta Aerospace, Denver, 1985-86, staff engr., 1986—; speaker in field. Mem. Nat. Mgmt. Assn., Am. Mgmt. Assn., Martin Marietta Mgmt. Assn., Career Women's Assn. Roman Catholic. Home: 2266 Thistle Ridge Circle Highlands Ranch CO 80126 Office: Martin Marietta Aerospace PO Box 179 Denver CO 80201

ORTEGO, GILDA BAEZA, librarian, information professional; b. El Paso, Tex., Mar. 29, 1952; d. Efren and Bertha (Singh) Baeza; m. Felipe de Ortego y Gasca, Dec. 21, 1986. BA, Tex. Woman's U., 1974; MLS, U. Tex., 1976; cert., Hispanic Leadership Inst., 1988. Pub. svcs. libr. El Paso Community Coll., 1976-77; ethnic studies libr. U. N.Mex., Albuquerque, 1977-81; br. head libr. El Paso Pub. Libr., 1981-82; dep. head libr. Mex.-Am. Svcs. Mex.-Am. Svcs., El Paso Pub. Libr., 1982-84; libr. Mex.-Am. Studies U. Tex. Libr., Austin, 1984-87; libr. Phoenix Pub. Libr., 1986-89; assoc. libr., west campus Ariz. State U., Phoenix, 1989—; speaker and cons. in field. Founding editor jour. La Lista, 1983-84; founding indexer Chicano Periodical Index, 1981-86; reviewer jour. Voice for Youth Advocates, 1989—; contbr. poetry and articles to books and jours. Mem. ALA, Ariz. State Libr. Assn. (pres. svcs. Spanish speaking Roundtable 1989-90), Reforma (pres. El Paso chpt. 1983, pres. Ariz. chpt. 1989-90), Unlimited Potential, Inc. (sec. bd. 1987-89), Mujer Inc. (treas. 1988-89), Hispanic Leadership Inst. Alumni Assn. Home: 5038 S Hardy #2120 Tempe AZ 85282 Office: Ariz State U Libr West Campus PO Box 37100 Phoenix AZ 85069

ORTENBERG, ELISABETH CLAIBORNE See CLAIBORNE, LIZ

ORTIZ, FRANCESCA, lawyer; b. San Antonio, Oct. 11, 1964; d. Carlos and Evelyn Grace (Castanon) O. BA, U. Tex., 1986; JD, Harvard U., 1989. Bar: Tex. 1989. Assoc. Jones, Day, Reavis & Pogue, Austin, Tex., 1989—. Author: Harvard Law Review jour., 1989, editor, 1987-88, exec. editor, 1988-89. Mem. ABA, Travis County Bar Assn., Tex. Young Lawyers Assn., Austin Young Lawyers Assn. Democrat. Home: 4911 Ave H Austin TX 78751 Office: Jones Day Reavis & Pogue 301 Congress Ave Ste 1200 Austin TX 78751

ORTIZ, IRMA, retired university administrator, interpreter; b. Calexico, Calif., May 28, 1922; d. Camilo Enrique and Emelina (Trujillo) O.; 1 adopted child, Kumari Mary Ruth Danda. AA, Imperial Valley Coll., 1942; BBA, Academia Coss y Leon, 1942. Cert. profl. sec., 1966. Stenographer U. Calif. Agrl. Extension, El Centro, 1942, sec., 1943-64; adminstrv. sec. U. Calif. Coop. Extension, El Centro, 1965-79, adminstrv. asst., 1980-86, ret.; speaker various high schs. and colls. Dir. Salvation Army, El Centro, 1968-79; chmn. Imperial Valley Coll. Community review com., Calif., 1977-78; pres. Imperial Valley Community Concert Assn., 1983-86; editor Imperial Arts Council, 1987-88; docent Imperial Valley Pioneers Mus., 1987—; sec. Imperial County Retired Employees Assn., 1988-89. Recipient Red Feather award Community Chest, El Centro, 1953; named Employee of Yr. Imperial County, 1969. Mem. Pilot Club (sec. western region 1968-69, 1st v.p. El Centro chpt. 1969-70), Beta Sigma Phi. Republican. Roman Catholic. Club: Euterpe (Mex.) (pres. 1945). Avocations: travel, reading, music, silvercraft, painting. Home: 918 Rockwood Ave Calexico CA 92231

ORTIZ, MELBA ANABEL, accountant; b. Rowe, N.Mex., Sept. 1, 1947; d. David and Rita (Ortiz) Padilla; m. Phillip R. Gomez, Feb. 14, 1967 (div. Oct. 1967); m. Lawrence Sabino Ortiz, Jan. 8, 1971; 1 child, Doreen. BA in Acctg., U. No. Iowa, 1980. Office mgr. Lazar of Santa Fe, 1967-71; acct.-auditor Mus. N.Mex., Santa Fe, 1971-76; bus. mgr. Assn. Coll., Univ. and Community Arts Adminstrs., Madison, Wis., 1977-79; acct. Bearing Distbrs., Inc., Waterloo, Iowa, 1980-81; bus. mgr. arts and lectrs. U. Calif., Santa Barbara, 1981-88, mgr. accounts receivable billing-cashier and collections, 1988—, mem. staff assembly, 1985-87; cons. Monte Farris Visual communications, 1984-85, El Freebird's Restaurant, Santa Barbara, 1987, PCPA Theaterfest, Santa Maria, 1987. Mem. U. Calif.-Santa Barbara Latina Network, 1985-87. Mem. Box Office Mgmt. Internat. (workshop leader San Antonio 1987, co-chmn. nat. standards and ethics com. 1988), U. Calif.-Santa Barbara Collections Mgrs., U. Calif.-Santa Barbara Staff Assn. (citation for excellence 1985). Office: U Calif 1311 Cheadle Hall Santa Barbara CA 93106

ORTIZ, MIRANDA RENEE, computer sales executive; b. Tulare, Calif., Jan. 28, 1962; d. Manuel Balestreous and Mary Helen (Torrez) O.; m. Harlod Lloyd Wyckoff II, June 29, 1979 (div. 1983); 1 child, Nathan Lloyd. BBA, Calif. State U., Fresno, 1986. Asst. sec. Acron Architects, Tulare, 1986-87; salesperson Bronzan's Sports World, Tulare, 1986-87; salesperson, asst. mgr. OnLine Connecting Point, Tulare, 1987—; cons. in field. Chairperson for student site counsel Palo Verde Sch., Calif. Mem. Visalia C. of C. Home: 5100 S Pratt Tulare CA 93274

ORTIZ-TRUSCOTT, MARGARITA, association executive; b. Santa Fe, June 15, 1942; d. Frank and Maria (Garcia) Ortiz Davis; m. Francis Charles Truscott, Jr. BA in Sociology, Temple U., 1968; AS, Mary Rogers Coll., Ossining, N.Y., 1965. Community organizer Archdiocese of N.Y., N.Y.C., 1964-66; caseworker Cath. Charities, Santa Fe, 1968-69; asst. exec. dir. Girl Scouts U.S.A. - Mile Hi Coun., Denver, 1970—. Treas.-sec. Las Mujeres - Lulac, Denver, 1981-84; active Colo. Women of Color, Denver, 1990—, Hispanics of Colo., Denver, 1986—; bd. dirs. Mi Casa Women's Resource Ctr., 1987—, pres. 1987-88. Recipient Adelante Mujer Hispana award, 1984. Mem. Leadership Denver Alumnae, Kiwanis (found bd. dirs. 1989—), Zonta (treas. 1989-90). Democrat. Roman Catholic. Office: Girl Scouts Mile Hi Council 400 S Broadway Denver CO 80209

ORTMANN, DOROTHEA, music educator; b. Balt., Jan. 12, 1912; d. Otto Rudolph and Margaret May (Donoho) Ortmann; m. Constantine Seletzky, Feb. 14, 1942 (dec.). Cert. in Piano, Peabody Inst., Balt., 1930, cert. in Harmony, 1934, artists diploma, 1935. Tchr. music Peabody Inst., Balt., 1931-41, Miami (Fla.) Conservatory of Music, 1942-45, Dorothea Ortmann-Seletzky Studio, Balt., 1946—; lectr. in field; judge Md. Fedn. of Music. Author: The Music of Otto Ortmann, 1984; composer of works for piano, violin and songs; concert pianist, 1925-61. Mem. Charles Village Civic Assn., Balt., 1976, Balt. Opera Guild. Recipient of Harold Randolph Meml. prize Peabody Inst., 1930. Mem. Charles Village Civic Assn. Republican. Episcopalian.

ORTNER, MARY JOANNE, pharmacologist; b. Windsor, Ont., Can., Nov. 10, 1946; d. Richard Edward and Joanne Carolyn (Cecile) O. BS, Calif. State U., L.A., 1968, MS, 1971; PhD, U. Hawaii, 1976; MBA, U. Conn., 1986. Sr. staff fellow NIH, Research Triangle Park, N.C., 1977-82; scientist, project mgmt. Boehringer Ingelheim Pharms., Inc., Ridgefield, Conn., 1982—. Contbr. articles to sci. jours. Nat. Rsch. Svc. award postdoctoral fellow NIH, 1976. Mem. AAAS, Am. Soc. Pharmacology and Exptl. Therapeutics, Inflammation Rsch. Soc., Skin Pharmacology Soc., N.Y. Acad. Sci., Project Mgmt. Inst., Smithsonian Assocs., Nat. Trust Hist. Preservation. Office: Boehringer Ingelheim Pharm 90 E Ridge Box 368 Dept R & D Adminstrn Ridgefield CT 06877

ORTON, SUSAN JOSEPHINE, lawyer; b. Bowie, Tex., Aug. 25, 1945; d. Oliver J. and Martha (Johnson) O.; m. O. Ray Baisden, Jr., May 5, 1968 (div. Feb. 1978); m. Lawrence J. Friedman, Aug. 1, 1981; children: Sarah Ann Friedman, Samuel Orton Friedman. BA, U. Tex., 1967; JD, U. Calif., San Francisco, 1974. Bar: Calif. 1974. Dep. atty. gen. Calif. Atty. Gen.'s Office, Sacramento, 1977—. Author: Cal. Codes Forms: Elections/Insurance, 1988. Named Outstanding Young Woman Am. Women Leaguers Sacramento, 1978. Mem. Women Lawyers Sacramento (pres. 1976). Office: Calif Atty Gen's Office 1515 K St Sacramento CA 95814

ORULLIAN, B. LARAE, banker; b. Salt Lake City, May 15, 1933; d. Alma and Bessie (Bacon) O.; cert. Am. Inst. Banking, 1961, 63, 67; grad. Nat. Real Estate Banking Sch., Ohio State U., 1969-71. With Tracy Collins Trust Co., Salt Lake City, 1951-54; sec. to exec. sec. Union Nat. Bank, Denver, 1954-57; exec. sec. Guaranty Bank, Denver, 1957-64, asst. cashier, 1964-67, asst. v.p., 1967-70, v.p., 1970-75, exec. v.p., 1975-77, also bd. dirs.; pres., chief exec. officer, dir. The Women's Bank N.A., Denver, 1977-88, chair, chief exec. officer, dir., 1989—, Equitable Bankshares of Colo., 1980—; vice chmn. Equitable Bank Littleton; vice chmn. bd., dir. Colo. and N.Mex. Blue Cross/Blue Shield, lectr. Treas. Girl Scouts U.S.A., 1981, 1st. nat. v.p., chair exec. com., 1987—, nat. pres., 1990—; bd. dirs., chair fin. Rocky Mountains Health Care Corp. Named to Colo. Women Hall of Fame, 1988, Colo. Entrepreneur of Yr., Inc. Mag. and Arthur Young and Co., 1989, Woman of the Yr., YWCA, 1989. Mem. Bus. and Profl. Women Colo. (3d Century award 1977), Inst. for Better Govt. (bd. dirs.), Colo. State Ethics Bd., Denver C. of C. (bd. dirs., chair state and local affairs), Am. Inst. Banking, Am. Bankers Assn. (mem. adv. bd. Community Bankers Coun.), Nat. Assn. Bank Women, Nat. Women's Forum, Com. of 200, Denver Partnership. Republican. Mormon. Home: 10 S Ammons St Lakewood CO 80226

ORUM, TERRELL BETH, marketing professional; b. Oakland, Calif., Nov. 26, 1961; d. William Allison Orum and Glenn (Keeler) Coxe. BA in Communications, Calif. State U., Fullerton, 1985, MA in Am. Studies, 1989. Retail Nordstrom, Costa Mesa, Calif., 1979-82; acct. exec. Orange Coast Mag., Costa Mesa, 1982-85; sr. acct. exec. Yellow Page, Fullerton, Calif., 1985-86; mktg. dir. Physician Care, Brea, Calif., 1986—; prin. Orum & Assocs., Brea, 1987—. Home: 2418 B Associated Rd Fullerton CA 92635 Office: Orum Assocs 603 S Valencia Ave Brea CA 92621

ORWIG, CHERIE LEE, corporate communications executive; b. Tiffin, Ohio, Sept. 9, 1948; d. Daniel James and Eldora Elizabeth (Hirschfield) O.; m. Duane Allen Ankney, June 12, 1971 (div. June 1979). BA, Bowling Green (Ohio) State U., 1970, MA, 1982. Social worker Lucas County Welfare Dept., Toledo, 1971-73; communications specialist Toledo Edison Co., 1973-75; vol. dir. Planned Parenthood of Toledo, 1975-78; dir. pub. rels. Riverside Hosp., Toledo, 1978-84; dir. editorial svcs. Miami Valley Hosp., Dayton, Ohio, 1984; v.p. communications div. Miami Valley Hosp., Dayton, 1984-87, v.p. corp. communications, 1987—; talk show hostess Sta. WGTE-TV, PBS, Toledo, 1977; mem. press advance First Lady of U.S., The White House, Washington, 1980; instr. Med. Coll. of Ohio, Toledo, 1980-83; mktg. cons. Pocket Quote, Toledo, 1980-83. Com. chair Toledo Festival of the Arts, 1981-84; loaned exec. United Way, Toledo, 1981; com. chmn., on air personality Sta. WGTE-TV Ann. Auction, Toledo, 1974-83; trustee Vis. Nurse Assn., Toledo, 1981-84. Mem. Am. Soc. for Hosp. Mktg. and Pub. Rels. (cert., regional dir. 1986-88, pres. 1990, Touchstone award 1986), Ohio Soc. Hosp. Pub. Rels. (pres. 1984), Internat. Assn. Bus. Communicators, Pub. Rels. Soc. Am. Democrat. Office: Miami Valley Hosp One Wyoming St Dayton OH 45409

ORWOLL, REBECCA LYNN, physician; b. Camden, N.J., May 10, 1949; d. Walter and Patricia Anne (Page) Schroth; m. Eric S. Orwoll, 1970 (div. 1988); children: Benjamin, Katherine; m. Peter J. Kiessling, 1990. AB cum laude, U. Mich., 1970; MA, U. Md., 1973; BS, Portland State U, ., 1975; MD magna cum laude, U. Oreg., Portland, 1979. Diplomate Am. Bd. Internal Medicine, Am. Bd. Hematology. Intern, resident in internal residence Oreg. Health Scis. U., Portland, 1979-82, fellow in hematology and med. oncology, 1982-84; pvt. practice Portland, Oreg., 1984—; clin. instr. Oreg. Health Scis. U., Portland, 1985—. Mem. AMA, Am. Soc. Clin. Oncology, Am. Heart Assn. (mem. council), Oreg. Med. Soc., Multnomah County Med. Soc., Alpha Omega Alpha. Democrat. Unitarian. Office: Hematology Clin 510 NE 49 Ste 421 Portland OR 97213

ORY, MARCIA GAIL, social science researcher; b. Dallas, Feb. 8, 1950; d. Marvin Gilbert and Esther (Levine) O.; m. Raymond James Carroll, Aug. 13, 1972. BA magna cum laude, U. Tex., 1971; MA, Ind. U., 1972; PhD, Purdue U., 1976; MPH, Johns Hopkins U., 1981. Rsch. asst. prof. U. N.C., Chapel Hill, 1976-77; from adj. asst. prof. to assoc. prof. sch. pub. health U. N.C., 1978-88; rsch. fellow U. Minn., Mpls., 1977-78; asst. prof. Sch. Pub. Health U. Ala., Bham, 1978-80; program dir. biosocial aging and health Nat. Inst. on Aging, Bethesda, Md., 1981-86; chief social sci. rsch. on aging Nat. Inst. on Aging, Bethesda, 1987—. Contbr. articles to profl. jours. Mem. several nat. task forces on aging and health issues. Recipient Dept. of Health and Human Svcs. award, 1984, 85, 88, Am. Men and Women of Sci., 1989. Mem. Gerentol. Soc. Am. (mem. program selection com. 1984-86), Am. Pub. Health Assn. (gov. coun. 1986-88, program chmn. 1986, chmn.-elect 1989—), Am. Sociol. Assn. (regional reporter 1984—, program com. 1986, nominations com. 1987), Soc. Behavioral Medicine (program chmn. pub. health track 1988-89, sci. liaison com. 1989), Assn. Health Svcs. Rsch., Phi Kappa Phi, Omicron Nu. Office: Nat Inst on Aging Bldg 32 5C32 Bethesda MD 20892

OSBORN, JACQUELINE ELIZABETH, water treatment company executive; b. Lexington, Nebr., Apr. 4, 1951; d. Samuel and Aurelie Bertha (D'orjo de Marchelovette) Janousek; 1 child, Aimee. Student, U. No. Colo. Asst. project mgr. Atascocita On Lake Houston, Houston, 1978-80; v.p. Walker Systems, Inc., Houston, 1980-86, DX Systems, Inc., Houston, 1986-90; owner Jacqueline E. Osborn & Assocs.; pres., prin., ind. cons. Dolphin Comml. Chem., Inc., 1990—. Guest lectr. ARC; mem. stewardship/fin. bd., lay hosp. visitation team LLUMC. Mem. NAFE, NSPI, NSPF, NRPA, Nat. Recreation and Pks. Soc., Tex. Recreation and Pks. Soc. (pres. comml. br. 1990—), Nat. Swimming Pool Found., Nat. Spa and Pool Inst., Phi Beta Kappa. Republican. Methodist. Home: 3707 Northaven Dallas TX 75229

OSBORN, JANET LYNN, information systems executive; b. Berea, Ohio, Dec. 25, 1952; d. Walter Martin and Mary Alice O. BS in Systems Analysis, Miami U., Ohio, 1975; MBA, U. Mich., 1984; postgrad., Universidad de las Americas, Puebla, Mex., 1974. Cons. mgmt. info. systems Arthur Andersen and Co., Cinn., 1975-77; systems analyst Consumers Power Co., Jackson, Mich., 1977-79; sr. systems analyst Consumers Power Co., Jackson, 1979-81; supr. analyst Consumer Power Co., Jackson, 1982, mgr. corp. systems, 1983-85, mgr. litigation systems, 1985-87, mgr. quality assurance and data adminstrn., 1988-89, mgr. info. and tech. planning and quality assurance, 1989—. Solicitor United Way, Jackson, 1983-84. Mem. Women's Info. Network, NAFE, Pi Mu Epsilon, Phi Kappa Phi, Delta Delta Delta. Office: Consumers Power Co 1945 W Parnall Rd Jackson MI 49201

OSBORN, JUNE ELAINE, pediatrician, microbiologist, university dean; b. Endicott, N.Y., May 28, 1937; d. Leslie A. and Dora W. (Wright) O.; divorced; children: Philip I. Levy, Ellen D. and Laura A. Levy (twins). B.A., Oberlin (Ohio) Coll., 1957; M.D., Western Res. U., 1961. Intern, then resident in pediatrics Harvard U. Hosp., 1961-64; postdoctoral fellow Johns Hopkins Hosp., 1964-65, U. Pitts. Hosp., 1965-66; practice medicine specializing in pediatrics Madison, Wis., 1966-84; dean Sch. Pub. Health U. Mich., 1984—, prof. epidemiology, pediatrics and communicable diseases, 1984—; mem. faculty U. Wis. Med. Sch., 1966-84, prof. pediatrics and microbiology, 1975-84, asso. dean Grad. Sch., 1975-84; mem. rev. panel viral vaccine efficacy FDA, 1973-79, mem. vaccines and related biol. products adv. com., 1981-85; mem. exptl. virology study sect. Div. Research Grants, NIH, 1975-79; bd. dirs. Stetler Research Fund Women Physicians, 1971-75; mem. med. affairs com. Yale U. Council, 1981-86; chmn. life scis. associateships rev. panel NRC, 1981-84; mem. U.S. Army Med. Research and Devel. Adv. Com., 1983-85; chmn. working group on AIDS and the Nation's Blood Supply, NHLBI, 1984-89; chmn. WHO Planning Group on AIDS and the Internat. Blood Supply, 1985-86. Contbr. articles to med. jours. Mem. task force on AIDS, Inst. of Medicine, 1986; mem. adv. com. Robert Wood Johnson Found. Health Svcs. Program, 1986—; mem. nat. adv. com. on the health of the pub. program pew and Rockefeller Founds.; mem. health promotion and disease prevention. bd. IOM, Global Commn. on AIDS World Health Orgn., 1988—; chmn. Nat. Commn. on AIDS, 1989—; trustee Kaiser Found., 1990—. Grantee NIH, 1969, 72, 74, 75; Grantee Nat. Multiple Sclerosis Soc., 1971. Fellow Am. Acad. Pediatrics, Am. Acad. Microbiology, Infectious Diseases Soc. Am.; mem. Soc. Pediatric Research, Am. Assn. Immunologists, Inst. Medicine. Office: U Mich Sch Pub Health Ann Arbor MI 48109

OSBORN, MICHELLE PYNCHON, journalist; b. N.Y.C., July 13, 1927; d. George Mallory Pynchon and Alice (Bennett) Dunnington; m. O'Neill Osborn, Aug. 16, 1949; children: Victoria Alice, Hugh O'Neill Pynchon, Ann Sayre, Julie Alexandra. AB, Smith Coll., 1948. Columnist Phila. Bull., 1965-69, editorial writer, 1969-70; cons. U.S. Commn. on Civil Rights, Washington, 1970-71; dir. pub. info. Bryn Mawr (Pa.) Coll., 1971-77; Bagehot fellow Columbia U., N.Y.C., 1977-78; reporter Wilmington (Del.) News-Jour., 1978-82; reporter USA Today, Arlington, Va., 1982-83, assignment editor Money sect., 1983-88; cover story editor USA Today, Arlington, 1988—. Home: 2127 California St NW Washington DC 20008

OSBORNE, AUDREY MAE, psychiatric social worker; b. Enumclaw, Wash., Dec. 12, 1935; d. Eric John and Vivian (Hinkleman) Stenholm; m. Edward S. Osborne, Jr., May 29, 1960 (div. 1981); children: Carolyn Osborne Glover, Krista, David. BA, U. Puget Sound, 1956. Lic. counselor, Wash. Psychiat. social worker Western State Hosp., Ft. Steilacoom, Wash., 1957-62, 71—; designated mental health profl. Pierce County Social Svcs., Tacoma, 1975—; guardian ad litem Pierce County Ct., Tacoma, 1989—. guest speaker Cop Talk, Sta. KMO, Tacoma, 1989. Mgr. jr. soccer team; leader Girl Scouts U.S.A., Tacoma. Mem. Wash. State Mental Health Profls., Chi Omega (coord. alumnae ann. art tea Tacoma 1970-80). Republican. Presbyterian. Office: Pierce County Social Svcs 88l1 S Tacoma Way Tacoma WA 98409

OSBORNE, CAROL ANN, lawyer; b. Erie, Pa., Aug. 26, 1938; d. Clarence Henry and Grace Louise (McLaughlin) Bronson; LL.B., Western State U., 1977, J.D., 1978; m. Dwight E. Osborne, Jr., Jan. 1, 1965 (div. July 1986); children—Dwight E., Joy Louise. Bar: Calif. 1978. Legal sec., Orange County, Calif., 1967-78; individual practice, Orange, Calif., 1978-83; assoc. with Maxine L. Zazzara, Downey, Calif., 1983-85; sole practice, Downey, Calif., 1985—; instr. Probate Paralegal Course, Cerritos Coll. Mem. ABA, Calif. Bar Assn., Los angeles County Bar Assn., Orange County Bar Assn., Southeast Bar Assn., Am. Bus. Women's Assn. (chpt. officer), Western State U. Alumni Assn., Nu Beta Epsilon. Club: Pico Rivera (sec. 1988-89). Lodge: Rotary. Republican. Office: 8221 3d St #307 Downey CA 90241

OSBORNE, GAYLA MARLENE, sales executive; b. Owenton, Ky., Aug. 9, 1956; d. Frederick Clay and Helen Beatrice (Mason) O. AAS, No. Ky. U., 1982, BS, 1986; cert. in Chinese Mandarin, Def. Lang. Inst., 1975. Pers. clk. Dept. Edn. State Ky., Frankfort, 1974; sec. Dept. Health, Edn., Welfare Nat. Inst. Occupational Safety Health, Cin., 1977-79; specialist sales promotion U.S. Postal Svc., Cin., 1980, coord. customer liaison, task force pub. image, account rep., 1986-87; reservation sale agt. Delta Airlines, 1987-89. Councilmember Florence City Coun., Ky. 1984-87; vol. Children's Home, Covington, 1982, 87. With USAF, 1974-76. Named to Hon. Order Ky. Cols. Mem. Disabled Am. Veterans, No. Ky. U. Alumni Assn., Nat. Assn. Postmasters U.S., Boone County Fraternal Order Police, Ky. Assn. Realtors, Nat. Bd. Realtors. Democrat. Baptist. Club: Fraternal Order Police. Home: 8395 Juniper Ln Florence KY 41042

OSBORNE, GAYLE ANN, corporate executive; b. Bossier City, La., Feb. 1, 1951; d. Walker Henry and Marjorie Evelyn (Cook) Pyle; m. Paul A. Huelsman, June 28, 1969 (div. Jan. 1976); children: Ginger, Paula; m. Luther L. Osborne, Sept. 10, 1976 (div. Aug. 1989). Sales assoc. Model City Real Estate, Midwest City, Okla., 1972-73; mgr. adminstrn. Equipment Renewal Co., Oklahoma City, 1973-76, Gulfco Industries, Inc., Casper, Wyo., 1976-77; v.p. B&B Tool and Supply Co., Inc., Casper, Wyo., 1977, 79, 81, pres., 1978, 80, 82; ptnr. Williston, N.D., 1983—, Osborne Leasing Co., Casper, Wyo., 1977—; pres. BOP Repair & Machine, Inc., Casper, Wyo., 1981—; ptnr. Pronghorn Trap and Skeet, Casper, Wyo., 1986—; owner Osborne Leasing Co. Mem. Casper Petroleum Club, Nat. Skeet Shoot Assn. (All Am. Skeet Team), Amateur Trapshooting Assn., Casper Skeet Club. Democrat. Office: B&B Tool & Supply Co Inc PO Box 2974 Casper WY 82602

OSBORNE, MARYHELEN, nurse; b. Mpls., Sept. 25, 1936; d. William H. Stewart and Mary H.T. (Stuart) Barquist; m. Lloyd D. Osborne, Sept. 13, 1957; children: Karen Lynn, Kevin Lee, Laura Jane. Diploma, St. Luke's Hosp. Sch. Nursing, Duluth, Minn., 1957; cert. in gerontology, St. Scholastic Coll., Duluth, Minn., 1982; BS in Nursing and Gerontology cum laude, U. Wis., Superior, 1987. R.N., Minn., Wis. Staff nurse St. Luke's Hosp., Duluth, 1957-68, Lakeshore Luth. Home, Duluth, 1973-77; staff nurse, supr. Park Point Manor, Duluth, 198-87, asst. head nurse, 1987-89; supr., staff RN Alzheimer's unit St. Francis Home, Superior, 1989—; RN, case mgr. gerontology The Duluth Clinic, 1989—. Mem. Am. Nurses Assn. (cert. in gerontology), St. Luke's Sch. Nursing Alumnae.

OSBORNE, THERESA JO, investment administrator; b. Seattle, Aug. 22, 1945; d. Stanley and Jean (Strazdas) Pospichal; m. Herbert L. Osborne Jr., June 3, 1967 (div. Feb. 1987); children: Amanda Jennifer, Maxwell Joseph. BFA in Art Printmaking, U. Nebr., Omaha, 1967; MFA in Arts Mgmt., Bklyn. Coll., 1982. Supr. art Burlington (N.J.) Twp., 1967-68, Harpswell Schs., Topsham, Maine, 1968-70; dir. spl. projects Borough of Queens City of N.Y.C., 1979-81, project coord. Bklyn. Bridge Centennial, 1981-82, dir. cultural affairs Borough of Queens, 1982-85; community coord. Bklyn. Acad. Music, 1980; exec. mgr., corp. sec. Live Oak Realty Corp., N.Y.C., 1985—. Trustee Old Stone House Gowanus, Bklyn., 1978, Flushing Meadows-Corona Park Corp., Queens, 1987-88, Black Am. Heritage Found., 1989—; mem. bd. mgrs. N.Y.C jr. League, 1984-85, N.Y. Drama League. Mem. NAFE, Chi Omega. Democrat. Roman Catholic. Club: Women's City (N.Y.C.). Home: 19 Ingram St Forest Hills Gardens NY 11375 Office: Live Oak Realty Corp 40 E 75th St Ste 1-A New York NY 10021

OSCAR, JOYCE ANNETTE, newscaster; b. Chgo., July 3, 1956; d. Edward Ambrose and Gertrude (Andrews) O. BA, Western Ill. U., Macomb, 1978. Copy writer advt. Sta. WFYR/RKO, Chgo., 1978-79; video journalist Cable News Network, Atlanta, 1980; reporter, anchor Sta. WJBF-TV ABC Affiliate, Augusta, Ga., 1980-83; news anchor Sta. WDEF-TV CBS Affiliate, Chattanooga, 1983-85; news reporter Sta. WSB-TV ABC Affiliate, Atlanta, 1985—. Talent, writer, producer Spot News Report, 1983, TV reporting, rotary, 1983. Vol. March of Dimes, Atlanta, 1986-87, pub. speaker United Way Agy., Atlanta, 1986-87; com. mem. Ga. Spl. Olympics. Recipient Spot News Reporting award, UP Internat. and W. Augusta Rotary, 1983, Gavel award Ga. Bar Assn., 1990, Gavel award Atlanta Bar Assn., 1990; Unicom Ednl. TV grantee, 1975-78. Mem. Ga. Assn. Newscasters, Soc. Profl. Journalists, Sigma Delta Chi, Sigma, Sigma, Sigma. Roman Catholic. Office: Sta WSB-TV 1601 W Peachtree St Atlanta GA 30309

OSCHIN, FRANCINE, journalist; b. Bklyn., Mar. 20, 1943; d. Albert and Goldie (Miller) Strauss; divorced; children: Sheryl, Danny, Karen, Kathy. AA, Los Angeles Valley Coll., 1965; BA, Calif. State U., Northridge, 1984, MA, 1986. Condr. slide show Friends of Hawaii Pub. TV, Honolulu, 1978-81, 1st v.p., 1978-80; corr. Leader Newspapers, Glendale, Calif., 1985-89; legis. dep. L.A. City Coun. 12th Dist., 1989—. asst., writer Office Pub. Affairs, Calif. State U., Northridge, 1985—; corr. sec. Birmingham High Sch. PTSA, Van Nuys, Calif., 1987-88. Mem. Soc. Profl. Journalists/Sigma Delta Chi, Calif. State U.-Northridge Alumni Assn., Calif. State U.-Northridge Journalism Alumni Assn., Greenpeace, Sierra Club, Cousteau Soc., Consumers Union, Kappa Tau Alpha, Phi Alpha Epsilon. Office: LA City Hall Rm 237 200 Spring St Los Angeles CA 90012

OSER, MARSHA, controller; b. N.Y.C.; d. Seymour Bookstaber and Jessie Lehmann. BS, Am. U., 1971; MBA, Frostburg U., 1981. Mgr. mgmt. info. Bechtel Corp., Gaithersburg, Md.; bus. mgr. Martin Marietta, Greenbelt, Md.; mgr. fin. analysis McDonnell Douglas, Rockwell, Md.; controller Mgmt. Systems Designers, Vienna, Va. Mem. MVHC (treas., bd. dirs.), Nat. Contract Mgmt. Assn. Home: 8400 Harron Valley Ct Gaithersburg MD 20879

OSERO, GLORIA JEAN, retail business owner, elementary school educator; b. Red Wing, Minn., Feb. 27, 1950; d. Bernard Walwin and Alice Mathilda (Peterson) Freier; m. Kenneth Lee Osero, Apr. 7, 1979; children: Ryan Blake, Brandon Tyler. BS in Elem. Edn. and Speech, U. Wis., River Falls, 1972. Cert. tchr. Tchr. Reedsburg (Wis.) Dist. Schs., 1972-73, Archdiocese of St. Paul and Mpls., 1973-78, West St. Paul (Minn.) Dist. Schs., 1978-79; case mgr. spl. edn. Roseville (Minn.) Dist.Schs., 1979-84; tchr. CorpusChristi Sch., Roseville, 1984-89; chmn. tchr. relicensure Corpus Christi, 1984-89. Contbr. articles to profl. jours. Tchr., Project Bus., Roseville, 1984-88. Mem. Nat. Assn. Female Execs., NEA, Minn. Edn. Assn. Lutheran. Home: 1010 Hill Ct Shoreview MN 55126

OSGOOD, BARBARA TRAVIS, conservationist, sociologist; b. Nyack, N.Y., Nov. 10, 1934; d. Donald Lovatt and Dorothy Catherine (Hammond) Travis; m. William Milne Osgood, Dec. 26, 1955 (div. 1985); children: Stephen Milne, Donald William. BS, Cornell U., 1956, PhD, 1980; MS, Lehman Coll., 1972. Lectr. Herbert H. Lehman Coll., Bronx, 1972-75; asst. prof. Cornell U., Ithaca, N.Y., 1978; staff scientist Coop. State Rsch. Svc., Washington, 1979; with Soil Conservation Svc., 1980—; asst. div. dir. Soil Conservation Svc., Washington, 1985-88; state conservationist Soil Conservation Svc., Somerset, N.J., 1988—. Co-author: (book chpt.) Yearbook of Agriculture, 1986, Conserving Soil, 1986. Flora Rose fellow Cornell U., 1977. Mem. Rural Sociol. Soc., Soil and Water Conservation Soc., Rotary, Phi Kappa Phi, Omicron Nu Hon. Soc. Methodist. Office: Soil Conservation Svc 1370 Hamilton St Somerset NJ 08873

O'SHAUGHNESSY, PATRICIA MARY, psychotherapist; b. Wilmington, Del., Mar. 21, 1949; d. Albert Charles and Grace Veronica (Nevins) Cereghino; m. M. L. O'Shaughnessy (div. 1990). BA in Psychology, St. Louis U., 1971; MSW, U. Tenn., 1977. Diplomate Nat. Assn. Social Workers. Crisis prog. dir. N.E. Community Mental Health Ctr., Memphis, 1973-76; social svcs. coordiantor New Horizons Inc., Batesville, Tenn., 1977-78; outpatient therapist/clin. supr. Middletown Area Mental Health Ctr., Middletown, Ohio, 1978-82; pvt. practice psychotherapy Franklin, Ohio, 1982—; co-founder S.W. Ohio Family Therapy Tng. Inst.; cons. in field. Columnist Middletown Community News, 1983-85. Bd. trustees Planned Parenthood Assn., Hamilton, Ohio, 1983-85; adv. bd. Juvenile Detention Ctr., Hamilton, 1983-85; trainer Miami U. Vol. Bd., 1983-85. Mem. Ohio Soc. Clin. Social Wk. (co-editor newsletter 1984-86). Home: 415 N Third St Hamilton OH 45011 Office: 6820 Roosevelt Ave Franklin OH 45005

O'SHAUGHNESSY, ROSEMARIE, clinical nutritionist; b. N.Y.C., Sept. 25, 1940; d. John O. and Maria Wellmann (Larranaga) Rao; m. Louis L. Feldman, May 3, 1980; children: Michelle Marie Ortiz, Chevonne Eileen Raggi, Melany Rose. BA, St. Mary's Coll., Notre Dame, Ind., 1961; MS, Donsbach U., 1978, PhD, 1979; postdoctoral, Union for Experimenting Colls. and Univs., Cin., 1987. Cert. clin. nutritionist. Pvt. practice clin. nutrition Orlando, Fla., 1979—; mem. adj. faculty Internat. U. for Nutrition Edn., 1987-88; expert witness for clin. nutritionists and nutritional cons. testimony before state legis. coms. State of Fla., Tallahassee, 1985-88; guest speaker various colls., univs., civic and profl. orgns. Interviewee numerous TV and radio programs. Fellow Am. Coun. Applied Clin. Nutrition; mem. Internat. and Am. Assn. Clin. Nutritionists (founder 1987, bd. dirs. 1987—, co-founder Fla. chpt. 1983, bd. dirs. Fla. chpt. 1986—, exec. dir. 1986—), Internat. Acad. Nutrition and Preventive Medicine (bd. dirs. 1987—), N.Am. Acad. Nutrition and Preventive Medicine. Republican. Roman Catholic. Home: 4062 Lake Conway Woods Blvd Orlando FL 32812 Office: 3203 Lawton Rd Ste 100 Orlando FL 32803

OSHINS, GLADYS BARBARA, advertising executive; b. N.Y.C., Sept. 10, 1935; d. Louis and Dorothy (Greenberg) Bernstein; m. Elliot Howard Oshins, Apr. 4, 1965. BA, Bklyn. Coll., 1956. Media supr. The Zlowe Co., Inc., N.Y.C., 1958-68; v.p. assoc. media dir. Marsteller, Inc., N.Y.C., 1968-80; v.p. media dir. Intermarco Advt., Inc., N.Y.C., 1980-83; sr. v.p. assoc. media dir. Della Femina McNamee, WRCS, N.Y.C., 1983—. Office: Della Femina McNamee WCRS Inc 350 Hudson St New York NY 10014

OSIGWEH, BRENDA JEAN, university professor; b. Manhattan, N.Y., June 25, 1957; d. Sylvester Jolley Sr. and Judith Elaine Blackwell; m. Chimezie A.B. Osigweh, Apr. 20, 1981; children: Amarachi, Nkechi and Ndidi. BA, Stillman Coll., Tuscaloosa, 1979; MA, Ohio State U., Columbus, 1980, PhD, 1984. Asst. prof. communication Northeast Mo. State U., Kirksville, Mo, 1982-85, Hampton U., Hampton, Va., 1986-87, U. Akron, Akron, Ohio, 1988—. Recipient Outstanding Young Woman Am., 1984, Univ. Fellow Ohio State U. Columbus, 1979-81, Who's Who Among Students in Am. U. and Coll., 1979. Mem. Speech Communication Assn, Women in Higher Edn. Democrat. Methodist. Office: Univ Akron Dept Communication Akron OH 44325

OSKEY, D. BETH, banker; b. Red Wing, Minn., Dec. 23, 1921; d. Alvin E. and Effie D. (Thompson) Feldman; student U. Wis., River Falls, 1939-41; B.A., Met. State U., Minn., 1975; grad. degree in banking, U. Wis., 1973, postgrad. in banking, 1977; student in interior decorating LaSalle Extension U., Chgo., 1970; m. Warren B. Oskey, Sept. 27, 1941; children—Jo Cheryl, Warren A., Peter (dec.), Jeffrey L. Officer, Hiawatha Nat. Bank, Hager City, Wis., 1959—, cashier, 1978-79, pres., 1979, chmn. bd., 1984—, exec. v.p., dir., sec. bd. dirs., 1959—, sec., mem. discount com.; with First Nat. Bank of Glenwood, Glenwood City, Wis., 1965— pres., exec. v.p., 1979—, dir., sec. bd., 1965—, chmn. bd., 1984—, sec., mem. discount com.; speaker on women in banking. Banking com. Vo-Tech Sch., Red Wing, Minn.; former officer civic orgns. Mem. Ind. Bankers Am., Wis. Bankers Assn., Am. Bankers Assn., Gen. Fedn. Women's Clubs Internat., Inc. (bd. dirs., pres. 1988—). Republican. Lutheran. Club: Minn. Fedn. Women's Clubs (v.p. 1983—, pres. dist. III 1978—, pres. elect 1986-88, pres. 1988—). Home: 1022 Hallstrom Dr Red Wing MN 55066 also: 1561 Leisure World Mesa AZ 85206 Office: Hiawatha Nat Bank Hager City WI 54014

OSLER, DOROTHY K., state legislator; b. Dayton, Ohio, Aug. 19, 1923; d. Carl M. and Pearl A. (Tobias) Karstaedt; BS cum laude in Bus. Adminstrn., Miami U., Oxford, Ohio, 1945; m. David K. Osler, Oct. 26, 1946; children: Scott C., David D. Mem. Conn. Ho. of Reps., 1973—. Mem. Greenwich (Conn.) Rep. Town Meeting, 1968—, Eastern Greenwich Women's Rep. Club, 1970—; sec. Conn. Student Loan Found., 1973-83, v.p., 1983-84; mem. Spl. Edn. Cost Commn., 1976-77, Sch. Fin. Adv. Panel, 1977-78, Edn. Equity Study Com., 1980-81, Commn. on Goals for U. Conn. Health Ctr., 1975-76; bd. dirs. ARC, 1975. Mem. Nat. Order Women Legislators (sec. 1987-89), Conn. Order of Women Legislators (sec. 1983-84, pres. 1985-86), LWV (pres. Greenwich chpt. 1965-67, sec. Conn. chpt. 1967-72), AAUW (dir. 1971-73), Mortar Board, Phi Beta Kappa, Alpha Omicron Pi. Republican. Christian Scientist. Bi-weekly columnist local newspaper, 1973-83.

OSLIN, KAY TOINETTE (K. T. OSLIN), singer; b. Crossett, Ark.. Student, Lon Morris Jr. Coll. Sang in folk trio; professional singing debut at Purple Onion, 1962; mem. road co. Hello, Dolly, also N.Y.C.; mem. cast Promise, Promises, revival West Side Story; songwriter; songs include Do Ya?, Round the Clock Lovin, Where Is A Woman To Go, Come Next Monday, Younger Men, others; albums: 80's Ladies, 1988 (Grammy award, Nat. Acad Rec. Arts and Scis. singles award 1988), This Woman, 1989. Recipient Grammy awards, Best Female Vocalist of Yr. Country Music Assn., 1988, Song of Yr. award 80's Ladies Country Music Assn., 1988, Best Female Country Vocalist award Acad. Country Music, 1989, Best Country song award for Hold Me, Nat. Assn. Rec. Arts and Scis., 1989. Office: Chip Peay Moress Nanas Golden 12424 Wilshire Blvd Ste 840 Los Angeles CA 90025*

OSMAN, BETTY BARSHAD, psychologist, author; b. N.Y.C., Sept. 1, 1929; d. Maurice S. and Rose B. (Bush) Barshad; m. Albert I. Osman, June 24, 1951; children: Richard Michael, Nancy Beth, Meg Jeanne. BA, Vassar Coll., 1951; MA, Columbia U., 1965, EdM, 1970; PhD, Fordham U., 1983. Lic. psychologist, N.Y. Social case worker Dept. Family and Child Welfare, Westchester County, N.Y., 1951-58; learning disabilities specialist White Plains (N.Y.) Pub. Schs., 1966-70; instr. Bank St. Coll. of Edn., N.Y.C.,

1970-75; vis. prof. Manhattanville Coll., Purchase, N.Y., 1984-89; psychologist Dept. of Psychiatry, White Plains Hosp. Med. Ctr., 1986—; pvt. practice Scarsdale, N.Y., 1966—; instr. grad. program Sarah Lawrence Coll., Bronxville, N.Y., 1986—; bd. dirs. Nat. Ctr. for Learning Disabilities, N.Y., chair, profl. adv. bd., 1978—; coun. Nat. Inst. Child Health and Human Devel., NIH, 1984-87; adv. com. children and adolescents Mental Health Assn., Westchester County, 1986—. Author: Learning Disabilities: A Family Affair, 1979, No One to Play With, 1982; contbr. articles to profl. jours. Second century initiative com. United Way of Am., Alexandria, Va., 1987—. Mem. Am. Psychol. Assn. (apptd. pres.'s com. on mental retardation 1990—, Disting. Psychologist award 1988), Internat. Acad. for Rsch. in Learning Disabilities, Internat. Neuropsychology Soc., Nat. Acad. for Advancement Sci., Assn. for Children and Adults with Learning Disabilities (disting. svc. award 1982), Orton Soc., Vassar Club (pres. 1972-75), Beach Point Club. Jewish. Office: White Plains Hosp Med Ctr Dept of Psychiatry Davis Ave at E Post Rd White Plains NY 10601

OSMAN, EDITH GABRIELLA, lawyer; b. N.Y.C., Mar. 18, 1949; d. Arthur Abraham and Judith (Goldman) Udem; m. Mitchel Osman, Nov. 21, 1971; children: Jacqueline, Daniel. BA in Spanish, SUNY, Stony Brook, 1970; JD cum laude, U. Miami, Fla., 1983. Bar: Fla. 1983, U.S. Dist. Ct. (so. dist.) Fla. 1984, U.S. Dist. Ct. (mid. dist.) Fla. 1988, U.S. Ct. Appeals (11th cir.) 1985, U.S. Supreme Ct. 1987, U.S. Ct. Mil. Appeals 1990. Assoc. Kimbrell & Hamann, P.A., Miami, 1984-90, Dunn, Dresnick & Lodish, P.A., Miami, 1990—. Mem. adv. com. for Implementation of the Victor Posner Judgement to Aid the Homeless. Mem. ABA (product liability com., corp. counsel com.), Fla. Bar Assn. (budget com. 1989—, voluntary bar liaison com. 1987—, spl. com. on formation of Ho. of Dels. 1988—, chmn. mid-yr. conv. 1989, mem. long range planning com. 1988—, numerous others), Dade County Bar Assn. (fed. ct. rules com. 1985-86, chmn. program com. 1988-89, 90-91), Nat. Coun. Bar Assn. Pres.'s (bd. dirs. 1990—), Fla. Coun. Bar Assn. Pres.'s (bd. dirs. 1988-89, treas. 1989-90, v.p. 1990-91), Fla. Assn. Women Lawyers (bd. dirs. 1985-86, v.p. Dade County chpt. 1986-87, pres. 1987-88, pres. elect Fla. chpt. 1988-89, pres. 1989-90), Women's Bar Assn. (dir. nat. conf. 1990—), Dade County Trial Lawyers Assn. Office: Dunn Dresnick & Lodish 2 Biscayne Blvd 2400 Miami FL 33131

OSMAN, MARY ELLA WILLIAMS, journal editor; b. Honea Path, S.C.; d. Humphrey Bates and Jennie Louise (Williams) Williams; student Coll. William and Mary, Ga. State Coll. for Women; A.B., Presbyn. Coll., 1939; B.S. in L.S., U. N.C., 1944; m. John Osman, Oct. 22, 1936. Asst. libr. Presbyn. Coll., Clinton, S.C., 1936-38, Union Theol. Sem., Richmond, Va., 1938-44; sr. cataloger, asst. libr. Rhodes Coll., Memphis, 1944-52; asst. test cities project Ford Found. Fund for Adult Edn., N.Y.C., 1952-57, assoc. dir. office of info., 1957-61, exec. asst. to pres., sec. to bd. dirs., 1960-61; asst. libr. AIA, Washington, 1962-68, asst. editor AIA Jour., 1969-72, assoc. editor, 1972-77, sr. editor, 1978-87. Mem. AIA (hon.), Chi Delta Phi, Kappa Delta. Presbyn. Contbr. to various mags. Home: 3600 Chateau Dr Apt #244 Columbia SC 29204 Office: AIA 1735 New York Ave Washington DC 20006

OSMOND, LYNN JOYCE, symphony orchestra manager; b. St. Catharines, Ont., Can., Mar. 31, 1957; d. George and Joyce Edith (Stanton) O. MusB with honors, Queens U., 1980; numerous courses and seminars in field. Adminstrv. asst. Assn. of Can. Orchs., Ont. Fedn. of Symphony Orchs., Toronto, 1980-81; exec. dir. Mississauga Symphony, Ont., 1981-83; youth orch. coord. for Ont., Ont. Fedn. Symphony Orchs., Toronto, 1981-84; festival coord. Ont. Youth Orch. Festival, 1983-85; gen. mgr. Thunder Bay Symphony Orch., Ont., 1983-85, Orch. London Ont., Can., 1985-88; gen. mgr. The Can. Stage Co., Toronto, 1988—; dir. Can. Assn. Youth Orchs., Banff, Alta.; mem. adv. bd. Performing Arts Mgmt. Confedn. Coll., Thunder Bay, 1984-86; bd. dirs. Performing Arts Ctr. for Tomorrow (PACT), London West Progressive Conservative Assn., 1986-88, London & Area Progressive Conservative Bus. Assn. Arts Mgmt. Tng. grantee Can. Council, 1984. Mem. Thunder Bay Press Club, Assn. Cultural Execs., Ont. Fedn. Symphony Orchs. (bd. dirs. 1986-88), Dirs. Club of London, Queen's U. Alumni Assn. (class agt., bd. dir.). Conservative. Anglican. Avocations: music, sports. Home: 585 Rochampton Ave, Toronto, ON Canada MYP 157

OSMOND, MARIE, singer; b. Ogden, Utah, Oct. 13, 1959; d. George and Olive O.; m. Brian Blosil, 1986; children: Stephen James, Jessica Marie, Rachel. Ed. pub. schs., pvt. tutors. Appeared with The Osmond family singing group from age 7, solo act, 1973—; co-star: Donny & Marie TV show, 1976-79, Donny & Marie Christmas Spl, 1979, Osmond Family Show, 1979, Osmond Family Christmas Show, 1980; star TV spl. Marie, 1981; record albums include (with Donny Osmond): Make the World Go Away, I'm Leaving It All Up To You; songs from their TV Show Goin Coconuts; solo albums include: Paper Roses, In My Little Corner of the World, Who's Sorry Now?, This Is The Way That I Feel, There's No Stopping Your Heart, 1985, I Only Wanted You, 1987, All In Love, 1988, Steppin' Stone, 1989; #1 singles include Meet Me in Montana (Best Country Duo of Yr. award with Dan Seals), 1986, You're Still New to Me, 1986, There's No Stoppin' Your Heart, 1986, I Only Wanted You, 1987; co-author: Fun, Fame, and Family, 1973; Marie Osmond's Guide to Beauty, Health, and Style, 1980. Recipient (with Donny Osmond) Georgie award for best vocal team Am. Guild Variety Artists, 1978. Mormon. *

OSORIO, ROSA, advertising executive; b. Pereira, Colo., Mar. 16, 1946; came to U.S., 1966; d. Jose J. and Ana (Ramirez) O.; m. Falcon (div 1982); children: Robert, Mary. Student, Idesco, Columbia, 1965, Union County Coll., N.J., 1987, Kean Coll., N.J. Export coord. The Singer Co., Elizabeth, N.J., 1979-84; advt. mgr. Heyco Molded Products, Inc., Kenilworth, N.J., 1985--. Mem: Bus. Profl. Advt. Assn. Democrat. Roman Catholic.

OSOWIEC, DARLENE ANN, psychologist, consultant, educator; b. Chgo., Feb. 16, 1951; d. Stephen Raymond and Estelle Marie Osowiec. BS, Loyola U., Chgo., 1973; MA with honors, Roosevelt U., 1980; postgrad., Calif. Inst. Integral Studies, 1982—; postgrad. in psychology, Saybrook Inst., San Francisco, 1985-88. Mental health therapist Ridgeway Hosp., Chgo., 1978; mem. faculty psychology dept. Coll. Lake County, Grayslake, Ill., 1981; counselor, supr. MA-level interns, chmn. pub. rels. com. Integral Counseling Ctr., San Francisco, 1983-84; clin. psychology intern Chgo.-Read Mental Health Ctr. Ill. Dept. Mental Health, 1985-86; cons. Gordon & Assocs., Oak Lawn, Ill., 1989—; lectr. psychology Daley Coll., Chgo., City Colls. Chgo., 1988-90; mem. faculty psychology dept. Moraine Valley Community Coll., Palos Hills, Ill., 1988-89. Ill. State scholar, 1969-73; Calif. Inst. Integral Studies scholar, 1983. Mem. Am. Psychol. Assn. (assoc.), Am. Assn. for Counseling and Devel., Am. Mental Health Counselors Assn., Am. Women in Psychology, Ill. Psychol. Assn. (affiliate), Calif. Psychol. Assn. (assoc.), NOW (chmn. legal adv. corps Chgo. 1974-76). Home: 6608 S Whipple St Chicago IL 60629-2916

OSSENBERG, HELLA SVETLANA, psychoanalyst; b. Kiev, Russia, June 10, 1930; came to U.S., 1957, naturalized, 1964; d. Anatole E. and Tatiana N. (Dombrovski) Donath; diploma langs. and psychology, U. Heidelberg (W. Ger.), 1953; M.S., Columbia U., 1968; cert. Nat. Psychol. Assn. Psychoanalysis, 1977; m. Carl H. Ossenberg, June 7, 1958. Sr. psychiat. social worker VA Mental Hygiene Clinic, N.Y.C., 1968-80, pvt. practice psychoanalysis, N.Y.C., 1975—; mem. Theodor Reik Cons. Center, 1978—; field instr. Columbia U., Fordham U. schs. social work. Mem. Nat. Assn. Social Workers, Acad. Cert. Social Workers (diplomate), Nat. Psychol. Assn. Psychoanalysis, Nat. Assn. Advancement Phychoanalysis (Am. Bds. Accreditation and Certification), Council Psychoanalytic Psychotherapists. Home: 820 West End Ave New York NY 10025 Office: 345 W 58th St New York NY 10019

OSSIP, BOBBI ANN, English educator; b. Cumberland, Md., Aug. 1, 1938; d. George and Jeanne Susan (Rosenstein) O. BA, U. Pitts., 1960, MLitt, 1962; postgrad., Barry U., Miami, Fla., 1967-68; EdD, Nova U., 1983. Pub. relations specialist Nat. Union Ins. Co., Pitts., 1962-63, Diplomat Hotel, Hollywood, Fla., 1964, Hume Smith Mickelberry Advt. Agy., Miami, 1964; from instr. to prof. English Miami-Dade Community Coll., Miami, 1964—, dir. sch. and coll. rels. Editor: Orientation Rev., 1983—. Mem. Fla. Assn. Community Colls. (chmn. fundraising 1988—), Nat. Orientation Dirs. Assn. (bd. dirs. 1982—), Hadassah, Phi Sigma Sigma (editor nat. mag., nat. pres. 1973-75, past nat. pub. relations chmn.). Jewish. Home: PO Box 402553 Miami Beach FL 33140 Office: Miami-Dade Community Coll 11380 NW 27th Ave Miami FL 33167

OSSOFSKY, HELEN JOHNS (MRS. ELI OSSOFSKY), psychiatrist; b. Phila., Dec. 7, 1921; d. William Calloway and Gertrude (Schindele) Johns; A.B., Mt. Holyoke Coll., 1943; student Women's Med. Coll. Pa., 1950-52; M.D., Johns Hopkins U., 1954; m. Eli Ossofsky, Aug. 8, 1950, (dec. Oct. 1950); m. Charles E. Iliff, 1987. Intern Osler Med. Service, Johns Hopkins, 1954-55, resident Pediatrics Cornell U., N.Y. Hosp., 1955-56, Pediatrics Johns Hopkins, 1956-57; research assoc. Johns Hopkins Sch. Hygiene and Pub. Health, 1957-59; asst. prof. Georgetown U. Sch. Medicine, 1959-66, assoc. prof. pediatrics, 1966-79; supervisory med. officer D.C. Dept. Pub. Health, 1959-62, med. cons. div. mental retardation, 1967-69; child psychiatry consultation practice, McLean, Va., 1966—. Cons., Inst. Child Health and Human Devel., NIH, Bethesda, Md., 1962-63; cons. in med. tng. div. chronic diseases USPHS, 1964-65; cons. Va. Assn. Children with Learning Disabilities, Psychiatric Inst. Washington, 1972-88; cons. treatment of psychiat. disorders task force Am. Psychiat. Assn., 1986-89; fellow Am. Acad. Pediatrics, 1975; lectr. Cath. U. Sch. Cardiovascular Nursing, 1959-79; mem. advisory council Cybernetic Research Inst. Mem. AMA, Washington Psychiat. Soc., Am. Psychiat. Assn., Johns Hopkins Med. and Surg. Assn., Phi Beta Kappa. Author: Tumors of the Eye and Adnexa in Infancy and Childhood, 1962; also articles in profl. jours. Address: 1333 Merrie Ridge Rd McLean VA 22101

OSSONT, MARGARET REBECCA, social services administrator; b. Newport News, Va, Sept. 28, 1948; d. George and Mary Beverly (Preston) Pilling; 1 child, Ashley Lauren. AS BA in Bus. Adminstrn., Ocean Co. Coll., Toms River, N.J., 1971; BS BA in Bus. Adminstrn., Ga. Court Coll., Lakewood, N.J., 1982; postgrad., Cen. Mich., McGuire AFB, N.J., 1987. Dir. Western Ctr., Jackson, N.J., 1974-85; promugated Inception of Ocean County Commn. on Women, Toms River, N.J., 1975-83; coordinator Life Mgmt. Program, Garden State Corrections, Yardville, N.J., 1985--; cons. Headstart Domestic Violence, 1977-80, preserto Dept. of Criminal Justice, Treton, 1979. Contbr. articles to profl. jours. Dir. initiator, Battered and Raped Program of Ocean County, 1975, chairperson HUD Housing Adv. Bd., 1977-79, Vol. for probationers, liaison Jackson Help Line Drugs and Crises, 1976-79, Forensic Mental Health Assn. Treatment Of Sex Offenders, 1988. Mem. Ocean County Tenant Orgn. (organizer-pres. 1979-80), Ocean County Commn. Status on Women. Roman Catholic. Home: 3 Deer Ln Jackson NJ 08527

OSTAP, MARTINE ELIZABETH, educator, librarian; b. New Brunswick, N.J., Mar. 31, 1959; d. Helen M. O.; BA with honors, in English, with honors in Am. Studies, U. Wyo., 1981, MA in Am. Studies, 1984; MA in English, U. Tex., El Paso, 1983; postgrad. U. N.Mex., 1984-86; MS in Library Sci., Fla. State U., 1989. Instr. English U. Tex., El Paso, 1981-83, research asst. English composition, 1982; teaching assoc. English, U. N.Mex., 1984-86; lectr. in English. U. Wyo., 1986-88. Contbr. to Jack London Newsletter. William Robertson Coe fellow, 1984. Mem. Omicron Delta Kappa. Home: 1271 N 17th St Laramie WY 82070

OSTBY, SANDRA JOSEPHINE, dietitian; b. Memphis, May 23, 1951; d. Joseph Smith Jr. and Viola Bernice (Childers) O.; m. Harold Burton Brackett, Apr. 14, 1973 (div. Sept. 1980). BS magna cum laude, U. Tenn., 1973; MS in Nutrition, Colo. State U., 1975; postgrad. bus. adminstrn., Memphis State U., 1988—. Dir. food svc. Santa Rosa Convalescent Ctr., Tucson, 1976-77; cons. dietitian Kennecott Copper Corp., Kearney, Ariz., 1977; clin. dietitian Boca Raton (Fla.) Community Hosp., 1978-80, Duke U. Med. Ctr., Durham, N.C., 1980-82; chief clin. dietitian John Umsted Hosp., Butner, N.C., 1982-84; cons. nutritionist Johnson & Johnson Co., New Brunswick, N.J., 1984; regional sales mgr. Practorcare, San Diego, 1984-85; corp.-adminstrv. dietitian Bapt. Meml. Hosp., Memphis, 1985-88; cons., dir. food svc. Trezevant Manor-Allen Morgan Nursing Ctr., Memphis, 1988—; speaker on nutrition and food svcs. to numerous state and local dietetic assns. and univs., 1984-85; internship instr. U. Tenn., Memphis State U., Memphis, 1987—. Edn. Professional Devel. Act fellow, 1974-75; recipient cert. of appreciation for outstanding and meritorious svc. to community City of Memphis, 1990. Mem. Am. Dietetic Assn. (preceptor Memphis 1988—), Am. Soc. for Hosp. Food Svc. Adminstrs. (treas. Memphis 1986-87), Memphis Dist. Dietetic Assn. , Omicron Nu, Phi Kappa Phi. Presbyterian. Home: 4766 Eaglecrest Dr Memphis TN 38117 Office: Trezevant Manor 177 N Highland Ave Memphis TN 38111

OSTENDORF, CAROLE GLORINE, health care facility executive; b. Little Falls, Minn., Sept. 6, 1948; d. Gilbert Frank and Monica Therese (Lange) O. BS, St. Cloud (Minn.) State U., 1973; M of Med. Sci., Emory U., 1980; MBA, U. Wis., Milw., 1987. Cert. phys. therapist. Staff phys. therapist McDowell (Ky.) Appalachia Regional Hosp., 1973-75; supr. Ebenezer Soc., Mpls., 1975-78; research asst. Emory U. Dept. Rehab., Atlanta, 1978-80; dir. phys. therapy Curative Rehab. Ctr., Milw., 1980-85, v.p., 1985—; mem. profl. adv. com. Kimberly Home Health, Milw., 1983-87. Active women's group Counseling Ctr., Milw., 1986-87; creator program for adult survivors of childhood sexual abuse, 1988. Mem. Am. Phys. Therapy Assn., Wis. Phys. Therapy Assn. (treas. 1984-85, v.p. 1985-87). Democrat. Office: Curative Rehab Ctr 1000 N 92d St Wauwatosa WI 53226

OSTENDORF, JOAN DONAHUE, fund raiser/volunteer; b. Boston, Dec. 9, 1933; d. John Stanley and Genevieve Catherine (Morrissey) Donahue; m. Edgar Louis Ostendorf, Feb. 10, 1962; 1 child, Mary Elizabeth. BA, Marymount Coll., Tarrytown, N.Y., 1956; postgrad., Boston U., 1956. Tchr. Boston pub. schs., 1956-57, Waltham (Mass.) pub. schs., 1957-62. Trustee Cleve. Inst. Music, 1984—, mem. trustees coordinating coun., 1989; mem. Jr. League Cleve., 1964, 1st v.p., 1972-73; founding mem. adv. coun. to pub. rels. com. Cleve. Mus. Arts, 1974-84; trustee women's com. Cleve. Orch., 1974, 1st v.p., 1975-76; mem. del. assembly United Way, 1977-87; chmn. benefits Vis. Nurse Assn., 1987-88, March of Dimes, 1982; trustee wommen's com. Univ. Hosps. of Case Western Res. U. Med. Sch., 1974—, also others. Mem. Longwood Cricket Club, Intown Club, Chagrin Valley Hunt Club. Republican. Roman Catholic. Address: 3425 Roundwood Rd Chagrin Falls OH 44022

OSTERBERG, BECKY, communications executive; b. Fargo, N.D., Sept. 11, 1946; d. Robert and Edna Mae (Smith) Huxtable; m. Robert C. Osterberg Jr., Jan. 20, 1979. BA in Journalism, Ind. U., 1969. Mgr. mdse. J.C. Penney & Co., Newport Beach, Calif., 1974-77; stockbroker Merrill Lynch, Fullerton, Calif., 1977-79; cons. communications Fin. Relations Bd., Chgo., 1979-81; v.p. fin. relations Burson-Marsteller, Chgo., 1981-83; dir. investor relations Ameritech, Chgo., 1983-86; v.p. communications Premark Internat., Chgo., 1986—. Mem. Nat. Investor Rels. Inst. (past. dir.). Republican. Office: Premark Internat Inc 1717 Deerfield Rd Deerfield IL 60015

OSTERMAN, CONSTANTINE E., elected legislative member; b. Acme, Alta., Can., June 23, 1936; m. Joe Osterman, Oct. 30, 1954; children: Theo, Kurt, Kim, Kelly, Joe Jr. MLA representing Three Hills constituency Alta. Legis. Assembly, 1979-82, 82-85, 86-89, 89—, party whip, mem. edn. caucus and agr. caucus coms., 1982-86, minister of consumer and corp. affairs, mem. social planning com. of cabinet, cabinet/caucus com. on legis. rev., agr. caucus com., 1986, minister of social svcs. and community health, 1986-89, minister career devel. and employment, chair econ. devel., 1989—; served select legis. com. to rev. surface rights issue, lead role in passing of Surface Rights Act, 1983. Active exec. bds. local ch., home and sch. assns., Carstairs, Alta., 1958—, surface rights area; commr., charter mem. Alta. Human Rights Commn., 1973-78; pres. Can. Assn. Statutory Human Rights Agys. Office: 620 Legislature Annex, Edmonton, AB Canada T5K 1E4

OSTERMAN-OLSON, KAREN, securities sales and financial consultant; b. Newark, Nov. 20, 1951; d. David and Harriet (Hirschoff) Rosenstein; m. Walter S. Olson, Apr. 9, 1984. BBA, Kent (Ohio) State U., 1972; MBA, No. Ill. U., 1981. Acct. Alexander Grant & Co., Chgo., 1973-74; tax acct. Interstate United Corp., 1974-77; asst. tax mgr. Chamberlain Mfg. Corp., Elmhurst, Ill., 1977-81; mgr. tax systems Data-Tax, Inc., Naperville, Ill., 1981-85; v.p., gen. mgr. IMD, Inc., 1985-86; fin. cons. Lisle, Ill., 1986—. Mem. Internat. Assn. for Fin. Planning. Republican. Office: 5915 Meadow Dr Lisle IL 60532

OSTERMEIR-NOSTRO, SHARON, chiropractor; b. N.Y.C., July 24, 1962; d. Walter Barthl and Mary Ann Rose (Ziefle) Ostermeir; m. John Paul Nostro, Oct. 10, 1987. AS, U. Bridgeport, 1982, BS, 1986; D of Chiropractic, N.Y. Chiropractic Coll., Old Brookville, 1986. Assoc. Office of Dr. Mystical DelGiorno, N.Y.C., 1986; ptnr. Commack (N.Y.) Chiropractic Care, 1986—; neurology resident N.Y. Chiropractic Coll., Waltham, Mass., 1989—. Mem. AAUW (v.p. program 1989-91), N.Y. Chiropractic Assn., Smithtown Bus. and Profl. Women's Network. Office: Commack Chiropractic Care 2171 Jericho Turnpike Commack NY 11725

OSTROM, CAROL MARIE, reporter; b. Seattle, June 27, 1947; d. Cameron Walthew and Eula Marie (Curry) O. BA in English Lit., U. Wash., 1970. Program asst. Sch. Medicine U. Wash., Seattle, 1970-73; asst. mgr. circulation Seattle Sun, 1974-75, reporter, asst. editor, 1974-77, editor, 1978-79; reporter, assoc. editor Willamette Week, Portland, Oreg., 1979-80; reporter features and news Seattle Times, 1980-83, reporter religion, 1983—. Recipient Excellence in Journalism awards Sigma Delta Chi, 1978-88; John S. Knight fellow Stanford U., 1984-85. Mem. Religion Newswriters Assn. (Supple award 1988). Office: Seattle Times Fairview Ave N & John St PO Box 70 Seattle WA 98111

OSTROW, EILEEN JOYCE, publisher; b. Detroit, June 21, 1949; d. Joseph Aaron and Doris Ostrow; m. Stanley Harold Feldman, May 25, 1989. BS in Spl. Elem. Edn.with distinction, U. Mich., 1971; MA in Edn. Exceptional Children Learning Disability, San Francisco State U., 1975; MA in English, Mills Coll., 1977. Cert. elem. tchr., jr. coll., adult sch. edn., spl. edn., English, Calif. Tchr. of educable mental retarded children Oakland Pub. Sch., 1971-74; typesetter West Coast Print Ctr., Berkeley, Calif., 1978-84; typographer Chevron Corp., San Francisco, 1985—; publisher, printer, editor Sea Urchin Press, Oakland, 1977—. Editor/publisher: Center Stage: An Anthology of 21 Contemporary Black-American Plays, 1981, Child of War & Revolution, 1983; contbr. articles to profl. jours.; exhibitor: Vancouver Arts of the Book Exhibiton, The Alcuin Soc., 1986. Mem., bd. dirs. Berkeley/Richmond Jew. Community Ctr., 1982-85. Recipient Small Press Grant Lit. Nat. Endowment for the Arts Program, 1980. Mem. Pacific Ctr. for the Book Arts (assoc. mem.). Office: Sea Urchin Press PO Box 10503 Oakland CA 94610-0503

OSTROW, RONA LYNN, librarian, educator; b. N.Y.C., Oct. 21, 1948; d. Morty and Jeane Goldberg; m. Steven A. Ostrow, June 25, 1972; 1 child, Ciné Justine. BA, CCNY, 1969; MS in LS, Columbia U., 1970; MA, Hunter Coll., 1975. Cert. libr., N.Y. Br. adult and reference libr. N.Y. Pub. Libr., N.Y.C., 1970-73, rsch. libr., 1973-78; asst. libr. Fashion Inst. Tech., N.Y.C., 1978-80; assoc. dir. Grad. Bus. Resource Ctr., Baruch Coll., CUNY, 1980—, assoc. prof., 1980—. Author: Dictionary of Retailing, 1984, Dictionary of Marketing, 1987; co-author: Cross Reference Index, 1989. Mem. ALA, Spl. Librs. Assn., Libr. Info. and Tech. Assn., Assn. Coll. and Rsch. Librs., Libr. Assn. CUNY, NAFE. Office: Baruch Coll GBRC Box 262 17 Lexington Ave New York NY 10010

OSTROWSKI, ELENA MARINA, construction management consultant; b. N.Y.C., June 3, 1962; d. Walter John Ostrowski and Clara Ernestina (Lluberes). AB, Smith Coll., Northampton, 1984. Facilities mgmt. project asst. Donaldson Lufkin & Jenrette, N.Y.C., 1984-85; constrn. project mgr. PJ Mech., N.Y.C., 1985-87; facilities mgmt. asst. treas. Morgan Guaranty Trust Co., N.Y.C., 1987—; cons.Nutravet Corp., Poughkeepsie, N.Y., 1986, Robert Abady Dog Food Corp., Poughkeepsie, 1986. Editor: The Secret is Out, 1987, The State of Animal Nutrition, 1988. Co-chmn. Smith Coll. Jr. Scholarship Com., N.Y.C., 1987. Mem. Am. Women Entrepreneurs; Smith Coll. Club. Republican. Roman Catholic.

OSTROWSKI, MARIA J., journalist; b. Joliet, Ill., Nov. 18, 1937; d. George and Helen (Argodale) Scoofakes; m. Robert Ostrowski, Oct. 17, 1961 (div. 1978); children: Vincent, Diana. BS in Journalism and Communications, U. Ill., 1959. Prodn. editor Encyclopaedia Britannica, Chgo., 1964-75; tech. editor AM Internat., Schaumburg, Ill., 1975-79; mng. editor Am. Med. Record Assn., Chgo., 1979-87; ass. editor U.S. League Savs. Instns., Chgo., 1987—. Mem. Chgo. Women in Pub. (sec. and chair mgrs. roundtable 1989), Chgo. Book Clinic, Women in Communications, Soc. Profl. Journalists, Ventura Users Group. Home: 1282 N Williams Dr Palatine IL 60067

OSTROWSKY, LAURA RUTH, healthcare adminstrator; b. Bronx, N.Y., Jan. 20, 1951; d. Jacob and Mildred (Kroos) O.; m. Edward Joseph Filemyr IV, Apr. 5, 1985. BA, Lehman Coll., 1973; AA, N.Y.C. Tech. Coll., 1979; M Urban Planning, Hunter Coll., 1984. Staff nurse Montefiore Med. Ctr., Bronx, 1979-82, adminstrv. resident office of v.p. planning, 1982-83; coordinator quality assurance Montefiore Med. Ctr., N.Y.C., 1983-85; dir. quality assurance Montefiore Med. Ctr., Bronx, 1985-88; dir. patient case mgmt. N.Y. Hosp. Cornell Med. Ctr., N.Y.C., 1988-. Bd. dirs. United Assn. Bedford Park, Bronx; mediator Bedford Mosholu. Mem. Nat. Assn. Quality Assurance Profl., N.Y. Assn. Quality Assurance. Office: NY Hosp Cornell Med Ctr 525 E 68 St New York NY 10021

O'SULLIVAN, EILEEN ANN, banker; b. Phila., May 7, 1956; d. Thomas and Elisabeth (Kiehl) O'S. Student, Ctr. for Fin. Studies, Fairfield, Conn., 1988. Teller trainee Beneficial Savs. Bank, Phila., 1974-75, jr. teller, 1975-80, teller #2, 1980-81, teller #3, 1981-82, head teller, 1982-84, mgmt. trainee, 1984-85, asst. mgr., 1975-87, mgr., 1987—. Co-chairperson Widener Day com. Widener Meml. Sch., 1987—; mem., speaker community workshops 35th Police Dist., 1986—, chairperson holiday meals program, 1988—; sec. Greater Broad and Olney Bus. Assn., 1984-88; assoc. mem. Phila. Orch. Soc., 1987—; mem. Smithsonian Inst., 1988—; mem. neighborhood improvement coun. Phila. Neighborhood Housing Svcs., 1989; mem. Earthwatch, 1990, Pa. Soc. for Prevention of Cruelty to Animals, 1990. Recipient Community Svc. award Phila. Police Dept., 1987, 88, 89. Mem. Nat. Space-L5 Soc. (life). Democrat. Roman Catholic. Office: Beneficial Savs Bank 330 Market St Philadelphia PA 19106

OSWALD, EVA SUE ADEN, insurance executive; b. Ft. Dodge, Iowa, Feb. 2, 1949; d. Warren Dale Aden and Alice Rae (Gingerich) Aspeslet; m. Bruce Elliott Oswald, Nov. 27, 1976. BBS, U. Iowa, 1972. With Great Am. Ins. Co., 1975—; v.p. mktg. div. Great Am. Ins. Co., Orange, Calif., 1987, v.p. profit ctr., 1988-90; ptnr. Vital Mgmt. & Cons. Corp., Mpls., 1990—. Mem. Nat. Assn. Ins. Women, State Guarantee Fund (bd. dirs. 1986-87). Methodist. Office: 3500 W 80th St Ste 255 Minneapolis MN 55431

OSWALD, GRETCHEN, lighting manufacturing company executive, industrial motor repairs and sales company executive; b. Pitts., Oct. 23, 1945; d. V.E. and Eleanor (Hook) O. BA, DePauw U., 1967. Pres. Shop Materials, Inc., Pitts., 1981—, Electric M&R Inc., Pitts., 1983—. Mem. World Affairs Council Pitts. Republican. Presbyterian. Clubs: Duquesne, Grow and Invest Now Investment (Pitts.). Office: Electric M&R Inc 2025 Milford Dr Pittsburgh PA 15102

OSZA, DEBRA EVANS, communications executive; b. South Bend, Ind., Mar. 3, 1954; d. Edward Farrell and Dola Mae (Carriger) Evans; m. David Allen Osza, July 12, 1975. BS in Bus. Adminstrn. and Mktg., St. Mary of the Woods Coll., 1990. Office mgr. Dairy Coun. of No. Ind., Inc., South Bend, 1977-85, info. specialist, 1985-87; dir. food svc. and spl. projects Am. Dairy Assn. of Ind., Indpls., 1987-89; communications dir. Milk Promotion Svcs. of Ind., Inc., Indpls., 1989—; chmn. spl. activities subcom. Ind. State Agr. Day Com., Indpls., 1989-90, chmn.-elect 1990-91. Contbr. articles to profl. jours. Mem. Women in Communications, Ind. Fedn. Bus. and Profl. Women (mem. state nominating com. 1985-86, rec. sec. Mishawaka chpt. 1986). Office: Milk Promotion Svcs Ind 9360 Castlegate Dr Indianapolis IN 46051

OTANI, PRISCILLA H. V., household products company executive; b. Tokyo, May 13, 1952; came to U.S., 1970; d. Montgomery and Fujiko (Takase) Jarmain; m. Michael Yochum, Dec. 28, 1978. BA, Mills Coll., 1974; MA, Columbia U., 1977. Benefits analyst Dean Witter Reynolds, San Francisco, 1980-81, mgr. retirement plans, 1981-89; mgr. benefits Shaklee Corp., San Francisco, 1989-90, dir. employee benefits, 1990—. Mem. Western Pension Conf. Office: Shaklee Corp 444 Market St San Francisco CA 94111

OTHELLO, MARYANN CECILIA, management consultant; b. N.Y.C., Oct. 23, 1946; d. Alphonse Reasum and Edith (Atwater) O. BS, St. Paul's Coll., Lawrenceville, Va., 1968; MS, Columbia U., 1972. Cert. adoption specialist. Family therapist crisis intervention Dept. Social Svcs., N.Y.C., 1968-72; dir. treatment team Abbott House, Irvington, N.Y., 1972-73; unit chief Manhattan State Psychiat. Facility, N.Y.C., 1973-75; asst. dir., dir. social svcs. St. Peter's Sch., Peekskill, N.Y., 1975-77; dir. Patchwork Svcs. for Children, Santa Ana, Calif., 1977-78; dir. adult and geriatric svcs. Cen. City Community Mental Health, L.A., 1978-79; trainer, facilitator Lifespring, Inc., San Rafael, Calif., 1978-80; sr. mgmt. cons. Nelson Cons. Group, Inc., Mpls., 1980—; cons. Calif. Dept. Edn., 1977; field instr. casework Hunter Coll. Sch. Social Work, N.Y.C., 1975-77; adj. instr. U. So. Calif., L.A., 1977-78; specialist career devel. Goal for It, L.A., 1977-82; mgmt. devel. cons. Mgmt. Dynamics, Irvine, Calif., 1980-82. Contbr. articles to profl. jours.; was interviewed twice on radio talk show As It Is, U. Calif., Irvine. Bd. dirs., presenter humanitarian awards L.A. Commn. on Assaults Against Women, 1985-87; facilitator Ch. of Religious Scis., Huntington Beach, Calif., 1981-83, NAACP, Urban League. Named one of Outstanding Young Women of Am., 1976, 81; N.Y. State Regent scholar, 1968; Marie Antoinette Canon fellow Columbia U., 1972. Fellow Child Welfare League Am. (Adoption Specialist plaque 1976-89); mem. NAFE, Smithsonian Instn., Nat. Soc. for Historic Preservation, Wadsworth Antheneum, Nat. Trust for Hist. Preservation, Assn. for Female Execs. Office: Nelson Cons Group Inc 14001 Ridgedale Dr Ste 300 Minneapolis MN 55343

OTHERSEN, CHERYL LEE, insurance broker, realtor; b. Bay City, Mich., Aug. 17, 1948; d. Andrew Julius and Ruth Emma (Jacoby) Houthoofd; m. Wayne Korte Othersen, Sept. 5, 1964; 1 child, Angela. Lic. ins., Mich. State U., 1980, lic. realtor, 1981. Owner, operator Glad Rags Boutique, Unionville, Mich., 1976-79; dept. mgr. Gantos, Saginaw, Mich., 1979-80; agt., bookkeeper Othersen Ins. Agy., inc., Unionville, 1979-81, v.p., 1981—; realtor Osentoski Realty Corp., Unionville, 1981—. Active Mich. chpt. Nat. Head Injury Found., Mich. chpt. Nat. Found. for Ileitis and Colitis, Nat. Mus. In The Arts, Nat. Trust for Hist. Preservation; vol. local Rep. campaigns, 1982, 84, 86; assoc. mem. Am. Mus. Natural History. Fellow (hon.) John F. Kennedy Libr. Found.; mem. Profl. Ins. Agts., Unionville Bus. Assn., Nat. Mus. Women in the Arts (charter). Mem. Moravian Ch. Club: Sherwood-on-the-Hill Country (Gagetown, Mich.). Home: 4483 S Unionville Rd Unionville MI 48767 Office: Othersen Ins Agy Inc 6639 Center St Unionville MI 48767

OTT, DANA BETH, professor, consultant; b. Holdrege, Nebr., Jan. 20, 1952; d. Harold Edward and Phyllis Viola (Losey) O. AA, Chaffey Coll., 1972; BS, Calif. State Polytech. U., 1974; MS, U. Nebr., 1976; PhD, Rutgers U., 1982. Asst. prof. Tex. A&M U., College Station, 1982-84; asst. prof. Mich. State U., East Lansing, 1984—, sensory cons., 1988—, dir. sensory lab., 1988—. Author: Applied Food Chemistry Laboratory Manual, 1987; contbr. articles to profl. jours. Am. Dietetic Assn. fellow, 1978, 79, Inst. Food Technologists fellow, 1977, 79; Mich. State U. tchr.-scholar, 1986. Mem. Inst. Food Technologists (alt. regional communicator 1986—, com. mem. regional sects. 1987—), ASTM, Am. Dietetic Assn. Home: 6248 Rothbury Way #6 East Lansing MI 48823 Office: Mich State U Dept Food Sci 139 Food Sci Bldg East Lansing MI 48824

OTT, HOLLY-BROOKS, fashion model, designer and talent agent; b. Baton Rouge, Feb. 14, 1956; d. Jack Leroy and Mary Caroline (Legere) O.; m. Clinton R. Hilderbrand, June 16, 1990. Student, La. State U., 1987—. Dir. sales and mktg. Prescott Murphy Agy., Baton Rouge, 1975-84; pres. The Holly-Brooks Ott Agy., Baton Rouge, 1986—, Sweet Dreams, Inc., Baton Rouge, 1990—, HBO/Modeling and Talent Mgmt., Baton Rouge, 1990—, The L.A. Connection, Baton Rouge, 1990—, Empress Lingerie & Sportswear, Baton Rouge, 1990—. Mem. NAFE, Women Bus. Owners Assn., Baton Rouge C. of C., Gov.'s Crewe Mardi Gras. Republican. Office: Holly-Brooks Ott Agy 1443 Delplaza Dr Ste 4 Baton Rouge LA 70815

OTT, RITA ANN, insurance executive; b. St. Charles, Mo., Oct. 15, 1961; d. Ned Robert and Geraldine Helen (Weingartner) Johnson. AS in Bus. Adminstrn., Florissant Valley Coll., 1989. Darkroom technician J.B. Photo, St. Charles, Mo., 1979-82; account payable mgr. St. Louis Foods Svc., Overland, Mo., 1982-89; cash balancing supr. Edward D. Jones & Co., St. Louis, 1989; claims mgr. Stieferman Bros. Van & Storage, St. Louis, 1989—. Mem. NAFE. Democrat. Roman Catholic. Home: 436 Blanche Dr Saint Charles MO 63303 Office: Roth Asbestos and Environ Cons 12395 Olive Blvd Saint Louis MO 63141

OTTAVIANO, DORIS BAGINSKI, librarian; b. Middletown, Conn., June 14, 1938; d. Edward Francis and Genevieve M. (Recko) Baginski; m. Thomas J., April 16, 1983. BA, U. Conn., Storrs, 1960; MSLS, Syracuse (N.Y.) U., 1963. Gen. asst. Hartford Pub. Library, Conn., 1960-61; grad. asst. Syracuse U., N.Y., 1961-63; reference libr. Enoch Pratt Free Libr., Balt., 1963-64, sr. reference libr., subject specialist, 1965-69; sr. subject cataloger Yale U. Libr., New Haven, 1969-70; head reference libr. US Naval War Coll., Newport, R.I., 1970—. Author Contr. Articles to Profl. Jours. 1985. Mem. Spl. Libr. Assn.(pres. 1988-89, R.I. chpt.), Am. Libr. Assn., New Eng. Libr. Assn., R.I. Libr Assn., Coalition of Libr. Advs., Beta Phi Mu (Libr. Sci. Honor Soc.), Bus. & Profl. Women's Assn. Home: 1485 Tower Hill Rd North Kingstown RI 02852

OTTINGER, MARY LOUISE, podiatrist; b. Valley City, N.D., July 8, 1956; d. Roy A. and Harriet A. (Noltimier) O. BS, N.D. State U., 1978; D of Podiatric Medicine, Scholl. Coll. Podiatric Med., Chgo. 1983. Resident in podiatric medicine J.A. Haley VA Hosp., Tampa, Fla., 1983-84; podiatrist Med. Ctr. Podiatry Group, Augusta, Ga., 1984—. Author: (with others) Podiatric Dermatology, 1986. Mem. Am. Podiatric Med. Assn., Ga. Podiatric Med. Assn., Am. Diabetes Assn., Am. Coll. Foot Surgeons (assoc.), AAUW, Network Augusta, Mensa, Toastmasters (treas. North Augusta 1987, pres. 1988, adminstrv. v.p. 1989, area gov. 1988). Methodist. Office: Med Ctr Podiatry Group 1515 Laney Walker Blvd Augusta GA 30904

OTTMAN, JOSEPHINE KENNEDY, financial software executive; b. Chgo., May 27, 1955; d. John Budlong and Joan (Kennedy) O. AB, Middlebury Coll., 1977; MBA, Columbia U., 1985. Mgr. Home Box Office, N.Y.C., 1978-83; fin. software exec. Thomson Fin. Networks Inc., Boston, 1986—. Mem. Middlebury Coll. Alumni Assn. (bd. dirs. 1986-88). Office: Thomson Fin Networks Inc 11 Farnsworth St Boston MA 02210

OTTMANN, JUDI, editor, writer; b. Pasadena, Calif., Oct. 7, 1959; d. Robert Donald and Ora Del (Schmitt) O. BJ, U. Tex., Austin, 1981. Asst. editor Austin City C. of C., 1981; asst. communications dir. and mng. editor Greater Houston Builders Assn., 1982-85; editor, writer St. Joseph Hosp., Houston, 1985—. Editor, writer DISCOVER Mag., 1989 (Healthcare Mktg. Report Silver award 1989). Fundraising campaign dir. Holy Covenant United Meth. Ch., Houston, 1986-87; vol. tutor Vols. in Continuing Edn. Program, Houston, 1990. Recipient Excalibur award Pub. Rels. Soc. Am. (Houston chpt.), 1990. Mem. Women in Communications, Internat. Assn. Bus. Communicators, Am. Soc. for the Prevention of Cruelty to Animals. Home: 1822 Barker Cypress Rd #607 Houston TX 77084 Office: St Joseph Hosp 1919 LaBranch St Houston TX 77002

OTTNEY, NANCY LOUISE, transportation specialist; b. Holden, W.Va., May 23, 1954; d. Otis and Julia Juanita (Preston) Lopresti; m. Richard K. Ottney, Oct. 7, 1989; 1 child, John Lopresti. Assoc. degree, Ashland (Ky.) Bus. Coll., 1975. Cert. MSHA instr.; dust cert., noise cert. methane cert., Ky underground mining cert., emergency med. technician, multimedia first aid instr. Legal sec. Charles M. Daniels, Atty.-at-Law, Greenup, Ky., 1974-76; probation and parole sec. State of Ky., Greenup, 1976-77; various positions Ky.-Ohio Transp. Co., South Shore, Ky., 1977-84, distbn. supr., 1984—. Mem. Coal Exch., Women in Networking, Propeller Club. Home: RR 1 Box 355 Greenup KY 41144 Office: PO Box 899 South Shore KY 41175

OTTO, CATHERINE NAN, clinical laboratory scientist; b. Stockton, Calif., Dec. 17, 1953; d. Edward Joseph Otto and Arlene Maud (Holmes)

Naylor. BS in Microbiology, Oreg. State U., 1976; BS in Med. Tech., Oreg. Health Scis. U., 1981; BA in French, Portland (Oreg.) State U., 1986, MBA, 1990. Cert. clin. lab. scientist, clin. lab. supr., clin. lab. specialist in hematology, med. technologist. Med. technologist night shift Ore. Health Scis. U., Portland, 1981-85; med. technologist night shift Bess Kaiser Med. Ctr., Portland, 1985, med. technologist hematology, 1985-86; lab. supr. div. med. office Kaiser Permanente, Portland, 1986-87, lab. supr. Vancouver Med. Office, 1987—. Bd. dirs. Friends of Ore. Pub. Broadcasting, Portland, 1985-88; mem. allied health subcom. Am. Cancer Soc., Portland, 1985-87. Mem. Assn. for Oreg. Med. Tech. (pres. 1986-87, bd. dirs. 1984-85, Mem. of Yr. 1989), Portland Dist. Soc. Assn. for Oreg. Med. Tech. (pres. 1983-84), Am. Soc. for Med. Tech. (chair region IX immunology/immunohematology scientific assembly 1984-87, vice chmn. 1987-88, chair 1990-91, trustee 1990—, commr. profl. and continuing edn. affairs 1989—), Am. Assn. Blood Banks, Am. Assn. Clin. Chemists, NAFE, Clin. Lab. Mgmt. Assn. , AAUW, Beaverton Internat. Tng. in Communication (sec. 1985-86).

OTTO, MARGARET AMELIA, librarian; b. Boston, Oct. 22, 1937; d. Henry Earlen and Mary (McLennan) O.; children—Christopher, Peter. A.B., Boston U., 1960; M.S., Simmons Coll., 1961; M.A. (hon.), Dartmouth Coll., 1981. Asst. sci. librarian M.I.T., Cambridge, 1963; Lindgren librarian M.I.T., 1964-67, acting sci. librarian, 1967-69, asst. dir., 1969-75, asso. dir., 1976-79; librarian of coll. Dartmouth Coll., Hanover, N.H., 1979—; pres., chmn. bd. Universal Serials and Book Exch., Inc., 1980-81; bd. govs. Rsch. Libr. Group, 1979—, trustee Howe Libr., Hanover, 1988—; mem. Brown Libr. Com.; trustee vis. com. U. Rochester Libr.; active ARL Com. on ARL Statis. Council on Library Resources fellow, 1974; elected to Collegium of Disting. Alumnus Boston U., 1980. Mem. ALA, Assn. Research Libraries (chmn. preservation com. 1983-85, bd. dirs 1985-87). Home: 16 Dresden Rd Hanover NH 03755 Office: Dartmouth Coll 115 Baker Meml Libr Hanover NH 03755

OTTO, (BERTHA) MARIE, educational administrator, educational consulting company executive; b. Houston, July 11, 1930; d. Robert Lillard and Bertha Irene (Allen) Davis; m. Robert Lee Otto, Jan. 7, 1950; children: Lois Ann Otto Buschmann, Barbara Jeane Otto Hunt, Robert Lee Jr. Student, Tex. Christian U., 1947-49, Hardin-Simmons U., summers 1947, 49, 54; BA in Speech, Drama and Edn., Sul-Ross State U., 1954; postgrad., U. Wyo., 1960-61, U. Calif., Santa Barbara, 1961-62, Calif. State U., Northridge, 1961-62, 64; MA, Calif. State U., Long Beach, 1969, postgrad., 1980-82. Lic. tchr., Tex., secondary tchr., Wyo., Calif.; lic. psychologist; lic. marriage and family counselor. Tchr. high schs., Tex., Wyo. and Calif., 1956-64; tchr., counselor Excelsior High Sch., Norwalk, Calif., 1964-66; counselor Neff High Sch., La Mirada, Calif., 1966-69; psychologist Huntington Beach (Calif.) Union High Sch. Dist., 1969-74, project mgr., dir. pupil pers., 1974-80, asst. supt., 1980-84, supt., 1984-88, supt. emeritus, 1988—; v.p. Poole-Young-Koehler Assocs. Inc., Long Beach, 1964-79; pvt. practice marriage and family counselor, Fountain Valley, Calif., 1970—; pres. Marie Ottos Assocs., Fountain Valley, 1979—; supr. student tchrs. Chapman Coll., Santa Ana, Calif., 1988—. Mem. Fountain Valley Human Svcs. Com., Huntington Beach Human Resources Commn., state planning com. Girl Scouts U.S., Worland, Wyo., 1959-61; pres. Spl. Edn. Local Plan Orgn., 1983-84; bd. dirs. Humana Hosp. Huntington Beach, Golden West Coll. Found., Huntington Beach, Huntington Beach Community Clinic, Orange County chpt. ARC, Santa Ana, Calif. No on Drugs, 1988—. Recipient numerous plaques, 1985—, including Fountain Valley Human Svcs. Com., 1979, City of Fountain Valley, 1975, 79, 88, City of Huntington Beach, 1988, Fountain Valley C. of C., 1988, City of Westminster, 1988, Orange Coast Coll., 1988, Golden West Coll., 1988, Ocean View Sch. Dist., 1988, Spl. Edn. Local Plan Orgn., 1984; named Woman of Yr., Soroptimist Club, Westminster, 1984, Disting. Alumnus, Grad. Sch. Edn. Calif. State U.-Long Beach, 1988. Home: 16689 Mt Hoffman Circle Fountain Valley CA 92708 Office: Huntington Beach High Sch Dist 10251 Yorktown Ave Huntington Beach CA 92646

OTTO-PRIMI, TERRE A., real estate executive and developer, interior designer; b. N.Y.C., Aug. 8, 1941; d. Sigfried S. and Ethyl (Goldstein) Alper; children: Regan Alexis, Tiffany Ariana, Dylan Richard. BA, Bennington Coll., 1963; postgrad., Columbia U., 1964, U. Geneva, 1960. Pres. Primiterre Assocs., Port Washington; communications mgr. Royal Rail, Port Washington, N.Y. Home: 82 Barkers Point Rd Sands Point NY 11050 Office: Royal Rail PO Box 1199 Port Washington NY 11050

OUALLINE, VIOLA JACKSON, psychologist; b. Edna, Tex., Oct. 17, 1927; d. S.R. Jackson and Myrtle Mae Wood; m. Charles M. Oualline Jr., Sept. 3, 1949; children—Stephen, Susan, Shari. B.S., U. Houston, 1949; M.S., North Tex. State U., 1962, Ph.D., 1975. Phys. therapist Hermann Hosp., Houston, 1948-49, pvt. practice, Austin, Tex., 1949-54, Miller Orthopedic Clinic, Charlotte, N.C., 1956-57; psychologist Dallas Easter Seal Soc., 1963-81, dir. psychology dept., 1981—; psychol. cons. Mesquite Independent Sch. Dist., Tex., 1974—, Duncanville Sch. Dist., Tex., 1974-76, Grand Prarie Ind. Sch. Dist., Tex., 1976-79. Mem. Am. Psychol. Assn., Tex. Psychol. Assn., Dallas Psychol. Assn., Am. Assn. Counseling Devel., Council for Exceptional Children, Chi Omega Mother's Bd. Patients' Advocations: reading; bicycle riding. Office: Dallas Easter Seal Soc 5701 Maple St Dallas TX 75229

OUELLETTE, JANE LEE YOUNG, biology educator; b. Charlotte, N.C., Dec. 29, 1929; d. James Thomas and Nancy Isabel (Yarbrough) Young; m. Armand Roland Ouellette, Aug. 3, 1951 (dec. Oct. 1984); children—Elizabeth Anne, James Young, Emily Jane, Frances Lee. B.A., Winthrop Coll., 1950; M.A., Oberlin Coll., 1952; postgrad. Coll. Medicine, Baylor U., 1974, U. Tex.-Houston, 1976-83, Tex. Woman's U., 1980-82. Lic. tchr., Tex. Tchr. Maria Regina High Sch., Hartsdale, N.Y., 1969-70, Spring Ind. Sch. System, Tex., 1972-78; coordinator biology program, instr., North Harris County Coll., Houston, 1979—. Mem. Internat. Assn. for Study of Pain, Internat. Pain Found., N.Y. Acad. Sci., AAAS, Internat. Chronobiol. Soc., People to People Internat. Democrat. Home: 1619 Big Horn St Houston TX 77090 Office: North Harris County Coll 2700 W Thorne Dr Houston TX 77073

OUJESKY, HELEN M., microbiology educator; b. Ft. Worth, Aug. 14, 1930; d. Steve and Lillie (Krivanek) Matusevich; m. Frank P. Oujesky, Dec. 27, 1951; children: Michael Jerome, David Franklin, Christopher Aaron. BA, Tex. State Coll. for Women, 1951; MA, Tex. Christian U., 1965; PhD, Tex. Women's U., 1968. Cert. profl. tchr., Tex. Chemistry/biology tchr. Ft. Worth Ind. Sch. Dist., 1951-63; grad. teaching asst. Tex. Christian U., Ft. Worth, 1963-65; grad. teaching Tex. Woman's U., Denton, 1965-68, asst. prof., 1968-73; assoc. prof. microbiology U. Tex. at San Antonio, 1973-80, prof. microbiology, 1980—; bd. dirs. Tex. Acad. Sci., 1980—. Contbr. numerous articles to profl. jours. Pres. Altrusa Club San Antonio, 1980-81; bd. dirs. Alamo Regional Acad. Sci. & Engring, San Antonio, 1986—, San Antonio Women's Celebration & Hall of Fame, San Antonio, 1985—. Named to San Antonio Women's Hall of Fame/Sci. & Technology, 1987; recipient Research contract Bur. Land Mgmt., 1977-79, Grants NSF, 1976, 77, 79, 80, 81. Fellow Tex. Acad. Sci.; mem. AAAS, AAUW (pres. 1985-87), Am. Soc. for Microbiology, Soc. for Indsl. Microbiology (com. mem. 1976), Sigma Xi (Alamo chpt. pres. 1985-86). Republican. Roman Catholic. Home: 604 Skyforest Dr San Antonio TX 78232 Office: U Tex at San Antonio 7000 NW Loop 1604 San Antonio TX 78285

OUNJIAN, MARILYN J., employment and training company executive; b. Harrisburg, Pa., Oct. 24, 1947; d. Stanley Wolf and Rebecca (Darrow) Freeman; m. Irving Henry Schwartz, Aug. 24, 1974 (dec. May 1975); 1 child, Jennifer; m. George Edward Ounjian, July 31, 1982; children: Jonathan, Kori. Student, U. Md. Pres. Today's People, Phila., 1973-81; chmn., founder, chief exec. officer Careers USA, Phila., 1981—; pres., chief exec. officer The Career Inst., Phila., 1981—. Mem. Rep. Senatorial Inner Circle; bd. dirs. Phila. Econ. Devel. Coalition. Mem. Cen. City Proprietors Assn., NAFE, Nat. Assn. Women Bus. Owners, Inst. Am. Entrepreneurs, Greater Phila. C. of C., Pa. C. of C., Assn. Venture Founders. Club: Gov.'s Del. Office: Careers USA 1825 JF Kennedy Blvd Philadelphia PA 19103

OUTHWAITE, LUCILLE CONRAD, ballerina, educator; b. Peoria, Ill., Feb. 26, 1909; d. Frederick Albert and Della (Cornett) Conrad; m. Leonard Outhwaite, Mar. 1, 1936 (dec. 1978); children—Ann Outhwaite Maurer, Lynn Outhwaite Pulsifer. Student, U. Nebr., 1929-30, Mills Coll., 1931-32; student piano, Paris, 1933-35, Legat Sch., London, 1934, N.Y.C. Ballet,

N.Y.C., 1936-41, Royal Ballet Sch., London, 1957-59. Tchr. ballet Perry Mansfield, Steamboat Springs, Colo., 1932, Cape Playhouse, Dennis, Mass., 1937-41, Jr. League, N.Y.C., 1937-41, King Coit Sch., N.Y.C., 1937-41; toured with Am. Ambassador Ballet, Europe and S. Am., 1933-35; owner, tchr. dance sch., Oyster Bay, N.Y., 1949-57. Producer, choreographer ballets Alice in Wonderland, 1951, Pied Piper of Hamlin, 1952. Author: Birds in Flight, 1984. Mem. English Speaking Union, Preservation Soc., Alliance Française, Delta Gamma. Republican. Episcopalian. Clubs: Mills Coll. Spouting Rock Beach, Clambake (Newport, R.I.). Office: Beachmound Bellevue Ave Newport RI 02840

OVER, JANA THAIS, computer specialist; b. Sangley Point, USN Sta., Philippines, Aug. 4, 1956; d. John James Jr. and Betty June (Pugh) O.; m. David Paul Harrington, Mar. 23, 1985. BA cum laude, Randolph-Macon Woman's Coll., 1978; MBA, Marymount Coll. Va., 1986. Rsch. asst., typist U.S. Dept. Treasury, Washington, 1978-82, computer programmer, analyst, Office Sec. Domestic Fin., 1982-85, computer specialist, Office Fiscal Asst. Sec., 1985—. Docent, U.S. Dept. Treasury, Office of the Curator, Washington, 1989—; mem. Choctaw Nation of Okla. Recipient Asian Studies award, Randolph-Macon Woman's Coll., Va., 1978, Award of Distinction in Cash Mgmt. U.S. Dept. Treasury, 1988. Mem. NAFE, Fed. ADP User's Group, Randolph-Macon Woman's Coll. Alumnae (treas. Washington chpt. 1982-83), Treasury Hist. Assn. (bd. dirs., treas. 1989—). Office: US Dept Treasury 1500 Pennsylvania Ave NW Washington DC 20220

OVERBAGH, VIRGINIA ANNE, media company executive; b. Caripito, Venezuela, Dec. 27, 1944; d. Charles Oron and Marjory Anne (Rendle) Vail; m. Wayne Jeffrey Overbagh, Jan. 11, 1964 (div. May 1972); children: Donald Wayne, Kristine Vail. Student, U. Colo., 1962-64. Dir. shows Denver Mdse. Mart, 1973-74; dir. sales and mktg. Holiday Inn Denver Downtown, 1974-78; mgr. pay TV Am. TV and Communications, Denver, 1978-79, gen. mgr. Denver HBO, 1980-82, corp. mktg. mgr., 1979-80; v.p. ops. S.W. Cable Am. TV and Communications, San Diego, 1982-84; v.p. mktg., programming and P.A. Nat. div. Am. TV and Communications, Denver, 1984-86, v.p. western operation-nat. div., 1986-87; v.p. western region mktg. The Disney Channel, Burbank, Calif., 1987—. Mem. So. Calif. Cable Assn. (bd. dirs. 1988—).

OVERBECK, LOIS MORE, humanities educator, researcher; b. Milw., Jan. 15, 1945; d. Thomas Irvin and Pearl (Eggebrecht); m. James Arwin, June 11, 1966; children: Kristen Sara, Andrew James, Jonathan Alex. BA, Beloit Coll., 1966; MA, U. Chgo., 1967; PhD, U. Pa., 1979. Instr. North Park Coll., Chgo., 1967-69; teaching fellow U. Pa., Phila., 1969-72; lectr. Claremont McKenna Coll., Claremont, Calif., 1977-80; asst. prof. Agnes Scott Coll., Atlanta; lectr. Ga. State U., Atlanta, 1984-86; asst. prof. Spelman Coll., 1986-88; rsch. assoc. Emory U. Grad. Sch., Atlanta, 1990—; cons. Beckett Festival Radio Plays, N.Y., 1985-89; dir. Beckett Atlanta, 1987. Editor: The Correspondence of Samuel Beckett; contbr. articles to profl. jours. V.p. Performance Gallery, Atlanta, 1987-88. Fellow Ford Found., Chgo., 1966-67; grantee Beckett Ga. Endowment for the Humanities, 1987, Nat. Endowment for the Humanities, 1987. Mem. S.E. Atlantic Modern Lang. Assn., Modern Lang. Assn., Assn. of Tchrs. of Advanced Composition, Am. Theatre Assn. Home: 517 Ridgecrest Rd NE Atlanta GA 30307

OVERHOLT, GAIL CLAIRE See KRENZER, GAIL CLAIRE

OVERMAN, AMEGDA NICOLE JACK, nematologist, researcher; b. Tampa, Fla., May 17, 1920; d. Nicholas George and Eloise (Urquhart) Jack; m. Richard Douglas Overman, July 5, 1953. BS, U. Tampa, 1942; MS, U. Fla., 1951. Instr. dept. chemistry U. Tampa, 1941-42; asst. in soil chemistry Gulf Coast Rsch. and Edn. Ctr., U. Fla., Bradenton, 1951-56; asst. soil microbiologist U. Fla., Gainesville, 1956-68, assoc. nematologist, 1968-73, nematologist, 1973-89, nematologist emerita, 1989—. Contbr. over 200 articles to rsch. publs. Vice-chmn. Bradenton City Planning and Zoning Commn., 1980—. Recipient rsch. award Fla. Fruit and Vegetable Soc., 1974. Mem. Fla. State Hort. Soc. (best paper award 1980, 84, 89, hon. mem. 1988), Orgn. Tropical Am. Nematologists (pres. 1975-76, Presdl. award 1985, hon. mem. 1989), Soc. Nematology (award for excellence 1982), Soil and Crop Soc. Fla. (pres. 1981-82), European Soc. Nematologists. Office: Gulf Coast Rsch Edn Ctr 5007 60th St E Bradenton FL 34203

OVERSTREET, SARAH GAYLE, newspaper columnist; b. Springfield, Mo., Oct. 21, 1951; d. Frank Daniel and Vermell (Pattillo) Keeslar. BS in Edn. and English, S.W. Mo. State U., 1974. Tchr. Ozark (Mo.) Pub. Schs., 1974-78; from reporter to columnist Springfield (Mo.) Newspapers, Inc., 1979-87; host pub. affairs program Telecable of Springfield, 1984-87; consumer reporter Sta. KSPR-TV, Springfield, 1987-89; columnist Newspaper Enterprise Assn., N.Y.C., 1987—. Home and Office: Rt 20 Box 2297 Springfield MO 65803

OVERTON, BETTY JEAN, college dean; b. Jacksonville, Fla., Oct. 10, 1949; d. Henry and Miriam (Gordon) Crawford; m. Joseph Alonzo Overton Jr., June 15, 1970 (divorced); children: Joseph Alonzo III, Jermaine Lamar. BA in English, Tenn. State U., 1970, MA in English, 1974; PhD in English, Vanderbilt U., 1980; student Inst. Ednl. Mgmt., Harvard U., 1990. Reporter Race Rels. Reporter Mag., Nashville, 1970-71; tchr. Met. Nashville Sch. System, 1971-72; instr., project dir. Tenn. State U., Nashville, 1972-76; asst. prof. Nashville State Tech. Inst., 1976-78, Fisk U., Nashville, 1978-83; assoc. dean. grad. sch. U. Ark., Little Rock, 1983-85, dean grad. sch., 1985—; instr. U. Tenn., Nashville, 1976-82 dir. rsch. sponsored programs, U. Ark., 1986-88; bd. dirs. Sci. and Info. Liason Office, 1984—. Bd. dirs. Ark. Sci. and Technology Authority, Little Rock, 1989—, Women's Project, 1986—, Ark. Pub. Policy Panel, 1988—, No. Bank Women's Adv. Bd., 1988—, Nashville Panel, 1974-83, Cen. Ark. Libr. Sys., 1990—, Ark. Coun. of Nat. Conf. Christians and Jews, Inc., 1990—; chair Bi-Racial Adv. Com. Little Rock Sch. Dist., 1987—. Am. Coun. Edn. fellow, 1981-82, W.K. Kellogg Found. fellow, 1988—. Mem. Nat. Coun. Tchrs. of English, Coun. Grad. Schs., Coun. So. Grad. Schs., Women Color United Against Domestic Violence (pres.), An. Assn. High Edn., Rotary, Alpha Kappa Alpha. Democrat. Roman Catholic. Office: Univ Ark Little Rock Grad Sch Office of the Dean 2801 S University Ave Little Rock AR 72204

OVERTON, HELEN PARKE (MRS. SAMUEL WATKINS OVERTON), Realtor; b. Memphis, Dec. 30, 1920; d. William and Pearl (Pinkston) Parker; m. Samuel Watkins Overton, Sept. 3, 1952; children—Helen Parke (Mrs. William Barron Brown), Napoleon Hill. Exec. sec. Memphis State U., 1941-43, Chgo. and So. Air Lines, 1943-46, Memphis Bd. Edn., 1948-50; dir. women's programs Sta. WHBQ-TV, Memphis, 1950-52. Pres., Beethoven Club, 1966-66, 72-78, 1988—, Mid-South Opera Guild, 1967-85; dir. auditions Mid-South region Met. Opera, 1960-71, mem. nat. council, 1960-71; chmn. Tenn. Arts Commn., 1968-70; bd. dirs. Opera Memphis, 1956—, Arts Appreciation, 1960-87, Tenn. Arts Commn., 1967-74. Mem. Sigma Alpha Iota, Alpha Gamma Delta. Clubs: Memphis Country (Memphis). Home: 5476 Collingwood Cove Memphis TN 38119

OVERTON, JANE VINCENT HARPER, biology educator; b. Chgo., Jan. 17, 1919; d. Paul Vincent and Isabel (Vincent) Harper; m. George W. Overton, Jr., Sept. 1, 1941; children: Samuel, Peter, Ann. AB, Bryn Mawr Coll., 1941, PhD, U. Chgo., 1950. Rsch. asst. U. Chgo., 1950-52, mem. faculty, 1952-89, prof. biology, 1972-89; prof. emeritus, 1989. Author articles embryology, cell biology. NIH, NSF research grantee, 1965-87. Home: 5648 Dorchester Ave Chicago IL 60637

OVERTON, ROSILYN GAY HOFFMAN, financial services executive; b. Corsicana, Tex., July 10, 1942; d. Billy Clarence and Ima Elise (Gay) Hoffman; m. Aaron Lewis Overton, Jr., July 2, 1960 (div. Mar. 1977); children: Aaron Lewis III, Adam Jerome. BS in Math., Wright State U., Dayton, Ohio, 1972, MS in Applied Econs. (fellow), 1973; postgrad. N.Y. U. Grad. Sch. Bus., 1974-76; Cert. Coll. Fin. Planning, 1987. Research analyst Nat. Security Agy., Dept. Def., 1962-67; bus. reporter Dayton Jour.-Herald, 1973-74; economist First Nat. City Bank, N.Y.C., 1974, A.T. & T. Co., 1974-75; broker Merrill Lynch, N.Y.C., 1975-80; asst. v.p. E.F. Hutton & Co., N.Y.C., 1980-84; v.p. nat. mktg. dir. investment products Manhattan Nat. Corp., 1984-86; pres. R.H. Overton Co., N.Y.C., 1986—; ptnr. Brown

& Overton Fin. Svcs., 1987—. Named Businesswoman of Yr., N.Y.C., 1976. Mem. Nat., N.Y. Assns. Bus. Economists, Nat. Fedn. Bus. and Profl. Women, Internat. Assn. Fin. Planning, Women's Econ. Roundtable, Gotham Bus. and Profl. Womens Club, Wright State U. Alumni Assn., Mensa, Zonta. Methodist. Office: 20 Exchange Pl New York NY 10005

OWEN, AMY, library director; b. Brigham City, Utah, June 26, 1944; d. John Wallace and Bertha (Jensen) O. BA, Brigham Young U., 1966, MLS, 1968. Systems libr. Utah State Libr., Salt Lake City, 1968-72, dir. reference svcs., 1972-74, dir. tech. svcs., 1974-81, dep. dir., 1981-87; dir., 1987—; serials com. chmn. Utah Coll. Libr. Coun., Salt Lake City, 1975-77, exec. sec., 1978-84, coun. mem. 1987—; mem. staff Gov.'s Utah Systems Planning Task Force, Salt Lake City, 1982; staff liaison Utah Gov.'s Conf. on Libr. and Info. Svcs., 1977-79, chair exec. planning com., 1990; mem. pres.'s adv. panel Baker & Taylor Co., Somerville, N.J., 1977-78; mem. adv. panel Nat. Commn. Libr. and Info. Svcs., 1985; Alumni Honor lectr. Coll. Humanities, Brigham Young U., 1990. Contbr. chpts. to books, also contbg. author various manuals; cons. and trainer in field. Coun. mem. Utah Endowment for Humanities, 1986—, vice chmn., 1987-88, chair, 1988-90; trustee Bibliographic Ctr. for Rsch., 1987—, vice-chmn. pers. com., 1988-89, chmn. pers. com., 1989-90, nominating com., 1984, v.p. bd. trustees, 1989—; mem. nominations com. Chief Officers of State Libr. Agys., 1987-88, stats. com., 1988—, state info. policy workshop com., 1988; mem. conf. program com. Fedn. of State Humanities Couns., 1988; mem. coop. pub. libr. data system task force Nat. Commn. on Libr. and Info. Svcs., 1988—; grant rev. panelist NEH, 1988, panel mem. reading and discussion groups, 1988; regional project mgmt. bd. mem. Intermountain Community Learning and Info. Ctr. Project, 1987-90; mem. adv. com. Brigham Young U. Sch. Libr. and Info. Svcs. Mem. Utah Libr. Assn. (pres. 1978-79, exec. bd. 1976-80, Spl. Svc. award 1989), Mountain Plains Libr. Assn. (rec. sec. 1979-80, fin. com. 1982-84, Disting. Svc. award 1989), ALA (bd. dirs. ASCLA div. 1984-86, fin. com. 1984-86, 89—, planning, orgn. and bylaws com. 1981-85, SLAS program com. 1984-86, pres. program com. 1986, exec. bd. mem., 1988-90; clene roundtable mem. com. 1984-86, nominations com. 1986-87, nat. adv. bd. office communications svcs., voices and visions project 1988-89; LITA div. Satellite Conf. Task Force mem. 1982; PLA div. editor column. 1987-89, PLA div. goals, guidelines and standards com. 1987-90, chair, 1990—, PLA pub. libr. data svc. adv. com. 1988—, PLA Kellogg Phase III EIC project adv. com. chair 1990—), ALA Office for Rsch. coop. pub. libr. data system adv. com. 1985-89), Phi Kappa Phi, Alpha Lambda Delta. Home: 4786 Naniloa Dr Salt Lake City UT 84117 Office: Utah State Libr 2150 S 300 W Ste 16 Salt Lake City UT 84115

OWEN, CAROL ELAINE, university administrator; b. Kingsport, Tenn., July 11, 1957; d. Carroll Cortland and Joy Elaine (Campbell) O. Student, Union U., Jackson, Tenn., 1975-78, U. Tenn., Martin, 1979; BS, Mid. Tenn. State U., 1980; MEd, Vanderbilt U., 1985. Asst. pub. rels. Bates, Campbell & Co., Union City, Tenn., 1980-81; communications officer Bapt. Sunday Sch. Bd., Nashville, 1981-84; mgr. campaign services Belmont Coll., Nashville, 1984-85, specialist corp. and found. relations, 1985-88, dir. annual giving, 1988-89; dir. field svcs. Samford U., Birmingham, Ala., 1989—; adj. faculty, vol. State Community Coll.; cons. mktg. research J. Robert Clark & Assocs., Memphis. Contbr. articles to profl. publs. Program leader Am. Cancer Soc., Nashville, 1987; leader conf. Tenn. Bapt. Conv., Nashville, Nat. Assn. Student Devel. Officers, Case 1989 Dist. III Planning Com. Mem. Nat. Soc. Fundraising Execs. (bd. dirs. Nashville chpt.), Nat. Assn. Student Devel. Officers (conf. leader), Coun. for Advancement and Support Edn. (scholar 1986), Nat. Assn. YMCA Devel. Officers (conf. leader), NSFRE (nat. conf. com. 1988), Nashville Area C. of C. (president's com. 1987-89), Rotary Internat., Zeta Tau Alpha, Sigma Alpha Iota, Alpha Psi Omega. Republican. Home: 3705 Buck Horn Cove Birmingham AL 35242 Office: Samford U 800 Lakeshore Dr Birmingham AL 35229

OWEN, CAROL THOMPSON, artist, educator; b. Pasadena, Calif., May 10, 1944; d. Sumner Comer and Cordelia (Whittemore) Thompson; m. James Eugene Owen, July 19, 1975; children: Kevin Christopher, Christine Celese. Student, Pasadena City Coll., 1963; BA with distinction, U. Redlands, 1966; MA, Calif. State U., L.A., 1967; MFA, Claremont Grad. Sch., 1969. Cert. community coll. instr., Calif. Head resident Pitzer Coll., Claremont, Calif., 1967-70; instr. art Mt. San Antonio Coll., Walnut, Calif., 1968—; dir. coll. art gallery Mt. San Antonio Coll., 1972-73. Group shows include Covina Pub. Library, 1971, U. Redlands, 1964, 65, 66, 70, 78, 88, Am. Ceramic Soc., 1969, others. Mem. Calif. Scholarship Fedn., Faculty Assn. Mt. San Antonio Coll., Coll. Art Assn. Am., Calif. Tchrs. Assn., Friends of Huntington Library, L.A. County Mus. Art, Heard Mus. Assn., Sigma Tau Delta. Republican. Presbyterian. Home: 534 S Hepner St Covina CA 91723 Office: Mt San Antonio Coll Grand Ave Walnut CA 91789

OWEN, CAROLYN SUTTON, teacher; b. Shreveport, La., Jan. 7, 1932; d. S.T. and Kathleen Willard (Judkins) Sutton; m. Donald Curtiss Owen, Aug. 6, 1955; children: Judith Kathleen Owen Moen, Kyle Curtiss. BA, La. Tech., 1953; MA, Tex. Woman's U., 1988. Cert. Tchr., Tex. Tchr. Calcasieu Parish, Lake Charles, La., 1953-54, Westlake, La., 1955-56; tchr. San Antonio Independent Sch. Dist., 1954-55, Dallas Independent Sch. Dist., 1967—. Mem. AAUW, NEA (life), Nat. Coun. Tchrs. English, Parent Tchr. Assn. Woodrow Wilson High, Tex. State Tchrs. Assn. Republican. Episcopalian. Home: 2952 Northaven Rd Dallas TX 75229 Office: Woodrow Wilson High Sch 100 S Glasgow Dallas TX 75214

OWEN, DEBORAH K., lawyer, federal official. BA, U. Md., 1972; JD, Harvard U., 1977. Atty. Piper & Marbury, 1977-79; minority counsel House Com. on the Judiciary, 1980-82; gen. counsel Senate Com. on the Judiciary, 1983-85; assoc. counsel to Pres. U.S. Govt., 1985-86; mng. ptnr. McNair Law Firm, 1986-89; mem. FTC, 1989—. Marshall scholar in polit. philosophy U. Edinburgh, Scotland, 1972-74. Office: FTC 6th & Pennsylvania Ave NW Washington DC 20580*

OWEN, KAREN MICHELLE, manufacturing executive; b. Garden City, Mich., Aug. 22, 1952; d. Leonard Arthur and Katrena Pickford (Floyd) Leonard; divorced; children: Joseph Paul, Nina Bloom. Student, Mich. State U., 1970-73, Eastern Mich. U., 1976-78; BBA, Western Mich. U., 1983. Dept. mgr. Meijer's Thrifty Acres Retail, East Lansing, Mich., 1973-74, Canton Ctr., Mich., 1974-75; insp. hydramatic Gen. Motors, Ypsilanti, Mich., 1975-76, specialized clk., 1976-77, supr. quality, 1977-79, gen. supr. quality, 1979; gen. supr. quality Gen. Motors, Three Rivers, Mich., 1979-84, asst. supr. mfg., 1984-87, supt. quality, 1987—. Leader Girl Scouts Am., Three Rivers, 1988—. Mem. NAFE, C. of C., Toastmasters, Beta Gamma Sigma. Republican. Home: 510 John Glenn Ct Three Rivers MI 49093 Office: Gen Motors 1 Saginaw Dr Three Rivers MI 49093

OWEN, PATRICIA ROSE, investment company executive; b. Chattanooga, Feb. 13, 1955; d. David G. and Elsie E. (Newman) Owen; m. Thomas J. Michel, Jan. 1990. AA, Broward Community Coll., 1974; BA, U. South Fla., 1976; MBA, Nova U., 1985. Cert. USCG ocean operator, 1983. Tchr. Dade County Sch. System, Miami, 1976-78; v.p. Securities Rsch. and Mgmt., Inc., Ft. Lauderdale, Fla., 1977-82, exec. v.p., 1982-84, dir., 1984—, pres., chief exec. officer, 1986—. Author numerous poems. Mem. Seven Seas Cruising Assn. (Ft. Lauderdale, Fla.), Cruising Assn. (London). Episcopalian. Office: Securities Rsch & Mgmt Inc 800 Corporate Dr Ste 602 Fort Lauderdale FL 33334

OWEN, SUZANNE, savings and loan executive; b. Lincoln, Nebr., Oct. 6, 1926; d. Arthur C. and Hazel E. (Edwards) O. BSBA, U. Nebr., Lincoln, 1948. With G.F. Lessenhop & Sons, Inc., Lincoln, 1948-57; with First Fed. Lincoln, 1963—; v.p., dir. personnel, 1975-81, 1st v.p., 1981—, sr. v.p., 1987—; mem. personnel bd. City of Lincoln, 1989—. Mem. Adminstrv. Mgmt. Soc. (past bd. dirs. local chpt.), Lincoln Personnel Mgmt. Assn., Lincoln Human Resources Mgmt. Assn., Phi Chi Theta. Republican. Christian Scientist. Clubs: Altrusa, Wooden Spoon, Twig Daniels Network (bd. dirs. 1987-88), Exec. Women's Breakfast Group, Pi Beta Phi Alumnae, Order of Eastern Star (Lincoln). Office: First Fed Lincoln 13th and N Sts Lincoln NE 68508

OWEN, TRACY LYNN, environmental engineer; b. Caribou, Maine, Apr. 14, 1961; d. Wilbert Paul and Jacquie Lynn (Hoy) O. BS in Archtl. Engring., U. Tex., 1983. Registered profl. engr. Tex. Engring. aide Water and Wastewater Utility, Austin, Tex., 1982-83, engring tech., 1983, engring. assoc. I., 1984, engring assoc. II, 1984-87, engring. assoc. III, 1987-88, engr. II, 1989—; mem. Water and Wastewater Standards com., Austin, 1983—, Package Plant Application Rev. com., Austin, 1985—. Contbr. articles to profl. jours. Facilitator Young Women in Leadership, Lyndon Baines Johnson High Sch., Austin, 1987—; mem. pub. rels. com. Austin Young Reps., 1989—. Recipient cert. of leadership Univ. YWCA, 1989. Mem. Water Pollution Control Fedn. Republican. Methodist. Office: City of Austin 625 E 10th St Austin TX 78701

OWENS, BARBARA ANN, telecommunications company manager; b. Memphis, Sept. 1., 1948; d. Harwood Casey and Anna Lou (Webb) Owens; m. Carroll Lynn Hughes, Feb. 24, 1978; 1 child, Kimberlyn Casey. B.S.Ed. summa cum laude, U. Tenn.-Knoxville, 1970; M.S. in Social Work, U. Tenn., 1975. Caseworker, supr. Tenn. Dept. Human Services, Knoxville, 1970-75; dir. social services ARC, Knoxville, 1975-77; bus. office supr. South Central Bell Tel. Co., Knoxville and Maryville, 1977-80; phone ctr. supr. South Central Bell, Maryville, Tenn., 1980-82; asst. staff mgr. BellSouth Services, Birmingham, Ala., 1983-87, Nashville, 1987—. Mem. Nat. Assn. Female Execs., Future Telephone Pioneers. Methodist. Clubs: Birmingham Big Orange. Avocations: personal computers; basketball; spectator sports. Home: 300 Ridgetop Ct Franklin TN 37064 Office: Bell South Services Rm 3-840 MSC Brentwood Data Ctr 402 Franklin Rd Brentwood TN 37027

OWENS, CHERYL LAURITA, funeral director, university program coordinator; b. Memphis, Feb. 2, 1957; d. Noble Hammett and Emma Laura (Buckner) O. BS, U. Tenn., Martin, 1982; MPA, Memphis State U., 1988. Lic. funeral dir., Tenn. Office clk. N.H. Owens and Son Funeral Home, Memphis, 1975-83, funeral dir., 1988—; substitute tchr. Memphis City Schs., 1984; testing adminstr., remedial devel. specialist Shelby State Community Coll., 1984-87; mus. interpreter Mud Island Miss. River, 1987; program coord. U. Tenn., 1988—. Active Memphis, Shelby County Children and Youth Coun., 1988. Mem. NAFE, Am. Biographical Inst. Hall Fame. Presbyterian. Home: 1857 S Parkway E Memphis TN 38114

OWENS, DONNA, former mayor; b. Aug. 24, 1936. Student, Stautzenberger Bus Coll. Past v.p. Lucas County Bd. Edn., Ohio; mem. Toledo City Council, 1980-84; mayor City of Toledo, 1984-89. Mem. Toledo-Lucas County Council for Human Services, Internat. Inst. Greater Toledo, Lucas County Improvement Corp., Toledo Area Employment and Tng. Consortium, St. Vincent Hosp. and Med. Guild, Ohio Sch. Bd. Assn., Assn. of Two Toledos, Toledo Econ. Planning Council, Criminal Justice Coordinating Council, Toledo Mus. of Art; mem. exec. com. Toledo Met. Area Council of Govts.; bd. dirs. pub. broadcasting WGTE-TV; bd. mgrs. West Toledo YMCA; bd. dirs. YMCA, Substance Abuse Service, Inc.; adv. bd. U.S. Conf. of Mayors. Recipient Legion of Leaders award YMCA, 1976; Community Service award Post 606 VFW. Office: care City of Toledo One Government Ctr Ste 2200 Toledo OH 43604*

OWENS, JEAN BATTS, school system administrator; b. Youngstown, Ohio, Nov. 27, 1928; d. Ellwood and Estelle (Hawthorne) Batts; m. Charles R. Owens Jr., May 26, 1956; children: Cheryl, Yvonne. AB, Morgan State U., 1950; MA, Columbia U., 1954; postgrad., John Hopkins U., NYU. Cert. English and adminstrn. and supervision. Tchr. English Balt. Pub. Schs., 1950-63, specialist English, 1963-66, project coord., 1966-68, asst. prin., 1968-73, regional specialist, 1973-75, asst. to regional supt., 1975-80, prin., 1980—; ass. prof. English Morgan State U., Balt., 1964-81. Support Morgan State U. Devel. Found., Balt., 1988-89. Recipient Disting. Svc. award Frederick Douglass Alumni Assn., 1983, 85, 89; Exxon fellow, 1975. Mem. ASCW, Pub. Sch. Suprs. and Adminstrs., Nat. Assn. Secondary Prins., Md. Assn. Secondary Prins., Melds Club, Alpha Kappa Alpha. Democrat. Presbyterian. Office: Frederick Douglass High Sch 2301 Gwynns Falls Pkwy Baltimore MD 21217

OWENS, LORRAINE LUCILLE, handwriting analyst, consultant; b. Pettus, Tex., Sept. 19, 1927; d. Bernard Phillip and Lucille Lillian (Newman) Hopkins; B.A. in Psychology, Ottawa (Kans.) U., 1977; m. George Erwin Owens, Feb. 5, 1947; children: Janet Lucille, George Erwin, David M., Lynn L. Ptnr. Allen and Owens, Kansas City, Mo., 1970-80; pres. Kaleidoscope Corp., Kansas City, Mo., 1980—; lectr., seminar speaker; psychology instr. Graphoanalysis Congress, Chgo., 1978-81; cons. with psychologist Lansing State Prison, Marillac Sch. Author: Different Ways to Describe Traits, 1976, Handwriting Analysis Dictionary, 1981, rev. edit., 1987, Dual Aspects of Traits, 1987, Trait Combinations, 1989. Bd. dirs. Marillac Sch., Kansas City, Mo., 1977-82; troop leader and organizer Mid Continent council Girl Scouts U.S., 1962-72. Mem. Internat. Graphoanalysis Soc. (cert. merit 1979), Nat. assn. Women Bus. Owners. Republican. Mem. Unity Ch. Home: 6300 Verona Shawnee Mission KS 66208 Office: 1524 Crystal Kansas City MO 64126

OWENS, SHELBY JEAN, electrologist, writer; b. Flintville, Tenn., Dec. 18, 1936; d. Harvey Chrethton and Emma Lucille (McDonald) Langford; m. David Randall Owens, Mar. 12, 1953 (div. Feb. 1970); children—Karen, Kristie, Kaylon; m. Richard Allen Brewer, May 26, 1977. Diploma Hoffman Electrolysis Inst., N.Y.C., 1968, postgrad. cert., 1972. Cert. clin. electrologist. Tech. typist Thiokol Chem. Corp., Huntsville, Ala., 1957-60; exec. sec. CFW Constrn. Co., Fayetteville, Tenn., 1961-65; pvt. practice electrolysis, Winchester, Tenn., 1968-70, Huntsville, 1970-77, Pensacola, Fla., 1975—. Author: About that Hair, 1989; founder, Hirsutes Anonymous Initiating Removal Reration, Inc., 1986—. Recipient Pres.'s award Am. Electrolysis Assn., 1984. Mem. Electrolysis Soc. Fla. (lobbyist 1979-86, pres. 1982-86), Am. Bus. Women's Assn. (Pensacola charter chpt.) (past pres., Woman of Yr. award 1984). Democrat. Avocations: sewing, writing. Home: 3801 N 12th Ave Pensacola FL 32503 Office: Owens Pub 213 E Brent Pensacola FL 32503

OWENS, SUSAN WEIR, emergency physician, consultant; b. Cin., Dec. 10, 1949; d. William Franklin and Dorothea (Hennigan) Weir; m. William Howard Owens Jr., June 6, 1976; children: Kathryn Anne, Charles Alexander. BS in Zoology, U. Ga., 1972; MD, Med. Coll. Ga., 1976. Intern anesthesiology and critical care medicine Georgetown U. Hosp., Washington, 1976-78, resident in emergency medicine, 1978-80; emergency physician Capital Emergency Assocs., P.A., Laurel, Md., 1980—; v.p. Capital Cons., Inc., Washington, 1988—; exec. editor Health Alert, Washington, 1988—; ptnr. Capital Emergency Assocs., P.A., 1982—, mem. exec. bd., 1985-87, bd. dirs.; chief emergency medicine Balt. County Gen. Hosp., Randallstown, Md., 1988—. Active mem. local and state Dem. Party, Md., 1976-84. Fellow Am. Coll. Emergency Physicians (counsellor 1983-88, mem. coun. steering com. 1985-87, chmn. key contact program, mem. govt. affairs com.); mem. AMA (del. young physicians sect., mem. key contact com.), Med. and Chirurg. Md. (chmn. young physician com. 1987—), Capital Hill Equestrian Soc., Trail Riders of Today, Md. Horsebreeders Assn., Carrollton Hounds Club. Home: Old Rolling Rd PO Box 250 Glenelg MD 21737 Office: Baltimore County Gen Hosp 5401 Old Court Rd Randallstown MD 21133

OWENS, VANASSA LYNN, nurse, massage therapist; b. Detroit, July 25, 1953; d. Jimmie Edward and Annie Elizabeth (King) Owens. Diploma in nursing, Harper Hosp. Sch. Nursing, 1974; diploma interior design, LaSalle U., 1979; BS, Siena Heights Coll., 1984; cert. in massage therapy, Stresage Coll., 1989. Cert. travel agt. Emergency nurse practitioner Detroit Receiving Hosp., 1975—; notary pub., owner VLO Enterprises, Detroit, 1979—; accessory designer, interior design cons. Transport Industries, Ga., 1979-83; interior designer Distinctive Designs/Med. Interiors, Detroit, 1979-85; dir. nurses New Detroit Nursing Ctr., 1986-87; flight nurse USAFR, Selfridge AFB, Mich., 1986—; admission coord. Detroit Receiving Hosp., 1988—. Mem. Emergency Nurses Assn., Am. Massage Therapists Assn., Nat. Notary Assn., Aerospace Med. Assn. (flight nurse sect.), NAFE, Nat. Flight Nurses Assn., Res. Officers Assn. Baptist. Home: 13030 Corbett Detroit MI 48213

OWEN-TOWLE, CAROLYN SHEETS, clergywoman; b. Upland, Calif., July 27, 1935; d. Millard Owen and Mary (Baskerville) Sheets; m. Charles Russell Chapman, June 29, 1957 (div. 1973); children: Christopher Charles, Jennifer Anne, Russell Owen; m. Thomas Allan Owen-Towle, Nov. 16, 1973. BS in Art and Art History, Scripps Coll., 1957; postgrad. in religion, U. Iowa, 1977. Ordained to ministry Unitarian-Universalist Ch., 1978. Minister 1st Unitarian Ch., San Diego, 1978—; pres. Ministerial Sisterhood, Unitarian Universalist Ch., 1980-82, Unitarian Universalist Svc. Com., 1983-85. Bd. dirs. Planned Parenthood, San Diego, 1980-86; mem. clergy adv. com. to Hospice, San Diego, 1980-83; mem. U.S. Rep. Jim Bates Hunger Adv. Com., San Diego, 1983-87; chaplain Interfaith AIDS Task Force, San Diego, 1988—. Mem. Unitarian Universalist Ministers Assn. (pres. 1989—). Office: 1st Unitarian Ch 4190 Front St San Diego CA 92103

OWINGS, MARGARET WENTWORTH, conservationist, artist; b. Berkeley, Calif., Apr. 29, 1913; d. Frank W. and Jean (Pond) Wentworth; m. Malcolm Millard, 1937; 1 child, Wendy Millard Benjamin; m. Nathaniel Alexander Owings, Dec. 30, 1953. A.B., Mills Coll., 1934; postgrad., Radcliffe Coll., 1935. One-woman shows include Santa Barbara (Calif.) Mus. Art, 1940, Stanford Art Gallery, 1951, stitchery exhbns. at M.H. De Young Mus., San Francisco, 1963, Internat. Folk Art Mus., Santa Fe, 1965. Commr. Calif. Parks, 1963-69, mem., Nat. Parks Found. Bd, 1968-69; bd. dirs. African Wildlife Leadership Found., 1968-80, Defenders of Wildlife, 1969-74; founder, pres. Friends of the Sea Otter, 1969—; chair Calif. Mountain Lion Preservation Found., 1987; trustee Environmental Def. Fund, 1972-83; Regional trustee Mills Coll., 1962-68. Recipient Gold medal, Conservation Service award U.S. Dept. Interior, 1975, Conservation award Calif. Acad. Scis., 1979, Am. Motors Conservation award, 1980, Joseph Wood Krutch medal Humane Soc. U.S., 1980, Nat. Audubon Soc. medal, 1983, A. Starker Leopold award Calif. Nature Conservancy, 1986, Gold medal UN Environment Program, 1988. Home: Grimes Point Big Sur CA 93920

OWINGS, RACHEL HARRIET (RAE OWINGS), graphic artist, illustrator, script writer; b. Bryn Mawr, Pa., July 8, 1926; d. Charles Croasdale and Rachel (Bulley) Trump; m. James Lee Owings, Nov. 1, 1947; children: Marjorie Lee, Charles Nathaniel, John Stanley. Student, Phila. U. Art, 1943-45. Children's tchr. art Phila. U. Art, 1944-46; designer custom needlepoint Sinkler Studio-Bryn Mawr Studio, Radnor and Bryn Mawr, 1948-52; illustrator, craft designer Jack and Jill mag., Phila., 1953-71; greeting card designer Abel Cards, Media, Pa., 1955-71; freelance TV illustrator and performer PBS TV, 1955—; freelance illustrator to music with various symphony orchs., Phila., Washington, Balt., 1955—; freelance sch. assembly performer, Phila., N.Y.C., Mass., Washington, 1955—; book illustrator Clark Davis/Vantage Press, Darnestown, Md. and N.Y.C., 1988-90. Illustrator, co-dir. ednl. TV series Gather 'Round, 1978, Teletales, 1985 (Golden Eagle ward Coun. on Internat. Non-Theatrical Events 1985); illustrator: As A Pup Grows Up, 1988, The Tooth Fairy Is Broke, 1989. Leader, trainer Girl Scouts U.S.A., Gladwyne, Pa., 1959-66; leader, counselor Boy Scouts Am., Gladwyne, 1961-70; Sunday sch. tchr. Presbyn. and Congl. chs., Gladwyne and Worcester, Mass., 1970-74; bd. dirs. Fairfax County Coun. Arts, Annandale, Va., 1973-76. Recipient Ohio State award Inst. for Edn. by Radio-TV, 1975, 88, bronze medal V.I. Film Festival, 1976, medal for 25 yrs. appearances with children's concerts Phila. Orch., 1988. Mem. Childrens Book Guild Wash. (chmn. speakers bur. 1985—). Home and Studio: 10214 Old Hunt Rd Vienna VA 22181

OWNBY, CHARLOTTE LEDBETTER, anatomy educator; b. Amory, Miss., July 27, 1947; d. William Moss and Anna Faye (Long) Ledbetter; m. James Donald Ownby, Sept. 6, 1969; children: Holly Ruth, Mary Faye. BS in Zoology, U. Tenn., 1969, MS in Zoology, 1971; PhD in Anatomy, Colo. State U., 1975. Instr. Okla. State U., Stillwater, 1974-75, asst. prof., 1975-80, assoc. prof., 1980-84, prof., 1984—; dept. head, 1990—; dir. Electron Microscope Lab. Okla. State U., Stillwater, 1977-87, head dept. physiol. scis., 1990—. Editor Proc. 9th World Congress Internat. Soc. Toxicology, 1989; editorial bd. Toxion, 1984—. NIH, USPHS grantee, 1984—. Mem. Okla. Soc. for Electron Microscopy (pres. 1977-78), Pan Am. Soc. on Toxinology (pres. 1984-95), Phi Beta Kappa, Phi Kappa Phi, Sigma Xi. Office: Okla State U Dept Physiol Scis 264 Vet Medicine Stillwater OK 74078

OWSLEY, MICHELE MALEK, aerospace engineer; b. Hackensack, N.J., Oct. 11, 1950; d. Leo Edward and Virginia (Brown) Malek; m. Robert Lamar Owsley, Sept. 20, 1974; 1 child, James Edward. BS in Aeronautical Engring., Rensselaer Poly. Inst., 1972; MS Aerospace Engring., Tex. A&M U., 1974. Aerospace engr. Boeing Comml. Airplane Co., Renton, Wash., 1974-77; aerospace engr. FAA, Ft. Worth, 1977-89, project mgr., 1985—. Mem. Experimental Aircraft Assn., Aircraft Owners and Pilots Assn. Club: Toastmasters (editor newsletter 1979-80). Home: 979 Trophy Club Dr Roanoke TX 76262 Office: FAA 4400 Blue Mound Rd Fort Worth TX 76193-0150

OWSNITZKI, GABRIELE ANNA J., marketing professional; b. Osnabrück, Fed. Republic of Germany, Mar. 5, 1957; came to U.S., 1960; d. Johannes Franz Karl and Theresia Paula (Richter) O. Student, Fairleigh Dickinson U., 1978—. Office, showroom mgr. Dynasty and Eterna, Mido Watches, N.Y.C., 1975-77; adminstrv. asst. Leber Katz Ptnrs., N.Y.C., 1977-78, Art Carved and Rosenthal Jewelry, N.Y.C., 1978-80; asst. product mgr. Art Carved Inc., N.Y.C., 1980-83, product mgr., 1983; dir. of merchandising Hirsch U.S.A., Inc., River Edge, N.J., 1983-87; brand mgr. Pulsar Time Inc., Mahwah, N.J., 1987—. Mem. Delta Mu Delta, Phi Zeta Kappa, Nat. Assn. Female Execs. Office: Pulsar Time Inc 1111 Macarthur Blvd Mahwah NJ 07430

OXFORD, SHARON M., insurance company executive; b. Ekalaka, Mont., Aug. 30, 1939; d. Price S. and Myrtle I. (Wilkoski) Purdum; m. James L. Oxford Jr., Sept. 7, 1958 (div. May 1973); children: James L. III, Dana Renee, Monica Lynn Oxford Jones; m. Ronald Butts, Jan. 1, 1990. Grad., Nat. Coll. Bus., Rapid City, S.D., 1958; student, Mesa (Ariz.) Community Coll., 1979-80. CPCU; cert. ins. counselor. Office mgr. Foster Fritchle Ins. Co., Colorado Springs, Colo., 1968-71, Mikes Ives Ins./Profl. Ins. Exchange, Colorado Springs, 1971-73; asst. to pres. Tolley-Weidman Ins. Co., Colorado Springs, 1973-76; with Home Ins. Co., Phoenix, 1976-78; mgr. adminstrn. Fred S. James & Co. Ariz., Phoenix and Tempe, 1978-84; v.p. Fred S. James & Co. Ariz., Tempe, 1984-85, sr. v.p., 1985—. Corr. sec. Young Reps., Colo. Springs, 1967; v.p. Colorado Springs chpt. Parents Without Ptnrs., 1975. Mem. Am. Inst. for Property and Liability Underwriters, Soc. Cert. Ins. Counselors, Jaycee Wives (pres. Colorado Springs chpt. 1970), Assoc. of Automated Mgmt. Republican. Office: Fred S James & Co of Ariz 1414 W Broadway Ste 200 Tempe AZ 85282

OXSEN, JO ANN, advertising account executive; b. Ellwood City, Pa., June 6, 1946; d. Harry Charles and Marjorie Ella (Liebendorfer) Miller; children: Jon David Gordon, Tammy Jo Gordon Smith; m. James H. Oxsen. Student, Ind. U., 1964-65, Mt San Antonio Coll., Walnut, Calif., 1976-79. Sales coordinator American's Cup Inc., City of Industry, Calif., 1982-83; advt. account exec. The Orange Coast Daily Pilot Newspaper, Costa Mesa, Calif., 1983—. Mem. Foundain Valley C. of C. Republican. Home: 17460 Dixie #10 Fountain Valley CA 92708 Office: Orange Coast Daily Pilot Newspaper 330 W Bay St Costa Mesa CA 92627

OZATO, KEIKO, microbiologist; b. Yamagata, Japan, Aug. 25, 1941; came to U.S., 1973; d. Masaru and Chiyo Naito; m. Igor Bert Dawid, Apr. 8, 1976. PhD, Kyoto (Japan) U., 1973. Rsch. fellow Carnegie Inst. of Washington, Balt., 1973-76; rsch. assoc. Johns Hopkins U., Balt., 1976-78; vis. assoc. Nat. Cancer Inst., Bethesda, Md., 1978-81; sr. staff fellow Nat. Inst. Child Health and Human Devel., Bethesda, 1981-83, rsch. microbiologist, 1983-85, sect. head, 1985—. Mem. Am. Assn. Immunologists, Internat. Soc. for Interferon Rsch. Office: Nat Inst Child Health and Human Devel NIH Lab Devel & Molecular Immunity Bldg 6 Rm 2A01 Bethesda MD 20892

OZAWA, MARTHA NAOKO, educator; b. Ashikaga, Tochigi, Japan, Sept. 30, 1933; came to U.S., 1963; d. Tokuichi and Fumi (Kawashima) O.; m. May 1959 (div. May 1966). BA in Econs., Aoyama Gakuin U., 1956; MS in Social Work, U. Wis., 1966, PhD in Social Welfare, 1969. Asst. prof. social work Portland (Oreg.) State U., 1969-70, assoc. prof. social work, 1970-72; assoc. rsch. prof. social work NYU, 1972-75; assoc. prof. social work Portland State U., 1975-76; prof. social work Washington U., St. Louis, 1976-85, Bettie Bofinger Brown prof. social policy, 1985—. Author: Income Maintenance and Work Incentives, 1982; editor: Women's Life Cycle: Japan-U.S. Comparison in Income Maintenance, 1989, Women's Life Cycle and Economic Insecurity: Problems and Proposals, 1989; editorial bd. mem. Social Work, Silver Spring, Md., 1972-75, 85-88, New Eng. Jour. Human

Charles Palermo, Apr. 1, 1961; 1 child, Donald Charles Jr. (dec.). BS in Secondary Edn., 1960. Cert. secondary and elem. edn. tchr., Tex. Art tchr. Dallas Ind. Sch. Dist., 1960-62, 65-67; asst. dir. freshmen orientation program North Tex. State U., Denton, summer 1969, dormitory dir. Oak St. Hall, 1968-71, tchr. part-time, 1970-77; substitute tchr. Denton Ind. Sch. Dist., 1975-78, tchr. 5th grade, 1979-87, art tchr., 1987—; tchr. kindergarten Kiddie Korral Pre-Sch., Denton, 1978-79; trained gifted tchr. Denton Ind. Sch. Dist.-Woodrow Wilson, 1980; grade level chmn. Woodrow Wilson Elem., Denton, 1980, Eva S. Hodge Elem., Denton, 1988—. Mem. Denton Humane Soc., 1982—, Denton Educators Polit. Action Com., 1984. Mem. NEA, Tex. State Tchrs. Assn., Denton Classroom Tchrs. Assn. (faculty rep. 1984-85), Denton Edn. Assn., Denton Area Art Edn. Assn. (program chmn. 1990-91), Greater Denton Arts Coun., PTA, Numismatic Assn., Denton Square Athletic Club, Denton Greater U. Dames Club (treas. 1970), Bus. and Profl. Women's Assn. (treas. 1990-91), Delta Kappa Gamma (treas. 1986-88). Democrat. Home: 1523 Pickwick Ln Denton TX 76201-1290

PALEY, RENEE E., service executive; b. Portsmouth, Va., Jan. 3, 1945; d. William Eisnitz and Eleanor (Schoolman) Wishengrad; m. Howard S. Paley, Mar. 21, 1965 (separated); children: Marisa Anne, William Martin. Student, Antioch Coll., 1961-62; BA in English Lit., NYU, 1965; postgrad., Hunter Coll., 1966-68. Asst. photo editor Modern Photography Mag., N.Y.C., 1965-66; English tchr. Jamaica (N.Y.) High Sch., 1967-68; reporter Community Newspapers, Glen Cove, N.Y., 1974-80; editor The Westbury (N.Y.) Times, 1980, The Roslyn (N.Y.) News, 1980-81, Glen Cove Record-Pilot, 1981-84; community rels. coord. The Community Hosp. at Glen Cove, 1984-86, dir. community rels., 1986-88; dir. communications Assn. of Nat. Advertisers Inc., 1988, v.p. communications, 1989-90, sr. v.p. communications, 1990—; newsletter editor Twin Rinks, Roslyn, 1975, Robert Half Internat., San Francisco, 1985—; travel editor Blvd. Mag., Greenvale, N.Y., 1986—; v.p. Hyphenates, Roslyn, 1985—. Scriptwriter, location coord. Word of Mouth, 1986; copywriter radio advertisements, 1985-87. Mem. adv. com. Glen Cove Sr. Citizens, 1985-88, vice chmn., 1988; mem. adv. com. Glen Cove Interagency Coun., 1984-88; pres. Greater Roslyn United Civic Assn., 1977, North Park Civic Assn., 1975; mem. Pub. Rels. Steering Com. Mem. Soc. Profl. Journalists, Am. Soc. Hosp. Mktg. and Pub. Rels., NAFE, Nassau-Suffolk Hosp. Coun. Pub. Rels., Healthcare Pub. Rels. Assn. Greater N.Y., World Fedn. Advertisers (pub. rels. steering com.), L.I. Press Club. Office: Assn Nat Advertisers 155 E 44th St New York NY 10017

PALIANI, MARY ANN, information center manager; b. Rochester, N.Y., Jan. 31, 1935; d. Angelo and Madeline (Serpico) P. BA in Biology, U. Rochester, 1956; MLS, Syracuse U., 1960; postgrad., Justus Liebig U., Giessen, Fed. Republic Germany, 1964-65; MBA, U. Colo., Denver, 1984. Lab. technician U. Rochester Med. Ctr., 1956-58; libr. trainee Rochester Pub. Libr., 1958-59, reference libr., 1960-62; Army libr. supr. U.S. Army Spl. Svcs. Br., Giessen, 1962-64; reference libr. N.Y. Pub. Libr., N.Y.C., 1965-68; libr. supr. Dow Chem. Rocky Flats Div., Golden, Colo., 1968-74, supr. info. svcs., 1974-75; libr. mgr. Rockwell Internat. Rocky Flats Div., Golden, 1975-89; info. ctr. mgr. EG & G Rocky Flats Inc., Golden, 1990—; spl. libr. rep. Colo. Coun. Libr. Devel., Denver, 1973-75. Loaned exec. Mile High United Way, Denver, 1980. N.Y. State Librs. Tng. grantee, 1959. Mem. Spl. Librs. Assn. (chpt. pres. 1970-71, vice chmn./chmn. nuclear sci. div. 1973-75), Am. Soc. for Info. Sci. (chpt. sec.-treas. 1972), Soc. Tech. Communications (chpt. sec. 1973-74), Beta Phi Mu, Beta Gamma Sigma. Home: 3630 Iris Ave B2 Boulder CO 80301 Office: EG & G Rocky Flats Inc PO Box 938 Golden CO 80402

PALINCSAR, ANNEMARIE SULLIVAN, educator; b. Monmouth, N.J., Jan. 30, 1950; d. Thomas Edward and Anne Marie (Leonard) Sullivan; m. John E. Palincsar, Aug. 2, 1975; 1 child, Danielle Marie. BS, Fitchburg (Mass.) State U., 1972; MS, U. Ill., 1974, PhD, 1982. Tchr. Sangamon Area Spl. Edn. Dist., Athens, Ill., 1971-76; adminstr. Sangamon Area Spl. Edn. Dist., Springfield, Ill., 1976-79; from asst. to assoc. prof. Mich. State U., East Lansing, 1983-89; assoc. prof. U. Mich., Ann Arbor, 1989—; author reading series MacMillan Pub. Co., N.Y.C., 1989—; cons. Coll. Bd., N.Y.C., 1986-88, Nat. Acad. Sci., Washington, 1987—, Children's TV Workshop, N.Y.C., 1988—. Co-editor: Strategic Teaching and Learning, 1987; contbr. articles to profl. jours. Mem. Ann Arbor PTO, 1987—. USOE fellow, 1974; NSF grantee, 1989, Office of Edn. Literacy grantee, 1989; Mich. State U. scholar, 1986. Mem. Am. Ednl. Rsch. Assn., Am. Psychol. Assn., Coun. for Exceptional Children, Nat. Reading Conf. Office: U Mich 610 E University Ann Arbor MI 48109

PALINSKY, CONSTANCE GENEVIEVE, hypnotherapist; b. Flint, Mich., May 31, 1927; d. George and Genevieve Treasa (Pisarski) Ignace; m. Joseph Palinsky, July 3, 1947; children: Joseph II, Mark Robert. Art student, Flint Inst. Arts, Oriental Artists Sch., others; numerous hypnosis studies including, Ethical Tng. Hypnosis Ctr., N.J. and Fla., Mid-West Inst., Hypnodye Found, Ill. and Fla. Cert. advanced master clin. and Ericksonian hypnotherapist. Owner, operator Palinsky Gallery of Art and Antiques, Flint, 1970-80; art lectr. Genesee County Grade Sch. System Flint Inst. Arts, 1972-74; owner, hypnosis cons. Hypno-Tech. Ctr., Flint, 1975-80; asst. mgr. Wethered-Rice Fine Jewelry, Flint, 1982-83; hypnotherapist, cons. Dailey Life Ctr., Flint, 1985-90; numerous radio shows and guest appearances, Flint, 1957-90, ABC Nat. Network, 1959, Flint Cable TV, 1972, others. Author: Constructive Personality Development, 1987, Secrets Revealed-How to Record Personal Tapes for Self-Improvement, 1990, The Magic of Photo Oil Coloring, 1990; one-woman show Dell's Artcraft Gallery, 1958; exhibited in group shows at Flint Inst. Arts, U. Mich., Purdue U., Lafayette, Ind., Flint Artist Market, Saginaw, Detroit and Grand Rapids, Mich., and Japan, others; contbr. articles to profl. jours., scripts and software in hypnosis field. Bd. dirs. The Chapel of The Angles Bldg. Fund for Lapeer County, 1974-75; pub. speaker various civic orgns. Named Oil Colorist of Yr. Profl. Photographers of Mich., 1959; recipient Pub. Svc. award Genesee County Sheriff's Dept., 1974. Mem. Internat. Soc. Profl. Hypnosis (regional v.p. 1977-79), Nat. Guild Hypnotherapists, Questers Antique Study Group (various offices including pres. 1972-90), Internat. Psychic Arts Rsch. (founder, pres. 1974-75), Flint Artist Market Group (program dir., treas.), Flint Soc. Arts and Crafts (v.p., pres. 1958-59), Quota Club, others. Republican. Roman Catholic. Home: 2362 Nolen Dr Flint MI 48504-4885

PALIT, HELEN MABEL VER DUIN, social service agency administrator; b. Detroit, May 12, 1948; d. Cornelius Bos and Helen Estelle (Masenhimer) Ver Duin; m. Satyajit Joy Palit, May 17, 1980. BA in Sociology, Psychology, Art, Tex. Tech. U., 1978, postgrad. in Sociology, 1979; PhD (hon.), Iona Coll., 1988. Producer, co-owner St. Nicholas Film Co., Lubbock, 1979-82; dir. Community Soup Kitchen, New Haven, Conn., 1980-82; exec. dir., founder City Harvest Inc., N.Y.C., 1982-90; founder, pres., chief exec. officer Am. Harvest Inc., Rye Brook, N.Y., 1990—. Mem. Select Com. on Hunger U.S. Ho. of Reps., 1985—, Inst. for Non-Profit Mgmt. Columbia U., 1988, Pres. Bush's 4th Point of Light, 1989. Nominated Esquire Mag. 400 Men and Women Under 40, 1985, 10 Americans Who Made a Difference Better Health and Living mag., 1987, Quintessential Women Town & country mag., 1986; recipient Roundtable for Women's Nat. award, 1987. Home: 36 Riverview Trail Croton-On-Hudson NY 10520 Office: Am Harvest Inc 4 International Dr #310 Rye Park NY 10573

PALLADINO-CRAIG, ALLYS, museum director; b. Pontiac, Mich., Mar. 23, 1947; d. Stephan Vincent and Mary (Anderson) Palladino; m. Malcolm Arnold Craig, Aug. 20, 1967; children—Ansel, Reed, Nicholas. BA in English, Fla. State U., 1967; grad., U. Toronto, Ont., Can., 1969; MFA, Fla. State U., 1978. Editorial asst. project U. Va. Press, Charlottesville, 1970-76; instr. English Inst. Franco American, Rennes, France, 1974; adj. instr. Fla. State U., Tallahassee, 1978-79, dir. Four Arts Ctr., 1979-82; dir. Univ. Gallery and Mus., Tallahassee, 1982—. Curator, editor and writer various articles and exhbn. catalogues, 1982—; gen. editor Athanor I-X, 1980—; paintings represented in Fla. Ho. of Reps., Barnett Bank and IBM Corp. Collections. Individual artist fellow Fla. Arts Coun., 1979. Mem. Am. Assn. Mus., Fla. Art Mus. Dirs. Assn. (sec. 1989—), Fla. Cultural Action Alliance, Phi Beta Kappa. Democrat. Home: 1410 Grape St Tallahassee FL 32303 Office: Fla State U Fine Arts Gallery & Mus 250 Fine Arts Bldg Tallahassee FL 32306

PALLOTTA, GINA M., psychologist; b. Santa Rosa, Calif., July 10, 1958; d. Henry and Delina (Zurlo) Plott; 1 child, Angela N. Smith. BA, Calif. State U., Stanislaus, 1983, MS, 1985; PhD, W. Va. U., 1990—. Intern Napa (Calif.) State Hosp., 1989-90; conducts workshops in field. Contbr. articles to profl. jours. Mem. Am. Psychol. Assn., Assn. for Advancement Behavior Therapy, Psi Chi (Nat. Svc. award 1985). Democrat. Office: Calif State Univ Psychology Dept Turlock CA 95380

PALLOTTI, MARIANNE MARGUERITE, foundation administrator; b. Hartford, Conn., Apr. 23, 1937; d. Rocco D. and Marguerite (Long) P. BA, NYU, 1968, MA, 1972. Asst. to pres. Wilson, Haight & Welch, Hartford, 1964-65; exec. asst. Ford Found., N.Y.C., 1965-77; corp. sec. Hewlett Found., Menlo Park, Calif., 1977-84, v.p., 1985—; bd. dirs. Overseas Devel. Network. Bd. dirs. N.Y. Theatre Ballet, N.Y.C., 1986—; allocations panelist United Way Bay Area, San Jose, Calif., 1988; bd. dirs. Miramonte Mental Health Svcs., Palo Alto, Calif., 1989. Mem. Women in Founds., No. Calif. Grantmakers, Peninsula Grantmakers. Home: 532 Marine World Pkwy #6203 Redwood Shores CA 94065 Office: William & Flora Hewlett Found 525 Middlefield Rd Ste 200 Menlo Park CA 94025

PALMER, ADA MARGARET, computer executive; b. Arkansas City, Kans., Feb. 8, 1940; d. Mark Lloyd Palmer and Eunice Elizabeth (Thompson) Palmer Schnitzer. AA, Colo. Woman's Coll., 1960; BA, George Washington U., 1962. Adv. sr. programmer Merrill Lynch, N.Y.C., 1969-72; systems analyst Tchrs. Ins. & Annuity, N.Y.C., 1972-77; systems specialist N.Y. Times, N.Y.C., 1977-81; computer cons. Applied Systems Resources, Inc., N.Y.C., 1981-82; asst. sec. Mfrs. Hanover Trust, N.Y.C., 1982—. Mem. AAUW, George Washington U. Alumni Club of N.Y.C. (pres.), Internat. Platform Assn., Fgn. Policy Assn. Republican. Presbyterian. Home: 201 W 85th St Apt 11 A New York NY 10024

PALMER, ASHLEY JOANNE, aerospace engineer; b. Chilliwack, B.C., Can., June 1, 1951; d. Roland Jack and Alice Jean (Gavin) P. BSME, Mich. Tech., 1978; MSME, U. Mich., 1981. Assoc. engr. Remington Arms Co., Ilion, N.Y., 1979-80; sr. engr. Boeing Co., Seattle, 1981-89, Rohr Industries, Inc., Chula Vista, Calif., 1989—; cons. Howland Enterprises, Santee, Calif., 1990; co. rep. Nat. Mil. Standards Body, Washington, 1990. Inventor in field. Recipient Pres.'s 100, Dir. Civilian Marksmanship, Camp Perry, Ohio, 1985, Disting. Rifleman, Dir. Civilian Marksmanship, Washington, 1986.

PALMER, BEVERLY BLAZEY, psychologist, educator; b. Cleve., Nov. 22, 1945; d. Lawrence E. and Mildred M. Blazey; m. Richard C. Palmer, June 24, 1967; 1 child, Ryan Richard. PhD in Counseling Psychology, Ohio State U., 1972. Lic. clinical psychologist, Calif. Adminstrv. assoc. Ohio State U., Columbus, 1969-70; research psychologist Health Services Research Ctr. UCLA, 1971-77; commr. pub. health Los Angeles County, 1978-81; pvt. practice clin. psychology Torrance, Calif., 1985—; prof. psychology Calif. State U., Dominguez Hills, 1973—. Reviewer manuscripts for numerous textbook pubs; contbr. numerous articles to profl. jours. Recipient Proclamation County of Los Angeles, 1972, Proclamation County of Los Angeles, 1981. Mem. Am. Psychol. Assn. Office: Calif State U- Dominguez Hills Dept Psychology Carson CA 90747

PALMER, CAROL ANN, psychotherapist, editor, writer, artist; b. Stamford, Conn., Sept. 20, 1949; d. Theodore Barclay and Mary Joan (Rekos) P. BA in English, Skidmore Coll., 1981. Lic. NASD-Series 7, 1985. Editorial asst. Jour. of Quantum Electronics Internat. Brotherhood Elec. and Electronics Engrs., N.Y.C., 1970-71; artists rep. Quinlan Artwork, Ltd., N.Y.C., 1971-73; picture researcher, mgr. color slide sect. The Bettmann Archive, N.Y.C., 1973-74; CETA grant welfare advocate MFY Legal Services, Inc., N.Y.C., 1976-77; dir. rsch. capital punishment project NAACP Legal Def. and Ednl. Fund, Inc., N.Y.C., 1977-84; SEC/NASD compliance officer First Realty Res. Inc., N.Y.C., 1984-85; stockbroker N.Y.C., 1985; proofreader, editor mergers and acquisitions dept. Morgan Stanley & Co., N.Y.C., 1986-89; pvt. practice psychotherapy Bklyn., 1986—; freelance editor, paralegal, illustrator, 1985—; co-producer, co-host TV program Cable Investors Digest, N.Y.C., 1984-86; counselor AIDS, N.Y.C., 1986—; psychotherapist, Bklyn., 1986—. Founding editor (newsletter) Death Row, U.S.A. Mem. St. Ann and the Holy Trinity Episcopal Ch., Bklyn., vol. stained-glass conservation studio project; founder The Palmer/Rekos Fund, 1989. Pitney Bowes scholar 1967; recipient Laurel Girls' award State of Conn., 1967. Mem. Nat. Coalition to Abolish the Death Penalty (bd. dirs. 1977-84), Am. Assn. for Counseling and Devel., Rotary. Democrat. Roman Catholic. Home: 62 Montague St Brooklyn NY 11201

PALMER, ETHEL SUSAN, technical information specialist; b. Bridgeport, Conn., July 31, 1943; d. Richard Barton and Ethel Braisted (Van Iderstine) Gethmann; m. John W.A. Palmer, Nov. 21, 1964 (div. 1986); children: Tamara K., Heather A. BS, Cornell U., 1965, MS in Genetics, 1969; MS in Library Sci., UCLA, 1982. Tech. info. specialist Chevron Oil Field Rsch. Co., La Habra, Calif., 1982—. Contbr. articles to profl. jours. Instr., Chevron Adopt-a-Sch. Program, La Habra, 1984—, program coord., 1989—. Recipient Cert. of Recognition, L.A. YWCA, 1986, Orange County YWCA, 1990; NSF grantee, 1979-82. Mem. Am. Soc. Info. Sci., Geosci. Info. Soc., Toastmasters. Home: 16124 E Rosecrans Ave Apt B La Mirada CA 90638 Office: Chevron Oil Field Rsch Co Po Box 446 La Habra CA 90633-0446

PALMER, HEIDI MARIE, health care manager; b. Danbury, Conn., Feb. 12, 1955; d. Joseph Edward Palmer and Christine Melanie (Schulze) Rella; 1 child, Nicole Santos. AS in Nursing, Mattatuck Community Coll., 1984; BA, Western Conn. State U., 1989. Lic. practical nurse, Conn. Staff nurse Waterbury (Conn.) Convalescent Ctr., Waterbury, 1979-82, Eastview Manor, 1982-83, Miller Meml. Community, Meriden, Conn., 1983-84; br. mgr. Kimberly Quality Care, Danbury, Conn., 1984-89. Commr. Commn. on the Status of Women, Danbury, 1988—; fundraiser Regional Hospice, Danbury, 1988—; mem. Tourette Syndrome Assn. Mem. NAFE, Danbury's Jaycees, Fraternal Order of Eagles (pre. 1984—, state officer 1982-85). Home: 62 Lake Breeze Dr Danbury CT 06811 Office: Kimberly Quality Care 57 North St Suite 313 Danbury CT 06810

PALMER, JANICE MARIE, psychologist, consultant; b. Boonville, Mo., Apr. 17, 1949; d. Herbert Edward and Wilma Louise (Grimes) Helmreich; m. May 23, 1969 (div. Oct. 1987); children: Russell, Christopher, Jonathan; 1 adopted child, Reanna. AA, Columbia (Mo.) Coll., 1969, BA in Psychology, 1984; MEd in Rehab. Counseling, U. Mo., 1986. Client svcs. coord. Coop. Sheltered Workshops, Marshall, Mo., 1986-87; social svc. worker State of Mo. Div. on Aging, Jefferson City, 1988; coord. intake svcs. Charter Hosp., Columbia, 1988; assoc. psychologist State of Mo. Dept. Corrections and Human Resources, Moberly, 1988—; cons. trainer State of Mo. Div. Family Svcs., Columbia, 1984—. Pres. Boone County Foster and Adoptive Parents, Columbia, 1984-86; advocate, pres. Mo. Foster and Adoptive Parents, Columbia, 1987-88. Democrat. Home: 852 Dometrorch Rd Rocheport MO 65279 Office: Moberly Tng Ctr for Men Box 7 Moberly MO 65270

PALMER, JO ANN, therapist; b. Laredo, Tex., Dec. 9, 1932; d. Joseph Arthur and Edna Lauraine (Crawford) Christopherson; m. James N. Palmer; children: Timothy, Gregory, Geofrey, Christine. BFA, Am. U., 1953; MA, U. South Fla., 1973, EDS, 1984. Therapist Tampa Heights Hosp., Tampa, Fla., 1973-78; supr. adol. project Fla. Mental Health Inst., Tampa, Fla., 1978-83; sch. counsel St. Lucie Co. Sch., Port St. Lucie, Fla., 1983-86; asst. project dir. Commn. Mental Health Svc., Gainesville, Fla. Contbr. articles to prof. jours. Facillitator, Parents United, Gainesville, Fla., 1987-89, Women Liberation Task Force. Democrat. Home: 3612 N W 53 Terr Gainesville FL 32608

PALMER, LINDA CONNER, sales professional; b. Lexington, Ky., Aug. 5, 1949; d. Walter Thomas and Anna Mark (Hendrix) Conner; m. Jeffrey Taylor Palmer, June 20, 1981. BS in Edn., No. Ill. U., 1971; postgrad., Morton Jr. Coll., 1967-69. Substitute tchr. Pub. Schs., DuPage County, Ill., 1971-72; asst. office mgr. B.A.M. Agy., Chgo., 1972-73; adminstrv. asst. Budget Rent-A-Car, Chgo., 1973-76, Mesirow & Co., Chgo., 1976-77; account mgr. Tellabs, Inc., Lisle, Ill., 1977-81, Oakland, Calif., 1981-86; ptnr. Palmer and Assocs., 1984—; area sales mgr. Reliable Electric/Utility Products, Oakland, 1986-88; sales rep. western area Homaco, 1989-90; regional sales mgr. Tollgrade Communications, 1990—. Republican. Roman Catholic.

PALMER, M. LESLIE, human resources specialist; b. Newport, R.I., Sept. 2, 1959; d. James Joseph and Mary Dorothy (Sullivan) P.; 1 child, Kevin Michael. BA in Psychology, Villanova U., 1981. Human resources coord. Narragansett Clothing co., Riverton, R.I. Home: 5 Summer St #2 Newport RI 02840 Office: Shake-A-Leg Inc PO Box 1002 Newport RI 02840

PALMER, NINA, public relations executive; b. Roaring Spring, Pa., Aug. 19, 1947; d. George Joseph and Helen Louise (Camp) P.; m. William Victor Sweeney, June 15, 1968; 1 child, Megan McDonnell. BA, Knox Coll., 1968; MA, U. Iowa, 1970. Research assoc. Carl Byoir & Assocs., N.Y.C., 1976-77, account exec., 1978-80, v.p., account supr., 1981-84, sr. v.p., mgmt. group supr., 1985-86; sr. v.p., gen. mgr. Doremus Porter Novelli, N.Y.C., 1986-87; exec. v.p., gen. mgr. Doremus Pub. Rels., N.Y.C., 1987-89, Gavin Anderson Doremus & Co., N.Y.C., 1990—; bd. dirs. Doremus & Co., N.Y.C., 1988—. Recipient Internat. Assn. Bus. Communicators award, 1984. Mem. Pub. Rels. Soc. Am. (Silver Anvil award 1979, 83). Home: 3 Peter Cooper Rd 8G New York NY 10010 Office: Doremus Pub Rels 120 Broadway New York NY 10271

PALMER, ROSE, foundation director, nurse; b. Pitts., Oct. 14, 1943; d. William Woodrow and Marion (Kuhn) Robbins; m. Anthony Joseph Palmer, (div. 1977); children: Tony, Kim; m. Alvin Phelps, 1985; stepchildren: Todd, Craig, Dean, Ryan, Mindy. AS in Nursing, Community Coll. Allegheny County, 1979; student, Carlow Coll., 1989. RN, Pa. Dir. SUPPORT, Pitts., 1979—. Legis. chair Allegheny County Transit Council, Pitts., 1985-87; candidate 45th legis. dist. Pa. Ho., 1988, 90; mem. steering com. Pitts. Women's Commn. Recipient Take Charge award Clairol, 1988. Mem. ABA (adv. bd. Child Support Advocacy Project 1987—), Nat. Child Support Coalition (treas. 1986—), Am. Acad. Family Mediators (assoc. 1986—), Family Mediation Coun. of Western Pa. (legis. com., bd. dirs.), Joint Family Law Coun. Pa., NOW, Women's Agenda Pa. Office: SUPPORT 429 Forbes Ave Ste 429 Pittsburgh PA 15219

PALMER-HASS, LISA MICHELLE, state official; b. Nashville, Sept. 4, 1953; d. Raymond Alonzo Palmer and Anne Michelle (Jones) Davies; m. Joseph Monroe Hass, Jr. BS in Bus. Adminstn., Belmont Coll., 1975; AA in Interior Design, Internat. Fine Arts Coll., 1977. Sec. to pres. Hermitage Elect. Supply Corp., Nashville, 1981-83; sec. to dir. Tenn. Dept. Mental Health and Mental Retardation, Nashville, 1984-86; transp. planner Tenn. Dept. Transp., Nashville, 1986—; interior designer Lisa Palmer Interior Designs, Nashville, 1977-84. Mem. Nat. Arbor Day Found. Recipient cert. of appreciation Tenn. Dept. Mental Health and Mental Retardation, 1986. Mem. Nat. Wildlife Fedn., Profl. Secs. Internat. (cert.), Nashville Striders Club, The Music City Bop Club. Republican. Mem. Disciples of Christ Ch. Office: Tenn Dept Transp Environ Planning Office 505 Deaderick St Suite 900 Nashville TN 37219

PALMIERI, JOANNE, hospital official, educator; b. Bklyn., June 5, 1956; d. Joseph and Mary Christine (Signore) P.; m. Stanley Peter Kokocki, Apr. 21, 1990. A.A.S., N.Y.C. Tech. Coll., 1981; cert., L.I. U., 1984; BS, St. Joseph's Coll., Bklyn., 1987; postgrad., St. Joseph's Coll., Maine, 1989—. Bus. rep. centralized ops. N.Y. Telephone Co., Bklyn., 1981-82; physician's asst. pvt. practice internist Bklyn., 1982-85; dir. quality assurance and risk mgmt. City Tech. Labs., 1985-87; quality assurance, risk mgmt. coord. Meth. Hosp., 1987-88; dir. risk mgmt. Community Hosp. Bklyn., 1988-89; clinic dir. S.I. (N.Y.) Hosp., 1989—; instr. med. program Kings Coll., Charlotte, N.C., 1990—; presenter Health Fair, N.Y.C. Bd. Edn., Bklyn., 1985; preceptor quality assurance and risk mgmt. SUNY Downstate Med. Ctr., Bklyn., 1987-88; instr. dental assisting program Coll. of S.I., 1989—. Mem. Nat. Assn. Quality Assurance Profls., Am. Pub. Health Assn., St. Jude Children's Research Hosp., Am. Soc. for Healthcare Risk Mgmt., Marine Park Civic Assn., Tau Phi Sigma. Roman Catholic. Home: 1920 Paces Landing Ave Rock Hill SC 29732

PALMISANO, CYNTHIA MARY, physician; b. Hinsdale, Ill., Jan. 27, 1954; d. William Leslie Sr. and Blanche Marie (Peska) Turek; m. Michael Palmisano, Dec. 16, 1972. BA, North Cen. Coll., Naperville, Ill., 1975; DO, Chgo. Osteo. Coll., 1981. Pvt. practice Elk Grove, Ill., 1981—. Office: 1080 Nerge Rd S103 Elk Grove IL 60007

PALMISANO, EDWINA MARGARET, real estate sales associate; b. East Orange, N.J., Sept. 28, 1943; d. Francis James and Edwina Parker (Marsh) Marron; m. Peter D. Mortimer, 1963 (wid. 1973); 1 child, Peter J.; m. John P. Palmisano, 1976. BA, Bloomfield Coll., 1973. Lic. real estate sales rep., N.J., 1972; N.Y. 1989;. Real estate sales rep. Better Homes & Gardens, Saddle River, N.J., 1986—, Murphy Realty, Better Homes & Gardens, Wyckoff, N.J., 1989; bd. dirs. Jersey Bank for Savings, Montvale. Mem. N.J. Assn. Realtors, Nat. Assn. Realtors, Million Dollar Club. Republican. Roman Catholic. Home: 122 Brewster Rd Wyckoff NJ 07481

PALMISANO, SHIRLEY ANN, small business owner; b. New Orleans, Feb. 22, 1944; d. Frank Joseph and Mary Louise (Austin) P. AA, St. Petersburg, Fla., 1969; BS, U. Wash., 1972; student, Calif. Culinary Acad., San Francisco, 1988. Lab. supr. U. Calif., San Francisco, 1976-86; chief owner Chez Jano, Forestville, Calif., 1988--. Recipient Danille Carlisle Walker award Calif. Culinary Acad., San Francisco 1988. Democratic.

PALSHO, DOROTHEA COCCOLI, publishing executive; b. Phila., June 9, 1947; d. John Charles and Dorothy Lucille (Decker) C.; m. Edward Robert Palsho; children: Christopher, Ryan, Erica (stepchild). BS, Villanova U., 1976; MBA, Temple U., 1977. With Dow Jones & Co., Princeton, N.J., 1977—; v.p. circulation Wall St. Jour. Named one of Class of Women Achievers YWCA Acad. of Women Achievers, 1985. Office: Dow Jones & Co Inc PO Box 300 Princeton NJ 08543*

PALSULICH, RONDA MARIE, accountant; b. Arvada, Colo., May 18, 1965; d. Richard Lynn Scotland and Joni Irene (West) Scotland Hill. BS in Bus. Adminstrn., Colo. State U., 1988. CPA, Colo. Theater mgr. Regency Theatre, Boulder, Colo., 1981-84; acad. asst. dept. acctg. Colo. State U., Ft. Collins, 1987-88; staff acct. Coopers & Lybrand, Denver, 1988-90; fin. asst. to chief exec. officer Jones Intercable Co., Englewood, Colo., 1990—. Instr. Jr. Achievement, Denver, 1989; vol. United Way Srs. Inc., Denver, 1989. Mem. Toastmasters. Republican. Home: 700 E Ellsworth Ave Apt 4 Denver CO 80209 Office: Jones Intercable Co 9697 E Mineral Ave Englewood CO 80112

PALUMBO, DIANE IRENE, lawyer; b. Bryn Mawr, Pa., Mar. 27, 1958; d. Joseph and Anna (Kuzma) Osifchok; m. Jeffrey John Palumbo, July 26, 1986. BA, Villanova U., 1980; JD, Pepperdine U., 1984. Bar: Calif. 1985, Pa. 1985, N.J. 1986, Okla. 1987. Elem. tchr. Archdiocese of Phila., 1980-81; assoc. Harvey, Pennington, Herting and Renneissen, Ltd., Phila., 1984-86, Nichols, Wolfe, Stamper, Nally & Fallis, Inc., Tulsa, 1986-89; ptnr. Nichols, Wolfe, Stamper, Nally & Fallis, Inc., 1990—. Pro bono counsel Tulsa Women's Resource Ctr., Tulsa U. and YWCA, 1986—. Named Vol. of Yr. YWCA, 1990. Mem. ABA, Tulsa Women's Lawyers Assn., Assn. of Trial Lawyers, Calif. State Bar Assn., Pa. State Bar Assoc., N.J. State Bar Assn., Okla. State Bar Assn. Republican. Roman Catholic. Office: Nichols Wolfe Stamper et al 124 E 4th St Ste 400 Tulsa OK 74103

PAMPUSCH, ANITA MARIE, academic administrator; b. St. Paul, Aug. 28, 1938; d. Robert William and Lucille Elizabeth (Whaley) P. BA, Coll. of St. Catherine, St. Paul, 1962; MA, U. Notre Dame, 1970, PhD, 1972. Tchr. St. Joseph's Acad., St. Paul, 1962-66; instr. philosophy Coll. of St. Catherine, St. Paul, 1970-76, assoc. acad. dean, 1979, acad. dean, 1979-84, pres., 1984—; Am. Council Edn. fellow Goucher Coll., Balt., 1976-77; bd. dirs. St. Paul Cos.; head Women's Coll. Coalition, 1988. Author: (book rev.) Philological Quarterly, 1976. Mem. adv. com. Instl. Leadership project, Columbia U., 1986—; dist. chmn. Rhodes Scholarship Selection com., Mo., Neb., Minn., Kans., N.D., S.D., 1987—; exec. com. Women's Coll. Coalition, Washington, 1985—. Mem. Council for Ind. Colls. (bd. dirs. 1987—), Am. Phil. Assn., Women's Econ. Roundtable, St. Paul C. of C. (bd. dirs. 1986—), Phi Beta Kappa. Roman Catholic. Clubs: St. Paul's Athletic (St. Paul), Women's (Mpls.). Office: Coll of St Catherine 2004 Randolph Ave Saint Paul MN 55105

PAMPY, EDNA THERESA, social worker; b. Long Prairie, Minn., Dec. 5, 1948; d. Anthony Aloysius and Olivia Helen (Klimek) P.; m. David Leo Sternitzke, May 20, 1989. BA, U. Minn., 1970; MSW, U. Iowa, 1981. Cert. clin. social worker, advanced clin. practitioner, pvt. practitioner. Fin. worker Hennepin County Econ. Assistance, Mpls., 1972-73; med. social worker Hennepin County Chest Clinic, Mpls., 1973-79; therapist Family & Children's Svc., Davenport, Iowa, 1980; rsch. asst. U. Iowa, Iowa City, 1980-81; family advocacy program coord. Army Community Svcs., Fort Lee, Va., 1982-84; therapist Scott County Mental Health Ctr., Shakopee, Minn., 1985-88; prin. social worker Hennepin County Child Protection, Mpls., 1984-89; counselor, cons. Personnel Performance Cons., Inc., Austin, Tex., 1989; cons. in field. Del. Dem. Farmer Labor Party, Mpls., 1976. Recipient Citation of Honor Hennepin County Bd. Commrs., 1989. Mem. Nat. Assn. Social Workers. Democrat.

PANAGOULIAS, PATRICIA ANN, nurse; b. Chgo., Sept. 22, 1951; d. Ray and Evelyn Frances (Kralicke) Huie; m. Steven Anthony Panagoulias, Sept. 19, 1987. AS, Triton Coll., River Grove, Ill., 1971, 80; BSN, Ill. Benedictine Coll., 1984. RN, Ill. Nurse Loyola U. Hosp., Maywood, Ill., 1980-81, Columbus Hosp., Chgo., 1982, U. Ill. Hosp., Chgo., 1982-86, 89—, West Suburban Hosp., Oak Park, Ill., 1986-88, Crescent Counties Found. for Med. Care, 1990—. Democrat. Roman Catholic. Home: 1614 Mayfair Ave Westchester IL 60154

PANAYI, LAURA POLITO, chemical technician; b. Hammond, Ind., Apr. 25, 1959; d. Thomas Anthony and Patricia Ann (Freeman) Polito; m. Peter Louis Panayi, July 16, 1984; children: Louis Peter, Thomas Peter. AAS in Supervision, Purdue U., Hammond, 1984, AAS in Chem. Tech., 1984; BSME, Purdue U., Westville, Ind., 1990. Sta. chem. technician No. Ind. Pub. Svc. Co., Hammond, 1979—. Mem. Nat. Assn. Female Execs. Home: 885 Meadowdale Ct Valparaiso IN 46383-9742 Office: NIPSCO PO Box 720M Gary IN 46401

PANCOAST, MARY SUSAN See SPRINGFIELD, MARY SUSAN

PANEK, JERI HERNDON, computer and public relations executive; b. Salt Lake City, June 15, 1939; d. Norman C. and Geraldine E. (Griffin) Herndon; ed. U. Utah; m. Larry H. Panek, Sept. 20, 1958 (div.); 1 son, Larry Brad. Public relations asst. Univac, Salt Lake City, 1961-69; dir. communications U. Utah, Salt Lake City, 1969-73; coordinator communications Sperry-Univac, Salt Lake City, 1973-74; electronic data processing communications coordinator Singer Bus. Machines Internat. Div., Brussels, Belgium, 1974-76; public relations and corp. planning mgr. Beehive Internat., Salt Lake City, 1977-80; program and sales mgr. Digistar computer graphics Evans & Sutherland Computer Corp., Salt Lake City, 1980—. Mem. Public Relations Soc. Am. (chmn. membership com., editor newsletter, chpt. treas. 1968—, v.p., immediate pas pres.), Assn. Computing Machinery (mem. conf. and symposia com. 1972-74), Internat. Planetarium Soc., Planetarium Assn. Can., C. of C. (aviation com.). Home: 1754 So Oak Springs Dr Salt Lake City UT 84108 Office: 580 Arapeen Dr Salt Lake City UT 84108

PANGBURN, PATRICIA DILLARD, public relations firm owner; b. Vineland, N.J., Oct. 15, 1933; d. Edgar Pugh and Sue (Atleson) D.; m. Newell Stephen Pangburn, Jr., June 16, 1956; children: Patricia Sue, Bradley. BS, U. Pa., 1955; MA, Western Mich. U., 1981. Sec., tissue lab. Hahnemann Med. Coll., Phila., 1955; educator Yeadon (Pa.) Pub. Schs., 1956, Willistown Twp. Pub. Schs., Paoli, Pa., 1956-57; acctg. technician U.S. Govt., Fort Huachuca, Ariz., 1958-59; pub. rels. dir. Glowing Embers Girl Scout Coun., Kalamazoo, Mich., 1969-73; community rels. dir. Goodwill Industries of S.W. Mich., Kalamazoo, 1976-81; asst. dir. pub. rels. Kalamazoo Coll., 1981-83; owner Pub. Rels. Svcs., Portage, Mich., 1984—. Chair Pvt. Industry Coun., Kalamazoo, 1990; mem. United Way Allocation Panel, Kalamazoo, 1987—; pres. Kalamazoo Ctr. for Ind. Living, 1985-87; bd. dirs. Glowing Embers Girl Scout Coun., Kalamazoo, 1988—. Mem. Women In Communication (past pres. 1985-86, Communicator of the Yr. award 1986), Portage Rotary, Kalamazoo C. of C. (bd. dirs. 1988—), Profl. & Exec. Assoc. Kalamazoo (past pres. 1988-89). Home: 1525 Greenview Portage MI 49002

PANICHI, MICHELE A., healthcare facility administrator; b. Phila., Dec. 12, 1959; d. Emil J. and Mary T. (Walsh) P. BS, U. Pa., Millersville, 1981. Lic. in nuclear medicine, N.J. Chief technologist nuclear medicine Rancocas Hosp., Willingboro, N.J.; dir. nuclear medicine W. Jersey Health System, Marlton, N.J. Mem. Soc. Nuclear Medicine (legis. govt. rels. com., cert.). Home: 21B E Daisy Ln Mount Laurel NJ 08054

PANICO, ALISON MARY, communications executive; b. N.Y.C., Apr. 10, 1967; d. Ralph and Rose (Trappani) P. BA, Tulane U., 1989. Exec. asst. ABC Capital Cities, N.Y.C., 1988-89; location intern Circle Films, New Orleans, 1989; acct. Fujisankei Communications, N.Y.C., 1989; asst. to unit mgr., producer NTV Internat. Corp., N.Y.C., 1989—; floor dir. Point of View, New Orleans, 1988-89. Active NOW, 1989. Mem. Media Bd. (chmn. 1988-89, mem. at large 1988). Home: 400 Stony Town Rd Manhasset NY 11030

PANNULLO, DEBORAH PAOLINO, quality assurance and productivity improvement director; b. Providence, Apr. 2, 1953; d. Joseph and Lena (Wilde) Paolino; m. Michael J. Pannullo, Apr. 23, 1971 (div. 1973); 1 child, Melissa Jean. BA in Econs., R.I. Coll., 1977; cert. in mfg. mgmt., Bryant Coll., 1982, MBA, 1987. Payroll analyst Bostitch/Textron, East Greenwich, R.I., 1977-79, cost analyst, 1979-80, U.S. mfg. coordinator, 1980-82, quality circles mgr., 1982-85; productivity mgr. Stanley-Bostitch, East Greenwich, 1985-87, dir. quality assurance-productivity improvement, 1987—; part-time instr. Bryant Coll.; cons. Sml. Bus. Devel. Ctr. Named outstanding Woman of Yr. WMCA, 1985. Mem. NAFE, Am. Soc. Quality Assurance, Internat. Assn. Quality Circles (pres. 1984-85, bd. dirs. R.I. chpt. 1985—), R.I. Technology Coun. (chairperson quality assurance sub-com.), Am. Soc. Quality Control (edn. com.), Delta Mu Delta. Roman Catholic. Home: 17 Hawkins St Greenville RI 02828 Office: Stanley-Bostitch Rt 2 East Greenwich RI 02818

PANOS SCHMITT, A(THANASIA) NANCY, marketing educator; b. Great Falls, Mont., Oct. 2, 1951; d. Alexander H. and Katherine (Papadrikopoulos) Panos; m. Gary Allen Schmitt, June 14, 1974; 1 son, Kyle Christopher. BS, U. Utah, 1974, MBA, 1979; MS, Va. Tech., 1976. Research specialist U. Utah, Salt Lake City, 1977-78; market adminstr. Mountain Bell Telephone Co., Salt Lake City, 1979-80; assoc. prof., chairperson mktg. dept. Westminster Coll., Salt Lake City, 1980—; owner, pres. Mktg./Mgmt. Inc., Salt Lake City, 1982—. Mem. Am. Mktg. Assn., Western Mktg. Assn., Salt Lake C. of C., Phi Beta Lambda, Phi Eta Sigma, Phi Sigma. Democrat. Greek Orthodox. Lodge: Zonta. Office: Westminster Coll Sch Bus 1840 S 1300 East Salt Lake City UT 84105

PANOWICZ, SISTER MARY KAY, print shop executive, health care administrator; b. Grand Island, Nebr., Mar. 29, 1948; d. Albin Eugene and Barbara (Pysczynski) P. BA with honors, Mt. Marty Coll., 1971; Master of Selected Studies, U. S.D., 1979. Adminstrv. asst. Mt. Marty Coll., Yankton, S.D., 1971-74, asst. dir. pub. rels., 1974-81, instr. art. dept., 1980-85; mgr. print shop Sacred Heart Convent, Yankton, 1981—; graphic art cons. Fedn. St. Gertrude, Crookston, Minn., 1979—. Two-person show of photographs, Mount Marty Coll., 1976, Bede Art Gallery, 1985. Trustee Sacred Heart Hosp., Yankton, 1982-89, chmn. bd. trustees, 1987-89; sec.-treas. bd. dirs. Benedictine Health System, Yankton, 1987—; sec. bd. dirs. Benedictine-Presentation Health Alliance, Yankton, 1987—. Mem. Coun. on Governance S.D. Hosp. Assn., Interchange. Democrat. Home: 1005 W 8th St Yankton SD 57078 Office: Convent Print Shop 1005 W 8th St Yankton SD 57078

PANTOJA, YVONNE MAGNO, diplomat; b. Belem, Para, Brazil, Nov. 9, 1926; came to U.S., 1972; d. Raymundo Da Silva and Odalea (Pantoja) Magno; m. Diego De Aldecocea Pantoja, Mar. 30, 1948 (div. July 1985); 1 child, Monica P. Student, U. of Rio de Janeiro, 1945-47; grad., Ministry of Fgn. Affairs Diplomatic Sch., Rio de Janeiro, 1957; cert. of proficiency in Eng., U. Mich., 1974; postgrad., Northwestern U., 1975, U. Calif., Berkeley, 1983-85, U. Houston, 1986. Vice consul Brazilian Consulate Gen., N.Y.C., 1959-62; consul Brazilian Consulate Gen., Chgo., 1974-76; 2nd sec. Brazilian Embassy & FAO, Rome, 1962-66; asst. to head of cultural dept. Ministry of Fgn. Affairs, Rio de Janeiro, 1966-67, head of documentation div., 1967-68; 1st sec. Brazilian Embassy, Copenhagen, 1969-72; consul Brazilian Consulate, Trieste, Italy, 1972-74, Houston, 1976-81, San Francisco, 1981-84. Translator: The Women of Brazil, 1946 (1st Literary prize in Brazil). Chrmn. of comm. for the study of the hist. of Brazil, Rio de Janeiro, 1969—; tchr. River Oaks Bapt. Ch. Internat. Program, 1985—. Decorated Cavalieri of the Italian order; Dannebrog comdr. (Denmark); Honor Cross (Copenhagen). Mem. Houston C. of C., Ladies' of the Houston Consular Corps. (sec. 1989), Japan Am. Soc., Christian Women's Club in Houston (chrmn. 1990). Baptist. Home: 1223 Post Oak Pk Dr Houston TX 77027

PANZONE, LISA MARIE GINA, tax consultant and specialist, financial planner, tax accountant; b. Phila., Feb. 26, 1960; d. Frank Vincent Sr. and Lisa Veronica (De Pierro) P. BA in Acctg., Glassboro (N.J.) State U., 1981; MS in Taxation, Widener U., 1983. CPA, Pa. Acct. Robert O'Connel & Co. (name now Touche Ross Co.), Phila., 1981; sr. acct., tax acct. Robert B. Burke, Phila., 1981-86; supr. sr. acct. Keystone Orgn., Phila., 1984-85; sr. tax acct. K.M.G. Main Hurdman, Phila., 1985-86; asst. tax dir. I.M.S., Inc., Phila., 1986-87; pvt. practice Phila., 1986—; tax specialist, co-owner Inches Off, Cherry Hill, N.J., 1985—; dir. ops. Cherry Hill Security Solutions, Mt. Laurel, N.J., 1988—. Vol. Community Accts., 1987—; treas., treas. Mt. Laurel Twp., 1984. Mem. Am. Soc. Women Accts., Contemporary Record Soc. (treas. Broomall, Pa. chpt. 1988—), GRASP (treas. Phila. chpt. 1988—). Home and Office: 12 B The Ellipse Mount Laurel NJ 08054

PAPALIA, DIANE ELLEN, human development educator; b. Englewood, N.J., Apr. 26, 1947; d. Edward Peter and Madeline (Borrin) P.; m. Jonathan Finlay, June 19, 1976; 1 child, Anna Victoria Finlay. A.B., Vassar Coll., 1968; M.S., W.Va. U., 1970, Ph.D. (NSF fellow), 1971. Asst. prof. child and family studies U. Wis., Madison, 1971-75; assoc. prof. U. Wis., 1975-78, prof., 1978-87, coordinator child and family studies, 1977-79; adj. prof. psychology in pediatrics U. Pa. Sch. Medicine, 1987-89; adj. prof. psychiatry svc. Meml. Sloan-Kettering Cancer Ctr., 1989—. Aukthor: (with Sally W. Olds) A Child's World: Infancy through Adolescence, 1975, 5th edit., 1990, Human Development, 1978, 4th edit., 1989, Psychology, 1985, 2d edit., 1988; contbr. articles to profl. jours. Am. Council on Edn. fellow, 1979-80; U. Wis. grantee. Fellow Gerontol. Soc.; mem. Am. Psychol. Assn., Soc. Research in Child Devel., Nat. Council Family Relations, Psi Chi. Home: 515 E 72d St Apt 20F New York NY 10021 Office: 410 E 62d St Rm 726 New York NY 10021

PAPE, PATRICIA ANN, psychotherapist, social worker; b. Aurora, Ill., Aug. 2, 1940; d. Robert Frank and Helen Louise (Hanks) Grover; children: Scott Allen, Debra Lynn. BA in Sociology, Northwestern U., 1962; MSW, George Williams Coll., 1979. Cert. addictions counselor, Ill.; lic. clin. social worker, sch. social worker, Ill. Pvt. practice family counseling, 1979—; coord. community resources DuPage Probation Dept., Wheaton, Ill., 1977-80; dir. The Abbey Alcoholism Treatment Ctr., Winfield, Ill., 1980-81; prin. Pape & Assocs., Wheaton, 1982—; dir. alcoholism counselor tng. program Coll. of DuPage, Glen Ellyn, Ill., 1982-87; Chgo. affiliate Employee Assistance Program, 1982—; cons. Luth. Soc. Services Ill., 1979-82. Contbr. articles to profl. jours. Mem. alcohol drug task force Ill. Synod Luth. Ch. Am., Chgo., 1985—. Named Woman of Yr., Entrepreneur Women in Mgmt., Oak Brook, Ill, 1986. Mem. Assn. Labor-Mgmt. Adminstrs. Cons. Alcoholism (women's issues com. 1984—), Acad. Cert. Social Workers, Am. Assn. Marriage Family Therapists, Nat. Assn. Soc. Workers, Women in Mgmt. Home: 26W360 Churchill Rd Winfield IL 60190 Office: Pape & Assocs 618 S West St Wheaton IL 60187

PAPE, PATRICIA JEAN, insurance company consultant, personnel consultant; b. Willimantic, Conn., Jan. 31, 1958; d. Robert Joseph and Mary Louise (Campbell) P. BS in Psychology cum laude, U. Hartford, 1983, postgrad., 1987—. Supr. career continuation services Cigna Corp., Hartford, Conn., 1983-85; mgr. planning and systems devel. Cigna Corp., Phila., 1985-87; sr. cons. Cigna Corp., Hartford, 1987-88, asst. dir., 1988—; outplacement cons., Phila., Hartford, 1985-89; human resources generalist, Hartford, 1989—. Co-author, editor co. manual, 1987. Mem. Am. Soc. Personnel Adminstrs., Phila. Fin. Assn., Nat. Assn. Female Execs., U. Hartford Alumni Assn. Republican. Home: 174 Mott Hill Rd East Hampton CT 06424 Office: Cigna Corp W 43 Hartford CT 06152

PAPEN, JULIA STEVENSON, food products company executive; b. Beaufort, S.C., May 21, 1910; d. Carl Frederick and Emma Stevenson; m. Frank O'Brien Papen, Apr. 22, 1942; 1 child, Michele Papen-Daniel. BA magna cum laude, U. S.C., 1931. Office mgr. Longview (Tex.) Coca-Cola Bottling Co., 1931-41, v.p., dir., 1960—; gen. mgr. Las Cruces (N.Mex.) Coca-Cola Bottling Co., 1941-44; office mgr. Frank O. Papen Ins. Agy., Las Cruces, 1944-57. Gov. appointed Regent N.Mex. State U., 1976-82; mem. Las Cruces Womens' Improvement Assn., Dona Ana Arts Council, Las Cruces, 1975-88; bd. dirs. Las Cruces Symphony Assn., 1983—. Named to Order of Holy Sepulchre Pope Pius XII, 1960. Mem. AAUW, Phi Beta Kappa, Beta Gamma Sigma. Democrat. Roman Catholic. Home and Office: 1857 Paisano Rd Las Cruces NM 88005

PAPINEAU, SANDRA LYNN, quality control engineer; b. Detroit, Sept. 2, 1964; d. Richard George and Jeanette (Beasley) Hill; m. Charles Gerard Papineau, Aug. 5, 1989. BS in Indsl. Engring., GMI Engring. and Mgmt. Inst., Flint, Mich., 1987. Vehicle systems engr. Cadillac Motor Co., Detroit, 1987-88; quality cons. Coopers & Lybrand, Detroit, 1888-89; fellow Ford Motor Co., Dearborn, Mich., 1989-90; quality engr. Lectron Products, Inc., Rochester, Mich., 1990—. Bd. dirs. Hugh O'Brian Youth Found., Mich., 1986-90. Mem. Soc. Automotive Engrs., Am. Soc. for Quality Control (cert.), Alpha Sigma Alpha. Home: 2157 Willow Circle Shelby MI 48315 Office: Lectron Products Inc 1400 S Livernois Rochester MI 48308-5020

PAPPAS, EFFIE VAMIS, English and business educator, writer; b. Cleve., Dec. 26, 1924; d. James Jacob and Helen Joy (Nicholson) Vamis; m. Leonard G. Pappas, Nov. 3, 1945; children: Karen Pappas Morabito, Leonard J., Ellen Pappas Daniels, David James. BBA, Western Res. U., 1948, MA in Edn., 1964, PhD in Edn., 1968; MA in English Lit., Cleve. State U., 1986. Cert. elem. and secondary tchr., Ohio. Tchr. elem. schs., Ohio, 1963-70; office mgr. Cleve. State U., 1970-72, adminstr. pub. relations, 1972-73; med. adminstr. Brecksville (Ohio) VA Hosp., 1974-78; lectr. English and bus. Cuyahoga Community Coll., Cleve., 1978—; lectr. bus. and communications Cleve. State U., 1980; participant Am. Inst. Chemists Del. to Republic of China, 1984, Inter-Cultural Exch. in the Soviet Union, 1989. Feature writer The Voice, 1970-78; editor, writer Cleve. State U. newsletter and mag., 1970-73. Den mother Brecksville chpt. Cub Scouts Am., 1960; mem. local council PTA, 1965-70; mem. St. Paul's Philoptohos-Friends of the Poor, North Royalton, 1985—; tchr. Sunday sch. United Ch. Christ, Brecksville, 1960-65, mem. choir, 1975-76; coun. sec. St. Paul's Ch., 1990—. Profl. devel. grantee Cuyahoga Community Coll., 1982. Mem. NAFE, NEA, Nat. Trust for Historic Preservation, Nat. Mus. Women in the Arts, Ohio Edn. Assn., Div. Active Retired Tchrs. Mem. United Ch. of Christ. Home: 8681 Brecksville Rd Brecksville OH 44141 Office: Cuyahoga Community Coll West Campus 11000 Pleasant Valley Rd Parma OH 44130-5199

PAQUIN, MARILYN JEAN, accountant; b. Milw., Dec. 21, 1940; d. Russel A. and Olive (Miller) Beierle; m. James E Paquin, July 25, 1965; children: Josette, Suzanne, Margot. AA, U. Md.; BS, SUNY, Albany, 1971. CPA, La. Various pub. rels. positions, 1960-65; acct. Slidell, La., 1978-82; sr. tax mgr. DeLoitte & Touche, New Orleans, 1982—; swim coach Pinewood Country Club, Slidell, 1979-81. Contbr. articles on taxation to tech. jours. Pres. St. Tammany Parish Swim League, 1983-85. Mem. La Soc. CPA's, Pinewood Country Club (bd. dirs. 1980-87), Cotillion Debutante Club, Ozone Camellia Club, Phi Kappa Phi, Sigma Chi Alpha. Republican. Home: 149 Rue Charlemagne Slidell LA 70461 Office: DeLoitte & Touche 201 St Charles Ave New Orleans LA 70170-4100

PARADIS, CAROL JEANNE, nurse, counselor; b. Providence, Dec. 15, 1944; d. Ralph Joseph and Jeannette Clarice (Langelier) Petrucci; m. Daniel Kirby Paradis, Sept. 5, 1970; children: Trent August, Scott LeMay. BS in Nursing, Boston U., 1966; M Nursing, UCLA, 1971. RN, Mass., Calif., R.I., Colo; cert. addictions counselor, Colo. Nurse Univ. Hosp., Boston, 1966-67, Peter Bent Brigham Hosp., Boston, 1967-68; sr. clin. nurse surg. intensive care and Children's Hosp. Long Beach (Calif.) Meml. Hosp. Med. Ctr., 1968-71; faculty chmn. and adminstrv. asst. Presbyn. Sch. Nursing, Denver, 1972-80; mem. faculty Delta (Colo.) Montrose Vocat.-Tech. Sch., 1982-84; staff nurse Montrose (Colo.) Meml. Hosp., 1984-86; program dir. Care Ctr. Montrose (Colo.) Hosp., 1986—, dir. nurses, 1987; cons. U. Denver Sch. Nursing, 1981-82. Speaker regional conf. Assn. Operating Rm. Nurses, 1974. Bd. dirs. Women's Resource Ctr., 1983-84; presenter Montrose Children's Mus., 1989; team mem. Montrose Community for Drug Free Colo., 1987—; leader local cub troop Boy Scouts Am.; active in various sch., ch. and communities activites. Recipient Bonnie Forquer award Nat. Coun. on Alcoholism and Drug Abuse, Mesa chpt., 1990. Mem. EAPA, Rocky Mountain Nurses Assn. (Colo. lobbyist Nurse Practice Act 1978), Friends of Nursing (scholarship coms. 1987—), Nurse Inc., Alpha Phi. Roman Catholic. Home: 64669 W Ranger Rd Montrose CO 81401

PARALEZ, LINDA LEE, technical writer, graphic designer; b. Raton, N.Mex., Oct. 29, 1955. AS, Amarillo Coll., 1975; student West Tex. State U., 1975-77, BBA, Century U., Beverly Hills, Calif., 1984, MBA, 1987; student Newport U. Sch. Law, 1988-89. Teaching asst. Amarillo (Tex.) Coll., 1974-75; drafter natural gas div. Pioneer Corp., Amarillo, 1975-76, sr. drafter exploration div. Amarillo Oil Co. 1976-77; drafting supr., engring. services supr., dir. speakers' bur. Thunder Basin Coal Co., Atlantic Richfield Co., Wright, Wyo., 1977-86; ptnr., tech. and adminstrv. cons. Rose Enterprises, 1986—; tech. writer Eaton Corp., Riverton, Wyo., 1986-88; cons. State Wyo. Office on Family Violence and Sexual Assault, Cheyenne, 1986-89; Diamond L Industires, Inc., Gillette, Wyo., 1986-88; tech. writer, pubs. cons. Thiokol Corp., Brigham City, Utah, 1987-89, design specialist space ops., 1989—. Bd. dirs. Campbell County Drafting Adv. Council, 1984-85; sec. bd. dir. exec. com. Am. Inst. Design and Drafting, 1984-85, tech. publ. chairperson, 1984-85. Named Most Outstanding Woman, Beta Sigma Phi, 1980, 81; recipient Woman in the Industry recognition Internat. Reprographics Assn., 1980; grand prize winner Wyo. Art Show with painting titled Energy, 1976. Mem. AAUW, NAFE, NOW, Am. Legion Aux., Ocean Research Edn. Soc., Gloucester, Mass. (grant proposal writer, 1984), Soc. Tech. Communications, 4-H Club. Author (poetry): God was Here, but He Left Early, 1976, Gift of Wings, 1980, Solo, 1987, 89; columnist, Wytech Digest; contbr. numerous articles to profl. jours. Home: 3159 N Holiday North Ogden UT 84414

PARAS, SOFIA DIMITRIA, counselor, author; b. Delaware, Ohio, Dec. 31, 1943; d. James Peter and Fotini Dimitria (Dellios) Stoycheff; m. Nicholas Andrew Paras, Dec. 8, 1968; 1 child, Alexandra Nicholas. BA, Ohio Wesleyan U., 1965; cert., Adelphi U., 1987. Tchr. Upper Arlington Schs., Columbus, Ohio, 1966-68; asst. tng. coord. personnel dept. Ohio State U. Hosps., Columbus, 1968-69, art fair coord., 1969; asst. tng. coord. personnel dept. New Eng. Deaconess Hosp., Boston, 1969-70; tng. coord. nursing dept. Meml. Hosp. of Sloan Kettering, N.Y.C., 1970-71; real estate salesperson Gen. Devel. Corp., 1971-72; adminstrv. asst. Ippocampos Maritime and Internship Fin. and Investments, Piraeus, Greece, 1976-81; office mgr. Internapa Fin. Svcs., Athens, Greece, 1981-86; adminstrv. dir. lawyer's asst. program Adelphi U., West Hempstead, N.Y., 1987-88, admissions counselor lawyer's asst. program, 1988—; cons. interior decorator hotel complex Paramount Tourist and Devel. Ltd., Paralimni, Cyprus, 1981-84; nat. nursing conf. coord. Meml. Hosp. Sloan Kettering, St. Louis, 1971. Editor Women's Internat. Club, Athens, 1978-84; author poetry and screenplays. Theatre dir. Am. Farm Sch., Salonica, Greece, 1974; program coord. choir recitals St. Nicholas Greek Orthodox, Babylon, N.Y., 1989—; v.p. Internat. Women's Orgn. of Greece, Salonica, 1973-74. Mem. NAFE, Nassau/Suffolk Neighborhood Network, L.I. Ctr. for Bus. and Profl. Women, Kappa Kappa Gamma, Theta Alpha Phi. Office: Adelphi U 307 Eagle Ave West Hempstead NY 11552

PARDEE, LENORA MAXINE, minister, director; b. Ravenswood, W.Va., July 1, 1937; d. Ross Erwin and Leora Inez (Brewer) Grimes; m. Pierre James Pardee, Sept. 4, 1957 (div. 1972); children: James, Martha Pardee Carlson, Robert. BS in Edn., Youngstown (Ohio) State U., 1967; MDiv, Pitts. Sem., 1986. Ordained to ministry Presbyn. Ch., 1986. With J.G. Pardee Co., Youngstown, 1967-72; tchr. East Liverpool (Ohio) City Sch., 1972-74; with computer dept. Hall China Co., East Liverpool, 1974-84; ministry, dir. Lake Erie Presbytery-Presbyn. Area Ministry, Sugargrove, Pa., 1985-87, Lehigh Presbytery-N.W. Ministry, Mahanoy City, Pa., 1987—; bd. dirs. ecumenical com. for continuing edn. MOravian Sem., Bethlehem, Pa., 1988—, Micah Project, Allentown, Pa. Commr. Boy Scouts Am., E. Liverpool, 1976-83. Mem. Mahanoy Area Administerial Assn. (pres. 1989—), AAUW. Democrat. Home and Office: 38 W Mahanoy Ave Mahanoy City PA 17948

PARDEE, MARGARET ROSS, violinist, violist, educator; b. Valdosta, Ga., May 10, 1920; d. William Augustus and Frances Ross (Burton) P.; diploma Inst. Mus. Art, Juilliard Sch. Music, 1940, grad. diploma, 1942, diploma Juilliard Grad. Sch., 1945; m. Daniel Rogers Butterly, July 5, 1944. Instr. violin and viola Manhattanville Coll. Sacred Heart, N.Y.C., 1942-54, Juilliard Sch., N.Y.C., 1942—, Meadowmount Sch. Music, Westport, N.Y., 1956-84, 88—, Bowdoin Coll. Music Festival and Sch., Maine, summer 1987; faculty Estherwood Sch. and Summer Festival, 1984-86; concert master Great Neck (L.I.) Symphony, 1954-85; adj. assoc. prof. music Queens Coll., Flushing, N.Y., 1978—; adj. assoc. prof. Adelphi U., Garden City, N.Y., 1979-83; adj. prof. SUNY, Purchase, 1980—; vis. prof. Simon Bolivar Youth Orch. and Conservatory, Caracas and Barquisimeto, Venezuela, 1988, 89, Conservatoria de la Orch. Nat. Juvenil, Caracas, Venezuela, 1988, 89; debut N.Y. Town Hall, 1952; toured U.S. as soloist and in chamber music groups; soloed with symphony orchs. in Miss., N.J., D.C. and N.Y.; mem. jury for internat. competitions; guest artist prof. 1st Internat. Festival for Young Violinists, Caracas, 1988. Recipient Merit award and citation for exceptional leadership ASTA, 1990. Bd. dirs. Meadowmount Sch. Music. Mem. Soc. for Strings (dir. 1965—), Associated Music Tchrs. League N.Y. (cert.), N.Y. State Music Tchrs. Assn. (cert., citation 1989), Music Tchrs. Nat. Assn., Am. Fedn. Musicians, Viola Research Soc. Office: care Juilliard Sch Lincoln Ctr Plaza New York NY 10023

PARDOE-RUSS, SUSAN MEREDITH, marketing executive; b. New Castle, Pa., May 6, 1948; d. Stephen C. and Frances E. (Simonsic) Meredith; m. Lawrence J. Pardoe, Apr. 28, 1972 (div. Oct. 1983); m. Timothy A. Russ, July 1, 1990. BS in Journalism cum laude, Ohio U., 1970; cert. exec. devel. program, U. Houston, 1982. Mktg. rep. advt. Chem. Abstract Services, Columbus, Ohio, 1970-71; free-lance copywriter, editor Hudson, Ohio and Los Angeles, 1971-76; mgr. advt. Automatic Sprinkler Corp. Am., Cleve., 1976-79; mgr. mktg. communications Norton Co., Akron, Ohio, 1979-82, dir. communications, 1982-90; v.p. communications GenCorp Automotive, Akron, 1990—. Mem. Internat. Advt. Assn., Bus. and Profl. Advertisers Assn. Office: GenCorp Automotive PO Box 3545 Akron OH 44309-3545

PARDUE, MARY LOU, biology educator; b. Lexington, Ky., Sept. 15, 1933; d. Louis Arthur and Mary Allie (Marshall) P. B.S., William and Mary Coll., 1955; M.S., U. Tenn., 1959; Ph.D., Yale U., 1970; D.Sc. (hon.), Bard Coll., 1985. Postdoctoral fellow Inst. Animal Genetics, Edinburgh, Scotland, 1970-72; assoc. prof. biology MIT, Cambridge, 1972-80; prof. MIT, 1980—; summer course organizer Cold Spring Harbor Lab., N.Y., 1971-80; mem. rev. com. NIH, 1974-78, 80-84, mem. nat. adv. gen. med. scis. council, 1984-88 ; mem. sci. adv. com. Wistar Inst., Phila., 1976—; mem. health and environ. research adv. com. U.S. Dept. Energy, 1987—. Mem. editorial bd. Chromosoma, Molecular and Cellular Biology, Cell Biol. Internat. Reports, Jour. Cell Biology Biochemistry; mem. editorial bd. mem. Annual Rev. of Cell Biology; contbr. articles to profl. jours. Recipient Esther Langer award Langer Cancer Rsch. Found., 1977, Lucius Wilbur Cross medal Yale Grad. Sch., 1989; grantee NIH, NSF, Am. Cancer Soc. Fellow AAAS, Nat. Acad. Scis., Am. Acad. Arts and Sci.; mem. Genetics Soc. Am. (pres. 1982-83), Am. Soc. Cell Biology (council 1977-80, pres. 1985-86), NRC (bd. on biology 1989—), Phi Beta Kappa, Phi Kappa Phi. Office: MIT Dept Biology 16-717 77 Massachusetts Ave Cambridge MA 02139

PAREKH, HEMA RATILAL, finacial execuitve; b. Valsad, Gujarat, India, Feb. 10, 1952; came to the U.S., 1975; d. Ratilal M. and Vasantben P. BBA, Bombay U., 1972, MS, 1974; MBA, Emory U., Atlanta, 1977. CPA. From

staff acct. to mgr. strategic planning First Tenn Nat. Corp., Memphis, 1977-84; sr. v.p. fin. adminstr. Sovran Bank, Memphis, 1984—; v.p. fin. Bankers Adminstrv. Inst., Memphis, 1988—, planning exec. inst. v.p. programs, Memphis, 1983. Mem. Nat. Assn. Accts., Coll. Mgmt. Accts., AICPA, AMA, Beta Gamma Sigma. Home: 411 Regis Cove Cordova TN 38018 Office: Sovran Bank 2670 Union Ave 4th Fl Memphis TN 38112

PARENT, MICHELLE SUSAN, management executive; b. Sidney, N.Y., Feb. 6, 1950; d. Louis Edward and Ruth Edna (Walker) P. AA, Broome Tech., Binghamton, N.Y., 1971; BA, State U. Coll., Brockport, N.Y., 1973; MEd, East Stroudsburg State Coll., 1979. Phys. edn. instr. Middletown (N.Y.) High Sch., 1973-76; from rental mgr. to asst. mgr. Golden Sands Club, Ocean City, Md., 1976-79; br. mgr. Anthony R. Diana Mgmt., Ocean City, Md., 1980-82; office mgr. Moisture Protection Systems Analysts, Inc., Mclean, Va., 1982-85; v.p. Moisture Protection Systems Analysts, Inc., Falls Church, Va., 1985-88; sales rep. Roofers Mart Capital Dist., Beltsville, Md., 1988-89, gen. mgr., 1989—. Mem. Washington Area Roofing Contractors Assn. (bd. dirs. 1989-90), Assoc. Roofing Contractors of Md., Constrn. Specifications Inst., Nat. Roofing Contractors Assn. Republican. Roman Catholic. Home: 3495 S Utah St Apt A1 Arlington VA 22206 Office: Roofers Mart Capital Dist 12120 Conway Rd Beltsville MD 20705-0817

PARETSKY, SARA N., writer; b. Ames, Iowa, June 8, 1947; d. David Paretsky and Mary E. Edwards; m. S. Courtenay Wright, June 19, 1976; children: Kimball Courtenay, Timothy Charles, Philip William. BA, U. Kans., 1967; MBA, PhD, U. Chgo., 1977. Mgr. Urban Rsch Ctr., Chgo., 1971-74, CNA Ins. Co., Chgo., 1977-85; writer, 1985—. Author: (novels) Indemnity Only, 1982, Deadlock, 1984 (prize Friends of Am. Writers 1985), Killing Orders, 1986, Bitter Medicine, 1987, Blood Shot, 1988, Burn Marks, 1990, also numerous articles and short stories. Pres. Sisters in Crime, Chgo., 1986-88; dir. Nat. Abortion Rights Action League Ill., 1987—. Named Woman of Yr. Ms mag., N.Y.C., 1987. Mem. Crime Writers Assn. (Silver Dagger award 1988), Mystery Writers Am. (v.p. 1989), Authors Guild, Chgo. Network. *

PARETZKY, YVONNE RUCKER, insurance brokerage company executive; b. Jenkintown, Pa., Oct. 15, 1949; d. William Henry and Opal Calivia (Jackson) Rucker; m. Kenneth Ira Paretzky, Apr. 8, 1978; children: Jessica Caitlin, Shannon Teresa, Johanna Naomi. BA, George Washington U., 1977. Corp. comm. staff Govt. Employees Ins. Co., Washington, 1976-78; sr. editor Bur. of Nat. Affairs, Inc., Washington, 1978-87; pres. Paretzky Info. Network, Inc., Bethesda, Md., 1987—; assoc. in risk mgmt. Ins. Inst. Am., 1988; instr. in field various seminars, classes; vis. instr. indsl. risk mgmt. Harare, Zimbabwe, 1988. Author: Guide to the London Insurance Market, 1988; contbg. editor: Chemical Safety Data Guide, 1987; author/editor: Loss Prevention and Control, 1978-87. Mem. Assn. Profls. in Risk-Related Disciplines (founding mem., mem. adv. bd. 1989—), Assn. of Profl. Ins. Women, Internat. Inst. Risk and Safety Mgmt. (London). Office: 6701 Democracy Blvd #300 Bethesda MD 20817

PARHAM, ELLEN SPEIDEN, nutrition professor; b. Mitchells, Va., July 15, 1938; d. Marion Coote and Rebecca Virginia (McNiel) Speiden; m. Arthur Robert Parham, Jr., Dec. 16, 1961; children: Katharine Alma, Cordelia Alyx. BS in Nutrition, Va. Poly. Inst., 1960; PhD in Nutrition, U. Tenn., 1967. Registered dietician. Asst. prof. to prof. No. Ill. U., DeKalb, Ill., 1966—; dir. coord. undergrad. program in dietetics. No. Ill. U., DeKalb, 1981-86, coord. grad. faculty in Human and Family Resources, 1985-87; cons. on nutrition various hosps., clins. and bus., Ill., 1980—; founder, dir. Horizons Weight Control Program, DeKalb, 1983—; co-chair Nutrition Coalition for Ill., 1989—. Bd. editors: Jour. Nutrition Edn., 1985—; contbr. articles to profl. jours. Mem. Am. Inst. Nutrition, Soc. Nutrition Edn., Am. Dietetic Assn., Am. Home Econs. Assn., No. Am. Assn. Study Obesity.

PARHAM, RUBY INEZ MYERS, civic worker, former educator; b. Tamaha, Okla., Nov. 4, 1914; d. Ola T. and Bursha Bell (Culver) Myers; B.S. in Edn., Northeastern State Coll., 1940, M.Teaching, 1955; m. Rufus K. McCollum, Dec. 31, 1937 (dec. Oct. 1966); m. Jewell A. Parham, June 10, 1973 (dec. Sept. 1987); stepchildren—Bill, Donal E., Ann (Mrs. Everett George), Garry. Tchr. rural schs., Haskell County, Stigler, Okla., 1934-38, Adair County, Stilwell, Okla., 1946-50, Cherokee County, Tahlequah, Okla., 1939-46, 50-66; tchr. Westville (Okla.) Jr. High Sch., 1966-77, ret., 1977. Vol., pres. Tahlequah City Hosp. Aux., 1982-83, 84-85, 85-86; vice chmn. Bapt. Women's Missionary Union, also past pres.; chmn. Nutrition Site Council, Tahlequah; mem. project council Cookson Hills Community Action Found., Inc.; adv. com. Helping Hands; precinct worker Republican party Recipient Oklahoma Bankers award, 1965. Mem. Nat., Okla. edn. assns., Tahlequah Sr. Citizens (bd. dirs.), Nat. Ret. Tchrs. Assn., Okla. Ret. Tchrs. Assn., Am. Assn. Ret. Persons, Am. Legion Aux., Northeastern State U. Alumni Assn. (life), Nat. Wildlife Assn., sr. Citizens Tahlequah, Kappa Kappa Iota (royal high lady Tahlequah, Okla., 1953-55), Delta Kappa Gamma. Clubs: Rebekah (noble grand 1959-60, jr. noble grand 1960-61, lodge dep. 1961-63, musician), Order Eastern Star (worthy matron 1979, organist, chmn. edn. com.). Home: 215 S College St Tahlequah OK 74464

PARIS, DONNA FRANCINE, accountant; b. Waterbury, Conn., Mar. 21, 1951; d. Bartholomew and Mary (Williams) Margiotta; m. Thomas Edward Paris, Aug. 7, 1972. BA, U. Conn., 1975; BS, Post Coll., 1989. Office mgr. The Lettercrafters, Inc., N.Y.C., 1980-84; owner Donna F. Paris Bookkeeping Svcs., Waterbury, 1984-89; acct. Deloitte Haskins & Sells, Waterbury, 1989-90, Pacowta & Hubbard, Waterbury, 1990—. Mem. Nat. Assn. Accts., Am. Soc. Women Accts., Post Coll. Alumni Assn. (bd. mem. 1989), Phi Kappa Phi, Phi Beta Kappa, Alpha Chi. Office: Pacowta & Hubbard One Exchange Pl Waterbury CT 06702

PARISEAU, PATRICIA, state senator; b. St. Paul, Aug. 10, 1936; d. James Martin and Mary Margaret (May) Wright; m. Kenneth Edward Pariseau, July 9, 1960; children: Susan M., Douglas C., Penny A., Linda D., Barbara J., Jacqueline. RN, Ravenswood Hosp. Sch. Nursing, Chgo., 1957. Staff nurse Ravenswood Hosp., Chgo., 1957-58, St. Joseph's Hosp., St. Paul., 1958-59, Office of Drs. Roy & Hilker, St. Paul., 1959-60; aide to U.S. Senator Rudy Boschwitz, St. Paul., 1982-88; mem. Minn. Senate, St. Paul., 1989—. Mem. adv. bd. St. Paul chpt. ARC, 1986-88; vol., officer Minn. Ind. Rep. Com., 1972-83; bd. dirs. Ind. Sch. Dist. 192, Farmington, Minn., 1976-79. Mem. Minn. Waterfowl Assn., Farmington C. of C., Dakota Arts Coun., Ducks Unltd., Eagles Aux., Am. Legion Aux. (sec. Farmington chpt.), VFW Aux., So. Dakota County Sportsmen Club. Office: Minn Senate 151 State Office Bldg Saint Paul MN 55155

PARK, JACQUELINE, investment banker; b. San Francisco, Aug. 4, 1951; d. Woonsun and Alice (Kim) P.; m. Jack Donald E. Webb, May 22, 1982; 1 child, Jayne-Louise. AA, City Coll., San Francisco, 1971; BA, San Francisco State U., 1973, MA in Spl. Edn., 1975. Budget adminstr. Standard Oil of Ohio, San Francisco, 1981-84; prin. The Webb Group, San Francisco, 1984-89, Pacific Capital Advisors, San Francisco, Burlingame, Calif., 1989—. Exec. bd. San Francisco-Seoul Sister City Com., 1988; founder Com. for Korean Art, San Francisco, 1989; mem. San Francisco State U. U.S.-Korea Inst., 1989. Mem. Profl. and Bus. Women's Orgn. (bd. dirs. 1989—), Internat. Assn. Fin. Planners. Office: Pacific Capital Advisors Bay Park Pla 577 Airport Blvd Ste 200 Burlingame CA 94010-2021

PARK, MARY CATHRYNE, educator; b. Bellefonte, Pa., June 18, 1918; d. James Theodore and Lucie Catherine (Coons) P. BA with hons., U. Pa., 1939, MA, 1942, PhD, 1947. Head market rsch. Scott Paper Co., Chester, Pa., 1944-48; assoc. prof. English and German Catawba Coll., Salisbury, N.C., 1950-52; assoc. prof. English Stetson U., Deland, Fla., 1952-55, Fla. So. Coll., Lakeland, 1955-60; prof. English Brevard Community Coll., Cocoa, Fla., 1960—; cons. in field; lectr. in field; prof. Fla. Inst. Continuing Edn. and Univ. Studies, Fla. Jr. Coll. TV Classroom, 1964—; adj. prof. grad. sch. bus. Fla. State U., 1964-70; adj. prof. English Shelton Coll. Cape Canaveral, Fla., 1970—, Rollins Coll., 1970—. Author: Testing, 1989; contbr. articles to profl. jours; creator TV series on preventive medicine, humaities series. Active Am. Cancer Soc., Brevard County YWCA, Salvation Army, Brevard County United Way, Brevard County Community Services Coun., Presbyn. Manor, and many others. Recipient William H. Meardy Tchr. of Yr. award Assn. Community Coll. Trustees, 1988. Classroom bldg. named in honor Brevard Community Coll., 1988. Mem. AAUW (founder, pres. local chpt.), Del. County Inst. Sci. and Fossil Club, So. Atlantic MLA, Am. Studies Assn., S.E. Am. Studies Assn., Space and Missile Pioneers, MLA, English Speaking Union, Fla. Acad. Scis., Charles Lamb Soc., Cap and Gown Soc., Rotary, Kiwanis, Sigma Pi Alpha, Alpha Psi Omega, Pi Gamma Mu, Sigma Tau Delta, Phi Delta Kappa, Delta Kappa Gamma. Republican. Presbyterian. Home: 450 Norwood St Merritt Island FL 32953 Office: Brevard Community Coll Cocoa FL 32922

PARKAS, IVA RICHEY, educator, historian, curator, paralegal; b. Comanche County, Tex., June 28, 1907; d. Andrew J. Richey and Pearl Lucretia (Kennedy) Richey; grad. Wayland Coll., 1927; B.A., Tex. Tech. U., 1935; M.Litt., U. Pitts., 1950; postgrad. UCLA, 1960, Pa. State U., 1961, U. Calif., Berkeley, 1962, Duquesne U., 1963, Carnegie-Mellon U., 1968; m. George Eduardo Parkas, May 5, 1945. Curator, historian Fort Pitt Blockhouse, Pitts., 1946-52, asst. curator-historian, 1964-84; tchr. U.S. history Pitts. sr. high schs., 1953-72; paralegal Allegheny County (Pa.) Law Dept., 1977-82. Del., White House Conf. on Children and Youth, Washington, 1960, 70, World Food Conf., Rome, 1974; U.S. Congl. Sr. Citizens intern, Washington, 1984. Named Disting. Alumnae, U. Pitts., 1978; recipient Valley Forge Classroom Tchr.'s medal, 1960. Henry Clay Frick Ednl. fellow; NDEA grantee; Greater Pitts. Air Force Squadron scholar, Pitts. Press scholar, 1960. Mem. NEA (life), AAUW (pres. Pitts. br. 1974-76), Hist. Soc. Western Pa., Western Pa. Council Social Studies (pres. 1969-71), DAR (regent Pitts. chpt. 1986-89), U. Pitts. Alumnae Assn. (bd. dirs. 1978—, v.p. 1984), Pa. Retired Pub. Sch. Employees Assn. (chairperson Am. revolution bicentennial 1974-76), Western Pa. Hist. Soc., Allegheny County Bicentennial Commn., Greater Pitts. Commn. for Women, Delta Kappa Gamma, Phi Alpha Theta. Editor: So Your Children Can Tell Their Children, 1976; contbr. articles on hist. subjects to newspapers, mags. Home: 5520 Fifth Ave C-5 Pittsburgh PA 15232

PARKE, MADELYN SARA (MINDY PARKE), insurance executive, educator; b. N.Y.C., Oct. 6, 1951; d. Edwin Daniel and Muriel (Cohen) P.; divorced; 1 child, Howard Silverman. BS cum laude, Queens Coll., 1972, MS magna cum laude, 1976. Educator N.Y.C. Bd. Edn., 1977-85; technician CIGNA Fin. Svcs., Tarrytown, N.Y., 1985-86; supr. Presdl. Life Ins., Nyack, N.Y., 1987-88, mgr., 1988—; tchr. adult edn. Pearl River, N.Y., 1987—; craftsperson County Charm, Nyack, 1987—; founder Presdl. Life Ins. Co. Vol. Program. Founder (co. newsletter) The Screaming Eagle. Bd. dirs. Friday Nite Alternative, Pearl River, 1987; founder vol. program Rockland County Infirmary. Regents scholar, N.Y., 1968. Mem. NAFE. Lodge: B'nai Brith (sec. Pomona Friendship N.Y. chpt. 1982).

PARKE, M(ARGARET) JEAN, business owner, editor; b. Akron, Ohio, Aug. 23, 1920; d. Lawrence William and Rosella (Washburn) Beat; m. Harry Morris Parke, July 25, 1942; children: Richard Blake, Catherine Jean. BA magna cum laude, U. Toledo, 1942, MA, 1959. Adminstrv. asst. Dist. Office Price Adminstrn., Toledo, 1943-45; editing cons. Century Press, Inc., Toledo, 1955-72; cons. women's progs. U. Toledo, 1973-75; reports editor Price-Waterhouse & Co., Cleve., 1976-78; fin. officer, ptnr. Parke Supply Co., Avon Lake, Ohio, 1980-86; co-owner, sec. Woodlark Farms, Inc., Georgetown, Ky., 1978—. Bd. trustees, past pres. Avon Lake Pub. Libr., 1981-90, Friends of the U. Toledo Libr., past pres. 1971-84; founding trustee Friends of Toledo-Lucas county Pub. Libr., 1970-73; bd. dirs. LWV, Sylvania, Ohio, Avon Lake; mem. Friends of Avon lake Libr. Jean Park conf. rm. named in her honor Avon Lake Pub. Libr., 1981. Mem. AAUW (past pres., bd. dirs. Toledo br. 1981-90, Ednl. Found. Prog. grantee 1981), Avon on the Lake Garden Club, U. Toledo Alumni Assn. (trustee, officer Blue T award 1981), Chi Omega Alumnae Toledo (officer), Chi Omega Alumnae Ohio (state bd. dirs. 1983-85, Outstanding Chi Omega Alumna 1982). Republican. Episcopalian. Home: 32821 Tanglewood Ct Avon Lake OH 44012

PARKER, ALICE, composer, conductor; b. Boston, Dec. 16, 1925; d. Gordon and Mary (Stuart) P.; widowed; children: David, Timothy, Katharine, Mary, Elizabeth. BA, Smith Coll., Northampton, Mass., 1947; MS, Julliard Sch., N.Y.C., 1949; MusD (hon.), Hamilton U., Clinton, N.Y. Arranger Robert Shaw Chorale, N.Y.C., 1948-66; freelance composer, condr. N.Y.C., 1960—; tchr., workshop leader Westminster Choir Coll., Princeton, N.J., summers 1972—; artistic dir. Melodious Accord, N.Y.C., 1985—. Composer 4 operas, 25 cantatas, 4 song cycles and numerous anthems and suites. Recipient Composer's Serious award ASCAP, 1968—, Spl. award Nat. Endowment Arts, 1975. Mem. Am. Choral Dirs. Assn., Am. Condrs. Guild, Hymn Soc. Am., Sigma Alpha Iota. Office: Melodious Accord Inc 801 West End Ave 9D New York NY 10025*

PARKER, ANNE VEREEN, furniture executive; b. Rockingham, N.C., Mar. 18, 1937; d. F. Lee Sr. and Gladys Elizabeth (Fields) P. Student, Kings Bus. Coll., 1956. Clk. typist Jefferson Standard Life, Greensboro, N.C., 1955-56; office mgr. Thomas P. Heritage Archtl. Engr., Greensboro, 1956-62; v.p., treas. Kindleys Office Furniture, Inc., Greensboro, N.C., 1962—. Vol. Red Cross, Greensboro, 1973-74, Am. Cancer Soc., Greensboro, 1980-90, Guilford County Dem. Party, Greensboro, 1987-90, Greensboro Urban Ministry, 1987-88; corr. sec. Dem. Women Guilford County, 1987-90; 2nd v.p. Dem. Women of Guilford County, 1990-91. Recipient Zoe Parks Barbee Svc. award Dem. Women Guilford County, 1989. Mem. NAFE, Nat. Assn. Profl. Saleswomen, Nat. Mus. Women in the Arts, Guilford County Dem. Women, Christian Women's Assn., Guilford's Women Network. Baptist. Home: 3741 Sagamore Dr Greensboro NC 27410 Office: Kindleys Office Furniture Inc 513 S Elm St Greensboro NC 27406

PARKER, BETTYE JEAN, real estate professional; b. Rossville, Ga., May 31, 1931; d. Leonard Virgle and Azalea (Miller) Burroughs; m. Edwin Carroll Parker, Oct 13, 1947; children: Elaine Parker Phibbs, Eileen Parker Sands, Edwin Paul, Susie Parker Deal, Polly Parker Wagoner. Diploma in bus., Edmondson Bus. Coll., 1947; student, U. Chattanooga, 1947-49, U. Tenn., Chattanooga, 1969-71. Tchr. Hamilton County Sch System, Chattanooga, 1963-68; prin., real estate broker Bettye Parker Realty Inc, Chattanooga, 1970—; pvt. practice real estate devel. and bldg. constrn. Chattanooga, 1951—; mem. legis. com. Chattanooga Bd. Realtors, 1987—, multiple listing service com., 1988, pub. rels. com., 1989. Exec. rep. Hamilton County Health Adv. Commn., 1981--; vice chmn. Scenic Cities Beautiful Commn., (Give a Hoot award) 1985--; chmn. bd. dirs. N.E. YMCA, Chattanooga, 1985-87, treas., 1988, vice chmn. bd. dirs., 1989; mem. signs and billboards task force com. Chattanooga Venture, 1986--; mentor U. Tenn.-Chattanooga Pilot Project for High Sch. Srs., 1987; advisor Youth in Govt. club Cen. High Sch., 1987; vol. chmn. Students Staying Straight-Project 714 Brown Mid. Sch., 1987--; life mem. PTA. Mem. Tenn. Assn. Realtors (profl. standard com. 1980-89), Am. Bus. Women's Assn. (pres. Lake Chickomauga chpt. 1979-80, Woman of Yr. award 1979), Small Bus. Council (steering com. 1986-88, fed., state, local affairs com. 1989), Greater Chattanooga Area C. of C. (bd. dirs. 1980-83, Disting. Citizen of Yr. award 1983), North 58 C. of C. (pres 1981, sec. 1988, dir. 1989), Chamber Outstanding Service award 1987). Methodist. Club: Tenn. Valley Patriots (v.p. 1986-87). Lodge: Civitan (pres. Riverland chpt. 1982—, Honor Key-Dist. Ms. Civitan award Appalachian dist. Riverland chpt. 1980, 83-84, Club Builder award, 1982, Civitan of Yr. award 1982, 87, dir. 1987—, lt. gov. Appalachian dist. 1988, Jr. Civitan Club Builder award 1988, Best Lt. Gov. award 1989). Office: Bettye Parker Realty Inc 4819 Hwy 58 N Chattanooga TN 37416

PARKER, BEVERLY J., fitness and nutrition consultant; b. Greenville, S.C., Aug. 2, 1953; d. Frederick Eugene and Martha Lorene (Starnes) Shupe; m. Robert L. Parker, Nov. 20, 1950. Student, Sullins Coll., Bristol, Va., 1978, HMH Ctr., Kingsport, Tenn., 1987; diploma in fitness and nutrition, Internat. Corrs. Schs., 1989. Instr., women's mgr. Alps Spa, Kingsport, 1975-78, Comsopolitan Spa, Kingsport, 1978-80; fitness cons. Kingsport, 1980-84, 86—; instr., mgr. Rythm 'n Bounce, Kingsport, 1984-85; instr., co-owner Tropic Tans & Fitness, Kingsport, 1985-86; model various mags., pageants, 1975—. Vol. Walk for Life, Kingsport, 1985-87, Walk for Multiple Sclerosis, Kingsport, 1984, 87, 88, Johnson City (Tenn.) Spl. Olympics, 1988—, Wheelchair Olympics, Johnson City, 1988—; mem. Contact Concern, Vol. Kingsport, Big Bros., Big Sisters. Named All Am. Beauty, Good Housekeeping Beauty Book, 1978, Saleswoman of Yr., Mrs. Tenn. State Pageant, 1985; nat. cover winner Sophisticate's Beauty Guide, 198l. Mem. NOW, NAFE, Am. Fitness Assn., Tec Camera Club, Kingsport Recreation Club, Moose. Baptist.

PARKER, CATHY JOAN, talent management company executive; b. Barrington, N.J., Oct. 28, 1937; d. Angelo A. and Philomena (Pomponio) DiDio; m. Norman J. Parker Jr., Feb. 11, 1961 (dec. May 1989); children: Norman III, Scott, John Jay. Pres. Cathy Parker Talent Mgmt., Voorhees, N.J., 1982—. Active Voorhees Dem. Club, Boy Scouts Am. Mem. NAFE, Nat. Assn. for Self-Employed, Nat. Conf. Pers. Mgrs. Roman Catholic. Office: PO Box 716 Voorhees NJ 08043

PARKER, CHERYL JEAN, career counselor, consultant; b. Kansas City, Kans., Feb. 3, 1948; d. Mildred Eileen (Mayer) Ross; m. Jack W. Parker, June 25, 1977; children: Brian Scott, Kimberly Michelle. BS, Kans. State U., 1970; MA, U. Mo., Kansas City, 1975; postgrad., Dept. Def. Info. Sch., 1984. Cert. tchr. Migrant tchr. Piper Unified Schs. 203, Kansas City, Kans., 1970-72; tchr. North Kansas City Pub. Schs., Kansas City, 1970-75; guidance counselor Excelsior (Mo.) Springs Pub. Schs., 1975-77; rsch. asst. foster parent rsch. project Coll. Human Ecology, Manhattan, Kans., 1977-78; test examiner 1st Inf. Div., Fort Riley, Kans., 1980-82; pub. affairs specialist 1st Inf. Div., Fort Riley, 1983-85; pers. clerk 3rd ROTC Div. Hdqrs., Fort Riley, 1982-83; tchr. Living Word Christian Sch., Manhattan, 1985-86; program mgr., career counselor Army Community Svcs., Army War Coll., Carlisle, Pa., 1987—; recording sec. Career Edn. Com., Excelsior Springs, 1975-77; career counselor personal contacts and referrals, Carlisle, 1986—; career counselor relocation/outplacement, U.S. Army, Carlisle, 1987—; job fair coord. Army Community Svcs., Carlisle, 1989—; guest speaker various clubs, confs., Carlisle, Excelsior Springs. Author: (with others, catalog) Foster Parent Resources, 1977-78; contbr. articles to profl. jours. Violinist Christ Community Ch. Orch., Camp Hill, Pa., 1986-89; mem. hospitality com. PTA, Carlisle, 1987-88; mem. Suggestion Awards Rev. Com., Fort Riley, 1983-85. Recipient Hollis award scholarship Kans. State U., 1968, Kansas City Star Newspaper, 1966-70. Mem. Carlisle Area Pers. Assn., Federally Employed Women (nomination chmn. 1989—), Federal Women's Program (program mgr. 1988-89, certificate 1989), Alpha Lambda Delta. Mem. Christian Ch. Home: 10566 Noland Rd Lenexa KS 66215

PARKER, DEBORAH L. ROBERTS, counselor; b. Meridian, Miss., Mar. 15, 1952; d. Bernice (Roberts) Pringle; m. Curtis Edward Parker, Nov. 25, 1972; 1 child, Shana. BS, U. So. Miss., 1978; MEd, Miss. State U., 1980. Lic. profl. counselor; nat. cert. counselor. Asst. PBX op., with client admissions dept. Weems Mental Health Ctr., Meridian, 1972-75, counselor children's svcs., 1981-86; career facilitator Meridian Pub. Schs., 1978-80; dir. gov.s youth grant Lauderdale County Juvenile Ctr., Meridian, 1980-81; adolescent counselor, case mgr. Laurel Wood Pscychiat. and Recovery Ctr., Meridian, 1986-89, adolescent program dir., 1989-. Named one of Outstanding Young Women of Am., 1983. Mem. AAUW, Am. Assn. for Counseling and Devel., Am. Assn. Clin. Mental Health Counselors, Alpha Lambda Delta, Delta Sigma Theta. Roman Catholic. Home: 411-45th Ct Meridian MS 39301 Office: Laurel Wood Psychiat & Recovery Ctr Hwy 39 N Meridian MS 39303

PARKER, DIANNA LYNN, economic and environmental analyst; b. Carthage, Ill., Oct. 18, 1960; d. Harold William and Nina Elizabeth (DePauw) Maynard; m. Blanc Airey Parker Jr., June 10, 1989. Cert., Northeast Mo. State U., 1980; BS, Drury Coll., Springfield, Mo., 1986; MBA, Southwest Mo. State U., 1989. Asst. mgr. Millstone Lodge and Restaurant, Gravois Mills, Mo., 1980-81; with accounts receivable dept. Drury Coll., 1981-84; adminstrv. asst. Hines Lumber Co., Springfield, 1984; econ. and environ. analyst Ledbetter, Toth and Assocs., Inc., Springfield, 1985—. Active Child Advocacy Coun., Springfield, 1987—; vol. Spl. Olympics, Springfield, 1980—. Named one of Outstanding Young Women Am., 1986; Kessler scholar Jaycees, 1978. Mem. NAFE, Alpha Sigma Lambda. Republican. Home: 104 Scott Wayne Dr Nixa MO 65714 Office: Ledbetter Toth and Assocs 2200 E Sunshine Ste 206 Springfield MO 65804

PARKER, EDNA G., judge; b. Johnston County, N.C., 1930; 1 child, Douglas Benjamin. Student, N.J. Coll. for Women (now Douglass Coll.); B.A. with honors, U. Ariz., 1953; postgrad., U. Ariz. Law Sch.; LL.B., George Washington U., 1957. Law clk. U.S. Ct. Claims, 1957-59; atty.-advisor Office of Gen. Counsel, Dept. Navy, 1959-60; trial atty. civil and tax div. Dept. Justice, 1960-69; adminstrv. judge Contract Appeals Bd., Dept. Transp., 1969-77; spl. trial judge U.S. Tax Ct., 1977-80, judge, 1980—. Mem. ABA, Fed. Bar Assn., D.C. Bar, D.C. Bar Assn., Women's Bar Assn., Nat. Assn. Women Lawyers of D.C., Nat. Assn. Women Judges. Office: US Tax Ct 400 2d St NW Washington DC 20217*

PARKER, ELENORE MYRNA, public relations executive; b. Boston, May 22, 1939; d. Max James Rosenberg and Sally Harriet Swartz; m. Robert Neal Parker, Aug. 7, 1960 (div. 1982); 1 child, Matthew Todd. BS in Edn., Boston State Coll., 1960, MS in Edn., 1966. Tchr. Long Beach Unified Sch. Dist., Calif., 1960-62, L.A. Sch. System, 1962-63, Cambridge (Mass.) Sch. Sys., 1963-67; mng. producer/ptnr. H & E Prodns., Dedham, Mass., 1964-77; account exec. Am. Prog. Bur., Chestnut Hill, Mass., 1977-81; pres. Good News! Public Relations, Dedham, 1982—; theatre reviewer Transcript Newspapers, Dedham, 1980—. Co-author: Jack and the Beanstalk, 1965, Beauty and the Beast, 1967, (both plays); contbr. articles to profl. jours. Mem. NOW, New Eng. Women Bus. Owners (bd. dirs. 1982-85), Smaller Bus. Assn. New Eng. (chmn. com. 1987), Publicity Club of New Eng., Charles River Wheelmen. Democrat. Office: Good News Pub Rels 850R Providence Hwy Dedham MA 02026

PARKER, GWEN COLE, chapter I supervisor; b. Kingstree, S.C., Nov. 4, 1949; d. David James Cole and JoAnn (Phillips) Griggs; m. Vernon W. Parker, Mar. 28, 1968 (dec. 1971); children: Stacey, Mart. BS, Francis Marion, Florence, 1978; EdS, U. S.C., Columbia, 1980, Student, 1987. Tchr., Prin., Supr., Superintendent. Tchr. Florence Sch. Dist. 3, Lake City, S.C., 1978-87; supr. Williamsburg County Schs., Kingstree, S.C., 1987--. Republican. Baptist. Address: Rte 2 Box 120-B Scranton SC 29591 Office: Cades-Hebron Sch. Rte 1 Box 58 Cades SC 29518

PARKER, GWENDOLYN D., computer programmer; d. Arthur J. and Juanita (Moore) Oates. BS, Western Conn. State U., 1982. Programmer analyst Am. Cyanamid Corp., Danbury, Conn.; sr. programmer analyst BAR Dun and Bradstreet, Norwalk, Conn.; sr. tech. support programmer date quality Dun and Bradstreet, Allentown, Pa. Mem. NAFE, SAS User Group. Home: 127 Valley Park S Bethlehem PA 18018

PARKER, GWENDOLYN HALL, teacher; b. Portsmouth, Va., Sept. 20, 1946; d. Joseph L. and Grace (Lewis) Hall; m. James M. Parker, Aug. 7, 1972; 1 child, Tasha Lynette. BS, Hampton (Va.) Inst., 1968, MA, 1972. Cert. English tchr., Va., N.C. Tchr. English Cen. High Sch., Gatesville, N.C., 1968-69, Ahoskie (N.C.) High Sch., 1969-70, C. Alton Lindsay Jr. High Sch., Hampton, 1970-85, Hampton High Sch., 1985—; advisor Hampton High Sch., 1987—. Sec. Victoria Pl. Civic Orgn., Hampton, 1984—; mem. Phyllis Wheatley br. Peninsula YWCA; mem. women's aux. east end Second Baptist Ch., Newport News, Va. Mem. Nat. Fed. Tchrs., Hampton Fed. Tchrs., Alpha Kappa Alpha (Newport News) (sec. 1980-84, treas. 1989—). Democrat. Baptist. Home: 504 Winona Dr Hampton VA 23661

PARKER, JEAN ELIZABETH, quality control engineer; b. St. Petersburg, Fla., Sept. 29, 1957; d. John Edward and Elizabeth Rose (Henneman) P.; m. Charles Wesley Paup, Apr. 2, 1977 (div. 1984); m. Keith Howard Knapp, June 27, 1986. AA cum laude, St. Petersburg Coll., 1977; BS cum laude, U. Tex., Dallas, 1980. Process engr., analysis and engring. supr. United Technologies Mostek, Carrollton, Tex., 1980-85; quality control engr., dept. mgr. MCE Semiconductor, West Palm Beach, Fla., 1985-89; quality assurance dept. mgr. mil. and med. optics/electronics Lenzar Optics, Riviera Beach, Fla., 1989—; owner, mgr. Mich. Christmas Trees, Jupiter, Fla., 1987—; cons. student tng., IEEE, West Palm Beach, 1988. Patentee, wafer inspection devices. Mem. Profl. Assn. Diving Instrs. Home: 121 Seabreeze Circle Jupiter FL 33477 Office: Lenzar Optics Corp 1006 W 15th St Riviera Beach FL 33404

PARKER, JOSEPHINE ANN, health science association administrator; b. Providence, July 18, 1952; d. Philip D'Ambra and Margaret Caulder; m. Richard Fulton Parker Jr., Aug. 6, 1977 (div. Nov. 1988); children: Caitlyn, Nathaniel, Brittany. Diploma in Nursing, St. Joseph's Hosp., Providence, 1971-73; BS in Nursing cum laude, Boston Coll., 1978; MS in Nursing, Boston U., 1980. Staff nurse surg. ICU St. Elizabeth's Hosp., Birghton, Mass., 1976-77; charge nurse Nashua (N.H.) Meml. Hosp., 1977-78; sr. nursing instr. Cath. Med. Ctr., Manchester, N.H., 1978-81; critical care instr. St. Joseph's Hosp., Nashua, 1981-86; med. sales rep. Searle Pharms. Inc., Chgo., 1986; dir. edn. Exeter (N.H.) Hosp., 1986-88; assoc. prof. dept. of nursing Rivier Coll., Nashua, 1988—; nurse mgr. Cath. Med. Ctr., Manchester, 1988—, coord. rsch. com., 1989—; adj. prof. dept. nursing U. N.H., Durham, 1987—; cons. N.H. Tech. Inst., Stratham, 1987—; ICU/CCU/CTU nurse mgr. rep. CMC ICU/CCU com., Manchester, 1988—. Developer cardiac arrest flow chart, 1982, pediatric resuscitation cards, 1982. Mem. Parent Tchr. Group, Bedford, 1989, Am. Heart Assn. Mem. Am. Assn. Critical Care Nursing (nat. and So. N.H. chpt., mem. at large program commn. 1988—), Am. Nurse Assn. Democrat. Roman Catholic. Home: 2 Westview Rd Bedford NH 03102

PARKER, JUDITH PATRICIA, counselor; b. Buffalo, Wyo., May 26, 1947; d. Stuart Milton and Margaret Imogen (Mastin) Hall; m. John Thomas Parker, Sept. 3, 1966 (div. July 1985); children: Christopher John, Patrick Mastin Parker; m. Robert Hughes Evans, Aug. 14, 1988. BA in Edn., Ea. Wash. U., 1968; MEd in Counseling, Whitworth Coll., 1984. Tchr. St. Mary's Sch., Spokane, Wash., 1968-70; parent educator Spokane Community Coll. Dist. 17, 1978-84; inside sales rep. Kaiser Aluminum, Spokane, 1984-87; spl. educator, program mgr. Spokane Pub. Schs. Dist. 81, 1987-89; vocat. counselor, regional mgr. Rehab. and Edn. Svc., Spokane, 1987—; chair steering com. Youth 2,000, Spokane, 1988-89; vocat. expert Social Security Office of Hearings and Appeals, Spokane, 1989—. Gov.'s commr. Wash. State Child Support Schedule Commn., Spokane, 1988-90; bd. dirs. SpokAnimal CARE, Spokane, 1988—. Mem. NOW, Spokane Club (chair house com. 1989—), Mu Phi Epsilon. Democrat. Office: Rehab and Evaluation Svcs W 222 Mission Ste 250 Spokane WA 99201

PARKER, JULIE ANN, mathematics educator; b. Dillon, Mont., Apr. 18, 1958; d. Clayborn James and Dorothy Ann (Woltermann) Anders; m. Keith Krom Parker, Sept. 7, 1985; children: Lynn Anders, Jenny Ann Burgstrom, Jacquelyn Elizabeth Burgstrom. AS, Western Mont. Coll., 1984, BS in Secondary Edn., 1984, cert. in elem. edn. with honors, 1986. Clk., typist USDA Forest Svc., Dillon, 1977-78; forestry aide USDA Forest Svc., Ennis, Mont., 1978; lab. asst. chem. dept. Western Mont. Coll., Dillon, 1984-86; substitute tchr. Dillon Pub. Sch. System, 1986; adj. math. faculty Western Mont. Coll., Dillon, 1985-86, temp. math. faculty, 1987—. Contbr. articles to profl. jours. Leader Girls Scouts Am. Recipient Howard Smith award Alpha Delta Kappa. Mem AAUW (v.p. 1989-90, pres. 1990-91, scholar), Am. Fedn. Tchrs., Mont. Acad. Scis., Mont. Coun. Tchrs. Math., Nature Conservancy, Women Western Mont. Coll. Democrat. Home: 933 S Washington Dillon MT 59725

PARKER, KATHLEEN, broadcast owner; b. Ortonville, Minn., May 23, 1948; d. L. R. and Barbara (Bruskin) Severin; m. John B. Parker, May 19, 1973. BA, Barnard Coll., 1970; MS, Columbia U., 1973; postgrad. Harvard U., 1988-90. Writer, AP, N.Y.C., 1973-74; journalist CBS Network News, Los Angeles, 1974; reporter, anchor woman Sta. KFMB-TV, San Diego, 1975-79; pres. Pacific Communications, South Lake Tahoe, Calif., 1979-82 ; owner, operator Sta. KOWL-AM, Inc., South Lake Tahoe, 1979-83, Island Communications Sta. KIKI-AM and KAMI-FM, Honolulu, 1980-89, Sta. KIKI Licensing Corp., Tokyo, 1981-89, Parker Communications Sta. KTCZ-FM and KTCJ-AM, Mpsl., 1984—, Desert Communications Sta. KXTZ-FM, Las Vegas, Nev., 1984—; Mountain Communications Sta. KLZE-FM, Mountain View, Calif., 1986-87; Delta Communications Sta. KHYL-FM and KAHI-AM, Sacramento, 1986—. Columbia U. fellow. Mem. Twin City Broadcasting Assn. (sec. 1984-85), Nat. Assn. Broadcastors, Minn. Zool. past bd. dirs.), Young Pres. Orgn. Avocations: art collecting, writing, walking. Office: The Parker Cos 2826 IDS Ctr Minneapolis MN 55402

PARKER, LINDA MARIAN BATES, university administrator; b. Cin., Feb. 23, 1944; d. Ernest Louis and Mary Elizabeth Bates; m. Breland Kennedy Parker, Nov. 24, 1946; children: Robbin, Brandon. BS, U. Dayton, 1965; MA, U. Cin., 1970. Market researcher Proctor & Gamble Co., Cin., 1965-67; tng. coord. Shillito's Dept. Store, Cin., 1968-70; head resident counselor U. Cin., 1971-75, assoc. dir. career planning and placement, 1975-76, assoc. vice provost student affairs, 1981-87, dir. career devel., 1987—. Pres., Black Career Women, Inc., Cin., 1977—; bd. dirs. Cin. Local Devel. Co., 1983-90; trustee Black Career Women's Resource Ctr., Inc., Cin., 1982—, WCET Pub. TV, Cin., 1974-75; pres. Jr. Alliance for Social and Civic Action, Cin., 1974; bd. dirs. Charter Com., 1979; mem. bicentennial tribute 100 Living Black Cincinnatians, 1988. Named Woman of Yr., Cin. Enquirer, 1983, One of 100 Top Black Bus. and Profl. Women in Am. Dollars and Sense mag., 1985; recipient Career Woman of Achievement award, YWCA, 1982, Unsung Heroine award Nat. Women's Conf. NAACP, 1982; Advocate award Women in Communications, 1982. Mem. Midwest Coll. Placement Assn. (chmn. affirmative action com., mem. assembly 1989). Roman Catholic.

PARKER, MARGARET MAIER, physician; b. Portland, Maine, Dec. 8, 1950; d. Paul and Miriam Deibler (Slack) M.; m. Robert Ingalls Parker, Nov. 2, 1974; children: Robert Ingalls Jr., Christopher Maier, Timothy Sumner, Matthew Paul. BS, Brown U., 1973, MD, 1977; cert. in critical care, 1987. Diplomate Am. Bd. Internal Medicine. Intern, resident Roger Williams Gen. Hosp., Providence, 1977-80; fellow critical care medicine NIH, Bethesda, Md., 1980-82, sr. staff physician, 1982—; assoc. clin. prof. medicine George Washington U., Washington, 1983—. Contbr. articles to profl. jours. Deacon Rockville Presbyn. Ch., 1985-88, elder, 1990—. Fellow ACP; mme. Am. Med. Women's Assn., Am. Fedn. Clin. Rsch., Soc. Critical Care Medicine. Republican. Presbyterian. Office: NIH Critical Care Medicine Dept Bldg 10 Rm 10D48 Bethesda MD 20892

PARKER, MARION DEAN HUGHES, home care service executive; b. Greenwich, Conn., July 21, 1911; d. Walter A. and Marion K. (Dean) Hughes; B.A., UCLA, 1932; m. Conkey P. Whitehead, Nov. 14, 1929 (div. Aug. 1933); m. Andrew Granville Pierce III, Oct. 21, 1933; m. Willard Parker, Oct. 5, 1939 (div. 1951); 1 child, Walter van Eps. Actress appearing in Broadway prodns. New Faces, Three Waltzes, I Must Love Someone, on tour in The Women, The Man Who Came to Dinner, Lady in the Dark; various night club engagements; appeared in motion picture All About Eve; TV appearances; owner, mgr. Marion Parker's Guys & Dolls, Scottsdale, Ariz., 1951-59; mng. dir., purchasing agt. shipboard gift and accessory shops Am. Export Lines, 1960-64; dir. spl. events ITT, N.Y.C., 1965-66; exec. dir. Assn. Operating Room Nurses, N.Y.C., 1965-66; asst. to v.p. in charge devel. Bennett Coll., Millbrook, N.Y., 1966-68; staff Park East Real Estate, 1968-70; pres. Home Care-Ring Svc., N.Y.C., 1970—; actress for TV and Comml. Mem. Women's Nat. Republican Club, N.Y.C., Manhattan East Rep. Club, N.Y.C.; sustaining mem. Rep. Nat. Com., 1981—. Mem. Screen Actors Guild, Actors Equity. Address: 301 E 78th St New York NY 10021

PARKER, MARJI WILBUR, contract specialist; b. Seattle, Aug. 15, 1931; d. Scott G. and Grace Pauline (Raney) Wilbur; m. Ivan Lincoln Parker, Dec. 26, 1960 (dec. Dec. 1969); children: Neil Ivan, Scott Douglas. BA, Whitman Coll., 1953; MA, Wash. State U., 1955. Tchr. Columbia Basin Community Coll., Pasco, Wash., 1955-64, dept. chmn., 1957-62; contract specialist U.S. Dept. Energy, Richland, Wash., 1973—. Mem. coun. Children's HOme Soc. Washington, Tri-Cities, 1973-75; trustee Columbia Basin Community Coll., 1975-80, pres. bd. trustees, 1979-80. Mem. Nat. Contract Mgmt. Assn., AAUW (br. pres. 1987—), Alpha Phi (chmn. 1972-74). Home: 605 Road 37 Pasco WA 99301 Office: US Dept Energy Richland Ops PO Box 550 Richland WA 99352

PARKER, MARTHA ANN, public relations specialist; b. Gainsville, Fla., Jan. 25, 1948; d. Morris Evans and Marian A. (Hickey) Paddick. BA in Communications, U. Ill., 1970; MS in History, U. R.I., 1988. Advt. asst., then advt. mgr. R.I. Hosp. Trust Nat. Bank, Providence, 1971-74; legis. asst. Congresswoman Pat Schroeder (D. Colo.), Washington, 1974-76; spl. asst. to dean Sch. Architecture U. New Haven, 1977-83; researcher Union Pacific Corp., Omaha, 1983-86; dir. pub. rels. Gorman & Assocs., Providence, 1986-88; account supr. pub. rels. FitzGerald & Co., Cranston, R.I., 1988-89, v.p. pub. rels., 1989—. Author book revs. for Master Plots, Groher Pub., 1979, 80, 81, 82. Mem. Pub. Rels. Soc. Am., Am. Hist. Soc., Orgn. Am. Historians. Office: FitzGerald & Co 1 Worthington Rd Cranston RI 02920

PARKER, PAMELA ANN, pharmaceutical company official, accountant; b. Hialeah, Fla., Feb. 7, 1962; d. Richard Hugh and Saundra (Dubbin) P. BS in Econs., U. Calif., Santa Barbara, 1983. CPA, N.Y. Staff acct. Jones, Parent, Wheeler & Wheeler, Santa Barbara, 1983-86; staff auditor I, Bristol-Myers Co., N.Y.C., 1986-87, staff auditor II, 1987-88, sr. auditor, 1988-89, fin. assoc., 1989—. Office: Bristol-Myers Co 345 Park Ave New York NY 10154

PARKER, PATRICIA HOLMES, communications educator; b. Astabula, Ohio, Dec. 31, 1936; d. Don Vern and Katherine (Timlin) P. BS in Edn., U. Dayton, 1965; MA, U. No. Colo., 1974, Loyola U., New Orleans, 1980; postgrad., Ohio U., 1984-87. Tchr. parochial schs., Ohio, Mo., 1957-65, Falls Church, Va., 1965-68, Denver, 1968-71; exec. coord. Archdiocesan Sisters' Coun., Denver, 1971-74; writer, producer Sta. WWL-TV, New Orleans, 1975-76; tchr. E.D. White High Sch., Thibodaux, La., 1981-82; instr. Loyola U., New Orleans, 1976-81; asst. prof. Cen. Mo. State U., Warrensburg, 1982-84; grad. asst. Ohio U., Athens, 1984-87; instr. dept. communication SUNY, Geneseo, 1987—; talk show host Sta. KMOS-TV, Warrensburg, 1982-83; mem. faculty Inst. for Religious Communication, New Orleans, 1976-79, Elderhostel, Athens, 1987. Writer, producer TV pub. svc. announcements and documentaries. Pres. Denver Sisters' Coun., 1969-70. Mem. Speech Communication Assn., Popular Culture Assn., Women in Communication, Religious Speech Communication Assn., N.Y. State Speech Communication Assn. Democrat. Roman Catholic. Office: SUNY Blake B 115 Geneseo NY 14454

PARKER, RUBY BRASTOW, telecommunications executive; b. Boston, June 11, 1947; d. Richard Brastow and Ruby (Stoddard) P. B.A., U. Mass., 1969; M.S., Central Conn. Coll., 1973. Tchr. Hartford Pub. Sch., Conn., 1969-74; counselor Haverhill Pub. Sch., Mass., 1974-81; with computer prodn. support dept. Honeywell, Waltham, Mass., 1981-83, telecommunications project analyst, 1983-86, mgr. data network adminstrn. and planning, 1986-89; sr. edn. specialist Bolt, Beranck & Newman Communications Corp., Cambridge, 1989—. Fellow NOW. Home: 10 Washington Ave Billerica MA 01821 Office: Bolt Berank & Newman Communications Corp 150 Cambridge Park Dr Cambridge MA 02140

PARKER, SARA ANN, librarian; b. Cassville, Mo., Feb. 19, 1939; d. Howard Franklin and Vera Irene (Thomas) P. B.A., Okla. State U., 1961; M.L.S., Emporia State U., Kans., 1968. Adult svcs. librarian Springfield Pub. Libr., Mo., 1972-75, bookmobile dir., 1975-76; coord. S.W. Mo. Libr. Network, Springfield, 1976-78; libr. developer Colo. State Libr., Denver, 1978-82; state librarian Mont. State Libr., Helena, 1982-88, State Libr. Pa., Harrisburg, 1988—; cons. and lectr. in field. Author, editor, compiler in field; contbr. articles to profl. jours. Sec., Western Council State Libraries, Reno, 1984-88, mem. Mont. State Adv. Council, 1983-88, Mont. Telecommunications Council, 1985-88, WLN Network Council, 1984-887, Kellogg ICLIS Project Mgmt. Bd., 1986-88. Inst. Ednl. Leadership Ednl. fellow, 1982; recipient Nature Conservancy Pres.'s award, 1989, PAECT Friends award, 1989. Mem. ALA, Chief Officers State Library Agys., Mont. Library Assn. (bd. dirs. 1982-88), Mountain Plains Library Assn. (sect. chmn. 1980, pres. 1987-88). Home: 931 N Front St #303 Harrisburg PA 17102 Office: State Libr Pa Box 1601 Harrisburg PA 17105

PARKER, SUSAN HUGGARD, public relations executive; b. N.Y.C., July 29, 1939; d. Bill C.W. and Margaret (Effinger) Huggard; m. Edward Parker, 1979 (div.); children: Julie Parker Marini, Cindy Parker Yates, Debbie; m. Charles Jeremy Sykes, Feb. 7, 1989. BA in English, U. Mich., 1961; MA in Media, Fairfield U., 1980. Lic. tchr. English. High sch. drama dir. Stamford (Conn.) Cath. High Sch., 1971-72; contbg. editor Stratford (Conn.) News, 1976-77; high sch. drama dir. Joel Barlow High Sch., Redding, Conn., 1978-80; tech. coord. Nat. CSS, Wilton, Conn., 1981-82; pub. rels. mgr. Intec Corp., Trumbull, Conn., 1982-83, Creative Output, Inc., Milford, Conn., 1983-84, Decision Resources, Inc., Westport, Conn., 1985-86; v.p. Inter Active Software, N.Y.C., 1988-90; pres. Market Makers Pub. Rels., Glen Cove, N.Y., 1987—. Mem. Pub. Rels. Soc. Am., Nat. Assn. Women Bus. Owners (L.I. chpt., chmn. membership 1989-90, v.p. 1990-91), Gamma Phi Beta. Unitarian. Office: Market Makers Pub Rels 40 Glen St Ste 1 Glen Cove NY 11542

PARKER, TREELA M(AY), army non-commissioned officer; b. Wise County, Va., Aug. 21, 1954; d. James Hobert and Bonnie F. (Begley) P. A.A., Cecil Community Coll., 1974; BS in Social Psychology with distinction, Park Coll., Parksville, Mo., 1983; MA in behavioral scis. Catholic U. Am., 1987. Enlisted as pvt. 1st class U.S. Army, 1975, advanced through grades to sgt. 1st class, 1984; legal clk. Hdqrs. 1st Maintenance Bn., Ludwigsburg, W. Ger., 1976-78; ops. specialist 235th Signal Detachment, Fort Monmouth, N.J., 1978-79; asst. noncommissioned officer-in-charge 209th Mil. Intelligence Bn., Yong San Seoul, Korea, 1979-80, Army community services Hdqrs. Installation Support Activity, Fort Monmouth, 1980-81; adminstrv. asst. to dir. of personal info. systems directorate Mil. Personnel Ctr., Alexandria, Va., 1981-83; chief top secret repository NATO Subregistry Army Materiel Command, Alexandria, 1983-87, also asst. instr. for phys. fitness test, 1984-86; recruiter U.S. Army, Carlisle, Pa., 1987—; mem. promotion selection bds., 1984-86, Soldier of Yr./Quarter Bds., 1984-86. Author NATO Subregistry Newsletter, 1984-86. Decorated Legion of Merit. Mem. Women's Army Corps Vet. Assn., Phi Theta Kappa. Avocations: horseback riding; reading; writing prose and poetry; dancing; theatre. Office: US Army Recruiting Office Suite 47 MJ Mall Carlisle PA 17013

PARKER, VIRGINIA ANNE, ranch administrator; b. Brockton, Mass., Apr. 24, 1918; d. John and Jennie (Krusas) Salus; student Bryant Stratton Coll., Boston, 1938, Columbia U., 1941; m. John Glendon Parker, Feb. 1942 (div. 1952); one dau., Deborah Anne. Sales supr. Reuben H. Donnelley Corp., N.Y.C., 1944-46; traveling sales rep. Elizabeth Arden Inc., N.Y.C., 1946-47; advt. salesperson Park East Pub. Co., N.Y.C., 1947-48; point of sale display work Parker Kleinhans Assos. and V.A. Parker Co., N.Y.C., 1950-55; merchandising coordinator WGBS Radio Sta., Miami, 1957-59; lighting cons. Verd-A-Ray Corp., Miami, 1960-63; string writer, advt. salesperson Palm Beach Post Times, Fla., 1963-65; advt. salesperson Avon Park Sun, Fla., and Sebring News, Fla., 1965-67; sales mgr. radio sta. WJCM, Sebring, Fla., 1967-69; office and advt. salesperson radio sta. WIPC, Lake Wales, Fla., 1967-69; office mgr., trustee asst., exec. sec. Griffith Ranch Inc., Okeechobee, Fla., 1969-80, semi-ret., 1980, now vol. worker with retarded and handicapped, also with ret. vol. sr. programs Nu-Hope. Mem. Bus. and Profl. Women Miami (2d v.p., rec. sec. 1958-60, state award for nat. security 1960), Parents Without Ptnrs. Fla. (news editor 1962-63). Club: Advt. Miami. Address: 415 Mat-Lo Ave PO Box 1112 Sebring FL 33871

PARKER, VIRGINIA LEE, municipal government administrator; b. Chgo., June 26, 1935; d. Charles Hines and Thelma (Scott) Thomas; m. Henri D. Parker, May 17, 1959 (div. 1967); children: Deborah A. Parker Anderson, Henri D. Jr. BS in Edn., Chgo. State U., 1973; postgrad., U. Chgo., 1973-74; MA in Bus Adminstrn., Gov.'s State U., University Park, Ill., 1978. Chief fiscal officer Ill. Gov.'s Office Human Resources, Chgo., 1973-75; chief acct. Ill. Dept. Children and Family Svcs., Chgo., 1975-80; bus. adminstr. Ill. Dept. Corrections, Joliet, 1980-83; dep. commr. Chgo. Dept. Health, 1983—. Bd. dirs. Chase House day care ctrs., Chgo., 5000 Cornell Condominium Assn., Chgo.; tutor Am. Adult Literacy Program, Chgo. Mem. Am. Soc. Pub. Adminstrs. (nat. coun. 1989—), Am. Pub. Health Assn., Ill. Pub. Health Assn., Chgo. State Alumni Assn., Nat. Assn. Mgmt. Accts., Gov. State Alumni Assn., Kappa Delta Phi. Office: Chgo Dept Health Rm 255 50 W Washington St Chicago IL 60602

PARKER-GRANT, BESS M., recruiter; b. Charlotte, N.C., Mar. 12, 1947; d. Gus and Eldora (Young) Parker; m. Reuben Ellis Brooks, Jan. 31, 1971 (div. Jan. 1987); children: Sean O'Neal, Reuben Ellis Jr.; m. Vincent P. Grant, Sept. 28, 1989. Student, Paul Lawrence Dunbar Bus. Sch., Balt., 1965. Clk.-typist Johns Hopkins Hosp., Balt., 1965-70, Levenson & Klein, Balt., 1970-71; sec. State of Md. Com. on Human Relations, Balt., 1971-84; recruiter USNR, Balt., 1984-88, recruiter-in-charge, 1988—. Mem. choir St. Francis Xavier Ch., Balt., 1979; reading tutor Brehms Ch. Balt., 1985, sch. adv. PTA Northeast Middle Sch. Balt., 1985. With U.S.N., 1984—. Mem. NAFE, Fed. Res. Assn., Fleet Res. Assn. Democrat. Roman Catholic. Office: Ft McHenry Baltimore MD 21230

PARKEY, PAULINE NELSON, librarian; b. Ocala, Fla., Mar. 28, 1932; d. W.L. and Gelene (Boyd) Nelson; m. Lawrence Edward Parkey, June 6, 1953; children: Linda Gail Parkey Dilworth, Joy Patrice Parkey Robinson, Vincente L. BS, Tenn. A&I U., 1954; MEd, Fla. A&M U., 1969, postgrad., 1980-89. Group social worker YWCA, Nashville, 1953-54; social worker outpatient clinic Fla. A&M Hosp., Tallahassee, 1956-57; sec. Fla. A&M U., 1957-69, libr. tech. asst. II, 1969-84, libr., 1984—, sec. Pharmacy Br. Libr., 1982-83. Editor: Summer Vacation Bible School, 1980, Army Family Support Group, newsletter, 1989. Vol. Nashville Dem. Com., 1951-53; street solicitor March of Dimes, Tallahassee, 1982. Recipient plaque Learning Tree Nursery, 1977, Summer Youth Enrichment, 1985, svc. pin Fla. A&M U., 1989, cert. United Black Network, 1983. Mem. ALA, Fla. Libr. Assn., Southeastern Libr. Assn., Med. Pharm. Assn., Calanthes, Zeta Phi Beta (undergrad. advisor 1958-76, plaque 1970). Home: 616 Howard Ave Tallahassee FL 32310 Office: Architecture Branch Libr Fla A&M U Tallahassee FL 32307

PARKHILL, MIRIAM MAY, librarian; b. Ada, Ohio, July 8, 1913; d. Thomas Jefferson Jr. and Cora Anita (Kemp) Smull; m. Edwin Hamilton Parkhill (div. July 1966); children: Diane Paget Parkhill (Mrs. Harlan K. Snouffer), Thomas Hamilton. AB, Ohio No. U., 1934; MA, Ohio State U., 1935; MA in Libr. Sci., U. Mich., 1963; student, Detroit Bus. Inst., 1937. Staff mem. Nat. Youth Adminstrn., Ada, 1937-38; asst. supr. Nat. Youth Adminstrn., Lima, Ohio, 1939-40; libr. staff mem. Ohio No. U., Ada, 1959-62, asst. libr., instr., 1963-68, catalog dept. head, asst. prof., 1969-72, catalog dept. head, assoc. prof., 1973-78, assoc. prof. emerita, 1980—. Vol. catalogue Ada Pub. Libr., 1980—. Mem. AAUW, DAR, Ohio Libr. Assn., Acad. Libr. Assn. of Ohio, Colonial Dames XVII Century, Hardin County Archaeol. and Hist. Soc., Alpha Phi Gamma, Zeta Tau Alpha. Republican. Presbyterian. Home: 301 S Main St Ada OH 45810

PARKIN, EVELYN HOPE, retired medical social worker; b. Owatonna, Minn., Aug. 2, 1910; d. Wilbur L. and Verta (Cowles) Parkin. BA, Carleton Coll., 1931; postgrad., U. Minn. Sch. Social Work, 1939-41. Desk attendant Mayo Clinic, Rochester, Minn., 1931-39; pediatric social worker U. Minn. Hosp., Mpls., 1941-45; supr. social svc. dept. Mayo Clinic, Rochester, Minn., 1945-53, dir. social svc. dept., 1952-75, staff mem., 1973-75, emeritus staff 1953-75, sec. Mayo Clinic Credit Union, 1958-65. Treas., Young mem., 1975—; sec. Olmsted County Rep. Com., 1953-55; bd. Rep.League, Rochester, 1952; sec. Olmsted County Rep. Com., 1953-55; bd. dirs. YWCA, Rochester, 1953-54, Minn. Heart Assn., 1959-64, Am. Heart Assn., N.Y.C., 1958-62; sec. Minn. Welfare Conf., 1954—. Honored for social work with open heart surgery patients, Fed. Republic Germany, 1975. Mem. Nat. Assn. Social Workers. Presbyterian. Home: 502 15th Ave SW Rochester MN 55902

PARKIN, SHARON KAYE, bookkeeper; b. Portland, Oreg., Nov. 21, 1940; d. Charles Edward and Beulah Elizabeth (Foraker) King; m. Russell Jerome Gartrell, Aug. 5, 1960 (div. Dec. 1971); children—Mark Russell, William Edward; m. Jack Edgar Parkin, Feb. 21, 1975. Student, Portland State U., 1959-60. Timekeeper, Sears, Roebuck & Co., Redmond, Wash., 1971-77; bookkeeper, acct. Bristol Bay Area Health Corp., Dillingham, Alaska, bookkeeper Whatcom Mental Health Corp., Bellingham, Wash., 1977-78, 82; bookkeeper Whatcom Counseling, 1978-80, Charlie's Marine, Juneau, Alaska, 1980-81, L & M Supplies, Dillingham, 1983—; owner, pres. Parkin Bookkeeping, 1984—; notary public State of Alaska, 1983—. Democrat. Mem. Christian Ch. Avocations: boating, fishing, hunting, traceling, crochet. Home: 10214 Goodnews Circle Anchorage AK 99515 Office: L & M Supplies PO Box 550 Dillingham AK 99576

PARKINSON, ANTOINETTE (TONI PARKINSON), public relations executive; b. Camden, N.J., Oct. 1, 1943; d. Anthony Vincent and Enes Marie (Guidarini) Parassio; divorced; children: Kim, Kris, Kraig. Grad., Peirce Sch. Bus. Adminstrn., 1963; BS in Pub. Relations, Pacific Western U., 1987. Adminstrv. asst., copywriter Neighborhood Publs., Collingswood, N.J., 1982-85; instr. Canterbury Press, Phila., 1983-85, v.p. nat. sales, 1984-85, pres., 1985; community liaison coordinator O'Brien Kreitzberg, Merchantville, N.J., 1985-86; pub. info. officer Camden County Solid Wate Mgmt., Camden, 1985-86; dir. mktg. Consolidated Fin. Mgmt., Clementon, N.J., 1986—; pub. rels. cons. IACREDT, Camden, 1987, Atlantic Beach Real Estate, Stone Harbor, N.J., 1986—, Ea. Resource Mgmt., Inc., Haddonfield, N.J., 1987; owner, pres. Parkinson Pub. Rels.; pub. info. officer Pollution Control Financing Authority of Camden County. Project coordinator (video) Recycling-The Winners Circle, 1987; columnist newspaper Camden County Record, 1986—;. Candidate Haddon Twp. Commrs., 1983, 87; press coord. Hart for Pres. campaign, Camden County, 1983; bd. dirs. Robin's Nest, Woodbury, N.J., 1986—, Garden State Rotary; chair Friends of Haddonfield Symphony, 1983-87. Mem. Pub. Relations Soc. Am., Pub. Relations Profls. of South Jersey, Nat. Assn. Female Execs., Cherry Hill C. of C., South Jersey C. of C., Am. Heart Assn. Home: 653 W Crystal Lake Ave Haddonfield NJ 08033 Office: Pollution Control Authority 608 Morgan Blvd Camden NJ 08104

PARKINSON, CLAIRE LUCILLE, climatologist; b. Bay Shore, N.Y., Mar. 21, 1948; d. C. V. and Virginia (Hafner) P. BA, Wellesley Coll., 1970; MA, Ohio State U., 1974, PhD, 1977. Rsch. asst. Inst. Polar Studies, Columbus, 1972-74; teaching asst. Ohio State U., Columbus, 1973-76; rsch. asst. Nat. Ctr. Atmospheric Rsch., Boulder, Colo., 1976-78; rsch. scientist Goddard Space Flight Ctr./NASA, Greenbelt, Md., 1978—; sci. colloquium com. mem. Goddard Space Flight Ctr., 1986—. Author: Breakthroughs, 1985; coauthor: Three-Dimensional Climate Modeling, 1986; lead author: Arctic Sea Ice, 1987 (Peer award 1988); assoc. editor Internat. Glaciological Soc., Cambridge, Eng., 1989—; contbr. articles to profl. jours. Vol. Spl. Olympics, Annapolis, Md., 1989; tutor Greenbelt Cares, 1989—. Recipient Charles Clifford Huntington award, Ohio State U., 1976; Exceptional Performance award, Goddard Space Flight Ctr., 1979; Group Achievement award, NASA, 1982; Best Paper award, Goddard Lab. Atmospheric Scis., 1984. Mem. Am. Polar Soc., Am. Meteorol. Soc. (history com. chmn. 1990), Internat. Glaciological Soc., Assn. for Philosophy of Math., Phi Beta Kappa. Home: 8345 Canning Ter Greenbelt MD 20770 Office: NASA Goddard Space Flight Ctr Code 971 Greenbelt MD 20771

PARKINSON, MARIA LUISA, entertainment employment executive; b. Burbank, Calif., July 27, 1951; d. Roy Wilbur (Parky) and Serafina Antonia (Sorzano) P. AA, Pasadena City Coll., 1973; student, Acad. Stage and Cinema Arts, Los Angeles, 1973-76, The Living History Center, Augoura, Calif., The Second City, 1989—. Career counselor Apple One Employment Agy., Marina Del Rey, Calif., 1977-80; career counselor Good People, Inc., Los Angeles, 1980-83, Friedman Personnel Agy., Inc., Los Angeles, 1983-84; owner Parkinson Entertainment Agy., Hollywood, Calif., 1984—; lectr. in field, 1978—. Sponsor Latin Legal Ctr., Santa Monica, 1987—; charter mem. Mus. Contemporary Art. Mem. SAG, Am. Film Inst., Women in Show Bus. (publicity chair), Acad. Sci. Fiction, Fantasy and Horror Films, Hollywood C. of C. (entertainment com.), Entertainment Coun., Count Dracula Soc. (bd. govs.). Democrat. Roman Catholic. Office: Parkinson Entertainment Agy 6525 Sunset Blvd 3d Fl Hollywood CA 90028

PARKS, ARVA MOORE, historian; b. Miami, Fla., Jan. 19, 1939; d. Jack and Anne (Parker) Moore; m. Robert Lyle Parks, Aug. 19, 1959 (div. May 1986); children: Jacqueline Carey, Robert Downing, Gregory Moore. Student, Fla. State U., 1956-58; BA, U. Fla., 1960; MA in History, U. Miami, Coral Gables, 1971. Tchr. Rolling Crest Jr. High Sch., West Hyattsville, Md., 1960-63, Miami Edison Sr. High Sch., 1963-64; grad. asst. U. Miami, Coral Gables, 1964-65; tchr. Everglades Sch. for Girls, Miami, 1965-66; cons., 1966-70; free-lance research historian Miami, 1970-86; adj. prof. U. Miami, Coral Gables, 1986-87; pres. Arva Parks & Co., Miami, 1986—; cons. thematic and interpretive research and design Hyatt Alhambra, Coral Gables, 1987-88, Colonnade Hotel, Coral Gables, 1987-88, Don Shula's Steak House, Miami Lakes, Fla., 1989—, Harry S. Truman Little White House, Key West, Fla., 1989—. Author: Miami the Magic City, 1981, The Forgotten Frontier, 1977; editor Tequesta, Jour. Hist. Soc. Fla., 1986. Bd. trustees, Miami-Dade Community Coll., 1984-90; bd. advs.,

Nat. Trust for Historic Preservation, 1984—, chairperson so region, 1990—; mem. Bi-Racial, Tri-Ethnic Adv. Bd., Miami, 1984—; exec. com. New World Sch. of Arts, Miami, 1986—; bd. mem. Louis Wolfson Media Histo ry Ctr., Miami, 1985—; community adv. Dade Heritage Trust, Miami, 1988—, Orange Bowl Com., 1989—. Recipient Am. History award DAR, 1987, Pathfinder's award Women's Com. 100, 1985, Outstanding Citizen award Coral Gables C. of C., 1983, Outstanding Preservationist award Dade Heritage Trust, 1983, Good Faith award Black Archives and Research Found., 1981, Mus. of Sci. award, 1981, Community Headliner award Women in Communications, 1980, Humanitarian award Urban League Guild, 1980, award City of Coral Gables Historic Preservation Bd., 1978; named to Alumni Hall of Fame Dade County Pub. Schs., 1985, Fla. Women's Hall of Fame, 1986, one of Women Who Made a Difference YWCA, 1988. Mem. Jr. League, Biltmore Club (bd. dirs.). Democrat. Methodist. Home and office: 1601 S Miami Ave Miami FL 33129

PARKS, CAROL LOUISE, marketing executive; b. Buffalo, June 20, 1963; d. Albert Worden and Alma Catherine (Copponex) P. BA in Sociology, SUNY. Sales rep. Town and Country Office Machines, Buffalo, 1985-87; sales coordinator Montreal Royal Leasing Ltd., Buffalo, 1986-88, sales mgr., 1988; owner Capital Mktg., Buffalo, 1988-89; ptnr. Universal Mktg. Concepts, Buffalo, 1989—; cons. Montreal Royal Leasing Ltd., Buffalo, 1989—. Mem. Alpha Clionian. Republican. Roman Catholic. Home: 190 Sanders Apt 7 Buffalo NY 14216 Office: Universal Mktg Concepts 4652 Genesee St Cheektowaga NY 14225

PARKS, DONNA MARIE, engineer; b. Phila., Aug. 18, 1959; d. Claude Edward and Edith Marie (Peppersack) P. BSEE, So. Ill. U., Carbondale, 1981; MBA, Webster U., St. Louis, 1986. Co-op engr. Gen. Electric, Marion, Ill., 1979; design engr. United Design Engring., St. Louis, 1980-81; sales engr. Lcomp Inc., St. Louis, 1981-84; mgr. DTLCC system engring. McDonnell Douglas, St. Louis. Mem. IEEE, Soc. Women Engrs., Internat. Soc. Parametric Analysis. Republican. Southern Baptist. Home: 11 Edgeworth Maryland Heights MO 63043

PARKS, JANET ELAINE, pharmacist; b. Watertown, S.D., Oct. 20, 1946; d. Dale O. and Della E. (Horn) P. BS, S.D. State U., 1970; MBA, U. Minn., 1981. Registered pharmacist, Minn., Iowa, Wis. Staff pharmacist St. Luke's Hosp., Duluth, Minn., 1970-81; fin. cons. Parks & Parks, Marshall, Minn., 1981-82; pharmacy cons. J. Parks, Mason City, Iowa, 1982-85; night pharmacist St. Joseph Mercy Hosp., Mason City, 1982-85; dir. pharmacy Tomah Meml. Hosp., Wis., 1985-86; pharmacy cons. Tomah Care Ctr., 1985-86; mgr. pharmacy computer ops. St. Nicholas Hosp., Sheboygan, Wis., 1986-89; pharmacist Walgreen's Pharmacy, 1989—; cons. Meadow View Manor Nursing Home, Sheboygan, 1987—. Fin. cons. Methodist Chs. Mem. AAUW, NAFE, Am. Soc. Hosp. Pharmacists (region sec. 1975), Nat. Assn. Future Women (photographer 1984), Phi Kappa Phi, Rho Chi. Methodist. Avocations: nature photography; needlecraft; cross-country skiing; bicycling; personal computers. Home: 1628 N 28th St Sheboygan WI 53081 Office: Walgreen's Pharmacy 3347 Kohler Memorial Dr Sheboygan WI 53081

PARKS, KARYN ANN, architect; b. Tulsa, June 14, 1955; d. Lloyd Lee and Mary Ellen (Scott) P.; m. Michael James Pickard, July 8, 1978 (div. Feb. 1986). BArch, Ariz. State U., 1978. Draftsman Brock & Craig Architects, Mesa, Ariz., 1978-79; project mgr. Dwayne G. Lewis Architects, Inc., Phoenix, 1979-82; pres., prin. Karyn A. Parks Architect, Inc., Scottsdale, Ariz., 1982—. Vol. Tempe Home Service, Ariz., 1986-87. Mem. AIA, Women Execs. Assn. Met. Phoenix (co-exec. dir.), Midtowners BPW. Republican. Office: Karyn A Parks Architect Inc 3428 E Indian School Rd Phoenix AZ 85018

PARKS, KIMBERLY SUE, public relations specialist; b. Wilmington, Ohio, Dec. 28, 1964; d. Richard Allen and Barbara Sue (Sielschott) Whetstone; m. Mark Samuel Parks, Sept. 16, 1989. BA in English, Wittenberg U., 1987; MA in Communication, U. Dayton, 1989. Communication asst. Community Hosp., Springfield, Ohio, 1987-89, acting dir. pub. rels., 1989-90, asst. dir. pub. rels., 1990—, also supr. desktop pub. dept., 1990—; hosp. liaison ptnrs. in edn. prog. Springfield, 1988—. Mem. pub. rels. com. Fighting Back Campaign, Springfield, 1989; youth advisor High St. United Meth. Ch., Springfield, 1988—; vol. counselor Ohio Kidney Found. Kappa Kidney Kamp, Belfontaine, 1988—. Mem. Ohio Hosp. Assn Pub. Relations Soc., Women in Communication Inc., Am. Heart Assn. (communication com., chair turkeywalk 1989), Wittenberg Coll. Honor Soc., Omicron Delta Kappa. Republican. Office: Community Hosp 2615 E High St Springfield OH 45501

PARKS, MARY IRENE, retailer; b. Asheboro, N.C., Apr. 19, 1919; d. Carl Clifton and Revella Rose (Strickland) Rollins; m. Albert Lee Parks, July 3, 1938; children—Albert Lee, Jr. (dec.), Rachel Yvonne White, Teresa Diana Cooper, Candace Susan Kirk, James Michael, Cynthia Revella Whitley. Bookseller Grandpa's House, Troy, N.C., 1963—. Baptist. Office: Grandpa's House Hwy 27 Rte 3 Box 292 Troy NC 27371

PARKS, MELANIE ANN, budget analyst; b. Pueblo, Colo., July 6, 1958; d. William Thomas and Barbara Jean (Chatham) Leonard; m. Floyd Mason Parks, Feb. 17, 1979. Student, U. So. Colo., 1976-78; BS in Mgmt., U. Utah, 1981. Dept. mgr. Grand Cen. Stores, Salt Lake City, 1981-82; asst. mgr. House of Fabrics, Denver, 1982; color analyst Stretch and Sew Fabrics, Denver, 1982-84; receptionist, sec. WestAm. Mortgage Co., Denver, 1984, budget analyst, 1984-85, pricing coordinator, 1985-86, jr. acct., 1986, fin. analyst, 1986-89; budget analyst City of Boulder, Colo., 1989—. Vice-chairperson Rep. precinct, Salt Lake City, 1981-82. Mem. Am. Bus. Womens Assn., Nat. Assn. Female Execs. Baptist. Office: City of Boulder Budget Office 1777 Broadway Boulder CO 80302

PARKS, ROBIN, editor; b. Downey, Calif., Mar. 7, 1957; d. Jerome Parks and Marjorie Lorraine (Thomas) Jones. Student, Calif. State U., Long Beach, 1980—. Asst. art dir. Andrews Printing Co., Inc., Lakewood, Calif., 1983-86; communications mgr. AIDS Project L.A., 1986-88; sr. editor St. Mary Med. Ctr., Long Beach, Calif., 1988—. Founding mem. bd. dirs. Friends of Women's Studies, Calif. State U., Long Beach, 1983—. Recipient Mercury award silver winner Nat. Media Conf. and Pub. Rels. Forum, 1989. Mem. Internat. Assn. Bus. Communicators (Bronze Quill award of excellence 1988, ACE award of merit 1989), Women in Communications, The Newspaper Guild, Pacific Coast Press Club (1990 Award of Excellence in writing), Radical Philosophy Assn., Soc. of Women in Philosophy, Am. Philos. Assn. (student membership com.), Pacific Coast Press Club (award for editorial excellence 1990). Democrat. Office: St Mary Med Ctr 1050 Linden Ave Long Beach CA 90813

PARKS, WILDA ALICE, chamber of commerce executive; b. Erie, Pa., Aug. 23, 1940; d. William Andrew and Irene Agnes (Smith) McKenna; m. LeRoy Dale Parks, June 27, 1960 (div. Apr. 1977); children: Gary Andrew, Jodi Parks Gruendler, Leon David. AA in Bus.-Human Svcs., Porterville Coll., 1982; BS in Orgn. Mgmt., U. San Francisco, 1986. Cert. activity dir., Calif. Reporter Philipsburg (Mont.) Mail, 1967-76, Porterville (Calif.) Recorder, 1976-77; activity dir. Hacienda Hosp., Porterville, 1976-84; exec. dir. Exeter (Calif.) C. of C., 1984-86, Hanford (Calif.) C. of C., 1986—; owner, operator Philipsburg Recreation Ctr., 1973-76. Author: Echoes, 1976. Pres., bd. dirs. Porterville Vol. Bur., 1977-82, Barn Theater, Porterville, 1982-88; bd. dirs. Kaweah Youth Svcs. Inc., Exeter, 1984-85, Tulare County United Way, Porterville, 1984-86; mem. Kings County Self Esteem Task Force, Hanford, 1988-89; bd. dirs., mem. exec. bd. Mt. Whitney coun. Boy Scouts Am., 1988—; mem. adv. coun. Fresno State U. Valley Bus. Ctr. Recipient legis. commendation Calif. Assembly, 1986. Mem. Am. Assn. C. of C. Execs., U.S. C. of C., Calif. Assn. C. of C. Execs. (bd. dirs. 1986—), Valley C. of C. Execs. (v.p. 1988-89, pres. 1989—), Tulare-Kings County C. of C. Execs. (cons. 1985—), South Valley Activity Dirs. Assn. (charter, pres. 1978-82), Calif. C. of C., Rotary, Quota Club (1st v.p Porterville 1982-84). Presbyterian. Office: Hanford C of C 213 W 7th St Ste l Hanford CA 93230

PARLIN, JODY A., psychotherapist, clinical consultant; b. Swampscott, Mass., Oct. 17, 1961; d. Arthur Warren and M. Deborah (Arnold) P. Student, Dartmouth Coll., 1979-82; MEd, Cambridge Coll., Boston, 1985. Cert. alcoholism counselor, Mass. Alcoholism counselor Fuller Meml. Hosp., South Attleboro, Mass., 1984-86; lead counselor High Point Treatment Facility, South Kingstown, R.I., 1986-87, clin. dir., 1987-89; pvt. practice, trainer-eating disorders specialist Jody Parlin and Assocs., Mahwah, N.J., 1989—; trainer R.I. Div. Substance Abuse, Warwick, 1986-89. Author: (pamphlets) Bulimia: A Complete Recovery Program, 1985, Guidelines for Health Living, 1989. Mem. Am. Anorexia-Bulimia Assn., Assn. Transpersonal Psychology, N.J. Assn. Alcohol and Drug Addiction Counselors (trainer 1989—). Home: 169 Grandview Ln Mahwah NJ 07430 Office: 6 East Main St Ramsey NJ 07446

PARMESE, BARBARA JEAN, medical organization executive, consultant; b. Hackensack, N.J., Sept. 21, 1954; d. Jack and Rose (Lodato) Insinga; m. Vincent James Parmese, Oct. 6, 1984. BS, Trenton State Coll., 1976; postgrad. William Paterson Coll., 1979-80. Health record analyst Hackensack Med. Ctr., 1976-79; quality assurance analyst Englewood Hosp., N.J., 1979-80; quality rev. mgr. Assn. Profl. Health Care Rev., Saddle Brook, N.J., 1980-82, asst. dir., 1982-83, exec. dir., 1983-85; v.p. North Jersey Physicians Rev., Parsippany, 1985—; mem. reimbursement adv. com. N.J. Dept. Health, Trenton, 1986.Mgr. campaign New Leadership for Hackensack ticket for City Coun., 1989. Home: 487 Kaplan Ave Hackensack NJ 07601 Office: North Jersey Physicians 120 Littleton Rd Parsippany NJ 07054

PARMET, HARRIET ABBEY, educator; b. Phila., July 22, 1928; d. Jacob and Belle Cecil (Popolow) Leibowitz; m. Sidney B. Parmet, June 7, 1950; children: Howard B., Jonathan L. AB, Temple U., 1950, MS, 1960; B in Hebrew Lit., Gratz Coll., 1979. Cert. secondary edn. tchr., Pa. Tchr. Hebrew Temple U., Phila., 1946-50, Beth Israel, Phila., 1946-51; tchr. English and social studies Gillespie Jr. High Sch., Phila., 1950-55; tchr. Hebrew and Jewish history Temple Beth El, Allentown, Pa., 1964-77; tchr. Hebrew and Israeli lit. Lehigh U., Bethlehem, Pa., 1976—; Hillel co-advisor, mem. exec. bd. Lehigh U., 1976—. Contbr. articles to profl. jours. Vice pres. Temple Beth El Sisterhood, Allentown, 1973-75; mem. exec. bd. Jewish Family Svc., Allentown, 1988—; bd. dirs. Women's Profl. Jewish Fedn., Allentown, 1973-75. Coolodge Colloquim fellow, 1986, Givat Haviva Rsch. fellow, 1987. Mem. Women's Studies Consortium, Lehigh Valley Assn. Ind. Colls., Am. Jewish Congress (pres. Allentown chpt. 1970), Assn. Jewish Studies, Nat. Assn. Hebrew Profs., Temple U. Alumni Assn., Gratz Coll. Alumni Assn., Hadassah (life). Home: 1118 N 28th St Allentown PA 18104 Office: Lehigh U Modern Lang Dept Coppee Hall-33 Bethlehem PA 18015

PARNESS, ANDREA MICHELLE, accounting firm owner, real estate developer; b. N.Y.C., Sept. 11, 1956; d. Jules Seymour and Theda M. (Rapaport) P.; m. David Jay Katz, Mar. 22, 1981; children: Jessie Rose, Emily Lauren. BA in Acctg., CUNY, 1978. CPA, N.Y., N.J. Internal auditor CIT Fin. Corp., N.Y.C., 1978-80, fin. analyst, 1980-81; sr. acct. Zimmerman & Co., N.Y.C., 1981-83; co-owner Intrator & Parness, Great Neck, N.Y., 1983-85; treas. MIF Assocs., Branford, Conn., 1983—, Banner Lodge Co., Moodus, Conn., 1985—; owner A. Parness Co., N.Y.C., 1985—; treas. Alpha Banner, Ltd., Moodus, 1987—; bd. dirs. Banner Lodge Co., MIF Assocs., Alpha Banner, Ltd. Pres. Deborah Group of Rockaway Pk. chpt. Hadassah, Queens, 1987; treas., fin. sec. of Rockaway Pk. chpt. of Hadassah, 1989—. Mem. AICPAs, N.Y. State Soc. CPAs, N.J. State Soc. CPA. Office: 533 Beach 132d St Belle Harbor NY 11694

PARR, CAROLYN MILLER, federal judge; b. Palatka, Fla., Apr. 17, 1937; d. Arthur Charles and Audrey Ellen (Dunklin) Miller: m. Jerry Studstill Parr, Oct. 12, 1959; children: Kimberly Susan, Jennifer Parr Turek, Patricia Audrey. BA, Stetson U., 1959; MA, Vanderbilt U., 1960; JD, Georgetown U., 1977; LLD (hon.), Stetson U., 1986. Bar: Md. 1977, U.S. Tax Ct. 1977, D.C. 1979, U.S. Supreme Ct. 1983. Gen. trial atty. IRS, Washington, 1977-81, sr. trial atty. office of chief counsel, 1982; spl. counsel U.S. Dept. Justice, Washington, 1982-85; judge U.S. Tax Ct., Washington, 1985—. Mem. ABA, Md. Bar Assn., Nat. Assn. Women Judges, D.C. Bar Assn. Republican. Office: US Tax Ct 400 2nd St NW Washington DC 20217

PARR, DORIS ANN, financial institution executive, consultant; b. Fergus Falls, Minn., July 10, 1933; d. Henry Fritzolf and Esther Marie (Ahlgren) Peterson; m. Mark Hoffman, 1949 (div. 1960); children: Cynthia Lee Davis, David Alan Hoffman; m. Harold R. Parr, 1961 (div. 1974). Student Am. Savs. and Loan Inst., 1965-66, Pioneer Nat. Title Ins. Co., 1969, Menlo Coll., 1975. Comml. loan officer Savbank Service Corp., Seattle, 1975-77; exec. v.p., mgr. Sound Savs. & Loan, Seattle, 1976-78; v.p. Queen City Savs. & Loan, Seattle, 1978-82; v.p., mgr. State Savs. & Loan Assn., Dallas, 1983-84; pres. Nat. Real Estate Mortgage Services Inc., Dallas, 1984—; instr. real estate law San Francisco City Coll., 1975. Recipient 1st Pl. Speech trophy Am. Savs. & Loan Inst., 1964. Mem. Assn. Profl. Mortgage Women (program chmn. Seattle chpt. 1969-70, program chmn. San Jose chpt. 1973-74, pres. 1975-76, Woman of Yr. 1979), U.S. Savs. and Loan League (consumer affairs and secondary market com.), Nat. Assn. Females Execs., Fed. Home Loan Bank Bd. (maj. comml. loan underwriter). Organized and managed 1st U.S. minority savs. and loan assn. Home: 2208 Canyon Valley Trail Plano TX 75023

PARR, SANDRA HARDY, health management company executive; b. Atlanta, Dec. 30, 1952; d. Raymond William Hardy and Ruth (Berry) Yancey; m. James Parr Jr., Apr. 14, 1978; 1 child, James Andrew Parr III. Student, Lurleen B. Wallace Jr. Coll., 1972. Sales adminstr. Etec Corp., Hayward, Calif., 1976-77; adminstrv. sec. Cities Svc. Co., Atlanta, 1977-82; sales and planning coord. Intermodal Transp. Co., Norcross, Ga., 1982-83; freelance temp. sec. Atlanta met. area, 1983-86; freelance word processor, cons. Amoco Container Co., Norcross, 1986-88; psychiat. rev. asst. Am. Psychiat. Assn., Atlanta, 1988-89; support svcs. mgr. Parkside Health Mgmt. Corp., Atlanta, 1989—. Del. internat. nursing conf., citizen ambassador program to People's Republic China, Seattle Washington People to People, Beijing, 1989, del psychiat. nursing delegation, Beijing, 1990; part-time exercise instr. Mem. NAFE. Home: 1253 Gatewood Dr Lawrenceville GA 30243 Office: Parkside Health Mgmt Corp 900 Circle 75 Pkwy Ste 1410 Atlanta GA 30339

PARRAMORE, BARBARA MITCHELL, educator; b. Guilford County, N.C., Aug. 29, 1932; d. Samuel Spencer and Nellie Gray (Glosson) Mitchell; m. Lyman Griffis Worthington, Dec. 23, 1956 (div. 1961); m. Thomas Custis Parramore, Jan. 22, 1966; children: Lisa Gray, Lynn Stuart. AB, U. N.C., Greensboro, 1954; MEd, N.C. State U., 1959; EdD, Duke U., 1968. Counselor, thcr. Raleigh City Schs., 1954-59, sch. prin., 1959-65; prof. dept. of curriculum and instrn. N.C. State U., 1970—; acad. specialist Office Internat. Edn., U.S. Info. Svcs., sec. sch. initatives prog., The Phillippines, 1987. Author: The People of North Carolina, 1972, 3rd edit. 1983. Mem. Raleigh Coun. of the Experiment in Internat. Living (hon. permanent mem.). Japan Inst. Social and Econ. Affairs fellow, 1980; N.C. AAUW award for juvenile lit., 1973. Mem. N.C. Coun. for Social Studies (pres. 1985-87), N.C. Assn. Supervision and Curriculm Devel., Assn. for Supervision and Curriculum Devel., Assn. Tchr. Educators, Delta Kappa Gamma, Kappa Delta Pi. Home: 5012 Tanglewood Dr Raleigh NC 27612

PARRAMORE, KATHERINE F., management training and development specialist; b. Columbus, Ohio, Oct. 29, 1959; d. Robert Walters and Margaret Ruth (Campbell) Foster; m. John Andrew Parramore, Oct. 7, 1989. BA in Communications, Ohio State U., 1982, MS in Edn., 1985; postgrad., Nat. U., 1987. Mgr. tng. Lagniappe Inns, Inc., Columbus, 1984-86; communications cons. The Logical Choice, Inc., Sacramento, 1986; mgmt. tng. and devel. specialist The Palmer Group, Ltd., Chgo., 1987-89; dir. tng. and devl. Enstar Splty. Retail Group, Inc., Montgomery, Ala., 1989—; bd. dirs. The Hartsfield Found., Jacksonville, Fla., 1987—. Coord. campaign sch. Ohio Republican Party, Columbus, 1983; adv. com. Nat. Multiple Sclerosis Soc., Columbus, 1983. Mem. Am. Soc. for Tng. and Devel., Nat. Assn. for Female Execs., MENSA. Republican. Presbyterian. Home: 3580 McGehee Pl S #503 Montgomery AL 36111

PARRATTO, NANETTE PAMELA, veterinarian; b. Phila., Apr. 24, 1956; d. Leonard Robert and Antoinette Nancy (Bracale) P. BS in Biology, Villanova U., 1978; DVM, U. Fla., 1985, PhD, 1988. Grad. rsch. asst. dept. pathology U. Fla., Gainesville, 1979-81, 85-87, lab. technician II dept. pathology, 1983-84, NIH trainee dept. pathology, 1987-88; assoc. veterinarian Gainesville, 1985-88, Charleston, S.C., 1989—; v.p. and dir. animal trials NBR-16, Ltd., Charleston, S.C., 1988—; adj. instr. dept. comparative/lab. animal medicine MUSC, Charleston, 1989—; cons. NBR-16, Ltd., Charleston, 1990. Contbr. articles to profl. jours. Mem. Vet. Cancer Soc., S.C. Assn. Vets., Trident Vet. Assn., AAAS, Am. Vet. Med. Assn.

PARRENT, JOANNE ELIZABETH, screenwriter, filmmaker; b. Detroit, July 22, 1948; d. Elton Laverne and Geraldine Elizabeth (Racine) P. Student, U. Mich., 1966-69; BA in Communications, UCLA, 1982. Founder, dir. Feminist Fed. Credit Union, Detroit, 1973-76; editor Chrysalis Mag., L.A., 1977; program developer Women's Community, Inc., L.A., 1978; asst. to pres. Screen Actors Guild, L.A., 1979-80; freelance writer, producer, dir. L.A., 1980—. Writer: (documentaries) The Workplace Hustle, 1980 (San Francisco Film Festival award, N.Y. Film Festival award), Sexual Shakedown, 1980, The Healing Force, 1983 (also dir.), Little Arkansas, 1985, 1988, (novel adaptation) Big Doc's Girl, 1987, (dramatic series) Susan B., 1989; writer, producer, dir.: (short films) Growing Healthy, 1986, AIDS, 1986, The Childhood Of Susan B. Anthony, 1987, Love is Feeding Everyone, 1988; co-writer (series) Alice & The Rainbow Rider, The Prophecy, 1981. Exec. sec., bd. dirs. Love Is Feeding Everyone (L.I.F.E.), Los Angeles, 1983—. Recipient Minority Bus. award Detroit Minority Bus. Assn., 1975; named Feminist of Yr. NOW, 1976. Mem. Writers Guild Am.-West. Democrat. Home: 9973 Durant Dr #1 Beverly Hills CA 90212 Office: The Artists Group 1930 Century Pk W #403 Los Angeles CA 90065

PARRINELLO, DIANE DAVIES, educator; b. West Warwick, R.I., Oct. 17, 1939; d. Stanley Duane and Catherine Margaret (Heelan) Davies; m. John Richard Parrinello, Apr. 28, 1962; children: Gregory, Timothy, Bethany, Matthew. BA, U. Rochester, 1961; MS in Edn., Nazareth Coll., 1987. Cert. tchr., N.Y. Biochem. research asst. Syracuse (N.Y.) U., 1962-64; presch. tchr. Jewish Community Ctr., Syracuse, 1964-65; co-owner, mgr. Spl. Creations, Rochester, N.Y., 1979-84; tchr. Winton Rd. Nursery Sch., Rochester, 1983—. Mem. women's council Meml. Art Gallery, Rochester, 1972—; coach Brighton Little League, Rochester, 1975-82; leader Camp Fire Girls, Inc., Rochester, 1975-78; bd. dirs., coach Brighton Soccer League, 1975-85; co-founder Brighton Girls Soccer League, 1976; active Friends of Strong Meml. Hosp. Mem. Nat. Assn. for Edn. Young Children (Rochester chpt.). Republican. Roman Catholic. Home: 334 San Gabriel Dr Rochester NY 14610 Office: Winton Rd Nursery Sch 220 Winton Rd South Rochester NY 14610

PARRISH, FAYRENE ELIZABETH, artist; b. Santa Monica, Calif., Sept. 20, 1936; d. Joseph Harrish and Fern (Loomis) Wright; m. Edward Witherill Parrish, Jr., Jan. 21, 1970. Student, San Diego State Coll., 1959-61, L.A. City Coll., 1962-64, UCLA, 1965-66, San Fernando City Coll., 1966-67, Santa Monica City Coll., 1973-74. Acting contractee Columbia Pictures/Screem Gems, Hollywood, Calif., 1962-64; actress, sculptress, gallery and art sch. founder Malibu Art Colony, L.A. area, 1965-75; owner Sea Gallery, Ventura County, Calif., 1975-80; owner, artist Parrish Studios, Ventura, Calif., 1977-82, Anacortes, Wash., 1982-. Docent N.W. Mus. Art, La Connor, Wash., 1988—; bd. dirs. Anacortes Arts Found., 1988—. Grantee Film Inst. Am., L.A., 1967. Mem. N.W. Watercolor Soc., N.W. Printmakers Soc. Republican. Roman Catholic. Office: Parrish Studios PO Box 317 Anacortes WA 98110

PARRISH, HELENSUE, education educator; b. Iowa City, Dec. 16, 1933; d. Ralph Wendell Lewis and Fern Amelia (Reedy) Rowland; m. William Ashley Stoppel, June 9, 1956 (div. 1970); children: Elizabeth Ann, William Lewis; m. William E. Parish, June 2, 1972. BA, Cornell Coll., 1956; MS, U. Mo., 1974. Home econs. sci. tchr. Martell (Iowa) High Sch., 1956-57; home econs. tchr. Mt. Vernon (Iowa) High Sch., 1958-62; clothing, textiles grad. asst. Univ. Mo., Columbia, 1970-72, clothing, textiles instr., 1972--75; owner, pres. City Goodwill Hostess, Starkville, Miss., 1982--. Author: Fit and Flattery for the over Fifties, 1974. Mem. Home Economists in Home and Community, Starkville, Miss.; pres. Com. on Status of Women, Miss. State U. Mem. AAUW (Miss. div. pres. 1988—), C. of C., Starkville Newcomers Club (sponsor). Presbyterian. Home: 703 Bonnie Rd Starkville MS 39759

PARRISH, MARY JEANNE, psychologist, nun; b. Nashville, Sept. 28, 1924; d. Charles Lee and Marguerite Patricia (Martin) P. BA in Math., Fontbonne Coll., St. Louis, 1951; MEd in Counseling, St. Louis U., 1956, MS in Psychology, 1963. Lic. psychologist, Mo.; cert. tchr., secondary adminstr., Mo. Nurse aid St. Thomas Hosp., Nashville, 1941-43; tchr. St. Stephen Sch., New Orleans, 1945-48, St. Vincent de Paul Sch., San Francisco, 1949-52, LaBoure High Sch., St. Louis, 1952-61; adminstr. Child Ctr. of Our Lady, St. Louis, 1963-66, Marillac Sch. and Residence, Kansas City, Mo., 1966-72; prin. LaBoure High Sch., St. Louis, 1972-74; cons. Daus. of Charit-West Cen., St. Louis, 1974-80; staff psychologist Kenrick Sem., St. Louis, 1980—; bd. dirs. Cath. Family Svcs., St. Louis, 1984—, Guardian Angel Settlement, St. Louis 1984; trustee DePaul Health Ctr., St. Louis, 1985—. Contbr. articles to psychiat. jours. Recipient key to city, Kansas City, 1972, New Orleans, 1975. Mem. Am. Psychol. Assn., Nat. Cath. Edn. Assn., Assn. Theol. Field Educators, Midwest Assn. Spiritual Dirs. Democrat.

PARRISH, NANCY ELAINE BUCHELE, lawyer, state senator; b. Cedar Vale, Kans., Nov. 9, 1948; d. Julian Milton and Vergie May (Bryant) Buchele; m. James Wesley Parrish, Jan. 31, 1970; children: Leslie Elgin, Tyler Jonathan, James Montgomery. BS in Edn., Kans. State U., 1970; MS in Spl. Edn., U. Kans., 1974; JD magna cum laude, Washburn U., 1984. Tchr., Topeka Public Schs., 1970-75; spl. edn. tchr. Topeka State Hosp., 1975-81; mem. Kans. Senate, 1980—; mem. edn. task force Council of State Govts., 1981-84; adv. bd. Boy's Club of Topeka, Kans. Action for Children; mem. fiscal affairs task force Nat. Council State Legislatures, 1985—; policy chmn. Senate Minority Party, 1985—. Bd. dirs. Family Svc. and Guidance Ctr., Topeka., Topeka North YMCA. Active Golden City Forum, Jr. League, Topeka; mem. adv. bd. Ct. Apptd. Spl. Advs., 1986—. Named one of Outstanding Women of Yr., Jaycees, 1979, 84. Mem. ABA, Kans. Bar Assn., Topeka Bar Assn., Topeka C. of C. (bd. dirs. 1988—). Office: State Senate Rm 403 Topeka KS 66612 also: 700 Jackson Ste 200 Topeka KS 66603

PARROTT, IDA T., school system administrator, researcher, counselor; b. L.A., Oct. 27, 1944; d. Cho Kim and Melba Kim (Ko) Bailey; m. Lawrence Allan Parrott, Apr. 25, 1970; 1 child, Henry Charles. AA, Reedley (Calif.) Jr. Coll., 1965; BA, Calif. State U., Fresno, 1967, MA, 1974; postgrad., U. So. Calif., L.A. Tchr. English Fresno (Calif.) Unified Sch. Dist., 1967-68; with Sanger (Calif.) Schs., 1968—, dist. counselor, 1986-90, project mgr., 1990—; mgr. football game project Sanger Unified Sch. Dist., 1990—; chmn. bd. Community TV Multi Media Ctr., Sanger, 1990—; chmn. Fresno Housing and Community Devel. Comm., 1990—. Mem. Cen. Calif. Polit. Action Com., 1985—; mem. exec. bd. Nat. Friends of Pub. Broadcasting, 1987—; charter season producer Calif. Shakespearean Festival, 1979. Recipient Cen. Calif. Patron of Youth award YMCA, 1987. Mem. Bus. and Profl. Women (legis. chmn. Cen. Calif. chpt. 1990—, pres. Sanger chpt. 1989—, Woman of the Yr.). Democrat. Roman Catholic. Home: 3802 E Huntington Blvd Fresno CA 93702 Office: 1905 Seventh St Sanger CA 93657

PARROW, JANICE ANN, veterinary technician; b. Davenport, Iowa, Oct. 29, 1954; d. Louis Ernest and Wanda Evangeline (Talbot) Gruenhagen; m. Kenneth Wayne Parrow, Oct. 24, 1976; 1 child, Laska Kristine. Student, Iowa State U., 1974; A in Applied Sci., Med. Inst. Minn., 1975. Cert. vet. tech., lab. animal tech. Vet. tech. Blue Cross Animal Hosp., Mpls., 1976-79; instr. Med. Inst. Minn., 1980-86; sr. lab. animal tech. Univ. Minn., 1987, vet. tech., 1987--. Adv. bd. Med. Inst. Minn., 1989. Mem. Minn. Assn. Vet. Technicians, N.Am. Vet. Technician Assn., Am. Assn. Lab. Animal Sci. Office: U Minn 1365 Gortner Ave Saint Paul MN 55108

PARRY, CAROL JACQUELINE, banker; b. Chgo., Apr. 12, 1941; d. Ralph G. and Estelle (Hoffman) Newman; m. John R. Fox, 1990. B.A., Tufts U., 1964; M.S.W., U. Conn., 1969; postgrad., Harvard U., 1984. Dir. program planning N.Y.C. Agy. for Child Devel., N.Y.C., 1971-72; cons. McKinsey & Co., N.Y.C., 1972-74; asst. commr. Spl. Svcs. for Children, N.Y.C., 1974-77; v.p., dist. head Chem. Bank, N.Y.C., 1978-80, sr. v.p., div. head, 1981-86, sr. v.p. nat. expansion program, 1985, sr. v.p. comml. sector, chmn. regional bank, 1985-87, head private banking, 1987-89; ptnr. Pers.

Corp. of Am., N.Y.C., 1989; mgmt. cons. N.Y.C., 1990; sr. v.p. bus. banking Mfrs. Hanover, 1990—; trustee Independence Savs. Bank. Bd. dirs. N.Y. Urban Coalition, Nat. Child Labor Com. Channel 13 adv. bd., N.Y. Landmarks Conservancy, Homes for the Homeless; chmn. N.Y. State Juvenile Justice Bd. Recipient Big WEAL award Women's Equity Action League, 1984. Home: 60 E 8th St New York NY 10003 Office: 60 E 8th St New York NY 10003

PARRY, PATRICIA GILMAN, hospital executive, consultant; b. N.Y.C., Jan. 9, 1942; d. Max and Gertrude (Weinberg) Gilman; m. Michael Norman Kahn, Dec. 23, 1962 (div. June 1973); children: Jennifer Lynn, Jason David; m. John Edward Parry, Aug. 28, 1977 (div. May 1989). BA in History, CCNY, 1963; postgrad. in non-profit mgmt., New Sch. for Social Research, 1987. Grants adminstr. SUNY, New Paltz, 1978-80; dir. sponsored funds SUNY, Purchase, 1980-81; dir. devel. Ulster Assn. for Retarded Citizens, Kinsgston, N.Y., 1983-86, Cornwall (N.Y.) Hosp., 1987—; cons. PGP Assocs., Cornwall, 1986—. Pres. Ulster County Ballet Guild, New Paltz, 1980-82; bd. dirs. Amos and Sarah Holden Home, Newburgh, N.Y., 1987-88. Mem. Nat. Assn. Fund Raising Execs., Nat. Assn. Hosp. Devel., Rotary. Democrat. Jewish. Home: 68 Laurel Ave Cornwall NY 12518 Office: Cornwall Hosp Laurel Ave Cornwall NY 12518

PARRY, RUTH ELAINE, health science specialist; b. Salisbury, Md., Apr. 10, 1952; d. Robert Owen and Margaret Elsie (Elburn) P. BA, Washington Coll., Chestertown, Md., 1974; MA, Conn. Coll., 1981; M in Adminstrv. Sci., Johns Hopkins U., 1983; JD, U. Md., 1989. Human factors scientist BDM Services Co., Ft. Ord, Calif., 1975-76; research coordinator sch. pub. health Johns Hopkins U., Balt., 1980-83; research assoc. sch. medicine U. Md., Balt., 1983-87; health sci. specialist dept. vet. affairs VA Med. Ctr., Perry Point, Md., 1987-90. Co-contbr. articles to profl. jours., 1983, 84, 88. Research and devel. com. mem. Md. High Blood Pressure Commn., 1983-86. Recipient Superior Performance awards VA, 1988, 89, 90, Outstanding Rating Certs., 1988, 89, 90, Cert. Appreciation, 1990. Mem. Am. Pub. Health Assn. (health law forum). Democrat. Home: 9900-I Tailspin Ln Baltimore MD 21220

PARSONS, GINGER SHELLENBERGER, educational administrator; b. Bluefield, Va., Feb. 21, 1950; d. William Henry and Gloria (Lynch) Shellenberger; m. Samuel Henry Parsons, June 29, 1988. BA, W.Va. U., 1972; MA in Edn., Lynchburg Coll., 1973. Elem. tchr. Portsmouth (Va.) City Schs., 1973-79, Raleigh County Schs., Beckley, W.Va., 1979-81; staff devel. specialist Lynchburg (Va.) City Schs., 1981—; mem. So. Assn. Accrediation Evaluation Team, 1986-88. Mem. visual arts bd. Lynchburg Fine Arts Ctr., 1983-86; vol. cons. Womans Resource Ctr., Lynchburg, 1986-87; pub. TV vol., Norfolk, Va., 1975-79, Beckley, 1979-81; mem. parish pastoral coun. St. Thomas More Cath. Ch., 1984-85; mem. riverfront revitalization com. Jr. League of Lynchburg, 1985—, editor Blaze, 1989-91. Mem. NEA, Va. Edn. Assn., Portsmouth Edn. Assn. (faculty rep., grievance rep. 1973-79), Lynchburg Edn. Assn. (exec. bd. 1984—, chmn. elections com. 1984-86, polit. action com. 1987-89), AAUW. Office: Paul Munro Elem Sch 4641 Locksview Rd Lynchburg VA 24503

PARSONS, HELGA LUND, writer; b. Seattle, Sept. 5, 1906; d. Gunnar and Marie Pauline (Vognild) Lund; m. Durwin David Algyer, June 6, 1937 (dec. 1971); children: Deanne Algyer Mathisen, Marilyn A. McIntosh-Virgil; m. James Stewart Parsons, Sept. 30, 1972 (dec. 1988). Grad., Columbia Coll. Expression, Chgo., 1926. Lead actress Repertory Playhouse, Seattle, 1929-34; assoc. prof. drama U. Wash., 1931-32; dir. apprentice group Repertory Playhouse, Seattle 1932-34; writer, anchor radio programs Bon Marche Dept. Store, Seattle 1933-35; v.p. creative dir. Norwegian Am. Mus., Decorah Iowa 1960-66. Author: Norway Travel Newspaper Series Seattle 1930, Concert Touring, Monodramas 1936, Novelized Version, Blondie and Dagwood King Features 1946; script writerserials include N.Y. Romance Evelyn Winters Career Alice Blair 1938-50; appeared in numerous plays. Mem. Norwegian Am. Mus. Decorah Iowa (hon. mem.), MIT, Naples Philharm. League, Viking Lodge High Point N.C. Republican.

PARSONS, JUDITH N., communications executive; b. Wilkes-Barres, Pa., Aug. 29, 1942; d. Ralph and Florence (Rauch) Nicholson; m. Raymond E. Parsons Jr., Sept. 22, 1967; children: Jennifer, Milissa, Allyson, Tara. BA, Wilkes Coll., 1964. Adminstrv. asst. LAPAC, Washington; exec. v.p. Medi-america, Inc., Lorton, Va.; campaign mgr. Author children's books, short stories and poetry. Mem. Direct Mktg. Assn. Libertarian. Office: 7214 Lockport Pl Lorton VA 22079

PARSONS, LYNDA A., state agency administrator; b. Marion, Iowa, Oct. 27, 1941; d. Theodore Alfred and Ada Dawn (Comley) P.; children: Michael Sheridan, Patrick Sheridan, Christopher Sheridan. Student, U. Wis., Eau Claire. Cert. real estate broker, Fla. Real estate salesperson Stephens Real Estate, Lawrence, Kans.; rightway agt., staff appraiser Kans. Dept. Transp., Topeka; sr. rev. appraiser Kaiser Engrs., Ft. Lauderdale, Fla.; chief rev. appraisal adminstrn. dist. IV Fla. Dept. Transp., Ft. Lauderdale. Past pres. PTA; co-chair Bloodmobile Food Svc.; dir., soloist Wesleyan Choir.; chair membership Eau Claire Presch., Newcomer's Club. Recipient Sr. Art award, Leadership award, Best Supporting Actress award. Mem. NAFE, Am. Inst. Real Estate Appraisers. Home: 6913 NW 4th Ct Plantation FL 33317

PARSONS, PATTY LEIGH, lawyer; b. Pocomoke City, Md., Feb. 20, 1954; d. E. Carmel Wilson (stepfather) and Evelyn Gay (Carter) Parsons-Wilson; m. Harry Dorman McKnett, May 24, 1980 (div. Dec. 1987). BA in Psychology, U. Md., Balt., 1976; JD, U. Balt., 1979. Bar: Md. 1981, U.S. Ct. Appeals (4th cir.) 1984. Residential counselor U. Md., Balt., 1973-76; adminstr. Juvenile Law Clinic, Balt., 1979-80; legal asst. Edelman & Rubenstein P.A., Balt., 1979-81; labor atty. Edelman & Rubenstein, P.A., Balt., 1981-85; labor atty. Abato, Rubenstein and Abato, P.A., Balt., 1985-87, ptnr., 1988-89; pvt. practice, 1989—. Drug counselor Open Arms Community Counseling Ctr., Balt., 1972-73. Recipient Md. Poetry Soc. award, 1972; Outstanding Adv. award, U. Balt., 1977-78. Mem. Md. State Bar Assn. (adv. bd. labor sect.), ABA (developing labor law com., labor and employment sect.), Indsl. Relations Research Assn., Coalition of Labor Union Women. Democrat. Home: 1309 Dartmouth Ave Baltimore MD 21234 Office: 101 W Ridgely Rd Ste 3A Lutherville MD 21093

PARSONS, VIRGINIA MAE, psychology educator; b. Milw., Oct. 27, 1942; d. John T. and Mable (Myers) Lakso; m. Ralph F. Parsons, Oct. 5, 1968; children: Ralph F. III, Robert, Jeanne. BA, U. Wis., Milw., 1964; MA, U. Iowa, 1967, PhD, 1970. Asst. prof. U. Wis.-Parkside, Kenosha, Wis., 1970-76; prof. psychology Carroll Coll., Waukesha, Wis., 1976—. Contbr. articles to profl. jours. NSF grantee, 1962-64, 72, 77, Carroll Coll., 1978, 80, 88. Mem. AAAS, Am. Psychol. Assn., N.Y. Acad. Sci., Sigma Xi, Psi Chi. Office: Carroll Coll 100 N East Ave Waukesha WI 53186

PARSONS-SALEM, DIANE LORA, lawyer; b. Arlington, Mass., Apr. 17, 1945; d. Hugh Crocker and Tryphena Grace (Reader) Parsons; 1 child, Nicole D. Salem. BA, Boston U., 1967; JD, Suffolk U., 1970. Bar: Mass. 1970, U.S. Dist. Ct. Mass. 1972, U.S. Supreme Ct. 1979. Atty. Allstate Ins. Co., Weston, Mass., 1970-72; assoc. Haig Der Manuelian, Boston, 1972-80; sr. assoc. real estate dept. Widett, Slater & Goldman, P.C., Boston, 1980-84; real estate atty. Friendly Ice Cream Corp., Wilbraham, Mass., 1984-87; asst. gen. counsel Hardee's Food Systems, Inc., Rocky Mount, N.C., 1987-90, dep. gen. counsel, 1990—. Mem. ABA, Mass. Bar Assn., Mass. Assn. Women Lawyers, Mass. Conveyancers Assn. Home: 724 Eagles Terr Rocky Mount NC 27804 Office: Hardees Food Systems Inc 1233 Hardees Blvd Rocky Mount NC 27802-1619

PARSONT, MINA RAINÈS-LAMBÉ, language teacher; b. Paris, France, Apr. 11, 1935; came to U.S., Jan. 1950; d. Léon and Anna (Lentzner) Rainès-Lambé; m. Michael Allen Parsont, July 4, 1959; children: Marc Sheldon, Todd Jamie. AA, Sacramento City Coll., 1954; BA with honors, U. Calif., Berkeley, 1956; postgrad., La Sorbonne, Paris, 1958; MAT in French, Colo. State U., 1966; postgrad., U. Md., 1975. Cert. secondary tchr., Md., Calif. Tchr. Spanish Sacramento Sr. High Sch., 1956-57; asst. English Ecole de Jeunes Filles, Suresnes, France, 1958; tchr. French Beverly Hills (Calif.) Elem. Sch., 1962-63; teaching asst., instr. Colo. State U., 1963-66; tchr. French, Spanish Montgomery County (Md.) Pub. Schs., 1971—; tchr. adult edn., Albany, Calif. and L.A., 1960-61, Montgomery County, 1972—; tutor French, 1955—. Creator (with others) Let's Talk Cards for fgn. lang. students. Recipient Disting. Fgn. Lang. Educator award, 1989; French Govt. scholar, 1987—. Mem. AAUW (winner scholarship 1955), Am. Assn. French Tchrs., Md. Fgn. Lang. Assn. (past bd. dirs.), Montgomery County Fgn. Lang. Assn., Greater Washington Assn. Fgn. Lang. Tchrs. (Disting. Fgn. Lang. Educator), Le Circle Français of Greater Washington, Na'amat USA. Office: Richard Montgomery High Sch 250 Richard Montgomery Dr Rockville MD 20852

PARTEE, BARBARA HALL, linguist, educator; b. Englewood, N.J., June 23, 1940; d. David B. and Helen M. Hall; m. Morriss Henry Partee, 1966 (div. 1971); children: Morriss M., David M., Joel T.; m. Emmon Werner Bach, Nov. 2, 1973. B.A. with high honors in Math., Swarthmore Coll., 1961; Ph.D. in Linguistics, MIT, 1965; DSc (hon.), Swarthmore Coll., 1989. Asst. prof. UCLA, 1965-69, assoc. prof., 1969-73; assoc. prof. linguistics and philosophy U. Mass., Amherst, 1972-73, prof., 1973—, head dept. Linguistics, 1987—; fellow Ctr. for Advanced Study in Behavior Scis., 1976-77. Author: (with Stockwell and Schachter) The Major Syntactic Structures of English, 1972, Fundamentals of Mathematics for Linguists, 1979; editor: Montague Grammar, 1976; co-editor: (with Chierchia and Turner) Properties, Types and Meaning, Vol. I: Foundational Issues, Vol. II: Semantic Issues, 1989; mem. editoral bd: Language, 1967-73, Linguistic Inquiry, 1972-79, Theoretical Linguistics, 1974—, Linguistics and Philosophy, 1977—. Recipient Chancellor's medal U. Mass., 1977; NEH fellow, 1982-83. Mem. NAS, Linguistic Soc. Am. (pres. 1986), Am. Philos. Assn., Assn. Computational Linguistics, Am. Acad. Arts and Scis., Sigma Xi. Home: 50 Hobart Ln Amherst MA 01002 Office: U Mass Dept Linguistics Amherst MA 01003

PARTHEMORE, JACQUELINE G., physician; b. Harrisburg, Pa., Dec. 21, 1940; d. Philip Mark and Emily (Buvit) Parthemore; m. Alan Morton Blank, Jan. 8, 1967; children: Stephen Eliot, Laura Elise. BA, Wellesley Coll., 1962; MD, Cornell U., 1966. Research edn. assoc., asst. prof. med. Veterans Adminstn. Hosp., San Diego, Calif., 1974-78; asst. prof. Sch. of Medicine U. Calif., San Diego, 1974-80; staff physician Veterans Adminstrn. Med. Ctr., San Diego, La Jolla, 1978-79; assoc. prof. medicine, 1980-85; asst. chief, med. service, staff physician Veterans Adminstrn. Med. Ctr., San Diego, La Jolla, 1979-80; acting chief, med. service Veterans Adminstrn. Med. Ctr., San Diego, 1980-81, chief of staff, 1984—; assoc. dean, prof. medicine Univ. Calif. San Diego Sch. Medicine, 1985—. Contbr. articles to profl. jours. Recipient Bullock's 1st Annaul Portfolio award, 1985, San Diego Pres.'s Council Woman of Yr. award, 1985, Calif. Women in Govt. award, 1985, YWCA Tribute to Women in Industry award, 1987. Mem. Endocrine Soc., Am. Fedn. Clin. Rsch., Am. Soc. Bone and Mineral, Nat. Assn. VA Chiefs of Staff (pres. 1989—). Office: VA Med Ctr 3350 La Jolla Village Dr San Diego CA 92122

PARTIER, SUSAN KALMUS, publicist; b. N.Y.C., Feb. 19, 1947; d. Allan H. and Jane (Wurzburger) Kalmus; m. Donald W. Partier, Sept. 30, 1973; children: Justin Allan, Jordan William. AA, Packer Collegiate Inst., Bklyn., 1967; BA, Finch Coll., N.Y.C., 1969. Publicity assoc. Family Circle Mag., N.Y.C., 1970-72; publicity mgr. New Am. Libr., N.Y.C., 1972-74; publicist Am. Freedom Train, San Francisco, 1975; event coord. Pickle Family Circus, San Francisco, 1977—, Wine Olympics, San Francisco, 1978-80, Oakland (Calif.) Ballet, 1978-80; publicity dir. Network, Inc., Berkeley, Calif., 1983; co-dir. Ropes 'N' Things, San Francisco, 1984-86; publicist, event coord. Caravan Stage Co., San Francisco, 1986; assoc. mgr. telemktg. Am. Conservatory Theatre, San Francisco, 1987-90; calendar editor Parents' Press, Berkeley, 1990—; cons. San Francisco Coun. Parent Participation Nursery Schs., 1982—, bd. dirs., 1984—; pres. Noe Valley Coop. Nursery Sch., 1982-83. Author: booklet, Publicity Handbook, 1988. Fundraiser Mantecca Pumpkin Festival, Xeregos Ballet, San Francisco, 1975. Mem. Media Alliance, No. Calif. Book Publicists Assn. Democrat. Home: 584 29th St San Francisco CA 94131

PARTON, DOLLY REBECCA, singer, composer, actress; b. Sevier County, Tenn., Jan. 19, 1946; d. Robert Lee and Avie Lee (Owens) P.; m. Carl Dean, May 30, 1966. Country music singer, rec. artist, composer, actress, radio and TV personality, star ABC-TV series Dolly, 1987; owner theme park Dollywood, established 1985. Radio appearances include Grand Ole Opry, WSM Radio, Nashville, Cass Walker program, Knoxville; TV appearances include Porter Wagoner Show, from 1967, Cass Walker program, Bill Anderson Show, Wilburn Bros. Show, Barbara Mandrell Show; rec. artist, Mercury, Monument, RCA , CBS record cos.; star movie Nine to Five, 1980, The Best Little Whorehouse in Texas, 1982, Rhinestone, 1984, Steel Magnolias, 1989; albums include Here You Come Again (Grammy award 1978), Real Love, 1985, Just the Way I Am, 1986, Portrait, 1986, Think About Love, 1986, Trio (with Emmylou Harris, Linda Ronstadt) (Grammy award 1988), 1987, Heartbreaker, Great Balls of Fire, Rainbow, 1988, White Limozeen, 1989; composer numerous songs including Nine to Five (Grammy award 1981, Acad. award nominee and Golden Globe award nominee 1981). Recipient (with Porter Wagoner) Vocal Group of Yr. award, 1968; Vocal Duo of Yr. award All Country Music Assn., 1970, 71; Nashville Metronome award, 1979; Am. Music award for best duo performance (with Kenny Rogers), 1984; named Female Vocalist of Yr., 1975, 76; Country Star of Yr., Sullivan Prodns., 1977; Entertainer of Yr., Country Music Assn., 1978; People's Choice award, 1980, 88; Female Vocalist of Yr., Acad. Country Music, 1980; Dolly Parton Day proclaimed, Sevier County, Tenn., designated Oct. 7, 1967, Los Angeles, Sept. 20, 1979; recipient Grammy awards for best female country vocalist, 1978, 81, for best country song, 1981, for best country vocal performance with group, 1987; co-recipient (with Emmylou Harris and Linda Ronstadt) Acad. Country Music award for album of the yr., 1987; named to Small Town of Am. Hall of Fame, 1988, East Tenn. Hall of Fame, 1988. Address: care Creative Artists Agy Inc 1888 Century Pk E Ste 1400 Los Angeles CA 90067*

PARTRIDGE, CONNIE R., advertising agency executive; b. Bklyn., Apr. 10, 1941; d. Nicholas and Teresa (Monteleone) Sorrentino; m. Vincent Richard Partridge, Dec. 17, 1960 (div. Aug. 1983); children: Jean Marie, Marianne, James. Student, Coll. New Rochelle (N.Y.), 1958-60; BA, Coll. Old Westbury, 1979. Sr. account exec. Finesse Promotions, Queens Village, N.Y., 1979-84; pres. Partridge Promotions, Wheatley Heights, N.Y., 1984—. Pres. Taukomas Sch. PTA, Wheatley Heights, N.Y., 1972-74; v.p. Half Hollow Hills Coun., Dix Hills, N.Y., 1974-76; campaign mgr. Half Hollow Hills Sch. Bd. Elections, 1978. Recipient Jenkins Meml. award N.Y. State PTA, 1974. Mem. Nat. Assn. Female Execs., Nat. Assn. Women Bus. Owners (L.I. chpt. founder 1985, corr. sec. 1986, v.p. 1989—), L.I. Ctr. Bus. and Profl. Women, Splty. Advt. Assn. Internat., Splty. Advt. Assn. Greater N.Y. Democrat. Roman Catholic. Office: 55 Waterford Dr Wheatley Heights NY 11798

PARTRIDGE, KATIE ANN, accountant; b. Wichita, Kans., June 26, 1958; d. William Baird and Joan (O'Rourke) P. BBA, Wichita State U., 1983. CPA, Kans. Bookkeeper Horton's Furniture, Inc., Wichita, 1979-84; acct. Bank IV Wichita, NA, 1984-89; contr. Stevens Enterprises, Inc., Wichita, 1989—. Vol., Kans. Spl. Olympics, Wichita, 1988—; mem. Children's Mus. Wichita, bd. dirs., 1989—. Named Outstanding Coach, Kans. Spl. Olympics, 1988; selected for Leadership 2000 program, 1990. Mem. Delta Gamma (pres. 1989—, Anchor Bright award 1990). Republican. Presbyterian. Home: 3444 E Douglas Apt 3 Wichita KS 67208 Office: Stevens Enterprises Inc 1130 Haskell Wichita KS 67213

PASAKARNIS, PAMELA ANN, worldwide diagnostics company executive; b. Pittsfield, Mass., May 11, 1949; d. Richard W. and Regina (Piskorski) Turner; m. Donald L. Pasakarnis, May 25, 1974; children: Seth M., Casey L. BA, Northeastern U., 1972; M.T., New Eng. Deaconess Hosp., Boston, 1973. Staff med. technologist New Eng. Deaconess Hosp., 1972-75, supr. clin. chemistry, 1975-77; tech. product supr. Corning Med. Co., Medfield, Mass., 1977-83, product mgr. clin. instrumentation, 1983-85; mgr. mktg. communications CIBA Corning Diagnostics Corp., Medfield, 1985-88, mgr. mktg. ops., 1988—. Mem. Am. Assn. Clin. Chemists, Clin. Lab. Mgrs. Assn., Biomed. Mktg. Assn., Am. Mgmt. Assn. Republican. Avocations: winemaking; fashion design; interior decorating; needlework. Home: 3 Partridge Ln Walpole MA 02081

PASAROW, REINEE ELIZABETH, food brokerage company owner; b. Glendale, Calif., Sept. 30, 1950; d. Homer Armand Beaulieu and Loy Fay (Card) Fender; m. Michael Robert Pasarow, Nov. 30, 1975; 1 child, Torin Michael Wade. BA, U. Calif., 1982. Freelance writer Pvt. Practice, 1982-85; v.p Pasarow Foods, Inc., Monterey Park, Calif., 1986-88; chief ops. officer Velling Pasarow Corbett, Inc., Monterey Park, 1986—. Contbg. author: Heading Towards Omega, 1987, The Human Animal, 1986; author numerous poems. Dir. Valley Interfaith Council, Chatsworth, Calif., 1984-86, Baha'i Rep. Interreligious Council So. Calif., Los Angeles, 1984-90, v.p. 1990; mktg. advisor Multiple Sclerosis Soc. of So. Calif., 1990. Baha'i. Office: Velling Pasarow Corbett Inc 9 Cupania Cir Monterey Park CA 91754

PASCHALL, PAMELA GENELLE, financial executive; b. Pasadena, Calif., June 18, 1949; d. James Edward and Mary Anita (Butler) P. BS, U. So. Calif., 1976; MBA, U. Conn., 1988. Asst. dir. fiscal services Pasadena (Calif.) Unified Sch. Dist., 1972-78; staff acct. George C. Troutman, C.P.A., Louisville, 1978-80; sr. staff acct. Celanese Water Soluble Polymers Co., Louisville, 1980-82; supr. gen. acctg. Celanese Splty. Resins. Co., 1983; mgr. fin. analysis Celanese Internat. Co., N.Y.C., 1984-86, Celanese Splty. Ops., 1986-87; mgr. acctg., ins. and credit Hoechst Celanese Corp., 1987-88, mgr. adminstrn., 1988-89, contr. Pampa (Tex.) plant, 1990—. Mem. AICPA, Ky. Soc. CPAs, Nat. Acctg. Assn. Home: PO Box 1501 Pampa TX 79066

PASCHYN, LISA JASEWYTSCH, financial executive; b. Cleve., Aug. 10, 1954; d. Walter and Joan (Halchak) J.; m. Oleh Roman Paschyn; children: Larissa I., Christina M. Student, Cleve. Inst. Music, 1975; BA, Cleve. State U., 1976. Cons. Dunn & Bradstreet, Cleve., 1975-80; statis. mgr. IRS, Cleve., 1980; mgr. Navy Fed. Credit Union, Cleve., 1980—. Dir. (album) MRIA..., 1977; author credit union tng. manual, 1984. Mem. Nat. Banking Inst., Internat. Credit Assn. NE Ohio, Ohio Credit Union League. Office: Navy Fed Credit Union 1240 E 9th St Cleveland OH 44199

PASCIUTI, MICHELE MAURA, microbiologist; b. Alexandria, Va., June 29, 1951; d. Richard Anthony and Lena Elvira (Frasca) P. AAS in Med. Tech., SUNY, Farmingdale, 1972; BS in Biology, SUNY, 1975; BS in Gen. Studies, Tex. Christian U., 1977; postgrad., C.W. Post Coll., 1984-86. Registered Med. Technologists. Med. technologists Microbiology and Serology Labs., Huntington (N.Y.) Hosp., 1975-78, Medi-screening Ctr., Syosset (N.Y.) Med. Ctr., 1975-80; sr. med. technologist Analytab Products, Plainview, N.Y., 1978-87; collateral worker, med. technologist Microbiology Lab., St. Johns Hosp., Smithtown, N.Y., 1981-88; microbiologist Good Samaritan Hosp., West Islip, N.Y., 1987—. Author numerous abstracts. Mem. Am. Soc. Microbiology. Roman Catholic. Home: 515 Lombardy Blvd Brightwaters NY 11718

PASCOE, PATRICIA HILL, writer, state legislator; b. Sparta, Wis., June 1, 1935; d. Fred Kirk and Edith (Kilpartrick) H.; m. D. Monte Pascoe, Aug. 3, 1957; children: Sarah, Ted, Will. BA, U. Colo., 1957; MA, U. Denver, 1968, PhD, 1982. Tchr. Sequoia Union High Sch. Dist., Redwood City, Calif. and Hayward (Calif.) Union High Sch. Dist., 1957-60; instr. Met. State Coll., Denver, 1969-75; instr. Denver U., 1975-77, 81, research asst. bur. ednl. research, 1981-82; tchr. Kent Denver Country Day, Englewood, Colo., 1982-84; freelance writer Denver, 1985—; commr. Edn. Commn. of the States, Denver, 1975-82. Contbr. articles to numerous publs. and jours. Pres. East High Sch. PTSA, Denver, 1984-85, Moore Budget Adv. Com., Denver, 1966-72; mem. legis. chair Colo. U. Alumni Bd., Boulder, 1987-89; del. Dem. Nat. Conv., San Francisco, 1984. Mem. Common Cause (bd. dirs. Denver chpt. 1986-88), Soc. Profl. Journalists, Phi Beta Kappa. Presbyterian. Home: 744 Lafayette St Denver CO 80218

PASCUAL, FELICITAS DORIS, fund raiser; b. Manila, Sept. 18, 1952; came to U.S., 1967; d. Florentino Jr. and Victoria (Salva) P.; 1 child, Michael R. Thorpe. Student, Pasadena (Calif.) City Coll., 1972, Fund Raising Sch., San Francisco, 1985. Cert. fund raising exec. Office mgr./specialist L.A. Unified Sch. Dist., 1970-80; dir. resource devel. Hawaii Loa Coll., 1980-85; devel. dir. Law Sch. U. Hawaii, 1980-85; devel. dir./fund raiser Am. Heart Assn., Hawaii, 1988—. Mem. Soroptimist, Nat. Soc. Fund Raising Execs. (bd. dirs. Aloha chpt. 1988—). Roman Catholic. Office: Am Heart Assn/ Hawaii Affil 245 N Kukui St #204 Honolulu HI 96817

PASCUAL, ROSA MONICA, banker; b. Miami, Fla., Oct. 15, 1961; d. Ignacio Dimas and Rosalin F. (De Paz) P. AS in Mktg. Mgmt., Broward Community Coll., Fla., 1982; BS in Profl. Studies, Barry U., 1988. Cert. profl. photographer N.Y. Inst. Photography, 1986. Clk.-typist Landmark Bank, Plantation, Fla., 1980-82, Spanish sec. I, 1982-83, new accounts rep. III, 1983-84, customer svc. rep. III, 1984-86; sr. customer svc. rep. C&S Nat. Bank, Ft. Lauderdale, Fla., 1986-87; ops. mgr. C&S Nat. Bank, Pompano, Fla., 1987; adminstrv. asst. Gold Coast Savs. Bank, Plantation, 1987, br. mgr., 1987-88, br. adminstr., 1988-90, systems and ops. officer, 1990—. Fla. Bankers Assn. scholar, 1982. Mem. Am. Inst. Banking (charter Tallahassee chpt.; ofcl. photographer 1985—, bd. dirs. Davie, Fla. 1986—, asst. mktg. dir. 1986—, edn. com. 1986—), Nat. Assn. Bank Women, Assn. Photographers Internat., Photog. Soc. Am., Plantation C. of C., Smithsonian Inst. Assocs., Nat.Trust for Historic Preservation. Democrat. Roman Catholic. Office: Gold Coast Savs Bank 1801 N Pine Island Rd Plantation FL 33323

PASDA, PATRICIA JEANINE, artist, educator; b. Bethlehem, Pa.; d. Joseph J. and Josephine D. Pasda. BFA, Kutztown State U., 1983; MFA, Syracuse U., 1987. Tchr. art Tempest Studios, Bethlehem, 1982—; freelance artist and illustrator Bethlehem, 1982—; colorist Marvel Comics Group, N.Y.C., 1986—; contbr. art work to Cetacean Soc., Westlands Inst., Nat. Wildlife Fedn., local PBS TV sta., auctions for fund, 1984—; condr. workshops for tchrs. Bethlehem Area Sch. Dist. Co-author, illustrator: The Music of Animals, 1989; one woman shows include Northampton County Area Community Coll., Bethlehem, 1982, The Wetlands Inst., Stone Harbor, N.J., 1982, Tiger's Cove Gallery, Bethlehem, 1988, 89; exhibited in group shows at Kutztown State U., 1982, Tempest Studios, Bethlehem, 1987, 89. Tchr. art Girl Scouts U.S.A., Boy Scouts Am., Bethlehem, 1982—. Recipient 1st place art award Tempest Studios, 1989; Syracuse U. scholar, 1987. Mem. Graphic Artists Guild, Cape May County Art Leage, Cetacean Soc., Assn. Sci. Fiction and Fantasy Art, Cousteau Soc., Am. Watercolor Soc. (assoc.), Ducks Unltd., Bethlehem Music Assn., Allies for Star Trek (contbg. artist, writer). Home: 3940 Dartmouth Dr Bethlehem PA 18017 Office: Tempest Studios 712 Main St Bethlehem PA 18017

PASEK, JUDITH ELEANOR, entomologist; b. Oak Park, Ill., Aug. 28, 1955; d. Albert Thomas and Dawn Eleanor (Smith) P. BS with distinction, U. Mich., 1977; MS, U. Mo., 1980; PhD, U. Nebr., 1987. Biol. technician Forest Svc. U.S. Dept. Agr., Montgomery, Ala., 1980, Ogden, Utah, 1980-82; rsch. entomologist Forest Svc. U.S. Dept. Agr., Lincoln, Nebr., 1982-89; supervisory entomologist Forest Svc. U.S. Dept. Agr., Rapid City, S.D., 1989—; adj. asst. prof. U. Nebr., Lincoln, 1987-89. Contbr. articles to profl. jours. Mem. Entomol. Soc. Am., Entomol. Soc. Can., Internat. Union Forestry Rsch. Orgns., Kans. Entomol. Soc., Mich. Entomol. Soc., Sigma Xi, Gamma Sigma Delta, Xi Sigma Pi. Office: US Dept Agr Forest Svc 501 E St Joe SDSMT Rapid City SD 57701

PASEK, MARY A., systems analyst; b. San Jose, Calif.. Student, San Jose State U., 1983. Computer ops. supr., prodn. control analyst, prodn. control scheduler Signetics, Sunnyvale, Calif.; prodn. control supr. Safeway, Oakland, Calif. Mem. NAFE, Phi Chi Theta (almuni group, program dir. collegiate chpt.). Office: 457 Roland Way Oakland CA 94621

PASEKOFF, MARILYN, actress; b. Pitts., Nov. 7, 1949; d. Sherman and Charlotte Pasekoff. BFA, Boston U.; studied with Theodore Kazanoff, Robert Hobbs, Maxine Klein, Evangeline Machlin, Joseph Gifford, Kenyon Martin, Therman Bailey, David Harris. Plays include: A View from the Bridge, The Rainmaker, After the Fall, (broadway) The Odd Couple, 1985, Godspell, 1975, (pre-broadway) Brain Child, 1974, (Off-broadway) Forbidden Broadway, 1983-84, 90, Showing Off, 1989, Professionally Speaking, 1986, May I'm Doing It Wrong, 1982, (resident) Straight Up With A Twist, 1987, Cole Porter Requests The Pleasure, 1985, Scrambled Feet, 1981, (film) Paul Mazursky's Scenes From A Mall, 1990. Mem. AFTRA, SAG, Actors' Equity Assn.

PASKINS-HURLBURT, ANDREA JEANNE, medical researcher; b. Eng., Apr. 26, 1943; d. Stanley and Jose Marie Betty Paskins; m. Douglas Herendenn Hurlburt, Sept. 7, 1968. BSc, McGill U., Montreal, Que., Can., 1965, MSc, 1970, PhD, 1974. Rsch. assoc. McGill, Montreal, 1974-77, Harvard Med. Sch., Boston, 1977—. Home: 12 Kenilworth St Newton MA 02158 Office: Harvard Med Sch 75 Francis St Boston MA 02115

PASLAWSKY, JEAN MARIE, telecommunications trainer and consultant; b. Pottsville, Pa., Sept. 18, 1957; d. Joseph Anthony and Eleanor Marie (Baddick) P. BA in English, Secondary Edn., Immaculata Coll., 1979. Tchr. English Muhlenberg (Pa.) Sr. High Sch., 1979-80; bus.-credit analyst Dun & Bradstreet, Inc., Phila., 1980-82; regional mgr. promotion, trainer sales dept. Durawood/Sears Kitchen Cabinets, Trevose, Pa., 1982-84; telecom system coord., trainer Standard Telecom, Phila., 1984-86; prin., ind. telecom system coord., trainer Jean M. Paslawsky & Assocs., Willow Grove, Pa., 1986—. Active Cath. Charities Appeal, Phila., 1983—; instr. Confraternity of Christian Doctrine program St. David's Parish, Willow Grove, 1985—; vol. Hatboro YMCA, 1982-83, Montgomery County Spl. Olympics, 1987—. Mem. Am. Soc. for Tng. and Devel., NAFE, Immaculata Coll. Alumnae Assn. (pres. 1983-85, assoc. editor, staff writer newspaper 1984-86, past pres. 1985-87, coord. telecom fund raising telethon 1985-87, alumnae bd. govs. del. 1983—), Alumni Assn. Marian High Sch. (com. mem., exec. bd., v.p.), Alpha Psi Omega, Lambda Iota Tau. Home and Office: 8 Knock-N-Knoll Circle Willow Grove PA 19090

PASQUALE, JOANNE EILEEN, gymnastics resource teacher; b. Monessen, Pa., July 2, 1940; d. Baldo Frank and Eileen Joanne (Von Bergen) Giannini; m. James Pasquale, Jan. 6, 1962 (div. 1981); children: Kimberly, Regina, Jami René. BS, Slippery Rock State Coll., 1962; MS, Northwestern State U., Natchitoches, La., 1963. Cert. tchr., Calif. Tchr. Anaheim (Calif.) Union High Sch. Dist., 1963-64; tchr. phys. edn. Westminster (Calif.) Sch. Dist., 1964-66; tchr. Sonora High Sch.-Fullerton (Calif.) Union High Sch. Dist., 1966-89; resource tchr. Colvis (Calif.) Unified Sch. Dist., 1989—; dir. Clovis Acad. Gymnastics and Dance, 1989—; judge Fedn. Internat. Gymnastics, Frankfurt, Fed. Republic Germany, 1974—; asst. tech. dir. women's gymnastics 1984 Olympics, L.A. Editor, scriptwriter practice video for gymnastics judges, 1986. Mem. U.S. Gymnastics Fedn. (regional tech. chmn. 1972—, women's tech. com., judge Pan Am. games 1979-83, asst. tech. dir. Pan Am. games 1987, judge 1987 world championships, Rotterdam, Netherlands, Svc. award 1989), Nat. Assn. Women's Gymnastics Judges, Nat. Fedn. State High Sch. Assn. (rules com. 1986, 87, 89). Roman Catholic. Home: 3126 Terry Ave Clovis CA 93612 Office: Clovis Unified Sch Dist 1450 Herndon St Clovis CA 93612

PASQUALE, ROSEMARIE DIANE, county official; b. Mt. Kisco, N.Y., Nov. 20, 1958; d. Rocco Joseph and Catherine Virginia (La Puma) C.; married. Cert. paralegal, Manhattanville Coll., 1979; BA, Pace U., 1980, MA, 1983; cert., Grantsmanship Tng. Ctr., L.A., 1988. Interviewer Nat. Jury Project, N.Y.C., 1979; asst. to assessor Village/Town of Mt. Kisco, 1980-83, asst. ct. clk., 1981-83; assessment records clk. Westchester County Tax Commn., White Plains, N.Y., 1983-84; mgmt. intern intergovtl. rels. County Exec.'s Office Westchester County, White Plains, 1984-85; asst. coord. adminstrv. affairs Exec.'s Office Westchester County, White Plains, 1985-86, exec. asst., dep. county exec. Exec.'s Office, 1986-89, asst. to county exec., 1989—. Vol. United Way, Westchester County, 1983-89, Am. Cancer Soc., Mt. Kisco, 1985, Am. Heart Assn., White Plains, 1985, 86. Civil Svc. Employees Assn. scholar, 1976. Mem. NAFe. Roman Catholic. Home: 24 East Ave Unit #2 Stamford CT 06902 Office: Westchester County Execs 148 Martine Ave 9th Fl White Plains NY 10601

PASQUARIELLO, ANGELA CATHERINE, health care administrator; b. Buffalo, N.Y., June 29, 1955; d. Julius and Maria (Cervera) P. BS in Pharmacy, Albany Coll., 1978; MBA, Union Coll., 1984, postgrad., 1987—. Pharmacist CUS Pharmacy, Inc., Schenectady, N.Y., 1978-85; mgr. A.W. Lawrence, Schenectady, 1985; mgr. prescription drug programs Empire Blue Cross and Blue Shield, Albany, N.Y., 1985-87; mgr.-audit Electronic Data Systems, Albany, 1987—; mem. CUS Pharmacy Adv. Panel, Woonsocket, R.I., 1981-84, N.Y. State Tech. ad hoc Pharmacy Adv. Panel, Albany, N.Y., 1982-86. Mem. Alumni Assn. Albany Coll. Pharmacy (Outstanding Young Alumni 1979, 2d v.p. 1985-86, 1st v.p. 1986-87, bd. dirs. 1987-88). Roman Catholic. Home: 345 Dolan Dr Schenectady NY 12306 Office: Electronic Data Systems 220 Washington Ave Exit Albany NY 12203

PASS, CAROLYN JOAN, dermatologist; b. Balt., May 14, 1941; d. Isidore Earl and Rhea (Koplowitz) P.; B.S., U. Md., 1962, M.D., 1966; m. Richard Malcolm Susel, June 23, 1963; children—Steven, Gary. Rotating intern USPHS Hosp., Balt., 1966-67; med. resident St. Agnes Hosp., Balt., 1967-68; dermatology resident and fellow U. Md. Sch. Medicine Hosps., 1968-71; pvt. practice specializing in dermatology, Balt. and Ellicott City, Md., 1971—; mem. staff James Lawrence Kernan, St. Agnes, South Baltimore Gen.; vol. dermatology clinics U. Md., St. Agnes hosps.; asst. clin. prof. dermatology U. Md. Sch. Medicine, 1978—; mem. exec. com. adv. bd. Nat. Program in Dermatology, 1975. Diplomate Am. Bd. Dermatology. Mem. AMA, Med. and Chirurgical Faculty Md., Balt. City Med. Soc. (del. 1974), Am. Women's Med. Assn., Am. Acad. Dermatology (award exhibit 1970), Soc. Investigative Dermatology, Md. Dermatology Soc. (sec.-treas. 1974-76, pres. 1976-77), Soc. Contemporary Medicine and Surgery, U. Md. Sch. Medicine Alumnae Assn. (bd. dirs. 1987—). Jewish. Clubs: Suburban Country (Balt.); Country Garden. Gourmet. Home: Timberlane 8410 Park Hts Ave Pikesville MD 21208 Office: Pine Heights Med Ctr Ste 301 1001 Pine Heights Ave Baltimore MD 21229

PASS, GAIL BERNICE, novelist; b. Toledo, Ohio, June 15, 1940; d. Arthur Ralph and Helen (Miller) P. Student, Smith Coll., Northampton, Mass., 1958-60; BA in Psychology with honors, U. Calif., Berkeley, 1962. Freelance writer Toledo, 1985-86, 90—; corp. communicator Trustcorp, Inc., Toledo, 1986-90. Author novels: Zoe's Book, 1976, Surviving Sisters, 1981; author TV documentary 19th Century Public Art, 1985. Mem. Women in Communications, Inc. Democrat. Jewish.

PASSEGGIO, NICOLE PHENICE, sales executive; b. N.Y., July 28, 1963; d. John Carl and Camille Dolores (Canzano) P. BA, Mt. Holyoke Coll., 1984. Sales rep. Lindenmeyr Paper Co., Long Island City, N.Y., 1984--. Religion tchr. Ch. of the Heavenly Rest, N.Y., 1985—, mem. newcomer com., participant women's class, 1988—. Mem. Women in Prodn., Mt. Holyoke Club, Canterbury Choral Soc. Episcopalian. Office: Lindenmeyr Paper Co 53-01 11th St Long Island City NY 11101

PASS KESLER, DELORES MERCER, business executive; b. Jacksonville, Fla., Sept. 20, 1940; d. S. Sherman and Margaret (Mixon) Mercer; children—Mark Gregory, Deborah Suzanne; m. Morton Kesler, 1988. Student Jacksonville U., 1961-63. Sec., A&P Co., Jacksonville, 1958-60; adminstrv. asst. Internat. Harvester, Inc., Jacksonville, 1961-69; gen. mgr. Underhill Agy., Inc., Jacksonville, 1969-77; pres. Conval-Aide Med. Staffing, Inc., 1977—, Associated Temp. Staffing, Inc. (name now ATS Svcs.), Jacksonville, 1978—, ; mem. Nat. Assn. Temp. Services (bd. dirs.), Jacksonville C. of C. (v.p. 1985, treas. 1986), Salvation Army (bd. dirs.), Com. of 200, Jacksonville Women's Network, UNF Found. (bd. dirs), United Way (bd. dirs.); recipient Eve award Fla. Pub. Co., Jacksonville, 1983, Top Mgmt. award Sales and Mktg. Execs. Jacksonville. Mem. N.E. Fla. Assn. Women Bus. Owners. Democrat. Methodist. Office: ATS Svcs Inc 3850 Beach Blvd Jacksonville FL 32207

PASTEN, LAURA JEAN, veterinarian; b. Tacoma, May 25, 1949; d. Frank Larry and Jean Mary (Slavich) Brajkovich; student Stanford U., 1970; BA in Physiology, U. Calif., Davis, 1970, DVM (regents scholar), 1974; postgrad. Cornell U., 1975. Veterinarian, Nevada County Vet. Hosp., Grass Valley Calif., 1975-80; pvt. practice vet. medicine, owner Mother Lode Vet. Hosp., Grass Valley, 1980—; affiliate staff Sierra Nevada Meml. Hosp.; lectr. in field. Bd. dirs. Sierra Svcs. for Blind. Mem. AVMA, Calif. Vet. Med. Assn. (exec. com., del.), Mother Lode Vet. Assn., Am. Animal Hosp. Assn. (Mother Lode Vet. Hosp. cited for excellence), Nat. Ophthal. Soc., Nat. Pygmy Goat Assn., Internat. Assn. for Arabians., Nat. Assn. Underwater Instrs., Denver Area Med. Soc., Internat. Vet. Assn. Am., Endurance Riding Soc. Republican. Lutheran. Club: Grass Valley Bus. Women. Author: (with Dr. Muller) Canine Dermatology, 1970; contbr. articles to profl. jours. Home: 15978 Shebley Rd Grass Valley CA 95945 Office: 11509 La Barr Meadows Rd Grass Valley CA 95949

PASTERNAK, KATHRYN ANN, filmmaker; b. Edmonton, Alta., Canada, Aug. 21, 1961; d. William Paul and Barbara Ellen (Wright) P. AB magna cum laude, Harvard U., 1985; cert., Sorbonne U., Paris, 1984. Post-prodn. coord. Leitmotif Films, N.Y.C., 1989, Apollo Assocs., N.Y.C., 1989; assoc. producer Visible Pictures, N.Y.C., 1989; asst. to agt. Creative Artists Agy., L.A., 1989-90; researcher, assoc. producer Nat. Geog. Soc. TV, L.A., 1990—. Worked on films including Rock on a Red Horse, 1988, Vienna is Different, 1989, For All Mankind, 1989, Terezin Diary, 1989, The Soul of Spain, 1990. Recipient Pulitzer Rsch. award Harvard U., 1984; grantee Robert Flaherty Film Seminar, 1989. Fellow Royal Soc. for Encouragement of Arts, Mfrs. and Commerce; mem. Internat. Documentary Assn., Ind. Feature Project West, Women in Film, Phi Beta Kappa. Home: 240 N Van Ness St Los Angeles CA 90004

PASTERSKI, DARIAN CHAG, systems analyst; b. Oakland, Calif., Mar. 23, 1955; d. Stephen S. and Mary Louise (Pacific) Chag; m. Walter Paul Pasterski III, Aug. 28, 1982; stepchildren: Walter Paul IV, Vickie Lynn. Student, U. So. Calif., 1973-77, Pierce Coll., L.A., 1977—; cert., UCLA, 1985. Med. asst., office mgr. A.E. Solomon, M.D., Inc., Beverly Hills, Calif., 1977-83; project coord. distbn. svcs. Mattel, Inc., Hawthorne, Calif., 1983-85, distbn. analyst, 1985, systems analyst info. resources, 1986, sr. systems analyst info. resources, 1987, specialist systems analyst info. resources, 1988-89, mem. tech. staff, 1989-90, PC application systems supr., 1990—. Mem. Telemktg. User Group, Assn. for Exec. Females. Republican. Roman Catholic. Office: Mattel Inc 5150 Rosecrans Ave Hawthorne CA 90250

PASTINE, MAUREEN DIANE, university librarian; b. Hays, Kans., Nov. 21, 1944; d. Gerhard Walter and Ada Marie (Hillman) Hillman; m. Jerry Joel Pastine, Feb. 5, 1966. AB, in English, Ft. Hays State U., 1967; MLS, Emporia State U., 1970. Reference librarian U. Nebr.-Omaha, 1971-77; undergrad. libr. U. Ill., Urbana, 1977-79; reference librarian, 1979-80; univ. libr. San Jose State U.-Calif., 1980-85; dir. librs. Wash. State U., Pullman, 1985-89, dir. cen. univ. librs. So. Meth. U., 1989—; mem. adv. bd. Foothill Coll. Libr. 1983-85; led ednl. del. librs. to People's Republic of China, 1985, Australia/New Zealand, 1986, Soviet Union, 1988. Co-author: Library and Library Related Publications: A Directory of Publishing Opportunities, 1973; asst. compiler: Women's Work and Women's Studies, 1973-74, 1975; compiler procs. Teaching Bibliographic Instruction in Graduate Schools of Library Science, 1981; editor: Integrating Library Use Skills into the General Education Curriculum, 1989; contbr. articles to profl. publs. Recipient Disting. ALumni Grad. award Emporia State U., 1986. Mem. ALA (chmn. World Book-ALA Goal awards jury 1984-85), Assn. Coll. and Rsch. Librs. (editorial adv. bd. BIS Think Tank 1982-85, chmn. bibliographic instrn. sect. 1983-84, editorial bd. Choice 1983-85, chmn. Miriam Dudley Bibliographic Instrn. Libr. of Yr. award com. 1984-85, 89, mem. task force on librarians as instrs. 1986—, chair task force internat. rels. 1987-89), Libr. Adminstrn. and Mgmt. Assn. (chmn. stats. sect. com. on devel., orgn., planning and programming 1982-83, sec. stats. sect. exec. com. 1982-83, mem. at large 1986—), ALA Library Instrn. Round Table (long range planning com. 1986—), ALA Libr. Rsch. Round Table, Wash. Libr. Assn., Pacific N.W. Libr. Assn., Phi Kappa Phi, Beta Phi Mu. Home: 8720 Hanford Dr Dallas TX 75243 Office: So Meth U Cen Univ Librs Fondren Libr Dallas TX 75275-0135

PATANELLI, DOLORES JEAN, physiologist; b. Elkhart, Ind., July 20, 1932; d. Michael and Concetta (Robina) P. BA, NYU, 1955, MS, 1958, PhD, 1962. Asst. to med. dir. population coun. Rockefeller U., N.Y.C., 1956-62; rsch. fellow Merck Inst. Therapeutic Rsch., Rahway, N.J., 1963-72; reproductive physiologist Ctr. Population Rsch., Contraceptive Devel. Br. Nat. Inst. Child Health, Bethesda, Md., 1972—; mem. regional health adv. commn. Health, Edn. and Welfare, N.Y.C., 1970-72;membership com. Soc. Study Reproduction, 1973-75, nominating com., 1980-81; mem. organizing com. testes workshop, 1973—. Editor: (book) Hormonal Control of Male Fertility, 1978; inventor (with others) Spiroxenone, 1972. Mem. N.Y. Acad. Scis., Endocrine Soc., Am. Assn. Anatomists, Am. Soc. Andrology, Am. Fertility Soc., Sigma Xi. Office: Nat Inst Child Health Ctr Population Rsch 6130 Executive Blvd Rm 600F Bethesda MD 20892

PATCH, LORRAINE MARIE, investment systems manager; b. Revere, Mass., Feb. 21, 1947; d. William Albert and Mary Rita (Gelardi) P.; B.A. magna cum laude in Mgmt. (Coll. Profl. Studies prize 1978), U. Mass., Boston, 1978; M.B.A., Suffolk U., 1981; Ed.M., Harvard U., 1986, postgrad.; 1 son, Derek Scott Burke. Benefits coord., money market bookkeeper State St. Bank and Trust Co., Boston, 1968-76; freshmen adv. U. Mass., Boston, 1976-77; customer svc. rep. First Nat. Bank Boston, 1977-78; analyst investment systems group TMI Systems Corp. (now SEI Corp.), (now Warrington Corp.), Lexington, Mass., 1980-81, staff cons., sect. mgr., 1981-82, mgr. investment mgmt. dept., 1983-86; tng. coord. Money Mgmt. Systems, Waltham, Mass., 1987-88; free-lance cons., Natick, Mass., 1988—. Mem. search com. for chancellor U. Mass., 1979, Spl. Edn. Adminstrn., Natick; coord. Spl. Edn. Parents Adv. Coun. of Natick; co-chmn. adv. coun. Cen. Mass. Regional Dept. Edn.; mem. Nat. Dropout Prevention Ctr. Network. Mem. Female Execs. Assn., Assn. Data Processing Trainers, Women in Mgmt. Network Assn. (co-founder 1981, treas. 1981-83), U. Mass. Alumni Assn. Suffolk U. Alumni Assn., NOW, Harvard Alumni. Home: 30 Bradford Rd Natick MA 01760

PATCHIS, PAULINE, handwriting expert, consultant; b. Pawtucket, R.I., Apr. 17, 1940; d. Alexander P. Patchis and Rose E. (Acquaviva) Jankowski. Grad., Warwick Police Acad., 1967. Cert. document examiner, R.I., Can. Exec. sec. to personnel dir. Ciba-Geigy Pharm. Co., Cranston, R.I., 1963-65; various ranks, then detective Warwick (R.I.) Police Dept., 1967-71; cons. jury selection, graphoanalyst Patchis and Wayne, Warwick, 1971—; lectr., instr. various orgns., 1971—. Contbr. articles to profl. jours. Mem. Nat. Forensic Ctr., Mass. Police Fraudulent Check Assn., Internat. Graphoanalysis Assn., NAFE, Internat. Graphoanalysis Soc. Inc. Home and Office: 67 S Fair St Warwick RI 02888

PATE, CHRISTINE NELSON, mortgage banker; b. Atlanta, Feb. 18, 1950; d. Julian Cary and Helen Clyde (Taylor) Pate. Student, St. Mary Coll., Raleigh, N.C., 1967-69, U. So. Fla., 1969-71. Loan processor Tampa (Fla.) Savs. & Loan Assn., 1969-73; owner, mgr. C.P. Smith Inc., Orlando, Fla., 1973-77; asst. sec., supr. Suburban Coastal, Tampa, 1979-82; asst. area v.p. Residential Fin. Corp., Tampa, 1982-84; asst. regional v.p. Great So. Mortgage Corp., Tampa, 1984-86; asst. v.p. Citizens and So. Mortgage Corp. Fla., Tampa, 1986—. Pres., v.p. Berkley Sq. Condo Assn., Tampa, 1985—; active Am. Cancer Soc., Tampa; contbr. Tampa Bay Performing Arts Ctr., 1985—. Recipient award Am. Legion, 1967. Mem. Mortgage Bankers Assn., Nat. Assn. Female Execs., Tampa Bd. Realtors, Savs. and Loan League, DAR. Republican. Episcopalian. Office: Citizens and So Mortgage Corp Fla 10050 N Florida Ave Suite 305 Tampa FL 33612

PATE, JACQUELINE HAIL, data processing company executive; b. Amarillo, Tex., Apr. 7, 1930; d. Ewen and Virginia Smith (Crosland) Hail; student Southwestern U., Georgetown, Tex., 1947-48; children: Charles (dec.), John Durst, Virginia Pate Edgecomb, Christopher. Exec. sec. Western Gear Corp., Houston, 1974-76; adminstr., treas., dir. Aberrant Behavior Ctr., Personality Profiles, Inc., Corp. Procedures, Inc., Dallas, 1976-79; dist. adminstrn. mgr. Digital Equipment Corp., Dallas, 1979—. Active PTA, Dallas, 1958-73. Mem. Internat. Assn. Facility Mgrs., Daus. Republic Tex. Methodist. Home: 1802 Lakecrest Ct Carrollton TX 75006 Office: Digital Equipment Corp 14131 Midway Rd Ste 800 Dallas TX 75244-3608

PATE, JOAN SEITZ, federal judge; b. Islip, N.Y.; d. Anthony and Frances Kowalski; m. Raymond Seitz (div.); children: Laura, Cherryl; m. Howard M. Pate, Dec. 9, 1961; stepchildren: Patricia, Barbara, Marsha, Peggy. BA, Ariz. State U.; JD, U. Ariz., 1974. Bar: Ariz. 1974, D.C. 1976, Ky. 1978; CPA, Ariz., Ky. Pvt. practice acctg. Phoenix, 1956-69; trial atty. U.S. Dept. Justice, Washington, 1974-78; ptnr. Goldberg & Simpson, Attys., Louisville, 1978-83; spl. trial judge U.S. Tax Ct., Washington, 1983—. Contbr. articles to profl. jours. Mem. ABA, Fed. Bar Assn. (bd. dirs. 1983-87), Ky. Bar Assn., Ariz. Bar Assn., D.C. Bar Assn., Order of Coif. Office: US Tax Ct 400 2d St NW Washington DC 20217

PATE, SHARON SHAMBURGER, educator; b. Kenosha, Wis., Mar. 30, 1957; d. Thomas Benjamin and Ruth (Penny) Shamburger; m. Johnny Lee Pate, July 23, 1976. BS, Miss. U. Women, 1975; MEd, Miss. State U., 1980. Cert. tchr., Fla. Mgr. Cato Dept. Stores, West Point, Miss., 1975-76; area mgr. Wal-Mart Stores, West Point, 1976; tchr. home econs. South Sumter High Sch., Bushnell, Fla., 1977-78; instr. community edn. Riverdale (Fla.) High Sch., 1982-84; substitute tchr., asst. to dean North Ft. Myers (Fla.) High Sch., 1982-84, tchr. home econs., 1978-80, 84—, instr. community edn., 1980-81, 84—; mgmt. trainee, J.C. Penney Co., Ft. Myers, 1980-81; sponsor, Future Homemakers Am., Cypress Lake High Sch., Ft. Myers, 1984—. Mem. Fla. Vocat. Assn., Lee County Vocat. Assn. Republican. Pentecostal. Home: 1324 SE 15th Pl Cape Coral FL 33910 Office: Cypress Lake High Sch 6950 Panther Ln Fort Myers FL 33910

PATEE, SUSAN, nurse; b. Toledo, June 23, 1944; d. Robert Osborn and Geraldine Marie Dickson; m. Eugene Oliver Patee, Aug. 26, 1967. Student, Toccoa Falls Bible Coll.; RN, Ga. Bapt. Hosp. Sch. Nursing, 1967. Charge nurse Luth. Hosp., Ft. Wayne, Ind.; charge nurse pediatrics Community Hosps. of Williams County, Bryan, Ohio; asst. dir. nursing Parkview Nursing Ctr., Edgerton, Ohio; nurse supr. Sacred Heart Home, Avilla, Ind. Mem. NAFE, Am. Family Assn., Concerned Women for Am. Baptist. Office: Sacred Heart Home 515 N Main St Avilla IN

PATEL, MARILYN HALL, federal judge; b. Amsterdam, N.Y., Sept. 2, 1938; d. Lloyd Manning and Nina J. (Thorpe) Hall; m. Magan C. Patel, Sept. 2, 1966; children: Brian, Gian. B.A., Wheaton Coll., 1959; J.D., Fordham U., 1963. Mng. atty. Benson & Morris, N.Y.C., 1963-65; sole practice N.Y.C., 1965-67, San Francisco, 1971-76; atty. Dept. Justice, San Francisco, 1967-71; judge Alameda County Mcpl. Ct., Oakland, Calif., 1976-80, U.S. Dist. Ct. (no. dist.) Calif., San Francisco, 1980—; adj. prof. law Hastings Coll. of Law, San Francisco, 1974-76. Author: Immigration and Nationality Law, 1974; also numerous articles. Mem. bd. of visitors Fordham U. Sch. of Law. Mem. ABA (litigation sect., jud. adminstrn. sect.), ACLU (former bd. dirs.), NOW (former bd. dirs.), Am. Law Inst., Am. Judicature Soc. (bd. dirs.), Calif. Conf. Judges, Nat. Assn. Women Judges (founding mem.), Internat. Inst. (bd. dirs.), Advs. for Women (co-founder). Democrat. Office: US Dist Ct 450 Golden Gate Ave PO Box 36060 San Francisco CA 94102*

PATERSON, LIN RICHTER, publisher, medical writer; b. Paterson, N.J., Apr. 15, 1936; d. Meyer and Evelyn (Letz) Notkin; m. Howard S. Richter, Dec. 27, 1955; children: Michael, Ronni; m. 2d Walter David Paterson, Aug. 26, 1982. B.A., Bryn Mawr Coll., 1957. Copy editor W.B. Saunders Co., Phila., 1957-58; free-lance med. editor Boston, 1958-65; med. editor Lahey Clinic Found., Boston, 1965-68; editor med. div. Little, Brown & Co., Boston, 1968-79, med. editor in chief, 1979-83; v.p., gen. mgr. book div. Appleton-Century-Crofts, East Norwalk, Conn., 1983-84; pres. Appleton & Lange (formerly Appleton-Century-Crofts), East Norwalk, Conn., 1984-89; pub. Scovill Paterson Inc., Norwalk, Conn., 1990—. Author: (with Fred Belliveau) Understanding Human Sexual Inadequacy, 1970. Democrat. Jewish. Office: Scovill Paterson Inc 28 Knight St Norwalk CT 06851

PATERSON, LINDA, farmer; b. Tacoma, July 8, 1951; d. Walter Meadow and Helen Irene (Price) P. Student, Everett (Wash.) Bus. Sch., 1970. Owner Paterson's Lazy Acre Tree Farm, Arlington, Wash., 1969—; travel assistance Auto Club of Wash., Everett, 1970-73; with Snohomish Health Dist., Everett, 1973-76, Snohomish County Assessor's Office, Everett, 1976-81. Mem. Puget Sound Christmas Tree Assn. Methodist. Home: 1315-188th St NE Arlington WA 98223

PATERSON, SHEILA, advertising agency executive; b. N.Y.C., Oct. 10, 1940; d. John and Sarah Agnes (Duncan) P. AB, Syracuse U., 1962; MBA, Pace U., 1975. Market research interviewer Procter and Gamble, Cin., 1962-63; media asst. to media supr. Dancer Fitzgerald Sample, N.Y.C., 1964-68; media planner to assoc media dir. Ted Bates (now Backer Spielvogel Bates, Inc.), N.Y.C., 1968-73, v.p., media dir., 1973-75, v.p., acct. exec., 1975-76, v.p., account supr., 1976; sr. v.p., exec. v.p. Backer Spielvogel Bates, Inc., N.Y.C., from 1976. Office: Backer Spielvogel Bates Inc 405 Lexington Ave New York NY 10174*

PATMORE, GERALDINE MARY (BOBBE PATMORE), real estate developer; b. Vancouver, B.C., Can.; came to U.S., 1968; d. Oscar Andrew and Geraldine Mary (Whalen) Jorgenson; m. Alan Max Patmore; children: Alan Barry, Paul Richard (dec.), Rosemary Anne Marta. Student, U B.C., Vancouver, Marylhurst Coll. Realtor George Beebe Co., Palm Springs, Calif., 1971-75; v.p. realtor Frank Bogert Co., Palm Springs, Calif., 1975-77; realtor West World Properties, Palm Springs, Calif., 1978-87; dir. sales Golden Mile Investment Co., Palm Springs, Calif., 1987—; pres. Patmore Assocs. Real Estate Investments, Palm Springs, 1989—. Charter mem. Child Help-USA (bd. dirs., desert chpt. 1976-80), Palm Springs; v.p. Humane Soc. Desert, Palm Springs, 1984-86; bd. dirs. SPCA-Animal Samaritans, Palm Springs, 1986—. Named Liaison Officer for work on sister city program between U.S. and Can. City of Palm Springs, 1973—. Mem. Palm Springs C. of C. (charter mem. sister city program 1972—), Nat. Bd. of Realtors (mem. Palm Springs Bd. Realtors 1972—), Internat. Council Shopping Ctrs. Roman Catholic. Clubs: Racquet (Palm Springs,Calif.), Vancouver Lawn Tennis and Badminton (B.C.). Home: 1466 Plato Circle Palm Springs CA 92264 Office: Golden Mile Investment Co 559 S Canyon Dr Ste B 212 Palm Springs CA 92264

PATON, MARY MARGARET, business executive; b. St. Louis, Feb. 18, 1918; d. William L. and Margaret (Brown) Paton; student pub. schs. Clk. typist Dun & Bradstreet, St. Louis, 1935-36; clk. typist, sec. Wm. A. Straub, Inc., Clayton, Mo., 1936-44, sec. to pres., 1947-53, corp. sec., 1950—, buyer, 1963—, supr. restaurant ops., 1953-72; with U.S. Civil Service, Army Air Base, Tonopah, Nev., 1944-46; sec. Parkside Realty Co., Clayton, 1950—; pres. Pro-Mir Garments, Ltd., St. Louis, 1971—. Presbyterian. Home: 8845 Burton Ave Saint Louis MO 63114 Office: 8282 Forsyth Blvd Clayton MO 63105

PATRICK, ANGELA ARLENE, lawyer, consultant; b. East Chicago, Ind., July 9, 1957; d. Arlie and Dorotha N. (Perry) P.; m. H. Douglas Nickels, Apr. 21, 1986; 1 child, Caitlin Michelle. BA in Govt. and Speech, Morehead (Ky.) State U., 1979; JD, U. Ky., 1982. Bar: Ky. 1982. With indsl. rsch. dept. Ky. Devel. Fin. Authority, Frankfort, 1979; real estate legal researcher Ky. Real Estate Rsch. Ctr., Lexington, 1979-82; assoc. White, Peck & Carrington, Mt. Sterling, Ky., 1982-83; pvt. practice Mt. Sterling, 1983—; legal cons. Humane Soc., Mt. Sterling, 1987—; chmn. Main St. Commn., Mt. Sterling, 1989—; adj. prof. real estate Morehead State U., 1985-88. Contbr. articles to profl. jours. Atty. City of Camargo, Ky., 1988. Mem. Ky. Bar Assn., Montgomery County Bar Assn., Mt. Sterling C. of C. Democrat. Home: 112 Elm Mount Sterling KY 40353 Office: Exchange Bank Bldg Ste 400 Mount Sterling KY 40353

PATRICK, DEBRA A., accountant; b. Manchester, N.H., Oct. 13, 1965; d. Norman Leo and Elise Lillian (Gagne) P. BS in Acctg., N.H. Coll., 1987. Acctg. trainee Va. Med. Ctr., Manchester; def. auditor Def. Contract Audit Agy., Lynn, Mass.; sr. acct. Philip E. Gleason, Bedford, N.H. Mem. NAFE, N.H. Soc. CPAs. Address: 3207C Arrowhead Cir Fairfax VA 22030 Office: Raffa & Assocs 1015 18th St NW Washington DC 20036

PATRICK, EDIE, small business owner; b. Winslow, Ariz., Feb. 10, 1935; d. Howard and Theda (Appling) Perkins; 1 child, Bill W. Metzger. Student, Phoenix Coll., Prinston Ill. Sch. Deep Muscle Therapy, 1970, Inst. Hypnosis, 1980, Ariz. Coll. of Electrolysis, 1982, Permaderm Acad. Permanent Make-up Implantation, 1987, Inst. of Skin Care, N.Y.C., 1979, Mesa Sch. Natural Healing, 1976. Therapist YWCA, Phoenix; client rep. Ariz. Creditors Bur., Phoenix; mgr. Cen. Creditors Assn., Flagstaff, Ariz.; pvt. practice electrolysis, skin care, hypnosis, body therapy Phoenix; med. records libr. Winslow (Ariz.) Meml. Hosp., 1955; with Beckwith & Lewis, MDs, Winslow, 1959; owner, operator Dance Sch., Winslow, 1962; credit mgr. Ariz. Gas Co., 1972. Author numerous songs. Mem. NAFE, Nat. Cosmetologists Assn., Ariz.

Assn. Profl. Hypnotherapist, Soc. for Med. Clin. Electrologists, Nat. Guild of Electrologists, The People Med. Soc., Nat. Health Fedn., Internat. Fund. for Animal Welfare, Astrology and Psychic Soc. Republican. Address: 3431 W Thunderbird Rd #13-404 Phoenix AZ 85023

PATRICK, GAIL DENISE, lawyer; b. Columbus, Ohio, July 24, 1954; d. David Bruce and Florence Marie (Ramsey) Patrick. AB, Wellesley Coll. (Mass.), 1976; JD, Capital U., 1979. Bar: Ohio 1979. Law clk. Franklin County Mcpl. Ct., Columbus, Ohio, 1978-79; tax auditor IRS, Detroit, 1979-80; staff atty. SEOLS, St. Clairsville, Ohio, 1980-82; staff atty. Legal Aid Soc. of Columbus, 1982-86, mng. atty. srs./institutionalized/handicapped unit, 1986—. V.p. Capitol U. Law Sch. Student Govt., Columbus, 1978-79. Nat. Merit Scholar, 1971. Mem. Assn. Trial Lawyers Am., Ohio State Bar Assn., Columbus Bar Assn., ABA, ACLU of Central Ohio (bd. dirs. 1983, 84). Club: Wellesley (Columbus; sec. 1982-84, pres. 1984-86). Home: 1313 Watkins Rd Columbus OH 43207 Office: Legal Aid Soc of Columbus 40 W Gay St Columbus OH 43215

PATRICK, JANE AUSTIN, association executive; b. Memphis, May 27, 1930; d. Wilfred Jack and Evelyn Eudora (Branch) Austin; m. William Thomas Spencer, Sept. 11, 1952 (div. Apr. 1970); children: Anthony Duke, Tonilee Candice Spencer Hughes; m. George Milton Patrick, Oct. 1, 1971. Student Memphis State U., 1946-47; BSBA, Ohio State U., 1979. Service rep. So. Bell Tel. and Tel., Memphis, 1947-52; placement dir. Mgmt. Pers., Memphis, 1965-66; pers. asst. to exec. v.p. E & E Ins. Co., Columbus, Ohio, 1966-69; Ohio exec. dir. Nat. Soc. for Prevention of Blindness, Columbus, 1969-73; regional dir. Ohio and Ky. CARE and MEDICO, Columbus, 1979-87; v.p. Career Execs. of Columbus, 1987—; lectr., cons. in field. Mem. choir 1st Community Ch., Columbus, Ohio State Univ. Hosp.'s Service Bd.; bd. dirs. Columbus Coun. on World Affairs, 1981—, sec., 1983-89, chmn. devel. com.; devel. dir., chmn. pers. com. Ohio Hunger Task Force, 1989—. Recipient commendations Nat. Soc. Prevention Blindness and Cen. Ohio Lions Eye Bank, 1973, Nat. Soc. Fund-Raising Execs., 1984, 85, Plaques for Service award Upper Arlington Pub. Schs., 1986. Mem. Non-Profit Orgn. Mgmt. Inst. (pres.), Nat. Soc. Fund-Raising Execs. (cert., nat. dir.), Pub. Rels. Soc. Am. (cert., membership com. chairperson), Ins. Inst. Am. (cert.), Mensa Internat., Columbus Dental Soc. Aux., Alpha Gamma Delta, Epsilon Sigma Alpha. Home: 2511 Onandaga Dr Columbus OH 43221

PATRICK, JUNE CAROL, psychiatrist; b. Charlotte, Mich., Aug. 29, 1932; d. John and Rachel Irene (Towe) Granstrom; m. Robert Bruce Patrick, Aug. 28, 1955 (dec. Jan. 1981); 1 child, Kathleen Ann. BA, U. Mich., 1954, MA, 1956; DO, Mich. State U., 1978. Diplomate Am. Bd. Psychiatry and Neurology. Staff psychiatrist Milw. County Mental Health Complex, Milw., 1982—; practice medicine specializing in psychiatry Milw. Psychiatric Hosp., Wauwatosa, Wis., 1982—; asst. clin. prof. psychiatry and mental health scis. Med. Coll. of Wis., Milw., 1983—. Mem. NOW, AMA, Am. Psychiat. Assn, Wis. Psychiat. Assn. (women's com. chmn. 1985-86), Am. Osteo. Assn.

PATRICK, PAMELA ANN, education educator; b. Mesquite, Tex., June 10, 1963; d. Gene Everett and Peggy Rose (Tanzy) P. AAS, Eastfield Coll., 1982; BA in English, East Tex. State U., 1987, MS in Edn., 1988. Sales clk. Sears, Mesquite, 1982-84; substitute tchr. various Ind. Sch. Dists., Tex., 1988—. Contbr. articles to profl. jours., 1987-88. Mem. Daus. of the Republic of Tex., DAR, United Daus. of the Condfederacy, Daus. of the Union Veterans of the Civil War, Dallas County Heritage Soc., Dallas Hist. Soc., Green County Hist. Geneal. Soc., Humane Soc. U.S., Phi Delta Kappa, Sigma Tau Delta. Republican. Methodist. Home: 3531 Palm Dr Mesquite TX 75150

PATRICK, SUE FORD, diplomat; b. Union Springs, Ala., Nov. 9, 1946; d. Oscar Ford and Mildred (Hunter) Ford Carter; m. Henderson M. Patrick, Dec. 24, 1973; 1 child, Lauren. BA, Coll. Notre Dame of Md., 1967; post-grad., U. Va., 1967-69, 70-72; MA, Boston U., 1982. Vice-consul Am. Consulate, Udorn, Thailand, 1973-74; desk officer Dept. State, Washington, 1976-78; 2d sec. U.S. Embassy, Nairobi, Kenya, 1978-81; 1st sec. Dept. of State, Washington, 1981-84; spl. asst. refugee programs Dept. State, Washington, 1984-85; 1st sec. polit. affairs U.S. Embassy, Abidjan, Ivory Coast, 1985-88; dep. chief of mission U.S. Embassy, Kigali, Rwanda, 1988—. Mem. Am. Fgn. Svc. Assn. Roman Catholic. Home and Office: Am Embassy Kigali DOS Washington DC 20521-2210 Office: BP28, Kigali Rwanda

PATRICK, THELMA JOYCE, programmer, analyst; b. Sibley, Iowa, May 26, 1935; d. Fredric Joseph and Anna (Klaassen) Abels; m. Arnold Charles DeJong, Mar. 28, 1953 (div. Dec. 1962); children: Steven Ray, Randal Dean, Daniel Gene (dec.), Brenda Sue DeJong McDonald; m. Larry Everet Patrick, Aug. 11, 1967 (div. Dec. 12, 1974; 1 child, Joel Channing. Student in programming, Iowa Tech., 1966; student, U. N.Mex., 1975-77, S.W. State Coll., Marshall, Minn., 1978-79, Metro State U., 1981-82. Clk. typist N.W. Iowa Power Coop., Le Mars, Iowa, 1963-65; programmer, analyst Albuquerque Pub. Sch. Adminstrn., 1967-69; systems analyst Rio Rancho (N.Mex.) Estates, 1969-71; methods analyst Albuquerque Nat. Bank, 1974-75; programmer, analyst Pub. Svc. Co. N.Mex., Albuquerque, 1975-77, Schwan's, Inc., Marshall, Minn., 1977-79; instr. Honeywell, Inc., Bloomington, Minn., 1979-82; cons. GE Info. Svcs., Rockville, Md., 1982-84; programmer, analyst City of Bellevue, Wash., 1984—. Vol. fundraiser Homeless Outreach Christian Adult Singles Together, Seattle, 1987—. Mem. Writer's Network. Republican. Mem. Reformed Ch. Am.

PATRICK MORALES, VITA JO, playwright, translator; b. New Brunswick, N.J., July 21, 1953; d. Charles Joseph and Mary (Coppola) Patrick; m. Guillermo Morales, Oct. 3, 1975; children: Guillermo Alejandro, Valentina Maria, Julian Charles, Maximilian Francis. BA in Italian Lit., Rutgers U., 1975; MA in Theater and Film, CUNY, 1989. Data processor N.Y.C. div. Am. Cancer Soc., 1975-76; freelance writer and translator N.Y.C., 1976-81; freelance legal proofreader and translator Curtis, Mallet-Prevost & Mosle, N.Y.C., 1981—. Author: play In The Name of the Father, 1978, Shared Music, 1979, The Final Tolling of the Bells, 1982, Michael, L.D., 1986, All God's Children, 1987, Mementos, 1987, Francis of Assisi, 1988. Mem. Millstone (N.J.) Hist. Commn., 1971-72; pres. Holy Cross Parents Assn., N.Y.C., 1983—. John Golden Fund grantee, 1987-88. Mem. Puerto Rican Traveling Theater, Profl. Playwrights Unit, Dramatists Guild, Sigma Iota. Democrat. Roman Catholic. Home: 662 10th Ave 4N New York NY 10036

PATRIE, CHERYL CHRISTINE, educator; b. Dobbs Ferry, N.Y., June 8, 1947; d. Edward F. and Antoinette C. (Patrie) P. B.A. in Edn., U. Fla., 1969; M.S. in Edn., U. Miami, 1979. Cert. assoc. master tchr., Fla. Tchr. Marion County Sch. Bd., Ocala, Fla., 1970, Dade County Sch. Bd., Miami, Fla., 1974—; bldg. union steward United Tchrs. Dade, 1979-89; faculty council Lorah Park Elem. Sch., Miami, 1979—, dropout prevention com., 1985, career lab. cons., 1983-85, Human Growth and Devel. cons., 1983—, comprehensive plan com., 1984—, phys. fitness co-chmn., 1984—; coordinator Quality Instrn. Incentives Program, 1984—; mem. Dade County Elem. Sch. Day Task Force, 1987-88. Mem. Crisis in Inner City task force United Tchrs. Dade, Miami, 1984-85. Named Tchr. of Yr., Lorah Park Elem. Sch., 1986. Mem. United Tchrs. Dade. (Disting. Service award 1984). Home: 1127 Robin Ave Miami Springs FL 33166 Office: Lorah Park Elem 5160 NW 31st Ave Miami FL 33142

PATRYN, ELAINE LILLIAN, real estate broker, life and health insurance salesperson; b. Phila., Sept. 14, 1937; d. Frank and Lillian Helen (Genga) Borgioni; divorced; 1 child, Steven James. B.S., Chestnut Hill Coll., 1959; postgrad. in acctg. and bus. law St. Joseph's Coll., Phila., 1960-61, Coll. for Fin. Planning, Denver, 1986. Engring. asst. Gen. Electric Co., Phila., 1959-61, math. technician, Santa Barbara, Calif., 1961-62, Reseda, Calif., 1964-65, King of Prussia, Pa., 1966-67; math. technician Space Tech. Lab., Redondo Beach, Calif., 1962-64; real estate broker Patryn Realty Corp., Ocala, Fla., 1980—; instr. Gold Coast Sch. Real Estate, Ocala, 1983-84. Mem. AAUW (treas. 1980-81), Nat. Assn. Female Execs. (dir. Marion County network 1985-86). Republican. Roman Catholic. Home: 525 Emerald Rd Ocala FL 32672

PATTEN, BEBE REBECCA, college dean, clergyman; b. Berkeley, Calif., Jan. 30, 1950; d. Carl Thomas and Bebe (Harrison) P. BS in Bible, Patten Coll., 1969; BA in Philosophy, Holy Names Coll., 1970; MA in Bibl. Studies New Testament, Wheaton Coll., 1972; PhD in Bibl. Studies New Testament, Drew U., 1976. Dean Patten Coll., Oakland, Calif., 1975—; presenter in field. Author: Before the Times, 1980, The World of the Early Church, 1990; author: (with others) International Standard Biblical Encyclopedia, rev. edit., 1983—. Active Wheaton Coll. Symphony, 1971-72, Drew U. Ensemble, 1971-75, Young Artists Symphony, N.J., 1972-75, Somerset Hill Symphony, N.J., 1973-74, Peninsula Symphony, 1977, 80-81, Madison Chamber Trio, N.J., 1973-75. Named one of Outstanding Young Women of Am., 1976, 77, 80-81, 82. Mem. Am. Acad. Religion, Soc. Bibl. Lit., AAUP, Internat. Biographical Assn..

PATTEN, CYNTHIA MARIE, educator; b. Pt. Gibson, Miss., June 29, 1956; d. Viola (Barber) Reynolds; m. Aaron Sr. Patten (div. 1986); children: Aaron Jr., Sharon Alicia, Travis. BS, Alcorn State U., 1978, MS, 1982. Tchr. Claibome County Sch., Pt. Gibson, 1977—, computer sci. cons., 1985-89. Mem. Miss. Math. Tchrs. Assn., Heroine of Jericho (sec. 1980—). Home: 103 Oriole Terr Natchez MS 39120

PATTEN, ETHEL DOUDINE, hematologist; b. N.Y.C., Feb. 21, 1942; d. Ethel (Campbell) Bruno; m. Bernard M. Patten, June 27, 1964; children: Allegra, Craig. BA, Barnard Coll., 1963; MD, N.J. Coll. Medicine, 1967. Diplomate Am. Bd. Internal Medicine, Am. Bd. Pathology. Intern USPHS Hosp., S.I., N.Y., 1967-68, resident in internal medicine, 1968-70; fellow in hematology NYU Med. Sch., N.Y.C., 1970-71, NIH, Bethesda, Md., 1971-72; fellow in blood banking Am. Nat. Red Cross, Washington, 1972-73; dir. blood bank U. Tex. Med. Br., Galveston, 1974—; assoc. prof. medicine and pathology U. Tex. Med. Br., 1974—. Contbr. sci. papers and abstracts to numerous publs. Sugreon, USPHS, 1967-73. Nat. Heart, Lung and Blood Inst. transfusion medicine grantee, 1985-90. Fellow ACP; mem. South Cen. Assn. Blood Banks (pres. 1981-82), AMA, Am. Assn. Blood Banks. Office: Blood Bank U Tex Med Br 114 McCullough St Galveston TX 77550

PATTERSON, BEVERLEY PAMELA GRACE, accountant; b. London, Feb. 6, 1956; came to U.S., 1975; d. Ernest Charles and Barbara (Wiseman) Patterson; children: Tamara, Russell, Stuart. AAS with honors, Tacoma Community Coll., 1978; BBA with honors, U. Puget Sound, 1980. CPA, Wash. Accounts payable clk. Hillhaven Corp., Tacoma, 1975-76, staff acct., 1980-83, acquisition analyst, 1984-86; contr., chief fin. officer Tacoma Luth. Home and Retirement Community, 1987—; cons. in field, 1984—. Vol. Make a Wish, Tacoma. Mem. AICPA, Tex. Soc. CPAs, Wash. Soc. CPAs, Nat. Assn. Accts., Am. Soc. Women Accts. (chairman, bd. dirs. Tacoma chpt., editorial bd. The Woman CPA mag. 1989—, pres.-elect 1990-91). Home: 4007 31st Ave NW Gig Harbor WA 98335 Office: Tacoma Luth Home & Retirement Community 1301 Highland Pkwy Tacoma WA 98406

PATTERSON, BEVERLY ANN GROSS, social services administrator; b. Pauls Valley, Okla., Aug. 5, 1938; d. Wilburn G. Jack and Mildren E. (Steward) Gross; m. Kenneth Dean Patterson, June 18, 1960 (div. 1976); children: Tracy Dean, Nancy Ann Patterson-McArthur, Beverly Jeanne Patterson-Wertman. AA, Modesto (Calif.) Jr. Coll., 1958; BA in Social Sci., Fresno (Calif.) State U., 1960; postgrad., Coll. Idaho, 1988—. Cert. secondary tchr., Calif., Idaho, lic. real estate agt., Idaho. Secondary tchr. Ceres and Modesto Calif., Payette and Weiser Idaho, Ontario Oreg., 1960-67; dir. vol. svcs. mental retardation and child devel. State of Idaho, 1967-70, cons. dir. vol. svcs. health and welfare, 1970-72; dir. Ret. Sr. Vol. Program, Boise, 1972-74; exec. dir. Idaho Nurses Assn., Boise, 1974-76; community svcs. adminstr. City of Davis, Calif., 1976-78; devel. dir. and fundraising Mercy Med. Ctr., Nampa, Idaho, 1978-85; exec. dir. St. Anphonsus Med. Ctr. Found., Boise, 1985-87; exec. dir. found. devel. and gift planning Idaho Youth Ranch, Boise, 1988—; founder Fellowship Christian Adult Singles, Boise, 1974; cons., exec. dir. Boise Hotline, 1988-90; cons., fundraising dir. Community Resources and Devel., 1990; co-dir., proprietor, ACOA workshop leader Child Within Concepts, Boise, 1987—; cons., coord. Rural Hosp. Edn. Consortium, 1988; cons. hosp. devel. and community resources Gritman Meml. Hosp., Moscow, Idaho, 1987-88; cons. conf. devel. State of Idaho, 1987-88. Coord. Idaho Golf Angels Open Pro-Am Tournament, Boise, 1989—; bd. dirs. Arthritis Found., Idaho, 1984-86, Idaho Mental Health Assn., 1985-87. Named Idaho Statesman, 1985; recipient Disting. Citizen award. Mem. Nat. Assn. for Hosp. Devel. (treas. 1980, accreditation chmn. 1984-86, conf. chmn. 1982, 85, charitable fundraising events coord. 1978—). Mem. Community Christian Ch. Home: 315 W Maple Meridian ID 83642 Office: Idaho Youth Ranch 1416 W Franklin St Boise ID 83702 Other Office: Child Within Concepts 2920 Raindrop Dr Boise ID 83706

PATTERSON, CINDY L., human resources specialist; b. Springfield, Mo., Dec. 8, 1956; d. Lyle A. and Georgia L. (Keeter) Wood. BSE cum laude, Sch. of the Ozarks, Pt. Lookout, Mo., 1983. Asst. pers. dir. Capital-Mercury Shirt Corp., Gassville, Ark., 1983—. Mem. NAFE, LWV, Bus. and Profl. Women (past pres. Mountain Home chpt., Young Careerist 1987), Ark. Fedn. Bus. and Profl. Women (past state membership chair, rec. sec.). Democrat. Baptist. Address: 337 N Walnut St Mountain Home AR 72653

PATTERSON, DAWN MARIE, educator, consultant; b. Gloversville, N.Y., July 30; d. Robert Morris and Dora Margaret (Perham) P.; m. Robert Henry Hollenbeck, Aug. 3, 1958 (div. 1976); children: Adrienne Lyn, Nathaniel Conrad. BS in Edn., SUNY, Geneseo, 1962; MA, Mich. State U., 1973, PhD, 1977; postgrad., U. So. Calif. and Inst. Ednl. Leadership. Librarian Brighton (N.Y.) Cen. Schs., 1962-67; asst. to regional dir. Mich. State U. Ctr., Bloomfield Hills, 1973-74; grad. asst. Mich. State U., East Lansing, 1975-77; cons. Mich. Efficiency Task Force, 1977; asst. dean Coll. Continuing Edn., U. So. Calif., Los Angeles, 1978-84; dean continuing edn. Calif. State U., Los Angeles, 1985—; pres. Co-Pro Assocs. Mem. Air Univ. Bd. Visitors, 1986—, Commn. on Extended Edn. Calif. State U. Calif., 1988—; Hist. Soc., Los Angeles Town Hall, Los Angeles World Affairs Council. Dora Louden scholar, 1958-61; Langworthy fellow, 1961-62; Edn. Professions Devel. fellow, 1974-75; Ednl. Leadership Policy fellow, 1982-83. Mem. AAUW (pres. Pasadena br. 1985-86), Am. Assn. Adult and Continuing Edn. (charter), Nat. Univ. Continuing Edn. Assn., Calif. Coll. and Mil. Educators Assn. (pres.), Los Angeles Airport Area Edn. Industry Assn. (pres. 1984), Kappa Delta Pi, Phi Delta Kappa. Republican. Unitarian. Club: Fine Arts of Pasadena. Lodge: Zonta. Office: 5151 State University Dr Los Angeles CA 90032

PATTERSON, DEBORAH-LEA, teacher; b. San Angelo, Tex., Sept. 29, 1951; d. Douglas Murray and Alice Mildred (Zoeller) Harris; m. Billy Ray Jacoby, June 10, 1972 (div. Jan. 1987); children: Jeffrey Douglas, Jinny Lenore; m. John William Patterson, Aug. 13, 1988. BS in Spanish and French, Angelo State U., 1972, BA in Elem. Edn., 1974, MAT in Elem. and Spl. Edn, 1977. Cert. early childhood, spl. edn. and bilingual tchr., Tex. Tchr. Eden (Tex.) Ind. Sch. Dist., 1972-76, San Angelo Ind. Sch. Dist., 1976-78, Big Spring Jr. Coll. Br., San Angelo, 1978-79, Grand Prairie (Tex.) Ind. Sch. Dist., 1986-89, Duncanville Ind. Sch. Dist., 1989—; cons. Devel. Learning Materials, Allen, Tex., 1989—. Western dance chair San Angelo Jr. League, 1982-86; pub. rels. chair San Angelo Symphony Soc., 1984-86. Mem. Tex. Classroom Tchr.'s Assn., San Angelo C. of C. (river events chair San Angelo chpt. 1983-85), Jr. Women's Club. Republican. Methodist. Home: 315 Meadowlark Duncanville TX 75137 Office: Alexander Elem Sch 510 Softwood Duncanville TX 75137

PATTERSON, ELIZABETH JOHNSTON, congresswoman; b. Columbia, S.C., Nov. 18, 1939; d. Olin DeWitt and Gladys (Atkinson) Johnston; m. Dwight Fleming Patterson, Jr., Apr. 15, 1967; children: Dwight Fleming, Olin DeWitt, Catherine Leigh. B.A., Columbia Coll., 1961; postgrad. in polit. sci., U. S.C., 1961, 62, 64. Pub. affairs officer Peace Corps, Washington, 1962-64; recruiter VISTA, OEO, Washington, 1965-66; state coord. Head Start and VISTA, OEO, Columbia, 1966-67; tri-county dir. Head Start, Piedmont Community Actions, Spartanburg, S.C., 1967-68; adminstrv. asst. Congressman James R. Mann, Spartanburg, S.C., 1969-70; mem. Spartanburg County Council, S.C., 1975-76, S.C. State Senate, S.C., 1979-86, 100th-102nd Congresses from 4th S.C. dist., S.C., 1987—. Trustee, Wofford Coll.; bd. dirs. Charles Lea Center, Spartanburg Council on Aging; pres. Spartanburg Democratic Women, 1968; v.p. Spartanburg County Dem. party, 1968-70, sec., 1970-75. Mem. Bus. and Profl. Women's Club, Alpha Kappa Gamma. Methodist. Office: Longworth Ho Office Bldg Rm 1641 Washington DC 20515 also: PO Box 5564 Spartanburg SC 29304

PATTERSON, FLORENCE GHORAM, real estate broker; b. Savannah, Ga., Mar. 20, 1936; d. Ernest and Ida (Robinson) Ghoram; m. Carl Patterson (div. 1986); children: Chrysetta Patricia, Carl Jr. Student, CCNY. Lic. real estate broker, N.Y. Mgr. Am. Express Credit Card, N.Y.C., 1958-59; asst. v.p. Citicorp, N.Y.C., 1967-84; exec. dir., founder Pamoja Internat. Cultural Exch., Inc., Helena, N.Y., 1982—; v.p. Parent Tchr. Support Group, Ft. Covington, N.Y., 1989—. Committeewoman Dem. Cen. Com., Suffolk County, N.Y., 1984; founder Deer Park (N.Y.) NAACP, 1968; v.p. United Civic Assn. Deer Park, 1982, pres., 1983-84. Recipient Cert. of Merit Universal Son and Daughters of Ethiopia, Inc., 1985, County Legislator, Babylon, N.Y., 1985, Proclamation County Exec., Suffolk County, 1985, Town of Islip, N.Y., 1986. Mem. NAFE, AMA, Nat. Trust for Hist. Presertion, Am. Mus. Natural History (hon. advisor), Am. Biog. Inst. Mem. Spiritual Ch. Home and Office: RR 2 Box 162 Smith Rd Brasher Falls NY 13613

PATTERSON, KATHERINE HULEN, pharmacist; b. Caracas, Venezuela, Dec. 21, 1947; d. Joseph T. and Antoinette (deLarroque) H.; m. Gary Wayne Patterson, May 31, 1969; children—Katherine Denise, Gary Wayne. B.F.A., U. Miss., 1969; B.S., U. Houston, 1980. Pharmacist, mgr. Superex Drugs, Houston, 1980-81, Walgreen Drugs, Houston, 1981-84, Gordon Drugs, Houston, 1984—. Mem. Spring Branch PTA, Houston, 1974—; sec. Spring Shadows Women's Club, 1973-74; rep. Spring Shadows Civic Assn., 1976-77. Mem. Am. Pharm. Assn., Tex. Pharm. Assn., Harris County Pharm. Assn. (bd. councillors 1984-86), Alpha Delta Pi. Republican. Roman Catholic. Clubs: U. Miss., Real Estate Investment (Houston). Avocations: swimming; tennis; reading; cooking. Home: 11196 NW Fifth Manor Coral Springs FL 33071

PATTERSON, LUCY PHELPS, educator; b. Dallas, Tex., June 21, 1931; d. John C. and Florence L. (Harllee) Phelps; A.B., Howard U., 1950; M.S.W., U. Denver, 1963; m. Albert S. Patterson, Nov. 25, 1950; 1 son, Albert Harllee. Tabulating machine operator supr. Dept. Commerce, Bur. Census, Washington, 1950-52, Dept. Navy, Bur. of Ships, Washington, 1952-54; caseworker dept. public welfare Dallas, 1954-61, casework supr., 1963-68; dir. Interagy. Project, Dallas, 1968-71; exec. dir. Dallas County Child Care Council, 1971-73; planning dir. Community Council of Greater Dallas, 1973-74; asst. prof. and field work coordinator N. Tex. State U., 1974-78; Ethel Carter Branham tenured prof. Bishop Coll., Dallas, 1978-88, dir. social work, 1978-88; pres., chief exec. officer Ednl. Transp. Inc., 1988—; cons. to Meth. Teaching Pathways, Pro EdVantage Systems, Giles Inst. Ednl. Excellence, Creative Learning Center, Rhodes Terrace Pre-sch., Head Start Consultation Register, Inst. Urban Studies, So. Meth. U. Councilwoman, City of Dallas, 1973-80; chairwoman Nat. Afro-Am. History & Culture Commn., 1985—; mem. adminstrv. bd., chairwoman bd. ch. and soc. com. St. Paul United Meth. Ch., 1987—. Recipient Outstanding Woman award Women's Center of Dallas, 1978, Public Service award Elite Newspaper, 1978; named Mother of Yr., 1979. Mem. Nat. Assn. Social Workers, Acad. Cert. Social Workers, Council on Social Work Edn., Tex. Assn. Coll. Tchrs., Nat. Assn. Black Social Workers, Dallas County Mental Health Assn., Nat. Alliance Sr. Citizens (pres. 1989—), Tex. Black Polit. Caucus, Tex. Assn. of Women Elected Ofcls., Women's Council of Dallas County, LWV, Nat. Council of Negro Women, Council on Consumer Edn., Nat. Polit. Congress Black Women, Exec. Women in Govt., Alpha Kappa Alpha. Republican. Club: Altrusa. Weekly columnist numerous pubs. including Post Tribune, 1973-80, The Dallas Weekly, 1973-80. Home: 2779 Almeda Dr Dallas TX 75216 Office: 1901 Industrial Blvd Colleyville TX 76034 also: PO Box 397976 Dallas TX 75339

PATTERSON, LYDIA ROSS, industrial relations specialist, consulting company executive; b. Carrabelle, Fla., Sept. 3, 1936; d. Richard D. Ross and Johnnie Mae (Thomas) Kelley; m. Edgar A. Corley, Aug. 1, 1964 (div.); 1 child, Derek Kelley; m. Berman W. Patterson, Dec. 18, 1981. BA, Hunter Coll., 1958. Indsl. rels. specialist U.S. Dept. Energy, N.Y.C., 1966-68; regional dir./mgr. Div. Human Rights State of N.Y., N.Y.C., 1962-66, 68-76; v.p. Bankers Trust Co., N.Y.C., 1976-87; pres., chief exec. officer Extend Cons. Svcs., N.Y.C., 1985—; v.p., mgr. Merrill Lynch and Co. Inc., N.Y.C., 1987—; seminar speaker Columbia U., Wharton Sch. Bus., Harvard U., Duke U., Cornell U., 1976-85; mem. Bus. Policy Rev. Coun., Exec. Leadership Coun. Bd. dirs. Project Discovery Columbia U., 1988, CUNY, Vocat. Edn. Adv. Coun., 1990. Mem. Am. Soc. Personnel Adminstrn., N.Y. and Nat. Urban League, Employment Mgrs. Assn., Fin. Women's Assn. (govt./community affairs com. 1986-87), Employment Dissemination of Info. Group Awareness Edn. Solving of Problems (bd. dirs. 1979—), Panel of Americans (bd. dirs. 1990). Office: 183 Rhododendron Dr Westbury NY 11590-6111

PATTERSON, MARIA JEVITZ, microbiology-pediatric infectious disease educator; b. Berwyn, Ill., Oct. 23, 1944; d. Frank Jacob and Edna Frances (Costabile) Jevitz; m. Ronald James Patterson, Aug. 22, 1970; children: Kristin Lara, Kier Nicole. BS in Med. Tech. summa cum laude, Coll. St. Francis, Joliet, Ill., 1966; PhD in Microbiology, Northwestern U., Chgo., 1970; D of Medicine, Mich. State U., 1984. Diplomate Am. Bd. Med. Examiners, Am. Bd. Pediatrics. Lab. asst., instr. med. microbiology for student nurses Med. Sch. Northwestern U., Chgo., 1966-70; postdoctoral fellow in clin. microbiology affiliated hosps. U. Wash., Seattle, 1971-72; asst. prof. microbiology and pub. health Mich. State U., East Lansing, 1972-77, assoc. prof., 1977-82, assoc. prof. pathology, 1979-82, lectr. dept. microbiology and pub. health, 1982-87, resident in pediatrics affiliated hosps., 1984-85, 86-87, clin. instr. dept. pediatrics and human devel., 1984-87, assoc. prof. microbiology-pub. health-pediatrics-human devel., 1987-90, prof., 1990—; med. dir. Pediatric Health Ctr. St. Lawrence Hosp., Lansing, Mich., 1987—; staff microbiologist dept. pathology Lansing Gen. Hosp., 1972-75; dir. clin. microbiology grad. program Mich. State U., 1974-8l, staff microbiologist, 1978-8l; postdoctoral fellow in infectious diseases U. Mass. Med. Ctr., Worcester, 1985-86; asst. dir. pediatrics residency Grad. Med. Edn. Inc., Lansing, 1987—; cons. Lansing Gen. Hosp., 1972-75, Mich. State U., 1976-82, Ingham County Health Dept., 1988; cons. to editorial bd. Infection and Immunity, 1977; presenter seminars. Contbr. chpt. to Med. Microbiology: Principles and Concepts, 1982, 2nd rev. edit., 1986; contbr. articles to profl. jours. and publs. Recipient award for teaching excellence Coll. Osteo. Medicine, Mich. State U., 1977, 79, 83, Disting. Faculty award Mich. State U., 1980, Woman Achiever award, 1985, excellence in pediatrics residency teaching award, 1988; grantee renal disease div. Mich. Dept. Pub. Health, 1976-82. Fellow Pediatric Infectious Diseases Soc., Am. Acad. Pediatrics; mem. AMA, Am. Soc. Microbiology, Am. Soc. Clin. Pathologists (affiliate, bd. registrant), South Cen. Assn. Clin. Microbiology, Infectious Diseases Soc. of Am., Mich. Soc. Infectious Diseases, Kappa Gamma Pi, Lambda Iota Tau. Roman Catholic. Home: 1520 River Terrace Dr East Lansing MI 48823 Office: Mich State Univ Microbiology/Pub Health East Lansing MI 48824

PATTERSON, MARJORIE SCOTT SELLERS, librarian; b. Decatur, Ala., Apr. 18, 1925; d. Clyde R. and Eula W. (Lewis) Scott; student Kansas City Met. Jr. Coll., Park Coll.; m. Leonard S. Sellers, Nov. 25, 1943 (div.); children: Carol, Steve, Mark; m. Thomas W. Patterson, 1983. Substitute and libr. asst. Oak Park Sr. High Sch., North Kansas City, Mo., 1968-71; periodicals bank coord. Kansas City Regional Coun. for Higher Edn., 1971-74; co-founder, dir. Mid-Am. inter-libr. svcs., interlibr. loans libr. Park Coll., Parkville, Mo., 1974-81; founder Access to Info. Svcs. Assos., 1981—; owner, operator Bell Rd. Barn Book, rare and out-of-print books, 1981-83; sec. Internat. Libr. Exch. Ctr., 1986—. Editor: The LOANER newsletter, 1974-80, Mid-Am. Shelflist newsletter, 1981—, The Dusty Shelf, 1986—, Family Focus newsletter, 1984—. Sec. Emerald-Hodgson Hosp Aux., 1987-89; mem. North Cen. Evaluation Com. Mem. Mo. Libr. Assn., Mountain Plains Libr. Assn., Oral History Assn., Park Coll. Hist. Soc., U. of the South Friends of the Libr., Park Coll. Friends of the Libr., Internat. Libr. Exch. Ctr., Sewanee Garden Club (sec. 1988-89). Methodist. Address: 210 Beard St SW Decatur AL 35601

PATTERSON, MARLA KATHERINE, nurse, naval officer; b. Billings, Mont., Dec. 18, 1950; d. Howard Chester and Cecelia Ann (Paluck) P. BSN, Mont. State U., 1973; diploma, Air Command and staff Coll., 1980; MA Health Care Adminstrn., Webster U., St. Louis, 1981; Naval Hosp. RN,

Mont. Commd. ensign USN, 1973, advanced through grades to comdr., 1990; staff nurse Billings Deaconess Hosp., 1973-74; staff nurse Naval Regional Med. Ctr., Bremerton, Wash., 1974-76, San Diego, 1976-78; staff nurse Naval Air Regional Med. Ctr., Pensacola, Fla., 1985-88; instr. Hosp. Corps Sch., Gt. Lakes, Ill., 1979-82; head operating room nursing dept. U.S. Naval Hosp., Naples, Italy, 1982-85, Naval Hosp., Twenty-Nine Palms, Calif., 1988—. Mem. Assn. Operating Room Nurses (cert.) Aircraft Owners and Pilots Assn., Nat. Assn. Sports Ofcls., NAFE, CAP (lt. col. 1963—), NRA (life), 99's. Democrat. Roman Catholic. Office: US Naval Hosp Twenty-Nine Palms CA 92278-5008

PATTERSON, P. J., accountant; b. Pana, Ill., June 7, 1950; d. Gordon G. and Doris (Stolte) Moore. Cert. tax practitioner. Acct. ADM, 1971-73, Ford Motor Co., 1973-74; asst. controller Union Iron Works, Decatur, Ill., 1974; acct. Caterpillar Co., Decatur, 1975; pvt. practice acctg., owner Patterson Acctg., Decatur, 1975—; speaker Networking Women convs., 1983-86. Bd. dirs. Boys Club, Decatur, 1985-87, Decatur Area Arts Council, 1985-87, 87—, Decatur Advantage, 1986, YWCA, Decatur, 1983-86. Mem. Ind. Accts. Assn. (treas. 1984), Nat. Assn. Income Tax Practitioners (pres. 1984—), Nat. Assn. Tax Practitioners, Nat. Assn. Income Tax Practitioners (pres. cen. Ill. chpt. 1984—), Assn. Bus. Women Am. (treas. 1982), Nat. Assn. Female Execs. (bd. dirs. 1983-86), Decatur C. of C. (Outstanding Bus. of Yr. award 1983). Republican. Baptist. Club: Decatur. Home: 315 Shoreline Pl Decatur IL 62526 Office: Patterson Acctg 1212 E Pershing Decatur IL 62526

PATTERSON, PAMELA JANE, audiologist; b. Passaic, N.J., Feb. 26, 1951; d. Robert and Marian M. Patterson. BS, Ohio State U., 1973, postgrad., 1973-74; MA, Kent State U., 1976. Audiologist E.N.T. Head and Neck Surgeons, Columbus, Ohio, 1975-76; audiologist Arnold D. Rubenfield M.D. & Assocs., New Kensington, Pa., 1976-80, bus. mgr., 1978-80; dir. audiological services Hearing Cons. for Industry, New Kensington, 1977-80; audiologist Cen. Ohio Hearing Aid Ctr., Reynoldsburg, 1980-83; pres. Micro Hearing Systems, Inc., Columbus, 1984—. Mem. Am. Speech and Hearing Assn., Auditory Soc. of Am., Ohio Hearing Aid Soc. Republican. Presbyterian. Home: 157 N Oak St London OH 43140 Office: Micro Hearing Systems Inc 15 Norton Rd Columbus OH 43228

PATTERSON, POLLY REILLY (MRS. W. RAY PATTERSON), retired communications company executive, civic worker; b. Wilkinsburg, Pa., 1912; d. Thomas L. and Margaret (Coughey) Reilly; m. W. Ray Patterson, Sept. 2, 1943. Student, U. Pitts. With Bell Telephone Co. of Pa., Pitts., 1925-71, clk., mgmt. positions, 1935-64, assoc. pub. rels. staff, 1965-71. Asst. treas. Allegheny County (Pa.) Soc. for Crippled Children, 1962-66, v.p., 1966-70; bd. dirs. Jr. Achievement, Inc., SW Pa., 1950-71, Pa. Soc. Crippled Children and Adults, 1960-68, Pitts. YWCA, 1964-72, Chatham Village Homes, Inc., 1973-76; mem. Allegheny County United Way, 1972—, nat. ho. of dels. Nat. Soc. for Crippled Children and Adults, 1965-67. Named Pitts. Advt. Woman of Yr., 1958, one of Pitts.'s Ten Outstanding Women, Pitts. Sun Telegraph, 1959; recipient Crystal Prism award Am. Advt. Fedn., 1972, 75. Mem. Assn. Pitts. Clubs (bd. dirs. 1946-81, pres. 1952-53), Altrusa Internat. (pres. Pitts. club 1950-51), Pitts. Advt. Club (v.p., sec. 1929-69), Pitts. Bus. and Profl. Women's Club, Telephone Pioneers Am. Home: 402 Olympia Rd Pittsburgh PA 15211

PATTERSON, VANESSA LEIGH, development executive; m. Stanley M. Patterson, Sept. 23, 1965; 1 child, Lee E. II. BA, SUNY, Albany, 1964; postgrad., Memphis State U., 1983-85. Project coordinator Holiday Inns, Inc., Memphis, 1978-79; supr., research corp. strategies div. Holiday Corp., Memphis, 1979-85; dir. research and records Fairleigh Dickinson U., Rutherford, N.J., 1985-89; devel. officer Kean Coll. N.J. Found., Union. Mng. editor Strategic News Review newsletter, Holiday Corp., 1984-85, Biomed. Research Zone Com. newsletter, 1985. Mem. Biomed. Research Zone com. of Memphis Ctr. City Commn., 1984-85, com. on info. tech. of William Carlos Williams Ctr. for Performing Arts, Rutherford, 1985-86. Mem. Am. Soc. Info. Scientists, Nat. Assn. Female Execs. (network dir. 1981-85), Council for Advancement and Support of Edn. Unitarian. Office: Kean Coll NJ Found Townsend Hall Union NJ 07083

PATTI, FRANCES MARIE, restaurateur; b. Milw., Feb. 17, 1934; d. Salvatore and Josephine (Pizzino) Librizzi; m. Domenic Patti, Oct. 23, 1954; children: Terri, Michael, Josephine, Pauline. Grad. high schs., Milw. Owner, mgr. Mr. D'o Pizza Restaurant, Milw., 1967—. Home: 7005 N Lombardy Ct Fox Point WI 53217

PATTI, JOSEPHINE MARIE, health science facility administrator; b. Buffalo, July 5, 1934; d. Joseph John and Caroline Mary (Mayer) P. BS, D'Youville Coll., Buffalo, 1964; MHA, Xavier U., Cin., 1974. Med. technologist Griffin Meml. Hosp., Kodiak, Alaska, 1964-70; asst. supr., sr. med. tech. A.B. Hepburn Hosp., Ogdensburg, NY, 1970-72; adminstrv. res. St. Joseph's Infirmary, Atlanta, 1973-74; adminstr. Kodiak (Alaska) Island Hosp., 1974-78; adminstrv. asst. St. Joseph's Hosp. Inc., Atlanta, 1978-79; asst. adminstr. St. Joseph's Hosp., 1979-80; dir., misson effective St. Joseph's Hosp., Atlanta, 1986-88, asst. v.p., 1988-90; v.p. mise effect St. Joseph's Hosp., 1990—; adminstr. Motherhouse, Grey Nuns of the Sacred Heart, Yardley, Pa., 1980-85; dir. St. Joseph's Mercy Care Corp., Atlanta; chairperson bd., bd. dir. Atlanta Community Health Prog. for the Homeless, 1988--, dir. South Central Health Planning and Devel. Inc., Anchorage Alaska, 1976-77. Mem. Lifelink of Georgia Adv. Bd., 1988, Atlanta Aids Rsch. Consortium, AIDS Rsch. Consortium Atlanta, 1988—; dir. North Atlanta Sr. Svcs., 1988, Grey Nuns of the Sacred Heart, Yardley 1954—. Mem. Am. Coll. Health Care Execs. Roman Catholic. Office: Saint Joseph's Hosp Atlanta 5665 Peachtree Dunwoody Rd Atlanta GA 30342

PATTI, SANDI, gospel vocalist; m. John Helvering; 4 children. Formerly with group First Call; performer, rec. artist. Albums include The Friendship Company, The Gift Goes On, Morning Like This, 1986, Make His Praise Glorious, 1988, The Finest Moments, 1989. Recipient Grammy awards for duo or group gospel performances, 1983, 85, 86, individual female gospel performance, 1986; named Artist of Yr. (5 times), Gospel Music Assn., Best Female Vocalist, 1982-88. Office: care Helvering Agy PO Box 2940 Anderson IN 46018*

PATTIE, JANE ANNE, freelance writer, photographer; b. Ft. Worth, Jan. 15, 1935; d. Robert A. and Juanita V. (Cahill) Rogers; m. Lyle Byron Pattie, Apr. 7, 1955; children: Sheryl Elise, Roger Byron. Docent, photographer Fossil Rim Wildlife Ctr. and Found., Glen Rose, Tex., 1988—. Author, photographer: Training Tips for Western Riders, 1972, Cowboy Spurs and Their Makers, 1991; assoc. editor: Kowa Voices vol. II, 1983; author, photographer over 2,000 mag. articles. Mem. Western Writers Am. (bd. dirs. 1979-80), Ft. Worth Westerners. Home: Rte 2 Box 49 Aledo TX 76008 Office: PO Box 121623 Fort Worth TX 76116

PATTISON-LEHNING, BARBARA JEANNE, marketing political consultant; b. Tacoma, Wash., Jan. 2, 1936; d. Richard Stanley and Elizabeth June (Miller) Bennatts; ;m. Thomas Wesley Lehning, Aug. 27, 1983; children: Mark, Scott, Kimberly, Trishawn. BA in Communications, U. Wash., 1972; MBA, Seattle U., 1979. Promotion dir. Sta. KIRO-TV, Seattle, 1960-67; editor TV Guide, Seattle, 1967-73; legis. asst. Seattle councilman Seattle, 1973-76; chmn. internat. conf. Assn. for Children with Learning Disabilities, Seattle, 1976; Ombudsman Wash. State Parent Community Relations Project, Seattle, 1976-89; cons. Rising Star Enterprise, Inc., Seattle, 1983—; small business owner, 1984-88. Author, producer videotapes and TV segments. Polit. strategist, campaign mgr. Re-elect Councilwoman V. Galle, Seattle, 1984, 89, Re-elect Councilwoman J. William, 1984, 89; state campaign mgr. Re-elect State Supt., King County field coord., 1984. Recipient Award of Merit, Wash. State Spl. Edn., 1983, 89; named Outstanding Citizen, Wash. Assn. Children, 1982. Mem. Wash. Press Assn. (sec. 1982-83, pres. 1983-84, cons., Woman of Achievement award 1984), Wash. Soc. for Intelligence Tng. (fund-raiser 1986, cons.), Wash. Generals, Gov.'s Com. Employment of Handicapped (chmn. pub. rels. and edn. coms. 1982-85, bd. dirs.), Variety Tent 46 (1st v.p., telethon chair, sec., v.p. 1982—), Seattle C. of C. (small bus. com. 1986, activist 1984—). Democrat. Home: 4331 Lake Wash Blvd NE #7311 Kirkland WA 98033

PATTON, DARLA JUNE EATON, law firm paralegal; b. Texarkana, Ark., May 22, 1948; d. Clarence Morris Eaton and Barbara June (Minshew-Eaton) Lauer; m. Daniel Courtney Patton; children: Rebecca June, Courtney Jane. Student, Texarkana Coll., 1966-69, East Tex. State U., 1970. Legal sec., paralegal Wheeler Watkins Law Firm, Texarkana, 1965-71, Russell Rolston Law Firm, Mt. Pleasant, Tex., 1973-76; sr. oil and gas lease analyst Dorchester Gas Corp., Dallas, 1981-83; sr. paralegal Locke Purnell Rain Harrell Law Firm, Dallas, 1983—. Mem. Nat. Assn. Legal Assts., State Bar Tex. (legal asst. div.), Legal Asst. Mgrs. Assn., Dallas Assn. Legal Assts., Tex. A&M U. Parents Assn., Chi Omega Parents Assn., Beta Sigma Phi. Republican. Methodist. Office: Locke Purnell Rain Harrell 2200 Ross Ave Ste 2200 Dallas TX 75021-6776

PATTON, JANET CLARA, university official; b. Mpls., Feb. 12, 1945; d. Howard John and Dorothy Clara (Draheim) Nelson; m. Ronald Paul Patton, Aug. 27, 1966; children: Jeffery, Jennifer, Jammie. BS, Emporia State U., 1968; MS, East Tex. State U., 1974, postgrad., 1989—. presenter Office Edn. Improvement Conf., Houston, 1986, 88, Arlington, Tex., 1989. Instr. bus. edn. Canton (Kans.) Sch. Dist., 1969-70; instr. office edn. Sherman (Tex.) Sch. Dist., 1972-76, Rains Sch. Dist., Emory, Tex., 1976-83, Commerce (Tex.) Sch. Dist., 1983-87; curriculum specialist East Tex. State U., Commerce, 1987—; presenter Office Edn. Improvement Conf., Houston, 1988, Arlington, Tex., 1989. Fellow Tex. Edn. Assn., 1982. Mem. Am. Vocat. Assn. (conf. presenter 1989), Tex. Bus. Edn. Assn. (dist. pres. 1988-89), Nat. Bus. Edn. Assn., Vocat. Office Edn. Tchrs. Assn. Tex., Tex. Computer Edn. Assn., Commerce C. of C. (Citizen award 1986), Delta Pi Epsilon (past pres., sec., treas.). Methodist. Home: 100 Briarwood Commerce TX 75428

PATTON, SHARI K., hypnotherapist; b. Chariton, Iowa, Apr. 13, 1951; widowed; children: Brian, Brett. PhD, Am. Inst. of Hypnotherapy, 1986. Founder, dir. Hypnosis Assocs. Inst., Des Moines; pvt. practice Des Moines; v.p. Nat. Soc. of Hypnotherapists; regional v.p. Nat. Bd. Hypnotic Anaesthesiology; cons. in field. Office: 1520 NW 107th St Des Moines IA 50322

PATY, MELISSA BROWN, nurse consultant; b. Dayton, Ohio, Sept. 21, 1951; d. Eugene Lee and Peggy Jean (Aikins) Brown; m. Ben Hooper Paty, Jr., Sept. 4, 1982. BS in Nursing, Vanderbilt U., 1973, MS in Nursing, 1974; Nurse Practitioner, Meharry Med. Coll, Nashville, 1976. Psychiat. clin. nurse specialist Mid. Tenn. Mental Health Inst., Nashville, 1974-82; pvt. practice psychotherapy Nashville, 1976-78; dir. forensic svcs. Tenn. Dept. Mental Health, Nashville, 1982-85; dir. nursing Vanderbilt Child and Adolescent Psychiat. Hosp., Nashville, 1985-87; nurse cons. Mid. Tenn. Mental Health Inst., Nashville, 1987—; clin. instr. psychiatry Vanderbilt U. Sch. Nursing, Nashville, 1987—; lectr. Med. Coll. Pa., Phila., 1988-89; dir. Suburban Home Health Bd., Nashville, 1985—. Mem. Vanderbilt Friends of Children's Hosp., Nashville, 1980—; mem. bd. advisors St. Andrews-Sewanne, Tenn., 1987—; pres. bd. dirs. Vanderbilt Sch. Nursing Alumni, Nashville, 1989—. Mem. Am. Nurses Assn., Nat. League Nursing, Tenn. Nurses Assn., Sigma Theta Tauu, Pi Beta Phi (chmn. Christmas Village 1989). Presbyterian. Home: 127 Page Rd Nashville TN 37205 Office: Vanderbilt U Sch Nursing Godchaux Hall Nashville TN 37212

PAUK, LARONNA, interior designer; b. San Antonio, Aug. 3, 1960; d. William H. and Sharon A. (Kendall) P. BA in Interior Design, Iowa State U., 1982. Space planner RMM, Inc., Chgo., 1982-83; planner, project mgr., v.p. Horn & Assoc., Inc., Chgo., 1983—. Office: Horn & Assoc Inc 223 W Erie Ave Chicago IL 60610

PAUL, ALICE, foundation executive; b. N.Y.C., Dec. 18, 1936; d. Lusha and Irene (Seplow) Nelson; m. HenryKurt Paul, June 28, 1956 (div. 1985); children: Karen Diane, Rachel Irene. BA, New Sch. Social Rsch., 1968. Program assoc. Joint Found. Support, N.Y.C., 1970-76; resource and info. coord. Neighborhood Stabilization Program N.Y.C. Commn. on Human Rights, 1976-78; exec. dir. Astella Devel. Corp., Bklyn., 1979-83, Uris Bros. Found., N.Y.C., 1983—; bd. dirs., v.p. Assn. Neighborhood Housing Devel., N.Y.C., 1981-83; pub. mem. N.Y. State Bd. Architecture, N.Y.C., 1982—; bd. dirs. Bklyn. in Touch, 1986—, Non-Profit Coordinating Com., N.Y.C., 1989—. Coord., Com. on Decent Unbiased Campaign Tactics, N.Y.C., 1984-86; bd. dirs., v.p. N.Y.C. Transit Authority Adv. Coun., 1986—. Mem. Women in Housing and Fin. (bd. dirs.), AIA, City Club N.Y. (trustee, com. chair). Democrat. Jewish. Office: Uris Bros Found 300 Park Ave New York NY 10022

PAUL, CAROL LYNN, hospital administrator; b. Garden City, Kans., Aug. 13, 1945; d. Owen Masters and Beulah May (Pocock) P.; 1 child, Carter Lee Marshall III. BA, U. Kans., 1967; MPH, Yale U., 1971. Coord. program planning Health Ins. Plan Greater N.Y., Flushing, 1972-76; dir. planning Morristown (N.J.) Meml. Hosp., 1978-81, asst. v.p. adminstrv. svcs., 1982-85, v.p. legal and external affairs, 1985—. Contbr. articles to profl. jours. Mem. Am. Coll. Health Care Execs., Am. Pub. Health Assn., Soc. for Hosp. Planning and Mktg. N.J., Assn. Yale Alumni in Pub. Health. Democrat. Office: Morristown Meml Hosp 100 Madison Ave Morristown NJ 07962

PAUL, CAROLYN M., company executive; b. Sacramento, June 8, 1932; d. Malcolm E. and Rosalina (Gomes) Mckenzie; m. F. Stan Paul, Dec. 12, 1926; children: Eric V., Karen E. Grad. high sch., Sacramento. From dental nurse to chmn. Tau Phi Lambda Sorority, Sacramento, 1951-63; pres. Hobrecht Lighting Co. Inc., Sacramento, 1963--. Republican. Roman Catholic.

PAUL, CHARLOTTE P., nursing educator; b. Clarendon, Tex., Jan. 13, 1941; d. William Clyde Peggram and Sibyl (Rattan) Jones; m. Robert M. Paul, Apr. 4, 1964; children: Peter, Lauraine. Diploma, St. Anthony's Hosp. Sch. Nursing, Amarillo, Tex., 1961; student, Amarillo Coll., 1958-65; BS, Syracuse U., 1972, MS, 1973, PhD in Edn. Adminstrn., 1979; postgrad., U. Tex., El Paso, 1983—. Nurse St. Anthony's Hosp., Amarillo, Tex., 1961-65; evening charge nurse Upstate Med. Ctr. SUNY, Syracuse, 1966-68, VA Hosp. Gen. Hosp., Syracuse, 1965-66; asst. to head nurse Meml. Hosp., Syracuse, 1966-68; nurse IV therapy Community-Gen. Hosp., Syracuse, 1968-72; instr. Syracuse Cen. Sch. System, 1972; asst. dir. insvc. edn. House of Good Samaritan Hosp., Watertown, N.Y., 1973-74; instr. SUNY Sch. Nursing, Syracuse, 1974-75, Syracuse U. Sch. Nursing, 1975-76; asst. dean Wright State U., Dayton, Ohio, 1977-79; assoc. prof. Edinboro U. Pa., 1979-86, prof., 1986—, chairperson dept. grad. studies, 1980-82, chairperson dept. nursing, 1987-89; coord. quality assurance William Beaumont Army Med. Ctr., Ft. Bliss, Tex., 1982-85; adj. assoc. prof. U. Tex., El Paso, 1982-85; cons. in field. Contbr. articles to profl. jours., papers in field. Bd. dirs. ARC, Syracuse, 1970-77, Erie County Emergency Mgmt. Agy.; chairperson-elect Lake Erie Higher Edn. Coun.; mem. Coun. on Aging Com. on Long Term Care, Dayton, 1977-78. Maj. USAR. Recipient Unit Citation award CAP, 1968; Gladys Post scholar, 1958-61, Rodney Horle scholar, 1971-72, Nellie Hurly scholar, 1971-72; HEW grantee, 1977, Wright State U. grantee, 1977-78, 77-82. Mem. AAAS, ANA, Nat. League for Nursing, Gerontol. Soc. Am., St. Anthony's Hosp. Sch. Nursing Alumni Assn., Syracuse U. Alumni Assn., N.Y. Acad. Sci., Am. Pub. Adminstrs., Nat. Acad. Polit. Sci., Am. Pub. Health Assn., Assn. Mil. Surgeons U.S., Nightengale Soc., Kiwanis (bd. dirs. Edinboro club 1987—, pres. 1988-89, v.p. 1987—), Sigma Theta Tau, Pi Lambda Theta (pres. local chpt. 1973-75). Republican. Office: Edinboro U Pa 133 Butterfield Hall Edinboro PA 16444

PAUL, ELLEN LOUISE, marketing professional, writer; b. Feb. 18, 1948. BA, U. Md., 1969, MA, 1975. Dir. communications Nat. Capital and Va's div. The Salvation Army, Washington, 1973-78; nat. dir. pub. relations Am. Assn. of Blood Banks, Washington, 1978; asst. world dir. pub. info. USO World Hdqrs., Washington, 1978-81, dir. direct mail, fin. devel., 1981-84; sales and mktg. exec. The Image Makers, Temple Hills, Md., 1982-88; freelance writer, prodn. mgr. Fairfax, Va., 1988—. Author textbooks McGraw-Hill; writer Radio Marti, NSF; contbr. articles to various publs. Recipient Toth award Pub. Relations Soc. Am., 1979, 80, Silver Anvil award 1979, 80; named Friendship Ambassador to Fed. Republic Germany. Home: 3500 Spring Lake Terr Fairfax VA 22030

PAUL, MARY MELCHIOR, management consultant; b. Tipton, Ind., Apr. 29, 1952; d. John A. and Inez Marie (Clark) Meyer; m. Jeffrey Paul, Sept. 27, 1987; 1 child, Regina. BS, U. Evansville, 1974; MBA, So. Ill. U., 1987. Mgr. The Children's Shops, St. Louis, 1980-86; cons., trainer Edison Bros. Stores, St. Louis, 1987; mgmt. devel. cons. Anheuser-Busch Cos., St. Louis, 1988—. Mem. Coro Found., Scott Joint Use, speakers bur. coun. Girl Scouts U.S.; mem. student leadership devel. mentoring program So. Ill. U., Edwardsville. Mem. Women's Commerce Assn. of St. Louis, Am. Soc. for Tng. and Devel., So. Ill. Network of Women, Women in Leadership Alumnae. Address: 530 Lafayette Belleville IL 62220

PAUL, SUSAN L., acupuncturist, nurse; b. N.Y.C., May 31, 1944; d. Ira Gerald and Charlotte May (Silverstein) L.; divorced; 1 child, Amanda Paul. BS in Nursing, Cornell U., N.Y.C., 1966; grad., Tri State Inst. Acupuncture, Stamford, Conn., 1986. RN, N.Y.; cert. Nat. Commn. for Cert. Acupuncturists. Nurse, hosp. supr. numerous orgns. and hosps., 1966-80, 85-87; pvt. practice N.Y.C., 1986—, New Hope, Pa., 1988—; presenter in field; mem. asst. faculty Tri State Sch. Acupuncture, 1986-87; internat. cons. on Herbal and Oriental medicine, India, France; field supr. Fgn. Health Svcs. of the Tibetan Refugee Alternative Health Care Project, 1990. Mem. Am. Assn. Acupuncture and Oriental Medicine, N.Y. State Assn. Profl. Acupuncturists. Home: 210 W 21st St New York NY 10011

PAULEY, JANE, television journalist; b. Indpls., Oct. 31, 1950; m. Garry Trudeau; 3 children. B.A. in Polit. Sci. Ind. U., 1971; D. Journalism (hon.), DePauw U., 1978. Reporter Sta. WISH-TV, Indpls., 1972-75; co-anchor WMAQ-TV News, Chgo., 1975-76; corr. NBC News, N.Y.C., 1976—; co-anchor The Today Show, NBC, N.Y.C., 1976-90; prin. writer, reporter NBC Nightly News, 1980-82, substitute anchor, 1990—; co-anchor Early Today, NBC, 1982-83; prin. corr. Real Life With Jane Pauley, NBC, 1990. Office: NBC News 30 Rockefeller Pla New York NY 10020*

PAULEY, JUDY RUTH, human service agency executive; b. Beatrice, Nebr., Oct. 15, 1943; d. Ernest R. and Thelma R. (Beasley) Bence; divorced; children: Gregory L., Anthony B. BS in Elem. Edn., U. Nebr., 1978. Elem. tchr. Milford (Nebr.) Sch., 1964-68; receptionist Coast Fed. Savs. & Loan Co., L.A., 1972-73; office supr. Temp. Employment Agy., Pasadena, Calif., 1973-74; activity aide Beatrice State Devel. Ctr., 1974-78, psychol. svcs. asst., 1979-80, mgr. mental retardation unit, 1980-84; vocat. case mgr. Jefferson County Community Ctr., Lakewood, Colo., 1984-85, resident supr., 1985-89, asst. and acting resident dir., 1989—. Mem. NAFE. Republican. Roman Catholic. Office: County Community Ctr 7456 W 5th St Lakewood CO 80226

PAULEY, RHODA ANNE, communications and mktg. exec.; b. Elizabeth, N.J., Nov. 26, 1939; d. Isadore and Jean Litin Manheim. BA magna cum laude, Smith Coll., 1961; postgrad. in Am. lit. Stanford U., 1961-63. Editorial asst. Edn. and World Affairs, N.Y.C., 1963-65; tech. writer Data Processing div. U.S. Life Ins. Corp., N.Y.C., 1965-67; dir. publs. and mktg. Diebold Group, Inc., N.Y.C., 1967-72; gen. mgr. Direct Mail/Mktg. Assn., Inc., N.Y.C., 1972-75; cons. on new bus. and orgn. devel., 1975-76; v.p. communications and clearinghouse Work Am. Inst., Scarsdale, N.Y., 1976-81; dir. communications svcs. Girl Scouts U.S., 1981-89; dir. communications YWCA, 1989—; chmn. com. for Liaison on Advt. and Sales Promotion, 1974. Chmn., Task Force on Employee-Mgmt. Rels. and Quality of Working Life, Transp. Rsch. Bd./NRC, 1979-82. Editor: The Student in Higher Education, 1968. Mem. Am. Mktg. Assn. (pres. not-for-profit coun.), N.Y. Women in Communications (v.p. pub. rels.). Home: 233 E 69th St New York NY 10021 Office: Girl Scouts US 830 3rd Ave New York NY 10022

PAULIK, MARY THERESA, municipal government official, researcher; b. Flushing, N.Y., Sept. 17, 1939; d. Joseph Percival and Gertrude Veronica (Mahony) Melanson; m. William Paul Paulik, Jan. 21, 1961. AA in Social Scis., Suffolk Community Coll., Brentwood, N.Y., 1979; BA in Human Rels., St. Joseph's Coll., Patchoque, N.Y., 1980; MPA, L.I. U., 1986. Teller, clk. Chase Manhattan Bank, Flushing, 1957-58; adminstrv. corp. sec. Ginn & Co./Ednl. Textbooks, N.Y.C., 1960-61, regional supervisory mgr., 1961-66; various per diem positions Writing/Rsch. Cos.-Bus. Firms, L.I., N.Y., 1967-70; adminstrv. sec. Town of Islip, Brentwood Water Dist., 1972-88, water dist. coord., 1988—; officer bus. and polit. orgns.; mem. environ. groups. Fundraiser United Way, Suffolk, N.Y., 1987-88, team coord., 1989—, assn. for retarded, 1987-88, unit coord., 1989—; fundraiser March of Dimes; mem. exec. bd. Bayshore Rep. Club, N.Y., 1989—, Islip Rep. Women, 1989—. Mem. AAUW (Islip chpt.), Bus. and Profl. Women (mem. exec. bd. Bay Shore chpt. 1989—), Cousteau Soc. (environmentalist), Nat. Audubon Soc., Nat. Geog. Soc. (environmentalist), Nat. Wildlife Soc. (environmentalist), Wilderness Soc., Sigma Iota Chi. Roman Catholic.

PAULINE, ROSEANN JUDITH, medical center official; b. Phila., Jan. 2, 1957; d. Ralph Rocco and Anna (Laverty) P. BA in Econs., St. Joseph's U., Phila., 1979; MBA, Widener U., 1988. Jr. buyer Lankenau Hosp., Phila., 1979-80, inventory control supr., 1980-81; asst. mgr. inside sales Dolbey Sci., Yeadon, Pa., 1981-85; sr. buyer Mercy Cath. Med. Ctr., Darby, Pa., 1985-86, mgr. cen. purchasing, 1986—; mem. med.-surg. com. Hosp. Purchasing Svc. Corp., Camp Hill, Pa., 1987—; mem. edn. com. Hosp. Cen. Svcs. Corp., Allentown, Pa., 1987-88. Mem. Am. Soc. for Hosps. Materials Mgmt., rec. sec. Southeastern Pa. chpt. 1988—, chmn. search and nominating com. 1988—), Delaware County C. of C., Phi Chi Theta, Phi Sigma Kappa. Republican. Roman Catholic. Office: Mercy Cath Med Ctr Lansdowne Ave and Baily Rd Darby PA 19023

PAULL, RACHEL KREBS, geology educator; b. Jan. 31, 1933; d. Lester John and Ruth Katherine (Sells) Krebs; m. Richard A. Paull, Mar. 6, 1954; children: Kay Marie, Lynn Ellen, Judith Ann. BS, U. Wis., 1954; MS, U. Wis., Milw., 1970; PhD, U. Wis., 1980. Instr. geology Alverno Coll., Milw., 1972-78; adj. prof. geology U. Wis., Milw., 1980—. Co-Author: (with Richard Paull) Geology of Wisconsin and Upper Michigan, 1977, (field guide) Wisconsin and Upper Michingan, 1980, Geologic Field Guides, 1988; contbr. sci. articles to profl. jours. Fellow Geological Soc. Am., Paleontological Soc., Soc. for Sedimentary Geology, Pander Soc. Office: U Wis Geosciences PO Box 413 Milwaukee WI 53201

PAUL-MICHELINI, JOAN B., company executive; b. N.Y.C., Apr. 28, 1934; d. Frank and Mary (Aidala) Vuozzo; m. Jerome Paul, June 6, 1954 (div. 1966); children: Leslie J., Jerome T., Cynthia A.; m. Gerald S. Michelini, Aug. 31, 1986; stepchildren: Karen Fraley, Donna Scardino, Lisa Michelini. BA in Bus. Adminstrn., Marymount Manhattan Coll., N.Y.C., 1980; MS, Cornell U., 1986. Supr. personnel/benefits Eutectic Corp., Flushing, N.Y., 1967-71; mgr. personnel/benefits Eutectic Corp., 1971-75; benefits analyst Colt Industries, N.Y.C., 1976-77; mgr. benefits adminstrn. Coltec Industries, 1977—. Republican. Roman Catholic. Home: 87 Fernwood Ln Roslyn NY 11576 Office: Coltec Industries Inc 430 Park Ave New York NY 10022

PAULO, MICHELE ANN, medical technologist; b. Pompton Plains, N.J., Dec. 5, 1963; d. Lauriano S. and Theresa M. (Kashmer) P. BS in Med. Tech., King's Coll., 1985. Coord. quality control, supr. hematology Bio-Reference Lab., Elmwood Park, N.J., 1985—. Mem. Am. Assn. Med. Technologists, N.J. Assn. Med. Technologists, Am. Soc. Clin. Pathologists.

PAULSHUS, DEBORAH LEE, typographer; b. Winnipeg, Man., Can., Jan. 8, 1955; d. Samuel and Bernice (Byra) Johnston; m. Jan Paulshus, Apr. 17, 1982. Student, Hochshule fur Musik und Darstellende Kunst, Salzburg, Austria, U. Redlands, Badlands, Calif.; BA, Calif. State U., San Bernardino, 1977. Music tchr. Temple City (Calif.) Sch. Dist, 1973-75; gen. office clk. Broadway Dept. Stores, L.A., 1976-80, asst. buyer, 1981-84, typographer, typesetter, 1984—; pvt. music tchr., Temple City, Calif., 1974-75; freelance typesetter, typographer, editor, 1988—. Home and Office: 100 E Alhambra Rd Alhambra CA 91801

PAULSON, JEANNETTE, film festival director; b. Pasadena, Calif.; d. Leo E. and Lucille J. (Bartholama) Butts; children: Bradley, Kelly Sutton, Holly. BS, Chaminade U., 1978; MA, U. Hawaii, 1988. Story teller Artist-in-the-Schs. Program, Dept. Edn. States of Oreg. and Hawaii, 1968-78; program dir. Jackson County Mental Health Assn., Medford, Oreg., 1973-74; producer, writer ednl. TV State of Hawaii, Honolulu, 1975-79; community relations officer East-West Ctr., Honolulu, 1980-83, film festival coordinator,

1980-89; dir. Hawaii, Palm Springs Film Festival, Honolulu, 1989—. Author: Touching a Season of Time, 1975; producer, writer (film) Taro Tales, 1979 (Best of West award 1979). Mem. adv. council Communications Dept. Chaminade U., 1986—; founder, dir. Storytelling Guild of So. Oreg., 1964-75; founder, dir. Children's Festival So. Oreg., 1966-73. Named one of Faces to Watch in the 1990's in Conchella Valley, Calif., one of 10 Individuals Who Made a Difference in Hawaii, 1988. Mem. Nat. Press Women (pres. Hawaii chpt. 1984-85), Women in Communications Inc. (v.p. 1982-85, Headliner award 1984).

PAULSON, LORETTA NANCY, psychoanalyst; b. Los Angeles, Nov. 5, 1943; d. Frank Morris and Rose (Kaufman) Fargo; m. Glenn Lewis Paulson, Dec. 27, 1970 (div. 1984). BA, U. So. Calif., 1966; MS in Social Work, Columbia U., 1969; cert. psychoanalyst, C.G. Jung Inst., N.Y.C. Cert. clin. social worker, N.Y., Conn. Pvt. practice psychoanalysis N.Y.C. and Wilton, Conn., 1976—; faculty, supr., vice chmn. Inst. Tng. Bd., chmn. evaluations com. Mem. Internat. Assn. for Analytical Psychology, Nat. Assn. for Accreditation of Psychoanalysis (mem. bd. dirs.), Nat. Assn. Social Workers (diplomate in clin. social work), N.Y. Assn. for Analytic Psychology (program com.). Democrat. Office: 6 Turtleback Rd Wilton CT 06897 Office: 334 W 86th St #1A New York NY 10024

PAUSTIAN, JODIE LEE, government official; b. Moline, Ill., June 2, 1957; d. Donald Bernhardt and Bobbie Nell (Wyers) P. BA, Western Ill. U., 1979. Substitute tchr. United Twp. Sch. Dist., East Moline, Ill., 1979-80; clk. Manpower Temp. Svcs., Moline, 1979-80; data entry clk. U.S. Army C.E., Rock Island, Ill., 1980-81; data entry clk. Hdqrs. U.S. Army Armament, Muntions and Chem. Command, Rock Island, 1981-82, tech. data clk., 1982-83, contract specialist, 1983-85; contract specialist McAlester (Okla.) Army Ammunition Plant, 1985-88; procurement analyst U.S. Army Concepts Analysis Agy., Bethesda, Md., 1988—; mem. exec. leadership devel. program Dept. Def., 1989-90. Recipient dir.'s award for excellence U.S. Army Concepts Analysis Agy., 1989. Mem. Nat. Contract Mgmt. Assn., AAUW (sec. 1985-87). Democrat. Methodist. Office: US Army Concepts Analysis 8120 Woodmont Ave Bethesda MD 20814-2797

PAUTH, PATRICIA RUTH, librarian; b. Rochester, N.Y., Feb. 14, 1936; d. Frank Alvin and Ruth Rose (Vose) P.; student Wittenberg U., Springfield, Ohio, 1953-56. Library asst. periodicals dept. Rush Rhees Library, U. Rochester (N.Y.), 1956-59; with Price Waterhouse, N.Y.C., 1959—, purchasing asst., 1959-63, reference librarian, 1963-72, asst. librarian, 1972-74, head librarian, 1974-85, mgr. info. services, 1985—. Mem. Spl. Libraries Assn., Am. Soc. for Info. Sci., DAR, Union Street Gardens Assn. (past treas., pres.). Home: 376 Union St Brooklyn NY 11231 Office: 153 E 53d St New York NY 10022

PAVEK, BRYN CARPENTER, director arts administration; b. Phoenix, Mar. 7, 1955; d. John Leon and Lenore Maxine (Stapp) Carpenter; m. Charles Christopher Pavek, Dec. 18, 1977. BFA in Theatre magna cum laude, Ariz. State U., 1977; student, U. Ariz., 1973. Freelance designer Phoenix, 1973-77; box office mgr. Ariz. State U. Theatre, Tempe, 1976; creative drama specialist City of Phoenix, summer 1976; box office ticketing asst. U. So. Calif., L.A., 1977; co. and stage mgr. Hartford (Conn.) Stage Co. Youth Theatre, 1978, adminstrv. mgr., 1979-80; budget analyst U.S. Naval Mil. Command, Arlington, Va., 1981; prodn. supr. Arlington County Visual & Performing Arts, 1981-84; dep. dir. McLean (Va.) Community Ctr., 1984-87; exec. dir. Reston (Va.) Community Ctr., 1987—; prodn. chair Southeastern Theatre Conf., Arlington, 1984; mem. Drug Free Recreation for Youth Task Force, Fairfax, Va., 1988—, Dogwood Edn. Task Force, Reston, 1989—. Mem. com. Fairfax County Coun. of the Arts, 1987—, Purple Sage Cluster Assn. Social Commn., Reston, 1988; mem. organizing com. Fairfax County Summit Youth Issues, 1989. Mem. Va. Assn. Female Execs., Cultural Alliance Greater Washington, Pk. and Recreation Assn. Democrat. Unitarian. Home: 12149 Purple Sage Ct Herndon VA 22070

PAVELKA, ELAINE BLANCHE, mathematics educator; b. Chgo.; d. Frank Joseph and Mildred Bohumila (Seidl) P.; B.A., M.S., Northwestern U.; Ph.D., U. Ill. With Northwestern U. Aerial Measurements Lab., Evanston, Ill.; tchr. Leyden Community High Sch., Franklin Park, Ill.; prof. math. Morton Coll., Cicero, Ill.; invited speaker 3d Internat. Congress Math. Edn., Karlsruhe, Germany, 1976. Recipient sci. talent award Westinghouse Elec. Co. Mem. Am. Edn. Research Assn., Am. Math. Assn. 2-Year Colls., Am. Math. Soc., Assn. Women in Math., Can. Soc. History and Philosophy of Math., Ill. Council Tchr. of Math., Ill. Math. Assn. Community Colls., Math. Assn. Am., Math. Action Group, Ga. Center Study and Teaching and Learning Math., Nat. Council Tchrs. of Math., Sch. Sci. and Math. Assn., Soc. Indsl. and Applied Math., Northwestern U. Alumni Assn., U. Ill. Alumni Assn., Am. Mensa Ltd., Intertel, Sigma Delta Epsilon, Pi Mu Epsilon. Home: PO Box 7312 Westchester IL 60154 Office: Morton Coll 3801 S Central Ave Cicero IL 60650

PAVKOV, JANET RUTH, state official; b. Wadsworth, Ohio, Aug. 7, 1939; d. George and Helen Rose (Pamer) P. RN, Mansfield (Ohio) Gen. Hosp., 1960; BS in Tech. Edn., U. Akron, 1972, MA in Family Life, 1976; cert. in nursing home adminstrn., Ohio State U., 1983. Lic. social worker; lic. nursing home adminstr., counselor; cert. activity cons./educator. Charge nurse obstet. dept. Mansfield Gen. Hosp., 1960; gen. practice office nurse P.O. Staker, M.D., Mansfield, 1961; operating room nurse Akron (Ohio) Gen. Hosp., 1961-70; charge nurse obstet. dept. Wayne Gen. Hosp., Orrville, Ohio, 1970-71; nursing faculty mem. North Cen. Tech. Coll., Mansfield, 1972-74, asst. chairperson nursing program, 1973-74; instr. St. Thomas Hosp. Sch. Nursing, Akron, 1974-77; nurse epidemiologist Alum Crest Nursing Home, Columbus, 1978-84, nursing supr., 1978-80; nursing home adminstr. Am. Health Care Facilities, Springfield and Canton, Ohio, 1986-89; health facilities standards rep. II dept. health State of Ohio, Akron, 1989-90; mgr. nursing svcs. Community Mental Health Ctr., Columbus, 1990—; vol. nurse and camp counselor Webster Springs (W.Va.) Camp, 1960-75, Palisades Camp, Pacific Palisades, Calif., 1963, Camp Massanetta, Harrisonburg, Va., 1978-79, 86; vol. nurse Prescott (Ariz.) Pines Camp, 1967, Oakwood Camp, Syracuse, Ind., 1968, Presbyn. Camp, Portland, Oreg., 1970; cons. McNeil Pharms., Spring House, Pa., 1982, 84, Assn. Developmentally Disabled Intermediate Care Facility forMentally Retarded, Columbus, 1983-85, Alum Crest Nursing Home, 1979-85; mem. ARC Vol. Nurse Div., 1958—, Nat. Council Nursing Home Nurses, 1979-84, Nat. Council Family Relations, 1975-84, Retired Sr. Vol. Program adv. council, 1975-77; instr. lic. practical nurse program Warren (Ohio) Pub. Schs., 1972; active Ohio Dist. 6 Mental Health Older Adult Council, 1977-84; staff nurse Eastland Care Ctr., Columbus, 1981-84; adminstr.-on-call nursing services Kimberly Pkwy. Group Home, Columbus, 1983-84, coordinator patient assessment and nursing services, 1983-84; counselor, shift leader emergency services Columbus Area Community Mental Health Ctr., Columbus, 1977-86, coordinator geriatric services, 1977-87, mem. quality assurance and peer rev. com., 1978-87; mem. adv. bd. home health care div. Health Care Personnel Assn., Inc., 1983-86; sec. Specialized Health Adminstrv. Resource Enterprises, 1983-85; chairperson Franklin County Mental Health Bd. Older Adult Task Force, 1984-87; mem. adv. com. Program 60 Ohio State U., 1984-87; workshop and seminar leader; adj. fellow Inst. of Life Span Devel. and Gerontology U. Akron, 1988—; lectr. in field. Editor: Ohio Gerontol. Soc. newsletter, 1984-85; mem. editorial adv. bd. Jour. Long Term Care Adminstrn., 1985-87; editorial asst. Ohio chpt. Am. Coll. Health Care Adminstrs. newsletter, 1985-87; contbr. articles to profl. jours. Instr. Sunday sch. Apostolic Christian Ch., 1958-83; mem. exec. com. Internat. Christian Friendship Group, 1965-79, mem. missionary com., 1980-83. Recipient Bronze medal Brit. Med. Soc., 1983, Staff award Franklin County Mental Health Bd., 1985. Mem. Am. Coll. Long Term Care Adminstrs., Am. Home Econs. Assn., Gerontol. Soc. Am., Ohio Gerontol. Assn., Cen. Ohio Geriatric Nurses Assn. (mem. program and planning com. 1979—, chairperson publicity com. 1980-81, sec. 1979-81, sec.-treas. 1981-84, mem. edn. com. 1983—), Mansfield Gen. Hosp. Alumnae Assn. (sec. 1960-61). Home: 169 G Brandywine Dr Westerville OH 43081 Office: Community Mental Health Ctr 1515 E Broad St Columbus OH 43205

PAVLICK, PAMELA KAY, nurse, consultant; b. Topeka, Aug. 16, 1944; d. Cy Pavlick and June Lucille (Arnold) Dull. Diploma nursing, St. Luke's Hosp., Kansas City, Mo., 1966; BA in Psychology magna cum laude, U. North Fla., 1982, MS in Health Adminstrn. summa cum laude, 1987. RN, Mo., Ill., Fla.; cert. ins. rehab. specialist; lic. rehab. providor, Fla. Clin. instr. St. Luke's Hosp., Kansas City, 1966-70; instr. lic. practical nursing Springfield (Ill.) Sch. Bd., 1970-72; nursing supr. Jacksonville Beach (Fla.) Hosp., 1972-74; pub. health nurse State of Fla., Ocala, 1974-76; dir. nursing Upjohn Health Care, Jacksonville, Fla., 1976-77, mem. adv. com.; med. rep. Travelers Ins. Co., Jacksonville, 1977-84; rehab. cons. Aetna Life & Casualty, Jacksonville, 1985—, rep. nurse cons. adv. coun., 1988-90. Mem. Am. Nurses Assn., Am. Assn. Rehab. Nurses, Nat. Assn. Rehab. Providers, Phi Kappa Phi. Republican. Episcopalian. Home: 1848 Willowood Dr Jacksonville FL 32225 Office: Aetna Life & Casualty PO Box 2200 Jacksonville FL 32203

PAVLIK, ELSA M., civic worker; b. Cleve., Apr. 6, 1943; d. Heinrich Sebastian and Olga Mary (Trampush) Felgemacher; m. Thomas Chester Pavlik Sr., Nov. 19, 1966; 1 child, Thomas Chester, Jr. BA, Case Western Res. U., 1967. V.p. Glor-el Real Estate Devel. Corp., Cleve., 1983-86; relocation transition cons. Realty One, Cleve., 1986—. Editor On Cue, 1982—. Mem. adv. bd. Fairmount Theatre of the Deaf, Cleve., 1982—, Cath. Social Services Cleve., 1986—; trustee Cath. Charities Corp., 1989—, United Way Assembly, 1989—, Cleve. Heritage Parks Assn., 1974-76, Beck Ctr. for The Cultural Arts, Lakewood, Ohio, 1985—, Hist. Sites Found., Cleve., 1985—. Named one of 100 Women of Achievement New Cleveland Woman Jour., 1988-89; recipient Mather Centennial award Case Western Res. U. Mem. NAFE, Susan B. Anthony Soc. Women Space, Internat. Platform Assn., Great Lakes Shakespeare Festival (pres. women's com. 1979-81, I Will award 1982, 86), Women's City Club (pres. 1987-89, Elsa M. Pavlik Vol. of Yr. Cleve. chpt.), Coll. Club West. Republican. Roman Catholic. Clubs: Women's City Cleve. (pres. 1987—), Coll. Club West (Rocky River). Office: Realty One Terminal Tower Ste 1415 Cleveland OH 44113

PAVLIK, LYNDA MCELROY, marketing manager; b. Irving, Ill., Feb. 26, 1939; d. Gerald Wilson and Mildred Louise (Lipe) McElroy; m. James Wm. Pavlik, July 18, 1959 (div. May 1985); children: Claire Cook, David James, Anne Louise; m. Frank Anthony Rouzée, Feb. 18, 1989. Student, Carthage Coll., 1956-59; BA, U. Wisconsin, 1972. Office mgr. WBCR Radio, Blacksburg, Va., 1959-61; tchr. Modern City Acad., Kumasi, Ghana, West Africa, 1961-62; admin. asst. UNESCO, Addis Ababa, Ethiopia, 1968-69; freelance writer Worcester, Mass. and River Falls, Wis., 1970-78; tech. editor Digital Equipment Corp., Marlboro, Mass., 1978-79; prodn. mgr. Digital Equipment Corp., Bedford, Mass., 1979-85; european pub. mgr. Digital Equipment Corp., Reading, England, 1985-88; mktg. mgr. Compound Document Architecture program Digital Equipment Corp., Nashua, N.H., 1988—. Contbr. several articles to prof. mags. Unitarian. Office: Product Marketing 10 Tara Boulevard Nashua NH 03062

PAVLOW, SHARA TOURSH, medical administrator; b. Miami, Fla., June 21, 1950; d. June R. (Toursh) P. BA, U. Miami, 1972; MA, U. N.C., 1975; postgrad., U. Miami, 1987. Reg. Emergency Med. Technician, Fla. Staff writer The Miami Herald, 1971-72; info. officer The N.C. Meml. Hosp., Chapel Hill, N.C., 1972-73; pub. info. dir. Heart Assn. of Greater Miami, 1973-74; sr. health planner Health Systems Agy. South Fla., Miami, 1974-78; asst. adminstrn. Jackson Meml. Hosp., Miami, 1978-81; dir. clin. affairs Sch. of Medicine, U. Miami, 1981-87; chief operating officer Healthcare Mgmt. Enterprises, Inc., Miami, 1988--; cons. South Fla. Emergency Med. Svcs. Coun., 1979-80, HEW, Washington, 1975-76; mem. adj. faculty Fla. Internat. U., 1975-79, St. Thomas U., 1987; coord. advanced trauma life support U. Miami Sch. Medicine, 1980-81; bd. dirs. F. Bratcher & Dancers. Bd. dirs. Sta. WLRN, various pub. radio, television stas.1988—. Home: 9002 SW 78th Pl Miami FL 33156

PAVONI, MARY MICHELLE, service executive, consultant, educator; b. Duluth, Minn., July 23, 1944; d. D.C. Mike and Jeanne Claire (LeNeau) Clark; m. Stephen Paul Bertrand (div. Jan. 1981); m. Lorenzo E. Pavoni, July 3, 1986; 1 child, Kathleen Claire. BS, Coll. of St. Scholastica, 1966. Dir. med. records dept. Poudre Valley Meml. Hosp., Ft. Collins, Colo., 1966-67, Charles T. Miller Hosp., St. Paul, 1967-70, Hennepin County Med. Ctr., Mpls., 1970-78, Henry Ford Hosp., Detroit, 1978-80, U. Ill. Hosp., Chgo., 1980-84; dir. med. records Mercy Hosp. and Med. Ctr., Chgo., 1984—; asst. clin. prof. med. records adminstrn. U. Ill., Chgo., 1980—. Mem. editorial rev. bd. Topics in Health Records Mgmt., 1987—. Mem. Am. Med. Record Assn. (editorial rev. bd. 1987—), Ill. Med. Record Assn. (pres. 1989-90), Chgo. Med. Record Assn. (pres. 1985-86, Disting. Mem. award 1988), Chgo. Assn. Parliamentarians. Democrat. Roman Catholic. Office: Mercy Hosp and Med Ctr Stevenson Expy and King Dr Chicago IL 60616

PAXMAN, GALE FREEMAN, lawyer, nurse; b. Cleve., Dec. 25, 1957; d. Marvin Stanley and Yolanda Claire (Dilgard) Freeman; m. John Terrence Paxman, Aug. 5, 1989. BSN, Syracuse U., 1979; JD, Case Western Res. U., 1989. Bar: Ga. 1989, Fla. 1990; RN, Ohio, Ga., Mass., Calif., Fla. Oper. rm. and office nurse E.N.T.-Head & Neck Surgery Assocs., Inc., Lakewood, Ohio, 1979, 87; clin. and charge nurse med.-surg. ICU Lakewood Hosp., 1979-82; sr. med. reviewer Blue Cross-Blue Shield-Medicare Mass., Boston, 1985; clin. and charge nurse cardiothoracic ICU Brigham and Women's Hosp., Boston, 1982-86; pvt. practice Savannah, Ga., 1989; assoc. Adams, Gardner & Ellis, Savannah, Ga., 1990—; med.-legal cons., Savannah, 1989—, West Palm Beach, Fla, 1990. Mem. AACCN, State Bar Ga., Savannah Bar Assn., Assn. Trial Lawyers Am., Nat. Health Lawyers Assn., Am. Assn. Nurse Attys. Home: 529 S Flagler Dr Apt 12H West Palm Beach FL 33401

PAXTON, ALICE ADAMS, artist, architect and interior designer; b. Hagerstown, Md., May 19, 1914; d. William Albert and Josephine (Adams) Rosenberger; m. James Love Paxton Jr., June 26, 1942 (div.); 1 child, William Allen III. Student, Peabody Inst. Music, Balt., 1937-38; grad., Parson's Sch. Design, N.Y., 1940; studies with J. Laurie Wallace, 1944-46; studies with Augustus Dunbier, 1947-48, Sylvia Curtis, 1949, Milton Wolsky, 1950, Frank Sapousek, 1951. Free-lance work archtl. renderings and interior design, N.Y., 1937-40; interior designer, designer spl. furnishings, muralist Orchard and Wilhelm, Omaha, 1940-42; tchr. art classes Alice Paxton Studio, Omaha, 1957-64; tchr. mech. drawing, archtl. rendering and mech. perspective Parson's Sch. Design, N.Y., 1937-40. Designer (interior) Chapel Boys' Town, Nebr., 1942; one-woman show of archtl. renderings Washington County Mus. Fine Arts, Hagerstown, 1944; exhibited group shows at Joslyn Mus., Omaha, 1943-44, Ann. Exhbn. Cumberland Valley Artists, Hagerstown, 1945; represented in permanent collections at No. Natural Gas Co. Bldg., Omaha, Swanson Found., Omaha; also pvt. collections; vol. designer, decorator: recreation room Omaha Blood Bank, ARC, 1943, recreation room Creighton U., 1943, lounge psychiat. ward Lincoln (Nebr.) Army Hosp., 1944; planner, color coordinator Children's Hosp., Omaha, 1947, painted murals, 1948, decorated dental room, 1950; designed Candy Stripers' uniforms; painted and decorated straw elephant bag presented to Mrs. Richard Nixon, 1960; contbr. articles and photographs to Popular Home mag., 1958. Co-chair camp and hosp. coms. ARC, 1943-45, mem. county com. to select and send gifts to servicemen, 1943-46; mem. Ak-Sar-Ben Ball Com., Omaha, 1946-48, Nat. Mus. Women in the Arts, The Md. Hist. Soc.; judge select Easter Seal design, Joslyn Mus., 1946; mem. council Girl Scouts U.S., Omaha, 1943-47; spl. drs. chmn. Jr. League, Omaha, 1947-48, chair Jr. League Red Cross fund dr., 1947-48; bd. dirs., vol. worker Creche, Omaha, 1954-56; mem. Omaha Jr. League; chmn. Jr. League Community Chest Fund Dr., 1948-50; co-chair Infantile Paralysis Appeal, 1944; numerous vol. profl. activities for civic orgns., hosps., clubs, chs., community playhouse, and for establishing wildlife sanctuary. Recipient three teaching scholarships Parson's Sch. Design, 1937-40, presdl. citation ARC activities, 1946, 1st prize Ann. Midwest Show Joslyn Mus., 1943. Mem. Associated Artists Omaha (charter), Am. Security Council (nat. adv. bd.), Internat. Platform Assn., U.S. Hist. Soc., Nat. Mus. Women in Arts (charter), Md. Hist. Soc. Republican. Episcopalian. Club: Fountain Head Country. Home: 300 Meadowbrook Rd Hagerstown MD 21740

PAXTON, LAURA BELLE-KENT, English language educator, management professional; b. Lake Charles, La., Feb. 8, 1942; d. George Ira and Gladys Lillian (Barrett) Kent; m. Kenneth Robert Paxton Jr., Jan. 2, 1962. BA, McNeese U., Lake Charles, 1963, MA in English, 1972; EdD, East Tex. U., 1983. cert. English, social studies instr., prin., supt., edml. adminstr., Ariz. Tchr. Darrington (Wash.) High Sch., 1966-70; English instr. Maricopa Community Coll., Phoenix, 1974—; migrant program instr. Phoenix Union High Sch., 1984-88; English instr. Embry-Riddle Aeronautical U., Luke AFB, Ariz., 1985-87; sales rep. Merrill Lynch Realty, Phoenix, 1985-88; co-owner Paxton Mgmt. Co., Phoenix, 1985—; Editor Ariz. corr. courses, 1987-88; presenter migrant worker program confs., 1987—; reviewer Prentice-Hall, 1985. Author: (books) A Handbook for Middle Eastern Dancers, 1978, The Kent Family History from 1787 to 1981, 1981, A Handbook of Home Remedies, 1981; contbr. articles, poems to mags., profl. jours. Mem. Everett, Wash. Opera Guild, 1966-70, Ariz. State U. Opera Guild, Tempe, 1978-80; mem. City of Darrington Council, 1969-70; ESL instr. Friendly House, Phoenix, 1978-79. Mem. NEA, Ariz. Edn. Assn., Ariz. English Assn., Ariz. Sch. Adminstrs., Ariz. Assn. Supervision and Curriculum Devel., Assn. Sch. Bus. Officials Internat., AWARE, Classroom Tchrs. Assn., Pre-Legal Soc. of McNeese U., Pi Kappa Delta, Phi Delta Kappa. Home: 8415 N 32d Ave Phoenix AZ 85051

PAYER, CAROLYN ANN, counselor; b. Lakewood, Ohio, June 28, 1934; d. James William and Maria (Heron) Kuliga; m. Allan Alexander Payer, Feb. 16, 1957; children: Cynthia Jeannette, Allan Mark, Shawn Alexander. Accounts receivable supr. Sheraton-Cleve. Hotel, Cleve., 1958-60; real estate counselor Realty One, Cleve. and Port Clinton, Ohio, 1967—. Author poems. Mem. Ottawa County Bd. Realtors (chairperson social com. Port Clinton chpt. 1990—, publicity com. 1990—), Pool League, Bowling League. Home: 426 E Perry St Port Clinton OH 43452 Office: Realty One 3336 NW Catawba Rd Port Clinton OH 43452

PAYNE, ANITA HART, reproductive endocrinologist, researcher; b. Karlsruhe, Baden, Germany, Nov. 24, 1926; came to U.S., 1938; d. Frederick Michael and Erna Rose (Hirsch) Hart; widowed; children: Gregory Steven, Teresa Payne-Lyons. BA, U. Calif., Berkeley, 1949, PhD, 1952. Rsch. assoc. U. Mich., Ann Arbor, 1961-71, asst. prof., 1971-76, assoc. prof., 1976-81, prof., 1981—, assoc. dir. Ctr. for Study Reprodn., 1989—; vis. scholar Stanford U., 1987-88; mem. reproductive biology study sect., NIH, Bethesda, Md., 1978-79, biochem. endocrinology study sect., 1979-83, population rsch. com. Nat. Inst. Child Health and Human Devel., 1989—. Assoc. editor Steroids, 1987—; contbr. book chpts., articles to profl. jours. Recipient award for cancer rsch. Calif. Inst. Rsch. Cancer, 1953, Acad. Women's Caucus award U. Mich., 1986. Mem. Endocrine Soc. (chmn. awards com. 1984-85, mem. nominating com. 1985-87, coun. 1988—), Am. Soc. Andrology (exec. coun. 1980-83), Soc. for Study Reprodn. (bd. dirs. 1982-85, sec. 1986-89, pres. 1989—). Office: U of Mich L1225/0278 Womens Hosp Ann Arbor MI 48108-0278

PAYNE, DEBORAH ANN, infosystems specialist; b. Weisbauden, Fed. Republic of Germany, Oct. 14, 1952; came to U.S., 1954; d. Robert Roswell and Paulene Ruth (Boone) P.; m. Dale Bruce Rickard, Dec. 22, 1974 (div. Mar. 1982); m. Richard Jay Atkinson, Nov. 2, 1989. Student, U. Hawaii, 1970-72; BA in Psychology, U. Okla., 1974; postgrad., Midwestern State U., Wichita Falls, Tex., 1979-80. Counselor Travelers Aid Soc., Oklahoma City, 1974-75; fin. aid counselor Allstate Bus. Coll., Dallas, 1976-79, dir. grad. placement, 1980-81; fin. aid counselor Midwestern State U., 1979-80; corp. tng. specialist AMF, Inc. subs. Minstar, Inc., Garland, Tex., 1981-85; computer tng. specialist Glendale, Calif., 1985-86; dist. sales mgr. AMF Bowling Cos., Inc. div. AMF, Inc., Houston, 1986-87; computer systems specialist Garland, 1987—, AMF Bowling Cos. Inc., Richmond, Va., 1989—. Mem. AAUW, Am. Bus. Women's Assn., Networking Women, Delta Gamma Alumnae Assn. Republican. Mem. Ch. Religious Sci.

PAYNE, DEBORAH ANNE, medical company officer; b. Norristown, Pa., Sept. 22, 1952; d. Kenneth Nathan Moser and Joan (Reese) Dewhurst; m. Randall Barry Payne, Mar. 8, 1975. AA, Northeastern Christian Jr. Coll., 1972; B in Music Edn., Va. Commonwealth U., 1979. Driver, social asst. Children's Aid Soc., Norristown, Pa., 1972-73; mgr. Boddie-Noell Enterprises, Richmond, Va., 1974-79; retail food saleswoman Hardee's Food Systems, Inc., Phila., 1979-81; supr., with tech. tng. and testing and computer depts. Cardiac Datacorp., Phila., 1981—. Mem. bd. advisers Am. Biog. Inst., 1989. Mem. NAFE, Delta Omicron (pres. Alpha Xi chpt. 1978-79, pres. Epsilon province 1980-85, chmn. Eastern Pa. alumni 1986-88, Star award 1979), Am. Soc. Profl. and Exec. Women. Republican. Office: Cardiac Datacorp 1429 Walnut St 2d Fl Philadelphia PA 19102

PAYNE, ELIZABETH ELEANORE, surgeon, otolaryngologist; b. Detroit, Mar. 17, 1945; d. Richard Franklin and Eleanore Grace (Dieterich) P.; 1 child from previous marriage, Julia Elizabeth Komanecky. Student, St. Olaf Coll., 1962-64; MD, U. Iowa, 1968. Cert. Am. Bd. Otolaryngology, Am. Acad. Otolaryngic Allergy; lic. in medicine, Minn., Iowa. Intern Phila. Gen. Hosp., 1968-69; resident gen. surgery U. Minn., Mpls., 1969-70; resident otolaryngology U. Minn., 1970-74, clin. asst. prof. dept. otolaryngology, asst. clin. prof. dept. family practice and community health; otolaryngologist, surgeon Affiliated Otolaryngologists, P.A., Mpls.; med. staff N. Meml. Med. Ctr., Mpls., Meth. Hosp., St. Louis Park, Minn. Contbr. articles to profl. jours. Mem. Hennepin County Med. Assn., Minn. State Med. Assn., AMA, Am. Acad. Otolaryngology Head and Neck Surgery, Minn. Acad. Otolaryngology Head and Neck Surgery, Am. Coll. Surgeons, Am. Acad. Otolaryngic Allergy, Minn. Acad. Medicine. Office: Affiliate Otolaryngologists 3366 Oakdale Ave N Ste 307 Minneapolis MN 55422

PAYNE, ILENE DELORES, federal agency administrator, program analyst; b. Bronx, N.Y., Apr. 23, 1946; d. Clyde Thomas Smith and Bessie (Grissom) Reeves; m. James D. Payne Jr., Oct. 5, 1974; 1 child, April Danielle. BA, Howard U., 1967. Intelligence rsch. analyst Library of Congress, Washington, 1967-70; legal technician U.S. Dept. of Justice, Washington, 1970-72; asst. dir. EEO U.S. Customs Svc., Washington, 1972-73; EEO specialist EEOC, Washington, 1973-75; fed. women's program mgr. Fed. Hwy. Adminstrn., Washington, 1975-80, chief internal EEO div., 1980-83, sr. state tng. officer, 1983—; mem. EEO curriculum com. U.S. Office Personnel Mgmt., Washington, 1981-89. Named One of Outstanding Young Women in Am., 1981; named to Hon. Order of Ky. COls., 1982. Office: Fed Hwy Adminstrn 6300 Georgetown Pike McLean VA 22101

PAYNE, JENNIFER LYNN, retail executive; b. Findlay, Ohio, Apr. 5, 1965; d. James D. and Barbara A. (McGee) P. BA, Findlay Coll., 1987. Pres. Gifts In Time, Inc., Findlay, 1986—. Pres. Young Reps. of Hancock County, 1989—; bd. dirs. Findlay Downtown Area Assn., 1987—; mem. United Way, 1987—. Mem. Hancock Leadership, Findlay/Hancock County C. of C. (showcase com., bus. com., communications com., ambassador 1987—). Republican. Office: Gifts in Time Inc 117 W Sandusky St Findlay OH 45840

PAYNE, LINDA COHEN, business owner; b. N.Y.C., Jan. 9, 1953; d. Gerald Theodore and Bianca (Joselson) Cohen; m. Stephen George Payne, Mar. 20, 1977. BA, Hunter Coll., 1981. Brokerage asst. Harris, Upham & Co., N.Y.C., 1974-75; dept. head cen. inquiry Standard & Poor's Corp., N.Y.C., 1976-87; owner, mgr. Payne Fin. Rsch., N.Y.C., 1988—. Mem. Spl. Libr. Assn., ALA, Libr. Mgmt. Assn. Home and Office: Payne Fin Rsch 85-99 98th St Woodhaven NY 11421

PAYNE, LORRAINE MARIE, marketing professional; b. Sherbrooke, Que., Can., Dec. 8, 1952; d. Marcel Joseph and Betty Cecilia (Larson) Gregoire; m. Robert Michael Payne, July 7, 1971 (dec. 1979); children: Jason Robert, Cory Steward; m. Patrick J. McKenna, Aug. 3, 1985. Student, Grant McKewan Coll., Edmonton, Alta., Can., 1975-77. Sr. copywriter Woodwards Ltd., Edmonton, 1977-79; advt. dir. Grove Pub., Edmonton, 1980-81; sr. dir. Mary Kay Cosmetics, Can., 1981-82; pub. affairs cons. Alta. Govt. Pub. Affairs Bur., Edmonton, 1982-86; v.p., ptnr. Williams & Wilson's PR Ltd., Edmonton, 1986; founder, ptnr. Payne Cook & Assocs. Inc.-Strategic Communications, Edmonton, 1986—; dir. pub. relations Edmonton Heritage Festival Assn., 1986-87; chmn. pub. relations Edmonton C. of C. Centennial '87 Com., 1987—. Author (column) Paynefully Thought Over, Edmonton Examiner, 1977-79; contbr. articles to profl. jours. Bd. dirs. Uncles at Large, Edmonton, 1980-82. Mem. Internat. Assn. Bus. Communications, Can. Pub. Rels. Soc. (accredited), Am. Mktg. Assn. (exec., founder No. Alta. chpt.). Progressive Conservative. Roman Catholic. Club: Toastmasters (founder Edmonton chpt. 1984). Office: Payne Cook & Assocs Inc, 1600 Royal LePage Bldg, Edmonton, AB Canada T5J 3N9

PAYNE, MABEL LOUISE, education administrator; b. Manhattan, N.Y., Oct. 24, 1949; d. Elaine Agusta (Phillips) P. BA in Social Scis., SUNY at Binghamton, 1971; MS in Counseling and Personnel Svcs., SUNY, Albany, 1974; MA in Orgnl. Psychology, Columbia U., 1987. Counselor, seminar coordinator N.Y.C. Tech. Coll., 1975-79; training specialist, career counselor Opportunities Industrialization Ctr. N.Y., 1979-82; prin., founder, career ednl. and organizational devel. cons. Resources Assocs., Bronx, N.Y., 1982—; adj. lectr. human svcs. dept., counselor recruiter La Guardia Community Coll., Long Island City, N.Y., 1984-87; assoc. edn. officer N.Y.C. Bd. Edn., 1987—, also mem. proposal rev. com.; assertiveness trainer cons. N.Y. State Commn. for Blind, N.Y.C., 1982-87. Mem. Orgn. Black and Hispanic Alumni SUNY-Binghamton. Office: NYC Bd Edn 110 Livingston St Rm 740 Brooklyn NY 11201

PAYNE, MELISSA ANNE, sales analyst; b. Arlington, Va., Mar. 14, 1964; d. Carroll James Payne and Frances (Cabaniss) Gentry. BBA, Morehead State U., 1986; MBA, Ball State U., 1987. Economic research analyst Indiana Natl. Bank, Ind., IN, 1987-88; sales analyst Ball InCon Glass Packaging, Muncie, Ind., 1988--; dir. Travel King Inc, 1988--. Vol., Spl. Olympics, Muncie, 1986, Pan Am. Games, Indpls., 1987. Mem. Natl. Assn. of Female Execs., Assn. of MBA Exec., Sigma Iota Epsilon, Beta Gamma Sigma. Republican. Protestant. Home: 211 N Greenbriar Muncie IN 47304

PAYNE, THERESA MAE, nurse, health educator; b. Harrisburg, Pa., Mar. 4, 1955; d. Roy Walter and Theresa Abigail (Mason) P. BSN, Coll. Mt. St. Joseph, Cin., 1978; MEd, Pa. State U., Middletown, 1987. Staff nurse Harrisburg Hosp.; asst. head nurse U. Va., Charlottesville, 1978-82; health edn. coord., nursing supr. Community Med. Assocs., Harrisburg, 1984—. Democrat. Roman Catholic. Office: 3544 N Progress Ave Harrisburg PA 17110

PAYNE PALACIO, JUNE ROSE, dietitian, educator; b. Hove, Sussex, Eng., June 14, 1940; d. Alfred and Doris Winifred (Blanch) Payne; m. Moki Moses Palacio, Nov. 30, 1968; children: Carmen, Dora Jean, Lurene, Michael. AA, Orange Coast Coll., Costa Mesa, 1958-60; BS, U. Calif., Berkeley, 1960-63; postgrad., Dietetic Registration Mills Co, Oakland, 1963-64; PhD, Kans. State U., Manhattan, 1980-83. Registered dietitian. Asst. dir. foodservice, residence hall Mills Coll., Oakland, Calif., 1964-66; staff dietitian Servomation-Bay Cities, Inc., Oakland, 1966-67; food svc. dir. Host Internat., Inc., Honolulu, 1967-73; instr. Kapiolani Community Coll., Honolulu, 1984—, U. Hawaii, Honolulu, 1973-80; dir. dietetics Straub Clinic & Hosp., 1973-80; instr. Kansas State U., Manhattan, Kans., 1980-83, El Camino & Santa Monica Colls., Santa Monica, Calif., 1984—; design cons. Clevenger Nutritional Svc., Santa Monica, 1984—; assoc. profr. Pepperdine U., Malibu, Calif., 1984—; instr. Ctr. Dietetic Edn., Woodland Hills, Calif., 1986--. Contbr. articles to profl. jours. Mem. Am. Dietetic Assn. (ho. dels., ethics com., AP4 rev. panel.). Republican. Episcopalian. Home: 24319 Baxter Dr Malibu CA 90265 Office: Pepperdine U Dept Nat Sci 24255 Pacific Coast Hwy Malibu CA 90265

PAYNE-PARSONS, SHARON LEE, management consultant; b. Chgo., Aug. 10, 1945; d. Steve and Shirley Florence (Johnson) Sawchuk; m. Edward Shier Parsons Jr., Feb. 14, 1981; Kimberly, Katharine, David. BS, U. Nev., 1977. Media dir. O'Brien Advt., Reno, 1978-81; ptnr. Mgmt. Devel. Assocs., Reno, 1981—. Pres. Nev. Alliance for the Arts, Reno, 1985-87; treas. Nev. Alliance Arts Edn., Las Vegas, 1985-88; panelist Am. Orch. Symphony League, Salt Lake City, 1986; bd. dirs. Very Spl. Arts of Nev., 1988—. Recipient Gov.'s Arts award Nev. State Council on the Arts, 1985. Mem. Reno Ad Club. Office: Mgmt Devel Assocs 115 W Plumb Ln Ste 206 Reno NV 89509

PAYSEUR, VICTORIA FELLAND, accountant; d. Wallace Maynard and Marjorie Rohease (Stowe) Felland; m. Gary Lee Leadmon, Aug. 18, 1973 (div. 1985); m. R. Ted Payseur, May 10, 1985. BA, Luther Coll., Decorah, Ia., 1973; MA, Wash. State U., 1975; MBA, Drake U., Des Moines, 1982. CPA, Iowa. Tax acct. Coopers & Lybrand, Des Moines, 1982-83; tax mgr. Peat Marwick, Des Moines, 1983-85; controller Simpson Coll., Indianola, Iowa, 1985-87, treas., 1987-89; v.p. for bus. and fin. Simpson Coll., Indianola, 1989—; mem. Way Up Planning Comm., Des Moines Iowa 1988--. Mem. NAFE, Cen. Assn. Coll. U. Bus. Offls., Nat. Assn. coll. U. Bus. Office. Democratic. Lutheran. Office: Simpson Coll 701 N Central St Indianola IA 50125

PAYTON, ANTOINETTE SHIELDS, realtor; b. Miles City, Mont., Mar. 9, 1926; d. Claude M. and Odie (Waddell) Shields; m. Robert J. Iholts, Mar. 30, 1946 (dec. Oct. 1957); children: Robert C., Marilyn Tracy; m. Donald Glen Payton, Dec. 5, 1959. BA, U. Mont., 1959; postgrad., U. Nev., 1960-71. Cert. tchr., libr., Nev.; lic. realtor, Nev. Tchr. Reno Pub. Schs., 1960-64; libr. Billinghurst Jr. High Sch., Pine Mid. Sch., Reno, 1964-85; realtor, co-owner, sec. Century 21 All Seasons, Reno, 1985—, also bd. dirs. Recipient Disting. Svc. award Washoe County Tchrs. Assn., 1985. Mem. AAUW, PTA (life Reno), Nat. Assn. Realtors, Nev. Assn. Realtors, Reno/Sparks Assn. Realtors, Alpha Delta Kappa (pres., treas. 1975-82), Beta Sigma Phi (life, officer 1950-90). Office: Century 21 All Seasons 1595 S Virginia Reno NV 89509

PAZANDAK, CAROL HENDRICKSON, professor of liberal arts; b. Mpls.; d. Norman Everard and Ruth (Buckley) Hendrickson; m. Bruce B. Pazandak (dec. 1986); children: David, Bradford, Christopher, Eric, Paul, Ann. PhD, U. Minn., 1970. Asst. dir. admissions U. Minn., Mpls., 1970-72, asst. dean liberal arts, 1972-79, asst. to pres., 1979-85, office of internat. edn., acting dir., 1985-87, asst. prof. to assoc. to prof. liberal arts, 1970—; vis. prof. U. Iceland, Reykjavik, 1984, periods in 83, 86, 87, 88, 89; exec. dir. Minn.-Iceland Adv. Com. U. Minn., 1984—; cons. U. Iceland, 1983—; co-chair Reunion of Sisters-Minn. and Finland Confs. Editor: Improving Undergraduate Education in Large Universities, 1989. Past pres. Minn. Mrs. Jaycees, Mpls. Mrs. Jaycees; bd. govs. St. John's Preparatory Sch., Collegeville, Minn.; former bd. trustees Coll. of St. Teresa, Winona, Minn.. Named to Order of the Falcon, Govt. of Iceland, 1990. Mem. Am. Psychol. Assn., Am. Coun. Edn. (former steering com. Nat. Identification Program for Women in Higher Edn. Adminstrn. 1983-86). Home: 1666 Coffman St #117 Saint Paul MN 55108 Office: U Minn CLA 101 Pleasant St SE Minneapolis MN 55455

PAZDAR, DONNA JEAN, personnel manager; b. Hartford, Conn., May 11, 1949; d. Walter Joseph and Frances Magdalen (Mierzejewski) Jedynak; m. John Stephen Pazdar, June 19, 1970; children: Craig Thomas, Eric John. AA, Greater Hartford Community, 1982; student, St. Joseph Coll., W. Hartford, Conn., 1984—, Williams Coll., 1986-88. Presentations designer Aetna Life & Casualty, Hartford, 1980-81; acctg. & statis. processor Aetna Life & Casualty, 1981-82, contract analyst, 1983-84, program asst. coll. relations, 1984-85; recruiter Conn. Bank & Trust Co., Hartford, 1985-86; asst. treas., mgr. staffing Conn. Bank & Trust Co., 1986-89; personnel mgr. Murtha, Cullina, Richter & Pinney, Hartford, 1989—; advisor Hartford Coll. for Women, 1987-89. Bd. dirs. Wethersfield (Conn.) Citizens Scholarship Found., 1988—. Mem. Nat. Assn. Bank Women (program chair 1988-89), Nat. Assn. for Female Execs., Assn. Legal Adminstrs. (editor chpt. newsletter 1990—, del to USSR legal mgmt. specialists 1990), Wethersfield Jr. Woman's Club (hon. mem., Outstanding Club Woman 1977), Conn. Jr. Women (pres. 1977-78, bd. dirs. 1986-88). Home: 80 Forest Dr Wethersfield CT 06109 Office: Murtha Cullina et al Asylum St at City Pl Hartford CT 06103

PAZNEKAS, SUSAN JENNIFER, information scientist; b. Chgo., Oct. 19, 1949; d. Charles Galen and Audrey (Ellsworth) Hammond; m. James Arrington, May 13, 1971 (div. Jan. 1974); m. William A. Paznekas, Sept. 30, 1989. BS, N.E. Ill. U., 1971; MLS, Rosary Coll., 1972. Asst. librarian Met. Sanitary Dist., Chgo., 1972-73, U.S. EPA, Chgo., 1973-76; acquisitions librarian U.S. Treasury Dept., Washington, 1976-78; asst. librarian U.S. Customs Svc., Washington, 1978-83; head. govt. reference svc. Pratt Library, Balt., 1983-89; pub. libr. cons. Md. State Dept. Edn., 1989—. Bd. mem. Fed. Hill Neighborhood Assn., Balt., 1986—. Mem. ALA, Md. Library Assn. (sec. 1989—). Home: 444 E Cross St Baltimore MD 21230 Office: Md State Dept Edn Div Libr. Devel and Svcs 200 W Baltimore St Baltimore MD 21201

PEABODY, JUDITH DUNNINGTON, philanthropist; b. Richmond, Va., May 6, 1930; d. Bradford H. and Elizabeth Taylor (Dunnington) Walker; m. Samuel Parkman Peabody, Mar. 31, 1951; 1 child, Elizabeth Taylor. Student, Bryn Mawr Coll., Columbia U. Bd. dirs. Dance Theatre of Harlem, Fresh Air Fund for Children, N.Y.C., N.Y. Shakespeare Festival; co-founder Reality House, N.Y.C.; vol. worker, fund-raiser Gay Men's Health Crisis. *

PEABODY, MARYANNE, management consultant; b. N.Y.C., July 26, 1946; d. Robert F. and Helen (Reilly) P.; m. Laurence J. Stybel, May 19, 1972; 1 child, Jennifer. Diploma in nursing, Bellevue Hosp. Sch. of Nursing, 1967; BS, Hunter Coll., 1971; MBA, So. Meth. U., 1974. RN. Dir. of clinics Planned Parenthood Assn. of N.E. Tex., Dallas, 1972-73; home health care coord. City of Boston Health and Hosps. Corp., 1974-75; profl. svcs. cons. Hillhaven, Inc., Lexington, Mass., 1975-81; v.p. Stybel, Peabody & Assocs., Inc., Boston, 1981—. Columnist Boston Bus. Jour.; contbr. articles to bus. and profl. jours. Elected mem. Wayland (Mass.) Bd. Health, 1985-89, chmn., 1986-88; bd. dirs. League Sch. of Boston, Newton, Mass., 1981-84, 90—, Newton, Wellesley, Weston, Needham Area Mental Health/Mental Retardation Bd., 1977-81. Hoblitzelle Found. scholar So. Meth. U., 1974. Office: Stybel Peabody and Assocs 8 Faneuil Hall Market Pl Boston MA 02109

PEACE, BARBARA LOU JEAN, education educator; b. Valdosta, Ga., Jan. 11, 1939; d. Billington Philip and Hattie Lougene (Dollar) Peace. Tenn, Temple U., 1961; MS, Fla. State U., 1963; postgrad., Valdosta State Coll., 1989. Receptionist ITT, Thompson Industries, Valdosta, Ga., 1961; child welfare worker Lowndes County Welfare Dept., Valdosta, 1962; supr. child welfare Muscogee County Dept. Family & Children Services, Columbus, Ga., 1963-66; dir. social worker Valdosta Headstart Program; tchr. Valdosta City Sch. System, 1966-73; tchr. advisor Valdosta Technical Inst., 1973--; advisor Vocational Indsl. Clubs, 1981-88, Valdosta Tech. Inst., 1980-88. Sponsor Am. Red Cross Blood Dr., Valdosta, 1984-88. Mem. Am. Vocational Assn., Ga. Vocational Assn., Vocational Ga. Assn., Vocational Edn. Spl. Needs Personnel, Action Travelers (bd. dirs. 1970—), Adventuretour Exchange Club (sponsor 1981-85). Republican. Baptist. Office: Valdosta Tech Inst Rte 1 Box 65 Valdosta GA 31602

PEACE, LISA BURK, systems programmer; b. San Diego, Jan. 31, 1960; d. Curtis R. and Karen (Schwab) Burk; m. Robert Dale Peace, June 1, 1985. AA, Chipola Jr. Coll., Fla., 1980; BS, U. West Fla., 1982. Computer systems analyst I, State of Fla., Tallahassee, 1982-83, II, 1983-84; programmer/analyst R.J. Kelly & Assocs., Tallahassee, 1985; systems programmer N.W. Regional Data Ctr., Tallahassee, 1985-90, Tallahassee Meml. Regional Med. Ctr., 1990—. Editor bull. Capital Chatter, 1985-86. Vol., Leon County Humane Soc., 1985. Mem. Am. Bus. Women's Assn. (bull. chmn. 1985-86, corr. sec. 1986-87), NAFE, Internat. Platform Assn., Nat. Systems Programmers Assn. Democrat. Avocations: sewing, knitting, jogging. Office: 1433 Miccosukee Rd Tallahassee FL 32308

PEACHEY, CATHY JEAN, writer; b. Newton Hamilton, Pa., Apr. 30, 1949; d. William Swanger and Helen Louise (Taylor) Houck; m. Leroy Aaron Peachey Jr., July 11, 1987; children: Jenny Leigh, Charles Martin, Chadwick Michael, Laura Jo, Amanda Beth. Student, Centre Bus., State Coll., Pa., 1987-88. Mgr. Unico Majik Markets, Lewistown, Pa., 1981-83; tank block assembler Falconer Lewistown, 1983-86; computer operator Houser Vending Co., State Coll., 1988; freelance writer Lewistown, 1988—. Troop leader Boy Scouts Am., Mifflen County, 1971-72, 78-79, 88—; mgr. poll workers Reps. To Elect State Reps., Mifflen County, 1988. Mem. Phi Beta Lambda (pres. and treas. 1987). Democrat. Methodist. Home: 2100 Rt 522 N Lewistown PA 17044

PEACHEY, GEORGIA A., government official; b. Bklyn., Feb. 16, 1928; d. Alfred Archer and Dorothy (Abrams) P. AA, N.Y. Community Coll., 1974; BA, Hunter Coll., 1980. Clerical asst. NIH, N.Y.C., 1955-60, IRS, N.Y.C., 1960-61; pers. asst. FDA, Bklyn., 1961-72; specialist devel. and staffing HHS, N.Y.C., 1972-80; mgr. equal employment fed. women's and Hispanic employment programs C.E. U.S. Army, N.Y.C., 1980-85, acting chief EEO officer C.E., 1985-87, chief EEO C.E., 1987—; leader, speaker Bklyn. Coll., 1982, workshop leader 1985; leader, speaker Hunter Coll., CUNY, 1982-83. Mem. adv. bd. Bklyn. Pub. Libr., 1986-90, CUNY Tech. Coll., Bklyn., 1989-91. Recipient U.S. Pres. Vol. Community Svc. award, 1983, N.Y. Fed. Exec. Bd. award, 1983, Nat. Sojourner Truth award Nat. Assn. Negro Bus. and Profl. Womens Club, 1984, numerous others. Mem. Fed. Employed Women (pres. N.Y.C. chpt. 1985-90, leader, speaker), Image (women's chmn. 1982-86, nat. pres.'s award 1983), Internat. Tng. Communication (served as chmn. various coms., speaker, installing officer, conv. soloist, Washington, 1977, Vancouver, B.C., 1987, pres. 1935-90, pres. club coun., conducted workshops), Am. Mgmt. Assn. Home: 47 McKeever Pl Apt 8D Brooklyn NY 11225

PEACO, JOYCE LORANE, elementary educator; b. Wilmington, Del.; d. James Wesley and Rosa Juanita (Petty) P. BA, Howard U., 1961; MA, U. Del., 1968; EdD, Nova U., 1984. Elem. tchr. Sarah Webb Pyle Sch., Wilmington, 1963, George Gray Sch., Wilmington, 1963-76, Shipley Sch., Wilmington, 1976-85, Lombardy Sch., Talleyville, Del., 1985—; cooperating tchr. Wilmington Pub. Sch. System, 1970, 80. Leader Chesapeake Bay Girl Scouts, Wilmington, 1969—. Recipient Green Angel award Chesapeake Girl Scouts, 1988, Outstanding Leader award Chesapeake Girl Scouts, 1988, Community Svc. award Martin Luther King Dinner Com., 1989. Mem. NEA, AAUW, Nat. Assn. Univ. Women, Kappa Delta Pi, Delta Kappa Gamma, Nat. Sorority Phi Delta Kappa Inc., Sigma Gamma Rho. Home: 8 Colony Blvd Wilmington DE 19802 Office: Brandywine Sch Dist c/o Lombardy Elem Sch 412 Foulk Rd Wilmington DE 19802

PEACOCK, JUDITH ANN See ERWIN, JUDITH ANN

PEACOCK, LARITA WILLIAMS, information systems specialist; b. Madisonville, Ky., Mar. 24, 1954; d. Charles Eugene and Clara Bell (Smith) Williams; m. Hubert Leonard Peacock, Jr., Aug. 30, 1980; 1 child, William Swinson. BA in Math., Princeton U., 1973; MBA, Stanford U., 1975. Systems analyst Exxon Corp., Florham Park, N.J., 1976-77, Exxon Chem. Co. U.S.A., Houston, 1977-79; project mgr. info. systems dept. Marriott Corp., Bethesda, Md., 1980-82, mgr. systems devel. Roy Rogers div., 1982-84, mgr. MIS info. systems dept., 1984-88, info. systems dir., 1988-90; assoc. dir. for data processing Nat. Edn. Assn., 1990—. Mem. NAFE, AAUW. Address: 20634 Neerwinder St Germantown MD 20874

PEACOCK, VALERIE LYNN, paralegal; b. Tallahassee, Nov. 6, 1962; d. William Stanley and Valerie Jo (Tate) P. AA with honors, Tallahassee Community Coll., 1982; BS in Bus. Communication, Fla. State U., 1986. Cert. legal asst., Ga. With Fla. House of Reps., Tallahassee, 1980-84; with office of registrar Fla. State U., Tallahassee, 1984-85; tchr. Leon County Sch. Bd., Tallahassee, 1986-87; legal asst. Dept. of Ins.-Receivership, Tallahassee, 1987-88, B.K. Roberts, Baggett, LaFace & Richard, Tallahassee, 1988; paralegal specialist criminal div. Fla. Atty. Gen., Tallahassee, 1988—; mem. adv. bd. Nat. Ctr. Paralegal Tng., Miami and Ft. Lauderdale, Fla., 1990—. Vol. missionary local church, Port-au-Prince, Haiti, 1985; mem. adminstrv. bd. local church, Tallahassee, 1988—; atty. gen. rep. Partners in Excellence, Tallahassee, 1990. Mem. Fla. Supreme Ct. Hist. Soc., Pi Kappa Phi, Phi Sigma Soc., Phi Theta Kappa. Republican. Office: Atty Gen Criminal Div The Capitol Tallahassee FL 32399-1050

PEAK, MYRA LEE, hazardous waste consultant and company executive; b. Jacksonville, Ill., June 30, 1954; d. Charles Marion and Marjorie Pauline (Kennedy) P.; m. Terry Lee Crowell, July 24, 1948. BA, Knox Coll., 1976; MS, Purdue U., 1979. Cert. surface coal mine foreman, Wyo., hazardous materials technician. Instr. Purdue U., W. Lafayette, Ind., 1976-79; rsch. asst. Colo. State U., Ft. Collins., 1979-80; chemist Front Range Lab., Ft. Collins., 1980; acad. counselor and instr. Purdue U., W. Lafayette, 1980-81; soil scientist Black Butte Coal Co., Point of Rocks, Wyo., 1981-82; field prodn. foreman Black Butte Coal Co., 1982-86; project mgr. MAECORP Inc., Homewood, Ill., 1987-89; pres. Peak Environ. Mgmt., Green River, Wyo., 1989—. Fundraiser Hyde Park Neighborhood Club, Chgo., 1989. Mem. Am. Soc. Agronomy, Soil Sci. Soc. Am., Women in Mgmt. (pub. relations chmn. 1988-89, Woman of Achievement award 1989), Hazardous Materials Mgrs., Gamma Sigma Delta. Office: Peak Environ Mgmt Inc PO Box 404 Green River WY 82935

PEALE, RUTH STAFFORD (MRS. NORMAN VINCENT PEALE), religious leader; b. Fonda, Iowa, Sept. 10, 1906; d. Frank Burton and Anna Loretta (Crosby) Stafford; m. Norman Vincent Peale, June 20, 1930; children: Margaret Ann (Mrs. Paul F. Everett), John Stafford, Elizabeth Ruth (Mrs. John M. Allen). AB, Syracuse U., 1928, LLD, 1953; LittD, Hope Coll., 1962; LHD (hon.), Judson Coll., 1988. Tchr. math. Cen. High Sch., Syracuse, N.Y., 1928-31; nat. pres. women's bd. domestic missions Ref. Ch. Am., 1936-46; sec. Protestant Film Commn., 1946-51; chmn. Am. Mother's Com., 1948-49; pres., editor-in-chief, gen. sec., chief exec. officer Found. for Christian Living, 1940—; nat. pres. bd. domestic missions Ref. Ch. in Am., 1955-56; mem. bd. N. Am. Missions, 1963-69, pres., 1967-69; mem. gen. program council Ref. Ch. in Am., 1968—; mem. com. of 24 for merger Ref. Ch. in Am. and Presbyn. Ch. U.S., 1966-69; v.p. Protestant Council N.Y.C., 1964-66; hon. chancellor Webber Coll., 1972—; co-editor, pub. Guideposts, N.Y.C., 1945—, pres., 1985—; pres. Fleming H. Revell, Old Tappan, N.J., 1985—. Appeared on: nat. TV program What's Your Trouble, 1952-68; Author: I Married a Minister, 1942, The Adventure of Being a Wife, 1971, Secrets of Staying in Love, 1984; co-editor, co-publisher, pres.: (with Dr. Peale) Guidepost mag, 1957—; co-subject with husband: film One Man's Way, 1963. Trustee Hope Coll., Holland, Mich., Champlain Coll., Burlington, Vt., Stratford Coll., Danville, Va., Lenox Sch., N.Y.C., Interchurch Center Syracuse U., 1955-61; bd. dirs. Cook Christian Tng. Sch., Lord's Day Alliance U.S.; mem. bd. and exec. com. N.Y. Theol. Sem., N.Y.C.; sponsor Spafford Children's Convalescent Hosp., 1966—; bd. govs. Help Line Telephone Center, 1970—, Norman Vincent Peale Telephone Center, 1977; mem. nat. women's bd. Northwood Inst., 1981. Named New York State Mother of Yr., 1963, Disting. Woman of Yr. Nat. Art Assn., Religious Heritage Am. Ch. Woman of Yr., 1969; recipient Cum Laude award Syracuse U. Alumni Assn. N.Y., 1965, Honor Iowans' award Buena Vista Coll., 1966, Am. Mother's Com. award religion, 1970, Disting. Svc. award Coun. Chs., N.Y.C., 1973, Disting. Citizen award Champlain Coll., 1976, Disting. Svc. to Community and Nation award Gen. Fedn. Women's Clubs, 1977, Horatio Alger award, 1977, Religious Heritage award, 1979, joint medallion with husband Soc. for Family of Man, 1981, Soc. Family of Man award, 1981, Alderson-Broaddus award, 1982, Marriage Achievement award Bride's Mag., 1984, Gold Angel award Religion in Media, 1987, Adela Rogers St. John Roundtable award, 1987, Disting. Achievement award Am. Aging, 1987, Paul Harris award N.Y. Rotary, 1989. Mem. Insts. Religion and Health (bd. exec. com.), Am. Bible Soc. (dir., v.p.), United Bible Soc. (v.p.), The Interchurch Ctr. (bd. dirs. 1957—, chair 1982-90), Nat. Coun. Chs. (v.p. 1952-54, gen. bd.; treas. gen. dept. United Ch. Women, vice chmn. broadcasting and film commn. 1951-55, program chmn. gen. assembly 1966), N.Y. Fedn. Women's Clubs (chmn. religion 1951-53, 57-58), Home Missions Coun. N.A. (nat. pres. 1942-44, nat. chmn. migrant com. 1948-51), Nat. League Am. Pen Women (hon. life), PEO, Alpha Phi (Frances W. Willard award 1976). Clubs: Sorosis (N.Y.C.) (pres. 1953-56, hon. life pres. 1975—); Lotos; Women's Nat. Republican (N.Y.C.). Office: Found for Christian Living 66 E Main St Pawling NY 12564

PEARCE, BETTY MCMURRAY, manufacturing company executive; b. Hastings, Nebr., Oct. 11, 1926; d. Frank Madry and Scereta (Mudd) McMurray; BS in Aerospace, U. Tex., Austin, 1949; 1 child, Karen A. Harsley. Draftsman, Koch & Fowler, Civil Engrs., Dallas, 1945-47; with LTV-APG-AMSD Corp., Dallas, 1949—, project engr., 1955-77, engring. project mgr., 1977-83, dir. engring., 1983-89, engring. mgr. advanced system concepts, 1989-90; program mgr. PAMPA 2000, 1990—; dir. LTV Fed. Credit Union, v.p. LTV Mgmt. Club; cons. Active Aux. St. Joseph's Hosp.; pres., St. Andrews Catholic Ch. Council, Fort Worth, 1977-78; mem. Bishop's Adv. Council Fort Worth Diocese, 1980-87, chmn. service com., 1980-81, pres., 1981-82, 84-85; mem. Allied Communities of Tarrant, 1982—. Mem. AIAA, Tech. Mktg. Soc. Am. Home: 2829 Princeton St Fort Worth TX 76109 Office: PO Box 225907 Dallas TX 75265

PEARCE, DRUE, state legislator; b. Fairfield, Ill., Apr. 2, 1951; d. H. Phil and Julia Detroy (Bannister) P. AB, Ind. U., 1973; MPA, Howard U., 1984. Sch. tchr. Clark County, Ind., 1973-74; curator Louisville Zoo, 1974-77; dir. Summerscene, Louisville, 1974-77; asst. v.p. Alaska Nat. Bank of the North, 1977-82; legis. aide to Alaska State Rep. John Ringstad, 1983; mem. Alaska Ho. of Reps., 1984-88; state senator Alaska Senate, 1988—. Mem. Alaska Resource Devel. Coun., Alaska Women's Polit. Caucus. Mem. DAR, Alaska C. of C. Republican. Home: 6035 Tanaina Dr Anchorage AK 99502 Office: Office of State Senate State Capitol Juneau AK 99811*

PEARCE, FRANCES JEAN, accountant; b. Norfolk, Va., Nov. 22, 1954; d. Andrew Wilson and Jessie Mae (Garrard) Pearce; m. Joel Woodrow Stalcup, Dec. 20, 1973 (div. June 1990); 1 child, Rebecca. Student, N.C. State U., 1982-85; BS in Acctg., Elon College (N.C.), 1987. CPA, S.C. Acct. McKnight, Frampton & Co., Charleston, S.C., 1987-89, Pratt-Thomas Welch & Co., CPA's, Charleston, 1989—. Mem. AICPA, S.C. Assn. CPA's. Lutheran. Home: 802-F Runaway Dr Mount Pleasant SC 29464 Office: Pratt-Thomas Welch & Co 157 E Bay St Charleston SC 29401

PEARCE, JANET DINKEL, foundation administrator; b. Toledo, Oct. 26, 1943; d. J. Edward and Betty (Richardson) Dinkel; m. James Erwin Pearce, Mar. 15, 1986. BA, Wittenberg U., 1965; MA, Ohio State U., 1968. Economic analyst Fed. Reserve Bank, Cleve., 1967-76; regional campaign dir. United Way Nat. Capital Area, Washington, 1976-79; exec. dir. United Way Adams County, Quincy, Ill., 1979-83; exec. v.p. United Way L.I., Melville, N.Y., 1983—. Contbr. articles to profl. jours. Mem. Jr. League, L.I. Episcopalian. Home: 5 Upper Dr Huntington NY 11743 Office: United Way LI 535 Broad Hollow Rd Melville NY 11747

PEARCE, JOAN DELAP, research company executive; b. Oakland, Calif., June 13, 1930; d. Robert Jerome and Wilhelmina (Reaume) DeLap; m. Gerald Allan Pearce, June 18, 1953; 1 child, Scott Ford. Student, U. Oreg., 1948-55. Research assoc. deForest Research, Los Angeles, 1966-78; dir. research Walt Disney Prodns., Burbank, Calif., 1978; assoc. dir. deForest Research, Los Angeles, 1978—; lighting dir. Wilcoxen Players, Beverly Hills, Calif., 1955-60, Theatre 40, Los Angeles, 1960-66. Bd. advisors Living History Ctr., Marin County, Calif., 1982-89, bd. dirs., 1989—. Mem. Am. Film Inst. Democrat. Avocations: photography; travel; theater; swimming. Home: 2621 Rutherford Dr Los Angeles CA 90068 Office: deForest Research Service Inc 1645 N Vine St Suite 701 Los Angeles CA 90028

PEARCE, JULIA LEE ANNE, hospital administrator; b. Seattle, Nov. 11, 1940; d. John Gilbert and Mildred Jeanette (Lagreide) McConnell; m. Charles Fulton Pearce, Dec. 18, 1966. BS, Loma Linda U., 1962, MS, 1965; postgrad., U. Calif., L.A., San Francisco, 1967-68; PhD, Columbia Pacific U., 1987. Cert. pub. health nurse. Head nurse surg. Loma Linda (Calif.) U. Med. Ctr., 1962-65; instr. nursing Atlantic Union Coll., South Lancaster, Mass., 1965-66; asst. prof. La Sierra Coll., Riverside, Calif., 1965-69; exec. dir. Salinas Valley Vis. Nurses, Salinas, Calif., 1970-72; clin. nurse III Guidance Clinic of Fla. Keys, Key West, Fla., 1972-73; nursing instr. Fla. Keys Community Coll., Key West, 1973-75; nursing mgr. mental health unit St. Helena Hosp., Deer Park, Calif., 1977-85, clin. nurse home health and Hospice, 1985-87, cons. women's health svc., 1988—; cons. Ukiah (Calif.) Adventist Hosp., 1989. Bd. mem. Crisis Help, St. Helena, 1978-83; mem. Napa County Commn. on Status of Women, 1989—. Mem. Nurses Assn. Am. Coll. Ob-Gyn, Assn. Seventh Day Adventists Nurses (sec.-treas. No. Calif. 1978-81), Nat. Assn. Female Execs., Loma Linda U. Sch. Nursing Alumni. Mem. Nurses Assn. Am. Coll. of Obstetricians & Gynecologists, Seventh Day Adventists Nurses (sec.-treas. No. Calif. 1978-81), NAFE, Loma Linda U. Sch. Nursing Alumni. Republican. Seventh Day Adventist. Home and Office: Butterfly Valley Ln Deer Park CA 94576

PEARCE, MARY MCCALLUM (MRS. CLARENCE A. PEARCE), artist; b. Hesperia, Mich., Feb. 17, 1906; d. Archibald and Mabel (McNeil) McCallum; A.B., Oberlin Coll., 1927; student John Huntington Inst., 1929-34, Cleve. Inst. Art, 1935-37, 54, Dayton Art Inst., 1946-49; m. Clarence A. Pearce, June 30, 1928 (dec.); children: Mary Martha (Mrs. William B. Robinson), Thomas McCallum. One woman shows at Cleve. Women's City Club, 1959, 69, Plymouth Harbor, Sarasota Fla., 1989, Cleve. Orch., 1967,

Cleve. Playhouse Gallery, 1968, 71, 76, 87, Van Wezel Hall, 1979, Sarasota (Fla.) Library, 1979, Hilton Leech Gallery, Sarasota, 1979, 80, 81, 86 Fed. Bank, Sarasota, 1980; exhibited in group shows at Oberlin Art Mus., Smithsonian Inst., Birmingham Mus. of Art, Am. Watercolor Soc., Cleve. Mus. Art, Foster Harmon Galleries, 1986, Fla. Watercolor Soc., Ala., 1988, Fla. Artist Group, 1989, Southeastern Watercolorists, 1989, many others: represented in pvt. collections: tchr. art, supr. pub. schs., Mayfield Heights, Ohio, 1927-28, Maple Heights, Ohio, 1928-30, Chagrin Falls, Ohio, 1938-39. Named best woman artist Ohio Watercolor Soc., 1955; recipient Bush Meml. award Columbus Gallery Fine Arts, 1962; nat. 1st prize for drawing Nat. League Am. Pen Women, 1966, 68; Littlehouse award Ala. Watercolor Soc., 1967; Wolfe award Columbus Gallery Fine Arts, 1971; awards Longboat Key Art Center, 1973, 75, 79-86; award Southeastern Art Soc., 1975; 2d prize Art League Manatee County, 1973, 90, 1st prize, 1988, Merit awards, 1975, 77, 88, 89; 3d prize Sarasota Art Assn., 1977, 78, hon. mention, 1989, Merit award, 1981, 85; 1st prize Venice (Fla.) Art League, 1979, 81, 82, 83, 86, 87, 2d prize, 1979, 80, 81, 89, 3d prize, 1978, merit award, 1985, 89; 1st prize Hilton Leech Gallery, 1981, 85, 1st prize Friends of Arts and Scis., 2d prize Suncoast Watercolor Soc., 1989; hon. mention Fla. State Merit award; Fla. West Coast Parade of prize winners, 1990, numerous others. Mem. Nat. League Am. Pen Women (treas. 1962), Am. (assoc.), Ala., Fla. watercolor socs. Republican. Congregationalist. Home: 5400 Ocean Blvd Apt 1401 Sarasota FL 34242

PEARL, HELEN ZALKAN, lawyer; b. Washington, Sept. 12, 1938; d. George and Harriet (Libman) Zalkan; m. Jason E. Pearl, June 27, 1959; children: Gary M., Esther H., Lawrence J. BA with hons., Vassar Coll., 1959; JD, U. Conn., 1978. Bar: Conn. 1978, U.S. Dist. Ct. Conn. 1978. Mkt. rsch. analyst Landers, Frary & Clark, New Britain, Conn., 1960-61; managerial statistician Landers, Frary & Clark, 1961-62; real estate salesperson Denuzze Co., New Britain, 1966-70; property mgr. self-employed New Britain, 1970-75; legal asst. Atty. Gen. Office, State of Conn., Hartford, 1978; assoc. Weber & Marshall, New Britain, 1978-83; ptnr. Weber & Marshall, 1983—; hearing officer Commn. on Human Rights & Opportunities, State of Conn., 1980—; spl. master State of Conn. Judicial Dept., 1986—. Rep. of City of New Britain to Cen. Conn. Reg. Planning Agy., 1973-75, 84—, chairperson 1990—; mem. bd. fin. and taxation City of New Britain, 1973-77; founder, commr. Conn. State Permanent Commn. on the Status of Women, 1975-82; others in past. Recipient Women in Leadership award, YWCA of New Britain, 1988, Book award for torts, Am. Jurisprudence, 1976, Econs. prize, Vassar Coll., 1959. Mem. AAUW (pres. 1970-72), Conn. Bar Assn. (family law sect., women and the law sect.), New Britain Bar Assn., League Women Voters (Conn. specialist 1987—), Hartford Vassar Club, Phi Beta Kappa. Democrat. Jewish. Home: 206 Hickory Hill Rd New Britain CT 06052 Office: Weber & Marshall PO Box 1568 New Britain CT 06050-1568

PEARL, JULIE CHAIKIN, lawyer; b. Detroit, May 23, 1960; d. Jack William and Faye (Chaikin) P. BA, Stanford U., 1981; MPA, Harvard U., 1986; JD, U. Calif., Hastings, 1987. Bar: Calif. 1988. Translator Internat. Interpreter's Svc., N.Y.C., 1981-82; founder, prin. artist Ont. Soft Sculpture Gallery, Toronto, Can., 1982-83; asst. to sr. producer ABC-News Nightline, London, 1986; spl. projects atty. Office Atty. Gen. of Calif., Sacramento, 1987-89, dep. atty. gen. major fraud unit, 1989—. Author: Symposium 87: White-Collar Crime, 1988; contbr. numerous articles to profl. jours. Mem. ABA, Calif. Bar Assn., Amnesty Internat., Stanford U. Alumni Assn., Harvard U. Alumni Assn., Calif. Women Lawyers. Office: Distr Atty's Office Spl Investigations Unit Sacramento CA 95814

PEARLMAN, DOROTHY RAE CARTER, civic worker, retired educator; b. Broadwell, Ill., Sept. 7, 1917; d. John and Corinne Winifred (Smith) Hanahan; m. Leroy Oliver Carter, May 17, 1936 (dec. May 1930); 1 child, David L.; m. Sidney Fred Pearlman, May 29, 1977; children: Vicki Liberman, Jonathan, Cathy Chatman. BS in Edn., Valdosta (Ga.) State Coll., 1961. Tchr. theatre and choral music Lowndes High Sch., Valdosta, 1961-75; tchr. theatre and coral music Valdosta Jr. High Sch., 1960-61; tchr. Valdosta Bd. Edn., 1953-57; ret., 1975. Charter mem. Valdosta Soup Kitchen, 1982; bd. dirs. Miss Valdosta Pageant; mem. Flint River coun. Girl Scouts U.S.A., 1989; organizer Love and Caring Aux. for Elderly, Valdosta, 1982; chmn. Lowndes-Valdosta Arts Commn., 1988-91; bd. dirs. Camp Relisto, 1984-90; mem. Drug Rehabilitatory Wholeway House, 1990—, Hadassah Sisterhood, 1986—. Named Tchr. of Yr., Lowndes County Bd. Edn., 1976, Outstanding Secondary Educator, State of Ga., 1976; recipient Super Hero award U. Ga., 1976, Woman of Excellence award Phoebee Punum Women's Ctr, 1989. Mem. Town and Country Garden Club (pres. 1986-88), Wymodausis Club (Women of Yr. award 1988, Super Star award 1990). Republican. Jewish. Home: 3326 Plantation Dr Valdosta GA 31602

PEARLMAN, FLORENCE SADOFF, social worker; b. N.Y.C., Dec. 26, 1928; d. Sam and Eva (Brunstein) Sadoff; BA, Barnard Coll., 1950; MSW, Wurzweiler Sch. Social Work, 1971; m. Donald Pearlman, June 22, 1947 (div. Feb. 1971); children: David J., Erica Lee (dec.). Editorial staff profl. jours., 1951-56; alumnae sec. Briarcliff Coll., Briarcliff Manor, N.Y., 1966-67; psychiat. social worker Westchester County (N.Y.) Mental Health Clinics, 1971; supr. Alcoholism Clinic, Yonkers, 1974-75, sr. social worker, 1986—. Mem. coms. Planned Parenthood-World Population, 1965-75, bd. dirs., 1966-72; active Planned Parenthood Westchester, 1962-80; bd. dirs. Assoc. Alumnae of Barnard Coll., 1975-78. Mem. Acad. Cert. Social Workers (diplomate in clin. social work), Nat. Assn. Social Workers (local bd. dirs. 1988—), Amateur Chamber Music Players, Am. Orthopsychiat. Assn. Democrat. Jewish. Club: The Bohemians. Home: 17 Cedar Road S Katonah NY 10536

PEARLMUTTER, A(NNE) FRANCES, secondary educator; b. Chelsea, Mass., Oct. 28, 1940; d. Albert and Esther Lea (Wool) Goldberg; m. Fishel A. Pearlmutter, Sept. 5, 1960 (dec. Oct. 1983); children: Barak, Nili; m. David Louis Blumenfeld, June 15, 1987. BS, Tulane U., 1962; MA, Case Western Res. U., 1967, PhD, 1969. Postdoctoral fellow Med. Coll. Ohio, Toledo, 1969-71, instr., 1971-73, asst. prof., 1973-80, assoc. prof., 1980-88; tchr. Horace Mann High Sch., Bronx, N.Y., 1989—. Home: 208 Victory Blvd New Rochelle NY 10804

PEARLMUTTER, FLORENCE NICHOLS, psychologist, therapist; b. Bklyn., Mar. 17, 1914; d. William and Marie Elizabeth (Rugamer) Griebe; m. Wilbur Francis Nichols, Aug. 17, 1940 (dec. 1967); 1 child, Roger F.; m. F. Bernard Perlmutter, June 17, 1969. BS, NYU, 1934, postgrad., 1965-75; MS, Yeshiva U., 1960. Psychologist P.P.P. Counseling Ctr., Northport, N.Y., 1967-69; therapist Robert E. Peck, M.D., Syosset, N.Y., 1969-75, Arthur J. Gross, M.D., Hicksville, N.Y., 1975—; Mem. NEA, Nassau County Psychol. Assn., AAUW, Kappa Delta Pi.

PEARMAN, MARY ANN, civic worker; b. Paris, Ill., Sept. 18, 1934; d. Lonnie and Mary (Englum) Mattingly; m. Ralph S. Pearman, Mar. 30, 1957; children: Ann, Matthew, Julie, Susan, Kay, John. BS in Music Edn., St. Mary-of-Woods (Ind.) Coll., 1956. Tchr. music pub. schs., Jasper, Ind., 1957; buyer Pearman's Clothing Store, Paris, 1980—. Organizer hosp. vols. Paris Jr. Woman's Club; chmn. Edgar County Positive Youth Devel. Com.; pres. Hosp. and Med. Found. Paris, Inc., 1982-89, bd. dirs., 1971—; music dir. St. Mary's Ch., Paris; mem., past pres. Paris Woman's Club; organizer Ecumenical Community Choir, Paris; mem. regional planning commn. Ill. Dept. Children and Family Svcs., Paris; cons. Ill. Positive Youth Devel. Grants. Named Outstanding Young Women of Am., 1968, Woman of Yr., Paris Woman's Club, 1975; recipient Alumni award Ill 4-H Club, 1965, Woman of Yr. award Beta Sigma Phi, 1974, Today's Woman award Covered Bridge coun. Girl Scouts U.S.A., 1987. Mem. Fedn. Women's Club, Cath. Daus. Am., Altar Soc. St. Mary's Parish. Republican. Home: 228 W Crawford St Paris IL 61944 Office: Pearman's Clothing Store 108 W Court St Paris IL 61944

PEARSALL, ROSELLEN DEE, insurance executive; b. Ft. Dix, N.J., Aug. 15, 1945; d. Raymond Donald and Rosemary (Dannenberg) P. BS in Nursing, U. Ky., 1967. RN U. Ky. Med. Ctr., Lexington, 1967-68; RN Cardiac Care Unit Cedars of Lebanon Hosp., Los Angeles, 1968-69; rehab. nurse cons. Employers Ins. of Wausau, Los Angeles, 1969-76; asst. v.p. rehab. services Fremont Compensation Ins. Co., Los Angeles, 1976—; ins. adv. bd. Casa Colina Inc., Pomona, Calif., 1984—. Recipient Cert. Achievement in Bus. and Industry Los Angeles YWCA, 1978, 80. Mem. Nat. Assn. Rehab. Profls. in the Pvt. Sector (legis. chair Calif.), Nat. Rehab. Assn. (pres. So. Calif. chpt. 1979-80, Outstanding Achievement award 1981), Rehab. Nurses Soc. (founding pres. 1972-74, Outstanding Services award 1980, Greatest Support award 1984-85), Ins. Rehab. Study Group. Club: Los Angeles Athletic. Office: Fremont Compensation Ins Co 1709 W 8th St Los Angeles CA 90017

PEARSON, DEBORAH ANN, psychologist; b. New Bedford, Mass., Apr. 23, 1957; d. Harry Jr. and Louise Agnes (Dalmar) P.; m. John Crawford Woodhouse II, Sept. 4, 1982. BA, Wesleyan U., 1979; MA, Rice U., 1982, PhD, 1986. Lic. psychologist, Tex. Rsch. asst. Rice U., Houston, 1979-82, Tex. Children's Hosp., Houston, 1983-86; vis. asst. prof. Rice U., Houston, 1986; asst. prof. U. Tex. Med. Sch., Houston, 1987—; adj. asst. prof. Rice U., Houston, 1988—; advisor Assn. of Retarded Citizens, Houston, 1989—; bd. dirs. Parents of Prematures, Houston, 1987—; cons. ADDH Assn., Houston, 1989—; reviewer Jour. of Experimental Child Psychology. Author: (with others) The Development of Attention: Research and Theory, 1990; contbr. articles to profl. jours. Elder St. Thomas Presbyn. Ch., Houston, 1986-88. Numerous rsch. grants, 1987-92. Mem. Am. Psychol. Assn., Am. Psychol. Soc., Houston Psychol. Assn., Soc. for Rsch. in Child Devel., S.W. Soc. for Rsch. in Human Devel., Tex. Psychol. Assn. Office: U Tex Med Sch 1300 Moursund Ave Houston TX 77030

PEARSON, LOUISE MARY, retired manufacturing company executive; b. Inverness, Scotland, Dec. 14, 1919 (parents Am. citizens); d. Louis Houston and Jessie M. (McKenzie) Lenox; grad. high sch.; m. Nels Kenneth Pearson, June 28, 1941; children—Lorine Pearson Walters, Karla. Dir. Wauconda Tool & Engring. Co., Inc., Algonquin, Ill., 1950-86; reporter Oak Leaflet, Crystal Lake, Ill., 1944-47, Sidelights, Wilmette, Ill., 1969-72, 79-82. Active Girl Scouts U.S.A., 1955-65. Recipient award for appreciation work with Girl Scouts U.S., 1965. Clubs: Antique Automobile of Am. (Hershey, Pa.), Vet. Motor Car (Boston), Classic Car of Am. (Madison, N.J.). Home: 125 Dole Ave Crystal Lake IL 60014

PEARSON, P. A. (LEE PEARSON), marine consultant; b. Phoenix, June 23, 1939; d. David Samuel and Margaret (Holtzman) Hamburger; divorced; 1 child, Stuart Deene. Student, Glendale Coll., 1963-64, Yacht Design Inst., 1975-76. Surveyor, cons. Lenders Yacht Mfrs. Ins. Co., 1974—; prin. Pearson Enterprises, Kemah, Tex., 1974-79, 1982—. Instr. USCG Aux. Mem. Soc. Naval Architects/Marine Engrs., Soc. Small Craft Designers, Am. Boat and Yacht Coun., Soc. Accredited Marine Surveyors (ethics com.), Boat U.S. Tech. Exch. (Most Outstanding Art award), Mensa. Democrat. Office: Pearson Enterprises PO Box 580547 Houston TX 77258

PEARSON, TONJA LEE, electronic company executive; b. Phoenix, Mar. 16, 1950; d. John W. and Shirlee Jean (Nelson) P.; m. Roland Edward Estes IV, Oct. 11, 1975 (div. Apr. 1989). BA, Ariz. State U., 1973; MBA, Tex. Christian U., 1983. Repair supr. Motorola, Ariz., 1969-76; scheduler Motorola, Tex., 1976-84; v.p. prodn. Vista Electronics, Cabot, Ark., 1984-85; safety and security mgr. Fleming Foods, Ft. Worth, 1985-87; prodn. planner Gen. Dynamic, Ft. Worth, 1987—; co-owner Printing Co., Arlington, Tex., 1984-89. Artist in watercolors; portfolio photographer; dress designer. Mem. Girl Scouts, Ft. Worth, 1984—, Woman's Haven Abused Women, Ft. Worth, 1984—, Alanon, Weatherford, Tex., 1986—. Mem. NAFE, Am. Mgmt. Assn. Democrat. Morman. Home: 516 Bois d'Arc Ln Weatherford TX 76086 Office: Gen Dynamics Electronic Mfg Ctr Fort Worth TX 76101

PEASE, CAROL HELENE, oceanographer; b. Bay City, Mich., Dec. 29, 1949; d. George Olson and Mernabelle Hattie (Laabs) P.; m. Alexander Jeffrey Chester, June 16, 1974 (div. May 1978); m. Bruce William Rummel, Oct. 28, 1989. Student, U. Mich., 1968-71; BS in Math., U. Miami, 1972; MS in Phys. Oceanography, U. Wash., 1975, MS in Meteorology, 1981; postgrad., U. Wash., Seattle, 1985. Rsch. asst. Arctic ice dyanamics joint expt. U. Wash., Seattle, 1972-75; oceanographer Pacific Marine Environ. Lab. Nat. Oceanic and Atmospheric Adminstrn., Seattle, 1975-78, sea ice project leader Pacific Marine Environ. Lab., 1978—. Contbr. articles to profl. jours. Mem. Arboretum Found., Seattle, 1975—, Seattle Art Mus., 1978—, Nat. Women's Polit. Caucus, Seattle, 1984—; sustaining mem. Friends of KUOW, KCTS Found., Seattle, 1978, 82. Recipient performance awards NOAA, 1977, 82, 85, 87, 88, 90, Adminstr.'s award, 1988. Mem. AAAS, Assn. Women in Sci., Am. Geophys. Union, Am. Meteorol. Soc. (session chair symposium meterology and oceanography N.Am. high latitudes 1984, mem. standing com. on polar meteorology and oceanography 1985-90, chmn. 1987-89, session chair, co-convener conf. on polar meteorology and oceanography 1988), Corinthian yacht Club, Valkyrien (sec. 1978-81), Daus. Norway. Office: Pacific Marine Environ Lab 7600 Sand Point Way NE Seattle WA 98115

PEASE, DENISE LOUISE, state bank regulator; b. Bronx, Mar. 15, 1953; d. William Henry Jr. and Louise Marion (Caswell) P. BA, Columbia U., 1978, postgrad., 1981-82; postgrad., Baruch Grad. Sch Pub Adminstrn., 1982-83, Institut Européen d'Administration des Affaires, 1990. Exec. spl. asst. to county exec. N.J. Office of the County Exec., County of Essex (N.J.), 1982-83; urban analyst III State of N.Y. Dept. Banking, 1983-86, exec. asst. to the supt. of banks, 1986-87; dep. supt. of banks State of N.Y. Dept. Banking, N.Y.C., 1987—; mem. N.Y. State Gov.'s Econ. Devel. Sub-cabinet. Adv bd. Cornell U. Coop. Extension; mgmt. program adv. bd. Sch. Bus. SUNY, 1990; mem. Alfred U. Devel. Com., mentoring program N.Y. State Women in Govt. Named in Salute to Outstanding African Am. Bus. and Profl. Women, Dollar & Sense Mag., 1990, one of Outstanding Young Women in Am., 1979-81; recipient N.Y. State Assembly Citation of Merit, 1988, Profl. Achievement award Nat. Assn. Negro Bus. and Women's Club, 1981; Nat. Urban fellow, 1982-83, Charles H. Revson fellow Columbia U., 1981-82. Mem. NAACP (life mem.), Nat. Coun. of Negro Women (life mem.), Coalition of 100 Black Women, Fin. Women's Assn. N.Y. (bd. dirs.). Office: NY State Banking Dept 2 Rector St 18th Fl New York NY 10006

PEASE, DORIS OWEN, magazine editor, artist; b. Eau Claire, Wis., Dec. 20, 1921; d. Lee F. and Irma Irmina (Ingram) Owen; m. Leon W. Pease, July 26, 1942; children: Terry, Steve, Gene, Mark, JoDee, LeAnn, Jon, Patti. Student, U. Minn., 1941-42, various art schs., Minn. Acct. Mpls. Star Jour. & Tribune, 1941-44; corr. West Cen. Daily Tribune, Willmar, Minn., 1952-57, New Ulm Daily Jour. and Redwood Falls Gazette, Minn., 1952-67; reporter, photographer, office mgr. Olivia (Minn.) Times Jour., 1967-70; asst. editor, advt. saleswoman Circulating Pines, Circle Pines, Minn., 1970-72; advt. sales cons. Osseo (Minn.) Press, 1972-74; owner, editor, pub. Dot Pub., Mpls., 1972-87; founder, editor Dancing USA Mag. and Entertainment Bits, Mpls., 1972—; exec. sec. Minn. Ballroom Operators Assn., 1975-88, Nat. Ballroom and Entertainment Assn., 1985-88. Exhibited in numerous group exhbns., Minn., 1970—; editor Minn. Palette News, 1974-80. Founder, bd. dirs. Renville County Art Ctr., Olivia, 1965-72; founder Newcomer Welcome Svc., 1968, 75; former leader, trainer, camp dir. Girl Scouts U.S.A.; pres. Coon Rapids Fine Arts Commn., 1988; bd. dirs. Banfill Locke Ctr. for Arts, 1980-82. Recipient Thanks Badge, Girl Scouts U.S.A., 1970, commendation Mayor of Coon Rapids, 1988. Mem. Artists del Norte (founder, pres. 1978-80, 84-85), Minn. Rural Artists Assn. (pres. 1981-84), North Star Watercolor Assn. Republican. Methodist. Home: 10870 Mississippi Blvd Coon Rapids MN 55433 Office: Dot Publs 10600 University Ave NW Minneapolis MN 55433

PEASE, ELEANOR THOMPSON (MRS. DONALD CARGILL PEASE), lawyer; b. Bucyrus, Ohio, Mar. 28, 1923; s. Edgar William and Mary (Bliss) Thompson; m. Donald Cargill Pease, Sept. 9, 1949; 1 child, William Thompson. BA, Vassar Coll., 1944; JD, Yale U., 1946. Bar: U.S. Dist. Ct. D.C. 1947, U.S. Ct. Appeals (D.C. cir.) 1947. Corp. lawyer E.I. Dupont Co., 1947-49. By-laws chmn. Jr. League, Wilmington, Del., 1951-53, bd. dirs., 1951-53, mag. chmn., 1959-60, edn. com., 1961-62; pres. Jr. League of Wilmington Sustainers Garden Club, 1969-70; by-laws chmn., bd. dirs. Del. Soc. Prevention Cruelty to Animals, 1950-52; day chmn. Winterthur Mus. Jr. League docents, 1955-61; del., class rep. Vassar Alumnae Council, 1954; parliamentarian Girl Scouts U.S., Wilmington, 1957, 59; pres. Del. Vassar Club, 1960-62; area chmn. United Fund, 1960-62; exec. com. Women's Coll. Info. Program, 1961; docent Del. Art Mus., 1961-63; mem. Cts. Task Force Del. Agy. to Reduce Crime, 1968-71. Bd. dirs. Vol. bur. Del. Welfare Council, 1950-52, Friends of John Dickinson Mansion, 1979-80. Mem. Del. Hist. Soc., Nat. Trust for Hist. Preservation, Nat. Soc. Colonial Dames Am. (bd. mgrs. 1973-79, pres. Del. chpt. 1976-79), Roger Williams Family Assn. Republican. Presbyterian. (deacon). Home: 804 Princeton Rd Westover Hills Wilmington DE 19807

PEASE, NORMA MAXINE FELTZ, retired clinical microbiologist; b. Kansas City, Kans., Mar. 13, 1925; d. Felix Carnot and Eva Marie (Muma) Feltz; m. Thomas Douglas Pease, July 9, 1953 (div. 1976); children: Thomas Christian, Norman Randall, Carnot Michael-Jon. BS, U. Denver, 1948; MS, U. Colo., 1951. Researcher biochemistry dept. U. Colo. Med. Ctr., Denver, 1948-54; med. technologist Wells F. Harvey, Denver, 1954-58; clin. microbiologist Swedish Hosp., Englewood, Colo., 1957-58; clin. microbiologist, instr. Med. Technologists Sch., Mercy Hosp., Denver, 1958-61; clin. microbiologist Children's Hosp., Denver, 1962-68, Swedish Am. Hosp., Rockford, Ill., 1968-70; microbiologist Marion Health and Safety, Rockford, 1973-80; med. technologist Winnebago Dept. Pub. Health, Rockford, 1981-87; activities asst. North Rockford Convalescent Home, 1986-89; ret., 1990; pvt. home health aide, Rockford, 1987—, Kelly Assisted Living, Rockford, 1989—; instr. microbiology Loretto Heights Coll., Denver, 1964. Pres. Winnebago County Heart Assn., 1967-70; vol. Rockford Mus. Ctr., North Rockford Convalescent Home. Mem. Am. Soc. Clin. Pathologists (cert. med. technologist, specialist in microbiology), Nat. Registry Microbiologists Am., Am. Acad. Microbiology, Colonial Dames 17th Century, Iota Sigma Pi, Alpha Lambda Delta, Beta Sigma Pi, Alpha Xi Delta. Roman Catholic. Home: 3108 Brendenwood Rd Rockford IL 61107

PEASLEE, MARGARET MAE HERMANEK, zoology educator; b. Chgo., June 15, 1935; d. Emil Frank and Magdalena Bessie (Cechota) Hermanek; m. David Raymond Peaslee, Dec. 6, 1957; 1 dau., Martha Magdelena Peaslee-Levine. A.A., Palm Beach Jr. Coll., 1956; B.S., Fla. So. Coll., 1959; med. technologist, Northwestern U., 1958, M.S., 1964, Ph.D., 1966. Med. technologist Passavant Hosp., Chgo., 1958-59, St. James Hosp., Chicago Heights, Ill., 1960-63; asst. prof. biology Fla. So. Coll., Lakeland, 1966-68, U. S.D., Vermillion, 1968-71; asso. prof. U. S.D., 1971-76, prof., 1976, acad. opportunity liaison, 1974-76; prof., head dept. zoology La. Tech. U., Ruston, 1976-90, assoc. dean, dir. grad. studies and rsch., prof. biol. scis. Coll. Life Scis., 1990—. Contbr. articles to profl. jours. Fellow AAAS; mem. Am. Inst. Biol. Scis., Am. Soc. Zoologists, S.D. Acad. Sci. (sec.-treas. 1972-76), AAUP, N.Y. Acad. Scis., La. Acad. Sci. (sec. 1979-81, pres. 1983), Sigma Xi, Phi Theta Kappa, Phi Rho Pi, Phi Sigma, Alpha Epsilon Delta. Home: PO Box 1573 Ruston LA 71273 Office: La Tech U Coll Life Scis Box 10198 Ruston LA 71272

PEAVLER, NANCY JEAN, editor; b. Kansas City, Mo., Dec. 19, 1951; d. Elmer Alfred and Ruth Lenoris (Peterson) Zimmerli; m. Craig Eugene Peavler, Dec. 6, 1975; 1 child, Matthew Dean. Assoc., Kansas City (Kans.) Community Coll., 1976. Staff writer The Kansas City Kansan, 1972-73; assoc. editor Capper's Stauffer Communications, Topeka, 1976-87, editor, 1987—. Den leader Cub Scouts; precinct com.-woman Shawnee County Rep. Party, Topeka, 1985-87. Mem. Women in Commucations, Beta Sigma Phi (chpt. v.p., 1979-80, sec. 1978-79). United Methodist. Office: Capper's 616 Jefferson St Topeka KS 66607

PECH, ROSE ANN, educator; b. Edwardsville, Ill., Oct. 16, 1942; d. Battista and Helen Justine (Menoni) Boccaleoni; m. James O. Pech, Oct. 23, 1965 (dec. Jan. 1974; 1 chid, Timothy James; m. Nelson K. Reese, May 15, 1976 (div. Apr. 1984). Student, So. Ill. U., Alton, 1960-62; BS with high honors, Ill. State U., Normal, 1964; postgrad., Northwestern U., Evanston, Ill., 1966; MS in Edn., No. Ill. U., DeKalb, 1968-72. Tchr. educable mentally handicapped Spl. Edn. Dist. Lake County, Gurnee, Ill., 1964-66, tchr. learning disabled, 1966-67; tchr. cons. Maine Twp. High Sch. Dist. 207, Des Plaines, Ill., 1967-69; itinerant tchr. learning disabled Spl. Edn. Dist. Lake County, Gurnee, 1969-70; substitute tchr. Glenbrook High Sch., Wheeling, Ill., 1971-73; instr. gen. ednl. devel. Coll. Lake County, Grayslake, Ill., 1973-76; tchr. learning disabled Lake Villa (Ill.) Sch. Dist. 41, 1976—; cons. Maine Twp. Diagnostic and Remedial Learning Ctr., Park Ridge, Ill., 1967-69; IFT rep. Lake County Inst. Adv. Com., Waukegan, Ill., 1988—; tchr. rsch. linker Am. Fedn. Tchrs,-Ill. Fedn. Tchrs. Local 504, Waukegan, 1988—; mem. Dist. 41 Curriculum Coun., Lake Villa, 1978-82, chmn., 1979-81. Youth ministry team chmn. United Protestant Ch. Grayslake (Ill.), 1983-89; vol. Am. Cancer Soc., Am. Legion, Chgo.-Lake Bluff Children's Home, Heart Fund, Salvation Army, Pub. Assitance to Deliver Shelter to Homeless, Lake County, Ill., 1988—. Spl. edn. fellow State Ill., 1966. Mem. Am. Fedn. Tchrs., Ill. Fedn. Tchrs., NEA, Ill. Edn. Assn., Lake Villa Fedn. Tchrs. (corr. sec. 1978-80, bldg. pres. 1983-84), Orton Dyslexia Soc., Kappa Delta Epsilon, Kappa Delta Pi, Women of the Moose. Home: 68 Wesley Ave Lake Villa IL 60046 Office: Lake Villa Sch Dist 41 133 McKinley Ave Lake Villa IL 60046

PECHULIS, ANN, business owner; b. Salem, Mass., Sept. 6, 1948; d. Myron Naczas and Cecelia Ann (Greto) Naczas. Student, Holyoke (Mass.) Jr. Coll., 1966-68. Various positions Conn. Bank & Trust Co., Hartford, 1974-84; sales assoc. Merrill Lynch Realty, Middletown, Conn., 1984-86; sales mgr. GMR Conn./Carriage Crossing Assocs., Cromwell and Middletown, Conn., 1986-88; pvt. practice cons. Conn., 1988-90; pres., owner, broker Nash Realty Inc., Cromwell, Conn., 1990—; cons. in field. Mem. Nat. Assn. Realtors, Conn. Assn. Realtors, C. of C. Home: 23 Lyman Dr Middletown CT 06457 Office: Nash Realty Inc 75 Berlin Rd Rt 72 Cromwell CT 06416

PECK, ANNE ELLIOTT ROBERTS, estates and trust specialist; b. N.Y.C., Dec. 17, 1935; d. James Ragan and Jane Ziegler (Elliott) Roberts; m. George Linn Davis, May 29, 1955 (div. Aug. 1967); children: James Roberts, Elliott Britton, George Linn Jr., William Vaughn (dec.); m. Robert Gray Peck III, Oct. 24, 1969; children: Andrew Adams, Matthew Canfield Roberts. BA in English with honors, Wellesley Coll., 1957; MA in English and Comparative Lit. with honors, Columbia U., 1966; postgrad. Villanova U., 1978-80, U. Bridgeport, 1988; Bus. Law and Corp. Fin. diploma, The Phila. Inst., 1988. Contbg. editor Newsfront mag., 1960-63; English tchr. The Masters Sch., Dobbs Ferry, N.Y., 1963-65; sports feature writer Westchester-Rockland newspapers, Gannett chain, White Plains, N.Y., 1969-70; corr., weekly column Knickerbocker News-Union Star, Capital Newspapers, Hearst chain, Albany, N.Y., 1971-73; pub. and exec. tax preparer H & R Block, Inc., Wayne, Pa., 1976-79; sr. estate planning trust officer Provident Nat. Bank-Trust div. PNC Fin. Corp., Phila., 1981-86; asst. v.p. estate planning dept., trusts and investments div. Mellon Bank (East) N.A., 1986-87; asst v.p., trust officer People's Bank, Stamford, Conn., 1987-88; estates paralegal asst. estates dept. Pepper, Hamilton and Scheetz, Berwyn, Pa., 1988-89; pres., ptnr. ChoirMaster, Inc., 1988—; estate and trusts paralegal adminstr. Blank, Rorre, Comisky and McCauley, Phila., 1989—. Mem. Mus. Art and Sci., Schenectady, N.Y., 1960-68; asst. producer Poetry, Channel 25-TV, N.Y.C.; bd. dirs., legis. chmn. Greenacres Sch. PTA, 1967-69; pub. rels. chmn. Planned Parenthood League, Schenectady; sec., parliamentarian N.Y. State Legis. Forum, 1971-73; pres. The Career Group, Phila., 1983-85; editorcongregation directory St. David's Ch., 1976, mem. exec. com. every-member canvass, 1977; ann. fair gates-keeper Episcopal Diocese Phila., 1974-80, rep. Merion Deanery; on-screen TV panel moderator Access, Channel 17, Albany-Schenectady-Troy, N.Y.; maj. gift solicitor Planned Parenthood Southeastern Pa., 1975-76; mem. plant sale exec. com. and Merry Malt com. Haverford Sch., 1976, 77; Rep. pollchecker Tredyffrin Twp., 1978, 79; majority insp. of elections Tredyffrin Twp. E-2, 1980—. Recipient prize Coll. Bd. Contest Mademoiselle mag., 1954, Prix de Paris, Vogue mag., 1957. Mem. DAR (bd. mgrs.-pub. rels. Phila. chpt., treas. 1983) Phila. Bicentennial Celebration com. 1987), AAUW (bd. dir. Schenectady 1971-73, legis. chmn. Valley Forge br., Albany-Schenectady br.), N.Y. State Women's Press Club (Capital dist. br.), Jr. League Phila. (sustaining, edn. com., child abuse ctr. com., bicentennial cookbook com., Waterworks Restoration com., 1984, bd. dirs. 1960-61), Schenectady Curling Club, Valley Forge Coun. Rep. Women, Mohawk Golf Club (Schenectady), Shenorock Shore Club (Rye, N.Y.), The Merion Cricket Club (Haverford, Pa.), Acorn Club (Phila.), Little Acorns Investment Club, Career Group (founder, chair 1983-85), Jeptha Abbott Chap (Bryn Mawr), Wellesley Alumnae (Phila.), Phila. Assn. Paralegal, Phila. Bar Assn. (probate and trust law sect., assoc., planning coun.), Chester County Estate Planning Coun., Little Egg Harbor Yacht Club (Beach Haven, N.J.), Jr. League of Phila. (sustainer, Waterworks Restoration com.). Episcopalian.

PECK, DIANNE KAWECKI, architect; b. Jersey City, June 13, 1945; d. Thaddeus Walter and Harriet Ann (Zlotkowski) Kawecki; m. Gerald Paul Peck, Sept. 1, 1968; children: Samantha Gillian, Alexis Hilary. BArch, Carnegie-Mellon U., 1968. Architect, P.O.D. Research & Devel., 1968, Kohler-Daniels & Assos., Vienna, Va., 1969-71, Beery-Rio & Assocs., Annandale, Va., 1971-73; ptnr. Peck & Peck Architects, Occoquan, Va., 1973-74, Peck, Peck & Williams, Occoquan, 1974-81; corp. officer Peck Peck & Assos., Inc., Woodbridge, Va., 1981—; chief exec. officer, interior design group Peck Peck & Assoc., 1988—. Work pub. in Am. Architecture, 1985. Vice pres. Vocat. Edn. Found., 1976; chairwoman architects and engrs. United Way; mem. Health Systems Agy. of No. Va., commendations, 1977; mem. Washington Profl. Women's Coop.; chairwoman Indsl. Devel. Authority of Prince William, 1976, vice chair, 1977, mem., 1975-79; developer research project Architecture for Adolescents, 1987-88; mem. inaugural class Leadership Am., 1988, Leadership Greater Washington. Recipient commendation Prince William Bd. Suprs., 1976, State of Art award for Contel Hdqrs. design, 1985, Best Middle Sch. award Coun. of Edml. Facilities Planners Internat., 1989; subject of PBS spl.: A Success in Howard Co. Mem. Prince William C. of C. (dir.). Republican. Roman Catholic. Club: Soroptimist. Research on inner-city rehab., adolescents and the ednl. environ. Office: 1924 Opitz Blvd Woodbridge VA 22191

PECK, ELLIE ENRIQUEZ, consultant, retired state administrator; b. Sacramento, Oct. 21, 1934; d. Rafael Enriquez and Eloisa Garcia Rivera; m. Raymond Charles Peck, Sept. 5, 1957; children: Reginaldo, Enrico, Francisca Guerrero, Teresa, Linda, Margaret, Raymond Charles, Christina. Student polit. sci. Sacramento State U., 1974. Tng. services coord. Calif. Div. Hwys., Sacramento, 1963-67; tech. and mgmt. cons., Sacramento, 1968-78; expert examiner Calif. Pers. Bd., 1976-78; tng. cons. Calif. Pers. Devel. Ctr., Sacramento, 1978; spl. cons. Calif. Commn. on Fair Employment and Housing, 1978; community svcs. rep. U.S. Bur. of Census, No. Calif. counties, 1978-80; spl. cons. Calif. Dept. Consumer Affairs, Sacramento, 1980-83, project dir. Golden State Sr. Discount Program, 1980-83; dir. spl. programs for Calif. Lt. Gov., 1983-90, ret., 1990; pvt. cons., 1990—; mem. Sacramento Community Svcs. Planning Coun., 1987—; chairperson Calif. Suprs.' Forum, 1966. Trustee, Stanford Settlement, Inc., Sacramento, 1975-79, hon. life trustee, 1979—; bd. dirs. Sacramento Emergency Housing Ctr., 1974-77; v.p. Comision Femenil Nacional, Inc., 1987—; del. Dem. Nat. Conv., 1976; mem. exec. bd. Calif. Dem. Cen. Com.; chairperson ethnic minority task force Am. Diabetes Assn. Recipient numerous awards, including Outstanding Community Svc. award Comuicaciones Unidos de Norte Atzlan, 1975, 77, Outstanding Svc. award, Chicano/Hispanic Dem. Caucus, 1979, Vol. Svc. award Calif. Human Devel. Corp., 1981, Dem. of Yr. award Sacramento County Dem. Com., 1987, Outstanding Advocate award Calif. Sr. Legis., 1988, Calif. Assn. of Home for Aging, 1989, Advocacy award, 1989, Resolution of Advocacy award, LULAC, 1989, Meritorious Svc. to Hispanic Community award Comite Patriotico, 1989, Meritorious Svc. Resolution award Lt. Gov. of Calif., 1989. Mem. Nat. Women's Polit. Caucas, Mexican-Am. Polit. Assn., Ombudsman Assn. (advocacy award), Hispanic C. of C. Club: Hispanic Dem. Sacramento County (v.p. 1982-83). Author U.S. Office Consumer Edn. publ., 1982, Calif. Dept. Consumer Affairs publ., 1981. Home: 2667 Coleman Way Sacramento CA 95818

PECK, MARIE JOHNSTON, Latin American area studies consultant; b. New Haven, Aug. 15, 1932; d. James Howard and Marie Anna Christina (Voigt) Johnston; m. Austin Monroe Peck, July 9, 1952 (div. 1959). AS, Larson-Quinnipiac, 1952; BA, U. N.Mex., 1968, PhD, 1974. Writer, coord. bilingual edn. coll. edn. U. N.Mex., Albuquerque, 1976-78; pres., owner Southwestern Images, Inc., Shawnee Mission, Kans., 1978—; Vis. scholar U. N.Mex., Albuquerque, 1983; vis. instr. Wofford Coll., Spartanburg, S.C., 1984; adj. instr. humanities Johnson County Community Coll., Overland Park, Kans., 1985-86, coord. Brown V. Topeka Conf., 1986; cons. Brown V. Topeka Project, Merriam, Kans., 1984-88; bd. dirs. Op. SER, Colorado Springs, Colo., Midcoast Radio, Inc., Kansas City; curriculum writer Albuquerque Pub. Schs., 1980-81. Contbr. articles to profl. jours. Mem. Internat. Trade Task Force Greater Kansas City. Fulbright scholar, 1981-82; Fgn. Lang. fellow HEW, 1967-71, Rsch. fellow Orng. Am. States, 1970. Mem. MLA, Latin Am. Studies Assn., Am. Assn. Tchrs. Spanish and Portugese, Midwest Assn. for Latin Am. Studies, Nat. Women's Studies Assn., Internat. Rels. Coun. (speakers bur. Kansas City 1986—), Internat. Trade Club Kansas City, Silicon Prairie Tech. Assn. Kansas City, Pacific Coast Coun. on Latin Am. Studies, Phi Beta Kappa. Home: care James H Johnston 4512 165th Ave NE Redmond WA 98052

PECK, PHYLLIS HAINLINE, educator; b. Clinton, Iowa, Mar. 14, 1921; d. Russell C. and Julia (Fairchild) Hainline; m. Albert Peck, Jan. 21, 1949; 1 child, Dana Russell. BA, Coll. of St. Catherine, 1942. Instr. in English and bus. Mt. St. Clare Coll., Clinton, 1955-74; instr. in bus. Clinton Community Coll., 1980-85; pvt. practice lectr. Clinton, 1972—; cons. Ea. Iowa Community Coll. Dist., Davenport, Iowa, 1984—; cons., lectr. U. Iowa, Iowa City, 1974-85; cons. in humanities Ea. Iowa Community Coll. Dist., 1984—. Author poems (Golden Poet, 1989, 90, Poet of Merit, 1989); contbr. articles to bus. periodicals. Recipient Main St. State award State of Iowa, 1988, Gov.'s Vol. award, 1989. Mem. P.E.O. (recording sec. 1986-87, chaplain 1987—), Profl. Secs. Internat. (hon., life), Alpha Delphian Lit. Soc. (sec. 1986-87, pres. 1987-88). Methodist. Home: 815 7th Ave S Clinton IA 52732

PECK, SUSAN, speech and language therapist; b. Bklyn., Aug. 31, 1948; d. Cornelius Lawrence and Loretta Agnes (Freligh) Cleary; m. Richard Carl Peck, Mar. 7, 1972; 1 child, Mary Catherine. BS in Speech, St. John's U., 1970. Lic. real estate salesman, N.Y. Speech therapist, dept. chair, tchr. Christ the King Elem. Sch., Commack, N.Y., 1970-72; supr. purchase planning Estee Lauder, Inc., Melville, N.Y., 1973-78; staff analyst Gen. Instrument Corp., Hicksville, N.Y., 1978-83; systems analyst ADP, Melville, 1983-85; mgr. info. systems R. A. Rodriguez, Inc., Garden City, N.Y., 1985-87; dir. personal computer ops., liaison healthforce Career Employment Services, Inc., East Meadow, N.Y., 1987; dir. data processing svcs., law clk. McSherry and Flynn Attys. at Law, Huntington, N.Y., 1988-89; speech and lang. therapist RCG Bd. Coop. Edn. Svcs., Castleton, N.Y., 1989—; v.p. Richard Peck Ltd., Shirley, N.Y., 1982—. Lector, extraordinary minister of eucharist St. Joseph the Worker Roman Cath. Ch., East Patchogue, N.Y., 1980-82; vol. Brookhaven (N.Y.) County Task Force, 1987. Scholar Touro Coll. Law, 1987-89. Mem. Nat. Assn. for Female Execs., Mensa. Republican.

PECORINO, DONNA MARIE, financial company administrator; b. Jersey City, N.J., Nov. 22, 1956; d. Patrick Martin and Marie Margaret (Burns) P.; m. Thomas M. Dack, Sept. 22, 1984. BS, Loyola Marymount U., Los Angeles, 1978; MA, San Diego State U., 1981. Customer service rep. Benham Capital Mgmt. Group, Palo Alto, Calif., 1980, stat. analyst, 1980-81, mgr., 1981-84, dir., 1984-87, v.p. adminstrn., 1987—. Mem. adv. bd. Agy. for Infant Devel. Mem. NAFE, Am. Soc. Profl. Women, Telecommunications Soc. Am., Risk Ins. Mgmt. Assn. Home: 38870 Altura St Fremont CA 94536 Office: Benham Capital Mgmt Group 1665 Charleston Rd Mountain View CA 94304

PECTOR, ELIZABETH ANN, physician; b. L.A., July 28, 1958; d. Robert Anthony and Barbara Anne (Boreczky) Fichtner; m. Scott Walter Pector, June 13, 1981. BA, Northwestern U., Evanston, Ill., 1979; postgrad., Washington U., St. Louis, 1979-81; MD, U. Chgo., 1984. Diplomate Am. Bd. Family Practice. Resident West Suburban Hosp. Med. Ctr., Oak Brook, Ill., 1984-87; physician Med First Physician Assocs., Chgo., 1987-88, Naperville (Ill.) Med. Assocs., 1989—; assoc. med. staff Edward Hosp., Naperville, 1989—. Mem. AAUW, AMA, Am. Acad. Family Physicians, Ill. State Med. Soc., Ill. Acad. Family Physicians, DuPage County Med. Soc., Phi Beta Kappa. Lutheran. Home: 1540 Ambleside Circle Naperville IL 60540 Office: Naperville Med Assocs 100 Spalding Dr Ste 408 Naperville IL 60540

PEDERSEN, JOYCE HELENA, English educator; b. San Francisco, June 26, 1928; d. Axel and Helena Dorothea (Gauzza) Hendry; m. Roy Clyde Gustafson, Sept. 27, 1952 (div. 1971); children: Dru, Lyn. BA, U. Calif., Berkeley, 1950; postgrad., San Francisco State U., 1951; MA in Teaching ESL, Norwich U., 1984. Cert. life teaching credential, reading specialist credential, Calif. Rsch. coord., graphic designer Project Care for Children, San Rafael, Calif., 1980-81; tchr., reading specialist, master tchr. Mill Valley (Calif.) Sch. Dist., 1963-77; instr. learning skills program Santa Rosa (Calif.) Jr. Coll., 1978-80; with Time Life Books/Japan, Osaka, 1981-83; instr. English Osaka Shoin Women's U., 1983-87, Tenri U., Tenri City, Japan, 1986-89, Nara (Japan) U., 1988-89, Sonoma State Am. Lang. Inst., Rohnert Park, Calif., 1990—; instr. English, ESL program Coll. of Marin, Kentfield, Calif., 1990—; Author: Believing Is Seeing, 1985, Good Morning Substitute, 1980, (travel guide) Passport U.S.A., 1988. Mem. Japan Assn. Lang. Tchrs., Japan Assn. Coll. English Tchrs., Japan Assn. U. Women. Democrat.

PEDERSON, CARRIE ANN, computer systems consultant; b. Port Townsend, Wash., Dec. 12, 1957; d. Joe Dell and Shirley Ann (Harris) Wall; m. Joseph Allen Bauer, May 5, 1979 (div. 1986); m. Roald Leif Pederson, May 23, 1987. AS in Computer Programming, So. Ohio Coll., 1981; cert. in data processing, Live Oaks Joint Vocat. Sch., Milford, Ohio, 1976. Programmer Procter & Gamble Co., Cin., 1976-87; systems analyst AMP Inc., Harrisburg, Pa., 1987-89; computer sys. cons. James Rich Computing, Corsicana, Tex., 1989—; prof. Navarro Coll., Corsicana, 1989—. Vol. Updowntowners, Cin., 1986-87; sponsor Ind. Order Odd Fellows Children's Home, Corsicana, 1989—. Mem. Newcomers Club (corr. sec. 1990). Democrat. Mem. Christian Ch. Home: 705 McKinney Corsicana TX 75110

PEDERSON, MAI, air force officer; b. Kuwait, May 27, 1960; d. Moheb Abbas-Helmy al Sadat and Amira. BSin Occupational Edn., Southern Ill. U., 1986; AAS in Pers. Adminstrn., Community Coll. Air Force, 1988; postgrad., Ga. Coll., 1988—. Telecommunications specialist Air Force Cryptologic Support Ctr., Kelly AFB, 1980-81; traffic analysis, telecommunications ops. specialist Air Force Communications Squadron, Norton AFB, 1981-82; info. systems ops. specialist Robins AFB, 1985-86, base career advisor, 1986—; asst. NCOICOF Reenlistment and Separations, 1990—. Vol. tchr. ESL, German Liaison Ops., 1983-85, Robins AFB, 1986; layleader Baha'i Faith, Robins AFB. Mem. Non-Commd. Officers Acad. Grad. Assn., Non-Commd. Officers Open Mess, Non-Commd. Officers Wives Club, Air Force Assn. (life), Non-Commd. Officers Assn. (life), Rambl'in Robins Volksmarch Club (pres. 1987—). Office: WR ALC/HRMPR Warner Robins AFB GA 31098

PEDERSON, MICHELE MARIE, computer engineer; b. Antigo, Wis., Dec. 9, 1962; d. Rudy John and Jeanette Ann P. BS in Computer Sci., U. Wis., Platteville, 1985. computer cons., 1984—. Oboist Dubuque (Iowa) Symphony Orch., 1984-86; project adminstr. Paper Machinery Corp., Milw., 1986-87; contract worker Bell Labs., Naperville, Ill., 1987; regional support rep. Ricoh Corp., Hillside, Ill., 1987-88, regional ops. mgr., 1988-89; sales engr. Ricoh Corp., Hillside, 1989—. Mem. NAFE. Office: Ricoh Corp 4415 W Harrison Ste 450 Hillside IL 60162

PEDRAM, MARILYN BETH, reference librarian; b. Brewster, Kans., Apr. 3, 1937; d. Edgar Roy and Elizabeth Catherine (Doubt) Crist; m. Manouchehr Pedram, Jan. 27, 1962 (Oct. 28, 1984); children: Jaleh Denise, Cyrus Andre. BS in Edn., Kans. State U., 1958; MLS, U. Denver, 1961. Cert secondary educator, Mo. 7th grade tchr. Clay Center (Kans.) Pub. schs., 1958-59, Colby (Kans.) Pub. Sch. System, 1959-60; reference libr. Topeka (Kans.) Pub. Libr., 1961-62, extension dept. head, 1963-64, reference libr., 1964-65; br. libr. asst. Denver Pub. Libr., 1965-67; reference libr. Kans. City (Mo.) Pub. Libr., Plaza Br., 1974-79, Kans. City (Mo.) Main Libr., Kansas City, 1979—. Mem. Mo. Libr. Assn., Kans. City Assn. Law Librs., Am. Assn. Retired Persons, Gluten Intolerance Group of N.Am., Celiac Spruce Assn., Kans. State U. Alumni Assn., Kans. City Online Users Group. Office: Kansas City Pub Libr 311 E 12th St Kansas City MO 64106

PEDRETTY, CATHERINE PARTAIN, education educator; b. Birmingham, Ala., May 25, 1928; d. Rufus Johnson and Flora Catherine (McIntyre) Partain; m. William Louis Pedretty, Sept. 11, 1949; children: Linda Catherine, Janet Evelyn, Donald William, Mark David. BA, U. Tenn., 1949; MA, U. So. Fla., 1973, PhD, 1987; postgrad., Fla. State U., 1978. Dept. chmn. Pinellas County Bd. Pub. Instrn., Clearwater, Fla., 1971-74, dept. chmn., dir. guidance, 1974—; Adv. Nat. Edn. Assn., Clearwater, 1986--. Mem. Pinellas County Tchrs. Assn., Nat. Edn. Assn., Fla. Assn. Schs., Educators in Industry. Democrat. Home: 3182 San Bernadino St Clearwater FL 34619 Office: Dunedin High Sch 1651 Pinehurst Rd Dunedin FL 34698

PEEBLES, ALLENE KAY, manufactured housing company executive; b. Waukegan, Ill., Feb. 9, 1938; d. Allan Laverne and Kathryn Bernice (McGill) Sedlmayr; m. William Ross Peebles, July 9, 1960; children: Ross William, Robb Allen, Raymond John, Renda Kay. BS with high honors, U. Wis., 1960, MS, 1967; grad., Realtors Inst., 1968. Cert. home economist. Tchr. Horicon (Wis.) High Sch., 1960-61, Oconomowoc (Wis.) High Sch., 1961-67; freelance writer, 1967-70; v.p. Luxury Homes, Inc., Watertown, Wis., 1970—, Plus Devel. Inc., Watertown, 1970—; co-developer Hidden Meadows Condominium Community, Watertown, 1976—; gen. ptnr. W and A Elderly Housing Ltd. Partnership, Watertown, 1988—; gen. ptnr. Sunrise Housing Ltd. Ptnrship., 1990—; builder new and rehab low-income housing, 1983—. Mem. Wis. Gov.'s Conf. on Family, 1980; chmn. adminstrv. bd. United Meth. Ch., Oconomowoc, 1974-77; chmn. family ministry Wis. Conf., United Meth. Ch.; membership chmn. Boy Scouts Am., 1984-90; chmn. Ams. abroad Am. Field Svc., Oconomowoc, 1982-87. Recipient Dist. award of Merit Potawatomi Area coun. Boy Scouts Am., 1986. Mem. NAFE, AAUW (pres. Oconomowoc 1983-85), Am. Home Econs. Assn., Wis. Home Econs. Assn. (parliamentarian 1988—), Nat. Home Economists in Bus. (internat. com. 1985-87, regional U.S. advisor 1990-92), Wis. Home Economists in Bus. (state chmn. 1987-88, Home Economist in Bus. of Yr. 1987), Nat. Assn. Realtors, Wis. Assn. Realtors, Waukesha Bd. Realtors, Wis. Manufactured Housing Assn. (bd. dirs. 1979-90, chmn. bd. 1985-88, Mem. of Yr. award 1986), Internat. Fedn. of Home Ecoms., Phi Kappa Phi, Phi Upsilon Omicron, Omicron Nu, Phi Lambda Theta. Republican. Home: 37788 Mapleton Rd Oconomowoc WI 53066 Office: Luxury Homes Inc Hidden Meadows Pkwy Watertown WI 53094

PEEBLES, LINDA M(AE), photographer; b. Toledo, May 3, 1950; d. William Russell Duckett and Gertrude LaVerne (Jones) Gruber; m. Ray Randall Peebles II, June 20, 1970; children: Nedra Allyn, Karla Marie. Student, St. Petersburg (Fla.) Jr. Coll., 1968-69, U. Toledo, 1969-71. Various positions Sta. WSPD-TV (now known as WTVG-TV), Toledo, 1970-76; sr. billing clk. Owens-Corning Fiberglass, Toledo, 1976-78; owner, photographer Peebles Photography, Sylvania, Ohio, 1979—. Trustee Sylvania Community Services, 1986—, Latchkey Program Sylvania; bd. dirs. First United Meth. Christian Nursery Sch., pres. 1985-86, 86—; adminstrv. bd. First United Meth. Ch., 1986—, Sylvania. Mem. Profl. Photographers Am., Profl. Photographers of N.W. Ohio (treas., v.p. 1983-87, pres. 1988-89), Profl. Photographers of Ohio (N.W. Ohio rep. 1987-88). Club: Highland Meadows Golf (Sylvania). Office: Peebles Photography 6625 Maplewood Sylvania OH 43560

PEEBLES, LUCRETIA NEAL DRANE, educational administrator; b. Atlanta, Mar. 16, 1950; d. Dudley Drane and Annie Pearl (Neal) Lewis; divorced; 1 child, Julian Timothy. BA, Pitzer Coll., 1971; MA, Claremont Grad. Sch., 1973, PhD, 1985. Special edn. tchr. Marshall Jr. High Sch., Pomona, Calif., 1971-74; high sch. tchr. Pomona High Sch., 1974-84; adminstr. Lorbeer Jr. High Sch., Diamond Bar, Calif., 1984—; co-dir. pre-freshman program, Claremont (Calif.) Coll., 1974; dir. pre-freshman program, Claremont Coll., 1975; cons., Claremont, 1983—. Author: Negative Attendance Behavior: The Role of the School, 1985. Active Funds Distbn. Bd.-Food for All, 1987—, Funds Distbn. Task Force-Food for All, 1986; mem. Adolescent Pregnancy Childwatch Task Force. Named Outstanding Young Career Woman Upland Bus. and Profl. Women's Club, 1978-79; Stanford U. Sch. Edn. MESA fellow, 1983, NSF fellow Stanford U., 1981, Calif. Tchrs. Assn. fellow, 1979, Claremont Grad. Sch. fellow, 1977-79, fellow Calif. Edn. Policy Fellowship Program, 1989-90. Mem. Assn. Calif. Sch. Adminstrs. (Minigrant award 1988), Assn. for Supervision and Curriculum Devel., Nat. Assn. Secondary Sch. Principals, Pi Lambda Theta. Democrat. Am. Baptist. Home: 725 Mansfield Dr Claremont CA 91711 Office: Lorbeer Jr High Sch 501 S Diamond Bar Blvd Diamond Bar CA 91765

PEEBLES, RUTH ADDELLE, secondary education educator; b. Livingston, Tex., Dec. 9, 1929; d. Andrew Wiley and Addelle (Green) P. BA, East. Tex. Baptist Coll., 1951; M of Religious Edn., Southwestern Baptist Seminary, Ft. Worth, 1955; MA, Sam Houston State U., 1968. Instr. of religion and Baptist student dir. Ea. N.Mex. U., Portales, 1955-58; Baptist student dir. Madison Coll., Harrisonburg, Va., 1958-60; youth dir. Garden Oaks Baptist Ch., Houston, 1960-62; history tchr. Livingston Ind. Sch. Dist., 1962-84; bd. dirs. Confederate Rsch. Ctr., Hillsboro, Tex., 1981—. Editor: Pictorial History of Polk County, Texas, 1976; author: There Never Were Such Men Before, 1987. Bd. dirs. Polk County Libr. and Mus., Livingston, 1980-83, Polk County Heritage Soc., 1987-89. Recipient Community Svc. award Polk County C. of C., 1980, Hist. Preservation awards Polk County Heritage Soc., 1987, Tex. State Hist. Commn., 1989. Mem. Daughters of the Republic of Tex., Tex. State Hist. Assn., Tex. State Hist. Found., Hood's Tex. Brigade Assn., Polk County Heritage Soc., Atascosito Hist. Assn., Fort Delaware Soc. Baptist.

PEEDEN, PAULA ZARBOCK, obstetrician/gynecologist; b. Fond du Lac, Wis., Oct. 8, 1958; d. Paul Gerhard and Carolyn Ann (Preston) Zarbock; m. Joseph N. Peeden Jr., Mar. 9, 1985; children: Sarah Katherine, Joseph Paul. BA, U. Tenn., 1980, MD, 1984. Intern Univ. Tenn. Dept. Ob-Gyn., Memphis, 1984-85, resident, 1985-88; Physician E. Tenn. Ob-Gyn. Assn., Knoxville, 1989—. Fellow Am. Coll. Ob-Gyn. (jr.); mem. East Tenn. Ob-Gyn. Soc., AMA, Knoxville Acad. Medicine, Mortarboard, Phi Beta Kappa, Alpha Omega Alpha, Omicron Delta Kappa. Lutheran. Home: 530 Arrowhead Knoxville TN 37919 Office: East Tenn Ob Gyn Assocs St Marys Hosp Emerald Ave Ste 805 Knoxville TN

PEEPLES, AUDREY RONE, association executive; b. Chgo., May 22, 1939; d. John Drayton and Thelma (Shepherd) Rone; m. Anthony Alonzo Peeples, Aug. 14, 1971; children: Jennifer Lynn, Michael Anthony. BA, U. Ill., 1961; MBA, Northwestern U., 1978. Trust adminstr. Continental Bank, Chgo., 1961-72; assoc. regional dir. Girl Scouts of U.S.A., Chgo., 1973-76; asst. exec. dir., then exec. dir. Girl Scouts of Chgo., 1976-87; exec. dir. YWCA Met. Chgo., 1987—. Mem. Chgo. Network, 1988—, adv. bd. Women In Bus. Yellow Pages, 1988—, Mus. of Sci. and Industry, Black Creativity Gala; bd. dirs. United Way Chgo., 1987—. Recipient St. Annes award, Archdiocese of Chgo., 1985, Black Rose award, League Black Women, Chgo., 1987. Mem. Chgo. Alliance Collaborative Effort (v.p. 1990—, bd. dirs. 1st Trust 1990—), Econ. Club Chgo., Chgo. Jack and Jill of Am. Democrat. Roman Catholic. Home: 9339 S Hoyne St Chicago IL 60620 Office: YWCA Met Chgo 180 N Wabash St Chicago IL 60601

PEERSCHKE, ELLINOR IRMAGARD BARBARA, hematopathologist, educator; b. Braunschweig, Fed. Republic of Germany, May 7, 1954; came to U.S., 1965; d. Heinz Herbert Otto and Barbara (Halberkann) P. BA, Rutgers U., 1975; PhD, NYU, 1980. Head clin. hematology labs U. Hosp., Stony Brook, N.Y., 1980—; asst. prof. pathology SUNY, Stony Brook, 1980-86, assoc. prof. pathology, 1986—; vis. scientist Weizmann Inst. Sci., Rehovot, Israel, 1980, 89; dir. grad. program pathology, SUNY, Stony Brook, 1987—; with hematology study sect. NIH, Washington, 1990—; faculty adviser EURECA, Stony Brook, BOCES, Stony Brook. Editor: Hematology Tech Sample, 1985-89, Thrombosis Research, 1990—; contbr. articles to profl. jours. NIH grantee, 1980—. Mem. Am. Soc. Hematology (platelet coun. 1987-90), Am. Soc. Clin. Pathologists, Internat. Soc. for Thrombosis and Hemostasis, N.Y. Acad. Scis. (faculty adviser), Soc. for Experimental Biology and Medicine, Am. Heart Assn. (peer review ctr. 1986—, grantee 1984-85), Harvey Soc., Sigma Xi, Phi Beta Kappa. Office: U Hosp Dept Labs L-3 SUNY Stony Brook NY 11794-7300

PEHFIELD, JANET HARBISON, editor; b. East Orange, N.J., Apr. 19, 1916; d. Harold and Evangeline (Dalrymple) German; m. E. Harris Harbison, Sept. 25, 1937 (dec. July 1964); children: John, Meg; m. Thornton Penfield, Jan. 7, 1970 (widowed). AB, Smith Coll., 1937; postgrad., Princeton (N.J.) Theol. Sem., 1957-59. Assoc. editor Presbyteray Life, Phila., 1959-72; adminstr. Princeton Theol. Svc., 1972-76. Author: (monthly column) Priscilla, 1957-76. Mem. Women in Communications, Inc., Assn. Ch. Press (hon. life). Home: 3120 David Brainerd Dr Jamesburg NJ 08831

PEIRCE, CAROLE, teacher; b. Oshkosh, Wis., June 11, 1943; d. Charles J. and Bernadette (Graf) P.; m. Jack McDowell, Nov. 18, 1982. BS, U. Wis., Oshkosh, 1965; MA, U. Wis., Madison, 1966. Instr. U. Wis. Ctr. System, Marinette & Fond Du Lac, 1966-70, Concordia Coll., Milw., 1970-71; tchr. of French Behavioral Rsch. Labs., Palo Alto, Calif., 1971-73; elem. tchr. Nido De Aguilas Internat. Sch., Santiago, Chile; elem. bilingual tchr. Alum Rock Sch. Dist., San Jose, Calif., 1978-87; elem. tchr. Huntsville (Ark.) Sch. Dist., 1987—; presentor Bay Area Sch. Dists. Calif. 1984-87; tchr. Alum Rock Sch. Dist. and State of Calif. San Jose, 1986-87; tchr., cons. Nat. Geog. Soc., 1990. Author Social Studies Review Article 1985. Recipient grant for Environmental Edn. State of Calif 1986. Mem. Nat. Council for Social Studies, Internat. Reading Assn., Ark. Sci. Tchrs., NEA, Computer Using Educators, Magna Cum Laude, Ozark Soc., Assn. for Supervision & Curriculum Devel. Home: Rte 1 Box 254 Huntsville AR 72738

PEIRCE, GEORGIA WILSON, public relations executive; b. Newton, Mass., Jan. 6, 1960; d. Norris Ridgeway and Anne (McCusker) P. BA, Duke U., 1982. Intern to Speaker of Ho. of Reps., Washington, 1981; prin. PR, Etc., Quincy, Mass., 1987—; cons. Mass. Group Insur. Commn., 1985. Contbr. articles to profl. jours. Mem. community rels. com. VNA/Hospice of the South Shore; mem. com. to elect Mondale-Ferraro, Mass.; speakers bur. coord., 1984; Dem. state del., 1982, 83. Recipient Ninth Wave awards, 1989, 1st Pl. in pub. rels. award, 1989, Merit Bell Ringer award Publicity Club of New Eng. Mem. NAFE, South Shore C. of C., Small Bus. Assn. of New Eng., Women's Golf Assn. Mass., Eastward Ho! Country Club, Chatham Club (club champion 1977-81), Wollaston Golf Club. Democrat. Roman Catholic. Home: 289 Thatcher St Milton MA 02186 Office: PR Etc PO Box 172 Quincy MA 02170

PELÁEZ, ARMANTINA R., religious educator; b. Havana, Cuba, Apr. 21, 1948; came to U.S., 1962; d. Armando and Argentina (Pérez) P. BA, Ladycliff Coll., Highland Falls, N.Y., 1973; MA in Religious Edn., Fordham U., 1977; Cert. Tng. in Psychoanalysis and Psychotherapy, Weschester Inst., 1987. Asst. child care worker St. Joseph's Home of Peekskill (N.Y.), 1968-70; assoc. dir. religious edn. St. Joseph's of Palisades Parish, Western N.Y. and N.J., 1973-75; sec. evangelization Diocese of Paterson (N.J.) Roman Cath. Ch., 1975-80; Hispanic Apostolate coordinator, asst. adminstr. to vicar of Hispanic ministries, 1980-84; coord. catechesis and religious edn. U.S. Dept. Edn., Washington, 1984-90; dir. tng. Poly. Inst. Fla., Miami, 1990—; vol. team mem. pastoral Hispanic youth ministry St. Augustine's Parish, Union City, N.J., 1979-84; cons. Latin Am. Program Wilson Ctr., Washington, 1982, Ctr. for Applied in Apostolate, 1981; authorized instr. parent and tchr. effectiveness tng., N.J.; psychotherapist Palisade Counseling Ctr., Rutherford, N.J., 1982-87, Lakeland Counseling Ctr., Dover, N.J., 1985-87; co-dir., psychotherapist Eirene Counseling Ctr., Union City, N.J., 1987-90. Contbr. numerous articles in English and Spanish. Chmn., nat. bd. dirs. Nat. Planning Council, 1974-75. Mem. Nat. Assn. for Women Religious, Found. of Thanatology (assoc.), Am. Soc. Psychical Research, Las Hermanas Nat. Orgn. (N.Y. coordinator 1970-72, N.Y. Upstate coordinator 1972-73, N.J. coordinator 1978-79), Nat. Assn. Advancement of Psychoanalysis and Am. Bds. for Accreditation and Certification Inc., Nat. Counseling and Devel. Assn. Clubs: N.Y. Road Runners, N.Y. Race Walking; N.J. Shore Athletic, N.J. Athletics Congress. Home: 7935 SW 8th St #68 Miami FL 33144 Office: Poly Inst Fla 11865 (H3) Coral Way Miami FL 33175

PELC, JO ANN, medical records director; b. Union City, Pa., July 5, 1956; d. Antoni Wincenty and Jennie Katherine (Bolas) P. BS in Health Records Adminstrn., U. Pitts., 1978. Registered record adminstr. Med. records adminstr. Womens Christian Assn. Hosp., Jamestown, N.Y., 1978-86; dir. med. records Deaconess Hosp. Cleve., 1986—; utilization info. svcs. adv. com. Hosp. Assn. N.Y. State, Buffalo, 1982-84; nursing home cons. Womens Christian Assn. Hosp., Jamestown, 1984-86. Adv. com. Cuyahoga Community Coll., Cleve., 1989—; decorations chmn. U. Pitts. Alumni Assn., Cleve., 1988, 89. Recipient Merit Scholarship U. Pitt., 1974-76, Senatorial Scholarship State of Pa., 1976-77. Mem. Ohio Med. Record Assn., Am. Med. Record Assn., Greater Cleve. Hosp. Assn. (med. records com. 1986—), Cuyahoga Community Coll. (med. record technology adv. com. 1989—). Roman Catholic. Office: Deaconess Hosp of Cleve 4229 Pearl Rd Cleveland OH 44109

PELCZARSKI, KAREN ANN, lawyer; b. New Bedford, Mass., Feb. 20, 1960; d. Alfred Joseph and Jane Theresa (Iwanski) P. BA cum laude, Wellesley Coll., 1982; postgrad., U. Pa., 1984-85; JD, Boston Coll., 1985. Bar: R.I. 1985, Mass. 1986, U.S. Dist. Ct. R.I. 1986, U.S. Dist. Ct. Mass. 1987, U.S. Ct. Appeals (1st cir.) 1989. Summer assoc. Sloane & Walsh, Boston, 1983, Murtha, Cullina, Richter & Pinney, Hartford, Conn., 1984; assoc. Hinckley, Allen, Snyder & Comen, Providence, 1985-87, Blish & Cavanagh, Providence, 1987—. Co-author: Tapping Officials' Secrets, R.I. Portion of Compendium, 1988. LDRC Annual Legal Survey of R.I. Libel Law, R.I. Portion, 1988. Founder The Music Sch., Inc., Providence, 1987, pres., 1989-90. Nat. Merit Spl. scholar Am. Express, 1978; recipient Outstanding Woman award YWCA, Providence, 1987. Mem. ABA, R.I. Bar Assn. (pub. relations com. 1986—), Mass. Bar Assn., R.I. Women's Assn., Mass. Women's Assn. Democrat. Roman Catholic. Office: Blish & Cavanagh Commerce Ctr 30 Exchange Terr Providence RI 02903

PELED, NINA, chemical executive; b. Padowa, Italy, Jan. 31, 1948; came to U.S., 1977; d. Eliezer and Sarah (Fischer) Schoengut; m. Sam Peled (div. 1984); 1 child, Ben. BS, Hebrew U., Jerusalem, Israel, 1970, MS, 1972, PhD, 1977; MBA, U. Houston, 1983. Cert. tchr., Israel. Instr. Hebrew U., 1972-77; asst. prof. Rice U., Houston, 1977-78; mgr. R & D Hycel, Houston, 1978-80; with Boehringer Mannheim, 1980-81, dir. quality assurance, 1981-83; dir. evaluations Boehringer Mannheim, Indpls., 1984—; chairperson Nat. Com. for Clin. Lab. Standards, Washington, 1987—. Author: Methods of Enzymatic Analysis, 1985; inventor bicarbonate assay; contbr. articles to profl. jours. Sgt. Israel Mil., 1965-67. Hebrew U. grantee, 1970-72. Mem. Am. Assn. for Clin. Chemists, Am. Diabetes Assn., Mensa. Democrat. Home: 1735 Park North Way Indianapolis IN 46260 Office: Boehringer Mannheim 9115 Hague Rd Indianapolis IN 46250

PELEJO-SUCH, PURITA P., retired nursing home executive; b. Manila, Philippines, Feb. 21, 1938; came to U.S., 1968; d. Fidel and Josefa (Penalosa) Pelejo; m. Domingo F. Such Jr., May 9, 1959; children: Rommelle Von, Hischellee, Ma. Lyndia, Domingo III. AA, U. of East, Manila, 1956; LLB, Lyceum Philippines, Manila, 1960. Bar: Philippines. Agt. Nat. Bur. Investigations, Manila, 1963-68; social case worker N.Y.C. Dept. Welfare, 1968-77; investigator N.Y.C. Inspector Gen's. Office; dir., owner Rivervale (N.J.) Manor, 1977-86, Long Branch (N.J.) Nursing Home, 1982-87, Purdom, Inc./ Milford Manor Nursing Home, West Milford, N.J., 1982-87, Brookside Manor, Inc., Wayne, N.J., 1980-86, Willowbrook, Inc., Wayne, 1980-86; pres. Purdom Found., Inc., 1985—. Mem. Catholic Golden Age, 1988—. Mem. Lic. Nursing Home Adminstrs., Philippine Bar Assn., Am. Assn. Retired Persons, Cursillo Club, Charismatic Club. Home: PO Box U Blairstown NJ 07825

PELL, PYRMA DAPHNE TILTON, civic worker; b. N.Y.C., Feb. 5, 1909; d. Newell Whiting and Mildred Olive (Bigelow) Tilton; student Queens Coll., London, 1921-26, Kunst Akademie, Vennia, Austria, 1927-28; m. John Howland Gibbs Pell, Sept. 3, 1929; children—Sarah Gibbs, John Bigelow. Active in preservation and restoration Fort Ticonderoga, N.Y., 1950-87 , also coordinator spl. events, 1950-87 ; treas. Friends of Chung Ang U., Korea, 1965-71, recipient spl. award, 1971. Recipient First award Historic Preservation, Garden Club Am., 1973. Mem. Am. Acad. Poets (co-founder), Colonial Dames Am., Assn. Churchill Fellows of Westminster Coll., Colony Club, Knickerbocker Club, Alpha Xi Delta. Christian Scientist. Address: Pelican Place Bellevue Ave Newport RI 02840

PELLEGRIN, DIANA JEANNE, educator; b. East Orange, N.J., Nov. 26, 1945; d. Robert Le Roy Jr. and Charlotte W. (Moore) Brackney; m. John Francis Pellegrin, June 18, 1967; children: Lisa, Richard. BA in Math., Occidental Coll., 1967; MS in Math., No. Ill. U., 1984. Cert. high sch. tchr., Calif., Ill. High sch. tchr. Carpinteria (Calif.) High Sch., 1968-69; computer programmer Motorola, Mesa, Ariz., 1969-71; part-time tchr. Lisle (Ill.) High Sch., 1978-79; math. tchr. Glenbard West High Sch., Glen Ellyn, Ill., 1979—; math. team coach North Suburban Math. League regional and state contests, Glenbard West High Sch., Glen Ellyn, 1986—. Deacon First Presbyn. Ch., Wheaton, Ill., 1987-90, part-time organist, 1989—; singer West Suburban Choral Union, Wheaton, 1987—; pres., singer Fine Arts Chorale, Geneva, Ill., 1978-87. NSF grantee Northeastern Ill. U., 1987, calculus grantee U. Ill., Champaign, 1989. Mem. AAUW, Ill. Coun. Tchrs. Math., Nat. Coun. Tchrs. Math., Met. Math. Club (Chgo.). Office: Glenbard West High Sch 670 Crescent Blvd Glen Ellyn IL 60137

PELLEGRINI, BERNADETTE, communications company official; b. Staten Island, N.Y., Nov. 17, 1966; d. John Louis and Angelina Anne (Colucci) P. BS, St. John's U., 1988. Mgr. ANR Salumeria, Inc., Staten Island, 1983-85; asst. dept. mgr. Macy's, Staten Island, 1985-88; computer lab. asst. St. John's U., Staten Island, 1986-88; mgr. N.Y. Telephone Co., N.Y.C., 1988—, software and system adminstr., 1990—. Active Cooley's Anemia Found., Staten Island, 1987—. Mem. Am. Math. Soc., Math. Assn. Am., Statis. Math. and Computer Sci. Club, St. John's U. S.I. Alumni Assn., St. John's U. Alumnae Assn., Am. Mgmt. Assn., Assn. of Mgmt. Women. Roman Catholic.

PELLEGRINI, LORA MARIE, legislative director; b. Norwood, Mass., May 5, 1960; d. Angelo J. Pellegrini and Grace M. (Vozella) Langill. BA in Govt., Wheaton Coll., 1982; JD, New Eng. Sch. Law, 1990. Office of gov. Lt. Gov. John Kerry, Boston, 1983-84; asst. legis. dir. Office Gov. Michael Dukakis, Boston, 1984—. State com. woman Mass. Dem. State Com., Boston, 1984—, chair, 1988—; chair Mansfield Dem. Town Com., 1988—. Democrat. Roman Catholic. Home: 24 Hillside Terr Mansfield MA 02048

PELLEGRINI, MARIA, biology professor; b. New Orleans, June 3, 1947; d. Sylvius and May (Renwald) P.; 1 child, Andrew Dervan. AB, Conn. Coll., 1969; PhD, Columbia U., 1974. Prof. biology U. So. Calif., L.A., 1977, chmn. dept. biology, 1988. Named Dreyfus Found. scholar, N.Y.C., 1979; Sloan fellow, Alfred P. Sloan Found., 1980. Mem. AAUP, Phi Beta Kappa, Sigma Xi, Phi Kappa Phi. Office: Univ Southern Calif AHF-107 Los Angeles CA 90089-0371

PELLEGRINO, LAUREN MARY, education educator; b. Warwick, R.I., Aug. 9, 1963; d. Gerard Richard and Carol Ann (Barto) P. BS, Syracuse U., 1985; MEd in Reading, Rhode Island Coll., 1987-90. Substitute tchr. Warwick (R.I.) Sch. Dept., 1985-87; reading specialist Barrington (R.I.) Sch. Dept., 1987-88; salesperson Jordan Marsh, Warwick, R.I., 1986-89; ins. adjuster Pilgrim-Pellegrino Adj. Co., Warwick, R.I., 1986-88; reading specialist, cons. Pawtucket (R.I.) Sch. Dept., 1988-89; reading specialist East Providence (R.I.) Sch. Dept., 1989—. Mem. NAFE, Assn. for Supervision and Curriculum Devel., Internat. Reading Assn. Roman Catholic. Home: 91 Bokar Rd Warwick RI 02886 Office: East Providence Sch Dept 80 Burnside Ave East Providence RI 02860

PELLEGRINO, VICTORIA GRAZZIELLA, marketing professional; b. Roma, Italy, May 5, 1962; came to U.S.A., 1970; d. Antonio and Maria Caterina (Surianello) P. Postgrad., Melrose Bty. Acad., 1980, American R.E. Acad., Waltham, Mass., 1981; BS, Boston Coll., 1984. Co-owner, prin. Monica Styles Hair Salon, Stoneham, Mass., 1980--; r.e salesperson Century 21 Small Real Estate, Malden, Mass., 1981-83; co-owner, founder Tantastix Suntanning Salon, Stoneham, Mass., 1984--; account exec. Allstates Air Cargo, Inc., E. Boston; nat. account exec. Exhibit Express Allied, Lexington, Mass., 1989--. Mem. Nat. Assn. Hairdressers, Nat. Assn. Realtors, Mass. Assn. Realtors, Middlesex Bd. Realtors, Internat. Exhibitors Assn. Home: 2 Barberry Ln North Reading MA 01864 Office: Exhibit Express Inc 189 Bedford St Lexington MA 02173

PELLER, MARCI TERRY, real estate executive; b. Upland, Pa., Nov. 5, 1949; d. Max Maclyn and Lucille Eugenia (Zucker) P. AA, Harcum Jr. Coll., Bryn Mawr, Pa., 1971. With sales dept. William H. Cartwright Real Estate, North Palm Beach, Fla., 1985—. Republican. Jewish. Home: 500 Bay S #709 Ocean City NJ 08226 also: 5420 N Ocean Dr Singer Island FL 33404 Office: William H Cartwright Real Estate 745 US Hwy 1 North Palm Beach FL 33408

PELLER, MARION, management consultant; b. Newark, Sept. 15, 1943; d. Bernard Oscar and Ruth (Silver) P.; m. Ronald David Tilden, Aug. 11, 1985. BS, Skidmore Coll., Saratoga Springs, N.Y., 1965; MA, U. Wash., 1967; EdD, U. Mass., 1976. Art specialist Berkeley (Calif.) Sch. Dists., 1965-67; comm. developer Peace Corp, Botswana, 1967-70; asst. prof. Leslie Grad. Sch. Edn., Cambridge, Mass., 1973-79; dir. tng. and organizational devel. Joseph Magnin, San Francisco, 1979-81; orgn. psychologist, v.p. Drake Beam Morin, Inc., San Francisco, 1981-86; pres., owner Peller Marion Assoc., Inc., San Francisco, 1986—; cons. Pacific Gas & Electric, San Francisco, 1986—, Wells Fargo, San Francisco, 1986—, Clorox, San Francisco, 1986—, Syntex, Palo Alto, Calif., 1986—; lectr. U. Mass. Simmons Coll., Antioch Coll. U. Calif., 1975-79; lectr., leader in residence Esalen Inst., Big Sur, Calif., 1988—. Author: When Success Is Not Enough, 1990; contbr. articles to profl. journs. Mem. exec. and personnel coms. Tiburon (Calif.) Community Congl. Ch., 1988—. Mem. Am. Psychol. Assn., Am. Art Therapy Assn. (registered), No. Calif. Human Resource Coun. Home: 150 Marguerite Ave Mill Valley CA 94941 Office: Peller Marion Assoc Inc 388 Market St Ste 500 San Francisco CA 94111

PELLER, MARY ELLEN CHENEY, mathematics educator; b. Laconia, N.H., Dec. 2, 1951; d. Thomas Perkins Cheney and Elaine Sinclair; m. Richard John Peller, Aug. 24, 1974; children: Ann Elizabeth, Michael Thomas. AB, Smith Coll., Northampton, 1973. Geology tchr. Northfield Mt. Hermon Sch., Northfield, Mass., 1973-75; math. tchr. Northfield Mt. Hermon Sch., Northfield, 1973—; asst. dir. student activities Mt. Hermon Sch., Northfield, 1974-75; dean of women Mt. Hermon Summer Sch., Northfield, asst. dir. summer sch., 1975-79; head math. dept. Mt. Hermon Summer Sch., 1984-89; dir. treas. NMH Campus Nursery Sch., Northfield, 1981-89; advisor Gill Sch. Advisory Com. Gill Mass., 1987—, Gill Elem. Sch. Task Force Gill, 1988—. Editor: AB Calculus, 1988. Leader Girl Scout Troop #450 Gill, 1986-88; head coach Gill Elem. Sch. Youth Soccer and Football, 1988—; com. chmn. Community Ctr., Mt. Hermon, 1973—; vol. Franklin Med. Ctr. Bd. Organized Work Greenfield, Mass., 1980—; Sunday sch. tchr. Trinity Congl. Ch., 1989—, leader Math. Sci. Club of Elem. Sch., 1989—. Recipient GTE Gift Fellowship GTE Corp., 1988-89, Culpepper Grant Culpepper Found., 1987-88, Acad. Dean's Award for Excellence in Teaching NMH, 1986. Mem. Mathwest, Nat. Council Tchrs. Mathematics. Ind. Congregational. Home: PO Box 95 Mount Hermon MA 01354 Office: Northfield Mt Hermon Sch Northfield MA 01360

PELLICCIOTTI, PATRICIA M., financial analyst, management consultant; b. Phila.. V.p., dir. regional sales EGR Commnications Inc., N.Y.C., 1975-77; pres. Pellicciotti Assocs., Northfield, N.J., 1977-83; registered rep. IDS/Am. Express, Mpls., 1981-85; v.p. Herzog, Heine, Geduld Inc., N.Y.C., 1984-85; pres. Fin. Cons. Group Inc., Phila., 1985—; registered rep. Rothschild Registry Inc., N.Y.C., 1986—; Founder, bd. dirs. Woman to Woman Seminars. Producer, hostess radio talk show WWDB-FM Woman to Woman, Phila.; author: Renting Money. Pres. bd., exec. dir. Upward Bound; bd. dirs. Girl Scouts U.S. Recipient Recognition award Vice Pres. George Bush. Mem. Mktg. Communications Execs. Internat. (past v.p.), Nat. Assn. Securities Dealers (registered rep., cert. real estate appraiser), Nat. Econ. Round Table, SBA (adv. Pres. Carter's Interagy. Task Force for Women, cons. Active Corp Execs.). Club: Toastmasters.

PELOQUIN, LORI JEANNE, clinical psychologist; b. Milw., Sept. 21, 1957; d. Wayne Joseph Peloquin and Jeanne Audrey (Ehlers) Driessen; m. Allen Theodor Retzlaff Jr., May 5, 1990. Student, U. Wis., Eau Claire, 1975-76; BA summa cum laude, U. Minn., 1978; MA, U. Rochester, 1982, PhD, 1985. Lic. psychologist, N.Y. Teaching asst. U. Rochester, N.Y., 1981-83, instr. psychology, 1984; instr. Univ. Affiliated Program for Devel. Disabilities U. Rochester Sch. Medicine and Dentistry, N.Y., 1984—; pvt. practice Rochester, 1985—; cons. Rochester Children's Nursery and Bd. Coop. Ednl. Svcs., Rochester, 1986-90, Hillside Children's Ctr., Rochester, 1985-87; planning coord. Crisis Intervention Program, Rochester, 1985-86; mem. steering com. Early Childhood Intervention Coun. Monroe County, 1989-90. Contbr. chpts. to books, articles to profl. publs. Mem. NOW, LWV. Mem. Psychologists for Social Responsibility, Rochester Area Assn. Clin. Psychologists (v.p. 1987-89, pres. 1989-90, exec. com. 1990-91), Genesee Valley Psychol. Assn., Coalition for Svcs. to Parents with Developmental Disabilities (com. chair 1985-90, coord. 1988-90), Am. Psychol. Assn., N.Y. State Psychol. Assn., Psi Beta Kappa. Office: 247 Park Ave Rochester NY 14607

PELOSI, EVELYN TYMINSKI, teacher; b. Chicopee, Mass., Dec. 6, 1938; d. Thomas John and Josephine (Kos) Tyminski; m. Stanford Salvatore Pelosi, Jr., Aug. 14, 1965; children: Sharon Marie, Steven Michael. BA, U. Mass., 1960; MS, U. N.H., 1963, PhD in Chemistry, 1965. Asst. prof. SUNY, Oneonta, 1967-68; chemistry tchr. Norwich (N.Y.) City Schs., 1977—; mem. Norwich City Sch. Dist. Instructional Coun., 1989—. Mem. Am. Chem. Soc. (high sch. coord. Norwich sect.). Office: Norwich High Sch Midland Dr Norwich NY 13815

PELOSI, NANCY, congresswoman; b. Balt., 1941; d. Thomas J. D'Alesandro Jr.; m. Paul Pelosi; children: Nancy Corinne, Christine, Jacqueline, Paul, Alexandra. Grad., Trinity Coll. Former chmn. Calif. State Dem. Com., 1981; committeewoman Dem. Nat. Com., 1976, 80, 84; elec. to U.S. Congress from 5th dist. Calif., 1987, re-elected to 101st, 102nd Congresses from 5th dist. Calif.; fin. chmn. Dem. Senatorial Campaign Com., 1987. Office: US Ho of Rep 1005 Longworth Bldg Washington DC 20515-0505

PELTON, ELOIS BLEIDT, physical education educator; b. Corpus Christi, Tex., Apr. 3, 1939; d. Hodge Lester and Valena (Lee) Bleidt; m. Scott Horton Pelton, July 23, 1961 (div. June 1967); 1 child, Shawn Scott. BS in Edn., U. Ark., 1961; MS in Edn., U. Central Ark., 1967; EdD, Northwestern State U. La., 1972. Phys. edn. tchr. East Side Jr. High Sch., Little Rock, 1963-65, Searcy (Ark.) Jr. High Sch., 1965-68; prof. phys. edn. Central Mo. State U., Warrensburg, 1968—; phys. edn. curriculum cons. Central Mo. State U., Warrensburg, 1965—. Mem. Park Bd., City of Warrensburg. Mem. AAHPER and Dance (nat. del. 1988—), Mo. Assn. Health, Phys. Edn., Recreation and Dance (pres. 1989, presidential award 1987). Home: 406 N Mulberry Warrensburg MO 64093

PELTON, TERRY LYNN, computer programmer; b. Orange, Calif., Nov. 6, 1950; d. John William and Billie Lou (Bomhoff) Bryant; m. R. Ballard, Oct. 10, 1976 (annulled 1982); m. Jeffery Scot Pelton, May 2, 1982; 1 child, Ida Yvonne. Student, Butte Coll., Oroville, Calif., 1972-77, Yuba Coll., Marysville, Calif., 1979-80; grad., Ctr. Ind. Living/Computer Tng., Berkeley, Calif., 1980; student, U. N.H., Burnwick, Maine, 1988. Cert. computer programmer, Calif. Computer operator U. Calif., Chico, 1976-78; key punch operator Beal AFB, Marysville, 1978-79; computer programmer U. Calif., Berkeley, 1980, Disabled Programmers Inc., San Jose, Calif., 1980-82; cons. Informatics Inc., Palo Alto, Calif., 1982-83; computer programmer Keystone Orgn., Phila., 1984-85; tech. support specialist Applied Data Rsch., Princeton, N.J., 1985-86; computer programmer, Supr. Shipbldg. USN, Brunswick, 1987—. Recipient Letter of Commendation, Am. Pres. Lines, San Mateo, Calif., 1983, cert. of appreciation and numerous other awards Disabled Programmers Inc., 1981. Mem. Am. Legion Aux., Navy Patrol Squad Spouse Club, Ctr. for Ind. Living/Computer Tng. Project, Epilepsy Found. Republican.

PELTON, VIRGINIA LUE, small business owner; b. Utica, Kans., Apr. 15, 1928; d. Forrest Selby and Nellie (Simmons) Meier; m. Theodore Trower King Jr., Oct. 27, 1956 (div.); m. Harold Marcel Pelton, July 11, 1970; children: Mary Virginia Joyner, Diana Jean. Student, Kans. State U., 1946-47, Ft. Hays U., 1947-48, Washington U., St. Louis, 1950-51. Instr. Patricia Stevens Modeling Sch., Kansas City, Mo., 1948-50; model various cos., Calif. and N.Y., 1951-53; fashion cons. Giorgio, Beverly Hills, Calif., 1967-68, Charles Gallay, Beverly Hills, 1975-77, Dorso's, Beverly Hills, 1977-79; buyer, mgr. giftware Slavick's, Laguna Hills, Calif., 1980-83; owner P.J. Secretarial Svcs., Laguna Hills, 1980—; v.p. H.P. Fin. Inc., Laguna Hills, 1983—. Editor Profl. Network newsletter, 1980—. Sec. Leukemia Soc. Am., Santa Ana, 1985—; mem. Laguna Beach Art Mus., 1986—. Mem. Profl. Network Assn. (sec. 1986—), Market Plus The Consumer Network, Saddleback C. of C., Laguna Hills Club, Kappa Delta. Republican. Methodist. Home: 24942 Georgia Sue Dr Laguna Hills CA 92653

PELTZ, LISA, telecommunications executive; b. L.A., Jan. 22, 1962; d. John Blake and Elizabeth Barrett (Brown) Ontario; m. Percy Peltz, Dec. 17, 1988. BBA, U. So. Calif., 1984; MBA, UCLA, 1986. Regional sales mgr. West Coast Communications, L.A., 1986-88; asst. dir. mktg. West Coast Communications, Van Nuys, Calif., 1988, mktg. dir., 1989—. Vol. L.A. Big Sisters, 1985-86; coord. young persons com. Van Nuys Luth. Ch., 1989—; coach Oakwood Park Dist., 1990—. Mem. Western Mktg. Assn., Women in Communications. Office: Werik Ctr 16045 Sherman Way Ste B Van Nuys CA 91406

PELUSO, RENEE IRENE, communications company executive; b. Akron, Ohio, Feb. 28, 1958; d. Antonio Leonino and Mary Lou Fritts; children: Angela, Alicia. BSBA, U. Akron, 1983. Sales rep. major accts. Xerox Corp., Akron, 1983-87, MCI Communications, Akron, 1987—. Mem. NAFE, Am. Inst. Cancer Rsch.

PELZ, CAROLINE DUNCOMBE, retired educational administrator; b. White Plains, N.Y.; d. David Sanford and Helena (Ebert) Duncombe; A.B., Barnard Coll., 1940; m. Edward Joseph Pelz, July 11, 1942; children—Caroline Pelz Elbow, Margaret L. (dec.), Patricia Pelz Hart, Sanford M. Adjustments supr. R.H. Macy & Co., N.Y.C., 1940-42; admissions interviewer Barnard Coll., 1960-63; alumni sec. Allen-Stevenson Sch., N.Y.C., 1967-70, admissions asst., 1969-70; adminstrv. asst. Ednl. Records Bur., N.Y.C., 1970-72; dir. admissions Grace Church Sch., N.Y.C., 1972-87. Trustee Barnard Coll., 1963-67. Mem. Barnard Coll. Alumnae Assn. (pres. 1963-66), Woman's Nat. Farm and Garden Assn. (scholarship chmn. N.Y.C. met. br. 1981—), English-Speaking Union. Republican. Episcopalian. Home: Box 395 S Main St Berlin NY 12022 Other: 55 E 87th St New York NY 10128

PELZ, ELAYNE FRANCES, data processing executive; b. L.A., Mar. 7, 1954; d. Paul and Flora (Sommers) Yampolsky; m. Bruce E. Pelz, July 13, 1974. BA in Slavic Langs., UCLA, 1975. Tax acct. Am. Med. Internat., Beverly Hills, Calif., 1981-84; configuration mgr. Ashton-Tate, Torrance, Calif., 1984—. Mem. L.A. Sci. Fantasy Soc. (bd. dirs. 1980—), So. Calif. Inst. for Fan Interests (bd. dirs. 1982—), Inst. for Specialized Lit. (treas. 1975—), Friends of English Regency (contbr.-editor Haut Ton newsletter 1981—). Home: 15931 Kalisher St Granada Hills CA 91344

PEMBERTON, DIRONDA LYNN See MIDDLETON, DIRONDA LYNN

PEMBERTON, ELIZABETH FAY, psychology educator; b. Wilmington, Del., Apr. 9, 1957; d. Wilfred Anderson and Carol Frances (Lundie) P. BA cum laude, Western Md. Coll., 1979; EdM, Harvard U., 1980; PhD, Pa. State U., 1985. Postdoctoral fellow, child lang. program U. Kans., Lawrence, 1985-87; postdoctoral fellow Boys Town Nat. Inst., Omaha, 1987-88; vis. asst. prof. devel. psychology U. Iowa, Iowa City, 1988—. Editor: Working Papers in Language Development, 2 vols., 1986-87; contbr. articles to profl. jours. Mem. Amnesty Internat., Washington, 1988—; foster parent Warwick (R.I.) Foster Parent Plan, 1989. Humanities fellow Pa. State U., 1983. Mem. Soc. Rsch. in Child Devel., Sigma Xi, Psi Chi, Lambda Iota Tau. Democrat. Office: U Iowa E-232 SSH Iowa City IA 52242

PEMBERTON, JOANNE JODY, legal administrator; b. Norwalk, Conn., Feb. 19, 1952; d. Joseph J. Jr. and Sandra J. (Constantino) Smith; m. Frank R. Pemberton, Apr. 8, 1978. BS in Elem. Edn., Western Conn. State U., 1973; postgrad., U. New Haven, 1975-77. With adminstrn. rsch. and devel. Pitney Bowes Inc., Stamford, Conn., 1975-80; mgr. office Starting Line, Saratoga Springs, N.Y., 1980-82; v.p. AMI, Computer Cons., Saratoga Springs, 1982-85; legal adminstr. Ferrara, Jones and Sipperly, Saratoga Springs, 1985—. Mem. Nat. Bus. Women's Leadership Assn., Saratoga County Mock Trial Program (co-ord. 1986—), NAFE, Saratoga Springs C. of C. (chmn. exec. dialogue com. 1982—). Republican. Roman Catholic. Home: 27 Northway Ct Saratoga Springs NY 12866 Office: Ferrara Jones and Sipperly 179 West Ave PO Box 396 Saratoga Springs NY 12866

PEMBERTON, MELISSIE COLLINS, elementary educator; b. Pembroke, Va., Dec. 25, 1907; d. Walter Wingo and Grace Moore (Musselman) Collins; m. Oakland Herbert Pemberton, May 17, 1930; children: Oakland Herbert Jr., Walter Scott, William Durwood. BA in Edn., George Washington U., 1962; MA equivalency, Md. Bd. Edn., 1968. Tchr. Giles County Bd. Edn., Newport, Va., 1925-30, D.C. Pub. Schs., Washington, 1945-47, Montgomery County Pub. Schs., Rockville, MD, 1955-59, 63-75; tchr. rep. Curriculum Materials Rev., Rockville, Md., 1967-68, Elem. Spl. Edn. Rev. and EvaluationCom. for Textbooks, Rockville, 1970; del. Montgomery Edn. Assn., Rockville, 1967. Leader Montgomery County Govt., Rockville, 1988; sponsor Rep. Nat. Com., Washington, 1988; radio operator U.S.A. Fed. Communications Commn., Washington, 1942. Named Civitan Internat. scholar, 1964. Mem. Bon Air Heights Civic Assn., Montgomery County Edn. Assn. (emeritus life mem. 1975), NEA, Md. State Tchrs. Assn., Pi Lamba Theta. Republican. Methodist. Home: 6208 Mac Arthur Blvd Bethesda MD 20816

PEÑA, HEATHER MARIA, internist; b. North Hampton, Mass., Sept. 30, 1955; d. Cesareo Dennis and Eloise Verna (Morrison) P. BS summa cum laude, Tufts U., 1977; MD, Harvard U., 1981. Intern, resident in internal medicine UCLA Hosp. and Clinics, 1981-84; staff physician Woodview Calabasas (Calif.) Hosp., 1983—, Oceanview Med. Group at Pritikin Long Ctr., Santa Monica, Calif., 1984—. Mem. Am. Heart Assn. Epidemiology Council. Mem. Am. Coll. Physicians (assoc.), Harvard Med. Hamilton-Hunt Soc., Phi Beta Kappa. Democrat.

PENARANDA, ELIZABETH ANNE, training analyst; b. Boulder, Colo., Oct. 11, 1943; d. Stanley Eugene and Laura Winona (Schwenk) Sprague. BA, Grinnell Coll., 1961; MA, Antioch U., 1979. Research psychologist Armed Forces Radiobiol. Rsch. Inst., Bethesda, Md., 1966-67, Naval Med. Research Inst., Bethesda, 1967-69; trainer Individual Psychology Assn., Wash., 1971-77; counselor Antioch Univ., Columbia, Md., 1977-79; tech. writer CSR, Inc., Wash., 1979-82; instl. technologist Indsl. Tng. Corp., Herndon, Va., 1982-86; mgr. course devel. Home Builders Inst., Wash., 1986-88; sr. tng. analyst Link Tng. Svcs. Div. CAE-Link Corp., Alexandria, Va., 1988—. Editor: Groups Under Stress Psychology Research in Sea Lab, 1968. Mem. Nat. Abortion Rights Action League, Wash., 1982. Mem. Nat. Orgn. for Women, Nat. Assn. Female Exec., Soc. Applied Learning Tech. Democrat. Office: Link Tng Svcs Div CAE-Link Corp 209 Madison St Alexandria VA 22314

PENCEK, MARY FAITH RUSSO, mathematics educator; b. Amsterdam, N.Y., June 22, 1958; ž. Joseph Santo and Therese Anne (Perron) Russo; m. Barry Donald Pencek, Sept. 22, 1984; children: Samuel Nicholas, James Barry, Andrew William. AA, DeKalb Community Coll., Atlanta, 1978; BS in Edn., Ga. State U., 1983; MEd, Kennesaw Coll., 1988. Tchr. Marietta (Ga.) Jr. High Sch., 1986—. Recipient Honor Tchr. award Atlanta Jour.-Constn. Newspapers, 1987. Mem. Nat. Coun. Tchrs. Math., Assn. for Supervision and Curriculum Devel., Phi Kappa Phi. Episcopalian. Home: 4653 N Springs Rd Kennesaw GA 30144 Office: Marietta Jr High Sch 340 Aviation Rd Marietta GA 30060

PENCSAK, PATRICIA SUSANNE, organization executive; b. Lexington, Ky., Nov. 21, 1963; d. Ray John and Nancy Elizabeth (Mumford) P. BBAA, NE La. U., 1985; M Sport Sci., U.S. Sports Acad., Daphne, Ala., 1987. Mgr. Baylor Ctr. for Health Promotion, Dallas, 1987-88, dir. health svcs., 1988-89; dir. aquatics and aerobics Ft. Worth YMCA-Downtown, 1989—. Mem. Assn. for Fitness in Bus., YMCA Assn. for Profl. Dirs. Office: Ft Worth YMCA-Downtown 512 Lamar Fort Worth TX 76102

PENDALL, MARIA HELGA, sales executive; b. Vienna, Austria, July 27, 1944; d. Francis Joseph and Helga Maria (Landesman) P. BA in English, Le Moyne Coll., 1968; postgrad., SUNY, Cortland, N.Y., 1968, 69. Cert. secondary edn. tchr., N.Y. Tchr. pub. schs. Syracuse, N.Y., 1968-72; sales rep. Atlantic-Richfield Co., Buffalo, 1972-73, Hills Bros. Coffee, Syracuse, 1973-79; sales supr. M&M/Mars Co., Syracuse, 1979-89, nat. promotion mgr., 1989; trade mktg. mgr. M&M/Mars Co., 1989—. Republican. Roman Catholic. Home: 5 Brentwood Ct Sparta NJ 07871 Office: M&M/Mars Co High St Hackettstown NJ 07840

PENDELL, JUDYTH WICKETT, insurance company executive; b. New Haven, Conn., Nov. 9, 1942; d. Kenneth Melvin and Anne Amrein (Crandall) Wickett; m. Thomas Gerow Pendell, Nov. 25, 1961 (div. Apr. 1979); children: Robert Gulian, Stephanie Wickett; m. Warren Bailey Azano, Jan. 16, 1988. BA, Vassar Coll., 1978; student, SUNY, Albany, 1978-80; M in Pub. and Pvt. Mgmt., Yale U., 1982. Commentator, producer Sta. WKIP Radio, Poughkeepsie, N.Y., 1974-80; mgr., dir. pub. policy issues analysis Aetna Life & Casualty Co., Hartford, Conn., 1982-87, asst. v.p. law, communications and pub. affairs, 1987—; mem. ins. adv. com. Inst. Civil Justice RAND Corp., Santa Monica, Calif., 1984—. Chmn. Dutchess County Exec.'s Task Force Emergency Housing, Poughkeepsie, 1980; pres., bd. dirs. Family Counseling Services, Poughkeepsie, 1969-73; bd. dirs. United Way of Dutchess County, Poughkeepsie, 1976-80, N.Y. State United Way, Albany, 1978-80. Mem. Issues Mgmt. Assn. Episcopalian. Club: Vassar (Hartford) (scholarship treas. 1985-87). Office: Aetna Life & Casualty 151 Farmington Ave Hartford CT 06107

PENDELL, SUE DAVIS, speech communication educator; b. Baton Rouge, Dec. 16, 1946; d. Frank B. and Elizabeth (Young) Davis. BS, Fla. State U., 1966; MA, Auburn U., 1970; PhD, U. Utah, 1976. Instr. speech U. Wis., La Crosse, 1971-73; asst. prof. speech communication, dir. speech extension U. Mo., Columbia, 1976-79; asst. then assoc. prof. speech communication Colo. State U., Ft. Collins, 1979—; faculty rep. Colo. Bd. Agr., 1988-90. Author: (with others) Speech Coursebook, 1986; contbr. articles to profl. jours. Cons. Ft. Collins Area United Way, 1986-88, bd. dirs., 1988—. Mem. Environ. Design Rsch. Assn., Internat. Communication Assn., Speech Communication Assn., Western States Communication Assn., Phi Kappa Phi. Office: Colo State U Dept Speech Communication 302 WH Fort Collins CO 80523

PENDLETON, ANDREA KAILO, editor; b. N.Y.C., Sept. 2, 1948; d. Norman Nathan and Marilyn Ruth (Waldman) Kailo; m. Alan Pendleton, Nov. 24, 1989. BA, Douglass Coll., 1970. Adminstrv. asst. to senate pres. Ill. State Senate, Chgo., 1970, U. Saskatchewan, Saskatoon, 1970-73; rsch. asst., editor Sci. Council Can., Ottawa, Ont., 1974-76; sr. editor Systems Cons., Inc., Washington, 1976-78; editor, dir. pub. affairs Nat. Conf. State Legislatures, Washington, 1978-83; dir. communications Nat. Council for Urban Eco. Devel., 1983-87; mng. editor Optical Soc. Am., Washington, 1987-89, editor, 1990—. Author: (with others) Implications of the Changing Age Structure of the Canadian Population, 1976; contbd. articles to profl. jours. Pres. Arena Stage Angels, Washington, 1982-84. Mem. Women in Communications, Inc. (pres. D.C. chpt. 1988-89). Democrat. Jewish. Home: 5111 Williamsburg Blvd N Arlington VA 22207 Office: Optical Soc Am 2010 Massachusetts Ave NW Washington DC 20036

PENDLETON, CAROLYN M., banker; b. Park City, Utah, May 17, 1941; d. Charles Henry and Sarah Madge (Petersen) John; children—Rick L. Dowden, Randy S. Dowden. Student U. So. Calif., UCLA, El Camino Coll. With Crocker Bank, Los Angeles, 1966-72, br. mgr., 1972-75, ops. officer, 1975-79, asst. v.p., account officer, 1979-81; asst. v.p. product devel. First Interstate Bank, Los Angeles, 1981-83; sr. v.p., mgr. comml. banking services Calif. Fed. Bank, Los Angeles, 1983—; banking advisor So. Calif. Regional Occupational Ctr., Torrance, Calif., 1973-81; instr. Jr. Achievement, Los Angeles, 1981-83; bd. govs. AIB, Los Angeles, 1971-75. Recipient Leadership award, YWCA, 1980. Mem. Nat. Assn. Female Execs, Nat. Assn. Bank Women, Big Sisters of Los Angeles. Republican. Mem. LDS Ch. Club: Los Angeles Athletic. Avocation: running. Office: Calif Fed Bank 5680 Wilshire Blvd Pla E Los Angeles CA 90036

PENDLETON, GAIL RUTH, newspaper editor, writer; b. Franklin, N.J., May 8, 1937; d. Waldo A. and Ruby (Bonnett) Rousset; m. John E. Tyler, Mar. 10, 1956 (div. 1978); children: Gwenneth, Victoria, Christine; m. Jeffrey P. Pendleton, Oct. 1, 1978. BA, Montclair (N.J.) State Coll., 1959; M in Div., Princeton (N.J.) Theol. Sem., 1973. Ordained minister Presbyn. Ch., 1974. Tchr. Epiphany Day Sch., Kaimuki, Oahu, Hawaii, 1956-58; editor Women's Sect. Daily Record, Morristown, N.J., 1959-62, reporter, 1963-65; tchr. Hardystown Twp. Sch., Franklin, 1968-69; asst. pastor First Presbyn. Ch., Sparta, N.J., 1973-74; reporter N.J. Herald, Newton, 1976-78, editor lifestyle sect., 1978—. Recipient Ruth Cheney Streeter award Planned Parenthood N.W. N.J., 1985. Mem. N.J. Press Assn. (family sect. layout award 1985, 87, 88, 89, 2nd feature columns award 1986), Zonta. Office: NJ Herald 2 Spring St Newton NJ 07860

PENDLETON, MARY CATHERINE, foreign service officer; b. Louisville, Ky., June 15, 1940; d. Joseph S. and Katherine R. (Toebbe) P. BA, Spalding Coll., 1962; MA, Ind. U., 1969. Cert. secondary tchr., Ky. Tchr. Presentation Acad., Louisville, 1962-66; vol. Peace Corps, Tunis, Tunisia, 1966-68; employment counselor Ky. Dept. for Human Resources, Louisville, 1969-75; gen. svcs. Am. Embassy, Khartoum, Sudan, 1975-77; counsular officer Am. Embassy, Manila, Philippines, 1978-79; adminstrv. officer Am. Embassy, Bangui, Cen. African Republic, 1979-82, Lusaka, Zambia, 1982-84; post mgmt. officer Dept. of State Bur. European and Can. Affairs, Washington, 1984-87; adminstrv. counselor Am. Embassy, Bucharest, Romania, 1987-89; with tng. dept. Indsl. Coll. of Armed Forces Nat. Def. U., Washington, 1989-90; dir. adminstrv. tng. div. Fgn. Svc. Inst., Arlingtonn, Va., 1990—. Bd. dirs. Am. Sch. of Bucharest, 1987-89. Named to Honorable Order of Ky. Cols., 1988. Mem. Women's Action Orgn. Democrat. Roman Catholic. Office: Dept State Washington DC 20520-5110 also: Fgn Svc Inst 1400 Key Blvd Arlington VA 22209

PENDLETON, THELMA BROWN, physical therapist, health service administrator; b. Rome, Ga., Jan. 30, 1911; d. John O. and Alma (Ingram) Brown; diploma Provident Hosp. Sch. Nursing, 1931; cert. Loyola U., 1942, Northwestern U., 1946; m. George W. Pendleton, Mar. 2, 1946; 1 son, George William. Pediatric nurse Rosenwald Found., Chgo., 1931-32; staff nurse Vis. Nurse Assn., Chgo., 1932-45; chief phys. therapy Provident Hosp., Chgo., 1946-55; phys. therapy cons. Parents Assn., Inc., Chgo., 1956-60; cons. United Cerebral Palsy of Greater Chgo.'s Pipers Portal Schs., 1961-63, dir., 1963-64; dir. phys. therapy svcs. LaRabida Children's Hosp. and Rsch. Ctr., Chgo., 1964-75; mem. nat. com. Joint Orthopedic Nursing Adv. Svcs., 1947-55; clin. supr., instr. programs in phys. therapy Northwestern U. Med. Sch., Chgo., 1947-55, 64-75; cons. United Cerebral Palsy, 1970-75; lectr. Japanese svc. com. on Cerebral Palsy, 1970; mem. Ill. Phys. Therapy Exam. Com., 1952-62. Recipient cert. of commendation CSC Cook County (Ill.), 1961, Citation of Merit, Wands Cerebral Palsy Unit, 1961. Mem. Am., Ill. phys. therapy assns., Provident Hosp. Nurses Alumni Assn. Democrat. Clubs: Tu-Fours Bolivia. Author: Low Budget Gourmet, 1977; (booklet) Patient Positioning, 1981; contbr. articles on phys. therapy and nursing to profl. jours.; contbr. to Am. Poetry Anthology (Golden Poet award for My Friend of Long Ago). Address: 2631 S Indiana Ave Chicago IL 60616

PENKA, ELOISE MARIE, physical therapist; b. Scott City, Kans., Oct. 18, 1960; d. Victor Eugene and Eleanor Lucy (Birzer) P. AA, Dodge City (Kans.) Coll., 1980; student, Ft. Hays State U., 1980-82; BS in Phys. Therapy magna cum laude, Wichita State U., 1984. Registered phys. therapist, Kans., Nebr., Colo., S.D., N.D., Minn., Iowa, Mo., Wyo., Okla., Mich. Agr. technician Penka Bros. Farms, Healy, Kans., 1974-84; phys. therapy technician St. Anthony Hosp., Hays, Kans., 1981-82, Agy. for Home Health Care, Wichita, Kans., 1983-84; staff phys. therapist Humana Hosp., Dodge City, Kans., 1984-87; field mgr. Nat. Therapeutic Assocs., Omaha, 1987—; pvt. contractor Mobile Agy. for SW Health, Garden City, Kans., 1984-87. Scholar Wichita State U., 1983-84. Mem. Am. Phys. Therapy Assn., Phi Kappa Phi. Democrat. Roman Catholic. Home: Rte 1 Box 33 Healy KS 67850 Office: Nat Therapeutic Assocs 11623 Arbor St Omaha NE 68144

PENN, LYNN SHARON, chemistry researcher; b. Iowa City, June 18, 1943; d. Robert Joseph and Dorothy Evelyn (Etsinger) Johnson; m. Arthur Leon Penn, June 24, 1968; 1 child, Ethan. AB, U. Pa., 1966; MA, Bryn Mawr Coll., 1970, PhD, 1974. Chemist Lawrence Livermore Nat. Lab., Livermore, Calif., 1974-78; sr. scientist Textile Rsch. Inst., Princeton, N.J., 1978-80, Ciba-Geigy Corp., Ardsley, N.Y., 1980-83; prin. scientist Midwest Rsch. Inst., Kansas City, Mo., 1983-86; rsch. prof. Polytechnic U., Bklyn., 1987—. Contbr. articles to profl. jours. Recipient rsch. funding, NSF, Washington, 1989-91. Mem. Am. Soc. Testing Materials, Soc. Adv. Materials and Process Engring., Fiber Soc., Adhesion Soc. (sec. 1982-90), Kappa Kappa Gamma. Jewish. Home: 31 Division Ave South Nyack NY 10960

PENN, PATRICIA A., human resource specialist; b. St. Louis; d. William H. Penn and Cansadie Brown. BA, Cen. Meth. Coll., Fayette, Mo., 1973; cert. in English, U. Mo., St. Louis, 1974; postgrad., So. Ill. U., Edwardsville. Cert. English and speech, theatre, communications tchr., Mo. Tchr. secondary sch. Ritenour Consolidated Sch. Dist., Overland, Mo., 1973-80; sr. human resource devel. rep. McDonnell Douglas Corp., St. Louis, 1980-85, mgmt. devel. rep., 1985—; presenter workshop and seminars on communication skills tng. and stress mgmt.; guest speaker in field; mem. Meth. study tour Mozambique, 1990. Winner United Meth. Women Essay contest. Mem. ASTD, Bd. Global Ministries (chair United Meth. ch. Mo. East Conf.), Cotillion de Leon, Inc. (chmn. pub. rels., Disting. Woman award 1984), Women in Leadership, Coro Found., Women in Networking, Cen. Meth. Coll. Alumni Assn. (bd. dirs. 1987—, chairperson ch. rels. conf. St. Louis chpt. 1988-89), Alpha Kappa Alpha. Methodist. Office: McDonnell Douglas Corp PO Box 516 Saint Louis MO 63166

PENN, PATRICIA W., educator; b. Richmond, Va., Aug. 4, 1953; d. Hugh G. and Peggy W. (Dymacek) Whitley; m. Robert Alan Penn, Aug. 16, 1975; children: Ginny, Lindsay. BS in English Edn., David Lipscomb U., Nashville, 1975; MEd in Reading, Va. Commonwealth U., Richmond, 1978. Cert. English edn. tchr. grades 5-12, reading specialist K-Adult, Kans., Va. Instr. lang. arts Hanover County Pub. Schs., Ashland, Va., 1975-80; reading specialist, spl. needs coord. Sherman Mid. Sch., Hutchinson, Kans., 1980—, Liberty Mid. Sch., Hutchinson. Named Davis Found. Educator of Yr. Mem. Internat. Reading Assn., Arkansas Valley Reading Assn., Kans. Reading Assn., Kans. Assn. Middle Level Edn., Phi Kappa Phi, Phi Delta Kappa. Mem. Ch. of Christ. Home: 2507 E 26th Ave Hutchinson KS 67502 Office: Liberty Mid Sch 200 W 14th Hutchinson KS 67501

PENNEY, ALEXANDRA, writer, editor-in-chief; m. Norman F. Stevens Jr.; 1 child. Grad., Smith Coll. Editor health and beauty Glamour mag.; editor at large Bantam Doubleday; editor-in-chief Self mag., 1989—. Author: How to Make Love to a Man, 1981, Great Sex, 1985, How to Keep Your Man Monogamous, 1989; contbr. articles to N.Y. Times Mag., Vogue, others. Office: Self Magazine Conde Nast Publs Inc 350 Madison Ave New York NY 10017*

PENNEY, NANCY SANFORD, educator; b. East Liverpool, Ohio, July 7, 1934; d. Ralph Lewis and Ruth Allis (Peterson) Sanford; m. David Paul Penney, June 2, 1956; children: D. Jeffrey, Lauri Penney Salverda. AB, Eastern Nazarene Coll., Wollaston Park, Mass., 1956; MA, U. Rochester, 1976; Cert. in Advanced Study in Adminstrn., SUNY, 1988. Rsch. tech. Boston U., 1956-58, United Fruit Co., Norwood, Mass., 1958-61; tchr. Monroe County Bd. Coop. Edn. Svcs., Fairport, N.Y., 1968-82, instrn. specialist, 1982—. Mem. Internat. Reading Assn., Nat. Council Tchrs. English, Assn. suprs. and Curriculum Devel., Delta Kappa Gamma. Office: Monroe County Bd Coop Ednl Svcs #41 O'Connor Rd Fairport NY 14450

PENNEY, SHERRY HOOD, university chancellor, educator; b. Marlette, Mich., Sept. 4, 1937; d. Terrance and B. Jean (Stoutenburg) Hood; m. Carl Murray Penney, July 8, 1961 (div. 1978); children: Michael Murray, Jeffrey Hood; m. James Duane Livingston, Mar. 30, 1985. BA, Albion Coll., 1959, LLD (hon.), 1989; MA, U. Mich., 1961; PhD, SUNY, Albany, 1972. Vis. asst. prof. Union Coll., Schenectady, N.Y., 1972-73; assoc. higher edn. N.Y. State Edn. Dept., Albany, 1973-76; assoc. provost Yale U., New Haven, Conn., 1976-82; vice chancellor acad. programs, policy and planning SUNY System, Albany, 1982-88; acting pres. SUNY, Plattsburgh, 1986-87; chancellor U. Mass., Boston, 1988—; chmn. bd. dirs. Nat. Higher Edn. Mgmt. Systems, Boulder, Colo., 1985-87; mem. commn. on higher edn. New Eng. Assn. Schs. and Colls., Boston, 1979-82, Middle States Assn. Schs. and Colls., Phila., 1986-88; mem. commn. on women Am. Coun. Edn., Washington, 1979-81, commn. on govt. rels., 1990—; bd. dirs. Boston Edison Co. Author: Patrician in Politics, 1974; editor: Women in Management in Higher Education, 1975; cons. editor Change mag. and Jour. Higher Edn. Mgmt.; contbr. articles to profl. jours. Mem. Partnership (Boston schs.), 1988—; trustee Berkeley Div. Sch., Yale U., 1978-82, John F. Kennedy Libr. Found.; bd. dirs. Albany Symphony Orch., 1982-88, U. Mass. Found., Amherst, 1988—, Mcpl. Rsch. Bur., Boston, 1990—; corp. mem. United Way, 1990—. Recipient Disting. Alumna award Albion Coll., 1978. Mem. Am. Assn. Higher Edn., Orgn. Am. Historians, Internat. Assn. U. Pres., Assn. Urban Univs. (nominating com.), Greater Boston C. of C. (bd. dirs.), Yale Club (N.Y.C.). Unitarian. Office: U Mass Harbor Campus Office of Chancellor Boston MA 02125-3393

PENNICK, LORAINE ANNE, accountant; b. New Haven, Mar. 18, 1954; d. Rocco W. Sr. and Mary C. (Cassella) Gargano; m. Edward David Pennick, July 12, 1980; children: Victoria Lee, Veronica Lynn. BS summa cum laude, U. New Haven, 1976; AS, So. Conn. State U., 1974; MBA, U. New Haven, 1987; C.P.A., Conn. Lic. real estate broker, Conn. Property mgr. Crestwood Mgmt., West Haven, Conn., 1973-78; sr. tax acct. Deloitte Haskins & Sells, New Haven, 1978-84; tax planning So. New Eng. Telephone Co., New Haven, 1984; tax mgr. LIGHTNET, New Haven, 1984-86; mgr. of acctg. and taxation SNET Systems, Inc., New Haven, 1986-88, dir. fin., 1989—; instr. Becker C.P.A. rev. course, Fairfield, Conn., 1982-86. Treas., RESPOND, New Haven, 1982-85; commr. West Haven Fair Rent Commn., 1982-84. Mem. Conn. Soc. C.P.A.s, Am. Inst. C.P.A.s, Conn. Estate and Tax Planning Council, Greater New Haven Jaycees (controler 1983-84, treas. 1985-86). Roman Catholic. Home: 430 Barton Dr Orange CT 06477 Office: SNET Systems Inc 367 Orange St New Haven CT 06511

PENNINGER, FRIEDA ELAINE, English educator; b. Marion, N.C., Apr. 11, 1927; d. Fred Hoyle and Lena Frances (Young) P. AB, U. N.C., Greensboro, 1948; MA, Duke U., 1950, PhD, 1961. Copywriter Sta. WSJS, Winston-Salem, N.C., 1948-49; asst. prof. English Flora Macdonald Coll., Red Springs, N.C., 1950-51; tchr. English Barnwell, S.C., 1951-52, Brunswick, Ga., 1952-53; instr. English U. Tenn., Knoxville, 1953-56; instr., asst. prof. Woman's Coll., U. N.C., Greensboro, 1956-58, 60-63; asst. prof., assoc. prof. U. Richmond (Va.), 1963-71; chair., dept. English Westhampton Coll., Richmond, 1971-78; prof. English U. Richmond, 1971—, Bostwick prof. English, 1987—. Author: William Caxton, 1979; compiler, editor: English Drama to 1660, 1976; editor: Festschrift for Prof. Marguerite Roberts, 1976. Fellow Southeastern Inst. of Mediaeval and Renaissance Studies, 1965, 67, 69. Mem. AAUP, New Chaucer Soc., Mediaeval Acad. Am., Southatlantic MLA. Democrat. Presbyterian. Home: 4312 Kensington Ave Richmond VA 23221 Office: U Richmond Richmond VA 23173

PENNINGTON, BEVERLY MELCHER, Small business owner; b. Vermillion, SD, Feb. 8, 1931; d. Cecil Lloyd and Phyllis Cecelia (Walz) M.; m. Glen D., Sept. 1, 1965 (dec. Aug. 1986); 1 child, Terri Lynn. BS, U. S.D., Vermillion, 1952. Enrolled agt. cert. IRS. Sec. budget dept. Bur. of Indian Affairs, Aberdeen, S.D., 1952-53, pvt. sec., 1953-54; pvt. sec. U.S. P.H.S. Indian Health, Aberdeen, 1954-55; adminstr. asst. U.S. Pub. Health Svc., Anchorage, 1955-58, U.S. Pub. Health, Dental Pub. Health, Washington, 1958-61, Dental Pub. Health, Wash., 1958-61; grant adminstr. Dental Pub. Health, 1961-65; co-owner Penn Mel Marina, Platte, S.D, 1965-74; co-owner Pennington Tax Service, Platte, 1974-86, owner, 1986—. Author Contr. Article to Profl. Jours. 1966-68. Mem. Platte's Women's Club, sec., 1965-68, pres., 1968-70, 89-90; mem. Libr. Bd., sec. 1982-85. Fellow: Am. Soc. Tax Profls.; mem. NAFE, Platte Comml. Club (v.p. 1989, pres. 1990-), U.S. C. of C. Wash., Dakota Cen. Com. Republican. Presbyterian. Office: Pennington Tax Svc 420 Main Platte SD 57369

PENNINGTON, JEANNE ROSE, broadcasting executive; b. Menominee, Mich., May 1, 1955; d. Elmer Burl and Doris Mary (De Keuster) P. BA in Communications cum laude, St. Norbert Coll., DePere, Wis., 1977. Comml. copywriter Sta. WFRV-TV, Green Bay, Wis., 1977-79; advt. dir. James H. White Realty, Green Bay, 1979-80; comml. copywriter Sta. WLUK-TV, Green Bay, 1980-85, promotion writer, producer, 1985-89; promotion dir. Sta. WNEP-TV, Scranton, Pa., 1989—. Big sister Big Bros./Big Sisters, Green Bay, 1978-86, pub. rels. chmn., 1978-86; vol., telethon producer Muscular Dystrophy Assn., Green Bay, 1987-89; sponsor refugee families, Green Bay, 1986-89; pub. rels chmn. Vol. Ctr., Green Bay, 1987-89; bd. dirs. Family Svcs., Scranton, 1990—, Vol. Action Ctr., 1990—, Interfaith Friends, 1990—; tutor Scranton Coun. on Literacy, 1990—. Recipient Addy award for advt. excellence, 1989, 88, 87, 84, 77, Newspaper award Gallery of Homes, 1979. Mem. NAFE, Broadcast Promotion Mktg. Execs. Roman Catholic. Home: Timber Falls Rt 6 Apt P-3 Blakely PA 18447 Office: Sta WNEP-TV 16 Montage Mountain Rd Moosic PA 18507

PENNY, JOSEPHINE B., retired banker; b. N.Y.C., July 7, 1925; d. Charles and Delia (Fahey) Booy; student Columbia U., Am. Inst. Banking; grad. Sch. Bank Adminstrn. U. Wis., 1975; m. John T. Penny, July 15, 1950 (div.); children—John T., Charleen Penny DeMauro, Patricia Penny Paras. With Prentice-Hall, N.Y.C., 1942-43; with Trade Bank & Trust Co., 1943-52, 61-70; with Nat. Westminster Bank U.S.A., 1970-85, v.p., dep. auditor, 1978-85. Mem. Bank Adminstrn. Inst. (chpt. dir. 1983-85), Inst. Internal Auditing, Nat. Assn. Bank Women (chpt. chmn. 1980-81). Home: 221A Manchester Ln Jamesburg NJ 08831

PENROSE, CYNTHIA C., health plan administrator, consultant; b. Manila, Philippines, Nov. 24, 1939; came to U.S., 1940; d. Douglas Lee Lipscomb Cordiner and Jane (Sturgeon) Edises; m. Douglas Francis Penrose, July 11, 1959 (div. 1981); children—Vicki Lynn, Lee Douglas; m. Alan Harrison Magazine, Aug. 30, 1984. B.A., U. Calif.-Berkeley, 1963; M.B.A., U. Santa Clara, 1977. Cert. social services. Vice pres and dir. employment Resource Ctr. for Women, Palo Alto, Calif., 1973-78; bus. planner Raychem Corp., Menlo Park, Calif., 1979; adminstrv. mgr. Electric Power Research Inst., Palo Alto, 1979-83; dir. ops. Utility Data Inst., Washington, 1984-85; dir. ops. Randmark, Inc., 1986-87; coordinator mkt. devel. for Mid-Atlantic States Kaiser Foundation Health Plan, Washington, 1987-88, asst. to assoc. regional mgr., 1988—; sr. ptnr. MB Assocs., Washington, 1983-88; bd. dirs. and treas. Unique Enterprises, Washington, 1985-87; sec. Wesley Property Mgmt. Co., 1987-89; bd. dirs. Wesley Housing Devel. Corp., 1988-89. Bd. dirs., v.p. LWV, Berkeley and Palo Alto, 1966-73; chmn. program adv. council Resource Ctr. for Women, Palo Alto, 1980-83; mem. Affirmative Action Adv. Com. Palo Alto, 1975-76. Mem. Exec. Women's Roundtable (Washington, founder), Peninsula Profl. Women's Network (v.p. 1981-82), U. Calif. Alumni Assn., AAUW (Bicentennial br. sec. 1986-88), Am. Soc. on Aging, Med. Group Mgmt. Assn., United Srs. Health Coop., LWV. Democrat. Episcopalian. Avocations: swimming; nutrition and health; reading. Home: 1302 Chancel Pl Alexandria VA 22314 Office: Kaiser-Permanente 4200 Wisconsin Ave Washington DC 20016

PENRY, NANCY SANDBERG, communications executive; b. Austin, Oct. 12, 1955; d. William David and Maxine (Wall) Alman; m. Harry Alan Sandberg, Dec. 27, 1974 (div. 1988); children: Christa Leigh, Clinton Alan; m. David Wayne Penry, Aug. 12, 1989. BS, U. Tex., 1976, MA, 1978, PhD, 1990. Med. sec. J.D. Cochrum, M.D., Austin, Tex., 1972-74; legal sec. Plaza 500 Inc., Austin, Tex., 1975-76; tchr. Stroman High Sch., Victoria, Tex., 1977-79; from cons., trainer to pres. Learning Cons. Inc., Victoria; tng. and devel. coord. ALCOA, Point Comfort, Tex., 1989—; lectr. U. Houston, Victoria, Tex., 1983-87; cons. E.I. DuPont, 1977—, U. Houston, 1979—, Union Carbide Corp., Seadrift, Tex., 1987—, Exxon Chem. U.S.A., 1988—. Sunday sch. tchr. Northside Baptist, Victoria, Tex., 1977-80. Mem. American Bus. Assn., Tex. State Tchrs. Assn., Tex. Classroom Tchrs. Assn., Speech Communication Assn., Alpha Lamba Delta, Pi Lambda Theta, Kappa Delta Pi. Office: ALCOA State Hwy 35 Point Comfort TX 77978

PENTA, LILY KIM, salon owner; b. Boston, Nov. 8, 1960; d. Chang C. and Ann Marie (Hayes) Kim; m. John Anthony Penta, Feb. 14, 1986; children: Cory, Colin. Grad. high sch., Boston. Buyer, salesperson Flair, Inc., Boston, 1979-80; salesperson Tannery Shoes, Boston, 1980-82, Brass Boot, Inc., Las Vegas, Nev., 1982; buyer, salesperson Rabbit's Foot, Inc., Newton, Mass., 1982-83; salesperson Jordan Marsh Co., Boston, 1983-85; mgr. Talal Shores, Inc., Boston, 1984-85; asst. mgr. Sola Shoes, Inc., Cambridge, Mass., 1986-87; mgr. J.P.'s Hair & Sun, Inc., Billerica, Mass., 1986—; instr. Tynan Sch. Gymnastics, S. Boston, 1979, Youth Enrichment Svcs., Boston, 1975-79. Democrat. Episcopalian.

PENTEK, MARION STANTON, educator; b. Earlville, N.Y., Apr. 16, 1931; d. Walter Lynn and Muriel Frances (Jelliff) Stanton; married June 6, 1953 (div. July 1973); children: Jeffrey Francis, Gregory John, Catherine Anne. BS, Wells Coll., 1952; MEd, SUNY, Geneseo, 1966; postgrad., U. S.C., 1978, NYU, Eng., Denmark, 1979. Various teaching positions, 1962-75; elem. tchr. St. Croix (U.S. V.I.) Country Day Sch., 1974-75, North Vista Sch., Florence S.C., 1975-76; instr. adults Darlington (S.C.) Career Ctr., 1977-80; admissions, tchr. Out-of-Door Acad., Sarasota, Fla., 1980-82; elem. tchr. Myrtle Beach (S.C.) Elem. Sch., 1982-83; dir. lower sch., elem. tchr. Coastal Acad., Myrtle Beach, 1984; instr. Job Tng. Partnerships Act Florence Darlington Tech. Coll., Florence, 1984-85; instr. learning disabilities Brunson Dargan Sch., Darlington, 1985-86; elem. tchr. Spring Elem. Sch., Darlington, 1986—; chairperson steering com. So. Assn. Schs. and Colls., Darlington, 1988-89; coord. Textbook Adoption Com., Darlington, 1989, Basic Skills Text Adminstrn., Darlington, 1986-89; co-instr. Grad.: Basic Skills Teaching Adults, Darlington, 1978-79; asst. tchr. St. Croix Country Day Sch., Christiansted, 1974-75, Planned Resource Ctr., Christiansted, St. Croix, 1974-75; tchr., asst. Penn Yan (N.Y.) Elem. Sch., 1962-65; tchr., LD East Aurora (N.Y.) Sch., 1967-73. Editor, compiler: (poetry anthology) Spring Breezes, 1989. Mem. Assn. Supervision and Curriculum Devel., NEA. Home: 2222 B Woodridge Ln Florence SC 29501

PENTLIN, SUSAN LEE, educator; b. Warrensburg, Mo., Feb. 9, 1947; d. James Arnold and Jean Marie (Flanery) Riddle; m. Floyd Clark Pentlin, June 12, 1971. BA, Cen. Mo. State, 1968; MA, U. Mo., 1970; PhD, U. Kans., 1977. Teaching asst. U. Mo., Columbia, 1969-70; assoc. prof. Cen. Mo. State U., Warrensburg, 1970—, acting dir. honors program, 1987-89; exchange tchr. Dom Gymnasium, Freising, Federal Republic of Germany, 1973-74; asst. instr. U. Kans., Lawrence, 1974; research assoc. Max Kade German-Am. Document Ctr., Lawrence, 1975; project advisor U. Honors Program Cen. Mo. State U., Warrensburg, 1986—. Author: (edited collection) The Teaching of German in America, 1988, numerous book revs.; editorial bd. Missouri Folklore Soc. Jour. Bd. dirs. Mo. Folklore Soc., 1980—, pres., 1982; Steering Com., Women's Equity Action League, Mo., 1984—; active Simon Wiesenthal Ctr., Los Angeles, 1981—, Johnson County Dem. Com., People for the Am. Way. Fulbright scholar U.S. Office Edn., 1973, 77; rsch. grantee Am. Coun. Learned Soc., 1979, Nat. Endowment Humanities, 1978. Mem. Am. Assn. Tchrs. of German, German Studies Assn., History of Edn. Soc., Nat. Assn. Holocaust Educators, Fulbright Alumni Assn., Anne Frank Inst. Office: Cen Mo State U 236J Martin Bldg Warrensburg MO 64093

PENTON, LILYMAE JOANNE, real estate developer; b. Forestburg, Tex., Jan. 9, 1933; d. Nicholas Leathers and Jessie Pauline (McGee) P. Grad. high sch., Phoenix, 1950. Sec. Valley Nat. Bank, Phoenix, 1950-54; asst. v.p. A.B. Robbs Trust Co., Continental Bank, Phoenix, 1954-68; sr. v.p. Murdock Devel., Phoenix, L.A., 1968—. Mem. Calif. Yacht Club. Republican. Home: 516 San Vicente #105 Santa Monica CA 90402 Office: Murdock Devel Co 10900 Wilshire #1600 Los Angeles CA 90024

PENZA, PATRICIA GERMAN, language educator; b. Oceanside, N.Y., Mar. 20, 1957; d. Joseph Edward German and Ann Theresa Larkin; m. Philip Anthony Penza, Aug. 14, 1982; children: Julienne Nicole, Michael Philip. AB, Coll. Holy Cross, Worcester, Mass., 1979; MA, Rhode Island Coll., Providence, 1986. Cert. language educator. Chair lang. dept. Xaverian Bros. High Sch., Westwood, Mass., 1979—. Participant Am. Host Found.; troop leader Girl Scouts. Mem. French Library of Boston, Holy Cross Club, Phi Sigma Iota. Democrat. Home: 2 Fieldstone Rd Foxborough MA 02035 Office: Xaverian Bros High Sch 800 Clapboardtree St Westwood MA 02090

PEPIN, CAROLAN, public relations executive. Bachelor's in Journalism, Marquette U. Pub. rels. specialist Quasar Electronics; pub. rels. mgr. William Hart Adler, Inc., Advt.; account exec. Daniel J. Edelmanm Inc., Chgo., 1980-85, v.p., from 1985, now sr. v.p. Office: Edelman Pub Rels 211 E Ontario Chicago IL 60611*

PEPIN, DEBBIE NEUHAUSER, superintendent of schools; b. Hartford, Conn., June 22, 1953; d. Albert Neuhauser and Nancy (Cawte) Beaverstock. BS, Keene (N.H.) State Coll., 1974; MEd, Am. Internat. Coll., Springfield, Mass., 1978; CAGS, U. Conn., Storrs, 1980; postgrad., SUNY, Albany and Buffalo, 1981-89. Cert. sch. dist. adminstr., sch. dist. adminstrn. elem. tchr., spl. edn. tchr. Spl. edn. tchr. Windsor (Conn.) High Sch., Windsor Sch. Dist., 1974-79; asst. prin. Kenmore East Sr. High Sch., Kenmore-Tonawanda (N.Y.) Schs., 1979-83; prin. Guilderland (N.Y.) High Sch., Gilberland Cen. Sch. Dist., 1983-89; supt. Greenville (N.Y.) Cen. Sch. Dist., 1989—; ednl. cons. Harvest Ednl. Labs., Newport, R.I., 1977—. Mem. Commrs. Adv. Coun. on Woman's Equity, N.Y. State Edn. Dept., 1988—. N.Y. State Edn. Dept.-Germany scholar, 1988. Mem. Assns. Supervision and Curriculum Devel., Am. Assn. Sch. Adminstrs., N.Y. Coun. Sch. Supts. Office: Greenville Cen Sch Dist Rt 81 Greenville NY 12083

PEPIN, YVONNE MARY, artist, writer; b. San Francisco, May 28, 1956; d. Arthur Henry and Mary Alice (Ratté) P. BA, Antioch U., 1982; postgrad., Fielding Inst., 1989—. Arts adminstr. Mendocino (Calif.) Art Ctr., 1978-85; founder, dir. Port Townsend (Wash.) Art Edn. Ctr., 1986—; dir. Blue Heron Gallery, Port Hadlock, Wash., 1989—. Author: Cabin Journal, 1984, Three Summers, 1986. Mem. AAUW.

PEPINSKY, PAULINE NICHOLS, psychologist, researcher; b. Baton Rouge, June 27, 1919; d. Irby Coghill and Pauline (Wright) Nichols; m. Harold Brenner Pepinsky, Aug. 27, 1943; 1 child, Harold Eugene. BA, La. State U., Baton Rouge, 1939, MA, 1941; PhD, U. Minn., 1949. Lic. psychologist, Ohio. Acting asst. prof. Mich. State U., East Lansing, 1946-48; from acting to asst. prof. Wash. State U., Pullman, 1948-51; rsch. assoc. Ohio State U. Rsch. Found., Columbus, 1952-61; sr. rsch. assoc. in social sci. Mershon Ctr. Ohio State U., Columbus, 1969—. Author: (with H.B. Pepinsky) Counseling: Theory and Practice, 1954; author chpts. in books; contbr. articles to profl. jours. Rosenwald Fund fellow, 1945-46; Fulbright scholar to Norway, 1961-62. Mem. Am. Psychol. Assn., Ohio Psychol. Assn., Cen. Ohio Psychol. Assn., Phi Kappa Phi, Pi Lambda Theta, Sigma Xi, Mortar Bd. Office: 519A Evergreen Circle Worthington OH 43088-3667

PEPPER, ADELINE, small business owner, writer; b. Madison, Wis.; d. John William and Emmeline (Able) P.; BA, U. Wis. Med. writer AMA, ACS; asst. advt. mgr. Mead Johnson & Co., Evansville, Ind., publicity dir. Com. on Care of Children in Wartime, Evansville, 1945; radio advt. writer Knox Reeves, Inc., Mpls.; pub. relations Pa. R.R. Centennial, 1946; advt. writer L. W. Frohlich Agy., N.Y.; med. advt. writer and designer E. R. Squibb & Sons, Ciba Pharm.; owner Pep, Inc., advt. service, 1956—. Vice pres. council Union County Extension Service, Rutgers U., 1980-81. Mem. N.Y. Acad. Scis., Theta Sigma Phi, Phi Kappa Phi. Author: Tours of Historic New Jersey (N.J. Tercentenary medal 1964), 1965, rev. edit., 1973; N.J. vol. Fodor's Guide to the U.S.A., 1966; The Glass Gaffers of New Jersey (award N.J. Assn. Tchrs. English 1972, award of Merit Am. Assn. State and Local History 1972), 1971. Contbr. articles on travel, history, and decorative arts to mags. and major met. newspapers. Pioneer in field of tech. writing for ethical pharm. and health products, subjects include Serpasil, Ritilin, Cortisone, Pablum, etc.

PEPPER, DOROTHY MAE, nurse; b. Merill, Maine, Oct. 16, 1932; d. Walter Edwin and Alva Lois (Leavitt) Stanley; m. Thomas Edward Pepper, July 1, 1960; children: Walter Frank, James Thomas. RN, Maine Med. Ctr. Sch. Nursing, Portland, 1954. RN, Calif. Pvt. duty nurse Lafayette, Calif.; staff nurse Maine Med. Ctr., Portland, Oakland (Calif.) Vets. Hosp.; pvt. duty nurse, dir. RN's Alameda County, Oakland. Mem. ANA, Calif. Nurses Assn.

PEPPER, MARY JANICE, educational consultant; b. Pearsall, Tex., Oct. 1, 1942; d. Muriel Newton and Jane (Harbour) Moore; m. Clifton Gail Pepper, Feb. 19, 1961; children: John David, James Newton, Jeffery Michael. Student, U. Tex., 1960, 65, 76. Bus. mgr. Natalia (Tex.) Independent Sch. Dist., 1967-71; statistician Tex. Edn. Agy., Austin, 1971-72; mgr. bookkeeping div. Tex. Ednl. Cons. Svc. Inc., Austin, 1972-76, adminstrv. v.p., 1976-82, v.p., chief oper. officer, 1982—; team tchr. edn. program. U. Tex., Austin, 1985; lectr. Tex. Assn. Secondary Sch. Prins., Austin, 1988. Editor: Sch. Fin. Newsletter, Update for Sch. Adminstrs. Sec. Community Indsl. Found., Natalia, 1969-71, Medina County Water Control and Improvement, Natalia, 1970-71; mem. adv. com. Tex. Edn. Agy. Mem. Tex. Assn. Sch. Bus. Ofcls. (instr. 1987-88), Mended Hearts. Baptist. Home: 1311 Quail Park Dr Austin TX 78758 Office: Tex Ednl Consultative Svcs Inc 1005 E Saint Elmo Rd Austin TX 78745

PERCIVAL, EVELYN M., communications executive; b. Ridgeland, S.C., July 1, 1953; d. Stepherson and Nellie Mae (White) Mitchell; m. Alex J. Percival, Jan. 24, 1988; 1 child, Alex J. Jr. BS in Math., Knoxville (Tenn.) Coll., 1975. Trainee IBM, Oak Ridge, Tenn., 1973; adminstrv. asst. ARA Food Svc., Columbia, S.C., 1975-77; traffic design engr. switched svcs. design So. Bell Telephone Co., 1977-86; asst. staff mgr. pricing and econs. BellSouth Svcs., Atlanta, 1986—; advisor explorer post 500 So. Bell Telephone, 1984-86. Pres. Area Future Pioneers, 1984-86, State Future Pioneers, 1985-86, Musical Choir, 1984-85; active Young Women Aux.; treas., mem. exec. com. March of Dimes, 1984-86; tutor Carver Elem. Sch.; pres., advisor Mt. Ephraim Bapt. Ch., founded singles ministry, 1988—; vol. United Way Atlanta; bd. dirs. Am. Kidney Fund, 1988—. Named one of Outstanding Women Am., 1985; recipient Dist. Award of Merit Explorers. Mem. S.C. State Coll. Alumni Assn., Columbia S.C. Speakers Bur., Am. Bus. Womens Assn. (Woman of Yr.), Toastmasters (ednl. v.p. BellSouth chpt. 1988, pres. 1989). Democrat. Home: 309 Heathrow Dr Riverdale GA 30274 Office: BellSouth Svcs 675 W Peachtree St NE Atlanta GA 30375

PERDUE, MARY HENDERSON, columnist, author; b. Concord, Mass., Mar. 27, 1941; d. Ernest Flagg and Mary (Stephens) Henderson; m. Francisco Jose Ayala, May 27, 1968 (div. 1985); children: Francisco Jose, Carlos Alberto; m. Franklin P. Perdue, July 31, 1988. BA, Harvard U., 1963; MPA, George Washington U., 1965. Mgmt. intern U.S. Treasury Dept., Washington, 1963-65; editorial coord. internat. div. Ency. Brit., N.Y.C., 1965-67; mgr. Ceres Farms, Sacramento, 1975—; hostess, producer show Coast to Coast Radio Network, San Francisco, 1980-81; columnist Capitol News, Sacramento, 1980—; hostess, producer show Sta. KXTV, Sacramento, 1980-88. Author: The Farmers' Cookbook, 1981, Frank Perdue: 50 Years of Building..., 1989. Mem. Am. Agri-Women (pres. 1987-89), Nat. Fedn. Bus. and Profl. Women, Nat. Speaker's Assn. Republican. Methodist. Home: 1529 Woodland Rd Salisbury MD 21801

PERDUE, THEDA, history educator, author; b. McRae, Ga., Apr. 2, 1949; d. James Howard and Ouida (Davis) P. AB, Mercer U., 1972; MA, U. Ga., 1974, PhD, 1976. From asst. prof. to assoc. prof. history Western Carolina U., Cullowhee, N.C., 1975-83; prof. history Clemson (S.C.) U., 1983-88, U. Ky., Lexington, 1988—; editor Indians of S.E., U. Nebr. Press, Lincoln, 1985—; cons. Smithsonian Instn., Washington, 1989; Fulbright lectr., N.Z., 1988. Author: Slavery and the Evolution of Cherokee Society, 1979, Native Carolinians, 1985, The Cherokee, 1988; editor: Nations Remembered, 1980, Cherokee Editor, 1983; mem. editorial bd. Jour. Women's History, 1988—. Newberry Libr. fellow, 1978, Rockefeller Found. fellow, 1980-8l. Mem. Am. Hist. Assn., Orgn. Am. Historians, Am. Soc. for Ethnohistory, So. Hist. Assn., So. Assn. for Women Historians (pres. 1985-86). Democrat. Office: U Ky Dept History POT 1715 Lexington KY 40506-0027

PEREC, ANN MARIE, accountant; b. Bridgeport, Conn., May 9, 1964; d. Tadeusz and Mary (Sajgovic) P. BS, Fairfield (Conn.) U., 1986. Adminstrv. asst. Leask and Leask, PC, CPA's, Fairfield, Conn.; sr. fin. assoc. MBI, Inc., Norwalk, Conn.; EDP sr. staff auditor People's Bank, Bridgeport, Conn.; adminstrv. mgr., acct. MATRICES Cons., Inc., Norwalk.

PEREIRA, JORGINA ANTUNES, data processing executive; b. Rio De Janeiro, Brazil, Aug. 12, 1944; came to U.S., 1974; d. Rafael and Maria Dolores Antunes Pereira; BA, Social Service Sch. Rio De Janeiro, 1970; BGS with emphasis in Computer Sci., Roosevelt U., 1978, M.S. in Info. Systems, 1985; m. Mark Louis Branham, Dec. 31, 1980. Head social work programs Paroquia Santa Cruz De Copacabana, Rio De Janeiro, 1971-73; participant council of internat. program Jane Addams Grad. Sch. Social Work, U. Ill., Chgo., 1974-75; trainee No. Trust Bank, Chgo., 1977-78, programmer, 1978-79, sr. programmer, 1979-80, tech. analyst, 1980-82, systems analyst, 1982-84; sr. systems analyst Montgomery Ward, 1984-86, assoc. tech. specialist, 1986-89, project leader, tech. specialist, 1989—. Pres. Coun. of Internat. Program for Social Workers, Chgo., 1987-89. Mem. Data Processing Mgmt. Assn. (bd. dirs.), Franklin Honor Soc. Home: 665 W Roscoe Chicago IL 60657 Office: 1 Montgomery Ward Plaza Chicago IL 60671

PEREIRA, LINDA CHRISTINE, car dealership executive; b. Boston, Apr. 14, 1966; d. Viriato Mascarenhas and Nancy Christine (Senna) P. BS, Boston Coll., 1988. Ops. mgr. Rite-Way Automotive, Inc., Kingston, Mass., 1988—. Mem. Ideal Club. Office: Rite Way Automotive Inc 157 Summer St Kingston MA 02364

PEREIRA, PATRICIA SUE, small business owner; b. Bellefonte, Pa., Oct. 1, 1960; d. John Daniel and Barbara Lou (McCool) Miller; m. Fernando Jorge Pereira, Jan. 1, 1960; children: Nicholas F., Chelsea E. Assoc. in Bus., Cen. Pa. Bus. Sch., 1980. Mgr. sales Ramada Inn, Mystic, Conn., 1980-81; dir. sales Ramada Inn, Portsmouth, R.I., 1980-81; adminstrv. asst. Imperial Wlev, Ashaway, R.I., 1982-86; owner, mgr. Klutter Kloset Consignments, Westerly, R.I., 1986—. Solicitor United Way, Ashaway, 1983, 85; supporter Juvenile Diabetes, Harrisburg, Pa., 1980; mem. citizens adv. coun. on link between diet, nutrition and cancer Am. Inst. for Cancer Rsch., 1985. Republican. Baptist. Home: 50 Charles Ave Charlestown RI 02813 Office: Klutter Kloset Consignment Shop 49 Beach St Westerly RI 02891

PERETTI, ELSA, jewelry designer; b. Florence, Italy, May 1, 1940. Tchr. French and Italian pvt. schs.; mem. staff Dado Torrigiani (Architect), Milan, Italy; fashion model Spain, France, Gt. Britain, U.S.; jewelry designer Halston, Giorgio Sant'Angelo, from 1969; designer jewelry accessories, perfume creator Tiffany & Co., N.Y.C., 1974—. Recipient Coty award, 1971, President's Fellow award R.I. Sch. Design, 1981, Fashion Group Night of the Stars award, 1986. Address: care Tiffany & Co 727 Fifth Ave New York NY 10022*

PERETTI, MARILYN GAY, volunteer management professional; b. Indpls., July 30, 1935; d. Philip E. and Harriet E. (Meyer) Woerner; children: Thomas A., Christopher P. BS, Purdue U., 1957. Nursery sch. lab. asst. Mary Baldwin Coll., Staunton, Va., 1957-58; tchr. 1st grade, nursery sch. No. Ill. area schs., 1958-61; asst. tchr. of blind Glenbard E. High Sch., Lombard, Ill., 1978-80; adminstrv. asst. Elmhurst Coll., 1980-81; dir. vol. svcs. DuPage Convalescent Ctr., Wheaton, 1981—. Bd. dirs. Lombard YMCA, 1977-83, pres. 1980; vol. Chgo. Uptown Ministry, 1979; rep. Our Developing World, 1989—; participant fact finding trips El Salvador, 1988, Honduras, 1989, Nicarugua, 1989. Mem. AAUW, Coun. Dirs. Hosp. Vols. Met. Chgo., DuPage Assn. Vols. Adminstrn., Assn. Vol. Adminstrn. Office: DuPage Convalescent Ctr Wheaton IL 60187

PEREZ, ANA C., school system administrator; b. Douglas, Ariz., Nov. 15, 1954; d. Henry F. and Aurelia (Torres) P. BA in Edn., Ariz. State U., 1976, MA of Edn., 1980, cert. in adminstrv., 1984. Cert. elem. tchr. 1976, spl. edn. tchr., 1976, elem. prin., 1984, Ariz. Tchr. Mesa (Ariz.) Unified Sch. Dist. #4, 1976-80, program specialist, 1980-84, prin., 1984-89; asst. dir. Chicago Pine Edn. Dist., North Branch, Minn., 1989—; Cons. Mesa Unified Sch. Dist. #4, 1980, 85-86; rep. Assn. Severe Handicapped. Author numerous curriculum programs. Bd. dirs., sec. Ariz. State Spl. Olympics, Tempe, Ariz. Named Outstanding Educator League of United Latin Am. Citizens, 1985, Outstanding Elem. Sch. Prin. League of United Latin Am. Citizens, 1988. Mem. Council for Exceptional Children, Mesa Assn. Retarded Citizens (Educator of the Yr. award 1984), E. Valley Civitan, Phi Kappa Phi, Phi Delta Kappa. Office: Chicago Pine Edn Dist North Branch Middle Sch North Branch MN 55046

PEREZ, ANNA, press secretary; b. N.Y.C.; m. Ted Sims; children: Anthony, Candace; 1 stepchild, Niambi. Student, Hunter Coll. Flight attendant United Airlines; various mktg. and communications positions West Coast; legis. aide to Senator Slade Gorton; press sec. to Rep. John Miller; regional press sec. George Bush campaign Rep. Nat. Conv., 1988; now press sec. to Barbara Bush. Office: Office of First Lady 1600 Pennsylvania Ave NW Washington DC 20500*

PEREZ, CECILIA C.A., management analyst, auditor; b. Agana Heights, Guam, July 7, 1946; m. Robert H. Perez, Sept. 11, 1965; children: Paul, Robert, F. Canice, Celeste-Maria. BBA, U. Guam, Mangilao, 1975. Exec. distbr. Noevir Products, Agana Heights; child care ctr. dir. Dededo, Guam; ptnr. Balance 3, Agana, Guam; mgmt. analyst U.S. Naval Sta., Agana. Recipient numerous community svc. awards. Mem. Guam Econ. Devel. Authority (sec. bd. dirs.). Home: 187 Tutajan Dr Agana Heights GU 96910 Office: PO Box 2035 Agana GU 96910 Also: Mgmt Control & Review Office U S Naval Station Box 152 FPO San Francisco CA 96630

PEREZ, GINGER SPRINKLE, newspaper official; b. Lexington, N.C., Feb. 6, 1962; d. Gilmer Ray and Pearl (Owen) Sprinkle. Student, Salem Coll., 1980=82; BA, U.N.C., 1984. Reporter, copy editor Pacific Daily News, Agana, Guam, 1985-86; reporter Highlander Pub., City of Industry, Calif., 1986-87; mgn. editor Observer-News- Enterprise, Newton, N.C., 1987-88; news copy editor Pacific Daily News, Agana, 1988-89, copy desk chief, 1989—. Mem. Soc. of Profl. Journalists, NAFE. Republican. Baptist. Office: Pacific Daily News PO Box DN Agana GU 96910 :

PEREZ, JULIE ANNA, audio engineer; b. Miami, Fla., Sept. 2, 1961; d. Miguel Angel and Dorothy Elizabeth (Headford) P. MusB, U. Miami, 1984. Audio engr. Ron Miller Quartet, Miami, 1980-84, Orange Bowl Com., Miami, 1982-84, Off The Wall Sound Co., Miami and Ft. Lauderdale, Fla., 1982-83, NBC, Inc., N.Y.C., 1984—; asst. music mixer (TV shows) Saturday Night Live, 1987—, Late Night with David Letterman Seventh Anniversary Spl., 1989; music mixer Late Night with David Letterman, summer 1989. Editor: Music Engring. Tech. newsletter, 1983; audio engr. TV talk-show Donahue, 1985-87 (Emmy nomination). Mem. Pub. Citizen Consumer Activists, Washington, 1987; contbr. Planned Parenthood Fedn. Am., 1986—, N.Y.C. Ballet; fellow Mus. Modern Art, Met. Opera Guild. Recipient Down Beat award Down Beat mag., 1982, Best Engineered Live Performance award Down Beat mag. Mem. Audio Engring. Soc., Nat. Acad. TV Arts and Scis. (Emmy nominee 1986), NAFE, Nat. Assn. Broadcast Employees and Technicians, Women in Music, Nat. Acad. Recording Arts and Scis., Soc. Motion Picture and TV Engrs. Democrat. Home: 110 Horatio St Apt 617 New York NY 10014 Office: NBC Inc 30 Rockefeller Pla New York NY 10112

PEREZ, KATHLEEN IRMA, nurse; b. Covington, Ky., May 10, 1951; d. Robert Charles and Irma Edna (Knasel) Loffink; m. E.A. Perez, Dec. 31, 1985. AA, Brevard Community Coll., 1971; BS in Nursing, U. South Fla., 1979, MS in Nursing, 1984. R.N., Fla. Staff nurse St. Joseph's Hosp., Tampa, Fla., 1979-80; asst. dir. nursing Woodlands Convalescent Ctr., Tampa, 1980-81; staff nurse Univ. Community Hosp., Tampa, 1981-84; staff nurse, rehab. nurse mgr., nursing resources coord. James A. Haley Vets. Hosp., Tampa, 1984-88; mgr. edn. and orgnl. devel. H. Lee Moffitt Cancer Ctr. and Rsch. Inst., Tampa, 1988—; cons. in field. Contbr. articles to profl. publs. Mem. Am. Nurses Assn. (coun. computer applications 1986—), Fla. Nurses Assn., NAFE, Sigma Theta Tau. Republican. Office: H Lee Moffit Cancer Ctr PO Box 280179 Tampa FL 33682-0179

PEREZ, LILLIAN, municipal and state arts and grants administrator; b. Manhattatn, N.Y., Mar. 3, 1957; d. Gilberto and Aida Luz (Velazquez) P. BA Polit. Sci., Spanish, Rutgers U., 1979; MPA in Pub. Fin. Mgmt., Am. U., 1985, MBA in Mgmt. and Industrial Rels., 1988. Cert. budget analyst. Community devel. intern Met. Washington Coun. Govts., Washington, 1983-84; fin. mgmt. intern IRS, Washington, 1984-85; program evaluator U.S. GAO, Washington, 1985-88; legis. and grants officer D.C. Commn. on the Arts and Humanities, Washington, 1988—; chair D.C. Congl. Art Competition Panel, Washington, 1989; mem. annual conf. planning com. Nat. Assembly State Arts Agencies, Washington, 1989-90, Inter-D.C. Grants-making Task Force, Washington, 1989; benefit com. mem. Capitol Women's Network. Author: Directory of Special Transportation Services, 1984, Information on EPA's Proposal to Delete Chemicals from Groundwater Monitoring USGAO, 1987; former co-editor, contbr. Guernica (Rutgers U. fgn. lang. publ.); contbr. articles to Art Lines. Mem. Nat. Coun. Puerto Rican Women, Washington, 1989; mem. Humane Soc. of U.S.; mgr. Flute Ensemble; panel mem. Loy Krathong Festival Competition. Full-time scholar Am. U., 1984-86. Mem. NAFE, Am. Soc. for Pub. Adminstrs., Nat. Network Grantsmakers, Coun. Govtl. Ethics Laws, Cultural Alliance Greater Washington.

PEREZ FARFANTE, ISABEL C., systematic zoologist; b. Guira, La Habana, Cuba, July 24, 1916; came to U.S., 1960; d. Gervasio and Isabel (Farfante) Perez; m. Gerardo Augusto Canet, Dec. 11, 1940; children: Gerardo Canet, Eduardo Canet. BS, U. La Habana, Cuba, 1938; MS, Radcliffe Coll., 1944, PhD, 1948. Asst. prof. Zool. U. Habana, La Habana, 1940-42; assoc. curator Mus. Comparative Zoology Harvard U., Cambridge, Mass., 1946-48; prof. zoology U. Habana, La Habana, 1948-60; dir. Centro Inv. Pesqueras, La Habana, 1959-60; assoc. in invertebrate zoology Mus. Comparative Zoology, Harvard U., Cambridge, 1961-69; scholar, instr. ind. study Radcliffe U., Cambridge, 1962-64; rsch. assoc. NMNH Smithsonian Inst., Washington, 1968—; carcinologist emeritus Nat. Marine Fisheries Svc., 1986—. Author: New Zoology, 1964; contbr. articles to profl. jours. Fellow John S. Guggenheim Meml. Found., 1942-44, Alexander Agassiz, Harvard U., 1944-45; grantee Woods Hole Oceanographic Inst. Mass., 1944-48; recipient Honorable Mention for best publ. in fisheries Nat. Marine Fisheries Svc., 1977, 80, 85, 87. Mem. Biol. Soc. Washington, Crustacean Soc., Sigma Xi, Phi Beta Kappa. Home: 8306 Whitman Dr Bethesda MD 20817

PEREZ-SPENCER, ELOISA, state official; b. Tempico, Mex., Sept. 28, 1935; came to U.S., 1940, father Am. citizen.; (parents Am. citizens.) d. Abraham Villareal and Julia (Suarez) Perez; m. Alan W. Spencer, May 1988 (div.); children: Linda, Eric, Tovi, Lisa. BA in Human Relations, Skidmore Coll., 1980; postgrad., Rutgers U., 1989—. Bilingual adminstrv. asst. SUNY, Dept. Puerto Rican Studies, Albany, 1975-80, SUNY, Hispanic and Italian Studies Dept., Albany, 1980-81; supr. certification, rev. & analysis bur. N.Y. State of Gen. Svcs., MWBD, Albany, 1982-89; supr. cert. N.Y. State Gov.'s Office, 1988—; chair Albany Human Rights Commn. Past pres., bd. dirs. Centro Civico Hispanoamericano, Albany, 1975-89; mem. NOW, Albany, 1986, N.Y. State Employment and Tng. Counc., 1978-82; past chair City of Albany Commn. of Human Rights; past mem. Coalition on Minority Employment, Albany Urban League; past chair Black and Hispanic Polit. Caucus of the Albany Area, Inc.; elder, choir mem. First Presbyterian Ch. Albany. With USAF, 1953-56. Recipient YWCA Outstanding Women's award, 1982, No. Region Black & Hispanic Caucus Youth award, 1978, Disting. Svc. award Centro Civico Hispanoamericano, 1978. Home: 42 Elm St Albany NY 12202

PERGAMENT, LISA DIANE, parent educator; b. Royal Oak, Mich., Dec. 26, 1960; d. Gerald Pergament and Miriam Sylvia Tait. BA, U. Mich., Ann Arbor, 1984. Padi Open Water Instr. Staff asst. Arbor Heights Ctr., Ann Arbor, Mich., 1982-83; rsch. asst. U. Mich., Ann Arbor, 1982-83; clk. X-ray Harper Hosp., Detroit, 1981-84; asst. scuba instr. U. Mich., Ann Arbor; rsch. asst. Achievement Rsch., Ann Arbor, 1983-84; deckhand Blackbeards Cruises, Fla., 1984-85; first mate cook, divemaster Sea Wolfe Charters, Clearwater, Fla., 1985-85; scuba instrn., sales Aquatic Adventures, Zephyrhills, Fla., 1985—; childcare parent educator New Life Dwelling Pl., Thonotosassa, Fla., 1986—. Mem. Am. Psychol. Assn., Instr. Profl. Assn. Diving Instr. Democrat. Jewish. Home: 5549 5th St Zephyrhills FL 34248

PERGANDER, MARY SUE, hospital executive; b. Hinsdale, Ill., Jan. 21, 1955; d. Orville E. and Betty J. (Price) Brown; m. James P. Pergander, Jan. 29, 1977; 1 child, Kristin Marie. BS in Food and Nutrition, No. Ill. U., 1976; MBA in Mgmt., Lake Forest Grad. Sch. Mgmt., 1984. Registered dietitian. Clin. dietitian St. Therese Hosp., Waukegan, Ill., 1977-79; asst. food svc. dir. Victory Meml. Hosp., Waukegan, 1979-84; dir. diagnostic imaging Victory Meml. Hosp., 1984-89, adminstrv. project dir., 1989—; pub. speaker AAUW, AABW, churches, librs., Lake County, Ill., 1979-88. Vol. Am. Cancer Soc., Waukegan, 1984-88. Mem. Am. Healthcare Radiology Adminstrs., Women in Mgmt. Lake County, Ill. Dietetic Assn. (chair tellers 1987, chair grants & awards 1987). Office: Victory Meml Hosp 1324 N Sheridan Rd Waukegan IL 60085

PERHACS, MARYLOUISE HELEN, musician, educator; b. Teaneck, N.J., June 15, 1944; d. John Andrew and Helen Audrey (Hosage) P.; m. Robert Theodore Sirinek, Jan. 27, 1968 (div. Jan. 1975). Student, Ithaca (N.Y.) Coll., 1962-64; BS, Juilliard Sch., 1967, MS, 1968; postgrad., Hunter Coll., 1976, St. Peter's Coll., Jersey City, N.J., 1977. Cert. music tchr., N.Y., N.J. Instr. Carnegie Hall, N.Y.C., 1966-69; program developer, coord., instr. urban edn. program Newburgh (N.Y.) Pub. Sch. System, 1968-69; adj. prof. dept. edn. St. Peter's Coll., Jersey City, 1976—; tchr. Indian Hills High Sch., Oakland, N.J., 1976, Jersey City Pub. Schs., 1976-77, N.Y.C. Pub. Sch., Bronx, 1980-84; pvt. tchr. Cliffside Park, N.J., 1976—; vocal music tchr. East Rutherford, N.J., 1990; singer, trumpeter Norwegian Caribbean Lines, 1981-82, Jimmy Dorsey Band, Paris and London, 1974; music tchr. Bergen County Spl. Svcs. Sch. Dist., 1990—. Singer with Original PDQ Bach Okay Chorale, N.Y.C., 1966, Ed Sullivan Show, N.Y.C., 1970, St. Louis Mcpl. Opera, 1970; singer, dancer actress (Broadway shows) Promises, Promises, 1969-71, Sugar, 1971-72, Lysistrata, 1972; trumpeter (Broadway shows) Jesus Christ Superstar, 1973, Debbie!, N.Y.C., 1976, Sarava!, 1979, Sophisticated Ladies, 1982, Fiddler on the Roof, 1981; writer, host series on women in music Columbia Cable/United Artists, 1984. Cons. to cadette troop Girl Scouts U.S., Jersey City, 1967-68. Mem. Am. Fedn. Musicians (mem. theater com. 1972—, chmn. 1973), Music Educator's Nat. Conf., N.J. Music Educators Assn., N.J. Sch. Music Assn., N.J. Edn. Assn., Actors Equity Assn., Internat. Trumpet Guild, Am. Fedn. TV and Recording Artists, Mu Phi Epsilon. Democrat. Episcopalian. Home and Office: 23 Crescent Ave Cliffside Park NJ 07010

PERI, BARBARA A., microbiology educator, consultant; b. Richmond, Calif., May 15, 1925; d. Walter George and Dorothy Gertrude (Webster) Miller; m. John Bayard Peri, July 21, 1946; children: Pamela Pazoles, Phyllis, Janet Gillies. BA, U. Calif., Berkeley, 1946; MS, U. Wis., 1948; PhD, U. Notre Dame, 1970. Instr. Valparaiso (Ind.) U., 1958-63, asst. prof., 1963-69, assoc. prof., 1969-74; rsch. assoc., asst. prof. Pritzker Sch. Medicine U. Chgo., 1974-84, rsch. assoc., assoc. prof. Pritzker Sch. Medicine, 1984-86; assoc. immunology prof. Harvard Med. Sch. Mass. Gen. Hosp., 1986-88; ret., 1988; freelance cons. Falmouth, Mass., 1988—; guest investigator Woods Hole (Mass.) Oceanographic Inst., 1989—. Mem. Am. Soc. for Microbiology, Am. Assn. Immunologists, Assn. for Gnotobiology (pres. 1990-91), LWV (observer corps Falmouth chpt.), Sigma Xi. Home: 2 Tortoise Ln Falmouth MA 02540

PERIGYI, JO-ANN KATHERINE, director of nursing; b. New Haven, Mar. 2, 1953; d. Arthur John Kelleher and Helen Katherine (Grady) Rohne; m. Carl Alexander Perigyi, July 14, 1984. A, Norwalk Community Coll., 1977; BS in Nursing, U. Bridgeport, 1986; MA in Nursing Orgn. Exec. Role, Columbia U., 1988, MA in Health Adminstrn., 1988. Lic. practical nurse Jersey Shore Med. Ctr., Neptune, N.J., 1972-75; nursing asst., RN Bentley-Gardens, West Haven, Conn., 1975-78; staff nurse., mgr. patient care Park City Hosp., Bridgeport, Conn., 1978-85; intake facilitator Hosp. Home Health Care Conn., New Haven, 1986; from asst. dir. nurses to dir. nurses Regis Multi Health Ctr. Inc., New Haven, 1986-89; dir. nurses Homestead Health Ctr., Stamford, Conn., 1989—. Mem. Am. Mgmt. Assn. Roman Catholic. Home: 654 Oldfield Rd Fairfield CT 06430 Office: Homestead Health Ctr 160 Glenbrook Rd Stamford CT 06902

PERINI, PATRICIA PAUL, television executive; b. N.Y.C., July 7, 1944; d. Bernard James and Ann (Hudlin) Paul; m. Robert Bryant Long, Apr. 19, 1986; m. Vincent Walker Perini, Feb. 10, 1969 (divorced); 1 child, Elizabeth M. Perini. BA, U. Tex., 1966; MA, Johns Hopkins U., 1967. Asst. to editor Delos Mag., Nat. Transl. Ctr., Austin, Tex., 1967-69; graphics designer Rep. Nat. Bank, Dallas, 1969; pub. info. dir. Sta. KERA-TV, Dallas, 1969-77, dir. creative svcs. and programming, 1977, v.p. broadcasting svcs., 1977-81, v.p. program devel. and prodn., 1981-83, v.p. programming, 1983-86; sr. v.p. programming, 1986—. Exec. producer Pub. Broadcasting System TV spls. The West of the Imagination, 1986 (Am. Film Festival award), Katherine Anne Porter, 1986, Jane Brody's Kitchen, 1987, The Fig Tree, 1987, Good Health from Hane Brody, 1987, Facing Evil with Bill Moyers, 1988. Adv. coun. bd. trustees Ft. Worth Art Mus., 1983—; trustee Greenhill Sch., 1983—; mem. leadership devel. subcom. Women and Minority Econ. Issues

Joint com. Dallas Citizens Coun. and C. of C., 1983-84; mem. task force adult edn. program goals com. Dallas Mus. Art, 1982-84; mem. Goals for Dallas, 1977-79; chmn. media adv. panel Tex. Commn. on Arts, 1983-84; trustee Tejas Girl Scout Coun., Dallas, 1986-89; mem. Gt. Performances Program Mgmt. Consortium, 1982-84; panelist Children's Media Panel, Nat. Endowment Humanities, 1983; pub. affairs evaluation panel Corp. Pub. Broadcasting, 1987, local program awards panel, 1987; mem. Leadership Dallas, 1980-81; adv. com. arts Magnet Sch. for Dallas Ind. Sch. Dist., 1978-83; mem. Charter 100. Mem. Exec. Women of Dallas (v.p. 1980-81), Nat. Assn. TV Programming Execs., Acad. TV Arts and Scis. (blue ribbon panel for prime time Emmys 1987), Dallas Communications Coun., Great Performances Program Mgmt. Consortium, Am. Inst. Food and Wine. Episcopalian. Office: Sta KERA-TV 3000 Harry Hines Blvd Dallas TX 75201

PERKINS, ANNE SCARLETT, state legislator; b. Balt., Sept. 29, 1937; d. William George and Anne (Edelen) Scarlett; children: Anne, Virginia. AB, Boston U., 1959; JD, U. Balt., 1979. Staff atty. Md. Advocacy Unit for Developmentally Disabled, Balt., 1979-81; elected mem. Md. Gen. Assembly, Annapolis, 1979—; adj. prof. Goncher Coll., Towson, Md., 1983. Recipient Disting. Service award Greenmount West Community Assn. and Balt. Braille Assn., 1981, Ann London Scott award for Legis. Excellence NOW, 1982, Award for Outstanding Legis. Leadership Md. Assn. for Housing and Redevel. Agys., 1983, Md. Victims Assistance Network award, 1984, Cert. Merit Md. Common Cause, 1984, Award for helping to eliminate domestic violence House of Ruth, 1985, Spl. award Women's Housing Coalition, 1985, Spl. awards Md. Child Care Assn., 1985, 86, Leadership award Gov.'s Housing Initiative Celebration com., 1986, Coop. Statesman award Md. Coop. Law Coalition, 1986, Legis. Excellence award House of Ruth, 1986, The Peabody Conservatory medallion, 1987. Democrat. Episcopalian. Home: 4110 Greenway Baltimore MD 21218 Office: 141 Lowe House Office Bldg 6 Gov Bladen Blvd Annapolis MD 21401-1991

PERKINS, BEVERLY ANN, private investigator; b. Winchester, Ky., Oct. 9, 1953; d. Virgil Sr. and Norma Jean (Haddix) Perkins; 1 child, Schtina Dyonne. B in Corrections, Ea. Ky. U., Richmond, 1989. Dep. jailer Clark County Detention Ctr., Winchester; sr. correctional officer U.S. Dept. Justuce, Fed. Bur. Prisons, Lexington, Ky.; owner, chief exec. officer, pvt. investigator Personnel Security Investigations, Winchester; founder former Vets. Coun. S.E. Fla.; specialized tng. in hostage negotions, applied criminology and media relations. Mem. Am. Legion, Am. Legion Aux., Disabled Am. Vets.; With U.S. Army, 1971-73. Named Vet. of Yr., 1983, hon. Sheriff, 1985; recipient Correctional Officer award, 1988. Mem. Am. Correctional Assn., Am. Fedn. Police, Ky. Chpt. Juvenile Justice Soc., KU Colonels Assn. (hon. 1975). Democrat. Baptist.

PERKINS, CHERYL ALICE, programmer analyst, real estate agent; b. Forest, Miss., July 17, 1956; d. Richard and Fannie Mae (Gresham) Gray; m. Kevin Isaac Perkins, Nov. 29, 1978; 1 child, Karl. BBA, Marian Coll., 1986. Mail carrier U.S. Post Office, Indpls., 1978-79; advanced sales asst. Jefferson Nat. Life Ins., Indpls., 1979-82, programmer, analyst I, 1982-85; programmer Nat. Vocat. Tech. Coll., Indpls., 1985-89; sr. programmer analyst Banc One, Indpls., 1989—. Presdl. scholar, 1978; Freedom of Choice grantee, 1978. Torchbearer United Way of Greater Indpls., 1984-85; mem. com. United Charities, 1984-85; bd. dirs. Dyslexia Remedial Assn., 1985, Neighborhood Belle Fellowship, 1988-89. Mem. Nat. Coun. Negro Women (liaison 1980-85), Data Processing Mgmt. Assn., Nat. Assn. Female Execs., Aglow Christain Women's Internat. (rec. sec. 1987—), Love Christian Fellowship, Agape Neighborhood Bible Fellowship (bd. dirs. 1988-89). Home: 4710 E 46th St Indianapolis IN 46226 Office: Banc One Indianapolis IN 46227

PERKINS, CHRISTINA WRAY, sales executive; b. Troy, Ohio, Apr. 15, 1946; d. Arthur Elmer and Anna Margaret (Wray) Smith; m. Charles Elliott, Nov. 1966, (div. 1970); 1 child, James Arthur. Waitress San Louis Bridge Restaurant, Oceanside, Calif., 1966-68; compositor Troy Daily News, Troy, Ohio, 1969-77; receptionist Electrolert, Tipp City, Ohio, 1977, lit. supr.; trade show mgr. Electrolert, Tipp City, 1977-84; asst. advt. mgr. Electrolert, 1977-84; prodn. mgr. Tricom, Inc., Dayton, 1984-87; nat. sales mgr. L.W. Milby, Inc., Tipp City, Ohio, 1987-.; cons. Inside Meeting Planning. Past Bd. dir. Ohio Valley Chpt. of Meeting Planners Internat., 1980-84, Big Brother Internat., 1970's. Recipient Hermes award Dayton AD Club, Dayton, 1980's. mem. Nat. Assn. Female Execs., Women in Mktg., Dayton Direct Mail Club, Dayton Ad Club, Dayton Sales and Mktg. Execs. (v.p. svcs.), Dayton Direct Mktg. Club (bd. dirs.) Office: LW Milby Inc 1701 Dalton Dr New Carlisle OH 45344

PERKINS, DEBORAH ANNE, interior designer; b. Mineola, N.Y., Mar. 8, 1954; d. Arthur Cudner and Maria (Risko) P. AAS in Interior Design magne cum laude, Chamberlayne Sch., Boston, 1975. Film admissions coord. Gen. Cinema Corp., Chestnut Hill, Mass., 1976-78; tchr. adult edn. Kennedy Community Sch., Cambridge, Mass., 1976; interior design cons. Jordan Marsh Co., Quincy, Mass., 1978-81; freelance interior designer Honduras, Central Am., 1981; sales rep. New Eng. territory LaFrance (S.C.) Fabrics, 1982-84; owner, designer The Design Studio, Watertown, Mass., 1985—; mem. Boston Soc. Architects Task Force for the Homeless, 1988—. Big Sister YWCA., Boston, 1985—; participant Grace Chapel Nursing Home Ministry, Lexington, Mass., 1989, Intermission Performing Arts, 1989-90. Mem. NAFE, Women Entrepreneurs Homebased, Am. Soc. Interior Designers, Alpha Nu Omega. Home and Office: 43 Capitol St Boston MA 02172

PERKINS, DEE ANN, real estate developer; b. Paris, Tenn., Aug. 15, 1968; d. Ed R. and Demetra (Scott) P. Student, Austin Peay State U., 1986-87; BS in Bus. cum laude, Bethel Coll., 1990. Clk. West and West Law Firm, McKenzie, Tenn., 1984-85; pres. The Perkins Corp., McKenzie, 1985-89; nat. award winner U.S. Achievement Acad., 1986, state chairperson Tenn. Better Sch. Effectiveness Prog., 1985. Active Carroll County Leadership, 1990; elder Presbyn. Ch. Named Tenn. Rep. Miss Young am. Nat. Pageant, L.A., 1985, presdl. scholar Austin Peay State U., Clarksville, Tenn., 1986, Bob Hope scholar Bethel Coll., 1989, Miss Tenn. Venus U.S.A. Nat. Pageant, Bridgeport, Conn., 1986. Mem. Rotary (youngest woman to join 1987, Rotarian of Yr. 1990), Gamma Beta Phi. Presbyterian. Home: 676 E Paris Ave Mckenzie TN 38201 Office: The Perkins Corp Highland Mall Ste 5 Mckenzie TN 38201

PERKINS, DOROTHY A., association executive; b. Weiser, Idaho, Aug. 13, 1926; d. Ross William and Josephine Stanford (Gwilliam) Anderson; m. Leonard Taylor Perkins, Nov. 16, 1948; children: Larry Taylor, Michael A., Drew A., Nancy. Grad. high sch., Boise, Idaho. Sec. Meadow Gold Dairies, Boise, 1944-46; sec. to supt. Idaho State Police, Boise, 1946-48, Idaho State Dept. Edn., Boise, 1952-56; sec. to maintenance engr. Idaho State Dept. Hwys., Boise, 1956-58; adminstrv. sec., asst. mgr. Casper (Wyo.) C. of C., 1962-72, exec. v.p., 1972—. Mem. Wyo. Ho. Reps., 1982—; leader girls 12-18 yrs. of age Casper Ch. Jesus Christ Latter Day Sts. Mem. Wyo. C. of C. Execs. (sec.-treas. 1978—, past pres.), Mountain States Assn. (bd. dirs. 1979—, past pres.), Wyo. Hwy. Users Found. (bd. dirs. 1978—). Republican. Home: 1014 Surrey Ct Casper WY 82609 Office: Casper Area C of C 500 North Ctr PO Box 399 Casper WY 82602

PERKINS, ESTHER ROBERTA, literary agent; b. Elkton, Md., May 10, 1927; d. Clarence Roberts and Esther Crouch (Terrell) P.; student West Chester State Tchrs. Coll., 1945-47, U. Del. Acct., S.I. duPont de Nemours & Co., Inc., Wilmington, Del., 1947-65; records specialist U. Del., 1966-78; partner Holly Press, Hockessin, Del., 1977-83; owner Esther R. Perkins Lit. Agy., Childs, Md., 1979—; author's agt. Mem. Cecil County Arts Council. Mem. Authors Guild, Nat. Writer's Club, DAR, Romance Writers Am., Mystery Writers Am. Author: Backroading Through Cecil County Maryland, 1978; Things I Wish I'd Said, 1979; Canal Town, Historic Chesapeake City, Maryland, 1983. Republican. Methodist. Home and Office: PO Box 48 Childs MD 21916

PERKINS, JULIE ANNE RATE, lawyer; b. Iowa City, Jan. 26, 1935; d. Edward Francis and Maude (Adams) Rate; m. Dwight Heald Perkins, June 15, 1957; children: Lucy Fitch, Dwight Edward, Caleb Blair. BA in Arts & Scis., Cornell U., 1957; LLB, Boston U., 1960. Bar: Mass., 1960, U.S. Dist.

Ct. Mass. 1982. Assoc. Foley, Hoag & Eliot, Boston, 1960-61; lectr., rsch. asst. Boston (Mass.) U., 1963-64; rsch. asst. Harvard U., Cambridge, Mass., 1964-66; staff atty. Cambridgeport Problem Ctr., Cambridge, 1981-86; assoc. Bastone Assocs., Boston, 1986—; corporator Belmont Savs. Bank, Boston, 1978—. Mem. Belmont (Mass.) Warrant Com., 1973-81 (chmn. 1978-81); elected town meeting mem. Town of Belmont, 1970—; elected mem. Belmont Dem. Town Com., 1984—. Mem. LWV (Belmont, pres. 1970-73), Mass. LWV (bd. dirs., legis. v.p. 1979-81, fin. v.p. 1977-79, fiscal policy chmn. 1973-77). Home: 64 Pinehurst Rd Belmont MA 02178 Office: Bastone Assocs 85 Devonshire St Boston MA 02109

PERKINS, LYNN MARIE, research assistant; b. Detroit, Dec. 6, 1963; d. Gerald Allan and Bobbie Jo (Justice) Shaffran; m. Brian Lynn Perkins, May 5, 1990. BS, Mich. State U., 1987. Rsch. asst. Wayne State U., Detroit, 1987-89, VA Med. Ctr.-West L.A., 1989—. Republican. Roman Catholic.

PERKINS, MARY LYNN, educator; b. Grenada, Miss., Jan. 23, 1954; d. Ralph Jamison and Myrtice Yvonne (Vanlandingham) P. BE, U. Miss., 1975, MEd, 1976. Cert. tchr. Tchr. Calhoun County Sch. System, Calhoun City, Miss., 1976—; pvt. tutor, Calhoun City, 1975-83; cheerleader sponsor Calhoun City Mid. Sch., 1979-80, social studies chair for Insructional Mgmt. Program, 1987—. Com. mem. Nat. Library Week Calhoun City Pub. Library, 1985—, chair, 1987—; mem. publicity div. Calhoun County chpt. Am. Cancer Soc., Pittsboro, Miss., 1986-87, mem.-at-large, 1987-88, treas. Calhoun County chpt., 1989-90; dist. III edn. dept. chmn. Miss. Fedn. Women's Clubs, Jackson, Miss., 1985-86, free enterprise dept. chmn., 1986-87. Named Outstanding Young Educator Calhoun City Jaycees, 1987; named one of Outstanding Young Women Am., 1984. Mem. Miss. Assn. Educators, Nat. Edn. Orgn., New Century Club (Calhoun City, com. mem. 1985—, pres. 1988-90), Phi Kappa Phi, Kappa Delta Pi. Baptist. Home: Rt 1 Box 210 Calhoun City MS 38916-9741 Office: Calhoun City Mid Sch PO Box 559 Calhoun City MS 38916

PERKINS, NANCY JANE, industrial designer; b. Phila., Nov. 5, 1949; d. Gordon Osborne and Martha Elizabeth (Keichline) P.; student Ohio U., 1967-68; BFA, U. Ill., Champaign, 1972. Indsl. designer Peterson Bednar Assoc., Evanston, Ill., 1972-74, Deschamps Mills Assocs., Bartlett, Ill., 1974-75; dir. graphic design Cameo Container Corp., Chgo., 1975-76; indsl. design cons. Sears Roebuck & Co., Chgo., 1977-88; cons. indsl. design, 1988—; founder Perkins Design Ltd.; indsl. design cons. co., 1979—; adj. prof. grad. design Seminar U. Ill. at Chgo., 1982, 88, instr. undergrad. design, 1984, 1988; adj. prof. Ill. Inst. Tech., 1987; juror Annual Design Rev. Indsl. Design mag., 1986; keynote speaker Soc. Automotive Engrs., 1980, Women in Design, 1982, 84, Meadow Club, 1983, U. Ill. Disting. Alumni Lecture Series, 1983, Human Factors Soc. Interface '85, 1985. Contbr. articles to profl. jours.; profiled in Indsl. Design mag., 1986. Co-leader Cadette troop DuPage County coun. Girl Scouts U.S., 1978-79. Recipient Outstanding Alumni award U. Ill. Alumni Jour., 1981. Mem. Indsl. Designers Soc. Am. (treas. Chgo. chpt. 1977-79, vice-chmn. 1979-80, chmn. 1981, dist. membership 1982, ann. conf. com. 1983, publs. 1985-86, dir.-at-large 1987-88, midwest dist. v.p. 1988-89, IDSA delegate Internat. Coun. of the Societies of Indsl. Design); speaker "Design in America Symposium," Nagoya, Japan, 1989. Patentee marine, automotive and consumer products. Home: 320 W Illinois #707 Chicago IL 60610 Office: 350 W Ontario Ste 200 Chicago IL 60610

PERKINS, PAULA MICHELLE, public relations professional; b. Opelousas, La., Dec. 3, 1955; d. Gerald Oswald and Doris Nell (Boagni) P. BFA, U. Southwestern La., 1977. Reporter Eunice (La.) Gazette, 1979-80, news editor, 1980-82; area editor Daily World, Opelousas, 1982-83; dir. pub. rels. Opelousas Gen. Hosp., 1983—. Mem. La. Hosp. Assn. (Pelican award 1984, 85, 87). Home: 460 S Market St Opelousas LA 70570 Office: Opelousas Gen Hosp 520 Prudhomme Ln Opelousas LA 70570

PERKINS, TAMMY JO, city official; b. Salem, Ohio, May 10, 1959; d. Glenn Wayne and Janet Elaine (Galbreath) P. BA, Drake U., 1981; MPA, U. Denver, 1982. Mgmt. intern City of Boulder, Colo., 1980; mgmt. intern City of Phoenix, 1982-83, mgmt. asst., 1983—; bd. dirs. City of Phoenix Deferred Compensation Bd., 1989—. Bd. dirs. Downtown Phoenix YMCA, 1986—; active Valley Leadership, Phoenix, 1986-87, Ariz. Women's Town Hall, Chandler, 1988-90. Mem. Am. Soc. Pub. Adminstrs., Ariz. City Mgmt. Assn. (exec. com. 1985), Ariz. Mcpl. Mgmt. Assts. Assn. (pres. 1985), Internat. City Mgmt. Assn., Renaissance Club, Phoenix City Club, Soroptimist Internat. Methodist. Office: City of Phoenix 251 W Washington 10th Fl Phoenix AZ 85003

PERKINS-CARPENTER, BETTY LOU, service executive; b. Rochester N.Y., Jan. 22, 1931; d. Edward C. and Bertha M. (Loeser) Kalmn; m. Floyd F. Perkins, Jan. 31, 1951 (div. 1979); children: Cheryl Lee, F. Scott; m. Marcellus Chipman Carpenter, Oct. 10, 1981. BS in Phys. Edn. Adminstrn., Empire State Coll., N.Y., 1979; MS in Early Childhood Edn. Adminstrn., Nova U., 1983. Tchr., coach Rochester YWCA, 1954-59, Perkins Swimming Sch., Penfield, N.Y., 1959-64; pres. Perkins Swim Club, Inc., Rochester, 1964—, Perkins Fit By Five, Inc., Rochester, 1969—, Child Fitness Prodns., Inc. d/b/a Sr. Fitness Prodns., Rochester, 1983—, Fit By Five Franchise Corp., Rochester, 1984—; diving coach Olympic Games, Montreal, 1976; mem. adv. com. N.Y. State Task Force Phys. Fitness and Sports, 1978-82; bd. dirs. U.S. Olympic Diving Com., 1976-80; cons. European sports facilities, 1969-83, Pres.'s Council on Phys. Fitness and Sports, 1986—; mem. adv. com. Community Savs. Bank, Rochester, 1976-79; mem. adv. bd. O.A.S.I.S. Author: The Fun of Fitness-A Handbook for the Senior Class, 1988, How to Prevent Falls-Introducing the Balance System, 1989; Am. editor: Teaching Babies to Swim, 1979; contbr. articles to profl. jours. Exec. producer audio-visual instructional materials. Served with USAF, 1948-51. Recipient Gold medal Inst. Achievement of Human Potential, Brazil, 1973; Mike Malone Meml. Diving award, 1977; Cady Diving award, 1977; named to Monroe County Athletes Hall of Fame, Rochester, 1979; named Sports Woman of Yr., U.S. Olympic Diving Commn., 1979, Citizen of Yr. Rotary, 1988. Mem. U.S. Diving Assn. (life, numerous offices), Rochester Assn. Edn. of Young Children, Nova U. Alumnae Assn., Genesee Valley Sports Medicine Coun., Oak Hill Country Club, Order Eastern Star (life). Republican. Avocations: swimming, cross-country skiing, reading, travel. Office: Perkins Swim Club 1606 Penfield Rd Rochester NY 14625

PERKS, BARBARA ANN MARCUS, psychologist; b. Wilson, Pa., July 1, 1937; d. Alfred M. and Lillian (Reibman) Marcus; B.S., Pa. State U., 1959; M.A., Columbia U., 1963; cert. in ednl. psychology Oxford (Eng.) U., 1965; postgrad. U. Oreg., U.S. Internat. U.; Ed.D., U. B.C., 1984; m. Anthony Manning Perks, Sept. 9, 1963. Tchr. gifted Hamden (Conn.) Sch. Dist., 1959-62; reading cons. Oxfordshire County, Littlemore, Eng., 1964-65; sch. psychologist Vancouver (B.C., Can.) Sch. Bd., 1972-76; supr. student tchrs. U. B.C., Vancouver, 1977-78, cons. Research Center, 1978-79, ednl. psychologist, child and family unit child psychiatry Health Scis. Centre Hosp., 1979-81, lectr., 1977—; instr. psychology Langara Coll., 1985; pvt. practice counseling and teaching, Vancouver, 1984—, counseling and sch. psychology, Burnaby, B.C., 1985—. Recipient Can. Daus. League award; Provincial Council of B.C. award, 1981, U. B.C. awards, 1980; Jonathan Rogers award, 1984; Univ. fellow, Dr. MacKenzie Am. Alumni scholar U. B.C., 1976; U. B.C. summer scholar, 1982; cert. psychologist, B.C. Mem. Am. Psychol. Assn., B.C. Psychol. Assn., Assn. Humanistic Psychology, Nat. Assn. Sch. Psychology, Am. Ednl. Research, N.Am. Soc. Adlerian Psychology, Am. Orthopsychiat. Assn., Mortar Bd., Pi Sigma Alpha, Pi Lambda Theta, Kappa Delta Pi. Clubs: Figure Skating (Vancouver, B.C., New Haven, Conn., Allentown, Pa.). Author research papers. Home: 4570 Glenwood Ave, North Vancouver, BC Canada V7R 4G5

PERL, TERI, computer educator; b. N.Y.C., Nov. 19, 1926; d. Nathan and Rose (Gross) Hoch; m. Martin L. Perl, June 24, 1927 (div. 1988); children: Jed, Anne, Matthew, Joseph. BA in Econs. Bklyn. Coll., 1947; postgrad., San Jose State U., Calif., 1969; PhD in Math Edn., Stanford U., Calif. 1979. Math. cons., resource tchr. Ventura Elem. Sch., Palo Alto, Calif., 1971-79; lectr. San Francisco State U., 1977-79; project assoc. Stanford (Calif) U., 1977-79; project assoc. lectr. U. Wis., Madison, 1979-80; dir. cofounder The Learning Co., Fremont, Calif., 1980-87; lectr. San Francisco State U. 1988; edn. cons. Teri Perl Assoc., Palo Alto, 1987—; contbr. editor SIG Tchr. Edn. Bulletin, Internat. Council for Computers in Edn., Eugene ORe. 1988—;

Bd. Mem. Assn. Women in Maths. Designer: Ednl. Software, Gertrude's Secrets, Puzzles, 1982, Math. Rabbit, 1986; author: Math Equals, 1978, Women, Numbers and Dreams, 1982. Mem. Computer Profls. for Social Responsibility, Palo Alto Calif., 1987--. Recipient Math Equals Citation CHOICE Mag. Am. Library Assn. Mem. Nat. Council Tchrs. Math, Internat. Council Computers in Edn., Calif. Math. Council, Assn. Women in Math, Women in Math Edn. Home and Office: 525 Lincoln Ave Palo Alto CA 94301

PERLESS, ELLEN, advertising executive; b. N.Y.C., Sept. 9, 1941; d. Joseph B. and Bertha (Messinger) Kaplan; m. Robert L. Perless, July 2, 1965. Student, Smith Coll., 1958-59, Bard Coll., 1959-62. Copywriter Doyle, Dane Bernbach, N.Y.C., 1964-70, Young & Rubicam, N.Y.C., 1970-74; creative supr. Young & Rubicam, 1974-76, v.p., creative supr., 1977, v.p., assoc. creative dir., 1978, sr. v.p., assoc. creative dir., 1979-84; v.p., assoc. creative dir. Leber Katz Ptnrs., 1984-85, sr. v.p., creative dir., 1986-87; sr. v.p., sr. creative dir. FCB/Leber Katz Ptnrs., N.Y.C., 1987--. Recipient 2 Clio awards, Andy awards, awards from Art Dirs. Club N.Y. Mem. One Club for Art and Copy. Club: Northeast Harbor Fleet of Maine. Home: 37 Langhorne Ln Greenwich CT 06831 Office: FCB/Leber Katz Ptnrs 767 5th Ave New York NY 10153

PERLICK, NANCY BETH, health services executive; b. Chgo., Aug. 18, 1944; d. Gene Roland and Joanne Catherine (Olender) Perlick. BA in Social Sci., Russell Coll., 1969; BS in Nursing, U. San Francisco, 1970; MHA, U. Wash., 1983. Clin. nurse intern St. Mary's Hosp. and Med. Ctr., San Francisco, 1970; staff nurse St. Joseph's Hosp. and Med. Ctr., Phoenix, 1970-73; charge nurse Mercy Hosp., Bakersfield, Calif., 1973-74; supr. nurse Mercy Hosp. and Med. Ctr., San Diego, 1974-81; adminstrv. intern Harborview Med. Ctr., Seattle, 1982; adminstrv. asst. St. Joseph's Hosp. and Med. Ctr., Phoenix, 1983-84; adminstrn. Barrow Neurol. Inst., 1984-85, v.p. Barrow Neurol. Inst. and Mental Health, 1986-88, v.p. neuroscis., 1988—; bd. dirs Ariz. Emergency Med. Systems, Inc., Phoenix, 1988, standing hosp. com.,1987, Mercy Hosp., 1983, v. chair 1988, St. John's Regional Med. Ctr., Oxnard, Calif., 1979-81; mem. Health Services Adv. Board-Sisters of Mercy, 1978-81, Grossmont (Calif.) Coll. Nursing Program Com., 1977-81, Cen. Ariz. Health Systems Agy. Contbr. articles to Jour. of Neurosurg. Nursing and other profl. jours. Bd. dirs. Ariz.-Mex. Commn., 1986, Cen. Ariz. Shelter Services, Phoenix, 1986, Community Housing Partnership, 1987, Human Devel. Council-Roman Catholic Diocese of Phoenix, 1986—, Phoenix Coalition for Health Care for the Homeless, 1986-89, Soc. Justice Commn.-Sisters of Mercy, 1985, Soc. Justice Com.-Sisters' Council-Roman Catholic Diocese of Phoenix, 1986—, Tule Devel. Corp., Bakersfield, Calif., 1983-86, Soc. Concerns Commn.-Sisters of Mercy, 1980-81, Peace and Justice Commn.-Roman Catholic Diocese of San Diego, 1979-81. Mem. Sisters of Mercy of Burlingame, Calif., Am. Assn. Neurosci. Nurses, Am. Mgmt. Assn., Health Svcs. Rsch. Assn., Mental Health Adminstrs. Assn., Health Care Fin. Mgmt. Assn., NAFE, Nat. League of Nurses, Sigma Theta Tau (Beta Gamma chpt.). Office: St Josephs Hosp and Med Ctr 350 W Thomas Rd Phoenix AZ 85013

PERLMAN, KAREN SUSAN, hospital administrator; b. Chgo., Sept. 12, 1943; d. Marvin and Florence Mae (Namowitz) P. BS in Edn., No. Ill. U., 1965; MFA, U. Wis., Madison, Wis., 1967; postgrad., Salzburg Acad. Arts, Salzburg, Austria, 1967, Santa Reparata Graphics Studio, Florence, Italy, 1973. Art educator various programs, L.I., N.Y., 1967-76; designer Industry, L.I., 1976-79; devel. cons. self-employed, various locations, 1979-89; dir. devel., pub. relations Peninsula Hosp. Ctr., Far Rockaway, N.Y., 1989—; bd. dirs. Bd. Suffolk County Office For Women, Islip, N.Y., 1988—. Author: New England Pickles, 1979. Editor: N.Y. State Manual for Child Custody, 1982, A Directory of Community Services, 1984; contbr. numerous articles to various mag. and jours. Bd. dirs. Huntington (N.Y.) Chpt. NOW, Polit. Task Force Chairperson NOW, Bd. Fin. Chairperson NOW, pres. NOW Alliance PAC of L.I., Selden, N.Y., 1987-88. Recipient Fellowship Skidmore Coll., 1974. Mem. Nat. Soc. Fund Raising, Execs. (publicity com. 1988), Nat. Assn. Female Execs., Nat. Hosp. Devel. Assn., Kiwanis, Exchange Club. Democrat. Office: Peninsula Hosp Ctr 51-15 Beach Channel Dr Far Rockaway NY 11691

PERLMAN, KATHERINE LENARD (KATO LENARD), organic chemist; b. Budapest, Hungary, July 18, 1928; came to U.S., 1963; d. Sandor and Lili (Fischer) Lenard; m. David Perlman, Aug. 18, 1968 (dec. 1980). Diploma chemistry, Eotvos U., Budapest, 1950, PhD, 1960. Rsch. chemist CHINOIN Pharms., Budapest, 1950-54; rsch. staff member Rsch. Inst. for Pharm. Industry, Budapest, 1954-62; Princeton (N.J.) U., 1963-68; rsch. assoc. U. Wis., Madison, 1968-69, assoc. scientist sch. pharmacy, 1969-81, sr. scientist biochemistry dept., 1981—. Contbr. numerous articles to profl. jours.; patentee in field. Mem. Am. Chem. Soc., Chem. Soc. London. Democrat. Home: 1 Chippewa Ct Madison WI 53711 Office: U Wis 420 Henry Mall Madison WI 53706

PERLMAN, RHEA, actress; b. Bklyn., Mar. 31; m. Danny DeVito, Jan. 8, 1982; children: Lucy Chet, Gracie Far, Jake. Grad., Hunter Coll. Has appeared in numerous Broadway plays; founder Colonades Theatre Lab., N.Y.C.; various roles in TV movies include I Want to Keep My Baby!, 1976, Stalk the Wild Child, 1976 Intimate Strangers, 1977, Having Babies II, 1977, Mary Jane Harper Cried Last Night, 1977, Like Normal People, 1979, Drop Out Father, 1982, The Ratings Game (cable), 1984, Dangerous Affection, A Family Again; TV series include Taxi, 1978-82, Cheers, 1982—; motion pictures include Love Child, My Little Pony, Enid is Sleeping. Recipient Emmy award for Outstanding Supporting Actress in a Comedy Series, 1984, 86. Address: CAA 9830 Wilshire Blvd Beverly Hills CA 90212*

PERLMAN, SANDRA LEE, playwright, consultant; b. Phila., June 18, 1944; d. Sidney Henry and Betty (Lee) P.; m. Henry Lewis Halem, Sept. 10, 1969; 1 child, Jessica Ariel. BA, Am. U., 1966. Actress sr. theatre Soc. Hill Theatre/Phila. Recreation, 1968; rsch. editor Prof. Harvey Littleton, Madison, Wis. 1968-69; speech and advt. writer Sta. WMTV-Channel 15, Madison, 1969; English tchr. Garfield High Sch., Akron, Ohio, 1969-72; producer, writer PBS Channels 45/49, Kent, Ohio, 1975-81; communications cons. Halem Studios, Kent, 1981—, chmn. bd., 1988—; promotions dir. Stas. NPR/WKSU-FM, Kent, 1985-87; playwright, dir. Massillon (Ohio) Mus., 1988-89. Editor: Glassblowing: A Search for Form, 1968. Bd. dirs. Bicentennial Commn., Kent, 1976, Kent Hist. Soc., 1977-87. Ohio Arts Coun. fellow, 1983, 86, Ohio Arts Coun./OHC fellow 1989. Mem. Ohio Theatre Alliance (bd. dirs., playwriting chair), Dramatists Guild , Ohio Arts Coun. (cochair new works panel 1987-89), First Internat. Women Playwrights Conf. (ops. dir. 1988). Democrat. Home: 429 Carthage Ave Kent OH 44240 Office: Halem Studios Inc 429 Carthage Ave Kent OH 44240

PERLMAN, SHARON TOBY, data processing executive; b. Bronx, Nov. 1, 1948; d. Sidney and Bertha (Steinberg) Yankowitz; m. Barry Steven, Feb. 1, 1969 (div. 1983); children: Adam Justin, Ryan Garrett. Student, Chamberlayne U., Boston, 1968. Salesperson Spangler Envelope Co., Phila., 1979-80; customer rel. mgr. NSA Arms, Cherry Hills, N.J., 1980-81; acct. mgr. EDP TEMPS, Bala Cynwyd, Pa., 1981-84, Am. Data Cons., Bensalem, Pa.; v.p. mktg. The Summit Group, Willingboro, N.J., 1985; v.p., owner The Support Group, Inc., Pa., 1986--. Mem. Nat. Assn. for Female Execs., Lower Bucks County C. of C., Cancer Soc.

PERLMUTTER, DIANE F., communications executive; b. N.Y.C., Aug. 31, 1945; d. Bert H. and Frances (Smith) P. Student, NYU, 1969-70; AB in English, Miami U., Oxford, Ohio, 1967. Writer sales promotion Equitable Life Assurance, N.Y.C., 1967-68; adminstrv. asst. de Garmo, Inc., N.Y.C., 1968-69, asst. account exec., 1969-70, account exec., 1970-74, v.p., account supr., 1974-76; mgr. corp. advt. Avon Products, Inc., N.Y.C., 1976-79, dir. communications Latin Am., Spain, Can., 1979-80, dir. brochures, 1980-81, dir. category merchandising, 1981-82, group dir. motivational communications, 1982-83, group dir. sales promotion, 1983-84, v.p. sales promotion, 1984, v.p. internat. bus. devel., 1984-85, area v.p. Latin Am., 1985, v.p. advtg. and campaign mktg., 1985-87, v.p. U.S. operational planning, 1987; cons., 1987-88; sr. v.p. Burson-Marsteller, N.Y.C., 1988—; chairperson ann. meeting Direct Selling Assn., Washington, 1982; v.p. Nat. Home Fashions League, N.Y.C., 1975-76; bd. dirs. Double L.P. Industries, Inc., 1988—. Founding bd. mem. Am. Red Magen David for Israel, N.Y.C.,

1970-75; mem. adv. coun. Miami Sch. Bus., 1986—, Miami Sch. Applied Scis., 1978-81. Mem. Advt. Women of N.Y., Women in Communications, Miami U. Alumni Assn. (pres., chair 1986), Atrium club (N.Y.C.), Beta Gamma Sigma. Office: Burson-Marsteller 230 Park Ave S New York NY 10003

PERLMUTTER, DONNA, newspaper music and dance critic; b. Phila.; d. Myer and Bessie (Krasno) Stein; m. Jona Perlmutter, Mar. 21, 1964; children: Aaron, Matthew. B.A., Pa. State U., 1958; M.S., Yeshiva U., 1959. Music and dance critic Los Angeles Herald Examiner, 1975-84, Los Angeles Times, 1984—; dance critic Dance Mag., N.Y.C.; music critic Opera News, N.Y.C., 1981—, Ovation Mag., N.Y.C., 1983—; panelist, speaker various music and dance orgns. Mem. Music Critics Assn. Home: 10507 Le Conte Ave Los Angeles CA 90024

PERLMUTTER, MARION, psychology educator; b. N.Y.C., Sept. 2, 1948; d. Frank and Eleanor L. (Lifschutz) P. BA in Psychology, Syracuse (N.Y.) U., 1970; MS in Ednl. Psychology, SUNY, Albany, 1971; PhD in Devel. Psychology, U. Mass., 1976. Asst. prof., prof., assoc. dir. Inst. Child Devel. Mpls., 1976-84; vis. scholar Max Planck Inst. Psychol. Study, Munchen, Fed. Republic Germany, 1984; prof. dept. psychology, rsch. scientist Inst. Gerontology and Ctr. Human Growth and Devel., U. Mich., Ann Arbor, 1985—; vis. fellow Ctr. for Advanced Studies, Andrus Gerontology Ctr., U. So. Calif., 1986, Max Planck Inst., Berlin, 1987; advisor Russell Sage Com. on Organizational Time Tables and Life Span Perspectives, 1987, Nat. Inst. Aging, Behavioral and Social Sci. Adv. Com., 1986—; traveling exhbn. cons. Am. Psychol. Assn., 1989—; chairperson grant rev. NIH Human Devel. and Aging Study Sect., 1984-85, NIMH Small Grant Study Sect., 1980-82. Author: (with E. Hall and M. Lamb) Child Psychology Today, 1982, 2d edit., 1986; (with E. Hall) Adult Development and Aging, 1985; (with A. Clarke-Stewart & S. Freedman) Life Long Development, 1988; editor: New Directions in Child Development; Children's Memory, 1980, Development and Policy Concerning Children with Special Needs; Minnesota Symposium on Child Psychology, 1983, Cognitive Perspective on Children's Social and Behavioral Development: Minnesota Symposium on ChildPsychology, 1986. Named Young Woman scholar U. Minn., 1982, Nat. fellow Brookdale Found., 1985-88. Fellow Am. Psychol. Assn. (awards com., exec. com., membership com., program com. div 20), Am. Psychol. Soc., Gerontol Soc. Am. (program chair); mem. AAAS, Am. Ednl. Rsch. Assn., Cognitive Sci. Soc., Internat. Soc. for Study of Behavioral Devel. (program chair), Internat. Soc. Twin Studies, Merill-Palmer Soc., Psychonomic Soc., Soc. for Rsch. in Child Devel. (chair program sect.). Democrat. Jewish. Home: 503 Detroit St Apt 2 Ann Arbor MI 48104 Office: U Mich 300 N Ingalls Ann Arbor MI 48109-2007

PERLOWITZ, VALERIE WIENSLAW, information systems executive, consultant; b. Queens, N.Y., Feb. 10, 1962; d. Arthur Eugene and Natalia (Pasichnyk) Wienslaw; m. William Bryan Perlowitz, July 25, 1987. BSEE in Computer Engring., Northeastern U., 1986. Cert. engr.-in-tng., Mass. Simulation engr. Sikorsky Aircraft, Stratford, Conn., 1986-87; engr. Bite, Inc., Manassas, Va., 1987-88; cons. Aerotek, Inc., Reston, Va., 1988-89, Comsys, Inc., Rockville, Md., 1989; pres. Reliable Integration Svcs., Inc., Fairfax, Va., 1989—. Mem. IEEE, Computer Soc. of IEEE, NAFE, Art Deco Soc. of Wash., Fairfax C. of C. Office: Reliable Integration Svcs Inc 12309 Fox Lake Ct Fairfax VA 22033

PERLSTEIN, BRENDA, real estate broker; b. Barnegat, N.J., Mar. 8, 1942; d. Bruno and Nellie (Taylor) Agnoli; m. Harry Perlstein (dec. 1970); children—Diana, Lisa, Sari, Bruno Perlstein. Student Real Estate Sch., Atlantic City, 1962; grad. N.J. Sch. of Dramatic Art and Voice, Fairhaven. Real estate broker, N.J. Pres., Pearl Realty, Bradley Beach, N.J., 1980—. Writer for local newspapers; also does voiceovers on commls. and radio. Mem. Nat. Bd. Realtors, N.J. Bd. Realtors, Monmouth County Bd. Realtors. Republican. Address: 704 Main St Asbury Park NJ 07712 also: Box 413 Bradley Beach NJ 07720

PERMAR, MARY ELIZABETH, real estate investor; b. Augusta, Ga., Mar. 18, 1956; d. Philip Howard and Doris (Maxwell) P. BS in Architecture, Clemson U., 1978; MArch, U. Ill., 1981, MBA, 1982. V.p., sec., treas. Assn. Student Chpts., AIA, Washington, 1978-79; with The Prudential Realty Group, 1982—; investment mgr. The Prudential Realty Group, Chgo., 1982-85; dir. acquisitions and sales The Prudential Realty Group, Newark, 1985-87; dir. acquisitions The Prudential Realty Group, Chgo., 1988—. Mng. editor CRIT The Archtl. Student Jour., 1978-79. Tutor Program for Underprivileged Children, Chgo., 1982-85; trustee Chgo. Acad. of Sci. Charles G. Rummel fellow U. Ill. Sch. Architecture, 1979-82. Mem. Nat. Assn. Indsl. and Office Pks., Execs. Club Chgo., Western Soc. Engrs. Republican. Presbyterian.

PERNICK, SANDRA ROSE, business executive; b. Chgo., Oct. 7, 1944; d. Karl and Diana (Matlin) Witt; m. Steven L. Pernick, Oct. 11, 1964; children—Kevin Michael, Kelly Andrew. B.A., Roosevelt U., Chgo., 1964. Corr. Time, Inc., 1964-66; tchr. emotionally handicapped children Chgo. Pub. Schs., 1966-68; pres. bd. dirs Orchard Village, Skokie, Ill., 1976—; pres. Direct Response Corp., Des Plaines, Ill., 1981-89; cons. Nat. Telemarketing, 1990—. Mem. mental health com. Nat. Council Jewish Women. Am. Telemarketing Assn. (bd. dirs. 1986—, pres. 1988), Chgo. Assn. Direct Mktg. (legis. com. 1986—), Nat. Assn. Retarded Citizens, Ill. Assn. Retarded Citizens.

PERNSTEINER, CAROL ANN, hotel executive; Mar. 16, Medford, Wis.; d. Alvin Anton and Lillian Therese (Spreen) P. BA, Marquette U., 1969. With The Sheraton Corp., 1971—; front office mgr. Sheraton Washington, D.C., 1979-81, resident mgr. Sheraton Hotel, St. Louis, 1981-88, gen. mgr., 1988—; Capt. Op. Brightside, St. Louis, 1984-86. Recipient Pres.'s award The Sheraton Corp., Washington, 1979, Divisional Pres.'s award St. Louis, 1985. Mem. Hotel and Motel Assn. Greater St. Louis (bd. dirs.), Mo. Hotel and Motel Assn. (bd. dirs.), Mo. Athletic Club, Downtown St. Louis Inc. (bd. dirs.). Republican. Avocations: violin, piano. Home: 428 Carswold Dr Clayton MO 63105 Office: Sheraton St Louis Hotel 910 N 7th St Saint Louis MO 63101

PERRAULT, DOROTHY ANN JACQUES, small business owner, nurse; b. New Orleans, Aug. 25, 1937; d. Alvin Joseph and Dorothy (Angelety) Jacques; m. Harry Joseph Perrault Jr., Oct. 24, 1959; children: Harry J. Perrault III, TroyLynne Ahmed, Sabrina. BSN, Dillard U., 1960. RN. Head nurse Sara Mayo Hosp., New Orleans, 1960; supr. Flint Goodridge Hosp., New Orleans, 1960-64; relief supr. Charity Hosp., New Orleans, 1964-69, nursing instr., 1969-70, supr., 1970-71, 1971-77, asst. dir., 1969-77; owner, pres. Perrault Kiddy Kollege, Inc., New Orleans, 1972—; pres. Deli Deluxe Catering Service, The Fashion Korner, New Orleans; bd. dirs. Coalition Child Care New Orleans, Nat. Assn. for Edn. Children, New Orleans, La. Fedn. Child Care, New Orleans; 1st v.p. Bayou Fed. Savs. & Loan Assn., 1980-87; mem. adv. bd. First Fed. Bank of New Orleans. Editor, chief of yearbooks and many orgnl. souvenir booklets; composer, dir., producer, stage mgr. children's theatrical plays. Bd. dirs. Am. Security Coun., New Orleans, 1979—, Pvt. Industry Coun., New Orleans, United Negro Coll. Fund, New Orleans, 1986—; mem. exec. com. La. League Good Govt., New Orleans, 1979; past pres. Nurses' Fedn. Charity Hosp.; 2 mayoral appointments Pvt. Industry Coun. and Bldg. Commn., 1984-88. Recipient Thomas Jefferson award Am. Inst. for Pub. Svc., 1978, award for achievement in child care Mayor of New Orleans, 1972—, La. Gov.'s award, 1983, 86, award La. Sec. of State, 1985, La. Sec. Commerce, 1985, Headstart program Total Community Action; named Disting. Alumni, Dillard U., 1985, One of Outstanding Bus. Women of Yr., Women in Forefront, 1986, numerous others. Mem. NAACP (life), Nat. Assn. Women (life), Friends of Armistead (life), AAUW, Dillard U. Profl. Orgn. Nurses (pres. 1988), Dillard U. Nat. Alumni Assn. (pres. 1981-83, founder perpetual scholarship fund), NAFE, Nat. Assn. Mgrs., New Orleans C. of C., Nat. Black Bus. League, Nat. Assn. Negro Bus. and Profl. Women's Club (Bus. Woman of Yr. award 1988), Nat. Coun. Negro Women (Presdl. award 1989), Zeta Phi Beta, Phi Delta Kappa (outstanding svc. award Theta chpt. 1989). Democrat. Roman Catholic. Club: Estelle Hubbard. Lodge: Knights of Peter Claver. Office: Perrault Kiddy Kollege Perrault Pla 6201 Chef Menteur Hwy New Orleans LA 70126

PERRAULT, PATSY ANN, advertising agency executive; b. Darrouzett, Tex., Mar. 30, 1939; d. Carson Lee and Mamie (Allen) Altmiller; m. Ronald Ray Weaver, Sept. 3, 1960 (div. July 1979); children: Leanne Weaver, Douglas Weaver; m. Thomas Burt Perrault, July 25, 1981. B.S., West Tex. State U., 1961, M.A., 1964. Program dir. Sta. KFMK, Houston, 1971-74; media buyer McCann-Ericksen, Houston, 1974-77; media planner Smith, Smith, Baldwin & Carlberg, Houston, 1977-78; media supr. Rives Smith, Baldwin & Carlberg, Houston, 1978-80; media mgr. Houston Coca-Cola Bottling, 1980-81; v.p., media dir. W. B. Doner, Houston, 1981-83; ptnr., exec. v.p. Taylor Brown & Barnhill (name changed to Taylor, Brown, Smith & Perrault 1989). Mem. adv. bd. bus. mktg. dept. Stephen F. Austin U. Mem. Houston Advt. Fedn., Assn. Women Radio & TV, Alpha Delta Pi. Republican. Mem. Assembly of God Ch.

PERREAULT, SISTER JEANNE, college administrator; b. Providence, Dec. 13, 1929; d. Alphonse and Malvina I. (Chevalier) P. BSEd, Cath. Tchrs. Coll., Providence, 1959; MS, Cath. U., Washington, 1968; EdD (hon.), Salve Regina Coll., Newport, R.I., 1990. Tchr. elem. sch. St. Ann Sch., West Warwick, R.I.; tchr. jr. high sch. St. John Jr. High Sch., West Warwick; tchr. high sch. Notre Dame High Sch., Berlin, N.H.; assoc. prof. Rivier Coll., Nashua, N.H., pres., 1980—; mem. Gov.'s Task Force for Edn. Mem. State of N.H. Post-Secondary Edn. Commn., Concord, Govs. Task Force Edn., New Hampshire. Mem. AAUP, Am. Coun. Colls., Assn. Cath. Colls. and Univs., New Eng. Assn. Chemistry Tchrs., N.H. Coll. and Univ. Coun.

PERRETTA, NANCY VROOMAN, medical insurance company representative; b. Oneonta, N.Y., Oct. 17, 1940; d. Harold Clute and Beatrice Evelyn (Thomas) Vrooman; m. Francis A. Perretta, Nov. 17, 1962; 1 child, Helenarose. Student, Stetson U., 1958-59; BA, Keuka Coll., 1962; postgrad., Wroxton (Eng.) Abbey, 1970; MS in Edn., SUNY, Oneonta, 1973. Editor women's news Daily Star, Oneonta, 1958; tchr. elem. grades Oneonta Pub. Schs., 1962-63, Cooperstown (N.Y.) Cen. Schs., 1965-66, Oneonta Jr. High Sch., 1966-78; dir. women's news Sta. WDOS, Oneonta, 1964-65; sales rep. Met. Life Ins. Co., Traverse City, Mich., 1978-80; account exec. Devoe Ins. Agy., New Milford, Conn., 1980-82, Crowe Ins. Agy., Stroudsburg, Pa., 1982-85; mktg. rep. Blue Cross Northeast Pa., Stroudsburg, 1985—; area news reporter Sta. WNBF-TV, Binghamton, N.Y., 1964-65. Bd. dirs. Ctr. for Devel. Disabilities, Stroudsburg, 1986-88; v.p. Pocono Raceway Ambs., Stroudsburg, 1988—; pres. Monroe unit Am. Cancer Soc., Stroudsburg, 1988-90. Mem. Nat. Assn. Females Execs., Pocono Mtns. C. of C. (bd. dirs. 1986—), Exec. Women's Coun. (co-chmn. 1987—), LWV (past bd. dirs. Oneonta and Stroudsburg). Republican. Roman Catholic. Clubs: Torch, Shawnee Country, Glen Brook Country (Stroudsburg). Home: Rd 4 PO Box 4006 Stroudsburg Pa 18360 Office: Blue Cross Northeast Pa 912 Main St Stroudsburg PA 18360

PERREWÉ, PAMELA LYNN, management consulting educator, researcher; b. Oak Park, Ill., Dec. 22, 1955; d. George and Lois Mae (Chadburn) P.; m. Frank Andrew Vickory, Apr. 20, 1985; children: Erin, Jenny, Andrew. Ba, Purdue U., 1978; MA, U. Nebr., 1980, PhD in Bus. Adminstrn., 1985. Assoc. prof. mgmt. Fla. State U., Tallahassee, 1984—. Guest editor: Jour. of Social Behavior & Personality, 1990—; contbr. articles to profl. jours. McKnight fellow Fla. Endowment Fund, 1989-90. Mem. Acad. of Mgmt., Am. Psychol. Assn., Beta Gamma Sigma. Home: 4943 Shannon Lakes E Tallahassee FL 32308 Office: Fla State U Coll of Bus Tallahassee FL 32306

PERRICK, CYNTHIA ALICE, bank officer; b. Sanford, Fla., Aug. 15, 1962; d. Frederick Jr. and Ethel Alice (Hoffman) P. AA, Daytona Beach Community Coll., 1981; BBA, Stetson U., 1988, postgrad., 1989—. Community desk coord. The News-Jour. Corp., DeLand, Fla., 1980-88; mgmt. assoc. Barnett Bank of Volusia County, DeLand, 1988-89; asst. v.p., comml. loan officer Barnett Bank of Volusia County, Ormond Beach, Fla., 1990—. Sec. Volusia Literacy Coun., Daytona Beach, Fla., 1988-89, bd. dirs., 1988-90; v.p., tutor West Volusia Literacy Coun., DeLand, 1987; charter mem. New Directions of Am. Cancer Soc., DeLand, 1989-90. Mem. DeLand Bus. and Profl. Women's Club (v.p. 1987-88, pres. 1988-89). Republican. Episcopalian. Home: 927 Marlboro Dr DeLand FL 32724 Office: Barnett Bank Volusia County 902 S Atlantic Ave Ormond Beach FL 32176

PERRIN, SARAH ANN, lawyer; b. Neoga, Ill., Dec. 13, 1904; d. James Lee and Bertha Frances (Baker) Figenbaum; LL.B., George Washington U., 1941, J.D., 1964; m. James Frank Perrin, Dec. 24, 1926. Bar: D.C. 1942. Assoc. atty. Mabel Walker Willebrandt, law office, Washington, 1941-42; atty. various fed. housing agys., 1942-69, asst. gen. counsel FHA, Washington, 1959-60, asst. gen. counsel HUD, Washington, 1960-69; sec. Nat. Housing Conf., Washington, 1970-80; rsch. cons. housing and urban devel., Palmyra, Va., 1970-76 ; acting sec. Nat. Housing Rsch. Coun., Washington, 1973-80; bd. dirs. Nat. Housing Conf., 1972—. Trustee Found. for Coop. Housing, 1975-80 ; mem. Blue Ridge Presbytery Div. Mission, Presbyn. Ch., 1979-80. Mem. ABA, Fed. Bar Assn., Women's Bar Assn. D.C. (pres. 1959-60), Nat. Assn. Women Lawyers, George Washington Law Assn., Charlottesville Area Women's Bar Assn., Fluvanna County Bar Assn., Phi Alpha Delta (internat. pres. 1955-57), Fluvanna County Hist. Soc. (pres. 1973-75, exec. com. 1985-89), Order Eastern Star. Home: Solitude Plantation Palmyra VA 22963

PERRINE, LYNN MARIE, health educator, nurse, insurance company professional; b. Cleve., Sept. 7, 1949; d. Scott Emerson and Mary Jane (Hocevar) Balmer; 1 child, Corinne Elizabeth; m. Donald Blair Perrine, Dec. 17, 1988. Student, U. Miami (Fla.), U. Wis., Oshkosh, 1967-68; AA, Miami-Dade Community Coll., 1974; diploma, Jackson Meml.Hosp.Sch. Nursing, Miami, 1975; student, Nova U. R.N. Staff nurse, SICU Jackson Meml. Hosp., Miami, 1975; staff nurse, asst. head nurse dialysis unit Luth. Med. Ctr., Miami, 1976-77; pvt. duty nurse Medox, Inc., Miami, 1978-79; staff nurse Am. Hosp., Miami, 1978-79, Bapt. Hosp. Miami, Inc., 1981-84; telemarketing specialist Solar Oriented Environ. Systems, Inc., Miami, 1984-85; sales rep. Complete Med. Svc., Dade County, Fla., 1985; dir. health promotion and wellness John Alden Life Ins. Co., Miami, 1985—; wellness cons., Burger King Corp., Miami, 1984-85, others; speaker, presenter, panelist in field; project reviewer, HHS, 1988—, Healthy People 2000; adv. com., Good Health is Good Bus. program, March of Dimes, Miami, 1986-87; exec. dir. Am. Health Resources Assn., 1990. Contbr. articles to newsletters. Mem. Soc. Prospective Medicine (bd. dirs.), Nat. Assn. Ins. Commrs. (past mem. health promotion and chem. abuse task force 1987), Wellness Coun. South Fla., Healthy Am. Fitness Leaders Assn. Republican. Home: 10017 SW 139th Pl Miami FL 33186 Office: John Alden Life Ins Co 7300 Corporate Ctr Dr Miami FL 33126-1208

PERRIS, ELIZABETH L., federal judge; b. 1951. AB, U. Calif.; JD, U. Calif., Davis. Admitted to bar, 1976. Bankruptcy judge U.S. Dist. Ct. Oreg. Office: US Dist Ct 900 Orbanco Bldg 1001 SW 5th Ave Portland OR 97204*

PERRONE, SUSANNE SAELI, advertising executive; b. Rochester, N.Y., Mar. 28, 1953; d. Anthony Joseph and Louise (Lynett) Saeli; m. John Joseph Perrone Jr., Aug. 20, 1982. Student, St. Bonaventure U., 1971-73; BS in Mktg., U. Colo., 1975. Advt., sales promotion mgr. First Fed. Savs. & Loan Assn., Rochester, 1976-80; v.p., gen. mgr. Arnold & Co., Inc., Rochester, 1980-87; pres. Perrone & Assocs., Rochester, 1987-88; v.p., mgmt. supr. Blair Advt., Rochester, 1988—; bd. dirs. Advt. Council of Rochester, Mktg. Communicators of Rochester, Blair Advt. Mem. Reserve Officers Assn. Ladies, Rochester, 1984—, Jr. League of Rochester, 1985—; adv. bd. Strong Childrens Med. Ctr., 1988—. Office: Blair Advt 96 College Ave Rochester NY 14607

PERRY, ANNA HAAS, programmer analyst; b. Salisbury, N.C., Aug. 28, 1943; d. William F. and Thelma A. (Haas) Peeler; m. Oliver H. Perry II, Mar. 19, 1961 (div. 1982); 1 child, Cathryn Anne. Student, Temple U., 1962. Programmer analyst UNISYS System Devel. Corp., McLean, Va., 1972-87; prin. programmer analyst Computer Based Systems Inc., Fairfax, Va., 1987—. CPR instr. ARC, Fairfax, 1980-87; adv. com. Franconia (Va.) Dist. Police, 1980-82; pres. Monticello Woods Civic Assn. Republican.

Presbyterian. Home: 8212 Cooper St Alexandria VA 22309 Office: Computer Based Systems Inc 2750 Prosperity Ave Ste 300 Fairfax VA 22031

PERRY, ANNE MARIE LITCHFIELD, educator; b. LaJunta, Colo., May 20, 1943; d. Robert Silas and Anne (Kennedy) Hovey; m. Franklin Haile Perry, Dec. 21, 1968; children: Kristina Marie, Tad Kennedy. BEd, Drake U., 1966; MA, U. Tex., 1969; PhD, Tex. A&M U., 1977. Grade sch. tchr., San Antonio, 1966-67, Austin, 1967-68; rsch. assoc. R & D. Ctr., U. Tex., Austin, 1968; grad. asst., instr. Tex. A&M U., 1969-70; kindergarten tchr., 1970-72; instr. U. St. Thomas, 1973-74; spl. edn. tchr., supr. Cypress-Fairbanks Ind. Sch. Dist., Houston, 1974-77, supr. gifted/talented, bilingual, English lang. devel. programs, 1977-80; mem. adj. grad. faculty U. Houston, 1979-80; lower sch. dir. curriculum and ednl. resources Kinkaid Sch., Houston, 1980-86, dir. young writers workshops, 1985—; tchr., chairperson lang. arts dept. Klein (Tex.) Intermediate Sch. Dist., 1986—; cons. gifted/talented edn., 1978—, teaching of writing, 1985—; vis. asst. prof. Tex. A&M U., 1988, 89. Author, photographer: Riders Ready, 1985; editor: Travels in Mexico and California (A.B. Clarke), 1988. Named Tchr. of Yr., Hancock Elem. Sch., 1975. Mem. NEA, Nat. Coun. for the Social Studies, Nat. Coun. Teachers of English, Assn. Supervision and Curriculum Devel., Tex. Coun. Social Studies, Tex. Assn. for Gifted and Talented, Tex. Computer Educators Assn., Tex. Joint Council of Tchrs. of English, Tex. State Tchrs. Assn., Tex. State Reading Assn. Presbyterian.

PERRY, ANNE WATERS, home economics educator; b. Rebecca, Ga., Feb. 12, 1933; d. Thomas McArthur and Emmie Louise (Haynie) Waters; m. Charles Eugene Perry, July 25, 1954; children: Connie, Cathy, Cindy, Chuck. BS, Ga. State Coll. for Women, 1954; M of Home Econs., U. Ga., 1961. Tchr. home econs. Bacon County, Alma, Ga., 1954-56, Berrian County, Nashville, Ga., 1956-67; tchr. elem. sch. Jefferson (Ga.) City Sch. System, 1957-58; tchr. home econs. Winder (Ga.) City System, 1958-60; tchr. secondary sch. Burke County, Midville, Ga., 1962-63, tchr. elem. sch., 1964, county extension agt., 1965—. Dir. Burke County 4-H Activities, Waynesbor, 1965-89; vice-chairperson Burke County Bd. Edn., 1985-89; adminstrv. chairperson Midville Meth. Ch. Mem. Nat. Assn. Extension Home Economists (disting. svc. award 1979), Am. Home Econs. Assn., Ga. Home Econs. Assn., Ga. Assn. Extension 4-H Agts. (bd. dirs. 1986-87, award 1986), Ga. Assn. Extension Home Economists (sec. 1986, disting. svc. award 1977), Ga. Home Econs. Assn., Nat. Assn. Extension 4-H Agts., Midville Woman's Club (pres.), Midville Garden (pres.), Town and Country Woman's Club, Epsilon Sigma Phi (past. pres., disting. svc. award). Democrat. Home: Rt 1 PO Box 146 Midville GA 30441 Office: Coop Extension Service Burke County Office Park W 6th St Waynesboro GA 30830

PERRY, BRENDA L., college administrator; b. New Bedford, Mass., Nov. 8, 1948; d. Frank Andrade and Mary Mendes; m. Clyde L. Perry, Jan. 18, 1965; children: Lisa Marie, Scott Anthony. AA, Middlesex Community Coll., Bedford, Mass., 1975; MA, Goddard Coll., 1977; BA, Stonehill Coll., 1981. Cert. alcohol and drug addiction counselor. Social worker Dorchester Child Devel. Ctr., Boston, 1971-75; coord. Mass. Advocacy Ctr., Boston, 1975-76; asst. dir. Roxbury Multi Svcs. Girls Residential Treatment Ctr., Boston, 1976-78, Commonwealth of Mass. Female Svcs. Dept. Youth, Boston, 1978-81; monitor evaluator Commonwealth of Mass. Dept. Social Svc., Boston, 1981-83; asst. dir. admissions Rollins Coll., Winter Park, Fla., 1983—. Poetry pub. in 1988 Anthology of Poems, Am. Poetry Assn. Bd. dirs. Seminole County Mental Health Assn., Altamonte Springs, Fla., 1983-85. Mem. Nat. Assn. of Wildlife Fedn., Smithsonian Inst., Nat. Arbor Day Found., Nat. Assn. of Black Sch. Educators, Nat. Assn. Coll. Admission Counselors, Nat. Assn. Fgn. Students, So. Assn. Coll. Admission Counselors. Democrat. Mem. Theosophical Soc. Home: 1310 Palm Dr Apopka FL 32703 Office: Rollins College Holt Ave Winter Park FL 32789

PERRY, CARRIE SAXON, mayor, former state representative; b. Hartford, Conn.. Student, Howard U. Mayor, City of Hartford, Conn.; former State rep. 7th Assembly Dist. (Conn.); exec. dir. Amistad House Inc., Conn.; adminstr. Community Renewal Team of Greater Hartford, Ambulatory Health Care Planning Inc., Hartford, Hartford Community Trainers, Conn. Welfare Dept.; mem. Exec. Bd. Greater Hartford Black Dems.; regional dir. Nat. Orgn. Black Elected Women Legislators, Nat. Black Caucus of State Legislators; corporator Oak Hill Sch. for the Blind, Hartford Pub. Library, Conn. Black and Hispanic Urban Inst.; mem. steering com. Our Neighborhood and St. Monica's Bldg. Fund; nominating chair permanent com. status Hartford Women, Fed. Dem. Women. Named Women of Yr. YMCA; recipient Outstanding Community Service award Black People's Union U. Hartford. Mem. NAACP (life), Nat. Orgn. 100 Black Women (pres. Hartford chpt.). Home: PO Box 3989 Old State House Sta Hartford CT 06103 Office: 550 Main St Hartford CT 06103*

PERRY, CYNTHIA NORTON SHEPARD, diplomat; b. Terre Haute, Ind., Nov. 11, 1928; d. George William and Flossie (Phillips) N.; m. George William Noton; m. 2d, James O. Shepard, Nov. 2, 1946 (div. June 1970); children: Donna Ross, James O. Jr., Milo Kent, Mark; m. 3d, James O. Perry Sr., Mar. 20, 1971; children: Paula Lucille, James O. Jr. BS in Polit. Sci., Ind. State U., 1967, DCL (hon.), 1987; EdD, U. Mass., 1972; LLD (hon.), U. Md., 1984. Sec. Nichols Investment Corp., Terre Haute, 1956-61; ednl. rep. Ohio region IBM Corp., Terre Haute, 1962-68; dir. tchrs. corps U. Mass., Amherst, 1968-71; assoc. prof. edn. Tex. So. U., Houston, 1971-74, dean internat. student affairs, 1978-82; cons., lectr., U. Nairobi U.S. Peace Corps, Kenya, 1974-76; staff devel. officer UN Econ. Com. for Africa, Addis Ababa, Ethiopia, 1976-78; chief edn. and human resource div. Agy. for Internat. Devel., Washington, 1982-86; U.S. amb. to Sierra Leone Freetown, 1986-89; U.S. amb. to Burundi Bujumbura, 1989—. Contbr. articles to profl. jours. Recipient Disting. Alumni award U. Mass., 1981, Ind. State U., 1987. Mem. Nat. Bus. and Profl. Women, Internat. Council for Ednl. Devel. (bd. dirs. 1984-86), Altrusan Soc. (bd. dirs. 1981-82), Delta Sigma Theta (pres. Houston chpt. 1982-83). Republican. Office: Am Embassy/Burundi Dept State 2201 C St NW Washington DC 20521-2100

PERRY, DIANNE FOSTER, marketing professional; b. Griffin, Ga., Apr. 11, 1948; d. Durward Lee and Bobbie Marie (Piper) G.; m. Steve Michael, Mar. 12, 1983. AA, Gordon Jr. Coll., 1968; BBA, U. Ga., 1970. Customer svc. rep. C&S Nat. Bank, Atlanta, 1971-73; consumer sales rep. Borden, Inc., Atlanta, 1973-75; mgr. of direct sales Best Food Div. CPC Internat, Atlanta, 1975—. Corp. Fundraising Com. Atlanta Dogwood Festival; active Mothers' March of Dimes, 1987-90. Mem. Food Mfr. Sales Exec. Club Atlanta (past pres.), Toastmistress Club, Atlanta Women's C. of C. Republican. Methodist. Home: 2478 Big Creek Ter Stone Mountain GA 30087 Office: 6055 Atlantic Blvd Ste F-1 Norcross GA 30071

PERRY, HOPE CRAIG, physician; b. Ft. MacPherson, Ga., Aug. 4, 1929; d. Frederick Stephen and Peggy (Lathem) Craig; m. Roger Hobart Perry, May 18, 1957; children: Elizabeth Hope, Stephen Roger. BA, Smith Coll., 1950; MD, Columbia U., 1954. Diplomate Am. Bd. Pediatrics. Asst. pediatrics, fellow The N.Y. Hosp., Cornell Med. Ctr., N.Y.C., 1955-58; pediatrician Tomp County Health Dept., Ithaca, N.Y., 1960-75; dir. Spl. Children's Ctr., Ithaca, 1962-65; med. dir. Planned Parenthood Tomp County, Ithaca, 1976-80; dep. dir. Cornell U. Health Svcs., Ithaca, 1980—; counselor health svcs. Tomp County Bd. Health, 1983—, Smith Coll. Northampton, Mass. 1987—. Mem. Soc. Adolescent Medicine, Am. Acad. Pediatricians, Am. Venereal Disease Assn., N.Am. Soc. for Pediatric and Adolescent Gynecology, Tomp County Med. Soc. (v.p., pres., sec. 1983-89). Office: Cornell U Health Svcs 10 Central Ave Ithaca NY 14853

PERRY, JACQUELIN, orthopedic surgeon; b. Denver, May 31, 1918; d. John F. and Tirzah (Kuruptkat) P. B.E., U. Calif., Los Angeles, 1940; M.D., U. Calif., San Francisco, 1950. Intern Children's Hosp., San Francisco, 1950-57; resident in orthopedic surgery U. Calif., San Francisco, 1951-55; orthopedic surgeon Rancho Los Amigos Hosp., Downey, Calif., 1955—; chief pathokinesiology Rancho Los Amigos Hosp. Med. Ctr., 1967—; chief stroke service Rancho Los Amigos Hosp., 1972-75; mem. faculty U. Calif. Med. Sch., San Francisco 1966—; clin. prof. U. Calif. Med. Sch., 1973—; mem. faculty U. So. Calif. Med. Sch., 1969—; prof. orthopedic surgery, 1972—; dir. polio and gait clinic, 1972—; Disting. lectr. for hosp. for spl. surgery and Cornell U. Med. Coll., N.Y.C., 1977-78; Packard Meml. lectr. U. Colo. Med. Sch., 1970; Osgood lectr. Harvard Med. Sch., 1978; Sumner

lectr., Portland, 1977; cons. USAF; guest speaker symposia; cons. Biomechanics Lab. Centinela Hosp., 1979—. Served as phys. therapist U.S. Army, 1941-46. Recipient Disting. Service award Calif. Assn. Rehab. Facilities, 1981, Pres.' award, 1984; Isabelle and Lenard Goldensen award for tech. United Cerebral Palsy Assns., 1981, Joe Dowling award, 1985, Profl. Achievement award UCLA, 1988, Amistad award Rancho Los Amigos Med. Ctr., Calif., 1990; named Woman of Year for Medicine in So. Calif. L.A. Times, 1959; Alumnus of Year U. Calif. Med. Sch., 1980. Mem. Am. Acad. Orthopedic Surgeons (Kappa Delta award for rsch. 1977), Am. Orthopedic Assn. (Shanks lectr. 1988), Western Orthopedic Assn., AMA, Calif., L.A. County med. socs., Am. Phys. Therapy Assn. (hon. Golden Pen award 1965), Am. Acad. Orthotists and Prosthetists (hon.), Scoliosis Rsch. Soc., LeRoy Abbott Soc., Am. Acad. Cerebral Palsy. Home: 12319 Brock Ave Downey CA 90242 Office: Rancho Los Amigos Med Ctr 7601 E Imperial Hwy Downey CA 90242

PERRY, JEAN LOUISE, educator; b. Richland, Wash., May 13, 1950; d. Russell S. and Sue W. Perry. BS, Miami U., Oxford, Ohio, 1972; MS, U. Ill., Urbana, 1973, PhD, 1976. Cons. ednl. placement office U. Ill., 1973-75; adminstrv. intern Coll. Applied Life Studies, 1975-76, asst. dean, 1976-77, assoc. dean, 1978-81, asst. prof. dept. phys. edn., 1976-81; assoc. prof. phys. edn. San Francisco State U., 1981-84, prof., 1984—, chmn. dept., 1981—. Named to excellent tchr. list U. Ill., 1973-79. Mem. AAHPERD (fellow research consortium, pres. 1988-89), Am. Assn. Higher Edn., Am. Ednl. Research Assn., Nat. Assn. Phys. Edn. in Higher Edn., Nat. Assn. Girls and Women in Sports (guide coordinator, pres.), Delta Psi Kappa, Phi Delta Kappa. Home: 3216 Sun Valley Ave Walnut Creek CA 94596 Office: San Francisco State U Dept Physical Edn 1600 Holloway Ave San Francisco CA 94131

PERRY, JOAN ANNE, investment company executive; b. Chgo., Mar. 1, 1951; d. Anthony John and Harriet (McGirr) P. BA in Biology, Denison U., 1973; MBA in Fin., Vanderbilt U., 1975. Mgr. nat. credit dept. N.C. Nat. Bank, Charlotte, 1975-77; investment banker Elkins & Co., Phila., 1977-82; devel. Barness Orgn., Phila., 1982-83; investment banker Alex Brown & Sons, Phila., 1984-85; pres. Perry Investments, Inc., Saratoga, Calif., 1985—; bd. dirs. Rotocare-Next Door, San Jose Repertory Theater. Bd. dirs. Frankford (Pa.) Hosp., 1986—. Mem. Rotary. Episcopalian. Office: Perry Investments Inc 1821 Saratoga Ave Ste 205 Saratoga CA 95070

PERRY, JOYCE LEE, real estate appraiser; b. Thomasville, N.C., May 1, 1945; d. Wesley Sherrill and Dorothy Mae (Hilton) Wood; m. John Roy Perry, Jr., Sept. 12, 1976. B, Ashemore Bus. Coll., 1964. Bookkeeper Brokers, Inc., Thomasville, 1964-72; payroll and bookkeeping Myrtle Desk Co., High Point, N.C., 1972-77, Car-Del Furniture, High Point, 1977-79; real estate appraiser Perry Appraisals, Thomasville, 1979—. Mem. N.C. Assn. Realtors, Nat. Assn. Realtors, Thomasville Bd. Realtors, Nat. Assn. Review Appraisers, Am. Assn. Cert. Appraisers, Internat. Inst. Valuers. Democrat. Methodist. Home and Office: 802 Lakeview Dr Thomasville NC 27360

PERRY, JUDITH LAURA, real estate company executive; b. Somerville, N.J., Sept. 1, 1939; d. Lambert E. Locke and Ruth Louise (Belles) Locke Baillie Thomas; m. Vincent Perry, Jan. 18, 1963 (div. 1967); children: Deborah, Alan, Lisa. With Pathmark Grocery Stores, Plainfield, N.J., 1961; sec. Kirby Sales, Scotch Plains, N.J., 1961-62, Howell Motors, Plainfield, 1967-68; real estate agt., then broker T.J. Bojum, North Plainfield, N.J., 1968-75; real estate broker, agt. Pioneer Agy., Martinsville, N.J., 1975-86, mgr., 1979-86; broker, owner Re/Max Preferred Profls., Bridgewater, N.J., 1986—. Mem. Nat. Assn. Realtors, N.J. Assn. Realtors (Million Dollar Sales Club), Somerset County Bd. Realtors, Morris County Bd. Realtors, Middlesex County Bd. Realtors, Hunterdon County Bd. Realtors. Office: Re/Max Preferred Profls 1311 Prince Rodgers Ave Bridgewater NJ 08807

PERRY, JULIA KAY, financial analyst; b. Rocksprings, Tex., Aug. 7, 1960; d. Paul Frederick and Gladys Regina (Hackl) P. Student, Rice U., 1977-80; BA in Musicology, SUNY, Albany, 1983; MBA in Fin., Rollins Coll., 1988. Lease analyst May Petroleum, Inc., Dallas, 1980-81; video libr. Warner Cable Communications, Dallas, 1981-82; beauty advisor Estee Lauder, Austin, Tex., 1984-86; fin. cons. Attys. Legal Svcs., Inc., Orlando, Fla., 1987-89; dir. info. systems Buddy MacKay for U.S. Senate, Orlando, 1988; adminstrv. asst. to campaign mgr. Hugh Parmer for U.S. Senate, Austin, Tex., 1989; acct., fin. analyst Mgmt. Co., Austin, 1989—; tech. mktg. cons. Schwartz Electo-Optics, Inc., Orlando, 1988-89. Vocalist Austin Choral Union; chmn. grants and fundraising com. Bach Festival Soc., Winter Park, Fla., 1987-89; bd. dirs., sec. Orlando Theatre Project, 1989; chmn. fin. com., bd. dirs. Orange County Dem. Com., 1988-89; mem. Dem. Leadership Coun. Network, Washington, 1989. Corp. Coun. scholar, 1986-88. Mem. Nat. Assn. Woman Cos., Word Perfect Support Group. Episcopalian. Office: Mgmt Co 1106 Clayton Ln Ste 400W Austin TX 78273

PERRY, KIMBERLY JEAN, environmental engineer; b. Meadville, Pa., Mar. 8, 1955; d. Robert Russell and Nancy Jean (Maurer) P.; m. Charles B. Manley, Oct. 17, 1987. BA, Vassar Coll., 1977; MS, Va. Poly. Inst. and State U., 1979. Engr. Sverdrup & Parcel & Assocs., Inc., St. Louis, 1979-81; quality assurance auditor Monsanto Co., St. Louis, 1981-86, sr. environ. engr., 1986-89; environ. specialist Monsanto Krummrich Plant, Sauget, Ill., 1989—. V.P., 1st Unitarian Ch., St. Louis, 1985-86, pres., 1986-87. Recipient Monsanto Achievement award, 1989; US EPA fellow, 1978-79. Mem. Am. Chem. Soc., Water Pollution Control Fedn., Soc. Women Engrs. Office: Monsanto Krummrich Plant 500 Monsanto Ave Sauget IL 62206

PERRY, MARGARET N., academic administrator; b. Waynesboro, Tenn., Apr. 23, 1940; m. Randy L. Perry; 2 children. BS in Home Econs., U. Tenn., Martin, 1961; MS in Nutrition, U. Tenn., Knoxville, 1963, PhD in Nutrition and Food Sci., 1965. NDEA fellow depts. food sci. and nutrition U. Tenn., Knoxville, 1961-64, part-time instr. dept. food sci. Coll. Home Econs., 1963-64, asst. prof. food sci. and food systems adminstrn., asst. to dean, 1966-68, asst. dean Coll. Home Econs., 1967-68, assoc. dean, 1968-73, dean for grad. studies, assoc. prof., 1973-79; assoc. v.p. for acad. affairs Tenn. Tech. U., 1979-86, dir. Joe L. Evins Appalachian Ctr. for Crafts, 1982-83; chancellor U. Tenn., Martin, 1986—; mem. exec. com. Council Grad. Schs. in U.S., Washington, 1974-77, chair nominating com., 1977; mem. exec. com. So. Conf. Grad. Schs., 1975-78; bd. dirs. Knoxville Early Child Devel. Ctr., 1975-78, corr. sec., 1976-77; apptd. mem. team Am. educators to visit and study univs. in Iraq, 1977; mem. Tenn. planning com. Identification Women in Higher Edn. Programs, Am. Council on Edn., 1978-86, chair, 1979-81, mem. Nat. Forum on Women in Higher Edn., Athens, Ga., 1978, mem. Commn. on Women in Higher Edn., Washington, 1979-82, resource person Nat. Forum on Women in Higher Edn., Princeton, N.J., 1981; rep. to N.E. U. Tech., Shenyang, Peoples Republic China, 1984; mem. internat. com. Am. Assn. State Colls. and Univs., 1986—; ofcl. visit and renewal sister univ. agreement Hirosaki U., Japan, 1989, English tng. Konohana-Gakuen High Sch., 1989; lectr. in field. Mem. editorial bd.: Grad. Programs and Admissions Manual, 1975-78; contbr. articles to profl. publs. Mem. U. Tenn. Alumni Bd. Govs., 1969-71, adv. com. Univ. Day Care Ctr., 1984-86, Tenn. 4-H Club Found., Inc., 1990, JOBS adv. coun. Dept. Human Svcs. State of Tenn., 1990, Tenn. Adv. Com., Lower Miss. Delta Devel. Commn., 1989—; chair Tenn. Tech. U. United Way Drive, 1979-82, dept. leader, 1983-86; tchr. Sunday sch. Collegeside Ch. of Christ, 1979-86; bd. dirs. Putnam County United Way, 1981-85; chair Weakley County United Way, 1987. Nat. Endowment for Arts grantee, 1979-83. Mem. Am. Assn. State Colls. and Univs. (state rep. 1989-90), Profl. and Organizational Devel. Networks in Higher Edn., Inst. Food Technologists, Am. Home Econs. Assn., Tenn. Home Econs. Assn., Am. Men and Women in Sci., Tenn. Women's Forum, Omicron Nu, Sigma Xi, Phi Kappa Phi, Omicron Delta Kappa, Delta Kappa Gamma. Club: U. Tenn. at Knoxville Faculty (bd. dirs. 1974-77). Home: Chancellor's Residence Martin TN 38238 Office: U Tenn 325 Adminstrn Bldg Martin TN 38238-5009

PERRY, MARSHA GRATZ, legislator, professional skating coach; b. Niagara Falls, N.Y., Dec. 9, 1936; d. William Henry and Margaret Edna (Barr) Gratz; m. Robert X. Perry, Jr., Jan. 28, 1961; children: Robert, Margarett, David. Student, Elmira Coll., 1954-57; BILR, Cornell U., 1959. Coll. recruiter Inmont, N.Y.C., 1959-61; skating dir. City of Bowie (Md.), 1971—; skating coach Benfield Pines Ice Rink, Millerville, Md., 1974—; mem. Md. Ho. of Dels.; summer hockey coach Washington Capitals, Landover, Md., 1986-89. Dist. dir., v.p., planning zoning dir. Crofton (Md.) Civic Assn., 1974-86; pres. West County Fedn. Community Assns. Hazardous Adv. Coun., 1986-87; mem. Md. Substance Adv. Coun., 1982-87. Named Citizen of Yr. Crofton Civic Assn., 1986. Mem. Assn. Women Legislators. Home: 1605 Edgerton Pl Crofton MD 21114 Office: Md Ho Reps Lowe Bldg Rm 215 Annapolis MD 21401

PERRY, MARY DEAN, music educator; b. Scranton, Pa., July 3, 1928; d. Michael Patrick and Florence Veronica (Costello) Dean; m. George Francis Perry, Aug. 28, 1963. BMus, Marywood Coll., Scranton, 1949, MA, 1953; postgrad., NYU, Juilliard Sch., Temple U., Eastman Sch. Music, Manhattan Sch. Music. Asst. prof. Marywood Coll., Scranton, 1949-77; dir. music Ch. of Our Lady of Snows, Clarks Summit, Pa., 1949-75, Ch. of St. Mary of Mt. Carmel, Dunmore, Pa., 1976—; prof. piano Clarks Summit, Pa., 1979—; co-organizer, co-dir. Coll. Without Walls prog., Marywood Coll., 1972, 73; judge Scranton Philharmonic Orch. Youth Competition, 1967-72; adjudicator Pa. Music Tchrs. Assn. Performance Festivals, 1980—. Arranger liturgical music, Mass for Easter, 1961, Mass for Christmas, 1962, 66, Mass for Pentecost, 1966. Mem. St. Peter's Cathedral Concert com., Scranton, 1990—. Recipient O'Reilly medal for outstanding achievement in music, Marywood Coll., 1949, Vicennial medal for disting. svc. as mem. of faculty Marywood Coll., 1969. Mem. AAUP, AAUW, Am. Musicol. Soc., Coll. Music Soc., Marywood Coll. Alumnae Assn., Pa. Music Tchrs. Assn., nat. Music Tchrs. Assn., Kappa Gamma Pi, Delta Epsilon Sigma, Delta Kappa Gamma. Democrat. Roman Catholic. Home: 109 Sturbridge Rd Clarks Summit PA 18411

PERRY, MARY-ELLEN, museum curator; b. Newark, Feb. 23, 1932; d. John Hayward and Mary Simpson (Alloway) Earl; m. Harold Edward Perry, July 17, 1971 (div. 1985). BA, Western Md. Coll., Westminster, 1953; MA, SUNY, Oneonta, 1965. Instr. Montclair Art Mus., N.J., 1954-59, curator, 1959-63; dir. Arnot Art Mus., Elmira, N.Y., 1965-72; curator The Strong Mus., Rochester, N.Y., 1972—; cons. Am. Assn. Mus., Wash. 1970—; mem. N.Am. Print Conf. Co-Author: Light of the Home, 1983; contbr. articles to profl. jours. Mem. City Hall Citizens Com., Rochester N.Y. 1982—; vol. GEVA Theatre, Rochester N.Y. 1985—, Landmark Soc. Western N.Y, Rochester, 1985—; chmn. Nat. Mus. Women in the Arts Upstate N.Y. Monroe County Wash. 1986—. Mem. Am. Assn. Mus., Mid-Atlantic Assn. Mus., Costume Soc. Am., Landmark Soc. Western N.Y., Nat. Trust. Democratic. Office: The Strong Mus 1 Manhattan Sq Rochester NY 14607

PERRY, MATILDA TONI, lawyer; b. Decatur, Ill.; d. Nathan Otis Perry and Elizabeth May Armstrong; m. Donald Harry Rubin, May 9, 1981; children: Michael, Deborah, Nikki, Brenda, Tom. BA, U. Nev., 1972; JD, U. Calif., Berkeley, 1975. Bar: Calif. 1975, U.S. Supreme Ct. 1980. Atty. Calif. State U., Long Beach, 1975-77; dep. county counsel Orange County, Calif., 1977-83; assoc. Rutan & Tucker, Costa Mesa, Calif., 1983-85; ptnr. Rutan & Tucker, Costa Mesa, 1986-87, Buchalter, Nemer, Fields & Younger, Newport Beach, Calif., 1988—. Mem. ABA, Calif. Bar Assn., Orange County Bar Assn., County Counsel Assn. (sch. law study sect.), Nat. Assn. Bond Lawyers.

PERRY, NANCY ESTELLE, psychologist; b. Pitts., Oct. 30, 1934; d. Simon Warren and Estelle Cecelia (Zaluski) Reichard; m. John Cleveland; children: Scott, Karen, Elaine; BS, Ohio State U., 1956, MA in Psychology, 1969, PhD in Psychology (EPDA fellow), 1973. Nurse, various locations, 1956-63; sch. psychologist Public Schs. Columbus (Ohio), 1970-72; human devel. specialist Madison County (Ohio) Schs., 1972-75; pvt. practice clin. psychology, cons. psychology, Worthington, Ohio, 1975-80; tchr. U. Wis. Sch. Nursing, Milw., 1980-88, Milw. Devel. Center, 1980-83; pvt. practice Assoc. Mental Health Services, 1983-87; dir., pvt. practice Glendale Clinic for Stress Mgmt. and Mental Health Clinics, 1987—; faculty Wis. Profl. Schs.; adj. faculty U. Wis., Milw. Ohio Dept. Edn. grantee, 1973-76. Mem. Wis. Psychol. Assn., Am. Psychol. Assn., Internat. Soc. Hypnosis, Internat. Soc. Study of Multiple Personality and Associated Disorders, Am. Assn. Marriage and Family Therapists. Home: 2210 Charter Mall Mequon WI 53092 Office: 5227 N Ironwood Rd Milwaukee WI 53217

PERRY, NANCY JO, investment company executive; b. Olean, N.Y., Dec. 12, 1931; d. Thomas Bronson and Doris Marjory (Bacon) White; student Gustavus Adolphus Coll.; grad. Bethesda Hosp. Sch. Nursing, St. Paul, 1952; m. Charles Robert Perry, Apr. 9, 1955; children—Elizabeth Perry Sewell, Charles Thomas, Nancy Marie. Asst. head nurse U. Colo. Gen. Hosp., 1953-55; co-owner, dir. Perry Gas Co., Perry Energy Co., Odessa, Tex., 1967-82; v.p. Perry Investments, Perry Found., 1982—; past sec.-treas. Perry Energy Co., Perry Gas Processors, Perry Gas Transmissions, Inc., PGP Gas Products, Inc., Rockies Oil and Gas Corp. Bd. dirs. Odessa Council on Alcoholism, Task Force on Women, Permian Basin Regional Coun. Alcohol & Drug Abuse, Our New Beginnings, halfway house for recovering alcoholic women, sec., 1982-86; pres. bd. dirs. West Tex. Pastoral Counseling Center; gov.'s appointee Tex. Commn. on Alcohol and Drug Abuse, 1985-89, adv. coun., 1989—. Presbyterian (elder). Home: 9 San Miguel Sq Odessa TX 79762 Office: PO Box 60380 Midland TX 79711-0218

PERRY, ROSE THERESA, printing and direct mail company executive; b. Maple Shade, N.J., Apr. 10, 1961; d. Thaddeus Anthony and Mary Sophia (Hatala) Nowakowski; m. Kenneth Allen Perry, Nov. 27, 1982; 1 child, Kyle Thomas Perry. BA in Communications, Glassboro (N.J.) State Coll., 1982. Advt. intern Serpente & Assocs., Mt. Laurel, N.J., 1981; editing supr. Lehigh ROCAPPI, Inc., Pennsauken, N.J., 1982-84; mfg. mgmt. trainee Donnelley/ROCAPPI, Inc., Cherry Hill, N.J., 1984-86, supr. in-house and offsite typesetting, 1986-87; planning, art mgr. Hibbert Group, Trenton, N.J., 1987-89, mgr. planning and printing, 1989—; mem. mgmt. com. Hibbert Group, 1990—; creative cons. Jazz Dir., 1987; co-owner Allied Med., 1989—. Writer publicity city coun. and mayoral campaigns, Burlington, N.J., 1980-88, Lumberton, N.J., 1988; campaign mgr. Lumberton twp. com. 1990. Garden State scholar, 1979-82. Mem. Nat. Assn. Female Execs., Gamma Tau Sigma. Democrat. Roman Catholic. Office: Hibbert Group 21 Muirhead Ave Trenton NJ 08638

PERRY-DANIEL, ANNIE VEE, minister; b. Rocky Mount, N.C., May 26, 1940; d. Levi Parson and Annie Mary (Powell) Perry; m. Jan. 23, 1965 (div. 1985); children: Dana Charlette, Corlisa Eugene, Barbara Ann. BA in Sociology, Morgan State U., Balt., 1980; MDiv, Howard U., Washington, 1983. Ordained to ministry, United Meth. Ch., 1983. Rsch. asst. Balt. City Schs., 1972-75; youth ministries coord. Christ United Meth. Ch., Balt., 1978-80; pastor Boundary United Meth. Ch., Balt., 1980-81; intern Simpson-Hamline United Meth. Ch., Washington, 1981-82; pastor Lewin United Meth. Ch., Balt., 1982-85, John Wesley United Meth. Ch., Glen Burnie, Md., 1985—; chaplain's asst. Morgan Christian Ctr., Balt., 1978-80; broadcaster Sta. WANN, Annapolis, Md., 1988; cons. in field; mem. Dist. Bd. Ordained Ministries, 1985—, Interfaith Com. on Jewish Christian Rels., 1988—, Bd. Higher Edn. and Campus Ministry, 1989—; featured writer Jour. Religious Thought, 1989; religious affairs editor Balt. Times, 1989—. Editor Annapolis Anchor, 1986-88; contbg. editor, A Jour. for Ministers, Sermon Starters, 1988. Charter mem. Meth. United for Peace with Justice, Balt., 1987. Cornish scholar, 1980, meritorious scholar Howard U., 1981, 82, United Meth. Crusade scholar, 1981, 82; Howard Stone Anderson fellow, 1981, 82. Democrat. Methodist. Office: John Wesley United Meth Ch 6922 Ritchie Hwy Glen Burnie MD 21061

PERRYMAN, ELIZABETH KAY, biology educator; b. Greenwood, Miss., Apr. 11, 1940; d. Hugh M. and Sarah Elizabeth (Campbell) P.; m. George E. Snow, Dec. 17, 1983. BS in Biology, Memphis State U., 1964; MS in Biology, Tex. Tech. U., 1967; PhD in Zoology, U. Ariz., 1972. Tchr. West Memphis (Ark.) High Sch., 1964-65; instr. Victoria (Tex.) Coll., 1967-69; prof. biology Calif. Poly. State U., San Luis Obispo, 1972—; vis. rsch. prof. U. Ariz., summers 1976, 77, 79, 90. Contbr. articles to sci. jours., chpts. to books. Faculty Rsch. Participation fellow Dept. Energy-Associated Western Univs., UCLA, 1978; Burroughs Wellcome grantee U. Leeds, U.K., 1981. Fellow AAAS; mem. Am. Soc. Zoologists, So. Calif. Soc. Electron Microscopy. Unitarian. Office: Calif Poly State U San Luis Obispo CA 93407

PERRYMAN, POLLY, manager technical operations; b. Hammond, Ind., Feb. 15, 1947; d. Joseph Robert Altenbach and Bertha Helen (Specht) Gephart; m. Lawrence A. Perryman, June 12, 1965 (div. 1974); children: Curtis, Leiha, Candice, Corey. Student Gov.'s State U., 1979; Assoc. Applied Sci., Joliet Jr. Coll., 1978. Computer operator Valley View Sch. Dist., Romeoville, Ill., 1978-80; mgr. data processing Village Communications, Romeoville, 1980-81; tech. writer Profl. Computer Resources, Oak Brook, Ill., 1981-82; owner, pres. Documentation Svcs., Inc., Romeoville, 1982-86; mgr. project support Sage Fed. Systems Inc., Rock Island, Ill., 1986-89; mgr. support svcs. Gumman Data Systems, Bethpage, N.Y., 1989—; dir. Indoco, Inc., Joliet. Contbr. articles to profl. jours. Precinct committeeman Republican Party, DuPage Twp., 1982—; mem. zoning bd. Village of Romeoville, 1978-82; bd. trustees Joliet Jr. Coll., 1977-78. Guest speaker Software Expo '84 Hitchcock Publishers, 1984. Mem. IEEE (working group for end-user manual standards 1984—), ISO JIC/1/WG2 System Documentation, U.S. del. nominee to ISO Plenary mtg., Amsterdam, 1988, Ill. Software Assn. and Ctr., Am. Bus. Women's Assn. (program chmn. 1982). Presbyterian. Avocation: collector clowns. Home: 125 Wa Wee Nork 6C Battle Creek MI 49017

PERRYMAN, THELMA DIANE, insurance underwriter; b. Tallahassee, Fla., July 14, 1952; d. Alexander and Gloria Mae (Ward) P. BS, Purdue U., 1976. With inside sales dept. Westinghouse Electric, Lima, Ohio; sr. underwriter Prudential Ins. Co., Houston; mgr. health underwriting Columbia Universal Life Ins. Co., Houston, Am. Nat. Ins. Co., Galveston, Tex. Fellow Life Mgmt. Inst., Mgmt. Inst. Soc.; mem. Internat. Claims Assn., Health Inst. Assn. Am., Nat. Assn. Security Dealers, Alpha Kappa Alpha (sec.). Home: 4006 Cedar Ridge Ct Houston TX 77082 Office: One Moody Pla Galveston TX 77550

PERSAILE, KERRI BULLARD, dietitian; b. Dallas, Mar. 25, 1960; d. Billy Dean Bullard and Joyce (Petty) Adkins; m. William Jeffrey Persaile, Aug. 8, 1987. BS in Dietetics, Harding U., 1981; MS in Instl. Mgmt., La. Tech. U., 1983. Registered dietitian. Clin. dietitian Warner Brown Hosp., El Dorado, Ark., 1983-85, Community Dialysis Ctr., El Dorado, 1984-85; instr. So. Ark. U., El Dorado, 1984, Baylor U. Med. Ctr., Dallas, 1985—. Mem. Am. Dietetic Assn. Republican. Home: 2569 El Cerrito Dallas TX 75228 Office: Baylor U Med Ctr 3500 Gaston Ave Dallas TX 75246

PERSCHBACHER, DEBRA BASSETT, lawyer; b. Pleasanton, Calif., Oct. 28, 1956; d. James Arthur and Shirley Ann (Russell) Bassett; m. Rex Robert Perschbacher, June 4, 1989. BA, U. Vt., 1977; MS, San Diego State U., 1982; JD, U. Calif., Davis, 1987. Bar: Calif. 1987, D.C. 1990, U.S. Dist Ct. (no. and ea. dists.) Calif. 1988, U.S. Ct. Appeals (9th cir.), 1988. Guidance counselor Addison Cen. Supr. Union, Middlebury, Vt., 1982-83, Milton (Vt.) Elem. Sch., 1983-84; assoc. Morrison & Foerster, San Francisco, 1986; jud. clk. to presiding justice U.S. Ct. Appeals (9th cir.), Phoenix, 1987-88; assoc. Morrison & Foerster, San Francisco, 1988—; tutor civil procedure, rsch. asst. U. Calif., Davis, 1985-87. Sr. articles editor U. Calif. Law Rev., Davis, 1986-87; editor, 1985-86. Mem. ABA (vice chair young lawyers div. ethics com. 1989—, exec. com., labor and employment law com. 1989-90) San Francisco Bar Assn. Democrat. Home: 307 Pimlico Dr Walnut Creek CA 94596 Office: Morrison & Foerster 345 California St San Francisco CA 94104

PERSKY, VICTORIA WEYLER, epidemiologist, internist; b. Providence, Mar. 30, 1945; d. Henry L.C. and Adelaide (Schwartz) Weyler; m. Joseph Jacob Persky; children: Daniel, Nicole. BA, Radcliffe U., 1966; MD, Albert Einstein Coll., 1971. Diplomate Am. Bd. Internal Medicine. Resident U. Ala., Birmingham, 1971-73, Montefiore (N.Y.) Hosp., 1973-74; fellow preventive cardiology Northwestern U., Chgo., 1974-75; assoc. Northwestern U., 1975-79, asst. prof., 1979-83; asst. prof. U. Ill., Chgo., 1983-87; assoc. prof. epidemiology U. Ill., 1987—; internist Erie Family Health Ctr., Chgo., 1975—. Contbr. articles to profl. jours. and chpts. to books. Bd. dirs. The Portes Ctr., 1983-84, Easter Seal Found., 1989. NIH grantee, 1984. Office: PO Box 6998 Chicago IL 60680

PERSON, DOROTHY EVELYN, genealogy educator; b. Battle Ground, Wash., Mar. 19, 1924; d. Ivan Llewelyn and Claire Inez (Spencer) Wooldridge; m. Vernon Lyle Person, Nov. 26, 1944; children: Pamela Rae, Renee Arlene, Timothy Ivan. AA, Clark Coll., 1960; BA, U. Portland, 1963, MA, 1968. Cert. tchr., Wash. Elem., jr. high tchr. Hockinson Sch., Brush Prairie, Wash., 1961-81, retired; tchr. lacemaking, Vancouver, Wash., 1982; tchr. genealogy Clark Coll., Vancouver, 1983—, tchr. history, 1989. Author: From a Forest Clearing, 1978, Leaves From Family Tree, 1978, Spencer Citings, 1986; co-author: Pioneer Stories, 1986. Pres. PTA, Battle Ground, 1962, Clark County Pioneers, 1989; judge Clark County Fair, 1973-85, Wash. County Fair, Oreg., Skamania Fair, Wash. Scholar Vancouver PTA, 1960. Mem. Ft. Vancouver Hist. Soc. (mem. com. 1965-66,85), Clark County Geneal. Soc. (lectr. 1980—), DAR (chpt. regent 1987—), Daughters of Pioneers (pres., sec. 1972-80). Clubs: Clark County Quilters (v.p. 1982-83), Volcano Lacemakers (pres., sec. 1981-87) (Vancouver); Columbia Stitchery Guild. Republican. Avocations: history and genealogy, needlework, lacemaking, quilting, sewing. Home: 30200 NE 123 Pl Battle Ground WA 98604

PERTHOU, ALISON CHANDLER, interior designer; b. Bremerton, Wash., July 22, 1945; d. Benson and Elizabeth (Holdsworth) Chandler; m. A.V. Perthou III, Sept. 9, 1967 (div. Dec. 1977); children: Peter T.R., Stewart A.C. BFA, Cornish Coll. Arts, 1972. Pres. Alison Perthou Interior Design, Seattle, 1972—, Optima Design, Inc., Seattle, 1986-89; treas. Framejoist Corp., Bellevue, Wash., 1973-90; pres. Classics: Interiors & Antiques, Inc., 1988—; cons. bldg. and interiors com. Children's Hosp., Seattle, 1976—; guest lectr. U. Wash., Seattle, 1980-81. Bd. trustees Cornish Coll. Arts, Seattle, 1973-80, sec. exec. com., 1975-77; mem. procurement com. Patrons of N.W. Cultural and Charitable Orgn., 1985—. Mem. Am. Soc. Interior Design, Seattle Tennis Club (house and grounds com. 1974-75), City Club (Seattle). Office: 4216 E Madison St Seattle WA 98112

PERU, ROSITA, broadcast executive. Former v.p. Univision Network; sr. v.p., dir. programming Univision Network, L.A., 1990—. Office: Univision Network 9200 Sunset Blvd Ste 1130 Los Angeles CA 90069*

PERYON, MARY CHARLEEN D., special education educator; b. Milw., Apr. 29, 1931; d. Raymond James Dolphin and Violet Selma Solheim Dolphin Berendes; m. Robert Edward Peryon, Nov. 21, 1953; children: Anne Marie Peryon Noonan, Robert Louis, Lynne Marie. BA in Biology, Clarke Coll., Dubuque, Iowa, 1953; cert. med. tech., St. Anthony Hosp. Sch. Med. Technology, Rockford, Ill., 1954; MEd in Clin. Reading, U. Guam, 1972; PhD in Spl. Edn., Utah State U., 1979. Cert. tchr. Ill., Iowa; cert. cons. Iowa; cert. sch. adminstr. Utah. Tchr. sci. LaGrange (Ill.) Schs., 1966-68, Washington Sr. High Sch., Mangiloa, Guam, 1968-70; asst. prof. edn. U. Guam, Mangiloa, 1970-71; reading specialist Dept. Edn. Territory of Guam, Agana, 1971-73, state curriculum cons., 1973-75; assoc. prof. reading and spl. edn. U. Guam, Mangiloa, 1975-85; assoc. prof. reading and learning disabilities Clarke Coll., Dubuque, 1985-86; spl. edn. cons. Keystone Area Edn. Agy., Dubuque, 1986-89; assoc. prof. spl. edn. U. Dubuque, 1989—; cons. in field. Author: Distar Teacher Aide's Handbook, 1974; co-auuthor: Reading Specialist's Handbook, 1973; mem. editorial bd. U. Guam Press, Manigloa, 1983-85; contbr. numerous articles to profl. jours. Recipient spl. award U.S. Dept. Def. Sch. Dist., Manila, 1976, Internat. Reading Assn. of Newark, 1975. Mem. Internat. Reading Assn. (pres. Guam chpt. 1973-74, chmn. Pacific area 1973-75), Phi Delta Kappa (historian 1977-78, 83-84), Chi Omicron Gamma (pres. 1982-84). Roman Catholic. Home: PO Box 127 Cascade IA 52033 Office: U Dubuque 2000 University Ave Dubuque IA 52001

PESCIOTTA, BARBARA PHYLLIS, pharmacy executive; b. Jersey City, Aug. 16, 1936; d. George Bishar and Evelyn Rose (Redvanly) Kedersha; m. Marshall Pesciotta, Aug. 18, 1957; children: Randy, Gary, Roy. BS, Douglass Coll., 1957. Cert. elem. tchr., N.J. Elem. tchr. Bergenfield (N.J.) Sch. System, 1957-61, Wayne (N.J.) Sch. System, 1975-78; v.p. Dover Pharmacy, Toms River, N.J., 1979—. Editor: (bull.) AAUW, Train of Thought, 1988-89. Vol. Chilton Meml. Hosp., Packanack Lake Aux., Pompton Plains, N.J., 1969-78. Mem. AAUW (treas. Toms River chpt. 1981-83, pres. 1986-88; nominating com. N.J. div. 1988-89, speakers bur. 1987-89). Avocations: gardening, walking. Home: 110 Woodridge Ave Toms River NJ 08755 Office: Dover Pharmacy 1245 Rt 166 Toms River NJ 08753

PESEK, DIANA LYNN, manufacturing executive; b. Newton Falls, Ohio, Nov. 17, 1950; d. John and Mary (Gasparek) Krupsa. BA cum laude, Case Western Res. U., 1973. Sales svc. mgr. Am. Printing and Label Co., Cleve.; gen. mgr. Mac Calla & Co., Inc., Phila.; estimating mgr. Thomas Press, Moorestown, N.J., Parker Printing Co., Trenton, N.J.; dir. jour. mfg. W.B. Saunders Co., Phila.; instr. lithography estimating. Active Big Bros./Big Sisters Phila. Mem. Graphic Arts Assn., Exec. Club. Home: 231 N Third St #510 Philadelphia PA 19106 Office: WB Saunders Co The Curtis Ctr Independence Sq W Philadelphia PA 19106

PESKIN-JACOBS, MARJORIE RUTH, business owner, instructor, consultant; b. Springfield, Mass., July 11, 1952; d. Samuel Benson and Jeanne-Roma (Frankel) Peskin; m. Paul Malcolm Jacobs, May 25, 1986; children: Raffi Hill, Matthew Hill, Sebastian Hill. BA, U. Colo., 1975; MEd, Antioch Coll., 1977. Tchr. Amesbury (Mass.) High Sch., 1977-78, North Middlesex Regional High Sch., Townsend, Mass., 1978-80; assoc. software engr. Avco Systems Div., Wilmington, Mass., 1980-81; tech. author Computervision Corp., Bedford, Mass., 1981-84; info. developer IBM Corp., Raleigh, N.C., 1984-85; resource editor Cullinet Software, Westwood, Mass., 1985-87; instr. Northeastern U., Boston, 1985—; owner Documentation and Design, Belmont, Mass., 1987—. Mem. Amnesty Internat., Boston, 1987-90, People for the Ethical Treatment of Animals, Washington, 1987-90, Belmont (Mass.) Dem. Town Com., 1989-90; area team leader Mass Choice, Belmont, 1989-90; town coord. Evelyn Murphy for Gov. Campaign, Boston, 1989-90. Mem. MLA, Boston Computer Soc., Soc. Tech. Communication. Jewish. Home and Office: 97 Elm St Belmont MA 02178

PESKOE, SONDRA HELANE, real estate executive; b. Phila., Sept. 30, 1955. AS in Acctg., Banking, Atlantic Community Coll., 1976; BS in Bus., Acctg., Stockton State Coll., 1982. CPA, N.J., Md. Acct. Robert R. Linzner and Co., CPA's, Atlantic City, 1978-79; project acct., office mgr. Rich-McBride Constrn. Co., Joint Venture, Atlantic City, 1979-80; fin. acct. Ramada Inc. dba Tropicana Hotel and Casino, Atlantic City, 1980-81, internal auditor, 1981-82; food and beverage ops. analyst Ramada Inc., Atlantic City, 1982-83; eastern regional controller Ramada Inc., Bethesda, Md., 1983-85; corp. controller Coakley and Williams, Inc., Greenbert, Md., 1985-88; sr. v.p., chief fin. officer NHP Property Mgmt. Inc., Washington, 1988-89; asst. v.p. Perpetual RE Svcs., Inc., Vienna, Va., 1989—; cons. MIC, Inc., Va., 1986-87; lectr. U. Md.-Eastern Shore, 1985. Assoc. Friends of the Kennedy Ctr., Washington, 1985—, Arena Stage Assocs., Washington, 1985-87; mem., singer Shir Chadash Chorale, Rockville, Md., 1985—; life mem. Hadassah, Washington, 1979. Fellow N.J. Soc. CPA's; mem. Am. Inst. CPA's, Md. Assn. CPA's, Controllers Council, Internat. Assn. Hospitality Accts., Nat. Assn. Accts., Richard Stockton State Coll. Alumni Assn. (life), Comml. Real Estate Women, Earthwatch. Club: Shaloma Hadassah (v.p. program 1979, v.p. edn. 1982).

PESTAINA, KAREN HELENA, newscaster, journalist; b. East Meadow, N.Y., Apr. 23, 1963; d. Basil Elman and Emma Helena (Flax) P. BA in Speech Communication and Broadcast Journalism, Penn State U., 1985. Licensed FCC. Producer WHLI-WKJY Radio, Hempstead, N.Y., 1985; sportswriter, news asst. WMCA-AM Radio, N.Y.C., 1986; new prodn. asst. WINS-AM Radio, N.Y.C., 1986-88; stringer WLIB-AM Radio, N.Y.C., 1986-87; reporter, assoc. producer Ecumedia News Svc., N.Y.C., 1986-87; chief editorial asst. ABC News Radio Networks, N.Y.C., 1988-89; news dir., anchor WNJR-AM Radio, Newark, 1989-90; fill-in-news anchor WBLS-FM, WLIB-AM, N.Y.C., 1989-90; per diem newswriter ABC News Radio Network, N.Y.C., 1990—; awards judge Nat. TV Acad., N.Y.C., 1987-90. Recognized for Best Radio News Feature North Jersey Press Club, 1990. Mem. Nat. Assn. Black Journalists, N.Y. Assn. Black Journalists, Am. Fedn. TV and Radio Artists, Writers Guild Am., Radio & TV News Dir. Assn., Nat. Black Media Coalition, Am. Women in Radio & TV (awards judge 1987-88). Episcopalian. Home: 117 Bennett Ave Hempstead NY 11550-2813

PESTANA, MARY HELEN, occupational therapist; b. Jersey City, Jan. 30, 1961; d. Francisco and Maria E. Pestana. BS, Kean Coll. N.J., 1984. Registered occupational therapist. Clin. student coord., supr. occupational therapy Bergen Pines Hosp., Paramus, N.J.; guest lectr. in occupational therapy Kean Coll. of N.J. Recipient Cert. of Appreciation Am. Heart Assn., 1989. Mem. Am. Occupational Therapy Assn., N.J. Occupational Therapy Assn. (Award of Merit in Practice 1989). Home: 159-61 St West New York NJ 07093 Office: Bergen Pines Hosp East Ridgewood Ave Paramus NJ 07652

PETERING, JANICE FAYE, hotel executive; b. Covington, Ky., Feb. 10, 1950; d. Edward Charles Petering Sr. and Shirley Ellen (McKenzie) Petering Brancucci. Student, Eastern Ky. U., 1969; cert., Ramada Mgmt. Inst., 1982. Cert. hotel adminstr. Night auditor Caesars Palace Hotel, Las Vegas, Nev., 1970-77; chief rack clk. Caesars Palace Hotel, Las Vegas, 1979-80, supr. accounts receivable, 1980-82, casino comptr., 1982-83, ops. comptr., 1983-85; exec. asst. to hotel mgr. Tropicana Hotel & Country Club, Las Vegas, 1977-79, hotel mgr., 1985-86; hotel mgr. MGM MArina Casino and Hotel, Las Vegas, 1986-87, dir. hotel ops., 1987—. Mem. Internat. Assn. Hospitality Accts., Las Vegas Hotel-Motel Assn., Las Vegas Hotel Mgrs. Assn., Network of Exec. Women in Hospitality. Roman Catholic. Office: MGM Marina Casino and Hotel 3805 Las Vegas Blvd S Las Vegas NV 89109

PETERS, BARBARA HUMBIRD, writer, editor; b. Santa Monica, Calif., Sept. 26, 1948; d. Philip Rising and Caroline Jean (Dickason) Peters. AA, Santa Monica Coll., 1971; BS, San Diego State U., 1976; postgrad. UCLA, 1981-82, 84. Gen. ptnr. Signet Properties, L.A., 1971-85; tech. editor C. Brewer & Co., Hilo, Hawaii, 1975-76; editor The Aztec Engineer mag., San Diego, 1976-77; regional publicist YWCA, San Diego, 1977-78; campaign cons. Rep. Congl. and Assembly Candidates San Diego; Pollster, Los Angeles Times, 1983; pres., dir. Humbird Hopkins Inc., L.A., 1978—; pub. rels. cons. ASCE, San Diego, 1975-76, Am. Soc. Mag. Photographers, San Diego, 1980. Author: The Layman's Guide to Raising Cane: A Guide to the Hawaiian Sugar Industry, 1975, The Students' Survival Guide, 1976, 2d edit. 1977. Mem. Mayor's Coun. on Librs., L.A., 1969; mem. Wilshire Blvd. Property Owners Assn., Santa Monica, 1972-78; docent Mus. Sci. and Industry, L.A., 1970; founding mem. Comml. and Indsl. Properties Assn., Santa Monica, 1982-89. Recipient Acting award Santa Monica Coll., 1970. Mem. Internat. Assn. Bus. Communicators, Sales and Mktg. Execs. Assn. Avocations: travel, opera, puns.

PETERS, BARBARA NANCY, highway safety administrator; b. White Plains, N.Y., Aug. 19, 1956; d. Henry S. and Barbara A. (Hannigan) P. BS in Edn., SUNY, Oneonta, 1978; MS in Spl. Edn., Coll. New Rochelle, 1979. Cert. tchr., N.Y. Tchr. spl. edn. White Plains Pub. Schs., 1978-79; tng. technician Westchester County Traffic Safety Dept., White Plains, 1979-81, instr. def. driving, 1983—, freedom of info. officer, 1986—. Editor newsletter, Westchester County Traffic Safety Dept., 1987—. Recipient Child Safety Program award Nat. Assn. Counties, 1981, Occupant Restraint Program award, 1985, Corp. Community Seat Belt Program award, 1987, Cost Effective Traffic Safety Communication Programs, 1988, Teddy Bears Child Trauma Victims Program, 1989. Mem. N.Y. State Assn. Traffic Safety Bds. (regional v.p. 1985-86, 1st v.p. 1986-88, pres. 1988—), N.Y. State Soc. Profl. Engrs. (scholastic guidance com. 1987—), Nat. Assn. Female Execs., TRANSCOM (pub. info. com. 1986—), N.Y. State Women in Traffic Safety (govs. council, regional dir. 1988—). Home: 295 Columbus Ave White Plains NY 10604 Office: Westchester County 148 Martine Ave White Plains NY 10601

PETERS, BERNADETTE (BERNADETTE LAZZARA), actress; b. Queens, N.Y., Feb. 28, 1948; d. Peter and Marguerite (Maltese) Lazzara. Student, Quintano Sch. for Young Profls., N.Y.C. Ind. actress, entertainer, 1959—. Appeared on TV series All's Fair, 1976-77; frequent guest appearances on TV including (ABC movie of week) David, 1988; films include The Longest Yard, 1974, Silent Movie, 1976, Vigilante Force, 1976, W.C. Fields and Me, 1976, The Jerk, 1979, Pennies from Heaven, 1981 (Golden Globe Best Actress award), Heart Beeps, 1981, Tulips, 1981, Annie, 1982, Slaves of New York, 1988, Pink Cadillac, 1989; stage appearances include The Most Happy Fella, 1959, Gypsy, 1961, This is Google, 1962, Riverwind, 1966, The Penny Friend, 1966, Curly McDimple, 1966, Johnny No-Trump, 1967, George M!, 1968, Dames at Sea, 1968, La Strada, 1969, W.C., 1971, On the Town, 1971, Tartuffe, 1972, Mack and Mabel, 1974, Sally and Marsha, 1982, Sunday in the Park with George, 1983, Song and Dance, 1985, Into the Woods, 1987; TV films David, 1988, Fall From Grace, 1990; rec. artist: (MCA Records) Bernadette Peters, 1980, Now Playing, 1981. Recipient Drama Desk award for Dames at Sea, 1968, Drama Desk award nomination, 1987, 88; Tony award nominee, 1971, 74, 85, Tony award for Song and Dance, 1986, Theatre World citation for George M!, 1968, Drama Desk award, 1986, Drama League award, 1986, Hasty Pudding Theatrical award, 1987 Woman of the Yr. Office: care Richard Grant & Assocs 8500 Wilshire Blvd Ste 520 Beverly Hills CA 90211

PETERS, CAROL BEATTIE TAYLOR (MRS. FRANK ALBERT PETERS), mathematician; b. Washington, May 10, 1932; d. Edwin Lucius and Lois (Beattie) Taylor; B.S., U. Md., 1954, M.A., 1958; m. Frank Albert Peters, Feb. 26, 1955; children—Thomas, June, Erick, Victor. Group mgr. Tech. Operations, Inc., Arlington, Va., 1957-62, sr. staff scientist, 1964-66; supervisory analyst Datatrol Corp., Silver Spring, Md., 1962; project dir. Computer Concept, Inc., Silver Spring, 1963-64; mem. tech. staff, then mem. sr. staff Informatics Inc., Bethesda, Md., 1966-70, mgr. systems projects, 1970-71, tech. dir., 1971-76; sr. tech. dir. Ocean Data Systems, Inc., Rockville, Md., 1976-83; dir. Informatics Gen. Co., 1983-89; pres. Carol Peters Assocs., 1989—. Mem. Assn. Computing Machinery, IEEE Computer Group. Home and Office: 12321 Glen Mill Rd Potomac MD 20854

PETERS, CHARLOTTE LESTYAN, landscape designer and contractor; b. Szarvas, Hungary, Feb. 2, 1942; came to U.S., 1955; d. John and Charlotte Barbara (Brozik) Lestyan; m. J. Richard Childers (div.) m. Jordan Holt Peters, May 6, 1978 (div.); children: Alexander M. Childers, Charlotte Elizabeth. BA, U. Ill., 1965; JD, DePaul U., Chgo., 1975. Atty. Continental Ill. Nat. Bank, Chgo., 1975-79, Rudnick & Wolfe, Chgo., 1979-80; landscape designer and contractor Charlotte Peters Gardens, Inc., Evanston, Ill., 1982—. Mem. Garden Club. of Evanston. Office: Charlotte Peters Gardens Inc 814 Ridge Terr Evanston IL 60201

PETERS, CHRISTINE MARIE, therapist; b. East St. Louis, Ill., Nov. 15, 1949; d. Evo and Loretta (Williams) DeAntoni; m. Norman E. Peters, 1969; children: Julie, Greg. BA in Behavioral Sci., Nat. Coll. Edn., Evanston, Ill., 1988; MA in Counseling Psychology, Liberty U., Va., 1989; postgrad., Univ. Sarasota. Therapist human svcs. DeKalb, Ill. Pres. Remove Intoxicated Drivers; created and developed a 24-hour crisis/victims assistance hot line. Mem. Nat. Assn. Substance Abuse and Alcoholism Counselors, Am. Psychol. Assn. Home: 633 Brickville Rd Sycamore IL 60178

PETERS, ELLEN ASH, state supreme court chief justice; b. Berlin, Mar. 21, 1930; came to U.S., 1939, naturalized, 1947; d. Ernest Edward and Hildegard (Simon) Ash; m. Phillip I. Blumberg; children: David Bryan Peters, James Douglas Peters, Julie Peters Haden. BA with honors, Swarthmore Coll., 1951, LLD (hon.), 1983; LLB cum laude, Yale U., 1954, MA (hon.), 1964, LLD (hon.), 1983; LLD (hon.), Georgetown U., 1984, Yale U., 1985, Conn. Coll., 1985, U. Hartford, 1855, N.Y. Law Sch., 1985; HLD (hon.), St. Joseph Coll., 1986; LLD (hon.), Colgate U., 1986, Trinity Coll., 1987, Bates Coll., 1987, Wesleyan U., 1987, DePaul U., 1988; HLD (hon.), Albertus Magnus Coll., 1990. Bar: Conn. 1957. Law clk. to judge U.S. Circuit Ct., 1954-55; assoc. in law U. Calif., Berkeley, 1955-56; prof. law Yale U., 1956-78, adj. prof. law, 1978-84; assoc. justice Conn. Supreme Ct., Hartford, 1978-84; chief justice Conn. Supreme Ct., 1984—; bd. dirs. Conf. Chief Justices. Author: Commercial Transactions: Cases, Texts, and Problems, 1971, Negotiable Instruments Primer, 1974; contbr. articles to profl. jours. Bd. mgrs. Swarthmore Coll., 1970-81; trustee Yale New Haven Hosp., 1981-85, Yale Corp., 1986—; conf. of Chief Justices, 1984—; hon. chmn. U.S. Constitution Bicentennial Com., 1986—; mem. Conn. Permanent Commn. on Status of Women, 1973-74, Conn. Bd. Pardons, 1978-80, Conn. Law Revision Commn., 1978-84. Recipient Ella Grasso award, 1982, Jud. award Conn. Trial Lawyers Assn., 1982, citation of merit Yale Law Sch., 1983, Pioneer Woman award Hartford Coll. for Women, 1988. Mem. ABA, Conn. Bar Assn., Am. Law Inst. (council). Office: Conn Supreme Ct Drawer N Sta A Hartford CT 06106

PETERS, FRANCES ELIZABETH, librarian; b. Phila., Nov. 25, 1915; d. Alexander and Sarah Mower (Scott) P. BSEd, U. Pa., 1936, MA in Latin, 1938; BSLS, Drexel Inst. Tech., 1940; MLS, Drexel U., 1966. Br. libr. Free Libr. Phila., 1951-52, 57-62, asst. in office of work with adults, 1953-57, asst. in art dept., 1945-48, asst. extension div., 1941-45; libr. Holiday mag. Curtis Pub. Co., Phila., 1948-51; asst. libr. Pedagogical Libr., Sch. Dist. Phila., 1962-63; libr. Cheltenham High Sch., Wyncote, Pa., 1963-66, Community Coll., Temple U., Phila., 1966-67; head libr. Pa. Coll. Podiatric Medicine, Phila., 1968-82, libr., 1982—. Mem. AAUW, DAR, Nat. Victorian Soc. (Phila. chpt.), Salvation Army Aux., Nat. Soc. U.S. Daus. 1812 (nat. chmn. Am. Mcht. Marine Libr. Assn. com.), Classical Assn. Atlantic States, Phila. Classical Assn., Hist. Soc. Pa., Cruiser Olympia Assn., Pa. Classical Assn., Pi Lambda Theta, Eta Sigma Phi, Beta Phi Mu, Phi Delta Gamma, Phi Kappa Phi. Republican. Baptist. Home: 600 E Cathedral Rd Apt H505 Philadelphia PA 19128 Office: Charles E Krausz Libr Pa Coll Podiatric Medicine Race at 8th St Philadelphia PA 19107

PETERS, JANE CATHERINE, farm management and investment administrator; b. Lincoln, Nebr., Oct. 16, 1939; d. Robin Alexander and Marie Catherine (Meyer) Spence; m. Alexander Roberts Peters, Feb. 14, 1959; children: Catherine Marie, Jane Louise. Student, Pensacola Jr. Coll., 1959-60; BA, Calif. State U., 1962; MS, Okla. State U., 1966. Cert. home economist, secondary tchr., Nebr. Instr. textiles Okla. State U., Stillwater, 1965-66; instr. textiles, interiors U. Nebr., Lincoln, 1970-72, catering mgr. Student Union, 1982-83; asst. coord., adult edn. Southeast Community Coll., Lincoln, 1982-83; Nebr. state fair judge Agrl. Extension Svc., Lincoln, 1966—; county 4-H judge Agrl. Extension Svc., Nebr., 1966—; farm mgr., investor Spence-Peters Family Crab Orchard, Bancroft, Nebr., 1975—. Bd. dirs. Jr. League of Lincoln, 1975—; past pres. P.E.O., Lincoln, 1958—, Colonial Dames XVII Century, 1973—, U. Nebr. Faculty Women's Club, Lincoln, 1966—, past pres.; bd. dirs. Lincoln Southeast High Sch. PTO, 1988, past pres. Mem. Am. Home Econs. Assn., Nebr. Home Econs. Assn., Lincoln Home Economists in Home and Community (past pres.), Am. Assn. of Textile Chemists and Colorists, Phi Kappa Phi, Pi Theta Kappa, Sigma Xi (assoc.), Phi Upsilon Omicron, Kappa Omicron Nu. Republican. Presbyterian. Home: 3235 S 29th St Lincoln NE 68502

PETERS, JANE KASTL, economic development professional; b. Charleston, W.Va., May 7, 1954; d. Karl George and Priscilla Jane (Richard) K.; m. Jerry Louis Peters, June 1, 1985; children: Kathleen Elyse, Stephen Kastl. BA in Polit. Sci., Miami U., 1976. Grant writer W.Va. Dept. Health, Charleston, 1977-78; research asst. Govs. Office Community & Indsl. Devel., Charleston, 1978-80, indsl. devel. rep., 1980-82; exec. dir. Jefferson County Devel. Authority, Charles Town. Bd. dirs. Shepherd Coll. Bd. Advs., Shepherdstown, W.Va., 1987—. Mem. Jefferson County C. of C. (bd. dirs. 1988—), So. Indsl. Devel. Council (bd. dirs. 1984-85), W.Va. Econ. Devel. Council (pres. 1985-86, bd. dirs. 1990—). Democrat. Roman Catholic. Office: Jefferson County Devel Auth PO Box 237 Charles Town WV 25414

PETERS, JANET J., clothing manufacturing company executive; b. Reading, Pa., Oct. 6, 1930; d. James Hubert and Dorothy Mary (Knoblanch) McElfatrich; m. Henry A. Peters; 1 child, Lisa Renee. Student June McAdam Coll. Vice pres. Vanity Fair Mills, Wyomissing, Pa.; v.p. VF Corp., Wyomissing, Pa. Chmn. Mother's Day Luncheon Mother's Day Council Am., N.Y.C., from 1980; bd. dirs., fundraiser Reading Community Coll., 1983—; active Factory for Sr. Citizens, Fleetwood, Pa., 1983—. Office: VF Corp 1047 N Park Rd Wyomissing PA 19610*

PETERS, JUDITH ROCHELLE, educator, administrator; b. Phila., July 16, 1951; d. John Bernard and Priscilla Jo (Johnson) P.; B.S. (Senatorial scholar), Pa. State U., 1973; postgrad. Temple U. Sch. Pharmacy, 1975-77; M.B.A., H.H.S.A., Cornell U., 1977. Supr., lifeguard Phila. Dept. Recreation, 1971-74; pharmacy intern Needle & Boonin, Zachian Bros. and Bell Family Pharmacies, Phila., 1976-79; mgr., partner Adero Pharmacy, Phila., 1980-83; sci. specialist Phila. Bd. Edn.; exec. dir. Urban Health Network Inc., 1984; bd. mgrs. YMCA of West Phila., 1985-88; contractor adminstr. BEBASHI, Phila., 1988—. Vol. Big Sisters Am., ARC, Phila.; elder, gospel choir Lombard Cen. Presbyn. Ch. USA, Phila. Mem. Nat. Assn. Health Svcs. Execs., Am. Public Health Assn., Pa. Assn. Notaries, United Presbyn. Women, Nat. Assn. Profl. and Exec. Women. Club: United Soul Ensemble.

PETERS, JUDY GALE, manufacturing company official, educator; b. Matoaka, W.Va., Dec. 13, 1941; d. Thomas Delbert and Vicie Clarice (Mundy) Hankins; m. Jesse Everitt Lobdell, Jr., Dec. 2, 1963 (div. Jan. 1975); 1 child, Jesse Everitt III; m. Kenneth Rae Peters, June 6, 1975 (div. Dec. 1984) 1 child, Kenneth Phillip. BS, Radford Coll., 1964. Tchr. county schs., Licking County, Ohio, 1964-73; with Hydrostrut Co., Newark, Ohio, 1974-76; buyer Anchor Coupling Co., Hebron, Ohio, 1976-78; expeditor Diebold Inc., Hebron, 1978-80, buyer, 1980-88, supr. purchasing, 1988—. Advisor 4-H Club Band, Licking County, 1965-67. Named Tchr. of Yr., Northridge Local Schs., 1972. Mem. Am. Choral Dirs., Diebold Mgmt. Club, Nat. Assn. Female Execs., Am. Soc. Profl. and Exec. Women. Club: Utica Music Boosters (Ohio). Lodge: Phythias. Avocations: reading, writing, dancing, bowling. Home: 3525 Johnstown Utica Rd Utica OH 43080

PETERS, KAREN RONELL, public administrator; b. Topeka, Kans., June 20, 1944; d. Ralph Keller and Mary Jean (Meyers) Wynn; 1 child, Lisa Renee. BA, U. Okla., 1966; MA in Spanish, Wichita State U., 1970; postgrad., U. Calif., Irvine, 1971-74, cert. in hazardous materials mgmt., 1986. Adminstrv. analyst I program planning div. County of Orange, Calif., 1976, adminstrv. analyst II program coordination div., 1976-79, staff analyst III program coordination div., 1979-80, mgr. adminstrv. services div. environ. mgmt. agy., 1980-84, sr. staff analyst hazardous material task force, 1984-86; mgr. hazardous materials program Orange County Fire Dept., 1986—; guest lectr. U. Calif., 1989. Co-chmn. issue briefing com. North Orange County chpt. NOW, 1983-84, state pres. Calif. 1979-81, chmn. polit. action task force, 1983-85, treas., 1983, numerous offices; sec. ERA-Orange County, 1982-83, treas. 1977-79; chmn. Community Devel. Coun., Inc., 1977-78, vice-chmn., 1976-77, chmn. project rev. and program devel. com., 1976-77; v.p., bd. dirs. Chateau Orleans Homeowners Assn., 1983-84, pres., 1977-78; active numerous polit. campaigns, 1976-84, prevention week activities Child Abuse Coun. Recipient numerous civic awards including Woman of Distinction award Soroptimist Internat. of Orange, 1989, Progress for Women award Santa Ana Coll., 1986, Cert. of Achievement for Leadership award North Orange County YWCA, 1986, Woman of Achievement award Women in Communications, Inc., 1983, Golden Key award Dem. Women Orange County, 1983, and many others. Mem. NOW, Calif. Hazardous Waste Assn., Calif. Chem. Waste Processors Assn., Am. Soc. for Pub. Adminstrn. (exec. coun. Orange County chpt. 1977-81, treas. 1978-79, chmn. task force 1976-77), U. Okla. Alumni Assn. (life), Wichita State U. Alumni Assn., Unitarian Soc. Orange County, Nat. Women's Polit. Caucus, Sigma Delta Pi. Home: 2525 N Bourbon St M-2 Orange CA 92665 Office: Orange County Fire Dept 180 S Water St Orange CA 92666

PETERS, KELLY BOYTE, clergywoman; b. Bartlesville, Okla., Oct. 12, 1958; d. Robert Howard and Barbara Ann (Stout) B.; m. David Alan Peters, June 18, 1983; children: Michael Eugene, Anne Elizabeth. BA, Kalamazoo Coll., 1980; MDiv, Vanderbilt U., 1983. Ordained minister Disciples of Christ Ch. Assoc. minister Cen. Christian Ch., Waco, Tex., 1983-85; edn. coord. Waco Rape Crisis Ctr., 1985-86; pastor First Christian Ch., Henry, Ill., 1986-88; assoc. minister Lakewood (Ohio) Congl. Ch., 1988—; freelance writer United Ch. News, Cleve., 1989—; com. mem. Continuing Edn. for Clergy, Cleve., 1988—. Co-author: Spiritual Growth, 1988; author: Holy Ground, 1990, Study Guide Ethics and Genetics, 1985. Pres. Inner City Ministry Bd. Dirs., Waco, 1986; sec. Bd. Dirs. Caritas of Waco, 1986. Democrat. Office: Lakewood Congl Ch 1375 W Clifton Blvd Lakewood OH 44107

PETERS, LAURIE JEAN, psychiatrist; b. Seattle, Calif., Apr. 26, 1943; d. Alan Emmett and Doris Anita (Hemrich) D.; m. Fitzgerald Peters, Dec. 14, 1964 (div. 1967); m. Thomas Lloyd Archer, Dec. 17, 1974; children: Theodore, Samuel, Amy; 1 adopted child, Nicolas Archer. BA, Stamford U., 1968; MD, U. Calif., San Diego, 1972. Intern U. Calif., San Diego, 1972-73, resident, 1973-75; mem. faculty dept. psychiatry USCD, La Jolla, Calif., 1975-80; clin. psychiatrist La Jolla, 1975-80, Roseville, Calif., 1980—; psychiatrist No. Calif. Surrogate Found., 1983—. Recipient American Friends of Psychiatry award, 1972.

PETERS, MERCEDES, psychoanalyst; b. N.Y.C.; student Columbia U., 1944-45; BS, L.I. U., 1945; MS, U. Conn., 1953; tng. in psychotherapy Am. Inst. Psychotherapy and Psychoanalysis, 1960-70; cert. in Psychoanalysis Postgrad. Ctr. For Mental Health; PhD in Psychoanalysis, Union Inst., 1989. Social worker various agys., pub. instns., 1945-63; staff affiliate, sr. psychotherapist Community Guidance Svc., 1960-75; affiliate Postgrad. Ctr. for Mental Health, 1974-76; pvt. practice psychotherapy, Bklyn., 1961—. Mem. LWV, NAACP. Cert. psychoanalyst Am. Examining Bd. Psychoanalysis; cert. mental health cons. Fellow Am. Orthopsychiat. Assn.; mem. Nat. Assn. Social Workers, Brooklyn Heights Mus. Soc., Postgrad. Ctr. Psychoanalytic Soc., Assn. For Psychoanalytic Self Psychology, N.Y. State Clin. Social Workers. Office: 142 Joralemon Brooklyn NY 11201

PETERS, MOLLY SAMUEL, obstetrician/gynecologist; b. Kerala, India, Mar. 17, 1958; came to U.S., 1965; d. Nagavara Koshy and Ammini (Alexander) Samuel; m. Albert Joseph, Sept. 24, 1988. BS, Columbia Union Coll., 1980; MD, Loma Linda U., 1984. Resident in family practice Rush-Presbyn. St. Luke Med. Ctr., Chgo., 1984-85; resident in ob-gyn. Geisinger Med. Ctr., Danville, Pa., 1985-89; staff ob-gyn. physician Neighborhood Health Ctr., Indpls., 1989—. Jr. fellow Am. Coll. Ob-Gyn. Office: Neighborhood Health Ctrs 3118 Bethel Ave Indianapolis IN 46203

PETERS, PAMELA SUE, family counselor; b. Cheyenne, Wyo., Dec. 6, 1956; d. Ernest Dane Peters and Twhila Marie (Robison) Dixon; m. Daniel Nelson Moss, Aug. 20, 1976 (div. Feb. 1984). B, Mt. Vernon Nazarene, 1979; M, U. Mo., Kansas City, 1983, cert. edl. specialist, 1986. Lic. profl. counselor, Mo. Counselor Community Counseling Service, Kansas City, Mo., 1983-84; pvt. practice counseling Kansas City, 1984—; family tng. counselor, vol. trainer Family and Childrens Services, Kansas City, Kans., 1986—; practicum instr. U. Mo., Kansas City, 1985; chairperson speakers bur. Wyandotte Coalition for Prevention of Child Abuse, Kansas City, Kans., 1986—. Mem. Hartford Family Inst., 1985—. Mem. Am. Assn. Counseling and Devel., Am. Assn. Milticultural Counseling and Devel., No. Assn. for Counseling and Devel., Mo. Assn. Multicultural Counseling and Devel. Home and Office: 2810 E 9th Kansas City MO 64124

PETERS, ROBERTA, soprano; b. N.Y.C., May 4, 1930; d. Sol and Ruth (Hirsch) P.; m. Bertram Fields, Apr. 10, 1955; children: Paul, Bruce. Ed. privately; Litt.D., Elmira Coll., 1967; Mus. D., Ithaca Coll., 1968, Colby Coll., 1980; L.H.D., Westminster Coll., 1974, Lehigh U., 1977; D.F.A., St. John's U., 1982; LittD, Coll. New Rochelle, 1989. Author: Debut at the Met; Met. Opera debut as Zerlina in Don Giovanni, 1950; recorded numerous operas; appeared motion pictures; frequent appearances radio and TV; sang at Royal Opera House, Covent Garden, London, Vienna State Opera, Munich Opera, West Berlin Opera, Salzburg Festival, debuts at festivals in Vienna and Munich; concert tours in U.S., Soviet Union, Scandinavian countries, Israel, China, Japan, Taiwan, South Korea, debut, Kirov Opera, Leningrad, USSR, sang at Bolshoi Opera, Moscow (1st Am. to receive Bolshoi medal). Named Woman of Yr. Fedn. Women's Clubs, 1964; honored spl. ceremony on 35th anniversary with the Met. Opera Co., 1985; was 1st Am. to receive Bolshoi medal. Home: Scarsdale NY 10583 Office: ICM Artists Ltd 40 W 57th St New York NY 10019

PETERS, ROBYN GOLDMAN, psychotherapist; b. St. Louis, Apr. 1, 1942; d. Sidney and Jacquelyn Rosetta (Forcheimer) Goldman; children: Todd A., Lisa Anne. BS in Elem. Edn., North Tex. State U., 1976, MEd, 1980; MS in Counseling, Prairie View A&M, 1986. Cert. alcohol & drug abuse, addictions counselor. Copywriter Van Winkle Motor Co., Dallas, 1970-72; copy writer Glenn Pub. Relations, Dallas, 1972-74; tchr. Dallas Ind. Sch. Dist., 1976-78, Plano (Tex.) Ind. Sch. Dist., 1978-80, Cypress Fairbanks Schs., Houston, 1980-85; psychotherapist domestic violence unit Harris County D.A.'s Office, Houston, 1986; coord. Optifast Program Cypress Fairbanks Med. Ctr., Houston, 1986-88; program therapist Spring Shadows Glen Psychiat. Hosp., Houston, 1988-90; pvt. practice, Houston, 1988-90—; speaker in field; therapist Alcohol Recovery Ctr., Boulder, Colo.

Mem. NOW, Am. Assn. Counseling Devel., Nat. Coalition Against Domestic Violence, Tex. Coun. Family Violence, Tex. Assn. Alcohol and Drug Abuse Counselors, Nat. Coun. Jewish Women, Bus. and Profl. Women Assn., Colo. Coalition for Domestic Violence, Colo. Addiction Counselors. Democrat. Home: 10307 Waving Fields Houston TX 77064

PETERS, TAMARA SUSAN, administrator; b. North Adams, Mass., Jan. 19, 1959; d. Francis A. and Helen M. (Mancuso) P. BA, BS, North Adams State Coll., 1980. Exec. dir. Northern Berkshire United Way, North Adams, Mass., 1980-81; dir. of devel. Shakepeare and Co., Lenox, Mass., 1981-82; acting exec. dir. Berkshire United Way, Pitts., 1982-83; pres. Tammy Peters and Assocs., Amsterdam, N.Y.; exec. dir. United Way Amstersdam N.Y. Inc., 1984--; cons. YWCA of Gloversville, N.Y., 1986-87; founder of ADD Cons. for FMCC, Inc., Johnstown, 1988—. Bd. mem. Touch Adv. Bd. of St. Marys Hosp., Amsterdam, 1989--, chmn. City of Amsterdam Chater 100th Anniversary, 1985. Named Citzen of the Year Rotary Club of Amsterdam, 1988. Mem. Profl. Adv. Coun. United Way of N.Y. State, Montgomery C. of C., Rotary (1st woman mem.). Roman Catholic. Home: 22 Green Acres Ln Hagaman NY 12086 Office: Polar Pla Rte 30N Amsterdam NY 12010

PETERS, TERESA WIDNER, computer systems manager, consultant; b. Knoxville, Tenn., June 11, 1959; d. Johnny Mack Widner and Wanda Faye (DeMarcus) Widner Rule; m. H. Wesley Peters, Mar. 18, 1982; 1 child, Erica Renee. BS in Mgmt.-Office Systems Concentration with honors, U. Tenn., 1985. Mktg. rep. Word Processing Systems, Inc., Oak Ridge, Tenn., 1985-86; service rep. Manpower Temporary Services, Knoxville, 1986; office automation cons. U. Tenn., Knoxville, 1986-89; mgr. Manpower Office Svcs. Ctr., Alcoa, 1990—. Mem. NAFE, Adminstrv. Mgmt. Soc. (v.p. mgmt. devel. greater Knoxville chpt. 1987—, bd. dirs., arrangements coord., photographer). Club: Knoxville Ski, Club LeConte. Home: PO Box 22073 Knoxville TN 37933 Office: Svcs Ctr 269 Cusick Rd Ste E Alcoa TN 37701

PETERS, VERA CONSTANCE ASTER HESS, real estate executive; b. Bklyn., Apr. 3, 1945; d. Charles H. and Erna Anna (Schoen) Aster. Student LDS Bus. Coll., 1958, U. Utah, 1961; m. Ted Peters, Nov. 23, 1980; children by previous marriage: Troy Dee, Tyrone Chad. Realtor, 1977-80; pres. Market Realty, Inc., 1980—; broker Eastern Airlines, 1985-87; product mgr., System One Corp., 1987—. Mem. Nat. Assn. Realtors, Salt Lake Bd. Realtors, Women's Coun. Realtors, LWV. Lutheran. Home: 501 Esplanade #104 Redondo Beach CA 90277

PETERS, VICKIE JANN, health care educator; b. Los Angeles, May 1, 1951; d. Edward and Elsie (Galyardt) Neuvert; m. Milan James Peters, June 24, 1972; 1 child, Milan Anthony. BS, Mount St. Mary's Coll., 1973; MS, Calif. State U., 1977, MA, 1978. RN. Adminstrv. dir. So. Calif. Orthopedic Research & Edn. Ctr., Van Nuys, Calif., 1987—; nursing faculty Calif. State U., Dominguez Hills, Calif., 1988—; nursing educator Valley Presbyn. Hosp., Van Nuys, 1973-87; cons. in field. Contbr. articles to profl. jours. Mem. The Cousteau Soc., Norfolk, Va., 1988. Mem. The Diabetes Educator Jour., AM. Assn. Diabetes Educators, Sigma Theta Tau, Phi Kappa Phi. Republican. Presbyterian. Home: 4228 Laurelgrove Ave Studio City CA 91604

PETERSBURG, LAURI LOTH, hospital financial manager; b. Dallas, Sept. 5, 1956; d. Robert Edward and LaNell (Musch) Loth; m. Bradley Floyd Petersburg, Oct. 6, 1979; children: Nicki, Alex. BS, Iowa State U., 1978. CPA, Iowa. Mgmt. trainee Northern Trust Bank, Chgo., 1978-79; fin. asst. North Iowa Med. Ctr., Mason City, 1980-81, chief fin. officer, 1981—. Mem. allocation com. United Way Cerro Gordo County, Mason City, 1984-86, bd. dirs. 1988-89; pres. Grace Luth. Ch., Hanlontown, Iowa, 1988, counsel mem., 1986-88; bd. dirs. Hospice N. Iowa, Mason City, 1988—, treas., 1989-90. Named Leader Lunch Honoree YWCA and Health One Corp., Mpls., 1987. Fellow Healthcare Fin. Mgmt. Assn. (advanced); mem. Iowa Soc. CPAs. Office: North Iowa Med Ctr 910 N Eisenhower Ave Mason City IA 50401

PETERSEN, ANNE CHERYL, college dean, educator; b. Little Falls, Minn., Sept. 11, 1944; d. Franklin Hanks and Rhoda Pauline (Sandwick) Studley; m. Douglas Lee Petersen, Dec. 27, 1967; children: Christine Anne, Benjamin Bradfield. BA, U. Chgo., 1966, MS, 1972, PhD, 1973. Asst. prof., rsch assoc. Dept. Psychiatry U. Chgo., 1972-80, assoc. prof., rsch. assoc., 1980-82; prof. human devel., head Dept. Individual and Family Studies Pa. State U., University Park, 1982-87, dean Coll. Health and Human Devel., 1987—; vis. prof., fellow Coll. End. and Devel. Psychology, Roosevelt. U., Chgo., 1973-74; cons. Ctr. for Health Adminstrn. Studies U. Chgo., 1976-78, Ctr. for New Schs., Chgo., 1974-78, Robert Wood Johnson Found. Mathtech, Inc., 1987— ; coord. clin. rsch. tng. program Michael Reese Hosp. and Med. Ctr., Chgo., 1976-80, dir. Lab. for Study of Adolescence, 1975-82; mem. faculty Ill. Sch. for Profl. Psychology, 1978-79; statis. cons. Coll. Nursing U. Ill. Med. Ctr., 1975-83; assoc. dir. health program MacArthur Found., 1980-82, also cons. health program, 1982-88; chair sr. adv. bd. NIMH, 1987-88. Reviewer Jour. of Youth and Adolescence, 1975-80, Devel. Psychology, 1979—, Sci., 1979, Jour. of Edn. Psychology, 1979—, Child Devel Devel., 1980—, Jour. Edn. Measurement, 1980, Ednl. Researcher, 1980—, Am. Ednl. Rsch. Jour., 1981—, Jour. of Mental Imagery, 1982—, Sex Roles, 1984—; cons. editor Psychology of Women Quarterly, 1978-82, assoc. editor, 1983-86; adv. editor Contemporary Psychology, 1985-86; editorial bd. various profl. jours. Bd. overseers Lewis Coll. Ill. Inst. Tech., 1980-82; mem. adv. bd. longitundinal data archive project Murray Ctr. Radcliff Coll., 1985—, sci. adv. bd., 1983—. Mem. NAS (nat. forum on the future of children and their families 1987—), AAAS, Am. Ednl. Rsch. Assn. (various offices), Am. Psychol. Assn. (chair task force on reproductive freedom 1979-81, program chair 1981-82, chair task force on long range planning 1986-89), Assn. Women in Sci., Behavior Genetics Assn., Psychometric Soc., Soc. for Rsch. on Adolescence (pres. elect 1988—, chair publ. com. 1986—). Home: 1338 Deerfield Dr State College PA 16803 Office: Pa State U Coll Human Devel 201 Henderson Bldg University Park PA 16802

PETERSEN, FRANKIE JOE, office manager; b. Troope, Tex., Oct. 7, 1933; d. Francis Harvey and Bessie Mae (Osborne) Simpson; m. Thomas John Kirby, Oct. 29, 1979 (div.); children: John Viktor Petersen. Student, Aurora U., 1949-51. Owner, operator Deckard Truck Co., Chgo., 1952; asst. to contr. Edgewater Inn, Mpls., 1962; asst. office mgr. Thriftway Foods, Oaks, Pa., 1979; office mgr., bookkeeper Tri County Roofing, Inc., Norristown, Pa. Fund raising Devon Horse Show, Valley Forge, Pa., 1975-83, Republican Group, Norristown, Pa., 1979--. Office: ACE Roofing & Sheet Metal 600 Markley St Norristown PA 19401

PETERSEN, MAUREEN JEANETTE MILLER, management information consultant; b. Evanston, Ill., Sept. 4, 1956; d. Maurice James and M. Joyce (Mielke) Miller; m. Gregory Eugene Petersen, July 7, 1984. BS in Nursing cum laude, Vanderbilt U., 1978; MS in Biometry and Health Info. Systems, U. Minn., 1984. Nurse U. Iowa Hosps. and Clinics, Iowa City, 1978-82; research asst. Sch. Nursing, U. Minn., Mpls., 1982-83; mgr. Arthur Andersen/Andersen Cons., Mpls., 1984—. Mem. Women in Biocomputing, Mensa. Methodist. Home: 1050 W County Rd C2 Roseville MN 55113 Office: Arthur Andersen 45 S 7th St Minneapolis MN 55402

PETERSON, ANNAMARIE JANE, medical record administrator; b. Eveleth, Minn., Aug. 9, 1936; d. Martin Henry and Agnes Elizabeth (Nyfors) Brown; m. Carl Dewane Peterson, Oct. 7, 1956 (div. Jan. 1968); children: Martine C. Peterson Trihey, Karin R. Peterson Harris, Carl Frederick (dec.). Student, Va. Jr. Coll., 1955, U. Minn., 1956; BA, Coll. of St. Scholastica, 1973. Pvt. practice interior design and drapery cons. Duluth and Two Harbors, Minn., 1966-72; dir. med. records Holy Family Hosp., Superior, Wis., 1973-75, Miller-Dwan Med. Ctr., Duluth, 1975—; clin. supr. Coll. of St. Scholastica, Duluth, 1973—; cons. St. Francis Nursing Home, Superior, 1975-78, Pk. Point Manor, Duluth, 1977-80, Polinsky Rehab. Ctr., Duluth, 1982-84; cons., com. mem. to develop med. transcription telecommunications project NorthSpan, Duluth, 1987—. Dem. Farmer Labor del., 1988; chmn. Lake County Devel. Commn., 1984—; mem. Lake County Housing and Redevel. Mgmt. Authority, 1984—, Knife River Community Coun., 1989—, Lake County Steering Com. for Blandin Community Leadership Program, 1989. Mem. Am. Med. Record Assn., Minn. Med. Record Assn. (nominating chmn. 1980, 89—, by-laws com. 1981, bd. dirs. 1987—), N.E. Minn. Med. Records Assn. (program chmn. 1977-79, pres. 1987—), Two Harbors Area C. of C., Altrusa Club of Duluth. Presbyterian. Home: Depot Campground Scenic Hwy 61 Knife River MN 55609 Office: Miller Dwan Med Ctr 502 E 2d St Duluth MN 55805

PETERSON, ANNE VIRGINIA, psychologist; b. Hartford, Conn., Jan. 24, 1948; d. Gustave Edward and Virginia (Denson) P. BA, Colby Coll., Waterville, Mass., 1970; MA, Cornell U., 1972; PhD, Ohio U., 1980. Lic. psychologist, Mass. Family worker Walker Sch., Needham, Mass., 1973-76; psychology intern Worcester (Mass.) State Hosp., 1979-80; psychology post-doctoral George Washington U. Health Plan, Washington, 1980-81; clin. psychologist U. Mass. Mental Health Svc., Amherst, 1981—, asst. dir. quality assurance, 1985—. Mem. Am. Psychol. Assn. Home: 44 Amity Pl Amherst MA 01002 Office: U Mass Mental Health Svc 127 Hills N Amherst MA 01003

PETERSON, APRIL LYNN, journalist; b. Chester, Pa., June 1, 1966; d. Gilbert Ernest and Charlotte A. (Brown) P. BA magna cum laude, Villanova U., 1988; student, Breadloaf Writer's Conf., Middlebury, Vt., 1989, Bucknell U., 1983. Freelance journalist East Penn Press, Emmaus, Pa., 1988—. Mem. Women in Communication, Amnesty Internat., Phi Beta Kappa, Phi Kappa Phi. Home: 5270 Javis Dr Emmaus PA 18049

PETERSON, BARBARA ANN, history educator; b. Portland, Oreg., Sept. 6, 1942; d. George Wright and Hope (Chatfield) Bennett; m. Frank Lynn Peterson, July 1, 1967. BA, BS, Oreg. State U., 1964; MA, Stanford (Calif.) U., 1965; PhD, U. Hawaii, Honolulu, 1978. Prof. history U. Hawaii, 1967—; chmn. social scis. dept. U. Hawaii, Honolulu, 1971-73, 75-76, asst. dean instrn., 1973-74; sabbatical teaching Asian and African history and world problems Chapman Coll. World Campus Afloat, 1974; tchr. European overseas exploration, expansion and colonialism U. Colo., Boulder, 1978; assoc. prof. continuing edn. and history U. Hawaii, Manoa, 1981; Fulbright prof. history Wuhan U., Rep. of China, 1988-89. Co-author: Woman's Place Is in the History Books, Her Story, 1620-1980, A Curriculum Guide for American History Teachers, 1980; author: Notable Women of Hawaii, 1984, America in British Eyes, 1988; mem. editorial bd. govs. American National Biography, 1989-90; contbr. articles to numerous profl. jours. Chairperson First Nat. Women's History Week, Hawaii, 1982; mem. State Commn. on Status of Women; mem. Coun. Bishop Mus. Recipient state proclamations Gov. of Hawaii, Mayor City of Honolulu, Outstanding Tchr. of Yr. award Wuhan (People's Republic China) U., 1988; Fulbright scholar, Japan, 1967, People's Republic China, 1988-89; NEH-Woodrow Wilson fellow, 1980. Fellow Internat. Biogl. Assn. (Cambridge, Eng. chpt.); mem. AAUW, Am. Studies Assn., Fulbright Alumni Assn. (founding Hawaii chpt., pres. 1984-88, nat. steering com. chairwomen Fulbright Assn. ann. conf., Honolulu 1990), Am. Hist. Assn. (numerous coms.), Hawaii Found. for History and Humanities (editorial bd. 1972-73), Hawaii Found. for Women's History, Hawaiian Hist. Assn., Nat. League Am. Pen Women (contest chmn. 1986). Home: 1341 Laukahi St Honolulu HI 96821 Office: U Hawaii 874 Dillinghem Blvd Honolulu HI 96817 also: East-West Ctr 1777 East-West Rd Honolulu HI 96848

PETERSON, BARBARA JO, public relations counselor; b. San Diego, Aug. 21, 1943; d. Warner Ernest and Opal Oneida (Weeks) P. Student, U. Houston, 1966, U. Ghana, West Africa, 1970-71; BA, UCLA, 1972, MA, 1975, postgrad., 1977. Jr. publicist Maslansky/Koenigsberg Pub. Rels., L.A., 1980; publicist Mahoney/Wasserman Pub. Rels., L.A., 1980; account exec. Scanlon, Skalsky, Menken Pub. Rels., L.A., 1981; assoc. Henri Bollinger Pub. Rels., L.A., 1982-85; ptnr. Peterson and Fisher Pub. Rels., L.A., 1986—. Editor: (mag.) World Series of Poker, 1984—. Chancellor's fellow UCLA, 1972. Mem. Women In Film, Publicists Guild of Am., Phi Beta Kappa, Phi Alpha Theta , Pi Gamma Mu. Republican. Greek Orthodox. Office: Peterson & Fisher Pub Rels 1800 N Argyle Ave Ste 407 Hollywood CA 90028

PETERSON, DIANE LYNN, rehabilitation specialist; b. Merrill, Wis., Sept. 6, 1955; d. Glen J. and Rosemarie (Kreis) Teskey; m. Steve A. Peterson, June 14, 1980; children: Lindsey Marie, Amanda Rae. BS in Phys. Therapy, U. Wis., LaCrosse, 1978; MS in Health Care Adminstrn., Cardinal Stritch Coll., Milw., 1989. Phys. therapist St. Joseph's Hosp., Marshfield, Wis., North Cen. Health Care Facilities, Wausau, Wis.; dir. rehab. svcs. Good Samaritan Health Ctr., Merrill. Bd. dirs. Our Way, Inc.; past v.p. bd. dirs. Hurd House, Merrill, Wis., 1987-88. Mem. Am. Phys. Therapy Assn. Home: 707 Cedar St Merrill WI 54452 Office: Good Samaritan Health Ctr 601 Center Ave Merrill WI 54452

PETERSON, HAZEL AGNES, consulting petroleum geologist; b. Houston; d. Howard Lynn, Sr., and Carrie Rice (Brown) P.; BA in Geology, NYU, 1939; MA in Geology, U. Tex., 1942; postgrad. various univs. Jr. subsurface geologist Shell Oil Co., Houston, 1942; subsurface geologist Texaco, Houston and Tulsa, 1942-44, Sun Oil Co., Dallas and Corpus Christi, Tex., 1944-52; supervising geologist Seaboard Oil Co. of Del., Dallas, 1952-54; pvt. practice cons. petroleum geologist, Dallas, Commerce and Denton, Tex., 1952—; instr. East Tex. State U., Commerce, 1958-67, asst prof., 1967-78; former water resources adv. City of Commerce. Mem. City of Commerce Planning and Zoning Commn., 1977-82, Bicentennial com. of the City of Denton, 1986-89. Rsch. grantee, U.S. Nat. Park Svc., 1959-61; faculty rsch. grantee East Tex. State U., 1960s. Mem. Am. Assn. Petroleum Geologists (cert. petroleum geologist), Dallas Geol. Soc., Dallas Geneal. Soc., DAR (regent 1983-85, parlimentarian 1985-88, state chmn. Tex. Woman's U. nursing scholarship fund 1985—, historian 1990—), Tex. State Soc. DAR, Huguenot Soc. of Founders of Manakin (parliamentarian Tex. state br. 1987-89, v.p. 1989—), Soc. New Eng. Women, Colonial Dames of XVII Century (charter; corr. sec.), Delta Zeta, Sigma Xi (hon.). Methodist. Rsch. profl. fields and local history; contbr. articles to various publs. Home and Office: 820 Hillcrest Denton TX 76201

PETERSON, J. RENEÉ, public relations professional; b. Houston, Jan. 7, 1966; d. Francis Kermit Dale and Juliana (Harrison) P. BA in English and BS in Journalism, Tex. Christian U., 1988. Dir. pub. rels. Arlington (Tex.) Family YMCA, 1988—; pub. speaker in field. Campaign coord. United Way, Ft. Worth, 1988, 89; fundraiser The 500, Inc., Dallas, 1989—; participant Leadership Arlington, 1989—. Mem. Women in Communications Inc. (co-chmn. career conf. 1989, student liaison 1990), Pub. Rels. Soc. Am. Roman Catholic. Home: 6060 Village Bend Apt 611 Dallas TX 75206 Office: Arlington Family YMCA 2200 S Davis Arlington TX 76013

PETERSON, JANE SCANLAND, real estate firm executive; b. Mineola, Mo., Dec. 18, 1935; d. Charles Boone and Pauline (Summers) Scanland; m. Robert Walter Peterson, July 27, 1957; children: Daniel Walter, David Scanland, John Christopher, Cheryl Dianne. B in Indsl. Studies, George Mason U., 1977. Tchr. Bonne Terre (Mo.) pub. schs., 1957-58; with sales dept. Cherner Lincoln Mercury, Tysons Corner, Va., 1977-79; sales rep. real estate VonMeister Georgelas, McLean, Va., 1979-81, The Phoenix Group, Vienna, Va., 1981-83, Ryan Lorey, Reston, Va., 1983-85; pres. Stratford Assocs., Inc., McLean, Va., 1985—; pres. LCIM, Fairfax, Va., 1985. Mem. No. Va. Assn. Realtors (bd. dirs. 1990, Top Producer award 1984). Presbyterian. Home: 1122 Duchess Dr McLean VA 22102 Office: Stratford Assocs Inc 1489 Chain Bridge Rd Ste 200 McLean VA 22101

PETERSON, JANE WHITE, nurse, anthropologist; b. San Juan, P.R., Feb. 15, 1941; d. Jerome Sidney and Vera (Joseph) Peterson; 1 child, Claire Marie. BS, Boston U., 1968; M in Nursing, U. Wash., 1969, PhD, 1981. Staff nurse Visiting Nurse Assn., Boston, 1964-66; prof. Seattle U., 1969—; chair dept. Community Health and Psychiatric Mental Health Nursing, 1988-89; sec. Coun. on Nursing and Anthropology, 1984-86; pres. Washington League of Nursing, Seattle, 1988—; pres. bd. Vis. Nurse Svcs., Seattle, 1988-90; contbg. cons. CSI Prodn., Okla., 1987; cons. in nursing WHO/U. Indonesia, Jakarta, fall, 1989. Contbr. articles to profl. jours. Mem. Seattle Art Mus., 1986—. Fellow: Soc. for Applied Anthropology; mem. Am. Anthropological Assn., Soc. for Med. Anthropology, Nat. League for Nursing, Am. Ethological Soc. Office: Seattle U Sch Nursing Broadway and Madison Seattle WA 98122

PETERSON, JANET BOLSTER, small business owner; b. Marblehead, Mass., Oct. 21, 1937; d. Charles Henry and Helen Vanderbilt (Bamford) Bolster. AA, Lasell Coll., Boston, 1952. Head pro Le Club Tennis Club, Milw., 1974-78; pres., owner, chief exec. officer Profl. Tennis Internat., El Cajon, Calif., 1978—; mktg. dir. San Diego Tennis Acad., 1980-83. Contbr. articles to profl. jours. Mem. Career Opportunities Panel, Milw., 1975-76. Mem. NAFE, U.S. Tennis Assn., Women's Tennis Assn., Nat. Cat Protection Soc., Zool. Soc. San Diego. Anglican. Home: 242 Van Houten El Cajon CA 92020 Office: PO Box 765 El Cajon CA 92022

PETERSON, JOLEEN PHYLLIS, probation officer; b. Somers Point, N.J., May 13, 1964; d. John Phillip and Joan Claudette (Motley) P. AS in Law Enforcement, Grambling State U., 1985, BS in Criminal Justice, 1986. Investigator Cape May County (N.J.) Probation Dept., 1986-88; probation officer Atlantic County Probation Dept., Atlantic City, N.J., 1988—. With ANG, 1987—. Mem. Am. Criminal Justice Assn.

PETERSON, KATHLEEN ANN, school psychologist; b. Erie, Pa., Jan. 28, 1951; d. Harry Melvin and Nathalie Jane (Summersgill) Edwards; m. David Rapp Peterson, June 23, 1972; 1 child, Jonathan David. BA in Psychology, Gannon Coll., Erie, 1972; MEd in Ednl. Psychology, Edinboro (Pa.) State U., 1974, cert. in sch. psychology, 1975; cert. in advanced study in adminstrn., SUNY, Buffalo, 1989. Nat. cert. sch. psychologist. Presch. tchr. Gertrude Barber Ctr., Erie, 1972-75; sch. psychologist Steubenville (Ohio) City Schs., 1976-78, Lancaster (N.Y.) Cen. Schs., 1979-80, Sweet Home Cen. Schs., Amherst, N.Y., 1980—; cons. Holland (N.Y.) Cen. Schs., 1984-85, Iroquois Cen. Schs., Elma, N.Y., 1984-85, Cynthia Clayton, M.D., East Aurora, N.Y., 1984-86. Mem., sec. long-range planning com. East Aurora Sch. Dist., 1987-90. Mem. Nat. Assn. Sch. Psychologists, N.Y. Assn. Sch. Psychologists, Phi Delta Kappa. Home: 299 S Grove St East Aurora NY 14052

PETERSON, KATHY MARIE, real estate executive; b. Burlington, Colo., Apr. 11, 1951; d. Marvin W. and Shirley M. (Revert) James; m. Dennis E. Wuthier, Aug. 13, 1972 (div. 1979); 1 child, Stacy M.; m. Kent M. Peterson, May 9, 1981. BBA, Colo. State U., 1972; BBA in Real Estate, Colo. U., 1981. Cert. real property adminstr. Real estate adminstr. United Banks of Colo., Inc., Denver, 1978-83; property mgr. Silverado Banking, Denver, 1983-84; property mgr. Field Real Estate Co., Denver, 1984-85, v.p. leasing, 1985, v.p. property mgmt., 1985-88, sr. v.p. property mgmt., 1988—; bd. dirs. Cherry Creek North. Sec. Colo. Bus. Energy Conservation, Denver, 1982-83. Mem. Bldg. Owners and Mgrs. Assn. (edn1. com. 1987—), Bldg. Owners and Mgrs. Internat. (real property adminstr. 1988), Soc. Real Property Adminstrn., Women in Comml. Real Estate. Republican. Baptist. Home: 1150 Lafayette St Denver CO 80218 Office: Field Real Estate Co 210 University Blvd Suite 600 Denver CO 80206

PETERSON, LISA LEE, beauty industry manager; b. Clark AFB, Philippines, Dec. 16, 1959; d. Wilbur Dean and Katherine (Lundgren) P. BS in Mktg. Mgmt. with ho, Radford U., 1978-82. Hairdresser Hair Pair, Md., 1979-82; market developer Playtex Inc., Stamford, Conn., 1982-85; dir. of edn. Beauty Group, Boston, 1985-87; reg. sales mgr. Conair corp., Stamford, 1987-88; regional sales mgr. Creative Hairdressers, Falls Church, Va., 1988-90, adminstrv. svc. mgr., 1990—. Mem. Delta Mu Delta. Republican. Lutheran. Home: 1641 Park Crest Circle Apt 101 Reston VA 22090 Office: Creative Hairdressers 2815 Hartland Rd Falls Church VA 22043

PETERSON, LOIS IRENE, transportation company executive; b. Falun, Kans., Mar. 25, 1935; d. Robert Theodore and M. LaVerne (Oleen) Dauer; m. Gerald L. Peterson, Mar. 13, 1955 (dec. May 1971); children: Dennis G., Linda Diane Peterson Johnson, Barbara Lynn Peterson Denny. Grad., Bell and Howell Internat. Acctg. Sch., Chgo., 1974; student, Brown-Mackie Coll., Salina, Kans., 1983. Co-owner Gerald's IGA Store, Falun, 1960-66; co-owner Gerald's Trucking Svc., Falun, 1966-71, pres., 1972—; sec.-treas. Wheat State Carriers Inc., Salina, 1985-88; asst. office mgr. Eldon's IGA Stores, Inc., McPherson, Kans., 1966-71; asst. office mgr. Smoky Hill Feedlot, Inc., Falun, 1971-86; bd. dirs. Kan. Motor Svcs., Inc.; speaker in field. Treas. Rural Water Dist. #1, Kans., 1972-75, bd. dirs., 1989; bd. dirs. Falun Drainage Assn., 1979. Mem. Kans. Motor Carriers Assn. (bd. dirs. 1979-82, 84—, Safety awards 1977-80, 82-88), Am. Trucking Assn. (state del. 1980-82). Avocations: photography, travel, reading, sewing. Home: Box 18 Falun KS 67442 Office: Gerald's Trucking Svc Falun KS 67442

PETERSON, LORNA INGRID, librarian; b. Buffalo, July 22, 1956; d. Raymond George and Sybil Odette (Lythcott) P. BA, Dickinson Coll., 1977; MSLS, Case Western Res. U., 1980. Reference libr. Wright State U., Dayton, Ohio, 1980-81; catalogr Ohio U., Athens, 1981-82; cataloger Iowa State U., Ames, 1983-85, libr. instr., 1985-89, bibliographic instrn. libr., 1989—; vis. asst. prof. Sch. Info. and Libr. Studies, SUNY/Buffalo, 1990—. Contbr. articles to profl. jours. Bd. dirs. YWCA, Ames, 1984-86. Mem. ALA, Iowa Libr. Assn. (chair communications com. 1984-86, chair membership com. 1987, co-chair 1987-88), Assn Coll. and Rsch. Libs. Office: SUNY-Buffalo 381 Baldy Hall Buffalo NY 14260

PETERSON, LYNN MARIE, immunologist; b. Milw., Dec. 28, 1953; d. Dorance and Audrey Mae (Mackie) P.; m. Lawrence Everett Dux, Aug. 28, 1976; children: Justin Peterson Dux, Erika Alena Dux. BS in Med. Microbiology, U. Wis., 1976. Cert. technologist in immunology, specialist in immunology Am. Soc. Clin. Pathologists. Lab. technologist dept. med. microbiology U. Wis., Madison, 1977-79; immunology technologist St. Joseph's Hosp., Milw., 1979-89, flow cytometrist, 1990—. Mem. Assn. Med. Lab. Immunologists, Wis. Histology Soc., Mensa. Roman Catholic. Home: N27 W22327 Burningwood Ln Waukesha WI 53186 Office: Franciscan Shared Lab St Joseph's Hosp 5000 W Chambers St Milwaukee WI 53210

PETERSON, MARIA CAROLINE, telecommunications executive; b. Hackensack, N.J., July 18, 1950; d. Carmine and Rose (Pisano) Zazzaro; m. John Peterson; children: Damon, Jessica. Grad. high sch., Orange, N.J. Phone ctr. mgr. AT&T, Parsippany, N.J., bus. performance mgr., asst. staff mgr. phone ctr. support. Mem. NAFE. Home: 22 Kensington Pl East Orange NJ 07017

PETERSON, MARY ALICE, medical technologist; b. Avella, Pa., Aug. 2, 1933; d. Clarence Raymond and Mary Sue (Ayers) Painter; m. Charles Robert Peterson, Jan. 26, 1957; 1 child, Caroline Sue. BS, Marietta Coll., 1955; Med. Technologist, Watts Hosp., Durham, N.C., 1956; MEd, Lehigh U., 1972. Supr. chemistry dept. Quincy (Mass.) City Hosp., 1957; med. technologist, educator Allentown (Pa.) Hosp., 1965-69; substitute tchr. Area Sch. Dists., Allentown, 1969-71; sci. tchr. Salisbury Twp. Schs., Allentown, 1971-76, Tehran (Iran) Am. Sch., 1976-78; supr. Balt. area office Md. Med. Lab., 1979-82; med. technologist, phlebotomy coordinator, St. Joseph Hosp., Towson, Md., 1982-89; pvt. practice, 1989—; mem. supts. adv. com. Tehran Am. Sch., 1977-78. Mem. ch. coun. Ascension Luth. Ch., Towson, 1986-89; mem. com. to organize and create Lehigh Valley Conservancy, Allentown, 1975; mem. Md. Com. for Responsible Corrections Policy. Mem. Am. Soc. Clin. Pathologists, AAUW (state pres. 1988-90, appointee pub. policy com. 1989—, award for community svc. 1986), LWV (coord. state lobby day 1986-88), Beta Beta Beta. Democrat. Home: 7400 Stanmore Ct Baltimore MD 21212 Office: St Joseph Hosp 7620 York Rd Towson MD 21204

PETERSON, MONICA (MONIQUE) (DOROTHY PETERSON), actress, singer, writer. Drama cert., Neighborhood Playhouse, N.Y.C., 1963, Jeff Corey Sch. Acting, 1967; student Sch. Music and Dance, Covent Garden, London, 1972; AA, Santa Monica Coll., 1983; BA, U. So. Calif., 1986. Editorial sec., writer Look mag., N.Y.C., 1964-66; asst. mgr. Venture Mag. Advt., N.Y.C., 1965-66; actress, singer, performer Wm. Morris Agy., Hollywood, Calif., 1967-70; contract player 20th Century Fox, 1967-70; contract singer, dancer, actress L.A. City Hall Theatre of Arts, 1975-80; staff writer SMC, L.A., 1981-83, newspaper editor, 1983-84; writer USC Newspaper, 1985-86; singer, actress, performer Agy. William Morris, London, Spain, Italy, Calif. Script analyst, editor, asst. casting dir. Inner City Cultural City, L.A., 1974-76; vol. Easter Seals, also vol. work for diabetics, homeless, needy, elderly and sick. Recipient Hollywood Star of Tomorrow award ABC, 1968, Overseas award USO, 1969, Two Thousand Women of Achievement award, Foremost Women in Communication Am. Pub. Co.

Mem. SAG (v.p. minority com. 1969-71, rep. Image award 1969-72), AFTRA, Women in Film, Equity. Democrat. Roman Catholic.

PETERSON, NADEEN, advertising agency executive; b. McKeesport, Pa., Dec. 3, 1934; d. Michael James and LaVerna Peal (Long) Powell; m. Robert Glenn Kilzer, Dec. 24, 1966; 1 son, Douglas Robert. Student, U. Fla., 1952-53. Copywriter Ellington & Co., N.Y.C., 1961-64; v.p., assoc. creative dir. Tatham-Laird, N.Y.C., 1964-65, Foote, Cone & Belding, Inc., N.Y.C., 1966-69; v.p., sr. assoc. creative dir. Norman, Craig & Kummell, N.Y.C., 1969-70, sr. v.p., creative dir., 1975-77; sr. v.p., creative dir. Doyle, Dane, Bernbach, Inc., N.Y.C., from 1978; sr. v.p. Saatchi & Saatchi DFS Compton, N.Y.C., exec. v.p., creative dir., exec. v.p., exec. creative dir., 1987-89, vice-chmn., exec. creative dir., 1989—; vice-chmn., exec. creative dir. Saatchi & Saatchi Advt., 1989. Recipient Matrix award, 1977; named 100 Best Brightest Women in Advt. Advt. Age, 1988. Office: Saatchi & Saatchi Advt 375 Hudson St New York NY 10014

PETERSON, NANCY ANN, real estate broker; b. Fargo, N.D., Sept. 18, 1947; d. Simar Kristian and Rhoda Alice (Anderson) Nelson; m. John William Peterson, Oct. 20, 1967 (dec. Aug. 1979); 1 child, Dauvin John. BS, Moorhead State U., 1979; student Real Conservatorio, Madrid, Spain, 1981. Cert. comml. investment mgr. Owner, pres. Circle Realtors Inc., Fargo, 1971—; bd. dirs. Town & Country Realty; Honorarium prof. Classical Guitar Moorhead State U. Bd. dirs. Plains Art Mus., Moorhead, Minn., 1983—, pres., 1987—; mem. devel. council Moorhead State U., 1987; treas. O'Rourke-Plains Mus., Moorhead, 1984-85, v.p., 1986-87; pres. O'Rourke-Plains Arts Assn., 1987-88; pres. Plains Art Mus., 1987-88; mentor Women's Network for Entrepreneuial Tng., 1989-90. Mem. Nat. Assn. Realtors, Fargo-Moorhead Bd. Realtors, Women's Council Realtors (pres. 1977), Fargo-Moorhead Home Builders, Linden Assoc., Fargo-Moorehead Black History Orgn. (com. dir. 1989), Women's Network for Entrepreneurial Tng. (mentor 1989-90). Lodge: Zonta. Avocations: classical guitar, fishing, scuba diving, skiing. Office: Cir Realtors Inc 1220 Main Ave Fargo ND 58103

PETERSON, NORMA JO, teacher; b. Knoxville, Tenn., Dec. 26, 1938; d. Henry Beecher and Dorotha (Gross) P. BS, U. Tenn., 1960; MA, E. Tenn. State U., 1976. Cert. Career Ladder Level III elem. tchr. Elem. tchr. Knox County-Halls Elem. Sch., Knoxville, 1960-63; adminstrv. asst. Southeastern Region-Ch. of the Brethren, Bridgewater, Va., 1963-64; dir. Children's Work Nat. Office-Ch. of the Brethren, Elgin, Ill., 1964-69; elem. tchr. Prince George's County-Seabrook Elem. Sch., Seabrook, Md., 1969-70, Kingsport (Tenn.) City Schs., Kingsport, 1970—. Recipient Outstanding Educator award, Kingsport City Schs., Tenn., 1986. Mem. NEA, Tenn. Edn. Assn., Kingsport Edn. Assn., Delta Kappa Gamma, Phi Kappa Phi, Pi Lambda Theta. Home: 4100 Prescott Dr Johnson City TN 37601

PETERSON, PAMELA WYNNE, broadcast producer and director; b. Columbia, Mo., June 17, 1949; d. John Edwin and Jane Cordelia (Scarbrough) P. BA, Cornell U., 1971. V.p. Sta. WVBR-FM, Ithaca, N.Y., 1969-71; studio and field engr. ABC Radio Network, N.Y.C., 1975-77; technician CBS TV Network, N.Y.C., 1977-81, mgr. tech. planning div., 1981-84; producer, dir. Sta. WMHT-Channel 17, Schenectady, N.Y., 1986-87; pres. ZPPR Prodns., Inc., N.Y.C., 1983—; cons. TL Electronics, N.Y.C., 1975—. Contbr. articles to profl. jours. Democrat. Office: ZPPR Prodns Inc 34 Gansevoort St New York NY 10014

PETERSON, PATTI MCGILL, college president; b. Johnstown, Pa., May 20, 1943; d. Earl Frampton and Helen Gertrude (Hershberger) McGill; m. Luther D. Peterson, Aug. 31, 1968; 1 son, Lars-Anders. B.A. in Polit. Sci., Pa. State U., 1965; M.A. in Polit. Sci., U. Wis., 1968, Ph.D. in Polit. Sci. and Ednl. Policy, 1974; cert. advance study, Harvard U., 1977; D.Litt (hon.), Le Moyne Coll., 1983. Asst. prof. polit. sci., dean of freshman women Schiller Coll., Ger., 1968-69; asst. prof. polit. sci. SUNY-Oswego, 1971-72, asst. to pres., adj. prof., 1972-77, v.p. acad. services and planning, assoc. prof., 1978-80; pres., prof. govt. Wells Coll., Aurora, N.Y., 1980-87, St. Lawrence U., Canton, N.Y., 1987—; bd. dirs. Nia. Mo. Power Corp. Author numerous articles in field. Trustee Nat. Women's Hall of Fame; dir. Security Mut. Life Ins. Co., OnBank; trustee Northwood Sch., Sta. WCNY-TV-FM; mem. bd. overseers The Nelson A. Rockefeller Inst. Govt., 1988—; trustee Assn. Am. Colls., 1987—; chmn. Pub. Leadership Edn. Network, 1983-85; mem. Gov.'s Com. on Vol. Enterprise, 1983-85; pres. Assn. Colls. and Univs., N.Y., 1984-86, Women's Coll. Coalition, 1983-85. Carnegie fellow Harvard U., 1977. Mem. Am. Council Edn. (chmn. com. on leadership devel. and acad. adminstrn. 1982-84), Am. Assn. Higher Edn., Middle States Assn. Colls. and Schs. (cons., chmn.). Home: Taylor House Aurora NY 13026 Office: St Lawrence U Canton NY 13617

PETERSON, PAULA MARIA, nurse; b. Sidney, Mont., Aug. 22, 1961; d. Gene Vernon Peterson and Ina Claire (Chandler) Pocha. AS in Nursing, Miles Community Hosp., Miles City, Mont., 1983; BS in Nursing, U. Tex., Arlington, 1986, postgrad., 1989—. RN, Tex.; cert. in advanced cardiac life support. Nurse asst. Community Meml. Hosp., Sidney, 1978-82; nurse Scott and White Meml. Hosp., Temple, Tex., 1983-86, Hugley Meml. Hosp., Ft. Worth, 1986-87; nurse ICU-CCU, All Saints Hosp.-Citiview, Ft. Worth, 1987—. Scholar VFW, 1979, Wayne Prevost Meml. scholar Savage (Mont.) Jaycees, 1979. Home: Rte 4 Box 368 Cleburne TX 76031

PETERSON, POLLY WIETZKE, educational psychologist; b. Flint, Mich., May 15, 1939; d. Mark Carl and Mary (Jones) Wietzke; m. David Leon Peterson, Aug. 30, 1962; children: David, Pirkko. BS, U. Mich., 1961; MA, Mich. State U., 1963, PhD, 1973. Tchr. U. Mich. Children's Psychiat. Hosp., Ann Arbor, 1961-62, asst. dir. sch., 1964-66; master tchr. dept. ednl. psychology U. Mich., Ann Arbor, 1964-66; asst. prof. ednl. psychology U. Miami, Coral Gables, Fla., 1966-68; asst. prof. pediatrics, dir. edn. psychology div. U. Miami, Fla., 1968-76; cons. Grupo Alfa, Casolar, Manzanillo, Mexico, 1977; EdD practicum advisor Nova U., Ft. Lauderdale, Fla., 1978—, sr. faculty Ctr. for Advancement Edn., 1980—; pvt. practice cons. Ft. Lauderdale, 1980—; exec. dir. Grand Traverse Area Child Care Council, Northwestern Mich. Coll., 1987-88; cons. Fla. Health and Rehab. Svcs. for Children and Youth Projects, 1988-89; cons. in field, 1988—. Contbr. articles to profl. jours., 1976—. Profl. pres. Ft. Lauderdale (Fla.) Jr. League, 1973, sustainer Jacksonville, 1984—; bd. dirs. Pub. TV of South Fla., 1976-79; vol. abuse prevention programs pub. schs., Mich., 1985-87; chmn. Benzie (Mich.) Family Advs., 1983-86; pres. bd. United Way, Benzie County, Mich., 1987-88. Mich. Dept. Pub. Health grantee, 1984, 85. Mem. Nat. Reading Assn., Nat. Assn. Educators Young Children, Council Exceptional Children, Delta Delta Delta. Republican. Congregationalist. Home: 335 Glen Lyon Dr Orange Park FL 32073

PETERSON, SALLY LU, communications executive; b. Waukegan, Ill., July 23, 1942; d. George C. and Luella Alice (Flood) P. BA, Govs. State U., Park Forest, Ill., 1983. V.p. Cabac TV, Gurnee, Ill., pres. Evangelist, founder, organizer TV ministry Calling Revival, 1977—, producer, dir. TV programming for Northern Ill., 1983—. Mem. Cabac Cable TV Producers of Lake County Ill. (pres. 1984, 88—), Order Ea. Star (Worthy Matron of Waukegan 209, 1968), Warren-Newport Woman's Afternoon Club of Gurnee (pres. 1982-84, 86-80). Home and Office: 33712 N O'Plaine Rd Gurnee IL 60031

PETERSON, SOPHIA, educator; b. Astoria, N.Y., Nov. 24, 1929; d. George Loizos and Caroline (Hofstetter) Yimoyines; m. Virgil Allison Peterson, Dec. 28, 1951; children: Mark Jeffrey, Lynn Marie. BA, Wellesley (Mass.) Coll., 1951; MA, UCLA, 1956, PhD, 1969. Instr. Miami U., Oxford, Ohio, 1961-63; with W.Va. U., Morgantown, 1966—, assoc. prof., 1972-79, prof., 1979—; co-dir. W.Va. Consortium for Faculty & Course Devel. in Internat. Studies, Morgantown. Author: monograph Monograph Series in World Affairs, 1979. Recipient CASE Prof. of the Yr. award Coun. for Advancement & Support of Edn., 1987, Outstanding Tchr. award W.Va. U. Coll. Arts & Scis., 1988, W.Va. U., 1988. Mem. Internat. Studies Assn. (v.p. Mid-Atlantic chpt. 1978-86), W.Va. Polit. Sci. Assn. (pres. 1984-85), AAAUP (pres. W.Va. U. chpt. 1976-78). Democrat. Home: 849 Vandalia Rd Morgantown WV 26505 Office: WVa U Dept Polit Sci Morgantown WV 26506

PETERSON, SUSAN KATHRYN, speech-language pathologist; b. Mountain View, Calif., Nov. 21, 1964; d. Lloyd Arthur and Frances Kathryn (Herriott) P. BS in Edn., Baylor U., 1986, MS with honors, 1987. Cert. clin. rehab. svcs., clin. competence. Resident asst. Baylor U., Waco, Tex., 1984-87; speech lang. pathologist Altos Speech, Lang. and Learning Ctr., Los Altos, Calif., 1987; area assoc., jr. paralegal Apple Computer, Inc., Cupertino, Calif., 1987-89; speech-lang. pathologist San Jose (Calif.) Unified Sch. Dist., 1989—. Leader, officer First Bapt. Ch., Los Altos, 1988—. Mem. Am. Speech Lang. Hearing Assn., Calif. Speech Lang. and Hearing Assn., Nat. Student Speech Lang. and Hearing Assn. (v.p. 1986-87), Tex. Student Speech Lang. and Hearing Assn. (v.p. 1987-88). Republican. Office: Randol Elem Sch 762 Sunset Glen Dr San Jose CA 95123

PETERSON, SUSAN VIETZKE, educator, researcher; b. El Reno, Okla., Oct. 13, 1960; d. Vernon H. and Mary (Swagerty) Vietzke; m. Alan Peterson, May 21, 1982. BA in Sociology, U. Okla., 1979, M in Human Rels., 1981; PhD in Home Econs., Okla. State U., 1984. Tutor U. Okla., Norman, 1980; news intern Sta. OETA-PBS, Oklahoma City, 1981; asst. producer Sta. KWTV-Channel 9 (CBS affiliate), Oklahoma City, 1981-82; human rels. cons. Indian-Meredian Vo-Tech Sch., Stillwater, Okla., 1983; tchr. kindergarten and English as second lang. McAllen (Tex.) Ind. Sch. Dist., 1986-87; instr. psychology and sociology Tex. State Tech Inst., Harlingen, 1987-89; asst. prof. child devel. and family studies Tarleton State U., Stephenville, Tex., 1989-90. Contbr. articles to profl. jours. Mem. Am. Home Econs. Assn. (New Achiever award 1989), Tex. Home Econs. Assn. (New Achiever award 1989), Am. Vocat. Assn. Mailing Address: RR 2 Box 100H Stratford OK 74872 Home: 1611 Vanderbilt #13 Stephenville TX 76401

PETERSON, SUSHILA JANE, dentist; b. New Delhi, June 4, 1952; d. James Carlyle and Audrey (Clinton) P. BS, Howard U., 1974, DDS, 1979. Assoc. dentist pvt. practice Silver Spring, Md., 1983-87; pvt. practice dentistry Washington, 1987—. Capt. U.S. Army, 1979-83; USAR Dental Corp, 1983-86. Mem. ADA, D.C. Dental Soc., Robert T. Freeman Dental Soc., AAUW, Alpha Kappa Alpha. Democrat. Roman Catholic. Home and office: 3816 8th St NW Washington DC 20011

PETERSON, VICKI JENKINS, social work educator; b. Wichita; d. William Harvard and Emelyne Bess (Gumm) Jenkins; m. Richard Herbert Peterson, Oct. 4, 1980; children—Erin, Michael, Chris. B.A., Duke U., 1971; M.S.W., U. N.C., 1980. Clin. social worker Western Carolina Ctr., Morganton, N.C., 1975-80, coordinator child and family services, 1980-83; exec. dir. Hospice Burke County, Morganton, 1983-84; dir. mktg. Mountain MicroSystems, Morganton, 1984-86 ; clinical instr. Sch. Social Work East Carolina U., Greenville, N.C., 1986—; instr. Western Piedmont Community Coll., 1985-86 ; cons. Morganton Area Psychologists and Attys., 1982-84; cons., trainer N.C. State Dept. Social Services. Steering com. Burke Soup Kitchen, Morganton, 1985-86 ; pres. bd. dirs. 1st Presbyn. Preschool Program, Morganton, 1985-86 ; pres. Durham Rape Crisis Ctr., N.C., 1975; lay reader St. Marys Episc. Ch., Morganton, 1983-86, St. Timothy's Episc. Ch., Greenville, 1987—; mem. program planning com., Greenville Community Shelter, 1987—. Named Outstanding Young Woman in Am. 1981, Outstanding Staff Mem. Western Carolina Ctr. 1982. Mem. Nat. Assn. Social Workers, Am. Assn. Mental Deficiency, N.C. Assn. Social Workers Mental Health, Assn. Retarded Citizens. Democrat. Episcopalian. Avocations: reading, travel. Home: 1900 E 6th St Greenville NC 27858 Office: East Carolina U Sch Social Work Greenville NC 27834

PETERSON PEREZ, EMILY LYNN, artist; b. Davenport, Iowa, Mar. 16, 1951; d. John Edwin and Jane Cordelia (Scarbrough) Peterson; m. Francisco Perez, Sept. 20, 1986. BFA in Illustration, Syracuse U., 1973, studies with Daryl Hughto, 1973, vis. artist studies with Milton Resnick, 1973. Owner, artist Peterson Perez Graphics, N.Y.C., 1980—; Freelance illustration, graphic and prodn. art for various orgns. including Nat. Resource Def. Coun., Nat. History Mag., Rodale Press, Stamford Ctr. for Arts, Time, Inc. Mags., others, 1975—; art instr. after sch. scholarship program Internat. Gallery, N.Y.C., 1987, Sarah Lawrence Sch., 1985; presenter graphic arts seminar N.Y.C. Found. for the Community of Artists, 1978. Exhibited in group shows at John Hawkes Pub., Milw., 1978, Internat. Gallery, N.Y.C., 1986, Esta Robinson Contemporary Art, N.Y.C., 1986; represented in pvt. and pub. collections. Mem. N.Y. Artists Equity Assn., Graphic Artists Guild, Syracuse U. Met. Alumni Club. Democrat. Studio: Peterson Perez Graphics 651 W 188th St #6P New York NY 10040

PETIET, CAROLE ANNE, clinical psychologist; b. Newport News, Va., Mar. 1, 1952; d. Gaston Kaleski and Ann (Snyder) Pettit Johnson; m. Lawrence Phillip Bischoff III, Dec. 29, 1973 (div. 1979); m. Robert Jomax Brooks, May 4, 1984 (div. 1989); 1 child, Niclole; stepchildren: Gregory, Randall. BS in Nursing, Baylor U., 1975; MA, Calif. Sch. Profl. Psychology, Berkeley, 1980, PhD, 1982. Lic. psychologist, Calif., Colo.; RN, Calif. Charge nurse Elizabeth Knutsson Hosp., Estes Park, Colo., 1975-76; nurse coordinator, staff nurse Alta Bates Hosp., Berkeley, Calif., 1976-83; pvt. practice psychotherapy, cons. Berkeley, Calif., 1982—; tng./clin. cons., rsch. cons. Phoenix Recovery Ctrs., Alameda, Calif., 1980-88; staff psychologist Kaiser Permanente Med. Ctr., Vallejo, Calif., 1982-84; sports psychology cons. Women's Ski Programs, Aspen, Colo., and B.C., Can., 1986—; coord. women's studies specialty, mem. adj. faculty Rosebridge Grad. Sch., Walnut Creek, Calif., 1986—; supr., mem. adj. faculty CSPP, Berkeley, 1986-89; intern Eden Youth and Family Svcs., Hayward, Calif., 1978-79, No. Calif. State Correctional Med. Facility, Vacaville, 1979-80, Kaiser Vallejo, 1980-81, Kaiser San Francisco, 1981-82; researcher in field. Contbr. articles, presentations to profl. publs. Scholar Baylor Hosp. Women's Aux., 1974, Soroptimists, 1981; recipient Am. Coll. Scholarship, 1979. Fellow Am. Orthopsychiat. Assn.; mem. Am. Psychol. Assn., Assn. Women in Psychology, World Fedn. Mental Health, NOW, Amnesty Internat., Wilderness Soc., Sierra Club, Colo. Mountain Club, Am. Friends of Tibet, Am. Women's Expedition to Mt. Kongur, China. Democrat. Office: 2340 Ward St Ste 105 Berkeley CA 94705

PETILLO, M. JOANN, analytical chemist, researcher; b. Balt., May 30, 1959; d. Frank and Carmen Marta (Fimiani) P. B.S. in Biology, Loyola Coll., Balt., 1981; postgrad. U. Balt. Analytical chemist Ecol. Analysts, Sparks, Md., 1982-83, Martin Marietta Corp., Balt., 1983-84; lab. mgr. Arundel Corp., Towson, Md., 1984—. Mem. Am. Concrete Inst., Soc. Applied Spectroscopy, Materials Research Soc., ASTM, Smithsonian Assocs., Nat. Assn. Female Execs. Democrat. Roman Catholic. Lodge: Sons of Italy. Avocations: jogging; raquetball; bicycling; piano. Home: 1612 Pinnter Rd Lutherville MD 21093 Office: The Arundel Corp 6806 Greenspring Ave Baltimore MD 21209

PETIT, LYNN ANN, school guidance counselor; b. Bklyn., Sept. 23, 1948; d. Richard George and Jean Margaret (Thurman) Berry; m. Thomas Lee Petit, July 4, 1981. BA, Notre Dame Coll., Cleve., 1970; MEd, Trenton State U., 1975. Cert. guidance counselor, Vt. Art tchr. Holy Name High Sch., Cleve., 1970-72, Hillsborough Middle Sch., Belle Meade, N.J., 1971-76; guidance counselor N. Country Union Jr. High Sch., Derby, Vt., 1976—. Author: (poems) Doubletake, 1973. Bd. advisors Lyndon State Coll., Lyndonville, Vt., 1988—. Home: RR 2 Box 384A Newport VT 05855 Office: N County Jr High Sch RR a Box 125 Derby VT 05829

PETO, ULRIKE ELIZABETH, import company executive; b. Wurbenthal, Tropau, West Germany, Apr. 25, 1944; came to U.S., 1971; d. Adolf and Irmgard (Merkel) Fritsch; m. Frank Desco Peto, Apr. 17, 1973; 1 child, Miranda Ursula. Grad. high sch., Nordlingen, West Germany. Apprentice Eisen-Fischer, Nordlingen, 1960-63, sec., showroom sales, 1963-70; exec. sec. Gittfried, Dachau, 1970-71, Otto Wolff, Houston, 1973-78; v.p. Sunbelt Trading Co., Houston, 1978—. Mem. Houston Grand Opera Guild, 1982—, Zoological Soc., Houston, 1986—; vol. Act for 8, Houston, 1982—. Mem. Tex. Assn. Steel Importers (pres. 1986-88, dir. 1982—, outstanding svcs. award 1988), Assn. of Women in the Metal Industry, Am. Inst. Internat. Steel (bd. dirs. 1990—). Roman Catholic. Office: Sunbelt Trading Co Inc 2000 Post Oak Blvd 1867 Houston TX 77056

PETRAKIS, JULIA WARD, small business owner; b. Englewood, N.J., Mar. 24, 1936; d. William Davis and Elizabeth (Shaw) Ticknor; children by previous marriage: Elizabeth Anne Kinnunen Stam, Allan Conrad III; m. Peter L. Petrakis, Jan. 2, 1988. BA in Biochemistry, Radcliffe Coll., 1958. Ct. reporter Miller Reporting, Washington, 1979-81; sec. Whittaker Corp., Arlington, Va., 1981-82; adminstrv. asst. Entre Computers, Tysons Corner, Va., 1982-84; bus. owner Facts on Line, Annapolis, 1984—; cons., researcher, book indexer, writer, and instr. in field. interviewer Harvard-Radcliff Colls., Cambridge, Mass., 1984-85; vol. Cancer Drive, Heart Drive, Annapolis, 1986-88; dir. Cape St. Claire Security Fund, Anapolis, Md., 1988-90. Home and Office: Facts OnLine 2020 Lake Heights Dr R301 Everett WA 98208

PETRAKIS-PAWSON, STELLA ROSE, nurse; b. San Juan, P.R., Mar. 5, 1948; d. Manuel Mark and Carmencita Eda (Diaz) Petrakis; m. Ivan Guy Pawson, Aug. 5, 1973 (div. 1990); 1 child, Laurence Gilmark. AB, Cornell U., 1970; BS, U. Calif., San Francisco, 1973; MS, U. Calif., 1978. RN, Calif. Oncology Cert. Nurse. Clin. nurse U.C.L.A., 1973-74; rsch. nurse U. Calif., San Francisco, 1974-77; oncology clin. nurse specialist VNA Alameda County, Oakland, Calif., 1977-84; clin. nurse specialist Pacific Presbyn. Med. Ctr., San Francisco, 1984—. Author: (booklet) Caring for the Cancer Patient at Home, 1985, '88. Non-salaried asst. prof. U. of Calif., San Francisco, 1982-; treas. Cub Scout Pack 14, San Francisco, 1987-90, asst. den leader Den 5, Cub Scout Pack 14, San Francisco, 1987-90. Named Spl. Vol. Am. Cancer Soc., San Francisco, 1977. Mem. Oncology Nursing Soc., Bay Area Oncology Nursing Soc. (co-chmn. Archives 1982—), Bay Area Vascular Access Network (v.p. 1988-89, pres. 1990—), Nursing Pain Assn. Democrat. Buddhist. Home: 387 Los Palmos Dr San Francisco CA 94127 Office: Pacific Presbyn Med Ctr 2351 Clay St San Francisco CA 94115

PETRARCA, PAMELA BETH, real estate developer; b. Chgo., June 9, 1956; d. Sheldon Sumner Simon and Pearl (Downey) Nugent; m. Justino Dante Petrarca, Aug. 4, 1979 (div. 1986). BA, U. Ill., 1978. Lic. real estate salesperson, Ill. Legal sec. Jenner and Block, Chgo., 1979-80, Hume, Clement, Brinks, Chgo., 1980-83; adminstrv. asst. Heizer Corp., Chgo., 1983-85; billing coordinator Kirkland and Ellis, Chgo., 1985-86; mgr. Office Park of Hinsdale, Ill., 1986-89; dir. devel. Janko Devel. Co., Naperville, Ill., 1989—. Event coord. Am. Cancer Soc., Glen Ellyn, Ill., 1989; mem. alumni coun. U. Ill. Mem. Oak Brook Jaycees (pres., Outstanding Dir. award 1988), Phi Sigma Sigma (dir. adminstrn. 1983-85, dir. extension 1985-88, Pyramid award 1983, Active Alumna award 1987). Home: 2118 Appaloosa Ct E Wheaton IL 60187 Office: Janko Devel 24W500 Maple Ave Ste 212 Naperville IL 60540

PETRAS, KATHLEEN ANN, nurse, emergency medical technician; b. Middletown, Conn., Mar. 17, 1958; d. Alois Francis and Arlene Gladys (Barrett) P. BA, York Coll. Pa., 1980; AS, Greater Hartford Community Coll., 1988. RN with critical care splty.; cert. advanced life support; cert. paramedic. Emergency med. tech., adminstr. Hunter's Meriden Ambulance Service, Conn., 1980-83, New Britain Emergency Med. Services, Inc., Conn., 1983-87, acting supr., 1987—. Senatorial intern Capitol Hill, Washington, 1975, Internat. Broadcast Systems, Inc., 1976-80; vol. Middlesex Assn. Retarded Citizens, 1980—. Named one of Outstanding Young Women Am., 1981. Fellow Am. Heart Assn.; mem. Nat. Assn. Female Execs., Conn. Assn. Women Deans, Adminstrs. and Counselors (award 1976). First female paramedic City of New Britain. Democrat. Methodist. Home: 77 Winding Brook Rd Bristol CT 06010 Office: New Britain Gen Hosp Intensive Care Unit 100 Grand St New Britain CT 06051 also: New Britain Emergency Med Svcs 153 Arch St New Britain CT 06051

PETRAUSKAS, HELEN O., automobile manufacturing company executive; b. 1944; married. BS, Wayne State U., 1966, JD, 1971. Chemist, group supr. Sherwin-Williams Co., 1966-71; various positions Ford Motor Co., Dearborn, Mich., 1971-79, asst. dir. emissions and fuel economy cert., 1979-80, dir. emissions and fuel economy cert., 1980-82, exec. dir. environ. and safety engring. and research staff, 1982-83, exec. dir. engring. and tech. staffs, 1983, corp. v.p. environ. and safety engring., 1983—. Office: Ford Motor Co Environ & Safety Engring American Rd Dearborn MI 48121*

PETRE, DONNA MARIE, county judge; b. Joliet, Ill., Apr. 21, 1947; d. James Jacob and Catherine (Hedrick) P.; m. Dennis Michael Styne, Sept. 4, 1971; children: Rachel Catherine, Jonathan James. BA, Clarke Coll., 1969; MA, Northwestern U., 1971; JD, U. Calif., San Francisco, 1976. Bar: Calif. 1976. Jud. clk. Calif. Ct. Appeals, San Francisco, 1976-77; instr. legal research and writing U. Calif. Hastings Coll. Law, San Francisco, 1976; dep. atty. gen. criminal appeals dept. State of Calif., San Francisco, 1977-80, consumer fraud dept., 1977-80; med. fraud dept. State of Calif., Sacramento, 1983-86; mcpl. ct. judge Yolo County Mcpl. Ct., Woodland, Calif., 1986-89; judge Yolo County Superior Ct., 1990—; adj. prof. trial practice U. Calif., Davis; mem. Marin County Bd. Suprs. Criminal Justice Commn., 1982; mem. adv. com. Jud. Coun. on Adminstrn. Justice in Rural Counties, 1988—. Mng. editor Hastings Constl. Law Quar., 1975-76. Mem., bd. dirs. Woodland Literacy Coun., 1986—. Mem. Calif. Judges Assn. (commn. studying problems with driving under influence of alcohol and drugs), Yolo County Bar Assn., Women Lawyers Calif., Sacramento Women Lawyers, AAUW, Bus. and Profl. Women's Assn. (co-chmn. legis. 1986—), LWV, Davis C. of C., Yolo C. of C., Woodland C. of C., West Sacramento C. of C. Republican. Office: Yolo County Superior Ct 725 Court St Woodland CA 95695

PETRIC, MARION LORNA, marketing director; b. Phoenix, May 20, 1965; d. Stanley and Mildred A. (Lesko) P. BS, Ariz State U., 1988. Asst. bookeeper Eagle Med. Svcs., Phoenix, 1986-89; sales mgr. Perception Pub., Phoenix, 1988-89; account exec. Computer Advantage, Phoenix, 1989—. Mem. NAFE, Toastmasters Internat. (adminstrv. v.p. Phoenix chpt.). Home: 3940 E Meadowbrook Phoenix AZ 85018

PETRIKIN, KATHLEEN MARIE, personnel executive; b. Chgo., May 2, 1955; d. Raymond William and Barbara Elaine (Justeson) Richardson; m. James Ronald Petrikin. BS in Psychology and Sociology, MacMurray Coll., 1977; MA, U. Tulsa, 1987, postgrad., 1987—. Word processor Arthur Andersen & Co., Chgo., 1977-78; sales asst., new account supr. Dean Witter Reynolds, Inc., Tulsa, 1978-79; sales asst., new account supr. Bus. Resources and Exec. Search, Tulsa, 1979, dir. personnel State Fed. Savs. and Loan, 1979-85; rep. Agrico Chem. Co., Tulsa, 1985-87; cons. Cambridge Court Services, Ltd., Tulsa, 1987-88; dir. human resources Okla. Practice Touch-Ross and Co., Tulsa, 1988-89; owner, operator Career Connection, Tulsa, 1989—. Leader Girl Scouts U.S.A., 1962-84. Recipient Award of Appreciation Girl Scouts U.S.A., Jacksonville, Ill., 1975. Mem. Inst. Fin. Edn. (pres. 1981-84), Tulsa Personnel Assn., Am. Soc. Personnel Adminstrn. Democrat. Roman Catholic. Lodge: Kiwanitas (bd. dirs. Tulsa 1982). Home: 6277 S Yorktown Pl Tulsa OK 74136 Office: Career Connection 4th Nat Bank Bldg Ste 1224 Tulsa OK 74119

PETRINE, DEBORAH LEIGH MARTIN, long term care executive; b. Roanoke, Va., Aug. 2, 1955; d. Gerald Corbin and Dorothy (King) Martin; m. James Gerard Petrine, June 27, 1981; children: Meghan Rachelle, James Bradford. BS in Mgmt., Va. Poly. Inst. and State U., 1978. Licensed nursing home adminstr.; cert. nursing home preceptor; licensed real estate agent, Va. Sec., receptionist HCMF Corp., Blacksburg, Va., 1975-77; adminstr.-in-tng. HCMF Corp., Blacksburg, 1977-78; adminstr.Grent Lox Hall Brent Lox Hall HCMF Corp., Chesapeake, Va., 1978-79; adminstr. Heritage Hall HCMF Corp., Blacksburg, 1979-82, area operations dir., 1982-87, v.p. operations, 1987—; adv. com. mem. Va. Poly. Inst. & State Univ. Ctr. for Gerontology, Blacksburg, 1984-85; bd. nursing home adminstrs. Va. Dept. Health Professions. Dir. Jaycees, Salem, Va., 1988—. Named Young Career Woman of the Year Bus. & Profl. Women's Assn., 1981. Mem. Va. Health Care Assn. (dist. sec. 1981-82). Office: HCMF Corp 3610 S Main St Blacksburg VA 24060 : 1480 S Main St Blacksburg VA 24060

PETROCCHI, LINDA ANN, management consultant; b. Ft. Worth, Jan. 8, 1958; d. Till A. and Jane E. (Bushmiller) P. MusB, Tex. Christian U., 1979; MA, NYU, 1982. Pvt. practice piano tutoring Ft. Worth, 1978-81; educator creative arts various locations, N.Y.C., 1982-85; mgmt. assoc. Citibank, Bklyn., 1985-87; office mgr. Bruce Kelly/David Varnell Landscape Architects, N.Y.C., 1987-88; pvt. practice mgmt. con. Petrocchi Assocs., Bklyn., 1988—. Author: Me and Mom. Mem. Am. Mgmt. Assn., Nat. Assn. Bank Women, NAFE, Am. Assn. Counseling and Devel., Ctr. Entrepreneurial Mgmt.

PETRUCCI, JUDITH B., lawyer; b. Chgo., Apr. 8, 1941; d. Robert Carl Bryan and Shirley (Kennedy) Bryan Moore; m. Fredric A. Petrucci, Oct. 26, 1963 (dec. July 1984), 1 child, Gina Lynn. A.B., Morton Coll., 1977; B.A., Lewis U., 1979; J.D., No. Ill. U., 1981. Bar: Ill. 1983, U.S. Dist. Ct. (no. dist.) Ill. 1983. Legal sec. Frank E. Mosetick, LaGrange, Ill., 1962-65, assoc., 1983-84; sole practice, Lyons, Ill., 1984—. Chmn. Lyons 4th of July Com., 1975, Crusade of Mercy, Lyons, 1975, Com. Against Home Rule, Lyons, 1978; leader West Cook Council Girl Scouts U.S., 1973-76; mgr. Lyons-McCook Little League, 1976-79; atty. No More Bars Com., Lyons, 1984; elected trustee Village of Lyons, 1987—. Mem. ABA, Ill. State Bar Assn., Chgo. Bar Assn., Du Page County Bar Assn., West Suburban Bar Assn. (bd. govs. 1988—), Ill. Trial Lawyers Assn., Women's Bar Assn., Ill. Roman Catholic. Club: St. Hugh Soc. Cath. Women. Home: 4521 S Cracow Lyons IL 60534 Office: 7949 W Ogden Ave Lyons IL 60534

PETRUS, JOAN KLINE, real estate executive; b. Schenectady, N.Y., June 2, 1941; d. Floyd John and Jane Ruth (Dorning) Kline; children: Michelle Joan, David George. BS in Psychology, Russell Sage Coll., Troy, N.Y., 1966; postgrad., Hollins (Va.) Coll. Dental asst. Dr. Samuel Feuer, Schenectady, 1962-64; tchr. Schenectady Sch. System; substitute tchr. Roanoke County (Va.)üSch. System, 1977-82; owner, mgr. J. Kline Properties, Roanoke, 1983—; substitute tchr. Salem City (Va.) Sch. System, 1989—. Pres. Docent Guild Roanoke Mus. Fine Arts, 1980-82. Republican. Home: 4826 Deerfield Rd Roanoke VA 24014 Office: PO Box 21712 Roanoke VA 24018-0173

PETRUSKA, MARILYN ROSE, sales executive; b. Denver, Apr. 1, 1955; d. Emmerich and Elisabeth (Braun) P. BA in History, Western State Coll., Gunnison, Colo., 1978; postgrad., U. Denver, 1987. Asst. residential mgr. Drexel Properties, Aurora, Colo.; account exec. showroom asst. sales rep. Cort Furniture Rental, San Diego; sales mgr. Fireplace Equipment of Colo., Westminster. Active in numerous community orgns. Mem. NAFE, Wood Energy West Inst. (bd. dirs.), Wood Heating Alliance Colo. (pres.), Met. Air Quality Coun. on Wood Burning Issues. Home: #14 Willowleaf Littleton CO 80217

PETRY, RUTH VIDRINE, educator; b. Eunice, La., Jan. 20, 1947; d. Adea and Ruth Alice (Fox) Vidrine; m. Carson Clinton Petry, June 19, 1976. BA, La. Coll., 1971; MEd, McNeese State U., 1984. Cert. tchr., La. Jr. high sch. tchr. Jefferson Davis Parish, Jennings, La., 1970-72; high sch. tchr. St. Tammany Parish, Mandeville, La., 1972-73, Jefferson Parish, Gretna, La., 1973-81; jr. high tchr. Acadia Parish, Crowley, La., 1981—; lang. arts tchr. Crowley Jr. High Sch., 1981—; writing assessment coord. Crowley Jr. High Sch., 1984-85, mem. faculty insvc. team, 1986-89, chmn. spelling bee, 1983-90; co-chmn. interim self study Crowley jr. High Sch. So. Assn., 1985-86. Co-sponsor Nat. Jr. Hon. Soc., 1984-90. Mem. Associated Profl. Educators La. (pres. Acadia chpt. 1988—), Acadiana Civitan Club of Lafayette, Delta Kappa Gamma (pres. XI chpt. 1988-90). Republican. Baptist. Home: 206 Bruce Lafayette LA 70503

PETTEY, SUSAN MARIE, health policy specialist, lawyer; b. Aurora, Ill., Nov. 20, 1949; d. Warren A. and Jeannette E. (Fixmer) P.; m. Roland M. Frye, Jr., Jan. 23, 1988. BA, U. Nebr., 1973; MPA, Northeastern U., 1978; JD, Am. Univ., 1984. Bar: Mass. 1985. Planning asst. N.E. Dept. Pub. Welfare, Lincoln, Nebr., 1973-74; legis. coord. Worcester Coun. on Aging, Worcester, Mass., 1974; program asst. Mass. Office Emergency Med. Svcs., Boston, 1974-76; asst. dir. ambulance regulation Mass. Dept. Pub. Health, Boston, 1976-77; dir. ambulance regulation Mass. Dept. Pub. Health, 1977-78; legis. analyst Health Care Financing Adminstrn., Washington, 1978-84; dir. govt. affairs Home Health Svcs. and Staffing Assn., Washington, 1984-86; dep. counsel Nat. Assn. for Home Care, Washington, 1986-88; dir. health policy Am. Assn. Homes for Aging, Washington, 1988—; mem. adj. faculty Cen. Mich. U., 1987—; presdl. mgmt. intern HHS, Washington, 1978-81. Mem. ABA, Nat. Health Lawyers Assn., Mass. Bar Assn., Women's Bar Assn. D.C., Women in Govt. Affairs. Home: 218 N Columbus St Alexandria VA 22314 Office: Am Assn Homes for the Aging 1129 20th St NW Ste 400 Washington DC 20036

PETTI, ANNMARIE, entrepreneur, former oil company executive; b. Yonkers, N.Y., Jan. 8, 1955; d. John B. and Santa (Conte) P.; m. Ralph Pane. BBA cum laude in Acctg., Pace U., 1976; MBA in Fin., St. Joseph's U., 1985. Various mgmt. positions Mobil Corp., N.Y. and Pa., 1976-87; co-owner, pvt. practice in consumer service bus. Mem. Pace U. Alumni Assn., Pace U. Soc. Acctg.

PETTI, YVETTE MARIE, nurse, consultant; b. Findlay, Ohio, July 26, 1963; d. Nicholas Alexander and Barbara Ann (Yunis) P. BSN, U. Toledo, 1985, MEd, 1988; postgrad., Wayne State U. Sch. Nursing, 1989—. RN, Ohio, Mich. Primary nurse U. Chgo. Med. Ctr., 1985-86; nursing instr. Med. Coll. Ohio Sch. of Nursing, Toledo, 1986—; nurse clinican, pub. educator St. Vincent's Med. Ctr., Toledo, 1988—; pvt. practice nursing and cardiovascular cons. Toledo, 1988-89; adolescent psychiat. nurse U. Mich. Hosps., Ann Arbor, 1989—; instr. Am. Heart Assn., Toledo, 1987—; teaching asst. Wayne State U., Detroit, 1989—; pvt. practice nurse cons. Vol. for homeless St. Vincent's Charity Work, Toledo, 1988—; vol. health days St. Vincent's High Sch., Toledo, 1988—. Am. Legion scholar, 1976-77, Nation League for Nursing scholar, 1983; U. Toledo fellow, 1986; recipient Medal of Honor, Am. Legion, 1976, 77, 78, 79. Fellow Nat. Alliance for Cardiovascular Technologists; mem. Am. Assn. Critical Care Nursing, Am. Heart Assn., Coun. Cardiovascular Nursing, Mich. Nurse's Assn., Phi Kappa Phi. Roman Catholic. Office: U Mich Hosps 1500 E Medical Ctr Dr Ann Arbor MI 48104

PETTIETTE, ALISON YVONNE, lawyer; b. Brockton, Mass., Aug. 16, 1952. Student Sorbonne, Paris, 1971-72; BA, Sophie Newcomb Coll., 1972; MA, Rice U., 1974; JD, Bates Coll., 1978. Bar: Tex. 1979, U.S. Dist. Ct. (so. dist.) Tex. 1980, U.S. Ct. Appeals (5th cir.) 1981. Ptnr. Harvill & Hardy, Houston, 1979-83; pvt. practice, Houston, 1983-84; assoc. O'Quinn & Hagans, Houston, 1984-86, Jones & Granger, Houston, 1986-88; pvt. practice, Houston, 1988—. Editor Houston Law Rev. U. Houston, 1976-78. Exercise instr. YWCA, Houston, 1976-81, U. St. Thomas, Houston. NDEA fellow Rice U., Houston, 1972-74; Woodrow Wilson scholar, Tulane U., New Orleans, 1972. Mem. ABA, Assn. Trial Lawyers Am., Tex. Trial Lawyers Assn., Houston Trial Lawyers Assn., Phi Delta Phi, Phi Beta Kappa.

PETTIGREW, DANA MARY, musician; b. Oklahoma City, Jan. 15, 1951; d. Richard Clester and Alice Butler (Sargent) P.; children: Marilyn Yvonne, Lonnie Dean Jr. Student, Oklahoma City U., 1966-68. Profl. performance musician Oklahoma City, 1965—; ind. agt. Pettigrew Ins. Agy., Oklahoma City, 1975—. Ch. organist Pa. Ave Christian Ch., 1979-89. Life Underwriter Tng. Council fellow, 1984. Mem. Oklahoma City Health Underwriters Assn. (bd. dirs., sec. 1986—, v.p. 1987, pres. 1989), Oklahoma City Life Underwriters Assn. (bd. dirs. 1984-85), Musicians Exch., NAFE, Okla. Country Music Assn., Profl. Ins. Agts. Assn., King County Assn. Health Underwriters, Cascade Assn. Life Underwriters, Kiwanis (sec. Renton chpt. 1988, 89, pianist 1987—). Republican. Mem. Christian Ch. Home and Office: 3511 NE 11th Pl Renton WA 98056

PETTIGREW, KAREN BETH, lawyer; b. Lubbock, Tex., July 26, 1948; d. Jim Moore and Wanda Beth (Chastain) P. B.A. with honors, Tex. Tech. U., 1970; J.D., So. Meth. U., 1974. Bar: Tex. 1974, U.S. Tax Ct., U.S. Dist. Ct. (so. and no. dists.) Tex. Staff mem. U.S. Senator John G. Tower, Dallas, 1970-71; law clk. U.S. Dept. Justice, Tax Div., Dallas, 1973-74; atty. Andrews & Kurth, Houston, 1974-80, Wyckoff, Russell, Dunn & Frazier, Houston, 1980-82, Morris, Tinsley & Snowden, Houston, 1982-84, Thelen, Marrin, Johnson & Bridges, Houston, 1984-86, ptnr., 1986—. Del. Tex. Rep. Conv., 1984; bd. dirs. Tex. Tech. U. Century Club, Houston, 1983-86, Bellaire Christian Ch., Houston, 1983; bd. dirs. Houston Red Raider Club, 1981—, v.p., 1986—; mem. Ladies Go-Texan com., 1984-86, Skybox com., 1985-86, Internat. com., 1987—, Houston Livestock Show and Rodeo (life mem.); trustee Theatre Under the Stars, 1987—. Acad. scholar Tex. Tech. U., 1966-70, So. Meth. U. Sch. Law, 1971-74. Mem. Houston Bar Assn., Tex. Bar Assn., ABA, Order of Coif, Phi Delta Phi, Phi Kappa Phi, Alpha Lambda Delta, Phi Alpha Theta, Phi Sigma Alpha. Republican (del. state conv. 1984). Mem. Disciples of Christ (deaconess 1983-86, pulpit com. 1986-87). Home: 3650 Glen Haven Houston TX 77025 Office: Thelen Marrin Johnson & Bridges 921 Main Ste 1700 Houston TX 77002

PETTIGREW, L. EUDORA, academic administrator; b. Hopkinsville, Ky., Mar. 1, 1928; d. Warren Cicero and Corrye Lee (Newell) Williams; children: Peter W. Woodard, Jonathan R. (dec.). B.Mus., W.Va. State Coll., 1950; M.A., So. Ill. U., 1964, Ph.D., 1966. Music/English instr. Swift Meml. Jr. Coll., Rogersville, Tenn., 1950-51; music instr., librarian Western Ky. Vocat. Sch., Paducah, 1951-52; music/English instr. Voorhees Coll., Denmark, S.C., 1954-55; dir. music and recreation therapy W.Ky. State Psychiatric Hosp., Hopkinsville, 1956-61; research fellow Rehab. Inst., So. Ill. U., Carbondale, 1961-63, instr., resident counselor, 1963-66, coordinator undergrad. ednl. psychology, 1963-66, acting chmn. ednl. psychology, tchr. corps instr., 1966; asst. prof. to assoc. prof. dept. psychology U. Bridgeport, Conn., 1966-70; prof., chmn. dept. urban and met. studies Coll. Urban Devel. Mich. State U., East Lansing, 1974-80; assoc. provost, prof. U. Del., Newark, 1981-86; pres. SUNY Coll. at Old Westbury, 1986—; cons. for research and evaluation Hall Neighborhood House Day Care Tng. Project, Bridgeport, 1966-68, coordinator for edn. devel., 1968-69; cons. Bridgeport Public Schs. lang. devel. project, 1967-68, 70; cons. research/evaluation U.S. Eastern Regional Lab., Edn. Devel. Center, Newton, Mass., 1967-69; assoc. prof. U. Bridgeport, 1970, Center for Urban Affairs and Coll. of Edn., Mich. State U., East Lansing, 1970-73; cons. Lansing Model Cities Agy., Day Care Program, Lansing, Mich., 1971; trustee L.I. Community Found.; program devel. specialist Lansing Public Schs. Tchr. Corps program, 1971-73; cons. U. Pitts., 1973, 74, Leadership Program, U. Mich. and Wayne State U., 1975, Wayne County Public Health Nurses Assn., 1976, Ill. State Bd. Edn., 1976-77; lectr. in field; condr. workshops in field; cons. in field. Tv/radio appearances on: Black Women in Edn, Channel 23, WKAR, East Lansing, 1973, Black Women and Equality, Channel 2, Detroit, 1974, Women and Careers, Channel 7, Detroit, 1974, Black Women and Work: Integration in Schools, WITL Radio, Lansing, 1974, others.; Contbr. articles to profl. jours. Recipient Diana award Lansing YWCA, 1977, Outstanding Profl. Achievement award, 1987, award L.I. Ctr. for Bus. and Profl. Women, 1988, Educator of Yr. 100 Black Men of L.I., 1988, Black Women's Agenda award, 1988, Woman of Yr. Nassau/Suffolk Coun. of Adminstrv. Women in Edn., 1989, Disting. Ednl. Leadership award L.I. Women's Coun. for Equal Edn. Tng. and Employment, 1989, L.I. Disting. Leadership award, 1990; named Outstanding Black Educator, NAACP, 1968, Outstanding Woman Educator, Mich. Women's Lawyers Assn. and Mich. Trial Lawyers Assn., 1975, Disting. Alumna, Nat. Assn. for Equal Opportunity in Higher Edn., 1990. Mem. AAAS, Nat. Assn. Acad. Affairs Adminstrs., Phi Delta Kappa. Office: SUNY-Old Westbury Box 210 Old Westbury NY 11568

PETTIGREW, SUSAN JILL, food chemist; b. Bridgeport, Conn., Oct. 18, 1956; d. David Alexander and Julia Vasiliki (Argeropoulos) P.; m. Kevin J. Curran, Sept. 19, 1987. BS, U. R.I., 1978; MS, Cornell U., 1981. Assoc. food scientist Gen. Foods Corp., White Plains, N.Y., 1980-82; sr. project leader Thomas J. Lipton, Englewood Cliffs, N.J., 1982-90; rsch. assoc. Nabisco Brands Inc., East Hanover, N.J., 1990—; Inventor flavored slush snack, 1987. Mem. Inst. of Food Technologists.

PETTIJOHN, JOYCE LORRAINE, pharmacist, educator; b. Portland, Oreg., Jan. 7, 1955; d. Elzo Irving and Verona Muriel (McKittrick) Pettijohn; B.S. with honors in Pharmacy, Oreg. State U., 1978; postgrad. in bus. adminstrn. U. Puget Sound, 1980-81. Pharmacy extern St. Vincent's Hosp., Portland, 1977; pharmacy intern Lakeshore Clinic Pharmacy, Kirkland, Wash., 1978; staff pharmacist Evergreen Pharm. Services, Kirkland, 1979-80, sr. staff pharmacist, 1981—; dir. Health Products, Inc., Kirkland, 1981-85. Lic. pharmacist, Wash., Calif., Oreg. Mem. Am. Pharm. Assn., Wash. Pharm. Assn., Seattle Women's Network, Internat. Platform Assn. Office: 402 6th St S Kirkland WA 98033

PETTINARI, CATHERINE JEAN, health service research director; b. Va., Minn., Oct. 28, 1943; d. Roberick Quentin and Geraldine Ann (Flagg) Johnson; m. Larry Selinker. BA, Coll. St. Scholastica, 1965; MA, U. Oreg., 1980; PhD, U. Mich., 1985. Asst. dir. med. records St. Paul Ramsey Hosp., 1965-66; asst. med. record adminstr. Hosp. U. Pa., Phila., 1969-70; instr. Eastern Ky. U., Richmond, 1971-73, Med. Record Tech., Anoka, Minn., 1975; program coordinator Oreg. State U., Corvallis, 1980-81; teaching, rsch. asst. U. Mich., Ann Arbor, 1981-85, research assoc., 1985-86; communication specialist Commn. on Profl. and Hosp. Activities, Ann Arbor, 1986-88; research dir. Inst. Maternal Child Health, Wayne State U., Detroit, 1989—; cons. Rockburn Inst., Elkridge, Md., 1988, ETA, Novi, Mich. Author: Task, Talk and Text in The Operation Room: A Study in Medical Discourse, 1988; contbr. article to profl. Vol. Dem. Election Campaign, Ann Arbor, 1988. Mem. Soc. of Applied Anthro., Am. Anthro. Assn., Assn. Applied Linguistics. Home: 2053 Yorktown Ann Arbor MI 48105

PETTIT, JOANNE MARIE, health facility administrator; b. L.A., Nov. 17, 1942; d. John Edgar and Dorothy Anita (Gowen) Berges; m. Ray Lindsey Pettit (div. 1968); 1 child, Lisa Marie. BA, Am. Inst. Hypnotherapy, 1986, PhD in Hypnotherapy, 1987. Cert. hypnotherapist. Hypnotherapist San Clemente (Calif.) Hypnosis Ctr., 1975-80; dir., owner Saddleback Valley Hypnosis Ctr., El Toro, 1980-90; lectr. various colls., orgns. and corps.; seminar leader workshop facilitator in uses of hypnosis and techniques for self-improvement. Author newspaper articles, hypnotherapy scripts, programs and tapes on hypnosis as a therapeutic tool. Active Orange County Fund for Environ. Def., Fountain Valley, Calif., 1980-90; vol. San Juan Citizens for Open Space, San Juan Capistrano, Calif., 1990. Mem. Calif. Coun. of Hypnotherapy, Hypnosis Examining Coun. Office: Saddleback Valley Hypnosis 22706 Aspan St Ste 400 El Toro CA 92630

PETTIT, MARGARET ESTA, broadcasting executive; b. Provo, Utah, July 22, 1926; d. Howard Hammil and Edith Susan (Cummins) Cann; student public schs.; m. Claud Martin Pettit, July 30, 1948; children—Ruth Elaine, Paul Martin. Co-owner, office supr. Sta. KEOS, Flagstaff, Ariz., 1960-61; co-owner, bookkeeper Sta. KWIV, Douglas, Wyo., 1965-74; co-owner, bookkeeper, program dir., office supr. Sta. KCMP, Brush Colo., 1976-82; dir. Custom Broadcasting Co., Denver; sec.-treas., dir. Ranchland Broadcasting Co.; dir., v.p. Better Day, Inc., Arvada, Colo. Bd. dirs. Jefferson Park Community Activity Assn., Denver, 1981-84, North Fed. Recreation, Denver, 1984—. Mem. Model T Ford Club. Baptist. Home and Office: 8320 W 66th Ave Arvada CO 80004

PETTIT, SARA L., legal administrator; b. Athens, Tenn., July 12, 1944; d. Raymond Lee and Louise (Smithson) P. BS, Middle Tenn. State U., 1966; JD, Nashville Law Sch., 1974. Purchasing assoc. Samsonite Corp., Denver; tchr. U. Tenn., Nashville; legal sec. Brown, Scott and Link, Attys., Nashville; adminstrv. asst. to chief justice U.S. Ct. Appeals (6th cir.), Nashville, 1977—. Vol. instr. local reading program; active Adult Literacy Coun. Mem. Civitan. Democrat. Home: 2011 Richard Jones Rd Q-14 Nashville TN 37215 Office: US Ct Appeals 303 Customs House 701 Broadway Nashville TN 37203

PETTIT, WENDY JEAN, advertising agency executive; b. Gary, Ind., Oct. 6, 1945; d. Wendell E. and Ethel (Binkley) Pettit. B.A., MacMurray Coll., 1967; M.S.B.A., Ind. U., 1978. Acctg. clk. J. Walter Thompson USA, Chgo., 1967-68, adminstrv. asst., 1968-72, personnel asst., 1973-74, fin. analyst, 1974-78, office services asst., 1978-79, acctg. dept. mgr., 1979—. Bd. dirs. Miller Citizens Corp., Gary, 1979-86, treas., 1979-82. Named Career Woman of the Year, Bus. and Profl. Women, Gary, 1967. Mem. Nat. Assn. Female Execs., Am. Mgmt. Assn., LWV. Methodist. Avocations: singing; piano; cooking. Home: 8000 Oak Ave Gary IN 46403 Office: J Walter Thompson USA Inc 900 N Michigan Ave Chicago IL 60611

PETTITT, BARBARA JEAN, pediatric surgeon; b. Niagara Falls, N.Y., Feb. 2, 1952; d. Robert Andrew and Joan Marilyn (Boore) P.; m. Richard Allen Schieber, May 24, 1981; children: Christine Pettitt Schieber, Lucy Pettitt Schieber. BA in Chemistry magna cum laude, Cen. Coll., Pella, Iowa, 1972; D of Medicine, Northwestern U., Chgo., 1976. Diplomate Am. Bd. Surgery with certificates of spl. competence in pediatric surgery and surg. critical care; lic. pediatric surgeon, Calif., Pa., Ga. Student fellow in rehab. medicine Rehab. Inst. Chgo., spring 1974; intern in straight surgery Los Angeles County-U. So. Calif. Med. Ctr., 1976-77, resident in gen. surgery, 1977-81; resident in pediatric surgery Childrens' Hosp. Pitts., 1982-84; asst. prof. surgery and pediatrics dept. Sch. Medicine Emory U., Atlanta, 1985-86; mem. staff Henrietta Egleston Hosp. for Children, Atlanta, 1985-86; mem. staff Grady Meml. Hosp., Atlanta, 1985—, dir. pediatric surg. svc., 1990—; clin. asst. prof. Sch. Medicine Emory U., 1986-87, instr., 1987—; instr. in ATLS, ACLS, PALS; active various coms. Henrietta Egleston Hosp. for Children, 1985-86; mem. resuscitation and respiratory care com. Grady Meml. Hosp., 1986; lectr., presenter many profl. and ednl. orgns., 1983—. Contbg. author: (with M. Rowe) Pediatric Surgery, 4th edit., 1986; contbr. articles to profl. publs. Vol. battered womens' hotline Womens' Resource Ctr., Decatur, Ga., 1988—; treas., bd. trustees DeKalb Choral Guild, Atlanta, 1987—. Rsch. grantee Rsch. Corp., summer 1971, NIH, 1983-84; Rollscreen full-tuition scholar, 1969-72; Ruth G. White scholar Calif. State P.E.O., 1974-75; 1st Prize Bernard Baruch Essay Contest, Am. Congress Rehab. Medicine, 1975; named Outstanding Young Woman of Yr., State of Pa., 1984, State of Ga., 1986. Fellow ACS; mem. AMA, Am. Med. Womens' Assn., Am. Truama Soc., Southeastern Surg. Congress, Am. Pediatric Surg. Assn., Assn. Women Surgeons, Med. Assn. of Ga., DeKalb County Med. Soc., Los Angeles County-U. So. Calif. Med. Ctr. Soc. Grad. Surgeons, Phi Delta Epsilon (pres. med. sch. chpt. 1974-75, undergrad. midwest regional coord. 1974-75, mem. nat. exec. com. 1976-80, nat. intern-resident liaison com. 1980-85, nat. constn. and bylaws com. 1986—, Isadore Pilot award Chgo. chpt. 1975, nat. svc. award 1976). Democrat. Episcopalian. Office: Emory Univ Sch Medicine Dept of Surgery 69 Butler St SE Atlanta GA 30303

PETTUS, NOREEN LOUISE, infosystem specialist; b. Phila., Dec. 3, 1962; d. Gene Arthur Pettus and C. Louise (Williams) Smith. BBA, Howard U., 1985. Cons. Cap Gemini Am., Phila., 1985-86; programmer/analyst John Hancock Healthplans, Inc., Phila., 1986-87; programmer, analyst Michelin Tire Corp., Spartanburg, S.C., 1987—. Mem. Digital Equipment Corp. Users Soc., NAFE, Corvision Users Soc., Howard U. Alumni Assn., I.S.S.C., Health Fitness Instrs. Club. Democrat. Baptist. Home: 1070 Hunt Club Ln Apt N Spartanburg SC 29301 Office: Michelin Tire Corp 1000 International Dr Spartanburg SC 29304

PETTY, JOYCE JONES, instructor, real estate broker; b. Little Rock, Jan. 1, 1945; d. Albert Lee and Julia Anna (Weekly) Jones; m. Pruitt Gordon Petty, Aug. 10, 1969; children: Pruitt Jr., Nicholas, Marc. BA, Philander Smith, 1966; MEd, Cleve. State U., 1979. Cert. work study coordinator, Cleve. Bd. Edn.; lic. real estate broker, Ohio. English tchr. Cleve. Bd. Edn., 1966-70, transition team leader, 1971-78; real estate agt. Heights Realty, Cleve. Heights, Ohio, 1972-79; work study coordinator Cleve. Bd. Edn., 1979—; real estate broker J. Petty Realty, Inc., Cleve. Heights, 1979—; drama dir., newspaper advisor Cen. Jr. High Sch., Cleve., 1966-74; honor soc. advisor Harry E. Davis Jr. High Sch., Cleve., 1982-86. Youth dir. First Bapt. Ch., Little Rock, 1964-66; active Beachwood PTA. Mem. Cleve. Area Bd. Realtors, Alpha Kappa Alpha. Democrat. Club: FNO Bridge (Cleve.). Home: 25830 Annesley Rd Beachwood OH 44122 Office: 2000 Lee Rd Suite 1 Cleveland Heights OH 44118

PETTY, PEGGY JOYCE, medical paralegal; b. Ft. Worth, Nov. 20, 1932; d. Julius Marcellus and Ruby Ozell (Quinn) Hirth; m. Glenn Royce Petty, Sept. 10, 1954 (dec.); children: Glenn, Jr., Kirk, Robert, Steven. Diploma, Parkland Hosp. Sch. Nursing, Dallas, 1953; BS in Health Care Adminstrn., East Tex. State U., 1982. Lic. RN, Tex. Supr. operating room Good Shepherd Hosp., Longview, Tex., 1960-61; head nurse labor and delivery The Methodist Hosp., Houston, 1968-73, supr. ob-gyn, 1978-81; dir. nursing Odessa Women's and Children's Hosp., Tex., 1975-77; chief oper. officer Fort Bend Community Hosp., Missouri City, Tex., 1983-86; nursing cons. Southwestern Gen. Hosp., El Paso, Tex., 1982-83. Pres., bd. dirs. Ft. Bend unit Am. Cancer Soc., Missouri City, 1984—; bd. dirs. Tex. for War on Drugs, Ft. Bend, 1985-86; Ft. Bend County Women's Refuge Ctr., 1984-86. Pres.'s scholar, 1981. Mem. Tex. Soc. Hosp. Nursing Svc. Adminstrs. Assn. Houston Area Nursing Svc. Adminstrs. (sec. 1985-87), Nat. Assn. Nurse Execs., Sigma Theta Tau. Republican. Baptist. Avocations: oil painting, golfing, tennis, aerobics. Home: 8719 Southwestern Blvd Apt 259 Dallas TX 75206 Office: Fulbright and Jaworski 2200 Ross Ave Ste 2800 Dallas TX 75201

PETTY, PRISCILLA HAYES, writer, columnist, producer; b. Nashville, Aug. 22, 1940; d. Anderson Boyd and Margaret Louise (Lauper) Hayes; m. Gene Paul Petty, Jan. 10, 1961; children: Eric, Damon, Boyd. BA in English, Vanderbilt U., 1962; student Russian Inst., Dartmouth Coll., 1965. Cert. tchr., Ohio. Tchr. English, Cin. Suburban Pub. Schs., 1962-65, head dept. English, tchr., 1971-79; newspaper columnist Cin. Enquirer, 1978-89, also syndicated newspaper columnist Gannett News Svc., Washngton, 1982-89; cons. Arthur Andersen & Co., 1981-82; writer United Western Corp., 1982; speaker W. Edwards Deming Seminars; cons. in field. Author: History of a Boardsman (oral history), 1979, Under a Lucky Star: The Story of Frederick A. Hauck, 1986, What's in It for You and the Firm: CEOs and Presidents Look at Community Involvement. Mem. Cin. Council World Affairs; chmn. Cin. Media-Bus. Exchange, 1983; founder, pres. bd. trustees Cin. Oral History Found., 1984—. Named Outstanding Tchr., Project Teach, Ohio Edn. Assn., 1978; recipient WICI Great Lakes Regional Communicators' award; Pulitzer Prize nominee for Harvard U. Bus. Rev. article. Mem. Women in Communications (Outstanding Communicator of Yr. 1985), Oral History Assn., Sigma Delta Chi. Home: 229 Oliver Rd Cincinnati OH 45215

PETTYJOHN, CAROL LAVONNE, genetic engineering company executive; b. Maple Creek, Sask., Can., May 13, 1940; came to U.S., 1948, naturalized, 1986; d. Glenn C. Pettyjohn and Ruth I. (Cox) Savchenko; m. Thomas Edward Hatfield, June 13, 1958 (div. 1964); 1 child, Tamra R.; m. Dan Franklin Black, Oct. 1, 1964 (div. 1971); children—Kelley S., Anthony G. Student Memphis State U., 1958-59, San Diego State U., 1960, Bapt. Meml. Hosp. Sch. Nursing, 1957-59, Atlanta Law Sch., 1963, U. Maine, 1976, Coll. DuPage, 1984. Staff nurse Erlanger Hosp., Chattanooga, 1961-62, DeKalb Gen. Hosp., Decatur, Ga., 1962-63; med. cons. Prudential Ins. Co., Atlanta, 1964-67, employment interviewer, 1967-71; personnel mgr. Montgomery Wards, Jacksonville, Fla., 1972-75; office mgr. Drs. Wildstein, Kaiser, Schlemann, Springvale, Maine, 1975-78; pres., owner Options Agy., Sanford, Maine, 1978-81; controller, product mgr., div. mgr. Immuno Genetics, Inc., Eldora, Iowa and Vineland, N.J., 1981-86; chief exec. officer, pres. PanoGen, Inc., 1986—; bus. cons. Sanford Fire Dept., 1979-81, Drs. Harrigan, Pollard, Peterlein, Schlemann, Kaiser, Buell, Bellevaun, 1978-81. Area coordinator NOW, Jacksonville, Fla., 1974-75, Portland, Maine, 1975-79; softball coach Little League, Sanford, 1977-82; mem. LWV, Sanford, 1978-79; bd. dirs. Big Bros./Big Sisters, Biddeford, Maine, 1979-80. Mem. NAFE(networkdir. 1985—), Nat. Agri-Mktg. Assn. (bd. dirs. 1987), Livestock Conservation Inst., Nat. Swine Improvement Fedn. (bd. dirs.), Eldora Amb. Club, Rotary. Democrat. Avocations: reading, softball, chess, music, fishing. Office: PanoGen Inc PO Box 496 Airport Rd Eldora IA 50627

PETYKIEWICZ, SANDRA DICKEY, editor; b. Detroit, Sept. 23, 1953; d. James Fulton and Alice Diane (Nowak) Dickey; m. Edward W. Petykiewicz, Oct. 17, 1981. BA, Cen. Mich. U., Mt. Pleasant, 1975. Reporter Big Rapids (Mich.) Pioneer, 1975, Midland (Mich.) Daily News, 1975-77; reporter Saginaw (Mich.) News, 1977-79, feature editor, 1979-80, asst. metro editor, 1980-81; copy editor Washington Post, 1981-82; asst. city editor Balt. News Am., 1982-83; metro editor Jackson (Mich.) Citizen Patriot, 1983-87, editor, 1987—; bd. dirs. Mich. Associated Press, 1987—, pres., 1990. Mem. Associated Press Mng. Editors, Am. Soc. Newspaper Editors, Soc. Profl. Journalists, Bus. Profl. Women's Club (editor newsletter 1985-86, Young Career Woman of Yr. award 1984), Sigma Delta Chi.

PETZEL, FLORENCE ELOISE, educator; b. Crosbyton, Tex., Apr. 1, 1911; d. William D. and A. Eloise (Punchard) P.; Ph.B., U. Chgo., 1931, A.M., 1934; Ph.D., U. Minn., 1954. Instr., Judson Coll., 1936-38; vis. instr. Tex. State Coll. for Women, 1937; asst. prof. textiles Ohio State U., 1938-48; asso. prof. U. Ala., 1950-54; prof. Oreg. State U., 1954-61, 67-75, 77, prof. emeritus, 1975—, dept. head, 1954-61, 67-75; prof., div. head U. Tex., 1961-63; prof. Tex. Tech U., 1963-67; vis. prof. Wash. State U., 1967. Effie I. Raitt fellow, 1949-50. Mem. Seattle Art Mus., Oreg. Art Mus., Textile Mus., Met. Opera Guild, San Francisco Opera Assn., Portland Opera Assn. Sigma Xi, Phi Kappa Phi, Omicron Nu, Iota Sigma Pi, Sigma Delta Epsilon. Author Textiles of Ancient Mesopotamia, Persia and Egypt, 1987; contbr. articles to profl. jours. Home: 625 NW 29th St Corvallis OR 97330

PETZOLD, CAROL STOKER, state legislator; b. St. Louis, July 28; d. Harold William and Mabel Lucille (Wilson) Stoker; m. Walter John Petzold, June 27, 1959; children: Ann, Ruth, David. BS, Valparaiso U., 1959. Tchr. John Muir Elem. Sch., Alameda, Calif., 1959-60, Parkwood Elem. Sch., Kensington, Md., 1960-62; legis. aide Md. Gen. Assembly, Annapolis, 1975-79; legis. asst. Montgomery County Bd. Edn., Rockville, Md., 1980; community sch. coordinator Parkland Jr. High Sch., Rockville, 1981-87; mem. Md. Ho. of Dels., Annapolis, 1987—. Editor Child Care Sampler, 1974, Stoker Family Cookbook, 1976. Pres. Montgomery Child Care Assn., 1976-78; mem. Md. State Scholarship Bd., Balt., 1978-87, chmn. 1985-87; chmn. Legis. Com. Montgomery County Commn. for Children and Youth, 1979-84; mem., v.p. Luth. Social Services Nat. Capitol Area, Washington, 1980-86. Recognized for outstanding committment to children U.S. Dept. HEW, 1980. Mem. AAUW (honoree Kensington br. 1971, honoree Md. div. 1981), Women's Polit. Caucus (chmn. Montgomery County 1981-83), Women's Caucus Md. Legislature, LWV. Democrat. Lutheran. Home: 14113 Chadwick Ln Rockville MD 20853

PEVAR, LINDA SUSAN, educator, public relations specialist; b. N.Y.C., Oct. 4, 1942; d. Bernard and Sophie (Zimmerman) Gershuny; m. Marvin Rechter, July 25, 1964 (div. Apr., 1980); children: Sharon, Alan, Michael; m. Ira Jeffrey Pevar, Feb. 14, 1982; stepchildren: Alyse, Brian. BS in Edn., CCNY, 1964; MS in Edn., Bklyn. Coll., 1969; postgrad., Broward Community Coll., 1973—. Lic. tchr., Fla., real estate salesman, Fla.; cert. tchr. common branches, N.Y. Tchr. P.S. 221, Bklyn., 1964-65; tchr. P.S. 104, Far Rockaway, N.Y., 1966-76, Pine Crest Preparatory Sch., Pine Crest Sch., Ft. Lauderdale, Fla., 1977-80; with pub. rels., discharge planning Am. Home Health Care, Plant, Fla., 1980-85; admissions coord. Broward Home Health Care, Ft. Lauderdale, 1986-90; prin., with pub. rels. Home Health Svcs. of South Fla., Ft. Lauderdale, 1990—; prin. Kids Today Clothing Store, Sunrise, Fla., 1989—. Author: (guidebook for children) More Than Meets the Eye, 1978. Task force mem. Temple Kol Ami, Plant, Fla. Mem. Discharge Planner's Broward County, Plant C. of C., Brandeis Women's Book Club. Jewish.

PEVERLY, LINDA PAULINE VAUGHAN, management development center administrator; b. Fairfield, Ill., July 28, 1941; d. Everett Paul and Inez Ladora (Simpson) Vaughan; m. Howard Ray Peverly, Mar. 28, 1964 (div. 1971); 1 child, A. Danielle. BS in Commerce, U. Ill., 1963, MEd in Bus. Edn., 1972, PhD in Adult Edn., 1987. Tchr. Clinton (Iowa) Job Corps, 1967-69; staff asst. Coll. of Commerce and Bus. U. Ill., Urbana, 1972-76, assoc. project dir., 1979-81; program coord. community svcs. U. North Tex., Denton, 1978-79; dir. Bus. and Econ. Inst. Danville (Ill.) Area Community Coll., 1981-85; asst. dean Sch. of Bus. Cen. Conn. State U., New Britain, 1985-89; assoc. dir. mgmt. devel. ctr. R.B. Pamplin Coll. of Bus. Va. Polytech. Inst. & State U., Blacksburg, 1990—. Mem. Soc. for Human Resource Mgmt., Am. Soc. for Tng. and Devel., Am. Assn. for Adult Continuing Edn., AAUW, Phi Delta Pi, Kappa Delta Pi. Democrat. Unitarian. Office: Va Polytech Inst & State U Pamplin Hall Blacksburg VA 24061

PEYTON, MARY JOHANNA, secondary educator; b. Salt Lake City, Apr. 15, 1946; d. John Edward and Ellen Bernice (Michaud) P. B in Music, U. Mont., 1968, M in Music Edn., 1969. Cert. secondary tchr., Calif. Elem. instr. music Ceres (Calif.) Unified Sch. Dist., 1969-71, instr. jr. high music, 1971-75, instr. jr. high English, 1975-84, instr. jr. high econs., 1984-86, coordinator career edn., 1984—, instr. ind. study, 1986—; cons. various edn. orgns., 1984—; trainer career edn. Nat. Diffusion Network, U.S. Dept. Edn., Washington, 1985—. Producer, writer film Project Ceres, 1985; speaker in field. Mem. NEA, Calif. Tchrs. Assn., Calif. Career Edn. Assn., Ceres Unified Tchrs. Assn. (faculty rep. 1969—, negotiations team 1979—, 2nd v.p. 1980, negotiations chair 1984—), Phi Delta Kappa. Republican. Roman Catholic. Home: 3128 Scenic Dr Modesto CA 95355

PFAELZER, MARIANA R., federal judge; b. 1926. AB, U. Calif.; LLB, UCLA, 1957. Bar: bar 1958. Assoc. Wyman, Bautzer, Rothman & Kuchel, 1957-78, ptnr., 1969-78; judge U.S. Dist. Ct. for Dist. Cen. Calif. Mem. Am. Bar Assn. Office: US Dist Ct 312 N Spring St Los Angeles CA 90012*

PFAELZER, MURIEL Z., communication specialist; b. Chgo., Dec. 15, 1926; d. William M. and Belle (Davis) Zavis; m. Laurence W. Pfaelzer, Jr., June 19, 1949 (dec. 1990); children: Anne Pfaelzer De Ortiz, Laurence W. III (dec.). AA, Stephen's Coll., 1946; B in Philosophy, U. Chgo., 1948. Art dept. mgr. Borg Warner Ednl. Systems, Arlington Heights, Ill., 1970-80, sr. editor, 1980-84; graphics prodn. mgr. Universal Tng., Northbrook, Ill., 1984—. Chmn. com. PTA, Northfield, Ill., 1963; chmn. library com. Village of Northfield, 1964; bd. dirs. Family Svc. of Winnetka (Ill.)-Northfield, 1965. Mem. LWV (v.p. Winnetka-Northfield chpt. 1966). Home: 344 Wagner Rd Northfield IL 60093 Office: Universal Tng 255 Revere Dr Northbrook IL 60062

PFAFFLIN, SHEILA MURPHY, psychologist; b. Pasadena, Calif., July 31, 1934; d. Leonard Anthony and Honora (Shields) M.; m. James Reid Pfafflin, Sept. 7, 1957. BA, Pomona Coll., 1956; MA, Johns Hopkins U., 1958, PhD, 1959. Mem. tech. staff AT&T Bell Labs., Murray Hill, N.J., 1959-75; dist. mgr. AT&T, Morristown, N.J., 1975-90; Chair sub com. on Women-Com. on Equal Opportunities in Sci. and Tech., NSF, Washington, 1981-85; mem. adv. coun. Math/Sci. Tchr. Supply and Demand, N.J. Dept. Higher Edn., 1982-83; mem. adv. bd. for Maths., Sci. and Computer Sci. Teaching Improvement Grants, N.J. Dept. Higher Edn., 1984-89. Co-editor: Expanding the Role of Women in the Sciences, 1978, Scientific-Technological Change & the Role of Women in Development, 1981, Psychology & Educational Policy, 1987; contbr. articles to profl. jours. Trustee Ramapo Coll. of N.J., Mahwah, N.J., 1984—; adv. bd. Project "SMART", Girls Clubs of Am., N.Y.C., 1984—, Consortium for Ednl. Equity, Rutgers U., New Brunswick, N.Y., 1983—; pres. Assn. for Women in Sci. Ednl. Found., Washington, 1982—. Fellow AAAS, N.Y. Acad. Scis., Am. Psychol. Assn.; mem. Assn. for Women in Sci. (pres. 1980-81, Women Scientist award, Met. Chpt., 1987), Phi Beta Kappa, Sigma Xi. Home: 173 Gates Ave Gilletee NJ 07933 Office: AT&T 1 Speedwell Ave West Rm 429 Morristown NJ 07962

PFAU, REBECCA HOULE, educator; b. Little Falls, Minn., June 16, 1959; d. Clayton Richard and Rachel Hannah (Tower) Houle; m. Paul Edward Pfau, May 30, 1987; 1 child, Christopher Arthur. BAS in Elem. Edn., U. Minn., Duluth, 1982; MS in Info. Media, St. Cloud State U., 1988. Lic. media generalist and tchr., Minn. Libr., computer coord. Washburn and Homecroft Elem. Schs., Duluth, 1984-85; audio visual technician Apollo High Sch., St. Cloud, Minn., 1985-86; grad. asst. St. Cloud State U., 1986, adj. instr., 1988; employee devel. paraprofl. Minn. Dept. Transp., Brainerd, 1986-88; instrnl. designer Dun and Bradstreet Software Svcs., Eagan, Minn., 1988—; mem. tech.-computer com. Duluth Pub. Schs., 1985; design cons. North Cen. ops. Prudential Ins. Co., Plymouth, Minn., 1986. Bd. dirs. Duluth Latch Key Prog., 1979-83. Recipient Dist. 3 Excellence award Minn. Dept. Transp., 1988; scholar Duluth Pub. Schs., 1985. Mem. Am. Soc. Tng. and Devel., Nat. Soc. for Performance and Instrn., Assn. for Devel. Computer-Based Instrnl. Sys., AAUW (life, issue chmn. 1983-84). Unitarian. Office: Dun & Bradstreet Software 3400 Yankee Dr Eagan MN 55122

PFEFFER, MARY GRAVES, accountant, educator; b. Stillwater, Okla., Oct. 14, 1951; d. Leo C. and Margaret B. (Cundiff) Graves; m. C. Jackson Pfeffer, May 25, 1984; children: Walter Christian, Lora Margaret. BS, Okla. State U., 1973, MS, 1974; PhD, U. N.Tex., 1987. CPA, Okla., Colo., Tex.; cert. mgmt. accct. Acctg. systems analyst Conoco, Ponca City, Okla., 1974-75; auditor D.H. Baldwin, Denver, 1975-76; acctg. coord. Frito Lay, Dallas, 1976-79; acctg. mgr. Xerox, Dallas, 1980-82; contr. Sunrise Systems, Inc., Carrollton, Tex., 1982-84; mem. faculty acctg. U. Tex., Dallas, 1987-89; asst. prof. acctg. U. Dallas, Irving, Tex., 1990—; cons. venture-backed cos., Carrollton, 1984—. Contbr. articles to profl. jours. Mem. adv. bd. Parker-Chase Child Devel. Ctr., Carrollton, 1988-89. Mem. AICPA, Inst. for Mgmt. Acctg., Tex. Soc. CPA's, Am. Women Soc. CPA's, Phi Kappa Phi. Methodist. Home: 2229 Arbor Crest Dr Carrollton TX 75007 Office: U Dallas GSM 1845 E Northgate Dr Irving TX 75062-4799

PFEFFER, PATRICIA IRENE HENDRYX, real estate agent; b. Kent, Ohio, Dec. 31, 1930; d. Dean I. and Irene (Hansen) Hendryx; children: Chaffee Dunelle, Jan Dedrie, Michelle Suzanne. Student, Kent State U., Akron (Ohio) U., Cleve. State U., Buffalo State U. Lic. realtor, Fla., Ohio; lic. daycare and nursery sch. dir. Founder, dir. Streetsboro (Ohio) Nursery Sch., Childs World of Ravenna, Ohio, Twin Lakes (Ohio) Nursery Sch. and Infant Ctr.; owner Akron Hydraulic, 1974-78; founder, pres. Childrens Environments, Inc., 1966-80; pres. Portage County (Ohio) Bd. of Realtors, 1980-89, dir., 1985-90; assoc. Century 21 Smiles Realty, Inc., Kent; sec. Ohio Day Care Assn., 1955-60; cons. Assn. for Advancement of Human Svcs., Tallmadge, Ohio, 1976; instr. swimming and water safety. Contbr. articles to profl. jours. Active PTA. Mem. NAFE, AFTRA, Nat. Assn. Realtors, Ohio Assn. Realtors, Fla. Real Estate Commn., Am. Guild Variety Artists, White Brotherhood. Office: 414 E Main St Kent OH 44240

PFEIFER, CATHERINE ILSE, advertising researcher; b. Green Bay, Wis., May 29, 1961; d. John Stephan and Elizabeth (Johnson) P. BA, Lawrence U., Appleton, Wis., 1983; MA, Marquette U., 1989; postgrad., U. Wis., Madison, 1989—. Sales rep. Computerworld, Appleton, 1983-84; software evaluator Computerland, Green Bay, 1984-85; software developer Info. Mgmt. Assocs., Appleton, 1984-87; rsch. analyst Hoffman York & Compton, Milw., 1987-88; teaching asst. Marquette U., Milw., 1989; pres. Giddyup Desktop, Madison, 1989—; lectr. writing seminars. Advertiser local charities; operator crisis telephone lines. Mem. Assn. Edn. in Journalism and Mass Communications, Kappa Tau Alpha, Phi Sigma Epsilon. Home: 746 W Main St Apt 201 Madison WI 53715

PFEIFFER, CHRISTINE JANET, English educator, writer; b. Syracuse, N.Y., May 11, 1951; d. Ralph Robert Pfeiffer and Mary Carol (Royer) Fleming. BS, Northwestern U., 1973, MS, 1974. Asst. dir. pub. rels. Nat. Coll. Edn., Evanston, Ill., 1974-78; editor, sr. editor Universal Tng. Systems Co., Northbrook, Ill., 1978-82; adj. instr. English Oakton Community Coll., Des Plaines, Ill., 1982—; freelance writer Chgo., 1982—; past treas. North Shore Pub. Rels. Club. Author: Poland: Land of Freedom Fighters, 1984, Germany: Two Nations, One Heritage, 1986, Chicago, 1989. Recipient awards for poetry. Mem. Ind. Writers Chgo., Women in Communications (past officer North Shore chpt.), Polish Arts Club Chgo. (bd. dirs. 1988—), Polish Am. Educators. Home and Office: 1821 W Leland Ave Apt 1 Chicago IL 60640

PFEIFFER, JANE CAHILL, former broadcasting company executive, consultant; b. Washington, Sept. 29, 1932; d. John Joseph and Helen (Reilly) Cahill; B.A., U. Md., 1954; postgrad., Cath. U. Am., 1956-57; LHD (hon.), Pace Coll., 1978, U. Md., 1979, Manhattanville Coll., 1979, Amherst U., 1980, Babson Coll., 1981; m. Ralph A. Pfeiffer, Jr., June 3, 1975. With IBM Corp., Armonk, N.Y., 1955-76, sec. mgmt. rev. com., 1970, dir. communications, 1971, v.p. communications and govt. relations, 1972-76, bus. cons., 1976-78; chmn. NBC, Inc., N.Y.C., 1978-80; bus. cons., 1980—; dir. Ashland Oil Co., Mony Fin. Svcs., Internat. Paper Co., J.C. Penney Co. Mem. pres.'s adv. com. White House Fellows, 1966, Pres.'s Gen. Adv. Commn. on Arms Control and Disarmament, 1977-80, Pres.'s Commn. Mil. Compensation, trustee Rockefeller Found., U. Md., Carnegie Hall, U. Notre Dame. White House fellow, Washington, 1966; recipient Achievement award Kapppa Kappa Gamma, 1974-80, Eleanor Roosevelt Humanitarian award N.Y. League for Hard of Hearing, 1980, Disting. Alumna award U. Md., 1975, Humanitarian award NOW, 1980, Centennial Alumna Medallion U. Md., 1988. Mem. Council on Fgn. Relations, Overseas Devel. Council. Club: Econ. of N.Y. Office: 90 Field Point Circle Greenwich CT 06830

PFEUFFER, HEIDI CHRISTINE, art gallery owner; b. Herrsching, Fed. Republic Germany, Feb. 13, 1947; came to U.S., 1981; d. German and Bettina (Krieg) P.; m. Maurice Lasnier, Apr. 1, 1982. BA, Maria Ward Gymnasium, Nurnberg, Fed. Republic Germany, 1969; MA in Linguistics, U. Munich, 1971. Fashion model, 1971-81; translator UNICEF, Paris, 1979-80; pres. HPL Prodns., Paris, 1979-81; owner, operator art gallery Graphics and Art, West Hollywood, Calif., 1983—. Active Mus. Contemporary Art, L.A. County Mus. Mem. West Hollywood C. of C., NAFE. Office: Graphics and Art 8652 Melrose Ave West Hollywood CA 90069

PFISTER, KARSTIN ANN, social services administrator; b. Phila., Apr. 26, 1955; d. Stephen John Dutch and Janis Loraine Runte; m. William Howard Pfister, July 10, 1979; 1 child, Caitlin Justine. BA, Cornell Coll., Mount Vernon, Iowa, 1977; MEd, George Mason U., Fairfax, Va., 1983; postgrad., Va. Poly. and State U., 1986, EdD, 1990. Cert. secondary sch. tchr.; lic. profl. counselor; Nat. Cert. Counselor. Instr. Nat. Meteorol. Inst., Kabul, Afghanistan, 1977-78; instr. faculty of medicine, faculty of letters Kabul U., 1978-79; program coord., counselor Pepperdine U., Malibu, Calif., 1979-81, Hdqrs. Marine Corps., Arlington, Va., 1981-87; dir. family svc. ctr. Hdqrs. Battalion, Hdqrs. Marine Corps., Arlington, Va., 1988—. Co-author: profl. jour. article. Mem. Am. Assn. for Counseling and Devel., Va. Counselors Assn., No. Va. Chpt. Clin. Counselors, Kappa Delta Pi, Phi Delta Kappa. Home: 13805 Cynthia Ct Manassas VA 22111 Office: Family Service Ctr HQBN HQMC Henderson Hall Arlington VA 22214

PFLEIDER, SHIRLEY JEAN, medical administrator; b. Rhinebeck, N.Y., Sept. 28, 1952; d. Earl Van Ness and Ellen Luella (Saulpaugh) Tallmadge; m. Frederick Warren Pfleider, Sept. 9, 1978; 1 child, Heather Ann. Student, Empire State Coll., New Paltz, N.Y. EEO counselor, facilitator Va. Med. Ctr., Castle Point, N.Y., fed. women's program mgr., med. administrv. asst., chief support svc. Leader Dutchess County coun. Girl Scouts U.S.A., 1981-82, del., 1982; mem. Nat. Com. to Preserve Social Security and Medicare, 1989-90. Mem. NAFE, Am. Mgmt. Assn., Federally Employed Women, Fed. Women's Program Mgr. Employee Assn. (pres.), Castle Point Employee Assn. Bowling League (pres. 1987-88). Home: 49 Channingville Rd Wappingers Falls NY 12590

PFUND, ROSE TOSHIKO, academic administrator; b. Honolulu, July 22, 1929; d. Toichi and Kame (Gibo) Omine. BA, U. Hawaii, 1951, MEd, 1978; PhD, U. Pitts., 1985. Sci. and tech. editor Water Rsch. Ctr. U. Hawaii, Honolulu, 1966-72, info. coord. Sea Grant Coll. Program, 1973-79, acting assoc. dir. Sea Grant Coll. Program, 1981-83, assoc. dir. Sea Grant Coll. Program, 1984—; mem. adv. com. Marine Affairs Hawaii State Legis., Honolulu, 1985-86, U. Hawaii Communications Council, Honolulu, 1987—. Editor Sea Grant Quar., 1979-89; contbr. articles to profl. jours. Mem. ESEA Title III/IV adv. council, Hawaii, 1970-79; pres. Hawaii PTA, Honolulu, 1976-78; state rep. com. status and role women United Meth. Ch., So. Calif.-Hawaii region, 1976-80, organizer, chair Asian Women's Caucus, 1977-80; mem. task force Gov.'s Ocean Resources Tourism Devel., 1987—. Hawaii state legis. grantee, 1975—. Mem. Am. Soc. Pub. Adminstrn. (nat. coun. 1987-90, exec. com. 1990, planning and evaluation com. 1987-88, chpt. devel. com. 1988-90 polit. issues com. 1989-90, chmn. environ. issues subcom. 1989-90), Acad. Polit. Sci., Western Govtl. Rsch. Assn., Soc. Risk Analysis. Office: U Hawaii Sea Grant Program 1000 Pope Rd MSB 220 Honolulu HI 96822

PHARES, LYNN LEVISAY, public communications executive; b. Brownwood, Tex., Aug. 6, 1947; m. C. Kirk Phares, Aug. 22, 1971; children: Margaret, Dele, Jessica. BA, La. State U., 1970. Asst. to advt. mgr. La. Nat. Bank, 1971-72; writer, producer, 1971-78; asst. v.p., account exec. Smith, Kaplan, Allen & Reynolds, Inc., Omaha; now v.p. pub. rels. Conagra, Inc., Omaha. Office: Conagra Inc 1 Conagra Dr Omaha NE 68102-5001*

PHARES, MARGUERITE LINTON, ballet educator, artistic director; b. Columbus, Ohio, Mar. 4, 1917; d. Henry Jehu and Viola Alice (Carmean) Linton; m. Hugh Kinzel Phares, Jr., June 6, 1941; children—Hugh III, Lisa Elaine. B.S. in Music Edn., Ohio State U., 1939. Profl. dancer, N.Y.C., 1939-41; ballet tchr. various schs. Glendale, Calif., 1941-43, Mt. Vernon, N.Y., 1944-47; prin. Marguerite Phares Sch. of Dance, Sacramento, Calif., 1947—; artistic dir. Phares Theatre Ballet, Sacramento, 1967—; choreographer ballets: Cinderella, 1977, 78; Sleeping Beauty, 1980, 85; Romeo and Juliet, 1984; regional dir. Internat. Ballet Competition, Jackson, Miss., 1981, regional field judge, Sacramento, 1982-83; subject of article Dance Tchr. Now mag., 1988. Recipient Outstanding Tchr. Plaudit award Nat. Dance Assn., 1978, Toast to Excellence award Sacramento Arts Mag., 1988 ; sleceted to represent Calif. in Young Americans Nat. Dance Festival. Mem. Pacific Regional Ballet Assn. Honor Co. (sec. 1977-79, pres. 1980-81), Delta Zeta (pres. 1954-55). Republican. Office: Marguerite Phares Sch Dance 4430 Marconi Ave Sacramento CA 95821

PHARIS, CLAUDIA CECILIA, small business owner; b. Phila., May 30, 1944; d. Clyde Anthony and Eula Mae (Faulkner) P. Student, Trinity Coll., Washington, 1962-65; BS in Physics, U. Hawaii, 1971; MBA, Harvard U., Boston, 1983. Policy analyst HUD, Washington, 1971-78, Office Mgmt. and Budget, Exec. Office of Pres., Washington, 1978-79; staff rep. budget com. Congressman William Gray, U.S. Ho. of Reps., Washington, 1979-80, U.S. Senate, Washington, 1980-81; dep. mng. dir. City of Phila., 1981; with strategic planning dept. 1st Nat. Bank Boston, summer 1982; exec. v.p. Royal Bus. Sch., N.Y.C., 1983-86; pres. Edu-Net, Media, Pa., 1987—; cons. State of Oregon, Salem. Harvard U. Grad. Sch. Design Loeb fellow. Club: Century (Boston). Home and Office: 420 Vernon St Media PA 19063

PHARIS, MARY EVANS, psychology educator; b. Milw., July 3, 1938; d. Silas McAfee and Lorraine (McManamy) Evans; m. David Bunsen Pharis, Aug. 6, 1966; children: Christopher, Michael. Student, Stanford U., 1956-58; BS, U. Wis., 1960; AM, U. Chgo., 1962; PhD, U. Tex., 1978. Lic. psychologist, Tex.; diplomate Am. Bd. Psychology. Case worker Scholarship & Guidance Assn., Chgo., 1962-66; coord. social work tng. Michael Reese Hosp. Psychiatry, Chgo., 1966-68; coord. spl. svc. Evanston Ind. Sch. Dist., Evanston, Ill., 1968-70; instr. Ill. Coll. and MacMurray Coll., Jacksonville, Ill., 1972-74; intern psychology Counseling Ctr. U. Tex., Austin, 1978-79; spl. asst. to chief Mental Health Study Ctr. NIMH, Adelphi, Md., 1980-81; asst. prof. U. Tex., Austin, 1981-84, assoc. prof. psychology, 1984—; pvt. practice Austin, 1984—; cons. in field. Author of book and contbr. chpts. to books; contbr. articles to profl. jours. Adv. com. family life Child and Family Svcs., Austin, 1982—; mem. com. capital area needs assessment project United Way, 1984; mem. Child and Adolescent Needs Task Force, Travis County, 1984; bd. dirs. Austin Teenage Parent coun., 1986-88. Fellow Lindsey Barbee, 1960-61, faculty U. Chgo., 1961-62, NIMH, 1976-78, Congrl. Sci., 1979-80, 82-84, Clara Pope Willoughby Centennial, 1985—. Mem. Ill. Soc. Clin. Social Work (founder), Am. Orthopsychiat. Assn., Am. Psychol. Assn. Tex. Psychol. Assn., Capital Area Psychol. Assn., Soc. Rsch. in Child Devel., Am. Bd. Profl. Psychology (life), Tex. Ex-Students Assn. (life), Stanford Alumni Assn. (life), Phi Kappa Phi (life). Home: 5400 Ridge Oak Dr Austin TX 78731

PHARIS, RUTH MCCALISTER, banker; b. San Diego, Feb. 13, 1934; d. William L. and Mary E. (Beuk) McC.; grad. Del Mar Coll., Corpus Christi, Tex., 1975-79; m. E. Edwin Pharis, Mar. 14, 1953; children—Beth, Tracey, Todd. Asst. cashier Parkdale State Bank, Corpus Christi, 1970-72, asst. v.p., 1972-76, v.p., 1976-79: v.p. Cullen Center Bank & Trust, Houston, 1979-81, sr. v.p., 1982—; instr. Am. Inst. Banking, 1977-79. Mem. adv. council Houston Community Colls. Mem. Am. Soc. Personnel Adminstrs., Bank Adminstrn. Inst. (v.p. Coastal Bend chpt. 1979), Nat. Assn. Bank Women (ednl. chmn. Coastal Bend group), Am. Inst. Banking (rep.), Tex. Bankers Assn. (council 1983-84), Coastal Bend Personnel Soc. (v.p.), Houston Personnel Assn., Corpus Christi C. of C. (mem. women's com. 1976-79). Republican. Baptist. Club: Order Eastern Star. Home: 5102 Wightman Ct Houston TX 77069 Office: 600 Jefferson St Houston TX 77001

PHARR, DORIS ANN, elementary counselor; b. Little Rock, May 20, 1951; d. James Henry and Eva Mae (Wadley) Reddick; m. Dennis Garland Pharr, Apr. 12, 1986; m. Roger D. Choate, June 12, 1970 (div. May 1982); children: Sharon Annette, Charles Brian. BSE, U. Cen. Ark., Conway, 1973, MS, 1985. Cert. tchr., Ark., counselor, Calif. Tchr. Pulaski County Spl. Sch. Dist., Little Rock, 1973-79, 82-87; counselor North Little Rock Pub. Schs., 1987-88, Rogers (Ark.) Pub. Schs., 1988-89, Stockton (Calif.) Unified Pub. Schs., 1989—; cons. Maumelle Pvt. Sch., 1986-87, Suicide Prevention Commn., North Little Rock, 1987—. Co-author: Tests Used in Psychological Evaluations, 1987. Dir. children's dept. Cedar Hts. Bapt. Ch., Morgan, Ark., 1986-89. Mem. NEA, NAFE, Ark. Ednl. Assn., Ark. Psychol. Assn., Ark. Assn. Counseling and Guidance, Calif. Assn. Counseling Devel., Calif. Sch. Counselor Assn., North Little Rock Classroom Tchrs. Assn., North Little Rock Counselors Assn. (co-pres. 1987-88). Office: 2245 E 11th Stockton CA 95206

PHARRIS, ANN MARIE, graphic artist; b. Manitowoc, Wis., Dec. 7, 1950; d. Charles ALexander and Caroline Marie (Wernecke) P.; m. Jeffrey James Collette, Aug. 5, 1953; children: John David Collette, Caroline Louise Collette. BA, U. Wis., 1972. Graphic artist Time Ins. Co., Milw., 1973, The Marban Co., Stone Bank, Wis., 1973-76, Ries Graphic, Butler, Wis., 1976-79; sole proprietor The Pharris Group, Milw. Lutheran. Home and Office: 8910C SW 20th Pl Fort Lauderdale FL 33324-6859

PHELAN, CAROLE MARY ROSS, minister, writer; b. Sydney, New South Wales, Australia, Dec. 30, 1925; came to U.S., 1962; d. Henry James and Elizabeth Maud (Shaw) Stevens; m. Christopher Joseph Phelan, Dec. 23, 1953; 1 child, Colin Michael Ross. BBA, Clarks Coll., London, 1942; DD, Philpots Sem., London, 1956. Sec. to dir. Archers Film Prodns., London, 1943-45; editorial asst. Hutchinson & Co., London, 1945-50; sec. to gen. mgr. Kemsley Newspapers, London, 1951-53; tchr. Philpots Sem., 1956-62; dir. edn. Universal Mind Sci. Ch., Long Beach, Calif., 1971-72; adminstr. Mountain View, Calif., 1972-74; treas.-sec., minister, tchr. Aquarian Horizon Centre, Los Angeles, Cupertino and Santa Barbara, Calif., 1975-86; pres., sec., minister, tchr. Los Angeles, 1987—. Author: Why Meditation?, 1988; contbr. articles on self-devel. and metaphysics to profl. jours. Home and Office: Aquarian Horizon Centre 10760 Rose Ave Suite 304 Los Angeles CA 90034

PHELAN, KAREN BARBARA, residence hall director, counselor; b. Torrington, Conn., June 14, 1953; d. George Vincent and Phyllis (Bishop) P. BA in Sociology, U. S.C., 1975; AS with honors, Northwestern Conn. Coll., 1977; MS in Edn. and Counseling, Cen. Conn. State U., New Britain, 1985. Ins. agt. George Phelan & Co., Torrington, 1980, 81-83, Litchfield County Agy., Torrington, 1983-85; residence hall dir. SUNY, Stony Brook, 1986-87; sec. Victor Temp. Svc., Farmington, Conn., 1987-88; residence hall dir. Green Mountain Coll., Poultney, Vt., 1988—; resident dir., best of both worlds coord. Russell Sage Coll., Troy, N.Y., 1990—. Sustaining mem. Rep. Nat. Com., Washington, 1978—. Mem. Am. Coll. Personnel Assn., Nat. Assn. Student Personnel Adminstrs., AAUW, Ins. Women of Litchfield County (v.p. 1983-85), Cath. Grads. Club of Hartford (v.p. 1984-86), Greater U.S.C. Alumni Assn. Home: Russell Sage Coll Box 1547 Troy NY 12180 Office: Russell Sage Coll Residence Program Office Troy NY 12180

PHELAN, MARY CLAIRE, librarian; b. East Cleveland, Ohio, Jan. 27, 1943; d. William Ignatius and Clara F. (Streisel) Walsh; m. William Thomas Phelan, Dec. 14, 1968; children: Michelle, Annemarie. BA, Ursuline Coll., 1965; MA, U. Chgo., 1967. Sci. libr. Abbott Labs., North Chicago, Ill., 1967-68; biology libr. U. Chgo., 1968-71; sci. bibliographer U. Manitoba, Winnipeg, Can., 1971-73; trustee Chelmsford (Mass.) Pub. Librs., 1976-78, Belmont (Mass.) Pub. Librs., 1982—. Mem. Mass. Libr. Trustees Assn., Spl. Librs. Assn., Am. Quilter's Assn. Home: 33 Taylor Rd Belmont MA 02178

PHELAN, PHYLLIS WHITE, psychologist; b. Harrisonburg, Va., Aug. 12, 1951; d. Shirley Lewis and Jean Elwood (Driver) White; m. Kenneth Edward Phelan, May 21, 1983. BA with honors, Coll. William and Mary, 1973, MA, 1977; PhD, U. Minn., 1984. Lic. cons. psychologist. Intern Ramsey Mental Health Ctr., St. Paul, 1983-84; psychologist Mental Health Clinics of Minn. P.A., St. Paul, 1983-84, Harley Clinics, Mpls., 1983-84; psychologist, dir. eating disorders program Primary Health Care, Bloomington, Minn., 1984-87; pvt. practice psychology St. Paul, 1987—; exec. dir. Eating Disorders Inst. for Edn. and Research, St. Paul, 1987—; instr. Continuing Edn. program, U. Minn., 1983-84, clin. asst. prof. dept. psychiatry, 1986—, clin. asst. prof. dept. psychology, 1989—. Contbr. articles to profl. jours. Coll. of William and Mary scholar, 1975-77; U. Minn. fellow 1981, 82-83. Mem. Am. Psychol. Assn., Minn. Psychol. Assn., Minn. Psychologists in Pvt. Practice, Minn. Women Psychologists. Home: 942 Summit Ave Saint Paul MN 55114 Office: 570 Asbury St Saint Paul MN 55105

PHELPS, CHRISTINE ELIZABETH, educational association administrator; b. Mpls., Nov. 11, 1959; d. Joseph Edward and Mary Ann (Ryan) Liedl; m. Ben L. Phelps, May 2, 1987; 1 child, Natasha Christine. BA, U. Iowa, 1982. Exec. asst. Synod of Lakes and Prairies, Mpls., 1982-84, communication asst., 1984-85, systems adminstr., 1985-86; systems coord. Am. Acad. Neurology, Mpls., 1985, mgr. edn. div., 1985—. Mem. NAFE. Office: Am Acad Neurology 2221 University Ave SE Minneapolis MN 55414

PHELPS, ERIN MARGARETTA, psychologist; b. Waynesville, Mo., Jan. 23, 1951; d. Richard Clayton and Ellen Margaretta (Beasley) P.; m. Richard Allen McElroy, Aug. 8, 1982. BA, Douglass Coll., 1973; EdM, Harvard U., 1974, EdD, 1981. Cons. Project Zero, Cambridge, Mass., 1979-83; lectr. Grad. Sch. Edn. Harvard U., Cambridge, 1979-84; sr. rsch. assoc., tech. dir. Murray Rsch. Ctr. of Radcliffe Coll., Cambridge, 1981—. Contbr. articles to profl. jours. Active town meetings, Arlington, Mass., 1987—; elected mem. town meetings. Mem. Soc. for Rsch. in Child Devel., Am. Ednl. Rsch. Assn., NOW, Am. Psychol. Assn., Am. Statis. Assn., Phi Beta Kappa. Office: Radcliffe Coll Murray Rsch Ctr 10 Garden St Cambridge MA 02138

PHELPS, FLORA L(OUISE) LEWIS, editor, anthropologist, photographer; b. San Francisco, July 28, 1917; d. George Chase and Louise (Manning) Lewis; m. C(lement) Russell Phelps, Jan. 15, 1944; children: Andrew Russell, Carol Lewis, Gail Bransford. Student, U. Mich.; AB cum laude, Bryn Mawr Coll., 1938; AM, Columbia U., 1954. Acting dean Cape Cod Inst. Music, East Brewster, Mass., summer 1940; assoc. social sci. analyst U.S. Govt., 1942-44; co-adj. staff instr. anthropology Univ. Coll., Rutgers U., 1954-55; mem. editorial bd. Américas mag. OAS, Washington, 1960-82, sr. editor, 1963-71, editor English edit., 1971-74, mng. editor, 1974-82, contbg. editor, 1982-89; N.J. vice chmn. Ams. Dem. Action, 1950; mem. Dem. County Com. N.J., 1948-49. Author articles in fields of anthropology, art, architecture, edn., travel; contbr. Latin Am. newspapers. Mem. AAAS, Am. Anthrop. Assn., Anthrop. Soc. Washington, Latin Am. Studies Assn., Soc. for Am. Archaeology, Soc. Woman Geographers. Home and Office: 3618 Albemarle St NW Washington DC 20008

PHELPS, SUZANNE, educational administrator; b. Tyler, Tex., Sept. 12, 1946; d. Julius Carl and Charm (Moseley) Norris; divorced, 1978; children: Melissa, Jennifer. BA, Baylor U., 1967, MS in Edn., 1980; postgrad., Tex. A&M U. Tchr. Midway Schs., Waco, Tex., 1967-68, Clear Creek Schs., League City, Tex., 1968-69, Jefferson County Schs., Denver, 1971-74, Robinson Schs., Waco, 1975-79, Temple (Tex.) Schs., 1979-80; edn. cons. Region XII Edn. Service Ctr., Waco, 1980-83; supr. math. Bryan (Tex.) Schs., 1983-85, dir., 1985—; mem. adv. com. Tex. Edn. Agy., Austin, 1985—; mem. steering com. TAMU Collaborative, 1987—. Tchr. First Baptist Ch., Bryan, 1984—. Mem. Assn. of Tex. Profl. Educators (treas. 1981-82, sec. 1982-83, v.p. 1983-84, chair legisl. com. 1984-85), Assn. of Supr. and Curriculum Devel., Bryan C. of C. (Leadership Brazos, 1986-87), Phi Delta Kappa, Delta Kappa Gamma. Home: 2913 Burning Tree Bryan TX 77802 Office: Bryan Ind Sch Dist 101 N Texas Ave Bryan TX 77801

PHIBBS, MARY ELLEN, educator; b. Bridgewater, Va., Oct. 25, 1924; d. Minor Cline and Mary Agnes (Shipman) Miller; m. Garnett Ersiel Phibbs, Aug. 18, 1945 (div. June 1972); children: Gerald Edwin, David Miller, Robert Lee. BA, Bridgewater Coll., 1945; MEd, U. Toledo, 1964; postgrad., NYU, 1965, Ariz. State U., 1971, U. Okla., 1972. Tchr. Bassett (Va.) High Sch., 1945-50, Maumee (Ohio) Jr. High Sch., 1964-69, Roosevelt Jr. High Sch., Glendale, Calif., 1969—; mem. Glendale Sci. Curriculum writing team, 1980-84. Mem. NEA, Calif. Tchrs. Assn., Glendale Tchrs. Assn., Nat. Sci. Tchrs. Assn. Democrat. Methodist. Home: 1650 Capistrano Ave Glendale CA 91208 Office: Roosevelt Jr High Sch 1017 S Glendale Ave Glendale CA 91205

PHIFER, CYNTHIA ANN, health facility administrator; b. Allentown, Pa., Dec. 10, 1960; d. Frederick A. and Annette A. (Barnack) Mihalow; m. Craig Phifer, Oct. 6, 1985. BS, Bloomsburg State Coll., 1981, MS, 1982; cert. health care adminstrn., Widener U., Chester, Pa., 1989; postgrad., Pa. State U. Speech/lang. pathologist Main Line Speech Cons., Haverford, Pa., 1982-84, Montgomery County Intermediate Unit #23, Norristown, Pa., 1982-85; clin. dir. speech/lang. pathology Montgomery Hosp. Med. Ctr., Norristown, 1985—. Mem. Am. Speech and Hearing Assn., Pa. Speech, Lang. and Hearing Assn. (profl. standards and practices com. 1990—), Northeast Pa. Speech and Hearing Assn., Southeast Pa. Speech and Hearing Assn. Office: Montgomery Hosp Powell and Fornance Sts Norristown PA 19401

PHILBRICK, KATHILYN DURNFORD, special education professional, humor consultant; b. Columbus, Ohio, July 2, 1948; d. Dewey Foster Jr. and Joanne (Fields) Durnford. BA in English, Ohio State U., 1970; MA in Mental Retardation, U. Cen. Fla., 1978; EdD in Ednl. Leadership, U. Fla., 1989. Cert. English tchr., tchr. of mentally retarded, adminstr., Fla. Tchr. educable mentally handicapped Orange County Schs., Orlando, Fla., adult edn. tchr., resource tchr., program cons. for mental handicapped programs; workshop leader, humor cons. Recognized for contributions to Spl. Olympics; recipient Alumni Profl. Achievement award U. Cen. Fla., 1990. Mem. Fla. Assn. Sch. Adminstrs., Assisting Women Through Access, Resources and Encouragement (founder Orlando chpt.), Assn. for Supervision and Curriculum Devel., Orange County Assn. for Mgmt. Personnel, Coun. for Exceptional Children (Adminstr. of Yr. 1989-90), Orange County Reading Assn., Assn. for Severely Handicapped, Orange County Artists League, Phi Delta Kappa. Home: 7753 Fox Knoll Pl Winter Park FL 32792 Office: Orange County Schs Dept Exceptional Edn 445 W Amelia Orlando FL 32801

PHILIPPBAR, DEBORAH DEBARR, retail executive, financial consultant; b. Grafton, W.Va., Dec. 18, 1951; d. Perry J. DeBarr and Mary Angela (Bevilocke) Stephenson; m. Mark Davies Philippbar, Feb. 28, 1986; 1 child, Kristan Angela. Student, Blue Ridge Coll., 1970-71, SUNY, Binghamton, 1981-83. Cert. fin. cons., ins. broker, N.Y., Conn., Va., Md., D.C. Fin., ins. cons. Binghamton, 1978-81; owner Faces and Things, Binghamton, 1980-82, Twice But Nice, Binghamton, 1980-82; fin. cons. Pat Ryan and Assocs., Chgo., 1983-86; bus. mgr. Tony March Buick, Hartford, Conn., 1986-89; dir. tng. F&I Alternatives, Inc., Springfield, Mass., 1988-89; exec. Royal Chevrolet, Sayre, Pa., 1990—; credit cons., Hartford, 1986—. Nat. Assn. Female Execs., Nat. Orgn. Fin. and Ins. Specialists. Republican. Baptist.

PHILIPS, BARBARA MURRAY, state legislator; b. Eveleth, Minn., Dec. 10, 1928; d. Gordon Howard and Pauline Bell (McCall) Murray; m. James Jerome May, July 17, 1950 (div. 1972); children: Cynthia McCall May, Daniel Howard May, Cathleen May Hoffman; m. Glen Franklin Philips, Mar. 21, 1975; stepchildren: Bruce, Wendy. BA, U. Wis., 1948; Degree in Elem. Edn., U. Minn., 1951; postgrad., U. Colo., Colorado Springs; grad., Jones Real Estate Coll., Colorado Springs, 1981. Cert. elem. tchr., real estate salesperson. Elem. tchr. Little Falls (Minn.) Pub. Schs., 1949-50, Mpls. Pub. Schs., 1950-52, Colorado Springs Sch. Dist. #11, 1972-75; mem. com. Precinct #59 Colo. State Legislature, 1974-88, sec. to commr. Dist. #2, 1977-82, vice-chmn. 17th Rep. Dist., 1977-82, leader "C" div. 17th Rep. Dist., 1982, chmn. 17th Rep. Dist., 1982-85, bonus mem. state cen. com., 1983-85, mem. fin. com., 1985-87, state rep. House Dist. #17, mem. edn. com., bus. affairs and labor coms., 1985—, vice-chmn. house appropriations com., 1987—, chmn. sunrise-sunset com., vice-chmn. house transp. com., mem. local govt. com., 1989—; del. to State Conv., 1974, 76, 82, 86, 88, to 3d Congl., 1978, to 5th Congl., 1982, 86, 88; mem. govt. ops. and pensions com. Nat. Conf. of State, 1989—; work in many campaigns, including 10th Senatorial, 3d Congl. and U.S. Senate; mem. Am. Legis. Exch. Coun. Vol. Goodwill Industries, 1975-76, Cancer Soc., Heart Fund; mem. Colorado Springs Bd. Adjustment, 1983-85; mem. El Paso County Adv. Com. to Dept. of Social Svcs., 1983-85. Mem. Nat. Fedn. Rep. Women, El Paso County Rep. Women, Pikes Peak Rep. Women (assoc. mem. Round Table, mem. MADD com. 1974—). Presbyterian. Home: 2822 Valley Hi Ave Colorado Springs CO 80910 Office: State Capitol Bldg Denver CO 80203

PHILLIPS, AMY, public relations conslutant; b. Suffern, N.Y., June 2, 1958; d. Maurice and Gladys (Baer) P. BFA, Jacksonville (Fla.) U., 1980; MFA, Fla. State U., 1982. Pub. rels. asst. Coconut Grove Playhouse, Miami, 1982-85; account exec. Spector Anker Pub. Rels., Miami, 1985; asst. program dir. Bus. Vols. for the Arts, Miami, 1986; pub. rels. cons. Hist. Mus. of So. Fla., Miami, 1986—, Gusman Ctr. for the Performing Arts, Miami, 1986—, Dade Community Found., Miami, 1988—. Contbr. articles to life style publs. Named Up and Comers award nominee Price Waterhouse and South Fla. Bus. Jour., 1990. Mem. Women in Communications, Inc., Pub. Rels. Soc. Am., Fashion Group Internat. (bd. dirs., program chairperson 1989-90), Greater Miami C. of C. (film and entertainment com. 1989-90, cultural action com. 1990-91, 1988 Grad. Leadership Miami), Generation After Simon Weisenthal Ctr. (bd. dirs.). Democrat. Jewish.

PHILLIPS, BARBARA RUTH, insurance company executive; b. Kansas City, Mo., Oct. 30, 1936; d. William Earl Daugherty and Ruth Augusta (Schultze) Woolfolk; divorced; 1 child, Hunter L. BS, U. Mo., 1961. Cert. tchr., Mo., Calif; lic. ins. agt., Tenn. Previously high sch. tchr. Mo. and Calif., 1958-62, 65-67; underwriting liaison The Travelers Ins. Group, San Francisco, 1963-64; claims adminstr. Conn. Gen. Ins., Seattle, 1964-65; adjuster Unigard Ins. Group, 1968-70; casualty claims dir. Zurich-Am. Ins. Group, Los Angeles, 1970-74; regional asst. to sales supt. Republic Nat. Life Ins., Los Angeles, 1974-82; corp. risk mgr. Rogers Group Inc., Nashville, 1983-87; dir. risk mgmt. Equicor-Equitable/Hosp. Corp. Am., Nashville, 1987—; co-chair Nat. Ins. Co. Industry Session, Boston, 1990—. Previously active Encino (Calif.) Hist. Park Found.; active Nashville Civil Justice Reform, Zoo Booster Assn., YWCA, Tenn. Roadbuilders Ins. Com. Mem. Am. Soc. Safety Engrs., Risk Ins. Mgrs. Soc. (sec. Nashville chpt. 1987-88, 1st v.p. 1988—, pres. 1989), Am. Mgmt. Assn., Nat. Assn. Ins. Women, NAFE. Office: Equicor Inc 1801 West End Ave Nashville TN 37203-2526

PHILLIPS, BETTY LOU (ELIZABETH LOUISE PHILLIPS), author; b. Cleve.; d. Michael N. and Elizabeth D. (Materna) Suvak; m. John S. Phillips, Jan. 27, 1963 (div. Jan. 1981); children: Bruce, Bryce, Brian; m. John D.C. Roach, Aug. 28, 1982. B.S., Syracuse U., 1960; postgrad. in English, Case Western Res. U., 1963-64. Cert. elem. and spl. edn. tchr., N.Y. Tchr. pub. schs., Shaker Heights, Ohio, 1960-66; sportswriter Cleve. Press, 1976-77; spl. features editor Pro Quarterback Mag., N.Y.C., 1976-79; freelance writer specializing in books for young people, 1976—; bd. dirs. Cast Specialties Inc., Cleve., The Children's Mus., Denver. Author: Chris Evert: First Lady of Tennis, 1977; Picture Story of Dorothy Hamill (ALA Booklist selection), 1978; American Quarter Horse, 1979; Earl Campbell: Houston Oiler Superstar, 1979; Picture Story of Nancy Lopez, (ALA Notable book), 1980; Go! Fight! Win! The NCA Guide for Cheerleaders (ALA Booklist), 1981; Something for Nothing, 1981; Brush Up on Your Hair (ALA Booklist), 1981; Texas ... The Lone Star State, 1989, Who Needs Friends? We All Do!, 1989; also contbr. articles to young adult and sports mags. Mem. Soc. Children's Book Writers, Delta Delta Delta. Republican. Roman Catholic. Home: 4 Random Rd Cherry Hills Village CO 80110

PHILLIPS, CAROL FENTON, pediatrician, associate dean; b. Bridgeport, Conn., Dec. 17, 1932; d. Laurance Edwin and Norma (Sullivan) Fenton; m. Charles Alan Phillips, Aug. 30, 1956; children: Michael, Cynthia, Catherine, Lynn. BS, Douglas Coll., 1954; MD, Yale U., 1958. Diplomate Am. Bd. Pediatrics. Intern in pediatrics Yale New Haven Hosp., 1958-59; resident in pediatrics Med. Ctr. Hosp. Vt., 1959-60, 66-68; rsch. assoc. Baylor Coll. Medicine, Houston, 1963-66; from instr. to assoc. prof. pediatrics Coll. Medicine U. Vt., Burlington, 1968-76, prof. pediatrics, 1976—, chmn. dept. pediatrics, 1983—, assoc. dean, 1985—. Assoc. editor: Report of Committee on Infectious Diseases, 1988; contbr. chpts. to books, articles to profl. jours. Fellow Infectious Diseases Soc., Pediatric Infectious Diseases Soc.; mem. Am. Acad. Pediatrics (sec. com. on infectious diseases 1985—), Am. Pediatric Soc., Pediatric Dept. Chairmen (exec. com. 1989—). Office: U Vt Burlington VT 05405

PHILLIPS, CAROLYN PATRICIA, telecommunications company official; b. Little Rock, Mar. 6, 1949; d. Andrew Jackson and Seartrice Bernice (Reid) P. BA, Ark. Coll., 1971. Neighborhood arts coord. Ark. Arts Ctr., Little Rock, 1971-73; bookstore clk. U. Ark., Little Rock, 1973-74; sales rep. Addison-Wesley Pub. Co., Reading, Mass., 1974-78, Southwestern Bell Telephone, Houston, 1978-81; sales specialist AT&T, Houston, 1981-87, asst. mgr., 1987—. Community vol. Houston Proud, 1985—; corp. team capt. March of Dimes, Houston, 1985-89; sec. assoc. bd. dirs. Arthritis Found., Houston, 1989. Mem. NAFE, Human Enrichment of Life Program (Young Black Achiever award 1989), Club MS. Democrat. Baptist. Office: AT&T 1360 Post Oak Blvd Ste 400 Houston TX 77056

PHILLIPS, CHERIE, publisher; b. Richmond, Va., June 14, 1950; d. James Iverson and Erline Rachel (Hall) P.; 1 child, Sean Patrick Fauls. Student, Va. Commonwealth U., Richmond, 1968-70, U. Md., College Park, 1989—. Pub. Spectrum Publs., Laurel, Md., 1984—. Author: Stick Exercises, 1984, 88, Alsharqi Dance, 1987, Alien Child, 1988; pub. Alsharqi Dancer, 1984—, Intellectual Spectrum, 1989—. Office: Spectrum Pubs PO Box 3006 Laurel MD 20708

PHILLIPS, COLETTE ALICE-MAUDE, public relations consultant, educator; b. St. Johns, Antigua, W.I., Sept. 20, 1954; d. Douglas Alfred Richard and Ionie Alice-Maude (Francis) P. AS, Grahm Jr. Coll., Boston, 1974; BS summa cum laude, Emerson Coll., Boston, 1976, MS, 1979. Editor in chief Govt. of Antigua, St. John's, news corr. Radio Antilles, Montserrat, W.I., TV talk show host Antigua Broadcasting Service, St. Johns, 1977-78; dir. pub. relations Patriot's Trail council Girl Scouts U.S.A., Boston, 1980-84; dir. pub. relations Cablevision of Boston, 1984-85; cons. pub. relations Royal Sonesta Hotel, 1985-87; instr. Stone Hill Coll., North Easton, Mass., 1982-85, Emerson Coll., 1984-86, Antioch Coll., 1986; pres. APR Co., 1985—. Mem. pub. info. com. Am. Cancer Soc., Boston, 1978—, chmn. 75th Anniversary com., 1987-88; v.p. Horizon for Youth, 1986—; mem. exec. com. Mus. Fine Arts Council, 1988, co-chair membership com.; cabinet mem. Finnegan for Boston Com., Boston, 1983; trustee Friends Boston Ballet, 1987—; bd. dirs. Urban League Eastern Mass., 1980—, Metro Council Ednl. Opportunity, Boston, 1981—, AIDS Action Com., 1987-88, Freedom House, 1989-92. Recipient Outstanding Alumni award Emerson Coll., 1983, United Way Agy. award for outstanding achievement in communication, 1981; named 100 Most Powerful in Boston Herald, 1987, 100 Most Influential Blacks in Boston, 1986, 87, 88, 89, 90, one of Ten Outstanding Young Leaders in Boston Jaycees, 1988, Faces to Watch in '88 Boston Mag, 100 Most Interesting Women in Boston, Boston Women mag., 1989. Mem. Pub. Relations Soc. Am., Mass. Assn. Mental Health (bd. dirs. 1984-87). Methodist. Home and Office: 41 Colborne Rd Brighton MA 02135

PHILLIPS, CONSTANCE GAISER, government lawyer; b. Toledo, Jan. 11, 1949; d. Charles William and Bernice Louise (Brauneck) Gaiser; children: Melissa Anne, Daniel Charles. BS, Bowling Green State U., 1972; JD, U. Louisville, 1978, LLM, 1988. Bar: Ky. 1979. Commd. maj. U.S. Army, 1980; tchr. Jefferson Ctr. for Handicapped, Toledo, 1972, Toledo Bd. Edn., 1972-76; acting v.p. Fort Knox (Ky.) Nat. Bank, 1976; legal clk. Skeeters & Bennett, Radcliff, Ky., 1976-78; sec. Stites, McElwain & Fowler, Louisville, 1979; corp. sec., advisor CoaLiquid, Inc., Louisville, 1979-80; faculty Elizabethtown (Ky.) Community /coll., 1979; mil. atty. U.S. Army, Ft. Monmouth, N.J., Republic of Panama, Honduras, 1980—; mil. atty. Office the Staff Judge Advocate, West Point, N.Y., 1984-87, Ft. Dix, N.J., 1988—; with LLM program JAG Sch., U. Va., Charlottesville, 1987-88. Sun. sch. tchr. various chs., 1972-84; group leader Ft. Monmouth, N.J. 4-H Club, 1981-83. Mem. Ky. Bar Assn., Pi Omega Pi. Republican. Lutheran. Club: Eastern Star (Waterville, Ohio). Office: Chief Mil Justice Office of the Staff Judge Advocate Fort Dix NJ 08640

PHILLIPS, DARLENE ANN, infection control manager; b. Springfield, Mass., July 24, 1951; d. Walter Theodore and Ann Christine (Morris) Kurman; m. George Stanley Phillips, Oct. 23, 1943. BS in Nursing, St. Anselm Coll., 1973; grad. course in surveillance, prevention and control of nosocomial infections U. Iowa, 1981; MS in Health Sci., Quinnipiac Coll., 1984. RN, Conn. Staff nurse gynecology Yale New Haven Hosp., 1974-75, staff nurse post-anesthesia care unit, 1975-81, staff nurse ambulatory surgery, 1977-80, infection control coordinator, 1981-83; nurse epidemiologist Holyoke Hosp., Mass., 1983-87; mgr. infection control Bay State Med. Ctr., Springfield, Mass., 1987-89, mgr. infection control, quality assessment, 1989—. Recipient Otis Clapp award Am. Assn. Occupational Health Nursing, 1985. Mem. NAFE, Assn. Practitioners Infection Control (New Eng. preceptor 1986-87), Area Health Edn. Ctr. Pioneer Valley, Sigma Theta Tau, Toastmasters (charter pres. Springfield club). Roman Catholic. Avocations: needlework, landscaping. Home: 158 Edgewood Rd West Springfield MA 01089 Office: PO Box 1633 Ste 252 Westfield MA 01086-1635

PHILLIPS, DEBRA SUE, physical therapist; b. Napoleon, Ohio, Jan. 19, 1957; d. Elmer B. and Rosalyn A. (Baker) Junge; 1 child, Nathan Robert. BS in Adapted Phys. Edn., Bowling Green State U., 1980, BA in Phys. Therapy, 1983; M of Spl. Edn., U. Toledo, 1988. Phys. therapist Henry County Schs., Napoleon, Ohio, 1983-86, 89; physical therapist Henry County Home Health, Napoleon, 1984-87; pediatric phys. therapist Henry County Bd. MR/DD, McClure, Ohio, 1983—; cons. pediatric phys. therapy Fulton County Bd. Mental Retardation and Devel. Disabilities, Wauseon, Ohio, 1985-89; ind. cons. phys. therapy, N.W. Ohio, 1987—. Participant Big Bros./Big Sisters, 1989; tchr. Sunday sch. St. Paul's Luth. Ch., Napoleon, 1985-89; mem. St. Paul's Parent-Tchr. League. Fed. Occupational and Phys. Therapy study grantee U. Toledo, 1986-88. Mem. Am. Phys. Therapy Assn., Northwestern Ohio Pediatric Spl. Interest Group, PTL. Home: V 405 SR108 Rte 1 Napoleon OH 43545

PHILLIPS, DOROTHY KAY, lawyer; b. Camden, N.J., Nov. 2, 1945; d. Benjamin L. and Sadye (Levinsky) Phillips; children: Bethann P., David M. Schaffzin. B.S. magna cum laude in English Lit., U. Pa., 1964; M.A., Family Life and Marriage Counseling and Edn., NYU, 1975; J.D., Villanova U., 1978. Bar: Pa. 1978, N.J. 1978, U.S. Dist. Ct. (ea. dist.) Pa. 1978, U.S. Dist. Ct. N.J., 1978, U.S. Ct. Appeals (3d cir.), 1984, U.S. Supreme Ct. 1984. Tchr., Haddon Twp. High Sch. (N.J.), and Haddon Heights High Sch. (N.J.), 1964-70; lectr., counselor Marriage Council of Phila.; lectr. U. Pa. and Hahnemann Med. Schs., profl. cons., lectr. Lankenau Hosp., Phila., 1970-75; atty. Adler, Barish, Daniels, Levin & Creskoff, Phila., 1978-79, Astor, Weiss & Newma, Phila., 1979-80; ptnr. Romisher & Phillips, P.C., Phila., 1981-86; prin. Law Office of Dorothy K. Phillips, 1986—; faculty Sch. of Law Temple U. Guest speaker on domestic rels. issues on radio and TV shows; featured in newspaper and mag. articles; contbr. articles to profl. jours. Mem. Rosenbach Found., Art Alliance, Phila.; bd. dirs. Philadanco; mem. Bus. and Profl. Women's Coalition of Fedn. Jewish Agys. Greater Phila., Bus. Women's Network. Mem. ABA, Assn. Trial Lawyers Am., Pa. Trial Lawyers Assn. (chair membership com. family sect. 1989-90), Pa. Bar Assn. (continuing legal edn. com. 1990-91), N.J. Bar Assn., Phila. Bar Assn. (chmn. early settlement program 1983-84, mem. custody rules drafting com. for Supreme Ct. Pa.), Phila. Trial Lawyers Assn., Montgomery County Bar Assn., Camden County Bar Assn., Tau Epsilon Rho Law Soc., Lawyers Club, Faculty Club. Office: 1608 Walnut St 10th Fl Philadelphia PA 19103

PHILLIPS, ELAINE LEE, psychologist, educator; b. Atlanta, Nov. 13, 1950; d. Irving Earl and Norma Nadine Young; m. Douglas Dean Chambers. BA summa cum laude, Western Mich. U., 1973, MA, 1975, PhD, 1986. Lic. psychologist, Mich. Sch. psychologist Eastern Svc. Dist., Galesburg, Mich., 1975-77; coord. Family and Children's Svcs. Barry County Mental Health, Hastings, Mich., 1977-82; psychologist Pheasant Ridge Ctr., Kalamazoo, Mich., 1982-83, Kalamazoo Regional Psychiat. Hosp., 1983-87; asst. prof. Western Mich. U., Kalamazoo, 1987—; cons. in field. Contbr. articles to profl. jours. Bd. dirs., Hospice Greater Kalamazoo, 1987—, mem. clin. records evaluation and rev. com., 1987—, program evaluation and adv. com., 1987—, chair bereavement evaluation com., 1989—. Grantee, Kalamazoo Consortium Higher Edn., 1989. Mem. Am. Psychol. Assn., Women in Psychology, Clinical Psychology, Am. Psychol. Assn. Office: Western Mich U Kalamazoo MI 49008

PHILLIPS, ELIZABETH FAYE, business manager; b. Las Vegas, June 8, 1934; d. Francis Clifford and Verna (Howell) Cravens; m. Lewis Edward Schofield, Apr. 10, 1952 (dec. 1978);l children: Michael Dennis, Michelle, Diane; m. Frank James Phillips, Aug. 6, 1983. AA in Acctg. with honors, Mesa Coll., 1988. Bus. mgr. Martin Chrysler-Plymouth, San Diego, 1971-80, Univ. Chrysler-Plymouth, San Diego, 1980-83, Bob Baker Volkswagen Crysler-Plymouth, Carlsbad, Calif., 1983-89, Bob Baker's All-Am. Chevrolet, El Cajon, Calif., 1989—. Democrat. Mormon. Office: All Am Chevrolet 900 Arnele St El Cajon CA 92020

PHILLIPS, ELIZABETH JOAN, marketing executive; b. Cleve., July 8, 1938; d. Joseph Tinl and Helen Walter; m. Erwin Phillips, June 1956 (div. 1960); 1 child, Michael A. B.A., Fordham U., 1980. Account exec. David Cogan Mgmt., N.Y.C., 1969-77; account exec. N.F.L. Films, N.Y.C., 1977-78; mgr. sports programs Avon Products, N.Y.C., 1978-83; v.p. Needham, Harper & Steers (now Needham, Harper Worldwide), N.Y.C., 1983-86; v.p. Ted Bates Event Mktg., N.Y.C., 1986-87; pres. Custom Event Mktg. subs. Ted Bates Advt. (now Backer, Spielvogel, Bates Worldwide) 1987—. adj. prof. NYU, N.Y.C., 1987—. Mem. exec. com. Vanderbilt YMCA, N.Y.C., 1976-84; ofcl. 1984 Olympic Games, L.A.; referee Women's Olympic Marathon, L.A., 1984; pres. Met. Athletics Congress, N.Y.C., 1980-83. Mem. Women's Sports Found. (bd. advisors 1983—). Club: N.Y. Road Runners (v.p., mem. exec. com. 1976—, pres. 1970—). Office: Custom Event Mktg Inc 633 3rd Ave 20th Fl New York NY 10017

PHILLIPS, ELIZABETH SNEDEKER, educator; b. New Castle, Del., Apr. 27, 1911; d. George and Eleanor Elizabeth (McCoy) Snedeker; m. Robert W. W. Phillips, Apr. 22, 1975. BS, U. Del., 1933, postgrad., 1989. Tchr. Del. Bd. of Edn., Wilmington, 1933-48; tchr. Fla. Bd. of Edn., Ft. Lauderdale, 1948-60, ret. Vice pres. awards, publicity and membership coms. Broward County (Fla.) chpt. Freedom Found. of Valley Forge, Ft. Lauderdale, 1982-89; treas. Coral Ridge Home Owners Assn., 1975-90. Named Outstanding Alumnus U. Del., 1983; recipient Medal of Merit U. Del., 1989. Mem. AAUW (Fla. state pres. 1971-73, , pres. Ft. Lauderdale br. 1964-67, 81-83), Broward County Ret. Tchrs., Sea Ranch Club (bd. dirs. 989—), Alpha Delta Kappa. Home: 5100 N Ocean Blvd #1006 Fort Lauderdale FL 33308

PHILLIPS, ELLEN HAYGOOD, educator; b. Greenville, Ala., Apr. 10, 1947; d. Joseph Edwin and Lucy (Seale) Haygood; m. Charles Nolen Wingett, June 24, 1966 (div. Apr. 1969); 1 child, Katherine Elizabeth Jeffries; m. Bruce Harrison Phillips, Dec. 19, 1981. BS, Troy State U., 1971; MEd, Auburn U., 1978; postgrad., U. Va., 1982. Speech and theatre dir. Pryor Jr. High Sch., Ft. Walton Beach, Fla., 1971-72; speech and theatre dir. Andalusia (Ala.) High Sch., 1972-74, Greenville (Ala.) High Sch., 1974-79; debate coach Vestavia High Sch., Birmingham, Ala., 1979-81; speech and theatre dir. Sandburg Intermediate Sch., Fairfax County, Va., 1981-89; English tchr. Lurleen B. Wallace Jr. Coll., Greenville, 1975-79, Whitman Intermediate Sch., Fairfax County, Va., 1989—; storytelling cons. Fairfax County Schs., 1988—; student govt. advisor, news liaison Whitman Intermediate Sch., Fairfax County, 1989. Contbr. articles to Mondays, Delta Kappa Gamma Internat. jour., 1988, Miss Mirabelle, Delta Kappa Gamma Internat. jour., 1989. Sec. Potomac Valley-River Bend, Fairfax County, 1987-89; pres. Mt. Vernon Woman's Club, Fairfax County, 1985-88. Named Outstanding Young Woman, State of Ala., 1976, Outstanding Educator, Jaycees, 1976, nominee Ala. Speech Tchr. of Yr., Ala. Speech Assn., 1980, nominee Va. Speech Tchr. of Yr., Va. Speech Assn., 1988; Storytelling Minigrantee, Fairfax County Schs., 1989. Mem. Am. Fedn. Tchrs., Nat. Assn. for the Perpetuation and Preservation of Storytelling, Delta Kappa Gamma (1st v.p.). Office: Walt Whitman Intermediate Sch 2500 Parkers Ln Alexandria VA 22306

PHILLIPS, EMILY SUSAN, admissions director; b. Elizabeth, N.J., May 20, 1960; d. Daniel T. and Vivian (Isaacson) P. BA, Barnard Coll., 1982; student, Mannes Coll. of Music, 1980-81. Music tchr. St. Hilda's and St. Hugh's Schs., N.Y.C., 1982-84; mgr. Automated Marking, Inc., N.Y.C., 1984-88; pvt. piano tchr. N.Y.C., 1980—; dir. admissions The Abraham Joshua Heschel Sch., N.Y.C., 1988—; cons. in field; cons. music The Dalton Sch., N.Y.C., 1989—. Composer musical: Cyclops, 1983. Home: 134 W 93rd St #2F New York NY 10025

PHILLIPS, GENEVA FICKER, editor; b. Staunton, Ill., Aug. 1, 1920; d. Arthur Edwin and Lillian Agnes (Woods) Ficker; m. James Emerson Phillips, Jr., June 6, 1955 (dec. 1979). B.S. in Journalism, U. Ill., 1942; M.A. in English Lit., UCLA, 1953. Copy desk Chgo. Jour. Commerce, 1942-43; editorial asst. patents Radio Research Lab., Harvard U., Cambridge, Mass., 1943-45; asst. editor adminstrv. publs. U. Ill., Urbana, 1946-47; editorial asst. Quar. of Film, Radio and TV, UCLA, 1952-53; mng. editor The Works of John Dryden, Dept. English, UCLA, 1964—. Bd. dirs. Univ. Religious Conf., Los Angeles, 1979—. UCLA teaching fellow, 1950-53, grad. fellow 1954-55. Mem. Assn. Acad. Women UCLA, Friends of Huntington Library, Friends of UCLA Library, Renaissance Soc. So. Calif., Samuel Johnson Soc. of So. Calif., Assocs. of U. Calif. Press., Conf. Christianity and Lit., Soc. Mayflower Descs. Lutheran. Home: 213 First Anita Dr Los Angeles CA 90049 Office: UCLA Dept English 2225 Rolfe Hall Los Angeles CA 90024

PHILLIPS, JOYCE MARTHA, human resources executive; b. Bridgeport, Conn., Dec. 18, 1952; d. Stephen and Shirley B. (Howard) Tabory; m. Glenn

L. Phillips, July 14, 1974. BA in English, Fairfield (Conn.) U., 1974; MS in Indsl. Relations, U. New Haven, 1982. Tchr. English and reading Fairfield Woods Jr. High Sch., 1975; asst. to v.p. mktg. Bunker Ramo Corp., Trumbull, Conn., 1975-76; rep. in investor relations Gen. Electric Co., Fairfield, 1976-77; specialist in manpower relations, 1977-79; specialist in employee benefits Gen. Electric Co., Bridgeport, Conn., 1979-80, specialist in employee relations, orgn. and staffing, 1980-84; mgr. hdqrs. personnel and office services Armtek Corp., New Haven, 1984-87, dir. compensation and benefits, 1987-89; v.p. human resources (div. sr. human resources officer) Citibank, N.Y.C., 1989—. Counsel Fairfield U. Alumni Adv. Coun. Mem. Conn. Personnel Assn. Office: Citibank 399 Park Ave New York NY 10043

PHILLIPS, JUDITH, real estate company executive; b. Denver, Mar. 3; d. Frank E. and Marjorie E. (Barclay) P. Student, U. Colo., 1960-61, Fullerton Jr. Coll., 1961-62, Colo. Mountain Coll., 1972-80. Lic. real estate broker, Colo. V.p. Vail (Colo.) Realty Inc.; broker Vail Assocs. Inc.; pres. JP Co., Vail, 1977-81, Denver Comml. Brokers, 1982-85; sr. mktg. exec. Previews Inc., Denver, 1985-87; pres. Estate Mktg. Group/Phillips Realty, Denver, 1987—; cons. Ridge at Castle Pines, Castle Rock, Colo., 1987—. Fundraiser Artreach, Denver, 1980-87; bd. dirs. Denver chpt. Cystic Fibrosis Found., 1987-89, Colo. Spl. Olympics, 1988—. Recipient awards for lyrics Am. Song Festival, Nashville, 1977—, grand prize Music City Song Festival, 1981. Mem. Nat. Assn. Realtors, Colo. Assn. Realtors (edn. com. 1988), Denver Bd. Realtors, Fedn. Internationale des Professions Immobilieres (pres. Colo. coun.), Citivan Club. Republican. Office: Estate Mktg Group 1021 E 9th Ave #127 Denver CO 80218

PHILLIPS, KELLY LYN, newspaper executive; b. Warwick, R.I., June 21, 1965; d. William R. and Linda C. (Greene) P. AA, Community Coll. R.I., Warwick, 1986. Mgr. classified advt. Kent County Daily Times, West Warwick, R.I., 1986, dep. advt. dir., 1988; mgr. classified advt. Community Newspapers of R.I., 1990—; co-owner, operator Resumés, Etc. Mem. NAFE, Assn. Newspaper Classified Adv. Mgrs., Humane Soc. U.S. Home: 26 Centennial St Coventry RI 02816

PHILLIPS, LINDA DARNELL ELAINE, nurse; b. Calgary, Alta., Can., July 23, 1940; came to U.S. 1964; d. Richard and Adeline Ruth (Kuch) Fredricks; m. Marion Rolley Phillips, June 25, 1960 (div. 1962). Cert. in nursing with honors, Broward Community Coll., Ft. Lauderdale, Fla., 1983. Exec. sec. Grandeur Motor Cars, Pompano Beach, Fla., 1975-80; charge nurse Las Olas Hosp., Ft. Lauderdale, 1983-85; nurse Med. Personnel Pool, Ft. Lauderdale, 1984-85; pvt. practice Ft. Lauderdale, 1985—; consultant nurse Waterford Point Condo, Pompano Beach, Fla. 1980—. Sponsor Children Internat., Kansas City, Mo. 1988-89. Mem. Nurses Assn. Address: 2910 NE 55th St Fort Lauderdale FL 33308

PHILLIPS, LOIS PLOWDEN, travel agent; b. Ft. Gaines, Ga., Dec. 30, 1927; d. Leonard Dale and Helen (Lindsay) Plowden; m. James Henry Phillips, Aug. 25, 1956 (div. Feb. 1959); 1 child, Jaye Dale. Student Ga. State Coll. for Women, 1946-48. Adminstrv. asst. U.S. Air Force, Warner Robins, Ga., 1950-56; asst. buyer Mut. Buying Syndicate, N.Y.C., 1957-59; owner, operator Junior Vogue, Macon, Ga., 1960-69; mgr. Lee-Roi, Atlanta and Highland, N.C., 1971-73; mgr., buyer Isakson's, Atlanta, 1974-76; owner, mgr., pres., Mercury Travel, Inc., Atlanta and Marietta, Ga., 1977—. Mem. Am. Soc. Travel, Prost Exec. Women. Republican. Clubs: Idle Hour (Macon, Ga.). Avocations: travel; gardening. Office: Mercury Travel Svc Inc 1325 Johnson Ferry Rd Marietta GA 30067

PHILLIPS, MARILYN CHENAULT, legal administrator; b. Mt. Vernon, Ill., Oct. 21, 1949; d. Nathan Bullock and Marguerite (Woodberry) Chenault; m. Tom Dee McFall, Aug. 29, 1969; children: Shannon, Nathan; m. 2d, Troy David Phillips, Aug. 14, 1981; stepchildren: Todd, Brittany. BS with honors, Okla. State U., 1970. Adminstrv. asst. Opticks, Inc. div. G. D. Searle, Dallas, 1977-78; office adminstr. Baker, Glast, Riddle, Tuttle & Elliott, Dallas, 1978-81; exec. dir. Haynes and Boone, Dallas, 1981—; lectr., instr. paralegal program So. Meth. U. Sch. Law, Dallas, 1981-85, lectr. law, 1988—. Lou Wentz scholar Coll. Bus., Okla. State U., Stillwater, 1969-70, also C.V. Richardson scholar, 1969-70; named Outstanding Office Mgmt. Grad., 1970. Mem. NAFE, Nat. Assn. Legal Adminstrs. (dir. of adminstrn. sect. 1979-85, mem. large firm adminstrn. sect. 1985—, com. mem. 1986-88, vice-chmn. 1989-90, chmn., 1990-91, chair in-house tng. task force, 1990-91, int. issues com. 1988-89, instr. law office adminstrn. course 1984, 87, pres. Dallas chpt. 1985-86), VS Legal Users Group (nat. bd. dirs. and v.p. 1985-88), Wang Legal Adv. Coun. Tech. Task Force (chair practicing law profitability conf. 1984, chair-at-large law firm tech. conf. 1990, co-chair VS legal users group conf. 1988). Methodist. Home: 6410 Northaven Rd Dallas TX 75230 Office: Haynes and Boone Law Firm 3100 NCNB Pla Dallas TX 75202

PHILLIPS, MARION GRUMMAN, author, civic worker; b. N.Y.C., Feb. 11, 1922; d. Leroy Randle and Rose Marion (Werther) Grumman; student Mt. Holyoke Coll., 1940-42; B.A., Adelphi U., 1981; m. Ellis Laurimore Phillips, Jr., June 13, 1942; children—Valerie Rose (Mrs. Adrian Parsegian), Elise Marion (Mrs. Edward E. Watts III), Ellis Laurimore III, Kathryn Noel (Mrs. Philip Zimmermann), Cynthia Louise (Mrs. Kenneth Gleason Jr.). Civic vol. Mary C. Wheeler Sch., 1964-68, Historic Ithaca, Inc., 1972-76, Ellis L. Phillips Found., 1960—; bd. dirs. North Shore Jr. League, 1960-61, 64-65, 68-69, Family Service Assn. Nassau County, 1963-69, Homemaker Service Assn. Nassau County, 1959-61. Author: (light verse) A Foot in the Door, 1965; The Whale-Going, Going, Gone, 1977; Doctors Make Me Sick (So I Cured Myself of Arthritis), 1979; editor: (with Valerie Phillips Parsegian) Richard and Rhoda, Letters from the Civil War, 1982, Wooden Shoes (F. M. Sisson), 1990, Irish Eyes (McTarsneys and Sissions), 1990; editor Jr. League Shore Lines, 1960-61, The Werthers in America-Four Generations and their Descendants, 1987; A B-Tour of Britain, 1986; contbr. articles on fund raising to mags. Episcopalian. Clubs: Hanover Garden, Creek, PEO Sisterhood. Home: Point of View RR1 Box 274 Sharon VT 05065

PHILLIPS, MARTHA HUGGINS, home economist; b. Lake City, S.C., Jan. 17, 1950; d. James Allison Jr. and Julia Louise (Baker) Huggins; m. Floyd Terry Phillips, Mar. 25, 1972 (div. 1983); children: Hayden Nicole, Nicholas Terry. BS in Home Econs., Limestone Coll., 1971; MEd in Personnel Services, Clemson U., 1977. Tchr. Dist. 7 Schs., Spartanburg, S.C., 1971-72; asst. county extension agt. Clemson Extension Svc., Spartanburg, 1972-75; assoc. county extension agt. Clemson Extension Svc., Spartanburg and Gaffney, S.C., 1975-82; sr. assoc. extension agt. Clemson Extension Svc., Gaffney, 1982-85, sr. county extension agt., 1985-89; area county extension agt. Clemson Extension Svc., Spartanburg, 1989—; del. S.C. to White House Conf. on Aging, 1981. Founder Parents of Preschoolers Charles Lea Ctr. for Mentally Handicapped, 1982—; chmn. legis com. McCarthy PTO; mem. Cannon United Meth. Women; tchr. Sunday sch. class; sec. Cherokee County Social and Health Orgns. Council, 1979, mem. project com., 1980-81, vice-chmn., 1983, chmn., 1984—, chmn. healthy mother/healthy baby network; chmn. nominating com. Am. Lung Assn., S.C., 1984, mem. Broad River adv. bd., 1984—, mem. program com., 1985, mem. state planning com., 1985; bd. dirs. vision for youth Clemson U., 1989—. Recipient State Communications award S.C. Assn. Extension Home Economists, 1974, Disting. Svc. award, 1988, Young Career Woman award Spartanburg County, 1976; named Outstanding Home Economist of Yr. Piedmont dist. S.C. Assn. Extension Home Economists, 1979. Mem. Nat. Assn. Extension 4-H Agts. (jr. editor news and views so. region, Disting. Svc. award 1988), S.C. Assn. Extension 4-H Agts. (participant state meeting 1983, pres. 1987-89, editor newsletter, historian 1989, chmn. nominating com. 1989, immediate past pres. 1989), Nat. Exec. Devel. Inst., Epsilon Sigma Phi (initiation com. 1980-81, screening and selection com. 1981-83, bd. dirs. Piedmont dist. 1989—). Democrat. Club: Town and Country Garden. Home: 280 Bramblewood Ln Spartanburg SC 29302 Office: Clemson Extension Svc PO Box 1010 Spartanburg SC 29304

PHILLIPS, MARYANN KATHERINE, real estate sales associate; b. Dayton, Ohio, Mar. 23, 1930; d. William and Dora Elizabeth (Thies) Kohnekamp; m. Robert Lee Phillips, Dec. 27, 1952; children: Daniel Lee, Kathryn P. Fielder, Thomas W. BA, Miami U., Oxford, Ohio, 1952; MEd, Oreg. State U., 1967. Rsch. assoc. Oreg. Rsch. Inst., Eugene, 1967-68; instr. Oreg. State U., Corvallis, 1968-75; asst. prof. and counselor Oreg. State U., 1975-84; sales assoc. Ridgepine, Inc., Sunriver, Oreg., 1984—; acting dean students Kings Coll., U. London, 1980. Mem. environ. com. Sunriver Owner's Assn., 1984-88, pub. wks. com. mem., 1989—. Mem. Grad. Realtors Inst., Nat. Assn. Realtors, Sunriver Area C. of C. (v.p. 1989), Century Club (pres. 1983), Million Dollar Club, Multi-Million Dollar Club, Women's Golf Club (statistician). Democrat. Office: Ridgepine Inc Sunriver Mall Box 3400 Sunriver OR 97707

PHILLIPS, MIRIAM ERNESTINE, civic worker; b. Haverhill, Mass., Mar. 11, 1918; d. William B. and Ermina Floride (Coburn) Faulcon; m. Oscar George Dudley Phillips, Dec. 19, 1954; children: Peter Joshua, Miriam Elaine. BA in Edn., U. Mass.-Boston, 1985; MA in English, U. Mass., Boston, 1987. Adminstrv. asst. Am. Bapt. Chs. of Mass., Boston, 1948-58. Contbr. articles to religious publs. Nat. denominational v.p. Church Women United, 1974-77, Northeast regional v.p., 1977-80, other nat. and state offices; mem.-at-large Gen. Council, Am. Bapt. Chs. USA, 1969-71, rep. to gen. bd., 1971-78, Participant study tour to People's Republic of China, 1978; mem. exec. com. Bd. Nat. Ministries; rep. to Nat. Council Chs., 1969-72, del. to World Council Chs., 1968; v.p. Am. Bapt. Chs. Mass., 1972, 73, 1st v.p., 1987—, chmn. ann. meeting com., mem. personnel com., mem. communications com.; nat. chmn. communications Am. Bapt. Women USA, 1964-68; trustee Mass. Bible Soc.; trustee Andover Newton Theol. Sch., 1969—, sec. bd. dirs., mem. coms.; commr. Medford Housing Authority, Mass., 1972—, chmn., 1974-75, 89—; co-founder Medford br. NAACP, chmn. press and publicity; bd. dirs. Middlesex-Cambridge Lung Assn., Family Service Assn. of Greater Boston, Resthaven Home. Recipient Valiant Woman award Ch. Women United, 1979, Walter Telfer award for Excellence in Supervision Andover Newton Theol. Sch., 1989. Avocation: travel. Home: 94 Monument St Medford MA 02155

PHILLIPS, NANCY CHAMBERS, social worker; b. Danville, Ky., Oct. 11, 1941; d. Alvia Jackson and Virginia Oradell Chambers; m. Eldon Franklin Phillips, Nov. 27, 1968 (div. 1984). BA, Georgetown Coll., 1962; MSW, U. Denver, 1968; postgrad. Tulane U., 1981-85. Tchr., Hazard (Ky.) High Sch., 1962-64; social worker Ky. Dept. Econ. Security, 1964-71; rehab. counselor Ky. Bur. Vocat. Rehab., 1971-72; team leader Cath. Social Services, Bureau, Ky., 1972-74; instr. U. Cin., 1972-77; vis. asst. prof. Fla. Internat. U., 1977-79; asst. prof. social work Idaho State U., Pocatello, 1979-81; rsch. asst. Child Welfare Tng. Ctr. Region VI, Tulane U., New Orleans, 1981-83; village mgr. Countryside Village, Belle Chasse State Sch., New Orleans, 1983-85; asst. supr. case mgmt. svcs. Office Mental Retardation/Developmental Disabilities, Dept. Health and Human Resources, Greater New Orleans Regional Svc. Ctr., 1985-86; social work cons. Depelchin Children's Ctr., Houston, 1986-87; cons. Vis. Nurses Assn. of Brazoria County, Inc., 1986-88, social svc. and hospice mgr., Nat. Med. Care, Inc., dialysis svcs. div. S.W. Houston Dialysis Ctr., med. social worker; med. social worker Dialysis Svcs. div. Bio-Med. Applications of S.W. Houston, S.W. Houston Dialysis Ctr., 1987-88; former mem. profl. adv. bd. Fla. Soc. Autistic Children, South Fla. Soc. Autistic Children, adv. council Ohio State U. Community Edn. Unit. Formerly active children's subcom. Dade and Monroe Counties Mental Health Bd., United Family and Children's Svcs., Family and Child Advocacy in Action Group. Recipient ednl. stipend Ky. Dept. Econ. Security, 1966-68, Nat. Cert. Recognition, South Fla. Soc. Autistic Children, 1979, Disting. Service award, 1979; named Ky. col. Mem. Nat. Assn. Social Workers. Home: 1017 San Felipe Angleton TX 77515 Office: Vis Nurses Assn Brazoria County 201 E Mulberry Ste 300 Angleton TX 77516-1779

PHILLIPS, PAMELA KIM, lawyer; b. San Diego, Feb. 23, 1958; d. John Gerald and Nancy Kimiko (Tabuchi) P. BA, The Am. U., 1978; JD, Georgetown U., 1982. Bar: N.Y. 1983, U.S. Dist. Ct. (so. dist.) N.Y. 83. Assoc. atty. Curtis, Mallet-Prevost, Colt & Mosle, N.Y.C., 1982-84; assoc. LeBoeuf, Lamb, Leiby & MacRae, N.Y.C., 1984—. Mng. editor The Tax Lawyer, Georgetown U. Law Sch., Washington, 1980-81. Mem. com. Halloween Benefit The Fresh Air Fund, N.Y.C., 1988-89. Am. Univ. scholar, Washington, 1976-78. Mem. ABA (mem. exec. com. young lawyer div. Young Lawyer Devel. Com.), Women's Bar Assn., Assn. of Bar of City of N.Y. (sec. Young Lawyers com. 1987-89, chmn. 1989—), Georgetown Club (N.Y.C.). Home: 107 E 36th St #3 New York NY 10016 Office: LeBoeuf Lamb Leiby & MacRae 520 Madison Ave New York NY 10022

PHILLIPS, PEARL RAPHELITA, real estate executive; b. Savanna La Mar, Westmoreland, Jamaica, Apr. 17, 1941; came to U.S., 1968; d. Hugh Lawrence Rance and Ada Louise (Mullings) Watson; m. Michael I. Phillips, June 9, 1962 (div. Sept., 1977); children: Karim Irving, Felitia Alssandra; m. Michael John Reardon, May 24, 1980. Student, Howard Community Coll., 1974-77, Am. U., 1984-86. Cert. real estate broker Grad. Real Estate Inst. Sr. sec. Nat. Coun. Cath. Men, Washington, 1968-69; exec. sec. Nat. Acad. Sci, Washington, 1969-71; sr. sec. President's Commn., Washington, 1971-72; exec. sec. Westinghouse Health System, Columbia, Md., 1972-76; adminstrv. group mgr. Price, Williams & Assocs., Silver Spring, Md., 1976-78; assoc. broker Merrill Lynch Realty, Silver Spring, 1977-81; pres. Pearl Properties, Silver Spring, 1982-86, Suitland, 1986—. Organizer Peoples Nat. Party, Linstead, Jamaica, 1966; founding mem. Jamaica Nat. Assn., Washington, 1969, sec. 1969-73. Mem. Internat. Real Estate Fedn., Nat. Assn. Realtors, Md. Assn. Realtors, Cen. Md. Bd. Realtors, Northern Va. Bd. Realtors, Montgomery Bd. Realtors, Prince George Bd. Realtors, D.C. Bd. Realtors. Office: Pearl Properties 4712 Suitland Rd Suitland MD 20746

PHILLIPS, PHYLLIS CATHERINE, realtor; b. Campbell, Ohio, July 14, 1935; d. Nellie J. Kosko; m. Eugene D. Phillips, Jan. 26, 1957; children: Mark P., Scott M. (dec.). Student, Youngstown (Ohio) U., 1952-53, 60-62; BS, Ohio State U., 1956; MEd, St. Francis Coll., Fort Wayne, Ind., 1971. Cert. elem. tchr., Ohio; lic. broker, Ohio, med. technologist, Calif. Med. tech. Children's Hosp., Washington, 1957, Youngstown Hosp. Assn., 1958-62; tchr. Youngstown Pub. Schs., Defiance, Ohio, 1962-65, Ayersville Local Schs., Defiance, 1965-74; realtor assoc. Strayer Realty, Inc., Defiance, 1978-80, Yoder's Realty, Defiance, 1980—; broker, realtor assoc. RE/MAX Realty of Defiance, 1986—. Active women's commn. Defiance Coll., Defiance Hosp. Aux. Martha Jennings Found. scholar, 1973-74. Mem. Mut. Improvement Circle, Am. Soc. Clin. Pathologists, Northwest Ohio Bd. Realtors, Nat. Assn. Realtors, Lions, Alpha Delta Kappa. Republican. Roman Catholic. Home: 212 Kettenring Dr Defiance OH 43512 Office: RE/MAX Realty of Defiance 516 Clinton St Defiance OH 43512

PHILLIPS, RENÉE ANN, computer business owner; b. Rochester, N.Y., Apr. 30, 1951; d. Wendell Maynard and Carmel (Lanzatella) P. Owner, opr. Info. Communication, Fairport, N.Y., 1984—, Fact Sheets, plus, Fairport, 1988—.

PHILLIPS, RUTH C., financial executive; b. Odum, Ga., June 17, 1935; d. Robert P. and Edna (Britt) Culpeper; m. Wiley Paul Phillips, Aug. 9, 1954; 1 child, Dorothy Kay. Attended Manatee Community Coll. and Bradenton (Fla.) Bus. Sch. With Peacock TV, Bradenton, 1953-55, Wyman Green & Blalock, Bradenton, 1955-66; fin. officer, asst. computer specialist Deschamps & Gregory Inc., Bradenton, 1966—. Mem. Nat. Assn. Female Execs., Credit Women's Assn. (sec.-treas. Bradenton area 1966-68). Democrat. Mem. Church of God. Office: Deschamps & Gregory Inc 1812 Manatee Ave W Bradenton FL 34205

PHILLIPS, SHARON KATHY, operations manager; b. Hollywood, Calif., Oct. 4, 1960; d. Fred and Joyce (Petersen) P. BA, Calif. State U., 1982. Sales asst. Bateman Eichler, Hill Richards, Calabasas, Calif., 1983-84, ops. mgr., 1984-89; sales asst. Bateman Eichler, Hill Richards, Westlake Village, Calif., 1990—. Mem. NAFE. Lutheran. Office: Bateman Eichler Hill Richards 31351 Via Colinas #205 Westlake Village CA 91362

PHILLIPS, SUSAN LYNN, ultra sonographer; b. Kingsport, Tenn., Dec. 9, 1955; d. Edward Adam Street and Leoria Linda (Caldwell) Phillips; m. Luther Barnett, July 25, 1981; children: Adam Lee, Amy Elizabeth. Student, East Tenn. State U., 1974-75; Registered Radiologic Technologist, Nave Paramedical Sch., Elizabethown, Tenn., 1977; Registered Diagnostic Med. Sonographer, Bomen Gray U., 1988. Radiol. technologist Indian Path Hosp., Kingsport, 1977-86, ultrasonographer, 1986--. Mem. Am. Soc. Diagnostic Med. Sonographers, Tenn. State Radiol. Technologists, East Tenn. Ultrasound Soc., Am. Inst. Ultrasound in Medicine. Republican. Home: 5013 Shannon Kingsport TN 37664 Office: Indian Path Hospital 2000 Brookside Drive Kingsport TN 37660

PHILLIPS-JONES, LINDA, consulting psychologist; b. South Bend, Ind.; d. Robert Milton and Priscilla Alicia (Tancy) Phillips; m. G. Brian Jones, Feb. 16, 1980; stepchildren: Laurie Darian Jones, Tracy Leigh Jones. BS, U. Nev., Reno, 1964; AM, Stanford U., 1965; PhD, UCLA, 1977. Lic. psychologist. Tchrs.' trainer Edn. Consultants Ltd. Internat. Tng. Consultants, Saigon, Vietnam, 1966-71; rsch. scientist Am. Insts. for Rsch., Palo Alto, Calif., 1979-83; sr. trainer, orgn. devel. cons. SRI Internat., Menlo Park, Calif., 1984-88; psychologist, cons. Coalition of Counseling Ctrs., Grass Valley, Calif., 1980—; cons., mem. adv. com. Clairol Nat. Mentor Program, N.Y.C., 1989—. Author: Mentors and Proteges, 1982; co-author: Men Have Feelings, Too!, 1988, A Fight to the Better End, 1989; contbr. articles to profl. jours.; editorial bd. Mentoring Internat., Vancouver, B.C., Can., 1989—. Recipient Civilian Svc. award Govt. of South Vietnam, 1971; grad. fellow UCLA, 1964-65, 72-77. Mem. Am. Psychol. Assn., Am. Soc. for Tng. & Devel. Office: Coalition Counseling Ctrs 13560 Gillum View Dr Grass Valley CA 95949

PHILLIPS-MADSON, ROBYN LYNN, osteopathic physician; b. Portland, Oreg., Feb. 12, 1953; d. Robert Owen and Dorothy Marie (Phillips) Phillips; m. Walter Joseph Madson, Dec. 29, 1978; children: Adam, Catherine. BS in Pharmacy, U. Wash., 1975; D.O., Mich. State U., 1979. Hosp. pharmacist Northwest Hosp., Seattle, 1975-77; intern Fifth Avenue Med. Ctr., Seattle, 1979-80; pvt. practice Seattle, 1980—; instr., cons. at home program Better Life Inst., Seattle, 1989—; pres. 4M Internat., network mktg. orgn., 1980—. Del. King County Rep. Conv., 1980, Snohomist County Rep. Conv., 1988; fundraiser Am. Heart Assn., 1982-83, East Seal Soc., 1986—, V.I.P.. Mem. King County Med. Soc., Am. Osteo. Assn., Wash. Osteo. Med. Assn., Crista Mothers Guild, U. Wash. Alumni Assn., Sigma Sigma Phi, Lambda Kappa Sigma, Phi Mu Alumnae Assn. Home: 22525 50th Ave SE Bothell WA 98021 Office: 1405 NW 85th St Seattle WA 98117

PHILPOT, KATHRYN ANN, aerospace company technical program manager; b. Salt Lake City, Mar. 29, 1958; d. Myron Charles and Patricia Sue (Rasmussen) P.; m. John Calvin Dobson, Aug. 20, 1983. BS in Materials Sci. and Engring., U. Utah, 1981; MS in Materials Sci. and Engring., U. Calif., Davis, 1985; MBA, U. Utah, 1987. Devel. engr. Longyear Co., Salt Lake City, 1981-83; tech. program mgr. Hercules Aerospace Div., Magna, Utah, 1985—. Mem. Soc. Advanced Materials Process Engrs., Am. Ceramic Soc., Tau Beta Pi, Beta Gamma Sigma. Office: Hercules Aerospace PO Box 98 Magna UT 84044

PHINNEY, BETH, Canadian legislator. Ed., McMaster U., Hamilton Tchrs. Coll. Tchr. Saltfleet, 1961-64, Montreal, Que., Can., 1964-67; tchr. ESL, 1968-74; with ministry of edn. Province of Que., 1974-79, spl. asst. to ministry of regional & econ. devel., 1981; real estate sales rep., 1982; mem. Ho. of Commons, Ottawa, Ont., Can., 1988—. Active Red Cross Soc., Girl Guides. Mem. Royal Can. Legion. Office: House of Commons, Parliament Bldgs, Ottawa, ON Canada K1A 0A6*

PHINNEY, JEAN SWIFT, psychology educator; b. Princeton, N.J., Mar. 12, 1933; d. Emerson H. and Anne (Davis) Swift; m. Bernard O. Phinney, Dec. 11, 1965; children: Peter, David. BA, Mass. Wellesley Coll., 1955; MA, UCLA, 1969, PhD, 1973. Asst. prof. psychology Calif. State U., L.A., 1977-81, assoc. prof. psychology, 1981-86, prof. psychology, 1986—. Editor: Children's Ethnic Socialization, 1987; contbr. articles to profl. jours. NIH grantee. Mem. Am. Psychol. Assn., Soc. for Rsch. in Child Devel., Soc. for Rsch. in Adolescence. Office: Calif State U Dept Psychology 2250 State University Dr Los Angeles CA 90032

PHINNEY, MARIANNE, linguistics educator; b. Fitchburg, Maine, July 31, 1954; d. Raymond Sheridan and Bertha (Maenpaa) P.; m. Peter George Liapis, July 18, 1981; 1 child, Anthony Raymond. BA in Anthropology and Linguistics, McGill U., Montreal, Que., Can., 1976; PhD in Linguistics, U. Mass., 1981. Rsch. fellow Smith Coll., Northampton, Maine, 1980-81; asst. prof. linguistics U. P.R., Mayagüez, 1982-85, U. Tex., El Paso, 1985—; reviewer NSF, Washington, 1985—. Contr. articles to profl. jours. Bd. dirs. St. Clement English Speaking Ctr., El Paso, 1987—; trustee sta. KCOS Pub. TV, El Paso, 1987-89; mem. S.W. Repertory Orgn., 1987—. Grantee U. Tex., 1986, U. P.R., 1982-84, rsch. grantee U. Tex., 1988; fellow NSF, 1977-80. Mem. AAUW (Young Scholar Recognition award 1989), Nat. Coun. Tchrs. English, Tchrs. English Speakers Other Langs. (contbg. editor newsletter and jour. 1989—), Linguistic Soc. Am. Democrat. Episcopalian. Office: U Tex- El Paso Dept Langs & Linguistics El Paso TX 79968

PHIPPS, DARLEEN MARIE, artist; b. Baraboo, Wis., June 13, 1929; d. Rudolph Frederick and Marie Amelia Rehbein; m. Robert Maurice Phipps, Aug. 23, 1952; children: David Marshall, Robert Maurice II, Christina Marie. High sch. grad., Baraboo, Wis.; student, Cuyahoga Valley Art Ctr., 1959. instr. Which Craft?, Creve Cour Mo., Downriver YMCA, Wyandotte, Mich., Roselawn Gallery, Pittsford, N.Y., Valley Manor, Rochester, N.Y. One-woman shows include Norfolk Gallery, Four Seasons Gallery, St. Louis, Hilton Gallery, Century Club, 1570 Valley Manor Gallery, AAUW House, Seven Artist's Gallery, Rochester, N.Y.; juried exhibits include Scarab Club Silver Medal Show, Detroit, Dreams and Fantasies Show, Cuyhago Falls, Ohio (juror's award 1986), Small Painting Exhibit, Ky. Highlands Mus., Ashland (purchase award 1987), Internat. Dogwood Festival, Atlanta, Still Life Now, New Haven, Conn., Bald Eagle Regional, others. Recipient Grumbacher award Beaux Arts, St. Louis, Best of Show award DuPage Art League, Wheaton, Ill., 1978, juror's award 48th Finger Lakes Exhbn. at Meml. Art Gallery, Rochester, N.Y., 1989. Mem. Penfield Art Assn., Rochester Art Club. Republican. Presbyterian. Home: 1118 Whalen Rd Penfield NY 14526

PHIPPS, DELORES CHERYL, county official; b. Hopkinsville, Ky., Sept. 2, 1946; d. Joseph W. and Frances Elaine (White) P. BS, Western Ky. U., 1966; MA, U. Ky., 1969; postgrad., Ohio State U., 1984. Cert. by Ohio Dept. Mental Retardation and Devel. Disabilities as supt.; qualified mental retardation profl. Social worker Bur. Employment Security, Div. Pub. Assistance, Hopkinsville, 1966-67; counselor Bur. Rehab. Svcs., Lexington, Ky., 1967-70; area supr. Bur. Rehab. Svcs., Covington, Ky., 1970-72; dir. Svcs., Tng. and Rehab. Ctr., Cin., 1972-73; rehab. dir. Clinton County Bd. Mental Retardation/Devel. Disabilities, Wilmington, Ohio, 1973-74; workshop dir. Franklin County Bd. Mental Retardation & Devel. Disabilities, Columbus, Ohio, 1974-77; asst. supt. Franklin County Bd. Mental Retardation and Devel. Disabilities, Columbus, Ohio, 1979-84; dir. residential svcs. Assn. for the Developmentally Disabled, Columbus, 1977-79; supt. Licking County Bd. Mental Retardation/Devel. Disabilities, Newark, Ohio, 1984—. Active Devel. Disabilities Planning Coun., Columbus, 1987—, Health Ins. Task Force, Columbus, 1988—, LWV, Newark, 1987—. Mem. Nat. Mgmt. Assn., Profl. Assn. for Retardation (pres. 1987-89, bd. dirs., Mem. of Yr. 1988), Assn. for Retarded Citizens, Ohio Mental Retardation and Devel. Disabilities Legis. Coalition (pres. 1988—, bd. dirs.), Supts. of County Bds. Assn. (trustee 1987—, bd. dirs., v.p. 1989-90). Democrat. Episcopalian. Office: Licking County Bd Mental Retardation/Devel Dis 65 W Church St Newark OH 43055

PHIPPS, SUSIE JONES, sales professional; b. Jacksonville, Fla., Aug. 27, 1950; d. Edward N. and Louann Deargentage (Jones) P.; children from previous marriage: Christine, Elizabeth. Student, Greenville Tech., 1974, Fla. Coll., 1978. Sales rep., br. mgr. Brockway, Standard, Tampa, Fla., 1974-83; dist. sales mgr. Package Supply & Equipment, Orlando, Fla., 1983-87; sales rep. Steeltin Can Corp., Balt., 1987—. Editor packaging newspaper. Mem. NAFE, Am. Bus. Women's Assn., So. Soc. Coating Tech. (sec.). Home: 1203 Athens Ct Bel Air MD 21014

PIANETTI, CATHERINE NATALIE, occupational therapist; b. Rock Spring, Wyo., June 4, 1909; d. Anthony and Anna Mary (Picco) P.; diploma Seattle Pacific Coll., 1932; B.A. in Edn., Central Wash. U., 1938; postgrad. U. Wash., 1940; cert. of proficiency in occupational therapy Mills Coll., 1945. Tchr., Wash. Public Schs., 1936-45; chief occupational therapist Marion (Ind.) VA Hosp., 1948-50, 54-69; head occupational therapist NP sect. Walter Reed Army Hosp., 1950, Valley Forge Army Hsop., 1952-53; chief occupational therapist Downey (Ill.) VA Hosp., 1953-54; ret., 1969; lectr. Ball State U., Purdue U., Marion and Anderson colls. Bd. dirs., sec., v.p. Family Service Orgn.; bd. dirs., treas., v.p Grant County Mental Health Assn.; bd. dirs. Blind Assn., Retarded Children Assn. Served from 1st lt. to capt., Womens Med. Specialists Corps., U.S. Army, 1950-53. Recipient Excellence in Communications with Pub. award, 1969, Mgrs. commendation on retirement, 1969. Mem. Am., Ind. occupational therapy assns., Am. Legion Aux. (1st and 2d vice comdr. Rainier Valley Post 139, 1971-72, comdr. 1976, comdr. Service Girls Post 1977, comdr. 1st Seattle Dist. 1978-79), 20 and 4, 8 and 40 (pres. 1976, chmn. 1979—), Pioneers of Columbia, Nat. Assn. Fed. Employees. Roman Catholic. Clubs: Seattle Womens Century (publicity chmn. rec. sec. Past Pres.'s Assembly 1974-75, treas. 1975-77, v.p. 1976-78, pres. 1979-81), DAV, Gen. Fedn. Womens' Clubs. Contbr. articles to profl. jours. Home: 4221 47th Ave S Seattle WA 98118

PIAZZA, MARGUERITE, opera singer, actress, entertainer; b. New Orleans, May 6, 1926; d. Albert William and Michaela (Piazza) Luft; m. William J. Condon, July 15, 1953 (dec. Mar. 1968); children: Gregory, James (dec.), Shirley, William J., Marguerite P., Anna Becky; m. Francis Harrison Bergthold, Nov. 8, 1970. MusB, Loyola U., New Orleans; MusM, La. State U.; MusD (hon.), Christian Bros. Coll., 1973; LHD honoris causa, Loyola U., Chgo., 1975. Singer N.Y.C. Ctr. Opera, 1948, Met. Opera Co., 1950; TV artist, regular singing star Your Show of Shows NBC, 1950-54; entertainer various supper clubs Cotillion Room, Hotel Pierre, N.Y.C., 1954, Las Vegas, Los Angeles, New Orleans, San Francisco, 1956—; ptnr. Sound Express Music Pub. Co., Memphis, 1987—; bd. dirs. Cemrel, Inc. Appeared as guest performer on numerous mus. TV shows. Nat. crusade chmn. Am. Cancer Soc., 1971; founder, bd. dirs. Marguerite Piazza Thanksgiving Gala for the Benefit of St. Jude's Hosp., 1976; bd. dirs. Memphis Opera Co., World Literacy Found., NCCJ; v.p., life bd. dirs. Memphis Symphony Orch.; nat. chmn. Soc. for Cure Epilepsy. Decorated Mil. and Hospittaler Order of St Lazarus of Jerusalem; recipient service award Chgo. Heart Assn., 1956, service award Fedn. Jewish Philanthropies of N.Y., 1956, Sesquicentennial medal Carnegie Hall; named Queen of Memphis, Memphis Cotton Carnival, 1973, named Person of Yr. La. Council for Performing Arts, 1975, named Woman of Yr. Am. Legion, named Woman of Yr. Italian-Am. Soc. Mem. Nat. Speakers Assn., Woman's Exchange, Memphis Country Club, Memphis Hunt and Polo Club, New Orleans Country Club, Summit Club, Beta Sigma Omicron, Phi Beta. Roman Catholic.

PICARD, PRISCILLA AOKI, pharmaceutical company executive; b. Woodland, Calif., Oct. 18, 1959; d. Jun and Kazie (Yoshida) Aoki; m. Larry Picard, D.D.S., Feb. 15, 1986. BA, Chapman Coll., 1981. Sr. merchandiser Max Factor & Co., L.A., 1981-83, sales rep., 1983-87; med. rep. Lederle Labs. div. Am. Cyanamid Co., L.A., 1987—. Mem. ADA Women's Aux., Lederle Labs. Gold Cup Club. Republican. Home: 5000 S Centinela Ave Apt 314 Los Angeles CA 90066 Office: Lederle Labs 2300 S Eastern Ave Los Angeles CA 90040

PICCARDI, MICHELLE MARIE, public relations supervisor; b. Pomona, Calif., Sept. 21, 1966; d. George Leonard and Sandra Ruth (Biggs) P. BA in Communications, Calif. State U. Fullerton, 1989. Sc. Orange (Calif.) Credit Svc., 1985-88; cable intern City of Walnut, Calif., 1988-90; supr. pub. rels. and cable City of Walnut, 1990—. Recipient Calif. State U. Fullerton Panhellenic Scholarship, 1987, Newport Beach Scholarship, 1988; named Greek Woman of the Yr. Nominee, 1988-89. Mem. Women In Communications, Alpha Delta Pi Alumnae (pres. 1988-89, Active of the Yr. 1988). Republican. Episcopalian. Home: 3352 Falcon Ridge Rd Diamond Bar CA 91765

PICCIONI, CONSTANCE ELISABETH, retired librarian; b. Boise, Idaho, Oct. 24, 1908; d. Christian Henry and Sophie (Goeke) Lehde; m. Claude Joseph Piccioni, June 14, 1942; children: Steven John, Gerold Claude, Kathryn Maria, Kristine Elise. BS in LS, U. Wash., 1930, BA in Sociology, 1931. Cert. libr., Wash. Acquisitions libr. U. Wash. Libr., Seattle, 1930-36, Oreg. State Coll. Libr., Corvallis, 1936-41, Mont. State U., Bozeman, 1957-67; chief camp libr. U.S. Army Spl. Svcs., Ft. Lewis, Wash., 1941-46; readers' advisor Santa Barbara (Calif.) Pub. Libr., 1948-52; cataloger Tacoma Pub. Libr., 1952-54, King County Pub. Libr., Seattle, 1954-57; acquisitions libr. Wash. State Libr., Olympia, 1967-72; ret., 1972. Author: New Ideas for the Mendery, 1936; co-author: Oregon State College Serial Publications, 1938. Driver Yellowstone County Coun. on Aging, Billings, Mont., 1973—; vol. St. Vincent Hosp., Billings, 1973—; reader tapes for handicapped Sch. Dist. 2, Billings, 1975—. Mem. AAUW (v.p. 1988-90), Bus. and Profl. Women (pres. 1968-69, v.p. 1980-81). Democrat. Roman Catholic. Home: 1823 Clark Ave Billings MT 59102

PICCOLA, MARY TERESA, clinical laboratory director, executive; b. Morristown, N.J., Oct. 5, 1950; d. Anthony Joseph and Josephine Ann (Romano) P. BA, U. South Fla., 1974. Cert. med. technologist. Technologist Damon Clin. Lab., Tampa, Fla., 1974-78; gen. supr. Smith/Kline Lab., Miami, Fla., 1978-81; spl. supr. Broward County Dist. Hosp., Ft. Lauderdale, Fla., 1981-86; dir. Cardinal Clin. Lab., Pompano Beach, Fla., 1986—; v.p. RN Corp., USA, dialysis svc. Nashville, 1989—; organizational cons. Acculab, Nashville, 1988; real estate cons. Ft. Lauderdale, 1980-90. Mem. Landings Residential Assn., Inc., Ft. Lauderdale, 1989. Mem. Am. Soc. Clin. Pathologists (assoc.), Clin. Lab. Mgmt. Assn., Phi Theta Kappa. Office: Cardinal Testing Lab 950 N Federal Hwy 304 Pompano Beach FL 33062

PICHE, STEPHANIE EMILIE, sales executive; b. Hialeah, Fla., Dec. 9, 1959; d. Joseph Etienne and Audrey Jane (Kurtz) P.; m. Ronald James Dennis, Apr. 1, 1982 (div. Feb. 1987); 1 child, Joseph David. BS, U. Nev., 1981. R.N., Nev., Utah; lic. real estate agt., Utah. Publisher's asst. Nev. Messenger, Las Vegas, 1974-76; sec. circulation Las Vegas Sun Newspaper, 1976-77; medical asst. Drs. Jacobs and Modaber, Las Vegas, 1977-79; lab asst. Sunrise Hosp., Las Vegas, 1979-81; nurse Dr. David Peterson, Orem, Utah, 1981-82; assoc. realtor Century 21, Provo, Utah, 1982-83; v.p. sales and mktg. Zion Worldwide Enterprises, Provo, Utah, 1983-84; mgr. regional sales Digital Tech. Internat., Orem, Utah, 1984-89; dir. sales ea. region Hyphen, Inc., Wilmington, Mass., 1989—; cons. publishing progams Buffalo 1984—. Area dir. fundraising. Am. Cancer Assn., Orem 1983-84. Mem. Buffalo Assn. Female Exec. (dir. 1987—), Nat. Assn. Female Exec. Republican. Roman Catholic. Clubs: Aviation (pres. 1976-77), Ski (sec. 1977-78). Home: 819 Second St B-218 Manchester NH 03102 Office: Hyphen Inc 187 Ballardvale St Wilmington MA 01887

PICKER, NELLY, soloist, educator; b. Vienna, Austria, Sept. 11, 1916; came to U.S., 1954; d. Anton and Henny Picker; 1 child, Daniela. Student, Vienna Acad., 1935; grad., Conservatory G. Verdi, Milan, 1939. Cert. tchr.; Singer British Army ENSA, Middle East, 1942-45, PBS (Palestine Broadcasting Svc.) Opera, 1939-52; tchr. Pub. Sch. System, Bklyn., 1957-67, Kearny, N.J., 1969-81; tchr. Studio for the Performer, Arlington, N.J., 1981—. Choral dir. Bel Canto Singers, Arlington, N.J., 1982—. Mem. Nat. Assn. Tchr. of Singing, Am. Choral Dir. Assn., Nat. Piano Tchr. Guild, Nat. Opera Assn. Home: 46 Exton Ave North Arlington NJ 07032 Office: Music Studio Performer 838 Kearny Ave Kearny NJ 07032

PICKERING, AVAJANE, specialized education facility executive; b. New Castle, Ind., Nov. 5, 1951; d. George Willard and Elsie Jean (Wicker) P. BA, Purdue U., 1974; MS in Spl. Edn., U. Utah, 1983, postgrad., 1985—. Tchr. Granite Community Edn., Salt Lake City, 1974-79; tchr. coordinator Salt Lake City Schs., 1975-85; co-dir., owner Specialized Ednl. Programming Service, Inc., Salt Lake City, 1976—; adj. instr. U. Utah, Salt Lake City, 1985—. Rep. del. Utah State Conv., also county conv.; vol. tour guide, hostess Temple Square, Ch. Jesus Christ of Latter-Day Saints, 1983—. Mem. Council for Exceptional Children, Assn. Children and Adults with Learning Disabilities, Delta Kappa Gamma. Home: 1595 S 2100 E Salt Lake City UT 84108 Office: 1760 South 1100 East Salt Lake City UT 84105

PICKERING, MARGARET HASTINGS, economist; b. Morgantown, W.Va., May 25, 1932; d. George Dewey and Jeannette (Smith) Hastings; m. Richard Carlyle Pickering, Aug. 25, 1963; children: Paula May, Andrew Hastings. BS, W.Va. U., 1954; MA, George Washington U., 1961. Rsch. asst. Bd. Govs. of Fed. Res. System, Washington, 1955-61, economist, 1969—; asst. to dir. bus. affairs W. Va. U., Morgantown, 1961-63; economist

U.S. Treasury Dept., Washington, 1964-69. Mem. Am. Econ. Assn. Home: 5109 N 37th St Arlington VA 22207 Office: Bd Govs of Fed Res System 20th & Constitution Aves Washington DC 20551

PICKETT, CHRISTINE SUE, human resources professional; b. Waltham, Mass., Sept. 30, 1955; d. Theodore R. and Mary Eleanor (Brown) P. BS, Seattle (Wash.) Pacific U., 1977; MS in Student Devel., Azusa (Calif.) Pacific Coll., 1979. Grad. asst. LaVerne (Calif.) U., 1977-78, Azusa Pacific Coll., 1978-79; dir. career planning U. Dubuque, Iowa, 1980-81; asst. dir. career planning No. Ariz. U., Flagstaff, 1981-84; human resources assoc. GTE Svc. Corp., Stamford, Conn., 1984-86; human resources rep. GTE Electronic Products Corp., Danvers, Mass., 1986-88; employee rels. rep. govt. systems div. GTE Corp. Inc., Colorado Springs, 1988—.

PICKETT, NANCY ELIZABETH, vocational rehabilitation consultant, government council executive; b. Barksdale AFB, La., Nov. 7, 1948; d. Richard Dewey and Evelyn (Weis) P.; m. Wendell Alfred Smith III, May 31, 1968 (div. 1976); children: Melinira Lynne, Wendell Alfred, IV. BA, Nicholls State U., 1970, MEd, 1972. Tchr. Cert. Vocat. expert; cert. rehab. counselor; qualified mental retardation profl.; lic. profl. counselor. St. Charles Sch. Bd., Luling, La., 1970-71; counselor, coordinator River Parishes Council Govt. Convent, La., 1973-74, exec. dir., Boutte, La., 1974-86; exec. asst. Centec Corp., New Orleans, 1986-87; vocat. rehab. cons. Crawford Health and Rehab., Metairie, La., 1987-89; mgr. Crawford Health and Rehab., Alexandria, 1989—; pres. pvt. industry council, LaPlace, La., 1981-83; pvt. practice trainer, cons., Boutte, La., 1979—; mem. adv. bd. La. Family Planning Program, New Orleans, 1976—. Editor: Directory Community Resources, 1977. Del. White House Conf. Families, Mpls., 1978, La. Gov.'s Conf. Libraries, Baton Rouge, 1978; founding bd. dirs. St. Charles Community Theatre, Luling, La., 1979-84; bd. dirs. v.p. S.E. La. Girl Scout Coun., New Orleans, 1978-83. Nat. Merit scholar, 1966. Mem. Am. Soc. for Tng. and Devel. (bd. dirs., treas. 1984, chmn. position referral 1983), NAFE, (charter), Service Delivery Area Dirs. Assn. Office: Crawford Health and Rehab 5208 Jackson St Ext Ste B Alexandria LA 71303

PICKETT, PATRICIA L., human resources specialist; b. Oak Park, Ill., Mar. 3, 1952; d. Peter L. and Rosemary (Berliner) P.; m. George D. Pickett, Jan. 18, 1980. BBA, U. North Fla., 1986. Pers. adminstr. Ships Supply, Inc., Jacksonville, Fla.; compensation benefits specialist UNIJAX, Inc., Jacksonville; employee benefits analyst Fla. Nat. Bank, Jacksonville; mgr. employee svcs. Fla. Community Coll.; compensation and benefits mgr. U. Med. Ctr. Mem. NAFE, Am. Mgmt. Assn., Am. Soc. Pers. Adminstrn., Jacksonville Compensation Assn. Democrat. Roman Catholic. Office: Univ Med Ctr 655 W 8th St Jacksonville FL 32209

PICKETT BARNES, SALLY, clinical nurse specialist; b. Dover, N.H., Oct. 31, 1958; d. James Francis and Addie (MacFarland) Pickett; m. Ronald S. Barnes, Oct. 28, 1989. BS Nursing, Boston Coll., 1980; MS, Boston U., 1985. Cert. in critical care nursing AACN, cert. clin. specialist; advanced cardiac life support instr. Primary nurse Univ. Hosp., Boston, 1980-85; critical care educator Malden (Mass.) Hosp., 1985-87; clin. specialist Salem (Mass.) Hosp., 1987-90; cons. Genentech, Inc., South San Francisco, 1990—. Bd. dirs. Mass. affiliate Northeast territory Am. Heart Assn., 1988—. Mem. AACCN (coun. clin. specialists), Am. Nurses Assn., Mass. Nurses Assn. (sec. dist. IV 1988-90). Home: PO Box 199 Rowby MA 01969

PICKFORD, SHIRLEY ROBERTA CLAY, computer and financial consultant; b. London, Aug. 17, 1949; d. Thomas R. and Maisey D. (Clay) P.; children: Clay, Christina. B.A. cum laude, Boston U., 1969; M.A., Brandeis U., 1972; Ph.D., Tex. A&M U., 1977. CPA, Fla.; lic. realtor, mortgage broker, securities broker, prin. ins. agt., Fla. Owner, fin. cons. Fin. Planning for Women Inc., Orlando, Fla., 1972-86, Integrated Fin. Svcs. Internat. Inc., Orlando, 1977—, also bd. dirs.; asst. prof. acctg. U. Cen. Fla., Orlando, 1977-81; assoc. prof. Fla. Atlantic U., Boca Raton, 1982-85; owner, computer cons. COMPSOL, Inc., Orlando, 1982—, also bd. dirs.; cons. Fla. Dept. Law Enforcement, 1978-80. Author: Accounting Principles, 1980-82. Fla. Dept. Law Enforcement grantee, 1980, 81. Mem. AICPAs, Am. Acctg. Assns., Electronic Data Processing Assn., Cen. Fla. Coun. for High Tech. (mem. capital rels. com.), Phi Kappa Phi, Beta Gamma Sigma, Alpha Beta Sigma, Fla. Exec. Women (founder, pres. 1980-81). Avocations: running, reading, music.

PICKLE, LINDA WILLIAMS, biostatistician; b. Hampton, Va., July 19, 1948; d. Howard Taft and Kathryn Lee (Riggin) Williams; 1 child from previous marriage, Diane Marie; m. James B. Pearson, Jr., Oct. 14, 1984. BA, Johns Hopkins U. 1974, PhD in Biostats., 1977; postgrad., George Washington U., 1986-87. Computer programmer Comml. Credit Computer Corp., Balt., 1966-69; systems analyst, computer programmer Greater Balt. Med. Ctr., Balt., 1969-72; grad. teaching asst. biostats. Johns Hopkins U., Balt., 1974-77; adj. asst. prof. div. biostats. and epidemiology Georgetown U. Med. Sch., Washington, 1983-88, assoc. prof. div. biostats and epidemiology, 1988—; dir. biostats. unit, V.T. Lombardi Cancer Rsch. Ctr., 1988—; biostatistician Nat. Cancer Inst. NIH, Bethesda, Md., 1977-88. Author: Atlas of U.S. Cancer Mortality Among Whites: 1950-80, 1987, Atlas of U.S. Cancer Mortality Among Nonwhites: 1950-1980, 1990; contbr. articles to med. and statis. jours. Sr. troop leader Girl Scouts U.S., 1981-83; sci. fair judge, 1983—. Mem. The Biometric Soc., Am. Statis. Assn., Soc. Epidemiological Research, Soc. Indsl. and Applied Math., Sigma Delta Epsilon (pres. Omicron chpt. 1984), Phi Beta Kappa. Office: Georgetown U Med Sch VT Lombardi Cancer Rsch Ctr 3800 Reservoir Rd NW Washington DC 20007

PICKLES, ANNE COURANZ, microbiologist, consultant; b. St. Louis, May 25, 1947; d. C. Edwin and Irene Nelda (Hackmann) Couranz; m. Donald Dale Pickles, Nov. 16, 1980; 1 child, Jeffrey Scott. BA, U. Mo., 1969. Bench microbiologist Sci. Assocs. Inc., St. Louis, 1970-73, chief microbiologist, 1973-87, dir. microbiology, 1987-90, v.p., 1990—. Sunday sch. tchr. Calvary Presbyn. Ch., St. Louis, 1981-86; vol. Wohlwend Sch. PTO, St. Louis, 1985-89; block capt. Am. Cancer Soc., St. Louis, 1987-89; vol. Cub Scouts Am., 1988-89. Mem. Am. Soc. for Microbiology, Parenteral Drug Assn. Office: Sci Assocs Inc 6200 S Lindbergh Blvd Saint Louis MO 63123

PICONE, EDITH, real estate company executive; b. Bklyn., Jan. 24, 1917; d. Amedeo and Domenica (Smilari) Moretti; m. John Picone, Jan. 24, 1952 (dec.); children—John Jr., Peter, Elisa. Grad. high sch., Bklyn. Buyer, Goldsmith Bros., N.Y.C., 1934-51; mgr. Bellmore Liquor Co., Greenwich, Conn., 1951-72; pres. John and John, Inc., Greenwich, 1972-77; gen. ptnr. PIC Assocs., Greenwich, 1977—. Republican. Roman Catholic. Lodge: Order Eastern Star (Matron 1949-52). Avocations: travel, cooking, philately.

PICON-VARNER, DORA AMALIA, neurologist; b. San Juan, P.R., Mar. 20, 1950; d. Guido F. Picon and Rosa L. Ramirez; children: Dora, Daphne, Dariush; m. Charles D. Varner, Feb. 13, 1986. BA, U. P.R., 1970; MD, U. Central del Este, San Pedro, R.D., 1982; postgrad., Wayne State U., Detroit, 1986, Wayne State U., 1987. From neurology resident to EEG fellow Wayne State U., Detroit, 1982-87; neurologist pvt. practice, Warren, Mich., 1987—; ethics com. Holy Cross Hosp., Detroit 1988—. Mem. AMA, American Acad. Neurology, Mich. State Med. Soc., Macomb County Med. Soc. Office: 234 Medical Circle Morehead KY 40351

PIECH, MARGARET ANN, mathematics educator; b. Bridgewater, N.S., Can., Apr. 6, 1942; d. Frederick Cecil and Margaret Florence (Laschinger) Garrett; m. Kenneth Robert Piech, June 19, 1965; children: Garrett Andrew, Marjorie Ann. BA, Mt. Allison U., Sackville, N.B., Can., 1962; PhD, Cornell U., 1967. Asst. prof. SUNY, Buffalo, 1967-72, assoc. prof., 1972-78, prof. math., 1978—; cons. NSF, Washington, 1980-83, Aspen Analytics, Buffalo, 1986—. Contbr. articles to profl. jours. Woodrow Wilson fellow 1962-63; grantee NSF, 1976—, U.S. Army Rsch. Office, 1985—. Mem. Am. Math. Soc., Assn. Computing Machinery, Apple Programmers and Developers Assn. Office: SUNY Diefendorf Hall Buffalo NY 14214

PIECHOWSKI, MARJORIE PAULINE, academic administrator; b. Redgranite, Wis., Mar. 28, 1939; d. Henry Edmund and Esther Margaret (Jakubowski) P. BA, Marquette U., 1961, MA, 1962; PhD, U. Wis., 1978. English tchr. Berlin (Wis.) High Sch., 1962-67; English lectr. U. Wis., 1967-

77; asst. prof. Marquette U., Milw., 1978-81, grant info. specialist, 1981-84; dir. sponsored program and rsch. DePaul U., Chgo., 1984—; cons. Eaton Corp., Milw., 1979-85, St. Luke Hosp.-Aurora Health Care, Milw., 1979—, U. Puerto Rico, 1988-89, Ill. State U., Bloomington, 1988-89. Bd. dirs. Milw. Cath. Symphony Bd., Milw., 1978-84, DePaul Com. Mental Health Ctr., Chgo., 1984—, Cen. States Univs., Inc. Chgo., 1985—, Women's Studies Adv. Coun., Chgo., 1986—. Fellow U. London, 1976, U. Wis., 1977-78. Mem. Soc. Rsch. Adminstrs. (midwest sec. 1988-89, exec. com. 1987—, editorial bd. 1985—), Nat. Coun. Univ. Rsch. Adminstrs. (midwest sec-treas. 1986-88, exec. com. 1988—). Office: DePaul U 243 S Wabash Ave Chicago IL 60604

PIEL, CAROLYN FORMAN, pediatrician, educator; b. Birmingham, Ala., Oct. 18, 1918; d. James R. and Mary Elizabeth (Dortch) Forman; m. John Joseph Piel, Aug. 3, 1951; children: John Joseph, Mary Dortch, Elizabeth Forman, William Scott. BA, Agnes Scott Coll., 1940; MS, Emory U., 1943; MD, Washington U., St. Louis, 1946. Diplomate Am. Bd. Pediatrics (examiner 1973-88, pres. 1986-87); diplomate Am. Bd. Pediatric Nephrology. Intern Phila. Gen. Hosp., 1946-47; resident Phila. Children's Hosp., 1947-49; fellow Cornell U. Med. Sch., N.Y.C., 1949-51; from instr. to assoc. clin. prof. Stanford U. Sch. Medicine, San Francisco, 1951-59; from asst. prof. to prof. Sch. Medicine, U. Calif., San Francisco, 1959-89, emeritus prof. 1989—. Author, co-author research articles in field. Bd. mem. San Francisco Home Health Service, 1977-83. Emeritus mem. Soc. for Pediatric Research, Am. Pediatric Soc., Am. Soc. for Pediatric Nephrology, Am. Soc. Nephrology, Western Soc. for Pediatric Nephrology (pres. 1960). Democrat. Presbyterian. Home: 2164 Hyde St San Francisco CA 94109 Office: Univ Calif-San Francisco San Francisco CA 94143

PIEPER, PATRICIA RITA, artist, photographer; b. Paterson, N.J., Jan. 28, 1923; d. Francis William and Barbara Margareth (Ludwig) Farabaugh. Student, Baron von Palm, 1937-39, Deal (N.J.) Conservatory, 1939, 40, Utah State U., 1950-52; m. George F. Pieper, July 1, 1941 (dec. May 3, 1981); 1 child, Patricia Lynn; m. Russell W. Watson, Dec., 9, 1989. One-woman shows include Charles Russell Mus., Great Falls, Mont., 1955, Fisher Gallery, Washington, 1966, Tampa City Libr., 1977, 78, 79, 80, 81, 83, 84, Ctr. Pl. Art Ctr., Brandon, Fla., 1985; exhibited in group shows Davidson Art Gallery, Middletown, Conn., 1968, Helena (Mont.) Hist. Mus., 1955, Dept. Commerce Alaska Statehood Show, 1959, Joslyn Mus., Omaha, 1961, Denver Mus. Natural History, 1955, St. Joseph's Hosp. Gallery, 1980, 82, 84-86; represented in pvt. collections. Pres. Bell Lake Assn., 1976-78, 79. Winner photog. competition Gen. Tel. Co. of Fla., 1979; recipient Outstanding Svc. award Bell Lake Assn., 1987, Meml. award Land O' Lake Bd. of Realtors, 1989; photography winner in top 100 out of 8,000 Nat. Wildlife Fedn. competition, 1986. Mem. Pasco County (Fla.) Water Adv. Coun., 1978—, chmn., 1979-82, 83-84, 86-88; gov.'s appointee to S.W. Fla. Water Mgmt. Dist., Hillsborough River Basin Bd., 1981-82, 84-87, vice chmn. 19888-89, sec., 1990-91; active Save Our Rivers program, 1982-84, 85-86, chmn., 1986; mem. adv. bd. Fla. Suncoast Expwy., 1988-90; pres. Bell Lake Assn., 1986, 87; mem. adv. bd. Tampa YMCA, 1979-80. Mem. Nat. League Am. Pen Women (v.p. Tampa 1976-78, Woman of Yr. award 1977-78), Tampa Art Mus., Ret. Officer's Wives Assn., Land O' Lakes C. of C. (bd. dir. 1981-82, Outstanding Svc. award 1980), Fla. Geneal. Soc., West State Archaeol. Soc. (distaff mem.), Ret. Officer's Assn., MacDill AFB, 1982—, Lutz Club, Land O' Lakes Women's Club. Home and Studio: PO Box 15 Land O' Lakes FL 34639

PIERCE, BENEDICT ENOL, social worker; b. Castries, St. Lucia, Mar. 23, 1942; came to U.S., 1955; d. Leon Joseph and Ionie (Mitchell) Williams; m. Allen Pierce, 1964; children: Gregory, Reginald. AAS, Bronx Community Coll., 1965; BA, CCNY, 1978; MSW, NYU, 1980. Cert. social worker, N.Y. Social worker St. Joseph Children Svc., Bklyn., 1980-82, social worker supr., 1982—, program dir., 1985—; counselor Enter Alcoholism Svcs., N.Y.C., 1988-89. Vol. Community Planning Bd., Bronx, N.Y., 1979; sec. Soc. for Advancement and Betterment of Children, 1968-78. Mem. Nat. Assn. Black Social Workers, Nat. Assn. Social Workers, N.Y. State Soc. Clin. Social Work (RSVCHO therapist), Network Orgn. Bronx Women. Democrat. Roman Catholic.

PIERCE, CAROL SHAFFER, medical educator; b. Lockport, N.Y., Mar. 4, 1938; d. Glenn H. and Dorothy M. (Peters) Shaffer; divorced. BS, Mt. Union Coll., 1960; MS, U. Chgo., 1963, SUNY, Buffalo, 1978; PhD, SUNY, Buffalo, 1981. Rsch. assoc. Argonne Cancer Rsch. Hosp., Chgo., 1963-65, Nat. Jewish Hosp., Denver, 1966, U.S. Dept. Agr., Washington, 1967-70, VA Med. Ctr., Buffalo, 1972-74; postdoctoral fellow Erie County Med. Ctr., Buffalo, 1980-82; asst. prof. SUNY, Buffalo, 1981-86, chmn. med. tech. dept., 1983-90, clin. assoc. prof., dir. grad. studies, 1986—. Contbr. articles to profl. jours. Mem. Am. Soc. Microbiology. Office: SUNY Buffalo/Med Tech Dept 462 Grider St Buffalo NY 14215

PIERCE, DEBORAH MARY, educator; b. Charleston, W. Va., Nov. 1, 1938; d. Edward Ernest and Elizabeth Anne (Trent) P.; m. Henry M. Armetta, Sept. 1, 1967 (div. 1981); children: Rosse Matthew Armetta, Stacey Elizabeth Pierce. Student, U. Tenn., 1956-59, Broward Jr. Coll., 1968-69; BA, San Francisco State U., 1977. Cert. elem. tchr., Calif. Pub. relations assoc. San Francisco Internat. Film Festival, 1965-66; account exec. Stover & Assocs., San Francisco, 1966-67; tchr. San Francisco Archdiocese Office of Cath. Schs., 1980-87; with The Calif. Study, Inc. (formerly Tchr's. Registry), Tiburon, Calif., 1988—; pvt. practice as paralegal San Francisco, 1989—. Author: (with Frances Spatz Leighton) I Prayed Myself Slim, 1960, Webster's Encyclopedia of Dictionaries. Pres. Mothers Alone Working, San Francisco, 1966, PTA, San Francisco, 1979, Parent Teacher Student Assn., San Francisco, 1984; apptd. Calif. State Bd. Welfare Community Rels. Com., 1964-66. Named Model of the Yr. Modeling Assn. Am., 1962. Mem. People Med. Soc., Assn. for Research and Enlightenment, The Course in Miracles, Commonwealth Club Calif. Democrat. Episcopal.

PIERCE, ELIZABETH GAY, civic worker; b. N.Y.C., Mar. 26, 1907; d. Martin and Julia (Stone) Gay; AB, Barnard Coll., 1929; m. William Curtis Pierce, June 19, 1929; children—Martin Gay, Elizabeth Gay (Mrs. Joseph S. Stout, Jr.), Josiah. Vol. worker Boston City Hosp., 1929-30, Community Service Soc., N.Y.C., 1931-32; mem. dependent children's sect. Welfare Council, N.Y.C., 1939-40; chmn. house com. North Shore Holiday House, Huntington, L.I., 1944, pres., 1945; co-chmn. thrift shop com. Knickerbocker Hosp., N.Y.C., 1957-64; mem. exec. com. of women's com. Legal Aid Soc., N.Y.C., 1958-59; mem. Women's Aux. Knickerbocker Hosp. (exec. com. 1960-64); adv. trustee Maine Citizens for Hist. Preservation, 1983-87; trustee Jones Mus. Ceramics and Glass, 1985-89. Mem. Soc. Colonial Dames in State N.Y. (bd. mgrs., 1962-67, corr. sec. N.Y. 1965-67, pres. 1967-70), Nat. Soc. Colonial Dames Am. (pres. 1972-76, nat. pres.), Soc. for Preservation New Eng. Antiquities (Maine council, former chmn. Marrett House), Mayflower Soc. N.Y. (sec. 1985-88), Daus. Founders and Patriots, Nat. Grange. Episcopalian. Club: Colony, Ch. (N.Y.C.). Home: Box 352 Rte 1 West Baldwin ME 04091

PIERCE, GRETCHEN NATALIE, investment company executive; b. Eugene, Oreg., July 7, 1945; d. Nils Bernard and Jewel (Bauman) Hult; m. Howard Walter Pierce, Dec. 26, 1970; children: Eric Nils, Hailey Lynn, . BA, U. Oreg., 1966. Rsch. analyst Boise (Idaho) Cascade Corp., 1966-68, mgr. divs., 1968-84, dir. info. adminstrn., 1984-86; pres., gen. mgr. Hult & Assocs., Eugene, 1986—; bd. dirs. Siuslaw Valley Bank, Florence, Oreg., Nat. Printing Corp., Seattle. Trustee U. Oreg., 1986, Sacred Heart Hosp., 1987, YMCA Endowment Fund, 1987. Mem. Profl. Women's Network, Oreg. Women's Forum, U. Oreg. Alumni (Disting. Alumni award 1984), Eugene C. of C. Republican. Lutheran. Lodge: Rotary. Office: Hult & Assocs 401 E 10th St Ste 500 Eugene OR 97401

PIERCE, HILDA RUBIN (HILDA HERTA HARMEL), painter; b. Vienna, Austria; came to U.S., 1940; m. S. Thomas Friedman, 1988; 1 child by previous marriage, Diana Rubin Daly. Student, Art Inst. of Chgo.; studied with Oskar Kokoschka, Salzburg, Austria. Art tchr. Highland Park (Ill.) Art Ctr., YWCA, Highland Park, Sandburg Village Art Workshop, Chgo., Old Town Art Center, Chgo.; owner, operator Hilda Pierce Art Gallery, Laguna Beach, Calif., 1981-85; dir. art workshops on cruise ships; guest lectr. major art museums and Art Tours in France, Switzerland, Austria, Italy. One-woman shows include Fairweather Hardin Gallery, Chgo.,

Sherman Art Gallery, Chgo., Marshall Field Gallery , Chgo.; exhibited in group shows at Old Orchard Art Festival, Skokie, Ill., Union League Club (awards), North Shore Art League (awards), ARS Gallery of Art Inst. of Chgo.; represented in numerous private and corporate collections; commissioned for all art work including monoprints, oils and murals for superliner Carnival Cruise Lines 70,000 ton megaliner M.S. Fantasy, 1990; contbr. articles to Chgo. Tribune Mag., American Artist Mag., Southwest Art Mag., SRA publs., others. Mem. Arts Club of Chgo. Office: Hilda Pierce Studio PO Box 7390 Laguna Niguel CA 92607

PIERCE, JANET KATHRYN, chemical dependency treatment facility executive; b. Texarkana, Tex., Nov. 4, 1948; d. George Dewey Jr. and Alice Ruby (Hatchett) Quillin; m. James Keith Evans, Aug. 27, 1966 (div. Mar. 1978); 1 child, Jeffrey Wade; m. John Louis Pierce, Dec. 24, 1985. AA, Richland Coll., 1974; BS in Edn. and Guidance, U. North Tex., 1976; MA in Psychology, Tex. Woman's U., 1983. Cert. alcohol and drug abuse counselor, Tex. Ednl. administr. Dallas Coun. on Alcoholism, 1980, adminstr. family edn., 1980-82; distl. alcohol svcs. coord. Tex. Commn. on Alcoholism, Arlington, 1982-84; contract counselor YWCA Women's Resource Ctr., Dallas, 1984; exec. dir. Chem. Awareness Coun. Park Cities, Dallas, 1984-85; program dir. Nexus, Inc., Dallas, 1985-88, exec. dir. 1989—; Children Are People, Inc., Mpls., 1984. Author: Career Shopper's Guide, 1980; columnist on substance abuse Woman's News, 1985. Facilitator Explore, Inc., Dallas, 1974-76. Mem. Nat. Assn. Alcohol and Drug Abuse Counselors (sec. Dallas chpt. 1984), Tex. Assn. Alcohol and Drug Abuse Counselors, Coalition Alcohol and Drug Abuse Leaders, Dallas Women's Coalition. Democrat. Methodist. Home: 65ll Deloache Dallas TX 75225 Office: Nexus Inc 8733 LaPrada Dr Dallas TX 75228

PIERCE, JANIS VAUGHN, insurance executive, consultant; b. Memphis, Dec. 23, 1934; d. Jesse Wynne and Dorothy Arnette (Lloyd) Vaughn; m. Gerald Swetnam Pierce, May 27, 1956; children; Ann Elizabeth Swetnam, John Willard. B.A., U. Miss., 1956, M.A., 1964 High sch. tchr., 1957-58; mem. faculty Memphis Univ. Sch.; Head-Ass. Memphis State U., 1968-75; agt. Aetna Life Ins. Co., Memphis, 1977-80, career supr., 1980—, mgr., 1983, supr. prime/career, 1984, chmn. Aetna Women's Task Force, 1980-85; coord. agy. tng. Specialist Union Cen. Life Ins. Co., Memphis, 1985-88, agt.; v.p., dir. Cons. System, Inc., bus. cons., 1975-84, pres., 1984—. Pres. Women's Resources Ctr., Memphis, 1974-77; sec. Tenn. chpt. Women's Polit. Caucus, 1975-76; bd. dirs., treas., mem. exec. com. Memphis YWCA, 1979—; mem. Memphis Area Transit Authority, 1982—, chmn. fin. and adminstrn. com., 1983—; pres., bd. dirs. The Support Ctr. Memphis, 1986—, Support Ctrs. Am., 1987—; mem. Tenn. adv. com. U.S. Civil Rights Commn., 1980-85, steering com. Big Break, 1978; mem. adv. bd. Porter Leath Children's Ctr., 1984—, bd. dirs. 1986—. Univ. scholar U. Miss. 1956; named Aetna Regionnaire, 1977-82, First Yr. Top Achiever, 1977; mem. Leadership Memphis, 1981. Mem. Million Dollar Roundtable, 1978, 79, Women Leaders Roundtable, Nat. Assn. Life Underwriters, Tenn. Life Underwriters Assn., Am. Pub. Transp. Assn. (governing bds. com. 1985—, sec. 1987-88, v.p. 1988—, mem. task force transp. for the handicapped, 1987, pres. 1989), Women's Life Underwriters Conf. (bd. dirs., pres. 1985), Memphis Life Underwriters Assn. (bd. dirs. 1982, edn. chmn. 1982, pub. svc. com. 1983, law and legis. chmn. 1984, pres. 1986), Memphis PTA Coun. 1971-72), Memphis Soc. CLUs, LWV, AAUW, Mortar Bd. (regional coord. 1972-78), Memphis C.L.U. assn., C. of C. (amb. 1980), Mortar Bd., Alpha Lambda Delta, Sigma Delta Pi, Le Bonheur Club (bd. dir.), Memphis State U. Women's Club (pres. 1978). Republican. Episcopalian. Home: 4743 Park Ave Memphis TN 38117 Office: Cons System PO Box 241579 Memphis TN 38124-1579

PIERCE, JUDY MARIE, corporate quality auditor; b. Springfield, Mo., Jan. 9, 1957; d. Judson Lee and Patricia (Strom) P. BS in Mgmt. and Mktg., Southwest Mo. State U., 1979. Lab. analyst Kraft Inc., Springfield, 1975-80; sr. systems engr. Kraft Inc., Glenview, Ill., 1980-85, developer, instr. computer courses, 1983-84, quality standards specialist, 1985-87; corp. quality auditor Kraft Gen. Foods, Glenview, Ill., 1985—. Deacon Presbyn. Ch., Mt. Prospect, Ill.; mem. Glenview Concert Band, Ill., 1988—. Mem. Am. Soc. for Quality Control (cert.), Pi Omega Pi (chaplain 1978-79). Democrat. Home: 10389 Dearlove Rd #1G Glenview IL 60025 Office: Kraft Gen Foods Kraft Ct Glenview IL 60025

PIERCE, MARIANNE LOUISE, merchant and investment banker, venture management executive, real estate financier, consultant; b. Atchison, Kans., Apr. 22, 1949; d. James Arthur and Marian Louise (Patton) P.; m. Woodrow Theodore Lewis Jr., June 23, 1973 (div. June 1981). Student, Barnard Coll.; AB, Columbia U., 1970, MBA, 1975. Dep. dir. N.Y. Model Cities, N.Y.C. 1971-73; assoc. corp. fin. Citibank Mcht. Banking, N.Y.C., 1975-77; sr. assoc. Booz Allen Hamilton, N.Y.C., 1977-82; dep. biotech. dir. Ciba Geigy A.G., Basel, Switzerland, 1982-85; pres. Life Scis. Assocs., Ltd., N.Y.C.; Conn.; Basel; Adelaide, Australia, 1985—; mng. ptnr. Patton, Pierce, Brandon & Co., 1986—. Author: (pamphlet) Developing Biotechnology Strategies for Multinational Corporations, 1985, Innovating Successful-Strategic Alliances, 1990. Mem. Brit. Biotech. Assn., Comml. Devel. Assn., Practicing Law Assn.

PIERCE BUCKELEW, CAROLYN ROSE, nursing educator; b. Norfolk, Va., May 23, 1946; d. William Patrick and Rose Veronica (McHugh) Pierce; m. Paul Thomas Buckelew, Mar. 7, 1969; 1 child, Heather Lael. BSN, Va. Commonwealth U., 1970; MA in Edn., Seton Hall U., 1978. RN, Va.; N.J.; cert. Nat. Bd. Cert. Counselors, clin. specialist adult psychiat and mental health nursing. Indsl. nurse United Engrs., Linden, N.J., 1970; staff nurse Carrier Found., Belle Meade, N.J., 1972, 73-74; instr. nursing Charles E. Gregory Sch. Nursing, Raritan Bay Med. Ctr., Perth Amboy, N.J., 1973—; cons. Ctr. for Life Dynamics, West Orange, N.J., 1984—, D. Loren Southern, MD, Princeton, N.J., 1989—; workshop speaker, 1980—. Vol. Health Fairs, East Brunswick, Old Bridge, N.J., 1975—, Hand-in-Hand, Middlesex Community Coll., Edison, N.J., 1986—, Cystic Fibrosis, East Brunswick, 1988; speaker family asthma program Am. Lung Assn., Freehold, N.J., 1982-87; sec. exec. bd. St. Thomas Parish Coun., Old Bridge, 1988—. Recipient vol. recognition award Marlboro Psychiat. Hosp., 1988. Mem. Assn. Diploma Schs. Profl. Nursing (nominations com. 1988-89, exec. bd. sec. 1989—). Home: 79 Hilliard Rd Old Bridge NJ 08857 Office: Charles Gregory Sch Nursing 530 New Brunswick Ave Perth Amboy NJ 08800

PIERCY, MARGE, poet, novelist, essayist; b. Detroit, Mar. 31, 1936; d. Robert Douglas and Bert Bernice (Bunnin) P.; m. Ira Wood, 1982. AB, U. Mich., 1957; MA, Northwestern U., 1958. Instr. Gary extension Ind. U., 1960-62; poet-in-residence U. Kans., 1971; disting. vis. lectr. Thomas Jefferson Coll., Grand Valley State Colls., fall 1975, 76, 78, 80; vis. faculty Women's Writers Conf., Cazenovia (N.Y.) Coll.; Elliston poetry fellow U. Cin., 1986. Author: Breaking Camp, 1968, Hard Loving, 1969, Going Down Fast, 1969, Dance the Eagle to Sleep, 1970, (with Bob Hershon, Emmett Jarrett and Dick Lourie) 4-Telling, 1971, Small Changes, 1973, To Be of Use, 1973, Living in the Open, 1976, Woman on the Edge of Time, 1976, The High Cost of Living, 1978, The Twelve-Spoked Wheel Flashing, 1978, Vida, 1980, The Moon Is Always Female, 1980, Braided Lives, 1982, Circles on the Water, 1982, Stone, Paper, Knife, 1983, Fly Away Home, 1984, My Mother's Body, 1985, Gone to Soldiers, 1987, Available Light, 1988, Summer People, 1989; (with Ira Wood) play The Last White Class, 1980, The Earth Shines Secretly: A Book of Days, 1990; poetry editor: Tikkun Mag., 1988—; essays Parti-Colored Blocks for a Quilt, 1982; editor: Early Ripening, 1987; adv. editor: APHRA, 1975-78, Poetry on the Buses, 1979-81; mem. adv. bd. Nat. Forum, 1979-83. Active Students for Dem. Soc., 1965-69, N.Am. Congress on Latin-Am., 1966-67, Movement for Dem. Soc., 1968-69, Women's Ctr. N.Y., 1969-71, Lower Cape Women's Ctr., 1973-76, New Jewish Agenda, 1986—, Internat. Bd. Israeli Ctr. for Creative Arts, 1986-88, mem. adv. bd., 1989—; cons. N.Y. State Coun. on Arts, 1971, Mass. Found. for Humanities and Coun. on Arts, 1974; mem. Writer Bd. 1985-86; bd. dirs. Transition House, Mass. Found. Humanities and Pub. Policy, 1978-85, Am. Ha-Yam, 1988—; gov.'s appointee to Mass. Cultural Coun., 1990—, Mass. Coun. on Arts and Humanities, 1986-89, Mass. Arts Lottery Coun., 1988-89; artistic adv. bd. Am. Poetry Ctr., 1988—; lit. adv. panel, poetry, Nat. Endowment Arts, 1989. James B. Angell scholar; Lucinda Goodrich Downs scholar; recipient Orion Scott award in Humanities; maj. and minor awards in poetry and fiction Avery Hopwood Contest, 1956, 57; Borestone Mountain Poetry award, 1968, 74; Lit. award Gov.

Mass. Commn. on Status of Women, 1974; Nat. Endowment Arts award, 1978; Faculty Assn. medal R.I. Sch. Design; Carolyn Kizer Poetry prize, 1986, 1990; Sheaffer Eaton-PEN New Eng. award for lit. excellence, 1989. Mem. PEN, NOW (Cape Cod chpt.), Authors Guild, Authors League, Writers Union, Poetry Soc. Am., Nat. Audubon Soc., Mass. Audubon Soc., New Eng. Poetry Club. Address: PO Box 1473 Wellfleet MA 02667

PIERIK, MARILYN ANNE, librarian; b. Bellingham, Wash., Nov. 12, 1939; d. Estell Leslie and Anna Margarethe (Onigkeit) Bowers; m. Robert Vincent Pierik, July 25, 1964; children: David Vincent, Donald Lesley. AA, Chaffey Jr. Coll., Ontario, Calif., 1959; BA, Upland (Calif.) Coll., 1962; cert. in teaching, Claremont (Calif.) Coll., 1963; MSLS, U. So. Calif., L.A., 1973. Tchr. elem. Christ Episcopal Day Sch., Ontario, 1959-60; tchr. Bonita High Sch., La Verne, Calif., 1962-63; tchr., libr. Kettle Valley Sch. Dist. 14, Greenwood, Can., 1963-64; libr. asst. Monrovia (Calif.) Pub. Libr., 1964-67; with Mt. Hood Community Coll., Gresham, Oreg., 1972—, reference libr., 1983—, chair faculty scholarship com., 1987—; mem. site election com. Multnomah County (Oreg.) Libr./New Gresham br., 1987; mem. adv. com. Mulnomah County Libr., Portland, Oreg., 1988-89; bd. dirs. Oreg. Episcopal Conf. of the Deaf, 1985—. Mem. com. to elect Polly Casterline commr., Multnomah County, 1985, Gussie McRobert mayor, Gresham, 1987; bd. dirs. East County Arts Alliance, Gresham, 1987—; vestry person, jr. warden St. Luke's Episcopal Ch., 1989-90; founding pres. and mgr. Mt. Hood Pops Community Orch. Recipient Jeanette Parkhill Meml. award Chaffey Jr. Coll., 1959, svc. award St. Luke's Episcopal Ch., 1983, 87, Edn. Svc. award Soroptimists, 1989. Mem. AAUW, NEA, Oreg. Edn. Assn., Oreg. Libr. Assn., Gresham Hist. Soc. Office: Mt Hood Community Coll Libr 26000 SE Stark Gresham OR 97030

PIERONEK, JOANN F., nurse; b. Hamtramck, Mich., July 9, 1939; d. Joseph and Mary (Socha) Winiarski; m. Richard Michael Pieronek, Oct. 14, 1961; children: Catherine Frances, Thomas Joseph, Patricia Marie. BSN, Mercy Coll., 1961; MSN, Wayne State U., 1975, postgrad. Staff Pieronek Photographics, Hamtramck, 1955—; assoc. prof. Mercy Coll., Detroit, 1975-86, dean div. of nursing, 1986—; cons. phys. assessment Mercy Hosp., Port Huron, Mich., 1982. Author, editor: (slide/tape) NDC Program, 1980; author: (research) Informed Consent, 1975. Mem. com. nat. alumni, Detroit, 1987, quality evaluation/med. staff com., Detroit, 1987. Recipient Sci. award Bausch and Lomb, Rochester, N.Y., 1957; Wayne State U. scholar, 1974; Mercy Coll. grantee, 1980. Mem. Am. Nurses Assn., Mich. Nurses Assn., Nat. Assn. Pro Life Nurses, Mich. Soc. Instructional Tech., Mich. Assn. Colls. of Nursing, Grosse Pointe Woods (Mich.) War Meml. Assn., Mercy Coll. Alumni Assn. Roman Catholic. Home: 1557 Lochmoor Blvd Grosse Pointe Woods MI 48236 Office: Mercy Coll-Detroit Sch Nursing 8200 W Outer Dr Detroit MI 48219*

PIERSANTE, DENISE, marketing executive; b. Detroit, Jan. 9, 1954; d. Joseph Lawrence and Virginia (Grunwald) P.; m. Wilfred Lewis Was II, June 7, 1975 (div. 1983). BA in Communications, Mich. State U., 1978. Tchr. Northwestern Ohio Community Action Commn., Defiance, 1979-80, counselor, 1980-82, job developer, 1982-83, Pvt. Industry Coun., Defiance, 1983, job developer coord., 1983-84, dir. pub. rels. and job devel., 1984-86; market master North Market, Columbus, Ohio, 1986-87, dir. mktg. Richard S. Zimmerman Jr., Columbus, 1987—; cons. Small Bus. Mgmt., Archbold, Ohio, 1985-87; promotion dir. Miss N.W. Ohio Pageant, Defiance, 1985-87, Uptowners Rib Fest, 1989; promotion dir. Gallery Jazz Series, 1988, organizer, Prism Awards Competition, 1987; scholarship auction, 1988; pub. relations coordinator Defiance County Social Svc. Agys., 1981-86. Author of various grants. Editor Job Tng. Partnership Act newsletter, 1984-86, (newsletter) North Market Soc., 1986-87. Defiance County Social Service Agys. newsletter, 1981-86; Value/Style Community News, 1987—. Organizer Auglaize River Race, Defiance, 1985. Nat. Merit scholar, 1972; recipient Am. Legion Citizenship award, 1969, 72. Mem. NAFE, Pub. Rels. Soc. Am., Am. Mktg. Assn., Jaycees (Jaycee of Month 1985), Columbus C. of C. (amb. level II 1989—), Bus. and Profl. Women (Defiance), Corps de Ballet (Columbus), Conductors (Columbus), Operation Operatics (Columbus). Home: 1010 Annagladys Worthington OH 43085 Office: 100 S 3d St Ste 414 Columbus OH 43215

PIERSON, HELEN HALE, educator; b. Lee County, Va., Aug. 5, 1941; d. James William and Genevieve (Dalrymple) Hale; widowed; children: Christine H., Michael B. BA, Westminster Coll., 1963; MEd, Indiana U. Pa., 1968; cert.community coll. tchr. Glendale Community Coll., 1983. Cert. tchr., Pa. Tchr. Sharon (Pa.) City Schs., 1963-66, York (Pa.) City Schs., 1966-67, Prince George's County Schs., Upper Marlboro, Md., 1967-81; office mgr. Creative Realty, Inc., Phoenix, 1983-85; tchr. Rio Salado Coll., Phoenix, 1983—, N.Am. Coll., Phoenix, 1985—; chairperson dept. bus. N.Am. Coll., Phoenix; dir. edn. Rio Salado Coll., 1990, speaker, dept. transp., 1989; tchr. Glendale Community Coll., 1990—. Recipient Outstanding Tchr. award Rio Salado Community Coll., 1990, Most Outstanding Tchr. award AZ Pvt. Sch. Assn., 1990. Mem. NCTE, Nat. Bus. Edn. Assn., Indiana U. Pa. Alumni Assn., Chi Omega Alumni Assn. Republican. Home: 2716 W Michelle Dr Phoenix AZ 85023 Office: N Am Coll 1777 W Camelback Rd Phoenix AZ 85015

PIERSON, KATHLEEN MARY, child care center administrator, consultant; b. Detroit, Apr. 17, 1949; d. Peter and Elsa (Stangh) Kornberger; m. David Alan Pierson, Aug. 23, 1980 (div. Nov. 1981). A.S., Macomb Coll., Mich., 1974; B.S., Central U. Mich., 1976. Model, Detroit, 1970-74, also piano player, lounges; horse jockey, Detroit, 1974-78; recreation therapist Rehab. Inst., Detroit, 1978-81; exec. dir. Kreative Korners, Warren, Mich., 1981—, founder Kreative Korners Adult Day Care Ctr., 1987; cons. low income child care centers Mich., 1986—. Bd. dirs. Macomb Coll., Warren, Mich., 1984—. Guest of Honor, Mich. Opportunity Soc., 1985, Easter Seal Soc., 1976; speaker United Found., 1987, 88. Mem. South Warren Community Orgn., Nat. Exec. Female Assn., Internat. Platform Assn. (speech competition). Lutheran. Avocations: Doberman breeding; playing classical music; horseback riding. Home: 34160 Ryan Rd Sterling Heights MI 48077 Office: Kreative Korners Inc 22021 Memphis St Warren MI 48091

PIERSON, MARGARET ROSALIND, dance educator, choreographer; b. Salt Lake City, Jan. 10, 1941; d. George Arthur and Eily (McKey) P. BA, Bennington (Vt.) Coll., 1963. Dancer Ruth Currier Co., N.Y.C., 1964, Charles Weidman Co., N.Y.C., 1965, Dancer's Theatre Co., N.Y.C., 1964-66; dancer, choreographer Valerie Bettis Dancer's Studio, N.Y.C., 1964-69; soloist Ballet Concepts, N.Y.C., 1966-71, Garden State Ballet, Newark, 1969-71; asst. prof. Mt. Holyoke Coll., South Hadley, Mass., 1971-75; assoc. prof. Ohio State U., Columbus, 1975—; dir. Ohio State U. Dance Co., Columbus, 1983—; Summer Inst. in the Arts, Columbus, 1990, dance coord., 1987—, choreographer of numerous works, 1963—. Recognized Greater Colls. Arts Coun., 1985, Ohio Arts Coun., 1986. Mem. Ohio Dance, Congress on Researching Dance, Alliance for Dance and Movement Arts (media chair 1986-87), Ohio Alliance for Arts in Edn. Office: Ohio State U Dept of Dance 1813 N High St Columbus OH 43206

PIETRS, FLORENCE, artist, investments and securities; b. Milw., Apr. 18, 1921; d. Walter John and Anna (Dutkiewicz) Jakubowski; m. Roman C. Pietrs, Sept. 27, 1941 (widowed Nov. 7, 1960); m. Thomas R., Ann F., Robert A., Michael J., Marcie L., Scott A. BS in Adminstrn., U. Wis., 1939; student, Dale Carnegie Inst., 1974; BFA, U. Minn., 1980. Mktg. rep. Schuster's, Gimbels, W.T. Grant, Milw. and Boston, 1937-38; office sec. Russel's Real Estate, Milw., 1939; sec. Internat. Harvesters, Milw., 1939-41; legal sec. credit office Ind. Atty.'s, Milw., 1940; invst. US Army Judge Adv., Chaffee, Ark., 1942-43; sec. Contracting for Post Salvage, Ft. Sill, Okla., 1943-44; credit interviewer Sears, Milw., 1953-55; apt. rentals U. Minn., Duluth, 1962—; artist Duluth, 1962—; cons. in field, Mpls., 1982—. Artis of paintings (hon. memtion 1946). Mem. task force, Pres. Reagen; sr. counselor C.I.O., 1972. Recipient Christian Mother's medal, Holy Ghost Ch., Milw., 1958; Merit medal, Pres. Reagan, 1986. Mem. Minn. State Sheriffs Assn. (hon.), Congress of Independent Operators (cert. sr. counselor), Senate Club. Republican. Home and Office: 1419 Waverly A Duluth MN 55803

PIETRUS, CAROL LYNN, company executive; b. Chgo., Sept. 15, 1948; d. Alfred E. and Nellie V. (Komperda) Cregier; m. Walter Nmn, May 4, 1968; 1 child, Tracey Aileen. High sch. grad., Chgo. Adminstrv. asst. Spector

Freight system, Inc., Bensenville, Ill., 1969-80; pres.'s asst. Kidco, Inc., Bensenville, Ill., 1980-82, Lauer Sbarbaro Assocs., Chgo., 1982-83, Cas Co., Lisle, Ill.; pres. The Office Extension, Inc., Chgo., 1987—, Originals Only, Inc., Ill., 1985-89, Money Mailer Greater Woodfield, Willowbrook, Ill., 1990—; speaker Direct Mail for Colls., Chambers & Conventions. Author: (office info. series) "If You Asked Me About...". mem. Profl. Assn. of Secretarial Svcs. (pres.1989), Nat. Network Women in Sales. Home: 26 W 471 Grand Ave Wheaton IL 60187 Office: Money Mailer Greater Woodfield 612 Executive Dr Willowbrook IL 60521

PIGNATELLI, DEBORA BECKER, vocational counselor, state legislator; b. Weehawken, N.J., Oct. 25, 1947; d. Edward and Frances (Fishman) Becker; m. Michael Albert Pignatelli, Aug. 22, 1971; children: Adam Becker, Benjamin Becker. AA, Vt. Coll., 1967; BA, U. Denver, 1969. Exec. dir. Girl's Club Greater Nashua, N.H., 1975-77; dir. tenant svcs. Nashua Housing Authority, 1979-80; vocat. counselor Comprehensive Rehab. Assocs., Bedford, N.H., 1982-85; specialist job placement Crawford & Co., Bedford, 1985—; mem. N.H. Ho. of Reps., Concord, 1986—, asst. minority leader, 1989—; mem. Appropriations Com.; del. Am. Young Polit. Leaders, Fed. Republic Germany, 1987. Mem. Nashua Peace Ctr., 1980—; asst. coach Little League Baseball, Nashua, 1987—; mem. steering com. Gephardt for U.S. Pres. campaign, N.H., 1987-88; del. to Dem. Nat. Convention, 1988. Mem. Nat. Order Women Legislators, N.H. Dem. State Com., N.H. Order Women Legislators. Democrat. Jewish. Office: Appropriations Com State House Rm 100 Concord NH 03301

PIHLAJA, MAXINE MURIEL MEAD, orchestra executive; b. Windom, Minn., July 19, 1935; d. Julian Wright and Mildred Eleanor (Ray) Mead; m. Donald Francis Pihlaja, Jan. 4, 1963; children: Geoffrey Blake, Kirsten Louise, Jocelyn Erika. BA, Hamline U., 1957; postgrad., Columbia U., 1957-58. Group worker Fedn. of Chs., L.A., 1956; case worker St. John's Guild Floating Hosp. Ship, N.Y.C., 1957-59; Y-Teen program dir. YWCA, Elizabeth, N.J., 1957-60, Boulder, Colo., 1964-65; spl. svcs. program and club dir. U.S. Army, Ingrandes and Nancy, France, 1960-62; music buyer, salesperson Guinn's Music, Billings, Mont., 1977-78, N.W. Music, Billings, 1978-79; office adminstr. Am. Luth. Ch., Billings, 1979-84; mgr. Billings Symphony Soc., 1984—; substitute tchr. Community Day Care and Enrichment Ctr., Billings, 1971-76. Dir. handbell choir 1st Presbyn. Ch., Billings, 1972—, Am. Luth. Ch., 1981-84, 1st English Luth. Ch., 1982—; mem. Billings Symphony Chorale, 1965—, bellissimo!, 1983—. Mem. Nat. Soc. for Fund Raising Execs. (sec. Mont. 1988), Mont. Assn. Female Execs., Am. Guild of English Handbell Ringers (state chair 1988—), Mont. Assn. Symphony Orchs. (treas. 1987—). Lutheran. Office: Billings Symphony Orch 104 N Broadway Ste 403 PO Box 602 Billings MT 59103

PIIRMA, IRJA, chemist, educator; b. Tallinn, Estonia, Feb. 4, 1920; came to U.S., 1949; d. Voldemar Juri and Meta Wilhelmine (Lister) Tiits; m. Aleksander Piirma, Mar. 10, 1943; children: Margit Ene, Silvia Ann. Diploma in chemistry, Tech. U., Darmstadt, Fed. Republic of Germany, 1949; MS, U. Akron, 1957, PhD, 1960. Rsch. chemist U. Akron, Ohio, 1952-67, asst. prof., 1967-76, assoc. prof., 1976-81, prof., 1981—, dept. head, 1982-85. Contbr. articles to profl. jours.; editor: Emulsion Polymerization, 1982. Recipient Extra Mural Rsch. award BP Am., Inc., 1989. Mem. Am. Chem. Soc. Home: 3528 Adaline Dr Stow OH 44224 Office: U Akron Akron OH 44325-3909

PIJAN, BARBARA ANNE, computer systems engineer; b. Chgo., Aug. 24, 1956; d. Bernard Gregory and Bernardine A. (Lear) P. BA, Reed Coll., 1981; MA, U. Chgo., 1985. Cert. in computer programming. Pvt. cons. practice San Francisco, 1986-88; personal computer systems analyst Itel Container, San Francisco, 1988-89, personal computer systems engr., 1989—. Author numerous astrological chart interpretations, 1984—; designer, instr. high altitude yoga program. Mem. Am. Fedn. Astrological Networks, Integral Yoga Tchrs. Assn. Buddhist. Office: Pijan Cons PO Box 613140 South Lake Tahoe CA 95761-3140

PIKE, CAROL JEAN, educator; b. Lancaster, Pa., Apr. 10, 1958; d. Leroy Enos and Jean (Somerford) Zimmerman; m. Mark Wayne Pike, Nov. 24, 1984; children: Matthew Wayne, Meghan Jean. BS in Health/Phys. Edn., E. Stroudsburg State Coll., 1980. Tchr. Sherman (Tex.) Ind. Sch. Dist., 1981—. Coach Spl. Olympics, Sherman, 1981—. Mem. AAHPER. Methodist. Home: 603 White St Whitesboro TX 76273 Office: Fred Douglas Sch 505 E College St Sherman TX 75090

PIKE, DANA ANN, nursery executive; b. Atlanta, June 16, 1965; d. William Leon and Margie Geraldine (Coleman) P. BA in Journalism, U. Ga., 1987. Co-owner, coord. advt., dir. human resources Pike Nurseries, Inc., Atlanta, 1987-; landscape cons. Zoo Atlanta, 1987—, Oakland Cemetery, Atlanta 1987—, Henrietta Egleston Hosp., Atlanta, 1987—. Editor, writer Pike's Peeks newsletter. Recipient outstanding achievement award Chevron Chem. Co., 1988. Mem. Am. Assn. Nurserymen (advt. awards 1985, 86, 87), Ga. Nurseryman's Assn. (Silver Spade award 1978-90), NAFE Greater Atlanta Nurserymen Assn., Met. C. of C., Young Careers, Atlanta Jr. League. Republican. Baptist. Office: 3935 Buford Hwy Atlanta GA 30345

PILCH, JANE ELIZABETH, technical representative; b. Pitts., Apr. 15, 1963; m. Ted Pilch Jr., Sept. 21, 1985. BSChemE, U. Pitts., 1985, MBA, 1991. Lab estimator Burrell Corp., Pitts., 1986-87, with tech. svc., 1987-89, outside tech. sales rep., 1989—. Asst. to researcher (book) Resource for Women Wanting Careers in Engineering & Computers, 1983. Mem. NAFE. Office: Burrell Corp 2223 5th Ave Pittsburgh PA 15219

PILEGGI, ELIZABETH MORGAN, biomedical engineer; b. Tarrytown, N.Y., May 21, 1957; d. Alfred Thomas and Elizabeth (Jennings) Morgan; m. Anthony John Pileggi, Nov. 19, 1983; 1 child, Nicole Denise. BA in Biology, Rosemont (Pa.) Coll., 1979; MS in Biomed. Enginering, Rutgers U., 1981. Quality assurance engr. for med. products E.I. Du Pont de Nemours & Co., Glasgow, Del., 1981-83, supr. product testing, 1983-85, supr. inventory mgmt., 1985-86, sect. supr. consumables, 1986-88, supr. inventory systems, 1988; supr. quality assurance and GMP's pharm. div. Good Mfg. Practices pharm. div. Miles Inc., West Haven, Conn., 1988-89; mgr. quality assurance standards Miles Inc., West Haven, Conn., 1990—. Fellow Grad. Profl. Opportunities Program, 1979. Mem. Internat. Soc. Pharm. Engrs., Good Mfg. Practices Tng. and Edn. Assn., NAFE, Tau Beta Pi. Republican. Home: 908 Monroe Turnpike Monroe CT 06468 Office: Miles Inc 400 Morgan Ln West Haven CT 06415

PILGRIM, DIANNE HAUSERMAN, art museum director; b. Cleve., July 9, 1941; d. John Martin and Norma Hauserman; divorced. BA, Pa. State U., 1963; MA, Inst. Fine Arts, NYU, 1965; postgrad., CUNY, 1971-74. Chester Dale fellow Am. wing. Met. Mus. Art, N.Y.C., 1966-68, researcher, 1971, rsch. assoc. Am. paintings and sculpture, 1972-73; asst. to dirs. Pyramide Galleries, Ltd., Washington, 1969-71, Finch Coll. Mus. Art, Washington, 1971; curator dept. decorative arts Bklyn. Mus., 1973-88, chmn. dept., 1988; dir. Cooper-Hewitt Mus., N.Y.C., 1988—; mem. adv. com. Gracie Mansion, N.Y.C., 1980; mem. design adv. com. Art Inst. Chgo., 1988—; mem. Hist. House Trust of N.Y.C., Mayor's Office, 1989—. Co-author, curator: (book and exhbn. catalogue) The American Renaissance 1876-1917, 1979, (book) The Machine Age in America 1918-1941, 1986 (Charles F. Montgomery prize Decorative Arts Soc.). Bd. dirs. Nat. Multiple Sclerosis Soc., N.Y.C., 1989. Mem. Art Table, Decorative Arts Soc. chpt. Soc. Archtl. Historians (pres. 1977-79). Office: Cooper-Hewitt Mus 2 E 91st St New York NY 10128

PILL, CYNTHIA JOAN, social worker; b. N.Y.C., Mar. 30, 1939; d. Alfred and Edna (Strauss) Fruchtman; BS cum laude, Jackson Coll., Tufts U., 1961; MS, in Social Work, Simmons Coll., 1963; PhD in Social Work, 1988; m. Robert Pill, July 29, 1961; children: Laura, Daniel, Karen. Clin. social worker Concord (Mass.) Family Service, 1965-78; coordinator family life edn. Family Counseling Service, Newton, Mass., 1979-83; pvt. practice clin. social work, Newton, Mass., 1979—; co-founder, clin. social worker Remarriage Counseling Collaborative, Newton, Mass., 1981-87; cons. Hospice of the Good Shepherd, Newton, Mass., 1979-84; rsch. advisor Smith Coll. Sch. for Social Work, Northampton, Mass., 1988—; adj. asst. prof. Simmins Coll. Sch. Social Work, Boston, 1989—. Vol. coordinator Hospice at Home, Sudbury,

Mass., 1986-88. Lic. ind. clin. social worker. Mem. Mass. Acad. Clin. Social Work, Inc., Nat. Assn. Social Workers, Register Clin. Social Workers (bd. cert. diplomate). Contbr. to profl. publs. Address: 14 Mason Rd Newton Center MA 02159

PILLAR, HEATHER RETA, photojournalist; b. Abington, Pa., Mar. 14, 1963; d. Walter Oscar and Mary Reta (O'Donnell) P. BS in Indsl. Mgmt., Carnegie Mellon U., 1985. Market researcher Herrmann Graphic Technologies, Pitts., 1983-85; researcher CBS Ednl. and Profl. Pub., N.Y.C., 1984; market researcher Ahlstrom Corp., Karhula, Finland, 1985; cons. Pirozzolo Co. Pub. Rels., Boston, 1986-89; pres. Heather Pillar Photography, Boston, 1989—; news photographer Beacon Communications, Acton, Mass., 1989—; new photographer UPI, Boston, 1987—. Tutor One with One, Quincy, Mass., 1986—; mem. CARE, Boston, 1986. Mem. Nat. Press Photographers Assn., Boston Press Photographers Assn. Home: 22 Maple St Waltham MA 02154

PILLING, JANET KAVANAUGH, lawyer; b. Akron, Ohio, Sept. 5, 1951; d. Paul and Marjorie (Logue) Kavanaugh; m. Martin Jolles, Mar. 6, 1987; children: Madeleine Sloan Langdon Jolles, Jameson Samuel Rhys Jolles. BA, Ohio Wesleyan U., 1973; JD, U. Mo., 1975; LLM, Villanova U., 1985. Bar: Pa. 1976, U.S. Tax Ct. 1976, U.S. Dist. Ct. (ea. dist.) Pa. 1976. Atty. Schnader, Harrison, Segal & Lewis, Phila., 1976-83; gen. counsel Kistler-Tiffany Cos. Schnader, Harrison, Segal & Lewis, Wayne, Pa., 1983—. Mem. Phila. Estate Planning Coun., Montgomery County Estate Planning Coun., Chester County Estate Planning Coun. Mem. ABA, Phila. Bar Assn. (probate sect., tax sect.), Pa. Bar Assn., Phi Beta Kappa, Phi Delta Phi. Office: Kistler Tiffany Cos 987 Old Eagle School Rd Ste 706 Wayne PA 19087

PILOT-PETERS, NORMA LOU, educational administrator, choir director; b. Mt. Clemens, Mich., Nov. 27, 1942; d. Arthur Louis and Elsie Lydia (Kempf) Ploetz; m. Louis Otto Peters Jr., Dec. 26, 1982; 1 stepchild, Mark Andrew. BA, Concordia Coll., 1966; Grad., Nat. Tchr's. Coll., Evanston, Ill., 1974; postgrad., Alverno Coll., 1981, U. Wis., Milw. Ordained to ministry Luth. Ch., 1977. Tchr. Elm Grove (Wis.) Luth. Sch., 1964-65; kindergarten tchr. Resurrection Luth. Sch., Chgo., 1966-67; tchr. University City (Mo.) Pub. Schs., 1967-68, Milw. Pub. Schs., 1969-78, Mo. Pub. Schs., University City, 1968-69; prin., founder, tchr. Holy Comforter Luth. Sch., Balt., 1978-81; prin. St. Peter's Christian Day Sch., Balt., 1981—; founder, master tchr., organizer Primary Individualized Learning Ctr., Allen Field Sch., 1969-71; Sunday sch. supr., dir. children's choir Christ Luth. Ch., 1989—; nat. rep. Luth. Schs.; mem. Md. Synod Lay Profl. Com., Balt., 1986-87. Mem. Luth. Prins. Conf., Balt., 1978—, speaker, 1982; founder, project dir. Learning Early to Achieve Potential Pre-Sch. Pub. Schs., Milw., 1971-76; speaker alternative edn. conf. Webster Coll., Webster Grove, Mo., 1971, Wis. Reading Conv., Milw., 1971, Luth. Spl. Edn. Dist., St. Louis, 1969; pres. Village Luth. Council; charter mem. Village Luth. Ch., Milw., 1967—. Mem. Evangelical Luth. Edn. Assn. (mem. div. edn. com. Md. synod 1988—, chmn. ad hoc com. Luth. schs. Md. synod 1989—), Am. Luth. Edn. Assn., Milw. Tchrs. Assn. Assn., Assn. Early Childhood Edn. Home: 3704 Delverne Rd Baltimore MD 21218 Office: St Peter's Christian Day Sch 7910 Belair Rd Baltimore MD 21236

PILOUS, BETTY SCHEIBEL, nurse; b. Cleve., July 30, 1948; d. Raymond W. and Dorothy E. (Groth) S.; m. Lee Alan Pilous, Sept. 11, 1970; 1 child. Diploma in nursing Huron Rd. Hosp., Cleve., 1970; BSBA, St. Joseph's Coll., 1989. RN, Ohio. Cert. med.-surg. nurse, nursing adminstr. Nurse Huron Rd. Hosp., Cleve., 1970-71, Hillcrest Hosp., Cleve., 1974-77; head nurse, relief supr. Oak Park Hosp., Oakwood, Ohio, 1977-81; head nurse med.-surg. Bedford Hosp., Ohio, 1981-87; dir. med.-surg. nursing Meridia Euclid Hosp., Euclid, Ohio; coord. hosp. info. system for nursing; former instr. ARC; chair nurse practice com. Am. Heart Assn.; mem. nursing standards com. Community Hosp. of Bedford. Mem. health and safety com. Twinsburg Schs., Ohio, 1984, mem. curriculum com., 1981-83; chairperson standards com. Community Hosp. of Bedford; former counselor jr. high youth 1st Congl. Ch., Twinsburg; adv. bd. Brecksville Rainbow Assembly for Girls. Mem. Ohio Citizen League Nursing Nurse Execs. Network (acting sec.), Ohio Hosp. Assn., Nat. League Nursing, Southeast Cleve. Mid Mgrs. Networking Group (initiated), Greater Cleve. Nurse Execs. Network Group, Order Eastern Star, Sigma Theta Tau, Iota Psi. Avocations: aerobics, hiking. Office: Euclid Hosp 18901 N Lake Shore Blvd Euclid OH 44143

PILSNER, JOYCE MARION, health services administrator; b. N.Y.C., Jan. 30, 1925; d. Sol and Estelle (Schaffle) Mayersohn; m. Harry Pilsner, Dec. 20, 1947; 1 child, Toby Jane. AB, Hunter Coll., 1944; MA, Columbia U., 1946. Tchr. N.Y.C., 1945-67; rsch. assoc. Inst. Community Studies Sarah Lawrence Coll., Bronxville, N.Y., 1968-69, asst. to dean faculty, dir. edn., 1968-70; rsch. assoc., field coordinator Consortium on Community Crises Cornell U., Ithaca, N.Y., 1970-71; adminstrv. dir. Riverdale Mental Health Clinic, Bronx, N.Y., 1971—. Group discussion leader Urban Systems Staff Devel. Ctr., Yonkers, N.Y., 1970; del., membership chmn., correspondence sec. Riverdale Community Coun.; mem. dist. bd. Comprehensive Health Planning Agy.; mem., sec. sub-regional com. Bronx Fedn. Mental Health and Mental Retardation Agys.; bd. dirs. Riverdale Sr. Ctr., 1974-82; v.p., bd. dirs. Coalition of Mental Health, Mental Retardation and Alcoholism Agys., 1975—; mem. Community Bd. 8, Bronx, 1975—, chmn. Health com., chmn. Youth com., 2d v.p., 1989; mem. community adv. bd. North Cen. Bronx Hosp., 1983-89, chmn. health, membership and nominating coms.; mem. Nat. Users Group, Info. Scis. Div. Nathan Kline Inst., 1984-87, exec. com., sec., 1985-86; borough outreach com. Greater N.Y. Fund/ United Way, 1985-89. Named Riverdalian of Yr., 1979; recipient Cert. of Meritorious Svc. N.Y.C. Mayor Edward I. Koch, 1986. Mem. Riverdale Mental Health Assn. (dir. 1965-71, chmn. pub. rels., editor newsletter), UN Assn. (dir. Riverdale chpt., chmn. publicity), Am. Assn.Univ. Women, LWV, Am. Orthopsychiat. Assn., Assn. Adminstrs. Mental Health and Mental Retardation Facilities (dir. 1974—), East Hampton Owners Ltd. (bd. dirs., v.p. 1986, pres. 1988), Alumni Assn., Inst. for Not-for-Profit Mgmt. (exec. com. 1987—). Home: 4721 Delafield Ave New York NY 10471 Office: Riverdale Mental Health Assn 5676 Riverdale Ave Bronx NY 10471

PINA, SHEILA MARTINES, regional tourist council administrator; b. Boston, Sept. 27, 1955; d. John Francis and Catherine Theresa (Martin) Sheehan; m. Ronald A. Pina, Sept. 2, 1988; 1 child, Kari Kay. BA magna cum laude, Southeastern Mass. U., 1977. Radio broadcaster Hall Communications, New Bedford, Mass., 1977-79; broadcast journalist Sta. WJAR TV, Providence, 1979-88; exec. dir. Bristol County Conv. & Visitors Bur., New Bedford, Mass., 1988—. Vice chair Govs. Adv. Coun. on Tourism, Mass., 1990; pres. Mass. Tourism Coalition, 1990; bd. dirs. New Bedford Theatre Festival, Inc., 1990. Recipient GTE Mktg. Excellence award GTE, 1990, Golden citation Am. Businesswoman Assn., 1988, Personal Achievement award Southeastern Mass. U. Alumni Assn., 1987; named Woman of Yr., YWCA, New Bedford, 1987. Mem. NAFE, Mass Tourism Coalition, New Eng. USA, Travel Rsch. Assn. Home: 70 N 2nd St PO Box BR 976 New Bedford MA 02740

PINAZZA, B(EVERLY) DIANE, respiratory therapist, administrator; b. Long Beach, Calif., June 2, 1961; d. Charles Saunders and Bernice (Morgan) Corrin; m. Darrell E. Pinazza, Mar. 9, 1985. Student, No. Ariz. U., 1980-81; cert. respiratory therapy, Biosystems Inst., Tempe, Ariz., 1982. Respiratory therapist Profl. Respiratory Care Svc., Phoenix, 1981-82, Bapt. Med. Ctr., Oklahoma City, 1982-84; home care therapist Foster Med., Oklahoma City, 1984-85; respiratory therapy supr. St. Anthony's Hosp., Oklahoma City, 1984—; clin. site instr., Francis Tuttle Vo-Tech. Sch., Oklahoma City, 1984—, Rose State Coll., Midwest City, Okla., 1984—. Mem. Nat. Bd. Respiratory Care, Okla. State Respiratory Care Bd., Alma Soc. for Adoptees' Rights. Republican. Office: Saint Anthonys Hosp 1000 N Lee St Oklahoma City OK 73109

PINCH, PATRICIA ANN, insurance agent; b. Port Hueneme, Calif., Oct. 8, 1947; d. William Claude and Lois (Monroe) Pinch; m. Vincent J. Lupo, Apr. 6, 1973 (dec. 1975). B.S. in Med. Tech., Med. Coll. Va., 1969. Human cytogenetic researcher Bklyn. Hosp., 1970-72; animal genetic researcher Mt. Sinai Hosp., N.Y.C., 1972-74; med. tech. supr., owner Vee-Jay Clin. Labs., Bklyn., 1974-86; supr. G.J.L. Clin. Lab., Amityville, N.Y., 1986-87; dist. agt. Prudential Ins., 1987—. Mem. Am. Soc. Clin. Pathologists. Roman Catholic. Office: 124 Kime Ave North Babylon NY 11703

PINCUS, ANN TERRY, television executive; b. Little Rock, Sept. 12, 1937; d. Fred William and Cornelia (Witsell) Terry; m. Walter Haskell Pincus, May 1, 1965; children: Ward, Adam, Cornelia Battle. BA, Vassar Coll., 1959. Reporter Ridder Pubs., Washington, 1963-66; freelance writer Washington, 1966-78; dir. info. select com. on U.S. population U.S. Ho. Reps., Washington, 1978-79; nat. publicist Nat. Pub. Radio, Washington, 1979-83; press sec. U.S. Sen. Charles Mathias, Washington, 1983-87; v.p. communications Stas. WETA-TV/Radio, Washington, 1987—; bd. dirs. Wildfowl Trust of N. Am., Graysonville, Md., Fgn. Student Service Council, Washington. Editor: Kennedy Center Cookbook, 1977; contbr. articles to profl. jours. Home: 3202 Klingle Rd NW Washington DC 20008 Office: WETA PO Box 2626 Washington DC 20013

PINCUS, DEBBIE SUE, psychotherapist; b. Glencove, N.Y., June 30, 1953; d. William and Reva (Napers) P.; m. Richard Ward, Sept. 24, 1989. BS magna cum laude, U. Bridgeport, 1975, MS, 1976. Tchr. Lerox Sch., N.Y.C., 1976-78, Horace Mann Barnard Sch., Riverdale, N.Y., 1978-1984; psychotherapist N.Y.C., 1983—; dir. counseling physician smoke stopping clinic Coll. Mt. St. Vincent, N.Y.C., 1984—. Author: Sharing, 1953, Interactions, 1987, Citizenship, Feeling Good About Yourself, 1989. Mem. Horatio St. Block Assn., 1990. Mem. Am. Assn. Counseling Devel. Home: 97 Horatio St #234 New York NY 10014

PINCUS, JEANETTE ENGEL, artist, educator; b. N.Y.C., Aug. 6, 1909; d. Henry and Jeanette (Frank) Engel; m. Jacob Theodore Pincus, Dec. 9, 1929 (dec. Nov. 1975); children: Theodore, Barbara Smiley. Student, Chgo. Acad. Art, 1928-30, Am. Acad. Art, Chgo., 1929, Chgo. Art Inst., 1926-30. Cert. art tchr., Calif. Ofcl. decorator Highland Park (Ill.) Community Ctr., 1950; tchr. Brandeis U. Extention, Highland Park, 1963; tchr. emeritus Saddleback Community Coll., 1970—. One woman shows include Chgo., 1958-70, Washington, 1970, Calif., 1970-90, Klutznik, Washington, 1970, Hillel House, Evanston, Ill., 1970, San Juan Mus., 1988; contbr. articles to profl. jours. Founder Suburban Fine Arts Ctr., Highland Park, 1963. Recipient artist awards Nat. League Am. Women, 1979-89, Internat. Art Challange, L.A., 1989, Kaleidoscope Internat., Irvine, Calif., 1989, 91. Home: 5378 B Sosiega Laguna Hills CA 92635

PINEAU, JOY VICTORIA, infosystems specialist; b. Chelsea, Mass., Aug. 6, 1957; d. Joseph Alyre and Delores (Rheault) P. Cert., N.E. Regional Vocat. Sch., Wakefield, Mass., 1975. Drafter BTU Engring., Billerica, Mass., 1975-76; tool designer GE Corp., Lynn, Mass., 1976-79; product specialist Computervision Corp., Bedford, Mass., 1979-81; applications engr. Computervision Corp., Charlotte and Orlando, N.C., Fla., 1981-84; regional applications systems specialist Computervision Corp., Dallas, 1984-89; applications engr. Advanced Graphics Systems, Dallas, 1989-90, Mfg. and Cons. Svcs. Inc., Dallas, 1990—. Author manual in field. With USNG, 1976-79. Republican. Roman Catholic. Home: 503 Anice Ln Euless TX 76039 Office: Mfg and Cons Svcs Inc 14755 Preston Rd Ste 726 Dallas TX 75240-7877

PINEDA, IRENE BASILIO, physician; b. Sto. Tomas, Pampanga, Philippines, Aug. 5, 1939; d. Saturnino C. Pineda and Consalacion Basilio; m. Andrew J. Stiber, Mar. 30, 1968; children: Jonathan, Jason. MD, U. Santo Tomas, Manila, Philippines, 1962. Diplomate Am. Bd. Obstetrics and Gynecology. Internship St. Clares Hosp., Schnectady, N.Y., 1963-64; residency St. Catherines Hosp., Bklyn., 1964-65, NYU Med. Ctr., N.Y., N.Y., 1965-68; pvt. practice in ob-gyn. N.Y.C., 1975—; clin. asst. prof. NYU Med. Ctr., N.Y.C., 1975—. Fellow Am. Coll. Obstetricians & Gynecologists, Bellevue Obstet. & Gynecol. Soc.; mem. Am. Fertility Soc., Med. Soc. of the County N.Y. Roman Catholic. Office: 220 E 30th St New York NY 10016

PINEGAR, MARTA CARLSON, management executive; b. Biloxi, Miss., May 7, 1955; d. Robert A. and Blanche (Brown) Carlson; 1 child, Carlson. BA, Fla. State U., 1976. Prodn. mgr. Highlander Publs., Industry, Calif.; sr. v.p. Praendex Pacific, Inc., La Canada, Calif. Mem. NAFE, Am. Mgmt. Assn. Home: 259 Saint Katherine Dr La Canada CA 91011

PINELLI, PATRICIA RUTH, real estate executive; b. Chgo., Feb. 28, 1929; d. Roland Beyer and Agnes Ann (Doolan) Lally; m. Henry Andrew Pinelli, Jan. 20, 1951; children: Kathleen Pinelli McAfee, Maureen Pinelli Jones, Dana, Charles. Student, Wright Jr. Coll., 1945-47, Ft. Lauderdale Coll., 1974. Sec. sales promotion Cadillac Motor Car Div., Chgo., 1949-54; realtor assoc. Glenview Realty, Ill., 1969-72, Cummings & Cohen Real Estate, Ft. Lauderdale, 1974-78, Cummings Realty, Ft. Lauderdale, 1978-79, Home Mktg. of Fla., Ft. Lauderdale, 1979-81, Cummings & Cohen Real Estate, Inc., Lauderdale-By-The-Sea, Ft. Lauderdale, 1981—. Area chmn. North Shore Mental Health Assn., Glenview, 1962; treas. Democratic Club of Galt Ocean Mile, Ft. Lauderdale, 1980. Named to Million Dollar Club, Am. Invesco, Chgo., 1980. Mem. Ft. Lauderdale Bd. Realtors (com. mem. 1978-82), Nat. Assn. Realtors, Fla. Real Estate Exchangors, Nat. Assn. Female Execs., Ft. Lauderdale Investment Div., Nat. Right to Life. Roman Catholic. Clubs: Suburban, Orchesis, Valley-Lo Sports. Avocations: swimming, golf, aerobics, bowling, travel. Office: Cummings & Cohen Real Estate Inc 2824 E Commercial Blvd Fort Lauderdale FL 33308-4206

PINES, CATHERINE DEIRDRE, clinical psychologist; b. Princeton, N.J., Aug. 13, 1955; d. David and Aronelle (Siegerman) P. AB with high honors, U. Mich., 1975; MA, Emory U., 1983, PhD, 1985. Registered clin. psychologist. Rsch. asst. Ypsilanti (Mich.) Area Community Svcs., 1976-77; staff psychologist Emory U. Counseling Ctr., Atlanta, 1979-81; clin. extern The Howard Sch., Atlanta, 1980-81; psychology trainee Siegel Inst., Michael Reese Med. Ctr., Chgo., 1981-84; clin. psychology resident Northwestern Meml. Hosp., Chgo., 1981-82; staff fellow Inst. of Psychiatry, Chgo., 1983-84; pvt. practice psychology Chgo., 1984—; staff psychologist DePaul U. Community Mental Health Ctr., Chgo., 1984—, coord. clin. tng., 1988—; course instr. Loyola U., Chgo., 1987; case cons. Siegel Inst., Michael Reese Med. Ctr., Chgo., 1988—; instr. to family practice residents Ravenswood Med. Ctr., 1989—. Contbr. articles to profl. jours. Bd. pres. Mo Ming Dance and Arts Ctr., Chgo., 1988—. Recipient Christian Bohr prize Bohr Family, Copenhagen, 1972. Mem. Am. Psychol. Assn., Ill. Psychol. Assn., Chgo. Assn. for Psychoanalytic Psychology, Phi Beta Kappa. Home: 524-3 Sheridan Sq Evanston IL 60202 Office: DePaul U Community Mental Health Ctr 2219 N Kenmore Rm 304 Chicago IL 60614

PINES, JUDITH AIELLO, advertising agency executive. Exec. v.p., gen. mgr. Scali, McCabe, Sloves, Inc., N.Y.C. Office: Scali McCabe Sloves Inc 800 3rd Ave New York NY 10022*

PINES, LOIS G., state legislator; b. Malden, Mass., 1940; m. Joseph Pines; 2 children. BA, Barnard Coll., 1960; JD, U. Cin. Law Sch., 1963. Corp. tax atty., 1964-72; alderman City of Newton, Mass., 1971-73; mem. Mass. Ho. of Reps., 1973-78; regional dir. New England Fed. Trade Commn., 1979-81; mem. Mass. State Senate, 1986—. Home: 40 Helene Rd Newton MA 02168 Office: Mass State Senate Boston MA 02133*

PINKHAM, ELEANOR HUMPHREY, university librarian; b. Chgo., May 7, 1926; d. Edward Lemuel and Grace Eleanor (Cushing) Humphrey; m. James Hansen Pinkham, July 10, 1948; children: Laurie Sue, Carol Lynn. AB, Kalamazoo Coll., 1948; MS in Library Sci. (Alice Louise LeFevre scholar), Western Mich. U., 1967. Pub. svcs. libr. Kalamazoo Coll., 1967-68, asst. libr., 1969-70, libr. dir., 1971—; vis. lectr. Western Mich. U. Sch. Librarianship, 1970-84; mem. adv. bd., 1977-81, also adv. bd. Inst. Cistercian Studies Libr., 1975-80. Mem. ALA, AAUP, ACRL (chmn. coll. libr. sect. 1988-89), Mich. Libr. Assn. (pres. 1983-84, chmn. acad. div. 1977-78), Mich. Libr. Consortium (exec. coun. 1974-82, chmn. 1977-78, Mich. Libr. of Yr 1986), OCLC Users Coun., Beta Phi Mu. Home: 2519 Glenwood Dr Kalamazoo MI 49008 Office: 1200 Academy St Kalamazoo MI 49007

PINKMAN, KAREN N., retail executive. A.Bus., Union County Coll., Cranford, N.J., 1973; student, Kean Coll., Union, N.J., 1974. With Macy's, N.Y.C., 1980, Bloomingdale's, N.Y.C., 1983, Carter Hawley Hale, N.Y.C., 1985; pres., owner Creative Retail Concepts, Westfield, N.J. Mem. Nat. Assn. Female Execs., Fashion Group Internat., Am. Women's Econ. Devel., Entrepreneurial Women's Network, NOW, Toastmasters (sec.). Democrat. Office: Creative Retail Concepts 503 S Chestnut St Westfield NJ 07090

PINKOWICZ, CHRISTINE ANN, arts administrator, fundraiser, theatre director, educator; b. York, Pa., Aug. 5, 1961; d. John Walter and Margaret Lucille (Burg) P. BA in English and Theater, Shippensburg (Pa.) U., 1983; MFA in Arts Adminstrn., Columbia U., N.Y.C., 1987; PhD in Theater, CUNY, 1988—. Tchr., dir. theatre The Mercersburg (Pa.) Acad., 1983-85; devel. and fundraising asst. N.Y. Theatre Workshop, N.Y.C., 1986-87, Circle Repertory Co., N.Y.C., 1986-87; devel. researcher People for Westpride, N.Y.C., 1987; asst. with real estate project Alliance Resident Theatres of N.Y., N.Y.C., 1987; dir. devel. Circle in Square Theatre, N.Y.C., 1987—; tchr. The Wood Sch., N.Y.C., 1990—; script evaluator Circle Repertory Co., N.Y.C., 1986-88; personal asst. Gloria F. Ross Tapestries, N.Y.C., 1986-88; fundraising cons. various not-for-profit theaters, N.Y.C., 1989—; dir. devel. Pieter Claesen Wyckoff House, Bklyn., 1989-90; editorial asst. Western European Stages, 1989—. Columbia U. scholar, 1985-87, CUNY scholar, 1989—. Mem. Alliance Resident Theatres (N.Y.C.), Devel. Profls. Roundtable, Nat. Coun. Tchrs. English, Met. Opera Guild, N.Y.C. Opera Guild, Assn. for Theatre in Higher Edn., Women in Fin. Devel., MLA. Lutheran. Home: 988 E 18th St Brooklyn NY 11230

PINKSTAFF, MARLENE ARTHUR, management consultant; b. Alma, Ark., Sept. 21, 1936; d. James Alexander and Ruby Jo (Fitzgerald) Arthur; m. Richard E. Pinkstaff, Sept. 2, 1955; children: Mark Richard, Jay Ralph. Student, McKendree Coll., 1957-58; AA, Claremore Coll., 1976; BS, U. Tulsa, 1979; postgrad., Okla. State U., 1981. Billing analyst A.S. Aloe Co., St. Louis, 1955-57; office mgr. McKendree Coll., Lebanon, Ill., 1957-58; exec. sec. Tri-State Ins. Co., Tulsa, 1958-59; analyst A.E. Staley Mfg. Co., Decatur, Ill., 1959-62; ptnr. Dick Pinkstaff Assocs., Tulsa, 1970-80; pres. PPW Cons. Group, Tulsa, 1980-82, Pinkstaff Consulting Assocs., Inc., Tulsa, 1982—; consulting dir. Aldersgate Presch., Tulsa, 1973-78; ptnr. Satellite Office Systems, Tulsa, 1983-84, owner, mgr., 1984-88. Co-author: Women at Work: Overcoming the Obstacles, 1979, Personal Skill Building for the Emerging Manager, 1979; contbr. articles to profl. jours. Mem. adv. coun. YWCA Women's Resource Ctr., Tulsa, 1981—; bd. dirs. Tulsa YWCA, 1983-89, United. Meth. Children's Home, Talequah, Okla., 1986—. Mem. Adminstrv. Mgmt. Soc. (cert., internat. v.p. mgmt. svcs. 1987-89, internat. v.p. profl. devel. 1989—, Amb. award 1988), Am. Soc. Tng. and Devel., Nat. Speakers Assn., Tulsa Women's Found., Nat. Assn. Women Business Owners. Methodist. Office: 3315 S Yale Ave Ste 200 Tulsa OK 74135

PINKSTON, ANITA SUE, elementary school educator; b. St. Louis, Oct. 14, 1960; d. Raymond and Sue (Wade) P. BS, Murray (Ky.) State U., 1982; MS, U. Tenn., Martin, 1990. Cert. elem. tchr., Tenn., Ky.; grades K-8 and libr. Substitute tchr. Weakley County Bd. Edn., Dresden, Tenn., Graves County Bd. Edn., Mayfield, Ky. Baptist. Home: Rt 1 Sedalia KY 42079

PINNEY, DIANE OLIVER, financial executive; b. Omaha, Dec. 29, 1941; d. Benine Albert and Christine Alice (Thoman) Oliver; m. Jerry Carlysle Pinney, Aug. 12, 1962; children: Katherine Ann Pinney Manuel, David Lars, Regina Sue. BA in Bus. Adminstrn., U. Wash., Seattle, 1978; MBA in Fin., Roosevelt U., Chgo., 1987. Sr. budget analyst Continental Telephone Co. N.W., Bellevue, Wash., 1979-82; controller Gen. Coun. on Fin. and Adminstrn. United Meth. Ch., Evanston, Ill., 1983-87, treas. Gen. Bd. Pensions, 1987—; treas. Bd. Higher Edn. and Campus Ministry, Chgo., 1988—; asst. pres. Conf. Coun. on Fin. and Adminstrn., Chgo., 1984-87. Chmn. com. on fin. First United Meth. Ch. Arlington Heights, Ill., 1984-88. Mem. Women in Mgmt., Nat. Assn. Accts. (dir. career devel. 1985-87), Rotary Club. Republican. Home: 645 N Douglas St Arlington Heights IL 60004 Office: Gen Bd Pensions 1200 Davis St Evanston IL 60201

PINSKER, ESSIE LEVINE, sculptor, former advertising and public relations executive; b. N.Y.C.; d. Harris and Sophia (Feldman) Levine; m. Sidney Pinsker; children: Susan Harris, Seth Howard. BA, Bklyn. Coll., 1940; postgrad., Art Students League, 1955, Columbia U., 1958, NYU, 1959, New Sch. for Social Research, Mus. Modern Art, 1970-71, Cambridge (Eng.) U., 1985. Former buyer Ohrbach's, N.Y.C., Arkwright, N.Y.C.; fashion model; former editor Woman's Wear Daily, N.Y.C.; former press. dir. Am. Symphony Orch., N.Y.C.; pres. Essie Pinsker Advt. Assocs., Inc., N.Y.C., 1960-82; guest editor Teen Merchandiser mag., Infant's and Children's Rev.; editor travel, beauty and fashion Woman Golfer mag.; lectr., instr. Fashion Inst. of Tech.; contbg. journalist N.Y. Times. One-woman shows include Bodley Gallery, N.Y.C., 1981, Vorpal Gallery, N.Y.C., 1987; exhibited in group shows at Met. Life, N.Y.C., 1969, Huntington (N.Y.) Art League, 1977, C.W. Post Ctr., Old Westbury, N.Y., 1978, North Shore Arts Ctr., Manhasset, N.Y., 1980, Allied Artists of Am., N.Y.C., 1980, Lever Bros., N.Y.C., 1982, Knickerbocker Artists, N.Y.C., 1982, Cadme Gallery, Phila., 1984, River Gallery, Westport, Conn., 1984, Clark Whitney, Lenox, Mass., 1985, Images Gallery, South Norwalk, Conn., 1987, Arco Internat. Art Fair, Madrid, 1988, Konstmassan Internat. Art Fair, Stockholm, 1988, Galleri Atrium, Stockholm, 1988, Galerie Atrium, Marbella, Spain, 1988, Feingarten Galleries, L.A., 1989, Nina Owen Ltd., Chgo., 1989, The Art Collector, San Diego, 1989, Galerie IlseLommel, Leverkusen, Fed. Republic Germany, 1989, Sandra Higgins Fine Art, London, 1989, Hampton Square Gallery, Westhampton Beach, N.Y., 1990; represented in permanent collections Everson Mus., Syracuse, N.Y., Aldrich Mus. Contemporary Art, Ridgefield, Conn., Okla. Art Ctr., Oklahoma City, Minn. Mus. Art, St. Paul, Mus. Arts and Scis., Daytona Beach, Fla., Vassar Mus., Poughkeepsie, N.Y., Mus. Modern Art, Warsaw, Poland, New Sch., N.Y.C., Pace U., N.Y.C., Necca Mus., Brooklyn, Conn., Lincoln Ctr. Fordham U., N.Y.C., Hinkhouse Collection, Eureka (Ill.) Coll., War Meml., Yehud, Israel, 1989, Rutgers Collection of Art, Camden, N.J.; represented in corp. collections Devon, Inc., N.Y.C., Judy Bond, Inc., N.Y.C., Regina Porter, Inc., N.Y.C., Paramount Group, Los Angeles, Joseph P. Day Realty Corp., N.Y.C., Rubenstein Planning Corp., N.Y.C., Queensboro Steel Corp., Wilmington, N.C., Southerland Tours, St. Croix, V.I., Robert D. Scinto, Inc., Shelton, Conn., Marriott Hotel, Minnetonka, Minn., Granard Communications Ltd., London, Tauxk Tours, Westport, Conn.; exec. producer film Pupae (Cine Eagle award 1973). Recipient Knickerbocker Artist's 24th ann. exhbn. sculpture award, Met. Life sculpture award. Mem. Nat. Mus. Women in the Arts, Internat. Sculpture Ctr., Artist's Equity, Fashion Group N.Y., Advt. Women N.Y., Fashion Coalition N.Y. Address: 8 Peter Cooper Rd New York NY 10010

PINSKER, PENNY COLLIAS (PANGEOTA PINSKER), television producer; b. Miami, Fla., Aug. 22, 1942; d. Theodore Peter and Agatha Madge (Bridgeman) Collias; m. Raymond Robert Elman, Feb. 19, 1962 (dec. 1967); 1 child, Alan; m. Lewis Harry Pinsker, Oct. 22, 1968. Grad. high sch., Miami, Fla. Operator So. Bell Telephone Co., Miami, 1960-67; asst. dir. pub. affairs Sta. WCKT-TV, Miami, 1968-70; dir. public affairs Sta. WOR-AM, N.Y.C., 1971-78; reporter documentary and consumer affairs Sta. WTFM, N.Y.C., 1978-81; dir. editorials and sta. services Sta. WWOR-TV, N.Y.C. and Secaucus, N.J., 1981-87; mgr. community affairs and spl. projects Sta. WWOR-TV, Secaucus, 1987—. Author, editor: (resource directory) Sta. WOR on Crime, 1982 (recipient George Washing Medal Honor Freedom Found.), The Changing Family, 1982 (recipient Broadcast Media award San Francisco State U., Emmy nominated), A Child is Missing, 1983 (recipient Broadcast Media award San Francisco State U., Emmy nominated), Taking the High Out of High School, 1984 (recipient Broadcast Media award San Francisco State U, Angel award Religion Media, Bronze medal Internat. TV and Film Soc.). Media advisor N.J. Crime Prevention Officers Assn.; mem. communication com. Am. Heart Assn. N.J. Affiliation; bd. dirs. Queensboro Soc. Prevention Cruelty Children, 1978-83; pub. mem. N.J. Gov.'s Task Force on Child Abuse and Neglect, 1988—; mem. communications com. Am. Cancer Soc.; bd. dirs. Hoboken Chamber Orch., 1989—. Recipient disting. service award N.J. Speech-Lang.-Hearing Assn., 1987, community service award Urban League Hudson County, 1986. Mem. Nat. Broadcast Editorial Assn. (bd. dirs. 1986-87), Nat. Broadcast Assn. Community Affairs, Nat. Assn. Female Execs., Advt. Council N.J. (bd. trustees 1986—). Home: Winterwood Farm 270 Kingwood-Locktown Rd Flemington NJ 08822 Office: Sta WWOR-TV 9 Broadcast Plaza Secaucus NJ 07094

PIOTROWSKI, DONNA LYNN, finance executive; b. L.I., Sept. 18, 1960; d. Albert and Linda Patricia (Burchins) Peters; 1 child, Noelle. AS in Bus. Adminstrn., SUNY, Suffern, 1084. Office mgr., restaurant mgr. Franco's Restaurant, Montvale, N.J.; accounts mgr. The Desk Set, Eatontown, N.J.; head fin. Ninja Inc., Hackensack, N.J. Mem. NAFE. Home: 21 Foxhill Rd Chestnut Ridge NY 10977

PIPER, CAROL ADELINE, councilman; b. Chgo., Jan. 28, 1924; d. John and Myra May (Hughett) Preston; m. Robert Donald Piper, Dec. 18, 1945; children: Stephen, Barbara, Bruce, Diane. BA, North Cen. Coll., Naperville, Ill., 1945. Asst. rsch. chemist Quaker Oats Co., Chgo., 1945; office mgr. H. & R. Block, Ridgewood, N.J., 1977-82; councilman City of Naperville, 1987—. Precinct committeewoman Naperville Rep. Com., 1956070; mem. Glen Rock Pub. Library Bd., 1975, Glen Rock City Council, 1977-82. Mem. LWV (pres. Glen Rock 1972-74). Home: 104 Devon Ln Naperville IL 60540 Office: City of Naperville 175 W Jackson Ave Naperville IL 60540

PIPER, PAT KATHRYN, state senator; b. Delavan, Minn., July 16, 1934; d. Claire I. and Geneva R. (Tibodeau) P. BA, Coll. St. Teresa, Winona, Minn., 1962; MA, Cath. U., 1972. Tchr. St. Augustine Sch., Austin, Minn., 1956-58, St. Francis Sch., Rochester, Minn., 1958-60, St. James (Minn.) Sch., 1960-61; catechist St. Catherine Sch. Ctr., Luverne, Minn., 1961-63, catechist, dir., 1964-67; catechist Area Ctr., Hayfield, Minn., 1963-64; dir. St. Ann's Ctr., Slayton, Minn., 1967-69, Christian Edn. Ctr., Austin, 1969—; mem. Minn. Ho. of Reps., 1982-84, 84-86, Senate State of Minn., 1986—. Contbr. articles to profl. jours. Active United Way, YMCA, Council for Hancicapped, Salvation Army. Mem. LWV, Bus. and Profl. Women. Mem. Democratic Farm Labor Party. Roman Catholic. Lodge: Zonta. Home: 800 1st Dr NW Austin MN 55912 Office: 301D 4th Ave NE Austin MN 55912

PIPPART-BROWN, JANE T., education educator; b. Hanover, Pa., Dec. 12, 1947; d. William H. and M. Lois (Reed) Theophel; m. Eric C. Pippart, June 14, 1969 (div. Nov. 1983); m. Peter A. Brown, June 16, 1987. BS in Music Edn., West Chester U., 1969; MusM, Holy Names Coll., 1979; postgrad., Liszt Acad., Budapest, Hungary, 1986. Tchr. Warwick Sch. Dist., Lititz, Pa., 1969-87; asst. prof. music edn. Towson (Md.) U., 1982, 83, 84; cons. MaCmillan Pub. Co., N.Y., 1983-87; asst. prof. West Chester (Pa.) U., 1987—; visiting prof. kodaly Messiah Coll., Pa., 1982, 84, 89; cons. in field. Condr. MENC Millersville U., 1982; contbr. to profl. jours. Vol. United Way, Lancaster County, 1981; condr. Lancaster City Children's Chorus; active Trinity Choir. Named Outstanding Young Women Ency. Brittanica, Outstanding Educator Internat. Kodaly Educators, 1985, 86. Mem. Actors Co. Pa. (actress 1977-81), Fulton Repertory Co., Music Educators Nat. Conf., Orgn. Am. Koday Educators (co-chmn. mems. at large), Kodaly Educators Ea. Pa. (sec., treas. 1976-83), Landis Valley Mus., Kiwanis. Republican. Lutheran. Home: 1522 Esbenshade Rd Lancaster PA 17601 Office: West Chester Univ West Chester PA 19383

PIRAINO, ANN MAE, educational association administrator, vocational rehabilitation counselor; b. Vancouver, Wash.; d. Elsworth Wallace Schmoeckel and Alice Marie (Blankenbickler) Avalos; m. Michael Salvatore, Nov. 19, 1983. BA in Edn., Seattle U., 1972; MA in Appl. Behavioral Sci., City U. Leadership Inst of Sea, 1987. Sec. to supt. Pasco (Wash.) Sch. Dist. No. 1, 1972-74; adminstrv. asst. Burns and Roe, Inc., Richland, Wash., 1974-81; exec. sec. UNC Nuclear Industries, Inc., Richland, Wash., 1981-83, Fairchild Semiconductor, Inc., Puyallup, Wash., 1984-87; instr. Eton Tech. Inst. (ETI), Federal Way, Wash., 1987-89; trainer, cons. Piraino Prodns., Wash., 1988—; seminar leader and cons. Profl. Secs. Internat. (PSI), Pullman/Spokane, Wash., 1985—; cons. Federal Way Women's Network & Career Devel. Network, Wash., 1985-88; employment coord. Bus. Computer Tng. Inst., 1990; adj. faculty Office Automation Griffin Coll. Editor: (newsletter) The Circuit Writer, 1985-87; editor, pub. assn. newsletter, Hear Ye, Hear Ye, 1986-88, Training Wheels, 1987—; role expert: competency study, ASTD Competency & Stds. Project, 1988. Co. rep. United Way/Fairchild Semiconductor, Wash., 1986; team co-leader March of Dimes/Fairchild Semiconductor, Wash., 1986; team leader March of Dimes/Town Criers Toastmasters, Wash., 1989. Named Sec. of the Yr., Pas-Ric-Ken/Sea Tac Chpts., PSI, Richland/Federal Way, Wash., 1979, 84; Sec. of the Yr., Wash.-Alaska Div. PSI, Spokane, 1980. Mem. NAFE, Am. Soc. Tng. and Devel. (chpt. v.p. 1988, pres. 1990), Federal Way Women's Network, Toastmasters (team leader town criers 1990), Xi Alpha Epsilon, Beta Sigma Phi (Woman of Yr. 1979-81). Home: 7022 190th Street Ct E Puyallup WA 98373

PIRSCH, CAROL MCBRIDE, state senator, customer relations administrator; b. Omaha, Dec. 27, 1936; d. Lyle Erwin and Hilfrie Louise (Lebeck) McBride; student U. Miami, Oxford, Ohio, U. Nebr., Omaha; m. Allen I. Pirsch, Mar. 28, 1954; children—Pennie Elizabeth, Pamela Elaine, Patrice Eileen, Phyllis Erika, Peter Allen, Perry Andrew. Former mem. data processing staff Omaha Public Schs.; former mem. wage practices dept. Western Electric Co., Omaha; former legal sec., Omaha; former office mgr. Pirsch Food Brokerage Co., Inc., Omaha; former employment supr. U.S. West Communications, Omaha, now mgr. customer relations; mem. Nebr. Senate, 1979—. Bd. dirs. Nebr. Developmental Disabilities Council, Omaha Pub. Libr., Meyer Rehab. Ctr.; past pres., bd. dirs. Nebr. Coalition for Victims of Crime. Recipient Golden Elephant award; Outstanding Legis. Leadership award Nat. Orgn. Victim Assistance, Keystoner of the Month award, Outstanding Legis. Efforts award YWCA. Mem. Orgn. U.S. West Women, Nat. Order Women Legislators, Tangier Women's Aux., VASA, Pilot Internat. Assn., N.W. Civic Club, Benson Rep. Women's Club, Bus. and Profl. Rep. Women Club, Recycle Omaha, Rotary. Office: State Capitol Lincoln NE 68509

PISCATELLI, NANCY MARIE, educator; b. Boston, Feb. 11, 1953; d. Joseph Murphy and Eleanor Elizabeth (Jeffers) Kelley; m. Thomas George Piscatelli, Apr. 17, 1976; 1 child, Thomas Joseph. BS, Bridgewater State Coll., 1975; MEd, Bridgewater State U., 1979, Boston Coll., 1977; EdD, Northeastern U., 1989. With sales Wm. Filenes & Sons Co., Boston, 1969-76; tchr. Boston Pub. Schs., 1975—; cons. Tchrs. Corp. Network, 1979-80. Author/editor: (handbook) The Paraprofessional Handbook, 1979; contbr. articles to profl. jours. Campaign worker Dem. Com., Quincy, Mass., 1975—; active sch. vol. pet project of Mrs. George Bush. Mem. Am. Fedn. Tchrs., Nat. Coun. Tchrs. Math., Internat. Reading Assn., Ea. Educators Rsch. Assn., Boston Tchrs. Union, Boston Computer Soc. Roman Catholic. Home: 16 Alvin Ave North Quincy MA 02171 Office: Boston Pub Schs 26 Court St Boston MA 02108

PISCITELLO, DENISE EMILY, advertising executive; b. San Fernando, Calif., May 25, 1948; d. Robert Francis and Dorothy (Johnson) Werner; m. Charles Michael Piscitello, Mar. 5, 1946; children: Michael Carmelo, Charles Robert. AA, Los Angeles Valley Coll., 1968; BA, Calif. State U., Northridge, 1970. Prodn. artist Audio Magnetics, Gardena, Calif., 1970-71, Glenco, Sepulveda, Calif., 1971-73, Typo Grafix Inc., Reseda, Calif., 1973-75; graphic artist asst. Indsl. Electronic Engrs., Van Nuys, Calif., 1975-77, graphic artist, 1977-82, advt. mgr., 1982—. Roman Catholic. Office: Indsl Electronic Engrs 7740 Lemona Ave Van Nuys CA 91405

PISULA, BETTYSUE, automotive company business analyst; b. Det., Jan. 29, 1932; d. Stephen and Mary (Bajzat) Csiszar; m. Harry John Pisula, June 17, 1961. Student, U. Mich., Dearborn, 1979-84, Sch. Bus., Det. Exec. sec. Ford Motor, Troy, Mich., 1950-86, bus. analyst, 1988—. Sec. City Beautiful Com., Dearborn Heights, Mich., 1988—. Mem. Mich. R.R. Club, Dearborn Heights Garden Club (v.p. programs and yearbook), Mich. Orchid Soc., Friends Matthaei Bot. Gardens. Home: 26333 Wilson Dearborn Heights MI 48127

PITASI, PAMELA JOAN, sales executive; b. N.Y.C., Nov. 3, 1961; d. William Allen and Joan Vivian (Carlsen) B. Student, Skidmore Coll., Saratoga Springs, N.Y., 1983. Ins. agt. Pa. Mut. Ins. Co., N.Y.C., 1983-84; adminstrv. asst. ISOETEC Communications, Darien, Conn., 1984-87; sales mgr. EXECUTONE Info. Systems, Darien, 1987—. N.Y. State Regent's scholar, 1979. Republican. Office: EXECUTONE Info Systems 6 Thorndal Circle Darien CT 06820

PITCHER, BARBARA KENT HICKEY, volunteer; b. New Haven, Mar. 28, 1921; d. William John and Marion Louise (Bradley) Hickey; m. Donald Torrey Pitcher, Nov. 14, 1942; children: Susan Ellan Haines, David Kent, Steven Torrey. Student, Bus. Coll., New Haven, 1938. Asst. Alumni Records Yale U., New Haven, 1937-38; secretarial asst. Treas. Office Yale U., New Haven, 1938-43, Alumni Records Yale U., New Haven; asst. photographic dept. Office Pub. Affairs Yale U., New Haven, 1985—. Pres. Missionary Soc. First Ch. of Christ, New Haven, 1966; regent DAR Mary Clap Wooster, New Haven, 1989. Republican. United Church of Christ. Home: PO Box 64 North Haven CT 06473

PITCHER, GEORGIA ANN, psychologist, educator; b. Indpls., Feb. 22, 1927; d. Arling Edgar and Lyda Lucille (Doty) Pitcher; m. Donald Aubrey Baker, Aug. 21, 1948 (div.); children: Catherine Lucille, Martha Ann, Susan Jane, Daniel Pitcher. BS, Butler U., 1948, MS, 1951; PhD, Purdue U., 1969. Asst. prof. Butler U., Indpls., 1964-68; asst. prof. Purdue U., West Lafayette, Ind., 1969-74; dir. psychol. svcs. St. Elizabeth Hosp., Lafayette, Ind., 1974-81; pvt. practice psychologist, Indpls., 1981—; asst. prof. pediatrics, sr. psychologist Riley Hosp. Child Devel. Ctr. Ind. U. Med. Ctr., Indlpls., 1990—; assoc. faculty Ind. U.-Purdue U. at Indpls., 1985—; med. cons. Social Security Adminstrn., 1986-88. Contbr. articles to profl. jours. Bd. dirs. United Cerebral Palsy of Ind., 1971—, chmn. com. human svcs., 1987—; mem. protective svcs. task force exec. com. State of Ind., 1976-77. Mem. Nat. Acad. Neuropsychology, Am. Psychol. Assn., Ind. Psychol. Assn., Am. Ednl. Rsch. Assn., Kappa Kappa Gamma. Democrat. Home: 3725 E Thompson Rd Indianapolis IN 46237 Office: 537 Turtle Creek South Dr Suite 14 Indianapolis IN 46227

PITCHER, HELEN IONE, advertising executive; b. Colorado Springs, Colo., Aug. 6, 1931; d. William Forest Medlock and Frankie La Vone (Hamilton) Tweed; m. Richard Edwin Pitcher, Sept. 16, 1949; children: Dushka Myers, Suzanne, Marc. Student, U. Colo., 1962-64, Ariz. State U., 1966, Maricopa Tech. Coll., 1967, Scottsdale Community Coll., 1979-81. Design draftsman Sundstrand Aviation, Denver, 1962-65; tech. illustrator Sperry, Phoenix, 1966-68; art dir. Integrated Circuit Engring., Scottsdale, Ariz., 1968-71, dir. advt., 1981—; advt. artist Motorola Inc., Phoenix, 1971-74; pres. Pitcher Tech. Pubs., Scottsdale, 1974-81. Profl. advisor Paradise Valley Sch. Dist., Phoenix, 1984—; mem. bd. advisors graphic arts dept. Ariz. State U., Tempe. mem. Nat. Audio Visual Assn., Bus. Profl. Advt. Assn. (treas. 1982-86), Direct Mktg. Club. Democrat. Mem. Ch. Christ. Office: Integrated Cir Engring Corp 15022 N 75th St Scottsdale AZ 85260

PITCHER, JUDITH MITCHELL, federal government agency division director; b. Stephenson County, Ill., July 9, 1941; d. James Edward Mitchell and Mabel Marie (Wiegmann) Crawford; m. Hugh Martin Pitcher, June 13, 1964 (div. 1974); children: Elizabeth Ann, Susan Reid; m. Ronald Aaron Eisenberg, Feb. 29, 1976 (div. 1983); 1 child, Mitchell David. BS in Maths., Newcomb Coll. Tulane U., 1963; PhD in Program Econs., Northwestern U., 1967, MA in Econs., 1968. Asst. Econometrics Rsch. Ctr., Evanston, Ill., 1963-65; instr. econs. evening Northwestern U., Chgo., 1966; instr. econs. Roosevelt U., 1966-67; lectr. econs., instr. statistics U. Ky., 1967-71; econ. cons. Jack Faucett & Assocs., Chevy Chase, Md., 1971-72; sr. economist, retail trade div. The Price Commn. Consumer Product Safety Commn., 1972-73; sr. economist. Bureau of Econ. Analysis, Washington, 1973-79; dir. spl. studies div. Consumer Product Safety Commn., Washington, 1979-88, dir., program analysis div., 1988—. Referee and ofcl. Montgomery County Md. Swim League, 1980—; social dir. exec. bd. Montgomery Single Parents, 1985; treas., 1986-87; mem. alumni admissions com. Tulane U., New Orleans, 1985-87. Mem. Am. Econ. Assn., Com. on the Status of Women in the Econs. Profession (exec. bd. 1976-77), Nat. Economists Club, Wash. Women Economists, Nat. Assn. Profl. & Exec. Women, Palisades Inc. (bd. dirs. 1982-89, sec. 1979-81), Omicron Delta Epsilon. Democrat. Home: 3314 Quesada St NW Washington DC 20015 Office: US Consumer Product Safety Program Analysis Div Econs Washington DC 20207

PITELKA, SANDRA LEA, office manager; b. Burbank, Calif., May 23, 1947; d. Albert Ely Sanders and Edith Carol (Jontra) Dijeau; m. Louis Frank Pitelka, Sept. 20, 1969; children: Erik Loren, Jessica Kristine. BA, U. Calif., Davis, 1969. Real estate broker Deemer/Pitelka Realty, New Gloucester, Maine, 1979-81; exec. asst. Oral-B Labs., Redwood City, Calif., 1985-87; office mgr. Greylock Mgmt., Palo Alto, Calif., 1987—. Office: Greylock Mgmt 181 Lytton Ave Suite 100 Palo Alto CA 94301

PITHAN, MAXINE HELEN, librarian; b. Aurelia, Iowa, Aug. 27, 1931; d. Henry Albert and Anna Sophia (Pingel) Roggow; m. Virgil John Pithan, Aug. 8, 1954 (div. Aug. 1972); children: Bernie Russell, Gregory John. BA in Phys. Edn. and Spanish, Buena Vista Coll., Storm Lake, Iowa, 1969; MA in Libr. and Mdeia, U. S.D., 1979. Tchr. phys. edn. and Spanish, St. Mary's High Sch., Storm Lake, 1969-70; libr. Manilla (Iowa) Community Sch., 1971-90, Anthon (Iowa)-Oto Community Sch., 1990—. Mem. Iowa Ednl. Media Assn., AAUW (v.p. program Denison, Iowa 1988-90). Lutheran. Home: 1507 3d Ave N Denison IA 51442 Office: Anthon-Oto Community Sch Anthon IA 51004

PITKAPAASI, ELIN LYDIA, construction executive; b. Phila., June 4, 1952; d. Unto and Wilma Helen (Koski) P.; (div. 1981). BA in Psychology, Calif. State U., Fullerton, 1980; postgrad., Drexel U., 1981-86. Sec. Constrn. Coordinated, Inc., Conshohocken, Pa., 1981-82, adminstrv. asst., 1982-83, asst. project mgr., 1983-85, project mgr., 1985—. Vol. coach AMBUCS Spl. Olympics, Conshohocken, 1988—; vol. Am. Assn. Emergency Med. Technicians, Orange County, Calif., 1975-77, CAP, Bryn Mawr, Pa. and Orange County, 1968-73. Democrat. Home: 1000 Conestoga Rd #C349 Rosemont PA 19010 Office: Constrn Coordinated Inc 101 E 8th Ave PO Box 508 Conshohocken PA 19428

PITMAN, JULIE AHRENS, advertising executive; b. Rochelle, Ill., Jan. 26, 1960; d. Theodore Walter and Roberta (McKinney) Ahrens; m. Christopher Gerald Pitman, Aug. 12, 1989. BA in Music, Colo. State U., 1983; postgrad., Houston Community Coll., 1986, Butler U., 1988—. Asst. mgr. Miller's Outpost, Houston, 1984-85; head sales asst. MMT Sales, Houston, 1985-87; media asst. Garrison, Jasper, Rose and Co., Indpls., 1987-88, media buyer, broadcast traffic mgr., 1988—. Active Indpls. Symphonic Choir, 1988—. Mem. Am. Women in Radio and TV. Republican. Presbyterian. Office: Garrison Jasper Rose and Co 8440 Woodfield Crossing 280 Indianapolis IN 46240

PITMAN, KARIN MARIE, architect; b. Stuttgart, Fed. Republic Germany, Mar. 7, 1961; d. Kenneth Maurice and Marilynn Sue (Holland) P. BArch, Ariz. State U., 1984. Registered architect, Ariz. Job capt. Allen & Philp Architects, Phoenix, 1984-85; designer Ellermann & Schick Architects, Phoenix, 1985-87; project mgr. James Abell & Assocs., Tempe, Ariz., 1987-88; project designer Cappello & Woker Architects, Phoenix, 1988-89; part-time instr., faculty assoc. Ariz. State U., Tempe, 1988-89; archtl. designer Habitat, Inc., Tempe, 1989-90; project architect James Abell & Assocs., Tempe, 1990—; pres. Pre-profl. Arhitecture Orgn., Ariz. State U., Tempe, 1980-81; v.p. Coll. Architecture Student Coun., Ariz. State U., Tempe, 1982-83. Illustrator: (student handbook) From Classroom to Market Place, 1988. Youth coord. Cath. Youth Alive in the Spirit, Phoenix, 1985-86; youth coord. life teen program Our Lady of Mt. Carmel Cath. Ch., Tempe, 1988-90. Phoenix Blueprint scholar, 1982. Mem. AIA (participant search for shelter 1987), Toastmasters Internat., Alpha Lambda Delta. Mailing Address: 3409 S Rural Rd #243 Tempe AZ 85282

PITOU, PENNY, travel agency owner, professional skier; b. Bayside, L.I., N.Y., Oct. 8, 1938; d. Augustus and Eulalie (Schaefer) Pitou; m. Egon Norbert Zimmermann, Feb. 19, 1961; children—Christian Egon, Kim Erik; m. Milo L. Pike, Sept. 1, 1981. Student Middlebury Coll., 1957. Cert. profl. ski instr., 1965. Operator, co-dir. Penny Pitou Ski Sch., Gunstock, N.H., 1961-68. Blue Hills, Mass., 1963-68; ski fashion cons. White Stag, 1960, 70, Montgomery Ward, J.C. Penney; coach girl's ski team Laconia High Sch., N.H., 1965-66; owner Penny Pitou Travel, Inc., Laconia, N.H., 1974—, Concord, N.H., 1979—, Plymouth, N.H., 1985-88, Wolfeboro, N.H., 1985-88, Portsmouth, N.H., 1986—; bd. dirs. Laconia People's Nat. Bank, 1967-68. Appeared various TV programs including What's My Line, To Tell the Truth, The Today Show; appeared numerous mag. covers; speaker various orgns.; mem. travel agts. adv. bd. Austrian Tourist Office. Chmn. bd. advisors Wildcat Winners Circle, U. N.H., 1981—; bd. dirs. Odyssey House, Portsmouth, 1985—, Greater Portsmouth Community Found., Futures Program, Portsmouth, Portsmouth Acad. Performing Arts. Recipient numerous awards including two silver medals Winter Olympics, Squaw Valley, Calif., 1960, New Eng. Council award, 1960, Nat. Ski Hall of Fame award, 1961; named Woman of Yr., Mademoiselle mag., 1965; rep. Pres. Gerald Ford as head of presl. del. at Olympics, Innsbruck, Austria, 1976. Home: 169 Potter Hill Rd Gilford NH 03246 Office: Penny Pitou Travel Inc 55 Canal St Laconia NH 03246

PITRONE, JEAN MADDERN, instructor, writer; b. Ishpeming, Mich., Dec. 20, 1920; d. William Courtney and Gladys Mae (Beer) Maddern; m. Anthony Pitrone, Oct. 26, 1940; children: Joseph, Jill, Anthony Jr., Joyce, John, Janet, Julie, Jane, Cheryl. Grad. high sch., Ishpeming. Short story instr. Writer's Digest Sch., Cin., 1971-89. Author: Trailblazer, 1969, Tangled Web: Legacy of Auto Pioneer John F. Dodge, 1989, Hud's: Hub of America's Heartland, 1990, others. Mem. Detroit Women Writers (pres. 1981-83). Republican. Roman Catholic. Home: 3878 Pare Ln Trenton MI 48183

PITTIUS, DOLORES GENEVIEVE, educator; b. Elizabeth, N.J., Dec. 15, 1932; d. Louis Valentine and Madeline Marcella (Monaghan) P. BS, Jersey City State Coll., 1954; MA, Seton Hall U., 1957, postgrad., 1970. Cert. tchr., prin., sch. adminstr., N.J.; enrolled agt. IRS. Tchr. Union (N.J.) Bd. Edn., 1954-56, Linden (N.J.) Bd. Edn., 1956-58; tchr. Keansburg (N.J.) Bd. Edn., 1959-67, 85—, sch. prin., 1967-85; income tax preparer, instr., office supr. H&R Block, Elizabeth, 1970—; playground dir. City of Elizabeth, 1953-64, arts and crafts supr., 1955-64; Head Start tchr., dir. Keansburg Bd. Edn., 1965-68, summer sch. dir., 1967-69. Mem. NEA, N.J. Edn. Assn., Keansburg Tchrs.' Assn. (sec. 1963-64, v.p. 1964-65, pres. 1965-66), N.J. PTA (life). Republican. Roman Catholic. Home: 208 Keats Ave Elizabeth NJ 07208 Office: Port Monmouth Rd Sch 140 Port Monmouth Rd Keansburg NJ 07734

PITTMAN, LAURA JANINE, title company executive, artist; b. Monmouth, Ill., Nov. 21, 1943; d. Lawrence E. and Betty Jean (Tucker) McKee; m. Thomas E. Ewinger Sr., Oct. 31, 1962 (div.); children: Thomas E. Jr., Desiree Michelle, Aimee Nicole; m. Kerwin Lee Pittman, Sept. 1, 1974. Grad. high sch., Biggsville, Ill. Buyer J.S. Schranm Co., Burlington, Iowa, 1961-62; sales advisor Ewinger Appliance Co., Burlington, 1963-70; designer Ferris Furniture, Galesburg, Ill., 1974; owner Wilhelmenas Health Spa, Burlington, 1970-72, Beavers Ltd., Galesburg, 1974-76; artist, owner Laura Janine Studios, Freeport, Ill., 1974—; customer rels. Bank Pecatonica, Ill., 1980-82—; pres., chairwoman bd. Northwestern Ill. Title Co., Inc., Freeport, 1982—. Bd. dirs. Freeport Art Mus., 1989—; fin. com. Embury Meth. Ch., Freeport, 1988—. Mem. Am. Land Title Assn., Ill. Land Title Assn., Rockford Bd. Realtors, Green County Bd. Realtors, Wis. Bd. Realtors, Freeport Bd. Realtors. Office: Northwestern Ill Title Co 116 W Exchange St Freeport IL 61032

PITTMAN, MARY GWENDOLYN B., educator; b. Jasper, Ala., Dec. 30, 1928; d. Vivian Collymore and Alice Ruth (McSheridan) Barrow; m. Albert Bertis Pittman, Oct. 14, 1950; children: Albert Bertis Jr., Faran, David, Sheridan (dec.). BS in Biol. Sci., Auburn U., 1950. Tchr. sci. Aiken (S.C.) County Schs., 1952-54; tchr. sci. York (S.C.) County Schs., 1960-65, Rock Hill, 1966-67; tchr. sci. Catawba Acad., Rock Hill, 1968-72, Union County Schs., Monroe, 1973-87. Precinct chmn. Monroe Rep. Cen. Com., 1985-86; active N.C. Wildlife Resources Commn. NSF scholar, 1969-70. Mem. NEA, Arbor Club, Waxnaw Scottish Soc., Internat. Garden Club (pres. 1963-64). Mem. Ch. of Christ. Home: 1601 Commodores Ct Surfside Beach SC 29575

PITTMAN, NATALIE ANNE, paralegal, society executive; b. Detroit, Apr. 17, 1952; d. George Jack and Catherine Helen (Platusich) Ochenski; children: Erik Garrett Pittman, Jason Christopher Pittman; m. John Robert Pittman, Dec. 16, 1977; stepchildren: Mark Allen, David Robert. AS with highest honors, Cen. Tex. Coll., 1985. Owner, mgr. pet store, Killeen, Tex., 1977-85; paralegal Silverblatt Law Office, Killeen, 1985—; corp. sec. Am. Budgerigar Soc., Inc., Killeen, 1986—; mem. adv. com. Legal Assistant's Program, Killeen, 1989—. Editorial advisor Know Your Pet-Budgerigars, 1987. Speaker legal assistant's program Cen. Tex. Coll., Killeen, 1986—; spokesman Concerned Citizens for Quality Edn., Killeen, 198l; pres. Peeble Sch. PTA, Killeen, 1984; mem. Killeen High Sch. Band Boosters, 1987—; umpire state softball tournaments, 1976; also active other polit. and civic orgns. Mem. State Bar Tex. (legal asst. div.), Nat. Notary Assn., Am. Budgerigar Soc. (bd. dirs. 1986—, Mem. of Yr. award 1988), Dallas-Ft. Worth Exhbn. Budgerigar Club (show sec. 1989), Heart 'O Tex. Exhbn. Budgerigar Club (founding). Republican. Roman Catholic. Home and Office: 1704 Kangaroo Ave Killeen TX 76543

PITTS, BONITA JANELL, television station official; b. Macon, Ga., June 27, 1964; d. Samuel Joseph and Jimmie (Black) P. BS in Communication Arts, Ga. So. Coll., 1986. Receptionist Sta. WGXA-TV, Macon, 1986, videographer, 1986-87, sales svc. dir., 1987-88; assoc. producer Tribune Creative Svcs., Atlanta, 1988-889; promotion producer Sta. WGNX-TV, Atlanta, 1989—; promotion coord. Jeff Malone Enterprises/Basketball Clinic, Macon, 1987-88. Mem. NAFE, Alpha Kappa Alpha. Methodist. Home: 536 Windmont Dr Atlanta GA 30329 Office: Sta WGNX-TV 1810 Briarcliff Rd NE Atlanta GA 30329

PITTS, WENDY JO, banker; b. St. Louis, Mar. 18, 1956; d. Joseph Max Michaels and Joan Eleanor (Weiss) Gutmann; m. Robert Brantson Pitts, Apt. 20, 1980 (div. Jan. 1988). Student, Ohio U., 1974-77. Supr. ops. No. Trust Co., Chgo., 1977-79; customer service rep. internat. banking Chase Manhattan Bank, N.Y.C., 1980-81; customer service rep. Allied Irish Bank, N.Y.C., 1981-82; br. mgr., officer United Counties Trust Co., Cranford, N.J., 1982-87, CenTrust Savs. Bank, Orlando, Fla., 1988—. Mem. Winter Park (Fla.) C. of C., Greater Orlando (Fla.) C. of C. Republican. Home: 420 Friar Rd Winter Park FL 32792 Office: Great Western Bank 1395 Semoran Blvd Casselberry FL 32707

PITURRO, MARLENE COHEN, managerial psychologist, business writer; b. N.Y.C., Mar. 17, 1947; d. Murray M. and Lillian (Urdang) Cohen; m. Frank P. Piturro, Oct. 31, 1972 (div. Oct. 1978); m. Howard M. Van Hyning, Nov. 20, 1983; children: Victoria, Kirk. BA summa cum laude, Adelphi U., 1968; MA, Fordham U., 1970, PhD, 1973; MBA in MIS, Iona Coll., 1982. Lic. psychologist, N.Y. State. Cons. Greer Woodycrest, Pomona, N.Y., 1979-81, Westchester Assn. for Retarded Citizens, White Plains, N.Y., 1981-84; internal cons. Mfrs. Hanover Trust, N.Y.C., 1984-86; seminar leader SUNY at Empire Coll., Hartsdale, N.Y., 1984—; freelance bus. writer N.Y. Times, Daily News, Working Woman, Westchester, 1986—; adj. prof. Cornell U. Sch. Indsl. and Labor Rels., Purchase, N.Y., 1988; coord. New Writers' Hotline, N.Y.C., 1989; designated writer Hong Kong Econ. Trade Office, 1989. Author: Business Finance, 1989; contbr. articles to various publs. Mem. Conscientious Mil. Tax Resistance Com., 1986—; mem. exec. bd. Legal Awareness Westchester, 1989. Regent's scholar Fordham U. scholar, NSF scholar, 1970, Writer's Circle award Electronic Networking Assn., 1989. Mem. Nat. Writers' Union, Westchester Assn. Women Bus. Owners (pres. 1982-84). Democrat. Mem. Soc. of Friends. Home and Office: 3 Wagner Pl Hastings-on-Hudson NY 10706

PITZER, BETTY BRAUN, social services administrator; b. Springfield, Ohio, Aug. 7, 1912; d. Frank J. and Alnora (Hagerman) Braun; m. Elwood Gilbert Pitzer, Oct. 2, 1936; children: Philip Elwood, Richard Alan. BA in Bus. Adminstrn., Wittenberg U., 1933. Asst. mgr. Baker's Cafeteria, Springfield, 1933-41; fin. sec. Credit Life Ins. Co., Springfield, 1933-41; pres. Ohio Assn. Alpha Delta Pi, Springfield, 1956-58; nat. treas. Alpha Delta Pi Sorority, Atlanta, 1963-79; assoc. dir. United Way Clark County, Springfield, 1965-69; exec. dir. Elderly United Springfield and Clark County, Springfield, 1969—; com. mem. Area Agy. on Aging, Dayton, Ohio, 1979-83, Ohio Gov.'s Conf. on Aging, Columbus, 1979-81, Home Care Adv. Com., Springfield, 1981-84, Ohio Commn. on Aging State Fair, Columbus, 1979-82; Clark County coord. White House Conf. on Aging, 1971. Pres. Adelphean Found., Atlanta, 1964-71; mem. fiscal rev. com. City of Springfield, 1982; mem. alumni coun. Wittenberg U., Springfield. Recipient Distinq. Alumna award Wittenberg U., 1975, gov.'s award State of Ohio, 1982, Svc. to Mankind award

Sertoma Club, Springfield, 1984, Meritorious Svc. award Community Hosp., Springfield, 1984, Hall of Fame award United Way Clark County, 1987. Mem. Ohio Assn. Sr. Ctrs., Ohio Citizens Coun. (policy bd.), Miami Valley Coun. on Gerontology, Zonta (pres. Springfield 1970-72), Alpha Delta Pi (Alumna of Yr. award 1987). Republican. Lutheran. Home: Ill Englewood Dr Springfield OH 45504

PIVNICKA, BARBARA MILLIKEN, public relations executive; b. Fremont, Nebr., Apr. 24, 1953; d. James Dale and Jane (Little) Milliken; m. Richard J. Pivnicka, Sept. 24, 1977. BA in English and Art History magna cum laude, U. San Francisco, 1975. Dir. pub. rels. Schwabacher/Frey Inc., San Francisco, 1977-79; dir. mktg. and pub. rels. Beier and Gunderson, Oakland, Calif., 1979-83; dir. pub. rels. Servamatic Systems Inc., San Ramon, Calif., 1983-86; mgr. pub. rels. Deloitte & Touche, San Francisco, 1986—. Editor Servamatic Jour., 1983, Roulac Register Newsletter, 1986—. Dir. Sanctuary for the Homeless, San Francisco, 1986—, The Support Ctr., San Francisco; mem. Arthritis Found., San Francisco, 1986—; mem. Learning Through Edn. in the Arts project, 1987—. Mem. Internat. Assn. Bus. Communicators, Am. Mgmt. Soc., Sales and Mktg. Execs. Assn. Republican. Roman Catholic. Home: 5530 Moraga Ave Piedmont CA 94611 Office: Deloitte & Touche 50 Fremont St San Francisco CA 94105

PIZIAK, VERONICA KELLY, physician; b. Oak Bluffs, Mass.; d. Sylvester John and Annie (Rogers) Kelly; m. Robert Piziak, Aug. 13, 1966. BS, U. Mass., 1963, MS, 1965, PhD, 1970; MD, U. Ky., 1976. Diplomate Am. Bd. Internal Medicine, Am. Bd. Endocrinology and Metabolism, Am. Bd. Med. Examiners. Rsch. assoc. div. endocrinology Univ. Fla. Coll. Medicine, Gainesville, 1970-73; rsch. assoc. dept. biochemistry U. Ky., Lexington, 1973-74; resident in internal medicine Akron (Ohio) Gen. Med. Ctr., 1976-79; fellow in endocrinology and metabolism U. Cin. Coll. Medicine, 1979-81; asst. prof. medicine and endocrinology Tex. A&M U., College Station, 1981-83, assoc. prof. medicine and endocrinology, 1983—; dir. Diabetes Ctr. Scott and White Clinic, Temple, Tex., 1985—, dir. Obesity Program, 1989—, dir. Med. Supply Store, 1987—, sr. staff physician, 1981—. Contbr. numerous articles to med. jours. Fellow ACP; mem. AMA, Tex. Med. Assn., Bell County Med. Soc. (exec. com.), Am. Men and Women of Sci., Am. Diabetes Assn. (local bd. dirs., regional profl. edn. com. 1986—, program coord. for ann. sci. meeting. 1987), Tex. Diabetes and Endocrine Assn. (chair regional profl. edn. com. 1989-90, exec. coun. 1981—, sec.-treas. 1986—), Endocrine Soc., So. Med. Assn. (chair medicine sect. 1986-87, vice-chair 1987-88, sec. medicine sect. 1990-93). Office: Scott and White Clinic 2401 S 31st St Temple TX 76508

PIZOR, KATHLEEN NATHANA, psychotherapist; b. Clarksburg, W.Va., Apr. 5, 1949; d. Lewis Preston and Eunice Elizabeth (Wilfong) Cox; m. James Clyde Pizor, June 10, 1972; children: Tovarich Kiev, Epiphany Elizabeth. BA, NYU, 1971; MA, Santa Clara U., 1986. Lic. marriage, family and child therapist, Calif. Tchr. Santa Clara (Calif.) Adult Edn., 1980-85; therapist Almaden Valley Youth Counseling, San Jose, Calif., 1984-85; instr. Nat. U., San Jose, 1987-88; pvt. practice, Los Altos, Calif., 1988—; mem. adv. bd. Santa Clara Sch. Dist., 1988-91. Contbr. articles to profl. jours. Leader Camp Fire, Sunnyvale, Calif., 1984-90; pres. Nursing Mother's Coun., 1978-79. Mem. Calif. Assn. Marriage and Family Therapy, Santa Clara U. Alumni Assn. (pres. counseling psychology div. 1990-91). Democrat. Methodist. Home: 20641 McClellan Rd Cupertino CA 95014 Office: 851 Fremont Ave Ste 214 Los Altos CA 94024

PIZZAMIGLIO, NANCY ALICE, performing company executive; b. Oak Park, Ill., Aug. 22, 1936; d. Howard Joseph and Marian Louise (Henne) Gilman; m. Ernest George Lovas, May 17, 1957 (div. Nov. 1976); children: Lori Dianne, Randall Gilman; m. Albert Theodore Pizzamiglio, Mar. 27, 1978. Student, North Tex. State U., 1955-56. Stewardess North Cen. Airlines, Chgo., 1956-57; receptionist Leo Burnett Advt. Agy., Chgo., 1957-59; office mgr. Judy Stallons Employment Agy., Oak Brook, Ill., 1973-75; mgr. and escort Prestige Vacations, Inc., Oak Brook, Ill., 1975-76; corp. dir. Al Pierson Big Band U.S.A., Inc., Aubrey, Tex., 1976—, Al Pierson, Ltd., Aubrey, Tex., 1978—; corp. pres. Gilman, Inc. Artists Mgmt., Aubrey, Tex., 1982—; owner Dancing Horse Ranch, Aubrey, Tex., 1983—; bus. mgr. Guy Lombardo's Royal Canadians, Aubrey, Tex., 1989—. Editor: (newsletter) Property Owners Assn., 1972-73; contbr. articles to profl. jours. Recipient expert award NRA, 1952. Mem. U.S. Lipizzan Registry (bd. dirs. 1986-89), Dallas Dressage Club (bd. dirs. 1988—), Am. Horse Shows Assn., Am. Quarter Horse Assn., U.S. Dressage Fedn. (qualified rider 1989, third-all breeds, first level 1989). Republican. Episcopalian. Home and Office: Rte 1 PO Box 149 Aubrey TX 76227

PLACE, DENISE LISETTE MARIE, administrator; b. Concord, N.H., June 13, 1961; d. Joseph Michael Wescott and Georgette Aline Marie (Dupont) Lavalliere. Student, U. N.H., Durham, 1979-83, BS in Bus. Adminstrn. Vice pres. AIESEC U.S., Inc., N.Y.C., 1983-84; mktg. mgr. asst. CODAREC, Brussels, Belgium, 1984; mgr. Francestown Village Store, 1985-88; adminstrv. asst. Dept. Quality Mgmt., Health N.E., Inc., Manchester, N.H., dept. adminstr., 1988—; session leader AIESEC, U.S. Regional Conf., Ohio, 1983; U. N.H., Durham; acct. rep. mktg. staff U. N.J. div., 1981, pres., 1982-83, chmn. Belgium Nat. Conv., 1984. Fundraiser N.H. Kidney Found., U. N.H., 1982; corp. fundraising session leader AIESEC U.S. Regional Conf., Boston, 1986; com. mem. employee pace-setter campaign United Way, 1988; exit poller CBS News, Manchester, 1988. Home: 313 Manchester St Manchester NH 03103

PLACEK, MARJORIE YOUNGBLOOD, health facility administrator; b. Cleve., Oct. 26, 1944; d. Melvin Anthony and Magdalene Anna (Suppan) Youngblood. BSN, Case Western Res. U., 1968; MSIA, Carnegie Mellon U., 1988; MN, U. Pitts., 1974, MNEd, 1980. RN, Pa. Staff devel. inst. Fairfax (Va.) Hosp.; asst. dir. nursing, dir. staff dvel./patient edn., dir. quality assurance West Penn Hosp., Pitts.; v.p. quality assurance Gen. Found., Lancaster, Pa.; speaker on quality improvement and quality assurance. Mem. allocations panel United Way Lancaster County, 1989-90, restructuring task force, 1990; strategic planning com. Lancaster-Lebanon Literacy Coun., 1989, bd. dirs. planning com., 1990. Cecilia A. Evans scholar. Mem. AAUW, ANA, NAFE, Am. Hosp. Assn., Am. Mgmt. Assn. Am. Mktg. Assn., Am. Coll. Healthcare Execs., Nat. League for Nursing, Sigma Theta Tau. Home: 3107 Dale Dr Lancaster PA 17601 Office: Lancaster Gen Hosp Found 555 N Duke St Lancaster PA 17603

PLACEK-ZIMMERMAN, ELLYN CLARE, educator, consultant; b. Chgo., Sept. 3, 1951; d. Clarence Joseph and Jerrine LaMarr (Ruhlow) Placek; m. Allan John Zimmerman, Aug. 10, 1974; 1 child, Alissa Jan. B.S., No. Ill., 1973, M.S., 1977, C.A.S., 1978, Ed.D., 1982. Tchr. Arlington Heights Pub. Sch., Ill., 1973-75, 75-76, dir. library and learning ctr., 1976-81, tchr. lang. arts and reading jr. high sch., 1981-84, tchr. kindergarten, 1984-86; prin. Pritchett Sch., Buffalo Grove, Ill., 1989—; dir. Ill. State grant "At Risk Program" for pre-sch. children, Cary Pub. Schs., 1986-87. mem. part-time faculty Coll. of Edn., Roosevelt U., Chgo., 1983-84, 88—; tchr. jr. high sch. studies, 1988; cons. in field; mem. steering com. Curriculum'90 Conf., De Kalb, Ill., 1985; lectr. in field; mem. registration com. Fall conf. IASCD, 1987; supr. student tchrs. Ill. State U., Normal, 1986, Roosevelt U., Chgo., 1988—. Contbg. author: Feeling Good About Food. Sec. Scarsdale Estates Homeowners Assn., Arlington Heights, 1983; hon. life mem. PTA. Mem. Ill. Assn. for Supervision and Curriculum Devel. (triple I arrangements com. 1988, registration com. for fall conf. 1987), Ill. Assn. Tchrs. of English (cons., speaker conf. 1984), Ill. Women Adminstrs. (publicity com. conf. 1985). Avocation: playing guitar, calligraphy. Home: 402 E Orchard Arlington Heights IL 60005 Office: Pritchett Sch Buffalo Grove IL 60089 also: Roosevelt U 430 S Michigan Ave Chicago IL 60605

PLACIENTE, SIONY ARANETA, dietitian; b. Manila, Philippines, Dec. 9, 1944; came to U.S., 1964; d. Ramon and Jacinta (Mercado) Araneta; m. Ramon M. Placiente, Oct. 28, 1967; children: Raymond John, Cynthia Araneta. BS, U. Santo Tomas, Manila, 1964; MS, NYU, 1967. Registered dietitian. Clin. and adminstv. dietitian Coney Island Hosp., Bklyn., 1965-66, St. John's Hosp., Queens, N.Y., 1966-67, Jersey City Med. Ctr., 1967-69, United Hosps., Newark, N.J., 1969-72; dir. dept. dietetics Montebello Hosp., Balt., 1972-88, Springfield Hosp., Sykesville, Md., 1988—; cons. dietitian Pleasant Manor Nursing Ctr., Balt., 1981—; owner Ray-Cyn's Restaurant, Balt., 1988—. Mem. Am. Dietetic Assn., Md. Dietetic Assn. Democrat. Roman Catholic. Home: 9107 Kilbride Rd Baltimore MD 21236 Office: Springfield Hosp. Rte 32 Sykesville MD 21784

PLAINE, LLOYD LEVA, lawyer; b. Washington, Sept. 3, 1947. BA, U. Pa., 1969; postgrad., Harvard U.; JD, Georgetown U., 1975. Bar: D.C. 1975. Legis. asst. to U.S. Rep. Disney Yates, 1971-72; ptnr. Sutherland, Asbill & Brennan, Washington. Fellow Am. Bar Found., Am. Coll. Probate Counsel; mem. ABA. Office: Sutherland Asbill & Brennan 1275 Pennsylvania Ave NW Washington DC 20004*

PLAISTED, CAROLE ANN, teacher; b. Meredith, N.H., Apr. 3, 1939; d. Morris Holman and Christina Martin (Dunn) P. BEd with honors, Plymouth (N.H.) Tchrs. Coll., 1960; MA, Columbia U., 1966; cert., N.Y. Inst. Photography, 1990. Cert. tchr., N.H. Tchr. Lang St. Sch., Meredith, 1960-61, Mechanic St. Sch., Laconia, N.H., 1961-62, Wheelock Lab. Sch., Keene, N.H., 1963—; summer tchr. Cheshire County Headstart, Hinsdale, N.H., 1965; tchr. children's lit. Keene State Coll., 1974, 75; classroom evaluator D.C. Health Co., Lexington, Mass., 1985-86; dist. trainer for drug edn. supervisory unit, Keene, 1988—. Author: The Graduates Speak, 1990; co-author curriculum materials; contbr. Kindergarten: A Sourcebook for School and Home, 1984. Trustee Reed Free Libr., Surry, N.H., 1988—; program chair Wheelock Sch. PTA, 1964-65. Named Outstanding Elem. Tchr. of Am., 1973. Mem. Associated Photographers Internat., Delta Kappa Gamma (corr. sec. Alpha chpt. 1972-76, state scholarship chmn. 1985—, Beta Alpha state scholarship 1989). Office: Wheelock Sch 340 Joslin Rd Surry NH 03431

PLAKANS, SHELLEY SWIFT, social worker, psychotherapist; b. Boston, Aug. 29, 1943; d. William Nye and Phyllis (Childs) Swift; m. John Joseph Guinan Jr. (div. 1975); children: Ashley, Lindsey Guinan, John Jeffrey, Daniel Plakans; m. John Plakans. AB, Wheaton Coll., 1965; MEd, Fitchburg (Mass.) State Coll., 1977; MSW, Simmons Sch. of Social Work, Boston, 1987. Lic. ind. clin. social worker, Mass. Staff psychologist Ayer (Mass.) Guidance Ctr., 1978-81; family therapist North Shore Community Mental Health Ctr., Salem, Mass., 1984-85; psychotherapist Boston-North Shore Assocs., Salem, 1985-90; clinician Caldwell Sch., Fitchburg, 1977-79; counselor Couryner, Guinan & Murray Counseling Assocs., Concord, Mass., 1979-81; social worker North Shore Children's Hosp., Salem, 1986-88, case mgr. Diagnostic Evaluation Ctr., North Shore Children's Hosp., 1988-90. Mediator Lynn (Mass.) Youth Resource Bur., 1986-87. Mem. Nat. Assn. Social Workers, Mass. Acad. Clin. Social Work, Inc. Office: 1 Pleasant Ln Marblehead MA 01945

PLANIT, JAN HOLLY, modeling agency executive; b. Bklyn., May 20, 1961; d. Harold and Marlene Kaplan; m. Michael Robert Planit, Nov. 22, 1989. BA, Ithaca Coll., 1983. Studio mgr. Maury Hammond Photography, Inc., N.Y.C., 1983-84; booking agt. Elite Models, Inc., N.Y.C., 1984-86, Wilhelmina Models, Inc., N.Y.C., 1987-89; account exec. Pluzynski Assocs., N.Y.C., 1986-87; v.p. Next Mgmt., Inc., N.Y.C., 1989—. Mem. N.Y. Fashion Guild (speaker 1990—). Office: Next Mgmt Inc 115 E 57th St Ste 1540 New York NY 10022

PLANK, DOROTHY DIANE GARLING, health facility administrator; b. Hazleton, Pa., Sept. 30, 1962; d. Karl Ronald and Doris Elaine (Zern) Garling; m. Michael Donald Plank, June 1, 1985. BS in Social Svc. and Spanish, Lebanon Valley Coll., Annville, Pa., 1984; MS in Gerontology, Va. Commonwealth U., 1987. Freelance writer Senior Citizens Gazette, Virginia Beach, Va., 1988-89; freelance writer, columnist The Va. Pilot-Ledger Star, Virginia Beach, 1988-89; DRG coord. Sentara Leigh Hosp., Norfolk, Va., 1989—. Contbr. numerous articles to newspapers. Sec. Norfolk Task Force on Aging, 1988—; mem. local human rights com. Ea. State Hosp., Williamsburg, Va., 1989—; bd. dirs. Women's Network Hampton Rds., 1988-89. Mem. Women's Network of Hampton Rds. (sec. 1988-90), NAFE, Gerontological Soc. Am., Am. Soc. Aging, So. Gerontological Soc., Va. Assn. Aging, Pi Gamma Mu, Phi Sigma Iota, Sigma Phi Omega. Home: 1336 Goose Landing Virginia Beach VA 23451

PLANT, MARETTA MOORE, public relations executive; b. Washington, Sept. 4, 1937; d. Henry Edwards and Lucy (Connell) Moore; m. William Voorhees Plant, June 14, 1959; children: Scott Voorhees, Craig Culver, Suzannah Holliday. BS in Bus. Adminstrn., U. Ark., 1959. Owner, mgr. Handcrafts by Maretta, Westfield, N.J., 1966-73; photographer M-R Pictures, Inc., Allendale, N.J., 1973-77; communications asst. United Way-Union County, Elizabeth, N.J., 1977-79; pub. rels. cons. Creative Arts Workshop, Westfield, 1977-81, Coll. Adv. Cons., 1983-89; community rels. coord. Raritan Bay Health Svcs. Corp., Perth Amboy, N.J., 1979-81; dir. pub. rels. St. Elizabeth Hosp., Elizabeth, N.J., 1981-86; dir. mkgt./communications Somerset Med. Ctr., Somerville, N.J., 1986-90; v.p. mktg. and pub. rels. Somerset Med. Ctr., Somerville, 1990—. Trustee Bridgeway House, Elizabeth, 1982-86, FarHills Race Meeting Assn., N.J., 1989—, mem. com.; mem. pub. rels. com. N.J. Hosp. Assn., Princeton, 1982-83, 89—, coun. auxs. 1988—, pub. rels. com., 1989—; committeewoman Union County Rep. Com., Westfield, 1983-85. Mem. NAFE, Pub. Rels. Soc. Am., Nat. Fedn. Press Women, N.J. Press Women (chmn. communications contest 1990—), Am. Soc. Hosp. Mktg. and Pub. Rels. (coun. mem. Region II, membership com.), N.J. Hosp. Mktg. and Pub. Rels. Assn. (corr. sec. 1984-86, pres. 1986-88), Internat. Platform Assn., Somerset City C. of C. (mag. com. 1988—), U. Ark. Alumni Assn., Summit-Westfield Assn., Delta Gamma, Coll. Women's (Westfield) Club, Soroptomists (internat., charter). Home: 118 Effingham Pl Westfield NJ 07090 Office: Somerset Med Ctr Rehill Ave Somerville NJ 08876

PLANT, MICHELE SUSAN, computer senior technical coordinator; b. N.Y.C., Dec. 1, 1959; d. Mark and Dorothy (Hirschberger) P. BS in Computer Sci., Quinnipiac Coll., 1982. Computer programmer, analyst Temple Computer Assocs., New Haven, 1980-81; instr. Quinnipiac Coll., Hamden, Conn., 1982-83; sr. programmer, analyst New Eng. Mgmt. Svcs., Inc., New Haven, 1981-85, Structured Technology Corp., New London, Conn., 1985; tech. coord. The Hardford (Conn.) Ins. Group, 1985-90, sr. tech. coord., 1990—. Recipient H.S. Geneen award, 1988. Mem. Internat. Soc. WANG Users. Office: Hartford Ins Group 1 Hartford Plaza Hartford CT 06115

PLANT, VALENTINA ANATOLIEVNA, computer sales executive; b. St. Paul, May 9, 1961; d. Anatoli and Nina (Isaeva) Swiridow; m. Michael William Plant, Nov. 28, 1981; 1 child, Stephanie Nicole. BA, U. Minn., 1982. Linguist Dept. Def., Ft. Meade, Md., 1984-85; instr. fgn. lang. Internat. Lang. Svcs., Mpls., 1985-86; internat. account mgr. Control Systems, Inc., St. Paul, 1986-90; western regional account mgr. Control Systems/Artists Graphics, St. Paul, 1990—; translator Assoc. Pubs., English Pravda, St. Paul, 1985-86; vol. Russian interpreter for local hosps., TV news and health svcs., 1985—. Mem. NAFE. Office: Artist Graphics 2675 Patton Rd Saint Paul MN 55113

PLANTE, PATRICIA R., academic administrator. Provost, v.p. acad. affairs Towson State U., Balt., until 1987; pres. U. So. Maine, Portland, 1987—. Office: U So Maine 96 Falmouth St Portland ME 04103*

PLANTS, HELEN LESTER, professor of engineering; b. Desloge, Mo., Mar. 9, 1925; d. Rolla Bertell and Margaret Cassandra (Stephens) Lester; m. Kenneth Dell Plants, Dec. 26, 1950; children: Frances, Kenneth Bertell, Edward Stephen, Lee DeGroot. BSCE, Mo. U., 1945; MSCE, W.Va. U., 1953. Registered profl. engr., W.Va. Petroleum engr. Amoco, Dallas, 1945; engr. Surveying Co., New Orleans, 1945-46; structural engr. Graham Cons. Engr. Co., Corpus Christi, Tex., 1946-47; prof. W.Va. U., Morgantown, 1947-82; sr. lectr. Kingston Poly., Kingston upon Thames, U.K., 1982-83; cons. Brighton (U.K.) Poly., 1983-84, UNESCO, Manila, Phillipines, 1980; dept. chair civil and archtl. engring. tech. Purdue U., Fort Wayne, Ind., 1985—; cons. in field, 1948-85; acad. advisor USN Acad., Annapolis, Md., 1976-80; chmn. Ednl. Rsch. and Methods, Washington, 1970-73. Author: An Introduction to Statics, 1975, Programmed Topics in Statics and Strength of Materials, 1966, Engineering Mechanics of Deformable Bodies, 1983. Fellow Am. Soc. Engring. Edn. (bd. dirs. 1974-76, v.p. 1975-76, Women in Engring. award 1988); mem. ASCE, NSPE, ASME, Soc. Women Engrs. Republican. Episcopalian. Home: 12 W Front St Morgantown WV 26505

PLASKET, CAROL MUELLER, psychologist; b. Rockville Centre, N.Y., Dec. 22, 1949; d. George R. and Eva Mae (Lehman) Mueller; m. Richard J. Plasket, July 21, 1974. Student, Rollins Coll., Winter Park, Fla., 1967-69; BA, U. Del., 1971; MEd, U. Va., 1972, PhD, 1978. Lic. psychologist, Pa.; cert. sch. psychologist, Pa., N.Y., N.J. Rsch. asst. U. Va., Charlottesville, 1972-74; psychology intern NIMH, Long Beach, N.Y., 1974-75; intern clin. psychology The Devereux Found., Devon, Pa., 1976-78; sch. psychologist Chester County Intermediate Unit, Coatesville, Pa., 1978-86; psychologist Redeemer Ctr., Meadowbrook, Pa., 1986-87; clin. psychologist The Devereux Found., Devon, 1987—; psychol. cons. Tredyffrin-Easttown Sch. Dist., Berwyn, Pa., 1978-88. Fellow Pa. Psychol. Assn.; mem. Am. Psychol. Assn., Phila. Soc. Clin. Psychologists. Home: 793 Tory Hollow Rd Berwyn PA 19312 Office: Career House Devereux 123 Old Lancaster Rd Devon PA 19333

PLASS, JANE PAULA, medical librarian; b. Elmhurst, Ill., Aug. 9, 1952; d. Erwin Ernst and Marion Jane (Kammeyer) P. AB, U. Ill., 1974, MS, 1975; OD summa cum laude, BS in Visual Sci., Ill. Coll. Optometry, 1984. Lic. optometrist, Ill., Wis. Grad. asst. in libr. U. Ill., Urbana-Champaign, 1974-75; libr. Va. Poly. Inst. and State U., Blacksburg, 1975-79; pvt. practice Chgo., Downers Grove, Ill., 1984-87; tech. svcs. libr. Nat. Coll. Chiropractic, Lombard, Ill., 1985-87, acting head libr., 1987-88; freelance indexer Villa Park, Ill., 1988—; head libr. Nat. Coll. Chiropractic, Lombard, Ill., 1988—; chmn. com. chiropractic subject headings Chiropractic Libr. Consortium, 1990. Author: Library Subject Headings for Visual Therapy and Developmental Vision Literature, 1984. Treas. After-Hours Weavers, Villa Park, 1987-88, chmn., 1988-89; program chmn. Ill. Prairie Spinners, Naperville, Ill., 1987-88, sec., 1990. Nikon scholar, 1981. Mem. Med. Libr. Assn., Health Sci. Librs. Ill., Online Audiovisual Catalogers, Am. Soc. Indexers, NAFE, Mensa, Handweavers Guild Am., Beta Sigma Kappa (Silver medal 1984), Phi Beta Kappa (jr. scholar 1972). Lutheran. Home: 2N181 Addison Rd Villa Park IL 60181 Office: Nat Coll Chiropractic 200 E Roosevelt Rd Lombard IL 60148

PLASSMAN, BRENDA LEE, neuroscientist; b. Grand Rapids, Mich., May 29, 1957; d. Harold H. and Joan C. (Palm) P.; m. Warren R. Jewett, Oct. 5, 1985. BA, Wittenberg U., 1979; MA, U. Ariz., 1985, PhD, 1986. Rsch. asst. U. Ariz., Tucson, 1982-84, teaching asst., 1981-85; postdoctoral fellow clin. neurophysiology unit Prince Henry Hosp., Sydney, N.S.W., Australia, 1987, cons. clin. neurophysiology unit, 1988-89. Contbr. articles to profl. jours. Resident advisor Wittenberg U., Springfield, Ohio, 1976-78; counselor Camarillo (Calif.) State Hosp., 1979. Wittenberg U. scholar, 1975. Mem. Phi Beta Kappa, Sigma Xi, Psi Chi.

PLATONI, KATHERINE THERESA, psychologist; b. Mount Kisco, N.Y., Apr. 28, 1952; d. Eugene Joseph and Sydell (Greenberg) P. BS in Psychology, Hobart and William Smith Coll., 1974; MEd, U. Miami, 1975; D in Clin. Psychology, Nova U., 1984. Lic. clin. psychologist, Va., Ohio. Vol. counselor Willard (N.Y.) State Hosp., 1971-74; vol. crisis coordinator Open Door Crisis Ctr., Miami, 1974-75; behavioral specialist Sunland Tng. Ctr., Opa Locka, Fla., 1976-77, specialist retardation tng. Staff Devel. Inst., 1977; tchr. spl. homebound edn. Dade County Assn. Retarded Citizens, Miami, 1977-78; behavioral specialist Village South Intensive Treatment Unit, Miami, 1977-78; clerical unit advisor Fellowship House, The Psycho-Social Rehab. Ctr., Inc., South Miami, 1978-80; intervention therapist newborn spl. care unit Jackson Meml. Hosp., Miami, 1981; research cons. Denver Research Inst., U. Denver, 1981-82; child psychologist Mental Health Svcs. of Clark County, Springfield, Ohio, 1987-88; clin. psychology intern William Beaumont Army Med. Ctr., El Paso, Tex., 1982-84; chief psychologist DeWitt ACH, Ft. Belvoir, Va., 1984-87; chronic pain psychologist Pain Ctr. Miami Valley Hosp., Dayton, Ohio, 1988—; clin. asst. prof. Wright State U., Dayton, 1988—; sr. clin. psychologist Optifast Program, Dayton, 1988—. Maj. USAR, 1989. scholarship Health Profls. U.S. Army, 1979. Mem. Am. Psychol. Assn., Am. Soc. Clin. Hypnosis, Soc. Clin. Exptl. Hypnosis, Ohio Psychol. Assn., Dayton Area Psychol. Assn. Presbyterian. Home: 2333 Colony Trail Xenia OH 45385 Office: Miami Valley Hosp 1 Wyoming St Dayton OH 45409

PLATTE, MARY KAY, television director and producer, writer; b. Newcastle, Wyo.; d. Vincent J. and Edith May (Wortman) F.; m. July 17, 1976; 1 child, Sabrina K. BS, S.D. State U., 1959; MA, Bowling Green U., 1960, PhD, 1981. Lifetime teaching cert. S.D., Calif. Community Colls.; FCC 1st class license. Dir. news Sta. KMHL-AM, Marshall, Minn., 1969-73; dir. pub. services Sta. KOTA-TV, Rapid City, S.D., 1973-74; asst. prof. Eastern Ky. U., Richmond, 1974-78; dir., producer bus. news Sta. WBGU-TV, Bowling Green, Ohio, 1978-81; assoc. prof. Walter Cronkite Sch. Ariz. State U., 1981-84; dir. TV Scottsdale (Ariz.) Coll., 1984-88; assoc. prof., artistic dir., chair dept. theater Wayland U., 1988—; dir. TV Manitou-Wabing Arts Ctr., Perry Sound, Ont., Can., 1988; exec. TV producer, dir. TeleVideo Edn. Projects, 1989—; instr. SW Minn. U., 1967-73; cons. in field; adv. radio magazine Sun Devil Persepctive. exec. dir.: An Evening With Words, 1967, Crossroad Sands (pre-Broadway presentation), 1983, numerous promotional videos, 1983; dir., producer various TV shows including Strokes and Strategies, 1984, Southwest Heritage series, 1986, also Am. Express Mgmt. program, 1987, and various radio series; producer numerous corp. video programs and workshops including Building Effective Video Centers, Communicating on TV, Making the Most of Media; producer, author: Today is Yesterday's Tomorrow (screenplay), 1978; author books Radio/TV Production, 1976, Beginning of Satellite Communication, pub. 1982, libretto for operas Karolee Fairaday, The Dinner, 1967, presented papers including TV in the Courtroom: Right of Access?, John Schlesinger: His Early Films; contbg. editor numerous profl. jours.; dir., actor, producer various theater groups. Dist. co-chair Dem. Party Minn. 1968; state dir. Higher Edn. Resource Services, Scottsdale, 1985—; mem. access bd. Ednl. TV, Phoenix. Recipient Addy award Am. Fed. Advertisers, 1977, award for excellence Gov. Babbitt Ariz., 1983, Golden award for excellence United Way Ariz. 1983, Recognition award Phoenix Ednl. Access Bd., 1987, Internat. Bus. Communication award, Critics Actor award, State playwriting award; grantee Kellogg Fine Arts, 1969-73, Bowling Green State U., 1978, Eastern Ky. U. (sabbatical), 1978, Ariz. State U., 1983, Ednl. Devel. Project, 1984, Senator's Cup, 1984, Lodestar, 1984, 88. Mem. Broadcast Edn. Assn. (vice chair history com., Nat. award, Nat. History award 1982), Women in Higher Edn. (pres. 1982-87), Speech Communication Assn. (state paper competition winner), Soc. Profl. Journalists, Ariz. Broadcast Assn. Convs., Nat. Assn. Ednl. Broadcasters (state mgrs. com., state adminstrs.), Pub. Rels. Soc. Am., Am. Film Inst., Am. Culture Assn., Internat. Communications Assn., AAUW, Women in Communications, Inc. (bd. dirs. Phoenix chpt., nominee Outstanding Woman in Ariz.), Internat. Ednl. Honors Soc., Sigma Delta Chi., Delta Kappa Gamma.

PLATTI, RITA JANE, educator, draftsman, author; b. Stockton, Calif., Aug. 29, 1925; d. Umbert Ferdinand and Concettina Maria (Natoli) Strangio; m. Elvin Carl Platti, July 27, 1955; 1 child, Kimberley Jane. Student, Dominican Coll., 1943-45; AB in Math, U. Pacific, 1947, postgrad., 1947-52, 68. Cert. sec. tchr., Calif. Farmer Escalon, Calif., 1943—; tchr. math St. Mary's High Sch., Stockton, 1947-49, 52, 54; chem. analyst Petri Winery, Escalon, 1949; draftsman Kyle Steel Co., Stockton, 1950-52; pvt. practice as draftsman Stockton, 1952-66; tchr. math Montezuma Sch., Stockton, 1956-57, Davis Elem. Sch., Stockton, 1957-58; with rental bus., 1958-81; tchr. math Amos Alonzo Stagg High Sch., 1961-80, Humphreys Coll., 1981-83, Hamilton Jr. High Sch., 1984—; real estate agt., 1979—. Author: Math Proficiency Plateaus, 1979; author, pub. Math Proficiency Plateaus Series, 1979-86; patentee. Mem. NEA, Calif. Tchrs. Assn. Democrat. Roman Catholic.

PLATZKER, MARJORIE ANN, interior designer; b. Providence, Mar. 12, 1942; d. James and Madeline (Bogin) Sanek; m. Arnold C.G. Platzker, June 9, 1963; children: David, Elizabeth. BS in Edn., Wheelock Coll., Boston, 1963; profl. designation in interior design, UCLA, 1979. Assoc. Kaneko/Laff Assocs., L.A., 1979-84; v.p. Stuart Laff Assocs., L.A., 1984-87; pres. Interior Design Inc., L.A., 1987—. Mem. Am. Soc. Interior Design, Women in Commercial Real Estate, Nat. Corp. Real Estate Execs., L.A. Hdqrs. Home: 654 Walther Way Los Angeles CA 90049 Office: Interior Design Inc 1440 S Sepulveda Blvd 216 Los Angeles CA 90025

PLAWECKI, JUDITH ANN, educator; b. E. Chicago, Ind., June 5, 1943; d. Joseph Lawrence and Ann Marilyn (Hamnik) Curosh; m. Henry Martin Plawecki, June 10, 1967; children: Martin H., Lawrence H. BS, St. Xavier Coll., Chgo., 1965; MA, U. Iowa, 1971; PhD, 1974. Asst. prof. Mt. Mercy Coll., Cedar Rapids, Iowa, 1971-73; asst. dept. chmn., assoc. prof., 1974-76; assoc. prof. U. Iowa, 1975-76; asst. dean, assoc. prof. U. Minn., 1976-81; acting dean, assoc. dean and prof. Univ. N.D., Grand Forks, 1981-82, dean and prof. nursing, 1982-83; dean and prof. nursing Lewis U., Romeoville, Ill., 1983-87, Univ. S. Fla., Tampa, 1987—. Univ. Iowa Fellow, 1973. Mem. Gerontol. Soc. Fla., Older Women's League, Nat. League Nursing, Am. Nurses Assn., Sigma Phi Omega, Sigma Xi, Sigma Theta Tau, Phi Lambda Theta. Office: Univ South Fla Coll Nursing 12901 Bruce B Downs Blvd Box 22 Tampa FL 33612

PLAYER, GERALDINE (JERI PLAYER), small business executive; b. Cleve., Mar. 26, 1952; d. Cornelius Millsape and Ola Mae (Maxie) Fisher; m. Van O. Player, Aug. 27, 1970 (dec. Mar. 1975); children—Ricardo T., Van O., Michelle. Student Sawyer Coll. Bus., Mayfield, Ohio, Virginia Marti Sch. Design, Lakewood, Ohio, Inst. Children's Lit., Conn., Case Western Res. U., Fall 1988. Owner, Jeri's Designs, Inc., Cleve., 1970—, Success Writers, Cleve., 1986—; fashion cons. Active adoptive parenting orgn. Mem. Nat. Assn. Female Execs. Club: Back Wall (Beachwood, Ohio). Lodge: Brotherhood (Bklyn.). Avocations: aerobics; photography; theatre; speech. Home and Office: 14217 Scioto Ave East Cleveland OH 44112

PLAYER, THELMA B., librarian; b. Owosso, Mich.; d. Walter B. and Grace (Willoughby) Player; B.A., Western Mich. U., 1954. Reference asst. USAF Aero. Chart & Info. Center, Washington, 1954-57; reference librarian U.S. Navy Hydrographic Office, Suitland, Md., 1957-58; asst. librarian, 1958-59; tech. library br. head U.S. Navy Spl. Project Office, Washington, 1959-68, Strategic Systems Project Office, 1969-76. Mem. Spl. Libraries Assn., D.C. Library Assn., AAUW, Canterbury Cathedral Trust in Am., Nat. Geneal. Soc., Internat. Soc. Brit. Genealogy and Family History, Ohio Geneal. Soc., Royal Oak Found., Daus. of Union Vets. of Civil War, Friends Folger Library. Episcopalian. Home: 730 24th St NW Washington DC 20037

PLEASANT, HELEN CAROLYN, health facility administrator; b. Mecklenburg County, Va., Feb. 26, 1945; d. Carter Thomas and Pearl Blanche (LeSueur) Stone. BS in Med. Tech., Med. Coll. Va., 1967; MA in Mgmt., U. Phoenix, 1985; postgrad., N.C. Meml. Hosp., 1970. Cert. med. tech. Lab. mgr. Sonora Lab. Svcs., Mesa, Ariz.; tech. dir. United Blood Svcs., Lubbock, Tex. Regional chmn. east valley Am. Cancer Soc., Phoenix, 1981-87. Mem. Clin. Lab. Mgmt., Am. Assn. Blood Banks, South Cen. Assn. Blood Banks. Home: 5018 27th St Lubbock TX 79407

PLECENIK, JEANNE TODD, accountant; b. Paterson, N.J., Nov. 16, 1955; d. David Robert and Eileen Rose (Crisbacher) McDougall; m. Richard Michael Plecenik, Sept. 25, 1982; children: Richard David, Karen Elizabeth. BBA in Pub. Acctg. magna cum laude, Pace U., 1981; postgrad., Marist Coll., 1987—. CPA, N.Y. Sales asst. Merrill Lynch, Pierce, Fenner & Smith, N.Y.C., 1976-77; exec. asst. The Barbuda Devel. Co., N.Y.C., 1977-80; staff acct. Arthur Young & Co., N.Y.C., 1981-83; prin. Jeanne T. Plecenik, CPA, Wappingers Falls, N.Y., 1983—; adj. lectr. Dutchess Community Coll., Poughkeepsie, N.Y., 1984—. Mem. Am. Woman's Soc. CPA's, N.Y. State Soc. CPA's, Nat. Alliance Homebased Businesswomen (treas. 1987-88), Poughkeepsie Bus. and Profl. Women's Club (chmn. fin. com. 1989-90, scholarship com. 1989-90, treas. 1990—). Roman Catholic. Home: 11 Helen Ave Wappingers Falls NY 12590 Office: PO Box 582 Hughsonville NY 12537

PLEMING-YOCUM, LAURA CHALKER, religion educator; b. Sheridan, Wyo., May 25, 1913; d. Sidney Thomas and Florence Theresa (Woodbury) Chalker; m. Edward Kibbler Pleming, Aug. 25, 1938 (dec. Nov. 1980); children: Rowena Pleming Chamberlin, Edward K. Pleming Jr., Sidney Thomas Pleming; m. William Lewis Yocum, Dec. 19, 1989. BA, Calif. State U., Long Beach, 1953, MA, 1954; postgrad., U. So. Calif., L.A., 1960-63; Rel. D., Grad. Sch. Theology, Claremont, Calif., 1968. Bible scholar 1st Ch. of Christ, Scientist, Boston, 1970-75; internat. lectr. Bibl. studies, 1953—; Bibl. lectr. Principia Coll., Elsah, Ill., 1968-90; adult seminar resource person, 1953—; lectr. Tours to Middle East, 1965—. Author: Triumph of Job, 1979; editor (newsletter) Bibleletter, 1968-84. Mem. Am. Acad. Religion, Soc. Bibl. Lit. & Exegesis, Am. Schs. Oriental Rsch., AAUP, Religious Edn. Assn., Zeta Tau Alpha (alumni pres. Long Beach chpt. 1960), Gamma Theta Upsilon (prs. Long Beach chpt. 1952).

PLESHETTE, SUZANNE, actress, writer; b. N.Y.C., Jan. 31; d. Eugene and Geraldine (Rivers) P.; m. Thomas Joseph Gallagher, III, Mar. 16, 1968. Student, Syracuse U., Finch Coll., Neighborhood Playhouse Sch. of Theatre. designer home furnishings and bed linens. Theatre debut in Truckline Cafe; star in Broadway prodns. Compulsion, The Cold Wind and the Warm, The Golden Fleecing, The Miracle Worker, Special Occasions; star TV series Bob Newhart Show, 1972-78, Suzanne Pleshette is Maggie Briggs, 1984; starred in TV series Bridges to Cross, 1986—, Nightingales, 1988-89; star 30 feature films including: The Birds, Forty Pounds of Trouble, If It's Tuesday This Must Be Belgium, Nevada Smith, Support Your Local Gunfighter, Hot Stuff, Oh God! Book II, 1980; TV movies include: Flesh and Blood, Starmaker, Fantasies, If Things Were Different, Help-Wanted Male, Dixie Changing Habits, One Cooks, The Other Doesn't, For Love or Money, Kojak, The Belarus File, A Stranger Waits, Alone In The Neon Jungle, Leona Helmsley: The Queen of Mean, 1990; writer, co-creator, producer two TV series.

PLESS, VERA, mathematics and computer science educator; b. Chgo., Mar. 5, 1931; d. Lyman and Helen (Blinder) Stepen; m. Irwin Pless, June 15, 1952 (div. 1980); children: Naomi, Benjamin, Daniel. PhB, U. Chgo., 1952; PhD, Northwestern U., 1957. Mathematician USAF, Lincoln, Mass., 1962-72; rsch. assoc. MIT, Cambridge, Mass., 1972-75; prof. math. U. Ill., Chgo., 1975—. Author: The Theory of Error Correcting Codes, 1989; contbr. articles to profl. publs. Mem. Am. Math. Soc. (chair nominating com. 1984), Math. Assn. Am., IEEE (bd. govs. 1985-89), Assn. Women in Math. Office: U Ill Morgan and Taylor Chicago IL 60680

PLEWINSKI, TERESA MARIA SAUER, physician; b. Poland; d. Gustav and Jadwiga (Bedynski) Sauer; naturalized, 1974; M.D., Wroclaw and Warsaw Med. Sch., 1951, Ph.D., 1966; m. Gustav L. Plewinski, Apr. 5, 1949; children—Magdalena, Michael. Intern, resident in internal medicine Columbus Hosp., N.Y.C., 1969-73; dep. surgeon-in-chief Children's Hosp., Warsaw, Poland, 1958-67; pediatric surgeon-in-chief Regional Hosp., Ho, Ghana, 1968; attending physician Cabrini Med. Center, N.Y.C., 1973—. Recipient Physician's Recognition award AMA, 1972, 75, 78. Fellow A.C.P., Am. Acad. Family Practice; mem. N.Y. Acad. Scis., Polish Inst. Arts and Scis. in Am. Research and publs. in med. field. Home: 10 Waterside Plaza New York NY 10010 Office: 242 E 19th St New York NY 10003

PLIMPTON, PAULINE AMES, civic worker; b. N. Easton, Mass., Oct. 22, 1901; d. Oakes and Blanche Ames; B.A., Smith Coll., 1922; m. Francis T.P. Plimpton, June 4, 1926; children: George Ames, Francis T.P., Oakes Ames, Sarah Gay. Pres., House of Industry, 1940-48; bd. dirs. Inst. World Affairs, 1940-74, Pub. Edn. Assn., 1933-44; chmn. United Campaign Fund for Planned Parenthood of Manhattan and Bronx, 1946-49; chmn. Planned Parenthood Fedn. Am. campaign, 1959-60, bd. dirs. 1959-67, 70-73; chmn. United Campaign, 1964; bd. dirs. Planned Parenthood of N.Y.C., 1965-74; rep. Western Hemisphere region Internat. Planned Parenthood Fedn., 1970-73; fund raiser, vol. coun. Philharm. Symphony Soc. N.Y., N.Y. Legal Aid Soc., ARC; mem. adv. coun. Friends of the Columbia Librs., 1986—. Recipient Planned Parenthood award for devoted service, 1969, Republican. Unitarian. Clubs: Cosmopolitan, River (N.Y.C.); Piping Rock Ausable (Adirondacks). Contbg. author, editor, compiler Orchids at Christmas, 1975, The Ancestry of Blanche Butler Ames and Adelbert Ames, 1977, Oakes Ames: Jottings of a Harvard Botanist, 1979, The Plimpton Papers: Law and Diplomacy, 1985, A Window on Our World: More Plimpton Papers, 1989. Home: 131 E 66th St New York NY 10021 also: 168 Chichester Rd Huntington NY 11743

PLIMPTON, PEGGY LUCAS, trustee; b. Burgaw, N.C., Nov. 3, 1931; d. David Nicholson and Margaret (MacMillan) Lucas; m. Hollis Winslow Plimpton, June 11, 1955; children: Victoria P. Babcock, Priscilla P. Morphy, Hollis Winslow Plimpton III. AB, Duke U., 1954. Tchr. Clinton (N.C.) Secondary Schs., 1954-55. Bd. trustees Carleton Williard Retirement Home, Bedford, Mass., 1968—; bd. dirs. Episcopal Ch. Women, 1968-78, Brigham & Women's Hosp., Boston, 1975—; pres. Boston Lying-In Hosp., 1970-72; chmn. Mass. Nat. Cathedral Assn., Boston, 1978-80, 1985-88; pres. bd. trustees Women's Ednl. and Indsl., Boston, 1980-83. Mem. New England Farm & Garden Club (bd. dirs. 1965—), Chestnut Hill Garden Club(bd. dirs. 1970-74), Jr. League (bd. dirs. 1970-76), Jr. League Garden Club (pres. 1981-83), Colonial Dames (bd. mgrs. 1983-89, Vincent Club, Chilton Club. Republican. Episcopalian.

PLISETSKAYA, ERIKA MICHAEL, biologist, physiologist; b. Leningrad, USSR, Dec. 8, 1929; came to U.S., 1980; d. Michael Israel and Amalia Zachary (Utevskaya) P. BS in Biology, State U., Leningrad, 1952, PhD in Physiology, 1958; DSc, Pavlov's Inst. Physiology Acad. Sci., USSR, 1972. Rsch. scientist Inst. Evolutionary Physiology Acad. Sci., Leningrad, 1958-79; rsch. assoc. dept. zoology U. Wash., Seattle, 1980-84, rsch. scientist III dept. zoology, 1984-89; prin. rsch. assoc. Sch. Fisheries U. Wash., 1989—. Author: Hormonal Regulation of Carbohydrate Metabolism in Lower Vertebrates, 1975; editor Evolution of Pancreatic Islets, 1977; assoc. editor Jour. Exptl. Zoology, 1990—; contbr. articles to profl. jours. Rsch. grantee NSF, 1985—. Fellow AAAS; mem. Am. Soc. Zoologists, Endocrine Soc., Fish Soc. Office: U Wash Sch Fisheries WH-10 Seattle WA 98195

PLITT, JEANNE GIVEN, librarian; b. Whitehall, N.Y., Aug. 27, 1927; s. Charles Russell and Anna Marie (Noyes) Given; student St. Lawrence U., 1945-47; AB, U. Md., 1940; postgrad. Am. U., 1960-61; MLS, Cath. U. Am., 1968; m. Ferdinand Charles Plitt, Jr., Jan. 19, 1952; children: Christine Marie, Charles Randolph. Libr. asst. Spl. Services div. U.S. Army, 1949-51; tchr. secondary schs., Md. and Va.; reference libr. Alexandria (Va.) Libr., 1967-68, asst. dir., 1968-70, dir., 1970—; chmn. librs.' tech. com. Coun. Govts., Washington, 1971-72, 80-81; chmn. No. Va. Libr. Networking Com. Active Little Theatre Group, Alexandria. Recipient Alexandria Pub. Service award, 1964, 74, recognition Am. Assn. Ret. Persons, 1990. Mem. ALA, Va. Libr. Assn. (legis. com. 1988—), Manuscript Soc., PTA, U. Md., Cath. U. alumni assns., Alexandria Assn., Urban League, Alexandria Hist. Soc. (dir. 1974—). Roman Catholic. Club: Zonta (sec. chpt. 1972-73, dir. 1988—). Office: Alexandria Libr 717 Queen St Alexandria VA 22314-2420

PLOPA, PATRICIA ANN, clinical psychologist; b. Detroit, Jan. 9, 1949; d. John and Jane (Miarecki) Gorski; m. Jeffrey David Plopa, Aug. 24, 1973; 1 dau., Lisa Michelle. B.A., Mich. State U., 1971; M.A., U. Detroit, 1976, Ph.D., 1977. Instr., U. Detroit, 1971-73; psychol. examiner, therapist Adult Psychiat. Clinic, Detroit, 1972-74; psychol. intern Children's Ctr. of Wayne County, Detroit, 1973-74, Sinai Hosp., Detroit, 1974-75; therapist, research asst. U. Detroit Psychology Clinic, 1972-77; therapist Project Headline: Family Counseling Ctr., Eastwood Clinic, Detroit, 1976-77; clin. psychologist Adult/Youth Devel. Services, Farmington, Mich., 1977-83; pvt. practice Maple Clinic, Birmingham, Mich., 1978-80, Northland Clinic, Southfield, Mich., 1980—; bd. dirs. Northland Clin., 1985—; cons. Marriage Growth Ctr., 1983—, St. Owen's Pastoral Minstry Program, Birmingham, 1987—; adj. faculty dept. psychology U. Detroit, 1986—.Mich. State Trustees scholar, 1967-71; U. Detroit teaching fellow, 1971-73. Mem. Mich. Soc. Clin. Psychologists (exec. com. council 1981-83, directory editor 1981-83), Mich. Psychol. Assn. (continuing edn. com. 1981-85), Mich. Soc. Psychoanalytic Psychology (program planning com. 1981-82), Am. Psychol. Assn., Nat. Register Health Service Providers in Psychology, Mich. Psychol. Assn., Mich. Soc. Psychoanalytic Psychology, Assn. for the Advancement of Psychoanalysis (program planning com. 1981-83), PTO (Conant bd. B.H. schs.), Phi Beta Kappa. Home: 4655 Pickering Rd Birmingham MI 48010 Office: 17117 W Nine Mile Rd Suite 1221 Southfield MI 48075

PLUM, DIANE WOODMAN, education educator; b. Edgewood Arsena, M.D., July 10, 1945; d. Clyde Edward and Ann Robbins, Woodman; m. Kenneth Darwin, May 13, 1967; 1 child Rebecca Ann. BS in Elem. Edn., W Va. U., 1967; MA in Spl. Edn. and Psychology, N.E. La. U., 1985. Tchr., math, title 1 Pasadena (Tex.) Ind. Sch. Dist., Tex., 1967-71; tchr., sixth grade East Baton Rouge Sch. Bd., La., 1972; tchr., dir. St. Johns Mini Sch. Day Care, Baton Rouge, 1974-78; tchr. third grade Ouachita Parish Sch. Bd., Monroe, La., 1978-79; tchr., spl. edn. Monroe (La.) City Sch. Bd., 1979—; chmn. spl. edn. dept. Carroll Jr. High, 1979—, Coun. for Exceptional Children, Monroe, La., 1986-87, So. Assn. Carroll Jr. High Sch., 1988—. Mem. NEA, Coun. for Exception children, La. Edn. Assn., Monroe City Edn. Assn., Monroe City Classroom Tchrs. Republican. Methodist. Home: 137 New Chapel Hill West Monroe LA 71291

PLUM, MARY ISABELLE, retired educator; b. Newton, Iowa, Feb. 29, 1920; d. Charles Wesley and Mary Frances (Kelly) P. BA, Grinnell Coll., 1941; MA, U. Iowa, 1963. Cert. tchr., Iowa. Bus., math. instr. Corwith (Iowa) High Sch., 1941-42, Newhall (Iowa) High Sch., 1942-45; bus. instr. Bus. Inst. Milw., 1945-47; exec. sec. Sch. Fine Arts and Iowa Meml. Union, Dir. U. Iowa, Iowa City, 1947-52, Dir. Hosp. Sch. of Handicapped Children, U. Iowa, Iowa City, 1952-54; prin. and bus., math. instr. Kalona (Iowa) High Sch., 1954-55; bus. edn. instr. Boone (Iowa) High Sch., 1955-64; bus. edn. instr. Marshalltown (Iowa) Community Coll., 1964-85, ret., 1985—. Ret. mem. NEA, Nat. Bus. Edn. Assn., Iowa State Edn. Assn. (hon.), Iowa Bus. Edn. Assn. (Disting. Svc. Scholarship award 1986), Delta Pi Epsilon. Roman Catholic. Home: 611 E South St 10A Marshalltown IA 50158

PLUMMER, MARCIE STERN, real estate broker; b. Plymouth, Mass., Oct. 28, 1950; d. Jacob and Rosalie (Adelman) Stern; m. John Dillon McHugh II, Oct. 8, 1974 (div.); 1 child, Joshua Stern; m. Louis Freeman Plummer Jr., Sept. 25, 1982; children: Jessica Price, Denelle Boothe. BA, Am. Internat. Coll., 1972, MAT in English, 1973, postgrad., 1974; postgrad., U. Conn., 1974; lic. real estate broker, Anthony Sch. Real Estate, Walnut Creek, Calif., 1985. Educator, chair dept. Windsor Locks (Conn.) Sch. Dist., 1972-74; educator, placement dir. Heald Bus. Coll., San Francisco, 1974-77; educator evening and day divs. Diablo Valley Coll., Pleasant Hill, Calif., 1975-77; real estate agt. Morrison Homes, Pleasant Hill, 1977-78; real estate agt., tract mgr. Dividend Devel., Santa Clara, Calif., 1978-81; real estate agt., broker, owner Better Homes Realty and Valley Realty, 1981-84; real estate broker, owner The Presád Co. Inc. subs. Better Homes Realty, Danville, Calif., 1984—. Better Homes Realty rep. for orgn. of Danville 4th of July Parade, City of Danville, 1984-88; publicist San Ramon Valley Little League, Alamo, Calif., 1986—; active Battered Women's Found., Contra Costa County, Calif., 1986—; active rep. voter registration, Walnut Creek, Calif., 1987—; mem. Civic Arts Coun., Walnut Creek, 1988—. Recipient numerous nat., state and regional awards in field. Mem. Bldg. Industry Assn. (Sales vol. award 1978-89), Sales & Mktg. Coun. (sponsor MAME awards banquet 1978-89, Gold sponsor 1986-88), Calif. Assn. Realtors, Contra Costa Bd. Realtors. Jewish. Home: 123 Erselia Trail Alamo CA 94507 Office: The Presád Co Inc 360 Diablo Rd Danville CA 94526

PLUMMER, ORA BEATRICE, nursing consultant; b. Mexia, Tex., May 25, 1940; d. Macie Idella (Echols); B.S. in Nursing, U. N.Mex., 1961; M.S. in Nursing Edn., UCLA, 1966; children—Kimberly, Kevin, Cheryl. Nurses aide Bataan Meml. Meth. Hosp., Albuquerque, 1958-60, staff nurse, 1961-62, 67-68; staff nurse, charge nurse, relief supr. Hollywood (Calif.) Community Hosp., 1962-64; instr. U. N.Mex. Coll. of Nursing, Albuquerque, 1968-69; sr. instr. U. Colo. Sch. Nursing, Denver, 1971-74; asst. prof. U. Colo. Sch. Nursing, Denver, 1974-76; staff assoc. III Western Interstate Commn. for Higher Edn., Boulder, Colo., 1976-78; dir. nursing Garden Manor Nursing Home, Lakewood, Colo., 1978-79; ednl. coordination Colo. Dept. Health, Denver, 1979—. Active Colo. Cluster of Schs.-faculty devel.; mem. adv. bd. Affiliated Children's and Family Services, 1977; mem. state instl. child abuse and neglect adv. com., 1984—; mem. planning com. State Wide Conf. on Black Health Concerns, 1977; mem. staff devel. com. Western Interstate Commn. for Higher Edn., 1978, minority affairs com., 1978, coordinating com. for baccalaureate program, 1971-76; active minority affairs U. Colo. Med. Center, 1971-72; mem. ednl. resources com. public relations com., rev. com. for reappointment, promotion, and tenure U. Colo. Sch. Nursing, 1971-76; regulatory tng. com., 1989—, gerontol. adv. com., Met. State Coll., 1989—; expert panel mem. Long Term Care Training Manual, HCFA, Balt., 1989. Mem. NAFE, Am. Soc. Tng. and Devel., Am. Nurses Assn., Colo. Nurses Assn. (affirmative action comm. 1977, 78, 79), Phi Delta Kappa. Contbr. articles in field to profl. jours. Office: 4210 E 11th Ave Denver CO 80013

PLUMMER, PATRICIA LYNNE MOORE, chemistry educator; b. Tyler, Tex., Feb. 26; d. Robert Lee and Jewell Ovelia (Jones) Moore; m. Otho Raymond Plummer, Apr. 10, 1965; children: Patrick William Otho, Christina Elisa Lynne. BA, Tex. Christian U., Ft. Worth, Tex., 1960; postgrad., U. N.C., 1960-61; PhD, U. Tex., 1964. Instr., Welch postdoctoral fellow U. Tex., Austin, 1964-66; postdoctoral fellow Dept. Chemistry, U. Ark., Fayetteville, 1966-68; rsch. assoc. Grad. Ctr., Cloud Phys. Rsch., Rolla, Mo., 1968-73; asst. prof. physics U. Mo., Rolla, 1973-77; assoc. dir. Grad. Ctr. Cloud Phys. Rsch., 1977-79, sr. investigator, 1980-85; assoc. prof. physics U. Mo., 1977-85; prof. dept. chem. physics U. Mo., Columbia, 1986—; internat. sci. advisor Symposium on Chemistry and Physics, 1982—. Assoc. editor Jour. of Colloid and Interface Sci., 1980-83; contbr. articles to profl. jours., chpts. to books. Rsch. grantee, IBM, 1990—, Air Force Office Rsch., 1989—, NSF, 1976-86, NASA, 1973-78; Air Force Office Rsch. summer fellow, 1988. Mem. Am. Chem. Soc., Am. Phys. Soc., Am. Geophys. Union, Sigma Xi (past pres.). Democrat. Baptist. Office: Univ of Missouri 314 Physics Bldg Columbia MO 65211

PLUNKETT, ANNE MARIE CECILIA, banker; b. Rochester, Minn., July 15, 1932; d. Eugene and Anna (Regan) Leddy; B.A., Manhattanville Coll., Purchase, N.Y., 1953; postgrad. Fordham U., 1953-54; m. Richard Harding Plunkett, July 12, 1958; children—Pamela, Patricia, Richard Harding, Julianne, Maureen. Instr. socio-econ. problems St. Marys Sch. Nursing, Rochester, 1957-58, 65-66; chmn. bd. Rochester Bank & Trust Co., 1973-82; v.p., sec. Midwest Video Electronics, Inc., Rhinelander, Wis., 1972-79; dir. Medelco, Inc., 1973-78. Pres., Olmsted County Lawyers Wives, 1959-60; leader Girl Scouts U.S.A., 1969-72; vol. tchr. St. Johns Religious Edn., 1972-75; founder Southeastern Minn. Regional Arts Coun., 1973; chmn. Minn. Arts Bd., 1974-75, bd. dirs., 1971-77; co-chairperson Minn. Bicentennial Commn., 1975-76; v.p., mem. finance com. United Way, Olmsted County, 1978, bd. dirs., 1976-78; chmn. subcom. on elementary edn. Rochester Sch. Dist. 535 Citizens Adv. Com. on Ednl. Facilities, 1976-77; bd. dirs., v.p. Friends of Mayowood, 1987-88; coord. Minn. Aesthetic Environment Program for Olmsted County, 1977; co-founder condrs. com. Rochester Symphony Orch., 1977; mem. Pres.'s Forum, Minn. Bible Coll., Rochester, 1977-79, bd. commr's adv. com. Minn. DNR, 1989—; mem. exec. com. Rochester Pres.'s Council, Coll. St. Teresa, Winona, Minn., 1977-78; adv. com. Agrl. Interpretative Center, Fairmont, Minn., 1979; 1st Dist. coordinator vol. activities Vice Pres. Walter F. Mondale, 1968; del. State Conv. from Olmsted County, Minn. Democratic party, 1974, 76, 78; nat. treas. U.S. Sen. Wendell R. Anderson Vol. Com., 1977-83; bd. dirs. AAU Rochester Swim Club, Family Consultation Center, Rochester YWCA, 1969-70, Lourdes High Sch. Devel. Fund; vol. Mondale for Pres. campaign, 1984; mem. Gov.'s Task Force Women's History Interperative Ctr., 1985—; v.p. Minn. Ornithologists Union, 1988—. Recipient Outstanding Vol. medal St. Marys Hosp., 1967, plaque of appreciation Olmsted County Bicentennial Commn., 1976, medallion and cert. of recognition Minn. Bicentennial Commn., 1976, cert. of appreciation Gov.'s Aesthetic Environ. Program, 1977. AAUW Ednl. Found. grantee, 1976. Mem. AAUW (founder Dayton Benefit for Scholarships 1955, dir. Rochester br. 1955-56, 75-77), Hospitality Inst. Tech. and Mgmt. (bd. dirs.), Rochester Banks Clearing House Assn. (chairperson 1977-78), Audubon Soc. (bd. dirs. Zumbro Valley chpt. 1987-88, v.p. 1988-89), Needlework Guild (v.p. 1986-87), Pres's. Club, T.S. Roberts Soc. of the Bell Mus. Natural History (charter 1989—). Assoc. editor jour. The Loon, 1987—. Home: 2918 SW 15th Ave Rochester MN 55902 Office: Rochester Bank & Trust Co Box 6478 Rochester MN 55903

PLUNKETT, MARYANN, actress; b. Lowell, Mass., 1953. Student, U. N.H. Co-founder Portland (Maine) Stage Co. Broadway debut in Agnes of God, 1983; other Broadway appearances include Sunday in the Park with George, Me and My Girl (Tony award for best actress in a mus. 1987). Office: care AFTRA 11 Beacon Boston MA 02136*

PLUNKETT, MELBA KATHLEEN, manufacturing company executive; b. Marietta, Ill., Mar. 20, 1929; d. Lester George and Florence Marie (Hutchins) Bonnett; student public schs.; m. James P. Plunkett, Aug. 18, 1951; children—Julie Marie Plunkett Hayden, Gregory James. Co-founder, 1961, since sec.-treas., dir. Coils, Inc., Huntley, Ill. Mem. U.S. C. of C., U.S. Mfg. Assn., Ill. C. of C., Ill. Notary Assn. Roman Catholic. Home: Rte 1 Sleepy Hollow Rd West Dundee IL 60118 Office: 11716 Algonquin Rd Huntley IL 60142

PLUNKETT, TAMMY JO, quality assurance professional; b. Salina, Kans., Oct. 11, 1958; d. Raymond Joseph and Leola Jean (Erickson) Gruber; m. Wayne L. Trickle, Nov. 5, 1977 (div. May 1987); children: Erin Amber, Laura Beth. Cosmetology degree, Acad. Hair Design, Salina, 1977; student, Kans. Coll. Tech., 1988-89. Lic. cosmetologist, Kans. Owner, operator Hair Designs by Tammy, Minneapolis, Kans., 1978-79; clk. Alco, Concordia, Kans., 1985-87; asst. mgr. Taco Grande, Inc., Concordia, 1987; quality assurance rep. Idelman Telemarketing, Salina, 1987-88; office mgr. Waste Mgmt. Salina, 1988—. Mem. NAFE, YWCA, North Salina Bus. Assn. (sec.-treas. 1990—, North Salina Clean-up 1989). Home: Rte 1 Box 42 Minneapolis KS 67467 Office: Waste Mgmt 1901 W Grand Salina KS 67401

PLUST, LOIS MARION, casino/hotel administrator; b. Trenton, N.J., May 31, 1954; d. John William and Josephine Theresa (Brovey) Pl. BA cum laude, Glassboro (N.J.) State U., 1976; MA, Rider Coll., 1980. Devel. specialist div. youth and family svcs. State of N.J., Trenton, 1976, adminstrv. analyst div. youth and family svcs., 1976-79, adminstrv. analyst II div. youth and family svcs., 1979-80; sr. procedures analyst personnel support Resorts Internat. Casino Hotel, Atlantic City, N.J., 1980-86, adminstr. human resources human resources dept., 1986-89, adminstr. internal communications employee svcs., 1989—; chairperson Inter-Casino Credit Unions, Atlantic City, 1986, chairperson supervisory com. Casino Hotel Employees Credit Union, 1984, 85, 86. Vol. fundraising activitis Am. Cancer Soc., Atlantic City, 1986—; chairperson Resorts Internat./Casino Hotel campaign United Way, Atlantic City, 1986, 87, 88, 89. Recipient Alan Angelo award United Way of Atlantic County, 1987. Mem. NAFE, Atlantic Area Bus. and Profl. Women (chairperson), 2000 Notable Am. Women for Community Achievement. Office: Resorts Internat Casino North Carolina & Boardwalk Atlantic City NJ 08404

PNAZEK, KAREN ANNE, advertising executive; b. Palos Township, Ill., Aug. 11, 1961; d. Thaddeus Charles and Lolita Beverly (Douglas) Pnazek. BS in Advt., U. Ill., 1983; postgrad. in bus., DePaul U., Chgo., 1985—. Retail display advt. sales exec. Chgo. Tribune, 1983-86; advt. and promotions dir. Milgram Kagan Corp., South Holland, Ill., 1986-87; advt. dir. La-Z-Boy Corp., Hammond, Ind., 1987; major accts. advt. exec. Penny Saver Publs., Tinley Park, Ill., 1988-90, Suburban Jours., St. Louis, 1990—; cons. Community Mktg. Cons., Stevens Point, Wis., 1988—. Contbr. poem to book (Hon. Mention award 1989). Vol. Orland Twp. (Ill.) Youth Commn., 1988-90, Children Learning Other Ways Naturally, Orland Twp., 1988-90; vol. mktg. cons. S. Suburban Arts Coun., Homewood, Ill., 1988. Mem. S. Suburban C. of C. Home: 741B Hawkmount Circle Chesterfield MO 63017 Office: Suburban Jours 1714 Deer Tracks Trail Saint Louis MO 63131

POBLETE, JOCELYN GUIA, information analyst, computer programmer; b. Manila, Philippines, Nov. 7, 1960; came to U.S., 1968; d. Nenita (Guia) Simon. BBA, U. Mass., 1984; MBA, Western New Eng. Coll., 1990. Prodn. controller Wang Labs., Inc., Holyoke, Mass., 1984-85, system technician II, 1985; programmer II Hartford (Conn.) Ins. Group, 1985-87; programmer Spalding Sports Worldwide, Chicopee, Mass., 1987-88, sr. programmer, 1988-89, info. analyst, 1989—. Co-founder, co-chmn. Profl. Woman's Support Group, 1990—. Mem. Data Processing Mgmt. Assn., Nat. Assn. for Female Execs., Theosophical Soc. Am. Office: Spalding Sports Worldwide 425 Meadow St Chicopee MA 01021

POBLETE, RITA MARIA BAUTISTA, physician; b. Manila, May 19, 1954; came to U.S., 1980; d. Juan Gonzalez and Rizalina (Bautista) Poblete. BS, U. Philippines, 1974, MD, 1978. Diplomate Am. Bd. Internal

Medicine. Intern, resident Wayne State U./Detroit Med. Ctr., 1982-85, fellow in infectious disease, 1986-87; fellow in infectious disease Chgo. Med. Sch./VA Hosp., North Chicago, Ill., 1985-86; fellow in spl. immunology U. Miami/Jackson Meml. Hosp., 1987-89; adj. clin. instr. Dept. of Med. U. Miami, 1989-90, asst. prof. medicine, 1990—; adj. clin. instr. dept. medicine U. Miami, 1989-90. Contbr. articles to med. jours. Mem. Am. Soc. for Microbiology, AMA. Office: U Miami Dept Medicine D90A Park Plaza East 901 NW 17th St Suite D Miami FL 33136

POCHAPIN, PAMELA SUSAN, public relations professional; b. Pitts., Oct. 1, 1961; d. Martin Arthur and Adrienne Marsha (Drapkin) P. Student, Edinboro U. Pa., 1979-80; BA, U. Pitts., 1983. Pub. rels. asst. Buhl Sci. Ctr., Pitts., 1983-85; pub. rels., publs. and edn. asst. Small Mfrs. Coun. (now SMC-Pa. Small Bus.), Pitts., 1985-86; pub. rels. coord. Vista Internat. Hotel, Pitts., 1986-88, Carlow Coll., Pitts., 1988-89; publicity and promotions coord. Buhl Sci. Ctr., Pitts., 1989—; media cons. Laser Images, Inc., Van Nuys, Calif., 1985-87. Mem. Women in Communications, Inc. (bd. dirs., pres. elect 1989-90, v.p. mktg. 1988-89, treas. 1987-88, pres. 1990-91). Democrat. Jewish. Office: Buhl Sci Ctr Allegheny Sq Pittsburgh PA 15212

PODAGROSI, KATY BLANCHE, municipal official, writer; b. Eagle Lake, Fla., May 5, 1935; ad. W.B. and Pina Ella (Self) Roberts; m. Ernest G. Podagrosi, Aug. 9, 1953; children: Victor, Rebecca, Jo-Ella, Andrew. BS, Ea. Ill. U., 1983; MPA, Sangamon State U., Springfield, Ill., 1988. Mng. editor The Rantoul (Ill.) Press, 1967-74; exec. dir. Rantoul Armed Svcs. YMCA, 1976-84; mayor, trustee Rantoul, 1984—; pres. Champaign (Ill.) County Mayor's Assn.,1986-87, Cen. Ill. Mayor's Assn., 1987-88. Author: NEIPSWAH, 1978. Chmn. United Way, Rantoul, 1973. Named Pub. Citizen of Yr. Cen. Ill Social Workers, 1973. Mem. Bus. and Profl. Women (pres. 1981, Outstanding Working Woman 1987), Ill. Mcpl. League (legis. com. 1985—). Office: Village of Rantoul 333 S Tanner Rantoul IL 61866

PODANY, AMY ELIZABETH, manufacturing executive; b. N.Y.C., Mar. 6, 1961; d. Albert and Stella T. (Wozniak) Stevens; m. John R. Podany, Sept. 22, 1984. BA, Seattle U., 1983; postgrad., Golden Gate U., 1990—. With aerospace manufacturing Rohr Industries, Riverside, Calif., 1985-89, material scheduler, 1987-88, project coord., 1988-89. Recipient Outstanding Svc. award ARC, 1990; recognized for outstanding svc. to community United Way; Seattle U. Alumni Assn. grantee. Mem. NAFE, LWV, Am. Prodn. and Inventory Control Soc., Assn. for MBA's. Home: 12410 Quail Ln Grand Terrace CA 92324

PODD, MARSHA DIANNE, small business owner, nurse; b. Washington, Apr. 14, 1951; d. John Francis and Gretchen (Green) P. BS in Child Devel., U. Calif., Davis, 1973; AA in Nursing, De Anza Coll., 1978. RN, Calif. Nurse Palo Alto (Calif.) Med. Clinic, 1973-78, St. Joseph Hosp., Orange, Calif., 1979-80, Diet Ctr., Petaluma, Calif., 1982-89; nurse Petaluma Valley Hosp., 1980-86; cons. Diet Ctr., Rexburg, Idaho, 1984-85; co-founder Health in Motion Prodns., 1987—. Nurse Vietnam Refugee Placement, Hamilton AFB, 1980; earthquake relief vol. ARC, San Francisco, 1989-90. Recipient award for one of top ten fastest growing Diet Ctrs. in U.S. and Can., 1987. Mem. Bay Area Diet Ctr. Assn. (pres. 1984, treas. 1987-88), U. Calif. Aggie Alumni Assn. Republican. Home: 1108 Susan Way Novato CA 94947

PODGOR, ELLEN SUE, lawyer, educator; b. Bklyn., Jan. 30, 1952; d. Benjamin and Yetta (Shilensky) Podgor. BS magna cum laude, Syracuse U., 1973; JD, Ind. U., Indpls., 1976; MBA, U. Chgo., 1987; LLM, Temple U., 1989. Bar: Ind. 1976, N.Y. 1984, Pa. 1987. Instr. Ind. U.-Purdue U., Indpls., 1975-76; law clk. Kroger, Gardis & Regas, Indpls., 1975-76; dep. prosecutor Lake County Prosecutor's Office, Crown Point, Ind., 1976-78, asst. county atty., 1981-83; ptnr. Nicholls & Podgor, Crown Point, 1978-87, instr. Temple U. Sch. Law, 1987-89; assoc. prof. law sch. St. Thomas U., Miami, Fla., 1989—. Assoc. editor Ind. Law Rev., 1975-76; contbr. articles to legal jours. Del. Ind. Dem. State Conv., 1982; bd. dirs. Lake County chpt. Am. Cancer Soc., 1982-83. Mem. ABA, Ind. Bar Assn., Nat. Assn. Criminal Def. Lawyers, Women Lawyers Assn. Lake and Porter County (past pres.). Democrat. Jewish. Office: St Thomas U Sch of Law 16400 NW 32d Ave Miami FL 33054

PODLES, ELEANOR PAULINE, state senator; b. Dudley, Mass., June 6, 1920; d. Francis and Pauline Magiera; student U. N.H.; m. Francis J. Podles, June 28, 1941; children: L. Patricia Podles Barrett, Elizabeth Lee Podles Keegan. Mem. N.H. Ho. of Reps., Concord, 1976-80; selectman City of Manchester, N.H., 1976-81, v.p., 1978-79; mem. N.H. State Senate, Concord, 1980—; asst. majority whip, mem. fin. com., chmn. public affairs com., public instns. health and welfare com. Del., N.H. Republican Conv., 1976, 78, N.H. Constl. Conv., 1984; pres. pro tem N.H. Senate, 1986—, chair jud. com., vice chair exec. com., senate fin. com., health and human services for pub. insts. com.; pres. Manchester Rep. Women's Club, 1979-80; bd. dirs. St. Joseph's Community Service, Manchester Vis. Nurse Assn.; state chmn. Am. Legis. Exchange Council. Mem. Am. Legis. Exchange Council, Orgn. Women Legislators, Manchester Vis. Nurse Assn. Club: Manchester Country. Home: 185 Walnut Hill Ave Manchester NH 03104 Office: N H State Senate Concord NH 03301

PODMOKLY, PATRICIA GAYLE, typesetting company professional; b. Chgo., May 15, 1940; d. Edwin Paul Baker and Frances (Williams) Popiela. Grad., Jones Comml. Sch., Chgo. Bookkeeper, sec. William C. Douglas & Ralph Falk II, Lake Forest, Ill., 1958—; owner Global Graphics, Inc., Elmhurst, Ill., 1988—. Roman Catholic. Home: 1002 W Muir Ave Lake Bluff IL 60044

POE, MERRY REX, insurance executive; b. Geneva, Ohio, Oct. 8, 1957; d. Glenn George and Ethel (Horvath) Rex; m. Gregory Scott Poe, July 25, 1981. B.S., Miami U., Oxford, Ohio, 1980. CPCU. Underwriter trainee Shelby Mut., Ohio, 1980-81; adminstrv. asst. Johnson & Higgins, Cleve., 1981-82; agt. Planned Ins. Counseling, Inc., Chesterland, Ohio, 1982—, v.p., 1982-88; ind. ins. agt. Rex-Poe Ins. Agy., Inc., 1988—, v.p., 1988—. Mem. Nat. Assn. Securities Dealers (lic., registered), Profl. Ins. Agts. Assn. Republican. Presbyterian. Office: Rex-Poe Insurance Agy Inc 12200 Sperry Rd Chesterland OH 44026

POE, (LYDIA) VIRGINIA, reading educator; b. Bklyn., Jan. 19, 1932; d. Harold Waldemar and Lydia Beatrice (Doswell) Lind; m. Harold Weller Poe, Sept. 11, 1954; children: Michael Lind, David Harold, Timothy Claude. BA, Beloit Coll., 1954; MEd, U. Southwestern La., 1961, EdS, 1972; EdD, U. So. Miss., 1983. Cert. tchr., Fla., La., Ill., Wis. Elem. tchr. Caroline Brevard Sch., Tallahassee, 1961-64; supervising tchr. Fla. State U., Tallahassee, 1962-64; elem., supervising tchr. Hamilton Lab. Sch., Lafayette, La., 1965-67; prof. reading U. Southwestern La., Lafayette, 1968—, head Dept. Curriculum and Instrn., 1987—, assoc. dir. Hawthorne Ctr. Spl. Edn. and communicative disorders, 1988—; co-originator field experiences U. Southwestern La., 1970—; observer in elem. sch. Ecole de Charlemagne, Nancy, France, 1967; cons. Lafayette Parish Schs., 1968—. Contbr. to book: Reading Research Review, 1984; contbr. articles profl. jours., 1985-87; presenter papers to profl. orgns. 1968—. Organizer Conf. on Women in Politics, Lafayette, 1976 (recipient scholarship 1974); treas. State of La. ERA United, 1977; organizer, pres. First Luth. Ch. Day Care Ctr., Lafayette, 1977-80. Recipient research grant, U. Southwestern U., 1986-87. Mem. Internat. Reading Assn., Am. Reading Assn., Coll. Reading Assn., AAUW, (fellowship contribution 1976), United Fedn. Coll. Tchrs., Phi Delta Kappa, Phi Kappa Phi, Kappa Delta Pi, Beta Sigma Phi. Democrat. Lutheran. Office: U Southwestern La USL Box 42051 Lafayette LA 70504

POETKER, FRANCES LOUISE, florist; b. Cin., Apr. 16, 1912; d. Charles Benjamin and Louise (Johnston) Jones; BA, Vassar Coll., 1933; MA, U. Cin., 1934; m. Joseph G. Poetker, Aug. 10, 1937. Buyer Mabley & Carew Dept. Store, Cin., 1933-35; former owner Jones the Florist, Cin., 1942-85, cons., 1985-87; lectr. in field; dir. Cin. Bell Telephone Co., Hospice of Cin., 1989—; co-chmn. flower decorations Winter Olympics, 1980 (silver medal); hostess Nat. Gov.'s Conf., Cin.; dir. profl. flower shows, N.Y. and France, commentator wedding shows; mem. Nat. Eisenhauer People to People expedition to China, 1987; cons. Cin. Zool. Botanical Gardens 1st flower and plant show. Mem. spl. dirs. com. Cin. Park Bd.; Appeared in Cin. Enquirer Bicentennial Flashback, Images Gallery Bicentennial Show; designer numerous floral settings for period mus. including U. Cin., Taft Mus.; designer Internat. Flower Show Peabody Mus., Salem, Mass.; lectr. Cooking With Flowers, 1987-88, mus. instruments; co-author: Wild Wealth, 1971, (newspaper column) Fun with Flowers, 1949—; hostess rev. of Tall Stacks Riverboat Reunion, Cin., 1988; mem. honors com. U. Cin.; founding mem. Nat. Mus. Women in the Arts, 1986, charter mem.; mem. Friends of Taft Mus., Cin. Mus. Natural History; friend of Nat. Arboretum Wildlife Protection Inst. Am.; mem. program com. Cin. Hist. Soc.; pres.'s com. Xavier U., Cin.; exec. com. Cin. Opera; Coll. Club of Cin. (hon mem.1986); v.p. Air Pollution Control League Cin.; adv. bd. Civic Garden Ctr.; bd. dirs. Bethesda Hosp., Cin.; mem. Cin. Beautiful Com. Recipient award of appreciation Dept. Agr., 1962, Sylvia award floral excellence, 1976; Belle Skinner Clark fellow, 1930; named Woman of Year, Cin. Enquirer, 1978; named to Floricultural Hall of Fame, 1967; Researcher, author: (guide) Symbolism of Plant Materials in Porcelain Collection Taft Mus. Cin., 1988. Mem. Am. Hort. Soc. (dir., chmn. 1982 conv., chmn. decorations N.Y.C. nat. meeting, Frances Jones Poetker award named for, 1988), Soc. Am. Florists (1st Century award 1982), Florists Transworld Delivery Assn. (commentator 1942—), Am. Acad. Florists (dir. emeritus), Allied Florists Assn. Cin., Profl. Florist Commentators Internat. (Tommy Bright award 1982), MacDowall Soc., McMicken Soc., N.C. Florists Assn. (mem. nat. com. on capital formation and estate taxation), Hillside Trust, Nature Conservency, Am. Music Scholarship Assn. (bd. dirs. 1987), English Speaking Union (Cin. chpt.). Lutheran. Clubs: Travel (pres., dir.), Women's, Symphony (lectr.), Banker's (Cin.); Garden of Am. (mem.-at-large), Town. Contbr. articles to mags.; designer food, fashion and floral illustrations for trade publs.; panelist weekly TV program Sunday Soul; actress, designer 3 syndicated movie shorts for Soc. Am. Florists; designer Florists Transworld Delivery and 3 florist shops, subject of various mag. articles. Home and Office: 1059 Celestial St Cincinnati OH 45202

POFFENBERGER, KATHRYN IONE, retired librarian, volunteer; b. Vincennes, Ind., Oct. 7, 1908; d. George Hirace and Mary Nell (Harber) Purcell; m. John Templeton Poffenberger (dec. 1954). BS, U. Indpls., 1930; MusM, Ind. U., 1951. Cert. libr., Ind.; cert. tchr., Ind. Tchr., libr. Pleasanville (Ind.) Pub. Schs., 1930-33, Glenwood (Ind.) Pub. Schs., 1933-36, Topeka (Ind.) Pub. Schs., 1936-41; tchr., libr. South Bend (Ind.) Community Schs., 1941-76, ret., 1976. Mem. Am. Assn. Ret. people (tax preparer 1976—), No. Ind. Hist. Soc. (mus. cataloging 1976—), AAUW (speaker), Nat. Ret. Tchrs. Assn., Ind. Ret. Tchrs. Assn., ALA, Ind. Libr. Assn., League Women Voters, Common Cause, Citizens Action Coalition, Am. Civil Rights Union, Mothers Against Drunk Driving, Met. Opera Guild.

POGER, JULIA PAULINE, linguist; b. Burlington, Vt., Dec. 24, 1962; d. Sidney Boris and Ruth Leah (Goldberg) P. Student, Middlebury Russian Sch., 1981, 84; Cert., Univ. de Nice, France, 1983; BA in French and Russian, U. Vt., 1984; Cert., Pushkin Russian Inst., Moscow, 1985; MA/Conf. Interpretation, Monterey Inst. Internat. Study, 1987. Freelance interpreter and translator, 1986—; Russian exhibit guide USIA Info. USA Exhibit, USSR, 1987-88; interpreter bus. negotiations, confs.; bd. dirs. S.T.B.F.P., Inc. (doing bus. as The Other Paper). Translator various articles, patents, speeches. Vol. Dem. Party, Vt. Mem. Am. Translators Assn. Democrat. Jewish.

POGGIOLI, FRANCES CONSOLO MOSTEL, educator, rehabilitation therapist; b. N.Y.C., Apr. 30, 1930; d. Anthony and Mary (Iannuzzi) Consolo; m. Irving Mostel, June 26, 1954 (dec. Aug. 1969); m. Lester John Poggioli, Oct. 27, 1974. B.B.A., St. John's U., Bklyn., 1952; M.S., L.I. U., 1959; postgrad. Buffalo U., U. Siena, 1973, Bklyn. Coll., 1974; doctoral equivalency, CUNY, 1974. Therapist VA Hosp., Bklyn., 1953-54; dir. N.Y. Sch. Industry, N.Y.C., 1954-57; lectr. L.I. U., Bklyn., 1959-62; bus. educator Heffley & Brown, Bklyn., 1963-65; prof. bus. and secretarial option Kingsborough Community Coll. of CUNY, Bklyn., 1965—, recruiter-advisor, 1973—, med. coordinator, 1972—; mem. employment com. bd. higher edn., CUNY, 1983, coordinator employment in med. field, Bklyn. and N.Y.C., 1971—. lectr. U. Siena, summer 1974. Author: (texts) Pitman Medical Shorthand Outlines, 1980; Gregg Medical Shorthand Outlines, 1980; Century 21 Medical Shorthand Outlines, 1981; Word Information Processing-Medical Projects, 1981, 84; also articles in med. and ednl. jours. Mem. Italian-Am. Adv. Com., Bklyn., 1983—. Fellow CUNY Bd. Higher Edn., 1983-84. Fellow Am. Assn. Rehab. Therapy (cert. rehab. therapist); mem. Eastern Bus. Edn. Assn. (conf. chmn. 1983). Roman Catholic (eucharistic minister). Avocations: research; writing; travel; languages; handcrafts. Office: 70A Independence Ct Yorktown Heights NY 10598

POGODIN, ARLYNE, executive recruiter data processing; b. Chgo., Jan. 21, 1947; d. Arnold M. and Bertha (Erkes) P.; B.A., DePaul U., 1980. Timekeeper Morris Handler Co., Chgo., 1964-70; compt., v.p. Lazar & Assocs. of Ill., Chgo., 1970-77; corp. sec., comptroller Interior Alterations, Inc., Chgo., 1977-86; pvt. practice fin. systems and computer analysis, 1986—; pres. Rly and Assocs. Inc., Chgo. Clubs: Mt. Sinai Hosp. Service, De Paul Century.

POGUE, MARY ELLEN (MRS. L. WELCH POGUE), youth and community worker; b. Fremont, Nebr., Oct. 27, 1904; d. Frank E. and Mary (Coe) Edgerton; m. L. Welch Pogue, Sept. 8, 1926; children: Richard Welch, William Lloyd, John Marshall. BFA, U. Nebr., 1926; studied violin with Harrison Keller, Boston, 1926-28, Kemp Stillings Master Class, N.Y.C., 1936-37. Mem. Potomac String Ensemble, 1947-80. Historian, Gov. William Bradford Compact, 1966—; vice chmn. Montgomery County (Md.) Victory Garden Ctr., 1946-47; pres. Bethesda Community Garden Club, 1946-48; bd. dirs. Montgomery County YWCA, 1946-50, 52-55. Recipient Outstanding Service award Bethesda United Meth. Ch., 1984, Cert. of Appreciation, Bethesda Community Garden Club, 1985, Outstanding Contbns. award Soc. Mayflower Descs. in D.C., 1985, 89. Mem. Mayflower Soc. (dir. D.C. 1950—), PEO (pres. 1957-59), Mortar Bd. Alumnae (pres. 1965-67, award 1986), Nat. Geneal. Soc., New England Hist. Geneal. Soc., Hereditary Order of Descs. Colonial Govs., Nat. Soc. Magna Charta Dames, Colonial Order of Crown, Sovereign Colonial Soc. Am. Royal Descent, Order of Descs. Colonial Physicians and Chirurgiens, Nat. Soc. Women Descs. Ancient and Hon. Arty. Co., Welcome to Washington Internat. Club, Ind. Agy. Women (assoc.), Capital Speakers Club, Kenwood Country Club, Delta Omicron Music. Methodist. Editor: Favorite Recipes of Mary Edgerton of Aurora, Nebraska, 1963; compiler, editor Edgerton Coe History, 1965. Home: 5204 Kenwood Ave Chevy Chase MD 20815

POHLMAN, JULIE M., sales executive; b. St. Louis, Sept. 12, 1959; d. Norman George and Mary A. (Pott) P. Student, S.E. State U., 1982, Mo. State U. Salesperson Sears Dept. Stores, St. Louis, 1976-79, Bluff City Beer Co., Cape Girardeau, Mo., 1980-82; sales rep. household div. Hoover Co., North Cantor, Ohio, 1983-87, sale mgr. comml. div., 1987—. Mem. NAFE, Nat. Housekeeper Assn., Bldg. Owners Mgmt. Assn. Office: The Hoover Co 3643 Green Pk Saint Louis MO 63125

POHLY, SUSAN KAY, sales and marketing executive; b. Angola, Ind., Feb. 20, 1946; d. Paul Theodore and Jean Winifred (Rawlinson) P.; m. Ken Cochran, July 6, 1968 (div. Sept. 1975); m. Cynthia Cochran, Steven Cochran. BA, Tex. Tech U., 1967; MEd, Tex. A&M U., 1975. Lic. profl. counselor; lic. in health maintenance orgn. Social worker Tex. Dept. Human Svcs., Dallas, 1967-69; lang. therapist Scottish Rite Hosp., Dallas, 1969-70; psychology instr. several colls., 1975-79; counselor McLennan Community Coll., Waco, Tex., 1975-78; psychologist Tex. Dept. Corrections, Gatesville, 1978-79; asst. warden Tex. Dept. Corrections, 1979-83; sales mgr. Chasewood Partnership, Dallas, 1983-86; sales mgr. Sanus Health Systems, Irving, Tex., 1986-87, dir. sales and mktg., 1987—. Guest therapist Am. Christian TV Network, Ft. Worth, 1986—. Named Finalist Rookie of Yr. Greater Dallas Sales & Mktg. Coun., 1985, Top Sales Cons., Mary Kay Cosmetics, 1983. Mem. Nat. Assn. Health Underwriters. Republican. Baptist. Home: 800 Stafford Dr Arlington TX 76012

POHORECKY, LARISSA ALEXANDRA, research scientist, neuropharmacologist; b. Cholm, Ukraine, Jan. 16, 1942; came to U.S., 1959; d. Roman and Maria (Chornij) Pohorecky; m. Adrian Dolinsky, Oct. 29, 1972. BS, U. Ill., Chgo., 1963; PhD, U. Chgo., 1967. Postdoctoral fellow MIT, 1967-70, rsch. assoc., 1970-71; asst. prof. Rockefeller U., N.Y.C., 1971-79; assoc. prof. Rutgers U., Piscataway, N.J., 1979-86, prof., 1986—; cons. Nat. Inst. Alcohol Abuse and Alcoholism, Rockville, Md., 1978—, Rsch. Council Can., 1980—. Editor: Stress and Alcohol Use, 1983; mem. editorial bd. Alcohol, Jour. Pharmacology and Exptl. Therapeutics, Jour. Studies on Alcohol, Alcoholism, Clin. and Exptl. Rsch. Alcohol. Recipient Career Devel. awards Nat. Inst. Alcohol Abuse and Alcoholism, 1976, 79. Mem. AAAS, Am. Soc. Pharmacology and Exptl. Therapeutics, Rsch. Soc. for Alcoholism, Internat. Soc. for Biomed. Rsch. on Alcoholism, Soc. for Neurosci., Sigma Chi. Office: Rutgers U Ctr Alcohol Study Piscataway NJ 08855-0969

POIANI, EILEEN LOUISE, mathematics educator, college administrator, higher education planner; b. Newark, Dec. 17, 1943; d. Hugo Francis and Eileen Louise (Crecca) P. BA in Math., Douglass Coll., 1965; MS in Math., Rutgers U., 1967, PhD in Math., 1971. Teaching asst., grad. preceptor Rutgers U., New Brunswick, N.J., 1966-67; asst. counselor Douglass Coll., New Brunswick, 1967, 69-70; instr. math. St. Peter's Coll., Jersey City, 1967-70, asst. prof., 1970-74, dir. of self-study, 1974-76, assoc. prof., 1974-80, prof., 1980—, asst. to pres., 1976-80; asst. to pres. for planning St. Peter's Coll., 1980—; chairwoman U.S. Commn. on Math. Instrn., NRC of NAS, Washington, 1983—; founding nat. dir. Women and Math. Lectureship Program, Washington, 1975-81, mem. adv. bd., 1981—; project dir. Consortium for the Advancement of Pvt. Higher Edn., Washington, 1986-88. Author: (with others) Mathematics Tomorrow, 1981; contbr. articles to profl. jours. Mem. Newark Mus., Nutley (N.J.) Hist. Soc.; trustee Nutley Free Pub. Libr., 1974-77, St. Peter's Prep. Sch., Jersey City, 1986—; active N.J. Supreme Ct. Fee Arbitration Commn., Trenton, 1983-86, N.J. Supreme Ct. Ethics Com., Trenton, 1986—; U.S. nat. rep. Internat. Congress on Math. Edn., Budapest, Hungary, 1988.; mem. statewide planning com. Nat. Conf. of Christians and Jews, 1988—; chair evaluation teams Middle States Assn. Colls. and Schs. Recipient Douglass Soc. award Douglass Coll., 1982; named Danforth Assoc., Danforth Found., 1972-86. Mem. Math. Assn. Am. (dir. lectureship program, chmn. various coms., gov. N.J. sect. 1972-79), Am. Math. Soc., AAUP, Nat. Coun. Tchrs. Math. (speaker 1974—), Soc. Coll. and U. Planning (mem. program com. 1989—, speaker nat. confs. 1988—), Phi Beta Kappa, Alpha Sigma Nu (hon.), Pi Mu Epsilon (1st woman pres. in 75 yrs. 1987—). Roman Catholic. Office: St Peter's Coll 2641 Kennedy Blvd Jersey City NJ 07306

POITRAS, NANCY LOU, educator; b. Hartford, Conn., May 24, 1944; d. Louis N. and Carolyn (Philbrick) P. BS in Social Sci., Cen. Conn. State Coll., 1966, MS in History, 1975; MA in Am. Studies, Pepperdine U., 1986. Cert. secondary tchr. Tchr. Berlin (Conn.) Pub. Schs., 1967-81; employee K-Mart Corp., Wethersfield, Conn., 1981-82; dept. chmn. history Parish Hill High Sch., Chaplin, Conn., 1982—; field researcher Berlin High Sch. and U. Conn. Alternative Edn., 1973, 74-81, Parish Hill High Sch. and U. Conn. Human Rights assessment for Conn. Dept. Edn., 1985-86; workshop participant for revision of Human Rights Manual, Dept. State, 1982-83, cons. to tchrs. on history edn., 1989; cons. State of Conn. Manual on Human Rights, 1986. Contbr. poetry to various publs. Adult leader girls Tri-Hi Y, YMCA Youth Club, Berlin, 1967-72; mem. steering com. Hartford chpt. NCCJ, 1986—; alumni rep. New Eng. region, coll. recruiter Pepperdine U. Fellow Ea. Coll., St. Davids, Pa., 1978, Am. Studies Alumni fellow, 1987; fellow Pepperdine U., 1981, 85,, Julian Virtue fellow, 1983; Conn. Coun. Humanities fellow, 1988. Mem. Conn. Edn. Assn. (state conv. rep. 1967-81, local contract negotiator 1973-79, grievance negotiator (1979-80, pres. 1980-81), Nat. Hist. Soc. (founding), Nat. Trust for Hist. Preservation, Conn. Coun. for Social Studies, Nat. Coun. for Social Studies (rsch. com. 1983-87), Alumni Assn. Cen. Conn. State U., Alumni Assn. Pepperdine U., Wilson Ctr. Assocs. (charter), NAFE, Womens Bus. and Profl. Club Hartford. Republican. Roman Catholic. Office: Parish Hill High Sch Parish Hill Rd Chaplin CT 06235

POKORNI, ORYSIA, musician; b. Ternopil, Ukraine, Aug. 4, 1938; came to U.S., 1951; d. Gregory and Olha (Moroz) Danylkiw; m. Paul Pokorni, Jan. 25, 1958; children: Daniel, Mark. Student, Cosmopolitan Sch. Music, 1962; AA, Truman Coll., 1984; BA, Northeastern U., 1989. Mgr. Internat. Theatre of Chgo., 1963—; asst. office mgr. Ravenswood Hosp., Chgo., 1980-83; radio announcer WEDC, Chgo., 1965-66; choir dir. Moloda Dumka Children's Choir, Chgo., 1981-85. Accompanist various choirs and soloists, 1960—; composer songs; music arranger for children's plays. Tchr. Sch. of Ukrainian Studies, Chgo., 1966—; active Ukrainian Women's League, Chgo., 1985. Mem. Ukrainian Congress Com. (chmn. spl. events com. 1984—), Nat. Geographic Soc. Home and Office: 4520 N Richmond Chicago IL 60625

POKRAS, SHEILA FRANCES, judge; b. Newark, Aug. 5, 1935; m. Norman M. Pokras, 1954; children: Allison, Andrea, Larry. Student, Beaver Coll., 1953-54; BS in Edn., Temple U., 1957; JD cum laude, Pepperdine U., 1969. Bar: Calif. 1970, U.S. Dist. Ct. D.C. 1970, U.S. Dist. Ct. Calif. 1970, U.S. Supreme Ct. 1975. Tchr. elem. and secondary schs. Phila. and Newark, 1957-59; pvt. practice law Long Beach, Calif., 1970-78; city councilwoman Lakewood, Calif., 1972-76; judge Long Beach Mcpl. Ct., 1978-85, L.A. Superior Ct., 1980—; supervising judge, 1986; del. Calif. State Dem. Cen. Com., 1975, Calif. State Conv., 1975. Advisor Jr. League, 1980—; mem. early childhood adv. bd. Long Beach City Coll.; bd. dirs. Long Beach Alcoholism Coun., 1979-80, Boys and Girls Club Am., 1981—, Long Beach Symphony, 1985, Jewish Community Fedn., 1982-86, past mem. community rels. com.; active Nat. Women's Polit. Caucus, LWV. Named Woman of Yr. NOW, Long Beach, 1984; recipient Torch of Liberty award B'nai B'rith Anti-Defamation League, 1974; honoree Nat. Conf. Christians and Jews, 1986. Mem. ABA, AAUW, Nat. Assn. Women Judges (dist. supr. 1986), Calif. Bar Assn. (judges div.), Calif. Judges Assn. (mem. ann. seminar com. 1981—), Mcpl. Cts. Judges Assn. (mem. Marshall com. 1979-80), L.A. County Bar Assn. (judges div., mem. arbitration com.), Women Lawyers Assn., L.A. (judges sect.), Women Lawyers Assn. Long Beach, Long Beach Legal Aid Found. (v.p. 1976-78), Long Beach Bar Assn. (active various coms., bd. govs. 1977-78, Judge of Yr. 1987), Long Beach C. of C. (bd. dirs.). Office: So Dist Superior Ct 415 W Ocean Blvd Long Beach CA 90802

POLA, ELIZABETH GRACE, securities analyst, portfolio manager; b. Boston, Aug. 16, 1956; d. Edward Stephen and Elizabeth Peel (Harkey) MacNeil; m. Nino A. Pola, Mar. 19, 1978; children: Stephanie, Stephen. BSBA, U. Fla., 1977; MBA, Emory U., 1979. Rate analyst Oglethorpe Power Corp., Atlanta, 1979-81; fin. analyst Souther Co. Svcs., Atlanta, 1981-82; security analyst Trusco Capital Mgmt., Atlanta, 1982—. Mem. Fin. Analysts Soc., Inst. Chartered Fin. Analysts, Atlanta Assn. Women in Securities.

POLAKAS, VICTORIA V., computer programmer; b. Binghamton, N.Y., Feb. 24, 1936; d. John Alexander and Brona Frances (Okoniewska) P. BA Polit. Sci., Syracuse U., 1957. Programmer USAF, Rome, N.Y., 1958-60, RCA Corp., Cherry Hill, N.J., 1960-68; cons./programmer Unisys, Blue Bell, Pa., 1968—. Mem. APICS, Pa. Hort. Soc., Alpha Omicron Pi (Phila. Alumni). Roman Catholic. Office: Unisys P O Box 500 Blue Bell PA 19424

POLAN, NANCY MOORE, artist; b. Newark, Ohio; d. William Tracy and Francis (Flesher) Moore; A.B., Marshall U., 1936; m. Lincoln Milton Polan, Mar. 28, 1934; children: Charles Edwin, William Joseph Marion. One-man shows include Charleston Art Gallery, 1961, 67, 73, Greenbrier, 1963, Huntington Mus. Art, 1963, 66, 71, N.Y. World's Fair, 1965, W.Va. U., 1966, Carroll Reese Mus., 1967; exhibited in group shows Am. Watercolor Soc., Allied Artists of Am., Nat. Arts Club, 1968-74, 76-77, 86, 87, Pa. Acad. Fine Arts, Opening of Creative Arts Center W.Va. U., 1969, Internat. Platform Assn. Art Exhibit, 1968-69, 72-74, 74, 79, 85-86, 88-90. Allied Artists W.Va., 1968-69, 86, Joan Miro Graphic Exhbn., Barcelona, Spain, 1970, XXI Exhibit Contemporary Art, La Scala, Florence, Italy, 1971, Rassegna Internazionale d'Arte Grafica, Siena, Italy, 1973, 79, 82, Opening of Parkersburg (W.Va.) Art Center, 1975, Internat. Platform Assn. Ann. Exhbn., 1979, others. Hon. v.p. Centro Studi e Scambi Internazionale, Rome, Italy, 1977; life mem. Huntington (W.Va.) Mus. Art. Recipient Acad. of Italy with Gold medal, 1979, 86; recipient Norton Meml. award 3d Nat. Jury Show Am. Art, Chautauqua, N.Y., 1960; Purchase prize, Jurors award, Watercolor award Huntington Galleries, 1960, 61; Nat. Arts Club for watercolor, 1969; Gold medal Masters of Modern Art exhbn., La Scala Gallery, Florence, 1975, gold medal Accademia Italia, 1984, 1986, diploma

Internat. Com. for World Culture and Arts, 1987, many others. Mem. DAR, Allied Artists W.Va., Internat. Platform Assn. (3d award-painting in ann. art exhbn. 1977), Allied Artists Am. (assoc.), Huntington Mus. Fine Arts, Tri-State Arts Assn. (Equal Merit award 1978), Sunrise Found., Pen and Brush (Grumbacher golden palette mem.; Grumbacher award 1978), Am. Watercolor Soc. (assoc.), W.Va. Watercolor Soc. (charter mem.), Am. Fedn. Arts, Nat. Arts Club, Leonardo da Vinci Acad. (Rome), Accademia Italia, Sigma Kappa. Episcopalian. Clubs: Vero Beach Arts (Fla.), Riomar Bay Yacht, Guyan Golf and Country (Huntington), Huntington Cotillion (charter mem.), Grand Harbor Club. Address: 2 Prospect Dr Huntington WV 25701 also: 2106 Club Dr Vero Beach FL 32963

POLANSKY, SHARON H., marketing professional. BA, NYU, 1972; MS, U. Ill., 1974; PhD, U. N.C., 1987. Editor Tea & Coffee Trade Jour., N.Y.C., 1974-76; news editor Lebhar, Friedman, N.Y.C., 1976-78; lifestyle editor Augusta (Ga.) Chronicle/Augusta Herald, 1978-82; asst. city editor Jacksonville (Fla.) Times Union, 1983-85; market researcher Chapel Hill, N.C., 1985-87; sr. rsch. dir. The Gallup Orgn., Princeton, N.J., 1987-89; v.p. Multi-sponsor Surveys, Inc., Princeton, 1989—. Office: Multi-sponsor Surveys Inc 244 Wall St Princeton NJ 08540

POLASCIK, MARY ANN, ophthalmologist; b. Elkhorn, W.Va., Dec. 28, 1940; d. Michael and Elizabeth (Halko) Polascik; B.A., Rutgers U., 1967; M.D., Pritzker Sch. Medicine, 1971; m. Joseph Elie, Oct. 2, 1973; 1 dau., Laura Elizabeth Polascik. Jr. pharmacologist Ciba Pharm. Co., Summit, N.J., 1961-67; intern Billings Hosp., Chgo., 1971-72; resident in ophthalmology U. Chgo. Hosp., 1972-75; practice medicine specializing in ophthalmology, Dixon, Ill., 1975—; pres. McNichols Clinic, Ltd.; cons. ophthalmology, Dixon Devel. Ctr.; mem. staff Katherine Shaw Bethea Hosp., Dixon, Dixon Developmental Ctr. Hosp. Bd. dirs. Sinissippi Mental Health Ctr., 1977-82. Mem. AMA, Ill. Med. Soc., Ill. Assn. Ophthalmology, Am. Assn. Ophthalmology, Alpha Sigma Lambda. Roman Catholic. Clubs: Galena Territory, Dixon Country. Office: 1700 S Galena Ave Dixon IL 61021

POLEMITOU, OLGA ANDREA, accountant; b. Nicosia, Cyprus, June 28, 1950; d. Takis and Georgia (Nicolaou) Chrysanthou. BA with honors, U. London, 1971; PhD, Ind. U., Bloomington, 1981. CPA, Ind. Asst. productivity officer Internat. Labor Office/Cyprus Productivity Ctr., Nicosia, 1971-74; cons. Arthur Young & Co., N.Y.C., 1981; mgr. Coopers & Lybrand, Newark, 1981-83; dir. Bell Atlantic Corp., Phila., 1983—; chairperson adv. coun. Extended Day Care Community Edn., West Windsor Plainsboro, 1987-88. Contbr. articles to profl. jours. Bus. cons. project bus. Jr. Achievement, Indpls., 1984-85. Mem. NAFE, AICPAs, Nat. Trust for Hist. Preservation, Ind. CPA Soc., N.J. Soc. CPAs (com. of mems. in industry and commerce), Princeton Network of Profl. Women (program bd. dir.). Home: PO Box 401 Princeton Junction NJ 08550 Office: Bell Atlantic 1880 John F Kennedy Blvd 4th Fl Philadelphia PA 19103

POLEN-DORN, LINDA FRANCES, communications executive; b. Cleve., Mar. 23, 1945; d. Stanley and Mildred (Kain) Neuger; m. Samuel O. Dorn; children: Lanelle, Brian, Adam, Dawn. BA cum laude, U. Miami, 1967. Reporter Miami (Fla.) News, 1966-67; writer Miamian Mag., 1967-68; dir. pub. rels. Muscular Dystrophy Assn., Miami, 1968-72; cons., adv. and pub. rels. Ft. Lauderdale, Fla., 1974-77; pub. rels. writer J. Cory and Assocs., Ft. Lauderdale, Fla., 1978-79; account supr. Maizner & Franklin, Fla., 1979-86; v.p., communications mgr. Glendale Fed. Bank, Fla., 1986—. Sustaining mem. Mus. Art., Ft. Lauderdale, 1986—, Philharmonic Soc., Ft. Lauderdale, 1987—. Mem. Internat. Assn. Bus. Communicators, Pub. Rels. Soc. Am., Women in Communications, Broward C. of C. (vice chmn. govt. affairs 1984-85). Office: Glendale Fed Bank 301 E Las Olas Blvd Fort Lauderdale FL 33301

POLEVOY, NANCY TALLY, lawyer, social worker; b. N.Y.C., May 27, 1944; d. Charles H. and Bernice M. (Gang) Tally; m. Martin D. Polevoy, Mar. 19, 1967; children: Jason Tally, John Gerald. Student, Mt. Holyoke Coll., 1962-64; BA, Barnard Coll., 1966; MS in Social Work, Columbia U., 1968, JD, 1986. Bar: N.Y. 1987. Caseworker unmarried mothers' service Louise Wise Services, N.Y.C., 1967, caseworker adoption dept., 1969-71; caseworker Youth Consultation Service, N.Y.C., 1968-69; asst. research scientist, psychiat. social worker dept. child psychiatry NYU Med. Ctr., N.Y.C., 1973-81; adv. ct. apptd. spl. advs. Manhattan Family Ct., N.Y.C., 1981-82; matrimonial assoc. Ballon, Stoll & Itzler, 1987, Herzfeld & Rubin, P.C., 1987-88; pvt. practice, N.Y.C.; cons. social work, 1981-86. Contbr. articles on early infantile autism to profl. jours. Mem. Parents' Adv. Bd. Riverdale Country Sch., 1988—; mem. program bd. Manhattan div. United Jewish Appeal Fedn., 1990—. Recipient French Govt. prize, 1963. Mem. Bar Assn. of City of N.Y., N.Y. State Bar Assn., Nat. Assn. Social Workers, Acad. Cert. Social Workers, Alumni Assn. Columbia U. Sch. Social Work. Home and Office: 1155 Park Ave New York NY 10128

POLIDORO, CAROLINE RUTH, marketing executive; b. Teaneck, N.J., Oct. 22, 1939; d. John and Henrietta (Secor) Lauber; m. Salvatore M. Polidoro, Apr. 4, 1959; children: Michele, Michael. Student, Data Tech Inst., 1989, Essex County Coll., West Caldwell, N.J., 1990. Sec. Gen. Motors Ins. Corp., Paterson, N.J., 1958-62, Channel Cos., Whippany, N.J., 1975-77; adminstr. Morgan Constrn. Co., Caldwell, N.J., 1979-83; sec., adminstrv. asst. Scanpro Instruments, Fairfield, N.J., 1983-88; v.p. mktg. and adminstrn. Scanpro/Lorentzen & Wettre U.S.A., Fairfield, 1988—, also sec. bd. dirs., 1989—. Sec. Democratic Assn., Roseland, N.J., 1980-84, Police Negotiating Commn. of Borrough of Roseland, 1976-77, Roseland PTA, 1968-70; active Roseland First Aid Squad, 1979-81. Mem. Nat. Assn. Female Execs., TAPPI. Home: 50 Cooper Ave Roseland NJ 07068 Office: Lorentzen & Wettre USA Inc 10 Madison Rd Fairfield NJ 07004

POLING, NORMA, principal; b. Independence, Mo.; d. Paul and Mabel Elizabeth (Gumersell) Erickson; m. Philip Eugene Poling, Apr. 13, 1951; children: Paula Wepprich, Kristen Ryan, Marta Poling-Goldenne, Douglas. BA in Edn., Ariz. State U., Tempe, 1953, MA in Edn., 1965. Cert. elem. tchr., Calif., Ariz. Faculty assoc. Ariz. State U., 1969-70; tchr. Palos Verdes (Calif.) Unified Sch. Dist., 1970-76; prin. Silver Spur Sch., Palos Verdes, 1976-79, Valmonte Sch., Palos Verdes, 1979-82, Lunada Bay Sch., Palos Verdes, 1982—; pres., chmn. supervisory com. Palos Verdes Fed. Credit Union, 1979-80, v.p., 1989-90. Treas. Palos Verdes Coordinating Coun., 1976-77; pres. congregation Ascension Luth. Ch., Rancho Palos Verdes, 1984-85; student recruiter Ariz. State U., Palos Verdes, 1980—. Recipient Community Achievement award South Bay Panhellenic, 1978; Kettering Found. fellow, 1985, 86, 88. Mem. Internat. Fedn. Univ. Women (participant Helsinki, Finland conf. 1989), Assn. Calif. State Adminstrs., Palos Verdes Adminstrs. Assn. (treas. 1987-88), AAUW (chmn. edn. conf. Helsinki, Finland 1987-88, 89), Alpha Delta Pi (pres. 1975-77, treas. 1977-79). Republican. Home: 68 Cottonwood Circle Rolling Hills Estate CA 90274 Office: Palos Verdes Unified Sch Dist 3801 Via la Selva Palos Verdes Estates CA 90274

POLINSKY, JANET NABOICHECK, state legislator; b. Hartford, Conn., Dec. 6, 1930; d. Louis H. and Lillian S. Naboicheck; BA, U. Conn., 1953; postgrad. Harvard U., 1954; m. Hubert N. Polinsky, Sept. 21, 1958; children: Gerald, David, Beth. Mem. Waterford 2d Charter Commn. (Conn.), 1967-68, Waterford Conservation Commn., 1968-69; Waterford rep. Town Meeting, 1969-71, SE Conn. Regional Planning Agy., 1971-73; mem. Waterford Planning and Zoning Commn., 1970-76, chmn., 1973-76; mem. Waterford Dem. Town Com., 1976—, del. State Dem. Conv., 1976, 78, 80, 82, 84, 86; mem. Conn. Ho. of Reps. from 38th Dist., 1977—, asst. majority leader, 1981-83, chmn. appropriations com., 1983-85, 87-89, ranking mem., 1985-87, minority whip, 1985-86, dep. speaker, 1989—. Trustee Eugene O'Neill Meml. Theatre Ctr., 1973-76, 81—; corporator, Lawrence and Meml. Hosps., 1987—; mem. New Eng. Bd. Higher Edn., 1981-83; mem. fiscal affairs com. Eastern Conf. Council of State Govts., 1983-88. Named Woman of Yr., Waterford Jr. Women's Club, 1977, Nehantic Women's Bus. and Profl. Club, 1979, Legislator of Yr., Conn. Library Assn., 1980. Mem. Order Women Legislators, Delta Kappa Gamma (hon.). Home: 19 E Neck Rd Waterford CT 06385 Office: Ho Reps Hartford CT 06106

POLIS, SHERI HELENE, marketing and education professional; b. Phila., Sept. 25, 1956; d. Joseph H. and Belle (Oslick) P. BA, Pa. State U., 1978; studied music, Neupauer Conservatory, Phila., 1978-84; MPA, Harvard U., 1985. Nat. sales coord. The Lowry Group, Westlake Village, Calif., 1980-85; dir. mktg. and ops. Travel Trust Internat., Washington, 1985-86; exec. dir. The Learning Annex, Phila., 1987-89; regional edn. dir. Bank Adminstrn. Inst., Voorhees, N.J., 1989—. Vocalist numerous performances throughout Pa. and N.J; contbr. numerous articles to profl. jours. Bd. dirs. Burlington County chpt. Am. Cancer Soc. Mem. NAFE, Am. Soc. Profl. and Exec. Women, Women in Communications Inc. Home: 1102 Sagemore Dr Marlton NJ 08053 Office: Bank Adminstrn Inst Pla 1000 Ste 202 Main St Voorhees NJ 08043

POLITE, EDMONIA ALLEN, consultant; b. Washington, June 22, 1922; d. Thomas Samuel and Narcissus Bertha (Porter) Allen-Sylvester; m. George Frederick Polite, Jan. 5, 1941; 1 child, Frederick Gartrell. BA, Roosevelt U., 1958; MEd, Loyola U., Chgo., 1966; PhD in Adminstrn. and Supervision, Purdue U., 1973; DDiv, Ea. U., Tampa, Fla., 1971, DEd in Psychology, 1972. Dir. Media Ctr., Chgo., 1958-69, 73-81; instr. media scis. Purdue U., West Lafayette, Ind., 1969-73; pres. Cons. Inc., Chgo. and Orlando, Fla., 1974—; dir. Community Tutoring Ctr., Chgo., 1974-80; dir. workshop U. Cen. Fla., 1987; cons. Lake Region Conf., Detroit, 1966, Librarians, Inc., Chgo., 1970-71. Author: In Passing, 1970, People Who Help Us, 1982. Founder South End Parents Council, Chgo., 1960, Humanitarian Profls., Chgo., 1974, Orlando, 1983—; bd. dirs. Salem House, Chgo., 1980—. Recipient Outstanding Service award Lions Club, Chgo., 1975, Outstanding Educator award Fla. Agrl. and Mech. U. Alumni Assn. Mem. Nat. Assn. Club Women (dir. archives 1980—), Ill. Audio Visual Assn., Phi Delta Kappa. Club: Successful Progressors (Orlando) (pres. 1983—). Avocations: writing, community service, counseling. Home and Office: PO Box 580459 Orlando FL 32858

POLITELLA, ELLEN SUE, president; b. Cuyahoga Falls, Ohio, Feb. 12, 1924; d. Bert Parker and Lucile (Wasson) Duke; m. Joseph Politella, Sept. 2, 1950 (dec. Jan. 1975). BA, Kent State U., 1950; AM, Oberlin Coll., 1960; student, Kent State U., 1964-70. Dir. christian edn. Christ Episcopal Ch., Shaker Hts, Ohio, 1952-58, St. Paul's Episcopal Ch., Akron, Ohio, 1960-62; instr. history Kent State Wadsworth Br., 1964-72, Wayne Coll. U. Akron Br., Orrville, Ohio, 1972-88; pres. Practical Devel. Systems Inc., Orrville, Ohio, 1989-. Contbr. articles to profl. jours. Mem. Nat. Speakers Assn., Ohio Speakers Forum (bd. dirs., newsletter editor 1988-), Am. Soc. for Training & Devel., Nat. Writers Club. Home and Office: PO Box 4 Orrville OH 44667

POLITOWICZ-HEIRES, THERESA, artist; b. Detroit, Mar. 3, 1953; d. Chester John and Mary Josephine (Barone) Politowicz; m. Vernon John Heires, May 1, 1981; children: Emily Rose, Meaghan Marie. BS, Western Mich. U., 1974. Grad. asst. Western Mich. U., Kalamazoo, 1974-75; manual arts therapist VA Hosp., Battle Creek, Mich., 1975-76; vocat. tchr. Davenport (Iowa) Sch. System, 1976-77; vocat. counselor Scott Community Coll., 1977-79; wood modelmaker, design staff mem. GM, Warren, Mich., 1979-81; freelance artist Iowa, Mich, 1981-89; artist Fountainhead Ltd. Editions, Edina, Minn., 1989—. Exhibited in one-woman and group shows: GM Design Staff, Warren, Mich., Waterfront Fesival, Easton, Md., Southeastern Wildlife Expo, Charleston, S.C., Midwestern Wildlife and Western Art Shows, 1981-89. Recipient 1st Place award N.C. Wildlife Fedn., 1988, craftman scholar U. Mich. Mem. Left Bank Art League, Nat. Women in Arts, Women Ducks Unltd. (art advisor 1986—), Epsilon Pi Tau (pres. 1973-74). Roman Catholic. Home: 2911 Cambridge Bett IA 52722 Office: Fountainhead 5301 Industrial Blvd Edina MN 55435

POLITY, LEDDY SMITH, preschool director; b. Wrightsville, Pa., Nov. 6, 1936; d. Michael Kenneth and Vivian Lentz (Birnstock) Smith; m. Richard Milton Polity, Sept. 15, 1956; children: Karen, Bruce, Jennifer. Student, Gettysburg (Pa.) Coll., 1954-56, Kean Coll., 1966-74. Cert. early childhood edn. Tchr. Little Folks Nursery Sch., Woodbridge, N.J., 1966-67; cofounder, tchr. Presbyn. Nursery Sch., Matawan, 1967; dir. Presbyn. Nursery Sch., 1982—; cons. community services bd. Brookdale Community Coll., 1977-82; workshop presentor, various community groups statewide. Contbr. articles to profl. jours.; appeared as TV panelist on N.Y. and N.J. talk shows. Mem. Sch. Aged Child Care Task Force, N.J. Dept. Human Services, 1983; ad hoc citizens adv. bd., N.J. Bur. of Licensing, 1981, 85, 86-87; Sunday sch. tchr., Cross of Glory Luth. Ch., Aberdeen, 1963-73, Sunday Sch. supt., 1974-76, vacation sch. dir., 1976-78; coordinator, Girl Scouts of U.S., Matawan, 1976-79; apptd. to Gov's. Child Care Adv. Council of N.J., 1984—. Mem. N.J. Shore Chpt. Assn. for Edn. of Young Children (pres. 1976-78), N.J. Assn. for Edn. of Young Children (lit. chmn. 1978-80, 1st v.p. 1980-82, state pres. 1982-84, exec. bd. advisor 1984-86), Assn. for Edn. of Young Children (state conf. planner, 1980, 81, 82). Home: 144 Idlebrook Ln Matawan NJ 07747 Office: Presbyn Nursery Sch 33 Hwy 34 Matawan NJ 07747

POLK, CAROL HURWITZ, real estate associate; b. Jersey City, Dec. 23, 1924; d. Felix Darwin and Lois (Marin) Hurwitz; m. Peter Polk, Oct. 20, 1945; children: Christopher, Robin. BA, Stanford U., 1945. Copywriter Nancy's Splty. Store, Hollywood, Calif., 1945; asst. prodn. mgr. Weinberg Advt., L.A., 1946-48; real estate assoc. Western Nat. Realtors, Sacramento, 1981-85, Conrad, Hunt & Assocs., San Clemente, Calif., 1985—. Mem. vol. bd. Mercy Hosp. Guild, Sacramento, 1955-80, also chmn. various coms.; vol. Dem. campaigns, Sacramento, 1950—. Mem. AAUW, Stanford U. Alumni Assn. (a founder jr. alumni L.A. 1946-47), Cap and Gown Soc. Jewish. Home: 2117 Ave Espada San Clemente CA 92672 Office: Conrad Hunt & Assocs 1000 S El Camino Real San Clemente CA 92672

POLK, EDWINA ROWAND, engineer, surveyor; b. Lakeland, Fla., Jan. 30, 1921; d. Charles Adrian and Edith Ruth (Gramling) Rowand; m. Virgil Isaac Polk, Jan. 2, 1949; 1 child, Edith. B.S. in Math., Fla. So. Coll., 1942; postgrad. The Citadel, 1943. Registered land surveyor, Fla. Draftsman U.S. Navy, Charleston, S.C., 1942-45; tchr. math. Brandon High Sch., Fla., 1945-46; draftsman Food Machinery, Lakeland, 1946-49; draftsman designer, 1949-63; designer Polk County, Bartow, Fla., 1963-76, asst. county engr., 1976-89, ret., 1989; tchr., mem. tech. com. Polk Community Coll., Winter Haven, Fla., 1966-69. Mem. Fla. Soc. Profl. Land Surveyors. Democrat. Baptist. Avocations: history; antiques; cooking. Home: 302 Ariana St Lakeland FL 33803 Office: Polk County Engring 168 W Main St Bartow FL 33830

POLK, MELANIE ROSA, engineering scheduler; b. Houston, Sept. 13, 1955; d. John H. and Ramona (Smith) P. Student Pearl River Jr. Coll., Poplarville, Miss., 1973-74, Jackson County Jr. Coll., Pascagoula, Miss., 1974-75, U. Houston, 1979-82. Prodn. control scheduler Ingalls Shipyard, Pascagoula, 1976-78; sr. engring. scheduler Brown & Root, Houston, 1978-84; sr. engring. scheduler Litton Data Systems, Pascagoula, 1984-85, sr. engring. scheduler, New Orleans, 1985-86; sr. research and devel. scheduler, sr. performance measurement analyst Litton Guidance and Control, Woodland Hills, Calif., 1986—. Contbr. to Best Loved American Poems, 1979, 80. Mem. Assn. Profl. Planners and Schedulers (treas. 1979-80), Nat. Assn. Female Execs. Avocations: scuba diving, sky diving, modeling, acting, traveling. Office: Litton Guidance and Control 5500 Canoga Ave Woodland Hills CA 91367

POLK, SUSAN LUZADER, anesthesiologist; b. Charleston, W.Va., June 16, 1944; d. Gilbert Brooks and Jean Linwood (Cook) Luzader; m. Lee Thomas Polk, Mar. 21, 1975; children: Angela, Adam. BS, Mich. State U., 1966; MD, W.Va. U., 1970; MEd., Northwestern U., 1986. Diplomate Am. Bd. Anesthesiology. Rotating intern Charleston Meml. Hosp., 1970-71; resident in anesthesiology U. Va., Charlottesville, 1971-74; instr. anesthesiology Vanderbilt U., Nashville, 1974-75; attending anesthesiologist Michael Reese Hosp., Chgo., 1975-85, dir. neuroanesthesia, 1978-85; asst. prof. anesthesia and critical care, dir. edn., chief sect. edn. U. Chgo., 1986—. Contbr. chapters to textbooks and articles to profl. jours. Mem. program devel. com. Cresent Counties Found. for Medical Care, Chgo., 1989—. Fellow Am. Coll. of Anesthesiologists, 1974. Mem. Am. Soc. Anesthesiologists (alt. del. 1986-), AMA, Ill. Medical Soc., Soc. for Edn. in Anesthesia (sec. 1985-), Ill. Soc. of Anesthesiologists (pres. 1989-90), Inter-Hosp. Study Group for Anesthesia Edn. (sec. 1985-). Office: Univ Chgo 5841 S Maryland Ave Chicago IL 60637

POLKING, KIRK DOROTHY, school administrator, freelance writer; b. Covington, Ky., Dec. 21, 1925; d. Henry C. and Mary (Hull) P. Student, U. Cin., Xavier U. Editorial asst. Writer's Digest & Modern Photography mags., Cin., 1945-50; asst. circulation mgr. Farm Quarterly mag., Cin., 1950-52, circulation mgr, 1952-57; freelance writer Cin., 1957-63; editor Writer's Digest, Cin., 1963-72, Artist's Market, Cin., 1972-75; dir. Writer's Digest Sch., Cin., 1976—. Author: Let's go with Lewis and Clark, 1963, Let's go with Henry Hudson, 1964, Let's Go See Congress at Work, 1966, Let's Go to an Atomic Energy Town, 1968, How to Make Money in Your Spare Time by Writing, 1971, The Private Pilot's Dictionary and Handbook, 1974, 86, Oceans of the World: Our Essential Resource, 1986. Mem. Women in Communications, Inc. (pres. Cin. chpt. 1976-77, 81-82), Nat. League Am. PEN Women (pres. 1982-85), Cin. Editors Assn. (pres. 1968-69). Democrat. Roman Catholic. Home: 529 Constitution Sq Cincinnati OH 45255 Office: F&W Publs Inc 1507 Dana Ave Cincinnati OH 45207

POLKINGHORNE, PATRICIA ANN, hotel executive; b. Galveston, Tex., Aug. 17, 1948; d. C.L. and Barbara Ann (Rathke) Hughes; children: Pamela, Christopher. Student, Sam Houston State Tchrs. Coll., Huntville, Tex. Catering mgr. Rodeway Inn, Denver; office mgr. sales dept. Hyatt Regency, Phoenix; asst. to v.p., treas., controller Continental Drilling, Okla. City; asst. to v.p. resort food and beverage The Pointe Resorts Inc., Phoenix; dir. adminstrn. S.W. Audio Visual, Inc. Mem. NAFE, Assn. for Info. Systems Profls. Republican. Episcopalian. Office: 1734 N 22d Ave Phoenix AZ 85009

POLKOW, LINDA ROSE, rehabilitation services administrator, occupational therapist; b. N.Y.C., Apr. 8, 1953; d. John Hans and Leonore (Hamburger) Schiff; m. Melvin Samuel Polkow, June 22, 1975; children: Eric Daniel, Jessica Gail. BS, NYU, 1975, postgrad. in pub. adminstrn., 1981—. Lic. occupational therapist. Dir. occupational therapy Burke Rehab. Ctr., White Plains, N.Y., 1975-84; rehab. services coordinator Barnert Meml. Hosp. Ctr., Paterson, N.J., 1984-86; pvt. cons. physicians offices Children's Aid Soc., N.Y., N.J., 1986-87; info. and referral specialist community outreach and pub. relations Health and Welfare Council Bergen County, Hackensack, N.J., 1988—; vis. guest lectr. various colls. and univs. Contbr. articles to profl. publs. Mem. Jewish Community Ctr., Paramus, N.J., 1982—; mem. aux. Bergen City Med. Soc., 1987—, Hackensack Med. Ctr., 1987—; vol. Health & Welfare Council Bergen County, 1988—; bd. govs. Jewish Community Ctr., Paramus, N.J., 1985—; mem. Yavneh Parents Assn., Aux. Paramus. Mem. Am. Occupational Therapy Assn., Vis. Nurses Assn. (utilization reviewer Westchester and White Plains chpts. 1980-84. Democrat. Jewish. Avocations: tennis, biking, camping, travel, reading.

POLLACK, ANN DAVIDSON, marketing executive; b. Newark, Mar. 21, 1958; d. Shepard Philip and Arlene (Harkavy) P. BA Psychology with honors, Vassar Coll., 1979; MBA, Dartmouth Coll., 1981. Product planning analyst Ford Motor Co., Dearborn, Mich., 1981-84; indsl. automation market mgr. Concurrent Computer Corp., Tinton Falls, N.J., 1985-87; product planning adminstr. Lexus div. Toyota Motor Sales, Torrance, Calif., 1988, market rsch. and planning mgr., 1988-89, product mktg. mgr., 1989—. Pres. Seaview Homeowners Assn., Neptune, N.J., 1986-87; bd. dirs. Monmouth County Arts Coun., Red Bank, N.J., 1986-87, N.J. Condominium Assns. Inst., Woodbridge, 1987. Mem. Am. Mktg. Assn., Advt. Rsch. Found., Phi Beta Kappa. Home: 3582 Bravata Dr Huntington Beach CA 92649 Office: Lexus Div Toyota Motors 19001 S Western Ave Torrance CA 90509

POLLACK, CAROL LOUGH, nurse, photojournalist; b. Wheeling, W.Va., Dec. 25, 1924; d. John J. and Mabel L. (Dague) Lough; RN, Ohio Valley Gen. Hosp., 1945; BS, Western Res. U., 1955; postgrad. Johns Hopkins U., 1962-63, Catholic U., 1965-66, NYU, 1949-50; m. Ronald Paul Pollack, Jan. 26, 1956; 1 son, John Ronald. Adminstr. charge nursing service Mt. Sinai Hosp., Cleve., 1953-57; instr. public health City of Cleve., 1957-59; instr. surgery Sinai Hosp., Balt., 1961-63; sch. nurse Franklin Sr. High Sch., Reisterstown, Md., 1964—; polit. reporter Times Newspapers, Baltimore County, Md., 1964-71; editor Northwest County News, 1971-75; editor Tribune, Reisterstown, 1976-77; photojournalist, feature writer Community Times, Randallstown News, Reisterstown, 1978-88; columnist Owings Mills (Md.) Times, 1988—. Pres. bd. trustees Luth. Community Cemetery, 1988—; sec. Reisterstown Community Corp.; v.p. Historic Reisterstown; chmn. Reisterstown Historic Room; mem. Baltimore County Gen. Hosp. Found. Bd.; mem. exec. bd. Humane Soc., Reisterstown; tchr. Sunday sch. Trinity Lutheran Ch., Reisterstown; mem. Baltimore County Landmarks Preservation Commn., 1982-88; hon. mem. Reisterstown Vol. Fire Co., Glyndon Vol. Fire Co. Recipient Meritorious Service award Nat. Hdqrs. CAP, 1979; named Woman of Year, Woman's Club Reisterstown, 1979; Outstanding Vol. Service award Baltimore County Public Library, 1982. Mem. Case Western U. FPB Alumni Assn., Bus. and Profl. Women, Delmarva Press Club, Am. Nurses Assn., Md. State Nurses Assn., Soroptimist, Federated Woman's Club of Glyndon. Author: Reisterstown, 1966, 9th rev. edit., 1976, 10th rev. edit., 1988; Reisterstown Volunteer Fire Company: 75th Anniversary History, and 20 minute VCR tape. Home: 303 E Cherry Hill Rd Reisterstown MD 21136 Office: 409 Washington Ave Towson MD 21204

POLLACK, FLORENCE ZAKS, management consultant; b. Washington, Pa.; d. Charles and Ruth (Isaacson) Zaks; divorced; children: Melissa, Stephanie. BA, Flora Stone Mather Coll., Western Res. U., 1961. Pres., treas. Exec. Arrangements, Inc., Cleve., 1978—. Lobbyist Ohio Citizens Com. for Arts, Columbus, 1975-83; mem. Leadership Cleve., 1978-79; trustee jr. com. Cleve. Orch., mem. pub. rels. adv. com.; trustee Great Lakes Theatre Festival, 1989-90; mem. pub. rels. adv. com., Cleve. Ballet, Dance Cleve., Jr. Com. of No. Ohio Opera Assn., Cleve. Opera, Shakers Lakes Regional Nature Ctr., Cleve. Music Sch. Settlement, Playhouse Sq. Cabinet, Cleve. Ctr. Econ. Edn., Cleve. Conv. and Visitors Bur., domed stadium adv. com. Named Idea Woman of Yr. Cleve. Plain Dealer, 1975, to Au Courrant list Cleve. Mag., 1979, one of Cleve.'s 100 Most Influential Women, 1985, one of 1988 Trendsetters Cleve. Woman mag. Mem. Cleve. Area Meeting Planning, Skating Club, Univ. Club, Women's City Club, Playhouse Club. Avocations: arts, travel, reading. Office: Exec Arrangements Inc 13221 Shaker Sq Cleveland OH 44120

POLLACK, JANE SUSAN, lawyer; b. Newark. BS, U. Pa., 1967; JD, Rutgers U., 1976; LLM, NYU, 1983. Bar: N.J. 1976, U.S. Dist. Ct. N.J. 1976, N.Y. 1982. Assoc. McCarter & English, Newark, 1976-82; labor counsel CBS, Inc., N.Y.C., 1982-84, broadcast counsel, 1984-87; asst. gen. counsel Athlone Industries, Inc., Parsippany, N.J., 1987—. Mem. ABA (entertainment and sports law com.), N.J. Bar Assn., Am. Corp. Counsel Assn., N.Y.C. Bar Assn., Phi Beta Kappa. Republican. Home: 280 Millburn Ave Millburn NJ 07041 Office: Athlone Industries Inc 200 Webro Rd Parsippany NJ 07054

POLLACK, JANET MARCIA, marketing communications specialist; b. N.Y.C., June 11, 1962; d. Herbert and Renee (Slotnick) P. BS in Mgmt., SUNY, Binghamton, 1984; MBA in Mktg., George Washington U., 1985. Asst. account exec. Graphic Harmony, Croton, N.Y., 1986-87; dir. mktg. and devel. YMCA, White Plains, N.Y., 1987—. Bd. dirs. Westchester Alzheimers Assn., 1988—; mem. United Way Vol. Svc. Bur., Westchester, 1988—. Mem. Women in Communications (bd. dirs. 1987—), White Plains Lions Club. Office: YMCA 250 Mamaroneck Ave White Plains NY 10605

POLLACK, JESSICA, account executive; b. Phoenix, Aug. 2, 1960; d. Sanford Pollack and Rhoda-Gale (Klein) P. BA in Psychology, U. Wis., 1982; CLU, Am. Coll., 1987; student, Marquette U., 1988-. Sales rep. Mutual of Omaha, Racine, Wis., 1982-84, Sentry Ins., Milw., 1984-88; account exec. Laub Group, Inc., Milw., 1988-89; treas., bd. dirs. Wis. Women Entrepreneurs, Milw., 1986-87; v.p., bd. dirs. Family Law Pro Se, Inc., Milw., 1988. Mem. Wis. Women Entrepreneurs, Nat. Assn. CLU & ChFC, Internat. Law Soc.

POLLACK, JILL SUSAN, communications executive; b. Cleve., July 26, 1963; d. Richard I. and Beverly C. (Perry) P. BA in Dramatic Arts, George Washington U., 1985. Traffic mgr. Power House Communications, Washington, 1985-86; asst. dir. mktg. and devel. Northlight Theatre, Evanston, Ill., 1986-88; sr. account exec. CM Communications, Chgo., 1988—. Vol. Names Project, Chgo., 1988; press rep. Pappas for Cook County Commr.,

Chgo., 1990. Mem. Women in Communications, Inc. (v.p. programming 1990—), Publicity Club of Chgo., Nat. Mus. Women in the Arts. Jewish.

POLLACK, LANA, state senator; b. Ludington, Mich., Oct. 11, 1942; d. Abbie and Genevieve (Siegel) Schoenberger; m. Henry Pollack, 1963; children: Sara (dec.), John. BA, U. Mich., 1965, MA, 1970; postgrad. Am. U., Am. Acad. Performing Arts, 1976.Instr. Washtenaw Community Coll., 1975-81; sr. adminstr. John Howard Compound Sch., Zambia, 1970-71; chmn. Ann Arbor Democratic Party (Mich.), 1975-77; mgr. campaign for State Senate, 1978, campaign for 2d Congl. Dist., 1980; regional coordinator gubernatorial campaign, 1981; mem. Mich. State Senate, 1983—; candidate for Congress, 1988. Trustee, Ann Arbor Bd. Edn., 1979-82. Democrat. Office: 465 Farnum Bldg Lansing MI 48909

POLLACK, MARY LOUISE, hotel executive; b. Phila., Nov. 15, 1949; d. Edward Latshaw and Mary Louise (Dempsey) Gruber; m. Stephen J. Pollack, May 15, 1977 (div. 1981). BA in English, Duke U., 1971; postgrad., Cornell U. Cert. tchr., Pa. Travel agt. G & O Travel, N.Y.C., 1977-80; sales mgr. Halloran House, N.Y.C., 1980-81; regional dir. Halloran Hotels, N.Y.C., 1981-83, nat. dir. sales, 1983-84; assoc. dir. mktg. Treadway Hotels and Resorts, Saddle Brook, N.J., 1984-85, dir. mktg., 1985-86, v.p. mktg., 1986-87, also bd. dirs.; dir sales and mktg. Eastern region Prime Mgmt., Fairfield, N.J., 1987-88; dir. sales and mktg. Balt. region Prime Mgmt., 1988-89, regional v.p., 1989—; with Treadway Inns Corp. Mem. Hotel Sales Mgrs. Assn. Internat., U.S. Tour Operators Assn., Am. Bus Assn., Meeting Planners Internat., Nat. Passenger Traffic Assn. (hotel com. 1986), Am. Soc. Travel Agts., Travel Industry Assn. Am. (planning com. 1983-84), Nat. Tour Assn. (conv. com. 1982-84, membership com. 1984, cert. com. 1986, mktg. com. 1987).

POLLACK, SYLVIA BYRNE, educator, researcher; b. Ithaca, N.Y., Oct. 18, 1940; d. Raymond Tandy and Elsie Frances (Snell) Byrne; divorced; children: Seth Benjamin, Ethan David. BA, Syracuse U., 1962; PhD, U. Pa., 1967. Instr. Women's Med. Coll. Pa., Phila., 1967-68; rsch. assoc. U. Wash., Seattle, 1968-73, rsch. asst. prof., 1973-77, rsch. assoc. prof., 1977-85, rsch. prof., 1985—; asst. mem. Fred Hutchinson Cancer Ctr., Seattle, 1975-79, assoc. mem., 1979-81; mem. study sect. NIH, Washington, 1978-79, 83-85. Contbr. numerous articles to profl. jours.; reviewer for profl. jours. Recipient rsch. grants Am. Cancer Soc., 1969-79, Nat. Cancer Inst., 1973—, Chugai Pharm. Co., Japan, 1985—. Mem. Am. Assn. Cancer Rsch., Am. Assn. Immunologists, Reticuloendothelial Soc., Soc. Devel. Biology, Women in Cancer Rsch. Office: Univ Wash SM-20 Seattle WA 98195

POLLARD, JENAL A., business owner; b. Okinowa, Japan, Nov. 17, 1961; d. Alvin Sterling and Jennie Mae (Winston) P. Student, Calif. Luth. Coll., 1979, Clark County Community Coll., 1980-81, Mesa Coll., 1984, Loop Coll., 1986. Salesperson Blvd. Mall, J.C. Penney, Las Vegas, Nev., 1978; teller, vault teller Nev. State Bank, Las Vegas, 1978-80; receptionist, sec. tax dept., word processor operator Deloitte Haskins & Sells, Las Vegas, 1980-83; word processor operator Deloitte Haskins & Sells, San Diego, 1983-84; owner Jenal Pollard Word Processing Svcs., San Diego, 1984-85, Chgo., 1985-86; exec. sec. various temp. agencies San Diego, Chgo., 1984-86; exec. sec. Nat. Assn. Realtors, Chgo., 1986-87; owner Jenal Pollard Word Processing Svcs., Las Vegas, 1987—. Office: Jenal Pollard Word Processing Svcs 2550 E Chandler Ave Ste 35 Las Vegas NV 89120

POLLARD, KATHRYN JANE, shopping center property management official; b. Alexandria, Minn., Nov. 2, 1951; d. Edward August and Jane Grace (Campbell) P. BS, Bemidji State U., 1974; MEd in Coll. Student Pers., U. Wis., La Crosse, 1981. Program dir. Student Ctr., instr. edn. dept. Moorhead (Minn.) State U., 1974-75; asst. dir. Student Ctr., U. Wis., Platteville, 1975-77; dir. confs., adult edn. counselor, instr. theatre arts dept. Viterbo Coll., La Crosse, 1978-81; mktg. dir. The Ctr. Cos.-Rosedale (Minn.) Ctr., 1983-89, The Ctr. Cos.-Valley View Mall, La Crosse, 1981-83; promotions mgr. BCE Devel. Properties Inc., St. Paul, 1989—. Contbr. articles to profl. publs. Chmn. parade-float com. St. Paul Winter Carnival, 1984—; mem. Roseville Community Band, 1985—; vol. Our Fair Carousel, St. Paul, 1989—. Recipient silver Effie award Am. Mktg. Assn., 1988, Andy award of distinction Advt. Club N.Y., 1988, Community Svc. award Minn. Found. for Better Hearing and Speech, 1988. Mem. Internat. Coun. Shopping Ctrs. (cert. mktg. dir., Maxi award 1989), Minn. Shopping Ctrs. Assn., Advt. Fedn. Minn. (Show award 1987), Roseville C. of C. (pres. 1987-88), St. Paul Downtown Coun. Roman Catholic. Home: 2670 Mackobin St Roseville MN 55113 Office: BCE Devel Properties Inc 1500 Meritor Tower 444 Cedar St Saint Paul MN 55101

POLLARD, MARCIA JEAN, automotive sales executive; b. Indpls., Nov. 4, 1951; d. Morris Dean and Bonnie Jean Pollard. AB, Ind. U., 1974; MS, Butler U., 1978. Tchr., coach Warren Twp. Met. Sch. Dist., Indpls., 1974-78; territory mgr. Fed.-Mogul Corp., Denver, 1982-85, sales program mgr., 1985-88; territory sales rep. Shell Oil Co., Indpls., 1978-82; account exec. Aeroquip Corp., Detroit, 1988—. Active Big Bros./Big Sisters Am.; vol. arbitrator Better Bus. Bur., Wellness Network Greater Detroit. Mem. NAFE, Soc. Automotive Engrs. Home: 222 W Lincoln Birmingham MI 48009

POLLARD, MARILYN BERGKAMP, utility company executive; b. Fowler, Kans., July 7, 1937; d. Frank Henry and Mary Magdalene (Kuhl) Bergkamp; 1 child, Darin. Student, U. Colo., Denver, 1962, U. Denver, 1968, Metro State Coll., Denver, 1969, Colo. Women's Coll., Denver, 1977. Ins. underwriter Laurin Jones Agy., Dodge City, Kans., 1955-60; legis. asst. State of Kans., Topeka, 1960-61; various positions Denver, 1961-76; asst. to pres. Pub. Service Co. of Colo., Denver, 1976-86, asst. to chmn. bd., chief exec. officer, pres., 1986-89, asst. to sr. v.p. and gen. counsel, 1989—. Mem. Pvt. Industry Coun., Denver, 1984-90; bd. dirs. Denver Jr. Achievement, 1979—, Colo. Found. Dentistry for Handicapped, 1985—, Am. Humanics, Denver, 1985—, Artreach, Denver, 1987—, Denver Civitan Club; incorporator, co-chmn. Colo. for Sensible Energy Policy, Denver, 1982; vice chmn. Denver Salvation Army, 1979—. Recipient Downtown Denver Career Woman award, 1974, Outstanding Achievement in Pub. Relations award, 1972. Club: Denver Press (bd. dirs. 1977-78). Office: Pub Svc Co Colo 550 15th Denver CO 80201

POLLARD, REBBECCA RAE, teacher; b. Hillsboro, Ohio, Jan. 18, 1952; d. Charles Tennyson Jr. and Jessie Lee (Day) Kreisher; m. Gerald Kay Pollard, Aug. 11, 1973; 1 child, Matthew Scott. AS in Chemistry, Ea. State Coll., Wilburton, Okla., 1971; BS in Sci. Edn., U. Okla., 1973; MEd, Northeastern State U., Tahlequah, Okla., 1978. Sci. tchr. Noble (Okla.) Jr. High Sch., 1973-75, Union Middle Sch., Tulsa, 1975-78, Iowa (La.) High Sch., 1978-79; sci. tchr. Union Jr. High Sch., Tulsa, 1979-81, gifted program coord., 1981—; acad. team coach, Union Jr. High Sch., Tulsa, 1984-87. Vol. Keating for Congress campaign, Tulsa, 1984; mem. Koinonia com., Patrian Ch., Tulsa, 1985-88. Mem. Nat. Sci. Tchrs. Assn., Okla. Assn. Gifted, Creative, Talented, Northeast Network for Gifted, Okla. Jubilee Chpt. of Sweet Adelines, Phi Delta Kappa. Republican. Office: Union Jr High Sch 5656 S 129th E Ave Tulsa OK 74134

POLLARD, SHIRLEY, personnel training director, consultant; b. Brunswick City, Va., July 8, 1939; 1 child, Darryl. Degree in bus. adminstrn., Upper Iowa U., 1978. Adminstr. East. Balt. Community Corp.; tng. coord. Balt. County Concentrated Employment Tng. Program; exec. dir. Park Heights Community Corp., Balt.; dir. Linkages, Inc., Balt. Contbr. articles to Afro Am. newspaper. Active Balt. Urban League, Balt. Welfare Rights Orgn.; pres. United Black Fund Balt., 1989—; founder, pres. Balt. County Polit. Action Coalition, 1982—; founder, dir. Linkages, Inc., 1980; founder, dir. Tng. and Placement Svcs., 1989; active United Svc. Orgn., Md. Minority Contractors Assn., U.S. Civil rights Mus. and Hall of Fame, Smithsonian Instn.; founder Arrican Am. Culture Ctr. Recipient Outstanding Achievement award Md. Minority Contractors Assn., Mayor's Citation, Martin Luther King Civil Rights award, 1987, Md. State Dept. Edn. award, 1987, Congl. Achievement award, Kool Achiever awards, 1990, Nat. Black Caucus Spl. award, 1990, Congrssional Achievement award, 1988; Mayor's citation, 1984. Mem. Am. Soc. Pers. Adminstrn., Am. Soc. Health/Manpower/Edn./Tng., Assn. for Providers Employment and Tng., NAACP (founder, pres. Randallstown chpt. 1988—), Balt. Coun. on Fgn. Affairs, Transafrica, USO, Md. Minority Contractors Assn. (Achievement award 1986, bd. dirs. 1984-89), Smithsonian Assoc. Office: PO Box 32051 Baltimore MD 21208

POLLITT, GERTRUDE STEIN, psychotherapist, clinical social worker; b. Vienna, Austria; came to U.S., 1949, naturalized, 1951; d. Julius and Sidoni (Brauch) Stein; m. Erwin P. Pollitt, Jan. 13, 1951 (dec. Aug. 1977). Social Service course Brit. Council, London, 1943-44; BA, Roosevelt U., 1954; MA, U. Chgo., 1956; LHD (hon.) World U., Ariz., 1986. Cert. Chgo. Inst. Psychoanalysis, 1963, diplomate clin. social work, 1987, diplomate Am. Bd. Clinical Social Work. Resident social worker Anna Freud Residential Nursery Sch., Essex, Eng., 1944-45; dep. dir. UN, U.S. Zone, Germany, 1945-48; psychiat. social worker Jewish Children's Bur., Chgo., 1955-63; pvt. practice as psychotherapist and/or clin. social worker, Glencoe, Ill., 1961—; cons. Winnetka (Ill.) Community Nursery Sch., 1962-63, North Shore Congregation Nursery Sch., 1966-69, Oakwood Home for Aged, Highland Park (Ill.) High Sch., 1979-80; instr. profl. devel. programs Chgo. Inst. for Psychoanalysis, 1982, Sch. Social Service Adminstrn., U. Chgo.; mem. core faculty Ctr. Psychoanalytic Studies; mem. faculty profl. devel. program Sch. Social Service Adminstrn., U. Chgo.; cons., supr. ongoing profl. study groups on clin. issues, 1984—. Contbr. articles to profl. jours. Bd. dirs. Glencoe Youth Service, Menninger Found. Fellow Am. Orthopsychiat. Assn.; mem. Nat. Assn. Social Workers (chmn. pvt. practice com. 1965-70), Ill. Soc. Clin. Social Workers (bd. dirs.), Acad. Cert. Social Workers. Home and office: 481 Oakdale Ave Glencoe IL 60022

POLLOCK, ALICE DIANE, Small business owner; b. Dodge City, Kans., May 14, 1939; d. Wallace Henry and Margaret Lois (Ludwick) Ott; m. William P. Morrison, Jr. (div. 1973); 1 child, Gregory Scott. AA, Scottsbluff Jr. Coll., Nebr., 1960. Cert. personnel cons. Sales mgr. Diamond Sales, Little Rock, Ark., 1967-73; real estate broker Oakmont Shores, Ridgedale, Mo., 1974-76; pers. E.A. Martin Co., Springfield, Mo., 1976-82; employment counselor Meadowmere Employment Agy., Springfield, 1982-86; mgr., owner First Place, Inc., Springfield, 1986--; adj. tchr. Phillips Jr. Coll., Springfield, 1990—. Cubmaster Boy Scouts Am., Willard, also bd. dirs. Ozarks coun.; bd. dirs. Willard Fire Protection Assn., 1984-86; chmn., fundraiser Ozarks Nat. Coun. on Alcoholism, Springfield, 1986; fundraiser Leukemia Soc., Make-A-Wish, Ronald McDonald House of Ozarks, Springfield, 1988; bd. dirs. pub. rels., chmn. fin. com., mem. pub. rels. com., ann. gift com., Jr. Achievement, Springfield, 1988-89; active Leadership Springfield, 1990—; com. chmn. Sta. KOZK, pub. TV, Springfield, 1988-89. Republican. Presbyterian. Office: First Place Inc 2200 E Sunshine #109 Springfield MO 65804

POLLOCK, KATHLEEN RORK, psychologist, consultant; b. Inglewood, Calif., Aug. 2, 1948; d. Elwood Cecil and Jacquelyn Dolores (Kilian) Rork; m. Kenneth L. Duber, June 14, 1968 (div. June 1989); children: Darrin, Matthew; m. Gregory Michael Pollock, Jan. 21, 1990. BA, Calif. State U., Northridge, 1975, 81; MA, Calif. Sch. Profl. Psychology, L.A., 1984, PhD, 1986. Lic. psychologist, Calif., Wash. Tchr. secondary edn., speech and debate coach L.A. City Schs., 1975-79; psychol. trainee Children's Bapt. Home/United Way Agy., Inglewood, 1982-83, San Fernando Valley Mental Health, Van Nuys, Calif., 1983-84; from intern in psychology to psychologist L.A. County Sheriff's Dept., 1984-87; exec. v.p., staff psychologist Duber Soc. Inc., Beverly Hills, Calif., 1986-88; pvt. practice psychol. cons. L.A. and Seattle, 1988—. Mem. Am. Psychol. Assn., Calif. Psychol. Assn., Wash. Psychol. Assn., Alpha Delta Pi. Home and office: 5340 W Mercer Way Mercer Island WA 98040

POLLOCK, MARSHA LEIBO, retailer; b. Jacksonville, Fla., June 2, 1942; d. Morris Leibo; m. Ronald L. Pollock, Aug. 19, 1962; children: Joy, Stacy, Lee. Student, U. Ga., 1960. Office worker Oxford Fin., Phila., 1962, Butler Shoe Corp., Atlanta, 1962-64; pre sch. tchr. Solomon Schechter Day Sch., Jacksonville, Fla., 1975-84; officer, bookeeper, cashier Leibo's Big and Tall Men's Shop, Jacksonville, Fla. Mem. Local Sch. Adv. Council, Dupont Jr. High, 1985-86, Wolfson High Sch., 1987-89, Nat. Council Jewish Women, Jacksonville, Fla., River Garden Hebrew Home, Jacksonville. Named Woman of Achievement Jewish Theological Seminary and Fla. Br. Women League, Miami, Fla., 1986. Mem. Women's Ort (past pres.), Jacksonville Jewish Ctr. Sisterhood (past pres.), Hadassah (past pres.), Delta Phi Epsilon. Home: 2452 Castellon Dr Jacksonville FL 32217 Office: 3522 Beach Blvd Jacksonville FL 32207

POLLOCK, MARTHA ISACSON, school social worker, therapist; b. N.Y.C., Dec. 8, 1951; d. Manus Isacson and Fay (Bryer) Rosenfeld; m. Larry D. Pollock, June 22, 1974; children: Benjamin, Alexander, Zachary. BA, Oklahoma City U., 1973; MSW, Washington U., St. Louis, 1977. Field coord. Okla. Assn. for Retarded Citizens, Oklahoma City, 1973-74; program dir. Macomb County Teen Health Program, Mt. Clemens, Mich., 1975-77; sch. social worker Utica (Mich.) Community Schs., 1977—; grief counselor, therapist D.S. Temrowski Funeral Home, Warren, Mich., 1981-84; grief counselor Mich. funeral homes, Detroit, 1981—. Contbr. articles to profl. jours. Entertainment dir. Colberry Hills Subdiv., Bloomfield Hills, Mich., 1988—; communicator Werner Erhard & Assocs., Detroit, 1989. Mem. Assn. Cert. Social Workers, Cert. Social Workers Mich., Psi Chi. Jewish. Home: 2763 Brady Dr Bloomfield Hills MI 48013 Office: Utica Community Schs 51401 Shelby Rd Utica MI 48087

POLLOCK, SHARON ROSE, management; b. Balt., Aug. 25, 1955; d. William Edward and Clare Virginia (Kirwan) Tabeling; m. Karl Graham Pollock, Oct. 24, 1986. BSBM, U. Coll. Md., Coll. Park, 1988; Postgrad., U. Coll., Md. Sec. Nat. Security Agy., Fort Meade, Md., 1973-77; budget program Nat. Security Agy., Ft. Meade, Md., 1977-79; printed circuit bd. Prodn. Control Specialist, Ft. Meade, Md., 1979-80; printing prodn. control specialist Nat. Security Agy., Ft. Meade, Md., indsl. prodn. control specialist, 1982-86; supr. spl. packaging ops. Nat. Security Agy., Md., 1986-87; sr. systems master planner Martin Marietta Aero and Naval Systems, Balt., 1987-89; project control specialist Systematic Mgmt. Svcs., Washington, 1989—. Religious edn. tchr. St. Marks Ch., Catonsville, Md. Mem. NAFE, Future Bus. Leaders Am., Exec. Women's Network, Club Balt. (pres. 1972-73), Toastmasters Internat., Club 1686, Kritikos, Phi Kappa Phi Honor Soc., Alpha Sigma Lambda Honor Soc. Republican. Roman Catholic. Home: 1-B Winesap Ct Baltimore MD 21228

POLLOCK, VICKI EILEEN, psychologist; b. Portland, Oreg., Apr. 24, 1956; d. Richard Edward and Margorie Helen (Smith) P. AB summa cum laude, Washington U., St. Louis, 1977; MA, U. So. Calif., 1982, PhD, 1985. Sr. research asst. Mo. Inst. Psychiatry, St. Louis, 1977-79; psychophysiol. lab. chief Psykologisk Institut, Copenhagen, 1979-80; data analyst Ctr. for Longitudinal Research, L.A., 1980-83, data coordinator, 1983-85; psychology intern Neuropsychiatric Inst., L.A., 1984-85; asst. prof. psychiatry (psychology) U. So. Calif., L.A., 1985—. Contbr. articles to profl. jours. Fellow Nat. Inst. Alcohol Abuse and Alcoholism, Washington, Grass Found. fellow, 1976. Soc. for Psychophysiol. Research, AAAS, Behavior Genetics Assn., Sigma Xi. Office: U So Calif 1934 Hospital Pl Los Angeles CA 90033

POLLOCK O'BRIEN, LOUISE MARY, public relations executive; b. Tarentum, Pa., Mar. 14, 1948; d. Louis P. and Amelia M. (Ballay) Pollock; m. Vincent Miles O'Brien. BS, Ind. U. of Pa., 1970. Tchr. Archbishop Wood High Sch., Warminster, Pa., 1970-75; spokesperson, publicist Calif. Olive Industry, Fresno, 1976-78; account exec. Ketchum Pub. Rels., N.Y.C., 1979-81, account supr., 1982-83, v.p., 1984, v.p., group mgr., 1985-88, sr. v.p., group mgr., 1988-89, dir. food mktg., sr. v.p., 1989—; mem. pub. relations adv. com. Mayor's Vol. Action Com., N.Y.C., 1986; mem. food service adv. bd. L.I. City Coll., Bklyn., 1987-88. V.p., fundraiser West 76th St. Block Assn., N.Y.C., 1982. Mem. Internat. Foodservice Editorial Council (v.p., bd. dirs. 1984-85). Democrat. Office: Ketchum Pub Rels 1133 Ave of the Americas New York NY 10036

POLON, LINDA BETH, educator, writer, illustrator; b. Balt., Oct. 7, 1943; d. Harold Bernard and Edith Judith Wolff; m. Marty I. Polon, Dec. 18, 1966 (div. Aug. 1983). BA in History, UCLA, 1966. Elem. tchr. Los Angeles Bd. Edn., 1967—; writer-illustrator Scott Foresman Pub. Co., Glenview, Ill., 1979—, Frank Schaffer Pub. Co., Torrance, Calif., 1981-82, Learning Works, Santa Barbara, Calif., 1981-82, Harper Row Co.; editorial reviewer Prentice Hall Pub. Co., Santa Monica, Calif., 1982-83. Author: (juvenile books) Creative Teaching Games, 1974; Teaching Games for Fun, 1976; Making Kids Click, 1979; Write up a Storm, 1979; Stir Up a Story, 1981; Paragraph Production, 1981; Using Words Correctly, 3d-4th grades, 1981, 5th-6th grades, 1981; Whole Earth Holiday Book, 1983; Writing Whirlwind, 1986; Magic Story Starters, 1987. Mem. Soc. Children's Book Writers. Democrat. Home: 1515 Manning Ave Apt 3 Los Angeles CA 90024 Office: L A Bd of Edn 980 S Hobart Blvd Los Angeles CA 90006

POLOSKI, PATRICIA ELIZABETH, elementary school educator; b. Ardmore, Okla., June 30, 1941; d. Anthony Charles and Hazel E. (Colbert) P. AA, St. Joseph Jr. Coll., 1960; BS, Mo. Western U., 1970; MS in Edn., Northwest Mo. State U., 1972, EdS in Adminstrn. and Supervision, 1985. Cert. tchr. elem. tchr., elem. prin., supt. Head tchr. Project Head Start, St. Joseph, Mo., 1965; tchr. St. James Sch., St. Joseph, 1961-70; prin. St. James Parochial Sch., St. Joseph, 1970-77; tchr. St. Joseph Sch. System, 1977-90, mem. 1st curriculum com., 1st instructional math. mgmt. com., sch.-wide discipline com., reading com., libr. skills com. PcD, & com. in charge vols., pub. sch. newspaper and yearbook, life mem. PTA. Named Outstanding Young Woman of Am., 1970, Outstanding Young Educator, 1972, Outstanding Young Leader of Am., 1985, 88, 89. Mem. ASCD, NAFE, NEA, Internat. Reading Assn., Mo. State Tchrs. Assn., St. Joseph City Tchrs. Assn. Home: 3501 Sacramento Saint Joseph MO 64507

POLSINELLI, ADELAIDE CLAUDIA LISA, real estate executive; b. N.Y.C., June 16, 1960; d. Emilio and Antonietta (Leva) P. BA in Pub. Adminstrn., NYU, 1983. With sales dept. Arthur Kahn Co., N.Y.C., 1978-85; with residential sales dept. Century 21 Realty, N.Y.C., 1985-86; with comml. sales dept., v.p. Bach Realty, N.Y.C., 1986—. Mem. N.Y. Bd. Realtors. Office: Bach Realty 18 E 48th St New York NY 10017

POLSTON, CAROLYN, manufacturing executive recruitment company; b. Kansas City, Mo., Jan. 20, 1946; d. Carsel Courtlin Whitenack and Loretta L. (Carlock) Brown; m. John A. Polston, Sept. 6, 1968 (div. Nov. 1973). BS in Psychology and Edn., Northeastern State U., 1969. Cert. personnel cons. Cons. Clarke Employment Svc., Tulsa, 1974-79; unit mgr., cons. Dunhill of Tulsa, 1979-90; sr. cons. refining and petrochem. industry Maxwell Search (formerly Dunhill of Tulsa), Tulsa, 1990—. Chmn. season ticket renewal Tulsa Opera Guild, 1987-88. Mem. Tulsa Engring. Soc., Cert. Personnel Cons. Soc. (charter), Okla. Assn. Pvt. Employment Svcs. (conv. chmn. 1976-77, sec. 1978). Office: Maxwell Search 8221 E 63d Pl Tulsa OK 74133

POLUMBAUM, JULIA BRUNER, real estate broker; b. N.Y.C., Sept. 22, 1910; d. Simon and Sarah (Kreigstein) Bruner; m. Richard Polumbaum, July 1, 1940; children: Peter, Douglas. Student, Columbia U., 1929-31; diploma, Am. Acad. Dramatic Arts, N.Y.C., 1933. Lic. real estate broker. Sales coord. First Nat. Real Estate Corp., N.Y.C., 1962-66; sales coord. Carlyle Constrn. Corp., N.Y.C., 1967-71; real estate broker Douglas Elliman Gibbons & Ives, N.Y.C., 1971-77, Julia Polumbaum Realty, N.Y.C., 1977—. Named for commitment to excellence N.Y. Times, 1989. Mem. Real Estate Bd. N.Y. Home: 220 E 72nd St New York NY 10021 Office: Julia Polumbaum Realty 220 E 72d St New York NY 10021

POLYÉ, MAUREEN ANN, corporate executive; b. N.Y.C., Sept. 20, 1956; d. William J. and Janice (Healy) P. BS, U. Rochester, 1978; postgrad., L.I. U. Cert. notary pub.; lic. real estate agt. Exec. asst. to pres. and chief exec. officer Travelsavers, Inc., Great Neck, N.Y., v.p. ops. Active fundraising com. Dominican Acad. Mem. NAFE. Home: 290 Community Dr Great Neck NY 11021

POMERANCE, DIANE LINDA, business owner, television/film producer; b. N.Y.C., July 3, 1951; d. Benjamin Louis and Gerda (Reider) Yapko; m. Norman Jerome Pomerance. BA, U. Mich., 1974, MA, 1976, PhD, 1979. Prodn. sec., asst. NBC Sports, N.Y.C., 1977-78; sales asst. NBC, N.Y.C., 1978; prodn. asst., assoc. dir. CBS, N.Y.C., 1978-79; assoc. dir. CBS, NBC and Sta. WNET, N.Y.C., 1978-83, freelance story analyst, reader, 1979-83; segment producer Sta. KTTV-Channel 11, L.A., 1983-84; v.p., account exec. Pub. Info. Network, L.A., 1984-85; exec. producer, co-owner 50/50 Prodns., L.A., 1985-87; exec. producer, owner Polaire Group, Inc., L.A., 1987—. Author: Katherine: A Woman of Vision, 1984. U. Mich. fellow, 1974-76. Mem. Dir.'s Guild Am., SAG, AFTRA, Internat. Documentary Assn., Women in Film, Book Publicists of So.Calif. (lectr., speaker L.A. chpt.), Speakers Press Bur. (lectr., speaker), Am. Film Inst. (seminar moderator, coord. L.A. chpt.), World Wildlife Fund, Greenpeace, Nat. Humane Edn. Soc., Am. Soc. for the Prevention of Cruelty to Animals. Office: Polaire Group Inc Ventura Pl Ste 340 Studio City CA 91604

POMERANTZ, CHERYL JEANNE, nurse, fashion designer; b. Elmhurst, Ill., Aug. 30, 1949; d. Charles Emil and Jeanne Marie (Diber) Mueller; m. Marc Abraham Pomerantz, June 8, 1986; child by previous marriage, Justin Nigel Koehler. AS, DuPage Jr. Coll., 1972; cert. in bio-feedback, Menninger Phys. Inst.; student, Oits Parsons Sch. Fine Art. RN, Ill. Staff nurse Rush-Presbyn. St. Luke's Hosp., Chgo., 1972-89; ind. fashion designer L.A., 1989—; med. dir. Vets. Leadership Conf., Chgo., 1982-84, assoc. med. dir., 1984-85. Contbr. to profl. publs.

POMERANTZ, LAURA, apparel company executive; b. 1948. V.p. Leslie Fay Cos., N.Y.C. Office: Leslie Fay Cos 1400 Broadway New York NY 10018*

POMERANTZ, RHODA SILVERSTEIN, geriatrician, internist, health center executive; b. Phila., May 6, 1937; d. Alexander Silverstein and Bertha (Joffe) Solomon; m. Marc A. Pomerantz, Aug. 14, 1958 (div. Jan. 1986); children: Lauren, Susan; m. Irwin I. Feinberg, Nov. 16, 1986; stepchildren: Susan, Michael, Jonathan, David, Steven. AB, U. Pa., 1958; MD, Women's Med. Coll., Phila., 1963; MPH, U. Ill., 1976. Diplomate Am. Bd. Internal Medicine, Am. Bd. Geriatric Medicine. Intern Presbyn. St. Luke's Hosp., Chgo., Calif., 1963-64; resident in internal medicine Presbyn. St. Luke's Hosp., Chgo., 1964-66, 68-69; mem. attending staff Tri-City Hosp., Oceanside, Calif., 1967, Mile Square Health Ctr., Chgo., 1969-72; mem. adj. attending staff Presbyn.-St. Luke's Hosp., Chgo., 1969-70, med. dir., assoc. adminstr. ambulatory care, 1969-72, asst. attending staff dept. internal medicine, 1970-74, assoc. attending staff internal medicine in preventive care, 1974-82; project dir. Johnston R. Bowman Health Ctr., 1972-76, med. dir., 1976-82; chief Sect. of Geriatric Medicine St. Joseph Hosp. and Health Care Ctr., Chgo., 1982—. Editor Geriatric Rehab. Series, 1980-81; mem. editorial bd. The Pharos, 1976, Ambulatory Medicine Alert, 1987. Fellow ACP, Am. Geriatrics Soc. (del. to AMA 1983—); mem. AMA, Gerontol. Soc. Am., Chgo. Geriatrics Soc., Phi Beta Kappa, Alpha Omega Alpha, Delta Omega. Home: 1315 Sutton Pl Chicago IL 60610 Office: St Joseph Hosp and Health Care Ctr 2900 N Lake Shore Dr Chicago IL 60657

POMERDY, CAROLINE SAUNDERS, management; b. Hartford, Conn., Feb. 14, 1960; d. Walter Saunders and Dorothy Ann (Entwistle) Pomeroy. BA, Lehigh U., 1982; MBA, Resellear Polytech., 1986. System mgr. New Departure Hyatt, Bristol, 1983-85; programmer, analyst Hamilton Standard, Windsor Locks, Conn., 1985-86; tech. cons. Hamilton Standard, Windsor Locks, 1986-87; project mgr. Lotus Devel. Corp., Cambridge, Mass., 1987-89; MIS mgr. Cayman Systems Inc., Cambridge, Mass., 1989—; adv. Jr. Achievement, Bristol Conn., 1983-84. Home: 1423 Commonwealth Ave #103 Brighton MA 02135 Office: Cayman Systems Inc 26 Landsdowne St Cambridge MA 02139

POMERENKE DASS, KELLY JOAN, travel agency manager; b. Rockville Ctr., N.Y., Jan. 8, 1961; d. Frederick William and Joan Ann (Kelly) Pomerenke; m. Lester William Dass, Oct. 31, 1951. AA, Nassau Community Coll., Uniondale, N.Y., 1981; BA, SUNY, Binghamton, 1983; postgrad., Queens Coll., 1990—. Reseacher austic children's unit SUNY, Binghamton, 1982-83; spl. edn. tchr. Woodward Mental Health Ctr., Freeport, N.Y., 1983; psychiat. asst. South Nassau Communities Hosp., Oceanside, N.Y., 1983-84; travel cons. Liberty Travel, Cedarhurst, N.Y., 1985-87; travel agy. mgr. Liberty Travel, Inc., Cedarhurst, 1987—. Home: 909 N Central Ave Woodmere NY 11598

POMPA, SUSAN JOY, medical products executive; b. Chgo., Oct. 14, 1951; d. Hy I. and Evelyn (Cohn) Kaplan; 1 child, Nicole. Student, Met.

Sch. Bus., Chgo., 1970-71. With med. records dept. Swedish Covenant Hosp., Chgo., 1971-74; dir. med. records Northwestern U. Med. Assocs., Chgo., 1974-75; research assoc. Am. Med. Records Assn., Chgo., 1975-76; dir. med. records HMO Rush Presbyn. St. Lukes Hosp., Chgo., 1977; pres., chief exec. officer S.J. Kaplan & Assocs., Inc., Lincolnwood, Ill., 1980—; cons., research assoc. health care grants, 1976—; cons. graphic arts dept. Niles West High Sch., Skokie, Ill., 1985. Patentee in field. Mem. Am. Med. Record Assn. (cert.). Office: SJ Kaplan & Assocs 7215 N Kildare Lincolnwood IL 60646

PONCHIO, MARY THOMAS, marketing professional; b. Lebanon, Ky., Jan. 3, 1954; d. Charles Damien and Mary Ruby (Hutchins) T.; m. John Michael Baute Sr., Sept. 1971 (div.); 1 child, John Michael II; m. Carlos R. Ponchio, June 20, 1983; 1 child, Steven Marcos. Student, U. Ky., Lexington, 1973-76, U. S. Ala., Mobile, 1976-77. Mgr. Champagne Interiors, Covington, La., 1977-79; editor, reporter St. Tammany News Banner, Covington, 1979-80; sec. Town of Mandeville, La., 1980; sales mgr. Rainbow Floor Covering, Covington; leasing mgr. Trosclair Assocs., Lafayette, La., 1981-82; tchr. pvt. tutor Brazil, 1982-85; free-lance writer Baton Rouge, 1985-86; mktg. asst. Kole Industries, Miami, 1986-88, mktg. dir., 1988-90; pres. Copywrite Svcs. Inc, Miami, 1990—. Reporter, writer newspaper Rio de Janeiro 1983-84. Mem. Printing Industry of S Fla. Office: Copywrite Svcs Inc 18524 NW 67th Ave Ste 247 Miami FL 33015

POND, ELAINE SKINNER, freelance writer; b. Ainsworth, Nebr., Sept. 11, 1909; d. Frederick Walter and Ezada Janet (Phelps) Skinner; m. Donald C. Pond, Mar. 13, 1948. Exec. sec. Kaiser Engrs., Oakland, Calif., 1945-48; agt., ownerPinole Agy. State Farm Ins. Co., Bloomington, Ill., 1949-76; freelance writer Pinole, Calif., 1977—. Contbr. numerous articles and columns to newspapers and mags. Named Disting. Civic Leader State of Calif. Mem. Nat. Press Club. Home: 3173 Estates Ave Pinole CA 94564

POND, GLORIA DIBBLE, educator; b. Merced, Calif., Mar. 10; d. Frank Burton and Joyce (Rickabaugh) D.; m. J. Lawrence Pond, Nov. 13, 1959; 1 child, Scott Lawrence. BA, Bennington (Vt.) Coll., 1960; MA, Wesleyan U., Middletown, Conn., 1968; Cert. Adv. Study, Wesleyan U., 1974. Editorial asst. Newsweek mag., N.Y.C., 1956, 58, 59, The Houston Chronicle, 1957; reporter, asst. editor The Rockland Independent, Suffern, N.Y., 1960-62; instr. New Haven U., 1967; from lectr. to prof. Mattatuck Community Coll., Waterbury, Conn., 1968—. Author: Succeed: Write Now, 1978, Write, Simply Write, 1979; contbr. articles to profl. jours. Founding chmn. Comprehensive Health Planning Coun., Cen. Naugatuck Valley, 1969-74; chmn. Conn. Siting Coun., New Britain, Conn., 1976—; mem. Conn. Energy Adv. Bd., Hartford, 1977—, Adv. Coun. to State Health Commr., 1986—; mem. Dem. Town Com., State Platform Com. Grantee, Wesleyan U., 1964-70. Mem. Conn. Libr. Assn. (scholar for libr. progs. 1988—), Conn. Humanities Coun. (scholar for community progs.), Western Conn. Bird Club (publicist 1985-90). Democrat. Office: Mattatuck Community Coll 750 Chase Pkwy Waterbury CT 06708

POND, PATRICIA ANN, travel agency executive; b. South Bend, Ind., Aug. 3, 1948; d. Frederick B. and Catherine L. (Keen) Stillwagon; m. Gary E. Pond, Apr. 18, 1968; children: Jonathon E., Heather A. Student, Ind. U., 1966-68. Pres. Skystream Airlines, Inc., South Bend, 1976-78, Plymouth (Ind.) Travel Ctr., Inc., 1981—. Mem. South Bend Art Ctr., 1988—. Mem. Internat. Assn. Travel Agys., Plymouth Area C. of C., New Buffalo (Mich.) Yacht Club. Office: Plymouth Travel Ctr Inc 208 N Water PO Box 420 Plymouth IN 46563-0420

POND, PHYLLIS JOAN, state legislator; b. Warren, Ind., Oct. 25, 1930; d. Clifford E. and Rosa E. (Hunnicutt) Ruble; m. George W. Pond, June 10, 1951; children: William, Douglas, Jean Ann. B.S., Ball State U., Muncie, Ind., 1951; M.S., Ind. U., 1963 . Tchr. home econs., 1951-54; kindergarten tchr., 1961—; mem. Ind. Ho. of Reps. from 15th Dist., 1978-82, from 20th Dist., 1982—, majority asst. caucus chmn. Del. Ind. State Rep. Conv., 1976, 80, 84, del., 1986, 88; alt. del. Rep. Nat. Conv., 1980. Mem. AAUW, New Haven Woman's Club. Lutheran.

PONDER, ANNELL, educator, consultant, researcher, nutrition and personal care products distributor; b. McDonough, Ga., Aug. 22, 1932; d. Arnold and Marie (Carmichael) P. BA magna cum laude, Clark Coll., 1955; MSW, Atlanta U., 1959, postgrad., 1983-84, 86; postgrad., Oral Roberts U., 1985-86, Cardinal Stritch Coll., 1989-90. Cert. early childhood, elem. and middle grades, Ga. Tchr., libr. Clayton County Sch. Systems, Jonesboro, Ga., 1955-57; field supr. citizenship edn. program United Ch. Christ and So. Christian Leadership Conf., N.Y.C. and Atlanta, 1962-67; instr. Atlanta U., 1967-68; tchr. Free For All Acad., Atlanta, 1971-72; subs. tchr. Atlanta Bd. Edn., 1977—, subs. sec., 1986—; tchr. sec. Lullwater Sch., Decatur, Ga., 1978; subs. tchr. DeKalb County Sch. Systems, Decatur, 1984—; substitute tchr. Univ. Sch. of Milw., 1990—; distbr. weight control, health, nutrition and personal care products Herbalife. Mem. NAFE, Alpha Kappa Delta, Alpha Kappa Mu. Address: 1521 W Kilbourn Ave #412 Milwaukee WI 53233

PONNÉ, NANCI TERESA, publisher; b. Chgo., May 10, 1958; d. Joseph Anthony and Irene Theresa (Nasadowski) P. BA, DePaul U., 1980. Actress, model Chgo., 1978—; pub. Chgo. Talent Directory, 1985—, Spotlight, 1989; speaker in field. Vol. Dems. to Re-elect Mayor Washington, 1987. Named Miss Chgo., recipient Spl. Judges award Miss America Scholarship Pageant, 1981-82; Goodman Sch. of Drama scholar, 1980. Mem. NATAS, Chgo. Conv. and Tourism Bur., Entrepreneurs Assn., Chgo. Advt. Club, Theatre Chgo. Affiliates. Roman Catholic. Home: 2215 E 83d St Chicago IL 60617 Office: Chgo Talent Directory 230 N Michigan Ave Chicago IL 60601

PONS, SILVIA TERESITA, banker; b. Havana, Cuba, Nov. 8, 1938; came to U.S., 1960; d. Joaquin and Maria Del Carmen (Ruiz) P. Student, U. Havana, Cuba, 1959. Clk. New Orleans Country Club, 1961-62; acctg. clk. La Grocers Co-op, Inc., New Orleans, 1962-73; v.p., cashier Pontchartrain State Bank, Metairie, La., 1973—. Mem. Fin. Women Internat. (group pres. 1981-82), Bank Adminstrs. Inst., Am. Bankers Assn., Club De Profesionales Cubanos. Roman Catholic. Office: Pontchartrain State Bank 3420 Severn Ave Metairie LA 70002

PONSER, MARILYN RUTH, real estate administrator; b. Newark, Ohio, May 29, 1952; d. Verlin and Freda Evelyn (Davis) Mathis; m. Gene Walter Ponser, Feb. 3, 1970; children: Rick Walter, Wanda Lynn. Student, Cen. Ohio Tech. Inst., 1974. Realtor Marilyn R. Ponser Real Estate, Newark, 1974—; weatherization aide Licking Econ. Action Devel. Study, Newark, 1983-87, energy auditor, 1985-88, weatherization program dir., 1987—. Treas. Hazelwood PTA, Newark, 1980-82, pres., 1982-84. Mem. Nat. Bd. Realtors, Ohio Bd. Realtors, Licking County Bd. Realtors, Nat. PTA, Lincoln PTA, Fairfield County Bd. Realtors. Office: 882 Garfield Ave Newark OH 43055

PONT, MARISARA, public relations executive; b. Rio Piedras, P.R., Oct. 29, 1941; d. Rafael Pont and Sara Marchese. BA in Humanities cum laude, U. P.R., 1962-63; MS in Libr. Sci., Columbia U., 1971. Asst. to libr. med. scis. campus U. P.R., Rio Piedras, 1964-72; spl. aide to Pres. Senate Commonwealth of P.R., San Juan, 1972; dep. aide in mgmt. Office of Gov. of P.R., San Juan, 1973, exec. aide to dir. of communications, 1973-74, dir. communications, 1974-76; pres. Plus Image Devel. and Pub. Rels., San Juan, 1977-86, Comstat/Rowland Pub. Rels., San Juan, 1986—; bd. dirs. Blue Shield Assn., San Juan; commr. Commn. for Hosting the 2004 Olympics in P.R., San Juan, 1988-89. Bd. dirs. Ballet of San Juan, 1985, Festival Cine San Juan, 1988-89, Mus. of Architecture, San Juan, 1988-89; Gov.'s Adv. Bd. Popular Dem. Party, San Juan, 1988. Mem. Assn. Profl. Pub. Rels. Practitioners of P.R. (pres. 1984-86), Pub. Rels. Soc. Am., Overseas Press Club P.R. (co-chmn. ann. award program 1981-89), P.R. Mfrs. Assn., P.R. C. of C. (pub. rels. award 1985), Bankers Club. Roman Catholic. Office: Comstat/Rowland Caparra Heights Sta 1506 FD Roosevelt Ave Caparra PR 00922

PONTIFLET, ADDIE ROBERSON, nursing educator; b. Decatur, Ga., Oct. 25, 1943; d. Emory Alexander and Emma Kate (Wilson) Roberson; m. Derrick Mayes, Dec. 12, 1965 (div. Apr. 1966); 1 child, Pamela Denise; m. Theodore Hubert Pontiflet, Nov. 17, 1972. RN diploma, Kings County Hosp. Ctr., Bklyn., 1964, nurse anesthetist diploma, 1973; BS, St. Joseph's Coll., 1975; MSEd, U. So. Maine, 1983. RN, Va.; lic. nurse practitioner, Va. Staff nurse Montifiore Hosp., Bronx, N.Y., 1964-66; head nurse Downstate Med. Ctr., Bklyn., 1967-68; in svc. instr. Kings County Hosp. Ctr., Bklyn., 1968-70; anesthetist Bklyn. Hosp., 1973-74; clin. instr. Ga. Bapt. Med. Ctr., Atlanta, 1976-80; assoc. dir. Mercy Hosp. Sch. of Anesthesia, Portland, Maine, 1980-86; asst. prof. nurse anesthesia Med. Coll. of Va.-Va. Commonwealth U., Richmond, Va., 1986—. Bd. dirs. YWCA, Portland, 1982-85, Last Stop Gallery, Richmond, 1988-89. Mem. Am. Assn. Nurse Anesthetists (cert.), Va. Assn. Nurse Anesthetists, Phi Delta Kappa. Office: Med Coll of Va Va Commonwealth U PO Box 226 MCV Sta Richmond VA 23298-0001

POOL, DEANNA, educator, satellite engineering group comptroller; b. Rabat, Morocco, North Africa, Apr. 21, 1942; came to U.S., 1975; d. Joseph and Perla (Dery) Amar; m. David Lynn Pool, Oct. 5, 1964; children—Nathaniel Dan, Michael Messod, Joel Eli. Student Universite de Rabat, 1960-61; diploma in Hispanic culture Centro Cultural Espanol, Rabat, 1960-61; diploma in Hispanic culture Centro Cultural Espanol, Madrid, Spain, 1964. Chief comml. liaisons and fgn. markets dept. Ministry of Commerce, Industry, Mines & Merchant Marine, Rabat, 1961-62; asst. to dir. fin. Caisse de Depot, 1962-64; co-owner, Marshall Tool and Die, Kansas City, Mo., 1975-77, Bio-Safe, Kansas City, 1977-80; co-owner, comptroller Satellite Engring. Group, Kansas City, 1980—; lectr. in Morocco, Honduras, Philippines, 1960-75; guest lectr., U. Mo.-Kansas City, 1984—; lectr. in field. Mem. Mo. Conservation Soc., Soc. Prevention Cruelty to Animals. Jewish. Avocations: Antiques, embroidery, reading. Home: 114 Hackberry Lee's Summit MO 64064 Office: Satellite Engring Group 6114 Connecticut Kansas City MO 64120

POOLE, GWENDOLYN BURTON, municipal agency administrator; b. Cin., Jan. 7, 1943; d. Samuel Carey and Catherine Jean (Cobb) Burton; 1 child, Dorene Jean Poole. BA, Mundelein Coll., Chgo., 1979; cert., Chgo. Coll. Commerce, 1969. Ct. transcriber U.S. Dist. Ct., Chgo.; adminstrv. officer U.S. Dept. Agriculture, Chgo.; sr. mgmt. analyst U.S. GAO, Chgo.; asst. chief fin. officer, dir. policies/internal controls Chgo. Housing Authority. Mem. Am. Mgmt. Assn., Nat. Assn. Accts., NAFE, Am. Assn. Individual Investors. Home: 341 Sherman Ave Evanston IL 60202

POOLE, JEAN WIGGINS, office manager; b. Cedartown, Ga., Mar. 4, 1942; d. William Webb and Frances Olice (Griffin) Wiggins; m. Samuel William Poole, June 24, 1963, (div. 1972); 1 child, Joseph Barron. Student, West Ga. Coll., 1959-61. Reservationist Eastern Air Lines, Atlanta and Tampa, Fla., 1963-65; travel cons. Internat. Travel Club, Charlotte, N.C., 1971-73; mgr. Gulliver's Travels, Inc., Charlotte, 1973-74; inventory clk. Burns Electronics (now Wells Fargo Alarm), Charlotte, 1974-78; dir., tariffs, reservations Sunbelt Airlines, Rome, Ga., 1979-80; adminstrv. asst. Civil Aeronautics Bd., Atlanta, 1980-82; exec. sec. Short Bros. USA, Inc., Arlington, Va., 1982-83; office mgr. Avmark, Inc., Arlington, 1983-85, Avitas, Inc., Reston, Va., 1985—. Mem. Mensa. Democrat. Home: 13305 Apgar Pl Herndon VA 22070 Office: Avitas Inc 1835 Alexander Bell Dr Reston VA 22091

POOLE, JOY LOUISE, museum administrator, curator; b. Council Bluffs, Iowa, July 29, 1955; d. Eugene and Helen Marie (Joy) P. BA in Mus. Studies, U. Colo., 1980. Mus. intern U. Colo. Mus., Boulder, 1977-80; oral history coord. Denver Mus. Natural History, 1980; park technician Nat. Pk. Svc., Ganado, Ariz., 1983-84; adminstr. Colo. Hist. Soc., Trinidad, 1984-87; mus. adminstr., curator City of Farmington, N.Mex., 1987—; cons. ednl. videos FOF Prodns., Washington, 1989-90. Mem. Santa Fe Nat. Hist. Trail adv. coun. Nat. Pk. Svc., 1988—; bd. dirs. Very Spl. Arts Festival, Trinidad, Colo., 1985, 86. Named Young Career Woman of the Yr., Bus. and Profl. Women's Assn., Trinidad, 1985. Mem. Am. Assn. Mus., Am. Assn. for State and Local History (Cert. of Commendation, 1988), Western History Assn., Mountain Plains Mus. Assn., Internat. Jazz Educators Assn., Santa Fe Trail Assn. (founder, incorporator 1985, v.p. of bd. 1986, bd. dirs. 1986—), NOW, AAUW (bd. dirs., by-law chair 1988-90). Office: Farmington Mus 302 N Orchard Farmington NM 87401

POOLE, RUTH WILLIAMS SWAIN, manufacturing executive; b. Anderson, Ind., May 8, 1945; d. John T. and Edie L. (Swain) Garrett; m. William N. Poole, Dec. 2, 1962; children: Raymond, Karen, Myra. AA, Ball State U., 1972, BS, 1976. Mil. pay clk. fin. ctr. U.S. Army, Indpls., 1966; mfg. supr. Delco Remy div. Gen. Motors Corp., Anderson, 1976—. Mem. Am. Bus. Womens Assn. (treas. 1983-84, sec. 1984-85, v.p. 1985-86, pres. 1988-89, Bus. Woman of Yr. 1989), NAFE. Home: 1711 Oakwood Dr Anderson IN 46011

POON, VIVIAN WEI MAN, accountant; b. Hong Kong, Nov. 30, 1961; came to U.S., 1976; d. Billy Y.B. and Anna K.Y. (Lui) P. BBA, U. Hawaii, 1982; postgrad., MACC, 1984. CPA. Sr. Peterson Sullivan and Co. CPAs, Seattle, 1984-88; sr. auditor Wash. Mut. Savs. Bank, Seattle, 1988-89; mgr. Benson and McLaughlin CPAs, Seattle, 1989—. Charles Hemeway scholar, 1980. Mem. AICPA (scholar 1983), Wash. Soc. CPAs. Home: 1743 NW 57th St #402 Seattle WA 98107

POOR, JANET MEAKIN, landscape designer; b. Cin., Nov. 27, 1929; d. Cyrus Lee and Helen Keats (Meakin) Lee-Hofer; m. Edward King Poor III, June 23, 1951; children: Edward King IV, Thomas Meakin. Student, Stephens Coll., 1947-48, U. Cinn., 1949-51, Triton Coll., 1973-76. Pres. Janet Meakin Poor Landscape Design, Winnetka, Ill., 1975—. Author, editor: Plants That Merit Attention Vol. I: Trees, 1984; contbr. articles to profl. jours. Participant in longe range planning City of Winnetka, 1978-82, archtl. and environ. bd., 1980-84, beautification commn., 1978-84, garden coun., 1978-82; adv. coun., sec. of agr. Nat. Arboretum, Washington; nat. adv. bd. Filoli, San Francisco; trustee Ctr. Plant Conservation at Arnold Arboretum, Jamaica Plain, Mass.; mem. adv. coun. The Garden Conservancy, 1989—; trustee Winnetka Congl. Ch., 1978-80. Recipient merit award Hadley Sch. Blind, 1972; named Vol. of Yr. Hadley Sch. Blind. Mem. Chgo. Hort. Soc. (chmn. bd. dirs. 1987—, medal 1984, gold medal garden design, exec. com., chmn. rsch. com., women's bd., designer herb garden Farwell Gardens at Chgo. Botanic Garden), Am. Hort. Soc. (bd. dirs., Catherine H. Sweeney award 1985), Garden Club Am. (chmn. nat. plant exchange 1980-81, chmn. hort. com. 1981-83, bd. dirs., 1983-85, corresponding sec. 1985-87, Horticulture award Zone X1 1981, Creative Leadership award 1986), Fortnightly Club, Garden Guild (bd. dirs.), Garden Club Am. (v.p. 1987-89). Republican. Home: 595 Cedar St Winnetka IL 60093 Office: Chgo Botanic Garden PO Box 400 Glencoe IL 60022

POOR, SUZANNE DONALDSON, advertising and public relations executive; b. Somers Point, N.J., Oct. 6, 1933; d. James Watt and Roberta (Radford) Donaldson; m. Richard Sumner Poor, Mar. 19, 1955 (div. Sept. 1983); children—Jonathan Scott, Jeffrey Sumner, Sara Suzanne. A.B., Mt. Holyoke Coll., 1955; M.A., Montclair State Coll., 1975; postgrad. NYU, 1977-83, Drew U. 1987—; photography student New Sch. Social Research, 1979-82. Reporter, copy writer WFLB, WFLB-TV, Fayetteville, NC., 1955-56; dir. public relations Montclair YMCA, N.J., 1965-69; dir. public relations Girl Scouts Greater Essex County, Montclair, 1969-74; assoc. pub. relations dept. Nat. League Nursing, N.Y.C., 1974; freelance public relations, photography, Montclair, 1974-76; dir. communications Insts. Religion and Health, N.Y.C., 1976-78; ptnr., pres. Miller/Poor Assocs., Verona, N.J., 1978—. Pres. bd. trustees Doubletree Gallery, Montclair, 1977-79; trustee Friends of N.J. Network. Mem. Am. Soc. Mag. Photographers, Am. Woman's Econ. Devel. Corp., Nat. Assn. Female Execs., Exec. Women N.J. (bd. dirs. 1980-83), Ad Club NJ (bd. govs. 1983—, editor Ad Talk, 1982—. Democrat. Episcopalian. Avocations: bicycling, swimming, tennis, furniture restoration. Home: 30 Plymouth St Montclair NJ 07042 Office: Miller Poor Assocs 280 Bloomfield Ave Verona NJ 07044

POPE, BARBARA SPYRIDON, federal agency administrator; b. Pitts., Nov. 10, 1951; d. Gus Arthur and Katherine (Soumas) Spyridon; m. James Selkirk Pope, Nov. 24, 1984; children: James Cantwell, Mary Katherine. BA, Vanderbilt U., 1973; postgrad., George Washington U., 1977-80. Indsl. counsellor Litton Industries, Pascagoula, Miss.; staff asst. SBA, Washington, 1974-79, exec. asst. to gen counsel, employee devel. specialist, 1980-82, acting chief of staff, spl. asst., 1982-86, dep. asst. sec. def. force mgmt. and personnel (family support, edn. and safety), 1986-89; asst. Sec. of the Navy manpower and res. affairs The Pentagon, Washington, 1989—. Mem. adv. bd. Charles Edison Youth Meml. Found., Washington, 1978-81. Scottish Rite fellow, George Washington U., 1979; named one of Outstanding Young Women Am., 1981; recipient Medal of St. Andrew Greek Orthodox Archdiocese of N. and S. Am., 1988, disting. pub. svc. award Sec. Def., 1989. Mem. Downtown Jaycees, Washington (bd. dirs. 1984-86). Republican. Greek Orthodox. Home: 5011 Wyandot Ct Bethesda MD 20816 Office: Office Sec Navy The Pentagon Washington DC 20301

POPE, DONNA, government official; b. Cleve., Oct. 15, 1931; d. John Emil and Marie Josephine (Thiel) Kolnik; m. Raymond Pope, Oct. 21, 1951; children: Candace Pope Wooley, Cheryl Pope Bosworth. Student public schs. Supr. election ofcls. dept. Cuyahoga County Bd. Elections, Cleve., 1965-68; mem. Ohio Ho. of Reps., 1972-81, minority whip; dir. U.S. Mint, Washington, 1981—. Mem. Exec. Women in Govt. Roman Catholic. Office: US Mint Dept Treasury 633 3rd St NW Washington DC 20220

POPE, INGRID BLOOMQUIST, artist, sculptor; b. Arvika, Sweden, Apr. 2, 1918; came to U.S., 1928; d. Oscar Emanuel and Gerda (Henningson) Broström; m. Howard Richard Bloomquist, Feb. 14, 1941 (dec. Nov. 18, 1982); children: Dennis Howard, Diane Cecile Connelly, Laurel Ann Shields; m. Marvin Hoyle Pope, Mar. 9, 1985. BA cum laude, Manhattanville Coll., 1979, MA in Humanities, 1981; MA in Religion, Yale Div. Sch. Yale U., 1984. Exhbns. include ManhattanvilleColl., Greenwich (Conn.) Art Soc., Greenwich Arts Coun., Yale Div. Sch., First Congl. Ch. of Stamford, Conn., First Ch. of Round Hill, Greenwich, Conn., Scarsdale (N.Y.), Congl. Ch., Ch. of Sweden, N.Y.C., St. Mary Ch., Greenwich. Past bd. dirs. N.Y.C. Mission Soc., Greenwich YWCA, Greenwich Acad. Mother's Assn.; trustee First Ch. Round Hill, Greenwich; pres. Ch. Women United, Greenwich, 1989—; bd. dirs. Greenwich Chaplaincy; mem. First Ch. of Round Hill. Mem. AAUW, Nat. Assn. Am. Pen Women, Yale Club (N.Y.C., Greenwich), Stanwich Club. Republican. Home: 538 Round Hill Rd Greenwich CT 06831

POPE, JANE LAIRD MILLER, health science association administrator; b. Lake City, Fla., Mar. 31, 1942; d. William Whitfield and Pearl (Laird) Miller; m. Fred Wallace Pope, Jr., Dec. 27, 1962 (div. 1985); children: Catherine Whitfield, Gregory Wallace. Cert. German, Army Lang. Sch., 1963; BA in English, U. Fla., 1968. Registrar, adminstrv. asst. Boston U. Grad. Sch., Heidelberg, Fed. Republic of Germany, 1966-67; adminstrv. asst. client rsch. mgmt. A.C. Nielsen Co., Chgo., 1967; med. records and student health svcs. asst. U. Fla., Gainesville, 1967-69; graphic artist HMS Visions, Inc., Palm Harbor, Fla., 1982-83, Bill McDermott Advt., Inc., Dunedin, Fla., 1983-86; freelance graphic artist Clearwater, Fla., 1986; exec. dir. Hunter Blood Ctr. Found., Inc., Clearwater, 1986—. Mem. Pinellas County Hist. Commn., Clearwater, 1976-77; chmn. bd. vols. Pinellas County Hist. Soc., 1975-76; treas., mem. met. bd. dirs. Suncoast Family YMCA, Clearwater, 1987—; mem. Leadership Tampa Bay, 1990; bd. dirs. Belleair Civic Assn., 1990. Exec. fellow U. South Fla. Inst. Govt. Mem. Nat. Soc. Fundraising Execs. (exec. bd., treas. Suncoast chpt. 9186—), Greater Clearwater C. of C. (bus. retention com. 1986), Leadership Pinellas (grad., co-chmn. aluumni assn., bd. dirs. 1989), Questers (Fla. sec. 1977), Kappa Delta. Home: 672 Poinsettia Rd Apt 20 Belleair FL 34616 Office: Hunter Blood Ctr Found Inc 424 Jeffords St Clearwater FL 34616

POPE, JANE LARUE, nurse educator; b. Boise, Idaho, July 17, 1929; d. James Alton and Luella (Sillivan) Weed; m. Henry Louis Pope Jr., Mar. 3, 1967 (dec. May 1986). Diploma in nursing, St. Marks Hosp., Salt Lake City, 1951; BS in Nursing, U. Utah, 1952; MS, U. Colo., 1960. RN, Utah, Calif., Ariz.; jr. coll. lifetime teaching credential, Calif. Nurse various hosps. in Utah and Idaho, 1952-58; instr. in psychiat. nursing Ariz. State U., Tempe, 1960-64; dir. of nursing Ariz. State Hosp., 1964-68; psychiat. nurse cons. Dept. Instns., Olympia, Wash., 1968; staff devel. project coord. Dept. Instns., Olympia, 1969-70; psychiat. nurse narcotic treatment project U. Calif., San Diego, 1974; program trainer, health svcs. specialist Atascadero (Calif.) State Hosp, 1977-78, dir. psychiat. nursing edn., 1978—; Nurse cons., reviewer Psychiatric Drug Guide, 1989. Contbr. articles to profl. jours. Grantee NIMH, 1965, 70. Republican. Episcopalian. Office: Atascadero State Hosp 10333 El Camino Real Atascadero CA 93423-7001

POPE, LILLIE, psychologist, educator, writer, consultant; b. N.Y.C., June 22, 1918; d. Isador and Annie (Chusid) Bellin; m. Martin Pope, June 27, 1947; children: Miriam, Deborah Judith. BA, CCNY, 1937, MS in Edn., 1941; PhD, NYU, 1969. Lic. psychologist, N.Y. Psychologist Bklyn. Jewish Hosp., 1957-64; psychologist day treatment program Infants Home of Bklyn., 1959-64; dir. Bur. Edn. & Tng. Job Orientation Neighborhoods, N.Y.C., 1964-65; dir. learning disability clinic Coney Island Hosp., Bklyn., 1965—, assoc. chief child psychiatry, 1986—; adj. assoc. prof. NYU, N.Y.C., 1968-72; adj. prof. Bklyn. Coll., 1972-47; cons., lectr. head start and spl. edn. programs, nationwide, 1956—; cons. New Theatre Bklyn., 1983—; mem. edn. adv. bd. Teaching Exceptional Children, Washington, 1980-86; chair adv. bd. McDonnell Ctr. for Learning, Bklyn., 1983—. Author: Guideline to Teaching Remedial Reading, 1968. Lectureships U. Anchorage, 1983; bd. dirs. New Theatre Bklyn., 1983—, Ezra Jack Keats Found., Bklyn., 1987—. NIMH fellow, 1968; United Cerebral Palsy Assn. grantee, 1969, N.Y.C. Bd. Edn. grantee, 1967—; recipient Mary Hornby award Atlantic Conf. Nova Scotia, 1981. Mem. Am. Psychol. Assn. (diplomate), Internat. Reading Assn., Coun. for Exceptional Children (Outstanding Svc. award 1990), Orton Soc., Multidisciplinary Acad. Clin. Edn. (charter), Assn. for Children with Learning Disabilities.

POPE, ROSLYN ELIZABETH, advertising consultant, concert pianist; b. Atlanta, Oct. 29, 1938; d. Rogers William and Ruth Pauline (Singleton) Pope; m. John W. Walker, May 17, 1960 (div. 1969); children: Rhonda Lynn, Donna Ruth. Certificat de Musique, L'Ecole Normale de Musique, Paris, 1959; BA in Music, Spelman Coll., 1960; MA in English Lit., Ga. State U., 1968; PhD in Humanities, Syracuse U., 1974. Asst. prof. religious studies Pa. State U., State College, 1974-76; chairperson div. humanities Bishop Coll., Dallas, 1976-79; dir. ethnic and intercultural relations U. Tex.-Arlington, 1979-81; advt. cons. Southwestern Bell Publs., Fort Worth, 1982—. Merrill scholar Spelman Coll., 1958-59, Kent fellow Danforth Found., Syracuse U., 1970-74, Univ. fellow Syracuse U., 1969-70. Democrat. Nichiren Shoshu Buddhist. Home: 7821 Acapulco Rd Fort Worth TX 76112

POPE, SUZETTE STANLEY, accountant; b. Florala, Ala., Sept. 15, 1925; d. Raymond T. and Vashti Viola (Williams) Stanley; m. W. Norelle Pope, June 22, 1947; children—Stephanie Suzanne, Brently Preston. A.S., Miami-Dade Community Coll., 1967; B.B.A. magna cum laude, U. Miami, 1969, M.B.A., 1971; Ed.S., U. Fla., 1976. Staff acct. Stuzin C.P.A.s; supr. acctg. staff Dade County Pub. Schs., Miami, Fla., 1969-75, chief acct. acctg. div., 1976-83, accounts payable div., 1983—. Contbr. articles to profl. publs. Bd. dirs. United Manpower Service, Inc., Miami, 1976-80; bd. dirs. United Home Care Service, 1981—; trustee Bay Oaks Home, 1981—. Named Outstanding Adminstr., Dade County Pub. Schs., 1982, Outstanding Bus. Woman Dade County, 1983, Outstanding Woman Vol., 1984, OUtstanding Bus. Woman of Dade County, 1984. Mem. AAUW (exec. bd., treas. 1988—), Assn. Sch. Bus. Officials (vice chmn. sch. finance com. 1985-88, vice chmn. internat. membership com. 1989—), Fla. Support Adminstr. Assn. (pres. 1987-88, bd. dirs. 1988—), Southeastern Assn. Sch. Bus. Ofcls., Fla. Assn. Sch. Bus. Ofcls. (vice chmn. Ad Hoc Sch. Acctg. Manual Com.), Fla. Fedn. Bus. & Profl. Women (exec. bd. 1988—), Fla. Sch. Fin. Coun., Am. Soc. Women Accts. (v.p. 1982-83), Coral Gables Bus. and Profl. Womens Club (v.p. 1984-85, del. state conv. 1985—, nat. conv. 1986—, 1st v.p., 1985-86, pres. 1986-87, bd. dirs. dist. 12 1988—, Woman of Yr. 1987, recipient Justice Cup award 1985), Fla. Assn. Sch. Adminstrs. (bd. dirs. 1986—), Fla. Support Adminstrs. Assn. (bd. dirs. 1982—, pres. 1987-88), Fla. Sch. Fin. Officers Assn. (pres. 1981), SE Assn. Sch. Bus. Officials (bd. dirs. 1981-83). Democrat. Baptist. Lodge: Soroptimist Internat. Miami (pres. 1981-83, bd. dirs. So. region 1984—, bd. dirs. 1984-88, treas. 1986-88, del. 1981—, treas. 1986-88, chmn. tng. awards program 1982-84). Home: 3925 NW 4th Terrace Miami FL 33126 Office: Dade County Pub Schs Room 602 1450 NE 2d Ave Miami FL 33132

POPE-MASSETTI, AUDREY LAURA, government agency director; b. St. Cloud, Minn., Apr. 4, 1951; d. Wheeler Henry and Laura Catherine (Scheeler) Pope; m. Richard Paul Massetti, Aug. 13, 1984. BA in Astrophysics, St. Cloud State U., Minn., 1980, BS in Geology, 1980; MS in Geodesy, Ohio State U., 1986. Ins. rep. Lincoln Nat. Life Ins. Co., Mpls., 1974-76; group ins. cons. Prudential Ins. Co., Mpls. 1976-78; geodesist defense mapping agy. Dept. Defense, Cheyenne, Wyo., 1982-86, Kwajalein, Marshall Islands, 1987—; geodesist/geodetic cons./office dir. Kwajalein Missile Range and associated users, 1987—. Mus. curator vol. Micronesian Handicraft Assn., Kwajalein, 1987—; vol. prosecutor, trial asst. Kwajalein Community Ct., 1990. Academic grantee St. Cloud State U., 1970-73. Mem. Am. Congress on Surveying and Mapping, Nat. Mgmt. Assn., Kwajalein Commodore Users Club, Kwajalein Women's Club, Yacht Club (Kwajalein)(editor newspaper), Scuba Club (Kwajalein). Roman Catholic. Club: Yacht (Kwajalein), Scuba (Kwajalein).

POPERA, SUSAN LOUISE, purchasing executive, customer service supervisor; b. West Covina, Calif., Nov. 7, 1957; d. Charles Frank and Iva Irene (Simkins) P. Quality control mgr. Scoobie Enterprises, Anaheim, Calif., 1975-76; mgr. McDonalds Restaurant, City of Industry, Calif., 1976-84; purchasing and traffic mgr. Coupon Clearing Svc., Costa Mesa, Calif., 1984-89, purchasing and traffic mgr., customer svc. supr., facilities mgr., 1986-90. Mem. Fountain Valley Jaycees (sec. 1989-90, v.p. 1990—, dist. sec./treas. 1990—). Republican. Methodist. Home: 306 S Sullivan SP 70 Santa Ana CA 92704

POPIELARZ, BEVERLY, advertising executive; b. Borger, Tex., Aug. 24, 1949; d. Leighton J.F. and Delores Martina (Rinker) Helm; m. Robert Philip Seppey, Aug. 14, 1975 (div. Dec. 1980); m. Donald Thomas Popielarz, Jan. 16, 1983; 1 child, Rachel Katherine. BA, Occidental Coll., 1971. V.p., personnel dir. Ogilvy & Mather, Los Angeles, 1971-83; sr. v.p., dir. human resources, ops. Foote Cone & Belding, Los Angeles, 1983—. Mem. Los Angeles Advt. Club. Office: FCB Los Angeles 11601 Wilshire Blvd Los Angeles CA 90025*

POPKIN, ELSIE DINSMORE, artist; b. Abington, Pa., Jan. 11, 1937; d. Archibald Alexander and Helen Smedes (Latta) Dinsmore; m. Mark Anthony Popkin, Dec. 20, 1961; children: Laird Alexander, Maurice Benjamin, Elizabeth Dinsmore. BFA, Cornell U., 1958; postgrad, NYU, 1960-68. Artist in residence Reynolda House Mus. Am. Art, Winston-Salem, N.C., 1975-78; cons. R.J. Reynolds Corp. Art Program, Winston-Salem, 1978-79; lectr. pastel workshops Reynolds House Mus. Am. Art, 1975—; tchr. workshops Sawtooth Ctr. Visual Design, Winston-Salem, 1982—; bd. dirs., sec. N.C. Vol. Lawyers for Arts, 1986—. One woman shows include Salem Coll. Fine Arts Ctr., Winston-Salem, 1980, Ward-Nasse Gallery, N.Y.C., 1975, 77, 82, 84, Lincoln Ctr. Gallery, N.Y.C., 1985, 86, Wyomissing (Pa.) Inst. Fine Arts, 1955, 86, Uptown Gallery, N.Y.C., 1986, 89, Herbert F. Johnson Mus. Cornell U., Ithaca, N.Y., 1988, Jennifer Moore Gallery, Greensboro, N.C., 1989, Winston-Salem Artist of Yr. Retrospective Sawtooth Ctr. Visual Design, 1989; Cardoza Sch. Law Yeshiva U., N.Y.C., 1989-90; illustrator: (symphony programs). Mem. alumni adv. coun. Coll. Architecture, Art and Planning Cornell U., 1975-80; artists rights activist; mem. Arts Advocates of N.C.; bd. dirs. Southeastern Ctr. Contemporary Art, Winston-Salem, N.C., 1975-79. Named Winston-Salems Artist of Yr., Sawtooth Ctr. Visual Design, 1989; fellow Yaddo, Saratoga Springs, N.Y., 1985, Va. Ctr. Creative Arts, Sweet Briar, 1983-85. Mem. Associated Artists Winston-Salem (pres. 1975-76), Artworks Gallery. Democrat. Jewish. Home: 740 Arbor Rd Winston-Salem NC 27104

POPKO, KATHLEEN MARIE, company executive; b. Holyoke, Mass., Oct. 28, 1943; d. Peter Anthony and Phyllis (Kisiel) P. BS in Nursing, Marillac Coll., 1968; Masters in Social Welfare, Brandeis U., 1973, PhD, 1975. Research assoc. Levinson Policy Inst., Brandeis U., Waltham, Mass., 1974-75; adj. asst. prof. Heller Sch., Brandeis U., Waltham, 1975-79; v.p. planning Mercy Hosp., Springfield, Mass., 1975-81; v.p. Sisters Providence, Holyoke, Mass.; project dir. Devel. Sisters Providence Health System, Holyoke, 1980-84; pres. Sisters Providence, 1985—. Author: Regulatory Controls, 1976. Chmn. bd. dirs. Consolidated Cath. Health Care, Chgo., 1985-88; bd. dirs. Cath. Health Assn., 1985-88; exec. com. Leadership Conf. Women Religious, 1986—, pres. 1990—. Home: 53 Mill St Westfield MA 01085 Office: Sisters Providence Gamelin St Holyoke MA 01040

POPOVIC, SANYA, political scientist, educator; b. N.Y.C., Sept. 20, 1962; d. Nenad and Tatyana Popovic. BA summa cum laude, Syracuse U., 1982; MA, MPhil, Columbia U., 1988. Vis. scholar MIT, Cambridge, 1987; commodities trainee Thomson McKinnon Securities, N.Y.C., 1987; instr. polit. sci. Barnard Coll. Columbia U., N.Y.C., 1988—. Vol. Carlsson Trust for Edn. and Assistance to Namibian/African Refugees, London. Soviet/ European Internat Security fellow, Ford Found., 1986. Mem. Am. Assn. for Advancement of Slavic Studies, Am. Polit. Sci. Assn., Phi Beta Kappa. Democrat. Russian Orthodox. Office: Columbia U Barnard Coll Dept Politics 3009 Broadway New York NY 10027

POPOVICH, JOANN MARGARET, quality assurance coordinator; b. Jamestown, N.Y., Apr. 15, 1952; d. John and R. Jean (Biggin) P. BS in Nursing, Loyola U., New Orleans, 1984; MS, U. So. Fla., 1988. Cert. poison info. specialist; cert. emergency nurse. Staff nurse WCA Hosp., Jamestown, N.Y., 1975-78, Hamot Med. Ctr., Erie, Pa., 1978-81; head nurse Tulane U. Hosp., New Orleans, 1981-85; poison info. specialist Tampa (Fla.) Gen. Hosp., 1985-89; med. nursing quality assurance coord. U. Rochester (N.Y.) Med. Ctr./Strong Meml. Hosp., 1989—. Recipient Sr. Mary Fortier award So. La. League for Nursing, 1984, Cross Keys Leonard G. Rozell award City Coll., Loyola U., New Orleans, 1984. Mem. N.Y. State Nurses' Assn., Emergency Nurses' Assn., Sigma Theta Tau. Home: 3246 Winton Rd So J-32 Rochester NY 14623 Office: Univ Rochester Med Ctr Elmwood Ave Rochester NY 14623

POPP, CAROL ADZICK, fashion retailer; b. St. Louis, Mar. 12, 1948; d. John Wesley and Eva (Chulick) Adzick; m. John William Popp Jr., June 20, 1970; children: John William III, Michael Adam, Jason Daniel, Ryan David. BE in Applied math., Vanderbilt U., 1970. Mktg. rsch. asst. So. New Eng. Telephone Co., New Haven, 1970-72, mktg. rsch. mgr., 1973-75; owner, mgr. Caprice Accessories, Columbia, S.C., 1989—. Vice-chmn. bd. trustees Ctr. for Cancer Treatment and Rsch., Richland Meml. Hosp., Columbia, 1986-87; officer, bd. trustees Friends of Libr., Richland County Librs., Columbia, 1990-91; vice-chmn. bd. trustees Heathwood Hall Episc. Sch., Columbia, 1990-91. Mem. Columbia Garden Club (2d v.p.-elect 1990-91), Columbia Med. Aux. (bd. dirs. 1980-90), Sandlapper Garden Club (pres. 1987, treas. 1985), Bookmark Book Club (pres.-elect 1990). Republican. Roman Catholic. Home: 1591 Woodlake Dr Columbia SC 29206

POPP, CHARLOTTE LOUISE, health development center administrator, nurse; b. Vineland, N.J., July 26, 1946; d. William Henry and Elfriede Marie (Zickler) P. Diploma in Nursing, Luth. Hosp. of Md., Balt., 1967; BA in Health Edn., Glassboro (N.J.) State Coll., 1972; MA in Human Devel., Fairleigh-Dickinson U., 1981. Cert. Sch. Nurse, N.J., Health Educator, N.J. Charge nurse Newcomb Hosp., Vineland, N.J., 1967-71; supr. Vineland Rehab. Ctr., 1971-72; charge nurse Bridgeton (N.J.) Hosp., 1972-73; dir. insvc. edn. Millville (N.J.) Hosp., 1973-76; dir. hosp. insvc. edn. Vineland Devel. Ctr. State of N.J., 1976-78; program asst. Vineland Devel. Ctr., 1978-87; dir. habilitation planning services State of N.J., Vineland Devel. Ctr., 1987—, lead program coord. Vineland Devel. Ctr. 1981—; exam proctor State of N.J. Bd. Nursing, Newark, 1973—. Editorial rev. bd. (jour.) Nursing Update, 1973-77. Instr. basic life support, Am. Heart Assn., bd. dirs. Tri-county chpt., 1979-83, South Jersey chpt., 1983—. Mem. Am. Nurses Assn., N.J. State Nurses Assn., Am. Assn. for Mental Retardation, South Jersey Inservice Exchange (life), Smithsonian Assn., Lutheran Hosp. of Md. Alumni Assn., Glassboro State Coll. Alumni Assn., Fairleigh-Dickinson U. Alumni Assn. Lutheran. Office: Vineland Devel Ctr 1676 E Landis Ave Vineland NJ 08360

POPP, PAMELA LYNN, healthcare system executive; b. Savannah, Ga., Feb. 13, 1962; d. Lloyd Ernest and Geraldine Ann (Hill) Weatherby; m. Timothy Daniel Popp, Nov. 29, 1986. BSBA, N.E. Mo. State U., 1980-83; MA in Health Svcs. Mgmt. and Legal Studies, Webster U., 1989; A in Mgmt., Ins. Inst. Am., 1989; postgrad., St. Louis U., 1990—. Credit inves-

tigator Sears, Roebuck & Co., St. Ann, Mo., 1979-80; admissions coord. N.E. Mo. State U., Kirksville, 1981-83; claims adjuster Liberty Mut. Ins. Co., Rockford, Ill., 1983-84; claims examiner Ill. State Med. Inter-Ins. Co., Chgo., 1984-86; healthcare supr. Alexsis Risk Mgmt. Svcs., St. Louis, 1986-87; corp. claims mgr. SSM Health Care System, St. Louis, 1987—; charter mem. Quality/Utilization/Risk Coordination Coun. for met. St. Louis area. Pershing acad. scholar N.E. Mo. State U., 1980. Mem. NAFE, St. Louis Assn. Healthcare Risk Mgrs. (pres. 1990). Mem. United Ch. of Christ. Office: SSM Health Care System 1031 Bellevue Ave Saint Louis MO 63117

POPP, ROSANNA KATHERINE, program director; b. Honolulu, Sept. 14, 1955; d. Gordon Franklin and Maryjean Kramer (Kiesow) P. Student, Piedmont Va. Community Coll. Sr. fiscal tech. U. Va., Charlottesville. Mem. NAFE, U. Va. Women's Faculty and Profl. Assn. Home: 125A N Baker St Charlottesville VA 22903

POPP, VIRGINIA GAIL, real estate developer; b. Balt., Sept. 10, 1944; d. LaMar John and Virginia Margaret (McComas) Campbell; m. Richard Lyell Guy, 1962 (div. 1964); children: Richard Jr., James (dec.); m. Lawrence Joseph Popp Jr., Feb. 10, 1973 (div. 1988); 1 child, JoElla; 1 stepchild, John. Grad. high sch., Towson, Md. Credit corr. Humble Oil Co., Balt., 1963-68; typist Charles J. Cirelli and Son, Inc., Severna Park, Md., 1969-70, from bookkeeper to adminstrv. asst., 1970-80, v.p. 1980-88; v.p. Tristate Devel. Corp., Severna Park, Md., 1988—, also bd. dirs.; v.p., bd. dirs. Cirelli Co., Severna Park, CJC Devel. Corp. Mem. Chpt. 81 Parents Without Ptnrs., Inc., Profl. Bookkeepers Assn. Am. Mem. Ch. of the Brethren Lodge: Ladies Aux. of the Moose.

POPPEN, JANET KLAWITER, accountant; b. Kansas City, Mo., Oct. 24, 1941; d. Harold Julius and Selma Elizabeth (Hilmer) Klawiter; divorced; children: Gavin, Ann. BA, U. Mo., Columbia, 1963; BS in Bus. Adminstrn., U. Mo., St. Louis, 1981. CPA. Staff acct. Lester Witte Co., St. Louis, 1981-82; tax supr. Rubin Brown Gornstein, St. Louis, 1982-84, KMG Main Hurdman, St. Louis, 1984-86; ptnr. Poppen & Wojcicki, CPAs (formerly Poppen & Duncan), St. Louis, 1986—; bd. dirs. Equitable Women. Officer Citizen's Adv. Council Lindberg Sch. Dist., St. :Louis, 1983-84. Named Woman of Recognition, Alliance, 1989. Mem. Am. Inst. CPA's, Mo. Soc. CPA's, St. Louis Soc. CPA's (treas. alliance 1987-88), Nat. Assn. Women Bus. Owners, Kirkwood C. of C. Mem. United Ch. Christ. Office: Poppen and Duncan 117 N Kirkwood Rd Suite 129 Saint Louis MO 63122

POPPER, PAMELA ANNE, finance company executive; b. Columbus, Ohio, Oct. 24, 1956; d. Edwin D. and Eleanor Ida P. Student Ohio State U. Assoc. dir. Conservatory of Piano, Columbus, 1974-79; v.p. The Window Man, Columbus, 1979-81; pres. Popper Brace Scott, Columbus, 1981-87; pres., chief exec. officer, The Popper Group, 1985-87; v.p., dir. Hamilton Fin. Corp., Columbus, 1983—; chmn. Netcare Found., 1986-89; pres., chief exec. officer Hamilton Capital Corp., Westerville, Ohio, 1987—; bd. dirs. Shelter One Group Corp., 1986—, Kaiser Devel., 1987—. Trustee Neoteric Dance Theatre, Columbus, 1985-87, Netcare Corp., Columbus, 1987-89, Columbus Contemporary Dance Theatre, 1987-88; dir., bd. dirs. Treemar Retreat, South Webster, Ohio, 1986-87, Ballet Met., Columbus, 1976-79; co-chmn. devel. com. Am. Heart Assn., Columbus, bd. trustees, 1989—; trustee Learning Juncture, 1988—; mem. bus. mktg. com. Jr. Achievement. Recipient Vol. award Netcare Corp., 1984; profl. sales awards. Mem. Nat. Assn. Profl. Saleswomen. Republican. Home: 338 Bristol Woods Ct Worthington OH 43085 Office: Hamilton Capital Corp 663 D Park Meadow Westerville OH 43081

POPPINO, JEAN LAVONNE, family nurse practitioner; b. Stilwell, Okla., July 25, 1938; d. Calvin N. and Geneva N. (Dannenberg) Stevens; m. Leonard S. Poppino, Dec. 28, 1957; children: Marty, J. Darlene. Diploma in Nursing, Sparks Meml. Hosp., 1960; cert. nurse practitioner, Okla. U. Health Sci. Ctr., 1978. RN, Okla. Obs. floor supr. St. Francis Hosp., Tulsa, 1960; supr. med. surg. floor Grand Valley Hosp., Pryor, Okla., 1961, supr. surgery, 1962, dir. nursing, 1962-65; office nurse Donald D. Collins, MD, Inc., Pryor, 1965-76, ind. family nurse practitioner, 1978-86; pediatric nurse practitioner Okla. State Dept. Health, Oklahoma City, 1986-87; continuing care coord. Grand Valley Hosp., Pryor, 1987—; cons., tchr. Okla. Dept. Health, Oklahoma City, 1986-87. Mem. Pryor Resource Bd., 1989; Dem. Roosevelt Elem. Sch. PTA. Mem. Am. Nurses Assn., Okla. Nurses Assn. (vice chmn. nurse practitioner div.), Acad. Nurse Practitioners, Dist. Nurses Assn. (pres., v.p., sec.-treas.). Democrat. Mem. Church of God. Home: Rte 2 Box 165 Pryor OK 74361 Office: Grand Valley Hosp Box 278 Pryor OK 74362

POPPY, CONSTANCE B., educator; b. Ean Claire, Wis., July 23, 1946; d. William Stanley and Florance Dorothy (Ciok) Kolasa; m. Roger William Poppy, Feb. 21, 1970 (div. 1990); children: Robert William, Lynne Frances. BA cum laude, Lakeland Coll., 1978; MA, Marian Coll., 1990. Tchr. Auburndale (Wis.) Sch. System, 1966-70, Milw. Sch. System, 1980-83, Howards Grove (Wis.) Sch. System, 1983—. Leader, 4-H, Sheboygan, Wis., 1985-89. Mem. Howards Grove Ednl. Assn. (v.p. 1987-88, pres. 1988-89), Interlake Reading Assn., Wis. Reading Assn. Reorganized Ch. of Jesus Christ of Latter-day Saints.

POPRICK, MARY ANN, psychologist; b. Chgo., June 25, 1939; d. Michael and Mary (Mihalcik) Poprick; B.A., De Paul U., 1960, M.A., 1964; Ph.D, Loyola U., Chgo., 1968. Intern in psychology Elgin (Ill.) State Hosp., 1961-62; staff psychologist, 1962; staff psychologist Ill. State Tng. Sch. for Girls, Geneva, 1962-63, Mt. Sinai Hosp., Chgo., 1963-64; lectr. psychology Loyola U. at Chgo., 1964-67; asst. prof. Lewis U., Lockport, 1967-70, assoc. prof., 1970-75, chmn. dept., 1968-72 (on leave 1972-73); postdoctoral intern in clin. psychology Ill. State Psychiat. Inst., Chgo., 1972-73; pvt. clin. practice David Psychiat. Clinic, Ltd., South Holland Ill., 1973-87; pvt. practice, South Holland, Ill., 1987—; assoc. sci. staff Riveredge Hosp., Forest Park, Ill., 1975-76; ltd. lic. practitioner dept psychiatry Christ Hosp., Oak Lawn, Ill., 1983—. Co-chmn. commn. on personal growth and devel. Congregation of 3d Order St. Francis of Mary Immaculate, Joliet, 1970-71; clin. resource person Cath. Archdiocese of Chgo., 1977-88. Mem. Am. Psychol. Assn. (rep. from Ill. 1985-88), Calif., Ill. (sec.-treas. acad. sect. 1975-77, mem. student devel. com. 1975-77, chmn. acad. sect. 1977-78, 78-79, mem. program com. 1977-78, sec. 1979-81, pres.-elect 1981-82, pres. 1982-83, past pres. 1983-84, chmn. program com. 1981-82, awards com. 1983-86, rep. Midwestern Psychol. Assn., Soc. for Sci. Study Religion, AAAS, Chgo. Assn. Psychoanalytical Psychology (rsch. com. 1988), Kappa Gamma Pi, Psi Chi (sec. 1964-65, pres. 1965-66). Home: 547 Marquette Ave Calumet City IL 60409 Office: 16284 Prince Dr South Holland IL 60473

PORCHER, CONNIE MITCHELL, secondary school educator; b. Dayton, Ohio, Sept. 18, 1950; d. Robert Earl and Janet Delphine (Hudnall) Mitchell; m. Melvin Lee Porcher, Apr. 14, 1973. BA, Ohio No. U., 1973; MA, Wright State U., 1980. Cert. tchr. Spanish and history, Ohio. Tchr. Spanish Wapakoneta (Ohio) Schs., 1973—; newspaper advisor Wapakoneta Sr. High Sch., 1986—. Author brochure and booklet. Recipient Tchr. Achievement award Ashland Oil Co., 1989, Golden Apple Achiever award, 1988. Mem. NEA, Ohio Edn. Assn., Wapakoneta Edn. Assn., Ohio Fgn.Lang. Assn. (pres. 1987—), Phi Delta Kappa. Home: 1555 Stockham Dr Piqua OH 45356 Office: Wapakoneta High Sch 1 W Redskin Trail Wapakoneta OH 45895

PORIS, RUTH GLORIA, small business owner; b. Bklyn., June 18, 1929; d. Charles and Gertrude (Estherson) Freedman; m. Robert William, July 13, 1951; children: John Bruce, Carol Jeanne, Michael Charles. BS, NYU, 1951; postgrad., Wayne State U., Detroit, 1965-66, Oakland Coll., Farm Hills Coll., 1972. Tchr. Essex Falls Pub. Schs., Essex Falls, N.J., 1951-55, Dayton Pub. Schs., 1960-62; substitute tchr. Detroit Pub. Schs., 1963-65; ceramic artist Art to Wear, Farmington Hills, Mich.; jeweler, author, publ. Art to Wear, Golden Hands Press, Farmington Hills, Mich., 1972—; workshop leader Art to Wear, 1984—. Author: Step by Step Beadstringing, 1984, Advanced Beadstringing, 1989. Recipient award Soc. N. Am. Goldsmiths, Mich. Soc. of Women Jewelers, Mich. Soc. of Silversmiths. Home and Office: 29505 Sugarspring Rd Farmington Hills MI 48018

PORRECA, ELIZABETH FAYE, company executive; b. Port Jefferson, Oct. 28, 1950; d. Oliver Barbour and Eleanor Rose (Fortney) Van Dyck; m. Arthur James, June 7, 1975. BS, C.W. Post Coll., 1973; MS, SUNY, Stonybrook, 1974. Cert. N.Y. State Permanent Teaching. Chem. educator Glen Cove HS, N.Y., 1974-75; sci. educator Brentwood Jr. High Sch., N.Y., 1975-76; Northeast regional mgr. Turner Assocs., Palo Alto, Calif., 1976-77; chem. edn. Kings Park HS, N.Y., 1978-80; inorganic rsch. chemist. PCK Technology, Melville, N.Y., 1980-83; systems analyst GSSD Harris Corp., N.Y., 1983-86; v.p. Dynamic Decor East, Ltd., Huntington, N.Y., 1986-88; pres. Health Weigh Gourmet, Phoenix, 1989-; co-chair safety com. PCK Technology, Melville, N.Y., 1981-83; chair PC users group, Harris Corp., Syosset, N.Y., 1984-86. Co-author: Techniques & Secrets of Hand Pinstriping; co-inventor: The Effect of Leaving Group on Product Proportions in the Ethanolysis of 2-Pentyl Derivatives, Synergism of MultiAdditives in Copper Plating. Episcopalian.

PORT, LOUISE A. M., small business owner. BS, Russell Sage Coll., Troy, N.Y., 1977; postgrad., Albany Sch. Law, 1979. Asst. v.p. fin. Freedlander The Mortgage People, Inc., Richmond, Va.; bus. systems mgr. Office Am., Inc., Richmond; pres. Cons. Plus, Inc., Richmond; pres. Shopping Spree Unltd., Inc., Richmond. Mem. NAFE, Am. Mgmt. Assn., Assn. for Systems Mgmt., Am. Assn. Individual Investors, Richmond Metro C. of C. Home: PO Box 35231 Richmond VA 23235

PORTER, BEATRICE, psychologist; b. Long Branch, N.J., Apr. 20, 1928; d. Kenneth and Mary (Eskew) Thomas; children: Bonnie, Dawn Tsushima, Christopher. AA summa cum laude, Nassau Community Coll., 1974; BA summa cum laude, Adelphi U., 1976; MA, SUNY, Stony Brook, 1978, PhD, 1981. Lic. psychologist, N.Y. Instr. Adelphi U., Garden City, N.Y., 1980-81; cons. Family Studies Ctr., Huntington, N.Y., 1982-84; dir. Island Psychol. Consulting, Miller Place, N.Y., 1982-84; pvt. practice Miller Place, 1982-88, Centereach, N.Y., 1988—; trainer Avanta Network & Antres, N.Y., Fla., 1987—, dir., 1988—; adj. faculty Gestalt Ctr. of L.I., Jericho, N.Y., 1987—; counseling ctr. SUNY, Stonybrook, 1989—. Mem. Am. Assn. of Marriage and Family Therapy (supr. 1988—); Am. Psychol. Assn., Nat. Register of Health Service Providers in Psychology, Assn. for Humanistic Psychology, Am. Orthopsychiatric Assn., Am. Family Therapy Assn., N.Y. State Psychol. Assn., Suffolk County Psychol. Assn., Avanta Internat. Tng. Network, Antres Tng. Assn., Delta Tau Alpha, Psi Chi. Democrat. Home: PO Box 606 Sound Beach NY 11789 Office: 3771 Nesconset Hwy Ste 101B Centereach NY 11720

PORTER, CATHERINE (KAY PORTER), therapist, business consultant; b. El Paso, Tex., Jan. 29, 1941; d. Horace Catlin and Lillian (Mier) P. BS, U. Tex., El Paso, 1962; MA, U. Houston, 1966; PhD, U. Oreg., 1972. Systems analyst Univac Corp., Houston, 1963-65; instr. in computers Houston Ind. Sch. Dist., Houston, 1965-67; rsch. assoc. computer ctr. Oreg. State U., Corvallis, 1967-74; asst. prof. U. Oreg., Eugene, 1974-82; pres. Porter Foster Sports & Orgnl. Cons., Eugene, 1983-88, Porter Performance Systems, Eugene, 1988—; sports psychologist U.S. Olympic Comm., Colorado Springs, Colo., 1987—, The Athletic Congress, Indpls., 1987—, U.S. Tennis Assn., Princeton, N.J., 1987—. Author: (with others) The Mental Athlete, 1986, Visual Athletics, 1990; contbr. articles to profl. jours. Mem. Assn. for Advance of Applied Sports Psychology, Eugene Bus. Women, Oreg. Track Club (bd. dirs. Eugene chpt. 1985—). Home: 2311 Columbia Eugene OR 97403 Office: Porter Performance Systems PO Box 5584 Eugene OR 97405

PORTER, CATHERINE M., artist; b. Rochester, Minn., Oct. 6, 1948; d. George Edward and Helen Elizabeth (Jaquet) P.; m. Jeffrey Charles Brown, Oct. 13, 1980. BA in Fine Arts, Coll. of New Rochelle, 1970. Freelance artist Weston, Conn., 1970-75, Lakeville, Conn., 1975-83, Colorado Springs, 1983—. Home: 6655 S Marksheffel Rd Colorado Springs CO 80925

PORTER, DAVENA YOUNG, nurse; b. Memphis, Feb. 20, 1950; d. Arnett Jr. and Ernestine (Jones) Young; m. Reginald Lawrence Sr. Porter, June 13, 1970; 1 child, Reginald Lawrence Jr. AS in Nursing, Memphis State U., 1977; student, Memphis Theol. Seminary, 1989—. RN, Tenn. Nurse Meth. Hosp., Memphis, 1977-79, St. Judes Children's Rsch. Hosp., Memphis, 1981-82, LeBonheur Children's Hosp., Memphis, 1982-83; quality assurance coordinator Elder Care Home Health Svcs., Memphis, 1981; dir. health svcs. LeMoyne Owen Coll., Memphis, 1981-82; health occupations coordinator Memphis City Schs., 1985-88; nurse adolescent psychiatry Mid South Hosp., 1979—, VA Med. Ctr., 1988—; adminstrv. supr. The Regional Med. Ctr., Memphis; lectr. in field. Asst. advisor to Young Adult Women's Auxiliary for the Progressive Nat. Bapt. Convention. Mem. Nat. Coun. Negro Women, NAACP, Am. Nurses Assn., Tenn. Nurses Assn., Memphis Nurses Assn. (membership com. 1989), Order of Foresters, Young Adult Women for the Progressive Nat. Bapt. Coswenhon (asst. adv.), Order of Foresters, Zeta Phi Beta. Baptist. Home: 3242 Brakebill Cove Memphis TN 38116

PORTER, DIXIE LEE, insurance executive, consultant; b. Bountiful, Utah, June 7, 1931; d. John Lloyd and Ida May (Robinson) Mathis. B.S., U. Calif. at Berkeley, 1956, M.B.A., 1957. Personnel aide City of Berkeley (Calif.), 1957-59; employment supr. Kaiser Health Found., Los Angeles, 1959-60; personnel analyst U. Calif. at Los Angeles, 1961-63; personnel mgr. Reuben H. Donnelley, Santa Monica, Calif., 1963-64; personnel officer Good Samaritan Hosp., San Jose, Calif., 1965-67; fgn. service officer AID, Saigon, Vietnam, 1967-71; gen. agt. Charter Life Ins. Co., Los Angeles, 1972-77, Kennesaw Life Ins. Co., Atlanta, from 1978, Phila. Life Ins. Co., San Francisco, from 1978; now pres. Women's Ins. Enterprises, Ltd.; cons. in field. Co-chairperson Comprehensive Health Planning Commn. Santa Clara County, Calif., 1973-76; bd. dirs. Family Care, 1978-80, Aegis Health Corp., 1977—, U. Calif. Sch. Bus. Adminstrn., Berkeley, 1974-76; mem. task force on equal access to econ. power U.S. Nat. Women's Agenda, 1977—. Served with USMC, 1950-52. C.L.U. Mem. C.L.U. Soc., U. Calif. Alumni Assn., U. Calif. Sch. Bus. Adminstrn. Alumni Assn., AAUW, Bus. and Profl. Women, Prytanean Alumni, The Animal Soc. Los Gatos/Saratoga (pres. 1987—), Beta Gamma Sigma, Phi Chi Theta. Republican. Episcopalian. Home and Office: PO Box 64 Los Gatos CA 95031

PORTER, DONNA VIOLA, nutritionist; b. Syracuse, N.Y., Apr. 16, 1950; d. Donald David and Viola Florence (Steck) P. BS in Foods and Nutrition, SUNY, Plattsburgh, 1971; PhD in Nutrition and Polit. Sci., Ohio State U., 1980. Therapeutic dietician Upstate Med. Ctr., Syracuse, 1972-73, Ohio State U. Hosp., Columbus, 1973-75; teaching assoc. Ohio State U., 1976-79; fellow Nat. Nutrition Consortium, Inc., Washington, 1979-80; Congl. sci. fellow AAAS, Washington, 1980-81; life scil. analyst Libr. of Congress, Washington, 1981-85, specialist in life sci., 1985—; project dir. food labeling NAS-Inst. Medicine, Washington, 1989-90. Recipient Disting. Alumni award SUNY, Plattsburgh, 1984, Disting. Young Profl. award Ohio State U., 1984, President's award D.C. Metro Area Dietetics Assn. 1987. Mem. Am. Dietetic Assn. (coord. legis. network 1980-87), Soc. for Nutrition Edn. (pub. policy adv. coun. 1985-88, chmn. jour. adv. bd. 1987-88), Phi Upsilon Omicron. Office: Libr of Congress LC-CRS-SPRD 413 Washington DC 20540

PORTER, DORIS M., program director; b. Reidsville, N.C., May 15, 1929; d. William Granville and Agnes Mae (Landreth) Mitchell; m. James S. Porter, Aug. 27, 1972; child. Guilford Coll. 1949; postgrad., Guilford Coll. Lic. real estate broker, N.C., lic. real estate appraiser, N.C. Nat. seminar dir. Nat. Sales, Greensboro, N.C.; v.p. James S. Porter Assocs., Inc., High Point, N.C.; owner Doris Porter Designs, Inc., Greensboro; community svcs. coord. Guilford Tech. Community Coll., Greensboro. Contbr. articles to profl. jours. Active in numerous vol. orgns. Mem. Nat. Assn. Real Estate Appraisers, Nat. Assn. Profl. Women, Nat. Press Card Assn., Nat. Stenciling Soc., Nat. Soc. Decorative Painters, Nat. Soc. Decopeurs, Nat. Soc. Early Am. Decorators, Order of the Amaranth (royal matron triad ct. #13 1970-71, grand assoc. conductress 1989-90, grand conductress 1990—). Methodist. Home: 4405 Williamsburg Rd Greensboro NC 27410

PORTER, ELISABETH SCOTT (LEEZEE PORTER), businesswoman, political worker; b. Mar. 23, 1942; d. Buford and Mary (Lowe) Scott; 1 child, Erin Lee; m. Lord Greenfield, June 1987. Student, Sweet Briar Coll., Pan Am. Bus. Sch. Pres. Antique and Contemporary Leasing, Inc., Washington; founder, dir. Women's Nat. Bank, Washington; mem. Bd. Trade,

Washington, Allied Bd. Trade, N.Y.C. Mem. fin. com. Diocese of Washington; mem. adv. bd. WAMU-FM, Washington; founder, profl. mem. Potomac chpt. Inst. Bus. Designers; active PTA; vestry mem. Grace Episcopal Ch., Washington; mem. Georgetown Citizens Assn., Leadership Washington, 1989—; mem. adv. bd. Elk Hill Farm, Va., Urban League; Democratic co-chmn. Women's Campaign Fund, Washington; mem. Dem. Women's Council; mem. bd. Women's Campaign Research Fund; trustee Maret Sch., Washington; bd. dirs. Champs Found. Mem. Washington C. of C., Nat. Assn. Women Bus. Owners, Georgetown Bus. and Profl. Orgn., Capitol Hill Assn. Bus. and Profls. Office: Antique and Contemporary Leasing Inc 709 12th St SE Washington DC 20003

PORTER, HAZEL REBECCA, entrepreneur, social worker; b. Hammond, La., Aug. 31, 1946; d. Hiram Wesley and Alzina Marie (Booker) Terry; m. Robert Porter; children:Tecoy Markee, Ellington Wesley. BA in Sci., U. Minn., 1983, cert. in aging, 1984. Social worker Presbyn. Home, Inc., St. Paul, 1983, St. Paul Pub. Housing, 1984; mgr. P&P Christian Bookstore, St. Paul, 1984-88; co-owner, mgr. Porgena's Clothing, St. Paul, 1984-88; mgr. P&P Robes & Ch. Supplies, St. Paul, 1984-88; owner P&P Robes & Ch. Supplies, Sacramento, Calif., 1988—; youth dir. Shiloh Bapt. Ch., St. Paul, 1978-88; treas. Blair Arcade Mchts. Assn., St. Paul, 1986-88; bd. dirs. Christian Married Couples, Sacramento. Author: play God's Uniform; author poetry. Co-chair structural com. matrons dept. N.B.C.A., Inc., 1989—; sec. Am. Cancer Soc., St. Paul, 1987-88; pres. Minn. State Minister's Wives, 1973-77; bd. dirs. Sacramento County Am. Cancer Soc., 1989—. Coll. of Home Econs. scholar, 1982, 83. mem. Christian Booksellers Assn., Interdenominational Minister's Wives, Phi Upsilon Omicron, Gamma Sigma Delta. Democrat. Baptist. Home: 9219 Camden Lake Way Sacramento CA 95624

PORTER, JOYCE KLOWDEN, theatre educator and director; b. Chgo., Dec. 21, 1949; d. LeRoy and Esther (Siegel) Klowden; m. Paul Wayne Porter, June 8, 1980; 1 child, David Benjamin. BA in Speech Edn., U. Ill., 1971; MA in Theatre, Northwestern U., 1972; postgrad., Northeastern U., Chgo., 1980, 89, Ill. State U., 1985—. Assoc. prof. theatre, play dir. Moraine Valley Community Coll., Palos Hills, Ill., 1972—; acting theatre coord., 1986-87; mem. adj. faculty Columbia Coll., 1988—; co-owner, tour organizer Chgo. Theatre/Arts Tours, Calumet City, Ill., 1988—; actress, 1972—. Mem. adv. bd. Oak Park (Ill.) Park Dist., 1983; co-chmn. Moraine chpt. Chgo. Area Faculty for Nuclear Freeze, Palos Hills, 1985-87; announcer for bilund Chgo. Radio Info. Svc., 1982-83; bd. dirs. Festival Theatre, Oak Park, 1989—. Mem. Assn. for Theatre in Higher Edn., Ill. Theatre Assn., Ill. Fedn. Tchrs., Nature Conservancy, Zeta Phi Eta. Office: Moraine Valley Community Coll 10900 S 88th Ave Palos Hills IL 60465

PORTER, LEAH LEEARLE, life scientist; b. Remington, Va., Sept. 19, 1963; d. James Wallace and Earline Yvonne (Moore) P. BS, U. Md., 1985; Student, Cornell U., 1986—. Biol. technician U.S. Dept. Agr., Beltsville, Md., 1981-85; agrl. cons. Md. Dept. Agr., College Park, 1985; cons. office mgr. Carpigraphics, Inc., Beltsville, 1985-86; grad. rsch. asst. Cornell U., Ithaca, N.Y., 1986—; cons. mktg. asst. Le Earle Enterprises, Ithaca, 1988—. Md. State Senate scholar, 1984-85; faculty grad. fellow Cornell U., 1986-87. Fellow N.Y. Acad. Scis.; mem. Soc. Nematologists, Assn. Women in Sci., Black Grad. and Profl. Students, Alpha Chi Sigma, Zeta Phi Beta. Democrat. Baptist. Office: Cornell U Dept Plant Pathology 334 Plant Sci Bldg Ithaca NY 14853

PORTER, MAXIENE HELEN GREVE, civic worker; b. Los Angeles; d. Henry Chris and Meyerl (Dixon) Greve; student U. So. Calif., 1928; m. Wellington Denny Palmer, Nov. 18, 1929 (dec. Mar. 1932); children—Virginia Palmer Stanhagen, Wellington Denny; m. 2d, Dale R. Porter, May 17, 1941. Accounting clk. Inglewood (Calif.) Sch. System, 1948-51; dep. tax collector City of San Luis Obispo (Calif.), 1963-65; acctg. clk. San Luis Obispo County Schs., 1965-66; asst. innkeeper Holiday Inn, Darien, Conn., 1967, Alexandria, Va.; innkeeper Holiday Inn, Falls Church, Va., 1973—; asst. gen. mgr. Darien Motor Lodge Assos.; tax cons. H & R Block, 1975-79, office mgr., 1976. Officer, Native Daus. Golden West, 1953—, state pres., 1959-60; chmn. various coms. Calif. Fedn. Womens Clubs, 1960-63; v.p. Bus. and Profl. Women, 1936-37; sec. Inglewood Coordinating Council, 1945-47, pres., 1947-48; pres., various other offices West Ebell Club, Los Angeles, 1947, 60-63; mem. public relations com. YWCA, Fairfax County, Va., 1967-68, Fairfax Hosp. Aux., 1967-68, spl. pub. com. Smithsonian Assn., 1967-68; sec.-treas. Pinecrest Citizens Assn., 1968, v.p., 1974; chmn. finance com. Va. Commn. Status of Women, 1973-75; docent vol. chmn. Green Spring Farm Park, Fairfax County, 1979-80; treas. Greater Falls Church Republican Womens Club, 1968-70, v.p., 1973-74, pres., 1975-76; treas. Va. Fedn. Rep. Women, 1968, parliamentarian, 1976-80; vice-chmn. Va. Nixon Inaugural Com., 1968-69; treas. Va. Women for Nixon, 1968; mem. Fairfax County Nixon for Pres. Com., co-chmn. Fairfax County Ladies for Lin—Gov.'s Campaign, 1969; mem. Fairfax County Rep. Com., 1968—, dist. chmn., 1974—, sec., 1975-76. Mem. Fairfax County C. of C. (legis., edn., polit. activities coms. 1973-74), Nat. Trust for Historic Preservation, Nat. Hist. Soc., Va., Metro (mem. program com., v.p 1972-73) motel assns., Am. Mgmt. Assn. Clubs: Toastmistress (treas. No. Va. 1975, organizer, charter pres. Falls Church 1977-78, pres., 1983-84 council extension chmn. 1977-78, council treas. 1979-80, council sec. 1980-81, council v.p. 1981-82, council pres. 1983-84, parliamentarian 1983-84 editor council newsletter 1978-79, regional awards chmn. 1984-85), Annandale Women's, No. Va. Fedn. Women's (registration chmn. 1980, conservation and energy com., scholarship com. 1982-84, pub. affairs chmn. 1984-86), Nat. Genealogy Soc., Maine Geneal. Soc., Harpswell Sounders, Orr's Island Libr. Assn. (chmn. membership com.), Harpswell Hist. Soc., Merriconeag Grange. Lutheran. Home: Lane Rd RR1 Box 140 Orr's Island ME 04066

PORTER, PATRICIA SUE, labor union administrator; b. Fort Scott, Kans., Aug. 29, 1933; d. Robert Milton and Inez Helen (Insley) Penn; m. Robert George Porter, Aug. 23, 1952; children: Stephen R., Paula S., Rudolph M. Student, Belleville (Ill.) Jr. Coll., 1954-55, No. Ill. U., 1965-67, Am. U., 1978-79. Sec. Sverdup & Parcel Engring., St. Louis, 1951-52; sales rep. Kay Andrews Real Estate, East St. Louis, Ill., 1953-59; sec. Am. Fedn. Tchrs., Chgo., 1961-62, St. Johns Luth. Ch., Rockville, Md., 1968-77, Human Resources Devel. Inst., Washington, 1978-79; apprenticeship dir. AFL-CIO Labor Inst., Washington, 1979-80; project dir. Jewish Labor Com., Washington, 1980—. Election judge Dem. Cen. Com., Rockville, 1977-79. Mem. Am. Fedn. Tchrs., Coalition Labor Union Women. Lutheran. Home: 13511 Oriental St Rockville MD 20853

PORTER, SUSAN SMITH, anesthesiology educator; b. Dayton, Ohio, Jan. 14, 1954; d. Donald Roy and Mary Lee (Smith) Smith; m. Charles Boyd Porter, May 31, 1980; children: Monica Leigh, Troy Thomas. BS, Colo. State U., 1976; MD, U. Kans., 1979. Diplomate Am. Bd. Anesthesiology. Intern Kans. U. Med. Ctr., 1979-80; resident in anesthesiology U. Tex. Health Sci. Ctr., San Antonio, 1980-82, instr. anesthesiology U. Kans. Med. Sch. Medicine, Kansas City, 1983-89, assoc. prof., 1989—; assoc. prof. U. Mo. Sch. Medicine, Kansas City, 1989—. Editor: Neuroanesthesia, 1989; contbr. articles to med. jours., chpt. to book. Mem. AMA, Am. Soc. Anesthesiology, Internat. Anesthesia Rsch. Soc., Soc. Neurosurg. Anesthesia and Critical Care (continuing editor 1983—), rsch. essay award 1983), Mortar Bd., Phi Beta Kappa, Alpha Omega Alpha, Pi Beta Phi. Republican. Episcopalian. Office: St Luke's Hosp Dept Anes 4400 Wornall Rd Kansas City MO 64111

PORTER, SYLVIA, writer; b. Patchogue, L.I. N.Y., June 18, 1913; d. Louis and Rose (Maisel) Feldman; m. Reed R. Porter, 1931; 1 child, Cris Sarah; 1 stepson, Sumner Campbell Collins; m. James F. Fox, 1979. BA magna cum laude, Hunter Coll., 1932; postgrad., NYU, 1933; 16 hon. degrees. Founder weekly news letter (Reporting on Govts.); assoc. N.Y. Post, 1935-77, N.Y. Daily News, 1978—; syndicated columnist L.A. Times Syndicate; chmn. Sylvia Porter Orgn., Inc., 1987—. Editor in chief: Sylvia Porter's Personal Fin. mag., 1983-89; author: How to Live Within Your Income, 1984, Sylvia Porter's Income Tax Guide, 1960—, How to Get More for Your Money, 1961, Sylvia Porter's Money Book-How to Earn It, Spend It, Save It, Invest It, Borrow It, and Use It to Better Your Life, 1975, paperback edit., 1976, Sylvia Porter's New Money Book for the 80's, 1979, paperback edit., 1981, Sylvia Porter's Your Own Money, 1983, Love and Money, 1985, Your Financial Security, 1988, Sylvia Porter's Your Finances

in the 1990s, 1990. Named one of Am.'s 25 Most Influential Women World Almanac, 1977-82; Woman of the Decade Ladies Home Jour., 1979. Mem. Phi Beta Kappa.

PORTER, VERNA LOUISE, lawyer; b. L.A., May 31, 1941. B.A., Calif. State U., 1963; JD, Southwestern U., 1977. Bar: Calif. 1977, U.S. Dist. Ct. (cen. dist.) Calif. 1978, U.S. Ct. Appeals (9th cir.) 1978. Ptnr. Eisler & Porter, L.A., 1978-79, mng. ptnr., 1979-86; pvt. practice law, 1986—; judge pro-tempore L.A. Mcpl. Ct., 1983—, L.A. Superior Ct., 1989—; mem. state of Calif. subcom. on landlord tenant law, panelist conv., mem. real property law sect. Calif. State Bar, 1983; speaker on landlord-tenant law to real estate profls., including San Fernando Bd. Realtors. Editorial asst., contbr. Apt. Owner Builder; contbr. to apt. Bus. Outlook, Real Property News, Apt. Age. Mem. ABA, L.A. County Bar Assn., L.A. Trial Lawyers Assn., Wilshire Bar Assn., Women Lawyer's Assn., Landlord Trial Lawyers Assn. (founding mem., pres.), da Camera Soc. Republican. Office: 2500 Wilshire Blvd Ste 1226 Los Angeles CA 90057

PORTER, VICKI S(HARON), lawyer, educator; b. Chgo., July 28, 1955; d. Simon Seymore and Renee Marilyn (Rossman) P. BA, U. Colo., 1976; JD cum laude, U. Miami, Coral Gables, Fla., 1979. Bar: Colo. 1980, U.S. Dist. Ct. Colo. 1980, U.S. Ct. Appeals (10th cir.) 1983; lic. real estate broker. Pvt. practive law Denver, 1979—; assoc. Holmes & Starr PC, Denver, 1979-80, Sterling & Simon PC, Denver, 1980-82, Sweig & Pockross, PC, Denver, 1983-84, Robinson, Waters, O'Dorsio & Rapson, PC, Denver, 1984; dir., assoc. Sterling & Miller, PC, Denver, 1984-86; spl. counsel Massey Burke & Showalter, PC and predecessor firms, Denver, 1986—; instr. U. Miami, Coral Gables, 1978-79; lectr. U. Denver, 1987-88, prof. Arapahoe Community Coll., Littleton, Colo., 1988-89. Contbr. articles to profl. jours. Apptd. as panel bankruptcy trustee by U.S. Trustee Dist. Colo., 1983—. Mem. ABA (mem. cabinet young lawyers sect. 1987-90, co-author, editor A Desk-Side Guide to the Rules of Bankruptcy 1986, 2d edit. 1988, moderator ann. meeting 1987, chairperson debtor-creditor relationships com. 1986-88), Colo. Bar Assn. (chmn. young lawyers sect. 1985-86, del. to ABA 1988—, author, speaker) Denver Bar Assn., Colo. Women's Bar Assn. (girls just wanna have fun com. 1988—, speaker), Colo. Women's C. of C. (gen. counsel 1988—), Bar and Gavel, Omicron Delta Kappa. Democrat. Jewish. Office: Massey Burke & Showalter PC 518 17th St Ste 1100 Denver CO 80202

PORTER-DAVIS, GAIL LORETTA, principal; b. Moline, Ill., June 19, 1952; d. Marvell and Clella M. (Williams) Porter; m. Dean Francis Davis, Feb. 27, 1982. BS in Elem. Spl. Edn., Western Ill. U., 1973, MS in Edn. Adminstrn., 1989. Cert. elem. and spl. edn. tchr., Ill. Tchr. 1st grade East Moline (Ill.) Pub. Schs. 1974; tchr. 1st grade and spl. edn. Rock Island (Ill.) Pub. Schs., 1974-88, dean of students, 1989-90; prin. Hawthrone-Irving Elem. Sch., 1990—. Mem. Am. Assn. Sch. Adminstrs., Ill. Women Adminstrs., Nat. Alliance Black Sch. Educators, Phi Delta Kappa, Alpha Kappa Alpha. Baptist. Home: 1528 30th Ave Moline Ill 61265

PORTMAN, CHERYL BETH, computer systems executive; b. Boston, Oct. 19, 1960; d. Arthur L. and Pearl (Hecht) P. BA in Sociology, Southeastern Mass. U., 1982. Proofreader O'Connor & Drew, CPA's, Braintree, Mass., 1982-83; data entry operator Kluwer Acad. Pub. Co., Norwell, Mass., 1983-85, computer operator, 1985-87, computer systems supr., 1987—. Mem. NAFE, Southeastern Mass. U. Alumni Assn. (dorm orientation com. 1978-82, student orgn. svc. 1978-82, tutor reading and writing ctr. 1978-82), Greepeace. Office: Kluwer Acad Pub Co l0l Philip Dr Norwell MA 02061

PORUCZNIK, MARY ANN, writer, editor, advertising and public relations consultant; b. Chgo., May 4, 1948; d. John Charles and Anna J. (Malec) P. B.A., St. Xavier Coll., Chgo., 1970; postgrad. Northwestern U., 1971-73, Triton Coll., 1981-82. Editor publs. CAC Ins. Co., Chgo., 1972-75, asst. dir. advt. and sales, 1975; advt. and sales promotion CNA Ins. Co., Chgo., 1975-77; dir. mktg. services N.Am. Co. Life and Health Ins., Chgo., 1977-81; gen. ptnr. Taurus Communications, Oak Park, Ill., 1981-86; profl. writer, Oak Park, 1986—. Mem. Ind. Writers Chgo. (pres. 1988—, bd. dirs. 1986, exec. sec. 1987-88), NAFE, Direct Mktg. Assn., VFW Aux., NOW (west suburban newsletter editor 1985-87, 89—, pres. 1987-88, treas. 1988—), Ill. NOW Times editor 1987), 19th Century Women's Club (chmn. literature dept. 1987-89), AAUW, Nat. Writers' Union. Avocations: filet crochet, camping, cooking, bridge, music. Address: 133 LeMoyne Pkwy Oak Park IL 60302

POSEN, MARION JABLON, advertising executive; b. St. Petersburg, Fla., Aug. 22, 1959; d. William W. and Winifred Francis (Jackson) Jablon; m. Philip James Posen, Sept. 10, 1988. BA, Auburn U., 1981. Comml. producer Sta. WCTV, Tallahassee, 1981-83; asst. promotion mgr. Sta. WBRC-TV, Birmingham, Ala., 1983-85; new promotion producer Sta. WMAR-TV, Balt., 1985-86; on-air promotion mgr. Sta. WCAU-TV, Phila., 1986-89, mgr. advt./promotion, 1989—. sec. Del. Valley Auburn Club, Phila., 1988-89. Mem. Broadcast Promotion/Mktg. Execs. (Gold award 1989), Phila. Nat. Acad. TV Arts and Scis., Women in Communications, Inc., Auburn U. Alumni, Kappa Alpha Theta. Office: Sta WCAU-TV City Ave and Monument Rd Philadelphia PA 19131

POSER, JOAN RAPPS, artists agent; b. Plainfield, N.J., Apr. 10, 1940; d. Mandel Max and Marion Davidson Rapps; m. Jay Sanford Poser, Nov. 15, 1964; children: Lester Philip, Toby Anne. BA, U. Conn., 1962. Self-employed travel cons. Lancaster, Pa., 1976-79; tchr. McDonogh Sch., Balt., 1982—; artist's agt. Joan E. Poser Assocs. Agts. in the Arts, Balt., 1978—. Pres. Lancaster Town Fair, 1974, Temple Beth El Sisterhood, 1973-77; campaign chair Bus. and Profl. Women, Assoc. Jewish Charities, Balt., 1985; spl. events chair Cultural Arts Inst. Chizuk Amuno Congregation, 1986-90, trustee, 1986-90. Mem. Hadassah. Democrat. Home: 8033 Strauff Rd Baltimore MD 21204

POSEY, ELSA, dance educator, artistic director; b. Huntington, N.Y., June 27, 1938; d. Jack Moody and Martha Edna (Kimmich) P.; children: Theo A. D. Novak, Thayer A. C. Novak. Student, Met. Opera Ballet Sch., N.Y.C., 1952-54, Ballet Russe de Monte Carlo, N.Y.C., 1954-56, Sch. Am. Ballet, N.Y.C., 1955-60, Am. Ballet Theatre Sch., N.Y.C., 1954-60, Dance Dept. 92d St., N.Y.C., 1952-58, Dance Notation Bur., N.Y.C., 1966. Co-dir. All About Dance Co., Huntington, N.Y., 1969-76; dir. Posey Dance Co., Huntington, 1976-79, artistic dir., 1981—; artistic dir. L.I. Ballet, Northport, N.Y., 1979-81; pres. Posey Sch. of Dance, Inc., Northport, 1953—, also dir., pres. Dance Edn. Svcs.of L.I., Inc., 1960—, also dir. Author: At Ease with Dance, 1979; staff writter Attitudes; reviewer Acad. Libr. Book Rev.; contbr. articles to profl. jours. Mem. Am. Dance Guild (founding mem., pres. 1983-84, bd. dirs. 1984—), Congress on Rsch. in Dance, Nat. Coalition for Edn. in arts (rep. 1987—), N.Y. Found. for Arts and Artists Roster, Dance Critics Assn., Soc. Dance History Scholars, Performing Arts Resources (adv. bd. 1986—), Nat. Dance Assn. (chmn. studio services com. 1980—), Am. Alliance Phys. Edn., Recreation and Dance. Avocation: sailing. Office: Posey Sch Dance PO Box 254 Northport NY 11768

POSEY, JUMETTA GAIL, investment banker; b. Denver, Dec. 24, 1954; d. Charles Limon and Joyce Lee (Wolf) P. Student, George Washington U., Washington. NASD lic. registered rep. Adminstr corp. fin. Denver, 1979-81; dir. corp. fin. J.W. Gant & Assocs., Inc., Denver, 1981-85; pres., founder Heritage Group, Ltd., Denver, 1985-88; co-founder, pres. Weldon Sullivan Carmichael & Co., Denver, 1988—. Bd. dirs., pres. Denver Housing Devel. Group, Inc.; mem. Colo. Black Roundtable; fin. chmn. and treqas. Com. to Elect Sharon Bailey for Denver pub. Sch. Bd.; gov.'s appointee to Hwy. Legis. Rev. Com. Mem. Nat. Assn. Securities Profls. (founding bd. dirs., conf. chmn.), Colo. Black C. of C. (bd. dirs.), Greater Denver C. of C. (grad. Leadership Denver prog.), NAFE. Office: Weldon Sullivan Carmichael 707 17th St 2901 Denver CO 80202

POSITANO, JILL MARIE, sales representative; b. Bristol, Conn., Aug. 27, 1965; d. Michael Andrew and Vivian Marie (Couture) P. BS in Mktg. Mgmt., Siena Coll., 1987. Sales rep. Am. Bank Stationery, Waterbury, Conn., 1987—. Mem. NAFE, Nat. Bank Stationery, Banking Women. Roman Catholic. Office: Am Bank Stationery 54 Great Hill Rd Watebury CT 06725

POSNER, ELEANOR, management; b. Bklyn., Sept. 23, 1942; d. Joseph and Edith Epstein; m. Robert M. Posner, Jan. 28, 1962; children: Jodi

Behrman, Dana, Jonathan. BA, Bklyn. Coll., 1965. Elem. sch. tchr. N.Y.C. Bd. Edn., Bklyn., 1965-74; dir. fin. Prestige Cosmetic Lab., Lindenhurst, N.Y., 1974-86; exec. mgr., sales, mktg. Lon Cosmetics Ltd., Lindenhurst, 1986—. Mem. PTA. Democrat. Office: Lon Cosmetics Ltd 165 S 10th St Lindenhurst NY 11757

POSNER, LINDA IRENE, corporate manager; b. Balt., Feb. 6, 1939; d. Morris and Rosabelle (Hankin) Rosen; m. Allan Bernard Posner, Dec. 29, 1957; children: Larry Gregg, Michael Glenn, Robert Ira. BA summa cum laude, Coll. of Notre Dame, 1989. Dir., lectr. Montgomery Ward's Fashion, Modeling and Charm Sch., Md., 1962-66; fashion and pub. rels. dir. Montgomery Ward, Md., 1966-75; freelance writer Balt., 1975-76; pres., co-owner Designer's Circle Ltd., Balt., 1976-78; TV writer, producer Dept. of Def., Ft. Meade, Md., 1979-87; TV mgr. Md Dept. of Def., Ft. Meade, 1980-87, sr. edn. and tng. mgr., 1987—; regional dir. The Fashion Group, Balt., 1972-74. Mem. com. March of Dimes, Balt., 1976-78; chairperson Combined Fed. Campaign Com., 1987, U.S. Savs. Bonds, 1989. Dept. of Def. scholar, 1987-88. Mem. Women in Communications, Human Resources Mgmt. Assn., AFTRA. Jewish. Home: 11008 Valley Heights Dr Owings Mills MD 21117

POSNER, TRACY, diversified industries executive; b. 1962. BS, Cornell U., 1983. With Southeastern Pub. Svc. Co., Miami, Fla., 1983—, now v.p., asst. sec., asst. treas., and also bd. dirs. Office: Southeastern Pub Svc Co 6917 Collins Ave Miami Beach FL 33141*

POSNIAK, SALLIE CECELIA, retail designer; b. Appleton, Wis., Mar. 2, 1934; d. Joseph Benjamin and Rebecca (Begin) P. Student, Ray Vogue Art Sch., Chgo., 1952-53, Chgo. Art Inst., 1954-57. Trimmer Marshall Fields, Chgo., 1957-58, asst. designer, 1958-61, designer, 1961-67, master designer, 1967-86, mgr. cen. design, 1986—. Office: Marshall Fields 111 N State St Chicago IL 60690

POSPISIL, EVA HOLDRIDGE, systems engineer; b. Hobbs, N. Mex., May 6, 1953; d. Earl Lee and Ruby Pearl (Bryan) Holdridge; m. Charles Henry Beecroft, Oct. 2, 1971 (div.); m. Francis Joseph Pospisil, Oct. 10, 1980. AS, Baylor U., 1977; BS, NYU, 1983; MS in Sci. Counseling Psychology with honors, Am. Technol. U., 1985, MS in Mgmt. Sci. with honors, 1986. Med. technician, instr. Acad. Health Sci., Fort Sam Houston, Tex., 1971-81; med. technician Darnall Army Community Hosp., Fort Hood, Tex., 1982-84; program analyst DOIM, Fort Hood, 1984-88; systems engr. Northern Telecom, Richardson, Tex., 1988-89, network mgr., 1989—; instr. Cen. Tex. Coll., Killeen, 1985-88, research mgr., 1984-85; owner, mgr. SUEDE, Copperas Cove, Tex., 1985—; cons. Mary Kay Cosmetics. Served with U.S. Army, 1971-81. Mem. Am. Med. Technicians, Tex. Assn. Counseling and Devel. Nat. Assn. Underwater Diving Instrs., Nat. Assn. Parachute Clubs, Nat. Assn. Hangliding, Copperas Cove C. of C., Epsilon Delta Phi. Democrat. Roman Catholic. Club: Fort Hood Parachute. Avocations: skydiving, scuba diving, water and snow skiing, racquetball. Home: 1329 Kesser St Plano TX 75023

POSSENTI, CHERYL ANN, lawyer; b. Yonkers, N.Y., Dec. 9, 1957; d. Vito Joseph and Catherine Margaret (Cooke) P.; m. Kenneth S. Zimmerman, May 7, 1983. BA, SUNY, Albany, 1978; JD, SUNY, Buffalo, 1982. Bar: N.Y. 1983, U.S. Dist. Ct. (we. dist.) N.Y. 1984. Assoc. Saperston & Day, P.C., Buffalo, 1982—, Cox, Barrell, Buffalo, 1983-87; judge moot ct. competition SUNY, Buffalo, 1985, 86, 89; atty., coach N.Y. State Bar Assn. Mock Trial Tournament, Buffalo, 1986-87. Mem. N.Y. State Bar Assn., N.Y. State Trial Lawyers Assn. Democrat. Office: Saperston & Day PC 1 Fountain Pla Buffalo NY 14203

POST, NANCY, organizational development executive; b. Bklyn., May 11, 1957; d. Joseph and Betty (Meltzer) P. BA, U. Pa., 1979; MA, Traditional Acupuncture Inst., 1984; cert., Houston Sch. for Psychotherapy, 1978. Diplomate nationally in acupuncture; lic. psychotherapist, Pa., Md. Dir. Health Wellness Project, Phila.; prin. investigator Facilitators, Inc., Las Vegas, Nev.; dir. faculty and rsch. Merriam Hill Ctr., Cambridge, Mass.; prin. Post Enterprises, Phila.; founder Systems Energetics. Grantee in field. Mem. Orgn. Devel. Network, Pa. Acupuncture Soc. Home: 616 W Upsal St Philadelphia PA 19144

POSTER-TAYLOR, TERRI LEE, marketing professional; b. Boston, Oct. 2, 1952; d. Harold Bernard and Sarah Lillian (Cristol) Poster; m. Barry Millman, Feb. 23, 1975 (div. Feb 1979); m. Clark Martin Taylor, Oct. 19, 1985. Student, Boston Conservatory of Music, 1970-73. Beauty advisor Revlon Co., N.Y.C., 1975-77; mktg. rep. V.H. Monette & Co., Smithfield, Va., 1977-78; sales mgr. Vidal Sassoon, Inc., Los Angeles, 1978-81; account exec. Sarvis & Assocs., Jacksonville, Fla., 1981-82; v.p.c. owner Exchange & Commissary Sales, Jacksonville, 1982-83; area mgr. Assoc. Temporary Staffing, Jacksonville, 1983-85; pres., owner Easy Info, Inc., Jacksonville, 1985-86; br. mgr. Ablest Temporary Services, Jacksonville, 1986-88; area mgr. Fla. Temporaries (name formerly Blue Arrow/Temporaries), Jacksonville, 1988-90; dir. mktg. O.P.T.I.O.N. Care, Jacksonville, 1990—; speaker in field. Bd. dirs. Jacksonville Urban League, 1987—, sec., 1989. Named Arlington Coun. Outstanding Mem. of Yr., 1988, Vol. of Month Jacksonville C. of C., 1988. Mem. Am. Soc. for Personnel Adminstrs., Adminstrv. Mgmt. Soc. (pres. 1985-86), Jacksonville C. of C. (chmn. area coun. main event 1987-88, sec., treas. Arlington coun. 1988, 90, bd. dirs. 1987-89, Ambs. 1989, pub. rels. chmn., svc. bd. tax 1989, chmn. Operation Y.O.U. 1990), Civitans (bd. dirs. Jacksonville 1985-86). Republican. Jewish. Office: OPTION Care 7302 Main St Jacksonville FL 32208

POST-GORDEN, JOAN CAROLYN, psychologist, educator; b. Oak Park, Ill., July 3, 1932; d. DeWitt T. and Mary Jane (Lewellen) Post; children: Gregrey Wayne, Jeffrey Scott, Kayle Lynn, Tamara Anne. BS, Manchester (Ind.) Coll., 1964; MS, U. Ga., 1967, PhD, 1970. Lic. psychologist, Colo. Tchr. Clarke County Schs., Athens, Ga., 1964-65; part-time asst. prof. Tex. Tech. U., Lubbock, 1968-69; instr. So. Colo. State Coll., Pueblo, 1970-71; asst. prof. U. So. Colo., Pueblo, 1971-76, assoc. prof., 1976-81, prof., 1981—; asst. to city mgr., Champaign, Ill., 1980-81; psychologist So. Cen. Ill. Devel. Dist., Flora, 1979-80; dir. scholarly and creative activities U. So. Colo., 1988—. Contbr. chpt. to book and articles to profl. jours. NDEA fellow, 1964-66, Danforth teaching fellow, 1978, faculty fellow Colo. State Div. Mental Health, 1986-87. Mem. Am Psychol. Assn., Soc. for Rsch. in Child Devel., Rocky Mountain Psychol. Assn., Psi Chi, Sigma Xi, Alpha Omicron Pi. Home: 1021 Ruppel #31 Pueblo CO 81001 Office: U So Colo Dept Psychology Pueblo CO 81001

POSTHUMA, HELEN MARIE, travel consultant; b. Bisbee, Ariz., Jan. 4, 1920; d. Harold Chamberlain and Harriet Elizabeth (Jones) Stull; m. Ynte Meindert Posthuma, June 28, 1941; children: Stephen Chamberlain, John Robert. BA in Spanish cum laude, Pomona Coll., 1941; postgrad., U. So. Calif., 1942. Tchr. Fontana (Calif.) Jr. High Sch., 1943; with rsch. dept. Aerojet Engring Co., Azusa, Calif., 1945; fashion model Copacahana Hotel, Rio de Janeiro, 1945; counselor Plaza Travel, Burbank, Calif., 1983—; bd. dirs. Art Ctr. Coll. Design, Pasadena, Calif. Mem. Huntington Meml. Clinic Aux., Pasadena, Altadena Guild Huntington Hosp. Mem. Am. Contract Bridge League, Pi Lambda Theta. Republican. Presbyterian. Home: 610 S Orange Grove Ave Pasadena CA 91105 Office: Plaza Travel 4020 W Magnolia Burbank CA 91505

POTASEK, MARY JOYCE, physicist, researcher; b. Mpls., Oct. 27, 1945; d. Chester and Millie P.; m. Karl W. Beeson, Jan. 22, 1977; 1 child, Jessica Elizabeth. BA in Math., Coll. St. Catherine, 1967; MS in Physics, U. Ill., 1970, PhD, 1974. Research asst. U. Ill., Urbana, 1970-74; research scientist Internat. Bus. Machines, Watson Research Ctr., Yorktown Heights, N.Y., 1974-75; NSF, AAUW postdoctoral fellow Princeton (N.J.) U., 1975-78; NATO postdoctoral fellow Max Planck Inst., Gottingen, West Germany, 1978-80; mem. tech. staff AT&T, Princeton, 1980-86, AT&T Bell Labs., Murray Hill, N.J., 1986-90, Columbia U., N.Y.C., 1990—. Contbr. articles to profl. jours. Mem. AAAS, Optical Soc. of Am., Am. Phys. Soc., Phi Beta Kappa, Pi Mu Epsilon. Home: 197 Dodds Ln Princeton NJ 08540

POTASH, JANICE SUE, accounting educator; b. Ft. Knox, Ky., Mar. 24, 1955; d. Robert S. and Madeline J. (Kirschner) Kraft; m. Steven Robert

POPE-MASSETTI, AUDREY LAURA, government agency director; b. St. Cloud, Minn., Apr. 4, 1951; d. Wheeler Henry and Laura Catherine (Scheeler) Pope; m. Richard Paul Massetti, Aug. 13, 1984. BA in Astrophysics, St. Cloud State U., Minn., 1980, BS in Geology, 1980; MS in Geodesy, Ohio State U., 1986. Ins. rep. Lincoln Nat. Life Ins. Co., Mpls., 1974-76; group ins. cons. Prudential Ins. Co., Mpls., 1976-78; geodesist defense mapping agy. Dept. Defense, Cheyenne, Wyo., 1982-86, Kwajalein, Marshall Islands, 1987—; geodesist/geodetic cons./office dir. Kwajalein Missile Range and associated users, 1987—. Mus. curator, vol. Micronesian Handicraft Assn., Kwajalein, 1987—; vol. prosecutor, trial asst. Kwajalein Community Ct., 1990. Academic grantee St. Cloud State U., 1970-73. Mem. Am. Congress on Surveying and Mapping, Nat. Mgmt. Assn., Kwajalein Commodore Users Club, Kwajalein Women's Club, Yacht Club (Kwajalein)(editor newspaper), Scuba Club (Kwajalein). Roman Catholic. Club: Yacht (Kwajalein), Scuba (Kwajalein).

POPERA, SUSAN LOUISE, purchasing executive, customer service supervisor; b. West Covina, Calif., Nov. 7, 1957; d. Charles Frank and Iva Irene (Simkins) P. Quality control mgr. Scoobie Enterprises, Anaheim, Calif., 1975-76; mgr. McDonalds Restaurant, City of Industry, Calif., 1976-84; purchasing and traffic mgr. Coupon Clearing Svc., Costa Mesa, Calif., 1984-89, purchasing and traffic mgr., customer svc. supr., facilities mgr., 1986-90. Mem. Fountain Valley Jaycees (sec. 1989-90, v.p. 1990—, dist. sec./treas. 1990—). Republican. Methodist. Home: 306 S Sullivan SP 70 Santa Ana CA 92704

POPIELARZ, BEVERLY, advertising executive; b. Borger, Tex., Aug. 24, 1949; d. Leighton J.F. and Delores Martina (Rinker) Helm; m. Robert Philip Seppey, Aug. 14, 1975 (div. Dec. 1980); m. Donald Thomas Popielarz, Jan. 16, 1983; 1 child, Rachel Katherine. BA, Occidental Coll., 1971. V.p., personnel dir. Ogilvy & Mather, Los Angeles, 1971-83; sr. v.p., dir. human resources, ops. Foote Cone & Belding, Los Angeles, 1983—. Mem. Los Angeles Advt. Club. Office: FCB Los Angeles 11601 Wilshire Blvd Los Angeles CA 90025*

POPKIN, ELSIE DINSMORE, artist; b. Abington, Pa., Jan. 11, 1937; d. Archibald Alexander and Helen Smedes (Latta) Dinsmore; m. Mark Anthony Popkin, Dec. 20, 1961; children: Laird Alexander, Maurice Benjamin, Elizabeth Dinsmore. BFA, Cornell U., 1958; postgrad, NYU, 1960-68. Artist in residence Reynolda House Mus. Am. Art, Winston-Salem, N.C., 1975-78; cons. R.J. Reynolds Corp. Art Program, Winston-Salem, 1978-79; lectr. pastel workshops Reynolds House Mus. Am. Art, 1975—; tchr. workshops Sawtooth Ctr. Visual Design, Winston-Salem, 1982—; bd. dirs., sec. N.C. Vol. Lawyers for Arts, 1986—. One woman shows include Salem Coll. Fine Arts Ctr., Winston-Salem, 1980, Ward-Nasse Gallery, N.Y.C., 1975, 77, 82, 84, Lincoln Ctr. Gallery, N.Y.C., 1985, 86, Wyomissing (Pa.) Inst. Fine Arts, 1955, 86, Uptown Gallery, N.Y.C., 1986, 89, Herbert F. Johnson Mus. Cornell U., Ithaca, N.Y., 1988, Jennifer Moore Gallery, Greensboro, N.C., 1989, Winston-Salem Artist of Yr. Retrospective Sawtooth Ctr. Visual Design, 1989; Cardoza Sch. Law Yeshiva U., N.Y.C., 1989-90; illustrator: (symphony programs). Mem. alumni adv. coun. Coll. Architecture, Art and Planning Cornell U., 1975-80; artists rights activist; mem. Arts Advocates of N.C.; bd. dirs. Southeastern Ctr. Contemporary Art, Winston-Salem, N.C., 1975-79. Named Winston-Salems Artist of Yr., Sawtooth Ctr. Visual Design, 1989; fellow Yaddo, Saratoga Springs, N.Y., 1985, Va. Ctr. Creative Arts, Sweet Briar, 1983-85. Mem. Associated Artists Winston-Salem (pres. 1975-76), Artworks Gallery. Democrat. Jewish. Home: 740 Arbor Rd Winston-Salem NC 27104

POPKO, KATHLEEN MARIE, company executive; b. Holyoke, Mass., Oct. 28, 1943; d. Peter Anthony and Phyllis (Kisiel) P. BS in Nursing, Marillac Coll., 1968; Masters in Social Welfare, Brandeis U., 1973, PhD, 1975. Research assoc. Levinson Policy Inst., Brandeis U., Waltham, Mass., 1974-75; adj. asst. prof. Heller Sch., Brandeis U., Waltham, 1975-79; v.p. planning Mercy Hosp., Springfield, Mass., 1975-81; v.p. Sisters Providence, Holyoke, Mass.; project dir. Devel. Sisters Providence Health System, Holyoke, 1980-84; pres. Sisters Providence, 1985—. Author: Regulatory Controls, 1976. Chmn. bd. dirs. Consolidated Cath. Health Care, Chgo., 1985-88; bd. dirs. Cath. Health Assn., 1985-88; exec. com. Leadership Conf. Women Religious, 1986—; pres. 1990—. Home: 53 Mill St Westfield MA 01085 Office: Sisters Providence Gamelin St Holyoke MA 01040

POPOVIC, SANYA, political scientist, educator; b. N.Y.C., Sept. 20, 1962; d. Nenad and Tatyana Popovic. BA summa cum laude, Syracuse U., 1982; MA, MPhil, Columbia U., 1988. Vis. scholar MIT, Cambridge, 1987; commodities trainee Thomson McKinnon Securities, N.Y.C., 1987; instr. polit. sci. Barnard Coll. Columbia U., N.Y.C., 1988—. Vol. Carlsson Trust for Edn. and Assistance to Namibian/African Refugees, London. Soviet/European Internat Security fellow, Ford Found., 1986. Mem. Am. Assn. for Advancement of Slavic Studies, Am. Polit. Sci. Assn., Phi Beta Kappa. Democrat. Russian Orthodox. Office: Columbia U Barnard Coll Dept Politics 3009 Broadway New York NY 10027

POPOVICH, JOANN MARGARET, quality assurance coordinator; b. Jamestown, N.Y., Apr. 15, 1952; d. John and R. Jean (Biggin) P. BS in Nursing, Loyola U., New Orleans, 1984; MS, U. So. Fla., 1988. Cert. poison info. specialist; cert. emergency nurse. Staff nurse WCA Hosp., Jamestown, N.Y., 1975-78, Hamot Med. Ctr., Erie, Pa., 1978-81; head nurse Tulane U. Hosp., New Orleans, 1981-85; poison info. specialist Tampa (Fla.) Gen. Hosp., 1985-89; med. nursing quality assurance coord. U. Rochester (N.Y.) Med. Ctr./Strong Meml. Hosp., 1989—. Recipient Sr. Mary Fortier award So. La. League for Nursing, 1984, Cross Keys Leonard G. Rozell award City Coll., Loyola U., New Orleans, 1984. Mem. N.Y. State Nurses' Assn., Emergency Nurses' Assn., Sigma Theta Tau. Home: 3246 Winton Rd So J-32 Rochester NY 14623 Office: Univ Rochester Med Ctr Elmwood Ave Rochester NY 14623

POPP, CAROL ADZICK, fashion retailer; b. St. Louis, Mar. 12, 1948; d. John Wesley and Eva (Chulick) Adzick; m. John William Popp Jr., June 20, 1970; children: John William III, Michael Adam, Jason Daniel, Ryan David. BE in Applied math., Vanderbilt U., 1970. Mktg. rsch. asst. So. New Eng. Telephone Co., New Haven, 1970-72, mktg. rsch. mgr., 1973-75; owner, mgr. Caprice Accessories, Columbia, S.C., 1989—. Vice-chmn. bd. trustees Fund for Cancer Treatment and Rsch., Richland Meml. Hosp., Columbia, 1986-87; officer, bd. trustees Friends of Libr., Richland County Librs., Columbia, 1990-91; vice-chmn. bd. trustees Heathwood Hall Episc. Sch., Columbia, 1990-91. Mem. Columbia Garden Club (2d v.p.-elect 1990-91), Columbia Med. Aux. (bd. dirs. 1980-90), Sandlapper Garden Club (pres. 1987, treas. 1985), Bookmark Book Club (pres.-elect 1990). Republican. Roman Catholic. Home: 1591 Woodlake Dr Columbia SC 29206

POPP, CHARLOTTE LOUISE, health development center administrator, nurse; b. Vineland, N.J., July 26, 1946; d. William Henry and Elfriede Marie (Zickler) P. Diploma in Nursing, Luth. Hosp. of Md., Balt., 1967; BA in Health Edn., Glassboro (N.J.) State Coll., 1972; MA in Human Devel., Fairleigh-Dickinson U., 1981. Cert. Sch. Nurse, N.J., Health Educator, N.J. Charge nurse Newcomb Hosp., Vineland, N.J., 1967-71; supr. Vineland Rehab. Ctr., 1971-72; charge nurse Bridgeton (N.J.) Hosp., 1972-73; dir. insvc. edn. Millville (N.J.) Hosp., 1973-76; dir. hosp. insvc edn. Vineland Devel. Ctr. State of N.J., 1976-78; program asst. Vineland Devel. Ctr., 1978-87; dir. habilitation planning services State of N.J., Vineland Devel. Ctr., 1987—; lead program coord. Vineland Devel. Ctr., 1981—; exam proctor State of N.J. Bd. Nursing, Newark, 1973—. Editorial rev. bd. (jour.) Nursing Digest, 1977. Instr. basic life support, Am. Heart Assn.; bd. dirs. Tri-county chpt., 1979-83, South Jersey chpt., 1983—. Mem. Am. Nurses Assn., N.J. State Nurses Assn., Am. Assn. for Mental Retardation, South Jersey Inservice Exchange (life), Smithsonian Assn., Lutheran Hosp. of Md. Alumni Assn., Glassboro State Coll. Alumni Assn., Fairleigh-Dickinson U. Alumni Assn. Lutheran. Office: Vineland Devel Ctr 1676 E Landis Ave Vineland NJ 08360

POPP, PAMELA LYNN, healthcare system executive; b. Savannah, Ga., Feb. 13, 1962; d. Lloyd Ernest and Geraldine Ann (Hill) Weatherby; m. Timothy Daniel Popp, Nov. 29, 1986. BSBA, N.E. Mo. State U., 1980-83; MA in Health Svcs. Mgmt. and Legal Studies, Webster U., 1989; A in Mgmt., Ins. Inst. Am., 1986; postgrad., St. Louis U., 1990—. Credit inves-

tigator Sears, Roebuck & Co., St. Ann, Mo., 1979-80; admissions coord. N.E. Mo. State U., Kirksville, 1981-83; claims adjuster Liberty Mut. Ins. Co., Rockford, Ill., 1983-84; claims examiner Ill. State Med. Inter-Ins. Co., Chgo., 1984-86; healthcare supr. Alexsis Risk Mgmt. Svcs., St. Louis, 1986-87; corp. claims mgr. SSM Health Care System, St. Louis, 1987—; charter mem. Quality/Utilization/Risk Coordination Coun. for met. St. Louis area. Pershing acad. scholar N.E. Mo. State U., 1980. Mem. NAFE, St. Louis Assn. Healthcare Risk Mgrs. (pres. 1990). Mem. United Ch. of Christ. Office: SSM Health Care System 1031 Bellevue Ave Saint Louis MO 63117

POPP, ROSANNA KATHERINE, program director; b. Honolulu, Sept. 14, 1955; d. Gordon Franklin and Maryjean Kramer (Kiesow) P. Student, Piedmont Va. Community Coll. Sr. fiscal tech. U. Va., Charlottesville. Mem. NAFE, U. Va. Women's Faculty and Profl. Assn. Home: 125A N Baker St Charlottesville VA 22903

POPP, VIRGINIA GAIL, real estate developer; b. Balt., Sept. 10, 1944; d. LaMar John and Virginia Margaret (McComas) Campbell; m. Richard Lyell Guy, 1962 (div. 1964); children: Richard Jr., James (dec.); m. Lawrence Joseph Popp Jr., Feb. 10, 1973 (div. 1988); 1 child, JoElla; 1 stepchild, John. Grad. high sch., Towson, Md. Credit corr. Humble Oil Co., Balt., 1963-68; typist Charles J. Cirelli and Son, Inc., Severna Park, Md., 1969-70, from bookkeeper to adminstrv. asst., 1970-80, v.p., 1980-88; v.p. Tristate Devel. Corp., Severna Park, Md., 1988—, also bd. dirs.; v.p. Cirelli Co., Severna Park, CJC Devel. Corp. Mem. Chpt. 81 Parents Without Ptnrs., Inc., Profl. Bookkeepers Assn. Am. Mem. Ch. of Brethren Lodge: Ladies Aux. of the Moose.

POPPEN, JANET KLAWITER, accountant; b. Kansas City, Mo., Oct. 24, 1941; d. Harold Julius and Selma Elizabeth (Hilmer) Klawiter; divorced; children: Gavin, Ann. BA, U. Mo., Columbia, 1963; BS in Bus. Adminstrn., U. Mo., St. Louis, 1981. CPA. Staff acct. Lester Witte Co., St. Louis, 1981-82; tax supr. Rubin Brown Gornstein, St. Louis, 1982-84, KMG Main Hurdman, St. Louis, 1984-86; ptnr. Poppen & Wojcicki, CPAs (formerly Poppen & Duncan), St. Louis, 1986—; bd. dirs. Equitable Women. Officer Citizen's Adv. Council Lindberg Sch. Dist., St. :Louis, 1983-84. Named Woman of Recognition, Alliance, 1989. Mem. Am. Inst. CPA's, Mo. Soc. CPA's, St. Louis Soc. CPA's (treas. alliance 1987-88), Nat. Assn. Women Bus. Owners, Kirkwood C. of C. Mem. United Ch. Christ. Office: Poppen and Duncan 117 N Kirkwood Rd Suite 129 Saint Louis MO 63122

POPPER, PAMELA ANNE, finance company executive; b. Columbus, Ohio, Oct. 24, 1956; d. Edwin D. and Eleanor Ida P. Student Ohio State U. Assoc. dir. Conservatory of Piano, Columbus, 1974-79; v.p. The Window Man, Columbus, 1979-81; pres. Popper Brace Scott, Columbus, 1981-87; pres., chief exec. officer, The Popper Group, 1985-87; v.p.; dir. Hamilton Fin. Corp., Columbus, 1983—; chmn. Netcare Found., 1986-89; pres., chief exec. officer Hamilton Capital Corp., Westerville, Ohio, 1987—; bd. dirs. Shelter One Group Corp., 1986—, Kaiser Devel., 1987—. Trustee Neoteric Dance Theatre, Columbus, 1985-87, Netcare Corp., Columbus, 1987-89, Columbus Contemporary Dance Theatre, 1987-88; dir., bd. dirs. Treemar Retreat, South Webster, Ohio, 1986-87, Ballet Met., Columbus, 1976-79; co-chmn. devel. com. Am. Heart Assn., Columbus, bd. trustees, 1989—; trustee Learning Juncture, 1988—; mem. bus. mktg. com. Jr. Achievement. Recipient Vol. award Netcare Corp., 1984; profl. sales awards. Mem. Nat. Assn. Profl. Saleswomen. Republican. Home: 338 Bristol Woods Ct Worthington OH 43085 Office: Hamilton Capital Corp 663 D Park Meadow Westerville OH 43081

POPPINO, JEAN LAVONNE, family nurse practitioner; b. Stilwell, Okla., July 25, 1938; d. Calvin N. and Geneva N. (Dannenberg) Stevens; m. Leonard S. Poppino, Dec. 28, 1957; children: Marty, J. Darlene. Diploma in Nursing, Sparks Meml. Hosp., 1960; cert. nurse practitioner, Okla. U. Health Sci. Ctr., 1978. RN, Okla. Obs. floor supr. St. Francis Hosp., Tulsa, 1960; supr. med. surg. floor Grand Valley Hosp., Pryor, Okla., 1961, supr. surgery, 1962, dir. nursing, 1962-65; office nurse Donald D. Collins, MD, Inc., Pryor, 1965-76, ind. family nurse practitioner, 1978-86; pediatric nurse practitioner Okla. State Dept. Health, Oklahoma City, 1986-87; continuing care coord. Grand Valley Hosp., Pryor, 1987—; cons., tchr. Okla. Dept. Health, Oklahoma City, 1986-87. Mem. Pryor Resource Bd., 1989; pres. Roosevelt Elem. Sch. PTA. Mem. Am. Nurses Assn., Okla. Nurses Assn. (vice chmn. nurse practitioner div.), Acad. Nurse Practitioners, Dist. Nurses Assn. (pres., v.p., sec.-treas.). Democrat. Mem. Church of God. Home: Rte 2 Box 165 Pryor OK 74361 Office: Grand Valley Hosp Box 278 Pryor OK 74362

POPPY, CONSTANCE B., educator; b. Ean Claire, Wis., July 23, 1946; d. William Stanley and Florance Dorothy (Ciok) Kolasa; m. Roger William Poppy, Feb. 21, 1970 (div. 1990); children: Robert William, Lynne Frances. BA cum laude, Lakeland Coll., 1978; MA, Marian Coll., 1990. Tchr. Auburndale (Wis.) Sch. System, 1966-70, Milw. Sch. System, 1980-83, Howards Grove (Wis.) Sch. System, 1983—. Leader, 4-H, Sheboygan, Wis., 1985-89. Mem. Howards Grove Ednl. Assn. (v.p. 1987-88, pres. 1988-89), Interlake Reading Assn., Wis. Reading Assn. Reorganized Ch. of Jesus Christ of Latter-day Saints.

POPRICK, MARY ANN, psychologist; b. Chgo., June 25, 1939; d. Michael and Mary (Mihalcik) Poprick; B.A., De Paul U., 1960, M.A., 1964; Ph.D., Loyola U., Chgo., 1968. Intern in psychology Elgin (Ill.) State Hosp., 1961-62; staff psychologist, 1962; staff psychologist Ill. State Tng. Sch. for Girls, Geneva, 1962-63, Mt. Sinai Hosp., Chgo., 1963-64; lectr. psychology Loyola U. at Chgo., 1964-67; asst. prof. Lewis U., Lockport, 1967-70, assoc. prof., 1970-75, chmn. dept., 1968-72 (on leave 1972-73); postdoctoral intern in clin. psychology Ill. State Psychiat. Inst., Chgo., 1972-73; pvt. clin. practice David Psychiat. Clinic, Ltd., South Holland Ill., 1973-87; pvt. practice, South Holland, Ill., 1987—; assoc. sci. staff Riveredge Hosp., Forest Park, Ill., 1975-76; ltd. lic. practitioner dept psychiatry Christ Hosp., Oak Lawn, Ill., 1983—. Co-chmn. commn. on personal growth and devel. Congregation of 3d Order St. Francis of Mary Immaculate, Joliet, 1970-71; clin. resource person Cath. Archdiocese of Chgo., 1977-88. Mem. Am. Psychol. Assn. (rep. from Ill. 1985-88), Calif., Ill. (sec.-treas. acad. sect 1975-77, mem. student devel. com. 1975-77, chmn. acad. sect. 1977-78, 78-79, mem. program com. 1977-78 sec. 1979-81, pres.-elect 1981-82, pres. 1982-83, past pres. 1983-84, chmn. program com. 1981-82, awards com. 1983-86, rep. Com. of ET and Minority Affairs 1988-89, rep. Cook County 1989—), Midwestern Psychol. Assn., Soc. for Sci. Study Religion, AAAS, Chgo. Assn. Psychoanalytical Psychology (rsch. com. 1988), Kappa Gamma Pi, Psi Chi (sec. 1964-65, pres. 1965-66). Home: 547 Marquette Ave Calumet City IL 60409 Office: 16284 Prince Dr South Holland IL 60473

PORCHER, CONNIE MITCHELL, secondary school educator; b. Dayton, Ohio, Sept. 18, 1950; d. Robert Earl and Janet Delphine (Hudnall) Mitchell; m. Melvin Lee Porcher, Apr. 14, 1973. BA, Ohio No. U., 1973; MA, Wright State U., 1988. Cert. tchr. Spanish and history, Ohio. Tchr. Spanish Wapakoneta (Ohio) Schs., 1973—; newspaper adviser Wapakoneta Sr. High Sch., 1986—. Author brochure and booklet. Recipient Tchr. Achievement award Ashland Oil Co., 1989, Golden Apple Achiever award, 1988. Mem. NEA, Ohio Edn. Assn., Wapakoneta Edn. Assn., Ohio Fgn.Lang. Tchrs., AAUW (program v.p. 1987-89, scholarship chmn. 1986-89), Piqua Hist. Soc. (pres. 1987—), Phi Delta Kappa. Home: 1555 Stockham Dr Piqua OH 45356 Office: Wapakoneta High Sch 1 W Redskin Trail Wapakoneta OH 45895

PORIS, RUTH GLORIA, small business owner; b. Bklyn., June 18, 1929; d. Charles and Gertrude (Estherson) Freedman; m. Robert William, July 13, 1951; children: John Bruce, Carol Jeanne, Michael Charles. BS, NYU, 1951; postgrad., Wayne State U., Detroit, 1965-66, Oakland Coll., Farm Hills Coll., 1972. Tchr. Essex Falls Pub. Schs., Essex Falls, N.J., 1951-55, Dayton Pub. Schs., 1960-62; substitute tchr. Detroit Pub. Schs., 1963-65; ceramic artist Art to Wear, Farmington Hills, Mich.; jeweler, author, publ. Art to Wear, Golden Hands Press, Farmington Hills, Mich., 1972—; workshop leader Art to Wear, 1984—. Author: Step by Step Beadstringing, 1984, Advanced Beadstringing, 1989. Mem. Soc. N. Am. Goldsmiths, Mich. Soc. of Women Jewelers, Mich. Soc. of Silversmiths. Home and Office: 29505 Sugarspring Rd Farmington Hills MI 48018

PORRECA, ELIZABETH FAYE, company executive; b. Port Jefferson, Oct. 28, 1950; d. Oliver Barbour and Eleanor Faye (Fortney) Van Dyck; m. Arthur James, June 7, 1975. BS, C.W. Post Coll., 1973; MS, SUNY, Stonybrook, 1974. Cert. N.Y. State Permanent Teaching. Chem. educator Glen Cove HS, N.Y., 1974-75; sci. educator Brentwood Jr. High Sch., N.Y., 1975-76; Northeast regional mgr. Turner Assocs., Palo Alto, Calif., 1977-78; chem. edn. Kings Park HS, N.Y., 1978-80; inorganic rsch. chemist. PCK Technology, Melville, N.Y., 1980-83; systems analyst GSSD Harris Corp., N.Y., 1983-86; v.p. Dynamic Decor East, Ltd., Huntington, N.Y., 1986-88; pres. Health Weigh Gourmet, Phoenix, 1989; co-chart safety com. PCK Technology, Melville, N.Y., 1981-83; chair PC users group, Harris Corp., Syosset, N.Y., 1984-86. Co-author: Techniques & Secrets of Hand Pinstripping; co-inventor: The Effect of Leaving Group on Product Proportions in the Ethanolysis of 2-Pentyl Derivatives, Synergism of MultiAdditives in Copper Plating. Episcopalian.

PORT, LOUISE A. M., small business owner. BS, Russell Sage Coll., Troy, N.Y., 1977; postgrad., Albany Sch. Law, 1979. Asst. v.p. fin. Freedlander The Mortgage People, Inc., Richmond, Va.; bus. systems mgr. Office Am., Inc., Richmond; pres. Cons. Plus, Inc., Richmond; pres. Shopping Spree Unltd., Inc., Richmond. Mem. NAFE, Am. Mgmt. Assn., Assn. for Systems Mgmt., Am. Assn. Individual Investors, Richmond Metro C. of C. Home: PO Box 35231 Richmond VA 23235

PORTER, BEATRICE, psychologist; b. Long Branch, N.J., Apr. 20, 1928; d. Kenneth and Mary (Eskew) Thomas; children: Bonnie, Dawn Tsushima, Christopher. AA summa cum laude, Nassau Community Coll., 1974; BA summa cum laude, Adelphi U., 1976; MA, SUNY, Stony Brook, 1978, PhD, 1981. Lic. psychologist, N.Y. Instr. Adelphi U., Garden City, N.Y., 1980-81; cons. Family Studies Ctr., Huntington, N.Y., 1982-84; dir. Island Psychol. Consulting, Miller Place, N.Y., 1982-84; pvt. practice Miller Place, 1982-88, Centereach, N.Y., 1988—; trainer Avanta Network & Antres, N.Y., Fla., 1987—, dir., 1988—; adj. faculty Gestalt Ctr. of L.I., Jericho, N.Y., 1987—; counseling ctr. SUNY, Stonybrook, 1989—. Mem. Am. Assn. of Marriage and Family Therapy (supr. 1988—), Am. Psychol. Assn., Nat. Register of Health Service Providers in Psychology, Assn. for Humanistic Psychology, Am. Orthopsychiatric Assn., Am. Family Therapy Assn., N.Y. State Psychol. Assn., Suffolk County Psychol. Assn., Avanta Internat. Tng. Network, Antres Tng. Assn., Delta Tau Alpha, Psi Chi. Democrat. Home: PO Box 606 Sound Beach NY 11789 Office: 3771 Nesconset Hwy Ste 101B Centereach NY 11720

PORTER, CATHERINE (KAY PORTER), therapist, business consultant; b. El Paso, Tex., Jan. 29, 1941; d. Horace Catlin and Lillian (Mier) P. BS, U. Tex., El Paso, 1962; MA, U. Houston, 1966; PhD, U. Oreg., 1972. Systems analyst Univac Corp., Houston, 1963-65; instr. in computers Houston Ind. Sch. Dist., Houston, 1965-67; rsch. assoc. computer ctr. Oreg. State U., Corvallis, 1967-74; asst. prof. U. Oreg., Eugene, 1974-82; pres. Porter Foster Sports & Orgnl. Cons., Eugene, 1983-88, Porter Performance Systems, Eugene, 1988—; sports psychologist U.S. Olympic Coms., Colorado Springs, Colo., 1987—; The Athletic Congress, Indpls., 1987—, U.S. Tennis Assn., Princeton, N.J., 1987—. Author: (with others) The Mental Athlete, 1986, Visual Athletics, 1990; contbr. articles to profl. jours. Mem. Assn. for Advance of Applied Sports Psychology, Eugene Bus. Women, Oreg. Track Club (bd. dirs. Eugene chpt. 1985—). Home: 2311 Columbia Eugene OR 97403 Office: Porter Performance Systems PO Box 5584 Eugene OR 97405

PORTER, CATHERINE M., artist; b. Rochester, Minn., Oct. 6, 1948; d. George Edward and Helen Elizabeth (Jaquet) P.; m. Jeffrey Charles Brown, Oct. 13, 1980. BA in Fine Arts, Coll. of New Rochelle, 1970. Freelance artist Weston, Conn., 1970-75, Lakeville, Conn., 1975-83, Colorado Springs, 1983—. Home: 6655 S Marksheffel Rd Colorado Springs CO 80925

PORTER, DAVENA YOUNG, nurse; b. Memphis, Feb. 20, 1950; d. Arnett Jr. and Ernestine (Jones) Young; m. Reginald Lawrence Sr. Porter, June 13, 1970; 1 child, Reginald Lawrence Jr. AS in Nursing, Memphis State U., 1977; student, Memphis Theol. Seminary, 1989—. RN, Tenn. Nurse Meth. Hosp., Memphis, 1977-79, St. Judes Children's Rsch. Hosp., Memphis, 1981-82, LeBonheur Children's Hosp., Memphis, 1982-83; quality assurance coordinator Elder Care Home Health Svcs., Memphis, 1981; dir. health svcs. LeMoyne Owen Coll., Memphis, 1981-82; health occupations coordinator Memphis City Schs., 1985-88; nurse adolescent psychiatry Mid South Hosp., 1979—, VA Med. Ctr., 1988—; adminstrv. supr. The Regional Med. Ctr., Memphis; lectr. in field. Asst. advisor to Young Adult Women's Auxiliary for the Progressive Nat. Bapt. Convention. Mem. Nat. Coun. Negro Women, NAACP, Am. Nurses Assn., Tenn. Nurses Assn., Memphis Nurses Assn. (membership com. 1989), Order of Foresters, Young Adult Women for the Progressive Nat. Bapt. Coswenhon (asst. adv.), Order of Foresters, Zeta Phi Beta. Baptist. Home: 3242 Brakebill Cove Memphis TN 38116

PORTER, DIXIE LEE, insurance executive, consultant; b. Bountiful, Utah, June 7, 1931; d. John Lloyd and Ida May (Robinson) Mathis. B.S., U. Calif. at Berkeley, 1956, M.B.A., 1957. Personnel aide City of Berkeley (Calif.), 1957-59; employment supr. Kaiser Health Found., Los Angeles, 1959-60; personnel analyst U. Calif. at Los Angeles, 1961-63; personnel mgr. Reuben H. Donnelley, Santa Monica, Calif., 1963-64; personnel officer Good Samaritan Hosp., San Jose, Calif., 1965-67; fgn. service officer AID, Saigon, Vietnam, 1967-71; gen. agt. Charter Life Ins. Co., Los Angeles, 1972-77, Kennesaw Life Ins. Co., Atlanta, from 1978, Phila. Life Ins. Co., San Francisco, from 1978; now pres. Women's Ins. Enterprises, Ltd.; cons. in field. Co-chairperson Comprehensive Health Planning Commn. Santa Clara County, Calif., 1973-76; bd. dirs. Family Care, 1978-80, Aegis Health Corp., 1977—, U. Calif. Sch. Bus. Adminstrn., Berkeley, 1974-76; mem. task force on equal access to econ. power U.S. Nat. Women's Agenda, 1977—. Served with USMC, 1950-52. C.L.U. Mem. C.L.U. Soc., U. Calif. Alumni Assn., U. Calif. Sch. Bus. Adminstrn. Alumni Assn., AAUW, Bus. and Profl. Women, Prytanean Alumni, The Animal Soc. Los Gatos/Saratoga (pres. 1987—), Beta Gamma Sigma, Phi Chi Theta. Republican. Episcopalian. Home and Office: PO Box 64 Los Gatos CA 95031

PORTER, DONNA VIOLA, nutritionist; b. Syracuse, N.Y., Apr. 16, 1950; d. David David and Viola Florence (Steck) P. BS in Foods and Nutrition, SUNY, Plattsburgh, 1971; PhD in Nutrition and Polit. Sci., Ohio State U., 1980. Therapeutic dietician Upstate Med. Ctr., Syracuse, 1972-73, Ohio State U. Hosp., Columbus, 1973-75; teaching assoc. Ohio State U., 1976-79; fellow Nat. Nutrition Consortium, Inc., Washington, 1979-80; Congl. sci. fellow AAAS, Washington, 1980-81; life sci. analyst Libr. of Congress, Washington, 1981-85, specialist in life sci., 1985—; project dir. food labeling NAS-Inst. Medicine, Washington, 1989-90. Recipient Disting. Alumni award SUNY, Plattsburgh, 1984, Outstanding Young Profl. award Ohio State U., 1984, President's award D.C. Metro Area Dietetics Assn., 1987. Mem. Am. Dietetic Assn. (coord. legis. network 1980-87), Soc. for Nutrition Edn. (pub. policy adv. coun. 1985-88, chmn. jour. adv. bd. 1987-88), Phi Upsilon Omicron. Office: Libr of Congress LC-CRS-SPRD 413 Washington DC 20540

PORTER, DORIS M., program director; b. Reidsville, N.C., May 15, 1929; d. William Granville and Agnes Mae (Landreth) Mitchell; m. James S. Porter, June 22, 1972,. Grad., Burlington (N.C.) Bus. Coll., 1949; postgrad., Guilford Coll. Lic. real estate broker, N.C., lic. real estate appraiser, N.C. Nat. seminar dir. Nat. Sales, Greensboro, N.C.; v.p. James S. Porter Assocs., Inc., High Point, N.C.; owner Doris Porter Designs, Inc., Greensboro; community svcs. coord. Guilford Tech. Community Coll., Greensboro. Contbr. articles to profl. jours. Active in numerous vol. orgns. Mem. Nat. Assn. Real Estate Appraisers, Nat. Assn. Profl. Women, Nat. Press Card Assn., Nat. Stenciling Soc., Nat. Soc. Decorative Painters, Nat. Soc. Decopeurs, Nat. Ear Am. Decorators, Order of the Amaranth (royal matron triad ct. #13 1970-71, grand assoc. conductress 1989-90, grand conductress 1990—). Methodist. Home: 4405 Williamsburg Rd Greensboro NC 27410

PORTER, ELISABETH SCOTT (LEEZEE PORTER), businesswoman, political worker; b. Mar. 23, 1942; d. Buford and Mary (Lowe) Scott; 1 child, Erin Lee; m. Lord Greenhel, June 1987. Student, Sweet Briar Coll., Pan Am. Bus. Sch. Pres. Antique and Contemporary Leasing, Inc., Washington; founder, dir. Women's Nat. Bank, Washington; mem. Bd. Trade,

Washington, Allied Bd. Trade, N.Y.C. Mem. fin. com. Diocese of Washington; mem. adv. bd. WAMU-FM, Washington; founder, profl. mem. Potomac chpt. Inst. Bus. Designers; active PTA; vestry mem. Grace Espiscopal Ch., Washington; mem. Georgetown Citizens Assn., Leadership Washington, 1989—; mem. adv. bd. Elk Hill Farm, Va., Urban League; Democratic co-chmn. Women's Campaign Fund, Washington; mem. Dem. Women's Council; mem. bd. Women's Campaign Research Fund; trustee Maret Sch., Washington; bd. dirs. Champs Found. Mem. Washington C. of C., Nat. Assn. Women Bus. Owners, Georgetown Bus. and Profl. Orgn., Capitol Hill Assn. Bus. and Profls. Office: Antique and Contemporary Leasing Inc 709 12th St SE Washington DC 20003

PORTER, HAZEL REBECCA, entrepreneur, social worker; b. Hammond, La., Aug. 31, 1946; d. Hiram Wesley and Alzina Marie (Booker) Terry; m. Robert Porter; children:Tecoy Markee, Ellington Wesley. BA in Sci., U. Minn., 1983, cert. in aging, 1984. Social worker Presbyn. Home, Inc., St. Paul, 1983, St. Paul Pub. Housing, 1984; mgr. P&P Christian Bookstore, St. Paul, 1984-88; co-owner, mgr. Porgena's Clothing, St. Paul, 1984-88; mgr. P&P Robes & Ch. Supplies, St. Paul, 1984-88; owner P&P Robes & Ch. Supplies, Sacramento, Calif., 1988—; youth dir. Shiloh Bapt. Ch., St. Paul, 1978-88; treas. Blair Arcade Mchts. Assn., St. Paul, 1986-88; bd. dirs. Christian Married Couples, Sacramento. Author: play God's Uniform; author poetry. Co-chair structural com. matrons dept. N.B.C.A., Inc., 1989—; sec. Am. Cancer Soc., St. Paul, 1987-88; pres. Minn. State Minister's Wives, 1973-77; bd. dirs. Sacramento County Am. Cancer Soc., 1989—. Coll. of Home Econs. scholar, 1982, 83. mem. Christian Booksellers Assn., Interdenominational Minister's Wives, Phi Upsilon Omicron, Gamma Sigma Delta. Democrat. Baptist. Home: 9219 Camden Lake Way Sacramento CA 95624

PORTER, JOYCE KLOWDEN, theatre educator and director; b. Chgo., Dec. 21, 1949; d. LeRoy and Esther (Siegel) Klowden; m. Paul Wayne Porter, June 8, 1980; 1 child, David Benjamin. BA in Speech Edn., U. Ill., 1971; MA in Theatre, Northwestern U., 1972; postgrad., Northeastern U., Chgo., 1980, 89, Ill. State U., 1985—. Assoc. prof. theatre, play dir. Moraine Valley Community Coll., Palos Hills, Ill., 1972—, acting theatre coord., 1986-87; mem. adj. faculty Columbia Coll., 1988—; co-owner, tour organizer Chgo. Theatre/Arts Tours, Calumet City, Ill., 1988—; actress, 1972—. Mem. adv. bd. Oak Park (Ill.) Park Dist., 1983; co-chmn. Moraine chpt. Chgo. Area Faculty for Nuclear Freeze, Palos Hills, 1985-87; announcer for blind Chgo. Radio Info. Svc., 1982-83; bd. dirs. Festival Theatre, Oak Park, 1989—. Mem. Assn. for Theatre in Higher Edn., Ill. Theatre Assn., Ill. Fedn. Tchrs., Nature Conservancy, Zeta Phi Eta. Office: Moraine Valley Community Coll 10900 S 88th Ave Palos Hills IL 60465

PORTER, LEAH LEEARLE, life scientist; b. Remington, Va., Sept. 19, 1963; d. James Wallace and Earline Yvonne (Moore) P. BS, U. Md., 1985; Student, Cornell U., 1986—. Biol. technician U.S. Dept. Agr., Beltsville, Md., 1981-85; agrl. cons. Md. Dept. Agr., College Park, 1985; cons. office mgr. Carpigraphics, Inc., Beltsville, 1985-86; grad. rsch. asst. Cornell U., Ithaca, N.Y., 1986—; cons., mktg. asst. Le Earle Enterprises, Ithaca, 1988—; rsch. asst. Nematologists, Assn. Women in Sci., Black Grad. and Profl. Students, Alpha Chi Sigma, Zeta Phi Beta. Democrat. Baptist. Office: Cornell U Dept Plant Pathology 334 Plant Sci Bldg Ithaca NY 14853

PORTER, MAXIENE HELEN GREVE, civic worker; b. Los Angeles; d. Henry Chris and Meyerl (Dixon) Greve; student U. So. Calif., 1928; m. Wellington Denny Palmer, Nov. 18, 1929 (dec. Mar. 1933); children—Virginia Palmer Stanhagen, Wellington Denny; m. 2d, Dale R. Porter, May 17, 1941. Accounting clk. Inglewood (Calif.) Sch. System, 1948-51; dep. tax collector City of San Luis Obispo (Calif.), 1963-65; acctg. clk. San Luis Obispo County Schs., 1965-66; asst. innkeeper Holiday Inn, Darien, Conn., 1967, Alexandria, Va.; innkeeper Holiday Inn, Falls Church, Va., 1973—; asst. gen. mgr. Darien Motor Lodge Assocs.; tax cons. H & R Block, 1975-79, office mgr., 1976. Officer, Native Daus. Golden West, 1953—, state pres., 1959-60; chmn. various coms. Calif. Fedn. Womens Clubs, 1960-63; v.p. Bus. and Profl. Women, 1936-37; sec. Inglewood Coordinating Council, 1945-47, pres., 1947-48; pres., various other offices West Elbell Club, Los Angeles, 1947, 60-63; mem. advisory bd. Inglewood Coordinating Council, 1945-47, 68, Fairfax Hosp. Aux., 1967-68, spl. pub. com. Smithsonian Assn., 1967-68; sec.-treas. Pinecrest Citizens Assn., 1968, v.p.; 1974; chmn. finance com. Va. Commn. Status of Women, 1973-75; docent vol. chmn. Green Spring Farm Park, Fairfax County, 1979-80; treas. Greater Falls Church Republican Womens Club, 1968-70, v.p., 1973-74, pres., 1975-76; treas. Va. Fedn. Rep. Women, 1968—, parliamentarian, 1976-80; vice-chmn. Va. Nixon Inaugural Com., 1968-69; treas. Va. Women for Nixon, 1968; mem. Fairfax County Nixon for Pres. Com., co-chmn. Fairfax County Ladies for Lin—Gov.'s Campaign, 1969; mem. Fairfax County Rep. Com., 1968—, dist. chmn., 1974—, sec., 1975-76. Mem. Fairfax County C. of C. (legis., edn., polit. activities coms. 1973-74), Nat. Trust for Historic Preservation, Nat. Hist. Soc., Va., Metro (mem. program com., v.p. 1972-73) motel assns., Am. Mgmt. Assn. Clubs: Toastmistress (treas. No. Va. 1975, organizer, charter pres. Falls Church 1977-78, pres., 1983-84 council extension chmn. 1977-78, council treas. 1979-80, council sec. 1980-81, council v.p. 1981-82, council pres. 1983-84, parliamentarian 1983-84 editor council newsletter 1978-79, regional awards chmn. 1984-85), Annandale Women's, No. Va. Fedn. Women's (registration chmn. 1968, conservation and energy com., scholarship com. 1982-84, pub. affairs chmn. 1984-86), Nat. Genealogy Soc., Maine Geneal. Soc., Harpswell Sounders, Orr's Island Libr. Assn. (chmn. membership com.), Harpswell Hist. Soc., Merriconeag Grange. Lutheran. Home: Lane Rd RR1 Box 140 Orr's Island ME 04066

PORTER, PATRICIA SUE, labor union administrator; b. Fort Scott, Kans., Aug. 29, 1933; d. Robert Milton and Inez Helen (Insley) Penn; m. Robert George Porter, Aug. 23, 1952; children: Stephen R., Paula S., Rudolph M. Student, Belleville (Ill.) Jr. Coll., 1954-55, No. Ill. U., 1965-67, Am. U., 1978-79. Sec. Sverdup & Parcel Engring., St. Louis, 1951-52; sales rep. Kay Andrews Real Estate, East St. Louis, Ill., 1953-59; sec. Am. Fedn. Tchrs., Chgo., 1961-62, St. Johns Luth. Ch., Rockville, Md., 1968-77, Human Resources Devel. Inst., Washington, 1978-79; apprenticeship dir. AFL-CIO Labor Inst., Washington, 1979-80; project dir. Jewish Labor Com., Washington, 1980—. Election judge Dem. Cen. Com., Rockville, 1977-79. Mem. Am. Fedn. Tchrs., Coalition Labor Union Women. Lutheran. Home: 13511 Oriental St Rockville MD 20853

PORTER, SUSAN SMITH, anesthesiology educator; b. Dayton, Ohio, Jan. 14, 1954; d. Donald Roy and Mary Lee (Smith) Smith; m. Charles Boyd Porter, May 31, 1980; children: Monica Leigh, Troy Thomas. BS, Colo. State U., 1976; MD, U. Kans., 1979. Diplomate Am. Bd. Anesthesiology. Intern Kans. U. Med. Ctr., 1979-80; resident in anesthesiology U. Tex. Health Sci. Ctr., San Antonio, 1980-82, instr. anesthesiology, 1982-83; asst. prof. anesthesiology U. Kans. Sch. Medicine, Kansas City, 1983-89, assoc. prof., 1989—; assoc. prof. U. Mo. Sch. Medicine, Kansas City, 1989—. Editor: Neuroanesthesia, 1989; contbr. articles to med. jours., chpt. to book. Mem. AMA, Am. Soc. Anesthesiology, Internat. Anesthesia Rsch. Soc., Soc. Neurosurg. Anesthesia and Critical Care (continuing editor 1983—, rsch. essay award 1983), Mortar Bd., Phi Beta Kappa, Alpha Omega Alpha, Pi Beta Phi. Republican. Episcopalian. Office: St Luke's Hosp Dept Anes 4400 Wornall Rd Kansas City MO 64111

PORTER, SYLVIA, writer; b. Patchogue, L.I., N.Y., June 18, 1913; d. Louis and Rose (Maisel) Feldman; m. Reed R. Porter, 1931; 1 child, Cris Sarah; 1 stepson, Sumner Campbell Collins; m. James F. Fox, 1979. BA magna cum laude, Hunter Coll., 1932; postgrad., NYU, 1933; 16 hon. degrees. Founder weekly news letter (Reporting on Govts.); assoc. N.Y. Post, 1935-77, N.Y. Daily News 1978—; syndicated columnist L.A. Times Syndicate; chmn. Sylvia Porter Group, Inc., 1987—. Editor in chief: Sylvia Porter's Personal Fin. mag., 1983-89; author: How to Live Within Your Income, 1984, Sylvia Porter's Income Tax Guide, 1960—, How to Get More for Your Money, 1961, Sylvia Porter's Money Book-How to Earn It, Spend It, Save It, Invest It, Borrow It, and Use It to Better Your Life, 1975, paperback edit., 1976, Sylvia Porter's New Money Book for the 80's, 1979, paperback edit., 1981, Sylvia Porter's Your Own Money, 1983, Love and Money, 1985, Your Financial Security, 1988, Sylvia Porter's Your Finances

in the 1990s, 1990. Named one of Am.'s 25 Most Influential Women World Almanac, 1977-82; Woman of the Decade Ladies Home Jour., 1979. Mem. Phi Beta Kappa.

PORTER, VERNA LOUISE, lawyer; b. L.A., May 31, 1941. B.A., Calif. State U., 1963; JD, Southwestern U., 1977. Bar: Calif. 1977, U.S. Dist. Ct. (cen. dist.) Calif. 1978, U.S. Ct. Appeals (9th cir.) 1978. Ptnr. Eisler & Porter, L.A., 1978-79, mng. ptnr., 1979-86, pvt. practice law, 1986—; judge pro-tempore L.A. Mcpl. Ct., 1983—; L.A. Superior Ct., 1989—; mem. state of Calif. subcom. on landlord tenant law, panelist conv., mem. real property law sect. Calif. State Bar, 1983; speaker on landlord-tenant law to real estate profls., including San Fernando Bd. Realtors. Editorial asst., contbr. Apt. Owner Builder; contbr. to Apt. Bus. Outlook, Real Property News, Apt. Age. Mem. ABA, L.A. County Bar Assn., L.A. Trial Lawyers Assn., Wilshire Bar Assn., Women Lawyer's Assn., Landlord Trial Lawyers Assn. (founding mem., pres.), da Camera Soc. Republican. Office: 2500 Wilshire Blvd Ste 1226 Los Angeles CA 90057

PORTER, VICKI S(HARON), lawyer, educator; b. Chgo., July 28, 1955; d. Simon Seymore and Renee Marilyn (Rossman) P. BA, U. Colo., 1976; JD cum laude, U. Miami, Coral Gables, Fla., 1979. Bar: Colo. 1980, U.S. Dist. Ct. Colo. 1980, U.S. Ct. Appeals (10th cir.) 1983; lic. real estate broker. Pvt. practive law Denver, 1979—; assoc. Holmes & Starr PC, Denver, 1979-80, Sterling & Simon PC, Denver, 1980-82, Sweig & Pockross, PC, Denver, 1983-84, Robinson, Waters, O'Dorsio & Rapson, PC, Denver, 1984; dir., assoc. Sterling & Miller, PC, Denver, 1984-86; spl. counsel Massey Burke & Showalter, PC and predecessor firms, Denver, 1986—; instr. U. Miami, Coral Gables, 1978-79; lectr. U. Denver, 1987-88, prof. Arapahoe Community Coll., Littleton, Colo., 1988-89. Contbr. articles to profl. jours. Apptd. as panel bankruptcy trustee by U.S. Trustee Dist. Colo., 1983—. Mem. ABA (mem. cabinet young lawyers sect. 1987-90, co-author, editor A Desk-Side Guide to the Rules of Bankruptcy 1986, 2d edit. 1988, moderator ann. meeting 1987, chairperson debtor-creditor relationships com. 1986-88), Colo. Bar Assn. (chmn. young lawyers sect. 1985-86, del. to ABA 1988—, author, speaker) Denver Bar Assn., Colo. Women's Bar Assn. (girls just wanna have fun com. 1988—, speaker), Colo. Women's C. of C. (gen. counsel 1988—), Bar and Gavel, Omicron Delta Kappa. Jewish. Office: Massey Burke & Showalter PC 518 17th St Ste 1100 Denver CO 80202

PORTER-DAVIS, GAIL LORETTA, principal; b. Moline, Ill., June 19, 1952; d. Marvell and Clella M. (Williams) Porter; m. Dean Francis Davis, Feb. 27, 1982. BS in Elem. Spl. Edn., Western Ill. U., 1973, MS in Edn. Adminstrn., 1989. Cert. elem. and spl. edn. tchr., Ill. Tchr. 1st grade East Moline (Ill.) Pub. Schs., 1974; tchr. 1st grade and spl. edn. Rock Island (Ill.) Pub. Schs., 1974-88, dean of students, 1989-90; prin. Hawthrone-Irving Elem. Sch., 1990—. Mem. Am. Assn. Sch. Adminstrs., Ill. Women Administrs., Nat. Alliance Black Sch. Educators, Phi Delta Kappa, Alpha Kappa Alpha. Baptist. Home: 1528 30th Ave Moline IL 61265

PORTMAN, CHERYL BETH, computer systems executive; b. Boston, Oct. 19, 1960; d. Arthur L. and Pearl (Hecht) P. BA in Sociology, Southeastern Mass. U., 1982. Proofreader O'Connor & Drew, CPA's, Braintree, Mass., 1982-83; data entry operator Kluwer Acad. Pub. Co., Norwell, Mass., 1983-85, computer operator, 1985-87, computer systems supr., 1987—. Mem. NAFE, Southeastern Mass. U. Alumni Assn. (dorm orientation com. 1978-82, student orgn. svc. 1978-82, tutor reading and writing ctr. 1978-82), Greepeace. Office: Kluwer Acad Pub Co l0l Philip Dr Norwell MA 02061

PORUCZNIK, MARY ANN, writer, editor, advertising and public relations consultant; b. Chgo., May 4, 1948; d. John Charles and Anna J. (Malec) P. B.A., St. Xavier Coll., Chgo., 1970; postgrad. Northwestern U., 1971-73, Triton Coll., 1987-82. Editor pubs. CAC Ins. Co., Chgo., 1972-75, asst. dir. advt. and sales, 1975; advt. and sales promotion CNA Ins. Co., Chgo., 1975-77; dir. mktg. services N.Am. Co. Life and Health Ins., Chgo., 1977-81; gen. ptnr. Taurus Communications, Oak Park, Ill., 1981-86; profl. writer, Oak Park, 1986—. Mem. Ind. Writers Chgo. (pres. 1988—, bd. dirs. 1986, exec. sec. 1987-88), NAFE, Direct Mktg. Assn., VFW Aux., NOW (west suburban newsletter editor 1985-87, 89—, pres. 1987-88, treas. 1988—, Ill. NOW Times editor 1987), 19th Century Women's Club (chmn. literature dept. 1987-89), AAUW, Nat. Writers' Union. Avocations: filet crochet, camping, cooking, bridge, music. Address: 133 LeMoyne Pkwy Oak Park IL 60302

POSEN, MARION JABLON, advertising executive; b. St. Petersburg, Fla., Aug. 22, 1959; d. William W. and Winifred Francis (Jackson) Jablon; m. Philip James Posen, Sept. 10, 1988. BA, Auburn U., 1981. Commi. producer Sta. WCTV, Tallahassee, 1981-83; asst. promotion mgr. Sta. WBRC-TV, Birmingham, Ala., 1983-85; new promotion producer Sta. WMAR-TV, Balt., 1985-86; on-air promotion mgr. Sta. WCAU-TV, Phila., 1986-89, mgr. advt./promotion, 1989—. sec. Del. Valley Auburn Club, Phila., 1988-89. Mem. Broadcast Promotion/Mktg. Execs. (Gold award 1989), Phila. Nat. Acad. TV Arts and Scis., Women in Communications, Inc., Auburn N.J. Alumni, Kappa Alpha Theta. Office: Sta WCAU-TV City Ave and Monument Rd Philadelphia PA 19131

POSER, JOAN RAPPS, artists agent; b. Plainfield, N.J., Apr. 10, 1940; d. Mandel Max and Marion Davidson Rapps; m. Jay Sanford Poser, Nov. 15, 1964; children: Lester Philip, Toby Anne. BA, U. Conn., 1962. Self-employed travel cons. Lancaster, Pa., 1976-79; tchr. McDonogh Sch. Balt., 1982—; artist's agt. Joan E. Poser Assocs. Agts. in the Arts, Balt., 1978—; Pres. Lancaster Town Fair, 1974, Temple Beth El Sisterhood, 1973-77; campaign chair Bus. and Profl. Women, Assoc. Jewish Charities, Balt., 1985; spl. events chair Cultural Arts Inst. Chizuk Amuno Congregation, 1986-90, trustee, 1986-90. Mem. Hadassah. Democrat. Home: 8033 Strauff Rd Baltimore MD 21204

POSEY, ELSA, dance educator, artistic director; b. Huntington, N.Y., June 27, 1938; d. Jack Moody and Martha Edna (Kimmich) P.; children: Theo A. D. Novak, Thayer A. C. Novak. Student, Met. Opera Ballet Sch., N.Y.C., 1952-54, Ballet Russe de Monte Carlo, N.Y.C., 1954-56, Sch. Am. Ballet, N.Y.C., 1955-60, Am. Ballet Theatre Sch., N.Y.C., 1954-60, Dance Dept. 92d St., N.Y.C., 1952-58, Dance Notation Bur., N.Y.C., 1966. Co-dir. All About Dance Co., Huntington, N.Y., 1969-76; dir. Posey Dance Co., Huntington, 1976-79, artistic dir., 1981—; artistic dir. L.I. Ballet, Northport, N.Y., 1979-81; pres. Posey Sch. of Dance, Inc., Northport, 1953—, also dir. pres. Dance Edn. Svcs.of L.I., Inc., 1960—, also dir. Author: At Ease with Dance, 1979; staff writer Attitudes; reviewer Acad. Libr. Book Rev.; contbr. articles to profl. jours. Mem. Am. Dance Guild (founding mem., pres. 1983-84, bd. dirs. 1984—), Congress on Rsch. in Dance, Nat. Coalition for Edn. in Arts (rep. 1987—), N.Y. Found. for Arts and Artists Roster, Dance Critics Assn., Soc. Dance History Scholars, Performing Arts Resources (adv. bd. 1986—), Nat. Dance Assn. (chmn. studio service com. 1980—), Am. Alliance Phys. Edn., Recreation and Dance. Avocation: sailing. Office: Posey Sch Dance PO Box 254 Northport NY 11768

POSEY, JUMETTA GAIL, investment banker; b. Denver, Dec. 24, 1954; d. Charles Limon and Joyce Lee (Wolf) P. Student, George Washington U., Washington. NASD lic. registered rep. Adminstr corp. fin. Denver, 1979-81; dir. corp. fin. J.W. Gant & Assocs., Inc., Denver, 1981-85; pres., founder Heritage Group, Ltd., Denver, 1988—. Bd. dirs. pres. Denver Housing Devel. Group, Inc.; mem. Colo. Black Roundtable; fin. commn. and treqas. Com. to Elect Sharon Bailey for Denver pub. Sch. Bd.; gov.'s appointee to Hwy. Legis. Rev. Com. Mem. Nat. Assn. Securities Profls. (founding bd. dirs., conf. chmn.), Colo. Black C. of C. (bd. dirs.), Greater Denver C. of C. (grad. Leadership Denver prog.), NAFE. Office: Weldon Sullivan Carmichael 707 17th St 2901 Denver CO 80202

POSITANO, JILL MARIE, sales representative; b. Bristol, Conn., Aug. 27, 1965; d. Michael Andrew and Vivian Marie (Couture) P. BS in Mktg. Mgmt., Siena Coll., 1987. Sales rep. Am. Bank Stationery, Waterbury, Conn., 1987—. Mem. NAFE, Nat. Assn. Banking Women. Roman Catholic. Office: Am Bank Stationery 54 Great Hill Rd Watebury CT 06725

POSNER, ELEANOR, management; b. Bklyn., Sept. 23, 1942; d. Joseph and Edith Epstein; m. Robert M. Posner, Jan. 28, 1962; children: Jodi

Behrman, Dana, Jonathan. BA, Bklyn. Coll., 1965. Elem. sch. tchr. N.Y.C. Bd. Edn., Bklyn., 1965-74; dir. fin. Prestige Cosmetic Lab., Lindenhurst, N.Y., 1974-86; exec. mgr., sales, mktg. Lon Cosmetics Ltd., Lindenhurst, 1986—. Mem. PTA. Democrat. Office: Lon Cosmetics Ltd 165 S 10th St Lindenhurst NY 11757

POSNER, LINDA IRENE, corporate manager; b. Balt., Feb. 6, 1939; d. Morris and Rosabelle (Hankin) Rosen; m. Allan Bernard Posner, Dec. 29, 1957; children: Larry Gregg, Michael Glenn, Robert Ira. BA summa cum laude, Coll. of Notre Dame, 1989. Dir., lectr. Montgomery Ward's Fashion, Modeling and Charm Sch., Md., 1962-66; fashion and pub. rels. dir. Montgomery Ward, Md., 1966-75; freelance writer Balt., 1975-76; pres., co-owner Designer's Circle Ltd., Balt., 1976-78; TV writer, producer Dept. of Def., Ft. Meade, Md., 1979-87; TV mgr. Md. Dept. of Def., Ft. Meade, 1980-87, sr. edn. and tng. mgr., 1987—; regional dir. The Fashion Group, Balt., 1972-74. Mem. com March of Dimes, Balt., 1976-78; chairperson Combined Fed. Campaign Com., 1987, U.S. Savs. Bonds, 1989. Dept. of Def. scholar, 1987-88. Mem. Women in Communications, Human Resources Mgmt. Assn., AFTRA. Jewish. Home: 11008 Valley Heights Dr Owings Mills MD 21117

POSNER, TRACY, diversified industries executive; b. 1962. BS, Cornell U., 1983. With Southeastern Pub. Svc. Co., Miami, Fla., 1983—, now v.p., asst. sec., asst. treas., and also bd. dirs. Office: Southeastern Pub Svc Co 6917 Collins Ave Miami Beach FL 33141*

POSNIAK, SALLIE CECELIA, retail designer; b. Appleton, Wis., Mar. 2, 1934; d. Joseph Benjamin and Rebecca (Begin) P. Student, Ray Vogue Art Sch., Chgo., 1952-53, Chgo. Art Inst., 1954-57. Trimmer Marshall Fields, Chgo., 1957-58, asst. designer, 1958-61, designer, 1961-67, master designer, 1967-86, mgr. cen. design, 1986—. Office: Marshall Fields 111 N State St Chicago IL 60690

POSPISIL, EVA HOLDRIDGE, systems engineer; b. Hobbs, N. Mex., May 6, 1953; d. Earl Lee and Ruby Pearl (Bryan) Holdridge; m. Charles Henry Beecroft, Oct. 2, 1971 (div.); m. Francis Joseph Pospisil, Oct. 10, 1980. AS, Baylor U., 1977; BS, NYU, 1983; MS in Sci. Counseling Psychology with honors, Am. Technol. U., 1985, MS in Mgmt. Sci. with honors, 1986. Med. technician, instr. Acad. Health Sci. Fort Sam Houston, Tex., 1971-81; med. technician Darnall Army Community Hosp., Fort Hood, Tex., 1982-84; program analyst DOIM, Fort Hood, 1988-89; systems engr. Northern Telecom, Richardson, Tex., 1988-89, network mgr., 1989—; instr. Cen. Tex. Coll., Killeen, 1985-88, research mgr., 1984-85; owner, mgr. SUEDE, Copperas Cove, Tex., 1985—; cons. Mary Kay Cosmetics. Served with U.S. Army, 1971-81. Mem. Am. Med. Technicians, Tex. Assn. Counseling and Devel. Assn., Nat. Assn. Underwater Diving Instrs., Nat. Assn. Parachute Clubs, Nat. Assn. Hangliding, Copperas Cove C. of C., Epsilon Delta Phi. Democrat. Roman Catholic. Club: Fort Hood Parachute. Avocations: skydiving, scuba diving, water and snow skiing, racquetball. Home: 1329 Kesser St Plano TX 75023

POSSENTI, CHERYL ANN, lawyer; b. Yonkers, N.Y., Dec. 9, 1957; d. Vito Joseph and Catherine Margaret (Cooke) P.; m. Kenneth S. Zimmerman, May 7, 1983. BA, SUNY, Albany, 1978; JD, SUNY, Buffalo, 1982. Bar: N.Y. 1983, U.S. Dist. Ct. (we. dist.) N.Y. 1984. Assoc. Saperston & Day, P.C., Buffalo, 1982—; Cox, Barrell, Buffalo, 1983-87; judge moot ct. competition SUNY, Buffalo, 1985, 86, 89; atty., coach N.Y. State Bar Assn. Mock Trial Tournament, Buffalo, 1986-87. Mem. N.Y. State Bar Assn., N.Y. State Trial Lawyers Assn. Democrat. Office: Saperston & Day PC 1 Fountain Pla Buffalo NY 14203

POST, NANCY, organizational development executive; b. Bklyn., May 11, 1957; d. Joseph and Betty (Meltzer) P. BA, U. Pa., 1979; MA, Traditional Acupuncture Inst., 1984; cert., Houston Sch. for Psychotherapy, 1978. Diplomate nationally in acupuncture; lic. psychotherapist, Pa., Md. Dir. Health Wellness Project, Phila.; prin. investigator Facilitators, Inc., Las Vegas, Nev.; dir. faculty and rsch. Merriam Hill Ctr., Cambridge, Mass.; prin. Post Enterprises, Phila.; founder Systems Energetics. Grantee in field. Mem. Orgn. Devel. Network, Pa. Acupuncture Soc. Home: 616 W Upsal St Philadelphia PA 19144

POSTER-TAYLOR, TERRI LEE, marketing professional; b. Boston, Oct. 2, 1952; d. Harold Bernard and Sarah Lillian (Cristol) Poster; m. Barry Millman, Feb. 23, 1975 (div. Feb 1979); m. Clark Martin Taylor, Oct. 19, 1985. Student, Boston Conservatory of Music, 1970-73. Beauty advisor Revlon Co., N.Y.C., 1975-77; mktg. rep. V.H. Monette & Co., Smithfield, Va., 1977-78; sales mgr. Vidal Sassoon, Inc., Los Angeles, 1978-81; account exec. Sarvis & Assocs., Jacksonville, Fla., 1981-82; v.p., owner Exchange & Commissary Sales, Jacksonville, 1982-83; area mgr. Assoc. Temporary Staffing, Jacksonville, 1983-85; pres., owner Easy Info, Inc., Jacksonville, 1985-86; br. mgr. Ablest Temporary Services, Jacksonville, 1986-88; area mgr. Fla. Temporaries (name formerly Blue Arrow/Temporaries), Jacksonville, 1988-90; dir. mktg. O.P.T.I.O.N. Care, Jacksonville, 1990—; speaker in field. Bd. dirs. Jacksonville Urban League, 1987—, sec., 1989. Named Arlington Coun. Outstanding Mem. of Yr., 1988, Vol. of Month Jacksonville C. of C., 1988. Mem. Am. Soc. for Personnel Adminstrs., Adminstrv. Mgmt. Soc. (pres. 1985-86), Jacksonville C. of C. (chmn. ara coun. main event 1987-88, sec., treas. Arlington coun. 1988, 90, bd. dirs. 1987-89, Ambs. 1989, pub. rels. chmn., svc. bd. tax 1989, chmn. Operation Y.O.U. 1990), Civitans (bd. dirs. Jacksonville 1985-86). Republican. Jewish. Office: OPTION Care 7302 Main St Jacksonville FL 32208

POST-GORDEN, JOAN CAROLYN, psychologist, educator; b. Oak Park, Ill., July 3, 1932; d. DeWitt T. and Mary Jane (Lewellen) Post; children: Gregrey Wayne, Jeffrey Scott, Kayle Lynn, Tamara Anne. BS, Manchester (Ind.) Coll., 1964; MS, U. Ga., 1967, PhD, 1970. Lic. psychologist, Colo. Tchr. Clarke County Schs., Athens, Ga., 1964-65; part-time asst. prof. Tex. Tech. U., Lubbock, 1968-69; instr. So. Colo. State Coll., Pueblo, 1970-71; asst. prof. U. So. Colo., Pueblo, 1971-76, assoc. prof., 1976-81, prof., 1981—; asst. to city mgr., Champaign, Ill., 1980-81; psychologist So. Colo. Mental Health Dist., Flora, 1979-80; dir. scholarly and creative activities U. So. Colo., 1988—. Contbr. chpt. to book and articles to profl. jours. NDEA fellow, 1964-66, Danforth teaching fellow, 1978, faculty fellow Colo. State Div. Mental Health, 1986-87. Mem. Am. Psychol. Assn., Soc. for Rsch. in Child Devel., Rocky Mountain Psychol. Assn., Psi Chi, Sigma Xi, Alpha Omicron Pi. Home: 1021 Ruppel #31 Pueblo CO 81001 Office: U So Colo Dept Psychology Pueblo CO 81001

POSTHUMA, HELEN MARIE, travel consultant; b. Bisbee, Ariz., Jan. 4, 1920; d. Harold Chamberlain and Harriet Elizabeth (Jones) Stull; m. Ynte Meindert Posthuma, June 28, 1941; children: Stephen Chamberlain, John Robert. BA in Spanish cum laude, Pomona Coll., 1941; postgrad., U. So. Calif., 1942. Tchr. Fontana (Calif.) Jr. High Sch., 1943; with rsch. dept. Aerojet Engring Co., Azusa, Calif., 1945; fashion model Copacabana Hotel, Rio de Janeiro, 1945; counselor Plaza Travel, Burbank, Calif., 1983—; bd. dirs. Art Ctr. Coll. Design, Pasadena, Calif. Mem. Huntington Meml. Clinic Aux., Pasadena, Altadena Guild Huntington Hosp. Mem. Am. Contract Bridge League, Pi Lambda Theta. Republican. Presbyterian. Home: 610 S Orange Grove Ave Pasadena CA 91105 Office: Plaza Travel 4020 W Magnolia Burbank CA 91505

POTASEK, MARY JOYCE, physicist, researcher; b. Mpls., Oct. 27, 1945; d. Chester and Millie P.; m. Karl W. Beeson, Jan. 22, 1977; 1 child, Jessica Elizabeth. BA in Math., Coll. St. Catherine, 1967; MS in Physics, U. Ill. 1970, PhD, 1974. Research asst. U. Ill., Urbana, 1970-74; research scientist Internat. Bus. Machines, Watson Research Ctr., Yorktown Heights, N.Y., 1974-75; NSF, AAUW postdoctoral fellow Princeton (N.J.) U., 1975-78; NATO postdoctoral fellow Max Planck Inst., Gottingen, West Germany, 1978-80; mem. tech. staff AT&T, Princeton, 1980-86, AT&T Bell Labs. Murray Hill, N.J., 1986-90, Columbia U., N.Y.C., 1990—. Contbr. articles to profl. jours. Mem. AAAS, Optical Soc. of Am. Am. Phys. Soc., Phi Beta Kappa, Pi Mu Epsilon. Home: 197 Dodds Ln Princeton NJ 08540

POTASH, JANICE SUE, accounting educator; b. Ft. Knox, Ky., Mar. 24, 1955; d. Robert S. and Madeline J. (Kirschner) Kraft; m. Steven Robert

Potash, May 28, 1978; children: Jamie Rebecca, Daniel Seth. BS in Bus. cum laude, Miami U., Ohio, 1977; MBA, Xavier U., 1982. CPA, Ohio. Staff acct., auditor Arthur Andersen & Co., Cin., 1977-78; acctg. supr. Children's Hosp. Med. Ctr., Cin., 1978-81; asst. prof. acctg. Miami U., Hamilton, Ohio, 1982-84, Marian Coll., Indpls., 1985-89; pvt. practice Carmel, 1989—. Campaign worker jud. polit. campaigns, Cin., 1972—; mem. Women's Am. Orgn. for Rehab Through Tng., Cin., 1982-85, Indpls., 1986—, treas., 1989-90, v.p. fundraising, 1990—; advisor Explorer post Boy Scouts Am., Kokomo, Ind., 1984. Mem. AICPA, Am. Acctg. Assn., Acctg. Rsch. Assn., Hadassah (bd. dirs. 1990—). Republican. Jewish.

POTEAT, CAROL MARTIN, educational administrator; b. Washington, Mar. 29, 1929; d. George William Martin and Hattie (Welsh) Fraction; widow; 1 child, Linda Michele. BS, Miner Tchrs. Coll., Washington, 1950; MA, Hunter Coll., 1963. Tchr. English, N.Y.C. Bd. Edn., 1961-70, coord. student affairs Springfield Gardens High Sch., 1970-73, prin. Middle Coll. High Sch., 1973-76, exec. asst. to exec. dir. div. high schs., 1976-78, dir. pupil personnel svcs., 1978-82, spl. asst. chief exec. for instrn., 1982-85, spl. asst. to chancellor, 1985-87, spl. asst. dep. chancellor for instrn. and devel., 1987—. Contbr. articles to various publs. Mem. adv. coun. Edwin Gould Group Homes, N.Y.C., 1978-81; pres. Lakeview Gardens Block Assn., West Hempstead, N.Y., 1980-82; bd. dirs. Project Double Discovery, Columbia U., N.Y.C., 1980—. Recipient Outstanding Svc. award Project Double Discovery, 1973, Leader in Edn. award N.Y.C. Adminstrv. Women in Edn., 1979, 85; scholarship given in her name Postal Worker's Union, 1978, Women Helping Women award Soroptimists Internat., 1989. Mem. Nat. Coun. Adminstrv. Women in Edn. (pres. 1986-88), Nat. Assn. Black Sch. Educators (policy commn.), Nat. Assn. Pupil Personnel Adminstrs., N.Y. State Assn. Pupil Svcs. Adminstrs. (pres. 1988-89), Delta Sigma Theta. Democrat. Episcopalian. Office: NYC Bd Edn 110 Livingston St Brooklyn NY 11201

POTTER, ANNE LOUISE, political scientist; b. Eugene, Oreg., Sept. 1, 1949; d. Daniel Oliver and Betty Louise (Harder) P.; BA, Reed Coll., 1971; MA, Stanford U., 1973, PhD, 1979. Vis. scholar Inst. Torcuato di Tella, Buenos Aires, Argentina, 1974-76; asst. prof. govt. Oberlin (Ohio) Coll., 1978-79; project mgr. Tech. Applications, Inc., Falls Church, Va., 1980-81; project mgr. Daedalean Assos., Inc., Woodbine, Md., 1981-82, Technology Applications, Inc., Falls Church, Va., 1982-84; owner Diversified Svcs. Group, 1984-88; founder, pres. Oreg. Rsch. and Cons. Group, Portland, Oreg., 1988—. Contbr. rsch. reports for U.S. Govt. and pvt. clients, articles to fin. publs. OAS rsch. fellow, 1976. AAUW dissertation fellow, 1975-76; Woodrow Wilson fellow, 1971-72; NSF grad. fellow, 1972-75. Mem. AAAS, N.Y. Inst. Sci., Am. Polit. Sci. Assn. (Gabriel A. Almond award), Women's Caucus for Polit. Sci., Acad. Polit. Sci., Oreg. Women's Polit. Caucus, Phi Beta Kappa.

POTTER, BARBARA ANN, educator; b. Freeport, Ill., Sept. 16, 1941; d. Nelson Thomas and Hazel Althea (Park) P. BA, Culver-Stockton Coll., 1965; MA, Goddard Coll., 1980. Cert. music tchr., Conn., Mo. Tchr. LeMo Pub. Sch. Dist., Lewistown, Mo., 1965-66, Henry County Regional Ind. Sch. Dist., Windsor, Mo., 1966-69; tchr. music Bristol (Conn.) Pub. Schs., 1969—. Author: Do It My Way: The Child's Way of Learning, 1977; Mem. editorial bd. The Orff Echo, 1987—. Fundraiser Easter Seals, Conn., 1984, 85; sec. Southington (Conn.) Arts Soc., 1988—. Mem. Am. Orff-Schulwerk Assn. Conf. (clinician nat. confs. Phoenix 1987, Chgo. 1987, Atlanta 1989, region V rep. for bd. of trustees 1983-87, pres. Conn. chpt. 1978-80). Home: 83 Parkview Dr Plantsville CT 06479-1933

POTTER, CAROLE ANN, broadcast executive; b. N.Y.C., Oct. 10, 1940; d. Theodore Benjamin and Beatrice (Weinberger) Lipshay; m. Allan Robbins Potter, May 1963 (div. 1968). BS in Pub. Communications, Boston U., 1962. Sr. unit publicist Am. Broadcasting Co., N.Y.C., 1967-76; asst. dir. pub. rels. United Airlines, N.Y.C., 1976-77; sr. acct. exec. Stone Assocs., N.Y.C., 1977-79; owner Potter & Co., N.Y.C., 1979-89; ptnr., v.p., creative dir. Alpert Prodns., N.Y.C., 1989—; travel/tour mgr. freelancer, China, Soviet Union, 1981-86. Author: Knock on Wood, 1984; contbr. articles to consumer mags. Democrat. Home: 355 E 72nd St New York NY 10021

POTTER, CYNTHIA M., educator; b. Balt., July 15, 1950; d. Percel Celon and Nancy Jane (Williams) Harris; m. Willis M. Potter, Oct. 11, 1975; 1 child, Shomaree. MS, Norfolk State U., 1979; postgrad., Old Dominion U., 1979; BA, Norfolk State Coll., 1983; postgrad., Hampton U., 1984. Cert. designated gifted alternative, inservice tng. program for mainstreaming, leadership skills. Summer enrichment art tchr. African Am. art Norfolk (Va.) Pub. Schs., photojournalist tchr., art tchr. Contbr. articles to profl. newsletters. Chair planning com. Ruth Winstead Diggs Scholarship Fund, Inc., 1988—; dir. minority concerns com. Va. Art Edn. Assn., 1990—. Recipient Cert. of Recognition, Superior Art Instrn. of Appreciation, 1989; fellow for travel study in West Africa; named Tidewater Elem. Art Tchr. of Yr., for Outstanding Svc., 1988. Mem. Nat. Art Edn. Assn., Nat. Conf. of Artists, Southeastern Va. Art Assn. Home: 3524 Silina Dr Virginia Beach VA 23452

POTTER, ELAINE CLARKE, sociology educator; b. Warren, Ohio, Jan. 31, 1935; d. Scot Butler Clarke and Lucy Jean (Spiers) Kellers; m. Ralph Miles, Potter, July 13, 1957; 1 child, Russell Alan. B.A. magna cum laude, Case Western Res. U., 1970; M.A., Kent State U., 1972. Office mgr. McGovern/Shriver Hdqrs., Euclid, Ohio, 1972; instr. sociology Ursuline Coll. for Women, Pepper Pike, Ohio, 1973-74; instr. sociology and soc. sci. Cuyahoga Community Coll., Parma, Ohio, 1975—. Mem. Am. Sociol. Assn., AAUP, North Central Sociol. Assn., Sociologists for Women in Soc., ACLU, NOW, Women's Internat. League for Peace and Freedom (pres. Cleve. chpt. 1975-76), Women Space (v.p. 1980), Phi Beta Kappa, Tri Beta. Democrat. Unitarian. Club: Sierra. Avocations: hiking; reading. Home: 2618 Brainard Rd Pepper Pike OH 44124 Office: Cuyahoga Community Coll West Campus 11000 Pleasant Valley Parma OH 44130

POTTER, ELIZABETH WALKER, rehabilitation services, human resources training and development executive; b. Mpls., Oct. 14, 1957; d. George Gholson and Teresa (Blatz) Walker; m. Carl Lynn Potter, June 1, 1984; 1 child, Julia Langdon. AA, Coll. of St. Benedict, St. Joseph, Minn., 1979; BS, U. Minn., 1981; MS, U. Wis., 1984. Cert. speech and lang. pathologist, Ohio. Speech pathologist Good Samaritan Hosp., Cin., 1985-89; pres. Potter Cons. Group, Cin., 1988—; adj. instr. U. Cin., 1988—; dist. mgr. Nova Care, Inc., 1990—. Contbr. articles to profl. jours. Named Woman Entrepreneur of Yr., Bus. Women's Showcase, Cin., 1989. Mem. N.Am. Speech and Hearing Assn., Employment Svcs. Profls. Network, Phi Kappa Phi. Office: 10979 Reed Hartman Hwy Cincinnati OH 45242

POTTER, EMMA JOSEPHINE HILL, language educator; b. Hackensack, N.J., July 18, 1921; d. James Silas and Martha Loretta (Pyle) Hill; A.B. cum laude with honors in Classics (scholar), Alfred (N.Y.) U., 1943; A.M., Johns Hopkins U., 1946; m. James H. Potter, Mar. 26, 1949. Tchr. Latin, Balt. County Public Schs., 1943-44; instr. French, Spanish, Balt. Poly. Inst., 1950-83; instr. Spanish adult edn. classes, 1946-48; treas. Bruno-Potter Inc., acctg. Trustee James Harry Potter Gold Medal, ASME. Mem. Johns Hopkins U., Alfred U. alumni assns., Internat. Platform Assn. Democrat. Roman Catholic. Club: Johns Hopkins U. Faculty. Home: 419 3d Ave Avon By The Sea NJ 07717

POTTER, JANET MARIE, inventory control manager; b. Pontiac, Mich., Aug. 29, 1967; d. Albert D. and Elsie M. (LaRue) P. Cert., South Coll., Savannah, Ga., 1989. Accounts payable clk. The Seabrook of Hilton Head (S.C.), Inc., 1985-86, accounts receivable supr., 1986-87; accounts receivable clk. The Cottages Resort and Conf. Ctr., Hilton Head, 1987-88; bookkeeper Fgn. Accents, Ltd., Hilton Head, 1988-89, inventory control mgr., 1990—. Mem. NAFE. Baptist.

POTTER, JUNE ANITA, small business owner; b. LaCrosse, Wis., Jan. 22, 1938; d. Christian John and Ethel Marie (Stafslien) Stefferud; m. James Oscar Potter, June 18, 1961; children: Jill Potter Rutlin, Todd. BA in Home Econs., St. Olaf Coll., Northfield, Minn., 1960; postgrad., U. Wis., Stout, 1964; MS in Edn., U. Wis., Menomonie, 1977. Sr. high home econs. tchr., FHA advisor Tomah (Wis.) High Sch., 1960-64, Black River Falls (Wis.) High Sch., 1971-83; free lance interior designer Warrens, Wis., 1964—; ptnr., mgr. James Potter Cranberry Marsh, Inc., Warrens, 1968—. Co-pubr.: Warrens Centennial Book, 1968, Cranberry Centennial Book, 1989. Active various charitable orgns.; bd. dirs. Warrens Cranberry Festival, 1984—; com. mem. Wis. Cranberry Growers Centennial, 1988—; mem. Warrens area Bus. Men's Orgn., 1990—. Mem. AAUW (v.p. 1989—), NAFE, Tomah Pkwy. Garden Club, Beta Sigma Phi (Nat. Orderof Rose, 1983, Silver Circle 1985, Girl of Yr., officer, com. mem. 1962). Lutheran. Home: RR 2 Box 12 Warrens WI 54666-9501

POTTER, LILLIAN FLORENCE, business executive secretary; b. Montreal, Que., Can., Oct. 19, 1912; came to U.S., 1934; naturalized citizen.; d. Thomas Joseph and Lily Rose (Robertson) Quirk; m. Theodore Edward Potter, July 20, 1932 (dec. Apr. 1980); children: Peter Edward, Stephen Thomas. Grad. high sch., Montreal, 1929, grad., 1931. Sr. sec. S.D. Warren div. Scott Paper Co., Westbrook, Maine, 1955-69, editor indsl. publ. S.D. Warren div., 1969-72; editor Nat. Antiques Rev. mag., Portland, Maine, 1972-77; exec. sec. Humboldt Portland Litho div. Humboldt Nat. Graphics, Inc., Fortuna, Calif., 1977—; free lance writer Guy Gannett Pub. Co., Portland, 1960-64. Author: (children's book) Once Upon an Autumn, 1984 (state 1st pl. award, nat. 3d pl. award); co-author: (textbook, tchrs. manual) Foundations of Patient Care, 1981; asst. editor, N.E. dist. The Secretary mag., Profl. Secs. Internat., 1960-62; editor Maine Chpt. Bull., 1963-64. Recipient George Washington Honors medal Freedoms Found., Valley Forge, Pa., 1964, Sec. of Yr. award Portland chpt. Profl. Secs. Internat., 1967, Outstanding Svc. award State of Maine Sesquicentennial, 1970, Outstanding Svc. award Island Pond (Vt.) Hist. Soc. 1978. Mem. Nat. Fedn. Press Women, Maine Media Women (pres. 1970-71, Woman of Yr. award 1973), Maine Writers and Pubs. Alliance, New Eng. Appraisers Assn., Portland Lyric Theater Club, Order Eastern Star (past matron, past pres.). Republican. Episcopalian. Home: 80 Payson St Portland ME 04102 Office: Humboldt Portland Litho 1600 Congress St Portland ME 04102

POTTER, NANCY DUTTON, psychologist; b. St. Joseph, Mo., Jan. 16, 1946; d. Paul Vernon and Rosa Lee (Hatfield) Dutton 1 child, Blakeslee Ann. BA, Pitzer Coll., 1968; MA, U. Kans., 1971; Ph.D., U. Mo., 1974; postgrad., Georgetown U., 1977-79. Lic. psychologist, D.C., Va. Chief clin. psychology Keesler AFB Med. Center, Miss., 1976-77; clin. psychologist Malcolm Grow Med. Center, Andrews AFB, Md., 1977-78; assoc. dir. Georgetown U. Counseling Ctr., Washington, 1978-79, acting dir., 1979-80, dir. internship tng., 1978-81; pvt. practice psychology Burke, Va., 1978—; chmn. ethics and profl. affairs Va. Acad. Clin. Psychology, Va., 1987-89. Bd. dirs. Family Counseling Agy., Biloxi, Miss., 1976. Served to maj. USAF, 1974-88. Mem. Am. Psychol. Assn., Am. Personnel and Guidance Assn., No. Va. Soc. Clin. Psychologists (v.p. 1984-86, pres. 1986-88). Home: 7400 Carath Ct Springfield VA 22153 Office: 8987 Cotswold Dr Burke VA 22015

POTTER, ROSEMARY LEE, educator; b. Miami, Fla., Nov. 22, 1938; d. Kenyon Molene and Virginia Catherine (Van Hemel) Lee; m. Robert Ellis Potter, Dec. 28, 1963; children: Robert Ellis II, Kenyon David (twins). BS, Maryville (Tenn.) Coll., 1960; MS, U. Tenn., 1963; EdD, U. Miami, 1973. Swimming instr. S.W. YMCA, Miami, 1956-62; tchr. Dade County Schs., Miami, 1960-62, 65-77, Hudson Sch. Dist., La Puente, Calif., 1963-65, Pinellas County Schs., Clearwater, Fla., 1977-90; project dir. Fla. classrooms online, Fla.-Eng. connection Office Tech. Fla. Dept. Edn., 1990—; cons. in field. Author: The Positive Use of Commercial Television with Children, 1975, Television in the Curriculum, 1984, Using Microcomputers for Teaching Middle School Reading, 1989. Scout coord. St. Petersburg Dist. United Meth. Ch., Clearwater, 1986—; mem. St. Paul United Meth. Ch. Mem. NEA, Internat. Reading Assn., Nat. Council for Families and TV, Pinellas Reading Coun. (dir. rsch. and legis. 1988—), Nat. PEN Women, Rachel/Lydia Cir. (co-chair 1988-89), Phi Delta Kappa. Office: Safety Harbor Middle Sch 125 7th St N Safety Harbor FL 34695

POTTER-HILL, LYNNE A., law librarian; b. Pasadena, Calif., Sept. 20, 1955. d. Robert Earl and Vivian Ann (Cox) P.; m. Gregory S. Hill, Apr. 14, 1985; children: Bricenna Elizabeth, Kathryh Ann, Kimberly Jeanne. BA, San Diego State U., 1976; MA, U. Denver, 1978; JD, Nat. U., 1984. Librarian, Ripey Car Mus., Denver, 1978; catalog librarian Western State Coll. Law, San Diego, 1978-79; law librarian Nat. U. Sch. Law, San Diego, 1979—; instr. legal research. Mem. ALA, Am. Assn. of Law Librarians, So. Calif. Assn. of Law Librarians. Office: Nat U Sch Law Libr 3580 Aero Ct San Diego CA 92123

POTTORFF, JO ANN, state legislator; b. Wichita, Kans., Mar. 7, 1936; d. John Edward McCluggage and Helen Elizabeth (Alexander) Ryan; m. Gary Nial Pottorff; children: Michael Lee, Gregory Nial. BA, Kansas State U., 1957; MA, St. Louis U., 1969. Elem. tchr. Pub. Sch., Keats and St. George, 1957-59; cons., elem. specialist Mid Continent Regional Edn. Lab., Kansas City, Mo., 1971-73; cons. Poindexter Assocs., Wichita, 1975; campaign mgr. Garner Shriver Congl. Camp, Wichita, 1976; interim dir. Wichita Area Rape Ctr., 1977; conf. coord. Biomedical Synergistics Inst., Wichita, 1977-79; real estate sales asst. Chester Kappelman Group, Wichita, 1979—; state rep. State of Kans., Topeka, 1985—. Mem. sch. bd. Wichita Pub. Schs., 1977-85; bd. dirs. Edn. Consol. and Improvement Act Adv. com., Kans. Found. for the Handicapped; mem. Children & Youth Adv. com. (bd. dirs.). Recipient Disting. Svc. award Kans. Assn. Sch. Bds., 1983, Outstanding Svc. to Sch. Children of the Nation award Coun. Urban Bds., 1984; Kans. State U. Alumni fellow, 1987. Mem. Leadership Am. Alumnae (bd. dirs., sec.), Found. for Agrl. in Classroom (bd. dirs.), Jr. League, Vet. Aux. (pres.), Chi Omega (pres.). Office: Chester Kappelman Group PO Box 8036St Wichita KS 67208

POTTS, BARBARA JOYCE, mayor; b. L.A., Feb. 18, 1932; d. Theodore Thomas and Helen Mae (Kelley) Elledge; m. Donald A. Potts, Dec. 27, 1953; children—Tedd, Douglas, Dwight, Laura. AA, Graceland Coll., 1951; grad., Radiol. Tech. Sch., 1953; grad. program for sr. execs. in state and local govt., Harvard U., 1989. Radiol. technician Independence Sanitarium and Hosp., Mo., 1953, 58-59, Mercy Hosp., Balt., 1954-55; city council mem.-at-large City of Independence, Mo., 1978-82, mayor, 1982-90; chmn. Mid-Am. Regional Coun., Kansas City, Mo., 1984-85; bd. dirs. Mo. Mcpl. League, Jefferson City, Mo., 1982-90, v.p., 1986-87, pres. 1987, 88; chmn. Mo. Commn. on Local Govt. Cooperation, 1985-90. Author: Independence, 1985. Mem. Mo. Gov.'s Conf. on Edn., 1976, Independence Charter Rev. Bd., 1977; bd. dirs. Hope House Shelter for Abused Women, Independence, 1982—; pres. Child Placement Svcs., Independence, 1972-89; trustee Independence Regional Health Ctr., 1982—, Nat. Women's Polit. Caucus, LWV, Park Coll., 1989—; mem. adv. bd. Greater Mo. Focus on Leadership; mem. adv. bd., steering com. Greater Mo. Focus on Leadership, 1989. Recipient George Lehr Meml award Com. for Lehr, 1989, Woman of Achievement award Mid-Continent Council Girl Scouts Am., 1983, 75th Anniversary Women of Achievement award Mid-Continent Council Girl Scouts, 1987, Jane Adams award Hope House, 1984, Community Leadership award Comprehensive Mental Health Services, Inc., 1984, Outstanding Community Svc. in Govt. award LWV, 1990; named Friend of Edn. Independence Nat. Edn. Assn., 1990. Mem. Am. Inst. Pub. Svc. (bd. nominators 1989). Mem. Reorganized Ch. of Jesus Christ of Latter-Day Saints. Home: 18508 E 30th Terr Independence MO 64057

POTTS, DARLA LYNN, protective services official; b. Sioux City, Iowa, Sept. 9, 1958; d. Merrill E. and Darlene Jane (Benton) P. BA in Criminal Justice, Morningside Coll., 1982. Youth worker Woodbury County Juvenile Detention Ctr., Sioux City, 1983; residential asst. Region IV Svcs., South Sioux City, Nebr., 1984; house mgr. Mid-Step Svcs., Inc., Sioux City, 1984—; employment clk. Job Svc. Iowa, Sioux City, 1977-78; asst. activity dir. Countyside Retirement Home, Sioux City, 1981. Vol. Am. Heart Assn., Sioux City, 1987, Mr. Goodfellow, Sioux City, 1988, Spl. Olympics, Sioux City, 1985; res. officer Woodbury County Sheriff's Posse, Sioux City, 1985—. Recipient gov.'s vol. award State of Iowa, 1989; A.W. Jones scholar, 1982. Mem. Iowa State Res. Law Officers Assn. (bd. dirs. dist. 4, 1988—, contbr. articles), AAUW (life), Order Eastern Star (Grand Cross of Color 1979). Republican. Methodist. Home: 2627 S Rustin Apt A-24 Sioux City IA 51106 Office: Mid-Step Svcs Inc 4303 Stone Ave Sioux City IA 51106

POTTS, JACKIE STEARNS, writer; b. Atlanta; d. Louis Grant and Ruth (Canada) Stearns. BA, Agnes Scott Coll.; MS, Emory U. Computer cons. U.S. Govt., Washington, 1965-75; computer graphics cons. U.S. Govt., Wash., 1975-82; pres. Worldwide Interface Designers, Columbia, M.D., 1982—; adj. prof., cons., adv. coun. Howard Community Coll., Columbia, 1987-. Author: Computer Aided Drafting and Design Using Autocad. Pres. Deering Woods Condominium Am., Columbia, 1987—. Mem. Data Processing Mgmt. Assn, Office Automation Soc. Internat. (vice chmn. 1981—). Home: Worldwide Interface Designers 5681 Harper Farm Columbia MD 21044

POU, LINDA ALICE, interior designer, architectural designer; b. Huntsville, Ala., Oct. 26, 1942; d. Louis and Lillian Maurice (Garvin) Grabensteder; m. Robert LeRoy Pou, Aug. 27, 1965; children: Susan Caroline, Stephanie Lynn. B of Interior Design, Auburn U., 1964; postgrad., Ecoles D'Art Americaines, 1964. Interior designer Martin Interiors, Huntsville, Ala., 1963, Blance Reeves Interiors, Atlanta, 1964-65, Loveman's Dept. Store, Huntsville, Ala., 1966, Southeastern Galleries, Charleston, S.C., 1967; draftsman Brown Engring., Huntsville, Ala., 1967-68, Naval Electronics Systems Command, S.C., 1968, Leland Engrs., Charleston, S.C., 1968-69; owner Drafting Svc., Mobile, Ala., 1977-78, The Design Svc., Prattville, Ala., 1980—. Composer songs include adult anthem, Sing for Joy, 1983, Sing Hallelujah to the Lord, He's the Rainbow in My Life, 1984; children's Lord of Harvest, 1984, Sing a Song to the Lord of Earth, 1985; compiler and editor book of poetry. Mem. jr. bd. Florence Crittendon Home for Unwed Mothers, Mobile, Ala., 1977-79, Prattville Planning Commn. 1980—, chmn. 1985-88, vice chmn. 1988—; mem. Prattville Hist. Re-devel. Authority, 1988-89. Mem. ASCAP, Greater Montgomery Homebuilders Assn., Spinners (treas. 1982-83), Prattville C. of C., Alpha Gamma Delta. Home: 591 Marlyn Dr Prattville AL 36067

POULIN-KLOEHR, LISA, bankruptcy consultant; b. Saigon, South Vietnam, Feb. 13, 1956; d. Normand and Joan Marie (Scileppi) Poulin; m. Clayton J. Kloehr. BA, Bucknell U., 1978; MBA, U. Pitts., 1986. permanent resident, 1968;. Asst. v.p. The Fidelity Bank, Phila., 1978-83; cons. Bus. Investigation Svcs. Coopers & Lybrand, Phila., 1983-85; sr. mgr. reorganization practice KPMG Peat Marwick, N.Y.C., 1986—. Mem. Am. Bankruptcy Inst., INSOL, Assn. Insolvency Accts. Republican. Roman Catholic. Office: KPMG Peat Marwick 345 Park Ave New York NY 10154

POULIOT, ASSUNTA GALLUCCI, business school owner and director; b. West Warwick, R.I., Aug. 14, 1937; d. Michael and Angelina (DeCesare) G.; Gallucci; m. Joseph F. Pouliot Jr., July 4, 1961; children: Brenda, Mark, Jill, Michele. BS, U. R.I., 1959, MS, 1971. Bus. tchr. Cranston High Sch., R.I., 1959-61; bus. dept. chmn. Chariho Regional High Sch., Wood River Junction, R.I., 1961-73; instr. U. R.I., Kingston, 1973-78; founder, dir. Ocean State Bus. Inst., Wakefield, R.I., 1977—; dir. Fleet Nat. Bank, 1985—; bd. mgrs. Bank of New Eng., 1984-85; speaker in field. Pres. St. Francis Women's Club, Wakefield, 1975; sec. St. Francis Parish Coun., Wakefield, 1980; mem. Econ. Devel. Commn., Wakefield, 1981-85; mem. South County Hosp. Corp., Wakefield, 1978—; fin. dir. Bus. and Profl. Women's Club, Wakefield, 1982-84; chmn. Ladies Golf Charity, 1985—. Mem. R.I. Bus. Edn. Assn. (newsletter editor 1979-81), New Eng. Bus. Coll. Assn. (sec. 1984-86, pres. 1985-87), R.I. Assn. Career and Tech. Schs. (treas., bd. dirs. 1979-86), Eastern Bus. Edn. Assn. (conf. leader), Nat. Bus. Edn. Assn. (conf. leader), Assn. Ind. Colls. and Schs. (conv. speaker, pub. rels. com., govt. rels. com.), R.I. Women's Golf Assn., Am. Cancer Soc., Phi Kappa Phi, Delta Pi Epsilon (pres., newsletter editor). Roman Catholic. Club: Point Judith Country. Avocations: golf; gardening. Home: 137 Kenyon Ave Wakefield RI 02879 Office: Ocean State Bus Inst Mariner Sq Boxes 1&2 140 Point Judith Rd Narragansett RI 02882

POULOS, CLARA JEAN, nutritionist; b. L.A., Jan. 1, 1941; d. James P. and Clara Georgie (Creighton) Hill; PhD in Biology, Fla. State Christian U., 1974; PhD in Nutrition, Donsbach U., 1979; D in Nutritional Medicine, John F. Kennedy U., 1986; Cert. in Diabetes Edn.; m. Themis Poulos, Jan. 31, 1960. Dir. rsch. Leapou Lab., Aptos, Calif., 1973-76, Monterey Bay Rsch. Inst., Santa Cruz, Calif., 1976—; nutrition specialist, Santa Cruz, 1975—; dir. nutritional svcs., health enhancement, lifestyle planning, Santa Cruz, 1983—; instr. Santa Cruz Extention U. Calif. and Stoddard Assocs. Seminars; cons. Biol-Med. Lab., Chgo., Nutra-Med Rsch. Corp., N.Y., Akorn-Miller Pharmacal, Chgo., Monterey Bay Aquaculture Farms, Threshhold Lab., Calif., Resurrection Lab., Calif. Recipient Najulander Internat. Rsch. award, 1971, Wainwright Found. award., 1979, various state and local awards. Fellow Internat. Coll. Applied Nutrition, Am. Nutritionist Assn., Internat. Acad. Nutritional Consultants; mem. Am. Diabetes Assn. (profl., pres. Santa Cruz chpt., editor newsletter The Daily Balance Santa Cruz chpt., sec. No. Calif. chpt.), AAAS, Internat. Platform Soc., Am. Heart Assn., Am. Public Health Assn., Calif. Acad. Sci., Internat. Fishery Assn. (health asct.), Am. Women's Bowling Assn., MUSE- Computer Users Group. Clubs: Toastmistress, Quota. Author: Alcoholism - Stress - Hypoglycemia, 1976; The Relationship of Stress to Alcoholism and Hypoglycemia, 1979; assoc. editor Internat. Jour. Bio-social Research, Health Promotion Features; contbr. articles to profl. jours. Office: 1595 Soquel Dr Suite 222 Santa Cruz CA 95065

POULSEN, FERN SUE, special events and public relations consultant; b. Chgo., Sept. 29, 1959; d. Herman and Renee (Greenberg) Bass; m. Gregory Carl Poulsen, May 5, 1953. Ba, N. Ill. U., 1981. Corporate communications staff coordinator Centel Corp., Chgo., 1981-86; mgr. special events Network Mktg. Group, Oak Brook, Ill., 1986-88; pres. Poulsen Promotions, Chgo., 1988—; cons. spl. events and pub. rels. Vol. Easter Seal Soc. and March of Dimes, Chgo., 1987-88, Penny Pullen Campaign Com., Park Ridge, Ill., 1981-83, Am. Cancer Soc., Des Plaines, Ill., 1983; exec. advisor Jr. Achievement, Chgo., 1982-83; active Lincoln Park Cen. Assn., Chgo., 1988. Named Outstanding Woman Student Leader N. Ill. U. Women's Faculty, 1980. Mem. Internat. Assn. Bus. Communicators, Ad-Net Chgo., Omicron Delta Kappa, Phi Kappa Phi. Home and Office: Poulsen Promotions 626 N Brookdale Schaumburg IL 60194

POUNCEY, MELINDA ALICE, pediatrician; b. Lafayette, La., Oct. 21, 1949; d. Cecil J. and Pauline (Reed) P. BS, La. State U., 1970; MD, Tulane U., New Orleans, 1975; postgrad., Northeastern State U., 1970-71. Resident in pediatrics U. Va. Hosp., Charlottesville, 1975-78; staff pediatrician Ochsner Clinic, New Orleans, 1978—; clin. faculty Tulane U. Med. Sch., New Orleans, 1978—; assoc. faculty Children's Hosp., New Orleans, 1979—; dir. pediatric residency tng. prog. Ochsner Clinic, New Orleans, 1987—. Recipient Owl Club Teaching award, Tulane Med. Sch., 1978, 79, 81. Mem. AMA, So. Med. Assn., Orleans Parrish Med. Assn., Tulane Pediatric Alumni Assn. (pres. 1986-87), Greater New Orleans Pediatric Soc., La. Med. Soc. (voting del. 1979—). Republican. Roman Catholic. Office: Ochsner Clinic 1514 Jefferson Hwy New Orleans LA 70121

POUND, NANCY E., marketing executive; b. Newark, Ohio, Nov. 8, 1952; d. Paul Franklin and Delcie Ruth (Gray) P.; m. John F. Heimovics, Jan. 2, 1982. BBA, Ohio U., 1974; postgrad., Cleve. State U., 1975-81; MBA, Kent State U., 1982. Asst. mgr. ops. rsch. Ohio Bell Telephone Co., Cleve., 1974-78, mgr. ops. rsch., 1978-81, mgr. budget system, 1981, mgr. bus. rsch., 1982, mgr. fin. analysis, 1983, mgr. rates and costs, 1983-85, dist. mgr. rate and access planning, 1985-86, dist. mgr. mktg. product mgmt., 1987-90, dist. mgr. bus. svc. ctrs., 1990—. Mem. leadership com. Medina County unit Am. Heart Assn., Medina, Ohio, 1988—, chairperson 1990—, mem. devel. com., Cleve., 1989-90. Mem. Am. Mktg. Assn., Women's City Club (long range planning com. 1988-89). Home: 3480 Allard Rd Medina OH 44256 Office: Ohio Bell Telephone Co 45 Erieview Pla Cleveland OH 44114

POUR-EL, MARIAN BOYKAN, mathematician; b. N.Y.C.; d. Joseph and Mattie (Caspe) Boykan; m. Akiva Pour-El; 1 dau., Ina. A.B., Hunter Coll.; A.M., Harvard U., 1951, Ph.D., 1958. Asst. prof. math. Pa. State U., 1958-62, asso. prof., 1962-64; mem. faculty U. Minn., Mpls., 1964—; prof. math. U. Minn., 1968—; mem. Inst. Advanced Study, Princeton, N.J., 1962-64; mem. coun. Conf. Bd. Math. Scis., 1977-82, trustee, 1978-81, mem. nominating com., 1980-82, chmn., 1981-82; lectr. internat. congresses in logic and computer sci., Eng., 1971, Hungary, 1967, Czechoslovakia, 1973, Germany, 1983, Japan, 1985, 88, China, 1987; lectr. Polish Acad. Sci., 1974; lecture series throughout Fed. Republic of Germany, 1980, 87, 89, Japan, 1985, 87, 90, China, 1987, Sweden, 1983; mem. Fulbright Com. on Maths., 1986-89. Author papers math. logic, analog computers, women in sci. Named to Hunter Coll. Hall of Fame, 1975; NAS grantee, 1966. Fellow

AAAS; mem. Am. Math. Soc. (coun. 1980-88, numerous coms., lectr. nat. meeting 1976, also spl. sessions 1971, 78, 82, 84, chmn. spl. sessions on recursion theory 1975, 84), Assn. Symbolic Logic, Math. Assn. Am. (nat. panel vis. lectrs. 1977—, lectr. nat. meetings 1982, 89), Phi Beta Kappa, Sigma Xi, Pi Mu Epsilon, Sigma Pi Sigma. Office: U Minn Dept Math Vincent Hall Minneapolis MN 55455

POUSADA, LIDIA, physician; b. Mt. Kisco, N.Y., July 21, 1957; d. Manuel and Maria Nieves (Mejuto) P.; m. Andrew Kemper Goodman, June 26, 1983 (div. Sept. 1986); 1 child, Sara Pousada Goodman; m. Wayne William Maibaum, Apr. 11, 1987; 1 child, Anna Pousada Maibaum. BS, CUNY, N.Y.C., 1978; MD, N.Y. Med. Coll., 1980. Diplomate Am. Bd. Internal Medicine. Student geriatric fellowship N.Y.U. Med. Sch., N.Y.C., 1978-80; resident, internal medicine Montefiore Med. Ctr., Bronx, N.Y., 1980-83, dir. geriatric unit, 1986-89; with nat. health svc. North Cent. Bronx Hosp., 1983-84, Morris Heights Health Ctr., Bronx, 1985; instr. City Coll. Med. Sch., N.Y.C., 1982-85; instr. Albert Einstein Coll. Medicine, Bronx, 1983-84, 86-89, asst. prof. medicine, 1988-89; dir. geriatric cons. svc. Montefiore Med. Ctr., 1987-89, dir. geriatric vol. program, 1988-89. Author: Geriatric Diagnostics, 1983, Emergency Medicine for the House Officer, 1986, Emergency Medicine for Nurses, 1989, Perioperative Medical Care of the Geriatric Patient, 1989. Recipient Physician Scholarship, Nat. Health Svc., 1978-80. Mem. Gerontol. Soc. Am., Am. Geriatric Soc., Am. Women's Med. Assn., Physicians for Social Responsibility. Office: Montefiore Med Ctr 111 East 210 St Centennial 3 Bronx NY 10467

POUSSAINT, RENEE FRANCINE, journalist; b. N.Y.C., Aug. 12, 1944; d. Christopher Wallace and Bobbie (Vance) P.; m. Henry J. Richardson III, Sept. 10, 1977. B.A., Sarah Lawrence Coll., 1966; M.A., UCLA, 1971; postgrad., Yale Law Sch., 1966-67, Ind. U., 1971-72; student, Sorbonne, Paris, 1964-65; hon. doctorate, Mt. Vernon Coll., Washington, 1985; cert., Columbia U. Journalism Sch., Michele Clark Fellowship Program for Minority Journalists, 1972. Program dir. AIESEC, N.Y.C., 1968-69; editor African Arts Mag., Los Angeles, 1969-71; reporter WBBM-TV, Chgo., 1974-76, CBS Network News, Chgo., 1976-78; anchorperson WJLA-TV, Washington, 1978—; dancer Jean Leon Destine Troupe, N.Y.C., 1966; translator U. Calif. Press, Los Angeles, 1970; tutor Operation Rescue, Washington, 1981—. Hon. dir. Nat. Kidney Found., Washington, 1981—; citizen advisor YWCA, Nat. Capitol Area, 1983—; co-chmn. Nat. Capital Area Lung Assn., 1982; membership chmn. Arthritis Found., 1981-82. Recipient Reporting award Ill. Mental Health Assn., 1976; recipient Reporting award Nat. Assn. Media Women, 1977, Broadcasting Excellence award AAUW, 1979, Emmy awards, 1979, 80, 81, 82, Broadcast award NAACP, 1980, Whitney Young Meml. award Washington Urban League, 1983. Mem. AFTRA, NAACP (life), Capitol Press Club. Office: Sta WJLA-TV 3007 Tilden St NW Washington DC 20008*

POW, JILL ANN, order fulfillment manager; d. John Alton and Sylvia Maxine (Payne) Stone; m. Steven W. Fitzerald, Mar. 17, 1972; (div. 1978); children: Jason Adam, Benjamin Michael Fitzgerald; m. David Kevin Pow, Aug. 24, 1985. BA (sociology), U. Mass., Boston, 1977-82. Admissions counselor U. Mass., Boston, 1982-82; supr. returns Wearguard, Inc., Norwell, Mass., 1982-84; asst. mgr. returns dept. WearGuard, Inc., Norwell, 1984-85; mgr. customer svc. Wearguard, Inc., Norwell, mgr. returns shipping, 1987-88; mgr. membership Nat. Fire Protection Assoc., Mass., 1988; mgr. order fulfillment Pot Pourri Collection, Inc., Medfield, Mass., 1982—. Mem. Mass. Sociological Assn., Internat. Customer Svc. Assn., Greater Boston Women's Network (sec. 1988-89), Toast Masters, Norwell, Mass., (v.p 1987-88). Office: Potpourri Collection Inc 120 N Meadows Rd Medfield MA 02052

POWELL, ANICE CARPENTER, librarian; b. Moorhead, Miss., Dec. 2, 1928; d. Horace Aubrey and Celeste (Brian) Carpenter; student Sunflower Jr. Coll., 1945-47, Miss. State Coll. Women, 1947-48; B.S., Delta State Coll., 1961, M.L.S., 1974; m. Robert Wainwright Powell, July 19, 1948 (dec. 1979); children: Penelope Elizabeth, Deborah Alma. Librarian, Sunflower (Miss.) Pub. Library, 1958-61; tchr. English, Isola (Miss.) High Sch., 1961-62; dir. Sunflower County Library, Indianola, Miss., 1962—; mem. adv. coun. State Instl. Library Services, 1967-71; mem. adv. bd. library services and constrn. act com. Miss. Library Commn., 1978-80, mem. pub. library task force, 1986—; mem. Pub. Library Standards Com., 1988—; mem. steering com. NASA community involvement program Miss. Delta Community Coll., 1990. Mem. ALA (speaker senate subcom. on illiteracy 1989), Miss. Library Assn. (exec. dir. Nat. Library Week 1975, steering com. 1976, chmn. Right to Read com. 1976, co-chmn., 1987, chmn. legis. com. 1979, chmn. intellectual freedom com. 1975, 80, mem. legis. com. 1973-86, chmn. membership com. 1982, pres. 1984, chmn. nominating com. 1986, chmn. election com. 1989, Peggy May award 1981), AAUW, Sunflower County Hist. Soc. (pres. 1983-87), Miss. Literacy Assn., Delta Coun., Sunflower County Literacy Coun. (treas.), State Adv. Coun. on Adult Edn. Methodist. Home: Box 310 Sunflower MS 38778 Office: Sunflower County Libr 201 Cypress Dr Indianola MS 38751

POWELL, BARBARA, clinical psychologist; b. Dexter, Mo., Apr. 25, 1929; d. Clarence Albert and Ethel (Mohrstadt) P.; B.A., Wellesley Coll., 1950; M.A., Columbia U., 1967; Ph.D., Fordham U., 1975; m. Richard W. O'Neill, Jan. 3, 1953 (div. 1966); children—Richard W., Susan P., Jennifer A., Julia K.; m. 2d, Charles J. McCarthy, May 13, 1967 (div. 1978); m. 3d, David S. Burt, June 16, 1983. Copywriter, Parade mag., 1951-52, McCall's, 1952-53; publicity dir. Silvermine Guild Art, New Canaan, Conn., 1964-66; reporter Bridgeport (Conn.) Post, 1964-69; psychologist Dunlap & Assos., Darien, Conn., 1966-67; dir. Guidance Center for Women, U. Conn., 1968-69; intern N.Y. Hosp., Westchester, 1972-73; psychologist St. Mary's in-the-field, Valhalla, N.Y., 1973-77, Behavior Therapy Inst., White Plains, N.Y., 1975-78; pvt. practice clin. psychology, Rowayton, Conn., 1976—; lectr. U. Conn., 1976-77; co-founder, assertive tng. leader Woman's Place, Darien. USPH grantee, 1970-71. Mem. Am. Psychol. Assn., Am. Assn. Marriage and Family Therapists, Am. Assn. Advancement Behavior Therapy, Soc. Clin. and Exptl. Hypnosis, Phi Beta Kappa, Sigma Xi. Author: Careers for Women after Marriage and Children, 1965; How to Raise a Successful Daughter, 1979; Overcoming Shyness, 1979; The Complete Guide to Your Child's Emotional Health, 1984; Alone, Alive and Well, 1985; Good Relationships Are Good Medicine, 1987. Address: 20 Covewood Dr Rowayton CT 06853 also: Mansion Beach PO Box 1036 Block Island RI 02807

POWELL, BETSY SUE, writer, producer; b. Warner Robins, Ga., Apr. 22, 1963; d. Richard Carl Jr. and Faye Irene (Goforth) Powell. ABJ, U Ga., 1985. Broadcast prodn. asst. Rich's Corp. Hdqrs., Atlanta, 1985-88; writer, producer B.P. Prodns., Atlanta, 1988—. Recipient award Internat. Radio Festival N.Y., 1989, 90. Mem. Advt. Club Atlanta (Addy award 1989, Telly award 1989), Ad II Atlanta, High Mus. Art. Democrat. Address: 205 Morningside Dr Warner Robins GA 31088

POWELL, CAROL CHRISTINE, restaurant owner; b. Seattle, Feb. 15, 1941; d. Benjamin Olaf and Lois Carol (Smith) Michel; m. William Fred Roth, Apr. 8, 1961 (div. Dec. 1972); children: Christine Roth Elliott, Fred Roth, Traci Roth; m. George Benjamin Powell, Dec. 22, 1972; children: Kathy Powell Rank, George Powell Jr. Grad. high sch., Seattle. Dishwasher Happy Chef, Cherokee, Iowa, 1978; dishwasher, waitress Randall's Cafe, Cherokee, 1978-79, mgr., 1979-82; owner, operator The Food Broker Restaurant, Cherokee, 1983-89; with Amway Network Mktg., 1988—. Mem. adv. com. Cherokee Sch. Mem. Cherokee C. of C. Democrat. Home and Office: 320 N 6th St Cherokee IA 51012

POWELL, CAROLYN WILKERSON, music educator; b. Hamburg, Ark., Oct. 9, 1920; d. Claude Kelly and Mildred (Hall) Wilkerson; m. Charles Luke Powell, Dec. 12, 1923; children: Charles Luke Jr., James Davis, Mark Wilkerson, Robert Hall. AB, Cen. Methodist, Fayette, 1942; MAT, U. N.C., Chapel Hill, 1970. Life Teaching Cert. Mo. Teaching Cert. N.C. Choral dir. Maplewood Richmond Heights Sch., St. Louis, 1943-45; pvt. piano tchr. Greensboro N.C. Area, Greensboro, 1951-63; organist Presbyterian and Methodist Ch., Greensboro, 1950-61; choral and humanities tchr. Page High Sch., Greensboro, 1963-67; choral dir. Githens Jr. High Sch., Durham, N.C., 1967-80; organist St. Peter's Episcopal Ch., Va., 1981-83; dir. Ch. Youth Choirs Greensboro, 1958-61; chmn. Dist. Choral Festival N.C. Dist., 1968-78; accompanist and music dir. Altavista Little Theatre Altavista, Va., 1981-83. Sunday and vacation schs., Grace Meth. Ch., Greensboro, Chapel of the Cross Episcopal, Chapel Hill, 1968-81; den mother Boy Scouts Am., Greensboro, 1951-67; mem. Chapel Hill Preservation Soc., Chapel Hill, 1981-87-89; vol., chapel organist, pediatric tutor N.C. Meml. Hosp., Chapel Hill, 1984-89. Mem. NEA, AAUW, Music Educators Nat. Conf., Nat. Federated Music Club Euterpe, Am. Organists Guild, Classroom Tchrs. Assn., Chapel Hill Country Club, Delta Kappa Gamma. Avocations: reading, golf, needlework, gardening, travel and antiques. Home: 2446 Honeysuckle Rd Chapel Hill NC 27514

POWELL, DIANA KEARNY, lawyer, poet; b. Washington, Apr. 15, 1910; d. William Glasgow and Alice Van Voorhees (Joline) P.; LL.B., Columbus U., 1940, LL.M., 1942; A.A., George Washington U., 1945; postgrad. Law Sch. Georgetown U., 1957. Admitted to D.C. bar, 1940, U.S. Supreme Ct. bar, 1959; practice law, Washington; contbr. poetry to various mags., 1930—; poetry recitations. Precinct chmn. Republican Party, 1965-68, co-chmn., 1972-75; mem. various campaign coms.; sec. Sodality Holy Name Soc. of St. Matthew's Cathedral, 1978-81, chmn. workshop com., 1975-81, 83-86, pres., 1981-83; mem. Republican Presdl. Task Force, 1982. Recipient various local and nat. poetry awards Nat. League Am. Pen Women; cert. of appreciation Anchor Mental Health Assn., 1975. Mem. ABA, Nat. Assn. Women Lawyers, Internat. Platform Assn., Saintpaulia Internat. Roman Catholic. Author: Selected Poems, 1986. Assoc. editor: Washington Vistas, 1953.

POWELL, DIANE ELAINE, healthcare official, lawyer; b. Ridley Park, PA, Sept. 25, 1955; d. George T. and Hilda D. (Eilenberg) P. BS, Bloomsburg U., 1976; JD, Widener U., 1989. CPCU; assoc. in risk mgmt.; assoc. in premium auditing. Premium auditor Liberty Mut. Ins. Co., Bala Cynwyd, Pa., 1977-79, PMA Group, Valley Forge, Pa., 1979-84; bus. cons. Broomall, Pa., 1984-88; mgr. risk and ins. Ea. Mercy Health System, Radnor, Pa., 1988-89; risk mgr. Beverly Enterprises, Virginia Beach, Va., 1990—. Mem. Soc. CPCU. Republican. Presbyterian. Office: Beverly Enterprises Corp E 3280 Virginia Beach Blvd Virginia Beach VA 23468-1000

POWELL, ELIZABETH, professional society administrator; b. Thorpe, W.Va., May 17, 1943; d. Thomas Powell and Frankie (Williams) Harris; m. Vernis Harris, Mar. 28, 1964 (div. Sept. 1982); children: Robert, Renee, Gregory. Student, W.Va. State U., 1961-63, Detroit Arbitration Sch., 1981. Postal clk. U.S. Postal Svc., Hempstead, N.Y., 1970-83; with Am. Postal Workers Union, Hempstead, 1970—, N.Y. State area v.p., 1981-83; nat. bus. agt. Am. Postal Workers Union, N.Y.C., 1983-89, N.E. regional coord., 1989—. Recipient numerous honors, awards. Mem. Nat. Coun. Negro Women, Coalition Labor Union Women, Post Office Women for Equal Rights, NAACP, Order of Eastern Star (conductress 1984—, assoc. matron 1989—). Democrat. Baptist. Office: Am Postal Workers Union 460 W 34th St 9th Fl New York NY 10001

POWELL, ERNESTINE BREISCH, retired lawyer; b. Moundsville, W.Va., Feb. 16, 1906; d. Ernest Elmer and Belle (Wallace) Breisch; student Dayton YMCA Law Sch., 1929; m. Roger K. Powell, Nov. 15, 1935; children—R. Keith (dec.), Diane L.D., Bruce W. Admitted to Ohio bar, 1929; tax analyst tax dept. Wall, Cassell & Groneweg, Dayton, Ohio, 1929-31; practiced law, 1931-40; gen. counsel for Dayton Jobbers and Mfrs. Assn., 1931-41; mem. firm Powell, Powell & Powell, Columbus, Ohio, 1944-86, ret. Ohio chmn. Nat. Woman's Party, Washington, 1950-51, nat. chmn., 1951-53, hon. nat. chmn. Pres. vol. activities com. Columbus State Sch., 1960-61, mem. bd. trustees, 1957-59. Mem. Nat. Assn. Women Lawyers, Am., Ohio, Columbus bar assns., Nat. Soc. Arts and Letters (pres. Columbus chpt. 1963-64), Nat. Lawyers Club (charter mem.), Nat. Mus. Women in Arts (charter mem.). Co-author: Tax Ideas, 1955; Estate Tax Techniques, 1956—. Editor-in-chief: Women Lawyers Jour., 1943-45. Office: 1382 Neil Ave PO Box 8010 Columbus OH 43201

POWELL, JOY LEE (BOK SIN LEE), shop owner, importer; b. Pyeong-Yang, Korea, Jan. 29, 1936; came to U.S., 1956, naturalized, 1962; d. Yong Joon and Chun Jai Lee; m. Jimmy Wayne Powell, Sept. 24, 1960; children: Chun Jai Lee, Miran Victoria. Student, Internat. Speech Coll., Pusan, Korea, 1952; Nat. U. Pusan, 1953-55, McMurry Coll., Abilene, Tex., 1956-58; BA, Wayland Bapt. U., Plainview, Tex., 1966; postgrad., Cent. State Coll., Okla., 1967-68. Cert. antique appraiser and consultant. Nurse, Rok Med. Sch., Pusan, 1950-53; news announcer Pusan Radio Sta., Korea, 1953; sec., choir organizer chaplain's office U.S. Army div. Hqdrs., Pusan, 1954-56, Meth. Mission, Pusan, 1955-56, U.S. A.S.C. Office, Floydada, Tex., 1958, Am. U., Washington, 1958-60; with Washington Post, U.S. Acad. Sci., 1960; with spl. study of prejudice among children grades 1 to 12 for Pub. Opinion and Propaganda, 1965-66; tchr. Oklahoma City Sch. Systems, 1968-70; head social studies dept. Dunjee High Sch., 1968; tchr. Spanish Carl Albert High Sch., 1969; owner Internat. Antiques, Upperville, Va., 1973—. Contbr. articles to profl. jours., (poetry) New Voices in American Poetry, 1978, poems and essays to Korean periodicals; charter mem. lit. mag. Mem. Mang Hiang, Internat. Platform Assn., NOW, Nat. Trust for Hist. Preservation, Smithsonian Assocs. Nat. Hist. Preservation, Nat. Bus. Assn., Better World Soc., Women's Mus., World Affairs Council Washington, NAFE, Internat. Student House. Avocations: art, painting, music, writing, swimming. Home and Office: PO Box 221 Upperville VA 22176

POWELL, KARAN HINMAN, university program administrator; b. Great Lakes, Ill., May 25, 1953; d. David Daniel and Mary Anne (Buretz) Hinman; m. David Leonidas Powell, Feb. 14, 1987. BS, We. Ill. U., 1975; MDiv, Loyola U., Chgo., 1981, B Sacred Theology (hon.), 1981. Cert. tchr., Ill. Tchr. St. Hugh Cath. Sch., Lyons, Ill., 1975-77; tchr. Lay Ministry Tng. Program, Chgo., 1980-81, Jackson, Miss., 1981-83; adminstr. Inst. Creation Centered Spirituality Mundelein Coll., Chgo., 1978-79; exec. dir. North Am. Forum Catechumenate, Washington, 1983-88; dir. Profl. Devel. Program, tchr. theol. studies, tng. cons. Georgetown U., Washington, 1988—; assoc. pastor Annunciation Cath. Ch., Columbus, Miss., 1981-83; cons. dioceses in U.S., Can., 1983—. Author: How to Form a Catechumenate Team, 1985; editor: Breaking Open the Word of God series, 1986-88, The Ninety Days, 1989; contbr. articles Cath. mags.; speaker Religious Edn. Congress, L.A., 1987-88, 90. Active on Blessed Sacrament RCIA Team, Alexandria, Va., 1984-86. Recipient tchr.'s scholarship State of Ill., 1971-75, cert. recognition KC, Columbus, Miss., 1982. Mem. Am. Soc. Tng., Devel., Soc. for Human Resource Mgmt., Assn. Creative Change, Assn. Psychol. Type, North Am. Forum Catechumenate (cons. 1982—), Cath. Edn. Future's Project (mem. com. 1985-88). Democrat. Office: Georgetown U Intercultural Ctr Ste 306 37th and O Sts Washington DC 20057

POWELL, M. ELAINE, state agency executive director; b. Waynesburg, Pa., Apr. 18, 1954; d. Grover Cleveland and Marie (Clarchick) P.; m. Jeffrey E.T. Bohm, June 6, 1981. BA in History and Econs., Denison U., Granville, Ohio, 1976; MA in Internat. Affairs, Johns Hopkins U., 1978; postgrad., Am. U. at Cairo, 1978. Fin. analyst Arabian Am. Oil Co., Houston, 1978-79, Dhahran, Saudi Arabia, 1979-81; budget analyst Office of Gov. of Tex., Austin, 1981-84, dir. div., 1984-87; telecommunications analyst Pub. Utility Commn., Austin, 1987-90; exec. dir. Tex. Incentive and Productivity Commn., Austin, 1990—. Exhibited in one-person photography show, 1989, group shows, 1987, 88. Candidate Bd. Employees Retirement System, Austin, 1989; del. U.S./USSR/Hungary Emerging Leaders Program, Columbus, Ind., 1989, U.S./Hungary Emerging Leaders Program, Budapest, Hungary, 1989; active in Austin Soc. Pub. Adminstrn., 1982-84, Leadership Tex., 1988; bd. dirs. Austin Women's Ctr., 1984-86. Nat. Merit scholar, 1972-76; recipient Nat Def. fellowship, Washington, 1977-78. Mem. Exec. Women in Tex. Govt., Women in Pub. Sector (v.p. 1989-90), Am. Ctr. for Internat. Leadership, Tex. Photographic Soc. (bd. dirs. 1987-88, sec. 1989), Women and Their Work, Leadership Tex. Alumnae Assn. (bd. dirs. 1989—), Phi Beta Kappa, Pi Beta Phi (alumnae co-chmn. 1988-89).

POWELL, MARJORIE ANN, school system administrator; b. Hannibal, Mo., May 15, 1933; d. Thomas Henry and Florence Margaret (Cribbs) Curtis; m. John Lawrence Powell, June 1, 1957; 1 child, Curtis Lawrence. BS in Edn., U. Mo., 1955. Cert. tchr., Mo. Tchr. high sch. Grandview (Mo.) Pub. Schs., 1955-57; pres. Dearborn (Mich.) City Coun., 1978-85; adminstr. adult and community edn. programs Dearborn Pub. Schs., 1987—. 1st runner-up for mayor City of Dearborn, 1985, 1st runner-up for state rep., 1986; mem. citizens adv. bd. U. Mich., Dearborn, 1984—; pres. Dearborn PTA Coun., 1975-77; trustee Henry Ford Hosp.-Fairlane, Dearborn, 1985—. Recipient Disting. Svc. award PTA Coun., 1975, Ruth Huston Whipple award Mich. Bus. and Profl. Women, 1983. Mem. Mich. Assn. Community and Adult Edn., Wayne and Monroe Counties Adult and Community Edn. Assn., AAUW, Bus. and Profl. Women, Rotary (Paul Harris fellow 1985). Republican. Methodist. Home: 240 N Waverly Dearborn MI 48128 Office: Dearborn Pub Schs 4824 Lois Dearborn MI 48126

POWELL, MARY LOUISE WELLS, psychology, educator; b. Asheville, N.C., July 7, 1935; d. John Kendall and Beatrice (Rice) Wells; m. Elton George Powell, June 21, 1969. AB, U. N.C., 1957, MS, 1964, PhD, 1976. Tchr. Myers Park High Sch., Charlotte, N.C., 1957-58; editorial rsch. asst. Time, Inc., N.Y.C., 1959-60; recreation and program dir. Spl. Svcs. U.S. Forces Europe, Fed. Republic Germany and France, 1960-62; resident adviser undergrad. women U. N.C., Chapel Hill, 1963-64, rsch. assoc. and asst. to project coord. State/Fed. Inst. for Profl. Devel., 1964-66; prof. organizational indsl. pers. psychology Appalachian State U., Boone, N.C., 1967—. NDEA fellow, 1966, NASA fellow, 1981. Mem. AAUW, Am. Psychol. Assn., Southeastern Psychol. Assn., N.C. Assn. Counseling and Devel., Assn. for Psychol. Type, N.C. Career Devel. Assn., Soc. for Human Resource Mgmt., Am. Soc. Tng. and Devel., Organizational Behavior Teaching Soc., Acad. of Mgmt., Pi Delta Phi. Home: 200 Anne Marie Dr Boone NC 28607 Office: Appalachian State U 112-A Smith Wright Hall Boone NC 28608

POWELL, MELANIE K., pharmacist; b. Evansville, Ind., June 29, 1957; d. Elmer Carl and Mary Ellen (Calvert) Seibert; m. David Wayne Powell, June 14, 1953; children: Hillary Ellen, Hayley Elizabeth. BS, Butler U., 1980. Staff pharmacist Welborn Bapt. Hosp., Evansville, Ind., 1980—. Mem. AAUW, So. Ind. Pharmacist Assn. (pres. 1986-87), Ind. Pharmacist Assn. Republican. United Ch. of Christ. Home: 11020 Upper Mt Vernon Rd Mount Vernon IN 47620 Office: Welborn Hospital 401 SE 6th St Evansville IN 47620

POWELL, PAMELA SUE, medical utilizaiton review company executive; b. Kansas City, Kans.; d. Urban Sidney and Katherine Ann (Gresik) P. AA, Maple Woods Coll., 1981; student, William Jewell Coll., Liberty, Mo., 1981; BA, U. Ariz., 1987. Lab. technician, med. asst. Frank and John Campobasso, Kansas City, Mo., 1979-85; provider contracts, processor Coop. Ariz. Preferred Providers, Tucson, Ariz., 1986—; lab. cons., Overland Park, Kans., 1982. Compiler data Jimmy Carter Campaign for Pres., Kansas City, 1976. Mem. Nat. Assn. Female Execs. Democrat. Roman Catholic. Office: Coop Ariz Preferred 5055 E Broadway Suite 204 D Tucson AZ 85711

POWELL, PEGGY JEAN, editor; b. La Grande, Oreg., June 29, 1933; d. Kenneth Gladstone and Clara Gertrude (Hercher) LaViolette; m. Donald Allan Powell, Sept. 14, 1957; children: Anthony Forrest, Alison Carol. BA, U. Calif., Berkeley, 1956; postgrad. Wayne State U., 1967. Writer Mademoiselle Mag., N.Y.C., 1955-56; reporter Berkeley Daily Gazette, 1956-57, Vancouver (B.C., Can.) Sun, 1957-59; freelance writer Calif., 1960-75; pvt. practice pub. rels. cons. Irvine, 1975-85; ptnr. Investor Communication Systems, Irvine, 1985-89; exec. editor The Investment Reporter, 1989—. Contbr. numerous articles to profl. and entertainment jours. Mem., docent, patron Newport Harbor Art Mus., Newport Beach, Calif., 1972-84; bd. dirs. Campus View Homeowners Assn., Irvine, 1976. Recipient Golden Orange award Orange County (Calif.) Advt. Fedn., 1981. Mem. Pub. Rels. Soc. Am., Orange County Chpt. Pub. Rels. Soc. Am. (3 Excellence awards 1984, 2 Excellence awards 1985), Publicity Club Am., U. Calif. Berkeley Alumni Assn., Prytanean Alumni Assn., Alpha Gamma Delta. Democrat. Unitarian. Office: Shareholder Communication Systems 1 Corporate Park Irvine CA 92714

POWELL, PEGGY NANCE, account executive, company executive; b. Balt., Dec. 10, 1940; d. Harding Peter Frizzell and Margaret (Nance) Webster. BA, Goucher Coll., 1965, MEd, 1966. Tchr. Garrison (Md.) Forest Sch., 1966-75; dir. programming Romper Room Enterprises, Inc., Balt., 1975-80; pres., owner Cookie Bank, Inc., Balt., 1980—; account executive Claster TV, Inc., Timonium, Md., 1985—. Mem. Balt. Country Club. Republican. Home: 131 E West St Baltimore MD 21230 Office: Claster TV Inc 9630 Deereco Rd Timonium MD 21093

POWELL, ROSALIE, home economist; b. Milw., Oct. 24, 1947; d. William and Daisy P.; BS, U. Wis., Stout, 1969, MS in Home Econs. Edn., 1974. Extension home economist U. Wis. Extension, Langlade County, 1969-74; Waukesha County, 1976—; instr. U. Wis.-Stout, Menomonie, 1975-76; asst. prof. dept. family devel. U. Wis. Extension, 1976-81, assoc. prof., 1981-87, chmn. family devel. dept., 1984—, prof., 1987—. Mem. Am. Home Econs. Assn., Wis. Home Econs. Assn., Nat. Assn. Extension Home Economists, Wis. Assn. Extension Home Economists, Soc. Nutrition Edn., Wis. Consumers League, Bus. and Profl. Women (chpt. pres. 1970-72), Am. Council on Consumer Interests, Gamma Sigma Sigma (nat. pres. 1975-77), Epsilon Sigma Phi. Club: Waukesha Altrusa. Home: 403 Sheffield Rd Waukesha WI 53186 Office: 500 Riverview Ave Waukesha WI 53188

POWELL, RUTH ANN, librarian, educator; b. Fairmont, W.Va., Feb. 22, 1939; d. Ben F. and Lela P. (Barb) P. BEd, Fairmont State Coll., 1961; MLS, Kent State U., 1967; postgrad., W.Va. U., 1970-80. Circulation libr. Fairmont State Coll., 1966-72, acquistion libr., 1972-76, tech. svcs. libr., 1976-88, tech. svcs. libr., reference, 1981-88, tech. svcs. libr., periodicals, govt., documents, 1989—; bd. govs. Adv. Council for Librs., 1978-79; chmn. program com. Govs. Conf. on Librs., 1978. Author: History of Fairmont State Coll. Libr., 1968; contbr. articles to profl. jours. Mem. ALA (state pres. adv. com. 1977-78), W.Va. Libr. Assn. (pres. 1977-78, mem. com. chmn.), Southeastern Libr. Assn. (mem. com. chmn. 1986-88), Pitts. Regional Libr. Council, Sigma Kappa, Delta Kappa Gamma (pres. 1984-86), Order of Eastern Star (worthy matron 1981-82, grand rep. Pa. 1984-86). Home: 126 Beach Lane Fairmont WV 26559 Office: Fairmont State Coll Locust Ave Fairmont WV 26554

POWELL, SHARON LEE, social welfare organization administrator; b. Portland, Oreg., July 25, 1940; d. James Edward Carson and Betty Jane (Singleton) Powell. BS, Oreg. State U., 1962; MEd, Seattle U., 1971. Dir. outdoor edn. Mapleton (Oreg.) Pub. Schs., 1962-63; field dir. Totem Girl Scout Council, Seattle, 1963-68, asst. dir. field services, 1968-70, dir. field services, 1970-72; dir. pub. relations Girl Scout Council of Tropical Fla., Miami, 1972-74; exec. dir. Homestead Girl Scout Council, Lincoln, Nebr., 1974-78, Moingona Girl Scout Coun., Des Moines, 1978—. Pres. agy dirs. assn. United Way of Cen. Iowa, Des Moines, 1987-88, mem. priorities com., 1986—, chairwoman agy. issues, 1989—; mem. priority goals task group United Way Found., Des Moines, 1985—; capt. Drake U. Basketball Ticket Dr., Des Moines, 1983-87; sec. Urbandale Citizens Schlarship Found., 1989—; mem. ad hoc long range planning com., Urbandale Schs., 1989. Mem. Assn. Girl Scout Execs. (chair nat. conv. 1985—, nat. bd. dirs. 1985-87, mem. nat. nominating com. 1982-84, nat. treas. 1987—), AAUW, Urbandale C. of C. (bd. dirs., chair edn. com.), Des Moines Obedience Tng. Club (treas. 1987—), Des Moines Golden Retriever Club, Chi Omega Alumni Assn. Democrat. Club: Altrusa (Des Moines) (treas. 1983-85, community service chair 1986-87). Office: Moingona Girl Scout Coun 10715 Hickman Rd Des Moines IA 50322

POWELL, SUSAN WOLFE, development center director; b. Orange, N.J., Mar. 1, 1942; d. Albert Lewis and Olga Katharine (Maurer) Wolfe; m. Benjamin N. Powell, Aug. 28, 1964 (div. 1989); 1 child, Amy Elizabeth. AB, Mt. Holyoke, 1964; MA, Rice U., 1973. Tchr. Grace Ch. Sch., N.Y.C., 1964-68, St. John's Sch., Houston, 1977-80; adminstr. Radcliffe Coll., Cambridge, Mass., 1968-70, Rice U., Houston, 1973-75; coordinator Washington County Mental Health, Bartlesville, Okla., 1988; dir. Profl. Devel. Ctr., Bartlesville, 1988—. Founder, co-chair Friends of the Schs., Bartlesville, 1982-87; edn. rep. Com. for Yr. 2000, Bartlesville, 1990. Mem. AAUW (Woman of Yr. award 1984), LWV (pres. 1985-86, Woman of Yr. award 1985), Nat. Staff Devel. Coun., Assn. Supervision and Curriculum Devel., Nat. Coun. States Inservice Edn., Okla. Women Ednl. Adminstrn., Bartlesville C. of C. (edn. com. 1989—), Mt. Holyoke Alumnae Assn. (bd. dirs. admission liaison 1988), Phi Delta Kappa. Republican. Presbyterian. Office: Profl Devel Ctr 4620 E Frank Phillips Blvd Bartlesville OK 74006

POWER, ELIZABETH HENRY, marketing consultant; b. Hickory, N.C., Sept. 28, 1953; d. William Henry Power and Katheryn Otis (Smith) Nelson. Cert. in creative writing, N.C. Sch. Arts, 1971; BA in Sociology, U. N.C., Greensboro, 1977. With adoption and foster home recruitment Davidson County Dept. Human Svcs., Nashville, 1980-81; behavioral cons. Nutri-System Weight Loss Ctr., Nashville, 1982-84; corp. sec., cons. Quantum Leap Cons., Inc., Nashville, 1984-86; v.p. mktg. Open Communication, Inc., Nashville, 1987-88; pres., owner E. Power & Assocs., Brentwood, Tenn., 1980-84, 86—; seminar presenter, 1977—; cons. GM/Saturn, 1988—. Author: Getting the Fat Out of Your Head So It Stays Off Your Body, 1987, Relocation, Survival and the South, 1989, If Change Is All There is, Choice Is All You've Got, 1990; co-author, editor: Circle of Love: Child Personal Safety, 1984. Vol. West Chester Women's Resource Ctr., West Chester, Pa., 1977; vol. instr. theology Lay Acad. Episcopal Diocese Western N.C., Asheville, 1976-77; mem. Burke County Coun. on Status of Women, Morganton, N.C., 1977-79, sec., 1978; vol. Western N.C. Flood Com., 1977-78; exec. dir. N.C. Rape Crisis Assn., Raleigh, 1979, Foothills Mental Health Ctr., Morganton, 1978-79; mem. task force, writer, convener, facilitator N.C. Gov.'s Conf. on Mental Health, 1979; trainer, vol. Rape House Crisis Ctr., Nashville, 1979-81; vol., trainer Rape and Sexual Abuse Ctr., Nashville, 1981-82, bd. dirs., 1981-82; mem. quality circles steering com. Tenn Dept. Human Svcs., 1980-81; program cons. Women's Resource and Assistance Program, Jackson, Tenn., 1981-82; vol. devel. cons. AGAPE Christian Counseling Ctr., Nashville, 1988. Recipient numerous awards N.C. Dept. Mental Health/Mental Retardation, 1979, State of N.C., 1979, Central Nashville Optimist Club, 1982, Waco YWCA, Waco, Tex., 1985. Mem. NAFE, Tenn. Orgn. Profl. Speakers, Tenn. Walking Horse Breeders' and Exhibitors' Assn., Pleasure Walking Horse Assn. of Tenn. Democrat. Home and Office: PO Box 2346 Brentwood TN 37027

POWER, JOANNE, neuropsychologist, business owner; b. Atlanta, Jan. 29, 1949; d. Joe Clarence and Martha Elizabeth (Powell) P.; m. Ivan Gray Prim III, June 6, 1970. BA, U. Ga., 1975, MEd, 1978, PhD, 1983. Lic. psychologist, Ga. Asst. prof. neurosurgery Med. Coll. of Ga., Augusta, 1984, asst. clin. prof. neurosurgery, 1984-87; pvt. practice Atlanta, 1984—; owner, dir. Atlanta Neurobehavioral Ctr., 1987—; bd. dirs., mem. profl. adv. bd. Ga. Chpt. Epilepsy Found. Am., Atlanta, 1988—. Contbr. articles to profl. jours. Mem. AAAS, Am. Psychol. Assn., Internat. Neuropsychol. Soc., Nat. Acad. Neuropsychology, N.Y. Acad. Scis. Office: Atlanta Neurobehavioral Ctr 6920 Jimmy Carter Blvd Norcross GA 30071

POWER, JOYCE HELENE, marketing consultant; b. Detroit, Apr. 30, 1946; d. Fredrick Bowen and Julia Jane (Oliphant) H.; (div. 1979); 1 child, Julia Lynne. BA, No. Ill. U., 1968; MA, U. Cin., 1971, EdD, 1975. Cons., pvt. practice Cin., 1970-75; pres. Power Learning Systems Inc., Cin., 1975—. Author: (workbooks) Computer Program, Pro-Grammar, 1987, Pro-Sentence, 1987. Mem. Orton Soc., Sierra Club, Alpha Lambda Delta.

POWER, KAREN ELIZABETH, accountant; b. Watertown, Mass., Jan. 8, 1966; d. Leo Francis and kathleen Anne (Sullivan) P. B, Boston Coll., Chestnut Hill, Mass., 1987. Telemarketing rep. Research Data, Farmington, Mass., 198184; research coordinator NE Field Facts, Farmington, Mass., 1982-87; sr. tennis counselor, instr. Chequessett Yacht & Country Club, Welfleet, Mass., 1985; sr. tennis instr. Villages at Ocean Edge Resort, Brewster, Mass., 1986; internship, asst. producer WCUBTV (Channel J), Needham, Mass., 1987; sales asst. Harrison Conf. Ctr., Wellesley, Mass., 1988; acct. rep. Harris /3m, Boston, Mass., 1988--. Recipient Boston Marathon award 1987; Named U.S.T.A. Nat. Tennis Family. Mem. U.S. Tennis Assn., New Eng. Lawn Tennis Assn.

POWER, MARIAN TRAINA, educator. BA in English, Bklyn. Coll., 1962; MS in Reading, Higher Ednl. Adminstrn., Syracuse U., 1971, EdD in Reading, Higher Ednl. Adminstrn., 1976. Cert. sch. dist. adminstr., sch. adminstr., supr. English secondary level. Tchr. English Willoughby Jr. High Sch., Bklyn., 1962-63, Lake View High Sch., San Angelo, Tex., 1963-64, Eisenhower Jr. High Sch., San Antonio, 1964-66, Phillips Ave Elem. Sch., Riverhead, N.Y., 1966-67; reading specialist, reading clinician Clary Jr. High Sch., Syracuse, N.Y., 1968-69; reading specialist, supr. cons. Syracuse U. Extension Program, N.Y.C., 1969-73, Jamesville (N.Y.) Dewitt Cen. Schs., 1969-73; dir. child research ctr., reading clin. SUNY, Oswego, 1973-74; dir. acad. supportive services, reading edn. undergrad. level Le Moyne Coll., Syracuse, 1974-77; dir. N.Y.C. Bd. Edn. Reading Div. Ednl. Planning and Support, 1977-80; author Random House Pub. Co., N.Y.C., 1980-83; asst. prof. Suffolk (N.Y.) County Community Coll., 1984—; dir. academic resource ctr. L.I. U. C.W. Post, Brookville, N.Y., 1987—; cons. Utica (N.Y.) Coll. Tech., 1987—. Contbr. articles to profl. jours. Home: 1980 Knollwood Ct Muttontown NY 11791 Office: LI Univ CW Post Brookville NY 11791

POWER, NORMA JEAN, hospital dietary administrator; b. Bluffton, Ind., June 22, 1928; d. John Raymond and Nettie May (Gilbert) Young; m. James Burton Power, June 28, 1950; children: Susan, Steven, J. Bradley. BSHE, Purdue U., 1950; MS, Mich. State U., 1976. Registered dietitian Am. Dietetic Assn. Tchr. Bd. of Edn., Saginaw, Mich.; home svc. advisor Consumers Power Co., Saginaw; dietitian Wells County Hosp., Bluffton, Ind.; dir. of dietary The Meml. Hosp., Owosso, Mich. Mem. AAUW, Dietetic Assn., Am. Soc. Hosp. Food Svc. Dirs., Gen. Fedn. Women's Club. Republican. Lutheran. Home: 5333 Lake Dr Owosso MI 48867 Office: The Meml Hosp 826 W King St Owosso MI 48867

POWER, SUSAN CANTRELL, arts and humanities consultant, studio owner; b. Toccoa, Ga., May 21, 1944; d. Fleming Mitchell Power and Cantrell Holcomb; m. Charles William Dubie, June 14, 1964 (div. 1972); children: Charles William Jr, Aimee Suzanne. BA, U. Ga., 1973, MA, 1975, PhD, 1982. Art cons. N.E. Ga. N.E. Ga. Cooperative Ednl. Svc. Agy., Winterville, 1978-82; dir. art and pub. rels. Jackson County Bd. Edn., Jefferson, Ga., 1982-84; state dir. arts and humanities Ga. Dept. Edn., Atlanta, 1984-88; owner Power Studios, Marietta, Ga., 1988—; rsch. assoc. The Lamar Inst., 1989—; bd. dirs. Ga. Endowment for Humanities, Atlanta, 1984-88. Author: (handbook/manual) Southeast Indians - Art and Culture, 1982, (handbook) Georgia Artists - State Collection, 1982; contbr. articles to profl. jours. Rsch. fellow D'Arcy McNickle Indian Ctr. Newberry Libr., Chgo., 1981; fellow Smith Cartography Ctr., Newberry Libr., 1986; NEH grantee, Scotland, 1990. Mem. Nat. Art Assn. Baptist. Home and Office: Power Studios 2090 Kolb Ridge Ct Marietta GA 30060

POWERS, DARYLE LYNN, sales and marketing executive; b. Summit, N.J., Dec. 15, 1960; d. Thomas Sheridan and Sarah Ann (McCullagh) P. BA, Rutgers U., 1983. With commodities exch. Fl. Brokers Assn., N.Y.C., 1983-84; retail mgr. Turlugreen, N.Y.C., 1984-85; acct. mgr. J. Rouff Enterprises, N.Y.C., 1985—. Vol. Svcs. for Children, N.Y.C., 1989. Mem. Club Premire. Democrat. Home: 1204 Washington St Hoboken NJ 07030 Office: J Rouff Enterprises 584 Broadway New York NY 10012

POWERS, DORIS HURT, engineering company executive; b. Indpls., Jan. 17, 1927; d. James Wallace Hurt Sr. and Mildred (Johnson) Devine; m. Patrick W. Powers, Nov. 12, 1950 (dec. 1989); children: Robert W. Powers, Jaye P. Billings, Laura S. Powers. Student, So. Meth. U., 1944-45; BS in Engring., Purdue U., 1949; postgrad., U. Tex., W. Tex., 1952-53, Ecole Normale Du Musique, Paris, 1965-68. Flight instr. Red Leg Flying Club, El Paso, Lawton, Okla., 1951-57; check pilot Civil Air Patrol, El Paso, Lawton, Okla., 1952-57; ground instr. Civil Air Patrol, Washington, Tex., Okla, 1957-61; exec. v.p. T&E Internat., Inc., Bel Air, Md., 1979-88, pres., 1989—; exec. v.p. T.E.I.S., Inc., Bel Air, 1979-88, pres., 1989—; pres. Shielding Technologies, Inc., Bel Air, 1987—. Recipient Svc. award U.S. Army, 1978, Cert. of Appreciation U.S. Army Test and Evaluation Command, 1988. Mem. Soc. of Women Engrs. (sr., v.p. 1977, treas. 1979, sec. rep. 1986-88, mentor 1986—, speaker 1978—), Engring. Soc. Balt. (speaker 1980—), 99's (pres. 1951-53), am. Soc. Indsl. Security, Civil Air Patrol (lt. maj. 1951-58), Am. Def. Preparedness Assn., Assn. of U.S. Army. Home: 6 McGregor Way Bel Air MD 21014

POWERS, JOANNE PATRICIA, software engineer, systems analyst, information scientist; b. Riverside, Calif., Jan. 9, 1953; d. Otis Kemp and Margaret Louise (Schaffer) P. BA in Math., BS in Computer Sci., U. Calif., Irvine, 1974; MBA in Mgmt., Calif. State U., Fullerton, 1987; postgrad., U. So. Calif., 1989—. Computer programmer Rockwell Internat., Anaheim, Calif., 1974-76, Los Angeles, 1976-77; lead software engr. Anaheim, 1978—, Seal Beach, Calif., 1987-90; software analyst Computer Sci. Corp., Santa Ana, Calif., 1977-78; prin. INFOPOWER, Santa Ana, 1990—. Sponsor Immigration and Refugee Ctr. St. Anselm's, Garden Grove, Calif., 1979-82; soprano in ch. choir. Mem. IEEE, NAFE. Nat. Mgmt. Assn., Planetary Soc., Assn. Computing Machinery, Beta Gamma Sigma. Democrat. Episcopalian. Home: 12292 Lesley St Garden Grove CA 92640 Office: Rockwell Internat 2600 Westminster Blvd Mail Code SJ62 Seal Beach CA 90740

POWERS, KATHLEEN ANNE, real estate manager, psychotherapist; b. Jersey City, Mar. 30, 1941; d. Cornelius Marshall and Christine Caroline (Waschman) Craig. BS in Bus. Mgmt., Otay Mesa Coll., 1975; MEd, Walden U., 1988. Cert. addictions profl., Fla., 1988-; ordained to ministry, 1973. Rebirthing trainer Cambell Hot Springs Tng. Ctr., Sierraville, Calif., 1980-83; mgr. Aquarian Healing Ctr., Naples, Fla., 1983-85; leasing agt. Bluehill Properties, Naples, 1984-86; alcohol and drug abuse counselor Serenity House, Ft. Myers, Fla., 1985-86; realtor, project mgr. Woodgate Realty, Inc., Naples, 1986-89; property mgr., pres. Meadowood Club Apts., Naples, 1989-90; faculty Acad. Real Estate Network, 1977-79. Mem. adv. bd. continuation edn. grant program U. Mass., Amherst, 1977-78; crisis coord. United Way, Augusta, Ga., 1979-80. Mem. Bldg. Mgrs. Internat., Fla. Assn. Realtors, Naples Area Bd. Realtors, Comml. Investment Real Estate Assn., Internat. Transactional Analysis Assn., Assn. Mental Health Adminstrs., Southwest Fla. Real Estate Exchangers, Unity, VFW Ladies Aux. Republican. Buddhist. Home: 40 9th Ave S Naples FL 33940

POWERS, LAURA BETH, physician; b. E. Chgo., Ind., Dec. 1, 1950. Student, Emory Coll., Atlanta, 1969-72; MD, Emory U. Sch. of Medicine, Atlanta, 1976. Ptnr. Knoxville Neurology Clinic, Knoxville, Tenn., 1982--; med. dir. St. Mary's Rehabcare Unit, Knoxville, 1988—; bd. dirs. St. Mary's Found. Chmn., Dept. of Medicine, St. Mary's Med. Ctr., Knoxville, 1989-91. Recipient: Phi Beta Kappa, Gamma Chpt., Emory U., 1972. Mem., Knoxville Acad. of Medicine, Am. Acad. of Neurology, Am. Med. Assn. Office: Knoxville Neurology Clinic 930 Emerald Ave Ste 815 Knoxville TN 37917

POWERS, MARY ANN, surgeon; b. Clovis, N.Mex., Apr. 23, 1959; d. Vernon Joseph and Sachiko (Tachihara) P. BS in Biochemistry, U. Calif., Davis, 1980; MD, Uniformed Svcs. U. Sch. Medicine, 1984. Diplomate Nat. Bd. Med. Examiners. Commd. lt. USPHS, 1980, advanced through grades to lt. comdr., 1988; intern in surgery Naval Hosp., San Diego, 1984-85; resident in surgery U. Calif., San Diego, 1985—; rsch. fellow dept. surgery Duke U. Med. Ctr., Durham, N.C., 1988-89. Contbr. articles to surg. and med. jours. Mem. AMA, Phi Delta Epsilon. Office: U Calif San Diego Med Ctr Dept Surgery 225 Dickinson St San Diego CA 92103

POWERS, REBECCA ELIZABETH, educator, writer; b. Bremerton, Wash., June 25, 1947; d. Norman Francis and Joan Marie (Tatham) P.; m. Lauren Charles Bathurst, Feb. 11, 1967 (div. Sept. 1990); children: Tobias, Adrian, Suzanne, Nate. AA, Olympic Coll., 1967; BA in Sociology and Anthropology, Western Wash. U., 1970; MFA in Creative Writing, Ea. Wash. U., 1988. Registrar Whatcom Mus. History and Art, Bellingham, Wash., 1971-73; rsch. and devel. assoc. Joy Martin Assocs., Davenport, Iowa, 1975-77; dir. elderly svcs. Project N.O.W., Rock Island, Ill., 1977-78; social svcs. planner Ea. Wash. Area Agy. on Aging, Spokane, Wash., 1980-81; free-lance grant writer Spokane, Wash., 1983-85; tchr. parapsychology Spokane Community Coll., 1983-84; instr. English Ea. Wash. U., Cheney, 1985-88; instr. creative writing, composition and lit. North Idaho Coll., Coeur d' Alene, 1987-88; rsch. and devel. assoc. for exec. devel. intensive program John Scherer and Assocs., Spokane, 1990—; judge creative writing Cen. Valley Schs., Spokane, 1988-89, Coeur d' Alene Poets, 1988. Bus. mgr., bd. dirs. Pioneer Sch. for Gifted, Veradale, Wash., 1984-85; vestrywoman Ch. of Holy Spirit, Veradale, 1987-89; chmn. evangelism and faith devel. dept. Episc. Diocese of Spokane; bd. dirs. Metaphys. Spriitual Ctr., Veradale, 1988. Democrat.

POWERS, SHIRLEY MARIE, banker; b. Miles City, Mont., Feb. 27, 1930; d. Emil Henry and Karen Elizabeth (Topp) Swanson; m. William Howard Powers Jr., Apr. 5,1952; children: Michael Howard, Thomas Mark. AAS, Coastal Carolina Community Coll, 1969; cert. Sch. Banking, U. N.C., Chapel Hill, 1978. Lic. real estate broker, N.C. Adminstrv. asst. Bank of N.C., Jacksonville, 1974-77; mortgage loan officer Bank of N.C., Raleigh, 1977-82; real estate lending officer N.C. Nat. Bank, Raleigh, 1983; asst. v.p. So. Nat. Bank N.C., Raleigh and Charlotte, 1983-86; v.p. So. Nat. Bank N.C., Charlotte, 1987—. Mem. Home Builders Assn. Charlotte (treas. women's coun. 1988). Democrat. Lutheran. Office: So Nat Bank NC 1263 Arow PIne Dr Ste 301 Charlotte NC 28273

POWERS-CRAIG, PAMELA ELISABETH, music educator; b. Parkersburg, W.Va., Dec. 2, 1962; d. Keith Wayland and Glada Clare (Hopkins) Powers; m. Russell Douglas Craig, Dec. 30, 1989. BA in Music Edn., Alderson-Broaddus Coll., 1985; postgrad, W.Va. U., 1990—. Cert. tchr., W.Va. Tchr. Jackson County Pub. Schs., Ravenswood, W.Va., 1985-86, Wood County Schs., Parkersburg, 1986—; dir. music St. Andrews' United Meth. Ch.,, Parkersburg, 1987—; pvt. instr. voice and piano, Parkersburg, 1986—; pvt. choreographer for area show choirs, Pa. and W.Va., 1985—. Mem. profl. choir and state ambs. The West Virginians. Mem. AAUW, Music Educators Nat. Conf., Am. Fedn. Tchrs., W.Va. Music Educators Orgn. Democrat. Baptist. Home: 4203 3d Ave Vienna WV 26105 Office: Edison Jr High Sch 1201 Hillcrest St Parkersburg WV 26101

POYNTER, MARION KNAUSS, publishing executive; b. Poughkeepsie, N.Y., Apr. 17, 1926; d. Louis Eugene and Rose (Arndt) Knauss; m. Nelson Paul Poynter, May 4, 1970 (dec. 1978). A.B., Vassar Coll., 1946. Librarian, Time, Inc., N.Y.C., 1949-51; research analyst U.S. Govt., Washington, 1952-60; editorial research analyst St. Petersburg Times, Fla., 1961-63, editorial asst./editorial writer, 1963-70, contbg. editor, 1970-78; dir. Times Pub. Co., 1970—, Poynter Inst. for Media Studies, 1970—. Mem. Women in Communications, Internat. Press Inst. Home: The Meadows Rte 5 Box 303 Warrenton VA 22186

POYNTER, MELISSA VENABLE, real estate broker; b. Bluefield, W.Va., July 11, 1949; d. Robert Vance and Lois Chapman (Smith) Venable; m. Dan D. Poynter, Jan. 16, 1975; 1 child, Melissa. BS, Pikeville (Ky.) Coll., 1971. Tchr. Floyd County (Ky.) Bd. Edn., Prestonburg, 1971-72; counselor Action Now, Inc., Louisville, 1972-73; exec. sec. Louisville Grocery, 1973-75; chief exec. officer Poynter Enterprises, Lexington, Ky., 1978—; residential broker Rector-Hayden Realtors, Lexington, 1977-87; co-owner, broker Ky. Fine Homes, Lexington, 1987-88; with Rector Hayden Realtors, Lexington, 1988—. Contbr. articles to profl. jours. Named 1989 Realtor of Yr., Lexington Bd. Realtors. Mem. Nat. Assn. Realtors (cert. nat. profl. standards instr. 1987—), Realtors Nat. Mktg. Inst. (cert. residential specialist Ky. chpt.), Ky. Assn. Realtors (chmn. profl. standards com. 1987-89), Lexington Bd. Realtors (chmn. grievance com. 1985-87, chmn. profl. standards standards com. 1987—, Realtor of Yr. 1989), Nat. Assn. Real Estate Appriasers (cert. real estate appraiser). Republican. Methodist. Club: Bluegrass Jr. Women's (Lexington) (legis. liaison 1978-82). Office: Rector-Hayden Realtors 2100 Nicholasville Rd Lexington KY 40503

POYTHRESS, STEPHANIE LYNN, editor, writer; b. Rockford, Ill., May 22, 1964; d. William Hull and Georgia Anne (Correnti) P. BA, Oakland U., Rochester, Mich., 1987. Freelance editorial asst. Aegis Group, Troy, Mich., 1986-89, freelance editor, 1988-89; freelance writer Stephanie Poythress, Inc., Rochester, 1987—; editor Entertainment Publs., Inc., Troy, 1990—; pub. rels. cons. Four Star Marble, Mt. Clemens, Mich., 1989—. Editor (airline newsletter) Spl. Agt., 1988-89, (automotive newsletter) New Dimensions, 1989; contbg. editor GMAC Quest mag., 1989-90; contbr. articles to numerous mags. Mem. Detroit Inst. Arts, 1989—. Mem. Internat. Women's Writing Guild, Women in Communications, Inc. Home: 53305 Cheshire Rochester MI 48064 Office: Entertainment Publs 2125 Butterfield Rd Troy MI 48084

POZNIAKOFF, RITA OPPENHEIM, education software consultant; b. Munich, Nov. 19, 1949; (parents Am. citizens); d. Lester and Pearl Tobia (Waldman) Oppenheim; m. Theodore A. Pozniakoff, Dec. 29, 1985. BS, Cen. Mo. State U., 1973. Dept. mgr. Venture Dept. Stores div. May Co., St. Louis, 1973-75; dist. sales mgr. Seven Up Co., St. Louis, 1975-76; account exec. Christmas Club A Corp., Easton, Pa., 1976-83, Bankers Systems Inc., St. Cloud, Minn., 1983-85; edn. svcs. rep. Control Data Corp., Mpls., 1985-86; edn. specialist Radio Shack bus. products Tandy Corp., Ft. Worth, 1986-87, dist. govt. and edn. mktg. mgr., 1987-88, area edn. mktg. mgr., 1988-89; mgr. govt. accounts Grid Systems Corp. div. Tandy Corp., Parsippany, N.J., 1989; sr. account rep. N.Y.C. schs. Unisys Corp., White Plains, N.Y., 1989-90; mktg. mgr. N.Y. schs. Jostens Learning Corp., Phoenix, 1990—. Republican. Home: 7004 Blvd East Guttenberg NJ 07093

PRACHT, IRENA, manufacturing company executive; b. Council Grove, Kans., Dec. 24, 1927; d. Berend Hiram and Amanda (Anderson) Bicker; student Kans. Agrl. Coll., 1945-46; m. Harold Ray Pracht, Oct. 23, 1948; children: Rae Ann Pracht Lowery, Gregory Ray, Rena Rochelle Pracht Coby, Glen Frederick. BS, Kans. State Coll., Emporia, 1949. CPA, Tex. Bookkeeper, Eby Constrn. Co., Wichita, 1951-52; partner Bell Sewing Centers, Tex., N.Mex., 1954-62, Tri State Sewing Machine Distbrs., Council Grove, Kans., 1962-68; staff acct. Mize, House & Reed C.P.A.s, Topeka, 1968-69; staff acct., gen. ledger supr., controller Farah, Inc., El Paso, 1969—; partner Pracht Enterprises, El Paso, 1975—; sec. treas. Vernon Investment Corp., El Paso, 1971—; v.p. dir. Tex. Pure Products, El Paso, 1981-86; Timber Made Playsets, Inc., El Paso, 1986-88. Mem. Tex. Soc. C.P.A.s, Theta Sigma Upsilon, Xi Phi. Home: 2813B Wong Pl El Paso TX 79936 Office: 8889 Gateway West El Paso TX 79925

PRAEGER, MARY WALLACE (POLLY PRAEGER), retired educator, civic worker; b. Bklyn., June 20, 1908; d. Edwin Chapin and Carolyn Dean (Foster) Wallace; m. Howard Albert Praeger, June 27, 1940; children: Pamela Praeger Kahl, Geoffrey. BA in English Lit., St. Lawrence U., 1929; MA in English Lit., Radcliff Coll., 1933; postgrad., U. Hawaii, 1934-35, Harvard U., 1938. Tchr. English, jr. high sch., Scotia, N.Y., 1929-32, Coxsackie (N.Y.) High Sch., 1932-33, Kamehameha Sch., Honolulu, 1934-36, Rye (N.Y.) High Sch., 1936-37; tchr. English, asst. dean Hathaway-Brown Pvt. Sch., Cleve, 1938-40. Contbr. articles to jours., mags. dir. vol. svcs. Binghamton State Hosp.; mem., pres. N.Y. State Libr. Trustees Assn., 1955-71; mem. nat. bd. Am. Libr. Trustees, 1968-70; pres. Hillcrest Libr., 1970-73, Broome County World Affairs Coun., Binghamton, 1958-60; bd. dirs. Binghamton Social Planning Coun., 1959-73; mem. Broome County Adv. Com. for Performing Arts; mem. citizens adv. com. Broome Tech. Community Coll.; bd. dirs., editor newsletter Transition House, 1987—; bd. dirs. Santa Barbara Parkinson Assn.; also numerous. Named One of Outstanding Women, Gov. State of N.Y., 1968, Woman of Yr. Hillcrest, 1970; recipient Velma Moore award N.Y. State Libr. Trustees, 1971, Hall of Fame award Am. Legion, Binghamton, 1970, vol. svc. award Valle Verde Retirement Home Coun., 1985, Alumni award St. Lawrence U., 1985. Mem. AAUW (v.p. 1977-78, named gift honoree 1984), LWV, Mortar Bd., Phi Beta Kappa, Tau Kappa Alpha. Presbyterian. Home: 900 Calle de los Amigos Apt N35 Santa Barbara CA 93105

PRAGACZ, SUSAN ANN, nurse, educator; b. Daggett, Mich., Dec. 22, 1952; d. Edward Theodore and Lorena Lily (Gagne) P.; m. Frederick Mark Barron, June 2, 1989. AA, Suomi Coll., Hancock, Mich., 1973; BS in Nursing, No. Mich. U., 1981, MS in Nursing, 1988. RN, Mich.; cert. in basic cardiac life support, advanced cardiac life support. Nurse ICU, Marquette (Mich.) Gen. Hosp., 1981-90, clin. nurse specialist ICU and Intermediate Care Unit, 1990—; clin. preceptor ICU-CCU, ICU rep. RN staff coun., Marquette Gen. Hosp., 1981-90; adj. asst. prof. dept. nursing No. Mich. U., Marquette, 1988—; cardiac rehab. technician No. Mich. U. Exercise Physiology Lab., 1988—; profl. lecture cons., 1984—. Mem. Am. Nurses Assn., Mich. Nurses Assn., Am. Assn. Critical Care Nurses (cert., conf. chmn. 1985, 86, sec. Lake Superior chpt. 1982-84, 88-90, pres. 1984-85, bd. dirs. 1985-90), Marquette-Alger Dist. Nurses Assn. (bd. dirs. 1985-86, 88-89). Office: Marquette Gen Hosp ICU 420 W Magnetic St Marquette MI 49855

PRÄGER-BENETT, NANCY ANN, artist; b. N.Y.C., Mar. 17, 1945; d. Sigmund Godfrey and Eleanor Pauline Prager; student MA program Syracuse U., 1961-62; BFA, Accademia de Belle Arte, Florence, Italy, 1965; B.A., Cooper Union Coll., 1968; m. Barry Lawrence Benett, June 19, 1966; children: Lara Christina, Andrew Bernard, Ariane Alison. Work exhibited in pvt. individual shows, also mus. and univ. group shows, U.S., Italy, France, Can., Turkey, Eng., Am. embassy, Turkish Mission to UN; represented in pvt. and corp. collections, U.S., Italy, Eng., Turkey, France, Can.; tchr. Black Emergency Cultural Coalition, Met. Mus., N.Y. prison systems; chmn. bd. Mannes Coll. Music; co-dir. program for disabled children Met. Mus. Art, 1987—, producer Dance program, Costume Inst., Met. Mus. Art.; bd. dirs. Acad. TV Arts and Scis., Am. Ballet Theatre II, Amalfi Coast Consortium, Georgetown U. Sch. of Languages and Linguistics, Am.-Italian Found. for Cancer Rsch.; dir. devel. and pub. rels. World Children's Day Found. Recipient Prix de Paris, 1975, Grand Prix Humanitaire de France, 1976. Mem. Am.-Scandinavian Found., Les Surindependants Societaire, Graphic Art Assn., Smithsonian Assocs., Met. Mus. Presbyterian. Club: Saltaire Yacht (dir. 1972-80, gov., bd. dirs.). Work noted in Artist USA Bicentennial, N.Y. Art Yearbook, Nouvelle Littaire, Art News Mag., Arts Mag.; author: Turkish Costumes in the Collection of the Costume Institute Metropolitan Museum of Art; editor Rsch. for Life jour.

PRAKUP, BARBARA LYNN, communications executive; b. Cleve., Oct. 6, 1957; d. Edward Vincent and Carol Marie (O'Hara) Reese; m. Gary M. Prakup, July 2, 1977; 1 child, Sarah Ellen. BA, Cleve. State U., 1979; MA, Cleve. State U., Ohio, 1981. Cert. Clinical Competence, Ohio. Speech therapist Keystone Local Sch. Dist., LaGrange, Ohio, 1981-82; lang. devel. spl. Cuyahoga County Bd. M.R., Cleve., 1982-86; sr. clinician InSpeech, Inc., Valley Forge, Pa., 1987—; speech pathologist Middleburg Heights, Ohio; dir. speech pathologists Litchfield Rehab. Ctr., Akron Gen. Med. Ctr., 1988—; owner Comprehensive Communication Specialists, Medina, Ohio, 1990—. Mem. Am. Sph. & Hrng. Assn., Aphasiology Assn. Ohio, Akron Regional Sph & Hrng Assn. Democrat. Roman Catholic. Office: Comprehensive Communication Specialists 750 E Washington St A-6 Medina OH 44256

PRALONG, SANDRA, publishing executive; b. Bucharest, Romania, Mar. 9, 1958; came to U.S. 1983; d. Fred A. and Sanda (Budis) DeGall; m. Christophe Pralong, Oct. 10, 1981 (dec. 1982). BA in Polit. Sci., U. Lausanne, Switzerland, 1980; MBA, U. Lausanne, 1981; MA in Law and Diplomacy, The Fletcher Sch., Medford, Mass., 1985. Lectr. econs. U. Niamey, Niger, W. Africa, 1981-82; mktg. cons. Les Marionnettes S.A., Lausanne, 1982; rsch. intern OECD, Paris, 1982-83; assoc. mktg. mgr. Newsweek, N.Y.C., 1985-86; mgr. spl. supplements Newsweek, 1986-88, dir. promotion, 1988—. Founder, pubr. newsletter, Easy Cooking with Great Chefs, 1988-89. Mem. Romanian Am. Com., N.Y.C., 1990. Mass. State Senate citation for outstanding contbn. to Commonwealth of Mass., 1983; Rotary Found. scholar, 1982. Republican. Greek Orthodox. Home: 222 W 14th St New York NY 10011

PRANKE, SUSAN ANN, army officer, educator; b. Green Bay, Wis., Oct. 18, 1957; d. William Eugene and Rosemary (Nienhaus) P. BS, U. Wis., La Crosse, 1980; student, Army Air Assault Course, 1979, French Commando Sch., 1986; grad., Dale Cornegie Course, 1989, grad. asst., 1990. Qualified parachute rigger. Commd. 2nd lt. U.S. Army, 1980, advanced through grades to capt., 1984; bn. asst. 105th supply and transport U.S. Army, Ft. Polk, La., 1981, brigade asst. adj. div. support command, 1981-83; materiel planner 29th area support group U.S. Army, Kaiserlautern, Fed. Republic Germany, 1985-86; co. commdr. 5th quartermaster detachment U.S. Army, Kaiserlavtern, Fed. Republic Germany, 1986-87; asst. prof. mil. sci. U. Mont., 1988—. Active Big Brothers/Big Sisters of Missoula, 1989—. Mem. Quartermaster Officers Assn., Western Mont. Officers Assn., Assn. U.S. Army (advisor). Roman Catholic. Home: 3811 Stephens Ave #40 Missoula MT 59801 Office: Mil Sci Dept Univ Mont Missoula MT 59812-1033

PRAST, LESLIE LOUISE, English educator; b. Pitts., Feb. 8, 1946; d. Willard Nelson and Frances Helen (Leslie) Thompson; m. Norman Edward Prast, Jan. 2, 1982; l child, Steven S. BA, Mich. State U., 1967; 0MA, Ind. U., 1969. Instr. English, U. P.R., Humacao, 1969-70, Frontisterion Mouyakou, Athens, Greece, 1970-71, Pierce Coll., Athens, 1971-75; prof.

English, Delta Coll., University Center, Mich., 1976—, dir. global and internat. edn., 1986-89; cons. ESL, Mich., 1979—; chmn. state and regional ESL and English confs., 1980—. Contbr. articles to profl. jours. Vol. Cystic Fibrosis, Bay City, Mich., 1983—. Recipient Leadership cert. Mich. Internat. Coun., 1980, Creative Change award Delta Coll. Faculty and Staff, 1987, Svc. award AAUP, 1987. Mem. Nat. Coun. Tchrs. English, Internat. Tchrs. English to Speakers Other Langs., Mich. Tchrs. English to Speakers Other Langs. (exec. bd. 1984-89, pres. 1986-88). Office: Delta Coll University Center MI 48710

PRATHER, LENORE LOVING, state supreme court justice; b. West Point, Miss., Sept. 17, 1931; d. Byron Herald and Hattie Hearn (Morris) Loving; m. Robert Brooks Prather, May 30, 1957; children: Pamela, Valerie Jo, Malinda Wayne. B.S., Miss. State Coll. Women, 1953; JD, U. Miss., 1955. Bar: Miss. 1955. Practice with B. H. Loving, West Point, 1955-60, sole practice, 1960-62, 65-71, assoc. practice, 1962-65; mcpl. judge City of West Point, 1965-71; chancery ct. judge 14th dist. State of Miss., Columbus, 1971-82; supreme ct. justice State of Miss., Jackson, 1982—; v.p. Conf. Local Bar Assn., 1956-58; sec. Clay County Bar Assn., 1956-71. 1st woman in Miss. to become chancery judge, 1971, and supreme ct. justice, 1982. Mem. Miss. State Bar. Assn., Miss. Conf. Judges, DAR, Rotary, Pilot Club, Jr. Aux. Columbus Club. Episcopalian. Office: Miss Supreme Ct PO Box 117 Jackson MS 39205

PRATHER, SUSAN LYNN, public relations executive; b. Melrose Park, Ill.; d. Horace Charles and Ruth Anna Paula (Backus) P.; divorced. BS, Ind. U., 1973, MS, 1975. Arts administr. Lyric Opera Chgo., 1975; jr. account exec. Morton H. Kaplan Assocs., Chgo., 1976-78, sr. account exec., 1978-81; account supr. Ketchum Pub. Relations, Chgo., 1981-83, v.p., 1983-87, v.p., group mgr., 1985-87; v.p., dir. pub. relations Cramer-Krasselt, Chgo., 1987—; cons. Skil Corp., Creda, Inc., Michael Reese Health Plan, Velamints, Citicorp Global Payments Div., S.W. Airlines NCH Promotional Svcs., Kellogg Co., Battle Creek, Mich., 1985—, Village of Rosemont, Ill., 1977—. Singer various recitals; founder, dir. Chgo. Sports Hall of Fame, 1978-81. Chmn. spl. projects Jr. Governing Bd. Chgo. Symphony Orch., 1986-88, mem. archives com., 1986—, long term planning com., 1987-89, press advance team Papal Visit to Chgo., 1978, White House Press Advance Team, Chgo., 1976-80. Mem. Pub. Relations Soc. Am. (bd. dirs. Chgo. chpt. 1987—), Internat. Pub. Relations Assn., Publicity Club (bd. dirs. 1986—, Merit award 1982, Golden Trumpet award 1987, Silver Trumpet award 1989). Lutheran. Home: 3950 N Lake Shore Dr Chicago IL 60613

PRATO, NANCY RUTTER HENRY, insurance consultant; b. Burlington, Vt., Feb. 4, 1935; d. William Rutter and Marjorie (Hodge) Henry; m. Raymond C. Prato, May 21, 1960; 1 child, William Henry (dec.). AS in Risk Mgmt. Cert. ins. cons. Asst. mgr. Arthur Murray Dance Studios, New Haven, 1954-60; numerous sales positions, 1960-75; sales rep. Sentry Ins., Concord, Mass., 1975-80; comml. agt. Mathog Group Ins., New Haven, 1980-83; sr. sales rep. A.A. Watson, Inc., Wethersfield, Conn., 1983-86; owner Nancy Henry Prato Ins. Mgmt. and Cons. Services, Hamden, Conn., 1987—; lectr. in field. Mem. Nat. Assn. Female Execs., Ind. Ins. Agts. Am., Underwriters Trng. Council. Republican. Home and Office: 80 Blue Trail Hamden CT 06518

PRATOLA, STEPHANIE, clinical psychologist; b. Wilmington, Del., Aug. 28, 1952; d. Michael B. and Mary C.E. (Di Stefano) P.; m. James R. Dalton, Aug. 25, 1973; children: Aaron, Andrew. BA, Gettysburg Coll., 1974; PhD, U. S.C., 1980. Lic. psychologist, Va. Resident-in-tng. Roanoke Valley Psychiat. Ctr., Salem, Va., 1980-81, staff psychologist, 1981-83, sr. clin. psychologist, 1983-85, children's clin. coord., 1985-88, children's program dir., 1988-89, supr., cons., 1989—; pvt. practice Roanoke, Va., 1989—. Mem. children's com. Roanoke Mental Health Assn., 1984—; mem. Roanoke Child Abuse Prevention Coun., 1984—. Mem. Am. Psychol. Assn., Southeastern Psychol. Assn., Va. Acad. Clin. Psychologists, Phi Beta Kappa. Episcopalian. Office: 2222 Electric Rd Ste 203 Roanoke VA 24018

PRATT, ALICE REYNOLDS, retired educational administrator; b. Marietta, Ohio, Oct. 5, 1922; d. Thurman J. and Vera L. (Holdren) Reynolds. BA, U. Okla., 1943. Reporter, high sch. tchr., 1944-50; asst. dir. Houston office Inst. Internat. Edn., 1952-58, dir. office, 1958-87, v.p., 1976-87, ret. 1987. Founding bd. govs. Houston Forum; mem. Houston Com. Fgn. Rels.; former bd. dirs., former v.p. Houston World Trade Assn.; founding mem. Japan Am. Soc. Houston; founding mem. Houston-Taipei Soc., pres., 1989—; founding mem. Stavanger Sister City Assn.; past nat. bd. dirs. Sister Cities Internat., Nat. Coun. Internat. Visitors; bd. dirs. So. Regional Office IIE Bd., Pan Am. Roundtable. Decorated Palmes Academiques (France), 1966; Order of Merit (Fed. Republic Germany), 1972; knight Order of Leopold II (Belgium), 1973; named Woman of Yr., Houston Bus. and Profl. Women, 1958; recipient Matrix award Theta Sigma Phi, 1961; Nat. Carnation award Gamma Phi Beta, 1976. Mem. Inst. Internat. Edn. (bd. dirs. So. office 1988—). Republican. Episcopalian.

PRATT, CHRISTINE, small business owner; b. Bluffton, Ind., June 9, 1961; d. Endre Francis and Marianne (Kertesz) S.; m. Joseph Caldwell, May 30, 1987. Student, Purdue U., 1983. Group supr. Margie Korshak Assn., Inc., Chgo., 1983-85; mktg. dir. Ronsley, Inc., Chgo., 1986; exec. pub. relations dir. Saffer, U.S.A., 1986-88. mem. Fashion Group, Publicity Club Chgo. Catholic. Office: Pratt Nolan Inc 1350 N Wells A-201 Chicago IL 60610

PRATT, DIANE ADELE, educator; b. Battle Creek, Mich., Oct. 24, 1951; d. John Robert and Kathleen Adele (Cooper) Dickert; m. Stephen Howard Pratt, Apr. 29, 1972; children: Eric Stephen, Elizabeth Adele. BS, Western Mich. U., 1972. Cert. elem. tchr., Ohio, Iowa. Elem. tchr. Berea (Ohio) Community Schs., 1973-76; ednl. cons. Kolbe Products, Inc., Phoenix and Scottsdale, Ariz., 1982-84; tchr. Lemon Tree Nursery Sch., Battle Creek, 1985-88; instr. Jr. Great Books, 1984-87; elem. tchr. Ft. Dodge (Iowa) Community Schs., 1976-78, substitute tchr., 1988-90, tchr., 1990—; exec. sec. Born Free Safari Club, Dodgen Industries, Humboldt, Iowa, 1988; contbg. assoc. Ft. Dodge Today mag., 1989; ednl. tutor, Battle Creek, Ft. Dodge, 1986-89; mem. adv. bd. Inst. for Instrnl. Svcs., Battle Creek, 1984-88; dir., instr. Battle Creek Presch. Enrichment Program, 1984; chmn. Ft. Dodge Supt.'s Community Com. To Study K-8 Curriculum, 1988-89, facilitator Community Com. K-3 Human Growth and Devel. Curriculum, 1989—; standing com. Early Childhood Adv. Bd., Ft. Dodge Sch., 1989—. Author, editor various newsletters. Mem., past chmn. bd. Christian edn. 1st Bapt. Ch., Ft. Dodge, 1978-79, 89, dir. children's choirs, 1988-90; membership chmn. Battle Creek Parents, 1981-83; neighborhood coord. mother's march March of Dimes, Battle Creek, 1981-83; troop leader Lakota coun. Girl Scouts U.S., 1988-90; pres. La Mora Park PTA, Battle Creek, 1985-87, Phillips Mid. Sch. PTA, Ft. Dodge, 1990—; sec., pres. Jr. Women's Club, Ft. Dodge, 1978-80; chmn. Duncombe Booster Club, Ft. Dodge, 1988—; bd. dirs. Main Stage Players Jr. Theater, Ft. Dodge; mem. steering com. Kids on Kampus, Iowa Cen. Community Coll., 1990—. Recipient Mem. of Yr. award La Mora Park PTA, 1987. Mem. AAUW (sec., pres. Battle Creek 1986-88), Fort Dodge Dodge Athletic Booster Club, Fort Dodge Pub. Libr. Friends of Libr. Home: 1851 9th Ave N Fort Dodge IA 50501

PRATT, E(LLEN) MARCELLA MORIN, designer; b. Trail, B.C., Can. (parents Am. citizens); d. Francis George and Rose Delima (Bousquet) Morin; student extension courses Wash. State Coll.; grad. Normal Coll., Victoria, B.C.; m. George Collins Pratt, Sept. 22, 1946. With art dept. Universal Internat. Pictures 1935-46; now home designer and decorator, Calif., Wash. Mem. Assistance League So. Calif., Canadian Red Cross (life), Navy League of the U.S. (life), Mary and Joseph League (life), Eisenhower Med. Aux. (founder, life mem.), Palm Desert, Calif., Desert Mus., Nat. Mus. of Women in the Arts (charter). Republican. Home: Box 427 Cathedral City CA 92234

PRATT, MARGARET WADE, information science executive; b. Kansas City, Mo., Apr. 5, 1925; d. Walter Wesley and Leone (Smith) P.; B.A., Washburn U., 1945; postgrad. in law Southwestern U. Dir. maternal and child health studies George Washington U., Washington, 1962-73; dir. maternal and child health studies project Minn. Systems Rsch., Inc., Washington, 1974-75; pres., project dir. Info. Sciences Rsch. Inst., Vienna, Va., 1976—. Mem. Am. Public Health Assn., Assn. MCH Programs.

PRATT, MARTHA LEE, nurse; b. Chattanooga, Tenn., Mar. 25, 1957; d. Joseph Hilliard and Thelma (Lee) Anders; m. Frank Martin Pratt, Jr., Dec. 9, 1977; children: Jessica Kristin, Andrew Brett. B.S. in Nursing, U. Ala.-Birmingham, 1979. Nurse's aide Univ. Hosp., Birmingham, 1977-79, staff nurse, 1979-80, charge nurse of burn dressing team, 1980—, speaker Burn Ctr., 1980—; researcher Robert Wood Johnson Found., Birmingham, 1985-88. Tchr. Valley Creek Baptist Ch., Hueytown, Ala., 1984-85. Recipient Clin. Excellent in Nursing U. Ala. Hosp., 1988. Mem. Am. Burn Assn., Nat. Burn Prevention Com. Democrat. Avocations: horseback riding, boating, camping, reading. Home: 149 Greenridge Rd Hueytown AL 35023 Office: University Hosp 619 S 19th St JT Room 1010A Birmingham AL 35233

PRATT, SHARRAN M., cosmetics company sales executive; b. Greeley, Colo., Sept. 22, 1940; d. Elmer Leroy and Mona Maire (Johnson) Fristrom; m. Robert Byron Pratt, Sept. 9, 1959 (div. Aug. 1976); children: Steven Robert, Lance Byron; m. Michael Allan Martin, May 12, 1990. BS in Biol. Sci., U. No. Colo., 1961, MA in English, 1966; AS in Women's Studies, Metro State Coll. Denver, 1977; AS in Computer Sci., Araphoe Community Coll., Littleton, Colo., 1983. Sales assoc. Jones Co., Greeley, 1960-62; tchr. Ten Sheep (Colo.) Pub. Schs., 1962-63, Weld County Re-1, Ft. Lupton, Colo., 1963-65, La Plata Sch. Dist., Durango, Colo., 1965-71, Jefferson County Schs., Lakewood, Colo., 1976-88, Summit Sch. Dist., Frisco, Colo., 1989-90; instr. Ft. Lewis Coll., Durango, 1969, Red Rocks Community Coll., Golden, Colo., 1987; sr. sales dir., beauty cons. Mary Kay Cosmetics, Dallas, 1971—. Editor, contbr. The Peak Experience, monthly newsletter, 1988-90. Mem. Summit County Rep. Com., 1989—. Mem. AAUW, Summit Hist. Soc., Summit Acad. Lutheran.

PRATT, SUZANNE GARRETT, physician; b. La Grange, Ga., Mar. 9, 1948; d. Roswell and Susie Turner (Keller) Garrett; m. Frank Graham Pratt III, Sept. 18, 1971; children: Frank Graham, Edward Garrett. BS summa cum laude, U. Ga., 1970; MD, Med. Coll. Ga., 1973. Diplomate Am. Bd. Ob-Gyn. Resident Med. Coll. Ga., Augusta, 1973-77; physician D.D. Eisenhower Army Med. Ctr., Ft. Gordon, Ga., 1977-79; practice medicine specializing in gynecology, Rome, Ga., 1980-89, pvt. practice limited to gynecology, 1989—; coord. ob-gyn family practice residency program Floyd Med. Ctr., Rome, 1983-84. Nat. Merit scholar U. Ga. Found., 1966-70. Fellow Am. Coll. Obstetricians and Gynecologists; mem. Floyd-Polk-Chattooga Med. Soc. (sec. 1982-84), AMA, Ga. Soc. Obstetricians and Gynecologists, Med. Assn. Ga., Endometriosis Assn. (bd. dirs., v.p. edn. and community rels. 1987-88), Zodiac, Phi Beta Kappa, Phi Kappa Phi. Avocation: reading. Home: 3 Hill Dale Ln SW Rome GA 30161 Office: Three Rivers Gynecology 909 N Fifth Ave Rome GA 30161

PRAWL, NANCY IRENE, county registrar; b. Kansas City, Mo., Feb. 26, 1942; d. Chester Earl and Martha Louise (Laverentz) Jacobs; m. Philip W. Prawl Sr., Aug. 30, 1989; 1 child, Penelope Ann. Sec. to probate judge Hiawatha, Kans., 1965-66; abstractor Finley & Miller, Attys., 1967-68; clk. County Treas., Hiawatha, Kans., 1976-77; registrar deeds Brown County (Kans.), Hiawatha, 1977—; treas. Northeast Kans. Emergency Med. Tech., 1985-86, pres., 1986-87; pres. Kansas Register of Deeds Assn., 1987-88. Disaster chmn. Brown County chpt. ARC, 1984-88, chpt. chmn., 1989—. Mem. Hiawatha Bus. and Profl. Women's Orgn. (pres. 1985-86, Woman of Yr. award 1983), Hiawatha High Sch. Alumni Assn. (treas. 1983—), Kans. Register of Deeds Assn. (treas. 1985-86), Kiwanis. Avocations: needlecrafts, reading. Home: PO Box 215 Hiawatha KS 66434 Office: Brown County Register of Deeds Office Courthouse Hiawatha KS 66434

PRAY, JANET LORRAINE, social work educator; b. Passaic, N.J., Nov. 18, 1939; d. Julius Van Riper and Lillian Frances (Flaig) P. BA, Montclair State Coll., 1961; MSW, Smith Coll., 1963; postgrad., Union Inst., 1988—. Diplomate in clin. social work. Social worker Cleve. Met. Gen. Hosp., 1963-65, social work supr., 1965-75, coord. edn., 1975-80; dir. social work program Gallaudet U., Washington, 1980—, assoc. prof. social work, 1985—, chmn. dept. sociology and social work, 1986-89, chmn. dept. social work, 1990—; cons. Evening Mental Health Clinic, Cleve., 1971-80. Contbr. articles on social work and deafness to profl. jours., chpts. to books. Bd. dirs. Family Life Ctr., Columbia, Md., 1981-84. Mem. Nat. Assn. Social Workes, Coun. on Social Work Edn., Am. Deafness and Rehab. Assn., Acad. Cert. Social Workers. Home: 6696 Drowsy Day Columbia MD 21045 Office: Gallaudet U Dept Social Work 800 Florida Ave NE Washington DC 20002

PRAY, MERLE EVELYN, nurse; b. Washington, Vt., Apr. 19, 1931; d. Clifton Clough and Dorothy Wadleigh Pray. BSN, Loyola U., Chgo., 1977; MS, U. Ill., Chgo., 1983; nursing diploma, N.H. Sch. Nursing, Concord, 1952. Planning area coord, community placement monitor, unit chief Ill. Dept. of Mental Health, Chgo.; clin. nurse specialist VA West Side Med. Ctr., Chgo., co-chair rsch. com.; adj. clin. instr. psychiat. nursing U. Ill., Chgo. Mem. INA, ANA (coun., cert. clin. specialist in adult psychiatry and mental health nursing), Psychiat. and Mental Health Nursing, Nat. Nurses Soc. on Addictions. Home: 175 E Delaware Pl Chicago IL 60611 Office: Vet Affairs West Side Med Ctr 820 S Damen Ave Chicago IL 60680

PRED, NANCY G., marketing professional; b. Morristown, N.J., Mar. 18, 1958; d. Gordon P. and Anne S. (Slesser) P. BA, Northwestern U., Evanston, Ill., 1980; MBA, U Mich., 1982. Mktg. asst. The Quaker Oats Co., Chgo., 1982-83, assoc. brand mgr., 1983-84; assoc. brand mgr. Kraft Inc., Glenview, Ill., 1984-85, brand mgr., 1985-88; group mktg. mgr. The Nutra Sweet Co., Deerfield, Ill., 1988-90; sr. category mgr. The Nutra Sweet Co., Skokie, Ill., 1990—. Recipient Outstanding Contbn. to Div. Performance Kraft-Grocery Products Div., Glenview, Ill., 1985. Democrat.

PREDMORE, MARIAN CORINNE, retired teacher, volunteer; b. Pittsburg, Kans., July 12, 1923; d. Robert W. and Retta S. Hart; m. William D. Predmore, Oct. 18, 1947; children: Richard L., Robert C. BA, Kans. State Coll., Pitts., 1944; MS, Kans. State U., 1948. Tchr. various secondary schs., Kans., 1944-56, Salina (Kans.) Pub. Schs., 1962-68; lectr. 1987-90. Editor: Informational Guide to Social Services in Saline County, 1974. Bd. dirs. Saline (Kans.) Girls Home, 1972-75; vol. Salina (Kans.) Day Care Ctr., 1970-72; docent Kans. Mus. of History, 1984—; mission chmn. United Meth. Ch., Silver Lake, Kans., 1988-90; v.p. LWV, Salina, 1970. Mem. AAUW (pres. Norton br. Kans., 1981-82). Home: 517 Mariner Silver Lake KS 66539

PREISS, MARILYN BRITON, interior designer; b. N.Y.C., Oct. 18, 1941; m. Sydney M.R. Preiss, Mar. 3, 1977 (dec. 1988). BFA, Pratt Inst., Bklyn. Designer Dallek Design Assocs., N.Y.C., 1970-72, Stanley Felderman, N.Y.C., 1972-74; systems planner R&G Affiliates, N.Y.C., 1974-77; mgr. design services InterRoyal, N.Y.C., 1977-79; sr. designer Wilke/Davis, N.Y.C., 1979-83; sr. project designer ODA/Shepard Martin, N.Y.C., 1983-85; design mgr. Mancini-Duffy, N.Y.C., 1985-89; owner, designer Briton/Preiss Assocs., N.Y.C., 1988—. Mem. Inst. Bus. Designers.

PREMEAUX, LANETTE LEA, national sales executive; b. Groves, Tex., Oct. 2, 1957; d. Joseph Abram Premeaux and Rosetta Ann (Richard) Hirsch. Student, Lamar U., 1977-79; AAS, North Harris County Coll., Houston, 1984. Payroll analyst Texaco, Inc., Houston, 1981-82; administrv. asst. Tex. Analytical Controls, Inc., Stafford, Tex., 1982-83; assoc. realtor Adam Investment Properties, Inc., Houston, 1982-86; nat. sales exec. TV Update div. Scripps Howard, N.Y.C., 1984—. Mem. NAFE, Tex. Real Estate Commn., State of Tex. Notary Pub. Commn. Roman Catholic. Home: 2423 Crescent Dr Groves TX 77619 Office: United Media/TV Update 200 Park Ave New York NY 10166

PRENDERGAST, CAROL UHLICH, educator, consultant; b. Mansfield, Ohio, Feb. 10, 1937; d. Wilford Dale and Ruby Lee (Barfield) Uhlich; m. Robert Lewis Prendergast, June 6, 1959; children: Lynn Prendergast La Chapelle, Robert Lewis Jr. BS, Fla. State U., 1959. From tchr. to administr. Montessori Child Devel. Ctr., Poway, Calif., 1978—. Mem. Am. Montessori Soc. (bd. dirs. N.Y.C. chpt. 1985—, treas. exec. coun. 1989—), Assn. Montessori Internat., San Diego Montessori Tchrs. Assn. (pres. 1980—), Nat. Assn. for Edn. Young Children, Montessori Adminstr. Coun. U.S.A. (coord. Area 1), N.Am. Montessori Tchrs. Assn. Republican. Baptist. Home: 16945 Vinaruz Pl San Diego CA 92128

PRESCOTT, ROBERTA WEINSTEIN, communication consultant; b. Hartford, Conn., June 13, 1937; d. Iver and Sarah (Bobrow) Weinstein; m. Marvin A. Prescott, June 17, 1956 (div. 1969); children: Jennifer, Laura, Emily. BS, Simmons Coll., 1959; diploma in drama, Hartford Conservatory, 1967. Sales rep. Dale Carnegie Courses, Hartford, Conn., 1972-75; pres. The Prescott Group, West Hartford, Conn., 1975—; Adj. prof. marketing U. Hartford Sch. Bus. Author tng. manuals: Speaking Made Easy, 1987, Image Made Easy, 1987, Speaking to the Media, 1988, Business Networking, 1988; exec. producer, author video tng. tape: Business Networking Made Easy, 1988. Chmn. bd. Greater Hartford Conv. and Visitors Bur., 1989—. Recipient Matrix Women of Yr. award Women in Communications Cen. Conn. Chpt. Mem. Am. Soc. for Tng. and Devel., Golf Club of Avon, Greater Hartford C. of C. (bd. dirs., chair womens exec. com.). Jewish. Office: The Prescott Group 345 N Main St West Hartford CT 06117

PRESGROVE, SHARON RUTH, state government administrator; b. Duncan, Okla., July 28, 1946; d. Lloyd Ray and Pearl Mae (Rupe) Wampler; m. Larry Glen Presgrove, Aug. 9, 1945. Assoc. Bus. Adminstrn., Oscar-Rose State Coll., 1975; postgrad. in acctg., Okla. Miss. Coll., 1983-85. Acct. Okla. Dept. Transp., Duncan, 1967-75, adminstrv. asst., 1975-86, div. office mgr., 1986—. Youth leader Seventh Day Adventist Ch., Duncan, 1979-81; speaker wildflower workshop, Cameron Coll., Lawton, Okla, 1981; sec. Duncan Firefighters Auxiliary, 1980—. Mem. NAFE, Bus. and Profl. Women, Okla. Soc. Cert. Pub. Mgrs., Okla. Hwy. Credit Union (bd. dirs. 1987—). Democrat. Home: 2109 Canary Ave Duncan OK 73533 Office: Okla Dept Transp 2205 S 81 Hwy Duncan OK 73533

PRESKA, MARGARET LOUISE ROBINSON, university president; b. Parma, N.Y., Jan. 23, 1938; d. Ralph Craven and Ellen Elvira (Niemi) Robinson; m. Daniel C. Preska, Jan. 24, 1959; children: Robert, William, Ellen Preska Steck. B.S. summa cum laude, SUNY, 1957; M.A., Pa. State U., 1961; Ph.D., Claremont Grad. Sch., 1969; postgrad., Manchester Coll., Oxford U., 1973. Instr. LaVerne (Calif.) Coll., 1968-75, asst. prof., assoc. prof., acad. dean, 1972-75; instr. Starr King Sch. for Ministry, Berkeley, Calif., summer, 1975; v.p. acad. affairs, equal opportunity officer Mankato (Minn.) State U., 1975-79, pres., 1979—; bd. dirs. No. States Power Co., Norwest Corp. Mankato, Minn. Wellspring, Southeastern Minn. Bus. Innovation Ctr. Pres. Pomona Valley chpt. UN Assn., 1968-69, Unitarian Soc. Pomona Valley, 1968-69, PTA Lincoln Elem. Sch., Pomona, 1973-74; mem. Pomona City Charter Revision Commn., 1972; chmn. The Fielding Inst., Santa Barbara, 1983-86; bd. dirs. Elderhostel Internat., 1983—, Minn. Agrl. Interpretive Ctr. (Farmam.), 1983—, Am. Assn. State Colls. and Univs., Moscow on the Mississippi - Minn. Meets the Soviet Union; nat. pres. Campfire, Inc., 1985-87; chmn. Gov.'s Coun. on Youth, Minn., 1983-86, Minn. Edn. Forum, 1984; mem. Gov.'s Commn. on Econ. Future of Minn., 1985—, NCAA Pres.'s Commn., 1986—, NCAA Cost Cutting Commn., Minn. Brainpower Compact, 1985; commr. Great Lakes Govs.' Econ. Devel. Coun., 1986, Minn Gov.'s Commn. on Forestry. Carnegie Found. grantee Am. Coun. Edn. Deans Inst., 1974; recipient Outstanding Alumni award Pa. State, Outstanding Alumni award Claremont Grad. Sch., YWCA Leader award 1982, Exch. Club Book of Golden Deeds award, 1987; named one of top 100 alumni, SUNY, 1985, Hall of Heritage award, 1988, Wohelo Camp Fire award, 1989. Mem. AAUW, LWV, Women's Econ. Roundtable, Mpls./St. Paul Com. on Fgn. Relations., Am. Council on Edn., Am. Assn. Univ. Adminstrs. Unitarian. Clubs: Benedicts Dance, Zonta. Lodge: Rotary. Home: 10 Sumner Hills Mankato MN 56001 Office: Mankato State U Box 24 South Rd & Ellis Ave Mankato MN 56002-8400

PRESLEY, JANET PASSIDOMO, advertising executive; b. Harrison, N.Y., Jan. 11, 1952; d. John A. and Gloria (Massaglia) Passidomo; m. Gregory Francis Presley, Sept. 16, 1984. BA, Manhattanville Coll., 1973; MBA, Columbia U., 1977. Account exec. Compton Advt., N.Y.C., 1977-79, The Marschalk Co., N.Y.C., 1979-80; v.p., mgmt. rep. BBDO, N.Y.C., 1980—. Office: BBDO NY 1285 Ave of the Americas New York NY 10019

PRESLEY, VIVIAN MATHEWS, junior college administrator; b. West Point, Miss., Oct. 12, 1952; d. Beatrus and Lula (Butler) Mathews; m. Dwight Presley, Sept. 12, 1971; 1 child, Julian. BA, Miss. State U., 1973, MA, 1975, Cert. Edn. Specialist, 1978, EdD, 1983. Counselor Coahoma Jr. Coll. (named changed to Coahoma Community Coll.), Clarksdale, Miss., 1975-80; title III coordinator Coahoma Jr. Coll., Clarksdale, Miss., 1981-82, asst. to pres., 1982-83, v.p., 1983—. Vice chairperson Miss. State Council on Vocat. Edn., Jackson, Miss., 1984. Named One of Outstanding Young Woman of Am., 1981, 84, 85, 88. Mem. Nat. Assn. Female Execs., Assn. Univ. Women, Nat. Council for Resource Devel., Psi Kappa Psi, Delta Sigma Theta. Democrat. Methodist. Home: 122 Crestline Apt 1301 Clarksdale MS 38614 Office: Coahoma Community Coll Rt 1 Box 616 Clarksdale MS 38614

PRESNELL, NADEAN ELIZABETH, social worker; b. Mpls., Apr. 18, 1936; d. Chester Emil and Ruth Theodora (Holmberg) Larson; m. Frank Lee Presnell, Nov. 17, 1962. BA, Augustana Coll., 1958; MSW, U. Minn., 1961. Case worker Ill. Dept. Children & Family, Chgo., 1962-63, Hillside Childrens Svc. Home, Rochester, N.Y., 1964-65; case work supr. Ill. Dept. Children & Family Svcs., Champaign, Ill., 1965-66; intake supr. Hillside Children's Home, Rochester, 1967-68; pvt. practice in therapy Dayton, Ohio, 1969-89. Mem. Nat. Assn. Social Workers, Acad. Certified Social Workers. Independent. Lutheran. Home and Office: 7431 Barr Circle Dayton OH 45459

PRESS, AIDA KABATZNICK, university administrator, editor; b. Boston, Nov. 18, 1926; m. Newton Press, June 5, 1947; children: David, Dina Press Weber, Benjamin Presskreischer. BA, Radcliffe Coll., 1948. Reporter Waltham (Mass.) News-Tribune, 1960-63; freelance writer, 1960-63; editorial cons. Mass. Dept. Mental Health, Boston, 1966-72; Waltham/Watertown reporter Boston Herald Traveler, 1963-70; dir. news and publs. Harvard Grad. Sch. Design, Cambridge, Mass., 1972-78; publs. editor Radcliffe Coll., Cambridge, 1978-81, dir., editor of publs., 1981-83, editor Radcliffe Quar., 1971—, dir. pub. info., 1983—. Contbr. articles to newspapers and mags. Recipient Publs. distinction Am. Alumni Coun., 1974, Top 5 Coll. Mag., Coun. for Advancement and Support of Edn., 1984; numerous other awards. Office: Radcliffe Coll 10 Garden St Cambridge MA 01238

PRESS, LINDA SEGHERS, biotechnology consultant; b. Jacksonville, Fla., Dec. 2, 1950; d. Joseph Wood and Jadwiga (Borusiewicz) Seghers; m. Jeffery Bruce Press, Dec. 21, 1976; children: Samantha Michelle, Michael Alexander. BS, Ohio State U., 1972, PhD in Chemistry, 1977; postgrad., N.Y. Med. Coll., 1981. Rsch. assoc. Internat. Paper Co., Tuxedo, N.Y., 1977-81, mgr. biochem. rsch., 1981-84; dir. biotech. Agr. Rsch. Ctr., FMC, Princeton, N.J., 1984-86; biotech. cons., Rocky Hills, N.J., 1986—. Structure editor Organic Reactions, 1988—; contbr. articles to profl. jours. Sec. Rocky Hill Community Group, 1987—; photographer Trinity Ch., Princeton, 1989—. Univ. fellow Ohio State U., 1971, 76. Home and Office: 716 Buckley Circle Penllyn PA 19422

PRESS, MICHELLE, editor; b. Memphis, Nov. 22, 1940; d. Sam and Rana (Cohen) Appelbaum; m. Robert Press, June 18, 1960 (div. 1965). B.A., New Sch. for Social Research, 1967. Tchr. U.S. Peace Corps, Malawi, Africa, 1962-64; copy editor Japan Quar., Tokyo, 1967-71; asst. editor Am. Scientist, New Haven, 1971-78, mng. editor, 1978-81, editor, 1981—. Office: Am Scientist 345 Whitney Ave New Haven CT 06511

PRESSBERG, GAIL, foundation executive; b. Bklyn., Apr. 26, 1949; d. David and Irma (Sanderson) P. BA, Hunter Coll., N.Y., 1971; MA, U. Md., 1990. Adminstr. P.E.N., N.Y.C., 1971-73; dir. tng. Am. Friends Svc. Com., Phila., 1973-77, dir. middle East progs., 1977-87; exec. dir. Found. for Middle East Peace, Washington, 1987—; pres. Sande Svcs., Md., 1990—; cons. in field. Co-author: A Compassionate Peace, 1982; author monograph: The Student's Guide to Hunter College, 1970. Bd. dirs. Am. Near East Refugee Aid, Washington, 1981-83, Grass Roots Internat., Boston, 1982-87; cons. Inst. for Peace and Internat. Security, Cambridge, Mass., 1986-90. Recipient Janet Lee Stevens award, U. Pa., 1986. Mem. NAFE, Women in Internat. Security. Democrat. Jewish. Office: Found for Middle East Peace 555 13 St NW #800 Washington DC 20004

PRESSLEY, JOYCE CAROLYN, clinical research analyst; b. Edneyville, N.C., Jan. 11, 1953; d. Merrimon Lewis and Barbara Lee (Gilliam) P. A.B. in Chemistry, Psychology, U. N.C., 1975; M.P.H. in Health Adminstrn., U. S.C., 1980. Asst. dir. emergency med. service Centralina Council of Govts., Charlotte, N.C., 1976-78; dir. emergency med. services Area IV EMS Program, Research Triangle, N.C., 1980-81; clin. research analyst Duke U., Durham, N.C., 1981—; bd. dirs. Carolina Cinema Corp.; mem. Triangle Cultural Arts Com. Author abstracts; contbr. articles to profl. jours. Docent bd. dirs. N.C. Mus. Art, Raleigh, 1984-85, chmn. library com.; del. N.C. Rep. Party, Chapel Hill, 1976-78. Acad. trainee HEW, 1978-80. Mem. Am. Heart Assn., S.C. Student Pub. Health Assn. (pres. 1978-79), Triangle Cultural Arts Com., N.C. Art Soc., Duke Faculty Club, LWV. Club: Duke Mgmt. Avocations: tennis, art. Office: Duke U Box 3860 Durham NC 27710

PRESSMAN, LISA JO, entrepreneur; b. Brookline, Mass., Jan. 7, 1963; d. Larry and Barbara (Karas) P. Student, Pedigree Inst., 1981. Owner Grooming by Lisa, Lynn, Mass., 1981—, Las Vegas East Casino, Lynn, 1983—; pres., owner TLC Videos Inc., Lynn, 1987—. Sponsor Girls Club Career Exploration Program, Lynn, 1982—; advisor North Shore Animal Relief Assn., Swampscott, Mass., 1983; pres. Am. Field Service Internat. and Intercultural Program, Lynn and N.Y.C., 1981—; advisor fireworks com. Muscular Dystrophy Assn., Lynn and Danvers, Mass., 1986-88. Recipient Citizenship award City of Lynn. Mem. North Shore C. of C., Mass. Dog Groomers Assn., Nat. Dog Groomers Assn., Nat. Fedn. Ind. Businesses. Democrat. Jewish. Home and Office: 30 Red Rock St Lynn MA 01902

PRESSMAN, THELMA, microwave company executive, consultant; b. N.Y.C., Apr. 10, 1921; d. William and Ida (Neckrich) Rosenson; m. Morris Pressman, May 17, 1942; children: Paul, Richard. Student, UCLA, 1073-77. Cert. coll. instr., Calif. Supr. new product testing Waste King Corp., Los Angeles, 1959-69; cons. Microwave div. Amana Corp., 1969-77; pres., owner Microwave Cooking Ctr., Encino, Calif., 1969—; dir. consumer edn. and services Sanyo Electric, Inc., 1971-87; instr., cookware designer Microwave Cooking Ctr., Encino, 1969—; microwave instr. Calif. State U., Northridge; currently spokesperson for Procter & Gamble Bounty Microwave Paper Towel, The Glass Packaging Inst. Author: The Art of Microwave Cooking, 1983 (selected by Library of Congress to be used as talking book for the blind, 1984), Microwave Cooking/Meals in Minutes, 1982, Microwave Magic, 1985, The Great Microwave Dessert Book, 1985, 365 Ways to Cook in Your Microwave, 1989; also New Product Cookbooks for Sears Roebuck & Co., 1977—; microwave columnist Bon Appetit mag., 1979-82; articles for newspapers and mags. throughout U.S. Mem. Mayor's Adv. Coun., L.A., 1979, Hadassah Club, Beverly Hills. Recipient trophy Sanyo Electric, Inc., 1985. Mem. Internat. Microwave Power Inst. (editor jour. 1975-77), Elec. Women's Round Table (pres. 1978-79), Am. Women in Radio and TV, Internat. Assn. Cooking Profls., AFTRA. Home and Office: 2193 La Paz Palm Springs CA 92264

PRESTAGE, JEWEL LIMAR, political scientist; b. Hutton, La., Aug. 12, 1931; d. Brudis L. and Sallie Bell (Johnson) Limar; m. James J. Prestage, Aug. 12, 1953; children—Terri, James, Eric, Karen, Jay. B.A., So. U., Baton Rouge, 1951; M.A., U. Iowa, 1952, Ph.D., 1954. Assoc. prof. polit. sci. Prairie View (Tex.) Coll., 1954-55, 56; assoc. prof. polit. sci. So. U., 1956-57, 58-62, prof., 1962—, chairperson dept., 1965-83, dean pub. policy and urban affairs, 1983-89; honors prof. of polit. sci. Banneker Honors Coll. at Prairie View U., 1989—; Chairperson La. adv. com. to U.S. Commn. on Civil Rights, 1975—; mem. nat. adv. council on women's ednl. programs U.S. Dept. Edn., 1980—; vis. prof. U. Iowa, 1987-88. Author: (with M. Githens) A Portrait of Marginality: Political Behavior of the American Woman, 1976; contbr. articles to profl. jours. Rockefeller fellow, 1951-52; NSF fellow, 1964; Ford Found. postdoctoral fellow, 1969-70. Mem. Am. Polit. Sci. Assn. (v.p. 1974-75), So. Polit. Sci. Assn. (pres. 1975-76), Nat. Conf. Black Polit. Scientists (pres. 1976-77), Am. Soc. for Pub. Adminstrn. (pres. La. chpt. 1988-89, mem. nat. exec. coun. 1989-90), Alpha Kappa Alpha. Home: 2145 77th Ave Baton Rouge LA 70807 Office: So Univ PO Box 125 Prairie View TX 77446-0125

PRESTERA, LAURETTA ANNE, newspaper executive; b. Newark, Dec. 15, 1947; d. George Anthony and Carmela (Sallustro) P. BA in Communications, Bridgewater State Coll., 1976; MBA in Mgmt., Fairleigh Dickinson U., 1983. Advt. sales rep. The N.Y. Times, N.Y.C., 1980-81, circulation sales rep., 1981-82, asst. mgr. circulation, 1982-83; home delivery mgr. The N.Y. Times, Torrance, Calif., 1983-84; S.W. mgr. The N.Y. Times, Dallas, 1984-85; west coast mgr. The N.Y. Times, Torrance, 1985-87; nat. sales dir. The N.Y. Times, N.Y., 1987—; treas. The N.Y. Times Distbn. Corp., N.Y. and Calif., 1984—. Recipient Pub. award The N.Y. Time, 1984. Mem. People for Ethical Treatment of Animals, San Francisco SPCA, L.A. SPCA, Cal-Western Circulation Mgrs., Am. Newspapers Pubs. Assn. Roman Catholic.

PRESTI, SUSAN MARIE, international trade consulting company executive; b. Poughkeepsie, N.Y., Feb. 6, 1959; d. Frank Patrick and Janet Marie (Vizdos); m. James Earl Woolford, Aug. 14, 1982, (div. Dec. 1986). BA in Polit. Sci. and Psychology, U. N.C., 1979; M Pub. Affairs, Princeton U., 1983. Intern Office of Senator Moynihan, Wash., 1979; project dir. N.C. Ctr. for Pub. Policy Research, Raleigh, N.C., 1980-81; intern Coun. on Fgn. Rels., N.Y., 1982; Presdl. mgmt. intern U.S. Dept. of Commerce, Washington; assoc. St. Maxens & Co., Washington, 1985-89, v.p., 1989—. Contbr. articles to profl. publs. Note, high school awards and merit scholarships are not included per Marquis style. Democrat. Office: St Maxens & Co 1140 Connecticut Ave NW Washington DC 20036

PRESTON, CECILIA MARIE RODGERS, information scientist, research consultant; b. Phila., May 16, 1954; d. Robert J. and Katherine J. (Semko) Rodgers; m. David J. Preston, May 20, 1978. BA, Glassboro State Coll., 1980; M Libr. Info. Scis., Rutgers U., 1983. Media specialist Brookdale Community Coll., Lincroft, Calif., 1978-82; info. specialist FMC Cen. Engring. Lab., Santa Clara, Calif., 1983-87; pres. Strategic & Competitive Rsch., Ventura, Calif., 1988—. Mem. Am. Soc. for Info. Scis. (pres. San Francisco Bay chpt. 1985-87), Assn. Ind. Info. Profls. (sec. bd. dirs. 1989—), Spl. Librs. Assn. Office: Strategic-Competitive Rsch PO Box 7817 Ventura CA 93006

PRESTON, DEBORAH, telephone company executive; b. Bronx, Nov. 21, 1953; d. Philip and Shirley (Loeb) Korn; m. Jay Wilson Preston. BA in Math., York U., 1977, MA in Math., 1979; MBA, Columbia U., 1983. Tchr. Greenwich (Conn.) Acad., 1979-81; office mgr. Ronan (Mont.) Telephone Co., 1983-87, v.p., 1988—. Bd. dirs., chmn., Mont. Folkhop, Ronan, 1989—; vice-chmn. Kicking Horse Job Corps Ctr., Community Rels. Com. Democrat. Jewish. Home and Office: Ronan Telephone Co 312 Main St Ronan MT 59864

PRESTON, FRANCES W., performing rights organization executive; children: Kirk, David, Donald. Hon. degree, Lincoln (Ill.) Coll. With BMI (Broadcast Music Inc.), Nashville, 1958—, v.p., 1964-85; sr. v.p. performing rights BMI (Broadcast Music Inc.), N.Y.C., 1985, exec. v.p., chief exec. officer, 1986, pres., chief exec. officer, 1986—, also bd. dirs. Mem. Film, Entertainment and Music Commn. Adv. Council State of Tenn., Leadership Nashville, John Work Meml. Found.; trustee Country Music Found., Inc.; mem. Commn. on White House Record Library, Carter adminstrn., Pres.'s Panama Canal Study Com., Carter adminstrn.; bd. dirs. Rock & Roll Hall of Fame; founding mem. Black Music Assn.; mem. adminstrv. council Confedn. of Internat. Socs. of Authors and Composers; v.p. Nat. Music Council; bd. dirs. Peabody Awards; hon. trustee Nat. Acad. Popular Music. Recipient Women's Equity Action League Achievement award; named to Gospel Music Hall of Fame. Mem. Country Music Assn. (life mem. bd. dirs., past chmn., past pres., Irving Waugh Award of Excellence), Nashville Symphony Assn. (past sec., bd. dirs.), Nat. Acad. Rec. Arts and Scis. (past bd. dirs. Nashville chpt.), Nashville Songwriters Assn. (life mem.), Gospel Music Assn. (life mem. bd., past chmn., past pres.), Am. Women in Radio and TV (past bd. dirs.). Presbyterian. Lodge: Rotary (1st woman mem. Nashville club). Office: Broadcast Music Inc 320 W 57th St New York NY 10019

PRESTON, LOYCE ELAINE, educator; b. Texarkana, Ark., Feb. 25, 1929; d. Harvey Martin and Florence (Whitlock) P.; student Texarkana Jr. Coll., 1946-47; B.S., Henderson State Tchrs. Coll., 1950; certificate in social work La. State U., 1952; M.S.W., Columbia U., 1956. Tchr. pub. schs., Dierks, Ark., 1950-51; child welfare worker Ark. Dept. Public Welfare, Clark and Hot Spring counties, 1951-56, child welfare cons., 1956-58; casework dir. Ruth Sch. Girls, Burien, Wash., 1958-60; asst. prof. spl. edn. La. Poly. Inst., Ruston, 1960-63; asst. prof. Northwestern State Coll., Shreveport, La., 1963-73; asst. prof. La. State U., Shreveport, 1973-79; ret., 1979. Chpt. sec. La. Assn. Mental Health, 1965-67, Gov's. adv. council, 1967-70; mem. Mayor's Com. for Community Improvement, 1972-76. Mem. AAUW (dir. Shreveport br. 1963-69), Acad. Cert. Social Workers, Nat. Assn. Social Workers (del. 1964-65, pres. North La. chpt., state-wide com. 1968-69), La Conf. Social Welfare, La. Fedn. Council Exceptional Children (pres. 1970-71), La. Tchrs. Assn. Home: 9609 Hillsboro Dr Shreveport LA 71118

PRESTON, NANCY LYNN, holding company official; b. Sparta, Mich., Feb. 25, 1960; d. Wendell Willis and Dorothy Margaret (Gray) Beuschel; m. Roger Max Preston, July 14, 1984. BA, Mich. State U., 1982; MBA, Western Mich. U., 1987. Petrochem. sales rep. Union Chem. Co., Cin., 1982-83; br. mgmt. trainee Mich. Nat. Bank, Lansing, 1983-84, fin. analyst I, 1984-85, fin. analyst II, 1985-86, budget coord., 1986-87; sr. fin. analyst Capital Holding Corp., Louisville, 1987-88, strategic planning analyst, 1988—. Mem. corp. com. United Way, Louisville, 1987, Fund for Arts, Louisville, 1988. Arnold E. Schneider MBA scholar, 1987. Mem. River City Bus. and Profl. Women, Beta Gamma Sigma, Alpha Mu Alpha. Republican. Lutheran. Home: 1113 Old Harrods Creek Ct Louisville KY 40223 Office: Capital Holding Corp 680 4th Ave Louisville KY 40202

PRESTON, PENNY HATCHER, television personality; b. Harlingen, Tex., Feb. 5, 1953; d. Gilbert Ray and Nora Sue (McLeod) Hatcher; m. Robert Tuck, June 18, 1971 (div. Feb. 1974); m. Charles Richard Preston, Mar. 25, 1983. Radio anchor, TV reporter KFPW-TV 40, Ft. Smith, Ark., 1976-77; weekend anchor assignment editor KTVP-TV 29, Fayetteville, Ark., 1977-80; weekend anchor, bur. chief KLMN-TV 24, Fayetteville, Ark., 1980-81; investigative reporter KTHV-Channel 11 TV, Little Rock, 1981-83; reporter Sta. WTVF-TV, Nashville, 1983-85; med. reporter KJRH-TV 2, Tulsa, 1985; news dir., news and sports anchor Sta. KTVT-TV, Ft. Worth, 1985—; guest lectr. journalism U. Ark., Little Rock, 1982. Recipient 1st place feature reporting award Ark. AP, 1983, Outstanding Achievement award Ark. UPI, 1983, Disting. Svc. award U. Ark.-Little Rock, 1983. Mem. World Tae Kwon Do Assn., Sigma Delta Chi, Kappa Tau Alpha. Home: 1904 Savoy Dr #178 Arlington TX 76006 Office: KTVT-Channel 11 5233 Bridge St Fort Worth TX 76103

PRESTON, SUSAN JEAN, university official, writer, journalist; b. Syracuse, N.Y., Dec. 3, 1950; d. Robert John and Jean Lois (Johnson) P. BA in English, Bucknell U., 1972. Reporter Herald-Jour./Am., Syracuse, 1972-77; press sec. U.S. Ho. of Reps., Washington, 1977-78; journalist Newhouse News Svc., Washington, 1978-81; dir. community rels. United Way Cen. N.Y., Syracuse, 1981-86; dir. corp. communications Sta. WCNY-TV-FM, Syracuse, 1986-89; sr. pub. info. coord. U. Medicine and Dentistry N.J., Newark, 1989—. Bd. dirs. Am. Heart Assn., 1986-88, Jr. League, Syracuse and Washington, 1976-83, Urban Ministry, 1984-87, Anorexia-Nervosa Support, 1984-86, Cen. N.Y. coun. Girl Scouts U.S.A., 1988-90; alumni class pres., regional admissions rep. Bucknell U.; community initiatives vol. United Way Cen. N.Y., 1987-90; pub. rels. chmn. CONTACT, 1987-90; mem. exec. com. Transitional Living Svcs., 1987-90; bd. dirs. United Cerebral Palsy and Handicapped Children's Assn., 1987-90, pres., 1988-90, also others. Recipient Community Svc. award Am. Heart Assn., 1986, Onondaga County Child Care Coun., 1988, advt. and promotion awards PBS, 1988, merit award Syracuse Advt. Club, 1989, Enable Pres.'s award, 1990. Mem. Bucknell U. Alumni Assn. (bd. dirs. 1981-87), LWV (bd. dirs. 1983-84), Mortar Bd. Roman Catholic. Office: U Medicine and Dentistry NJ 30 Bergen St Newark NJ 07107

PRESTON, WENDY ANN, research pharmacist; b. Oneonta, N.Y., July 17, 1956; d. Keith Gerald and Cynthia Mary (Wescott) P. BS, Albany Coll. Pharmacy, 1979; PhD, Purdue U., 1984. Registered pharmacist, N.Y. Rsch. pharmacist Lederle Labs. div. Am. Cyanamid Co., Pearl River, N.Y., 1984-87, group leader Lederle Labs. div., 1987—. Contbr. articles to profl. jours. Vol. Rockland County Jail Ministry, New City, N.Y., 1986-87; mem. Nat. Right to Life Com., Inc., Washington, 1986—; bd. dirs. Rockland Pregnancy Counseling Ctr., 1986—, chair, 1989—. USP fellow U.S. Pharmacopeial Conv., 1983-84. Mem. Am. Assn. Pharm. Scientists, Am. Pharm. Assn., Lederle Employees Recreation Assn. Winter Tennis (pres. 1987-88). Republican. Baptist. Home: 8 Lenox Ct #804 Suffern NY 10901 Office: Lederle Labs div Am Cyanamid Co N Middletown Rd Pearl River NY 10965

PRESTON-STUBBS, TISH, health organization specialist; b. Alexandria, Va., Mar. 12, 1952; d. George W. and Mary Alice (Barrett) Preston; m. James W. Stubbs, Jr., Nov. 6, 1982. BA, Mich. State U., 1974; MA, Wayne State U., 1978. Cert. DDI instr. Tchr. Waterford (Mich.) Twp. Schs.; mgr. edn. and tng. Riverside Osteo. Hosp., Trenton, Mich.; dir. edn. and tng. Akron (Ohio) City Hosp.; sr. assoc. Henry Ford Health System, Detroit. Instr. Smoke Stoppers. Mem. NAACP (life), Am. Soc. for Edn. and Tng., Mich. Soc. for Edn. and Tng., Mich. Soc. for Healthcare Edn. and Tng., Assn. for Quality and Participation, Mich. Women's Found. (bd. trustees 1989—). Office: 31780 Telegraph Rd Ste 2 Birmingham MI 48010

PRESTRIDGE, PAMELA ADAIR, lawyer; b. Delhi, La., Dec. 25, 1945; d. Gerald Wallace Prestridge and Peggy Adair (Arender) Martin. BA, La. Poly. U., 1967; M in Edn., La. State u., 1968, JD, 1973. Bar: U.S. Dist. ct. (mid. dist.) La. 1975, U.S. Dist. Ct. (so. dist.) Tex. 1982, U.S. Ct. Appeals (5th cir.) 1982, U.S. Dist. Ct. (ea. dist.) Tex. 1984. Law clk. to presiding justice La. State Dist. Ct., Baton Rouge, 1973-75; ptnr. Breazeale, Sachse & Wilson, Baton Rouge, 1975-82, Hirsch & Westheimer P.C., Houston, 1982—; bd. dirs. The Actors Workshop, Houston, 1988—. Counselor Big Bros./Big Sisters, Baton Rouge, 1968-70; legal cons., bd. dirs. Lupus Found. Am., Houston, 1984—; bd. dirs. Quota Club, Baton Rouge, 1979-82, Speech and Hearing Found., Baton Rouge, 1981-82; bd. dirs. The Actors Workshop, Houston, 1988—. Named one of Outstanding Young Women Am., 1980; named Outstanding Profl. Woman Houston, 1984. Mem. ABA, La. Bar Assn., Tex. Bar Assn., Houston Bar Assn., Assn. Trial Lawyers Am., Phi Alpha Delta, La. State U. Student Bar Assn. Democrat. Eckankar. Home: 908 Welch Houston TX 77006 Office: Hirsch & Westheimer PC 700 Louisiana #2550 Houston TX 77002

PRESTWIDGE, KATHLEEN JOYCE, biologist, educator, consultant, researcher; b. N.Y.C., Jan. 7, 1927; d. Hubert Lenard and Inez G. (Espin) P. BA, Hunter Coll., 1949; MA, Bklyn. Coll., 1957; PhD, St. John's U., 1970. Jr. high sch. tchr. N.Y.C., 1956-59; instr. to prof. Bronx Community Coll. CUNY, 1959-87, ret., 1987, resident prof., 1987-90; mem. adv. bd. Community Rev. CUNY Faculty, 1980—. Author: (poems) Wisdom Teeth, 1973, Bits and Pieces, 1976; sci. columnist N.Y. Voice, 1982-85. Pres. bd. dirs. Hodson Community Ctr., Inc., Bronx, 1981—. Fellow N.Y. Acad. Scis.; mem. Internat. Women's Writers Guild, Sigma Xi. Home: 162-01 77th Rd Flushing NY 11366 Office: Bronx Community Coll 181 St & Univ Ave Bronx NY 10453

PRESTWOOD, DEBORAH LYNN, air traffic control specialist; b. Greensboro, N.C., Sept. 5, 1952; d. Carey Cleve Caudill and Muriel Elaine (Taylor) Caudill Johnson; (div. 1980); children: Curtis E. Jr., Carrie L. BS summa cum laude, Embry-Ridle Aero. U., 1989. Lic. pilot. Personnel clk. Carter Machinery, Salem, Va., 1972-74; sec. VA Hosp., Biloxi, Miss., 1976-78; adminstrv. specialist Miss. Army Nat. Guard, Gulfport, 1978-84; air traffic control specialist FAA, Gulfport, 1984—; chmn. facility adv. bd. FAA, 1988-89. Pres., Gulfport Ladies Ch. Softball League, 1983-84; mem. Grace Meml. Bapt. Singles coun., 1986-89. Mem. Aero Club (sec., v.p., pres. 1982-84), Aviation Explorers (adv. 1989-), Nat. Air Traffic Contrs. Assn. (sec. local chpt.). Republican.

PRETLOW, CAROL JOCELYN, fashion and communications consultant; b. Salisbury, Md., Nov. 9, 1946; d. Kenneth H. and Vivian Virginia (Hughes) P. B.A., Fisk U., 1976; M.A., Norfolk State U., 1982; postgrad. Antioch Law Sch., 1984-85, Am. U., 1988—. Fashion columnist The Smithfield Times (Va.), 1977-80; talk show hostess Sta. WAVY-TV, 1978-81; fashion editor Tidewater Life Mag., 1979; reporter, asst. news dir. Sta. WNSB News, Norfolk, Va., 1980-81; press sec. Com. to Elect Fred D. Thompson Jr. Treas. Isle of Wight County, 1981; ind. fashion cons., Smithfield, Va., 1982—, publicist, 1987—; fashion reporter Sta. WRAP Radio, Norfolk, 1986-87; fashion coord. Theresa's Boutique, Franklin, Va., 1989—; adj. prof. communication Paul D. Camp Community Coll., Franklin, 1986-87; entertainment fashion editor Citizens Press Am. Newspaper, Portsmouth, Va.; fashion publicist, cons. Carrie's House of Fashion, Smithfield, Va.; Va. Coord. Sesquitricentennial Celebration, Isle of Wight County, 1984. Home: RR3 Box 697 Smithfield VA 23430

PREUSS, EVA SILVIA, software distributing company executive; b. Solothurn, Switzerland, Mar. 17, 1955; came to U.S., 1986; d. Helmut Robert and Ruth (von Felten) P. MBA, U. St. Gallen (Switzerland), 1979, PhD in Bus. Adminstrn., 1986. Cons. Walter G. Abeggler & Ptnrs., Zurich, Switzerland, 1979-81; mktg. mgr. Albay AG, Zurich, 1981-82; cons. Zurich and Munich, 1982-85; product mgr. Ansa Software, Belmont, Calif., 1986-87; dir. datebase product mgmt. Borland Internat., Belmont, 1987-89, mng. dir. European distbn., 1989—. Office: Borland Internat 1800 Green Hills Rd Scotts Valley CA 95066

PREVOST, MARY LYNN, lawyer, law association executive; b. Decatur, Ill.; d. Raymond Lynn and Edith Lydia (Munro) Braden; children: Denise, Nancy, Jeffrey. BA, Evergreen State Coll., 1979; JD, U. Puget Sound, 1982. Bar: Wash. 1982. Legal intern Owens, Weaver, Davies, Mackie & Lyman, Olympia, Wash., 1981; mgmt. analyst State of Wash., Olympia, 1982; staff cons. Office Fin. Mgmt., State of Wash., Olympia, 1982-85, exec. policy analyst, 1985-86, on spl. assignment for comparable worth study Office of Gov., 1985-87; exec. policy analyst Office of Gov. State of Wash., Olympia, 1986-88; exec. dir. Conf. Western Attys. Gen., San Francisco, 1988—; mem. adv. com. Highline Community Coll. Legal Asst. Program, Midway, Wash., 1977-78; student coordinator Wash. Bar Assn. Conf. on Adoption Legislation, Tacoma, 1981. Program coordinator Rotary Internat. Dist. Conf., Olympia, 1980. Evergreen Found. scholar, 1979. Mem. Wash. Bar Assn. (legis. com. 1987-89, Centennial com. 1988, task force on minorities in the profession 1988), ABA, Governmental Lawyers (pres. 1986-87), Wash. Women Lawyers. Methodist. Office: Conf Western Attys Gen 121 2d St 4th Fl San Francisco CA 94105

PRICE, ALICE I., service company executive; b. Charlottesville, Va., Feb. 3, 1949; d. Robert Huntington and Alice Isabel (Valle) Knight; 1 child, Rita Michael. BA, UCLA, 1982, MBA, 1982. Owner, mgr. Rocky Mt. Housing, Denver, 1972-74; organizational cons., Los Angeles, 1977-82, Don't Ask Computer Software, Inc., Los Angeles, 1982-83; lit. agt. Peter Livingston Assocs., Boulder, Colo., 1983-88; cons. ABC TV, Los Angeles, 1978—, Lorimar Prodns., Los Angeles, 1977-79, Foote, Cone & Belding/Honig, Los Angeles, 1980, Microsystems Cons. Group, Los Angeles, 1980-82; guest lectr. Colo. Lang. Arts Soc., 1986; vol. writing tchr. Boulder County Pub. Schs., 1984—; fed. and state election judge, 1986-87; expert witness in publ. cases, 1987. Co-author: (with Gillian Rice) Together Again, 1987; contbg. author: The World's Great Contemporary Poems, 1981; contbg. author, editor: How to Get a Man to Make a Commitment, 1985, Personal and Social Responsibility, 1989; editor: Gray Eagles, 1986, Rebecca Wood's Encyclopedia of Whole Foods, 1986, Professional Design with Quark XPress, 1990; seminar leader: "How to Get your Book Published, 1987—. Dem. del., Colo., 1972, 76; Colo. State Arbitrator 20th Judicial Dist., 1988—. Mem. Ind. Lit. Agts. Assn., Inc., Am. Film Inst., Colo. Chautauqua Assn., Denver Art Mus., Boulder C. of C., Boulder Hist. Soc., U. Denver Writing Inst. (bd. dirs.), Colo. Authors' League (bd. dirs.), Denver Woman's Press Club, Sierra Club, Phi Beta Kappa, Psi Chi, Pi Gamma Mu. Club: Pres.'s. Office: 2978 Eagle Way Boulder CO 80301

PRICE, ANDREA RENEE, hospital administrator; b. Flint, Mich., June 16, 1959; d. Clifford and Clara (Jones) P. BA in Lit., Sci. and Arts, U. Mich., 1981; MHA, Tulane U., 1984. Adminstrv. resident D.C. Hosp. Assn., Washington, 1983-84; mgr. ambulatory care services DataCom Systems Corp., Washington, 1984-85; admission/registration interviewer George Washington Hosp., Washington, 1985; adminstrv. fellow Children's Hosp., Washington, 1985-86, asst. to exec. v.p., 1986, acting dir. planning and mktg., 1986-87, asst. v.p. adminstrv. svcs., 1986-89, v.p. profl. svcs., 1989—; speaker in field; preceptor George Washington Sch. Bus., 1987; presiding officer Am. Coll. Healthcare Execs., Chgo., 1988, pres., bd. dirs., chair, corp. sponsor women's forum, 1987—. Mem. Lupus Found., Washington, 1983—. Recipient Excellence in Healthcare Industry award Bus. Exchange Network, Washington, 1987. Mem. Am. Pub. Health Assn., Am. Soc. Healthcare Risk Mgmt., Nat. Assn. Health Services Execs. (bd. dirs. D.C. chpt., sec. 1987, membership chair, mem. program com.), Soc. Ambulatory Care Profls., Alpha Kappa Alpha, Zeta Chi Omega. Democrat. Baptist. Home: 47 Mich Ave NE Washington DC 20002 Office: Children's Hosp Nat Med Ctr 111 Mich Ave NW Washington DC 20010

PRICE, ANGELA LYNN, production professional, former non-commissioned military officer; b. Shelbyville, Tenn., Sept. 22, 1965; d. Larry D. and Dorothy Louise (McCart) Ferrell; m. Rolan Michael Price. Student, U. Md., 1986. Track vehicle repairer U.S. Army D Co. 4th Support BN, Nurberg, W. Germany, 1984-87; maintenance supr. U.S. B Co. 24th Support, Ft. Stewart, Ga., 1987-90; with prodn. dept. Am. Nat. Can Co., Shelbyville, Tenn., 1990—. Author: (poem) New Am., 1987, World of Poetry, 1988. Recipient NCO Initiative award, 1987. Republican. Baptist. Home: PO Box 3616 Fort Stewart GA 31314

PRICE, BARBARA ANN, educator; b. Detroit, Apr. 21, 1951; d. Leon Frederick and Pearl (Weiner) Block; m. Kenneth Hanley Price, July 8, 1973; 1 child, Benjamin Jacob. BA, Mich. State U., 1972; MEd, Tex. Woman's U., 1978. Cert. reading specialist. Tchr. high sch. Eaton Rapids (Mich.) High Sch., 1972-73; tchr. jr. high sch. Arlington (Tex.) Ind. Sch. Dist., 1973-80, 87—; tchr. Tarrant County Jr. Coll., Ft. Worth, 1983-86; tchr. middle sch. Ft. Worth Ind. Sch. Dist., 1986-87. Mem. AAUW, Internat. Reading Assn., NEA, Tex. State Tchrs. Assn., Arlington Reading Assn. Democrat. Jewish. Home: 2109 Rocky Branch Arlington TX 76012 Office: Shackelford Jr High 2000 N Fielder Arlington TX 76013

PRICE, CAROLE RUNYAN, hospital administrator; b. Covina, Calif., Feb. 3, 1937; d. Willard Ahab and Maude H. (Brubaker) Runyan; divorced; children: Devin, Jennifer. BA, Pomona Coll., 1958; JD, U. Santa Clara, 1977. Tchr. West Covina (Calif.) Sch. Dist., 1958-61, Mill Valley (Calif.) Sch. Dist., 1961-62, San Carlos (Calif.) Elem. Sch. Dist., 1962-63; sec. Stanford (Calif.) U., 1969-71, legal asst., 1973-79, assoc. staff counsel, 1979-81; asst., then assoc. dir. Stanford U. Hosp., 1981-88; dir. physician svcs. and risk mgmt. Stanford U. Hosp., 1988—; lectr. Stanford U. Sch. Medicine, 1983—. Contbr. articles to profl. publs. Mem. Am. Soc. Healthcare Risk Mgmt., Assn. Western Hosps., Healthcare Forum, Am. Pub. Health Assn. Democrat. Office: Stanford U Hosp 300 Pasteur Dr Stanford CA 94305

PRICE, DEBRA, associate manager; b. Elizabeth, N.J., Nov. 4, 1958; d. Clifford Thomas and Myrtle Edith (Kuhlmann) P. BA in Psychology, Douglass Coll., 1980; MS in Indsl. Relations/Human Resource, Rutgers U., 1982. Intern human resources Johnson & Johnson, New Brunswick, N.J., 1980, Supermarkets Gen. Corp., Woodbridge, N.J., 1980-81; research asst. Ctr. for Human Resources Rutgers U., New Brunswick, 1981-82; methods analyst AT&T Bell Labs. Corp. Methods, Short Hills, N.J., 1982-83; asst. fin. svc. specialist AT&T Bell Labs. Fin., Short Hills, 1983-84; compensation analyst, salary adminstr. AT&T Bell Labs, Short Hills, 1984-87, supr. working funds, 1987-89; assoc. mgr. AT&T, Basking Ridge, N.J., 1989—. Mem. N.Y.C. Opera Guild, 1988, Union County Arts Soc., Rahway, N.J., 1988, The Nature Conservancy, 1988. Mem. NAFE, N.J. Skin Diving Club, Dosils Scuba Club. Home: 13 Linda Ln Clark NJ 07066 Office: AT&T 295 N Maple Ave Basking Ridge NJ 07920

PRICE, GAIL ELIZABETH, research firm executive; b. Jacksonville, Fla., 1940; d. Roy Melvin Price and Claire Elizabeth (Baxter) Lee; m. William Pershing Geiger (div. 1982); children: Richard, Stuart, Terri; m. Jerome A. Rossman, June 25, 1988. BS, U. Md., 1962. Rsch. asst. CIA, Langley, Va., 1958-62, 70-82, Griffith & Werner, Hollywood, Fla., 1982-84; prin. G. E. Price & Assocs., Ft. Lauderdale, Fla., 1984—. Mem. Exec. Women's Club, Ft. Lauderdale Profl. Women's Club. Republican. Baptist. Office: GE Price & Assocs 2455 E Sunrise Blvd Ste 811 Fort Lauderdale FL 33304-3111

PRICE, HELEN LAURA, life insurance company official; b. Suffield, Conn., Sept. 16, 1930; d. Alexander and Eva (Grabowski) Kosinski; m. Daniel D. Price, Oct. 7, 1950. Grad. high sch., Suffield. Clk.-typist Conn. Light & Power, Enfield, 1949-65; broker Chestnut Realty, Suffield, 1965-67; with Hamilton Standard, Windsor Locks, Conn., 1968-70; claim examiner Conn. Gen. Life Ins. Co., Bloomfield, 1971—; flower arranger The Flower Arrangers, Suffield, 1988-89; constable Town of Suffield, 1988—. Mem. Suffield Dem. Town Com., 1986; fund raiser Dems. for Congress, Suffield, 1986, Dems. for Selectman, Suffield, 1988, 90; del. 6th Congl. Dist., Suffield, 1988, Sheriff's Conv., Suffield, 1990. Home: 261 Halladay Ave Suffield CT 06078 Office: Conn Gen Life Ins Co Hartford CT 06152

PRICE, HOLLISTER ANNE CAWEIN, airline project administrator, interior design consultant; b. Memphis, Feb. 11, 1954; d. Madison Albert Cawein and Billie Jeanne (Roberts) Stewart; m. James H. Price, Jr., Oct. 21, 1978 (div. 1985). BA in Communications and Fine Arts, Memphis State U., 1988. Office mgr. Bruce Motor Co., Memphis, 1975-76; br. mgr. Cen. States Agy., Memphis, 1976-78; facility coord. Fed. Express Corp., Memphis, 1978-86, corp. interior designer, project mgr., 1986—; design cons. Smart Shoppes, Inc., Hardy and Trumann, Ark., 1985-86; Fed. Express dept. coord. interior design student interns Memphis State U. Dept. leader Ch. Sch. Edn. Program, Cen. Ch., 1984-85; mem. Arts Svcs. League for Greater Memphis Area, 1986—; active Very Spl. Arts Coun. for Handicapped, Memphis, 1987—. Mem. Nat. Assn. Female Execs., Duration Club (Memphis), Delta Gamma Alumnae. Republican. Episcopalian. Avocations: scuba diving, horseback riding, biking, antique collecting. Office: Fed Express Corp Dept 1870 PO Box 727 Memphis TN 38194

PRICE, JACQUELINE S., small business owner; b. L.A., Oct. 25, 1952; d. Fred R. and Sonia (Elmer) Price. AA, Pierce Coll., 1972; BA, Calif. State, Northridge, 1977. Set decorator motion picture industry Hollywood, Calif.; owner Nip It In The Bud, North Hollywood, Calif. Patentee in field. Recipient honors in broadcasting for commls. and news writing; grantee in behavior and communications. Mem. AFL-CIO, Burbank C. of C., Environ. com. Burbank, Acad. TV Arts and Scis., Am. Hypnosis Assn. Home: 12706 Califa St North Hollywood CA 91607

PRICE, JANIS, medical center administrator; b. N.Y.C.; d. Marvin Howard and Helen (Saks) Davidson; m. H. Laurence Price, May 28, 1972; children: Sarah Lynn, David Matthew. BA, SUNY, Brockport, 1972. Accredited admitting mgr. Admissions clk. U. Mich. Med. Ctr., Ann Arbor, 1972-74, patient rep., 1974-76, admissions supr., 1976-82, asst. admitting mgr., 1982-85, admissions mgr.-psychiatry, 1985-89, asst. dir. psychiatry, 1989—; speaker in field. Contbr. articles to profl. jours. Recipient JFK Good Citizenship award Reader's Digest, 1968. Mem. Nat. Assn. Hosp. Admissions Mgrs. (nomination chmn. 1989—, Doris Gleason Publ. award 1989), Hosp. Admitting Mgrs. of S.E. Mich. (pres. 1985-89, newsletter editor 1989—), Med. Group Mgmt. Assn., Acad. Practice Assembly, Adminstrs. in Acad. Psychiatry (contbg. newsletter editor). Jewish.

PRICE, JEANNINE ALLEENICA, clinical psychologist; b. Cleve., Oct. 29, 1949; d. Q. Q. and Lisa Denise (Wilson) Ewing; m. T. R. Price, Sept. 2, 1976. BS, Western Res. U., 1969; MS, Vanderbilt U., 1974; MBA, Stanford U., 1985. Cert. alcoholism counselor, Calif. Health Service coordinator Am. Profile, Nashville, 1970-72; exec. dir. Awareness Concept, San Jose, Calif., 1977-80; mgr. employee assistance program Nat. Semiconductor, Santa Clara, Calif., 1980-81; mgmt. cons. employee assistant programs; counselor Awareness Concept, 1989—. Mem. Gov.'s Adv. Council Child Devel. Programs. Mem. Am. Bus. Women's Assn., NAFE, AAUW, Coalition Labor Women, Calif. Assn. Alcohol counselors, Almaca. Author: Smile a Little, Cry a Lot, Gifts of Love, Reflection in the Mirror, The Light at the Top of the Mountain, The Dreamer, The Girl I Never Knew, An Act of Love, Walk Toward the Light.

PRICE, JOANNE, financial executive; b. Louisville, May 23, 1938; m. James E. Price, Feb. 10, 1979; children: Rosemarie, Donna Jean, James, Robert, John, Elke. BS, U. Md., 1988. Asst. controller Wald, Harkrader, and Ross, Washington; controller The Sporting Club, McLean, Va.; fin. dir. Words and Co., Washington; Pres. Hansel and Gretel Nurseries and Child Devel. Ctr.; v.p. fin. ops. Info. Resources Mgmt. cons. Corp. Active St. Labre Indian Sch. Mem. Nat. Assn. Legal Adminstrs., Am. Inst. Profl. Bookkeepers, Univ. Md. Alumni Assn. (charter), Phi Kappa Phi, Alpha Sigma Lambda, Century Club. Presbyterian. Home: 15301 Surrey House Way Centreville VA 22020 Office: Cherrydale 6072 Franconia Rd Alexandria VA 22310

PRICE, LEIGH, banker; b. Malin, Oreg., Feb. 6, 1941; d. Clarence Loraine and Nina Ellen (Kamping) P.; m. Richard D. McNabb, 1958 (div. 1963); children: Brian, Leigh Ann; m. Ronald D. Stein, 1969 (div. 1988). BA magna cum laude in Psychology, UCLA, 1980, MBA in Mgmt., 1982. Analyst Standard Oil Co., Tulsa, 1967-69; programmer/analyst Honeywell, Inc., Mpls., 1969-73; sr. systems analyst Fabri-Tek, Inc., Mpls., 1974-77; pres. Price & Assocs., Mpls., 1978-79; sr. cons. MRG Assocs., L.A., 1981-83; exec. v.p., chief operating officer Prescription Health Svcs., L.A., 1984-85; v.p., mgr. First Interstate Bank, L.A., 1985-88; v.p. Md. Nat. Bank, Balt., 1988—. Del. Minn. Dem. Conv., 1972; chmn. Parent/Sch. Bd. Coun., Edina, Minn., 1975; pres. Friends of L.A. Opera, 1980-81; v.p. Guild Opera Co., L.A., 1983-85; exec. v.p. Opera Guild So. Calif., 1984-85, pres., 1985-87, parliamentarian, 1987-88. Unitarian. Office: MNC Info Svcs PO Box 987 Baltimore MD 21203

PRICE, LINDA ANNE, mortgage company administrator, sales associate; b. Frederick, Md., May 13, 1961; d. John Olan and Ruby (Hanson) P. BA, Western Md. Coll., 1983; postgrad., U. Md., 1989. Settlement adminstr. Standard Fed. Savs., Gaithersburg, Md., 1984-85; loan processor Ryland Mortgage Co., Columbia, Md., 1985-86, br. supr., 1986-89, quality assurance mgr., 1989—; sales assoc. Paul Harris Stores, Columbia, 1988-89. Com. mem. div. of camping United Meth. Ch., Balt., 1988. Recipient Morris Unger scholarship Western Md. Coll., 1979. Mem. NAFE, J.C. Bodyworks. Republican. Home: 5035-1 Green Mountain Cir Columbia MD 21044

PRICE, LINDA MARGARET, psychologist, educator; b. Chgo., May 19, 1946; d. Nicholas Aloysius and Lorraine Mary (Consamus) Herrig; m. Donald Allen Price, Jan. 3, 1971. B.S., U. Wis., Stevens Point, 1973; MS, No. Ill. U., DeKalb., 1976; PhD, U. Utah, 1979. Lic. psychologist, Utah. Tchr. lit. Richards High Sch., Tallahassee, Fla., 1973-75; psychologist Granite Mental Health, Salt Lake City, 1979-83, Salt Lake Mental Health, Salt Lake City, 1983-85; pvt. practice Salt Lake City, 1980—; assoc. prof. U. Utah, Salt Lake City, 1985—; cons. Agrophobia Group, Salt Lake City, 1984-85; mem. exec. bd. Norman S. Anderson Award, Salt Lake City, 1990—. U. Nebr. doctoral fellow, Lincoln, 1976. Mem. Am. Psychol. Assn., Utah Psychol. Assn. (bd. dirs. 1982-85, advocacy com.), Utah Soc. Clin. Hypnosis. Home: 1746 E Herbert Ave Salt Lake City UT 84108 Office: 182 S 600 E Ste 203 Salt Lake City UT 84102

PRICE, LUCILE BRICKNER BROWN, retired civic worker; b. Decorah, Iowa, May 31, 1902; d. Sidney Eugene and Cora (Drake) Brickner; B.S., Iowa State U., 1925; M.A., Northwestern U., 1940; m. Maynard Wilson Brown, July 2, 1928 (dec. Apr. 1937); m. 2d, Charles Edward Price, Jan. 14, 1961 (dec. Dec. 1983). Asst. dean women Kans. State U., Manhattan, 1925-28; mem. bd. student personnel adminstrn. Northwestern U., 1937-41; personnel research Sears Roebuck & Co., Chgo., 1941-42, overseas club dir. ARC, Eng., Africa, Italy, 1942-45; dir. Child Edn. Found., N.Y.C., 1946-56. Participant 1st and 2d Iowa Humanists Summer Symposiums, 1974, 75. Del. Mid Century White House Conf. on Children and Youth, 1950; mem. com. on program and research of Children's Internat. summer villages, 1952-53; mem. bd. N.E. Iowa Mental Health Ctr., 1959-62, pres. bd., 1960-61; mem. Iowa State Extension Adv. Com., 1973-75; project chmn. Decorah Hist. Dist. (listed Nat. Register Historic Places); trustee Porter House Mus., Decorah, 1966-78, emeritus bd. dirs., 1982—; participant N. Cen. Regional Workshop Am. Assn. State and Local History, Mpls., 1975, Midwest Workshop Hist. Preservation and Conservation, Iowa State U., 1976, 77; mem. Winneshiek County (Iowa) Civil Service Commn., 1978-87; rep. Class of 1940 Northwestern U. Sch. Edn. and Social Policy, 1986-88. Recipient Alumni Merit award Iowa State U., 1975, Cert. of Appreciation Iowa State U. Extension, 1988. Mem. Am. Coll. Personnel Assn., (life), Am. Overseas Assn. (nat. bd.; life), AAUW (life mem., mem. bd. Decorah; recipient Named Gift award 1977), Nat. Assn. Mental Health (del. nat. conf. 1958), Norwegian-Am. Mus. (life, Vesterheim fellow), Winneshiek County Hist. Soc. (life, cert. of appreciation 1984), DAR, Pi Lambda Theta, Chi Omega. Designer, builder house for retirement living. Home: 508 W Broadway Decorah IA 52101

PRICE, MARILYN JEANNE, fund raising and management consultant; b. N.Y.C., Jan. 24, 1948; d. George Franklin and Mary Anastasia (Barnishin) Lawrence; student Temple Bus. Sch., 1964-66; student U. Md., 1973-74; 1 child, Kimberly Jean. Asst. to sr. printing and paper buyer ARC, Washington 1965-67; conf. planner for classified mil. confs. Nat. Security Indsl. Assn., Washington, 1967-69; fund devel. office asst. Nat. Urban Coalition, Washington, 1970; direct mail/membership coordinator Common Cause, Washington, 1970-72; mgr. direct mail fund raising Epilepsy Found. of Am., Washington, 1973-76; exec. v.p. Bruce W. Eberle & Assocs., Vienna, Va., 1977-81; pres. Response Dynamics, Inc., Vienna, Va., 1981-83; v.p. The Best Lists, Inc., Vienna, 1981-83; pres. The Creative Advantage, Inc., Fairfax, Va., 1983—, Creative Mgmt. Services, Inc., Fairfax, 1987—; cons. in field. Asst. to Young Citizens for Johnson, 1964; vol. Hubert Humphrey campaign, 1968, George McGovern campaign, 1972. Recipient Silver Echo award, Direct Mail/Mktg. Assn. Internat. competition for mktg. excellence, 1980. Mem. Nat. Soc. Fund Raisers, Direct Mail Mktg. Assn., Non-Profit Mailers Fedn., Assn. Direct Response Fundraising Council (bd. dirs., treas.), Direct Mktg. Club. Home: 9614 Lindenbrook St Fairfax VA 22031 Office: The Creative Advantage 9401 Lee Hwy Suite 205 Fairfax VA 22031

PRICE, NANCY CHANCE, personnel director; b. Wichita, Kans., Sept. 24, 1953; d. William G. and Doris A. (Blank) Chance; m. Robert J. Price, May 19, 1979 (div. Apr. 1983). Postgrad., Ark. State U., Jonesboro, 1972, U. Ark., Little Rock, 1980. Probation Officer. Caseworker Prosecuting Atty's. Office, Little Rock, 1979, div. head, Hot Check div., 1983; probation officer Pulaski County Mcpl. Court, Little Rock, 1983-85; research cons. Ark. Adult Probation Commn., Little Rock; reg. dir. Mcpl. Court Probation Svcs., Little Rock, 1987--; cons., fundraiser Ark. Special Olympics, Little Rock, 1988. Author: Policy & Procedures Manual for Adult Probation Officers, 1987, Orientation Manual for Vols. in Court, 1988, Community Resource Manual, 1987. Campaign Com. Bill Watt Cpt. Mcpl. Judge, Little Rock, 1983; Chmn. Sid Newcomb Campaign Justice of Peace, Little Rock, 1984; Fundraising Chmn. Congressman Bill Ramsey, Little Rock, 1989; Com. Chmn. Senator Joe Yates Toast & Roast, Little Rock, 1988. Recipient Community Svc. award City of Little Rock, 1984. Mem. Ark. Criminal Justice Assn., Adult Probation & Parole Officers Assn., CAP CASI, Internat. Chili Soc. Democrat. Roman Catholic. Home: 4605 N Hickory North Little Rock AR 72116

PRICE, NANCY P., cellist; b. Sioux City, Iowa, Jan. 10, 1932; d. Axel and Naomi (Swanson) Pierson; m. Phillip Rennick, Oct. 30, 1952 (div. Dec. 1966); m. Robert W. Price, June 17, 1967; children: Lynn, Gaile, Bruce, Nancy Jane. BS in Psychology, Northwestern U., 1957; MA in Library Sci., U. Chgo., 1985. Cellist Gaska String Quartet, South Bend, Ind., 1967—; prin. cellist Elkhart (Ind.) Symphony, 1970-78; cellist South Bend Symphony, 1978—; pvt. tchr. cello. Author various children's books based on songs, 1985. Mem. Am. String Tchrs. Assn., Amateur Chamber Music Soc., Audubon Soc. Democrat. Presbyterian. Office: Oaklawn Ctr 2600 Oakland Ave Elkhart IN 46517

PRICE, PHYLLIS ELIZABETH, insurance executive; b. Blacksburg, Va., June 13, 1949; d. Patrick Henry and Ina Virginia (Graham) P. Student, Radford Coll., 1967-69. Student loan processor U. N.C., Chapel Hill, 1969-71; typist Aetna Life and Casualty, Knoxville, Tenn., 1971-76, supr., 1976-83; from clk to supr. Aetna Life and Casualty, Atlanta, 1983-88, supt., 1988—. Pub. poet. Office: Aetna Life and Casualty 9 Piedmont Ctr Atlanta GA 30505

PRICE, REINE IRENE, educational administrator; b. Natchitoches, La., Sept. 6, 1950; d. Robert Lee and Neva Lucille (Uhl) Merriam; m. Michael Clinton Price, Aug. 11, 1973; children—Autumn Irene, Gabriel Clinton. B.S. in Edn., Bowling Green State U., 1971; M.S. in Edn., U. Central Ark., 1982; MEd in gifted edn. U. Ark., 1986; MS in Ednl. Leadership U. Cen. Ark., 1989. Cert. elem. tchr., Ark., cert. biology, gifted and reading specialist, cert. elem. prin. and supr. Tchr. Oregon Pub. Schs., Ohio, 1971-72, Immaculate Conception Sch., North Little Rock, Ark., 1974-77; dir. plan edn. North Little Rock Br., 1973-74; reading specialist U. Central Ark., Conway, 1982-83; reading specialist Dardanelle Pub. Schs., Ark., 1983-84, coordinator spl. services, 1984-85; prin. East End Elem. Sch., Bigelow, Ark., 1985-87, Wilson Elem. Sch. Little Rock Dist., 1987—; tutor, Mayflower, Ark., 1981-83; cons. in field; program developer, coordinator Spl. services 1st Gifted Preschool tied to pub. sch. in Ark., 1984-85; mem. Ark. Gov.'s Sch. Staff, summer 1986. Ch. organist Brumley Baptist Ch., Conway, Ark., 1976-81, youth dir., 1977-80. Recipient Martha Ann Jones Service award Arkawasans for Gifted and Talented Edn., 1989. Mem. Internat. Reading Assn., North Central Reading Assn. Council (sec. 1985-86), Agate Council Educators, Prin.'s Roundtable, Ark. Assn. Ednl. Adminstrs., Ark. Gifted and Talented Edn. (bd. dirs., v.p. membership 1986—), Assn. Supervision and Curriculum Devel., Women's Missionary Union (pres. 1978-79, sec. 1979-80), Kappa Delta Pi, Phi Delta Kappa. Democrat. Lodge: Order Eastern Star. Avocations: sewing; needlework; crafts; boating; reading. Home: RR 1 Box 152 Houston AR 72070 Office: Wilson Elem Sch 4015 Stannus Rd Little Rock AR 72204

PRICE, RENATA FRANCES, government official; b. Allentown, Pa., Aug. 28, 1946; d. Wilbur Francis and Patricia Ann (Maynes) P. BS, U.S. Mil. Acad., 1968; MBA, Fairleigh Dickinson U., 1983. Commd. 2d lt. U.S. Army, 1968, advanced through grades to capt., 1970; resigned, 1977; mech. engr. U.S. Army Armament Rsch. Devel. and Engring. Ctr., Picatinny Arsenal, N.J., 1977-83, system project engr., 1983-85, system project officer, 1985-87, chief anti-armor br., 1987-88, chief tank ammunition br., 1988-89; dep. dir. Close Combat Armament Ctr., 1989—; U.S. subgroup leader Working Party with U.K., 1981-85; U.S. armament chmn. Rsch. Program with Fed. Republic Germany, 1982-85; U.S. rep. NATO Panel Armament Experts, Brussels, 1983-85; presentor, speaker in field; chmn. Fed. Women's Program Com., 1988-89. Patentee in field. Recipient Rsch. and Devel. Achievement award U.S. Army, 1980, Comdr.'s award Armament Rsch. Devel. and Engring. Ctr., 1987. Mem. Am. Def. Preparedness Assn., Federally Employed Women, NOW (del. nat. conf. 1988-90, v.p. Morris County chpt. 1989). Office: US Army Armament Rsch Devel Attention SMCAR-CC Picatinny Arsenal NJ 07806-5000

PRICE, ROSALIE PETTUS, artist; b. Birmingham, Ala.; d. Erle and Ellelee (Chapman) Pettus; A.B., Birmingham-So. Coll., 1935; M.A., U. Ala., Tuscaloosa, 1967; m. William Archer Price, Oct. 3, 1936. Painter in watercolors, casein, oil and acrylic; one man shows include: Samford U., 1964, Birmingham Mus. of Art, 1966, 73, 82-83, Town Hall Gallery, 1968, 75, South Central Bell, 1977; instr. Birmingham (Ala.) Mus. Art, 1967-70, Samford U., 1969-70. Bd. dirs. Birmingham Mus. of Art, 1950-54, vice chmn., 1950-51; bd. trustees Birmingham Music Club, 1956-66, rec. sec., 1958-62; mem. Springfield (Mo.) Art Mus. Recipient purchase award Watercolor USA, 1972; named to Watercolor USA Honor Soc., 1986. Mem. Nat. Watercolor Soc., Nat. Soc. Painters in Casein and Acrylic (W. Alden Brown Meml. award 1970, Joseph A. Cain Meml. award 1983), Birmingham Art Assn. (pres. 1947-49, Little House on Linden purchase award 1968), So. Watercolor Soc., Watercolor Soc. Ala. (sec. 1948-49), La. Watercolor Soc., Pi Beta Phi. Episcopalian. Clubs: Jr. League of Birmingham (chmn. art com. 1947-50), Window Box Garden. Home: 300 Windsor Dr Birmingham AL 35209 Office: 2132 20th Ave S Birmingham AL 35223

PRICE, SELMA BROWN, educator; b. Hodges, Ala., Nov. 26, 1915; d. William Daniel and Mamie (Swink) Brown; m. Samuel McGowan Price; children: Samuel M., Alice P. Mcgill. Student, Hackleburg Bus. Coll., Greenwood, S.C., 1937, Peterson's Bus. Coll., Greenwood, S.C., 1937; BA in Edn., Newberry Coll., 1974. Bookkeeper Boyd's Clothing, Greenwood, 1938-42, Western Electric, Balt., 1942-45; sec., treas. Cooner's Inc., Newberry, S.C., 1945-81; tchr. Newberry City Schs., 1975—; part-time position Wal-Mart Store, Inc. Tutor S.C. Literacy Assn., Vocat. Ctr., Newberry, 1980; active Newberry County Family YMCA. Sunday sch. tchr. Mem. AAUW, Hist. Soc., United Daus. Assn., Good Sam Camping Club. Republican. Baptist. Home: PO Box 326 Newberry SC 29108

PRICE, SHERRI ANN, protective services professional; b. Quantico, Va., July 28, 1953; d. J.M. Claunch and Lorraine (Hobein) Coffee; m. Thomas B. Price, Mar. 11, 1978; 1 child, Brian. BS in Law Enforcement, Sam Houston State U., Huntsville, Tex., 1977; M of Liberal Arts, So. Meth. U., 1983. Cert. probation officer Tex. Dep. Office of Sheriff, County of Dallas, 1975-76; adminstrv. asst. Dallas County Criminal Ct. #5, Dallas, 1976-78; investigator Unviersity Park Police Dept., Dallas, 1978-85; supr. Dallas County Adult Probation Dept., 1985—. V.p. Dallas Lawyer's Wives Club, 1990; active Richardson (Tex.) Rep. Women's Club, 1980—, v.p. 1990—. Named one of Outstanding Young Women of Am., 1982. Mem. Tex. Probation Assn. Methodist. Office: Adult Probation Dept 2627 Zelrich Dallas TX 75229

PRICE, STEFANIE JEAN, corporate professional; b. New Paris, Ohio, July 14, 1958; d. M. James and Leatrice J. (Muckridge) Arnett; m. Philip P. Price, July 15, 1978; children: Rebecca Lee, BJ. A. in Sec., Ind. Bus. Coll., Richmond, Ind., 1979. Receptionist/teller Second Nat. Bank, Richmond, Ind., 1977; clk. Richmond Water Works Corp. Inc., Richmond, 1977-79; jr. acct. Am. Water Works Co., Inc., Richmond, 1979-80; bookkeeper Phil's Phix-It Shop, Eaton, Ohio, 1978—; treas. Arnett Tool, Inc., New Paris, Ohio, 1980—. Mem. St. Clair Squares Square Dance Club (treas.), Nat. Honor Soc. Ch. of the Brethren. Office: Arnett Tool Inc 217 W Main St PO Box 40 New Paris OH 45347-0040

PRICE, TERESA A., vocational rehabilitation specialist; b. Lawrenceburg, Tenn., Apr. 4, 1965; d. Dorris Ray and Betty (McClanahan) P. BSW, Middle Tenn. State U., 1986; grad., Correction Acad., Tullahoma, Tenn., 1987. Cert. First Aid, CPR. Spl. events/grant coord. Martin Meth. Coll., Pulaski, Tenn., 1988; correctional counselor Dept. of Correction, State of Tenn., Clifton, 1987-88; vocat. rehab. counselor II State of Tenn., Columbia, 1988—; low vision and rehab. counselor trainer CEU's U. Tenn., Knoxville, Auburn (Ala.) U., Miss. State U., Starkville. Precinct del. Lawrence County Dem. party, mem. exec. bd., 1983—; vol. day care ctrs., nursing homes, EMR children, Girl Scouts, Fire Dept. Roy Kumpe fellow AEB Enterprise AR for the Blind. Mem. Assn. of Educators and Rehabilitators for Blind and Visually Impaired, Nat. Rehab. Assn., AR Enterprise for the Blind, Lawrence County Coun. of Community Clubs (sec.). Democrat. Methodist. Home: Rte 4 Box 409 Lawrenceburg TN 38464 Office: State of Tenn Vocat Rehab PO 457-6011 Mount Pleasant Pike Columbia TN 38401

PRICE BODAY, MARY KATHRYN, choreographer, small business owner; b. Fort Bragg, N.C., May 20, 1945; d. Max Edward and Katharine (Jordan) P.; m. Les Boday (div. 1982); children: Shawn Leon Boday, Irmali Ferecho Boday; m. Richard A. Weil, May 1, 1986. BFA, U. Okla., 1968, MFA, 1970. Soloist dancer Mary Anthony Dance Co., N.Y.C., 1971-74, Larry Richardson Dance Co., N.Y.C., 1971-73; dancer Pearl Lang Dance Co., N.Y.C., 1971-73, Gaku Dance Theater, N.Y.C., 1972-74; ballet mistress and dancer St. Gallen Ballet, Switzerland, 1974-75; dancer, tchr. Zurich Ballet, Switzerland, 1975-76; asst. prof. U. Ill., Champaign-Urbana, 1976-79; artist-in-residence Cornish Inst., Seattle, 1979-80; pres. The Dance Work, Inc., Seattle, 1981-90, Erie, Pa., 1990—; dir. dance dept., asst. prof. Mercyhurst Coll., Erie, Pa., 1990—; tchr. Harkness Ballet N.Y., Mary Anthony Dance Sch., Zurich Ballet, Nat. Acad. Arts Ill., Jefferson High Sch. Performing Arts Portland, also choreographer; tchr. Summer Dance Lab.; choreographer Mary K. Price Dance Co., U. Ill., Nat. Acad. Arts, Cornish Inst., Seahurst Ballet; tchr. Kneeland Workshops, Port Townsend, Wash., 1988; tchr., co-dir. Kneeland Seminars, Las Vegas, Nev., Port Townsend, summers 1989, 90, Oklahoma City U., summer 1990. Choreographer 3 ballets Ballet Co. St. Gallen, 1988, dance concert Mary & Friends, Seattle, 1990. Outstanding Dancer award U. Okla., 1968; named one of Outstanding Young Women of Am., 1977.

PRICE-LEE FATT, PATRICIA ANN, automobile leasing consultant; b. Danville, Va., June 19, 1954; d. William Oliver and Bessie Carolyn (Keene) P. Cert. data entry Braxton Bus. Sch., Richmond, Va., 1973; cert. computer ops. data analysis Mgmt. Info. Systems Office, San Antonio, 1980. Ordained to ministry Ch. Gospel Ministry, 1986, ordained bishop, 1988. With data entry dept. Va. Dept. Taxation, Richmond, 1985; telephone surveyor Stan Parris Campaign for Gov., Richmond, 1985; telephone sec. Sleepy Time & Wakeup, Richmond, 1984-89; founder For Sale Rep. Only, 1989—; writer, salesman, pres. Sister Starfire & Co., Richmond, 1982—; automobile leasing cons. Trans Leasing, Richmond, 1986—; beauty cons. Avon, Richmond, 1981-89; distbr. Amway, Richmond, 1980-83; radio/telephone operator FCC, Richmond, 1983—. Contbr. to World of Poetry, 1985 (Golden Poet award 1986, 87, 88, 89), American Poetry Anthology, 1986. Fund raiser Crop Walk for Hunger, Richmond, 1982, Elks Lodge 15, 1985; chpt. mem. Muscular Dystrophy Assn., 1987-89; active Marshall Clemon for Gov. Campaign, 1989—; mem. Crusade for Voters, Richmond, 1982, Friendship Force of Richmond, 1987—; voters registrant Office of City Registrar, Richmond, 1983; mem. Republican Presdl. Task Force, 1985—, Muscular Dystrophy Assn. Served with U.S. Army, 1979-81. Recipient Unsung Hero award Met. Bus. Shoppers Guide, Richmond, 1985. Mem. Internat. Platform Assn., Nat. Assn. Female Execs. (network dir. 1985), Liberian Aux. Assn. (hon. internat. hostess 1983—), NAACP (vets. affairs and armed forces com. 1982), Nat. Com. to Preserve Social Security and Medicare, Smithsonian Assocs., Songwriters of Am. (life), Internat. Platform Assn. Republican. Buddhist. Club: Dollywood Ambassador. Avocations: photogrpahy; theater; aerobics; reading; stamp collecting. Home: 225 Laurel Fork Dr Richmond VA 23225

PRICE-RABAH, KELLY ANN, marketing professional; b. Riverdale, Md., Jan. 9, 1963; d. James Logan and Marlene Patricia (Rinckenberger) Price; m. Mazen M. Rabah, Oct. 29, 1988. BA in Communication, Miami U., Oxford, Ohio, 1985; postgrad., U. Mich., 1989—. Sales rep. Procter & Gamble Distbn. Co., Southfield, Mich., 1985-88; mgr. key accounts Nabisco Brands, Cin., 1988-89; exec. dir. mktg. Nat. Coun. Alcoholism and Other Drugs, Southfield, 1989—. Vol. ARC, 1988—, local hosp., 1989—. Recipient scholarship Wayne State U., Detroit, 1989. Mem. Lansing Area Grocery Mfr. Reps. (bd. dirs. 1985-86, pres. 1986-88), Nat. Assn. Social Workers, Young Reps., Jr. League of Birmingham, Mich., Toastmasters, Sigma Sigma Sigma (alumnae del. 1985—, Pollack Grad. Study grant 1990), Omicron Delta Kappa. Roman Catholic.

PRICHARD, ELIZABETH ROBINSON, social worker, civic worker; b. N.Y.C., Oct. 20, 1915; d. Harold Grant and Kathryn Virginia (Robinson) P.; B.A., Adelphi U., 1943; M.S., Columbia U. Sch. Social Work, 1947. Home service worker ARC, Bklyn. and N.Y.C., 1943-45, 47-48; social worker N.Y. U., Bellevue Pilot Home Care Project, N.Y.C., 1948-49; asst. dir. social service Columbia-Presbyn. Med. Center, N.Y.C., 1949-54, dir. social services, 1954-81; asst. prof. clin. social work Coll. Physicians and Surgeons, Columbia U., 1957-81; mem. profl. adv. bd. for social work Found. Thanatology, 1970—, mem. exec. com., 1974—. Trustee Greater N.Y. chpt. Myasthenia Gravis Found., 1981—, nat. bd. dirs., 1986—; participant seminar on death Columbia U.; lectr. Brookdale Inst. Aging, Columbia U. Ret. Faculty Projet; mem. New York County Democratic Com. Mem. Nat. Assn. Social Workers, Acad. Cert. Social Workers, Nat. Conf. Social Welfare, Am. Pub. Health Assn., AAAS, N.Y. Acad. Scis., Columbia U. Sch. Social Work Alumni Assn. Clubs: Women's City (health com. 1981—), City. Editor 6 books, including 5 books on death and dying; contbr. articles on social work and care of terminally ill to profl. publs.

PRICHARD, NANCY BEVILLE, art educator; b. Langdale, Ala., Aug. 22, 1952; d. Lee Harlan and Margaret (Bowers) Beville; m. Bruce Prichard. BS in Art, Va. Polytechnic Inst., 1974; MS in Art, Radford U., 1977. Cert. art tchr., elem. art specialist, Va. Tchr. Va. Beach (Va.) City Pub. Schs., 1977-87; tchr. artistically gifted Old Donation Ctr. for Gifted and Talented, Va. Beach, 1987—; art instr. Va. Wesleyan Coll., Va. Beach, 1985-87; adj. faculty Old Dominion U., Norfolk, Va., 1987. Exhibited in group and one-woman shows Piedmont Craftsmen, 1987-88, Va. Beach Arts Ctr., 1988, Hermitage Mus., 1987. Mem. NEA, Va. Edn. Assn., Nat. Art Edn. Assn., Va. Art Edn. Assn., Va. Assn. for Gifted, Norfolk Soc. Arts, Tidewater Artists Assn. (bd. dirs. 1984-86, v.p. 1985-86). Home: 2604 Chubb Lake Ave Virginia

Beach VA 23455 Office: Old Donation Ctr for Gifted 1008 Ferry Plantation Rd Virginia Beach VA 23455

PRICKETT, NANCY MIRIAM, physical therapist; b. Mount Holly, N.J., Apr. 17, 1950; d. Phillip D. and Miriam Ann (Yoos) P. BS, West Chester (Pa.) State U., 1972; M in Phys. Therapy, Baylor U., 1973; MPA, Cen. Mich. U., 1982. Lic. phys. therapist, N.J., Pa., Colo. Phys. therapist Fitzsimons Army Med. Ctr., Denver, 1973-76; phys. therapy instr. Christian Med. Coll., Vellore, India, 1977-79; phys. therapist Schieffelin Leprosy Rsch. and Tng. Ctr., Karigiri, India, 1976-79, Hand Rehab. Ctr., Phila., 1980; cons., surveyor N.J. Dept. Health, Trenton, 1980-82; supr. phys. medicine and rehab. Del. Valley Med. Ctr., Bristol, Pa., 1982-83; dir. rehab. Luth. Home at Moorestown, N.J., 1983-86; pvt. practice Aspen Phys. Therapy, Mt. Holly, N.J., 1986—. Ch. coun. sec. St. Paul's Luth. Ch., Mt. Holly, 1989-90. Major USAR, 1972—. Decorated Commendation medal. Mem. Am. Phys. Therapy Assn., Res. Officers Assn., Assn. Mil. Surgeons, U.S. Army Alumni Assn. (Outstanding Alumni 1990). Home: 27 Ridge Ave Mount Holly NJ 08060

PRIDE, PORTIA DUKE, pharmaceutical representative; b. Amory, Miss., Sept. 19, 1964; d. Pinson Duke Pride and Hortense (Lavender) Parks. BBA, U. Miss., 1985. Mgr., sales rep. AC3 Computing Products Ctr., Jackson, Miss., 1986-87; pharmaceutical rep. Hoffmann-La Roche Inc., Greenville, Miss., 1987—. Mem. NAFE, Miss. Pharmacists Assn., Old Miss Alumni Assn. (recruiting 1988—), Delta Gamma (pres. Miss. Delta chpt. 1989—). Baptist. Home and Office: 481 Cypress Ln #B109 Greenville MS 38701

PRIELIPP, PAULINE LOUISE, accountant; b. Tecumseh, Mich., Aug. 19, 1957; d. Carl Fredrick and Irene Anna (Bexten) P. BA magna cum laude, Siena Heights Coll., 1979; MS in Acctg., Ea. Mich. U., 1986. Acct. Chelsea (Mich.) Community Hosp., 1979-82, acctg. services supr., 1982-83, budget and cost analyst, 1983-84, budget analyst, 1984-87, mgr. acctg., 1987—. Mem. Health Care Fin. Mgmt. Assn. Office: Chelsea Community Hosp 775 S Main St Chelsea MI 48118

PRIEST, EVA LOUISE, organization executive; b. Indpls., May 16, 1935; d. Jesse L. and Laura May (Reed) P.; m. William F. Fisher (div. 1964); 1 child, David L. BS in Psychology, U. So. Ind., 1977; postgrad., George Mason U., 1977-79. Aquatic dir. YMCA, Indpls., 1962-66; dir. safety svcs. ARC, Evansville, Ind., 1966-72; asst. nat. dir. ARC, Washington, 1972-80; exec. dir. Coun. Nat. Coop. Aquatics, Indpls., 1980—; cons. Can. Red Cross Soc., Ottawa, Ont., 1977—, Ind. Conv. and Visitors Bur., Indpls., 1984—; bd. dirs. Nat. Forum Adv. of Aquatics, Ft. Lauderdale, Fla., 1980—. Author: Adapted Aquatics, 1977; founder, editor Nat. Aquatic Jour., 1985—; contbr. articles to profl. jours. Cons. field svc., mem. water safety com. ARC, Indpls., 1986—. Mem. AAHPER and Dance (adv. com. 1987—), Psi Chi, Alpha Chi. Home: 3654 N Mitchner St Indianapolis IN 46226 Office: Coun Nat Coop Aquatics 901 W New York St Indianapolis IN 46223

PRIESZ, CONNIE JOAN, teacher; b. Mpls., Jan. 6, 1956; d. Jerry Jerome and Edna Lenore (Ayer) Lamon; m. Arthur W. Priesz Jr. BA in Phys. Edn. and Elem. Edn., Augsburg Coll., 1978; MS in Curriculum Instrn., Mankato (Minn.) State U., 1988. Tchr. phys. edn. and health Orono Sch. Dist. 278, Long Lake, Minn., 1978—, coach high sch. gymnastics, 1979—; coach high sch. track Orono Sch. Dist. 278, Long Lake, Minn., 1982-88; supr. traveling students Sch. Dist. 278 and Isabella Environ. Learning Ctr., Washington, 1983—. Vol. twin study U. Minn., Mpls., 1973—; coach track and field Spl. Olympics, Mpls., 1985—; ride mgr. St. Judes Children's Hosp., Loretto, 1986—; instr. AIDS, ARC, Mpls., 1988—. Recipient 5-Yr. Svc. Pin Minn. ARC, 1984, Qualified Rider award U.S. Dressage Fedn., 1987, U.S. Nat. Internat. Arabian Horse Assn. Dressage Competition, 1986, Canadian Nat. Internat. Arabian Horse Assn. Dressage Competition, 1990; Top Ten, Internat. Arabian Horse Assn. Nat. Competitive Ride; various athletic awards. Mem. NEA, Minn. Edn. Assn., Minn. State High Sch. Coaches Assn. (clinician 1982), Minn. State Girl's Gymnastics Judges Assn. (clinician), Orono Edn. Assn. (meet and conf. membership com. 1979—), North Cen. Assn. Colls. and Schs. (validation team Albert Lea, Minn. chpt. 1983). Home: Rt 1 Box 177A Montrose MN 55363 Office: Orono Sch Dist 278 685 Old Crystal Bay Rd Long Lake MN 55356

PRIETO, CORINE, geophysicist; b. El Paso, Tex., Sept. 26, 1946; d. Manuel M. and Angela (Zapata) P. BS in Physics and Math., U. Tex., El Paso, 1968; MS in Applied Physics, U. Toronto, Ont., Can., 1974. Geophysicist Mobil Oil Corp., Dallas, 1968-71, sr. geophysicist, 1973-76; exploration supr. Superior Oil Co., Houston, 1976-82; pres. Integrated Geophysics Corp., Houston, 1982—. Bd. dirs. Spaulding for Children, 1988—. Named Houston Bus. Woman of Yr., Tex. Exec. Women, 1983. Mem. Soc. Exploration Geophysicists, Geophys. Soc. Houston (chmn. potential fields sect. 1980-83). Office: Integrated Geophysics Corp 1502 Augusta Dr Suite 390 Houston TX 77057

PRIETTO, CAROLE ANNE, library assistant; b. L.A., Jan. 11, 1962; d. William Albert Jr. and Charlotte Marilyn (Mercurio) P. BA, U. Calif., Santa Barbara, 1984; MA, U. Calif., L.A., 1987. Libr. asst. UCLA Archives, 1986—. Mem. Am. Classical League. Democrat. Roman Catholic. Office: UCLA Archives 134 Powell Libr Los Angeles CA 90024

PRIGMORE, MARALEE SANDS, construction engineer; b. Kansas City, Mo., July 22, 1930; d. Virgil J. and Edith (Plimmer) Sands; m. Edward Parks Prigmore, Oct. 28, 1949; children: Suzette Rexford, Margaret Michele Prigmore Van Cleave. Projects mgr. Rad Daniel Corp., Memphis, 1963-67; pres. Maralee Prigmore, Contractor, Memphis, 1967-76, Maralee Prigmore, Inc., Gen. Contractor, Memphis, 1974-76; constrn. engr. McDonald's Corp., New Orleans, 1977—; pres., owner Heritage Hist. Homes, 1984—. Bd. dirs. Symphony League, Fine Arts Festival, Birmingham, Ala., 1956-58, Needs Children's Lunch Program, Memphis, 1968-70; mem. Air. Svc. Commn. Memphis, 1972-77; bd. dirs. Family Svc. Assn. Memphis, 1972-75; del. Rep. Conv., 1972, 76; pres. Rep. Women, Memphis, 1974; mem. fin. com. Election Sen. Bill Brock, Tenn., 1976; mem. Nat. Civic Affairs Com., Washington, 1973-76. Mem. Nat. Home Builders. Presbyterian. Home: 2631 Prytania St New Orleans LA 70130

PRILLWITZ, DIANE PATRICIA, purchasing executive; b. L.I. City, N.Y., Sept. 23, 1958. Student, Brookdale Community Coll., Lincroft, N.J., 1984—. Cert. purchasing mgr. Expeditor Wheelock, Inc., Long Branch, N.J., 1976-79, purchasing asst., 1979-81, jr. buyer, 1981-84, buyer, 1984-88, sr. buyer, 1988—. Mem. Nat. Assn. Purchasing Mgmt., Purchasing Mgmt. Assn. Central Jersey, World Wildlife Fund, Nat. Wildlife Fedn., Jack La Laane Club. Lutheran.

PRIMAVERA, ANNE MARILYN, educational administrator; b. Webb City, Mo., Sept. 1, 1944; d. James William and Catherine Mary (Costello) Gerard; m. Louis H. Primavera, Aug. 27, 1966; children: James, William. BA, St. John's U., 1966, postgrad., 1985—; MS, Hofstra U., 1974, diploma in ednl. adminstrn., 1981. Secondary reading cons. Massapequa (N.Y.) High Sch., 1966-67; elem. tchr. Our Lady of Lourdes, Massapequa Park, N.Y., 1971-74; asst. prof. St. Francis Coll., Bklyn., 1975-76; secondary tchr. English, Brentwood (N.Y.) Sch. Dist., 1974-79, secondary reading cons., 1979-88, secondary adminstr., 1988—; v.p. Gerardi Corp., N.Y.C., 1975—. Mem. Assn. for Supervision and Curriculum Devel., Am. Fedn. Tchrs., Internat. Reading Assn., Nat. Orgn. on Legal Problems in Am., Sch. Adminstrs. Assn. N.Y. State, Univ. Club (Hempstead, N.Y.). Democrat. Roman Catholic. Home: 1799 Collins St Seaford NY 11783 Office: Brentwood Sch Dist 1st St and 5th Ave Brentwood NY 11717

PRIMAVERA, JOANNE MARTINA, vocational education administrator; b. Langley, Wash., Sept. 17, 1940; d. Victor and Anna Ethel (Peters) P.; m. Donald E. McClain, Sept. 10, 1960 (div. Mar. 1967). BS in Home Econs. Edn., U. Wash., 1964, MEd, 1972; PhD in Vocat. Edn. Adminstrn., U. Mo., 1978. Cert. home economist. Tchr. home econs. Mukilteo (Wash.) Sch. Dist., 1965-68, Fed. Way (Wash.) Sch. Dist., 1968-75; asst. dir. curriculum devel. lab. U. Mo., Columbia, 1976; rsch. asst. Ellis & Assocs., College Park, Md., 1977; vocat. edn. adminstr. Renton (Wash.) Vocat. Tech. Inst., 1977—; adj. prof. Seattle Pacific U., 1981—. Contbr. articles to profl. jours. Bd. dirs. King County YMCA, Seattle, 1979-82, Child and Family Resource Ctr., Seattle, 1985-87; community rep. Puget Power, Bellevue, 1981; mem. Policy Coun. Head Start, King County, 1985-87. U.S. Dept. Edn. fellow, 1975-77. Mem. Nat. Coun. Vocat. Adminstrs. (bd. dirs. 1985-87), Family Opportunity Coun. (co-chair), Student Bar Assn. U Puget Sound, Assn. for Supervision and Curriculum Devel., Nat. Assn. Edn. Young Children, Wash. Coun. Vocat. Adminstrs. (pres. 1981-82), Wash. Vocat. Assn. (pres. 1983-84), Wash. Home Econs. Assn. (pres. 1988), Bellevue Athletic Club. Home: 7951 129th Pl SE Renton WA 98056

PRIMM, DARLENE BELL, psychologist; b. Columbia, Tenn., June 3, 1960; d. Robert Dallas and Flora Jane (Tidwell) Bell; m. Thomas M. Primm, Mar. 25, 1989. BA, Freed Hardeman Coll., Henderson, Tenn., 1982; M of Marriage and Family Therapy, Tex. Christian U., 1984, MS, 1985. Lic. psychol. examiner, Tenn.; cert. sch. psychologist. Psychol. asst. Abilene State Sch., 1984-85; psychol. examiner Clover Bottom Devel. Ctr., Nashville, 1985-86; pvt. practice Nashville, 1986—. Mem. Am. Psychol. Assn. Home: 1507 Grandview Dr Nashville TN 37215

PRIMO, MARIE NASH, shopping center executive; b. Clarksburg, W.Va., Dec. 10, 1928; d. Frank and Josephine (DiMaria) Nash; student pub. schs. Clarksburg; m. Joseph C. Primo, Sept. 27, 1953; 1 dau., Joan E. Sec., Nat. Bank Detroit, 1945-46; exec. sec. Cutting Tool Mfrs. Assn., Detroit, 1946-50; adminstrv. asst. Irwin I. Cohn atty., Detroit, 1950-84; mgr. Bloomfield (Mich.) Shopping Plaza, 1959—; North Hill Center, Rochester Hills, Mich., 1957—; Drayton Plains Shopping Center (Mich.), 1958-84; South Allen Shopping Center, Allen Park, Mich., 1953-77, Huron-Tel Corner, Pontiac, Mich., 1977—; officer, dir., numerous privately held corps. Mem. steering com., treas. Univ. Liggett Antiques Show, 1971-76, advisory com., 1977-80; mem. parents' com. Wellesley Coll., 1979-1981. Mem. Founders Soc. Detroit Inst. Arts, Women's Econ. Club, Mich. Humane Soc., Detroit Sci. Center, Detroit Zool. Soc., Smithsonian Assos., Hist. Soc. Mich., Grosse Pointe War Meml. Assn., Grosse Pointe Pub. Library Assn., Mich. Opera Theatre Guild. Roman Catholic. Home: 1341 N Renaud Rd Grosse Pointe Woods MI 48236 Office: 1631 1st National Bldg Detroit MI 48226

PRINCE, ANTOINETTE ODETTE, visual artist, art educator; b. Watertown, N.Y., Mar. 18, 1946; d. Clarence Oliver and Marion Eva (Moffatt) Odette; m. George Mather Prince, Aug. 5, 1976 (div. 1981). Grad., Boston Mus. Sch., 1981-82; postgrad., Harvard U., 1986—. Painting instr. Boston Mus. Sch., 1981-82, 86; painting instr. Exptl. Coll. Tufts U., Medford, Mass., 1986; dir. Loading Dock Gallery, 1982-83; painting instr. Cambridge (Mass.) Art Assn., 1983-85, instr. painting, drawing and art, 1984—; freelance painting instr., 1984-90; dir., instr. Prince Workshops for Artists; coord. Art Talk, Cambridge Art Assn., 1983-85, bd. dirs. Recipient Traveling Scholars award Mus. Fine Arts, 1982; Pub. Action for Arts grantee, 1985. Studio: 6 Vernon St Somerville MA 02145

PRINCE, CATHERINE MORAN, marketing executive; b. Toledo, Ohio, Nov. 16, 1945; d. Edward Richard and Margaret Irene (Vickers) Moran; m. John Franklin Prince, Feb. 4, 1967 (div. 1986); children: John Edward, Julie Elizabeth. BS, U. Toledo, 1967. Tchr. Sandusky (Ohio) pub. schs., 1967-69; tutor Canton, Mich., 1978-84; research analyst Devel. Rsch. Assocs., Inc., Canton, 1984-88, v.p., 1988—; field rep. U.S. Dept. Labor, Detroit, 1986. Mem. housing task force S.E. Mich. Council Govts., Detroit, 1988—, community and econ. devel. adv. council, 1988—; chmn. Canton Twp. Zoning Bd. Appeals, 1988—; vice chmn. Canton Twp. Planning Commn., 1985-87; mem. Oakwood Hosp. Adv. Bd., 1983—. Mem. League Women Voters (bd. dirs. 1986-89). Roman Catholic. Home: 44431 Newburyport Canton MI 48187 Office: Devel Rsch Assocs Inc 42180 Ford Rd #304 Canton MI 48187

PRINCE, CYNTHIA ANN, management analyst; b. Washington, Feb. 27, 1953; d. Edward Robinson and Era Mae (Prince) Wall. BSW, Norfolk (Va.) State U., 1977; MA in Mental Health, U. D.C., 1981. Adminstrv. asst. HUD, Washington, 1979-83; forms mgmt. officer Dept. Def., Washington, 1983-87; asst. office mgr. AT&T, Washington, 1987-88; cosmetic cons. Biotherm Skincare/Fashion Fair Cosmetics, Washington and N.Y.C., 1985—; mgmt. analyst Def. Logistics Agy., N.Y.C., 1988—; organizer Fed. Women's Program, N.Y.C., 1989—; speaker in field. Author various pamphlets. Mem. Fed. Women's Program (vice-chair 1989—), Bus. Forms Mgmt. Assn. Democrat. Roman Catholic. Home: 2892 Pitkin Ave Brooklyn NY 11208

PRINCE, JACQUELYNNE BOLANDER, nurse, consultant; b. Norfolk, Va., July 4, 1955; d. Jack C. Bolander and Particia (Loud) Bolander Melvin; m. John Martine Prince, Jr., Oct. 1, 1977; children:Emily Alene, John Ryland, Christopher. B.S., Med. Coll. of Va., 1978; M.S., Tex. Woman's U., 1985. Registered critical care nurse. Staff nurse Med. Coll. of Va., Richmond, 1978-80; asst. nurse coordinator Parkland Hosp., Dallas, 1980-82, supr., 1982-83; head nurse N.C. Meml. Hosp., Chapel Hill, 1983-85; coord. critical care edn. Wise Appalachian Regional Hosp., Wise, Va., 1985-86; coord. continuing edn. Norton (Va.) Community Hosp., 1986—; cons. in field. Contbr. articles to profl. publs. Instr. Advanced Cardiac Life Support, Am. Heart Assn., Dallas, Chapel Hill, N.C., 1980—; chmn. bd. dirs. Wise Sch. Dance; v.p. PTA. Mem. Assn. Critical Care Nurses (bd. dirs.), Am. Nurses Assn., North Atlantic Nursing Diagnosis Assn., N.C. Meml. Collaborator Practice Com., Wise County Med. Soc. Auxilliary (pres.), Parkland Woman's Club (project svc. chmn. 1980-83). Baptist. Avocations: skiing, quilting, reading, running. Home: 704 Ridge Ave Norton VA 24273 Office: Norton Community Hosp 100 15th St NW Norton VA 24273

PRINCIPAL, VICTORIA, actress; b. Fukuoka, Japan, Jan. 3, 1950; d. Victor and Ree (Veal) P.; m. Harry Glassman, 1985. Attended, Miami-Dade Community Coll.; studied acting with Max Croft, Al Sacks and Estelle Harman, Jean Scott, Royal Acad. Dramatic Arts. Worked as model, including TV comml. appearances; film debut in The Life and Times of Judge Roy Bean, 1972; other movie appearances include Vigilante Force, Earthquake, I Will I Will For Now, The Naked Ape; TV film appearances include Last Hours Before Morning, 1975, Fantasy Island, 1977, The Night They Stole Miss Beautiful, 1977, Pleasure Palace, 1980, Not Just Another Affair, 1982, Naked Lie, 1989, Blind Witness, 1989, Sparks, 1990; became theatrical agt., 1975; appeared in TV series Dallas, 1978-87; other TV appearances include Sixty Years of Seduction, Mistress, 1987. Author: The Body Principal, 1983, The Beauty Principal, 1984, The Diet Principal, 1987. Office: care Alan Nierob Rogers & Cowan Ste 400 10000 Santa Monica Blvd Los Angeles CA 90067

PRINCZ, JUDITH, publishing executive. BA, Wheaton Coll., 1974. Retail circulation asst. Family Media, 1975-76; asst. mgr. direct mail Redbook, 1977; asst. mgr. direct mail, subscription mgr. Women Sports, 1977; circulation mgr. Sport mag., 1978-79; circulation dir. Weight Watcher's, 1979-83; assoc. pub. Am. Baby mag., N.Y.C., 1983-89, pub., 1989—. Office: Am Baby 475 Park Ave S New York NY 10016*

PRINDLE, CHERYL H., public relations and sales executive; b. Paintsville, Ky., Sept. 8, 1960; d. Lloyd and Phyllis (Greene) Hackworth; m. James R. Prindle, Sept. 10, 1980. AA, Alice Lloyd Coll., 1980; BSBA, Am. Internat. Coll., 1985; postgrad., Cambridge Coll. Computer cons. Indsl. Residential Security, Southampton, Mass.; computer lab. instr. Am. Internat. Coll., Springfield, Mass.; mgmt. cons. Northampton, Mass.; exec. dir. Mirage Studios, Northampton, Mass. Producer Teenage Mutant Ninja Turtles. Mem. NAFE, Nat. Assn. of Self-Employed, Am. Mgmt. Assn., Data Processing Mgmt. Assn. (treas. 1985). Office: Mirage Studios 26 Center St Northampton MA 01060

PRINGLE, BARBARA CARROLL, state legislator; b. N.Y.C., 1939; d. Nicholas Robert and Anna Joan (Woloshinovich) Terlesky; m. Richard D. Pringle, Nov. 28, 1959; children: Christopher, Rhonda. Student, Cuyahoga Community Coll. With Dunn & Bradstreet, 1957-60; precinct committeewoman City of Cleve., 1976-77; elected mem. Cleve. City Council, 1977-81; mem. Ohio Ho. of Reps., Columbus, 1982—, vice chmn. pub. utilities com., ins. com., econ. affairs and fed. rels. com.; chair fin.-edn. subcom., mem. hwy. and pub. safety com., small bus. com., aging and housing com. Vol. Cleve. Lupus Steering Com.; vol. various community orgns. Mem. Nat. Order Women Legislators. Democrat. Home: 708 Timothy Ln Cleveland OH 44109

PRINGLE, DORA ROBERTA, nurse; b. Waldwick, N.J., Sept. 23, 1921; d. James Arthur and Olive May (Conklin) Lamb; m. Fulton Knight Singleton I, Oct. 24, 1942 (dec. 1959); children: Fulton Knight II, Diane J., William Edward, Pamela Ann; m. William Broadbent Pringle, Oct. 12, 1971 (dec.); 1 stepchild, Janice Pringle. Grad., Bklyn. Meth. Sch. Nursing, 1942; BS in Health Care Adminstrn., U. Santa Monica, 1984. RN, N.J. With Pascack Valley Hosp., Westwood, N.J., 1975—; rehab. nurse community health care projects Pascack Valley Hosp., Westwood, 1983—; lectr. in field. Advocate pub. hearings N.J. Legis. Newworking Com., Trenton, 1984-86; adv. bd. Hayden Rehab. Agy., 1983-86. Mem. N.J. Assn. RNs (chmn. legis. com. 1984—), Nat. Assn. Rehab. Nurses (legis. com. 1986—), N.J. Assn. Rehab. Profls. Pvt. Sector, N.Y. Neurosci. Nurses. Republican. Methodist. Club: Pascack Valley Hosp. Stroke Recovery (coordinator). Home: 79 Riverdale St Hilsdale NJ 07642 Office: Pascack Valley Hosp Old Hook Rd Westwood NJ 07675

PRINOS, MONIQUE E., financial services executive; b. N.Y.C., Aug. 13, 1957; d. John and Aspasia (Mavros) P. BS in Psychology, Mercy Coll., 1979. Cert. in personnel mgmt. Employee benefits adminstr. Helmsley-Spear, Inc., N.Y.C., 1981-86; asst. benefit mgr. Mut. of Am., N.Y.C., 1986—. Corp. coord. WalkAmerica, The March of Dimes; rsch. bd. of advisors ABI. Mem. NAFE, Daus. of Penelope. Greek Orthodox. Home: 4705 Henry Hudson Pkwy Riverdale NY 10471

PRINS, LAVONNE KAY, systems programmer; b. Sibley, Iowa, Feb. 28, 1957; d. Henry Simon and Katherine (Schram) P. BA, S.W. State U., Marshall, Minn., 1982; postgrad., Mankato (Minn.) State U., 1982-84. Instr. math. Mankato State U., 1982-84; computer operator Sathers, Round Lake, Minn., 1985; law records analyst ITT Consumer Fin. Corp., St. Louis Park, Minn., 1985-86; systems programmer Metaphor, Eden Prairie, Minn., 1987-89; pres. Ablazon Unltd. Inc., Plymouth, Minn., 1990—; sr. systems programmer Health Risk Mgmt., Edina, Minn., 1989—. Sgt. U.S. Army, 1975-79. Mem. Nat. Systems Programmers Assn. Republican. Mem. Reformed Ch. in Am. Home: 3567 N Pilgrim Ln Plymouth MN 55441

PRIOLI, MARY GRACE, educator; b. Newark, Sept. 29, 1916; d. Michael Mariano and Angelina (De Cicco) Feravolo; m. Peter Albert Prioli, Apr. 20, 1969. BA, Rutgers U., 1959; MA, Seton Hall U., 1961, postgrad., 1961. Cert. tchr., N.J. Asst. to dean Rutgers U., Newark, 1950-59; adviser to women students Newark colls. Rutgers U., 1959-64; dir. acad. svcs. Grad. Sch. of Bus. Rutgers U., Newark, 1964-69, with bur. community svcs., 1969-77, ret., 1977; adviser Delta Phi Delta, Newark, 1950-64, Panhellenic Assn., Newark, 1950-64. Contbr. article to profl. jour. Del. Civic Club Coun., Newark; mme. Newark Mus., Spring Lake (N.J.) Hist. Soc., 1989—; bd. dirs., nat. bd. dirs. Newark YM-YWCA, 1964-71. Mem. Coll. Woman's Club of Essex County (pres. 1968-70, bd. dirs. 1978-80, Paul Revere Silver bowl), Peter Clan of Lee (Lady Mary), Woman's Club of Spring Lake (pres. 1990—), Spring Lake Garden Club, Spring Lake Golf Club, Soroptimists Internat. (pres. 1976-77, Plaque). Home: 218 Ocean Rd Spring Lake NJ 07762

PRISK, PATRICIA, nurse, computer programmer and analyst; b. Troy, N.Y., Nov. 6, 1944; d. Harold George and Mary Alice (Murphy) Connor; m. William Prisk; children: William, Sandra, Kimberly, Rebecca, Sharon. Student, Hudson Valley Community Coll., 1962; RN, Samaritan Hosp. Sch. Nursing, 1965. Staff nurse Samaritan Hosp., 1965, Mt. Sinai Hosp., Hartford, Conn., 1966-69, Johnson Meml. Hosp., Stafford Springs, Conn., 1972-74; supr. Riverside Health Care Center, 1974-76; dir. nursing Middletown (Conn.) Health Care Center, 1976-81, staff nurse, 1981-82; staff nurse Lorraine Manor, Hartford, 1981-82; computer programmer Aetna Life and Casualty Co., Hartford, 1982-83; systems analyst Hartford Ins. Co., 1983—; lectr., cons. in field. Office: 1 Hartford Plaza Hartford CT

PRITCHARD, BARBARA ELLEN, clinical psychologist; b. Phoenix, Sept. 27, 1952; d. James Willard Angelo and Evelyn Amelia (Ritter) Bakke; m. W. Douglas Pritchard, Jan. 12, 1979 (div. 1984). Student, Occidental Coll., 1970-71; BA with highest distinction, U. Ariz., 1978, MA, 1983, PhD, 1990. Clin. psychology extern Catalina Mountain Juvenile Inst., Tucson, 1979-80; clin. psychology extern Southern Ariz. Mental Health Ctr., Tucson, 1980-81; clin. psychology extern U. Ariz. Health Scis. Ctr., Tucson, 1981-82, clin. psychology intern, 1983-84, postdoctoral fellow, 1984-85; chief psychol. svc. Marana (Ariz.) Community Clinic, 1984-85; coord. eating disorders program Palo Verde Hosp., Tucson, 1985-86, psychology assoc., 1986-88; clin. dir. Optifast Program, Tucson Med. Assocs., 1986—; cons. The Haven Residential Placement for Women, Tucson, 1984-85, So. Ariz. Mental Health Ctr., Tucson, 1981-82, Tucson Med. Ctr.-Lifegain Program, 1986-88, Sonora Desert Hosp., Tucson, 1990; presenter, invited speaker in field. Contbr. articles to profl. jours. Acad. scholar Occidental Coll., 1970-71, Gen. Resident scholar U. Ariz., 1974-75, Class scholar U. Ariz., 1978, NIMH scholar, 1978-79. Mem. Am. Psychol. Assn., Ariz. State Psychol. Assn., Phi Beta Kappa. Democrat. Home: 5702 E S Wilshire Tucson AZ 85711 Office: 2122 N Craycroft Ste 118 Tucson AZ 85712

PRITCHARD, LOIS RUTH BREUR, engineer; b. Paterson, N.J., Mar. 26, 1946; d. George L. and Ruth Margaret (Farquhar) Breur; m. Bruce N. Pritchard, Aug. 10, 1968 (div. May 1982); children: John Douglas, Tiffany Anne; m. Robert H. Krause, 1984. Student, Keuka Coll., 1964-65; BS in Chemistry cum laude, Fairleigh Dickinson U., 1980; postgrad., Stevens Inst. Tech. With dept. R & D UniRoyal, Wayne, N.J., 1966-68, Jersey State Chem. Co., North Haledon, 1968-69, Inmont, Clifton, N.J., 1969; from chemist to sr. analyst Lever Bros., Edgewater, N.J., 1976-80; process engr. Bell Telephone Labs., Murray Hill, N.J., 1980-84, RCA, Somerville, N.J., 1984-86; sr. engr. electron beam lithography ops. Gain Electronics Corp., Somerville, 1986-88; cons. Pritchard Assocs., Budd Lake, N.J., 1988—; presenter profl. papers for profl. confs. Patentee package design. Troop leader, trainer, cons. Bergen County council Girl Scouts U.S., 1969-80, troop leader Morris Area council, 1980-83, head com. Mt. Olive twp., 1980-81; den leader, den leader coach, trainer Boy Scouts Am., 1973-76. Mem. AAAS, AAUW, NAFE, IEEE, Components, Hybrids, and Mfg. Tech. Soc. (semicondr. tech. subcom. electronic components conf. program com. 1981-86), Soc. Photo-Optical Instrumentation Engrs., Am. Soc. for Quality Control, Soc. Women Engrs., Am. Chem. Soc., Am. Inst. Chemists, Assn. Women in Sci., Internat. Platform Assn., Mensa, Phi Omega Epsilon. Republican. Episcopalian.

PRITCHARD, MARY D'ERCOLE, teacher; b. Seneca Falls, N.Y., Jan. 8, 1940; d. Pasquale Antonio and Italia Louis (DeRousi) D'Ercole; m. Richard Timken, Sept. 5, 1959 (div. 1964); m. Alun Pritchard, Aug. 8, 1965; children: Michael Arthur, Amy Marie. Student, Mynderse Acad., Seneca Falls,, N.Y., 1957; BS, SUNY at Cortland, 1961; student, SUNY at Albany, 1983. Cert. Tchr., N.Y., Iowa, S.D. Tchr. Ballston Spa Sch. System, N.Y., 1961-62; tchr. Sioux City Sch. System, 1962-63, Vermillion Sch. System, S.D., 1963-64, Shenenedowa Cen. Sch., Elnora, N.Y., 1964-65; sub. tchr. Schenectady Sch. System, N.Y., 1968-78; dir. teen pregnancy network Human Service Planning Council, N.Y., 1978-80; ednl. cooordinator Refreshing Spring Day Care Ctr., Schenectady, N.Y., 1980-83; asst. dir. day care Campus Children Ctr., Albany, N.Y., 1983-85; dir. Carol A. Dunigan Day Care Ctr., Albany, N.Y., 1985-86; tchr. Schenectady Sch. System, N.Y., 1987—. Campaign Worker Dem. Party, Schenectady, N.Y., 1988—; chair of allocation panel United Way, Schenectady, 1988; rels. chairperson Cancer Soc., Schenectady, 1989; sec. YWCA, 1983-84; treas. Coop. Extension, 1986—; deacon, Presbyn. Ch., 1988—; vol. usher Saratoga Performing Arts Ctr., 1969—, Capital Repertory Theater, 1984—, Empire Ctr. for Performing Arts, 1989—. Mem. Am. Assn. U. Women (Pres. 1985-86), WMHT Ednl. T.V. Station, Delta Kappa Gamma, Bus. & Profl. Women Club Schenectady N.Y. Democrat. Home: 1670 Wendell Ave Schenectady NY 12308 Office: Yates Creative Arts Magnet Sch Salina ST Schenectady NY 12308

PRITCHARD, SARAH MARGARET, librarian; b. Boston, Feb. 8, 1955; d. Wilbur Louis and Kathleen Hunton (Moss) P.; m. Timothy John Brennan, Aug. 20, 1977. BA, U. Md., 1975; MA in French, U. Wis., 1976, MLS, 1977. Intern Libr. Congress, Washington, 1977-78, reference specialist in women's studies, 1978-88, head microform reading rm., 1988-90; sr. program officer Assn. Rsch. Librs., Washington, 1990—; acad. libr. mgmt. intern Coun on Libr. Resources Princeton U., N.J., 1988-89; editorial advisor Women's Rsch. and Edn. Inst., Washington, 1987—. Editor: The Women's

Annual, 1983-84, 1984; contbr. articles to profl. jours. Wis. Alumni Rsch. Found. fellow, 1975-77. Mem. ALA (chair machine assisted reference sect. 1986-87, chair women's studies sect. 1989-90, coun. 1990—), Nat. Women's Studies Assn. Democrat. Home: 1708 Noyes Ln Silver Spring MD 20910 Office: Assn Rsch Librs 1527 New Hampshire Ave NW Washington DC 20036

PRITT, CHARLOTTE J., state legislator; b. Jan. 2, 1949. BS, MA, Marshall U. Dir. Mountain State Press; mem. W.Va. Ho. of Dels., 1984-86; state senator W.Va. Senate, 1988—. Mem. AAUW, W.Va. Writers, Nat. Coun. Tchrs. of English, Sierra Club. Presbyterian. Home: Rte 5 Box 346-C Charleston WV 25312*

PRIVOTT, JO A., real estate agent; b. Ahoskie, N.C., Jan. 19, 1953; d. Joseph and Ethel Faye (Minton) Andrusia; m. Steven David Privott, June 25, 1972 (div. Apr. 1983); 1 child, David Joseph. Grad., Realtor's Inst. Va., 1985. Cert. residential specialist. Sales assoc. Hometown Properties, Inc., Herndon, Va., 1984-87; sales assoc., assoc. broker Merrill Lynch Realty, Herndon, 1987; assoc. broker RE/MAX, 1988—. Mem. Realtors Active in Politics, Fairfax, Va., 1985—. Mem. No. Va. Bd. Realtors (speakers program 1986-88, profl. edn. subcom. 1987, profl. courtesy 1987), Nat. Assn. Realtors (instr. mid-yr. conv. 1987), Va. Assn. Realtors, Realtors Nat. Mktg. Inst. (council course promo subcom. 1987-88, council spl. events com. 1987-88), Women's Council Realtors. Republican. Home: 7 Awsley Ct Sterling VA 22170 Office: RE/MAX 20 Pidgeon Hill Dr #201 Sterling VA 22170

PROCIDANO, MARY ELIZABETH, psychologist, educator; b. New Rochelle, N.Y., Apr. 1, 1954; d. John D'Arge and Dorothy Diane (Utter) P.; m. Stephen Anthony Buglione, Aug. 9, 1986; 1 child, Daniel Stephen. BS summa cum laude with honors, Fordham U., 1976; PhD, Ind. U., 1981. Lic. psychologist. Research asst. Fordham-Yale Prison Research Project Fordham U., 1974-76; research asst. N.Y. State Psychiat. Inst., 1975; teaching asst. psychology Ind. U., Bloomington, 1976-79, assoc. instr., 1979-80; intern in clin. psychology Inst. of Living, Hartford, Conn., 1980-81; asst. prof. Fordham U., Bronx, N.Y., 1981-90, asst. chair psychology dept., 1984-87, chair Inst. Rev. Bd. for Protection of Human Subjects, 1986—, assoc. prof., mem. faculty senate, 1990—, also mem. coll. coun. and various coms., advisor; article reviewer for profl. and scholarly jours. Cons. editor Jour. of Personality and Social Psychology; contbr. articles and chpts. to profl. and scholarly jours. and books. Faculty fellow Fordham U., 1990; rsch. and faculty devel. grantee Fordham U. Mem. Am. Psychol. Assn., Ea. Psychol. Assn., Assn. for Advancement Behavior therapy, Soc. for Behavioral Medicine, Phi Beta Kappa, Sigma Xi, Psi Chi. Roman Catholic. Office: Fordham Univ Dept Psychology Bronx NY 10458

PROCOPE, ERNESTA GERTRUDE, insurance broker; b. Bklyn., Feb. 9; d. Clarence and Elvira Forster; m. John L. Procope, July 3, 1954. Student, Bklyn. Coll., Coll. Ins., Pohs Inst. Ins.; LLD (hon.) Adelphi U., Marymount Manhattan Coll., 1987, HHD (hon.) Morgan State U., 1978. Pres. E.G. Bowman Co. Inc., N.Y.C., 1953—, also chief exec. officer; dir. Avon Products, Inc., Chubb Corp., Columbia Gas Systems Inc.; panelist corp. governance and advancement of women Women's Bur., U.S. Dept. Labor, 1981; ambassador 10th Anniversary Independence Celebration, Republic of Gambia, 1975. Trustee N.Y. Zool. Soc., Cornell U., dir. adv. council Gov.'s office Mgmt. and Productivity, 1984—, Bus. Adv. Bd., 1984—. Recipient achievement award Thelma T. Johnson Meml. Scholarship Fund, 1972, bus. achievement award Intercracial Council for Bus. Opportunity, 1973, Community Service award F & M Schaefer Brewing Co., 1974, Sojourner Truth award Negro Bus. and Profl. Women's Club, Inc., 1974, Bus. Achievement award Nat. Bus. League, 1976, Catalyst award Women Dirs. of Corps., 1977, Torch of Liberty award Anti-Defamation League, 1990; named Bus. Person of Yr. Urban Bankers Coalition, 1990; honored as disting. black woman in corp. role Nat. Council Negro Women, Inc., 1981, also others. Mem. Nat. Assn. Ins. Brokers, Nat. Assn. Ins. Women, Women's Forum, Alpha Kappa Alpha (hon.). Presbyterian. Club: Cosmopolitan. Office: EG Bowman Co Inc 97 Wall St New York NY 10005

PROCOPIO, DIMPLE OZELLA, electronics company executive; b. Elizabethton, Tenn., Aug. 22, 1940; d. John Paul and Lena Jane (Cooke) Greer; m. Paul R. Beck, May 27, 1967, (div. June 1980); children: Paul J., Brian R.; m. Vincent Joseph, Aug. 14, 1982; children: Barry J., Mark. Student, AMA, NY, 1985, NCR, Columbus, 1988, Tex. Instrument, Columbus, 1988. Personnel specialist Alsco Aluminum, Akron, Ohio, 1956-65; sypr. advt. B.F. Goodrich Co., Akron, Ohio, 1965-71; computer specialist Brennan and Howard, Akron, Ohio, 1972; dir. Mid-Am. region Arrow Electronics, Inc., Dublin, Ohio, 1972-89, v.p. Mid-Am. region, 1990—. Mem. Nat. Assn. Female Exec. Republican. Home: 7655 Brandon Way Dr Dublin OH 43017

PROCTOR, BARBARA GARDNER, advertising agency executive, writer; b. Asheville, N.C.; d. William and Bernice (Baxter) Gardner; B.A. Talladega Coll., 1954; m. Carl L. Proctor, July 20, 1961 (div. Nov. 1963); 1 son, Morgan Eugene. Music critic, contbg. editor Down Beat Mag., Chgo., from 1958; internat. dir. Vee Jay Records, Chgo., 1961-64; copy supr. Post-Keyes-Gardner Advt., Inc., 1965-68, Gene Taylor Assos., 1968-69, North Advt. Agy., 1969-70; contbr. to gen. periodicals, from 1952; founder Proctor & Gardner Advt., Chgo., 1970—, now pres., chief exec. officer. Mem. Chgo. Urban League, Chgo. Econ. Devel. Corp. Bd. dirs. People United to Save Humanity, Better Bus. Bur. Cons. pub. relations and promotion, record industry. Recipient Armstrong Creative Writing award, 1954; awards Chgo. Fedn. Advt. Clubs, N.Y. Art Dirs. Club. Woman's Day; Frederick Douglas Humanitarian award, 1975; named Chgo. Advt. Woman of Year, 1974. Mem. Chgo. Media Women, Nat. Assn. Radio Arts and Sci., Women's Advt. Club, Cosmopolitan C. of C. (dir.), Female Execs. Assn., Internat. Platform Assn., Smithsonian Instn. Assos. Author TV documentary Blues for a Gardenia, 1963. Office: Proctor & Gardner Advt 111 E Wacker Dr Chicago IL 60601*

PROCTOR, DEBORAH SUZANNE, educational information-radio station executive; b. Huntington, N.Y., May 9, 1951; d. Ralph George and Mary Carol (Gulick) Procopio. BSEE, N.C. State U., 1973. Pres. Ednl. Info. Corp., Raleigh, N.C., 1973—; gen. mgr. Sta. WCPE, Raleigh, 1978—; chmn. tech. interconnect subcom. N.C. Pub. Radio Adv. Com., Raleigh, 1988—. Mem. NAFE, IEEE, Soc. Broadcast Engrs. (cert. profl. broadcast engr.), Triangle Soc. Broadcast Engrs. Office: Sta WCPE PO Box 828 Wake Forest NC 27588

PROCTOR, PATRICIA ANN PEZANOWSKI, accountant; b. North Tarrytown, N.Y., Apr. 4, 1958; d. Joseph and Joan (Strieder) Pezanowski; m. Alan S. Proctor, Oct. 4, 1981; 1 child, Douglas Alan. BS in Acctg., U. Bridgeport, 1980; cert. in computer literacy, So. Meth. U., 1986. Acct. Briar Electric, Inc., Croton-on-Hudson, N.Y., 1980-81; acct., cash mgmt. analyst Exxon Office Systems Co., Stamford, Conn., 1981-83; sr. staff acct. United Technologies Bldg. System, Irving, Tex., 1983-85; fin. acct. Dresser Industries, Inc., Dallas, 1985—. Volleyball coach YMCA, Arlington, Tex., 1985; recruiter U. Bridgeport, 1985—. Mem. Nat. Assn. Accts., Soc. Women Accts., Am. Bus. Women's Assn., U. Bridgeport Alumni Assn., U. Bridgeport Acctg. Roundtable, Toastmasters (CTM), Omega Phi Alpha. Republican. Roman Catholic. Office: Dresser Industries Inc 1600 Pacific Dallas TX 75201

PROCTOR, SALLIE EARLE, sales and marketing executive; b. Winston Salem, N.C., Dec. 15, 1950; d. Richard Culpepper and Daisy Bethea (Chamness) P. BA, Vanderbilt U., 1972; MBA, Emory U., 1979. Asst. dir. cash control Sugar Mountain Co., Banner Elk, N.C., 1972-74; psychiat. counsel Med. U. S.C., Charleston, 1974-77; credit analyst commercial loan svcs. N.C. Nat. Bank, Charlotte, 1979-80, trust rep. corp. trust bus. devel., 1980-81, trust officer corp. trust bus. devel., 1981-83, asst. v.p. corp. trust bus. devel., 1983-85, v.p., mgr. Fla. corp. trust new bus., 1985-86; v.p., dir. mktg. Nat. Property Advisors, Atlanta, 1986-87; 1st v.p. Mitchell Hutchins Asset Mgmt., N.Y.C., 1987—; mem. investment com. PaineWebber Properties, Inc., N.Y.C., 1988—. Fund raiser Heart Assn., United Way, Arts and Sci. Coun., Charlotte, 1980-86; active Jr. League, Atlanta, Charlotte, 1979-87, N.Y.C., 1988. Mem. Asns. Investment Mgmt. Sales Execs., N.C. Soc. N.Y., Grandfather Golf and Country Club (Linville, N.C.), Charlotte C. of C., Kappa Alpha Theta, Beta Gamma Sigma, Beta Alpha Psi. Republican. Methodist. Office: Mitchell Hutchins Asset 1285 Ave of Americas New York NY 10019

PROEFROCK, VICKI GAITHER, psychometrist; b. Bloomington, Ill., Sept. 18, 1947; d. Harold Victor and Grace Lucille (Phelps) Gaither; m. David Wayne Proefrock, June 20, 1970; children: Amy, Benjamin. Student Western Ill. U., 1965-66, Memphis State U., 1976-78; BA, Augusta Coll., 1982. Med. technician Mercy Hosp., Urbana, Ill., 1967-72; med. technician Med. Coll. Ga., Augusta, 1972-74, psychometrist, 1980-87; research chemist U. Tenn. Ctr. Health Scis., Memphis, 1975-80. Contbr. articles to profl. jours. Vice pres. Augusta Coll. Women, 1983-84; mem. ways and means com. Assn. Parents of Gifted, Columbia County, Ga., 1983-84; chmn. Friends of Ezekiel Harris; mem. Columbia County Dem. Com., 1982—; mem. Ga. Dem. Com., 1982—; mem. adv. bd. Ga. Regional Hosp., Augusta, 1984—; mem. Community Leadership Program, Columbia, 1986—; exec. dir. Richmond County Hist. Soc., 1989—. Recipient de Treville award for hist. article Richmond County Hist. Soc., 1982, Modern Traditional Homemaker award State of Ga., 1987, Golden Key award Augusta Coll. Found. for Community Service, 1987; named to Outstanding Young Women Am., U.S. Jaycees, 1983, 84; named Modern Traditional Homemaker for State of Ga.; nat. merit scholar Western Ill. U., 1965. Mem. Augusta Area Psychol. Assn. (assoc.), Hist. Augusta, Augusta Coll. Alumni Assn. (bd. dirs. 1983—, Golden Key award 1987). Unitarian. Avocations: aerobic dancing; baking; historical research. Home: 4684 Oakley Pirkle Rd Martinez GA 30907 Office: Med Coll Ga Dept Pediatrics BIW 848 Augusta GA 30912

PROFITA, KAREN JENSEN, sales executive; b. Hammond, Ind., May 20, 1959; d. Larrie Oliver and Joan Mae (Bakota) J. m. William Keith, Sep. 5, 1987. BS, La. State U., 1982. Admin. asst. for publ. rels. 19th JDC Clerk of Ct., Baton Rouge, 1980-82; acct. exec. AT&T Info. Systems, Baton Rouge, 1982-83; field coord. People for Gov. Dave Treen, Baton Rouge, 1983; account exec. Johnson/McGehee Advt., Baton Rouge, 1984; pres./founder Modular Info. Systems, Baton Rouge, 1984-86; sales mgr. La. Network, Baton Rouge, 1986—. Author/Producer Record for All Time, 1980 (1st Place 1981). advance person White House-Office of the V.P. U.S. 1981-83, Photographer La. Spl. Olympics, Hammond, La. 1985, photographer U.S. Sports Festival- Local Com., Baton Rouge 1985, event coord. various polit. campaigns Baton Rouge, 1981--. Office: La Network 263 Riverside Mall 5th Fl Baton Rouge LA 70801

PROGULSKE-FOX, ANN, microbiology educator; b. Springfield, Mass., Dec. 10, 1951; d. Donald Robert and Eunice Miller (Hopler) Progulske; m. William David Fox, Aug. 13, 1983. BS, S.D. State U., 1974; PhD, U. Mass., 1983; postgrad., U. Conn. Health Ctr., 1983-84. Instr.-in-residence U. Conn. Med. Sch., Farmington, 1983-84; asst. prof. Coll. of Dentistry U. Fla., Gainesville, 1984-89, assoc. prof., 1989—, dir. PhD program, 1986-90, asst. prof. Coll. of Medicine, 1985-89, assoc. prof., 1989—; v.p. ZZ Fox Enterprise, Orange park, Fla., 1987—; cons. NIH, Bethesda, Md., 1987—, Am. Dental Assn., Chgo., 1988—. Co-author: Oral Microbiology and Immunology, 1988, Contemporary Oral Biology, 1990; contbr. articles to profl. publs.; patentee in field. Vol. Am. Cancer Soc., Gainesville, 1987—; jr. warden vestry St. Anne's Episcopal Ch., Keystone Heights, Fla., 1988—. NIH fellow, 1983; NIH grantee, 1985; recipient Periodontal Disease Rsch. Ctr. award NIH, 1985, Biotech. Rsch. award NSF, 1987. Fellow Assn. Am. Pathologists; mem. Am. Soc. Microbiology, Internat. Assn. for Dental Rsch., Am. Assn. for Dental Rsch., Am. Assn. Exec. Women, Am. Assn. Oral Biologists, Dental Guild. Democrat. Episcopalian. Office: U Fla JHMHSC Dept Oral Biology Box J-424 Gainesville FL 32610-0424

PRONTNICKI, JANICE, pediatrician; b. Bayonne, N.J., Aug. 30, 1960; d. Raymond Isadore and Margaret (Zavada) P.; m. Leonard DenBleyker, June 1, 1985. BS in Biology, St. Peter's Coll., 1981; MD, NYU, 1985. Diplomate Am. Acad. Pediatrics. Intern in pediatrics Thomas Jefferson U. Hosp., Phila., 1985-86, resident, 1986-88, chief resident, 1987-88; fellow devel. disabilities U. Medicine and Dentistry of N.J., New Brunswick, 1988-90. Recipient clin. fellowship grant United Cerebral Palsy Assn., 1988, 89. Mem. Am. Acad. Cerebral Palsy and Devel. Medicine, Soc. Devel. Pediatrics, Soc. Behavioral Pediatrics, Alpha Omega Alpha. Office: Robert Wood Johnson U Hosp 1 Robert W Johnson Pl CN19 New Brunswick NJ 08903-0019 also: Hunterdon Pediatric Assocs Flemington NJ

PROPP, GAIL DANE GOMBERG, computer consulting company executive; b. N.Y.C., Mar. 22, 1944; d. Oscar and Goody (Rosenburgh) Dane; BA in Econs., Barnard Coll., 1965; m. Ephraim Propp; children: Eric Wesley, David Marc, Anna Michelle. Instr., programmer IBM Corp., N.Y.C., 1965-66; systems and programmer analyst R.S. Topas Co., N.Y.C., 1966-67; dir. systems and programming Abercrombie & Fitch Co., N.Y.C., 1967-69; dir. corp. data processing and MIS, 1969-77; founder, 1977, since pres. Met Data Systems, Inc., N.Y.C., 1977—; founder, pres. Datatype Internat. Inc, 1982—; assoc. dir. Burns Archive of Hist. Med. Photographs, N.Y.C., 1979—. Bd. overseers Bar-Ilan U., Israel; mem. adv. bd. KIRUV. Mem. Internat. Coun. Computers in Edn., Women in Info. Processing, Assn. Systems Mgmt., Data Processing Mgmt. Assn., Assn. Systems Mgmt., Assn. Inst. Cert. Systems Profls., Photog. History Soc. Am., Photog. Historic Soc. N.Y. Contbr. articles to profl. jours. Office: 919 3d Ave New York NY 10022

PROPST, CATHERINE LAMB, biotechnology company executive; b. Charlotte, N.C., Mar. 10, 1946; d. James Pinckney and Eliza Mayo (Mills) P. BA magna cum laude, Vanderbilt U., 1967; M of Philosophy, Yale U., 1970, PhD, 1973. Head microbiology div. GTE Labs., Waltham, Mass., 1974-77; various mgmt. positions Abbott Labs., North Chgo., Ill., 1977-80; v.p. rsch. and devel. Ayerst Labs., Plainview, N.Y., 1980-83; v.p. rsch. and devel. worldwide Flow Gen. Inc., McLean, Va., 1983-85; pres. and chief exec. officer Affiliated Sci. Inc., Ingleside, Ill., 1985—; vis. prof. genetics, U. Ill., Chgo.; bd. dirs. several cos. Author and editor: Computer-Aided Drug Design, 1989; contbr. articles to profl. jours. Named to Outstanding Working Women in the U.S., 1982; recipient many sci. and bus. awards. Fellow Soc. for Indsl. Microbiology (bd. dirs. 1990—); mem. Am. Soc. Microbiology, AAAS, Nat. Wildlife Fedn., Phi Beta Kappa, Sigma Xi. Episcopalian. Office: Affiliated Sci Inc PO Box 437 Ingleside IL 60041

PROSSER, DEBORAH L., sales executive; b. Indpls., Jan. 1, 1954; d. Robert Glenn and Clara Joy (Lumpkin) Hazel; m. Larry Dean Prosser, May 24, 1986. Supr. Wabash Life Ins. Co. Denver; sales coord. Kidney-Wood Co., Inc., Indpls. Mem. Life Office Mgmt. Assn. Home: RR 1 Box 606 Clayton IN 46118 Office: 1501 W Market St Indianapolis IN 46222

PROSSER, LISA LYNN, security systems company executive; b. Indpls., May 18, 1955; d. Samuel Benjamin and Norma Rose (Opell) Phillips; m. Edgar Royal Prosser III, Nov. 25, 1978; children: Lucas Tye, Audra Lynn, Emma Katheryn. Grad. high sch., Indpls. Legal sec. Hoosier State Press Assn., Indpls., 1973-76; cosmetic artist Glemby Internat., Columbus, Ohio, 1976-77; regional supr. Glemby Internat., Cleve. and Boston, 1977-78; real estate sales rep. Realty World Real Estate, Portsmouth, Va., 1978-79; sales rep. Gen. Alarm Co., Inc. div. Dictograph Security Systems, Indpls., 1980—; sales mgr., v.p. Gen. Alarm Co., Inc. div. Dictograph Security Systems, 1982—, co-owner, 1986—; v.p., corp. sec. Gen. Emergency Monitoring Co., Indpls., 1985—. Mem. Am. Soc. Indsl. Security, Internat. Crime Prevention Practitioners, Nat. Crime Prevention Inst., Builders Assn. Greater Indpls. Republican. Presbyterian. Office: Gen Alarm Co 1803 N Meridian St Indianapolis IN 46202

PROTHERO-SMITH, JOY EDDETTE, education educator; b. Oskaloosa, Iowa, Oct. 3, 1952; d. Edward George and Wilda Geneva (Richardson) Prothero; m. William F. Smith, Dec. 22, 1984 (div. Jan. 1990); children: Holly, Heather. BA, William Penn Coll., Oskaloosa, 1974; MS in Edn., Drake U., 1985, EdD, 1989. Cert. tchr. with endorsements, Iowa. Tchr. Twin Cedars Community Schs., Bussey, Iowa, 1974-85; prof. edn. William Penn Coll., 1985—. Officer Mahaska County Rep. Cen. Com., 1980—. Mem. Internat. Reading Assn., Assn. Tchrs. Educators, Assn. Curriculum and Instrn., Phi Delta Kappa (v.p. 1990-91). Presbyterian. Home: RR 3 Box 203 Oskaloosa IA 52577 Office: William Penn Coll 201 Trueblood Ave Oskaloosa IA 52577

PROTIC, DUSHICA BABICH, lawyer; b. Belgrade, Yugoslavia, Feb. 22, 1958; came to U.S., 1967; d. Dushan J. and Zorica (Markovic) Babich; m. John R. Protic, June 11, 1988. BA, Cornell U., 1979; JD, Fordham U., 1983. Bar: N.Y. 1984. Staff atty. SEC, N.Y.C., 1984-86; assoc. Weil, Gotshal & Manges, N.Y.C., 1986—. Editor, contbr. Fordham Internat. Law Jour., 1982-83. Office: Weil Gotshal & Manges 767 Fifth Ave New York NY 10153

PROVENCHER-KAMBOUR, FRANCES, public relations executive; b. Exeter, N.H., Apr. 22, 1947; d. Roger Arthur and Josette Marguerite (Camus) Provencher; m. Benjamin C. Ryder, Apr. 12, 1969 (div. Mar. 1979); 1 child, Tiffany Nicholas; m. Edward S. Kambour, Dec. 27, 1988. BA, U. N.H., 1969. Clk. typist, editorial asst. U.S. Embassy, Moscow, 1964-65; asst. editor Durham (N.H.) Advertiser, 1965-69; assoc. editor Kaman Aerospace Corp., Bloomfield, Conn., 1970-71; publs. editor The Hartford Ins. Group (Conn.), 1974-76; pub. rels. cons. Fran Ryder Assocs., Farmington, Conn., 1976-78; pub. rels. account exec. Shailer Davidoff Rogers, Inc., Fairfield, Conn., 1978-80; sr. account exec. Creamer Dickson Basford, Inc., Hartford, Conn., 1980-83; account group mgr., account exec. Spiro & Assocs., Phila., 1983-84, v.p., assoc. pub. rels. dir., 1984-85; sr. v.p. pub. rels. LSGE Advt. Inc., Avon, Conn., 1985-87; v.p. corp. communications Wondriska Assocs., Farmington, Conn., 1987-88; pres. The Kambour Co., Raleigh, N.C., 1988—. Translator: The Cogito in Edmund Husserl's Phenomenology, 1969. Founder, The Art Guild, 1975; bd. dirs. Parent's Assn., Hartford Sch. Ballet, 1982-83, U. Conn. Found., 1986—. Recipient Gold Quill awards Internat. Assn. Bus. Communicators, 1974. Mem. Pub. Rels. Soc. Am. (accredited, bd. dirs. 1980-88, 90—, mem. Counselors Acad. 1982—, assembly del. 1987-88, spl. commendation 1985). Republican. Congregationalist. Office: The Kambour Co 518 W Jones St Raleigh NC 27603

PROVIS, DOROTHY L(OUISE), artist, sculptor; b. Chgo., Apr. 26, 1926; d. George Kenneth Smith and Ann Hart (Day) Smith Guest; m. William H. Provis Sr., July 28, 1945; children: Timothy A., William H. Jr. Student Sch. Art Inst., Chgo., 1953-56, U. Wis.-Milw., 1967-68, 69-70. Sculptor Port Washington, Wis., 1963—; pres. bd. dirs. West Bend Gallery of Fine Arts, Wis., 1984-86, bd. dirs., 1987-89; speaker, presenter in field. Author, lobbyist Wis. Consignment Bill, Madison, 1979; panelist Women's Caucus for Art Conf., Phila., 1983; mem. adv. bd. Percent for Art Pro., 1985-87, Wis. Arts Bd. Wis. Arts Bd. Designer-Craftsmen grantee, NEA, 1981. Mem. Coalition of Women's Art Orgns. (del. to continuing com. Nat. Women's Conf. 1979, panelist conf. 1981, v.p. for membership/nominations, 1981-83, pres. 1983-85, nat. pres. 1985-87, 89—, v.p. communications 1987-89, editor CWAO newsletter 1985—), Wis. Painters and Sculptors (pres. 1982-84, editor newsletter 1982-85), Wis. Women in Arts (legis. liaison 1978-80), Nat. Women's Studies Assn. (conf. presenter 1988), Artists for Ednl. Action (corr. 1979-85), Wis. Designer Craftsmen, Women's Caucus for Art (panelist 1981, 83, 86, 87, conf. com. panelist 1987, presenter 1989), Chgo. Artists Coalition. Home and Studio: 123 E Beutel Rd Port Washington WI 53074

PROVOST, ELEANOR, judge; b. Schenectady, N.Y., Aug. 22, 1947; d. Roger Provost and Evelyn (Palme) P.; m. Al Costa, Aug. 5, 1978. BA, U. Calif., Berkeley, 1969; JD, New Eng. Sch. Law, 1975. Bar: Calif. 1976. Pvt. practice San Francisco, 1976-77; dep. dist. atty. Tuolumne County, Sonora, Calif., 1977-82; judge Groveland, Calif., 1982—; sem. leader Judges coll., Berkeley, Calif., 1988—, Mcpl. & Justice Cts. Inst., San Diego, 1986. Mem. adv. group Sonora Community Hosp., 1983—; mem. Jail Expansion Com., Sonora, 1988; pres. Friends of Libr., Sonora, 1987. Mem. Calif. Bar Assn., Calif. Judges Assn., Tuolumne County Bar Assn. Democrat. Office: 4th Dist Justice Ct PO Box 496 Groveland CA 95321

PROVOST, RHONDA MARIE, nurse anesthetist; b. Quincy, Mass., Sept. 13, 1948; d. John Stanley and Roberta Adelaide (Tangstrom) P. RN, Quincy City Hosp. Sch. Nursing, 1969, Nurse Anesthetist, 1971; BS, George Washington U., 1982. Cert. registered nurse anesthetist. Staff anesthetist, instr. Children's Hosp. Med. Ctr., Boston, 1971-77; staff anesthetist George Washington U. Med. Ctr., Washington, 1977-78; dir. Sch. of Anesthesia, New Eng. Med. Ctr. Hosp., Boston, 1978-79; staff anesthetist Kaiser-Permanente Med. Group, Redwood City, Calif., 1979-88, chief anesthetist, 1988-89, Santa Rosa, Calif., 1989—; freelance anesthetist Pregnancy Counseling Ctr., San Jose, Calif., 1983-84, Plastic Reconstructive Ambulatory Ctr., Los Altos, Calif., 1984-85; treas. Specific Publs., Inc., 1983. Co-author: Indoor Exercise Book, 1981, Advanced Indoor Exercise Book, 1982, Feeling Fit in Your Forties, 1986; also articles; TV race commentator 2d Ann. Manila Internat. Marathon, 1983. Sec. bd. dirs. Grant Ave. Condominium Owners Assn., Palo Alto, Calif., 1984, v.p. bd. dirs., 1985. Mem. Am. Assn. Nurse Anesthetists, Calif. Assn. Nurse Anesthetists. Roman Catholic. Avocations: triathletics, piano, snow skiing, water skiing, horseback riding. Home: 7050 Guisti Rd Forestville CA 95436 Office: The Permanente Med Group 401 Bicenntenial Way Santa Rosa CA 95403-2192

PRUDHOMME, LISA ANN, statistician, researcher; b. New Orleans, Oct. 5, 1960; d. Oliver Theophile and Beverly May (Rodriguez) P. BS in Biol. Scis., U. New Orleans, 1982; MS in Biometry, La. State U., New Orleans, 1985. Rsch. assoc. dept. medicine La. State U., New Orleans, 1985-87, rsch. assoc. dept. biometry and genetics, 1987-88; assoc. statis. Boots Pharms. Inc., Shreveport, La., 1988—. Mem. Am. Agrl. Econs. Assn., Am. Statis. Assn., Beta Beta Beta, Phi Eta Sigma, Alpha Theta Epsilon. Democrat. Roman Catholic. Home: 8501 Millicent Way Shreveport LA 71115

PRUETT, DONNIE RAY, sales executive; b. Denton, Tex., Apr. 17, 1948; d. Harold Ray and Jackie Lou (Malone) P. AA in Bus., Temple Jr. Coll., 1968. Account mgr. Gen. Foods Corp., Houston, 1975-80; exec. recruiter Search Unltd., L.A., 1980-84; account rep. Shade Foods, Inc., L.A., 1984-89; nat. sales dir. Clarendon Flavor Engring., L.A., 1989—. Recipient basketball scholarship Temple Jr. Coll., 1966; named Tex. All-Star Basketball Player, Amateur Athletic Assn., 1966, Miss Temple Jr. Coll., 1967. Mem. Bakery Prodn. Club (chmn. greeter com. 1989-90). Home: 963 Hedges Dr Corona CA 91720 Office: Clarendon Flavor Engring 3300 7th St Rd Louisville KY 40216

PRUETT, HELEN GORHAM, home economist; b. Cardwell, Mo., Nov. 9, 1919; d. Zeron T. Gorham and Beckie Lou (Warren) Gorham Hart; m. Finis Q. Pruett, May 4, 1945; 1 child, Beckie Ann. BS in Edn., S.W. Mo. State U., 1941; cert., Mo. U., Columbia, 1941. Voc. home economics tchr. Ava (Mo.) High Sch., 1941-43; home economist, supr. Chr. Hansen's Lab., St. Louis, 1943-46; home economist, dem. Brown Supply Co., St. Louis, 1949-57; home economist & mgr. consumer affairs Milnot Co., St. Louis, cons., 1958-88. Author: Tested and Tasted Economical Recipes, 1961, 2nd Editon, 1963, New and Favorite, 1965, Great Food Ideas and 2nd Edition, 1983-88. Mem. Mo. Vocat. Adv. Bd., Pkwy. Dist. Adv. Bd. Mem. Am. Home Econs. Assn., Mo. Home Economists Assn. (Table Honors award 1981), St. Louis Home Economist Bus. (chmn. 2 terms). Democrat. So. Baptist. Home: 9523 W Milton Saint Louis MO 63114

PRUETT, RHEA ROELIE HOFMAN, personnel manager; b. Bakkeveen Friesland, The Netherlands, Oct. 14, 1955; d. Henry J. and Minnie J. (Doller) Hofman; m. Raymond M. Pruett, Aug. 29, 1981. AAS with highest honors, Davenport Coll., Grand Rapids, Mich., 1987. Mil. pers. specialist U.S. Army, 1975-78; mil. pers. technician Mich. Army N.G., Wyoming, 1978-87; chief pers. svc. ctr. Mich. Army N.G., Lansing, 1987—. Mem. NAFE, N.G. Assn. Mich. (bd. dirs.), N.G. Assn. U.S. Address: 2500 S Washington St Lansing MI 48913

PRUITT, ALICE FAY, mathematician, engineer; b. Montgomery, Ala., Dec. 17, 1943; d. Virgil Edwin and Ocie Victoria (Mobley) Maye; m. Mickey Don Pruitt, Nov. 5, 1967; children: Derrell Gene, Christine Marie. BS in Math., U. Ala., Huntsville, 1977; postgrad. in engring., Calif. State U., Northridge, 1978-79. Instr. math. Antelope Valley Coll., Quartz Hill, Calif., 1977-78; space shuttle engr. Rockwell Internat., Palmdale, Calif., 1979-81; programmer, analyst Sci. Support Svcs. Combat Devel.-Experimentaton Ctr., Ft. Hunter-Liggett, Calif., 1982-85; sr. ops. rsch. systems analyst LTV Missiles and Electronics Group, Dallas, 1985—. Mem. DeSoto (Tex.) Coun. Cultural Arts, 1987-89. Mem. AAUW (sch. bd. rep. 1982, phone chmn. 1987-89, legal advocacy Fund Chairperson 1989—), Phi Kappa Phi. Republican.

Methodist. Office: LTV Missiles-Electronics PO Box 650003 MS WT-52 Dallas TX 75254-0003

PRUITT, CINDY KAY, maintenance technician; b. Dallas, Oct. 28, 1957; d. John H. Moore and Patricia Wallace Zimmerman; 1 child, Tom I. White III; m. Anthony E. Pruitt, Dec. 27, 1980; children: T. J. Dillon, Timothy J. W. AAS, Mt. View Community Coll., Dallas, 1989. Gen. office clk. Tex. Indsl. Accident Bd., Dallas, 1974-77; data entry operator Olan Mills, Dallas, 1977-78; adminstrv. asst. Marshall & Sons Ind., Arlington, Tex., 1978-79; sales mgr. Gem Exchange Inc, Dallas, 1979-80; letter carrier U.S. Postal Svc., Irving, Tex., 1980-86; maintenance technician U.S. Postal Svc., Irving, 1986—. Author: (children's musical) Caleco Key the What's in it for Me CAT, 1986, (poetry) What Is A Teacher, 1987; composer: (wong) No Greater Love, 1988. Vol. Dem. Congressional Campaign, 1978; den leader Boy Scouts of Am., Cedar Hill, Tex., 1981-82; dir. Children's Ch. Airport Irving, Tex., 1983-85. Recipient scholarship Dallas County Community Coll. Dist, 1988. Mem. Phi Theta Kappa. Republican. Home: PO Box 783 Cedar Hill TX 75104 Office: US Postal Svc 125 W 23rd Irving TX 75060

PRUITT, DOROTHY J. GOOCH, educational administrator; b. Granville County, N.C., June 10, 1935; d. Edgar N. and Lorine (Henley) Gooch; m. William Leonard Pruitt, July 22, 1958. BS, East Carolina U., 1956; MEd, U. N.C.-Chapel Hill, 1971; sixth yr. cert. Nova U., 1984, EdD, 1985. Home econs. tcr. Granville County Schs., Oxford, N.C., 1956-69; cons. State Dept. Pub. Instrn., Raleigh, N.C., 1972-82; prin. Granville County Schs., 1982—. Bd. dirs. N.C. Sch. Bd. Assn., Raleigh, 1980-82; chmn. Granville County Bd. Edn., 1979-82; v.p. Jr. Woman's Club, Oxford, 1965-66 (named Club Woman of Yr. 1965). Named Granville County Prin. of Yr., 1987-88. Mem. N.C. Assn. Sch. Adminstrs., Am. Sch. Curriculum Devel. Assn., Am. Sch. Curriculum Assn., Am. Ednl. Research Assn., N.C. Future Homakers of Am. (hon.), Alpha Delta Kappa (corr. sec. 1970). Baptist. Home: 106 Country Club Dr Oxford NC 27565 Office: Granville County Schs 223 College St Oxford NC 27565

PRUITT, INA, artist, gallery owner; b. Kalispell, Mont., Dec. 25, 1905; d. Andrew Jackson and Amelia Catherine (Hartsook) Collins; m. Veltie Pruitt, Aug. 13, 1925; children: Ina, Veltie, David, Janice. Student, Eugene (Oreg.) Bible U., 1923, U. Oreg., 1923. Artist, owner Ina Pruitt Art Gallery, Springfield, Oreg.; Judge Dept. Traditional Art, Oreg. State Fair, 1963-64, Ann. Mission Mill Art Show, Salem, Oreg., 1985. Painter working in oils; illustrator: (poems by E.J. Gilstrap) Round the Fireplace, Undaunted Pioneers; 75 one-woman shows in 5 states, 1959, State Capital Bldg., 1963-66; works include portrait Barry Goldwater, 1964, lithographs, poems, sketches in Steene Mountain Heritage Scrapbook, 1982. Recipient 1st award 1st and 2d Artists' Showcase, Eugene, 1960-61, 1st Favell Mus. Western Heritage award, 1977, 1st award for Amazing Grace Seattle Art Show, 1980; named Oreg. Artist of Yr., 1985; subject of radio progam Stories of Pacific Powerland, 1969. Mem. Women in the Arts (Washington) (charter). Republican. Mem. Ch. of Christ. Address: 88830 Ross Ln Springfield OR 97478

PRUITT, NANCY LOUISE, educator; b. Phila., Feb. 24, 1953; d. Walter E. and Dorothy (Barnes) P.; m. Marvin E. Neas, Mar. 2, 1979 (div. Aug. 1987). BA, Gettysburg Coll., 1975; MA, Wake Forest U., 1977; PhD, Ariz. State U., 1983. Assoc. prof. biology Colgate U., Hamilton, N.Y., 1983—. Contbr. articles to profl. jours. Grantee Rsch. Corp., Hamilton, N.Y., 1986, 87, NSF, Hamilton, 1987. Mem. Am. Physiol. Soc., AAAS, Am. Soc. Zoologists, Upstate MacIntosh Users Group. Office: Colgate U Dept Biology Hamilton NY 13346

PRUNIER, CHANTAL, real estate executive and advisor; b. Beaune, France, Nov. 10, 1956; came to U.S., 1978; d. Roger and Monique (Barrault) P.; m. Michael Elmore Grindon, June 29, 1983; children: Alexandra Marie, Casey. B. in Econs. and Bus., Ecole Superieure de Commerce, Dijon, France, 1977; MBA, Harvard U., 1980; broker's license, NYU, 1987. Cert. in real estate mgmt. and devel. Product mgr. Becton Dickinson, Rutherford, N.J., 1980-82; dir. mktg. Western Union, Upper Saddle River, N.J., 1982-84; v.p. LaSalle Ptnrs., N.Y.C., 1984—. Mem. Cedar Knolls Community Assn., Bronxville, N.Y., 1989. Mem. Real Estate Bd. N.Y., Urban Land Inst. (Washington). Democrat. Roman Catholic.

PRUSSIN, BARBARA KAHN, instructor; b. N.Y.C., June 10, 1942; d. Joseph and Toby (Grubel K.; m. Richard Alan Prussin, Dec. 8, 1937; children: Jodi Karin, Shari Lynn. U. Bridgeport, Bridgeport, 1963; MS, U. Bridgeport, 1970, Student, 1982. Reading tchr. Norwalk Pub. Sch., Norwalk, Conn., 1963-65; chpt. 1 tchr. Norwalk Pub. Sch., Norwalk, 1974-76, Fairfield Pub. Sch., Fairfield, Conn., 1976—; lang. arts, spec. edn. tchr. New Canaan Country Sch., New Canaan, Conn. Hospice Vol., Fairfield Visiting Nurses Assn., Fairfield, Conn., 1980-81. Mem. Elisabeth Kubler-Ross Ctr., Conn. Assn. for Children with Learning Disabilities. Democrat. Jewish. Office: New Canaan Country Sch PO Box 997 New Canaan CT 06840

PRUSSING See BURDEN, JEAN

PRUSSING, LAUREL LUNT, county official, auditor; b. N.Y.C., Feb. 21, 1941; d. Richard Valentine and Maria (Rinaldi) Lunt; m. John Edward Prussing, May 29, 1965; children: Heidi Elizabeth, Erica Stephanie, Victoria Nicole Johanna. AB, Wellesley Coll., 1962; MA, Boston U., 1964; postgrad., U. Calif., San Diego, 1968-69, U. Ill., 1970-76. Economist Arthur D. Little, Cambridge, Mass., 1963-67, U. Ill., Urbana, 1971-72; mem. county bd. Champaign County, Urbana, 1972-76, county auditor, 1976—; mem. local audit adv. bd. Office Ill. Compt., Chgo., 1984—. Contbr. to Illinois Local Government: A Handbook, 1989. Founder, treas. Com. for Intelligent Tax Reform, Urbana, 1982—, Com. for Elected County Exec., Urbana, 1986—; treas. Unity '88 for Dukakis-Bentsen, Urbana, 1988. Mem. Govt. Fin. Officers Assn. U.S. and Can. (com. on acctg., auditing and fin. reporting, 1980-88, fin. reporting award 1981-88, disting. budget award 1986), Nat. Assn. Local Govt. Auditors (charter), Ill. Assn. County Auditors (pres. 1984-85), LWV. Democrat. Home: 2106 Grange Dr Urbana IL 61801 Office: Office County Auditor 212 E Main St Urbana IL 61801

PRUTER, MARGARET FRANSON, encyclopedia editor; b. Oak Pk., Ill., Jan. 16; d. Frederick G. and Margaret K. (Svoboda) Franson; m. Robert D. Pruter, July 22, 1972; 1 child, Robin. AB, Rosary Coll., 1961; MA, Northwestern U., 1965. Asst. editor Am. People's Encyclopedia, Chgo., 1961-62; rsch. assoc. Am. Med. Assn., Chgo., 1962-63; asst. editor New Standard Encyclopedia, Chgo., 1964-66, assoc. editor, 1966-75, sr. editor, 1975—; exec. dir.Militaria Archives, Elmhurst, Ill., 1972—. Co-author: DuPage Roots, 1985 (Ill. State Hist. Publ. award 1986). Commr. Elmhurst (Ill.) Hist. Commn., 1981—; bd. dirs. DuPage County Hist. Soc., Wheaton, Ill., 1982—, DuPage County Sesquicentennial Com., 1988-89. Mem. AAUW, Organ. Am. Historians, Nat. Trust Hist. Preservation, Am. Studies Assn., Ill. Hist. Soc., Elmhurst Hist. Soc., Chgo. Hist. Soc., Chgo. Architecture Found., Byrd's Nest Chapel Questers, Pi Gamma Mu. Office: Standard Ednl Corp 200 W Monroe St Chicago IL 60606

PRUTZMAN, PENELOPE ELIZABETH, educator; b. Vancouver, Wash., Apr. 25, 1944; d. Delbert Daniel and Jessie May (Lowry) P. BA in Sociology, CUNY, 1975; diploma, Grand Diplôme Cooking Sch. Tchr. Mt. Carmel-Holy Rosary Sch., N.Y.C., 1968—. Active Vol. Services for Children, N.Y.C., 1980-83. Recipient 10 Yr. Service to Cath. Schs. of Harlem award Office of Supt. Sch. Archdiocese of N.Y., 1979, 20 Yrs. to Cath. Sch. award Archdiocese of N.Y., 1986; named one of Outstanding Elem. Tchrs. of Am., 1974. Mem. Fedn. Cath. Tchrs. (exec. council 1974—, negotiating com., Cert. of Honor 1982), Nat. Cath. Edn. Assn., Reading Reform Found. Democrat. Episcopalian. Home: 35-25 34 St C44 Astoria NY 11106 Office: Mt Carmel-Holy Rosary Sch 371 Pleasant Ave New York NY 10035

PRUZAN, IRENE, arts administrator, music educator, flutist, marketing specialist; b. Watertown, N.Y., Jan. 3, 1949; d. John Edward and Esther (Coahn) P.; m. Charles G. Ullery, Jan. 30, 1972 (div. 1978); m. Charles Robert Freeman, May 20, 1988. Student, U. Ariz., 1966-68; MusB, U. So. Calif., 1971; postgrad., San Francisco State U., 1972-74, U. Minn., 1976-80. Tchr. flute, coach chamber music MacPhail Ctr. for Arts, U. Minn., Mpls., 1976-85, coordinator instrumental music, 1978-81, program dir. instrumental music, 1982-85, div. head of programs, 1985-86; regional dir. Music On The Move, Inc., Valley Cottage, N.Y., 1986-87; pres. Music On the Move Minn., Inc., St. Paul, 1987—; founding mem. Crocus Hill Trio, 1976—; faculty Nat. Music Camp, Interlochen, Mich., 1983, 84; cons. edn. and festival Ordway Music Theatre, St. Paul, 1985-87; mgr. Sartory String Quartet, Mpls., 1986—; developer numerous master classes. Writer teaching materials for flute. Mem. Ariz. Chamber Orch., Tucson, 1967, San Gabriel (Calif.) Symphony, 1968-71; extra player St. Paul Chamber Orch., 1977—; competition judge Women's Assn. Minn. Orch., Mpls., 1982—; bd. dirs. Twin Cities Friends of Chamber Music, 1982—; organizer German jazz residency USIA, Minn. and Wis., 1986; cons., program dir. Young Audiences Minn., Mpls., 1986-88. Mem. Nat. Flute Assn. (dir. mktg. 1987—), Minn. Alliance for Arts in Edn., Twin Cities Musician's Union. Office: Music On The Move Minn Inc PO Box 4125 Saint Paul MN 55104

PRYATEL, HOLLY ANN, compensation and benefits executive; b. South Bend, Ind., Apr. 1, 1948; d. Frank John and Lillian May (Holley) P. B in History, Am. U., 1971, MBA, 1977. Cert. compensation profl., employee benefits specialist. Employee rels. specialist COMSAT, Washington, 1978-79, pers. info. specialist, 1979-81, supr. personnel systems and records, 1981-82, mgr. compensation and benefits adminstrn., 1982-83, compensation cons., 1983-84; mgr. compensation and benefits Ctr. for Naval Analyses, Alexandria, Va., 1984-88, Dialcom Inc. now BT Tymnet Inc., Rockville, Md., 1988-90; mgr. benefits CONTEL Fed. Systems, Chantilly, Va., 1990—; publicity chairperson Va. Am. Soc. Personnel Adminstrs. Conf., 1989. Mem. Washington Personnel Assn. (v.p. 1988-90), Washington Tech. Personnel Forum (bd. dirs. 1990—), Nat. Coun. Career Women (career day com. 1984, nominating com. 1988-89, v.p. programs 1990—), Washington Area Recreation and Employee Svcs. Coun. (v.p. 1979). Republican. Lutheran. Home: 14905 Bradwill Ct Rockville MD 20850 Office: Contel Fed Systems 15000 Conference Center Dr PO Box 10814 Chantilly VA 22021-3808

PRYOR, BRENDA ROGERS, tax executive; b. Jonesboro, Ark., Sept. 28, 1952; d. J. Richard and Vida Mae (Lawrence) Rogers; m. John Thomas Pryor, May 10, 1980; children: Kristen Leigh, Rachel Lynn. BBA in Acctg., Memphis State U., 1974. CPA, Tenn., Ark. Tax sr. Arthur Andersen & Co., Memphis, 1974-78; tax mgr. Price Waterhouse, Little Rock, 1978-81; treas. Jacuzzi, Inc., Little Rock, 1981-88; tax dir. Dillard Dept. Stores, Little Rock, 1988—. Bd. dirs. Suzuki Inst., Little Rock, 1988. Mem. Ark. Fin. Execs. Inst. (v.p. 1987-88, pres. 1988-89), Am. Soc. Women Accts. (pres. Cen. Ark. chpt. 1979-80). Methodist. Office: Dillard Dept Stores Inc 900 W Capitol Little Rock AR 72203

PRYOR, CAROL GRAHAM, obstetrician-gynecologist; b. Savannah, Ga.; d. Louis O.J. Manganiello, June 11, 1950; children: Carol Helen Manganiello, Victoria Manganiello Mudano. AB, Ga. Coll., 1943; MD, Med. Coll. Ga., 1947. Rotating intern City Hosps., Balt., 1947-48; asst. resident pathology Baroness Erlanger Hosp., Chattanooga, 1948; intern. obstetrics City Colls., Balt., 1949; coll. physician Ga. State Coll. for Women, Milledgeville, Ga., 1949-50; resident obstetrics City Hosps., Balt., 1950-51; asst. resident gynecology Univ. Hosp., Balt., 1951-52; sr. resident ob-gyn. Univ. Hosp., Augusta, Ga., 1952; pvt. practice ob-gyn. Augusta, 1952—. Mem., former pres. Iris Garden Club, Augusta; mem. coun. on maternal and infant health State of Ga., Atlanta, 1981—; mem. edn. found. AAUW, 1961-63, state iv. pres., br. pres., 1963-65. Recipient Cert. of Achievement-Community Leadersip, Ga. div. AAUW, 1982; named Med. Woman of Yr., Ga. br. 51 Am. Med. Women's Assn., 1961. Fellow Am. Coll. Surgeons (1st woman mem. Ga. chpt. 1956); mem. AMA, Richmond County Med. Soc., So. Med. Assn., So. Surg. Congress, Delta Kappa Gamma. Democrat. Methodist. Office: 2316 Wrightboro Rd Augusta GA 30904

PRYOR, KAREN WYLIE, biologist, writer; b. N.Y.C., May 14, 1932; d. Philip Gordon Wylie and Sally Ondeck; m. Taylor A. Pryor, June 25, 1954 (div. 1973); children: Tedmund, Michael, Gale; m. Jon M. Lindbergh, May 14, 1983. BA in English, Cornell U., 1954; postgrad., U. Hawaii, 1957-59, NYU, 1977-79, Rutgers U., 1979-82. Founder, curator Sea Life Park Oceanarium, Honolulu, 1960-71; copywriter Fawcett-McDermott, Honolulu, 1973-76; drama critic Honolulu Advertiser, 1971-75; free lance writer, 1963—, marine mammal cons., 1970—; sci. advisor U.S. Tuna Found., Washington, 1976-82; cons. NSF, NASA, Nat. Geographic Soc., 1976—; commr. Marine Mammal Commn., Washington, 1984-87. Author: Nursing Your Baby, 1963, rev. edit. 1973, Lads Before the Wind: Adventures in Porpoise Training, 1975, Don't Shoot the Dog! The New Art of Teaching and Training, 1984 (Excellence in Media award Am. Psychol. Assn. 1984), How to Teach Your Dog to Play Frisbee, 1985, (with K.S. Norris) Dolphin Societies: Discoveries and Puzzles, 1989; editor: Phil Wylie's Stories of Florida Fishing, 1990, (with Gale Pryor) Nursing Your Baby Today, 1990; contbr. articles to profl. jours. Mem. Internat. Marine Amimal Trainers Assn., Authors Guild, Marine Mammal Soc. (charter mem.), Soc. Women Geographers, Cosmopolitan Club. Home: 44811 SE 166 St North Bend WA 98045

PRYOR, LAUREL MAE, risk management consultant; b. Burlington, Vt., Aug. 4, 1956; d. Lewis A. and Barbara A. (Graves) P. BSN, Keuka (N.Y.) Coll., 1979. Staff/charge RN Genessee Hosp., Rochester, N.Y., 1979-80, staff nurse CCU, 1980-81; nursing supr. North Cumberland Meml. Hosp., Bridgton, Maine, 1981-83, 87-88, head nurse, 1988-90, acting dir. nursing, 1989; asst. head nurse Maine Med. Ctr., Portland, 1983-84; risk mgmt. rep. PHICO Ins., Mechanicsburg, Pa., 1990—. Active Maine Citizens for Quality Health Care, Augusta, 1989. Mem. ANA, Maine State Nurses Assn. Home: Ingalls Hill Rd Bridgton ME 04009 Office: PHICO Ins Co One Phico Dr PO Box 85 Mechanicsburg PA 17055

PRYOR, LORI LOU, advertising executive; b. Searcy, Ark., May 20, 1964; d. Neale Thomas and Treva (Terrell) P. BA in Bus. Mgmt., Harding U., 1986. Personnel mgmt. First Comml. Bank, Little Rock, 1987-88; catering mgr. The Little Rock Club, 1988-89; advt. account exec. KKYK Radio Sta., Little Rock, 1989—; catering cons. to Little Rock Club. Dir. pub. rels. Hugh O'Brien Youth Found., Little Rock, 1989-91. Named to Outstanding Young Women of Am., 1988. Mem. Cen. Ark. Radio Assn., Pub. Rels. Soc. Am., Jr. Chamber of Little Rock. Republican. Mem. Ch. of Christ. Office: KKYK Radio Station PO Box 4189 Little Rock AR 72214

PRZELOMSKI, ANASTASIA NEMENYI, retired newspaper editor; b. Cleve., Dec. 11, 1918; d. Ernest Nicholas and Anna (Ress) Nemenyi; m. Edward Adrian Przelomski, July 4, 1946. A.B., Youngstown State U., 1939; M.Ed., U. Pitts., 1942. Tchr. Youngstown Pub. Sch., Ohio, 1939-42; reporter Vindicator, Youngstown, 1942-57, asst. city editor, 1957-73, city editor, 1973-76, mng. editor, 1976-88, ret., 1988. Named Woman of Yr., Youngstown Bus. and Profl. Women's Club, 1977, bus. category Woman of Yr., YWCA, 1986; recipient Community Service award Youngstown Fedn. Women's Clubs, 1981, Woman of Yr. award YWCA, 1983; named to Ohio Woman's Hall of Fame, 1986. Mem. AP Mng. Editors Assn., UPI Ohio Editors Assn. (bd. dirs. 1984-88), Ohio Assn. AP, Ohio Soc. Newspaper Editors, Youngstown State U. Alumni Assn. (trustee 1978-83), Catholic Collegiate Assn., Phi Kappa Phi. Republican. Roman Catholic. Home: 2261 Cordova Ave Youngstown OH 44504

PRZYBYLOWICZ, CAROLYN LYON, controller, personnel administrator; b. Clare, Mich., Jan. 18, 1947; d. Aaron Eugene and Alice Marie (Fall) Prout; m. Stanley George Lyon, July 13, 1968 (dec. May 1971); children: Lori Anne Lyon, Jamie Lynn Lyon; m. Dennis Karl Hunt, Jan. 1975 (div. Nov. 1977); 1 child, Julie Marie Hunt Przybylowicz; m. Arthur Roy Przybylowicz, Nov. 3, 1979. Cert. acctg., Lansing Bus. U., 1965. Bank teller Citizens Bank & Trust, Rosebush, Mich., 1965-68; bookkeeper, sec. Doyle & Smith P.C., Lansing, Mich., 1968-74; legal sec. Foster, Swift, Collins & Coey P.C., Lansing, 1974-79; mgr. office ARC, Lansing, 1979-81; controller, personnel adminstr. Mich. Protection & Advocacy Service, Lansing, 1981-88; bus. adminstr. White, Beekman, Przybylowicz, Schneider & Baird, P.C., Okemos, Mich., 1988—. Vol. bookkeeper Citizens Alliance to Uphold Spl. Edn., Lansing, 1977-79; coordinator bingo IHM Sch., Lansing, 1979-80; mem. St. Casimir Christian Service, Lansing, 1981-84, chairperson, 1983-84; eucharistic min., 1987—; bd. dirs. Immaculate Heart of Mary Sch., Lansing, 1977-80; vol. Ingham County chpt. Am. Cancer Soc., 1989—. Democrat. Roman Catholic. Office: White Beekman Przybylowicz Schneider & Baird PC 2214 University Park Dr Ste 200 Okemos MI 48864

PUCHTLER, HOLDE, histochemist, pathologist, educator; b. Kleinlosnitz, Germany, Jan. 1, 1920; came to U.S., 1955; d. Gottfried and Gunda (Thoma) P. Cand. med., U. Würzburg, 1944; Md, U. Köln, 1949; MD, U. Küln (Germany), 1951. Rsch. assoc. U. Köln, 1949-51; resident in pathology U. Küln, 1951-55; rsch. fellow Damon Runyon Found., Montreal, Que., Can., 1955-58; rsch. assoc. Med. Coll. Ga., Augusta, 1959-60, asst. rsch. prof., 1960-62, assoc. rsch. prof., 1962-68, prof., 1968—. Assoc. editor Jour. Histotechnology, 1982—; mem. editorial bd. Histochemistry, 1977—; contbr. articles to profl. jours. Honored at Symposium on Connective Tissues in Arterial and Pulmonary Diseases, 1980. Fellow Am. Inst. Chemists, Royal Microscopical Soc.; mem. Royal Soc. Chemistry, Am. Chem. Soc., Histochem. Soc. Gesellschaft Histochemie, Anatomische Gesellschaft, Ga. Soc. Histotech. (hon.). Office: Med Coll Ga Dept Pathology Augusta GA 30912-3600

PUCKETT, BARBARA CHANDLEY, freelance writer; b. Kansas City, Kans., Feb. 14, 1935; d. John Stothers and Edythe Raechel (Jones) Chandley; m. Robert Hugh Puckett, Dec. 23, 1964; 1 child, Sarah Anne. AA, Stephens Coll., 1955. Reporter Kansas City (Mo.) Star, 1956-58, asst. soc. editor, 1958-63, asst. women's page editor, 1963-64. Leader 4-H Club, Terre Haute, Ind., 1980—; mayoral appointee Bd. Assocs. to Archtl. Commn. Terre Haute Civic Improvement, 1974-76; bd. dirs. Terre Haute Woman's Symphony Assn.; bd. dirs., pres. Terre Haute YWCA, 1970-76; bd. dirs., pub. rels. chmn. Alternatives for Learning and Living Sch. Nursery Bd., 1984—. Mem. Women in Communication, Inc., P.E.O., Columbia Club, MVP Club, Hyannis (Mass.) Yacht Club (assoc.). Home: 122 Marigold Dr Terre Haute IN 47803

PUCKETT, BOBETTE LINN, insurance agency executive; b. Kans. City, Mar. 30, 1959; d. Robert Roy and Kathleen Ann (Renick) P. BBA in Ins. and Mgmt. Scis., U. Iowa, 1981. Cert. ins. counselor (CIC). Comml. property underwriter Chubb Ins. Co., Chgo., 1981-82, multiline comml. underwriter, 1982-83, sr. comml. underwriter, 1983-84; account exec. The Alper Agy., Chgo., 1984--; cons. Calif. Shirt Co. Windsports, San Diego, 1984--. Mem. Exec. Guild, Chgo., 1987--. Mem. Chartered Property, Casualty Underwriters, Alpha Phi. Republican. Office: The Alper Agy 60 W Superior Chicago IL 60610

PUCKETT, CHRISTINE STARLING, magazine editor; b. Guntersville, Ala., Nov. 19, 1922; d. Dalton Georgia and Pearl (Williams) Starling; m. George Wells Puckett, Sept. 6, 1946; children: Samuel Dalton, William Glenn, Thomas Carle. BA in English, U. Ala., Tuscaloosa, 1975, MA in Secondary Edn., 1977, AA in Secondary Edn., 1979. Sec., acct. Puckett & Co., Inc., Gadsden, 1946-85; mng. editor Unknowns mag. Abri Publs., Atlanta, 1984—, audio-visual mgr., 1986—; owner, mgr., artist CEE Star, greeting cards co., Gadsden; owner Ram-Star Prodns. Contbr. poetry and fiction to various publs.; patentee food product. Named Woman of Yr., Ala. Fedn. Bus. and Profl. Women, 1987. Mem. ASCAP, NAFE, Altrusa, Order Eastern Star, Beta Sigma Phi (life, pres. Gadsden 1957). Republican. Home and Office: 1403 Bellevue Dr Gadsden AL 35901

PUCKO, DIANE BOWLES, public relations executive; b. Wyndotte, Mich., Aug. 15, 1940; d. Mervin Arthur and Bernice Letitia (Shelly) Bowles; m. Raymond J. Pucko, May 22, 1965; children: Todd Anthony, Gregory Bowles. BA in Sociology, Bucknell U., Lewisburg, Pa., 1962. Accredited in pub. rels. Asst. to pub. rels. dir. Edward C. Michener Assocs., Inc., Harrisburg, Pa., 1962-65; advt./pub. rels. coord. Superior Switchboard & Devices, Canton, Ohio, 1965-66; editorial dir. women's svc. Hutchins Advt. Co., Inc., Rochester, N.Y., 1966-71; pres. Editorial Communications, Rochester and Elyria, Ohio, 1971-77; mgr. advt. and sales promotion Tappan Air Conditioning, Elyria, 1977-80; mgr. pub. affairs Kaiser Permanente Med. Care Program, Cleve., 1980-85; corp. dir. pub. affairs Keystone Health Plans, Inc., Camp Hill, Pa., 1985-86; v.p., dir. client planning Young-Liggett-Stashower, Cleve., 1986; v.p., dir. pub. rels. Marcus Pub. Rels., Cleve., 1987—; mgr., role model Women in Mgmt. Field Placement program, Cleve. State U., 1983—; prof. advisor Pub. Relations Student Soc. of Am., Kent State U., 1988—. Bd. dirs., chmn. pub. rels. com. Assn. Retarded Citizens, Cleve., 1987—. Recipient MacEachern award Acad. Hosp. Pub. Rels., Des Moines, 1985, Bell Ringer award Community Rels. Report, Bartlesville, Okla., 1985, Woman Profl. Excellence award YWCA, Cleve., 1984. Mem. Pub. Rels. Soc. Am. (dir. 1983-85, 86—, mem. counselors acad. 1986—, Silver Anvil award 1985), Press Club Cleve. (dir. 1989—, v.p. 1990), Cleve. Advt. Club, Women's City Club Cleve. Republican. Methodist. Home: 656 University Ave Elyria OH 44035 Office: Marcus Pub Rels 25700 Science Park Dr Cleveland OH 44122

PUDNEY, BETTY ANN, state official; b. Oneonta, N.Y., May 6, 1931; d. Cecil Loren and Mary Harriet (Lawless) P. BS in Journalism, Northwestern U., Evanston, Ill., 1953; postgrad., Cornell U., 1955-56. Asst. publicity dir. Harper & Bros. (now Harper & Row), N.Y.C., 1959-62; edn. editor Nat. Instructional TV Libr., N.Y.C., 1962-64; special researcher for pub. rels. Cunningham & Walsh, N.Y.C., 1964; reporter Nat. Lutheran Ch. in Am., N.Y.C., 1965; pub. information dir. Div. Employment Opportunities, Mobilization for Youth, N.Y.C., 1965-73; asst. rsch. scientist Narcotic and Drug Rsch., Inc., N.Y.C., 1974-76; dir., Concerns of Children Campaign Odyssey Inst., N.Y.C., 1977; tax compliance agt. N.Y. State Dept. Labor, Unemployment Div., Bronx, 1977-79; staff analyst, Office Appraisal Rsch. N.Y.C. Dept. Fin., 1979-80; investigator N.Y. State Liquour Authority, N.Y.C., 1980—. Co-author: (monograph) The Utilization of Industrial Advisory Committees to Increase Employment Opportunities, 1973 and others. Mem. Coalition Labor Union Women, 1980—, Pub. Employees Fedn., AFL-CIO. Mem. Assn. State Liquor Enforcement Agys. (sec. 1988—). Liberal. Lutheran. Home: 315 E 77th St New York NY 10021 Office: NY State Liquor Authority 250 Broadway New York NY 10007

PUENTES, SONIA, paralegal; b. P.R., Nov. 25, 1940; d. Manuel and Rosa (Morell) Velazquez; children: Hipolito, Dennise, Jose Manuel, Nancy, Sonia Margarita, James, Rosa Milagros, Marcus, Sylvia. Student, U. P.R., 1963. Office mgr., sr. paralegal Paul E. Bleifer, Ft. Lee, N.J. Recipient Valores Humanos, Valores de Am. Mem. NAFE. Address: 185 Bridge Plaza N Fort Lee NJ 07024

PUFF, JEAN ELLINGWOOD, civic worker; b. Evanston, Ill., July 25, 1924; d. Lloyd and Margaret (Brown) Ellingwood; m. Henry b. Puff, June 10, 1950; children: James Raymond, Margaret Elizabeth. BA, Northwestern U., 1945, BS in Nursing, 1947. Nurse, student health svc. Northwestern U., Evanston, Ill., 1947-48; pres. Gov. Wentworth Arts Coun., N.H., 1973-81 ; bd. dirs. Wolfeboro (N.H.) Playhouse, 1975-82; gov. Wentworth Arts Coun.; vol. Delta Gamma vision screening, Buffalo, 1960-65, Buffalo Philharmonic, 1959-69; mem. Huggins Hosp. Aid (Wolfeboro), Friends of Music of the Smithsonian Instn. Mem. Northwestern U. Med. Sch. Alumni Assn., Northwestern U. Alumni Assn., Rep. Women's Fedn., Wolfeboro Garden Club, Delta Gamma. Presbyterian. Home: Box 743 Springfield Point Wolfeboro NH 03894

PUFFER, BARBARA WARZECHA, corporate communications specialist; b. Phila., June 29, 1951; d. Stanley George and Barbara Jean (Maloney) Warzecha; m. Thomas R. Puffer. BA in Journalism, U. Bridgeport, 1972; MA in Corp. and Polit. Communications, Fairfield U., 1976. Suburban reporter New Haven Register, 1973; advt. asst. Union Trust & Co., New Haven, 1973-76; mgr. pub. rels. Phoenix Mut. Life, Hartford, Conn., 1976-84, 85; mgr. corp. pub. rels. So. New England Tel., New Haven, 1977-84; mgr. advt. Sonecor Systems div. So. New England Tel., New Haven, 1984-85; mgr. corp. communications Barnes Group, Inc., Bristol, Conn., 1985—; freelance writer, 1973—; assoc. producer CBS Network Sports, N.Y.C., 1977, 78. Event dir., Internat. Spl. Olympics, 1979—; vice chmn. exec. bd., pub. edn. chmn. Conn. Spl. Olympics, 1979-81, 88—; bd. corporators, mem. devel. and mktg. com., Am. Sch. for Deaf, 1986—; exec. bd., Bristol, Plymouth, Burlington United Way, 1986-90, Bristol Girls Club Family Ctr., 1987-90, Exceptional Cancer Patients, 1988. Named Communicator of Yr., Conn. chpt. Internat. Assn. Bus. Communicators, 1975, 83. Mem. New Eng. Assn. for Bus., Industry and Rehab., Conn. Pvt. Industry Coun. (mktg. com. greater New Haven sect. 1980), Nt. Panel Consumer Arbitrators, New Haven Better Bus. Bur., Internat. Assn. Bus. Communicators (accredited, pres. Conn. 1979-80, internat. exec. bd. 1985-89), Guilford Boat Owners.

Republican. Roman Catholic. Office: Barnes Group Inc 123 Main St Bristol CT 06010

PUFFER, NANCY PLACEK, small business owner; b. Chgo., Dec. 18, 1933; d. Bohumir and Agnes (Kilinski) Placek; m. Bruce M. Puffer, May 7, 1955 (div.); children: Robert B., Michael D., Timothy D., James A. BE, Northwestern U., 1955; postgrad., Ea. Mich. U., 1969-73. Tchr., elem. counselor Avondale Sch. Dist., Auburn Heights, Mich., 1969-73; owner, mgr. Swan Creek X-mas Tree Plantation, St. Charles, Mich., 1978-84; ltd. ptnr. Swan Creek X-mas Tree Plantation, St. Charles, 1984—; owner, mgr. Wheels of Fountain Hills (Ariz.) Transp. Svc., 1988—. Founder, co-chairperson Concerned Ariz. Voters, Phoenix, 1988-90; mem. gov. bd. Fountain Hills Schs., clerk, 1988-89; mem. Concerned Women for Am., Ariz., 1988—; bd. dirs. Ariz. Coord. Coun. Rep. Women, 1989—; mem. trunk & tusk com. Ariz. State Rep. Party, Phoenix, 1990; founder, counselor The Group, Bloomfield Hills, Mich., 1971-72; crusade chmn. Am. Cancer Soc., 1975 (Oakland County, Mich. chpt., Gold Key award, Best Yr. Ever award). Mem. Nat. Coun. Social Studies, Nat. Assn. Supervision and Curriculum Devel., Ariz. Sch. Bds. Assn. (delegate), Northwestern Alumni Club of Phoenix. Presbyterian. Home: 11043 Indian Wells Fountain Hills AZ 85268

PUFFER, SHEILA MARILYN, business administration educator; b. Edmonton, Alta., Can., Sept. 10, 1953; d. Kenneth Ross and Ellen Nina (Hendry) P; m. James Hugh Fraser, Oct. 11, 1974; children: Douglas Hugh, Carol Ellen. BA, U. Ottawa, 1974, MBA, 1979; PhD, U. Calif., Berkeley, 1985. Personnel adminstr. Govt. of Can., Ottawa, Ont., 1973-79; asst. prof. bus. adminstr. SUNY, Buffalo, 1984-88; asst. prof. bus. adminstrn. Northeastern U., Boston, 1988—; fellow Russian Rsch. Ctr. Harvard U., Cambridge, Mass., 1990—. Co-author: Behind the Factory Walls: Decision Making in Soviet and U.S. Enterprises, 1990; contbr. articles to bus. publs. Mem. Acad. Mgmt., Am. Psychol. Assn. Home: 12 Wildwood St Winchester MA 01890 Office: Coll Bus Northeastern U 325 Hayden Hall Boston MA 02115

PUGH, CLAUDIA ANN, accountant; b. San Bernardino, Calif., May 31, 1947; d. Claude Aaron and Loyce Lillian (Brown) Norton; m. Lloyd Douglas Martin, Feb. 26, 1966 (div. Nov. 1975); children: John Eric, Christopher Scott; m. William Reibert Pugh, Dec. 6, 1975. AS Magna Cum Laude, Lord Fairfax Coll., Middletown, Va., 1986. Sales rep. Sta. WFFV-FM radio, Middletown, 1974-75; sales clk. Winchester (Va.) Book Gallery, 1975-76; acctg. clk. Southland Corp., 1976; owner, ptnr. Bayliss Market and Gift Shop, Winchester, 1976-81; asst. to controller Arthur Fulton, Inc., Stephens City, Va., 1982-83; sec. treas. Pugh Enterprises, Inc., Wincester, 1983—; sec., treas. Borror and Pugh Enterprises, Inc., Winchester, 1984—; pres. Uniglobe Ultimate Travel Inc., Winchester, 1988—. Mem. Nat. Assn. Female Execs. Democrat. Club: Exchange (Shenandoah Valley). Home: 217 Davis Ave Leesburg VA 22075 Office: Uniglobe Ultimate Travel Inc 121 Weems Ln Winchester VA 22601

PUGH, JUNE BLANKENSHIP, nurse, consultant; b. Atlanta, Mar. 19, 1938; d. Tommie Walls and Helen Constance (Cofield) Blankenship; m. James Leland Pugh, Mar. 30, 1961; children: Jennifer Lynn, Janet Lorraine. BSN, Emory U., 1960; MS, U. Colo., 1962. Instr. Sch. Nursing Emory U., Atlanta, 1962-64; in-svc. dir. Ga. State Mental Health Inst., Atlanta, 1966-68; instr. nursing svc. VA Med. Ctr., Nashville, 1970-79, clin. specialist alcohol treatment program, 1979-88, nursing resource coord., 1988—; adj. faculty mem. Vanderbilt Sch. Nursing, Nashville, 1972—; cons. in field. Author: (with others) Nurse Manager, 1979; contbr. articles to profl. jours. Vol. Am. Cancer Soc., Nashville, 1989—. Mem. Tenn. Nurses Assn. Republican. Methodist. Office: Nashville VA Med Ctr 1310 24th Ave S Nashville TN 37212

PUGH, NELDA JORDAN, business administrator educator; b. Birmingham, Ala., Aug. 5, 1935; d. Gordon Brookins and Nell (Jones) Jordan; m. Tillman William Pugh Jr., Dec. 18, 1954; children—Gordon Irwin, Tillman W., III (dec.). B.S., Samford U., 1955; M.A., U. Ala., 1961; postgrad., Cumberland Sch. Law, 1970-1972; Ed.D., Nova U., 1981. Instr. Jefferson County, Birmingham, 1965-69; educator Jefferson State Coll., Birmingham, 1969—; speaker Civic orgns., Birmingham, 1980—; active Ala. Symphony Assn., 1985—; capt. Heart Sunday Drive, Birmingham, 1988; sponsor Women on the Way, Birmingham, 1979-83; coordinator Ala. Bus. Communication Assn., 1983. Editor newsletter Jordans Journeys, 1980—; textbook editor. Seminar coordinator Winners Circle, Jamaica, 1981, YMCA, Birmingham, 1980. Mem. Nat. Bus. Law Assn., Am. Bus. Communication Assn. (proceedings reviewer 1984), Nat. Bus. Edn. Assn., Women's Com. of 100 for Birmingham, Inc., Depta Pi Epsilon. Republican. Baptist. Club: Internat. Toastmistress (treas., pres., v.p., sec., del., 1976—). Avocations: genealogy, needlework. Home: 3723 Brookwood Rd Birmingham AL 35223-1538 Office: Jefferson State Coll 2601 Carson Rd Birmingham AL 35215

PUGLISI, ANGELA AURORA, educator, consultant, artist; b. Messina, Italy, Jan. 28, 1949; came to U.S., 1954, naturalized, 1980; d. Vittorio and Carmela (Alizzi) P. B.A. cum laude, Dunbarton Coll., 1972; M.F.A., Cath. U., 1974, M.A. in Art History, 1976, M.A. in Modern Langs and Lit., 1977, Ph.D. in Comparative Lit., 1983. Art instr. Cath. U., Washington, 1974-84, lectr. modern langs., 1984-85; cons., writer U.S. Dept. Edn., Washington, 1983-85; faculty arts/cultural Georgetown U., Washington, 1986—; asst. to dean Am. U., 1988; various exhbns. of works, 1972-84. Author poetry: Nature's Canvas, 1984, Homage, 1984, Sonnet I, 1985, Primavera, 1986, Ocean Waves, 1986, Sand Dunes, 1986, The Sun's Journey, 1986, Prelude, 1987, Jet d'Eau, 1987; Woodland Revisited, 1988; art work in pvt. collections. Founding mem. Italian Cultural Ctr., Washington; bd. dirs. Edn. Enterprises. Mem., Cath. Acad. Scis. (academician), Nat. Mus. of Women in Arts (charter), Corcoran Gallery Art Assocs. Republican. Roman Catholic. Avocations: writing, sculpting.

PUHVEL, SIRJE MADLI, medical scientist, skin biologist, educator; b. Tallinn, Estonia, July 26, 1939; came to U.S., 1960; d. George Jüri and Tiina (Toodo) Hansen; m. Jaan Puhvel, June 4, 1960; children: Peter J., Andres J., Markus J. BA, UCLA, 1961, PhD, 1963. Postdoctoral fellow div. dermatology UCLA Sch. Medicine, 1963-65, asst. rsch. immunologist, 1965-68, asst. adj. prof., 1968-73, assoc. adj. prof., 1973-78, adj. prof., 1978—. NIH rsch. grantee, 1974-77, 77-80, 80-84, 81-84, 85—. Mem. Soc. Investigative Dermatology (western sect. counselor 1978-80, chmn. 1980-81), Am. Fedn. Clin. Rsch., Calif. Found. Dermatol. Rsch. Home: 15739 High Knoll Rd Encino CA 91436 Office: UCLA Sch Medicine Div Dermatology Los Angeles CA 90024

PULAS, ELAINE COMER, information resources specialist; b. South Boston, Va., Oct. 11, 1952; d. Fauntly David and Alma Lucy Ann (Frazier) Comer; m. Demetrios George Pulas Jr., June 25, 1977; children: Christina Alexandra, Stephanie Elaine. AAS, No. Va. Community Coll., Annandale, 1980; diploma, Va. Computer Coll., 1972; cert., USDA, 1981, Am. Grad. U., 1987. Programmer Computer Data Systems, Inc., Bethesda, Md., 1972-75; with House Info. Systems, Washington, 1975—, mgmt. and evaluation officer, 1981-88, project officer, 1989—. Mem. rep. House Dist. Office Task Force, 1987-89. Recipient Good Citizenship award Am. Legion, 1971, Ten Yr. Svc. award U.S. Ho. of Reps., 1986. Mem. Congl. Staff Club, NAFE. Democrat. Baptist. Office: House Info Systems H2-628 House Annex 2 Washington DC 20515

PULITANO, CONCETTA NORIGENNA, corporate professional; b. Sicily, Italy, June 16, 1941; came to U.S., 1947, naturalized, 1948; d. Umberto and Benedetta (Triassi) Norigenna; student public schs., North Miami, Fla.; m. Francis Joseph Pulitano, Dec. 29, 1962; children: Maria Anne, Margaret Theresa, Angela Marie. Sec., Ka-Line Pool Products, Hialeah, Fla., 1959-61, Westinghouse, Balt., 1961, Bendix Communications, Balt., 1961-63; student council moderator, sec., learning center coordinator Cathedral Sch., Balt., 1974-83; sec., word processor operator Md. Agy., Balt., 1983-85, adminstrv. asst., 1988—; exec. sec. Comp-U-Staff, Inc., 1985-88; adminstrv. asst. Md. Agy., Balt., 1988-89; office mgr. Ga. Pacific Corp., 1989—. Democrat. Roman Catholic. Club: Valley Country.

PULITZER, EMILY S. RAUH (MRS. JOSEPH PULITZER, JR.), art consultant; b. Cin., July 23, 1933; d. Frederick and Harriet (Frank) Rauh. A.B., Bryn Mawr Coll., 1955; student, Ecole du Louvre, Paris, France, 1955-56; M.A., Harvard, 1963. Mem. staff Cin. Art Mus., 1956-57; asst. curator drawings Fogg Art Mus., Harvard, 1957-64, asst. to dir., 1962-63; curator City Art Mus., St. Louis, 1964-73; mem. painting and sculpture com. Mus. Modern Art, 1975—; chmn. visual arts com. Mo. Arts Council, 1976-81; co-chmn. fellows Fogg Art Mus.; mem. bd. Inst. Mus. Services, 1979-84; commr. St. Louis Art Mus., 1981-88, vice chmn., 1988. Bd. dirs. 1st Street Forum, St. Louis, 1980—, Mark Rothko Found., 1976-88; bd. dirs. arts in transit com. Bi-State Devel. Agy., vice chmn., 1987—; mem. ovwr-seers' com. to visit Harvard Art Mus., 1990—. Mem. Am. Fedn. Arts (dir. 1976-89), St. Louis Mercantile Libr. Assn. (bd. dirs. 1987—), Women's Forum of Mo. Home: 4903 Pershing Pl Saint Louis MO 63108

PULLEN, PENNY LYNNE, state legislator; b. Buffalo, Mar. 2, 1947; d. John William and Alice Nettie (McConkey) P.; B.A. in Speech, U. Ill., 1969. TV technician Office Instructional Resources, U. Ill., 1966-68; community newspaper reporter Des Plaines (Ill.) Pub. Co., 1967-72; legislative asst. to Ill. legislators, 1968-77; mem. Ill. Ho. of Reps., 1977—, chmn. ho. exec. com., 1981-82, minority whip, 1983-87, asst. minority leader, 1987—; mem. Pres.'s Commn. on AIDS Epidemic, 1987-88; mem. Ill. Goodwill Del. to Republic of China, 1987; del. Rep. Nat. Conv, 1984; mem. Republican Nat. Com., 1984-88; bd. dirs. Legal Svcs. Corp. Del. Atlantic Alliance Young Polit. Leaders, Brussels, 1977; summit conf. observer as mem. adhoc Women for SDI, Geneva, 1985; active Maine Twp. Mental Health Assn.; mem. Nat. Coun. Ednl. Rsch., 1983-88. Recipient George Washington Honor medal Freedoms Found., 1978, Dwight Eisenhower Freedom medal Chgo. Captive Nations Com., 1977, Outstanding Legislator awards Ill. Press Assn., Ill. Podiatry Soc., Ill. Coroners Assn., Ill. County Clks. Assn., Ill. Hosp. Assn., Ill. Health Care Assn.; named Ill. Young Republican, 1968, Outstanding Young Person, Park Ridge Jaycees, 1981, One of 10 Outstanding Young Persons, Ill. Jaycees, 1981. Mem. Am. Legis. Exchange Council (dir. 1977—, exec. com. 1978-83, 2d vice chmn. 1980-83), DAR. Lodge: Kiwanis. Office: Dist Office 22 Main St Park Ridge IL 60068

PULLIAM, FRANCINE S., real estate broker and developer; b. San Francisco, Sept. 14, 1937; d. Ralph C. Stevens and Frances I. (Wilson) Sarno; m. John Donald Pulliam, Aug. 14, 1957 (div. Mar. 1965); 1 child, Wendy; m. Terry Kent Graves, Dec. 14, 1974. Student, U. Ariz., 1955-56, U. Nev., Las Vegas, 1957. Airline stewardess Bonanza Airlines, Las Vegas, 1957; real estate agt. The Pulliam Co., Las Vegas, 1958-68, Levy Realty, Las Vegas, 1976-76; real estate broker, owner Prestige Properties, Las Vegas, 1976—; importer, exporter Exports Internat., Las Vegas, 1984—; Citicorp Bank. Bd. dirs. Las Vegas Bd. Realtors, Fedn. Internation Realtors, Las Vegas Taxi Cab Authority, Nat. Kidney Found., Citizens for Pvt. Enterprises, Assistance League, Sen. Chic Hecht Adv. Bd., Better Bus. Bur., Cancer Soc., Easter Seals, Economic Research Bd., Children's Discovery Museum, New Horizons Ctr. for Children with Learning Disabilities, Girl Scouts, Home of the Good Shepard, St. Jude's Ranch for Homeless Children. Mem. Las Vegas C. of C. Republican. Roman Catholic. Office: Prestige Properties 601 S Ranch Rd Ste A5 Las Vegas NV 89106

PULLIAM, JUDITH HARRIS, country club executive; b. Memphis, Dec. 7, 1934; d. Wiley Chasteen and Irene Randle (Hodges) Harris; student Memphis State U., 1952-53, seminars U. Tenn., Nashville, 1971-76, Tenn. State U., 1978-81, Vanderbilt U., 1982, Gourmet's Oxford (Eng.) Center for Mgmt. Studies, 1982, Lo Scaldavivande Cooking Sch., Rome, 1983; m. Leslie Doss, Jr., 1953 (div. 1973); children: Leslie Walter III, Randle Elizabeth; m. W. Cary Pulliam Jr., Nov. 10, 1989. Sec., receptionist James W. Stewart, investor, Dixie Oil Co., 1971-75; food svc. dir. The Webb Sch., Bell Buckle, Tenn., 1976-83; mgr. Plantation Country Club, Pharr, Tex., 1983-87; gen. mgr. Graymere Country Club, Columbia, Tenn., 1987—; mem. 3d Nat. Conf. Nutrition, 1980, Nat. Food Policy Conf., Washington, 1982. Pres. Hillwood Presbyn. Ch. Women, Nashville, 1968-70; mem. Nashville Symphony Guild. Mem. Colonial Dames Am. (chpt. dir. 1981-83), Ladies Hermitage Assn. (life), Cheekwood Fine Arts Ctr., Assn. Tenn. Antiquities, Nat. Assn. Female Execs., Club Mgrs. Assn. Am. Internat. Wine Soc., Orgn. Women Execs. (v.p. 1986-87), DAR, Zonta Club (chpt. bd. dirs. 1986-87), Alpha Gamma Delta. Contbr. to The Webb Cookbook, 1977, 79. Home: 917 Hillcrest Columbia TN 38401 Office: Graymere Club Country Club Ln Columbia TN 38401

PULLIAM, SUSAN ELISE, quality assurance laboratory technician; b. Harrisonville, Mo., Sept. 9, 1953; d. James Emery and Eleanor Virginia (Jones) Courtney; children: W. Dean Doll, Shelbi Linnae Eliane Pulliam. Student, State Fair Community Coll., Sedelia, Mo., 1973. Receiving inspector Kansas City div. Allied Signal, Kansas City, Mo., 1980-88; travel cons. Exec. Travel Inc., Leawood, Kans., 1989; quality assurance lab technician I Marion Merrell Dow, Kansas City, Mo., 1989—. Author: Middle of Seven, 1982, Letter To My Brasilian Daughter, 1986; composer numerous songs and lyrics; author numerous poems. Mem. Internat. Adoptive Parent, Mo. Citizens for Life. Mem. ASCAP, BMI. Home: Oak Tree Ridge Rt 1 Box 30H Harrisonville MO 64701

PULLO, BARBARA JEAN, cooking instructor; b. Millville, N.J., Apr. 6, 1935; d. Michael and Rosa (Orfanella) Stanle; m. Daniel Thomas Pullo, May 25, 1957; children: Barak, Sabrina, April. Student, Culinary Inst., Hyde Park, N.Y., 1976. Owner, operator cooking sch. Suffern, N.Y., 1975-86; chef, food stylist Food Emporium, Rye Brook, N.Y., 1986—; food stylist, N.Y.C., 1987—. Author: Cooking With Class, 1980. Exec. com. Helen Hayes Hosp., N.Y., 1986—. Mem. Am. Heart Assn., Women in Food Svc. Jehovah's Witness. Home and Office: 30 Scenic Dr Suffern NY 10901

PULLON, KELLEY LAYNE, medical records professional, marketing specialist; b. Chattanooga, July 28, 1962; d. Jimmy Layne Ervin and Lucille (Brown) Burnette; m. Michael David Pullon, Dec. 30, 1988. BS in Records Adminstrn., U. Tenn. Ctr. Health Scis., 1985. Supr. coding, abstracting, assembly Bapt. Med. Ctr., Memphis, 1985-86; mgr. perinatal data systems U. Tenn., Memphis, 1986-88; dir. med. records Decatur (Ga.) Hosp., 1988; mktg. specialist HBO & Co., Atlanta, 1989—; med. records cons., 1988—. Mem. Am. Med. Record Assn., Tenn. Med. Record Assn., Ga. Med. Record Assn., Ga. Utilization Rev. Com., Atlanta Med. Record Assn., Young Reps. Methodist.

PULS-JAGER, ELIZABETH ANNE, insurance company executive; b. Troy, N.Y., July 19, 1934; d. Patrick Vincent and Elizabeth (Alliry) Costello; m. Earl J. Puls, June 15, 1957 (div. Jan. 1982); children: Mary E., Ellen C., Michael J., Kathleen M.; m. Linn B. Jager, Feb. 7, 1988. RN, St. Mary's Hosp. Sch. Nursing, Amsterdam, N.Y., 1954; BS in Nursing, Marquette U., 1956; BA in Sociology, Elmhurst Coll., 1972; MA in Counseling, Psychology, Alfred Adler Inst., Chgo., 1987. RN, Ill., N.Y., Wis.; lic. ins. rep. Staff nurse St. Mary's Hosp., Amsterdam, 1953-54; head nurse, med. ward St. Joseph's Hosp., Milw., 1955-58; dir. health svcs., health edn. Ill. Benedictine Coll., Lisle, 1972-81; owner, agent State Farm Agy., St. Charles, Ill., 1981—; bd. dirs. Zonta Internat., St. Charles, Geneva and Batavia, Ill., Women-In-Networking, St. Charles. Bd. dirs. United Meth. Women, Baker Ch. Mem. AAUW. Home: 14 Southgate Course Saint Charles IL 60174 Office: Betty Puls State Farm Ins 700 S Randall Rd Ste 15 Saint Charles IL 60174

PUMO, DOROTHY ELLEN, biologist, educator; b. Charleston, W.Va., Oct. 27, 1951; d. Benjamin J. and Mabel M. (Konschott) P. BS, U. Mich., 1973, MS, 1974, PhD, 1976. Teaching asst. in biology and cell biology U. Mich., Ann Arbor, 1974-75, rsch. asst., 1975-76; rsch. assoc. U. Colo., 1976-78; rsch. assoc. U. Vt., 1978-79, 81, NIH post-doctoral trainee, 1980; asst. prof. biology Hofstra U., Hempstead, N.Y., 1981-87, assoc. prof. biology, 1987—, program dir. human cytogenetics, 1988—. NIH grantee, 1989, 90, 83-86, NSF grantee, 1987, 82-83, N.Y. State Health Rsch. Coun. grantee, 1982-83. Mem. AAAS, Soc. for Study of Evolution, Am. Soc. Mammologists. Office: Hofstra U Biology Dept Gittleson Bldg Hempstead NY 11550

PUMPHREY, JANET KAY, editor; b. Balt., June 18, 1946; d. John Henry and Elsie May (Keefer) P. AA in Secondary Edn., Anne Arundel Community Coll., Arnold, Md., 1967, AA in Bus. and Pub. Adminstrn., 1976. Office mgr. Anne Arundel Community Coll., 1964—; mng. editor Am. Polygraph Assn., Severna Park, Md., 1973—; archives researcher Am. Polygraph Assn., Severna Park, 1973—. Editor: (with Albert D. Snyder) Ten Years of Polygraph, 1984, (with Norman Ansley) Justice and the Polygraph, 1985, A House Full of Love, 1990. Mem. Rep. Nat. Sustaining Com. Mem. NAFE, Am. Polygraph Assn. (hon.), Md. Polygraph Assn. (affiliate), Internat. Platform Assn., Anne Arundel County Hist. Soc., Alumni Assn. Anne Arundel Community Coll. Republican. Methodist. Home: 3 Kimberly Ct Severna Park MD 21146 Office: Am Polygraph Assn PO Box 1061 Severna Park MD 21146

PUNAK, DEBRA LYNN, corporate auditor; b. Milw., June 22, 1959; d. John and Katherine Elizabeth (Huebner) P. Cert., Reids, 1988. Hotel detective Marc Pla., Milw., 1979-80, Hyatt Regency, Milw., 1980-81; detective Gimbels, Milw., 1980-81, downtown supr., 1981-83, regional mgr., 1983-84; asst. security mgr. Neiman Marcus, Bal Harbor, Fla., 1984-86; asst. dir. loss and prevention Charles A. Stevens, Chgo., 1986-88; regional loss and prevention mgr. Ann Taylor, Northbrook, Ill., 1988-90. Mem. Am. Soc. Indsl. Security, Security Trainers of Am., NAFE, Inst. Internal Mgrs. Home: 1316 W Grange Ave Milwaukee WI 53221 Office: Ann Taylor 2500 North Mayfair Rd Wauwautosa WI 53226

PUNG, ROSALYN ALYCE (ROSIE), nurse; b. Shelbyville, Ind., May 3, 1948; d. William O. and Dorothy Alice (Roupp) Hill; m. Ronald J. Pung, Aug. 25, 1984; 1 child, Bradley Scott Smith. ASN, Ind. U., 1969, BSN, 1983, MSN, 1985. Head nurse Winona Hosp., Indpls., 1976; hemodialysis staff nurse renal dept. Ind. U. Med. Ctr., Indpls., 1976-78, hemodialysis home nurse coordinator renal dept., 1978=79, adult dialysis units nursing dir. renal dept., 1979-85; clin. lectr. Ind. U. Sch. Nursing, Indpls., 1985, 88; nurse analyst Associated Group Blue Cross/Blue Shield of Ind., 1985-88; project SIHO office mgr. Southeastern Ind. Health Orgn., Columbus, 1987-88; relief mgr. Community Hosp. South (formerly Univ. Heights Hosp.), Indpls., 1988-90; nurse med. cons. Holland and Holland Law Firm, Indpls., 1988-90; relief house supr. McPherson Hosp., Howell, Mich., 1990—; clin. instr. Henry Ford Community Coll., Dearborn, Mich., 1990—; hemodialysis cons. HCFA project System Scis., Inc., Washington, 1980-81; hemodialysis cons. Cobe Labs., Denver, 1984, Travenol Labs., Chgo., 1983. Author: (with others) Nursing Theorists and Their Work, 1986. Mem. Am. Nephrology Nurses Assn., Nat. Assn. Exec. Women, Ind. State Nurses Assn., Am. Nurses Assn., Sigma Theta Tau. Home: 3260 Ravinewood Dr E Milford MI 48382

PURCELL, ANN MARIE C., marketing executive; b. Harvey, Ill., Feb. 20, 1957; d. Carlo Leo and Lucille Lillian (Colletti) Allegro; m. Fredrick William Purcell, June 29, 1980; children: Carly Allegro, Gianna Cecile. BS, Loyola U. Chgo., 1979; postgrad. Keller Grad. Sch. Mgmt. Lab. instr. Loyola U., Chgo., 1977-79; rsch. technician Travenol Labs., Inc., Morton Grove, Ill., 1979-80, rsch. asst., 1980, rsch. assoc., 1980-81; product specialist Fenwal Labs. div. Travenol Labs., Inc., Deerfield, Ill., 1981-85, product mgr., 1985—. Mem. Women's Aux. to Dental Soc. Loyola U. Dental Sch., NAFE, Phi Kappa Omega Alumnae (a founder), Tri Beta. Roman Catholic. Home: 1921 Tano Ln Mount Prospect IL 60056

PURCELL, ELAINE IRENE (ELAINE IRENE SCHOCK), banker; b. Pottsville, Pa., Nov. 13, 1946; d. Salem Henry and Ethel Mae (Howells) Schock; m. Jerome James Purcell, June 27, 1969 (div. July 1984). BS in Math., Bloomsburg U., 1968; JD, Duquesne U., 1981; MBA in Fin. and Acctg., Columbia U., 1983. Cert. tchr., Pa. Math. tchr. Pottsville Area High Sch., 1968-69, Keystone Oaks Sch. Dist., Pitts., 1969-81; credit trainee 1st Nat. Bank Chgo., 1983-84; corp. banking officer 1st Nat. Bank Chgo., N.Y.C., 1984-86, asst. v.p., 1987-88; v.p. 1st Nat. Bank Chgo., 1988—. Mem. Women in Cable, Pa. Bar Assn., NAFE, Internat. House, Bklyn. Acad. Music. Office: 1st Nat Bank Chgo 153 W 51st St New York NY 10019

PURCELL, MARY HAMILTON, educator; b. Ft. Worth; d. Joseph Hants and Letha (Gibson) Hamilton; m. William Paxson Purcell, Jr., Dec. 28, 1950; children: William Paxson III, David Hamilton. BA, Mary Hardin-Baylor Coll., 1947; MA, La. State U., 1948. Instr., dept. speech and dramatic arts Temple U., Phila., 1948-53, 60-61; part-time instr. speech Cushing Jr. Coll., Bryn Mawr, Pa., 1966-78. Pres., Pa. Program for Women and Girl Offenders, 1968-73; pres. Nether Providence Parent Tchr. Orgn., 1975-76; treas. Virginia Gildersleeve Internat. Fund Univ. Women, 1975-81; bd. dirs. Citizens Crime Commn. of Phila., 1976—; mem. Wallingford-Swarthmore Dist. Sch. Bd., 1977-83; bd. dirs. Nat. Peace Inst. Found., 1983-86, Big Bros./Big Sisters of Am., 1985-90, Pa. Women's Campaign Fund, 1985-88; bd. dirs. Ministers and Missionaries Fund, 1985—, Am. Bapt. Conv., 1986—. Named Outstanding Alumna Mary Hardin-Baylor Coll., 1972, Disting. Dau. Pa., 1982; recipient Zeta Phi Eta award excellence in communications, 1983. Mem. AAUW (Pa. div. pres. 1968-70, v.p. middle Atlantic region 1973-77, program v.p. 1979-81, pres. 1981-85, rep. to UN, 1985-89), Internat. Fedn. Univ. Women (1st v.p. 1986-89, pres. 1989—), Speech Assn. Am., Pi Kappa Delta, Pi Gamma Mu, Delta Sigma Rho, Alpha Psi Omega, Alpha Chi. Democrat. Baptist. Home: 9 Oak Knoll Dr Wallingford PA 19086

PURCELL, MARY LOUISE GERLINGER, educator; b. Thief River Falls, Minn., July 17, 1923; d. Charles and Lajla (Dale) Gerlinger; student Yankton Coll., 1941-45, Yale Div. Sch., 1949-50, NYU, summer 1949; MA (alumni fellow), Tchrs. Coll. Columbia, 1959, EdD, 1963; m. Walter A. Kuyawski, June 9, 1950 (dec. July 1954); children: Amelia Allerton, Jon Allerton; m. 2d, Dale Purcell, Aug. 26, 1962. Teen-age program dir., YWCA, New Haven, 1945-52; dir. program in family rels., asst. prof. sociology and psychology Earlham Coll., Richmond, Ind., 1959-62, conf. coord. undergrad. edn. for women, 1962; chmn. div. home and community Stephens Coll., Columbia, Mo., 1962-73, chmn. family and community studies, 1962-78, dir. Learning Unltd., continuing edn. for women, 1974-78, developer course The Contemporary Am. Woman, 1962, cons., 1962; prof., Auburn (Ala.) U., 1978-88, prof. emerita, 1988—, head dept. family and child devel., 1978-84, spl. asst. to v.p. acad. affairs, 1985-86. chmn. search com. for v.p. acad. affairs, 1984; vis. prof. Ind. U. Summer Sch., 1970. Cons. student personnel svcs., Trenton (N.J.) State Coll., 1958-59, 61. Recipient Alumni Achievement award Yankton Coll., 1975. Mem. AAUW, Am. Home Econs. Assn. (bd. dirs. 1967-69, chair 1st subject matter unit 1969, family relations and child devel. sect. 1986-89), Groves Conf. on Family, Nat. Council Family Relations (dir., chmn.-elect affiliated councils, 1981-82, chmn., 1982-84, nat. program chmn. 1977, chmn. film awards com., chmn. spl. emphases sect., bd. dirs., Ernest G. Osborne award for excellence in teaching 1979), Delta Kappa Gamma. Presbyterian. Contbr. articles to coll. bulls., jours. Home: 120 Belden St Falls Village CT 06031

PURCELL, MICKI NOLAN, personnel service executive; b. Washington, Apr. 13, 1953; d. Bernard A. and Theresa (Hagan) Nolan; m. Joseph F. Purcell, Apr. 21, 1979; children: Jennifer, Anthony. Ed. pub. schs., Bowie, Md. V.p. Washington Internat. Secretarial Exch., 1973-79; pres. MNP Pers. Svc., Beverly Hills, Calif., 1979-88, Newport Beach, Calif., 1988—. Mem. Nat. Assn. for Personnel Cons. Republican.

PURCELL, NANCY LOU, fashion boutique co-owner; b. Reading, Pa., Nov. 26, 1934; d. Russel Louis Button ad Helen Geneve (Wichrowski) Shuker; m. John Joseph Crimmins, Dec. 19, 1953; (div. 1982); children: John B. Crimmins, Mark A. Crimmins, Cathy A. Crimmins; m. Grant S. Purcell, May 20, 1989. Sec. US Navy, NH Security Agy., Wash., 1952-55, Harvard U., Cambridge, Mass., 1956-58; personnel mgr. 3B's Corp., Columbia, S.C., 1972-75; mgr., buyer Card N Such, Columbia, S.C.; mgr., trainer Casual Corner, Columbia, 1979-82; dist. mgr. Casual Corner, 1982-85; co-owner, buyer Grant Purcell, Hilton Head, S.C., 1985--; wardrobe cons. Pvt. Practice, Charleston, S.C., 1981--; cons. S. Bell Mktg. SCN Bank, Bankers Trust Bob Capes Realty, Christian Women's Assn, Profl. Women's Club, Columbia, 1981--. Mem. Nat. Orgn. for Women, Christian Women, Bus. Profl. Women. Democrat. Protestant. Office: Grant Purcell 191 Meeting St Charleston SC 29401

PURDY, HELEN CARMICHAEL, librarian; b. Miami, Jan. 17, 1920; d. James B. and Alice Cornelia (Brown) C.; m. Joseph Lynn Purdy, Feb. 12, 1946 (div. Aug. 1971). AB, U. Miami-Coral Gables, 1943; MS, Fla. State U.-Tallahassee, 1957. Asst. dept. head U.S. Censorship, Miami, 1944-45; library asst. catalog dept. U. Miami, Coral Gales, 1946-56, cataloger, 1957-60, Fla.

cataloger, 1961-77/78, head archives and spl. collections dept., 1978, 79-90, ret., 1990, senator Faculty Senate, 1967-71, mem. coun., 1969-71; mem. Women's Adv. Com. on Acad. Affairs, Coral Gables, 1972-81. Mem. Citizens Crime Watch, Miami, 1980—; mem. Republican Nat. Com., Washington, 1981—; mem. Republican Party of Fla., Tallahassee, 1983—. Mem. ALA, Southeastern Library Assn., Fla. Library Assn. (div. vice chmn. 1958-59, chmn. 1959-60), Soc. Fla. Archivists, Miami Pioneers. Beta Phi Mu. Episcopalian. Lodge: Zonta Internat. Home: 5824 SW 50th St Miami FL 33155 Office: Univ Miami Library Coral Gables FL 33124

PURICELLI, MARJORIE GIBSON, retired government official, consultant; b. Opelika, Ala., Jan. 11, 1923; d. Frederick Meyer and Lottie Belle (Hearn) Gibson; student U. Ala., 1965, 66, Macon Jr. Coll., 1968-71; m. Russell Antonio Puricelli, May 17, 1984; children by previous marriage: William Guy Walter, Ralph Gibson Walter. Contract negotiator trainee Robins AFB, Ga., 1966-68, contract negotiator, 1968-71; fin. analyst HUD, Birmingham and Washington, 1971-75; contract price analyst U.S. Army, Washington, 1976-77; contract price analyst U.S. Marine Corps, Albany, Ga., 1977-80, head contracts support br., contracts div. Marine Corps Logistics Base, Albany, Ga., 1980-84, br. head value analysis engring. data mgmt. br., office competition advocate, 1984-86; ret., 1986; v.p. MARCON Cons.; ptnr. Amare Stained Glass Co. Vice pres. Woman's Caucus, HUD, 1975. Recipient Sustained Superior Performance award U.S. Marine Corps, 1978. Mem. Nat. Contract Mgmt. Assn., Fed. Mgrs. Assn. Home: 466 Church St NE Dawson GA 31742

PURKEY, RUTH ELANE, insurance agency executive; b. Upper Sandusky, Ohio, Apr. 4, 1936; d. Charles William Henry and Avah Alice (Wilson) Butcher; m. Wallace D. Purkey, Jr., Apr. 17, 1955; children: Robin Sue Purkey VanGorder, Justin Neal. Grad. high sch., Millbury, Ohio. Ins. agt. Purkey Ins. Agy., Northwood, Ohio, 1967—, v.p., sec., treas., 1976—; speaker on youth substance abuse to various groups and orgns. Mem., v.p. PTA Genoa Schs., Ohio, 1968-70; club adviser 4-H Clubs Am., Ottawa County, Ohio, 1968-73; bd. dirs., treas. Friends of Library of Genoa, 1972-75; chmn. Village Bikeway Com., Genoa, 1972-76; facilitator Parents Helping Parents, Inc., Toledo, 1985-89, mem. exec. bd., 1986; cons. Wood County Juvenile Ct. Adv. Bd., 1985—, Wood County Schs. Without Drugs Community Action Bd., 1987—; mem. Nat. Fedn. Parents for Drug-Free Youth, 1983—; mem. Chem. Abuse Reduced through Edn. and Svcs. Agy. of Lucas County, 1988—, former exec. bd. dirs., 1988-89; mem. Parents Resource Inst. Drug Edn., 1986—, Region V of U.S. Atty.'s Force Prevention Drug and Alcohol Abuse, 1987. Recipient Jefferson award, 1988. Mem. Profl. Ins. Agts., NAFE, Fedn. Women's Clubs (bd. dirs. Genoa 1973-76). Republican. Methodist. Club: Belle Ami (Genoa) (sec. 1969-70, v.p. 1972-73). Avocations: distance swimming, cross-country skiing, American Indian pottery. Home: 1524 Red Bud Dr Northwood OH 43619 Office: Purkey Ins Agy Inc 3401 Woodville Rd Ste B Northwood OH 43619

PURRINGTON, SUZANNE TOWNSEND, chemistry educator; b. N.Y.C., Apr. 30, 1938; d. Edward Nicoll Townsend and Eleanore T. (Vietor) Rutherfurd; m. Alfred L. Purrington III, Aug. 24, 1963; children: Alfred Nicholas, John Vietor, Elizabeth Grimes. BA, Wheaton Coll., 1960; MA, Radcliffe Coll., 1962; PhD, Harvard U., 1963. Instr. Duke U., Durham, N.C., 1963-65; asst. to assoc. prof. Shaw U., Raleigh, N.C., 1965-68; assoc. prof. N.Y. Inst. Tech., Old Westbury, N.Y., 1968-70; with chemistry dept. Peace Coll., Raleigh, 1972-77; vis. asst. prof. N.C. State U., Raleigh, 1976-78, asst. prof., 1978-85, assoc. prof., 1985—. Mem. N.C. Am. Chem. Soc. (sec., treas. 1974-75, chmn. 1977, alternate councilor 1988-91). Episcopalian. Office: Dept Chemistry NC State U Raleigh NC 27695

PURVIS, WENDY KIM, wholesale distribution executive; b. Abilene, Tex., Aug. 11, 1964. BS, Tex. Christian U., 1986. Area sales mgr. Dillard's Inc., Ft. Worth, 1986-88, asst. buyer, 1988-90, Liz Claiborne specialist, 1990—. Mem. NAFE, Jr. League of Ft. Worth, Phi Upsilon Omicron (v.p. 1988-89). Republican. Presbyterian.

PUSEY, ELLEN PRATT, home economist; b. Milford, Del., Aug. 27, 1928; d. Algeo Newell and Ruby Newton (Boorman) Pratt; m. William W. Pusey, June 12, 1950; children: William W., Patricia A., Cynthia L., Daniel N. BS, U. Md., 1950, MS, 1951. Camp dietitian N.Y. Herald Tribune Fresh Air Fund Camps, 1947; supr. cafeteria Roosevelt Hosp., N.Y.C., 1948; supt. sch. cafeterias, Seaford, Del., 1964; field faculty home economist Md. Coop. Ext. Svc., Wicomico County, Md., 1967—. Chmn. lower shore coun. Am. Lung Assn., Md., 1978-79; pres. U. Md. Coll. Human Ecology Alumni Bd., 1988-89. Named one of 10 Outstanding Women Wicomico County, Commn. for Women, 1989. Mem. Am. Home Econs. Assn., Md. Home Econs. Assn., Nat. Assn. Extension Home Economists, Md. Assn. Extension Home Economists, Tri-County Home Econs. Assn. (chmn. 1973), Nutrition Jour. Club of Eastern Shore, Phi Kappa Phi, Alpha Xi Delta, Soroptimists Club (pres. 1978, 2d v.p. 1989, South Atlantic region Women Helping Women award 1989). Presbyterian. Home: 301 W Federal St Snow Hill MD 21863 Office: PO Box 1836 Salisbury MD 21802

PUSKAR, KATHRYN ROSE, nurse, educator; b. Akron, Ohio, Apr. 7, 1946; d. Stanley William and Virginia (Roberts) McKavish; m. George Paul Puskar, Aug. 28, 1969; 1 child, Stacey. Diploma in nursing, Johnstown Mercy Sch. Nursing, 1966; BS, Duquesne U., 1969; MS in Nursing, U. Pittsburgh, 1971, MPH, 1978, DrPH, 1981. RN. Mem. faculty U. Ill., Chgo., 1976-78; cons. Westmoreland Coll., Greensburg, Pa., 1976; clin. specialist McKeesport (Pa.) Hosp., 1971-73; dir. mental health clinic Frick Hosp., Mt. Pleasant, Pa., 1974-76; asst. prof. U. Pitts., 1980—; cons. Southwood Hosp., 1984-86, VA Med. Ctr., Pitts., 1985—. Contbr. articles to profl. jours.; editor profl. jour. Cons. Newcomers Club, Pitts., 1985-87. NIMH fellowship. Mem. Am. Nurses Assn. (cert. psychiat. specialist), Pa. Nurses Assn., Sigma Theta Tau. Republican. Roman Catholic. Home: 1795 Robson Dr Pittsburgh PA 15241 Office: U Pitts Sch Nursing 367 Victoria Pittsburgh PA 15261

PUTANSU, PATRICIA JOAN, office manager; b. Detroit, July 10, 1934; d. Norman K. and Anna Bernice (Sawicki) King; m. Don. L. Putansu, Aug. 30, 1958 (dec. Jan. 23, 1977). Student, Madonna, Livonia, Mich., 1978. Bookkeeper Baker Simmons & Co., Detroit, 1952-57; adminstrv. asst. Neumann Engring., Madison Heights, Mich., 1957-62; sec., treas. Mack Pattern Works, Inc., Detroit, 1962-82; office mgr. Shapiro Mold, Inc., Livonia, Mich., 1983—. Mem. Farmington Art Found. (treas. 1970-87, sec. 1987-90. trustee 1967—), Farmington Artist Club. Roman Catholic. Office: Shapiro Mold Inc 30880 Industrial Rd Livonia MI 48150

PUTNAM, BARBARA DEYO, nurse; b. Brattleboro, Vt., Oct. 28, 1926; d. Harold E. and Grace B. (Thomas) Deyo; m. Richard B. Putnam, Jr., Dec. 11, 1949; children—Richard B., III, Alan E., Jeffrey S. Nurse Springfield Hosp. Tng. Sch. for Nurses, 1945-48. Oper.rm. staff nurse Brattleboro (Vt.) Meml. Hosp., 1948-51, asst. night supr., 1961-68, coord. discharge planning, 1980-88 ; office nurse ob-gyn, 1968-72; pub. health nurse Brattleboro Pub. Health Nursing, 1973-78. Staff vol. nurse ARC, 1985—, bd. dirs. Windham County Area, 1986—; den mother Boy Scouts Am.; pres. PTA, Acad. Sch., Brattleboro, 1960; co-organizer Brattleboro chpt. United Ostomy Assn., Inc.; active Vt./New Hampshire chpt. Continuity of Care, Am. Assn. Continuity Care, rses Assn., Nat. Rifle Assn., Brattleboro Sportsmen, Am. Assn. Ret. Persons.

PUTNAM, BONNIE BEAN, marketing executive; b. Rockville Centre, N.Y., Dec. 20, 1955; d. David Charles and Betty Lou (Simonin) Bean; m. William Shields Putnam, Oct. 29, 1978; 1 child, William Shields Jr. A.B. in Econ., Duke U., 1978, A.B. in Can. Studies, 1978, M.B.A., 1983. Material and acctg. mgmt. assoc. Western Elec. Co., Winston-Salem, N.C., 1978-79, material planning specialist, Greensboro, N.C., 1979-80; rate design adminstr. GTE of S.E., Durham, N.C., 1980-83; market rsch. analyst Northern Telecom, Rsch. Triangle Park, N.C., 1983, product mgr., 1983-84, mgr. market rsch. and bus. planning, 1984-85, mgr. contract svcs., San Ramon, Calif., 1985-86, regional mktg. mgr., 1987, dir. product mktg., 1988—, dir. customer svc., 1989—. Author research papers. Bd. dirs. Fuqua Sch. Bd., Durham, 1985—. Exec. scholar GTE of S.E., 1981. Mem. Am. Mktg. Assn., Women in Telecommunications. Republican. Avocations: cooking, alpine skiing, interior design. Home: 1908 Cedar St Durham NC 27707 Office: No Telecom Dept 2210 PO Box 13010 Research Triangle Park NC 27709

PUTNAM, CONSTANCE ELIZABETH, communications consultant, writer; b. Hanover, N.H., Mar. 2, 1943; d. William Frederick and Mildred Margaret (Best) P. BA, Reed Coll., Portland, Oreg., 1965, MAT, 1966. Tchr. Marshall High Sch., Portland, Oreg., 1965-67, Catlin Gabel Sch., Portland, 1967-70, Gymnasium Fuer Jungen and Maedchen, Duderstadt, Fed. Republic of Germany, 1971; instr. Paedagogische Hochschule Niedersachsen, Hildesheim, Fed. Republic of Germany, 1971-73; editor Houghton Mifflin Co., Boston, 1974-83; program dir. Northeastern U., 1983-85; pres. Fairfield Communication Cons., Concord, Mass., 1985—; instr. Harvard U. Ctr. for Lifelong Learning, Cambridge, Mass., 1981-89; NEH seminar dir. Iona Coll. New Rochelle, N.Y.C., 1984. Author: Books German Today 1&2 Tests 1982; Author Contb. Articles to Profl. Jours., Mags., Newspaper. 1978. Mem. Concord Fair Housing Com., Concord-Carlisle Human Rights Coun., West Concord Depot Citizen's Adv. Com. Recipient Incentive award Graphic Arts Found., Rochester, N.Y., 1984. Mem. Nat. Writers Union, Soc. for German Am. Studies, Concord Art Assn. (Disting. Artist award 1987). Democrat. Home: 111 Hayward Mill Rd Concord MA 01742

PUTNEY, MARY ENGLER, federal auditor; b. Overland, Mo., May 1, 1933; d. Bernard J. and Marie (Kunkler) Engler; children: Glennon (dec.), Pat Michael, Michelle. Student Fontbonne Coll., 1951-52; AA, Sacramento City Coll., 1975; BS in Bus., Calif. State U., 1981; CPA, Calif. Asst. to acct. Mo. Research Labs., Inc., St. Louis, 1953-55, sec. to controller, 1955-56, adminstrv. asst. to pres., 1958-60; sec. to mgr. Western region fin. Gen. Electric Co., St. Louis, 1960-62; sec. to regional v.p. agrl. loans Crocker Nat. Bank, Sacramento, 1962-67, asst. credit analyst No. region, 1967, sec. to v.p. and mgr. capital office, Sacramento, 1967-72; student tchr. Sacramento County Dept. Edn., 1979-81; acctg. technician East Yolo Community Services Dist., 1983; mgmt. specialist USAF Logistics Command, 1984; staff auditor office Insp. Gen., U.S. Dept. Transp., 1984—. Mem. Sacramento Community Commn. for Women, 1978—, rec. sec., 1980-81, bd. dirs., 1980—; mem. planning bd. Golden Empire Health Systems Agy. Mem. Nat. Assn. Accts. (dir., newsletter editor), Fontbonne Coll. Alumni Assn., AAUW (fin. officer 1983—), Assn. Govt. Accts. (chpt. officer), Am. Soc. Women Accts., Beta Gamma Sigma, Beta Alpha Psi. Roman Catholic. Club: Arden Hills Swim and Tennis. Home: 2616 Point Reyes Way Sacramento CA 95826 Office: US Dept of Transp Office Insp Gen Room 287 PO Box 1915 Sacramento CA 95809

PUTZ, CHRISTINE, financial executive, accountant; b. Palmer, Mass., Feb. 4, 1950; d. Anthony Charles and Stephanie Veronica (Niemiec) P. Student Salem State Coll., Springfield Tech. Coll.; B.S. in Bus. Adminstrn., Western New Eng. Coll., 1979. Chief acct. Wing Meml. Hosp., Palmer, 1969-79; field acct. Hillhaven Corp., Lexington, Mass., 1979-83; fin. dir. Bus. Mgmt., Malden, Mass., 1983-87; cons. Melrose VNS, Mass., 1983-87; contr. Nashua (N.H.) Brookside Hosp. div. Psychiatric Inst. Am. Hosp., 1987—. Mem. Healthcare Fin. Mgmt. Assn., NAFE. Roman Catholic. Avocations: outdoor activities, sports reading, work. Office: Nashua Brookside Hosp Nashua NH 03063

PUTZRATH, RESHA MAE, toxicologist; b. Camden, N.J., Sept. 9, 1949; d. Franz Ludwig and Pearl (Robins) P.; m. Lawrence Smedley Olson, May 13, 1978. BA in Physics cum laude, Smith Coll., 1971; MS in Biophysics, U. Rochester, 1974, PhD in Biophysics, 1978. Diplomate Am. Bd. Toxicology. Rsch. fellow Med. Sch. Harvard U., Boston, 1977-79, fellow Sch. Pub. Health, 1979-81; cons. U.S. Environ. Protection Agy., Washington, 1981-82; assoc. scientist Nat. Acad. Scis., Washington, 1982-83; sr. assoc. ENVIRON Corp., Washington, 1983-86, project mgr., 1986—; mem. faculty Found. for Advanced Edn. in Scis., NIH, Rockville, Md., 1982-86; exec. dir. Acad. Toxicol. Scis., Washington, 1983-84; mem. FDA Planning Bd., Washington, 1984-86. Author: Elements of Toxicology and Chemical Risk Assessment, 1986. Nat. evaluator NSTA-NASA Space Shuttle Student Involvement Project, Washington, 1982-86. Mem. Am. Coll. Toxicology, Biophys. Soc., ASTM, Environ. Mutagen Soc., Assn. for Women in Sci. (nat. councilor Washington chpt. 1989—, v.p. 1982-83, pres. 1985-87), Phi Beta Kappa. Home: 3223 N St NW Washington DC 20007 Office: ENVIRON Corp 4350 N Fairfax Dr Ste 300 Arlington VA 22203

PYLE, SUSAN CLINARD, administrative specialist; b. High Point, N.C., Nov. 11, 1960; d. Robert Winfred and Elaine (Sells) Clinard; m. Nicholas Ayrault Pyle, Dec. 18, 1982; 1 child, Sophie Spencer. BSBA, U. N.C., 1982. Account exec. Robert Pyle & Assocs., Inc., Washington, 1985-86; cons. Minority Bus. Devel. Ctr., Washington, 1986-89; assoc. Perot Systems Corp., Vienna, Va., 1989—. Active Jr. League, Washington, 1986-89, N.C. State Soc., Washington, 1985—, Nat. Coun. Career Women, 1985-87, Columbia Hist. Soc., 1986-87. Mem. City Tavern Club. Republican. Methodist. Home: 1734 10th St NW Washington DC 20001 Address: PO Box 25001 Washington DC 20007

PYLES, CAROL DELONG, dean, health sciences, consultant, educator; b. Oil City, Pa., Apr. 6, 1948; d. William J. and Doris (Gresh) DeLong; m. Richard Pyles, Mar. 26, 1980; 1 child, Whitney Dawn. BS, Alderson-Broaddus Coll., Philippi, W.Va., 1966-70; MS, Tex. Woman's U., 1982-85; MA, W. Va. U., 1972-73, PhD Edn., 1974-80. RN, W.Va., Tex.; cert. health edn. specialist; lic. profl. counselor; nat. cert. counselor. Instr. of Nursing Fairmont (W.Va.) State Coll., 1971-73, asst. prof. of Nursing Edn., 1973-76, asst. Dean of Com. Coll., 1976-78; cons. and adj. faculty Salem Coll., Clarksburg, W.Va., 1978-81; prof. of nursing, chmn. Div. of Health Careers Fairmont (W.Va.) State Coll., 1978-81; officer Allied Health Houston Com. Coll. System, 1981-83, chmn. div. of Sales, Mktg. & Mgmt., 1983-85; dean Coll. Spl. Arts & Scis., prof. health edn. adminstrn. Cen. State U., Edmond, Okla., 1985-87; Dean Coll. of Health, Physical Edn. & Recreation Eastern Ill. U., Charleston, Ill., 1987—, prof. of Health Studies, 1987—; pres. cons. seminar devel., P & P Assoc., Inc., Houston; coun. pvt. practice for marriage, life crises, behavior & image problems. Author: articles for Issues in Higher Edn.; articles, Ind. State U. Press 1988. Chmn. Indsl. Comm., Charleston (Ill.) Recreation Ctr. 1989; bd. dirs. Am. Red Cross, east Coles County Chpt., Reg. United Way, Coalition Against Domestic Violence. Named Personality of Am. 1986, Outstanding Young Leader in Allied Health, 1984, Most Outstanding Young Women of Am., 1983; recipient Svc. award Am. Cancer Soc., 1984. Mem. Am. Council of Edn. Nat. Identification Program, Am. Assn. of Coll. for Tchrs. Edn. Inst. Rep., Am. Assn. for Health, Physical Edn., Recreation & Dance, Ill. Assn. for Health, Physical Edn., Recreation & Dance, Ill. Assn. for Prof. Preparation in Health, Physical Edn. and Recreation, Rotary Internat., Rotary Club. Office: Coll Health Physical Edn Eastern Ill U Lantz Rm 164 Charleston IL 61920

PYLES, SUSAN KAY, radio station executive; b. Mt. Clemens, Mich., Apr. 29, 1954; d. Paul James Pyles and Charlotte Ettalene Snowden. BA cum laude, U. South Fla., 1976. Copy writer Denton & French, Tampa, Fla., 1977-79, asst. account exec., account exec., 1979-81; account rep. J. Walter Thompson, Atlanta, 1981-82; account exec. Liller Neal, Atlanta, 1982-83; account exec. The Bloom Agy., Dallas, 1983-85, sr. account exec., 1985-86, v.p., account supr., 1986-89; sales and mktg. dir. Sta. KSPN-FM, Aspen, Colo., 1989—. Mem. Women's Forum, Aspen. Mem. Phi Kappa Phi. Home: PO Box 8264 Aspen CO 81612 Office: Sta KSPN-FM 305L AABC Aspen CO 81611

PYNN, HELEN WEST, retired banker; b. Poughkeepsie, N.Y., Oct. 13, 1936; d. Leslie Alten and Margaret Walsh (Hughes) West; m. Malcolm David Pynn, Feb. 11, 1978. BFA, Cornell U., 1958. Unit ops. mgr. Lissone Lindeman, U.S.A., N.Y.C., 1958-62; sales mgr. Havas Exprinter, S.A., N.Y.C., 1962-65, operation and sales mgr., 1972-77; mgr. Citibank, N.A., N.Y.C., 1965-70, Bronxville, N.Y., 1979-82, Rye, N.Y., 1982-87; pres. Clara Laughlin Travel, N.Y.C., 1977-79. Editor The Meteor newsletter, 1976, Fedn. News newspaper, 1977-78; contbr. articles to Citibank newsletter; paintings exhibited at Cornell U. (Gold Star 1957, 58). Bd. dirs. Phelps Mgml. Hosp., Tarrytown, N.Y., 1987; chmn. nurse's aides Bellevue Hosp., ARC, N.Y.C., 1959-61; guide, vol. Rancho De Las Golondrinas. Mem. Hist. Santa Fe Found., Southwestern Assn. on Indian Affairs, Mus. of N.Mex. Found., Santa Fe Country Club. Republican. Roman Catholic. Home: 1251 Seville Rd Santa Fe NM 87501

PYSZ, DONNA MARIE, educator; b. Derby, Conn., Dec. 9, 1952; d. Gino Salvatore and Antoinette (Conte) DiMauro; m. Robert Pysz, Aug. 1, 1975; 1 child, Robert Jr. BS in Teaching, Western Conn. State Coll., 1974; MS in Counseling, U. Bridgeport, 1977; postgrad., So. Conn. State U., 1982-84. Tchr. Lincoln Sch., Derby, 1974-77, Derby Middle Sch., 1977-81, Bradley Sch., Derby, 1981-85, Derby Upper Sch., 1985—; adminstrv. intern Bradley Sch., Derby, 1983-84; tchr. Adult Basic Edn., Derby, 1981-82, Derby Bd. Edn., 1973-74; supr. Derby Recreational Program, 1970-73. Sec. Cath. Family Svcs., Ansonia, Conn.; treas DiMauro for Mayor com.; vol. United Way, New Haven, 1988-89; bd. dirs. Lower Naugatuck Valley Mental Health Ctr., Inc. Recipient Ofcl. citation Conn. Senate, 1989, Mini grant United Illuminating Conservation of Energy. Mem. ASCD, Adminstrn. and Supervision Assn., Conn. Edn. Assocs., Nat. Edn. Assocs., Conn. Sci. Tchrs. Assn., Phi Delta Kappa, Delta Kappa Gamma. Democrat. Roman Catholic. Home: 21 Gilyard St Seymour CT 06483 Office: Derby Upper School Nutmeg Avenue Derby CT 06418

QUADT, SUZANNE MARIE, sales and marketing executive; b. Phila., May 2, 1947; d. George Joseph and Mary Anne (Poniatowski) Cummings; m. Robert Paul Quadt, Aug. 3, 1968; David Paul, Rachel Anne. BA in Govt. Politics, George Mason U., 1977; MBA in Mktg., Marymount Coll., 1982. Dir. sales, mktg. Info. Concepts, Inc., Washington, 1982-83; sales, sr. mkt. planner, devel. Hazeltine Corp., Reston, Va., 1984-86; v.p. internat. sales and mktg. Computers Anyware, Inc., McLean, Va., 1986-87; dir. fed. mktg. Bus. Computer Solutions, Inc., Vienna, Va., 1987; owner, pres. Internat. Advantage, Inc., Vienna, 1988—; cons. various bus., not-for-profit and polit. orgns., Washington; bd. dirs. Health Systems Agy., No. Va., 1982; chmn. Group Residential Facilities Commn., Fairfax, Va., 1979-81; mem. criminal adv. bd. NOVA Planning Dist. Commn., 1977-78. Campaign worker, local, state, nat. campaigns, Va., 1970-82; campaign mgr. Barbara Weiss for State Dele., Va., 1977; chmn., Minority Affairs Standing com., Fairfax, 1972-79, Dem. Party Steering com., 1972-79; bd. dirs., Fedn. Civic Assns., Fairfax County, 1975-76; v.p., bd. dirs., YWCA, 1976-77, chmn. pub. policy and social action com., 1978-79. Mem. NAFE, Washington Internat. Trade Assn., Va. Internat. Trade Assn., Fairfax County C. of C., Software Pubs. Assn., Nat. Assn. Women Bus. Owners, Am. Mktg. Assn., Nat. Mus. Women in the Arts, Women in Internat. Trade, Delta Epsilon Sigma. Roman Catholic. Home: 6423 Lakeview Dr Falls Church VA 22041 Office: Internat Advantage Inc 8375 Leesburg Pike #133 Vienna VA 22180

QUALLS, CORETHIA, archaeologist; b. Sparta, Tenn., Jan. 17, 1948; d. Malcolm Talmadge and Lucille (Jackson) Qualls. BA, Marlboro Coll., 1970; MPhil, Columbia U., 1980, PhD, 1981. Exec. curator Mus. of Archaeology of Staten Island, 1981; asst. prof. St. John's U., S.I., 1981-82; cons. curator Queens Mus., N.Y., 1982-83; cons. curator Kuwait Nat. Mus., 1984-86; curatorial advisor for archaeology, Bahrain Nat. Mus., 1987—; archaeologist Columbia U., 1970-74, NYU Inst. Fine Arts, 1972-73, 84, Johns Hopkins U., 1974, Fulbright prof. archaeology, 1985-86. Dir. excavations Hamad Town, Bahrain, 1985-86. Editor: Seals of the Marcopoli Collection, vol. 1, 1984; contbr. articles to profl. jours. Columbia U. fellow, 1970-74; Am. Schs. Oriental Rsch. fellow, 1973-74. Mem. Am. Inst. Archaeology, Am. Oriental Soc., Am. Schs. Oriental Rsch., Inst. Nautical Archaeology, Brit. Sch. Archaeol. in Iraq, Oriental Club of N.Y.C., Egypt Exploration Soc., Am. Soc. Profl. and Exec. Women, Nat. Assn. Bus. and Profl. Women, NAFE. Roman Catholic.

QUALTROUGH, MARY LOUISE, physical therapist; b. Rochester, N.Y., Nov. 4, 1941; d. Vincent E. and Marjorie Ann (Blycostin) LaValle; m. John David McPherson, Sept. 26, 1965 (div. 1976); 1 child, Michael John; m. Robert Dale Qualtrough, Feb. 16, 1978. BS in Phys. Therapy, St. Louis U., 1963; Cert. in Gerontology, St. John's Fisher Coll., 1987; MPA, SUNY, Brockport, 1987. Lic. phys. therapist, N.Y. Staff phys. therapist St. Ann's Home, Rochester, 1963-65, 68-76, Millard Filmore Hosp., Buffalo, N.Y., 1965-68; sr. staff phys. therapist St. Mary's Hosp., Rochester, 1976-77; cons. phys. therapist St. Joseph's Convent Infirmary, Rochester, 1979-81; clin. coord. Rochester Gen. Hosp., 1980-89; staff phys. therapist VA Hosp., Canandaigua, N.Y., 1989-90; dir. rehab. svcs. Hill Haven Nursing Home, Webster, N.Y., 1990—; phys. therapy rep. Rochester Gen. Hosp., 1982-89; com. mgr. utilization rev. bd. of Genesee Region Home Care Assn., Rochester, 1987-89. Com. mem. Finger Lakes Health Systems Agy. Coun., Rochester, 1988-90. Recipient Ella Hollister award for Outstanding Human Svc., social work dept. Rochester Gen. Hosp., 1984. Mem. NAFE, Nat. Campers and Hikers Assn. Home: 1352 Stanton Lane Rochester NY 14617 Office: Hill Haven Nursing Home 1550 Empire Blvd Rochester NY 14580

QUARLES, DENISE MARIE, state agency administrator; b. Detroit, Jan. 26, 1950; d. Leon George McDonald and Dorothy Kimble Booker; m. Larry Quarles, June 20, 1970 (div. 1983); m. Alvin Leonidus Whitfield, May 11, 1985. BS in Sociology, Eastern Mich. U., 1971; MA in Sociology, U. Detroit, 1977. Probation agent Mich. Dept. Corrections, Detroit, 1971-74, parole agent, 1974-77, community services liason, 1977, corrections ctr. supr., 1977-79; asst. dep. warden Marquette br. prisons Mich. Dept. Corrections, 1979-81; adminstr. Riverside Reception Ctr., Mich. Dept. Corrections, Ionia, 1981; dep. dir. probation services Mich. Dept. Corrections, Detroit, 1981-83; prison warden Huron Valley Women's Facility, Mich. Dept. Corrections, Ypsilanti, 1983-85, Riverside Correctional Facility, Mich. Dept. Corrections, Ionia, 1985-87, G. Robert Cotton Correctional Facility, Ionia, 1987-88; dep. dir. Bur. of Field Svcs., Mich. Dept. Corrections, Lansing, 1988—; del. People to People internat. conf., criminal justice del. to China, Japan, Hong Kong, 1987, USSR, 1989. bd. dirs. Big Brothers/Big Sisters, Marquette, 1980, Lansing, 1989—. Named one of Young Career Women of 1980, Bus. and Profl. Women's Club, Marquette. Mem. Mich. Corrections Assn. (life, sec. 1977-78, v.p. 1978-79, pres. 1979-80), Am. Corrections Assn. (del. assembly 1988-90). Office: Mich Dept Corrections Bur of Field Svcs PO Box 30003 Lansing MI 48909

QUARLES, MARY VIRGINIA, education union consultant; b. Nashville, Nov. 12, 1940; d. Chester Lew and Virginia Estelle (Cooper) Q. BA, Miss. Coll., 1962; MA, Fla. State U., 1970. Tchr. recruiter Brevard County Schs., Titusville, Fla., 1962-76; dir. Fontana/Chaffey UniServ, Calif., 1976-78, Cen. Wis. UniServ Council-West, Wausau, Wis., 1978—. Older children dir. Park Ave. Bapt. Ch., Titusville, Fla., 1970-73; Sunday Sch. dir. Calvary Bapt. Ch., Schofield, Wis., 1985-86, 1st Bapt. Ch., Wausau, 1986—. Experienced Tchr. fellow Fla. State U., 1970. Mem. Indsl. Relations Research Assn., AAUW, Fla. Teaching Profession div. NEA (bd. dirs. 1974-76), Sigma Tau Delta. Democrat. Home: 726 N 1st Ave Wausau WI 54401 Office: Cen Wis UniServ Council-West PO Box 1606 Wausau WI 54402-1606

QUARRY, MARY ANN, chemist; b. Phila., June 27, 1953; d. James Joseph and Violet Mary (Varano) Q. BS in Chemistry, Villanova U., 1975, PhD in Chemistry, 1984. Analytical chemist ARCO Chem., Glenolden, Pa., 1979-80; tech. specialist E.I. du Pont de Nemours & Co., Wilmington, Del., 1981-84, rsch. chemist, 1984-89, group leader, 1989—. Contbr. articles to profl. jour. Recipient student award Am. Inst. Chemists, 1975. Mem. Am. Chem. Soc., Chromatography Forum Delaware Valley (1st pl. student symposium 1981), Am. Guild Organists, MENSA, Sigma Xi. Republican. Roman Catholic. Office: E I du Pont de Nemours & Co PO Box 80400 Rm 2273 Wilmington DE 19880-0400

QUARTARO, LINDA SCHMIDT, lawyer; b. Fond du Lac, Wis., July 21, 1963; d. David John and Janet Margaret (Altman) S. BA, U. Wis., 1985; JD magna cum laude, Pepperdine U., 1988. Bar: Wis. 1988, U.S. Dist. Ct. (ea. and we. dists.) Wis. 1989. Assoc. Ives, Kirwan & Dibble, L.A., summer 1986, Gibson, Dunn & Crutcher, L.A., summer 1987, Mulcahy & Wherry, Milw., 1988-89, Shneidman, Myers, Dowling & Blumenfield, Milw., 1989—; lectr. Milw. Area Tech. Coll., Marquette U., 1990. Editor: Pepperdine U. Law Rev., 1987-88. Mem. Am. Trial Lawyers Assn. Republican. Lutheran. Office: Shneidman Myers et al PO Box 442 Milwaukee WI 53201

QUARTERMAN, ELSIE, ecology educator; b. Valdosta, Ga., Nov. 28, 1910; d. David Sinclair Quarterman and Alla (Irene) Peek. AB, Valdosta State, 1932; AM, Duke U., 1941, PhD, 1949. Tchr. Ga. Pub. Schs., 1932-43; instr. Vanderbilt U., Nashville, 1943-48, asst. prof., 1948-52, assoc. prof., 1952-60, prof., 1960-76, prof. emerita, 1976—. Contbr. articles to profl. jours. Mem. Assn. Southeastern Biologists (v.p. 1958-59, treas. 1959-62, pres. 1966-67, Meritorious Teaching award 1988), Nature Conservancy (bd. dirs. Tenn. chpt. 1984-90, Oak Leaf award 1981, Sol Feinstein Conservation award 1982). Democrat. Presbyterian.

QUARTON, JEAN ELSA RULF, psychologist, hypnotherapist; b. Hartford, Conn., Mar. 29, 1942; d. Walter Otto and Elsa Margareta (Blume) Rulf; m. David T. Quarton, Aug. 25, 1973 (div.); m. Conrad L. Bergendoff, Feb. 9, 1980. BFA, R.I. Sch. Design, 1964; MA in Home Econs., U. Iowa, 1968, PhD, 1974. Lic. psychologist, Ill.; cert. advanced clin. hypnotherapist Staff psychologist Riverside Retreat, 1974-76; pvt. practice clin. psychology, Rock Island, Ill., 1976-81; clin. cons. to Quad-cities Indsl. Employee Assistance Programs, Internat. Harvester, 3M, John Deere, J.I. Case, Rock Island arsenal, Army C.E., 1977-81; pvt. practice clin. psychology, LaGrange Park, Ill., 1982—; cons. Quad-Cities Alcoholism Info. Ctrs., 1977-80, Davenport (Iowa) Sch. System, 1977-78; staff psychologist ACP, Chgo., 1982-84; pres. Accredited Affiliated Psychologists, P.C.; clin. cons. Gen. Motors, Reuben Donnelley, Continental Bank, AT&T, United Airlines, McDonald's; adj. prof. psychology Augustana Coll., Rock Island, 1977; mgr. Chgo. Psychol. Assn. Telephone Answering Svc., 1985—. Mem. Quad-cities Career Women's Network, 1978-81, keynote speaker, 1978; lectr. in field. Spl. Rsch. asst. U. Iowa, 1970-73. Mem. Rock Island Psychol. Assn. (sec. 1980-81), Chgo. Psychol. Assn. (chmn. newsletter com. 1982-83, editor newsletter 1982-83, sec. 1983-85, pres. 1986-87, chmn. program com. 1985-86), NOW, Bus. Networking Soc. (bd. dirs. Chgo. 1983—). Lutheran. Club: Bus. and Profl. Women's (chmn. pub. rels. 1983-84, named Woman of Achievement 1983), Movers and Shakers in Feminist Thought and Action (co-chair). Contbr. articles to profl. jours. Home and Office: 537 S 10th Ave La Grange IL 60525 Office: Accredited Affiliated Psychologists 230 N Michigan Ave Ste 3200 Chicago IL 60601

QUASIUS, CHIYOKO TANINARI, accountant; b. Hiroshima, Japan, Aug. 12, 1948; came to U.S., 1977; d. Isao and Chidori (Yamasaki) Taninari; m. Robert Thomas Quasius, July 22, 1957; 1 child, Marie Elizabeth. Assoc. Sci., South Ga. Coll., 1978; BSBA, Christopher Newport Coll., 1981; MBA, Old Dominion U., 1985. Tour guide for non-Japanese Japan Travel Bur., Hiroshima, 1969-74; project mgr.'s sec. Kaiser Engring., Hiroshima, 1974; freelance interpreter Hiroshima, 1974-76; asst. to project mgr. Shipping Mgmt. S.A.M., Hiroshima, 1976-77; sr. acct. Peat Marwick Main & Co., N.Y.C., 1987-90; tax cons. Price-Waterhouse, N.Y.C., 1990—. Translator: Hiroshi Oshima Biography. 1st v.p. Denbigh Lioness Club, Newport News, Va., 1986-87. Japan Soc. scholar U. New Orleans, 1979; Univ. fellow Old Dominion U., 1984. Home: 1388 Omara Dr Union NJ 07083

QUAST, FLORENCE EDWINA, nurse; b. Somerville, Mass., Apr. 24, 1937; d. Joseph Frank and Florence Irene (Tinkham) Follomon; children: Kenneth, Katherine, Joseph, Erika. Postgrad., Somerville Sch. Nursing, 1958; BS, Simmons Coll., Boston, 1962, New England Coll., Henniker, N.H., 1984. RN, N.H. Nurse supr. Knox County Meml. Hosp., Barbourville, Ky., 1960-65; charge nurse St Josephs Hosp., Nashua, N.H., 1975--; pres. N.H. Mobile Home Owners and Ten. Assn., Concord, 1987—; bd. dis. N.H. Community Loan Fund, Concord, N.H., pres. Souhegan Valley Mfr. Housing Coop, Milford, N.H., 1986--. Organizer Mobile Home Owners and Tenant Assn., Concord, N.H., 1986—, pres. 1987—. Republican. Methodist. Home and Office: 7 Town and Country Pk Milford NH 03055

QUAYLE, MARILYN, wife of vice president of U.S.; b. 1949; d. Warren and Mary Alice Tucker; m. J. Danforth Quayle, Nov. 18, 1972; children: Tucker, Benjamin, Corinne. BS in Polit. Sci., Purdue U., 1971; JD, Indiana U., 1975. Pvt. practice atty. Huntington, Ind., 1974-76. Office: Old Exec Office Bldg Rm 258 Washington DC 20500*

QUEOFF, PAMELA FRANCES, risk management professional; b. Menominee, Mich., Oct. 25, 1952; d. Joseph Arnold and Jane Mildred (Reiswitz) Phelps; m. Robert Thomas Leemon, Aug. 22, 1970 (div. 1977); m. Thomas James Queoff, Jan. 3, 1981. BBA in Fin. with honors, U. Wis., Madison, 1984, MBA in Risk and Ins., 1985. Dist. acctg. clk. Wis. Pub. Svcs. Corp., Green Bay, 1971-80; risk mgr. Graebel Movers, Inc., Wausau, Wis., 1985-86; dir. risk mgmt. Wausau Paper Mills Co., 1986-89; pres. Queoff Assocs., Inc., Wausau, 1989—. Mem. Ris. and Ins. Mgmt. Soc., U. Wis. Bus. Alumni, Bus. and Profl. Women, Women in Bus., Wis. River Valley Acctg. Assn., Wausau Area C. of C., Merrill Concert Assn., Altrusa Club Wausau (com. chair 1988—), Mid Wis. Risk Mgrs. (chair 1988—), Beta Gamma Sigma. Roman Catholic. Office: Queoff Assocs Inc 300 3d St PO Box 6068 Wausau WI 54402-6068

QUERBES, BETTY-LANE SHIPP, interior designer, real estate agent; b. Mayersville, Miss.; d. Byron Cadmus and MaryLucille (Lane) Shipp; m. Andrew C. Querbes Jr., Dec. 21, 1950; children: Renee Lane, Andrew IV, Maura Colette. Student, Centenary Coll., 1949-51, La. State U., Shreveport, 1971-73. Designer, salesperson Dunn Furniture Co., Inc., Shreveport, La., 1976; interior designer, buyer Dunn Furniture Co., Inc., 1977-82, advertising specialist, 1978-82; columnist, feature writer The Times, Shreveport, 1974-87; co-owner, designer Prothro-Querbes Interior Design, Shreveport, 1982—; real estate salesperson, Andrew Querbes, Jr., Inc., Shreveport, 1975—. Mem. orgnl. com. Live Oak Retirement Ctr., Shreveport; active Lay Resources Task Force First Meth. Ch. of Shreveport, 1989—; sec. La. chpt. Am. Lung Assn., 1987-90, v.p., 1990—; mem. Commn. for Bi-Centennial of Constn. of U.S., 1987-91; chmn. Mayor's Com. to Fight Veneral Disease, Shreveport; pub. rels. specialist Shreveport Mental Health Assn.; v.p. Caddo Bossier Day Care Assn.; pres. Jr. League Shreveport, 1970-71; acquisitions chmn. Spring Street Mus., 1988-90, chmn. bd. dirs., 1990—. Mem. DAR (Pelican chpt.), Nat. Soc. Colonial Dames in Am. (sec. Shreveport com. 1987-90), Shereveport Med. Soc. (tobacco com.), Demoiselle Club Shreveport (past sec., chmn.), Cotillion Club Shreveport (gen. chmn. 1977), Chi Omega Alumnae (past-pres.). Democrat. Methodist. Home: 321 Corinne Circle Shreveport LA 71106 Office: Prothro Querbes 7035 Sand Beach Blvd Shreveport LA 71105

QUICK, CAROLYN MAY, nurse administrator; b. Providence, June 20, 1938; d. Arland Reuben Merchant and Helen Veronica (Barbour) De Ve; m. Ronald. BS, St. Mary's Coll., 1978. Head nurse ICU, Roger Williams Gen. Hosp., Providence, 1960-63; pharmacology research asst. Shell Research & Devel., Salida, Calif., 1964-66; operating room nurse Dr. Med. Ctr., Modesto, Calif., 1965-66; staff nurse St. Joseph's Hosp., Eureka, Calif., 1966-67, Columbus (Ga.) Med. Ctr., 1967-68; nursing supr. Meml. Hosp. Assocs., Modesto, 1972-76, nurse educator, 1976-80, asst. v.p., dir. nursing, 1980-89; v.p. nursing Meml. Med. Ctr., Modesto, 1989—. Patron, Modesto Symphony Orchestra, 1973--, troop leader, Muir Trail Girl Scout Council, Modesto, 1975-77, mem. Mayor's Council, Pub. Relations. Mem. N. Cen. Calif. Nursing Council, Calif. Soc. Nursing Service Admistrn, Calif. Soc. Nursing Service Adminstr. Legis. Com. Democrat.

QUIGLEY, BEHNAZ ZOLGHADR, educator, consultant; b. Tehran, Iran, Nov. 17, 1944; came to U.S., 1968, naturalized, 1978; d. Hamid and Behjat (Shoaibi) Zolghadr; m. Herbert Gerald Quigley, Aug. 24, 1968; children: Narda, Paran. Diploma in Edn., Tchrs. Tng. Coll., Tehran, 1964; BA, U. Tehran, 1968; MBA, U. D.C., 1975; PhD, U. Md., 1987. Tchr. secondary sch. Ministry of Edn., Tehran, 1964-68; instr. in bus. Strayer Coll., U. D.C. Washington, Prince George's Community Coll., Md., U. Md., College Park, 1975-87; asst. prof. bus. adminstrn. Mt. Vernon Coll., Washington, 1977-88, assoc. prof., 1983—, chmn. dept. bus. adminstrn., 1978—; aide to chief economist Iranian Econ. Mission, 1974; freelance cons. World Trade Assocs., Distbn. Systems, co-owner, freelance cons. Univ. Systems Assocs., Inst. Curriculum Devel., Mid. East Inst., 1975-80. Author several books; coeditor: Management Systems: Contemporary Perspectives; contbr. articles to profl. jours. Faculty devel. grantee Mt. Vernon Coll., Mid. East Inst. Mem. Nat. Assn. Female Execs. (bd. dirs. Washington area chpt.), Assn. MBA Execs., Am. Acctg. Assn., Acad. Mgmt., Am. Soc. for Pub. Adminstrn., U. D.C. Alumni Assn., U. Md. Alumni Assn. Democrat. Home: 5 Canfield Ct Potomac MD 20854 Office: 2100 Foxhall Rd Washington DC 20007

QUIGLEY, RUTH HELEN, entrepreneur; b. Hutchinson, Kans., Feb. 4, 1935; d. John Baird and Zelda (Marks) Q. BA, Smith Coll., 1953; MBA, Stanford U., 1956. Investment analyst Wells Fargo Bank, San Francisco, 1956-59, De Vegh & Co., N.Y.C., 1960-62, Ralph E. Samuels & Co., N.Y.C., 1962-64; v.p. Mitchell, Hutchins, San Francisco, 1964-67, Irving Lundborg & Co., San Francisco, 1967-70; pres. Quigley, Friedlander & Co., San Francisco, 1983-86, Joan Quigley Enterprises, San Francisco, 1988—; Bd. dirs. GT Global Growth Funds, San Francisco. Mem. San Francisco Rep. Finance Com., 1974—; bd. dirs. ARCS Found., Inc., No. Calif. Chpt., 1976—. Mem. San Francisco Security Analysts Soc. Home: 1055 California St San Francisco CA 94108

QUIGLEY-WOLF, ANNA MARIE HELEN, organizational development consultant; b. Phila., Aug. 15, 1950; d. William Joseph, Jr. and Elizabeth (Harkins) Ailes. BA, Point Park Coll., Pitts., 1972; postgrad. Temple U., Phila.; MA, Antioch U., Phila., 1984. Ednl. resource specialist Community Coll. Phila., 1972-74; edn. coordinator Penn Mut. Life Ins. Co., Phila., 1974-76, human resource cons., 1976-81; adminstr. orgn. devel. RCA Service Co., Cherry Hill, N.J., 1981-85; mgr. orgn. devel. and compensation The Lehigh Press, Inc., Pennsauken, N.J., 1985-89, dir. corp. human resources, 1989—; chmn. Women's Resource Group, Phila., 1980-81; speaker in field. Mem. Orgn. Devel. Network, Am. Soc. Tng. and Devel., Nat. Assn Female Execs., Human Resource Planning Soc., Am. Compensation Assn.

QUILTER, JOAN MARY, school system administrator; b. Waterbury, Conn., Jan. 12, 1928; d. Thomas George and Sally Ann (Sakocius) Q. BS in Math. Edn., Boston U., 1958; MA in Counseling, Fairfield U., 1960, cert. in sch. psychology, 1962; PhD in Child Study and Sch. Psychol. Services, St. John's U., Jamaica, N.Y., 1978. Lic. psychol. examiner, counselor, math. tchr., adminstr., Conn. Elem. tchr. St. John Baptiste Sch., N.Y.C., 1955-56, St. Patrick Sch., Stoneham, Mass., 1956-59; math. tchr. Crosby High Sch., Waterbury, Conn., 1959-64; psychol. examiner Waterbury Pub. Schs., 1964-68, sch. psychologist, 1968-70; dir. spl. services Sch. Dist. 15, Middlebury and Southbury, Conn., 1970—; adj. prof. Post Coll., Waterbury, 1978—, Sacred Heart U., Fairfield, 1987—. Mem. STS Program Rev. Com., Southbury, 1986—; bd. dirs. Child Guidance Clinic, Waterbury, 1987—, sec., 1988—; bd. dirs. Family Svcs. Waterbury, 1987—; commr. Commn. for People with Disabilities, Waterbury, 1987—; early edn. adv. bd. Post Coll., Waterbury, 1987—. Mem. Am. Psychol. Assn., Am. Assn. Mental Retardation, Am. Assn. Sch. Adminstrs., Am. Assn. Counseling and Devel., Coun. Exceptional Children, Assn. Suprs. Curriculum Devel., Litchfield County Dirs. Assn., Conn. Assn. Pupil Pers. Adminstrs. (treas. 1984-86), AAUW (v.p. 1984—), Quota Club (sec. Waterbury 1980-81, v.p. 1981-83, pres. 1983-85, treas. 1985-87, lt. gov. 5th dist. Quota Internat. 1986-87, gov. 1987-89, internat. chair of hearing and speech com., 1988-90), Delta Kappa Gamma (chair membership com. 1982-84). Democrat. Roman Catholic.

QUINDEL, DARLENE JEAN, manufacturing executive; b. Janesville, Wis., Oct. 7, 1944; d. Harry F. and Dorothea E. (Peche) Marquardt; m. Vernon C. Ryan, Apr. 18, 1964 (dec. 1980); children: David C., Michael S.; m. Gary K. Quindel. AA in Bus., Spencerian Bus. Coll., Milw., 1964; postgrad., Elgin (Ill.) Community Coll., 1974; MA in Supervision, Mima Coll., Elgin, 1980. Customer svc. mgr., prodn. scheduler Union Carbide Corp., Streamwood, Ill., 1967-76; plant mgr. Parker Seal/GNP Ops. div. Parker Hannifin Corp., Naples, Fla., 1976—; cons. indsl. div. State of Fla. Sch. System, 1983-84; dir. Southwest Fla. Pvt. Industry Coun., Naples, 1988—. Mem. Am. Bus. Women Am., Nat. Assn. Bus. Execs., Am. Soc. Testing and Materials, Southwest Fla. Mfrs. Assn., Am. Soc. Exec. and Profl. Women, Econ. Devel. Coun. (chmn. 1987-88, award 1986). Republican. Lutheran. Office: Parker Seal/GNP Ops 1429 Don St Naples FL 33942

QUINLAN, CLAIRE, educational administrator; b. Westerly, R.I., Oct. 3, 1929; d. William James and Mary Cecilia (Murray) Q. BA, U. R.I., 1951; MA, U. No. Colo., 1961, PhD, 1964; MBA, Calif. State U., Sacramento, 1986. English tchr. Jeffersonville (Vt.) High Sch., 1952-53, Rangely (Colo.) High Sch., 1953-58; social studies, English tchr. Babcock Jr. High Sch., Westerly, 1958-59; English tchr. Westminster (Colo.) High Sch., 1959-60; psychometrist U. No. Colo., Greeley, Colo., 1960-61; asst. prof. U. No. Colo., Greeley, 1961-64, assoc. dean, psych. svcs., 1964-69; v.p. for student affairs Jamestown (N.D.) Coll., 1969-75; administr. program evaluation and rsch. Dept. of Edn., Sacramento, Calif., 1975—. Recipient Fulbright scholarship, USA Office of Edn., India, 1977. Mem. Am. Edn. Rsch. Assn., Am. Assn. for Counseling & Devel., Assn. for Measurement and Evaluation in Counseling & Devel., Nat. Coun. on Measurement in Edn., Pi Lambda Theta. Roman Catholic. Office: Dept of Education 721 Capitol Mall Sacramento CA 95814

QUINLAN, LIZ W. (ISADORA QUINLAN), public relations executive; b. N.Y.C., Dec. 30, 1937; d. A. Ralph and Mary Ella (Darbee) Wexler; m. Robert J. Quinlan, Aug. 6, 1966. A.B., Vassar Coll., 1959. Assoc. editor Macmillan Pubs., N.Y.C., 1962-65, Reader's Digest Almanac, N.Y.C., 1965-67; publs. editor Assn. of Jr. Leagues, N.Y.C., 1968-72, 76-80, dir. communications, 1980—; cons. pub. rels., N.Y.C., 1972-80; mem. rev. com. Ind. Sector/Ad Coun. Nat. Voluntarism Ad Campaign, 1982-83; rep. to subcom. of Presdl. Task Force for Pvt. Sector Initiatives, 1982. Contbr. articles to mags., and assn. jours. Mem. governing com. Off-the-Record Series, Fgn. Policy Assn., N.Y.C., 1977-85. Recipient cert. of merit Art Dirs.' Club, 1970. Pub. Rels. Soc. Am., Mem. Women in Communications, Alumnae/Alumni of Vassar Coll. (dir. 1982-86, pres. 1986—), DAR (Maj. Jonathan Lawrence chpt.), Vassar of N.Y. Club (dir. 1972-79, pres. 1976-79), Cosmopolitan Club. Home: 200 East End Ave New York NY 10128 Office: Assn Jr Leagues Internat Inc 660 First Ave New York NY 10016

QUINN, BARBARA ANN, athletics administrator; b. Freehold, N.J., Jan. 13, 1933; d. Walter Stanley and Mary (Craig) Harris; B.S. in Health and Phys. Edn., Ursinus Coll., 1955; M.A., Trenton State Coll., 1968. Dir. phys. edn. for girls Charles Ellis Sch., Newtown Square, Pa., 1956-60; instr. phys. edn. Pennsbury Schs., Yardley, Pa., 1960-63, Exeter Twp. High Sch., Reading, Pa., 1963-66, Hartwick Coll., Oneonta, N.Y., 1966-68; asst. prof. phys. and health edn. Madison Coll., Harrisonburg, Va., 1968-71; instr. phys. edn. Whitemarsh Jr. High Sch., Plymouth Meeting, Pa., 1971-74; dir. women's intercollegiate athletics U. Nev., Las Vegas, 1974-76; dir. women's intercollegiate athletics Simpson Coll., Indianola, Iowa, 1977-78; dir. women's athletics U. N.C., Asheville, 1978-81; dir. women's intercoll. athletics SUNY, Cortland, 1981-84; fitness dir. St. Joseph's Hosp., Asheville, N.C., 1985—; instr. phys. edn. Asheville-Buncombe Community Coll., 1989—; site dir. Western Region, Women's U.S. Olympic Basketball Trials, Las Vegas, 1976, U.S. Volleyball Assn. Coaches Clinic, Simpson Coll., 1977; chmn. selection com. Va. State Lacrosse Tournament, 1970-71; mem. selection com. So. Dist. Lacrosse Tournament, 1970-71; coach So. dist. team U.S. Women's Lacrosse Assn. Nat. Tournament, 1971; mem. women's soccer com. Nat. Collegiate Athletic Assn. 1982-84, chmn. NE region; participant 5th Nat. Inst. Girls' Sports Advanced Basketball Coaching, 1969. Mem. AAHPER (sec. coll. div. N.Y. State chpt. 1967), Va. Women's Lacrosse Assn. (chmn. nominations com. 1970-71), Nat. Assn. Coll. Athletic Dirs., N.Y. Assn. Intercollegiate Athletics for Women (chair ethics and eligibility com. 1982). Address: RD 3 Box 238 Bear Branch Rd Mars Hill NC 28754

QUINN, CHERI LYNNE, director of education, researcher, educator; b. Bakersfield, Calif., Mar. 7, 1949; d. Charles Hunter and Lillian Frances (Sides) Sawders; m. John Francis Quinn Jr.; children: Shannon Marie, Patrick Shawn, Erin Frances. BS, San Jose (Calif.) State U., 1977; MS, Okla. State U., Stillwater, 1983; EdD, Okla. State U., 1989. Cert. social studies and lang. arts tchr., Okla. Tchr. social studies Agra (Okla.) High Sch., 1979-83, Empire High Sch., Duncan, Okla., 1984-87; asst. to dir. of tchr. edn. Cameron U., Lawton, Okla., 1987-90; chair dept. edn., dir. tchr. edn. Dickinson Coll., Carlisle, Pa., 1990—; citizen bee coord. Close-Up Found., Duncan, 1986-87. Del. Okla. Dem. Conv., Oklahoma City, 1984. Okla. State Regents for Higher Edn. grantee, 1983-84. Mem. Am. Assn. for Colls. of Tchr. Edn. (instl. rep. 1987-90), Assn. Tchr. Educators (commn. on substitute teaching 1990—), Okla. Assn. of Tchr. Educators (pres. elect 1990—), Assn. for Supervision and Curriculum Devel., Okla. Women in Edn. Adminstrn. Office: Dickinson Coll Bosler 204 Box 1773 Carlisle PA 17013-1773

QUINN, CHRISTINE AGNES, radiologist; b. Cleve., Sept. 23, 1946; d. Paul Leo and Estelle Christine Q.; m. Paul C. Janicki, July 11, 1970; children: Sarah Christine, Megan Alexandra. B.A., Marquette U., 1967; M.D., Med. Coll. Pa., 1971. Diplomate Am. Bd. Radiology. Intern, St. Luke's Hosp., Cleve., 1971-72; resident in diagnostic radiology Cleve. Clinic Found., 1972-75, radiologist, 1975-81; radiologist Marymount Hosp., Cleve., 1981—. Trustee Am. Cancer Soc. Mem. Radiol. Soc. N. Am., Am. Coll. Radiology, Soc. Nuclear Medicine, Ohio Med. Soc., Cuyahoga County Med. Soc., AMA. Contbr. to CRC Handbook Series, Vol. II, 1977; contbr. articles to profl. jours. Home: 2781 Sherbrooke Rd Shaker Heights OH 44122 Office: 12300 McCracken Rd Cleveland OH 44125

QUINN, CLAIRE KOFFLER, marketing executive; b. Hammond, Ind., July 21, 1959; d. Carl Albert Quinn and Constance (Dittmann) Koffler; m. Patrick G. Quinn, Mar. 24, 1989. BSBA, U. Ark., 1981; MBA, U. Pa., 1983. Mktg. asst. Gen. Mills, Mpls., 1983, asst. product mgr., 1984, product mgr., 1986-88; dir. mktg. CIBA Vision, Atlanta, 1988—. Fellow AAUW, 1982-83. Mem. Wharton Club. Home: 6417 Rosecommon Dr Norcross GA 30092 Office: CIBA Vision 2910 Amwiler Ct Atlanta GA 30360

QUINN, EMILY STEIFLE, historical house manager; b. Greensboro, N.C., June 15, 1946; d. James Riley and Rubye (Martin) Steifle; m. David Hazel Quinn, June 14, 1969; children: Duncan, Collin. BA, Wake Forest U., 1968. Cert. secondary edn. French tchr. Tchr. of French St. Genevieve-of-the-Pines, Asheville, N.C., 1969-70; head start tchr. Head Start Program, Asheville, N.C., 1970-71; psychometrist Ga. Inst. Tech., Atlanta, 1971-72, libr. asst., 1972-73; asst. dir., house mgr. Smith-McDowell House, Asheville, 1984—. Bd. dirs., sec. WCQS-FM Pub. Radio, Asheville, 1979-84. Mem. AAUW (treas. 1977-79, pres. 1983-84, nominee for ednl. found. scholarship 1984), Nat. Trust for Hist. Preservation, Hist. Preservation Found. of N.C., Preservation Soc. of Asheville and Buncombe County. Baha'i Faith. Home: 38 Imperial Ct Asheville NC 28803 Office: Smith-McDowell House 283 Victoria Rd Asheville NC 28801

QUINN, JANE BRYANT, journalist; b. Niagara Falls, N.Y., Feb. 5, 1939; d. Frank Leonard and Ada (Laurie) Bryant; m. David Conrad Quinn, June 10, 1967; children—Matthew Alexander, Justin Bryant. B.A. magna cum laude, Middlebury Coll., 1960. Assoc. editor Insiders Newsletter, N.Y.C., 1962-65, co-editor, 1966-67; sr. editor Cowles Book Co., N.Y.C., 1968; editor-in-chief Bus. Week Letter, N.Y.C., 1969-73, gen. mgr., 1973-74; syndicated financial columnist Washington Post Writers Group, 1974—; contbr. fin. column to Women's Day mag., 1974—; contbr. NBC News and Info. Service, 1976-77; bus. corr. WCBS-TV, N.Y.C., 1979, CBS-TV News, 1980-87; contbg. editor Newsweek mag., 1978—. Author: Everyone's Money Book, 1979, 2d edit., 1980. Mem. Phi Beta Kappa. Office: Newsweek Inc 444 Madison Ave New York NY 10022

QUINN, JULIA PROVINCE, civic worker; b. Franklin, Ind., Feb. 23; d. Oran Arnold and Lillian (Ditmars) Province. B.A., Franklin Coll., 1937; M.S., Smith Coll., 1939; m. Robert William Quinn, Jan. 21, 1942; children: Robert Sean, Judith Ditmars. Caseworker, student supr. Community Svc. Soc., N.Y.C., 1939-44; caseworker community rsch. Family Svc. Soc., New Haven, 1946; social worker in rsch., dept. preventive medicine Yale U. Sch. Medicine, New Haven, 1946-49; rsch. asst. dept. preventive medicine Vanderbilt U. Sch. Medicine, Nashville, 1969-70. Bd. dirs. Tenn. Bot. Gardens and Fine Arts Ctr., 1976-81, Friends of J. F. Kennedy Ctr., 1976-81, Family and Children's Svc., Nashville, 1977-83, Friends of Cheekwood, 1966-81, Nashville Symphony Assn., 1978-85, Tenn. Performing Arts Found., 1979—; bd. dirs. Nashville Opera Assn., 1983—, chmn. pub. rels., 1985—, Nashville Opera Guild, charter mem., bd. dirs.; chmn. pub. rels. Friends of the Tenn. Performing Arts Ctr., 1985—, charter mem., 1986—; chmn. pub. rels. Friends of Cheekwood, 1966-68, 72-74, 76-78, Tenn. Performing Arts Found., 1978-85, Family and Children's Svc., 1978-83; founder Friends of the Family & Children's Svc., charter mem., 1989—; founder Tenn. Arts Found., charter mem., 1989—; mem. adv. bd. Vanderbilt Ctr. for Fertility and Reproductive Rsch., 1981-85. Recipient Nashville Vol. Activist award Cain-Sloan and Germaine Monteil, 1979. Mem. Nat. Assn. Social Workers, Acad. Cert. Social Workers, Ladies Hermitage Assn., Vanderbilt Med. Ctr. Aux., Nashville Area C. of C. (cultural affairs com. 1979-85). Democrat. Presbyterian. Clubs: Smith Coll., Centennial (Nashville); Vanderbilt Garden, Vanderbilt Woman's. Contbr. articles to social work and med. jours. Home: 508 Park Center Dr Nashville TN 37205

QUINN, KELLY, urban planner; b. Pitts., Oct. 10, 1962; d. Michael Thomas and Kristin (Hoch) Q. BA, UCLA, 1984; M of City Planning, MIT, 1986. Asst. project mgr. Mass. Capital Planning Ct. Unit, Boston, 1986-87, project mgr. mental health team, 1987-88; dep. dir. Ct. Facilities Unit, 1988—; co-chairperson bus. planning subcom. Adaptive Environments, Inc., Boston, 1989—. Mem. Planner's Network, UCLA Club of Boston (founding mem, treas.), Phi Beta Kappa.

QUINN, MARY HOPE, financial analyst; b. N.Y.C., Feb. 14, 1941; d. Frank Edward and Catherine Agnes (Berrill) Q. A.B., Mt. St. Agnes Coll., 1964; Ed.M., U. Ga., 1973; M.B.A., Loyola Coll., Balt., 1976. Chartered fin. analyst. Instr. Mt. de Sales High Sch., Macon, Ga., 1964-69; adminstr. St. Vincent's Acad., Savannah, Ga., 1970-72, Mercy High Sch., Balt., 1973-75; v.p. Mercantile Trust Co., Balt., 1976-83; dir. fin. Sisters of Mercy, Silver Spring, Md., 1984—; Trustee Loyola Coll., Balt., 1982—, Mt. Aloysius Jr. Coll., Cresson, Pa., 1980—; mem. pastoral council Archdiocese of Balt., 1977-80; mem. sch. bd. St. Vincent's Acad., Savannah, Ga., 1974-80; bd. dirs. Mount St. Agnes Ctr., Balt., 1977-82; mem. investment com. Sisters of Mercy Nat. Office, Silver Spring, 1980—. R. J. Reynolds fellow, 1970. Mem. Fin. Analysts Fedn., Fin. Mgmt. Assn., Assn. Governing Bds. of Colls. and Univs., Washington Soc. Investment Analysts, Washington Assn. Money Mgrs., Phi Kappa Phi, Kappa Delta Pi, Alpha Sigma Nu. Democrat. Roman Catholic. Home: 1111 University Blvd W Silver Spring MD 20902 Office: Sisters of Mercy of the Union 1320 Fenwick Ln Silver Spring MD 20910

QUINN, RITA MARIE, lawyer; b. Boston, Aug. 31, 1929; d. Joseph Patrick and Helen Veronica (Griffin) Sullivan; m. Robert Clarke Quinn, Apr. 11, 1953 (dec. 1969); children: Deborah, Susan, Michael, Maureen, Robert, Stephen. BA, U. Mass., 1974; JD, Suffolk U., 1985; Cert. in Mgmt., Simmons Coll., 1987. Owner, mgr. Atlantic Coast Vending CO., Sommerville, Mass., 1969-77; manpower specialist U.S. Dept. Labor, Boston, 1977-82; chief contract ops. Def. Logistics Agy., Burlington, Mass., 1982—. Mem. Arlington (Mass.) Town Meeting, 1987—. Mem. Mass. Bar Assn., Nat. Contracts Mgmt. Assn. Home: 205 Jason St Arlington MA 02174 Office: Def Logistics Agy DCASR 495 Summer St Boston MA 02210

QUINN, SALLY, journalist; b. Savannah, Ga., July 1, 1941; d. William Wilson and Bette (Williams) Q.; m. Benjamin Crowninshield Bradlee, Oct. 20, 1978; 1 child, Josiah Quinn Crowninshield Bradlee. Grad., Smith Coll. Reporter, Washington Post, 1969-73, 74—; co-anchorperson CBS Morning News, N.Y.C., 1973-74. Author: We're Going to Make You a Star, 1975, (novel) Regrets Only, 1986. Address: 3014 N St NW Washington DC 20007

QUINN, SUSAN GIBSON, optometrist; b. Warren, Ohio, Feb. 13, 1958; d. Harry Wayne and Sarah (Tufaro) Gibson; m. Thomas Gerard Quinn, May 8, 1982; children: Brian David, Kathryn Claire. OD, Ohio State U., 1982. Clin. optometrist Livingston Ave. Vision Ctr., Columbus, Ohio, 1982-84, Health One HMO, Columbus, 1984-86; pvt. practice Athens, Ohio, 1983—; low vision cons. Bur. Svcs. for Visually Impaired, Athens, 1984—, Southeastern Ohio Regional Resource Ctr., Athens, 1985—; vision cons. Hickory Creek Nursing Home, The Plains, Ohio, 1983-86. Chmn. Athens Friends and Newcomers Gourmet Club, 1987; adv. bd. mem. Athens County Sheltered Workshop for the Mentally Retarded and Developmentally Delayed, 1987—; co-chmn. med. div. United Way, Athens, 1989. Mem. Am. Optometric Assn. (charter, low vision sect.), Ohio Optometric Assn. (awards com., long-range planning com. 1989—, treas. zone 6 1989—), Civitan (pres. Athens chpt. 1989-90, Rookie of Yr. 1988, Outstanding Svc. award 1989). Republican. Roman Catholic. Office: 530C W Union St Athens OH 45701

QUINN, TERESA MOSS, lawyer; b. Logan, Utah, Apr. 27, 1952; d. Harold J. and Shirley (Farrer) Moss; m. John B. Quinn, Aug. 28, 1974. BA magna cum laude, Pomona Coll., Claremont, Calif., 1973; JD, Boston U., 1978. Bar: Calif. 1979. Research asst. Boston Univ., 1975; law clk. Gaston Snow & Ely Bartlett, Boston, 1977; assoc. Milbank, Tweed, Hadley & McCloy, N.Y., 1979; ptnr. Lillick & McHose, Los Angeles, 1983. Exec. Com. Bus. Law Section of Calif. State Bar, chairperson 1987-88, adv. 1987--; chairperson Fin. Instn. Com., 1984-85; adv. Inst. Corp. Council,. Mem. ABA, Calif. Bar Assn., L.A. County Bar Assn., Barristers Law Assn., Women Lawyer's Assn. L.A. Democrat. Home: 344 S Hill Ave Pasadena CA 91106 Office: Lillick & McHose 725 S Figueroa St Los Angeles CA 90017

QUINNETTE, PATRICIA ANN, purchasing agent; b. Ind., Dec. 9, 1939; d. Forrest H. and Fannie M. (McQuiston) Walker; m. Robert L. Quinnette, Dec. 28, 1956; children: Richard Lee, Debra Jo, Timothy Michael, Steven Robert. Grad., Porter Bus. Coll., Indpls., 1957; student, Ind. U., Indpls. Clinic clk. Wishard Meml. Hosp., Indpls.; sec., receptionist Litho Press, Inc., Indpls.; receptionist Gen. Supply and Tool, Indpls.; purchasing mgr. div. health and hosp. corp. Marion County Health Dept., Indpls.; buyer Winona Meml. Hosp., Indpls. Mem. NAFE, Nat. Purchasing Inst., Contract Mgrs. Assn., Purchasing Mgrs. Assn., Cen. Ind. Artists Assn. Roman Catholic. Home: RR 2 Box 225A1 Pittsboro IN 46167

QUINN-SKOROS, JUDITH, city manager, personnel director, administrator; b. Detroit, May 2, 1949; d. Joseph Francis and Helen Marie (Yates) Quinn; m. Steven S. Skoros, Dec. 30, 1977. BA, U. Detroit, 1971, MA, 1972. Adminstrv. asst. City of Oak Park, Mich., 1974-80, dir. personnel, 1980-82, asst. city mgr., personnel and labor rels., 1982—. Mem. Am. Assn. Pub. Adminstrs. (bd. dirs.), Assn. Internat. City Mgmt. Assocs., Internat. Personnel Mgmt. Assn., Pub. Risk Mgmt. Assn., Mich. Pub. Employees Labor Rels. Assn., Antique Auto Club, LWV, Detroit Symphony, Friends of Greenfield Village. Roman Catholic. Home: 19060 Beverly Rd Birmingham MI 48009 Office: City of Oak Park 13600 Oak Park Blvd Oak Park IL 48237

QUINTANA, MARIA DEL ROSARIO, toxicologist, health facility administrator; b. Havana, Cuba, Mar. 23, 1958; came to U.S., 1970; d. Manuel and Juana Maria (Alfonso Q.; m. Efren Leal, Dec. 23, 1978 (div. Oct. 1985); 1 child, Aymee Marie. AA, Miami-Dade Community Coll.-North, 1978; BS in Med. Tech., Fla. Internat. U., 1980. Med. technician Jackson Meml. Hosp., Miami, 1979-80; med. technologist Cedars Med. Ctr., Miami, 1980-85; toxicologist Cen. Med. Lab., Inc., Miami, 1985-87; chemistry/toxicology supr. Nat. Health Labs., Miami, 1987-89; mgr. ops. and pathology svcs. Jackson Meml. Hosp., Miami, 1989—; med. tech. cons., provider for lab. continuing edn., Miani. Mem. Am. Soc. Clin. Pathologists (cert. med. technologist). Roman Catholic.

QUIRK, BARBARA LONG, medical center executive, nurse; b. Kansas City, Mo., July 31, 1935; d. Anthony James and Nelle G. (Martin) Long; .m Patrick G. Quirk (div.); 1 child, Erin Christine. Diploma in nursing, St. Luke's Hosp., 1956; BSN, U. Kans., 1965, M in Nursing, 1972; PhD in Edn., U. Mo., 1984. RN, Kans., Mo. Staff nurse St. Luke's Hosp., Kansas City, 1958-65; sch. nurse Kansas City Bd. Edn., 1965-70; clin. nurse specialist Kans. U. Med. Ctr., 1972-75; adminstrv. asst. Truman Med. Ctr. West, 1975-78; dir. nursing Truman Med. Ctr. East, 1978-85, assoc. adminstr., 1985—; asst. prof. U. Mo. Sch. Medicine, Kansas City, 1976—, asst. prof. grad. studies, 1977—; mem. adj. faculty Avila Coll., Kansas City, 1986—; assoc. sci. med. and dental staff Truman Med. Ctr., Kansas City, 1980—. Contbg. author: Sexual Counseling & The Health Professional, 1978. Chmn. adv. bd. vocat. tech. program for LPN's Kansas City Bd. Edn., 1979—; mem., vice chmn. Joint Commn, Accreditation for Health Care Orgns., 1989—, PTAC com. for LTC, 1989—. Mem. Am. Hosp. Assn. (rep.), Mo. Orgn. Nurse Execs. (bd. dirs. 1981-83, 87-89, pres.-elect 1989-90, pres. 1990—), Greater Kansas City Area Nursing Adminstrs. (pres. 1982-83, sec.-treas. 1985-86), Acad. Health Professions (bd. dirs. 1980-88), Sigma Theta Tau. Roman Catholic. Office: Truman Med Ctr East 7900 Lees Summit Rd Kansas City MO 64139

QUIRK, DONNA HAWKINS, financial analyst; b. Chgo., Sept. 29, 1955; d. Martin Francis and Monica Mae (Hesslau) Hawkins; m. John James Quirk, Dec. 5, 1981; children: Martin Patrick, Mary Kathleen, Colleen Monica. BS in Commerce, DePaul U., 1977, M.B.A., 1982. With Jewel Food Stores, Melrose Park, Ill., 1977—, acctg. mgr., 1980-85, fin. analyst, 1985—. Mem. Assn. M.B.A. Execs., Nat. Assn. Female Execs., Twice as Nice Mothers of Multiples, Beta Gamma Sigma, Delta Mu Delta. Roman Catholic. Home: 5046 N Mason Ave Chicago IL 60630 Office: Jewel Food Stores 1955 W North Ave Melrose Park IL 60160

QUIRK, GAIL ELIZABETH MANZ, community services administrator; b. Phila., Dec. 25, 1929; d. Erwin Christian and Ruth Agnes (Pope) Manz; m. Virgil Porter Quirk, Feb. 14, 1953; children: Susan Crawford, Alexander Johnson, Elizabeth Pope Quirk Wood, Caroline Manz Quirk Flacinski, Sarah Porter, Nancy Stiles Quirk Cameron. BS in Art Edn., Kutztown U., 1951. Elem. art supr. Wilson Sch. Dist., Easton, Pa., 1951-53; agy. dir., chief exec. officer Oak Manor, Inc., St. Marys, Pa., 1975—; bd. dirs. Tri-County Home Health Agy., St. Marys, 1972-81. Cadette-sr. leader Keystone Tall Tree council Girl Scouts U.S., 1969-74, calendar chmn., 1972-74; mem. charity ball com. Andrew Kaul Meml. Hosp. Aux., St. Marys, 1964-66. Recipient Disting. Svc. cert. Am. Legion, 1987. Mem. Am. Assn. for Mental Retardation, Pa. Assn. for Mental Health-Mental Retardation Providers, AAUW, Cath. Daus. Am., Assn. Retarded Citizens Pa., Pa. Assn. Resources for People with Mental Retardation, Assn. Retarded Citizens Elk County, Elk County Cursillo (St. Marys). Republican. Roman Catholic. Avocations: genealogy, interior decorating, painting. Home: 828 Johnsonburg Rd Saint Marys PA 15857 Office: Oak Manor Inc 129 N Michael St Saint Marys PA 15857

QUIROGA, ALICIA ESPINOSA, physiatrist; b. Manila; d. Eugenio Rillo and Felisa Padiernos (Espinosa) Q. BS, U. Philippines, 1969, MD, 1973. Rotating intern Philippine Gen. Hosp., Manila, 1973-74, resident dept. pediatrics, 1975-77; resident dept. phys. medicine and rehab. U. Md., Balt., 1977-80; fellow Children's Hosp. Nat. Med. Ctr., Washington, 1980-81, George Washington U. Hosp., Washington, 1980-81; attending physiatrist, asst. prof. U. Md. Sch. Medicine, Balt., 1981-86; attending physiatrist Sinai Hosp. of Balt., 1986-87; chief rehab. medicine svc. VA Med. Ctr., Augusta, Ga., 1987—. Fellow Am. Acad. Phys. Medicine and Rehab.; mem. Assn. Acad. Physiatrists. Home: 3408 Kerry Pl Augusta GA 30909-2716 Office: VA Med Ctr 2460 Wrightsboro Rd Augusta GA 30910

QUIST, JEANETTE FITZGERALD, television production educator, choreographer; b. Provo, Utah, July 4, 1948; d. Sherman Kirkham and Bula Janet (Anderson) Fitzgerald; m. G. Steven Quist; children: Ryan, Amy, Michelle, Jeremy. Student, U. Redlands, Calif., 1970; BA, Brigham Young U., 1971; postgrad., Calif. State U., Riverside, 1972, Calif. State U., San Bernardino, 1973. Host, co-producer children's show PBS Sta. KBYU-TV, Provo, 1968-69; buyer ready to wear J.C. Penney & Co., Redlands, 1969-71; tchr. spl. reading program Fontana (Calif.) Elem. Sch. Dist., 1971-73; owner, choreographer Jeanette Quist Creative Dance, Tri Cities, Wash., 1975-79; owner, tchr. Dance Studio, Gridley, Calif., 1979-81; producer, instr. Butte Coll., Oroville, Calif., 1986—; asst. producer Kate Knight Prodn. Co., Chico, Calif., 1987; with video prodn. Gridley Sch. Dist., 1987-88; choreographer Kaleidoscope Mus., Gridley, 1988, "South Pacific", Oroville, 1989—. Producer, editor promotional video Butte Police Acad., 1986, commls. Butte Coll., 1987—, producer instructional video, 1989-90; producer, dir. telecourse Interior Designer, 1988—; producer, hostess TV talk show Crossroads, 1988—; choreographer Fantasticks, 1990, Amahl and the Night Visitors, 1990;. State judge Miss Am. Contest, Provo, 1968; 1st v.p. Friends of the Library, Gridley, 1988—; chairperson Regional Fine Arts Festival, Tri Cities, 1978; mem. PTA, Oroville, 1984-85. Mask Club scholar Brigham Young U., 1967. Mem. Butte County Arts Coun. (spl. com. 1986), Kaleidoscope Arts Coun., AAUW (mem. v.p. 1989—). Republican., Ch. of Jesus Christ Latter-day Saints.

QUITEVIS, MINDA ALTEA, sales executive; b. Bacolod, Philippines, Apr. 25, 1937; came to U.S., 1967; d. Lazaro Onang and Estelita (Villar) Altea; m. Hilario P. Quitevis, Aug. 14, 1968; 1 child, Richard Joseph. BS in Pharmacy, Uno Recoletos, Bacolod City, Philippines, 1960; BS in Edn., Notre Dame, Jolo, Philippines, 1966. Pharmacist Farmacia San Benito, Zamboanga, Philippines, 1960-61, New Life Drug Store, Zamboanga, 1961-62, Universal Pharmacy, Zamboanga, 1962-64, San Antonio Drugstore, Jolo, Philippines, 1964-67; sci. tchr. Notre Dame, Jolo, 1964-67; pharmacy clk. Get Pharmacy, San Francisco, 1967-68; rep. Avon, San Francisco, 1968-81; med. claims examiner Blue Shield Calif., San Francisco, 1971-81; sales dir., Cadillac dir. Mary Kay Cosmetics, San Francisco, 1983—; jeweler Minda's Jewelry, San Francisco, 1981—. Editor, pub. Minda's Goldmines, 1983-89. Mem. Fayco. Roman Catholic. Home: 397 Moscow St San Francisco CA 94112 Office: Mindas Goldmines 163 El Camino Real South San Francisco CA 94080

RAAB, SUSAN SALZMAN, public relations executive; b. Springfield, Mass., Sept. 11, 1958; d. Bernard Benson and Glenda (Ring) Salzman; m. David Martin Raab, June 24, 1984; children: Brian, Jeffrey, Joshua. BA in English, U. Conn., 1980. Promotion asst. Bantam Books, N.Y.C., 1980-81; publicist for juvenile books Dell Pub., N.Y.C., 1981-83; publicity mgr. Scholastic Inc., N.Y.C., 1983-85; account exec. Shimer Von Cantz, Phila., 1985-86; pres., founder Raab Assocs., Rose Valley, Pa., 1986—. Author: An Author's Guide to Children's Book Promotion, 1988; contbr. articles to various publs. Mem. Assn. Booksellers for Children (assoc.), Pubs. Publicity Assn., NAFE. Home and Office: 19 Price's Ln Rose Valley PA 19065

RABEN, GAIL, consulting company executive; b. Kansas City, Mo., Oct. 14, 1945; d. David and Frances (Brand) Levitch; m. Ronald J. Raben, Aug. 11, 1968; children: Lisa, Cori. BS, U. Ariz., 1967, MEd, 1968; MEd, Wash. U., St. Louis, MSW, 1979. Prin. Gail Raben Cons. Svcs., Austin, Tex. Bd. dirs. The Women's Fund, 1990. Mem. NAFE. Home and Office: 4410 Silent Trail Austin TX 78746

RABINOWITZ, REBECCA SUSAN, health executive; b. N.Y.C., Jan. 19, 1953; d. Bernard and Ann Hoch (Kubie) R.; m. Frank M. Calabrese, June 7, 1981. AB in Sociology, Washington U., St. Louis, 1975, MSW (Comprehensive Care Corp. fellow), George Warren Brown Sch. Social Work, 1977; cert. Rutgers U., 1979. Chief psychiat. social worker alcohol treatment program Inst. Psychiatry, Northwestern Meml. Hosp., Chgo., 1977-78; exec. adminstr., spl. health cons. Atlantic Chem. Corp., Nutley, N.J., 1978-79; asst. to dir. Madeleine Borg Counseling Svcs., N.Y.C., 1980-81; chief therapist/asst. program coord. CAREUNIT, Buena Park, Calif., 1981-82; pvt. practice psychotherapy, cons. alcohol, Montclair, N.J., 1979—; exec. dir. N.J. Alcoholism Assn., 1982—; dir. pub. rels. Jersey City Med. Ctr., 1983-86; pres. Christ Hosp. Found., Jersey City, 1986-87; exec. v.p. Beth Health Care Found., Newark, N.J., 1987-90; exec. v.p. Environ. Ptnrs., Inc., Naples, Fla., 1990—; condr. alcoholism in-svc. workshops. Active in numerous polit. campaigns, local, and nat. Mem. AAUW, Nat. Soc. Fund Raising Execs. (bd. dirs. N.J. chpt.), Nat. Assn. Hosp. Devel., Greater Naples C. of C., Alumni-Parents Assn. Washngton U. (local coord.), LWV (Collier County).

RABLEN, MADELINE JEAN, interior designer; b. Bklyn., Oct. 31, 1914; d. George Henry and Eva May (Goode) Keller; m. William Henry Rablen, June 1, 1935; children: Nancy, Susan. Student, Adelphi U., Garden City, N.Y. Stylist Nassau Wayside Shop Inc., Rockville Centre, Amityville, N.Y., 1939-52, Rablen Shelton Internat. Inc., Ft. Lauderdale, 1953-65; furniture designer Mills-Burnett Inc., Hialeah, Fla., 1960-65, Guild Furniture Inc., Miami, Fla.; v.p. Rablen-West Interiors Inc., Vero Beach, Fla., 1965-73; v.p., treas. The Rablens of Ormond, Fla., 1973—. Mem. Nassau Women's Club (Pres., Founder 1939-41), Am. Soc. Interior Designers, Kappa Kappa Gamma Adelphi U., Halifax River Yacht Club Daytona Beach Fla. Republican. Presbyterian. Home and Office: 70 Riverside Dr Ormond Beach FL 32074

RABURN, JOSEPHINE, librarian, educator; b. Norman, Okla., Dec. 6, 1929; d. Albert E. and Josephine D. (Hudson) Riling; m. James Winston Raburn, Sept. 29, 1950; children: Catherine Anne Heller, Dora Lynn Greenleaf. BS, U. Okla., 1950, MLS, 1964, PhD, 1981. Library asst. Spl. Services, Ft. Sill, Okla., 1962-63, reference, adminstrv. librarian, 1964-66; reference and circulation librarian Morris Sweatt Tech. Library, 1966-67; spl. instr. U. Okla. Sch. Library Sci., 1966-67; reference librarian Cameron Agrl. and Mech. Jr. Coll., 1967-68; instr. Cameron U., Lawton, Okla., 1968-72, asst. prof., 1972-81, assoc. prof., 1981-85, prof., 1985—, dept. chmn., 1982-83, head lang. arts div., 1983-87; dean sch. Liberal Arts, 1987—; trustee Lawton Pub. Library, 1973-86; pres. bd., 1973-76, also systems analyst; adv. com. library tech. asst. program Rose State Coll., Oklahoma City, 1986-88; cons., lectr. in field. Contbr. articles to profl. jours., chpts. to books. Mem. mammography bd. Meml. Hosp., 1979-81, sec., 1979-80. Recipient Disting. Faculty award Cameron U., 1976; Helen Olander scholar, 1979. Mem. ALA, Okla. Library Assn. (sec. Sequoyah children's book award com. 1985-86, chmn., 1987-88), Okla. Orgn. Ednl. Tech., Assn. Ednl. Communications and Tech., Adolescent Lit. Assn., AAUW, Friends of Library, Beta Phi Mu (pres. Lambda chpt. 1973), Phi Kappa Phi, Delta Kappa Gamma (pres. Xi chpt. 1986-88), Alpha Delta Kappa. Democrat. Methodist. Home: 511 NW 40th St Lawton OK 73505 Office: Cameron U Lawton OK 73505

RABY, NANCY E., marketing company executive; b. Brockton, Mass.; d. Stanley B. and Eileen E. (Blackburn) R. BA, Cardinal Cushing Coll., Brookline, Mass., 1962; MBA, Anna Maria Coll., Paxton, Mass., 1983. Lic. real estate broker, Mass.; notary pub.; cert. in hotel-motel mgmt. Dir. Cen. Networking Assocs., Milton, Mass.; dir. grad. bus. programs Anna Maria Coll.; owner, pres. Mktg. Cen., Milton. Mem. NAFE (regional networking dir.), Exec. MBA Coun., South Shore C. of C. (small bus. com.), Plymouth C. of C., Worcester C. of C. (mem. edn. com.), Exec. Suite Network.

RACENSTEIN, JODY MEG, psychosocial rehabilitation counselor; b. Chgo., Aug. 28, 1963; d. Norton Nathan and Rhoda Lenore (Siegel) Gold; m. Michael Jay Racenstein, May 28, 1988. BS, U. Ill., 1985; MA, Loyola U., Chgo., 1988. Crisis hotline vol. Prairie Ctr. for Substance Abuse, Champaign, Ill., 1983-84; vol. asst. instr. Loyola Day Sch., Chgo., 1984; site dir., edn. asst., recreation instr. North Suburban Spl. Recreation Assn., Highland Park, Ill., 1985-87; psychology intern Evanston (Ill.) Hosp. Outpatient Psychiatry, 1986-87; mental health worker Northwestern Meml. Hosp. Inst. of Psychiatry, Chgo., 1987-88; psychosocial rehab. counselor Transitional Living Ctrs. for L.A. (Calif.) County Inc., 1988—; part-time rsch. assoc. U. Calif. L.A. (Calif.) Psychology Dept., 1990—. Mem. Am. Psychol. Assn., Am. Assn. for Counseling & Devel., Coun. for the Exceptional Child, Alpha Lamba Delta, Phi Eta Sigma, Golden Key Nat. Honors Soc. Jewish. Home: 11050 Strathmore Dr #326 Los Angeles CA 90024

RACICOT, CATHY LEE, moving company executive; b. Kingston, N.Y., Nov. 22, 1950; D. Robert Ennist Racicot and Eva Catherine (Lukasz) Racicot Helfmann. AS, Ulster County Community Coll., Stone Ridge, N.Y., 1979; BA in Communications, U. Miami, 1981. Cert. moving cons. Telemktg. specialist Ryder Truck Rental, Inc., Miami, Fla., 1987; mktg. svcs. rep. Ryder Move Mgmt., Inc., Miami, Fla., 1987-88; nat. account rep. Ryder Move Mgmt., Inc., Birmingham, Mich., 1988—. Vol. Boys Clubs Miami, 1985-86, March of Dimes Walk-A-Thon, 1987-88, Cropwalk-Stop World Hunger, Farmington, Mich., 1989. Bateman scholar, 1980-81. Mem. Nat. Assn. Female Execs., Am. Bus. Women Assn., Profl. Women in Sales and Mktg. (v.p. programs 1988). Office: Ryder Move Mgmt Inc 31100 Telegraph Suite 240 Birmingham MI 48010

RACINE, JEAN DORINE, banker; b. Portland, Oreg., May 23, 1944; m. Bill F. Racine; children: Carmell R., Tawna L. Student, Inst. Fin. Edn., Portland, 1976-83, Portland State U., 1981-82, N.W. Intermediate Banking Sch., Portland, 1987, IFE Asset/Liability Sch., 1989. Bookkeeper escrow closing Bump & Meyer Real Estate, Hillsboro, Oreg., 1965-66; sec. Forest Grove br. Wash. Fed. Savs. Bank, Hillsboro, 1966-70, with loan dept., loan closing, loan svc., 1971-75, mgr. Aloha br., 1975-76, v.p. personnel, 1976-83, v.p. adminstrn., 1983-89, sr. v.p., 1989—; bd. dirs. Washington Fed. Ins. Corp., Hillsboro, Washington Fed. Svc. Corp., Hillsboro, Ward Cook, Inc., Portland; bd. dirs. Oreg. Fin. Inst. Edn. Assn. Bd. dirs. Hillsboro Downtown Bus. Assn.; former sch. bd. chmn. Groner Elem., Hillsboro. Mem. Pacific N.W. Personnel Mgmt. Assn., Western Pension Conf., Oreg. League Fin. Insts. (personnel com.). Office: Wash Fed Savs Bank 314 E Main St Hillsboro OR 97123

RACKERS, CLETA LOUISE, analytical chemist; b. St. Joseph, Mo., Nov. 30, 1950; d. Cletus Robert and Melva C. (Wilkenson) R.; m. Kenneth W. Shepherd, July 29, 1972 (div. 1977). BS, U. Tex., Arlington, 1976. Lab. technician Okla. State U., Stillwater, 1969-70, Analytical Biochemistry Labs., Columbia, Mo., 1970-72; chemist Southwestern Med. Labs., Dallas, 1974-76, Mobil R & D Corp., Dallas, 1976-78, 79—; tchr., Colo. State U., Ft. Collins, 1978-79. Patentee in field. Del., Tex. Rep. Conv., Dallas, 1979-80; literacy vol., Dallas Pub. Libr., 1987—. Mem. Mensa. Roman Catholic. Home: 13551 Shahan St Farmers Branch TX 75234 Office: Mobil R & D Corp 13777 Midway St Dallas TX 75244-4312

RADCLIFFE, BEVERLY LOUISE, council director, consultant; b. Reading, Pa., Apr. 26, 1942; d. Frank Edmund and Katherine Emma Mae (Kohler) R.; m. Helmut Franz Pfanner, Sept. 16, 1966 (div. Aug. 1988); children: Heidi Louise, Eric Franz, Marta Katrin. BA, Gettysburg (Pa.) Coll., 1964; MEd, Kutztown (Pa.) U., 1968; PhD, Purdue U., 1985. Cert. secondary edn. tchr., Nebr. Tchr. German Reading Sr. High Sch., 1964-66; tchr. English second lang. HBLA für wirtschaftliche Frauenberufe, Linz, Austria, 1976-78; teaching asst. Purdue U., W. Lafayette, Ind., 1979-82; lectr. U. N.H., Durham, 1983-86; cons. Nebr. Dept. Edn., Lincoln, 1986-88; dir. mediated fng. lang. program Instructional Materials Coun., Lincoln, 1988—, exec. dir., 1989—; cons. Nebr. Japanese-by-Satellite Project, Lincoln, 1988—; student tchr. supr. U. Nebr., Lincoln, 1988-89. Contbr. articles to profl. jours. Fulbright scholar, Austria, 1976-78; Deutscher Akademischer Austauschdienst grantee, 1985. Mem. Computer Assisted Lang. Learning and Instrn. Consortium, Nebr. Fgn. Lang. Assn. Home: 3135 Puritan Ave Lincoln NE 68502 Office: Instructional Materials Coun 920 O St Lincoln NE 68508

RADDI-WALSH, ANTOINETTE MARIE, advertising agency executive; b. Chgo., Dec. 27, 1954; d. Anthony Nicolas and Delores Beatrice (Bronieck) Anatra; m. Mario Raddi, June 17, 1972 (div. 1983); children: Nicole Marie, Christina Maria; m. George Albert Walsh, Nov. 8, 1989. Grad. high sch. Owner Raddi Ent. d.b.a. Fonzie's, Chgo., 1975-81; promotion coordinator Pepsi-Cola Gen. Bottlers, Chgo., 1982-83; media buyer Genadco Advt. Agy., Chgo., 1983-88; reg. account exec. Genadco Advt. Agy., 1988-89; gen. mgr. Genadco Advt. Agy., Rolling Meadows, Ill., 1990—. Chief editor People in Gen. mag., 1988—. Recipient Effie award, Pepsi Cola U.S.A., 1988. Roman Catholic. Home: 304 S Redfield Ct Park Ridge IL 60068 Office: Genadco Advertising Agency 3501 Algonquin Rd Rolling Meadows IL 60008

RADER, (M.) ELIZABETH, accountant; b. Knoxville, Tenn., May 7, 1951; d. Charles Edward and Eleanor (Wall) R.; m. Donald Floyd McKee. BA summa cum laude, Rice U., 1973; MBA, Tulane U., 1975. CPA, Tex., N.Y. From staff auditor to audit mgr. Arthur Andersen & Co., Houston, 1975-81; securities profl., acctg. fellow U.S. SEC, Washington, 1981-83; audit mgr. nat. office Touche Ross & Co., N.Y.C., 1983-84, audit ptnr. Fin. Services Ctr., 1984—; exchange exec. Pres.'s Commn. on Exec. Exchange, 1983-84. Thomas J. Watson fellow, 1973-74; recipient John Burnis Allred award Tex. Soc. CPA's, 1975. Mem. AICPA, Am. Acctg. Assn. (SEC liaison com. 1985-86), Fin. Women's Assn. of N.Y., Swedish-Am. C. of C., Phi Beta Kappa, Beta Gamma Sigma. Methodist. Club: Roton Point (Rowayton, Conn.). Office: Deloitte & Touche One World Trade Ctr 93d Floor New York NY 10048

RADER, HANNELORE, library director, consultant; b. Berlin, Germany, Dec. 19, 1937; d. Henry H. and Talia E. (Tramontin) Busch; widowed; 1 child, Ingrid M. BA in Russian, U. Mich., 1960, MA in Libr. Sci., 1968, MA in German Lit., 1971; Degree in Ednl. Leadership, Eastern Mich. U., 1978. Children's librarian Washington D.C. Pub. Libr., 1960-62; asst. humanities librarian Eastern Mich. U., Ypsilanti, 1968-70, orientation librarian, 1970-76, coord. edn., psychology div., 1976-80; libr. dir. learning ctr. U. Wis.-Parkside, Kenosha, 1980-87; dir. univ. libr. Cleve. State U., 1987—; evaluator, libr. instr. Ball State U., Muncie, Ind., 1983; evaluator for self study Calif. State U.-L.A. Libr., 1989, CCNY Libr., 1989. Contbr. articles to numerous jours. Recipient Walter H. Kaiser award Mich. Libr. Assn., 1977, Disting. Alumnus award U. Mich. Libr. Sch., 1984; fellow Coun. Libr. Resources, 1975-76; USIA and West German Libr. grantee, 1987. Mem. Assn. Coll. and Rsch. Librs. (pres., bd. dirs. 1985-88), ALA (coun. mem. 1980-84, 88—), Ohio Libr. Assn., Am. Assn. Higher Edn., Spl. Libr. Assn., Women's City Club, Rotary. Office: Cleve State U Libr 1860 E 22d St Cleveland OH 44115

RADER, MELODEE ANN, oil company executive; b. Mesa, Ariz., Nov. 22, 1961; d. Archie Leroy and Gloria Jean (Ramos) R. Student, No. Ariz. U., 1979-81; BS, San Jose State U., 1984; MBA, San Diego State U., 1987. Facilities analyst Mobil Oil Corp., Fairfax, Va., 1987; terminal supr. Mobil Oil Corp., East Providence, R.I., 1988-89; asst. mgr. plant ops. area 47 Mobil Oil Corp., Schaumburg, Ill., 1989; asst. mgr. plant ops. area 46 Mobil Oil Corp., Vienna, Va., 1989—. Fellow NAFE; mem. San Diego State Alumnae. Home: 3902 Golf Tee Ct #302 Fairfax VA 22033

RADFORD, LINDA ROBERTSON, psychologist; b. Winnipeg, Man., Can., Nov. 6, 1944; came to U.S., 1954; d. William and Edith Aileen (Wheatley) Robertson; m. F. Richard Radford, Mar. 5, 1965 (div. 1967); 1 child: Drew Richard. BA, Seattle Pacific U., 1970; MEd, U. Wash., 1972, PhD, 1980. Lic. psychologist. Dir. support svcs. Highline-West Seattle Mental Health Clinic, 1973-75; rsch. asst. in human affairs Battelle, Seattle, 1976-80, rsch. scientist, 1982-87; sr. cons. Martin Simmonds Assoc., Seattle, 1980-82; pres., owner R.R. Assocs., Seattle and Miami, 1982—; vis. sr. assoc. Joint Ctr. for Environ. and Urban Problems, North Miami, Fla., 1986-88; cons. Health Ministry Govt. of Thailand, Bangkok, 1989—. Contbr. articles to profl. jours. Community Mental Health Ctr fellow, Seattle, 1972-73. Mem. Am. Psychol. Assn., ASTD, N.Y. Acad. of Sci. Office: R R Assocs/Peer Group Influences Inc 9764 W Bay Harbor Dr Bay Harbor Island FL 33154

RADICE, ANNE-IMELDA, museum director; b. Buffalo, Feb. 29, 1948; d. Lawrence and Anne (Marino) R. A.B., Wheaton Coll., (Mass.), 1969; M.A., Villa SchiFanoia, Florence, Italy, 1971; Ph.D., U. N.C., 1976; M.B.A., Am. U., 1984. Asst. curator Nat. Gallery of Art, Washington, 1972-76; archtl. historian U.S. Capitol, Washington, 1976-80, curator Office of Architect, 1980-85; dir. Nat. Mus. Women in the Arts, 1985-89; chief div. of creative arts USIA, 1989—. Contbr. articles to profl. jours. Home: 2311 Connecticut Ave NW Washington DC 20024 Office: USIA 301 4th St NW Washington DC 20547*

RADICE, SHIRLEY ROSALIND, educator; b. Newark, June 2, 1935; d. Gerald Alexander and Pauline Deborah (Baitz) Deitz; m. Richard Charles Radice, Dec. 17, 1955; children: Carol, Richard Neil. BA, Kean Coll., Union, N.J., 1960, MA, 1963; EdD, Rutgers U., 1985. Tchr. Edison (N.J.) Bd. Edn., 1960-64, 70—, trainer, 1990—; mem. grant com. N.J. Dept. Higher Edn., 1988-90; lectr. Rutgers U., 1989—; ednl. cons. Contbr. articles to profl. jours. Grantee Ford Found., 1966, State of N.J., 1973. Mem. Nat. Tchrs. Assn. (del. 1980-87), N.J. Tchrs. Assn., Edison Tchrs. Assn. (co-chmn. legis. com. 1975-76), Kappa Delta Phi.

RADIN, LAURA LEVINE, state official; b. N.Y.C., Aug. 24, 1944; d. Samuel Archie and Ray (Tessler) L; m. Kalman David Radin, June 15, 1965 (div. 1972); m. Rodney Leinberger, June 25, 1988; B.S., CCNY, 1965; M.A., Columbia U., 1978. Employment interviewer N.Y. State Dept. Labor, N.Y.C., 1965-67, vocat. counselor, 1967-70, supervising interviewer, 1970-76, employement security mgr., 1976-80; environ. programs specialist Port Authority of N.Y. and N.J., N.Y.C., 1984, hazardous materials specialist, 1984, asst. mgr. Lincoln Tunnel, 1986, mgr. pub. services div. Tunnels Bridges and Terminals Dept., 1984—. Co-author: Creativity: A Human Resource, 1984. Mem. Women's Equity-Port Authority N.Y. and N.J., Women's Transp. Sem., City Coll. Alumni Assn. Bronx High Sch. Sci. Alumni Assn. Democrat. Jewish. Avocations: piano playing; tennis; skiing; travel. Office: Port Authority NY and NJ One World Trade Ctr Room 71W New York NY 10048

RADOJCSICS, ANNE PARSONS, librarian; b. Mansfield, Ohio, Mar. 23, 1929; d. Richard Walbridge Parsons and Iva Pearl (Ruth) Kemp; m. Joseph Michael Radojcsics, July 8, 1950; children: Kurt Joseph, Jo Anne Radojcsics Kent. Diploma, Bethel Woman's Coll., Hopkinsville, Ky., 1949; BS, Miss. State U., 1972, MEd, 1974. Cert. secondary tchr., Miss. Chemist Humphries Borg-Warner Co., Mansfield, 1950-53; asst. reference libr. Mansfield Pub. Libr., 1953-59; libr. media specialist Verona (Miss.) Sch., 1970—, supr. computer lab., 1985—; supr. Verona computer lab., 1985—; supr. libr. Guntown (Miss.) Sch., 1988-89, Shannon (Miss.) Sch., 1988—; chmn. assessment project Miss. Libr.-Miss. Dept. Edn., Jackson, 1986—; mem. Miss. Edn. TV Adv. Coun., 1985-89, 90—; region 1 coord. Miss. Conf. on Librs. and Info. Svcs., 1990. Author: Clay Tablets to Media Centers: Library Development from Ancient to Modern Times, 1975. Bd. dirs., v.p. SAFE, Inc., Tupelo, Miss., 1978—; mem. Lee County Adult Literacy Task Force, Tupelo, 1987—; schs. chmn. Target Tupelo, 1981-85. Mem. ALA, Miss. Profl. Educators Lee

County (pres. 1990—), Mississippians for Ednl. Broadcasting, Miss. Ednl. Computer Assn., Miss. Libr. Assn. (project chmn. com. on sch. librs. 1989, awards chmn. 1987-88), AAUW (pres. Tupelo chpt. 1977-81, Miss. div. 1984-86), Apple Computer User Group (co-organizer). Democrat. Episcopalian. Home: 3 Michael St Carr Vista Tupelo MS 38801-8608 Office: Verona Sch 272 College St Verona MS 38879

RADOVIC, CAROL ANN, choreographer, educator; b. Ypsilanti, Mich., Aug. 9, 1940; d. John Lewis and Mary Vivian (Altherr) Keeney; m. Jack Laurel Scharp, June 14, 1958; children: Kathryn Elaine, Mark Aaron; m. Srecko Radovic, Nov. 15, 1989. Student ballet, Randazzo Studio, Ypsilanti, 1950-60, Harkness, Joffrey, Briansky and Eglevsky Schs., N.Y.C., 1960-83; student U. Mich., 1977; Pereslavic, Danilova Mme. Darvash, N.Y.C., 1982; Russian Tchrs. tng. Jugen Schneider (ABT-NYC), Janina Cunova (Australian Ballet Co.), Bolshoi Ballet Sch., Moscow. Tchr. ballet Chapelle Sch., Ypsilanti, 1968; owner, dir. C.A.S. Ballet Theatre Sch., Ann Arbor, Mich., 1975—; dance dir., mem. steering com. Explorer Scouts, Boy Scouts Am., 1981; dir. Ann Arbor Ballet Theatre, Adrian Coll. Ballet Acad.; regional field judge Nat. Ballet Achievement Fund, 1983. Choreographer 17 prodns. including: Carnival of the Animals, 1982, Midsummer Night's Dream, 1982, Carmen, 1983, Beauty and the Beast, 1983, Nutcracker, 1983. Ruth Mott Fund grantee, 1983; invited guest USSR Ministry of Culture festival, 1989. Mem. Mich. Dance Assn., Washtenaw Council for Arts. Presbyterian. Office: Ann Arbor Ballet Theatre 548 Church St Ann Arbor MI 48104

RAE, BARBARA JOYCE, executive; b. Prince George, B.C., Can., May 17, 1930; d. Alfred and Lottie Kathleen (Davis) Holmwood; m. George Suart, Feb. 14, 1984; children: Jamie, Glenn, John. MBA, Simon Fraser U., Burnaby, B.C., 1975. Pres., chief exec. officer Adia Can., Ltd., Vancouver, B.C., 1953—; bd. dirs. B.C. Telephone Co., Seaboard Life Ins. Co., Microtel Ltd., Microtel Pacific Rsch., Sta. KCTS 9 Seattle Pub. TV, Royal Trust Adv. Com. Chancellor Simon Fraser U., 1987—; mem. Jud. Appointments Com., B.C., 1988—, Nat. Adv. Coun. Imagine Campaign, 1988—, Premier's Econ. Adv. Coun., B.C., 1987—; gen. chmn. United Way Lower Mainland, 1987, Salvation Army Red Shield Vancouver campaign, 1986; bd. dirs. Vancouver Bd. Trade, 1972-76. Recipient Simon Fraser U. Outstanding Alumnae award, 1985, Vancouver YWCA Bus. Woman of Yr. award, 1986, West Vancouver Achievers award, 1987, B.C. Entrepreneur of Yr. award, 1987. Home: 2206 Folkestone Way #3, West Vancouver, BC Canada V7S 2X7 Office: Simon Fraser U, Office of Chancellor, Burnaby, BC Canada V5A 1S6

RAEBURN, VICKI PEARTHREE, publishing executive; b. Duluth, Minn., Jan. 5, 1947; d. M.J. and Jean (Rutter) P.; m. Charles Fredrick Raeburn, June 23, 1968; children: Robert Warren, Katherine Elizabeth. BA, New Coll., 1968; PhD, Yale U., 1972. Asst. prof. Vassar Coll., Poughkeepsie, N.Y., 1972-78; exec. editor Columbia Univ. Press, N.Y.C., 1978-81; planning analyst McGraw Hill, N.Y.C., 1982-83; with Standard & Poor's/McGraw-Hill, N.Y.C., 1983—, v.p. bus. devel. div., 1987-89, v.p., gen. mgr., 1989—; dir. E. Coast sales div. DRI/McGraw-Hill, N.Y.C., 1986-87. Office: Standard & Poor's 25 Broadway New York NY 10009

RAEDER, MYRNA SHARON, lawyer, educator; b. N.Y.C., Feb. 4, 1947; d. Samuel and Estelle (Auslander) R.; m. Terry Oliver Kelly, July 13, 1975; children: Thomas Oliver, Michael Lawrence. BA, Hunter Coll., 1968; JD, NYU, 1971; LLM, Georgetown U., 1975. Bar: N.Y. 1972, D.C. 1972, Calif. 1972. Spl. asst. U.S. atty. U.S. Atty.'s Office, Washington, 1972-73; asst. prof. U. San Francisco Sch. Law, 1973-75; assoc. O'Melveny & Myers, L.A., 1975-79; assoc. prof. Southwestern U. Sch. Law, L.A., 1979-82, prof., 1983—. Coord., bd. dirs. Mothers' Support Group Womens Lawyers Assn. of L.A., 1987—. Prettyman fellow Georgetown Law Ctr., Washington, 1971-73. Author: Federal Pretrial Practice, 1987, ALI, 1989. Mem. ABA (chmn. com. on fed. rules and criminal procedure criminal justice sect. 1987, trial evidence com. litigation sect. 1980—), Assn. Am. Law Schs. (com. on sects. 1984-87 , chairperson women in legal edn. sect. 1982), Order of Coif, Phi Beta Kappa. Office: Southwestern U Sch Law 675 S Westmoreland Los Angeles CA 90005

RAEZER, SALLIE STEWART, software company executive; b. N.Y.C., May 11, 1951; d. John Larry and Margaret Ann (Thompson) Stewart; m. John Raezer, Aug. 18, 1984; children: John Kenneth, Julie Rebecca. BA, Bucknell U., 1973. Programmer to systems analyst Sperry Univac, Blue Bell, Pa., 1973-75; systems analyst Prudential Ins. Co. Am., Dresher, Pa., 1975-76; systems engr. Datapoint Corp., Bala-Cynwyd, Pa., 1976-78; v.p., bus. design architect Finpac Corp., Narberth, Pa., 1978-89, bd. dirs., sec., 1984—; founder, software architect SR Designs, Narberth, 1989—; founder SR Investment Co., Narberth, Pa., 1984—. Mem. Soc. Indsl. and Applied Math., Bucknell U. Alumni Assn. (trustee 1978-83). Club: Island Heights (N.J.) Yacht. Home: 107 Foxhall Ln Narberth PA 19072 Office: SR Designs 230 Windsor Ave Narberth PA 19072

RAFAELS, DIANE, marketing director; b. Kingsport, Tenn., Aug. 7, 1940; d. John Claude and Sarah Katherine (Piety) Catron; m. David Michael Deans, Oct. 25, 1957 (div. Sept. 1975) children—Juliana Susan, Leslie Gloria; m. Umberto Rafaels, Mar. 28, 1985. A.A., Sullins Coll., Bristol, Va., 1959. Cert. mktg. dir. Assoc. account exec. Ehrich-Manes Advt., Bethesda, Md., 1974-76; asst. mall mgr. Kettler Bros., Gaithersburg, Md., 1976-79; mktg. dir. Farber Co., Pompano Beach, Fla., 1979-80, Springfield Mall, Va., 1980-83; communications mgr. MD-IPA, Rockville, Md., 1983; dir. mktg. Chas. E. Smith Cos., Arlington, Va., 1983—; mem. adv. bd., dir. MD-IPA, Rockville; cons., Publicity & Media Resources, Falls Church, Va. Contbr. articles to profl. jours. and mags. Chmn. communications com. Fairfax County Arts Council, Va., 1982-83; publicity com. Internat. Children's Festival-Wolftrap, Vienna, Va., 1982-83, mktg. com. chair, 1985-86. Recipient Vol. Recognition awards Fairfax County Fire Dept., 1983, N. Va. Lung Assn., 1983, United Way, 1982-83. Mem. Internat. Council Shopping Ctrs., Women in Advt. and Mktg., Washington Ad Club, Fairfax County C. of C. (communications com. 1981-84), Arlington County C. of C. (communications com. 1984-85), Montgomery County C. of C. (communications com. 1983). Democrat. Methodist. Clubs: Jr. Women's of Rockville (pres. 1972-73), Jr. Clubs (Md. state dir. 1974-76), Contemporary (v.p. 1984-86). Avocations: reading, needlework. Office: Chas E Smith Cos 2345 Crystal Dr Arlington VA 22202

RAFF, BEVERLY STEIN, foundation administrator; b. N.Y.C., Nov. 15, 1933; d. Samuel and Rose (Deutsch) Stein; m. Joseph Raff, Apr. 11, 1954; children: Marla Lynn, Garry Scott. BS, Bellevue Sch. Nursing, 1955; MA, NYU, 1967, PhD, 1976. Asst. prof. SUNY, Farmingdale, 1967-71; assoc. prof. Adelphi U., Garden City, N.Y., 1971-78; v.p. profl. svcs. March of Dimes Birth Defects Found., White Plains, N.Y., 1978—; v.p. bd. dirs. NCC Certification Corp. Co-author Maternity Nursing, 1982, Quick Reference to Marternity Nursing, 1989; mem. editorial bd. Issues in Health Care of Women, N.Y.C., 1985—. Bd. dirs. Alliance of Genetic Support Group, Washington, 1985, Family Aide, Inc., Hicksville, N.Y., 1985-87. Fellow Am. Acad. Nursing; mem. Nurses Assn. of Am. Coll. Ob-Gyns. (vice chair dist. II 1982-84), Am. Nurses Assn. (councils, coms. 1985-87, Perinatal Nurse of Yr. 1986), Nat. Perinatal Assn. Office: March of Dimes Birth Defects Found 1275 Mamaroneck Ave White Plains NY 10605

RAFF, SANDRA BETH, internist; b. N.Y.C., June 9, 1947; d. Edward and Claire (Barcham) R. BA, NYU, 1967; MD, N.Y. Med. Coll., 1971. Diplomate Am. Bd. Internal Medicine. Rotating intern Beth Israel Med. Ctr., N.Y.C., 1971-72, resident-in-internal medicine, 1972-74; fellow in diabetes and metabolism Sch. Medicine NYU, N.Y.C., 1974-76; asst. prof. internal medicine U. Ala. Sch. Medicine, Tuscaloosa, 1976-77, U. Conn. Sch. Medicine, Hartford, 1977-79; practice medicine specializing in diabetes and endocrinology Cromwell, Conn., 1980-84, Middletown, Conn., 1984-90; assoc. med. dir. Aetna Life & Casualty, Hartford, 1990—; attending physician Middlesex Meml. Hosp., Middletown, 1978—; instr. clin. medicine NYU Sch. Medicine, 1974-76; cons. Elmcrest Psychiat. Hosp., Portland, Conn., 1983-90; physician advisor Conn. Peer Rev. Orgn., 1984—; bd. dirs. M.D. Health Plan, New Haven. Contbr. articles to med. jours. Bd. dirs. Greater Middletown Chorale, 1986-88. Mem. AMA, ACP, Am. Soc. Internal Medicine, Am. Diabetes Assn. (diabetic camp com. 1980—), Psi Chi, Delta Phi Epsilon. Office: 151 Farmington Ave Aetna MA 3 Hartford CT 06457

RAFFEL, ANGELA, educator, consultant, lecturer; b. White Plains, N.Y., Oct. 2, 1919; d. Ralph and Mary (Paulding) Ferraro; m. Glenn M. Kelly, Aug. 28, 1943 (dec. Apr 1954); 1 child, Cynthia Kelly McWilliams; m. Leon Raffel, Dec. 21, 1963 (dec. Feb. 1984). BA cum laude, Coll. of White Plains, 1940; MA, NYU, 1943; diploma, U. Bridgeport, Conn., 1979, EdD, 1989. Cert. humanities tchr., N.Y., Conn. Tchr. Portchester High Sch., N.Y., 1954-61; tchr., chair English dept. Greenwich (Conn.) High Sch., 1961-81; tchr. Scarsdale (N.Y.) High Sch., 1984—; cons. Nat. Humanities Faculty, Atlanta, 1979-88, Greenwich High Sch., 1978—. Mem. Phi Delta Kappa, Delta Kappa Gamma (sec. State of Conn. 1985). Home: 701 Abbey Ln Valley Cottage NY 10989

RAFFERTY, GENEVIEVE KENNEDY, social service agency administrator; b. Davenport, Iowa, Jan. 21, 1922; d. Thomas Cyril and Mabel Veronica (Finefield) Kennedy; B.A., St. Ambrose Coll., 1942; postgrad. U. Iowa, 1972; m. Daniel J. Rafferty, Aug. 22, 1942 (dec. 1984); children—Daniel D., Michele M., Genevieve, Thomas K., Eileen M., Margaret M., Sheila M. Real estate saleswoman Manhard Realty, Moline, Ill., 1950-59; substitute tchr., Rock Island, Ill., 1963-67; head start tchr. Rock Island-Scott County Dept. Social Services, 1966; public welfare worker Scott County Dept. Social Services, Davenport, Iowa, 1967-72; exec. dir. Info., Referral and Assistance Service, Rock Island, 1972—; mem. Travelers Aid Internat.; chair Rock Island Housing Authority; mem. Quad-City Council on Crime and Delinquency, 1977-80; mem. Rock Island County Council on Alcoholism, 1976-82; chairperson CETA Adv. Bd., 1982-84, bi state metropolitan planning comn. 1986—; steering com., Quad-City Vision for the Future, 1987; bd. dirs. Quint-City Drug Abuse. Named Social Worker of Yr. Quad-City, Nat Assn. Social Workers, 1973. Mem. Nat. Assn. Social Workers, Iowa Council Info. and Referral Providers, Nat. Conf. Social Welfare, Ill. Welfare Assn., NOW, Ill. Alliance Info. and Referral Services (dir.). Republican. Roman Catholic. Office: 2002 3d Ave Rock Island IL 61201

RAFOTH, MARY ANN, psychology educator; b. Cin., Apr. 12, 1957; d. Robert Anthony and Providence Elizabeth (Gagliardo) Kinkemoeller; m. Bennett Alan Rafoth, July 28, 1979; children: Henry David, Paige Elizabeth. BS in Edn., Miami U., Oxford, Ohio, 1979; MEd, U. Ga., 1981, PhD, 1984. Lic. psychologist, Ga., Ill., Pa. Tchr. Princeton High Sch., Cin., 1979-80; coord. psychol. svcs. Clarke County Schs., Athens, Ga., 1982-84; sch. psychologist County Sch. Edn. Coop., Champaign, Ill., 1984-85; asst. prof. psychology dept. Ea. Ill. U., Charleston, 1985-87; asst. prof. ednl. psychology dept. Indiana U. of Pa., Indiana, Pa., 1987—. Author: (monograph) Study Skills, 1990. Mem. Nat. Assn. Sch. Psychologists (cochair retention subcom. children's svc. com. 1988-89, pre-sch. cons.), Am. Psychol. Assn., Coun. on Learning Disabilities, Assn. Sch. Psychologists of Pa. Office: Ind U Pa Ednl Psychology 246 Stouffer Hall Indiana PA 15705

RAGAN, ELIZABETH HOFFMAN, retired business executive; b. Albemarle, N.C., Nov. 11, 1916; d. Joseph Filson and Lilly Bassett (Carter) Hoffman; cert. bus. adminstrn. High Point Coll., 1937; m. Herbert Tomlinson Ragan, Oct. 14, 1939 (div. Sept. 1985); 1 son, Herbert Tomlinson. Head bond dept. Sunflower Ordnance Works, Hercules Powder Co., DeSota, Kans., 1942-45; sec.-treas. Ragan-Carmichael, Inc., High Point, N.C., 1956-74, Staple Products, Inc., High Point, 1956-74, R & C Holding Co., Inc., High Point, 1956-74, sec. Ragan Hardware Co., Inc. (merger), High Point, 1974-82; trustee Ragan-Hardware, Inc., Profit Sharing Trust and Pension Trust, 1974-82. Cellist, N.C. Symphony, 1932-35. Mem. adv. bd. Maryfield Nursing Home, 1975-79; bd. visitors High Point Coll., 1979-82; mem. exec. bd. Friends of Guilford Coll. Library, 1980-82. Mem. High Point Community Concert Assn. (bd. dirs. 1987-90, treas. 1988-89), Soc. of Friends (organist, choir dir.), High Point Hist. Soc. (dir. 1977-81, pres. 1979-80). Author: (compiler) The Lineage of the Amos Ragan Family, 1976. Home: 1825 Country Club Dr High Point NC 27260

RAGAN, MARY ALICE, health insurance professional; b. Seattle, Apr. 16, 1961; d. William Henry and Alice (Achorn) Fetherston. BA, Mt. Holyoke Coll., 1983. Adminstrv. asst. Lincoln Nat. Life Ins. Co., Phoenix, 1985-86; employee benefits rep. Provident Life and Accident Ins. Co., Phoenix, 1986-88; life and health account exec. Ariz. Trust Co., Tucson, 1989-90; health ins. specialist Physicians Mut. Ins. Co., Tucson, 1990—. Mem. NAFE, Aztec Toastmasters. Home: 11141 E Prince Rd Tucson AZ 85749

RAGAN, SUSAN MCLAREN, health care information industry executive; b. N.Y.C., July 5, 1952; d. John Bernard and Doris Carolyn (Lynch) McLaren; m. Richard Maurice Ragan, Mar. 15, 1977; 1 child, Richard Maurice Jr. BA, Skidmore Coll., Saratoga Springs, 1974. Secondary Edn. Tchrs. Cert. (NY). Exec. train-asst. buyer Macy's, N.Y.C., 1974-76; merchandise mgr. Macy's, Garden City, N.Y., 1976-78; buyer Macy's, N.Y.C, 1978-79; sales rep. dist. field rep. Procter & Gamble, Wayne, Pa., 1980-81; unit mgr. Procter & Gamble, Boston, 1981-84, N.Y.C., 1984-85; area sales mgr. Procter & Gamble, N.Y.C., 1986-87; field sales mgr. Procter & Gamble, Cin., 1987-88; v.p. sales and mktg. Vanguard Direct, Inc., N.Y.C., 1988-89; dir. field svcs. IMS Am., Ltd./Dun & Bradstreet, Inc., Totowa, N.J., 1989—; cons. The Vanguard Group-Printing Co's N.Y.C., 1988—. Vol. Am. Cancer Soc., N.J. Chpt., 1988, 89. Mem. Am. Mgmt. Assn., Direct Mktg. Assn., Skidmore Alumni. Republican. Roman Catholic. Home: 11 Franklin Pl Maplewood NJ 07040

RAGGI, REENA, federal judge; b. Jersey City, May 11, 1951; d. Edward J. and Tina (Navarchi) R.; m. David W. Denton, May 14, 1983; 1 child, David. BA, Wellesley Coll., 1973; JD, Harvard U., 1976. Bar: N.Y. 1977. U.S. atty. Dept. Justice, Bklyn., 1986; ptnr. Windels, Marx, Davies & Ives, N.Y.C., 1987; judge U.S. Dist. Ct. (ea. dist.) N.Y., Bklyn., 1987—. Office: US Courthouse 225 Cadman Pla E Brooklyn NY 11201

RAGGIO, OLGA, museum curator, educator; b. Rome, Italy, Feb. 5, 1926; d. Enrico and Renee (Levine) R. Diploma, Internat. Library Sch., Vatican, 1947; Ph.D., U. Rome, 1949; postgrad., N.Y. U., 1951-52. With Met. Mus. Art, N.Y.C., 1950—; assoc. rsch. curator Met. Mus. Art, 1966-68, curator Western European arts, 1968-71, chmn. dept. European sculpture and decorative arts, 1971—; adj. asso. prof. Inst. Fine Arts, N.Y. U., 1964-68, adj. prof., 1968—. Author works in field. Am. Council Learned Socs. fellow, 1962-63, Metro. Mus. Art. Trustee fellow, 1969-70, Am. Acad. in Rome Resident in Art History, 1983-84. Mem. Coll. Art Assn. Am., Renaissance Soc. Am., Am. Assn. Museums, Internat. Com. Mus. Orgn. Roman Catholic. Office: Met Mus Art Fifth Ave & 82nd St New York NY 10028

RAGHAVAN, VEENA, promotion executive; b. Greenwich, Con., Oct. 11, 1938; d. Hardit Singh and Prakash (Bhagat) Malik; m. Jai Dev, July 6, 1960; children: Sarita Malik, Surekha Nedyam. Attended, Geneva U., Switzerland, 1960. Feature writer & reader in French All India Radio, New Delhi, 1967-68; info. officer Norwegian Embassy, New Delhi, 1967-70, Embassy of Peru, New Dehli, India, 1971-72; admin. officer Pan Am. GSA, Bombay, India, 1975-76; asst. to sr. ptnr. Leon Weill & Mahony, N.Y.C., 1976-80; dir. spl. projects and promotion Davis Publs., Inc., N.Y.C., 1980—. Contbr. articles to profl. jours. Office: Davis Publs Inc 380 Lexington Ave New York NY 10168-0035

RAGINS, NAOMI, psychiatrist, psychoanalyst, educator; b. Chgo., Apr. 23, 1926; d. Oscar B. and Ida (Kraus) R.; m. Mark Goldsmith, July 31, 1955. PhB, U. Chgo., 1946, BS, 1947, MD, 1951; grad., Pitts. Psychoanalytic Inst., 1967. Diplomate Am. Bd. Neurology and Psychiatry. Rotating intern U. Chgo. Clinics, 1951-52, resident in adult/child psychiatry, teachiang fellow, 1952-55, 56-57; with U. Pitts., 1956—, asst. prof. child psychiatry, 1960-63, clin. assoc. prof. in child psychiatry, 1964—; faculty Pitts. Psychoanalytic Inst., 1969—, tng. and supervising psychoanalyst and child analysis supr., 1971—. Author: book chpt. Contributions of Child Analysis to Child Psychiatry, 1987; contbr. articles to profl. jours. Mem. Internat. Psychoanalytic Assn., Am. Psychoanalytic Assn., Am. Psychiat. Assn., Am. Acad. Child Psychiatry, Assn. for Child Psychoanalysis, Am. Orthopsychiat. Assn., Physicians for Social Responsibility, United Mental Health Svcs., Amnesty Internat., ACLU. Office: 4716 Ellsworth Ave Cathedral Mansions Ste 118-119 Pittsburgh PA 15213

RAGLAND, ALWINE MULHEARN, judge; b. Monroe, La., July 28, 1913; m. LeRoy Smith, 1947 (dec.); children—LeRoy, Caroline Smith Christman; m. 2d, L. Percy Ragland, Mar., 1978. A.A., Principia Coll., St. Louis; J.D., Tulane U., 1935. Bar: La. 1935. Sole practice, Tallulah, La., 1935-74; mem. firm Mulhearn & Smith, 1972-74; judge 6th Jud. Dist. Ct., Lake Prvidence, La., 1974—; atty. for inheritance tax collector Madison Parish, La., 1968-74; former city atty., Delta, La.; temporary judge La. Ct. Appeals (2d cir.), 1976. Charter bd. dirs. Silver Waters council Girl Scouts U.S.A.; past pres. Band Boosters Assn. Tallulah High Sch., Tallulah High Sch. PTA; past dist. dir., past bd. dirs, lay reader 1st Ch. Christ Scientist, Vicksburg, Miss.; past bd. dirs. Delta Christian Sch. Mem. ABA, La. Bar Assn., 6th Jud. Bar Assn., La. Def. Counsel Assn. (jud. assoc. mem.), Am. Judges Assn., La. Judges Assn., Am. Judicature Soc., La. Council Juvenile and Family Ct. Ct. Judges (past pres.), Nat. Council Juvenile Ct. Judges, So. Juvenile Ct. Judges, Assn. Trial Lawyers Am., La. Trial Lawyers Assn., Family Conciliation Cts. and Services, Nat. Juvenile Ct. Service Assn., La. Conf. Social Welfare, Practicing Law Inst., Nat. Assn. Women Judges, La. Assn. Def. Counsel. Home and Office: PO Box 392 Lake Providence LA 71254

RAGLE, JOANNE FEIGER, educator; b. St. Louis, May 5, 1948; d. Francis Sibley Feiger and Katherine (Combs) Feiger-Young; m. John D. Ragle, Jan. 2, 1987. BA, U. Ill., 1970; MEd, U. Miss., 1974; postgrad., U. Tex., 1985-86. Cert. tchr., Ill., Miss., Tex. Tchr. various pub. schs., 1970-71, 72-85, U. Miss., Oxford, 1971-72, Frontier Community Coll., Fairfield, Ill., 1984-85; program coord. Miller-Keys Assocs., Austin, Tex., 1986; communication rsch. cons. U. Tex. Coll. Communications, 1986-87; lang. arts tchr. Pflugerville (Tex.) Middle Sch., 1987—, chmn. lang. arts. dept., 1988—; Spanish tchr. Flugerville High Sch., 1990—; advisor State of Tex.Textbook Adv. Com., 1989; tchr., trainer Pflugerville Independent Sch. Dist., 1989—. Youth advisor, mem. com. University United Meth. Ch., Austin, 1985-88. Mem. Am. Assn. Tchrs. Spanish and Portuguese, Nat. Coun. Tchrs. English, Central Tex. Coun. Tchrs. English, Phi Beta Kappa, Kappa Kappa Gamma (chmn. adv. bd. 1986-88). Home: 11901 Dove Haven Dr Austin TX 78753 Office: Pflugerville High Sch 1300 W Pecan Pflugerville TX 78660

RAGONA-SIDES, LAURENE CECILIA, marketing executive; b. Bklyn., Apr. 20, 1955; d. Francis John and Ruth (Albrecht) Ragona; m. C. David Sides III, Oct. 17, 1987. BS, Tex. Christian U., 1977, MEd, 1980. Vocat. counselor Goodwill Industries, Ft. Worth, 1980-81; coordinator Tarrant County Learning Ctr., Ft. Worth, 1981-82; plato analyst Control Data Corp., Mpls., 1982-84, plato ednl. cons., 1984-86, product line mgr., 1986-88; product mktg. mgr. AmeriData, Inc., Mpls., 1989—. Mem. mktg. and membership com. YMCA, Mpls., 1988—; corp. div. rep. United Way, Mpls., 1986. Mem. Eden Prairie Profl. Women's Network (newsletter com. 1988—), Tex. Rehab. Assn. Democrat. Roman Catholic. Home: 9440 Garrison Way Eden Prairie MN 55347 Office: AmeriData Inc 10200 51st Ave N Plymouth MN 55442

RAGONE, THERESE VICTORIA, transportation executive; b. Bklyn., Oct. 13, 1935; d. James Vincent and Celeste Marie (Pizzani) R.; m. Harold Anthony Castellano, Sept. 15, 1956 (div. 1971); children: Michele, Harold Jr., James, Suzanne, Victoria. Student, Suffolk Community Coll., 1971-74, 78. Single copy rep. Newsday, Inc., Melville, N.Y., 1978-79, single copy supr., 1979-81, transp. field supr., 1981-82, asst. transp. foreman, 1982—. Home: 175 Main Ave 114 Wheatley Heights NY 11798 Office: Newsday Inc Pinelawn Rd Melville NY 11747

RAGSDALE, BERTHA MAE See KOLB, BERTHA MAE

RAGSDALE, SHARON DORISE, nursing home administrator; b. Somerville, N.J., July 10, 1953; d. Leonard Gordon and Dorise Lorraine (Cook) Ragsdale; 1 child, James Kelley Robert Cook. BS in Secondary Edn. and Communications, Temple U., 1976; cert. in nursing home adminstrn., George Washington U., 1988. Lic. nursing home administr., Del., N.J., cert. communications tchr., Pa., N.J. 9th and 10th grade tchr. Delran (N.J.) High Sch., 1978-79; bus. office mgr., adminstr.-in-tng. Rainbow Nursing Ctr., Bridgeton, N.J., 1984-88; asst. exec. dir., health ctr. adminstr. Forwood Manor, Wilmington, Del., 1988-90; billing mgr. United Hosp., Inc., Elkins Park, Pa., 1990—. Active League Women Voters, Wilmington, 1989—. Mem. Gerontology Inst. N.J., Del. Health Care Facilities Assn. Office: United Hosps Inc 60 E Township Line Rd Elkins Park PA 19117

RAGUSEO, LORRAINE ANNE, public relations company executive; b. Bklyn., Feb. 3, 1955; d. John Joseph and Geraldine T. (Cardlin) R.; m. Peter J. McCarthy, Oct. 17, 1987. BA, Fordham U., 1977. Asst. account exec. Geltzer & Co., N.Y.C., 1979-81; v.p. Kanan, Corbin, Schupak & Aronow, Inc., N.Y.C., 1981-84; assoc. The Wiener Group, N.Y.C., 1985-88; v.p., group dir. Dunwoodie Communications, N.Y.C., 1988—; cons. EAM Copy & Creative, Bklyn., 1989—. Mem. Advt. Women N.Y. (pub. rels. mgr. Addy awards 1989), Publicity Club N.Y. Office: Dunwoodie Communicationss 122 E 42d St Ste 2200 New York NY 10168

RAHBAR, ZITA INA, health insurance executive; b. Kaunas, Lithuania, Mar. 15, 1937; came to U.S. 1949; d. Stasys and Ona (Eitkeviciute) Carneckas; m. Vytautas Dudenas, June 20, 1960 (div. 1965); m. 2d, Darius Rahbar, Mar. 26, 1970. B.A. St. Xavier Coll., Chgo., 1957; postgrad. in physiology U. Chgo., 1957-59, M.B.A., 1978. Mng. editor Lyons & Carnahan div. Meredith Corp., Chgo., 1960-68, mgr. program planning, 1968-73; exec. cons. George S. May Co., Chgo., 1973-75; sr. cons. planning Blue Shield Assn., Chgo., 1975-76, dir. corp. planning Blue Shield/Blue Cross Assn., 1976-78, sr. dir. program devel. and implementation, 1978-81, v.p. mktg. Blue Cross Calif., Los Angeles and Oakland, Calif., 1981-87; pres., Creative Mktg. Solutions, 1987—. Bd. dirs. Bethune Ballet, Los Angeles, 1982—; mem. com. Orgn. Women Execs., Los Angeles, 1982—; cofounder Women in Pub., Chgo., 1965; mem. NOW, Town Hall Calif., Chgo. Council Fgn. Relations, World Affairs Council Los Angeles. Fellow U. Chgo., 1957-58. Mem. Am. Mgmt. Assn., Am. Mktg. Assn., AAAS, Republican. Roman Catholic. Home: 912 Blue Spring Dr Westlake Village CA 91361

RAHJA, JEAN MARIE, elementary school teacher; b. Frederick, S.D., May 18, 1929; d. George Gordon and Mary Florence (Christie) Elliott; m. Gilbert Rahja, Nov. 1, 1947; children: Robert Andrew, Daniel George, Patricia Ann Rahja Van Gerpen. Student, U. N.D., 1968-69; BS, No. State U., 1972, MS, 1972. Sixth grade tchr. Aberdeen (S.D.) Pub. Schs., 1972—; Bd. mem. S.D. Social Studies Coun., 1990; Textbook Commn. Nat. Coun. for Social Studies, 1989. Mem. AAUW, Nat. Coun. Geog. Edn. (George F. Cramm fellowship commn., 1988, merit tchr. award, Pitts., 1981), Delta Kappa Gamma, Phi Delta Kappa. Republican. Lutheran. Home: 610 23 Ave N E Aberdeen SD 57401 Office: Howard Hedger Elem Sch 815 N 2nd St Aberdeen SD 57401

RAHM, SUSAN BERKMAN, lawyer; b. Pitts., June 25, 1943; d. Allen Hugh and Selma (Wiener) Berkman; m. David Alan Rahm, Nov. 23, 1972; children: Katherine, William. BA with honors, Wellesley Coll., 1965; postgrad., Harvard U., 1966-68; JD, NYU, 1973. Bar: N.Y. 1974, D.C. 1988. Assoc. Marshall, Bratter, Greene, Allison & Tucker, N.Y.C., 1973-81, ptnr., 1981-82; ptnr. Kaye, Scholer, Fierman, Hays & Handler, N.Y.C., 1982—. Editor: New York Real Property Service, 1987. Bd. dirs. Girls Club Am., 1989—; mem. aux. bd. Mt. Sinai Hosp., N.Y.C., 1976-78; mem. Com. of 1000, N.Y.C., 1987—. Recipient cert. of outstanding svc. D.C. Redevel. Land Agy., 1969, She Knows Where She's Going award Girls' Clubs of Am., 1987. Mem. ABA, Assn. of Bar of City of N.Y., N.Y. State Bar Assn. (real property law com., co-chmn. on real estate devel.), Am. Coll. Real Estate Lawyers. Office: Kaye Scholer Fierman Hays & Handler 425 Park Ave New York NY 10022

RAIKOW, RADMILA BORUVKA, scientist; b. Prague, Czechoslovakia, Mar. 20, 1939; came to U.S., 1957; d. Svatopluk and Pavla (Erba) Boruvka; m. Robert Jay Raikow, June 10, 1966; children: David Francis, Steven Boruvka. BA, NYU, 1961; MA, CUNY, 1965; PhD, U. Calif., Berkeley, 1970. Rsch. assoc. U. Hawaii, Honolulu, 1970-71; instr. U. Pitts., 1983-85; rsch. assoc. Allegheny Gen. Hosp., Pitts., 1978-80; assoc. scientist Allegheny-Singer Rsch. Inst., Pitts., 1980-83, scientist, 1983—; asst. prof. pathology and lab. U. Pa. Med. Coll., 1990—. Contbr. articles to profl. jours. NYU scholar, 1957-61; NIH trainee, 1966-70. Mem. AAAS, Am. Assn. for Cancer Rsch., Soc. for Exptl. Biology and Medicine, Assn. for Rsch. in Vision and Ophthalmology, Clin. Immunology Soc. Home: 1229 Winterton St Pittsburgh PA 15206 Office: Allegheny-Singer Rsch Inst 320 E North Ave Pittsburgh PA 15212

RAIM, ELLEN, lawyer; b. Miami, Fla., Apr. 27, 1958; d. Jerome Abraham and Nina Claire (Ellenbogen) R. BA, Brown U., 1979; JD, U. Miami, 1982. Bar: Fla. 1982, Calif. 1983, Wash., 1986, D.C. 1987. Assoc. Wicker Smith, Ft. Lauderdale, Fla., 1982-83; contract negotiator United Airlines, Burlingame, Calif., 1983-85; assoc. Hopkins & Carley, San Jose, Calif., 1985-90, Phelen Marrin Johnson & Bridges, San Jose, 1990—; judge pro tem Small Claims Ct., San Jose, 1985—; settlement judge pro tem Superior Ct., San Jose, 1985—. Bd. dirs. Northside Theater, San Jose, 1988-90. Mem. ABA, Santa Clara County Labor Lawyers Assn. (exec. com. 1990—), Calif. Bar Assn., Wash. State Bar Assn., D.C. Bar Assn., Fla. Bar Assn. Office: Thelen Marrin Johnson & Bridges San Jose CA 95113

RAIMAN, GAIL ANN, educational association administrator; b. Chgo., May 27, 1951; d. Robert Joseph and Cecile Marcelle (Scharfenberg) R.; m. Robert Daniel Hynes Jr. BA, Kalamazoo (Mich.) Coll., 1973. Asst. Office of V.P. Designate Gerald R. Ford, Washington, 1973, Office of V.P. Gerald R. Ford, Washington, 1973-74; pers. asst. to counselor Pres. Gerald R. Ford, Washington, 1974-77; dir. office of info. Hollins Coll., Roanoke, Va., 1978-82; producer, host pub. affairs program WDBJ-TV, Roanoke, 1979-82; dir. pub. rels. Trinity Coll., Washington, 1982-83; asst. dir. communications Am. Textile Mfrs. Inst., Washington, 1983-88; v.p. pub. affairs Nat. Assn. Ind. Colls. and Univs., Washington, 1988—. Mem. Pub. Rels. Soc. Am., Am. Women in Radio and TV, Coun. for Advancement and Support of Edn. Office: Nat Assn Ind Colls & Univs 122 C St NW Ste 750 Washington DC 20001

RAIMOND, ROSE, hospital administrator; b. Bklyn., Mar. 27, 1929; children: Gloria, Jane. AAS, Orange County Community Coll., Middletown, N.Y., 1965; BS, SUNY, Oneonta, 1973; MPS, New Sch. for Social Rsch., 1983. RN; cert. sch. nurse-tchr. Asst. dir. nursing Community Gen. Hosp. of Sullivan County, Harris, N.Y., 1978-80, dir. utilization rev., 1980-87, med. staff coord., 1987-88, assoc. adminstr., 1988—; past v.p. utilization rev. affiliate No. Met. Hosp. Assn. Mem. Nat. Assn. Quality Assurance Profls., N.Y. Assn. Quality Assurance Profls., Assn. Operating Room Nurses. Address: Box 245 Harris NY 12742-0245

RAIMONDO, BEVERLY NICKELL, data processing company executive; b. Lexington, Ky., Feb. 24, 1946; d. William Rice and Frances Louise (Jinkins) Nickell; m. Anthony Neal Raimondo, Apr. 24, 1976; children: Christa Nickell, Laurel Dana. BA in Edn., U. Ky., 1968, MSLS, 1969; postgrad. Xavier U., 1974-78. Librarian, IBM Corp., Lexington, 1969-75, edn. coordinator, 1975-79, mgr., 1979-81, project mgr., 1982-84, adminstrv. asst., 1984-86, plans and controls mgr. 1987-88, instr. mgmt. devel., 1988—; seminar instr. U. Ky. Community Edn., Lexington, 1981-83. Co-chmn. March of Dimes Mother's March, Lexington, 1984; mem. Fayette County Schs. task force for excellence in edn., 1984-85; mem. Blue Grass Trust for Historic Preservation, 1981—, Leadership Lexington, 1983-84; bd. dirs. Lexington Children's Theatre, 1985—, pres. 1987-88; bd. dirs. YWCA, 1987—, v.p., 1989-90, pres. 1990—. Recipient IBM IPD Achievement award, 1982. Mem. Profl. Women's Forum, Ky. Library Assn., U. Ky. Alumni Assn., Beta Phi Mu (pres. 1974). Republican. Christian Science. Clubs: Cotillion, Spindletop Hall. Avocations: boating, sailing, reading, spectator sports. Home: 1327 Strawberry Ln Lexington KY 40502

RAINES, BETTY LYNN, social service administrator; b. Ft. Benning, Ga., Oct. 28, 1957; d. Jesse Dewey and Bertha (Cross) Johnson; m. Calvin N. Raines, May 1, 1982; children: Candice, Kristen. BS in Edn., Auburn (Ala.) U., 1979, MEd, 1982. Instr. recreation dept. City of Phenix, Ala., 1976-77; therapist Vets. Hosp., Tuskegee, Ala., 1978-79; tchr. Opelika (Ala.) City Schs., 1980; counselor E. Ala. Mental Health, Opelika, 1981; dir. Older Ams. Coun., Macon, Ga., 1982—; coun. mem. Houston County (Ga.) Coun. on Aging, 1982—. Mem. Perry (Ga.) Sr. Citizens Benefit Com., 1988-, Community Leadership Program, Perry and Warner Robins, Ga., 1989-; vol. distbr. Macon Food Bank, Perry, 1982-; active Christmas Program Perry Pal Program, 1982-; campaing worker local and state elections, 1988; lobbyist Older Ams. Coun., Atlanta, 1989-; bd. dirs., Friends of Perry Hosp.; choreographer music program Westfield Sch. and Perry High Sch., 1982-84; mem. Houston County Leadership Program, 1989. Mem. AAUW (bd. dir. internat. relationships 1987—). Democrat. Episcopalian. Home: 116 Dogwood Dr Warner Robbins GA 31088 Office: Older Ams Coun 538 First St Macon GA 31201

RAINES, JO-ANN RYAN, cooperative educational director; b. N.Y.C., June 4, 1948; d. James Henry Ryan and Vevette Yvonne (Morales) Ryan Lewis; m. Rudolf Lawrence Raines, June 14, 1980; children: Aisha, Dana, Felicia, Christopher. B.A. in Social Scis., St. John's U., Jamaica, N.Y., 1969; M.A. in Adult Edn. Columbia, U., 1976; cert. in mktg. and mgmt. Trenton State Coll., 1984. Lic. in real estate sales, N.J. Ednl. cons. N.Y. Tel., N.Y.C., 1969-76; staff mgr. AT&T, Bedminster, N.J., 1976-84; real estate salesperson Bea M. Scott Realty, East Orange, N.J., 1985-88, Coldwell Banker Real Estate, Maplewood, N.J., 1988-89; asst. dir. Div. Coop. Edn. N.J. Inst. of Tech., Newark, 1989—; career cons., South Orange, N.J., 1985. Mem. South Orange/Maplewood Awareness Coun., 1982—; bd. dirs. Gardens Nursery Sch., N.Y.C., 1978-81, Assn. Retarded Citizens for Essex County, N.J., 1983—. Mem. NAFE, Nat. Assn. Realtors, Phi Delta Kappa, Sigma Delta Pi, Delta Sigma Theta (v.p. chpt. 1968-69). Democrat. Roman Catholic. Avocations: reading, aerobics, travel. Home: 357 Irving Ave South Orange NJ 07079 Office: NJ Inst Tech Div of Coop Edn University Heights Newark NJ 07102

RAINEY, CHRISTINE ROSE, pharmacist, company executive; b. Detroit, Dec. 23, 1952; d. Percy Elmer and Nadine Marie (Papke) R. BS, Wayne State Coll., 1977. Reg. pharmacist, preceptor. Chief pharmacist Community Pharmacy, Inc., Whitmore Lake, Mich., 1977-78; staff pharmacist Perry Drug Stores, Troy, Mich., 1978; pharmacy dept. mgr. Perry Drug Stores, Waterford, Mich., 1978-79; asst. store mgr. Perry Drug Stores, Troy, 1979-81; pharmacist, store mgr. Perry Drug Stores, Novi, Mich., 1981-84, pharm. buyer, 1984-90; pharm. buyer Nat. Wholesale Drug Co., Taylor, Mich., 1990—; bd. dirs. Whitmore Lake Health Clinic, 1977-78. Mem. Mich. Pharmacists Assn., Oakland County Pharmacists Assn., Wayne State U. Pharmacy Alumni Assn. (bd. govs.). Office: Nat Wholesale Drug Co 21405 Trolley Dr Taylor MI 48180

RAINEY, JEAN OSGOOD, public relations executive; b. Lansing, Mich., Apr. 5, 1925; d. Earle Victor and Blanche Mae (Eberly) Osgood; m. John Larimer Rainey, Nov. 29, 1957; children: Cynthia, John Larimer, Ruth. Grad., Lansing Bus. U., 1942. Pub. rels. dir. Nat. Assn. Food Chains, Washington, 1954-59; v.p. pub. rels. Manchester Orgns., Washington, 1959-61; ptnr. Rainey, McEnroe & Manning, Washington, 1962-73; v.p. Manning, Selvage & Lee, Washington, 1973-79, pres. Washington div., 1979-84, sr. counsellor, 1985—; owner Jean Rainey Assocs., Washington, 1986-87; sr. v.p. Daniel J. Edelman Inc., 1987—. Author: How to Shop for Food, 1972. Pres. Hyde Home and Sch. Assn., Washington, 1969-71; co-chmn. Nat. Com. for Reelection of the Pres., 1972. Mem. Pub. Rels. Soc. Am. (accredited), Am. Women in Radio and TV (pres. Washington chpt. 1962-63, mem. nat. bd. 1963-65), Am. News Women's Club (pres. 1973-75). Republican. Episcopalian. Clubs: City Tavern, International; Capitol Hill (Washington). Home: 4000 Cathedral Ave NW Apt 120B Washington DC 20016 Office: Edelman Pub Rels 1420 K St NW Washington DC 20005

RAINEY, MARY TERESA, advertising executive; b. Dunbarton, Scotland, May 24, 1955; came to U.S., 1983; d. Peter Logue and Margaret (McClure) R. MA in Psychology with honors, U. Glasgow, Scotland, 1976; PhD in Psychology, U. Aston, Birmingham, Eng., 1978. $D; account planner T.B.W.A., London, 1978-80; sr. account planner Gold, Greenlees, Trott, London, 1980-83; dir. account planning Chiat/Day, L.A., 1983-84; v.p., dir. account planning Chiat/Day, San Francisco, 1985-87; v.p., corp. dir. account planning Chiat/Day, N.Y.C., 1988—. Named one of Hundred Best and Brightest Women in Advt., Advertising Age mag., 1989. Mem. Am. Advt. Fedn. (maj. market mem.), Am. Mktg. Assn. (exec., judge Effie awards 1988, Grand Effie award 1985, Gold Effie award 1986), Am. Mgmt. Assn., Advt. Rsch. Found. (mem. com. copy rsch. coun. 1988—), Advt. Women N.Y., Groucho Club. Democrat. Roman Catholic. Office: Chiat/Day Inc 79 Fifth Ave New York NY 10003

RAINEY, MILLICENT ANN, accademic administrator; b. Durham, N.C., June 24, 1944; d. Octavious Hooker and Elouise (Watson) Crisp; m. Charles William Rainey III, Aug. 9, 1969; 1 child, Letitia Rochelle. BS, Winston Salem State U., 1966; MA, N. C. State U., 1974; postgrad., Duke U., 1976, U. Calif., 1978. Cert. academic adminstr.;. Tchr. Orange County Schs., Hillsborough, N.C., 1965-66, Person County Schs., Roxboro, N.C., 1966-67, Richmond County Schs., Rockingham, N.C., 1967-69; tchr. Orange County Schs., Hillsborough, 1969-74, elem. supr., 1974-78, dir. instr., 1978-84, asst. supt., 1984--. Editor: (book) Orange Pealings, 1977-84. author:(handbook) Chapter 1. Bd. dirs. Student Tchr. Placement, Hillsborough, Sch. of Dance,. Fellow N.C. Sch. Bd. Assn.; mem. N.C. Assn. Compensatory Educators, Am. Assn. Sch. Adminstrs., N.C. Assn. Sch. Adminstrn., Alpha Kappa Alpha, Phi Delta Kappa. Democrat. Baptist. Home: PO Box 544 Hillsborough NC 27278 Office: Orange County Schs 200 E King St Hillsborough NC 27278

RAINS, CATHERINE BURKE, bank executive; b. Richmond, Va., Oct. 31, 1959; d. Michael Evan and Marthann (Coleman) Burke; m. Cal Rains II, Jan. 24, 1981. Student Polit. Sci., U. Tenn., Knoxville, 1977-81; BA in Polit. Sci. with high honors, U. West Fla., 1982. Sr. loan servicer First Mutual Savings & Loan, Pensacola, Fla., 1983-84; escrow officer First Am. Title Co., Yuma, Ariz., 1984-85; asst. v.p., branch mgr. The Hammond Co., Honolulu, Hi, Newport Beach, Calif., 1985-89; br. mgr. Bank of Am., Irvine, Calif., 1989—. Swimming instr. ARC, Knoxville, Tenn., 1979; bible sch. tchr., Naval Air Station, Pensacola, Fla., 1984; 1st place runner in March of Dimes Walkathon, 1985, Am. Cancer Soc. Marathon, 1985. Mem. Golden Key, Gamma Beta Pi, Phi Kappa Phi, Pi Sigma Alpha, Alpha Delta Pi (exec. v.p. 1979-80, scholarship chmn. 1978, named Outstanding Young Women 1986). Republican. Episcopalian. Home: 31590 Jewel St South Laguna CA 92677 Office: Bank of America Irvine CA 92720

RAINS, MARY JO, banker; b. Konawa, Okla., Oct. 27, 1935; d. Albert Wood and Mary Leona (Winfield) Starns; student Okla. Sch. Banking, 1969, Seminole Jr. Coll., 1970-72, E. Central State U., 1978-79, Okla. State U., 1987, Pontotoc County Adult Vocat. Tech. Ctr., 1987; diploma Am. Inst. Banking, 1981, 83; m. Billy Z. Rains, June 17, 1956; 1 son, Nicky Z. Accounting div. Universal C.I.T., Oklahoma City, 1953-56; cashier Okla. State Bank (name changed to Bancfirst), Konawa, 1957-89, sr. v.p., customer svc. officer, 1989—. Sec. 1st Baptist Ch., Konawa, 1969-79, mem. budgeting com., 1982—. Mem. Okla. Bankers Assn. (dir. women's div. 1974-76), Konawa C. of C., Am. Legion., Order Eastern Star. Home: RR 2 PO Box 28 Konawa OK 74849 Office: PO Box 156 Konawa OK 74849

RAINSONG, TOVAH, advanced systems worker, writer; b. Albert Lea, Minn., Mar. 17, 1950; d. Richard Patrick and Barbara Ann (Johnson) Crumb; m. Charles Collins, Mar. 1, 1980 (div. Sept. 1, 1980). BS in Recreation and Park, U. Minn., 1973. Forest worker Dept. of Natural Resources, Quilcene, Wash., 1977; motor winder NW Electric Apparatus, Inc., Port Townsend, Wash., 1978-81; union factory labor Champion Internat. Bldg. Products, Seattle, 1982; freelance The Painter Sisters, Seattle, 1983; apprentice carpenter Keiwitt & Grice Constrn., Seattle, 1984; shelving installer Design Shelving, Seattle, 1984-85; freelance Seattle, 1985-87; project mgr. Edelstein Advt. Shop, Seattle, 1986-88; integral fuel cell sealer Boeing Co., Seattle, 1989—. Buddhist. Home: 7003 Mary Ave NW Seattle WA 98117

RAITT, BONNIE LYNN, singer, musician; b. Burbank, Calif., Nov. 8, 1949. Student, Radcliffe Coll. Performer blues clubs, East Coast; concert performer tours in Britain, 1976, 77; albums include: Bonnie Raitt, 1971, Give It Up, 1972, Takin' My Time, 1973, Streetlights, 1974, Home Plate, 1975, Sweet Forgiveness, 1977, The Glow, 1979, Green Light, 1982, Nine Lives, 1986, Nick of Time, 1989. Recipient numerous Grammy nominations; four Grammy awards, 1990: album of the year, best rock vocal performance, best female pop vocal performance, best traditional blues performance (with John Lee Hooker). Office: PO Box 626 Los Angeles CA 90078*

RAIZEN, SENTA AMON, educational researcher; b. Vienna, Austria, Oct. 28, 1924; came to U.S., 1940; d. John and Helen (Krys) Amon; m. Abraham A. Raizen, Apr. 18, 1948; children: Helen S., Michael B., Daniel J. BS, Guilford Coll., 1944; MA, Bryn Mawr, 1945; Tchr. Cert., U. Va., 1960. Cert. tchr. Rsch. chemist Sun Oil Co., Norwood, Pa., 1945-48; rsch. asst. Nat. Acad. Scis., Washington, 1960-62; assoc. program dir. NSF, Washington, 1962-69, spl. asst., 1969-72; sr. researcher The Rand Corp., Washington, 1972-74; assoc. dir. Nat. Inst. Edn., Washington, 1974-78; ind. cons. Washington, 1978-80; study dir. Nat. Acad. Scis., Washington, 1980-88; dir. Nat. Ctr. for Improving Sci. Edn., Washington, 1988—; cons. Nat. Ctr. for Edn. Stats., Washington, 1987—, Nat. Opinion Rsch. Ctr., Chgo., 1988—, State Dept. Edn./Calif. and Mich., 1989—; adv. bd. Ctr. for Policy Rsch. in Edn., Rutgers U., N.J., 1988—, Ctr. for Rsch. on Elem. Subjects, East Lansing, Mich., 1988—. Editor several ency. articles, books and reports in field; contbr. articles to profl. jours. Pres. Cooperative Nursery Sch., Arlington, Va., 1953-57; leader Brownies, Girl Scouts, U.S. and Cub Scouts, Boy Scouts, Am., Arlington, 1958-64. Recipient grants NSF, 1984-88, U.S. Dept. Edn., 1980-82, fellowship for grad. study, NSF, 1944-45, Meritorious Svc. award, 1968. Fellow AAAS; mem. Am. Chem. Soc., Am. Ednl. Rsch. Assn. Home: 5513 N 31st St Arlington VA 22207 Office: Nat Ctr Improving Sci Edn 1920 L St NW Washington DC 20036

RAKICH, DAWN MICHELE, optometrist; b. Steubenville, Ohio, June 8, 1956; d. Duke and Florence (Banda) R.; m. Felix J. Martinez. OD, So. Coll. Optometry, 1983. Optometrist San Antonio Eye Assocs., 1984-86; pvt. practice optometry San Antonio, 1986—. Recipient Contact Lens award, Bauch & Lomb, 1982. Mem. Am. Optometric Assn., Tex. Optometric Assn., Bexar County Dist. Optomtric Soc. (treas. 1987), Gold Key (internat. treas. 1982-83), Omega Delta (pres. 1982, outstanding Omega Delta 1983), Zonta Internat. (San Antonio) (bd. dirs. 1986—). Eastern Orthodox. Home: 7315 Clear Rock San Antonio TX 78255 Office: 2267 NW Military Hwy San Antonio TX 78213

RAKOV, BARBARA STREEM, marketing executive; b. Bklyn., Jan. 4, 1946; d. Harold B. and Claire (Colbert) Streem; m. Harris J. Rakov, Nov. 20, 1970 (div. Mar. 1972). BS, Boston U., 1967; postgrad. NYU, 1972-74. Market rsch. analyst, product mgr., mktg. mgr. J.B. Williams, N.Y.C., 1967-77; mktg. mgr. Del Labs., Farmingdale, N.Y., 1977-78; product mgr., sr. product mgr., asst. to office of pres., dir. mktg. and sales Benelux countries, v.p. group mktg., dir., dir. new products, v.p. bus. devel. Joseph E. Seagram & Sons, 1978—, N—. Mem. L'Ordre des Coteaux de Champagne, Les Gastronomes de la Mer, Am. Mgmt. Assn. Avocations: tennis, skiing, squash, reading, water skiing. Home: 415 E 52d St New York NY 10022 Office: House of Seagram 375 Park Ave New York NY 10152

RAKOW, CANDACE DEMLER, nursing services administrator; b. Lebanon, Pa., Apr. 5, 1947; d. Lewis Frederick and Arline Claire (Hertzog) Demler; m. William W. Rakow, June 22, 1973 (div. 1988); children: Jennifer, Christopher. Diploma in nursing, Lancaster (Pa.) Gen. Hosp. Sch., 1968; BS in Nursing, Lebanon Valley Coll., Annville, Pa., 1972; MS in Psychology, U. Pa., Millersville, 1981. Registered nurse cert. in operating room nursing and sch. nursing. Supr. Cedar Haven, Lebanon, 1968-69; oper. room nurse Atlantic City (N.J.) Hosp, Franklin Med. Ctr., San Francisco, 1969-71; oper. room nurse post-anesthesia care Lancaster Gen. Hosp., 1971-72; oper. room nurse Hershey (Pa.) Med. Ctr., 1972-74; exec. dir. Lebanon County Homemaker Svc., Lebanon, 1974-76; operating room nurse Swedish Med. Ctr., Englewood, Colo., 1976; asst. dir. nursing, dir. operating room svc. Parkview Episcopal Hosp., Pueblo, Colo., 1976-81; staff nurse Hahnemann Hosp., Phila., 1981-82; staff nurse oper. room and neo-intensive care unit Children's Hosp., San Diego, 1982-85; adminstr. women's and infants pediatric oncology and cen. adminstrv. nursing svcs. The Allentown (Pa.) Hosp., Lehigh Valley Hosp. Ctr., 1985—. Active Jr. League Pueblo, 1982-84, Jr. League San Diego, 1984-85. Named Boss of Yr., Am. Bus. and Profl. Women, Pueblo, 1981. Mem. Nurses Assn. of Am. Coll. Obstetricians and Gynecologists, Assn. Operating Room Nurses, Pa. Perinatal Assn. (bd. dirs. 1986—, chair program com. 1988—). Democrat. Roman Catholic. Home: 1622 Elm St Lebanon PA 17042 Office: The Allentown Hosp 1627 Chew St Allentown PA 18102

RAKOWSKI, BARBARA ANN, principal; b. Flint, Mich., Jan. 24, 1948; d. Casimir Anthony and Harriet Ann (Craft) R.; BS, Central Mich. U., 1971, MS, 1978. Tchr. langs. and scis. Sts. Peter and Paul Area High Sch., Saginaw, Mich., 1971-79, chmn. dept. fgn. langs., 1974-79; instr. high sch. program field studies Central Mich. U., Beaver Island, Mich., 1973-81; prin., tchr. Beaver Island Community Schs., 1979-84; biologist, chair dept. sci. Sacred Heart Acad., Mt. Pleasant, Mich., 1984-89; principal Holy Familiy Middle Sch., Bay City, Mich., 1989—; cons. sci. Mich. Dept. Edn., Lansing, 1987—; mem. exec. bd. Project Learning Tree, Escanaba, Mich., 1988—. Mem. Mich. Sci. Tchrs. Assn., Sci. Edn. in Middle Sch. (cadre), Activities to Integrate Math and Sci. (cadre), Byzantine Catholic. Home: 1301 4th St Bay City MI 48708 Office: Holy Family Middle Sch 1503 Kosciuszko Ave Bay City MI 48708

RALEY, CHERI ELAINE, sales and marketing executive; b. Jacksonville, Fla., Mar. 30, 1951; d. Harvey and Helen (Bowen) Lottman; m. Donald Keith Raley, Jan. 16, 1970 (div. Oct. 1980); 1 child, Brian. Grad. high sch., Jacksonville, Fla.; cert. in bus. and real estate, Houston Community Coll.; cert. in middle mgmt., ITT, 1988. Fashion coordinator Montgomery Ward, Houston, 1970-76; freelance model Ben Shaw Studios, Houston, 1970-76; leasing cons. R&B Enterprises, Houston, 1976-80; sales, tng., mktg. and advert. mgr. ITT Employer Svcs., Encino, Calif., 1980-88; dist. mgr. Remedy Personnel Svcs., San Diego, 1988. Exhibited in group show Brushworks Gallery, San Diego, Zimm's Emporium, San Diego. Recipient Personal Progress award and Outstanding Performance award Dale Carnegie Inst., 1987, also Human Rels. award; cert. of appreciation Senator Campbell's Conf. on Women. Mem. Personnel Indsl. Rels. Assn., Calif. Assn. Temp. Svcs., Am. Soc. Tng. and Devel., San Diego C. of C., San Diego Employers Assn., San Diego Art Assn., Skits R Us. Office: Remedy Personnel Svcs 5430 Clairmont Mesa Blvd San Diego CA 92117

RALKE-KAHN, GINA LIN, social worker; b. Los Angeles, Aug. 6, 1958; d. Clifton Dee Ralke and Leona Clair (Alcantara) Berge; m. Peter Andrew Kahn; 1 child, Alexandra Simone. BA, UCLA, 1983; MS in Counseling, Loyola Coll., Towson, Md., 1988; MSW, U. Md., Balt., 1988. Child therapist UCLA Young Autism Project, Los Angeles, 1981-83; mental health worker Sheppard & Enoch Pratt Hosp., Towson, Md., 1984-85; social work intern North Charles Gen. Hosp., Balt., 1986-87, psychology intern, 1986-87; social work intern Villa Maria Childrens Residential Treatment Ctr., Timonium, Md., 1987-88; social worker, family therapist Sheppard & Enoch Pratt Hosp., Towson, 1988—. Alternate mem. Foster Care Review Bd., Balt., 1988-89. Mem. Nat. Assn. Social Workers, Am. Psychol. Assn. Democrat. Unitarian. Home: 3 Alcan Ct Towson MD 21204 Office: Sheppard & Enoch Pratt Hosp 6501 N Charles St Towson MD 21204

RALPH, DEBORAH MALONE, social services administrator, educator; b. N.Y.C., Aug. 4, 1951; d. Richard Ernest Sr. and Lottie Mae (Richardson) Malone; m. Hilroy Walton Ralph, Aug. 2, 1975; children: Jamaal, Marcus. BS with honors, SUNY, Buffalo, 1972; MSW, Columbia U., 1974. Lic. social worker, N.Y. Psychiat. social worker Arthur C. Logan Meml. Hosp., N.Y.C., 1974-77; asst. exec. dir. Community Participation Ednl. Program, N.Y.C., 1976-79; acting social work supr. Bronx Lebanon Hosp., N.Y.C., 1979-84; supr. clin. services Dept. Juvenile Justice City N.Y., 1979—, mem. Com. Women's Concerns, 1985; active project mgr. Nat. Video Conf. Sch. Social Work, Va. Commonwealth U., Richmond, 1988—; adj. prof. Coll. New Rochelle, N.Y.C., 1979—, adj. mem. faculty CCNY Sophie Davis Sch. Biomed. Edn., 1978-79; vis. prof. Tchr.'s Coll. Inst. Urban Minority Edn. Columbia U., N.Y.C., 1986, guest speaker Sch. Social Work, 1985; mem. field work adb. bd. Sch. Social Work NYU, 1986—. Mem. YMCA; site dir. after sch. program Glen Allen Elem. Sch., North Richmond and Richmond, Va., 1990; dir. 13th dist. juvenile and domestic rels. ct. Stepping Stone Group Home, Richmond, 1988—. Columbia U. scholar, 1972; recipient Innovations award Dept. Juvenile Justice Ford Found., Boston, 1986. Mem. Nat. Assn. Social Workers (cert.), Assn. Black Social Workers, Nat. Juvenile Detention Assn. Office: Va Commonwealth U Sch Social Work 1001 W Franklin St Box 2027 Richmond VA 23284-2027

RALPH, JEAN DOLORES, retired education educator, consultant; b. Detroit, Sept. 6, 1923; d. Alfred Heath and Genievieve (Taber) Smith; m. Fred A. Ralph, May 4, 1946 (dec. June 1979); children: Nancy Jean, Ellen Sue, Marty. BA, Ea. Mich. U., 1946; MA, Wayne State U., 1961; edn. specialist, U. Mich., 1973; EdD, Nova U., 1981. Cert. gifted elem. and secondary English tchr., adminstr., supr., reading specialist, Mich., Ariz., Fla. Elem. tchr. pub. schs., Harper Woods, Farmington, Mich., 1954-61; elem. prin. Farmington Pub. Schs., 1961-73; curriculum writer Nogales (Ariz.) Pub. Schs., 1973-74; elem. prin. Miami (Ariz.) Pub. Schs., 1974-75; adminstr. Tucson Hebrew Acad., 1975-76; adminstr., tchr. Santa Cruz Sch. Dist. 28, Nogales, 1976-77; dir. edn. Eckerd Wilderness Camps, Brooksville, Fla., 1977-78; prof. edn. Eckerd Coll., St. Petersburg, Fla., 1978-79; adminstr. edn. program Nova U., Orlando, Fla., 1981-86, prof. edn., 1986-89; adj. prof. Ea. Ariz. Coll., Gila County, 1974-75; tchr. gifted Orange County Schs., Orlando, 1979-83, tchr. lang. lab. for migrant children, 1983-86, Chpt. I coord., tchr. reading, 1986-89; edn. cons. Ency. Brit., 1969-73, Ariz. Dept. Edn., Phoenix, 1973-77; reading cons. Holt Winston Rinehart, 1973-75. Mem. Nat. Coun. Tchrs. English, Internat. English Reading Assn., Coun. Exceptional Children, Assn. Supervision and Curriculum Devel. Home: Rte 1 Box 754 Morganton GA 30560

RALPH, JO ANN M., insurance executive; b. Jersey City, Mar. 9, 1957; d. Leon and Lillian (Opalach) Mrowicki; m. Daniel Ralph, Apr. 7, 1979. CPCU; cert. ins. counselor. Ins. sec. Edward L. Salmon Agy., Inc., Farmingdale, N.J.; comml. account underwriter Fireman's Fund Ins. Co., San Rafael, Calif.; casualty underwriter Ins. Co. North Am., Piscataway, N.J.; v.p. Redden Agy. Inc., Fair Haven, N.J. Named N.J. Ins. Woman of Yr., 1989. Mem. NAFE, Nat. Assn. Ins. Women (regional com. chmn., mem. nat. com., officer), Soc. CPCU, Soc. CIC. Office: PO Box 262 Fair Haven NJ 07704

RALSTON, CLARICE MCDUFFIE, nurse; b. Tampa, Fla., Feb. 11, 1932; d. Welbourne Clifton and Louise Teresa (Sellers) McDuffie; R.N. diploma Gordon Keller Sch. Nursing, 1953; m. William Kent Ralston, Mar. 12, 1954; children—Diana Lynn (dec.), Stephen Kent. Staff nurse Jackson Meml. Hosp., Miami, Fla., 1953-54, New Braunfels (Tex.) Gen. Hosp., 1954-55; nurse supr. Wichita Falls (Tex.) State Hosp., 1971-84, retired, 1984; endl. coord. in-svc. tng. Care Manor Nursing Home, Burkburnett, Tex. Mem. Am. Nurses Assn. (cert. gerontol. nurse), Tex. Nurses Assn. (charter mem. continuing edn. program), Fla. State Student Nurses Assn. (charter), Tex. Pub. Employees Assn., Air Force Sgts. Assn. Aux. Am. Legion Aux. Democrat. Methodist. Club: Order Eastern Star. Research on hygiene for elderly patients. Home: 815 Preston St Burkburnett TX 76354 Office: Care Manor Nursing Home 608 Red River Expwy Burkburnett TX 76354

RALSTON, JAN ELIZABETH, computer program analyst; b. Pitts., Mar. 25, 1963; d. Robert Eugene and Dess Alyene (Bell) R. BS in Computer Sci., Pa. State U., 1985; postgrad., Nat. Technol. U., Ft. Collins, Colo., 1988-89. Computer tape libr. Gulf Oil Rsch. Ctr., Harmarville, Pa., 1982; pre-profl. programmer software mfg. IBM, Kingston, N.Y., 1984, assoc. programmer software engring., 1985-86, sr. assoc. programmer VM operating system, 1986—. Republican. Home: 7 Rondout Harbor Port Ewen NY 12466 Office: IBM Kingston 49YA-908 Neighborhood Rd Kingston NY 12401

RAMALEY, JUDITH AITKEN, academic administrator, endocrinologist; b. Vincennes, Ind., Jan. 11, 1941; d. Robert Henry and Mary Krebs (McCullough) Aitken; m. Robert Folk Ramaley, Mar. 1966 (div. 1976); children: Alan Aitken, Andrew Folk. BA, Swarthmore Coll., 1963; PhD, UCLA, 1966; postgrad., Ind. U., 1967-69. Rsch. assoc., lectr. Ind. U., Bloomington, 1967-68, asst. prof. dept. anatomy and physiology, 1969-72; asst. prof. dept. physiology and biophysics U. Nebr. Med. Ctr., Omaha, 1972-74, assoc. prof., 1974-78, prof., 1978-82, assoc. dean for rsch. and devel., 1979-81; asst. v.p. for acad. affairs U. Nebr., Lincoln, 1980-82; prof. biol. scis. SUNY, Albany, N.Y., 1982-87, v.p. for acad. affairs, 1982-85, acting pres., 1984, exec. v.p. for acad. affairs, 1985-87; exec. vice chancellor U. Kans., Lawrence, 1987-90; pres. Portland State U., Portland, Oreg.,

1990—; mem. endocrinology study sect. NIH, 1981-84; cons.-evaluator North Cen. Accreditation, 1978-82, 1989-90; mem. reculation biology panel NSF, 1979-82; mem. Ill. Commn. Scholars, 1980-90. Co-author: Progesterone Function: Molecular and Biochemical Aspects, 1972; Essentials of Histology, 8th edit., 1979; editor: Covert Discrimination, Women in the Sciences, 1978; contbr. articles to profl. jours. Bd. dirs. Family Svc. of Omaha, 197982, Albany Symphony Orch., 1984-87, mem. exec. com., 1986-87; bd. dirs. Urban League Albany, 1984-87, 2d v.p., mem. exec. com., 1986-87; bd. dirs. Upper Hudson Planned Parenthood, 1984-87, Capital Repertory Co., 1986-89; chmn. bd. dirs. Albany Water Fin. Authority, 1987; mem. exec. com. United Way Douglas County, 1989-90; mem. adv. bd. Emily Taylor women's Resource Ctr., U. Kans., 1988-90. NSF grantee, 1969-71, 71-77, 75-82, 77-80, 80-83. Fellow AAAS; mem. Endocrine Soc. (chmn. edn. com. 1980-85), Soc. Study Reprodn. (treas. 1982-85), Soc. for Neuroscis., Am. Physiol. Soc., Nat. Assn.State Univs. and Land Grant Colls. (mem. senate 1986-88), Am. Council on Edn. (chmn. commn. on women in higher edn. 1987-88), Signum Laudis. Office: Portland State Univ PO Box 751 Portland OR 97207

RAMANATHAN, ROHINI BALAKRISHNAN, banker; b. New Delhi, India, Nov. 4, 1952; came to U.S., 1972, naturalized, 1984; d. Mayuram Srinivasa Venkata and Gnanam (Sundaresan) Subramanian; m. Balakrishnan Ramanathan, July 4, 1977; children—Karthik Shankar, Ashwin Kalyan. B.A. with honors, Jesus and Mary Coll., New Delhi, 1972; M.S., Fed. City Coll., 1974; Ed.D., Boston U., 1979. Sr. media intern Fed. City Coll., Washington, 1973-75; media specialist Fashion Inst. Tech., N.Y.C., 1979-80; sr. mgmt. cons. N.Y.C. Health and Hosps., 1981-82; mgr. computer based tng. Chem. Bank, N.Y.C., 1983-88; dir. computing ctr. St. Johns U., Jamaica, N.Y., 1988-89; pres., creative dir. Images Internat. Contbr. articles to profl. jours. Editor, broadcaster news programs. Bd. dirs. ethnic fellowships Queens Coll. Grad. Library Sch., N.Y., 1980-83. N.Y.C. Police Commisioner's Asian Am. Adv. Coun. (co-chmn.); cons. Asian-Am. Ctr. Queens Coll., N.Y.; trustee Carnatic Music Acad. of N.A., N.Y.C., 1979-80. Mem. Asian Indian Women in Am. (founder 1981, editor News 1981-83), Fedn. Indian Assns. (chmn. publicity 1980-82, v.p. N.Y.C. 1986-87), Bharathi Soc. (sec. 1979-80, pres. 1988-89), Avocations: Vocal South Indian classical and other Indian light music, writing, sports. Home and Office: 171 Harris Dr Oceanside NY 11572

RAMBERG, DOROTHY CATHLEEN, juvenile court administrator; b. Northwood, N.D., Nov. 16, 1923; d. Theodore Oliver and Alma J. (Strom) Fladager; m. E. Robert Ramberg, Sept. 8, 1946; children: John Michael, David Allen, Gary Steven. Cert., Coll. Juvenile Justice, Reno, autumn 1975; cert. probation officer, Nat. Coll. Juvenile Justice, Charleston, S.C., 1986; cert., Erickson Mediation Inst., Bismarck, N.D., 1988. Clk./typist, policy writer Implement Dealers Mut. Ins. Co., Grand Forks, N.D., 1943-49, rate clk., 1943-46, asst. fire ins. underwriter, 1946-48, underwriter, 1953-59; underwriter Citizens Ins. Agy. subs. Hartford Mut. Ins. Co., Chgo., 1949-51; office mgr., sec. to dir. med. social svcs. Ill. Rsch. Hosp., Chgo., 1951-53; sec. Juvenile Ct. N.E. Cen. Jud. Dist., Grand Forks, 1953-59, asst. juvenile supr., 1969-74, juvenile supr., office adminstr., 1974—; served on numerous panels on juvenile ct. topics; past mem. jud. tng. com. Juvenile Ct. N.E. Cen. Jud. Dist.; participant 2nd Nat. Conf. Juvenile Justice, New Orleans, 1975, N.D. Conf. Social Welfare, 1969—. Pres. Lincoln PTA, Grand Forks, 1967; active N.D. Dental Aux., 1954—; pres. Tuesday Night Twilight League, Grand Forks, 1980-81, Thursday Golf League, Grand Fors, 1983-84. Recipient Cert. of Appreciation, Lions, Grand Forks, 1981, Cert. of Participation, Strait, Grand Forks, 1981. Mem. N.D. Juvenile Ct. Assn. (pres., liaison to Children and Family Svcs. div. Dept. Human Svcs. 1981-83), Elks Aux. Lutheran. Home: 4698 Belmont Rd Grand Forks ND 58201 Office: Juvenile Ct NE Cen Jud Dist 201 S 4th St PO Box 993 Grand Forks ND 58206

RAMBO, SYLVIA H., federal judge; b. Royersford, Pa., Apr. 17, 1936; d. Granville A. and Hilda E. (Leonhardt) R.; m. George F. Douglas, Jr., Aug. 1, 1970. BA, Dickinson Coll., Carlisle, Pa., 1958, JD, 1962; LLD (hon.), Wilson Coll., Chambersburg, Pa., 1980. Bar: Pa. 1962. Atty. trust dept. Bank of Del., Wilmington, 1962-63; pvt. practice Carlisle, 1963-76; public defender, then chief public defender Cumberland County, Pa., 1976; judge Ct. Common Pleas, Cumberland County, 1976-78, U.S. Dist. Ct. Middle Dist. Pa., Harrisburg, 1979—; asst. adj. prof. law Dickinson Sch. Law, 1973, 76, 77. Mem. Nat. Assn. Women Judges, Pa. Trial Lawyers Assn., Phi Alpha Delta. Democrat. Presbyterian. Office: US Dist Ct PO Box 868 Harrisburg PA 17108

RAMIREZ, LINDA SUE, nuclear medicine professional; b. Akron, Ohio, Mar. 27, 1955; d. Dennis Sterling and Helen Teresa (Haas) Keller; m. Arthur Fernando Ramirez, Oct. 17, 1980; children: Gina Marie, Kellie Lynn. BA in Allied Health, Hiram (Ohio) Coll., 1988. Technologist Robinson Meml. Hosp., Ravenna, Ohio, 1975-83, supr. nuclear medicine, 1983—. Catechist Holy Family Parish, Stow, Ohio, 1988—. Mem. Soc. Nuclear Medicine (cert. technologist. Roman Catholic. Office: Robinson Meml Hosp 6847 N Chestnut St Ravenna OH 44266

RAMIREZ, MARIA C(ONCEPCIÓN), educational administrator; d. Ines and Carlota (Cruz) R. BA, Incarnate Word Coll., San Antonio, 1966; MEd, U. Tex., Austin, 1979; postgrad., S.W. Tex. State U., San Marcos, 1980. Cert. elem. tchr., bilingual tchr., supr. Elem. tchr. regular and bilingual Edgewood Ind. Sch. Dist., San Antonio, 1966-69; elem tchr. regular and bilingual Austin (Tex.) Ind. Sch. Dist., 1969-74, bilingual program coord., 1974-89, instructional coord., 1989—. Mem. NAFE, Nat. Assn. for Bilingual Edn., Tex. Assn. for Bilingual Edn., Austin Area Assn. for Bilingual Edn., Austin Assn. for Pub. Sch. Adminstrs., Hispanic Pub. Sch. Adminstrs.

RAMIREZ-COBLAZO, LOURDES, marketing specialist; b. N.Y.C., Feb. 11, 1962; d. Jose Anthony and Irma Iris (Alvarado) Ramirez. BS, Iona Coll., 1989. Fin. aid officer Pace Bus. Sch., Yonkers, N.Y., 1982-83; with accounts payable Celanese Fibers Ops., N.Y.C., 1983-84, budget coord., 1984; sr. invoice coord. Amax Base & Precious Metals, Greenwich, Conn., 1984-86; contracts adminstr. Amax Metal Products, Greenwich, 1987-88; sales and contract adminstr. Amax Metals Refining Operation, Greenwich, 1988-89; sales and mktg. devel. specialist Climax Performance Metals, Greenwich, 1989—. Mem. Am. Mktg. Assn. (profl.), Am. Mgmt. Assn., NAFE. Office: Climax Performance Metals Amax Ctr PO Box 1700 Greenwich CT 06836

RAMO, VIRGINIA M. SMITH, civic worker; b. Yonkers, N.Y.; d. Abraham Harold and Freda (Kasnetz) Smith; B.S. in Edn., U. So. Calif., D.H.L. (hon.), 1978; m. Simon Ramo; children—James Brian, Alan Martin. Nat. co-chmn. ann. giving U. So. Calif., 1968-70, vice chmn., trustee, 1971—, co-chmn. bd. councilors Sch. Performing Arts, 1975-76, co-chmn. bd. councillors Schs. Med. and Engring.; vice-chmn. bd. overseers Hebrew Union Coll., 1972-75; bd. dirs. The Muses of Calif. Mus. Sci. and industry, UCLA Affiliates, Estelle Doheny Eye Found., U. So. Calif. Sch. Medicine; adv. council Los Angeles County Heart Assn., chmn. com. to endow Chair in cardiology at U. So. Calif.; vice-chmn., bd. dirs. Friends of Library U. So. Calif.; bd. dirs., nat. pres. Achievement Rewards for Coll. Scientists Found., 1975-77; bd. dirs. Les Dames Los Angeles, Community TV So. Calif.; bd. dirs., v.p. Founders Los Angeles Music Center; v.p. Los Angeles Music Center Opera Assn.; v.p. corp. bd. United Way; v.p. Blue Ribbon-400 Performing Arts Council; chmn. com. to endow chair in gerontology U. So. Calif.; vice chmn. campaign Doheny Eye Inst., 1986. Recipient Service award Friends of Libraries, 1974; Nat. Community Service award Alpha Epsilon Phi, 1975; Disting. Service award Am. Heart Assn. 1978; Service award U. So. Calif.; Spl. award U. So. Calif. Music Alumni Assn., 1979; Life Achievement award Mannequins of Los Angeles Assistance League, 1979; Woman of Yr. award PanHellenic Assn., 1981; Disting. Service award U. So. Calif. Sch. Medicine, 1981; U. So. Calif. Town and Gown Recognition award, 1986; Asa V. Call Achievement award U. So. Calif., 1986; Phi Kappa Phi scholarship award U. So. Calif., 1986. Mem. UCLA Med. Aux., U. So. Calif. Pres.'s Circle, Commerce Assos. U. So. Calif., Cedars of Lebanon Hosp. Women's Guild (dir. 1967-68), Blue Key, Skull and Dagger.

RAMOS, CARMEN R., psychiatrist; b. San Juan, P.R., Nov. 28, 1948; d. Francisco and Carmen (Vega) R. Student, Coll. of Notre Dame Md., 1966-68; BS, Boston U., 1970; MD, SUNY, Buffalo, 1974. Diplomate Am. Bd. Psychiatry and Neurology. Fellow in neurology and neurophysiology SUNY, Buffalo, 1972; Am. Cancer Soc. fellow in neurology and neurophysiology Maida Hosp., London, 1972; resident in psychiatry Tulane U. Sch. Medicine, New Orleans, 1974-77, resident in child psychiatry, 1980-81, 87; pvt. practice New Orleans, 1977-82, 1988—; chief inpatient psychiatry VA Hosp., New Orleans, 1982-85; dir. adolescent unit S.E. Hosp., Mandeville, La., 1985-86. Bd. dirs. YWCA, New Orleans, 1990—. Fellow Am. Orthopsychiat. Assn.; mem. Am. Acad. Child and Adolescent Psychiatry, Am. Psychiat. Assn., Am. Soc. Adolescent Psychiatry, Am. Med. Women's Assn., La. Psychiat. Assn. Office: 3801 N Causeway Blvd Metaire LA 70002

RAMOS, LINDA MARIE, endoscopy technician; b. San Jose, Calif., July 8, 1961; d. Albert Sequeira and Catherine Marie (Souza) Vieira; m. John Bettencourt Ramos, June 12, 1982. AA, De Anza Coll., 1986; BA, St. Mary's Coll. Calif., Moraga, Calif., 1988. Cert. gastrointestinal clinician. Endoscopy technician O'Connor Hosp., San Jose, 1979—; instr. aerobic, Mountain View, Calif., O'Connor Hosp., San Jose, Calif. Contbr. articles to profl. jours. Vol. O'Connor Hosp., 1975-79; active campaign Santa Clara City Council, 1980-81. Fellow Irmandade Da Festa Do Espirito Santo (sec. 1974-82, queen 1975-76), Soc. Gastrointestinal Assts., No. Soc. Gastrointestinal Assts., Soc. Espirito Santo of Santa Clara, Luso Am. Fraternal Fedn. (state youth pres. 1979-80, youth leader local coun. Santa Clara Mountain View 1979-87, scholar, 1979, founder, organizer Mountain View-Santa Clara chpt. 1980, pres. local region 1980-84, state 20-30 pres. 1984-85, state dir. youth programs 1988—). Republican. Roman Catholic. Home: 1101 Civic Center Dr 10 Santa Clara CA 95050 Office: O'Connor Hosp 2105 Forest Ave San Jose CA 95126

RAMOS, LUCIE ELLEN TEMPLIN, mechanical engineer, automotive executive; b. Royal Oak, Mich., Mar. 19, 1959; d. Robert James and Ellen Norine (Mulvihill) Templin; m. John Albert Ramos, June 28, 1986. BSME, U. So. Calif., 1981; MSMSE, Stanford U., 1985. Registered profl. engr., Mich. Sr. assoc. engr. Gen. Tech. Div. IBM, Manassas, Va., 1981-85; assoc. adminstr. Delco Moraine Div. Gen. Motors, Dayton, Ohio, 1985-86; sr. project engr. Advanced Engring. Staff GM, Warren, Mich., 1986—; Inventor: Feed bowl alignment fixture, 1982; co-inventor: transparent stop alignment jig, 1983. Mem. Tau Beta Pi. Home: 1003 Fremont Ave Menlo Park CA 94025 Office: Gen Motors AES 30300 Mound Rd Mfg Bldg B/MD-54 Warren MI 48090-9040

RAMOS, OLGA LETICIA, dialysis technician; b. Laredo, Tex., Sept. 3, 1956; d. Jesus and Eida Amparo (Salazar) R. Quimico Pharm. Biology, U. Autonoma de Coahuile, Mex., 1979. Lab. technician Dr. V.H. Mata Clinic, Laredo, 1980-85; dialysis technician Laredo Kidney Ctr., 1982-84, dialysis re-use technician, 1984-89, asst. dialysis chief technician, 1989—. Home: 204 Maguey Dr Laredo TX 78041

RAMP, MARJORIE JEAN SUMERWELL, civic worker; b. Kansas City, Mo., July 20, 1924; d. Walter Francis and Helen Louise (Nichols) Sumerwell; m. Floyd Lester Ramp, Sept. 4, 1948; children: David L., Sandra Jean, Paul F., Cheryl Louise. BS in Nursing Edn., U. Minn., 1948. RN, Minn. Instr. nursing edn. U. Minn., Mpls., 1948-50; adminstrv. asst. to assn. minister Western Res. Assn. of Ohio Conf. United Ch. of Christ, Cleve., 1983-85. Former chmn. hunger task force Ohio Conf. of United Ch. of Christ, moderator, 1981-82, moderator West. Res. Assn., 1976-77, mem. nat. exec. coun., N.Y.C., 1983-89, mem. nat. bd. for world ministries, 1971-82; past bd. dirs. Western Res. coun. Girl Scouts U.S.; nat. sec. Campaign for UN Reform, Washington, 1987—; pres. Cleve.-Volgograd Ptnr. Cities, 1988—; coord., co-founder Richfield-Wolfach Twin City Program, 1970—; mem. numerous local and nat. peace groups. Recipient Golden Trefoil award Western Res. coun. Girl Scouts U.S.A., 1972; named Outstanding Women of Ohio Conf., Gen. Synod United Ch. of Christ, 1985. Mem. World Federalist Assn. (chmn. Ohio 1985—), Delta Kappa Gamma (hon.). Home: 3948 Humphrey Rd Richfield OH 44286

RAMPINO, MARJORIE, corporate manager; b. N.Y.C., Aug. 2, 1949; d. Joseph and Constance Rampino; m. Richard Johnson, Nov. 25, 1978 (div. Mar. 1980). BA, Hunter Coll., CUNY, 1974; M Graphoanalysis, Internat. Graphoanalysis Soc., 1989. Kindergarten tchr. Dept. Edn., N.Y.C., NSW, Australia, 1975-77; rep., analyst, programmer Olivetti Corp., 1977-79; sales support rep. Standard & Poors, N.Y.C., 1980-81, applications cons., 1981-82, sales support supr., 1982-84, sales support mgr., 1984-87, dir. Blue List ops., 1987-89, gen. mgr., 1989—. Vol. Cath. Big Sisters, N.Y.C., 1985—. Mem. Internat. Graphoanalysis Soc. (treas. N.Y. chpt. 1988-89), N.Y. Women's Mcpl. Bond Club, Am. Mensa. Home: 25-65 32d St Astoria NY 11102 Office: Standard & Poors 25 Broadway New York NY 10004

RAMSAY, JANICE SUSAN, computer programmer, analyst; b. Nashville, Ark., Aug. 20, 1952; d. Reginald Carlyle and Jesse Evelyn (Hill) R. BA in English, Ariz. State U., 1977. With data ops. Maricopa County Govt., Phoenix, 1973-82, programmer analyst I, 1982-84, programmer analyst II, 1984-86; sr. programmer analyst Peralta Community Colls., Oakland, Calif., 1986—. Author: Recovery Techniques, 1984, User-Friendly FAMS, 1985. Active Sierra Club, World Wildlife. Mem. Assn. for Women in Computing, No. Calif. Profls., Assn. Systems Mgmt. Home: 1715 Grand St Alameda CA 94501 Office: East Bay Mcpl Utilities Dist PO Box 24055 Oakland CA 94623

RAMSAY, PATRICIA LEYDEN, academic support administrator; b. Virginia, Minn., Oct. 5, 1935; d. Ralph Calvin Leyden and Marion (Imo) Kelly; m. O. Bertrand Ramsay, Apr. 12, 1962; 1 child, C. Sean. AA, Stephens Coll., 1954; BA, U. Mo., 1956; MA, Ind. U., 1957. Instr. fgn. langs., dir. lang. lab. Mary Baldwin Coll., Staunton, Va., 1957-59; asst. prof., dir. lang. lab. U. Pacific, Stockton, Calif., 1960-62; instr. ESL Kendall Coll., Evanston, Ill., 1964-65; media asst. Eastern Mich. U., Ypsilanti, 1974-80, supr. instructional support ctr., 1980-86, coordinator instructional support ctr., 1986—; mem. planning com. Instructional Support Ctr., Eastern Mich. U., 1978-80. Pres. bd. trustees 1st Unitarian Ch., Ann Arbor, Mich., 1976-78. Mem. Internat. Assn. Learning Labs., Nat. Assn. Devel. Edn., Assn. Edn. Communications Tech., Midwest Coll. Learning Ctr. Assn., Mich. Assn. Computer Users in Learning, Phi Theta Kappa, Phi Beta Kappa. Office: Eastern Mich U ISC 102 Univ Library Ypsilanti MI 48197

RAMSEY, ELIZABETH M(APELSDEN), physician, placentologist; b. N.Y.C., Feb. 17, 1906; d. Charles Cyrus and Grace (Keys) Ramsey; grad. Bishop's Sch., LaJolla, Calif.; BA, Mills Coll., 1928; fellow Inst. Internat. Edn., Hamburg, Germany, 1928-29; MD, Yale U., 1932; DSc, Med. Coll. Pa., 1965; m. Hans Alexander Klagsbrunn, Jan. 27, 1934. Intern, asst. resident New Haven Hosp., 1932-34; asst. pathology Yale U., 1933-34; asso. pathology George Washington U., 1934-41, professorial lectr., 1941-55; asst. chief Office Med. Info., NRC, 1942-45; guest investigator dept. embryology Carnegie Inst., Washington, 1934-51, research assoc. and pathologist, 1951-63, staff mem. placentalogy and pathology, 1963-71, research assoc., 1976—; Mamie A. Jessup vis. prof. ob-gyn. U. Va. Sch. Medicine, 1972-76; Bartholomew Mosse Meml. lectr. Rotunda Hosp., Dublin, Ireland, 1970; professorial lectr. ob-gyn. Georgetown U. Sch. Medicine, 1981—. Bd. dirs. Nat. Symphony Orch., 1949—, 2d v.p., 1952-55, mem. exec. com., 1955-64, 67-68, 73-79, chmn., 1955-61, pres. women's com., 1950-52; trustee Cathedral Choral Soc., 1967-81, 83—. Recipient Alumna of Year citation Bishop's Sch., 1960, Lewis prize Am. Philos. Soc., 1970, diplome d'Honneur, Federation Internationale de Gynecologie Infantile et Juvenile, 1972. Hon. fellow Chgo. Gynec. Soc.; mem. Audubon Naturalist Soc. Central Atlantic States (dir. 1961-64), Am. Assn. Anatomists (exec. com. 1963-66, v.p. 1974-76), Am. Coll. Obstetricians and Gynecologists (hon. assoc., recipient disting. service award 1976, named to Hall of Fame 1985), Am. Gynecol. Obstet. Soc. (hon.), Perinatal Research Soc. (charter), Soc. Gynecologic Investigation (hon., recipient Pres.'s Disting. Scientist award 1987), AAAS, Acad. Med. Scis. (Cordoba, Argentina) (acad. fgn. corr.), Soc. Perinatal Obstetricians, Deans Coun. Yale U. Sch. Medicine, Phi Beta Kappa, Sigma Xi. Episcopalian. Club: City Tavern. Author: The Placenta of Laboratory Animals and Man, 1975; (with Martin W. Donner) Placental Vasculature and Circulation, 1980; The Placenta, Human and Animal, 1982; mem. editorial bd. Placenta jour., Trophoblastic Research jour. Contbr. to profl. jours. Home: 3420 Quebec St NW Washington DC 20007 also: Salem Farm Rt 1 Box 600 Purcellville VA 22132

RAMSEY, INEZ LINN, librarian, educator; b. Martins Ferry, Ohio, Apr. 25, 1938; d. George and Leona (Smith) Linn; m. Jackson Euguene Ramsey, Apr. 22, 1961; children—John Earl, James Leonard. B.A. in Hist. SUNY-Buffalo, 1971; M.L.S., 1972; Ed.D. in Audiovisual Edn., U. Va., 1980. Librarian Iroquois Central High Sch., Elma, N.Y., 1971-73, Lucy Simms Elem. Sch., Harrisonburg, Va., 1973-75; instr. James Madison U., Harrisonburg, 1975-80, asst. prof., 1980-85; assoc. prof. 1985—; mem. Va. State Library Bd., Richmond, 1975-80; cons.; librarian, book reviewer Harrisonburg-Rockingham County Assn. for Retired Citizens. Contr. to Enclopedia, articles to profl. jours.; author (with Jackson E. Ramsey): Budgeting Basics, Library Planning and Budgeting; project dir. Oral (tape) History Black Community in Harrisonburg, 1977-78; storyteller, puppeteer. Mem. Harrisonburg Republican City Com., 1981-83. Recipient spl. citation for service Va. Readathon Program, Harrisonburg, 1977; rsch. grantee James Madison U., Harrisonburg, 1981, Commonwealth Ctr. State Va., 1989. Mem. ALA, Am. Assn. Sch. Librarians, Assn. Edn. Communications, Tech., Children's Lit. Assn., Puppeteers Am., Nat. Assn. Preservation and Perpetuation of Storytelling, Va. Ednl. Media Assn. (sec. 1981-83, citation 1983 pres. 1985-86, Educator of Yr. award 1984-85, Meritorious Service award 1987-88), Phi Beta Kappa (pres. Shenandoah chpt. 1980-81), Children and Young Adults Round Table (exec. bd. 1977-80), Va. Library Assn., Beta Phi Mu. Home: 282 Franklin St Harrisonburg VA 22801 Office: James Madison U Dept Ednl Resources Harrisonburg VA 22807

RAMSEY, JULIE D., financial executive; b. Nashville, Feb. 27, 1966; d. William Jerome and Frances Marie (Barnes) Dodd; m. Ronnie Ramsey, July 19, 1986. BA cum laude, Maryville (Tenn.) Coll., 1988. Accounts payable, vacation relief Ryder Truck Rental, Inc., Nashville, 1985, 86; sales assoc. Lerner, Inc., Maryville, 1986-87; front-line pers. First Fed. Savs. and Loan, Maryville, 1987-88; budget analyst Dept. of Energy, Oak Ridge, 1988—. Div. rep. Combined Fed. Campaign. Mem. Federally Employed Women (v.p. Oak Ridge chpt.), Alpha Gamma Sigma. Presbyterian. Home: Rte 1 Box 338 White Wing Rd Lenoir City TN 37771 Office: Box 2001 Oak Ridge TN 37831

RAMSEY, LUCILLE AVRA, community relations organization administrator; b. N.Y., Mar. 3, 1942; d. Albert and Mazie (Gordon) Miller; m. Charles Allen Ramsey, April 1, 1936; children: Ramsey, Jacqueline, Aaron (dec.). BS, U. San Francisco, 1986. Office mgr. Quicksilver Products Inc., San Francisco, 1962-66; exec. sec. Far West Lab. for Educ. Rsch. and Devel., San Francisco and Berkeley, Calif., 1966-68; office mgr. The Ark Pub. Co., Tiburon, Calif., 1973-75; adminstrv. asst. Nat. Coun. Jewish Women, San Francisco, 1979-80; asst. to the chief Tiburon Fire Protection Dist., 1980; exec. dir. Zionist Orgn. Am., San Francisco, 1980-87; asst. dir. Bay Area Coun. for Soviet Jews, San Francisco, 1987-89; exec. dir. Jewish Community Rels. Coun., Oakland, Calif., 1989—; leader first ever interreligious task force to the USSR. Author: Concerns of the Jewish Community 1930's/1970's. Civic organizer, planner, chairperson Marin County Clergy Group, San Rafael, Calif., 1975-79. Democratic. Jewish. Office: Jewish Community Rels Coun 401 Grand Ave Ste 500 Oakland CA 94610

RAMSEY, PAMELA PRATT, advertising executive; b. Columbus, Ohio, Aug. 27, 1961; d. John Eli and Leona Mae (Longshore) Pratt; m. Bruce Mitchell Ramsey, May 21, 1983. Student, U. Fla., 1981; BSA, Fla. Atlantic U., 1983. Account exec., media buyer, copywriter Mktg. Cons. Inc., West Palm Beach, Fla., 1981-84; dir. account svcs. Lawrence, Prather and Welsh, West Palm Beach, 1984-85; v.p., dir. account svcs. Hanna, Ramsey & Co., Inc., West Palm Beach, 1985-89; v.p., account exec. M.B.I. Advt./Mktg., Palm Beach Gardens, Fla., 1989—. Mem. communications com. Pvt. Sector Initiatives, West Palm Beach, 1983-84, Adopt-A-Family, West Palm Beach, 1986—, chmn. bd. dirs., 1988—; mem. art in pub. places com. City of West Palm Beach, 1990-93. Recipient Up and Comers award South Fla. Bus. Jour., 1988, 89. Mem. AMA, Ad Club of Palm Beaches, Nat. Assn. Female Execs., Beta Gamma Sigma. Home: 7791 Nemec Dr S West Palm Beach FL 33406 Office: MBI Advt/Mktg 11000 Prosperity Farms Rd Ste 302 Palm Beach Gardens FL 33410

RAMSEY, REVA SNELSON, retired banker; b. Leicester, N.C., Mar. 4, 1934; d. Alonzo Ambrose and Ethel Clementine (Hawkins) Snelson; m. Garrett Charles Ramsey, Aug. 7, 1954; 1 child, Gary Philip. Student, Blanton's Bus. Coll., Asheville, N.C., 1952, Am. Inst. Banking, Asheville, 1970, Wilson Learning Corp., Winston-Salem, N.C., 1976. Personal and comml. loan officer, personal banker Wachovia Bank & Trust Co. Developed personal banker lending manual. Bd. dirs., treas. Meals on Wheels of Asheville and Buncombe County. Mem. Am. Bus. Women's Assn., Am. Inst. Banking. Baptist. Address: 101 Sunset Ridge Leicester NC 28748

RAN, SHULAMIT, composer; b. Tel Aviv, Oct. 21, 1949; came to U.S., 1963; Studied composition with, Paul Ben-Haim; student, Mannes Coll. Music, N.Y.C., 1963-67. With dept. music U. Chgo., 1973—, prof. music; composer-in-residence Chgo. Symphony Orch., 1990—. Compositions include 10 Children's Scenes, 1967, Structures, 1968, 7 Japanese Love Poems, 1969, O the Chimneys, 1970, 3 Fantasy Pieces, 1972, Ensembles for 17, 1975, Sonata Brevis, 1975, Double Vision, 1977, Piano Concerto, 1977, For an Actor: Monolog for Clarinet, 1978, Apprehensions, 1979, Private Game, 1979, Fantasy-Variations, 1980, Excursions, 1980, A Prayer, 1982, Verticals, 1983, Sonata-Waltzer, 1983; composer, and soloist for 1st performances Capriccio, 1963, Symphonic Poem, 1967, Concert Piece, 1971. Recipient Acad. Inst. Arts and Letters award, 1989. Office: U Chgo Dept Music 5801 S Ellis Ave Chicago IL 60637*

RANCOUR, JOANN SUE, nurse; b. Elyria, Ohio, Nov. 10, 1939; d. Joseph and Ann (Donich) Sokol; diploma M.B. Johnson Sch. Nursing, 1960; BS in Profl. Arts, St. Josephs Coll., N. Windham, Maine, 1981; student in psychology Alfred Adler Inst., Chgo., 1976—, Lorain County Community Coll., 1973-75, Ursuline Coll., Cleve., 1976, Baldwin Wallace Coll., 1982; m. Richard Lee Rancour, July 29, 1961; children: Kathleen Ann, Donna Marie. RN. Staff nurse Elyria Meml. Hosp., 1960-62, 72-75, head nurse psychiat. unit, 1975-79; sec.-treas. Alfred Adler Inst. Cleve., 1978-79; nurse Lorain County Juvenile Detention Home, Elyria, 1980; nurse VA Med. Center, Brecksville, Ohio, 1981—; mem. Cleve. VA nursing bioethics com. Active PTA, yearbook com., 1969-70, co-chmn. ways and means, 1971; Democratic poll worker, 1971-72; sec. St. Mary's Confrat. Christian Doctrine Program, 1970-71. Mem. Am. Nurses Assn. (cert. generalist practitioner psychiat. and mental health nursing practice), Ohio Nurses Assn., Lorain County Dist. Nurses Assn., Nurses Orgn. of VA (NOVA), N.Am. Soc. Adlerian Psychology. Roman Catholic. Home: 205 Denison Ave Elyria OH 44035

RAND, JOELLA M., nursing educator; b. Akron, Ohio, July 9, 1932; d. Harry S. and Elizabeth May (Miller) Halberg; m. Martin Rand; children: Craig, Debbi Stark. BSN, U. Akron, 1961, MEd in Guidance, 1968; PhD in Higher Edn. Adminstrn., Syracuse U., 1981. Staff nurse Akron Gen. Hosp., 1953-54; staff-head nurse-instr. Summit County Receiving, Cuyahoga Falls, Ohio, 1954-56; head nurse psychiat. unit Akron Gen. Hosp., 1956-57; instr. psychiatric nursing Summit County Receiving, Cuyahoga Falls, 1957-61; head nurse, in-service instr. Willard (N.Y.) State Hosp., 1961-62; asst. prof. Alfred (N.Y.) U., 1962-76, assoc. prof., assoc. dean, 1976-78, acting dean, 1978-79, dean, 1979-89, dean coll. profl. studies, 1989-90, prof. nursing, 1990—; cons. N.Y. State Regents Program for Non-Collegiate Sponsored Instrn., 1984, Collegiate Programs for N.Y. State Dept. Edn., 1985. Recipient Teaching Excellence award Alfred U., 1977, Mary E. Gladwin Outstanding Alumni award Akron U. Coll. Nursing, 1983. Mem. N.Y. State Coun. of Deans (treas. 1984-88), Genesee Regional Consortium (v.p.), Sigma Theta Tau (treas. Alfred chpt. 1984-85), Genesee Valley Edn. Com. (chair 1984-86). Office: Alfred U Div Nursing 3690 East Ave Rochester NY 14618

RAND, MARTHA ELIZABETH, mental health clinician; b. N.Y.C., Nov. 30, 1950; d. Arthur and Jean (MacNeish) R.; m. David Louis Ryzman, Apr. 20, 1986. BA, CUNY, 1972; cert. in dance and movement therapy, Inst. of Sociotherapy, N.Y.C., 1978; MA, New Sch. for Social Rsch., N.Y.C., 1982; diploma, Swedish Inst., 1985; M in Social Work, Fordham U., 1990. Adj. prof. yoga and dance Queensborough Community Coll., Queens, N.Y., 1978, 80; dep. dir. communications and spl. projects N.Y. State Spl. Prosecutor for Health, Social Svc. and Welfare, N.Y.C., 1978-79; instr. phys. edn. YWCA., N.Y.C., 1981-82, Human Rels. Ctr. New Sch. for Social Rsch., 1980-82;

ptnr. Help Yourself Assocs., N.Y.C. and Montclair, N.J., 1981—; recreation dir. Coler Hosp., N.Y.C., 1985-86; ptnr. Lively Earth Yoga Studio, N.Y.C., 1984-85; staff clinician inpatient and intermediate care program eating disorders unit St. Clare's Hosp., Boonton, N.J., 1986—; ptnr. Lively Earth Yoga Studio, N.Y.C., 1984-85; dance therapist Very Spl. Arts N.J., 1989. Mem. Am. Massage Therapy Assn., Internat. Assn. Eating Disorder Profls. (cert. eating disorder therapist), Am. Group Psychotherapy Assn.

RANDALL, CLAIRE, church executive; b. Dallas, Oct. 15, 1919; d. Arthur Godfrey and Annie Laura (Fulton) R. A.A., Schreiner Coll., 1948; BA, Scarritt Coll., 1950; DD (hon.), Berkeley Sem., Yale U., 1974; LHD (hon.), Austin Coll., 1982; LLD, Notre Dame U., 1984. Assoc. missionary edn. Bd. World Missions Presbyterian Ch., U.S., Nashville, 1949-57; dir. art Gen. Council Presbyterian Ch., U.S., Atlanta, 1957-61; dir. Christian World Mission, program dir., assoc. dir. Ch. Women United, N.Y.C., 1962-73; gen. sec. Nat. Council Ch. of Christ in U.S.A., N.Y.C., 1974-84; nat. pres. Ch. Women United, N.Y.C., 1988—. Mem. Nat. Commn. on Internat. Women's Yr., 1975-77, Martin Luther King Jr. Fed. Holiday Commn., 1985. Recipient Woman of Yr. in Religion award Heritage Soc., 1977; Empire State Woman of Yr. in Religion award State of N.Y., 1984; medal Order of St. Vladimir, Russian Orthodox Ch., 1984. Democrat. Presbyterian. Home: 155 W 68th St New York NY 10023

RANDALL, HERMINE MARIA, power plant engineer; b. Vienna, Austria, July 22, 1927; came to U.S., 1948; d. Heinrich Georg Adametz and Maria Antonia (Paul) Safranek; m. May 25, 1948 (div. 1975); children: George Eugene, Dorothy Maria. Lic. 1st class stationary engr., Mass. Shift supr. Stony Brook Generating Sta. Mass. Mcpl. Wholesale Electric Co., Ludlow, 1980-82; chief engr. power plant U. Mass., Amherst, 1982-87, mgr. utility generation and distbn., 1987-90, acting dir. engring., 1990—. Recipient spl. achievement award Region I, U.S. Dept. Labor, 1980, Chancellor's Citation U. Mass., 1990, Citation for Outstanding Performance, Commonwealth of Mass., 1990. Mem. Nat. Assn. Power Engrs. (pres. Springfield chpt. 1989-90), Assn. Energy Engrs. Republican. Home: 4 Pope's Way Hadley MA 01035 Office: U Mass Phys Plant Amherst MA 01003

RANDALL, LINDA L., nurse; b. Williamson, W.Va., Nov. 5, 1945; d. Opal Ferne (Chapman) C.; diploma St. Mary's Hosp. Sch. Nursing, Huntington, W.Va., 1966; postgrad. W.Va. U., 1969, Marshall U., 1971, St. Joseph's Coll., North Windham, Maine, 1978, U. Central Fla., 1982—; cert. emergency nurse; m. Steven Edward Randall, Oct. 12, 1974. Charge nurse ICU and CCU, St. Mary's Hosp., Huntington, 1966-68; supr. ICU and CCU, Drs. Meml. Hosp., Huntington, 1968-73; team leader CCU, Community Hosp., Springfield, Ohio, 1973-74; charge nurse Urbana (Ohio) Care Center, 1974, dir. nursing services, 1974-78; dir. nursing services The Palms Health Care Center, Sebring, Fla., 1978-79; asst. head nurse, emergency and employee health services Ringling Bros., Barnum & Bailey Circus World, Orlando, Fla., 1979-80; asst. charge nurse emergency dept. Halifax Hosp. Med. Center, Daytona Beach, Fla., 1980-82; supr. operating room and post anesthesia Daytona Beach (Fla.) Gen. Hosp., 1982-83; head nurse emergency dept. Community Hosp. of Bunnell (Fla.), 1983-84; charge nurse emergency dept. Fla. Hosp. Med. Ctr., Orlando, 1984-86; occupational health nurse Repco Inc., Orlando, 1986-90; corp. nurse mgr. Am. Automobile Assn., Heathrow, Fla., 1990—; mem. trauma staff Daytona Beach Internat. Speedway, 1981-86; program dir. SW div. W.Va. Heart Assn., 1969-73; bd. dirs. Ohio Hi-Point Joint Vocat. Sch. Allied Health Fields. Recipient Dr. Frist Humanitarian award Hosp. Corp. of Am., 1984. Mem. Nat. League Nursing, Am., Fla. nurses assns., Emergency Dept. Nurses Assn., Am. Heart Assn. (basic life support instr. 1981, advanced cardiac life support 1982), Am. Assn. Critical Care Nurses, Am. Assn. Occupational Health Nurses, Fla. Assn. Ocupational Health Nurses, Defenders of Wildlife, Fla. Audubon Soc., Fla. Wildlife Found., Nat. Audubon Soc., Nat. Wildlife Found., Fla. Wildlife Assn., Cousteau Soc. Republican. Roman Catholic. Home: 435 Tulane Dr Altamonte Springs FL 32714 Office: Am Automobile Assn Internat Hdqrs Heathrow FL 32714

RANDALL, LINDA LEA, biochemist, educator; b. Montclair, N.J., Aug. 7, 1946; d. Lowell Neal and Helen (Watts) R.; m. Gerald Lee Hazelbauer, Aug. 29, 1970. BS, Colo. State U., 1968; PhD, U. Wis., 1971. Postdoctoral fellow Inst. Pasteur, Paris, 1971-73; asst. prof. Uppsala (Sweden) U., 1975-81; assoc. prof. Washington State U., Pullman, 1981-83, prof. biochemistry, 1983—; guest scientist Wallenberg Lab., Uppsala U., 1973-75; study section NIH, 1984-88. Editorial bd. Jour. of Bacteriology, 1982—; co-editor: Virus Receptors Part I, 1980; contbr. articles to profl. jours. Recipient Eli Lilly Award in Microbiology and Immunology, Am. Soc. Microbiology, Am. Assn. Immunologists, Am. Soc. Exptl. Pathology, 1984, Faculty Excellence Award in Rsch., Washington State U., 1988, Disting. Faculty Address, 1990. Mem. Am. Microbiol. Soc., AAAS, Am. Soc. Biol. Chemists, Protein Soc. Office: Washington State U. Biochemistry/Biophysic Dept Pullman WA 99164-4660

RANDALL, LOLLY (PRISCILLA RANDALL), manufacturers' representative; b. Boston, Aug. 15, 1952; d. Raymond Victor and Priscilla (Richmond) R.; m. Harold Glen Middleton, Dec. 7, 1983; children: Priscilla Eva. B. Arts and Scis., U. Colo., 1973. Asst. to dir. pub. relations Pepsi Cola Co., Mpls., 1975; sales rep. DiCosta Knits, Ltd., San Francisco, 1975-76, Lilli Ann Corp., San Francisco, 1976-78; owner Lolly & Co., Seattle, 1978—; dir. 6100 Bldg. Assn., Seattle, 1981. Mem. Pacific N.W. Toy Assn. (pub. relations officer 1981-82, founding mem. 1981). Republican. Episcopalian. Avocations: volunteer work in field of recovering alcoholics, skiing. Home: 418 SW 189th St Seattle WA 98166 Office: Lolly & Co 6100 4th Ave S #355 Seattle WA 98108

RANDALL, LYNN ELLEN, librarian; b. Chgo., Oct. 10, 1946; d. Ward W. and Hazel A. (Nettles) R. BA, King's Coll., 1970; MA, Seton Hall U., 1973; MLS, Rutgers U., 1978. Libr. N.J. Inst. Tech., Newark, 1970-75; libr. dir. N.E. Bible Coll., Essex Fells, N.J., 1975-81; reference libr. Seton Hall U., South Orange, N.J., 1983-85; dir. libr. services Berkeley Sch., West Paterson, N.J., 1985-89, libr. dir. Caldwell Coll., 1989—; reference librarian, instr. Morris (N.J.) County Coll., 1981-83. Mem. Union County (N.J.) Heritage Commn., 1975-76. Mem. Middle States Assn. Bible Colls., Am. Assn. Bible Colls. (evaluator 1977, 79, 84), ALA (treas. Libr. Instrn. Round Table 1989—), N.J. Libr. Assn. (chair automated libr. services com. 1986-88, conf. program 1987—, chair exhibits com. 1989—, editor newsletter 1982-84, 87-89), N.J. Libr. Network (pres. Region II 1987-89), Assn. Coll. and Research Librs. (com.). Co-author: N.J. Online Directory, 1983. Editor N.J. Librs., fall 1984, spring 1986. Home: 173 Ridge Rd Apt #H7 Cedar Grove NJ 07009

RANDALL, PATRICIA MARY, temporary employment firm executive; b. Boston, June 12, 1948; d. Alfred Earl Randall and Evangeline A. (McHugh) Freitag; m. Richard Paul James, June 26, 1982 (div. 1989); children: David, Jennifer; m. Scott Darren Graff, Jan. 1, 1990. BA in Philosophy, Bridgewater (Mass.)State Coll., 1980. Owner, mgr. The Indoor Garden, Brockton, Mass., 1972-78; dining room mgr. Red Coach Grill Cambridge, Mass., 1981-82, Boston Ramada, Allston, Mass., 1982-85; br. mgr. The Resource Group, Cambridge, 1985—. Roman Catholic. Home: PO Box 1361 Cambridge MA 02238 Office: The Resource Group 122 Mount Auburn St Cambridge MA 02238

RANDALL, PRISCILLA RICHMOND, travel executive; b. Arlington, Mass., Mar. 19, 1926; d. Harold Bours and Florence (Hoefler) Richmond; m. Raymond Victor Randall, Mar. 2, 1946; children: Raymond Richmond, Priscilla Randall Middleton, Susan Randall Geery. Student, Wellesley Coll., 1943-44; Assoc., Garland Coll., 1946; student, Winona State U., 1977-81. Pub. relations dir. Rochester Meth. Hosp., Rochester, Minn., 1960-69; dir. pub relations Sheraton Rochester, 1969-71; pres. Med. Charters, Rochester, 1970-75, Ideas Unltd., Rochester, 1969-77; chief exec. officer Randall Travel, Rochester, 1977-89; pres. Randall Travel Delray, Delray Beach, Fla., 1989—; pres. Bar Harbour Apts. Inc., Delray Beach, 1989. Editor, Inside Story, 1960-69, Rochester Meth. Hosp. News, 1960-69; producer Priscilla's World, 1972-75. Pres. Rochester Meth. Hosp. Aux., 1957-59, Downtown Bus. Assn., Rochester, 1985. Recipient Woman of Achievement Bus. YWCA, Rochester, 1983, Golden Door Knob, Bus. and Prfl. Women, Rochester, 1979. Mem. Inst. Cert. Travel Agts. (life), Assn. Retail Trvel Agts. (life, nat. bd. 1988-90, sec. to bd. 1988-90, sec.-treas. Croton on Hudson N.Y. chpt. 1989) Am. Soc. Travel Agts., Pacific Area Travel Agts., Minn. Exec. Women in Travel, Assn. Retail Travel Agts. Home: 86 MacFarlane Dr 2C Delray FL 33483

RANDALL, RUTH EVELYN, state commissioner, educator; b. Underwood, Iowa, Mar. 4, 1929; d. Oluf and Lillie Martha (Bondo) Larsen; m. Robert Dale Randall (dec.); children—Robert, Mark, Diane. Teaching cert., Dana Coll., Blair, Nebr., 1949; B.S., U. Omaha, 1961; M.S., U. Nebr.-Omaha, 1968, Ed.S., 1972; Ed.D. in Ednl. Adminstrn., U. Nebr.-Lincoln, 1976. Various teaching positions Iowa and Nebr., 1949-67; elem. prin. Omaha Pub. Schs., 1967-75; asst. prin. Horace Mann Pub. Sch., Omaha, 1976-78; asst. supt. Rosemount Ind. Sch. Dist., Minn., 1978-81, dep. supt., 1981, supt., 1981-83; commr. of edn. State of Minn., St. Paul, 1983—; mem. Tandy Ednl. Grants Rev. Bd., planning group for Nat. Bd. Cert. of Profl. Tchrs., Carnegie Corp., Minn. State High Sch. League; mem. Nat. Bd. for Profl. Teaching Standards; lectr. in field. Mem. editorial adv. bd. Electronic Learning mag.. T.H.E. Journal; contbr. articles to profl. jours. Mem. exec. com. Minn. Acad. Excellence Found., adv. council for Mentally Retarded and Physically Handicapped, Higher Edn. Adv. Council, Horace Mann League of U.S., Minn. Women's Edn. Council, Jr. Achievement Bd., Citizens League, Sci. Mus., Blue Ribbon Campaign for Child Survival, Elem. Sch. Ctr., Minn. Permanent Sch. Fund. Adv. com., Sta. KTCA Channel Two, Luth. Women's Caucus, Commn. on New Luth. Ch.; bd. dirs. Luth. Brotherhood Mut. Fund Bd.; mem. North Cen. Regional Edn. Lab. Bd., Nat. Adv. Panel Ctr. on Effective Secondary Schs.; trustee Tchrs. Retirement Assn.; mem. nat. adv. bd. Pub. Agenda Found.; mem. edn. adv. council Carnegie Corp., N.Y.; sec. Minn. Bd. Edn.; ex-officio mem. Minn. Indian Affairs Council; mem. Minn. High Tech. Council; mem. adv. bd. Bush Pub. Schs. Exec. Fellows; mem. Edn. Commn. of States; mem. bd. advisors Close Up, Young Writer's Contest Found. (hon.); bd. dirs. Global Perspectives in Edn. Inc., Council Chief State Sch. Officers, 1987—, SEARCH Inst., Agy. for Instrnl. Tech., Minn. Job Tng. Ptnrship. Iowa Farm Bur. scholar Dana Coll., 1947-49; Franklin E. and Orinda M. Johnson fellow U. Nebr.-Lincoln, 1975-76; Bush Pub. Schs. Exec. fellow, 1980-81; recipient appreciation award Apple Valley C. of C., 1983, Award U. Nebr. Lincoln, 1983, Disting. Alumnus award Dana Coll., 1984. Mem. Council of Chief State Sch. Officers (bd. dirs.), Am. Forum (bd. dirs.), Minn. Valley Bus. and Profl. Women's Club (Woman of Yr. 1982), Minn. Assn. Supervision and Curriculum Devel. (award for contbns. to Am. Edn. 1988), Minn. Assn. Sch. Adminstrs., Adminstrv. Women in Edn. Minn., LWV, AAUW, Upper Midwest Women in Edn. Adminstrn., Nat. PTA (life), Omaha Edn. Assn. (Human Relations award 1978), Women Execs. in State Govt. (founding), Nat. Council Adminstrv. Women in Edn., Am. Edn. Research Assn., Am. Assn. Sch. Adminstrs., Assn. Supervision and Curriculum Devel., Minn. Council for Gifted and Talented, Minn. Women's Econ. Roundtable, Minn. Soc. Fine Arts, Travelers Soc., U. Nebr.-Omaha Alumni (Achievement award 1987, recipient distinguished alumnus award, 1987), U. Nebr. Alumni Assn. (life), Dana Coll. Alumni Assn., Phi Delta Kappa, Delta Kappa Gamma. Mem. Democratic Farm Labor Party. Lutheran. Home: 8738 Summer Wind Bay Woodbury MN 55125 Office: Edn Dept 712 Capitol Sq Bldg 550 Cedar St Saint Paul MN 55101

RANDALL, RUTH JEAN, advertising agency executive; b. N.Y.C., May 7, 1937; d. Rudolph Harold and Rose (Mass) Gordon; m. Bob Randall, Mar. 11, 1962 (div. Sept. 1976); children: Julia, Edward. BA, NYU, 1958. Mng. editor New Am. Library, N.Y.C., 1964-68; editor-in-chief The Women's Guide to Books, N.Y.C., 1974-77; dir. N.Y. Office The Word Guild, Cambridge, Mass., 1977-79; editorial prodn. mgr. Viking Penguin Inc., N.Y.C., 1979-85; exec. v.p. The Studio Inc., Stamford, Conn., 1985—. Editor: The Women's Guide to Books, 1974. Democrat. Office: The Studio Inc 750 Summer St Stamford CT 06901

RANDALL, RUTH LEWIS, retired librarian; b. Westport, Conn., Sept. 4, 1916; d. Edward Rust and Susan (VanVliet) Lewis; m. Charles Kyle Randall, Nov. 15, 1941; children: Judith Louise, Sylvia Joyce Randall Perucci, Susan Elaine Randall Shlaes. BA, Nebr. Wesleyan U., 1938; MLS, Columbia U., 1939. Head juvenile dept., cataloger Hastings (Nebr.) Pub. Libr., 1939-41; clk. hist. sect. USDA, Washington, 1944-45; pres. Friends of Martha Washington Libr., Fairfax County, Va., 1954-66; libr. Fairfax County Pub Libr., Va., 1969-81; ret., 1981. Chmn. Groveton Travelers, Alexandria, 1978—; patient driver United Community Ministries, Fairfax County, 1983—; mem. Mt. Vernon United Meth. Ch., 1953—. Mem. AAUW (pres. Mt. Vernon chpt. 1986), Am. Assn. Ret. Persons (edn. sec. Mt. Vernon chpt. 1986—), United Meth. Women (pres. 1959-61), Alpha Gamma Delta (Old Dominion Alumnae club 1942—, pres. 1955-56). Democrat. Methodist. Home: 1909 Paul Spring Rd Alexandria VA 22307

RANDALL, SHERRI LEE, accountant; b. Burlington, Vt., Dec. 21, 1959; d. Robert Dale and Carolyn Sue (Ferguson) Schaffner; m. Cleve Hadley Randall, Feb. 11, 1981. BBA with high honors, Idaho State U., 1985. CPA, Idaho. Staff acct. Price Waterhouse, Anchorage, 1985-87; acct. Little-Morris, Boise, Idaho, 1987—; mem. acctg. alumni adv. panel Idaho State U., Pocatello, 1989-90. Vol. coord. Caribou Nat. Forest, Pocatello, 1984; treas., chmn. fin. com. Assn. for Retarded Citizens ada County, Boise. Scholar Idaho State U., 1983-84, Crawford-Moore Found., 1984. Mem. AICPA, Idaho Soc. CPA's, Phi Kappa Phi, Beta Gamma Sigma, Beta Alpha Psi. Office: Little-Morris 350 N 9th St Ste 200 Boise ID 83701

RANDLE, ELLEN EUGENIA FOSTER, opera, classical singer, educator; b. New Haven, Conn., Oct. 2, 1948; d. Richard A.G. and Thelma Lousie (Brooks) Foster; m. Ira James William, Mar. 7, 1947 (div. 1972); m. John Willis Randle. Student, Calif. State Coll., Sonoma, 1970; studied with Boris Goldovsky, 1970; student, Grad. Sch. Fine Arts, Florence, Italy, 1974; studied with Tito Gobbi, Florence, 1974; student, U. Calif., Berkeley, 1977; BA in World History, Lone Mountain Coll., 1976, MA in Performing Arts, 1978; studied with Madam Eleanor Steber, Graz, Austria, 1979; studied with Patricia Goehl, Munich, Fed. Republic Germany, 1979; postgrad., U. San Francisco, 1989—, MA, 1990. instr. East Bay Performing Art Ctr., Richmond, Calif., 1986, Chapman Coll., 1986. Singer opera prodns. Porgy & Bess, Oakland, Calif., 1980-81, LaTraviata, Oakland, Calif., 1981-82, Aida, Oakland, 1981-82, Madame Butterfly, Oakland, 1982-83, The Magic Flute, Oakland, 1984, numerous others; performances include TV specials, religous concerts, musicals; music dir. Natural Man, Berkeley, 1986; asst. artistic dir. Opera Piccola, Oakland, Calif. Art commr. City of Richmond, Calif. Recipient Bk. Am. Achievement award. Mem. Music Tchrs. Assn., Nat. Council Negro Women, Nat. Assn. Negro Musicians, Calif. Arts Fedn., Calif. Assn. for Counseling and Devel. (mem. black caucus), The Calif.-Nebraskan Orgn., Inc., San Francisco Commonwealth Club, Gamma Phi Delta. Democrat. Mem. A.M.E. Zion Ch. Home: 5314 Boyd Ave Oakland CA 94618

RANDO, RAE, manager; b. Paterson, N.J., Apr. 12, 1956; d. Frank J. and Rachel R. (Turpstra) R.; m. Dimitri Voicechovski, Nov. 6, 1976; 1 child, Nikolai Alekseі. B.S. in Bus. Adminstrn. candidate Thomas A. Edison State Coll., 1985—; cert. Katharine Gibbs Sch., 1974-76. Tenant/landlord adminstr. Claridge House, Verona, N.J., 1976-79, Paragon Enterprises, West Orange, N.J., 1979-81; account rep. Sci. Mgmt., Parsippany, N.J., 1981-82, mgr. temporary services, 1982-86, mgr. major accounts, 1986-88, br. mgr., 1988—. Canvas vol. Greenpeace, 1980—; trustee North Jersey Psychotherapeutic Inst., 1983-85 , treas., 1984-85. Avocations: astronomy, skiing, birding, wildlife conservation. Roman Catholic. Home: Jennings Rd Milton NJ 07438 Office: Sci Mgmt Corp 2001 Rt 46 Waterview Plaza Parsippany NJ 07054

RANDOLPH, BEVERLEY, production stage manager; b. Norristown, Pa., Aug. 26, 1951; d. Robert Lyman Kratz and Sarah Randolph (McDonnell) DaCosta. BFA magna cum laude, Ithaca Coll., 1973. Prodn. stage mgr.: Jerome Robbins' Broadway, N.Y.C., 1988-90, Kiss of the Spider Woman, 1990, Cabaret, N.Y.C., 1988, Galla Opening of Ky. Ctr. Performing Arts, Loisville, 1983, Follies in Concert, Lincoln Ctr., 1985, Grind, 19855, End of the World, Washington and N.Y.C.; prodn. supr. Queenie Pie, Duke Ellington Musical, Phila., Washington, 1987, Uptown It's Hot, Phila., 1985-86; prodn. stage mgr. A Doll's Life, L.A., N.Y.C., 1982, Merrily We Roll Along, N.Y.C., 1981; stage mgr. Chapter Two. Stage mgr. Nat. Inst. of Music Theatre, N.Y.C., 1986-87; participant Broadway Cares. Mem. Actors Fund (life), Actor's Equity Assn., League of Profl. Theatre Women.

RANDOLPH, DEBORAH JEAN GREENWAY, data processing executive; b. Anderson, S.C., Sept. 17, 1951; d. Charles Corbett and Ruth Marcelia (Ham) Greenway; m. Randall Scott Randolph, June 14, 1980; 1 child, Jordan Vance. BA in Journalism, U. S.C., 1973, BS in Computer Sci., 1979. Data processing supr. Giant Cement Co., Columbia, S.C., 1973-78; data processing mgr. Greater Carolinas Ins. Co., Columbia, 1979-80; asst. dir. data processing Providence Hosp., Columbia, 1980-85; dir. computer services Richland Sch. Dist. 2, Columbia, 1985—. Named Outstanding Young Woman in Am., 1985. Mem. NAFE, Data Processing Mgmt. Assn., Common IBM Users Group, Ednl. Software Uers Inc. (bd. dirs. 1988-89). Democrat. Methodist. Home: 4010 Linwood Rd Columbia SC 29205 Office: Richland Sch Dist Two 6831 Brookfield Rd Columbia SC 29206

RANDOLPH, EVONNE P., real estate investor; b. Austin, Tex., Aug. 27, 1941; d. Alexander and Delia (Mea) Patterson; m. Philip L. Randolph, June 7, 1986; children: Debra L. Donahue, Laura A. Massey, Richard D. Austin. BA in Bus., Coll. of Mainland, Texas City, 1980; Bus. courses, Corr. Sch., Houston, 1988; real estate, Real Estate Sch., Webster, Tex., 1989. Mgr. Holiday Inn, Lamarque, Tex., Bayview Hotel, Hawaii; rsch. asst. IGT, Chgo.; pvt. practice real estate investing Texas City. Mem. Hotel Mgmt. Assn. Republican. Home: 1002 Broadway San Leon TX 77539 Office: Rt 1 Box 1605 Dickinson TX 77539

RANDOLPH, PATRICIA DOLVIN, educator; b. Washington, Ga., Oct. 27, 1940; d. James Hamilton and Louise (Glasure) Dolvin; m. Edward Fairfax Randolph Jr., June 15, 1962 (div. May 1980); children: Peyton O'Fallon, James Key, Edward Fairfax III. BA cum laude, Vanderbilt U., 1962; MA in Religion, Gannon U., 1977; postgrad., U. Dayton, 1976-78, Grad. Theol. Union, Berkeley, Calif., 1978-79. Assoc. editor The Peanut Press, Dayton, Ohio, 1977-78; chair of bd., treas. Peanut Pub., Dayton, 1978; tchr. Presentation High Sch., San Francisco, 1979—, chair theology dept., 1985—. Freelance writer newspaper column, 1977-78. NEH grantee, 1985, Assisi and Siena, Italy, 1989; honoree San Francisco Star Tchr. project, 1990. Mem. Nat. Cath. Edn. Assn., Nat. Assn. Secondary Sch. Prins. (div. student activities). Democrat. Roman Catholic. Home: 412 Forbes Ave San Rafael CA 94901 Office: Presentation High Sch 2350 Turk Blvd San Francisco CA 94118

RANDOLPH, SHIRLEY WILSON, nurse, communications consultant; b. Scottsburg, Ind., Nov. 21, 1945; d. Porter Ebenezer and Mary Katherine (Hall) W.; m. Gariel DeLane Randolph, Aug. 26, 1967; children: Gariel DeLane Randolph II, Kathryn DeShele Randolph. BS, U. Tenn., 1967; AA, U. Charleston, 1978. Cert. Image Cons. Home econ. United Fuel Gas Co., Charleston, W.Va., 1967-68; substitute tchr. Mason County Schs., Point Pleasant, W.Va., 1969-70; vocat. home econ. tchr. Kanawha County Schs., Charleston, W.Va., 1970-71; sewing instr. Kanawha County Schs., Charleston, 1971-77; RN St. Francis Hosp., Charleston, 1978-79; communications cons. Women's Coun. Ctr., Charleston, 1984-88; RN Charleston Area Med. Ctr., 1979—. Camp Nurse, Kanawha County 4-H, Camp Virgil Tate, W.Va., 1983; Red Cross Nurse, Am. Red Cross Cen. W.Va. Chpt., Charleston, 1982-86. Mem. AAUW (trainer, Vol. Leadership Tng. 1986—; W.Va. pres. elect 1988-90; W.Va. Program v.p. 1987-89; W.Va. treas. 1986-87; W.Va. Legis. Program Chmn. 1985-86), Home Econ. in Homemaking (pres. 1987-89), 4-H (asst. leader 1981-89, photography leadership award, Kodak 1980), Soc. Profl. Engrs. Aux. (office 1970-82), Vol. Alumni Network. Home: 722 Chappell Rd Charleston WV 25304

RANDOLPH, WILLENE JOYCE, computer specialist; b. Lebanon, Ill., Feb. 7, 1935; d. Rudolph Mitchell and Cleo (Gant) Davis; m. Scott Roosevelt Randolph, Feb. 2, 1952; children—Craig, Teresa, Keith and Kathy (twins). B.A., Stephens Coll., 1985. Sec., USAF, Scott AFB, Ill., 1958-63, computer programmer, 1963-69; computer specialist U.S. Army, St. Louis, 1969-72; data processing instr. State Community Coll., East St. Louis, Ill., dir. computer services/plan and research 1976-81; data processing mgr.Bd. Edn., 1981-82; computer systems analyst, program mgr. Fed. Govt., U.S. Army, St. Louis, 1982—; mem. Ford Found. Adv. Bd., 1984—, St. Louis Community Coll. adv. bd., 1986-87. Pres., Jack and Jill Am., East St. Louis, 1979; editor newsletter St. Paul Bapt. Ch., East St. Louis, 1982—; precinct committeewoman East St. Louis Precinct 33, 1983. Recipient Outstanding Performance award USAF, 1963; Fed. Women's Program Mgr. of Year award, 1984-86; Spl. Act award U.S. Army, 1982-84; award of Merit Top Ladies of Distinction, 1984. Mem. Blacks in Govt. (v.p. 1984-85), Federally Employed Women (workshop presenter), Data Processing Mgrs. Assn., Ill. Bus. Edn. Assn., St. Louis Fed. Women's Program Council. Republican. Avocations: travel, reading. Home: 490 N 33d St East Saint Louis IL 62205 Office: US Army ALMSA 210 N Tucker Blvd Saint Louis MO 63188

RANDS, BETTY ANN, guidance counselor; b. Palatka, Fla., Sept. 24, 1931; d. Amos Newell and Miriam (Smith) Wyllys; children: Karen Yvette Rands Bock. Student, Fla. So. U., 1949-51; BSPE, U. Fla., 1953, MEd, 1973; postgrad., U. N.Fla., 1978. Phnys. edn. tchr./coach Duval County Sch. Bd., Jacksonville, Fla., 1953-59; tchr. L.A. City Schs., Hollywood, Calif., 1959-68; tchr., coach Putnam County schs., Palatka, Fla., 1968-70; health sci. tchr. Duval County Sch. Bd., Jacksonville, 1970-73; dean girls Duval County Sch. Bd., 1974-79, guidance counselor, 1979—; instr. various classes adult edn. Mobile maid Ron Reagan Gov. campaign, 1965-66; del. Calif. St. Gen. Com. Rep. Party, 1966-68; campaign worker various Rep. candidates, 1968—. Mem. Beaches and Jacksonville Bd. Realtors, Duval County Reading Coun., Fla. Assn. Counseling and Devel., Duval County Assn. Elem. Counselors, Am. Bus. Women's Assn. (edn. chmn. 1981-83), Am. Contract Bridge Assn. Methodist. Home: 1823 Oak Grove Cir Jacksonville Beach FL 32250

RANEY, MIRIAM DAY, actress; b. Florence, S.C., Sept. 30, 1922; d. Lewis Griffith and Iola Lewis (Edwards) Day; m. Robert William Raney, Mar. 31, 1946 (div. Sept. 1976); children: Robert William Jr., Miriam, Kevin Paige, Megan. BSM in Voice, Music Edn., U. N.C., Greensboro, 1939-43; student (summers), Julliard Sch. Music, 1942-43; BA in Music History, U. Ark., Little Rock, 1978-81; Certificate, Adam Roarke Film Actors Lab., Irving, Tex., 1989. Singing chorus N.Y. Center Opera Co., 1943-44; understudy, singing chorus Oklahoma, Theater Guild, N.Y.C., 1944-45; ingenue lead Connecticut Yankee, Geosan Subway Cir., N.Y.C., 1945; understudy, singing chorus Up In Central Park, Michael Todd, N.Y.C., 1945-46; guest singer NBC Radio, N.Y.C., 1944, CBS Radio, N.Y.C., 1945; actress in commls., Little Rock, 1988-89, Unsolved Mysteries, TV, Hot Springs, Ark., 1989. Author: slide, sound show Ark. Women in Music, 1982; composer, lyricist: The Bend and the Willows, 1982, Ballad of Petit Jean, 1983. Ch. soloist, various protestant chs., Little Rock, 1946-55; music dir., leader Ouachita Girl Scout Coun., Little Rock, 1963-70; choir mem. Pulaski Heights United Meth. Ch., Little Rock, 1970-76; mem. Speakers Bur. Coalition of Womens Clubs for ERA, Little Rock, 1974-75; bd. dirs. Local 266, AFM, Little Rock, 1980-83. Named Illustrious Alumna, U.N.C. at Greensboro, 1945; recipient Thanks Badge, Girl Scouts U.S., Ouachita Coun., Little Rock, 1965. Mem. AAUW (Little Rock legis. com. 1973-79, program com. 1973-79, state rep. for cultural interests 1976-79), Musical Coterie (Little Rock), Cen. Ark. Guild of Organists (pres. student chpt. 1977-80). Democrat. Home: 707 Pleasant Valley Dr #2 Little Rock AR 72207

RANKAITIS, SUSAN, artist; b. Cambridge, Mass., Sept. 10, 1949; d. Alfred Edward and Isabel (Shimkus) Rankaitis; m. Robbert Flick, June 5, 1976. B.F.A. in Painting, U. Ill., 1971; M.F.A. in Visual Arts, U. So. Calif., 1977. Rsch. asst., art dir. Plato Lab., U. Ill., Urbana, 1971-75; art instr. Orange Coast Coll., Costa Mesa, Calif., 1977-83; chair dept. art Chapman Coll., Orange, Calif., 1983-90; Fletcher Jones chair in art Scripps Coll., Claremont, Calif., 1990—; represented by Meyers/Bloom Gallery, Santa Monica, Calif., Gallery Min, Tokyo; assoc. prof. art, chair Chapman Coll.; overview panelist visual arts Nat. Endowment for Arts, 1983, 84. One-man shows include L.A. County Mus. Art, 1983, Internat. Mus. Photography, George Eastman House, 1983, Gallery Min of Tokyo, 1988, Meyers/Bloom Gallery, Santa Monica, 1989; represented in permanent collections U. N.Mex. Art, Santa Monica Coll., Ctr. for Creative Photography, UCLA, Mus. Modern ARt, Santa Barbara Mus. Art, L.A. County Mus. Art, Mpls. Inst. Arts, San Francisco Mus. Modern Art, Security Pacific Bank, Mus. Modern Art, Lodz, Poland, Nat. Mus. Am. Art. Active Friends of Photography, 1985-88, mem. adv. bd. trustees. Nat. Endowment for Arts fellow, 1980, 88, Chapman rsch. fellow 1984-87, U.S./France fellow, 1989;

Djerassi resident, 1989; recipient Graves award in the humanities, 1985. Mem. Coll. Art Assn., Los Angeles Inst. Contemporary Art, Los Angeles County Mus. Art, Friends of Photography, Center Creative Photography, Calif. Council Fine Arts Deans. Gallery: Myers/Bloom Gallery 2112 Broadway Santa Monica CA 90404-2912 Office: Scripps Coll Art Dept 1031 Columbia Claremont CA 91711

RANKIN, BONNIE LEE, insurance executive; b. Lancaster, Pa., June 27, 1953; d. E. Lee and Mary Jane (Weaver) R.; m. Michael Cornwell, July, 1978 (div. May 1987). BA in Liberal Arts, Millersville (Pa.) U., 1975. Cert. ins. counselor, 1986; CPCU. Claim adjuster Nationwide Ins. Co., Phila., 1975-76; comml. underwriter Nationwide Ins. Co., Harrisburg, Pa., 1976-78; sr. comml. underwriter Harleysville (Pa.) Mut. Ins. Co., 1978-79, tng. coord., 1979-81, br. underwriting mgr., 1981-84; with Worcester (Mass.) Ins. Co. subs. HMIC, 1984—, asst. v.p., 1987-89, v.p., 1989—. Mem. adv. bd. Mechs. Hall, Worcester, 1987—. Mem. Soc. Chartered Property Casualty Underwriters (dir. candidate devel. 1985-87), Greater Valley Forge Soc. Chartered Property Casualty Underwriters (founder, bd. dirs. 1983-84), Pa. Assn. Mut. Ins. Cos. (edn. com. chmn. 1980-82), Ins. Soc. Phila. (mem. faculty 1980-84), Ins. Inst. Am. (mem. grading bd. Malvern, Pa. 1981-84), MENSA, Audubon Soc., Sierra. Republican. Methodist. Office: Worcester Ins Co 440 Main St Worcester MA 01608

RANKIN, DIANNE MARY, accountant, financial planner; b. Mineola, N.Y.; d. David Jay and Rose Mary (Ruggerio) Keller.; m. Eric Lynn Rankin, Nov. 18, 1972; 1 child, Derek. BA., U. Louisville, 1969. CPA, N.J.; cert. fin. planner; registered investment adviser; cert. tax. profl. Stewardess Pan Am. Airways, 1969-72; material contr. RCA, Somerville, N.J., 1972-75; pvt. practice acctg., Flemington, N.J., 1975—; investment adviser SEC, 1982; instr. tax preparation, Flemington, 1976-78. Mem. Delaware Twp. Mcpl. Utilities Authority, 1979—. Dean's scholar U. Louisville, 1969. Author: Financial Planning, 1984, Tax Reform, 1987, Personal Financial Planning and Tax Guide, 1990. Mem. Nat. Soc. Pub. Accts., Nat. Tax Tng. Inst. Address: 174 Ferry Rd Flemington NJ 08822

RANKIN, DORREEN WINNIE, marketing representative, consultant; b. Pitts., Jan. 4, 1965; d. Robert Marcella Dana Rankin and Katherine Marie (Jordan) Dotson. AS in Acctg., Robert Morris Coll., 1984, BSBA in Mgmt., 1988. Asst. advt. bus. mgr. Gimbels Dept. Store, Pitts., 1984-86; broker's asst. Kidder, Peabody & Co., Inc., Pitts., 1986-87; collector Kaufmann's, Pitts., 1987-88; office and mktg. mgr. Rain Soft Water Treatment, Greensburg, Pa., 1988-90; sr. mktg. rep. United Tech. Svcs., Monroeville, Pa., 1990—. Mem. Residents Advocating Good Environment, Blairsville, Pa., 1989-90; mem., leader Help Get the Kids Off the Street, Pitts., 1989—; v.p. fin. Minority Student Union, 1988; pres. Cornerstone Scholarship Fund, 1990—. Omega scholar, 1982; recipient Cert. of Achievement, Residents Advocating Good Environment, 1990. Mem. NAFE, Data Processing Mgmt. Assn., Robert Morris Coll. Alumni Assn. (chpt. founder, leader). Republican. Baptist. Office: United Tech Svcs 200 James Pl Ste 200 Monroeville PA 15146

RANKIN, HELEN CROSS, cattle rancher, guest ranch executive; b. Mojave, Calif; d. John Whisman and Cleo Rebecca (Tilley) Cross; m. Leroy Rankin, Jan. 4, 1936 (dec. 1954); children—Julia Jane King Sharr, Patricia Helen Denvir, William John. A.B., Calif. State U.-Fresno, 1935. Owner, operator Rankin Cattle Ranch, Caliente, Calif., 1954—; founder, pres. Rank Ranch, Inc., Guest Ranch, 1965—; mem. sect. 15, U.S. Bur. Land Mgmt.; mem. U.S. Food and Agrl. Leaders Tour China, 1983, Australia and N.Z., 1985; dir. U.S. Bur. Land Mgmt. sect. 15. Pres., Children's Home Soc. Calif., 1945. Recipient award Calif. Hist. Soc., 1983, Kern River Valley Hist. Soc., 1983. Mem. Am. Nat. Cattlemen's Assn., Calif. Cattlemen's Assn., Kern County Cattlemen's Assn., Kern County Cowbelles (pres. 1949, Cattlewoman of Yr. 1988), Calif. Cowbelles, Nat. Cowbelles, Bakersfield Country Club, Bakersfield Raquet Club. Republican. Methodist. Office: Rankin Ranch Caliente CA 93518

RANKIN, JOANNA MARIE, astronomy educator; b. Denver, Mar. 10, 1942; d. Robert McCordy and Julia Bernice (Pelsor) R.; life ptnr. Mary Rose Fillmore. BS, So. Meth. U., 1965; MS, Tulane U., 1966; PhD in Astrophysics, U. Iowa, 1970. Asst. prof. astronomy dept. Cornell U., Ithaca, N.Y., 1974-78; acting head computer dept. Arecibo (P.R.) Obs., 1976; sr. rsch. assoc. history dept. Ctr. for Radiophysics and Space Rsch., Cornell U., Ithaca, 1978-80; assoc. prof. physics dept. U. Vt., Burlington, 1980-88, prof. physics and astronomy physics dept., 1988—; organizer Internat. Astron. Union Colloquium 128, Lagow, Poland, 1990; organizer, participant in internat. astron. collaborations with astronomers, India, USSR, Poland, 1985-90; lectr. in field. Contbr. articles to profl. jours. Bd. dirs. Vt. Pro-Choice, 1987—; activist Women's Internat. League for Peace and Freedom, Burlington, Vt., 1981-86; mem. War Resister's League, N.Y.C., 1982—; supporter Lesbian Herstory Archives, N.Y.C., 1987—; creator, collector polit. poster art show, 1983-85. Recipient NASA traineeship U. Iowa, 1966-70; Van Allen/Link fellow astron. dept. U. Iowa, 1970; named finalist Kellogg Nat. fellow Kellogg Found., 1984, U.S./India fellow Fulbright Found., 1990; rsch. grantee NSF, 1972, 73, 78, 90. Mem. Internat. Astron. Union, Am. Astron. Soc., Fedn. Am. Scientists, Am. Women in Sci., Sci. for the People, Nat. Women's Studies Assn. Office: U Vt Physics Dept A-405 Cook Bldg Burlington VT 05405

RANKIN, JOCELYN DAVIS, veterinarian; b. Mt. Kisco, N.Y., June 6, 1955; d. Donald W. and Evelyn (Gagnon) Davis; m. Bruce Michael Rankin, Oct. 1, 1988. BS, U. N.H., 1977; DVM, N.Y. State Coll. Vet. Medicine, 1986. Cert. in vet. medicine. Animal health technician Bedford Animal Hosp., Mt. Kisco, 1977-82; assoc. vet. Animal Hosp. Pittsford, Rochester, N.Y., 1986-89, Old Canal Vet. Clinic, Plainville, Conn., 1989—. Equine Experience scholar N.Y. State Thoroughbred Racing Assn., N.Y. State Coll. Vet. Medicine, 1984. Fellow Phi Zeta, Alpha Zeta; mem. Am. Animal Hosp. Assn., Am. Vet. Med. Assn., N.Y. State Vet. Med. Soc., Gennessee Valley Vet. Med. Assn., Conn. Vet. Med. Assn., Hartford County Vet. Med. Assn., Alpha Psi (social chair Ithaca chpt. 1983-84, alumni sec. 1983-85). Democrat. Episcopalian. Home: 123 E Country Squire Dr Cromwell CT 06416 Office: Old Canal Vet Clinic 49 E Main St Plainville CT 06062

RANKIN, KITTY V., textile sales representative; b. Charlotte, N.C., Nov. 21, 1953; d. Richard Eugene and Julia Wilson (Pancake) R. Student, Converse Coll., 1972-74; BS, U. Ga., 1977; AA, N.C. Vocat. Textile Sch., Belmont, 1982; postgrad., Phila. Coll. Textiles and Sci., 1983. Mktg. coord, designer Thomas Taylor and Sons, Hudson, Mass.; textile sales rep. United Elastic Corp., Stuart, Va., Elastic Corp. Am., Columbiana, Ala. Mem. NAFE, GAIN.

RANKIN, SYBIL ZOE, dental hygienist; b. Bklyn., Nov. 11, 1943; d. Milton and Elsie (Levinson) Finkelstein; m. Steven Alan Rankin, Aug. 14, 1966; children: Jennifer, Shari. AAS, N.Y.C. City Coll., 1963. Dental hygienist Coney Island Hosp., Bklyn., 1963-64, Dr. M. Zimmerman, Bklyn., 1963-65, Dr. Moskowitz, Bklyn., 1965-69, Dr. Golterman, Staten Island, N.Y., 1976—; sec., treas. S.A. Rankin Electric, Bklyn., 1982—. Leader Girl Scouts U.S., Staten Island, 1974; mem. exec. bd. P.T.A., Staten Island, 1971-77, sec., 1980-82 booster leader Wagner High Sch., Staten Island, 1983. Fellow Am. Dental Hygiene Assn.; mem. Five Boro Contraction Assn., Alziheimers Assn., MADD. Jewish. Home: 174 Harold St Staten Island NY 10314

RANKS, ANNE ELIZABETH, retired elementary and secondary educator; b. Omaha, June 10, 1916; d. Salvatore and Concetta (Turco) Scolla; m. Harold Eugene Ranks, Aug. 20, 1955 (dec.). B in Philosophy, Duchesne Coll., Omaha, 1937; MA, Creighton U., 1947. Tchr. Good Shepherd Parochial HighSch., Omaha, 1937-38, St. Benedicts High Sch., Omaha, 1938-39, Omaha Pub. Schs., 1939-81. Pres. women's div. Dem. Cen. Com., Nebr.; chmn. Gov.'s Profl. Practices Commn. Nebr., 1938-39; vol. Bergan-Mercy Hosp., Omaha, 1980-86, mem. aux. bd., 1985-86; vol. Saddleback Hosp., Laguna Hills, Calif., 1989-90; bd. dirs. Sylvia Tischhauser Scholarship Found., 1989—; mem. bd. dirs. Saddleback Valley Ednl. Found., 1990—. Mem. AAUW (v.p. Laguna Hills br. 1988-90), NEA (pres. dept. Classroom tchrs. Nebr. chpt. 1956-57), Omaha Edn. Assn. (v.p. 1960-62), Calif. Ret. Tchrs. (corr. sec. div. 42, 1988-89, v.p., 1989—), Coun. Cath. Women Club (v.p. Laguna Hills chpt. 1988-89), Womens Club, Cath. Daus. Ct. (recording sec. Lake Forest, Calif. ct. 1988-90), Orange Diocesan Coun. Cath. Women Calif. (bd. dirs. 1989—), Nebr. State Edn. Assn. (exec. bd. dirs. 1965-70), Cath. Daus. of the Am. (regent Omaha ct. 1980), Phi Delta Gamma (pres. local chpt. 1985-86).

RANNEY, HELEN MARGARET, physician, educator; b. Summer Hill, N.Y., Apr. 12, 1920; d. Arthur C. and Alesia (Toolan) R. AB, Barnard Coll., 1941; MD, Columbia U., 1947; ScD, U. S.C., 1979. Diplomate: Am. Bd. Internal Medicine. Intern Presbyn. Hosp., N.Y.C., 1947-48, resident, 1948-50, asst. physician, 1954-60; practice medicine specializing in internal medicine, hematology N.Y.C., 1954-70; instr. Coll. Phys. and Surg. Columbia, N.Y.C., 1954-60; assoc. prof. medicine Albert Einstein Coll. Medicine, N.Y.C., 1960-64, prof. medicine, 1965-70; prof. medicine SUNY, Buffalo, 1970-73; prof. medicine U. Calif., San Diego, 1973-90, chmn. dept. medicine, 1973-86, Disting. physician vet. adminstr., 1986—. Fellow AAAS, ACP; mem. NAS, Inst. Medicine, Am. Soc. for Clin. Investigation, Am. Soc. Hematology, Harvey Soc., Am. Assn. Physicians, Am. Acad. Arts and Scis., Phi Beta Kappa, Sigma Xi, Alpha Omega Alpha. Office: VA Med Ctr (11-F) 3350 La Jolla Village Dr San Diego CA 92161

RANSOM, BUNNIE JACKSON, corporate executive, professor; b. Louisburg, N.C., Nov. 16, 1940; d. Burnall James and Elizabeth (Day) Hayes; m. Maynard H. Jackson, Dec. 29, 1965 (div.); children: Elizabeth, Brooke, Maynard III; m. Raymond L. Ransom, Apr. 25, 1979; 1 child, Ray Yvonne. BS, N.C. Coll., 1961; MS, N.C. Cen. U., 1970. Instr. Bennett Coll., Greensboro, N.C., 1962-63; rsch. asst. N.C. fund, Durham, 1964-65; with EEO Atlanta, 1965, program coord., 1967, dir. planning, 1967-70; pres. First Class, Inc., Atlanta, 1975—; part-time prof. Ga. State U., Atlanta, 1981—; artists mgr. Atlanta Artists Records, Atlanta, 1983—. Mem. Nat. Assn. Media Women, Nat. Assn. Market Developers (exec. dir.), Atlanta Bus. League, Atlanta Womens Network, NAACP (bd. dirs. Atlanta chpt. 1989—), Public Relations Soc. Am., Nat. Assn. Black Journalists, Links, Jack & Jill, Delta Sigma Theta (pres. 1970-72). Democrat. Baptist. Home: 1272 Oakcrest Dr SW Atlanta GA 30311 Office: First Class Inc 1422 W Peachtree St NW Atlanta GA 30309

RANSOM, JANET RUTH, nurse; b. Shawnee, Okla., Jan. 2, 1951; d. Jack Linzy Ransom and Geneva Rose (Helms) Eddy; m. Robert R. Riggs, May 18, 1973 (div. July 1984). Diploma, St. Anthony Sch. Nursing, Oklahoma City, 1973; BS in Profl. Arts, St. Joseph's Coll., North Windham, Maine, 1988. RN, Okla. Charge nurse South Community Hosp., Oklahoma City, 1973-80, 81-83, head nurse, 1980-81, asst. head nurse, 1983-87, coord. risk mgmt., 1987—. Vol. healthcare fairs, 1990; instr. CPR, Am. Heart Assn., 1974-75. Named Nurse of Yr., South Community Hosp., 1981. Fellow Am. Assn. Critical Care Nurses; mem. Assn. Cardiovascular Nursing (treas. 1975). Democrat. Roman Catholic. Office: South Community Hosp 1001 SW 44th St Oklahoma City OK 73159

RANSOM, MARGARET PRISCILLA, government official; b. Jackson, N.C., Sept. 17, 1947; d. Lister and Argentina (Lockhart) R.; BS, N.C. A&T State U., 1969; M.A., Central Mich. U., 1981. IRS agt. various locations, 1969-76, exempt orgns. analyst, Washington, 1976-82, group mgr., Balt., 1982-89, asst. br. chief, Washington, 1989—. Recipient Communications and Services to Public award IRS, 1971, Disting. performance awards, 1982, 85-89, group award for program accomplishments, 1983, 87, Outstanding Supr. for Balt. Dist. IRS, 1989. Mem. Nat. Assn. Female Execs., Assn. Improvement of Minorities in Internal Revenue Service, Federally Employed Women, Profl. Mgrs. Assn., Delta Sigma Theta.

RANTA AHO, MARTHA HELEN, teacher, retired; b. Poplar, Wis., July 12, 1923; d. John and Aurora (Aho) Ranta; m. Wayne August Aho, Dec. 19, 1942 (dec. June 1978); children: Dennis Wayne, Marla Jane Thibodeau. BS in Elem. Edn., U. Wis., Superior, 1968, MS in Teaching, Elem. Edn., 1977, postgrad., 1979-86; postgrad., U. Wis., Duluth, Minn., 1980-89, Coll. of St. Scholastica, 1978. Cert. elem. tchr., Minn. Tchr. kindergarten Ind. Sch. Dist. #709, Duluth, 1968-75; tchr. first grade ISD #709, Duluth, 1975-89, master tchr., 1978-89, ret., 1989. Mentor tchr. Kenwood Elem. Sch., 1987-89, vol. storyteller, 1989-90; vol. Family Svc. St. Luke's Hosp., 1990; tchr. leader, insvc. sessions, 1972-80; docent St. Louis County Hist. Soc.- Depot Mus., Duluth, 1989-90. Recipient trophy and award Wis. Indianhead Dist. of Garden Club, Superior, 1959. Mem. Duluth Area Ret. Educators Assn., Am. Assn. Univ. Women, Am. Assn. Ret. Persons, Minn. Hist. Soc., Univ. for Srs., Parent Tchr. Student Assn. (hon. life 1988), Delta Kappa Gamma. Democrat. Lutheran. Home: 2722 E 1st St Duluth MN 55812

RANTS, CAROLYN JEAN, academic administrator, teacher; b. Hastings, Nebr., Oct. 3, 1936; d. John Leon and Christine (Helzer) Halloran; m. Marvin L. Rants, June 1, 1957 (div. July 1984); children: Christopher Charles, Douglas John. Student, Hastings Coll., 1954-56; BS, U. Omaha, 1960; MEd, U. Nebr., 1968; EdD, U. S.D., 1982. Tchr. elem. Ogallala (Nebr.) Community Sch., 1956-58, Omaha Pub. Schs., 1958-60, Hastings Pub. Schs., 1960-64, Grosse Pointe (Mich.) Community Schs., 1964-67; asst. prof., instr. Morningside Coll., Sioux City, Iowa, 1974-82, dean for student devel., 1982-84, v.p. for student affairs, 1984—. Mem. new agy. com., fund distbn. com. United Way, Sioux City, 1987—, Iowa Civil Rights Commn., 1989—; bd. dirs. Leadership Sioux City, 1988—, Siouxland Y, Sioux City, 1985—, pres., 1988. Mem. Iowa Women in Ednl. Leadership (pres. Sioux City chpt. 1986), Nat. Assn. Student Personnel Adminstrs., AAUW (corp. rep.), Nat. Assn. for Women Deans, Adminstrs. and Counselors, P.E.O. (pres. Sioux City chpt.), Iowa Student Personnel Adminstrn. (profl. devel. chair Iowa chpt. 1988-89), Tri-State Women's Bus. Conf. (treas., planning com. Sioux City chpt. 1987-89), Quota Club (com. chair Sioux City chpt. 1987-89, Siouxland Woman of the Yr. 1989), Sertoma (all offices, gov., regional dir.). Republican. Methodist. Home: 2904 S Cedar #4 Sioux City IA 51106 Office: Morningside Coll 1501 Morningside Ave Sioux City IA 51106

RANUCCI, MARGUERITE CULLEN, financial executive; b. Trenton, N.J.; d. Eugene Joseph and Mildred (Cullen) R. BA, Anna Maria Coll., Paxton, Mass.; MEd, Trenton (N.J.) State Coll.; MBA, Pepperdine U. Comml. loan officer Crocker Bank, L.A., 1978-85; fin. analysis officer McDonnell-Douglas, Long Beach, Calif., 1986-87, 1st Interstate Bank, L.A., 1987-89, Security Pacific Bank, L.A., 1989—.

RAPHAEL, LOUISE ARAKELAIN, mathematician; b. N.Y.C., Oct. 24, 1937; d. Aristakes and Antionette (Sudbeaz) Arakelian; m. Robert Barnett Raphael, June 12, 1966 (div. 1985); children: Therese Denise, Marc Philippe. BS in Math., St. John's U., 1959; MS in Math., Cath. U., Washington, 1962; PhD in Math, Cath. U., 1967. Asst. prof. math. Howard U., Washington, 1966-70, vis. prof., 1981-82, assoc. prof., 1982-86, prof., 1981—; assoc. prof. Clark Coll., Atlanta, 1971-79, prof., 1979-82; vis. assoc. prof. MIT, Cambridge, 1977-78, vis. prof., 1989-90. Contbr. 28 articles to rsch. jours. Program dir. NSF, Washington, 1986-88; acting adminstrv. officer Conf. Bd. Math. Scis., 1985-86. Grantee NSF, 1975-76, 79-81, 89—, Army Rsch. Office, 1981-89, Air Force Sci. Rsch., 1981-82. Mem. AAAS, Am. Math. Soc. (com. mem.), Math. Assn. Am. (chmn. minorities in math. task force 1988), Soc. Indsl. and Applied Math., Sigma Xi. Democrat. Roman Catholic. Office: Howard U Dept Math Washington DC 20059

RAPHAEL, MARYANNE JEANNE D'ARC, author; b. Waverly, Ohio, Mar. 18, 1938; d. Vincent Ignatius and Doris Louise (Brown) Patterspn; m. Lennox Allison Raphael, May 19, 1961 (div. 1972); 1 child, Raphael Azariah. BA with honors, Ohio U., 1959; postgrad., The Sorbonne, Paris, France, 1960, U. Brazil, 1961, NYU, 1963-64. Social dir. USAF Svc. Club, Hahn, Fed. Republic Germany, 1960-61; tchr. Latin Am. Inst., N.Y.C., 1962-63; editor Prentice Hall, Inc., N.Y.C., 1963-64; editorial asst. Women's Day Mag., N.Y.C., 1964-65; tchr. Alternative U., N.Y.C., 1965-66, Frederick Douglas High Sch., N.Y., 1965-66, U. of the Streets, N.Y.C., 1968-73; women's studies tchr. New Sch. for Social Rsch., N.Y.C., 1971-72; activities dir. Pike Manor Nursing Home, Piketon, Ohio, 1982; book reviewer Writer's Lifeline, Ontario, Canada, 1978—, tchr. interpretor St. James Mission Circle, 1988—, language tchr. CoWorkers of Mother Teresa, Tijuana, Mex., 1989—. Author: Une Annee a Paris, 1960, Your Psychic Powers, the Key to Success, 1974, How to Survive as a Freelance Writer, 1974, Akita, A Dog for All Seasons, 1974, An Interview with Anais Nin, 1980, How to Survive as a New Age Writer, 1988; editor, pub. Writers World/Bhakti Press, Hilo, Hawaii, 1979-82, Writer's World Press, Encinitas, Calif., 1982—. Bd. dirs. YMCA Women's Ctr., Family Crisis Shelter, Hilo, Hawaii, 1978-79, Pike County Community Action, coordinator St. Mary's Ctr., Waverly, Ohio, 1982-84. Mem. NAFE, Nat. Writers Club, Shawnee U. Poets Cir., San Diego Christian Writers' Guild, Cath. Women, San Luiz Rey Prayer Group. Democrat. Home and Office: 444-113 N El Camino Real Encinitas CA 92024

RAPIN, ISABELLE, physician; b. Lausanne, Switzerland, Dec. 4, 1927; d. Rene and Mary Coe (Reeves) R.; m. Harold Oaklander, Apr. 5, 1959; children: Anne Louise, Christine, Stephen, Peter. Physician's Diploma. Faculte de Medicine, U. Lausanne, 1952, Doctorate in Medicine, 1955. Diplomate Am. Bd. Psychiatry and Neurology. Intern in pediatrics N.Y. U. Bellevue Med. Center, 1953-54; resident in neurology Neurol. Inst. of N.Y., Columbia-Presbyn. Med. Center, 1954-57, fellow in child neurology, 1957-58; mem. faculty Albert Einstein Coll. Medicine, Bronx, N.Y., 1958—; prof. neurology and pediatrics Albert Einstein Coll. Medicine, 1972—; attending neurologist and child neurologist Einstein Affiliated Hosps., Bronx.; Mem. Nat. Adv. Neurol. and Communicative Disorders and Stroke Coun., NIH, 1984-88. Contbr. chpts. to books, articles to med. jours. Fellow Am. Acad. Neurology; mem. Internat. Child Neurology Assn. (sec.-gen. 1979-82, v.p. 1982-86), Am. Neurol. Assn. (v.p. 1982-83), Child Neurology Soc. (Hower award 1987), Internat. Neuropsychology Soc., AAAS, N.Y. Acad. Scis., Assn. Research in Nervous and Mental Diseases (v.p. 1986). Office: Albert Einstein Coll Medicine 1410 Pelham Pkwy S Bronx NY 10461

RAPOPORT, JUDITH, psychiatrist; b. N.Y.C., July 12, 1933; d. Louis and Minna (Enteen) Livant; m. Stanley Rapoport, June 25, 1961; children: Stuart, Erik. BA, Swarthmore Coll., 1955; MD, Harvard U., 1959. Lic. psychiatrist. Cons., child psychiatrist NIMH/St. Elizabeth's Hosp., Washington, 1969-72; clin. asst. prof. Georgetown U. Med. Sch., Washington, 1972-82, clin. assoc. prof., 1982-85, clin. prof. psychiat., 1985—; med. officer biol. psychiatry br. NIMH, Bethesda, Md., 1976-78, chief, child mental illness unit, biol. psychiat. br., 1979-82, chief, child psychiatry lab. of clin. scis., 1982-84, chief, child psychiatry div. intramural rsch. programs, 1984—; prof. psychiatry George Washington U. Sch. Med., Washington, 1979—; cons. in field. Author: (non-fiction) The Boy Who Couldn't Stop Washing, 1989 (best seller literary guild selection 1989), Childhood Obsessive Compulsive Disorder, 1989. Fellow Am. Psychiat. Assn., Am. Acad. Child Psychiat.; mem. Ea. Psychol. Assn., D.C. Psychiat. Assn., Am. Psychopath. Assn. Home: 3010 44th Pl NW Washington DC 20016 Office: NIMH Bldg 10 Rm 6N240 Bldg 10 Rm 11C205 Bethesda MD 20892

RAPOPORT-LEVY, SUSAN MARILYN, advertising executive; b. Balt., Nov. 5, 1950; d. Leonard and Jeanne (Mendelsohn) R.; m. Alan Jonathan Levy, Oct. 29, 1988. BA with honors, U. Md., 1973. TV prodn. asst. Md. Ctr. for Pub. Broadcasting, Balt., 1974-76; med. sales rep. Bio-Nuclear Assays, Inc., Balt., 1976-79; advt. account rep. Sta. WQSR-FM, Balt., 1981-84, Image Mgmt., Washington, 1984, News Am., Balt., 1985-86, Home Team Sports, Washington, 1986-87, Donnelley Directory, Balt., 1987—. Capt. neighborhood fundraising drive Mental Health Assn., Balt., 1986-88. Mem. Advt. Assn. Balt., Diadem. Democrat. Jewish. Home: 5 Rhodes Pl Baltimore MD 21093 Office: Donnelley Directory 110 West Rd Baltimore MD 21204

RAPP, DOROTHY GLAVES, cancer research scientist; b. Sheffield, Eng., Aug. 14, 1943; came to U.S., 1972; d. Herbert Henry and Evelyn (Self) Glaves; m. Robert Andrus Rapp, Sept. 9, 1978. BSc, U. London, 1965; PhD, U. Nottingham, Eng., 1969. Rsch. asst. Unilever, Bedford, Eng., 1965-66; rsch. officer Cancer Rsch. Campaign, Nottingham, 1966-72; cancer rsch. scientist Roswell Park Cancer Inst., Buffalo, 1972—. Office: Roswell Park Cancer Inst 666 Elm St Buffalo NY 14263

RAPP, MARTHA BRUNE, communications executive; b. Springfield, Ill., July 28, 1950; d. Reynold William and Camille (Frainer) Brune; m. James Anthony Rapp,. BS in Communications, U. Ill., 1972. Staff reporter The Rock Island Argus, Ill., 1972; lifestyle editor The Belleville News Democrat, Ill., 1972-74; pub. relations assocs Blessing Hosp., Quincy, Ill., 1974-76; pub. relations dir. St. Mary Hosp., Quincy, Ill., 1977-84; pub. relations specialist Quincy, Ill., 1985-86; mgr. communications Harris Corp. Broadcast Division, Quincy, Ill., 1986-89, mgr. mktg. communications, 1989—. Mem. Quincy Symphony Women's Bd., Ill., 1981-86, United Way of Adams. Mem. Pub. Relations Soc. Am. (accredited). Republican. Roman Catholic.

RAPP, SUE CAROL STORER, small business owner, writer; b. Springfield, Ohio, Aug. 24, 1939; d. John Earl and Irene Mae (Beedy) Storer; m. William H. Johnson, June 24, 1958 (div. 1961); m. Thomas Alan Rapp, Feb. 3, 1962; 1 child, Tami Sue. Grad. high sch., Bellefontaine, Ohio, 1957. Bookkeeper United Telephone Co., Bellefontaine, 1957-58; exec. sec. Barber Colman Co., Rockford, Ill., 1958-64; supr., head cashier Laurentide Fin., Seaside, Calif., 1962-63; office mgr. Certified Water Co., Byron, Ill., 1981-82; owner, operator Rapp's Water Treatment, Byron, 1982-87; owner Sta. WCR Studio, Byron, 19889—. Author: From Somewhere Within, 1986, (poetry) Seasons fo Love, 1988; author short stories, numerous poems; composer songs; profl. songwriter, freelance writer Ogle County Life, Oregon, Ill., 1988—; author polit. and social reform papers. Com. chair Rockford area Muscular Dystrophy Assn., 1983-87. Mem. Nat. Water Quality Assn., Am. Soc. Composers, Authors & Pubs., Ill. WritersInc., World of Poetry (12 Certificate of Merit awards, Golden Poet award 1985, 86), Am. Poetry Assn., Byron C. of C.

RAPPAPORT, MARGARET M., psychologist, author, consultant; b. Buffalo, Nov. 16, 1947; d. Leo J. and Marie L. (Fischle) Williams; m. Herbert Rappaport, Oct. 20, 1969; children: Amanda, Alexander. BA, U. Buffalo, 1967; MA, SUNY, 1969; PhD, MD, U. Colo., 1971. Adj. faculty Temple U., Phila., 1974—; exec. dir. Inst. for Parent/Child Svcs., Phila., 1978—; physician Rappaport Assocs., Phila., 1974—; prof., researcher Univ. Dar es Salaam, Tanzania, 1970-74; program dir. Frontrunners, 1978—; child care/devel. cons. to media especially TV, 1984—; program dir. First Steps, 1986—. Author books and articles on parenting and family life, monographs on existential psychology. Mem. NOW, AAUP, Nat. Assn. for Edn. of Young Children, Del. Valley Assn. for Edn. of Young Children, Phila. Cricket Club, Cosmopolitan Club. Republican. Home: 509 E Sedgwick St Philadelphia PA 19119

RAPPORT, ROBIN SCHUMAN, communications executive; b. Phila., Oct. 9, 1954. BS in Visual and Performing Arts, Syracuse U., 1975; MA in Media and Communications, NYU, 1979, doctoral candidate, 1990—. Talent mgr. Jarrett Mgmt. Inc., 1979-80; assoc. producer Atlantic City Alive TV broadcast, 1981; communications dir. All Star Advt. Agy., N.J., 1981-84; corp. communications specialist Empire Blue Cross and Blue Shield, N.Y.C., 1984—. Writer, editor for various publs. Herbert Lehman fellow, 1975-79; recipient PADI cert. 1987, PADI Advanced cert., 1990. Home: 300 Mercer St #31-A New York NY 10003

RARICK, JEANNE TOSH, moving company executive; b. Rochester, Pa., June 23, 1944; d. Bernard Thomas and Emma Jean (Pickrell) Everly; m. Alexander Rex Tosh, Mar. 20, 1965 (dec. May 1969); m. John Robert Rarick Jr., Dec. 21, 1975. AB in Bus. Communications, Pa. State U., Monaca, 1973. Sec. Tosh Moving & Storage, Rochester, Pa., 1963-65, officer mgr., 1965-68, owner, 1968-74; operation mgr. Century Moving & Storage, Hartford, Conn., 1974-75; office mgr. Parks Moving & Storage, Inc., Warrendale, Pa., 1975-83; customer svc. mgr. Grabel Moving & Storage, Inc., Ambridge, Pa., 1983-87; dir. claims Parks Moving & Storage, Inc., Warrendale, Pa., 1987—. Pres. Bridgewater Borough coun., 1988—; pres. Beaver County Borough Assn., 1990-92. Mem. Beaver Jr. Womans Club (treas. 1979-80), Delta Nu Alpha (del. 1984-85). Republican. Methodist. Home: 1020 Mulberry St Bridgewater PA 15009-3030 Office: Parks Moving & Storage Inc 740 Commonwealth Dr Pittsburgh PA 15086

RASBERRY, SHAROL BARTA, accountant, management executive; b. Red Cloud, Nebr., Oct. 15, 1947; d. Allen James and Orfa Irene (Copley) Barta; m. Robert E. Rasberry, Dec. 29, 1968; children: Kimberly, Robert E. BBA, U. Nebr., 1969. CPA, Kans. Tax prin. Arthur Young & Co., Wichita, Kans., 1969-79; dir. taxes CWG Enterprises, 1979-80; exec. v.p. fin. Capital Enterprises, 1980—; bd. dirs. Inst. Logopedics. Bd. dirs. YWCA,

1978, Accent on Kids, 1983—, Wichita area coun. Girl Scouts U.S., 1986—; Leadership 2000, 1986; mem. Wichita Jr. League, 1985—. Mem. AICPA, Kans. Soc. CPAs, Wichita C. of C. Beta Gamma Sigma. Republican. Avocation: skiing. Home: 8501 Tipperary Wichita KS 67206 Office: Capital Enterprises Inc 300 N Main St Ste 200 Wichita KS 67201

RASCH, ELLEN MYRBERG, biophysics educator; b. Chicago Heights, Ill., Jan. 31, 1927; d. Arthur August and Helen Catherine (Stelle) Myrberg; m. Robert W. E. Rasch, June 17, 1950; 1 son, Martin Karl. PhB with honors, U. Chgo., 1945, BS in Biol. Sci., 1947, MS in Botany, 1948, PhD, 1950. Asst. histologist Am. Meat Inst. Found., Chgo., 1950-51; USPHS postdoctoral fellow U. Chgo., 1951-53, rsch. assoc. dept. zoology, 1954-59; rsch. assoc. Marquette U., Milw., 1962-65, assoc. prof. biology 1965-68, prof. biology, 1968-75, Wehr Disting. prof. biophysics, 1975-78; rsch. prof. biophysics East Tenn. State U., John H. Quillen Coll. Medicine, Johnston City, 1979—; interim chmn. dept. cellular biophysics, 1986—. Mem. Wis. Bd. Basic Sci. Examiners, 1971-75, sec. bd., 1973-75. Recipient Postdoctoral fellowship USPHS, 1951-53, Research Career Devel. award, 1967-72; Teaching Excellence award Marquette U., 1975; Kreeger-Wolf vis. disting. prof. in biol. sci. Northwestern U., 1979. Fellow AAAS, Royal Microscopic soc.; mem. Am. Microscopical Soc., Am. Soc. Cell Biology, Am. Soc. Zoologists, Am. Soc. Ichthyologists and Herpetologists, The Histochem. Soc., Phi Beta Kappa, Sigma Xi. Contbr. articles to various publs. Home: 1504 Chickees St Johnson City TN 37604 Office: East Tenn State U Biophysics Dept Box 15 130A Johnson City TN 37614-0002

RASKIN, FLORENCE BRAAF, hospital administrator; b. N.Y.C., Aug. 6, 1957; d. Harvey and Claire (Mintzis) B. BA, Cornell U., 1979; MPH, U. Calif., Berkeley, 1982, MBA, 1983. Rsch. asst. Meml. Sloan Kettering Cancer Ctr., N.Y.C., 1979-80; staff asst. Alameda County Health Care Agy., Oakland, Calif., 1981; cons. City of Berkeley Health Dept., 1982; asst. mktg. project Alta Bates Corp., Berkeley, 1982-83; asst. v.p. strategic planning St. Luke's Hosp., San Francisco, 1983-86; adminstrv. asst. to physician in chief Kaiser Found. Hosp., Hayward, Calif., 1986; asst. administr. Kaiser Found. Hosp., Hayward, 1986—. Mem. ACLU, Bay Area Health Care Planners (treas. 1988—), Health Care Execs. No. Calif. (symposium chair 1990). Office: Kaiser Found Hosp 27400 Hesperian Blvd Hayward CA 94545

RASMUSSEN, CAREN NANCY, hospital executive; b. Fort Riley, Kans., July 7, 1950; d. Stanley Junior and Katherina Wilhelmina (Wagner) R. AAS, Grand Rapids Jr. Coll., 1970; BS, U. Md., 1977. Med. sec., Walter Reed Army Med. Ctr., Washington, 1970-72, sec. procurement, 1972-76, contract specialist, 1976-79, 81-84; contract specialist Kadena Air Base, Okinawa, 1979-81; procurement analyst Walter Reed Med. Ctr., 1984—, sr. contracting specialist, 1988—. Fellow Nat. Assn. Female Execs.; mem. Nat. Contract Mgmt. Assn. Democrat. Avocations: photography; stamp collecting; gardening; travel. Home: 17514 Longview Ln Olney MD 20832 Office: Walter Reed Army Med Ctr Directorate of Contracting Washington DC 20307

RASMUSSEN, EVIE WEBB, financial institution executive; b. Wurzburg, Franken, Fed. Republic of Germany, June 18, 1952; came to U.S., 1956; d. Robert Daniel and Rosemarie Franziska (Scheidermeier) Webb; m. Terry James Rasmussen, Dec. 29, 1973; 1 child, John Robert. Student, Mt. Hood Community Coll., Portland, Oreg., 1983-84, Claremont Coll., Pamona, Calif., 1984-86. Clk. Unishops Inc., Portland, Oreg., 1969-71; teller Tigard (Oreg.) Community Fed. Credit Union, 1980-81; auditor Nat. Credit Union Adminstrn., Portland, 1981-83; chief exec. officer United Assn. NW Federal Credit Union, Portland, 1983—. Vol. Portland Easter Seals, 1986—, Nat. Fedn. for Blind, 1987. Credit Union Nat. Assns. scholar 1984. Mem. Nat. Assn. Female Execs., Credit Union Womens Assn., Oregon Credit Union League (scholarship com. 1983—), budget com. 1986—), bd. dirs. dir.-at-large, 1987, bd. dirs. Columbia chpt. 1985—), Smithsonian Assocs. Club: Toastmasters (Portland) (treas. 1987—). Office: United Assn NW Fed Credit Union 2111 NE 43d Ave Portland OR 97213

RASMUSSEN, JULIE SHIMMON, cellist, educator; b. Aberdeen, S.D., June 3, 1940; d. George Barr and Clara (Lange) Shimmon; m. Frederick Robert Rasmussen, Apr. 1, 1961 (div. May 1971). BMusic, Ind. U., 1963; MEd, U. Fla., 1967. Cert. tchr., Fla. Coord. music Bradford County Sch. Bd., Starke, Fla., 1965-68; tchr. Duval County Sch. Bd., Jacksonville, Fla., 1968-69, community edn., 1972-79, program devel., 1979—; master tchr. Clay County Sch. Bd., Orange Park, Fla., 1969-72; facilitator, mem. planning com. Duval County Sch. Bd., Jacksonville, 1985-86. Grant writer in ednl. areas, 1979—. Com. mem. Jacksonville Community Coun., Inc., 1973; cellist Jacksonville Symphony, 1963-65; tech. asst. Arts Assembly of Jacksonville, Inc., 1979-82; mem. Cummer Art Gallery, Jacksonville, 1983; bd. dirs. YWCA, 1986; active Resource Devel. Assistance Program Com. for Vol. Jacksonville, 1986—. Recipient Little Red Schoolhouse award Fla. Dept. Edn., 1977-78, Sense of Community award Duval County Community Edn., 1979; Internat. String Congress grantee Musician's Union, 1961. Mem. Fla. Ednl. Rsch. Assn., Pi Kappa Lambda, Phi Delta Kappa, Kappa Delta Pi (parliamentarian 1985-86). Democrat. Lutheran. Club: Pilot. Avocations: physical fitness, jogging, swimming, cycling, psychology. Home: 3946 St John's Ave Jacksonville FL 32205 Office: Duval County Sch Bd 1701 Prudential Dr Adminstrn Bldg 2d Fl Jacksonville FL 32207

RASMUSSEN, KATHLEEN ANNE, legal assistant; b. Hammond, Ind., Sept. 16, 1958; d. Thomas Jefferson II and Agnes Margaret (Mannion) Golden; m. Dan L. Rasmussen, Feb. 22, 1978 (dec. Dec. 1978). BS in Justice and Pub. Safety, Auburn U., 1985, MPA, 1986, MS in Justice and Pub. Safety, 1987, M.Polit. Sci., 1988. Cert. legal asst. technician, legal asst. administr. Legal asst. Johnson and Thorington, Attys. at Law, Montgomery, Ala., 1985-86; legal asst. Office of Gen. Counsel Ala. State Dept. Edn., Montgomery, 1986-90; legal asst. Ala. Dept. Econ. and Community Affairs, Montgomery, 1990—; chmn. curriculum com. Auburn U. at Montgomery, 1984—; legal asst. adv. com. Auburn U. Blood drive coord. ARC, Montgomery, 1987—; campaign worker United Way campaign, Montgomery, 1987—; contbr. Friends of the Libr., Montgomery, 1986—; mem. Disabled Am. Vets., Montgomery, 1981—; charter mem. Montgomery Mus. Fine Arts, 1987—, Ala. Shakespeare Festival, Montgomery, 1989, Montgomery Women Civitan, 1990—. With U.S. Army, 1976-81. Vice Chancellor's Acad. Achievement scholar Auburn U., 1983, 84. Mem. Nat. Assn. Legal Assts., Ala. Assn. Legal Assts., Montgomery County Bar Assn. (legal asst. sect., continuing legal edn. com. 1987—, treas. 1990, chmn. membership com. 1990), NAFE, Assn. Fed. Investigators, Am. Soc. for Pub. Adminstrn. (bd. dirs. 1985—, newsletter com. 1985—), Die Hard Cub Fan Club Chgo., Auburn U. Alumni Assn., Civitan (charter mem. Montgomery Women club 1990—), Lambda Alpha Epsilon (pres., sec. Auburn chpt. 1984—), Phi Theta Kappa, Alpha Phi Sigma, Omicron Delta Kappa, Pi Sigma Alpha. Republican. Roman Catholic. Office: Ala Dept Econ Community Affairs Legal Section 3465 Norman Bridge Rd Montgomery AL 36106

RASOR, DORIS LEE, educator; b. Gonzales, Tex., June 25, 1929; d. Leroy and Ora (Power) DuBose; m. Jimmie E. Rasor, Dec. 27, 1947; children: Jimmy Lewis, Roy Lynn. BS, Abilene (Tex.) Christian U., 1949. Part-time sec. Abilene Christian Coll., 1946-50; sec. Radford Wholesale Grocery, Abilene, 1950-52; tchr. Odessa (Tex.) High Sch., 1967—. Author play: The Lost Pearl, 1946. Recipient Am. Legion award, 1946. Mem. AAUW, Classroom Tchrs. Assn., Tex. Tchrs. Assn., NEA, Tex. Bus. Educators Assn., Alpha Delta Kappa (pres. 1976-78). Ch. of Christ. Home: 3882 Kenwood Odessa TX 79762 Office: Odessa High School 1301 N Dotsy Odessa TX 79760

RASPER, DEBORAH YOUNG, health science facility administrator; b. Bluffton, Ind., Dec. 24, 1950; d. Jacques Edward and Eleanor (Shafer) Young; m. Alan Frank Rasper, Apr. 5, 1975. BS, U. Cin., 1973; MHA, Xavier U., 1980. Dietitian's asst., dietetic trainee Provdence Hosp., Cin., 1973-74; adminstrv. dietitian The Christ Hosp., Cin., 1974-79; exec. asst., dir. transition St. Francis, St. George Hosp. Inc., Cin., 1979-82; adminstrv. dir. Mgmt. Dynamics, Inc., Cin., 1982-84; asst. administr. Univ. Clin. Hosp., Cin., 1984-88, CareUnit Hosp., Cin., 1988-90; v.p. clin. svcs. Margaret Mary Community Hosp., Batesville, Inc., 1990—. Mem. Adv. Com. Dietetic Intership Christ Hosp., 1980—; mem., chmn. St. John's Learning Ctr. Bd.,

1985—. Mem. Am. Coll. Healthcare Exec., Tri. State Health Administr. Forum, Am. Hosp. Assn. Home: 2660 Cyclorama Dr Cincinnati OH 45211

RATAJCZAK, HELEN VOSSKUHLER, immunologist; b. Tucson, Ariz., Apr. 9, 1938; d. Maximillian Philip and Marion Harriet (Messer) Vosskuhler; m. Edward Francis Ratajczak, June 1, 1959 (div. 1968); children—Lorraine, Eric, Peter, Eileen. B.S., U. Ariz., 1959, M.S., 1970; Ph.D., 1976. Asst. research scientist U. Iowa Coll. Medicine, Iowa City, 1976-78; instr. U. Pitts., 1978-80; research assoc., 1980-81; asst. prof. Loyola U. Coll. Medicine, Maywood, Ill., 1981-83; research immunologist Ill. Inst. Tech., Research Inst., Chgo., 1983-86, staff immunologist, 1986-88, sr. immunologist, 1988—; instr. Ill. Inst. Tech., 1988—. Fellow Am. Thoracic Soc., 1974-76, NIH, 1978; grantee Loyola U., 1981. Mem. Am. Thoracic Soc., Am. Assn. Immunologists, Chgo. Assn. Immunologists (sec./treas. 1986-88), N.Y. Acad. Scis., AAAS, Soc. Toxicology, Internat. Soc. for Chronobiology, Daus. Am. Colonists, Sigma Xi, Kappa Kappa Gamma. Republican. Roman Catholic. Avocations: Piano playing; sewing; baking. Office: IIT Rsch Inst 10 W 35th St Chicago IL 60616

RATCLIFF, SUELLEN, employment manager; b. Peoria, Ill., Nov. 6, 1956; d. Harold Boardman and Betty Lee (Swisher) R. BA in Psychology, Baylor U., 1978. Employment coordinator Fox and Jacobs, Dallas, 1979-81; recruiter A.D.P., Dallas, 1982; mgr. recruiting Uccel Corp., Dallas, 1982-87; area employment mgr. Digital Equipment Corp., Dallas, 1987—. Vol. Children's Mental Health and Retardation, Peoria, summers 1974-78; bd. dirs. SW High Tech. Coop. Office: Digital Equipment Corp 4851 LBJ Freeway Suite 1100 Dallas TX 75244

RATCLIFFE, ANN ELIZABETH, health care service representative; b. Norton, Va., Apr. 24, 1963; d. Thomas L. Ratcliffe and Jacqueline A. Tinsley-Ratcliffe. BS in Health Sci. Edn., U. Fla., 1985. Mem. support staff Environ. Scis., Engring., Gainesville, Fla., 1985-86; counselor, case worker Mental Health Svcs., Gainesville, 1986-87; office mgr. Baringer-Springer Group, PA, Gainesville, 1987-89; account svc. rep. Humana Helath Care Plans, Ormond Beach, Fla., 19909—. Mem. NAFE, Am. Alliance Health, Phys. Edn., Recreation & Dance, Am. Coll. Health Assn., World Wildlife Fund, Environ. Def. Fund, Eta Sigma Gamma. Republican. Methodist. Home: PO Box 1447 Daytona Beach FL 32115-1447 Office: Baringer Springer Group PA 3700 NW 91st St #C100 Gainesville FL 32606

RATCLIFFE, KATHLEEN MARY, marketing professional; b. Chgo., Jan. 19, 1958; d. Robert Henry and Kathleen Mary (Cummins) R. With Albert's Hosiery Stores, Inc., 1976-82; supr. trainee Albert's Hosiery Stores, Inc., Houston and Schaumburg, Ill., 1980-81; area supr. Albert's Hosiery Stores, Inc., Washington, 1981-82; dir. Carbondale (Ill.) Conv. and Tourism Bur., 1982-85; conv. sales exec. St. Louis Conv. and Visitors Commn., 1985-89; dir. mktg. Radisson Hotel, Denver, 1989—. Mem. Humane Soc. U.S., Washington, 1988-89, People for Ethical Treatment of Animals, Washington, 1988—, Greenpeace, 1987—. Mem. St. Louis Area Meeting Planners Internat. (bd. dirs. 1987—, Supplier of the Yr. 1988, 89), Meeting Planners Internat. (rels. com. Dallas chpt. 1988—), Ill. Coun. Conv. and Visitor Burs. (sec., chair legis. com. 1983-85), Ill. Dept. Commerce and Community Affairs (exec. adv. com. dept. tourism Springfield, Ill. chpt. 1984-85), Ill. Soc. Assn. Execs. (Svc. award 1984), Nat. Assn. Profl. Saleswomen, Profl. Conv. Mgmt. Assn., Greenpeace, Cardondale C. of C. (auction yard sale com. 1988-89). Democrat. Office: Radisson Hotel Denver 1550 Court Pl Denver CO 80202

RATCLIFFE, SHIRLEY PENDLETON, real estate broker, communications executive; b. Blountville, Tenn., Mar. 30, 1932; d. Paris Lee and Elizabeth Armetta (Gammon) Pendleton; m. Robert Issac Ratcliffe, Jan. 26, 1952 (div. Apr. 1970); children—Paula, Louise, Darby. Student U. Ky., 1952, East Tenn. U., 1962-63; grad. Grad. Realtors Inst. Lic. broker, Tenn., Va., N.C. Broker, Pendleton Real Estate, Blountville, 1970—; v.p. Mount Empire Devel. Co., Kingsport, Tenn., 1971-74, Pendleton Land Co., Blountville, 1975—; pres. Tenn. Radio Telephone, Kingsport, 1982—, Cell-Tel of Knoxville, Kingsport, 1985—; chmn. Cellular One, Tri-Cities, Washington, 1984-85; pres. Ragtime Investments, Kingsport, 1978—. Vol. Contact Concern, Kingsport, 1978—; mem. Sullivan County Republican Exec. Bd., Tenn.; bd. dirs. Sullivan County LWV. Methodist. Clubs: Ridgefields Country, Ridgefield Garden. Lodge: Order Eastern Star. Avocations: golf; tennis; bridge. Home: 536-B Fleetwood Ct Kingsport TN 37660 Office: Pendleton Real Estate PO Box 253 Main St Blountville TN 37617

RATH, LILLIAN VICTORIA, toy manufacturing executive; b. Pitts., Oct. 1, 1952; d. Frank Eugene and Lillian Brandon (Spang) R.; m. Ole Raff, Dec. 4, 1988. BS, Cornell U., 1975; MBA, Wharton U. Pa., 1980. CPA. CPA Coopers and Lybrand, Pitts., 1975-78; with American Express, N.Y.C., 1979; sr. finance mgr. Walt Disney Prodns., Los Angeles, 1980-84; pres. Today's Kids, Dallas, 1984—; dir. Spang and Co., Butler, Pa., 1982—, Assoc. Industries of Ark., Little Rock, 1986—, Toy Mfg. Assn., N.Y.C., 1987—. bd. dirs. Sparks Regional Hosp., Ft. Smith, Ark., 1987—. Republican. Home: 6412 Lafayette Way Dallas TX 75230 Office: Today's Kids 13630 Neutron Rd Dallas TX 75244

RATH, MARI KAYE, litigation consultant; b. Elgin, Ill., Sept. 10, 1958; d. Lester Herman and Marsilia Marie (Parrucci) R. BBA, Western Ill. U., 1979. CPA, Ill. Acct. Arthur Andersen & Co., Chgo., 1980-81; exec. litigation cons. Peterson & Co., Chgo., 1981-90; owner, operator K's Auction Svc. and ACD Apparel, 1989—; owner K's Auction Svc., Classic Auto Body. Named one of Outstanding Young Women of Am., 1987. Mem. Am. Inst. CPA's, Ill. Soc. CPA's, Ill. Auctioneers Assn. (sec.-treas. 1988—), Nat. Auctioneers Assn. Roman Catholic. Home: 38 W 196 US 20 Elgin IL 60123 Office: Peterson & Co 310 S Michigan Suite 1900 Chicago IL 60604

RATHFELDER, MARY L., administrating assistant; b. Tiffin, Ohio, July 26, 1932; d. Samuel G. and Ruth L. (Mills) Anglemyer; m. Irvin M. Rathfelder, Jan. 27, 1951; children: Norman, Marti. AS, Tiffin (Ohio) U., 1984. Adminstrv. asst. Ohio Bell Telephone Co., Fremont, 1954-84; sec. Sandusky Valley Ctr., Fremont, Ohio, 1985-90. Bd. dirs. St. Apptd. Spl. Advocate for Children, Seneca County, Tiffin, Ohio, c hairperson pers. com., 1989-90; vol. Hayes Presdl. Libr., Spiegel Grove, Fremont, Ohio, 1990—, Meml. Hosp., Fremont, 1990—. Mem. Pioneers of Am. (sec., treas.), Joint Commn. on the Accreditation of Health Care Orgns., Task Force Compensation Com., Am. Legion (aux.), Ea. Star. Home: 5496 N CR #15 Green Springs OH 44836

RATHJÉ, JUDY CHRISTINE, health science facility administrator; b. Bklyn., Nov. 4, 1952; d. James A. and Margaret Agnes Smith; 1 child, Sheri Christine. AAS in Nursing, Hudson Valley Community Coll., Troy, N.Y., 1973; BS in Nursing and Psychology, SUNY, Albany, 1987; postgrad. in bus. adminstrn., Calif. Coast U., 1987. RN. Scrub nurse, 1st asst. Dr. Metin Koluksuz, Schenectady, N.Y., 1974-77; staff nurse, relief head nurse St. Clare's Hosp., Schenectady, 1973-77; dir. rev. programs Profl. Standards Rev. Orgn., Inc., Albany, 1977-79; quality assurance coordinator Martha's Vineyard Hosp., Oak Bluffs, Mass., 1979-80; sr. nurse St. Peter's Hosp., Albany, 1980-84; nurse mgr. Rensselaer Poly. Inst., Troy, 1982-84; dir. nursing and patient services Samaritan Hosp., Troy, 1984-88; program coordinator, adj. faculty Cornell U., Albany, 1985-87; dir. nursing consultative services Hosp. Assn. N.Y. State, Albany, 1988—; cons. in health care mgmt. Mem. Am. Orgn. Nurse Execs., Am. Mgmt. Assn., Bus. and Profl. Women's Assn., Northeastern N.Y. Nursing Service Adminstr.'s Assn., Nat. League for Nursing. Democrat. Office: Hosp Assn NY State Albany NY 12207

RATHJE, RHONDA JEAN, community affairs executive; b. Chgo., Aug. 28, 1958; d. Victor Dean and Rae Jean (Henzen) R. BA in Journalism and Speech, Iowa State U., Dallas, 1980; MA in Interdisciplinary Studies, U. Tex., Dallas, 1988. With GTE S.W., 1980—; pub. affairs mgr. GTE S.W., Irving, Tex., 1988-89, mgr. community affairs, 1989—; adv. dir. Straight, Inc., Irving. Mem. pub. rels. com. Vol. Ctr. of Dallas, 1989-90. Named Woman of Yr., Plano (Tex.) C. of C., 1989. Mem. Women in Communications, Inc., Pub. Rels. Soc. Am. (bd. dirs. membership com. 1990—). Republican. Lutheran. Office: GTE-SW 290 E Carpenter Fwy Irving TX 75062

RATHKE, DEBRA ANN, hospital executive; b. Toledo, Aug. 14, 1953; d. Earl S. and Dolores Rose (Gregor) Arthurs; m. Daniel Karle Rathke, June 26, 1981; 1 child, Devin James. BS, U. Toledo, 1975, MS, 1976, MEd, 1976, MA, 1983; postgrad., Cornell U., 1978. Planning assoc. Health Planning Assn. Northwest Ohio, Maumee, 1977-82; dir. planning Flower Meml. Hosp., Sylvania, Ohio, 1982-85; dir. planning and mktg. Flower Meml. Hosp. & Crestview of Ohio, Sylvania, 1985—. Mem. Ohio Soc. Hosp. Planning and Mktg. (bd. dirs., pres.-elect 1989-90, pres. 1990), Ohio Hosp. Assn., Soc. Hosp. Planning and Mktg. of Am. Hosp. Assn., Toledo Planning Forum (bd. dirs. 1990), Hosp. Coun. Northwest Ohio (chmn.-elect planning dirs. com.), Alpha Kappa Delta, Pi Gamma Mu, Alpha Omicron Pi Alumnae (officer Theta Psi Corp. Bd. 1984-86). Roman Catholic. Office: Flower Meml Hosp 5200 Harroun Rd Sylvania OH 43560

RATHKE, SHEILA WELLS, advertising and public relations executive; b. Columbia, S.C., Aug. 9, 1943; d. Walter John and Elizabeth Marie (McLaughlin) Wells; m. David Bray Rathke, Sept. 1966 (div. Apr. 1977); 1 child, Erinn Michele. BA summa cum laude, U. Pitts., 1976, postgrad., 1976-77. Loan coord. Equibank, Pitts., 1961-65; office mgr. U.S. Steel Corp., Pitts., 1966-70; sr. v.p., gen. mgr. Burson-Marsteller, Pitts., 1977—, also bd. dirs.; adviser Exec. Report Mag., Pitts., 1986-88; instr. Slippery Rock Coll., Pitts., 1984-85. Trustee U. Pitts., 1986—, ann. giving fund drive, 1989—; bd. dirs. Vocat. Rehabil. Ctr., 1987—, Freewheelers, 1989—. Named one of Outstanding Young Women of Am., 1977. Mem. Pitts. Advt. Club (bd. dirs. 1988—, pres. 1990), Female Execs. Am., Alpha Sigma Lambda (charter). Home: 15 Marquette Rd Pittsburgh PA 15229 Office: Burson-Marsteller 1 Gateway Ctr Pittsburgh PA 15222-1433

RATLIFF, DONNA LEE, corporate treasurer; b. Manhattan, N.Y., Nov. 21, 1946; d. Josiah William and Edith Mae (Peruzzi) Davis; m. Ronald Wayne Ratliff, Apr. 16, 1966; children: Lisa Ann, Colleen Marie, Brock Wayne. Bookkeeper Downtown Motors, Canton, Ohio, 1964-65, title clk., 1965-66; credit clk. 1st Nat. Bank Pa., Erie, 1971-73, loan asst., 1973-76, internal auditor, 1976-78; acctg. mgr. Budget Rent-A-Car, Houston, 1978-79; sec.-treas. Gill Services, Inc., Houston, 1979-84; controller Santa Fe Supply Co., Inc., Houston, 1984-85; treas. GNI Group Inc., Webster, Tex., 1985—. Pres. Greengate Swim Team, Spring, Tex., 1984. Mem. Nat. Assn. Female Execs., Nat. Notary Assn. Home: 6619 Lynngate Dr Spring TX 77373 Office: GNI Group Inc 1001 Fannin Ste 4656 Houston TX 77002

RATLIFF, LEIGH ANN, pharmacist; b. Long Beach, Calif., May 20, 1961; d. Harry Warren and Verna Lee (Zwink) R. D in Pharmacy, U. Pacific, 1984. Registered pharmacist, Calif., Nev. Pharmacist intern Green Bros. Inc., Stockton, Calif., 1982-84, staff pharmacist Thrifty Corp., Long Beach, Calif., 1984-85, head pharmacist, 1986-87, pharm. buyer, 1987—. Mem. Pacific Alumni Assocs., Nat. Trust for Hist. Preservation, Friends of Rancho Los Cerritos; treas. Bixby Knolls Ter. Homeowners Assn., 1988-90; vol. Docent Rancho Los Cerritos Hist. Site, 1988—. Mem. NAFE, Am. Pharm. Assn., Am. Inst. History Pharmacy, Calif. Pharmacist Assn., Lambda Kappa Sigma. Republican. Methodist. Avocations: creative writing, horseback riding, fishing, house plants, painting. Home: 3913 Virginia Rd #301 Long Beach CA 90807 Office: Thrifty Corp 3424 Wilshire Blvd Los Angeles CA 90010

RATNER, LILLIAN GROSS, psychiatrist; b. N.Y.C., Aug. 18, 1932; d. Herman and Sarah (Widelitz) Gross. BA, Barnard Coll., 1953; postgrad. U. Lausanne (Switzerland), 1954-56; MD, Duke U., 1959. Diplomate Bd. Pediatrics, Am. Bd. Psychiatry and Neurology, Am. Bd. Child Psychiatry; m. Harold Ratner, Feb. 4, 1961; children: Sanford Miles, Marcia Ellen. Intern Kings County Hosp., Bklyn., 1959-60, resident, 1967-70, fellow in child psychiatry, 1969-70, psychiatrist devel. evaluation clinic, 1970-72; resident Jewish Hosp., Bklyn., 1960-62, fellow in pediatric psychiatry, 1962-63; physician in charge pediatric psychiat. clinic Greenpoint (N.Y.) Hosp., 1964-67; pvt. practice psychiatry, Great Neck, N.Y., 1970—; clin. instr. psychiatry Downstate Med. Ctr., Bklyn., 1970-74, clin. assoc. prof.; lectr. in psychiatry Columbia U., 1974—; psychiat. cons. N.Y.C. Bd. Edn., 1972-75, Queens Children's Hosp., 1975—; mem. med. bd. Camp Sussex (N.J.), 1963—, Saras Ctr., Great Neck, N.Y., 1977—. Fellow Am. Acad. Pediatrics, Am. Acad. Psychiatry, Am. Acad. Child Psychiatry; mem. Am. Psychiat. Assn., Nassau Psychiat. Assn., Bklyn. Psychiat. Assn., Bklyn. Pediatric Soc. (sr. mem.), Nassau Pediatric Socs., Soc. Adolescent Psychiatry, N.Y. Coun. Child Psychiatry, Soc. Clin. and Exptl. Hypnosis, Am. Med. Women's Assn. (pres. Nassau), AMA, N.Y., Kings County med. socs., Am. Soc. Clin. Hypnosis, N.Y. Soc. Clin. Hypnosis (past pres.), Internat. Soc. for Study of Multiple Personality and Dissociation (founder, pres. L.I. component study group). Home and Office: 55 Bluebird Dr Great Neck NY 11023

RATNER-GANTSHAR, BARBARA GRACE, education association administrator; b. Phila., Nov. 7, 1933; d. Jules and Samuella (Isadora) Ratner; m. Martin Gantshar, June 1961 (div. 1984); children: Judith Susan Claire, Lois Nichole Merraine, David Joseph. MS, Simmons Coll., 1985. Project dir. Boston Family Inst., Brookline, Mass., 1982-84; exec. dir. Summer's World Ctr. for the Arts, Worcester, Mass., 1985-87; assoc. dir. of devel. Am. U., Washington, 1987-88; dir. devel. Harford Day Sch., Bel Air, Md., 1988-90; cons. Alzheimer's Disease Ctr., Falls Ch., Va., 1988, The Galleries, Wellesley, Mass., 1984-85, The Etz Chaym Ctr., Balt., 1990. Author: A Beacon Was Hoisted in Boston, 1975, Philadelphia: The City and the Bell, 1976. Apptd. commr. Harford County Commn. for Women, Bel Air, 1989; bd. mem. Sexual Assault-Spousal Abuse Resource Ctr. Mem. AAUW, LWV, Nat. Soc. of Fundraising Execs., Mass. and R.I. Antiquarian Booksellers Assn. (fair coord. 1978-79). Democrat. Jewish. Home: 114 Oakmoore Ct Bel Air MD 21014

RATTERREE, TINA GAYE, teacher; b. Murray, Ky., July 17, 1963; d. Allen Brice and Frances Christine (Williams) R. BS in Elem. Edn., Murray State U., 1985, MEd, 1987. Cert. tchr., reading specialist, Ky., Libr. Sci. Endorsement, 1989. Elem. tchr. Murray (Ky.) Headstart, 1987-88, Murray Elem. Sch., 1988—; trainer Math. Manipuatives Workshops; writing cons. Purchase Area Writing Project, summer 1990. Tchr. Grace Bapt. Ch., Murray, 1986-88; co-chairperson Am. Edn. Week, 1988; fund raiser PTO Fund, 1987-89; treas. Murray Edn. Assn., 1988-89. Grantee Murray Found. of Excellence, 1988-89. Mem. Internat. Reading Assn. (sec. 1987-90), AAUW (sec. 1986-88). Baptist. Home: 712 Elm St Murray KY 42071

RATTLEY, JESSIE MENIFIELD, former mayor, educator; b. Birmingham, Ala., May 4, 1929; d. Alonzo Menifield; m. Robert L. Rattley; children: Florence, Robin. BS in Bus. Edn. with hons., Hampton U., 1951; postgrad., Hampton Inst., IBM Data Processing Sch., LaSalle Extension U. Tchr. Huntington High Sch., Newport News, Va., 1951-52; owner, operator Peninsula Bus. Coll., Newport News, 1952-85; hosp. administr. Newport News Gen. Hosp. from 1986; elected mayor of Newport News, 1986-90. Mem. Nat. League of Cities, bd. dirs., 1975, 2d v.p., 1977, 1st v.p., 1978, pres. 1979, active various coms. and task forces; active many adv. bd., coms., State Dem. Party. Recipient Cert. of Merit Daus. of Isis, 2d annual Martin Luther King, Jr. Meml. award Old Dominion U., Sojourner Truth award Nat. Assn. of Negro Bus. and Profl. Women's Clubs, Cert. of Appreciation NAACP. *

RATTY, TESS MCBRIDE, media executive; b. Billings, Mont., July 20, 1944; d. Murray Wallace and Patricia Jean (Franzen) McBride; m. Raymond W. Nunn, Apr. 24, 1964 (div. 1969); children: Shannon McBride Waibel, Amy McBride Nunn; m. Brian Dudley Ratty, Dec. 4, 1971. Student, Calif. Coll. Arts and Crafts, Oakland, 1962-65; BS, Portland (Oreg.) State U., 1988. Mgr. advt. prodn. Meier & Frank, Portland, 1967-69; asst. mgr. advt. Pendleton Woolen Mills, Portland, 1969-74; corp. v.p. Media West, Inc., Beaverton, Oreg., 1974—. Exec. producer spl. interest videos, 1986, 87 (Double 5-Star award Video Choice Mag. 1988). Bd. dirs. Northwest Pilot Project, Portland, 1984-86; pres. bd. dirs. Beaverton Arts Commn., 1988-89; chmn. Art in the Marketplace, Beaverton, 1987; trustee Parry Ctr. for Children, Portland, 1987—; judge Oreg. Jr. Miss Scholarship, Eugene, 1986; adv. Metro Pub. Art Adv. Panel, 1987—; active in Edn. Svc. Dist. County of Washington, Oreg., 1987—. Recipient Vol. award Beaverton Arts Commn., 1987, 88. Mem. NAFE, Oreg. Media Producers Assn., Portland Advt. Fedn. (Nat. Addy award nat. fedn. 1972), Portland State Alumni Assn., Portland C. of C., Washington County Hist. Soc., Nat. Mus. Women in the

Arts (charter Beaverton sister cities chpt.). Republican. Office: Media West Inc 10255 SW Arctic Dr Beaverton OR 97005

RAUB, FRIEDA WRIGHT, community worker; b. New Brunswick, Can., May 7, 1912; came to U.S., 1936; d. Ira B. and Mabel Oranda (Mitton) Wright; m. Archie Maxwell Raub, Aug. 5, 1936 (dec. 1987); children: Richard Albert, Edward Dwight. Student, Tchrs. Coll., Fredericton, Can., 1928-30; BS in Edn., Upsala Coll., 1953. Tchr. pub. schs. Can., 1930-36; pres. Franklin Elem. Sch., East Orange, N.J., 1951-52, Clifford Scott High Sch., East Orange, N.J., 1957-58; tchr. schs. N.J. & Md., 1957-77. Bd. dirs. YWCA, East Orange, N.J., 1954-57, treas., 1957-58; trustee United Fund West Essex County, N.J.; chmn. publs. Essex County PTA, 1957-60; chmn. fund raising drs., N.J., Md., 1954-77; mem. Bd. Pub. Librs., Bethesda, Md., 1972-77, Monroe County, N.C., 1989—; v.p. Central Rep. Com., Montgomery County, Md., 1972-77; precinct chmn. Eureka Precinct Monroe County, N.C., 1984—; pres. Whispering Pines Assn., N.C., 1981-82. Mem. Civic Club Southern Pines (v.p., pres. 1982-86), Garden Club (v.p. 1980—). Republican. Presbyterian. Home: 325 A Pine Ridge Dr Whispering Pines NC 28327

RAUB, MARGARET JANE, mathematics educator; b. Youngstown, Ohio, Mar. 16, 1948; d. Karl and Marie Theresa (Herrlich) R. AB, Youngstown State U., 1971; MA, Cleve. State U., 1980. Tchr. Cardinal Mooney High Sch., Youngstown, 1971-73, St. Joseph Acad., Cleve., 1973-78; tchr., chair math. dept. Strongsville (Ohio) High Sch., 1978—; instr. Capital Univ., Columbus, Ohio, 1980—. Author: (with others) Focus on Functions, 1985. Martha Holden Jennings Found. scholar, 1984; Woodrow Wilson Found. fellow, 1985, NASA Newmast fellow, 1987, Pimm fellow Oberlin Coll., 1989; recipient Presdl. award NSF, 1986. Mem. Nat. Coun. of Tchrs. of Maths., Greater Cleve. Coun. of Tchrs. of Maths. (bd. dirs 1986—, pres. 1989), Coun. Tchrs. of Maths., Ohio Coun. Tchrs. Maths. (bd. dirs. N.E. Ohio chpt. 1988—), Phi Kappa Phi, Delta Kappa Gamma. Democrat. Roman Catholic. Office: Strongsville High Sch 20025 Lunn Rd Strongsville OH 44136

RAUCH, KATHLEEN, retail executive; b. Franklin Square, N.Y., Oct. 30, 1951; d. William C. and Marian (Shull) R.; BA., U. Rochester, 1973; M.A. in L.S., U. Mich., 1974; postgrad. N.Y.U., 1981-82. Media specialist Sutton (Mass.) Sch., 1974-76; program cons. Advanced Mgmt. Rsch. Internat. N.Y.C., 1976-79; pub. rels. cons., N.Y.C., 1979; pres. N.Y. chpt. NOW, N.Y.C., 1979-80; computer programmer Blue Cross/Blue Shield of Greater N.Y., N.Y.C., 1981-82; computer programmer analyst Fed. Res. Bank of N.Y., 1983-84; systems officer Citibank, N.A., 1984-85; systems analyst Fed. Res. Bank of N.Y., 1986-89; pres. Panorama Videos, 1989—; computer and children's libr. East Meadow (N.Y.) Pub. Libr., 1989—. Mem. NOW (dir. pub. rels. N.Y.C. chpt. 1978, v.p. programs 1978, chmn. bd. 1981, founding mem., sec. Svc. Fund, N.Y.C. chpt. 1981), Lambda Legal Def. and Edn. Fund. Mem. Assn. for Women in Computing (v.p. membership 1984, exec. v.p. 1985, treas. 1986, mem.-at-large 1987, pres. 1988), L.I. Computer Assn., L.I. Ladies' Soccer League, Nassau Libr. Assn., Suffolk Libr. Assn., N.Y. State Libr. Assn., Caths. for a Free Choice, Greenpeace.

RAUCH, MARY LAURISSA, infosystems specialist; b. San Antonio, Feb. 5, 1952; d. Laurence Walter and Mary Katherine (Becherer) B.; m. Robert Gary Rauch, Aug. 11, 1973; children: Andrea Marie, Regina Lynn. MBA, U. Iowa, 1982; BS in Chem., St. Ambrose U., 1974. Prodn. controller Eagle Signal, Davenport, Iowa, 1974-77; materials coor. Bear Mfg., Rock Island, Ill., 1977-80; materials mgr. Star Forms, Inc., Rock Island, Ill., 1980-85; dir. Star Forms Aquis Corp., Moline, Ill.; v.p. info. systems Bowater Communication Papers, Inc., Moline, 1986—. Mem. Data Processing Mgmt. Assn., NAFE. Roman Catholic. Home: 2 Windy Point Rock Island IL 61201 Office: Bowater Comm Papers Inc 4414 River Dr Moline IL 61265

RAUCH, ROXANE SPILLER, marketing executive, writer; b. New Rochelle, N.Y., June 11, 1935; d. Jesse Bernard and Hazel (Cooley) Spiller; m. Arthur Irving Rauch, Aug. 19, 1962 (div. Sept. 1977); children: David Spiller Rauch, Janine Beth Rauch. AB cum laude, Bryn Mawr Coll., 1957. Adminstrv. asst. I. Miller, N.Y.C., 1957; asst. publicity dir., fashion coord. Peck & Peck, N.Y.C., 1957-59; publicity and advt. dir. Suzy Perette, N.Y.C., 1959-61; campaign coord. N.Y. Conv. & Visitors Bur., 1961-64; assoc. exec. dir. N.Y.C.: Fashion Capital of the World, Inc., 1975-76; pres. TLP, Inc., N.Y.C., 1976-77; mktg. cons. Taubman Cos., Bloomfield Hills, Mich., 1977, 79-87; corp. pub. rels. dir. Simplicity Pattern Co. Inc., N.Y.C., 1978; dir., chief exec. officer Lifestyles People, Ltd., N.Y.C., 1987—; TV fashion advisor (on-camera) J. Walter Thompson's Cableshop, N.Y.C., 1982; co-dir., co-producer nat. fashion shows, 1980-81; fashion pub. rels. and advt. cons. NY Sportswear Assn., Fashion Capital (NYC), Cox & Co., Odette Barsa, Ohrbach & Benjamin, N.Y.C., 1970-77. Co-author: Country Inns New York State, 1984; contbr. articles to Tennis Midwest, 1984; columnist New Fla. mag., 1981-82. Travel spokesperson N.Y. State Dept. Commerce, 1985; TV feature reporter news dept. Sta. WSNL-TV, Channel 67, Central Islip, L.I., N.Y., 1985-86. Recipient First Place, Honorable Mention outstanding shopping ctr. advt. Chgo. Area Mktg. Dirs. Orgn., 1988, Cert. Hospitality N.Y. State C. of C., 1988. Mem. Internat. Coun. Shopping Ctrs., The Fashion Group, Bryn Mawr Club N.Y., Purveyors Club Greater N.Y. (hotel/restaurant cons. 1987—). Office: The Lifestyles People Ltd 1235 Park Ave Ste 4C New York NY 10128

RAUSEO, JANET C., architect; b. Riverhead, N.Y., July 28, 1963; d. Arthur H. and Doris I. (Jacobsen) Kremer; m. Lawrence John Rauseo, Aug. 15, 1987. BArch., Cooper Union, 1986. Design architect Philip Birnbaum & Assoc. PC, N.Y.C., 1986-89, Costas Kondylis Architects, P.C., N.Y.C., 1989—. Exhibitions include Aedes Deutsches Architektur Mus., Berlin, Vienna, and others.

RAVENS, CATHERINE ELIZABETH, public affairs specialist; b. Boston, Jan. 21, 1930; d. John Joseph and Elizabeth Mary (Pontuso) Tesorero; m. Fred Joseph Ravens Jr., June 9, 1951; children: Fred Joseph III, Margaret Perkins, David, Jean Ravens Phalen, Thomas M., Robert E. AA, Burdett Coll., 1949, Northeastern U., 1988. With U.S. Army Corps. Engrs., Anchorage, 1951-52; sec. U.S. Army Corps. Engrs., Waltham, Mass., 1978-84; intern pub. rels. U.S. Army Corps. Engrs., Waltham, 1984-85, pub. affairs specialist, 1985—. Editor Yankee Engr. newsletter U.S. Army Corps Engrs., 1988—; contbr. articles to profl. jours. Treas. St. Timothy Guild, Norwood, Mass., 1975-76; capt. tennis team, Town of Norwood, 1977-78, elections officer, 1982; com. mem. Campfire Girls Am., Norwood, 1965; asst. leader Girl Scouts U.S.A., 1973; den mother Cub Scouts Boy Scouts Am., 1972. Recipient Ofcl. Commendation U.S. Army Corps Engrs., 1982, Letters of Appreciation 1981, 83, 84. Roman Catholic. Club: Dartmouth Womens, St. Timothy Guild. Home: 72 Croydon Rd Norwood MA 02062 Office: US Army Corps Engrs 424 Trapelo Rd Waltham MA 02254-9149

RAVIN, MONA CLAIRE, counselor; b. Newark, Aug. 16, 1939. Student, Douglass Coll., New Brunswick, N.J., 1957-59; BSN, Columbia U., 1962; MSN, U. Pa., 1971; EdD, U. So. Calif., 1989. RN, Alaska, N.Y. Vis. nurse Vis. Nurses Assn. Eastern Union County, Elizabeth, N.J., 1962-64; pub. health nurse Fairbanks (Alaska) Health Ctr., 1967-69; instr. U. Pa., Phila., summer 1973; asst. prof. Alaska Meth. U., Anchorage, 1973-76, U. Alaska, Anchorage, 1976-80; pvt. practice kinlein counselor Anchorage, 1979—; bd. dirs., v.p. I Care Patient Support Network, Inc., Anchorage. Author: Forging A New Profession: The Practice of Kinlein, 1971-86, 1989; Editor, co-founder Journal of Kinlien, 1981-83; contbr. articles to profl. health jours. Named Outstanding Leader in Nursing in Alaska award Dist. 1 Alaska Nurses Assn., 1980. Mem. Nat. Soc. for Kinlein. Office: Kinlein Counselors 207 E Northern Lights Blvd Ste 110 Anchorage AK 99503

RAVITZ, ELENE BECKY, computer programmer; b. Montclair, N.J., Dec. 19, 1964; d. Lester and Florence (Snyder) R. BS, Montclair State Coll., Upper Montclair, N.J., 1987. Programmer, input clk. Montclair State Coll. Fin. Aid Office, Upper Montclair, 1983-87; programmer analyst N.J. Prudential Ins. Co. Am., Roseland, N.J., 1987—; student advisor N.J. Student Adv. Com., N.J. Bd. Higher Edn., Trenton, 1986-87. Democrat. Jewish. Office: Prudential Ins Co Am 3 Becker Farm Rd Roseland NJ 07068

RAWLINGS, MARY, escrow company executive; b. Lansing, Mich., Nov. 17, 1936; d. Frederick Thomas and Anna (Bondy) Belbeck; m. Richard M. Rawlings, Feb. 11, 1967 (div. 1985); children—Bonita Rawlings Walker, Mary Rawlings Rios, R. Patrick. Student, So. Calif. Sch. Escrows, Los Angeles, 1956-57, Pierce Coll., Woodland Hills, Calif., 1959-60. Vice pres., gen. mgr. Manhattan Mortgage Co., North Hollywood, Calif., 1962-66; mgr. San Fernando Valley Escrow Co., Calif., 1966-67; v.p., mgr. Golden West Escrow Co., Panorama City, Calif., 1967-77; pres. The Escrow Office, Inc., Woodland Hills, 1977—; bd. dirs. Escrow Agt.'s Fidelity Corp., Newport Beach, Calif., 1983-87, chmn., 1985-87; instr. Pierce Coll., 1978-80; appointed by Mayor Tom Bradley to Van Nuys Airport Citizens Adv. Council, 1987. Mem. 99's Inc. (Women Pilot of Yr. 1984), Calif. Escrow Assn. (bd. dirs. 1977-87), San Fernando Valley Escrow Assn. (pres. 1977). Avocations: flying; air racing. Office: The Escrow Office Inc 21228 Ventura Woodland Hills CA 91364

RAWLINS, CAROL LYNNE STANLEY, publisher; b. Portsmouth, Ohio, Nov. 26, 1940; d. Frank B. and Kathleen (Van Meter) Rolf; m. Larry Clinton Stanley (div. 1969); children: Larry Clinton Jr., Patricia Lynne. BS, Ohio State U. Owner Harbor Isle Mgmt., Pitts., 1972-80; real estate The Kroger Co., Columbus, Ohio, 1964-71; owner Tri State Marine Surveyors, Pitts., 1974—; pub. Synapse Pubis. Inc., Pitts. Animal Rescue League Western Pa., Pitts., 1982—; The Cousteau Soc., 1987—. Mem. Nat. Assn. Desk Top Pubs. Methodist. Office: Synapse Pubis Inc 1420 Centre Ave Ste 116 Pittsburgh PA 15219

RAWLINS, LINDLEY TOWNSEND, stockbroker; b. Greenwich, Conn., Apr. 16, 1950; d. Murray Morgan and Joyce (Wesley); m. James Alexander Mitchell; children: Morgan, Cuyler. BA, Am. U., 1972; postgrad., Adelphi U., 1982. Acct. exec. Hipp Waters, Stamford, Conn., 1973-77; stockbroker, v.p. Dean Witter Reynolds, Greenwich, Conn., 1977—. Mem. Cert. Fin. Planners (internat. bd. standards and practice). Home: 114 June Rd Stamford CT 06903 Office: Dean Witter Reynolds 3 Pickwick Pla Greenwich CT 06830

RAWLINS, PATTI LYNN, nurse; b. Jacksonville, Fla., May 26, 1960; d. Hershel and Nita Lou (Waters) R. Assoc. Sci., Fla. Jr. Coll., 1981; postgrad., U. N. Fla., 1984-89. RN, Fla. Nursing aide St. Lukes Hosp., Jacksonville, 1978-81; staff nurse Jacksonville (Fla.) Wolfson Children's Hosp., 1981-87, shift charge nurse, 1987—. Mem. NAFE, Phi Kappa Phi, Sigma Theta Tau Internat. Baptist. Home: 7946 Mendoza Dr Jacksonville FL 32217 Office: Jacksonville Wolfson Childrens Hosp 800 Prudential Dr Jacksonville FL 32207

RAWLINSON, VICTORIA FAIRCHILD, information systems specialist; b. Newton, Mass., Nov. 27, 1959; d. Paul Elmer and Sheila Margaret (Fairchild) R. BS in Math., U. Vt., 1981; MS in Engring. Mgmt., Northeastern U., 1988. MIS programmer, then computer analyst Liberty Mut. Ins., Portsmouth, N.H., 1981-84; MIS sr. programmer analyst Codman and Shurtleff, Inc. (a Johnson and Johnson Co.), Randolph, Mass., 1984-86; MIS systems analyst Codman and Shurtleff, Inc. (a Johnson and Johnson Co.), 1987—, MIS project leader, 1986—; bus cons. Jr. Achievement, Boston, 1987—; Quincy (Mass.) Sch. System, 1987; computer cons., JK Project Svcs., Arlington, Va., 1988—, Dragonfly Info. Svcs., Arlington, Va., 1989. Mem. Computer Mus. Assn., Mothers Against Drunk Driving, Ellis Island Found.

RAWSKI, EVELYN SAKAKIDA, history educator; b. Honolulu, Feb. 2, 1939; d. Evan T. and Teruko (Watase) Sakakida; m. Thomas G. Rawski, Dec. 16, 1967. B.A., Cornell U., 1961; M.A., Radcliffe Coll., 1962; Ph.D., Harvard U., 1968. Asst. prof. history U. Pitts., 1967-72, assoc. prof., 1973-79, prof. history, 1980—. Author: Agricultural Change and the Peasant Economy of South China, 1972, Education and Popular Literacy in Ch'ing China, 1979; co-author: Chinese Society in the Eighteenth Century, 1987; co-editor: Popular Culture in Late Imperial China, 1985; Death Ritual in Late Imperial and Modern China, 1988. NEH fellow, 1979-80, Chinese Studies fellow Am. Coun. Learned Socs./Sci. Rsch. Coun., 1989, Guggenheim Meml. Found. fellow, 1990; Am. Coun. Learned Socs. grantee, 1973-74. Mem. Assn. for Asian Studies (mem. China-Inner Asia Coun., vice chair 1976-79), Econ. History Assn. Home: 5317 Westminster Pl Pittsburgh PA 15232 Office: U Pitts Dept History Pittsburgh PA 15260

RAY, ALICE LOUISE RANEY NELSON, cosmetics consultant, secondary school educator; b. Brinkley, Ark., June 3, 1934; d. Jeff Davis and Edith Vestal (Blaylock) Raney; children: Phil, Mark, Blanton, Emily, Craig. BA, Miss. Coll., Clinton, 1955; MS, Miss. State U., Meridian. Cert. gifted children tchr., Miss. High sch. biology tchr. Lamar Found. Sch., Meridian, Miss., Meridian Pub. Schs.; image cons. Beauti-Color Cosmetics. Div. dir. March of Dimes, Meridian, Miss., 1987-89; vol. ARC. Mem. AAUW, Am. Bus. Womens Assn., Nat. Ass. Jr. Auxs. (chmn. nat. scholarship com. 1985-86, regional dir. 1980-81). Baptist.

RAY, ANNIE LEE, retired educator, sales professional; b. Shawmut, Ala., Sept. 15, 1922; d. Augustus Lee and Annie Mae (Smith) Golden; m. Jacob Hubert Ray, Mar. 18, 1945; children: Brenda Smith, Rosalind Golden Winslett. AB, Howard Coll. (now Samford U.), 1945; ed., So. Bapt. Theol. Sem., Louisville, 1946-47; MEd, Auburn U., 1961; cert. specialist in spl. edn., U. Ala., Tuscaloosa, 1973. Tchr. elem. and secondary schs. Ala. and Ky., 1945-46, Webb, Ala., 1952-55; spl. edn. tchr. Talladega (Ala.) Jr. High Sch., 1955-58, Tallasee High Sch., 1958-61, Columbus (Ga.) Bd. Edn., 1961-65, Graham Sch., Talladega, Ala., 1965-70, Ala. Sch. for Deaf, Talladega, 1970-79; spl. edn. tchr. of deaf and multiple handicapped Bullock County Bd. Edn., Union Springs, Ala., 1979-84; ind. dealer and distbr. Nat. Safety Assocs., Talladega, 1989—; tchr. sch. accreditation team Union Springs Elem. Sch., 1983-84. Recipient Cert. of Appreciation, City of Union Springs, 1984. Mem. NEA, Ala. Edn. Assn. (tchr. coll. accreditation team 1980, local sec. 1975-76), Concerned Women of Am., Pace Literary Soc., Delta Kappa Gamma (recording sec. 1988-89). Republican. Baptist. Home and Office: 368 Pinehurst Dr Talladega AL 35160

RAY, BARBARA ANN, computer products distributing company executive; b. N.Y.C., July 9, 1952; d. Nicholas Salvatore and Catherine Eva (Schaller) Marino; m. Richard Rade, Aug. 25, 1974 (div. Jan. 1977); m. Gregory Alan Ray, Oct. 29, 1983 (div. Sept. 1989); 1 child, Jason. BA in Psychology cum laude, St. John's U., 1974. Adminstrv. asst. Bowne Time Sharing, Inc., N.Y.C., 1974-76; supr. word processing Kaye, Scholar, N.Y.C., 1976-77; customer svc. rep. Daconics/Xerox, Inc., N.Y.C., 1977-78; mktg. specialist Wordstream, Inc., N.Y.C., 1978-79; sales rep. Wang Labs., Inc., Stamford, Conn., 1979-83, br. mgr., 1983-87; owner, mgr. Barbara A. Ray & Assocs., Econocom agts., Westport, Conn., 1987—; bd. dirs. PCT Group, Inc., Danbury, Conn. Mem. NAFE. Republican. Home and Office: 91 Kings Hwy South Westport CT 06880

RAY, BEATRICE THOMAS, management; b. Suffolk, Va., Nov. 15, 1950; d. James William and Betty Anne (Nurney) Thomas; m. Noel Wallace Ray, Nov. 24, 1973; 1 child, Beatrice Arlene. BS in Mgmt. Info. Sci., Christopher Newport Coll., 1973; MS in Adminstrn., George Washington U., 1976, Cert. in Data Processing, 1981. Computer programmer City of Newport News, Newport News, Va., 1973-76; computer auditor Ala. Gas Corp., Birmingham, Ala., 1976-77; systems analyst United Chair Co., Leeds, Ala., 1977-79; sr. systems analyst Vulcan Materials Co., Birmingham, 1979-80, mgr. info. svcs., 1980-87, mgr. info. svcs. support, 1987—. Night Circle leader Asbury United Meth. Women, Birmingham, 1987-88 (nominating chmn., 1987-88, mem. nominating com., 1989—); adminstrv. council mem. at large Asbury United Meth. Ch., Birmingham, 1987-88. Mem. Nat. Mgmt. Assn. (sec. 1982-83, v.p. 84-85, pres. 85-86, leadership award, 1987), NAFE, Network Birmingham, Toastmasters Internat. (Birmingham, competent toastmaster award, 1989). Home: 2848 Berkeley Dr Birmingham AL 35242 Office: Vulcan Materials Co Metroplex One Dr Birmingham AL 35209

RAY, CAROLYN MARIE, bank executive; b. Pittsfield, Ill., Oct. 24, 1933; d. Emmett Edward and Lena Mae (DeHart) Dunham; m. Gordon Lee Ray, July 22, 1956; children: Gwendolyn Lee, Garold Lynn, Geoffrey Otis, Gregory Edward. BS, U. Ill., 1956; postgrad., Am. Inst. Banking, 1986, Ill. State U., 1988. Office mgr. Kanartex Corp., Galesburg, Ill., 1974-78; teller

Abingdon (Ill.) Bank & Trust Co., 1978-79, sec. to pres., 1979-84, loan ops., 1984-85, cashier, 1985-90; asst. v.p. First Illini Bank (formerly Abingdon Bank), Abingdon, 1990—. Editor: History of Abingdon, 1968. Asst. treas. City of Abingdon, 1987—, mem. human resources com., 1990—. Mem. Fin. Women Internat. (pub. affairs chair 1988—), Delphian Club (pres. 1987-89), Jr. Woman's Club (pres. 1962-63), Woman's Club (pres. 1987-89). Home: 406 N Pennsylvania Abingdon IL 61410 Office: First Illini Bank 101 N Main PO Box 72 Abingdon IL 61410

RAY, DORATHEA HAMMERS, retail needlework executive; b. Diboll, Tex., Apr. 28, 1917; d. James Franklin and Maude Augusta (Baines) H.; m. Walter Emery Ray, July 12, 1940 (dec. Mar. 1989); children—Dorathea Bryan Ray Lyons, James Clayton. Student Tex. Woman's U., 1935-38. Analyst, Dupont, Orange, Tex., 1948-82. Columnist, Opportunity Valley News, 1984—; designer hand-made fashions. Chmn. nominating com. Southeast Tex. Womens Comm., Beaumont, 1985; mem. Orange County Sesquicentennial Commn., 1984-87, Tri-Cities Clean Up commn., 1987—; Riverfront Plaza Assn., First Bapt. Ch., chair pub. relations com., 1984—; assoc. dir., pub. relations com. Miss Orange County Scholarship Pageant; bd. dirs. local chpt. Am. Cancer Soc. Mem. Nat. Needle Work Assn., Tex. Fedn. Bus. and Profl. Women's Clubs (best dist. dir. 1972), Greater Orange Area C. of C. (bd. dirs. 1983-89, chmn. beautification com. 1983—), Tex. Fedn. Bus. and Profl. Women's Club (chair bicentennial). Democrat. Baptist. Avocations: knitting; reading; crafts. Home: 1213 W Wrenway St Orange TX 77630

RAY, JUDY SELF, marketing consultant; b. Neosro, Mo., June 23, 1946; d. Dan J. and Madge Lee (Hager) Self; m. Charles E. Smith, May 8, 1965 (div. 1974); 1 child, Jennifer Charlene; m. John Wallace Ray, June 20, 1974; stepchildren: Donna Sue, Vickie Kay, Wendy Ann. Student, Columbus Coll., 1965, Brunswick Jr. Coll., 1975, Chattahoochee Valley State Coll., 1975-76. Operator So. Bell, Columbus, Ga., 1964-66, service rep., 1966-71, 79-87, service cons., 1987—; service rep. Southern Bell, Phenix City, Ala., 1972-74, 75-79; sec. Brunswick (Ga.) Jr. Coll., 1975; trainer/facilitator Communications Workers Am., Columbus, 1984-87, So. Bell, Columbus, 1984-87; tng. course developer So. Bell, 1985-87. Contbr. articles to profl. jours. Vol. campaign com. Sen. Danny Corbett, Phenix City, Ala., 1982, 83, 86; poll worker State of Ala., Russell county, 1982—; legis. sec. Communications Workers Am., 1988—; vol. CWA Charity Golf Tournament, 1986—; sec., mem. exec. com. Russell County Ala. Dems., 1990—. Mem. Am. Bus. Women's Assn. (treas. 1987-88, v.p. 1988-89, pres. 1989-90, sec. 1990—, woman yr. 1990), NAFE, Telephone Pioneers Am. Democrat. Mem. Assembly of God Ch. Office: So Bell 1251 13th St Columbus GA 31994

RAY, SARA BRADSHAW, insurance executive, entertainment consultant; b. Stillwater, Okla., Sept. 28, 1964; d. Gerald Edward and Jeanette (Foster) Bradshaw; m. Steven Lamont Ray, Feb. 4, 1989. BS in Merchandising, Okla. State U., 1986. Asst. store mgr. Coach Leatherware, Dallas, 1986-87; comml. underwriter USF&G Ins. Co., Oklahoma City, 1987-88; prin., comml. lines specialist Bradshaw Agy., Inc., Stillwater, 1988—. Bd. dirs. Stillwater Med. Ctr. Found. Named Outstanding Young Woman of Am. Nat. Businesswomen Am., 1982, Young Careerist Bus. and Profl. Women, Oklahoma City, 1988. Mem. Nat. Soc. Cert. Ins. Counselors, Ins. Women Oklahoma City, Stillwater C. of C. (ambassador chair, community image com. 1989), Chi Omega. Democrat. Baptist. Office: Bradshaw Agy Inc PO Box 1717 Stillwater OK 74076

RAY, SUSANNE GETTINGS, counselor; b. Marietta, Ohio, July 20, 1938; d. Lewis B. and Reina Ashton Gettings; m. John W. Ray; children: Nancy Ann, Susan Christy. BS in Nursing, Case Western Res. U., 1960; MEd in Community Counseling, Ohio U., 1987. Staff nurse Cleve. Vis. Nurse Assn., 1960-61; sr. nurse Columbus (Ohio) Pub. Health Nursing Svc., 1962-64; founder, mgr. healthcare program Muskingum County (Ohio) Children's Svcs., 1972-76; spl. svcs. coord. Muskingum County Head Start, Zanesville, Ohio, 1979-85; clin. counselor Six County Mental Health Ctr., Zanesville, 1987—. Stephen Minister Ch. Sch. tchr. Cen. Presbyn. Ch.; founder, coord. SAFE; bd. dirs. Ohio Head Start Handicap Assn., Community Against Rape Edn. and Svc., Eastside Community Ministry; adv. bd. Avondale Youth Ctr. program Muskingum County Head Start. Recipient various profl. and community awards. Mem. Am. Assn. Counseling and Devel., Sigma Theta Tau, Chi Sigma Iota. Home: 1245 East Dr Zanesville OH 43701 Office: Six County Mental Health Ctr 2845 Bell St Zanesville OH 43701

RAYBURN, MARGARET, state legislator; b. North Powder, Oreg., Apr. 5, 1927; d. John Alexander and Pearl Leanel (Wicks) Shaw; m. Glenn Albert Rayburn, July 19, 1946; children: Jeffery John, Mary Jane Victoria Rayburn Ahlbeck. BA, Eastern Wash. U., 1949. Elem. tchr. Harriett Thompson Elem. Sch., Grandview, Wash., 1949-63; jr. high tchr. Grandview Jr. High, 1963-76, counselor, 1976-83; mem. Wash. Legislature, 1985—; chair Agr. Comm., Olympia, Wash., 1987—, Edn. Commn., Olympia, 1985—, Local Gov. Comm., Olympia, 1985—. Bd. dirs. Crisis Ctr., Sunnyside, Wash., 1979-89. Named Outstanding Elected Official Grandview C. of C., 1985. Mem. AAUW, Dem. Club, Fedn. Women's Club, Delta Kappa Gamma (pres. 1974-76). Home: Rte 3 Box 3799 Grandview WA 98930 Office: 1610 S Euclid Rd John OBrien Bldg #335 Olympia WA 98504

RAYL, INDIA, marketing executive; b. Chateauroux, France, May 1, 1956; d. Rommie Clarence and Peggeanne (Moore) Walker; m. Robert Richard Rayl Jr., June 19, 1982; children: Brandon Joseph. Student, Mesa Coll., San Diego, 1982-85, U. San Diego, 1988-89; cert. in direct mktg., San Diego State Univ., Univ. San Diego, 1990. Brand mgr. Undergear Catalog, San Diego, 1983; dir. custonr relations Internat. Male, San Diego, 1977-86; catalog dir. ACA Joe, San Diego, 1986-87; media mgr. Internat. Male-Hanover House Ind., San Diego, 1988; gen. mgr. Petco-Animal City, San Diego, 1988-89; mktg. mgr. More Direct Health Products, 1989—; new bus. cons. Gift Baskets, Inc., San Diego, 1988. Editor various catalogs. Mem. Nat. Assn. Female Execs., Nat. Assn. Mil. Spouses, San Diego Direct Mktg. Club. Office: More Direct Health Products 6351-E Yarrow Dr Carlsbad CA 92009

RAYMOND, DOROTHY GILL, lawyer; b. Greeley, Colo., June 2, 1954; d. Robert Marshall and Roberta (McClure) Gill; m. Peter J. Raymond, June 8, 1974. BA summa cum laude, U. Denver, 1975; JD, U. Colo., 1978. Bar: Conn. 1978, Colo. 1981. Assoc. Dworkin, Minogue & Bucci, Bridgeport, Conn., 1978-80; counsel Tele-Communications, Inc., Englewood, Colo., 1980-88; v.p., gen. counsel WestMarc Communications, Inc., Denver, 1988—. Mem. Colo. Assn. Corp. Counsel (pres. 1987), Am. Corp. Counsel Assn. (sec., dir. Colo. chpt. 1988—), Sports Car Club Am. (nat. champion ladies stock competition 1981, 85, 86, 88). Office: WestMarc Communications Inc 4643 S Ulster St Ste 400 Denver CO 80237

RAYMOND, JUNE FERGUSON, oncological nurse; b. Endicott, N.Y., Apr. 9, 1931; d. David Rogers and Ruth (Whitesell) Ferguson; m. Raymond G. Gibson, June 1954 (div. 1956); m. John S. Raymond, Sept. 6, 1957; children: Margaret E., John D. Diploma, Wilson Meml. Hosp. Sch. Nurses, Johnson City, N.Y., 1952; BS in Nursing Edn., Syracuse U., 1955. Instr. med. and surgical nursing, Ob-Gyn nursing Wilson Meml. Hosp., 1955-59, staff nurse United Health Svcs., 1981—. Bd. dirs. Am. Cancer Soc., Binghamton, N.Y., 1980-88; choir dir. Christ The King Luth. Ch., Vestal, N.Y., 1989—. Recipient scholarship C.S. Wilson Meml. Hosp., 1952. Mem. C.S. Wilson Meml. Hosp. Sch. of Nursing Alumnae, C.S. Wilson Meml. Hosp. Aux., Syracuse U. Alumnae, Broome County Nurses Assn., N.Y. State Nurses Assn., Am. Nursing Assn., Sigma Theta Tau. Republican. Home: 8 Normandy Ct Binghamton NY 13903

RAYMOND, SANDRA L., elementary school educator; b. Washington, Mar. 14, 1944; d. Glenn David and Esther Francis (Smith) Thompson; m. Philip John Raymond, Apr. 8, 1967; children: Brian Jon, Bradley Glenn. BS, U. Md., 1966; postgrad., Trinity Coll., Am. U., U. Western Md. Cert. elem. tchr., Md. Spl. edn. tchr. 7th and 8th grades, now tchr. 2d grade and coord. Montgomery County Pub. Schs., Rockville, Md., 1990—; tchr. 2d grade, primary sci. coord. Archdiocese of Washington. Mem. nursery sch. coun. YMCA; mem. parents coun. Bullis Sch. Greater Washington, 1988-90, bd. dirs. 1988—. Mem. NEA, Md. State Edn. Assn., Montgomery County Edn. Assn., Nat. Cath. Educators Assn. Address: One Meadowcroft Ct Gaithersburg MD 20879

RAYMOND, SUSAN GRANT, sculptor; b. Denver, May 23, 1943; d. Edwin Hendrie and Marybelle (McIntyre) G; m. Macpherson Raymond Jr., Aug. 18, 1967 (div. Mar. 1987); children: Lance Ramsay, Mariah McIntyre. BA in English, Cornell U., 1965; MA in Anthropology, U. Colo., 1968. Curator of anthropology Denver Mus. of Nat. History, 1968-71, contract artist, 1976-77, 79, 81, 83; instr. in anthropology U.S. Internat. U., Steamboat Springs, Colo., 1971-73. Sculpted monumental bronze sculpture for Littleton Colo., 1987, Vail, Colo., 1986, inspirational sculpture Childrens Hosp., 1977, diorama figures for Denver Mus. of Nat. History, 1971, 76, 77, 79, 81, 83; other prin. works include sculptures Routt Meml. Hosp. 1977, U. Denver, 1982, Craig Hosp. 1984, Lakewood Westernaires, 1984, Stonegate swimming hole, Scottsdale, 1989. Mem. Nat. Ski Patrol, 1965-75; bd. dirs. Tread of Pioneers Mus., Steamboat Springs, 1971-87. Recipient Maurice Hexter award Nat. Sculpture Soc., 1984, Art Castings award N. Am. Sculpture Exhibition, 1982, Summerart award Steamboat Springs Arts and Humanities, 1984; winner 10th Mountain Div. Monumental Sculpture Competition at Ft. Drum, Lake Placid, N.Y., 1990.

RAYMUS, TONI MARIE, real estate executive, newspaper publisher; b. Stockton, Calif., Feb. 11, 1957; d. Antone Edward and Marie Fatima (Medeiros) R.; m. Andrew Sephos, Oct. 1, 1989. BA, U. Pacific, 1979; postgrad., Richmond Coll., London, 1980. Gen. asst. Manteca (Calif.) News, 1977-79, asst. to pub., 1980-82, entertainment editor, 1980-82; pub. Ripon (Calif.) Record, 1982—; v.p. fin. Raymus Devel. & Sales, Inc., Manteca, 1984—. Chairwoman Jr. Miss Scholarship Program, Manteca, 1980—; commr. Juvenile Justice Commn., Stockton, 1981-82; dir. Mateca Boys and Girls Club, 1982—, pres., 1988—. Mem. Manteca Builders Assn., Builder's industry Assn. of Delta (dir. 1987—, sec. 1990—), Calif. Pubs. Assn., Ripon C. of C. Republican. Roman Catholic. Club: Venture (Manteca) (v.p. 1981-82). Office: Raymus Devel & Sales 544 E Yosemite Ave Manteca CA 95336

RAYNOR, SHERRY DIANE, association administrator; b. Escanaba, Mich., Aug. 18, 1930; d. James Christopher and Ebba (Ebbesen) Nevans; married, 1949 (div. 1955); children: Robert Storrer, Christine Storrer, Sandra Storrer; married, 1959 (div. 1972); children: Ebba Raynor, Nels Raynor, Beatrice Raynor. BA, Mich. State U., 1965, MA, 1967. Cert. elem. tchr., in spl. edn., Mich., Mass. Pres., founder, dir. Blind Children's Fund (formerly Internat. Inst. for Visually Impaired, 0-7, Inc.), East Lansing, Mich. and Auburndale, Mass., 1978—; supr., initiator Perkins Presch., Watertown, Mass., 1979-80; coordinator, initiator Perkins Infant/Toddler Program, Watertown, 1980-83; project dir. Project Outreach USA, Newton, Mass., 1983-84; dir., founder Infant Program for Visually Impaired, IISD, Mason, Mich., 1972-79; chmn. ICEVH Subcom. Presch. Blind Children, 1987; pres. 1st Internat. Symposium on Infant and Presch. Visually Handicapped Infants and Young Children, Internat. Inst. for Visually Impaired, 0-7, Inc., Israel, 1981, 2d Internat. Symposium, Netherlands Antilles, 1983; mem. standing com. Annual Internat. Seminars on Presch. Blind. Author: (with others) (books for parents of blind children) Get a Wiggle On, 1975, Move It, 1977, (book for tchrs. of blind children) Mainstreaming Preschoolers: Children with Visual Handicaps, 1985. Mem. Assn. for Edn. and Rehab. of Blind and Visually Impaired (chairperson div. VIII Infants and Preschoolers 1984-86, Pauline M. Moor award 1986), Nat. Assn. Parents of Visually Impaired (1986 award for exemplary practice), Internat. Council for Exceptional Children, Internat. Council for Edn. of Visually Handicapped, World Blind Union, Am. Council for the Blind, Assn. Childhood Edn. Internat., Nat. Fedn. Blind. Lodge: Zonta.

RAYNOR, SUSANNE, chemical physics educator; b. Phila., May 18, 1948; d. William McLean and Susanne Louise (Chambers) R.; m. Louis H. Kipnis, Dec. 28, 1972. BS, Duke U., 1970; PhD, Georgetown U., 1976. Grad. fellow Georgetown U., Washington, 1971-78; rsch. assoc. U. Toronto, Ont., Can., 1978-80, Harvard U., Cambridge, Mass., 1980-82; asst. prof. chem. physics Rutgers U., Newark, 1982-88, assoc. prof., 1988—; collaborator Los Alamos (N.Mex.) Nat. Lab., 1984—. Contbr. articles to profl. jours. Recipient Outstanding Tchr. award Rutgers U. Alumni Assn., 1986; grantee N.J. Dept. Higher Edn., 1985-88, Rsch. Corp., 1986-87. Mem. Am. Chem. Soc. (grantee Petroleum Rsch. Fund 1988-90), Am. Phys. Soc. Office: Rutgers U Dept Chemistry Newark NJ 07102

RAZENSON, HELEN LOUISE, banker; b. Oceanside, N.Y., Mar. 23, 1954; d. Charles Peter and Evelyn Ruth (Marquis) Kerns; M. Charles Harvey Razenson, Apr. 9, 1978; children: William Francis, Thomas Samual. AA, Nassau Community Coll., Garden City, N.Y., 1974; BS in Acctg., N.Y. Inst. Tech., 1976; MBA, Adelphi U., 1981. Acctg. specialist, asst. v.p. fin. control div. Citibank/Citicorp, N.Y.C., 1975-85, asst. v.p., v.p. N. Am. investment bank div., 1986—. Mem. Grace Luth. Evang. Ch. Choir, North Bellmore, N.Y., 1964-86. Mem. Bethpage (N.Y.) Fire Dept. Ladies Aux. Democrat. Home: 47 Elliott Dr Hicksville NY 11801 Office: Citibank 55 Water St 44th Fl New York NY 10043

REA, ANN HADLEY KUEHN, public information officer; b. Arlington, Va., Oct. 14, 1962; d. Alvin Henry Kuehn and Barbara Ann (Schmall) Schanzenbach; m. Burt Richard Rea, June 30, 1990. BA in Communications, Va. Poly. Inst. & State U., Blacksburg, 1984; postgrad., Georgetown U., Washington, 1990—. Desk asst., prodn. asst. ABC News, Washington, 1986-88; media/info. officer Embassy of Australia, Washington, 1988—. Mem. NAFE. Episcopalian. Home: 4401 Lee Hwy Apt 51 Arlington VA 22207 Office: Embassy of Australia 1601 Massachusetts Ave NW Washington DC 20036

REA, KATHRYN POLLYANNA, management consultant, data processing consultant; b. Los Angeles, Aug. 23, 1957; d. Virginia (Robinson) Rea. BS, SUNY, Albany, 1981; Cert. in Data Processing, U. Calif., 1983. Real estate agt. Beverly Hills, Calif., 1977-80; real estate broker Beverly Hills, 1980—; pres., chmn. bd. The Consulting Edge, Inc., Beverly Hills, 1983—; project mgr. and advisor banking automation The Cons. Edge, Inc., Beverly Hills, 1984—, instr. data communications, systems analysis and design seminars, 1984—, developer fin. models related to automation, assessment of automation for comml. banking, 1985—; cons. in electronic data interchange The Consulting Edge, Inc., Beverly Hills, 1986—, developer numerous long-range systems plans, 1987—. Author: Data Communications For Business, 1987; contbr. articles to profl. jours. Mem. IEEE, Nat. Computer Graphics Assn., Assn. for Computing Machinery. Office: The Cons Edge Inc 9107 Wilshire Blvd Ste 320 Beverly Hills CA 90210

REA, NORMA, telecommunications executive, small business owner; b. Berea, Ohio, July 16, 1958; d. James and Mary (Roberts) R. Student, Tri-City Community Coll., Parma, Ohio. Pres. Wilmington Cellular Telephone Corp., Cleve.; controller Clepro, Inc., Cleve.; chmn. Wilmington (N.C.) Cellular Ptnr.; president, chief exec. officer Cellular One of Costal Carolina, Wilmington; only woman in U.S. FCC licensed to own and operate cellular phone co. Mem. Home Builders Assn., Wilmington C. of C., Cape Fear Sales and Mktg. Club.

READ, SISTER JOEL, college president. BS in Edn., Alverno Coll., 1948; MA in History, Fordham U., 1951; hon. degrees, Lakeland Coll., 1972, Wittenburg U., 1976, Marymount Coll., 1978, DePaul U., 1985, Northland Coll., 1986, SUNY, 1986. Former prof., dept. chmn. history dept. Alverno Coll., Milwaukee, Wis.; pres. Alverno Coll., 1968—; pres., Am. Assn. for Higher Edn., 1976-77; mem. Council, Nat. Endowment for the Humanities, 1977-83; bd. mem., Edn. Testing Service, Neylan Commn.; past pres., Wis. Assn. Ind. Colls. and Univs.; chmn., Commn. on the Status of Edn. for Women, Am. Assn. Colls., 1971-77; bd. dirs., mem. exec com. Greater Milwaukee Comm.; mem. exec. com. GMC Edn. Trust; bd. dirs. F and M Bank. First recip. Anne Row Awd., Harvard U. Grad Sch. Edn., 1980. Mem. Rotary. Office: Alverno Coll 3401 S 39th St Milwaukee WI 53215-4020

READ, SUSAN C., advertising agency executive. Past sr. v.p. J. Walter Thompson, N.Y.C.; exec. v.p., exec. creative dir. Lintas: N.Y., N.Y.C., 1986-90; co-dir. creative svcs. N. W. Ayer Inc., N.Y.C., 1990—. Office: N W Ayer Inc Worldwide Pla 825 8th Ave New York NY 10019*

READER, MARY RAE, architect, architectural firm executive; b. Waukesha, Wis., Aug. 31, 1952; d. Ray and Helen (Breidenbach) Mackey; 1 child, Adrienne. Student, U. Tex., 1970-73; BA in Architecture, U. Md., 1979. Registered architect in Va., Md., DC, Tenn., N.J. Architect intern Donald F. Nalley, Potomac, Md., 1974-75, Sullivan, Almy, Inc., Bethesda, Md., 1979-80, GMR Ltd., Gaithersburg, Md., 1980-82; architect Berkus Group, Washington, 1983; pres. Archtl. Design Group, Alexandria, Va., 1983—; mem. Va. State Bd. Architects, Profl. Engrs., Land Surveyors and Cert. Landscape Architects, 1987—; sec., treas. Mid-Atlantic Region of the Nat. Coun. Archtl. Review Bds., 1988—. Recipient numerous home design awards from profl. orgns. Mem. AIA, Nat. Coun. Archtl. Registration Bds., Washington Women in Architecture, Alexandria C. of C., Nat. Trust for Historic Preservation, No. Va. Bldg. Industry Assn., Suburban Md. Bldg. Industry Assn., Nat. Assn. of Home Builders. Office: Archtl Design Group Inc 403 N Henry St Alexandria VA 22314

READY, ELIZABETH M., state legislator; b. Burlington, Vt., Oct. 7, 1953; m. John H. McLain; 3 children. BA, U. Vt. Selectman Town of Lincoln, Vt.; state senator Vt. Senate, Montpelier, 1989—; regional planning commr.; educator. Home: RD 1 Box 2018 Bristol VT 05443 Office: Vt State Senate Montpelier VT 05602*

REAGAN, BERNIDA, lawyer; b. Corona, Calif., Apr. 17, 1954; d. John Walter and Lillian Owens (Davis) R.; m. James William Head, Sept. 10, 1988. Student, UCLA, 1976, JD, 1979. Bar: Calif. Staff atty. Legal Aid Found. L.A., 1980-83, sr. atty., 1983-86; dir. litigation Pub. Counsel, L.A.; exec. dir. Berkeley Community Law Ctr., Calif., 1988—; lectr. UCLA, 1982-83. Mem. bd. Fed. Emergency Mgmt. Agy., Oakland, Calif. 1988. Named Lawyer of Yr. Nat. Conf. Black Lawyers 1988. Mem. Black Women Lawyers.

REAGAN, MAUREEN, political worker; b. 1941; d. Ronald Reagan and Jane Wyman; m. 2d, David Sills; m. 3d, Dennis Revell, 1981. Chair U.S. del. to UN Conf. on Status of Women, Nairobi, Kenya; co-chmn. Rep. Nat. Com., 1987-89. Author: First Father, First Daughter: A Memoir, 1989. Active in Rep. polit. work. Office: care Rep Nat Com 310 1st St SE Washington DC 20003*

REAGAN, NANCY DAVIS (ANNE FRANCIS ROBBINS), wife of former President of U.S.; b. N.Y.C., July 6, 1923; d. Kenneth and Edith (Luckett) Robbins; step dau. Loyal Davis; m. Ronald Reagan, Mar. 4, 1952; children: Patricia Ann, Ronald Prescott; stepchildren: Maureen, Michael. BA, Smith Coll.; LLD (hon.), Pepperdine U., 1983; LHD (hon.), Georgetown U., 1987. Contract actress, MGM, 1949-56; films include The Next Voice You Hear, 1950, Donovan's Brain, 1953, Hellcats of the Navy, 1957; Author: Nancy, 1980; formerly author syndicated column on prisoner-of-war and missing-in-action soldiers and their families; author: (with Jane Wilkie) To Love a Child, (with William Novak) My Turn: The Memoirs of Nancy Reagan, 1989. Civic worker, visited wounded Viet Nam vets., sr. citizens, hosps. and schs. for physically and emotionally handicapped children, active in furthering foster grandparents for handicapped children program; hon. nat. chmn. Aid to Adoption of Spl. Kids, 1977; spl. interest in fighting alcohol and drug abuse among youth: hosted first ladies from around the world for 2d Internat. Drug Conf., 1985; hon. chmn. Just Say No Found., Nat. Fedn. of Parents for Drug-Free Youth, Nat. Child Watch Campaign, President's Com. on the Arts and Humanities, Wolf Trap Found. bd. of trustees, Nat. Trust for Historic Preservation, Cystic Fibrosis Found., Nat. Republican Women's Club; hon. pres. Girl Scouts of Am. Named one of Ten Most Admired Am. Women, Good Housekeeping mag., ranking #1 in poll, 1984, 85, 86; Woman of Yr. Los Angeles Times, 1977; permanent mem. Hall of Fame of Ten Best Dressed Women in U.S.; recipient humanitarian awards from Am. Camping Assn., Nat. Council on Alcoholism, United Cerebral Palsy Assn., Internat. Ctr. for Disabled; Boys Town Father Flanagan award; 1986 Kiwanis World Service medal; Variety Clubs Internat. Lifeline award; numerous awards for her role in fight against drug abuse. Address: 11000 Wilshire Blvd Los Angeles CA 90024*

REAGAN, SALLY A., health facility administrator; b. Harrisburg, Pa., Nov. 27, 1945; d. Francis A. and Betty (Buglman) R. BS, Bloomsburg U., 1966; EdM, Temple U., 1970; PhD, U. Pitts., 1973; postgrad., Duquesne U., 1971. Psychologist pvt. practive Allentown, Pa.; exec. dir. Horizon Hosp., St. Louis; assoc. exec. dir. Humana Woman's Hosp., Tampa, Fla.; exec. dir. Bayview Hosp., Corpus Christi, Tex. Mem. NAFE, Costal Pend Area Hosp. Coun. (pres.) Health Care Corpus Christi (sec. bd. trustees), Am. Psychol. Assn., Am. Assn. Family Therapists. Office: Houston Internat Hosp 6441 Main St Houston TX 77030

REAL, SISTER CATHLEEN CLARE, college president; b. Kewanee, Ill., June 1, 1934; d. John Thomas and Catherine Cecelia (Breen) R. BA in Math. and Chemistry, Marycrest Coll., Davenport, Iowa, 1957, LHD (hon.), 1985; MA in Math., St. Louis U., 1959; PhD in Math., U. Iowa, 1968. From instr. to asst. v.p. for acad. affairs to pres. Marycrest Coll., 1958-75; chair dept. math. Schenectady (N.Y.) County Community Coll., 1975-77; asst. acad. dean Barat Coll., Lake Forest, Ill., 1977-79; v.p. for acads. Coll. of St. Mary, Omaha, 1979-84, acting pres., 1983-84; pres. Siena Heights Coll., Adrian, Mich., 1984—; bd. dirs. Adrian State Bank. Bd. dirs. United Way, Adrian, 1985-, Goodwill-LARC, Adrian, 1986-, legatus Mich. chpt., 1988-, Citizens Gas, Adrian, 1990—. Recipient Anti-Defamation award Omaha Anti-Defamation League, 1983. Mem. Am. Assn. Higher Edn. Democrat. Roman Catholic. Lodge: Zonta. Office: Siena Heights Coll 1247 E Siena Heights Dr Adrian MI 49221-1796

REAL, MARGARET ANNE, pharmaceutical executive, internist; b. Kewanee, Ill., June 24, 1931; d. John Thomas and Catherine (Breen) R. BA, Marycrest Coll., 1953; MS, State U. of Iowa, 1955; MD, Ill. Coll. Medicine, Chgo., 1965. Diplomate Nat. Bd. Internal Medicine. Asst. dir. Abbott Labs., North Chicago, Ill., 1975, 1980-81; dir. med. dept. Berlex Labs., Cedar Knolls, N.J., 1981-84; dir. clin. devel. Wyeth Labs., Radnor, Pa., 1984-86; sr. dir. med. affairs Adria Labs., Dublin, Ohio, 1986-90; clin. asst. prof. Dept. Internal Medicine, Div. Cardiology, Columbus, Ohio, 1990. Mem. AMA, Am. Med. Womens Assn., Am. Heart Assn. Home: 72 E North St Worthington OH 43085 Office: Ohio State U Hosps Cardiology Div 1654 Upham Dr Columbus OH 43210

REAP, SISTER MARY MARGARET, college president; b. Carbondale, Pa., Sept. 8, 1941; d. Charles Vincent and Anna Rose (Ahern) R. BA, Marywood Coll., Scranton, Pa., 1965; MA, Assumption Coll., Worcester, Mass., 1972; PhD, Pa. State U., 1979. Elem. tchr. St. Ephrem's, Bklyn., 1966-67; secondary tchr. South Catholic High Sch., Scranton, Pa., 1967-69, Maria Regina High Sch., Uniondale, N.Y., 1969-72; mem. faculty Marywood Coll., Scranton, Pa., 1972-86, dean, 1986-88, pres., 1988—; vis. tchr. Mainland China, Wuhan, 1982, Marygrove Coll., Detroit, 1979; bd. dirs. Moses Taylor Hosp., Lourdesmont Sch. Contbr. articles to profl. jours. Recipient bilingual fellowship Pa. State U., 1976-79, Local Chpt. Svc. award UN, 1984; named Northeast Woman, Scranton Times, 1986, Outstanding Alumna, Pa. State Coll. Edn., 1989. Mem. Coun. Ind. Colls., Am. Assn. Cath. Colls., C. of C. (bd. dirs.), Phi Delta Kappa (Educator of Yr. award 1990).

REARDON, ANNA JOYCE, emeritus physics educator; b. East St. Louis, Ill., Jan. 22, 1910; d. John Leo and Julia Gertrude (Galvin) Reardon. AB, Coll. St. Teresa, Winona, Minn., 1930; MS, St. Louis U., 1933, PhD in Physics, 1937. Instr. math. and phys. edn. high schs. in Minn. and Mo., 1930-35; instr. physics and math. Ursuline Coll., New Orleans, 1936-37, Mt. St. Scholasica Coll., Atchison, Kans., 1937-39, Loretto Hts. (Colo.) Coll., 1939-40; Coll. St. Teresa, Winona, Minn., 1940-41; instr. physics Woman's Coll., U. N.C., Greensboro, 1941-42, from asst. prof. to assoc. prof., acting head dept. physics, 1942-475, assoc. prof., head dept. physics, 1947-49; prof., head dept. physics U. N.C., Greensboro, 1949-65, prof. physics, 1965-75, emeritus prof. physics, 1975—; cons. Moses H. Cone Meml. Hosp., Greensboro. Contbr. articles to profl. jours. Mem. lay adv. bd. Sacred Heart Coll., Belmont, N.C., 1964-70, bd. visitors, 1970-87. Recipient Disting. Svc. award N.C. Sci. Tchrs. Assn., 1985. Mem. AAAS, Am. Assn. Physics Tchrs., AAUS, Am. Phys. Soc., Cath. Hist. Soc. N.C. (charter), NEA, N.Y. Acad. Sci., N.C. Acad. Sci., N.C. Edn. Assn., Photog. Soc. Am., So. Assn. Sci. and Industry, George Eastman House Assocs., Mus. Natural History, Albertus Magnus Guild Sigma Xi, Delta Kappa Gamma, Sigma Pi Sigma. Home: 1105 Dover Rd Greensboro NC 27408

REARDON, GERALYN ANNE, cheerleading executive; b. Everett, Mass., Apr. 24, 1959; d. James Francis and Rita Virginia (Bernard) R.; m. Michael Richard Marchant, June 5, 1982 (div. Dec. 1987). Student, Emmanuel Coll., Boston, 1977-81. Dir. Allstar Promotions, Everett, 1984-86; pres. Profl. Cheerleading Instrs., Everett, 1986-88; ptnr., chief exec. officer Internat. Cheer Ltd., Inc., Fayetteville, N.C., 1988—; dir. Allstar/Stuntstar/Dancestar Cheerleading Clinics, 1986—; creator, dir. Nat. Cheerleading Judges Cert. Program, 1988—, Cheerleading Coaches Ednl. Program, 1988—; instr. Nat. Cheerleading Coaches Conf., Fayetteville, 1988-89; nat. lectr., 1989—; creator Ptnr. Stunt Challenge; creator, tournament dir. CanAm Challenge Cup; judge Nat. Collegiate Championship, Dallas, 1987, Nat. High Sch. Championship, Dallas, 1987; cons. Nat. Cheerleaders Assn., Dallas, 1988. Author: The Power Concept, 1989, (TV project) Over The Rainbow, 1989; designer Cheer Wear, 1989, The Partner Stunt Challenge, 1989; patentee in field; contbr. articles newspapers and mags. Organizer Project Bread, Boston, 1985; tchr. Meth. Ch. Sch., Fayetteville, 1989; vol. Children's Hosp., Boston (Outstanding Contbr. award 1984-86); bd. advs. New England Sports Mus., 1985-87. Cited for Outstanding Contbn. to Youth Mass. Gov. Michael Dukakis, 1986, Outstanding Achievement Mass. Speaker of House George Keverian, 1986, Outstanding Contbn. to Cheerleading Evening Mag. and The Good Day Show, 1986; recipient Superstar Sports award WNEV-TV, Boston, 1987. Mem. NAFE, New Eng. Coaches Assn. (founder, pres. 1985-87), United Spirit Alliance Cheer Coaches (founder, pres. 1987-88), Fayetteville C. of C., Blue Gold Club.

REASER, FREDA BRIGHT, author; b. Boston, Sept. 27, 1929; d. Harry and Julia (Mintz) Sternfield; 1 child, Victoria. Student, Boston U. Coll. Music, 1946-50. Editor RCA Victor Records, N.Y.C., 1957-60; copywriter BBDO, N.Y.C., 1960-63; copy group head MGM Pictures, N.Y.C., 1963-65; assoc. creative dir. Product Devel. Workshop, N.Y.C., 1966-67; advt. cons. film industry N.Y.C., London, 1967—. Author: Options, 1982, Decisions, 1984, Infidelities, 1986, Singular Women, 1988. Democrat.

REASONER, ELIZABETH DIANE, public relations specialist; b. Birmingham, Ala., Nov. 1, 1949; d. George Wilburn and Martha Overton (Eason) Fulmer; m. Richard Merle Reasoner, Feb. 10, 1968; children: Richard Michael, Robert Mark. AS, Southwest Bapt. U., 1978; BA, Ottawa (Kans.) U., 1985; postgrad., Ga. State U., 1989. Substitute tchr. Liberty County Sch. Dist., Bristol, Fla., 1975-76; with dean's office Southwest Bapt. U., Bolivar, Mo., 1977-78; sec., adminstrv. asst. Midwestern Bapt. Theol. Sem., Kansas City, Mo., 1978-87; pub. rels. specialist Ga. Bapt. Conv., Atlanta, 1987—; coord. workshops and musical prodns. Midwestern Bapt. Theol. Sem., Kansas City, 1981-84. Editor: Georgia Baptist Digest, 1990; author, editor publicity material, Ga. Bapt. Conv., 1990—, (newsletter) CenterLines, 1989—. Youth dir. Lake Mystic Bapt. Ch., Bristol, 1974-76; associational music dir. Applachacola Assn., Liberty County, Fla., 1975; music dir. Liberty County Early Learning Ctr., 1974. Recipient Cert. of Merit, The Naval Officers Wives League, Pensacola, 1964, Svc. award Midwestern Singers, Kansas City, 1987; named one of Outstanding Young Women Am., 1982. Mem. Bapt. Pub. Rels. Assn., NAFE, Tau Pi Epsilon (pres. 1972-73). Home: 5022 Abbey Ln Lilburn GA 30247 Office: Ga Bapt Conv 2930 Flowers Rd S Atlanta GA 30341

REAST, DEBORAH STANEK, ophthalmology center administrator; b. Phila., Feb. 25, 1955; d. Chester Joseph and Thelma Sylvia (Hop) S. AA, Gwynedd Mercy Coll., 1975; Cert. Mgmt., Villanova U., 1987. Billing clk. Ophthalmic Assocs., Lansdale, Pa., 1971-75, exec. sec., 1975-80, ops. mgr., 1980—; treas., bd. dirs. Montgomery County Chpt. Profl. Secs. Internat. Author numerous poems. Ch. organist Corpus Christi Parish, Gwynedd, 1970-86, Saint Marie Goretti Parish, Hatfield, 1986—. Mem. Am. Mgmt. Assn., Pa. Assn. Notaries, The Wine Connection Bucks. Democrat. Roman Catholic. Office: Ophthalmic Assocs 1000 N Broad St Lansdale PA 19446

REAVIS, VIOLA LEA SCHUBERT, educator; b. Miami, Okla., July 11, 1927; d. Joe and Rose Lea (Van Horn) Schubert; m. Robert E. Reavis, Sept. 27, 1946; children: Edwin R., Loretta J., Kieran, Robert II. A.A., Okla. Northeastern A&M Coll., 1973; B.S., Pittsburgh State U., Kans., 1975, M.S., 1961, EDS in Higher Edn., 1987 . Sec. Miami Pub. Schs., Okla., 1968-69, tchr., 1979—; tchr. Wyandotte Pub. Schs., Okla., 1977-79. Treas. Republican Women, 1975. Mem. NEA, Okla. Edn. Assn., Miami Classroom Tchrs. Assn., AAUW (pres. 1988-90), Delta Kappa Gamma (scholarship 1985, 86, v.p. 1988-90), Beta Sigma Phi, Epsilon Sigma Alpha. Roman Catholic. Avocations: needlepoint; sewing.

REBENTISCH, SUSAN WEBSTER, radio management consultant; b. Los Angeles, Apr. 24, 1943; d. Maurie E. and Judy A. (Peairs) Webster; m. Edward H. Rebentisch, Dec. 4, 1974. AA, Parsons Sch. Design, 1965; cert. N.Y. Inst. Photography, 1982; BS in Bus. Mgmt., Mercy Coll., 1988. Office mgr. Travelworld Inc., N.Y.C., 1970-73; sales rep. Brit. Caledonia Airways, N.Y.C., 1973-74; mgr. Egyptian tours Lindblad Travel Inc., N.Y.C., 1975-77; v.p., adminstrv. mgr. The Webster Group, N.Y.C., 1977—. Co-author: St. Luke's Church Sesquicentennial Celebration 1986. 4-H program asst., Coop. Extension 4-H, Mahopac, N.Y., 1982-88, leader photography and communications 1979-89, chmn. Putnam County 4-H Fair 1984, chmn. 4-H Publicity, 1979—, chmn. spl. events 1986-90; sr. warden St. Luke's Ch., 1986-90 Recipient Outstanding Leader award Kodak, 1982. Mem. S.E. Hist. Soc., Photog. Soc. Am., Nat. Assn. Female Execs., Internat. Radio and TV Soc., Delta Mu Delta Honor Soc. Avocations: photography, gardening.

REBILAS, JANET MARIE, human resources manager; b. El Paso, Tex., July 9, 1958; d. Henry Raymond and Graceanna Theresa (Hair) R. BS in Commerce, Rider Coll., 1980; MS in Mgmt., Trenton State Coll., 1986. Auditor III N.J. Div. Bldg. & Constrn., Trenton, N.J., 1980-83; adminstrv. analyst II N.J. Gen. Svcs. Adminstrn., 1983-87; mgmt. improvement specialist II N.J. Gen. Svcs. Adminstrn., Trenton, 1987-89; adminstrv. analyst I N.J. Gen. Svcs. Adminstrn., 1989—; N.J. Gen. Svcs. Adminstrn. rep. Treasury Suggestion Awards Com., Trenton, 1985—, Treasury Affirmative Action Com., Trenton, 1987—, Treasury Internal Controls Com., Trenton, 1989—. Mem. Princeton Ski Club, N.J. Sierra Club, Delta Sigma Pi (pres. Princeton alumni chpt. 1987-88). Office: NJ Gen Svcs Adminstrn 135 W Hanover St CN039 Trenton NJ 08625

RECCA, THERESA MARIE, administrative assistant; b. Bklyn., Nov. 2, 1948; d. Francis Charles and Vincenzia Sylvia (Conigliaro) Pellegrini; divorced, Nov. 1982; children: Joanna Marie, Dianna Marie, Frank Joseph. BA, Bklyn. Coll., 1971. Adminstrv. asst. Bendix Corp., N.Y.C., 1968-69; exec. sec. to pres. R.E.A. Air Express, N.Y.C., 1969-71; v.p. R&R Computer Analysts, Staten Island, N.Y., 1972-78; exec. asst. to pres. SeaView Hosp. and Home, Staten Island, 1979-81; asst. to exec. Milbank, Tweed, Hadley & McCloy, N.Y.C., 1981-89; exec. sec. adminstrn. Rockefeller Family & Assocs., N.Y.C., 1989-90; exec. asst. to chmn. Associated Merchandising Corp., N.Y.C., 1990—; fin. cons. Sea View Hosp and Home Aux., 1980-82. Mem. Oakwood Heights Civic Assn., Staten Island, 1971—; treas. Sea View Hosp. and Home Aux., 1981-82, co-leader Tough Love group, 1987—. Democrat. Roman Catholic. Home: 94 Tysens Ln Staten Island NY 10306 Office: Associated Merchandising Corp 1440 Broadway New York NY 10018

RECHTZIGEL, SUE MARIE (SUZANNE RECHTZIGEL), child care center executive; b. St. Paul, May 27, 1947; d. Carl Stinson and Muriel Agnes (Oestrich) Miller; m. Gary Elmer Rechtzigel, Aug. 20, 1968 (div. Feb. 1982); children: Brian Carl, Lori Ann. BA in Psychology, Sociology, Mankato (Minn.) State U., 1969. Lic. in child care, Minn. Rep. ins. State Farm Ind. Co., Albert Lea, Minn., 1969-73; free-lance child caretaker Albert Lea, Minn., 1973-78; owner, dir. Lakeside Day Care, Albert Lea, Minn., 1983—; asst. Hawthorne Sch. Learning Ctr., Albert Lea, 1978-83. Mem. New Residents and Newcomers Orgn., Albert Lea, 1970—, past. pres.; asst. pre-sch. United Meth. Ch., Albert Lea, 1975-78, tchr. Sunday sch., 1976-80, tchr. Bible sch., 1980-85; active Ascension Luth. Ch., 1976-80. Mem. Freeborn Lic. Day Care Assn. (v.p. 1986, pres. 1987), AAUW (home tour 1977, treas. 1980-81), Bus. and Profl. Women, YMCA, Albert Lea Art Ctr. Republican. Club: 3M Families. Home and Office: 1919 Brookside Dr Albert Lea MN 56007

RECORDS, SUSAN FRANCES, publishing manager and editor; b. Kansas City, Mo., Apr. 8, 1943; d. John Williams and Eleanor Allen (Jeffrey) R.; m. Charles John Harrison, Aug. 11, 1965 (div. Mar. 1983); 1 child, Richard Jeffrey. Student, U. Colo., 1961-62; BA in Journalism, U. Okla., 1965. Advt. asst. Norman (Okla.) Transcript, 1965-68; prodn. asst. Williams Printing Co., Atlanta, 1972-73; freelance writer, editor Oklahoma City, 1975-80; copy editor Economy Co., Oklahoma City, 1980-82; prodn. asst. Denver Reese Typographics, Oklahoma City, 1982-83; mng. editor Jour. Okla. State Med. Assn., Oklahoma City, 1983—. Recipient 1st prize Sandoz Pharms. Nat. Med. Journalism Competition, 1987, Spl. award, 1989, honorable mention, 1990. Mem. Coun. Biology Editors, Am. Med. Writers Assn., Internat. Assn. Bus. Communicators, Women in Communication Inc., Sierra Club, Nature Conservancy. Office: Jour Okla State Med Assn 601 NW Expressway Oklahoma City OK 73118

RECTOR, MARGARET HAYDEN, writer; b. Azusa, Calif., May 23, 1916; d. Floyd Smith and Anna Martha (Miller) Hayden; m. Robert Wayman Rector, Aug. 25, 1940; children: Cleone Ann Rector Black, Robin Rector Krupp, Bruce Hayden. BA, Pomona Coll., 1938; postgrad., Columbia U., 1942-46, UCLA, 1959-66, U So. Calif., L.A., 1959-65. .Mem. advt. staff Curt Wagner, Redondo Beach, Calif., 1957-67; house reporter Am. Home Mag., N.Y.C., 1942-46, House Beautiful Mag., N.Y.C., 1942-46; author children's books Grossmont Press, San Diego, 1974-76; freelance writer L.A., 1940—. Author: Norton and Gus, 1976, other children's books, Alva-That Vanderbilt-Belmont Woman, 1990. Dem. organizer, Annapolis, Md., 1946-56; sec. Redondo Beach Homeowners Assn., 1960-64; v.p. Palos Verdes (Calif.) Arts Assn., 1962-64. Mem. AAUW (life), PEN, Dramatists Guild (life), Women in Film (house hostess), Women in Theatre (playwriting award 1988), UCLA Faculty Wives, First Stage Theater Group, Surfwriters Club (pres., historian). Home: 10700 Stradella Ct Los Angeles CA 90077

REDD, J. DIANE, professional fund raiser and grants management executive; b. Beckley, W.Va., Apr. 10, 1945; d. Robert Fountain and Lillian (Fitts) Redd. B.S., W.Va. State Coll., 1967. Instr. bus. subjects Paterson (N.J.) Bus. Edn., 1967-68; with U. Medicine and Dentistry N.J., Newark, 1968—, adminstrv. asst. research and sponsored programs, 1968-73, asst. dir. health edn., 1973-76, sr. devel. officer, 1976-79, asst. dir. devel., 1979-83, chief devel. and alumni affairs, 1983-89; dir. devel. Planned Parenthood Fedn. Am., Inc, N.Y.C., 1989—. Mem. priorities com., devel. com. United Way of Essex and West Hudson, Newark, 1983-85; chmn. human resources com. Community Adv. Bd., U. Medicine and Dentistry N.J., Newark, 1978-82. Recipient Recognition of Achievement award Young Women of America, Inc., Montgomery, Ala., 1979, Black Achiever award YMWCA, 1986. Mem. Council Advancement and Support of Edn., Nat. Soc. Fund Raising Execs. Inc. (cert., trustee), Assn. Am. Med. Colls., Exec. Women N.J. (trustee, chmn. scholarship com.), Women in Fin. Devel., Consortium of Devel. and Alumni Profls. of Greater N.Y. Democrat. Office: Planned Parenthood Fedn of Am 810 7th Ave New York NY 10019

REDD, KATHRYN JANE, retail executive; b. Lafayette, Ind., Aug. 14, 1958; d. Joseph Martis and Jean (Gay) R. Student, Ball State U., 1976-78. Co-mgr. The Limited Stores, Inc., Columbus, Ohio, 1978-81; store mgr. Chas A. Stevens, Chgo., 1981-84, Banana Republic, Washington, 1985-88; dist. mgr. Paul Harris Stores, Inc., Indpls., 1984-85, Ralph Lauren Corp., N.Y.C., 1988—; pres. Retail Devel. Group, Burke, Va., 1987-88. Vol. Bush Election Com., N.Y.C., 1988. Mem. Nat. Assn. for Female Execs. Republican. Episcopalian. Home: 310 W 80th Street #3E New York NY 10024

REDD, MARY ANN, data systems operator; b. Chgo., Oct. 10, 1956; d. Edgar Gilbert Sr. and Florence (Payne) Bolden; m. Reginald Gilbert Redd Sr., Feb. 1, 1975; children: Reginald G. Jr., Diana M. Grad. high sch., Chgo., 1974. With word processing/acctg. Norell Inc., Chgo., 1984-87; data operator Harris Trust and Savs., Chgo., 1987—. Mem. 69th and 70th Sts. Block Club, Chgo. Mem. NAFE, Ryerson leaders Cir. (Bronze award 1990). Home: 6940 S Wallace Chicago IL 60621

REDDELL, PATTI JEAN, pediatrician; b. Fort Riley, Kans., Apr. 21, 1959; d. Eugene Baxter and Joanne (Harris) R. BS, McNeese U., 1981; MD, La. State U., 1985. Intern U. Tex., Galveston, 1985-86, resident, 1986-88; with gen. pediatrics dept. Kelsey-Seybold Clinic, Houston, 1988—; staff physician St. Luke's Hosp., Houston, 1988—, Tex. Children's Hosp., Houston, 1988—. La. State Bd. Regents scholar, 1977-81, Ben Goldsmith MD scholar, 1981. Fellow Am. Acad. Pediatrics; mem. AMA Women's Assn., AMA, Tex. Med. Assn., Harris County Med. Soc., Tex. Pediatric Soc., Phi Mu (scholar 1981). Republican. Methodist. Office: Kelsey-Seybold Clinic 830 Gemini Ave Houston TX 77058

REDDEN, BETTE JO, federal agency administrator; b. Helena, Mont., Sept. 9, 1936; d. Rueben Anton Quenzer and Helen Marion (Miller) Neumann; m. Robert David Wilmer, Apr. 13, 1954 (div. Nov. 1962); m. Lance Gordon Redden, Mar. 19, 1965. Cert. career counselor. With IRS, 1960—; program analyst ARC audit IRS, San Francisco, 1975-78; chief quality assurance br. IRS, Fresno, Calif., 1985—; mem. several task forces IRS, Ogden, Utah, 1968, Washington, 1969, Fresno, 1971, chairperson fed. women's program, 1974-75, career coach, 1974—, instr. mgmt. practices, 1980—. Mem. adv. bd. Fresno City Coll., 1981—. Home: 5083 E Townsend Fresno CA 93727

REDDITT, NINA BELLE, property management executive; b. Kinston, N.C., Apr. 26, 1923; d. Leonidus Bryan and Nina Belle (Harris) R. AA, Blackstone Coll. for Girls, 1943; BA, U. N.C., 1948. Enlisted USN, 1944, advanced through grades to chief petty officer, 1970, ret., 1977; v.p. Rampage Corp., Greenville, N.C., 1977—. Mem. women's studies adv. coun., Pitt Community Coll., Greenville, 1980-86; sec. Pitt County Women's Commn., Greenville, 1987-89. Mem. Am. Bus. Women's Assn. (pres. Triangle chpt. 1976-77, pres. Pirate Charter chpt. 1980-81, sec. 1981-82, pres. 1982-83), Women's Network, NAFE, Nat. Assn. Women Vets., Inc. (charter), Fleet Res. Assn., Retired Enlisted Assn., WAVES Nat., Navy League U.S., Vietnam Vets. Am., Doll Lovers Club, Intrepids. Democrat. Mem. Christian Science Ch. Home: 610 E 10th St Greenville NC 27858

REDDY, ELLEN LOUISE, banker; b. Cleve., Oct. 27, 1961; d. Richard Lyons and Elizabeth (Rohrer) R. BA, Mount Holyoke Coll., 1983; MBA, U. Chgo. Grad. Sch. of Bus., 1990. Cert. Cash Mgr. 2nd v.p. Chase Manhattan Bank, N.A., N.Y.C., 1984-89; assoc. Merrill Lynch & Co., N.Y.C., 1990—. Vol. Meml. Sloan-Kettering Cancer Ctr., N.Y.C., 1986-87. Mem. Nat. Corp. Cash Mgmt. Assn., Mount Holyoke Club of N.Y. (bd. dirs. 1985-88). Home: 395 South End Ave #7H New York NY 10280

REDE, DEBORAH F., systems administrator; b. Yuba City, Calif., May 30, 1952; d. Gordon L. and Doris I. (Gates) Ginn; m. Jack P. Rede, May 1, 1970; children: Jason A., Isaac J., Seth A. Student, Am. River Coll., Sacto, Calif., 1983-85, Sacramento City Coll., Sacto, Calif., 1988-89. Mgr's. sec. Mutual of N.Y. Ins., Sacramento, 1975-78; personnel asst. Employment Devel. Dept., Sacramento, 1978-84; acctg. mgr. Rollins Burdick Hunter Ins., Sacramento, 1984-86; budget analyst Sec. of State's Office, Sacramento, 1986-89; system adminstr. Stephen P. Teale Data Ctr., Sacramento, 1989—; Chmn. Personnel Users Group, Sacramento, 1989. Mem. NAFE. Office: Stephen P Teale Data Ctr 2005 Evergreen St Sacramento CA 95813

REDFIELD, LISA CLAIRE, journalist; b. St. Albans, N.Y., Dec. 5, 1950; d. Ernest S. and Eleanor D. (Soneson) R. BA, Marietta Coll., 1973, Calif. State U., 1983. Asst. writer Santa Ana (Calif.) Coll., 1982-83; editor, reporter Orange (Calif.) City News, 1983-85; adminstrv. asst. Epsicopal Svc. Alliance, Mission Viejo, Calif., 1985-89; freelance writer N.J., 1989—; reporter Courier-Post, Cherry Hill, N.J., 1990—. Scripps Howard Internship award Calif. State U., Fullerton, 1983; recipient Sky Dunlap award Santa Ana Coll., 1990. Mem. Women in Communications, Inc. Episcopalian.

REDFIELD, RUE JEAN, sales representative; b. Neptune, N.J., Oct. 30, 1962; d. Robert G. and Joan Redfield. AS, Harcum Jr. Coll., 1983. Animal health tech. Shrewsbury Animal Hosp., Tinton Falls, N.J., 1983-85; telemktg. supr. Summit Hill Labs., Navesink, N.J., 1985-87, telemktg. mgr., 1987-88; account exec. Fulton Vet. Supply, Syosset, N.Y., 1988—. Roman Catholic. Home: 1390 Ocean Ave Sea Bright NJ 07760

REDGRAVE, LYNN, actress; b. London, Eng., Mar. 8, 1943; d. Michael Scudemore and Rachel (Kempson) R.; m. John Clark, Apr. 2, 1967; children: Benjamin, Kelly, Annabel. Ed., Queensgate Sch., London, Central Sch. Speech and Drama, London. Theatrical appearances include Midsummer Night's Dream, The Tulip Tree, Andorra, Hayfever, Much Ado About Nothing, Mother Courage, Love for Love, Zoo, Zoo, Widdershins Zoo, Edinburgh Festival, 1969, The Two of Us, London, 1970, Slag, London, 1971, A Better Place, Dublin, 1972, Born Yesterday, Greenwich, 1973, Hellzapoppin, N.Y., 1976, California Suite, 1977, Twelfth Night, Stratford Conn. Shakespeare Festival, 1978, The King and I, St. Louis, 1983, Les Liaisons Dangereuses, L.A., 1989, The Cherry Orchard, L.A., 1990, Three Sisters, London, 1990; Broadway appearances include Black Comedy, 1967, My Fat Friend, 1974, Mrs. Warren's Profession, 1975, Knock, Knock, 1976, St. Joan, 1977, Sister Mary Ignatius Explains It All, 1985, Aren't We All?, 1985, Sweet Sue, 1987; film appearances include Tom Jones, Girl With Green Eyes, Georgy Girl (Recipient N.Y. Film Critics award, Golden Globe award, Oscar nomination for best actress 1967), The Deadly Affair, Smashing Time, The Virgin Soldiers, Last of the Mobile Hotshots, Mrs. Warren's Profession, Don't Turn the Other Cheek, Every Little Crook and Nanny, Everything You Always Wanted to Know About Sex, The National Health, The Happy Hooker, The Big Bus, Sunday Lovers, Morgan Stuart's Coming Home, Getting It Right; TV appearances include: The Turn of the Screw, Centennial, 1978, The Muppets, Gauguin the Savage, Beggarman Thief, The Seduction of Miss Leona, Rehearsal for Murder, 1982, Walking On Air, The Fainthearted Feminist (BBC-TV), 1984, My Two Loves, 1986, The Old Reliable, 1988, Jury Duty 1989, Whatever Happened to Baby Jane, 1990; guest appearances include Carol Burnett Show, Evening at the Improv and Steve Martin's Best show Ever, Circus of the Stars; co-host nat. TV syndication Not for Women Only, 1977—; nat., TV spokesperson Weightwatchers, 1984—; TV series include House Calls, 1981, Teachers Only, 1982, : Chicken Soup, 1989; albums: Make Mine Manhattan, 1978, Cole Porter Revisited, 1979; video: (for children) Meet Your Animal Friends, Off We Go, Off We Go Again: author: This is Living, 1990. Named Runner-Up Actress, All Am. Favorites, Box Office Barometer 1975; recipient Sarah Siddons award as Chgo.'s best stage actress of 1977, 1978. Office: care John Clark PO Box 1207 Topanga CA 90290

REDGRAVE, VANESSA, actress; b. London, Jan. 30, 1937; d. Michael and Rachel (Kempson) R.; m. Tony Richardson, Apr. 28, 1962 (div.); children: Natasha Jane, Joely Kim. Student, Central Sch. Speech and Drama, London, 1955-57. Prin. theatrical roles include Helena in Midsummer Night's Dream, 1959, Stella in Tiger and the Horse, 1960, Katerina in The Taming of the Shrew, 1961, Rosaline in As You Like It, 1961, Imogene in Cymbeline, 1962, Nina in The Seagull, 1964, Miss Brodie in The Prime of Miss Jean Brodie, 1966; other plays include Cato Street, 1971, Threepenny Opera, 1972, Twelfth Night, 1972, Anthony and Cleopatra, 1973, Design for Living, 1973, Macbeth, 1975, Lady from the Sea, 1976, 78, 79, The Aspern Papers, 1984, The Seagull, 1985, Chekhov's Women, 1985, The Taming of the Shrew, Antony and Cleopatra, Ghosts, 1986, Touch of the Poet, 1988, Orpheus Descending, 1989, A Madhouse in Goa, 1989, Three Sisters, 1990; film roles include Leonie in Morgan-A Suitable Case for Treatment, 1965 (Best Actress award Cannes Film Festival 1966), Sheila in Sailor from Gibraltar, 1965, Anne-Marie in La Musica, 1965, Jane in Blow Up, 1967, Guinevere in Camelot, 1967, Isadora in Isadora Duncan, 1968 (Best Actress award Cannes Film Festival); other films include The Charge of The Light Brigade, 1968, The Seagull, 1968, A Quiet Place in the Country, 1968, Daniel Deronda, 1969, Dropout, 1969, The Trojan Women, 1970, The Devils, 1970, The Holiday, 1971, Mary Queen of Scots, 1971, Murder on the Orient Express, 1974, Winter Rates, 1974, 7 per cent solution, 1975, Julia, 1977, Agatha, 1978, Yanks, 1978, Bear Island, 1979, Playing for Time, 1980, My Body My Child, 1981, Wagner, 1982, The Bostonians, 1984, Wetherby, 1985, Steaming, 1985, Prick Up Your Ears, 1987, Comrades, 1987, Consuming Passions, 1988, King of the Wind, 1989, Diceria dell'intore, 1989; TV film and miniseries appearances include Snow White and the Seven Dwarfs, 1985, Three Sovereigns for Sarah, 1985, Peter the Great, 1986, Second Serve, 1986, A Man For All Seasons, 1988; Author: Pussies and Tigers, 1964. Bd. govs. Central Sch. Speech and Drama, 1963—. Decorated comdr. Order Brit. Empire; recipient Drama award Evening Standard, 1961, Best Actress award Variety Club Gt. Brit., 1961, 66, Best Actress award Brit. Guild TV Producers and Dirs., 1966, Golden Globe award, 1978, Acad. award for best supporting actress, 1977, Emmy award for best actress in limited series or special, 1980. *

REDICAN, LOIS D., owner small business, therapist; b. Portsmouth, Va., Nov. 16, 1944; d. Norman J. and Edna M. (Lemieux) Lemay; children: Michelle, Patrick, Ryan. BA, Bridgewater State Coll., 1979. Owner, mgr., therapist Synergic Weight Loss Ctr., Brockton, Mass. Mem. Am. Chem. Soc. Home: 495 Wesstgate Dr Brockton MA 02401

REDICK, EVA JANE, piano educator; b. Grand Island, Nebr., Jan. 14, 1901; d. Hans Peter and Blanche (Crocker) Johnson; divorced; 1 child, Victoria. Student, U. Wash., 1918-19, U. So. Calif., 1932, 37, UCLA, 1939; studied with T. Bennett, 1933-37. Pvt. tchr. piano L.A. and Beverly Hills, Calif., 1927-89; ret., 1989; mem. faculty Sherwood Sch. Music, Chgo., 1954-89. Author: Eva Redick Piano Improvising Book I, 1962, Book II, 1982, Piano Playtime; patentee piano practice glove; recitalist Bel Air Hotel, Beverly Hills, 1961-89. Eva Redick Day proclaimed City of Beverly Hills, 1988; recipient Cert. of Appreciation Commendation L.A. County, 1988. Mem. Nat. Music Tchrs. Assn., Nat. Guild Piano Tchrs., Music Tchrs. Assn. Calif. (pres. West Los Angeles County br. 1960-62). Republican. Home and Office: 9933 Young Dr Beverly Hills CA 90212

REDLEAF, IRENE JACKLIN, business executive; b. N.Y.C., Dec. 16, 1940; d. Irving and Carol (Storch) Jacklin; m. David A. Redleaf, Sept. 8, 1960; children: Barbara, Joan, Richard. BA cum laude, NYU, 1961. Placement counselor Gilbert Lane Personnel, N.Y.C., 1967-75; v.p. spl. svcs. Merrill Lynch, N.Y.C., 1975—; pres. Dacion Corp., N.Y.C., 1985—. Sec. Fleetwood Tennis Assn., Great Neck, N.Y., 1988—. Mem. Great Neck Hadassah, B'nai B'rith, Phi Beta Kappa. Democrat. Jewish. Office: Dacion/Merrill Lynch 225 Liberty St New York NY 10080-6106

REDLER, SHERRY PRESS, audiologist; b. N.Y.C.; d. Martin M. and Elsie (Opin) Press; B.A., Adelphi U., 1954; M.S., So. Conn. State Coll., 1971, postgrad., 1976-79; children—Michael, Steven, Lynda. Speech pathologist Roslyn (N.Y.) Public Schs., 1954-56; tchr. drama Rollins Coll., Winter Park, Fla., 1961-63; personnel counselor Internat. Bus. Assn., Pitts., 1965; speech pathologist Fairfield (Conn.) Public Schs., 1968-75, ednl. audiologist, 1976—; clin. audiologist Rehab. Center, Bridgeport, Conn., 1975-76; sign lang. instr. Bridgeport Rehab. Center, 1976-78, Staples High Sch., Westport, Conn.; instr. So. Conn. State Coll., New Haven, 1976—; lectr., cons. in field; ind. evaluator of programs for hearing impaired; author, project dir. Title IV Fed. Grant, Conn., 1976-80; mem. Conn. State Task Force to assess services provided to mentally retarded, 1981—; author, project dir. sch. audiology program, Conn., 1981. Trustee Congregation B'Nai Israel, 1985—, chmn. older adult com.; mem. com. to revise hearing screening guidelines, Conn., 1987, State Conn. com. to establish guidelines for services to hearing impaired children, 1988—; mem. commn. on community rels., urban issues com., 1989—; mem. commn. on the elderly. Mem. Am. Acad. Audiology, Conn. Speech and Hearing Assn. (co-chmn. com. on edn. hearing impaired 1976—), NEA, Conn. Edn. Assn., Fairfield Edn. Assn., Am. Speech and Hearing Assn., Am. Ednl. Audiology Assn. (1st v.p. 1986—, pres. 1987-88). Home: 28 Lockwood Circle Fairfield CT 06430 Office: 60 Thompson St Fairfield CT 06430

REDMAN, GLORIA DIANE, communications executive; b. Omaha, Jan. 7, 1940; d. Augusta Redman Montgomery. BA in engring., George Pepperdine U., 1962; MA in Polit. Sci., U. N.C., 1982; fellow, Harvard U., 1985. Cert. Armed Forces Electronic Communications. Commd. 2nd. lt. U.S. Army, 1964, advanced through grades to col., retired, 1987; pub., legis. officer State Dept. U.S. Govt., Washington; dir. bus. devel., sr. systems analyst Automation Rsch. Systems, Alexandria, Va.; v.p., dir. communications, info. Advanced Resource Technologies, Inc., Alexandria. Active Smithsonian Inst., Nat. Geographic Soc. Decorated Legion of Merit; recipient Am. Legion award. Mem. NAFE, Harvard Alumni Assn., U. N.C. Alumni Assn. Office: Advanced Resource Technologies 4401 Ford Ave Ste 460 Alexandria VA 22302

REDMOND, GAIL ELIZABETH, petroleum company executive; b. Milw., July 28, 1946; d. George Foote and Doris Ruth (Roethke) R.; student Coll. St. Catherine, 1964-66; BS magna cum laude, Utah State U., 1968. Tchr. pub. schs., Milw., 1968-70; staff coordinator Med. Personnel Pool, Milw., 1973-76; corp. manpower devel. mgr. Clark Oil & Refining Corp., Milw., 1976-80; sr. advisor communications, employee benefits Conoco, Inc., Ponca City, Okla., 1980-81, coordinator profl. recruiting, 1981-82, coordinator employee benefit communications, 1982-84, asst. mgr. Phase II Job Eval. Project, 1984-86, coordinator job evaluation, 1986-87; dir. employee relations and job evaluation, 1987-90; employee rels. cons. E.I. duPont de Nemours, Wilmington, Del., 1990—. With USNR. Mem. Naval Enlisted Res. Assn., Phi Kappa Phi. Office: EI duPont de Nemours Co 1007 Market St Wilmington DE 19806

REDMOND, LULA MOSHOURES, family therapist; b. Asheville, N.C., Feb. 3, 1929; d. Christopher John and Rosa Marie (Blankenship) Moshoures; m. John Gerald Redmond, Oct. 9, 1949 (dec. Aug. 1974); children: John Christopher, Thomas Michael, Anne Redmond Fishel. Student, Coker Coll., 1945-46; RN, Duke U., 1949; BS in Nursing, George Mason U., 1976; MS, U. Md., 1978; postgrad. Georgetown Family Ctr., Georgetown U., 1978-81. Counselor Navy Relief Soc., Hawaii, Guam, Brunswick, Maine, Washington, 1957-68; psychiat./pediatric instr. Arlington (Va.) Hosp., 1975-76; coordinator community adult edn. program Mt. Vernon Community Mental Health, Alexandria, Va., 1978-80; family therapist, edn. dir. Hospice Care Inc., Seminole, Fla., 1980-81; pvt. practitioner family therapy Clearwater, Fla., 1980—; chief exec. officer Crime Victims Ctr., Inc., 1989; mem. faculty Assn. for Death Edn. and Counseling Inc., Washington, 1979-83, bd. dirs., 1981—, coordinator internat. conf. 1979-81; program case cons. Hospice Programs, 1980-83; founder, dir. Homicide Survivors Group Treatment program, 1985; lectr. Nat. Orgn. for Victim Assistance, Nat. Victim Ctr., 1988, 89. Author: Surviving When Someone You Love Was Murdered: A Professional's Guide to Group Grief Therapy for Families and Friends of Murder Victims, 1989. Chmn. edn. com. Mental Health Assn. Pinellas County, Clearwater, 1981-82, v.p., 1982-84; bd. dirs. Homicide Survivors Group Inc. Pinellas County, 1986—. Recipient Victim Services award Pinellas County Victims Rights Coalition, 1987, Nat. Service award Assn. for Death Edn. and Counseling, Inc., 1988, Tribute to Women in Bus. and Industry award, 1989; NIMH fellow, 1976. Mem. Am. Nurses Assn., Nat. Hospice Orgn., Sigma Theta Tau, Alpha Chi, Phi Kappa Phi. Republican. Roman Catholic. Office: Psychol Consultation & Edn Svcs PO Box 6201 Clearwater FL 34618

REDROW, ELINOR MARY, psychologist; b. Washington, July 14, 1938; d. Allan Raymond and Mary Elizabeth (Turner) R.; 1 child, Sean Patrick. BA in English Lit., Assumption Coll., 1962, MA in Psychology, 1970, cert. in psychology, 1972. Lic. psychologist, Mass. Dir. vols. Worcester (Mass.) County Extension Svc., 1961-62; svc. rep. N.E. Telephone Co., Worcester, 1962-63; reporter Ansonia (Conn.) Evening Sentinel, 1964; social worker Mass. Dept. Pub. Welfare, Webster, 1965-70; psychologist Grafton (Mass.) State Hosp., 1970-72, Valley Adult Counseling Svc., Milford, Mass., 1972—; psychometrist Douglas (Mass.) Pub. Schs., 1984-87; emergency svc. clinician Valley Adult Counseling Svc./Psychiat. Emergency Svc., Milford, 1987-90. Roman Catholic. Home: 451 Carpenter Rd Whitinsville MA 01588

REDRUELLO, ROSA INCHAUSTEGUI, municipal department executive; b. Havana, Cuba, Dec. 6, 1951; came to U.S., 1961, naturalized, 1971; d. Julio Lorenzo and Laudelina (Vazquez) Inchaustegui; m. John Robert Redruello, Dec. 14, 1972; 1 child, Michelle. AA, Miami-Dade Community Coll., 1972; BS, Fla. Internat. U., 1974. Cert. systems profl. With Fla. Power & Light Co., Miami, 1975-81, records analyst, 1981-84, sr. records analyst, 1984-87, office mgr. Miami Beach Sanitation Dept., 1987—; cons. United Bus. Records, Miami, 1985—. Editor South Fla. Record newsletter, 1983-86; editor, producer Files Mgmt. video tape, 1984-85. Rotary Club scholar, 1970. Mem. Assn. Records Mgrs. and Adminstrs. (chpt. chmn. bd. 1985—, chpt. mem. of yr. 1985), Assn. for Info. and Image Mgmt., Exec. Female, Nuclear Info. and Records Mgmt. Assn. (Appreciation award 1985). Republican. Roman Catholic. Avocations: swimming, jazzercise, reading. Office: Miami Beach Sanitation Dept 1100 Washington Ave Miami Beach FL 33139

REDSHAW, PEGGY ANN, molecular biologist, educator; b. Beardstown, Ill., Sept. 4, 1948; d. Francis Benjamin and Margaret Annabel (Lee) R.; m. Jerry Bryan Lincecum, Sept. 28, 1985. BS, Quincy Coll., 1970; PhD, Ill. State U., 1974. Postdoctoral fellow St. Louis U. Med. Sch., 1974-77; asst. prof. Wilson Coll., Chambersburg, Pa., 1977-79; from asst. to prof. Austin Coll., Sherman, Tex., 1979—; adv. com. Project Kaleidoscope, Washington, 1990—. Mem. Am. Soc. Microbiologists, AAAS. Office: Austin College 900 N Grand Ste 61565 Sherman TX 75090

REE, RHONDA See ANDERSON, RONNI

REECE, BETH PAULEY, commodities broker; b. Warsaw, Ind., June 4, 1945; d. Lester Elden and Genevene (Walter) Pifer; m. Gyle Barry Reece, June 20, 1987. BA, Grace Coll., 1967. Grain trader, hedger Cen. Soya Inc., Ft. Wayne, Ind., 1973-82; account exec. ACLI Internat. Inc., Chgo., 1982-83; account exec., hedger Cen. States Enterprises, Ft.Wayne, 1983-84; account exec. Stotler & Co., Chgo., 1984-89, LaSalle Brokerage Inc., Chgo., 1989—. Mem. Nat. Futures Assn., Art Inst. of Chgo., Met. Club. Republican. Presbyterian. Home: 227 E Delaware Apt 5C Chicago IL 60611 Office: LaSalle Div Refco 111 W Jackson Ste 1700 Chicago IL 60604

REECE, CYNTHIA ANN, petroleum engineer; b. Alliance, Ohio, Mar. 20, 1956; d. Karl Junior and Marie Louise (Stertzbach) Betz; m. David Paul Reece, May 27, 1983 (div. 1986). BS in Petroleum Engring., Marietta Coll., 1978; postgrad., U. Tex., 1979-80. Project engr. Maraflood project Marathon Co., Robinson, Ill., 1975; roustabout Marathon Prodn., Bay City, Tex., 1976; offshore drilling engr. Chevron Co., Lafayette, La., 1977; project engr. East Tex. drilling ops. Exxon Co. U.S.A., Midland, 1978-79; sr. engr. South Tex. Drilling ops. Exxon Co., U.S.A., Corpus Christi, 1980-83; supervisory drilling engr. South Tex. Drilling Ops. Exxon Co., U.S.A., 1983-84, supervisory drilling engr. Houston Drilling Ops., 1984-86; sr. supervisory engr. prodn., div. supr. Exxon Co., U.S.A., Midland, Tex., 1986-90, ops. supt. prodn., 1990—; div. chmn. Petroleum Industry, 1990. Co. coord. Corpus Christi United Way, 1984; campaign sect. leader Midland United Way, 1987, 88, 89; big sister Midland Big Bros./Big Sisters, 1987—. Mem. NAFE, NSPE (sec.-treas. spl. ops. study group 1988-89, chmn. 1989-90, bd. dirs. 1990—), Tex. Soc. Profl. Engrs., Rotary, Phi Beta Kappa, Pi Epsilon Tau, Omicron Delta Kappa, Kappa Mu Epsilon. Office: Exxon Co USA SWD Prodn Bldg B 25 Desta Dr Midland TX 79702

REECE, KATHLEEN D., recreational facility executive; b. Winston-Salem, N.C., May 23, 1954; d. Oscar Edwin and Louise K. (Hall) R. Student Art, N.C. State U., 1976; student Culinary Arts Restaurant Mgmt., Wilkes Community Coll., Wilkesboro, N.C., 1981. Chef Roaring Gap (N.C.) Country Club; owner, mgr. Catering By George, Sparta, N.C.; asst. gen. mgr. Plaza Club, Bradenton, Fla.; asst. gen mgr. Foryth Country Club, Winston Salem, N.C; gen. mgr. Winchester (Va.) Country Club, Carolina Trace Country Club, Sanford, N.C. Contbr. articles to profl. jours. Active Say No to Drugs, Am. Cancer Soc., Multiple Sclerosis Soc. 1st place Best Presentation Menu Design Fla. Food Show. Mem. CMAA, NRA, NAFE. Office: Carolina Trace Country Club PO Box 2100 Sanford NC 27330

REECE, WANDA G., engineer, writer; b. Tuscaloosa, Ala., June 21, 1956; d. James Elton and Mattie Lou (Keating) R. BA, U. Ala., Tuscaloosa, 1977; MA, U. Ala., 1981. News corr. Birmingham (Ala.) Post Herald, The New York Times, N.Y.C.; assoc. editor Kentron Internat., Houston, Pickens County Herald, Sumter County Jour.; tng. engr. space sta. Teledyne Brown Engring., Huntsville, Ala. Author: Univ. of Alabama-Tuscaloosa, A Search for Love, Vengeance Is Mine. Active Huntsville Engr., Sci. and Tech. Com. Recipient Scripps-Howard Found. award, 1981, 1st place writer's contest Randall House Publs., 1982; named to Internat. Cultural Diploma of Honor, 1990; Paul "Bear" Bryant Acad. Scholarship, U. Ala. (1st recipient), 1974. Mem. AIAA (first woman chmn. of Ala./Miss. sect., chmn. AIAA/ASTD tng. and simulation conf., missile and space reunion com., many other coms., spl. citation award 1990, Martin Schilling award 1990, Engr. of Yr. Ala./Miss. sect. 1988), NAFE, Nat. Space Soc., Am. Soc. Tng. and Devel., Soc.

Profl. Journalists, Kappa Tau Alpha, Sigma Delta Chi. Home: 6315-D Madison Pike Huntsville AL 35806

REED, AMY, magazine publishing company executive; b. Cedar Rapids, Iowa, Mar. 17, 1960; d. Robert LeRoy and Beth (Winks) Reed; m. Paul LeRoy Roberts, Feb. 7, 1981 (div. Apr. 1989); children: Leah Elizabeth, Benjamin Michael. Student mktg.-pub. rels., U. Iowa. Sales asst. for creative svcs. Cedar Rapids Gazette, 1979; exec. asst. to pres. United Vintners, San Francisco, 1979-80; regional dir. TransDesigns, Atlanta, 1982-84; corp. art cons. CornerHouse Gallery, Cedar Rapids, 1985-86; sr. account exec. Area Bus. Mag., Waterloo, Iowa, 1986-87, pub., pres., chief exec. officer, 1987-89, mkgt. dir., 1989-90; account exec. Pepco., Cedar Rapids, Iowa, 1990—. Contbr. articles to profl. publs. Mem. Cedar Rapids Arts Coun. Mem. Profl. Women's Network, Nat. Orgn. Women Bus. Owners, Adminstrv. Mgmt. Soc. Office: Pepco Litno Inc PO Box 489 3351 Square D Dr SW Cedar Rapids IA 52406

REED, BARBARA LEE, teacher; b. N.Y.C., Feb. 10, 1942; d. Max Charles and Edna (Semryck) Bauman; m. Joel I., Aug. 2, 1964; children: Jill Stacey, Glen Eric. BA, Queens Coll., 1962; postgrad., N.Y.U., 1962, Harvard U., 1962; MS, City U. of N.Y., 1965. Tchr. N.Y.C. Sch. System, 1962-67, Mt. Olive Sch. System, N.J., 1975—; mem. educational steering com., Mt. Olive Jewish Ctr., N.J., 1972-78. treas. Mt. Olive Parent Tchr's. Assn., 1986-87. mem. Nat. Council of Tchrs. of Mathematics.

REED, BERENICE ANNE, art historian, artist, government official; b. Memphis, Jan. 1, 1934; d. Glenn Andrew and Berenice Marie (Kallaher) R. BFA, St. Mary-of-the-Woods Coll., Ind., 1955; MFA in Painting and Art History, Istituto Pio XII, Villa Schifanoia, Florence, Italy, 1964. Cert. art tchr., Tenn. Comml. artist Memphis Pub. Co., 1955-56; arts adminstr., educator pub. and pvt. instns., Washington, Memphis, 1957-70; arts adminstr. Nat. Park Svc., 1970-73; mem. staff U.S. Dept. of Energy, Washington, 1973-81, U.S. Dept. Commerce, Washington, 1983-84, Exec. Office of the Pres., Office of Mgmt. and Budget, Washington, 1985; with fin. mgmt. svc. U.S. Treasury Dept., Washington, 1985—; cons. on art and architecture in recreation AIA, 1972-73; artist-in-residence St. Mary-of-the-Woods Coll., Ind., 1965; guest lectr. instr. Nat. Sch. Fine Arts, Tegucigalpa, Honduras, 1968; mem. exec. com. Parks, Arts and Leisure Project, Washington, 1972-73; researcher art projects, Washington, 1981-83. Bd. dirs. Am. Irish Bicentennial Com., 1974-76; advisor Royal Oak Found. Recipient various awards for painting. Mem. Soc. Woman Geographers, Nat. Soc. Arts and Letters, Ctr. for Advanced Study in Visual Arts, Art Barn Assn. (bd. dirs. 1973-83). Roman Catholic. Home: PO Box 34253 Bethesda MD 20827 Office: Dept Treasury Fin Mgmt Svc 401 14th St SW Washington DC 20227

REED, CAROLYN BREEDING, psychologist; b. Tenn., Aug. 16, 1945; d. Robert L. and Joyce (Keck) Breeding; m. John Kenneth Baker; 1 child, Maguire. BS with honors, Tex. Christian U., 1967, MA, 1968; PhD, U. Fla., 1979. Sch. counselor Leon County, Tallahassee, 1970-72; dir. rsch. and evaluation Hillsborough County, Tampa, Fla., 1972-78; pvt. practice Psychol. Svcs. Assocs., Tampa, 1979—. Author, producer: (cassette tape) Stop Smoking - Hypnosis, 1988; contbr. articles to profl. jours. Pres. Vol. Ctr., Tampa, 1970-76; past pres. Ctr. for Women, Tampa. Woodrow Wilson fellow, 1967. Mem. Am. Psychol. Assn., Am. Soc. Clin. Hypnosis, Am. Assn. Sex Educators, Counselors and Therapists, Network Exec. Women (past pres.), Athena Soc. (pres.), Phi Kappa Phi. Democrat. Office: 3333 W Kennedy Blvd Ste 104 Tampa FL 33609

REED, DENISE JEAN, restauranteur; b. Akron, Ohio, Jan. 30, 1951; d. John Davey and Gladys Mae (Bressler) Brooks; m. Earl Lee Reed, Aug. 24, 1968 (div. Sept. 1977); children: Dale Edward, David Lee; m. Richard Allen Guth, Sept. 30, 1978 (div. May 1987). AS in Restaurant Mgmt., Akron U., 1984, student, 1986—. Cook, server Deerfield (Ohio) Circle Pump, 1966-67; assembler Cleve. Electronics, Macedonia, Ohio, 1969-70; cook, server, dishwasher, prep cook, cashier East Park Restaurant, Ravenna, Ohio, 1972-80; car hop, cashier, cook, server East Park Drive-In, Ravenna, 1978-80; cook, prep cook, dishwasher Bavarian Haus I, Kent, Ohio, 1980-81; owner, operator Patterns & Pins, Ravenna, 1981-84; cook, prep cook, salad bar attendent, dishwasher Casey's Restaurant, Kent, 1982-83; asst. mgr. L&K Restaurant, Macedonia, 1984; mgr. Country Manor Family Restaurant, Kent, 1984-89; restaurant mgr. Emro Mktg. subs. Marathon Oil, Springfield, Ohio, 1989—. Mem. Internat. Food Service Execs. Assn. (sec. U. Akron chpt. 1982-83, pres. 1983-84, scholar 1983-84), Nat. Assn. Female Execs. Democrat. Methodist. Home: 250 McKinney Blvd Kent OH 44240 Office: Emro Mktg 2525 N Limestone Springfield OH 45503

REED, DIANE GRAY, business information service company executive; b. Trion, Ga., Sept. 5, 1945; d. Harold and Frances (Parker) Gray; m. Harry Reed, Oct. 2, 1982. Student, Jacksonville U., 1963-64, Augusta Coll., 1972-74; BS, Ga. State U., 1981. Various mgmt. positions Equifax Svcs., Inc., Atlanta, 1964-72, field rep., 1972-74, tech. rep., 1974-79, mgr. systems and programs, 1979-84, dir. tech., 1984-86, asst. v.p., 1986-89; v.p. info. tech. sector Equifax Svcs., Inc., 1989—; presdl. adv. council Equifax Svcs., Inc., Atlanta, 1984—; cons. Ga. Computer Programmer Project, Atlanta, 1984-86, spkr. Oglethorpe U. Career Workshop, Atlanta, 1986. Bd. dirs. Atlanta Mental Health Assn., 1985—, Atlanta Women's Network, pres. elect 1989; bd. dirs. United Way Bd. Bank, Atlanta, 1984-86; chairperson EquiFax United Way Campaign, 1988-89; vol. Cobb County Spl. Olympics, Marietta, Ga., 1984-87; mem. adv. coun. Coll. Bus. Adminstrn. Ga. State U. mgmt. info. systems industry adv. bd. U. Ga.; mem. Girl Scouts Friendship Circle. Named Woman of Achievement 1987 Atlanta YWCA. Mem. Women in Info. Processing, Inst. Computer Profls. (cert.), Soc. Info. Mgmt., Internat. Women's Alliance, Ga. State Alumni, LWV, Atlanta Yacht Club, Kiwanis Internat. (bd. dirs. Atlanta Buckhead chpt.). Office: Equifax Svcs Inc 1600 Peachtree St NW Atlanta GA 30309

REED, DIANE MARIE, psychologist; b. Joplin, Mo., Jan. 11, 1934; d. William Marion and Olive Francis (Smith) Kinney; married; children: Wendy Robison, Douglas Funkhouser. Student, Art Ctr. Col., Pasadena, Calif., 1951-54; BS, U. Oreg., 1976, MS, 1977, PhD, 1981. Lic. psychologist. Illustrator J.L. Hudson Co., Detroit, 1954-56; designer, stylist N.Y.C., 1960-70; designer, owner Decor To You, Inc., Stamford, Conn., 1970-76; founder, exec. dir. Alcohol Counseling and Edn. Svcs., Inc., Eugene, Oreg., 1981-86, clin. supr., 1986; clin. supr. Christian Family Svcs., Eugene, 1986-87; pvt. practice Eugene, 1985—. Evaluator Vocat. Rehab. Div., Eugene, 1982—; alcohol and drug evaluator and commitment examiner Oreg. Mental Health Div., 1981-86. Mem. Am. Psychol. Assn., Oreg. Psychol. Assn., Lane County Psychol. Assn. (pres. 1989-90), Alcohol and Drug Profls. Assn., C2 Investors (treas. 1987-88), Altair Ski and Sport, Oreg. Track. Republican. Office: 5 E 24th Ave Eugene OR 94705

REED, EDITH THERESA, actuary, employee benefits consultant; b. N.Y.C., Aug. 16, 1927; d. John James and Carolyn (Siebert) R. B.A., St. Joseph's Coll., 1949; postgrad. U. Mich., 1949-50. Actuarial asst. George B. Buck Cons. Actuaries, Inc., N.Y.C., 1950-57, asst. actuary 1957-74, assoc. cons. actuary, 1974-79, cons. actuary, 1979—. Fellow Conf. Actuaries in Pub. Practice; mem. Internat. Actuarial Assn., Am. Acad. Actuaries, Actuarial Soc. Greater N.Y. (formerly Actuaries Club N.Y.), Internat. Platform Assn., NAFE, Am. Soc. Profl. and Exec. Women, Kappa Gamma Pi. Roman Catholic. Home: 300 E 40th St New York NY 10016 Office: George B Buck Cons Actuaries Inc 1 Pennsylvania Pla New York NY 10121

REED, ELIZABETH WAGNER, biologist; b. Baguio, PI, Aug. 27, 1912; came to U.S., 1916; d. John Ovid and Catherine (Cleland) Wagner; m. James Otis Beasley, Sept. 17, 1940 (dec. 1942); 1 child, John Wagner Beasley; m. Sheldon Clark Reed, Aug. 20, 1946; children: Catherine Reed, William Reed. BA, Ohio State U., 1933, MA, 1934, PhD, 1936. Researcher on fungicides Ohio State U., Columbus, 1936-37; biology instr. Atlantic Christian Coll., Wilson, N.C., 1938-40; researcher Ohio State Rsch. Found., Columbus, 1943-44; asst. prof. Vassar Coll., Poughkeepsie, N.Y., 1944-45; asst. prof. rsch. drosophila Ohio Wesleyan U., Delaware, 1945-46, Harvard U., Cambridge, Mass., 1947-48; researcher Dight Inst., Mpls., 1948-65; asst. prof. Minn. Math. and Sci. Teaching, Mpls., 1966-69; with pub. sch. system St. Paul, Mpls., 1969-73; lectr. biology U. Minn., Mpls., 1960-69; asst. prof. Macalester Coll., St. Paul, 1967-68, Hamline U., St. Paul, 1973. Author: (with others) Mental Retardation, 1962; contbr. articles to profl. jours. Active NOW, St. Paul, 1980—, Nat. Abortion Rights, St. Paul, 1980—, Nature Conservancy, St. Paul, 1980—, Minn. Hort. Soc., St. Paul, 1981—, Zero Population Growth, St. Paul, 1978—. Fellow AAAS; mem. Women in Sci., Sigma Delta Epsilon, Phi Beta Kappa, Sigma Xi. Congregationalist. Home: 1588 Vincent St Saint Paul MN 55108

REED, GAIL S. (NINA REED), psychoanalyst; b. N.Y.C., Apr. 21, 1943; d. Jeff B. and Helen L. Simon; m. Thomas Alexander Reed, Oct. 1, 1965; children: William Trowbridge, Danielle Alexandra. AB, Bryn Mawr Coll., 1964; MA, Yale U., 1970, PhD, 1976; cert. psychoanalysis, Nat. Psychol. Assn. for Psychoanalysis, 1985. Adj. lectr. dept. English CUNY, 1970-77, U. Conn., Stamford, 1976-78; pvt. practice psychoanalysis and psychotherapy N.Y.C., 1978—; mem. faculty, tng. analyst Nat. Psychol. Assn. for Psychoanalysts, 1985—; co-chair extension div. course on methods in applied psychoanalysis N.Y. Psychoanalytic Inst., N.Y.C., 1989—; founder Group for the Study of Psychoanalytic Process, Inc., Haddonfield, N.J., 1988—; mem. faculty Inst. for Psychoanalytic Tng. and Rsch.; founder, pres. group for the study of the psychoanalytic process. Contbr. articles to profl. jours. Woodrow Wilson Found. fellow, 1964; recipient Recent Grad. Jour. Prize, Jour. Am. Psychoanalytic Assn., 1985. Mem. Internat. Psychoanalytical Assn., N.Y. Freudian Soc., Inst. Psychoanalytic Tng. and Rsch., Internat. Assn. for History Psychoanalysis. Office: 1199 Park Ave New York NY 10128

REED, HELEN BERNICE, artist; b. Watsonville, Calif., Dec. 22, 1917; d. Harry James and Loretta Elizabeth (Morgan) Aguirre; m. Clarence Varnick Reed, Sept. 8, 1944 (dec. Aug. 1988). Grad. high sch., Watsonville. Demonstrator Long Beach (Calif.) Art Assn., 1984; lectr., demonstrator Muckenthaler Cultural Ctr., Fullerton, Calif., 1984; juror Nat. Date Festival, Indio, Calif., 1987, Lakewood (Calif.) Art Guild, 1984; demonstrator San Bernardino (Calif.) Art Assn., 1984, Whittier (Calif.) Art Assn., 1984; art instr. Fullerton, 1967—. Exhibited in group shows with The Nat. Watercolor Soc., Stockholm, 1972, Farmington, N.Mex., Grants Pass, Ores., Sponake, Wash., 1985, Am. Watercolor Soc., N.Y.C., 1979, Springville (Utah) Mus., 1983; art represented in books, 1986, 88. Recipient Strathmore Paper award Okla. Watercolor Soc., 1984, Arches Paper Cash award Watercolor West, 1984, Purchase award Tex. Fine Arts Assn., 1974. Mem. Watercolor West Transparent Watercolor Soc. (bd. dirs. 1979-84), Nat. Watercolor Soc. Republican.

REED, JANE GARSON, consultant, accounting educator; b. Cleve., Jan. 11, 1948; d. Joseph John Guzowski and Irene Sophie (Dominic) Garson; m. Wayne Ellis Reed, May 17, 1969; children: Craig Michael, Kevin Matthew. BBA magna cum laude, Baldwin Wallace Coll., 1977; MBA in Mgmt., Case Western Res. U., 1983. CPA, Ohio. Letter carrier U.S. Postal Service, Brecksville, Ohio, 1966-76; sr. asst. acct. Deloitte, Haskins & Sells, Cleve., 1977-78; sr. corp. auditor White Motor Corp., Beachwood, Ohio, 1979-81; instr. acctg. Cuyahoga Community Coll., Parma, 1981-82; ind. contractor State of Wash., Olympia, 1982-84; dir. fin. The Montefiore Home, Cleveland Heights, Ohio, 1985-86; controller, bus. mgr. Western Res. Human Services, Inc., Akron, Ohio, 1986-87; lectr. mgmt. acctg. U. Akron, 1987-88; controller Multi-Care Mgmt. Co., Beachwood, 1988-89; asst. prof. Baldwin-Wallace Coll., Berea, Ohio, 1989—. Fin. sec. to bd. dirs. Prince of Peace Luth. Ch., Medina, Ohio, 1978-79; mem. budget and fin. com. Wooster (Ohio) dist. office United Meth. Ch., 1983-84; mem. Brunswick High Sch. Band and Choir Boosters, 1984-90; cub scout leader Boy Scouts Am., Brunswick, 1978-79; agt. Trinity High Sch. Alumni; mem. fin. com. Brunswick United Meth. Ch., 1988-89. Mem. AICPAs, Am. Women's Soc. CPAs, Ohio Soc. CPAs, Nat. Assn. Accts., Soc. for Advancement Mgmt. (chpt. pres. 1976-77). Methodist. Home: 1254 Hadcock Rd Brunswick OH 44212 Office: Baldwin Wallace Coll Div Bus Berea OH 44017

REED, JEAN SALAS, educational administrator; b. Torreon, N.Mex., Aug. 30, 1940; d. Ross Ray and Cora (Lopez) Salas; m. Cliff A. Reed, July 19, 1974. B.A. in Social Scis., Siena Heights Coll., 1969; M.A. in Ednl. Adminstrn., U. N.Mex., 1972, Edn. Specialist in Ednl. Adminstrn., 1974. Counselor Jobs for Progress, Albuquerque, 1971-72; tchr. Los Lunas Pub. Sch., N.Mex., 1972; edn. specialist N.Mex. State Dept. Edn., Santa Fe, 1973-75; prin. Harrington Jr. High Sch., Santa Fe, 1975-78, Capshaw Jr. High Sch., Santa Fe, 1978-86; asst. supt. elem. edn. Santa Fe Pub. Schs. 1986-88, asst. supt. instrn., 1988—; resident advisor Job Corp Ctr. for Women, Albuquerque, 1971-72; prin. Holy Rosary Sch., Albuquerque, 1970-71; tchr. Co. of Mary Schs., Los Angeles, 1965-70. Bd. dirs. Cancer Soc., Santa Fe, N.Mex., 1982-85. Mem. Nat. Assn. Secondary Sch. Prins., N.Mex. Sch. Adminstrs. (mem. bd. 1981-85, pres. 1986-87), N.Mex. Assn. Secondary Sch. Prins. (pres. 1981-82, honors for excellence program 1984), Phi Delta Kappa, Delta Kappa Gamma (pres. 1982-84, edn. scholar 1980). Democrat. Roman Catholic. Home: 1915 Camino Lumbre Santa Fe NM 87501 Office: Santa Fe Pub Schs 610 Alta Vista Santa Fe NM 87501

REED, JOELLEN, state government administrative assistant; b. Winchester, Ky., May 18, 1953; d. Joe F. and Betty (Haggard) R. BS in Elem. Edn. and Early Childhood, Ea. Ky. U., 1975, MA Rank I, 1981. Tchr. elem. sch. Clark County Schs., Winchester, 1975-85; cons. Ky. Dept. Edn., Frankfort, 1985-86, dir. recognition div., 1986, ombudsman, 1986-88, liaison to edn. and humanities cabinet, 1988; adminstrv. asst./advance for Gov. of Ky., Frankfort, 1988—. Chmn. Clark County Heart Fund, 1970, 74, co-chmn., 1971, 77, 78; advisor Frontier Chpt. ARC, 1976-78; vol. Clark County Hosp., 1968-70; program coordinator Coll. and U. Partnership Program, 1981; asst. leader Girl Scouts U.S., 1973-74; sponsor youth club Fannie Bush Elem. Sch., 1978, ARC youth club, Leadership Ky., 1986; mem. Winchester Art Guild, Clark County Assn. for Handicapped Citizens; local chmn. Tchrs. on Target for Dems., 1983; mem. Dem. Women's Club Ky., 1984—, state page Dem. Nat. Convention, 1984; pres. Aplastic Anemia Found, 1981, Bapt. Young Women, 1976-81; mem. council Women's Missionary Union, 1976-81; mem. various coms. Cen. Bapt. Ch.; bd. dirs. Hospice of Clark County, 1983, Big Bros./Big Sisters of Winchester, 1981-85, Leadership Winchester, Winchester Council for the Arts, Winchester Jaycees, Leadership Ky. Alumni Assn., 1984-89. Named One of Outstanding Young Women of Am., 1984, 87, Outstanding Young Career Woman, Clark County Bus. and Profl. Women, 1978, Outstanding Young Leader Winchester Jaycees, 1988; recipient Heart Assn. Family award State of Ky., 1977, Women of Achievement award YWCA of Lexington, 1987. Mem. Ea. Ky. U. Alumni Assn. (life), U. Ky. Alumni Assn. (assoc., bd. dirs. local chpt. 1986—), Mended Hearts, Inc., Kappa Delta Pi. Home: 526 S Maple St Winchester KY 40391 Office: Office of Gov State Capitol Bldg Frankfort KY 40601

REED, LARITA DIANE, accountant, controller, consultant; b. Chgo., Sept. 26, 1960; d. Henry Michael and Joyce Marie (Hinton) R.; m. Gregory Anthony Clark, June 18, 1988. BBA, Loyola U., Chgo., 1982. Asst. auditor Peat Marwick Main, Chgo., 1982-83, sr. auditor, 1983-84; asst. contr. McCormick Pl., Chgo., 1984-86, contr., 1986—. Mem. fin. com. Unity Fellowship Missionary Bapt. Ch., Chgo., 1978-88. Named one of Up and Coming Black Bus. and Profl. Women Dollars & Sense Mag., 1988. Fellow Leadership Greater Chgo.; mem. AICPA, Nat. Assn. Black Accts. (scholarship 1982, student affairs 1986-88), Ill. CPA Soc.. Democrat. Baptist. Office: McCormick Pl 2301 S Lake Shore Dr Chicago IL 60616

REED, MARCIA MCCLAIM, registered nurse; b. Salem, Mar. 1, 1944; d. James A. and Esthen M. (Marshall) McClain; m. James H. Reed, June 26, . BS in Nursing, Capital U., 1967. Lic. registered nurse;. Staff registered nurse Lake County Mem. Hosp., Painesville, Ohio, 1968; house supr. N.C.C.L. Hosp., Salem, Ohio, 1969-72; dir. GMN Tri County Family Planning, Cambridge, Ohio, 1974-76; staff registered nurse Mem. Hosp. Sandusky Co., Fremont, Ohio, 1976-79; patient care dir. St. Charles Hosp., Oregon, Ohio1979--. Mem. Sigma Theta Tau Inc. Methodist. Office: St Charles Hosp 2600 Navarre Ave Oregon OH 43616

REED, MARGARET CAROL, nurse; b. Frankfort, Ky., Nov. 29, 1935; d. Regis Francis and Margaret Frances (Moore) Whitehead; m. Clyde E. Reed, May 9, 1964 (div.); children—Suzanne, Rebecca Lynn. Diploma, Nazareth Sch. Nursing, 1958. Registered nurse, Ky.; lic. ins. rep., Ky. Head nurse critical care unit, intensive care unit King's Daus. Hosp., Frankfort, Ky., 1970-77; sr. regional adminstr. Ky. Peer Rev. Orgn., Louisville, 1977-81; dir. Assoc. Care Service, 1983-85; health care cons., 1985—; chief exec. officer Reed Enterprises, 1989—. Pres. Franklin County (Ky.) Republican Women, 1966, 78; 4th v.p. Ky. Fedn. Rep. Women, 1979; activities dir. Good Shepherd Parish Council, 1976, 77, 78, 89; staff senate Rep. Leadership Ky. Gen. Assembly, 1988; Rep. candidate for treas. State of Ky., 1987; eucharistic minister Good Shephard Parish. Mem. Ky. Nurses Assn. (bd. dirs. polit. action com., 1979). Roman Catholic. Office: PO Box 1141 Frankfort KY 40602

REED, MARSHA LEE, personnel agency executive, consultant; b. Pitts., Sept. 8, 1953; d. Milton and Ruth (Farber) Denmark; m. David P. Reed, Sept. 4, 1977; children—Diane, Robert. B.Gen. Studies, Ohio U., 1975. Cons. Devonshire Personnel, Garden Grove, Calif., 1977-79, Mgmt. Recruiters, Miami, Fla., 1979-80; unit mgr. Dunhill Personnel, Miami, 1980-82; owner, pres. Markett Personnel, Miami, 1982—. Mem. Nat. Assn. Personnel Cons., Nat. Assn. Female Execs., Nat. Assn. Female Bus. Owners, Fla. Assn. Personnel Cons., Bus. and Profl. Women, Greater Miami Jewish Fedn., Kappa Delta (social chmn. 1973-75), Kappa Delta Alumni Assn. Democrat. Club: Hadassah (Miami). Avocations: reading; piano playing. Home: 8818 Castleford Ln Cincinnati OH 45242 Office: Markett Pers 11430 N Kendall Dr Miami FL 33176

REED, MARY LOU, state legislator; m. Scott Reed; children: Tara, Bruce. BA, Mills Coll. Mem. Idaho State Senate, 1985—; coord. Com. for Fair Rates. Mem. North Idaho Alliance for Women. Democrat. Office: 10 Giesa Rd Coeur d'Alene ID 83814*

REED, MERIAN LYNN, small business owner, realtor; b. Ottumwa, Iowa, July 1, 1947; d. Jimmie Lee and Elizabeth JoAnn (Bottorf) Summy; m. Gerald Eugene Reed, June 9, 1967; children: Michelle Lynn, Christopher Gerald. Student, Ea. Ill. U., Parkland Coll.; grad., Grad. Realtors Inst. Lic. real estate broker, mortgage broker. Pres., owner Exec. Realty Group Ltd., Champaign; owner, ptnr. Reed Co. Constrn., Champaign. Mem. NAFE, Nat. Assn. Realtors, Nat. Assn. Homebuilders. Address: PO Box 3966 Champaign IL 61821

REED, ROBERTA GABLE, biochemist; b. Balt., Sept. 18, 1945; d. George Young and Margaret Hannah (Withers) Gable. BS, Lebanon Valley Coll., 1967; MA, Wesleyan U., 1969; PhD, Ga. Wesleyan U., 1971. Postdoctoral fellow U. N.C., Chapel Hill, 1971, Rsch. Triangle Inst., Durham, N.C., 1971-72; instr. SUNY, Oneonta, 1972-73; rsch. assoc. Mary Imogene Bassett Hosp., Cooperstown, N.Y., 1973-75, rsch. biochemist, 1975—. Author chpts. in books. Mem. Am. Chem. Soc., Am. Soc. for Biochemistry and Molecular Biology, Am. Assn. for Clin. Chemistry, Nat. Acad. Clin. Biochemistry. Office: Mary Imogene Hosp One Atwell Rd Cooperstown NY 13326

REED, ROSEMARY, training educator, consultant; b. Worcester, Mass., Dec. 11, 1952; d. George Albion and Rosa Mae (Duncan) R. B.S. in Speech, Emerson Coll., 1974; M.Ed., Worcester State Coll., 1976; postgrad. U. Mass., 1980; M.B.A., Anna Maria Coll., 1986. Cert. tchr., Mass. Communication instr. Suffolk U., Boston, 1976-78, 81-83, Fitchburg State Coll., Mass., 1978-80; edn. adminstr. Option Program, Haverhill, Mass., 1981-83; edn. dir. Stetson Sch., Barre, Mass., 1983-85; corp. recruiter Positions Inc., Westborough, Mass., 1985; tchr. Butler Ctr., Westborough, 1985—; tng. mgr. Future Products, Worcester, 1986-87; tng. cons. A-Z Vacuum Mart, Worcester, 1987—. Author, editor accreditation programs. Recipient Horace Mann Teaching grant, 1987, 88; named Tchr. of Yr., Bur. of Instl. Schs., 1988. Mem. NAFE, Internat. Platform Assn., Assn. Supervision & Curriculum Devel., Corrections Edn. Assn., Lions. Avocations: acting, reading, vegetarian cooking, program development research. Home: 12 Shore Dr Spencer MA 01562 Office: Bulter Ctr PO Box 01562 Westborough MA 01581

REED-BIGNALL, NANCY LOUISE, probation officer; b. Borger, Tex., Oct. 16, 1954; d. Thomas Lee Jr. and Marguerite L. (Landers) Reed; m. John Robert Bignall, Sept. 22, 1973; 1 child, Eric Alan Bignall. BS, San Jose State U., 1977. Social worker County of Kern, Ridgecrest, Calif., 1983-90, probation officer, 1990—. Bd. dirs. Home Health Adv. Coun., Ridgecrest, 1984-87, Hi-Desert Child Abuse Prevention Coun., Ridgecrest, 1990, Mosquite Infant Care Adv. Coun., Ridgecrest, 1990. Mem. AAUW. Republican.

REEDER, VIRGINIA LEE (VIRGINIA LEE FOSTER), educator; b. Tuskahoma, Okla., Jan. 25, 1929; d. Clarence William and Alice (King) Foster; m. Walter Lee Reeder, July 24, 1950; children: Ralph Wesley, Alice Jean. BA, U. Redlands, 1974; MS, Pepperdine U., 1976. Elem. tchr. Harbor City Pub. Schs., 1960-61, First Bapt. Sch., Compton, Calif., 1961-64, Compton Unified Sch., 1980—; head start tchr. Compton Community Youth Ctr., Compton, 1964-76, Charles R. Drew Sch., Compton, 1976-80; tchr. early childhood edn. Compton Coll., 1974-80; tchr. 3d grade gifted program Compton Unified Schs., 1980—. Democrat. Baptist. Home: 11919 E 161st St Norwalk CA 90650

REEGER, MARIE ANN, chiropractor; b. Greensburg, Mar. 8, 1956; d. Robert Earl and Mary Angeline (Capparelli) R. AS, Mt. Ida Jr. Coll., Newton Ctr., 1978; chiropractic prerequisite, New Coll. Calif., San Francisco, 1983; chiropractic, Life Chiropractic Coll. West, San Lorenzo, 1987. Drafting clk. West Penn Power, Greensburg, 1974-76; flight attendant Delta Air Lines, Atlanta, 1978-83; chiropractic intern Swampscott Family Chiropractic, 1987-88, Corcetti Chiropractic Clinic, Murrysville, 1988; prin. Dr. Marie A. Reeger, Chiropractor, Narragansett, R.I., 1988—. Mem. Internat. Chiropractic Assn., Am. Chiropractic Assn., Massachusetts Chiropractic Soc., Rhode Island Chiropractic Soc., C. of C.; South County Women's Network, Nat. Assn. for Women Exec. Roman Catholic. Office: 30 Mariner Sq Narragansett RI 02882

REELS, DONNA MARIE, industrial government security executive; b. Cookeville, Tenn., Mar. 13, 1948; d. Haskel Moore and Edna Mae (Flatt) R. Grad high sch. Cert. in nat. security. Spl. security officer SRI Internat (formerly Stanford Research Inst.), Arlington, Va., 1972-79; security mgr. SRI Internat., Arlington, Va., 1979--. Sgt. U.S. Army, 1966-69. Recipient James S. Cogswell Outstanding Indsl. Security Achievement award, Dept. of Def., 1988; decorated A.C.M. with one oak leaf cluster. Mem. Nat. Classification Mgmt. Soc., Am. Soc. Indsl. Soc. Presbyterian. Home: 1200 S Arlington Ridge Rd Arlington VA 22202 Office: SRI Internat 1611 N Kent St Arlington VA 22209

REES, DIANE DEMURO, lobbyist, public relations consultant; b. Muskegon, Mich., Jan. 8, 1939; d. Robert Guydon and Elizabeth (Hradsky) DeMuro; m. Thomas F. Rees, 1960 (div. Dec. 1984); children: Elizabeth, Dana, Andrew. BA in English, U. Colo., 1964, MA in English Lit., 1969. Reporter Colorado Springs (Colo.) Gazette Telegraph, 1959-60; reporter, librarian Star-Jour.-Chieftain, Pueblo, Colo., 1960; writer U. Colo. Conf. Bur., Boulder, 1967-73; pres. sec. to Congressman Donald G. Brotzman, Boulder, 1973-74; Rep. caucus pres. sec. Colo. Ho. of Reps., Denver, 1975-76; legis. research dir. AMAX, Inc., Golden, Colo., 1976-79; dir. state govtl. affairs AMAX, Inc., Golden, 1979-85; lobbyist, pub. relations cons. Friendly Persuasion, Boulder, 1985—; cons. in field. Chmn. Boulder County Young Republicans, 1971; sec. Boulder County Rep. Com., 1972-73; mem. Colo. Rep. Cen. Com., 1972-80; active numerous congl., state and local Rep. campaigns; mem. exec. com. Colo. Pub. Expenditures Council, 1985—; bd. dirs. Boulder Pow Wow Rodeo, 1972-74, Colo. Mining Assn., 1982—, Ft. Howard Found., 1990—. Mem. Internat. Rodeo Writers (sec. 1972-73, pres. 1973-75). Home and Office: 783 Cypress Dr Boulder CO 80303

REES, FRANCES IRENE, management and professional education consultant; b. Douglas, Ariz., Oct. 11, 1942; d. Hugh Eldred and Carmen Emily (Kennedy) Mayfield; m. David Evans Rees, Aug. 29, 1980; 1 child, Lauren Emily. BA, UCLA, 1964; MusM, U. Ariz., 1975, MBA, 1980. Cert. in prodn. and inventory mgmt. Am. Prodn. and Inventory Control Soc. Tchr. pub. schs., Long Beach, Anaheim, Santa Ana, Calif., 1964-68; tchr. Rabat (Morocco) Am. Sch., 1971-72; exec. sec. Kaiser Exploration Co., Tucson, 1972-73; dir. admissions and scholarships Sch. Music, U. Ariz., Tucson, 1973-80; tng. mgr. Digital Equipment Corp., Phoenix, 1980-85; cons., The Netherlands, 1986-88; cons., owner Rees & Assocs., Phoenix, 1989—; mem.

adv. coun. Ctr. for Exec. Devel., Ariz. State U., Phoenix, 1982; chmn. orgn. devel. task force Am. Soc. for Tng. and Devel., Phoenix, 1982-83; developer seminars on facilitator tng., cons. skills, workshop on bus. writing skills, numerous others. Mem. Soc. for Intercultural Edn., Tng. and Rsch. Home and Office: 2302 W Lompoc Circle Mesa AZ 85202

REESE, DANA ELIZABETH, real estate executive; b. Greenwood, S.C., Sept. 18, 1955; d. Richard Black and Jacquelyn Nenice (Hulsey) R. Grad. high sch., Greenwood. Cert. paramedic. Owner Great Southern Glass Works, Crystal River, Fla., 1979—; pres. Crystal River Trading Co., 1984-87; owner, mgr. Glen Aire Apts., Crystal River, 1985—. Mem. Rainbow River Conservation, Inc., Dunnellon, Fla., 1984—; firefighter, paramedic, bd. dirs., lt. Connell Heights Vol. Fire Dept., Crystal River, 1986—. Mem. SE Drag Boat Assn. (first team fire inwater rescue specialist team). Home and Office: 129 SE Paradise Point Crystal River FL 32629

REESE, DEBORAH DECKER, writer; b. Milw., Aug. 12, 1950; d. Ernst and Sophia (Karolewicz) Decker; m. Clyde William Reese, Oct. 22, 1983; 1 child, Robert Ernst. Student, U. Wis., Milw., 1980-83. Author: Rutherford: The Life of a Racer, 1989; author greeting cards; contbr. articles to profl. jours. Mem. Author's Guild, Internat. Freelance Photographer's Orgn., Nat. Writer's Club, Beta Phi Gamma. Democrat. Roman Catholic. Home and Office: 4858 S Hoyt St Littleton CO 80123

REESE, LYDIA JANE, legislative and government relations specialist; b. Washington, Pa., Dec. 12, 1960; d. John Byron and Judith Marlene (Keeney) R. BA, Alderson-Broaddus Coll., 1982. With ticket sales Combined Airlines Ticket Office, Washington, 1982-83; legis. rels. cons. Charles G. Botsford Assocs., Washington, 1983—; sales agt. Maggie Dickins Realty, Inc., Arlington, Va., 1987—. Mem. N. Ten Mile Bapt. Ch., Amity, Pa., 1972—; asst. campaign mgr. Gates for Congress, Franklin, Vt., 1988. Mem. Helicopter Assn. Internat. (chmn. legis. com. 1986—, Cert. of Appreciation 1989), Aero Club of Washington, Internat. Aviation Club, Am. League of Lobbyists, Am. Def. Preparedness Assn., Alexandria (Va.) Jaycees, U.S. Nat. Fedn. Bus. and Profl. Women's Clubs. Republican. Home: 6044 Chicory Pl Alexandria VA 22310 Office: Charles G Botsford Assocs 1730 M St NW Ste 911 Washington DC 20036

REESE, MARTHA GRACE, minister, lawyer; b. Newark, Ohio, Feb. 27, 1953; d. John Gilbert and Louella Catherine (Hodges) R.; m. William Pulliam Harman; children: Benjamin Victor Harman, Elizabeth Lang Harman. BA with high distinction, DePauw U., 1975; JD magna cum laude, Ind. U., 1980; MDiv, Christian Theol. Sem., 1989. Bar: Ind. 1980, U.S. Dist. Ct. (so. dist.) Ind. 1980, U.S. Ct. Appeals (7th cir.) 1981. Law clk. U.S. Dist. Ct. (so. dist.) Ind., 1980-82; ordained to ministry Christian Ch. (Disciples of Christ), 1989; assoc. Baker & Daniels, Indpls., 1982-83; ptnr. Wilson, Hutchens & Reese, Greencastle, Ind., 1984-86; interim assoc., regional minister , The Christian Ch. in Ind. (Disciples of Christ), 1988-89; sr. pastor Carmel (Ind.) Christian Ch. (Disciples of Christ), 1989—; cons. Lilly Endowment, Inc., 1989—. Steering com. Ind. Leadership Celebration, 1983—; profl. adv. com. Buchanan Counseling Ctr., 1989—. Mem. Carmel Ministerial Assn., Phi Beta Kappa, Theta Phi. Home: 3942 N Delaware St Indianapolis IN 46205

REESE, MILDRED LYONS, civic leader, retired educator; b. New Orleans, July 28; d. Colman and Emily Eleanor (Carter) Lyons; m. Lorenzo Joshua Reese. BA, Dillard U., 1942; MSW, Atlanta U., 1952; postgrad., Columbia U. Tchr. New Orleans Pub. Schs., 1938-49, asst. prin., 1950-51, sch. social worker, 1952-63, prin., 1964-77; part-time program dir. Area Agy. on Aging, New Orleans, 1978-79; ednl. specialist New Orleans, 1979-82; asst. to the pres. Urban League of Greater New Orleans, 1982-85. Author: America and Us, 1975; contbr. articles to profl. publs. Youth adv. com. Youth Study Ctr., New Orleans, 1983-86; co-chairperson Citizens Com. Against Crime, New Orleans, 1978; mem. Mayor's Com. Found. for Edn., New Orleans, 1988; pres. Neighborhood Assn., New Orleans, 1983-89; del. Internat. Women's Yr., Houston, 1976; bd. dirs. New Orleans Coun. on Aging, Family Svcs. of Greater New Orleans, Mayor's Found. for Edn., Inc.; adv. com. U. New Orleans; active Mainstream Against Illiteracy. Recipient Merit award of PTA, New Orleans, 1959, 62, 66, 74, PTA award Convent Elem. Sch., 1976, 89, Whitney M. Young, Jr. award Urban League of Greater New Orleans, 1983, Unsung Heroine award New Orleans Links, Inc., 1989, New Orleans Pub. Svc. Appreciation award, 1989; named 1st Citizen of the Learning Soc., U. New Orleans, 1988. Democrat. Baptist. Home: 2625 Prentiss Ave New Orleans LA 70122

REESE, MONA LYN, composer; b. Morris, Minn., Aug. 24, 1951; d. Robert James and Lillian Evangeline (Fugleberg) R.; 1 child from previous marriage, Greer Reese Davis. BA with honors, U. Minn., Morris, 1969-73; postgrad., U. Kans., 1974-76. Instr. Golden Valley (Minn.) Luth. Coll., 1976-86, West Bank Sch. Music, Mpls., 1976-83; freelance composer Mpls., 1976—; music arranger for Kinder Konzerts, Minn. Orch., 1986—. Mem. American Soc. of Composers, Authors, Publishers, Minn. Composers Forum, Acad. of St. Cecelia. Episcopalian. Home and Office: 3301 Girard Ave S Minneapolis MN 55408

REESE, NORMA CAROL, psychologist; b. Biloxi, Miss., Oct. 26, 1946; d. Virgil Stephen and Lila Mae (Shelton) Tatom; m. John Jay Reese, June 5, 1965 (div. Mar. 1983); children: Cher LeAnne, James Steven. AA in Psychology, Dade County Jr. Coll., Kendall, Fla., 1971; BS in Psychology, U. Miami, 1973; MS and PhD in Psychology, U. So. Miss., 1976. Lic. cons. psychologist, Minn., N.D. Rsch. asst. NASA Lang. Rsch. Lab., Coral Gables, Fla., 1971-73; psychology instr. U. So. Miss., Hattiesburg, 1975-76, Grambling (La.) State U., 1976-78; clin. psychologist II Lake Charles (La.) Mental Health Ctr., 1979-83; tng. cons. Human Rels. Cons., Lake Charles, 1983-86; clin. dir. Grafton (N.D.) State Sch., 1986-89; dir. psychol. svcs. State Devel. Ctr., Grafton, 1989—; ind. contractor, cons. psychol. svcs. Harley Residential Svcs. (name changed to Applied Behavioral Cons., Inc. 1990), Roseville, Minn., 1990—; dir. Sexual Health Project, Devel. Disabled/Mentally Retarded, State Dept. Human Svcs., Grafton, 1989—. Author: The Bulletin of the Psychonomic Soc., 1975-76; author/cartoonist The Worm Runner's Digest, 1975-80. Freedom writer Amnesty Internat., Midwest, 1989; founding mem. Sexual Health Coalition of N.D., 1990. Named Silver Knight candidate, art, Miami (Fla.) Herald News, 1965; nominated Profl. of the Yr., La. Assn. Retarded Citizens, Lake Charles, 1983. Mem. N.D. Psychol. Assn., Minn. Psychol. Assn., Soc. Sci. Study of Sex, Am. Assn. Mental Retardation (sec./treas. N.D. chapter, 1991), The Assn. for Severely Handicapped. Republican. Methodist. Office: The Developmental Ctr West 6th St Grafton ND 58230-7000

REESER, DENISE LOUISE, data management director; b. Allentown, Pa., Nov. 19, 1957; d. Roland Joseph and Orella Amanda (Christman) Doncses; m. Ronald Wayne Reeser; children: Zachary Ellsworth, Dana LeAnn. BS in Health Adminstrn., Pa. State U., 1979; MBA in Finance, Temple U., 1986. Dir. data mgmt. Sacred Heart Health Care System, Allentown, Pa., 1979—. Mem. Health Care Info. & Mgmt. Systems Soc., Electronic Computing Health Orgn., Pa. Health Care Info. & Mgmt. Systems Soc., NAFE, Lehigh Valley Computer Systems Assn.

REESER, SHIRLEY SCHULZ, school counselor; b. Edgerton, Wis., Apr. 11, 1935; d. William August Schulz and Edith Mathilda (Schlichting) Maves; m. Robert Delmar Reeser, Sept. 1, 1956 (div. Aug. 1970); 1 child, Victoria Anne Reeser Montgomery. AA, Palos Verdes (Calif.) Coll., 1955; BA, U. So. Calif., L.A., 1957, MS, 1970; PhD, Golden State U., L.A., 1983. Ordained to ministry; lic. elem. tchr., sch. counselor. Tchr. Torrance (Calif.) Unified Sch. Dist., 1958-62, Hawthorne (Calif.) Sch. Dist., 1962-87; asst. minister, minister Inst. Spiritual Awareness, Woodland Hills, Calif., 1984-87; instr. Nat. U., L.A., 1988; grad. asst. U. Calif.-Dominguez HIlls, Carson, 1989-90; sch. counselor Hawthorne Schs., 1987—; spl. trainer Calif. Tchrs. Assn., 1989. Author: Handbook for Holistic Learning, 1983. Leader Campfire Girls, Rolling Hills Estates, Calif., 1968-70; pres. bd. Ch. of Religious Sci., L.A., 1976-78; sec. bd. Inst. Religious Sci., Woodland Hills, Calif., 1978-85. Recipient spl. award Yukon Sch. and PTA, Hawthorne, 1989, awards for dedicated svc. Ch. of Religious Sci., L.A., 1978, Inst. Spiritual Awareness, Woodland Hills, 1980. Mem. Nat. Teachers Assn., Calif. Tchrs. Assn., Hawthorne Elem. Tchrs. Assn. (v.p. 1985-87). Home: 2519 Vanderbilt Ln 2 Redondo Beach CA 90278

REEVES, A. SUE WINDSOR, academic administrator; b. Oxford, Miss., Mar. 1, 1947; d. Alton Eugene and Mary Emma (Haney) Windsor; m. Johnny Lafayette Reeves Jr., Nov. 1, 1969; children: Ashley Renee, Lesley Windsor, Douglas Stephens. BA in Edn., U. Miss., 1969; MEd, La. State U., 1972. Cert. tchr., La. Tchr. Jackson (Miss.) Pub. Schs., 1969-71; profl. vol. Nat. Assn. Jr. Aux., Slidell, La., 1979-87; tchr. St. Tammany Parish Schs., Slidell, 1981-83; dir. infant youth services Slidell Meml. Hosp., 1984, dir. community relations, 1984-85, dir. women's ctr., 1985-87, dir. physician recruitment, 1985-87, dir. physician services, 1987-90; regional physician recruitment coord. Am. Med. Internat., New Orleans, 1986-88; dir. physician svcs. Slidell (La.) Meml. Hosp., 1989-90; asst. chair for adminstrn. U. N.C. Sch. Nursing, Chapel Hill, 1990—; mem. com. Women's Health Found. La.; healthcare cons., 1989—; healthcare cons., 1989—. Project designer Vol. Coordinating Ctr., 1983, bd. dirs., 1983-88; exec. dir. Women's Health Found., 1987-88; mem. gala com. Lukemia Soc. Am., 1989; founding bd., v.p. Women's Health Care Exec. Network, New Orleans, 1988—. State La. grantee, 1982. Mem. NAFE, Nat. Assn. Jr. Aux. (Martha Wise award 1984, nat. com. woman 1982-87), Am. Coll. Healthcare Execs., Am. Mgrs. Ob-Gyn, Med. Group Mgmt. Assn., Slidell Panhellenic, Camellia Club, Le Cotillion Club, Pinewood Country Club., Univ. Women's Club, Phi Kappa Phi, Phi Mu. Republican. Club: Camellia (Slidell), Le Cotillion, Pinewood Country. Home: 601 Airport Rd #1 Carriage Row Chapel Hill NC 27514 Office: U NC Sch Medicine Dept Ob-Gyn CB #7570 Chapel Hill NC 27599

REEVES, CARLA MARIANNE, nurse, midwife; b. San Francisco, June 25, 1949; d. Robert Dwight and Irma Marianne (Nelson) R. BS in Nursing, U. Md., Balt., 1971; MS in Nursing, U. Ky., 1975. RN, Ariz., Calif.; cert. nurse midwife, Ariz., Calif. Commd. officer U.S. Army, 1967-77; commd. officer USAF, 1978, advanced through grades to maj., 1971-83; nurse, midwife USAF Hosp. Luke, Luke AFB, Ariz., 1978-84, sr. nurse, midwife, 1985-88; sr. nurse, midwife Regional Med. Ctr., Clark Air Base, The Philippines, 1984-85; ret., 1988; nurse, midwife S.W. Women's Health Svcs., Phoenix, 1988—; pvt. duty-clinic nurse Homemakers Upjohn, Santa Maria, Calif., 1978; ob-gyn nurse practitioner Planned Parenthood Santa Barbara (Calif.), Inc., 1978. Decorated Meritorious Svc. medal with oak leaf cluster. Mem. Am. Coll. Nurse Midwives (cert.), Nurses Assn. of Am. Coll. Obstetricians and Gynecologists, Am. Pub. Health Assn., World Wildlife Fund, Ariz. Humane Soc., Doris Day Animal League, Cousteau Soc. Home: 9609 N 34th Dr Phoenix AZ 85051 Office: SW Women's Health Svcs 2850 N 24th St Ste 500B Phoenix AZ 85008

REEVES, CHARLOTTE TEEL, health services coordinator; b. Durant, Okla., Mar. 16, 1955; d. Hayes Gerald and Lillie Opal (Stilwell) Teel; m. Barry Ray Reeves, Jan. 3, 1953. BS in Psychology, Southeastern U., 1977, BS in Sociology, 1977, BA, 1977. Activities dir. Texoma Campfire Coun., Durant, 1977-78; spl. needs. coord. Community Action Program, Frederick, OKla., 1978-79; handicapped child specialist Project Head Start, Durant, 1979-83, health svcs. coord.; dir. for handicapped Big Five Community Svcs., Durant, 1979-89; cons. Big Five Head Start Program, Durant, 1981-89; cons. on nutrition, dental and medical health to Head Start Program grantees for Info. Scis. Rsch. Inst. and Region VI Pub. Health Svcs., Dallas and Vienna, Va., 1989. Mem. Nat. Head Start Staff Assn., Okla. Head Start Staff Assn., Okla. Community Action Dirs. Assn., Optomists, Jaycees (Durant chpt.), Newcomers Club, Durant Country Club. Democrat. Home: 4743 Melisa Dr Durant OK 74701 Office: Big Five Community Svcs PO Box 1577 Durant OK 74702

REEVES, LUCY MARY, teacher; b. Pewamo, Mich., July 2, 1932; d. Lavaldin Edgar and Marian S. (Lee) Hull; m. Walter Emery Reeves, Jan. 21, 1922. BS, Western Mich. U., Kalamazoo, 1965; postgrad., Western Mich. U., 1965-75. Tchr. Country Sch. One Room, Matherton, Mich., 1956-57, Ionia, Mich., 1957-58, Belding, Mich., 1958-62, Saranac, Mich., Belding, Mich., 1965; tchr. Belding (Mich.) Area Schs., 1965--. Mem. NEA, Mich. Edn. Assn., Belding Area Edn., Profl. Businesswomen's Assn.

REEVES, PATRICIA RUTH, heavy machinery manufacturing company executive; b. Bklyn., Mar. 26, 1931; d. Maurice G. and Ethel Helen (Kessler) Der Brucke m. Cedric E. Reeves, June 22, 1952. BA, Adelphi U., 1952. Chief of records sect. Hydrocarbon Rsch., Inc., N.Y.C., 1952-65; lead sec. C.F. Braun & Co., Murray Hill, N.J., 1965-69; exec. sec. Wilputte Corp., Murray Hill, N.J., 1969-75, adminstrv. asst., 1975-79, sales coord., 1979-81, pers. adminstr., 1981-82; sales coord. Krupp Wilputte Corp., Murray Hill, N.J., 1982-84; pers. adminstr. Somerset Techs., Inc., N.J., 1984-85, pers. mgr., 1985—. Pres. Mountain Jewish Community Ctr., Warren, N.J., 1976-77, bd. dirs., 1972-81. Mem. NAFE, AAUW, Women's Network Cen. N.J. (v.p., editor newsletter 1981-83, career assistance coord. 1984-85, membership chmn. 1986—), Am. Soc. Pers. Adminstrs. (sec. 1986-88, v.p. 1988-89), Soc. Human Resources Adminstrn. (pres. Cen. N.J. chpt. 1989-90), Community Indsl. Rels. Orgn. (treas. 1985-88, chmn. 1988-90). Jewish. Home: 89 Knollwood Dr Watchung NJ 07060 Office: Somerset Techs Inc Weston Canal Rd Somerset NJ 08873

REEVES-DARBY, VONDA GAIL, gastroenterologist, physician; b. Collins, Miss., Sept. 19, 1958; d. Andrew Carnegie and Cleoria (Sanders) R.; m. Alvin Darby, June 18, 1988; 1 child, Galen Ashton. BS, Millsaps Coll., 1978; MD, Meharry Med. Coll., Nashville, 1982. Intern, then resident U. Tex. Med. Br., Galveston, 1988—; dir. AIDS program Tex. Dept. of Corrections, Galveston, 1986-88; liaison physician U. Tex. MB Liason Physician, Galveston, 1986-88; fellow Dept. Gastroenterology, Galveston, 1988—. Mem. NAACP, ACP (assoc.) , AMA, Nat. Med. Assn., Tex. Med. Assn., Am. Soc. Internal Medicine, Am. Gastroent. Assn., Galveston County Med. Assn., Alpha Kappa Alpha. Democrat. Methodist. Office: Div Gastroenterology Rt G-64 Substation 1 Galveston TX 77550

REEVES-KAZELSKIS, CAROLYN, education educator; b. Wellington, Tex., June 20, 1941; d. Harold Joseph and Bertha Mae (Carter) Keller; m. T. Glen Reeves, Sept. 2, 1960 (div. 1977); children: Rhea Ann, Harold Lynn; m. Richard Kazelskis, May 17, 1985; stepchildren: Kathy, Kim. BS, East Tex. State U., 1968; MEd, Miss. State U., 1970, EdD, 1973. Tchr. Kiddie Kollege, Commerce, Tex., 1966-68, Starkville (Miss.) Pub. Schs., 1969-74; dir. tchr. corps U. Southern Miss., Hattiesburg, 1979-81, assoc. prof., 1981—, mem. faculty senate, 1989—; cons. Choctaw Tribe, Philadelphia, Miss., 1974-88, Miss. Dept. Edn., Jackson, 1983-88. Author and editor: The Choctaw Before Removal, 1985; author tng. manuals; contbr. chpts. to books and articles to profl. jours.; editor; Miss. Reading Jour., 1985—. U.S. Office Edn. grantee, 1974-81. Mem. Am. Ednl. Rsch. Assn., Internat. Reading Assn., Mid-South Ednl. Rsch. Assn. (bd. dirs. 1981-84, v.p. 1984, pres. 1985), So. Assn. Children Under Six. Episcopalian. Home: 208 Beverly Ln Hattiesburg MS 39402 Office: Univ Southern Miss SS Box 5057 Hattiesburg MS 39406

REGALMUTO, NANCY MARIE, small business owner, psychic consultant; b. Bay Shore, N.Y., Aug. 24, 1956; d. Antonio J. Jr. and Agnes C. (Dietz) R. Student, SUNY, Stony Brook. Sales mgr. Fire, Inc., Hempstead, N.Y.; sports handicapper Red Hot Sport, J. Dime Sports, Diamond Sports, Hicksville, N.Y.; small bus. owner Bellport, N.W.; cons. in fields of med., fin., personal and animal clairvoyancy. Columnist Daily Racing Form; appeared on numerous TV programs. Mem. NAFE. Home and Office: 18 Woodland Park Rd Bellport NY 11713

REGAN, ANN ELLEN, computer scientist; b. Mineola, N.Y., Dec. 18, 1962; d. James J. and Mary E. (Deegan) R. BS in Computer Sci., Ariz. State U., 1985; MS in Computer Sci., Northwestern U., 1988. Jr. programmer Comsystems div. SAIC, San Diego, 1981-85; systems analyst, programmer Computer Scis. Corp., San Diego, 1985-86; computer scientist Four Pi Systems, San Diego, 1988—. Mem. Assn. for Computing Machinery, Am. Assn. for Artificial Intelligence, Calif. Scholastic Fedn. (life), Upsilon Pi Epsilon. Office: Four Pi Systems 10905 Technology Pl San Diego CA 92128

REGAN, ANN KENNEDY (PAT REGAN), state legislator; b. Chgo., 1923; d. Thomas Carey and Katherine (Knight) Kennedy; m. Thomas Patrick Regan; children: Kate, Thomas Joseph, Ann, Margaret. BS, Ill. Inst. Tech., 1948; MS, Ea. Mont. Coll., 1963. Tchr. Castle Rock Jr. High Sch.; mem. Mont. Ho. of Reps., 1973-74; mem. from dist. 31 Mont. State Senate, 1975-85, mem. from dist. 47, 1985—. Recipient Women of Achievement award Billings Bus. and Profl. Women. Mem. LWV, NOW, Nat. Edn. Assn., Billings, Mont. Edn. Assn. Home: 204 Mountain View Billings MT 59101*

REGAN, ELLEN FRANCES (MRS. WALSTON SHEPARD BROWN), ophthalmologist; b. Boston, Feb. 1, 1919; d. Edward Francis and Margaret (Moynihan) R.; A.B., Wellesley Coll., 1940; M.D., Yale U., 1943; m. Walston Shepard Brown, Aug. 13, 1955. Intern, Boston City Hosp., 1944; asst. resident, resident Inst. Ophthalmology, Presbyn. Hosp., N.Y.C., 1944-47, asst. ophthalmologist, 1947-56, asst. attending ophthalmologist, 1956-84; instr. ophthalmology Columbia Coll. Physicians and Surgeons, 1947-55, asso. ophthalmology, 1955-67, asst. clin. prof., 1967-84. Mem. Am. Ophthal. Soc., AMA, Am. Acad. Ophthalmology, Assn. Research Ophthalmology, N.Y. Acad. Medicine, N.Y. State Med. Soc., Mass. Med. Soc., River Club. Home: Tuxedo Park NY 10987 Office: Box 632 Tuxedo NY 10987

REGAN, MARDEE HAIDIN, editor; b. Barberton, Ohio, Sept. 23, 1949; d. Mark V. Haidin and Gladys D. (Galehouse) Hilgert; m. Gary Lee Regan, Aug. 22, 1979. BA, Ohio State U., 1971. Assoc. editor Food & Wine Mag., N.Y.C., 1980-84, columnist, 1984—; mng. editor Chocolatier Mag., N.Y.C., 1984; assoc. Beard Glaser Wolf, N.Y.C., 1976-79; cons. Ketchum Communications, N.Y.C., 1989—; kitchen cons. Food & Wine Mag., N.Y.C., 1989—. Author: Aunt Freddie's Pantry, 1983, Great Desserts, 1988, Great Recipes for Great Weekends, 1990. Mem. Roundtable for Women, Am. Inst. Wine and Food, Hemlock Soc. (bd. dir. 1988-90). Home: 131 W 28th St 4D New York NY 10001 Office: Ketchum Communications 1133 6th Ave New York NY 10036

REGAN, MURIEL, small business owner; b. N.Y.C., July 15, 1930; d. William and Matilda (Riebel) Blome; m. Robert Regan, 1966 (div. 1976), 1 child, Jeanne Salmon. BA, Hunter Coll., N.Y.C., 1950; MLS, Columbia U., 1952; MBA, Pace U., N.Y.C., 1982. Post librarian US Army, Okinawa, 1952-53; researcher P.F. Collier, N.Y.C., 1953-57; asst. libr. to libr. Rockefeller Found., N.Y.C., 1957-67; dep. chief librarian Manhattan Community Coll., N.Y.C., 1967-68; librarian Booz Allen & Hamilton, N.Y.C., 1968-69, Rockefeller Found., 1969-82; prin. Gossage Regan Assocs., Inc., N.Y.C., 1980—; dir. NY Met. Reference and Research Library Agy., 1988--, cons. Libraries, Info. Ctrs. Mem. ALA, Spl. Librs. Assn. (pres. 1989-90), Archons of Colophon, N.Y. Libr. Club. Home: 792 Columbus Ave New York NY 10025 Office: Gossage Regan Assocs Inc 25 W 43rd St New York NY 10036

REGAN, SUZANNE MARIE, marketing executive; b. Camden, N.J., May 11, 1950; d. Cornelius Joseph and Jeannette (Way) R.; B.S., U. Conn., 1972; M.B.A., Drexel U., 1978; m. Ronald L. Feldberg, Apr. 10, 1976; children: Matthew Regan, Michael Regan. Acctg. procedures analyst Campbell Soup Co., Camden, N.J., 1972-74, mktg. rsch. analyst, 1974-77, asst. mktg. mgr. Swanson div., 1977-78, mktg. mgr. Swanson div., 1978-81, mktg. dir. Pet Food unit, 1981-85, pres., gen. mgr. Pet Food unit (Champion Valley Farms) 1985-87, gen. mgr. refrigerated deli unit, 1987-88, gen. mgr. Marie's Salad Dressing, 1988—. Mem. Am. Mgmt. Assn., NAFE. Home: 6 Hidden Acres Dr Voorhees NJ 08043 Office: Campbell Pl Camden NJ 08101

REGASPI, LISA FORD, interior designer; b. Decatur, Ga., Sept. 13, 1961; d. Hardie Braden and Betty Faye (Ryan) Ford; m. Guillermo Prudencio DeAusen, Nov. 4, 1989. A Interior Design, Southern Coll., Orlando, Fla., 1985; AA, Brevard Community Coll., 1987; B Interior Design, Fla. State U., 1988. Floral designer, mgr. Flower Boutique, Titusville, Fla., 1980-85; interior designer, sales Meehan's, Melbourne, Fla., 1985-86; interior designer Thomas W. Ruff & Co., Orlando, 1988—. Author: (poem) Shooting Star, 1981. Mem. Interior Design Assn. Fla., Orlando Landmark Def., Inc., Golden Key (Outstanding Scholastic Achievement award 1988). Republican.

REGELIN, LOUISE O., lawyer; b. Juneau County, Wis., Nov. 13, 1940; d. George Emil August and Genevieve Jenette (Phaff) R.; m. C. James Dunigan, July 3, 1972 (div. July 1978); m. Everett David Sherman, Nov. 5, 1981. BS, U. Wis., La Crosse, 1962, MS, 1969; postgrad., So. Ill. U., 1963-64, 66; JD, U. Idaho, 1979. Bar: Idaho 1979, U.S. Supreme Ct. 1989; cert. tchr., Wis., Wash., Tenn. Libr. Tomah (Wis.) High Sch., 1962-63, Marathon (Wis.) High Sch., 1964-65, Mt. Horeb (Wis.) High Sch., 1965-68, Stewart County High Sch., Dover, Tenn., 1973-76; dir. Learning Ctr., State of Wash. Green Hill Sch., Chehalis, 1969-72; staff atty. Idaho Legal Aid Svcs., Lewiston, 1979-80; pvt. practice Grangeville, Idaho, 1980-84; ptnr. Swayne & Regelin, Moscow, Idaho, 1984-89; pvt. practice, Moscow, 1989—; lectr. bus. law Wash. State U., Pullman, 1989—. Vice chmn. Latah County Dem. Cen. Com., Moscow, 1988-90. Mem. LWV (bd. dirs. Idaho chpt. 1987-89), AAUW (chair div. Ednl. Found. Programs 1988-90, pres. div. 1990-92), Idaho Bar Assn. (family law and bankruptcy sects.), Am Bankruptcy Inst., Idaho Women Lawyers (pres. 1989—), Moscow C. of C. (com. chmn. 1988-90), Idaho Women's Network, Older Women's League, Kiwanis (bd. dirs. Moscow chpt. 1988-90), Phi Alpha Delta (dep. internat. justice 1984—). Episcopalian. Home: PO Box 9512 Moscow ID 83843-0120

REGINI, JUDITH L., infosystems specialist; b. La Marque, Tex., Nov. 13, 1953; d. Henry Thomas and Nell Beatrice (McNary) Shields; m. Alvine H. Regini, June 29, 1973. ABA, Coll. of the Mainland, Texas City, Tex., 1989; student, U. Houston. Tng. coord. Am. Nat. Ins. Co., Galveston, Tex. Contbr. articles to newsletters, jours. Choir dir. Our Lady of Lourdes Ch., Hitchcock, Tex., 1986—. Fellow Life Office Mgmt. Assn.; mem. Data Trainers S.E. Tex. (v.p. publs. 1988, v.p. facilities 1990), Phi Theta Kappa. Roman Catholic. Home: PO Box 532 Hitchcock TX 77563 Office: Am Nat Ins Co One Moody Pla #721 Galveston TX 77550

REGISTER, ANNETTE ROWAN, reading teacher; b. Doctors Inlet, Fla., Apr. 5, 1931; d. Ernest Ambors and Frances Perlena (Monroe) R.; Henry Ira Register, Oc. 31, 1954; 1 child, Andrew Henry. RN, Grnville Gen.Hosp.Sch.of Nursi, Greenville, 1948-51; BS, Tex. Woman's U., Denton, 1954; MEd, U. Fla., Gainesville, 1959; SEd, Fla. State U., 1983. Instrn. dir. nursing edn. Alachua Gen. Hosp., Gainesville, Fla., 1955-57; pub. sch. tchr. Okaloosa County, Ft. Walton Beach, Fla., 1966-; v.p., Internation Training in Communication Ft. Walton Beach, Fla.,. Pres. United Meth. Women, Ft. Walton Beach, Fla., 1985-87; pres. Okaloosa Reading Coun., 1976-80. Mem. Phi Delta Kappa (1st v.p.). Methodist. Office: Okaloosa County Sch Bd 10 Lowery Pl SE Fort Walton Beach FL 32548

REGISTER, PENELOPE WARREN, lawyer; b. Decatur, Ala., Dec. 7, 1956; d. Seymour Arnold Spiegelman and Sara Jean (Warren) Nichols; m. William Wood Register, Jr., Aug. 8, 1981. BA, Southwestern U., Memphis, 1979; JD, Vanderbilt U., 1982. Bar: Tenn. 1982, R.I. 1985. Assoc. Waring Cox, Memphis, 1982-84; ptnr. Tillinghast Collins & Graham, Providence, 1984—. Bd. dirs. Elizabeth Buffam Chase House, Warwick, R.I., 1989, Rape Crisis Ctr., Cranston, R.I., 1989. Mem. Nat. Assn. Bond Lawyers, Govt. Fin. Officers Assn., R.I. Bar Assn. (chmn. mcpl. law com. 1988-90). Episcopalian. Office: Tillinghast Collins & Graham 1 Old Stone Sq Providence RI 02903

REGUERO, MELODIE HUBER, chief financial officer; b. Montebello, Calif., May 10, 1956; d. Adam W. and Helen Carolyn (Antrim) Huber; m. Edward Anthony Reguero, Oct. 3, 1987. BA in Econs. magna cum laude, UCLA, 1978; M in Bus. Taxation, U. So. Calif., 1983. CPA, Calif. Mem. tax audit staff Arthur Young & Co., Los Angeles, 1978-80; sr. mem. Singer, Lewak, Greenbaum & Goldstein, Los Angeles, 1980-82; tax suprr. Coldwell Banker & Co., Los Angeles, 1983-84; fin. analyst, acquisitions specialist Coldwell Banker Residential Group, Newport Beach, Calif., 1984-86; fin. svcs. profl. The Acacia Fin. Group, Newport Beach, Calif., 1986-88; chief fin. officer, owner Fin. Engring. Concepts, Inc., Irvine, Calif., 1988—, Worldwide Investment Network, Inc., Irvine, 1989—; treas. Champions Choice, Inc., Anaheim, Calif., 1980—. Active, Center Club, Costa Mesa, 1989—, Ctr. 500 Performing Arts, Costa Mesa, 1989—. Mem. AICPA, IAFP, Calif. Soc. CPAs (pres. 1980—), Irvine C. of C., Racquet Club of Irvine, Delta Gamma. Republican. Office: Worldwide Investment Network Inc 8001 Irvine Ctr Dr Ste 1200 Irvine CA 92718

REGULES, ROXANNE, school system administrator; b. Monterey, Calif., Sept. 17, 1955; d. Miguel Valenzuela and Maria Regules. AA, Monterey Peninsula Coll., 1974; BA, San Jose State U., 1976, MA, 1980. Cert. tchr. Spanish, sch. adminstr. Tchr. Salinas (Calif.) City Sch. Dist., 1976-78, resource tchr., 1978-82; coordinator spl. projects Santa Rita Union Sch. Dist., Salinas, 1982-86; dir. aux. and spl. projects Alisal Union Sch. Dist., Salinas, 1986-89; bilingual cons., 1986—; tchr. adult edn. Monterey Peninsula Unified Sch. Dist., Salinas, 1980-82, dir. aux. and spl. projects, 1989—; tchr. Pacific Grove (Calif.) Unified Sch. Dist., 1984-86; cons. State Dept. Edn., Sacramento, 1986-87, pvt. contracts for various sch. dists., Monterey, 1980—; part-time faculty mem. Bethany Bible Coll., 1988—. Bd. dirs. Door to Hope, Salinas, 1987-88; tchr. Monterey Assembly of God Ch., 1970-82, bd. dirs., 1987—. Named Outstanding Supr. of Yr., Monterey County Youth Employment Service, 1983-84, Outstanding Educator of Yr., Salinas Woman's Jaycees, 1984; Monterey Peninsula Coll. Inst. Fgn. Studies scholar, 1973. Mem. Calif. Assn. Sch. Adminstrs., Calif. Assn. Compensatory Edn. (regional rep. 1983-86), Assn. Supervision and Curriculum Devel., Asilomar Regional Reading Conf. (pres. elect 1986—, bd. dirs. 1984—), Salinas C. of C., Phi Delta Kappa, Delta Kappa Gamma. Democrat. Lodge: Soroptimists. Home: 1055 Johnson Ave Monterey CA 93940 Office: Monterey Peninsula Unified Sch Dist 700 Pacific St Monterey CA 93940

REGULSKI, JANICE STEELE, community volunteer; b. Oakland, Jan. 26, 1928; d. Thomas S. and Milbrun J. (Atchison) Steele; m. Lee T. Regulski, Nov. 19, 1926; children: Susan, Kurt, Doris, Mark. BA, Cornell U., 1949. Mem. Cornell U. Coun., Ithaca, 1983-89, Cornell Adv.-Admissions, Ithaca, 1977-87. Mem. LWV (pres. Pinellas County chpt. 1988-89), Cornell Alumnia Assn. (pres. Suncoast Area chpt. 1980-81), AAUW, Libr. Found. (sec. 1980-83).

REHA, ROSE KRIVISKY, business educator emeritus; b. N.Y.C., Dec. 17, 1920; d. Boris and Freda (Gerstein) Krivisky; m. Rudolph John Reha, Apr. 11, 1941; children: Irene Gale, Phyllis. BS, Ind. State U., 1965; MA, U. Minn., 1967, PhD, 1971. With U.S. and State Civil Service, 1941-63; tchr. pub. schs., Minn., 1965-66; teaching assoc., instr. U. Minn., Mpls., 1966-68; prof. Coll. Bus., St. Cloud (Minn.) State U., 1968-85, prof. emeritus, 1985—, chmn. bus. edn. and office adminstrn. dept., 1982-83; adj. prof. profl. and bus. communication Fla. Atlantic U., Boca Raton, Fla., 1989-90; cons., lectr. in field. Reviewer of bus. communications and consumer edn. textbooks; contbr. articles to profl. jours. Camp dir. Girl Scouts U.S.A., 1960-62; active various community fund drives; sec., mem. relicensure rev. Com. Minn. Bd. Teaching Continuing Edn., 1984-85. Recipient Achievement award St. Cloud State U., 1985, St. Cloud State U. Research and Faculty Improvement grantee, 1973, 78, 83. Mem. Am. Vocat. Assn., Minn. Econ. Assn., Minn. Women of Higher Edn., NEA, Minn. Edn. Assn. (pres. women's caucus 1981-83, award 1983), St. Cloud U. Faculty Assembly (pres. 1975-76), St. Cloud State U. Grad. Council (chmn. 1983-85), Pi Omega Pi (sponsor St. Cloud State U. chpt. 1982-85), Phi Chi Theta, Delta Pi Epsilon, Delta Kappa Gamma. Jewish. Home: 3671 Eviron Blvd Lauderhill FL 33319 Office: St Cloud State U Coll Bus Saint Cloud MN 56301

REHAGEN-HUFF, ANDREA LEE, career consulting, outplacement company executive, consultant; b. St. Louis, Nov. 20, 1949; d. Clemens John and Margaret Mary (Sheridan) Rehagen; m. S. Michael Huff, Jan. 11, 1969; 1 child, Jeffrey Michael. B.A. in Sociology, So. Ill. U., 1971; M.A. in Counseling, Washington U., St. Louis, 1975. Career counselor State of Ill., Granite City, 1971-73; counselor RHS, Inc., St. Louis, 1973-75, Womanhelp, San Francisco, 1975-77; dir. career devel., career cons. Career Planning Services/Woman's Way, San Rafael, Calif., 1977-80; pres., career cons. CareerWorks, San Francisco, 1980—. Mem. Am. Soc. Tng. and Devel. (chmn., founder career devel. div. 1979-81), No. Calif. Human Resources Council, Women Entrepreneurs, Career Planning and Adult Devel. Network. Democrat. Avocations: collector of early 20th century art and furnishings, collectible antique jewelry. Office: CareerWorks 100 Spear St Ste 850 San Francisco CA 94105

REHM, PATRICE KOCH, physician; b. DeSoto, Mo., Nov. 23, 1954; d. James Clarence and Eleanor (Koch) R. BA in Chemistry, U. Mo., 1977; MD, Yale U., 1981. Diplomate Am. Bd. Radiology, Am. Bd. Nuclear Medicine. Intern in medicine Waterbury (Conn.) Hosp., 1981-82; resident in radiology Yale New Haven Hosp., 1982-83, 84-85, fellow in neuroradiology, 1985-86, fellow in nuclear medicine, 1986-87; resident in radiology SUNY Upstate Med. Ctr., Syracuse, 1983-84; clin. assoc. Cleve. Clinic, 1987-88, staff physician, 1988-89; staff physician Presbyn. Hosp., Charlotte, N.C., 1989—. Author: (chpt.) Brain Imaging, 1990. Mem. Am. Coll. Radiology, Am. Coll. Nuclear Physicians, Radiologic Soc. N.Am., Soc. Nuclear Medicine. Office: Mecklenburg X-Ray Assn PO Box 221249 Charlotte NC 28222

REHRMANN, EILEEN MARY, legislative delegate; b. Chester, Pa., Nov. 30, 1944; d. Victor Casmir and Anne (Quinn) Marchlik; m. Joseph Anthony Rehrmann, July 3, 1965; children: William, Mary Anne, Kristine, Robert. Student, Immaculata Coll., Phila., 1962-65. Town commr. Town of Bel Air (Md.), 1979-82; mem. Md. Ho. of Dels., 1982—; del. 1980 Dem. Conv., Bel Air, 1980; mem. appropriations com. Law Enforcement Transp. Sub-Com. Chairperson Harford County Del. Named Outstanding State Legislator Assembly Govtl. Employees; recipient Service award Md. Troopers Assn., Appreciation award No. Md. Assn. for Retarded Citizens. Mem. Women Legislators of Md. (pres. 1989), Md. Mcpl. League (pres. 1981, Disting. Service award, Md. Police Chief's award, 1988, Md. Child Care Assn. award, 1989). Roman Catholic. Office: 103 N Main St Bel Air MD 21014

REIBMAN, JEANETTE FICHMAN, state senator; b. Ft. Wayne, Ind., Aug. 18, 1915; d. Meir and Pearl (Schwartz) Fichman; m. Nathan L. Reibman, June 20, 1943; children: Joseph M. Edward D., James E. AB, Hunter Coll., 1937; LLB, U. Ind., 1940; LLD, Lafayette Coll., 1969; hon. degree, Lehigh U., 1986, Wilson Coll., 1974, Cedar Crest Coll., 1977, Moravian Coll., 1990. Bar: Ind., 1940, U.S. Supreme Ct. 1944. Pvt. practice law Ft. Wayne, 1940; atty. U.S. War Dept., Washington, 1940-42, U.S. War Prodn. Bd., Washington, 1942-44; mem. Pa. Ho. of Reps., 1956-66, Pa. State Senate, Harrisburg, 1966—; chmn. com. on edn. Pa. State Senate, 1971-81, minority chmn., from 1981; mem. Edn. Commn. of the States. Trustee emeritus Lafayette Coll.; bd. mem., Pa. Med. Coll., Pa. Higher Edn. Assistance Agy., Pa. Coun. on Arts, Camphill Schs. Recipient Disting. Dau. of Pa. award and medal Gov. Pa., 1968, citation on naming of Jeanette F. Reibman Adminstrn. Bldg., East Stroudsburg State Coll., 1972, Pub. Svc. award Pa. Psychol. Assn., 1977, Jerusalem City of Peace award Govt. Israel, 1977; named to Hunter Coll. Alumni Hall of Fame, 1974. Mem. Hadassah (Myrtle Wreath award 1976), Sigma Delta Tau, Delta Kappa Gamma, Phi Delta Kappa, Order Ea. Star. Democrat. Jewish. Office: 711 Lehigh St Easton PA 18042 also: Pa State Senate State Capitol Harrisburg PA 17120

REIBMAN-MYERS, FRANCINE LEE, corporate executive; b. N.Y.C., Dec. 5, 1949; d. Abe and Katherine C. (Glass) Reibman; m. Jay H. Myers, May 31, 1980; 1 child, Benjamin Alexander Reibman-Myers. B.A. cum laude, CUNY. Assoc. dir. Nat. Student Lobby, Washington, 1972-74; dir. govt. ops. Continental Mktg., Washington, 1972-74; acting dir. vets. affairs CUNY, 1974-75; chmn. bd. Culpepper, Inc., 1983—, Millburn, N.J., 1983-86; pres. Fran Reibman & Assocs., Millburn, 1976-77; cons. House Select Com. on Aging, 1977-78, Triathalon Products, Inc., 1985-86, cons. Mennen Med. Inc., 1985-87; cons., DAL Svcs., Inc., 1987-89; dir. dept. clin. engring. U. Med. Dentistry of N.J., 1987—; pres. Electro Diagnostics subs. Culpepper, 1989—. Contbr. articles to profl. jours. Patentee rehab. gym, 1985. Candidate for N.Y. State Assembly, 1972; adv. People to Rehabilitate and Integrate the Disabled, 1973-78; sec. Coun. on Internat. Rels. for UN, 1972-73; Democratic county com. person, Queens, 1972-74; bd. govs. Queensborough Pres.'s Council for Tenants, 1972-73; mem. Carter/Mondale White House Transition Team, 1976; trustee N.J. Zool. Soc., 1990. Mem. Am. Assn. Advancement of Med. Instrumentation, N.J. Assn. Clin. Engrs., NAFE (bd. dirs. North Jersey chpt. 1988-89). Jewish. Avocations: horseback riding, golf, sailing, building, reading.

REICH, EILEENE ELIZABETH, chemical company executive; b. Pitts., Jan. 3, 1953; d. John Patrick and Eileen Mae (Horgan) R. B in Chemistry, Washington & Jefferson Coll., 1974; postgrad., Lehigh U., 1981-83. Chemist Mobay Chem. Co., Pitts., 1974-78, tech. sales rep., 1978-79; tech. sales rep. Air Products & Chems. Inc., Allentown, Pa., 1979-80, mktg. mgr., 1980-81, product mgr., 1981-83; mgr. mktg. devel. Arco Chem. Co., Newton Square, N.J., 1983-88, project mgr., 1988—; adv., cons. in field. Contbr. articles to profl. jours. Fund raiser Big Bros./Big Sisters of Burlington County, Riverton, N.J. 1987—; vol. Walnut St. Theatre, Phila., 1988—. Recipient Suppliers award Nat. Home Furnishings Assn., 1986, 87. Mem. Soc. Plastics Industry (chmn. 1981—), Waterbed Retailers Assn., Nat. Assn. Bedding Mfrs., Home Furnishings Mgrs. Assn. Republican. Roman Catholic. Office: Arco Chemical 3801 West Chester Pike Newton Square NJ 19073

REICH, GLORIA CAROLYN, association executive; b. Seattle, Nov. 18, 1932; d. Harry James Erickson and Fleta Elizabeth (McNaughton) Smith; married. Student, Reed Coll., 1950-52; BS in Psychology, Portland State U., 1980, MS in Psychology, 1982, PhD in Urban Studies, 1988. Social worker Pa., 1953-54; bank clk., trainer U.S. Nat. Bank, Portland, Oreg., 1954-60; community vol. Portland, 1960-75; vol. coord. Aging Program, Portland, 1974-76; chief exec. officer Am. Tinnitus Assn., Portland, 1976—. Contbr. articles to profl. jours. Pres. Community Music Ctr., Portland, 1970-72. Mem. Deafness Rsch. Centurions, Nat. Voluntary Health Assn., Am. Psychol. Soc., Oreg. Psychol. Assn. for Applied Psychology, Bio-feedback Internat. Tinnitus Study Group. Democrat. Office: Am Tinnitus Assn 1618 SW 1st Ave #417 Portland OR 97201

REICH, JOANNE LEE, business and marketing consultant; b. Oakland, Calif., Aug. 30, 1945; d. Herbert and Wanda Jane (Porter) R. B.A., UCLA, 1967; postgrad. Babson Coll., 1988. Programmer analyst, cons. various orgns., Los Angeles, 1969-73; sr. programmer analyst Compata, Inc., Canoga Park, Calif., 1973-75; systems engr. Data Gen. Corp., El Segundo, Calif., 1975-78; project mgr., bus. planning Honeywell Info. Systems, Billerica, Mass., 1978-82; bus. planning cons. Wang Labs., Inc., Lowell, Mass., 1982-86; project mgr., mktg. support mgr. Direct Products div. Data Gen. Corp., Westboro, Mass., 1986—; market research cons. Micro Tech. Research, Chelmsford, Mass., 1984—. Mem. Am. Mgmt. Assn., Nat. Assn. Female Execs. Avocations: oil painting, drawing, community theater production activities. Office: Data Gen Corp 4400 Computer Dr Westboro MA 01580

REICH, OLIVE BUERK, artist, educator; b. Bklyn., Mar. 1, 1935; d. Percival G. and Olive (Wirth) Buerk; m. Daniel Oehler Reich, Aug. 4, 1956; children: Peter, Robin, Daniel. BA, Mt. Holyoke Coll., 1956. Tchr. water color technique Olive Reich Studio, Bklyn., 1970—, Aquarelle Studio, Shelter Island, N.Y., 1983-86, Polytech. Preparatory Inst., Bklyn., 1987; cons. art Union Ch., Bay Ridge, Bklyn., 1984-87, Reich Paper Co., Bklyn, 1986-88, Meta Catering Corp., Bklyn., 1987-88. Illustrator book God's Summer Cottage, 1980, Chronicle of Shelter Island Churches, 1983, Shelter Island Yacht Club, 1986. Pres. Bay Ridge Festival Arts., Bklyn, 1978-80. Mem. Nat Assn. Women Artists, Artists Equity, Contemporary Artists Guild (corr. sec. 1980-87), Audabon Artist, Salmagundi Club (N.Y.C.), Catharine Lorillard Wolfe Art Club (1st v.p. 1982). Home: 36 79th St Brooklyn NY 11209 Office: Olive Reich Studio 7518 Third Ave Brooklyn NY 11209

REICH, ROSE MARIE, art teacher; b. Milw., Dec. 24, 1937; d. Valentine John and Mary Jane (Grochowski) Kosmatka; m. Kenneth Pierce Reich, July 13, 1968; 1 child, Lance Pierce. BA, Milw. Downer Coll., 1959; MA, U. Wyo., 1967. Art tchr. Oconomowoc (Wis.) Area Schs., 1959—. Mem. Oconomowoc Edn. Assn., NEA, AAUW (v.p. membership 1989—), Delta Kappa Gamma (past pres.). Roman Catholic.

REICHENBACH, M. J. GERTRUDE, university program director, retired, consultant; b. Heerlen, Limburg, The Netherlands, Aug. 18, 1912; came to U.S., 1946; d. Jan Hubert Emile and M.J. Gertruda (Cardaun) Consten; m. Joseph Winfield, May 7, 1946; children: Paul Joseph, Peter David, Miriam Johanna, Eric Emile, Ingrid Gertrude. MA in English, U. Utrecht, The Netherlands, 1936; postgrad., Post Grad. Sch., The Netherlands, 1942-43; MA in German, U. Pa., 1971. English tchr. St. Clara Coll., Heerlen, The Netherlands, 1940=46; coord., originator Dutch studies U. Pa., Phila., 1969-87, cons. Dutch programs, 1987—; cons. Dutch programs Syracuse (N.Y.) U., 1987—. Co-editor presentations and lectures, 1985. Recipient John Adams medal The Netherlands Govt., 1976; named Officer in the Order of Orange Nassou, The Netherlands Govt., 1986, Officer in the Crown Order of Belgium, Belgian Govt., 1987. Mem. AAUW, Internat. Assn. Netherlandic Studies, Am. Assn. Netherlandic Studies, Netherlands Soc. Phila. (chmn. lectures, mem. exec. bd. 1988—), Netherland Am. Assn. Delaware Valley (mem. exec. bd. 1988—), Assn. Advancement of Dutch Studies, Can. Assn. English Netherlandic Studies, Am. Translators Assn. Republican. Roman Catholic. Home: 3031 W Coulter St Philadelphia PA 19129

REICHERT, CHERYL MCBROOM, pathologist, research consultant; b. Great Falls, Mont., Sept. 4, 1946; d. Harold and Arlyne (Cohn) R.; m. Sherwood McBroom Jr., 1964 (div. 1971); children: Scott, Cari. BS, Coll. of Great Falls, 1969; MS, U. Mich., 1971, PhD, 1974, MD, 1976. Diplomate Am. Bd. of Med. Examiners. Resident in anatomic pathology Nat. Cancer Inst., Bethesda, Md., 1977-79; resident in clin. pathology NIH, Bethesda, 1979-80, surgical pathologist, chief autopsy service, 1981-85; pathologist Sibley Meml. Hosp., Washington, 1985-86; cons. Digene Corp., College Park, Md., 1985—, Nat. Cancer Inst., Bethesda, 1985-88; pathologist Columbus Hosp., Great Falls, 1987—; cons. McLaughlin Research Inst., Great Falls, 1987—; clin. assoc. prof. Uniformed Services U. of Health Scis., Bethesda, 1983-86; teaching fellow dept. biochemistry U. Mich., Ann Arbor, 1969-74; presenter Pres. Reagan's Nat. Cancer Adv. Bd., Washington, 1983. Contbr. 50 articles to profl. jours. Mem. profl. edn. com. Am. Cancer Soc.; bd. dirs. Ann Arbor Child Care and Devel. Served as lt. comdr. USPHS, 1977-80. Named Outstanding Young Women of Yr., State of Mich., 1973. Mem. U.S. Acad. Pathologists, Mont. Pathologists Soc. (pres. 1989-90), Glens Med. Soc., Alpha Omega Alpha. Home: 51 Prospect Dr Great Falls MT 59405

REICHERT, NURY VANDELLOS, journalist, fundraiser; b. Barcelona, Catalonia, Spain, Nov. 14, 1929; came to the U.S., 1946; d. Jose Antonio and Maria (Frontera) Vandellos; m. Otto E. Reichert-Facilides; children: Mark, Kent, Christina, Christopher. BA in Psychology, Barnard Coll., 1951. Editor Overseas Weekly, Frankfurt, Fed. Republic Germany, 1954-57; recreational dir. USAF, Wiesbaden, Fed. Republic Germany, 1952-54; research editor Saturday Evening Post, Phila., 1958-61; mktg. dir. Reichert-Facilides P.C., Phila., 1974-84; exec. dir. The Global Interdependence Ctr., Phila., 1986—; cons. R-F Assocs., Phila., 1986—. citizen com., Pub. Edn. Bd., Phila, 1974-80; bd. United Way Phila.. Mem. AAUW, Internat. City Com., Penn Faculty Club. Democrat. Home: 6 Summit Pl Philadelphia PA 19128 Office: Global Interdependence Ctr 3814 Walnut St Philadelphia PA 19104

REICHGOTT, EMBER DARLENE, lawyer, state senator; b. Detroit, Aug. 22, 1953; d. Norbert Arnold and Diane (Pincich) R. BA summa cum laude, St. Olaf Coll., Minn., 1974; JD, Duke U., 1977, postgrad, Coll. of St. Thomas, 1988—. Bar: Minn. 1977, D.C. 1978. Assoc., Larkin, Hoffman, Daly & Lindgren, Bloomington, Minn., 1977-84; counsel Control Data Corp., Bloomington, Minn., 1984-86; atty. The Gen. Counsel, Ltd., 1987—; mem. Minn. State Senate, 1983—, senate majority Whip, 1990—; chmn. Legis. Commn. on Econ. Status of Women, 1984-86; Vice chmn. Senate Judiciary Com., 1983-86, Senate Edn. Com., 1987-88; chmn. tax subcom. on econ. devel., 1987—; chmn. civil law div. Jud. Com., 1989—; trustee, bd. dirs. N.W. YMCA, New Hope, Minn., 1983-88; Greater Mpls. Red Cross, 1988—, United Way Mpls., 1989— . Youngest woman ever elected to Minn. State Senate, 1983; recipient Woman of Yr. award North Hennepin Bus. and Prof. Women, 1983, Award for Contbn. to Human Svcs., Minn. Social Svcs. Assn., 1983, Clean Air award Minn. Lung Assn., 1988, Disting. Svc. award Mpls. Jaycees, 1984, Minn. Human Rights award, 1989; named One of Ten Outstanding Young Minnesotans, Minn. Jaycees, 1984, Policy Advocate of Yr. NAWBO, 1988, Woman of Achievement Twin West C. of C., 1989. Mem. Minn. Bar Assn. (Pro Bono Publico Atty. award 1990), Hennepin County Bar Assn., Corporate Counsel Assn. (v.p.), Minn. Bar Assn. Mem. Minn. Democratic Farmer-Labor Party (del. nat. Dem. conv. 1984, state exec. com. 1980-82). Home: 7701 48th Ave N New Hope MN 55428

REICHMAN, DAWN LESLIE, lawyer, teacher, deputy sheriff; b. Portsmouth, Va., Feb. 15, 1951; d. Stanley J. and Ernestine Enid (Kaiserman) Greif; m. James Richard Smith, Apr. 27, 1975 (div. July 1978); m. Victor I. Reichman, Nov. 24, 1979; children: Mark Heath, Margo Ilene, Shelley Renee. BA, U. Calif., L.A., 1972; cert. dep. sheriff, Sheriff Acad., 1974; JD, Whittier Coll., 1988. Bar: Calif. 1988, U.S. Dist. Ct. (ea. and cen. dists.) Calif. 1988. Dep. sheriff L.A. County Sheriff's Dept., 1973-81; substitute tchr. Palmdale (Calif.) Sch. Dist., 1988—; pvt. practice law Palmdale, 1988—; alt. def. counsel, 1990—. Spokesperson Ana Verde Homeowners Assn., Palmdale, 1989—; mem. Alpha Charter Guild of Antelope Valley Hosp. Mem. Antelope Valley Bar Assn., Los Angeles County Bar Assn., Calif. Trial Lawyers Assn., Antelope Valley Legal Found., AAUW, Phi Alpha Delta. Office: 1305 E Palmdale Blvd Ste 4 Palmdale CA 93550

REICHMAN, LEAH CAROL, artist; b. Kansas City, Mo., Aug. 9, 1951; d. Julian and Charlotte Mignon (Bobrecker) R.; m. David Cohen, June 7, 1987. Student, Oxbow Sch. Painting, Saugatuck, Mich., 1970; BS, U. Wis., Milw. and Madison, 1973; student, Whitney Mus. of Am. Art, 1973; MA in Studio Art, Hunter Coll., CUNY, 1980. Tchr. St Ann's Acad., Bklyn., 1974, Children's Aid Soc., N.Y.C., 1978; asst. tchr. Internat. Play Group for Children, N.Y.C., 1980. Group exhnbs. include U. Wis., Madison, 1973, O.K. Harris Gallery, N.Y.C., 1974, Three Mercer St. Store, N.Y.C., 1975, Womanart Gallery, N.Y.C., 1977, Soho Art Fair, N.Y.C., 1977, One Hundred Dollar Gallery, N.Y.C., 1978, Nat. Mus. of Spain, Bilbao, 1981, Los Derachos Humanos, 1983, Mail Art De Warande, Belgium, 1984. Democrat. Jewish. Studio: PO Box 55 Canal St Station New York NY 10013

REICHMAN, ROSE EHRINPREIS, communications executive; b. Detroit, Aug. 18, 1942; d. Jacob and Anna (Fox) E.; m. Lee Brodersohn Reichman, Oct. 9, 1965; children: Daniel, Deborah. BA, U. Mich., 1964; MA, NYU, 1969. Tchr. various high schs., Berkely (Mich.), Santa Cruz (Boliva), N.Y.C., 1964-69; freelance writer N.Y.C., 1971-76; writer bus. devel. Parsons Brinckerhoff Quade & Douglas, Inc., N.Y.C., 1976-78, mgr. communications, 1978-83, v.p., dir. communications, 1983-89; pres. Reichman Frankle Inc., Ft. Lee, N.J., 1990—. Pres. Classic Ballet Co. N.J., Closter, 1971-73; bd. dirs. Arts Ctr. No. N.J., New Milford, 1980-84. Mem. Nat. Pub. Rels. Commn., Am. Cons. Engrs. Coun., Soc. Am. Mil. Engrs., Internat. Assn. Bus. Communicators (N.Y. Excellence award 1981), Soc. Mktg. Profl. Svcs. (Nat. Communications awards 1985, 86), Women Exec. Pub. Rels. (v.p. 1988-89, pres. 1989-90), Women Exec. Pub. Rels. Found. (pres. 1987-89), Gotham Town House Coop. (v.p. 1989). Democrat. Jewish. Home: 2 Brook Rd Tenafly NJ 07670 Office: Reichman Frankle Inc 1355 15th St Ste 270 Fort Lee NJ 07024

REICHMANIS, ELSA, chemist; b. Melbourne, Victoria, Australia, Dec. 9, 1953; came to U.S., 1962; d. Peteris and Nina (Meiers) R.; m. Francis Joseph Purcell, June 2, 1979; children: Patrick William, Elizabeth Anne. BS in Chemistry, Syracuse U., 1972, PhD in Chemistry, 1975. Postdoctoral intern Syracuse (N.Y.) U., 1975-76, Chaim Weiemann rsch. fellow, 1976-78; mem. tech. staff AT&T Bell Labs., Murray Hill, N.J., 1978-84, supr. radiation sensitive materials and applications, 1984—; mem. panel on advanced matls. Japanese Tech. Evaluation Prog., NSF, Washington, 1986, mem. com. to survey matls. rsch. opportunities and needs for electronic industry, Nat. Rsch. Coun., 1986. Editor: The Effects of Radiation on High Tech Polymers, 1989, Polymers in Microlithography, 1989; patentee in field; contbr. numberous articles to profl. jours. Mem. Am. Chem. Soc. (mem.-at-large polymer materials sci. and engring. div. 1986—), Soc. for Photo-optical Engrs., AAAS. Office: AT&T Bell Laboratories 600 Mountain Ave 1A261 Murray Hill NJ 07090

REICHTER, BARBARA F(AST), interior designing company executive; b. Haviland, Ohio, July 23, 1935; d. William Clayton and Marie (Stiebeling) Fast; m. Richard A. Reichter, Feb. 16, 1957; children: Bradley A., Lizabeth R. BS in Edn., Otterbein Coll., 1957; cert., N.Y. Sch. Interior Design, 1977. Tchr. Edwards AFB, Calif., 1957-59, Dayton, Ohio, 1959-60; founder Barbara Reichter Interiors, N. Andover, Mass., 1977-78; pres., chmn., founder Andover Interior Designs, 1978—; participant Lawrence Gen. Hosp. Showhouse, 1982, Ladies of Merrimack Tour of Homes, 1983-87, 88—, Boston Jr. League Showhouse, 1986, N. Shore Jewish Community Ctr. Showhouse, 1988, 90. Contbr. articles to profl. jours. Mem. The Hay Scales Exch., Inc., N. Andover, 1970—; mem. adv. bd. N. Andover Community Ctr., 1970-77. Mem. ASID, Greater Lawrence C. of C., YWCA Women's Network Assn., N. Andover Country Club (golf com. 1978-82). Republican. Home: 1 Coolidge Rd Andover MA 01810 Office: Andover Interior Designs 63 Park St Andover MA 01810

REID, BONNIE LEE, junior high school principal; b. St. Louis, Jan. 30, 1937; d. William Charles Lovrenic and Fern Lee (Swingler) Reiman; m. Thomas James Fitzsimmons, Aug. 16, 1958 (div. Aug. 1966); children: Susan Lee, Scott James; m. Donald Francis Reid, Nov. 18, 1966; stepchildren: Christopher Kearns, Donald Francis Jr., Connie Ann, Britton Anthony, Douglas Nye. BE, U. Mo., 1958; MA in Adminstrn., Washington U., St. Louis, 1977, postgrad., 1978-80. Cert. tchr., Mo.; cert. secondary adminstr., Mo. Tchr. Webster Groves (Mo.) High Sch., 1958-60; tchr., dept. chmn. Parkway Sch. Dist., Chesterfield, Mo., 1971-81, asst. prin., 1982-83, assoc. prin., 1984, interim prin., 1985; prin. Parkway E. Jr. High Sch., Chesterfield, 1986—; mem. governance com. Gov.'s Conf. Edn., 1978; prin. Nat. Secondary Sch. Recognition Sch., 1986-87. Team leader Danforth Found. Marginal Students Responsive Schs. Consortium, 1989—; mem. mid. sch. task force Boy Scouts Am. Fellow Prin.'s Acad.; mem. Nat. Assn. Secondary Sch. Prins., Assn. Supervision and Curriculum Devel. (consortium sch. team leader 1986-89), Nat. Middle Sch. Assn. (conf. edn.), Mortar Bd., Mo. State Future Tchrs. Am., Parkway Ind. Community Tchrs. Assn. (pres. 1976-78), Greater St. Louis Tchrs. Assn. (pres. 1977-78), Delta Kappa Gamma, Kappa Alpha Theta, Pi Lambda Theta, Phi Sigma Iota, Kappa Epsilon Alpha, Sigma Rho Sigma. Republican. Presbyterian. Office: Pkwy E Jr High Sch 181 Coeur De Ville Creve Coeur MO 63141

REID, CAROL ANN, legal administrator; b. Albuquerque, Dec. 27, 1938; d. Jesse Taylor and Florence Adeline (Isaacs) R.; children: Lindsey Guinan, Lee Taylor White, Lane Reid White. BA, U. N.Mex., 1973, MBA, 1983. Tchr. Albuquerque Pub. Schs., 1973-85; pvt. practice cons. Albuquerque, 1973—; bus. mgr. Cottonwood Treatment Ctr., Los Lunas, N.Mex., 1987-90; legal adminstr. Atkinson & Kelsey, Albuquerque, 1990—; cons. in field. Campaign mgr. state senator, Albuquerque, 1980; ward chmn. Rep. Party, 1984-86; speaker City Speaker's Bur., Albuquerque, 1987—; arbitrator Better Bus. Bur., Albuquerque, 1988—. U. N.Mex. fellow, 1981. Methodist. Home: 520 Sanchez Rd NW Albuquerque NM 87107 Office: Atkinson & Kelsey PO Box 3070 Albuquerque NM 87090

REID, CHERYL SOLED, clinical geneticist; b. Jersey City, July 30, 1953; d. Howard and Irma Soled; m. Randall James Reid, Mar. 6, 1982; children: Benjamin and Rebecca (twins). SC.B., Brown U., 1975; MD, CMDNJ-Rutgers Med. Sch., 1979. Cert. Nat. Bd. Med. Examiners, Am. Bd. Med. Genetics, Am. Bd. Pediatrics. Intern, resident pediatrics Montefiore Hosp. Med. Ctr., Bronx, N.Y., 1979-82; fellow genetics John F. Kennedy Inst. and pediatric genetics unit dept pediatrics John Hopkins U., Balt., Md., 1982-85; head div. genetics Cooper Hosp./Univ. Med. Ctr., Camden, N.J., 1985—; dir. clin. genetics sch. ostopathic medicine UMDNJ, Camden, N.J., 1985-90; asst. prof. pediatrics UMDNJ Robert Wood Johnson Med. Sch., Camden, 1985—; dysmorphologist So. N.J. Fetal Loss Program, Camden, 1987—; cons. N.J. State Dept. Health Newborn Biochem. Screening Program, 1985—, Underwood Meml. Hosp., Woodbury, N.J., 1986—, Kennedy Meml. Hosps./ Univ. Med. Ctr., Stratford, Washington Twp., Cherry Hill, N.J., 1987—, Meml. Hosp. Burlington County, Mt. Holly, N.J., 1987—, W. Jersey Health Systems, Voorhees, Marlton, Camden, N.J., 1987—, Our Lady of Lourdes Med. Ctr., Camden, 1987—, Deborah Heart and Lung Ctr., Browns Mills, N.J., 1987—, Atlantic City Med. Ctr., 1986—, Zurbrugg Meml. Hosp., Willingboro, N.J., 1989—; genetics cons. Cooper Regional Cleft Palate Program, Camden, 1985—. Contbr. articles to profl. jours.; abstractor in field. Med. adv. bd. Little People Am., Inc; med. adv. com. Billy Barty Found. Grantee NIH. Fellow Am. Acad. Pediatrics; mem. AMA, Am. Soc. Human Genetics, Am. Cleft Palate Craniofacial Assn., Soc. Craniofacial Genetics, Human Genetics Assn. N.J. (sec. 1987-88), Middle Atlantic Regional Genetics Network, Alpha Omega Alpha. Jewish. Office: Cooper Hosp Univ Med Ctr Dept Pediatrics 3 Cooper Plaza Camden NJ 08103

REID, DONNA JOYCE, television and film executive; b. Springfield, Tenn., June 25, 1954; d. Leonard Earl Reid and Joyce (Robertson) Kirby; m. Kenneth Bruce Sadler, June 26, 1976 (div. Apr. 1980); m. John Christopher Moulton, Oct. 18, 1987. Student, Austin Peay State U., Clarksville, Tenn., 1972-75. Show writer, producer WTVF-TV (CBS affiliate), Nashville, 1977-83, promotion producer, 1983-85, on-air promotion mgr., 1985-86; gen. mgr. Steadi-Film Corp., Nashville, 1986—. Big sister Buddies of Nashville, 1981-87. Named to Honorable Order of Ky. Cols. John Y. Brown, Gov., 1980; recipient Significant Svc. award ARC, 1982, Clara Barton Communications award, 1983. Mem. NAFE, Nat. Assn. TV Arts and Scis., Nat. Film Inst. Methodist. Office: Options Internat 1110 17th Ave S Nashville TN 37212

REID, DOROTHY-MARIE, nursing director; b. N.Y.C., July 10, 1937; d. Clifford Thaedeus and Lillian Louisa (Taitt) Butte; m. John Henry Jr. Reid, Mar. 15, 1958 (div. 1969); children: Randee Cecile, John H. III, Jacqueline Marie. Assoc. in Nursing, NYU, 1958; BS summa cum laude, Mercy Coll., Dobbs Feiry, N.Y., 1981. RN, N.Y. Head nurse Bellevue Hosp., N.Y.C., 1958-61; supr., asst. dir. nursing Deepdale Hosp., Littleneck, N.Y., 1964-72; dir. nursing New Rochelle (N.Y.) Nursing Home, 1972-74, Sprainbrook Manor, Scarsdale, N.Y., 1974-76, Meth. Home for the Aged, Riverdale, N.Y., 1976-81, Bay Harbor Rehab., Lomita, Calif., 1983-85, Jewish Home for Aging, Reseda, Calif., 1986—; nurse cons. Country Villa Corp., Culver City, Calif., 1981-83; nurse cons., quality assurance regional dir. Summit Health Corp., L.A., 1985-86. Contbr. articles to profl. jours. Mem. edn. task force Beverly Found., Pasadena, Calif., 1988-89. Recipient Citizen award Firefighter Assn., New Rochelle, 1975, Community Svc., Pierce Coll., 1989. Mem. Nat. League Nursing, Am. Coll. Health Care Adminstrs., Westchester Assn. for Long Term Care Dirs. (co-chmn. 1974-75), Alpha Chi. Democrat. Office: Jewish Home for the Aging 18855 Victory Blvd Los Angeles CA 91335

REID, INEZ SMITH, lawyer, educator; b. New Orleans, Apr. 7, 1937; d. Sidney Randall Dickerson and Beatrice Virginia (Bundy) Smith. BA, Tufts U., 1959; LLB, Yale U., 1962; MA, UCLA, 1963; PhD, Columbia U., 1968. Bar: Calif. 1963, N.Y. 1972, D.C. 1980. Assoc. prof. Barnard Coll. Columbia U., N.Y.C., 1972-76; gen. counsel youth div. State of N.Y., 1976-77; dep. gen. counsel HEW, Washington, 1977-79; inspector gen. EPA, Washington, 1979-81; chief legis. and opinions, dep. corp. counsel Office of Corp. Counsel, Washington, 1981-83; corp. counsel D.C., 1983-85; counsel Laxalt, Washington, Perito & Dubuc, Washington, 1986-90, ptnr., 1990—; William J. Maier, Jr. vis. prof. law W.Va. U. Coll. Law, Morgantown, 1985-86. Author: Together Black Women, 1972; contbr. articles to profl. jours. and pubis. Bd. dirs. Homes and Ministries Bd. United Ch. of Christ, N.Y.C., 1978-83, vice chmn., 1981-83; chmn. bd. govs. Antioch Law Sch., Washington, 1979-81; chmn. bd. trustees Antioch U., Yellow Springs, Ohio, 1981-82; bd. trustees Tufts U., Meford, Mass., 1988—, Lancaster (Pa.) Sem., 1988—; bd. dirs. Capitol Hill Hosp. Recipient Emily Gregory award Barnard Coll., 1976, Arthur Morgan award Antioch U., 1982, Service award United Ch. of Christ, 1983, Disting. Service (Profl. Life) award Tufts U. Alumni Assn., 1988. Office: Laxalt Washington Perito & Reid 1120 Connecticut Ave NW Ste 1100 Washington DC 20036

REID, JOAN EVANGELINE, lawyer, stockbroker; b. Mich., Apr. 22, 1932; d. August W. and Evangeline R. (Brozeau) Rogers; m. Belmont M. Reid. AA in Bus., San Jose State U., 1951; JD, McGeorge Sch. Law, 1989. Bar: Nev.; lic. realtor, life, disability and annuity ins. Officer, dir. Lifetime Fin. Planning Corp., San Jose, Calif., 1967-77, Lifetime Realty Corp., San Jose, 1967-77; co-founder, officer, dir. Belmont Reid & Co., San Jose, 1960-77; officer, corp. counsel, dir. JOBEL Fin. Inc., Carson City, Nev., 1980—. Past sec., treas. Nev. Fedn. Rep. Women; charter pres. Santa Clara Valley Rep. Women Federated; past v.p. Carson City Rep. Women's Club. Mem. First Jud. Dist. Bar Assn., Washoe County Bar Assn., NAFE, State Bar Nev., Carson City C. of C., Soroptomist (past pres. Carson City club). Address: PO Box 3676 Carson City NV 89702

REID, KATHERINE LOUISE, artist, educator, author; b. Port Arthur, Tex., Mar. 25, 1941; d. Clifton Commodore and Helen Ross (Moore) Reid. BA, Baylor U., 1963; postgrad. in design and illustration, Kans. City Art Inst., 1964; MEd, U. Houston, 1973; cert. supervision U. Houston-Clear Lake City, 1980; postgrad. San Jacinto Coll., 1982. Cert. art educator, profl. supr., Tex. Litho reproduction artist Hallmark Cards, Kansas City, Mo., 1963-64; tchr. art high sch. Pasadena Ind. Sch. Dist. (Tex.), 1964-77, supr. art, gifted and talented and photography, 1977-85; supr. art and photography InterAct, 1985—; head crafts, asst. dir. winter discovery program-ski camp Cheley Colo. Camps, Denver, Estes Park, 1967-74; staff artist, media workshop, Tex. Edn. Agy., Austin, summer 1961; art enrichment tchr. Port Arthur Ind. Sch. Dist. (Tex.), summer 1961; head crafts Camp Waluta, Silsbee, Tex., summer, 1960. Author: Through Their Eyes, 1988-89. Mem. Friends of Fine Arts-Baylor U., Waco, Tex., 1981—; mem. Scholastic Art awards Regional Bd., Houston, 1978-84, Tex. Edn. Agy. Art Leadership Inst., 1989, 90; bd. dirs. Houston Council Student Art Awards, Inc., 1984—. Named Tchr. of Yr. Pasadena Ind. Sch. Dist., 1975; Outstanding Secondary Educator of Am., 1975; Tex. Art Educator of Yr., 1985. Mem. Tex. Art Edn. Assn. (rep. editor newsletter 1982-85, chmn. supervision div. 1982-83, v.p. membership 1978-80, chmn. pub. info. com., regional chmn. youth art month 1980-82; regional chmn. membership com. 1976-78, pres. elect 1987), Tex. Alliance for Arts Edn. (bd. vice chmn. 1984-86, treas. 1988-90), Nat. Art Edn. Assn. (conv. com. 1977, 85), Houston Art Edn. Assn. (sec. 1969), Nat. Assn. for Supervision and Curriculum Devel., Delta Kappa Gamma (2d v.p. 1984-86). Baptist. Home: 106 Ravenhead Houston TX 77034

REID, LAURA MARCELLA, marketing executive; b. Vidalia, Ga., July 25, 1952; d. Robert Hugh and Lanette Marie (Haar) R. Student, Monticello Jr. Coll., 1970-71; BA, U. Ga., 1974. Bookkeeper First Nat. Bank, Vidalia, Ga., 1975-76; travel agt. Ship 'n Shore Travel, Macon, Ga., 1976-77; acting dir. of admissions, asst. dir. admissions Wesleyan Coll., Macon, 1977-79; admissions couselor Ga. Inst. Tech., Atlanta, 1979-81; market devel. mgr. Coca-Cola USA, Atlanta, 1981—; proprietor The Little House, Savannah, Ga., 1987—. Vol. DAR, Ga., 1970—, High Mus., Atlanta, 1978-86, Jr. League DeKalb County, Inc., Decatur, Ga., 1984-86, Jr. League Savannah, 1986—, bd. dirs., transfer chmn., 1989-90, party chmn., 1990; bd. dirs. Hist. Savannah Found., Ga., 1988—; trustee Ga. Hist. Preservation, 1980—, Telfair Mus., 1986—; mem. jr. com. Atlanta Symphony, 1982-86; chmn. gift shop Festival of Trees, 1989; advisor mus. shop Hist. Savannah-Davenport House, 1989—; co-chmn. bazaar St. John's Episcopal Ch., 1989, chmn. women's programs, 1990—. Named Hon. State Pres. Ga. Soc. CAR, 1971. Mem. NAFE, Savannah Area C. of C., Ga. Hist. Soc., Phi Theta Kappa, Alpha Delta Pi. Episcopalian. Home: 631 E Victory Dr Savannah GA 31405 Office: The Little House 107 E Gordon St Savannah GA 31401

REID, NANCI GLICK, health care professional; b. Brookline, Mass., Sept. 22, 1941; d. Robert Louis and Esther (Shostack) Green; m. Ronald Jay Coleman, July 5, 1962 (div. Sept. 1969); 1 child, Lori Sue; m. Alan Marshall Glick, Jan. 12, 1976 (div. Oct. 1978); 1 child, Staci Alison; m. Raymond Augustus Reid, Feb. 15, 1985. AS, Garland Jr. Coll., Boston, 1960; student, Harvard U. Extension, 1961, 64, 65; BS, Northeastern U., 1983, postgrad. in bus. adminstrn., 1989—. Cert. clin. lab. sci., clin. lab. specialist in cytogenetics. Research technician Children's Hosp., Boston, 1961-63; sr. research technician, med. technician New Eng. Med. Ctr., Boston, 1963-65, 67-69; cytogeneticist supr. Carney Hosp., Boston, 1969-84; instr. medicine Med. Sch. Tufts U., Boston, 1969-86; systems analyst Cognos/Coulter Corp., Waltham, Mass., 1976-77; med. technologist Milton (Mass.) Hosp, 1978-83, Mass. Eye and Ear, Boston, 1983-84; lab. mgr. Harvard Community Health Plan, Braintree, Mass., 1985-88; chairperson com. continuing edn. Harvard Community Health Plan, Boston, 1986-88; quality control mgr. Oncolab Inc., Boston, 1988—; presenter abstracts at 12th and 13th Internat. Hematology Soc. Confs. Contbr. articles to profl. jours. Vol. human body discovery space program Mus. Sci., 1990. Mem. Assn. Cytogenetic Technologists (pres. 1976-78), Am. Soc. Med. Tech. (lectr.), Mass. Ski Club (supr. 1989—), Plymouth Yacht Club, Pythian Sisters Club (sec., editor 1966-67), Sigma Epsilon Rho (v.p. 1987-88, former treas.). Republican. Jewish. Home: 70 Flintlocke Dr Plymouth MA 02360

REID, NATALIE, language and writing specialist; b. Oakland, Calif., Mar. 8, 1947; d. Harold and Gloria (Schleifer) R.; m. Charles Edward Wood, May 19, 1985; children: DoShik Wood, Thomas Wood. BA, U. Calif., Berkeley, 1968; MA, San Francisco State U., 1974. Cert. coll. instr., Calif. Instr. ESL U. Calif., Berkeley, 1974-77; pres. Natalie Reid Assocs., San Francisco and Southborough, Mass., 1977—; cons. HUD, San Francisco, 1977—, Mortgage Bankers Assn., Washington, 1983—, Reed Pub. (USA) Inc., Newton, Mass., 1986—, Gillette, Boston, 1987—. Author: America Grows Young, 1981; co-author: Dictionary of English Phrasal Usage, 1985. Mem. Worcester (Mass.) Com. Fgn. Rels. Mem. NAFE, Nat. Writers Union, Assn. Profl. Writing Cons., Nat. Edn. Assn.

REID, ROSEMARY ANNE, insurance agent; b. Portland, Maine, June 15, 1951; d. Kenneth Bruce and Mary (Hollywood) R.; m. Ronald E. Walls, May 7, 1977 (div. Mar. 1986); children: Rachel A., Tate A. BS in Edn., U. South Maine, Portland, 1973. V.p. ins. Gruntal and Co., Inc., Portland, 1987—; pvt. practice Portland, 1973—. Town councilor Cape Elizabeth, 1990—. Recipient 10 Yrs. Nat. Quality, 10 Yrs. Nat. Sale Achievement award, 1979-89 Nat. Assn. of Life Underwriters. Mem. Million Dollar Round Table (life and qualifying mem., Top of the Table, 1984, 86), South Maine Assn. Life Underwriters (bd. dirs. 1985—, officer 1987—, pres. 1989-90, regional v.p., pub. svc. chair, life underwriter polit. action com. 1990), Life Underwriter Tng. Coun. (chairperson 1986-87), Maine Assn. Life Underwriters (bd. dirs. 1989—). Roman Catholic. Office: PO Box 927 Portland ME 04104

REID, RUTH HANFORD, communications company executive, writer; b. Hartford, Conn., June 16, 1938; d. Edwin Christie and Linda Margaret (Richards) Hanford; m. Gerald J. Reid, June 13, 1959 (div. Jan. 1975); children: Margaret, Jerry, Mary E., Tricia. Student, Trinity Coll., U. Conn.; cert., IBM Mgmt. Sch., 1986. Contract underwriting asst. The Travelers, Hartford, 1956-57; group underwriting asst. Conn. Gen., Bloomfield, Conn., 1958-59; free lance pub. relations, free lance writer Hartford, 1968-70; editor Guider Mag.-Hartford, 1970-71; communications dir. United Way of Greater Hartford, 1971-77; assoc. exec. dir. United Way Services, Cleve., 1977-85; pres. Ruth Reid & Co., Cleve., 1985—; chmn. market rsch. United Way of Am., Alexandria, Va., 1978-84, vice chmn. communications, 1982-84, chmn. conf. communications program, 1984. Contbr. articles to profl. jours. Campaign coord. U.S. Rep. Toby Moffett, Suffield, Conn., 1976; active mem. Leadership Cleve., 1983—, various arts and service orgns., Cleve.; chmn. Mayor's Award for Volunteerism Pub. Rels., Cleve., 1985-86; v.p. mktg. Ohio chpt. Nat. Osteoporosis Found., 1989—. Recipient over 100 awards for communications programs and materials, films, advt., publs., 1975—. Mem. Advt. Club. Home: 3266 Braemar Rd Shaker Heights OH 44120 Office: Ruth Reid & Co 700 W Saint Clair Ave Ste 320 Cleveland OH 44113

REID, SUE TITUS, law educator; b. Bryan, Tex., Nov. 13, 1939; d. Andrew Jackson Jr. and Loraine (Wylie) Titus. BS with honors, Tex. Woman's U., 1960; MA, U. Mo., 1962, PhD, 1965; JD, U. Iowa, 1972. Bar: Iowa 1972, U.S. Ct. Appeals (D.C. cir.) 1978, U.S. Supreme Ct. 1978. From instr. to assoc. prof. sociology Cornell Coll., Mt. Vernon, Iowa, 1963-72; assoc. prof., chmn. dept. sociology Coe Coll., Cedar Rapids, Iowa, 1972-74; assoc. prof. law. U. Wash., Seattle, 1974-76; exec. assoc. Am. Sociol. Assn., Washington, 1976-77; prof. law U. Tulsa, 1978-88; dean, prof. law Sch. Criminology Fla. State U., Tallahassee, 1988-90; prof. pub. adminstrn., dir. devel. Fla. State U. Coll. Social Sci., 1990—; acting chmn. dept. sociology Cornell Coll., 1965-66; vis. assoc. prof. sociology U. Nebr., Lincoln, 1970; vis. disting. prof. law and sociology U. Tulsa, 1977-78, assoc. dean 1979-81; vis. prof. law U. San Diego, 1981-82; mem. People-to-People Crime Prevention Del. to People's Republic of China, 1982; George Beto Prof. criminal justice Sam Houston U., Huntsville, Tex., 1984-85; lecture/study tour of Criminal Justice systems of 10 European countries, 1985; cons. Evaluation Policy Rsch. Assocs., Inc., Milw., 1976-77, Nat. Inst. Corrections, Idaho Dept. Corrections, 1984, Am. Correctional Inst., Price-Waterhouse. Author: (with others) Bibliographies on Role Methodology and Propositions Volume D - Studies in the Role of the Public School Teacher, 1962, The Correctional System: An Introduction, 1981, Crime and Criminology, 4th ed., 1985, 5th ed., 1987, 6th ed., 1990, Criminal Justice: Procedures and Issues, 1987, 2nd ed., 1990, Criminal Law, 1989; editor (with David Lyon) Population Crisis: An Interdisciplinary Perspective, 1972; contbr. articles to profl. jours. Recipient Disting. Alumni award Tex. Woman's U., 1979; named One of Okla. Young Leaders of 80's Oklahoma Monthly, 1980. Mem. Am. Correctional Assn., Am. Soc. Criminology, Acad. Criminal Justice Scis. Office: Fla State Univ 635 Bellamy Bldg School Criminology Tallahassee FL 32306

REIDA-ALLEN, PAMELA ANNE, nursing administrator, consultant; b. Fitchburg, Mass., June 8, 1944; d. Alvah Michael Reida and Sirkka Margaret (Anttila) Kao; m. Dennis Alan Joaquin, 1967 (div. 1973); children: Joshua, Amy, Sebastian; m. Yahya Radazar, Oct. 1983 (dec. Sept. 1987); m. Loyall C. Allen. BA in English, Philosophy, Calif. State U., Los Angeles, 1966; RN diploma with honors, Leominster (Mass.) Hosp., 1976; BS in Nursing cum laude, Fitchburg (Mass.) State Coll., 1982; MS magna cum laude, Lesley Coll., 1986. Substitute tchr. Fitchburg Pub. Schs., 1966-67; social worker N.Y.C. Dept. Social Services, N.Y.C., 1967-68; news correspondent The Lowell (Mass.) Sun, 1969-71; nurse lab., delivery Leominster Hosp., 1976-77A; inservice coordinator Birchwood Manor Nursing Home, Fitchburg, 1977, asst. dir. nursing, 1977-78, dir. nursing, 1978-80; dir. nursing Naukeag Hosp., Ashburnham, Mass., 1980-84; asst. dir. nursing Beech Hill Hosp., Dublin, N.H., 1984-87, dir nursing, 1987—, chair utilization rev. com., 1985—; mem. adv. council allied health majors Mass. Regional Vocat. Sch., Fitchburg, Mass., 1977-84; with Area Speakers Bur., Fitchburg, 1980-84, vice chair Quality Assurance Program, 1988; cons. Quality Healthcare Resources, Inc. subs. Joint Commn. on Accreditation of Hosps. Vol. Family Planning, Fitchburg, 1981-82; del. Intercity Mgmt. Council, Fitchburg, 1980-84. Mem. NAFE, Tri-City Nursing Home Assn. (pres. 1978-80), Nat. Nurses Assn., N.H. Nurses Assn. (program com. 1985—), Greater Fitchburg C. of C., N.H. Orgn. Exec. Nurses, N.H. Quality Assurance Assn. Office: Beech Hill Hosp Old Harrisville Rd Dublin NH 03461

REID-BILLS, MAE, editor, historian; b. Shreveport, La.; d. Dayton Taylor and Bessie Oline (Boles) Reid; m. Frederick Gurdon Bills (div.); children: Marjorie Reid, Nancy Hawkins, Frederick Taylor, Virginia Thomas, Elizabeth Sharples. AB, Stanford U., 1942, MA, 1965; PhD, U. Denver, 1977. Mng. editor Am. West mag., Tucson, Ariz., 1979-89; cons. editor Fulcrum Pub., Inc., Golden, Colo., 1989—. Gen. Electric fellow, 1963, William Robertson Coe fellow, 1964. Mem. Orgn. Am. Historians, Am. Hist. Assn., Phi Beta Kappa, Phi Alpha Theta.

REIDY, CAROLYN KROLL, publisher; b. Washington, May 2, 1949; d. Henry August and Mildred Josephine (Mencke) Kroll; m. Stephen Kroll Reidy, Dec. 28, 1974. BA, Middlebury Coll., 1971; MA, Ind. U., 1974, PhD, 1982. Various positions to mgr. subs. rights Random House, Inc., N.Y.C., 1975-83, assoc. pub., 1987-88; dir. subs. rights William Morrow & Co., N.Y.C., 1983-85; v.p., assoc. pub. Vintage Books, N.Y.C., 1985-87, pub., 1987-88; pub. Anchor Books, Doubleday & Co., N.Y.C., 1988; pres., pub. Avon Books, N.Y.C., 1988—. Mem. Women's Media Group, Pubs. Lunch Club. Office: Avon Books 105 Madison Ave New York NY 10016

REIDY, ELLEN TERESA, counselor, therapist; b. Elmira, N.Y., Aug. 3, 1962; d. Richard Vincent and Teresa (Beirne) R. BA in Psychology and Sociology, Boston Coll., 1984; MS in Counseling, SUNY, Brockport, 1988. Cert. counselor, N.Y. Interior designer Victor Furniture, Rochester, N.Y., 1985; daycare dir. YMCA, Rochester, 1986-87; guidance counselor Greece Athens High Sch., Rochester, 1987; casework counselor Hillside Children's Ctr., Rochester, 1987—, student intern supr., 1989-90; pvt. therapist, Rochester; co-therapist for eating disorders, Rochester. Mem. Jr. League Rochester, Nat. Honor Soc. Home: 46 Elmerston Rd Rochester NY 14620

REIF, LORALYN, marketing consultant; b. Long Beach, Calif., Jan. 11, 1961; d. Robert Paul and Lola Deon (Murphy) R. BS in Communications, Calif. State U., Fullerton, 1985. Account coord. Basso & Assocs., Newport Beach, Calif., 1983-85; account supr. Zuckerman Pub. Rels./Advt., Santa Ana, Calif., 1985-88; prin. Reifined Mktg. Concepts, Newport Beach, 1988—; bd. dirs. Ctr. 500, Costa Mesa, 1988—, sec., 1990—. Mem. NAFE. Office: Reifined Mktg Concepts 5160 Birch St Ste 100 Newport Beach CA 92660

REIFENRATH, DOROTHY ANN, nurse; b. Kentland, Ind., July 7, 1922; d. Herman and Mary (Rheude) Diedam; m. John B. Reifenrath, Sept. 14, 1946; children: Carol A. Mallett, Thomas J., John B., Michael D., James C. Student, St. Elizabeth Sch. Nursing, Lafayette, Ind., 1943, Cath. U., 1944, Purdue U., 1974, St. Mary of the Woods Coll., Terre Haute, 1977. Obstet. supr. St. Elizabeth's Hosp., Lafayette, 1943-46; nurse, office adminstr. Drs. Ira Cole and Charles Rutherford, Lafayette, 1960-70; geriatric nurse Am. Health Care, Lafayette, 1971-72; instr. practical nursing Ind. Vocat. Tech. Coll., Lafayette, 1972-86; pub. health nurse City of Lafayette, 1986—. Chmn. bd. health City of Lafayette, 1972-87; vol. ARC, 1968—; bd. dirs. Am. Cancer Soc., 1950-55; active St. Elizabeth Hosp. Aux., 1947—, Hist. 9th St. Assn., YWCA. Mem. Nat. League for Nursing Edn., Community Aids Resource Assn., Sagamore Bus. and Profl. Women, Cath. Nurses, St. Elizabeth Alumni Assn. Democrat. Home: 609 S 9th St Lafayette IN 47901 Office: City Lafayette Health Dept 20 N 6th St Lafayette IN 47901

REIFF, DOVIE KATE, urban planner; b. Birmingham, Ala., Nov. 5, 1931; d. Roy Humes and Lou Ada (Erwin) Petty; m. Donald Allen Reiff, Dec. 25, 1956 (div. Dec. 1977); children: Donna Lynn Reiff Jayanathan, Benjamin Lyle, Johanna Carol. BArch, U. Pa., 1954, M in City Planning, 1969, postgrad. in city and regional planning, 1975. Registered architect, Pa. Architect Oskar Stonorov Architect, Phila., 1954-57; research asst. Inst. Environ. Studies, Phila., 1967-68; sr. planner Montgomery County Planning Commn., Norristown, Pa., 1969-71; urban planner Wallace McHarg Roberts & Todd, Phila., 1971-74; research analyst Del. Valley Regional Planning Commn., Phila., 1974-77; recreation planner U.S. Heritage Conservation and Recreation Service, Phila., 1977-80; community planner U.S. Gen. Services Adminstrn., Phila., 1980-85; vol., urban planner U.S. Peace Corps, Kathmandu, Nepal, 1986-87; program devel. planner Chattanooga Neighborhood Enterprise Inc., 1987-88; environ. planner dept. urban planning City of Birmingham, 1989—; mem. exec. com. Phila. chpt. Am. Inst. Planners, 1970-75; bd. dirs. Phila. chpt. AIA, 1978-79, mem. architects in govt. com., Washington, 1984-85. Participant nat. conf. Pres.'s Com. on Employment of Handicapped, Washington, 1974-76; regional del. Gov.'s Council on Handicapped, Hrrisburg, Pa., 1975; vol. Laurel House Women's Shelter, Norristown, Pa., 1985, GSA Adopt a Sch. Program, Phila., 1985; vol. Birmingham Ptnrs. in Edn., 1990; mem. Birmingham Hist. Soc., Cahaba River Soc. Brunner grantee AIA, N.Y.C., 1974. Mem. Am. Inst. Cert. Planners, Am. Planning Assn., Nat. Trust for Hist. Preservation, Sierra Club. Republican. Office: City of Birmingham Dept Urban Planning City Hall 5th Fl Birmingham AL 35203

REIFF, PATRICIA HOFER, space physicist; b. Oklahoma City, Mar. 14, 1950; d. William Henry and Maxine Roth (Hoffer) R.; m. Thomas Westfall Hill, July 4, 1976; children: Andrea Hofer, Adam Reiff, Amelia Reiff. Student, Wellesley Coll., 1967-68; BS, Okla. State U., 1971; MS, Rice U., 1974, PhD, 1975. Cert. secondary tchr., Okla., Tex. Rsch. assoc. space physics and astronomy dept. Rice U., Houston, 1975, asst. prof. space physics and astronomy dept., 1978-81, asst. chmn. space physics and astronomy dept., 1979-85, assoc. rsch. sci., 1981-87, sr. rsch. scientist, 1987—; resident rsch. assoc. Marshall Space Flight Ctr., Huntsville, Ala., 1975-76; adj. asst. prof. Rice U., 1976-78, adj. assoc. prof., 1983; mem. sci. team Atmosphere Explorer Mission, Dynamics Explorer Mission, Gobal Geospace Sci. Mission, Comet Rendezvous/Asteroid Flyby Mission; cons. Houston Mus. Natural Sci., 1986—; adv. com. on atmospheric scis. NSF, Washington, 1988—; mem. strategic implementation study panel NASA, Washington, 1989—; exec. com. George Observatory, Houston, 1989—, others. Designer Sundial/Solar Telescope, 1989; editor scientific newspaper, 1986; contbr. articles to profl. jours. Trustee, Citizens' Environ. Coalition, Houston, 1978—, pres. 1980-85; mem. air quality com. Houston/Galveston Area Coun., 1980-83, Green Ribbon Com., City of Houston, 1981-83; active coms. Macedonia United Meth. Ch., 1988—. Named rsch. fellow Nat. Acad. Sci./Nat. Rsch. Coun., 1975, Outstanding Young Women of Am., 1977, 80; recipient grant NSF, Houston, 1990-92. Mem. Am. Geophys. Union (fin. com. 1980-82), Am. Meterol. Soc. (coun. 1985-88), Wellesley Club, Internat. Union of Geophys. (del. 1975, 81, 83, 89). Office: Rice Univ/Ctr Space Physics 6100 S Main St Houston TX 77257-1892

REIGSTAD, RUTH ELAINE, lay worker, retired physical therapy consultant; b. Mpls., Apr. 26, 1923; d. Olin Spencer and Amanda Sophia (Fjelstad) R. BA, St. Olaf Coll., Northfield, Minn., 1945; cert., U. Minn., 1947. Lic. phys. therapist, Wash. Phys. therapist Crippled Childrens's Sch., Jamestown, N.D., 1948-52; phys. therapist, clin. instr. Shriners Hosp., U. Minn., Mpls., 1955-58; phys. therapist Rehab. Center, Albuquerque, N.M., 1958-60, Brit. Nat. Health Service, London; phys. therapy cons. State Health Dept., Olympia, Wash., 1961-73, cons., 1961-74; lay worker Good Shepherd Luth. Ch., Olympia, 1972-75; various coms. mem. Christ Luth. Ch., Tacoma, Wash., 1980—; Vol. Children Health Svcs. and Pub. Health of Wash. 1974—; bd. dirs. Morningside Rehab. Orgn., Olympia, Wash., PAVE rehab. orgn. Bd. dirs. Wash. State Phys. Therapy Assn., 1965-68. With USCG, 1943-45. Recipient Fellowship award Nat. Easter Seal Soc. Chgo. 1949; Scholarship award US Pub. Health Service Wash. 1962-64. Mem. Am. Phys. Therapy Assn. (life), Am. Pub. Health Assn., Am. Acad. Religion, Luth. Brotherhood Fraternity and Benevolent Orgn. (bd. dirs. Pierce County), Air Force Assn. (exec. coun. Pierce County, 1985—). Mem. Evang. Luth. Ch. Am. Home: 400 Wheeler S #207 Tacoma WA 98444

REILEY, MAME CARRIGAN, service executive, political consultant; b. Newport News, Va., Dec. 24, 1952; d. Bernard Campbell and Joan (Carrigan) R. BA in Liberal Arts, Sacred Heart Coll., 1974; cert., Cornell U., 1977. Asst. mgr. Watergate Hotel, Washington, 1975-83; real estate agt. Watergate Mgmt., Washington, 1980-84; dir. mktg., producer spl. events Courtesy Assocs., Washington, 1983-90; campaign mgr. Jim Moran for Congress, Alexandria, Va., 1990—; guest lectr. Am. U., Washington, 1987; bd. dirs. Rte One Corridor Housing. Mem. fin. com. Dem. Nat. Com., Washington, 1983, Va. State Cen. Com., 1989— 1st v.p. Washington chpt. Internat. Spl. Events Soc. Mem. Washington Performing Arts Soc. (chmn. pub. relations com. 1985-89). Club: Nat. Dem. Home: 8506 Wagon Wheel Rd Alexandria VA 22309 Office: 501 Slaters Ln Ste 17 Alexandria VA 22314

REILING, CECILIA POWERS, hospital chaplain; b. Boston, Mar. 23, 1926; d. Edward Thomas and Delia (Hehir) Powers; m. Thomas Leonard Reiling, Nov. 11, 1960; stepchildren—Elizabeth, Kathleen, Mary, Eileen. B.A., Northeastern U., 1964, M.A., 1973; M.Ed., Boston U., 1979. Instr., advisor Chamberlayne Jr. Coll., Boston, 1964-73; instr. Bryant Coll., North Smithfield, R.I., 1973-79; chaplaincy vol. Sherrill House, Boston, 1972-79, researcher, 1977-79; program dir., v.p. College Club, Boston, 1970-72; chaplaincy vol. Martin Meml. Hosp., Stuart, Fla., 1980—. Mem. Am. Sociol. Assn., Mass. Sociol. Soc., Christian Sociol. Soc., Assn. for Clin. Pastoral Edn. Republican. Roman Catholic. Clubs: Stuart Yacht and Country (Fla.); Kittansett (Marion, Mass.). Avocations: golf, music. Home: 4264 SE Fairway E Stuart FL 34997

REILLY, COLLEEN MARIE, utility executive; b. Ledyard, Iowa, Apr. 3, 1957; d. Bernard W. and Mary Ann (Haag) R. BS, Iowa State U., 1979. Assoc. dir. communications Iowa Farm Bur., West Des Moines, Iowa, 1979-80; reporter Sta. KGAN-TV, Cedar Rapids, Iowa, 1980-84; dir. coll. rels. Kirkwood Coll., Cedar Rapids, 1984-85, asst. to pres. for community rels., 1985-87; mgr. corp. communications Iowa Electric Light & Power, Cedar Rapids, 1987—; cons. Iowa Acad. Sci., Cedar Falls, 1985-86. Grad. Leadership for 5 Seasons, Cedar Rapids, 1986-87, Leadership Iowa, Des Moines, 1988-90, bd. dirs., 1989—; mem. Iowa Bd. Optometry Examiners, 1988—; bd. dirs. Salvation Army, 1989—, Cedar Rapids Symphony, 1990—, Indian Creek Nature Ctr., 1987—; mem. adv. bd. Cedar Rapids Silver Bullets. Recipient bronze award Fin. World mag., 1988, award of excellence Women in Communications, 1988, 1st place award Advt. Fedn. Cedar Rapids, 1990. Mem. Pub. Rels. Soc. Am. (accredited), Cedar Rapids Pub. Rels. Assn., Jr. League Cedar Rapids (officer 1989—), Rotary. Home: 1136 27th St NE Cedar Rapids IA 52402 Office: Iowa Electric Light & Power 200 1st St SE Cedar Rapids IA 52406

REILLY, CYNTHIA FAITHE, comptroller; b. Norfolk, Va., Sept. 29, 1952; d. Vernon Gilbert and Emma Sue (Crosley) Bailey; m. Larry Gwen Harcum, June 29, 1974 (div. 1979); 1 child, Heather Lynne; m. John Brendon Reilly, Dec. 18, 1987. Student, Tidewater Community Coll., Old Dominion U.

Teller Bank of Va. Eastern, Norfolk, 1972-74; traffic dept. sec. Evans Products Co., Chesapeake, Va., 1974-75; sr. acct. Thomas M. Perry & Co., Virginia Beach, Va., 1975-81; paraprofl. Goodman & Co., Norfolk, 1983-87; compt. Aam Inc., Chesapeake, Va., 1987-90, Dyna-Fax Ltd., Virginia Beach, Va., 1990—; owner CJ Assocs., Virginia Beach, 1988—. Democrat. Methodist. Home: 2258 Wake Forest St Virginia Beach VA 23451 Office: Dyna-Fax Ltd Business Park Dr Virginia Beach VA 23462

REILLY, CYNTHIA MARIE, marketing communications executive; b. Detroit, Aug. 9, 1960; d. Ronald Earl and Jacqueline E. (Moeller) Hamel; m. James Charles Reilly, Oct. 18, 1986; 1 child, Jacqueline Elizabeth. BS in Edn., Winona State U., 1982. Mktg. communications specialist Hayssen Mfg. Co., Sheboygan, Wis., 1983-86; sales rep. Procter & Gamble Co., Oakbrook, Ill., 1986-87; mgr. mktg. communications U.S. Marine Power Mfg. Co., Hartford, Wis., 1987—. Mem. Bus. and Profl. Advt. Assn. Republican. Lutheran. Office: US Marine Power Mfg Co 105 Marine Dr Hartford WI 53027

REILLY, JOAN RITA, nursing administrator, educator, nurse; b. Evanston, Ill., Apr. 4, 1947; d. Thomas A. and Elmira E. (McCauley) R. BSN, U. Mich., 1969; MSN, U. Colo., Denver, 1972, postgrad., 1974. Pediatric nurse practitioner U. Chgo., Wyler Hosp., 1975-77; sch. nurse spl. edn. Chgo. Pub. Schs., 1986—, sch. nurse coord. spl. svcs., 1986—; pediatric nurse cons. U. Colo., John F. Kennedy Child Devel. Ctr., 1972-74; adj. prof. U. Ill., 1981—; seminar dir., Chgo., 1981—. Contbr. articles to profl. jours.; contbr. to profl. books. Bd. dirs. Family and Children's AIDS Network. Angel scholar, 1969; recipient Shirley Titus award, 1972. Mem. ANA, Ill. Nurses Assn., Sch. Nurses Assn., Interdivisional Coun. Nurse Practitioners, Sigma Theta Tau. Home: 2020 Lincoln Pk W Apt 5J Chicago IL 60614 Office: Medicalt Sch Health 1819 W Pershing Rd Ste 5CN Chicago IL 60609

REILLY, LOIS ANN PELCARSKY, educator; b. Cleve., Feb. 25, 1941; d. William Paul and Eleanor (Mikulski) Pelcarsky; m. Anthony Eugene Reilly, June 19, 1980; children: Michael, Diane, David. BS in Edn., Baldwin-Wallace Coll., Berea, Ohio, 1962; MEd, Kent State U., 1970. Cert. reading specialist, permanent tchr., Ohio. Elem.-jr. high sch. tchr., reading specialist South Euclid-Lyndhurst (Ohio) Schs., 1962-74; ednl. cons. Scott, Foresman & Co., Glenview, Ill., 1974-75, Laidlaw Bros. Pubs., River Forest, Ill., 1978-81; reading cons. Pub. Schs. Cleveland Heights and University Heights, Ohio, 1975-76, Solon (Ohio) Schs., 1976-77; ednl. cons. Chgo. Sun-Times, 1981-84; elem. tchr. Solomon Schechter Day Sch., South Euclid, Ohio, 1984-87; jr. high sch. tchr. St. Joseph-Collinwood Sch., Cleve., 1988—; seminar presenter, 1974—; bd. dirs. South Euclid-Lyndhurst Tchrs. Credit Union, 1969-74. Contbr. articles to various publs. V.p. Women's Christian Fellowship League, 1990-91; pres. Forest Hill Presbyn. Ch., Cleveland Heights, 1987-89. Mem. AAUW (v.p. 1976-78, sec. 1980-81, newsletter editor 1981-82, v.p 1988-90), Cleve. Coll. Club, Irish Am. Club East. Home: 343 Royal Oak Blvd Richmond Heights OH 44143

REILLY, M. SUZANNE, school superintendent, consultant; b. Lakewood, N.J., June 5, 1941; d. James Russell and Margaret Katherine (Sallay) Hyres; m. Frank Richard Reilly, June 9, 1962; children: Jonathan F., Joshua J. BA, Trenton (N.J.) State Coll., 1963; MEd, Rutgers U., 1966, postgrad., 1981—; MA, Fairleigh Dickenson U., 1976. Succesively elem. tchr., title I tchr., title I head tchr., coordinator of funded programs Jackson (N.J.) Bd. Edn., 1963-84, dir. funded programs and community services, 1984-88, dir. funded programs and staff devel., 1988-89; supt. Millstone Twp. Sch. Dist., Clarksburg, N.J., 1989—; cons. Instructional Tng. Assocs., Howell, N.J., 1981—. Mem. PTO, DAV, N.J. Assn. Fed. Program Adminstrs. (pres.), Jackson Twp. Adminstrs. Assn. (pres.), N.J. Assn. Sch. Adminstrs. (exec. com.), Assn. Supervision and Curriculum Devel., N.J. Edn. Assn. (women in edn. com.), NE Coalition Ednl. Leaders. Unitarian. Club: Cruzers Soccer (Jackson). Office: Millstone Twp Sch Dist 18 Schoolhouse Ln Clarksburg NJ 08510

REILLY, SUSAN MOIRA, personnel research psychologist; b. Newark, July 1, 1948; d. James Harry and Eileen (Moran) R. BA, Coll. Notre Dame of Md., Balt., 1970; MA, Loyola Coll., Balt., 1977; PhD, Fordham U., 1985. Lic. sch. psychologist, Md. Sch. psychologist Balt. City Pub. Schs., 1972-80; teaching fellow, asst., cons. Fordham U., Bronx, N.Y., 1980-84; personnel rsch. psychologist U.S. Office Personnel Mgmt., Washington, 1985—; psychometrician, cons. Md. Dept. Edn., Balt., 1974-80; vis. asst. prof. Davidson (N.C.) Coll., 1985; adj. prof. Kean Coll. N.J., Union, 1985; cons. on testing and rsch. design, 1988—; sec. Balt. City Assn. Sch. Pscyhologists, 1977-78. Vol. Piarist Fathers Latin Mission, Tabasco, Mex., 1977-80, House of Ruth homeless shelter, Washington, 1986-87. Mem. Am. Psychol. Assn. (program com. 1990—), Am. Psychol. Soc., Nat. Coun. Measurement in Edn., Am. Ednl. Rsch. Assn., Northeast Ednl. Rsch. Assn. (program com. 1985), Va. Alliance for Mentally Ill, Sigma Xi, Phi Kappa Phi. Democrat. Roman Catholic. Office: US Office Personnel Mgmt 1900 E St Washington DC 20415

REILLY, THERESA, business educator; b. N.Y.C.; d. Bernard and Bridget (Smyth) R. BA, Ohio Dominican Coll., 1949; MA, Fordham U., 1953, PhD, 1957. Cert. bus. tchr., N.Y. Adj. prof. Pace U., N.Y.C., 1980-85; asst. prof. Briarcliff Coll., Briarcliff Manor, N.Y.; prof. bus. Queens Community Coll. CUNY, Bayside; prof. emerita CUNY, 1961-80. Author: Legal Secretary's Word Finder and Desk Book, 1974, Secretary's Guide to Correct English Usage, Punctuation, Spelling and Word Division, 1979. Mem. AAUW, Am. Irish Hist. Soc., Nat. Bus. Edn. Assn., Asia Soc., Cath. Actors Guild, Delta Pi Epsilon, Delta Kappa Gamma. Address: 70 St Andrews Dr Pinehurst NC 28374

REIMER, SUSAN MARTIN, lawyer; b. Long Beach, Calif., Aug. 7, 1953; d. Ival Eugene and Ernestine (Flinn) Martin; m. Robert A. Reimer, Aug. 21, 1982. Student Clemson U., 1971-73; J.D., John Marshall Law Sch., Savannah, Ga., 1979. Bar: Ga. 1979. Legal asst. Moss Creek Devel. Corp., Hilton Head, S.C., 1974-76, Sea Pines Plantation, Hilton Head Island, 1976-78, Bouhan, Williams & Levy, Savannah, 1979; assoc. Stephen E. Curry, Augusta, Ga., 1980-82; pvt. practice, Augusta, 1982-85, 87—; assoc. Paine, Dalis, Smith & McElreath, P.C., Augusta, 1985-86. Pres., dir. Central Savannah River coun. Girl Scouts U.S.A., 1983-86; mem. In Focus Baptist Ch.; bd. dirs. YWCA Augusta, 1989-90. Mem. ABA, Augusta Bar Assn. (sec.), Ga. Bar Assn., Ga. Trial Lawyers Assn., Nu Beta Epsilon (Frat. Achievement award 1979). Home: 3307 Thread Needle Ct Augusta GA 30907 Office: 505 Courthouse Ln Augusta GA 30901

REINARZ, KAREN NIELSEN, entrepreneur, publishing company executive; b. Horsens, Denmark, Apr. 6, 1941; came to U.S., 1948; d. Kurt Ejvind and Luise (Koch) Nielsen; m. Robert Charles Reinarz, Dec. 27, 1961; children: Robert Charles, Kristine Reinarz Parks. Student, U. Calif., Berkeley, 1959-60, San Diego State U., 1960-62, U. Tex., Austin, summer 1963. Model Mary Webb Davis "Living Look", Los Angeles and London, 1959-68; founder, mng. editor Mission Pub. Co., Mission Viejo, Calif., 1968—; owner Bright Ideas, Greenwich, Conn., 1975-84; v.p., sec.-treas. R.C. Reinarz and Co., Inc., San Antonio, 1981-86; ptnr., gen. mgr. C.W. Ranch Enterprises, Sisterdale, Tex., 1986—; cons. Atlantic Mgmt. Services, San Antonio, 1986-88. Founder Ednl. Media Ctr. Thousand Oaks (Calif.) Sch. Dist., 1972-73; mem. fin. com. Greenwich Acad., 1981-82, chairperson renovation com., 1983; mem. gardening com. Brunswick Boys Sch., Greenwich, 1978-80. Recipient 2d pl. award Nat. Crewel Contest Phila. Mus., 1976. Mem. Internat. Simbrah Congress (founder). Republican.

REINER, CAROL CURNOW, paralegal; b. Latrobe, Pa., Dec. 24, 1959; d. Joseph William and Jean Holter (Campbell) Curnow; m. Dennis M. Reiner, Oct. 24, 1987. BS, W.Va. Wesleyan U., 1982. Counselor Southwest Communities, Pitts., 1982-84; telemarketer Fed. Investors, Pitts., 1984-85; paralegal Papernick & Gefsky, P.C., Pitts., 1985—. Mem. Pitts. Paralegal Assn., Nat. Paralegal Assn. Republican. Methodist. Home: 103 Valleyview Rd Lawrence PA 15055 Office: Papernick & Gefsky PC 1 Oxford Ctr 34th Floor Pittsburgh PA 15219

REINER, RORI ELLEN, public relations executive; b. Bronx, N.Y., Mar. 7, 1962; d. Jerry and Frieda Ethel (Meyers) Tolkov; m. Barry Phillip Reiner, Aug. 24, 1985. BBA in Mktg., Iona Coll., 1984. Account exec. Dante Personnel, N.Y.C., 1985-88; account coord. Fleishman-Hillard, N.Y.C., 1988-89; account exec. GTFH Pub. Rels., N.Y.C., 1989—. Mem. Women in Communications, Inc., Pub. Rels., Soc. Am., Radio and TV New Dirs. Assn. Home: 363 E 76th New York NY 10021 Office: GTFH Pub Rels 114 Fifth Ave New York NY 10011

REINERT, PAMELA ANN, social services agency administrator; b. Pipestone, Minn., Dec. 28, 1952; d. Louis Ilse Bickford and Marcella M. (Oye) Hoisington; m. Roger Leo Reinert, Mar. 14, 1970; children: Roger, Aarron, Yolanda, Rosa, Karina, Simone. BA, S.W. Minn. State Coll., 1973; postgrad., Mankato State U., 1974; MA, Coll. St. Thomas, St. Paul, 1982. Lic. ind. clin. social worker. Behavior cons. Robert E. Milton Home, Redwood Falls, Minn., 1972-73; tchr. Renville Co., Olivia, Minn., 1973-74; coord. spl. edn. Region 6E Headstart Program, Cosmos, Minn., 1974-75; therapist WCCSC, Willmar, Minn., 1975; adoption specialist Crossroads, Mpls., 1976-84; founder, exec. dir. Building Families through Adoption, Dawson, Minn., 1984—; co-founder Project Love, Willmar, 1983; cons. Grief Counseling, Mpls., 1987—. Contbr. articles to profl. jours. Treas. Nat. Coalition to End Racism, 1988—; coord. Heal the Children, 1987—. Project Hometown Am. grantee, 1986. Mem. Nat. Assn. Social Workers, N.D. Social Workers Assn. Lutheran. Office: 4565 Pioneer Trail Medina MN 55340

REINERTSON-SAND, MARY ANN, library professional; b. Grand Forks, N.D., Apr. 2, 1959; d. Robert James and Louise Georgene (Swanson) Reinertson; m. Thomas Richard Sand, June 13, 1980. BS in Elem. Edn., U. N.D., Grand Forks, 1981, BS in Library Sci., 1984; MLS, U. Ala., 1990. Cert. tchr., N.D., Minn.; N.D. media specialist. Substitute tchr. Grand Forks Pub. Schs., 1981-84; library asst. Grand Forks Pub. Library, 1984-85; geology librarian U. N.D., Grand Forks, 1985—. Recipient Meritorious Svc. award U. N.D., 1989. Mem. ALA, N.D. Library Assn. (jr. mem. round table sect. pres-elect 1989-90), Cen.-Red River Valley Library Assn., Mt. Plains Library Assn. Office: Geology Library U ND Box 8068 University Sta Grand Forks ND 58202

REINGANUM, JULIE LOUISE, international marketing, entrepreneur; b. Chgo., May 2, 1955; d. Carrol Harrison and Maurine Judith (Scheckman) R. BA, Vassar Coll., 1977; MA, Johns Hopkins U., 1979; MBA, Stanford (Calif.) U., 1984. Corr. Mainichi Shimbum, Washington, 1978-79; program assoc. Nat. Commn. on U.S.-China Rels., N.Y.C., 1979-82; dir. mktg. devel. Pacific Telesis Internat., San Francisco, 1984-86; mng. dir. Kamsky Assocs., N.Y.C., 1986-88; founder, mng. dir. Pacific Rim Resources, Inc., San Francisco, 1988—; bd. dirs. Arts Pacific, Mpls.; mem. cons. team Stanford U., 1989-90. Chairperson Internat. Speakers Forum, Stanford, 1983-84; mem. Shanghai friendship com. City of San Francisco, 1989—. Ill. State scholar, 1973; recipient Helen Dwight Reid award Vassar Coll., 1977; Margaret Peabody fellow Johns Hopkins U., 1978; Milton L. Roberts grantee Stanford U., 1982. Mem. NAFE. Office: Pacific Rim Resources 201 Spear St Ste 1600 San Francisco CA 94105

REINHARD, SISTER MARY MARTHE, educational organization administrator; b. McKeesport, Pa., Aug. 29, 1929; d. Regis C. and Leona (Reese) R. AB, Notre Dame Coll.; MA, U. Notre Dame. Asst. prin. Regina High Sch., Cleve., 1960-62, prin., 1963-64; prin. Notre Dame Acad., Chardon, Ohio, 1965-72; pres. Notre Dame Coll. of Ohio, Cleve., 1973-88; dir. devel. Sisters of Notre Dame Ednl. Ctr., Chardon, 1989—. Campaign chairperson United Way Svcs., 1985, v.p.-at-large, 1987, trustee 1985—; trustee, mem. exec. com. NCCJ, Cleve., 1987; chairperson edn. div. United Way Campaign; bd. dirs. Centerior Energy, 1984—. Named one of 100 most influential women in Cleve. Women's City Club, 1983, one of 79 most interesting people in Cleve. The Cleve. mag., 1979. Mem. Area and Clergy Bus. for Dialogue. Roman Catholic. Home and Office: 13000 Auburn Rd Chardon OH 44024

REINHARDT, CHERYL LYNN, healthcare executive; b. Neenah, Wis., Mar. 26, 1960; d. Ruben Paul and Marjorie E. (Beyer) Popp; m. Glenn John Reinhardt, Oct. 13, 1984. B Bus., U. Wis., Oshkosh, 1982; MS, U. Wis., Milw., 1988. Customer rep. GMAC, Milw., 1982-87; supr. internal control Wis. Health Orgn., Milw., 1987-88; med. mgmt. analyst PrimeCare Health Plan, Milw., 1988—. Mem. Am. Coll. Health Care Execs., Assn. Health Care Execs., NAFE. Republican. Lutheran. Office: PrimeCare Health Plan 1233 N Mayfair Rd Milwaukee WI 53226

REINHART, BETTY LOUISE, marketing firm owner; b. Elgin, Ill., Oct. 25, 1943; d. Sherman Leroy and Louise Margreta (Underhill) Holman; m. Charlie E. Glover, June 8, 1968 (div. Jan. 1985); m. Walter Lee Reinhart, Mar. 16, 1985; children: Bessie Louise Glover, Deborah Charlene Glover Daniel. Student, St. Mary's, N.Y.C., 1960; student, So. Ill. U., 1963. Lic. practical nurse. With nursing hosps., Pinehurst, N.C., 1968-80; dir. nursing Seven Lakes Rest Home, West End, N.C., 1981-83; interior design Cruise Ships, Miami, Fla., 1984-87; owner mktg. firm W.L.R. Enterprises, Inc., Coral Springs, Fla., 1986—; tchr. psychic awareness, stress mgmt., Coral Springs, 1983—. Author: Life of a Psychic, 1987, Working Woman's Cookbook, 1989. Mem. Calif. Astrology Assn. (life), NAFE, Am. Film Inst. Home: 2533 NW 82nd Terr Coral Springs FL 33065 Office: WLR Enterprises Inc PO Box 9116 Coral Springs FL 33075

REINHART, KAREN BOYLL, real estate financial analyst; b. Mt. Clemens, Mich., Nov. 8, 1962; d. Ralph Glen and Rose Marie (Hernacki) Boyll; m. Gerald Francis Reinhart, may 29, 1987. BA in Acctg., Mich. State U., 1984; postgrad. in bus. mgmt., U. Mich., 1987—. CPA, Mich.; lic. real estate broker, Mich. Sr. auditor Coopers and Lybrand, Detroit, 1984-86; sr. fin. analyst Kojaian Properties, Inc., Bloomfield Hills, Mich., 1987—; adj. instr. U. Mich., Walsh Coll. Mem. Mich. Assn. CPAs, Comml. Real Estate Women, Mich. State U. Alumni, Real Estate Round Table, Inc. Republican. Roman Catholic.

REINHART, KAY ELLEN, arts marketing professional; b. Port Washington, Wis., Sept. 20, 1946; d. John L. and Betty (Morrison) Rahmlow; m. Carl F. Reinhart III, Nov. 25, 1967 (div. 1972); m. Charles E. Ziff, May 29, 1976; 1 child, Emily Lambert Ziff. Student, U. Wis., Madison, 1964-66; BFA, U. Wis., Milw., 1969. Exec. asst. Nikolais-Louis Found., N.Y.C., 1969-71; art editor Harcourt Brace Jovanovich, N.Y.C., 1972-79; bus. mgr., corp. sec. Ziff Mktg. Inc., N.Y.C., 1981—; owner, artist Open East Pottery, Cobble Hill, Bklyn., 1975—. Editor (screenplay) The Winning Sky; (novel) This Ascending Dust, 1983. Mem. NAFE, Nat. Mus. Women in the Arts, Warren Pl. Assn. (treas.), Conn. Craftsmen, Greenpeace, Coop. Am. Office: Ziff Mktg Inc 126 Fifth Ave New York NY 10011

REINING, BETH LAVERNE (BETTY REINING), public relations consultant, journalist; b. Fargo, N.D.; d. George and Grace (Twiford) Reimche; student N.D. State Coll., U. Minn., Glendale Community Coll., Calif. State Coll., Carson; 1 dau., Carolyn Ray Toohey Hiett; m. Jack Warren Reining, Oct. 3, 1976 (div. 1984). Originated self-worth seminars in Phoenix, 1970-76; owner Janzik Pub. Relations, 1971-76; talk show reporter-hostess What's Happening in Ariz., Sta. KPAZ-TV, 1970-73; writer syndicated column People Want to Know, Today newspaper, Phoenix, 1973; owner JB Communications, Phoenix, 1976-84; owner, pres. Media Communications, 1984—; freelance writer; tchr. How to Weigh Your Self-Worth courses Phoenix Coll., Rio Solado Community Coll., Phoenix, 1976-84; instr. pub. rels. Scottsdale (Ariz.) Community Coll., 1987; muralist, works include 25 figures in med. office. Founder Ariz. Call-A-Teen Youth Resources, Inc., pres., 1975-76, v.p., 1976-77, now bd. dirs. Recipient awards including 1st pl. in TV writing Nat. Fedn. Press Women, 1971-88, numerous state awards in journalism Ariz. Press Women, 1971-76, Good Citizen award Builders of Greater Ariz., 1961. Mem. Ariz. Press Women (1st place award 1988), No. Ariz. Press Women (pres. 1983), Nat. Fedn. Am. Press Women, Pub. Relations Soc. Am., Phoenix Pub. Relations Soc., Nat. Acad. TV Arts and Scis., Phoenix Valley of Sun Convention Bur., Verde Valley C. of C. (bd. dirs., tourism chmn. 1986-87, Best Chair of Yr. award 1986), Phoenix Metro C. of C. Cottonwood C. of C. (chmn. of Yr. award, 1986). Inventor stocking-tension twist footlet, 1962. Club: Phoenix Press. Office: PO Box 10509 Phoenix AZ 85064

REINING, KAREN M., nurse; b. Phila., Nov. 13, 1960; d. Karl H. and Una M. (Morrisroe) R. BSN, Holy Family Coll., 1984. RN, Pa.; cert. critical-care nurse. Asst. nurse mgr., staff nurse no. div. Albert Einstein Med. Ctr., Phila.; staff nurse PACU Thomas Jefferson U. Hosp., Phila., nursing care coord. Mem. Am. Assn. Critical-Care Nurses, Pa. Assn. Post-Anesthesia Nurses, Am. Soc. Post-Anesthesia Nurses, Sigma Theta Tau.

REINKE, DORIS MARIE, retired teacher; b. Racine, Wis., Jan. 12, 1922; d. Otto William Reinke and Louise Amelia Goehring. BS, U. Wis., Milw., 1943; MS, U. Wis., Whitewater, 1967. Tchr. kindergarten Elkhorn (Wis.) Area Sch. System, 1943-69, bldg. prin., 1968-70, summer sch. dir., 1974, grade 2 tchr., 1970-84, primary dept. chmn., 1971-84, administrv. asst., supervising tchr., 1957-83, student tchr., 1984, ret., 1984; oriented experience tchr. Program Area Sch. System, Elkhorn, 1966; pres. Elkhorn Edn. Assn., 1949-50; rep. dist. State Kindergarten Conf., Oshkosh, Wis., 1966; participant early edn. conf. State Early Edn. Conf., Egle River, Wis., 1968, 75. Co-author: Elkhorn, 1976; Author: 1887 Bldg., 1987, Webster Notes, 1989. Bd. dirs. Food Pantry, Elkhorn, 1985-88, RSVP Vol. Food Pantry, Elkhorn, 1987; del., dist. constn. conv., Evang. Luth. Ch. Am., Beloit, Wis., 1987; com. mem., Luth. Ch., Elkhorn, 1987; chmn. sch. centennial, Elkhorn, 1987. Recipient Wis. Edn. Research, West Bend, Wis., 1966, Outstanding Elem. Tchrs., Wash., 1973, Wis. Dept. Edn., Madison, 1980. Mem. Nat. Ret. Tchrs. Walworth County (v.p. 1988), Walworth County Hist. Soc. (treas. 1985-89), Alpha Delta Kappa (state pres. 1968-70, 76-78). Home: 516 N Wisconsin St Elkhorn WI 53121

REINKE, TWILA O'SUCH, crisis interventionist, educator; b. Perth Amboy, N.J., Oct. 10, 1942; d. Michael and Dorothy (Larsen) O'Such; m. Roger Richard Reinke, July 3, 1979 (div. Apr. 1980); 1 child, Lisa. BA, U. Fla., 1963, MEd, 1964; EdM, Columbia U., 1972, EdD, 1974. Cert. elem. and early childhood, administrn. and supervision, emotional disturbed mental retardation., Fla. Tchr. mentally retarded Sunland Tng. Ctr., Gainesville, Fla., 1965-70; recreation coord. Philanthropic League, N.Y.C., 1971; adminstrv. asst. Am. Assn. Mental Deficiency, Washington, 1972; asst. prof. North Ga. Coll., Dahlonega, 1973-75, U. Nev., Reno, 1975-80; tchr. emotionally handicapped Palm Beach County Sch. System, Pahokee, Fla., 1982-85; crisis interventionist Palm Beach County Sch. Bd., West Palm Beach, Fla., 1985—; pass convenor Nova U., Ft. Lauderdale, Fla., 1988—; adj. prof. Nova U., Ft. Lauderdale, 1987—; cons. Nev. State Dept. Project Child Fund, 1975-77, Stewart Indian Sch., Carson City, Nev., 1978-79, Duckwater (Nev.) Shoshone Indian Reservation, 1979, Assn. for Retarded Citizens, West Palm Beach, 1988-89. Speaker Sta. KOLO-TV Network Attitudes, Reno, 1977, Sta. KONE, Reno, 1977; mem. Pks. and Recreation Environ. Restoration Project, Stuart, Fla., 1989. Mem. Coun. for Exceptional Children (chmn. com. 1970-90), Am. Assn. on Mental Deficiency (chmn. com. 1969-78), Nat. Soc. Profs., NEA, AAUW (corp. rep. 1976-78), Washoe County Edn. (sec. adv. bd. 1977), AAUP. Democrat. Lutheran. Home: 865 SE St Lucie Blvd Stuart FL 34996

REINSCHMIEDT, ANNE TIERNEY, nurse; b. Washington, Mar. 6, 1932; d. Edward F. and Frances (Palmer) Tierney; m. Edwin Ruben Reinschmiedt, Sept. 20, 1959 (div. 1961); 1 child, Kathleen Frances Tierney. BS, Cen. State U., Edmond, Okla., 1975; postgrad., Oklahoma City U. Sch. Law, 1987—. RN, Calif., Okla.; lic. nursing home adminstr. Nurse San Jose (Calif.) Hosp., 1952-55; owner, operator Hominy Studio, 1960-62; dir. nurses, lab and x-ray, technician, adminstr. Hominy (Okla.) City Hosp., 1961-63; nurse Jackson County Dept. Health, Altus, Okla., 1963-65; adminstr. Propp's Inc., Oklahoma City, 1965-80; nursing homes cons. Propps & Self, Oklahoma City, 1965—; pres. Shamrock Health Care Ctr., Bethany, Okla., 1981—; operator Lakeview Lodging Residential Care Facility, 1981—; adult edn. instr., med. aide technicians East Central U., Ada, Okla., 1987-89; cons. in field. Author: Recovery Room Procedures, 1958. Mem. Jackson County (Okla.) Draft Bd., 1965-70. Lt. USN, 1955-60. Mem. Am. Nurses Assn., Nat. Assn. Residential Care Facilities (sec., bd. dirs. 1983-85), Okla. Assn. Residential Care Facilities (founding pres. 1981-87, bd. dirs. 1981—), Beta Sigma Phi, Phi Alpha Delta (vice justice, exec. bd. 1988-90). Republican. Roman Catholic. Office: Shamrock Health Care Box 848 Bethany OK 73008

REIS, MURIEL HENLE, lawyer, broadcast executive; b. N.Y.C.; d. Frederick S. and Mary (Meyers) Henle; m. Arthur Reis Jr., Sept. 25, 1953; children: Arthur Henle, Diane Mary, Pamela Robin. BA, Vassar Coll., 1946; LLB, Columbia U., 1949. Bar: N.Y. 1950, U.S. Ct. Appeals (2d cir.) 1959. Asst. gen. counsel ABC, N.Y.C., 1950-52; from asst. gen. counsel to assoc. gen. counsel Metromedia Inc., N.Y.C., 1956-86; v.p. WNEW, N.Y.C., 1974-86; v.p., legal affairs Fox TV Sta. Inc., N.Y.C., 1986—. Mem. Assn. of Bar of City of N.Y., Internat. Soc. Radio and TV Execs. Home: 1136 Fifth Ave New York NY 10128 Office: Fox TV Sta Inc 205 E 67th St New York NY 10021

REISMAN, JUDITH A., educational institute executive; b. Hillside, N.J., Apr. 11, 1935; MA in Speech Communication, Case Western Res. U., 1976, PhD in Speech Communication, 1980. Faculty dept. anthropology and sociology and sch. of edn. Haifa U., Israel, 1981-83; rsch. prof. sch. edn. Am. U., Washington, 1983-85; founder Inst. Media Edn., 1985—; cons., reviewer grant proposals audio-visual drug programs for youth Dept. Edn., 1987; rsch. design cons. Alcohol and Tobacco Media Analysis in Mainstream Mags. Dept. HHS, 1987-90; cons., field reviewer Drug Free Youth Sch. Candidates Dept. Edn., 1988; lectr., adj. prof. George Mason U., Va., 1990; expert witness. Author: Images of Children, Crime and Violence in Playboy, Penthouse and Hustler; contbr. articles on U.S. Supreme Ct. cases to profl. jours.; rsch. cited in U.S. Supreme Ct. cases. Co-recipient Scholastic Mag. awards: Dukane award, 1982, Gold Camera award, 1982, Silver Screen award 1982, Filmstrip of Yr. award, 1981-82, Silver Plaque award, 1982; Family Svc. Assn. Am. 1st pl. award local TV series, 1974; Best of 1965 award, 1965. Mem. AAAS, Am. Assn. Composers, Authors and Pubs., Internat. Communication Assn., N.Y. Acad. Scis., Soc. Sci. Study Sex, Nat. Black Child Devel. Inst. Office: Inst Media Edn PO Box 7404 Arlington VA 22207

REISNER, RUTH TORREY, ambulance service executive; b. Olean, N.Y., Sept. 23, 1951; d. Adrian L. and Ethelruth (Keller) Torrey; m. Walter L. Reisner II, Feb. 14, 1975; children: Jeffrey Paul, Janet Marie, Adriann Torrey. Diploma, St. James Mercy Sch. Nursing, Hornell, N.Y., 1972. RN, N.Y. Nurse St. Francis Hosp., Olean, 1972-87; pres., owner Trans Am Ambulance Svcs., Inc., Olean, 1983—; CPR instr. Am. Red Cross, Buffalo, N.Y., 1983-90, Am. Heart Assn., Jamestown, N.Y., 1989-90. Mem. DAR, Olean C. of C. Episcopalian. Home: 1658 Olean Portville Rd Olean NY 14760 Office: Trans Am Ambulance Svc Inc 305 N 8th St Olean NY 14760

REISS, CAROL SHOSHKES, immunology educator; b. Boston, Mar. 14, 1950; d. Milton Abraham and Lila (Topal) Shoshkes; m. Paul Petigrow, Aug. 25, 1971 (div. 1976); m. David Simon Reiss, June 5, 1977; children: Steven M., Joshua S. AB, Bryn Mawr (Pa.) Coll., 1972; MS, Sarah Lawrence Coll., 1973; PhD, CUNY, 1978. Postdoctoral fellow Harvard U., Boston, 1978-81, instr. pathology dept., 1981-83; asst. prof. pathology dept. Med. Sch., 1981-83, assoc. prof. pathology dept., 1983-88; assoc. prof. pathology dept. Harvard Med. Sch. Harvard U., Boston, 1988—; assoc. prof. pediatric oncology div. Dana Farber Cancer Inst., Boston, 1980—; lectr. Found. of Microbiology, 1990—. Assoc. editor: Jour. Immunology, 1989—. Recipient Jr. Faculty Rsch. award Am. Cancer Soc., 1984, New Investigation award USPHS, 1981. Mem. Am. Assn. Immunologists, Assn. for Women in Sci., Am. Soc. for Microbiology, Am. Soc. for Virology, NIH (experimental virology study sect. 1987—). Democrat. Jewish. Office: Dana Farber Cancer Inst 44 Binney St Boston MA 02115

REISS, ELAINE SERLIN, advertising agency executive, lawyer; b. N.Y.C., Oct. 27, 1940; d. Morris and Dorothy (Geyer) Serlin; m. Joel A. Reiss, Sept. 1, 1963; children: Joshua Adam, Naomi Lee. B.A., N.Y. U., 1961, LL.M., 1973; LL.B., Columbia U., 1964. Bar: N.Y. 1965. Mgr. legal dept. Doyle Dane Bernbach Advt., 1965-68; mgr. legal clearance dept., then v.p., mgr. legal dept. Ogilvy & Mather, N.Y.C., 1968-78; sr. v.p., mgr. legal dept. Ogilvy & Mather, Inc., N.Y.C., 1978-82, gen. counsel, sec. U.S. bd. dirs., 1982—, exec. v.p., 1985—; gen. counsel Ogilvy Group Inc., N.Y.C., 1988—, sec., 1989—; industry adv. seminar series on children Georgetown U. Law Sch., 1978-79; mem. part-time faculty NYU Tisch Sch. Arts, 1982—. Recipient Matrix award in advt. N.Y. Women in Communications, 1987. Mem. Am. Assn. Advt. Agencies (chmn. legal com. 1979-81), ABA (com. on corp. law depts.), Assn. Bar City N.Y., Legal Aid Soc. (bd. dirs.). Office: Ogilvy & Mather Advt Worldwide Pla 309 W 49th St New York NY 10019

REITAN, RACHEL ELSA, nurse; b. Sioux City, Iowa, Dec. 8, 1964; d. Phillip Jennings and Ruth Elsie (Grethen) R. Student, U. So. Calif., L.A., 1983-85; BSN, Luther Coll., 1987. Clin. nurse I UCLA Med. Ctr., 1988; clin. nurse II Cedars Sinai Med. Ctr., L.A., 1988; charge nurse Charter Pacific Hosp., Torrance, Calif., 1988-89; pub. relations staff Gen. Motors, Torrance, Calif., 1989—. Recipient 3d Pl. Ribbon, State of Wis., 1982; recipient Trophy, City of Decorah, 1983. Mem. NAACP (asst. bd. dirs. Beverly Hills, Calif. chpt. 1988—), Calif. Nurses Assn., Phi Sigma Kappa, Alpha Beta Psi (treas. Decorah chpt. 1987). Democrat. Lutheran. Home: 341 S Doheny Dr #5 Beverly Hills CA 90211 Office: Marketing & Fin Mgmt Inc Canoga Ave Woodland Hills CA 98212

REITER, ELAINE MARY, state agency administrator; b. Ellsworth, Minn., July 21, 1928; d. Jacob Nicholas and Esther Suzanne (Kappes) R.; BS in Bus. Adminstrn., Marquette U., Milw., 1953; MEd in Counseling, U. Mo., Columbia, 1967, MPA, 1976. Personnel asst. Square D Co., Milw., 1953-56; exec. asst. Psychol. Svc. Corp., St. Louis, 1957-63; svcs. mgr. Psychol. Assos., St. Louis, 1963-64; counselor Mo. Employment Svc., St. Louis, 1964-68; dep. dir. Mo. Office Aging, Jefferson City, 1968-72; cons. adult svcs. to State of Mo., 1973-76; regional adminstr. Mo. Div. Family Svcs. and Aging, 1977-81, alternative svcs. adminstr. Mo. Div. Aging, 1981—; bd. dirs. Nat. Com. for the Prevention of Elder Abuse, 1988—; mem. nat. protective svcs. task force Adminstrn. Aging, 1982; del. White House Conf. Aging, 1971. Recipient various svcs. awards. Mem. AAUW, Am. Public Welfare Assn. (chmn. membership Mo. chpt. 1976-77), Mo. Assn. Social Welfare (dir. 1975-82, exec. com. 1976-79, chmn. aging task force 1975-80, chmn. Kansas City div. 1981-82), Nat. Coun. on Aging, Geront. Soc., Mo. Assn. Prevention Adult Abuse, Am. Soc. on Aging, Mid-Am. Congress Aging, Lakewood Club, Zonta. Roman Catholic. Office: Div of Aging 2701 W Main PO Box 1337 Jefferson City MO 65102

REITZ, BARBARA MAURER, freelance writer, poet; b. Teaneck, N.J., Dec. 26, 1931; d. William Ritschy and Ruth Gunhild (Noren) Maurer; m. William Stanley Reitz, Jr., Sept. 15, 1956; children: William Stanley III, David Stewart. BA in English, Bucknell U., 1953. Sec. UN, N.Y.C., 1953-54; sec. to pres. Charles Scribner's Sons, N.Y.C., 1954-56; freelance writer Chillicothe, Ohio, 1987—, poet, 1949—. Contbr. articles to local newspapers. Campaign mgr., creative dir. W.S. Reitz Jr. for City Coun. Pres., Chillicothe, 1987, 89. Mem. AAUW (pres. Chillicothe br. 1988—), Bucknell Alumni Assn. (class reporter 1968-83), Chillicothe Tennis Assn. (sec.-treas. 1973-82), Sigma Tau Delta (pres. 1952-53), Pi Delta Epsilon, Alpha Lambda Delta, Pi Beta Phi. Republican. Presbyterian (elder 1981—). Home: 675 Hilltop Ct Chillicothe OH 45601

REITZ, JEANNE GEIGER, mathematics educator; b. New Orleans, Feb. 2, 1941; d. George Thomas and Leonora Agnes (Ziifle) Geiger; m. Ronald Charles Reitz, Jan. 23, 1965; children: Erica Anne, Pieter Brett. BS, La. State U., 1963. Research asst. Tulane Med. Sch., New Orleans, 1963-64; tchr. Jefferson Parish Sch. Dist., Gretna, La., 1965-66; sales rep. Jacobson's, Ann Arbor, Mich., 1966-67; tchr. Novi (Mich.) Schs., 1967-68, Washoe County Sch. Dist., Reno, 1982—; mem. testing com. Washoe County Schs., 1987—; mem. equity in math. adv. bd. U. Nev., Reno, 1987-88; with publicity Chapel Hill Sch. Art Guild, 1971-74. Bd. dirs. Nev. Opera Assn., Reno, 1987—, Young Audiences No. Nev., Reno, 1981-83; dist. dir. Met. Opera Nat. Council, Reno, 1985-86. Mem. NEA, AAUW (sec. 1981-83, 86-88), Washoe County Tchrs. Assn. (Disting. Performance award 1987), Washoe County Math. Assn. (newsletter editor 1987-88), Faculty Wives U. Nev. Club (sec., 2nd v.p.). Republican. Roman Catholic. Home: 3237 Susileen Dr Reno NV 89509 Office: Swope Mid Sch 901 Keele Dr Reno NV 89509

REITZ, STEPHANIE KAREN, journalist; b. Grosse Pointe, Mich., July 22, 1968; d. Robert Elwin Reitz and Pamela Rae (Granger) Haggerty. BA in Journalism, Mich. State U., 1990. Staff reporter Lake Orion (Mich.) Rev., 1983-86, Mich. State News, East Lansing, 1986-88; govt. reporter Mansfield (Mass.) News, 1989; police reporter Allentown (Pa.) Morning Call, 1989; sports reporter Lansing (Mich.) State Jour., 1990—; copy editor Detroit News, 1990—; pres. MSU Journalism Adv. Com., 1990—. Editor-in-chief MSU Found. Prospectus, 1986-88. Vol. Am. Cancer Soc., Southfield, 1987-89. Recipient Golf Writer's Excellence award Golf Writers Assn. Am., 1988, 89, Commentary award Detroit Press Club, 1990. Mem. Women in Communications Inc., Soc. Profl. Journalists (pres. 1987-89). Home: 1410 Loraine Ave Lansing MI 48910

REIZIAN, LEE MALVINA, television and radio producer, recording artist; b. Franklin at Amherst, Mass., Aug. 14, 1962; d. Albert Vincent and Takoohy Quinn (Kenoian) Reizian. BA, U. Mass., 1982. Freelance publicist Boston and N.Y.C., 1982-85; producer Ogilvy & Mather, N.Y.C., 1985—; writer and singer N.Y.C., 1984—. Producer music video Sweet Talk, 1989. Vol. tchr. Easter Seals, Boston, 1980-82; producer video United Way Tri-State, N.Y., 1989. Mem. ASCAP (assoc.), Amnesty Internat. Mem. Armenian Apostolic Ch. Office: Ogilvy & Mather Advt 309 W 49th St 8th Floor New York NY 10019

RELIGA, SHARILYN JEAN, electronics executive, fingerprint analyst; b. Whittier, Calif., Dec. 14, 1957; d. John James and Stella Gertrude (Pavlis) R.; m. Patrick A. Tafoya, Nov. 14, 1982 (div. Mar. 1987). BS in Biology, U. Calif., Santa Cruz, 1979. With Sumware, Laguna Beach, Calif., 1980-81; installation coord. Am. Med. Internat., Marina Del Rey, Calif., 1981-82; systems analyst, support mgr. Systems Unlimited, Huntington Beach, Calif., 1982-84; software-system engr. De La Rue Printrak, Anaheim, Calif., 1984-88, mgr. system support-tech. ops., 1988—. Democrat. Home: 20 Snowberry Irvine CA 92714 Office: De La Rue Printrak 1250 N Tustin Anaheim CA 92807

REMAK, JEANNETTE ELIZABETH, quality control executive; b. Queens, N.Y., Nov. 23, 1952; d. Bela Alexander and Helen (Almassy) R. Student, N.Y. Inst. Photography, 1971-72; student, Sch. Visual Arts, N.Y.C., 1972-73, CUNY, 1973-76. Cert. photo finishing engr. Photo Mktg. Assn. Prodn. mgr. Rembrandt Color Labs., Jamaica, N.Y., 1976-80; builder, operator Fast Photo, N.Y.C., 1980-83; prodn. mgr. Jackson Photo, N.Y.C., 1983-86; quality control mgr. Universal Photo, N.Y.C., 1986—. Paintings exhibited at Internat. Art Challenge Art Show, Calif., 1987; paintings included in (book) American Artists an Illustrated Survey, 1990. Contbg. mem. USAF Art Program, NASA Art Program. Mem. Soc. Photofinishing Engrs., Am. Soc. Sci. Fiction Fantasy Artists, Challenger Ctr. for Edn. (sponsor).

REMETA, ESTHER MARIE, chiropractor; b. N.Y.C., July 23, 1960; d. Daniel and Gerd Margareta (Steinholtz) R. BS in Biology, Rutgers U., 1982; BS in Anatomy, Nat. Coll. Chiropractic, Lombard, Ill., 1984; D Chiropractic, Nat. Coll. Chiropractic, 1986. Chiropractic physician Lichtenstein Chiropractic Ctr., Scotch Plains, N.J., 1987; physician, ptnr. N.W. Chiropractic Clinic, Banner Elk, N.C., 1988—. Mem. N.C. Chiropractic Assn., Am. Chiropractic Assn., Banner Elk C. of C., Boone C. of C., Sacro Occipital Technique Soc., Delta Tau Alpha (pres. 1984, v.p. 1985). Home: Rte 1 Box 354 B Banner Elk NC 28604 Office: Northwest Chiropractic Cln Rte 1 Box 354 B Banner Elk NC 28604

REMETZ, CAROL LOUISE, accountant; b. Lancaster, Pa., Apr. 8, 1956; d. George and Bernadine (Michael) R. Cert. radiology, Lancaster Gen. Hosp. Sch., 1976; BS in Acctg., Villanova (Pa.) U., 1989. Radiologic technologist Georgetown U. Hosp., Washington, 1976-83, Pa. Hosp., Phila., 1983-85; acct. Meridian Acctg., Phila., 1985-89; tax adminstr. J.P. Morgan, N.Y.C., 1989—. Mem. Am. Soc. Women Accts., Phi Kappa Phi, Alpha Sigma Lambda. Democrat. Roman Catholic.. Home: 235 Watkins St Philadelphia PA 19148

REMICK, LEE (MRS. WILLIAM RORY GOWANS), actress; b. Quincy, Mass., Dec. 14, 1935; d. Frank E. and Margaret (Waldo) R.; m. William A. Colleran, Aug. 3, 1957 (div. 1969); children: Kate, Matthew; m. William Rory Gowans, Dec. 18, 1970. Student, Barnard Coll., 1953. Broadway debut in Be Your Age, 1953; other plays include: Anyone Can Whistle, 1964, Wait Until Dark, 1966, Bus Stop, London, 1974, I Do, I Do, 1983, Follies in Concert, 1985; films include: A Face in the Crowd, 1956, The Long Hot Summer, 1957, Anatomy of a Murder, 1959, Wild River, 1959, Sanctuary, 1960, Experiment in Terror, 1961, Days of Wine and Roses, 1961, The Wheeler Dealers, 1962, Baby The Rain Must Fall, 1963, Hallelujah Trail, 1965, No Way to Treat a Lady, 1967, The Detective, 1968, Hard Contract, 1969, Loot, 1972, A Delicate Balance, 1973, Hennessy, 1974, The Omen, 1976, Telefon, 1977, The Europeans, 1979, The Competition, 1980, Tribute, 1980; appeared in TV prodns.: Jennie, Lady Randolph Churchill, 1975; TV mini-series Wheels, 1978, Ike, 1979; other TV films include: Haywire, 1980, The Women's Room, 1981, The Letter, 1982, Mistral's Daughter, 1984, Rearview Mirror, 1984, The Snow Queen, 1985, Toughlove, 1985, Follies in Concert, 1986, Of Pure Blood, 1986, Eleanor in Her Own Words, 1986, Nutcracker, 1987, Money, Murder, Madness, 1987, The Vision, 1988, A Bridge to Silence, 1989, Around The World in 80 Days, 1989, Dark Holiday, 1989. Address: care Internat Creative Mgmt 8899 Beverly Blvd Los Angeles CA 90048

REMIGNANTI, ANITA ESPOSITO, psychologist; b. Bridgeport, Conn., July 15, 1953; d. Fred George and Natalie Teresa (Rubino) Esposito; m. Drew Curtis Remignanti; children: Kirk, Ben, Laine. BA, Ind. U., 1975; MEd, Ga. State U., 1976; EdD, Rutgers U., 1979. lectr. U. N.H. Lectr. Middlesex Community Coll., Middleton, Conn., 1980; psychologist Psychology Assocs., Plymouth, Mass., 1983-88, Seacoast Family Practice, Portsmouth, N.H., 1988—; lectr. on world peace and child rearing, various churches, schs., and civic orgns. Contbr. articles to profl. jours. Mem. Women for Internat. Peace & Arbitration (editor The Peace Maker 1989—), Am. Psychol. Assn. Mem. Bahai Faith. Home: 10 Meader Ln Durham NH 03824

REMLEY, AUDREY WRIGHT, educational administrator, psychologist; b. Warrenton, Mo., Dec. 26, 1931; d. Leslie Frank and Irene Lesetta (Graue) Wright; m. Alvin Remley, Mar. 25, 1951; children: Steven Leslie, David Mark. AA, Hannibal-LaGrange Coll., 1951; BS in Edn. cum laude, U. Mo., 1963, MA, 1969, PhD, 1974. Lic. psychologist, Mo. Asst. prof. psychology Westminster Coll., Fulton, Mo., 1969-74, assoc. prof., 1975-88, prof., 1988—, prof., assoc. dean faculty, 1989—, chmn. dept. psychology, 1975-78, dir. counseling svcs., 1975-79, dir. student devel., 1979-80, dir. acad. advising and counseling svcs., 1980-88 ; cons. OVID Bell Press, 1988—; mem. adv. bd. Callaway Community Hosp., 1988—; bd. dirs. Serve, Inc., Fulton, 1989—. Recipient Outstanding Young Woman of Am. award Jaycettes, 1965; NDEA fellow, 1968. Mem. Am. Assn. Counseling and Devel., Am. Coll. Personnel Assn. (exec. council 1982-85, co-editor ACPA Developments, 1984-87, v.p. state divs., 1987-89, treas.-elect 1990—, Outstanding State Div. Leader 1982), Mo. Coll. Personnel Assn. (pres. 1981-82), Am. Psychol. Assn., Mo. Psychol. Assn. (lic.), Kiwanis (exec. bd. 1989—). Presbyterian. Avocations: singing; antique collecting; knitting. Office: Westminster Coll 501 Westminster Ave Fulton MO 65251-1299

REMOL, THERESA ANNE, rental manager; b. Watonga, Okla., June 19, 1952; d. J. Russell and Lexina McKay (Conway) Swanson; m. John Collinge Remol, Dec. 29, 1973 (div. Oct. 1981); 1 child, Justin Iver. BS, William Woods Coll., 1974. Lic. real estate broker. Bookkeeper Jetty East Condominium, Destin, Fla., 1979-81; rental property supr. Seascape Resort, Destin, 1981-83; rental mgr. The Islander Condominium, Destin, 1983—; Mem. Emerald Coast Improvement Coun., Ft. Walton Beach, Fla., 1989-90. Bd. dirs., sec. Destin Little League, 1985—; sec. Destin Village Players, 1981-84; mem. Com. for Good Govt., Destin, 1986-90. Mem. Destin C. of C., Ft. Walton C. of C. (bus. rep. 1988—), Destin Lioness Club (sec. 1981-84), Jr. League of Ft. Walton Beach. Republican. Mem. Christian Ch. Home: 21 Rue d'Etretat Destin FL 32541 Office: The Islander 502 Gulfshore Dr Destin FL 32541

REMOLADOR, PHYLLIS LIEBERMAN, human resources systems specialist; b. Passaic, N.J., Oct. 17, 1950; d. J. Murray and Lillian (Biller) Lieberman; m. Felipe A. Remolador, July 19, 1975. BA in Psychology, Douglass Coll., 1972; cert., NYU, 1973, U. So. Calif., 1988; MBA, Rutgers U., 1985. Rsch. asst. Harvard U., Cambridge, Mass., 1973-76; mgr., programmer, system architect New Eng. Telephone, Boston, 1978-80; programmer John Hancock Mut. Life, Boston, 1976-78; dist. mgr. computer systems AT&T, Morristown, N.J., 1981-89, div. mgr. human resources, 1990—. Mem. Human Resources System Profls., Assn. for Women in Computing, Am. Contract Bridge League, Beta Gamma Sigma. Office: AT&T 1 Speedwell Ave W Morristown NJ 07960

RENCEHAUSEN, LINDA MARY, safety manager; b. Springfield, Mass., Feb. 1, 1950; d. Victor Frank and Lorraine Ruth (Perusse) Antienowicz; 1 child, Will. BS in Microbiology, Ariz. State U., 1977. Microbiology technician Armour-Dial, Phoenix, 1976; histology technician Phoenix Meml. Hosp., 1977-78; soils technician U.S. Forest Service, Flagstaff, Ariz., 1979; secondary sch. tchr. Logan (N.Mex.) Schs., 1980-81, Ft. Sumner (N.Mex.) Schs., 1981-83; industrial hygienist Westinghouse Electric Co., Carlsbad, N.Mex., 1984-89; mgr. safety and plant prodn. Westinghouse Elec. Co., Carlsbad, N.Mex., 1989—. Assoc. safety profl. Served with USMC, 1968-70. Mem. Am. Soc. Safety Engrs., Am. Indsl. Hygiene Assn., Bd. of Cert. Safety Profls. Republican. Roman Catholic. Home: 2835 Western Way Carlsbad NM 88220 Office: Westinghouse Electric PO Box 2078 Carlsbad NM 88221

RENDAL, CAMILLE LYNN, artist; b. San Jose, Calif., Apr. 1, 1955; d. Lloyd Eugene and Madelyn (Bruno) R. BFA, Otis Parsons Sch. Design, L.A., 1981. Art educator, dept. chmn. Crossroads Sch. for the Arts & Scis., Santa Monica, Calif., 1981-88; profl. artist L.A., 1984—. Artist posters; created commemorative postage stamp Halley's Comet, 1985. Recipient Kay Neilsen Young Talent award, L.A. County Museum of Art, 1980, Cert. for Inspired Teaching, Nat. Found. for Advancement in Arts, N.Y.C., 1989; scholarship Parsons Sch. Design, L.A., 1980, 81. Mem. NOW, Rosicrucian Order. Democrat.

RENDELL, RUTH BARBARA, novelist; b. Feb. 17, 1930; d. Arthur Grasemann and Ebba Kruse; m. Donald Rendell, 1950; 1 son. Student, Loughton County High Sch., Eng. Author: From Doon with Death, 1964, To Fear a Painted Devil, 1965, Vanity Dies Hard, 1966, A New Lease of Death, 1967, Wolf to the Slaughter, 1967, The Secret House of Death, 1968, The Best Man to Die, 1969, A Guilty Thing Surprised, 1970, One Across Two Down, 1971, No More Dying Then, 1971, Murder Being Once Done, 1972, Some Lie and Some Die, 1973, The Face of Trespass, 1974, Shake Hands for Ever, 1975, A Demon in my View, 1976, A Judgement in Stone, 1977, A Sleeping Life, 1978, Make Death Love Me, 1979, The Lake of Darkness, 1980, Put on by Cunning, 1981, Master of the Moor, 1982, The Speaker of Mandarin, 1983, The Killing Doll, 1984, The Tree of Hands, 1984, An Unkindness of Ravens, 1985, Live Flesh, 1986 (Gold Dagger award Crime Writers Assn. Eng.), Heartstones, 1987, Talking to Strange Men, 1987, The Veiled One, 1988, The Bridesmaid, 1989, Ruth Rendell's Suffolk, 1989; (as Barbara Vine) A Dark-Adapted Eye, 1986, A Fatal Inversion, 1987, The House of Stairs, 1988; short stories The Fallen Curtain, 1976, Means of Evil, 1979, The Fever Tree, 1982, The New Girl Friend, 1985 (Edgar Allen Poe award Mystery Writers Assn. Am.), Collected Short Stories, 1987. Recipient Arts Council Nat. Book award, 1981. Address: Nussteads, Polstead, Suffolk England*

RENDER, ARLEEN, ambassador. Formerly dep. chief of mission Accra, Ghana; mem. Sr. Seminar Dept. of State; amb. to The Gambia, 1990—. Address: Embassy of U S, Banjul Dept of State Washington DC 20521-2070*

RENDER, ROBYN ROBERTS, data processing executive; b. Cin., Aug. 28, 1953; d. Lucius G. and Edna (Green) Roberts; m. Michael B. Render; children: Michael B. II, Rae Marie. BS in Info. Systems, U. Cin., 1978. Lic. real estate assoc., N.J. Programmer LeBlond, Inc., Cin., 1975-76; programmer, analyst AT&T Long Lines, Cin., 1976-79; mgr. systems devel. AT&T Communications, Piscatawat, N.J., 1980-86; dir. adminstrv. data processing U. Cin., 1986—; recruiter minority programmers AT&T Communications, Morristown, N.J., 1984-85; co-owner Experience Dance Theater, Cin., 1977-79; real estate relocation referrals Wiechert County Realtors, Hillsborough, N.J., 1984-85. Mem. Black Women's Leadership Caucus, Cin., 1977-78; panelist Career Devel. Workshop, Cin., 1988. Mem. CAUSE. Office: U Cin 2900 Reading Rd ML 149 Cincinnati OH 45206

RENDL-MARCUS, MILDRED, artist, economist; b. N.Y.C., May 30, 1928; d. Julius and Agnes (Hokr) Rendl. BS, NYU, 1948, MBA, 1950; PhD (Dean Bernice Brown Cronkhite fellow 1950-51), Radcliffe Coll., 1954; m. Edward Marcus, Aug. 10, 1956. Economist, GE, 1953-56, Bigelow-Sanford Carpet Co., Inc., 1956-58; lectr. econs. evening sessions CCNY, 1953-58; rsch. investment problems in tropical Africa, 1958-59; instr. econs. Hunter Coll. CUNY, 1959-60; lectr. econs. Columbia U., 1960-61; rsch. econ. devel. Nigeria, West Africa, 1961-63; sr. economist Internat. div. Nat. Indsl. Conf. Bd., 1963-66; asst. prof. Grad. Sch. Bus. Adminstrn., Pace Coll., 1964-66; assoc. prof. Borough of Manhattan Community Coll., CUNY, 1966-71, prof., 1972-85; vis. prof. Fla. Internat. U., 1986; prin. MRM Assocs., Rendl Fine Art; corp. art econ. cons.; fine arts appraiser; participant Internat. Economical Meeting, Amsterdam, 1968, Econs. of Fine Arts in Age of Tech., 1984, Internat. Economic Assn. N.Am., Laredo, Tex., 1987-88, Soc. Southwestern Economists, San Antonio, 1988, New Orleans, 1989, Dallas, 1989, S.W. Soc. Economists, 1990, Western Econ. Assn. Internat., 1990, Ind. U. Pa., 1990. Exhibited New Canaan Art Show, 1982, 83, 84, 85, New Canaan Soc. for Arts Ann., 1983, 85, New Canaan Arts, 1985, Silvermine Galleries, 1986, Stamford Art Assn., 1987, Women in the Arts at Phoenix Gallery, Group Show, N.Y.C., 1988, Parkview Point Gallery, Miami Beach, Fla., 1982-89, Art Complex, New Canaan, 1988-89; group shows include Lever House, N.Y.C., 1990, Cork Gallery, Lincoln Ctr., N.Y.C., 1990, Women's Caucus for Art, San Antonio, 1990; symposium participant Sienna, Italy, 1988, South Fla. Art Ctr., Miami Beach, 1990; contbr. articles to Women in the Arts newsletter, 1986-87, Coalition Womens Art Orgns., 1986-87. Bd. dirs. N.Y.C. Coun. on Econ. Edn., 1970—; mem. program planning com. Women's Econ. Roundtable; participant Eastern Econ. Assn., Boston, 1988, Art and Personal Property Appraisal, NYU, 1986-88. Recipient Disting. Svc. award CUNY, 1985. Fellow Gerontol. Assn.; mem. Internat. Schumpeter Econs. Soc. (founding), Am. (vice chmn. ann. meeting 1973), Met. (sec. 1954-56) econ. assns., Indsl. Rels. Rsch. Assn., Audubon Artists and Nat. Soc. Painters in Casein (assoc. 1987-88) Allied Social Sci. Assn. (vice chmn. conv. 1973), AAUW, N.Y.C. Women in Arts, Women's Econ. Roundtable, NYU Grad. Sch. Bus. Adminstrn. Alumni (sec. 1956-58), Radcliffe Club, Women's City Club (art and landmarks com.). Author: (with husband) Investment and Development of Tropical Africa, 1959, International Trade and Finance, 1965, Monetary and Banking Theory, 1965; Economics, 1969; (with husband) Principles of Economics, 1969; Economic Progress and the Developing World, 1970; Economics, 1978; also monographs and articles in field. Econ. and internat. rsch. on industrialization less developed areas, internat. debtor nations and workability of buffer stock schemes, pricing fine art; columnist economics of art Women in Art. Home: 928 West Rd New Canaan CT 06840 Office: Art Complex PO Box 814 New Canaan CT 06840 also: 7441 Wayne Ave Miami Beach FL 33141

RENEAU, SUSAN CAMPBELL, marketing professional; b. Jacksonville, N.C., July 15, 1952; d. Frederick Hollister and Amy (Strohm) Campbell; m. William John Reneau, Apr. 6, 1974; children: John, Robert, Richard. BA magna cum laude, U. No. Colo., 1974; MS in Bus. and Pub. Rels. with honors, Am. U., 1987. Reporter numerous newspapers and jours., Calif., 1976-88; mktg. dir. Colo. Big Game Trophy Records, 1980—; pub. info. officer No. Va. Community Coll., Annandale, Va., 1983-88; mktg., publs. dir. Am. Assn. of Community and Jr. Colls., Washington, 1988-90; mktg., publs. dir. Am. Assn. Community and Jr. Colls., Washington 1988-90; pub. rels. cons., Va., Calif., 1979-88; cons. Dulles Internat. Airport, Va., 1987, Prince William County Supr., Va., 1985-88, Reston Devel., Va., 1987, Smithsonian Inst., Washington, 1979, So. Trinity Area Rescue, 1979-83. Co-author: Colorado's Biggest Bucks and Bulls, 1984, Adventures of Moccasin Joe: Scarhead the Crazy Scout, 1990. Mem. ASAE, Press Club, Women in Pub. Rels., Soroptimist Internat. (v.p. 1986-90, sec. 1985 Woodbridge chpt.). Republican. Presbyterian.

RENEGAR, LAURA ESTELLE, behavioral health therapist; b. Spartenburg, S.C., Feb. 8, 1964; d. Elmer G. and mary Dellora (Rouse) R. BS in Psychology, No. Ariz. U., Flagstaff, 1986, MA in Psychology, 1988. Behavioral health therapist Inst. Human Svcs., Scottsdale, Ariz., 1988—; pain and stress cons. Phoenix Humana Hosp., 1989—; vol. Ariz. State Hosp., Phoenix, 1989—. Mem. Am. Psychol. Assn. (assoc.), Phi Kappa Phi (life). Democrat. Presbyterian. Office: Cathie S O'Connell Phd PC Ctr Med Clinic 4444 N 32nd ST Ste 150 Phoenix AZ 85018

RENER, JACQUELINE KATHLEEN, accountant; b. Bitburg, Ger., May 7, 1959; came to U.S. 1961; d. William Herman and Theresa Jeanne (Wise) R. BS in Fin., Ind. State U., 1982. Acct. City of Terre Haute, Ind., 1983-87; acctg. mgr. Knapp Office Supply & Equip., Terre Haute, 1987-88; acctg. asst./personnel asst. Data Label, Inc., Terre Haute, 1988—. Mem. White River Park State Games orgnaizing com., reg. support and fin. chmn. Mem. Am. Soc. Women Accts., Nat. Fedn. Bus. and Profl. Women's Clubs. Democrat. Roman Catholic. Address: 1032 Helen Ave Terre Haute IN 47802

RENFRO, MAXINE JUNE, consumer shows producer; b. Grand Rapids, Mich., Feb. 11, 1927; d. Archie Dennis and Gertrude Fern (Nelson) Korb; m. Robert David Kaley, Mar. 1947; 1 child, Mark; m. Harry Edward Renfro, June 1, 1959; children: Daniel Nelson, Todd Ryan, Kevin Dennis. Grad. high sch., Traverse City, Mich. From sec. to treas. Indpls. Boat, Sport and Travel Show, 1972-86, pres., 1986—; pres. Renfro Prodns., Indpls., 1985—. Pres. Fishers, Ind. council PTA, 1968, United Meth. Women, 1980-83; treas. United Meth. Ch., Fishers, 1977-79. Recipient cert. of appreciation Ind. Wild Turkey Fedn., 1983, cert. of appreciation Ind. Bass Fedn., 1986, 87, 88, 89, Ind. Bass'n Gals, 1989. Mem. Internat. Sport Show Producers Assn., Internat. Assn. Travel Exhibitors, Am. Fishing Tackle Manufacturers Assn., Nat. Assn. Consumer Shows, Indpls. C. of C. Republican. Office: Indpls Boat Sport Travel Show 2511 E 46th St #E-2 Indianapolis IN 46205

RENFROE, JANICE MARIE, association executive; b. Redlands, Calif., Feb. 8, 1954; d. Robert Francis and Verna Marie (Carter) McVein; m. William Thomas Renfroe, Jr., Apr. 2, 1988; children: Cameron Robert, William Thomas III. BA in Art History, Portland State U., 1989. Grant program rep. HUD, Portland, Oreg., 1976-83; grant project mgr. Oreg. Exec. Dept., Salem, 1983; grant program officer Portland Community Devel., 1983-86; grant projects coord. Oreg. Dept. Environ. Quality, Portland, 1986-87; grants officer Oreg. Art Inst., Portland, 1987-89; exec. dir. N.W. Print Coun., Portland, 1989—. Bd. dirs. Portland French Am. Sch. Mem. Nat. Soc. Fund Raising Execs., Am. Assn. Mus., Coll. Art Assn., Willamette Valley Devel. Officers, Assn. Art Historians, NAFE.

RENICK, CAROL BISHOP, insurance planning company executive; b. Arlington, Mass., June 5, 1956; d. Francis Joseph and Mary Ruth (Robinson) Bishop; m. Lawrence A. Balboni, May 5, 1979 (div. 1982); m. Gary L. Renick, Jan. 31, 1986. Student anthropology, Harvard U., 1983-85, 87—. Mgr. Larson Ins., Arlington, 1979-85, v.p., 1987-88; mgr. Merrill Lynch Realty Ins. Svcs., Boca Raton, Fla., 1985-87; pres. Essex Ins. Planners, Haverhill, Mass., 1988—. Vol. Mus. Sci., Boston, 1988; tutor Mass. Campaign for Literacy, 1988—. Mem. Profl. Ins. Agts., Inc. Democrat. Roman Catholic. Office: Essex Ins Planners PO Box 1552 Haverhill MA 01831

RENICK, MICHELE DIANE, account executive; b. Miami, Oct. 15, 1963; d. Ralph Appearson and Elizabeth (Henry) R. AA in Communications, Dean Jr. Coll., 1983; BS, Fla. Internat. U., 1986. Licensed notary public. Event coord. Fla. Internat. U., Miami, 1985-86; mgr. Sunset Harbour Marina, 1987-88; promotions asst. Penrod's Beach Club, Miami Beach, 1988-89; mktg. coord., acct. exec. Holiday Inn, Miami Beach, 1989—; Mem. Hotel Mktg. Assn. Fla., NAFE, Am. Cancer Soc., Miami Beach C. of C., North Dade C. of C. Mem. Hotel Mktg. Assn. Fla., NAFE, Miami Beach C. of C., North Dade C. of C. Roman Catholic. Home: 1579 NE 104th St Miami Shores FL 33138

RENICK, SUSAN GARNER, school system administrator; b. Birmingham, Ala., Nov. 30, 1945; d. John Chester and Eloise (Fisher) Garner; m. Robert

Renick, Oct. 2, 1975 (div. Nov. 1984). BS, U. Montevallo, 1969; MA with honors, U. Ala., 1975; Cert., U. No. Colo., 1976, Fla. Internat. U., 1979. Cert. exceptional student edn. adminstr., Fla., IRLEN screener. Tchr. vocat. edn. Jefferson County Pub. Schs., Hewitt-Trussville, Ala., 1969, reading tchr. for mentally retarded, 1974-75; tchr. learning disabilitites Dade County Pub. Schs., Miami, Fla., 1975-77, specialist exceptional student placement, 1977-78, dir. exceptional student, 1978—; assoc. prof. Nova U., 1989; ednl. cons. emotionally disturbed children Charter Hosp., Miami, 1987; awards chmn. Broader Opportunities for Learning Disabled, 1986-89; bd. dirs. Fla. Diagnostic Learning Resources Ctr., Miami; area rep. to feeder pattern adv. bd. NMB Feeder Pattern Prin.'s Coun.; various appointments Fla. Dept. Edn., including com. chmn. tchr. of yr. selection com., chmn. office employee of yr. Com. mem. Miami-Metro Action Plan, 1986—, Very Spl. Art Commn., 1988-89; mem. Greater Miami Drug Coun., 1987; chmn. North Cen. area campaign United Way, 1987; adv. bd. Coun. Exceptional Children, 1988-89; advisor hearing impaired commn. State Dept. Edn., 1988-89; designer, implementer crisis intervention psychol. team north area DCPS;. Recipient Awards of Appreciation, 1975—. Mem. Fla. Assn. Sch. Adminstrs., Coun. Exceptional Children (com. mem. Spl. Olympics, Birmingham area 1973-75, region coordinating prin. of yr., 1990), Assn. for Children with Learning Disabilities, Dade Assn. Sch. Psychologists, Fla. Council Adminstrs. Spl. Edn., U. Montevallo Alumni Assn., Family Christian Assn. Am., Phi Delta Kappa (hon.). Democrat. Office: Dade County Pub Schs Region II Adminstrv Office 14027 NE 16th Ct Miami FL 33181

RENIKOFF, ELIZABETH THERESE, marketing executive; b. Mpls., Aug. 16, 1964; d. Patrick Gregory Fairley and Leanne Kay (Solem) Clipper; m. Richard Alan Renikoff, May 14, 1961. BA in Mktg. and Mgmt., Augsburg Coll., 1988. Phone banker Norwest Bank Mpls., 1983-85; analyst technician Target Stores, Inc., Mpls., 1985-87; cost acct. adminstrv. asst. Honeywell, Inc., Golden Valley, Minn., 1987-88; mktg. product mgr. GE Capital Fleet Svcs., Eden Prairie, Minn., 1988—. Intern, Visitation Parochial Sch., Mpls., 1988, Instrumentation Svcs., Golden Valley, 1988. Mem. Am. Mktg. Assn. Lutheran. Office: GE Capital Fleet Svcs 3 Capital Dr Eden Prairie MN 55344

RENKAR-JANDA, JARRI J., paint manufacturing executive; b. Chicago Heights, Ill., Feb. 26, 1951; d. Eugene N. and RoseMarie (Morgenson) Zar; m. Leonard F. Renkar (div.); 1 child, Sandra R.; m. James E. Janda. Student, Northeastern Ill. U., 1978, Harper Jr. Coll., 1978, Mundelein Coll., 1979-80. Acctg. clk. Wittek Mfg., Chgo., 1970-73; credit clk. McKesson Chem., Chgo., 1973, purchasing agt., 1973-76; product supply mgr. Gen. Paint and Chem., Cary, Ill., 1976-78; purchasing mgr. Glidden Coatings and Resins, Chgo., 1978-80, Columbus and Oakwood, Ga., 1980-84; purchasing mgr. paint div. Ace Hardware Corp., Matteson, Ill., 1984-87, materials mgr. paint div., 1987—. Counselor Shelter for Battered Women, Gainesville, Ga., 1982. Mem. Chgo. Paint and Coating Assn. (buyers com. 1985-87), Chgo. Soc. Coatings (mfg. com. 1986-87), Chgo. Paint and Coatings Assn. (golf com. 1986-88). Office: Ace Hardware Corp Paint div 21901 S Central Ave Matteson IL 60443

RENKENS, MADELINE A., lawyer. BA, U. Rochester, N.Y., 1973; MLS, Queens Coll., 1974; JD cum laude, Fordham U., 1979. Bar: N.Y. 1980, Conn. 1981, Wash. 1984, Alaska 1986, U.S. Dist. Ct. Alaska, U.S. Dist. Ct. (so. dist.) N.Y., U.S. Dist. Ct. (we. dist.) Wash., U.S. Ct. Appeals (9th cir.), U.S. Supreme Ct. Tchr., library media specialist Southampton (N.Y.) Pub. Schs., 1974-76; law clk. U.S. Dept. Justice, 1978-79, trial atty. anti-trust div., 1979-82; assoc. Willkie Farr & Gallagher, N.Y.C., 1982-84, Barokas & Martin, Seattle, 1984-87; pvt. practice Snohomish, Wash., 1987—. Mem. adv. bd. Snohomish Police Dept.; bd. dirs. Everett (Wash.) Rowing Assn. Mem. Snohomish Hist. Soc., Snohomish County Hist. Soc., USCG Aux. Home and Office: 329 Ave C Snohomish WA 98290

RENNE, LOUISE HORNBECK, city attorney; b. Pitts., Aug. 26, 1937; d. Lewis Alvin and Anne (Bartrem) Hornbeck; m. Paul A. Renne, July 11, 1959; Christine, Anne. BA, Mich. State U., 1958; postgrad. law, Harvard U., 1958-59, U. Pa., 1959-61; JD, Columbia U., 1961. Bar: Calif. 1964, D.C. 1961, U.S. Supreme Ct. 1969. With broadcast bur., office gen. counsel FCC, 1961-64; assoc. Peterson & Barr, San Francisco, 1964-66; dep. atty. gen. State of Calif., San Francisco, 1966-77; pres. Calif. Women Lawyers, San Francisco, 1977-78; mem. bd. Suprs., San Francisco, 1978-86; city atty. San Francisco, 1986—; lectr. Golden Gate U., U. San Francisco. Office: Office of City Atty Room 206 City Hall San Francisco CA 94102 Home: 3725 Jackson St San Francisco CA 94115

RENNICK, HILDA MAY, retired educator; b. Kansas City, Kans., Nov. 24, 1902; d. Shelby Hudson and Charlotte (Morris) R. BS in Edn., Kans. State U., 1935; MA in Edn., U. Mo., Kansas City, 1950. Cert. primary tchr. Classroom tchr. Kansas City (Kans.) Pub. Schs., 1920-72. Author: Jiffy to Jenna, 1990. Vol. storyteller. Named One of Kans. Outstanding Citizens, 1975. Mem. NEA (life), AAUW (life), Nat. Parent Tchr. Assn. (life), Kans. State Retired Tchr. Assn. (life), Kans. Tchr. Assn., DAR, Daus. of Am. Colonists (treas.), Magna Charta Dames (life).

RENNICK, KYME ELIZABETH WALL, lawyer; b. Columbus, Ohio, Dec. 27, 1953; d. Robert Leroy and Julie (Allison) Wall; m. Ian Alexander Rennick, Oct. 15, 1983; 1 child, Daniel Alexander. BA, Centre Coll., 1975; MA, Ohio State U., 1978; JD, Capital U., 1982. Bar: Ohio 1982, U.S. Dist. Ct. (no. and so. dists.) Ohio 1983. Legal intern Ohio Dept. Natural Resources, Columbus, 1981-83, gen. counsel, 1983-86, chief counsel, 1986—. Editor: Baldwin's Ohio Revised Code Annotated, Title 15 Conservation of Natural Resources, 1984. Mem. ABA, Columbus Bar Assn. Presbyterian. Office: Ohio Dept Natural Resources Fountain Sq Bldg D-3 Columbus OH 43224

RENNINGER, JANE FRANCES, military officer; b. Quakertown, Pa., May 29, 1943; d. John Louis and Marion Myrtle Renninger. BS in Math., Pa. State U., 1965; MS in Computer Sci., Naval Postgrad. Sch., 1975. Commd. ensign USN, 1965; advanced through grades to capt., 1984. Mem. NAFE, U.S. Naval Inst., Pa. State U. Alumni Assn. (life). Office: USN Computer and Telecommunications Sta San Diego CA 92135-5110

RENSE, PAIGE, editor, publishing company executive. Student, Calif. State U., Los Angeles. Editor-in-chief Archtl. Digest, Los Angeles, 1970—; sr. v.p., also bd. dirs. Knapp Communications Corp. Recipient Nat. Headliner Women in Communications award, 1983, Pacifica award So. Calif. Resources Coun., 1978, Editorial award Dallas Mkt. Ctr., 1978, Golden award Chgo. Design Resources Svc., 1982, Agora award, 1982, Outstanding Profls. in Communications award, 1982, Trailblazers award, 1983, ; named Woman of Yr. Los Angeles Times, 1976, Woman of Yr. Muses, 1986; named to Interior Design Hall of Fame. Office: Archtl Digest 5900 Wilshire Blvd Los Angeles CA 90036

RENSHAW-ZEASON, CHERYL R., nurse paralegal; b. Oakland, Calif., Aug. 11, 1952; d. Waverly D. and Shirley J. (Parson) Krueger; m. William F. Zeason, June 16, 1990; children: Scott, Jenna. Diploma in Nursing, Meth. Hosp., Peoria, Ill., 1973; BS, St. Francis, Joliet, Ill., 1982. Cert. paralegal, psychiatric and mental health nurse. Med./surgical staff nurse St. Mary's Hosp., Decatur, Ill., 1973-80; emergency nurse Victory Hosp., Waukegan, Ill., 1980-83; acute psychiatric nurse North Chgo. (Ill.) Med. Ctr., 1983-86, acute psychiatric head nurse, 1986-89; claims analyst Coronia Corp., Des Plaines, Ill., 1989-90; nurse paralegal Sussman, Selig, Ross, Chgo., 1990—. Home: 10405 West Ford Ave Zion IL 60099

RENT, CLYDA STOKES, academic administrator; b. Jacksonville, Fla., Mar. 1, 1942; d. Clyde Parker Stokes Sr. and Edna Mae (Edwards) Shuemake; m. George Seymour Rent, Aug. 12, 1966; 1 child, Cason Lynley. BA, Fla. State U., 1964, MA, 1966, PhD, 1968. Asst. prof. Western Carolina U., Cullowhee, N.C., 1968-70; asst. prof. Queens Coll., Charlotte, N.C., 1972-74, dept. chair, 1974-78, dean Grad. Sch. and New Coll., 1979-84, v.p. for Grad. Sch. and New Coll., 1984-85, v.p. acad. affairs, 1985-87, v.p. community affairs, 1987-89; pres. Miss. U. for Women, Columbus, 1989—; cons. Coll. Bd., N.Y.C., 1983-89; sci. cons. N.C. Alcohol Rsch. Authority, Chapel Hill, 1976-89. Author rsch. articles in acad. jours.; speeches pub. in Observer; mem. editorial bds. acad. jours. Trustee N.C. Performing Arts Ctr., Charlotte, 1988-89, Charlotte County Day Sch., 1987-89; bd. visitors Johnson C. Smith U., Charlotte, 1985-89; exec. com. bd. dirs. United Way Allocations and Rev., Charlotte, 1982-88; bd. advisors Charlotte Mecklenburg Hosp. Authority, 1985-89; bd. dirs. Jr. Achievement, Charlotte, 1983-89; chmn. bd. dirs. Arts and Sci. Coun., Charlotte, 1987-88; Danforth assoc. Danforth Found., St. Louis, 1976-88. Named Prof. of Yr. Queens Coll., 1978-79; grantee Ford Found., N.Y.C., 1981. Mem. Am. Sociol. Assn., So. Sociol. Soc. (state membership chair 1978-79), N.C. Assn. Colls. and Univs. (exec. com. 1988-89), N.C. Assn. Acad. Officers (sec.-treas. 1987-88), N.C. Sociol. Soc. (bd. dirs., exec. com. 1973-76), Conf. So. Grad. Schs. (planning com. 1981-84), University Club (Jackson, Miss.) Old Waverly Country Club (West Point, Miss.), Rotary (1st female mem. Columbus chpt.). Office: Miss U Women Office of Pres PO Box W-1602 Columbus MS 39701*

RENTER, LOIS IRENE HUTSON, librarian; b. Lowden, Iowa, Oct. 23, 1929; d. Thomas E. and Lulu Mae (Barlean) Hutson; m. Karl A. Renter, Jan. 3, 1948; children: Susan Elizabeth, Rebecca Jean, Karl Geoffrey. BA cum laude, Cornell Coll., Mt. Vernon, Iowa, 1965; MA, U. Iowa, 1968. Tchr. Spanish, Mt. Vernon High Sch., 1965-67; head libr. Am. Coll. Testing Program, Iowa City, Iowa, 1968-89, ret. 1989; vis. instr. U. Iowa Sch. Library Sci., 1972—. Mem. Spl. Libraries Assn., Phi Beta Kappa. Methodist. Home: 1125 29th St Marion IA 52302

RENTERIA, CHERYL CHRISTINA, federal agency administrator; b. Corpus Christi, Tex., May 11, 1944; d. C.J. and Nazelle (Smart) Casey; m. Carlos Raymundo Renteria, Oct. 17, 1975; children: Crissa Cybele, Cori Renee. Grad. Inst. U.S. & World Affairs, Am. U., 1965; BA, Tex. Christian U., 1966. Inventory mgmt. specialist Tinker AFB, Oklahoma City, 1966-67; with U.S. Dept. HUD, 1967—; chief housing programs region VI U.S. Dept. HUD, Ft. Worth, 1988—. Pres. Dallas Office Orgn. Women, 1974-75; treas. Fed. Women's Program coun., Dallas, 1977-78; bd. dirs. Ballet Guild Ft. Worth, 1984-88, treas. 1985, v.p. 1986-88; bd. dirs. lectr. series U. Tex., Arlington, 1987—, Dance Theatre Arlington, 1987—, Planned Parenthood North Tex., 1988-90. Smith scholar, 1966. Mem. Exec. Women in Govt. (pres. 1989-90), Fed. Bus. Assn., Arlington Fine Arts Coun., Internat. Sister Cities, Arlington Opera Assn., Friends Univ. Tex. Libr., Symphony Soc. Tarrant County (editor newsletter 1984), Jr. Woman's Club Decortique (v.p. 1977), Woman's Club of Ft. Worth, Delta Gamma (pres. house corp. 1985, 86, bd. dirs. 1987—, chair Province leadership seminar 1987, corres. 1984). Home: 1115 Montreau Ct Arlington TX 76012 Office: US Dept HUD PO Box 2905 Fort Worth TX 76113-2905

RENTZEL, CATHARINE RASMUSSEN, catalog and electronic publishing consultant; b. Quonset Point, R.I., June 29, 1951; d. John E. and Catherine (Clark) Rasmussen; m. Christopher H. Rentzel, May 25, 1974 (div. Dec. 1988); children: Kelly, Lynn, Christin. BA, Sweet Briar (Va.) Coll., 1973. Legal asst. U.S. Congress, Washington, 1973-75; game mgr., pub. rels. So. Meth. U., Dallas, 1979-83; computer trainer Vroom, Inc., Dallas, 1985—, cons., acct. mgr., 1988—; cons. Jr. League Dallas, 1988-90, Ctr. for Non Profit Mgmt., Dallas, 1985-87; speaker, sem. coord. Direct Mktg. Assn., N.Y.C., 1990; coord., cons. mail order catalog Am. Eagle Outfitters, 1988. Vol. Jr. League Dallas, 1982—, Highland Park United Meth. Ch., Dallas, 1982—. Mem. Phi Beta Kappa. Office: Vroom Inc 2200 N Lamar #205 Dallas TX 75202

REPKO, CHERYL BEATRICE, lawyer; b. Cleve., Mar. 2, 1951; d. John Paul and Beatrice Julia (Skala) R. BA in English, Mich. State U., 1973; JD, U. Denver, 1984. Bar: D.C. 1985. With U.S. Dept. Justice and IRS, various locations, 1978—; with office of dist. counsel IRS, Denver, 1986—. Contbr. articles on chronic fatigue and immune dysfunction syndrome. Co-founder, Chronic Fatigue Syndrome Rsch. Found. Inc., Denver, 1988, bd. dirs., sec., 1988-89. Mem. Mich. State U. Alumni Assn. Democrat. Roman Catholic. Home: 1149 Columbine St Apt 204 Denver CO 80206

REPLOGLE, KATRINIA SUE, research chemist; b. Morristown, N.J., Oct. 19, 1956; d. Joe Oliver and Mary Martha (McCurdy) R. AB, Mt. Holyoke Coll., 1978; MS, Cornell U., 1981, PhD, 1984. Rsch. chemist E.I. Du Pont de Nemours & Co., Towanda, Pa., 1984-90, staff rsch. chemist, 1990—. Mem. Am. Chem. Soc., AAUW, Phi Beta Kappa, Sigma Xi (assoc.). Office: EI Du Pont de Nemours & Co RD 1 Box 15 Towanda PA 18848

REPP, JOAN MERCEDES, librarian; b. N.Y.C., Oct. 24, 1930; d. Paul Francis and Anna Crescentia (Stock) McIntyre; m. Victor E. Repp, Sept. 3, 1949; children: Anna, James. BS, State Tchrs. Coll., Oswego, N.Y., 1951; MEd, U. Md., 1954; AMLS, U. Mich., 1974. Cert. elem. educator. Tchr. Arlington County (Va.) Schs., 1951-57, Perrysburg (Ohio) Pub. Schs., 1968-69; from instr. English and libr. to head cataloging dept. Bowling Green (Ohio) State U., 1972-82, chmn. access svc., 1983-87, dir. access svcs., 1987—; cons. State Libr. Ohio, Columbus, 1980-83; workshop dir. N.W. Libr. Dist., North Cen. Libr. Consortium, Ohio Ednl. Libr. and Media Assn., Ohio, Dade County Libr. Assn., 1984. Contbr. articles to profl. jours. Svc. unit dir. Girl Scouts of Am., Toledo, Ohio, 1963-67; mem. Environ. Health Coun. Ohio and Mich., 1964; cons. Ronald McDonald House, Toledo, 1987—. Mem. AAUP, ALA, Acad. Libr. Assn. Ohio, Assn. Coll. and Rsch. Librs., Libr. Adminstrn. and Mgmt. Assn., Resources and Tech. Svcs. Assn., Mensa, Beta Phi Mu, Kappa Delta Pi. Office: Bowling Green State U Jerome Libr Bowling Green OH 43403

REPPERT, NANCY LUE, county official; b. Kansas City, Mo., June 17, 1933; d. James Everett and Iris R. (Moomey) Moore; m. James E. Cassidy, 1952 (div.); children: James E., II, Tracy C. Student Cen. Mo. State U., 1951-52, U. Mo., Kansas City, 1971-75; cert. legal asst., Rockhurst Coll., Kansas City, Mo., 1980; cert. risk mgr., 1979. With Kansas City (Mo.) chpt. ARC, 1952-54, N. Cen. region Boy Scouts Am., 1963-66, Clay County Health Dept., Liberty, Mo., 1966-71, City of Liberty, 1971-80; risk mgr. City of Ames (Iowa), 1980-82; risk mgr. City of Dallas, 1982-83; dir. Dept. Risk Mgmt., Pinellas County, Fla., 1984—; mem. faculty William Jewell Coll., Liberty, 1975-80; vis. prof. U. Kans., 1981; adj. prof. public sci. masters program U. So. Fla., 1990; seminar leader, cons in field. Lay minister United Meth. Ch., 1965—; dir. youth devel. Hillside United Meth. Ch., Liberty; co-chmn. youth dir. Collegiate United Meth. Ch. scouting coord. Palm Lake Christian Ch., Exec. Fellow U. South Fla., mem. Coun. of Ministries; advancement chmn. Mid-Iowa Coun. Boy Scouts Am., membership chmn. White Rock Dist. coun., health and safety chmn. West Cen. Fla. coun., 1985—; scouting coord., chmn. youth dept., bd. dirs., pastor's cabinet, diaconate Palm Lake Christian Ch., 1987—; skipper Sea Explorer ship, 1986—. Recipient Order of Merit, Boy Scouts Am., 1979, Living Sculpture award, 1978,79; Svc. award Rotary Internat., 1979; Exec. fellow U. South Fla., 1988. Mem. NAFE, Am. Mgmt. Assns., Internat Platform Assn., Risk and Ins. Mgrs. Soc., Pub. Risk & Ins. Mgmt. Assn., Am. Soc. Profl. & Exec. Women, Am. Film Inst., U.S. Naval Inst., Nat. Inst. Mcpl. Law Officers. Author: Kids Are People, Too, 1975. Pearls of Potentiality, 1980; also articles. Home: Blind Pass Marina 9555 Blind Pass Rd St Petersburg Beach FL 33706 Office: 400 S Ft Harrison Clearwater FL 34616

REPPERT, SUSANNA REBECCA, herbal gift shop wholesale/retail executive; b. Mechanicsburg, Pa., June 4, 1962; d. Byron Leibold and Bertha Ottylia (Peplau) R. B Social Sci., Pa. State U., 1985. Sales clk. The Rosemary House, Inc., Mechanicsburg, 1972-82, mgr., 1982—, v.p. corp., 1985—; lectr., cons. and tour dir. Editor Master Sprouts, 1989—; contbr. articles and photographs to profl. jours. Intern Nat. Herb Garden, Nat. Arboretum, Washington, 1988; state sec. Pa. State Master Gardners, Pa. State Extension, 1989—. Mem. Internat. Herb Growers and Marketers Assn., Herb Soc. Am., Pa. Cumberland Garden Club. Republican. Home: 116 S Market St Mechanicsburg PA 17055 Office: The Rosemary House Inc 120 S Market St Mechanicsburg PA 17055

REPS, CONSTANCE PECK, foreign language professional, educator, retired; b. Birmingham, Mich., Oct. 30, 1921; d. Raymond Henry and Lila Parmenter (Burnett) Peck; m. John William Reps, June 26, 1948; children: Martha Christine, Thomas William. AB, Kalamazoo Coll., 1943; MA, Brown U., 1944. Cert. life tchr., Mich., N.Y. Lang. tchr. Birmingham High Sch., 1943; cryptographer U.S. Army, Washington, 1944; instr. French, Spanish Kalamazoo Coll., 1945-46; asst. prof. French Drury Coll., Springfield, Mo., 1946-48; instr. French Triple-Cities Coll. of Syracuse U. (name now SUNY), Endicott, 1948-50; pvt. tutor French Ithaca, N.Y., 1952-70; tchr. French Boynton Jr. High Sch., Ithaca, 1962-65. Pres. Ithaca High Sch. PTA, 1969-70; candidate Ithaca Sch. Bd., 1971; v.p. Cornell Campus Club, 1976-77, pres., 1977-78; vol. U.S. Rep. Matthew McHugh, Pub. Libr. Book Sale; sec., bd. dirs. Upstairs Gallery 1987-90; bd. dirs., 2d v.p. Tompkins Community Hosp. Aux., 1990—. Mem. AAUW (pres. 1957-58, cultural affairs chmn., chmn. ednl. project for pub. schs.), P.E.O. (chpt AF), Hangar Theatre Support Orgn. (chmn. opera trips, pres. 1979, 80, 81), Phi Kappa Alpha, Alpha Lambda Delta.

RESCH, MARY LOUISE, educational administrator, social services counselor; b. David City, Nebr., Oct. 26, 1956; d. Ernest John and Mary Jean (Roelandts) Cermak; m. Eugene Joseph Resch, Apr. 28, 1979. BS in Psychology, SUNY, Albany, 1984; MS in Counseling and Edn. with high honors, U. Wis., Platteville, 1986. Enlisted U.S. Army, 1974, advance through ranks to sgt., 1982; bomb disposal tech. U.S. Army, Ft. Riley, Kans., 1977-79, Platteville, 1982-85; bomb disposal instr. U.S. Army, Indian Head, Md., 1979-80; resigned U.S. Army, 1985; intern in family advocacy Army Community Service U.S. Army, Ft. Belvoir, 1986; sr. counselor, child therapist Community Crisis and Referral Ctr., Inc., Waldorf, Md., 1986-87; adminstr. Walter Reed Army Med. Ctr. USDA Grad. Sch., Washington, 1987-88; contract mgr. USDA Grad. Sch., Ft. Jackson, N.C., 1988—; instr. family advocacy Army Community Service, Ft. Belvoir, 1986; human services cons., Washington, 1986-87; on-site adminstr. USDA Grad. Sch., Washington, contract mgr., 1988—; adj. instr. Park Coll., Coker Coll., Ft. Jackson, S.C. Mem. NAFE, Am. Assn. for Counseling and Devel., Am. Mental Health Counselors Assn., Mil. Educators and Counselors Assn., Nat. Contract Mgmt. Assn., Assn. of U.S. Army. Democrat. Lutheran. Home: 6305 Saye Ct Columbia SC 29209 Office: USDA Grad Sc 4600 Edn Svc Office Bldg Fort Jackson SC 29207

RESNICK, ALICE ROBIE, state supreme court justice; b. Erie, Pa., Aug. 21, 1939; d. Adam Joseph and Alice Suzanne (Spizarny) Robie; m. Melvin L. Resnick, Mar. 20, 1970. Ph.B., Siena Heights Coll., 1961; J.D., U. Detroit, 1964. Bar: Ohio 1964, Mich. 1965, U.S. Supreme Ct. 1970. Asst. county prosecutor Lucas County Prosecutor's Office, Toledo, 1964-75, trial atty., 1965-75; judge Toledo Mcpl. Ct., 1976-83, 6th Dist. Ct. Appeals, State of Ohio, Toledo, 1983-88; instr. U. Toledo, 1968-69; judge Ohio Supreme Ct., 1989—. Trustee Siena Heights Coll., Adrian, Mich., 1982—; organizer Crime Stopper Inc., Toledo, 1981—; mem. Mayor's Drug Coun.; bd. dirs. Guest House Inc. Mem. ABA, Toledo Bar Assn., Lucas County Bar Assn., Nat. Assn. Women Judges, Am. Judicature Soc., Toledo Women's Bar Assn., Toledo Mus. Art, Internat. Inst. Toledo. Roman Catholic. Home: 2407 Edgehill Rd Toledo OH 43615 Office: Supreme Ct Office 30 E Broad St Columbus OH 43215

RESNICK, CAROL LYN, sales executive; b. Wheeling, W.Va.; d. Edward M. and Annette (Graff) R.; m. Donald Joseph Swartz, Feb. 6, 1990. BEd, Pa. State U., 1968; MEd, U. So. Calif., L.A., 1971. Product mgr. RCA, Hamburg, Germany, 1973-76; mgmt. cons. Alexander Proudfoot Co., Palm Beach, Fla., 1977-81; with Hallmark Cards, Kansas City, Mo., 1982—, sales devel. mgr., 1989—. Bd. dirs. Manchester Humane Soc., Manchester, 1980-83. Mem. NAFE, Greenpeace, World Wildlife Fedn., Wilderness Soc., Internat. Counsel Shopping Ctr. Developers. Home: 41 Belmar Ct Sewell NJ 08080

RESNICK, CYNTHIA BILT, speech and language pathologist; b. Bklyn., Mar. 8, 1946; d. Murray and Helen Francis (Rubin) Bilt; m. Jerry Resnick, June 17, 1967 (dec. 1972). BA cum laude, Marymount Manhattan Coll., 1976; MS in Speech Pathology, Tchrs. Coll., Columbia U., 1978. Lic. speech pathologist, N.Y., Mass. Trainee in speech and lang. clin. pathology Marymount Manhattan Coll., N.Y.C., 1975, Columbia U., N.Y.C., 1976-77, Kennedy Child Study Ctr., N.Y.C., 1977, Beth Abraham Hosp., Bronx, N.Y., 1977; speech and lang. clinician L.I. Jewish-Hillside Med. Ctr., New Hyde Park, N.Y., 1977; tchr. speech and hearing handicapped Good Shepherd Sch., Inwood, N.Y., 1977-78; mem. staff Bur. Speech Improvement, N.Y.C. Bd. Edn., 1978; speech/lang. pathologist and coord. speech/lang. svcs. Lorge Sch., N.Y.C., 1978-80 Summit Sch., N.Y.C., 1980; speech/lang. cons. Forest Hills Nursing Home, 1980-85; speech/lang. cons. Coll. Nursing Home, Flushing, N.Y., 1983-85; pvt. practice, Rego Park, N.Y., 1981—. Recipient hon. mention for acad. excellence in speech sci., Marymount Manhattan Coll., N.Y.C., 1976; citizenship award Roosevelt Prep. Sch., Stamford, Conn., 1963. Mem. Am. (cert.), N.Y. State Speech and Hearing Assns., Mass. Speech Lang. Hearing Assn., Speech Communication Assn. Address: 94-11 59 Ave Ste A7 Rego Park NY 11373

RESNICK, DEBRA B., clinical psychologist; b. Montreal, June 30, 1955; came to U.S., 1981; d. Frank and Sorryl (Cohen) Hoffer; m. Jerome H. Resnick, Aug. 5, 1981; children: Justin, Jonathan. BA, McGill U., 1977; MA, Temple U., 1979; D in Psychology, Hahnemann U., 1986. Lic. psychologist Que., Pa. Staff psychologist Allan Meml. Inst., Montreal, 1980-81; sr. clin. instr. Hahnemann U., Phila., 1986-89, staff psychologist, 1986-89; adj. clin. asst. prof. Widener U., Chester, Pa., 1989—; pvt. practice Elkins Pk., Pa., 1989—; psychology cons. Inpatient Psychodiagnostic Assessment, 1988—. Ad Hoc adv. com. to supt. Sch. Dist. of Cheltenham Twp., Elkins Pk., 1988. Mem. Am. Psychol. Assn., Pa. Psychol. Assn., Que. Corp. Psychologists, Phila. Soc. Clin. Psychologists. Jewish. Home: 328 Marvin Rd Elkins Park PA 19117

RESNICK, STEPHANIE, lawyer; b. N.Y.C., Nov. 12, 1959; d. Ronald and Diane Gross. AB, Kenyon Coll., 1981; JD, Villanova U., 1984. Bar: Pa. 1984, N.J. 1984, U.S. Dist. Ct. (ea. dist.) Pa. 1984, U.S. Dist. Ct. N.J. 1984. Assoc. Cozen and O'Connor, Phila., 1984-87, Fox, Rothschild, O'Brien & Frankel, Phila., 1987—. Active Vols. for the Indigent Program, Phila., 1987—; mem. investigative div. Commn. Jud. Selection and Retention, Phila., 1988—. Mem. ABA, Pa. Bar Assn. (disciplinary bd. study com.), Phila. Bar Assn., N.J. Bar Assn. Home: 2 Independence Pl Apt 1505 Philadelphia PA 19106 Office: Fox Rothschild O'Brien & Frankel 2000 Market St 9th Fl Philadelphia PA 19103

RESNIK, ANNA GARFINKEL, financial executive; b. Antwerp, Belgium, Jan. 18, 1951; came to U.S., 1953; d. Simon and Sonia (Tenzer) Garfinkel; m. Bruce Lee Resnik, Apr. 19, 1974; children: Simon, David. BA, Barnard Coll., 1972; MBA, Columbia U., 1974. CPA, N.Y. Staff acct. Arthur Andersen Co., N.Y.C., 1974-75; analyst CitiBank, N.Y.C., 1975-77; exec. v.p. fin. wine subs. The Seagram Co. Ltd., N.Y.C., 1977-88; asst. v.p. fin. Home Ins. Co., N.Y.C., 1989—; bd. dirs. alumni bd., Columbia U., 1987—. Mem. Maplewood (N.J.) Devel. Commn., 1985—. Mem. AICPAs, Planning Forum, Fin. Women's Assn., Columbia Bus. Sch. Club N.Y.C. (v.p. 1980—), Acad. Women Achievers (elected). Republican. Jewish. Home: Maryland Rd Maplewood NJ 07040 Office: Home Ins Co 59 Maiden Ln New York NY 10038

RESS, ERICA LESLIE, advertising creative director; b. N.Y.C., June 21, 1950; d. Irwin Ress and Marcia (Fierstein) Tullman. BA, Am. U., 1971. Jr. writer Daniel & Charles, N.Y.C., 1973-75; writer Grey Advt., N.Y.C., 1975-78; sr. writer Young & Rubicam, N.Y.C., 1978-83; v.p., copy supr. Epstein/Raboy, N.Y.C., 1983-84; v.p., group head Saatchi & Saatchi DFS, N.Y.C., 1984-85; v.p. Wells, Rich & Greene, N.Y.C., 1986; sr. v.p., assoc. creative dir. Lintas: N.Y., N.Y.C., 1987-89; sr. v.p., creative dir. Grey Advt., N.Y.C., 1989—; tchr. The Sch. of the Visual Arts, N.Y.C., 1976—. Writer, performer (comedy team) Radio Waves. Recipient numerous awards for print, radio and TV advt. Mem. Advt. Women of N.Y. (chair career conf.). Office: Grey Advt 777 3d Ave New York NY 10017

RETTBERG, BARBARA CAROL, chemist; b. Elizabeth, N.J., Nov. 6, 1941; d. Heinrich Wilhelm and Barbara Lilian (Braterís) R. BA, Notre Dame Coll., Staten Island, 1963; MS, Rutgers U., 1966. Technician Atlantic Powdered Metals, Elizabeth, N.J., 1964-65; sr. research analyst Merck and Co., Rahway, N.J., 1965-88; pres. Rettberg Assocs., Inc., Elizabeth, 1989—. Asst. dir. Blessed Sacrament Ch. Choir, Elizabeth 1985—; bd. dirs. Choral Art Soc. N.J., Westfield, N.J. 1980—. Mem. Am. Chem. Soc., North Jersey Chromatography Group (com. mem. 1989-90), Kappa Gamma Pi. Democrat. Roman Catholic. Home and office: 402 Washington Ave Point Pleasant Beach NJ 08742

RETTGER, MARY ANN, elementary educator; b. St. Marys, Pa., July 12, 1951; d. George Edward and Isabel Ann (Sarginger) Rettger. BS in Elem. Edn., Villa Maria Coll., Erie, Pa., 1973; cert. in religious edn., Gannon U., Erie, 1985. Cert. elem. tchr., Pa. Tchr. St. Mary's (Pa.) Parochial Sch., 1971—; homebound tchr. St. Mary's Area Sch. Dist., 1987. Mem. AAUW (life, legis. chmn. 1985). Democrat. Roman Catholic.

RETTIG, CAROLYN FAITH, educator; b. Tarentum, Pa., June 30, 1951; d. William and Jennie Annetta (Lear) Ambrose; m. Gary Alan Rettig, July 10, 1985. BS in Edn., Ind. U. Pa., 1973; MA in Student Personnel, Slippery Rock U., 1988. Cert. English tchr. jr. high, secondary schs. Jr. high tchr. Saxonburg and Butler, Pa., 1974-75; English tchr. Butler Area High Sch., 1975-76; assessor community needs Butler County Community Coll., Pa., 1977-78; tchr. English Butler Area Sch. Dist., 1978—, speech and debate coach, 1979-84, curriculum writing coord., 1986-87; chmn. English dept. Butler Intermediate High Sch., 1986-88; chmn. English dept. Butler Intermediate High Sch., 1986-88; coord. fin. aid counselor practicum Butler County Community Coll., 1988. Publisher high sch. student art and literary mag., 1988—. Mem. Butler Edn. Assn., Pa. State Edn. Assn., NEA. Democrat. Lutheran. Home: 261 Fisher Rd RD 1 Cabot PA 16023 Office: Butler Intermediate High Sch 151 Fairground Hill Rd Butler PA 16001

RETZER, MARY ELIZABETH HELM, retired librarian; b. Balt.; d. Francis Leslie C. and Edna (Smith) Helm; m. William Raymond Retzer, June 28, 1945; children: Lesley Elizabeth, April Christine. BA, Western Md. Coll., 1940; MA, Columbia U., 1946; postgrad., George Washington U., Ind. U., U. Ill., Ill. State U., Bradley U.; PhD, Western Colo. U., 1972. Mem. faculty Rockville (Md.) Bd. Edn., 1940-47, elem. supr., 1945-47; mem. staff Peoria Pub. Libr., 1957-63, homebound libr., 1961-63; cons., organizer libr. Bergan High Sch., 1964-67; condr. libr. sci. course in reference Bradley U., 1966—; libr. Hines Elem. Sch., 1963-66, Roosevelt Jr. High Sch., 1966-69; head media ctr. Manual High Sch., Peoria, Ill., 1969-83. Instr. water safety courses ARC, 1938—; pres. women's bd. Salvation Army, 1952-54; pres. Peoria Nursery Sch. Assn., 1953-54; mem. legis. action com. Ill. Congress PTA, 1955-56; mem. Crippled Children's Adv. Com., Peoria, 1957-60; active various community drives; mem. women's adv. bd. Peoria Jr. Star, 1970-73. Mem. AAUW, NEA, ALA, Ill. Edn. Assn., Peoria Edn. Assn., Ill. Libr. Assn., Ill. Valley Librs. Assn. (pres. 1971-72), Ill. Assn. Media in Edn. (cert. com. 1973—), Ill. Audiovisual Assn., Internat. Platform Assn., Order Ea. Star, Ill. State U. Adminstrs. Club, Willowknolls Country Club, Sarasota Yacht Club. Republican. Presbyterian. Home: 1317 W Moss Ave Peoria IL 61606 also: 5676 Pipers Watte Sarasota FL 34235

RETZKE, MELANIE JAYNE, computer systems analyst; b. Columbus, Ohio, Dec. 31, 1952; d. Franklin Albert and Dorothy Viola (Payne) R. BS in Edn., Va. Poly. Inst. & State U., 1974; postgrad., Old Dominion U., 1978-80; AS summa cum laude, Tidewater Community Coll., 1985; postgrad., Hood Coll., 1988—. Tchr. Mecklenburg County Pub. Schs., Palmer Springs, Va., 1974-76; supr. aquatics Virginia Beach (Va.) YMCA, 1976-78; tchr. health and phys. edn. Holy Trinity Cath. Sch., Norfolk, Va., 1978-82; sec. Smith & Tolerton, P.C., Norfolk, 1983-85; systems analyst Clin. Ctr. NIH, Bethesda, Md., 1985—; computer cons., analyst Escalation Cons., Gaithersburg, Md., 1987-88. Mem. Nat. Assn. for Female Execs. Republican. Lutheran. Home: 19933 Sweet Gum Circle #32 Germantown MD 20874 Office: NIH 9000 Rockville Pike Bldg 10 Info Systems Dept Bethesda MD 20892

REUBEN, BETTY GENE, Entrepreneur; b. Newberry, S.C., Nov. 2, 1943; d. George Benjamin and Annie Lee (Burton) R. BA, Fordham U., N.Y.C., 1980. From control agt. to passenger svc. mgr. American Airlines, Queens, NY, 1967-83; office mgr., adminstrv. asst. Mark Nicholes Assocs., N.Y.C., 1983-84; asst. to dir. The Hambros Orgn., Ltd., N.Y.C., 1984-85; owner Reuben's Pub. Co., N.Y.C., The Ad Agy., N.Y.C., 1985--, PC Unlimited, 1988--. Author: Touch Me If You Can, 1988. Mem. United Way of N.Y.C.; fund-raiser, div. dir. N.Y.C. Combined Municipal Campaign. Democrat.

REUDER, MARY E(ILEEN), retired psychology and statistics educator; b. Mpls., Mar. 12, 1923; d. Leo Aloysius and Mary Agnes (McGuire) R.; m. Marvin Alvin Iverson, July 11, 1953 (dec. Dec. 1979); children: Carol Mary, Kent Gery. BA, Coll. St. Catherine, St. Paul, 1944; MA, Brown U., 1945; PhD, U. Pa., 1951. Lic. psychologist, N.Y. Asst. instr. psychology U. Pa., Phila., 1946-51; work mgmt. specialist U.S. Naval Ammunition Depot, Ft. Mifflin, Pa., 1951-52; rsch. psychologist pers. br. Adj. Gen.'s Office, Dept. Army, Washington, 1952-54; instr. psychology Queens Coll., CUNY, Flushing, 1957-62, asst. prof., 1962-66, assoc. prof., 1966-71, prof., 1971-86, chmn. dept., 1984-85, chmn. acad. senate, 1982-85, prof. emerita, 1986—; mem. grad. faculty CUNY, 1977-86; mem. adv. bd. Dushkin Press, Guilford, Conn., 1975-84; cons. NATO postdoctoral fellowships NSF, Washington, 1978; cons., manuscript peer reviewer Acad. Psychology Bull., 1980-85, Jour. Profl. Psychology, 1986—. Contbr. articles to profl. jours. and encys., also monographs, chpt. to book. Cons. com. on rsch. and evaluation Nassau coun. Girl Scouts U.S.A., 1971-74. Grantee NSF, 1964, Sigma Xi, 1962. Fellow N.Y. Acad. Scis., Am. Psychol. Assn. (pres. divs. 1 and 36 1987-88, exec. com. div. 1 1981-87, div. 36 1979—, coun. reps. div. 36 1980-83), Ea. Psychol. Assn. (adminstrv. coord. 1961-67, 70), Psychometric Soc., Biometric Soc., Am. Statis. Assn., AAAS; mem. Queens Coll. Faculty Club (past bd. dirs., v.p.), U. Pa. Club L.I. (bd. govs. 1980—), Brown U. Club L.I., Sigma Xi (grantee 1962, regional lectr. 1977-86, nat. bd. dirs. 1972-75, 77), Alpha Sigma Lambda, Pi Gamma Mu, Delta Phi Lambda, Kappa Gamma Pi, Alpha Pi Epsilon, Psi Chi. Democrat. Roman Catholic. Home: Po Box C Shohola PA 18458 Office: CUNY Queens Coll Dept Psychology Flushing NY 11367

REUSS, PRISCILLA A., marketing executive; b. Delaware County, Pa., Aug. 13, 1946; d. Robert J. and Virginia (Fox) Wright; m. Calvin Ira Ruess, Nov. 18, 1967; children: Laura Noreen, Philip Glenn. BS, East Stroudsburg U.; postgrad., Villanova U., West Chester U. Customer svc. mgr. Pier Angeli Co., Edgemont, Pa., telemktg. mgr.; br. mgr., mgr. mktg. support Eczel Corp., Phila.; dir. communications product mgmt. and product mgmt. Unisys Corp., Blue Bell, Pa. Hospice vol. Delaware County (Pa.) Meml. Hosp. Recipient Award for Citizenship Am. Legion. Mem. NAFE, Unysis Women's Group. Home: 77 S Brighton Ave Upper Darby PA 19082 Office: Unisys Corp Offices PO Box 500 MS HA 228 Blue Bell PA 19424

REUTER, CAROL JOAN, insurance company executive; b. Bklyn., June 1, 1941; d. Michael John and Elizabeth Lucille (Garmer) R. BA, St. John's U., 1962. Exec. dir. N.Y. Life Found., N.Y.C., 1979-89, asst. v.p., 1984-89; sec. N.Y. Life Found., 1989-90; pres. N.Y. Life Found., N.Y.C., 1990—; corp. v.p. N.Y. Life Ins. Co., N.Y.C., 1990—. Mem. exec. com. Conf. Bd. Contbns. Coun. (chmn.), N.Y. Contbns. Adv. Group (former chmn.), United Way of Am. (mem. corp. assocs.), United Way of Tri-State (vice-chmn., mem. corp. adv. com.), Found. Ind. Higher Edn. (nat. corp. adv. com., former chmn., nominating com.), Met. N.Y. (mem. adv. com. Philanthropic Adv. Svc.). Named Acad. of Women's Achievers, YWCA, 1987. Republican. Roman Catholic. Office: NY Life Ins Co 51 Madison Ave New York NY 10010

REUTER, JEANETTE MILLER, psychologist, educator; b. Sheboygan, Wis., Sept. 9, 1921; d. Arthur Herbert and Evangeline Miller; m. Louis Frederick Reuter, Feb. 1, 1943; children: Louis Frederick IV, Katherine Evan Reuter, James Arthur. BS, U. Wis., 1944; MS, Case Western Res. U., 1959, PhD, 1962. Diplomate Am. Bd. Profl. Psychology, Am. Bd. Profl. Neuropsychology; lic. psychologist, Ohio. Lectr. U. Md., Heidleberg, Fed. Republic of Germany, 1962; clin. psychologist USAF Hosp., Weisbaden, Fed. Republic of Germany, 1962-63; psychologist IV Sagamore Hills (Ohio) Children's Psychiat. Hosp., 1964-65; asst. prof. psychology Kent (Ohio) State U., 1965-70, assoc. prof. psychology, 1970-75, prof. psychology, 1975-78; prof. emerita, 1988—; pres. Kent (Ohio) Devel. Metrics, 1982—; cons. psychologist Hattie Larlham Found., Mantua, Ohio, 1974—; prin. investigator handicapped children's early edn. program U.S. Dept. Edn., 1974-82; rsch. conss. Inst. Dexeus, Barcelona, Spain, 1985—, Free U. Amsterdam, The Netherlands, 1988—; apptd. by gov. Ohio Interagy. Early Intervention Coun., 1987-89. Contbr. articles to profl. jours. Bd. dirs., program chair Ardmore, Inc., Akron, Ohio, 1986—. Recipient Disting. Teaching award Kent State U., 1973, Pres.'s medal, 1987. Mem. Am. Psychol. Assn., Soc. Behavioral Pediatrics, Soc. for Rsch. in Child Devel., Am. Assn. for Mental Retardation. Democrat. Home: 7551 Diagonal Rd Kent OH 44240 Office: Kent Devel Metrics 1325 S Water St Kent OH 44240

REUTER, WILMA SANBORN, credit bureau manager; b. Lime Springs, Iowa, Mar. 15, 1922; d. Harold Moar and Anna Johannah (Sorensen) Sanborn; m. James Henry Reuter, Apr. 15, 194 (div. Mar. 1979); 1 child, Janyce Kaye Webb. Ltd. teaching cert., Preston Tchrs. Tng. Sch., Preston, Minn., 1941. Rural sch. tchr. Stewartville Rural Sch., Stewartville, Minn., 1941-43; engr. planning N. Am. Aviation, Inglewood, Calif., 1943-45; clerical position MGM Studio, Culver City, Calif., 1945-47; mgr. The Credit Bur., Kankakee, Ill., 1947—; sec. Kankakee Area Consumer Credit Assn., 1962-87; mem., past pres. Kankakee Credit Women Internat., 1948-88. Mem. Tri County Bd. Pvt. Industry Coun., Kankakee, 1982—; charter mem. Women in Bus. div. Kankakee C. of C., 1982-85; div. head, worker United Way, Kankakee, 1983-87; bd. dirs., sec., meml. chmn. Kankakee chpt. Ill. Heart Assn. Named Woman of Yr. 1960s, Boss of Yr., 1977, Kankakee Credit Women Internat. Mem. Working Women's Coun. Assn. Credit Burs. Ill. (pres. 1986-87), Kankakee Emblem Club (pres.), Beta Sigma Phi (1960s Girl of Yr. Gamma Rho chpt. 1963). Home: 1465 Budd Kankakee IL 60901 Office: The Credit Bureau 119 East Ct Kankakee IL 60901

REUTHE, MARJORIE SNYDER, orthodontist; b. Canadian, Tex., Apr. 16, 1914; d. Edward Henry and Nona Agnes (Alexander) Snyder; m. John Julius Reuthe, July 29, 1939; children: John Edward, Susan Kay Reuthe Gatten. Student, Park Coll., 1931-33; DDS, Baylor U., 1937; MS in Orthodontics, Northwestern U., 1939. Pvt. practice South Bend, Ind., 1939-83; ret., 1983. Contbr. articles to profl. jours. Bd. dirs. St. Joe County Scholarship Found., South Bend; trustee First Presbyn. Ch., 1983-86. Fellow Am. Coll. Dentists, Internat. Coll. Dentists; mem. AAUW, ADA, Am. Assn. Orthodontists, Ind. State Assn. Orthodontists (past sec.-treas.), Angle Assn. Orthodontists (past pres. Mid-West comp.), St. Joe County Dental Assn., Ind. State Dental Soc. (Disting. Svc. award 1988), DAR (chaplain, sec., regent 1987-89), South Bend Altrusa Club (charter), Internat. Svc. Club, Omicron Kappa Upsilon. Home: 51880 Lilac Rd South Bend IN 46628

REUTHER, ROSANN WHITE, advertising agency executive; b. Nashville, Nov. 24, 1943; d. Wiley Butler and Mildred Elizabeth (Little) White; student George Peabody Coll., 1961-64; m. Peter Martin Reuther, Oct. 3, 1964. Advt. copywriter WHMA Radio, Anniston, Ala., 1964-65, Bapt. Sunday Sch. Bd., Nashville, 1965-72, Thomas Nelson Pubs., Nashville, 1972-73; account exec. Holder-Kennedy Pub. Relations, Nashville, 1973-74; pub. relations dir. T. Nelson, Nashville, 1974-75; pension adminstr. Wood, Bateman, Nord, Assos., Nashville, 1975-76; owner, pres. In-Vision Advt. and Pub. Relations, Nashville, 1976—; lectr. Tenn. State U., 1978-79; part-time instr. Nashville State Tech. Inst.; faculty Tenn. Entrepreneur Forum, 1984. Worker, Carter for Pres. campaign, Tenn., 1976. Recipient Paul M. Hinkhous award of excellence in advt., 1974. Mem. Nashville Advt. Fedn. (bd. dirs. 1986-88), Am. Women in Radio and TV (pres. Nashville chpt. 1981-82, dir. dist. B, 1982-83), Hist. Waverly Place Neighborhood Assn. (pres. 1988-89). Baptist. Home: 1908 Elliott Ave Nashville TN 37204 Office: PO Box 41161 Nashville TN 37204

REVAK, BLAIRANNE, physician; b. York, Pa., June 3, 1943; d. John Blair and Annabelle (Hamm) Hoover; m. David John Revak; children: Heather, Celestia, Charles, Matthew, Shally. BS, Susquehanna U., 1965; MD, Women's Med. Coll. Pa., 1969. Intern Germantown Hosp., Phila., 1970; pvt. practice Bloomsburg, Pa., 1971-89; physician Navajo Area Indian Health Svc., Crownpoint, N.Mex., 1981-83, Bloomsburg (Pa.) U., 1984—; cons. ARC, Columbia County, Pa., 1985—. Mem. AMA, AAUW, Am. Med. Women's Assn. (com. med. edn.), Pa. Med. Soc. (com. edn. and sci., chmn. commn. bioethics 1989-90). Republican. Lutheran. Home: PO Box 258 Pine St Orangeville PA 17859 Office: Penn Glenn Ave Bloomsburg PA 17815

REVER, BARBARA L., medical educator, consultant, researcher; b. Bklyn., Dec. 18, 1947. B.A., Barnard Coll., 1969; M.P.H., U. Calif.-Berkeley, 1970; M.D., N.Y. Med. Coll., 1974. Diplomate Am. Bd. Internal Medicine, Splty. Nephrology. Intern, Los Angeles County Hosp., U. So. Calif., 1974-75; resident in internal medicine, Los Angeles County Hosp., 1975-76, Kaiser Found. Hosps., Los Angeles, 1976-77; fellow in nephrology U. Calif., L.A. Sch. Medicine, 1978-80, specialist in Nephrology, Salinas Valley Dialysis Services, Inc., also chmn. bd.; founder, chmn. bd. Cen. Coast Health Enhancement Ctr., Salinas, Calif; chmn. bd. Cen. Coast Weight Reduction Program; spl. cons. Calif. State Dept. Pub. Health, summer 1970; research assoc. Dept. Community and Preventive Medicine, N.Y. Hosp. Coll., summer 1971; instr. biology and physiology Community Health Medic Tng. Program, Indian Health Service Hosp., N. Mex., summer 1972; asst. prof. medicine, asst. dir. renal transplantation div. nephrology UCLA, 1980-81. Office: 230 San Jose St Ste 50 Salinas CA 93901

REVILLE, JOANN M., airport management representative; b. Buffalo, Sept. 4, 1946; d. Joseph H. and Luella (Harnick) Miller; m. Joseph M. Reville, Mar. 28, 1981; children: Kara Ann, Brittany Erin. BA in Psychology/Sociology with honors, SUNY, Buffalo, 1978, cert. in human resources mgmt., 1979; postgrad. in bus., SUNY. Exec. sec. Goodrich Tire and Rubber Co., Washington, 1964, Blue Cross Western N.Y., Buffalo, 1965-70; pub. relations asst. Gen. Motors Corp., Buffalo, 1970-73; adminstrv. asst. Erie County Dept. Mental Health, West Seneca, N.Y., 1975; grant asst. State Tchrs. Coll., Buffalo, 1976-78; exec. sec. Interstate United Corp., Tonawanda, N.Y., 1978-81; mgmt. rep. Niagra Frontier Transp. Authority, Buffalo, 1981—. Mem. Erie County Dem. Women; notary public State of N.Y.: election inspector Erie County. Mem. IASS, AAAE, N.Y. State Airport Mgrs. Assn. (N.E. chpt.), Am. Assn. Airport Execs., Variety Women (Buffalo), Tent #7, Alpha Kappa Delta (zeta chpt.). Democrat. Roman Catholic. Home: 85 Coolidge Rd Buffalo NY 14220 Office: Greater Buffalo Internat Airport Niagara Frontier Transp Authority Buffalo NY 14225

REVIS-YEOMAN, ALEXIS, communications executive; b. Washington, Aug. 7, 1957; d. Alex and Bettye (Matthews) Revis; m. Felix Yeoman, June 6, 1987. BA, Am. U., 1979. Producer Sta. WJLA-TV (ABC affiliate), Washington, 1975-78, 85; producer, writer Sta. WRC-TV (NBC affiliate), Washington, 1978-81, Sta. WHMM-TV (PBS affiliate), Washington, 1981-83, Warner Amex Qube, Columbus, Ohio, 1983-84; producer Essence Communications, Inc., N.Y.C., 1984-85; dir. R&D Eli Prodns., Inc., Washington, 1985-87; dir. communications State's Atty.'s Office Prince George County, Upper Malboro, Md., 1987—; TV producer, writer, Washington, 1985—; pub. rels. cons., Washington, 1987—. Recipient Emmy award NATAS, 1978, 79. Fellow Pub. Rels. Soc. Am., Capital Press Club, Nat. Coalition of 100 Black Women (v.p. 1987-90). Democrat. Roman Catholic. Office: Office States Atty 14735 Main St Upper Marlboro MD 20772

REWEY, PAMELA SUE, lobbyist; b. Wausau, Wis., Sept. 15, 1946; d. Clemens Stanley and Arleen Joyce (Sicklinger) Wadzinski; m. Michael Wayne Rewey, Aug. 12, 1967; children: M. Wade, Brianna, Nathaniel, Rachel. BS, U. Wis., 1969, MS in Edn. Adminstrn., 1988. Cert. secondary edn. tchr./administr., Wis.; cert. YMCA tchr. Tchr. of English Wausau (Wis.) Sch. Dist., 1968-69, Wisconsin Rapids (Wis.) Sch. Dist., 1969-71; program dir. Stevens Point (Wis.) Area YMCA, 1978-85, asst. exec. dir., 1985-88; account exec. Wood Communications, Inc., Madison, Wis., 1987-88; mng. dir. YMCA of Met. Madison, 1988-89; legis. svcs. Wis. Assn. Sch. Bds., Madison, 1989—; state dir. Wis. YMCA Youth in Govt., 1988—; bd. dirs. Wis. Alliance for Arts Edn., Madison; mem. DPI/NCREL Policy: Report Cards on the Schs., Madison, 1989—; sr. dir. Nat. Bd. YMCAs, 1984. Contbr. articles to profl. jours. Mem. Stevens Point Sch. Bd., 1978-88, pres. 1979-84; founder/mem. Portage County Commn. on Women, Stevens Point, 1978-85; parent adv. coun. Madison Met. Sch. Dist., 1988—. Recipient Wellness Commn. award Portage County, 1987, Citation by the Senate, Wis., 1987. Mem. Madison East Rotary (dist. youth exch. officer), Women In Communications, Inc. (bd. dirs. 1988-89), League of Women Voters (pres. 1975-77). Democrat. Roman Catholic. Office: Wis Assn Sch Bds 122 W Washington Madison WI 53703

REYES-WILSON, EDNA LUISA, psychologist, educator; b. El Paso, Tex., June 24, 1952; d. Luis and Selsa (Gavaldon) Reyes; m. Eddie Wilson, Nov. 22, 1980; 1 child, Felipe Luis. BA, U. Tex., 1979, MA, 1984; PhD, N.Mex. State U., 1990. Lic. profl. counselor. Clinician El Paso Ctr. for Mental Health & Retardation, 1980-82; therapist Family Svc. of El Paso, 1985-88; pvt. practice counselor El Paso, 1989—; instr. El Paso Community Coll., 1989—. Mem. adv. com. project redirection Teen Pregnancy Prevention, El Paso, 1987—; mem. adv. com. client self support program Tex. Dept. Human Svcs., Austin, 1986—. Mem. Am. Psychol. Assn., El Paso Psychol. Assn., Am. Assn. Marriage and Family Therapy, El Paso Assn. Marriage and Family Therapy. Roman Catholic. Office: 1301 N Oregon El Paso TX 79902

REYNES, WENDY WARNER, publishing company executive; b. Boston, Sept. 29, 1944; d. Philip Russell and Elizabeth (Patton) Warner; A.A., Conn. Coll., 1966; m. Jose (Tony) Antonio Reynes, III, Apr. 26, 1969; children: Jose (Tad) Antonio, Gabrielle Elizabeth. With Foote, Cone, Belding, N.Y.C., 1966-68; advt. sales rep. Cosmopolitan Mag., N.Y.C., 1968-69, Co-Ed Mag., N.Y.C., 1969-70; asst. product mgr. Avon Products, N.Y.C., 1970; advt. sales rep. Mag. Networks, N.Y.C. and Chgo., 1970-72; midwest mgr. advt. sales Girl Talk Mag., Chgo., 1972-75; div. mgr. advt. sales Pattis Group, Chgo., 1975-79; pres. Reynes & Assocs., Inc., 1979—, Sales Unltd., Inc., 1985-86. Bd. dirs. Multiple Sclerosis, 1974-79, St. Joseph's Sch. PTA, 1979-80, Marriage Encounter, 1976—; active Jr. League Greenwich, Conn., 1965-67, Jr. League N.Y.C., 1967-75; mem. cen. coun. New Trier High Sch., 1987—. Mem. Agate Club (dir.), Advt. Assn., Women's Advt. Club Chgo. (co-chmn.), Chgo. Advt. Club, Wilmette Tennis Club, East Bank Club, Women's Advt. Club of Chgo., Winnetka Yacht Club (bd. dirs. 1989—), Winnetka Women's Club (bd. dirs. 1989—). Home: 460 Ash St Winnetka IL 60093

REYNOLDS, ALVA-INEZ, manufacturing company executive; b. Douglas, Ga., Oct. 31, 1933; d. Daniel Beamon and Alva (Flanders) Smith; children from previous marriage: Leon Paulk, Linda Paulk Tanner, James Paulk; m. Don Wayne Reynolds, June 13, 1973. Grad. high sch., Douglas. Lic. realtor, Fla. Order dept. sec. Steiner Co., Chgo., 1956-64; so. controller Cable Raincoats Co., Douglas, 1964-70; so. regional mgr. Sosine Mohawk Co., Statenville, Ga., 1970-78; office mgr. Pan Am. Gyro-Tex., Jasper, Fla., 1978-80; asst. gen. mgr. Gen. Laminates Corp., Jasper, 1980-86; pres., mgr. Sunshine Products Corp., Jasper, 1986-88; mgr. Suwanne Swifty Convenience Food Store, Live Oak, Fla., 1988-89; correctional officer Hamilton Correctional Inst. State of Fla. Dept. of Corrections, 1989—; substitute tchr. Hamilton County High Sch. and Adult Vocat., 1989—. Mem. NOW, Nat. Assn. Women Bus. Owners, Nat. Assn. Female Execs., Am. Assn. Retired Persons, Jasper C. of C. Democrat. Baptist. Home: Rt 4 Box 99 Jasper FL 32052

REYNOLDS, ELAINE MARIE, talent agency director; b. Quonset Pt., R.I., Oct. 15, 1963; d. Roger George and Nancy Lorraine (Wawro) Atchison. AA, St. Johns River Coll., 1982; BA, Samford U., 1983. Licensed Agency Dir., Fla. Dept. of Regulations. Regional mktg. dir. Regis Hotels, Birmingham, Ala., 1983-85; mktg. advisor Richway Dept. Stores, Atlanta, Ga., 1985-86; promotions dir. Gas Leisure and Entertainments, Cheltenham, England, 1986-87; cons. Natural Resources Mktg., Cheltenham, England; agy. dir. Sessions Modeling and Talent Agy., Jacksonville, Fla., 1988--; mktg. cons. Aggio Graphic Design Inc. Jacksonville, 1988-89, Bristol, England 1987-89, Spolin Studios, Bristol, 1987—. Mem. Inst. of Mktg., Inst. of Sales and Mktg., Fla. Motion Picture and TV Assn. (v.p., mem. state board 1989—), Jacksonville C. of C. (ambassador 1988—), Phi Theta Kappa Honor Soc. (pres. 1981-82). Republican. Catholic. Home: 3355 Claire Ln #1508 Jacksonville FL 32223 Office: Sessions Modeling and Talent Agy 8258 Arlington Expwy Jacksonville FL 32211

REYNOLDS, GARNET LULYAN, speech pathologist, communications specialist; b. California, Pa., Aug. 16, 1940; d. William Rex and Garnet Wilda (Dias) R.; m. Francis Sinko, Sept. 5, 1959 (div.); m. Charles L. Ilvento, Dec. 29, 1982. BS, Calif. State Coll., 1960; MS, Fla. State U., 1967, PhD, 1977. Supr. Communication Disorders Dade County Pub. Schs., Miami, Fla., 1969-73; asst. prof., audiology, speech pathology Fla. State U., Tallahassee, 1974-77, Sch. Medicine, U. Miami, 1978-80; dir. clin. tng. U. Miami, Coral Gables, Fla., 1977-81; research speech pathologist VA, Miami, 1982-86; dir. The Speech-Voice-Lang. Ctr., Miami, 1982—; pres. A Positive Communication Image, Coral Gables, 1984—; cons. Am. Express-Latin Am., Coral Gables, 1985—; speech pathologist VA Hosp., Miami, 1988. Author: Speech-Facial Acceptability and Self-Concept, 1981, Foibles and Follies of Speech Therapy in Cleft Palate Speakers; editor Fla. Lang. Jour., 1980. Fundraiser Young Reps., Dade County, 1981. Recipient Dedicated Service award Nat. Council Bds. of Examiners of Speech and Hearing, 1983, Dedicated Service award Fla. Adv. Council Speech and Hearing, 1980, Outstanding Service award VA, Miami, 1984. Mem. Am. Speech, Lang., and Hearing Assn. (cert. clin. competence), Fla. Lang. Speech and Hearing Assn. (editor 1980-82), Am. Cleft Palate Assn., Am. Women in Radio and TV (sec. 1986-87, v.p. 1987-88, pres. 1988-89), Soroptimists (pres. Coral Gables chpt. 1989—), Kappa Delta Pi, Alpha Delta Kappa. Republican. Methodist. Home: 10725 SW 128 Terr Miami FL 33176

REYNOLDS, GAYLE MARIE, cultural organization administrator; b. Cleve., Dec. 30, 1943; d. Oscar Lee and Margaret Mae (Johnson) R. BA in Communications, Baldwin-Wallace Coll., 1974. Exec. dir. March of Dimes N.E. Fla., Jacksonville, 1974-78, United Travel Systems, Inc., Jacksonville, 1979-81; v.p. ops. Jr. Achievement, Jacksonville, 1982—; state edn. liason Fla. Jr. Achievement, Colorado Springs, Colo., 1988—. Campaign coordinator Mayors Race, Jacksonville, 1987. Mem. Sales and Mktg. Execs. (chmn. scholarship sem. com. 1985-86, 88-90) AAUW (mem.-at-large), Kappa Delta Pi. Roman Catholic. Home: 3208 Crosby Ln Jacksonville FL 32216 Office: Jr Achievement Jacksonville FL 32207

REYNOLDS, GINGER FAY, healthcare company executive; b. Jackson, Miss., July 14, 1950; d. Neville Scott and Mabel Fay (Covington) R. Diploma, Miss. Gulf Coast Jr. Coll. (formerly Perkinston (Miss.) Jr. Coll.), 1969, Bates Bus. Coll., 1970; BSBA in Acctg., U. So. Miss., 1973. With Stallworth Furniture Co., Pascagoula, Miss., 1969-71; asst. sec. U. So. Miss., Hattiesburg, 1972-73; office acct. South Miss. Home Health Found. Inc. (formerly S. Miss. Home Health and Rehab. Agy. Inc.), Hattiesburg, 1973, comptr., 1973—, sec., 1976—, comptr., sec.-treas., 1987—; sec.-treas. Health Care Enterprises Inc., Hattiesburg, 1985—. Vol. Am. Cancer Soc., Hattiesburg, 1984, 85. Mem. U. So. Miss. Alumni Assn., Miss. Gulf Coast Jr. Coll. Alumni Assn. Republican. Baptist. Office: South Miss Home Health Inc PO Box 16929 Hattiesburg MS 39404-6929

REYNOLDS, HELEN ELIZABETH, service executive; b. Minerva, N.Y., Aug. 30, 1925; d. Henry James and Margurite Catherine (Gallagher) McNally; m. Theodore Laurence Reynolds, Feb. 27, 1948; children: Laurence McBride, David Scott, William Herbert. BA, SUNY, Albany, 1967; MA, Union Coll., Schenectady, N.Y., 1971. Owner, mgr. Schafer Studio, Schenectady, 1970-73; co-owner, v.p. Reynolds Chalmers Inc., Schenectady, 1971—; program coordinator Schenectady County, 1980-81; adminstr. Wellspring House of Albany, N.Y., 1981—; cons., examiner N.Y. State Civil Service, Albany, 1971-81; mem. adv. council SBA, Washington, 1978-80. Mem. planning bd. Town of Niskayuna, N.Y., 1977-81, town councilwoman, 1986—; co-chairwoman Great N.E. Festival on the Mohawk River, 1989; bd. dirs. HAVEN, Schenectady, 1978-81; bd. dirs. Schenectady YWCA. Named Woman Vision, 1986, 87, Today's Woman, 1987, Schenectady YWCA. Mem. Antique and Classic Boat Soc. (bd. dirs. 1974—, Disting. Service award 1979), Assn. Adminstrs. Independent Housing (pres. 196-88), Inst. Real Estate Mgmt., Am. Mgmt. Assn., Lake George (N.Y.) Assn. Club: N.Y. State Women's Press. Lodge: Zonta (pres. 1981-82). Home: 2262 Cayuga Rd Schenectady NY 12309 Office: Wellspring House Albany Washington Ave Extension Albany NY 12203

REYNOLDS, KATHRYN ANNE, accountant; b. Kalamazoo, July 31, 1957; d. Ronald Louis and Patricia Anne (Mathers) Blaul; m. Lee Michael Reynolds, Aug. 4, 1979; children: Daniel, Stephani, Joseph. Student, McHenry Community Coll., 1975-76, Knox Coll., 1976-77; BBA in Acctg. magna cum laude, U. Wis.-Whitewater, 1979. CPA, Wis. Intern Arthur Anderson & Co., Milw., 1979; mem. staff Baillies, Denson, Erickson & Smith, CPAs, Lake Geneva, Wis., 1980-82, sr. acct., 1983-84; contr. Rubidell Recreation Inc., Elkhorn, Wis., 1984—. Rotary exchange student, France, 1973-74. Mem. AICPA, NAFE, Wis. Inst. CPAs, Nat. Assn. Accts., Beta

Alpha Psi, Phi Gamma Nu. Home: Powers Lake Rd Rte 1 PO Box 585 Genoa City WI 53128 Office: Rubidell Recreation Inc 39 N Washington St Elkhorn WI 53121

REYNOLDS, KLARA BOYNTON, real estate executive; b. Portsmouth, Ohio, Oct. 18, 1942; d. Howard E. and Mary Katherine (Smith) Rapp; m. Joseph Roger Boynton, Mar. 22, 1964 (dec. July 1986); children: Katherine L., Kristina L.; m. Thomas B. Reynolds, Oct. 24, 1987. BS, Ohio State U., 1964; MA, Marshall U., 1988. Owner, mgr. Scioto Rental Mgmt. Co., 1971—; ptnr. KB Properties, Ohio, 1989—, KBR Constrn. Co., 1989—. Pres. AAUW, Portsmouth, 1972-74; sec. Coop. Extension Adv., Portsmouth, 1975-85; adv. 4-H, Portsmouth, 1972-85. Mem. Am. Home Econ. Assn., W.Va. Home Econ. Assn., Ohio Home Econ. Assn., Am. Paint Horse Assn., Ohio Paint Horse Club, Ohio State U. Alumni Assn. (sec. Scioto County 1989).

REYNOLDS, LOLA SULLIVAN, lawyer; b. New Rochelle, N.Y., Apr. 25, 1955; d. James Francis and Lola Joan (Blank) Sullivan; m. Timothy Gerard Reynolds, Mar. 15, 1980; children: Timothy Gerard Jr., Terence Sullivan, Kieran Patrick. BA, Trinity Coll., Washington, 1977; JD, Fordham U., 1980. Bar: N.Y. 1981, U.S. Dist. Ct. (so. and ea. dists.) N.Y. 1981, U.S. Dist. Ct. N.J. 1981, U.S. Ct. Appeals (2d and 3d cirs.) 1984, U.S. Supreme Ct. 1984. Assoc. gen. counsel The Hearst Corp., N.Y.C., 1980—. Active Friends and Neighbors Club, Mineola, N.Y. Mem. N.Y. State Bar Assn., Assn. of Bar of City of N.Y., Guild of Cath. Lawyers, Phi Beta Kappa. Republican. Roman Catholic. Home: 185 Pomander Rd Mineola NY 11501 Office: The Hearst Corp Office Gen Counsel 959 8th Ave New York NY 10019

REYNOLDS, MARJORIE LAVERS, educator; b. Collingwood, Ont., Can., Jan. 10, 1931; d. Henry James and Laura (Wilson) Lavers; m. John Horace Reynolds, Aug. 17, 1963; children: Steven, Mark. BA, U. Toronto, 1953; MS, U. Minn., 1957; PhD, U. Wis., 1964; AS, State Tech. Inst. Knoxville, 1982. Registered dietitian; cert. sec. tchr. Rsch. dietitian Mayo Clinic, Rochester, Minn., 1957-59; rsch. dietitian Cleve. Met. Gen. Hosp., 1959-60; rsch. assoc. U. Tenn., Knoxville, 1963-66; instr. Ft. Sanders Sch. Nursing, Knoxville, 1967-76, State Tech. Inst., Knoxville, 1982-88; substitute secondary sch. tchr. Knox County Schs., Knoxville, 1989—. Contbr. articles to biochem. and nutrition jours.; newletter editor Juvenile Diabetes Found., Knoxville, 1985—. Sec. Midway Rehab. Ctr., Knoxville, 1987—; mem. LWV, Knoxville, 1965—. Mem. Knoxville Dist. Dietetic Assn. (pres. 1971-72, Outstanding Dietitian 1973-1974), Tenn. Dietetic Assn. (pres. 1973-74, Outstanding Dietitian 1973-74), Omicron Nu. Democrat. Presbyterian. Home: 7112 Stockton Dr Knoxville TN 37909

REYNOLDS, MARY TRACKETT, political scientist; b. Milw., Jan. 11, 1913; d. James P. and Mary (Nachtwey) Trackett; m. Lloyd G. Reynolds, June 12, 1937; children: Anne Reynolds Skinner, Priscilla Reynolds Roosevelt, Bruce. BA, U. Wis., 1935, MA, 1935; postgrad. (Rebecca Green fellow), Radcliffe Coll., 1935-36; PhD (U. fellow, Barnard fellow), Columbia U., 1939. Rsch. asst. Littauer Sch. Harvard U., 1938-39; instr. Queens Coll., 1939-40; instr. Hunter Coll., 1941-42, lectr., 1945-47; assoc. in polit. sci. Johns Hopkins U., 1942-43; lectr. Conn. Coll., 1947-48, asst. prof., 1948-50; asst. prof. U. Bridgeport, 1950-51; rsch. assoc. in econs. Yale U., 1961-67, vis. lectr. in English, 1973-82; meml. lecture Joyce Centennial, 1982. Author: Interdepartmental Committees in the National Administration, 1940, Joyce and Nora, 1964, Source Documents in Economic Development, 1966, Joyce's Debt to Dante, 1968, Two Essays on James Joyce, 1970; Joyce and D'Annunzio, 1976, Joyce and Dante: The Shaping Imagination, 1982, A Companion to Joyce Studies, 1984, Vico, Dante and Joyce, 1987, Joyce and Pirandello, 1987, Joyce's Shakespeare, 1990, Mr. Bloom and the Lost Vermeer, 1989; contbr. articles to profl. jours. Rsch. asst. Pres.'s Com. Adminstrn. Mgmt., 1936; sr. economist Nat. Econ. Com., 1940; adminstrn. asst. Glenn L. Martin Aircraft Co., Balt., 1942-43; editorial asst. pub. adminstrn. com. Social Sci. Rsch. Coun., 1944-45; cons. Nat. Def. Adv. Commn., 1949, Nat. Mcpl. Assn., 1956, Orgn. Econ. Cooperation and Devel., Paris, 1964, U.S. State Dept.-AID 1965. Mem. AAUP, LWV, Am. Polit. Sci. Assn., Dante Soc. Am., James Joyce Found. (editorial bd. Quar. 1985—), Conn. Acad. Arts and Scis. (coun. 1988-89), New Haven Hosp. Aux. (bd. dirs.), Elizabethan Club (sec.-treas. 1984-89, bd. incorporators 1986-89), Grolier Club, Appalachian Mountain Club. Home: 4000 Cathedral Ave Apt 147-B Washington DC 20016 Office: Yale Sta Box 604 New Haven CT 06520

REYNOLDS, MOIRA DAVISON, writer; b. Bangor, No. Ireland, June 22, 1915; parents Am. citizens; d. Asa Francis and Marjorie Racy (Bolton) Davison; m. Orland Bruce Reynolds, Sept. 4, 1954; 1 child, Ronald Davison. BA, Dalhousie U., 1937; AM, Boston U., 1949, PhD, 1952. Cert. med. technologist. Med. technologist Quincy (Mass.) City Hosp., 1939-42; chief technologist Faulkner Hosp., Boston, 1942-46; rsch. med. technologist Wayne U., Detroit, 1946-48; mem. cancer rsch. team Boston U., 1952-62; head lab. dept. Porter Hosp., Middlebury, Vt., 1963-68; freelance writer, 1969—. Author: Margaret Sanger, 1981; Uncle Tom's Cabin and Mid-19th Century U.S., 1983; Nine American Women of the 19th Century, 1988; also mag. articles. Bd. dirs. Mich. div. Am. Cancer Soc., 1978-83; mem. health facilities and agys. adv. com. State of Mich., 1980-85; trustee Peter White Pub. Library, Marquette, Mich., 1983-90. Recipient Pres.'s award for Disting. Citizenship No. Mich. U., 1979; Mich. Coun. for Arts writer-in-residence, 1980—. Mem. Am. Assn. for Clin. Chemistry (pres. N.E. sect. 1957-58), Am. Assn. Cancer Rsch., AAUW (pres. Marquette br. 1989—), Zonta Internat. (pres. Marquette club 1978-79). Home: 225 E Michigan Marquette MI 49855

REYNOLDS, NANCY BRADFORD DUPONT (MRS. WILLIAM GLASGOW REYNOLDS), sculptor; b. Greenville, Del., Dec. 28, 1919; d. Eugene Eleuthere and Catherine Dulcinea (Moxham) duPont; m. William Glasgow Reynolds, May 18, 1940; children: Kathrine Glasgow Reynolds, William Bradford, Mary Parminter Reynolds Savage, Cynthia duPont Reynolds Farris. Student, Goldey-Beacom Coll., Wilmington, Del., 1938. One-woman shows include Rehoboth (Del.) Art League, 1963, Del. Art Mus., Wilmington, Caldwell, Inc., 1975, Wilmington Art Mus., 1976; exhibited group shows Corcoran Gallery, Washington, 1943, Soc. Fine Arts, Wilmington, 1937, 38, 40, 41, 48, 50, 62, 65, NAD, N.Y.C., 1964, Pa. Mil. Coll., Chester, 1966, Del. Art Ctr., 1967, Met. Mus. Art, N.Y.C., 1977, Lever House, N.Y.C., 1979; represented in permanent collections Wilmington Trust Co., E.I. duPont de Nemours & Co., Children's Home, Inc., Claymont, Del., Children's Bur., Wilmington, Stephenson Sci. Ctr., Nashville, Lutheran Towers Bldg., Travelers Aid and Family Soc. Bldg., Wilmington, Bronze Fountain Head, Longwood Gardens, Kennett Square, Pa. Guide; contbr. articles to profl. jours. Organizer vol. svc. Del. chpt. ARC, 1938-39; chmn. Com. for Revision Del. Child Adoption Law, 1950-52; pres. bd. dirs. Children Bur. Del.; pres., trustee Children's Home, Inc.; del. regent Gunston Hall Plantation, Lorton, Va.; mem. adv. com. Longwood Gardens, Kennett Sq., Pa.; garden and grounds com. Winterthur (Del.) Mus.; mem. rsch. staff Henry Francis DuPont Winterthur Mus., 1955-63. Recipient Confrerie des Chevaliers du Tastevin Clos de Vougeot-Bourgogne France, 1960; Hort. award Garden Club Am., 1964, medal of Merit, 1976; Dorothy Platt award Garden Club of Phila., 1980; Alumni medal of merit Westover Sch., Middlebury, Conn. Mem. Pa. Hort. Soc., Wilmington Soc. Fine Arts, Mayflower Descs., Del. Hist. Soc., Colonial Dames, League Am. Pen Women, Nat. Trust Hist. Preservation. Garden Club of Wilmington (past pres.), Garden Club of Am. (past asst. zone 4 chmn.), Vicmead Hunt Club, Greenville Country Club, Chevy Chase Club (Washington), Colony Club (N.Y.C.). Episcopalian. Address: PO Box 3919 Greenville DE 19807

REYNOLDS, NANCY REMICK, editor, writer; b. San Antonio, July 15, 1938; d. Donald Worthington and Edith (Remick) R.; m. Brian Rushton, June 25, 1983; 1 child, Ehren T. Park. Student, Sch. Am. Ballet, 1951, 53-61, Juilliard Sch. Music, 1957, Martha Graham Sch. Contemporary Dance, N.Y.C., 1959, U. Sorbonne, Paris, 1962; BA in Art History, Columbia U., 1965; postgrad., Goethe Inst., Prien, Fed. Republic Germany, 1972, U. Chgo. and Sarah Lawrence Coll., 1974-77. Dancer N.Y.C. Ballet, 1956-61; editor Praeger Pubs., N.Y.C., 1965-71; dir. rsch. book Choreography by George Balanchine: A Catalogue of Works, N.Y., 1979-82 (pub. 1983); dir. rsch. pub. TV spl. Balanchine, N.Y., 1983-84; assoc. editor Internat. Encyclopedia of Dance, 1982—; dir. Critics' Notebook project, 1986-90; mem. publ. com. Congress on Rsch. in Dance, 1977-78; mem. nat. adv. coun. II Internat. Ballet Competition, Jackson, Miss., 1982; oral historian for The Dance Collection, N.Y. Pub. Library, 1977-78; co-pub. Twentieth-Century Dance in Slides, 1978—. Author: Repertory in Review: Forty Years of the New York City Ballet, 1977 (De la Torre Bueno prize 1977), The Dance Catalog: A Complete Guide to Today's World of Dance, 1979, co-author: In Performance: A Companion to the Classics of the Dance, 1980; editor: Movement and Metaphor: Four Centuries of Ballet (Lincoln Kirstein), 1970, Dance as a Theatre Art: Source Readings in Dance History from 1581 to the Present (Selma Jeanne Cohen), 1974, School of Classical Dance (V. Kostrovitskaya and A. Pisarev), 1978; contbr. (book) Ballet: Bias and Belief, "Three Pamphlets Collected" and Other Dance Writings of Lincoln Kirstein, 1983, also numerous articles and revs. to Dancing Times, Ballet News, Playbill, ArtsLine, Dancemag., N.Y. Times, Ency. Britannica., others. Ford Found. Travel and Study grantee, 1974. Mem. Dance Critics Assn. (pres. 1986-87), Soc. Dance History Scholars, Soc. for Dance Rsch. in affiliation with Nat. Resource Ctr. for Dance, Am. Soc. for Theatre Rsch., Internat. Fedn. for Theatre Rsch. in affiliation with Societe Internat. des Bibliotheques et Musees des Arts du Spectacle. Home: 9 Prospect Park W Brooklyn NY 11215

REYNOLDS, NINA LOUISE, nurse; b. Long Beach, Calif., Mar. 10, 1934; d. Quincy Arthur and Evie Lorraine (Boykin) Roberts; m. Craig Byron Reynolds; children: Dennis E., Michael H., Patricia S. AA, RN, Pasadena City Coll., 1976. Nurse surg. service Meth. Hosp. of So. Calif., Arcadia, 1976, staff nurse surg. ICU, 1977-79, head nurse surg. ICU, 1979-80; rev. mgr. PSRO, 1980-81, dir. profl. services, 1981-82, exec. dir., 1982-84; with Los Angeles dist. ops./rev. Calif. Med. Rev., Inc., 1984-86; dir. quality assurance CIGNA Healthplans of Calif., 1986—; lectr., author. Youth coordinator Pasadena (Calif.) council Girl Scouts U.S.A., 1964-74; mem. Pasadena Election Bd., 1964—. youth leader Congl. Ch., 1964-74. Cert. advanced life support in CPR, critical care R.N. Mem. Assn. Critical Care Nurses, Nat. Critical Care Inst., Alpha Gamma Sigma, Delta Gamma Omega, Sigma Phi Nu. Congregationalist. Home: 3870 Mayfair Dr Pasadena CA 91107

REYNOLDS, ROSALIE DEAN, chemistry educator; b. Jacksonville, Ill., Mar. 8, 1926; d. Eldridge Ashlen and Evalena (Martin) Sibert; m. Joseph Franklin Reynolds, June 26, 1948. AB, Ill. Coll., Jacksonville, 1947; MS, U. Wyo., 1950, PhD, 1953. Grad. asst. U. Wyo., Laramie, 1948-51; technician U. Wyo., 1951-52, instr., 1952-53, asst. prof., 1955-60; postdoctoral fellow U. Colo., Boulder, 1953-54; lectr. U. So. Calif., L.A., 1954-55; assoc prof. chemistry No. Ill. U., DeKalb, 1960-68; prof. chemistry No. Ill. U., 1968-81, prof. emeritus chemistry, 1981—; cons. in field. Contbr. articles to profl. jours. Recipient Excellence in Teaching award, No. Ill. U., 1968, Honors Tchr. of Yr., 1977; Disting. Citizen, Ill. Coll., Soroptimist Grad. award, 1953. Mem. Am. Chem. Soc., Ill. Coll. Alumni Assn. (bd. dirs. 1962-67, 77-81, alumni trustee 1976-81), Sigma Xi, Iota Sigma Pi, Gamma Sigma Epsilon. Home: 1852 Perry Ct Sycamore IL 60178

REYNOLDS, SALLIE BLACKBURN, civic volunteer, editor; b. Kansas City, Mo., Feb. 9, 1940; d. Anton and Sallie Churchill (Blackburn) Zajic; m. Jeffrey Calhoun Loker, Mar. 25, 1959 (div. May 1965); children: Toni Lynne, Michael David, Kathryn Lee Simpson; m. Everett Lee Reynolds, Mar. 29, 1969. Student, William Jewell Coll., 1959, BA magna cum laude, 1977; student, U. Mo., Kansas City, 1966-67, Kansas City Art Inst., 1966-70. Cert. tchr., Mo. From clk. to sec. Hdqrs. Strategic Air Command, Offutt AFB, Omaha, 1960-62; sec., wage and hr. law enforcement asst. wage hr. div. U.S. Dept. of Labor, Kansas City, 1963-68, exec. sec. to regional manpower adminstr., 1968-71, spl. asst. to regional exec. staff mem., 1971-72, mgmt. asst. Office of Regional Dir., 1972-73; from. clk. to sec. air carrier dist. office FAA, Kansas City, 1978-81; from clk. typist to sec. regional personnel officer Bur. of Reclamation, U.S. Dept. of Interior, Boulder City, Nev., 1982-84; editorial asst. div. of planning Bur. of Reclamation, Boulder City, 1984-86; ret., 1986. Editor (newsletter) Laurie Fine Art, 1989—. Ofcl. commr., sec., corr. Clay County (Mo.) Bicentennial Commn., 1974-76; mem. Ozark Brush and Palette, Inc., Camdenton, Mo., 1987—, editor newsletter, 1988-89; v.p., sec. Clay County Hist. Soc., 1972—; mem. Friends of Mo. State Archives, 1990, Nat. Wildlife Fedn. Recipient 1st Pl.award NSDAR Am. Heritage Contest, 1990. Mem. DAR (pub. rels. chmn., recording sec., archives chmn. Camdenton chpt. 1985—), Phi Epsilon of Phi Beta Kappa. Presbyterian. Home and Office: Rte 1 Box 95A Versailles MO 65084

REYNOLDS, SUSAN ELIZABETH, marketing professional; b. Carlisle, Pa., Dec. 12, 1950; d. Harold Kenneth and Elizabeth (Holman) R. BS, Western Mich. U., 1973, postgrad., 1974-75. Systems engr. IBM, Lansing, Mich., 1977-81; regional mktg. support rep. IBM, Detroit, 1982-83, systems engring. mgr., 1984-85, area systems support mgr., 1985-86, resource programs mgr., 1986-87, area mktg. mgr., 1987; asst. to v.p. and area mgr. IBM, Southfield, Mich., 1987-88; br. mgr. IBM, Youngstown, Ohio, 1988—. Judge retriever field trials Am. Kennel Club. Recipient Grand prize photograph contest Dog's USA, 1985, Nat. Photography awards, 1985-88. Mem. Youngstown C. of C. (bd. dirs.), Rotary, Birmingham Community Women's Club, Wolverine Retriever Club, Buckeye Retriever Club. Republican. Lutheran. Office: IBM 250 Federal Pla E Youngstown OH 44503

REYNOLDS, SUSAN JEAN, food scientist, journalist; b. London, Ky., Nov. 10, 1954; d. Richard Samuel and Darlene Marie (Goehring) R. BS in Home Econs., Tenn. Technol. U., 1976; MS in Food Sci., U. Tenn., 1977. Cert. home economist; lic. dietitian, Ga. Co-editor publs. Tenn. Technol. U. Alumni Assn., Cookeville, 1975-76; foods and nutrition specialist Ala. Coop. Extension Svc., Auburn, 1977-82; extension foods specialist U. Ga. Coop. Extension Svc., Athens, 1982—; trainer, cons. Tex. Coop. Extension Svc., College Station, 1989; host, author TV series So Easy To Preserve, 1988. Author: So Easy To Preserve, 1984; editor Foodways to Better Health newsletter, 1984-87; writer over 25 brochures. Youth counselor United Meth. Ch., Auburn and Athens, 1979-86, missions chmn., Athens, 1987; pub. rels. chmn. Am. Cancer Soc. Aux., Athens, 1986-87; advisor Mortar Bd., U. Ga., 1987—; historian Classic City Christmas Community Celebration, Athens, 1988, 89. Mem. Inst. Food Technologists (sec. extension sect. 1988-89), Am. Home Econs. Assn., Internat. Fedn. for Home Econs., Greater Athens Single Profls. (organizer), Palladia, Epsilon Sigma Phi, Phi Kappa Phi (sec. U. Ga. 1989—). Home: 120 E Rutherford St Athens GA 30605 Office: U Ga Coop Extension Svc Hoke Smith Annex Athens GA 30605

REYNOLDS, W(YNETKA) ANN, university system administrator, educator; b. Coffeyville, Kans., Nov. 3, 1937; d. John Ethelbert and Glennie (Beanland) King; m. Thomas H. Kirschbaum; children—Rachel Rebecca, Rex King. BS in Biology-Chemistry, Kans. State Tchrs. Coll., Emporia, 1958; MS in Zoology, U. Iowa, Iowa City, 1960, PhD, 1962; DSc (hon.), Ind. State U., Evansville, 1980; LHD (hon.), McKendree Coll., 1984, U. N.C., Charlotte, 1988, U. Judaism, L.A., 1989; DSc (hon.), Ball State U., Muncie, Ind., 1985, Emporia (Kans.) State U., 1987; PhD (hon.), Fu Jen Cath. U., Republic of China, 1987. Asst. prof. biology Ball State U., Muncie, Ind., 1962-65; asst. prof. anatomy U. Ill. Coll. Medicine, Chgo., 1965-68, assoc. prof. anatomy, 1968-73, research prof. ob-gyn, from 1973, prof. anatomy, from 1973, acting assoc. dean acad. affairs Coll. Medicine, 1977, assoc. vice chancellor, dean grad. coll., 1977-79; prof. ob-gyn Ohio State U., Columbus, 1979-82, prof. anatomy, 1979-82, provost, 1979-82; chancellor Calif. State Univ. system, Long Beach, 1982-90, prof. biology, 1982—; cons. and lectr. in field; prof. biology Calif. State U., Dominguez Hills, 1982—; hon. prof. biol. scis. San Francisco State U., 1982—; clin. prof. ob/gyn. UCLA, 1985—; chair exec. coun. of chief acad. officers Am. Coun. Edn., 1981-82, bd. dirs. coun., 1982-85; chair Econ. Literacy Coun. Calif., 1983-83; mem. Nat. Commn. for Excellence Tchr. Edn., 1984-85, Nat. Commn. Excellence in Ednl. Adminstrn., 1985-86, Nat. Commn. Continuing Higher Edn. Leadership, 1985-88; co-chair Fed. Task Force on Women, Minorities and Handicapped in Sci. and Tech., 1987—; adv. bd. Congl. Black Caucus Inst. Sci., Space and Tech., 1987—; mem. Nat. Coun. Devel. Edn., 1987—; bd. dirs. Regional Rsch. Inst. So. Calif., 1984-87; co-chair Humanitas Coun. L.A. Ednl. Partnership, 1986-89; bd. dirs. GTE Calif., Maytag Corp., Abbott Labs., Am. Electric Power Co. Contbr. chpts. to books, articles to profl. jours; assoc. editor Am. Biology Tchr., 1964-67. Active numerous civic activities involving edn. and the arts; chair Econ. Literacy Coun. Calif., 1983-89; bd. dirs. Am. Council for the Arts, 1986—, Calif. Econ. Devel. Corp., 1984—; trustee Internat. Life Scis. Inst.-Nutrition Found., 1987—, Southwest Mus., L.A., 1986—, L.A. County High Sch. For Arts Found., 1985—; mem. arts in edn. adv. bd. NEA, 1989—. Recipient Disting. Alumni award Kans. State Tchrs. Coll., 1972, Calif. Gov.'s Award for the Arts for an Outstanding Individual in Arts in Edn., 1989, Prize award Cen. Assn. Obstetricians and Gynecologists, 1968; NSF Predoctoral fellow, 1958-62, Woodrow Wilson Hon. fellow, 1958; named Honoree Women's Employment Options Conf., Pasadena, 1983, Women's Opportunity Week, North San Diego County, 1983. Fellow Calif. Acad. Scis., Am. Coll. Obstetricians and Gynecologists (assoc.); mem. AAAS, Am. Assn. Anatomists, Am. Diabetes Assn., Am. Soc. Zoologists, Am. Assn. for Higher Edn. (bd. dirs. 1984—), Endocrine Soc., Perinatal Research Soc., Soc. Exptl. Biology and Medicine, Soc. Gynecologic Investigation (sec./treas. 1980-83), Am. Assn. State Colls. and Univs. (nat. commn. role and future of state colls. and univs. 1985-87), Nat. Assn. Systems Heads (pres. 1987-88), Calif. C. of C. (bd. dirs. 1990—), Sigma Xi. Office: City U NY 535 E 80th New York NY 10021

REYNOLDS SHAW, MARY ANNE, special education teacher; b. Hanover, N.H., Apr. 23, 1947; d. Earl Wesley and Anne Virginia (McDermott) Reynolds; m. Robert Thomas Shaw, June 19, 1980; children: Marissa, Elizabeth, Christian, Virginia, Lincoln, Ormacinda. BS, So. Ill. U., 1969, postgrad., 1977-79, 88—; MS, No. Ill. U., 1972. Cert. elem. and spl. edn. tchr., Ill. Tchr. spl. edn. primary grades Carpentersville (Ill.) Sch. Dist., 1969-70; tchr. English high sch. DeKalb (Ill.) Sch. Dist., 1970-71; tchr. primary grades Marissa (Ill.) Sch. Dist., 1971-73; tchr. spl. edn. jr. high sch. Zeigler-Royalton (Ill.) Sch. Dist., 1973-76; asst. prin. Crete-Monee Jr. High Sch., Park Forest South, Ill., 1976-77; spl. educator Dept. Corrections Ill. Dept. Corrections, Menard, 1979—. Active on sch. bd. Marissa Sch. Dist., 1987-91, rm. mother, 1984-89; asst. leader Brownies, Marissa, 1988-89; asst. leader Girl Scouts Am., Marissa, 1985-89. Recipient fellowship No. Ill. U., DeKalb, 1969-70, doctoral fellowship So. Ill. U., Carbondale, 1977-79. Mem. Am. Correctional Edn. Assn., AAUW (pres., editor yearbook Sparta chpt. 1988-89), DAR (regent Marissa chpt. 1988—, editor yearbook 1986—, program presenter 1984-89), Marissa Women's Club (chmn. edn. 1980-87, program presenter 1979-89), Phi Delta Kappa, Kappa Delta Phi. Republican. Presbyterian. Home: 320 S Park Marissa IL 62257 Office: Menard Correctional Ctr Sch Bldg Menard IL 62259

REZENTES, CYNTHIA KIM LEN, engineering specialist, electrical engineer; b. Honolulu, Apr. 9, 1952; d. Kirkwood Joseph and Betty Rose (Saylor) R.; m. Anthony J. Steflik , Apr. 9, 1983 (div. June 1989). BSEE, Gonzaga U., 1974; MSEE, U. N.Mex., 1975. With IBM Corp., 1976—; lab. engring. mgr. IBM Corp., Boulder, Colo., 1979-89, Tucson, 1990—. Home: 8750 E Saddleback Dr Tucson AZ 85749

RHEA, MARCIA CHANDLER, accountant; b. Columbia, S.C., Apr. 27, 1956; d. Foster Frazier and Virginia Elizabeth (Goude) Chandler; m. Randall W. Rhea, Aug. 23, 1980. AA, Bauder Coll., Atlanta, 1975; BA magna cum laude, Coll. of Charleston, S.C., 1981; postgrad., CPA studies. Cert. tax practice ptnr., notary pub., S.C. Acct. Foster F. Chandler, Acctg., St. John's Island, S.C.; writer, producer U.S. Army C.E., Charleston, 1984; mng. ptnr. Care/Share Prodns., Charleston. Author: (books) Does It Have to Happen Again?, From Hell's Angel to Heaven's Saint; contbr. articles to mags. and profl. jours.; producer various films. Adult tchr. Ashley Rivers Bapt. Ch. Recipient Outstanding Acad. Achievement award Coll. of Charleston. Mem. Am. Soc. Notaries, S.C. Motion Picture TV Assn., Script Writers of S.C., Inc., Acctg. Assn., Coll. of Charleston Alumni, Film Soc. Coll. Charleston (bd. dirs.), Phi Kappa Phi, Phi Mu. Republican. Baptist. Office: 3226 Maybank Hwy Ste 1 PO Box 508 Johns Island SC 29455

RHEDIN, JUDITH A., lawyer; b. San Marcos, Tex., July 19, 1948; d. James Porter and Ethel Louise (Belcher) Washington; m. Peter Bjorn V. Rhedin, May 19, 1971 (dec. 1976). B Profl. Studies, Pace U., N.Y.C., 1985; JD/MSc. in Judicial Admin, U. Denver, 1987. Asst. passage adminstr. Interair Luftfahrt Service Duesseldorf Internat. Airport, W. Germany, 1973-77; profl. actress TV Stage, U.S.A., Europe, 1977-82; asst. to Mrs. Lee Hart 1988 Campaign, Denver, 1987; research asst. U. Denver Coll. Law; law clerk, judge Colo. Court of Appeals, Denver, 1988; asst. dir. narcotics control unit N.Y.C. Dept. Housing Preservation and Devel., 1988--. Co-Author: Denver Journal of Internat. Law and Policy; contbr. articles to law jours. Mem. Coalition of 100 Black Women, N.Y.C. 1989. Recipient Commencement award Pace U., 1985, Distinguished Service award Sam Cary Bar Assn., Denver 1985. Mem. Nat. Acad. TV Arts and Sci., Am. Assn. U. Women, U. Denver Coll. Law, Nat. Bar Assn., Alpha Kappa Alpha, Phi Gamma Mu. Democrat. Episcopal. Office: NYC Dept Housing Preservation 75 Maiden Ln Rm 412 New York NY 10038

RHEE, SUSAN BYUNGSOOK, educator, counselor; b. Seoul, Korea, Oct. 16, 1937; came to U.S., 1956; d. Kap Soo and Heung Soon (Kim) Lee; m. Charles Hangtai Rhee, Mar. 17, 1961 (dec. 1987); children: Ronald E., Sandra H., Robert Y. BA in Sociology, MacMurray Coll., 1960; MS in Counseling Psychology, George Williams Coll., 1971; postgrad., No. Ill. U., 1987—. Nat. cert. counselor and nat. cert. career counselor. Counselor, career specialist Counseling and Human Rels. Ctr. George Williams Coll., Downers Grove, Ill., 1971-82; part-time dir. career counseling Ball Found., Glen Ellyn, Ill., 1979-81, cons., 1981-85; assoc. prof., counselor Coll. of DuPage, Glen Ellyn, Ill., 1938-89, prof., 1989—. Mem. adv. bd. Korean-Am. Community Svc., Chgo., 1989—. Mem. Am. Assn. Counseling and Devel. (conv. chair 1988, women's com. 1989, 90—, Cert. of Recognition 1988), Am. Assn. Multicultural Counseling and Devel. (chair multicultural concerns 1985, 86, 87), Ill. Assn. Multi-Cultural Counseling and Devel. (pres. 1989-90), Ill. Assn. for Counseling and Devel. Conv. (chair human rels. com. 1985, 86, conv. co-chair 1989), Phi Beta Kappa, Phi Gamma Mu, Kappa Delta Pi. Home: 3605 Buckthorn Ln Downers Grove IL 60515 Office: Coll of DuPage 22d Lambert St Glen Ellyn IL 60137

RHEINSTEIN-PITTARD, LINDA CAROL, marketing professional; b. L.A., Sept. 15, 1956; d. Frederic and Patricia (Horn) Rheinstein; m. William Blackburn Pittard, Aug. 16, 1986: 1 stepson, Colby Pittard. Pres. Autographics, Inc., Hollywood, Calif.; dir. Electric Paint, Inc., Hollywood; v.p. The Post Group, Inc., Hollywood. Nominated TV Emmy award; recipient BDA Svc. awards. Mem. AWRT, BDA BPME, NCGA, Acad. TV Arts and Scis.. Home: 6335 Homewood Ave Hollywood CA 90028

RHIND, LISA KAY, communications and public relations specialist; b. Detroit, Feb. 10, 1965; d. Christopher George and Janice Kay (Remo) R. BA in Social Sci. Prelaw, Polit. Sci., Mich. State U., 1987, MA in Social Sci., 1989. Sales cons. Zales Jewelers, Inc., Okemos, Mich., 1986-87; cons. Mich. Coalition on Smoking or Health, Lansing, Mich., 1988; student asst III Ctr. for Environ. Health Scis., Mich. Dept. Pub. Health, Lansing, 1987-89; chief info. resource unit vet. health promotion sect. Mich. Dept. Pub. Health, Lansing, 1989—; intern personnel unit Office of Gov., Lansing, 1986-87. Editor, author: (annual report) Michigan Agent Orange Program, 1989, 90; editor, contbr. (quar. newsletter) The Hourglass, 1989-90, (program brochure) Mich. Agent Orange Program, 1989—. Tutor Boys and Girls Club Lansing, 1989—; vol. press unit Office of Gov., Lansing, 1987-88. Mem. Women in Communications Inc. (sec. Lansing profl. chpt. 1990—), NAFE, Mich. Assn. for Info. Specialists. Home: 1210 2A Runaway Bay Dr Lansing MI 48917

RHINE, JENNIE, judge; b. Washington, Sept. 14, 1939; d. Henry Rhine and Jessica Irene (Buck) Wildman; 1 child, Derek M. Rusch. Student, Harvey Mudd Coll., 1957-59; BA, San Francisco State U., 1964; JD, U. Calif. Hastings Coll. Law, San Francisco, 1969. Employment security officer Calif. Dept. Employment, San Francisco, 1964-67; Reginald Heber Smith fellow San Francisco Neighborhood Legal Assistance, San Francisco, 1969-70, San Mateo County Legal Aid, Redwood City, Calif., 1970-71; ptnr. Rhine & Morgan, Berkeley, Calif., 1972-75; pvt. practice Berkeley, 1975-88; adminstrv. law judge Calif. Agr. Labor Rels. Bd., Occidental, 1977-83; hearing officer Office of Citizen Complaints, San Francisco, 1985-88; judge Alameda County Mcpl. Ct./Berkeley-Albany Jud. Dist., Calif., 1989—; Mem. adv. bd. Nat. Jury Project, Oakland, Calif., 1980—; mem. substance abuse subcom. Jud. Coordinating Commn., Alameda County, Calif., 1989—, chair gender bias subcom., 1990—. Mem. adv. bd. Sta. KPFA Radio, Berkeley, 1983—; vice chair, bd. dirs. Pacifica Found., Berkeley, 1986—. Reginald Heber Smith fellow, 1969; named one of Outstanding Young

Women in Am., 1972. Mem. Nat. Assn. Women Judges, Calif. Judges Assn., Nat. Lawyers Guild (pres. San Francisco chpt. 1974-75), Alameda County Bar Assn. Democrat. Office: Berkeley Albany Mcpl Ct 2120 Martin L King Jr Way Berkeley CA 94704

RHOADES, BARBARA LYNN, administrative services coordinator; b. Davenport, Iowa, May 6, 1949; d. Mark Thomas and Helen Evelyn (McGuire) Canum; m. Gregory G. Peterson, Apr. 13, 1968 (div. Oct. 1976); children: Scott Peterson, Blair Peterson; m. Gary Townsend, Oct. 21, 1978 (dec. Oct. 1980); stepchild, Rachel Townsend; m. Daniel Paul Rhoades, May 9, 1981; stepchildren: Daniel Blake, Heidi Lyn. Assoc., Black Hawk Coll., 1987. Bookkeeper, filer 1st Nat. Bank of the Quad-Cities, Rock Island, Ill., 1967-68, night supr., 1971-72; proof operator Davenport Bank & Trust Co., 1976-80; head proof dept. Uptown Nat. Bank, Moline, Ill., 1980; bldg. sec., MasterCard sec. Davenport Bank & Trust Co., 1980-81; staff asst. Congressman Lane Evans, Moline, 1984-85; adminstrv. asst. to pres. Stokeld Health Svcs. Corp., Moline, 1985-88, C & B Consulting Group, St. Louis, 1988-89; supr. adminstrv. svcs. Invitron Corp., St. Louis, 1989—. Home: 2752 Wintergreen Florissant MO 63033 Office: 4649 Le Bourget Saint Louis MO 63134

RHOADES, NANCY ANN, air force officer; b. Fort Campbell, Ky., June 16, 1959; d. Glen Lee and Mary Josephine (Lasell) R. BS in Astro Engring., U.S. Air Force Acad., 1981; MS in Aero. and Astronaut. Engring., Stanford U., 1985. Commd. 2d lt. U.S. Air Force, 1981, advanced through grades to capt., 1985; satellite test engr. space div. Los Angeles, 1981-84; instr. dept. astronautics U.S. Air Force Acad., Colorado Springs, Colo., 1985-88, office of the sec. Air Force Spl. Projects, 1988—. Recipient Medal of Merit, Nat. Air Force Assn., 1985; named Colorado Springs Mil. Woman of Yr., Gazette Telegraph newspaper, 1987. Mem. Air Force Assn., Am. Astronautical Soc., Soc. Women Engrs. Avocations: aerobics, long distance running, sewing. Home: 13429 Glasgow Pl Hawthorne CA 90250 Office: PO Box 92960 Worldway Postal Ctr Los Angeles CA 90009

RHOADES, SYLVIA EILEEN, educator; b. L.A., Aug. 6, 1936; d. Reni Sylvanus and Aili Maria (Haigler) Berry; m. Joseph Welles White, Jan. 29, 1974 (dec. May 1980); m. Harold Emerson Rhoades, Aug. 20, 1989. BA, Pepperdine Coll., L.A., 1958, MA, 1963. Kindergarten tchr. Braddock Dr. Elem. Sch., L.A., 1960-82, pre-kindergarten tchr., 1982—. Recipient 4 1st place awards in ceramics Art Show Commn. Pomona, Calif., 1979. Mem. Am. Guild of English Handbell Ringers, Four Tones Quartet, Marching Handbell Choir. Republican. Church of Christ. Home: 862 Galloway St Pacific Palisades CA 90272

RHOADS, NANCY GLENN, trial lawyer; b. Washington, Oct. 15, 1957; d. Donald L. and Gerry R. R.; m. Robert A. Koons, June 23, 1984. BA, Gettysburg Coll., 1980; JD, Temple U., 1983. Bar: Pa., U.S. Dist. Ct. (ea. dist.) Pa. 1983. Rsch. asst. Prof. Mikochick, Phila., 1982-83; law clk. Phila. Ct. of Common Pleas, 1983-85; assoc. Post and Schell P.C., Phila., 1985—. Co-author: Aging and the Aged: Problems, Opportunities, Challenges, 1980. Vol. Spl. Olympics. Mem. Phila. Bar Assn. (civil judicial procedures rules com.), Pro Bono Work, Phi Beta Kappa, Phi Alpha Theta, Pi Delta Epsilon, Eta Sigma Phi. Home: Gwynedd Knoll 1374 Tanglewood Dr Gwynedd PA 19436 Office: Post and Schell PC 1800 JFK Blvd 19th Fl Philadelphia PA 19103

RHOADS, SHEILA LUBIN, French educator; b. L.A., June 11, 1946; d. David and Martha (Prochnik) Lubin; m. Donald Perry Rhoads, Jan. 5, 1969; children: Emma, Perry, John, Anna. Diploma, U. Dijon, France, 1966, U. Grenoble, France, 1967; BA in French and German, UCLA, 1968, MA in French, 1970. Tchr. French Westridge Sch. for Girls, Pasadena, Calif., 1970-73; supr. teaching program French and German Mt. St. Mary's Coll. and Hamilton High Sch., L.A., 1974; tchr. French L.A. City Sch. Dist., 1975-81; instr. French San Bernardino (Calif.) Valley Coll., 1984-87, 89—, instr. French evening div., 1984—; tchr. French Rim of the World High Sch., Lake Arrowhead, Calif., 1988-89; tchr. English as a second lang. Belmont Community Adult Sch., 1975-81. Bd. dirs. Arrowhead Lake Assn., Calif., 1984-87, mem. lake ops. com., 1984-88; asst. dir., instr. Lake Arrowhead Elem. Sch. Ski Club, 1982-86; co-founder, asst. dir., ski team coach Mary Putnam Henk Intermediate Sch. Ski Club, 1987-88, instr., 1989—. Mem. AAUW, Alliance Francaise, San Bernardino-Riverside (acad. rep. 1985, leader book club div. 1985—), Am. Assn. Tchrs. French. Home: 675 Grass Valley Rd Lake Arrowhead CA 92352 Address: PO Box 8094 San Bernardino CA 92412-8094

RHODEHAMEL, SHARON MAE, electrical engineer; b. Portland, Ind., Dec. 12, 1944; d. Charles W. and Florence M. (Heidegger) Coldren; 1 child, Rex. BS, Purdue U., Ft. Wayne, Ind., 1968; MS, Purdue U., 1972; grad., Charmaine Finishing, Modeling, 1989; tech. assoc., GTE North Telephone Ops., Ft. Wayne, Ind., 1989. Cert. profl. secondary tchr., Ind. Math tchr. Smith Green Community Schs., 1968-72; co-owner, operator Ray's Svc. Ctr., Churubusco, Ind., 1971-80; math. tchr. Ft. Wayne Community Schs., 1972-74; clk., treas. Town of Crubusco, Ind., 1984; instr. math. Purdue U., Ft. Wayne, Ind., 1981-84; sr. engr. GTE North Telephone Ops., North Ft. Wayne, Ind., 1984—. Past pres. Churubusco Vol. Fire Dept. Aux. Mem. IEEE, SIAM, OES (past matron), Purdue Alumni, Beta Sigma Phi.

RHODES, ANN L(OUISE), construction company executive; b. Ft. Worth, Oct. 17, 1941; d. Jon Knox and Carol Jane (Greene) R.; student Tex. Christian U., 1960-63. V.p. Rhodes Enterprises Inc., Ft. Worth, 1963-77; owner-mgr. Lucky R Ranch, Ft. Worth, 1969—, Ann L. Rhodes Investments, Ft. Worth, 1976—; pres., chmn. bd. ALR Enterprises, Inc., Ft. Worth, 1977—; pres. Sunergos Prodn. Co. div. ALR Enterprises, Inc., 1983—. Bd. dirs. Tarrant Coun. Alcoholism, 1973-78, hon. bd. dirs., 1978—; bd. dirs. N.W. Tex. coun. Arthritis Found., 1977-84; adv. bd. Stage West, 1987—; bd. dirs. Circle Theater, 1987—; bd. govs. Ft. Worth Theatre, 1989—; exec. com. Tarrant County Rep. Party, 1964-69. Recipient various svc. awards. Mem. Jr. League Ft. Worth, Addison and Randolph Clark Soc. Tex. Christian U., Alpha Psi Omega, Kappa Kappa Gamma. Episcopalian. Office: Ridglea Bank Bldg Ste 908 Fort Worth TX 76116

RHODES, ANN MARIE, academic administrator, lawyer; b. Waterloo, Iowa, July 1, 1953; d. John Paul and Kathleen (Kennedy) R.; m. Steven Paul Miller, May 30, 1980; children: Kathleen Kennedy, Elizabeth Rhodes. BS, Coll. St. Teresa, 1975; MA, U. Iowa, 1976, JD, 1982. Bar: Iowa 1982. Instr. Mt. Mercy Coll., Cedar Rapids, Iowa, 1976-77; clin. nursing specialist U. Iowa Hosps. and Clinics, Iowa City, 1977-79, supr. nursing, 1979-82, clin. nursing specialist, 1982-83, asst. to dir., 1983-87; asst. v.p. fin. and univ. svcs. U. Iowa, Iowa City, 1987—; adj. asst. prof. mgmt. and adminstrv. law U. Iowa, 1982—. Author: Nursing and the Law, 1984 (named Book of Yr. 1984); contbg. editor Health Care Supr., 1983-85, Topics in Hosp. Law, 1985—; columnist Am. Jour. Maternal Child Nursing, 1985—. Health care advisor to U.S. Senator Tom Harken, 1984—; bd. dirs. Iowa City Domestic Violence Intervention Project, 1989—, Iowa Hwy. Rsch. Bd., 1989—. Mem. ABA, Iowa Bar Assn. (com. on liason with other profls. 1985—), Johnson County Bar Assn., Am. Acad. Hosp. Attys., Am. Soc. Law and Medicine. Democrat. Roman Catholic. Club: Altrusa (Iowa City). Home: 2238 Bancroft Dr Iowa City IA 52240 Office: U Iowa 101 Jessup Hall Iowa City IA 52242

RHODES, BEVERLY ANISOWICZ, bursar, sports columnist, educator; b. Northampton, Mass., Oct. 18, 1947; d. Chester Stanley and Christine Constance (Szarkowski) Anisowicz; m. Francis C. Rhodes, Jr., June 17, 1989. AA, Greenfield Community Coll., 1971; BA magna cum laude, U. Mass., 1973; MS, Antioch-New Eng. Grad. Sch., 1988; postgrad. U. Mass., 1988—. Bursar, Smith Coll., Northampton, Mass., 1977-88, mgmt. cons., 1988—, instr. Antioch-New Eng. Grad. Sch., 1987—, Greenfield Community Coll., 1987-88, Sch. for Internat. Tng., 1989—; columnist Pro Football Weekly, Chgo., 1979-88, The Recorder, Greenfield, Mass., 1988—; free-lance writer, 1981—; pres. Investments Unlimited, Northampton, 1976, 78-80; treas. Town of Whately, Mass., 1988-89; sports talk show host various Mass. radio stas., 1982-84. Author: Beefcake and Lifeslices, 1986. Mem. Nat. Assn. Accts. (v.p. communications 1975-78), Nat. Football League Players Assn. (founder, bd. dir. of career transition program 1989—), Phi Beta Kappa. Avocations: whale watching, interspecies communication, scuba diving, photography. Home and Office: RFD 1 16 Laurel Mountain Rd Haydenville MA 01039

RHODES, CHRISTINE ELISE, medical editor, writer; b. Munich, Sept. 19, 1952; came to U.S., 1954; d. Alfred H. and Martina (Donner) R.; m. E. Michael Geiger, Nov. 29, 1987. BS in Nutrition, Lehman Coll. CUNY, 1979; MS, Columbia U., 1983. Asst. editor PW Communications, N.Y.C., 1976-79; asst. to banquet mgr. Plaza Hotel, N.Y.C., 1979-80; copy editor Biomed. Info., Inc., N.Y.C., 1979-80; asst. program specialist Fed. Feeding Program/USDA, N.Y.C., 1980; editor-in-chief Jour. Practical Nursing, N.Y.C., 1982-84; sr. assoc. editor Diagnosis mag., Oradell, N.J., 1984-87; copy chief Benefit Communications Svcs./Equicor, Inc., N.Y.C., 1987-88; sr. editorial dir. med. communications Edelman Pub. Rels., N.Y.C., 1988-90; dir. publs. Row Pubs., N.Y.C., 1990—; presenter workshops in field. Democrat. Office: Park Row Pubs 1457 Broadway New York NY 10036

RHODES, CYNTHIA STRAHLER, communications company manager; b. Allentown, Pa., May 28, 1947; d. George Robert and Janet Gordon Strahler; student Ursinus Coll., 1965-66, U. Md., 1970, Lafayette Coll., 1982-89; m. Robert Wesley Rhodes, Oct. 22, 1966; children—Danielle Renee, Robert Carver. Supr. network engring. AT&T Long Lines, 1972-75, market adminstr., 1975-78, supr. spl. communications project, 1978-79, supr. service costs, Bedminster, N.J., 1979-81, staff supr. tariff planning and adminstrn., 1981-82, staff mgr. interstate tariff implementation, 1982-86, staff mgr. interstate strategic access costs, 1986-89, regulatory case mgr. custom designed integrated svcs., Bridgewater, N.J., 1989—. Mem. NAFE. Republican. Moravian. Office: 131 Morristown Rd D145 Basking Ridge NJ 07920

RHODES, ELIZABETH JOAN, public relations executive; b. Hartford, Conn., Jan. 30, 1955; d. Elton Dibble and Dorothy C. (Woods) R.; m. Gregory D. Morell, Sept. 11, 1982; 1 child, Clayton R. Student, Franklin & Marshall Coll., 1972-74; BA in Am. Studies, George Washington U., 1977. Asst. account exec. Sontheimer & Co., N.Y.C., 1978-81; account exec. Ruth Morrison Assocs., N.Y.C., 1981-83; account supr. Ketchum Pub. Rels., N.Y.C., 1983-85; v.p. Dorf & Stanton Communications, Stamford, Conn., 1985-90; pres. Rhodes-Morell Communications, West Redding, Conn., 1990—. Bd. dirs. March of Dimes, Fairfield County, 1986-88, spl. event publicist, 1986-88. Mem. Women in Communications, Inc. (bd. dirs. 1986-88, Matrix award 1987), Fairfield County Pub. Rels. Assn.

RHODES, GINNA LOIS, supervisor education; b. Flagstaff, Ariz., Jan. 5, 1936; d. Edgar W. Cheves and Helen A. (Willis) Olson; m. Jay W. Rhodes, Feb. 5, 1966. BA in Edn., Ariz. State U., 1960, MA in Edn., 1967; postgrad., East Tex. State U., 1973, North Tex. State U., 1975, U. Tex., El Paso, 1984. Cert. tchr. Tex., profl. supr., provisional high sch., Eng. and indsl. arts. Tchr. Irving (Tex.) Ind. Sch. Dist., 1966-71, English cons. K-12, 1971-76; co-owner Ginna's Card Nook, Ginna's Inkwell, Crown Printing, 1976-89; tchr. El Paso Ind. Sch. Dist., 1979-82; supr. secondary English, journalism and speech Ysleta Ind. Sch. Dist., El Paso, 1982—; adjunct asst. prof. U. Tex., El. Paso, 1984—. Contbr. articles to newspapers and profl. jours. Mem. ASCD, Paso Del Norte ASCD, Nat. Coun. Tchrs. of English, Tex. Coun. Tchrs. of English (treas. 1985-86, v.p. for programs 1987-88, pres.-elect 1990—), Tex. Coun. of Women Sch. Execs., Conf. for Secondary Sch. Eng. Dept. Chmn., Phi Delta Kappa, Alpha Delta Kappa. Office: Ysleta Ind Sch Dist 9600 Sims El Paso TX 79925

RHODES, HELEN LOUISE, insurance underwriter; b. L.A., Sept. 3, 1946; d. Dale Albert and Frances Marion (Nelson) Riley; 1 child, Wendy Meredith. BA, UCLA, L.A., 1968. Assoc. underwriting. Underwriter Western Employers, Fullerton, Calif., 1977-81; deputy underwriter GIGNA, Orange, Calif., 1981-82; field underwriter mgr. Argonaut, San Diego, 1982-86; underwriter supr. Safeco, Fountain Valley, Calif., 1986-90; casualty underwriter supr. Kemper, Industry, Calif., 1990—. Home: 2637 Amherst Ave Fullerton CA 92633 Office: Kemper 17800 Castleton St Industry CA 91748

RHODES, HELEN MARY, real estate broker, educator; b. Fort Branch, Ind., Jan. 12, 1921; d. Henry A. and Anna J. (Herr) Wirth; m. David A. I, May 3, 1952; children: David A. II and Brooke Anthony. Grad., Lockyear Coll., 1939; cert., Real Estate Inst., 1981. Grad. Realtors Inst. Clk. War Dept., Washington, 1942-44; stenographer OSS, Washington (D.C.), 1944-45; clk. Dept. of Fgn. Svc., London, 1945-46; asst. sales mgr. printing and advt. Keller Crescent Co., Evansville, Ind., 1946-52; stenographer Indpls. Air Procurement, Evansville, 1952-53; asst. media dir. Grant Advt., 1953-56; freelance writer, 1955-70; prin. real estate Columbus, Ohio, 1970—; real estate instr. Columbus State Community Coll., 1977—. Author: Josie's Bedtime Stories, 1966; writer Chicago Heights Star, Ill., 1961-61; contbr. articles to profl. jours. Pub. rels. officer Sauk Village, Ill., 1962. Mem. Nat. Assn. Realtors, Ohio Assn. Realtors, Columbus Bd. Realtors, Columbus Real Estate Exchangers, Ohio Comml. Real Estate Assn., Nat. Real Estate Educators Assn. (charter), Ohio Real Estate Educators Assn., Women's Coun. of Realtors.

RHODES, JUDITH CAROL, microbiologist, mycologist; b. Tulsa, Okla., Jan. 27, 1949; d. George Newton and Bonnie Beatrice (Gates) R. BS in Med. Tech., U. Okla., 1971, MS in Microbiology, 1973; PhD in Microbiology and Immunology, UCLA, 1980. Diplomate Am. Bd. Med. Microbiology; cert. med. technologist, clin. lab. technologist. Rsch. assoc. Mayo Clinic, Rochester, Minn., 1973-74; clin. lab. technologist UCLA Hosp. and Clinics, 1974-80; postdoctoral fellow NIH, Bethesda, Md., 1980-82; asst. prof. U. Cin., 1982-87, assoc. prof., 1987—; dir. mycology lab. Univ. Hosp., Cin., 1982—, assoc. dir. clin. microbiology, 1985—; cons. VA Med. Ctr., Cin., 1990—. Author book chpt. in field; editorial bd. Infection and Immunity jour., 1990-92. Recipient Dalldorf fellowship Infectious Diseases Soc. of Am., 1980-82, rsch. grants, NIH, 1988-91, 90-95. Mem. Am. Soc. Microbiology (Found. for Microbiology lectr. 1989-90), Am. Soc. Clin. Pathology (assoc. mem.), Internat. Soc. for Human and Animal Mycology, Med. Mycol. Soc. of the Ams., Mycol. Soc. Am., South Cen. Assn. Clin. Microbiology. Democrat. Presbyterian. Office: Dept Pathology/Lab Medicine Univ Cincinnati Cincinnati OH 45267-0529

RHODES, SUSAN E., pharmaceutical executive; b. Springfield, Mo., Jan. 25, 1954; d. Alan Duryea and Joyce Blaine (Pine) Sutherland. AA, Santa Fe Community Coll., Gainesville, Fla., 1973; BA, U. of South Fla., 1976; mgmt. and supr. program, Wilmington Coll., 1983. Clin. rsch. asst. Janssen Pharms., Piscataway, N.J.; clin. rsch. assoc. DuPont Pharms., Wilmington, Del., Schering Rsch Key Pharms., Miami; sr. clin. rsch. assoc. and asst. project mgr. Clin Rsch. Internat., Rsch. Triangle Park, N.C.; group leader, project mgr. Clin Rsch. Internat., Rsch. Triangle Park, asst. bus. devel. mgr. Mem. NAFE, NOW, Assocs. of Clin. Pharmacology, Psi Chi. Home: 102 Old Maple Ln Durham NC 27713

RHODES, VALERIE RUTH, accountant; b. Valdosta, Ga., Oct. 25, 1961; d. Arthur and Mary Frances (Crawford) Moore. BSBA in Acctg., Boston U., 1983; Cert. in Computer Programming and Systems Analysis, Northeastern U., 1988. Acct. mut. funds State St. Bank, Quincy, Mass., 1983-85; acct. Blue Cross/Blue Shield, Boston, 1985-86, supr. acctg. control, 1986-88; staff acct. Coopers and Lybrand, Boston, 1988-90, sr. assoc., 1990—. Mem. Nat. Assn. Female Execs. Home: 251 Belmont St #2B Brockton MA 02401 Office: Coopers and Lybrand 1 PO Sq Boston MA 02109

RHODES, VICTORIA ELIZABETH, assistant film director; b. Los Angeles, Jan. 7, 1957; d. Augustus Hulon and Winifred Elizabeth (Cash) R. BA, U. So. Calif., Los Angeles, 1978. Tchr. math. John Burroughs Jr. High Sch., L.A., 1978-80; freelance asst. dir. motion picture prodn. L.A., 1980—; spokesperson Asst. Dirs. Tng.Program, Los Angeles, 1988—. Contbr. to book. Mem. choir Ch. Christian Fellowship, L.A., 1983-85. Recipient Cert. Commendation, City of Los Angeles, 1987. Mem. Dirs. Guild Am. (award 1986), U. So. Calif. Cinema-TV Alumni Assn., Alpha Kappa Alpha Sorority (Ebony Excellence award-Women of the 80's Mu Beta Omega chpt. 1987). Democrat. Congregationalist. Home: 4031 Wade St Unit A Los Angeles CA 90066

RHODIG, LORI L., chemist; b. Omaha, Nov. 3, 1958; d. Fred F. and Janet R. (Kuker) Anderson; m. Brian S. Rhodig, June 24, 1981; 1 child, Joshua Nicholas. BS in Chemistry, Creighton U., Omaha, 1981; postgrad., U. Nebr. at Omaha, 1988--. Chemist V.P.O., Omaha, 1981-83; quality control mgr. Smith-Kime Animal Health Products, Omaha, 1983--; methods review com. AOAC, Arlington Va., 1988--. Co-author: Contbr. article to profl. jours. 1984. Mem. Am. Chem. Soc., Assn. Offl. Analytical Chemists, Am. Inst. Chemists. Roman Catholic. Office: Smith Kline Animal Health 4444 S 76th Circle Omaha NE 68127

RHULE, IMOGENE GRETCHEN, English language educator; b. Akron, Ohio, Apr. 17, 1941; d. Lloyd Merrill and Rosa Alice (Edwards) Tate; m. Dwayne Lloyd Rhule, Aug. 5, 1972; children: Chris, Phil, Ann, Gretchen. BA, Anderson U., 1969; MA, Ball State U., 1976. Tchr. Pendleton Heights High Sch., Pendleton, Ind., 1969-81; lectr. Anderson (Ind.) U., 1984—; dir. Writing Ctr. Anderson (Ind.) U., 1987—. Author essays; speaker in field. Sec. Gateway N.W. Agy., Anderson, 1984-89. Mem. Ind. Tchrs. of Writing (sec. 1987-89), Alpha Delta Kappa (chpt. pres. 1986-88, regional pres. 1988-90, state sec. 1990—). Mem. Ch. of God. Home: 3713 W 1000 S Pendleton IN 46064 Office: Anderson U 1100 E 5th St Anderson IN 46012

RIABOV, DARELLE DEE LAKE, marketing professional; b. Detroit, Nov. 26, 1951; d. William Thomas Lake and Virginia Blair (Torbert) Sigler; m. John Riabov, July 16, 1983. BS, U. Del., 1973. Secondary edn. tchr., Del. Secondary edn. tchr. Brandywine Sch. Dist., Claymont, Del., 1975-83; technical mktg. assoc. W.L. Gore & Assocs., Eklton, Md., 1983-87; dir. sales and mktg. Hamm & Assocs., Wilmington, Del., 1987-90; dir. mktg. St. Francis Hosp., Wilmington, 1990—. Mem. New Castle County Civic League, Wilmington, 1988-89. Mem. Gov's Commn. on Families, Bus. Industry Edn. Alliance, Del. C. of C. (svc. com.), U. Del. Human Resources Alumni Assn., Wilmington Women in Bus. (past pres.). Home: 18 Eden Rd Landenberg PA 19350

RIBAR, DIXIE LEE, nurse, educator; b. Albia, Iowa, June 22, 1938; d. Eugene Guy Clark and Margaret Ellen (Edwards) De Joode; m. John David Ribar, Aug. 22, 1959 (div. 1981); children: Michael, Christopher, Patrick. Diploma, St. Joseph Hosp. Sch. Nursing, Ottumwa, Iowa, 1959; BSN, U. Dubuque, 1987, MSN, 1990—. RN, Iowa; cert. emergency room nurse; cert. emergency med. technician, Iowa. Staff nurse Ottumwa Hosp., 1959-60; surg. staff nurse Jane Lamb Hosp., Clinton, Iowa, 1960-67; dur. nursing ICU-CCU Jane Lamb Health Ctr., Clinton, Iowa, 1967-79, dir. cardiac rehab., 1980-86, ednl. instr., 1986—; instr. edn. Samaritan Health Ctr., Clinton; internat. edn. cons. Am.-Mideast Ednl. and Tng. Svcs., 1989—; contractual instr. med. svcs. Emergency Learning Resources Ctr., U. Iowa Hosp., Iowa City, 1976—, Ea. Iowa Community Coll., Davenport, Iowa, 1978—, Marycrest Coll., Davenport, 1986—; paremedic River Cities Ambulance Co., Clinton, 1987—; presenter in field. Contbr. articles to profl. jours. Bd. dirs. Clinton County Heart Assn., 1976—; coordinator emergency med. technician program Clinton Fire Dept., 1980-88; med. missionary 1st Congl. Ch. Clinton, Ghana, 1983. Mem. Emergency Nurses Assn., Iowa Emergency Nurses Assn., Am. Nurses Assn., Iowa Nurses Assn., Iowa Hosp. Assn. Republican. Roman Catholic. Home: 511 Melrose Ct Clinton IA 52732 Office: Samaritan Health System 1410 N 4th St Clinton IA 52732

RIBBLE, ANNE HOERNER, information representative; b. Balt., Oct. 30, 1932; B.A., Smith Coll., 1954; M.A., Harvard U., 1955; m. John C. Ribble, July 26, 1974; tech. asst. IBM, N.Y.C., 1958-63, editor, Armonk and White Plains, N.Y., 1969-75, mgr. editorial services data processing div., White Plains, 1976-77, program adminstr. systems communications div., N.Y.C., 1977-78, staff tech. edn., fed. systems div., Houston, 1978-80, info. rep., 1980-87, staff info. systems Integration div., 1988—. Bd. dirs. Stanley Isaacs Community Center, N.Y.C., 1968-72; mem. United Way allocations com., Houston, 1989—. Mem. Internat. Assn. Bus. Communicators (pres. Houston chpt. 1982, community rels. dir. 1989-90). Home: 6200 Willers Way Houston TX 77057 Office: IBM 3700 Bay Area Blvd Houston TX 77058

RIBBY, ALICE MARIE, nurse; b. Lowell, Mich., Oct. 16, 1943; d. Merle Levi and Merleen Maude (Gooden) Bickford; m. Robert Allen Ribby, Nov. 25, 1961; children: Bobette Morgan, Mylie Wasylewski, Joseph R. Ribby, Barbara A. Ilten. AS in Nursing cum laude, Lansing Community Coll., 1976. RN, Mich. Nurse ICU Ingham Med. Ctr., Lansing, Mich., 1976-81; nurse hemo and peritoneal dialysis Sparrow Hosp., Lansing, Mich., 1983-84; head nurse, dir. Continuous Ambulatory Peritoneal Dialysis Program Community Dialysis Ctr., Jackson, Mich., 1984-87; registered nursein adolescent psychiatry unit St. Lawrence Hosp., Diamondale, Mich., 1990; therapist intern Inst. Attitude and Behavior Modification, Lansing, 1990; cons. Foote Hosp., Jackson, 1985. Lectr. (video tape) Continuous Ambulatory Peritoneal Dialysis, 1985. Founder, dir. One Another's Support Group. Mem. Am. Assn. Critical Care Nurses. Republican.

RIBELIN, ROSEMARY BINGHAM, college bookstore and campus center administrator; b. Indpls., Ind., Aug. 8, 1933; d. Remester Alexander and Joy Dorothy (Reed) Bingham; m. Richard Grant Ribelin, Aug. 16, 1957; children—Pamela Joy, Karen Sue. Student Indpls. schs. sec. to mgr. Phoenix Mut. Life Ins., Indpls., 1952-61, office supr., 1971-76; sec. to pres. Franklin Coll., Ind., 1976-79, bookstore/campus ctr. dir., 1979—. Leader Hoosier Capital council Girl Scouts U.S.A., 1965-75; canvasser Multiple Sclerosis Soc., Am. Cancer Soc., Am. Heart Assn., 1965-77; canvasser Channel 20 Pub. Broadcasting Service, Indpls., 1968; active com. mem. J. K. Lilly School PTA, Indpls., 1965-75, pres., 1972; canvasser United Fund, Indpls., 1968-75, pres., 1971. Moneyraiser, poll worker Republican Party, Indpls. Deacon, Sunday Sch. tchr. and supt. First Presbyn. Ch. of Franklin. Named a Go-Getter Channel 20, 1987. Mem. Philanthropic Nat. Soc., Delta Theta Tau (treas. Lambda Eta chpt. 1981-82, v.p. 1982-83, pres. 1983-85), Assn. Ind. Coll. Stores (treas. 1987—). Lodges: Daus. of Nile, Order Eastern Star, Oriental Shrine. Avocations: Hooking rugs, reading, crocheting, playing cards, embroidery. Office: Franklin Coll Bookstore Campus Ctr Franklin IN 46131

RICARDO-CAMPBELL, RITA, economist, educator; b. Boston, Mar. 16, 1920; d. David and Elizabeth (Jones) Ricardo; m. Wesley Glenn Campbell, Sept. 15, 1946; children: Barbara Lee, Diane Rita, Nancy Elizabeth. BS, Simmons Coll., 1941; MA, Radcliffe Coll., 1945, PhD, 1946. Instr. Harvard U., Cambridge, Mass., 1946-48; asst. prof. Tufts U., Medford, Mass., 1948-51; labor economist U.S. Wage Stabilization Bd., 1951-53; economist ways and means com. U.S. Ho. of Reps., 1953; cons. economist, 1957-60; vis. prof. San Jose State Coll., 1960-61; sr. fellow Hoover Instn. on War, Revolution, and Peace, Stanford, Calif., 1968—; lectr. health svc. adminstrn. Stanford U. Med. Sch., 1973-78; bd. dirs. Watkins-Johnson Co., Palo Alto, Calif., Gillette Co., Boston, 1978-90; dir. mgmt. bd. Samaritan Med. Ctr., San Jose. Author: Voluntary Health Insurance in the U.S., 1960, Economics of Health and Public Policy, 1971, Food Safety Regulation: Use and Limitations of Cost-Benefit Analysis, 1974, Drug Lag: Federal Government Decision Making, 1976, Social Security: Promise and Reality, 1977, The Economics and Politics of Health, 1982, 2d edit., 1985; co-editor: Below-Replacement Fertility in Industrial Societies, 1987, Issues in Contemporary Retirement, 1988; contbr. articles to profl. jours. Commr. Western Interstate Commn. for Higher Edn. Calif., 1967-75, chmn., 1970-71; mem. Pres. Nixon's Adv. Coun. on Status Women, 1969-76; mem. task force on taxation Pres.'s Coun. on Environ. Quality, 1970-72; mem. Pres.'s Com. Health Services Industry, 1971-73, FDA Nat. Adv. Drug Com., 1972-75; mem. Econ. Policy Adv. Bd., 1981-90, Pres. Reagan's Nat. Coun. on Humanities, 1982-89, Pres. Nat. Medal of Sci. com., 1988—; bd. dirs. Ind. Colls. No. Calif., 1971-87, Mt. Pelerin Soc., 1988—; mem. com. assessment of safety, benefits, risks Citizens Commn. Sci., Law and Food Supply, Rockefeller U., 1973-75; mem. adv. com. Ctr. Health Policy Rsch., Am. Enterprise Inst. Pub. Policy Rsch., Washington, 1974-80; mem. adv. coun. on social security Social Security Adminstrn., 1974-75; bd. dirs. Simmons Coll. Corp., Boston, 1975-80; mem. adv. coun. bd. assocs. Stanford Libr., 1975-78; mem. coun. SRI Internat., Menlo Park, Calif., 1977—. Mem. Am. Econ. Assn., Mont Pelerin Soc. (bd. dirs. 1988—), Phi Beta Kappa. Home: 26915 Alejandro Dr Los Altos Hills CA 94022 Office: Stanford U Hoover Instn Stanford CA 94305

RICCI, CAROLYNE YOUNGBLOOD, print shop owner; b. Westville, Okla., Jan. 11, 1951; d. Gifford Dewitt and Beatrice Louise (Owens) Youngblood; m. John James Ricci Jr., May 1, 1980 (div. June 1983); 1 child, Jared James. Student, Ea. N.Mex. U., 1969-70. File clk. Scott & White Hosp., Temple, Tex., 1971; office mgr. Dr. Gifford Youngblood, Clovis,

N.Mex., 1972-75; owner Red Door Women's Wear, Clovis, 1975-77; apprentice contractor Gentry Real Estate, Clovis, 1977; office mgr. Rendering Plant, Clovis, 1980-81; ops. mgr. Sta. KMCC-TV, Clovis, 1981-83; salesperson Desert Beauty Supply, Tuscon, 1984-85; owner Pronto Printing, Tuscon, 1985—. Mem. Jr. League of Tucson, 1987—, Working Women's Expo, mem. State Pub. Affairs Com.; Tucson Bus. Com. for the Arts, 1987—, sponsor Women's Expo, 1989-90; chair Art Smarts Conf.; mem. adv. bd. Young Audiences, Friends of the Ballet, Nat. Safety Coun.; mem. So. Ariz. Adv. Bd.; mem. steering com. Tucson Bus. Coalition; trustee Ballet Ariz.; mem. active fundraising events Multiple Sclerosis; chair parish events St. Philips Episcopal Ch.; Heart Ball com. Am. Heart Assn.; charter mem. Paws Assistance League. Mem. NAFE, Nat. Assn. Quick Printers, Quick Printers in Tuscon (mem. steering com. 1987), Rincon Exch. Club, Exec. Women Internat., Resources for Women, Tucson C. of C., Tucson Racquet Club, Porsche Club Am., Alpha Delta Pi Alumnae (past pres.). Republican. Club: Greeters. Office: Pronto Printing 7020 E Broadway Tucson AZ 85710

RICCI, DEBRA PATRICIA, assistant principal; b. Port Chester, N.Y., July 31, 1951; d. John Joseph and Velma May (Dellner) R.; m. Richard F. Gomberg, Aug. 12, 1973 (div. July 1979); m. Alva D. Henehan Jr., May 27, 1989; stepchildren: Jama L., Nathan B. AA, Miami (Fla.) Dade Community Coll., 1971; BA in Edn., U. South Fla., 1973; MS, Nova U., 1978. Cert. elem. edn. tchr. and sch. prin., Fla. Tchr. 2d grade St. Lucie County Schs., Ft. Pierce, Fla., 1973-81, primary edn. specialist, 1982-86, asst. prin., 1987—. Mem. Treasure Coast Pvt. Industry Coun., Ft. Pierce, 1986-88, St. Lucie County Dem. Exec. Com., 1975-84; pres., mem. Treasure Coast Cen. Labor Coun., Ft. Pierce, 1974-88, Ft. Pierce br. AAUW, 1976-88, Friends of St. Lucie County Libr., 1985-89, Libr. Adv. Bd., 1986—. Mem. Fla. Assn. Sch. Adminstrs., St. Lucie County Adminstrs. Assn., Nat. Assn. Elem. Sch. Prins., Phi Delta Kappa. Roman Catholic. Home: 916 Skylark Dr Fort Pierce FL 34982 Office: Chester A Moore Elem Sch 827 N 29th St Fort Pierce FL 34947

RICCIARDI, PATRICE JOAN, relocation executive; b. Albany, N.Y., Mar. 15, 1956; d. Dominic L. and Joan M. (Caulkins) R.; m. Donald R. Ragaini, May 23, 1981; 1 child, Krista Elise. AA, AS, Hudson Valley Community Coll., 1973; BS cum laude, Siena Coll., 1975; postgrad., Ga State U., 1982-84. Dist. sales mgr. Duracell Products Co., Bethel, Conn., 1975-79, nat. sales coord., 1979-84; with PHH Homequity, Danbury, Conn., 1979—, mgr. client rels. and real estate svcs., 1984-88; dir. home mgmt. P.H.H. Homequity, Danbury, Conn., 1988-90; facilitator quality svc. teams PHH FleetAm., Hunt Valley, Md., 1990—; speaker Employees Relocation coun., Washington, 1990; panel mem. Telecommuting Conf., N.Y.C., 1987. Contbr. articles to profl. jours. Mem. Fuller Rd. Ladies Aux., Siena Coll. Alumni Assn. Home: 38 Whippoorwill Rd Bethel CT 06801 Office: PHH FleetAm 307 International Circle Hunt Valley MD 21031

RICE, ANNE, author; b. New Orleans, Oct. 14, 1941; d. Howard and Katherine (Allen) O'Brien; m. Stan Rice, Oct. 14, 1961; children: Michele (dec.), Christopher. Student, Tex. Woman's U., 1959-60; BA, San Francisco State Coll., 1964, MA, 1971. Author: Interview with the Vampire, 1976, The Feast of all Saints, 1980, Cry to Heaven, 1982, The Vampire Lestat, 1985, The Queen of the Damned, 1988, The Mummy or Ramses the Damned, 1989, (as A.N. Roquelaure) The Claiming of Sleeping Beauty, 1983, Beauty's Punishment, 1984, Beauty's Release, 1985, (as Anne Rampling) Exit to Eden, 1985, Belinda, 1986. Office: care Simon & Schuster 1230 Ave of the Americas New York NY 10020*

RICE, ARGYLL PRYOR, Hispanic studies and Spanish educator; b. Va.; d. Theodorick Pryor and Argyll (Campbell) R. BA, Smith Coll., 1952; MA, Yale U., 1956, PhD, 1961. Spanish instr. Yale U., New Haven, 1959-60, 61-63; asst. prof. Spanish, Conn. Coll., New London, 1964-67, assoc. prof., 1967-72, prof., 1972—, chair dept. Hispanic Studies, 1971-74, 77-84. Author: Emilio Ballagas: poeta o poesia, 1967, Emilio Ballagas, Latin American Writers III; editor in chief Carlos A. Solé, Charles Scribner's Sons, 1989. Mem. MLA, Am. Assn. Tchrs. of Spanish and Portuguese, New Eng. Coun. Latin Am. Studies, Phi Beta Kappa. Avocations: music, tennis. Home: 133 Cliffmore Rd West Hartford CT 06107

RICE, BARBARA SLYDER, mathematics educator; b. Chambersburg, Pa., Dec. 19, 1937; d. Solomon Brake and Stella Nell (Cetnarowski) Slyder; m. Laurence Bliss Rice, June 23, 1963; children: Cynthia, Catherine, Corey, Gordon. AB, Clark U., 1959; MA, U. Va., 1961, PhD, 1965. Tchr. Hunterdon Cen. High Sch., Flemington, N.J., 1959; mathematician U.S. Bur. Standards, Washington, 1961; adj. prof. Fla. Inst. Tech., Melbourne, 1963-73; assoc. prof. math. Ala. A&M U., Huntsville, 1975—; mem. Ala. Com. for Leading Math. into 21st Century, 1990—. Mem. Am. Math. Soc., Math. Assn. Am., Ala. Assn. Coll. Tchrs. Math. (pres. 1990—, test writer 1984-90). Republican. Office: Ala A&M U Dept Math PO Box 326 Normal AL 35762

RICE, CLAIRE JANE, banker, auditor; b. Phenix, Va., Sept. 17, 1959; d. Millard Berger and Harriet Ann (Willson) R. BS, Va Poly. Inst. and State U., 1981, BA, 1982; grad., Va. Sch. Bank Mgmt., 1989. Asst. bank examiner State Corp. Commn., Richmond, Va.; auditor Cen. Fidelity Bank, Lynchburg, Va.; auditor, compliance officer Farmers Nat. Bank, Appomattox, Va.; lic. and apptd. agt. Va. Farm Bur. Ins., Richmond, Va. Mem. Nat. Assn. Bank Women, Inc., Am. Inst. of Banking, Va. Bankers Assn. (compliance com. young bankers sect.), Va. Assn. Community Banks (community bankers for compliance cert.). Presbyterian. Home: Rt 1 Box 210 Phenix VA 23959 Office: PO Box 2098 Appomattox VA 24522

RICE, DAPHNE SWEATMAN, software developer; b. Cumming, Ga., Dec. 30, 1962; d. Crafton Lamar and Velma Grace (Moss) Sweatman; m. Keith Edward Rice, Apr. 4, 1987. Student, Gainesville (Ga.) Jr. Coll., 1982, 83, Berry Coll., Rome, Ga., 1980-81; BS in Computer Sci., U. Ga., 1984. Programmer/analyst Constrn. Data Control, Inc., Atlanta, 1984-90; ind. contractor Atlanta, 1990—. Mem. Marietta Jaycees (bd. dirs. 1986-87, v.p. individual devel. 1987-88, chaplain 1988-89, St. Jude program 1989-90), Bapt. Young Women. Baptist. Home and Office: 1805 Peachtree Rd Cumming GA 30130 Office: Constrn Data Control Inc 3675 Crestwood Pkwy Suite 400 Atlanta GA 30136

RICE, DOROTHY PECHMAN (MRS. JOHN DONALD RICE), medical economist; b. Bklyn., June 11, 1922; d. Gershon and Lena (Schiff) Pechman; m. John Donald Rice, Apr. 3, 1943; children: Kenneth D., Donald B., Thomas H. Student, Bklyn. Coll., 1938-39; B.A., U. Wis., 1941; D.Sc. (hon.), Coll. Medicine and Dentistry N.J., 1979. With hosp., and med. facilities USPHS, Washington, 1960-61; med. econs. studies Social Security Adminstrn., 1962-63; health econs. br. Community Health Svc., USPHS, 1964-65; chief health ins. rsch. br. Social Security Adminstrn., 1966-72, dep. asst. commr. for rsch. and statistics, 1972-75; dir. Nat. Ctr. for Health Stats., Rockville, Md., 1976-82; prof. Inst. Health & Aging U. Calif., San Francisco, 1982—; developer, mgr. nationwide health info. svcs. Contbr. articles to profl. jours. Recipient Social Security Adminstrn. citation, 1968, Disting. Service medal HEW, 1974, Jack C. Massey Found. award, 1978. Fellow Am. Public Health Assn. (domestic award for excellence 1978, Sedgwick Meml. medal, 1988), Am. Statis. Assn.; mem. Inst. Medicine, Assn. Health Scvs. Rsch. (President's award 1988), Am. Econ. Assn., Population Assn. Am., LWV. Home: 1055 Amito Ave Berkeley CA 94705 Office: U Calif Sch Nursing N631 San Francisco CA 94143-0612

RICE, ELIZABETH FISCHER, financial executive; b. Highland Park, Ill., Mar. 25, 1953; d. Thomas Clark and Nancy (Knight) Fischer; m. Larry Alan Rice, Feb. 25, 1984. BA, Coe Coll., 1975; MBA, Northwestern U., 1977. Fin. analyst Xerox Corp., Rochester, N.Y., 1977-81, plant controller, Oak Brook, Ill., 1981-85, program fin. mgr., Rochester, 1985—. Mem. Nat. Assn. Female Execs., Xerox Mgmt. Assn. (pres. 1987-88, bd. dirs. 1988—), Omicron Delta Epsilon, Delta Delta Delta. Republican. Episcopalian. Avocations: racquetball, running, reading. Home: 134 Beckwith Terr Rochester NY 14610 Office: Xerox Corp 800 Phillips Rd Webster NY 14580

RICE, ELLEN FRANCES, counselor; b. Gettysburg, Pa., May 14, 1941; d. John Stanley and Grace Luene (Rogers) R. BA in English, Gettysburg Coll., 1964; MA in Christian Edn., Wheaton (Ill.) Grad. Sch., 1966; MS in Guidance and Counseling, Nova U., 1973. Cert. tchr., Fla. Dir. Christian edn. Greenville Community Reformed Ch., Scarsdale, N.Y., 1966-69; tchr. St. Mark's Episcopal Sch., Ft. Lauderdale, 1969-70; youth dir. First United Meth. Ch., Ft. Lauderdale, 1972-74; vocat. counselor Christian Counseling Ministries, Pompano Beach, Fla., 1986-87; individual therapy Counseling & Cons. Assocs., Pompano Beach, 1987—. Sec., bd. dirs. Ctr. of Pastoral Counseling and Human Devel., Ft. Lauderdale, 1973-78, Lago Mar Place, 1983—;-vol. North Ridge Gen. Hosp. Aux., Ft. Lauderdale, 1977-81; mem. nat. bd. Med. Coll. Pa., Phila., 1976-82. Mem. Am. Assn. for Counseling and Devel., Am. Mental Health Counselors Assn., Nat. Career Devel. Assn., Ft. Lauderdale Yacht Club, Lago Mar Beach Club, Delta Gamma. Home: 1750 S Ocean Ln Fort Lauderdale FL 33316 Office: Counseling & Cons Assocs 351 S Cypress Rd Ste 307 Pompano Beach FL 33060

RICE, FERILL JEANE, writer, civic worker; b. Hemingford, Nebr., July 4, 1926; d. Derrick and Helen Agnes (Moffatt) Dalton; m. Otis LaVerne Rice, Mar. 7, 1946; children: LaVeria June McMichael, Larry L. Student, U. Omaha, 1961. Dir. jr. and sr. choir Congl. Ch., Tabor, Iowa, 1952-66; tchr. Fox Valley Tech. Inst., Appleton, Wis., 1970-77; dir. activity Family Heritage Nursing Home, Appleton, Wis., 1972-75, Peabody Manor, Appleton, Wis., 1975-76. Editor: Moffatt and Related Families, 1981; asst. editor (mag.) Yester-Year, 1975-76; contbr. articles to profl jours. Chmn. edn. Am. Cancer Soc., Fremont County, 1962, 63, 64; founder Mothers Club Nishna; 1st pres. valley chpt. Demolay Boys. Mem. DAR, Internat. Carnival Glass Assn., Heart Am. Carnival Glass Assn., Nat. Cambridge Collectors, Heisey Collectors Am., Inc., Iowa Fedn. Women's Clubs (Fremont county chmn. 1964, 65, 66, 67, 7th dist. chmn. library services 1966-67), Tabor Women's Club (pres. 1962, 63, 64), Jr. Legion Aux. (founder, 1st dir. 1951-52), Fenton Art Glass Collectors Am., Inc. (co-founder 1977, sec., editor newsletter 1976-86, editor, sec. 1988—), Mayflower Soc., John Howland Soc., Ross County Ohio Geneal. Soc., Iowa Geneal. Soc., Dallas County Mo. Geneal. Soc., Imperial Collectors Am., Tiffin Glass Collectors, Clay County (Ind.) Geneal. Soc., Vinton County (Ohio) Geneal. Soc., Fenton Finders of Wis. (chpt #1, pres. 1988-90), Greentown Collectors. Republican. Methodist. Lodge: Order of Eastern Star (worthy matron 1959, 64), Rainbow for Girls (bd. dirs. 1964), Internat. Order Jobs Daughters (honored queen 1945). Home: 302 Pheasant Run Kaukauna WI 54130 Office: Rice Enterprises & Rice & Rice 1665 Lamers Rd PO Box 305 Little Chute WI 54140

RICE, GRETA JACQUELYNN, sales executive; b. Cin., Nov. 22, 1959; d. Robert and Dorothy Mae (Lindsey) R. BS, U. Cin., 1982. Lic. tchr., Ohio. Camp counselor West Cin. Summer Program, 1977, group leader, 1978, sect. leader, 1979-81; videx operator Montgomery Ward, Cin., 1982-83; tchr. multihandicapped Cin. Bd. Edn., 1982-86; sales account exec. Eastman Kodak Co., Whittier, Calif., 1985—. Recipient Kodak Regional All-Star; U. Cin. scholar. Mem. Nat. Assn. Market Developers, Nat. Assn. Exec. Women, Am. Fedn. Tchrs., Jaycees, Delta Sigma Theta (chmn. Teen Lift, 1986, chmn. Teen Pregancy Seminar, 1987—, Outstanding Service award). Democrat. Prebyterian. Office: Eastman Kodak Co 1462 Wilson Ave Perris CA 92370

RICE, HEIDE INGEBORG, anesthesiologist; b. New Orleans, Dec. 21, 1950; d. Clarence Hagler and Ingeborg (Rabe) R. MusB., Curtis Inst., 1972; MusM., Manhattan Sch. Music, 1974; MD, U. Ala., Birmingham, 1981. Diplomate Am. Bd. Anesthesiology. Gen. sugery intern U. Ala., Birmingham, 1981-82; resident anesthesiology U. Ala., 1982-85, anesthesiology fellow pediatrics, 1985; anesthesiology fellow pediatrics Emory U., Atlanta, 1986; anesthesiologist Children's Hosp. Ala., Birmingham, 1986-89; staff anesthesiologist Walker Regional Med. Ctr., Jasper, Ala., 1989—; asst. prof. anesthesiologist U. Ala., Birmingham, 1986-89; anesthesiologist So. Anesthesia Assocs. PC, Jasper, Ala., 1989—. Pres., founder Soc. for Med. Scis. and Music, Birmingham, 1987—. Mem. Am. Soc. Anesthesiologists, Internat. Anesthesia Rsch. Soc., Soc. for Neurosurgical Anesthesia & Critical Care, Soc. for Pediatric Anesthesia, AMA, Alpha Omega Alpha. Republican. Presbyterian. Home: 1903 Overton Dr Jasper AL 35501 Office: So Anesthesia Assocs PC Med Arts Tower 3400 Hwy 78 Ste 204 Jasper AL 35501

RICE, JENNIFER SUSAN, nonprofit organization administrator; b. Houston, Jan. 18, 1951; d. Myer and Rose (Forrest) R. BA with honors, U. Tex., Austin, 1972, MA in Communications, 1974. Dist. exec. dir. Am. Cancer Soc., Austin, Tex., 1974-75, br. dirs., Miami, Fla., 1975-76; dir. public info./rsch. Urban League Greater Miami, 1976-77; mental health planning cons., communications coord. Miami Jewish Home and Hosp. for Aged, 1977-79; dir. public rels. and devel. James Archer Smith Hosp., Homestead, Fla., 1979-81; assoc. dir. N.J. region Deborah Hosp. Found., Browns Mills, N.J., 1981-83; mktg. mgr. West Coast Reply-o/Kennedy Sinclair, Wayne, N.J., 1983-84; exec. dir. Ocean County Coll. Found., Toms River, N.J., 1984-87; dir. devel. Community Home Health Svcs. Phila., 1987-88; dir. cash collections Fedn. Jewish Agys. Greater Phila., 1988—. Mem. public edn. com. Am. Cancer Soc.; mem. Child Abuse Task Force, Mental Health Assn. NIMH fellow, 1972. Mem. Public Rels. Soc. Am., Nat. Assn. Hosp. Devel., Nat. Soc. Fund Raising Execs. (pres. mid-state N.J. chpt., bd. dirs. Delaware Valley chpt.), Fla. Hosp. Assn., South Fla. Hosp. Public Rels. Assn., Internat. Assn. Bus. Communicators (pres. S. Fla. chpt.), Phi Kappa Phi. Home: 7013-B McCallum St Philadelphia PA 19119 Office: Fedn Jewish Agys 226 S 16th St Philadelphia PA 19102

RICE, KATHLEEN MARIE, nurse; b. Pitts., Feb. 21, 1960; d. Martin Robert and Mary Helen (McFarren) Corcoran; m. Harold Rice, Mar. 6, 1981 (div. June 1988). Diploma in nursing, Mercy Hosp. Sch. Nursing, 1980. RN, Pa.; cert. critical care RN, Am. Assn. Critical Care Nurses. Staff nurse Mercy Hosp., Pitts., 1980-88, 1980-88, 87—, profl. clin. nurse II, 1988--; mem. Appropriateness of Nurse Quality Practice group Mercy Hosp. Active Sheraden PTA. Mem. Am. Assn. Critical Care RN, Parents Without Ptnrs. Democrat. Roman Catholic. Home: 3113 Fadette St Pittsburgh PA 15204 Office: Mercy Hosp 1400 Locust St Pittsburgh PA 15219

RICE, LINDA JOHNSON, publishing executive; d. JOhn J. and Eunice Johnson; m. Andre Rice, 1984. Grad., Northwestern U., 1987. With Johnson Pub. Co., 1980—, past v.p. and asst. to pub., pres., 1987—, also chief oper. officer. Office: Johnson Pub Co Inc 820 S Michigan Ave Chicago IL 60605*

RICE, LINDA TILLMAN, professional volunteer; b. Orlando, Fla., June 3, 1943; d. Thomas John and Stella Frances (Block) Tillman; m. James T. Rice. Student Valencia Community Coll., Orlando, 1973-74, Fla. Jr. Coll., Jacksonville, 1976-78, U. North Fla., 1983-84; student Luther Rice Sem., 1986—. Exec. sec. to mgr. advance systems engring. Martin Marietta Aerospace Corp., Orlando, 1963-69; exec. sec. to pres., also office mgr., fashion coordinator and writer Act II Jewelry Inc., Orlando, 1969-76; legal asst., sec. Howell, Howell, Liles, Braddock & Milton, Jacksonville, Fla., 1976-78; exec. asst. to owners and developers Regency Sq. Shopping Center, Jacksonville, 1978-79; free-lance legal sec. and asst., Jacksonville, 1979-80; adminstrv. asst. to sr. v.p. human resources and labor relations Seaboard System R.R., Jacksonville, 1980-85. Hospitality chmn., v.p. Women of Jacksonville Art Mus., 1977-80, publicity chmn., 1981-82; mem. St. Luke's Hosp. Aux. and Endowment Bd., Nat. Rep. Com., Jacksonville Humane Soc. Aux. Mem. Rep. Nat. Com. Nat. Secs. Assn. (asst. treas. 1973-74, sec. 1974-75), Women's Guild Jacksonville Mus. Arts and Scis., Nat. Assn. Ry. Bus. Women (pres. 1984-85, parliamentarian 1986-87, publicity chmn. 1987-88). Recipient Dist. VI Railway Bus. Woman of Yr., 1986. Mem. Capitol Hill Women's Club. Episcopalian. Home: 10754-8 Scott Mill Rd Jacksonville FL 32223

RICE, MARIAN RUTH, academic administrator; b. Phila., June 24, 1931; d. Charles and Rae (Zuchovitz) Coopersmith; m. Stuart Alan Rice, June 1, 1952; children: Barbara Ellen, Janet Ann. BS in Chemistry, Bklyn. Coll., 1952; AM in Chemistry, Harvard U., 1954, PhD in Chemistry, 1958. Rsch. assoc. dept. chemistry U. Chgo., 1957-58, lectr. phys. sci., 1962-67, rsch. assoc. biophysics dept., 1968-70; sci. tchr. U. Chgo. Lab. Schs., 1971-82; exec. assoc. AAAS, Cambridge, Mass., 1982—; abstractor Chem. Abstracts, Midwest Ctr., 1958-62; freelance editor Harper & Row, N.Y.C., 1969-76. Editor: Proceedings of the University of Chicago Conferences on Liberal Education No. 1: Undergraduate Education in Chemistry and Physics, 1986; contbr. articles to profl. jours. NIH fellow, 1955-56. Mem. Phi Beta Kappa, Sigma Xi. Office: AAAS 5801 S Kenwood Ave Chicago IL 60637

RICE, MELANIE AILENE, singer, entertainer; b. Phila., Nov. 4, 1957; d. Anthony Joseph and Marie Rose (Ranere) R. BA in Music, Glassboro (N.J.) State U., 1980. Pres. Melanie Rice Entertainment; account exec. The Entertainment Group, Phila., 1990—; pres. Melanie Rice Entertainment, Absecon, N.J., 1987—. Opening act for entertainers including Smokey Robinson, Shecky Greene, David Brenner; background singer Joe Piscapo, Grover Washington Jr., Bobby Rydell, others; performed for radio/TV commercials, casinos. Co-chair March of Dimes Golf Tournament, Atlantic City, N.J., 1987. Recipient John Phillip Sousa Music award, 1975; winner 1975 N.J. State Jr. Girls Golf Championship. Mem. Am. Fedn. Musicians, Assn. Research and Enlightenment. Democrat. Roman Catholic. Home and Office: 274 Mattix Run Absecon NJ 08201

RICE, PATRICIA ANN, consultant; b. Aldrich, Mo., Aug. 24, 1946; d. William Wayne and Wilda Mae (Lowery) Rice; m. children: Jessica Jean Rice, Clifford Wayne Rice, Jacqueline Marie Rice, Alicia JoAnne Rice. A.A., Southwest Baptist U., Bolivar, Mo., 1966; B.A., Southwest Mo. State U.; postgrad. Calif. State U.-Fullerton. Office mgr. Patscheck-Veiga Constrn. Co., Tustin, Calif., 1972-75; asst. to controller Richards West Co., Newport Beach, Calif., 1976-78; acctg. supr. Warner Lambert Co., Anaheim, Calif., 1978-80, supr. fin. analysis and planning, 1980; mgr. fin. control Pepsi Cola, Torrance, Calif., 1980-82; sr. fin. adminstr. Microdata Corp., (name changed to McDonnell Douglas Computer Systems Co.), Newport Beach, Calif., 1982-86, gen. acct. mgr. Printronix, Irvine, Calif., 1986-88; sr. cons. Deloitte & Touche, Costa Mesa, Calif., 1988—. Bd. dirs. Real Reasons Homes for Abused Children. Mem. NAFE, Am. Prodn. and Inventory Control Soc., Am. Mgmt. Assn., AAUW, NOW (chpt. program chmn. 1977), LaLeche League (chpt. publicity chmn. 1972-73), Lifestyles Internat. Democrat. Roman Catholic. Home: 7720 B El Camino Real Ste 155 Rancho La Costa CA 92009 Office: Deloitte & Touche 695 Town Center Dr Ste 1200 Costa Mesa CA 92626

RICE, PATRICIA BIRCH, accountant; b. Walden, N.Y., July 23, 1949; d. Abner H. and Dorothy A. (Gillespie) Birch; m. Donald W. Rice, Feb. 14, 1969; children: Corinna A., Derek W. BS, Murray State U., 1979. CPA, Ky. Acct. Reed & Co., Mayfield, Ky., 1983—. Author: Love Betrayed, 1987, Indigo Moon, 1988, Silver Enchantress, 1988, Lord Rogue, 1989, Cheyenne's Lady, 1990, Love Forever After, 1990. Exec. bd. Purchase Area Arts Coun., Mayfield, 1987—. Mem. AAUW, Romance Writers Am., AICPA, Ky. Soc. CPAs, Mayfield C. of C. (treas., dir. 1988—. Home: 237 N 6th Mayfield KY 42066

RICE, RAMONA GAIL, physiologist, phycologist, educator, consultant; b. Texarkana, Tex., Feb. 15, 1950; d. Raymond Lester and Jessie Gail (Hubbard) R.; m. Carl H. Rosen. BS, Ouachita U., 1972; MS, U. Ark., 1975, PhD, 1978; postgrad. Utah State U., 1978-80. Undergrad. asst. Ouachita U., Arkadelphia, Ark., 1970-72; grad. teaching asst. U. Ark., Fayetteville, 1972, 77-78, grad. rsch. asst., 1973-77; asst. rsch. scholar, scientist Fla. Internat. U., Miami, 1980-85; rsch. coord. in biology, Pratt Community Coll., Kans., 1985-87, faculty, 1985—; adj. instr. Miami Dade Community Coll., 1984-85, Wichita (Kans.) State U., 1986-88. Contbr. articles to profl. jours. Judge Pratt County Sci. Fairs, Dade County Sci. Fair, Fla., 1981-85, Barber County Sci. Fairs; tchr. Sunday Sch. First Baptist Ch., South Miami, Fla., 1982-85, leader girls in action, 1982-83, youth chaperone, 1982-85; patron Pratt Community Concert Series. Grantee NSF, 1981-83, Am. Biog. Inst. Disting. Leadership award, 1987. Fla. Dept. Environ., 1981-83, EPA, 1983-85, So. Fla. Rsch. Ctr., Everglades Nat. Park, 1983-86. Mem. AMA, Ninescah Valley Med. Soc. Aux., Pratt Higher Edn. Assn. (sec. 1987-88), Fla. Acad. Scis., AAAS, Phycological Soc. Am., Soc. Limnology and Oceanography, Epsilon Sigma Alpha (Epsilon Pi chpt. recording sec. 1989-90, publicity com. 1988-89, philanthropic com. 1988-90, zone publicity co-chmn. 1989-90, v.p. 1990—, zone 12 auditor 1990—, Kans. state bd. road runner zone 12 1990—), Delta Kappa Gamma, Sigma Xi. Democrat. Avocations: pianist, crochet, needlework, photography, reading. Office: Pratt Community Coll Dept Biol Scis Pratt KS 67124

RICE, REBECCA ANNE, healthcare executive; b. Dayton, Ohio, Aug. 6, 1952; d. Gilbert August and Betty Lee (Morrison) Neubauer; m. William Charles Rice, Jr., Aug. 31, 1974; children: David Alexander and Matthew Neubauer. BS, U. Cin., Cin., 1974; MA, Wright State U., Fairborn, 1984. Dir. operations Upper Valley Med. Ctr., Piqua, Ohio, 1987--; campus adminstr. Dettmer Hosp., Troy, 1985-87; dir. prof. services Piqua Mem. Med. Ctr., Piqua, 1978-85, dir. dietary; exec. com. bd. mem. Miami County Mental Health Assoc. Piqua,, 1987--; long term care com. mem. Miam Valley Health Impr. Coucil, Huber Heighs, Ohio, 1987--; bd. mem. Soc. Advancement Mgmt. Western Ohio, 1988--. Author: Quality Assurance Jour., 1984. Cub Scout Asst. Cub Scout Pack 136 Vandalia, 1988-89; Mem. Women in Networking (Troy C. of C.) Troy, 1987--. Recipient Am. Bus. Women of Year Am. Bus. Women's Assoc. Piqua, 1988. Mem. Am. Dietic Assoc., Am. Coll. Health Care Exec. Republican. Episcopalian. Home: 980 W Alkaline Springs Rd Vandalia OH 45377 Office: Upper Valley Med Ctr 3130 N Dixie Hwy Troy OH 45373

RICE, RUTH DIANNE, psychologist; b. Oklahoma City, Mar. 29, 1924; d. Isaac Benson and Lela (Ward) R.; children: Sheri, Cynthia, Paul. BA summa cum laude, East Tex. State U., 1965, MA, 1966; PhD, U. Tex., Austin, 1975. Rsch. dir. Tenn. Sch. for Girls, Nashville, 1966-67; rsch. asst. Learning Disabilities Project, Greeley, Colo., 1967-68; dir. Psychol. Svcs. Ctr., Harlingen, Tex., 1968-69, Child Study Team, Dallas, 1971-72; asst. prof. U. Tex., Dallas, 1975-76; rsch. dir. Cradle Care, Inc., Dallas, 1975—; pvt. practice Dallas, 1980—; adj. prof., East Tex. State U., Commerce, 1976-78; lectr. in infant stimulation and birth trauma, various hosps. and clinics, U.S., Europe, China, Can. Developer stimulation techniques for premature infants; contbr. articles to profl. publs. Recipient honors in infant devel., U. Helsinki, Finland, 1983, honors in infant programs, Esotera, Munich, 1988. Mem. Pre and Perinatal Psychology Assn. (adv. bd.), Am. Assn. Marriage and Family Counselors. Democrat. Home: 6455 Meadow Rd Dallas TX 75230

RICE, SUE ANN, education administrator, industrial and organizational psychologist; b. Ponca City, Okla., Sept. 17, 1934; d. Alfred and Helen (Revard) R. BS in Edn., U. Okla., 1956; MA, Cath. U., 1979, PhD, 1988. Ensign USN, 1958, advanced through grades to comdr., 1973; adminstr., asst. staff, comdr. in-chief Pacific Fleet, Honolulu, 1958-61; head edn. div. Naval Air Sta., Lemoore, Calif., 1961-63; instr., acad. dir. Women Officers' Sch., Newport, R.I., 1963-66; head. tng. div. Naval Command Systems Support Activity, Washington, 1966-70; head, ops. support sec., comdr.-in-chief Lant, Norfolk, Va., 1970-74; sr. U.S. rep. NATO, subgroup 5 orgn. JCS, Washington, 1974-77; head vocation office Archdiocese of Washington, 1977-78; ret. USN, 1977; con. Notre Dame Inst., Arlington, Va., 1989—, dean of students, 1990—; lectr. Cath. U. of Am., Washington, 1983-84; bd. dirs. Villa Cortona Apostolic Ctr., Bethesda; cons. Notre Dame Inst., Arlington. Tech. reviewer Personnel Administration, 1964; editor (newsletter) Vocation News, 1978. Conoco scholarship Continental Oil Co., 1952-56; recipient Meritorious Svc. medal Pres. of U.S., 1977, rsch. grant Cath. U., Sigma Xi, 1986. Mem. Washington Acad. Scis., Cath. War Vets (post vice comdr.), Lay Women's Assn. (nat. bd. dirs.), Potomac Ch. Human Factors Soc. (assoc.). Roman Catholic. Office: PO Box 1541 Falls Church VA 22041

RICE, SUSAN JOETTE, nurse; b. Topeka, Nov. 15, 1946; d. Claude Harvey and Martha May (McClellan) R.; student Pasadena Nazarene Coll., 1964-66; BS in Nursing, Calif. State U., L.A., 1969, MSN, 1982; postgrad Cambridge Grad. Sch. Psychology, L.A., 1985—. Staff nurse Children's Hosp. L.A., 1969-75, asst. head nurse, 1972-74, nurse mgr., 1974-75; nursing unit coord. newborn and neonatal intensive care nurseries, perinatal clinician Glendale (Calif.) Adventist Med. Center, 1976-78; neonatal clin. specialist Huntington Meml. Hosp., Pasadena, 1981-85; staff nurse mental health unit Glendale Adventist Med. Ctr., 1985—; practicum field placement Treatment Ctrs. Am. Panorama City, Calif., 1988-89; intern Life PLUS Treatment Ctr., Panorama City, 1988-89, Wright Inst., L.A., 1989—. Vol. counselor Pasadena Mental Health Ctr., 1985-88. Mem. Am. Assn. Critical Care Nurses, Calif. Perinatal Assn., Calif. State Psychol. Assn., Nat. Assn. Neonatal Nurses, Pasadena Area Psychol. Assn. Republican. Mem. Nazarene Ch. Home: 133 E Pamela Rd Monrovia CA 91016

RICE-SIMMONS, CATHRYN FATIMA, communications educator; b. Seattle, Aug. 24, 1954; d. Leighton Charles and Marie Anne (Vitalech) Rice; m. Keith Charles Simmons, Dec. 20, 1986. AA, Tacoma (Wash.) Community Coll., 1984; BA in Communications/Theatre Arts (hons), U. Puget Sound, Tacoma, 1986; MA in Communication Studies, U. Calif., Santa Barbara, 1988. Reporter, news editor Collegiate Challenge, Tacoma, 1982-84; teaching asst. I.E.L.I., Pacific Luth. U., Tacoma, 1984; prog. asst. Assoc. Students, U. Puget Sound, 1984-85; editor arts and features The Trail, Tacoma, 1984-85; newswriter pub. rels. U. Puget Sound, 1985-86, teaching asst., 1985-86; teaching asst. U. Calif., Santa Barbara, 1986-88; communications instr. Brooks Inst. Photography, Santa Barbara, 1990—. Precinct leader Dem. Party, Goleta, Calif., 1988. Mem. Speech Communication Assn., Women in Communications (membership chmn. 1989). Office: Brooks Inst Photography 801 Alston Rd Santa Barbara CA 93108

RICH, CYNTHIA GAY, teacher; b. Jamestown, N.Y., Feb. 16, 1945; d. Alpheus T. and Gloria (Adler) Gable; m. David G. Rich, Aug. 26, 1967. BA in Elem. Edn., SUNY, Fredonia, 1967, MS in Elem. Edn. and Remedial Reading, 1971; EdD in Elem. Edn., Remedial Reading and Early Childhood, SUNY, Buffalo, 1989. Cert. tchr. elem., remedial reading, N.Y. Tchr. Ft. Carson (Colo.) Sch., 1967-68, Frewsburg (N.Y.) Cen. Sch., 1968—; cheerleading advisor Frewsburg Cen. Sch., 1977-79. Vol. Am. Cancer Soc., Am. Heart Assn., Mental Health Assn.; mem. Parent, Student and Tchr. Assn., 1968—; mem. ednl. commn. First United Meth. Ch., Jamestown, N.Y. Mem. AAUW (rec. sec., chairperson numerous programs, del. to conv.), Bus. and Profl. Women, Internat. Reading Assn. (presenter New Orleans conf. 1986, Phila. conf. 1989), Green Thumb Garden Club, Order of Ea. Star, Shriners Aux., Consistory Aux., Soc. for Prevention Cruelty to Animals, Kiwanis (Disting. Kiwanian 1990), Kiwanis Wives, Phi Delta Kappa (life, Educator of Yr. 1988, Researcher of Yr. 1988), Delta Kappa Gamma, Pi Lambda Theta. Home: 15 E Pearl St Falconer NY 14733

RICH, ELAINE SOMMERS, writer; b. Plevna, Ind., Feb. 8, 1926; d. Monroe and Effie (Horner) Sommers; m. Ronald L. Rich, June 14, 1953; children: Jonathan, Andrew, Miriam, Mark. BA, Goshen Coll., 1947; MA, Mich. State U., 1950. Asst. prof. Goshen (Ind.) Coll., 1947-49, 1950-5; instr. Bethel Coll., Newton, Kans., 1953-66; lectr. Internat. Christian U., Tokyo, 1971-78; instr. English Findlay (Ohio) Coll., 1986-89; free-lance writer Raleigh, N.C., 1990—; mem. Commn. on Edn. Gen. Conf. Mennonite Ch., 1980—. Author: Breaking Bread Together, 1958, Hannah Elizabeth, 1964, Tomorrow Tomorrow Tomorrow, 1966, Am I This Countryside?, 1981, Mennonite Women: A Story of God's Faithfulness, 1983, Spiritual Elegance: A Biography of Pauline Krehbiel Raid, 1987, Prayers for Everyday, 1990; contbr. articles to profl. jours. Democrat. Home: 112 S Spring St Bluffton OH 45817

RICH, HILDA ATLAS, professional travel consultant; b. Houston, Jan. 19, 1929; d. Max and Mary (Yellin) Atlas; m. Hershel Maurice Rich, Sept. 7, 1947; children: Morton, Renie Rich Carniol, Sharon. BA with distinction, Rice U., 1948. Sec., treas. Phil Rich Fan Mfg. Co., Houston, 1947-1980; pres. Rainbow Tours & Travel, Houston, 1982—; pres. Atlas Investments, Houston, 1975—. Bd. trustees, Hebrew Immigrant Aid Soc., 1978—, Jewish Fed. Greater Houston, 1980—, Houston Met. Ministries, 1980—. Mem. Houston Exec. Women in Travel, Houston C. of C. Democrat. Jewish. Office: Rainbow Tours & Travel 720 N Post Oak Rd Ste 100 Houston TX 77024

RICH, JUDITH G. HEMPHILL, insurance agent, small business owner; b. Murphy, N.C., June 23, 1947; d. Ray Mauney and Mary Grace (Colwell) Hemphill; m. Sidney F. Rich, July 3, 1965 (div. 1970); 1 child, Cary R. Student Kennesaw Coll., 1977-78. Lic. ins. agt., real estate agt. Sales rep. Combined Ins. Co., Chgo., 1972-76; policy service rep. Prudential Property and Casualty Ins., Atlanta, 1976-77; sales rep. Fran Hale Ad Agy., Marietta, Ga., 1977-79, Atlantic and Pacific Life Ins., Atlanta, 1979-80; dist. sales mgr. Mut. of Omaha, College Park, Ga., 1980-84; sales rep. Hagan & Assocs., Marietta, 1984-87, also bd. dirs.; prin. Rich Life and Health Agy., Smyra, 1987—. Recipient awards Combined Ins., 1973, 74-75 Mut. of Omaha, 1982-83. Mem. Ins. Women of Cobb County (pub. relations chmn. 1986—, bd. dirs. 1986-87, instr. pub. speaking class 1989). Mem. Ch. of God. Avocation: collecting old family photographs, gardening.

RICH, LINDA SUE, public relations executive, trainer; b. Nashville, Feb. 26, 1945; d. Paul and Ruby D. (Johnson) Smith; m. David Lee Rich, Sept. 4, 1964; children: David Lee II, Derrick Lee, Daniel Lee. Student, Indpls. Sch. Arts, 1964, Cumberland Sch., Winning Image, 1987-88, The Bus. Woman's Tng. Inst., Nashville, 1988-90, Tenn. Real Estate, 1988, 1989. Sec., receptionist Wiley Mobile Homes, Nashville, 1964-69; office mgr. Schlotte, Norman, Cain Architects, Nashville, 1969; officer Mortgage Am. Corp., Nashville, 1970-79; dir. grad. placement Nashville Aut Diesel Coll., Inc.; exec. com. Nashville Auto Diesel Coll., Inc., 1979—; cons. with schs. and companies across the U.S. in regard to hiring graduates. Speaker to Schs. and Bus. all across the U.S.; vol. Met. Pub. Schs., Margo Jacobs Top Pageants; exec. state dir. The Mrs. Tenn. Nat. U.S. Pageant. Recipient Mrs. Tenn. Career & Bus. Women awards, 1988, Good Friends award Met. Pub. Schs.; named Mrs. Tenn. Nat. U.S., 1990. Mem. Nat. Assn. Trade and Tech. Schs., Nat. Assn. Female Execs., Southern Assn. Student Employment Adminstrs., Notary At Large, State Tenn., The Bus. Woman's Tng. Inst., Fla. Assn. Accredited Pvt. Schs. Home: 1109 Greenfield Ave Nashville TN 37216 Office: Nashville Auto Diesel Coll 1524 Gallatin Rd Nashville TN 37206

RICH, LUCILLE MARY, distribution company administrative assistant; b. Duluth, Minn., Feb. 4, 1930; d. Louis and Theresa (Maniella) R. BA, UMD Marquette, Duluth, Minn., 1950. Cert. notary pub. Distbn. mgr. Zenith Interstates Newspaper Co., Duluth, Minn.; exec. sec. North States Supply Corp., Duluth. Mem. Nat. Assn. Exec. Secs., Am. Soc. Profl. Exec. Women, Nat Polinsky Rehab. Ctr. and Italian-Am. Aux. Roman Catholic. Home: 1819 Kenwood Ave Duluth MN 55811

RICH, ROSAN, textiles manufacturing executive; b. Sebastopol, Calif., June 1, 1946; d. Emil John and Betty Ceclia (Garcia) Duckhorn; 1 child, Eric. Student, Calif. State U., Sonoma, Rohnert Park, 1964-67. Claims supr. Blue Cross No. Calif., Oakland, 1971-76; treas. Bridge Pubs., L.A., 1980-82; plant mgr. EZ Sportswear, Chatsworth, Calif., 1985-88; v.p. mfg. EZ Sportswear, Chatsworth, 1988—. Mem. NAFE, NRA, Am. Apparel Mfg. Assn., Chatsworth C. of C. (indsl. coun. 1989-90). Democrat. Roman Catholic. Office: EZ Sportswear 9419 Mason Ave Chatsworth CA 91311

RICH, S. JUDITH, public relations executive; b. Chgo., Apr. 14; d. Irwin M. and Sarah I. (Sandock) R. BA, U. Ill., 1960. Staff writer, reporter Economist Newspapers, Chgo., 1960-61; asst. dir. pub. relations and communications Council Profit Sharing Industries, Chgo., 1961-62; dir. advt. and pub. relations Chgo. Indsl. Dist., 1962-63; account exec., account supr., v.p., sr. v.p., exec. v.p. and nat. creative dir. Daniel J. Edelman Inc., Chgo., 1963-85; exec. v.p., dir. Ketchum Pub. Rels., Chgo., 1985-89, exec. v.p., exec. creative dir. USA, 1990—. Mem. Pub. Relations Soc. Am. (Silver Anvil award, judge Silver Anvil awards), Counselors Acad. of Pub. Relations Soc. Am. (exec. bd.). Club: Publicity (Chgo.) (7 Golden Trumpet awards). Home: 2500 N Lakeview Dr Chicago IL 60614 Office: Ketchum Pub Rels 142 E Ontario St Chicago IL 60611

RICH, SARAH M., physical educator educator; b. Stamford, Conn., Nov. 2, 1940; d. William Nelson and Mary (Stepnowska) R. BS, U. Conn., 1962, MA, 1972; PhD, Tex. Womans U., 1981. Cert. therapeutic recreation specialist, phys. edn. tchr., N.Y. Phys. edn. tchr. Stillwater (N.Y.) Cen. Sch., 1962-66, Am. Community Sch., Beirut, Lebanon, 1966-71; grad. asst. U. Conn., Storrs, 1971-72; with Ithaca (N.Y.) Coll., 1972—; dir. travel Tompkins County Sr. Citizens, Ithaca, 1988—; dir. Sta-home Care, Ithaca, 1990—. Contbr. author: Adapted Physical Education and Sport, 1989; contbr. articles to profl. jours. ESL tchr. Cornell Womens Club, Ithaca, 1989—; team member United Way, Ithaca, 1987-89; coach Mavericks Beep baseball team, Ithaca, 1987—. Mem. Am. Alliance for Health, Phys. Edn., Recreation and Dance, Am. Therapeutic Recreation Assn., Nat. Consortium Phys. Edn. and Recreation for Handicapped, Nat. Recreation and Park Assn., Zonta Internat. (vice chmn. 1981—). Methodist. Home: 103 Kendall Ave Ithaca NY 14850 Office: Ithaca Coll 35 Hill Ctr Ithaca NY 14850

RICHARD, ANITA LOUISE, entrepreneur; b. Willard, N.Y., June 22, 1951; d. Marvin Gerald and Illene (Rosenberg) Isaacson; m. J.E. Richard, May 16, 1981: stepchildren: Christine, Chad. Student, U. Fla., 1969-70, CUNY, Bklyn., 1972-74, Barnard Baruch U., 1974-76; BA magna cum laude, Golden Gate U., 1981. Mktg. mgr. Exxon Office Systems, N.Y.C., 1976-77; program mgr. Exxon Office Systems, Dallas, 1977-78; br. mgr. Exxon Office Systems, Pasadena, Calif., 1978-79; br. sales mgr. Exxon Office Systems, Century City, Calif., 1979; mgr. regional sales program Exxon Office Systems, Marina Del Rey, Calif., 1979-81; mktg. mgr. Exxon Office Systems, San Francisco, 1981-82; product mgr. Wells Fargo Bank, San Francisco, 1984; mng. prin. J. Richard and Co., Montara, Calif., 1984—. Mem. Am. Mgmt. Assn., Am. Compensation Assn., Group Health Assn. Am., No. Calif. Human Resource Coun., No. Calif. Health Care Mktg. Assn., Practicing Law Inst. Republican. Jewish. Clubs: Los Angeles Athletic. Office: 1301 Main St PO Box 779 Montara CA 94037

RICHARD, ANN BERTHA, nursing administrator; b. Hartford, Conn., Mar. 21, 1944; d. Victor Charles and Theresa (Gasper) R.; children: Elena Burinskas, Judith Burinskas. Diploma, Capital City Sch. Nursing, Washington, 1965; BSN summa cum laude, U. Hartford, Bloomfield, Conn., 1982; MS, U. Conn., 1986. RN, Conn.; cert. nurse adminstr., med.-surg. nurse. Staff nurse D.C. Gen. Hosp., Washington, 1965-66; staff nurse Hartford Hosp., 1972-73, asst. head nurse, 1973-74, head nurse, 1974-83, nutritional support clinician, 1983-85; total nursing care project cons. Hosp. of St. Raphael, New Haven, 1986-88, assoc. dir. gen. surg. nursing and spltys., 1986-88; v.p. for nursing svcs. Manchester (Conn.) Meml. Hosp., 1988—. Contbr. chpt. to book. Passini scholar, 1985. Mem. CLN (bd. dirs. 1990—), Am. Nurses Assn. (nursing adminstrn. coun. 1986—), New Eng. Orgn. Nurse Execs., Conn. Nurses Assn. (govt. rels. com. 1984-88), Conn. Orgn. Nurse Execs. (nominating com. 1986-88), Am. Coll. Healthcare Execs., Sigma Theta Tau (program com. 1986-88, nominating com. 1988-89), Alpha Chi. Office: Manchester Meml Hosp 71 Haynes St Manchester CT 06040

RICHARD, COLLEEN MARY, telephone company executive; b. Providence, Dec. 15, 1964; d. Eugene Francis and Dolores Ann (Sheridan) R. BA Speech Communication magna cum laude, Boston Coll., 1986. Asst. mgr. Decision Rsch. Co., Brighton, Mass., 1985-87; purchasing asst. Coastal Property Mgmt. Corp., Boston, 1987-89; mgr. New England Telephone, Brockton, Fitchburg, Mass., 1989—; mgr. Directory Assistance Svc. Perception Com., Fitchburg, 1990—; mem. Vol. Inspection Program, Brockton, 1989—. Mem. Nat. Coun. Alcoholism, 1988—. Mem. NAFE, Boston Coll. Alumni Assn., Alpha Sigma Nu. Roman Catholic. Office: New England Telephone 365 Main St Fitchburg MA 01402

RICHARD, DARLENE DOLORAS, direct marketing consultant, writer and speaker; b. Mansfield, Ohio, Jan. 4, 1946; d. Charles Alvertis and Marjorie Elaine (Foster) Swander; m. David Allen Richard, Aug. 14, 1965 (div.). AA in Comml. Art, Famous Artist Sch., 1964; BA in Edn., Ohio State U., 1969. Asst. to contr. Johnstown Properties, Atlanta, 1978-79; adminstrv. mgr. TCG Communications Group, Atlanta, 1979; promotional dir. Am. Health Cons., Atlanta, 1979-83; pres. Direct Mktg./R&D Internat., Atlanta, Buffalo (N.Y.), Australia, 1982—, Slight Edge Enterprises, 1983—, Marine Midland Bank, Buffalo, 1985-88, Access Computing Pty. Ltd., Victoria, NSW, Australia, 1988—. Mem. Bus. Womens Adv. Com., Newsletter Assn. Am., Direct Mktg. Assn., Inner Circle, Telemktg. Coun., Fin. Coun., Australian Direct Mktg. Assn., T.A.C.T.A. (Sidney), Bank Mktg. Assn., Am. Soc., Am. C. of C., Buffalo C. of C., Am. Inst. Banking, Am. Assn. Profl. Cons., Am. Cons. League, Am. Soc. Profl. and Exec. Women, Atlanta Profl. Women's Network, Atlanta Women Entrepreneurs, Atlanta C. of C., Printing Assn. Ga., Printing Industries of Am., Direct Mktg. Assn. of N. Tex., Southeast Direct Mktg. Club, Humane Soc. U.S., Kangaroo Protection Agy., Smithsonian Inst., NAFE, AAUW, Am. Mgmt. Assn., Internat. Oceanographic Found, Creative Problem Solving Inst. (alumni), Creative Edn. Found. (bd. dirs.). Republican. Clubs: Seven Seas Sailing, Studio Arena Acting, Atlanta Advt., Melbourne and Sydney Direct Mktg., SWAP. Address: Direct Mktg R&D Ltd 2316 Delware Ave Ste 136 Buffalo NY 14216

RICHARD, ELAINE, educational therapist; b. N.Y.C., Apr. 24, 1930; d. Jacob Michael and Mildred (Levenstein) Simon; m. Jack Richard, Apr. 11, 1954; children: Mark Steven, Susan Richard Weiller. BA, St. Lawrence U., 1950; MA, Columbia U., 1981. Cert. spl. edn. tchr., N.Y. Psychiat. social worker Ralph S. Banay, M.D., N.Y.C., 1950-54, 61-66; asst. to headmaster Dalton Sch., N.Y.C., 1967-70; asst. to prin. Horace Mann Elem. Sch., N.Y.C., 1970-72; dir. admissions Calhoun Sch., N.Y.C., 1972-80; ednl. cons. Ethical Culture Schs., N.Y.C., 1980-81; pvt. practice as ednl. therapist N.Y.C., 1981—; bd. dirs. Ind. Schs. Admissions Assn. Greater N.Y., 1974-80. Mem. N.Y. Orton-Dyslexia Soc., Assn. for Children with Lrng. Disabilities. Home and Office: 501 E 79th St New York NY 10021

RICHARD, LAURA ANN, aerospace engineer; b. Oak Harbor, Wash., Feb. 28, 1961; d. Roy Austin and JoAnn Gayle (Green) R. BA in Environ. Sci., U. Calif., 1983; BS in Aerospace Engring., San Diego State U., 1986. Structural engr. Space Systems div. Gen. Dynamics, San Diego, 1987—. Mem. AIAA (young mems. sect. treas., program arrangements com. 1984—), San Diego State Coll. Engring. Alumni Assn. (bd. dirs. 1987—). Home: 1242 Hidden Mountain Rd El Cajon CA 92019 Office: Gen Dynamics PO Box 85990 MZC38830 San Diego CA 92138

RICHARD, MARLENE JOAN, nutritionist; b. Hartford, S.D., Apr. 3, 1932; d. Edwin John and Grace Jane (Hilton) Johnson; m. John Joseph Richard, Apr. 7, 1956. BS, S.D. State U., 1954. Analyst Experiment Stn. Biochemistry, S.D. State U., Brookings, 1951-54; analytical chemist Ames (Iowa) Lab of the Atomic Energy Commn., 1954-58; research assoc. Nutritional Physiology Group Animal Sci. Dept., Iowa State U, Ames, Iowa, 1959–; mem. Nutritional Sciences Council, Ames Iowa, 1975--. Articles to profl. jours. Vol. Meals on Wheels, 1974-82, mem., sec. Parish Council, St. Cecilia Parish, 1972-76, planner Midnight Madness Running Annual Event, Ames Iowa, 1979-80. Recipient Profl. and Sci. Excellence award Iowa State U., 1989. Mem. Am. Oil Chemist's Soc., Sigma Xi, Iota Sigma Pi. Democrat. Roman Catholic. Home: RR 1 Box 18 Ames IA 50010 Office: Iowa State U 313 Kildee Hall Ames IA 50011

RICHARD, SANDRA CLAYTON, business educator; b. Athens, Tex.; d. Chester Armendale and Lola Hybernia (Clayton) R. AA, Trinity Valley Community Coll.; BBA, U. Tex., 1958, MBA, 1959, PhD, 1968. Instr. Am. U. of Beirut, 1959-61, asst. prof., 1968-74, vis. assoc. prof., 1978-81; asst. prof. Haile Selassie I U., Ethiopia, 1965-66, U. Mo., St. Louis, 1966-67; vis. assoc. prof. U. Notre Dame, 1974-77, Calif. State U., Long Beach, 1977-78; assoc. prof., chmn., div. bus. adminstrn. Laredo (Tex.) State U., 1981—; prodn. and inventory control cons. Mathes Mfg. Co., Athens, 1958, U.N. Indsl. Devel. Orgn., Vienna, Austria, 1968; mgmt. devel. programs Pakistan Indsl. Devel. Corp., Karachi, 1963, Beirut, Bahrain, Qatar, 1970-74, 78-81. Contbr. articles to profl. jours. Mem. Leadership Laredo, 1985—; founding bd. mem. Laredo Regional Food Bank, 1982—; bd. mem. Animal Protective Soc., Laredo, 1982—; mem. steering com. Am. for Justice in the Middle East, Beirut, 1980-81. Named Outstanding Ex-Student Trinity Valley Community Coll., Athens, 1983; Fulbright grad. research grantee, Karachi, 1962-63. Mem. Soc. for Internat. Devel., Acad. Internat. Bus., Acad. Mgmt., Internat. Trade and Fin. Assn. (bd. dirs.), Tex. Assn. Mid. East Scholars, AAUP, Animal Air Transp. Assn., Phi Kappa Phi. Office: Laredo State U 1 W Washington St Laredo TX 78040

RICHARDELLA, LILLIE PARKER, administrative manager; b. Los Angeles, Aug. 12, 1952; d. Emmet Elwin and Darlene Margaret (Kochen) Parker; m. Roland George Richardella, May 27, 1978; 1 child, Christopher. BA, Calif. State U., Long Beach, 1973; postgrad., Cambridge (Eng.) U., 1974-76. Research asst., contract analyst Gen. Revenue Sharing, Orange County, Calif., 1977-79; assoc. exec. dir. YWCA, Oklahoma City, 1979-81; coordinator WORKHAWAII, Honolulu Job Tng. Program, Honolulu, 1983-84, acting chief planner, 1984, contracts mgr., 1985, chief of ops., 1985-86, adminstr., 1986-87; cons. Pub. Econ. Devel. Job Tng. Program, Honolulu, pvt. tng. programs. Author: (handbook, slideshow) Contributions of American Women to the Professions, 1981; project dir.: (video tape) Give Me a Break, 1986 (recipient Nat. Assn. Countries Youth Projects awd, 1986). Organizer, Mayor's Mobilization Task For Vets., Honolulu, 1985; fund raiser, treas., Lt. Govs. Conf., Honolulu, 1986; spokesperson, Network of Mktg. Women and YWCA, Honolulu, 1985-87. Recipient Fulbright scholarship, 1974, Pres'. Scholarship, Calif. State U., 1970-73. Mem. Hawaii Visitors Bur. (edn. and tng. com.), U.S. Dept. Edn. (adv. council Windward Dist. Exemplary Program), U.S. Dept. of Labor and Indsl. Relations (adv. council Sch. to Work Transition Ctr.), Network of Mktg. Women, YWCA, Nat. Women's Polit. Caucus (exec. dir. 1987-89, internat. women's forum exec. dir.), Alpha Lamda Delta, Phi Kappa Phi. Republican. Roman Catholic. Office: Nat Women's Polit Caucus 1275 K St NW Suite 750 Washington DC 20005

RICHARDS, ANN WILLIS, state official; b. Waco, Tex., Sept. 3, 1933; d. Cecil and Ona Willis; m. David Richard; children: Cecille, Daniel, Clark, Ellen. B.A., Baylor U., 1954; postgrad., U. Tex., 1957. Tchr. Austin Ind. Sch. Dist., Tex.; mgr. Sarah Weddington Campaign, Austin, Tex., 1972, adminstrv. asst., 1973-74; county commr. Travis County, Austin, 1977-82; state treas. State of Tex., Austin, from 1983; chairperson Tex. Depository Bd., Austin, from 1983; elected gov. of Tex., 1990; mem. State Banking Bd. Tex., from 1982; ex-officio mem. Tex. Senate Interim Com. on Agy. funds Mgmt., 1982, Joint Select Com. on State Fiscal Policy, 1982; mem. Austin Transp. Study, Tex., 1977-82, Capital Indsl. Devel. Corp., Austin, Tex., 1980-81, Spl. Commn. Delivery Human Services in Tex., 1979-81, Tex. Criminal Justice Adv. Bd., 1981-82, Pres.'s Adv. Com. on Women, 1979. Author (with Peter Knobler): Straight From the Heart, 1989. Mem. com. strategic planning Dem. Nat. Com., 1983; keynote speaker Dem. Nat. Conv., 1988. Named Woman of Yr. Tex. Women's Polit. Caucus, 1981, 83. Mem. Nat. Assn. State Treas. Office: Treasury Dept PO Box 12608 Capitol Sta Austin TX 78711*

RICHARDS, BRIGID, educator, artist; b. Limerick, Clare, Ireland, Sept. 17, 1950; came to U.S., 1951; d. Bridie (Walsh) Scanlon; m. John S. Richards, Dec. 25, 1976 (div. Jan. 1989); children: Sean, Ryan. BA, U. Wis., 1972; MS, Dominican Coll., 1987; postgrad., U. San Francisco, 1989—. Cert. tchr., learning handicapped, Calif. Resource specialist Richmond (Calif.) Unified Sch. Dist., 1987—; graphic artist, copywriter Calif. Pacific Advt., Petaluma, Calif., 1984-86. Mgr. Media Savages Softball, San Francisco, 1988-89. Mem. Coun. for Exceptional Children, Am. Art Therapy Assn., Media Alliance, NEA. Home: 525 Heather Way San Rafael CA 94903 Office: DeAnza High Sch 5000 Valley View Rd Richmond CA 94803

RICHARDS, CARMELEETE A., corporate computer trainer; b. Springport, Ind., Feb. 8, 1948; d. Gordon K. and Virginia Christine (New) Brown; 1 child, Annasheril. BS in Edn., Southwestern State Coll., Weatherford, Okla., 1971; postgrad., Ashland (Ohio) Coll., 1981—. Cert. tchr., Ohio. Tng. mgr. Computer Depot, Columbus, Ohio, 1984-85; corp. trainer, exec. sales Litel Telecommunications, Worthington, Ohio, 1987-89; communications cons. Telemarketing Communications of Columbus, Ohio, 1988-89; corp. computer tng. O/E Learning, Troy, Mich., 1989—. Pres. PTA, 1981-82. Recipient Outstanding Participation award Dorothy Carnegie Pub. Speaking. Mem. NAFE, Am. Soc. for Tng. and Devel., Columbus Computer Soc., Kappa Delta Pi. Baptist.

RICHARDS, CHRISTINE-LOUISE, music publisher, artist, author; b. Radnor, Pa., Jan. 11, 1910; d. Joseph Ernest and Catherine (Fletcher) R.; student pvt. schs., art schs., N.Y.C., Munich, Ger. One-woman shows: Stockbridge, Mass., 1947, 48, 52, 53, Oneonta, N.Y., 1960, 61; group shows include: Stockbridge Art Assn., 1931-32; represented in collections, Calif., Mass., N.Y.; owner, founder, pres. Blue Star Music Pub. Co., Pittsfield, Mass., 1946—, now Morris, N.Y. Dep. dir. gen. Internat. Biog. Centre. Recipient Silver medal Internat. Inst. Community Service, Cambridge, Eng., gold medal Internat. Parliament U.S.A., prize of Golden Centaur, others; fellow World Lit. Acad. Fellow Internat. Biol. Assn. (dep. dir. of Americas); mem. Phila. Art Alliance, Am. Fedn. Musicians (hon. life), Nightingale-Bamford Alumni Assn., Academia Italia delle arte e del Lavoro (2 gold medals, hon. diploma Master of Painting), Met. Mus. Art, Audubon Soc., Nat. Assn. Composers USA, Emergency Aid of Pa., Pa. Acad. Fine Arts, Nat. Mus. Women in Arts, Acad. Natural Scis., Friends of Library Bryn Mawr Coll., Phila. Mus., Friends N.Y. Pub. Library, Pa. Hort. Soc., Am. Hort. Soc., Bklyn. Bot. Gardens, Met. Opera Guild, Glimmerglass Opera Theatre, Nat. Trust, Nat. Arbor Day Found., Save the Redwoods, Smithsonian Inst., Nat. Wildlife Fedn., Nature Conservency, Greenpeace, Doll Artisans Guild. Club: Peale (Phila.). Avocations: grand opera, dolls, photography, gardening, handicrafts. Author and Illustrator: The Blue Star Fairy Book of Stories for Children; The Blue Star Fairy Book of More Stories for Children; The Blue Star Fairy Book of New Stories for Children, 1980; Branches, 1983. Composer: (song) What Makes Me Dream of You, 1950, numerous others. Contbr. portrait to Artists U.S.A., 1970-71, 76. Address: Springslea PO Box 188 Morris NY 13808

RICHARDS, DEBORAH DAVIS, health educator, editor; b. St. Augustine, Fla., Dec. 19, 1943; d. Philip A. and Ann (Winship) Davis; m. James Lincoln Richards, June 12, 1965 (div. Aug. 1984); 1 child, Christine. BA, Wellesley Coll. (Mass.), 1965. Vol., Peace Corps, India, 1966-67, tng. assoc., 1967; clinic dir. Planned Parenthood, Washington, 1968-69; co-founder, dir. Action for Child Transp. Safety, N.Y.C., 1972-82; computer tech. analyst, Buckner News Alliance, Seattle, 1981-87; newsletter writer, editor Am. Acad. Pediatrics, Evanston, Ill., 1981—; editor Nat. Child Passenger Safety Assn., Washington, 1983-87; health educator Harborview Injury Prevention and Research Ctr., 1987-89; child safety, editorial cons., 1989—; mem. nat. hwy. safety adv. com. U.S. Dept. Transp., 1979-83; cons. Nat. Hwy. Traffic Safety Adminstrn., Washington, 1981-83. Author and narrator (ednl. film) Don't Risk Your Child's Life, 1978, revised, 1980, 83; author, editor (program manual) Protecting Our Own, 1983, rev. 1988. Mem. Nat. Child Passenger Safety Assn. (sec. bd. dirs. 1985-86, regional rep. 1981-83, 88-89), L.A. Area Child Passenger Safety Assn., Am. Trauma Soc., Washington State Pub. Health Assn. Democrat. Unitarian. Clubs: The Mountaineers, Wellesley (Seattle).

RICHARDS, DONNA NELL, recreational therapist; b. Dublin, Ga., Dec. 28, 1959; d. Aaron Isaah Richards and Ruby Nell (Richards) Dawkins. BA in Recreation Therapy, Ga. Coll., 1982; MEd in Guidance and Counseling, West Ga. Coll., 1989. Lic. therapeutic recreation specialist, Ga. Asst. occupational therapist VA Med. Ctr., Dublin, 1980, lab. asst., phlebotomist, 1981; subs. tchr. N.W. Laurens Elem. Sch., Dublin, 1981; outdoor edn. assn. Ga. Coll., Milledgeville, 1982; intern in recreation therapy So. Med., Dublin, 1982; mgr. recreation therapy dept. South Ga. Med. Ctr., Valdosta, 1982-84; activity therapist Cobb Douglas Mental Health Ctr., Marietta, Ga., 1984—; cons., 1984-87. Vol. Cobb County Emergency Aid Program, Marietta, 1986-87. Mem. Ga. Recreation and Park Soc., Day Treatment Ctr. Ga., Atlantic Alumni Club Ga. Coll. Democrat. Baptist. Home: Rt 11 Box 110 Toonigh Rd Canton GA 30114 Office: Cobb/Douglas Mental Health 260 Hawkins Store Rd Kennesaw GA 30144

RICHARDS, GINA RUE, marketing executive; b. Austin, Tex., Oct. 11, 1963; d. George Tunney and Evelyn Pearl (Smith) Richards. Student, U. Tex., Austin, 1981-83; student, Austin Community Coll., 1981-88. Adminstrv. technician II Gov.'s Office, State of Tex., Austin, 1981-84; adminstrv. technician III Atty. Gen.'s Office, State of Tex., Austin, 1984-85; paralegal Atty. Gen.'s Office, State of Tex., 1985; mktg. adminstr. TECOM (govt. contractor), Austin, 1985-86; editor, mktg. adminstr. Tex. Med. Assn., Austin, 1986-87; contract mgr., corp. security officer Tech. Support Svcs., Inc., Austin, 1987-90, dir. mktg., 1990—. Vol. Rape Crisis Prevention Ctr., Austin, 1987—. Mem. NAFE, NOW, Nat. Abortion Rights Action League,

Tex. Abortion Rights Action League. Republican. Methodist. Office: Tech Support Svcs Inc 12116 A Jekel Circle Austin TX 78727

RICHARDS, JANE AILEEN, rehabilitation nursing consultant; b. Oakland, Calif., Oct. 19, 1948; d. John Donald and Mary Dolores (Peters) R. BS in Nursing, U. San Francisco, 1970; MS in Nursing, San Jose State U., 1976. RN; cert. ins. rehab. specialist. Staff nurse ICU Mills Meml. Hosp., San Mateo, Calif., 1970-73; asst. head nurse ICU, 1973-76, edn. specialist, 1976-80, mgr. acute rehab. ctr., 1980-83; rehab. nursing cons. J.R. Assocs., San Mateo, 1983—; nurse cons. Calif. State Dept. Corps., 1989—. Pres. United Cerebral Palsy Assn., Mt. View, Calif., 1983-85, 79-82, bd. dirs., vice chmn. vol. devel. com., N.Y.C., 1989—. Mem. Assn. of Rehab. Nurses, Calif. Assn. Rehab. Profl., Nat. Rehab. Assn., Rehab. Ins. Nurse Group (pres. 1987-89), Sigma Theta Tau (Alpha Gamma chpt.). Republican. Avocations: golf, camping. Home and Office: JR Assocs 456 Mariner's Island Blvd Suite 210 San Mateo CA 94404

RICHARDS, JESSIE POLLARD, postmaster; b. Montvale, Va., July 12, 1927; d. Jesse Witt and Julia Ethel (Smith) Pollard; m. Cecil Richards, Oct. 2, 1948; children: Cecilia, Jackolyn, Julia Ann, Ted. Student, Berea Coll., 1947-48. Tchr.'s aid Montvale Elem. Sch., 1944-45; clk. Bromena Grocery, Montvale, 1945-46; bookkeeper Walters Printing Co., Roanoke, Va., 1948-50; clk. U.S. Postal Svc., Montvale, 1961-68, postmaster, 1968-88; bd. dirs., sec., treas., Montvale Water Co... Tchr. adult classes, Montvale Meth. Ch.; past bd. dirs., Montvale Library; driver, crew mem. Montvale Rescue Squad, 1970-90; past pres., Montvale PTA. Mem. Nat. League Postmasters (editor 1977-87, v.p. 1977, 88—). Democrat. Methodist. Home: PO Box 123 Montvale VA 24122 Office: US Postal Svc US Rte 460 Montvale VA 24122

RICHARDS, JUDITH G., business service owner; b. Kalamazoo, Oct. 20, 1939; d. Robert H. and Mary R. (Slumkoski) Richards. A.A.S., Ferris State U., 1960. Legal sec. Bush & Bush, Sturgis, Mich., 1965-77; owner Executives Bus. Svc., Sturgis, 1978-87; pres. Exec. Suites and Svcs., Inc., Kalamazoo, 1987—; Mich. bus. rep. Job Tng. Coordinating Council, 1987—. Bd. dirs. ARCH Rehab. Facility, 1975-87; city commr. Sturgis City Commn., 1983-87. Methodist. Avocations: travel; sailing; gourmet cooking. Office: Exec Suites and Services Walnut Woods Centre 5955 W Main St Kalamazoo MI 49009

RICHARDS, KATHERINE MARY, librarian; b. Longview, Wash., Oct. 31, 1941; d. William Robert and Tessie Margaret (Winn) Enright; m. Joe McCall Richards, June 30, 1961 (div. 1966). BA, Marylhurst Coll., 1964; MLS, Ind. U., 1968; cert., Johns Hopkins U., 1969. 73, Cath. U. Am., 1968-69, Columbia U., 1981. Asst. librar. Dental Sch. U. Oreg., Portland, 1965-67; asst. hist. libr. Med. Sch. Yale U., New Haven, 1969-70; hist. libr. Health Sci. U. Med., Balt., 1970-77; mgr. libr. Emergency Care Rsch. Inst., Plymouth Meeting, Pa., 1978-79; dir. libr. Cooper Med. Ctr., Camden, N.J., 1979-80; assoc. libr. N.Y. Hist. Soc., N.Y.C., 1981-84; libr. Metro. Mus. Art, 1985; assoc. libr. Univ. Club, 1986-88; asst. dir. libr. svc., Drew U., L.A., 1988—; mem. preservation com. Rsch. Libr. Group, Stanford, Calif., 1983-84, mem. pub. svcs. com., 1983-84. Sec. Trentcentun Corp., Bronx, N.Y., 1983, pres., 1983-86 ; bd. dirs. NOW Md. State, 1975-76, Balt. chpt., 1974-76. Fellow Johns Hopkins U., 1968. Mem. ALA, Spl. Libr. Assn. (adv. bd. N.Y.C. 1983-88, sec.-treas. Mus. of Art and Humanities of N.Y.C. 1983-87), Am. Printing History Assn., Am. Assn. History of Medicine. Republican. Unitarian. Home: 1505 Purdue Ave Los Angeles CA 90025

RICHARDS, LACLAIRE LISSETTA JONES (MRS. GEORGE A. RICHARDS), social worker; b. Pine Bluff, Ark.; d. Artie William and Geraldine (Adams) Jones; B.A., Nat. Coll. Christian Workers, 1953; M.S.W., U. Kans., 1956; postgrad. Columbia U., 1960; m. George Alvarez Richards, July 26, 1958; children—Leslie Rosario, Lia Mercedes, Jorge Ferguson. Diplomate Clin. Social Work; cert. gerontologist. Psychiat. supervisory, teaching, community orgn., adminstrv. and consultative duties Hastings Regional Ctr., Ingleside, Nebr., 1956-60; supervisory, consultative and adminstrv. responsibilities for psychiat. and geriatric patients VA Hosp., Knoxville, Iowa, 1960-74, field instr. for grad. students from U. Mo., EEO counselor, 1969-74, 78-90, com. chmn., 1969-70, Fed. women's program coordinator, 1972-74; sr. social worker Mental Health Inst., Cherokee, Iowa, 1974-77; adj. asst. prof. dept. social behavior U. S.D.; instr. Dept. of Psychiatry U. S.D Sch. of Medicine, Augustana Coll., 1981-86; outpatient social worker VA Med. and Regional Office Center, Sioux Falls, S.D., 1978—; EEO counselor. Mem. Knoxville Juvenile Adv. Com., 1963-65, 68-70, sec., 1965-66, chmn., 1966-68; sec. Urban Renewal Citizens' Adv. Com., Knoxville, 1966-68; mem. United Methodist Ch. Task Force Exptl. Styles Ministry and Leadership, 1973-74, mem. adult choir, mem. ch. and society com.; counselor Knoxville Youth Line program; sec. exec. com. Vis. Nurse Assn., 1979-80; canvasser community fund drs., Knoxville; mem. Cherokee Civil Rights Commn.; bd. dirs., pub. relations, membership devel. and program devel. cons. YWCA, 1983-85; bd. dirs. Family Svc. Agy., 1989-90. Named S.D. Social Worker of Yr., 1983. Mem. NAACP (chmn. edn. com. 1983-85), AAUW (sec. Hastings chpt. 1958-60), AMA Aux., Nat. Assn. Social Workers (co-chmn. Nebr. chpt. profl. standards com. 1958-59), Acad. Cert. Social Workers, S.D. Assn. Social Workers (chmn. minority affairs com., v.p. S.E. region 1980, pres. 1980-82 exec. com. 1982-84, mem. social policy and action com.), Nebr. Assn. Social Workers (chmn. 1958-59), Seventh Dist. S.D. Med. Soc. Aux., Coalition on Aging. Methodist (Sunday sch. tchr. adult div.; mem. commn. on edn.; mem. Core com. for adult edn.; mem. Adult Choir; mem. Social Concerns Work Area). Home: 1701 Ponderosa Dr Sioux Falls SD 57103

RICHARDS, MARTA ALISON, lawyer; b. Memphis, Mar. 15, 1952; d. Howard Jay and Mary Dean (Nix) Richards; m. Jon Michael Hobson, May 5, 1973 (div. Jan. 1976); m. 2d, Richard Peter Massony, June 16, 1979 (div. Apr. 1988); 1 child, Richard Peter Massony, Jr. Student Vassar Coll., 1969-70; AB cum laude, Princeton U., 1973; JD, George Washington U., 1976. Bar: La. 1976, U.S. Dist. Ct. La. 1976, U.S. Ct. of Appeals (5th cir.) 1981, U.S. Supreme Ct. 1988. SAssoc. Phelps, Dunbar, Marks, Claverie & Sims, New Orleans, 1976-77; assoc. counsel Hibernia Nat. Bank, New Orleans, 1978; assoc. Singer, Hutner, Levine, Seeman & Stuart, New Orleans, 1978-80, Jones, Walker, Waechter, Poitevent, Carrere & Denegre, New Orleans, 1980-84; ptnr. Mmahat Duffy, & Richards, 1984, Montgomery, Barnett, Brown, Read, Hammond & Mintz, 1984-86, Montgomery, Richards & Ballin, 1986-89, Gelpi, Sullivan, Carroll and Laborde, 1989—; counsel Maison Blanche Inc., Baton Rouge, 1990—; lectr. paralegal inst. U. New Orleans, 1984-89, adj. prof., 1989—. Contbr. articles to legal jours. Treas. alumni coun. Princeton U., 1979-81. Mem. ABA, La. State Bar Assn., Fed. Bar Assn., New Orleans Bar Assn., Princeton Alumni Assn. New Orleans (pres. 1982-86). Republican. Episcopalian. Home: 7813A Jefferson Pl Blvd Baton Rouge LA 70809 Office: Maison Blanche Inc 1500 Main St Baton Rouge LA 70821

RICHARDS, MILDRED RUTH, health-care administrator; b. Sterling, Colo., Feb. 5, 1933; d. Frederick and Amalia Luft; student Northeastern Jr. Coll., U. No. Colo., St. Louis U., Colo. Women's Coll.; children—Valerie Jo Richards Hettinger, Renae Ruth Richards. Co-owner Fish's Profl. Pharmacy, Sterling, 1967-70: acct. Ceres Land & Cattle Co., Sterling, 1970-75; acct. Monfort of Colo., Greeley, 1975-77; adminstr. Meml. Hosp. of Greeley, 1977-84, also bd. dirs.; adminstr. Oakhurst Towers Adult Congregate Living Community, Denver, 1987—. Trustee, No. Colo. Osteo. Hosp. Found.: active disaster com. City of Greeley. Mem. Am. Hosp. Assn., Am. Osteo. Hosp. Assn. (trustee 1981—, com. small and rural hosps. 1981—, pres. 1982, 83, 84), Colo. Hosp. Assn., Colo. Osteo. Hosp. Assn. (sec.-treas. 1980-84), N. Central Colo. Hosp. Adminstrs. Council (pres. 1982), Larimer/Weld Counties Hosp. Planning Council, Colo. Small and Rural Hosp. Task Force, TONACK (Osteo.) Assn. (sec.-treas. 1982, v.p. 1983, pres. 1984), People to People Internat./AHA goodwill ambassador to Australia and N.Z. 1981), Greeley C. of C. (city improvement com. 1984)m contract negotiator, Devel. of Craig-Meeker, Colo. Health Care/Bus. Alliance and Preferred Physician Orgn., 1985-87); adminstr. Oakhurst Towers, Denver, 1987—, Phi Sigma Alpha. Lutheran. Contbr. articles to profl. pubs. Office: 8030 E Girard Ave Denver CO 80231

RICHARDS, RHODA ROOT WAGNER, civic worker; b. Phila., Oct. 2, 1917; d. Edward Stephen and Rhoda Earley (Root) Wagner; student U. Pa., 1937-39; A.A., Wildcliff Jr. Coll., 1938; m. J. Permar Richards, Jr., May 18, 1940; children: Patricia A.V. Richards Cosgrave, J. Permar III. Profl. artist; founder, chmn. Hosp. Corps, Navy League Service, 1941-43; chmn. ARC Nurses Aide Corps, Jacksonville, Fla., 1944-45, Long Beach, Calif., 1945-46; founder, chmn. Fiesta Benefits, Hahnemann Hosp., 1950-57; former chmn. jr. com. Met. Opera; bd. dirs. Phila. Lyric Opera Co.; chmn. Ring for Freedom Republican Campaign of S.E. Pa., 1960; pres. Emergency Aid of Pa., 1961-64; v.p. bd. dirs. Inglis House, Phila., 1977-82; pres. women's bd. Phila. div. Am. Cancer Soc., 1978-81, hon. life mem.; founder, chmn. Community Activities Calendar, 1970-80; gen. chmn. 1st Ann. Washington Crossing Assembly, 1978; trustee Baldwin Sch.; co-chmn. fundraising com. Ambulatory Service Pavilion, Presbyn.-U. Pa. Med. Center; vice chmn. Women's Commn. for Bicentennial, 1976; bd. dirs., mem. Appleford Commn. Parsons-Banks Arboretum; bd. dirs. St. Johns Settlement House, 1954-86, Vol., chmn. women's bd. Phila. div. Am. Cancer Soc., 1978-86; vol. Phila. chpt. Lupus Found., 1980-81; mem. Delaware Valley women's bd. Freedoms Found. at Valley Forge; past v.p. women's assn., past chmn. fin. com., chmn. centennial spl. event and gen. com. for the celebration Bryn Mawr Presbyn. Ch.; hon. col. corps of cadets Valley Forge Mil. Acad. and Jr. Coll.; founder, chmn. Rittenhouse Preservation Coalition, 1982—; founder, v.p., asst. treas. Preservation Coalition of Greater Phila., 1984—; mem. Hospitality, Phila. Style; chmn. bd. dirs. Emergency Aid of Pa. Found., chmn. 75th anniversary celebration, fin., long range planning, investment coms. Recipient Crusade award Am. Cancer Soc., 1976; spl. award for community service St. John's Settlement House, 1977; Florence A. Sanson award for patriotism, 1986; named Disting. Dau. of Pa., 1985. Mem. Phila. Mus. Art, Pa. Acad. Fine Arts, Woodmere Art Gallery, Hahnemann Hosp. Women's Assn. (Phila. chpt.), DAR, Daus. of the Cincinnati, Dames of Loyal Legion, Nat. Soc. Colonial Dames of XVII Century, Dames Sovereign Mil. Order Temple of Jerusalem, Honolulu Mus. Art, Geneal. Soc. Pa., Am. Hist. Soc., Nat. Trust for Historic Preservation, Smithsonian Instn., Friends of Independence Hall, Friends of Hist. Cliveden, Andalusia Friends. Clubs: Sedgeley, Cosmopolitan, Peale, Safari, Bald Peak Colony. Home: 1250 Lafayette Rd PO Box 608 Bryn Mawr PA 19010

RICHARDS, SUSAN MARIE (SUSAN MARIE WOS), microbiologist, researcher; b. Buffalo, Dec. 2, 1955; d. Anthony Lucas and Florence Angeline (Woloszyn) Wos; 1 child, Derek Anthony. BA, SUNY, Buffalo, 1977, MA, 1980, PhD, 1983. Med. lab. technician Erie County Med. Ctr., Buffalo, 1974-79; rsch. technician N.Y. State Dept. Health, Albany, 1979-83; postdoctoral fellow Wadsworth Ctr. Labs./Rsch., Albany, 1983-84; rsch. microbiologist E.I. duPont de Nemours & Co., Wilmington, Del., 1984-87; staff scientist Integrated Genetics, Inc., Framingham, Mass., 1987-89; sr. scientist Genzyme/Integrated Genetics, Inc., Framingham, 1989—; presentor nat. sci. meetings, 1980—. Author (column) Infectious Disease Inst. News, 1982; also articles, chpts. Vol. E.J. Meyer Meml. Hosp., Buffalo, 1973-74, Friends of Saratoga Performing Arts Ctr., N.Y., 1981-82. N.Y. State Regents scholar SUNY, Buffalo, 1973-77. Mem. Am. Soc. Microbiology, N.Y. Acad. Sci., Buffalo Collegium of Immunology, Am. Soc. Virology, Sigma Xi. Avocations: travel, microcomputers, photography. Office: Genzyme Corp 1 Mountain Rd Framingham MA 01701

RICHARDSON, BARBARA CONNELL, transportation research scientist; b. N.Y.C., Dec. 29, 1947; d. John Joseph and Joan Marie (Tobin) Connell; m. Rudy James Richardson, Aug. 23, 1970 (div. Dec. 1984); 1 child, Anne Elizabeth. BA, SUNY, 1969; SM, MIT, 1973; PhD, U. Mich., Ann Arbor, 1982. Programmer/analyst The Phys. Review, Upton, N.Y., 1969-70; transp. planner Mass. Exec. Office of Transp. and Constrn., Boston, 1973-74; transp. research officer Greater London Council, 1974-75; assoc. research scientist and dir. transp. planning and policy Univ. Mich., Ann Arbor, 1975-86; pres. Richardson Assocs., Inc., Ann Arbor, 1983—. Contbr. numerous articles on transp. to profl. jours. Mem. Transp. Research Bd., Am. Assn. for Advancement Sci., Soc. Automotive Engrs., Kappa Mu Epsilon, Signum Laudis, Sigma Xi. Roman Catholic. Office: Richardson Assocs Inc 325 E Eisenhower Pkwy Ste 106 Ann Arbor MI 48108

RICHARDSON, BARBARA JEAN ACKER, marketing executive; b. Cambridge, Mass.; d. Robert H. and Irene A. (Reed) Acker; m. William Gordon, May 24, 1958; children: Kenneth, William Jr., Bradford. Student, Mesa Community Coll., 1975-78. Prodn. liaison Ambassador Internat., Tempe, Ariz., 1976-78, asst. mgr. print, 1978-79, mgr. print svcs., 1979-82; mgr. print and advt. svcs. Ambassador Internat./CPS, Phoenix, 1982-89; dir. print svcs., chmn. postal affairs com. CPS Direct Mktg. Inc., Phoenix, 1989-90; western div. graphics/print mgr. Advo-System Inc., Scottsdale, Ariz., 1990—. Mem. Direct Mktg. Assn., Third Class Mailers Assn., Phoenix Direct Mktg. Club, Phoenix Postal Customer Coun. (adv. coun. 1987-89). Republican. Home: 3406 E Woodland Dr Phoenix AZ 85044 Office: CPS Direct Mktg Inc 7822 S 46th St Phoenix AZ 85044

RICHARDSON, BETTY KEHL, nurse administrator, researcher, therapist; b. Jacksonville, Ill., Mar. 24, 1938; d. Alfred Jason and Hilda (Emmons) Kehl; m. Joseph Richardson, June 27, 1959 (div. 1980); children: Mark Joseph, Stephanie Elaine. BA in Nursing, Sangamon State U., 1975, MA in Adminstrn., 1977; MS in Nursing, Med. Coll. Ga., 1980; PhD in Nursing, U. Tex., 1985. Cert. advanced nursing adminstrn. Staff Lincoln Land Community Coll., Springfield, Ill., 1978-79; acting dir. nursing MacMurray Coll., Jacksonville, Ill., 1979-81; charge nurse Shoal Creek Hosp., Austin, Tex., 1981-83; adminstr. children and adolescent programs Shoal Creek Hosp., Austin, 1989-90; nursing dir. Austin State Hosp., 1983-89; therapist San Marcos (Tex.) Treatment Ctr., 1990—; asst. prof. Sangamon State U., Springfield, 1981-82. Contbr. several articles to profl. jours. Pres. PTA, 1968. Named Outstanding Nurse Passavant Hosp., 1958; recipient Plaque for Outstanding Leadership Austin State Hosp., 1989; Paul Harris fellow. Mem. ANA, Ill. State Geneal. Soc., Assn. Play Therapy, Rotary, Sigma Theta Tau, Phi Kappa Phi. Methodist. Home: 5207 Doe Valley Ln Austin TX 78759 Office: San Marcos Treatment Ctr PO Box 768 San Marcos TX 78667-0768

RICHARDSON, BOBBI, interior designer, executive; b. Evansville, Ind., July 1, 1945; d. Julius John and Anna Louise (Griggs) Steinkamp; children: Amy Griggs Richardson, Michael Lawrence Richardson. Student Lockyear Bus. Coll., 1963, U. So. Ind.; AA, Ivy Tech. Coll., 1989. Exec. sec. Citizens Nat. Bank, Evansville, Ind., 1964-69; legal sec. Newkirk, Keane, Kowalczyk & Leal, Ft. Wayne, Ind., 1971-72; sec. Mead Johnson & Co., Evansville, 1977-78; med. staff coordinator Deaconess Hosp., Evansville, 1978-85, cons., 1985-86; exec. dir. Share-In Care, Inc., Evansville, 1985; owner, pres. Bus. Interiors, Evansville, 1985—; cons. Builders' Spltys., Evansville, 1984—. Mem. Am. Entrepreneur Assn., Nat. Assn. Female Execs., Network of Evansville Women, Women in Networking (recorder, historian 1985-87, sec. 1985-87), Interior Design Club (v.p. 1987-88, pres. 1988-89). Republican. Roman Catholic. Avocations: skiing, reading, travel. Home and Office: Bus Interiors 10110 Lindar Ln Evansville IN 47712

RICHARDSON, DEANNA RUTH, microbiologist; b. Columbus, Ohio, Jan. 7, 1956; d. Raymond and Anna Mary (Underwood) R. BS, Ohio State U., 1978. Lab tech. Ohio Dept. Agr., Reynoldsburg, Ohio, 1978-81, lab technologist, 1981-86, microbiologist, 1986—. Mem. Neighborhood Civic Assn., 1983-87, Columbus Zoo, Nat./Internat. Wildlife Fedns., Smithsonian Inst. Mem. Ohio Valley Inst. of Food Technologists, Vet. Microbiologists Assn., Ohio State U. Alumni Assn., Franklin County Alumni Club. Home: 6267 Barberry Hollow Columbus OH 43213 Office: Ohio Dept Agr Labs 8995 East Main St Reynoldsburg OH 43068

RICHARDSON, DOROTHY VIRGINIA, accountant; b. Bennington, Okla., Sept. 26, 1937; d. William Lycurgus and Mittie Mae (Richardson) Ray; student Eastern Okla. A&M, 1955-56; B.B.A., U. Alaska, 1974; m. Charles Howard Richardson, Dec. 28, 1958; children—Charles Timothy, Michael Todd. Asst. acct. Peat, Marwick, Mitchell & Co., Omaha, 1975-76; gen. acct. U. Alaska Statewide System, Fairbanks, 1976; asst. bus. mgr. Geophys. Inst., Fairbanks, 1976-77; dir. grant and contract services U. Alaska, Fairbanks, 1977-80; controller Alaska Legal Services Corp., Anchorage, 1980-81; bus. mgr. div. community colls., rural edn. and extension U. Alaska, Anchorage, 1981-83; assoc. controller U. Fla., Gainesville, 1983-89; dir. sponsored projects Va. Polytech. Inst. and State U., 1989—. Active Cub Scouts, Mothers March of Dimes, PTA; pres. Alachua County Geneal. Soc., 1984-86, Am. Cancer Soc. Served with USAF, 1957-59. Mem. Am. Inst. C.P.A.s, Soc. Research Adminstrs., Council on Govtl. Relations, Nat. Council Univ. Research Adminstrs. Office: Va Tech 203 Burruss Hall Blacksburg VA 24061

RICHARDSON, ELAINE M., federal government official; b. Boston, May 4, 1954; d. Albert S. and Phyllis E. (Brosnahan) R. BA, Regis Coll., 1976; MBA, George Washington U., 1985. Staff asst. Edward W. Brooke, U.S. Sen., Boston, Mass.; exec. asst. Edward W. Brooke, U.S. Sen., Washington; office mgr. Congressman Bill Green, Washington; risk mgmt. analyst Fed. Savings & Loan Ins. Corp., Washington; asst. dir. mktg. Fed. Deposit Ins. Corp. Div. Fed. Savings & Loan Ins. Corp., Washington. Mem. NAFE, Women in Govt. Relations, Women In Housing and Fin. Office: 801 17th St NW #659 Washington DC 20006

RICHARDSON, ELEANOR ELIZABETH, marketing professional; b. Durham, N.C., Jan. 16, 1948; d. Thurman Eugene Hogan and Flora Elizabeth (Pope) Teele; m. Fredrick Glenn Richardson, July 16, 1977; children: Glenn, David, Tammy. BS in Bus., Liberty U., 1990, MBA, 1990. Banking officer State Bank Raleigh, 1977-79, Ft. Knox (Ky.) Nat. Bank, 1980-82, Am. Express, Augsburg and Heidelberg, Fed. Republic Germany, 1982-83; dep. registrar U.S. Army-Europe Vehicle Registry, Heidelberg, 1983-88; mktg. dir. Dept. Def., Ft. Bragg, N.C., 1989—. Mem. Ft. Knox Sch. Bd., 1981-82; pres. Home Health Care Sr. Citizens, Fayetteville, N.C., 1990—. Mem. NAFE, Ft. Bragg Officers Club,. Republican. Home: 3516 Gowan Ln Fayetteville NC 28311 Office: Directorate Pers Community Affairs Knox St Fort Bragg NC 28307

RICHARDSON, EMELINE HILL, retired archaeology educator; b. Buffalo, June 6, 1910; d. William Hurd and Emeleen Howe (Carlisle) Hill; m. Lawrence Richardson, Jr., May 28, 1952. AB, Radcliffe Coll., 1932, AM, 1935; PhD, Harvard U., 1939. From instr. to assoc. prof. Wheaton Coll., Norton, Mass., 1942-49; vis. lectr. Yale U., New Haven, 1955-65; prof. classical archaeology U. N.C., Chapel Hill, 1968-79; ret., 1979; vis. prof. Stanford U., Palo Alto, Calif., 1962; vis. lectr. Inst. Fine Arts, NYU, 1967; dir. NEH Summer Session for Coll. Tchrs., Rome, summer 1979; Norton lectr. Archaeol. Inst. Am., N.Y.C., 1976-77. Author: The Etruscans, Art and Civilization, 1964, Etruscan Votive Bronzes, 1983. Recipient Disting. Achievement award Radcliffe Coll. Alumnae Assn., 1966,, Dignitario, Ombra della Sera, Assn. pro Volterra (Italy), 1980; grantee Am. Philos. Soc., 1958, U. N.C., 1975. Fellow Am. Acad. in Rome, Am. Acad. Arts and Scis.; mem. German Archaeol. Inst. (corr.). Democrat. Mem. Soc. of Friends.

RICHARDSON, FREIDA LARAMY, retired educator, free lance writer, civic worker; b. Chateaugay, N.Y., Aug. 14, 1912; d. Fred Chester and Martha Ann (Shepard) Laramy; m. Francis John McNulty, Dec. 2, 1950 (dec. Sept. 1979); children: Suzanne Kay, Patrick Jon; m. Edwin Lyle Richardson, Nov. 28, 1985. BS, SUNY, Potsdam, 1950. Cert. tchr., N.Y. Tchr. kindergarten Perry Street Sch., Johnstown, N.Y., 1939-44, Margaretville (N.Y.) Cen. Sch., 1944-46; tchr. Massena (N.Y.) Schs., 1947-50; ret., 1950; hostess Elderhostel-Star Lake (N.Y.) Campus, 1989-90. Nursery tchr. St. Raymond's Cath. Ch., Raymondville, N.Y., 1983-85; vol. local polit. campaign, 1988; camp counselor Girl Scouts, Vt., 1943, leader, Raymondville, N.Y., 1963-65. Mem. AAUW (program chmn. 1983, dir. LIFT 1984—), Am. Assn. Ret. Persons (pub. rels. com. St. Lawrence County 1987—), Rod and Gun Club (Massena), Order Eastern Star (matron 1977, historian 1990). Republican. Home: Box 35 Stark Rd Raymondville NY 13678

RICHARDSON, HART MIDDLETON, computer programmer; b. Sumter, S.C., Dec. 28, 1943; d. Ellis Spear Middleton and Anne Hooe (Rust) Patteson; m. Thomas W. Richardson, Jan. 23, 1965; children: Amanda Hart, Elizabeth Anne. BA in Econs., Conn. Coll. for Women, 1964. Programmer trainee Am. Nat. Bank and Trust Co., Morristown, N.J., 1966-67, programmer, 1967-69; sr. programmer Somerset Trust Co., Somerville, N.J., 1969-72; programmer analyst First Nat. Bank Cen. Jersey, Somerville, 1972-73, S.T.C. Computer Services, Raritan, N.J., 1973-78; sr. cons. Vital Computer Resources, Trenton, N.J., 1978-85; sr. programmer, analyst Baker and Taylor Co., Bridgewater, N.J., 1985—. Treas. Pattenburg United Meth. Ch., N.J., 1985-89; active Union Twp. Hist. Soc., N.J. Hunterdon Art Ctr., Clinton, N.J., Clinton Hist. Mus. Republican. Home: RD 1 Box 610 Asbury NJ 08802 Office: Baker & Taylor 652 E Main St Bridgewater NJ 08807-0920

RICHARDSON, JEAN MCGLENN, civil engineer; b. Everett, Wash., Nov. 15, 1927; d. Clayton Charles and Marie Elizabeth (Mellish) McGlenn; BSCE, Oreg. State U., 1949; registered profl. engr., Ala., Oreg.; m. William York Richardson, II, June 11, 1949; children: William York III, Paul Kress II, Clayton McGlenn. Engr., Walter Schoel Engring. Co., Birmingham, Ala., 1950-54; office engr. G.C. McKinney Engring. Co., San Jose, Calif., 1972-74; civil design leader Harland Bartholomew & Assocs., Birmingham, 1974-78, Rust Engring. Co., Birmingham, 1978-82; owner, prin. Jean Richardson and Assocs. Inc., 1983-88; cons. engr. Rust Internat. Corp., 1988—, Fed. Emergency Mgmt. Agy., 1986—; women's engring. del. to China and USSR, 1984; counselor to female students on engring. as a career; regional chmn. Mathcounts, 1986-88; math. vol. pub. schs. Mem. NSPE, Soc. Women Engrs. (sr. sect. rep. to nat. bd.), Ala. Soc. Profl. Engrs. (pres. Birmingham chpt., state dir., state chmn. Mathcounts), Alpha Phi. Republican. Episcopalian. Clubs: Inverness Country, Women's Golf Assn. Office: 1905 Indian Lake Dr Suite 3 Birmingham AL 35244

RICHARDSON, LINDA WALKER, college activities director; b. Palestine, Tex., June 10, 1941; d. Woodward Watson and Argen (Nelms) Walker; m. Burl Burton Richardson, Nov. 30, 1963; children: Andrew C., Amy L. BJ, Sam Houston State U., 1962. Reporter, photographer Rusk (Tex.) Cherokeean, 1962-63, Jacksonville (Tex.) Jour., 1962-63, Palestine (Tex.) Herald-Press, 1963-64; area reporter Houston Chronicle and Hempstead (Tex.) News, 1965-69; broker Texas Heritage Realtors, Bryan, Tex., 1979—; coord. new student confs. Tex. A&M U., College Station, 1989—; owner Greenfield Hair Designs, Bryan, 1987—. Mem. Bryan City Coun. War on Drugs, 1989; leader Bible Study Fellowship, Bryan, 1978-82, tchr. adult women's Bible class, 1982—. Mem. Bryan-College Station Bd. Realtors (chmn. grievance com. 1989—), A&M Mother's Club (historian 1989—), Extension Svc. Club (pres., 1979), Bryan-College Station C. of C. Baptist. Office: Tex A&M U Office Admissions and Records College Station TX 77843-0100

RICHARDSON, MARILYN GOFF, small business owner, artist; b. Taunton, Mass., Sept. 9, 1934; d. Laurence Warren and Beatrice Cornelia (Rogers) Goff; m. Winthrop Horton Richardson Jr., July 18, 1959; children: Keith Warren, Kendra Lee. BFA, Boston U., 1956; MS, Cen. Conn. U., 1965. Cert. elem., secondary edn. tchr., Conn. Art tchr. New Britain (Conn.) Pub. Schs., 1956-63; elem. tchr. Lakeview Sch. Dist., San Angelo, Tex., 1959-60; prin. Wickettwood Arts & Graphs, Coventry, Conn., 1980—. Graphic artist: Bicentennial Cookbook, 1976, Plan of Development, 1978, Recipes from Coventry's First 275 Years, 1987, Exclusively Rhubarb Cookbook, 1988; works exhibited in galleries in Taos, N.Mex., Nat. Juried Show, Women Art, 1985, Springfield, Chicopee and Falmouth, Mass., Hartford, Glastonbury, Willimantic, New Haven, and Manchester, Conn., and N.Y.C.; one woman shows at Casey-Greene Gallery, Willimantic, 1986, The Artery, Ellington, Conn., 1986, Gallery 24, Conn. Pub. TV, Hartford, 1988. Sec., vice chmn. Coventry Zoning Bd. Appeals, 1969-74; chmn. Coventry Planning Commn., 1974-80; adv. com. supply chmn. Children's Sch. Sci., Woods Hole, Mass., 1976-90; com. mem. Booth and Dimock Meml. Libr., Coventry, 1982-83; mem. Falmouth Art Guild, 1982—, Glastonbury Art Assn., 1985—, Springfield Art Assn., 1985—, Mystic Art Assn., 1990—, Windham Regional Arts Coun., 1986—; organizing mem. Coventry Arts Commn., 1986-88. Mem. AAUW (membership com. Storrs-Willimantic chpt. 1977-79, cultural com. 1985-87), Ct. Guild Craftsmen, Nat. Soc. Tole & Decorative Painters, Inc. Republican. Protestant. Home and Office: 252 Wrights Mill Rd Coventry CT 06238

RICHARDSON, MARION WACHTER, title insurance company executive; b. Jamaica, N.Y., Oct. 7, 1947; d. Raymond Charles and Marion Isabel (Heid) Dezendorf; m. Edwin H. Wachter, Nov. ll, 1967 (div. 1973); 1 child, Eric; m. Frank K. Richardson, Apr. 6, 1980. Grad. high sch., Yonkers, N.Y. Clk. USLife Title Ins. Co. (acquired by Title USA Ins. Corp., White Plains, N.Y., 1966-70, 73-77; adminstrv. asst. USLife Title Ins. Co. (acquired by

Title USA Ins. Corp.), N.Y.C., 1977-79; v.p., mgr. Title USA Ins. Corp. (acquired by TRW Inc.), N.Y.C., 1979—. Mem. Rockland County Builders Assn. (assoc. bd. dirs. 1984-85, Assoc. of Yr. award 1985), NAFE. Office: Title USA Ins Corp NY 2 New Hempstead Rd New City NY 10956

RICHARDSON, MARTHA, nutrition analyst; b. Noble, La., Apr. 22, 1917; d. Alexander M. and Olive (Barlow) R.; A.B., U. Mo., 1938, Ph.D., 1953; M.S., Kans. State U., 1939. Dietitian, William Newton Meml. Hosp., Winfield, Kans., 1940-42, Molly Stark Sanatorium, Canton, Ohio, 1942-47; asst. dir. residence halls, instr. home econs. U. Mo., 1947-50, instr. home econs., 1951-53; head of foods and nutrition U. Utah, 1953-55; nutrition analyst Agrl. Research Service, Washington, 1955-80. Named Disting. Alumna, U. Mo., 1968. Fellow AAAS; mem. Am. Dietetic Assn., Am. Home Econs. Assn., Am. Med. Writers Assn., Am. Inst. Food Techologists, Am. Chem. Soc. Am. Assn. Cereal Chemists, Am. Forestry Assn., AAUW, N.Y. Acad. Scis., Sigma Xi, Gamma Sigma Delta, Phi Upsilon Omicron, Sigma Delta Epsilon. Contbr. articles to profl. jours. Home: 403 Russell Ave #309 Gaithersburg MD 20877

RICHARDSON, MELISSA ANN, government contract specialist; b. Ft. Worth, Aug. 11, 1954; d. Hullie Cabot and Mary Louise (Fluellen) Dixon Burns; m. Alfred Lamar Nichols, Aug. 23, 1975 (div. Mar. 1980); 1 child, Joycelyn Capri; m. Donald Leroy Richardson, Aug. 5, 1988; stepchildren: Donald Leroy Jr., Christopher. BA, Columbus (Ga.) Coll., 1979; MBA, Frostburg State U., 1989. Billing clk. Champion Internat. Paper Co., Columbus, 1974-76; teller Inf. Credit Union, Ft. Benning, Ga., 1977-78; procurement specialist U.S. Army Med. Rsch. and Devel. Command, Ft. Detrick, Md., 1984—; med. technologist Frederick (Md.) Meml. Hosp., 1980-84, Md. Med. Labs., Columbia, 1985-86; mem. publicity and programs coms. Fed. Women's Program, 1982-84, 86-88. Mem. program and fin. coms. Family Life Ctr., Frederick, 1987—; mem. Polit. Umbrella Group, Frederick, 1987—; vice chmn. Black Employment Program, Ft. Detrick, 1988—; mem. Frederick County Bd. Edn. Ethics Panel, 1989—. With U.S. Army, 1978-84. Recipient Young Careerist award Frederick Bus. and Profl. Women, 1989. Mem. NAFE, Negro Bus. and Profl. Women. Democrat. Baptist. Home: 6732 Sandpiper Frederick MD 21701 Office: Army Acquisition Activity Bldg 820 Fort Detrick MD 21701

RICHARDSON, MIDGE TURK, magazine editor; b. Los Angeles, Mar. 26, 1930; d. Charles Aloysius and Marie Theresa (Lindekin) Turk; m. Hamilton Farrar Richardson, Feb. 8, 1974. BA, Immaculate Heart Coll., L.A., 1951, MA, 1956; postgrad., U. Calif., Santa Barbara, Duquesne U., U. Pitts. Mem. Immaculate Heart Community, Roman Catholic Ch., 1948-66; asst. to dean Sch. Arts, NYU, 1966-67; coll. editor Glamour mag., N.Y.C., 1967-74; editor-in-chief Co-Ed mag.; also editorial dir. Forecast and Co-Ed mags., N.Y.C., 1974-75; editor-in-chief Seventeen mag., N.Y.C., 1975—; lectr. Tishman seminars Hunter Coll., N.Y.C., 1975-77. Host, guest TV and radio programs.; Author: The Buried Life: A Nun's Journey, 1971, Gordon Parks: A Biography for Children, 1971; also articles. Bd. dirs. YMCA, N.Y.C., 1972-73, Timothy Dwight Sch., 1979-83, Girl Scout council Greater N.Y., 1979-82; life trustee Internat. House. Recipient award Outstanding Women in Pub., 1982. Mem. Am. Soc. Mag. Editors, Fashion Group, Women's Forum Inc. Democrat. Clubs: River, Meadow. Office: Seventeen Mag 850 3rd Ave New York NY 10022

RICHARDSON, PATRICIA FOGARTY, editor; b. St. Petersburg, Fla., Mar. 31, 1933; d. George Clarence and Thelma Marguerite (Hickman) Fogarty; m. Richard Edward Richardson, Mar. 24, 1953; children: Kathlyn Patricia Richardson Vaughn Vargas, Diane Elizabeth. BA, U. South Fla., 1965. Editor (periodical) Florida Voter, 1987—; editor, designer, producer (books) Study and Action, 1989, Recollections: History of LWVF 1939-1989, 1989, Our Florida Government, 1990. Mem., chmn. St. Petersburg Community Improvement Projects Com., St. Petersburg, 1975-81; mem. Govs. Coun. on State Housing Needs, Fla., 1980-81, Gov's Coun. on Farmworker Affairs, Fla., 1980-86. Mem. LWV of Fla. (dir. 1975-81, 87—, 1st v.p. 1981-83), LWV of St. Petersburg Area (pres. 1973-75, 85-87). Democrat. Christian Science. Home: 1912 Bonita Way S Saint Petersburg FL 33712

RICHARDSON, REGINA JO, travel consultant and coordinator; b. Indpls., Aug. 30, 1949; d. James J. and Juanita J. (Noel) Malad; m. William L. Richardson, Apr. 20, 1969 Idiv. 1986); children: Jamise Jo, William, James. AA, Ind. U.-Purdue U., Indpls., 1983. Gen. mgr., sec., treas. Jim Malad Tours, Inc., Indpls., 1979—; mktg. rep. Caesars World, Las Vegas, Nev., 1988—; pres. Quality Coal, Inc., Indpls., 1985—; owner Regina Richardson Enterprises, Indpls., 1989—. Bd. dirs. Midwest Amputee Assn., Indpls., 1989—. Roman Catholic. Office: Jim Malad Tours Inc 2511 E 46th St Ste B Indianapolis IN 46205

RICHARDSON, RITA FAYE, company executive; b. Blytheville, Ark., July 19, 1951; d. Delbert J. Anderson and E Juanita (Bynum) Carter; m. Kevin Richardson. Student, Ark. State U. Office adminstr. Gene Roebuck Ins. Agy., Jonesboro, Ark., 1976-80; adminstrv. asst. Eversmeyer & Assoc. Fin. Planners, Okla., 1980-81; office adminstr. Gene Roebuck Ins. Agy., Jonesboro, 1981-85; pres. Profl. Communication Services, Jonesboro, 1985-. Author: Pending Completion, 1989. Mem. Southern Mktg. Execs., Jonesboro, 1989-. Mem. Nat. Assn. For Female Execs., Insight Club. Republican. Office: Profl Communication Svc 3212 E Nettleton Ave Jonesboro AR 72401

RICHARDSON, RUTH GREENE, social worker; b. Washington, Mar. 30, 1926; d. Arthur Alonzo and Ruth Naomi (Conway) Greene; m. Frederick D. Richardson, June 7, 1968; 1 child, Arthur William Boler. BS, St. Louis U., 1948; MSW, Washington U., St. Louis, 1950. Exec. dir. Anna B. Heldman Community Center, Pitts., 1962-64; assoc. dir. Hillhouse Assn., Pitts., 1964-67; assoc. dir. Dixwell House, also supr. group work services in community schs., New Haven, 1967-69; exec. dir. Three Rivers Youth Inc., Pitts., 1969—; adv. bd. Sch. Social Work, U. Pitts., 1979-80; pres. Assn. Residential Youth Care Agys., 1973-77; pres., bd. dirs. Pa. Council Vol. Child Care Agys., 1973-78; asst. v.p. Allegheny Children and Youth Services Council, 1974-76; bd. dirs. Children's Council Western Pa.; adv. council Booth Home; bd. dirs. Nat. Assn. Homes for Children, Campfire Boys and Girls, 1988, South Arts. Recipient Social Assistance award Pitts. region Women's Am. ORT, 1975, Internat. Yr. of Child award region III, HEW, 1979; Jurors award Images I Pitts. Black Artists William Pitt Union Gallery U. Pitts, 1986, Purchase prize Images III Waterworks, 1st prize in water color South Arts Sr. Citizen Show, Purchase prize Community Coll. Show, Ann. Svc. award Children's Coun. Western Pa., 1990. Mem. Child Welfare League Am., Nat. Assn. Social Workers, Pitts. Watercolor Soc., Midwest Watercolor Soc., Pa. Soc. Watercolor Painters, Black Adminstrs. in Child Welfare, Creative Lens, Visions (v.p.). Presbyterian. Paintings exhibited in Pitts. region. Home: 641 Robinwood Dr Pittsburgh PA 15216 Office: 2039 Termon Ave Pittsburgh PA 15212

RICHARDSON, SANDRA KAY, psychotherapist; b. Des Moines, June 5, 1959; d. Donald Sieg Richardson and Charlotte Anne (Hartwell) Gee. BA in Psychology, U. No. Iowa, 1981; MS in Clin. Psychology, North Tex. State, 1984. Cert. psychol. assoc., divorce and family mediation, Tex. Rsch. assoc. dept. psychology North Tex. State, Denton, 1981-83; staff psychologist Dallas County Mental Health/Mental Retardation, 1983-85, East Tex. Regional Mental Health/Mental Retardation, Canton, 1985-87; psychol. assoc. Southwest Psychol. Svcs., Dallas, 1987-89, Priority Systems, Dallas, 1987-89, Motivational Assocs., Dallas, 1989—. Mem. Am. Psychol. Assn. (assoc.), Tex. Psychol. Assn. (assoc.), Dallas Psychol. Assn. (assoc.), Toastmasters Internat. (1st place area 34 humorous speech contest 1989, 3d place so. div. humorous speech contest 1989, ednl. v.p. Downtowner's Club 1989, pres., 1989), 500, Inc., USA Film Assn. Office: Motivational Assocs 13760 Noel Rd Ste 236 Dallas TX 75214

RICHARDSON, SANDRA LORRAINE, educator; b. Ypsilanti, Mich., Feb. 5, 1947; d. Alfred Jack and Marianna (Boersema) O'Key; m. Frank Raymond Richardson, Dec. 27, 1969; 1 child, Elaine Ellen. BS, Eastern Mich. U., 1969. Tchr. Eaton Rapids (Mich.) Schs., 1969-70, Salinas (Calif.) Schs., 1970-71, Paso Robles (Calif.) Elementary Schs., 1971-72, San Luis Coastal Schs., San Luis Obispo, Calif., 1972—; mentor tchr. San Luis Coastal, San Luis Obispo, Calif., 1985-88, GATE coord., 1988-89, dept. chmn. 1988—; adjunct prof. Calif. Poly State U., San Luis Obispo, 1988-89; cons. Self-esteem Workshops, San Luis Obispo, 1988—. Author: Touch and Feel ABC, 1974; contbr. articles to profl. jours. and mags., poetry to Nat. Poetry Press. Pres. Coun. for Exceptional Children, San Luis Obispo, 1973-74; life mem. Friends of the Libr., San Luis Obispo. Recipient Calif. Reading Assn. award, San Luis Obispo br., 1985. Mem. AAUW (pres. San Luis Obispo, Calif. 1981-82, honored with scholarship in her name 1989), NEA, Nat. Coun. Tchrs. of English, Calif. Tchrs. Assn., San Luis Coastal Tchrs. Assn. Office: San Luis Coastal Unified Sch Dist 1499 San Luis Dr San Luis Obispo CA 93401

RICHARDSON, SHIRLEY MAXINE, public relations director; b. Rising Sun, Ind., May 3, 1931; d. William Fenton and Mary (Phillips) Keith; m. Arthur Lee Richardson, Feb. 11, 1950; children—Mary Jane Hamm, JoDee Mayfield, Steven Lee Richardson. Personnel mgr. Mayhill Pubs., Knightstown, Ind., 1967-87, prodn. mgr., 1975-87, editor, 1967-87; info. staff, assoc. editor Ind. Farm Bur., Inc., 1987-89, dir. info. and pub. rels., 1989—. Mem. Newspaper Farm Editors of Am., Am. Agrl. Editors' Assn., Profl. Journalists of Am. Republican. Avocations: traveling; reading; boating; quilting. Home: 366 E Carey St Knightstown IN 46148 Office: 130 E Washington St Indianapolis IN 46206

RICHARDSON, SUSAN LYNN, hospital business manager and personnel director; b. Warren, Pa., Mar. 31, 1964; d. James Lowell and Elizabeth Francis (Juliano) Richardson; m. Stephen Eugene Krauss, Mar. 15, 1964. BS in Bus. Mgmt., Maryville Coll., 1986. Apt. mgr. Century Three Property Mgmt., St. Louis, 1987; bus. mgr., personnel dir. CPC Weldon Spring Hosp., St. Charles, Mo., 1987—. Democrat. Roman Catholic. Home: 7745 Gannon Dr 1st Fl University City MO 63130 Office: CPC Weldon Spring Hosp 5931 Hwy 94 S Saint Charles MO 63303

RICHART, VICTORIA BETTY, social services agency administrator; b. N.Y.C., Nov. 1, 1937; d. Francisco Richart Cervera and Victoria (Pla Carbonell) de Richart. BA, Marymount Coll., 1960; MA, MEd, Columbia U., N.Y.C., 1979, EdD, 1982. Asst. Quaker Oats Co., N.Y.C., 1960-61; adminstr. Careers Inc., N.Y.C., 1961-63; tchr. Pub. and Pvt. Schs., N.Y. and Mex., 1963-69; sr. project assoc. Columbia U., N.Y.C., 1979-80; dir. N.H. Dept. of Edn., 1980-85; mgmt. tng. dir. Bd. of Edn. Personnel, N.Y.C., 1985-87; dep. adminstr. N.Y.C. Human Resource Adminstrn., 1987-89; dir. Casita Maria, Inc., N.Y.C., 1989—. Mem. action audit com. YWCA; mem. Wall St. chpt. Image, N.Y.C., 1986—; active 100 Hispanic Women. Mem. NAFE, Assn. for the Advancement of of Internat. Edn., Nat. Coalition for Sex Equity in Edn. (mem. steering com. 1983-86), Nat. Assn. Bilingual Edn., NAACP, Am. Edn. Rsch. Adminstrn. (presentee 1983). Home: 160 E 88th St New York NY 10128

RICHEIMER, MARY JANE, retired teacher; b. Massillon, Ohio, Oct. 20, 1913; d. Thomas Carl and Nellie (Bea) R. AB, Lake Erie Coll., 1936; MA, Kent State U., 1951; postgrad., Northwestern U., 1960, U. London, 1968-69. Asst. libr. Lake Erie Coll., Painesville, Ohio, 1936-37; tchr. Edmund Jones Jr. High Sch., Massillon, 1937-45, Washington High Sch., Massillon, 1945-51; libr. New Trier High Sck., Winnetka, Ill., 1951-53; tchr., chmn. dept. English Evanston (Ill.) Twp. High Sch., 1953-74; mem. classified advt. staff Pioneer Press, Wilmette, Ill., 1975-82; now ret.; summer sch. instr. lit. for adolescents, Northwestern U., Evanston, 1960; mem. nat. bd. tchrs. of English, Scholastic mags., N.Y.C., 1960—; vol. libr. Evanston Hosp. Med. Libr., 1989—. Author: A Century of Education, 1947; co-author: Planning My Future, 1961; contbr. poetry, articles to various publs. Mem. AAUW, Evanston Hosp. Women's Aux., Nat. Ret. Tchrs. Assn., North Shore Ret. Tchrs. Assn., Viewers for Quality Television. Republican. Episcopalian. Home: 601 Trinity Ct Evanston IL 60201

RICHENS, MURIEL WHITTAKER, counselor, educator; b. Prineville, Oreg.; d. John Reginald and Victoria Cecilia (Pascale) Whittaker; children: Karen, John, Candice, Stephanie, Rebecca. BS, Oreg. State U.; MA, San Francisco State U., 1962; postgrad., U. Calif., Berkeley, 1967-69, U. Birmingham, Eng., 1973, U. Soria, Spain, 1981. Lic. elem. tchr., sch. adminstrn., pupil pers. svcs., marriage, child and family counselor, Calif. Instr., counselor Springfield (Oreg.) State U., San Francisco State U., Coll. San Mateo, Calif., San Mateo High Sch. Dist., 1963-86; therapist AIDS health project U. Calif., San Francisco, 1988—; pvt. practice family therapist San Mateo; guest West German-European Acad. seminar, Berlin, 1975. Lifeguard, ARC. postgrad. student Ctr. for Human Communications, Los Gatos, Calif., 1974, U. P.R., 1977, U. Guadalajara (Mex.), 1978, U. Durango (Mex.), 1980, U. Guanajuato (Mex.) 1982. Mem. U. Calif. Berkeley Alumni Assn., Am. Contract Bridge League (life master, cert. instr., tournament dir.), Women in Communications, Computer-Using Educators, Commonwealth Club, Pi Lambda Theta, Delta Pi Epsilon. Republican. Roman Catholic. Home and Office: 847 N Humboldt St Apt 309 San Mateo CA 94401-1451

RICHERSON, MODESTA DORSETT, artist, lecturer; b. Coolidge, Tex., Jan. 4, 1905; d. William Brockman and Maude Lilian (Ives) Dorsett; m. Doss Richerson, Aug. 28, 1930 (dec. 1974); children: William Doss, Vallie Jean Richerson Medlin. BA, North Tex. State U., 1929; MA, Kansas City (Mo.) Art Inst., 1950; postgrad., La. Tech. U., Rome and Florence, Italy, 1983. Tchr. art Dallas Pub. Schs., 1928-30, Barstow Girls Sch., Kansas City, 1948-50; instr. art Hallmark Greeting Card Co., Kansas City, 1938-45; designer Mid West Embroidery Co., Kansas City, 1951-62; pvt. tchr. art; art lectr. to clubs and various orgns., 1950—. Murals executed Cen. Ch., Kansas City, 1950, Truman Med. Ctr. Chapel, Kansas City, 1979. Pres., charter mem. Mid Winter Art Fair, Kansas City, 1965—. Named Woman of Yr., Am. Bus. Women, Kansas City, 1964, Caring Person, Caring mag., 1989; recipient citation Truman Med. Ctr. Bd., 1984. Mem. AAUW, Nat. League Am. Pen Women (past pres. Kansas City-Westport, past mem. nat. art bd.), Greater Kansas City Art Assn. (life, past pres.), PIlot Club (pres. Kansas City 1962-63, Dist. Sweetheart award 1983), Kansas City C. of C. (life). Methodist. Home: 7916 Ward Parkway Pla Kansas City MO 64114

RICHESIN, JILL DAWN, psychotherapist; b. Jacksonville, N.C., Nov. 1, 1964; d. Henry Harrison and Donna Jean (Adams) Stacy; m. Thomas Bruce Richesin, May 16, 1987. BA, East Tenn. State U., 1987, MA, 1989. Lic. psychol. examiner, Tenn. Grad. asst. East Tenn. State U., Johnson City, 1987-89, rsch. cons., 1990; outpatient therapist Holston Mental Health Ctr., Kingsport, Tenn., 1989-90; psychol. examiner, therapist Behavioral Cons., Johnson City, 1990—; office asst. Peggy Cantrell, Ph.D., Johnson City, 1987-89; presenter symposia on eating disorders, Tucson, Ariz., 1989; adj. faculty East Tenn. State U., 1990—. Mem. Intermountain Psychol. Assn., C.A.P.S., T.P.A., Phi Kappa Phi, Psi Chi, Gamma Beta Phi. Methodist. Home: 1300 Greenfield Dr Johnson City TN 37604 Office: Behavioral Cons 100 W Unaka Ave Johnson City TN 37604

RICHEY, SARA JOSEPHINE, physician; b. San Francisco, Feb. 27, 1950; d. Sabino Joseph and Alice Laura (Gamlen) D'Amico; m. Karl Everett Richey, Sept. 2, 1973; children: Talitha Sara, Priscilla Helen, John Sabino. Student, U. Calif., San Diego, 1978-81, MD, 1985. Diplomate Nat. Bd. Med. Examiners. Med. and surg. intern U. Calif., San Diego, 1985-86; resident in ob./gyn. Stanford (Calif.) U. Hosp., 1986-87; med. staff Redwood Med. Group, Redwood City, Calif., 1987—, St. Catherine Hosp., Half Moon Bay, Calif., 1987—, Sequoia Hosp., Redwood City, 1989—; Educator, Sequoia High Sch. Dist., Redwood City, 1987—. Named Profl. Vol. of Yr., San Mateo chpt. Am. Cancer Soc. Mem. AMA. Democrat. Office: Redwood Med Group 2900 Whipple Ave Redwood City CA 94062

RICHKUS, PETA NAYLOR, marketing executive; b. Manila, July 1, 1947; came to U.S. 1949; d. Arthur Samuel and Patricia Martha (Fanning) Naylor; m. William Albert Richkus (div.); 1 child, Rebecca Fanning; m. Randolph Burlin Rosencrantz, Jan. 18, 1985. Student, U. Calif., San Diego, 1965-68; BA with honors, U. R.I., 1970; MBA magna cum laude, U. Balt., 1980. Rsch. analyst Balt. County Econ. Devel. Commn., Towson, Md., 1980; regional mktg. rep. Buchart-Horn, Inc., Balt., 1980-82; v.p., dir of mktg. Buchart-Horn, Inc., York, Pa., 1987—; pvt. practice mktg. cons. Balt., 1984-86; mktg. assoc. Kidde Cons., Inc., Balt., 1983-85; pvt. practice real estate agt. Miami, Fla., 1985-86; dir. of mktg. Instiform East, Inc., Landover, Pa., 1986; cons. in field; bd. dirs. Afro-Am. Newspapers, Balt. Chair com. LWV, Balt., 1979-80; bd. dirs. Balt. City Pub. Wks. Mus., 1990—, Balt. City Cons. Evaluation Bd., 1990—. Mem. Soc. Am. Mil. Engrs. (conf. chair 1989-90, Svc. award 1989), County Engs. Assn. Md. (chair legis. com. 1983-84, Cert. of Appreciation 1984). Home: 2718 St Paul St Baltimore MD 21218 Office: Buchart-Horn Inc 55 S Richland Ave York PA 17404

RICHMAN, GERTRUDE GROSS (MRS. BERNARD RICHMAN), civic worker; b. N.Y.C., May 16, 1908; d. Samuel and Sarah Yetta (Seltzer) Gross; B.S., Tchrs. Coll. Columbia U., 1948, M.A., 1949; m. Bernard Richman, Apr. 5, 1930; children—David, Susan. Vol. worker Hackensack Hosp., 1948-70; mem. bd. dirs. YM-YWHA, Bergen County, N.J., 1950-75, bd. mem. emeritus, 1975—; chmn. Leonia Friends of Bergen County Mental Health Consultation Center, 1959; founder, hon. pres. Bergen County Serv-A-Com., affiliated with women orgns. Div. Nat. Jewish Welfare Bd.; v.p. N.J. sect. Nat. Jewish Welfare Bd., 1964-71; hon. trustee women's div. Bergen County United Jewish Community; mem. adv. council Bergen County Office on Aging, 1968-83, reappointed, 1984—; mem. Hackensack Bd. Edn., 1946-51; mem. pub. relations com. Leonia Pub. Schs., 1957-58; N.J. del. White House Conf. on Aging, 1971; trustee Mary McLeod Bethune Scholarship Fund; v.p. Bergen County nat. women's com. Brandeis U., 1966-67. Recipient citation Nat. Council Jewish Women and YWCA in Bergen County, 1962; citation Nat. Jewish Welfare Bd., 1964, Harry S. Feller award N.J. Region, 1965; 14th Ann. Good Scout award Bergen council Boy Scouts Am., 1977; Woman Vol. of Distinction, Bergen County council Girl Scouts, 1979; Human Relations award Bergen County sect. Nat. Council Negro Women, 1982; recipient Gov.'s award, 1988, Cert. of Commendation County Exec. and the Bergen County Bd. of Chosen Freeholders, 1989; honored at testimonial United Jewish Community Bergen County, 1987. Mem. Kappa Delta Pi.

RICHMAN, JOAN F., television consultant; b. St. Louis, Apr. 10, 1939; d. Stanley M. and Barbara (Friedman) R. B.A., Wellesley (Mass.) Coll., 1961. Asst. producer WNDT, N.Y.C., 1964-65; researcher CBS News, N.Y.C., 1961-64; researcher spl. events unit CBS News, 1965-67; mgr. rsch. CBS News (Rep. and Dem. nat. convs.), 1968; assoc. producer CBS News, 1968, producer spl. events, 1969-72; sr. producer The Reasoner Report, ABC News, 1972-75; exec. producer CBS Sports Spectacular, 1975-76; exec. producer weekend broadcasts CBS News, 1976-81, v.p., dir. spl. events, 1982-87, v.p. news coverage, 1987-89; fellow Inst. Politics, John F. Kennedy Sch. Govt., Harvard U., 1990. Recipient Nat. TV Acad. Arts and Scis. Emmy award for CBS News space coverage, 1970-71, 71-72; Alumnae Achievement award Wellesley Coll., 1973. Mem. Nat. Acad. TV Arts and Scis., Council on Fgn. Relations, Wellesley Coll. Alumnae Assn. (pres. class of 1961, 1966-70). Home: 133 W 81st St New York NY 10024 also: Box 74 Tinicum Creek Rd Erusinna PA 18920

RICHMAN, PHYLLIS CHASANOW, newspaper editor; b. Washington, Mar. 21, 1939; d. Abraham and Helen (Lieberman) C.; m. Alvin Richman, June 5, 1960 (div. 1984); children—Joseph, Matthew, Libby. B.A., Brandeis U., 1961; postgrad., U. Pa., 1961-63, Purdue U., 1966-70. Restaurant critic Washington Post, 1976—, exec. food editor, 1980-88, food critic, 1988—. Author: Barter, 1976, Best Restaurants, 1980, 82, 85, 89. Mem. Washington Ind. Writers (adv. bd.), Nat. Press Club, Les Dames D'Escoffier (bd. dirs.). Home: 2118 O St NW Washington DC 20037 Office: Washington Post 1150 15th St NW Washington DC 20071

RICHMAN, SELMA, microbiologist; b. Bklyn.; d. Joseph and Leah (Kennis) R. B.S., Bklyn. Coll.; M.A., Cen. Mich. U., 1979. Successively lab. technician Queens Gen. Hosp., Jamaica, N.Y.; jr. microbiologist Cumberland Hosp., Bklyn.; asst microbiologist Queens Hosp. Ctr., Jamaica; prin. microbiologist Coney Island Hosp., Bklyn., 1965—; lectr. Scientists in Sch. program N.Y. Acad. Scis.; judge sch. sci. fairs, N.Y.C.; cons. in field. Author: Case Study on Aeromonas Hydrophila, 1982. Mem. NAFE, Am. Soc. Clin. Pathologists, Am. Soc. Microbiology, Med. Mycology Soc. Am. Avocations: knitting, tennis, racquetball, swimming, music. Office: Coney Island Hosp 2601 Ocean Pkwy Brooklyn NY 11235

RICHMAN, VICTORIA S., hotel, real estate consultant; b. Boston, June 21, 1959; d. Justin Lewis and Susan (Kadison) R. BA, Brown U., 1981; MBA, U. Pa., 1985. Lic. in real estate sales. Pvt. investigator Pinkerton Security Service, Boston and Providence, R.I., 1980-81; bus. analyst Hibernia Nat. Bank, New Orleans, 1981-83; hotel real estate cons. Stephen W. Brener Assocs., Inc., N.Y.C., 1985—; sponsor's rep. Ann. Hospitality Investment Conf., N.Y.C., 1985—. Interviewer nat. alumni sch. program Brown U., New Orleans and N.Y.C., 1981—. Mem. Nat. Assn. Female Execs., Ednl. Inst. of Am. Hotel and Motel Assn. Clubs: Brown, Wharton (N.Y.C.).

RICHMOND, DINA RAE, education educator; b. Shawnee, Okla., Apr. 29, 1929; d. Jack H. Williams and Bertha B. (Megehee) McNair; children: Gregory,. BA in Edn., U. Cen. Okla., 1952; MA in Edn., S.W. Tex. State U., San Marcos, 1977. Tchr. Cotton County Ind. Sch. Dist., Randlett, Okla., 1952-53, Terrell County Ind. Sch. Dist., Sanderson, Tex., 1967-71, Luling (Tex.) Ind. Sch. Dist., 1971-87, Lexington (Tex.) Ind. Sch. Dist., 1987-90, Brenham Ind. Sch. Dist., 1990—. Mem. NEA, Tex. State Tchrs. Assn., Delta Kappa Gamma. Democrat. Baptist. Home: 3902 E 29th St Apt E-6 Bryan TX 77802

RICHMOND, PHYLLIS ALLEN, library and information science educator; b. Boston, Jan. 5, 1921; d. Charles Francis Hitchcock and Alberta (Currie) Allen; m. James Hugh Richmond, Sept. 24, 1949 (dec. 1951). B.A., Western Reserve U., 1942; M.A., U. Pa., 1946, Ph.D., 1949; M.S. in Library Sci., Western Reserve U., 1956. Curator of history Rochester, N.Y. Mus., 1943-47; research asst. to dir. Welch Inst. Johns Hopkins U., Balt., 1952; librarian U. Rochester, N.Y., 1955-68; prof. Syracuse U., N.Y., 1969, Case Western Reserve U., Cleve., 1970-84; vis. prof. UCLA, 1985, Columbia U., 1986; speaker, U.S., Can., Europe, 1960—; cons. to profl. groups, 1965—. Author: Precis for North American Usage, 1982; co-editor Theory of Subject Analysis: A Sourcebook, 1985; mem. editorial bd. Internat. Classification, Germany, 1970-84; contbr. articles to profl. jours. Mem. ALA (recipient Margaret Mann citation 1978), Am. Soc. for Info. Sci. (recipient award of merit 1972, Pioneer Info. Sci. award 1987), History of Sci. Soc., Am. Radio Relay League. Republican. Presbyterian. Home: 6628 Aintree Park Dr Apt 202 Cleveland OH 44143

RICHMOND, ROCSAN, television producer, inventor; b. Chgo., Jan. 30, 1945; d. Alphonso and Annie Lou (Combest) R.; divorced; 1 child, Tina S. Student, Wilson Jr. Coll., 1963, 2d City Theatre, Chgo., 1969, Alice Liddel Theatre, Chgo., 1970. Lic. 3d class radio/tel. operator FCC. Vegetarian editor Aware mag., Chgo., 1977-78; investigative reporter, film critic Chgo. Metro News, 1975-81; producer, talk show host Sta. WSSD Radio, Chgo., 1980-81; dir. pub. rels. IRMCO Corp., Chgo., 1981-82; pub. rels. agt., newsletter editor Hollywood (Calif.) Reporter newspaper, 1985-86; exec. producer Donald Descendent's Prodns., Hollywood, 1985—, (TV show) Future News, 1985—. Inventor invisible drapery tieback. Jehovah's Witness. Office: PO Box 665 Hollywood CA 90078

RICHOLSON, SANDRA LEHMAN, editor; b. Meadville, Pa., Dec. 25, 1951; d. Elmer Benjamin and Helen Louise (Hetrick) Lehman; m. Byron Bradford Richolson, Sept. 3, 1977; children: Bradford A., Ann R. BJ, U. Mo., Columbia, 1975. Asst. pub. info. officer Mo. Dept. Agr., Jefferson City, 1975-77; publs. mgr. St. Louis Community Coll., 1977-85; reporter, copy editor Wolfe Publs., Rochester, N.Y., 1986-87; editor T&E News, 1987-89; editor Image World mag. Rochester Inst. Tech., 1989—. Contbr. articles to profl. jours. Recipient Silver Anvil award Pub. Rels. Soc. Am., 1980. Home: 2 Terrace Dr Fairport NY 14450 Office: Rochester Inst Tech 1 Lomb Memorial Dr Rochester NY 14623

RICHTER, BARBARA ANN, social work educator, personnel director; b. St. Louis, Dec. 11, 1943; d. Peter W. and Ann (Meserve) Salsich; m. Michael A. Richter, Aug. 22, 1964; children: Michael Jr., Tricia, Christopher, Jennifer, Joshua. BSW, U. Mo., St. Louis, 1981; MSW, Washington U., 1982. Cert. ACSW. Foster parent St. Louis County Juvenile Ct., St. Louis, 1972-76; acting dir. group home Youth Emergency Svcs., St. Louis, 1979-80; social worker Child Guidance Clinic, St. Louis, 1980-83; assoc. exec. dir. Edgewood Children's Ctr., St. Louis, 1983-87; faculty Meramac Community Coll., St. Louis, 1987—; faculty social work Washington U., St. Louis, 1987—; v.p. personnel Children's Factory, Inc., St. Louis, 1987—; pres., mem. regional adv. coun. Dept. Mental Health, St. Louis, 1985-90. Author:

Suffer the Children, 1980. Mem. bd. Nerinx Hall High Sch., St. Louis, 1988-90; bd. dirs. Youth Emergency Svcs., St. Louis, 1977-88; allocations panel United Way Greater St. Louis, 1988-90. Mem. Nat. Assn. Social Workers (treas. Mo. chpt. 1986-90). Democrat. Roman Catholic. Office: Childrens Factory Inc 505 N Kirkwood Rd One Brookings Dr Saint Louis MO 63122

RICHTER, DORIS LOUISE, teacher; b. Martin, S.D., Apr. 18, 1935; d. Edgar W. and Rhoda E. (Jackson) Gardner; m. Wendelyn Richter, June 3, 1960 (div. Jan. 1977); children: Michael J., Pamela J., Suzanne L. BS in Edn., Black Hills State Coll., 1969. Tchr. Erskine Elem., Sturgis, S.D., 1969—. Mem. S.D. Edn. Assn., Nat. Edn. Assn. Republican. Lutheran. Home: RR #2 Box 198 Whitewood SD 57793

RICHTER, JUDITH ANNE, pharmacology educator; b. Wilmington, Del., Mar. 4, 1942; d. Henry John and Dorothy Madelyn (Schroeder) R. BA, U. Colo., 1964; PhD, Stanford U., 1969. Postdoctoral fellow Cambridge (Eng.) U., 1969-70, U. London, 1970-71; asst. prof. pharmacology and neurobiology sch. medicine Ind. U., Indpls., 1971-78, assoc. prof. sch. medicine, 1978-84, prof. sch. medicine, 1984—; vis. assoc. prof. U. Ariz. Health Sci. Ctr., Tucson, 1983; mem. biomed. rsch. rev. com. Nat. Inst. on Drug Abuse, 1983-87. Mem. editorial bd. Jour. Neurochemistry, 1982-87; contbr. numerous articles to sci. jours. Scholar Boettcher Found., 1960-64; fellow Wellcome Trust, 1969-71. Mem. AAAS, Am. Soc. for Pharmacology and Exptl. Therapeutics (exec. com. neuropharmacology div. 1989-92), Am. Soc. for Neurochemistry, Internat. Soc. for Neurochemistry, Soc. for Neurosci., Women in Neurosci., Phi Beta Kappa, Sigma Xi. Office: Ind U Sch Medicine 791 Union Dr Indianapolis IN 46202-4887

RICHTER, LINDA DALE, occupational therapist, management consultant; b. Ft. Collins, Colo., Jan. 11, 1949; d. Kenneth Dale and Dorothy Lenore (Ward) R.; m. Robert Allan Manuel, Dec. 31, 1988. BS, Colo. State U., 1972, MS, 1984, postgrad., 1990—. Dir. occupational therapy Mercy Med. Ctr., OshKosh, Wis., 1973-74; dir. occupational therapy Poudre Valley Hosp., Ft. Collins, Wis., 1974-88, dir. work ctr., 1987-88; developer, pvt. cons. mgmt. tng. for health care mgrs. Bldg. Bridges, Ft. Collins, 1986—; owner, dir. Life Achievement Systems, Ft. Collins, 1989—; loaned exec. United Way campaign Poudre Valley Hosp., 1986-88; mem. affiliate faculty Colo. State U., Ft. Collins, 1985-89, 90, postgrad. field work rep., 1985-88. Mem. Am. Occupational Therapy Assn., World Fedn. Occupational Therapists, Ft. Collins Soc. of Head Injury Found. (pres. 1988), Nat. Head Injury Found. (bd. dirs. Denver chpt. 1988—), Colo. Occupational Therapy Assn. Republican. Office: Life Achievement Systems 343 W Drake Rd Ste 105 Fort Collins CO 80526

RICHTER, MARY JANE, school administrator, consultant; b. Red Bank, N.J., Oct. 17, 1937; d. Ross Eckman and Esther Jackson (Herr) Wiley; m. John Edward Richter, Aug. 11, 1956; children: Jacqueline Richter-Menge, Andrea Ross. BS, U. Del., 1980, postgrad., 1982—. Cert. tchr., Del. Dir. Little Sch., Dover, Del., 1975-89. Pres. Kent Gen. Hosp., Dover, Dover Acad., 1982—; trustee Del. Fedn. Retarded Children, Wilmington, 1978—; v.p., bd. dirs. Kent Gen. Hosp.; pres. Second Nat. Bd.; apptd. Kent County Tech. Vocat. Sch. Dist. Bd.; tchr. Del. Tech. Community Coll., Dover. Mem. alumni bd., chpt. coord. U. Del. Mem. AAUW, NEA Young Children, Del. Assn. Edn. Young Children, Internat. Reading Assn., Omicron Nu. Republican. Lutheran. Club: Dover Century. Avocations: tennis, fitness, reading. Home: 733 Oak Dr Dover DE 19901 Office: Little Sch Inc 308 N Queen St Dover DE 19901

RICHTER, ROBERTA BRANDENBURG (MRS. PAUL J. RICHTER), business educator; b. Osborn, Ohio, Dec. 29, 1911; d. Warren F. and Mary M. (Davis) Brandenburg; student Miami-Jacobs Coll., 1930, Wittenberg U., 1930-31, Coll. Music, U. Cin., 1931-32, U. Dayton, 1954, 64; B.S., Miami U., Oxford, Ohio, 1958, M.Ed., 1959; postgrad. Wright State U., 1966-70; doctoral candidate Ohio State U., 1969; m. Jean Paul Richter, Oct. 6, 1934; 1 son, James Paul. Bus. mgr. T.D. Peffley, Inc., 1929-32; sec., prodn. mgr. Delco Products div. Gen. Motors, 1932-34; exec. sec. LWV, 1935-38; buyer Elder & Johnston Dept. Store, 1938-40; ct. reporter Common Pleas Ct. Montgomery County, 1940-46; adminstrv. asst. Ch. Fedn. Greater Dayton, Ohio, 1946-50; audio-visual cons. schs., chs. Twyman Films, 1950-53; office mgr. Nadlin Law Offices, 1953-58; instr. stenotype, office practice Miami-Jacobs Coll., Dayton, 1941-48; tchr. stenotype, guidance counselor Stebbins High Sch., Dayton, 1958-82; vocat. guidance coordinator Mad River Planning Dist., Montgomery County, Ohio, 1968-73. Instr. stenotype for ct. reporting Wright State U., Dayton, 1970-87; cellist Cin. Symphony Orch.; dir. Lang. Unlimited, Inc., Lake Forest, Ill. Supt., tchr., adviser youth div. Grace United Meth. Ch., Dayton, 1942-72, sec. adminstrv. bd., 1940-80, sec. emeritus, 1980—, council on ministries, 1972-74, past pres. Excel Club, circle leader, hospitality chmn., pres. homebuilders class, program chmn., laywoman chmn. Christian higher edn.; instr., counselor Camp Miniwanca, Am. Youth Found., 1949-68. Mem. Am., Ohio, Miami Valley personnel and guidance assns., Nat., Ohio bus. tchrs. assns., Am., Ohio sch. counselor assns., Nat., Ohio edn. assns., Nat. Vocat. Guidance Assn., Dayton Area Bus. Soc. (v.p. 1969-82), Nat. Shorthand Reporters Assn., Delphian Soc. (past pres.), Pub. Speaker Bur., Council World Affairs, AAUW, LWV (past pres. and treas., nat. officer), Internat. Platform Assn., World Trade Club (1st woman), Greater Dayton C. of C., Bus. and Profl. Women (past pres.), Pi Omega Pi. Clubs: Order Eastern Star, Progressive Mothers (chmn. program Dayton 1969-70). Author ednl. handbooks, pamphlets. Contbr. articles to profl. jours.; lectr. in field. Home: care James P Richter 645 E Westminster Lake Forest IL 60045

RICHTERS, TRACY ANN, sales executive; b. St. Louis, Nov. 29, 1960; d. Robert Erwin and Doris Mildred (Niehaus) R.; m. Robert Bruce Kerr, Mar. 12, 1988. BA in Spanish and BS in B, SE Mo. State U., 1984; postgrad., U. Dallas. Sales rep. Procter & Gamble, Oklahoma City, 1984-85; dist. field rep. Procter & Gamble, Dallas, 1985, unit mgr., 1985-89, project mgr. SW div. package soap and detergents, 1989—. Mem. Nat. Assn. Female Execs. Republican. Office: PO Box 1910 Dallas TX 75221

RICKARD, CAROLYN LUCILLE, educator; b. Colorado Spgs., Colo., Aug. 26, 1937; d. Irving Edwin and Viola Esther (Essman) Sims; m. Kenneth Allan Rickard, Sept. 2, 1961 (div. 1977); children: Kenneth Allan, Keith Andrew. BS, Iowa State U., 1959; MA, Colo. Coll., 1986. Kindergarten tchr. Colorado Springs Sch. Dist. #11, 1960-66, 1st grade tchr., 1966-82, 2nd grade tchr., 1982-86, 4th grade tchr., 1986—; curriculum writer math., sci. and social studies Colo. Springs Sch. Dist. #11. Neighborhood leader El Paso County Rep. Party, Colorado Springs, 1968, office vol., 1978. Mem. Unified Teaching Profl. Assn., Kindergarten Tchrs. Assn., PhiKappa Phi, PsiChi, Omicron Nu. Republican. Congregationalist. Office: Penrose Elementary Sch 4285 Nonchalant Cr S Colorado Springs CO 80917

RICKARD, KATHRYN WRIGHT, dentist; b. Houma, La., Aug. 11, 1957; d. Raymond Hermit and Garnett (Austin) Wright; m. William Douglas Rickard, July 15, 1984; children; Andrew Douglas, Graham Patrick. BS, La. Tech. U., 1979; DDS, U. Tenn., Memphis, 1983. Pvt. practice Memphis, 1983—. Choir dir., mem. contemporary Christian ensemble, mem. chancel choir, mem. Seekers group Bartlett Meth. Ch., 1988—. Mem. ADA, Tenn. Dental Assn., Memphis Dental Soc., Alpha Chi Omega Alumni. Republican. Home: 3899 Windy Trail Cove Bartlett TN 38135 Office: 100 N Main St Ste 2331 Memphis TN 38103

RICKARD, REBECCA ANN, club executive; b. Oklahoma City, Mar. 25, 1952; d. Robert Edward and Helen Clydella (Lewis) R. BA, Oklahoma City U., 1974. Desk clk. Oklahoma City Tennis Ctr., 1971-74; desk clk./saleswoman Cts. Tennis Club, Oklahoma City, 1974-76; mgr./buyer Greens Country Club, Oklahoma City, 1976-82, Walnut Creek Country Club, Oklahoma City, 1982-86, Santa Fe Club, Oklahoma City, 1988—; mem. adv. staff Tennis Industry mag., 1987; advisor recreational devel. com. Oklahoma City Jr. Coll., 1979-80. Mem. U.S. Racquet Stringers Assn. Republican. Presbyterian.

RICKARD, RUTH DAVID, history and political science educator; b. Germany, Feb. 20, 1926; came to U.S., 1940; d. Carl and Alice (Koch) David; m. Robert M. Yaffee, Oct. 1949 (dec. 1959); children: David, Steven; m. Norman G. Rickard, June 1968 (dec. 1988); 1 stepson, Douglas. BS cum laude, Northwestern U., 1947, MA, 1948. Law editor Commerce Clearing House, Chgo., 1948; instr. history U. Ill., Chgo., 1949-51; instr. extension program U. Ill., Waukegan, 1960-67; instr. history Waukegan (Ill.) Schs., 1960-69; prof. western civilization, polit. sci. Coll. of Lake County, Grayslake, Ill., 1969—; mem. Inter-Univ. Seminar on Armed Forces and Soc. Author: History of College of Lake County, 1987 (honored by City of Waukegan, 1987); also articles; speaker on various ind. radio and TV programs. Scholar Freedoms Found. Am. Legion, Valley Forge, Pa., 1967. Mem. AAUW (pres. Waukegan chpt. 1955-57, scholarship named for 1985), LWV (charter, v.p.), Coll. Lake County Fedn. Tchrs., Phi Beta Kappa. Office: Coll of Lake County Waukegan IL 60085

RICKARD-RIEGLE, BARBARA KATHERINE, journalist, newscaster; b. Los Angeles, May 1, 1931; d. Thomas and Katherine Elizabeth (Blackburn) Rickard; student pvt. schs., Santa Rosa, Calif.; Irvine Valley Coll. (hon.), 1988; children—Katherine, Karen, Christopher, Melissa, Richard. Editor, Phenix City (Ala.) Herald, 1957-58; news broadcaster, editor WRBL-Radio-TV, Columbus, Ga., 1958-62; polit. reporter Esquire Broadcasting Co., Sta. WQXI, Atlanta, 1962-63; news commentator Sta. WAII-TV, Atlanta, 1962-63; polit. writer, columnist Los Angeles Herald Examiner, 1963-66; Congressional news sec., Washington, 1966-67; news writer, guest broadcaster Stas. KNXT, KABC-TV, Hollywood, Calif., 1964-67; broadcaster, women's news editor Sta. KNX-CBS, 1967-71; news broadcaster, producer, reporter, bur. chief Westinghouse Broadcasting Corp., Sta. KFWB, Hollywood, 1971-87; lectr., media cons., writer, 1987—; guest broadcaster Pub. Broadcasting System, Sta. KCOP, 1975—; propr., pres. Calico Feature Prodns., Anaheim, Calif., 1969—; instr. journalism Calif. State U., Fullerton, 1972-73. Republican candidate for Calif. State Assembly, 1976. Named Journalist of Year, Cypress Coll., 1980; recipient Angel of Distinction award City of Los Angeles, 1973, John Swett Journalist of Yr. award Calif. Tchrs. Assn., 1974, 79. Mem. Am. Women in Radio and TV (chpt. pres. 1982-83; chairperson bus. and industry forum Ednl. Found. 1979), Nat. Women's Polit. Caucus, Investigative Reporters and Editors, Orange County Press Club (dir. 1979-85, pres. 1984-85), Women in Communications (award 1979), Pioneer Broadcasters W., Soc. Profl. Journalists, Author: The Long Hot Summer of 1962; Something is Missing: The Majority Sex, 1971; Dinner for One: Soupçon for Singles, 1977. Home and Office: 2512 W Chain Ave Anaheim CA 92804

RICKER, NANCY LEE, school program administrator; b. Lincoln, Nebr., Oct. 31, 1940; d. Howard Clyde and Leora May (Frenzen) Renier; m. Larry G. Ricker, June 9, 1962 (div. June 1984); children: Daniel L., Robert Renier. BS in Edn., Tex. Tech. U., 1962. Life cert. elem. tchr., Tex. Elem. tchr. Wichita (Kans.) Ind. Sch. Dist., 1962-64, Crowley (Tex.) Ind. Sch. Dist., 1964-69; ednl. cons. Parenting Guidance Ctr., Ft. Worth, 1981-83, dir. vols., 1983—; cons. area ind. sch. dists., Tex., 1988—. Cons. various civic orgns., Tarrant County, Tex., 1983-88; dir. Tex. Sch. Vol. Programs, 1989—, Streams and Valleys Exec. Com., Ft. Worth, 1981—; bd. dirs. Camp Carter YMCA, Ft. Worth, 1988—, Ft. Worth Clean City, Inc., 1983-88, Ft. Worth Opera, 1979-80; active Jr. League Ft. Worth, 1979—. Mem. Nat. Assn. Partnerships in Edn., Delta Gamma Alumnae (province XI officer, past pres.). Democrat. Presbyterian. Office: Adopt-A-Sch Fort Worth Ind Sch Dist 3210 W Lancaster Fort Worth TX 76107

RICKETTS, DEBORAH ANN, film research company executive; b. Phila., Mar. 5, 1952; d. Glenn L. and Catherine June (McDowell) R. BA, Temple U., 1975; MLS, Drexel U., 1977. Adult libr. Free Libr. Phila., 1977-79; law libr. Smaltz & Neelley Profl. Law Corp., L.A., 1979-80; film libr. Hawthorne (Calif.) Libr., 1980-81; rsch. libr. N.Y. Pub. Libr., N.Y.C., 1981; script analyst Dino De Laurentis Corp., N.Y.C., 1981-83; freelance script supr. for commls., features N.Y.C., 1983, freelance film researcher for features, documentaries, 1983-89; founding ptnr. CineQuest, N.Y.C., 1988—; judge Internat. Emmy Awards, N.Y.C. Mem. Ind. Feature Project, Am. Ind. Video and Filmmakers, Women in Film. Office: CineQuest 625 Broadway 12th Fl New York NY 10012

RICKEY, ROBERTA NATALIE, auditor; b. Chgo., June 4, 1951; d. Alexander Roman and Natilie (Jakacki) Sadlowski; m. Michael Alan. BS, Northern Ill. U., 1973; MBA, De Paul U., 1978. Cert. Fraud Examiner. Auditor U.S. Dept. Health & Human Services, Chgo., 1973-75, Fed. Aviation Adminstrn., Chgo., 1975-78, Office Child Support Enforcement, Chgo., 1978-82; auditor supr. U.S. Environ. Protection Agy., Chgo., 1982-86; auditor mgr. U.S. Dept. Office Inspector Gen., Chgo., 1986--. Recipient bronze award, U.S., 1987. Mem. Assn. Govt. Accts., Inst. Internal Auditors.

RICKIN, SHEILA ANNE, personnel executive; b. N.Y.C., Oct. 13, 1945; d. Louis and Ethel (Schmukler) Bernstein; BA, CCNY, 1966; postgrad. N.Y.U.; MBA, Pace U., 1988. Research asst. pre-baccalureate program CCNY, 1966-68; placement counselor Elaine Revell, Inc., N.Y.C., 1968; adminstr. asso. to chief exec. officer Planned Parenthood Fedn. of Am., N.Y.C., 1969-74; personnel mgr. Family Circle Mag./N.Y. Times Mag. Group, 1974-87; sr. human resources rep., Drexel Burnham Lambert, 1987-88; asst. v.p., dir. pers. and adminstrn. Oppenheimer Mgmt. Corp., 1989—. Mem. Am. Compensation Assn., Am. Soc. Pers. Adminstrs., Am. Mgmt. Assn., Am. Soc. Tng. and Devel. (securities industry group), N.Y. Human Resources Planners, N.Y. Pers. Mgrs. Assn. (program com.), Mag. Pubs. Assn. (pers. com. 1978-87). Office: Oppenheimer Mgmt Corp 2 World Trade Ctr New York NY 10048-0669

RIDDIFORD, LYNN MOORHEAD, zoologist, educator; b. Knoxville, Tenn., Oct. 18, 1936; d. James Eli and Virginia Amalia (Berry) Moorhead; m. Alan Wistar Riddiford, June 20, 1959 (div. 1966); m. James William Truman, July 28, 1970. AB magna cum laude, Radcliffe Coll., 1958; PhD, Cornell U., 1961. Research fellow in biology Harvard U., Cambridge, Mass., 1961-63, 65-66, asst. prof. biology, 1966-71, assoc. prof., 1971-73; instr. biology Wellesley (Mass.) Coll., 1963-65; assoc. prof. zoology, U. Wash., Seattle, 1973-75, prof., 1975—; mem. study sect. tropical medicine and parasitology NIH, Bethesda, Md., 1974-78; mem. Competitive Grants panel USDA, Arlington, Va., 1979, 89; mem. regulatory biology panel NSF, Washington, 1984-88; chmn. adv. com. SeriBiotech, Bangalore, India, 1989—. Contbr. articles to profl. jours. Mem. editorial bd. profl. jours. NSF fellow, 1958-60, 61-63; grantee NSF, 1964—, NIH, 1975—, Rockefeller Found., 1970-79, USDA, 1978-82, 89—; fellow John S. Guggenheim, 1979-80, NIH, 1986-87. Fellow AAAS, Royal Entomol. Soc.; mem. Am. Soc. Zoologists (pres. elect 1990), Am. Soc. Biochem. and Molecular Biology, The Internat. Ctr. for Insect Physiology and Ecology (governing coun., chmn. program com. 1989—), Entomol. Soc. Am., Am. Soc. Cell Biology, Soc. Devel. Biology. Methodist. Home: 16504 51st Ave SE Bothell WA 98012 Office: U Wash Dept Zoology Seattle WA 98195

RIDDLE, CONSTANCE CHRISTINE, educational administrator, consultant; b. Wichita, Kans., Oct. 7, 1923; d. Chester Victor and Evalyn Eugenia (Billinger) Stippich; m. George Archibald Riddle, Jr., June 25, 1944; children—George Archibald III, Michael Christopher, Penelope Diane, David Payne. B.A. in Journalism, U. Okla., 1944; postgrad. in edn. U. Houston, 1968, M.Ed. in Curriculum and Instrn., 1970. Tchr. 3d grade Houston Ind. Sch. Dist., 1963-67, tchr. minimally brain injured, 1967-71, diagnostic tchr., 1972-74, chmn. adv. com., 1973-74, adminstrv. supr., 1974-79, tng. coordinator spl. edn., 1975-79, program adminstr., 1980-82, asst. dir. proposal devel., 1982-85, mem. adv. bd. Vols. in Pub. Schs., 1984—; exec. dir. Literacy Advance, Houston, 1985—; cons. Am. Women in Radio/TV, Houston, 1983, Shearer Pub. Co., 1986. Author, editor. Developing Motor Skills, 1979; Reading Management System, 1979; co-author, editor Parent Education Workshop Modules, 1983. Bd. dirs. Houston chpt. Am. Heart Assn., 1961-72; pres., bd. dirs. Literacy Advance Houston, 1979-81; Tex. rep. South Central Literacy Action, 1985—; chmn. nat. long range planning com. Laubach Literacy Action, 1985-87; treas. Tex. Adult Literacy, Laubach, 1989—, steering com., 1987—; steering com. Tex. A&M Adult Learning and Literacy Clearinghouse, 1988—; mem. Mayor of Phila.'s Conf. on Urban Literacy; chmn. Literacy Providers-Houston Read Commn., 1988, chmn. nominating com., 1988-89; presenter 1st Conf. on Adult and Adolescent Literacy, Internat. Reading Assn. Flotilla comdr. U.S. Coast Guard Aux., Seabrook, Tex., 1984-85. Recipient Bell Ringer award Literacy Advance Houston, 1982-84. Mem. Women in Communications (exec. com. 1983-84), Houston Profl. Adminstrs. (exec. com. 1982-83), Assn. United Way Execs. (sec. 1989), Altrusa (v.p. 1989-90, literacy chmn. Dist. 9 1990), Delta Kappa Gamma (scholar 1974, pres. 1976-78), Phi Delta Kappa, Kappa Delta Pi. Home: 5238 Ariel Houston TX 77096 Office: Literacy Advance of Houston Inc 4545 Bissonnet Ste 125 Bellaire TX 77401

RIDE, SALLY KRISTEN, scientist, former astronaut; b. Los Angeles, May 26, 1951; d. Dale Burdell and Carol Joyce (Anderson) R.; m. Steven Alan Hawley, July 26, 1982 (div.). B.A. in English, Stanford U., 1973, B.S. in Physics, 1973, Ph.D. in Physics, 1978. Teaching asst. Stanford U., Palo Alto, Calif.; researcher dept. physics Stanford U.; astronaut candidate, trainee NASA, 1978-79, astronaut, 1979-87; on-orbit capsule communicator STS-2 mission Johnson Space Ctr. NASA, Houston; on-orbit capsule communicator STS-3 mission NASA, mission specialist STS-7, 1983, mission specialist STS-41G, 1984; sci. fellow Stanford (Calif.) U., 1987-89; dir. Calif. Space Inst. of U. Calif. San Diego, La Jolla, 1989—; prof. Physics U. Calif. San Diego, La Jolla, 1989—; mem. Presdl. Commn. on Space Shuttle, 1986. Author: (with Susan Okie) To Space and Back, 1986. Office: Calif Space Inst A-021 U Calif San Diego La Jolla CA 92093

RIDEOUT, JANET LITSTER, chemist; b. Bennington, Vt., Jan. 6, 1939; d. John Ramage and Elizabeth Dinwiddie (Dewey) Litster; m. Ralph L. Rideout Jr., Mar. 3, 1973. AB, Mt. Holyoke Coll., 1961, MA, 1963; PhD, SUNY, Buffalo, 1968. Rsch. chemist exptl. therapy dept. Burroughs Wellcome Co., 1968-70, sr. rsch. chemist exptl. therapy dept., 1970-79, group leader exptl. therapy dept., 1979-83, group leader organic chemistry dept., 1983-88, asst. div. dir. organic chemistry div., 1988—; bd. dirs. Burroughs Wellcome Employee Credit Union, 1981—, treas., 1985-87, sec. 1987-89, pres., 1983-85. Editor: Nucleosides, Nucleotides and Their Biological Applications, 1983; patentee in field. Allied Chem. fellow, 1966-67; Skinner Found. fellow, 1962; Dupont study grantee, 1961. Fellow Am. Inst. Chemists (life); mem. Am. Chem.Soc., N.Y. Acad. Scis. Office: Burroughs Wellcome Co 3030 Cornwallis Rd Research Triangle Park NC 27709

RIDEOUT, PHYLLIS MCCAIN, university official, educator; b. Macon, Ga., Sept. 15, 1938; d. Wayne Eugene and Lois Stone (Rollins) McC.; m. William Milford Rideout, Jr., Mar. 10, 1961; children: Christina Lynn, William Milford III, Julie Linda. AB in Modern European Lit., Stanford U., 1961; MA in English, Fla. State U., 1973, PhD in Humanities, 1981. Cert. community coll. life teaching credential, Calif. Teaching asst. Fla. State U., Tallahassee, 1974-75; program coord. humanities U. So. Calif., L.A., 1981-82; program adminstr. Norris Comprehensive Cancer Ctr., U. So. Calif., L.A., 1983-86; adminstrv. dir. U. So. Calif., L.A., 1986-89, assoc. dir. for adminstrn. and edn., 1989—, clin. instr. preventive medicine Sch. Medicine, 1989—. Leader, trainer Girl Scouts U.S.A., Tallahassee and Los Alamitos, Calif., 1975-81; bd. dirs. jr. and sr. high schs. PTA's, Los Alamitos, 1977-81; bd. dirs. Cancer Coalition Calif., 1986—. Mem. AAUW, Nat. Assn. Women Deans, Counselors and Adminstrs., Cancer Ctr. Adminstrs. Forum (exec. com. 1987-1991, U. So. Calif. Women in Mgmt. (bd. dirs. 1986-89, 90-91), Stanford U. Alumni Assn. (life), Stanford Profl. Women (pres., bd. dirs. 1982-85), Stanford Club Los Angeles County (bd. dirs. 1985-88). Office: U So Calif Norris Comprehensive Cancer Ctr 1441 Eastlake Ave Los Angeles CA 90033-0800

RIDER, MARILYN ANN, stockbroker; b. Conrad, Mont., Dec. 15, 1941; d. Louis E. and Emmi V. (Markuson) Schroer. Diploma acctg., Gt. Falls (Mont.) Comml. Coll., 1960. CPA, Wash.; m. Joe Raunig, Jan. 2, 1960 (div. 1971); children: Christina M., Rodney B., Brett R.; m. Lloyd D. Keith, Apr. 19, 1972 (dec. July 1973); m. 3d, Bruce A. Rider, Dec. 10, 1977 (div. 1979); 1 child, Marc D.; m. David R. Corn, Nov. 24, 1989. Engaged in acctg., 1960-74, 75-77; owner Keith Enterprises, Chester, Mont., 1974-75; account exec. Merill Lynch, Pierce Fenner and Smith, Spokane, 1977, asst. v.p., fin. cons.; v.p. investments Prudential Bache, 1987—; tchr. courses in field. Mem. core team New Life. Mem. Wash. Soc. CPAs, Am. Women's Soc. CPAs, Spokane Duplicate Bridge Club (bd. dirs. 1976). Roman Catholic. Home: N 7927 Pine Meadow Nine Mile Falls WA 99026

RIDER, QUILA OWENS, nurse midwife; b. Bisbee, Ariz., Dec. 17, 1942; d. Hadley Hugh and Margaret (Urguhart) Hicks; m. George R. Mason, June 2, 1960 (div. Apr. 1980); children: Carrie L., Cynthia A., Mason, Cheri L. Naudin. AA, Golden West Coll., 1975; AS, Cypress (Calif.) Coll., 1977. Nurse-midwife FHP Inc., Fountain Valley, Calif., 1989—; cons., expert testifier State of Calif., 1989—; chief exec. officer Womens Health Resources Creation of Alternatives for Women's Health, 1989—. Mem. Alliance for Survival, Orange County, Calif., 1988—, Poverty Law Ctr., Montgomery, Ala., 1987, Pub. Citizen, Washington, 1985. Mem. Internat. Assn. Parents and Profls. for Alternative in Childbirth, Am. Coll. Nurse-Midwife (chair pub. rels. com. 1988-90), Consortium for Nurse Midwifery, Inc. (bd. dirs. Torrance, Calif. chpt. 1990—), ACLU, NOW. Home: 35156 Camino Capistrano Capistrano Beach CA 92624

RIDGE, HELEN SOPHIE, electrical contractor, nurse practitioner; b. N.Y.C., Apr. 13, 1932; d. Adolf William and Elfrieda (Nachtigale) Reimer; m. James Ridge, Nov. 22, 1951 (dec.); children: James, William A., Patricia A., Kelly K. Student, Luth. Med. Ctr., Bklyn., 1949-51; Assoc in Nursing, Suffolk Community Coll., 1968; BS in Nursing, SUNY, Stony Brook, 1974. Cert. elec. contractor. Operating room nurse St. John's Smithtown (N.Y.) Hosp., 1968-78; owner, pres. James T. Ridge & Sons Inc., East Northport, N.Y., 1970—. Mem. Suffolk County Elec. Contractors Assn. Republican. Roman Catholic. Home: 30 Hayes Hill Dr Ft Salonga NY 11768 Office: James T Ridge & Sons Inc 39 Doyle Ct East Northport NY 11731

RIDGWAY, HELEN JANE, chemist, consultant; b. Ft. Worth, Aug. 10, 1937; d. Ralph Pope and Virginia Leah (Link) R. AS, Arlington (Tex.) State Coll., 1957; BA, North Tex. State Coll., Denton, 1959; MS, Baylor U., Waco, Tex., 1963, PhD, 1968. Rsch. asst. Wadley Rsch. Inst., Dallas, 1960-68; sr. investigator Wadley Insts. Molecular Medicine, Dallas, 1968-86, chmn. chemistry, 1986—; cons. Helena Labs., Beaumont, Tex., 1986—. Contbr. articles to sci. jours. AAUW scholar, 1955, 56. Fellow Internat. Soc. Hematology; mem. Am. Chem. Soc., Am. Heart Assn. (coun. on thrombosis).

RIDGWAY, ROZANNE LEJEANNE, foreign policy executive; b. St. Paul, Aug. 22, 1935; d. H. Clay and Ethel Rozanne (Cote) R.; m. Theodore E. Deming. B.A., Hamline U., 1957, LL.D. (hon.), 1978; LL.D. (hon.), George Washington U., 1986. Career diplomat U.S. Fgn. Svc., 1957-89; amb. to Finland, 1977-80; counselor of the Dept. State, Washington, 1980-81; spl. asst. to sec. state, 1981; amb. to German Dem. Republic, 1982-85; asst. sec. state Europe and Can., 1985-89; pres. The Atlantic Coun. of U.S., Washington, 1989—; bd. dirs. 3M Corp., RJR Nabisco, Union Carbide Corp., Berlitz Internat., Inc., Bell Atlantic, Citicorp. Trustee Hamline U.; bd. dirs. Am. Inst. Contemporary German Studies, Inst. for East-West Security Studies. Recipient Profl. awards Dept. State, 1967, 70, 75, 81, 89 Joseph C. Wilson internat. rels. achievement award, 1982, Sharansky award Union Couns. Soviet Jewry, 1989, Grand Cross of the Order of the Lion, Finland, 1989; named Person of Yr., Nat. Fisheries Inst., 1977, Knight Comdr. of the Order of Merit, Fed. Republic Germany, 1989, U.S. Presdl. Citizens Achievement medal, 1989. Fellow Nat. Acad. Pub. Adminstrn.; mem. Met. Club. Office: The Atlantic Coun of The US 1616 H St Washington DC 20006

RIDILLA, ANDREA JAYNE, oboist, educator; b. Latrobe, Pa., Feb. 23, 1956; d. Andrew Joseph and Theresa Marie (Kozenko) R. MusB, Oberlin Conservatory of Music, 1978, The Juilliard Sch., 1980; MusM, The Julliard Sch., 1981. Artist faculty N.Y. State Summer Sch. the Arts, Saratoga Springs, N.Y., 1984-87; prin. oboe R.I. Philharmonic, Providence, 1982-84; lectr. U. Nev., Las Vegas, 1984-87; prin. oboe Las Vegas Symphony, 1984-87; assoc. prof. music Miami U., Oxford, Ohio, 1987—. Named to Jury Annual Concours Que. Conservatores of Music, 1989; grantee Ohio Arts Coun., 1990, Western States Arts Found., 1987, Arts Midwest Found., 1990. Mem. Am. Fedn. Musicians, Internat. Double Reed Soc., Pi Kappa Lambda. Roman Catholic. Home: 639 W Chestnut St #11 Oxford OH 45056

RIDINGS, DOROTHY SATTES, communications executive; b. Charleston, W.Va., Sept. 26, 1939; d. Frederick L. and Katharine E. (Backus) Sattes; m.

Donald Jerome Ridings, Sept. 8, 1962; children—Donald Jerome, Matthew Lyle. Student, Randolph-Macon Woman's Coll., 1957-59; BSJ, Northwestern U., 1961; MA, U. N.C.-Chapel Hill, 1968; D.Pub. Svc. (hon.), U. Louisville, 1985; LHD (hon.), Spalding U., 1986. Reporter Charlotte Observer, N.C., 1961-66; instr. U. N.C. Sch. Journalism, 1966-68; freelance writer Louisville, 1968-77; news editor Ky. Bus. Ledger, Louisville, 1977-80, editor, 1980-83; communications cons., editor, 1983-86; mgmt. assoc. Knight-Ridder Inc., Charlotte, N.C., 1986-88; pres., publisher The Bradenton (Fla.) Herald, 1988—; adj. prof. Night Div. U. Louisville, 1982-83; copy editor Washington Post, summer 1967; v.p. Nat. Mcpl. League, 1985-86; bd. dirs. com. on Constl. System, Nat. Com. Against Discrimination in Housing, 1982-87, Com. for Study of Am. Electorate; mem. Ind. Sector, 1983-86; mem. exec. com. Leadership Conf. Civil Rights, 1982-86. Pres. LWV U.S., 1982-86, 1st v.p. 1980-82, human resources dir., 1976-80, chair edn. fund, 1982-86, 1st vice chair, 1980-82, trustee, 1976-80, pres. Louisville/Jefferson County, 1974-76, bd. dirs. 1969-76; trustee Citizens Research Found., 1982-84; mem. Gov.'s Council Ednl. Reform, 1984-85; chair Prichard Com. Acad. Excellence, 1985-86; bd. dirs. Leadership Ky., 1984-87, Leadership Louisville, 1983-86, Louisville YWCA, 1978-80, Jr. League Louisville, 1972-74; mem. Gov.'s Commn. Full Equality, 1982-83; mem. state adv. council U.S. Commn. Civil Rights, 1975-79; mem. steering com. Task Force for Peaceful Desegregation, 1974-75; elder 2d Presbyn. Ch., 1972-75, 78-81; mem. adv. council on ch. and soc. United Presbyn. Ch. in USA, 1978-84. Recipient Leadership award Nat. Assn. Community Leadership Orgns., 1986, Alumnae Achievement award Randolph-Macon Woman's Coll., 1985, Disting. Citizens award Nat. Mcpl. League, 1983. Mem. ABA (accreditation com.), Jud. Coun. Fla., Am. Judicature Soc. (bd. dirs.), Benton Found. (bd. dirs.), Ford Found. (trustee). Home: 3412 Avenida Madera Bradenton FL 34210 Office: PO Box 921 Bradenton FL 34206

RIDINGS, SUSAN ELIZABETH, social worker; b. Bethlehem, Pa., July 6, 1949; d. Charles Frederick Schmidt and Eleanor Martin Jenico; m. Edward Haslam Ridings, Aug. 28, 1971; children: Alexis Katherine, Adam Edward. BSW, Pa. State U., 1971. Caseworker Pa. Dept. Welfare, Phila., 1973-78; bus. mgr. Vallement Surg. Assocs., Lewistown, Pa., 1987—. Pres. bd. dirs. Community Counseling Ctr., Lewistown, 1986-88, Mifflin County Children and Youth Svcs., Lewistown,1 990—; pres. elect Lewistown Hosp. Aux., 1989; bd. trustees Mifflin County Libr. Assn., 1988; co-founder Teen Parenting Prog., Lewistown, 1985; bd. dirs. Mifflin-Juniata Assn. of the Blind, Lewistown, 1987—. Mem. AAUW (named outstanding woman 1985), Alpha Omicron Pi. Home: 1 Pine Ln Lewistown PA 17044 Office: Vallemont Surgical Assocs 100 Stine Dr Lewistown PA 17044

RIDLEN, LILLIAN MAY HEIGLE, public relations, sales and marketing executive, writer, inventor; b. New Orleans, Nov. 15, 1946; d. Joseph Manuel and Lillian Mae (Theriot) H.; m. Larry Vinson Ridlen, Dec. 28, 1968; children: Larry V. Jr., Kenneth C., Jennifer C. Degree in Nursing, Orleans Parish Sch. Practical Nursing, 1969. Nurse So. Bapt. Hosp., New Orleans, 1970-72; pres. Sunshine & Co., LaPlace, La., 1983-86, The Gift Gallery, LaPlace, 1984-85; v.p. La. Bartending Inst., Kenner, Baton Rouge and New Orleans, 1986-87; dir. La. Bartending Inst., 1987-89; pub. rels. officer, sales and mktg. dir. Universal Fast Foods of LaPlace, Chalmette and Marrero, 1989—; nurse St. Charles Manor Nursing Ctr., 1989—; owner, pres. Ton-Lil Pub. Co., LaPlace, 1990—. Author: A Sampling of Southern Cooking, 1985, A Home Study Course in Bartending, 1989; composer, lyricist songs; lyricist Tony's Song for artist Wayne Presley; inventor Santa's Snack Pack; writer poetry. Organizer Mothers for Safe Edn. St. John the Bapt. Parish, La., 1984. Mem. NAFE. Democrat. Roman Catholic.

RIDLEY, BETTY ANN, educator, church worker; b. St. Louis, Oct. 19, 1926; d. Rupert Alexis and Virginia Regina (Weikel) Steber; m. Fred A. Ridley, Jr., Sept. 8, 1948; children: Linda Drue Ridley Archer, Clay Kent. BA, Scripps Coll., Claremont, Calif., 1948. Christian Sci. practitioner, Oklahoma City, 1973—; Christian Sci. tchr., 1983—; mem. Christian Sci. Bd. Lectureship, 1980-85. Found. Bibl. Research and Preservation Primitive Christianity. Mem. Jr. League Am. Home: 7908 Lakehurst Dr Oklahoma City OK 73120 Office: 3000 United Founders Blvd Suite 100-G Oklahoma City OK 73112

RIDOLFI, LORETTA ELIZABETH, state official; b. Trenton, N.J., Mar. 12, 1933; d. John J. and Elizabeth (Teringer) Barabas; m. Benjamin F. Ridolfi, Jr., Feb. 19, 1955; children: Cynthia, Lisa, Benjamin. BS in Pharmacy, Phila. Coll. Pharmacy and Sci., 1954; postgrad., Rutgers U., 1981, Trenton State Coll., 1989. Reg. pharmacist, N.J., Pa. With various pharmacies Mercer County, N.J., 1954-80; field rep. health N.J. Dept. Health, Trenton, 1980-83, pub. health rep., 1983-84, program specialist, 1984-85, 1988—, community service officer, 1985—. Contbr. articles to profl. jours. Chmn., Impaired Pharmacists Program of N.J., Trenton, 1987-89; sec. Impaired Pharmacists Network Dist. II, 1986—; bd. dirs. Am. Cancer Soc., Mercer County, 1983—, lay del. from Mercer County; mem. staff N.J. Drug Abuse Adv. Council, 1985-89. Mem. Am. Pharm. Assn., N.J. Pharm. Assn. (pres. 1980-81, Frederick B. Kilmer Meml. award 1987), Soc. Mercer County Pharmacists (pres. 1975-76, James E. Delahanty Meml. award 1984, A.H. Robins Hygeia award 1982, others), Phila. Coll. Pharmacy and Sci. Alumni Assn., Communication Workers Am. Democrat. Roman Catholic. Club: Compassionate Friends. Home: 163 Highland Ave Yardville Heights NJ 08620 Office: NJ Dept Health CN 362 Trenton NJ 08625-0362

RIECKEN, ELLNORA ALMA, music teacher; b. Delaware, Ohio, Mar. 21, 1934; d. William Emil and Alma Ellanora (Gollner) R. BA cum laude, Millsaps Coll., 1955; M in Music, Fla. State U., 1957; grad., U. Miami, 1986-87. Tchr. Filer Jr. High, Hialeah, Fla., 1956-72; choral dir. H. Mann Jr. High, Miami, Fla., 1972-74; music tchr. Olympia Heights Elem., Miami, 1974-80; music. tchr. Melrose Elem., Miami; tour mem. Kjelson Summer Chorale, Miami, 1970; performing mem. Civic Chorale of Greater Miami, 1970--; dept. rep. Melrose Faculty Council, Miami, 1984-87. Composer: 5 Incidental Songs for Christmas All Over the Place by J. Martin, 1986. panel speaker Soroptimist Club Regional Conv., Atlanta, 1960; credentials chmn. Venture Club Nat. Conv., Miami, 1964; team lay speaker Sunshine Via De Cristo Retreat, Miami, 1984. Mem. Venture Club (treas. 1965), Music Educators Nat. Conf., Fla. Music Educators Assn., Dade County Music Educators Assn., Am. Choral Dirs. Assn., Fla. Elem. Music Educators Assn., United Tchrs. of Dade County, United Meth. Women (circle vice chmn. 1987-89). Democrat. Home: PO Box 660177 Miami Springs FL 33266 Office: Melrose Elem Sch 3050 NW 35th St Miami FL 33142

RIEDEL, JOYCE LUCKE, data processing executive; b. Clinton, Iowa, May 1, 1953; d. Fred and LaVera (Reimer) Lucke; m. Thomas E. Riedel, June 25, 1977; 1 child, Brian E. BS, Iowa State U., 1975; MBA, Ill. Benedictine Coll., 1980. Programmer Montgomery Wards, Chgo., 1975-77; sr. programmer McDonald's Corp., Oak Brook, Ill., 1977-78, programmer analyst, 1978, systems analyst, 1979-80, mgr., 1980-83, programming staff dir., 1983—. Leader Girl Scouts U.S., Naperville, Ill., 1975-77, coun. del. 1978-80, fin. com. 1982-83, bd. dirs. 1980-83, Wider Opportunites com. 1980-85; fin. com. Christ Luth. Ch., Clarendon Hills, Ill., 1986-89; zone chairperson Homeowners Assn., 1988—. Mem. Nat. Computer Graphics Assn.

RIEFKOHL, GLORIA ROSANGELES, pediatrician; b. Hato Rey, P.R., Dec. 23, 1959; d. Jorge Eduardo and Carmen Gloria (Rey) R.; m. Virginio Rodriguez, June 6, 1985 (div. May 1989). BS magna cum laude, U. P.R., 1981; MD, Ponce Sch. Medicine, 1985; postgrad., U. Miami, 1989—. Resident in pediatrics St. Agnes Hosp., Balt., 1985-88; pvt. practice West Palm Beach, Fla., 1988-89, Belle Glade, Fla., 1989—; instr. neonatal resuscitation, 1989; mem. Nat. Health Svc. Corps, HRS-Belle Glade, 1989—. Pres. Explorer med. post Boy Scouts Am., Hato Rey, 1978-80. Mem. AMA, Am. Acad. Pediatrics, Am. Hosp. Assn. Roman Catholic. Home: 603 Lakeview Dr E West Palm Beach FL 33411 Office: HRS-Carl L Brumback Ctr PO Box 934 Belle Glade FL 33430

RIEGER, AUDREY F., psychologist; b. Chgo., Nov. 22, 1920; d. Malvin and Alfrieda (Ritter) Flesham; m. Martin M. Rieger, July 4, 1943; children: Pamela Sherman, Dean Rieger. BA, U. Ill., 1942; AM, U. Chgo., 1943, PhD, 1948. Lic. psychologist, N.J.; sch. cert. psychologist. Psychologist agencies Chgo., 1944-48; psychologist Robert McMurry Co., Chgo., 1946-52; psychologist nursery schs., cons. Chgo., Englewood, N.J., 1953-60; instr. Fairleigh Dickinson U., Teaneck, N.J., 1955-58; psychologist sch. systems N.J., 1959-86; pvt. practice psychologist Morris Plains, N.J., 1986—. Bd. dirs. Planned Parenthood, Bergen County, N.J., 1962-67; com. mem. YMHA, Bergen County, 1962-67. Mem. Am. Psychol. Assn. Jewish. Home and office: 304 Mountain Way Morris Plains NJ 07950

RIEGLE, LINDA B., federal judge; b. 1947. BS, Shepherd Coll., Shepherdstown, W.Va.; JD, Union U., Albany, N.Y. Admitted to bar, 1978. Bankruptcy judge U.S. Dist. Ct. Nev., Las Vegas. Office: US Dist Ct 300 Las Vegas Blvd S Las Vegas NV 89101*

RIEKER, ANNE ELLORA, judge, humanitarian; b. Elmira, N.Y., Sept. 27, 1923; d. Eric Wendell and Viola Della (Hinkley) Phillips; m. Thomas Henry Rieker, Nov. 6, 1943; children: Constance Anne, Carla Anne, Thomas Eric. AS, Hershey Jr. Coll., 1943; student, Washburn U., 1958-59, U. Nev., 1982, 85. Dir. recreation therapy Extended Care Facility, Andover, N.J., 1967-70; exec. dir. Office on Aging, Sussex County, N.J., 1970-74; surrogate judge County of Sussex, Newton, N.J., 1975-89; mem. N.J. State Juvenile Delinquency/Commn., 1987—, N.J. State and Local Expenditure and Revenue Policy Commn., 1987-89, Local Govt. Policy Com. N.J. Dept. Pers. and Civil Svc., 1987-89. Trustee Knoll Heights Sr. Citizens Housing, Sparta, N.J., 1975-86; chmn. March of Dimes, Morristown, N.J., 1978-79; bd. dirs. Vis. Nurses Assn. Sussex County, Sparta, N.J., 1983—, pres., 1988—; chmn. govt. div., Sussex County United Way, 1985—, mem. allocation com., bd. dirs., 1988—; mem. N.J. Assembly Local Govt. Affairs Adv. Coun., 1988—, Sussex County Communities in Transition Planning Com., 1988—. Named Outstanding Citizen of Yr., VFW, 1975; recipient Vol. award March of Dimes, 1981, 82, 83, 84, 85. Mem. N.J. Assn. County Officers (pres. 1979-81), Nat. Coll. Probate Judges, Nat. Judges Assn., N.J. Assn. Counties (4th v.p. 1985, pres. 1987), N.J. Bar Assn. (assoc.), N.J. Assn. Elected Women Ofcls. (bd. dirs. 1981-83), Soroptomist (internat., v.p. 1985), Newton Country. Democrat. Espsicopanian. Avocations: music, golf, handcrafts, travel. Office: Hall of Records 4 Park Pl Newton NJ 07860

RIELY, CAROLINE ARMISTEAD, physician, medical educator; b. Washington, Feb. 1, 1944; d. John William and Jean Roy (Jones) Riely. AB, Mt. Holyoke Coll., 1966; MD, Columbia U., 1970. Diplomate Am. Bd. Internal Medicine. Med. intern Presbyn. Hosp., N.Y.C., 1970-71, resident in medicine, 1971-73; fellow in liver disease Yale U., New Haven, 1973-75, asst. prof., 1975-80, assoc. prof., 1980-88; prof. medicine U. Tenn., Memphis, 1988—. Asst. editor Am. Jour. Gastroenterology. Fellow ACP, Am. Coll. Gastroenterology; mem. Am. Assn. Study Liver Disease, Internat. Assn. Study Liver, N.Am. Soc. for Pediatric Gastroenterology and Nutrition. Home: 1756 Central Ave Memphis TN 38104 Office: U Tenn 951 Court Ave Rm 555D Room 555D Memphis TN 38163

RIELY, PHYLLIS ELEANOR, microbiologist, consultant; b. Welshfield, Ohio, Jan. 25, 1918; d. Clifford James and Ethel (Corliss) Brunton; student Capital U., 1936-39; grad. Sch. Med. Tech. Huron Rd. Hosp., 1941; m. Charles T. Riely, Nov. 28, 1942 (div.); children—Terrence, Patricia, Maura, Shawn. Systems microbiologist Fairchild Hiller Co., Farmingdale, N.Y., 1960-66; life support coordinator Pall Corp., Glen Cove, N.Y., 1966-69; mgr. med. product devel. Internat. Paper Co., Tuxedo, N.Y., 1969-71; dir. med. products East-West Med. Products Co., Hauppage, N.Y., 1971-73; mgr. biomed. regulatory affairs Pall Corp., Glen Cove, 1973-74; mgr. microbiol. devel. Marion Labs., Kansas City, Mo., 1974-81; mgr. tech. edn. Marion Sci. div. Marion Labs., Kansas City, Mo., 1981-82; biomed. cons., 1984-88; sr. scientist Inst. Biogerontology Rsch., 1988—. Mem. Am. Soc. Microbiology, Royal Soc. Health, Soc. Neurosci. Republican. Methodist. Patentee in field; author book; contbr. articles to profl. jours. Home: 13373 Plaza Del Rio Blvd Apt 7738 Peoria AZ 85381

RIEMAN, LETICIA LINDA, media relations and marketing executive, consultant; b. N.Y.C., Apr. 21, 1951; d. Joseph and Felisa (Bauza) Nebbiai; m. Peter Hayes Rieman, Feb. 9, 1971. Student, Inst. New Cinema Artist, N.Y.C., 1973; BA, Hunter Coll., 1979. Publicist Arthur Rubine Pub. Rels., N.Y.C., 1973-78; assoc. producer, producer Metromedia, N.Y.C., 1979-82; communications officer U.S. Com. for UNICEF, N.Y.C., 1982-83; pres. L.L. Rieman Communications, N.Y.C., 1983—; consulting v.p. media rels. and mktg. Mostel & Taylor Securities, Inc., N.Y.C., 1986—; judge Blue Ribbon Panel for Emmys NATAS, 1979-80, Internat. Film and TV Festival of N.Y. 31st annual awards, 1988; cons. United Cerebal Palsy Video Therapy, 1984-85, Assn. of Indian Ams., 1987-89; exec. producer spl. events; lectr. Learning Annex Video Production, 1986-88; backup lectr. The New Sch. for Social Rsch., 1986-88. Assoc. producer, producer numerous TV Pub. Affairs programs, 1980 (Emmy 1983); photographer Am. Image News Svc., Washington, 1988-89. Mem. Environ. Def. Fund, 1988-89, Sierra Club Def. Fund, 1988-89, Nat. Humane Soc., 1988-89, People for Ethical Treatment of Animals, 1988-89. Mem. NATAS (assoc. producer Emmys 1980-81), Internat. Assn. Bus. Communication, Internat. Freelance Photographers Orgn., Nat. Acad. Cable Programming. Theosophist. Home: 153 E 57th St New York NY 10022

RIEMCKE, KATHRYN ELIZABETH, retired educator; b. Connell, Wash., Mar. 31, 1922; d. Leo Clement and Mina Adele (Collins) Crossland; m. Wesley Allen Ketcham, July 9, 1942 (dec. Apr. 1965); children: Milton Leo, Roger Allen; m. Charles A. Riemcke, Aug. 19, 1967. BA, Cen. Wash. U., 1959; MA, Holy Name Coll., 1979. Cert. tchr. K-12, Wash. Tchr. Prosser (Wash.) Jr. High Sch., 1959, Highlands Jr. High Sch., Kennewick, Wash., 1959-64, Yakima (Wash.) Dist. 7, 1965-80. Pres., Yakima Community Concert Assn., 1984—; bd. dirs. Yakima Symphony Orch., 1986—; vol. ARC, Yakima; vocal music tchr. Yakima Acad. Arts; music dir. Bel Canto Choral Soc., Yakima, 1980-83. Mem. Altrusa Club (pres. 1989-90), Yakima Country Club (pres. women's div. 1987-88). Republican. Episcopalian.

RIEMER, DELILAH, physician, consultant; b. Bklyn., Aug. 28, 1910; d. Moses Joseph and Sophia (Isacson) R.; m. Abraham Daniel Rubenstein, Dec. 26, 1937; children: Joel Jay, David Harvey, Susan Sophia Albright. BS, Tufts U., 1931; MD, Med. Coll. of Pa., 1936. Intern Univ. Hosp., Boston, 1936-37; jr. physician Boston Dispensary, 1937-47; physician-in-charge blood program ARC, Boston, 1942-45; ward physician VA Hosp., Bedford, Mass., 1948-53, chief phys. medicine and rehab., 1953-63; dir. John T. Berry Rehab. Ctr., North Reading, Mass., 1963-79; med. dir. Whittier Rehab. Hosp., Haverhill, Mass., 1979-83; pvt. practice cons. Newton Centre, Mass., 1983—; med. dir. Newburyport Chronic Hosp., 1979-83; cons. Shaughnessy Rehab. Hosp., 1983-85. Contbr. articles to profl. jours. Bd. dirs. Jewish Meml. Hosp., Roxbury, Mass., 1980—. Mem. Am. Psychiat. Assn., Am. Congress Rehab. Medicine (Bronze medal 1954), Mass. Med. Soc. Home and Office: 164 Ward St Newton Centre MA 02159

RIENNER, LYNNE CAROL, publisher; b. Pitts., Aug. 3, 1945; d. David and Molly (Rice) R. B.A., U. Pa., 1967. Exec. v.p., assoc. publisher, editorial dir. Westview Press Inc., Boulder, Colo., 1975-84; pres. Lynne Rienner Pub. Inc., Boulder, Colo., 1984—; pub. cons. various orgns.; lectr. U. Denver Pub. Inst., 1981-84; panelist nat. meetings. Mem. Soc. Scholarly Pub., Assn. Am. Pubs. (exec. coun. Internat. div.). Office: Lynne Rienner Pub Inc 1800 30th St Ste 314 Boulder CO 80301

RIERDAN, JILL E., psychology educator; b. Boston, Apr. 6, 1945; d. Walter and Dorothy (Keaveney) R. BA, Clark U., 1967, MA, 1970, PhD, 1974. Instr. in psychology U. Mass., Boston, 1973-74; asst. prof. psychology Mass. Wellesley Coll., 1974-80; postdoctoral fellow West Haven (Conn.) VA Hosp., 1977-78, lectr., 1982—; rsch. assoc. Wellesley Ctr. for Rsch. on Women, 1982—. Office: Wellesley Ctr Rsch on Women Dept of Psychology Wellesley MA 02181

RIES, CAROLE ELIZABETH, children's theatre director; b. Watertown, S.D., Nov. 4, 1940; d. Clifford Bernard and Lillian Mary (Manthei) R.; m. Gerd Walter Hensen, Dec. 6, 1963 (div. Sept. 1985); children: Christopher Walter, Shannon Elizabeth. BS, S.D. State U., 1963. Exec. sec. Memphis Little Theatre, 1964-66; vol., 1966-74; tchr. Whitehaven (Tenn.) Meth. Day Sch., 1974; adminstrv. dir. Theatre Memphis, 1975-89; exec. dir. Ft. Lauderdale (Fla.) Children's Theatre, 1989—; grants panelist in theatre S.C. Arts Commn., 1990—. Actress community theatre. Pres. Memphis chpt. NOW, 1973-74. Mem. Women in Communications, Inc., Women's Profl. Network, Interested Mems. for the Performing Arts Ctr., Southeastern Theatre Conf., Tenn. Theatre Assn. Democrat. Roman Catholic. Home: 1123 N Andrews Ave Fort Lauderdale FL 33311 Office: Childrens Theatre 640 N Andrews Ave Fort Lauderdale FL 33311

RIESCO, NANCY, educator; b. Chgo., July 14, 1943; d. Anthony J. and Mildred (Masters) Summins; m. Antonio Orestes Riesco, Aug. 24, 1967; 1 child, Lara Maria. BA, No. Ill. U., 1966; MA, U. Salamanaca, Spain, 1976. Cert. secondary tchr., Ill. Tchr. Spanish, Oak Park (Ill.)-River Forest High Sch., 1966, Arlington High Sch., Arlington Heights, Ill., 1966-68; tchr. English, Chgo. Pub. Schs., 1969-70; tchr. Spanish, Barrington (Ill.) High Sch., 1970—; tchr. Round Lake Summer Bilingual Program, Round Lake Beach, Ill., summer 1981. Cand. for state rep., 54th Legis. Dist. of Ill., 1990. Mem. NAFE, NSDAR (founding charter mem. Sarah's Grove chpt.)Am. assn. Tchrs. Spanish and Portuguese, Ill. Coun. on Teaching Fgn. Langs. (charter, presenter 1988-89, newsletter liaison 1989-90), Nat. Abortion Rights Action League. Democrat. Home: 355 W Miner St Arlington Heights IL 60005 Office: Barrington High Sch 616 W Main St Barrington IL 60010

RIESMAN, EVELYN THOMPSON, freelance writer; b. Brookline, Mass., Feb. 14, 1912; d. Maurice Dekay and Lilian (Hastings) Thompson; m. David Riesman, July 15, 1936; children: Paul (dec.), Jennie, Lucy, Michael. BA in English, Bryn Mawr (Pa.) Coll., 1935. Editor jour. consumers div. U.S. Dept. Labor, Washington, 1935-36; Author: (with others) Conversations in Japan, 1967; author: (short stories) New World Writing, 1955, Southwest Review, 1958, Univ. Kans. City Rev., 1959; contbr. articles to profl. jours. Democrat. Unitarian. Home: 49 Linnaean St Cambridge MA 02138

RIESS, DOROTHY YOUNG, internist; b. Atlanta, Dec. 9, 1931; d. Roy Wallace and Dorothy (West) Young; m. Louis Riess, July 4, 1971 (div. 1987); children: Louis Andrew, John Charles. BMus, U. Okla., 1953, MD, 1969. Intern French Hosp., San Francisco, 1969-70; resident Huntington Hosp., Pasadena, Calif., 1970-73; pvt. practice Pasadena, 1973—. Editor, pub. Better Health Newsletter, 1984—; contbr. articles to profl. publs. Mem. Pasadena Med. Soc. (pres. 1987-88), L.A. County Med. Assn. (CMA del. 1987—), L.A. County Physicians Art Soc. (pres. 1981). Republican. Presbyterian. Office: 2750 E Washington Blvd #270 Pasadena CA 91107

RIFE, PATRICIA ELIZABETH, interdisciplinary liberal arts educator, writer; b. Abington, Pa., Mar. 6, 1957; d. Edward Franklin and Anne (Kirk) Rife. BS in Social Ethics, Grand Valley State U., Allendale, Mich., 1978; PhD in Social History of Sci., Union Inst., Cin., 1983; postgrad., MIT and Harvard, 1981. Tng. program coordinator Human Resources Assocs., Ann Arbor, Mich., 1984-85; adj. faculty in humanities Nat. U., Oakland and Sacramento, Calif., 1986-88; curriculum cons. communications and liberal studies John F. Kennedy U., Orinda, Calif., 1987-88; sr. lectr. Hutchins Sch. Liberal Studies Sonoma State U., Rohnert Park, Calif., 1987—; pres. Ednl. Consortium, Greenbrae, Calif., 1987—; instr. grant writing San Francisco, Napa and Sacramento community colls., 1987—; lectr. Exploritorium Sci. Mus., San Francisco, 1989; producer Worldwide Media, San Rafael, Calif., 1984-87. Author: Lise Meitner: The Life and Times of a Pioneering Woman Physicist 1878-1968, 1990; author oral history rev., book revs.; producer, dir. ednl. wideo Chain Reaction: Dawn of the Nuclear Age. Mem. Israel Women Tech. Conf. Swedish Inst. grantee, 1981, 88, NSF travel grantee, 1989; History of Sci. Unaffiliated scholar, 1987; recipient Young Writers award Detroit News, 1970. Mem. ACLU, History of Sci. Soc. (Unaffiliated Scholars award 1986), Greenpeace, Nat. Assn. Female Execs. Office: Sonoma State U Hutchins Sch. Liberal Stud Rohnert Park CA 94928

RIFFE, CONNIE DIANNE, information systems training manager; b. Galipolis, Ohio, Sept. 14, 1957; d. Frank Eugene and Lois Marie (Noonkester) R. Grad., J. Sargeant Reynolds Community Coll., 1990. Sec. Commonwealth of Va. Dept. Planning and Budget, Richmond, 1975-78; personnel sec. Commonwealth of Va. Dept. Info. Tech., Richmond, 1978-79, personnel asst., 1979, asst. personnel mgr., tng. coordinator, 1979-84, tng. & career devel. mgr., 1984—. Mem. Richmond Info. Systems Educators (sec. 1984, program chairperson 1986-87, v.p. 1989-90, pres. 1990—), Richmond Large Users Group, Data Processing Mgmt. Assn. (mem. edn. com. 1987—), Am. Soc. Tng. and Devel., Richmond Volleyball Club, Assn. Psychol. Type. Office: Commonwealth of Va Dept Info Tech 110 S 7th St 3d Fl Richmond VA 23219

RIFFONE, DIANNA LYNN, fundraising executive; b. Plainview, N.Y., Jan. 15, 1965; d. Edward Andrew and Joyce Lynn (Schiller) R. BA, NYU, 1987. Account exec. Burson-Marsteller, N.Y.C., 1987-89; devel. assoc. Catalyst, N.Y.C., 1989—. Office: Catalyst 250 Park Ave S New York NY 10003

RIFKIND, ARLEEN B., physician, researcher; b. N.Y.C., June 29, 1938; d. Michael C. and Regina (Gottlieb) Brenner; m. Robert S. Rifkind, Dec. 24, 1961; children—Amy, Nina. B.A., Bryn Mawr Coll., 1960; M.D., NYU, 1964; Lic. M.D., N.Y. Intern Bellevue Hosp., N.Y.C., 1964-65, resident, 1965; clin. assoc. Nat. Inst. Child Health and Human Devel. Endocrine br. Nat. Cancer Inst., 1965-68; research assoc., asst. resident physician Rockefeller U., 1968-71; asst. prof. medicine Cornell U. Med. Coll., N.Y.C., 1971-82, assoc. prof. medicine, 1983—, asst. prof. pharmacology, 1973-78, assoc. prof., 1978-82, prof., 1983—; chmn. Gen. Faculty Council Cornell U. Med. Coll., 1984-86, Nat. Inst. Environ. Health Scis. Rev. Com., 1985-86; mem. toxicology study sect. Nat. Inst. Health, 1989—. Contbr. articles to profl. jours. Chmn. Friends of the Library, Jewish Theol. Sem. Am., 1984-86. mem. bd. Library Corp, 1982— ; trustee Dalton Sch., 1986—; mem. Environ. Health and Safety Coun. Am. Health Found., 1990— . Recipient Andrew W. Mellon Tchr.-Scientist award, 1976-78; USPHS spl. fellow, 1968-70, 71-72. Mem. Endocrine Soc., Am. Soc. Clin. Investigation, Am. Soc. Pharmacology and Exptl. Therapeutics, AAAS, Soc. Toxicology. Office: Cornell U Med Coll Dept Pharmacology 1300 York Ave New York NY 10021

RIFMAN, EILEEN NISSENBAUM, music educator; b. Bklyn., June 10, 1944; d. Jack and Sarah (Bednarsh) Nissenbaum; m. Samuel Sholom Rifman, Aug. 12, 1972; children: Edward, Aimee. MusB, Manhattan Sch. Music, 1966, M Music Edn., 1967; MusM, Ind. U., 1970; cert., Fontainebleau, France, 1967. Music specialist N.Y.C. Pub. Sch. System, 1966-67; instr. Long Beach (Calif.) City Coll., 1970-72, Immaculate Heart Coll., Hollywood, Calif., 1971-74, Univ. Judaism, Hollywood, 1973-74; co-coord. Community Sch. Performing Arts, L.A., 1974-82, instr., 1973-83; pvt. piano tchr. Manhattan Beach, Calif., 1963—. Performer Pratt Inst., Clinton Hill Symphony, N.Y.C., 1962, WNYC-FM, 1964. Chair Cultural Arts Com., Manhattan Beach, 1985-86; bd. dirs. Hermosa Beach (Calif.) Community Ctr., 1990—. Mem. AAUW, Music Tchrs. Assn., Nat. Fedn. Music Clubs (adjudicator 1970). Home: 1700 Lynngrove Dr Manhattan Beach CA 90266

RIFNER, LOIS JEAN, clinical child psychologist; b. Rushville, Ind., Apr. 30, 1947; d. Ben Orison and Luella Elizabeth (Kinney) R.; m. Vincent Anthony Mabert, June 16, 1973 (div. 1975). BA, Ind. U., 1970; PhD, Ohio State U., 1977. Lic. psychologist, Ind. Clin. psychology intern Case Western Res. U., Cleve., 1974-75; staff psychologist Akron (Ohio) Child Guidance Ctr., 1975-78, South Cen. Community Mental Health Ctr., Bedford, Ind., 1978-84; pvt. practice Bedford, 1982—; adj. prof. Ind. U., Bloomington, 1984. Bd. dirs. The Villages, Inc., Topeka, Kans., 1980—; bd. dirs., v.p. The Villages of Ind., Inc., Bloomington, 1979—; sec., pres. Lawrence Interfaith Endeavor food pantry, Bedford, 1986-89; founding mem. Domestic Violence Intervention Network, Bedford, 1989—. Mem. Am. Psychol. Assn., Ind. Psychol. Assn. (div. sec. 1988-90), Psi Iota Xi (nat. editor 1988-89). Office: 1429 J St Ste B PO Box 213 Bedford IN 47421-0213

RIGAUD, MARIE-CLAUDE, psychiatrist; b. Port-Au-Prince, Haiti, Jan. 24, 1939; came to U.S. 1964; d. Antoine Dolbrise and Charlotte (Aarons) Saint-Jean; m. Andre Rigaud, Sept. 30, 1961; children: Carl, Ralph, J-Philippe, Cassandre, Joseph, Claudine. Bachelor, Pensionnat Sterose de Lima, Haiti, 1956; MD, U. Haiti, 1962; MPH, U. Ill., Chgo, 1988. Diplomate Am. Bd. Psychiatry and Neurology. Resident in pub. health, Plaisance, Haiti, 1962-63, Pont-Sonde, Haiti, 1963-64; resident in psychiatry Seton Psychiat. Inst., Balt., 1966-69, sr. staff supr., 1970-73; house physician in medicine and obstetrics Provident Hosp., Balt., 1965-66; staff psychiatrist

Spring Grove State Hosp., Balt., 1969-70; med. dir. Psychiat. Day Hosp., Seton Inst., 1971-73; practice medicine, specializing in psychiatry, 1973—; psychiat. cons. to med. dept. and EAP program, Western Electric Co., Aurora, Ill., 1979-85; assoc. med. dir. Psychiat. substance Abuse Rev., Republic RSB, Naperville, Ill., Cardiac Rehab. Program, Copley Meml. Hosp., Aurora; med. staff Mercy Ctr. for Health Care Svcs., Aurora; cons. HMO Ill., Blue Cross Blue Shield; lectr. in field. Fellow Am. Psychiat. Assn.; mem. Ill. Psychiat. Soc., Am. Psychiat. Soc., Assn. Haitian Physicians Abroad (past pres.). Roman Catholic. Home: 13 Mossfield Ct Aurora IL 60506 Office: PO Box 2816 Aurora IL 60507

RIGELWOOD, DIANE COLLEEN, insurance adjuster, administrator; b. Savannah, Ga., Apr. 24, 1950; d. William Howell III and Ruth Colleen (Treanor) Bridges; m. Frank DeWayne Rigelwood; 1 child, Stephanie Michelle Rigelwood Metzger. Student, Savannah Tech., 1968-69. Bookkeeper Nat. Heritage Group, Savannah, 1972-74; ins. adjuster Gab Bus. Svcs., Inc., Savannah, 1974-86, Cramer Johnson White & Assocs., Savannah, 1986-89, Gay & Taylor, Savannah, 1989—. Pres. Isle of Hope PTA, Savannah, 1978. Mem. Nat. Assn. Ins. Women Internat. (Savannah chpt.), Savannah Claims Assn. Republican. Office: Gay & Taylor Inc 320 Montgomery Crossroads Savannah GA 31406

RIGGLEMAN, SHIRLEY EVELYN, school system supervisor; b. Wellsburg, W.Va., Oct. 5, 1934; d. Eugene Clifford and Elma Maxine (Cook) Jeans; m. Ronald James Riggleman, July 17, 1956; 1 child, Rhonda Jean Riggleman Sartoris. BS in Elem. Edn., Kent (Ohio) State U., 1956; MS in Elem. Edn., U. Pitts., 1971; postgrad., U. Dayton, Ohio, 1970, U. Steubenville, Ohio, 1980. Cert. tchr., Ohio. Tchr. elem. Toronto (Ohio) City Schs., 1956-81, tchr. jr. high, 1981-87, supr. curriculum, 1985-87, ret., 1987. Mem. Toronto Svcs. Com., 1990—; pres. Lidramu, Toronto, 1972-74; pres., chmn. ARC, Steubenville, 1987-90. NDEA fellow Kent State U., 1969; Annie Webb Blanton scholar, 1970; Hilda Maehling Found. grantee, NEA, 1986, Martha Holden Jennings Found. grantee, 1986. Mem. Ohio Edn. Assn., Ohio Ret. Tchrs. Edn. Assn., Toronto Edn. Assn. (pres., treas., bldg. rep., negotiations chairperson 1960-87), Ea. Ohio Tchrs. Assn. (pres. 1975-76), Literacy Coun. (adult tutor Upper Ohio Valley chpt. 1987—), AAUW (pres. 1988-90), Dyer County Club Women's Golf Assn. (pres. 1988-90), Riverview United Meth. Women (pres. 1985-90, Outstanding Svc. award 1988), Delta Kappa Gamma (pres. 1980-82, Annie Webb Blanton award 1971). Republican.

RIGGS, ANNA CLAIRE, metals service company executive; b. Danville, Ind., Jan. 22, 1944; d. Leland Wesley and Mary Alice (Miller) Cox; m. Michael Ross Riggs, Dec. 10, 1983; 1 child, Matthew. B.S. in Edn., Ind. U., 1966. Credit tng. and promotion mgr. L.S. Ayres, Indpls., 1966-74, cons., credit dept., 1984; credit ops. mgr. Burdine's, Miami, Fla., 1974-77; br. mgr. Centaur Metals, Indpls., 1977-85; gen. mgr. Copper & Brass Sales, Indpls., 1985—, Louisville, 1989—; promotion dir. Ind. Jersey Cattle Club. Children's choir dir. and Sun sch. tchr. United Meth. Ch., Danville, Ind. Mem. Nat. Assn. Female Execs., Am. Jersey Cattle Club (exec. com., all am. 1990), Beta Sigma Phi (pres., advisor). Avocations: traveling, sewing, reading. Home: 107 Martin Dr Danville IN 46122 Office: Copper & Brass Sales 8002 Woodland Dr Indianapolis IN 46278

RIGGSBEE, JACQUELINE SUE, personnel and staffing professional; b. Apex, N.C., Aug. 27, 1950; d. Edward Jackson and Peggy Allen (Stone) R. Grad., Hardbarger Bus. Coll., 1969; Student, N.C. State U., 1983, Meredith Coll., 1983. Lic. real estate salesman. Sec. Wake County Pub. Schs., Raleigh, N.C., 1969-74; legal sec. Poyner, Geraghty, Hartsfield & Townsend, Raleigh, 1974-75; exec. sec. Crabtree Valley Shopping Ctr., Raleigh, 1975-80; office mgr., exec. sec. Pennington Assocs., Inc., Raleigh, 1980-81; adminstrv. sec. V N.C. State U., Raleigh, 1981-82; adminstrv. asst II N.C. State U., 1981-88; supr. adminstrv. svcs. dept. contracts adminstrn. SAS Inst. Inc., Cary, N.C., 1988—; instr. Cen. Carolina Tech. Coll., Sanford, 1980; customer svc. rep. Thalhimer's Dept. Stores, Raleigh, 1985—; personnel cons. Smith & Assocs., Cary, 1989; bookkeeper Woodcock TV, Sumter, S.C., 1988—. Bd. dirs. YWCA Wake County, Raleigh, 1983-84, Wake County Mental Health Assn., 1988; gov.'s appointee N.C. Assembly on Women and Economy, 1983; foreman Fed. Grand Jury, U.S. Dist. Ct. (ea. dist.) N.C., 1987-89. Named Career Woman of Yr., Raleigh Bus. and Profl. Women's Club, 1984. Fellow Cert. Profl. Sec. Acad.; mem. Profl. Secs. Internat. (pres. Raleighchpt. 1979-80, 87-88, N.C. pres. 1983-84, Outstanding Mem. award 1977, Sec. of Yr. award 1980), Wolfpack Club, Zonta Club Raleigh, NAFE, Wake County Mental Health Assn. Nat. Notary Assn. Democrat. Baptist. Home: 5602 E Falls of Neuse Rd Raleigh NC 27609 Office: SAS Inst Inc SAS Campus Dr Cary NC 27513-2414

RIGGSBY, DUTCHIE SELLERS, education educator; b. Montgomery, Ala., Oct. 26, 1940; d. Cleveland Malcolm and Marcelia (Bedsole) Sellers; m. Ernest Duward Riggsby, Aug. 25, 1962; 1 child, Lyn. BS, Troy (Ala.) State Coll., 1962, MS, 1965; postgrad., George Peabody Coll., 1968; EdD, Auburn U., 1972. Cert. tchr., Ala., Ga.; cert. libr., Ga. Tchr. Montgomery Pub. Sch.s, 1962-63, Troy City Schs., 1963-67; instr. Auburn (Ala.) U., 1968-69; asst. prof. Columbus (Ga.) Coll., 1972-77, assoc. prof., 1978-83, prof., 1983—; visiting prof. U. Puerto Rico, Rio Piedras, 1972, 73; cons. schs. Columbus and Ft. Benning, Ga., 1980—; leader various workshops, 1989. Photographer: (book) Families, Professionals and Exceptionality, 1986, (textbook) Counseling Parents of Exceptional Children, 1986; contbr. more than 75 articles to profl. jours., 1968-87. Educator internal aerospace CAP, Maxwell AFB, 1980—. Recipient STAR Tchr. award Nat. Sci. Tchrs. Assn., Washington, 1968. Mem. Nat. Congress on Aviation and Space Edn. (dir. spl. promotions 1986—), World Aerospace Edn. Org., Ga. Assn. Instructional Tech. (bd. dirs. 1982-84), Phi Delta Kappa (pres. Chattahochee Valley chpt. 1986-87, Svc. award 1989). Baptist. Home: 1709 Ashwood Ct Columbus GA 31904-3009 Office: Columbus Coll Sch Edn Columbus GA 31993-2399

RIGHTHAND, VERA FAY, virologist; b. Pittsfield, Mass., Sept. 4, 1930; d. Benjamin and Nellie (Maizen) R. BA, U. Rochester, 1952; PhD in Microbiology, Rutgers U. Jr. biologist Am. Cyanamid Co., Stamford, Conn., 1952-55; rsch. asst. Rockefeller U., N.Y.C., 1955-59; predoctoral fellow Inst. Microbiology Rutgers U., New Brunswick, N.J., 1959-63; from instr. to asst. prof. SUNY, Buffalo, 1963-68; assoc. prof. Wayne State U., Detroit, 1968—, dep., chmn. dept., 1975-78; v.p. faculty senate Wayne State U. Sch. of Medicine, 1977-78, coun. mem. univ. faculty, 1983-87; cons. NIH, 1981; speaker at numerous nat. and internat. meetings in field. Author textbook chpts. in microbiology/virology; contbr. articles to profl. jours. Rsch. grantee NIH, 1970—, NSF, 1984-86, Children's Leukemia Found. of Mich., 1970-74; recipient merit awards Wayne State U. Fellow Acad. for Microbiology; mem. Am. Soc. for Microbiology (councilor 1984-88, treas. Mich. br. 1989—, exec. com. 1984—), Soc. Gen. Microbiology, Am. Soc. Virology, AAAS. Office: Dept Immunol & Microbiology Wayne State Univ Sch Med 540 E Canfield Ave Detroit MI 48201

RIGHTS, EDITH MARIE ANDERSON, librarian; b. Kearney, Nebr., Sept. 27, 1927; d. Frans Leander and Ruth Mary (Gitchel) Anderson; m. Robert Matthew Rights, Aug. 21, 1949; children: David Leander, Bruce Theodore, John Christian. BA, Bethany Coll., 1950; MA, Montclair State Coll., 1962; MS in Libr. Sci., Columbia U., 1983. Acting libr. Bethany Coll. Libr., Lindsborg, Kans., 1948; part-time staff Montclair (N.J.) State Coll., 1950-52; part-time staff mem. Upsala Coll., East Orange, N.J., 1966-68; libr. Montclair Art Mus., 1968—; seminar panelist grad. sch. Rutgers U., New Brunswick, 1980; libr. cons. Parrish Art Mus., Southampton, 1983. Curator, author (exhibition and catalog) Ex Libris: Selected Bookplates of Arthur Nelson Macdonald, 1986, The Bookplate Work of David McNeely Stauffer, 1990, (book) The Bookplates of A.N. Macdonald, 1986. Co-chairperson Art in Sussex County (N.J.), 1980-82; chairperson Art Librs. Soc. N.J., 1970-72, 80-82. Recipient 1st prize 4th Annual Exbn., Sumi-e Soc. N. Am., N.Y.C., 1966. Mem. Art Librs. Soc. N. Am., Spl. Librs. Soc., ALA (Coll. and Rsch. Librs.), N.J. Libr. Assn., Bookplate Soc. London. Republican. Lutheran. Home: 33 Brookfield Rd Upper Montclair NJ 07043 Office: Montclair Art Mus 3 S Mountain Ave Montclair NJ 07042

RIGO, MARION LEE BENNETT, interior designer, business owner; b. Hot Springs, Ark., Sept. 22, 1948; d. Jim Boss Bennett and Elma (Ferguson) Rhoades; m. Michael Maurice Rigo; children: Clifford Craig Smith, Donald Lee Smith, Amy Michelle Rigo. BS in Criminal Justice, Brenau Coll., 1983; grad. planning and design, Art Inst. of Atlanta, 1989. Patrol officer Cobb County Dept. Pub. Safety, Marietta, 1976-80; state trooper Ga. Dept. Pub. Safety, 1980-84; coord. security Lockheed-Ga., Marietta, 1984-86, engring. property analyst, 1986-88; mgr., interior designer Rigo's Antiques & Interior Design, Marietta, 1987—. Family coun. mem. Marietta Health Ctr., 1988—; troop leader N.W. Ga. Girl Scouts U.S. coun., Marietta, 1988-90; mem. Marietta City Coun., 1990—; bd. dirs. Crime Victims Adv. Coun., Marietta Bd. Lights and Water. Mem. NAFE, Cobb County C. of C. (mem. convention and tourism steering com.), Exec. Connection Cobb County C. of C. (mem. mng. com.), Am. Bus. Women's Assn. (pres. 1987), Nat. League Cities and Communities. Home: 67 Oakmont Dr Marietta GA 30064 Office: Rigo's Antiques & Interior Design Marietta GA 30060

RIGSBY, ROSEANNE CAROLE, veterinarian; b. Greenville, Ky., Sept. 4, 1956; d. James Bryan and Hazel Annette (Tooley) R. BS, Mich. State U., 1979, DVM, 1983. Veterinarian Lapeer (Mich.) Animal Hosp., 1983-84, Westcott Vet. Care Ctrs., Detroit, 1985-87, Shaker Vet. Hosp., Latham, N.Y., 1987-89, North Clarksville (Tenn.) Animal Clinic, 1989—. Mem. Am. Vet. Med. Assn., Am. Animal Hosp. Assn.

RIGSBY, SHEILA G., accounting firm executive; b. Macon, Ga., June 13, 1955; d. David Wendell and Carolyn (Canington) Goree; children: Jason, Ryan. Student, Macon Coll., 1979. Tax preparer Better Income Tax Svc., Macon; acct. Bass Tool and Indsl. Supply, Macon, Padgett Bus. Svc., Macon; owner Ind. Acctg. Svcs., Macon. Mem. NAFE, GAPA, NFIB, NSTP. Office: 4000 Mercer University Dr Macon GA 31204

RIIKONEN, NANCY COOPER, municipal government industrial waste professional; b. Fitchburg, Mass., May 25, 1938; d. Urho Emil and Laila Onerva (Kallio) R.; m. Gary David Cooper, Nov. 25, 1961 (div. 1980); children: Jessica Elizabeth, James Courtney. AA with honors, Mesa Community Coll., 1977; BA with honors, Nat. U., San Diego, 1982. Lab tech. pretreatment program City of San Diego, 1980-81, chemist pretreatment program, 1981-82, inspector pretreatment program, 1982-86, permits supr. pretreatment program, 1986-87, compliance sect. supr. pretreatment program, 1987—. Author, editor: Indsl. Waste Inspection Guide. Mem. Calif. Water Pollution Control Assn. (cert. chmn. for area inspection 1988—), House of Finland (pres. houses of pacific rels. 1987, 88, newsletter editor 1985—). Democrat. Home: 2944 Bancroft St San Diego CA 92104 Office: SanDiegoIndsl Waste Program 2799 Caminito Chollas San Diego CA 92105

RIKLEEN, LAUREN STILLER, lawyer; b. Winthrop, Mass., Apr. 29, 1953; d. Joseph Stiller and Elaine Lillian (Brodie) Stiller; m. Sander A. Rikleen, May 25, 1975. Student, Clark U., 1971-73; BA, magna cum laude, Brandeis U., 1975; JD, Boston Coll., 1979. Bar: Mass. 1979, U.S. Dist. Ct. Mass. 1980, U.S. Ct. Appeals (1st cir.) 1980, U.S. Supreme Ct. 1985. Asst. dir. Flaschner Jud. Inst., Boston, 1979-81; atty. enforcement div. EPA, Boston, 1981-82, Office Regional Counsel, 1982-84; asst. v.p. for negotiations Clean Sites, Inc., Alexandria, Va., 1984-87; asst. atty. gen. Mass. Dept. of the Atty. Gen., 1987-88; chair environ. practice area Bowditch & Dewey, Worcester and Framingham, Mass., 1988—; lectr., author environ. law. Mem. Wayland Planning Bd., Mass., 1980-83; mem. Met. Area Planning Coun., Boston, 1980-84; bd. dirs. Metrowest Leadership Acad., 1989—; bd. vis. Clark U., 1989—; pres. Metrowest Harvest, Women's Independence Network. Mem. ABA (natural resources com.), Boston Bar Assn. (environ. sect.), Soc. Profls. in Dispute Resolution. Democrat. Office: Bowditch & Dewey 205 Newbury St Framingham MA 01701

RILEY, ALICE HEISKELL, social services administrator, management consultant; b. Phila.; d. James Theodore and Alice (Heiskell) Harris; m. William L. Watkins, Dec. 19, 1946 (div. Aug. 1954); children: Teresita L. Watkins Dorrall, William L. Jr.; m. Raymond E. Riley, Nov. 11, 1962 (dec. May 1985). BA in History, Glassboro (N.J.) State Coll., 1973; MPA, Cen. Mich. U., 1978; postgrad., Princeton U., 1978-79. Adminstrv. asst. Johnson & Johnson, New Brunswick, N.J., 1966-69, community relations specialist, 1969-72; field rep. N.J. Dept. Civil Service, Trenton, 1972-73; field coordinator Div. of Youth and Family Services, Trenton, 1974-77, 1979-87, adminstrv. analyst, 1987—; asst. dep. commr. N.J. Dept. of Banking, Trenton, 1977-79; cons. Higher Edn. Assistance, Albany, N.Y., 1978—, Wanda Webster Stansbury Assoc., Trenton, 1979-84; cons. in field; banking rep. Fed. Exec. Bd. of Minority Bus. Enterprise, 1977-79. Coordinator Womens Polit. Caucus, Burlington County, N.J., 1974-77; mem. rules com. Dem. Nat. Conv., Washington, 1978. Fellow Am. Soc. of Pub. Adminstrs., Am. Mgmt. Assn., Alpha Kappa Alpha; mem. Nat. Polit. Congress, League of Women Voters (chmn. human resources 1968), Minority Womens Network (co-chair, chair 1987—), 100 Black Women of South (chair econ. devel. 1986), Sigma Iota Epsilon. Republican. Roman Catholic. Home: 139 Country Club Ln Willingboro NJ 08046 Office: Div Youth & Family Services 1 S Montgomery Trenton NJ 08625

RILEY, CATHERINE IRENE, state senator; b. Balt., Mar. 21, 1947; d. Francis Worth and Catherine (Cain) R. BA, Towson State U., 1969. Bacteriologist Balt. City Hosp., 1969-72; legis. aide Md. Ho. of Dels., Annapolis, 1973-74, mem., 1975-82; mem. Md. State Senate, Annapolis, 1982—; cons. Md. State Div. Alcoholism Control, 1973; mem. House Environ. Matters Com., 1975-82; mem. Spl. Joint Com. Energy, 1977-83, chmn., 1978-79, 1980-83; mem. So. Legis. Conf. Energy Com. 1978, Environ. Com., 1983—, vice chmn., 1985—, chair senate fin. com., 1987—, joint budget & audit com., 1988—; mem. So. Environ. Resource Coun., 1978, Power Plant Siting Adv. Com., 1977—, State of Md. Energy Conservation Bd., 1978-83, Fire Safety Subcom., 1981-83; mem. BiState Cheasapeake Bay Commn., 1981-83, chmn. 1982; chmn. Forest Land Task Force, 1981-84, Budget and Taxation Senate Com., 1983-86, Subcom. Edn., Health, and Human Resources, 1983-86, Nat. Conf. State Legis. Energy Commn., 1983—; senate chmn. adminstrv. exec. and legis. review com., 1983-86, Ho. of Dels. mem. 1978-82; various state govt. coms. and subcoms. Contbr. articles to profl. jours. Mem. adv. com. State Edn. Policy Seminars Adv. Com., 1983—, Protective Svcs. to Children and Families, 1983—; exec. bd. Balt. Area Coun. Boy Scouts Am., 1983—; hon. chmn. Am. Cancer Soc., 1982-83; mem. Harford County Child Protection Coun., 1978-80, vice chmn. 1980; mem. Harford County Coun. Community Svcs., 1976—, Harford County legis. del., 1975-82, chmn. 1976, 1980-82; mem. Md. Order Women Legislators, 1975—, sec. 1976-79; mem. adv. bd. Susquehanna State Park, 1975—; mem. Joppatowne Womens Club, 1975—, No. Md. Assn. for Retarded Citizens, Inc., 1975—, Upper Cheasepeake Watershed Assn., Inc., 1975—. Recipient Disting. Svc. award Md. State Troopers, 1980, Community Svc. award, United Way, 1978, Disting. Svc. award Jaycees, 1976, Liberty award Harford Christian High Sch., 1975, Cert. of Appreciation Md. Mcpl. League, 1984, William P. Coliton Outstanding Community Svc. award Johns Hopkins U., 1985, Outstanding Alumni award, 1989; named Young Dem. of Yr. State of Md., 1975, Women of Yr. Soroptimist Club, 1980; Guide State Govt. Toll fellow, 1987, other state and civic awards. Mem. Towson State U. Alumni Assn. (admissions coun. 1975—, chmn. fund drive 1980), Md. Jaycee Women, Izaak Walton League. Office: Md State Senate Annapolis MD 21401

RILEY, DOLORES MARIE, educational administrator; b. Ft. Thompson, S.D., Nov. 18, 1941; d. Richard LaRoche and Violet Margaret (Langdeau) Rekow; m. Michael L. Riley, Oct. 12, 1973; children: Michael, Tamara Hill, Terry Pexa, Lanny Pexa, Nicole P. BS in Elem. Edn., Black Hills State, 1977; MA in Edn., Western State Coll., 1979. Tchr. Rapid City (S.D.) Area Sch. Dist., 1977, dir. Indian edn., 1978, dir. bilingual edn., 1981-82; tchr. Logan Utah Dist., 1983-84; tchr. Salt Lake City Schs., 1984-85, elem. prin., 1985—; proposal reviewer D.C. Dept. Edn., Washington, 1977-82, 83, 85; evaluator U. N.D., Grand Forks, 1984-85; cons. Ute Tribe, Ft. Duchesne, Utah, 1981, Sioux Tribe, Lower Brule, S.D., 1982, Hopi Tribe, Oraibi, Ariz., 1984; adj. instr. U. Utah, 1985—. Mem. gov.'s Commn. on Status of Women in Utah, 1988, S.D. State Commn. on Human Relations, 1973. Fellow Utah Prins. Acad.; mem. Nat. Assn. Elem. Prins., Salt Lake Assn. Sch. Adminstrs. (treas. 1986-87), Utah Assn. Tchr. Edn., Assn. Supervision and Curriculum Devel., Utah Women in Adminstrn. (pres. 1989-90), Phi Delta Kappa. Republican. Office: Salt Lake City Sch 400 N 200 W Salt Lake City UT 84103

RILEY, DOROTHY COMSTOCK, state supreme court chief justice; b. Detroit, Dec. 6, 1924; d. Charles Austin and Josephine (Grima) Comstock; m. Wallace Don Riley, Sept. 13, 1963; 1 child, Peter Comstock. B.A. in Polit. Sci., Wayne State U., 1946, LL.B., 1949; LLD (hon.), Alama Coll., 1988. Bar: Mich. 1950, U.S. Dist. Court (ea. dist.) Mich. 1950, U.S. Supreme Court 1957. Atty. Wayne County Friend of Court, Detroit, 1956-68; ptnr. Riley & Roumell, Detroit, 1968-72; judge Wayne County Circuit, Detroit, 1972, Mich. Ct. Appeals, Detroit, 1976-82; justice Mich. Supreme Court, Detroit, 1982-83, 85-87; chief justice Mich. Supreme Court, Lansing, 1987—; mem. U.S. Jud. Conf. Commn. on State-Fed. Court Relations; chmn. tort reform com. Conf. of Chief Justices; bd. dirs. Nat. Ctr. for State Cts. Co-author manuals, articles in field. Mem. adv. com. Citizenship Edn. Study, 1946-50. Recipient Disting. Alumni award Wayne U. Law Sch., 1977; Headliner award Women of Wayne, 1977; Donnelly award, 1946. Mem. ABA (family law sect. 1965—; vice chmn. gen. practice sect. com. on juvenile justice 1975-80; mem. jud. adminstrn. sect. 1973—, standing com. on fed. ct. improvements), Am. Judicature Soc., Fellows Am. Bar Found., Mich. State Bar Found., State Bar Mich. (civil liberties com. 1954-58, young lawyers sect. 1956-60, family law sect. 1966—), Detroit Bar Assn. (pub. relations com. 1955-56, author com. in Action column, Detroit Lawyers 1955, chmn. friend of ct. and family law com. 1974-75), Nat. Women Judges Assn., Nat. Women Lawyers Assn., Women Lawyers Assn. Mich. (pres. 1957-58), Karyatides, Pi Sigma Alpha. Republican. Roman Catholic. Club: Women's Econ. Office: Mich Supreme Ct PO Box 30052 Lansing MI 48909*

RILEY, DOROTHY ELAINE, nursing home administrator; b. Boston, July 4, 1944; d. Daniel Thomas and Josephine Marie (Durken) Horgan; m. Timothy John Riley, Feb. 3, 1968; children: Timothy John Jr., Christopher John, Shannon Marie. BS in Nursing, Boston Coll., 1966; MS in Nursing, U. Wis., Milw., 1977. Cert. advanced nursing adminstr. Staff nurse various hosps., 1969-75; dir. nursing Samaritan Home, West Bend, Wis., 1975-76; mem. nursing faculty Marquette U., Milw., 1977-79; asst. dir. nursing Outagamie County Health Care Ctr., Appleton, Wis., 1979-80; mem. nursing faculty U. Wis., Oshkosh, 1980-83; nursing svc. adminstr. Brown County Mental Health Ctr., Green Bay, Wis., 1983-88, nursing home adminstr., 1988—; mem. adv. com. N.E. Tech. Coll., Green Bay, 1985—, U. Wis., Green Bay, 1986—, U. Wis., Oshkosh, 1987—. Lt. Nurses Corps USN, 1966-69. Named Nurse of Yr., Appleton Dist. Nurses Assn., 1984. Mem. Wis. Nurses Assn. (bd. dirs. 1984-86, sec. 1986-88), Green Bay Nurses Assn. (bd. dirs. 1986-89, pres. elect 1989-90, pres. 1990—), Sigma Theta Tau. Roman Catholic. Office: Brown County Mental Health Ctr 2900 St Anthony Dr Green Bay WI 54311

RILEY, FRANCENA, nurse, noncommissioned army officer; b. New Smyrna Beach, Fla., May 5, 1957; d. Willard Harrell and Jacqueline Delores (Griffen) R.; 1 child, Daniel Albert Cross. AA, U. Md., Heidelberg, Fed. Republic Germany, 1987. Enlisted U.S. Army, 1980, advanced through grades to staff sgt., 1985, parachutist; practical nurse Keller Army Hosp., West Point, N.Y., 1981; bn. tng. noncommd. officer 34th Med. Bn., Ft. Benning, Ga., 1988-89, practical nurse 2d Mobile Army Surg. Hosp., 1989—; practical nurse Walter Reed Army Med. Ctr., Washington, 1982-84; practical nurse, then nursing supr. 913th Med. Detachment, Kaiserslautern, Fed. Republic Germany, 1984-86; wardmaster surgery clinic Army Regional Med. Ctr., Landstuhl, Fed. Republic Germany, 1987. Baptist. Home: 104 Leonard St Apt B Fort Benning GA 31905 Office: 2d MASH 34th Med Bn Fort Benning GA 31905-5000

RILEY, GLENDA, history educator; b. Cleve., Sept. 9, 1938; d. George F. and Lillian B. (Knafels) Gates; 1 child, Sean Gates. BA, Western Res. U., 1960; MA, Miami U., Oxford, Oxio, 1963; PhD, Ohio State U., 1967. Instr. Denison U., Granville, Ohio, 1967-68; vis. asst. prof. Ohio State U., Columbus, 1968-69; successively asst. prof. history, assoc. prof., prof., dir. women's studies program, 1981-86, U. No. Iowa, Cedar Falls, 1969—. Author: Frontierswomen: The Iowa Experience, 1981; Women and Indians on the Frontier, 1984; Inventing the American Woman, 1985, The Female Frontier, 1988. Contbr. articles on women's history to profl. jours. NEH pilot grantee, 1980-81, NEH summer fellow, 1984, Huntington Libr. fellow, 1988-89; Fulbright scholar, 1986-87, Huntington Libr. fellow, 1988-89; recipient Palladin Writing award Mont. Hist. Soc., 1984; named AMUW Prof. Marquette U., 1990; named to Iowa Women's Hall of Fame, 1990. Mem. Orgn. Am. Historians, Nat. Coun. Pub. History, Nat. Women's Studies Assn., Am. Assn. State and Local History (Award of Merit, 1986), Western History Assn. (nominating bd. 1984-86), Rotary. Avocations: photography, travel, hiking, biking. Home: 3908 Heritage Rd Cedar Falls IA 50614 Office: U No Iowa Dept History Cedar Falls IA 50614

RILEY, LISA MARIE, business analyst; b. Hastings, Minn., Oct. 27, 1961; d. James Edward and Sophie Ester (Rosenberger) R. Staff auditor corp. fin. audit div. Honeywell Inc., Mpls., 1984-85, lead auditor corp. fin. audit div., 1985-87; product line acct. indsl. controls div. Honeywell Inc., Ft. Washington, Pa., 1987-88, mfg. resource planning II program mgr. indsl. controls div., 1988-89, exec. bus. analyst, 1989—. Chairperson United Way Drive, Ft. Washington, 1988-89. Democrat. Roman Catholic. Office: Honeywell Indsl Automation and Controls 16404 N Black Canyon Hwy Phoenix AZ 85023

RILEY, MATILDA WHITE (MRS. JOHN W. RILEY, JR.), science administrator, emeritus sociology educator; b. Boston, Apr. 19, 1911; d. Percival and Mary (Cliff) White; m. John Winchell Riley, Jr., June 19, 1931; children: John Winchell III, Lucy Ellen Riley Sallick. A.B., Radcliffe Coll., 1931, M.A., 1937; D.Sc., Bowdoin Coll., 1972; L.H.D. (hon.), Rutgers U., 1983. Rsch. asst. Harvard U., 1932; v.p. Market Rsch. Co. Am., 1938-49; chief cons. economist WPB, 1941; rsch. specialist Rutgers U., 1950, prof., 1951-73, dir. sociology lab., chmn. dept. sociology and anthropology, 1959-73, emeritus prof., 1973—; Daniel B. Fayerweather prof. polit. econ. and sociology Bowdoin Coll., 1974-81, prof. emeritus, 1981—; assoc. dir. Nat. Inst. on Aging, 1979—; mem. faculty Harvard U., summer 1955; staff assoc., dir. aging and society Russell Sage Found., 1964-73, staff sociologist, 1974-77; chmn. com. on life course Social Sci. Rsch. Coun., 1977-80; sr. rsch. assoc. Ctr. for Social Scis., Columbia U., 1978-80; adv. bd. Carnegie Aging Soc. Project, 1985-87; mem. Commn. on Coll. Retirement, 1982-86; vis. prof. NYU, 1954-61; cons. Nat. Coun. on Aging, Acad. Ednl. Devel.; mem. study group NIH, 1971-79, Social Sci. Rsch. Coun. Com. on Middle Years, 1973-77; chmn. NIH Task Force on Health and Behavior, 1986—; cons. WHO, 1987—; Winkelman lectr. U. Mich., 1984; Selo lectr. U. No. Calif., 1987; Disting. lectr. Southwestern Social Scis. Assn., 1990. Author: (with P. White) Gliding and Soaring, (with Riley and Toby) Sociological Studies in Scale Analysis, 1954, Sociological Research, vols. I, II, 1964, (with others) Aging and Society, vol. I, 1968, vol. II, 1969, vol. III, 1972, (with Nelson) Sociological Observation, 1974, Aging from Birth to Death: Interdisciplinary Perspectives, 1979, (with Merton) Sociological Traditions from Generation to Generation, 1980, (with Abeles and Teitelbaum) Aging from Birth to Death: Sociotemporal Perspectives, 1982, (with Hess and Bond) Aging in Society, 1983; editor: AIDS in an Aging Society, 1989; co-editor: Perspectives in Behavioral Medicine: The Aging Dimension, 1987; (with J.W. Riley) The Quality of Aging, 1989; The Annuals jour., 1989; editorial com.: Ann. Rev. Sociology, 1978-81, Social Change and the Life Course, Vol. 1, Social Structures and Human Lives, (with B. Huber and B. Hess) Sociological Lives, 1988, (with M. Ory and D. Zablotsky) AIDS in and Aging Society: What We Need to Know, 1989; contbr. articles to profl. jours. Fromer trustee The Big Sisters Assn. Recipient Lindback Rsch. award Rutgers U., 1970, Social Sci. award Andrus Gerontology Ctr., U. So. Calif., 1972, Radcliffe Alumnae award, 1982, Commonwealth award 1984, Kesten Lecture award U. So. Calif., 1987, Sci. Achievement award Washington Acad. Scis., 1989, Disting. Sci. award, 1989; fellow Advanced Study in Behaviorial Scis., 1978-79; Matilda White Riley award in rsch. and methodology established in her honor Rutgers U., 1977; Matilda White Riley prize established Bowdoin Coll., 1987. Fellow AAAS (chmn. sect. on social and econ. scis. 1977-78); mem. Inst. Medicine of NAS (sr.), Acad. Behavioral Medicine Rsch., Am. Sociol. Assn. (exec. officer 1949-60, v.p. 1973-74, pres. 1986, chmn.-elect sect. on sociology of aging 1988, Disting. Scholar in Aging 1988), Am. Assn. Public Opinion Rsch. (sec.-treas. 1949-51, Disting. Svc. award 1983), Eastern Sociol. Soc. (v.p. 1968-69, pres. 1977-78, Disting. Career award 1986), Soc. for Study Social Biology (bd. dirs. 1986—), Am. Acad. Arts and Scis., D.C. Sociol. Soc. (co-pres. 1983-84), Sociol. Rsch. Assn., Internat. Orgn. Study Human Devel., Am. Philos. Soc. (membership lectr. 1987), Phi Beta Kappa,

Phi Beta Kappa Assocs. Home: 4701 Willard Ave Apt 1607 Chevy Chase MD 20815 Office: NIH Nat Inst on Aging 9000 Rockville Pike Bethesda MD 20205

RILEY, PATRICIA YVONNE, veterinarian; b. El Paso, Tex., June 12, 1958; d. James Earl Jr. and Maria del Refugio (Trivizo) R. BS in Biology, U. Tex., El Paso, 1979; BS in Vet. Sci., Tex. A&M U., 1981, DVM, 1982. Relief vet. local clinics, El Paso, 1982-83; instr. El Paso Community Coll., 1982-83; assoc. vet. Eastwood Animal Clinic/El Paso Vet. Hosp., 1983-84, Animal Def. League Clinic, San Antonio, 1984-86, N.W. Vet. Hosp., Austin, Tex., 1986—. Troop leader Rio Grande coun. Girl Scout U.S., El Paso, 1976-79, troop leader, adult trainer and adminstr., 1982-84, adult vol., 1984—; riding instr. Girl Scout U.S. Nat. Ctr. West, Tensleep, Wyo., 1987. Josephine Clardy Fox scholar U. Tex., 1977-79; named Neighborhood Vol. of Yr., Rio Grande Girl Scout Coun., 1984. Mem. Am. Vet. Med. Assn., Capital Area Vet. Med. Assn., Phi Kappa Phi, Beta Beta Beta, Phi Zeta. Roman Catholic. Office: NW Vet Hosp 3817 Dry Creek Austin TX 78731

RIMBACH, EVANGELINE LOIS, music educator; b. Portland, Oreg., June 28, 1932; d. Raymond Walter and Viola Clara (Gaebler) Rimbach. BA, Valparaiso (Ind.) U., 1954; MMus, Eastman Sch. Music, Rochester, N.Y., 1956; PhD, Eastman Sch. Music, 1967; student, Pacific Luth. U., Parkland, Wash., 1950-52. Vocal music instr. Goodwin Jr. High Sch., Redwood City, Calif., 1956-57; music instr. Calif. Concordia Coll., Oakland, Calif., 1957-62; prof. music Concordia Coll., River Forest, Ill., 1964—, chmn. dept., 1989—. Contbg. editor: Church Music, 1965-80; editor book: Johann Kuhrau: Magnificat, 1980; contbr. articles to profl. jours. Bd. dirs. Civic Symphon of Oak Park-River Forest, 1974-80, concert com. chmn., 1976-78, prog. annotator, 1976-80; mem. choir Grace Luth. Ch., River Forest, 1964—. AAUW postdoctoral fellow, 1969-70; DAAD grantee, Munich, 1980; recipient Rose of Honor award, Sigma Alpha Iota, 1987. Mem. Am. Musicol. Soc., Am. Recorder Soc., Luth. Edn. Assn., Sigma Alpha Iota. Republican. Lutheran. Home: 1115 Bonnie Brae River Forest IL 60305 Office: Concordia College 7400 Augusta St River Forest IL 60305

RINALDI, HEIDI ABUABARA, telecommunications specialist; b. Bogota, Colombia, Jan. 9; came to U.S., 1971; d. Fuad and Gloria (Rodriguez) Abuabara; m. Mark Anthony Rinaldi, Nov. 15, 1986; 1 child, Bryanna Marie. AA, Oakland Community Coll., Farmington, Mich., 1985; student, Xavier U., Cin., 1989—. Adminstrv. asst. C. Itoh & Co., Ltd., Farmington, Mich., 1982-87; supr. telecommunications Chiquita Brands Internat., Cin., 1987—. Named Ky. Col., State of Ky., 1988. Mem. Toastmasters Internat. (pres.). Office: Chiquita Brands Internat 250 E 5th St Cincinnati OH 45202

RINALDO, HELEN, interior designer; b. Manville, N.J., July 5, 1922; d. Zigmond and Kate (Szymanski) Ossowski; student summer and evening classes N.Y. Sch. Interior Design, 1964; student N.Y. U., 1964, Somerset County (N.J.) Coll., 1975-76; m. Nicholas Rinaldo, Feb. 7, 1948; children—Linda Ann, Lorraine Ann. Interior designer W. & J. Sloane, Red Bank and Short Hills, N.J., 1981, Lord & Taylor, Paramus, N.J., 1974; owner Rinaldo Interiors, Scotch Plains, N.J., 1959-65; designer local firms; speaker career day local sch. Mem. Hist. Commn. Twp. of Branchburg (N.J.), until 1982. Mem. Allied Bd. Trade (N.Y.C.), Internat. Platform Assn. Home and Office: 69 Partridge Ln Cherry Hill NJ 08003

RINCK, ELIZABETH APPEL, editor; b. Indpls., Apr. 14, 1961; d. Wilbur Lewis and Myrna Jeanne (Pipes) Appel; m. Jeffrey Bliss Rinck, May 11, 1985. BS, Butler U., 1983. Asst. editor Internat. Computer Programs, Indpls., 1982; coord. community rels. John County Meml. Hosp., Franklin, Ind., 1983-85; editor Children's Playmate Children's Digest Mag., Indpls., 1985—. Bd. advisors Young Writer's Contest Found., McLean, Va., 1985—. Mem. Soc. Profl. Journalists, Ednl. Press Assn. Am. Office: Children's Better Health Inst 1100 Waterway Blvd Indianapolis IN 46220

RINEHART, KATHRYN ANN, principal; b. Eaton, Ohio, Nov. 15, 1948; d. Eugene Warner and Alice Kathryn (Eagle) Donson; m. Charles Edward Rinehart, Dec. 26, 1969. BS in Edn., Miami U., 1969, MEd, 1982, postgrad., 1982-85. Cert. local supt., high, middle, and elem. sch. prin., elem. tchr., vocat. home econs. tchr. Vocat. home econs. tchr. Twin Valley Local Schs., West Alexandria, Ohio, 1969-85; community edn. supr. Twin Valley Local Schs., West Alexandria, 1983-90, middle sch. prin., 1985-90. Author: (manual) Community Education, 1983; (curriculum guide) Career Education, 1985; editor, writer: Entrepreneurship, 1982. Active Preble County Lit. Coun., Eaton, Ohio, 1989. Mem. NAFE, ASCD, Nat. Assn. Elem. Sch. Adminstrs., Nat. Assn. Secondary Sch. Adminstrs., Ohio Assn. Elem. Sch. Adminstrs., Ohio Assn. Secondary Sch. Adminstrs., Ohio Community Edn. Assn. (Gold award 1987, v.p. 1989-92), Ohio Elem. Prins. (county rep. 1987-89). Home: 4496 Sharpsburg Rd Eaton OH 45320

RINEHART, NITA, state senator; b. Tex. BA, So. Meth. U. Mem. Wash. State Ho. of Reps., 1979-82; mem. Wash. State Senate, 1983—, vice chmn. edn. com., mem. rules, ways and means, govtl. ops. coms. Bd. dirs. Planned Parenthood of Seattle. Mem. LWV, Bus. and Profl. Women. Democrat. Office: State Senate Olympia WA 98504 Home: 4515 51st Ave NE Seattle WA 98105*

RING, ANNE CECELIA, advertising executive; b. N.Y.C., Feb. 21, 1964; d. John E. and Janet F. (Tregoning) D'Andrea; m. David Vincent Ring, June 24, 1989; 1 child, Ellen Cecelia. BA in English, Providence Coll., 1986; MA in Communications, Fordham U., 1990. Acct. exec. Popper Stron Communications, Harrison, N.Y., 1986-89; advt. sales mgr. Popper Stron Communications, Harrison, 1987-88, sales, mktg. mgr., 1988—; cons., speaker in field. Contbr. articles to profl. jours. Recipient Golden Apple Success award Westchester City C. of C., 1989. Mem. Women in Communications (v.p. communications 1989-90), Women in Sales (v.p. pub. 1988-90), Am. Cancer Soc. (bd. dirs. 1988-90), Am. Lung Assn. (spl. events coun.), NAFE. Roman Catholic. Home: 10 Prospect St #5 Norwalk CT 06850

RINK, KATHLEEN CLARE, insurance company official; b. Hinsdale, Ill., Feb. 8, 1954; d. Virgil William and Patricia Jane (Donahue) R. B.A., St. Mary's Coll., Notre Dame, Ind., 1976; J.D., DePaul U., 1979; LL.M. in Estate Planning, U. Miami, 1980. Bar: Ill. 1979; C.L.U., 1985, Chartered Fin. Cons., 1987; cert. fin. cons., Ill. Trust adminstr. State Nat. Bank, Evanston, Ill., 1981-82; assoc. dir. advanced underwriting The Equitable, Oak Brook, Ill., 1982-85; advanced underwriting cons. N.Y. Life, Bannockburn, Ill., 1985-89, asst. v.p. compliance, 1989-90; speaker estate planning various profl. orgns. Co-author play: Naperville Live, 1981. Mem. ABA, Ill. Bar Assn. Roman Catholic.

RINK, LINDA, railroad executive; b. Trenton, N.J., May 30, 1951; d. Evald and Hildegard (Romet) R. BA, Harvard U., 1973; MBA, U. Pa., 1976. Asst. brand mgr. Quaker Oats Co., Chgo., 1977-79; nat. product mgr. Seagram Distillers, Joseph E. Seagram & Sons, N.Y.C., 1979-82; dir. mktg. Westmount Enterprises div. J.E. Seagram & Sons, N.Y.C., 1982-85; cons., Phila., 1985-89; dir. r.r. svcs. devel. Amtrak, Washington, 1989—. Presdl. scholar, 1969. Mem. Phi Beta Kappa, Beta Gamma Sigma.

RINKE, LYNN THERESE, nurse, home care consultant; b. Detroit, Sept. 14, 1955; d. Leonard John and Ellen (Dakoske) R. BS in Nursing, Wayne State U., 1977; MS, U. Mich., 1980. Pub. health nurse Vis. Nurse Assn. Met. Detroit, 1977-80, nursing supr., 1980-81, dist. dir., 1981-86; dir. div. of accreditation for home care & community health Nat. League Nursing, N.Y.C., 1986-87; v.p., chief operating officer Vis. Nurse Assn. of Met. Detroit, 1987—; fellow Nat. League Nursing, Robert Wood Johnson Pub. Policy, Washington, summer 1979; intern Health Care Financing Adminstrn., HHS, Washington, summer 1980. Recipient Nightingale award in nursing adminstrn., 1990. Mem. Nat. League Nursing, Am. Pub. Health Assn., N.Y. Counties Registered Nurse Assn., Sigma Theta Tau (small research award grant Rho chpt. 1979). Roman Catholic. Home: 3345 Wiscasset Apt 109 Dearborn MI 48120

RINKER, RUBY STEWART, foundation administrator; b. Dayton, Ohio, June 11, 1936; d. Encle Stewart and Addie (Hamilton) Stewart-Smith; children from previous marriage: William Bertram Klawonn, Elizabeth Lynn Dennis, William Stewart-Bradley Klawonn; m. Marshall E. Rinker Sr., Aug. 27, 1987. MA of Adminstrn. and Supervision, Fla. Atlantic U., 1978. Human relations counselor Palm Beach County Sch. System, West Palm Beach, Fla., 1974-84; adminstrv. asst. Bohmfalk Estate, Palm Beach, Fla., N.Y.C, Newport, R.I., 1984—; hon. counselor U.S. Naval Acad., U.S. Air Force Acad. Trustee Bohmfalk Charitable Found. Mem. Phi Delta Kappa. Home: 561 Island Dr Palm Beach FL 33480

RINSKY, JUDITH LYNN, foundation administrator, educator consultant; b. Sept. 12, 1941; d. Allen A. Lynn and Sophie (Schwartz); m. Joel C. Rinsky, Esq., Jan. 29, 1963; children: Heidi Mae, Heather Star, Jason Wayne. BA in Home Econs., Montclair State Coll., 1963. Notary pub., N.J. Tchr. home econs. Florence Ave. Sch., Irvington, N.J., 1963-66; substitute tchr. Millburn-Short Hills Sch. System, 1978-82, 85—, sr. citizen coord., 1982-87; respite care coord. Essex County Respite Care, East Orange, N.J., 1988-90; edn. and aging cons., 1990—; bd. mem. adv. com. gerontology Seton Hall U., 1984-90; coord. Mayor's Adv. Bd. St. Citizens, Millburn-Short Hills, 1982-87. Pres. Deerfield Sch. PTA, 1979-80, Millburn High Sch. PTA, 1983-85; co-chmn. Charles T. King Student Loan Fund dinner dance, 1981; mem. Handicapped Access Study com. 1983-85; bd. dirs. Coun. on Health and Human Svcs., 1985-90, mem., 1985—. Mem. Lake Naomi Assn. (chmn. sailing com. 1981), N.J. Home Econs. Assn., Am. Home Econs. Assn., Rotary (chairperson Interact Club 1987—, pres.-elect Millburn chpt. 1990—), Notary Pub. N.J., Millburn Rotary (bd. dirs. 1987—). Home: 23 Winthrop Rd Short Hills NJ 07078

RIO, LINDA KAREN, electrical engineer; b. Hollywood, Fla., Oct. 5, 1964; d. Victor and Grace R. MusB, U. Miami, Coral Gables, Fla., 1986. Process engr. Philips and DuPont Optical Co., Grover, N.C., 1986-87; process, research and devel. engr. Memory Tech, Inc., Plano, Tex., 1987—. Mem. NAFE, Audio Engring. Soc. Office: Memory Tech Inc 2800 Summit Ave Plano TX 75074

RIOLO-QUINN, LISA, therapist; b. Mineola, N.Y., May 16, 1963; d. Jack and Jean Ann (Voege) Riolo; m. Robert H. Quinn, June 22, 1985. BS in Physical Therapy, Quinnipiac Coll., 1985; MEd Motor Learning, Temple U., 1988; postgrad., U. Conn., 1989—. Staff physical therapist Moss Rehab. Hosp., Phila., 1985-88; research physical therapist New Medico Assocs., Plantsville, Conn., 1988-1989; asst. prof. phys. therapy Quinnipiac Coll., Hamden, Conn., 1989—; cons. Bryn Mawr Rehab. Ctr., Phila., 1987-88; contract phys. therapist Patient and Restorative Care Assn., 1987; speaker U. Conn., 1988-89, Springfield Coll., Beaver Coll., Hahnemann U., Temple U.; presenter profl. confs. Contbr. articles to profl. jours. Mem. Conn. Phys. Therapy Assn. (sec.), Neuro Devel. Treatment Assn., Am. Phys. Therapy Assn., Conn. Traumatic Brain Injury Assn. Home: 5 E Lake Dr Middletown CT 06457 Office: Quinnipiac Coll Mt Carmel Ave Hamden CT 06518

RIORDAN, CAROL CAMPBELL, producer; b. Fresno, Calif., May 15, 1946; d. Alexander Boyle and Jeanne Carol (Yarnell) Campbell; m. Samuel Gresham Riordan, May 27, 1966; children; Loren Jeremy, Rachel Elisabeth. AA, San Diego City Coll., 1976; BA, Union Inst., 1986; postgrad., San Diego State U. Instr., dir. San Diego Jr. Theatre, 1963-66, Actor's Lab., San Francisco, 1966-68; costume designer Playhouse Interplayers Theatres, San Francisco, 1966-68, Stage 7 Dance Theater, San Diego, 1981-83; producer TV edn. County Edn. Office, San Diego, 1974-76; producer, dir. Community Video Ctr., San Diego, 1976-78, program mgr., 1978-79; designer-in-residence Three's Co. and Dancers, San Diego, 1976-89, also bd. dirs., 1981; media producer TV San Diego State U., 1982—; cons. in field;. Producer, dir. TV, Poems of Wonder and Magic, 1986 (Emmy award, Best of West award, Western Ednl. Soc. Telecommunications, ITVA Excellence award), The Fearless Vampire Dressers, 1984 (Best of West award 1985); author: (with others) Framework and Instructional Units for Teaching CCTV, 1980, The Fall of The House of Ushers, 1986 (Best of West Spl. Merit award 1987, ITVA award of Merit 1986). Mem. Environ Def. Fund, environ. adv. com. for Congressman Duncan Hunter, 1982-84; mem. peer rev. panel San Diego Pub. Arts Coun., 1988. Grantee Calif. Coun. Humanities, 1988, N. County Community TV Found., 1985; recipient Best Supporting Actress award San Dieguito Little Theatre, 1975-76, various awards for costumes Annual San Diego Renaissance Festival, Tech. award San Dieguito Little Theatre, 1975-76. Mem. Women in Film, Nat. Acad. TV Arts and Scis. (bd. govs. San Diego chpt. 1989—), Internat. TV Assn., Sierra Club (off shore oil com. 1982), Greenpeace Internat. Zen Buddhist. Office: San Diego State U Media Tech Svcs San Diego CA 92182-0524

RIORDAN, FRANCIS ELLEN, linguist, French literature educator emerita; b. Solomon, Kans., Oct. 24, 1915; d. Patrick Francis and Ella (Barret) R.; AB, Marymount Coll., 1936; MA, Cath. U. Am., 1945, PhD, 1952. Joined Sisters St. Joseph, 1937; directress St. Mary Acad., Silver City, N.Mex., 1950-51; prin. Luckey High Sch., Manhattan, Kans., 1951-53, Cathedral High Sch., Salina, Kans., 1953-57; prof. French, chmn. fgn. langs. dept. Marymount Coll., Salina, 1962-83, chmn. humanities div., 1980-83, dir. interdisciplinary program, 1973-76; mem. faculty Northwestern Coll., Orange City, Iowa, 1983-84, Ctr. for Peace Concerns, 1984—, Bethany Coll., Lindsborg, Kans., 1985-86. Author: Concept of Love in the French Catholic Literary Revival, 1952, The Brave Walk Single File, pagent, 1959; co-editor The Sea Remains (Jean Sulivan), 1988. Mem. coordinating com. State of Kans. Women's Meeting, 1977. Lang. dept. fellow Cath. U., 1948-49. Mem. Am. Assn. Tchrs. of French, Kappa Gamma Pi. Home: 108 N Estates Dr Salina KS 67401

RIPLEY, VICKIE CORBETT, hospital pharmacist; b. Bailey, N.C., June 17, 1950; d. Bobby Jones and Mary Lou (Ayers) Corbett; m. Robert Kenyon Ripley Jr., Aug. 5, 1972. BS in Pharmacy, U. N.C., 1973; paramedic cert., Nash Community Coll., Rocky Mount, N.C., 1987. Registered pharmacist, N.C. Pharmacy intern Madison (Wis.) Gen. Hosp., 1974-75; staff pharmacist Nash Gen. Hosp., Rocky Mount, 1975-76, Southside Pharmacy, Inc., Spring Hope, N.C., 1976-86, Raper Drugs, Inc., Rocky Mount, 1980-86; dir. pharmacy Community Hosp. Rocky Mount, 1986—; practitioner, instr. U. N.C. Chapel Hill Sch. Pharmacy, 1987—; instr. paramedic pharmacology Nash Community Coll., 1988—; instr. basic life support Community Hosp. Rocky Mount, 1988—. Mem. Gibson Meml. Chancel Choir, Spring Hope, 1978—, Rocky Mount Civic Chorus, 1980-82, Drug Awareness in Spring Hope; mem. bd. advisors Nash County Civic Chorus, Spring Hope, 1982-84; vol. paramedic Strong Creek Fire Rescue, Inc., Rocky Mount, 1985-88. Mem. N.C. Pharm. Assn., N.C. Soc. Hosp. Pharmacists, Am. Soc. Hosp. Pharmacists, Am. Pharm. Assn., Spring Hope Hist. Assn., AHEC (Area L pharmacy adv. bd.), Kappa Epsilon. Democrat. Methodist. Home: PO Box 185 Spring Hope NC 27882 Office: Community Hosp Rocky Mount 1031 Noell Ln Rocky Mount NC 27804

RIPPER, RITA JO (JODY RIPPER), financial executive; b. Goldfield, Iowa, May 8, 1950; d. Carl Phillip and Lucille Mae (Stewart) Ripper; B.A., U. Iowa, 1972; M.B.A., N.Y.U., 1978. Contracts and fin. staff Control Data Corp., Mpls., 1974-78; regional mgr. Raytheon Corp., Irvine, Calif., 1978-83; v.p. Caljo Corp., Des Moines, Iowa, 1983-84; asst. v.p. Bank of America, San Francisco, 1984—. Vol. and alt. del. Republican Party, Edina, Minn., N.Y.C., 1975—; vol. Cancer, Heart, Lung Assns., Edina, N.Y.C., Calif., 1974-78, 84—; Lita, 1986—. Mem. Internat. Mktg. Assn., World Trade Ctr. Assn., Acctg. Soc. (pres. 1975-76), Engring. Club of San Francisco, Mensa, Beta Alpha Psi (chmn. 1977-78), Phi Gamma Nu (v.p. 1971-72) Presbyterian. Clubs: Corinthian Yacht, Mt. Tamalpai Racquet. Home: 242 Baywood Dr Newport Beach CA 92660-7132 Office: Bank of Am 2 Embarcadero Ctr San Francisco CA 94111

RIPPY, FRANCES MARGUERITE MAYHEW, English educator; b. Ft. Worth, Sept. 16, 1929; d. Henry Grady and Marguerite Christine (O'Neill) Mayhew; m. Noble Merrill Rippy, Aug. 29, 1955 (dec. Sept. 1980); children: Felix O'Neill, Conrad Mayhew, Marguerite Hailey. BA, Tex. Christian U., 1949; MA, Vanderbilt U., 1951, PhD, 1957; postgrad., U. London, 1952-53. Instr. Tex. Christian U., 1953-55; instr. to asst. prof. Lamar State U., 1955-59; asst. prof. English, Ball State U., Muncie, Ind., 1959-64; assoc. prof. English, Ball State U., 1964-68, prof., 1968—, dir. grad. studies in English, 1966-87; editor Ball State U. Forum, 1960-89; vis. asst. prof. Sam Houston State U., 1957; vis. lectr., prof. U. P.R., summers 1959, 60, 61; exch. prof. Westminster Coll., Oxford, Eng., 1988; cons.-evaluator North Central Assn. Colls. and Schs., 1973, commn.-at-large, 1987—; cons.-evaluator New Eng. Assn. Schs. and Colls., 1983. Author: Matthew Prior, 1986; contbr. articles to profl. jours., encys., chpts. to anthology; contbr. to Dictionary of Literary Biography. Recipient McClintock award, 1966; Danforth grantee 1964, Ball State U. Rsch. grantee, 1960, 62, 70, 73, 76, 87, 88, 89, 90 Lilly Library Rsch. grantee, 1978; Fulbright scholar U. London. Mem. MLA, Coll. English Assn., Ind. Coll. English Assn. (pres. 1984-85), Johnson Soc. Midwest (sec. 1961-62), AAUP, Nat. Council Tchrs. English, Am. Soc. 18th Century Studies. Home: 4709 W Jackson St Muncie IN 47304

RISER, BRENDA DENICE, pharmacist, educator; b. Fresno, Calif., May 24, 1962; d. Charles D. and Violet Lucille (Swigart) R.; m. Marc C. Costo, July 28, 1985 (div. June 1990). AA, Fresno City Coll., 1982; PharmD, U. Pacific, 1985. Lic. pharmacist, Calif. Oncology pharmacist O.P.T.I.O.N. Care, Fresno, 1985; pharmacist Homedco, San Diego, 1986-88; pharmacy mgr. Vons, San Diego, 1986—; adj. prof. U. Pacific, Stockton, 1988—; cons. Lumé, Salt Lake City, 1989—. Mem. Le Tip. Republican. Office: Vons No 81 13255 Black Mountain Rd San Diego CA 92129

RISHEL, PEGGY LYNN, nonprofit organization executive; b. Leesville, La., Dec. 29, 1951; d. Allen James and Neva Louise (Coghill) Young; m. Jon Lester Rishel, Dec. 16, 1972. AS in Graphic Arts Tech., Springfield Tech. Comm. Coll., 1982; student, SUNY, Plattsburgh, 1970-71, Utica Sch. Commerce, 1973. Entertainer, singer, 1971-78; bus. mgr., ptnr. Glimmerglass Prodns., Chicopee, Mass., 1985—; med. transcriptionist radiology dept. Baystate Med. Ctr., Springfield, Mass., 1978-81, sec. to dir. media svcs. dept., 1981-84, sec. to dir. med. physics dept., 1984-88; exec. asst. Corp. for Pub. Mgmt., Springfield, 1988—; cons. in graphic svcs. Glimmerglass Prodns., 1985—. Mem. exec. com. Western Mass. chpt. March of Dimes, Springfield, 1988-89. Mem. NAFE, Greater Springfield C. of C. Office: Corp for Pub Mgmt 82 Maple St Springfield MA 01020

RISICA, VIRGINIA JEAN, psychologist; b. Queens, N.Y., June 21, 1957; d. John Phillip and Erma Margaret (Cantus) R. BA in Psychology, St. John's U., Jamaica, N.Y., 1979, MA Explt. Psychology, 1981, PhD in Clin. Psychology, 1987. Lic. psychologist, N.Y. Extern in psychology Mercy Hosp., Rockville Centre, N.Y., 1982-83, Creedmoor Psychiat. Ctr., Queens Village, N.Y., 1982-83, Oceanside (N.Y.) Counseling Ctr., 1983-84; intern in psychology NYU Med. Ctr./Rusk Inst. Rehab. Medicine, N.Y.C., 1984-85; staff psychologist N.Y.C. Police Dept., Rego Park, N.Y., 1986—; presenter Oceanside Counseling Ctr., 1984; presenter colloquim at St. John's U., 1989. Recipient Cert. of Excellence, St. John's U., 1978. Mem. Am. Psychol. Assn. (presenter conv. 1987), N.Y. State Psychol. Assn., Nassau County Psychol. Assn., Queens County Psychol. Assn., Coalition Hosp. and Instl. Psychologists. Democrat. Roman Catholic. Home: 95-22 94th St Ozone Park NY 11416 Office: NYC Police Dept Psychol Svc One Lefrak City Pla 15th Fl Rego Park NY 11368

RISING, SUZANNE, copywriter; b. El Paso, Tex., May 23, 1964; d. Ernest Eugene and Nancy Orene (Goston) R. BS, U. Tex., 1986, BJ, 1988; MA, E. Tex. State U., 1989. Copywriter E. Tex. State U. Creative Svcs., Commerce, 1987-88; sr. copywriter Holt, Rinehart & Winston, Inc., Ft. Worth, Tex., 1989—. WICI scholar, 1988; Dallas Press Club scholar, 1988. Mem. Women in Communications, E. Tex. State U. Alumni Assn., Soc. for Creative Communications, U. Tex. Ex-Students Assn., Alpha Chi Omega. Republican. Methodist. Office: Holt Rinehart & Winston 301 Commerce St #3700 Fort Worth TX 76102

RISLEY, EDYTH C., petroleum geologist; b. Little Rock, Oct. 12, 1928; d. Elmer J. and Lillie L. (McNeill) R.; student Randolph-Macon Woman's Coll., 1945-47; B.S., So. Meth. U., 1949; postgrad. U. Colo., 1949; M.S., Stanford U., 1951. Jr. geologist McAlester Fuel Co., Magnolia, Ark., 1949; geologist Continental Oil, Midland, Tex., 1951-56; sr. geologist, cons. McCord & Assocs., Dallas, 1957-63; sr. sci. reference librarian Dallas Public Library, 1963-75; hdqrs. staff geologist Holly Corp., Dallas, 1975-77; sr. geologist Ray Holifield & Assos., Dallas, 1977-85, cons. geologist, 1977—. Mem. Am. Assn. Petroleum Geologists (ho. of dels. 1981-84, rec. sec. 1983-84), Dallas Geol. Soc. (sec. 1979-80), West Tex. Geol. Soc., Nat. Audubon Soc., Energy Club of Dallas, Pi Beta Phi. Contbr. publs. in field. Home and Office: 2905 University Blvd Dallas TX 75205

RISLEY, KATHRYN HANFORD, design consultant, fashion designer; b. Waterville, Maine, June 30, 1954; d. John Hollister and Mary (Kring) R. BFA in Apparel Design, RISD, 1977. Pres., designer Kathryn Risley Ltd., Middletown, Conn., 1980-83; assoc. designer Gil Aimbez for I.E.I. Industries, N.Y.C., 1984; designer Carole Little for St. Tropez West, L.A., 1985; head knitwear designer St. Michel Sportswear, N.Y.C., 1986, Indesign, N.Y.C., 1987; design dir. Apparel Imports-Gerard Works, N.Y.C., 1988-89; cons., owner, mgr. Knit Solutions, N.Y.C., 1989—. Democrat. Home and Office: 72 E 3d St Apt 4B New York NY 10003

RISNES, MARILYN LOUISE NEITZERT, educator; b. Huron, S.D., Mar. 22, 1935; d. Herman and Lillian Julia (Delvaux) Neitzert; m. Lawrence Martin Risnes Jr., June 6, 1959 (div. Nov. 1975); children: Bruce Douglas, Wayne LeRoy, Gloria Lynn. BA, St. Cloud U., 1963; MA, St. Mary's Coll., 1978; PhD in clin. hypnotherapy, Am. Inst. Hypnotherapy, 1989; postgrad., Hamline U. Cert. elem. tchr., hypnotherapist. Waitress Bar Harbor Supper Club, Brainerd, Minn., 1952-55; tchr. Dist. 31 Rural Schs., Owatonna, Minn., 1954-57, Elizabeth Gardner Sch., Mound, Minn., 1957-59, Spl. Dist. No. 1, Mpls., 1968-89; tchr. gifted and talented students Spl. Dist. No. 1, 1989—; sales rep. Stanley Home Products, Mpls., 1962-64, World Book Ency., Mpls., 1988—; psychotherapist Internat. Transactional Analysis Inst., Mpls., 1974-76; front desk clk. Tyrol Motor Inn, Estes Park, Colo., 1987; asst. tchr. Baldwin Girls Sch., Bangalore, India, 1980; cons. Personal Dynamics Inst., Performax Systems Internat., Youth Devel. Inst., Mpls., 1980-87. Den mother Boy Scouts Am., Mpls., 1970-73; vol. life enhancement counselor, Minn. AIDS Project, 1989-90; cert. Laubach reading instr. Minn. Adult Literacy Project. U.S. Dept. Edn. study grantee, 1972. Mem. NEA, Internat. Med. and Dental Hypnotherapy Assn., Internat. Graphoanalysis Soc., Minn. Edn. Assn., Mpls. Edn. Assn., Minn. Fedn. Tchrs. (union rep.), Mental Health Assn. of Minn., Educators Social Responsibility, ACLU, Women Against Mil. Madness, Ams. for Legal Reform, Peace with Justice Cen. Am., Assn for Supervision and Curriculum Devel., Nat. Bd. for Hypnotherapy and Hypnotic Anaesthesiology, Internat. Graphoanalysis Soc., 1990. Democrat. Mem. Ch. Religious Sci. Lodge: Moose. Home: 143 Cecil St SE Minneapolis MN 55414 Office: Marcy Open Sch 1042 18th Ave SE Minneapolis MN 55414

RISTUCCIA, PATRICIA ANN, microbiologist; b. N.Y.C., Aug. 10, 1954; d. Joseph John and Ann (Fesco) R. BS, St. John's U., 1976, MS, 1983. Clin. chemist Meml. Sloan Kettering Cancer Ctr., N.Y.C., 1976-79, St. Vincent's Med. Ctr., S.I., 1979-82; rsch. microbiologist Winthrop U. Hosp., Mineola, N.Y., 1982-85; dir. microbiology rsch. Therapeutic Rsch. Inst., Sarasota, Fla., 1985—. Author: (with others) Antimicrobial Therapy, 1984, The Nursing Clinics of North America Infections in the Compromised Host, 1985, Prevention and Control of Nosocomial Infections, 1987. Mem. Am. Soc. for Microbiology, Am. Soc. of Clin. Pathologist, Nat. Certification Agy. for Med. Lab. Personnel. Republican. Roman Catholic. Office: Therapeutic Rsch Inst 2709 Floyd St Sarasota FL 34239

RITCH, KATHLEEN, diversified company executive; Harbor Beach, Mich., Jan. 23, 1943; d. Eunice (Spry) R.; B.A., Mich. State U., 1965; student Katharine Gibbs Sch., 1965-66. Exec. sec., adminstrv. asst. to pres. Katy Industries, Inc., N.Y.C., 1969-70; exec. sec., adminstrv. asst. to chmn. Kobrand Corp., N.Y.C., 1970-72; adminstrv. asst. to chmn. and pres. Ogden Corp., N.Y.C., 1972-74; asst. sec., adminstr. office services, asst. to chmn. Ogden Corp., N.Y.C., 1974-81, corporate sec., adminstr. office services, 1981-84, v.p., corporate sec., adminstr. office services, 1984—; part-owner Unell Mfg. Co., Port Hope, Mich., 1966-87. Mem. Am. Soc. Corporate Secs. Home: 500 E 77th St New York NY 10162 Office: Ogden Corp Two Pennsylvania Pla New York NY 10121

RITCHEY, SHERRY YEARICK, managing editor; b. Lewistown, Pa., Oct. 15, 1947; d. Richard Frederick Yearick Sr. and Atha Jane (Clugh) Workinger; m. Dennis Russell Ritchey, Sept. 23, 1972; children: Joshua Cushing, Russell Clugh. AA in English, York Coll., 1969, student, 1989—; student,

Ariz. State U., 1965-66, Messiah Coll., 1969-70. Exec. sec. Dun & Bradstreet, Harrisburg, Pa., 1970-71; office mgr. Grant Co., York, Pa., 1971-75; ins. mgr. Pa. and Atlantic Seaboard Hardware, Harrisburg, 1975-77; freelance York and Harrisburg, 1980-82; typographer Gen. Graphic Svcs., York, 1982-86, typog. computer markup supr., 1986, plant supr., 1986-87; mng. editor Northwoods Publs., Inc., Harrisburg, 1987—. Mem. Nat. Assn. Exec. Women, Pa. Outdoor Writers, Eastern Star (worthy matron starlight #508, 1990—). Democrat. Home: 7127 Salem Park Circle Mechanicsburg PA 17055

RITCHIE, DEBORAH CAMPBELL, technical writer; b. Grove City, Pa., Jan. 24, 1950; d. Wilbur D. and Jean (Montgomery) Campbell; m. Kenneth W. Lengel, June 24, 1967 (div. Jan. 1972); m. David J. Ritchie, Oct. 5, 1974. Student, Grove City Coll., San Jose State Coll. Spl. projects dir. Grove City Area Sch. Dist., 1978-80; editor SPI, N.Y.C., 1980-81; manuscript editor TSR, Lake Geneva, Wis., 1981-83; sr. writer Coleco, West Hartford, Conn., 1983-85, Ashton-Tate, East Hartford, Conn., 1986-89, Cadkey, Manchester, Conn., 1990—; documentation cons. Cuno, Inc., Meriden, Conn., 1988-90, CNF Industries, Meriden, 1990—, Meca Ventures, Inc., Westport, Conn., 1989-90, Spinaaker Software Cambridge, Mass., 1989—. Contbg. editor Hartford Monthly mag., 1988—; co-author: Multimate Users Guide, 1986, Using Multimate Advantage, 1987. Mem. Nat. Abortion Rights League, Planned Parenthood. Democrat. Home: 64 Tunxis Village Dr Farmington CT 06032 Office: Cadkey 440 Oakland St Manchester CT 06040-2100

RITCHIE, KAREN, advertising agency executive. Former sr. v.p. Campbell-Ewald Co. (formerly Lintas: Campbell Ewald), Warren, Mich.; sr. v.p. McCann-Erickson/Detroit, Troy, Mich., 1989—. Office: McCann-Erickson/Detroit 755 W Big Beaver Rd Troy MI 48084*

RITCHIE, MARIE P., financial executive; b. Murfreesboro, Tenn., Aug. 23, 1937; d. Walter Hershel and Lillian Birdette (Eads) Pope; m. Dean Lenair Ritchie, May 1, 1987. Student, Belmont Coll., Nashville, U. Tenn., Knoxville. Notary pub., Tenn. Fiscal and budget dir. Alcoholic Beverage Commn.; dir. payroll and budget State of Tenn.-Middle Tenn. Health Inst., Nashville; dir. payroll and revenues Inter-State Constrn. Co., Nashville; dir. fgn. banks dept. 3d Nat. Bank, Nashville; fiscal and budget dir. Tenn. Alcoholic Beverage Commn., Nashville; owner Ritchie Enterprises Interior Design. Tchr. Sunday sch., Bible sch. Two Rivers Baptist Ch., Nashville. Mem. Internat. Pers. Mgmt. Assn. (treas. conf. Tenn. chpt. 1990), Murfreesboro Bus. and Profl. Women (1st v.p.), Women's Aux. to Tenn. Assn. of Rescue Squads (1st v.p., treas. 1990), Capitol Club. Democrat. Office: 226 Capitol Blvd Ste 300 Nashville TN 37243-0755

RITCHIE, PEGGY LOU, state deputy warden; b. Rugby, N.D., Dec. 13, 1945; d. Donald Mayo and Phyllis Georgine (Carlson) Hakanson; 1 child, Christopher Barrett. BS in Edn., U. N.D., 1968, MS in Counseling/Guidance, 1977; MBA, U. Phoenix, 1987. Educator various pub. schs., 1965-79; exec. dir. Centre, Inc., Fargo, N.D., 1978-80, La Clinica del Pueblo Behavioral Health Ctr., Superior, Ariz., 1980-82; assoc. dir. Inter-Mountain Behavioral Health Assn., Miami, Ariz., 1980-82; psychol. assoc. II Ariz. State Prison Complex, Florence, 1982-84, asst. dep. warden, 1984-86; dep. warden Ariz. State Prison Complex Douglas-Gila Unit, 1986-87; assoc. warden spl. mgmt. unit Ariz. State Prison Complex, Florence, 1987; dep. warden Arizona State Prison Complex Perryville-Santa Maria Unit, 1987—; lectr. U. N.D., Grand Forks, 1985; guest speaker Los Nosotros Hispanic Women's Conf., Cochise Coll., Douglas, 1987, 88; correctional programs specialist Nat. Inst. Corrections Acad., Boulder, Colo. Vol. for the arts in Phoenix and Scottsdale, Ariz. Internat. Halfway House Assn. scholar, Denver, 1979; Gov.'s Award for Outstanding Women of Yr. State of Ariz., 1985. Mem. Ariz. Coun. on Prevention, LWV, NEA, N.D. Edn. Assn., Minn. Community Correctional Assn., PACE, IHHA, NOW, Community Arts Coun., Am. Correctional Assn., Tucson Crime League (hon.), Assn. on Programs for Female Offenders, Jazz in Ariz., Delta Zeta. Home: 1989 19th St #D Boulder CO 80302

RITCHLIN, MARTHA ANN, occupational therapist; b. Jacksboro, Tex., Oct. 20, 1953; d. Carl Alton and Julia Ann (Jones) Rumage; m. Roger James Ritchlin; children: Carl Allen, Julie Marie. BS, Tex. Women's U., 1976, postgrad., 1977. Occupational therapist Wichita Gen. Hosp., Wichita Falls, Tex., 1977-79; dir. occupational therapy Red River Hosp., Wichita Falls, 1979-83, Bethania Regional Health Care Ctr., Wichita Falls, 1983-87; occupational therapist Girling Home Health, Wichita Falls, 1984-85, Wichita Home Health, Wichita Falls, 1984-86, Outreach Home Health Svcs., Seymour, Tex., 1987—, N. Tex. Easter Seal Rehab. Ctr., Wichita Falls, 1988—; owner, therapist Community Occupational Therapy Svcs., Wichita Falls, 1988—; cons., speaker Muscular Dystrophy Assn., Wichita Falls, 1986, Advantage Sr. Citizens Club, Wichita Falls, 1988, Stroke Club, 1986; cons., activity dir. Clay County Hosp., Henrietta, Tex., 1986-87. Cons., vol. Wichita County Juvenile Detention Svcs., Wichita Falls, 1980; mem. task force State Task Force on Assistive Tech., Tex., 1989—. Named Notable Women of Tex., 1985. Mem. Tex. Occupational Therapy Assn., Am. Occupational Therapy Assn., World Fedn. Occupational Therapy. Methodist. Home: 4845 Colleen Wichita Falls TX 76302 Office: 1901 10th St Wichita Falls TX 76301

RITCHOTTE, RITA ELIZABETH, educator; b. Warwick, R.I., May 22, 1926; d. Romeo Joseph and Diana Henriette (Chartier) R. BA in Clothing and Textiles, Rivier Coll., 1958; MS, U. R.I., 1972, U. R.I., 1983. Tchr. Presentation of Mary Sch., North Providence, R.I., 1958-62; tchr. St. Charles Sch., Dover, N.H., 1962-64, St. John the Evangelist, Hudson, N.H., 1964-65, St. Joseph Sch., Woonsocket, R.I., 1965-70; prof. textiles Rivier Coll., Nashua, N.H., 1972—. Mem. N.H. Home Econs. Assn. (student advisor 1984—), Am. Home Econs. Assn., Omicron Nu. Roman Catholic. Office: Rivier Coll 429 Main St Nashua NH 03060

RITSCH, LISA CATHARINA, city revitalization director; b. Spartanburg, S.C., Mar. 8, 1961; d. Frederick Field Jr. and Jeannette (McClung) R. BA in Sociology, Converse Coll., 1983, BA in Art History, 1983; MA in Hist. Preservation, Middle Tenn. State U., 1990. Intern Pa. Bur. for Hist. Preservation, Harrisburg, 1984; project mgr. Gaffney (S.C.) Main St. Corp., 1985-87; exec. dir. Downtown Statesville (N.C.) Devel. Corp., 1987-88, Main Street Beaufort (S.C.), USA, 1988—; speaker various civic groups and orgns.; resource team cons. S.C. Downtown Devel. Assn. Bur., Gaffney, Chester, Woodruff, 1987-90. Coord. Beaufort Christmas Parade, 1989-90, Downtown Water Festival, 1988—, Beaufort Tree Lighting Ceremony, 1988—; vol. Heart Fund Golf Tourn., Beaufort, 1989; speaker United Way; bd. dirs. Trash/Litter Control for Beaufort County, 1989—. Recipient fellowship Mus. of Early So. Decorative Arts, Winston-Salem, 1982; named Cherokee County Bus. Woman, Gaffney (S.C.) Ledger, 1987, Young Career Woman, Bus./Profl. Women's Orgn., Beaufort, 1989, Regional Young Career Woman, dist. Bus./Profl. Women's Orgn., 1990. Mem. Am. Bus. Woman's Assn. (mem. of month award 1990), Lions, Nat. Trust for Hist. Preservation. Democrat. Presbyterian. Office: Main Street Beaufort USA PO Box 501 Beaufort SC 29901

RITSON, DONNA DIANE, communications administrator; b. Chgo., Feb. 22, 1955; d. Raymond Bernard and Elaine Marion (Englund) Nietschmann; m. Scott Campbell Ritson, Feb. 25, 1978; 1 child, Evan Ray-Bernard; 1 stepchild, Carrie Stewart. B.S. with honors, Roosevelt U., Chgo., 1983; postgrad., 1983—; cert. bus. communicator. Sec. Baxter-Travenol Labs., Deerfield, Ill., 1973-76, advt. asst., 1976-80, conv. coordinator, 1980-83; communications coordinator Angus Chem. Co., Northbrook, Ill., 1983-84, communications mgr., 1984—. Mem. Bus. Profl. Advt. Assn., Nat. Assn. Female Execs., Am. Mktg. Assn. Club: Chgo. Yacht. Avocations: skiing, sailing, scuba diving, boating. Home: 1084 Old Colony Rd Lake Forest IL 60045 Office: Angus Chem Co 2211 Sanders Rd Northbrook IL 60062

RITTENHOUSE, RONNI, psychotherapist; b. Bklyn., Apr. 20, 1947; d. William and Roslyn (Silberstein) Orenstein; m. Harvey Triebwasser, Apr. 6, 1968 (div. 1974); m. Paul R. Hedges, May 6, 1988. BA, Adelphi U., 1968; MS, CUNY, 1969; cert. advanced study, W.Va. U., 1979; PhD, Pacific Western U., 1988. Lic. cert. social worker, cert. addictions counselor, lic. profl. counselor; diplomate Am. Bd. Med. Psychotherapists. Shift supr. Youth Svc. Systems, Fountain Valley, Calif., 1971-74; addictions counselor Dept. of Health, Morgantown, W.Va., 1974-79; psychotherapist, adminstr. No. Panhandle Behavioral Health Ctr., Wheeling, W.Va., 1979-86; psychotherapist Wheeling Clinic, 1986—. Columnist The Chemical Column News-Register, Wheeling Intelligencer, Wheeling News-Register, 1983-88. Mem. W.Va. Assn. Alcoholism and Drug Abuse Counselors (bd. dirs. 1982-84, 86-88, oral examiner cert. bd. 1983—). Jewish. Office: Wheeling Clinic 58 16th St Wheeling WV 26003

RITTER, ANN L., lawyer; b. N.Y.C., May 20, 1933; d. Joseph and Grace (Goodman) R. B.A., Hunter Coll., 1954; J.D., N.Y. Law Sch., 1970; postgrad. Law Sch., NYU, 1971-72. Bar: N.Y. 1971, U.S. Ct. Appeals (2d cir.) 1975, U.S. Supreme Ct. 1975. Writer, 1954-70; editor, 1955-66; tchr., 1966-70; atty. Am. Soc. Composers, Authors and Pubs., N.Y.C., 1971-72, Greater N.Y. Ins. Co., N.Y.C., 1973-74; sr. ptnr. Brenhouse & Ritter, N.Y.C., 1974-78; sole practice, N.Y.C., 1978—. Editor N.Y. Immigration News, 1975-76. Mem. ABA, Am. Immigration Lawyers Assn. (treas. 1983-84, sec. 1984-85, vice chair 1985-86, chair 1986-87, chair program com. 1989-90, chair speakers bur. 1989-90, chair media liaison 1989-90), N.Y. State Bar Assn., N.Y. County Lawyers Assn., Assn. Trial Lawyers Am., N.Y. State Trial Lawyers Assn., N.Y.C. Bar Assn., Watergate East Assn. (v.p., asst. treas. 1990—). Democrat. Jewish. Home: 47 E 87th St New York NY 10128 Office: 420 Madison Ave New York NY 10017

RITTER, DARLENE MAE, English educator; b. Tilden, Nebr., May 15, 1925; d. Ernest and Olga Louise (Johnson) R. BS, U. Nebr., 1949, MA, 1979; MA, U. No. Colo., 1958. Elem. tchr. North Bend and Wisner Pub. Schs., Nebr., 1944-48; tchr. English Fremont (Nebr.) Pub. Secondary Sch., 1949-62, 63-64; Fulbright prof. Reggio Emilia, Italy, 1962-63, Reykjavik, Iceland, 1966-67; prof. English, Midland Luth. Coll., Fremont, 1964-66, 67—; lectr. Nebr. Com. for Humanities, Lincoln, 1987—. Editor: Letters of Louise Ritter, 1979; contbr. articles to profl. jours. Recipient Zimmmerman Outstanding Tchr. award Midland Luth. Coll., 1989. Mem. Western Lit. Found., Cather Found., Neihardt Found., Altrusa (com. mem. Fremont), Sigma Tau Delta (no. regent 1980—). Republican. Mem. United Ch. of Christ. Home: 2061 N Hancock Fremont NE 68025 Office: Midland Luth Coll 900 Clarkson Fremont NE 68025

RITTER, KAREN A(NNE), state legislator; b. Shirley, Mass., Feb. 28, 1953; d. James P(ierce) and Faye E(ileen) (Morrissey) R. Cert. legal asst., Northampton County Area Community Coll., 1978. Legal sec. Brennen and Gross, Allentown, Pa., 1971-75, Gross and Brown, Allentown, 1975-76; exec. sec. The Goodman Co., Allentown, 1976-77, legal asst., 1977-78; mgr., co-owner Allen Abstract Inc., Allentown, 1978-81; br. mgr. Indsl. Valley Title Ins. Co., Allentown, 1981-83; mgr. Associated Abstract Inc., Allentown, 1983-84, Realty Abstract Inc., Allentown, 1984-86; mem. Pa. Ho. of Reps., Harrisburg, 1986—. Alt. del. Dem. Nat. Conv., N.Y.C., 1980, del., San Francisco, 1984, Atlanta, 1988; local coord. Ted Kennedy for Pres. com., Allentown, 1980; mem. Allentown City Council, 1982-86, v.p., 1982; mem. Allentown Art Mus., 1982—; bd. dirs. Lehigh Valley Dem. Assn., 1985—, pres. 1988—; bd. dirs. The Program for Female Offenders, Allentown, 1985-86, Girls Club of Allentown, 1985—; lector Trinity Meml. Luth. Ch., Allentown, 1987—. Mem. Pa. Elected Women's Assn., Pa. Fedn. Dem. Women, LWV. Lodge: Altrusa (pres. local chpt. 1983-85). Office: 932 Union Blvd Allentown PA 18103

RITTER, KATRINA DANIA, sales representative; b. Fort Collins, Colo., Dec. 13, 1963; d. John Thomas and Karen Dania (Christensen) R. BA, Gustavus Adolphus Coll., 1986. Sales rep. Deluxe Check Printers, Boise, Idaho, 1987—. Mem. Fin. Women Internat., Nat. Assn. Bank Women, Capital Jaycees. Home: 912 Benjamin Ln Boise ID 83704

RITTER, TERESA G., management consultant; b. Rochester, N.Y., Oct. 9, 1951; d. Paul W. and Gladys V. (Clarke) Miller; m. Charels J. Ritter, Aug. 10, 1973; children: Paul J., Amy G. BA, Nazareth Coll., 1973; MBA, U. R.I., 1983. Personnel asst. Women & Infants Hosp., Providence, 1974-75; med. records supr. R.I. Group Health Assn., Providence, 1975-77, asst. dir. personnel, 1977-82; project dir. Bryan Assocs., Inc., Providence, 1983—; adj. faculty R.I. Coll., Providence, 1984-86. Editor co. newsletter, 1976-81 (2nd pl. publs. United Way 1981). Mem. employment subcom. Gov.'s Adv. Commn. on Women, 1979-81; speaker, panelist Project Equality R.I., Providence, 1979-81, Youth Motivation Task Force, 1980-82. Mem. Soc. Human Resources Mgmt., Personnel Assn. R.I. (sec. 1979-80, treas. 1980-81, v.p. 1981-82, pres. 1985-86), Internat. Assn. Bus. Communicators (officer, v.p. 1979-80).

RITTER, VEDA IRENE, insurance company executive, civic worker, private investor; b. Weatherford, Tex., Aug. 11; d. Wesley Marion and Callie Ann (Hudlow) Hill; m. Chauncey Hirsch Ritter, July 16, 1943 (dec. Dec. 1981). Student, Barnes Bus. Sch., 1934-35, Denver U. Sch. Commerce, 1935-36. Assoc. Ritter Ins. Agy., Denver, 1935—, owner, 1966—; pvt. investor in stocks and bonds. Bd. dirs. Friends of Pub. Library, 1950; active vol. Vis. Nurse Assn., Denver, 1956—; 1st v.p. Republican Assocs., 1960, mem. Colo. fin. com., 1964, alt. del. Nat. Conv., 1960. Presbyterian. Clubs: Denver Press, Cherry Hills Country, Brown Palace, Denver Athletic. Lodge: Ladies of Rotary. (dir. 1950).

RITZEMA, JEAN HART, psychologist; b. Morgantown, W.Va., June 10, 1948; d. Floyd Ralph and Doris June (Lough) Hart; m. Robert James Ritzema, Nov. 27, 1970; children: James Nathan, Elliot Hughes. BA, Calvin Coll., 1966; MA, Kent State U., 1979; cert. advanced study, East Carolina U., 1987. Lic. psychol. assoc.; nationally cert. sch. psychologist. Pvt. practice Fayetteville, N.C., 1982-85; head psychol. svcs. St. Pauls (N.C.) City Schs., 1986-87; sch. psychologist Cumberland County Schs., Fayetteville, 1987-88; therapist Christian adolescent in-patient program Cumberland Hosp., Fayetteville, 1989—. Com. chmn. LWV, Jackson, Mich., 1978. Nat. Merit scholar, 1966-70. Mem. Nat. Assn. Sch. Psychologists, N.C. Sch. Psychologists Assn., Cumberland County Mental Health Assn. (bd. dirs. 1986—). Baptist. Home: 620 Hermosa Ct Fayetteville NC 28304 Office: Cumberland Hosp Melrose Rd Fayetteville NC 28314

RITZER, TERI ANN, editor trade publication; b. L.A.; d. Stanton Eli and Evelyn Claire (Dugas) Lobree; m. Herb William Ritzer, Sept. 25, 1976 (div. Apr. 1989). BA in Journalism, U. So. Calif., 1974. Publicity asst. Universal Amphitheatre and Tour, L.A., 1975-77; editor The Tolucan, weekly newspaper, Toluca Lake, Calif., 1977-79; dir. nat. publicity Universal Pictures, L.A., 1984-86; bus. editor, sr. film reporter Hollywood Reporter, L.A., 1980-84, editor, 1986—. Mem. Soc. Profl. Journalists, Publicists Guild Am. Roman Catholic. Office: Hollywood Reporter 6715 Sunset Blvd Los Angeles CA 90028

RITZU, BARBARA JEAN, electronics company administrator; b. Cleve., July 25, 1951; d. Frank Charles and Laureen Catherine (Donelon) Pilny; m. Jeremy Allen Ritzu, Nov. 10, 1948; 1 child, Laura Katheryn. Cert. real estate, Lakeland Community Coll., 1986, student, 1986—. Expediter Gould Inc. Ocean Systems Div., Cleve., 1977-78, buyer, 1978-80, sr. buyer, 1980-83; sr. buyer Picker Internat. Inc., Highland Heights, Ohio, 1983-84, major subcontracts adminstr., 1984-88, mgr. subcontracts, 1988-90, mgr. purchasing MRI div., 1990—; cons. Project Bus., Cleve., 1981-83, 86-89. Democrat. Roman Catholic. Home: 4775 Highland Dr Willoughby OH 44094 Office: Picker Internat Inc 595 Miner Rd Highland Heights OH 44143

RIVERA, ANA DELIA, accountant, food service manager; b. Morovis, P.R., Dec. 30, 1928; d. Juan Antonio and Domitila (Delgado) R. BBA, U. P.R., 1950. Acct., mgr. Maquinaria Cafetalera, Inc., Bayamon, P.R., 1954—. Treas. Art Students League, San Juan, P.R., 1979-82, Mujeres Artistas De P.R., San Juan, 1983—. Recipient Gold medal Artistic Ceramic Competition, 1979. Mem. AAUW. Home: PO Box 2411 Bayamon PR 00621 Office: Maquinaria Cafetalera Inc Rd #2 Bayamon PR 00619

RIVERA, CARMEN M., small business owner; b. San Juan, Puerto Rico, May 2, 1962; d. Carmelo and Francisca (Corchado) Castro; m. Luis A. Rivera, Jan. 30, 1982; children: Luis II, Michael, Julius. Student, Elizabeth Seton Coll., St. John U., N.Y.C. Pres. Sweetheart Lingerie Co., Bronx, N.Y., N.Y. Assn. Female Bus. Owners Corp., Bronx, Rivera & Assocs. Devel. Corp., Bronx. Mem. NAFE.

RIVERA, CHITA, actress, singer, dancer; b. Washington, Jan. 23, 1933; d. Pedro Julio Figuerva del Rivero; m. Anthony Mordente. Student, Am. Sch. Ballet, N.Y.C. Broadway debut: Call Me Madam, 1952; appeared on stage in: Guys and Dolls, Can-Can, Seventh Heaven, Mister Wonderful, West Side Story, Father's Day, Bye Bye Birdie, Three Penny Opera, Flower Drum Song, Zorba, Sweet Charity, Born Yesterday, Jacques Brel is Alive and Well and Living in Paris, Sondheim-A Musical Tribute, Kiss Me Kate, Ivanhoe, Chicago, Bring Back Birdie, Merlin, Jerry's Girls, 1985, The Rink, 1984 (Tony award 1984), Can-Can, 1988; performs in cabarets and nightclubs around world; starred in: film Sweet Charity, 1969; numerous TV appearances include The New Dick Van Dyke Show, 1973-74, Kennedy Ctr. Tonight-Broadway to Washington!, Pippin. Office: care Actors Equity Assn 165 W 46th St New York NY 10036*

RIVERA GRACIA, MARIA TERESA, nursing administrator; b. Vega Baja, P.R., Sept. 11, 1946; d. Preferido Rivera Ray and Antonia Gracia Santiago; m. Jose Joaquin Rivera Ortiz, Nov. 10, 1973; children: Jose Joaquin III, Jose Joaquin IV, Maritere. MS in nursing, U. P.R., 1987. Staff nurse in gen. surgery ward Tchr.'s Hosp., San Juan, P.R., 1970-75, head nurse, 1975-77, supr. emergency dept., 1977-78, nursing edn. coordinator, 1978-82, nursing dept. adminstr., 1982—; instr. in nursing edn. Met. U., San Juan, 1982—. Vice pres. parents' com. Boy Scouts Am., San Juan, 1988—. Fellow P.R. Nursing Adminstr. Assn., P.R. Profl. Nurses Coll.; mem. Horticultive Soc. Office: Tchrs Hosp GPO 4708 San Juan PR 00936

RIVERMAN, RYLLA CLAIRE, health association administrator; b. Brewster, Wash., Apr. 16, 1955; d. Francis William and Helen Edna (Caldwell) Hicks; m. Brian Matthew Riverman, Nov. 2, 1985. BS in Nursing, Walla Walla Coll., 1978. RN. Nurse Portland (Oreg.) Adventist Med. Ctr., 1978-80; dir. pub. affairs Seaside (Oreg.) Gen. Hosp., 1980-82; pub. affairs assoc. Providence Child Ctr., Portland, 1982-83; utilization rev. coordinator St. Vincent Hosp., Portland, 1983-88; dir. internal ops. Metrocare Adminstrv. Svcs., 1988—; lectr. Portland Community Coll., 1983—, Walla Walla Coll., 1983-85, 87, Portland Bus. Group on Health, 1987. Contbr. articles to profl. jours. Mem. Pacific St. Neighbor Watch, Portland, 1986—, Mansfield (Wash.) Grange # 883, 1976—, World Forestry Ctr., Portland, 1986—; chairperson employee fundraising United Way, 1986-87. Recipient Merit award St. Vincent Med. Found., Portland, 1986, U.S. flag for community service, U.S. Senate, Washington, 1982. Mem. Am. Bd. Quality Assurance and Utilization Rev. (diplomate), NW Healthcare Roundtable (v.p. 1984-85, pres. 1985-87, bd. dirs. 1987—, Merit award 1988). Republican. Home: 612 NE 144th Ave Vancouver WA 98684 Office: Metrocare Adminstrv Svcs Inc 12655 SW Center Beaverton OR 97005

RIVERS, BONNIE MCFARLANE, brokerage house executive; b. Bronxville, N.Y., Aug. 19, 1945; d. John Andrew and Frances Darden (Sanders) McF.; (div.) 1 child, Sharon Lynn Jones; m. Alonzo Burrell Rivers, Jan. 31, 1987. Student, Emory U., 1962-63, U. Calif., 1963-64; BBA, Ga. State U., 1966. Analyst fin. Atlantic Steel Co., Atlanta, 1966-67, Minis and Co., Savannah, Ga., 1968-69; v.p. Montag and Caldwell Inc., Atlanta, 1972-79, Robinson-Humphrey Co., Atlanta, 1979-83, J.C. Bradford and Co., Nashville, 1983-85; v.p., food industry analyst Salomon Bros. Inc., N.Y.C., Atlanta, 1985—; trustee, treas. Atlanta Soc. Fin. Analysts, 1982-83. Contbr. articles to profl. jours. Fund raiser, group leader Atlanta Arts Alliance, 1976-78. Fellow Fin. Analysts Fedn.; mem. N.Y. Soc. Security Analysts Inc., Inst. Chartered Fin. Analysts, Consumer Analysts Group N.Y. Office: Salomon Bros Inc 133 Peachtree St Ste 5000 Atlanta GA 30303

RIVERS, HELENE, freelance writer; b. San Francisco, July 14, 1916; d. Walter Allen and Eva (Graff) R. BA, U. Calif., Berkeley, 1938. Copy girl San Francisco Chronicle, 1942-43, reporter women's pages, 1943-53, editor, 1953-56; writer, editor This World, San Francisco, 1956-82, freelance writer book sect., 1982—. Recipient Black Cat trophy San Francisco Press Club, 1976. Mem. AAUW, San Francisco-Oakland Newspaper Guild, Media Alliance, Mechanics Libr. (life), Marin Soc. Artists, Calif. Tennis Club (past editor), Press Club (first woman bd. dir.). Democrat. Home: 368 Via Hidalgo Greenbrae CA 94904

RIVERS, JESSIE MAE, chemist, eucator; b. Chgo., Aug. 31, 1933; d. Charlie Hill and Eula (White) Cunningham; m. Willie Rivers,. Student, Palmer Writers Sch., 1974. Writer Palmer Writers Sch., Mpls., 1972-74; mgr. Jackson Pk. Hotel, Chgo., 1957-62, Herman Roberts Motel, Chgo., 1962-68; private duty Chgo., 1984-88. Home: 640 W Briar Pl Chicago IL 60657

RIVERS, JOAN, entertainer; b. N.Y.C., June 8, 1933; d. Meyer C. Molinsky; m. Edgar Rosenberg (dec.), July 15, 1965; 1 child, Melissa. BA, Barnard Coll., 1958. Formerly fashion coordinator Bond Clothing Stores. Debut entertaining, 1960; mem. From Second City, 1961-62; TV debut Tonight Show, 1965; Las Vegas debut, 1969; nat. syndicated columnist Chgo. Tribune, 1973-76; creator: CBS TV series Husbands and Wives, 1976-77; host: Emmy Awards, 1983; guest hostess: Tonight Show, 1983-86; hostess The Late Show Starring Joan Rivers, 1986-87, Hollywood Squares, 1987—, (morning talk show) Joan Rivers (Daytime Emmy award 1990), 1989—; originator, screenwriter TV movie The Girl Most Likely To, ABC, 1973; other TV movies include: How to Murder A Millionaire, 1990; cable TV spl. Joan Rivers and Friends Salute Heidi Abromowitz, 1985; film appearances include The Swimmer, 1968, Uncle Sam, The Muppets Take Manhattan, 1984; co-author, dir.: (films) Rabbit Test, 1978 (also acted), Spaceballs, 1987; actress: theatre prodn. Broadway Bound, 1988; recs. include: comedy album What Becomes a Semi-Legend Most, 1983; author: Having a Baby Can be a Scream, 1974; The Life and Hard Times of Heidi Abromowitz, 1984, (autobiography with Richard Meryman) Enter Talking, 1986; debuted on Broadway (play) Broadway Bound, 1988. Nat. chmn. Cystic Fibrosis, 1982—, benefit performer for AIDS, 1984. Recipient Cleo awards for commls., 1976, 82; named Woman of Yr., Harvard Hasty Pudding Soc., 1984. Mem. Phi Beta Kappa. Office: care Dorothy Melvin DTM Mgmt 145 S Fairfax Ave Ste 201B Los Angeles CA 90036*

RIVERS, JOAN NADIA, graphics designer; b. Santa Ana, Calif., Nov. 1, 1944; d. Hubert Murray and Alix (Bredé) Brown; m. David Allen Rivers, Sept. 3, 1965; 1 child, Kristan David. BFA, U. Tex., 1978. Staff artist Sta. KLRN/KLRU TV, Austin, Tex., 1975-78; art dir. J. Walter Thompson Co., N.Y.C., 1979-81; designer Steck-Vaughn Pub. Co., Austin, 1982-83, Tex. Instruments, Austin, 1984-85; designer, owner Rivers Graphic Design, Austin, 1985—. Author, illustrator cartoon: Word Processing and Info. Systems mag., 1980-83. Recipient Cert. Recognition Nat. Assn. Ednl. Broadcasters, 1977-78, Best of Show award Internat. Assn. Bus. Communicators, 1986, Cert. Merit Printing Industries Am., 1986. Mem. Am. Inst. Graphic Arts, Austin Graphic Arts Soc. (award of Excellence 1986), Soc. Tech. Communication (Achievement award 1986). Democrat.

RIVERS, MARIE BIE, broadcasting executive; b. Tampa, Fla., July 12, 1928; d. Norman Albion and Rita Marie (Monrose) Bie; m. Eurith Dickinson Rivers, May 3, 1952; children—Eurith Dickinson, III, Rex B., M. Kells, Lucy L., Georgia. Student, George Washington U., 1946. Engaged in real estate bus., 1944-51, radio broadcasting, 1951—; chairperson part owner Sta. WGUN, Atlanta, 1951-87, Stas. KWAM and KRNB, Memphis, Sta. WEAS, Savannah, Ga., Stas. WGOV and WAAC, Valdosta, Ga., Sta. WSWN-, Belle Glade, Fla.; owner, chairperson Sta. WXOS, Islamorada, Fla.; chairperson The Gram Corp. subs. Dee Rivers Group, Ocala; pres. real estate com. Creative Christian Concepts Corp., 1985, Ocala, 1986; cons. Deesown, Inc., Suncoast Broadcasting Inc.; owner Laser Acceptance Corp., 1988. Author: A Woman Alone, 1986; contbr. articles to profl. jours. Youth dir. Fla. Appaloosa Horse Club, 1972—. Mem. Fla. Assn. Broadcasters (bd. dirs.), Kappa Delta. Republican. Roman Catholic. Clubs: La Gorce Country (Miami Beach, Fla.); Coral Reef Yacht (Coconut Grove, Fla.); Sweetwater Country (Orlando, Fla.). Office: Laser Acceptance Corp PO Box 158 Indian Rocks Beach FL 34635

RIVET, LAURIE JEAN, healthcare administrator; b. Detroit, Jan. 9, 1955; d. Nelson Louis and Jacqueline G. (LaBelle) R. BA in Psychology and Bus., U. md., 1982; MBA in Mktg. and Internat. Bus., U. St. Thomas, 1987. Exec. sec. Niagara Machine and Tool Works, Buffalo, N.Y., 1974-78; fgn. svc. sec. U.S. Dept. State, London, 1978-80, East Berlin, 1980-82; dir. adminstrv. and fin. svcs. Hermann Affiliated Hosp. System, Houston, 1982-87;

dir. Diabetes and Nutrition Ctrs. and Family Medicine U. Tex. Med. Br., Galveston, 1988—; cons. Office and Computer Systems, Houston, 1990—. Mem. Health Svcs. Mktg. Soc. (sec. 1989-90), Med. Group Mgmt. Assn., Am. Mgmt. Assn., Bus. and Profl. Women (pres. elect 1990-91), Med. Adminstrs. of Tex., NAFE, Am. Diabetes Assn., Am. Assn. Diabetes Educators. Office: UTMB Diabetes & Nutrition 700 University Blvd #302 Galveston TX 77550

RIVLIN, ALICE MITCHELL, economist; b. Phila., Mar. 4, 1931; d. Allan C. G. and Georgianna (Fales) Mitchell; m. Lewis Allen Rivlin, 1955 (div. 1977); children: Catherine Amy, Allan Mitchell, Douglas Gray; m. Sidney Graham Winter, 1989. B.A., Bryn Mawr Coll., 1952; Ph.D., Radcliffe Coll., 1958. Mem. staff Brookings Instn., Washington, 1957-66, 69-75, 83—; dir. econ. studies Brookings Inst., 1983-87; dir. Congl. Budget Office, 1975-83; dep. asst. sec. program coordination HEW, Washington, 1966-68, asst. sec. planning and evaluation, 1968-69; Staff Adv. Commn. on Intergovtl. Relations, 1961-62; bd. dirs. UNISYS Corp., Union Carbide Corp. Author: The Role of the Federal Government in Financing Higher Education, 1961, (with others) Microanalysis of Socioeconomic Systems, 1961, Systematic Thinking for Social Action, 1971, (with others) Economic Choices 1987, 1986; (with others) The Swedish Economy, 1987, (with others) Caring for the Disabled Elderly: Who Will Pay?, 1988. Bd. dirs. Coun. on Fgn. Rels. Wilderness Soc. MacArthur fellow, 1983-88. Mem. Am. Econ. Assn. (nat. pres. 1986). Office: Brookings Inst 1775 Massachusetts Ave NW Washington DC 20036

RIZK, CHRISTINE MARIE, medical group administrator; b. Pitts., Jan. 9, 1953; d. Angelo Francis Marino and Shirley Mae (Kelly) Andonisio; m. Wafa I. Rizk, Sept. 2, 1972 (div. 1981); children: Tarek Nathan, Stephanie Wedad, Alia Nicole. Student, Seton Hall U., 1970-71, U. Pitts., 1973-74; BSBA, Marywood Coll., 1976; MPA, Carnegie Mellon U., 1985. Owner, prin. Physicians Bus. and Mng. Svcs., Irwin, Pa., 1974-79; clinic adminstr. Whittaker Health Svcs., Saudia Arabia, 1979-81; svc. mgr. Allegheny Gen. Hosp., Pitts., 1981-84; bus. cons. Microsota, St. Paul, 1984-85; mktg. cons. Keyart, Greensburg, pa., 1985-87; bus. mgr. Oakland Neurosurg. Assoc., Pitts., 1987—; cons. in field. Co-author videos, pamphlet in field. Bd. dirs., v.p. Irwin YMCA, 1976-82, Orchard Performing Arts, Delmont, Pa., 1982-88; mem. Westmoreland Choral Soc., Greensburg, Pa., 1988—. Mem. Am. Mgmt. Assn., Am. Mktg. Assn., Assn. Patient Acct. Mgrs., Med. Group Mgrs. Assn. Democrat. Roman Catholic. Home: 810 Pennsylvania Ave Irwin PA 15642 Office: Oakland Neurosurg Assocs 3471 5th Ave Ste 811 Pittsburgh PA 15213

RIZZO, MARY ANN FRANCES, international trade executive, former educator; b. Bryn Mawr, Pa., Jan. 11, 1942; d. Joseph Franklyn and Armella Louise (Grubenhoff) R. BA magna cum laude (N.Y. State scholar), Marymount-Manhattan Coll., 1963; MA (fellow), Yale U., 1965, PhD (Lounsbury-Cross fellow), 1969; postgrad. Harvard U., 1979. Instr. Romance langs. and lit. Yale U., New Haven, 1966-70; asst. prof. Finch Coll., N.Y.C., 1971-73; v.p. Joseph F. Rizzo Co., Fla., 1969-87; owner, pres., 1987—; minister of the Word coordinator, Our Lady of Perpetual Help Ch., Scottsdale, Ariz., 1986—; mem. bd. adv. Assn. Internat. des Etudiants en Sciences Economiques et Commerciales, Ariz. State U. Vice chmn., charter mem. bd. regents Catholic U. Am. Mem. Am. Assn. Tchrs. of Italian, MLA, Am. Assn. Univ. Profs. Italian, Am.-Italy Soc., Il Circolo Italian Cultural Club (Palm Beach, Fla.), Fgn. Trade Coun. Palm Beach County (charter mem.), World Affairs Coun. of Ariz., Scottsdale C. of C. (internat. bus. devel. com.), Trade Coun., Scottsdale C. of C., Alpha Chi. Republican. Roman Catholic (community council 1972-74). Clubs: Marriott Mountain Shadows Country, Harvard Bus. Sch. Greater N.Y., Yale (N.Y.C. and Phoenix); Alliance Francaise (Phoenix); Yale of Palm Beaches; Cercle Français de Palm Beach (Fla.); Ariz. Harvard Bus. Sch. Translator: From Time to Eternity, 1967; bibliographer: Italian Literature-Roots and Branches, 1976. Home: Villa Serein 2170 Ibis Isle Rd Palm Beach FL 33480 also: 5665 N 74th Pl Scottsdale AZ 85250 Office: 7436 E Stetson Dr Suite 180 Scottsdale AZ 85251 also: PO Box 1376 Lake Worth FL 33460

RIZZO, TERRIE LORRAINE HEINRICH, health and fitness executive; b. Oneonta, N.Y., Dec. 15, 1946; d. Steven Joseph Heinrich and Grace Beatrice (Davis) Chamberlin; m. Michael Louis Rizzo, Dec. 28, 1968; 1 child, Matthew Michael. BA, Pa. State U., 1968; MA, Johns Hopkins U., 1971. Tchr. Balt. County Sch. System, 1968-79; asst. dir. univ. rels. U. Md., Catonsville, 1980-81; exec. dir. Aerobic Danse de Belgique, Brussels, 1981—; pres. Eurobics Inc., Sunnyvale, Calif., 1984-86; aerobics dir. Green Valley Health Clubs, San Jose, Calif., 1985; pres. Personally Fit, 1986—; asst. dir. health improvement program Stanford U., Palo Alto, Calif., 1990—; cons. Belgian Ministry Sport, Sabena Airlines, others; lectr., syndicated columnist, 1986—. Author: Sittercise, 1985, How To Keep Fit While You Sit, 1988, Stress Relief Through Exercise, 1988; contbr. articles to profl. jours. Pres. Internat. Study Group, Brussels, 1983-84. Named Marketeer of Yr. Am. C. of C. in Belgium, 1987; recipient Outstanding Alumni award Pa. State U., 1990. Mem. Internat. Dance Exercise Assn., Assn. for Fitness in Bus., Aerobics and Fitness Assn. Am., Pa. State Alumni Assn. (bd. dirs. 1979-88, nat. alumni coun. 1990—), Brussels and Sunnyvale C. of C., San Francisco VCB, Mensa, Pi Gamma Mu, Phi Alpha Theta. Democrat. Roman Catholic. Clubs: Am. Women's (Brussels) (dir. 1983-84); San Jose Quota (bd. dirs. 1986-87). Avocations: traveling, oenology, gourmet cooking. Home: 19755 Lanark Ln Saratoga CA 95070 Office: 137 E Fremont Ave Sunnyvale CA 94087

ROACH, BONNIE LEE, educator; b. Columbus, Ohio, Aug. 10, 1957; d. Marvin Harold and Barbara Lee (Philips) R. BA, Vassar Coll., Poughkeepsie, N.Y., 1979; MLHR, Ohio State U., 1980, PhD, 1984. Asst. prof. mgmt. U. Ill., Champaign/Urbana, 1985-88, Ohio U., Athens, 1988—. Editorial bd. Jour. Mgmt. Sys., 1989—; contbr. articles to profl. jours. Recipient Grad. Student Alumni award, Ohio State U., 1984. Mem. Acad. Mgmt., Assn. Mgmt., Indsl. Rels. Rsch. Assn. Office: Ohio U Dept Mgmt Sys 107 Copeland Hall Athens OH 45701

ROACHE, FIONA ALEXANDRIA, foundation administrator; b. Stretford, England, Dec. 8, 1961; came to U.S., 1977; d. Ruel Alexander and Dorothy Patricia (Brown) R. BBA, U. Miami, Coral Gables, Fla., 1981. Asst. acctg. Broward Ednl. Ctr., Ft. Lauderdale, Fla., 1982-83; adminstr. life, health Ossip-Harris Ins. Co., Miami, Fla., 1984-85; writer grants Juvenile Diabetes Found., N.Y.C., 1985, asst. mgr. major gifts, 1986, mgr. chpt. ops., 1986-87, asst. dir. field ops., mktg., 1987—. Mem. NAFE, Nat. Assn. Fund Raising Execs., Women Fin. Devel. Roman Catholic.

ROATH, ALANE ELIZABETH, sales representative; b. Aurora, Colo., July 29, 1964; d. Sterling and Marie Esther (Betts) R. BS in Mktg., S.W. Mo. State U., 1986. Sales rep. 3-M Co., Bloomington, Ill., 1987-88; account rep. Hallmark Cards, Kansas City, Mo., 1988—. Vol. Persoinal Assistance Phone Help, Bloomington 1988. Mem. Nat. Assn. Female Execs., Am. Mktg. Assn. Home and Office: 33 E 53d St Kansas City MO 64112

ROBB, LYNDA JOHNSON, writer; b. Washington, Mar. 19, 1944; d. Lyndon Baines and Claudia Alta (Taylor) Johnson; m. Charles Spittal Robb, Dec. 9, 1967; children: Lucinda Desha, Catherine Lewis, Jennifer Wickliffe. BA with honors, U. Tex., 1966. Writer, McCall's mag., 1966-68; contbg. editor Ladies Home Jour., 1968-80; lectr. bd. dirs. Reading Is Fundamental, 1968—, Lyndon B. Johnson Family Found., 1969—; mem. Woodlawn Found., White House Fellows Regional Selection Bd., Va. State council on Infant Mortality, Nat. Commn. to Prevent Infant Mortality; chmn. Pres.'s Adv. Com. for Women, 1979-81; chmn. Va. Women's Cultural History Project, 1982-85; bd. dirs. Nat. Home Library Found., Ford Theatre; chmn. Va. Women's Cultural History Project, 1982—; mem. So. Govs. Task Force on Infant Mortality; mem. adv. bd. Commn. Presdl. Debates. Mem. Nat. Wildflower Research Ctr., Zeta Tau Alpha. Democrat. Episcopalian.

ROBBERSON, JULIA DELORES, education educator; b. Springfield, Mo., Sept. 18, 1931; d. James Isaac and Sarah Josephine (Vaughan) R. AA, Stephens Coll., Columbia, Mo.; BS, U. Mo., 1960, MEd, 1964. Pysical edn. tchr. Point Loma High Sch., San Diego, 1960-62; equitation dir. William Woods Coll., Fulton, Mo., 1963-64; assoc. prof. Mo. Valley Coll., Marshall, 1964-77; tchr. spl. edn. Green County Spl. Edn., Springfield, Mo., 1977-78; coord. recreation and leisure svcs. Lambs Inc., Libertyville, Ill., 1978—. co-author: Camp Counseling, 1977. Bd. mem. Wheeling Park Dist., 1983-89; State of Ill. head softball coach, Internat. Spl. Olympics, Notre Dame, 1987. Mem. Am. Assn. for Health, Physical Edn., Recreation, Am. Park and Recreation Assn., Ill. Park and Recreation Assn., Delta Kappa Gamma. Home: 294 Second St Wheeling IL 60090

ROBBINS, ANN TURNER, school system administrator; b. Athens, Ala., Aug. 23, 1940; d. Frank Patterson and Ora Lee (Rose) Turner; m. James Woodrow Robbins, Oct. 28, 1956; children—James Woodrow, Joseph Howell II. B.S. in Elem. Edn. cum laude, Samford U., 1969, M.S. in Elem. Edn., 1972; advanced degree in edn. leadership U. Ala.-Birmingham, 1978. Cert. tchr. grades 1-8, cert. ednl. adminstr. kindergarten-12, Ala. Tchr. Vestavia Elem. Sch., Ala., 1969-71; tchr. Pizitz Middle Sch., Vestavia, 1972-77, tchr., adminstrv. asst., 1977-78; prin. Edgewood Elem. Sch., Homewood, Ala., 1978—. Recipient Outstanding Prin. award U. Montevallo. Mem. Homewood Prins. Assn. (v.p. 1984-86), Ala. Assn. Elem. Sch. Prins. (dist. IV v.p. 1986-87, pres. 1987-88), Nat. Assn. Sch. Prins., Ala. Assn. Sch. Adminstrs., Ala. Council Sch. Adminstrs. Suprs., Assn. Supervision and Curriculum Devel., Women Educators Network, Montevallo In-Service Ctr. (adminstr. governing bd.), Ala. Council Computer Edn., Kappa Delta Pi. Republican. Baptist. Avocations: cooking; reading; physical fitness. Office: Edgewood Elem Sch 901 College Ave Homewood AL 35209

ROBBINS, ANNE FRANCIS See REAGAN, NANCY DAVIS

ROBBINS, CHRISTINE PATRICIA, artist, designer, creative director, educator; b. Montclair, N.J., Jan. 9, 1954; d. Frederick James Nabkey and Eleanor Maroon; m. Andrew Richard Magdanz (div. Feb. 1984); m. K.C. Lambert, July 18, 1987. BA with honors, U. Wis., 1975, MA with honors, 1976; MFA, Calif. Inst. Arts, 1988. Assoc. curator Art Mus. Assn. Am., San Francisco, 1977-1981; prin. Max Almy Prodns., Oakland, Calif., 1981-84; exec. editor, pub. G.A.S. jour., Corning, N.Y., 1984-88; artist, designer Robbins Design, San Francisco, 1980—; creative dir. Digifilm, Oakland, 1988-90; design prin. Western Influence Studios, Berkeley, Calif., 1976-80; cons. fine arts design, San Francisco, 1981—, Art Programs, San Francisco, 1981-82, Calif. Arts Council, Sacramento, 1981—, Craft and Folk Art Mus., Los Angeles, 1985; video instr. U. Calif., Berkeley, 1988, 89. Numerous internat.pub. and private collections, exhibitions and publications. Recipient 1st place Calif. State Art Exhibn., 1982, 1st place Women Design Internat., N.Y.C., 1983, 1st place internat. competition, 1983. Mem. Am. Film Inst., Glass Art Soc. (bd. dirs. 1984-88), Image Techs. (bd. advisors 1986—), Women in Dirs. Chair, Commonwealth Club. Democrat. Home: 1537 18th St San Francisco CA 94107

ROBBINS, JANE BORSCH, library and information science educator; b. Chgo., Sept. 13, 1939; d. Reuben August and Pearl Irene (Houk) Borsch; 1 child, Molly Warren Robbins. B.A., Wells Coll., 1961; M.L.S., Western Mich. U., 1966; Ph.D., U. Md., 1972. Asst. prof. library and info. sci. U. Pitts., 1972-73; asso. prof. Emory U., Atlanta, 1973-74; cons. to the bd. Wyo. State Library, 1974-77; asso. prof. La. State U., Baton Rouge, 1977-79; dean La. State U. (Sch. Library and Info. Sci.), 1979-81; prof., dir. Sch. Library and Info. Studies U. Wis., Madison, 1981—. Author: Public Library Policy and Citizen Participation, 1975, Public Librarianship: A Reader, 1982, Are We There Yet?, 1988, Libraries: Partners in Adult Literacy, 1990; contbr. numerous articles to profl. jours.; editor: Library and Information Science Research, 1982—. Mem. ALA (councilor 1976-80), Am. Soc. Info. Sci., Assn. for Library and Info. Sci. Edn. (dir. 1979-81, pres. 1984), Wis. Library Assn. (pres. 1986). Democrat. Episcopalian. Office: U Wis Sch Libr & Info Studies Madison WI 53706

ROBBINS, JANET EDITH, social work administrator; b. Detroit, Jan. 15, 1955; Lyon Herbert and Lois Mildred (Burton) R.; m. Richard Andrew Hopkins, De. 31, 1977. BS with distinction, U. N.Mex., 1978; M in Social Work Adminstrn., Rutgers U., 1989. Program asst. Las Vegas (N.Mex.) Campus Community Ministry, 1975-76; asst. dir. Project Hold State of Fla., Jacksonville, pub. assistance eligibility specialist, social rehab. specialist, child support investigator, vocat. rehab. specialist, 1979-84; coord. of tng. Prairie Freedom Ctr., Sioux Falls, S.D., 1984-85; personnel supr. Kelly Svcs., Inc., Somerville, N.J., 1985-86; accounts exec. Pitney Bowes, Inc., Lawrenceville, N.J., 1986-88; community problem solving specialist Somerset United Ways, Somerville, 1988-89; dir. social work and discharge planning Hunterdon Med. Ctr., Flemington, N.J., 1989—; chairperson Suffrage Anniversary Celebration Event, Albuquerque, 1978, Somerset County Child Care Alliance, Somerville, 1988—, Teen Esteem Curriculum Com., Somerville, 1988—, planner, Human Svcs. Mgmt. Inst., New Brunswick, N.J., 1988—; mem. consumer adv. coun. United Telephone Co. N.J., Inc., 1990—. Founder, Pres. U. N.Mex. Women's Studies Student Assn., 1977-78; founder, Women Who Love Too Much Support Group, Bridgewater, N.J., 1987—; pres. Southwestern Right to Choose, Albuquerque, 1977-79. Fellow Nat. Assn. Social Workers, Inst. on Research for Women, Union for Concerned Scientists, Physicians for Social Responsibility; mem. NOW. Democrat. Unitarian Universalist. Home: 2 Wythe Circle Neshanic Station NJ 08853

ROBBINS, JOAN RAFF, real estate executive; b. Newark; d. Morry and Florence (Lubin) Raff; m. Jay Howard Robbins, Apr. 15, 1961; children—Jonathan David, Jeffrey Michael, Joshua Benjamin. A.A. in Nursing, Fairleigh Dickinson U., 1960; grad. Realtors Inst. Md., 1980. RN. Dir. nursing Bethesda-Silver Spring Nursing Ctr., Chevy Chase, Md., 1967-69; real estate sales Snider Bros., Inc., Potomac, Md., 1976-79; sales mgr. Lewis & Silverman, Potomac, 1980-81, Peck Properties, Potomac, 1981-83; broker of record Joan Robbins Realty, Bethesda, Md., 1983—; sales mgr. Merrill Lynch Realty, Montgomery County, Md., 1988-90; sales mgr. Coldwell Banker Real Estate, Potomac, Md., 1990—; lectr. sales incentive, mktg. techniques, 1977-84. Mem. Nat. Assn. Realtors, Md. Assn. Realtors, Realtors Nat. Mktg. Inst. (cert. real estate broker), Montgomery County Bd. Realtors (Top 1st Yr. licensee 1977, Million Dollar Sales Club 1979, profl. standards com. 1984—), Nat. Assn. Female Execs. Republican. Jewish. Avocations: swimming; reading; antique collecting; creative artwork/graphics. Home: 8209 Gainsborough Ct W Potomac MD 20854 Office: Coldwell Banker Real Estate 10220 River Rd Potomac MD 20854

ROBBINS, JUDITH HOFFMAN, municipal official; b. L.A., Feb. 24, 1937; d. Richard John and Ruth Janet (Lofthouse) Hoffman; m. Marcus Page Robbins, Jr., June 25, 1961; children: Andrew Page, Janet Elizabeth. BA, Stanford U., 1958; MPA, Suffolk U., 1982. Mem. Attleboro (Mass.) Charter Commn., 1971-73; councilman-at-large City of Attleboro, 1974-89, coun. pres., 1984-89; dir. Massachusetts Bay Transp. Authority, Boston, 1983—; coord. spl. com. on pay equity Mass. Ho. of Reps., Boston, 1985-89. Pres. Celebrity Nights of Attleboros; bd. dirs. Plymouth Bay coun. Girl Scouts U.S.A., Sturdy Meml. Hosp., Attleboro, 1980-89; pres. Little Folks Coop. Nursery Sch., Attleboro, 1970-71. Mem. ASPA, Am. Pub. Transit Assn., Mass. Mcpl. Assn. (bd. dirs. 1981-84), Mass. Mcpl. Councillors Assn. (pres. 1984), Women's Transp. Seminar, LWV, AAUW, Stanford U. Alumni Assn., Phi Beta Kappa, Kappa Alpha Alpha. Congregationalist. Home and Office: 20 Ashton Rd Attleboro MA 02703

ROBBINS, MARTHA HELEN, corporate administrator; b. La Junta, Colo., Sept. 27, 1952; d. Richard Carl and Ruth Janet (Staman) R. BA, Drake U., 1972, M Pub. Adminstrn., 1973. Health planner Gov.'s Office for Planning and Programming, Des Moines, 1973-75, dir. health manpower project, 1975-77; dir. resources devel. Western Colo. Health Systems Agy., Grand Junction, 1977-78; planning specialist Colo. Hosp. Assn., Denver, 1978-79; chief operating officer Davis Inst. on Aging, Denver, 1979-80; asst. adminstr. The Children's Hosp., Denver, 1980-84; v.p., co-owner Med. Systems for Bus. and Industry, Inc. dba Clinicare, Denver, 1981-90; corp. staff specialist Rocky Mountain Child Health Services, Inc., Denver, 1984-86; gen. and mng. ptnr. 5400 Investment Co., Denver, 1985—; v.p., co-owner Work Rite of Colo., Inc., Denver, 1985—; gen. and mng. ptnr. Work Rite Ltd., Denver, 1986—; adminstr. MSBI/Clinicare Employee Benefit Trust, Denver, 1987-90; instr. pub. adminstrn. Drake U., Des Moines, 1974; speaker in field, 1974—; cons. in field, 1980—. Contbr. articles to profl. jours. Orch. mem. Des Moines Symphony, 1969-73, Des Moines Met. Operas, Indianola, Iowa, 1969-76; mem. Colo. Nursing Needs Assessment Panel, Denver, 1974-78; vice chairperson adv. bd. Colo. Hosp. Commn., Denver, 1977-78; vol. Hospice of St. John, Denver, 1987—, bd. dirs. 1988—, sec. bd. dirs., 1989—; vol. instr. econs. program Jr. Achievement, 1987—. Named one of Outstanding Young Women of Am., 1978. Mem. Am. Soc. for Pub. Adminstrn. (chairperson task force on affirmative action Capitol chpt. 1975-77), Colo. Safety Assn., Colo. Motor Carriers' Assn., Denver C. of C., Colo. Masters Swimming Assn., Denver Athletic Club (budget and fin. com. 1988-89), Phi Beta Kappa. Republican. Home: 10220 W Alamo Place Littleton CO 80127 Office: MSBI/Clinicare 4665 Paris St #A-148 Denver CO 80239

ROBBINS, NANCY SLINKER, volunteer; b. New Kensington, Pa., Jan. 28, 1923; d. Charles Morris and Nancy Grace (Moore) Slinker; m. James Bingham Murray, Aug. 1, 1946 (div. 1959); m. Daniel Harvey Robbins, Nov. 21, 1964; children: Nancy Caroline, Christina. BA, Westminster Coll., 1945; grad., U. Pitts., 1946. Cert. tchr. Pa. Tchr. Lower Burrell Sch., New Kensington, 1945-48; asst. buyer Gimbel's, Pitts., 1951-53, buyer, 1953-57; buyer La Salle's, Toledo, 1957-61, Sibley's, Rochester, N.Y., 1961-66. Editor: Fan Fare, 1980-81. Pres. bd. Woman's Edn. and Indsl. Union, Rochester, 1973-76, Women's Coalition for Downtown, Rochester, 1982-84, Ronald McDonald Ho., Rochester, 1986-90; chmn. Pub. TV Auction, Rochester, 1980. Recipient Jefferson award Am. Inst. Pub. Svc., 1988, Forman Flair award for outstanding volunteerism, 1990. Home: 35 Schoolhouse Ln Rochester NY 14618

ROBBINS, NINA, loan officer; b. St. Petersburg, Fla., May 14, 1965; d. James William and Ethel (Young) R. Mortgage clk. First Fidelity Bank Corp., Burlington, N.J., 1984-87; loan counselor PHH US Mortgage Corp., Cherry Hill, N.J., 1987—. Mem. Rep. Presdl. Task Force, Washington, 1989. Republican. Office: PHH US Mortgage Corp 55 Haddonfield Rd Cherry Hill NJ 08002

ROBBINS, SALLY ANN, inventory control professional; b. Cairo, Ill., Mar. 25, 1946; d. Ivan Lester and Lucille Margaret (Fries) Watson; m. Alvin Gene Robbins, June 30, 1962; children: Teena Maree Robbins Wellence, Kimberly Sue Robbins Zale. Machinist, union steward Greenwald Surg. Instruments, Lake Station, Ind., 1966-75; mgr. McDonalds Restaurant Mgmt. Corp., Michigan City, Ind., 1975-81; assembly supr. Task Force Tips, Inc., Valparaiso, Ind., 1981—. Youth leader United Pentecostal Ch. Mem. Am. Mgmt. Assn., Order Eastern Star. Office: 2800 E Evans Ave Valparaiso IN 46383

ROBBINS-WILF, MARCIA, English educator; b. Newark, Mar. 22, 1949; d. Saul and Ruth (Fern) Robbins; m. Leonard A. Wilf, June 21, 1970; 1 child, Orin. Student, Emerson Coll., 1967-69, Seton Hall U., 1969, Fairleigh Dickinson U., 1970; BA, George Washington U., 1971; MA, NYU, 1975; postgrad., St. Peter's Coll., Jersey City, 1979, Fordham U., 1980; MS, Yeshiva U., 1981, EdD, 1986; postgrad., Monmouth Coll., 1986. Cert. elem. tchr., N.Y., N.J., reading specialist, N.J., prin., supr., N.J., adminstr., supr., N.Y. Tchr. Sleepy Hollow Elem. Sch., Falls Church, Va., 1971-72, Yeshiva Konvitz, N.Y.C., 1972-73; intern Wee Folk Nursery Sch., Short Hills, N.J., 1978-81, dir. day camp, 1980-81, tchr., dir., owner, 1980-81; adj. prof. reading Seton Hall U., South Orange, N.J., 1987, Middlesex County Coll., Edison, N.J., 1987-88; asst. adj. prof. L.I. U., Bklyn., 1988, Pace U., N.Y.C., 1988—; ednl. cons. Cranford High Sch., 1988; presenter numerous workshops; founding bd. dirs. Stern Coll. Women Yeshiva U., N.Y.C., 1987; adj. vis. lectr. Rutgers U., New Brunswick, N.J., 1988. Chairperson Jewish Book Festival, YM-YMHA, West Orange, N.J., 1986-87, mem. early childhood com., 1986—, bd. dirs., 1986—; vice chairperson dinner com. Nat. Leadership Conf. of Christians and Jews, 1986; mem. Hadassah, Valerie Children's Fund, Women's League Conservative Judaism, City of Hope, assoc. bd. bus. and women's profl. div. United Jewish Appeal, 1979; vol. reader Goddard Riverside Day Care Ctr., N.Y.C., 1973; friend N.Y. Pub. Library, N.Y.C., 1980—; life friend Millburn Pub. Library, N.J., 1980—. Co-recipient Am. Heritage award, Essex County, 1985; recipient Award Appreciation City of Hope, 1984, Profl. Improvement awards Seton-Essex Reading Council, 1984-86, Cert. Attendance award Seton-Essex Reading Council, 1987. Mem. N.Y. Acad. Scis. (life), N.J. Council Tchrs. English, Nat. Council Tchrs. English, Am. Ednl. Research Assn., Coll. Reading Assn. (life), Assn. Supervision and Curriculun Devel., N.Y. State Reading Assn. (council Manhattan), N.J. Reading Assn. (council Seton-Essex), Internat. Reading Assn., Nat. Assn. for Edn. of Young Children (life N.J. chpt., Kenyon group), Nat. Council Jewish Women (vice chairperson membership com. evening br. N.Y. sect. 1974-75), George Washington U. Alumni Club, Emerson Coll. Alumni Club, NYU Alumni Club, Phi Delta Kappa (life), Kappa Gamma Chi (historian). Club: Greenbrook Country (Caldwell, N.J.); George Washington Univ. Home: 242 Hartshorn Dr Short Hills NJ 07078 also: 1640 Vauxhall Rd Union NJ 07083

ROBERGE, JILL QUIGLEY, editorial director; b. Englewood, N.J., Feb. 7, 1955; d. Charles Joseph and Constance (Osberg) Quigley; m. John Philip Roberge, Sept. 25, 1982; 1 child, Kelly Richard. BA, Franklin Pierce Coll., 1977. With Tech Com Ptnrs., Wilton, Conn., 1985—; editorial dir. Tech Com Ptnrs., Wilton, 1989—. Asst. coach little league and basketball, Monroe, Conn., 1988-90. Mem. Am. Med. Writer's Assn. Home: 182 Jockey Hollow Rd Monroe CT 06468 Office: Tech Com Ptnrs 11 Grumman Hill Rd Wilton CT 06897

ROBERGE, M. SHEILA, state legislator; b. Manchester, N.H.; m. A. Roland Roberge; 2 children. Ed. St. Anselm's Coll. Mem. N.H. Senate, 1985—; chmn. Manchester, N.H., Rep. com., 1979-80; del., Rep. Nat. Conv., 1980, 84; Rep. nat. committeewoman from N.H.; vice-chmn., Rep. Nat. Com., 1980-88. Roman Catholic. Office: Rep Nat Com 310 1st St SE Washington DC 20003*

ROBERSON, CAROLYN A., educator; b. McComb, Miss., Jan. 12, 1950; d. Vernon and Christine (Alexander) Williams; m. Sylvester Roberson, June 17, 1975; 1 child, Carol Syleste. BS, Abilene Christian U., 1972; MS with honors, Chgo. State U., 1978, MS in Guidance and Counseling, 1987; postgrad. in policy studies, Loyola U., Chgo., 1985—. Cert. spl. educator, bus. educator, phys. edn. instr. Tchr. phys. edn. and health Waukegan (Ill.) Sch. Dist., 1972-75; phys. edn. coordinator, asst. activities dir. Hamlin House, Chgo., 1975-76; mental health therapist Ridgeway Hosp., Chgo., 1976-77; adaptive phys. tchr. phys. therapy dept. Spalding High Sch., Chgo., 1977-78; tchr. emotionally and mentally handicapped Blue Island (Ill.) Sch. Dist., 1978-79; tchr. emotionally disturbed Ray Graham Assn., Des Plaines, Ill., 1980; tchr. EMH, TMH, phys. edn., health Spalding High Sch., Chgo., 1980—, acting asst. prin. in charge of discipline, 1983-84, discipline counselor, 1984-85, sch. disciplinarian PE Dept. Spalding High Sch., 1985-86; tchr. of the handicapped Chgo. Bd. Edn., 1985—. Grantee for teaching sci. to handicapped U. Chgo., 1984-85; recipient Inst. Psychoanalysis Scholarship award, 1982-83, 83-84, Grad. Scholarship award Chgo. State U., 1986-87. Mem. Assn. Supervision and Curriculum Devel., Coun. of Basic Edn., Am. Assn. Counseling and Devel., Coun. of Exceptional Children, Ill. Assn. Health, Phys. Edn. and Recreation, NAACP, Phi Delta Kappa. Mem. Ch. of Christ. Home: 10216 S LaFayette St Chicago IL 60628 Office: Spalding High Sch 1628 W Washington Chicago IL 60612

ROBERSON, GLENDA F., professor; b. Dubach, La., July 28, 1942; d. Garland H. and Adele C. R.; children: Jamie K. Norwood, Jennifer K. Broussard. BS, La. Tech. U., 1965; MEd, Tex. Woman's U., 1971, EdD, 1979. Tchr. Grapevine (Tex.) Ind. Schs., 1969-78; asst. prof. West Ga. Coll., 1981-85; assoc. prof. U. Tex., Tyler, 1986—. Mem. Organisation Mondiale pour L'Education Prescolaire (Tex. liason rep. 1989—), Am. Assn. for the Edn. of Young Children, Assn. for Childhood Edn. Inernat., Phi Delta Kappa (rsch. rep. 1989—). Office: University of Texas 3900 University Blvd Tyler TX 75701

ROBERSON, KIM ELIZABETH, real estate broker; b. Seattle, Sept. 20, 1955; d. Frank Tracey and Zetta Elizabeth (Jacobson) R. BS in Nursing, Seattle U., 1977. Commd. 2d lt., U.S. Army, 1977, advanced through grades to maj., 1980; asst. head nurse, Frankfurt-W.Ger., 1980-81, chief nurse Health Clinic, 1981-83, clin. staff nurse, San Francisco, 1983-85,; house supr. Seattle VA Med. Ctr., 1985-87; occupational health nurse, Boeing Aerospace Co., Seattle, 1987-89 sales assoc. Kamas Realty, Inc, 1988—; co-chairperson dept. nursing quality assurance com., 1980-81; mem. affiliate faculty Am. Heart Assn., San Francisco, 1984-85. Maj. USAR, 1989—. Avocations: kayaking, study of wines, music, reading, travel. Home: 8730 Wabash Ave S Seattle WA 98118

ROBERSON, LORIANN, psychologist, educator; b. Mpls., Sept. 1, 1955; d. John Brady and Sara Jean (Sells) R. BA, U. Minn., 1977, PhD, 1984. Instr. Hubert H. Humphrey Inst. of Pub. Affairs U. Minn., 1982-83; rsch. psychologist Personal Decisions Rsch. Inst., Mpls., 1984; asst. prof. Psychology Dept. NYU, 1984—. Contbr. articles to profl. jours. Active Interparish Coun., Trinity Ch., N.Y.C., 1989-90. Awarded Social Sci. Rsch. Coun. Dissertation fellow, U.S. Dept. Labor, 1983; winner S. Reins Wallace award, Soc. for Indsl. and Orgnl. Psychology, 1985. Mem. Assn. Black Psychologists, Ea. Psychol. Assn., Acad. of Mgmt., Soc. for Indsl. and Organiztional Psychology. Office: Psychology Dept NYU 6 Washington Pl New York NY 10003

ROBERSON, MARIAN HOLBROOK, volunteer association adminstrator; b. Cornwall, N.Y., Jan. 28, 1937; d. Willard Ames and Helen Hoyle (Herr) Holbrook, m. Richard Word Roberson, June 7, 1986. Student, Wellesley (Mass.) Coll., 1954-56; MusB, So. Meth. U., 1956-59. Editorial asst. Izaak Walton League of Am., Arlington, Va., 1974-76, conservation assoc., 1977-80, sr. conservation assoc., 1980-82, dir. leadership devel., 1982-88; Washington rep. Patton Cons. Svcs., 1988—. Chmn. Haiti Task Force, St. Patrick's Episc. Ch., Washington, 1984-87; bd. dirs. Hannah House Shelter for Women, Washington, 1985-87, Cathedral Choral Soc., 1985—. Mem. Assn. for Vol. Adminstrn. (chmn. pub. issues com. 1985-87, bd. dirs. 1985-87), Am. Soc. for Tng. and Devel., Am. Soc. Assn. Execs. Republican. Home: 5015 Fulton St NW Washington DC 20016 Office: Patton Cons Svcs 5015 Fulton St NW Washington DC 20016

ROBERSON, VICKY SUE, treasurer; b. Great Bend, Kans., Sept. 28, 1946; d. Floyd Paul and Josephine Delores (Brown) Bell; m. Wayne Leon Roberson, Mar. 25, 1966 (div. 1971); 1 child, Dale Leon. Student, Southwest Assemblies of God Co, Waxahachie, Tex., 1966, Hutchinson Jr. Coll., 1966, Tulsa Jr. Coll., 1974-79; BS, Southwest Mo. State U., Springfield, 1981. Asst. cashier Southwest Tulsa (Okla.) Bank, 1976-79; deferred gift processor Oral Roberts Evang. Assn., Tulsa, 1981-84; city treas. City of Sapulpa, Okla., 1984--. Democrat. Home: 4328 E 66th St Apt 45 Tulsa OK 74136 Office: City of Sapulpa PO Box 1130 Sapulpa OK 74067

ROBERTS, ADELE MARIE (DEDE ROBERTS), public relations executive; b. El Paso, Tex., Sept. 6, 1941; d. George Silk and Adele Freeman (Clay) Howard; m. William Andrew Roberts III, Aug. 2, 1963 (dec. Nov. 1973); children: Janet Lynn, Sandra Kay (dec.). Student, U. Tex., 1959-60; BS in Journalism, Tex. Tech U., 1963. Sales promotion Southwestern Life Ins., Dallas, 1968-70, Popular Dry Goods Co., El Paso, Tex., 1970-71; acct. exec. Mithoff Advt., El Paso, 1971-74, Van Dyke & Assocs., Denver, 1974-77, Sam Lusky Assocs., Denver, 1977-79; owner, mgr. D.R. Communications, Denver, 1979-83; mktg. pub. relations dir. YWCA Met. Dallas, 1983-87; dir. pub. info. North Tex. chpt. Arthritis Found., Dallas, 1987-89; account exec. membership devel. Greater Dallas C. of C., 1989; assoc. dir. pub. rels. and sales S.W. Mus. Sci. and Tech./ The Sci. Pl.; chairperson Dallas C. of C. adv. bd. Social Svcs. & Edn. Magnet Sch., 1983—. Copywriter various ads and videos (1st place fashion copywriting Am. Advt. Fed., outstanding pub. relations, pub. service campaign). Co-chmn. pub. relations Dallas welcoming com. Republican Nat. Conv., 1983-84; v.p. pub. relations Turtle Creek Assn., Dallas, 1984-86; mem. media com. speaker's bur. Arthritis Found., Dallas, 1983—; chmn. media steering com. Dallas Ind. Sch. Dist., 1988—. Recipient Outstanding Achievement award United Way Dallas, 1986, award of excellence Dallas Press Club, 1987 for annual report YWCA, award of excellence Dallas Press Club, 1987 for assn. image video, YWCA 1983-87; finalist Matrix award Women In Communications, 1989. Mem. Pub. Relations Soc. Am., No. Tex. Pub. Relations Soc. Am., NAFE, Speakers Bur. and Media Com., Turtle Creek Assn. (v.p. pub. relations)Dallas C. of C. (media com., media com. 1987-88), East Dallas C. of C. (pub. relations com., auction com. 1987—), Dallas Art Mus., Dallas Arboretum, Altrusa Club (2nd v.p. pub. relations), Beta Sigma Phi (v.p. 1970-71). Episcopalian. Home: 7324 Skillman #201 Dallas TX 75231 Office: Arthritis Found N Tex Chpt 2824 Swiss Ave Dallas TX 75204

ROBERTS, ANN M., management consultant; b. Tulsa, Apr. 3, 1954; d. Richard E. and Evelyn Irene (Breslin) Mahan. BS, U. Tulsa, 1978. Legal sec. Woodson & Gasaway, Tulsa, 1970-73, Ungerman Grabel & Ungerman, Tulsa, 1974-76, Boone, Ellison & Smith, Tulsa, 1976-77, Gable & Gotwals, Tulsa, 1977-78, Andrews, Davis et al, Oklahoma City, 1978-79; dir. admissions Oklahoma City U. Sch. Law, 1979-80; legal asst. McAfee & Taft, Oklahoma City, 1980-81; legal adminstr. Fellers, Snider, Blankenship, Bailey & Tippens, Oklahoma City, 1982-89; pvt. practice mgmt. cons., 1989—; speaker Oklahoma City U. Sch. Law Seminar, 1985, 89. Mem. ABA, Cen. Okla. Assn. Legal Assts. (pres. 1984-85), Assn. Legal Adminstrs.

ROBERTS, BARBARA, state official; b. Corvallis, Oreg., Dec. 21, 1936; m. Frank Roberts, 1974; children—Mark, Michael. Mem. Multnomah County Bd. Commrs., Oreg., 1978; mem. Oreg. Ho. of Reps., 1981-85; sec. of state State of Oreg., from 1985, elected gov., 1990. Mem. Parkrose Sch. Bd., 1973-83. Office: Office of Sec State 136 State Capitol Salem OR 97310

ROBERTS, BARBARA HAHN, computer engineer; b. Cin., May 15, 1942; d. Robert Simpson and Helen Sophia (Shead) Hahn; m. Arthur Adams Roberts, Mar. 26, 1965; children: John Arthur, Jennifer Hahn. BS in Math. cum laude, Clark U., 1964; MS in Math., George Mason U., 1974; postgrad., Va. Poly. and State U., 1974-78; MSEE, Worcester Poly. Inst., 1990. Asst. prof. No. Va. Community Coll., Fairfax, 1974-80, adminstrv. intern to pres., 1978-79; math analyst Goddard Space Flight Ctr., Greenbelt, Md., 1980-84; systems engr. GTE Corp., Westboro, Mass., 1984-88; mem. tech. staff The MITRE Corp., Bedford, Mass., 1988—; ednl. cons. Lt. Gov. Charles S. Robb, Fairfax, 1978. Contbr. articles to profl. jours. Chairperson senate No. Va. Community Coll., Fairfax, 1978-79; statis. cons. Va. Dem. Party, Fairfax, 1979. NSF fellow Clark U., 1962-64. Mem. IEEE (sr., participant budget com. ASSP Mini. Conf. 1989), Soc. Women Engrs., Simulation Computer Soc. (chairperson/session leader summer conf. 1990). Phi Beta Kappa, Phi Delta Kappa, Phi Sigma Tau, Sigma Phi Sigma. Office: The MITRE Corp Burlington Rd Bedford MA 01730

ROBERTS, BARBARA JEAN, civilian military employee; b. Burley, Idaho, Apr. 28, 1934; d. Arthur Lincoln and Matilda Jane (Sabin) R. BA, Idaho State U., 1969, M in Teaching Biol. Sci., 1972. Cert. elem. tchr., Idaho. Sr. lab. asst. Idaho State U., Pocatello, 1970-79, lab. mat. supr., 1979-89; coord. vol. job bank Davis Monthan AFB, Tucson, 1989—; cons. Terminally Unique Cons. Svc., Pocatello, 1970—; mem. transitional student scholarship com. Davis Monthan AFB, 1987-89, vol. employment info. specialist, publicity coord. employment and edn. fair com., 1990. Impartial reviewer Idaho Persn. Commn.; mem. State of Idaho Women's Commn., 1986-89, steering com. Evan for Senate, Bannock County, 1986; active Stalling for Congress, Bannock County, 1984; dir. Idaho State U. Gallery exhibit for Nat. Women's History Month, 1987. mem. NAFE, Nat. Assn. Sci. Material Mgrs., Am. Chem. Soc., Idaho Pub. Employees Assn. (chpt. v.p. 1985), Idaho Mediation Assn. (steering com. ea. Idaho network), Idaho State U. Profl. Women, Sweet Adelines (show and pub. chair 1979-80), Nat. and Tucson Ret. Officer's Aux., Davis Monthan AFB Ret. Officer's Wives Club. Democrat. Home: 711 N 6th #503 Pocatello ID 83201

ROBERTS, BETTY JO, librarian, speech therapist; b. Ft. Worth, Tex., Nov. 11, 1927; d. Harry Pulliam and Mamie Josephine (Parker) Easton; m. Robert Lester Roberts Jr.; children: Jo Lu Roberts Johnson, Lee Ann Foster. Graduate, Polytechnic high sch., Fort Worth, Tex., 1945; student, Tex. State Coll. Women, Denton, 1945-47, Tex. Wesleyan Coll., 1950-51; BS, S.W. Tex. State U., San Marcos, 1952. Tchr. Milton H. Barry Sch. for Physical Rehab., Houston, United Cerebral Palsy Ctr., Ft. Worth, Tex., San Marcos Pub. Schs., Tex., 1952-53; supr. practice tchrs. SW Tex. State Tchrs. Coll., 1952-53; tchr. Waco (Tex.) Ind. Schs., 1953-54; speech therapist Provide Crippled Children's Hosp., Waco; tchr. phonics, creative art Latin Am. Ctr., Waco, 1961-69; ch. librarian Trinity United Methodist Ch., Waco, 1979-88; ch. lib. Cen. United Methodist Ch., Waco, Tex., 1988--. Compilor, Editor: Swedishes and More 1984. Mem. YWCA Waco, Tex. 1954, Assn. Childhood Assn. Waco, Tex. 1954, Tex. Mem. Ch. and Synagogue Libr. Assn., Internat. Browning Soc., Browning Library, Baylor U. Waco Tex., Am. Speech and Hearing Assn., Gem & Mineral Soc. Club Waco Tex., Cokebury Libr. Assn., United Meth. Women. Democrat. Methodist.

ROBERTS, BLANCHE ELIZABETH, cash management sales executive; b. Chgo., Apr. 23, 1955; d. Leroy Edison Jones and Alexandra Mary (Hoover) Johnson; m. Charles Scott Roberts, Nov. 23, 1985; children: Alexis Cleo, Charles Scott Jr. BA in Chemistry and Math., Dartmouth Coll., 1977; MBA in Internat. Bus., DePaul U., Chgo., 1983. Rsch. asst. Gillette Co., Boston, 1974; Spanish tchr. Universidad de Granada/Dartmouth, Granada, Spain, 1978; English/drama tchr. Instit. Chileno NorteAmer., Santiago, Chile, 1978-79; English tchr. Herald's Inst., Rio de Janeiro, 1979; commissioned salewoman Charles of the Ritz Cosmetics, Chgo., 1980-81; exec. asst. Freedom Systems, Chgo., 1981-82; internat. cons. No. Trust Co. Bank, Chgo., 1982-85; with internat. sales First Nat. Bank Chgo., 1985-87; sales mgr. LaSalle Nat. Bank, Chgo., 1987—. Recording sec. Vis. Nurses Assn., Chgo., 1989—, bd. dirs., 1988—; bd. dirs. VNA Ventures, Chgo., 1989—. Named Chgo.'s Up and Coming Bus. Profl., Dollars and Sense Mag., 1988. Mem. Nat. Corp. Cash Mgrs. Assn. (cert. cash mgr. 1987), El Circulo Espanol Hanover (bd. dirs. 1976-77). Home: 5448 S Cornell Chicago IL 60615 Office: LaSalle Nat Bank 120 S LaSalle Chicago IL 60603

ROBERTS, CAROL ANTONIA, county commissioner, real estate associate; b. Miami, Fla., June 22, 1936; d. Milton R. and Betty Shirley (Pallot) Klein; m. Aug. 9, 1953; children: David, Jonathan, Mark, Stephen, Scott, Pamela. Student, Tuft U., 1953-54, Palm Beach (Fla.) Jr. Coll., 1960-62, Palm Beach Atlantic Coll., 1971-72. Host radio program Sta. WPBR, Palm Beach, Fla., 1976-83; co-founder Denman Roberts & Ross, West Palm Beach, Fla., 1978-80; pres. Sunshine Acad. Press, Inc., West Palm Beach, 1978—; pres., broker VIP Mgmt. and Realty, Inc., West Palm Beach, 1980—. Commr. City of West Palm Beach, Fla., 1975, 77, 82, 84, vice mayor, 1976-77, 84-85, mayor, 1985-86; chair Palm Beach County Bd. Commrs., 1987, 88; bd. dirs., chair women's div. Palm Beach County Comprehensive Community Mental Health Ctr. Bd., 1978-80, Jewish Fedn. Palm Beach County, 1978-80, Palm Beach Inst. Med. Rsch., Goodwill Industries, Cities in Schs., Anti-Defamation League, Adopt-A-Family; vice chair Tri-County Rail Authority, chmn. mktg. com.; vice chair Solid Waste Authority, 1977-78; chair Art in Pub. Places, Artificial Reef com., Intracoastal Waterway com.; co-chair Water Resources Mgmt. Adv. Bd.; vice chair Fla. League of Cities Intergovtl. Rels. com.; mem. Palm Beach Sports Authority, So. Fla. Mental Health Consortium, Treasure Coast Regional Planning Coun.; mem Fla. Crime Prevention Commn., 1985. John and Mabel Ringling Mus. Art grantee, Norton Art Gallery grantee, U. Mus. grantee, U. Fla. grantee, Tufts U. grantee, Fla. A&M U. grantee; named Woman of the Yr., Bus. and Profl. Women Palm Beaches, 1985, Leading Lady in Mcpl. Govt., Network Connection, 1985; recipient Appreciation award Tri-County Nat. Bus. League, 1985, Woman of the Yr. award Temple Beth El Sisterhood, 1986, Disting. medal Palm Beach Atlantic Coll., 1986, Disting mem. of Pres. Coun. U. Fla.; inducted into Fla.'s Hall of Fame, 1986. Mem. Fla. League of Cities (vice chair intergovtl. rels. com.), Fla. Assn. Counties (social svcs. policy com.), Fla. Assn. Counties Bd. Dirs., Nat. Assn. Counties (intergovtl. rels. com.), South Fla. Mental Health Consortium. Democrat. Jewish. Home: 6708 Pamela Ln West Palm Beach FL 33405 Office: 301 N Olive Ave West Palm Beach FL 33401

ROBERTS, CAROL JOY, goverment administrator; b. Paducah, Tex., July 21, 1953; d. Charles Gene Bragg and Anita Joy (Bates) Hurta; m. Glen Earl Roberts, Jan. 4, 1975 (div. Nov. 1979). BA in Psychology, U. Tex., 1974. Contract specialist NASA, Houston, 1974-77; collections supr. U.S. Dept Edn., Dallas, 1977-80, lender examiner, 1980-84; chief, fin. mgmt. sect. U.S. Dept Edn., Washington, 1984-86, chief, guaranteed student loan policy br., 1986-87, chief, guaranteed student loan ops. br., 1987—. Baptist.

ROBERTS, CELIA ANN, librarian; b. Bangor, Maine, Feb. 6, 1935; d. William Lewis and Ruey Pearl (Logan) R.; A.A., U. Hartford, 1957, B.A., 1961; postgrad. So. Conn. State Coll., 1963—. With catalog, acquistion and circulation depts. U. Hartford Library, 1956-65; librarian Simsbury (Conn.) Free Library, 1965; reference librarian Simsbury Public Library, 1969—. Tchr. ballet classes, 1965-66; ballet mistress Ballet Soc. Conn., Inc., 1968-70; with corps de ballet Conn. Opera Assn., 1963-64; active in prodns. Simsbury Light Opera Assn., 1964, 69. Mem. ALA, Conn. Library Assn., Simsbury Hist. Soc., Ont. Geneal. Soc., New Eng. Historic and Geneal. Soc., AAUW (past pres. Greater Hartford br.), Pro Dance, DAR (Abigail Phelps chpt.), Conn. Soc. Genealogists, Soc. Mayflower Descs. Conn., Dance Masters Am. Universalist. Office: 725 Hopmeadow St Simsbury CT 06070

ROBERTS, DIANA KAYE, accountant; b. Independence, Mo., Mar. 14, 1959; d. Charles Mitchell Villines and Betty Jane (Mead) Crandall; m. Robert Lee Roberts Jr., May 16, 1980; children: Valerie Marie, Rosemary Kaye. Cert. tax preparer, Mr. Tax. of Am., 1979, Nat. Tax Tng. Sch., 1981, H&R Block, 1986; enrolled agt., IRS. Ins. agt. Mutual of Omaha, Kansas City, Mo., 1979; pres. Roberts Acctg. and Tax Svc., Independence, 1979—. Editor Internat. Quill and Scroll, Independence, 1973-76. Mem. Bicentennial Liaison Com., Independence, 1975-76; cons. Pentecostal Ch. of God in Christ, Kansas City, 1986-90. Mem. NAFE, Nat. Soc. Pub. Accts., Ind. Accts. Soc. Mo. (sec. 1987-88), Concept Therapy Inst. (navigator 1989—), Mo. Assn. Tax Practitioners, Independence C. of C. Office: Roberts Acctg and Tax Svc 6516 Independence Ave Kansas City MO 64125

ROBERTS, DORIS EMMA, epidemiologist, consultant; b. Toledo, Dec. 28, 1915; d. Frederic Constable and Emma Selina (Reader) R. Nursing diploma, Peter Bent Brigham Sch. Nursing, Boston, 1938; B.S., Geneva Coll., Beaver Falls, Pa., 1944; M.P.H., U. Minn., 1958; Ph.D., U. N.C., 1967. Staff nurse Vis. Nurse Assn., New Haven, 1938-40; sr. nurse Neighborhood House, Millburn, N.J., 1942-45; supr. Tb Baltimore County Dept. Health, Towson, Md., 1945-46; Tb cons. Md. State Dept. Health, 1946-50; cons., chief nurse Tb program USPHS, Washington, 1950-57; cons. div. nursing USPHS, 1958-63; chief nursing practice br. Health Resources Adminstrn., HEW, Bethesda, Md., 1966-75; adj. prof. Sch. Pub. Health, U. N.C., 1975-84; cons. WHO. Mem. Pub. Citizen, Inc. Served with USPHS, 1945-75. Recipient Distinguished Alumna award Geneva Coll., 1971; Distinguished Service award USPHS, 1971; Outstanding Achievement award U. Minn., 1983. Fellow Am. Pub. Health Assn. (v.p. 1978-79, Distinguished Service award PHN sect. 1975, Sedgwick Meml. medal 1979); mem. Inst. Medicine of Nat. Acad. Scis., Common Cause, Delta Omega. Home: 6111 Kennedy Dr Chevy Chase MD 20815

ROBERTS, DOROTHY HYMAN, accessory company executive; b. N.Y.C., Dec. 6, 1928; d. Edgar C. and Theresa M. (Marks) Hyman; B.A., Conn. Coll., 1950; m. Paul M. Roberts, June 18, 1950 (dec.); children—Lynn, Steven; m. Paul M. Cohen. With Echo Design Group, Inc. (formerly Echo Scarfs, Inc.), N.Y.C., 1950—, pres., 1978—. Mem. The Fashion Group. Office: 10 E 40th St New York NY 10016

ROBERTS, EILEEN DORIS FRAHM, graphic designer, illustrator; b. N.Y.C., June 3, 1933; d. Walter Frederick and Gertrude May (Meyer) Frahm; m. Stanton Harvey Roberts, Jr., Sept. 13, 1953; children—Jodi Lynn, Stanton Harvey, Brent Walter. Student Pratt Inst., 1951-52, SUNY-Buffalo Coll. for Tchrs., 1952-54, Albright Art Sch., 1952-54, N.Y. Sch. Interior Design, 1965, Mira Costa Coll., 1971-73, Palomar Jr. Coll., 1979, U. Calif.-San Diego, 1984. Comml. artist Art Design Assocs., Mountainview, Calif., 1959-60; illustrator Ford Found., N.Y.C., 1964-65; craft coordinator Recreation Dept. City of Carlsbad, Calif., 1972; math. aide Oceanside Unified Sch. Dist., Calif., 1976-78; owner, artist Roberts Design Studio, Carlsbad, 1977—; art dir. Evergreen Nursery, San Diego, 1988—; art cons. gifted children Oceanside Pub. Schs., 1973-74. Designer, illustrator: Self-Hypnosis, A Guide To, 1983, May Centers Safety Book, 1983; painter: Misty (best of show award 1969); 1st woman contbr. to Combat Art Program USMC, Quantico, Va., 1967—. Arts and crafts assn. Prince William County Fair, Va., 1967-68; artist-in-residence Oceanside Bicentennial Com., 1975-76; chmn. Meet the Americans, Oceanside, 1975-76; mem. San Diego Art Inns, Oceanside, 1975-76; mem. San Diego Art Inst. Mem. Nat. League Am. Pen Women, Book Publicists of San Diego. Avocations: hiking; bicycling; painting; jogging; cooking; reading. Home and Office: Roberts Design 12527 Kestrel St San Diego CA 92129

ROBERTS, ELIZABETH DIXON, retired educator; b. Independence, Calif., May 25, 1925; d. John Wardle and Luceal (Root) Dixon; m. Clyde Martin Roberts, Jan 27, 1945; children: Keith Alan, Ann Elizabeth. AB, Fresno State U., 1946. Tchr. L.A. Ind. Sch. Dist., 1947-49, San Angelo (Tex.) Ind. Sch. Dist., 1958-81; ret., 1981. Chmn. children's edn. 1st United Meth. Ch, 1977. Mem. AAUW (pres. San Angelo 1974-76, named scholarship award 1983), P.E.O. (pres. 1987-89), NEA, Tex. State Tchrs. Assn., Tex. Classrm. Tchrs. Assn., PTA (award Tex. Life Mem. 1984), Delta Kappa Gamma (pres. Alpha Beta Chpt. 1976-78, Achievement award 1977).

ROBERTS, ERICA SUE, infosystems specialist; b. N.Y.C., Nov. 30, 1960; d. Joel S. and Rene (Farkas) Balsam; m. James J. F. Roberts, Nov. 28, 1982. B.A., NYU, 1981. Cert. info. system auditor. EDP auditing specialist Blue Cross-Blue Shield, N.Y.C., 1981; EDP auditor Dean Witter Reynolds, N.Y.C., 1982, Hazeltine Corp., Greenlawn, N.Y., 1983-84, L.I. Savs. Bank, Centereach, N.Y., 1984-85, Norton Co., Worcester, Mass., 1985-87, Ocean Spray Cranberries, Lakeville, Mass., 1987—. N.Y. State Regents scholar, 1977. EDP Auditors Assn. (program dir. New England chpt.), Profl. Women Greater Worcester (treas.), NAFE, NYU Alumni Assn. Office: 1 Ocean Spray Dr Lakeville MA 02349

ROBERTS, GAYLE ANN, pharmacist; b. Tacoma, Apr. 4, 1953; d. Abner J. and Lyle L. (Van Winkle) R. BS in Pharmacy, Wash. State U., 1976. Resident in hosp. pharmacy Rhode Island Hosp., Providence, 1976-77, staff pharmacist, 1977-78; pharmacy mgr. Bi-Lo Pharmacy, Tacoma, 1978-85, Tacoma/Pierce County Health Dept., 1985-89; pharmacist Allenmore Hosp., Tacoma, 1989—. Bd. dirs. Lakewood Players, Tacoma, 1988-89; mem. Jr. League of Tacoma, 1986-89, steering com. for follies 89, 1988-89. Mem. Am. Pharm. Assn. Lutheran. Home: 2536 Narrows Dr #18 Tacoma WA 98406 Office: Allenmore Hosp Pharmacy 19th and Union Sts Tacoma WA 98405

ROBERTS, GERRY REA, music educator, organist; b. Brady, Tex., Nov. 13, 1940; d. Willie Melvin and Mary Catherine (Brown) Howard; m. Leslie Wayne Templeton, July 28, 1961 (div. Feb. 1977); children: Todd Wayne, Gwen Marie; m. Harold James Roberts Jr., Sept. 24, 1977. Student, Sam Houston State U., 1959-60; MusB, U. Houston, 1962, postgrad., 1964-65; postgrad., North Tex. State U., 1966, Stephen F. Austin U., 1983, East Tex. State U., 1984, Memphis State U., 1984, 85, Las Vegas U., 1985. Cert. music tchr., 1-12, Tex., elem. tchr., 1-6, Tex.; cert. Orff-Schulwerk levels I, II, III. Music tchr. Deer Park (Tex.) Ind. Sch. Dist., 1962-63, Dallas Ind. Sch. Dist., 1963, Richardson (Tex.) Ind. Sch. Dist., 1964-68; kindergarten tchr. Houston Ind. Sch. Dist., 1971, tchr. 1st grade, 1974-78; tchr. music Klein (Tex.) Ind. Sch. Dist., 1978-90; church organist Garden Villas Bapt. Ch., Houston, 1955-59, Fourth Church of Christ Scientist, Houston, 1960-63, South Park Bapt. Church, Houston, 1962-63, Westshore Meth. Ch., Richardson, Tex., 1964-67; substitute organist Bethany Meth. Ch., Houston, 1971-75, dir. children's choir, 1971-74; organist Lakewood Meth. Ch., Houston, 1979-81, Windwood Presbyn. Ch., Cypress, Tex., 1982-90, others. Pianist, musical dir. 1960 Playhouse, 1979; pianist prodns. Klein Forest High Sch., 1984, 85, 86, Klein High Sch., 1987, 88, 89; singer Houston Symphony Chorale, 1960-62, Richardson Choral Club, 1963-64, Jeffrey Ross Chorale, 1988-89, Tomball (Tex.) Community Chorus, 1988-90. Organist St. Paul's Presbyn. Ch., 1975-77, Lakewood Meth. Ch., Houston, 1979-81, Windsood Presbyn. Ch., Cypress, Tex., 1982-90. Recipient Tex. Pianist 2nd Pl. award Tex. Music Tchrs. Assn, 1959; Jesse Jones Foundation scholar, 1959; Sam Houston State U. scholar, 1959, U. Houston scholar, 1960. Mem. Tex. Music Educators Assn., NEA, Tex. State Tchrs. Assn., Klein Educators Assn., Music Educators Nat. Conf., Am. Guild Organists, Gulf Coast Orff-Schulwerk Assn., Am. Orff-Schulwerk Assn., Sigma Alpha Iota (pres. U. Houston chpt. 1961-62, v.p. Houston Alumni chpt. 1971-72, Sword of Honor 1972). Republican. Home and Office: Rte 1 Box 799 Harrah OK 73045

ROBERTS, HELEN WYVONE, city official; b. Kirksville, Mo., Jan. 9, 1934; d. William Lawrence and Lectie Beryl (Boley) Chitwood; m. Philip C. Roberts, Jan. 9, 1952 (div. 1976); children—Christy, Cheryl, Gayla. Secretarial degree Chillicothe Bus. Coll., 1951; B.S., Lindenwood Coll., 1983. Exec. sec. McDonnel-Douglas Aircraft, St. Louis, 1962-65, Transit Homes, Inc., Greenville, S.C., 1970-76; exec. sec. City of St. Peters, Mo., 1976-79, asst. planning and devel. coordinator, 1979-81, adminstrv. asst. to city adminstr., 1981-84, purchasing agt., 1984, asst. to city adminstr., 1985-89; asst. city adminstr., mgr. staff support svcs., 1989—. Mem. Nat. Assn. Female Execs., Internat. Cities Mgmt. Assn., Am. Mgmt. Assn., Am. Bus. Women's Assn., Lindenwood Coll. Alumni Assn., Alpha Sigma Tau. Baptist. Avocations: horseback riding; sports; reading. Home: 329 Karen St Saint Charles MO 63301 Office: City of St Peters PO Box 9 Saint Peters MO 63376

ROBERTS, JANICE LYNN, economist; b. Pine Bluff, Ark., Dec. 31, 1959; d. James Clifton and Deloris Diane (Strivers) Roberts. BA, U. Ark., Pine Bluff, 1981; MPA, U. Ark, Pine Bluff, 1985, U. S.C., 1986; PhD, U. S.C., 1989. Cert. economist. Economist Dept. Agri. Soil Conservation Service, Little Rock, Ark., 1979-85, U.S. Army Corps. of Engrs., Los Angeles, 1985-- . Mem. Nat. Female Exec., Wash., 1982--; v. chairperson Fed. Women Program, Los Angeles, 1987-; mem. NAAP; treas. Blacks in Govt., Los Angeles,. Named Outstanding Young Women of Am., 1988-89, U.S. Congressional Advisor, 1981. Mem. NAFE, Nat. Assn. Economist, Gamma Sigma Sigma. Democrat. Baptist. Home: PO Box 851 Los Angeles CA 90053 Office: U S Army Corps Engrs 300 N Los Angeles CA 90053

ROBERTS, JEAN, registered nurse; b. Middletown, Conn., Apr. 12, 1947; d. Willard H. and Dorothy (Woolley) R.; m. Gary W. Kyle, Aug. 28, 1972 (div. 1978); children: Ashleigh Sheridan, Beverly Arden; m. Donald James Henry, Dec. 31, 1986. BS in Nursing, Boston U., 1969; MS in Nursing, UCLA, 1972. RN, Calif. Clin. nurse IV UCLA, L.A., 1969-76; dir. nursing Mesa Vista Hosp., San Diego, 1978—; mem. Edgemor Profl. Review, Sartee, Calif., 1989—; adv. bd. San Diego City Nursing, 1982—; mem. Sharp Home Health Care Bd., San Diego, 1985—. Author: (with others) Manual for Professional to teach Behavior Modification, 1976. Mem. Dir. of Nursing Coun., Sigma Theta Tau. Democrat. Home: 1095 Helix Village Dr El Cajon CA 92020 Office: Mesa Vista Hosp 7850 Vista Hill Ave San Diego CA 92123

ROBERTS, JEAN REED, lawyer, business executive; b. Washington, Dec. 19, 1939; d. Paul Allen and Esther (Kishter) Reed; m. Thomas Gene Roberts, Nov. 26, 1958; children: Amy, Rebecca, Nathanial. AB in Journalism, U. N.C., 1966; JD, Ariz. State U., 1973. Bar: Ariz. 1974. Sole practice, Scottsdale, Ariz., 1975-84; founding ptnr. Simon, Reeves & Roberts, 1985—; legal dir., advisor to gov. Ariz.-Mex. Commn., 1980-89; judge pro tem Superior Ct., Maricopa County, Ariz., 1979—. Editor: Scottsdale Bar Practice Manual, 1981. Sec. Charter 100 Phoenix, 1983-84; bd. dirs. Ariz. Ctr. for Law in Pub. Interest, 1988; chmn. Bd. of Adjustment, Town of Paradise Valley, 1984—. Mem. ABA, State Bar Ariz. (founder art law sect. 1979-81), Scottsdale Bar Assn. (dir. 1980-82), Ariz. Bar Assn., Soroptimist (pres.). Democrat. Jewish. Home: 6655 E Hummingbird Ln Paradise Valley AZ 85253 Office: Reeves & Roberts 7110 E McDonald Dr Ste A-1 Scottsdale AZ 85253

ROBERTS, JOAN ELLEN, arts and entertainment management consultant; b. N.Y.C., Jan. 15, 1944; d. Carl and Elizabeth (Levine) Spitz; m. Samuel Smith Roberts, Nov. 16, 1963 (div. 1973); children: Nancy Anne, Pamela Susan. Student, Boston U., 1961-63; B of Profl. Studies, Empire State Coll., 1983; MA, Montclair State Coll., 1985. Musical dir. Port Chester (N.Y.) Youth Theatre, 1963-65; various positions Elmwood Theatre, Nyack, N.Y., 1965-73; music tchr. Rockland Country Day Sch., Congers, N.Y., 1971-73; musical theatre dir. Camp Oguago, Andes, N.Y., 1978-82; mgr., adminstrv. asst. Woodstock (N.Y.), Playhouse, 1985-86; performer various clubs, resorts and restaurants, N.Y., 1972—; realtor, assoc. Yvonne B. Curran Real Estate, Kingston, N.Y., 1986—; tutor theatre Empire State Coll., New Paltz, N.Y., 1987—; cons. Byrdcliffe Theatre Festival, 1987—; tchr. Town Ramapo Cultural Ctr., Suffern, N.Y., 1971-74; house mgr. Woodstock Playhouse, summer 1984; tchr. vocal, music, dir. music theatre Kingston High Sch., 1988-89; vocal music tchr., dir. music theatre Onteora High Sch., 1989; exec. dir. Ulster Performing Arts Ctr., Kingston, N.Y., 1990—. Mem. Actors' Equity Assn., Phi Kappa Phi. Alpha Sigma Alpha. Jewish. Club: Woodstock Golf.

ROBERTS, JUDITH MARIE, librarian, educator; b. Bluefield, W.Va., Aug. 5, 1939; d. Charles Bowen Lowder and Frances Marie (Bourne) Lowder Alberts; m. Craig Currence Jackson, July 1, 1957 (div. 1962); 1 son, Craig, Jr.; m. 2d, Milton Rinehart Roberts, Aug. 13, 1966 (div. 1987). B.S.,

Concord State Tchrs. Coll., 1965. Librarian, Cape Henlopen Sch. Dist., Lewes, Del., 1965—. Pres. Friends of Lewes Pub. Library, 1986—; chmn. exhibits Govs. Conf. Libraries and Info. Services, Dover, Del., 1978; mem. Gov.'s State Library Adv. Council, 1987—. Mem. ALA, NEA, Del. State Edn. Assn., Sussex Help Orgn. for Resources Exchange (pres. 1984-85), Del. Library Assn. (pres. 1982-83), Del. Learning Resources Assn. (pres. 1976-77). Methodist. Home: 42 DeVries Circle Lewes DE 19958 Office: Cape Henlopen High Sch Kings Hwy Lewes DE 19958

ROBERTS, KAREN See WALKER, KAREN

ROBERTS, KATHLEEN JOY DOTY, educator; b. Jamaica, N.Y., Apr. 19, 1951; d. Alfred Arthur and Helen Caroline (Sohl) Doty; B.A. in Edn., Queens Coll., 1972, M.S. in Spl. Edn., 1974; cert. of advanced study in ednl. adminstrn. Hofstra U., 1982; m. Robert Louis Roberts, Nov. 24, 1974; children: Robert Louis, Michael Sean, Kathleen Meagan. Health conservation tchr. Woodside Jr. High Sch., Woodside, N.Y., 1973-77; coord. spl. edn. dept., Ridgewood (N.Y.) Jr. High Sch., 1977-81; adminstrv. asst., health coord., compliance coord., resource tchr. Grover Cleveland High Sch., Ridgewood, N.Y., 1981—. Cert. N.Y. State Dept. Mental Hygiene; cert. sch. adminstr., math. tchr., N.Y.; lic. spl. edn. supr., ednl. adminstr., legis. chmn. Fairfield and McKenna PTA. Mem. NEA, N.Y. State Tchrs. Assn., Council for Exceptional Children, Soc. Mayflower Descs. AAUW, Colonial Daus. of 17th Century (pres. 1985—), nat. chmn. hist. activities com. 1988—), Nat. Soc. DAR, Pilgrim Edward Doty Soc. Republican. Author: Closed Circuit Television and Other Devices for the Partially Sighted, 1971. Home: 52 Hicksville Rd Massapequa NY 11758 also: Lake Ariel PA Office: Grover Cleveland High Sch 2127 Himrod St Ridgewood NY 11385

ROBERTS, KAY K., department director; b. Salem, Ill., Aug. 22, 1940; d. Keith Emerson and Helen Edith (Griffin) Kehl; m. John A. Roberts, Aug. 22, 1965; children: Sherrill Page, Stacy Robin. BS, Pitts. State U., 1963; postgrad., U. Mo., Columbia. Tchr. Wichita (Kans.) Pub. Sch., 1963-64, Coltey Coll., Nevado, Mo., 1965; rsch. asst. Family Commn. Medicine U. Mo., Columbia, 1970-81; county ct. judge Boone County, Columbia, 1981-84; legis. liaison to Gov. John Ashcroft, Jefferson City, Mo., 1984-86; dept. dir. Boone County Nat. Bank, Columbia, 1986—. Contbr. articles to profl. jours. Mem. County Planning and Zoning com., Columbia, 1975-81; Rep. campaign com., Columbia, 1978, regional chair for Gov. Ashcroft, 1988. Recipient Columbia Pub. Sch. Outstanding Svc. award, 1976, Svc. award Boone Retirement Ctr., 1982, Mo. Assn. Counties, Outstanding Svc. award State Mo., 1983. Mem. Mo. Bankers Assn., Columbia C. of C., PEO, Kiwanis. Republican. Methodist. Office: Boone County Nat Bank PO Box 678 Columbia MO 65205

ROBERTS, KAYE VIRGINIA, service company executive; b. Newnan, Ga., Feb. 19, 1958; d. Julian Floyce and Sara Virginia (Roesel) R. Student, Berry Coll., 1976-77; BSBA, Ga. Coll., 1980; MS, Ga. State U., 1984. Funding adminstr. Algemene Bank Nederland, N.V., Atlanta, 1980-83; office mgr., contr. Response Media Products, Inc., Atlanta, 1983-88; dir. mktg. and fin. Calmic, Inc., Atlanta, 1989—. Mem. Brit. Am. Bus. Group, Atlanta Hist. Soc., Alpha Delta Pi. Methodist.

ROBERTS, KRISTI SMITH, psychologist; b. Long Beach, Calif., Sept. 9, 1946; d. Wallace Burton and Viola (Heinen) Smith; m. Dennis Richard Brightwell, Mar. 8, 1983; children: Adrienne Wallace, David Johnston. BA, U. Ariz., 1968, MS, 1972; PhD, U. Mo., 1979. Lic. psychologist, Mo., Fla. Chief therapist West Ctr. Tucson (Ariz.) Gen. Hosp., 1972-73; program dir. CareUnit, San Jose, Calif., 1973-74; coord. client svcs. employee assistance program U. Mo., Columbia, 1975-79, asst. prof., 1977-85; program coord. VA Hosp. Alcoholism Program, Columbia, 1979-85; clin. dir. VA Hosp. Alcoholism Program, Tampa, Fla., 1985-89; area alcohol and drug abuse coord. Fla. Biodyne, Tampa, 1989—. Contbr. articles to profl. jours. Mem. Am. Psychol. Assn. Episcopalian. Home: 4306 Gainsborough Ct Tampa FL 33624 Office: Biodyne 4010 Boy Scout Blvd Ste 240 Tampa FL 33607

ROBERTS, LILLIAN, educator, school system administrator; b. Albuquerque, Dec. 1, 1927; d. John Wagner and Mattie Rebecca (Beaty) Thomas; m. Vernie Roberts, Aug. 28, 1953 (dec. Sept. 13, 1980); children: Albert, Kenneth, Constance Marie. BA, Calif. State U., Stanislaus, 1964; MA, Fresno (Calif.) Pacific Coll., 1979. Cert. elem. tchr., Calif. Mgr., co-owner Vernie's Barber Shop and Cocktail Lounge, Merced, Calif., 1955-66; tchr. Merced City Sch. Dist., 1962-72, resource tchr., 1972-77, coordinator consolidate programs, 1977—, preschool prin., 1981—; pvt. music tchr., Merced, 1960-65; adult edn. tchr. Merced Union High Sch. Dist., 1965-66; chief attendance officer Merced City Sch. Dist., 1981—, affirmative action officer, 1981-86; adj. instr. Merced Community Coll., 1983-86, seminar leader Early Childhood Devel., 1985, Early Childhood Edn., 1989, 90. Mem. Merced County LWV, 1971—, Merced Community Concerts, 1972-79, Merced Area Dems., 1972—, Unitarian Universalists Assn. of Merced County, 1967—, Muir Trail Girl Scout Council, Merced, 1979-80, 15th Cong. Dist. Constituents Adv. Com., 1987—, Calif. State U. Acad. Adv. Council, Stanislaus, 1980, Merced Masterworks Chorale, 1980-85; proctor Merced County Acad. Decathalon; mem. com. Children's Svc. Netork of Merced County, 1983—, chairperson 1986—, bd. dirs. Mem. NEA, Calif. Tchrs. Assn. Merced City Tchrs. Assn., Assn. Calif. Sch. Adminstrs., Merced Sch. Employees Fed. Credit Union (credit com. 1972-77, bd. dirs 1977-84), Nat. Assn. for the Edn. Young Children, Calif. Assn. for the Edn. Young Children. Office: Merced City Sch Dist 444 W 23d St Merced CA 95340

ROBERTS, MARGOT MARKELS, business executive; b. Springfield, Mass., Jan. 20, 1945; d. Reuben and Marion (Markels) R.; children—Lauren B. Phillips, Debrah C. Herman. B.A., Boston U. Interior designer Louis Legum Furniture Co., Norfolk, Va., 1965-70; buyer, mgr. Danker Furniture, Rockville, Md., 1970-72; buyer W & J Sloane, Washington, 1972-74; pres. Bus. & Fin. Cons., Palm Beach, Fla., 1976-80, Margot M. Roberts & Assocs., Inc., Palm Beach, 1976—; dealer 20th century Am. art and wholesale antiques Margot M. Roberts, Inc., Palm Beach, 1989—; v.p., dir. So. Textile Services Inc., Palm Beach. Pres. Brittany Condominium Assn., Palm Beach, 1983-87; v.p. Palm Beach Civic Assn., 1983-88, South Palm Beach Pres.'s Assn., 1984-88; vice chmn. South Palm Beach Planning Bd., 1983-88. Mem. Nat. Assn. Women in Bus., Palm Beach C. of C. Republican. Office: Margot M Roberts & Assocs Inc 3575 S Ocean Blvd #211 Palm Beach FL 33480

ROBERTS, MARIE DYER, computer systems specialist; b. Statesboro, Ga., Feb. 19, 1943; d. Byron and Martha (Evans) Dyer; BS, U. Ga., 1966; student Am. U., 1972; cert. systems profl., cert. in data processing; m. Hugh V. Roberts, Jr., Oct. 6, 1973. Mathematician, computer specialist U.S. Naval Oceanographic Office, Washington, 1966-73; systems analyst, programmer Sperry Microwave Electronics, Clearwater, Fla., 1973-75; data processing mgr., asst. bus. mgr. Trenam, Simmons, Kemker et al, Tampa, Fla., 1975-77; mathematician, computer specialist U.S. Army C.E., Savannah, Ga., 1977-81, 83-85, Frankfurt, W. Ger., 1981-83; ops. rsch. analyst U.S. Army Contrn. Rsch. Lab., Champaign, Ill., 1985-87; data base adminstr., computer systems programmer, chief info. integration and implementation div. U.S. Army Corps of Engrs., South Pacific div., San Francisco, 1987—; instr. computer scis. City Coll. of Chgo. in Franfurt, 1982-83. Recipient Sustained Superior Performance award Dept. Army, 1983. Mem. Am. Soc. Hist. Preservation, Data Processing Mgmt. Assn., Assn. of Inst. for Cert. Computer Profls., Assn. Women in Computing, Assn. Women in Sci., NAFE, Am. Film Inst., U. Ga. Alumni Assn., Sigma Kappa, Soc. Am. Mil. Engrs. Author: Harris Computer Users Manual, 1983.

ROBERTS, MARJORIE HELEN, marketing and public relations executive; b. Port Chester, N.Y., Feb. 23, 1938; d. George and Blanche (Mulwitz) Goldowitz; m. Arthur W. Roberts, Aug. 23, 1959 (div. Aug. 1967); children: Scott Eric, Allison. BA in Journalism, U. Mich., 1959. Lic. real estate broker, N.Y. Reporter and editor Gannett Westchester Newspapers, Port Chester, N.Y., 1955-60; fin. adminstr. Investors Diversified Svcs., White Plains, N.Y., 1969-73; real estate adminstr. Schulman Realty Group, White Plains, 1973-78; exec. v.p. R.S. Silver & Co., Greenwich, Conn., 1978-89; freelance writer, editor. med. columnist Women's News, Westchester, N.Y., 1981—; dir. mktg. pub. rels. Matthew J. Warshauer Architects, PC, Hawthorne, NY, 1989-90; contbr. articles to mags. and newspapers. Mem. Harrison Archtl. Rev. Bd., N.Y., 1979-87, Harrison Com. Cable TV, 1977-79; bd. dirs. Home for Mentally Retarded, Harrison, 1982-87, Westchester Symphony, 1983-86. Home: 101 River West Greenwich CT 06831

ROBERTS, MARJORY LOUISE, editor, writer; b. Detroit, Feb. 8, 1963; d. George Allen and Eleanor Jane (Heilbronner) Roberts. BA in Mag. Journalism, Psychology, Syracuse U., 1985. Sci. writer Syracuse Post-Standard, N.Y., 1985; editorial asst. The Horse Digest, Leesburg, Va., 1985; rsch. reporter Psychology Today, Washington, 1985-87, staff writer, 1988; assoc. editor, health editor Psychology Today, N.Y.C., 1989; assoc. editor U.S. News and World Report, Washington, 1989—. Contbr. Planned Parenthood, N.Y.C., 1989. Recipient Allan H. Lytel Tech. Writing award, Syracuse U., 1985. Office: US News and World Report 2400 N St NW Washington DC 20037

ROBERTS, MARY BELLE, clinical social worker; b. Akron, Ohio, Sept. 27, 1923; d. Joseph Gill and Inez Wilson (Garvey) Roberts; BS, U. Mich., 1948, MSW, 1950. Cert. social worker, Md., lic. clin. social worker, Fla. Instr. dept. psychiatry U. Ala. Med. Coll., 1950-53; psychiat. social worker div. mental hygiene Ala. Dept. Pub. Health, 1950-52, acting dir., dir., 1952-53; sr. psychiat. social worker bur. mental health div. community svc. Pa. Dept. Welfare, 1954-55; cons. psychiat. social work community svc. br. NIMH, USPHS, HEW, 1955-64; pvt. practice psychiat. social work, 1964-68; caseworker Family Svc., Miami, Fla., 1968-70, Family and Childrens Svc., Miami, 1971-75; casework cons. United Family and Childrens Svcs., Miami, 1975-85; clin. social worker Family Counseling Svcs., Miami, 1985-90. Home: 8126 SW 105th Pl Ocala FL 32676

ROBERTS, MARY MARJORIE S., educator; b. Buffalo, Mo., Sept. 16, 1923; d. Ray Henderson and Grace (Sweaney) Southard; m. Joseph Franklin Roberts (dec. Jan. 1987); 1 child, Mary Jo. BS in Edn., U. Mo., 1954, MEd, 1956, DEd, 1967. Cert. elem. and secondary tchr., Mo. Tchr. Dallas County, Buffalo, 1941-45, Buffalo Sch. System, 1948-51; asst. in edn. U. Mo., Columbia, 1952-53; instr. edn. U. Mo., 1953-67, asst. prof. edn., 1967-86. Contbr. articles to profl. jours.; editor: (jour.) Delta Kappa Gamma, 1972-74. Pres. Kings Daus., Columbia; moderator Presbyn. Women, Columbia, 1988—; exec. bd. Koinonia House, Columbia, 1989—; mem. Fed. Rep. Women, Columbia, 1988—. Mem. AAUW (pres. 1975-77), Columbia Garden Club, DAR (columbian chpt., regent 1989—), United Daus. Confederacy, Daus. Am. Colonists, Pi Lambda Theta (pres. 1957-59). Republican. Presbyterian. Home: 1000 Bourn Ave Columbia MO 65203

ROBERTS, MARY VESLEY, interior designer/decorator; b. Omaha, June 24, 1939; m. Peter Roberts, Sept. 19, 1981; children from previous marriage: Chip, Scott, Sally. Student, U. Fla., 1957-60. Model Jantzen Inc., Portland, Oreg., 1958-60; stewardess Northwest Airlines, Washington, 1961-62; interior decorator 800 House Furniture & Design, Portland, 1973-74; prin. Mary Roberts Interiors, Oswego, Oreg., 1975—; decorator Christiensen Motor Yacht Corp. Fund raiser Oreg. Mus. Sci. and Industry, March of Dimes; mem. Jr. League of Portland, 1973—. Republican. Roman Catholic.

ROBERTS, NANCY, educator; b. Boston, Jan. 25, 1938; d. Harold and Annette (Zion) Rosenthal; m. Edward Roberts; children: Valerie, Mitchell, Andrea. AB, Boston U., 1959, MEd, 1961, EdD, 1975. Elem. tchr. Sharon (Mass.) Pub. Schs., 1959-63; asst. prof. Lesley Coll., Cambridge, Mass., 1975-79; assoc. prof. Lesley Coll., 1980-83, prof., 1983—; research assoc. MIT, Cambridge, 1976-79; mem. nat. steering com. Nat. Edn. Computing Conf., Eugene, Oreg., 1979—, chair steering com., 1989; dir. Lesley Coll. Ctr. for Math., Sci. and Tech. in Edn., 1990—. Author: Dynamics of Human Service Delivery, 1976, Practical Guide to Computers in Education, 1982, Computers in Teaching Mathematics, 1983, Introduction to Computer Simulation, 1983 (J.W. Forrester award 1983), Integrating Computers into the Elementary and Middle School, 1987, Computers and the Social Studies, 1988, Integrating Telecommunications into Education, 1990; mem. editorial bd. Jour. Ednl. Computing, 1983—; editor Computers in Edn. book series, 1984—. Mem. Computer Policy Com., Boston, 1982-84, mem. adv. bd. Electronic Learning, 1989—; bd. dirs. Computers for Kids, Cambridge, 1983-85; apptd. by Gov. Dukakis to State Ednl. Tech. Adv. Coun., 1990—. NSF grantee, 1985—. Mem. System Dynamics Soc. (bd. dirs. policy com. 1987-89). Republican. Jewish. Home: 17 Fellsmere Rd Newton MA 02159 Office: Lesley Coll 29 Everett St Cambridge MA 02138-2790

ROBERTS, NIGRA LEA See SINK, NIGRA LEA

ROBERTS, SALLY JOANN, relocation company executive; b. Terre Haute, Ind., Jan. 31, 1938; d. Frances Wayne and Berniece Ernestine (Scanlon) Hatfield; m. Ronald Leroy Roberts, June 8, 1957; children—Terri Lynn, Timothy Lee, Cynthia Ann, Christopher Allen. Student Ind. State U., 1955-57. Relocation mgr. Employee Transfer Corp., Chgo., 1977-79; mgmt. cons. C21 No. Ill. Region, Rosemont, 1979-80; v.p. Baird & Warner, Chgo., 1980-83; v.p., co-owner Profl. Relocation, Oak Brook, Ill., 1983-85; pres. Profl. Relocation, Bloomingdale and Oak Brook, Ill., 1985—; bd. mem. I.C.R. Referral Network, Kansas City, Kans., 1981-83; mem. adv. bd. Am. Bound Pubs., L.A., 1986—. Author: Homebuyers Guide, 1980, Relocation, 1981-85. Mem. Nat. Assn. Realtors (life mem. million dollar sales 1977, cons. Chgo. 1983-86), Employee Relocation Council (com. mem. 1981-85), Relocation Dirs. Council (com. mem. 1981-85), Chgo. Assn. Commerce and Industry. Republican. Lutheran. Avocations: sailing, golfing, bridge. Office: Profl Relocation Group 261 E Lake St Bloomingdale IL 60108 also: 2000 Spring Rd Oak Brook IL 60521

ROBERTS, SANDRA BROWN, realty company executive; b. Boston, May 26, 1939; d. Frederick Thomas and Christine (Peyton) Brown; m. Joseph Peter Roberts, Aug. 26, 1962 (div. May 1984); children: Christine, Joseph, Paul. B.A., Boston Coll., 1981. Lic. real estate broker, Mass. Owner, mgr. real estate, Wellesley, Mass., 1963—; pres. Riverview Realty, Wellesley, 1970—; comml. realtor, Boston, 1974—; cons. Berkshire Hathaway, New Bedford, Mass., 1983—; asst. to pres. BHR, Inc., New Bedford, 1988—. Founder, pres., bd. dirs. Friends of Ft. Washington, Inc.; active Friends of Boston Ballet, 1983—. Mem. DAR (Boston Tea Party chpt. regent 1983-84, 84-85). Navy League of U.S., New Eng. Hist. Geneal. Soc. Republican. Roman Catholic. Club: College (Boston). Lodge: Order of Crown of Charlemagne (life mem.), Order of Lafayette (bd. dirs.). Home: 52 Kenilworth Rd Wellesley MA 02181 Office: BHR Inc 51 River St Wellesley MA 02181

ROBERTS, SHEILA POWE, communication executive; b. N.Y.C., Jan. 12, 1947; d. Forrest Alfred Powe and Dorothy Lee (Watkins) Moore; m. Walter M. BBA, Pace U., N.Y.C., 1978; Asssoc. in Risk Mgmt., Ins. Institute of Am., Malvern, 1978. Ins. mgr. The Lionel Corp., N.Y.C., 1969-78; dir. risk mgmt. & ins. Columbia Pictures, Inc., N.Y.C., 1978-84; dir., risk mgmt & ins. Time Inc., N.Y.C., 1984-89; exec. v.p. Paretzky Info. Network, Inc., Bethesda, Md., 1989—; pres., Risk Research Institute dba N.Y. Chpt., Risk & Ins., 1983-84;. Recipient Black Achievement award NY YMCA-Harlem Div., N.Y.C., 1981. Mem. Risk & Ins. Mgmt. Soc. Inc. (dep. mem.), Am. Risk & Ins. Assn. (bd. dirs.), Ins. Edn. Coun. N.Y. (founding mem.), Assn. Profls. in Risk-Related Disciplines (founding mem., sec.). Home: 17809 Cottonwood Terr Gaithersburg MD 20877 Office: Paretzky Info Network Inc 6701 Democracy Blvd Ste 300 Bethesda MD 20817

ROBERTS, SUZANNE HELEN, insurance professional; b. Elizabeth, N.J., May 3, 1946; d. William E. and Irene (Boganski) Gleason; m. George W. Roberts Jr.; children: George W. III, Kelly I. Roberts Moore. AB in Edn., U. Mich., 1982. Customer svc. rep. Provident Life and Accident Ins. Co., Chattanooga, Tenn., 1987—. Mem. AAUW (assoc. treas. Chattanooga chpt. 1988—), Freedoms Found. Valley Forge (treas. Chattanooga chpt. 1988—). Home: 2800 Igou Ferry Rd Soddy-Daisy TN 37379 Office: Provident Life, Acc Ins Co 1 Fountain Sq Chattanooga TN 37402

ROBERTS-ATWATER, BEVERLY, psychology educator; b. Jacksonville, Fla., Feb. 16, d. Joseph Roberts and Alfeta (Graham) Love; m. Tony Atwater, Dec. 20, 1980. BA, Fisk U., 1974; MA, NYU, 1976; PhD, Mich. State U., 1984. Lic. psychologist, Mich. Psychometrist Rsch. Assocs. Menlo Park, Atlanta, 1975-76; cons., analyst Mental Health Bd., Miami, Fla., 1976-80; asst. prof. psychology dept. psychiatry Mich. State U., East Landing, 1984—, dir. out-patient clinic, 1988-89; psychologist Vanderjagt and Howard Assocs., Okemos, Mich., 1985—; asst. dir. residency Fairlawn Ctr. Psychiat. Hosp., Pontiac, Mich., 1984-87. Grantee NIMH, 1975; Janie Moristen scholar Mich. State U., 1980; doctoral fellow Mich. State U., 1980, William T. Grant fellow Nat. Med. Found., 1990. Mem. Am. Psychol. Assn., Mich. Psychol. Assn., Infant Mental Health Assn., Urban League, NAACP, Delta Sigma Theta. Democrat. Baptist. Home: 1832 Chester Rd Lansing MI 48912 Office: Vanderjagt and Howard Assocs 2248 E Mount Hope Rd Okemos MI 48864

ROBERTS-KING, CATHERINE STEPHANIE, purchasing manager; b. Bklyn., June 29, 1962; d. Carl Edward and Dorothy Denise (DeGazon) Roberts; m. James Alfred King II. BSE, Wharton Sch., 1983. Intern Chase Loan Officer Credit Program, N.Y.C., 1982, Goode for Mayor Campaign, Phila., 1983, Princeton (N.J.) U. Plasma Physics Lab., 1984; assoc. buyer paper div. Procter & Gamble Co., Cin., 1984-85, purchasing mgr. health, personal care, beauty care div., 1985-86; resident purchasing mgr. buckeye cellusose and specialties div. Procter & Gamble Co., Memphis, 1986-88; purchasing mgr. packaged soap div. Procter & Gamble Co., Cin., 1988—; dir. Cin. Restoration, Inc., Cin., 1986—. Vol. Rainbow Coalition, Bklyn., 1984, Carl Roberts for Assembly, Bklyn., 1984, Sch. Dist. Campaign, Cin., 1986; intern Goode for Mayor Campaign, Phila., 1983; advisor Jr. Achievement, Cin., 1986. Named to Honor Soc. Black Undergrad. Assn. U. Pa., 1983. Mem. Nat. Black MBA Assn., Zeta Phi Beta. Democrat. Roman Catholic. Office: Procter & Gamble Co PO Box 599 Cincinnati OH 45201

ROBERTSON, CHRISTINE, education administrator; b. Ames, Iowa, Oct. 20, 1949; d. Howard Robert and Winifred (Wolters) Cushman; m. Fred Paul Robertson, Nov. 24, 1970 (div. Nov. 1984); children: Megan, Rusty. BEd, Iowa State U., 1971; MEd, U. Cin., 1987. Cert. elem. tchr., reading specialist, gifted and talented tchr., elem. supr., Nebr., Ga., Ohio. Tchr. Johnson-Brock (Nebr.) Schs., 1972, Auburn Rural Schs., 1972-73, Cobb County Schs., Marietta, Ga., 1973-79; tchr. Cin. Pub. Schs., 1980—, assoc. supr. elem. edn., 1989—; tchr. LaBelle Elem. Sch., Marietta, 1974-79, Linwood Acad., Cin., 1980-89; developer enrichment writing, reading program Linwood Acad., Cin., 1987—. Mem. adminstrv. bd., chmn. edn. com. St. Phillips Meth. Ch., Marietta, 1973-79, Cherry Grove Meth. Ch., Cin., 1980-87; mem. adv. council Ayer Elem. Schs, Cin., 1984-86. Martha Holden Jennings Found. scholar, 1986-87. Mem. Internat. Reading Assn., Assn. Suprs. and Curriculum Devel., Cin. Assn. Adminstrs. & Suprs., Ohio Elem. Adminstrs. Assn., Ohio Valley Talented and Gifted Assn., PTA, Nat. Tchr. of Math., Nat. Tchrs. of English, Early Childhood Edn., Phi Kappa Delta. Home: 7137 Woodridge Dr Cincinnati OH 45230 Office: Cin Bd of Edn 320 E Ninth ST Cincinnati OH 45202

ROBERTSON, ELIZABETH ANN, nurse; b. Phila., Jan. 21, 1943; d. Joseph Hamilton and Edna Atkinson (Clayton) R. Diploma in nursing, Presbyn. Sch. Nursing, Phila., 1963; BS in Nursing, Villanova U., 1969, MEd, 1976. RN, Pa. Operating room staff nurse Presbyn.-U. Pa. Med. Ctr., Phila., 1963-66; staff nurse Taylor Hosp., Ridley Park, Pa., 1966-69; mem. nursing faculty Presbyn. Sch. Nursing, Phila., 1969-79; substitute sch. nurse Lower Merion (Pa.) Sch. Dist., 1980-83; nurse counselor Phila. Child Guidance Clinic, 1980-83; staff nurse Haverford Community Hosp., Havertown, Pa., 1983—. Vol. nurse African Evangelical Fellowship Mission, Zambia, 1971. Mem. Pa. Nurses Assn., Presbyn. Sch. Nursing Alumnae Assn. (rec. sec. 1975-79, bd. dirs. 1989). Republican. Home: 400 Glendale Rd Unit D-44 Havertown PA 19083

ROBERTSON, HEATHER ANNE LAURE, educator; b. Burbank, Calif., Apr. 14, 1956; d. Thorington Blair and Janine R.; m. Tom Mason Headrick; 1 child, Cori; m. Stephen Hale Lindsey, June 17, 1983; 1 child, Julianne. BA, Calif. State U., L.A., 1980, MA, 1988. Instr. Kaiming English Pusiban, Taipei, Taiwan, Republic of China, 1979; testing coord. Am. culture and lang. program Calif. State U., L.A., 1981-83; program coord. Calif. State U./Am. Culture and Lang. Prog., 1984-87, instr., 1980—; cons. Culture Edn. Bus. Network, L.A., 1984-86; corp. sec. Internat. Resource Assocs., L.A., 1986-88; v.p., corp. sec. Lindsey-Ramme, Inc., Glendale, Calif., 1989. Author: Bridge to College Success, 1990. Credit com. Calif. State U. Fed. Credit Union, 1985. Recipient Pres.'s Achievement award, Calif. State U., 1986, Outstanding Univ. and Community Svc. award, 1989. Mem. Calif. Tchrs. of English to Speakers of Other Lang. (L.A. reg. conf. site chmn. 1982, 83, 87), Tchrs. of English to Speakers of Other Lang. Democrat. Office: Calif STate U Bldg L 5151 State University Dr Los Angeles CA 90032

ROBERTSON, JACQUELINE LEE, entomologist; b. Petaluma, Calif., July 9, 1947; d. John Lyman and Nina Pauline (Klemenok) Schwartz; m. Joseph Alexander, Sept. 12, 1970 (div. Jan. 1978). BA, U. Calif., Berkeley, 1969, PhD, 1973. Registered profl. entomologist. Research entomologist USDA Forest Service, Berkeley, 1970—. Editor Jour. Econ. Entomology, 1982—; contbr. articles to profl. jours.; patentee lab. device, 1982. Mem. Entomol. Soc. Am., Entomol. Soc. Can., AAAS. Democrat. Office: US Forest Service PSW Sta 1960 Addison St Berkeley CA 94704

ROBERTSON, JEANNE CHORLEY, sales representative, physical education educator; b. Chgo., Feb. 6, 1949; d. Joseph H. and Laura (Lilley) Chorley; 1 child, April Dawn. BA in Polit. Sci./Phys. Edn., East Carolina U., Greenville, 1976. Sales rep. Oxford Chem., Atlanta, 1977—; tchr. phys. edn. Martin Community Coll., Williamston, N.C., 1989—; instr. Robersonville (N.C.) Parks and Recreation, 1989—, La Moulin Rouge, Williamston, N.C., 1989—; cater staff Kelly's, Nags Head, N.C., 1988—. County mgr. Howard Lee for Gov., Pitt County, N.C., 1975. Internat. Relief Agt., Safe the Children, Lebanon, 1982, Emergency Relief Vol., ARC, Charleston, 1989. Mem. Martin Hist. Soc. (exec. bd.). Democrat. Baptist. Home and Office: 902 Woodlawn Dr Williamston NC 27892

ROBERTSON, JEWELL LEWIS, investment company executive; b. Lelia Lake, Tex., Mar. 17, 1911; d. Earnest Luther and Margaret Mae (Reeves) Lewis; m. Charles Andrew Robertson, Dec. 31, 1950 (dec. May 1976). Student, Clarendon (Tex.) Jr. Coll., 1929; grad., Amarillo (Tex.) Bus. Coll., 1930; student, Amarillo Coll., 1978. Sec., bookkeeper Rolla V. Cartwright Ins., Amarillo, 1930-36; sec. to gen. mgr. Farm Security Adminstrn., Amarillo, 1936-42; paymaster, banker Pantex Ordnance Plant, Amarillo, 1942-45; sec. to pres. Oil Devel. Co. Tex., Amarillo, 1945-48, Maynard Sash and Door Co., Amarillo, 1948-50; sec. to sales mgr. Graham Plow Co., Amarillo, 1950-59; exec. dir. Tex. Panhandle Home Builders Assn., Amarillo, 1959-70; adminstrv. asst. Tex. State Tech. Inst., Amarillo, 1970-72; br. office adminstr. Edward D. Jones & Co., Amarillo, 1972—. Recipient Mem. Devel. awards Nat. Assn. Home Builders, Washington, 1963, 64, 65. Mem. Nat. Asns. Female Execs., Fin. Planners Assn., Amarillo Fedn. Women's Clubs(v.p. 1955-56), Amarillo Coun. Garden Clubs (sec. 1960), Amarillo C. of C. (program chmn. women's div. 1963), Daus. of the Nile, Order Eastern Star. Home: 2803-B W 27th St Amarillo TX 79109 Office: Edward D Jones & Co 2414-4 Lakeview Dr Amarillo TX 79109

ROBERTSON, JOSEPHINE-LESLIE, cosmetologist; b. Henderson, Tex., Mar. 25, 1948; d. Josephus Leslie and Lorene (Smith) Leslie-Brown; m. Roy Lincoln Robertson, Aug. 6, 1962 (dec. Dec. 1969). AA, L.A. City Coll., 1972. Cosmetologist L.A. Community Coll., 1978-80; with Bethany Community Coll., L.A., 1980-82; fashion designer Bethany Community Coll., 1983-85; owner, cosmetologist Josie's, L.A. Mem. Tuskegee Airmen Assn. (award funds com. L.A. chpt. 1974—, Merit award 1988). Home and Office: 2640 S Harvard Blvd #6 Los Angeles CA 90018

ROBERTSON, MARIAN ELLA (MARIAN ELLA HALL), handwriting analyst; b. Edmonton, Alta., Can., Mar. 3, 1920; d. Orville Arthur and Lucy Hon (Osborn) Hall; m. Howard Chester Robertson, Feb. 7, 1942; children: Elaine, Richard. Student, Willamette U., 1937-39; BS, Western Oreg. State U., 1955. Cert. elem., jr. high. tchr., supt. (life) Oreg.; cert. graphoanalyst. Tchr. pub. schs. Mill City, Albany, Scio and Hillsboro, Oreg., 1940-72; cons. Zaner-Bloser Inc., Columbus, Ohio, 1972-85, assoc. cons., 1985-89; pres. Write-Keys, Scio, 1980—; tchr. Internat. Graphoanalysis Soc., Chgo., 1979; instr. Linn-Benton Community Coll., 1985-89. sr. intern 5th Congl. Dist. Oreg., Washington, 1984, mem. sr. adv. council; precinct committeemem. Rep. Cen. Com., Linn County, 1986, alt. vice-chair, 1986, parliamentarian, 1988—; candidate Oreg. State Legis., Salem, 1986. Mem. Altrusa Internat. (internat. chmn. 1985-86, chmn. pub. rels. 1989—, corr. sec. 1990-91), Internat. Platform Assn. Republican. Mem. Soc. of Friends. Home: 37929 Kelly Rd Scio OR 97374 Office: Write-Keys PO Box 54 Jefferson OR 97352

ROBERTSON, MELVINA, construction company executive; b. Guilford, Mo., June 3, 1934; d. Charlie Gale and Christina Gertrude (Nelson) Turner; m. Ponnie Leonard Robertson, June 3, 1955; children: Raymond Edward, Richard Leonard. Student, Cen. Mo. State Coll., 1966. Mgr. Knowles Restaurant, Kansas City, Mo.; v.p. P.L. Robertson Concrete Found. Co., Inc., Ozark, Mo.; pres. P.L. Robertson Concrete Found. Co., Inc. Mem. Rose Soc. of Ozark, Nat. Audubon Soc. Reorganized Ch. of Jesus Christ of Latter-day Saints.

ROBERTSON, MINTA CAROL, health care administrator; b. Charleston, W.Va., Feb. 2, 1949; d. Oliver Wendell and Minta Ruth (Davis) Halstead; m. Gerald Wayne Robertson Sr., Feb. 20, 1946; children: Troy, Eric, Gerald Jr., Mark, Cheri. AA, Salem Coll., 1973; B. Health Adminstrn., Fla. Atlantic U., 1987. RN, Fla. Head nurse Grafton (W.Va.) City Hosp., 1973-75, Kettering (Ohio) Med. Ctr., 1975-76; nurse supr. Hialeah (Fla.) Hosp., 1976, Humana Hosp. South Broward, Pembroke Park, Fla., 1977-78; adminstrv. coordinator Southeastern Med. Ctr., North Miami, Fla., 1976-77; assoc. nursing svc. Dr.'s Hosp., Hollywood, Fla., 1978-80; evaluations supr. James M. Jackson Meml. Hosp., Miami, Fla., 1980-82; dir. quality assurance Bascom Palmer Eye Inst., Miami, Fla., 1982—; lectr. Southeastern Hosp. Conf., Nashville, 1989; cons. in field. Author: Quality Assurance and You, 1985; author pub. rels. booklet; co-author: Current Incidents of Infection Following Intraocular Surgery, 1989. Mem. NAFE, Nat. Assn. Quality Assurance Profls., Am. Assn. Infection Control Practitioners, Nat. Assn. Risk Mgrs., Fla. Hosp. Assn., Dade County Assn. Quality Assurance (sec. 1986), Optimists (internat. lt. gov. 1986, pres. Miramar chpt. 1985-86). Home: 4100 SW 137th Ave Miramar FL 33024 Office: Bascom Palmer Eye Inst 900 NW 17th St Miami FL 33136

ROBERTSON, SANDRA DEE (GRAEN), accountant; b. Denver, Nov. 7, 1953; d. Fredrick Philip Arthur Graen and Dorothea Stone (Bell) Kohler; m. Charles E. Robertson Jr., Aug. 4, 1973 (Jan. 1985); 1 child, Daniel Philip. BS in Bus. cum laude, U. Colo., 1980. CPA, Colo. Staff acct. Brock, Cordle & Assocs., CPA's, Boulder, Colo., 1980-82; corp. tax acct. Storage Tech. Corp., Louisville, Colo., 1983-87; state tax supr. RJR Nabisco, Inc., Atlanta, 1987-89; mgr. Ernst & Young CPA's, Atlanta, 1989—. Served with U.S. Army, 1972-75. Mem. Am. Inst. CPA's, Colo. Soc. CPA's, Beta Gamma Sigma. Democrat. Club: Toastmasters. Home: 2074 Arbor Forest Dr Marietta GA 30064

ROBERTSON, SARA ELIZABETH, editor; b. Kansas City, Mo., July 7, 1956; d. Earl Edward Robertson Jr. and Mona Belle Williams Lyda; m. Stephen G. Phillips, Oct. 8, 1988. AB, Stanford U., 1978; M in Internat. Affairs, Columbia U., 1984. Tchr. English Agy for Agrl. Research and Devel., Bogor, Indonesia, 1978-79; prodn. mgr., publicity dir. The Asia Record, Palo Alto, Calif., 1979-80; tchr. English Beijing (People's Republic China) Metallurgical Inst. Mech. and Elect. Tech., 1980-82; editor coun. on fgn. rels. Fgn. Affairs mag., N.Y.C., 1985-88; mgr. pub. affairs Washington State Centennial Commn., Seattle, 1989—. Democrat. Home: 1702 Lake Washington Blvd Seattle WA 98122 Office: Coun on Fgn Relations 111 W 21st 1001 Fourth Ave Pla 12th Fl Olympia WA 98504

ROBEY, KATHLEEN MORAN (MRS. RALPH WEST ROBEY), civic worker; b. Boston, Aug. 9, 1909; d. John Joseph and Katherine (Berrigan) Moran; B.A., Trinity Coll., Washington, 1933; m. Ralph West Robey, Jan. 28, 1941. Actress appearing in Pride and Prejudice, Broadway, 1935, Tomorrow is a Holiday, road co., 1935, Death Takes a Holiday, road co., 1936, Left Turn, Broadway, 1936, Come Home to Roost, Boston, 1936; pub. relations N.Y. Fashion Industry, N.Y.C., 1938-43. Mem. Florence Crittenton Home and Hosp., Women's Aux. Salvation Army, Gray Lady, ARC; mem. Seton Guild St. Ann's Infant Home. Mem. Christ Child Soc., Fedn. Republican Women of D.C. English-Speaking Union. Republican. Roman Catholic. Clubs: City Tavern, Cosmos (Washington), Nat. Woman's Republican. Home: 4000 Cathedral Ave NW Washington DC 20016

ROBFOGEL, SUSAN SALITAN, lawyer; b. Rochester, N.Y., Apr. 4, 1943; d. Victor and Janet (Rosenthal) Salitan; m. Nathan Joshua Robfogel, July 12, 1965; children: Jacob Morris, Samuel Salitan. BA cum laude, Smith Coll., 1964; JD, Cornell U., 1967. Bar: N.Y.1967, U.S. Dist. Ct. (we. dist.) 1968, U.S. Ct. Appeals (2d cir.) 1971, U.S. Supreme Ct. 1971, U.S. Dist. Ct. (no. dist.) 1974, D.C. 1982. Asst. corp. counsel, then sr. asst. corp. counsel City of Rochester, N.Y., 1967-70; assoc. Harris, Beach & Wilcox, Rochester, 1970-75; ptnr. Harris, Beach, Wilcox, Rubin & Levey, Rochester, 1975-85; ptnr., chair health svcs. practice Nixon, Hargrave, Devans & Doyle, Rochester, 1985—; panel mem., Fed. Svc. Impasses Panel, Washington, 1983—; mem., chair Data Protection Rev. Bd., Albany, N.Y., 1984—. Bd. dirs., Alfred (N.Y.) U. Recipient Brockport Coll. Found. Community award, 1989. Fellow Am. Bar Found.; mem. ABA (ho. of dels.), N.Y. State Bar Assn., Washington D.C. Bar Assn., Monroe County Bar Assn. (Rodenbeck award 1988), Rochester Area C. of C. (trustee). Home: PO Box 39508 Rochester NY 14604 Office: Nixon Hargrave Devans Doyle PO Box 1051 Rochester NY 14603

ROBICHAUD, PHYLLIS IVY ISABEL, artist, educator; b. Jamaica, West Indies, May 16, 1915; came to U.S., 1969, naturalized, 1977; d. Peter C. and Rose Matilda (Rickman) Burnett; grad. Tutorial Coll., 1933, Kingston, Jamaica, Munro Coll., St. Elizabeth, Jamaica, 1946; student Central Tech. Sch., Toronto, Ont., Can., 1960-63, Anderson Coll., Can., 1968-69; m. Roger Robichaud, July 22, 1961; children by previous marriage—George Wilmot Graham, William Henry Heron Graham, Mary Elizabeth Graham Watson, Peter Robert Burnett Graham. Sec. to supr. of Agr., St. Elizabeth, 1940-50; loans officer and cashier Confederation Life Assn., Kingston, 1950-53; tchr. art Jamaica Welfare Ltd., 1963; tchr. art recreation dept. New Port Richey, Fla., 1969-77; tchr. art Pasco Hernando Community Coll., New Port Richey, 1977—; demonstrator various organizations including West Pasco Art Guild, New Port Richey, Ace Artists, New Port Richey; propr., mgr. Band Box Dress Shop, Kingston, Jamaica, 1954-57; numerous one-woman shows of paintings including various banks, libraries, Kingston, 1963-64, 67, Toronto, 1968, New Port Richey, 1969, 70, 73, 76, Tampa, Fla., 1974, 75, 76, Omaha Cattle Company restaurant, Clearwater Fla., 1982, Mus. Pasco Hernando Community Coll., New Port Richey, Fla., 1989; numerous group shows, latest being: Sweden House, Tampa, 1977-78, Chasco Fiesta, New Port Richey, 1977, Magnolia Valley Golf and Country Club, New Port Richey, 1978, W. Pasco Art Guild, New Port Richey, 1978, 79, Indian Rocks Beach, 1985, Hernando Community Coll. at the Mus. of the Coll., 1989, other cities in Fla.; executed murals, New Port Richey and Kingston; represented in permanent collection New Port Richey C. of C., also pvt. collections. Patron, St. Alban's 4H Club, 1942; sec. Sunday sch. Ch. of Eng., Kingston, 1937-39. Recipient award T. Eaton Co. of Can., 1961, cert. of merit, Mayor of New Port Richey, 1976, appreciation award New Port Richey Recreation Dept., 1977; award Fla. Heart Fund. Mem. Nat. League Am. Pen Women (v.p. Tampa br. 1978-80, dir. 1969—), West Pasco Art Guild (Blue ribbons 1978, 79), Fla. Fine Arts Guild. Republican. Roman Catholic. Address: 7032 Lenox Dr New Port Richey FL 34653

ROBILLARD, RENEE JEAN, medical editor; b. Van Nuys, Calif., Jan. 17, 1952; d. Robert Gregory and Lila Mae (Peregrine) Robillard. BA, Boston U., 1974; MA, U. B.C., 1976; postgrad., Tex. A&M U., 1978-80. Editor Editorial Svc./U. Tex. Med. Br., Galveston, 1981-84; sr. editor Hospi Medica and Medilab, Westport, Conn., 1984-85; manuscript editor New Eng. Jour. Medicine, Boston, 1985-88; med. writer, editor dept. surgery St. Elizabeth's Hosp., Boston, 1988—; part-time tchr. Galveston Coll., 1980-83, Fairfield (Conn.) U., 1985, Northeastern U., Boston, 1987. Asst. editor: Medical Microbiology, 1985; freelance writer and editor. Mem. Am. Med. Writers Assn. (sec. S.W. chpt. 1983-84), Council Biology Editors. Home: 1415 Commonwealth Ave Apt 101 Brighton MA 02135 Office: St Elizabeth's Hosp Dept Surgery 736 Cambridge St Brighton MA 02135

ROBINETTE, BETSYE HUNTER, school psychologist; b. Nashville, Sept. 30, 1960; d. Gerald Sylvan and Eleanor Louise (Felts) Hunter; m. Michael David Robinette, Aug. 13, 1988. BS, Va. Poly. Inst. and State U., 1982; MA cum laude, Wheaton (Ill.) Coll., 1984; postgrad., U. Tenn. Lic. psychol. examiner, cert. sch. psychologist, Tenn.; cert. psychologist, Ky. Adolescent counselor Mercy Ctr., Aurora, Ill., 1983-84; mental health technician Glendale Heights (Ill.) Community Hosp., 1984; staff psychologist Cumberland River Comprehensive Care Ctr., Harlan, Ky., 1985-86; psychotherapist Family Svc. Ctr., Asheville, N.C., 1987; psychol. examiner Overlook Mental Health Ctr., Knoxville, Tenn., 1987-88; sch. psychology intern Cherokee Mental Health Ctr., Morristown, Tenn., 1989-90; sch. psychologist Knox County Schs., Knoxville, Tenn., 1990—; crisis intervention worker RAFT, Inc. Crisis Intervention, Blacksburg, Va., 1981-82; grad. asst. Wheaton Coll., 1984, U. Tenn., Knoxville, 1988-89; clinic coord. U. Tenn., 1989. Missionary Campus Crusade for Christ, Tokyo, 1982; tchr. 1st Bapt. Ch., Morristown, 1989-90; mem. Cedar Springs Presbyn. Ch. Mem. Am. Psychol. Assn., Nat. Assn. Sch. Psychologists, Tenn. Assn. Sch. Psychologists, Christian Assn. Psychol. Studies, Phi Kappa Phi, Psi Chi (v.p. 1981-82). Presbyterian. Home: 1624 Summerhill Dr Knoxville TN 37922

ROBINETTE, SHEREE, construction executive; b. Tampa, Fla., Mar. 12, 1957; d. William J. and Patricia Ann (Gearhart) R. AA Hillsborough Community Coll., 1977; BA in Acctg. U. South Fla., 1980. Mgr. Fontaine Supply, Tampa, 1977-80; owner,mgr. Tampa Accessory Corp., 1980—. Mem. Constrn. Trade Assn., Nat. Assn. Women in Constrn., Nat. Assn. Profl. Estimators . Republican. Baptist. Avocations: ballet, swimming, cycling. Office: Tampa Accessory Corp 5688B W Crenshaw St Tampa FL 33634

ROBINS, CARA LEIGH, public relations professional; b. Elmhurst, Ill., Oct. 27, 1963; d. Bert V. and Ruth R. (Holter) R. BFA summa cum laude, Ohio U., 1985. Mktg. coord. Delta Svc.Plans Ins. Co., Ga., Calif, 1986; pub. and profl. rels. dir. Delta Svc. Plans Ins. Co., Atlanta, 1986—. Mem. NAFE, Atlanta C. of C., Pub. Rels. Soc. Am. Office: Delta Svc Plan Ins Co 3405 Piedmont Rd Ste 400 Atlanta GA 30305

ROBINS, JERI LYNN NAGLER, marketing official; b. Cleve., May 19, 1961; d. Leon Gregory and Elise (Charness) Nagler; m. Steven Neal Robins, June 11, 1988. BS in Info. Systems-Bus., Carnegie-Mellon U., 1983; SM in Mgmt., MIT, 1988. Quality assurance analyst Kendall Co., Boston, 1983-84, corp. fin. analyst, 1984-86, home health care analyst, 1986; strategic-market planner Codex Corp. subs. Motorola Co., Canton, Mass., 1988-89; mktg. asst. Welch's, Concord, Mass., 1989-90, asst. product mgr., 1990—. Mem. Delta Delta Delta. Office: Welch's 100 Main St Concord MA 01742

ROBINS, LEE NELKEN, medical educator; b. New Orleans, Aug. 29, 1922; d. Abe and Leona (Reiman) Nelken; m. Eli Robins, Feb. 22, 1946; children: Paul, James, Thomas, Nicholas. Student, Newcomb Coll., 1938-40; B.A., Radcliffe Coll., 1942, M.A., 1943, Ph.D., 1951. Mem. faculty Washington U., St. Louis, 1954—, prof. sociology in psychiatry, 1968—; prof. sociology Washington U., 1969—; former mem. Nat. Adv. Council on Drug Abuse, Pres.'s Commn. on Mental Health task panels; expert adv. panel mental health WHO.; Salmon lectr. N.Y. Acad. Medicine, 1983. Author 3 monographs; editor 10 books; assoc. editor N.Am. Methods in Psychiatric Research; mem. editorial bd. Psychol. Medicine, Am. Pub. Health, Child Psychology and Psychiatry, Devel. and Psychopathology; contbr. articles to profl. jours. Recipient Research Scientist award USPHS, 1970-90; Pacesetter Research award Nat. Inst. Drug Abuse, 1978; Radcliffe Coll. Grad. Soc. medal, 1979; Research grantee NIMH; Research grantee Nat. Inst. on Drug Abuse; Research grantee Nat. Inst. on Alcohol Abuse and Alcoholism. Fellow Am. Coll. Epidemiology, Royal Coll. Psychiatrists (hon.); mem. World Psychiat. Assn. (treas. sect. com. on epidemiology and community psychiatry), Am. Sociol. Assn., Internat. Sociol. Assn., Inst. of Medicine, Internat. Epidemiological Assn., Soc. Epidemiol. Rsch., Am. Psychopathol. Assn. (Paul Hoch award 1978, pres. 1987-88), Am. Pub. Health Assn. (Rema Lapouse award 1979), Soc. Life History Rsch. in Psychopathology, Am. Coll. Neuropsychopharmacology. Office: Washington U Dept Psychiatry Med Sch Saint Louis MO 63110

ROBINS, MARJORIE MCCARTHY (MRS. GEORGE KENNETH ROBINS), civic worker; b. St. Louis, Oct. 4, 1914; d. Eugene Ross and Louise (Roblee) McCarthy; AB, Vassar Coll., 1936; diploma St. Louis Sch. Occupational Therapy, 1940; m. George Kenneth Robins, Nov. 9, 1940; children—Carol Robins Von Arx, G. Stephen, Barbara A. Robins Foorman. Mem. Mo. Libr. Commn., 1937-38; mem. bd. St. Louis Jr. League, 1945, 46; mem. bd. Occupational Therapy Workshop of St. Louis, 1941-46, pres., 1945, 46; mem. bd. Ladue Chapel Nursery Sch., 1957-60, 61-64, pres. bd., 1963, 64; past regional chmn. United Fund; past mem. St. Louis Met. Youth Commn., St. Louis Health and Welfare Coun.; bd. dirs. Internat. Inst. of St. Louis, 1966-72, 76—82, 83—, sec., 1968, v.p., 1981; bd. dirs. Mental Health Assn. St. Louis, 1963-70, Washington U. Child Guidance and Evaluation Clinic, 1966-78; bd. dirs. Cen. Inst. for Deaf, 1970—, v.p., 1975-76, pres., 1976-78; bd. dirs. Met. St. Louis YWCA, 1954-63, 64-74, pres. bd., 1960-63, trustee, 1977—; mem. nat. bd. YWCA, 1967-79, nat. v.p., 1973-76; vol. tchr. remedial reading clinic St. Louis City Schs., 1968-71; trustee John Burroughs Sch., 1960-63, John Burroughs Found., 1965-80, Roblee Found., 1972—, Nat. YWCA Retirement Fund, 1979-88; bd. dirs. Gambrill Gardens United Meth. Retirement Home, 1979-85, Thompson Retreat and Conf. Center, 1981-87; bd. dirs. Springboard to Learning Inc., 1980—, v.p., 1980—. Mem. Archeol. Inst. Am. (bd. dirs., treas. St. Louis chpt. 1985-87). Clubs: Vassar (sec. and pres. 1939-40), Wednesday (dir. 1968-70, 77-79, 80-81) (St. Louis). Home: 45 Loren Woods Saint Louis MO 63124

ROBINS, ROSEMARY GAY, Egyptologist; b. Fleet, England, June 28, 1951; came to U.S., 1988; d. John Maurice and Alison (Gerrish) Robins; m. Charles Cameron Shute, Sept. 6, 1980. BA in Chinese with honors, U. Durham, England, 1972, BA in Egyptology with honors, 1975; DPhil, U. Oxford, England, 1981; PhD, U. Cambridge, England, 1982. Rsch. fellow in Egyptology Cambridge U., 1979-83; hon. rsch. fellow U. Coll., London, 1984-88; affiliated lectr. U. Cambridge, 1987-88; asst. prof. art history Emory U., Atlanta, 1988—; curator Egyptian art Emory Mus. Art and Archaeology, Atlanta, 1988—. Author: Egyptian Painting and Relief, 1986, (with Charles Shute) Rhind Mathematical Papyrus, 1987; contbr. numerous articles to profl. jours. Mem. Egypt Exploration Soc., Internat. Assn. Egyptologists, Am. Rsch. Ctr. in Egypt, Archaeol. Inst. Am., Coll. Art Assn. Office: Emory U Art History Dept Atlanta GA 30322

ROBINS, SUSAN LYNNE, stock brokerage official; b. Flushing, N.Y., Apr. 28, 1953; d. Joseph and Miriam (Gansky) Sandler; m. Larry Allen Robins. BA magna cum laude, Beaver Coll., 1975; MS, U. Pa., 1977. Mgr., counselor Pounds and Inches Weight Reducing Ctrs., Inc., Cherry Hill, N.J., 1975-76; dir. child abuse prevention program Phila. Dept. Human Svcs., 1977-87; mgr. mgmt. devel. Merrill Lynch, Princeton, N.J., 1987—; pvt. therapist, Phila., 1984-87; instr. Community Coll. Phila., 1977-78. Bd. dirs., Parents Anonymous Pa., Harrisburg, 1985—. Grantee, HHS, 1980-82. Mem. Am. Soc. Tng. and Devel., Orgnl. Devel. Network. Office: Merrill Lynch 800 Scudders Mill Rd Plainsboro NJ 08543

ROBINSON, ALIX IDA, microbiology educator, researcher; b. Ft. Worth, Oct. 26, 1937; d. Marvy Young and Ida Goldie (Glickman) R.; m. Byron Allen Bassel, Dec. 30, 1960 (div. 1983). BA, U. Tex., 1959, PhD, 1964. Rsch. assoc. U. Ill., Urbana, 1964; postdoctoral fellow U. Göteborg (Sweden) Med. Sch., 1965; instr. in anatomy SUNY Upstate Med. Ctr., Syracuse, N.Y., 1966-68, microbiol. rsch. assoc., 1968-71, asst. prof., 1971-75; assoc. prof. microbiology SUNY Health Sci. Ctr., Syracuse, 1975—; N.E. rep. basic sci. edn. forum Assn. Am. Med. Coll., Washington, 1989, coordinating com. women in medicine, 1988—. Contbr. articles to profl. jours. Vol. numerous community orgns., Syracuse, 1980—; senator faculty senate SUNY, 1987-93, v.p./sec., 1990-92; pres. SUNY Faculty Women's Caucus, 1986—; bd. dirs. Sta. WAER Broadcast Svc., Syracuse U., 1987-89, Temple Soc. Concord, Syracuse, 1989—; bd. dirs. Upstate Day Care Ctr., Syracuse, 1987—, pres., 1990-91. NIH postdoctoral fellow, 1964-65; recipient Rsch. Career Devel. award, 1968-72; rsch. grantee, 1973-76, NSF grantee, 1981-88; Blinken fellow SUNY, 1989. Mem. Am. Soc. Microbiology, Am. Soc. Cell Biology, Assn. for Women in Sci., Sigma Xi. Democrat. Jewish. Office: SUNY Health Sci Ctr Dept Microbiology Syracuse NY 13210

ROBINSON, ANGELA TOMEI, medical technologist; b. Bklyn., June 5, 1957; d. Leo James and Nina Angela T.; m. John C. Robinson, Sept. 27, 1987. BS, St. John's U., 1979, MS, 1985. Exec. sec. Stead-fast Temporaries, Inc., N.Y.C., 1975-79; med. technologist Winthrop-U. Hosp., Mineola, N.Y., 1979—, coord., founder Nat. Med. Lab. Week, contbr. newsletter, 1981—; coord., founder Nat. Med. Lab. Week Winthrop-U. Hosp. Newsletter, Mineola, 1981—; lectr. guest seminar C.W. Post Coll., Westbury, N.Y., 1986—; chmn. com. to petition salary increases Winthrop-U. Hosp., 1987-90. Author: (poetry) Our World's Best Loved Poems, 1984 (2d place merit cert. 1983). Contbr. articles to profl. jours. Singer Blessed Sacrament Ch. Choir, Bklyn., 1971-73; mem. Mothers Against Drunk Driving, 1985-87, Nat. Rep. Congl. Com., 1984-86, Am. Health Found., 1986-87, DAV, 1984-87; fundraiser Statue of Liberty/Ellis Island Found., 1985-86, Hands Across Am., 1986. Recipient cert. of merit N.Y. State Senate, 1985, citation Gov. N.Y. State. Mem. Am. Soc. Clin. Pathologists (registered), Empire State Assn. Med. Tech. (chmn. govt. liaison com., state bd. dirs. 1988—, Outstanding Med. Tech. Student 1979, Nassau/Suffolk chpt. founding officer 1985-86, bd. dirs., seminar moderator, 1985-87, pres.-elect 1986-87), Nat. Honor Soc., Nat. Bus. Honor Soc., Empire State Assn. Med. Tech., Theta Phi Alpha (alumni chmn. 1976-77, marshal/parliamentarian 1977-78, alumni/collegiate rep. 1986-87), Pres. Soc. Alumni Assn.

ROBINSON, ANGELINA MASSARI, lawyer; b. San Antonio, Mar. 27, 1962; d. Franklin Stephen and Virginia Anne (Bunnell) Massari; m. David B. Robinson. BA, Vanderbilt U., 1984; JD, Washington U., St. Louis, 1987. Bar: Fla. 1988. Assoc. Maguire, Voorhis & Wells, P.A., Orlando, Fla., 1987—. Contbr. articles to profl. jours. Mem. Fla. Bar Assn., Orange County Bar Assn., Cen. Fla. Assn For Women Lawyers, Jr. League Orlando (Winter Park), Order of Barristers, Phi Delta Phi. Republican. Roman Catholic. Home: 507 Sheridan Blvd Orlando FL 32804 Office: Maguire Voorhis & Wells P A 2 S Orange Pla Orlando FL 32804

ROBINSON, ANNETTMARIE, entrepreneur; b. Fayetteville, Ark., Jan. 31, 1940; d. Christopher Jacy and Lorena (Johnson) Simmons; m. Roy Robinson, June 17, 1966; children: Steven, Sammy, Doug, Pamela, Olen. BA, Edison Tech. U., 1958; BA in Bus., Seattle Community Coll., 1959. Dir. perss. Country Kitchen Restaurants, Inc., Anchorage, 1966-71; investor Anchorage, 1971—; cons. Pioneer Investments, Anchorage, 1983—, M'RAL, Inc. Retail Dry Goods, Anchorage, 1985. Mem. Rep. Presdl. Task Force, Washington, 1984—, Reps. of Alaska, Anchorage, 1987; mem. chmn. round table YMCA, Anchorage, 1986—. Named Woman of Yr. Lions, Anchorage, 1989, marksman first class Nat. Rifle Assn., 1953. Mem. NAFE, Spenard Lion's Aux. (past pres.).

ROBINSON, CARI SUZANNE, library director; b. Nashville, Nov. 21, 1956; d. William Allen and Nan (Fussell) Robinson. BA, David Lipscomb Coll., 1979; M of Library Sci, Vanderbilt U., 1981. Cert. M.L.S. Conservation clk. Am. Gen. Life Ins. Co., Nashville, 1982-83; library dir. Dickson (Tenn.) County Pub. Library, 1983--. Bd. dirs. Dickson County Lit. Council, Dickson County Adult Edn. Planning Com. Mem. Tenn. Library Assn., Southeastern Library Assn., Tenn. Architects, Beta Phi Mu. Office: Dickson County Pub Library 305 Hunt St Dickson TN 37055

ROBINSON, CARLAN MARIE, psychologist; b. Norfolk, Va., Aug. 29, 1944; d. Ralph Carlan Robinson and Frances (Fluker) Anderson; divorced; 1 child, Julie Marie Restivo. BA, NYU, 1972, MA, 1975, PhD, 1977. Lic. psychologist, N.Y., Calif., Hawaii. Clin. instr. med. sch. NYU, N.Y.C., 1978-81; sr. psychologist outpatient clinic VA Hosp., L.A., 1981-82; acting head adult svcs. Hawaii Dept. Mental Health, Honolulu, 1982-83; pvt. practice Psychol. Svcs. Hawaii, Honolulu, 1982—; clin. instr. U. Hawaii Med. Sch., Honolulu, 1982—; affiliate prof. staff Queen's Hosp., Honolulu, 1982—; sr. psychologist forensic team dept. mental health State of Hawaii, Honolulu, 1989—; cons. in field. Author: Breaking Up, Moving On..., 1989; contbr. articles to profl. jours. Mem. med. bd. Alztheimers Diseases and Related Diseases, Honolulu, 1981—; stroke bd. Hawaii Heart Assn., 1990—, guild mem. Honolulu Acad. Arts, 1988—, Honolulu Symphony Guild, 1982—. Recipient Founder's Day award NYU, 1972, University Honors scholar NYU, 1972; postdoctoral fellow NIMH NYU Med. Sch., 1978-80. Mem. Am. Psychol. Assn., Hawaii Psychol. Assn., Internat. Women's Writing Guild, Nat. Register Mental Health Providers, Hawaii Yacht Club, Psi Chi. Mem. Soc. of Friends. Home: 1739-C Ala Moana Blvd Honolulu HI 96815 Office: 700 Bishop St Ste 1902 Honolulu HI 96816

ROBINSON, CARLOTA NILSON, business owner; b. Austin, Minn., June 7, 1939; d. Alfred Alvin and Gwyneth Emily (Gustafsson) Norton; m. Joe B. McCawley, Jr., (div.); m. Roy E. Nilson, Oct. 10, 1970 (div.); m. Paul Robinson, Mar. 10, 1980. Grad. high sch., Austin, Minn. Dir. Sta. KICA-TV, Clovis, N.Mex., 1958; with Sta. WHOO-Radio, Orlando, Fla., 1958-59, Sta. WLCY-Radio, St. Petersburg, Fla., 1963-67; owner Creative Outlet of Fla., Inc., St. Petersburg, Tampa, 1967—; claims rep. Travelers Ins. Co., Orlando, Tampa, 1965-76. Author: Dream Come True Family Cookbook, 1967. Mem. pub. rels. com. Fla. State Fair, Tampa, Fla., 1967. Mem. Internat. Assn. Fairs and Expositions. Office: Creative Outlet of Fla Inc 5809-20 Ave S Tampa FL 33619-5457

ROBINSON, CAROLE ANN, insurance executive; b. Omaha, Dec. 21, 1935; d. Harry B. and Mildred (Daley) Baker; widowed Mar. 1989; 1 child, Pamela Fleming. Clk. BlueCross/Blue Shield Colo., Denver, 1969-70; mgr. BlueCross/Blue Shield Colo., 1970-72, asst. to treas., 1972-74, dir., 1974-79, treas., 1980-86, sr. v.p., treas., 1986—; v.p., treas., chief investment officer Rocky Mountain Health Care (Holding Co.), Denver, 1986—; bd. dirs. TRIAD Health Mgmt. Co., Denver, Rocky Mountain Life Ins. Co., Denver, Occupational Health Mgmt. Svcs., Denver. Mem. investment com. City and County of Denver, 1988. Mem. Colo. Cash Mgmt. Assn., Nat. Cash Mgmt. Assn., Life Office Mgmt. Assn. (treasury ops. com. 1985—). Republican. Office: Rocky Mountain Health Care 700 Broadway Denver CO 80273

ROBINSON, CAROLINE J., credit examiner; b. Easley, S.C., May 17, 1963; d. Alfred B. and Margot (Juette) R. BA, Randolph-Macon Woman's Coll., 1985; postgrad., Emory U. Bus. merger and acquisition consulting asst. Ted Harris, Inc., Lynchburg, Va.; reservationist Litchfield Co., Pawleys Island, S.C.; asst. mgr., buyer Robinson Co., Inc., Easley; credit examiner Farm Credit Adminstrn., McLean, Va. Mem. NAFE, Randolph-Macon Woman's Coll. Alumnae Assn. (bd. dirs. 1989—), Atlanta Hist. Soc. (v.p.), Jr. League Atlanta.

ROBINSON, CATHALEEN STARN, development executive; b. Pleasantville, N.J., Nov. 20, 1940; d. Charles Sheppard and Sophie Emma (Hess) Starn; m. Neil Wentworth Robinson, Sept. 28, 1973 (dec. Oct. 1976). Grad. high sch., Pleasantville, 1958. Sec. and asst. treas. Starn's Markets Inc., Somers Point, N.J., 1959-73; pres. Robinson Enterprises, Inc., Killington, Vt., 1973—, Robinwood Pipeline Inc., Killington, 1988—; bd. dirs. Alpine Pipeline Co. Bd. dirs. Vt. Achievement Ctr., Rutland, 1979-88; auditor towns of Sherburne, Killington, 1983-88. Mem. Vt. Rep. Club. Baptist. Clubs: Rutland Country; Woodstock Country; Atlantic City Country;Sherburne Women's; Ch. Women United (pres. 1986, 87). Home: Robinwood-Star Rt Killington VT 05751 Office: Robinson Enterprises Inc Robinwood-Star Rt Killington VT 05751

ROBINSON, CATHERINE LAUER, business consultant; b. Titusville, Pa., Nov. 5, 1948; d. William A. and Frances (Zdarko) Lauer; m. James W. Robinson, May 25, 1968 (div. 1981); 1 child, Melissa C. Robinson. Student Jamestown Bus. Coll., N.Y., 1966-68, George Mason U., No. Va. Community Coll., 1972-73, 90—. Payroll clk. Cyclops Spl. Steel Co., Titusville, 1969-70; payroll specialist U.S. Dept. Navy, Washington, 1971-74; payroll liaison U.S. Dept. State, Washington, 1974-78; health liaison specialist HEW, Washington, 1978-79; grants specialist Dept. Edn., Washington, 1979-83; procurement analyst U.S. Marshals Svc., McLean, Va., 1983-85, program mgr., 1985-88; pres. C.L. Robinson & Assocs., 1988—. Presdl. apptd. U.S. Dept. Energy, 1989-90. Recipient Outstanding Performance award U.S. Dept. Edn., 1982, Outstanding Performance award U.S. Marshals Svc., 1983-86; named Outstanding Young Woman of Yr., 1983. Mem. NAFE, Internat. Biographical Centre (hon., mem. adv. coun. 1989—), Bus. and Profl. Women's Assn. Episcopalian. Avocations: swimming, walking, sight seeing, travel. Home: 7041 Alicent Pl McLean VA 22101 Office: US Dept Energy L'Enfant Pla Forrestall Bldg Washington DC 20585

ROBINSON, CATHY, retail manager; b. Denison, Iowa, June 1, 1951; d. Teddy Junior and Ruth F. (Paulsen) Cornelius; m. Billy Don Turner, July 3,

1975 (div. Dec. 1979); 1 child, Michelle Suzanne; m. Gary L. Robinson, June 24, 1989. BA, U. Iowa, 1973. Asst. store mgr. Casual Corner, Houston, 1975-77, store mgr., 1977-80, dist. mgr., Tampa, Fla., 1980-81, regional mgr., Tampa, 1981—; bd. dirs., sec. Galleria Mall, Houston, 1979-80. Mem. Nat. Assn. Female Execs., Gamma Phi Beta. Lutheran. Avocations: water skiing, skiing, snorkeling, softball. Office: Casual Corner 3302 W Buffalo Ave #1022 Tampa FL 33607

ROBINSON, CHERYL ANN, registered nurse; b. Buffalo, Feb. 18, 1946; d. James Erskine Robinson and Helen Marie (Tsybulsky) Applestein; m. William DeDario, Apr. 26, 1972 (div. 1981); children: Jennifer Denise, Marc Anthony. Grad., Meyer Meml. Hosp. Sch. Nursing, Buffalo, 1966; nurse practitioner, Meharry Med. Coll., Nashville, 1982-83; BS, Coll. St. Francis, Joliet, Ill., 1990. RN, N.Y. Nurse, head nurse Erie County Med. Ctr., Buffalo, Nev., 1966-70, So. Nev. Meml. Hosp., Las Vegas, 1970-72; field nursing supr. Upjohn Health Care Svcs., Las Vegas, 1976-80; utilization rev. coord. N. Las Vegas Hosp., N. Las Vegas, Nev., 1980-81; hosp. rev. mgr. Nev. Profl. Standards Rev. Orgn., Reno, 1981-83; claims/risk investigator Vanderbilt U. Med. Ctr., Nashville, 1983-84; mgr. health care rev. Corroon & Black Benefits, Inc., Nashville, 1984-87; dir. med. svcs. Equicor Health Plan, Inc., Nashville, 1987; utilization mgmt. specialist Equicor, Inc., Nashville, 1988, dir. utilization, 1989-90; utilization mgmt. specialist Aetna Health Plans, San Diego, 1990—; profl. adv. com. mem. Ptnr's Home Health, Inc., Nashville. Contbr. articles to profl. jours. Mem. Jacques Cousteau Soc., 1975, Greenpeace, 1988. Mem. Middle Tenn. Utilization Mgmt. Quality Assurance Profls. (v.p. 1985, pres. 1986), Nat. Assn. Quality Assurance Profls., Tenn. Soc. for Quality Assurance Profls. Episcopalian. Office: Aetna Health Plans 7676 Hazard Center Dr 10th Fl San Diego CA 92108

ROBINSON, COZY MORRIS, retired educator, association executive; b. Johnstown, Pa.; d. Dennis and Mamie (Rucker) Morris; m. John C. Robinson, Apr. 28, 1946; children: JoAnn Cozy, Judith Ann, John C. Jr. BA, Lycoming Coll., 1961; MA, Bucknell U., 1980. Cert. in elem. edn., secondary edn., English, Spanish, social studies. Pub. sch. tchr. Williamsport (Pa.) Area Sch. Dist., 1961-75; parochial sch. tchr. Diocese of Scranton, Williamsport, 1973-74; remedial tchr. Muncy (Pa.) Correctional Instn., 1974; dir. Robinson Edn. Cons. Svc., Williamsport, 1972-76; grad. asst. Bucknell U., Lewisburg, Pa., 1977-80; mem. Pa. legis. com. Am. Assn. Ret. Persons, Harrisburg, 1987—; consumer adv. com. Keystone Peer Rev. Orgn., Harrisburg, 1988—. Author 2 books. Bd. dirs. Bethune Douglas Community Ctr., Williamsport, 1957-76; chmn. Greater Williamsport Coordination Com. for Housing, 1959-61. Order Eastern Star grantee, 1958. Mem. AAUW (life), Lycoming County Ret. Pub. Sch. Employees Assn. (life), Prince Hall Affiliation (dist. dep. 1983-85), Order Eastern Star (grand matron). Mem. African Meth. Episcopal Ch. Home: 509 Lycoming St Williamsport PA 17701

ROBINSON, DORIS HERBERT, psychologist, educator, cable TV producer/host, corporate executive; b. Waterbury, Conn., Nov. 26, 1942; d. Hence David and Cynthia (Mott) Herbert (div.); children: Kheesa Lauren, Harold Oscar Jr. (Robby). BA, Fisk U., 1964; MEd, Rutgers U., 1971. Cert. tchr., N.J. Tchr. Evergreen Sch., Plainfield, N.J., 1964-69; counseling psychologist Rutgers U., New Brunswick, N.J., 1969-81; corp. mgr. Bell Labs./Bell Communications Rsch. (Bellcore), Piscataway, N.J., 1981—; cable TV producer, host Piscataway Community TV Ctr., 1988—, Dialogue With DorisTalk/Talent Show; mem. Cen. N.J. Jack & Jill, Inc., New Brunswick, 1983, Piscataway Calbe TV Adv. Commn., 1989. Mem. Crossroads Theater, New Brunswick, N.J., subscription com., Piscataway subcapt., 1989; bd. dirs. YWCA Cen. N.J., 1990. Mem. Alpha Kappa Alpha (co-founder, 1st grad. advisor Iota Psi undergrad., charter mem.), Nu Xi Omega. Methodist. Home: 103 Coventry Circle Piscataway NJ 08854

ROBINSON, ELAINE DIANE, public affairs executive; b. N.Y.C., Feb. 13, 1940; d. William Emanuel and Sylvia (Eisenberg) Robinson; m. Leonard Adler, June 12, 1960 (div. 1979); children: Mona Jane, Sari Michele. BA, Queens Coll, 1960; MBA, Adelphi U., 1982. Mem. zoning bd. appeals, consumer protection bd. Town of Huntington, N.Y., 1972-76; legislator Suffolk County, Hauppauge, N.Y., 1976-78; with L.I. Lighting Co., Hicksville, N.Y., 1978-87; mgr. nuclear info. Boston Edison Co., Plymouth, Mass., 1987—. Mem. Phi Beta Kappa, Delta Mu Delta. Office: Boston Edison Co Rocky Hill Rd Plymouth MA 02360

ROBINSON, EMMA CALLOWAY, senior citizen's advocate; b. Red Ash, W.Va., Feb. 19, 1896; d. Anthony Tuschan and Janie Elizabeth (Beasley) Calloway; m. Robert Lee Robinson; children: Geraldine Elizabeth, Evelyn Robinson Jones, Francine Robinson Jackson. Tchr.'s degree, Storer Coll., Harpers Ferry, W.Va., 1917; AB in Edn., W.Va. State Coll., 1940; MA in Edn., W.Va. U., 1949. Cert. elem. tchr., W.Va. Tchr. Fayette (W.Va.) Pub. Schs., Raleigh County (W.Va.) Pub. Schs. Del. White House Conf. on Aging, Washington, 1971—; life mem. Rep. Presdl. Task Force, 1988—; bd. dirs. Martin Luther King, Jr. Community Coll., Mt. Hope, W.Va.; guest speaker numerous orgns. Mem. NEA, W.Va. Edn. Assn., Nat. Caucus and Ctr. on Black Aged, W.V.a Edn. Assn., Am. Assn. Ret. Persons. Baptist. Home: 101 Madison St Mount Hope WV 25880

ROBINSON, EVELYN LOUISE, protective services official, counselor; b. New Orleans, June 15, 1933; d. Joseph Smith and Blanche Scott; m. Leroy Robinson, July 28, 1955; children: Alaric Vincent, Frank Joseph. BS, So. U., 1955; postgrad., UCLA, 1957; MSW, La. State U., 1972. Cert. social worker, La. Tchr. Charlotte Mitchell High Sch., Bossier Parish Sch. Bd., Bossier City, La., 1955-58; sec. Capitol Jr. High Sch., Baton Rouge, 1959-66; supr. detention home and probation officer family ct. Parish of East Baton Rouge, La., 1966-88; mgr. detention home City Police Juvenile Detention Ctr. City of Baton Rouge, 1988, counselor City Police Juvenile Detention Ctr., 1990—; presenter seminars, sch. programs. Contbr. to profl. publs. Active Mt. Zion 1st Bapt. Ch. Mem. AAUW, La. Juvenile Detention Assn., Nat. Juvenile Detention Assn., Zeta Phi Beta.

ROBINSON, FLORINE SAMANTHA, marketing professional; b. Massies Mill, Va., Feb. 4, 1935; d. John Daniel and Fannie Belle (Smith) Jackson; m. Frederick Robinson (div. 1973); children: Katherine, Theresa, Freda. BS, Morgan State U., 1976; postgrad., U. Balt., 1977-81, Liberty U., 1987. Writer, reporter Phila. Independent News, 1961-63; free lance writer, editor Balt., 1963-71; asst. mng. editor Williams & Wilkins Pubs. Inc., Balt, 1971-76; mktg. rep., then mktg. mgr. NCR Corp., Balt., 1977—; assoc. minister, trustee Christian Unity Temple, Balt., 1976—; bd. dirs. Armstrong & Bratcher, Inc., Balt. Editor: Stedman's Medical Dictionary, 1972; contbr. articles to profl. jours. Active PTA, Balt., 1963-65; bd. dirs. Howard Park Civic Assn., Balt., 1967—; leader, cons. Girl Scouts USA, 1970-73. Recipient Excellence in Research award Psi Chi, 1976. Mem. Mid-Atlantic Food Dealers Assn., Am. Soc. Notaries, NAFE, Internat. Platform Assn. Democrat. Club: Edelweiss. Lodge: Order Eastern Star. Home: 3126 Howard Park Ave Baltimore MD 21207

ROBINSON, GLYNNE, photographer, writer; b. Fredericksburg, Va., Feb. 23, 1934; d. Frederick Hampden and Jessie (Maguire) Robinson; children: Elizabeth, William, Katherine. AB, Wells Coll., 1956; postgrad. in history of art Columbia U., 1957; postgrad. in journalism NYU, 1975; photography student, The New Sch., 1967, 71, of Ansel Adams, Yosemite, Calif., 1968, Paul Caponigro, Bethel, Conn., 1969-71. Cert. media specialist, N.Y.C. Bd. Edn. With news and publicity dept. Riverdale Neighborhood House, 1974-76; staff photographer, The Reporter, publ. Ethical Culture Schs., N.Y.C., 1974-76; condr. photostudy project, N.Y.C. pub. sch., 1974-75; guest lectr. U. Maine, 1979; condr. photog. workshop for jr. high sch. students sponsored by N.Y. Pub. Libr., 1973; pub. The Lakeville (Conn.) Jour., The Millerton (N.Y.) News. Works appeared in publs. including N.Y. Times, Washington Post, N.Y. Daily News, Christian Sci. Monitor, Village Voice, San Francisco Chronicle, L.A. Times, Asia, Am. Heritage; featured in Women At Their Work, 1977; author: Writers in Residence, 1981; one-woman photog. shows Soho Photo Gallery, N.Y.C., 1974, Wells Coll., 1973, N.Y. Pub. Libr., 1973; participant group exhibits: Riverdale Neighborhood House, N.Y.C., 1968, Guild Hall, Easthampton, N.Y., 1970, Soho Photo Gallery, 1973, Wells Coll., 1974-75, Carnegie House, N.Y.C., 1978, Cosmopolitan Club, N.Y.C., 1976, Community Gallery Met. Mus. Art, 1976. Mem. Am. Soc. Mag. Photographers. Club: Cosmopolitan. Home: 15 E 91st St Apt 11C New York NY 10128

ROBINSON, GRETCHEN ELIZABETH, dietitian, corporate consultant; b. Pitts., Nov. 10, 1937; d. William Parks and Elizabeth (Grossman) Yant; m. William L. Robinson, July 29, 1961; children: Todd W., Staci E. BA in Biology, Coll. of Wooster, Ohio, 1959; BS in Foods and Nutrition, Pa. State U., State College, 1961; MS in Nutrition, Ind. U., 1964. Clinical asst. dietitian Lima (Ohio) Meml. Hosp., 1961-63; county extension agt. Union County, Columbus, 1963-68; program dir. Ohio No. U., Ada, 1968-70; pvt. practice dietary cons., 1970-73; dietitian Mary Rutan Hosp., Bellefontaine, Ohio, 1973-75; corp. dietitian Health Care Facilities, Inc., Lima, 1975—; area coord. Cons. Dieticians in Health Care Facilities, Ohio, Ind., Ky., W.Va., Ill., Tenn., 1988-90, chair Ohio chpt., 1986-88. Officer Ada Coop. Nursery, 1980; pres. Ada Jr. Civic League, 1975. Mem. AAUW (pres. Ohio div. 1985-87), Ohio No. U. Women (pres.), Meadowink Farms Inc. (sec., treas.). Republican. Lutheran. Home: 608 Conley Ada OH 45810 Office: HCF Inc 2615 Ft Amanda Rd Lima OH 45804

ROBINSON, INGRID B., medical management company executive; b. Neuenhagen, Niederbann, Germany, Feb. 5, 1939; came to U.S., 1963; d. Johannes Antonsious and Margot Martha E. (Grundmann) Wawersig; children: Karen A. Robinson-Smith, Joan S. Robinson-Raisle, Pamela J. B Hotel and Restaurant Mgmt., Le Ecole du Hotel, Lausanne, Switzerland, 1956; MBA, Dickerson Coll., Carlisle, Pa., 1970. Gen. mgr. 1863 Holiday Inn, Gettysburg, Pa., 1964-69; owner, mgr. Batzen House Hotel-Restaurant, Fayetteville, Pa., 1970-72; unit svc. coord. Central Bapt. Hosp., Lexington, Ky., 1975-77; office mgr. Pulmonary Assocs., Lexington, 1979-82; med. cons. Lexington, 1983-88; pres. IBR Svcs. Inc., Lexington, 1988—; presentor U. Ky. Med. Ctr., Lexington, 1988-89; mem. faculty Humana Symposium, Lexington, Louisville, 1989; lectr. Third Party Reimbursement, Cen. Ky., 1985-90. Author: Effective Collection Management, 1988, Liability in the Medical Office, 1988, Maximum Reimbursement, 1989; editor IBR Newsletter, 1988, 89, 90. Mem. Profl. Womens Orgn., Better Bus. Bur., Nat. Arts and Letters Soc. (awards chmn. 1984), C. of C. Republican. Office: IBR Svcs Inc 811 Corporate St Ste 202 Lexington KY 40503

ROBINSON, JACQUELINE CARTER, teacher; b. Norfolk, Va., Mar. 13, 1944; d. James William and Cornelia Francis (Graves) Andrews; m. Linwood G. Robinson, Nov. 24, 1965 (div. 1990); children: John Allen, Elizabeth Anne. BS, Longwood Coll., 1966; MS, SUNY, New Paltz, 1973. Cert. tchr., N.Y. Tchr. Fishkill Plains-Wappingers (N.Y.) Central Sch. Dist., 1967-73, Krieger-Poughkeepsie (N.Y.) Sch. Dist., 1987—; chmn. bd. dirs. New Hackensack Nursery Sch., Wappingers, 1973-79; substitute tchr. Wappingers Sch. Dist., 1986-87. Vol. Meals on Wheels, Wappingers Falls, N.Y., 1981-87; leader Boy Scouts Am., POughkeepsie, 1981-83, Girl Scouts U.S.A., Poughkeepsie, 1986-88; Sunday sch. tchr. New Hackensack Reformed Ch., Wappingers Falls, 1972-89, deacon, elder, 1986—. Recipient Tchr. of Yr. award New Hackensack Reformed Ch. Mem. Mid-Hudson Reading coun., Am. Fedn. Tchrs., N.Y. State Tchrs. Assn., POughkeepsie Tchrs. Assn., United Tchr. Assn., AAUW. HOme: 45 Spring Rd Poughkeepsie NY 12601 Office: Krieger Sch 265 Hooker Ave Poughkeepsie NY 12603

ROBINSON, JAN, software company executive; b. Kansas City, Mo., June 8, 1945; d. Leonard Stuart and June (Barker) R.; widowed 1980. BA, U. Colo., 1966. Officer Colo. Nat. Bank, Denver, 1966-68; cons. Bank of Am., San Francisco, 1968-70, 78-80; owner Janco Systems, Kalispell, Mont., 1971-76; dir. mgmt. info. systems Shortstop Markets, Benicia, Calif., 1977-79; pres. JALAN, Spokane, 1980—; edn. adminstr. Am. Inst. Banking, Denver, 1967-68. computer advisor Santa Rosa (Calif.) Jr. Coll., 1979-80; dir. fin. Benicia Homeowners, 1977-79, Interplayers Theatre, Spokane, 1984-86; faculty mem. advanced computer tech. Nat. Jud. Coll. Univ. Nev. Mem. Kalispell C. of C., Wash. Assn. Sheriff's & Police, Assn. Wash. Cities, Nat. Assn. Female Execs., Calif. State Sheriff's Assn (assoc.). Republican. Presbyterian. Home: S 168 Coeur D'Alene #E303 Spokane WA 99204 Office: JALANInc S 140 Arthur Ste 400 Spokane WA 99202

ROBINSON, JANE HASTY, cosmetics consultant; b. London, Ky., Dec. 5, 1947; d. George Robert and Virginia Lelan (Durham) Hasty; m. Harold Wayne Robinson, June 2, 1967; 1 child, Leah Lynn. Cert. med. secretary, Sue Bennett Coll.; student, Fugazzi Bus. Coll., 1966. Keypunch operator Appalachian Computer Svc., London, Ky.; sec. 1st United Meth. Ch., London, Ky.; receptionist Scissor Wizards, London, Ky.; beauty cons. Mary Kay Cosmetics, Dallas. Mem. NAFE, Beta Club. Republican.

ROBINSON, JANET ANDREWS, development administrator; b. Salt Lake City, Aug. 17, 1935; d. James William and Katherine (Nicol) A.; m. George Thomas Heisel, Jan. 31, 1971 (div. Aug. 1979); children—Andrea Eileen, John Michael; m. John Glass Robinson, Dec. 4, 1980 (div. Dec. 1986). B.S., U. Utah, 1957. Adminstrv. asst. St. Luke's Hosp., Phoenix, 1963-66; manpower planner Health Council of Monroe County, Rochester, N.Y., 1966-67; dir. rev. Genesee Regional Health Planning Council, Rochester, 1969-73; dir. devel. Highland Hosp., Rochester, 1980—; bd. dirs. Blue Shield Rochester, treas., 1979-85; bd. dirs. Rochester Hosp. Services, Rochester, 1979—, chmn., 1983-85; bd. dirs. Highland Hosp., Rochester, 1979—, v.p., 1981-84. Bd. dirs. The David Hochstein Meml. Music Sch.; mem. exec. com. YMCA. Author manuals. Mem. exec. com. Nat. Soc. for Fund Raising Execs. (bd. dirs. 1983—). Republican. Roman Catholic. Club: Genesee Valley (Rochester). Avocations: squash, golf, tennis, music, art. Home: 69 Green Valley Rd Pittsford NY 14534 Office: Highland Hosp Found 1000 South Ave Rochester NY 14620

ROBINSON, JENNIFER MILNER, mortgage banker; b. Sylacauga, Ala., July 12, 1963; d. John Donald and Clara Jean (Boulware) Milner; m. Mark Hamilton Robinson, Jan. 3, 1987. BBA, U. Montevallo, Ala., 1985. Ops. asst. mgr. K Mart, Scottsboro, Ala., 1985-86; pers. tng. mgr. K Mart, Huntsville, Ala., 1987; account exec. Tenn. Valley Press, Decatur, Ala., 1987-89; loan processor 1st Cen. Mortgage, Saginaw, Mich., 1990—. Mem. AAUW (exec. bd. 1987-89, voter registraation 1988). Republican. Baptist.

ROBINSON, JOAN, education educator; b. White Plains, N.Y., Aug. 28, 1963; d. Joseph Franklin and Mattie Ann (Chapman) R.; children: Jovan R., Derrick C., Gian D. BS, Merry Coll., 1987. Respite counselor Westchester Ass. for Retarded Citizens, White Plains, 1986-87; educ. cons. sales Early Learning Ctr., White Plains, 1987; crisis counselor Children's Village, Dobbs Ferry, N.Y., 1986-87, sociotherapist; psych. counselor Med. Ctr. of Cen. Ga., Macon, 1987-88; edn. cons. Discovery Toys, White Plains, 1985-87; proprietor Heavens Little Creations, White Plains, Juana Prodns., Scarsdale. Mem. Mt. Vernon Community Choir, Calvary Bapt. Ch.; vol., Union Child Day Care Ctr., Victim Info. Bur.'s Children's Village Program. Mem. NAFE, Entrepreneurs Am., Cen. Westchester Audubon Soc., Westchester Assn. Women Bus. Owners. Republican. Home: 60 Gibson Ave White Plains NY 10607

ROBINSON, JOAN EILEEN, retired volunteer program director; b. Albion, N.Y., Apr. 24, 1937; d. John Dewey and Helen Elizabeth (Lanagan) R. BS, SUNY at Geneseo, 1959; MS, Syracuse U., 1966. Cert. tchr. Elem. tchr. Clifton Springs (N.Y.) Cen. Sch., 1959-65; grad. asst. Syracuse (N.Y.) U., 1965-66; dir. ind. study program Niskayuna (N.Y.) Pub. Schs., 1966-69; assoc. in edn. com. N.Y. State Edn. Dept., Albany, N.Y., 1969-71; regional sales mgr. Rud Clarke Co., Albany, N.Y., 1971-72; account coord. Gen. Electric Corp. Mkt. Com., Schenectady, N.Y., 1973-86; dir. Ret. Sr. Vol. Program of Cape Cod, Hyannis, Mass., 1988-; cons. ind. study program Kettering Found., 1971-72. One person show of photography Schenectady Pub. Library, 1984. Vol. photographer ARC, Schenectady, 1967-80, Habitat for Humanity, Brewster, Mass., 1989—. Mem. Nat. Assn. of Ret. Sr. Vol. Program Dirs. (sec./treas.), New England Ret. Sr. Vol. Program Coun., Mass. Assn. of Ret. Sr. Vol. Program Dirs. (Cape Cod Literacy Coun. 1990—). Home: PO Box 1136 Mashpee MA 02649 Office: Retired Sr Vol Program 48 Camp St Unit 5 Hyannis MA 02601

ROBINSON, JOAN MCCUEN, nursing administrator; b. Detroit, Dec. 13, 1953; d. Norman Warner and Patricia (Shoemaker) McCuen; children: Erica Lindsay, Kelly Martina. BA with highest honors, U. Fla., 1975, BS in Nursing, 1977; MS in Nursing, U. Tex., Houston, 1983. Coord. adolescent psychiat. unit Spring Shadows Glen Hosp., Houston, 1981-82; psychiat. instr. Hermann Hosp., Houston, 1983-86, systems mgr. pediatrics and obstetrics, 1986; dir. nursing Charter Kingwood Hosp., Houston, 1986-87; dir. nursing and ancillary svcs. Houston Internat. Hosp., 1987—; clin. asst. prof. Health Sci. Ctr., U. Tex. Sch. Nursing, Houston, 1985—; mem. nurse researcher coun. Tex. Med. Ctr., 1987—; mem. referral devel. bd. First City Bank, 1988; mem. psychiat. nursing coun. U. Tex., Houston, 1985—. Mem. Houston Bus. Forum, 1989. Lt. Nurse Corps, USNR, 1989—. Mem. Houston Assn. Psychiat. Nurses (v.p. 1985), Houston Orgn. Nurse Execs., Sigma Theta Tau. Unitarian. Home: 4341 Mildred St Bellaire TX 77401

ROBINSON, KAREN ANDREA, investment banker, consultant; b. N.Y.C., June 8, 1953; d. Kenneth Andrew and Carolyn Elizabeth (Smith) R. BA, Fairleigh Dickinson, 1971-75, MPA, 1976-78. Planning assoc. Regional Health Planning Coun., Newark, 1976-78; sr. edn. officer Health Systems Agy., Phila., 1978-82; sr. legis. asst. Hon. John Heinz U.S. Senate, Washington, 1980-82; cons. Phila., 1982-83; dep. dir. dept. Housing & Community Devel. City of Camden, NJ, 1983; chief of staff office of mayor City of Camden (N.J.), NJ, 1984; operations chief Hon. James J. Florio US Congress, Stratford, NJ, 1984-85; v.p. Van Kampen Merritt Inc., Phila., 1985--; cons. The White House (Carter/Mondale), Washington, 1979-80, Mondale/Ferraro Campaign, Washington, 1983-84, The Mandela Tour, 1990; pres. 1260 Housing Corp., Phila., 1988-90. Chmn. Regular Democrats for the 90's, Camden, N.J.; mem. fin. com. Wilson for Phila. Mayor, Casey for Pa. Gov., Florio for Gov. Office: Van Kampen Merritt Two Penn Center Pla Ste 1600 Philadelphia PA 19102

ROBINSON, KAREN ANN, marketing executive; b. Roswell, N.Mex., Nov. 15, 1957; d. Conard Roe and Shirley Maxine (Donahey) Shelnut; m. Raymond Lee Robinson Jr., Dec. 5, 1987. BA in Econs. and Polit. Sci., U. Redlands, Calif., 1980. Exec. trainee, dept. mgr. May Co., L.A., 1980, div. sales mgr., 1981; mgr. phone ctr. Pacific Bell/AT&T, L.A., 1982-83; regional sales mgr. AT&T, L.A., 1983-85; mgr. strategic planning AT&T, Basking Ridge, N.J., 1985-86; nat. applications mgr. AT&T, Atlanta, 1986-87; v.p. strategic planning Ernest Telecom, Atlanta, 1988; v.p. sales and mktg. Nat. Data Corp., Atlanta, 1989—; speaker in field. Contbr. articles to profl. jours. Mme. Sales and Mktg. Execs. of Atlanta, NAFE. Presbyterian. Office: Nat Data Corp National Data Pla Atlanta GA 30329

ROBINSON, KAREN R., nurse; b. Grafton, N.D., Mar. 22, 1948; d. Howard J. and Clarine O. (Larson) R. Diploma in nursing, St. Luke's Hosp. Sch. Nursing, Fargo, N.D., 1969; BS in Nursing, U. Ky., 1977; MS, Tex. Woman's U., 1982; postgrad., U. Tex., Austin. RN, N.D. Day nursing supr., infection control nurse VA Med. Ctr., Fargo, asst. chief nursing svc. Contbr. to profl. publs.; inventor. Myrtle & Earl Walker Found. scholar, 1989, Lola Wright Found. Centennial Nursing scholar, 1990. Mem. Am. Nurses Assn., Am. Assn. Critical Care Nurses, Midwest Nursing Rsch. Soc., U. Ky. Alumni Assn., YWCA (Disting. Leadership award 1984, 86, 90, Women of Yr. 1990), Soc. Advancement of Modeling in Role-Modeling, Jr. League, Bus. and Profl. Women's Club (treas. 1984-85, sec. 1986). Methodist. Office: VA Med Ctr 2101 Elm St Fargo ND 58102

ROBINSON, LINDA GOSDEN, communications executive; b. L.A., Jan. 10, 1953; d. Freeman Fisher and Jane Elizabeth (Stoneham) Gosden; m. Stephen M. Dart (div. June 1977); m. James Dixon Robinson III. Student, UCLA, 1970-72; BA summa cum laude in Psychology, U. So. Calif., 1978. Dep. press sec. Reagan Presdl. Campaign, L.A., 1979; press sec., dir. pub. relations Rep. Nat. Com., Washington, 1979-80; dir. pub. affairs U.S. Dept. Transp., Washington, 1981-83; ptnr. pub. and govt. affairs Heron, Burchette, Ruckert & Rothwell, Washington, 1983; dep. to spl. envoy Office of the Pres., N.Y.C., 1985; sr. v.p. corp. affairs Warner Amex Cable Communications, N.Y.C., 1983-86; pres., chief exec. officer Robinson, Lake, Lerer & Montgomery, N.Y.C., 1986—; bd. dirs. Revlon Group, Inc., N.Y.C., Coro Found., N.Y.C., Bozell, Jacobs, Kenyon & Eckhardt, N.Y.C., N.Y. Hist. Soc., N.Y.C., Andrews Group, Inc., N.Y.C. bd. trustees The N.Y. Hist. Soc., N.Y.C., Del. Rep. Nat. Conv., 1985; mem. YMCA. Mem. Women Achievers Acad., Nat. Women's Econ. Coun., Phi Beta Kappa. Republican. Clubs: Lake Waramaug, Washington (Conn.).

ROBINSON, LOIS HART, retired public relations executive; b. Freeport, Ill., Aug. 9, 1927; d. Seril N. and Cora (Stabenow) Hart; m. Noel M. Henze, Nov. 15, 1947 (div. 1964); m. Jack Fay Robinson, July 16, 1968; children: Susan Henze Bentley, Cynthia Henze Berkeley, Charles Henze. Student Oakton Community Coll., 1976-77, Northwestern U., 1977-81. Med. sec. Freeport Meml. Hosp., 1945-47; sec. No. Ill. Corp., 1947-49; adminstrv. asst. to supt. schs. Community Sch. Dist. 303, St. Charles, Ill., 1962-68; exec. sec. Bell & Howell Co., Chgo., 1969-73, supr. corp. rels., 1973-79, mgr. corp. communications, 1979-85, mgr. corp. communication svcs., 1985-88; pres., dir. Bell & Howell Found., 1983-88; free-lance writer, Evanston, Ill., 1989—. Recipient Effie award Am. Mktg. Assn., 1983. Bd. dirs. Christ Temple Shelter for Homeless. Mem. Chgo. Women in Philanthropy, Corp. Volunteerism Coun. Mem. Internat. Assn. Bus. Communicators, Nat. Soc. Fund Raising Execs. Congregationalist. Home: 2614 Lincolnwood Dr Evanston IL 60201

ROBINSON, LORNA JANE, marketing executive; b. N. Tonawanda, N.Y., Jan. 28, 1957; d. Lawrence Esdras and Irene Nancy (Sachuk) Cyr. AS in Bus. Methods, SUNY, Buffalo, 1983, BS in Bus. Adminstrn., 1987. Credit clk. Nat. Assn. Credit Mgmt., Buffalo, 1975-77; sec. to v.p. The Sample, Inc., Buffalo, 1977-78; credit rep. Liberty Nat. Bank and Trust, Buffalo, 1978-79, Spencer Kellogg Div. Textron, Buffalo, 1979-82; sr. customer svc. rep. Spencer Kellogg/NL Chems., Buffalo, 1982-86; account exec. WYRK-FM, Buffalo, 1986, Genigraphics Corp., Phila., 1986—. Roman Catholic. Home: 5153 Judson Dr Bensalem PA 19020 Office: Genigraphics Corp 3 Ben Franklin Pkwy Philadelphia PA 19102

ROBINSON, MARGARET VIRGINIA, personnel director; b. Charleston, W.Va., Jan. 27, 1951; d. Charles Elba and Naomi Virginia (Roberts) R. AS, W.Va. Inst. Tech., 1972; BA, Morris Harvey Coll., 1977; postgrad., W.Va. Coll. Grad. Studies, 1977—. Sec. W.Va. Div. Vocat. Rehab., Charleston, 1972-76, personnel asst., 1976-79, personnel specialist, 1979-82, chief of personnel adminstrn., 1982-83; asst dir. personnel W.Va. Dept. Edn., Charleston, 1983-89, asst. dir. higher edn. personnel, 1989—; cons. W.Va. Com. for the Prevention of Child Abuse, Charleston, 1988—. Active United Way of the Kanawha Valley, 1988, Community Council of the Kanawha Valley, St. Andrew United Meth. Ch. and others. Named to Outstanding Young Women of Am., 1983. Mem. Civitan Internat. (gov. W.Va. dist. 1984-85, dist. dir. 1982-83, 85-86, recipient Disting. Gov. award, 1985-86, Disting. Lt. Gov. award, 1981-82, Honor Key 1982), Capitol City Civitan Club (pres. 1980-81), W.Va. Jr. Civitans (chmn. 1985-89), W.Va. Internat. Personnel Mgmt. Assn. (pres. 1988-89), Mid-Atlantic Region Nat. Rehab. Assn. (pres. 1982-83), W.Va. Rehab. Assn. (pres. 1980-81), W.Va. Rehab. Adminstrn. (pres. 1979-80), Order of Eastern Star. Democrat. Home: 2741 Lincoln Ave Saint Albans WV 25177 Office: WVa Higher Edn Cen Office 1018 Kanawha Blvd E Ste 700 East Bldg 6 Rm 348 State Capitol Charleston WV 25301

ROBINSON, MARIETTA SEBREE, lawyer; b. Platteville, Wis., Dec. 26, 1951; d. Herbert Thomas and Agnes Marie (Traver) Sebree; m. Lloyd Peniston Jones III (div. 1981; m. James Kenneth Robinson, Aug. 14, 1983. BA, U. Mich., 1973; JD, UCLA, 1978. Bar: Calif. 1978, Mich. 1979, U.S. Dist. Ct. (ea. dist.) Mich. 1980, U.S. Ct. Appeals (6th cir.) 1983. Data processing mktg. rep. IBM, 1973-75; atty. Bank of Bermuda, Hamilton, 1978-79, Dickinson, Wright, Moon, VanDusen & Freeman, Detroit, 1979-84; atty./shareholder Sommers, Schwartz, Silver & Schwartz, Southfield, Mich., 1985-89; pvt. practice law Detroit, 1989—; trustee Dalkon Shield Claiments' Trust, Richmond, Va., 1989—, State of Mich. Bldg. Authority, Lansing, 1985-89; mem. Rep. of State Bar Rep. Assy., 1984-85; lectr. in field. Contbr. articles to profl. jours.; contbg. author: Evidence in America, The Federal Rules in the States, 1987, Introducing Evidence, A Practical Guide for Michigan Lawyers, 1988. Mem. ABA, Assn. Trial Lawyers Am., Mich. Trial Lawyers Assn., Women Lawyers of Mich., Detroit Bar Assn., Oakland Bar Assn., Women Lawyers of Am., Wayne County Bar Assn. Democrat. Office: 407 E Fort St #101 Detroit MI 48226

ROBINSON, MARILYN PLATT, book company executive; b. Bklyn., Mar. 2, 1936; d. Herman and Ann (Itzkowitz) Platt; m. David Arnold Robinson, Dec. 29, 1957; 1 child, Rachel Jennifer. BS, NYU, 1957; MS, Hunter Coll., 1961. Cert. tchr., N.Y., N.J. Tchr. N.Y.C. Schs., 1957-58; tchr. Linden (N.J.) Schs., 1959-64; customer rep. Baker & Taylor Books,

Somerville, N.J., 1978-86, contract adminstr., 1987—; substitute tchr. Bridgewater (N.J.) Schs., 1975-78. Borden scholar Borden Found., 1957. Mem. AAUW (treas. 1967-69, fellowship chmn. 1979-80, community affairs chmn. 1987-89), Omicron Nu (sec. 1959-60). Home: 15 Wight St Bridgewater NJ 08807 Office: Baker & Taylor Books 50 Kirby Ave Somerville NJ 08876-0734

ROBINSON, MARLENE BEATRICE, communications consultant; b. Syracuse, N.Y., July 7, 1934; d. Louis Elon and Jasmine Lucille (Zuckerman) Muller; m. Louis Robinson, Aug. 28, 1955 (dec. 1985); children: Wendy Linda, Donna Gail Robinson Tabas. BS magna cum laude, Syracuse U., 1955. CLU. Theatrical dir. Syracuse (N.Y.) U. Children's Theater, 1953-55; sound dir. Royer Cartoon Film Co., Syracuse, 1954-55; copywriter Aetna Ins. Co., Harford, Conn., 1955-56; spl. agt. Prudential Ins. Co., Harrison, N.Y., 1976-77; dir. agys. Gerber Life Ins. Co., White Plains, N.Y., 1977-80; pres., chief exec. officer Speech-Coach, Inc., Scarsdale, N.Y., 1986—; v.p., dir. Westchester Women's Fed. Credit Union, White Plains, 1981-83; workshop leader Westfair Office 2000 Bus. Expo, White Plains, 1989; bd. dirs. Phoenix Theatre Co., N.Y.C. and Dobbs Ferry; lectr. and speaker in field. Funds mgr. Democratic Family Ct. Election, Westchester, N.Y., 1987. Mem. Sales and Mktg. Execs. N.Y. and Westchester, Nat. Speakers Assn. (judge, evaluator 1989—), Am. Soc. Tng. and Devel., Westchester C. of C., Assn. Personal Image Cons., Westchester Assn. Women Bus. Owners, Women in Communications, Am. Mgmt. Assn., Westchester County Assn., Women in Mgmt., Town Club Scarsdale (mem. sr. housing com. 1984—), Rotary (educator and trainer youth exchange program 1989—), Phi Kappa Phi, Zeta Phi Eta. Democrat. Jewish. Office: Speech Coach Inc PO Box 331 H Scarsdale NY 10583

ROBINSON, MARY E. GOFF, retired historian, researcher; b. East Providence, R.I., Jan. 3, 1925; d. Newell Darius and Eva Agnes (Crane) Goff; m. Charles Albert Robinson, July 30, 1954; 1 child, Thomas Goff (dec.). BA, Wheaton Coll., Norton, Mass., 1947. Cataloger, fine arts Chester County Hist. Soc., West Chester, Pa., 1973-76. Author: (monograph) Newell D. Goff, 1990; co-author: (monograph) Ada Clendenin Williamson, 1983, (history) The Ingalls, The Hoyts, 1990; editor: (autobiography) A Quiet Man From West Chester, 1974. Mem. Jr. League, Providence, 1957-62, The Providence Athenaeum, 1955-63, Providence Preservation Soc., 1959-63; active Brandywine Conservancy, Phila. Orch., Winterthur Mus., Nat. Mus. Women in Arts. Mem. AAUW, Chester County Hist. Soc. (bd. dirs. 1974-80), R.I. Hist. Soc., Chester County Art Assn., Hershey's Mill Country Club.

ROBINSON, MARY LOU, federal judge; b. Dodge City, Kans., Aug. 25, 1926; d. Gerald J. and Frances (Pierce) Strueber; m. A.J. Robinson, Aug. 28, 1949; children: Rebecca Aynn Gruhlkey, Diana Ceil, Matthew Douglas. B.A., U. Tex., 1948, LL.B., 1950. Bar: Tex. 1949. Sole practice Amarillo, 1950-55; judge County Ct. Potter County, Tex., 1955-59; judge (108th Dist. Ct.), Amarillo, 1961-73; assoc. justice Ct. of Civil Appeals for 7th Supreme Jud. Dist. of Tex., Amarillo, 1973-77; chief justice Ct. of Civil Appeals for 7th Supreme Jud. Dist. of Tex., 1977-79; U.S. dist. judge No. Dist. Tex., Amarillo, 1979—. Named Woman of Year Tex. Fedn. Bus. and Profl. Women, 1973. Mem. Nat. Assn. Women Lawyers, ABA, Tex. Bar Assn., Amarillo Bar Assn., Delta Kappa Gamma. Presbyterian. Office: US Dist Ct Box F 13248 Amarillo TX 79189

ROBINSON, MILDRED ANN, accountant; b. Okmulgee, Okla., Feb. 27, 1938; d. John and Opal (Kelly) Carr; m. Keith C. Hall (div. 1971); 1 child, Vicki R. Hall Davis; m. Clarence W. Robinson, May 4, 1973; stepchildren: Clarence W. Jr., Ruth, Rita. BS in Adminstrn., U. Pittsburg, Kans., 1960. With State Compensation Ins., Denver, 1960—, underwriter, acct. II, 1971-75, acct. III, 1975-79, 1979--. Tchr. Sunday sch., coord. sisters Ch. of Christ, Denver. Home: 2351 Monaco Pkwy Denver CO 80207 Office: State Compensation Ins 600 Grant Denver CO 80203

ROBINSON, MINNIE LENETHA, science educator, real estate executive; b. Clinton, Miss., Nov. 21, 1939; d. I.L. and Aurdurey (Smith) R. BS, Alcorn State U., 1964; postgrad., Chgo. State U., 1965-67; MA, De Paul U., Chgo., 1976, adminstrv. cert., 1988. Cert. tchr., Ill., Miss.; lic. real estate broker. Sci. instr. Chgo. Bd. Edn., 1964—; with North Side Real Estate Bd., 1985-87, Chgo. Real Estate Assn., 1988-89; rsch. cons. Profl. Rsch. Svc., Chgo., 1988—. Recipient Phenomenal Achievement award Sci. and Math. Initiatives for Learning Enhancement (SMILE) Program NSF, 1989. Mem. NAFE, Am. Fedn. Tchrs. of AFL-CIO, Chgo. Tchrs. Union, Kappa Delta Pi. Democrat. Baptist. Home: 15616 Woodlawn E South Holland IL 60473

ROBINSON, NAN SENIOR, foundation executive; b. Salt Lake City, Jan. 11, 1932; d. Clair Marcil Senior and Lillian (Worlton) Senior Davis; m. David Zav Robinson; Sept. 6, 1954; children: Marc S. Robinson, Eric S. Robinson. BA with hons., Mills Coll., 1952; MA, Harvard U., 1953. Spl. asst. to undersec. Dept. Housing and Urban Devel., Washington, 1966-69; asst. to the pres. U. Mass. Statewide System, Boston, 1970-73, v.p. for planning, 1973-78; dep. commr. Conn. Bd. Higher Edn., Hartford, 1978-81; v.p. adminstrn. The Rockefeller Found., N.Y.C., 1981-90; mem. governing coun. Rockefeller Archive Ctr., Pocantico Hills, N.Y., 1986-89; com. mem. Coun. on Founds. N.Y. Regional Assn. Grantmakers, 1985-89; mem. nat. advisory panel on governance Carnegie Found. for the Advancement of Teaching, Princeton, N.J., 1980-82. Trustee, chmn. fin. com. Inst. for Current World Affairs, Hanover, N.H., 1987-90; trustee Calif. Sch. Profl. Psychology, San Francisco, 1985—. Recipient Centennial award Am. Assn. U. Women Hartford Br., 1981; named Women of Yr. Hartford YWCA, 1980. Mem. Soc. for Coll. and U. Planning (com. chmn. 1985-86, nominating com. 1980-85, regional rep. 1975-77), Harvard Club, Phi Beta Kappa. Home: 10 Washington Mews New York NY 10003

ROBINSON, NELL BRYANT, nutrition educator; b. Kopperl, Tex., Oct. 15, 1925; d. Basil Howell and Lelia Abiah (Duke) Bryant; m. Frank Edward Robinson, July 14, 1945 (dec.); 1 child, John Howell Robinson. B.S., N. Tex. State U., 1945; M.S., Tex. Woman's U., 1958, Ph.D., 1967. Registered dietitian, Tex. Tchr. Comanche High Sch., Tex., 1945-46, Kopperl High Sch., Tex., 1946-48; county extension agt. Agrl. Extension Service, Tex., 1948-56; prof. nutrition Tex. Christian U., Fort Worth, 1957—, chmn. dept. nutrition and dietetics, 1985—; chmn. coun. on edn. div. Edn. Accreditation/Approval, 1989-90. Pres., bd. dirs. Sr. Citizens Svcs. of Greater Tarrant County, 1990. Contbr. chpt. to book. Named Top Prof., Tex. Christian U. Mortar Bd., 1978. Mem. Am. Dietetic Assn. (del. 1983-88, ethics com. 1985-88, coun. edn. 1988-90), Am. Home Econs. Assn., Tex. Dietetic Assn. (pres., 1972-73, Disting. Dietitian 1981), Tex. Home Econs. Assn. (pres. 1978-80, Home Economist of Yr. 1975). Club: Fort Worth Women. Lodge: Order Eastern Star. Home: 5729 Wimbleton Way Fort Worth TX 76133 Office: Tex Christian U PO Box 32869 Fort Worth TX 76129

ROBINSON, PAMELA ELAINE, commentator; b. N.Y.C., July 22, 1963; d. Paul Rhodes and Carole (Daniel) R. BA in Communications/Policy Studies, Syracuse U., 1985. Affiliate rels. station rep. Unistar Radio Network, N.Y.C., 1985-88; exec. producer talkshow WMCA-AM N.Y. Alan Colmers Show, N.Y.C., 1988-89; talkshow producer ABC Talkradio Network, N.Y.C., 1989—. Mem. Internat. Radio TV Soc., Am. Women in Radio and TV, Inc.

ROBINSON, PATRICIA LEE, investment specialist; b. Macon, Ga., May 24, 1942; d. Joseph Michael and Ruth Lee (Martin) R.; children: Scarlett, Christopher Bell. B in Gen. Studies, George Washington U., 1981; cert., N.Y. Stock Exch. Investment exec. Ferris & Co., Washington, E.F. Hutton Internat., Washington; investment broker Legg Mason Wood Walker, Alexandria, Va. Fund raiser Pub. Support for Arts; gala com. Torpeda Factory Art Ctr., Alexandria, 1990. Roman Catholic. Home: 8253 Doctor Craik Ct Alexandria VA 22306

ROBINSON, ROB, publishing company executive; b. Chgo., June 17, 1955; d. Joseph Ross and Charlotte Evelyn (Harchanko) R. BA, No. Ill. U., 1977. Account exec. Meldrum & Fewsmith, Inc., Chgo., 1978-81; sales rep. Jack O'Grady, Inc., Chgo., 1981-82, Leigh Communications, Inc., Chgo., 1982; sales rep. Midwest region Modern Metals Pub. Co., Chgo., 1982-83; regional sales mgr. Morgan-Grampian Pub. Co., Chgo., 1983-86, Cahners Pub. Co., Des Plaines, Ill., 1986—; bd. dirs. Am. Advt. Fedn. 6th Dist. Hon. appointee rsch. bd. advisors The Am. Biog. Inst.. Mem. Electronic Young Tigers, Women in Electronics (bd. dirs. 1985—), Bus. and Profl. Advt. Assn. (co-chmn., benefit officer, bd. dirs.), Women's Ad Club of Chgo. (co-chmn. ADDY com. 1982—, co-chmn. ednl. benefit 1980—, officer, bd. dirs.), Surface Mount Tech. Assn. (officers, bd. dirs.), Sigma Kappa (1st v.p. 1976-77, chpt. historian 1975-76). Republican. Roman Catholic. Club: The Athletic Congress. Home: 26501 Alicante Mission Viejo CA 92691 Office: Cahners Pub Co 18818 Teller Ave Ste 170 Irvine CA 92715

ROBINSON, SALLY ANNE, clinical psychologist; b. Gassoway, W.Va., Aug. 13, 1923; d. Roland Robert and Malinda Bell (Hurt) R. AB, Marshall U., 1949, MA, 1950; MA, George Washington U., 1957, EdD, 1975. Lic. psychologist, Md., D.C. Elem. tchr. Wayne (W.Va.) County Pub. Schs., 1950-51, Fairfax (Va.) County Pub. Schs., 1952-53, Prince Georges County Schs., Upper Marlboro, Md., 1953-58; high sch. tchr. Carrol County, Westminster, Md., 1958-59; asst. prof. Alliance Coll., Cambridge Springs, Pa., 1959-60; elem. tchr. Prince Georges County Schs., Upper Marlboro, 1960-66; clin. psychologist D.C. Pub. Schs., Washington, 1966—; pvt. practice Bowie, Md., 1975—. With WAVES, 1943-46. Mem. AAUW, Am. Psychol. Assn., Coun. Sch. Officers. Republican. Baptist. Home: 2908 Belair Dr Bowie MD 20715

ROBINSON, SALLY WINSTON, artist; b. Detroit, Nov. 2, 1924; d. Harry Lewis and Lydia (Kahn) Winston; m. Eliot F. Robinson, June 28, 1949; children: Peter Eliot, Lydia Winston, Sarah Mitchell. BA, Bennington Coll., 1947; student Cranbrook Acad. Art, 1949; grad. Sch. Social Work, Wayne U., 1948, MA, 1972; MFA, Wayne State U., 1973. Psychol. tester Detroit Bd. Edn., 1944; pyschol. counselor and tester YMCA, N.Y.C., 1946; social caseworker Family Service, Pontiac, Mich., 1947; instr. printmaking Wayne State U., Detroit, 1973—. One person shows U. Mich., 1973, Wayne State U., 1974, Klein-Vogol Gallery, 1974, Rina Gallery, 1976, Park McCullough House, Vt., 1976, Williams Coll., 1976, Arnold Klein Gallery, 1977; exhibited group shows Bennington Coll., Cranbrook Mus., Detroit Inst. Art, Detroit Artists Market, Soc. Women Painters, Soc. Arts and Crafts, Bloomfield Art Assn., Flint Left Bank Gallery, Balough Gallery, Detroit Soc. Women Painters, U. Mich., U. Ind., U. Wis., U. Pittsburg, Toledo Mus., Krannert Mus.; represented in permanent collections, Detroit, N.Y.C., Birmingham, Bloomfield Hills; tchr. children's art Detroit Inst. Art, 1949-50, now artistic advisor, bd. dirs. drawing and print orgn. Bd. dirs. Planned Parenthood, 1951—, mem. exec. bd., 1963—; bd. dirs. PTA, 1956-60, Roeper City and Country Sch., U. Mich. Mus. Art, 1978; trustee Putnam Hosp. Med. Research Inst., 1978; mem. Gov.'s Commn. Art in State Bldgs., 1978-79; mem. art and devel. coms. So. Vt. Art Ctr., 1987-88; mem. vol. com. Marie Selby Gardens. Mem. Detroit Artists Market (dir. 1956—), Bennington Coll. Alumnae Assn. (regional co-chmn. 1954), Detroit Soc. Women Painters, Birmingham Soc. Women Painters (pres. 1974-76), Bloomfield Art Assn (program co-chmn. 1956), Founders Soc. Detroit Inst. Art., Village Women's Club (Birmingham, Mich.), Women's City Club (co-ordinator art shows Detroit 1950), Garden Club, Am. Club (Bennington, Vt., Sarasota, Fla.), Cosmopolitan (N.Y.C.). Unitarian. Home: 7 Monument Circle Old Bennington VT 05201 also: 840 N Casey Key Rd Osprey FL 34229

ROBINSON, SANDRA DEE, financial company executive, consultant; b. Dallas, Nov. 8, 1960; d. G.W. and Claudine (Carpenter) R. BS in Bus. and Pub. Adminstrn., U. Tex., 1982. Dir. mgmt. info. svcs. Richardson Savs. & Loan, Dallas, 1982-86; asst. v.p. Am. Banc Svs., Dallas, 1986-87; sr. systems analyst Murray Savs., Dallas, 1987; sr. cons. Ferguson & Co., Irving, Tex., 1987-88; v.p. First Pinnacle, Inc., Dallas, 1988—; owner SDR Cons., Dallas, 1986—. Mem. Concerned Women of Am., Washington, 1985. Home: 2116 Rose Cliff Ln Carrollton TX 75007

ROBINSON, SANDRA LAWSON, pediatrician, educator; b. New Orleans, Mar. 22, 1944; d. Alvin James Lawson and Elvera (Stewart) Martin; m. Carl Robinson; children: Michael, Carla. BA, Howard U., 1965, MD, 1969; MPH, Tulane U., 1977. Intern in pediatrics Children's Hosp. Nat. Med. Ctr., Washington, 1969-70, resident in pediatrics, 1970-71; resident in pediatrics, fellow in ambulatory care U. Calif.-San Francisco, San Francisco Gen. Hosp., 1971-72; coord. minority affairs La. State U. Med. Ctr., 1979; med. dir. Neighborhood Health Clinics, New Orleans, 1973-77; dir. ambulatory care and outpatient svcs. Charity Hosp., New Orleans, 1977-81; dir. ambulatory care svc. Children's Hosp. New Orleans, 1981-84; sec. and state health officer La. Dept. Health and Human Resources, Baton Rouge, 1984-88; clin. asst. prof. pediatrics La. State U. and Tulane U. Schs. Medicine, 1974—; adj. asst. prof. Tulane U. Sch. Pub. Health and Tropical Medicine, 1977—; mem. bd. adminstrs., 1989—; mem. subcom. on community health HHS. Recipient Region V award Howard U. Alumni, Outstanding Leadership award Morehouse Coll. Sch. Medicine, 1986, Outstanding Community Svc. award Black Orgn. Leadership Devel., Outstanding Svc. award Tangipahoa Voters League, Woman's Day Honor award Mt. Zion United Meth. Ch.; named Woman of Yr. NABSW, 1987. Mem. New Orleans Med. Soc., Pediatric Soc. of New Orleans, Tulane Women's Assn., Orleans Parish Women's Med. Assn., New Orleans Grad. Med. Assembly, Ambulatory Pediatric Soc., Nat. Med. Assn. (Scroll of Merit award 1987), La. Women's Network, Inc., Assn. State and Terr. Health Ofcls., Internat. Women's Forum, Delta Sigma Theta (Community Svc. award, Pub. Svc. award). Democrat. Roman Catholic. Avocations: skiing, reading.

ROBINSON, SARAH BONHAM, artist, educator, therapist; b. Somerville, N.J., Mar. 16, 1939; d. Robert Daniel and Eleanor Cammann (McMurtry) Bonham; m. Bruce Mitton Robinson, Aug. 28, 1961 (div. 1975); children: Christopher Day, David Brooke, Megan Louise, Andrew Cornell. BA, Wilson Coll., 1961; MFA, U. Pa., 1962; art edn. cert. Kean Coll., 1979. Asst. art instr. Wilson Coll., Chambersburg, Pa., 1960-61; art educator Newark Acad., Livingston, N.J., 1966-68; adj. instr. Rutgers U., New Brunswick, N.J., 1967; art therapist J.E. Runnells, Berkeley Heights, N.J., 1974; creative arts therapist dept. psychiatry Elizabeth Gen. Med. Ctr. (N.J.), 1974—, dir. activity therapy, 1976—, clin. chief partial hosp., 1978-85, chmn. quality assurance psychiatry 1980-83, asst. dir. rehab. services, 1983-87; art therapy cons. Children's Specialized Hosp., Mountainside, N.J., 1976—. Producer, editor film strip: Changes, 1974. Illustrator: Miller-Cory Colonial Cooking, 1975. Paintings exhibited in eastern U.S., 1960—, including World's Fair 1965. Artist, Miller-Cory Hist. Orgn., Westfield, N.J., 1969-79; artist, mem. Sane, Union County, N.J., 1969—. Woodrow Wilson fellow, 1961. Mem. Am. Assn. Partial Hosps., N.J. Assn. Partial Hosps. (regional chmn. 1983-87, co-founder), N.J. Assn. Rehab. Facilities, N.J. Psychiat. Rehab. Assn. Democrat. Home: 235 Sinclair Pl Westfield NJ 07090 Office: Elizabeth Gen Med Ctr 925 E Jersey St Elizabeth NJ 07201

ROBINSON, SHANNON, state legislator. BA, JD, U. N.Mex. Atty.; mem. N.Mex. State Senate. Democrat. Home: 716 Indiana SE Albuquerque NM 87108*

ROBINSON, (NANCY) SHARLEEN, information systems specialist; b. Chattanooga, Nov. 13, 1950; d. William Thomas and Gilberta Marlin (Austin) Gribble; m. Larry Joe Robinson, June 3, 1978. Student, Tomlinson/BTI, 1975, Chatanooga State U., 1978, 80, Dalton Coll., 1984, 85. Asst. mgr. Payless Shoe Source, Chattanooga, 1970-75; needlecraft, ladieswear custom designer Chattanooga, 1975-78; asst. bookkeeper Rossville (Ga.) Bank, 1978-79; mgr. svc. delivery info. systems Family and Children's Svcs. Chattanooga, 1979—. Recipient cert. of appreciation Ross Bus. and Profl. Women's Club, 1982, cert. of honor Am. Bible Soc., 1986. Mem. Assn. Records Mgrs. and Adminstrs. (charter chpt., treas. 1981-82, edn. com.), Am. Svc. Info. Soc., Nat. Assn. Govt. and Archival Records Adminstrs. Republican. Presbyterian. Home: 146 Valley Breeze Trail Rossville GA 30741 Office: Family and Childrens Svcs 300 E 8th St Chattanooga TN 37403

ROBINSON, THERESA STONE, computer/infosystems engineer; b. Binghamton, N.Y., Sept. 20, 1954; d. Jack K. and Mary Ann (Mahoney) Stone; m. Howard G. Robinson, Nov. 17, 1979 (div. 1984). BS, SUNY, Oneonta, 1976; MS, SUNY, Binghamton, 1982; AAS, Broome Community Coll., Binghamton, 1984; MS, Boston U., 1989. Educator Binghamton Pub. Schs., 1976-84; sr. software specialist Digital Equipment Co., Marlboro, Mass., 1984-86, sr. software engineer, 1986-90, engring. ops. mgr., 1990—. Mem. NAFE. Republican. Roman Catholic.

ROBINSON, V. YVONNE, hospital nursing administrator; b. Stuttgart, Ark., Dec. 18, 1939; d. Guy Wacthel Robinson and Norma Louise Hospodarsky; m. William J. Flanigan. Student, Harding Coll., 1957-58, U. Ark., Fayetteville, 1958-59; BS in Nursing, U. Ark., Little Rock, 1961; MS in Edn., U. Cen. Ark., 1973. RN, Ark. Staff nurse U. Ark. Med. Ctr., Little Rock, 1961-62, supr. clin. rsch. ctr., 1962-73; asst prof. nursing U. Ark., Little Rock, 1973-79; asst. chief trainee VA Med. Ctr., Little Rock, 1979-80; asst. chief nursing svc. VA Med. Ctr., Syracuse, N.Y., 1980-81; assoc. chief nursing svc VA Med. Ctr., Hines, Ill., 1981-83; chief nursing svc. VA Med. Ctr., Tucson, 1983-84; assoc. chief nursing svc. J.L. McLellan VA Hosp., Little Rock, 1984—; cons. Ark. League Nursing, Conway, 1973; cons. insvc. edn. Ark. Children's Hosp., Little Rock, 1973-74. Contbr. articles to profl. publs. Named one of Outstanding Young Women of Am., 1974. Mem. Am. Nurses Assn. (mem. coun. nursing adminstrn. 1986—), Ark. State Nursing Assn., Nurses Orgn. of the VA, Sr. Citizen's Activities Today (bd. dirs. 1986—), Sigma Theta Tau. Home: 2517 Arkansas Valley Dr Little Rock AR 72212

ROBINSON, VIOLET MARIE, social worker; b. Morrisdale, Pa., Feb. 17, 1935; d. Howard Lyod and Iva Susan (Moyer) Hubler; m. Franklin Elmer Robinson, Apr. 9, 1954; children: Susan M. Robinson Kelonis, Carl, Morry, Richard. Student, Philipsburg (Pa.) State Hosp., 1953-54; BA in Human Rels., U. Pitts., Bradford, 1987. Child protective caseworker McKean County Children Svcs., Smethport, Pa., 1987; social worker Cath. Social Svcs., Cin., 1988; child protective caseworker Dearborn County Welfare State of Ind., Lawrenceburg, 1988—; social worker Family Out Reach Program div. New Life Youth Svcs., Cin. Republican. Methodist. Home: 23115 Salt Fork Rd Lawrenceburg IN 47025 Office: Family Outreach Program 1527 Madison Rd 2d Fl Cincinnati OH 45206

ROBISON, BARBARA ANN, newspaper editor; b. Portland, Oreg., July 15, 1933; d. Louis Keith and Marjorie (Work) R.; 1 child, Nancy. Student, Coll. Idaho, 1951-54, U. Utah, 1968-70. Reporter Caldwell (Idaho) News Tribune, 1951-54; sports editor LaGrande (Oreg.) Evening-Observer, 1954-55; reporter Idaho Daily Statesman, Boise, 1955-57; asst. women's editor Tacoma (Wash.) News Tribune, 1958-59; lifestyle editor Salt Lake Tribune, 1967—. Mem. Salt Lake Exchange Club, 1986—. Episcopalian. Home: 4210 Caroleen Way Salt Lake City UT 84124 Office: Salt Lake Tribune Box 867 Salt Lake City UT 84110

ROBISON, CAROLYN LOVE, librarian; b. Orlinda, Tenn., Aug. 9, 1940; d. Fount Love and Martha Desha (Jones) R. BA, Denison U., 1962; MLS, Emory U., 1965; PhD, Ga. State U., 1982. Tchr. Dag Hammarshjold Jr. High Sch., Wallingford, Conn., 1962-64; asst. librarian, lectr. Architecture Library Ga. Inst. Tech., Atlanta, 1965-67; head circulation Ga. State U., Atlanta, 1967-71, asst. librarian, 1971-75, assoc. librarian, 1976—. Active Friends of Atlanta-Fulton County Pub. Library, 1981—. Mem. ALA, Southeastern Library Assn., Ga. Library Assn., Am. Assn. Univ. Professors, Delta Kappa Gamma, Phi Kappa Phi, Kappa Delta Pi. Republican. Presbyterian. Home: 1057 Capital Club Circle Atlanta GA 30319 Office: Ga State U 100 Decatur St SE Atlanta GA 30303

ROBISON, JOYCE JUNE, realtor; b. Chgo., June 13, 1945; d. Steven Michael and Roseann Florence (Cerny) Lesniak; m. Charles Edward Robison, July 11, 1964; children: Jeffrey Charles, Laura Christine. Student, Lorain County Community Coll., 1983-84, Cleve. State U., 1985. Licensed Real Estate Agent, Sales Assoc., Relocation Counselor. Sec. Radio Industries/TRW, Des Plaines, Ill., 1963-65; office mgr. William Rainey Harper Coll., Palatine, Ill., 1969; exec. sec. LorTec Electronics, North Ridgeville, Ohio, 1978-79; spl. edn. asst. North Ridgeville City Schs., 1979-83; exec. dir. North Ridgeville Arts Coun., 1983—; realtor, mem. adv. coun. Realty One, North Ridgeville, 1986—; speaker in field. Leadership rep. Nat. Community Leadership Conf., Providence, 1988; mem. Leadership Lorain County (Ohio) Class of 1985; facilitator, bd. mentors Pub. Svc. Inst., Lorain County Community Coll., 1989; levy steering com. Lorain County Mental Health Svcs., 1987; organizer North Ridgeville First Night Festival; bd. dirs. Leadership Lorain County, 1986. Recipient Leadership award No. Ridgeville Arts Council, 1987, Rookie of the Year award Realty One, 1987, Cert. of Recognition Leadership Lorain County, 1984. Mem. NAFE, Lorain County Women's Network, Lorain County Bd. Realtors, Leadership Lorain County Alumni Assn. (pres. 1986, bd. dirs. 1985-90), North Ridgeville C. of C., Mills Creek Women's Club. Roman Catholic. Home: 33040 Leafy Mill Ln North Ridgeville OH 44039 Office: Realty One 36178 Center Ridge Rd North Ridgeville OH 44039

ROBISON, JUDY KAY, nursing home administrator; b. Rosebud, Tex., Mar. 26, 1947; d. Edwin Jerry and Mildred Nadine (Tawater) Slovacek; m. James Harold Cunningham, Mar. 19, 1971 (div. Aug. 1976); 1 child, Jena Cassidie; m. Donnie Ray Robison, Dec. 20, 1976 (div. July 1982). Student LaSalle Extension U., 1966, U. Tex., 1976; AAS, McLennan Community Coll., 1980. Designer Green Flower Shop, Rosebud, 1961-65; exec. sec. Gary Job Corps Ctr., San Marcos, Tex., 1965-74; asst. adminstr. Rosebud Med. Services, 1975-77, adminstr., 1977-82; Community adminstr. Hosp. Assn. of Tex., Inc., Rosebud, 1982—. Mem. Med. Products Research Panel, 1985—; adv. bd. Foodservice Research Ctr., 1984, Temple Jr. Coll., Tex., 1982, 85, R-L Ind. Sch. Dist., 1979—; TV telethon coordinator Easter Seal Soc., 1985. Recipient Friend to Edn. award Tex. State Tchrs. Assn., 1986. Mem. Am. Coll. Nursing Home Adminstrs., Rosebud C. of C. (dir. 1990—). Clubs: Rosebud Ex-Students (sec., treas. 1982—), Rosebud-Lott Booster (sec. 1989). Avocations: music, horticulture, tennis, skiing, dancing. Home: 530 E Ave G Rosebud TX 76570 Office: Community Hosp Assn Tex Inc Heritage House Corner of College and Ave F Rosebud TX 76570

ROBISON, SUSAN MILLER, psychologist, educator, consultant; b. Chgo., Nov. 15, 1949; d. William Louis and Constance Mary (Maloney) Miller; m. Philip Dean Robison, Dec. 27, 1969; 1 child, Christine Alyssa. BS, Loyola U., Chgo., 1967; MS, Ohio U., 1969, PhD, 1971. Lic. psychologist, Md. Asst. prof. psychology Ohio U., Lancaster, 1970-72; prof. psychology Coll. Notre Dame, Balt., 1972—; pvt. practice Ellicott City, Md., 1982—; leadership cons. Nat. Coun. Cath. Women, Washington, 1987—. Author: Sharing Our Gifts, 1987, Thinking and Writing Across the Disciplines, 1989, Discovering Our Gifts, 1989. Troop leader Girl Scouts U.S.A., Ellicott City, 1982-85, mem. adv. bd. Girl Scouts Central Md., 1987-88; mem. adv. bd. Archdiocese of Balt., 1986. Mem. Am. Psychol. Assn., Am. Assn. Sex Educators, Counselors and Therapists, Assn. for Advancement Behavior Therapy. Home: 3725 Font Hill Dr Ellicott City MD 21043

ROBLE, CAROLE MARCIA, accountant; b. Bklyn., Aug. 22, 1938; d. Carl and Edith (Brown) Dusowitz; m. Richard F. Roble, Nov. 30, 1969. MBA with distinction, N.Y. Inst. Tech., 1984. CPA, Calif., N.Y. Compt. various orgns. various orgns., 1956-66; staff acct. ZTBG CPA'S, L.A., 1966-67; sr. acct. J.H. Cohn & Co., Newark, 1967-71; prin. Carole M. Roble, CPA, South Hempstead, N.Y., 1971-90; ptnr. Roble, Libman & Cohen, CPAs, Baldwin, N.Y., 1990—; speaker, moderator Found. for Acctg. Edn., N.Y., 1971-87; lectr. acctg. various schs. including New Sch., Queens Coll., Empire State Coll., Touro Coll., N.Y. Inst. Tech., N.Y.C., 1971-82. Guest various N.Y. radio and TV stas. Treas. Builders Devel. Corp. of L.I., Westbury, N.Y., 1985; dir. Women Econ. Devels. of L.I., 1985-87. Recipient Sisterhood citation Nat. Orgn. Women, 1984, 85, cert. of Appreciation Women Life Underwriters, 1988, Women in Sales, 1982, 84; named top Tax Practitioner Money Mag., 1987. Mem. AICPAs, Am. Acct. Assn. (auditing sect.), Am. Soc. Women Accts. (pres. N.Y. chpt. 1980-81), Am. Woman's Soc. CPAs, Nat. Conf. CPA Practitioners (trustee L.I. chpt. 1981-82, sec. 1982-83, treas. 1983-84, v.p. 1984-85, 1st v.p. 1985-86, pres. 1986-87, nat. nominating com. 1983-84, 88-89, nat. continuing profl. edn. chmn. 1988-90, edn. chmn. 1988—), Calif. Soc. CPAs, N.Y. State Soc. CPAs (bd. dirs. Nassau chpt. 1981-86, bd. dirs. profl. devel., 1982-86, sec., mem. fin. acctg. standards com. 1990—), Kiwanis (program chmn. County Seat chpt. 1989-90). Home: 626 Willis St South Hempstead NY 11550

ROBLES, ROSALIE MIRANDA, teacher; b. L.A., Oct. 30, 1942; d. Richard and Carmen (Garcia) Miranda; m. Ralph Rex Robles, July 12, 1986; children: Gregory, Eric, Karen. BA, Calif. State Coll., L.A., 1964;

postgrad., Northridge State Coll. Playground supr. L.A. City Schs., 1961-64; elem. tchr. Montebello (Calif.) Unified Schs., 1964—; rep. Montebello Credit Union, 1973-75, Bilingual Com., 1983-88; chmn. Sch. Site Coun., 1980-83. Chmn. Monterey Park Christmas Food Baskets, 1973-88; mem., boys coord., girls coord. Am. Youth Soccer; chmn. Boy Scouts Am., 1980-85; mem. exec. bd. PTA, 1978, 80, 85, 87, pres. 1990—. Recipient Hon. Svc. award PTA, 1979, Hon. Svc. Continuing award PTA, 1982. Roman Catholic.

ROBOHM, PEGGY ADLER, writer, researcher, literary consultant, illustrator; b. N.Y.C., Feb. 10, 1942; d. Irving and Ruth (Relis) Adler; m. Jeremy Abbott Walsh, June 1, 1962 (div. Dec. 1968); children: Tenney Whedon, Avery Denison; m. Richard A. Robohm, Dec. 24, 1976; stepchildren: Erick John, Kurt William, Kim Alene (Mrs. John L. Moore). Student, Bennington Coll., 1959-60, Columbia U., 1962. Illustrator, author childrens books, 1958—; agt. Jan J. Agy., Inc., N.Y.C., 1981-82; freelance talent scout Cuzzins Mgmt., N.Y.C., 1982-83; personal mgmt. and pub. rels. cons. Madison, Conn., 1983—; investigative researcher, writer, lit. cons., 1986—. author, illustrator: The Adler Book of Puzzles and Riddles, 1962, The 2nd Adler Book of Puzzles and Riddles, 1963, Metric Puzzles, 1977, Math Puzzles, 1978, Geography Puzzles, 1979; author: Hakim's Connection, 1988; co-author: Skull and Bones: The Skeleton in Bush's Closet?, 1988; illustrator numerous books including (Humane Soc. of U.S. pubs.) Pet Care, 1974, Caring for Your Cat, 1974, Hot and Cold, 1959, Numbers New and Old, 1960, Do a Zoomdo, 1975, Reading Fundamentals for Teen-Agers, 1973; graphic designer various book covers, posters, co. logos: PR, Sweetie, Baby, Cookie, Honey (with Freddie Garson), 1986; researcher Passion and Prejudice: A Family Memoir (Sallie Bingham), 1989; cons. The President's Private Eye: The Journey of Detective Tony U. From N.Y.P.D. to the Nixon White House(Anthony Ulasewicz with Stuart McKeever), 1990; cons., researcher Bush's Boys Club: Skull and Bones, 1990; cons. Spy Saga (Philip H. Melanson), 1990; contbr. Lies of Our Times. Founder Shoreline Youth Theater, Inc., 1979, mem. adv. bd., 1981-86; bd. dirs. The Greens Condominium Assn. of Branford, Conn., 1975-78, Arts Council of Greater New Haven, 1971-73, Planned Parenthood of Greater New Haven, 1972-73, Assassination Archives and Rsch. Ctr., Washington, 1990—; v.p., bd. dirs. Pub. Info. Rsch., Washington, 1989. Mem. Nat. Conf. Personal Mgrs., Dramatists Guild, Authors League of Am., Assasination Archives and Rsch. Ctr., Inc. (bd. dirs. Washington chpt. 1990—), Conn. Soc. Genealogists, Inc., Yale Club of New Haven. Home and Office: Connections 45 Lawson Dr Madison CT 06443

ROBOLD, ALICE ILENE, mathematician; b. Delaware County, Ind., Feb. 7, 1928; d. Earl G. and Margaret Rebecca (Summers) Hensley; m. Virgil G. Robold, Aug. 21, 1955; 1 son, Edward Lynn. B.S., Ball State U., 1955, M.A., 1960, Ed.D., 1965. Substitute elem. tchr. Am. Elem. Sch., Augsburg, Germany, 1955-56; instr. Ball State U., Muncie, Ind., 1960-61; teaching fellow Ball State U., 1961-64, asst. prof. math. scis., 1964-69, assoc. prof., 1969-76, prof., 1976—. Mem. Nat. Council Tchrs. Math., Ind. Council Tchrs. Math., AAUP, U.S. Metric Assn., Sch. Sci. and Math. Assn., Pi Lambda Theta. Mem. Ch. of God. Office: Ball State U Dept Math Scis Muncie IN 47306

ROBSON, BARBARA BAKER, linguist; b. Salt Lake City, May 6, 1942; d. George Whitman and Georgia Elizabeth (Gilchrist) Baker; m. Roy Anthony Robson, Mar. 25, 1966; 1 child, David Anthony. BA, U. Utah, 1963; PhD, U. Tex., 1971. Asst. prof. U. Wis., Madison, 1971-754; rsch. assoc., div. dir. Ctr. for Applied Linguistics, Washington, 1975—; presenter workshops in field, 1975—. Author texts in field; contbr. articles to profl. publs. Vol. Mondale Presdl. Campaign, Washington, 1984, Sta. WETA, pub. radio, Washington, 1985—. Mem. Linguistic Soc. Am., Jane Austen Soc. N.Am., Bronte Soc., Am. Mgmt. Assn., Phi Beta Kappa, Phi Kappa Phi. Democrat. Office: Ctr for Applied Linguistics 1118 22d St NW Washington DC 20037

ROBSON, DEBORAH RUTH, editor, consultant, artist, writer; b. Evanston, Ill., Nov. 6, 1948; d. William Wallace and Allene (Reich) R.; 1 child, Rebekah Ellen Robson May. Student, Carleton Coll., 1966-69, U. Iowa, 1970-71; BA, U. Wash., Seattle, 1972; MFA, Goddard Coll., 1978. Freelance editorial cons., 1972—; editor U. Mass., Amherst, 1979-80, Shuttle Spindle & Dyepot/HGA, West Hartford, Conn., 1985-86, Interweave Press, Loveland, Colo., 1986—; chmn. bd. Arts Extension Inst., Amherst, 1986—. Author short stories; contbr. articles to profl. jours. Corr. clk. Ft. Collins Meeting Religious Soc. of Friends, 1990—. Office: Interweave Press 201 E Fourth St Loveland CO 80537

ROBSON, SUSAN LUCILLE, nurse; b. Chgo., Dec. 24, 1951; d. John Henry and Katherine (Hendershot) Rapp; m. Raymond John Robson, Dec. 16, 1972; 1 child, Ainsley Marie. AS, Rochester (N.Y.) Inst. Tech., 1972; student, Elmhurst (Ill.) Coll., 1976; Nursing Diploma, St. Francis, Trenton, N.J., 1985; student, Edison State Coll., Trenton, N.J., 1985—. RN, N.J., Pa. Med. photographer U. Chgo., 1972-73; chem. supr. Berey Photo, Des Plaines, Ill., 1973-75; rsch. technician Gould, Inc., Rolling Meadows, Ill., 1975-76, Union Camp Corp., Princeton, N.J., 1977-80; RN St. Francis Med. Ctr., Trenton, N.J., 1985-87, Holy Redeemer Hospice, Phila., 1987-88; med. reviewer Independence Blue Cross, Phila., 1988—; dir. Emergency Care, Levittown (Pa.) Rescue Squad, 1979-83. Photographer (jour.) Mag. of DAR, 1980. Instr. ARC, Langhorne, Pa., 1978, Am. Heart Assn., Bucks County, Pa., 1978; Rep.committeewoman, Bucks County, Pa., 1981; staff officer USCG aux., 1982. Mem. DAR (Outstanding Jr. of Am., mem. Pa. 1985, Outstanding Young Woman of Am. 1983, Outstanding Persons of Am.). Home: 46 Hydrangea Rd Levittown PA 19057 Office: Independence Blue Cross 1333 Chestnut St Philadelphia PA 19101

ROBSON, SYBIL ANN, film producer; b. Tulsa, Dec. 8, 1956; d. John Nicholas and Alma Robson. BFA, So. Meth. U., 1979. Anchor, reporter Sta. WRR-AM Radio, Dallas, 1976-78; researcher Sta. WFAA-TV, Dallas, 1977-78; polit. researcher ABC News, Paris, 1978-79; anchor, reporter Sta. KOLR-TV, Springfield, Mo., 1979-80, Sta. WFMY-TV, Greensboro, N.C., 1980-83, Paramount Pictures, L.A., 1983-86; investor Robson Investments, L.A., 1982—; film producer Bernhard/Robson Entertainment, L.A., 1987—, 1988—. Mem. Earth Communications Office; mem. com. Hollywood Women's Politica. Mem. Am. Film Inst., Ind. Feature Project, Women in Film, Environ. Media Assn., Sigma Delta Chi.

ROBY, CHRISTINA YEN, data processing specialist, instructor; b. Shanghai, China; came to U.S., 1980; d. Hai Zhou and Yun Qui (Zhang) Yen; m: Ronald L. Roby; 1 child, Colin H. BS, Jiao-Tung U., Shanghai, 1957; MS, U. Balt., 1986. Lic. engr., Peoples Republic of China. Chief mech. engr. Shenyang Valve Rsch. Inst., China, 1958-1980; computer system operator U. Balt., 1984, rsch. asst., 1984-86; sales assoc. V. F. Assocs., Inc., Balt., 1986-88; system analyst Computer Data Systems, Inc., Rockville, Md., 1988-89; data processing specialist Dept. of Health and Mental Hygiene, Balt., 1989—; instr. Community Coll. of Balt., 1986, 88; cons. Nat. Ins. Agency, Balt., 1988. Author: Guide to Using MS-DOS, 1988; contbr. author Japanese-Chinese Electrical Mechanical Industry Dictionary, 1980; transl., editor Analysis of Gas, Impurities and Carbide in Steel, 1961; contbr. articles to profl. jours. Vol. tchr. Chinese Lang. Sch., Balt., 1985-86; lectr. Internat. Festival Exh bn., 1986; vol. tutor U. Balt., 1983. Recipient Cert. of appreciation Chinese Language Sch., Balt., 1986. Mem. NAFE, Sci. and Tech. Assn., Beta Gamma Sigma, Delta Mu Delta.

ROCHA, MARILYN EVA, clinical psychologist; b. San Bernardino, Calif., Oct. 23, 1928; d. Howard Ray Gonding and Laura Anne (Johanson) Walker; m. Hilario Ursala Rocha, Mar. 25, 1948 (dec. Feb. 1971); children: Michael, Sherry, Teri, Denise. AA, Solano Jr. Coll., 1970. BA, Sacramento State U., 1973, MA, 1974; PhD, U.S. Internat. U., 1981. Psychologist, Naval Drug Rehab. Ctr., U.S. Navy, San Diego, 1975-85, chief psychologist, 1983-84; staff clin. psychologist Calif. Youth Authority No. Reception Ctr. Clinic, 1985—; dir. Self-Help Agys., San Diego. Author short story. Vol. counselor Hamonium, San Diego, 1976-77; SMRC Planning Group Scripps/Miramar Ranch, 1982-85; leader Vacaville council Cub Scouts Am., Calif., 1957-62, 4-H, also Brownie's. Mem. Calif. Scholastic Fedn., PTA (hon. life), Am. Psychol. Assn., Am. Assn. Suicidology, Bus. and Profl. Women, Delta Zeta. Democrat. Unitarian. Home: 4919 Gastman Way (Birch Cottage) Fair Oaks CA 95628

ROCHE, SISTER DENISE ANN, college president; b. Buffalo, Sept. 17, 1942; d. Vincent Joseph and Mary Elizabeth (Crehan) R. B.A., D'Youville Coll., 1967; M.A., Boston U., 1968; Ph.D., U. Mass., 1977. Tchr., Our Lady of Fatima Grade Sch., L.I., N.Y., 1964-66; instr. D'Youville Coll., Buffalo, 1968-71, asst. prof., 1975-78, assoc. dean for continuing studies, 1978-79, pres., 1979—; teaching assoc. U. Mass.-Boston, 1972-75; mem. adv. bd. Business First, Buffalo, 1985—; bd. dirs. Key Bank Western N.Y. Trustee Marygrove Coll., Detroit, 1981-87; bd. dirs. Child and Family Svcs., 1985—, City of Buffalo Bd. of Ethics, 1989; chmn. coll. and univ. div. United Way Appeal, Buffalo, 1983—. Named Citizen of Yr. N.Y. Soc. Profl. Engrs., 1984, Woman of Yr. Girl Scouts U.S., 1987; recipient Pub. Service award SUNY-Buffalo Alumni Assn., 1985, Brotherhood award in religion NCCJ, 1986, Recognition award SUNY, 1986, Chancellor Charles P. Norton award , 1988, Edn. award So. Christian Leadership Conf., 1989. Mem. Ind. Coll. Fund N.Y., Western N.Y. Consortium Higher Edn. (v.p.), Western N.Y. Regional Edn. Ctr. for Econ. Devel., Greater Buffalo Area C. of C., Zonta. Roman Catholic. Home: 320 Porter Ave Buffalo NY 14201

ROCHESTER, DIANA, advertising professional; b. Manhattan, N.Y., July 11, 1944; d. Joseph George and E. Delora (Broyles) Brown; m. David Andrew Rochester; children: Steven Andrew, William David. Student, Berkeley Coll., East Orange, N.J., 1964, RVCC, 1988. Asst. media mgr. Simms & McIvor, Bound Brook, N.J., 1987-88; media mgr. Simms & McIvor, Branchburg, N.J., 1988—. Mem. NAFE, N.J. Bus. Women's Assn. Home: 1804 Middle Rd Martinsville NJ 08836 Office: Simms & McIvor Inc 3121 Rte 22 E Somerville NJ 08876

ROCHIRA, NANCY MARY, public housing administrator; b. Lawrence, Mass., May 1, 1944; d. Walter Richard and Anna (Kuchuruk) Kibildis; m. Joseph Rochira, Nov. 25, 1962 (dec. Jan. 1984); 1 child, Teresa Anne. Cert. McIntosh Bus. Sch., 1962, pub. housing mgr., 1979; lic. real estate rep. State N.H., 1985; student N.H. Coll., 1975, 77, U. N.H., 79, 85, Castle Jr. Coll., 1984, Inst. for Practicing Real Estate, 1985, 87, Quantum Ednl. Acctg., 1987, Computer Support Services Tng., 1987. Receptionist, exec. sec. Supervisory Union, Atkinson, N.H., 1961-68; sales assoc. Salem-Derry Cable Co., Salem, N.H., 1971; asst. to mgr. Lancelot Assos., Salem, 1974; exec. dir. Salem Housing Authority, 1974—, sec. bd. commrs., 1974—. Area leader Heart Fund, 1980-81; mem. Salem Assn. Retarded Citizens, Salem, 1975—; mem. adv. com. Town and Country Theatre, 1985; Greater Salem Human Services Council, 1984; sec. Help the Handicapped Club, 1975—. Recipient Cert. of Recognition, Green Thumb Nat. Farmers Union, 1980, Cert. of Recognition, N.H. Housing Commn., 1978, Cert. Recognition Am. Cancer Soc., 1985. Mem. N.H. Assn. Exec. Dirs., N.H. Assn. Housing Authorities (sec.-treas. 1987—), NAFE, Nat. Assn. Housing and Redevel. Ofcls. (cert. 1987, sec. N.H. chpt. 1987-88). Avocations: swimming; gardening; cooking. Home: 117 Haverhill Rd Salem NH 03079

ROCHWARGER, MICHELLE, business consultant; b. Buffalo, Mar. 7, 1955; d. Leonard and Arlene Jean Rochwarger. BA, U. Wis., 1977; MBA, U. San Francisco, 1981. Family case worker Salvation Army, Buffalo, 1977; social worker crisis intervention Eric County (N.Y.) Office of Aging, Buffalo, 1977-78; dir. We. Inst. for Tchrs. United Way, Buffalo, 1979; congl. asst. Office Congressman Burton, San Francisco, 1979-80; corp. loan officer Wells Fargo Bank, San Francisco, 1981-83, asst. v.p., tng. mgr., 1983-85; fin. svcs. cons. Omega Performance Corp., San Francisco, 1985-87; pres. Strategic Resources: Cons. Connection, Inc., San Francisco, 1987—; cons. Citicorp, San Francisco, 1980-81; mgr. corp. fitness challenge program Wells Fargo Bank, 1983. Bd. dirs. Big Bros./Big Sisters of San Francisco, 1983-86, Florence Crittendon Soc., San Francisco, 1984-86, Ct. Appointed Spl. Advs., San Francisco, 1983-85. Recipient Community Support award United Way, 1984. Mem. NAFE, San Francisco Advtg. Club, Nat. Soc. Performance and Instrn. Democrat. Jewish. Office: Strategic Resources Inc 2040 Polk St Suite 281 San Francisco CA 94109 also: 135 Delaware Ave Ste 200 Buffalo NY 14202

ROCK, AMELIA SIRIANNI, retired educational administrator; b. Ellwood City, Pa.; d. Antonio and Mary (Gualtieri) Sirianni; m. Salvatore Rock, June 6, 1940; children: Geraldine, Gloria. BA, Geneva Coll., Beaver Falls, Pa., 1936; MEd, U. Miami, 1965; EdD, Nova U., 1975. Cert. tchr., Pa., Fla. Tchr. French and English, Ellwood City Pub. Schs., 1937-42; elem. tchr. Dade County Pub. Schs., Miami, Fla., 1948-51; curriculum asst. Fineberg Elem. Sch., Miami Beach, Fla., 1952-56; asst. prin. Lorah Park Elem. Sch., Miami, 1956-60, Gladeview Elem. Sch., Miami, 1960-65; prin. Bethune Elem. Sch., Miami, 1965-70, Redondo Elem. Sch., Miami, 1970-84; ret., 1984; adj. prof. U. Tenn., Knoxville, summers 1965-70, Miami Dade Commuity Coll., 1964, U. Miami, 1964; cons. Dade County Pub. Schs., 1961-65, in-svc. instr., 1965-70. Mem. AAUW, Fla. Ret. Tchrs. Assn., Miai Ret. Tchrs. Assn., Am. Assn. Ret. Persons, Nat. Order Sons of Italy (sec. edn. com. 1988), Phi Delta Kappa. Democrat. Roman Catholic. Home: 13270 SW 68th St Miami FL 33183

ROCK, CHERYL LYNNE POORE, dental hygienist, consultant, educator; b. Columbus, Ohio, Oct. 12, 1957; d. Jack Jennings and Margaret Louise (Beamer) Poore; m. Michael Charles Rock, June 27, 1981; children: Erin Lynne, Lisa Michele. AS, U. Cin., 1977, BS, 1979, MEd, 1980. Dental hygienist Thomas R. McLaughlin, DDS, Ormond Beach, Fla., 1980-81; substitute tchr. Mainland Sr. High Sch., Daytona Beach, Fla., 1980-81; dental hygienist Robert B. Hammond, DDS, Daytona Beach, 1981, Ronald I. Spritzer, DDS, Cin., 1977-85, Peter H. Schwenkmeyer, DDS, Cin., 1979-82; instr. in dental hygiene U. Cin., 1981-85; dental hygienist Warren V. Wingate, DDS, Springfield, Ohio, 1984-85; curriculum cons. U. Ky., Lexington and, Saudi Arabia, 1984; cons., coord. Sinclair Community Coll., Dayton, Ohio, 1986-87; dental hygienist Timothy A. McDuffee, DDS, Columbus, 1989-90, Dale R. Bauer, DDS, Dublin, Ohio, 1990—; com. mem. Ohio State Dental Bd., 1990—; instr. in CPR, ARC, Cin., Dayton and Columbus, 1977—, New Haven, 1988-89; curriculum cons. Aramco-Dental Hygiene Sch., Saudi Arabia, 1984. Named Outstanding Young Woman of Am., 1982. Mem. Am. Dental Hygienists Assn. (assoc.), Ohio Dental Hygienists Assn. (assoc., chairperson continuing edn. com. 1987-88), Acad. Dental Hygiene (bd. dirs.), Dayton Dental Hygienists' Assn. (pres., v.p. 1985-88), Cin. Dental Hygienists Assn. (pres., v.p. 1982-84), New Haven Dental Hygienists' Assn. (treas. 1988-89), Kappa Delta Pi, Sigma Phi Alpha. Home: 4629 Bridle Path Ln Dublin OH 43017

ROCK, HEIDI MARIE, educator, researcher; b. Cleve., Aug. 16, 1957; d. Heinz George and Marianne (Zieg) R. BA, Cleve. State U., 1982, MEd, 1985; PhD, U. Chgo. Cert. secondary edn. tchr., Ohio. Tchr. Cleveland Bd. of Edn., 1982-87, curriculum developer, 1985-87; rsch. assoc.Coll. Urban Affairs Cleve. State U., 1986—; rsch. asst. Wayne State U., Detroit, 1988; supr. MST teaching program U. Chgo., 1988—, coord. adminstrn. workshop dept. edn., 1989-90; conf. coord. Ctr. for Sch. Improvement, 1990—; ednl. cons. dept. rsch., evaluation and planning Chgo. Bd. Edn., 1989—; mem. editorial com. Adminstr.'s Notebook, Chgo., 1989-90. Author (with others) (chpt.) Race and Inner City Education, 1990, Policy Prescriptions for Inner City Education, 1990, Education as an Economic Development Resource, 1990. Crisis intervention counselor RVA, Chgo., 1990—. Mem. Am. Ednl. Rsch. Assn., Phi Delta Kappa (historian 1989,90, v.p.membership com. 1990—), Phi Alpha Theta, Pi Lamda Theta. Office: 4812 S Kimbark Chicago IL 60615

ROCK, LYDIA G., company executive, financial aid consultant; b. N.Y.C., Dec. 22, 1952; m. Randy R. Rock, May 17, 1984; 1 child, Brian. BA cum laude, Queens Coll., 1977. Credit analyst ITT, N.Y.C., 1979-80; v.p. E.C.M., Inc., fin. aid servicing co., Wantagh, N.Y., 1984—; cons. Hunter Bus. Sch., Hicksville, N.Y., 1987—. Co-editor Saw Mill Log, 1989-90. Mem. coms. Alley Pond Environ. Ctr., Douglaston, N.Y., 1984—, editor cookbook, 1988; bd. dirs. PTA, North Bellmore, N.Y., 1990, bd. dirs., v.p. of fundraising. Regent's scholar Queens Coll., 1970. Office: ECM Inc 3681 Carrollton Ave Wantagh NY 11793

ROCK, SABRA LEIGH, temporary employment agency executive; b. Henderson, N.C., Oct. 4, 1952; d. Hobert Lee and Edna Lee (Pitman) Burleson; m. Jack Patton Burleson, Dec. 4, 1969 (div.); children: Tammy Lynn, Christina Lynn; m. Brendan James Rock, Nov. 4, 1982. AS, Mayland Community Coll., Spruce Pine, N.C., 1977; student, Fla. State U., 1978, DeKalb Coll., Atlanta, 1985, Dale Carnegie Sch., Morganton, N.C., 1989. Sec. Mead Corp., Atlanta, 1983-85, adminstrv. asst., 1985-88; office mgr. Personnel, Inc., Marion, N.C., 1988-90; regional mgr. Personnel, Inc., Spartanburg, S.C., 1990—. Youth choir dir. Mt. Carmel Bapt. Ch., Spruce Pine. Mem. NAFE, Downtown Bus. Assn., McDowell County C. of C., Burke County C. of C., Mitchell C. of C. Office: Personnel Inc 10-C S Main St Marion NC 28752

ROCKALL, DIANE MARGARET, librarian, consultant; b. Detroit, Dec. 16, 1945; d. John Joseph Dunn and Shirley Lena (Book) Dunn Cunningham; m. Arthur Allison Rockall. BA in Journalism, Wayne State U., 1970, MLS, 1977. Cataloguer reference dept. Detroit News, 1968-71, photo classifier, 1971-77, asst. supr. reference dept., 1977-80, head reference dept., 1980-87; library cons. Rockall Ltd., Northville, Mich., 1987—; cons. Info. Rsrh. Svc., Bloomfield, Mich., 1989; archivist Northville Hist. Soc., 1990. Co-author: Step By Step Through Northville, 1989; dir. oral history audio tapes Northville Oral History Project, 1990; contbr. articles to profl. jours. Speaker, Friends for a New Community Library, Northville, 1990. Recipient Spirit of Detroit award Detroit city Council, 1979; LWV grantee, 1989. Mem. AAUW, Friends of Northville Pub. Library, Detroit Press Club, Wayne Library Sci. Alumni (pres., v.p., editor), Spl. Libraries Assn. (pres., bd. dirs.), Northville Hist. Soc., LWV (pres. Northville 1990), Women of Wayne (western v.p. 1989-90). Mem. United Ch. of Christ.

ROCKEFELLER, SHARON PERCY, broadcast executive; b. Oakland, Calif., Dec. 10, 1944; d. Charles H. and Jeanne Dickerson Percy; m. John D. Rockefeller IV; children: John, Valerie, Charles, Justin. BA cum laude, Stanford U.; LLD (hon.), U. Charleston, 1977, Beloit Coll., 1978; LHD (hon.), West Liberty State Coll., 1980, Hamilton Coll., 1982, Wheeling Coll., 1984. Founder, chmn. Mountain Artisans, 1968-78; pres. Stas. WETA-TV-FM, Washington; bd. dirs. Corp. Pub. Broadcasting, Washington, chmn., 1981-84; bd. dirs. W.Va. Edn. Broadcasting Authority. Mem.-at-large Dem. Nat. Conv., del., 1976, 80, 84; bd. dirs. Rockefeller Bros. Fund. Office: care Corp Pub Broadcasting 1111 16th St NW Washington DC 20036*

ROCKLEN, KATHY HELLENBRAND, lawyer, banker; b. N.Y.C., June 30, 1951; d. Samuel Henry and Sheila (Kurzrok) Hellenbrand; m. R. Michael Rocklen, Aug. 26, 1972 (div. June 1978). BA, Barnard Coll., 1973; JD magna cum laude, New England Sch. Law, 1977. Bar: N.Y. 1978, U.S. Dist. Ct. (so. and ea. dists.) N.Y. 1982, U.S. Dist. Ct. (no. dist.) Calif. 1985. Assoc. Weiss, Rosenthal, N.Y.C., 1977-79; interpretive counsel N.Y. Stock Exchange, N.Y.C., 1979-81; asst. counsel Bradford Nat. Corp., N.Y.C., 1981-84; asst. v.p. E.F. Hutton & Co. Inc., N.Y.C., 1984, v.p., 1985, 1st v.p., 1986; v.p., gen. counsel and sec. S.G Warburg (U.S.A.) Inc., N.Y.C., 1986-90; counsel Rogers & Wells, N.Y.C., 1990—. Office mgr. Com. to elect Charles D. Breitel Chief Judge, N.Y., 1973. Named one of Outstanding Young Women in Am., 1976. Mem. ABA, N.Y. Women's Bar Assn., Assn. Bar City N.Y. (2d century com. 1982-85, sec. 2d century com. 1985-86, mem. sex. and law com. 1982-85, young lawyers com. 1979-82, corp. law com. 1986-89, spl. com. drugs and law 1986—, fed. legis. com. 1989—, chair fed. legis. com. 1990—), Athletic and Swim Club. Home: 153-29 82d St Howard Beach NY 11414 Office: Rogers & Wells 200 Park Ave New York NY 10166

ROCKMAN, ILENE FRANCES, librarian, teacher, consultant; b. Yonkers, N.Y., Nov. 9, 1950; d. Leon and Margaret (Klein) R.; m. William A. Skahen, Mar. 19, 1988. BA, UCLA, 1972; MS in L.S. U. So. Calif., 1974; MA, Calif. Poly. State U., 1978; PhD, U. Calif.-Santa Barbara, 1985. Librarian, Wash. State U., Pullman, 1974-75, Calif. Poly. State U., San Luis Obispo, 1975—; adj. prof. Cuesta Coll., San Luis Obispo, 1982-85; abstracter Women Studies Abstracts, Rush, N.Y., 1976—. Contbr. articles to profl. jours.; editor, Reference Services Rev., 1987—; co-author: BLISS--Basic Library Information Sources and Svcs., 1989. Del. Democratic Nat. Conv., 1984. Recipient scholarship Calif. PTA, Los Angeles, 1973. Mem. ALA, Calif. Library Assn. (mem. council 1983-86), Assn. Coll. and Research Libraries, Am. Ednl. Research Assn., Total Library Exchange (pres. 1979-80), Library Assocs. Calif. Poly. State U. (exec. sec. 1981-83).. Office: Calif Poly State U San Luis Obispo CA 93407

ROCKMORE, SYLVIE MARIE, French educator; b. Nice, France, Nov. 13, 1945; came to U.S. 1969; d. Henri J. and Anne-Marie Tschann; m. Tom Rockmore, 1971; children: Christophe, Marc. Baccalaureat, Lycee A Calmette, Nice, 1965; licence es-lettres, U. Nice, 1969; MA in English, Vanderbilt U., 1971, PhD in Comparative Lit., 1974. Lectr. Quinnipac Coll., Hamden, Conn., 1974-87; lectr. Duquesne U., 1987-88, asst. prof. of French, 1988-89; asst. prof. Chatham Coll., 1990—; vis. lectr. comparative lit. Pa. State U., Monaca, 1990. Mem. Am. Assn. Tchrs. French, MLA, Am. Montessori Assn., Beckett Soc. Office: Chatham Coll Pittsburgh PA 15232-2814

ROCKOFF, SHEILA G., nursing educator, health facility administrator; b. Chgo., Mar. 15, 1945; d. Herbert Irwin and Marilyn (Victor) R.; divorced. ADN, Long Beach City Coll., 1966; BSN, San Francisco State Coll., 1970; MSN, Calif. State U.-Los Angeles, 1976; postgrad., Nova U., 1989—. RN, pub. health nurse, nursing instr., health facility supr., Calif. Staff nurse Meml. Hosp., Long Beach, Calif., 1966-67, Mt. Zion Med. Ctr., San Francisco, 1967-69; instr. nursing Hollywood Presbyn. Med. Ctr., Los Angeles, 1970-74; nursing supr. Orthopedic Hosp., Los Angeles, 1974-76; instr. nursing Ariz. State U., Tempe, 1976-78; nurse supr. Hoag Meml. Hosp., Newport Beach, Calif., 1977-78; nurse educator U. Calif.-Irvine and Orange, Calif., 1978-80, Santa Ana Coll. (Calif.), 1980-89, dir. health svcs., 1989—; nurse educator Rancho Santiago Community Coll., Santa Ana Campus; nurse cons. Home Health Care Agy., Irvine, 1983; educator/cons. Parenting Resources, Tustin, Calif., 1985—. Mem. Calif. Nurses Assn. (chmn. com. 1970-73), Health Svcs. Assn. Calif. Community Colls., Am. Heart Assn., Nat. League for Nursing, Am. Cancer Soc., Phi Kappa Phi. Democrat. Jewish. Home: 13834 Comanche Tustin Ranch CA 92680 Office: Rancho Santiago Community Coll 17th at Bristol Santa Ana CA 92706

ROCKWELL, ELIZABETH DENNIS, financial planner; b. Houston; d. Robert Richard and Nezzell Alderton (Christie) Dennis. Student Rice U., 1939-40, U. Houston, 1938-39, 40-42. Purchasing agt. Standard Oil Co., Houston, 1942-66; asst. sec. Heights Savs. Assn., Houston, 1967-70, asst. v.p., 1970-75, v.p. mktg., 1975-82; sr. v.p., fin. planner Oppenheimer & Co., Inc., Houston, 1982—; 2d v.p. Desk and Derrick Club Am., 1960-61; instr. Coll. of Mainland, Texas City, Tex.; instr. Downtown Coll. and Continuing Edn. Ctr., U. Houston; mem. Dean's adv. bd. U. Houston, alumni bd. 1987—, treas., 1988, mem. found. bd. bus. coll., 1989—. Bd. dirs. ARC, 1985—, Houston Heights Assn., 1973-77, 85—, U. Houston Coll. of Bus. Found., 1989—; active Houston Jr. League, 1986-87. Named Outstanding Woman of Yr., YWCA. Mem. Am. Savs. and Loan League (state dir. 1973-76, chpt. pres. 1971-72; pres. S.W. regional conf. 1972-73; Leaders award 1972), Savs. Inst. Mktg. Soc. Am. (Key Person award 1974), Inst. Fin. Edn., Fin. Mgrs., Soc. Savs. Instns., U.S. Savs. and Loan League (com. on deposit acquisitions and adminstrn.), Spring Branch Meml. C. of C., Internat. Platform Assn., Houston Heights Assn. (charter, dir. 1973-77), Houston North Assn., Harris County Heritage Soc., Rice U. Bus. and Profl. Women, River Oaks Bus. Womens Exchange Club, U. Houston Bus. Womens Assn. (pres. 1986). Club: Forum. Author articles on retirement planning, tax planning and tax options. Home: 3617 Yoakum Blvd Apt #4 Houston TX 77006 Office: Oppenheimer & Co Inc 333 Clay St Ste 4700 Houston TX 77002

RODDY, MARITA, marketing professional; b. Norwalk, Conn., Feb. 28, 1954; d. Michael Joseph and Margaret Agnes (Sullivan) R.; m. Harry Alburn Kendall, Oct. 6, 1979 (div. 1988); children: Jennifer Lynn, Kristina Leigh; m. Patrick John Nolan, Sept. 17, 1988; 1 stepchild, Rebecca J. BS cum laude, Stonehill Coll., 1976; MBA, Pepperdine U., 1983. With GTE, 1976—; mkt. strategies mgr. telephone ops. div GTE, Dallas, 1989—; mem. leadership coun. GTE, 1990; speaker in field. Mem. Stuart McKinney's Youth Adv. Bd., Fairfield, Conn., 1971-73; vol. Little Okas Montessori Sch. Fund Raising Coms., 1988-89; mem. Colleyville Elem. PTA. Recipient GTE Leadership award, 1987; named Conn. Dept. Edn. scholar, 1972. Mem. NAFE, Sacred Heart Acad, Alumni Assn., Thousand Oaks Racquet Club. Republican. Roman Catholic. Home: 811 Laurel Oaks Ln Colleyville TX 76034 Office: GTE Tel Ops 4500 Fuller Dr Irving TX 75038

RODEHEAVER, OLAH ANITA, county official; b. Houston, Sept. 27, 1923; d. Charles Lee and Olah Hunter (West) Robertson; m. James Harvey Rodeheaver, Nov. 1, 1943; children: Margaret Dianne Rodeheaver Dupont, Nancy Ruth Rodeheaver Luksa. Grad. John H. Reagan High Sch., Houston. Exec. asst. to clk. Harris County, Houston, 1961-78, clk., 1979—; mem. faculty Internat. Ctr. Election Law and Adminstrn., 1985. Bd. dirs. New Directions, Inc., Houston, 1982—; mem. adv. panel Fed. Elections Commn., 1987—, adminstrv. bd. Collins United Meth. Ch., Houston, 1984—. Recipient Outstanding Achievement to Community and Mankind award Ethel Ransom Literary Club, 1985. Mem. Internat. Assn. Clks. Recorders, Election Ofcls. and Treas. (past pres., 2d v.p. 1985), County and Dist. Clks. Assn. Tex. (co-chmn. legis. com. 1979-89, chmn. 1989—, County Clk. of Yr. 1989), Nat. Assn. Counties. Democrat. Lodge: Order Eastern Star. Avocations: fishing, crocheting, enjoying children and grandchildren. Home: 4514 Mountwood St Houston TX 77018 Office: County Clk PO Box 1525 1001 Preston St Houston TX 77251

RODENBAUGH, MARCIA LOUISE, educator; b. Pitts., Nov. 11, 1942; d. F. Thomas and Lucy Indiana (Fry) Wimer; m. John Anthony Lee, Mar. 21, 1964 (div. Nov. 1971); m. Richard Allan Rodenbaugh, Aug. 3, 1975 (div. Dec. 24, 1989); stepchildren: Ken, Tiffany, Tricia. B.A. in Edn., Westminster Coll., New Wilmington, Pa., 1964, M.Ed. in Remedial Reading, 1966. Tchr., North Hills Sch. Dist., Pitts., 1964-70, Cen. Bucks Schs., Doylestown, Pa., 1970—. Author children's books: Marci Books (set of 6), 1983—. Pres. Maple Leaf Day Care Ctr. Bd., Warminster, Pa., 1971; pres. Wesley Coll. Parents Assn., Dover, Del., 1985-86. Mem. Pa. Edn. Assn., NEA, Central Bucks Edn. Assn., NAFE, AAUW. Republican. Presbyterian. Avocations: skiing, sailing, writing, piano, church choir. Home: 7-16 Aspen Way Doylestown PA 18901 Office: Cen Bucks Sch Dist 315 W State St Doylestown PA 18901

RODENBIKER, JO ANN, chamber of commerce executive; b. Devils Lake, N.D., May 25, 1954; d. Edward C. and Mary Eleanor (Graham) Wilcox; m. Ronald James Rodenbiker, Sept. 11, 1976; children: John, Luke, Mark, Paul, Mary Jo. BS in Agrl. Econs., N.D. State U., 1977. Devel. specialist North Cen. Planning Coun., Devils Lake, 1977-83; program adminstr. N.D. Office Intergovtl. Assistance, Bismarck, 1984-86; dep. dir. N.D. Econ. Devel. Commn., Bismarck, 1986-89; exec. v.p. Devils Lake Area C. of C., 1989—; small bus. adv. com. Bismarck State Coll., 1987—. Active Rock Lake (N.D.) Sch. Bd., 1984. Named one of five Outstanding Young North Dakotans, 1987. Mem. N.D. Indsl. Devel. Assn., N.D. Planning Assn. (sec.-treas. 1987-88), Jaycee Women (pres. 1982). Roman Catholic. Office: Devils Lake Area C of C Box 879 Devils Lake ND 58301

RODENBUSH, REBECCA LYNN, financial consultant; b. Benton, Ill., Sept. 11, 1948; d. Kenneth Monroe and Anne (Shapkoff) R.; m. Lawrence Wayne Shook, Sept. 6, 1969 (div. Sept. 1973); 1 child, Jennifer Anne. BA, San Diego State U., 1972. Fin. analyst Univ. Hosp. of U. Calif., San Diego, 1974-77; personnel cons. M. David Lowe, Houston, 1978-81; fin. cons. Dean Witter Reynolds, San Diego, 1981-83, Sutro and Co., San Diego, 1983-84, Merrill Lynch, San Diego, 1984-89, Shearson Lehman Hutton, Bellevue, Wash., 1989—. Mem. Rep. Nat. Com. Mem. Zoolog. Soc. San Diego. Methodist. Office: Shearson Lehman Hutton 411 108th Ave NE Bellevue WA 98004

RODERICK, SUE SCHOCK, health sciences executive; b. Muskogee, Okla., Oct. 28, 1937; d. Willie Orville and Dona Leona (Gordon) Perry; m. Kenneth Robert Schock, Nov. 22, 1955 (div. 1971); m. John Kenneth Roderick, Aug. 9, 1981. BS with distinction, San Jose (Calif.) State U., 1970; MS, San Jose State U., 1973; M in Pub. Adminstrn., U. So. Calif., 1982, D in Pub. Adminstrn., cert. in gerontology, 1984. cert. tchr., Calif. Sr. citizens dir. City of San Jose, 1968-72; chief gerontology Kings View Mental Health Ctr., Visalia, Calif., 1972-74; cons. on aging State of Calif., Sacramento, 1974-76; dir. edn. Calif. Assn. Health Facilities, Sacramento, 1976-77; exec. dir. Hillhaven Found., Tacoma, Wash., 1977-83; pres. Med. Ednl. Svcs. Devel., Alameda, Calif., 1979—; asst. v.p. planning and research Am. Bapt. Homes of the West, Oakland, Calif., 1984—; cons. St. Mary's Hosp., San Francisco, 1973-74, Hillsdale Manor, Inc., San Mateo, Calif., 1973—; bd. dirs. St. Peter's Adult Day Care Ctr., San Leandro, Alameda County Long Term Care Planning Coun.; co-founder Shades of Gray: Perspective in Aging, Alameda, 1987. Contbr. articles to profl. jours. Chi Kappa Rho scholar San Jose State U., 1970, U. So. Calif.-Gerontology Ctr. scholar, 1971-74. Mem. Am. Soc. on Aging, Gerontol. Soc. Am., Intercare, Am. Assn. of Homes for Aging, Am. Coll. Health Care Adminstrs., Calif. Specialists on Aging, Calif. Assn. Homes for Aging. Democrat. Home: 3406 Redhook Ln Alameda CA 94501 Office: Am Bapt Homes of the West 400 Roland Way Oakland CA 94621

RODGERS, ALICE LYNN, marketing research executive; b. Mt. Clemens, Mich., Nov. 23, 1942; d. Albert William and Margaret Dorothy (Small) Kockentiet; m. Larry W. Rodgers, June 8, 1963. BS magna cum laude, Rider Coll., 1975. Mng. editor Jour. Consumer Research, Chgo., 1975-78; sr. cons. assoc. Mgmt. Horizons, Columbus, Ohio, 1978-81; pres., founder Rodgers Mktg. Research (formerly Mktg. Programs and Services), Canton, Ohio, 1981—. Dir., author numerous research publs.; contbr. articles on retailing and mktg. to profl. jours. Bd. dirs. New Communities, Columbus, 1982—; mem. Akron (Ohio) Regional Devel. Bd. Recipient Award of Merit, Garden Industry Am., 1981, cert. of appreciation Retail Bakers Assn., 1986. Mem. Am. Mkgt. Assn. (trustee Akron chpt. 1986-90, Outstanding Achievement award San German Collegiate chpt. InterAm. U., P.R. 1988), Assn. Consumer Rsch., Qualitative Rsch. Cons. Assn., Mktg. Rsch. Assn., Sales and Mktg. Execs. Assn., Canton C. of C. Office: 4575 Edwin Dr NW Canton OH 44718

RODGERS, ANTOINETTE YVETTA, mental health therapist; b. Richmond, Va., Oct. 22, 1959; d. Lester Blaine and Phyllis Beniece (Washington) R.; m. Gregory Lawrence Farmer, Nov. 26, 1983; 1 child, Bradford. BS, U. Pitts., 1982, MS, 1986, postgrad., 1987—. Rsch. assoc. Western Psychiat. Inst. and Clinic, Pitts., 1982-86, specialty counselor, 1986-89; mental health therapist Turtle Creek (Pa.) Valley Mental Health/Mental Retardation, 1989—; cosn. The Pressley Ridge Schs., Pitts., 1989—; instr. U. Pitts. (Pa.) Sch. of Social Work, 1990. Contbr. articles to profl. jours. Scholarship Assn. of Negro and Profl. Women's Club, 1978. Mem. Am. Psychol. Assn. (assoc.). Home: 1129 Woodbine St Pittsburgh PA 15201 Office: Turtle Creek Valley MH/MR 519 Penn Ave Turtle Creek PA 15145

RODGERS, DIANA LOUISE, Engineer; b. Ft. Collins, Colo., Nov. 18, 1962; d. John Paul Rodgers and Jerry Lea (Williamson) Hoddinott. Student, Tidewater Com. Coll., 1982; BS, Old Dominion U., 1985; MA, U. Va., 1987. Research asst., statistician U. Va. Hosp., Charlottesville, 1986-87; engr. Bell Atlantic, Wash., 1987--. Co-Author Researcher Med. Jour. Article, 1987. Vol. Nat. Zoo. Wash. 1987--. Home: 9039 Sligo Creek Pkwy #1609 Silver Spring MD 20901

RODGERS, LESLIE CLEGG, regional sales manager; b. Longview, Tex., Sept. 16, 1952; d. Theodore Nelson and Beth Lynn (Miller) Clegg; m. Alan Kent Farnsworth, Jan. 30, 1973; (div. 1977); m. Leven Lee Rodgers, Feb. 23, 1983. BS, U. Tex., Austin, 1975. Dietitian St. Davids Hosp., Austin, Tex., 1975-76, Parkland Hosp., Dallas, 1976-77; asst. food service dir. Hockaday Sch., Dallas, 1978-80; sales rep. Sysco Food Systems, Dallas, 1980-85; sales rep. Kraft Foodsvc., Dallas, 1985, major account mgr., 1985-86, dist. sales mgr., 1986-88, regional sales mgr., 1988—. Recipient Torch Bearer Club Outstanding Sales & Profit Achievement Sysco Foods Corp. Headquarters, Houston, 1983. Republican. Presbyterian. Office: Kraft Food Svc 9650 Chartwell Dallas TX 75243 : Kraft Foodsvc 950 S Shiloh Garland TX 75042

RODGERS, MARY COLUMBRO, university chancellor, English language educator; b. Autora, Ohio, Apr. 17, 1925; d. Nicola and Nancy (DeNicola) Columbro; m. Daniel Richard Rodgers, July 24, 1965; children: Robert, Patricia, Kristine. A.B., Notre Dame Coll., 1957; M.A., Western Res. U., 1962; Ph.D., Ohio State U., 1964; postgrad. Fulbright scholar, U. Rome, 1964-65; Ed.D., Calif. Nat. Open U., 1975, D.Litt., 1978. Tchr. English Cleve. elem. schs., 1945-52, Cleve. secondary schs., 1952-62; supr. English student tchrs. Ohio State U., 1962-64; asst. prof. English U. Md., 1965-66; assoc. prof. Trinity Coll., 1967-68; prof. English D.C. Tchrs. Coll., 1968—; pres. Md. Nat. U., 1972—; chancellor Am. Open U., 1965—; dean Am. Open U. Acad. Author numerous books and monographs, latest works include: A Short Course in English Composition, 1976, Chapbook of Children's Literature, 1977, Comprehensive Catalogue: The Open University of America System, 1978-80, Open University of America System Source Book, V, VI, VII, 1978, Essays and Poems on Life and Literature, 1979, Modes and Models: Four Lessons for Young Writers, 1981, Open University Structures and Adult Learning, 1982, Papers in Applied English Linguistics, 1982, Twelve Lectures on the American Open University, 1982, English Pedagogy in the American Open University, 1983, Design for Personalized English Graduate Degrees in the Urban University, 1984, Open University English Teaching, 1945-85: Conceptual History and Rationale, 1985, Claims and Counterclaims Regarding Instruction Given in Personalized Degree Residency Programs Completed by Graduates of California National Open University, 1986, The American Open University, 1965 t0 1985: History and Sourcebook, 1986, New Design II: English Pedagogy in the American Open University, 1987, The American Open University, 1965 to 1985: A Research Report, 1987, The American Open University and Other Open Universities: A Comparative Study Report, 1988, Poet and Pedagogue in Moscow and Leningrad: A Travel Report, 1989, Foundations of English Scholarship in the American Open University, 1989, Twelve Lectures in Literary Analysis, 1990, others. Fellow Catholic Scholars; mem. Poetry Soc. Am., Nat. Council Tchrs. English, Am. Ednl. Research Assn., Pi Lambda Theta. Roman Catholic. Home and Office: Coll Heights Estate 3916 Commander Dr Hyattsville MD 20782

RODGERS, NANCY LUCILLE, corporate executive; b. Denver, Aug. 22, 1934; d. Francis Randolph and Irma Lucille (Budy) Baker; student public schs.; m. George J. Rodgers, Feb. 18, 1968; children by previous marriage: Kellie Rae, Joy Lynn, Timothy Francis, Thomas Francis. Mgr., Western Telearm, Inc., San Diego, 1973—; pres. Rodgers Police Patrol, Inc., San Diego, 1973-80; br. mgr. Honeywell Inc., Protection Services div., San Diego, 1977-80; pres. Image, Inc., Image Travel Agy., Cairo, Egypt, 1981-83, Western Solar Specialties, 1979-80; founder, pres. Internat. Metaphysicians Associated for Growth through Edn., San Diego, 1979; founder, dir. Point Loma Sanctuary, 1983-86; co-founder, producer Zerciee Prodns. Unltd., 1986—, co-founder, producer, dir. mktg., 1986—. Bd. dirs. Cen. City Assn. Named Woman of Achievement Cen. City Assn., 1979. Mem. Nat. Assn. for Holistic Health, Am. Bus. Women's Assn. (Woman of Yr. 1980), Am. Union Metaphysicians, Philae West (co-owner, mgr.). Republican. Clubs: Am. Bashkir Curly Registry, Bashkir Curly Breeder.

RODIN, JUDITH SEITZ, psychology educator; b. Phila., Sept. 9, 1944; d. Morris and Sally R. (Winson) Seitz; m. Nicholas Niejelow, Feb. 12, 1978. A.B., U. Pa., 1966; Ph.D., U. Columbia, 1970. Asst. prof. psychology NYU, 1970-72; assoc. prof. Yale U., 1973-78, prof., dir. grad. studies, 1979-84, Philip R. Allen prof. psychology, medicine and psychiatry, 1984—, chmn. dept. psychology, 1989—; chmn. John D. and Catherine T. MacArthur Found. Rsch. Network on Health-Promoting and Health-Damaging Behavior, 1984—. Author: (with S. Schachter) Obese Humans and Rats, 1974, Exploding the Obesity Myths, 1982; editor: Appetite Jour., 1979—; contbr. articles to profl. jours. Fellow Woodrow Wilson Found., 1966-68, John Simon Guggenheim Found., 1986-87; grantee NSF, 1975—, NIH, 1979—. Fellow Am. Psychol. Assn. (bd. sci. affairs 1979-82), AAAS, Soc. Behavioral Medicine; mem. Inst. Medicine, Am. Acad. Arts and Scis., Acad. Behavioral Medicine Research, Eastern Psychol. Assn. (exec. bd. 1980-83, pres. div. 38 health psychology 1982-83, Outstanding Contbn. award 1980, Disting. Sci. award 1977), Phi Beta Kappa, Sigma Xi (pres. Yale chpt. 1986-87). Office: Yale U Box 11A Yale Sta New Haven CT 06520

RODIN-NOVAK, SHEILA KAREN, theater director; b. Chgo., May 7, 1947; d. Shabtai Harold and Ruth Francis (Rohde) Rodin; m. Lawrence A. Novak, Sept. 17, 1981; children: Raymond, Gregory, Gail. Student, No. Ill. U., 1964-68, Goodman Sch. Drama, 1967-69. Dir. sta. svcs. Internat. Digisonics Corp., Chgo., 1970-74; freelance dir. various theaters Chgo., 1970—; asst. dir. live shows Fred Niles, Chgo., 1974-75; dir. live shows Motivation Media, Glenview, Ill., 1975-80; pres., owner, dir. Sheila Rodin Creative Svcs., Chgo., 1980—; artistic dir. Performers Arena, Chgo., 1986-87; founder, artistic dir. The Original Theatre Co., Chgo., 1987-90; co-founder, co-owner Stand-Ins, Inc., 1990—. Mem. Actors Equity Assn., Nat. Assn. Women Bus. Owners, Women in Bus., Equity Library Theatre (mem. new plays com. 1980—). Democrat. Jewish. Office: 2736 N Hampden Ct #101 Chicago IL 60614

RODIS, MONICA, personnel consultant; b. Urbana, Ohio, Oct. 14, 1953; d. Thomas C. and Jeanne E. (Palmer) R. BA in History, Kean Coll., 1975. Acct. exec. Gardiner Stein & Franke Advt., Chgo., 1978-79; acct. sec. Hill & Knowlton, N.Y.C., 1979-83; prodn. coord. Lane Bryant, N.Y.C., 1983-85; exec. asst. Haley Assocs., N.Y.C., 1985-87; adminstrv. mgr. Heidrick & Struggles, N.Y.C., 1987-88; personnel cons. Norman Locke Assoc., Inc., N.Y.C., 1989—; adj. faculty Katharine Gibbs Sch., 1990—. Republican. Home: 111 Hicks St Apt 9R Brooklyn Heights NY 11201

RODMAN, ANGELA FAYE, telecommunications research executive; b. Arlington, Va., Apr. 3, 1963; d. John Ivan and Wanda Faye (Smith) Slane; m. Edward Ford Rodman, Oct. 12, 1985; 1 child, Andrew Ford. AS in Info. Systems/Computer Sci. with high honors, Chattanooga State Tech. Community Coll., 1983; BS in Math., Computer Sci., Monmouth Coll., 1987, postgrad., 1987-88; MS in Computer Sci., Fairleigh Dickinson U., 1990. Tech. assoc. AT&T Bell Labs., Holmdel, N.J., 1983-84; staff technologist Bell Communications Rsch., Red Bank, N.J., 1984-87; sr. staff technologist Bell Communications Rsch., Red Bank, 1987—. Music software developer (book) Animation, Games and Sound for the IBM PC, 1983. Mem. Monmouth County Rep. Exec. Com., 1989-90; chairperson so. coun. Future Pioneers, 1990-91. Mem. Digital Equipment Computer Users Soc., Phi Theta Kappa. Republican. Episcopalian. Home: 501 Oxford Way Neptune Township NJ 07753

RODMAN, CYNTHIA WILLETT, food products executive; b. Norfolk, Va., Feb. 21, 1960; d. David B. and Carol (Willett) R. AB, Mt. Holyoke Coll., 1982. Brand asst. Procter & Gamble Co., Cin., 1982-83, asst. brand mgr., 1983-85; product mgr. Kellogg Co., Battle Creek, Mich., 1985-87, group product mgr., 1987-89; mktg. dir. Kellogg Co., Battle Creek, 1989—. Club: Mt. Holyoke of Western Mich.(sec.). Home: 3704 Tartan Circle Portage MI 49002

RODMAN, SUE ARLENE, wholesale Indian crafts company executive, artist; b. Fort Collins, Colo., Oct. 1, 1951; d. Marvin F. and Barbara I. (Miller) Lawson; m. Alpine C. Rodman, Dec. 13, 1970; 1 child, Connie Lynn. Student Colo. State U., 1970-73. Silversmith Pinel Silver Shop, Loveland, Colo., 1970-71; asst. mgr. Traveling Traders, Phoenix, 1974-75; co-owner, co-mgr. Deer Track Traders, Ltd., Loveland, 1975-85, exec. v.p., 1985—. Author: The Book of Contemporary Indian Arts and Crafts, 1985. Mem. U.S. Senatorial Club, 1982-87, Rep. Presl. Task Force; mem. Civil Air Patrol, 1969-73, 87—, personnel officer, 1988—. Mem. Internat. Platform Assn., Nat. Assn. Female Execs., Indian Arts and Crafts Assn., Native Am. Art Studies Assn., Inc., Western and English Sales Assn. Baptist. Club: Crazy Horse Grass Roots (S.D.). Avocations: museums, recreation research, fashion design, reading, flying. Office: Deer Track Traders Ltd PO Box 448 Loveland CO 80539

RODNICK, AMIE BOWMAN, lawyer; b. Paris, Nov. 4, 1953; d. David and Elizabeth (Amis) Rodnick; m. Lawrence Mark Smith, June 20, 1975. Student, Sarah Lawrence Coll., 1972; BA (with honors), U. Tex., 1975, JD, 1978. Asst. attorney gen. Attorney Gen. Office, Austin, 1979-84; ptnr. Cox & Rodnick, Austin, 1984—. City council mem. City of Rollingwood, Tex., 1984-88, bd. dirs. United Action for the Elderly, Inc. (pres. 1987—). Mem. Travis Co. Bar Assn., Austin Young Lawyers, Travis County Women Lawyers. Democrat. Home: 8 S Peak Rd Austin TX 78746 Office: Cox & Rodnick 507 W 7th St Austin TX 78701

RODOVICH, ARLENE GUYOTTE, administrator, small business owner; b. Springfield, Mass., Mar. 21, 1935; d. Walter L. Guyotte and Dorothy (Hawley) Bigelow; m. Robert F. Rodovich, Sept. 30, 1955; 1 child, Heidi E. Pepyne. AA, Greenfield (Mass.) Community Coll., 1977. Cert. property mgr. Sec., bookkeeper Gordon E. Ainsworth Assocs., South Deerfield, Mass., 1954-60; from jr. clk. to dir. U. Mass. Property and Inventory Control, Amherst, 1966—; owner Conway (Mass.) Bus. Service, 1958—. Author: (manual) Property Management, 1972. Chmn. fin. com., zoning bd. appeals, Conway, 1975—. Mem. Nat. Property Mgmt. Assn. (v.p. profl. devel. 1987—, v.p. fin. 1988, pres. 1989-90, Property Person of the Yr. 1984, Property Person of the Yr. Eastern region 1986), Mass. Fedn. Bus. and Profl. Women (2d v.p. 1986—, 1st v.p. 1987-88, pres. elect 1988—, pres. 1989-90). Home: Ashfield Rd Conway MA 01341 Office: U Mass Goodell Bldg Amherst MA 01341

RODRIGUEZ, CARMEN MARTA, federal executive; b. Humacao, Jan. 18, 1943; d. Jose A. and Marta R. AS, Cath. U., P.R., 1963. Bank clk. Commercial Loans Dept., 1963-66; sec. Banco de Ponce, 1966-68; exec. sec. Steffens & Santoni, Inc., Puerto Rico, 1968-71, Lawrence Systems, Inc., Hosp. San Carlos, Inc., 1975-76, Hosp. San Pablo, 1976-83; sec. IMCS Div., 1983-85; exec., personel sec. Internat. Mgmt. Cons. Svcs. div. Coopers & Lybrand, Washington, 1985-87, exec. sec. resource mgmt. group, 1987—; instr. MCA Modelling Acad., San Juan, 1974-75. Mem. Profl. Secs. Internat. (treas. San Juan 1982-83), NAFE, LANAO Cath. U., Pablicosas. Republican. Roman Catholic.

RODRIGUEZ, LILIAN TERESA, marketing director; b. Miami, Fla., Sept. 17, 1969; d. Joaquin Ambrosio and Gladys Adela (Gonzalez) R. Student, Internat. Fine Arts Coll., 1986-87; student, Miami Dade Community Coll., 1988, U. Miami, Fla., 1989. Traffic asst. Associated Graphic Prodns., Miami, 1984-85; exec. sec. Baldwin Sackman & Assocs., P.A., Coconut Grove, Fla., 1985-87; dir. mktg. Baldwin Sackman & Assocs., P.A., 1987—; dir. submittals Baldwin Sackman & Assocs., Am. Inst. Architects Design Awards, 1987-89. Mem. Bush 1988 Electoral Campaign, Miami, 1988, Reagan 1980 Electoral Campaign, 1979, Reagan 1984 Electoral Campaign, 1983. Mem. NOW, Nat. Assn. Female Execs., Coconut Grove C. of C., AIA (Miami chpt., profl. affiliate mem.), Ctr. for Fine Arts. Republican. Roman Catholic. Home: 3026 Day Ave Coconut Grove FL 33133

RODRIGUEZ, LORRAINE DITZLER, biologist, consultant; b. Ava, Ill., July 4, 1920; d. Peter Emil and Marie Antoinette (Mileur) D.; m. Juan G. Rodriguez, Apr. 17, 1948; children: Carmen, Teresa, Carla, Rosa, Andrea. BEd, So. Ill. U., 1943; MS, Ohio State U., 1944; PhD, U. Ky., 1973. Asst. nutritionist OARDC, Wooster, Ohio, 1944-49; postdoctoral fellow U. Ky., Lexington, 1973-74, pesticide edn. specialist, 1978-89; pvt. cons. Lexington, 1974-79, 89—. Author ext. publs. in field; co-author rsch. publs. and book chpts. in field. Leader 4-H, Lexington, 1962-68. Named Outstanding 4-H Alumni Woman, Ky., 1969. Mem. Vegetation Mgmt. Assn. Ky. (chmn. adv. bd. 1985-89), Am. Chem. Soc. Democrat. Roman Catholic. Home: 1550 Beacon Hill Rd Lexington KY 40504

RODRIGUEZ, MARIA A., counseling educator; b. Coamo, P.R., Aug. 16, 1953; d. Angel Manuel Rodriguez and Cesarea (Reyes) Serrano. MS, EdS, SUNY, Albany, 1977, PhD, 1986; MA, New Sch. for Social Rsch., 1990. Permanent cert. in guidance, N.Y. Vocat. counselor Human Resources Ctr., Albany, 1977-78; project dir. Capital Dist. Psychiat. Ctr., Albany, 1978-79; mem. faculty Boricua Coll., N.Y.C., 1979-80; counselor, tutor Fashion Inst. Tech., N.Y.C., 1981-82; asst. prof. counseling Hunter Coll. CUNY, 1982—; lectr. SUNY, Albany, 1978; adj. asst. prof. La Guardia Community Coll., Long Island City, N.Y., 1988-89; book reviewer coll. div. Scott, Forsman and Co., 1988, McGraw-Hill Pub. Co., 1989. Contbr. articles to profl. jour. and newsletter. Bd. dirs. Practicing Attys. for Law Students, N.Y.C., 1989—. Recipient Outstanding Adj. Faculty award La Guardia Community Coll., 1988; named One of 100 Hispanic Influentials, Hispanic Bus. mag., 1988. Mem. APA, AACD, Hispanic Nat. Bar Assn. (chmn. edn. com. 1987—), Nat. Puerto Rican Network. Office: Hunter Coll Dept Acad Skill 695 Park Ave 927 EB New York NY 10021

RODRIGUEZ, MARIA TERESA, dentist; b. Havana, Cuba, Feb. 7, 1951; d. Luis Enrique and Maria Rosa (Rodriguez) R. AA in Dental Hygiene, Fairleigh Dickinson U., 1971, BS in Dental Hygiene, 1973; MS, Columbia U., N.Y.C., 1975; DMD, U. Medicine & Dentistry N.J., 1983. Dental hygienist Michael R. Torre, DDS, West New York, N.J., 1973-74; clin. and didactic instr. Bergen Community Coll., Paramus, N.J., 1975-79; pvt. practice West New York, 1983—; sch. dentist West N.Y. Bd. Edn., 1983—. Recipient Leadership award N.J. Dental Sch., 1983, Pediatric Dentistry award Am. Soc. Dentistry for Children, 1983. Mem. ADA, N.J. Dental Assn. (del. North Brunswick, N.J. chpt. 1983—), Am. Soc. Dentistry for Children, Hudson County Dental Soc. (sec. 1985-87, v.p. 1987-88, pres. 1990—). Republican. Methodist.

RODRIGUEZ, RUTH ANN, city and county official; b. Denver, Dec. 11, 1949; d. Benjamin and Wanda Lee (Kirkpatrick) R. BA in Polit. Sci., U. Colo., 1973, MPA, 1975. Planner Adams County, Brighton, Colo., 1975-76; county mgr. Park County, Fairplay, Colo., 1976-78; cir. rider city mgr. Town of Georgetown, Colo., 1978-79, town adminstr., 1979; asst. mgr. community affairs Mt. Emmons project Amax, Inc., Gunnison, Colo., 1979-81; sr. assoc. BMLL, Inc., Boulder, Colo., 1981-83; mgmt. cons. City of Evanston, Colo., 1983; exec. dep. mgr. City and County of Denver, 1984—; asst. mgr. parks and recreation City of Denver, 1986-87. Mgr. Bronco Super Bowl Celebration, Denver, 1987, 88. Named Best Bureaucrat, Westword, news and arts weekly, Denver, 1986. Mem. Internat. City Mgrs. Assn. Democrat. Roman Catholic. Home: 1625 Larimer St Apt 2004 Denver CO 80202 Office: City and County of Denver 1437 Bannock St Rm 377 Denver CO 80202

RODRIGUEZ, SOLANGE B., electrical engineer, biomedical engineer; b. Ponce, P.R., Nov. 3, 1962; d. Ernesto and Maria (Smith) R. AS in Engring. Sci., Broward Community Coll., Ft. Lauderdale, Fla., 1984; BS in EE, U. Miami, 1987; postgrad., Boston U. and U. Md., 1988—. Aerospace engring. tech. NASA, Kennedy Space Ctr., Fla., 1985; systems engr. WWMCCS Info. Systems div. GTE Govt. Systems Corp., Mass., 1987-89; systems engr. Strategic Systems div. GTE Govt. Systems Corp., Westborough, Mass., 1989—. Mem. Soc. Women Engrs., Internat. Neural Network Soc., Fla. Bd. Realtors. Republican. Roman Catholic. Home: 10 Linwood St #106 Malden MA 02148

ROE, ALLIE JONES, technical writer; b. Greenville, S.C., Dec. 3, 1950; d. James Richard and Allie McGreg (Singletary) Jones; m. Eugene Bartlett Roe, Aug. 29, 1970 (div. 1986); 1 child, David Michael. AB in English, Valdosta State Coll., 1972; MA in Journalism, Ohio State U., 1982. Instr. II State of Ga. Health Svcs., Valdosta, 1972-74; prodn. asst. Easton (Md.) Publ. Co., 1974-75; sec. office of radiation safety Emory U., Atlanta, 1977-79; asst. mgr. classified The Booster Newspaper, Columbus, Ohio, 1980-81; editorial aide Battelle Columbus Labs., 1983-84; publs. coord. specialist Battelle Project Mgmt. Div., Columbus, 1984-85, adminstv. coord., 1985-87; free-lance editor Am. Ceramic soc., Westerville, Ohio, 1988; tech. writer, editor Resource Internat., Westerville, 1988-89; tech. writer Cons. & Designers, Winter Park, Fla., 1989—. Vol. Am. Heart Assn., Columbus, 1984-88, Am. Cancer Soc., Columbus, 1986-88. Mem. Women in Communications, Inc. (v.p. projects 1986-87, chair job placement com. 1987-89), Nat. Mus. for Women in the Arts (charter 1988—), Phi Kappa Phi. Methodist. Home: 3732 E Grant St Orlando FL 32812

ROE, RADIE LYNN, bank officer; b. Stuart, Fla., Nov. 14, 1962; d. Albert R. III and Martha Katherine (Brooks) Krueger; 1 child, Travis; m. Dan C. Roe, May 24, 1990. AB, Ga. Wesleyan Coll., 1984; postgrad., U. Cen. Fla. Tchr. English Brevard County Sch. System, Melbourne, Fla., 1984-86; bank officer, tng. dir. First Nat. Bank and Trust, Stuart, 1987-90; dir. Christian edn. First Presbyn. Ch., Stuart, Fla., 1990—; prof. English Indian River Community Coll., 1990—. Mem. Am. Inst. Banking, NAFE. Republican. Presbyterian. Home: 2808 SE Buccaneer Circle Port Saint Lucie FL 34952 Office: 1715 NW Pine Lake Dr Stuart FL 34994

ROEHM, CAROLYNE J., fashion designer; b. Jefferson City, Mo., May 7, 1951; d. Kenneth Smith and Elaine C. (Beaty) Bresee; m. Axel Roehm, June 3, 1978 (div. 1981); m. Henry Raymond Kravis, Nov. 23, 1985. BFA, Washington U., St. Louis, Mo., 1973. Designer Kellwood Co., N.Y.C., 1974-75; asst. designer Oscar de la Renta Ltd., N.Y.C., 1975-85; designer, owner Carolyne Roehm, Inc., N.Y.C., 1985—; design critic Fashion Inst. of Tech., N.Y.C., 1986, Parsons Inst., N.Y.C., 1988; mem. Fashion Group, 1988. Mem. of assn. Met. Opera, N.Y.C., 1988—; chairperson N.Y.C. Ballet

Gala, Met. Opera Gala, 1987-88, Winter Antiques Fair for Eastside Settlement House, 1988; co-chair Fête de Famille (Aids), 1988-89, Sta. WNET TV Silver Anniversary Ball, 1988; patron Lions of Performing Arts Dinner N.Y. Pub. Libr., 1989; co-sponsor embassy benefit ball French Am. Found. for Med. Rsch., 1987. Recipient Key to City St. Louis C. of C., 1988, Dallas C. of C., 1988, New Orleans C. of C., 1988, Chgo. Fashion awards, 1988; named Woman of Achievement Girl Scouts U.S., 1988, The Girls' Club, 1988. Mem. Coun. Fashion Designers (pres. 1989—), N.Y. Pub. Libr. (bd. trustees), Carnegie Hall (steering com.), Kappa Kappa Gamma. Republican. Office: 550 7th Ave 8th Fl New York NY 10018

ROEHM, MARYANNE EVANS, university dean; b. Vigo County, Ind., Nov. 29, 1925; d. Herbert and Fern Evans; m. Joseph L. Roehm, Aug. 10, 1947. BS, Ind. State U.-Terre Haute, 1953, MS, 1957; MS in Nursing, Ind. U., Bloomington, 1965, EdD., 1966. Instr. nursing, asst. dir. Sch. Nursing, Union Hosp., Terre Haute, 1946-55; assoc. dir. edn. Sch. Nursing, St. Anthony Hosp., Terre Haute, 1957-64; asst. and assoc. prof. nursing Ind. State U., 1966-70, dir. continuing edn., 1970-78, dean Sch. Nursing, 1977—; mem. Ind. State Bd. Nursing Registration and Nursing Edn., 1978-81, pres., 1980-81; mem. adv. com. hypertension project Vigo County Health Dept., 1981; mem. health occupations adv. com. Ind. Vocat. Tech. Coll., 1970—. Mem. Vigo County Home Citizens Com., Ind., 1970—; mem. Vigo County Blood Donor Council, 1980; vice precinct committeeman Vigo County. Recipient Outstanding Leadership award Ind. div. Am. Cancer Soc., 1982. Mem. Ind. State Nurses Assn. (Cert. of Recognition 1978, named Outstanding Nurse Educator 1959), Ind. League for Nursing, Am. Nurses' Assn., AAUP, Am. Assn. Coll. Deans, Midwest Alliance on Nursing, Ind. Council Baccalaureate and Higher Degree Deans and Dirs., Ind. Council Assoc. Degree Deans and Dirs. Home: Rte 22 Box 561 Terre Haute IN 47802 Office: Ind State U Sch Nursing Terre Haute IN 47809*

ROEHRIG, KARLA LOUISE, food science and nutrition educator, consultant; b. Sycamore, Ill., Aug. 18, 1946; s. James H. and Louise (King) Reed; m. Frederick K. Roehrig, Aug. 19, 1967. BS, U. Ill., Urbana, 1967; PhD, Ohio State U., 1977; postgrad. Ind. U. Sch. Medicine, Indpls., 1978. Research asst. Ohio State U., Columbus, 1967-75, research assoc., 1975-77, asst. prof., 1978-83, assoc. prof. dept. food sci. and nutrition, 1983—; Showalter P.D. fellow Ind. U. Sch. Medicine, Indpls., 1977-78; mem. research adv. council Columbus Zoo, 1984—; mem. peer rev. bd. Am. Diabetes Assn. for Ohio, Am. Heart Assn. for Ohio, Cen. Ohio Diabetes Assn. Author: Carbohydrate, Biochemistry and Metabolism, 1984. Trustee Columbus Zoo, 1984—; troop leader Seal of Ohio council Girl Scouts U.S., 1968-72; neighborhood vol. March of Dimes, Columbus, 1982, 83. Burroughs Wellcome, grantee, Scotland, 1981; grantee NIH, USPHS. Mem. Biochem. Soc., Am. Diabetes Assn., N.Y. Acad. Scis., Am. Inst. Nutrition, Am. Soc. Biolog. Chemists, Jr. Opean Ct. Club (sec. 1983-84), Sigma Xi (Ohio chpt. pres. 190-91), Gamma Sigma Delta, Sigma Delta Epsilon. Avocations: computer architecture, gourmet cooking. Presbyterian. Office: Ohio State U Dept Food Sci and Tech 122 Vivian 2121 Fyffe Rd Columbus OH 43210

ROEHRKASSE, PAULINE CATHERINE HOLTORF, retired educator; b. Malmo, Nebr., Sept. 14, 1909; d. Jurgen Heinrich and Wiebke (Knuth) Holtorf; m. Raymond Roehrkasse, June 11, 1935; children: Paula Joan Knepper, Claire Rae Eason, Kathryn Grace Trebelhorn. Grad. in Music, Luther Jr. Coll., Wahoo, Nebr., 1929; BS in Edn., U. Nebr., 1967; postgrad., Kearney State U., Nebr., 1970. Tchr. Grand Island (Nebr.) pub. schs., 1951-72; pipe organist Trinity Luth. Ch., 1938-53. Author: A Flowering: A Festival, 1984. Vice pres. Cen. States Coalition on Aging, 1989-90; elected U.S. Silver Haired Senator from Nebr., 1988—; sec. Nat. Silver Haired Congress steering com., 1985—; publicity chmn. Nat. Coun. Silver Haired Legislators, 1985—. Mem. AAUW (legis. chmn., prog. chmn.), Am. Assn. Retired Persons (prog. chmn. 1983-85, legis. chmn. 1985—), Retired Tchrs. Assn., Alpha Delta Kappa (pres. Epsilon chpt.). Democrat. Lutheran. Home: 503 S Broadwell Ave Grand Island NE 68803

ROEMER, ELAINE SLOANE, real estate broker; b. N.Y.C., Apr. 23, 1938; d. David and Marion (Frauenthal) Sloane; m. David Frank Roemer, June 21, 1959; children: Michelle Sloane Wolf, Alan Sloane. BBA, U. Fla., 1959; MEd, U. Miami, 1960. Cert. tchr., Fla.; lic. real estate broker, Fla. Tchr. math. Dade County Pub. Schs., Miami, 1959-80; tchr. math and bus. Miami Dade Community Coll., 1968-80; tchr. edn. Fla. Internat. U., Miami, 1977-80; real estate broker Miami, 1978—; mortgage broker, Miami, 1986—; speaker in field. Contbr. articles to profl. jours. Organizer, officer Colonial Dr. Homeowners Assn., Miami, 1965; mem., officer Dade County Polit. Action League for Unincorporated Areas, Miami, 1965-68; chmn. women's com. state's atty.'s campaign, Miami, 1968. Mem. Kendall-Perrine Bd. Realtors, Fla. Assn. Realtors, Nat. Assn. Realtors, NEA, Fla. Edn. Commn., Classroom Tchrs. Assn., Dade County Edn. Assn., Fla. Coun. Tchrs. of Math., Fla. Bus. Edn. Assn., Assn. Classroom Educators, Dade County Assn. Ednl. Adminstrs., Assn. Supervision and Curriculum Devel., Alpha Delta Kappa, Kappa Delta Pi. Home: 7705 SW 138th Terr Miami FL 33158 Office: 15950 SW 96th Ave Miami FL 33157

ROENISH, DANA D., real estate executive; b. New Brunswick, N.J., Dec. 12, 1955; d. Arthur and Rae (Yaw) De M. Grad. real estate sch., Profl. Sch. Bus., Union, N.J., 1986. Cert. real estate agt. Clk. typist County Food Stamps N.J. Welfare Dept., New Brunswick, 1974-75; sec. County Prosecuter's Office, New Brunswick, 1975-76; claims examiner Blue Cross/Blue Shield N.J., Princeton, 1976-81; exec. sec., adminstrv. asst. Action Temps, Inc., New Brunswick, 1981-82; NE/SE regional sales asst. Osborne Computer Corp., Monmouth Junction, N.J., 1982-84; north/cen. regional sales asst. Fujitsu Microsystems Am., Iselin, N.J., 1984-86; real estate agt. Sun Realty, Inc., Woodbridge, N.J., 1986-88; adminstr. office Rothe-Johnson Assocs., Edison, N.J., 1986-88; real estate agt. Century 21-Golden Post Realty, Bound Brook, N.J., 1988—; office mgr. Met. Glass Co., Inc., Metuchen, N.J., 1988—; freelance bookkeeper, math tutor. Mem. Ambassadors for Friendship. Matawan, N.J., 1974. Mem. Nat. Assn. Female Execs., Middlesex, Hunterdon, Morris, and Somerset County Bds. Realtors, N.J. Soc. Archtl. Adminstrs., Nat. Soc. Archtl. Adminstrs. Home: 260 Grant Ave Piscataway NJ 08854 Office: Met Glass Co Inc 255 Forrest St Metuchen NJ 08840

ROEPER, NOLA CHARLENE, radio and television personality; b. Bethesda, Md., Mar. 22, 1950; d. Charles August and Susan (Zavacky) R. BFA, U.S.I.U., 1972. Actress, writer Film and Television, 1973; founder and artistic dir. Lexington Repertory Theatre, Ky., 1979-83; host WZZU The Morning Zoo, Raleigh, N.C., 1983-85, WPIX Best Talk In Town, N.Y.; radio personality WNEW Radio, N.Y., 1985--; founder, chief exec. officer Venus Nat. Video; co-founder, chief exec. officer World Radio One. Mem. Guttman Breast Cancer Inst., N.J. Lung Assn., United Negro Coll. Fund. Recipient Broadcaster award N.Y. State Broadcasters, 1987; Folio award, 1988. Home and Office: 300 E 93rd New York NY 10128

ROEPKE, NANCY JEAN, investment company executive; b. Arlington, Va., Jan. 16, 1955; d. Duane Henry and Helen (Smeltzer) R. Student, Radford (Va.) Coll., 1973-77. Staff asst. Capitol Investors, Ltd., Alexandria, Va., 1979-82; adminstr. DeRand Corp. Am., Arlington, 1982-88; sec. Bankwest Corp., Denver, 1977—; pres., bd. dirs. Pace Investments, Inc., Washington, 1988-90; sec., treas., bd. dirs. Pace Holdings, Inc., Washington, 1988-89, United Gibralter Corp. Del., Inc., Washington, 1987—, Unocam, Inc., Washington, 1987—; gen. securities prin. Washington Investment Corp., 1990. Mem. Rep. Party Va., Alexandria, 1989; active Columbia Bapt. Ch., Falls Church, Va.; handbells dir. chancel choir Children's Special Edn. Sunday Sch. Dept. Named to Outstanding Young Women Am., 1984, 88. Home: 4845 W Braddock Rd #202 Alexandria VA 22311 Office: United Gibraltar Corp Del Inc 600 N Hampshire Ave NW #450 Washington DC 20037

ROERDEN, CHRIS (CLAIRE ROERDEN), editor, business owner, consultant; b. N.Y.C., Aug. 28, 1935; d. Marion Smolin; m. Harold H. Roerden (div. 1985); children: Ken, Doug. BA in English summa cum laude, U. Maine, 1969, MA in English, 1971. Mem. pub. rels. staff Shell Oil Co., N.Y.C., 1952-55; asst. to pub. rels. dir. Interchem. Corp., N.Y.C., 1956-59; staff editor Newkirk Assocs., Albany, N.Y., 1960-62; instr. in English U. Maine, Portland, 1969-71; mentor Empire State Coll., SUNY, Rochester and Syracuse, N.Y., 1973-74; exec. dir. Wis. NOW, 1978-81; mng. editor CPA Digest, Brookfield, Wis., 1983; owner Edit It, Brookfield, 1985—; speaker and trainer in field. Author: Collections From Cape Elizabeth, 1965, Open Gate: Teaching in a Foreign Country, 1990. Mem. Mensa Internat., Soc. for Tech. Communication, Women in Communication, Inc. (bd. dirs. 1988), Women Bus. Owners of Wis., Wis. Bus. Womens Coalition (bd. dirs. 1988—), Wis. Womens Network (founding mem.), Alliance of Metro. Milw. (bd. dirs. 1989—), Brookfield C. of C., Brookfield Civic Music Assn. (v.p. 1989—). Office: Edit It 3225 Hillcrest Dr Brookfield WI 53045

ROES, NANCY BENNETT, controller; b. Freeport, N.Y., Jan. 9, 1954; d. John Joseph and Elizabeth Anne (Howell) Bennett; m. Nicholas A. Roes, Nov. 26, 1977. BS, U. Bridgeport, 1976. Bookkeeper North Atlantic Ins. Co., Syossett, N.Y., 1976-79; chief fin. officer NAR Assocs., Saddle River, N.J., 1977—; office mgr. Ridgewood (N.J.) Ford, 1979-84; mgr. bus. Higgins Buick, Ridgewood, 1984—; cons. Winfo., Hohokus, N.J., 1979—, Tchr. Update, Inc., Belmont, Mass., 1983—, NAR Prodn., Barryville, N.Y., 1986; office mgr. Pistilli Ford, Paramus, N.J. Office: NAR Assocs PO Box 205 Saddle River NJ 07458

ROESCHLAUB, JEAN MARIAN CLINTON, restaurant chain executive; b. Berkeley, Calif., June 1, 1927; d. Clifford E. and Nelda M. (Patterson) Clinton; m. David J. Davis III, June 26, 1946 (dec. 1963); children: David J. Davis IV, Diane Davis Ciardy, Burce Clinton Davis; m. Ronald Curtis Roeschlaub, Jan. 9, 1965; 1 child, Ronald W. AA, Stephens Coll., 1944. Civilian cons. on loan Q.M. Gen., 1944-45; co-owner, exec. v.p. Clinton's Restaurants, Inc., operators Clinton's Cafeterias, Los Angeles, 1944—; bd. dirs. Glendale Fed. Savs. and Loan Assn. Chmn. bd. curators Stephens Coll.; bd. dirs. Assistance League of So. Calif.; mem. aux. bd. Braille Inst. Am., Los Angeles. Mem. Nat. Restaurant Assn., Calif. State Restaurant Assn., Los Angeles Country Club. Republican. Presbyterian. Home: 222 Monterey Rd #1606 Glendale CA 91206 Office: 515 W 7th St Los Angeles CA 90014

ROESINGER, ANNA LORETTA, financial executive; b. Jersey City, July 16, 1951; d. Edward J. and Anna L. (Fern) R.; 1 child, Rochelle Marie. BA in English, Jersey City State, 1980. Instr. Edison Job Corps, Edison, N.J., 1979-85; adminstrv. asst. Exec. Images, Watchung, N.J., 1987-89; chief exec. officer, owner E.Z. Acctg., Berkeley Heights, N.J., 1986—; advisor Vocat. Indsl. Club of Am., N.J., Pa., 1979-86. Pres. Am. Legion Aux., Spotswood, 1981. Mem. NAFE. Roman Catholic. Home: 170 Caldwell Rd Laurenceville GA 30245 Office: EZ Acctg PO Box 41 Berkeley Heights NJ 08902

ROESKE, ARLYS MAE, graphic artist, researcher; b. Jamestown, N.D., May 17, 1934; d. Emil Arthur and Clara Anna Roeske. AA, Los Angeles Trade Tech., 1961. Nurse Sch. for Mentally Retarded Children, Denver, 1958; nurse Hollywood (Calif.) Presbyterian Hosp. Nursery, 1959-61; drafting aid Calif. Hwys., Eureka and Stockton, Calif., 1961-63; delineator Calif. Forestry Dept., Sacramento, 1963-65; drafts person, designer for BART Tudor Engrng. Co., San Francisco, 1965-68; delineator Caltrans, San Francisco/Sacramento, 1968-75; sr. graphic artist Calif. Franchise Tax Bd., Sacramento, 1976—; ind. distbr. Light Force Co.; ptnr. Toward a Healthier State. HM3, USN, 1952-56. Mem. Sacramento Womens Network, Sacramento Art Dir. & Artist Club. Democrat. Lutheran. Home: 937 Fremont Blvd West Sacramento CA 95605

ROESSER, JEAN WOLBERG, state legislator; b. Washington, May 8, 1930; d. Solomon Harry Wolberg and Mary Frances Brown; m. Eugene Francis Roesser, Aug. 3, 1957; children: Eugene Jr., Mary, Anne. BA, Trinity Coll., Washington, 1951; postgrad. in econs., Cath. U. of Am., 1951-53. Congl. relations asst. U.S. Info. Agy., Washington, 1954-58; news reporter for Montgomery County Council Suburban Record, 1983-86; elected mem. Md. Gen. Assembly, Annapolis, 1986—; mem. Md. Ho. Dels. constl. and adminstrv. law com., spl. com. on Drug and Alcohol Abuse; mem. Md. Gen. Assembly Women's Legis. Caucus. Contbr. articles to polit. jours. Former pres. Montgomery County Fedn. Rep. Women, Potomac Women's Rep. Club; former 3d v.p. Md. Fedn. Rep. Women; ; founding mem. Montgomery County Arts Council. Mem. West Montgomery County, Germantown, Greater Darnestown citizens assns., Gaithersburg and Upper Montgomery County C. of C., Germantown C. of C., Potomac C. of C. Republican. Roman Catholic. Home: 10830 Fox Hunt Ln Potomac MD 20854 Office: Lowe House Office Bldg Annapolis MD 21401

ROESSLER, P. DEE, lawyer, former municipal judge, educator; b. McKinney, Tex., Nov. 4, 1941; d. W.D. and Eunice Marie (Medcalf) Powell; m. George L. Roessler, Jr., Nov. 16, 1963; (div. Dec. 1977); children: Laura Diane, Trey. Student Austin Coll., 1960-61, 62-64, Wayland Bapt. Coll., 1961-62; BA, U. West Fla., 1968; postgrad. East Tex. State U., 1975, U. Tex.-Dallas, 1977; JD, So. Meth. U., 1982. Bar: Tex. 1982, U.S. Dist. Ct. (ea. dist.) Tex. 1983, U.S. Dist. Ct. (no. dist.) Tex. 1983. Tchr., Van Alstyne Ind. Sch. Dist., Tex., 1968-69; social worker Dept. Social Services, Fayetteville, N.C., 1971-73, Dept. Human Services, Sherman and McKinney, Tex., 1973-79, 81; assoc. atty. Abernathy & Roeder, McKinney, Tex., 1982-85, Ronald W. Uselton, Sherman, 1985-86, program coordinator Collin County Community Coll., McKinney, 1986—; judge City of McKinney Mcpl. Ct., 1986-89; mem. Collin County Shelter for Battered Women, 1984-86, chmn., 1984-85; v.p. Collin County Child Welfare Bd., 1986, pres. 1987-88, treas. 1989; Rep. jud. candidate Collin County, 1986; chmn. bd. Tri County Consortium Mental Health Mental Retardation, 1984-85; mem. Tex. Area 5 Health System Agy., 1979; mem. Collin County Mental Health Adv. Bd., 1978-79; trustee Willow Park Hosp., HCA, 1987-88. Mem. Collin County Bar Assn. (criminal justice sub-com. 1987-88), Collin County Women's Bar (chmn. 1984-85), Plano Bar Assn., Tex. Mcpl. Cts. Assn. Baptist. Avocations: dancing, tennis, golf, reading, writing. Home: 2118 Chippendale St McKinney TX 75069 Office: Collin County Community Coll 2200 University McKinney TX 75070

ROETTGER, DORYE, human resources development consultant, speaker, trainer; b. Utica, N.Y., Oct. 22, 1932; d. Albert Frank and Marion Emma (Farber) Rutger. Student, Ithaca Coll., 1949-51; MusB, Univ. Extension Conservatory, Chgo., 1955; PhD, U. Ea. Fla., 1972. Cert. tchr., Calif. Concert musician, 1955-80; founder, dir. Festival Players Calif., 1957—; freelance writer, 1960—; editor Ind. News Bur., 1967—; cons. human resources development L.A. Police Dept., 1984-90; pub. rels. cons., L.A. County Parks and Recreation, 1969; musicologist, Inner City Cultural Ctr., L.A., 1963-73; vis. prof., Immaculate Heart Coll., L.A., 1970-71; in-svc. trainer, L.A. Unified Sch. Dist., 1973—; creator numerous music and art programs for children. Author: Creative Innovators, 1988; syndicated columnist, Bridging the Culture Gap, 1971—; contbr. articles to profl. publs. Fine arts chmn. Explorers div. Boy Scouts Am., 1972-74; pres. Silver Lake Protective and Betterment Assn., 1980—; intern Coro Found., 1987. Mem. Nat. Speakers Assn., Internat. Platform Assn., Nat. Writers Club, Nonprofit Mgmt. Assn., Pub. Interest Radio and Television Ednl. Soc., AARP (legis. com. 1984-88), Toastmasters Internat., Order Eastern Star. Christian Scientist. Home and Office: 38909 De Longpre Ave Los Angeles CA 90027

ROETTINGER, RUTH LOCKE, retired educator; b. Newport, Ky., Nov. 1, 1904; d. William Dodsworth and Bessie B. (Horner) R. BA, Asbury Coll., 1926; MA, U. Ky., 1927, Radcliffe Coll., 1933; PhD, U. N.C., 1956. Tchr. polit. sci. Winthrop Coll., Rock Hill, S.C., 1927-29, 30-31, 37-52, Mills Coll., Oakland, Calif., 1934-37, U. N.C., 1952-56, Sweet Briar Coll., 1956-57; dir. fellowship program AAUW, Washington, 1958-70, ret. Author: The Supreme Court and State Police Power, 1930-56, A Study in Federalism, 1957. Mem. Montgomery County Md. Commn. for Women, 1975-78. Mem. Am. Polit. Sci. Assn., So. Polit. Sci. Assn., Am. Acad. Polit. and Social Sci., Am. Soc. Internat. Law, S.C. Hist. Soc., Soc. for the Right to Die (bd. dirs.), Pi Sigma Alpha, Pi Gamma Mu, Phi Alpha Theta. Home: 3305 Shepherd St Chevy Chase MD 20815

ROFÉ, BARBARA DALE, insurance company executive; b. N.Y.C., Dec. 1, 1946; d. Hyman and Julia (Smilowitz) Cossin; div.; 1 child, Erik Lewis. BA, Bklyn. Coll., CUNY, 1968, MS, 1971. Fellow Life Mgmt. Inst., CLU, ChFC. Tchr. N.Y.C. Bd. Edn., 1968-72; employment counselor Allied Personnel, Houston, 1972; mgr. sales and ops. Key-Data, Inc., Houston, 1973-74; supr., ops. unit mgr. Allstate Ins. Co., Houston, 1974-77; regional tng. coord., acctg. control mgr., planning mgr. Allstate Life Ins. Co., Atlanta, 1977-84; mng. claim tng. Provident Life and Accident Ins. Co., Chattanooga, 1984-85, dir. tng. and communication, 1985—; mgmt. cons., free-lance trainer, 1979-84. Mem. Am. Soc. Tng. and Devel., Nat. Soc. Performance and Instrn. Jewish. Office: Provident Life & Accident Ins Co One Fountain Sq Chattanooga TN 37402

ROFFEY, LEANE ELIZABETH, research systems analyst programmer; b. Chgo., Mar. 17, 1949; d. Joseph Andrew and Ethel Antoinette (DeSalvo) Accomando; m. Arthur Roffey, 1972 (div. 1973). B.A., Wayne State U., 1972. Indsl. cons. Computype Corp., Ann Arbor, Mich., 1976-77; project leader Manufacturing Data Systems, Ann Arbor, 1978-80; info. mgmt. supr. First Variable Life Ins. Co., Little Rock, 1980-82; programmer/analyst First Pyramid Life, Little Rock, 1982-83, Ark. Blue Cross and Blue Shield, Inc., Little Rock, 1983-85, Am. Security Life Ins. Co., San Antonio, 1985-90; rsch. sr. analyst Metrica, Inc., 1990—. Fellow Life Mgmt. Inst.; mem. Mensa, Phi Theta Kappa. Republican. Episcopalian. Avocations: vocal coach, classic car restoration, auto racing.

ROGALSKI, LOIS ANN, speech and language pathologist; b. Bklyn., Dec. 17, 1947; d. Louis J. and Filomena Evelyn (Maro) Giordano; m. Stephen James Rogalski, June 27, 1970; children: Keri Anne, Stefan Louis, Christopher James, Rebecca Blair. BA, Bklyn. Coll., 1968; MA, U. Mass., 1969; PhD., NYU, 1975. Lic. speech and lang. pathologist, N.Y. Speech, lang. and voice pathologist Rehab. Ctr. of So. Fairfield County, Stamford, Conn., 1969, Sch. Health Program-P.A. 481, Stamford, 1969-72; pvt. practice speech, lang. and voice pathology Sch. Health Program-P.A. 481, Scarsdale, N.Y., 1972—; cons. Bd. Coop. Ednl. Svcs., 1976-79, Handicapped Program for Preschoolers for Alcott Montessori Sch., Ardsley, N.Y., 1978—; rsch. methodologist Burke Rehab. Ctr., 1977. Mem. profl. adv. bd. Found. for Children with Learning Disabilities, 1978—; bd. dirs. United Way of Scarsdale-Edgemont, 1988-89. Fellow Rehab. Svcs. Adminstrn., 1968-69; N.Y. Med. Coll., 1972-75. Mem. N.Y. Speech & Hearing Assn., Westchester Speech & Hearing Assn., Am. Speech, Hearing & Lang. Assn. (cert. clin. competence), Coun. for Exceptional Children, Assn. on Mental Deficiency, Am. Acad. Pvt. Practice in Speech Pathology & Audiology (bd. dirs., treas. 1983-87, pres. 1987-89), Internat. Assn. Logopedics & Phoniatrics, Sigma Alpha Eta. Office: PO Box 1242 Scarsdale NY 10583

ROGAN, ELEANOR GROENIGER, cancer researcher, educator; b. Cin., Nov. 25, 1942; d. Louis Martin and Esther (Levinson) G.; m. William John Robert Rogan, June 12, 1965 (div. 1970); 1 child, Elizabeth Rebecca. AB, Mt. Holyoke Coll., 1963; PhD, Johns Hopkins, 1968. Lectr. Goucher Coll., Towson, Md., 1968-69; rsch. assoc. U. Tenn., Knoxville, 1969-73; rsch. assoc. U. Nebr. Med. Ctr., Omaha, 1973-76, asst. prof., 1976-80, assoc. prof. Eppley Inst. and U. Nebr. dept. pharm. scis., 1980-90, prof., 1990—. Contbr. articles to profl. jours. Activist, Common Cause, Omaha, 1974—. Predoctoral fellow USPHS, Johns Hopkins U., 1965-68. Mem. AAAS, AAUP, ASBMB, Am. Assn. Cancer Rsch., Am. Soc. Biochem. Molecular Biology. Democrat. Roman Catholic. Home: 8210 Bowie Dr Omaha NE 68114 Office: U Nebr Med Ctr Eppley Inst 600 S 42d St Omaha NE 68198-6805

ROGEL, MARY JOSEPHINE, psychologist; b. Alliance, Ohio, Dec. 7, 1951; d. John and Josephine T. (Pandin) R. BA, Mt. Union Coll., Alliance, Ohio, 1972; MA, U. Chgo., 1973, PhD, 1976. Instr. psychology Roosevelt U., Chgo., 1974-79; rsch. analyst Ctr. for Urban Affairs, Northwestern U., Evanston, Ill., 1979-80; asst. prof. psychology St. Xavier Coll., Chgo., 1980-83; mem. faculty clin. rsch. tng. program in adolescence Michael Reese Hosp. and Med. Ctr., Chgo., 1982-83; rsch. assoc. dept. psychiatry U. Chgo., 1982-83; project dir., prin. investigator adolescent decision making Michael Reese Hosp. and Med. Ctr., Chgo., 1978-85; assoc. Chgo. Assocs. Social Rsch., 1980-85; program evaluator State of Ill. Dept. Mental Health & Devel. Disabilities, Chgo., 1985-87; pvt. cons. Health and Behavioral Rsch. and Program Evaluation, Chgo., 1987—; presenter profl. presentations, workshops. Contbr. articles to profl. jours., chpts. to books. Grantee MacArthur Found., Chgo., 1981-83, HEW, Chgo., 1976-78; postdoctoral fellow Michael Reese Hosp. & Med. Ctr., Chgo., 1978-79, U. Chgo., 1975-76, 76-78. Mem. Am. Psychol. Assn., Ill. State Acupuncture Assn. Office: 1525 E 53d St Ste 516-3 Chicago IL 60615

ROGELL, IRMA ROSE, harpsichordist; b. Malden, Mass.; d. M. Edward and Sara (Freedman) Rose; A.B., Radcliffe Coll.; student Wanda Landowska; m. Bernard C. Rogell (dec. 1964); children—Gerald, Gillian, Michael. Profl. debut Boston Jordan Hall, 1960; N.Y. debut, 1961; soloist with symphony orchs. including: Boston Symphony Orch., Brazil Symphony; European concert tours; radio-TV appearances; rec. artist Titanic Records, Protone; mem. faculty CUNY, 1973-78, Ethical Culture Sch. of N.Y.; guest lectr.-recitalist at various colls. and univs.; vis. faculty mem. Longy Sch. Music, Cambridge, Mass., New England Conservatory. Mem. Coll. Music Soc., Piano Tchrs. Congress N.Y. Jewish. Club: Harvard (N.Y.C.). Home and Studio: 31 Devon Rd Newton Center MA 02159

ROGERS, ADRIANNE ELLEFSON, physician, researcher, educator; b. Aberdeen, Wash., Feb. 18, 1933; d. Raymond Carl and Gretchen Lucille (Hodges) Ellefson; m. Hartley Rogers J.r, Aug. 6, 1954; children: Hartley Raymond, Campbell David Kinsey, Caroline Rebecca. AB magna cum laude, Radcliffe Coll., 1954; MD with honors, Harvard U., 1958. Diplomate Am. Bd. Pathology, Am. Bd. Toxicology. Intern in medicine Beth Israel Hosp., Boston, 1958-59; rsch. fellow pathology dept. Mallory Inst. Harvard U. Med. Sch., Boston, 1960-65; rsch. assoc. MIT, Cambridge, Mass., 1965-72, sr. rsch. scientist, 1972-86; staff pathologist Univ. Hosp., Boston, 1982; asst. prof. pathology, assoc. chair Sch. of Medicine Boston U., 1984, 85—; lectr., instr. in pathology Harvard U. Med. Sch., 1964-88; assoc. pathologist Boston City Hosp., 1979, 85—; with Wellman Inc., Land, Ohio, 1975—; toxicology cons. Kimberley Clark Inc., Neenah, Wis. and Cleve., 1986—; chair grants rev. panel Am. Inst. Cancer Rsch., Washington, 1984—; bd. sci. counselors Nat. Toxicology Program, Research Triangle Park, N.C., 1986-90. Contbr. numerous articles to profl. jours. Mem. Mystic River Watershed Assn., Arlington, Mass., 1975—; trustee Forsyth Dental Ctr., Boston, 1987—. Mem. Am. Assn. Pathologists, Fedn. Am. Soc. for Exptl. Biology, Am. Inst. Nutrition, New Eng. Soc. Pathologists, Am. Assn. for Cancer Rsch., Soc. of Toxicology. Office: Boston U Sch of Medicine 80 E Concord St Boston MA 02118-2394

ROGERS, BETTY GRAVITT, research company executive; b. Valdosta, Ga., June 24, 1945; d. Jim Aldine and Ruby Romell (Mann) Gravitt; m. Ennis Odean Rogers, May 8, 1967; children: Catheryne, Charles, Elizabeth, Susanne. Student, Fla. Community Coll., Jacksonville, 1988. Chief exec. officer Info. Rsch. Ctr., Inc., Jacksonville, 1982—; co-mgr. Sizes Unltd., The Ltd., Tampa, Fla., 1984-85. Mem. Plan and City Bus. and Profl. Women's Club, Phi Theta Kappa, Beta Phi Gamma. Democrat. Methodist. Home: 17443 Eagle Bend Blvd Jacksonville FL 32226

ROGERS, BRENDA GAYLE, educational administrator, educator, consultant; b. Atlanta, July 27, 1949; d. Claude Thomas and Louise (Williams) Todd; m. Emanuel Julius Jones, Jr., Dec. 17, 1978; children: Lavelle, Brandon. BA, Spelman Coll., 1970; MA, Atlanta U., 1971, EdS, 1972; PhD, Ohio State U., 1975; postgrad. Howard U., 1980, Emory U., 1986. Program devel. specialist HEW, Atlanta, 1972; research assoc. Ohio State U., Columbus, 1973-75; asst. prof. spl. edn. Atlanta U., 1975-78, program adminstr., 1978—, CIT project dir., 1977—; tech. cons. Dept. Edn., Washington, 1978-88; due process regional hearing officer Ga. State Dept Edn., Atlanta, 1978-84, adv. bd., 1980-84; mem. parent adv. coun. APS, 1988—; cons. program devel. Ga. Respite Care, Inc., 1988-89; mem. exec. bd., treas. PTA Stone Mountain Elem. Sch., 1989—. Mem. Ga. Assessment Project com., Atlanta Pub. Schs. Adv. Council, 1986— ; bd. dirs. S.W. Montessori Sch., Atlanta, 1980, Malibu Civic Assn., College Park, Ga., 1977-78; mem. Grady Meml. Hosp. Community Action Network, Atlanta, 1982-83. Recipient disting. service award Atlanta Bur. Pub. Safety, 1982, award Atlanta Pub. Sch. System, 1980, 82, 83; fellow Ohio State U., 1972-74, Howard U., 1980; mem. Assn. for Retarded Citizens, Council for Exceptional Children, NAFE, Phi Delta Kappa, Phi Lambda Theta. Democrat. Roman Catholic. Avocation: gourmet cooking. Office: Atlanta U 233 James P Brawley Atlanta GA 30314

ROGERS, DEBORAH LYNN, psychologist; b. Wichita, Dec. 24, 1951; d. Robert Earl and Marion Louise (Jones) Fulton; m. Joseph Dirk Rogers, Feb. 17, 1978; 1 child, Casondra Victoria. BS, U. Wyoming, 1981; MA, U. No. Colo., Greeley, 1981; PhD, U. Texas, 1988. Personnel rsch. psychologist AF Human Resources Lab., San Antonio, 1981-84; manpower policy analyst Office of Sec. of Def. State of D.C., Washington, 1988—; cons. in field. Active Falls Church PTA, 1988—. With USAF, 1984-88. Fellow Inter-Univ. Seminar on Armed Forces and Soc.; mem. Am. Psychol. Assn., Assn. Human Resources Mgmt. and Organizational Behavior, Acad. of Mgmt., Am. Mgmt. Soc. Office: OASD (FM&P) Accession Policy Dir Rm 2B271-The Pentagon Washington DC 20301-4000

ROGERS, DIANE ELIZABETH, psychotherapist, program coordinator; b. Holyoke, Mass., Apr. 24, 1948; d. Alexander Sidney and Rachel (Imatt) R.; m. Joseph Michael Long, Oct. 26, 1977 (div. 1980); 1 child, Daniel. BA, U. Fla., 1970, MEd, 1973, EdS, 1973, PhD, 1982. Lic. mental health counselor, Fla.; cert. addictions profl.; diplomate Am. Bd. Med. Psychotherapists. Substance abuse counselor Fla. Correctional Instn., Lowell, 1973-77; instr. Community Counseling Ctr., Bronson, Fla., 1978-79; pvt. practice Alcohol and Drug Abuse Counslng Ctr., Gainesville, Fla., 1980-83; mem. faculty dept. pediatrics U. Fla., Gainesville, 1983-86; dir., counselor New Leaf Counseling Ctr., Gainesville, 1987-90; program coord. new start program drug-free beginnings for moms and babied Sacred Heart Gen. Hosp., Eugene, Oreg., 1990—; provider employee assistance program City of Gainesville, 1988-90; cons. Health Techs, Inc., Jacksonville, Fla., 1982—. Vol. VISTA, Broward County, Fla., 1970-71. Mem. Am. Pub. Health Assn., Am. Assn. Counseling and Devel., Nat. Women's Studies Assn., Nat. Assn. Perinatal Addiction, Rsch. and Edn., NOW, Sierra Club, Greenpeace, Cousteau Soc., Aububon Soc., AAUW, World Wildlife Fund. Jewish. Home: 2571 Erin Way Eugene OR 97401 Office: Sacred Gen Hosp New Start Program 950 Patterson Eugene OR 97401

ROGERS, DOLORES MCMANUS, training company executive; b. Bellflower, Calif., Mar. 31, 1936; d. Joseph John and Thelma Joanne (Hinds) McManus Miller; m. Michael Creighton Rogers, Nov. 26, 1971; children—Michael Creighton II, Eric Grinnell, Blake Lawrence. m. Clinton Lewis Byers, Jr., Aug. 2, 1958 (div. Mar. 1971). B.S., UCLA, 1957. Sales promotion staff Georgia Bullock, Inc., Los Angeles, 1957-62, v.p. sales promotion, 1962-66; dir. sales promotion Travilla, Los Angeles, 1966-71; owner, mgr. Exec. Assocs., Sherman Oaks, Calif., 1975—. Bd. dirs. Coldwater Counseling Ctr., Studio City, Calif., 1974-76; rec. sec. Las Donas, Los Angeles, 1979—. Mem. Am. Soc. Tng. and Devel., Fashion Group, AAUW. Republican. Episcopalian. Clubs: Sherman Oaks C. of C., UCLA Alumni Assn., Kappa Kappa Gamma. Avocations: cooking; reading; travel; golf; needlework. Home: 3906 Stone Canyon Rd Sherman Oaks CA 91403 Office: Exec Assocs 15015 Ventura Blvd Sherman Oaks CA 91403

ROGERS, FRANCES ARLENE, biology educator; b. Northfield, Minn., Jan. 24, 1923; d. Charles James and Mary Gertrude (Still) Ritchey; m. Rodney A. Rogers, July 1, 1956; children: Robert Allen, William David. BA, Drake U., 1944; MS, U. Chgo., 1946; PhD, U. Iowa, 1953. Instr. biology Earlham Coll., Richmond, Ind., 1946-49, U. Iowa, Iowa City, 1951-53; asst. prof. Cornell Coll., Mt. Vernon, Iowa, 1954, Shimer Coll., Mt. Carroll, Ill., 1955-56; lectr. and acting asst. prof. Drake U., Des Moines, 1956-69, asst. prof. to prof., 1969—; mem. Sci. Educator's Tour of sch./univs. in Europe and Russia, Iowa Acad. Sci., 1972. Author: Outline Text of Comparative Anatomy, 1983. Bd. dirs. Calvin Retirement Community, Des Moines, 1988—, sec., 1990—; judge oral presentations Hawkeye Sci. Fair, Iowa, 1969-90. Recipient sci. faculty profl. devel. grant, NSF, 1977-78. Mem. Assn. Midwest Coll. Biology Tchrs., Iowa Acad. Sci., Sigma Xi, Delta Kappa Gamma, Phi Beta Kappa (pres. 1981-82, sec. 1987— Gamma of Iowa chpt.), Mortar Bd. Democrat. Presbyterian. Home: 4203 40th St Des Moines IA 50310 Office: Biology Dept Drake Univ Des Moines IA 50311

ROGERS, GINGER (VIRGINIA KATHERINE MCMATH), dancer, actress; b. Independence, Mo., July 16, 1911; d. William Eddins and Lela Emogene (Owens) McMath; m. Edward Jackson Culpepper (div.); m. Lew Ayers (div.); m. Jack Briggs (div.); m. Jacques Bergerac (div.); m. G. William Marshall (div.). Ed. pub. schs. Began as a child dancer, 1926; appeared in motion pictures, 1930—; starred in Broadway prodn: Girl Crazy, 1929-30; danced with Fred Astaire in Flying Down to Rio, 1933, has co-starred with Astaire in numerous motion picture prodns. including Roberta, Shall We Dance, Top Hat, Gay Divorcee, Follow the Fleet, Swing Time; other movie appearances include Teenage Rebel, Twenty Million Sweethearts, Change of Heart, Chance at Heaven, The Sap from Syracuse, Sitting Pretty, Young Man of Manhattan, Star of Midnight, Top Hat, In Person, Golddiggers of 1933, Stage Door, Vivacious Lady, Having a Wonderful Time, O Men O Women, Harlow, Carefree, The Story of Vernon and Irene Castle, Bachelor Mother, Fifth Avenue Girl, Primrose Path, Lucky Partners, Kitty Foyle (Acad. award for Best Actress, 1940), Tom, Dick and Harry, Roxie Hart, The Confession, The Major and The Minor, Tales of Manhattan, Once Upon a Honeymoon, Lady in the Dark, Tender Comrade, I'll Be Seeing You, Week-end at the Waldorf, Heartbeat, Magnificent Doll, It Had to Be You, Barkleys of Broadway, Perfect Strangers, Storm Warning, The Groom Wore Spurs, We're Not Married, Monkey Business, Forever Female, Dreamboat, Twist of Fate, Black Widow; TV appearances include Perry Como Show, Bob Hope Show; star stage plays Hello Dolly, 1965, Mame, 1969; dir. play Babes in Arms, 1987. *

ROGERS, GLENNA JOAN, media relations executive; b. Terre Haute, Ind., May 25, 1947; d. Glenn Norman and Joan (Smith) Felling; m. George E. Rogers, May 25, 1975. BS, Ind. State U., 1970. Real estate assoc. Meneely-Williams, Terre Haute, 1980-85; corp. conf. coord. Unidynamics Corp., Stamford, Conn., 1982-85; media rels. exec. GTE Corp., Stamford, Conn., 1985—; bd. dirs. GTE Employees Assn., IABC Westfair. Mem. Westchester/Fairfield County Meeting Planners. Mem. Delta Gamma. Republican. Presbyterian. Club: Ind. State U. Century. Home: 1330 High Ridge Rd Stamford CT 06903

ROGERS, HEIDI, office supervisor; b. Danville, Ind., Oct. 12, 1963; d. James R. and Sue A. (Whited) R. BS in Bus., Ind. U., Indpls., 1986. Office supr. Rhoades Beverage Co., Inc., Plainfield, Ind. Mem. NAFE, Ind. U. Alumni Assn. Home: 419 S Carr Rd Plainfield IN 46168

ROGERS, HELEN EVELYN WAHRGREN, newspaperwoman; b. Tacoma, Jan. 24, 1924; d. John Sigurd and Emma Elina (Carlson) Wahrgren; B.A., U. Wash., Seattle, 1946; m. Charles Dana Rogers, July 24, 1948. Mem. editorial staff Holiday mag., Phila., 1946; civilian public relations writer, Ft. Lewis, Wash., 1946-47; asst. society editor Tacoma News Tribune-Sunday Ledger, 1947-51, radio-TV editor-columnist, 1951-86. Author: What's Your Line? vol. I: Delila Sprague Sherburne Harrington: Her Ancestors and Descendants. Mem. Newspaper Guild, Wis. Geneal. Soc., Tacoma-Pierce County Geneal. Soc., U. Wash. Alumni Assn. Democrat. Lutheran. Home and Office: 2906 N 24th St Tacoma WA 98406

ROGERS, IRENE, librarian; b. Yonkers, N.Y., Oct. 12, 1932; d. Franklyn Harold and Mary Margaret (Nealy) R.; B.S. in Edn., New Paltz State Tchrs. Coll., 1954; M.L.S. (N.Y. State Tng. grantee), Columbia U., 1959. Tchr., West Babylon (N.Y.) Sch. System, 1954-57, Yonkers Sch. System, 1957-58; reference librarian Yonkers Pub. Library, 1959-67, adult services coordinator, 1967-73, asst. library dir., 1973—. Mem. Mayor's Adv. Com. Consumer Edn., Yonkers, 1970—; active United Way of Yonkers; mem. curriculum adv. com., report card revision com. Office Supt. Schs., 1982; mem. Yonkers unit Am. Cancer Soc. West Library System grantee, 1966. Mem. ALA, Westchester, N.Y. library assns., Soroptimists (pres. 1978-79, 80-81, sec. dist. I North Atlantic region), Bus. and Profl. Women's Club (pres. Yonkers chpt. 1989-90). Home: 41 Amackassin Terr Yonkers NY 10703 Office: 7 Main St Yonkers NY 10701

ROGERS, ISABEL WOOD, religious studies educator; b. Tallahassee, Aug. 26, 1924; d. William Hudson and Mary Thornton (Wood) R. BA, Fla. State U., 1945; MA, U. Va., 1947; MRE, Presbyn. Sch. Christian Edn., 1949; PhD, Duke U., 1961; DD (hon.), Austin Coll., 1986; LLD (hon.), Westminster Coll., 1988; LHD, Centre Coll., 1989. Campus min. 1st Presbyn. Ch., Milledgeville, Ga., 1949-52; campus chaplain Ga. Coll., Milledgeville, 1952-61; prof. of applied Christianity Presbyn. Sch. Christian Edn., Richmond, Va., 1961—; elder Ginter Pk. Presbyn. Ch., Richmond, 1976-79, 89—; moderator of Gen. Assembly, Presbyn. Ch. U.S.A., 1987-88; lectr. Presbyn. chs. Author: The Christian and World Affairs, 1965, In Response to God, 1969, Our Shared Earth, 1980, Sing A New Song, 1981. Vol. Richmond Community Action Program, 1968-75, YWCA, Women's Advocacy Program, 1982—; bd. dirs. Presbyn. Outlook Found., Richmond, 1987—. Du Pont fellow U. Va., 1946. 47, Kearns fellow Duke U. Mem. Soc. Christian Ethics, Phi Kappa Phi, Phi Beta Kappa. Democrat. Home and Office: Presbyn Sch Christian Edn 1205 Palmyra Ave Richmond VA 23227

ROGERS, JACQUELINE, therapist, drug and alcohol educator; b. Milw., Nov. 8, 1960; d. John Stubblefield and Betty Jane (Christie) R. BA in Psychology, U. Wis., 1983, MS in Ednl. Psychology, 1987. Mem. bindery personnel Color Corps. of Am., Milw., 1979-82; with United Parcel Svc., Milw., 1983; telephone salesperson Spic & Span, Inc., Milw., 1984-85; security guard Marshall & Ilsley Bank, Milw., 1985-86; customer svc. rep. Security Savs. & Loan, Milw., 1985-86; drug and alcohol therapist Multi-Cultural Counseling Svcs., Milw., 1988; drug and alcohol counselor Social Devel. Commmn., Milw., 1988-89; psychotherapist outpatient clinic Sinai Samaritan Med. Ctr., Milw., 1989—; deviser, developer night treatment program Multi-Cultural Counseling Svcs., 1988. U. Wis.-Milw. fellow, 1986-87. Mem. NAFE, U. Milw. Alumni Assn. Democrat. Roman Catholic. Office: Sinai Samaritan Med Ctr 2000 W Kilbourn Ave Milwaukee WI 53233

ROGERS, JANE HOOKS, insurance agent; b. Princeton, Ky., Feb. 15, 1941; d. Samuel Forest and Margaret (Cook) Hooks; m. Don R. Rogers, June 20, 1959; 1 child, Joel Craig. BS magna cum laude, Murray State U., 1971, MA in Edn., 1972. Office mgr., legal sec. Edward H. Johnstone Law Offices, Princeton, Ky., 1960-67; office mgr. Dist. Office Frank A. Stubblefield U.S. Congress, Murray, Ky., 1967-73; instr. U. Ky., Paducah Community Coll., 1973-75; instr., coord. of coop. & experiential edn. Murray (Ky.) State U., 1975-80; ins. agt. Jane Rogers State Farm Ins., Murray, Ky., 1980—; cons. U. South Fla. Coop. Edn. Ctr. Mem. Murray Civic Music Assn., 1980—, sec., treas. 1990. Mem. AAUW (pres. Murray, Ky. 1987-89), Murray Life Underwriters' Assn. (pres. 1985), Coop. Edn. Assn. of Ky. (oustanding contbn. award 1977, pres. 1979-80), Gideons Internat. Aux. (pres. Murray, Ky 1986). Democrat. Baptist. Home: 1205 Dogwood Dr E Murray KY 42071 Office: Jane Rogers State Farm Ins PO Box 408 305 N 12th St Ste B Murray KY 42071

ROGERS, JANSIE, art and decorating company executive; b. Lenoir, N.C., Feb. 22, 1939; d. Raymond L. and Ruth (Henley) Setzer; m. G.R. Walter Rogers, June 23, 1963; widowed; children: Rob, Sharon. BA, James Madison U., 1961. Cert. custom decorator. Pub. sch. tchr., Baltimore County, Md., 1960-63, Perryville, Md., 1975-77; custom decorator Transart Industries, Woodstock, Ga., 1977-78, design dir., 1978-82, nat. dir. Trans Designs, Woodstock, 1982—. Bd. dirs. YMCA, Nat. Multiple Sclerosis Soc., Arthritis Found. Recipient awards including trips abroad, mink coats, diamonds TransDesigns, 1977-86. Mem. The Female Exec., Am. Bus. Women's Assn., LWV, Howard County C. of C. Democrat. Avocations: tennis, racquetball. Home and Office: 7554 Weatherworn Way Columbia MD 21046

ROGERS, JILL SUZANNE, broadcast journalist; b. Enid, Okla., May 5, 1968; d. Clarence James and Janice Kay (Herbert) R. BA in Journalism, U. Okla., 1990; postgrad., Stanford (Calif.) U., 1990—. With talk show Sta. KXLS, Enid, 1986-87; performer Six Flags Over Tex., Dallas, 1987-88, Six Flags Over Am., Chgo., 1988-89; broadcast journalist Sta. WKY, Oklahoma City, 1989—. Officer Young Reps., Norman, Okla., 1989—. Mem. Am. Assn. Coll. Broadcasters, Women in Communications, Inc. (sec. Norman chpt. 1988-89), Radio and TV Network Club (sec. Norman chpt. 1988—). Home: 2701 Wildwood Enid OK 73703

ROGERS, JUDITH LONG, wholesale distribution executive; b. Virginia Beach, Va., Dec. 4, 1955; d. Raymond Egerton and Nancy Marie (Gouldman) L. BA in Edn., Ariz. State U., 1977. Tchr., coach Scottsdale (Ariz.) High Sch.; asst. dir. field svcs., exec. dir. Am. Cancer Soc., Phoenix and Tucson; area sales mgr. Ray Long Ltd., Am. Kitchens, Phoenix; v.p. Cardinal Cabinets Ltd., Phoenix. Mem. Ariz. Community Found., Valley Leadership Phoenix, 1988-89, Leadership Tucson, 1986; chmn. tng. Jr. League of Phoenix. Mem. Nat. Soc. Fund Raising Execs., Nat. Kitchen and Bath Assn. Republican. Home and Office: PO Box 1316 Bigfork MT 59911

ROGERS, JUDITH W., District of Columbia chief judge. AB cum laude, Radcliffe Coll., 1961; LLB, Harvard U., 1964; LLM, U. Va., 1988. Bar: D.C. 1965. Law clk. Juvenile Ct. D.C., 1964-65; asst. U.S. atty. D.C., 1965-68; trial atty. San Francisco Neighborhood Legal Assistance Found., 1968-69; atty. U.S. Dept. Justice, 1969-71; gen. counsel Congl. Commn. on Organization of D.C. Govt., 1971-72; coordinator legis. program Office of Dep. Mayor D.C., 1972-74, spl. asst. to mayor for legis., 1974-79, corp. counsel, 1979-83; assoc. judge D.C. Ct. Appeals, 1983-88, chief judge, 1988—; mem. D.C. Law Revision Commn., 1979-83, Mayor's Commn. on Crime and Justice, 1982, vis. com. Harvard Law Sch., 1984-90; trustee Radcliffe Coll., 1982—; mem. grievance com. U.S. Dist. Ct. for D.C., 1982-83. Bd. dirs. Wider Opportunities for Women, 1972-74, Friends of the D.C. Superior Ct., 1972-74. Fellow ABA; mem. D.C. Bar Assn., Phi Beta Kappa. Office: DC Ct Appeals 500 Indiana Ave NW 6th Fl Washington DC 20001

ROGERS, JUDY ANN, health facility professional; b. Temple, Tex., July 23, 1954; d. Thelbert Douglas and Jewel Etta (Myles) R. BS in Health Professions, Southwest Tex. State U., 1988. Respiratory therapy technician Scott & White Hosp., Temple, 1975-798, Olin E. Teague VA Med. Ctr., Temple, 1979-88; dir. recreational therapy Behavioral Health Ctr., Temple, 1989-90; mental health technician Cedar Crest residential treatment ctr. Hosp. Corp. Am., Belton, Tex., 1990—. Mem. NAFE, NRA, NOW, Am. Film Inst., Sheriff's Assn. Tex., Belton C. of C. (mil. affairs com.). Republican. Episcopalian. Home: 1305 S 13th St Temple TX 76504 Office: HCA Cedarcrest 3500 S IH 35 Belton TX 76513

ROGERS, JULIE DOWDLE, mortgage company executive; b. Chgo., Oct. 5, 1949; d. John Anthony and Julie (McGuire) Dowdle; m. Geoff Rogers, Nov. 26, 1971 (div. Sept. 1976); children: Geoffrey Jr., Spencer. MBA, DePaul U., 1986; BS in Psychology, Loyola U., Chgo., 1972. Lic. real estate broker, Ill. 1978. Sales person to v.p. Norkett & Assocs., Winnetka, Ill., 1975-80; sec. to real estate officer First Ill. Bank, Evanston, 1980-85; underwriter to acting dir. Fed. Home Loan Mortgage, Chgo., 1985-88; pres. Cole Taylor Mortgage Co., Wheeling, Ill., 1989—.

ROGERS, KRISTA JANE FRITZ, writer, editor; b. Perry, Iowa, June 17, 1956; d. C. Wayne and Ethel Mae (Hendrickson) Fritz; m. Barry Bristow Rogers, Oct. 4, 1980; children: Benjamin James, Katherine Alice. BS with distinction, Iowa State U., 1979. Pub. rels. rep. Westinghouse Elec. Corp., Pitts., 1979-80; employee communications coord. Thermo King, Mpls., 1980-83; freelance writer Hutchinson, Kans., 1983-85; editor Ergosyst Assocs./Report Store, Lawrence, Kans., 1985-87; freelance writer Prairie Village, Kans., 1987—. Contbr. articles to mags. Recipient Communications awards United Way, Mpls./St. Paul, 1981-82. Mem. Women in Communications, Inc. (local officer 1989—, communications award Midwest region 1990), P.E.O., Mortar Bd., Kappa Delta Alumni, Chi Epsilon, Tau Beta Pi, PHi Kappa Phi, Alpha Pi Mu. Presbyterian. Home and Office: 4712 W 70th St Prairie Village KS 66208

ROGERS, MAE DAVIS, interior designer; b. Robbins, N.C., Nov. 26, 1938; d. Clarence Webster and Carlyne Sanders Davis; m. W. Ray Rogers, Oct. 24, 1958; children: Gwynn R. Taylor, Sharon R. Sheller, Lori R. Brasfield, Pamela J. Diploma, Sheffield Sch. Interior Design, N.Y.C., 1989. Cert. interior designer. Indsl. nurse Internat. Latex, La Grange, Ga., 1959-60, W.R. Bean & Son, Inc., Atlanta, 1960-62; mgr. Roger Williams Piano Studio, Atlanta, 1968-70; sales recruiting and tng. Fly-In Concept, Atlanta, 1971; sales investment cons. IDS, Inc., Atlanta, 1974-75; ptnr. Davis Furniture Co., Sanford, N.C., 1985-88; owner The Fountainhead, Sanford, 1989—. Nursing scholar, Robbins, N.C., 1956. Mem. Nat. Assn. Self-Employed, Interior Home Furnishing Rep. Assn., NAFE. Republican. Baptist. Home: 103 McLeod Dr Sanford NC 27330

ROGERS, MARGARET ELLEN JONSSON, civic worker; b. Dallas, Aug. 7, 1938, d. John Erik and Margaret Elizabeth (Fonde) Jonsson; ed. Skidmore Coll., 1956-57, So. Methodist U., 1957-60; children: Emily, Erik, Laura. Civic worker, Dallas; dir. KRLD radio, Dallas, 1970-74; dir. 1st Nat. Bank, Dallas, 1976-85, vice-chmn. dirs. trust com.; trustee Meth. Hosps., 1972-82, mem. exec. com., 1977-82, corp. bd. mem., 1990—; dir., vice chmn. Lamplighter Sch., 1967—; past mem. vis. com. dept. psychology MIT; mem. vis. com. Stanford U. Libraries, 1984—; bd. dirs. Winston Sch., 1973-85; bd. dirs., mem. exec. com. Episcopal Sch., 1976-83; bd. dirs. Callier Center Communication Disorders, 1967-90, v.p., 1974—; chmn. Crystal Charity Ball; active Stanford Centennial Campaign (co-chmn. nat. major gifts com.), bd. dirs., past mem. Children's Med. Center, Hope Cottage Childrens' Bur., Baylor Dental Sch., Dallas Health and Sci. Mus., Dallas YWCA, Day Nursery Assn.; mem. devel. bd. U. Tex., Dallas, 1988—, bd. govs. The Dallas Found., 1988—, trustee So. Meth. U., 1988—, vis. com. Dedman Coll., 1989—; life trustee Dallas Mus. Art; mem. collectors com. Nat. Gallery Art. Margaret Jonsson Charlton Hosp. of Dallas named in her honor, 1973. Mem. Internat. Council Mus. of Modern Art., Ctr. for Strategic and Internat. Studies., mem. steering com. Stanford Centennial Campaign, 1986-89, co-chmn. major gifts com., 1986-89; pres. MJC Fund, Jonsson Found., Susan G. Komen Found, 1988— (mem. steering com.); trustee Southern Meth. U., U. Tex., Dallas; mem. adv. bd. Tiffany & Co., Dallas, 1987, Dallas Breakfast Group. Republican. Club: Dallas Women's, Tower, Crescent, Brook Hollow Golf, Dallas County.

ROGERS, MARGARET RURIKO, infosystems support specialist; b. Fukuoka, Japan, July 12, 1968; came to U.S., 1968; d. William Charles and Ruriko (Ishikawa) R. Student, St. Mary's Hosp. Sch. Nursing, Waterbury, Conn., 1985-86. Mgr. St. Croix Islander Svcs., Christiansted, U.S. Virgin Islands, 1986-87; receptionist, accounts payable clk. Terumo Corp., Piscataway, N.J., 1987-88; product support coord., tech. assoc. Computer Integration Assocs., Inc., Old Bridge, N.J., 1988-89; tech. support coord. voice response products Performance Software Inc., West Caldwell, N.J., 1989-90; systems design rep. Siemens/Tel Plus, South Plainfield, N.J., 1990—. Mem. NAFE. Republican. Home: 60 Eton Way Somerset NJ 08875

ROGERS, MARTHA, marketing educator; b. Tallahassee, Apr. 30, 1952; d. John Lewis and Ruby Ann (Madsen) R.; m. J. Stuart Bertsch, 1988. BA magna cum laude, Birmingham So. Coll., 1974; MA, U. New Orleans, 1979; PhD, U. Tenn., 1983. Advt. copywriter Loveman's, Birmingham, Ala., 1973-74; advt. copywriter Maison Blanche, New Orleans, 1974-76, copy chief advt. dept., 1976-78, advt. dir., 1978; asst. prof. mktg. Bowling Green (Ohio) State U., 1981—; instr. Meadows-Draughon Coll., New Orleans, 1976, U. Tenn., 1981; speaker in field; cons. Elder-Tech Market Assocs., 1983-85, Whitman Ford, Temperance, Mich., 1984-85, Am. Assn. Advt. Agys., N.Y.C., 1985—, Aspen Grill & Cafe, 1985-86, Am. Hair Replacement Systems, Cleve., 1986—, others. Contbr. articles to profl. jours. Recipient Seklemian Advt. award Seklemian Found., 1975, 76; Karl A. Bickel fellow, 1979-80, 80-81; named Master Tchr. Bowling Green State U., 1987. Mem. Acad. Mktg. Sci., Am. Acad. Advt., Am Advt. Fedn. (bd. govs. 1988—), Am. Collegiate Retailing Assn., Am. Mktg. Assn., Assn. Educators in Journalism and Mass Communication, Nat. Advt. Rev. Bd., Phi Beta Kappa, Phi Kappa Phi, Kappa Tau Alpha. Office: Bowling Green State U Dept Mktg Bowling Green OH 43403-0266

ROGERS, NATALIE, psychologist; b. Rochester, N.Y., Oct. 9, 1928; d. Carl Ransom and Helen (Elliott) R.; m. Lawrence Howard Fuchs, June 5, 1950 (div. Oct. 1970); children: Janet Pearl, Frances Sarah, Naomi Ruth. AA, Stephens Coll., Columbia, Mo., 1946; BA, DE Pauw U., 1948; MA, Brandeis U., 1960. Lic. psychologist, Mass. Psychologist Counseling Ctr., U. Hawaii, Honolulu, 1965-66, Cambridge (Mass.) Guidance Ctr., 1964-65, Children's Hosp., Boston, 1967-68, North Shore Family Therapy Inst., Boston, 1970-71, Coll. Mental Health Ctr., Brookline, Mass., 1970-71; pvt. practice, Santa Rosa, Calif., 1974—; workshop facilitator, Europe, Latin Am., Japan, USSR, 1975—; founder, dir. The Person Centered Expressive Therapy Inst., Santa Rosa, 1984—. Author: Emerging Woman: A Decade of Midlife Transitions, 1980; contbr. articles to profl. jours. Bd. dirs. Resources for Creativity and Consciousness, Santa Rosa. Radcliffe scholar Bunting Inst., Cambridge, 1966-67. Mem. APA, Assn. Humanistic Psychology (bd. dirs.), Assn. Transpersonal Psychology. Democrat. Home: 1515 Riebli Rd Santa Rosa CA 95404 Office: Resources for Creativity PO Box 6518 Santa Rosa CA 95406

ROGERS, PEGGY JEAN, health services administrator; b. Houston, Nov. 13, 1944; d. Oscar Franklin and Margaret Jane (McGowen) R. BA, U. Houston, 1966; MPH, U. Tex., 1973, PhD, 1982. Research asst. Tex. Rsch. Inst. Mental Scis., Houston, 1968-72; health program coordinator SW Ctr. Urban Research, Houston, 1972-75; research asst., evaluator Houston Ind. Sch. Dist., 1975-76; research assoc. U. Tex. Med. Sch. Psychiatry, Houston, 1976-77, U. Tex. Med. Br. Edn., Galveston, Tex., 1977-82; dir. health promotion Hermann Hosp., 1982-83; cons., lectr. U. Houston, 1983-86; chief health planning Houston Dept. Health and Human Services, 1984--; adv. bd. mem. Houston Internat. Hosp., 1985-86, bd. mem. Health Services Mktg. Soc., 1986-88, mem. Tex. Econ. and Demograpghic Assn., 1986--, health profl. adv. com., March of Dimes Birth Defects, 1987--, Houston. Mem. Forum Club of Houston, 1986--, Internat. Bus. Network C. of C., 1987-88. Mem. Am. Pub. Health Assn., Women Profls. in Gov., Fedn. Houston Profl. Women (prog. chair, 1985, v.p. 1986), Sigma Xi-Sci. Research Soc. Home: 715 Peden Houston TX 77006

ROGERS, RUTH FRANCES, retired microbiologist; b. Chgo., Nov. 5, 1925; d. Frank Joseph and Ruth Elizabeth (Abbott) Kucera; m. James Alvin Rogers, June 17, 1950; children: Kenneth James, David Wayne. BS, U. Ill., 1948. Microbiologist No. Rsch. Ctr., USDA, Peoria, Ill., 1963-85; ret., 1985. Contbr. articles to profl. jours. Recipient Sustained Superior Performance award USDA, 1984. Methodist.

ROGERS, SELETA JUSTINE, education coordinator; b. Griffin, Ga., Apr. 11, 1950; d. Grady Francis and Mary Justine (Hall) Rogers; m. Robert Kenneth Jernigan, Nov. 21, 1970 (div. Dec. 1975). BA, Ga. Southwestern Coll., 1972; BS in English, Columbus Coll., 1978; MEd in Library Edn., U. Ga., 1982. Inventory control Thompson-Hayward Chem. Co., Americus, Ga., 1974-77; clerical aide Marion County Bd. Edn., Buena Vista, Ga., 1970-73, tchr.'s aide, 1977-78, tchr., 1978-79; tchr. Crisp County Bd. Edn., Cordele, Ga., 1979-80, media specialist, 1980-86; edn. coordinator Ga. Dept. Edn., Atlanta, 1986—. Founder, instr. mountain style clogging Dixieland Cloggers, 1976-86, Muckalee Mudstompers, 1977-85, Satin Belles, 1978-80. Mem. Ga. Assn. for Instructional Tech. (bd. dirs. 1980—, exec. bd. 1989-90), Ga. Library Assn., Ga. Library/Media Assn., ALA, Assn. for Ednl. Communications and Tech., Soc. Sch. Librarians Internat., Ga.'s Finest Cloggers. Methodist. Office: Ga Dept Edn Suite 2054 Twin Towers East Atlanta GA 30334

ROGERS, SHARON J., library administrator; b. Grantsburg, Wis., Sept. 24, 1941; d. Clifford M. and Dorothy L. (Beckman) Dickau; m. Evan D. Rogers, June 15, 1962 (div. Dec. 1980). BA summa cum laude, Bethel Coll., St. Paul, 1963; MA in Libr. Sci., U. Minn., 1967; PhD in Sociology, Wash. State U., Pullman, 1976. Lectr., instr. Alfred (N.Y.) U., 1972-76; assoc. prof. U. Toledo, 1977-80; assoc. dean Bowling Green (Ohio) State U. Librs., 1980-84; univ. libr. George Washington U., Washington, 1984—, asst. v.p. acad. affairs, 1989—; mem. Online Computer Libr. Ctr. Users Coun., 1985—, pres. 1989-90, mem. rsch. adv. com., 1990—. Contbr. articles to profl. jours. Bd. dirs. ACLU, Toledo, 1978-84. Jackson fellow U. Minn., 1964-65; NSF trainee Wash. State U., 1969-72. Mem. ALA (exec. coun. 1987—, pub. com. 1989-90, chair 1990), Assn. Coll. and Rsch. Librs. (pres. 1984-85), Am. Sociol. Assn., Washington Rsch. Libr. Consortium (bd. dirs. 1987-90,), Universal Serials and Book Exch. (bd. dirs., treas. 1987). Office: George Washington U Gelman Libr 2130 H St NW Washington DC 20052

ROGERS, SUSAN (SUE ROGERS), data processing consultant; b. Jonesboro, Ark., Aug. 22, 1949; d. Eric J. Jr. and Suzanne (Payne) R.; m. Joseph Edward Aldrich, July 3, 1974 (div. Mar. 1985). BS in Math, U. Ark., 1975. Cert. computer programmer. Chief programmer State Ark. Dept. Fin. and Adminstrn., Little Rock, 1973-76; programmer, analyst Dillards Dept. Stores, Little Rock, 1976-77; mem. profl. staff Cutler-Williams Inc., Dallas, 1977-79; sr. tech. cons. Sterling Software (formerly Informatics Gen.), Dallas,

1979-86; pvt. practice cons. Dallas, 1986-87; programmer, analyst Fed. Res. Bank, Dallas, 1988-89; pvt. practice Dallas, 1989—; tchr. jewelry making Dallas Community Coll., 1988—. Exhibitions at State Fair of Tex., 1985-87, Plano Art Assn., 1985, Arlington Art Assn., 1986, North Lake Coll., 1987. Vol. arts and crafts program Dallas County Juvenile Detention Ctr. Mem. Tex. Designer and Craftsmen (exhibition 1986), Craft Guild of Dallas, Bead Soc. of Dallas, North Tex. Enamelist Guild, North Tex. Herb Club, Mensa. Home and Office: 2925 Seymour Dallas TX 75229

ROGERS, TAMARA ANN, French, Latin and dance educator; b. Hillsboro, Ohio, Mar. 27, 1947; d. Roy Steele and Anna Mary (Murray) R.; m. John Arthur Rosberg, Aug. 31, 1968 (div. 1985); children: Mariya Aryn, Jordis Amanda. BA, Denison U., 1969; postgrad., U. Minn. Cert. Tchr., Minn. Tchr. French Centennial High Sch., Champaign, Ill., 1969-72; tchr. Eisenhower High Sch., Hopkins, Minn., 1972-75, Blake Upper Sch., Mpls., 1975-76; staff pilot program for children Alliance Francaise, Mpls., 1977-78; tchr. Hopkins Sch., Minn., 1978-80, Minnetonka East Jr. High Sch., 1980-82, Art Ctr. Minn., Wayzata, Minn., 1983-84, St. Louis Park (Minn.) High Sch., 1984, Woods Acad., Maple Plain, Minn., 1984-88, Roosevelt High Sch., Mpls., 1988—; head dance dept. tch. Art Ctr. Minn., Wayzata, 1981-87; dir. tchr. dance Three Flights Up dance studio, Excelsior, Minn., 1983-85; dir., choreographer, tchr. Fidgety Feet Repertory Group, Twin Cities Minn., 1981—; model Kimberly Franson Agy., Mpls., 1987—; mem. Dance Edn. Devel. Project for Minn. Moderator of deacons local Presbyn. Ch., 1990. Democrat. Home: 3616 Tonkawood Rd Minnetonka MN 55345

ROGERS, WILMA MESSER, retired educator; b. Jacksonville, Fla., Oct. 15, 1931; d. William and Ruth Esther (Lockett) Messer; m. Lorain Winston Rogers, Aug. 14, 1954 (dec. 1986); children: Winston Bernard, Marlene Denise, William Earl. BS, Hampton (Va.) U., 1953; MS, Nova U., Ft. Lauderdale, Fla., 1980. Cert. tchr., Fla. Tchr. J.R.E. Lee Elem. Sch., South Miami, Fla., 1953-59; first grade tchr. Liberty City Elem. Sch., Miami, Fla., 1959-66, 72-88, kindergarten tchr., 1972-88, Headstart program tchr., 1966-72; supervising tchr. Early Childhood Program Miami Dade Community Coll., 1975-77; ret., 1988; vol. Child Watch, Miami, 1982; mem. edn. component Metro-Miami Action Plan, 1979-81. Assoc. editor The Krinon jour., 1980. Dep. registrar Met. Dade County elections, Miami, 1990. Recipient numerous citations for excellence in teaching Top Ladies of Distinction, Inc. Mem. NAACP, Nat. Congress Parents and Tchrs. (membership chair Liberty City Elem. PTA 1973-78), Dade County Retired Tchrs. Assn., Fla. Retired Educators Assn., Dem. Women's Club Dade County, Dem. Black Caucus Fla., Nat. Coun. Negro Women (pres. 1985-86, Svc. award 1983, 88), Greater Miami Opera, Miami-Dade Nat. Panhellenic Coun. (recording sec. 1985-87, Svc. award 1988), B.O.L.D., Inc., Phi Delta Kappa (nat., recording sec. 1976-77, Svc. award 1988), Zeta Phi Beta (fin. sec. 1983-87, Svc. award 1983-87). Baptist. Home: 2017 NW 55th Ter Miami FL 33142

ROGGOW, DIANE LYNN, telecommunications marketing manager; b. Cochabamba, Bolivia, Feb. 9, 1957; came to U.S., 1963; d. Zelma Joy (Divers) R.; m. Kim Lance Thorne, May 20, 1978 (div. April 1983). BBA, U. Denver, 1988. Adminstrv. asst. Mobile Premix Concrete, Inc., Denver, 1978; adminstr. Mr. Steak, Inc., Denver, 1979; regional account coordinator AT&T Teletype Corp., Denver, 1980-85; adminstrv. mgr. US Sprint, Denver, 1986-88; mktg. mgr. US Sprint, Kansas City, Kans., 1988—. Mem. Nat. Assn. Female Execs. Republican. Home: 4519 W 72d St Prairie Village KS 66208 Office: 8140 Ward Pkwy Kansas City MO 64114

ROGOZINSKI, TINA MARIE, pharmaceutical company marketing executive; b. Oklahoma City, Dec. 10, 1962; d. Leonard Peter and Mildred Helen (Little) R. B.S. in Internat. Mktg., Quinnipiac Coll., 1984, cert. in export mktg., 1983. Advt. coordinator Healthkraft, Inc., Danbury, Conn., 1983-85; mktg. mgr. Tishcon Corp., Westbury, N.Y., 1985-87; owner Unistar Mktg. Group Inc., 1986—. Contbr. poems to mags. Conn. State scholar, 1980. Mem. NOW, NAFE, Am. Women Entrepreneurs, Internat. Platform Assn. Avocations: writing, tennis, skiing. Home: PO Box 10194 Westbury NY 11590 Office: Unistar Mktg Group 30 Charm City Dr Jefferson NY 11776

ROGUS, PAMELA L., recreational facility executive, geriatric social worker; b. Ft. Pierce, Fla., Mar. 1, 1952; d. Victor A. and Marion E. (McNally) Blackmer; m. Randall T. Rogus, June 28, 1975; children: Richard Randall, Michael Franklin. BS in Psychology, Fla. So. Coll., 1974. Cert. gerontologist. Geriatric social worker State of Fla.-DHRS, Ft. Pierce, 1975-85; coord. ACLF licensure div. Health and Rehabilitative Svcs. State of Fla., Ft. Pierce; co-owner Ga. Mountain Madness Cabins, Helen, 1985—, Ocean Side Pharmacy, Ft. Pierce, Fla. Mem. NAFE, Am. Bus. Women's Assn., Ga. Hospitality and Travel Assn., White County C. of C., Helen C. of C. Home and Office: PO Box 308 Helen GA 30545

ROHE, MARIA THERESA, marketing executive, consultant; b. Buffalo, Apr. 8, 1959; d. John and Thereza (Fazekas) Ribarits; m. Michael P. Rohe, July 25, 1987. BA, Canisius Coll., 1981; MBA, Am. Grad. Sch. Internat. Mgmt., 1984. Account exec., industry cons. AT&T, Dallas, 1984—. Office: AT&T 5525 LBJ Frwy Dallas TX 75240

ROHN, ELIZABETH G., banker; b. Hartford, Conn., May 25, 1948; d. Charles Alonzo and Julie (Gelston) Harrington; m. Douglas Jerome Gregor (div. 1980); m. William John Rohn, Aug. 29, 1980. AA, Hartford Coll. for Women, 1968; BA, U. Ill., Chgo., 1971; MBA, U. Minn., 1975; cert. in exec. program-Sloan Mgmt., MIT, 1988. Coord. svc. TIES-Computer Coop., St. Paul, 1971-73; mgr. svcs. Metro-II Computer Coop, Mpls., 1976-78; sr. cons. Plante & Moran-CPA/Mgmt. Cons., Southfield, Mich., 1979-82; sr. cons. Fed. Nat. Mortgage Assn., Washington, 1982-83, asst. to chief exec. officer and chmn. bd., 1983-84, dir. mortgage acquisition, 1984-86, v.p. mortgage ops., 1987-88; v.p., mgr. consumer lending Mellon Bank (East), Phila., 1988-89; v.p. mortgage products mid-atlantic region Mellon Bank, 1990—. Office: Mellon Bank 7th and Market Sts Philadelphia PA 19101-7899

ROHRBOUGH, LINDA JANDECKA, computer center administrator; b. Akron, Ohio, Dec. 7, 1947; d. Clyde William and Dorothy Jean (Nine) Jandecka; m. Gene L. Rohrbough; 1 child, Zachary William. AAS, U. Akron, 1967, BSBA, 1971. Data contr. U. Akron (Ohio) Computer Ctr., 1970-72, sec. to dir., 1972-75, computer svcs. coord., 1975—. Bd. dirs. Firestone Pk. Citizens Council, Akron, 1980—, newsletter editor Akron, 1984-87. Mem. NOW. Republican. Baptist. Home: 217 N Firestone Blvd Akron OH 44301 Office: U Akron Computer Ctr 302 E Buchtel Ave Akron OH 44325

ROHREN, BRENDA MARIE ANDERSON, psychologist; b. Kansas City, Mo., Apr. 18, 1959; d. Wilbur Dean and Katheryn Elizabeth (Albright) Anderson; m. Lathan Edward Rohren, May 10, 1985; 1 child, Amanda Jessica. BS in Psychology, Colo. State U., 1983; MA in Psychology, Cath. U. Am., 1986. Mental health therapist, sr. case mgr. Rappahannock Area Community Svcs. Bd., Fredericksburg, Va., 1986-88; mental health therapist, case mgmt. supr. Rappahannock Area Community Svcs. Bd., 1988; rsch. assoc. Inst. Medicine, NAS, Washington, 1988-89; supr. adult psychiat. program Lincoln (Nebr.) Gen. Hosp., 1989, program supr. mental health svcs., 1989—; computer cons., Syscon Corp., Washington, 1983-84. Active Lincoln Mental Health Coalition. Active duty USN, 1981-86. Mem. NAFE, NOW, Am. Psychol. Assn. (assoc.), Nat. Alliance for Mentally Ill, Internat. Assn. Psychosocial Rehab. Svcs., Nebr. Psychol. Assn. (assoc.), Am. Legion Auxiliary. Democrat. Roman Catholic. Home: 3821 S 33d St Lincoln NE 68502 Office: Lincoln Gen Hosp 2300 S 16th St Lincoln NE 68502

ROHRER, EDNA (DOLLY ROHRER), weight loss franchise executive; b. Sturgis, Mich., Sept. 2, 1942; d. David W. Eberhard and Martha (Troyer) Horowitz; m. Lloyd R. Rohrer, Sept. 29, 1961 (div. July 1977); 1 child, JoDee L. Grad. high sch., Sturgis. Receptionist, sec. Rapa Electric Inc., Allegan, Mich., 1961-76; adminstrv. asst. Allegan Med. Clinic, 1978-81; sales rep. Say Cheez, White Pigeon, Mich., 1981-82, Met. Ins. Co., Battle Creek, Mich., 1982-85; account rep. Met. Ins. Co., Kalamazoo, 1987-89; sales rep., asst. mgr. N.Am. Benefit Assocs., Kalamazoo, 1985-87; mgr. Riko, Inc. (doing bus. as Formu-3 Internat.), Lansing, Mich., 1989—. Fellow Life Underwriter Tng. Coun. Home: 190 Grand Manor Grand Ledge MI 48837 Office: Riko Inc/Formu-3 Internat 3238 W St Joseph Lansing MI 48917

ROIGER, LORI ANN, controller; b. Mankato, Minn., Mar. 29, 1962; d. Richard Carl Frey and JoAnn Idella (Carlson) Priller; m. Donald James Roiger, Oct. 6, 1984; children: Jennifer Elizabeth, Courtney Marie. AA, St. Cloud State U., 1984. Store mgr. Books Plus, New Hope, Minn., 1981-84; accounts payable clk. Vandura Mktg., Burnsville, Minn., 1984-85; accounts payable rep. Midwest Systems, Inc., Burnsville, 1985-86; accounts payable analyst Condura Mktg. Corp., Burnsville, 1986—, controller, 1989—. Recipient Bus. Career Devel. Program award Mpls. chpt. Exec. Women Internat., 1980. Democrat. Lutheran. Home: 18025 180th Ct Farmington MN 55024 Office: Condura Mktg Corp 701 Ladybird Ln Burnsville MN 55337

ROITMAN, JUDITH, mathematician; b. N.Y.C., Nov. 12, 1945; d. Leo and Ethel (Gottesman) R.; m. Stanley Lombardo, Sept. 26, 1978; 1 child, Ben Lombardo. BA in English, Sarah Lawrence Coll., 1966; MA in Math., U. Calif., Berkeley, 1971, PhD in Math., 1974. Asst. prof. math. Wellesley (Mass.) Coll., 1974-77; from asst. prof. to prof. math. U. Kans., Lawrence, 1977—. Author: Introduction to Modern Set Theory, 1990; contbr. articles to profl. jours. Grantee NSF, 1976-87, faculty U. Kans., 1977-89. Mem. Assn. Symbolic Logic, Am. Math. Soc., Assn. Women in Math. (pres. 1979-81).

ROJAS, KRISTINE BRIGGS, insurance underwriter; b. Pocatello, Idaho, July 25, 1947; d. Fergus Jr. and Shirley (Tanner) Briggs; divorced; children: Anthony Ted, Nancy Kristine. Student, Idaho State U., 1965-66. Ops. clerical coord. Farmers Ins. Group, Pocatello, 1971-81; svc. rep. All Seasons Ins. Agy., Ventura, Calif., 1982; sr. comml. underwriting asst. Royal Ins. Co., Ventura, 1982-85; sr. comml. lines underwriter Andreini & Co., Ventura, 1985-88; large comml. account unit coord. Frank B. Hall, Inc., Oxnard, Calif., 1988—. Editor (bulletin) News Waves, 1985-87; artist various works specializing in charcoal portraits. Mem. NAFE, Ins. Women Ventura County (treas. 1987-88, v.p. 1988-90, pres. 1990—, bd. dir. 1986-87, Woman of Yr. 1989-90), Nat. Assn. Ins. Women. Republican. Baptist. Home: 1021 Center Rd Somis CA 93066 Office: Frank B Hall Inc 2500 Vineyard Oxnard CA 93030

ROLAND, CATHERINE DIXON, entrepreneur; b. Andalusia, Ala., Mar. 9, 1936; d. Charles and Thelma (Chapman) Dixon; m. Henry F. Roland, Dec. 16, 1966 (div. Nov. 1976); 1 child, Charles H.; stepchildren: Bill, Vickie Roland Little. Student, Huntingdon Coll., 1954-56; BS, Auburn U., 1956-59; MA in History, U. Ala., Tuscaloosa, 1965-66. Sec. Dixon Lumber Co., Inc., Andalusia, 1969-74, v.p., 1974-78; land and timber owner, mgr. Catherine D. Roland & Co., Andalusia, 1978—; owner Sta. WCTA, Andalusia, 1947-75; owner, bd. dirs. D & G Devel. Property, Ltd., Perth, Australia, 1967—, So. Nat. Corp. Covington County Bank, Andalusia, 1985—, mem. women's adv. council, 1980—. Chmn. Thelma Dixon Found., Andalusia, 1981—; mem. Rep. Senatorial Inner Circle, Washington, 1980—, 2d Congl. Com., Montgomery, Ala., 1980—, Andalusia Pub. Library Friends, Inc., 1981—; mem. adv. council Mises Inst. Auburn (Ala.) U., Auburn and Washington, 1983-85, Coll. Bus. Auburn U., 1987—; mem. Com. of 100 Huntingdon Coll., 1978, bd. trustees, 1978—, vice chmn. bd. trustees, 1986—; bd. dirs. Women Health, Birmingham, Ala., 1978-82, Andalusia Hosp., Inc. 1980-82, Health Services Found., 1982—. Named one of Outstanding Young Women of Am., 1965, Countess of Huntingdon Coll., Montgomery, 1978; recipient Commendation for Outstanding Service and Leadership, Huntingdon Coll., 1980; elected to Huntingdon Coll. Hall of Honor, 1980. Mem. Bus. Adv. Council Auburn U. Sch. Bus., Forest Farmers Assn., Ala. Wildlife Fedn., Andalusia Area C. of C., Auburn Alumni Assn., Huntingdon Coll. Alumni Assn. (chmn. Andalusia area chpt. 1983—), Am. Legion, Nat. Soc. Magna Charta Dames of Phila., DAR, Nat. Soc. Colonial Dames XVII Century, Ams. of Royal Descent, Study Club. Methodist.

ROLAND, ELEANOR JOYCE, nurse educator, researcher; b. LaGrange, N.C., Feb. 14, 1940; d. Willie Edward Sr. and Mamie Clara (Jenkins) Simmons; m. Lewis Roland, May 28, 1961; children: Leslie, Lorecia, Lisa. BS in Nursing, Winston-Salem (N.C.) State U., 1961; cert. in anesthesia, Danville (Va.) Meml. Hosp., 1966; MS in Nursing, Seton Hall U., 1977; MS in Psychology, N.C. State U., 1986, postgrad., 1981—. RN, N.C., N.J. Instr. nursing Lincoln Hosp. Sch. Nursing, Durham, N.C., 1961-63; nurse anesthetist East Orange (N.J.) Gen. Hosp., 1967, Crippled Children's Hosp., Newark, 1967-69, St. Mary's Hosp., Orange, N.J., 1972-76, Coll. Medicine & Dentistry, Newark, 1977-78; asst. prof. nursing U. N.C., Chapel Hill, 1978-83, lectr. in nursing, 1985-89; with Rsch. Triangle Inst., Research Triangle Park, N.C., 1990—; coord. pain clinic Coll. Medicine & Dentistry, Newark, 1977-78; coord. registered nurses program U. N.C., Chapel Hill 1980-81. Bd. dirs. Orange County Mental Health Assn., Chapel Hill, 1985-87; v.p. PTA Coun. Chapel Hill Schs., 1986-87, Planned Parenthood Orange County, 1987—. Mem. Am. Nurses Assn., Alpha Kappa Mu, Sigma Theta Tau, Delta Sigma Theta (historian jours. 1988-89, pres. 1990—). Democrat. Methodist. Home: 413 Overland Dr Chapel Hill NC 27514 Office: Rsch Triangle Inst Ctr For Social Rsch & Policy Analysis PO Box 12194 Research Triangle Park NC 27709

ROLAND-SCHERZER, LISA JOY, bank training director; b. Newark, Oct. 30, 1956; d. Jack and Natalie (Molin) Roland. Student, Inst. Internat., Madrid, 1977; BA, Douglass Coll., 1978; postgrad., Kean Coll., 1980. Cert. Spanish tchr., N.Y. Tchr. Union (N.J.) High Sch., 1978-81; customer service mgr. People Express Airlines, Newark, 1981-82, corp. tng. mgr., 1982-84; city mgr. O'Hare Airport People Express Airlines, Chgo., 1984-86; sr. tng. mgr. Citibank N.Am., N.Y.C., 1986-87, asst. v.p., dir. teller tng., 1988-89, dir. design and devel., 1989—; cons. Nancy Weed Assocs., San Francisco, 1986-87. Gymnastics instr. Summer Enrichment Program, Union; mgr. Cabaret Theatre Soc., New Brunswick. Mem. Am. Soc. Tng. and Devel. Democrat. Jewish.

ROLFE, BELINDA, pharmacist; b. Hartselle, Ala., June 1, 1960; d. Perry Ray and Julia Ann (Johnson) R. Student, Auburn U., 1978-79; AA in Edn., Calhoun Coll., 1980; BS in Pharmacy, Samford U., 1984. Registered pharmacist, Ala. Pharmacy extern Reynold's Pharmacy, Birmingham, Ala., 1982-84, Weldon's Pharmacy, Hueytown, Ala., 1984, Princeton Hosp.-Birmingham Med. Ctr., Hueytown, Ala., 1984; pharmacy intern Big B Drugs Inc., Roebuck, Ala., 1984-85, pharmacist, 1985—; pharmacy cons. Bradford Group, Birmingham, 1986-88. Mem. Am. Pharm. Assn., Ala. Pharm. Assn., Lambda Kappa Sigma, Alpha Omicron Pi. Roman Catholic. Home: 2075 Montreat Circle Birmingham AL 35216 Office: Big B Drugs No 58 Highway 31 S Pelham Plaza Pelham AL 35124

ROLL, BARBARA HONEYMAN, anthropologist; b. Portland, Oreg., Apr. 4, 1910; d. Arthur and Carlotta (Parker) Honeyman; m. Scott Alexander Heath, Dec. 23, 1953 (dec. July 1974); m. George Frederick Roll, Mar. 5, 1977. BA, Smith Coll., 1932, LHD (hon.), 1989. Exec. sec. Const. Lab. P&S Med. Ctr., N.Y., 1948-51; rsch. assoc. U. Oreg. Med. Sch., Portland, Oreg., 1951-53; cons. U. Oreg. Sch. Health and Phys. Edn., Eugene, Oreg., 1957-68, Dr. Margaret Mead AMNH, N.Y., 1966-75; rsch. assoc. U. Pa. Mus., Phila., 1975—; instr. anthropology Community Coll., Monterey, Calif., 1966-74; vis. scholar Inst. Anthropology, Moscow, 1967, 1975. Contbr. articles to profl. jours. Fellow AAAS, Am. Assn. Anthropology, NY Acad. Scis.; mem. Coun. Human Biol., Am. Assn. Phys. Anthropology, Inst. Intercultural Studies (sec. 1980-83). Home: 26030 Rotunda Dr Carmel CA 93923

ROLL, MARGUERITE S., writer; b. Cleve., Aug. 7, 1927; d. Norwood Wendell and Gladys Myrl (Spies) Swallen; m. Lyle Charles Roll, Apr. 24, 1971 (dec.). BA cum laude, Syracuse (N.Y.) U., 1948, cert. in journalism, 1948; postgrad., Universite de Lausanne, Switzerland, 1951; student, U. Oxford, Eng., 1989. Reporter Enquirer and News, Battle Creek, Mich., 1945; writer W.K. Kellogg Found., Battle Creek, 1947; advt. prodn. expeditor Clark Equipment Co., Battle Creek, 1948-50; advt. mgr. Battle Creek Food Co., 1951-53; advt. staff asst. Kellogg Co., Battle Creek, 1952-61, legal adminstrv. asst., 1961-71. Sec., bd. dirs. Bay Village Condominium Assn., Battle Creek, 1981-82. Swiss fellow Inst. Internat. Edn., 1950-51. Mem. Women's Athletic Club of Chgo., Marco Polo Club, Paradise Valley Country Club, Battle Creek Country Club.

ROLLAND, DONNA JOSEPHINE, state official; b. Chgo., May 8, 1952; d. Frederick R. Sr. and Doris C. (Howard) R. BA, So. Ill. U., 1974; postgrad., Chgo. State U., 1976. Cert. instr., trainer, 1989. Dir., mgr. employee relations task force Tex. Atty. Gen., Austin, 1989, asst. to title IV-D, dir. child support enforcement, agy. trainer, meeting planner, 1987-89; instr. Austin Community Coll. Vol. Hospice, 1989; exec. bd. Austin Adopt-A-School, 1985-86. Recipient award for significant contbns. in field of HRD, Shares of Appreciation award, Pres.'s award Austin Community Coll.; named one of Outstanding Women of Am., 1982. Mem. ASTD (v.p. external affairs), NAFE, MPI, Mktg. Fedn. Am. (mem. HRD/UTA adv. coun.), Meeting Planners Internat. (program com.), Austin Choral Union(bd. dirs. 1985-86). Roman Catholic. Address: 510A Cutty Trail Austin TX 78734 Office: Atty Gen Office 210 Barton Springs Austin TX 78711

ROLLBERG, JEANNE NORTON, education educator; b. Jacksonville, Fla., Oct. 31, 1957; d. James Thomas and Joan Wade (Jennings) N.; m. Charles Anthony Rollberg, Aug. 4, 1956. BA, Wesleyan Coll., Macon, Ga., 1979; MA in Journalism, U. Mo., 1980. Stringer Dayton (Ohio) Daily News, 1981; asst. news dir. KAMU-TV/FM, Tex. A&M U., College Station, 1981-82, news dir., 1983; asst. prof. U. Ark., Little rock, 1983—; pub. affairs show producer KLRE-KUAR/FM, Little rock, 1987—; gen. asst. rep. part time KTHV-TV, Little Rock, 1984, 89—. Recipient 1st PlacePub. Affairs award Ark. AP, 1989; named winner talk show Am. Women Radio & TV, Inc., 1989. Mem. Assn. Edn. Journalism & Mass Communications, Soc. Profl. Journalists,Broadcast Edn. Assn., Ark. Press Women, Internat. Communication Assn. Office: U Ark 2801 S University Little Rock AR 72204

ROLLE, ESTHER, actress; b. Pompano Beach, Fla.. Student, Spellman Coll., Hunter Coll., New Sch. for Social Research. Dancer, Shogola Obola Dance Co., then mem., Negro Ensemble Co.; off-Broadway debut The Blacks, 1962; London stage debut God is a (Guess What?), 1969; numerous stage appearances include: Macbeth, Amen Corner, Blues for Mister Charlie, Don't Play Us Cheap; toured Scandinavia in stage prdn. The Skin of Our Teeth; toured Australia, New Zealand in stage prdns. Black Nativity; other stage prdns. The Member of the Wedding, 1988; films include To Kill a Mockingbird, 1963, Nothing But a Man, 1964, The Learning Tree, 1969, Cleopatra Jones, 1973, Driving Miss Daisy, 1989; regular on: TV series Maude, 1972-74, One Life to Live, 1972-74, Good Times, 1974-77, 78-79; TV appearances include Dinah's Place, N.Y.P.D., Like It Is, East Side, West Side; appeared in: TV movie Summer of My German Soldier, 1979 (Emmy award 1979); recipient Image award, NAACP. Hon. chmn. Pres.'s Com. on Employment of Handicapped.; Grand Marshall Cherry Blossom Festival, Washington, 1975. Named Woman of Yr.; 3d World Sisterhood, 1976; recipient NAACP leadership award, 1990. Address: care Triad Artists 10100 Santa Monica Blvd Los Angeles CA 90067*

ROLLINS, DONNA L., bank executive; b. Panama, July 13, 1959; d. Charles J. and Beryl A. (Hinds) R. Student, Rutgers U. 2d v.p., asst. treas., supr. MIS Chase Manhattan Bank, N.Y.C. Mem. 100 Coalition of Black Women (editor employment newsletter), Nat. Economist Club. Office: 101 Park Ave 28th Fl New York NY 10178

ROLNICK, DIANE MICHELLE, public relations executive; b. Long Beach, Calif., Aug. 12, 1964; d. Matthew and Betty Marie (Williamson) R. BA in Journalism, Calif. State U., 1986. Nat. field rep. Delta Zeta Sorority, Oxford, Ohio, 1986-88; asst. account exec. The Amies Group, Irvine, Calif., 1988-89; account exec. GCI Group, L.A., 1989—. Advisor Long Beach Greek Housing Adv. Bd., 1989, Delta Zeta House Corp., Long Beach, 1989, Delta Zeta Sorority Nat. Rush Com., Oxford, 1988—. Mem. Young Pub. Relations Profls., Delta Zeta. Republican. Mem. Christian Ch. Home: 11291 Mac St Garden Grove CA 92641 Office: GCI Group 6100 Wilshire Blvd #840 Los Angeles CA 90048

ROMACK, SOPHIE MARIE, labor relations representative; b. Warren, Ohio, Feb. 12, 1945; d. Nick and Virginia (Miller) Blahu; m. Donald Zane Romack, Sept. 21, 1963 (div. May 1972); children: Victoria Marie Torres, Andrea Lynn Romack. BBA, Kent State U., 1983. With stationary bd./prodn. Packard Electric/GM, Warren, 1964; desk clk. Packard Electric/GM, 1964-81, sick leave claims approver, 1981-85, transfer coord. med. placement, 1985-88, sr. labor rels. rep., 1988—; cons. Project Bus., Jr. Achievement, 1989—. Pres. League Women Voters, Trumbull County, Ohio, 1989; instr. Labaugh Lit. Soc., Mahoning County, Ohio, 1987; arbitrator Mahoning Better Bus. Bur., Mahoning County, 1985—. Mem. AAUW (mentor 1989—), Nat. Ass. Exec. Women, Profl. Connection (steering com.), Trumbull Indsl. Mgmt. Assn., Trumbull Personnel Mgmt. Assn., Kent State Alumni Assn. Democrat. Eastern Orthodox. Home: 6430 Woodview Leavittsburg OH 44430 Office: Packard Electric Div Gen Motors 408 Dana St Warren OH 44482

ROMAIN, MARGARET ANN, accountant; b. Mercer, Pa., Jan. 1, 1940; d. Peter Paul and Susie Ann (Murcko) Kutcher; m. Joseph Romain Jr.; children: Lucretia Ann, Kimberly Rose, Annette Marie. Student, Youngstown State U., 1957-58, 68-69, LaSalle Extension U., Pa. State U., Alliance Coll. Cert. graphoanalyst. Bookkeeper Mort-Bohn & Assocs., CPA, 1960-62, D.G. Reed & H. Hudson, PA, 1962-64; asst. office mgr. J.V. McNicholas Transfer Co., 1965-66; ptnr. Reed-Romain & Assocs., 1966-70; pvt. practice acctg., 1970-76; ptnr. Romain-Pendel & Assocs., 1976-78, R-P Computer Services, 1976-80, Romain Pendel Office Rental, 1976-80; pvt. practice acctg., 1978-87; ptnr. Romain & Swanson, P.C., 1987—. Editor: Pennsylvania Accountant, 1980-84. Asst. treas. St. John's Episcopal Ch., 1974-75; mem. exec. bd. Episcopal Churchwoman, 1977-78; leader 4-H Club. Mem. Nat. Soc. Pub. Accts., Nat. Assn. Enrolled Agts. (sec. Pa. chpt. 1972-73), Pa. Soc. Pub. Accts. (state sec. 1978—), Pa. Soc. Enroleld Agts. (pres. 1972-74, exec. dir. 1975-87), Ohio soc. Enrolled Agts., Internat. Graphoanalysis Soc., Shenango Valley C. of C., Saddlemates Saddle Club (Transfer, Pa., treas. 1979), Quota Club, Baldwin Organ Club (Sharon, Pa., pres. 1969), Butler Area Dairy Goat Club. Democrat.

ROMAN, LINDA ANNE, marketing and insurance company executive; b. Milw., June 10, 1947; d. Frank Paul abd Mildred Dattner (Trapp) R. BFA, U. Wis., Milw., 1971; A in Bus. Mgmt., Marquette U., 1987. Cert. in time mgmt., leadership skills svcs. and sales seminars. Benefits analyst Johnson Controls, Milw., 1974-78; claims adminstr. Employee Benefit Claims of Wis., Milw., 1978-83, Nat. Ins. Svcs., Brookfield, Wis., 1982-83; sr. accounts exec. Prime Care Health Plan, Wauwatosa, Wis., 1983—. Mem. NAPS, NAFE. Address: 1233 N Mayfair Rd #301 Wauwatosa WI 53226

ROMAN, MARY BROUMAS, management; b. Wash., Mar. 12, 1932; d. John Constantino and Demetra (Papaliou) Broumas; m. David Allen Watson, June 10, 1954 (div. 1979); 1 child, Robert Allen. BSc., U. Md., 1954. Cert. Tchr., Fla. Tchr. kindergarten City of Balt., 1954-58; tchr. music in elem. and kindergarten Pine Crest Prep., Ft. Lauderdale, Fla., 1962-79; dir. pub. relations devel. Coral Ridge Min. for D. James Kennedy, Ft. Lauderdale, Fla., 1979-82; assoc. dir. s. region Living Bibles Internat. Dr. Ken Taylor, Ft. Lauderdale, Napervill, Fla., Ill.; exec. dir., producer The Joy of Music T.V. Series - Diane Bish, Ft. Lauderdale, Fla., 1985—. Worker Republican Party, Ft. Lauderdale Fla. 1964-68; Mem. Women's League Voters, Ft. Lauderdale Fla. 1967; Bd. Dirs. YMCA, Ft. Lauderdale Fla. 1970-73. Republican. Presbyterian. Office: The Joy of Music Inc 560 East McNab Rd #105 Pompano Beach FL 33060

ROMAN, VALERIE ANN, data processing executive; b. Saugus, Mass., July 24, 1956; d. George Anthony and Esther (Theodore) Anthonakes; m. Anthony Michael Roman, Oct. 2, 1982; children: Matthew Michael, David Michael. BA, Wellesley Coll., 1978. Chief dept. consumer expenditures, system analysis and design Census Bur., Washington, 1978-85; dir. data processing City of Cambridge, Mass., 1985—. Mem. Nat. Assn. Female Execs., Assn. System Mgrs., Mass. Mcpl. Data Processing Assn., Phi Beta Kappa. Home: 32 Blossom Rd Windham NH 03087 Office: City of Cambridge 795 Massachusetts Ave Cambridge MA 02139

ROMANANSKY, MARCIA CANZONERI, book company executive; b. Bklyn., Apr. 22, 1941; d. Nicholas C. and Ellen (Zukas) Canzoneri. BA in History, Coll. of Misericordia, Dallas, Pa., 1962; MLS, Pratt Inst., 1969; MA in Edn., Seton Hall U., 1973; postgrad. Fairleigh Dickinson U., 1980—. Acquisitions libr. St. Peter's Coll., Jersey City, 1963-68; sch. libr. Roselle (N.J.) High Sch., 1968-72; selection libr. Baker & Taylor, Somerville, N.J., 1972-74, chief libr., 1974-80, asst. mgr. program services, 1980-81, mgr. program svcs., 1981-87, dir. pub. libr. mktg., 1987-88; v.p. Yankee Book Peddler, Contoocook, N.H., 1988-89; dir. collection devel. svcs. Blackwell NAm., Blackwood, N.J., 1989—. Contbr. articles to profl. jours. Mem. publicity com. Showhouse, Aux. Muhlenberg Hosp., Plainfield, N.J., 1982, 84. Mem. ALA (tech. svcs. com. 1982-84), Beta Phi Mu. Home: care Blackwell NAm Inc 1001 Fries Mill Rd Blackwood NJ 08012 Office: Blackwell NAm Inc 1001 Fries Mill Rd Blackwood NJ 08012

ROMAN-BARBER, HELEN E., mining company executive; b. Dec. 20, 1946. LLB, U. Paris, 1971, M of Internat. Law, 1972. Chmn., chief exec. officer Denison Mines Ltd. and Roman Corp. Ltd., Toronto, Ont., Can.; chmn. bd. Lawson Mardon Group Ltd., Standard Trust Co. Office: Denison Mines Ltd, S Tower Royal Bank Pla, Toronto, ON Canada M5J 2K2 also: Lawson Mardon Group Ltd, 6711 Mississauga Rd, Mississauga, ON Canada L5N 2W3

ROMANELLO, KAARENLEE, food company official; b. Lawrence, Mass., Nov. 24, 1956; d. Martin Thomas Caughey and Ellen Joan (Sillars) Bell; m. T. MacDonald, June 24, 1978 (div. 1988); 1 child, Craig Vernon; m. Joseph Michael Romanello. Student, Salem (Mass.) State Coll., 1974-76. Customer svc. rep. Rohtstein Corp., Woburn, Mass., 1976-78; customer svc. rep. SS Pierce (name changed Kraft SS Pierce 1987), Woburn, 1978-79, asst. buyer, 1979-84; buyer SS Pierce (name changed Kraft SS Pierce 1987), Peabody, Mass., 1985—, editor What's Cookin newsletter, 1986-87; model Clothes Closet, Reading, Mass., 1986-89. Baptist. Home: 156 Salem St Reading MA 01867 Office: Kraft SS Pierce Inc 1 Technology Dr Peabody MA 01960

ROMANELLO, MARGUERITE MARIE, librarian; b. San Francisco, Feb. 14, 1939; d. Antonio Joseph and Josephine Remilda (Magliano) R. BA cum laude, Lone Mountain Coll., 1960, MA, 1961. Cert. secondary tchr. and librarian, Calif. Instr. Portola Jr. High Sch., San Francisco, 1961-74, Abraham Lincoln High Sch., San Francisco, 1978-81; libr. Francisco Jr. High Sch., San Francisco, 1974-75, instr., 1975-78; libr., media specialist Raoul Wallenberg Traditional High Sch., San Francisco, 1981—; judge U.S. Acad. Decathalon, San Francisco, 1988, 89. Author: MOSAIC, 1975, (play) Scenes from Sense and Sensibility, 1986; editor San Francisco Guitar Soc. Newsletter, 1975-76; exhibitor Festival of Needlework, San Francisco, 1979. Founder, curator Raoul Wallenberg Mus., San Francisco, 1981—; active in Community Adv. Coun., San Francisco, 1968-70, KRON Community Adv. Com., San Francisco, 1985—, Adopt-A-Sch. Program, San Francisco, 1988—, San Francisco Opera Guild. Grantee Office of Supt., San Francisco, 1972, Calif. State Assembly, Sacramento, 1988. Mem. Jane Austen Soc. North Am. (chmn. membership 1986-89), Assoc. Alumni of Sacred Heart, Alpha Psi (treas. Alpha Delta Kappa chpt. 1978-80). Roman Catholic. Home: 15 Red Rock Way #N301 San Francisco CA 94131 Office: Wallenberg High Sch 40 Vega St San Francisco CA 94115

ROMANO, JO ANN PATRICE, public relations executive; b. Bronx, N.Y., Sept. 6, 1963; d. Richard Joseph and Joan Ann (Looney) Murtha; m. Kevin P. Romano. BS in Mktg., SUNY, Plattsburgh, 1985; postgrad., Careers for Women, 1986. Governess, household mgr. Coppotelli's Residence, Southampton, N.Y., 1983-84; resident asst. SUNY, Plattsburgh, 1984-85; jr. account exec. Ultra Mag., N.Y.C., 1985-86; sales rep. Citicorp, N.Y.C., Rockland, 1986-87; account exec. Am. Office Dealer, N.Y.C., 1987-88, Harry Levine Assocs., Inc., N.Y.C., 1988—. Counselor Crisis Ctr., Plattsburgh, 1983. Mem. Am. Mktg. Assn., NAEF, Omicron Delta Kappa. Roman Catholic. Office: Harry Levine Assocs Inc 345 Park Ave New York NY 10154

ROMANO, PAULA JOSEPHINE, laboratory director; b. Rochester, N.Y., Mar. 19, 1940; d. James Richard and Christine (Loboglio) R. AB, Cath. U. Am., 1961; PhD, Duke U., 1975. Instr. dept. pediatrics Georgetown U., Washington, 1976-79; dir. histocompatibility lab. Found. for Blood Rsch., Scarborough, Maine, 1979-81; dir. histocompatibility lab Milton S. Hershey Med. Ctr. Pa. State U., Hershey, Pa., 1981—; asst. prof. pathology and pharm. Milton S. Hershey Med. Ctr. Pa. State U., Hershey, 1981—; sci. adv. staff Maine Med. Ctr., Portland, 1980-81; asst. prof. biology U. So. Maine, Portland, 1980-81. Contbr. to book chpt. and articles to profl. jours. Fellow USPHS, Washington, 1971-74, NIH, Bethesda, Md., 1975-76. Mem. Am. Soc. Histocompatibility (regional lab. inspector 1980—, standards com. 1985—), United Network Organ Sharing (histocompatibility com. 1989—), Del. Valley Transplant Program (adv. coun. 1989—), Am. Bd. Transplant Coords. (adv. com. 1990). Republican. Roman Catholic. Office: M S Hershey Med Ctr PO Box 850 Hershey PA 17033

ROMANO, SHARON MARIE, financial executive; b. Rochester, N.Y., Mar. 19, 1952; d. Andrew A. and June M. (Kruse) R.; m. Joseph L. Petrelli, Nov. 4, 1969; children: Victoria, Joseph Jr. Dir. religious edn. St. Timothy Parish, Columbus, Ohio, 1982-86; office mgr. Govtl. Casualty Insur. Co., Dublin, Ohio, 1986-87; v.p., treas. Demotech, Inc., Columbus, 1987—, also chairperson of bd.; agt. Acceleration Nat. Insur., 1987—. Vol. Girl Scouts of U.S., Columbus, 1982, Am. Cancer Soc., Columbus, 1986—; mem. St. Timothy Sch. Bd. Edn., 1982-86, office of youth ministry, 1983—. Roman Catholic. Office: Demotech Inc 2941 Donnylane Blvd Columbus OH 43235

ROMANOFF, MARJORIE REINWALD, educator; b. Chgo., Sept. 29, 1923; d. David Edward and Gertrude (Rosenfield) Reinwald. Student, Northwestern U., 1941-42, 43-45; B.Ed., U. Toledo, 1947, M.Ed., 1968, Ed.D., 1976; m. Milford M. Romanoff, Nov. 6, 1945; children: Bennett Sanford, Lawrence Michael, Janet Beth (dec.). Tchr., Old Orchard Elem. Sch., Toledo, 1946-47, McKinley Sch., Toledo, 1964-65; substitute tchr., Toledo, 1964-68; instr. Mary Manse Coll., Toledo, 1974; instr. children's lit. Sylvania (Ohio) Bd. Edn., 1977; supr. student tchrs. U. Toledo, 1968-73, 85—, instr. advanced communications, 1977, researcher, 1973-74, instr. Am. Lang. Inst., 1978—; part-time asst. prof. elem. edn. Bowling Green (Ohio) State U., 1978—. Presenter numerous workshops and demonstrations in children lit. and analysis of tchr. behavior, 1976—; mem. rsch. com. Am. Language Inst. U. Toledo, 1985-89, asst. prof. elem. edn. in lang. arts 1985-87. Trustee Children's Svcs. Bd., 1974-76; pres. bd. Cummings Treatment Ctr. for Adolescents, 1978-80; mem. Crosby Gardens Adv. Bd., 1976-82, Community Planning Coun., 1980-84, Citizens Rev. Bd. of Juvenile Ct., 1979—; mem. allocations com. Mental Health and Retardation Bd., 1980-81; mem. Bd. Jewish Edn., 1976—, pres., 1982-84; mem. Jewish Family Svc., 1978-85, v.p., 1980-85; mem. allocations com. Jewish Welfare Fedn., 1980, 89; bd. dirs. Family Life Edn. Coun., 1984—, sec., 1988—; mem. allocations com. Jewish Fedn., 1989-90. Named One of Ten Women of Yr. St. Vincent's Hosp. Guild, 1985. Mem. Tchrs. English to Speakers Other Langs. (presenter 1986), Am. Assn. Supervision and Curriculum Devel., Am. Edn. Rsch. Assn., Nat. Soc. for Study Edn., Toledo Assn. Children's Lit., Nat. Coun. Jewish Women, Orgn. Rehab. and Tng., Hadassah (chpt. pres. regional bd. 1961-64), Northwestern U. Alumni Assn., Phi Kappa Phi, Phi Delta Kappa, Kappa Delta Pi (pres./faculty adv. 1971-75), Pi Lambda Theta (chpt. pres. 1978-80, nat. com. 1979-84). Democrat. Home: 2514 Bexford Pl Toledo OH 43606 Office: U Toledo DCCE 1006 Toledo OH 43606

ROMANT-SOLIS, JANICE ANNE, sales and marketing executive; b. New Orleans, Oct. 24, 1944; d. Salvador and Lorraine (Demazelier) Romant; m. Ray E. Solis, Jan. 30, 1965; children: Ray E. Solis Jr., Janice Lorraine, John Charles. AA, Skyline Jr. Coll., 1974; BA, San Francisco State U., 1976, postgrad., 1976. Employment counselor Employment Devel. Dept., San Mateo, Calif., 1966-73; career developer Employment Devel. Dept., San Mateo, 1966-75; with rsch. and stats. dept. Employment Data and Rsch., San Francisco, 1973-75; fund developer for social svc. programs Ala. County Tng. and Employment Bd./Assn. Community Action Programs, Hayward, Calif., 1975-78; work incentive program counselor, pres. Fashion Dynamics Inc., Foster City, Calif., 1982-86; pres. mktg. and sales Solex Enterprise, Inc., Foster City, Calif., 1987—; trained, devel. nutrition and health oriented distributorship to approximately 7 million annually; pres. distributorship for health and life style itmes Solex Corp., 1987—. Creator "Calif. Kid of Yr." award "Pros for Kids" San Mateo, 1986; fund raiser, chairperson Leukemia Curathon, Ctr. For Ind. Disabled, Mexican Earthquake Relief Fund San Francisco, 1983-86. Named Bus. Woman of Yr. award Am. Bus. Women's Assn. Burlingame, Calif., 1985; elected to San Mateo County Hall of Fame Bd. of Trustees Redwood City (Calif.), 1986; recipient Two Million Dollar Bus. award, 1987, Six Million Dollar Bus. award, 1988, 89. Mem. Nat. Speakers Assn., NAFE, Am. Bus. Women's Assn. (speaker), Direct Sales Assn. Am. (speaker, trainer, cons.), Foster City (Calif.) C. of C., San Jose (Calif.) C. of C. Republican. Roman Catholic.

ROMBERG, LESLIE HOLMES, international marketing management company executive; b. Bklyn., Aug. 11, 1941; d. Alton Butler and Margaret Nichol (Arnett) H.; m. Jon Word Blaschke, 1966 (div. 1968); m. Conrad Louis Romberg, Jan. 6, 1985; 1 stepchild, Allison Romberg. Student, Baylor Coll. Dentistry, 1959-60, U. Tulsa, 1962-64; BS in Chemistry and Biology, Cen. State U., Edmond, Okla., 1966; PhD in Biochemistry, U. Okla., 1968. Head internat. ops. New Eng. Nuclear Corp., Boston, 1969-77 (name now DuPont-NEN); sales engr. Tracor Analytic, Des Plaines, Ill., 1977-79; internat. mktg. and product mgr. Zoecon Industries, Dallas, 1979-80; owner, operator Tex-Am. Internat., Dallas, 1980—; ptnr. Twin Assocs. Engring. Cons., Olten, Switzerland. V.p. Richardson Unitarian Ch., 1985-86, pres., 1986-87, bd. dirs. 89-91, sec. 1988-89; bd. dirs. Greenhill Parents Assn., 1987-88; founder Greenhill Former Parents' Assn., 1988. Mem. Dallas C. of C., Rowlett C. of C., North Dallas Network Career Women, Tex. Assn. Bingo Licensees (pres. 1989-90), Diamond Connection Internat. Republican. Home and Office: PO Box 549 Rowlett TX 75088

ROMEO, LUCILLE MARMOLEJO, psychologist; b. El Paso, Tex., Jan. 8, 1944; d. Ramon and Maximina (Lucero) Marmolejo; m. James P. Romeo, Jan. 12, 1963; children: Richard J., Christopher J. AA in Mental Health, Catonsville Community Coll., 1976; BA, Antioch U., Columbia, Md., 1978; MS, Loyola Coll., Balt., 1982; D of Psychology, U. Denver, 1986. Lic. profl. counselor, marriage and family therapist. Counselor Youth Svc. Bur., Westminster, Md., 1978-83; pscyholgist intern El Paso Guidance Ctr., 1985-86; clin. dir. Adolescent unit Sun Valley Regional Hosp., El Paso, 1986-88, family therapist, 1988-89; psychologist El Paso, 1989—; cons. Tex. Dept. Human Svcs., El Paso, 1987—, Tex. Dept. Human Svcs., El Paso, 1987—; Sun Valley Regional Hosp., El Paso, 1989—; family therapy cons. Tex. Tech. Med. Sch., El Paso, 1988—; adj. faculty U. Tex. El Paso Nursing Dept., 1987—. Bd. mem. Tennis West, El Paso, 1989-90. Mem. Tex. Psychol. Assn., Am. Psychol. Assn. (assoc.), Acad. of Psychologists (bd. dirs.), El Paso Psychol. Soc. (bd. dirs.), El Paso Assn. for Marriage and Family Therapy (pres. 1990—, treas. 1989-90). Office: 1810 Murchison #301 El Paso TX 79902

ROMEO, NANCY C., health care executive; b. Bklyn., Apr. 22, 1956; d. John Salvatore and Christine Marie (LaSala) R.; divorced; 1 child, Maria Elizabeth. BS in Nursing, Hartwick Coll., 1978; M in Pub. Adminstrn., Pace U., 1986. Staff nurse Peekskill (N.Y.) Community Hosp., 1973-78, No. Westchester Hosp., Mt. Kisco, N.Y., 1978-80; pediatric nurse Westchester County Med. Ctr., Vahalla, N.Y., 1980-82; staff supr. Marrs Extended Care Facility, Shrub Oak, N.Y., 1984-85; supr. home health care Westchester County Health Dept., Peekskill, 1982-85, West Jersey Home Health Care, Marlton, N.J., 1985-86; dir. patient services West Jersey Home Health Care, Marlton, 1986; dir. quality assurance Found. Health Preferred Plan, Short Hills, N.J., 1986-88; v.p. Found. Health Preferred Plan, Short Hills, 1987—; healthcare cons. Princeton, N.J., 1988—; v.p Consumer Health Network, Maplewood, N.J., 1988-90, owner, pres., chief exec. officer, 1990—; lectr. in field; career advisor Hartwick Coll., Oneonta, N.Y., 1987—, mem. career planning adv. panel. Recipient Achievement award Nat. Assn. Counties, 1985. Mem. NAFE, N.J. Assn. Female Exec. (bd. dirs.), Am. Coll. Health Care Execs., Am. Coll. Utilization Rev. Physicians, Nat. Assn. Quality Assurance Profls., Soc. Ambulatory Profls., Home Health Assembly N.J., N.Y. Nurses Assn., N.J. Home Health Assembly. Republican. Roman Catholic. Home and Office: 238 Elmwood Ave Maplewood NJ 07040

ROMERO, NANCY LYNN, account executive; b. Syracuse, N.Y., June 3, 1958; d. Donald Joseph and Cecelia (Koster) R. BA, St. Bonaventure U., 1980, MBA, 1987. Resident asst. St. Bonaventure U., Olean, N.Y., 1979-80, asst. to dean, 1984-87; resident mgr. U. So. Calif., L.A., 1980-81; office mgr. Stutzman Inc., L.A., 1981-84; claims adjuster Workers Compensation Fund, L.A., 1983-84; sr. account exec. Barnett Assocs., Garden City, N.Y., 1987—. Mem. N.Y.C. Assn. Unemployment Tax Orgns. (pres. regional chpt. 1989—), St. Bonadventure U. Alumni Assn. (pres. 1987—). Democrat. Roman Catholic. Home: 89 Colonial St East Northport NY 11731 Office: Barnett Assocs 61 Hilton Ave Garden City NY 11530

ROMERO, THERESA HAZELDINE, auditor; b. Las Vegas, N.Mex., Dec. 22, 1959; d. Frank and Delphy Bernice (Baca) R. BBA in Acctg. Mgmt., Coll. Santa Fe, N.Mex., 1981. Acct. Coll. Santa Fe Bus. Office, 1977-81; bookkeeper Great Western Devel., Santa Fe, 1981-85; fin. auditor I N.Mex. Health and Environ. Dept., Santa Fe, 1981-83, fin. auditor II, 1983-88, audit mgr., 1988—; mem. statute com. Govt. Auditor's, Santa Fe, 1989—; mem. joint audit efforts N.Mex. Govt. Auditor's, Santa Fe, 1989—. Mem. Assn. Govt. Accts. (nat. awards com. 1988-89, local pres. 1985-86, chpt. svc. award 1989), inst. Internal Auditors (v.p. 1989—), Coll. Santa Fe Alumni Assn. Democrat. Roman Catholic. Home: 2732 Paseo de Tularosa Santa Fe NM 87505 Office: N Mex Health & Environ Dept 1190 St Francis Dr Santa Fe NM 87503

ROMERO WHEELER, ROSANNA MARIE, architect; b. Mexico City, Oct. 4, 1953; (parents Am. citizens); d. Robert and Bernice Eloise (Blanding) Romero; m. Joseph Chester Wheeler, May 1, 1982; children: Sean Joseph, Robert Brett, Kendra Marie. B Environ. Design, Tex. A&M U., 1977. Registered architect, Tex. Architect Andres Aldrege, Dallas, 1977-81, HOK, Dallas, 1981-82, DiGiammatoe & Assocs., cons. architect, Dallas, 1983-85; pvt. practice, Irving, Tex., 1985—. Mem. AIA. Roman Catholic.

ROMÉY, ROBERTA, publishing executive; b. N.Y.C., Jan. 2, 1953; d. Samuel Wesley and Bertha (Simmons) R.; divorced; 1 child, Tiffanie. Cert. media specialist studies, Inst. New Cinema Artist, 1979; cert. paralegal studies, York Coll., 1985, cert. real estate, 1988. Pres. Fantazia Travel and Transp., N.Y.C., 1981—, Rome Print Pub., N.Y.C., 1986-87; pub., editor Special Affairs Events and Nightlife Network Calendar, N.Y.C., 1987—; dir. Spl. Affairs Network Parties, N.Y.C., 1987—; program coordinator Press/Media Extravaganza Queens County, 1986—; pres. Special Affairs public relations, pub. in-house mag. Chmn. publicity Queens County United Negro Coll. Fund, 1986—; bd. dirs. Neighborhood Housing Services Jamaica, 1985—, Anderson Creative Arts Ctr., N.Y.C., 1978—; vol. N.Y. Urban League Nat. Conv., Black Spectrum Theatre Co. (outreach referral specialist 1977-79). Named Bus. Woman Yr., HUN-E Enterprises, Queens, 1983. Mem. 100 Black Women, SST Entertainment (bd. dirs. 1978—), Struggle Shop Theatre. Democrat. Baptist. Home: 168-22 127th Ave Jamaica NY 11434 Office: Fantazia Travel & Transp 165-48 Baisley Blvd Jamaica NY 11434

ROMICK, JOYCE TRUDEAU, educator; b. Plattsburgh, N.Y., Jan. 23, 1939; d. Norman Samuel and Lurena (Flemming) Trudeau; m. Ronald Virgil Romick, Jan. 3, 1959; children: Cynthia Lynne, Norman Charles. BS in Early Childhood Edn., SUNY, Plattsburgh, 1959, MS in Elem. Edn., 1964; EdS in Reading Edn., Ariz. State U., 1970. Cert. tchr., Ariz., Wash. Tchr. Heartwood Elem. Sch., Tacoma, Wash., 1960-62, Tolleson (Ariz.) Grammar Sch., 1963, Cartwright Elem. Sch., Phoenix, 1963—; intermediate rep. for lang. arts curriculum Consortium Sch. Dists., Phoenix, 1975-77; mem. cadre corps Ariz. Dept. Edn., 1977-79; presenter workshops on creative musical activities. Contbr. articles to Boston Bull., 1982-83. Mem. fin. com. Shepherd of the Valley United Meth. Ch., Phoenix, 1985-90. Mem. Alpha Delta Kappa (state historian 1984-86, 90—, state treas. 1988-90), Phi Delta Kappa. Republican. Office: Cartwright Sch Dist 3401 N 67th Ave Phoenix AZ 85031

ROMIG, MOLLY JANE, publishing executive; b. Massillon, Ohio, Dec. 6, 1962; d. Robert Lee Meese and Sarah Jane (Shook) Valentine; m. Bruce C. Romig, Feb. 20, 1982 (div. Mar. 1987). Student, R. G. Drage Vocat. Sch., 1979-81. Cert. paralegal. Legal sec. The Okey Law Firm, Canton, Ohio, 1981-83; legal sec. Atty. John S. Kuhn, Canton, 1983-88, paralegal, 1987-88; paralegal Roetzel & Andress, Akron, Ohio, 1988; dir. publs. Profl. Reports Corp., Canton, 1988—. Mem. Northeastern Paralegal Assn., Stark County Legal Secs. Assn. (v.p. 1984), Red Lantern Sqs. (Brewster, Ohio). Home: 430 9th St NE Massillon OH 44646 Office: Profl Reports Corp 4571 Stephen Circle NW Canton OH 44718

ROMOFF, JOYCE WEIZER, lawyer; b. Phila., Dec. 4, 1954; d. Samuel and Esther (Segal) W. BBA, Temple U., 1976; JD, Villanova U., 1979. Bar: Pa. 1979. Legal intern Del. City Legal Asst. Assn., Darby, Pa., 1978-79; gen. counsel, sec. Zinman Group subs. and affiliates, Jenkintown, Pa., 1979-82; gen. counsel, asst. sec. Mut. Fire, Marine and Inland Ins. Co. subs. and affiliates, Phila., 1982-87, Underwriters Mgmt. Ins. Co., Phila., 1987-88; assoc. Griffith & Burr, P.C., Phila., 1989—; arbitrator Phila. Ct. Common Pleas, 1985—. Active Phila. Acad. of the Fine Arts, 1988—. Mem. ABA, Pa. Bar Assn., Phila. Bar Assn., Mensa, Lawyers Club (Phila). Republican. Jewish. Office: Griffith & Burr PC 101 W City Ave Bala-Cynwyd PA 19006

ROMZEK, BARBARA S(UE), public administration educator; b. Mt. Clemens, Mich., Aug. 3, 1948; d. Lawrence John and Theresa Agnes (Kociba) R.; m. David Alan Greenamyre, May 19, 1984; 1 child, Wallis Greenamyre Romzek. BA, Oakland U., 1970; MA, Western Mich. U., 1972; PhD, U. Tex., 1979. Asst. instr. U. Tex., Austin, 1977-79; asst. prof. polit. sci. U. Kans., Lawrence, 1979-85, rsch. assoc. Ctr. for Pub. Affairs, 1981-84, assoc. prof. pub. adminstrn., 1985—, chairperson Dept. Pub. Adminstrn., 1988—; cons. pub. affairs various local, state, nat. and internat. orgns., 1980—; interim dir. human resources Bd. Pub. Utilities, Kansas City, Kans., 1986. Contbr. articles to profl. publs. Recipient Redford prize U. Tex., 1977; dissertation fellow AAUW, Washington, 1978-79. Mem. Am. Polit. Sci. Assn. (pub. adminstrn. sect. chairperson 1988-89, mem. exec. coun. 1986—, mem. Gaus award com. 1989—), Am. Soc. Pub. Adminstrn. (governing bd. Kans. chpt. 1983-84, active award com. 1987—), Acad. Mgmt. (Levine award com. 1989), Nat. Assn. Schs. of Pub. Affairs and Adminstrn. (exec. coun. 1990—, dissertation award com. 1988-89, commn. on peer rev. and accreditation 1989—, chairperson com. 1989, rsch. com. 1987—, joint task force on local govt. edn. and internat. City Mgmt. Assn. 1987—), League Kans. Mcpls. (spl. com. on future 1989), Pi Alpha Alpha (nat. coun. 1989—). Office: Dept Pub Adminstrn Univ Kans 318 Blake Lawrence KS 66045

RONALD, PAULINE CAROL, school system administrator; b. York, Yorkshire, Eng., Feb. 28, 1945; came to U.S., 1966; d. Peter Vincent Leonard and Doris Annie (Clark) Hume-Shotton; m. James Douglas Ronald, July 16, 1966 (div. 1986); 1 child, Alexia Denise. Diploma, Harrogate Sch. Art, Yorkshire, 1965, U. New Castle, Upon Tyne, 1966; MA, Ball State U., 1977. Cert. art tchr., Ind. Art tchr. Knightstown (Ind.) Schs., 1966-67, Dunkirk (Ind.) Schs., 1967-68, Richmond (Ind.) High Sch., 1968—; part time tchr. Ind. U., East Richmond 1974-84; set painter Richmond Civic Theatre. Exhibited in numerous group shows; illustrator History of Wayne County, History of Centerville. Coach State Acad. Fine Arts Team Champions for 1988, 2d Pl. for the stateg, 1989; bd. dirs. Richmond Mus. Art, Richmond Civic Theatre. Recipient Best Set awards, also numerous awards for drawing and painting. Mem. NEA, Ind. State Tchrs. Assn. Home: 417 S 20th St Richmond IN 47374

RONAN, ELENA VINADÉ (MRS. WILLIAM JOHN RONAN), real estate broker; b. Havana, Cuba; d. Ricardo Poblet and Virtudes (Alpérez-Inclán) Vinadé; B.A., N.Y. U., 1943; m. William John Ronan, May 29, 1939; children—Monica Ronan Nourie, Diana Ronan Quasha. Broker Douglas, Elliman, Gibbons & Ives, N.Y.C., 1976-88, assoc. broker Sotheby's Internat. Realty, 1988—; pres. Comillas Corp., N.Y.C., 1982-88. Clubs: Cosmopolitan, Maidstone (East Hampton, L.I.), Knickerbocker, Winged Foot Golf, Creek. Home: 655 Park Ave New York NY 10021 Office: 980 Madison Ave New York NY 10021 also: Villa La Pointe du Cap, Au de la Corniche St Ju Cap, Ferrat France

RONEY, MICHELE MARIE, advertising executive; b. Detroit, Sept. 12, 1964; d. Henry Alfred and Julia Francesca (Pirolli) Mollicone; m. Timothy Dwight Roney, June 2, 1989. BFA, Mich. State U., 1986. Keyliner Detroit Art Svcs., Troy, Mich., 1986; graphic coord. ADVO Systems, Inc., Livonia, Mich., 1986-87; account exec. Pub. Corp. Am., Troy, 1987, v.p., account supr., 1987-88, sr. v.p., 1988-90; dir. promotional planning Mars Advt. Co., Southfield, Mich., 1990—. Mem. NAFE, Adcraft Club Mich. Home: 28611 Franklin River Dr Apt 206 Southfield MI 48034

RONGO, LUCILLE LYNN, medical center executive; b. N.Y.C., Sept. 15, 1958; d. Vincent Frank and Lucy Ann (Guilano) R. BS, Mercy Coll., Dobbs Ferry, N.Y., 1984. Asst. supr. accounts receivable Montefiore Med. Ctr., Bronx, 1978-81, asst. mgr. accounts payable, 1981-83, payroll mgr., 1983-87, spl. funds mgr., 1987—. Mem. NAFE, Am. Payroll Assn., Healthcare Fin. Mgmt. Assn. Avocations: drying, preserving and framing flowers; collecting miniatures; art; dance, skiing. Home: 4219 Baychester Ave Bronx NY 10466 Office: Montefiore Med Ctr 111 E 210th St Bronx NY 10466

RONISH, CHERYL ANN, small business owner; b. Detroit, Oct. 5, 1957; d. Loris E. and Barbara Ann (Frantz) Withers; m. Walter V. Ronish Jr., June 26, 1976. Grad., ITT Peterson Sch. Bus., Seattle, 1976; AA, Olympic Coll., Bremerton, Wash., 1988; postgrad., U. Wash., 1989. Legal sec. Wilson Platt Johnson & Irwin, Port Angeles, Wash., 1976-77, Niichel, Rutz & Johnson, Port Angeles, 1977-80, Rusing & Platte, Bellingham, Wash., 1980-83; legal asst. Richard R. Stocking, Port Orchard, Wash., 1983-84; legal asst., bookkeeper Brody & Reynolds, Bremerton, 1984-89; owner, operator word processing and sec. svc., Orange, Calif., 1989—. Mem. Greenpeace, Sierra Club. Office: Excellence in Processing 19082 Country Hollow Orange CA 92669

RONKARTZ, PATRICIA ELLEN, gifted education educator, graphic artist; b. Bay St. Louis, Miss., Aug. 15, 1959; d. Dwight Aurther and Ellen Colleen (Goancke) Payne; m. Stephen Mark Ronkartz, June 9, 1989. BFA in Comml. Art, Miss. U. for Women, 1981, BFA in Art Edn., 1983; MEd, U. S.W. La., 1987; postgrad., Inst. Children's Lit., Redding Ridge, Conn. Cert. gifted edn. and art tchr., computer operator. Engraver, trophy designer Al Summy Signs, Bay St. Louis; graphic artist Columbus (Miss.) Mfrs.; tchr. gifted students grades 6-8 Acadia Parish Schs., Crowley, La. Mem. NAE, La. Assn. Educators, Acadia Assn. Educators (v.p.), Assn. for Gifted and Talented, Prof. Assn. Tchrs. of Gifted and Talented, Crowley Bus. and Profl. Women, Delta Kappa Gamma. Home: 436 Webster St Bay Saint Louis MS 39520 Office: Crowley Middle Sch 401 W Northern Ave Crowley LA 70526

RONNFELDT, JACQUILINE CAROLINE, nurse educator; b. Fremont, Nebr., July 9, 1950; d. Melvin Christian and Leona M.M. (Jensen) Holtorf; m. John H. Ronnfeldt, Nov. 18, 1977; 1 child, John Christian. BS in Nursing, U. Nebr., Omaha, 1972; MA in Adult Edn., U. Nebr., Lincoln, 1979. Staff and charge nurse Nebr. Psychiat. Inst., Omaha, 1972-73; staff nurse med. ICU, VA Med. Ctr., Omaha, 1973-74; instr. nursing VA Med. Ctr., Lincoln, 1974-80; coord. nursing and gerontology North Cen. Regional Med. Edn. Ctr., Mpls., 1980-84; assoc. chief nursing edn. VA Med. Ctr., Seattle, 1984-86, American Lake VA Med. ctr., Tacoma, 1986-88; mgr. nursing edn., acting dir. orgn. devel. Multicare Med. Ctr., Tacoma, 1988—; adj. instr. U. Wash., Seattle, 1984-88; cons. edn. program planning and ind. learning activities, Federal Way, Wash., 1984—. Contbr. articles to profl. publs. Mem. clin. adv. bd. assoc. degree in nursing program Highline Community Coll., Des Moines, Wash., 1986—; mem. adv. bd. Seattle Pacific U. Sch. Nursing, 1988—; instr. CPR, South King County, 1988—; mem grad. program adv. bd. Pacific Luth. U., Parkland, Wash., 1989. Recipient performance award VA Med Ctr., Mpls., 1982, achievement award, American Lake VA Med. Ctr., 1987. Mem. Am. Nurses Assn. (cert. in nursing adminstrn., writer test questions cert. exam. for nursing adminstrn. 1987), Am. Soc. Healthcare Edn. and Tng. (pres. Cascade chpt. 1987-88, treas. 1988-89), Am. Legion Aux., Sigma Theta Tau. Lutheran. Home: 1617 SW 324th Pl Federal Way WA 98023 Office: Multicare Med Ctr PO Box 5299 Tacoma WA 98405-0986

RONSTADT, LINDA MARIE, singer; b. Tucson, July 15, 1946; d. Gilbert and Ruthmary (Copeman) R. Rec. artist numerous albums including Evergreen, 1967, Evergreen Vol. 2, 1967, Linda Ronstadt, The Stone Poneys and Friends, Vol. 3, 1968, Hand Sown, Home Grown, 1969, Silk Purse, 1970, Linda Ronstadt, 1972, Don't Cry Now, 1973, Heart Like a Wheel, 1974, Different Drum, 1974, Prisoner In Disguise, 1975, Hasten Down the Wind,

1976, Greatest Hits, 1976, Simple Dreams, Blue Bayou, 1977, Living in the U.S.A, 1978, Mad Love, Greatest Hits Vol. II, 1980, Get Closer, 1982, What's New, 1983, Lush Life, 1984, For Sentimental Reasons, 1986, Trio (with Dolly Parton, Emmylou Harris), 1986, 'Round Midnight, 1987, Canciones de Mi Padre, 1987, Cry Like a Rainstorm-Howl Like the Wind, 1989; starred in Broadway prodn. of Pirates of Penzance, 1981, also in film, 1983, off Broadway as Mimi in La Boheme, 1984. Recipient Am. Music award, 1978, Grammy awards, 1975, 76, 87, 88, (with Emmylou Harris and Dolly Parton), 89 (with Aaron Neville), Emmy award 1988, Acad. of Country Music award, 1987, 88. Office: care Peter Asher Mgmt Inc 644 N Doheny Dr Los Angeles CA 90069

ROOD, HOPE THORNTON THOMPSON, educator; b. Stamford, Conn., Aug. 29, 1933; d. Hervey and Priscilla (Robinson) Thompson; m. John Nugent Cullen, Oct. 31, 1953 (div. Sept. 1985); children: Priscilla Cullen Kovalsky, John Nugent Jr., Jeffrey Sanford, David Thomas, Hope Anne, Virginia Cullen Rush, Peter, Mark, Matthew, Sarah Hervey; m. Harold Edward Rood, Dec. 27, 1986. Student, Vassar Coll., 1951-52; BA, Alvernia Coll., 1977; MEd, Millersville U., 1981; MSW, Temple U., 1989. Cert. home and sch. visitor, tchr. mentally and phys. handicapped. Substitute tchr. Berks County Intermediate Unit, Reading, Pa., 1977-83, social worker, 1983-89, spl. edn. tchr. learning disabilities, 1989—. Mem. Nat. Assn. Social Workers Inc., AAUW, Assn. for Children with Learning Disabilities, Phi Delta Kappa. Methodist. Home: 335 Reading Ave Shillington PA 19607

ROOF, BETTY SAMS, physician; b. Columbia, S.C., Apr. 13, 1926; s. Grover Melton Saunders and Lucinda Wood (Sams) R.; m. Herman Hugh Fudenberg (div.); children: Drew Douglas, Brooks Roberts, David Melton, Hugh Haskell. BS, U. S.C., Columbia, 1944; MD, Duke U., 1949. Diplomate Am. Bd. Internal Medicine, Am. Bd. Endocrinology and Metabolism. Vol. vis. investigator Rockefeller Inst., N.Y.C., 1949-50; intern Presbyn. Hosp., N.Y.C., 1950-51, asst. resident, 1951-53, asst. physician, 1953-55; attending physician Francis Delafield Hosp., N.Y.C., 1954-55; clin. and research fellow dept. medicine Mass. Gen. Hosp., Boston, 1955-56, research fellow dept. pathology, 1957-58; research fellow Harvard U., 1955-56; research assoc. dept. microbiology and pathology Rockefeller Inst., 1958-59; asst. research physician Cancer Research Inst. U. Calif., San Francisco, 1962-63, assoc. research physician, 1967-71, lectr. medicine, 1971-74, assoc. clin. prof., 1974; assoc. prof. medicine Med. U. S.C., 1974-80, prof., 1980—, asst. dean, 1989—. Mem. Library Bd., Mill Valley, Calif., 1965-68; mem. Tamalpais Nursery Sch. Bd., Mill Valley, Calif., 1968. Am. Cancer Soc. trainee, 1953-55; grantee Am. Cancer Soc., USPHS, Koebig Trust Fund; USPHS fellow, 1949-50. Mem. Am. Assn. Cancer Research, Western Soc. Clin. Research, Endocrine Soc., Internat. Endocrine Soc., Am. Soc. for Bone and Mineral Research, Charleston Med. Soc., ACP, Am. Fedn. Clin. Research, So. Soc. Clin. Investigation, Waring Library Soc., Soc. for Destitute Widows and Children of Dec. Physicians, Pilot Club of Charleston (S.C.) (v.p., 1988-89, pres. 1990-91), Phi Beta Kappa, Alpha Omega Alpha. Contbr. articles to profl. jours. Home: 675 Fort Sumter Dr Charleston SC 29412 Office: Med U SC 171 Ashley Ave Charleston SC 29425

ROONEY, CAROL BRUNS, dietitian; b. Milw., Dec. 20, 1940; d. Edward G. and Elizabeth C. (Lemke) Bruns; m. George Eugene Rooney Jr., July 1, 1967; children: Steven, Sean. BS, U. Wis., 1962; MS, U. Iowa, 1965. Intern VA Med. Ctr., Hines, Ill., 1962-63; resident in dietetics VA Med. Ctr., Iowa City, 1963-65; dietitian nutrition clinic VA Med. Ctr., Hines, 1965-67, 69-70, chief clin. dietetics, 1970-71, chief adminstrv. dietetics, 1971-73; clin. dietitian VA Med. Ctr., Memphis, 1967-68; asst. chief dietetic service Zablocki VA Med. Ctr., Milw., 1974-85, chief dietetic service, 1985—; adj. lectr. Loyola U. Coll. Dentistry, Maywood, Ill., 1969-72; investigator nutrition VA/Med. Coll. Wis., Milw., 1975—, co-dir. ann. clin. nutrition symposium, Milw., 1979—; chairperson task force on ration allowance VA, Washington, 1977-84, mem. dietetic service spl. interest users group, Washington, 1983-85, chairperson tech. adv. group region IV, 1986; mem. dietetic intership adv. bd. St. Luke's Hosp., Milw., 1983-87; lectr., speaker in field, 1965—. Author videocassette, 1976; editor: Nutrition Principles and Dietary Guidelines for Patients Receiving Chemotherapy and Radiation Therapy, 1980; contbr. articles to profl. jours., 1978—. Mem. profl. edn. com. Milw. South unit Am. Cancer Soc., 1976-86, bd. dirs. Milw. South unit, 1984-86, Milw. Div., 1986-87, Wis. div., 1987—, media spokesperson, 1983—, del. to Milw. div., 1984-85, bd. dirs. Milw. div., 1986-87, mem. organizational and expansion com. Milw. div., 1986-87, profl. edn. com. Milw. div., 1986-87, Wis. div., 1987—, mem. taking control com. Wis. div., 1987—, chair nutrition Wis. div., 1989—; mem. med. adv. com. YMCA Met. Milw., 1985—. Recipient Disting. Service award Am. Cancer Soc. Milw. South unit, 1980, Women of Achievement award Girl Scouts Milw. Area, 1987, Leadership award VA, 1989; Paralyzed Vets. Am. research grantee, 1981-83. Mem. Am. Dietetic Assn. (registered, practice groups in mgmt. responsibilities in health care delivery, in gerontoloy nutrition 1980—, in dietetics in phys. medicine and rehab. 1983—, in clin. nutrition mgmt. 1987—, amb., nat. media spokesperson 1983-89, Outstanding Service award 1983-89), Wis. Dietetic Assn. (co-chairperson div. mgmt. practice 1976-77, chairperson 1977-78, bd. dirs. 1981-83, 87—, council on practice 1982-83, coordinating cabinet 1984—, pres. 1988-89, chmn. nominating com. 1989-90, chmn. long range planning com. 1989-90, Wis. Medallion award 1986), Milw. Dietetic Assn. (community nutrition and clin. dietetics and research coms. 1975-76, chairperson ad hoc com. for nutrition and oncology patient 1976-79, clin. dietetics and research study group 1981-90, chairperson 1983-85, pres. 1982-83, by-laws com. 1983-84, chairperson policies and procedures com. 1983-87, pub. relations com. 1983-87, chairperson nominating com. 1984-85), Fed. Execs. Asssn. Home: 18230 LeChateau Dr Brookfield WI 53045 Office: Zablocki VA Med Ctr 5000 W National Ave Milwaukee WI 53295

ROONEY, GAIL SCHIELDS, college administrator; b. St. Francis, Kans., Feb. 15, 1947; d. Fred Harlan and Darlene Mary (Saint) Schields; m. Thomas Michael Rooney, June 27, 1970; children: Shane Michael, Shauna Meghan. BA, U. Colo., 1969; MS, George Williams Coll., 1974; PhD, U. Ill., 1982. Asst. dir. Spl. Svcs. Program Cleve. State U., 1970-71; admissions counselor George Williams Coll., Downers Grove, Ill., 1972-73; coord. of career exploration ctr. Women's Programs Cuyahoga Community Coll., Cleve., 1973-76; vis. asst. prof. Sch. Clin. Medicine U. Ill., Champaign, 1981-82; counselor, instr. Cuyahoga Community Coll., Cleve., 1982-84, dir. counseling, career and psychol. svcs., 1984-85; dir. career, counseling and health svcs. Briar Cliff Coll., Sioux City, Iowa, 1985-88, v.p. for student devel., 1988—; adj. instr., counselor edn., Wayne (Nebr.) State Coll., 1988; program, presenter Myers Briggs Type Indicator, Sioux City, 1986-90. Bd. dirs. Gordon Chem. Dependency Ctr., Sioux City, 1986-89; program adv. coun. St. Luke's Gordon Recovery Ctr., Sioux City, 1989-90. Mem. Am. Psychol. Assn. (div. counseling psychology and psychology of women), Am. Assn. of Counseling and Devel., Nat. Assn. of Student Personnel Adminstrs. Home: 52 Red Bridge Dr Sioux City IA 51104 Office: Briar Cliff Coll 3303 Rebecca St Sioux City IA 51104

ROOS, KAREN LOUISE, physician, educator; b. Pittsburgh, Pa., Sept. 6, 1956; d. David Jules and Marjorie Lois (Flynn) R.; m. Robert M. Pascuzzi, March 26, 1983; children: Anna Marie, Janice Kristina. BS in Biology, U. Pitts., 1977; MD, Hahnemann Med. Coll., Phila., 1981. Diplomate Am. Bd. Psychiatry and Neurology. Resident in neurology U. Va., Charlottesville, 1982-85; asst. prof. Neurology Ind. U., Indpls., 1985—. Home: 4736 Clarkston Ct Zionsville IN 46077

ROOS, SONYA INGRID, interior designer, educator, business owner; b. London, Oct. 24, 1940; came to U.S., 1945; d. Henry S. and Emily (Reich) Rosenfeld; m. Leo Roos, Jan. 29, 1961; children: Joel, Lori, Robin. AS in Interior Design, West Valley Coll., 1980; BA, Newark State Tchrs. Coll., 1971; student, CUNY, 1958-61. Cert. tchr., N.J.; lifetime credential Calif. coll. instr. in interior design. Interior designer Creative Interiors, San Jose, Calif., 1980-81; part-time instr. in interior design West Valley Coll., Saratoga, Calif., 1980-85, Saddleback Community Coll., Mission Viejo, Calif., 1986—; dir. interior design dept. Forma Decor, Newport Beach, Calif., 1985-86; interior designer Rolf Broms & Assocs., Laguna Niguel, Calif., 1986—, designer, owner, 1990—; part-time instr. Orange Coast Community Coll., Costa Mesa, Calif., 1986-89, Rancho Santiago Coll., Santa Ana, 1988-90; guest lectr. pvt. orgns. Mem. Am. Soc. Interior Designers (assoc.), Int. Soc. Inter. Designers (assoc.), AAUW, Soroptimists, Hadassah. Home: 1404 Morningside Dr Laguna Beach CA 92651

ROOSE, CHARLENE JOANN, mobile home community manager; b. Lansing, Mich., Feb. 14, 1950; d. Charles Eldon and Vera Jean (Omans) R.; 1 child, Gordon Scott. Cosmetologist, M.J. Murphy Acad., Lansing, 1968. Lic. cosmetologist. Waitress Ikey Joe's Restaurant, E. Lansing, Mich., 1966-67; cosmetologist Arlette Beauty Salon, Lansing, 1968-69, Parson's Beauty Salon, Lansing, 1969-71, Casey's Beauty Salon, Lansing, 1971-72; sub-contractor Tri-County Painting, Laingsburg, Mich., 1972-81; gen. labor Electro-Wire Inc., Mason, Mich., 1981-83; asst. mgr. Joe's Furnace Cleaning, Lansing, 1983-86; branch mgr. Joe's Furnace Cleaning, Troy, Mich., 1986-87; community mgr. Champion Home Communities, Parma, Mich., 1988-89, Choice Properties, Inc., Benton Harbor, Mich., 1989—. Mem. Nat. Huntington's Disease, Lansing, 1972-76. Mem. Nat. Assn. Female Execs.

ROOT, ANN RENEE, marketing educator; b. Berkeley, Calif., Dec. 11, 1959; d. Dale William and Mildred Jean (Robbins) R. BS, U. Calif., Berkeley, 1981; MBA, U. Mich., 1986, PhD, 1989. Sales clk. Lee Frank Jewelers, Berkeley, 1979-81; asst. dept. mgr. Bullocks Dept. Store, Walnut Creek, Calif., 1981-82, asst. personnel mgr., 1982; ins. mgr. Formosa Plastics, Florham Park, N.J., 1982-83; project mgr. J-M Mfg., Stockton, Calif., 1983-84; teaching and rsch. asst. U. Mich., Ann Arbor, 1985-89; asst. prof. U. Notre Dame, Ind., 1989—; cons. Chrysler Motors, Detroit, 1987-89, U.S. West, Denver, 1988. Editor: Survey of Mktg. Rsch., 1988. Dykstra teaching fellow U. Mich., 1988-89, Phelps fellow, 1986-89, Calif. Alumni scholar, 1979-80, Herrick Found. grantee, 1990. Mem. Am. Mktg. Assn., Calif. Alumni Assn., U. Mich. Alumni Assn., Order Golden Bear, Ladies Notre Dame, Beta Gamma Delta, Alpha Omicron Pi. Office: U Notre Dame Sch Bus Notre Dame IN 46556

ROOT, KATHLEEN JEAN, auditor; b. Republic of Korea, Sept. 1, 1964; came to U.S., 1964; d. Robert E. and Jong S. (Kim) R. AA, Ocean County Coll., 1984; BA, Rutgers U., 1987; postgrad., Fairleigh Dickinson U., 1989—. Registered series 7 rep. Customer svc. rep. Merrill Lynch, Pierce, Fenner & Smith, Somerset, N.J., 1987-88; sr. asst. auditor United Jersey Bank Fin. Corp., Hackensack, N.J., 1988—. Mem. NAFE. Democrat. Home: 409 Hackensack St Carlstadt NJ 07072 Office: UJB Fin Corp 241 Moore St Hackensack NJ 07602

ROPER, MARYANN, administrator of government cancer research agency; b. Bayonne, N.J., July 17, 1949; d. Edward Felix and Helen Dolores (Maryanski) Jedziniak; m. William Lee Roper, Jan 14, 1978; 1 child, William Lee Jr. BA, U. Del., 1971; MD, Pa. State U., Hershey, 1975. Diplomate Am. Bd. Pediatrics. Intern, then resident dept. pediatrics U. Colo., Denver, 1975-77; fellow U. Ala., Birmingham, 1977-81, asst. prof. medicine and pediatrics, 1982; pediatrician Levine, Johnston, Birmingham, 1983-84; sr. investigator Nat. Cancer Inst. NIH, Bethesda, Md., 1985-86, spl. asst. to dir. Nat. Cancer Inst., 1986-87, acting dep. dir. Nat. Cancer Inst., 1987-89, dep. dir. Nat. Cancer Inst., 1989—. Author: (with others) Principles and Practice of Pediatric Oncology; contbr. articles to profl. jours. Bd. dirs. Exodus, Washington, 1989—. Recipient Spl. Recognition award HHS, Washington, 1989; Jr. Faculty Clin. fellow Am. Cancer Soc., 1982-83. Fellow Am. Acad. Pediatrics. Republican. Office: Nat Cancer Inst 9000 Rockville Pike Bldg 31 Bethesda MD 20892

ROPP, ANN L., health facility administrator; b. Cin., June 24, 1939; d. William Howard and C. Louise (Kloecker) R. Diploma in nursing, Good Samaritan Hosp. Sch. Nursing, Cin., 1960; BA, U. Minn., 1970; postgrad., Coll. St. Francis, Joliet, Ill., 1985. Cert. in maternal-child nursing. Clin. nurse specialist Fairview Southdale Hosp., Edina, Minn.; dir. nursing St. Mary's Hosp., Mpls.; nursing cons. Mpls.; dir. maternal-child nursing svcs. Riverside Med. Ctr., Mpls. Author: Guidelines for Education and Practice for Intrapartum Nurses. Mem. NAACOG (pres.-elect), Am. Coll. Healthcare Execs., Sigma Theta Tau (hon.).

ROPP, CARRIE LYNN, window and floor covering contractor; b. Santa Ana, Calif., Aug. 19, 1961; d. Earl Wayne and Judith Ann (Holasek) R. Cert. dental asst., Oreg. Inst. of Tech., 1980; student, Cen. Oreg. Community Coll., 1982, Orange Coast Coll., 1984. Dental asst. Dr. H.H. Kemple DDS, Bend, Oreg., 1980-84; asst. adminstr. Pridemark Ins. Co., Costa Mesa, Calif., 1984-85; acctg. adminstr., systems mgr. Sheward & Son & Sons, Newport Beach, Calif., 1985-88; sr. accounts payable rep. The Baldwin Co., Irvine, Calif., 1988-89; bookkeeper, systems mgr. Sheward & Son & Sons, Newport Beach, Calif., 1989—. Vol. Multiple Sclerosis Soc., 1990—. Republican. Lutheran.

ROQUE, BARBARA BOYD, university program administrator; b. Cumberland, Md., Sept. 22, 1943; d. Robert William and Elinor (Boyd) Fink; m. Magno P. Roque, June 10, 1963; children: Robert Magno, Steven Vincent. RN, Johns Hopkins U., 1964; AA, Allegany Community Coll., Cumberland, 1979; BS, Frostburg (Md.) State U., 1982; JD, U. Pitts., 1985. RN, head neonatal intensive care Mt. Sinai Hosp./Chgo. Med. Sch., 1964-65; intern Sta. WTBO/WKGO, Cumberland, 1979; with State's Attys. Office, Cumberland, 1984; paralegal instr. Sch. of Law George Washington, Cumberland, 1985-86; dir. coll. advancement Allegany Community Coll., Cumberland, 1988—, instr., 1988-89; mem. devel. orgn., pub. rels. com. Md. Community Coll., 1988—; bd. dirs. Western Md. Area Health Edn. Ctr., Cumberland, Allegany Health Rights, Cumberland. Author poem. Nurse blood mobile ARC, Cumberland, 1964; vestry mem. Emmanuel Episcopal Ch., Cumberland, 1988. Allegany Community Coll. scholar, 1979. Mem. Am. Nursing Assn., AAUW, LWV, Cumberland C. of C. (bd. dirs. 1989), Rotary. Democrat. Office: Allegany Community Coll Willowbrook Rd Cumberland MD 21502 Home: 612 Crest Dr Cumberland MD 21502

ROQUEMOUR, GRAYSON, communications consultant; b. High Point, N.C., July 22, 1942; d. Charles Victor and Edna (Burgess) Webb; 1 child, Pharron Roquemour Webb. AB, George Washington U., 1964; MLS, U. Md., 1970. Med. libr. cert. Mktg. and media dir. Century 21 Geiger Real Estate, Tampa, Fla., 1979-81; founder, owner, pres., mktg. and media cons. Grayson Roquemour, Inc., Loganville, Ga., 1982—; lectr., guest speaker, seminar organizer. Contbr. articles to profl. jours.; pub. zoning update newsletter. Consumer adv. and activist environ. protection and zoning reform; mem. Ga. Conservancy Water Quality Task Force; organizing mem. Ga. Strategic Lawsuits Against Pub. Participation Coalition, land use planning Walton County Pub. Interest Rsch. Group; founder Gwinnett County Water Issues Coalition; founding mem. Corridor Area Residents Assn. Mem. George Washington U. Alumni Assn. (Atlanta area rep. fundraiser). Republican. Baptist.

RORISON, MARGARET LIPPITT, reading consultant; b. Wilmington, N.C., Feb. 6, 1925; d. Harmon Chadbourn and Margaret Devereux (Lippitt) R. AB, Hollins Coll., 1946; MA, Columbia U., 1956; Diplôme de langue, L'Alliance Française, Paris, 1966; postgrad. U. S.C., 1967-70, 81—. Market and editorial researcher Time, Inc., N.Y.C., 1949-55; classroom and corrective reading tchr. N.Y.C. public schs., 1956-65; TV instr. ETV-WNDT, Channel 13, N.Y.C., 1962-63; grad. asst., TV instr. U. S.C., Columbia, 1967-70; instrnl. specialist in reading S.C. Office Instrnl. TV and Radio, S.C. Dept. Edn., Columbia, 1971-81; reading cons. S.C. Office Instructional Tech., 1982—. Active Common Cause. Mem. AAUW, Internat. Reading Assn., Am. Ednl. Rsch. Assn., Assn. Supervision and Curriculum Devel., Nat. Soc. Study of Edn., Phi Delta Kappa, Delta Kappa Gamma. Episcopalian. Author instrnl. TV series: Getting the Word (So. Ednl. Communications Assn. award 1972, Ohio State award 1973, S.C. Scholastic Broadcasters award 1973), Getting the Message, 1981. Home: 460 S 23rd St Wilmington NC 28403

RORKE, MARCIA LYNNE, research firm executive; b. Albany, N.Y., Nov. 17, 1942; d. Gerald Dean and Bernice Elizabeth (Ferguson) Bouton; m. Jerome Alan Grad, Sept. 1966 (div. Jan. 1971); m. John Joseph Rorke, III, May 3, 1980; children: Blys Lien Grad, John Joseph. BA, U. Denver, 1969, MA, 1975. Pres., Mohawk Research Corp., Rockville, Md., 1979—; research asst. dept. mass communications U. Denver, 1967-69; instr. dept. history Trinity Coll., Burlington, Vt., 1971-72; research asst. spl. edn. program U. Vt., Burlington, 1971-73; writer/editor Behavior Assocs., Tucson, Ariz., 1973-74; research social scientist Social Systems Research and Evaluation Div. and Ctr. for Social Research and Devel., Denver, 1975-79; treas., dir. Inventors Council Chgo., 1983-86; dir. Ind. Bus. Assn. Ill., 1983-86; cons. The World Bank, Washington, 1977-79, U.S. AID, Dept. State, Washington, 1978, Entrepreneurship Inst., Columbus, Ohio, 1977-79, Owens-Corning Fiberglas, Granville, Ohio, 1977-78, Coler Engring. Co., N.Y.C., 1977-81. Contbr. articles to profl. jours. Mem. alumni exec. bd. Am. Field Service Internat. Scholarships, N.Y.C., 1971-73, exchange student scholar, 1960. Mem. Lic. Execs. Soc. (chmn. small bus. com.), Product Devel. Mgmt. Assn. Office: Mohawk Research Corp 915 Willowleaf Way Rockville MD 20854

ROSA, ELAINE MARIA, esthetician, nutritionist; b. N.Y.C., Feb. 11, 1940; d. Herman Ernst August and Sally Katy (Lazarow) Draeger; m. Edward Thomas Boyle, Aug. 20, 1966 (div. 1977); children: Michele H., Donna A.; m. Nemesio da Silva Rosa, Aug. 8, 1984. AA (with hons.), S.D. City Coll., 1983; postgrad., Tai Chi Inst., San Diego, Calif., 1983. Esthetician Adrien Arpel, San Diego, Calif., 1983-84, Christine Valmay, San Diego, Calif., 1984-85, Aida Grey, San Diego, Calif., 1985-86, Personal Appearances Inc., San Diego, 1985—. Makeover Artist, Newspaper, San Diego Symphony Orch., 1985, Petite Style, 1988, author, Forecast for Faces, Eyes Have It, 1987. Mem. San Diego Cosmetology Assn. Democrat. Jewish. Home: 1844 Parrot St San Diego CA 92105

ROSA, MARGARITA, lawyer, state agency official; b. Bklyn., Jan. 5, 1953; d. Jose and Julia (Mojica) R.; 1 child, Marisol Kimberly Rosa-Shapiro. BA in History cum laude, Princeton U., 1974; JD, Harvard U., 1977. Bar: N.Y. Assoc. Rosenman & Colin, N.Y.C., 1977-79, Rabinowitz & Boudin, N.Y.C., 1981-84; staff atty. Puerto Rican Legal Def. Edn. Fund, N.Y.C., 1979-81; teaching fellow Urban Legal Studies program CUNY, 1984-85; gen. counsel N.Y. State Div. Human Rights, N.Y.C., 1985-88, exec. dep. commr., 1988-90, commr., 1990—; bd. dirs. Pub. Interest Law Found., NYU Law Sch., 1982-84. Bd. dirs. N.Y. Civil Liberties Union, 1981-86, Lower East Side Family Union, N.Y.C., 1982-84. Lombard Assn. fellow Office of U.S. Atty., So. Dist. N.Y., 1975; Revson teaching fellow Charles Revson Found., 1984-85; recipient Hispanic Women Achievers award N.Y. State Gov.'s Office Hispanic Affairs, 1990. Office: NY State Div Human Rights 55 W 125th St New York NY 10027

ROSA, VICKY LYNN, health facility administrator; b. Spokane, Wash., Oct. 3, 1953; d. Richard and Marilyn Ann (Kennedy) Smythe; m. Antonio Rosa, May 2, 1981; 1 child, Victoria Elise. Student, Wishard Hosp., Indpls., 1977; BS in Health Arts, Coll. St. Francis, Joliet, Ill., 1983, MS in Health Adminstrn., 1990. Cert. instr. BLS. Asst. head nurse CCU St. Francis Hosp., Beech Grove, Ind.; info. specialist Ind. Poison Ctr., Indpls.; mgr. patient care Meth. Hosp. EMTC, Indpls.; ctr. mgr. Metro Health/Meth. Hosp., Indpls.; Mem. Am. Coll. Healthcare Execs. Address: 4925 Young Ave Indianapolis IN 46201

ROSADO, PATRICIA VIRGINIA, wholesale distribution executive; b. Madrid, Apr. 21, 1958; came to U.S., 1961; d. William and Juanita (Reyes) R.; m. Timothy Long, July 3, 1975 (div. Nov. 1982); 1 child, Tiffany Linn. Cert. in cosmetology, Allure Career Coll., Tucson, 1976. Owner Long's Beauty Svc., Tucson, 1979-84; dir. esthetics The Headline Hair Design, Helena, Mont., 1984-85; owner Quality Beauty & Health, Las Vegas, Nev., 1985-88; dist. mgr. Aveda Corp., Las Vegas, 1988-89; nat. dir. sales Aveda Corp., Tucson, 1989-90; v.p. sales dept. Caesar's Beauty Products, Torrance, Calif., 1990—; cons. Aveda Corp., Mpls., 1985—. Mem. Toastmasters. Office: Caesars Beauty Products 3230 Fujita St Torrance CA 90505

ROSADO, PEGGY MORAN, actress, singer, dancer, educator; b. Canton, Ohio, Apr. 16, 1946; d. Clarence Ellsworth and Mabel Cecilia (Kearns) Moran; student Northwestern U.; B.S., Kent State U.; M.A., Hunter Coll., 1969; student Arthur Mitchell's Dance Theatre of Harlem, 1971, Am. Ballet Theatre, 1972-74; m. Richard Robert Garcia di Magpiong, Apr. 7, 1979. Dir., lead dancer New World Dancers Inc., N.Y.C., 1971—; dance tchr. performing arts program Franklin K. Lane High Sch., Bklyn., 1970-71; dance tchr., choreographer Lincoln Sq. Community Center, N.Y.C., 1971-76, 81—; tchr. singing La Guardia High Sch., Lincoln Ctr., 1985—, stage dir., Opera Workshop choreographer, 1986— ; emergency dancer Arthur Mitchell's Dance Theatre of Harlem, 1976—; student head NBC Theatre Workshop, N.Y.C., 1960-61; film appearances Serpico, Dog Day Afternoon, Nunzio, Prince of the City, Ragtime, So Fine, Cotton Club; TV series Fame; choreographer New World Journey, 1971, The Creation, 1982, Glück's Orfeo and Euridice, La Guardia High Sch., 1987, Purcell's Dido and Aeneas, 1988. Mem. Actors Equity Assn., Screen Actors Guild, AFTRA, AGVA, Assn. Am. Dance Cos., Am. Indian Community House. Roman Catholic. Home and Office: 345 W 58th St New York NY 10019

ROSAMOND, SANDRA PAULINE (SANDI ROSAMOND), educator; b. Oklahoma City, July 22, 1947; d. Benjamin Franklin and Opal Pauline (Wilson) Creason; m. Marvin Lee Cooke, Dec. 23, 1967 (div. 1979); 1 child, Francis Wesley Cooke; m. Freedus Edward Rosamond, Mar. 17, 1984. BS in Edn., Cen. State U., Okla., 1969; MS in Family Relations and Child Devel., Okla. State U., 1977, postgrad., 1986—. Cert. educator, vocat. educator, Okla. Tchr. Oklahoma City Pub. Schs., 1969-70, Ctr. Sch. Dist., Kansas City, Mo., 1970-72; adminstrv. asst. Grad. Sem., Phillips U., Enid, Okla., 1974-75; tchr. pre-sch. Meml. Dr. United Meth. Ch., Tulsa, 1975-77; officer probation Juvenile Bur. Okla. Dist. Ct., Tulsa, 1977-81, fiscal officer, 1981-82; tchr. Liberty Mounds Schs., Mounds, Okla., 1982-83; tchr. L.E. Rader Juvenile Ctr., Sand Springs, Okla., 1983-86, chairperson tchrs., 1983-86, tchr. intensive treatment, 1986-89; tchr., program devel. specialist U. Okla. Nat. Resource Ctr. for Youth Svcs., Tulsa, 1989—; owner Sandi's Crochet Originals; grant reader Okla. State Bd. Edn., Oklahoma City, 1985; presenter workshops and seminars at nat. confs. Author: Detention Worker Curriculum; contbr. articles to profl. jours. Chairperson, with curriculum devel. sexuality com. Okla. United Meths., Oklahoma City, 1974-77, bd. dirs. placement and adoption bd., 1975-78; mem. rewrite com. Okla. State Dept. Vocat./Tech. Edn. in Home and Community Services, 1988; nat. trainer Advanced Course for Residential Child Care Workers, 1989—, Mng. Aggressive Behavior, 1989—. Mem. Nat. Juvenile Detention Assn., Am. Soc. for Tng. and Devel. (chpt. sec. 1989), Assn. for Supervision and Curriculum Devel., Okla. Assn. Children's Instns. and Agencies, Inc. (exec. bd. dirs.), Child Care Workers Okla. (cert. com.) Omicron Nu, Beta Sigma Phi. Democrat. Home: 14806 W 18th Pl Sand Springs OK 74063 Office: U Okla Nat Resource Ctr 202 W 8th St Tulsa OK 74119-1419

ROSAR, VIRGINIA WILEY, librarian; b. Cleve., Nov. 22, 1926; d. John Egbert and Kathryn Coe (Snyder) Wiley; m. Michael Thorpe Rosar, April 8, 1950 (div. Feb. 1968); children: Bruce Wiley, Keith Michael, James Wilfred. Attended, Oberlin Coll., 1944-46; BA, U. Puget Sound, 1948; MS, C.W. Post Coll., L.I.U., Greenvale, N.Y., 1971. Cert. elem. and music tchr., N.Y.; cert. sch. library media specialist, N.Y. Music programmer Station WFAS, White Plains, N.Y., 1948; prodn. asst. NBC-TV, N.Y.C., 1948-50; tchr. Portledge Sch., Locust Valley, N.Y., 1967-70; librarian Syosset (N.Y.) Schs., 1970-71, Smithtown (N.Y.) Schs., 1971—; pres. World of Realia, Woodbury, N.Y., 1969-86; founder Cygnus Pub., Woodbury, 1985-87. Active local chpt. ARC, 1960-63, Community Concert Assn., 1960-66, Leukemia Soc. Am., 1978—. Mem. Suffolk Sch. Library Media Assn., AAAS, N.Y. Acad. Scis., Am. Mus. Natural History (assoc.), Am. Library Assn., L.I. Alumnae Club of Pi Beta Phi (pres. 1964-66). Republican. Presbyterian. Home: 10 Warrenton Ct Huntington NY 11743 Office: Smithtown Elem Sch Lawrence Ave Smithtown NY 11787

ROSATI, BETH A., systems engineer; b. New Brunswick, N.J., Mar. 28, 1964; d. Mark D. Rosati. BA, Alma Coll., 1986; student, L'Alliance Francais, Paris. Mem. inventory/traffic control staff Broder Bros., Oak Park, Mich.; systems engr. Electronic Data Systems Corp., Southfield, Mich. Mem. NAFE. Home: 10536 W Braemar Dr Holly MI 48442

ROSBROW-REICH, SUSAN R., psychologist; b. Wilmington, Del., Apr. 1, 1946; d. James Manuel and Miriam Faith (Berger) Rosbrow; m. Kenneth I. Reich; children: Elizabeth, Jennifer. BA cum laude, U. Pa., 1968; MS, Columbia U., 1970; PhD, Adelphi U., 1974. Lic. psychologist, Mass. Dir. Ednl. Program on Drugs, New Hyde Park, N.Y., 1972-73; family therapist therapeutic instrn. ctr. Bronx State Hosp., Albert Einstein Med. Coll., N.Y., 1972-73; intern in clin. psychology Harvard U. Health Svcs. Ctr./Cambridge (Mass.) Guidance Ctr., 1973-74; psychologist Chelsea Clinc, Erich Lindemann Mental Health Ctr., Boston, 1974-75; asst. in psychology Dept. Psychiatry Mass. Gen. Hosp., Boston, 1975-77; cons. psychologist Harvard

U. Health Svcs., Cambridge, 1976—; pvt. practice Cambridge, 1974-81, Belmont, Mass., 1981—; cons. supr. Harvard U. Health Svcs., Cambridge, 1976—, Mass. Gen. Hosp., Boston, 1975-77; editorial staff Psychoanalytic Inst. of New England, Boston, 1988—. cons. psychologist Women's Counseling and Resource Ctr., Cambridge, 1974-75. Bella Williams scholarship U. Pa., 1964-68. Fellow Mass. Psychol. Assn.; mem. Am. Psychol. Assn., Am. Psychol. Assn. (affiliate), Mass. Assn. for Psychoanalytic Psychology, Nat. Register of Health Care Providers in Psychology. Home and Office: 54 Elizabeth Rd Belmont MA 02178

ROSCHE, MARY ELLEN, health care management consultant; b. Balt., June 25, 1949; d. John Joseph and Margaret E. (McCourt) R. BS in Med. Tech., Towson State U., 1971; specialist blood bank, Johns Hopkins Hosp., Balt., 1974; MBA in Health Care, Loyola Coll., Balt., 1982. Cert. med. technologist and blood bank specialist. Lab technician Union Meml. Hosp., Balt., 1969-71; med. technologist Good Samaritan Hosp., Balt., 1971-73; med. technologist Johns Hopskins Hosp., Balt., 1973-74, lead med. technologist, 1974-83; blood bank chief technologist Barnes Hosp., St. Louis, 1983-84, assoc. dir., 1984-88; pvt. practice cons. Balt., 1988—; radiology adminstr. Sinai Hosp., Balt., 1989—. Contbg. author: Principles and Practices of Quality Control in Blood Bank, 1980. Vol. Am. Heart Assn., Balt., 1988, Md. Assocs. for Dyslexic Adults & Youth, Inc., Balt., 1989. Mem. Am. Assn. Blood Banks (quality control com. mem. 1975-77), Am. Blood Commn. (commonality in blood banking com. 1974-76), Am. Soc. for Apheresis (bd. dirs. 1984-87), Md. Assn. Health Care Execs., Clin. Lab. Mgmt. Assn. (bd. dirs. 1985-87). Roman Catholic. Home and Office: 435 Alabama Rd Towson MD 21204

ROSCHER, NINA MATHENY, chemistry educator; b. Uniontown, Pa., Dec. 8, 1938; d. Charles Kenneth and Wilma Pauline (Solomon) Matheny; m. David Roscher, Dec. 27, 1964. BS in Chemistry, U. Del., 1960; PhD in Chemistry, Purdue U., 1964. Phys. chemist Nat. Bur. of Standards, 1958-61; rsch. and teaching asst. Purdue U., West Lafayette, Ind., 1960-64, fellow in chemistry, instr. chemistry, 1964-65; instr. U. Tex., Austin, 1965-67; sr. staff chemist Coca-Cola Export Corp., 1967-68; asst. prof. Douglass Coll., Rutgers U., The State U., 1968-74, asst. dean, 1971-74; dir. acad. adminstrn. Am. U., Washington, 1974-76, assoc. prof. chemistry, 1974-79, prof., 1979—, assoc. dean grad. affairs Coll. Arts and Scis., 1976-79, vice-provost acad. svcs., 1979-82, vice provost for acad. affairs, 1982-85, dean faculty affairs, 1981-85; program dir. sci. edn., NSF, 1986—; lectr. in field. Contbr. articles to profl. jours. Standard Oil fellow, 1961-62, David Ross fellow, 1963-64, Rutgers U. Rsch. Fund, Biomed. Support grantee. Fellow AAAS, Am. Inst. Chemists (profl. opportunities for women com., pres. dist. inst. chemists 1978-79, sec. 1976-77, fin. com. 1983-87, exec. com., bd. dirs. 1986); mem. Am. Chem. Soc. (treas. Monmouth county sect. 1970-72, chmn. 1974, profl. programs planning and coord. com. 1976-78, adminstrv. com. 1981-89, Gen. Motors scholar 1956-60, Virgil F. Payne award, numerous others), N.Y. Acad. Scis., AAUA, Assn. Women in Sci., Soc. Applied Spectroscopy, Scientific Manpower Commn. Profls. in Sci. a. Home: 10400 Hunter Ridge Dr Oakton VA 22124 Office: Am Univ Dept Chemistry Washington DC 20016-8014

ROSE, ANITA CARROLL, retired educator; b. New Bedford, Mass., Oct. 14, 1922; d. Louis Arthur and Aline (Chicoine) Carroll; m. Anthony E. Rose, Sept. 24, 1955 (dec.); children: Anthony David, Stephen Arthur. BA, Southeastern Mass. U., 1971; MAT, R.I. Coll., 1975. Exec. sec. Berkshire-Hathaway, Inc., New Bedford, 1941-55, New Bedford Cancer Soc., 1956-59; tchr. French and English New Bedford Pub. Schs., 1971-88; ret., 1988. Pres. New Bedford Jr. Women's Club, 1950-51; v.p. Cath. Women's Club, 1957-59, del. Coun. of Women's Orgns., 1989—; pres. Fairhaven Mothers' Club, 1967-69, book chmn. 1989—; mem. Fairhaven Town Meeting, Mass., 1965—; trustee Millicent Libr., Fairhaven, 1980—; rec. sec. Fairhaven Improvement Assn., 1982—; sec. Fairhaven Rep. Town Com., 1980—; bd. dirs. St. Anne Credit Union, New Bedford, 1988—, mem. adv. coun. Coastline Elderly Svc. Inc., 1988—; del. Mass. Rep. Conv., 1974, 82, 86, 90; mem. YWCA, Old Dartmouth Hist. Assn., Friends of the Zeiterion Theatre. Mem. AAUW (pres. Coll. Club New Bedford Inc. 1983-85, 1st v.p. 1989—, del. nat. conv. 1981, 83, 85, chmn. nominating com. Mass. div. 1988—), Tri-County Music Assn. (bd. dirs. 1988—), Southea. Mass. U. Alumni Assn., R.I. Coll. Alumni Assn., Southea. Mass. Assn. of Social Studies, New Bedford Glass Soc., Mil. Order of the World Wars, Am. Ex-Prisoners of War, St. Joseph's Couples' Club (pres. 1987-88), Fairhaven Colonial Club (2nd v.p. 1988—). Home: 49 Laurel St Fairhaven MA 02719

ROSE, BARBARA BLANCHARD, antique dealer; b. Evanston, Ill., Jan. 28, 1927; d. William and Elizabeth (Corey) Blanchard; m. William Richard Rose, June 19, 1948; children: Peter, Susan, Michael. BA, Colo. Coll., 1945; postgrad. Northwestern U., 1946, Mich. Coll. Mining and Tech., 1948. Copy writer Needham Louis & Brorby, Chgo., 1946; clk. Northwestern U., Evanston, Ill., 1947-48; owner Compass Rose Antiques, Geneva, Ill., 1971—. Mem. sch. bd. Dist. 4, Dist. 220, Barrington, Ill., 1960-65, 71-76, 80-84; bd. dirs. Barrington Youth Services, 1986—, Family Service South Lake County, 1985—. Mem. League Women Voters. Republican. Presbyterian. Office: Compass Rose Antiques 402 State St Geneva IL 60134

ROSE, BARBARA ELAINE, transportation services company official; b. Snyder, Tex., Aug. 20, 1951; d. Joe and Ruth (Tedder) R.; 1 child, Simon Cody. Student, Tarrant County Jr. Coll., Hurst, Tex., 1969-71. Receptionist Tex. Rangers Baseball Club, Arlington, 1972-73; jr. exec. S.W. Crysler-Plymouth, Dallas, 1973-78; saleswoman Caraven Refrigerated Cargo, Irving, Tex., 1978-84, Alterman Transp. Lines, Dallas, 1984-85; sales rep. Aero Precision, Arlington, Tex., 1985-87, Jenco Electronics, Grand Prairie, Tex., 1987-88, FFE Transp. Svcs., Inc., Dallas, 1988—. Campaigner Arlington Dem. Com., 1988. Mem. Transp. Club Dallas, NAFE, NOW, Am. Bus. Womens Assn. Baptist. Office: FFE Transp Svcs Inc 318 Cadiz St Dallas TX 75265

ROSE, CANDACE KORNER, company executive; b. Coral Gables, Fla., Aug. 31, 1956; d. Robert David and Jean (Bain) Korner; m. John Butterworth Rose, Aug. 12, 1979; children: David Finley, Catherine Jean. AA, Miami Dade Community Coll., 1977; postgrad., Appalachian State U., Boone, N.C., 1978-80. HUD closing agent Korner & McIntyre, Coral Gables, Fla., 1982-84; real property, paralegal, office mgr. Robert D. Korner Atty., Coral Gables, Fla., 1984—; v.p. Trail Title, Inc., Miami, 1985—. Dir.: (play) You're A Good Man Charlie Brown, 1987; Tech. dir. (play) Oh Jonah, 1988. Dir. Players for the Prince, Coral Gables United Meth. Ch., 1987, right fielder, 1987—, Sunday sch. tchr., 1985—. Mem. Alpha Psi Omega. Republican. Methodist. Office: Trail Title Inc 4505 W Flager St #201 Miami FL 33134

ROSE, CHERYL ROMPREY, counseling psychologist; b. Laconia, N.H., Nov. 15, 1949; d. Thomas Adrian Romprey and Vera Irene (Swift) Curry; m. Clinton Richard Rose, Nov. 26, 1981; children: Cydney Ryanne, Chandler Randall. BS, Plymouth State Coll., 1971; MEd, Wayne State U., 1976; PhD, Brigham Young U., 1981. Lic. profl. counselor, Ala. Treatment adminstr. Odyssey House, Salt Lake City, 1975-76; dir. counseling and guidance Jordan Sch. Dist., Copperton, Utah, 1976-81; counselor Family Counseling Ctr., Mobile, Ala., 1982—; counselor Lyons Park Evaluation and Counseling Ctr., Mobile, Ala., 1983-84; supr. practice and grad. students U. South Ala., Auburn, 1983—, instr. edn. svc., 1985—; staff mem. Doctors Hosp., Mobile, 1990. Contbr. articles to profl. jours. Trainer, instr. Contact Mobile, 1985—; presentor Barton Acad.-Mobile Sch. Dist., 1984; pres. Community Health Fairs, Mobile, 1982—; group leader Community Activities Workshop, Mobile, 1982—. Capt. U.S. Army, 1971-74. Decorated Army Commendation medal; Lakes Region scholar, 1967. Mem. Am. Psychol. Assn., Mobile Assn. Psychologists. Democrat. Roman Catholic. Clubs: New Mobilians, St. Andrews County. Avocations: golf, creative writing, sports. Home: 105 E Claridge Rd Mobile AL 36608 Office: Family Counseling Ctr 6 S Florida St Mobile AL 36606

ROSE, DEBORAH ELIZABETH, auditor, consultant, accountant; b. Toledo, July 21, 1956; d. James David and Marlene Frances (Roach) R. BBA, U. Mo., 1978, MS, 1979. CPA, Kans., Mo.; cert. internal auditor, fraud examiner. Cost acct. Vendo Co., Overland Park, Kans., 1976-77, tax acct., 1977-78; contr. Vet. Labs., Lenexa, Kans., 1978; staff mgr. Ernst & Whinney, Kansas City, 1979-85; sr. mgr. Price Waterhouse, Oklahoma City, 1985-86; audit mgr. Mut. Benefit Life, Kansas City, 1986—; treas. Exec. Source, Inc., Kansas City, 1986—; bd. dirs. Ins. Internal Auditors Group, Hartford, Conn.; cons. in field. Fellow Life Officer's Mgmt. Inst.; mem. AICPA, Mo. Soc. CPAs, Inst. Internal Auditors, Nat. Assn. Cert. Fraud Examiners (mem. ins. fraud com.), EDP Auditors Assn., Chi Omega (pres. 1977-78, treas. 1980-86). Office: Mut Benefit Life 2323 Grand Ave Kansas City MO 64108

ROSE, DEBORAH JANE, financial planner; b. San Francisco, Apr. 14, 1954; d. Leonard L. Rose and Charlene (Reynolds) Lewis. BS summa cum laude, U. Houston, 1983. Asst. mgr. Home Savs., Houston, 1977-79; mgr. bus. devel. Commonwealth Savs., Houston, 1979-80; pension cons. Houston, 1980-82; regional pres. Gibraltar Savs., Houston, 1982-86; v.p. br. adminstrn. BancPlus, Houston, 1986-87; fin. adviser Rose Fin. Group, Houston, 1988—. Mem. speakers bur. Houston Livestock Show and Rodeo, Houston, 1986—. Mem. Fedn. Houston Profl. Women (dir. ways and means com. 1987, pres. 1989—), Am. Bus. Women's Assn. (program chmn. 1984), Houston C. of C. (life, vice chmn. membership com. 1985-87), Leadership Houston Class VI (grad. Kiwanis). Republican. Home: 3525 Sage #1012 Houston TX 77027 Office: Rose Fin Group 4265 San Felipe 7th Floor Houston TX 77027

ROSE, DENISE BEYE, insurance company executive; b. Portsmouth, Va., Oct. 22, 1953; d. Fred Lewis and Donna Kathleen (Luing) Beye; B.A., U. Ark., 1974; m. Andy Murray Rose, Nov. 23, 1979. With Nationwide Ins., Denver, 1974-75; with Ins. Co. of N.Am., 1975-77, bond underwriter, Dallas, 1976-77; resident mgr. states of Tenn., Ky., Lawyers Surety Corp., Nashville, 1977-85, ind. agy. mgr. Allstate Ins. Co., 1985-87; sr. mktg. mgr. Nat. Grange Mut. Ins. Co., 1987—. Cert. profl. ins. woman, cert. ins. counselor licensed agt.; CPCU. Mem. Nat. Assn. Ins. Women, Tenn. Ins. Assn., Insurers of Tenn., Surety Assn. Nashville, Profl. Ins. Agts. Tenn. (sec. 1989), NAFE, Ark. Alumni Assn. Republican. Baptist. Club: Tenn. 1752 (v.p. 1980, pres. 1981, sec.-treas. 1982-84, treas. 1985-86, bd. dir. 1989-92). Home: 3705 Waterford Way Antioch TN 37013

ROSE, EDITH SPRUNG, lawyer; b. N.Y.C., Jan. 7, 1924; d. David L. and Anna (Storch) Sprung; m. David J. Rose, Feb. 15, 1948; children—Elizabeth Rose Stanton, Lawrence, Michael. B.A., Barnard Coll., 1944; LL.B., Columbia U., 1946. Bar: N.Y. 1947, N.J. 1973. Adminstr., Practising Law Inst., N.Y.C., 1947-48; ptnr. Smith, Lambert, Hicks & Miller, Princeton, N.J., 1974-88; counsel to Drinker, Biddle & Reath, Princeton, 1988—. Mem. ABA, N.J. Bar Assn., Princeton Bar Assn., Women's Law Caucus of Mercer County. Club: Princeton (N.Y.C.). Home: 201 Lambert Dr Princeton NJ 08540 Office: 100 Palmer Sq PO Box 627 Princeton NJ 08540

ROSE, ELAINE OLGA, small business owner, artist; b. Pawtucket, R.I., Mar. 31, 1943; d. Thomas and Olga Ann (Rabchenuk) Graiko; m. Guiteau Lanoue, 1984; children: Tamara, Nicole Lanoue. Student, U. Tenn., 1974. Supr. claims Chesapeake Life Ins., Balt., 1973-75; supr. ins. Kelsey-Seybold, Houston, 1975; pres. Artist's Touch, Inc., Houston, 1976—. Pub. posters Westheimer Festival, 1979—; exhibitor Internat. Art Exhbn., N.Y.C., 1984—, Artexpo Calif., 1986-89; numerous commns. Recipient cert. for contbn. Houston Sch. for Deaf, 1981-82, Merit award Notable Women Tex., 1984, Tex. Star award Channel 8 Auction, 1987. Mem. Art League Houston, Water Color Soc. (so. chpt.), Profl. Picture Framers Assn., Art Dealers Assn., Nat. Artists Equity Assn., Nat. Mus. Women in Arts. Republican. Mem. Assemblies of God. Office: Artists Touch Inc 8800 K Bissonnet St Houston TX 77074

ROSE, ELIZABETH (PATRICIA H. BURKE), author, environmental poisoning specialist, satirist; b. N.Y.C., Sept. 18, 1941; d. William James and Bernadine S. (Ryan) Burke; children: Kimberly, Dana. Nurse, Lenox Hill Hosp. Sch. Nursing, 1962; BA summa cum laude, U. Redlands, 1976. Asst. head nurse emergency room N.Y.C., 1963-66; head nurse San Pedro (Calif.) Hosp., 1968-69; pub. Butterfly Pub. Co., Santa Monica, 1985; radio and TV personality L.A., 1985—; founder Candida Anonymous, Santa Monica, 1985; cons. health profls. Author: Lady of Gray: Healing Candida-The Nightmare Chemical Epidemic, 1985, 2d edit. 1987, 3d edit. 1989, Sainthood and Single Motherhood, 1990. N.Y. State Regents scholar, 1959. Mem. UCLA Alumni Assn. (life), Ind. Writers So. Calif., Womens Nat. Book Assn., Pubs. Mktg. Assn., Cousteau Soc., L.A. County Mus. Art, Better World Soc. (recipient internat. world leader award, Cambridge, Eng. 1989), Nat. Abortion Rights League, Calif. Abortion Rights League, Coalition Against Malathion Spraying, Tesla Soc., L.A. Blue Book Club, Sierra Club. Office: Elizabeth Rose Prodns 2210 Wilshire Blvd Suite 845 Santa Monica CA 90403

ROSE, GAIL ELAINE, wholesale trade company manager; b. Chgo., Sept. 14, 1949; d. Edward Vincent and Ollove Lorraine (Ruska) Ruzicka. AAS, Morton Coll., 1969; BA, Nat. Coll. Edn., Evanston, Ill., 1984. Dental asst. Merrill Shepro, D.D.S., LaGrange Park, Ill., 1968-71; dental asst. instr. Morton Coll., Cicero, Ill., 1969-71; dental asst. Bernard C. Marker D.D.S., Niles, Ill., 1971-73; adminstrv. asst. KYB Corp. Am., Oak Brook, Ill., 1973-78, adminstrv. mgr., Lombard, Ill., 1978-87, dir. adminstrv. dept., 1987-90, v.p. adminstrn., 1990—. Mem., assoc. Ill. Sheriffs' Assn., 1982-86; mem. Republican Nat. Com., Washington, 1980—. Mem. Am. Mgmt. Assn., Internat. Platform Assn., Nat. Assn. Female Execs., Japan Am. Soc. Chgo. Roman Catholic. Lodge: Women of Moose. Avocations: phys. fitness, bicycling, reading. Office: KYB Corp Am 901 Oak Creek Dr Lombard IL 60148

ROSE, JACKIE MICHELLE, computer consultant; b. Phila., Jan. 21, 1954. BS in Phys. Edn. and Biol. Scis., U. Md., 1975; cert. in computer programming, Camden County Coll., 1979; MBA in Mktg., Temple U., 1986. Supplemental and substitute tchr., asst. gymnastics coach Cherry Hill (N.J.) Bd. Edn., 1975-79; with retail ops. div. Navy Aviation Supply Office, Phila., 1979-83, with activity mgmt. div., 1984-85, with systems devel. div., 1985-87; cons. Info. Ctr., Phila. Newspapers Inc., 1987—. Recipient plaque of appreciation Chief Naval Res., 1983, Naval Air Sta., Willow Grove, Pa., 1983. Mem. Beta Gamma Sigma, Phi Alpha Epsilon. Home: 166 Upton House Maple Shade NJ 08052 Office: 400 N Broad St Philadelphia PA 19130

ROSE, JANET LUCILLE, sales executive; b. Goldsboro, N.C., July 23, 1954; d. Conway Joel and Lew (Langston) Rose; m. Murray MacIntyre Lumpkin, Dec. 22, 1978; children: Collier Lewis, Kathryn Rose. BS, Salem Coll., Winston, N.C., 1972-76; student, Bowman Gray Sch. Medicine-Wake, N.C., 1976-78. Cert. Physician Asst., N.C. Physican asst. Salem Coll. Infirmary, Winston, 1978-79; instr. med. asst. program, head coach women's varsity tennis Rochester Community Coll., Minn., 1980-83; med. sales rep. Mead Johnson Pharm. (div. Bristol-Myers U.S. Pharm. Group), Evansville, Ind., 1985-87, sr. med. sales rep., regional sales trainer pharm. and nutritional group, 1987-88; dist. sales mgr. Mead Johnson Pharm. (div. Bristol-Myers U.S. Pharm. Group), Ill., 1988—. Student Mem. Goldsboro City Schs. Bd. Edn., N.C. 1972; pres. Salem Coll. Student Govt., Winston, 1976. Recipient Pfohl award Salem Coll., Winston-Salem, 1976. Fellow Am. Acad. Physician Assts. Democrat. Methodist. Home and Office: 410 Tearose Place Leesburg VA 22075

ROSE, JOANNA SEMEL, cultural board member; b. Orange, N.J., Nov. 22, 1930; d. Philip Ephraim and Lillian (Mindlin) Semel; m. Daniel Rose, Sept. 16, 1956; children: David S., Joseph B., Emily, Gideon G. Cert. Shakespeare Inst., U.K., 1951; BA summa cum laude, Bryn Mawr Coll., 1952; postgrad. St. Hilda's Coll., Oxford U., 1953. Chmn. adv. bd. Partisan Rev., N.Y.C.; chmn. Am. Friends of St. Hilda's Coll.; former pres. bd. dirs. current bd. dirs. Paper Bag Players, N.Y.C.; current bd. dirs. Poets and Writers, Inc., N.Y.C., Guild Hall, East Hampton, N.Y., Nat. Dance Inst., N.Y.C., British Inst., N.Y.C., Musical Theatre Works, N.Y.C., Eldridge St. Project, N.Y.C., Ctr. for Visual History, N.Y.C. Assoc. fellow Berkeley Coll., Yale U. Bryn Mawr European fellow Oxford U., 1952-53. Mem. Cosmopolitan Club, Bryn Mawr Club (N.Y.C.). Home: 895 Park Ave New York NY 10021

ROSE, JUNE H., healthcare financial executive; b. N.Y.C., Aug. 15, 1949; d. Henry Frank and Regina (Hoffman) R. BA in English, NYU, 1970, MBA in Fin., 1985; postgrad. in speech, Northwestern U., 1970-71. Hosp. care investigator N.Y.C. Health and Hosps. Corp., 1971-77, unit mgr., 1977-78, project dir., 1978-83, sr. systems analyst, 1983-84, supervisory systems analyst, 1984-85, sr. mgmt. cons., 1985-86, asst. dir. revenue ops., 1986-87, dir. revenue ops., 1987—. Joint Industry Bd. Electric Industry Teman Meml. scholar, 1966-70, N.Y.C. Mayor's Grad. scholar, 1984; Northwestern U. fellow, 1970-71. Mem. N.Y. Area SAS Users Group, N.Y.C. HHC SAS Users Group (chmn. 1984-85), Beta Gamma Sigma. Home: 60 Gramercy Park N New York NY 10010 Office: NYC Health and Hosps Corp 230 W 41st St New York NY 10036

ROSE, KAREN EVANS, banker; b. Chicago Heights, Ill., Mar. 14, 1959; d. Robert Jr. and Lois Ellen (Herr) Evans; m. William Cudebec Rose, May 25, 1985; children: Michelle Rebecca, William Robert. AB cum laude, Harvard Coll., 1981; MBA, U. Pa., 1985. Planning analyst Mobil Sekiyu K.K. (Mobil Oil Japan), Tokyo, 1981-83; mktg. rsch. cons. Atlantic Fin. Fed. Savs., Bala Cynwyd, Pa., 1984-85; asst. to chief fin. officer MBNA Am. Bank, N.A., Newark, Del., 1985-86, mgr. new product devel., 1986-87, dir. sales, 1987-88, v.p. fin., 1988—. Mem. Beta Gamma Sigma. Presbyterian.

ROSE, MARTHA REA, sales representative; b. New Rochelle, N.Y., Feb. 11, 1938; d. Clarence Dessler and Mary Ann (Brown) Rose; m. James Pryor, Jan. 15, 1968 (div. 1979); children: Debroah Charliste, Darmane Delray, Tanika Surette Carson. Lic. nurse, N.Y. Charge nurse L.I. Nursing Home, Flushing, N.Y., 1968-71; inservice instr. L.I. Nursing Home, 1969-71; with nursing New Rochelle Hosp., New Rochelle, N.Y., 1955-81; sit mgr. assistance Greater Centennial Homes, Mt. Vernon, N.Y., 1983-87; lady attendant Holmes Meml. Funeral Chapel, N.Y.C., 1986—; sales rep. S. Bklyn. Casket Co., N.Y.C., 1988—; inservcie edn. instr. Met. Nursing Home Assn., Flushing, 1969-71. Pres. Greater Centennial Tenants Coun., Mt. Vernon, 1987; sec. United Coun. Ch., Mt. Vernon, 1981; notary Dept. State Office, N.Y. Mem. Nat. Assn. Female Execs., Royal Princess Club, Order of Eastern Star. Democrat. Jewish. Home: 69 W 5th St Mount Vernon NY 10550 Office: South Brooklyn Casket Co 2491 Frederick Douglas Blvd New York NY 10030

ROSE, SHEILA PHILLIPS, data processing executive; b. Columbus, Ga., Feb. 6, 1952; d. Stanley Rudolph and Carol Justyne (Fellows) Phillips. Student, Meadows Bus. Coll., 1975, IBM GSD Customer Edn., 1978-79. Cert. data processor, cert. systems profl. Data processing mgr. Columbus Packaging, Inc., 1978-81, Rossmark Specialty Products, LaGrange, Ga., 1981-82, Lummus Industries, Columbus, 1983-84; dir. mgmt. info. systems Control Laser Corp., Orlando, Fla., 1984-88; mgr. systems and programming Universal Studios Fla., Orlando, 1988—. Mem. NAFE, Data Processing Mgmt. Assn., Assn. for Inst. for Cert. Computer Profls., Mu Alpha Theta. Democrat. Baptist. Home: 2514 Lakeway Br Dr Orlando FL 32809 Office: Universal Studios Fla 1000 Universal Studios Pla Orlando FL 32819

ROSE, SHIELA ANNE, technical products consultant; b. Missoula, Mont., Feb. 27, 1954; d. Robert Sayre and Coralie Mae (Segraves) R. Student, U. Mont., 1972-73; BA Spl. Studies in Counseling and Nutrition, Graceland Coll., Iowa, 1976; postgrad. in counseling, Mont. State U., 1978-79, Cheyenne Aero Tech., Wyo. Records specialist Gallatin County, Mont., 1978-79; prodn. supr. High Country News, Bozeman, Mont., 1979-81; prodn. specialist Insty-Prints, Bozeman, 1981-82; press supr. Star Printing, Gillette, Wyo., 1982-83; owner Rose Enterprises, Wright, Wyo., 1983—; tech. writing/publs. cons. space div. Morton Thiokol Inc. Wasatch Ops., Brigham City, Utah, 1987-89; tech. writing cons. printer products div. Eaton Corp., Riverton, Wyo., 1986-87; bus. plan cons. Diamond "L" Industries Inc., Gillette, 1986-87, Allstar Video Inc., Gillette, 1985; subcontractor Amax Coal Co., Gillete, 1986-89; tech. svcs./drafting cons. Thunder Basin Coal Co., Wright, Wyo., 1983-86. Active Nat. Coalition Against Sexual Assault. Mem. NAFE, Associated Photographer's Internat., Wright Aea C. of C. Avocations: graphic, arts/phtography. Office: Rose Enterprises 2551 Whitetail Dr Antelope Valley Gillette WY 82716

ROSE, SISTER CECILIA, healthcare management administrator; b. Point Marion, Pa., Apr. 16, 1925; d. Fred Hazard and Yvonne Augusta (Bellette) R. BS in Nursing, Cath. U., 1952; MEd, Boston Coll., 1958; cert., St. Louis U., 1978. Instr. nursing Catherine Laboure Sch. Nursing, Boston, 1952-61, dir., 1962-63; dir. sch. nursing St. Mary's Hosp., Troy, N.Y., 1961-62, St. Vincent's Hosp., Bridgeport, Conn., 1965-69, St. Vincent's Med. Ctr., Jacksonville, Fla., 1969-71; dir. St. Vincent's Community Mental Health Ctr., Jacksonville, 1971-75; asst. adminstr. Sacred Heart Hosp., Cumberland, Md., 1975-78, pres., chief exec. officer, 1978-87; v.p. St. Agnes Hosp., Balt., 1987—; sec., bd. dirs. Providence Hosp., Washington, 1981—; bd. dirs. St. Vincent Med. Ctr., Jacksonville, S.S. Cooper Corp., Del., Anne Plume Herron Found., Norfolk, Va. Chmn. Associated Cath. Charities, Cumberland, Md., 1983-84; mem. Roundtable for the Future, Western Md., 1983-87; bd. dirs. Consultation Ctr., Balt., 1989. Fellow Am. Coll. Healthcare Execs.; mem. Am. Soc. Healthcare Risk Mgmt., Nat. Assn. of Quality Assurance Profls. Roman Catholic. Home and Office: St Agnes Hosp 900 Caton Ave Baltimore MD 21229

ROSE, SUSAN CAROL, restaurant executive, chef, consultant; b. Rochester, N.Y., Jan. 29, 1942; d. Frederick Raymond Smith and Grace Eunice (Read) Smith Drum; m. Larry Anthony Rose, Jan. 5, 1963 (div. Jan. 1976); children: John David, Karen Michelle Haines, Patricia Anne. Student, Monroe Community Coll., Rochester, 1959-60; cert. exec. steward, Innisbrook Resort, 1976; student, St. Petersburg Jr. Coll., Tarpon Springs, Fla., 1978-80, Pinellas Voc. Tech., 1987—. With Blue Cross-Blue Shield, Rochester, 1959-67; from coffee service mgr. to exec. steward Innisbrook Resort, Tarpon Springs, 1974-84; catering team supr. Bon Appetit Restaurant, Dunedin, Fla., 1984, Bounty Caterers, Dunedin, 1984; asst. mgr. trainee Wendy's Internat., Largo, Fla., 1984; store mgr. Long John Silver's, Largo, 1984-85; exec. steward, banquet chef, room service mgr., cons. Sandestin Beach Hilton, Destin, Fla., 1985; day mgr. Shells Restaurant, Clearwater, Fla., 1986-87; sous chef, kitchen mgr. Saltwaters Seafood Grille, Palm Harbor, Fla., 1987; exec. steward Adam's Mark Caribbean Gulf Resort, Clearwater Beach, 1987—; garde manger 94th Aero Squadron Restaurant, Las Fontanas Restaurant; cons. restaurant mgmt. Mem. Nat. Assn. Female Execs., Hospitality Industry Assn., Smithsonian Inst. Assocs., Holiday Inn Priority Club, Internat. Travel Club, Encore Travel Club, Clearwater Jaycees. Democrat. Roman Catholic. Home: 1162 Jackson Clearwater FL 33515 Office: Adam's Mark Caribbean Gulf Resort Gulfview Blvd Clearwater Beach FL 34616

ROSE, VELMA ANNETTE, accountant; b. Aurora, Colo., Dec. 18, 1953; d. William Wood and Merlinda Aga (Sheifer) Middleton. BS in Acctg. magna cum laude, U. Colo., 1976, MBA, 1977. CPA, Colo. Sr. auditor Arthur Anderson & Co., Oklahoma City, 1977-80, Peat, Marwick, Mitchell & Co., Denver, 1980-82; mgr. audit Lehman, Butterwick & Co., Lakewood, Colo., 1982-84; controller Regional Transp. Dist., Denver, 1984, fin. dir., 1984-86; dir. budget Denver Pub. Schs., 1986-87, exec. dir. budgetary services, 1987-90, chief fin. officer, 1990—; mem. fin. policies and procedures com. Colo. Bd. Edn., 1986—; bd. dirs., treas. Colo. Sch. Dists. Self Ins. Pool, 1988—; asst. sec.-treas. Denver Pub. Schs., 1988—. Clarinetist Jewish Community Ctr. Orch., Denver, 1980-86. Mem. AICPA, Colo. Soc. CPAs, Govt. Fin. Officers Assn., (reviewer mem. budget awards program 1985—), Council Great City Schs. Bus. Ofcls., Colo. Assn. Sch. Execs. (bd. dirs. 1987-89). Democrat. Jewish. Home: 1928 S Cherry St Denver CO 80222 Office: Denver Pub Schs 900 Grant St Denver CO 80203

ROSE (PIERCE), MARJORIE VIRGINIA, retired educator, retired human services provider; b. Wichita, Kans., Nov. 26, 1926; d. William Otis and Marquerite H.L. (Sherman) Pierce; m. John Riley Rose, Mar. 19, 1945; children: Marguerite Rowe, Alvin C. Rose, Joseph E. Rose, Russell Rose. BA, Friends U., 1962; MS, Emporia State U., 1969. Cert. tchr., spl. edn.-trainable-educable, reading specialist. Tchr. Dist. 259 Stanley Sch., Wichita, 1962-63; tchr. Dist. 353, Madison/Washington, Wellington, Kans., 1963-65; tchr. trainable retarded Dist. 353 Spl. Edn., Wellington, 1965-73; substitue Dist. 259, Wichita, 1973-74; tchr. autistic class Inst. of Logopedics, Wichita, 1974-75, tchr. severly retarded, 1975; tchr. activities of daily living Kans. Elks Tng. Ctr., Wichita, 1980-82, group home provider, 1969-89; house parent in-residence under direction of Kans. Elks Tng. Ctr., Wichita,

1969-89. Author (poetry book) Rough Roads have Beautiful Roses, 1980; author (book of metrics, film strip) Millli Meter Maid, 1975. Recording sec. Area Retarded Citizens, Wichita, 1981-83 (cert. appreciation); pres. South Wind chpt. Am. Bus. Women's Assn., Wichita, 1988-89; tchr. sunshine class St. Lukes United Meth. Ch., Wichita, 1975—; vol. Good Neighbors Nutrition Program, Wichita, 1987-89; tambourine player Goldenairs Orch., Wichita, 1987—; team mem. United Way, Wichita, 1978; vol. Masonic Home, 1987-89 (certificate); substitute house mgr. 10th St. Adult Group House Kans. Elks Tng. Ctr., 1990. Named Woman of Yr. Am. Bus. Women's Assn. Southwind chpt., 1990. Mem. Coun. for Exceptional Child, White Shrine Jerusalem (worthy high priestess), Amaranth Ct. #4 Friendship (faith 1984, asst. conductress), Rebekah-Queen City (chaplain 1989), Order of Ea. Star (martha 1987—, care home visitor Ivy Leaf 1990—), ACATIA White Shrine (queens attendant 1990—, worthy high priestess 1988-89). Republican. Methodist. Home: 339 N Elizabeth Wichita KS 67203

ROSE-HAYES, KARLA LAVON, political consultant; b. Phillips, Tex., Aug. 21, 1947; d. Buster LeRoy and Elna Lavon (Ostrom) Caviness; children: Stephen Brent Turner, Lane Randall Rose, Lydsy Caviness Rose; m. Joseph William Hayes Jr., Sept. 23, 1987. Student, Okal. U., 1965-66, West Tex. State U., 1967-68, El Centro Coll., 1975-76. Ptnr., polit. cons. Panhandle Polit. Cons., Amarillo, Tex., 1988—; cons. Tex. State Bd. Edn., Amarillo, 1989—; aerobic and fitness instr., 1981—. Bd. dirs. Am. Heart Assn., 1983-85, Rape Crises-Domestic Violence Com., 1986-87; mem. staff Campaign to Re-Elect Bill Clements, 1986; conv. devel. dir. Amarillo C. Of. C., 1987; publicity chair Panhandle Disting. Women's Svc. award, 1988; del. Tex. Rep. Conv., 1988-90; mem. exec. bd. Rep. Women, 1988-89; lobbyist Child Abuse, Battered Women, War on Drugs, Oil and Gas rules, Head Injury Fedn, 1985—. Mem. Amarillo Sympnay Guild, Downtown Merchants Assn. (pres. 1984-85), Women's Forum (publicity chmn. 1988-89), Amarillo Women's Network, Am. Mktg. Assn. (program com. 1987-88), Amarillo Art Alliance, Alpha Phi. Republican. Methodist. Home and Office: 3412 Danbury Amarillo TX 79109

ROSELL, SHARON LYNN, physics and chemistry educator, researcher; b. Wichita, Kans., Jan. 6, 1948; d. John E. and Mildred C. (Binder) R. BA, Loretto Heights Coll., 1970; postgrad., Marshall U., 1973; MS in Edn., Ind. U., 1977; MS, U. Wash., 1988. Cert. profl. educator, Wash. Assoc. instr. Ind. U., Bloomington, 1973-74; instr. Pierce Coll. (name formerly Ft. Steilacoom (Wash.) Community Coll.), 1976-79, 82, Olympic Coll., Bremerton, Wash., 1977-78; instr. physics, math. and chemistry Tacoma (Wash.) Community Coll., 1979-89; instr. physics and chemistry Green River Community Coll., Auburn, Wash., 1983-86; researcher Nuclear Physics Lab., U. Wash., Seattle, 1985-88; asst. prof. physics Cen. Washington U., Ellensburg, 1989—. Mem. Math. Assn. Am., Am. Assn. Physics Tchrs. (rep. com. on physics for 2-yr. colls. Wash. chpt. 1986-87, v.p. 1987-88, pres. 1988-89), Am. Chem. Soc., Internat. Union Pure and Applied Chemistry (affiliate). Democrat. Roman Catholic. Home: Rte 5 Box 880 Ellensburg WA 98926 Office: Cen Wash U Physics Dept Ellensburg WA 98926

ROSEN, BETH DEE, traveling agency executive; b. N.Y.C., June 27, 1945; d. Walter and Anne (Goodman) Werfel; m. Martin H. Rosen, June 9, 1968. BA, Queens Coll., 1967, MA, 1970. Tchr. N.Y.C. Bd. Edn., 1967—; lectr. City U. N.Y., 1971-73; pres. Uniglobe Rainbow Travel Inc., Middletown, N.J., 1982—; dir. Uniglobe Rainbow Travel Sc., 1983-87. Columnist "The Courier" newspaper, Middletown, N.J. Office: Uniglobe Rainbow Travel 500 Hwy 35 Union Sq Middletown NJ 07701

ROSEN, CAROL ZWICK, physicist; b. N.Y.C., Jan. 6, 1932; d. Frank and Mae (Kleinberg) Zwick; m. David Edward Golden, Mar. 18, 1956 (div. July 1962); 1 child, Richard Jonathan; m. Bernard Rosen, Oct. 27, 1962; children: Rachel Elizabeth, (adopted) Richard Jonathan. BS in Chemistry, Bklyn. Coll., 1953; MS in Physics, NYU, 1955; PhD in Physics, Stevens Inst. Tech., Hoboken, N.J., 1965. Rsch. assoc. IBM Columbia U., N.Y.C., 1965-67; rsch. assoc. Stevens Inst. Tech., 1967-70; editor Am. Inst. Physics, N.Y.C., 1970-73; asst. prof. York College CUNY, Queens, 1974-75; staff physicist Am. Phys. Soc., N.Y.C., 1975-76; scientist Johnson and Johnson, Skillman, N.J., 1976-79; project mgr. Airco Suerconductor, Cateret, N.J., 1979; digital engr. computer specialist Alvarod Tech. Inc., Fairlawn, N.J., 1980-83; physicist Plessey Electronics (formerly Sugar-Kearfott), Wayne, N.J., 1984—; adj. prof. Queens Coll., CUNY, 1975-76; cons. Am. Inst. Physics, N.Y.C., 1988—. Patentee in field; sr. editor: American Institute of Physics and Pyroelectricity, 1990. Host mom KIDS of Bergen County, Inc., Hackensack, N.J., 1987—. Mem. Am. Phys. Soc., N.Y. Acad. Scis., Metall. Soc., Am. Electroplaters and Finishers Soc., Soc. of Women Engrs. (pres. 1973, v.p. 1972), Sigma Xi. Office: Plessey Electronics Corp 164 Totowa Rd CN 975 Wayne NJ 07474-0875

ROSEN, MRS. JOSEPH E. See BLOCK, JANET LEVEN

ROSEN, KAREN, interior designer; b. N.Y.C., Jan. 14, 1946; d. Leon D. and Beatrice (Willett) Miller; 1 child, Meredith Lauren. Student Boston U., 1964-66; B.S. in Elem. Edn., NYU, 1968; cert. N.Y. Sch. Interior Design, 1971. Pres., KMR Design Group, Inc., N.Y.C., 1973—; color cons. to various mfrs. in design field; interior design work ranges from residential to pub. and comml.; designer custom furnishings; guest lectr. various coll. and real estate seminars; numerous radio and TV appearances; work featured in several major design mags. and newspapers. Recipient S.M. Hexter award for best residential interior, 1981. Mem. Internat. Soc. Interior Designers. Office: KMR Design Group Inc 27 E 63d St Ste 1B New York NY 10021

ROSEN, LESLIE APRIL, nutritionist; b. Bklyn., Dec. 29, 1954; d. Sidney and Lillian Lee (Fierstein) R. BS in Nutrition, Cornell U., 1977; MS in Nutrition and Pub. Health, Columbia U., 1979. Dietitian asst. Kings Pk. (N.Y.) Psychiat. Ctr., 1977-78; dietitian, supr. Margaret Tietz Ctr. for Nursing Care, Jamaica, N.Y., 1978-80, chief therapeutic dietitian, 1980-83; chief clin. dietitian Highland Care Ctr., Jamaica, N.Y., 1983-85, Mencrah Home and Hosp. for the Aged, Bklyn., 1985-86; dir. dietetics L.I. Jewish Med. Ctr. Manhasset (N.Y.) Div., 1986-87; dir. food svc. River Manor HRF, Bklyn., 1987; chief clin. dietitian Mariott Corp./Nyack (N.Y.) Hosp./Jewish Inst. Geriatric Care, New Hyde Park, 1987-90; asst. dir. nutrition Bronx (N.Y.) Lebanon Hosp. Ctr., 1990—; cons. dietitian Phoenix House Programs, N.Y.C., 1985-86. Pres. Tenants Assn. Bd. Dirs., Great Neck, N.Y., 1987, treas., 1988-89. Mem. Am. Dietetic Assn., L.I. Dietetic Assn. Democrat. Jewish. Home: 1275 Fifteenth St Fort Lee NJ 07024

ROSEN, RHODA, obstetrician-gynecologist; b. Trenton, N.J., Jan. 17, 1933; d. Max and Gussic (Thierman) R.; m. Seymour Kanter, Aug. 19, 1956; children: Cynthia, Gregg, Lawrence, Brad. BA, U. Pa., 1954, MD, 1958. Diplomate Am. Bd. Obstetrics and Gynecology. Intern Albert Einstein Phila. Med. Ctr., 1958-59, resident, 1959-62; clin. prof. ob-gyn. Temple U. Med. Sch., Phila.; assoc. staff gyn. exec. com. Albert Einstein Med. Ctr., Phila.; attending physician Rolling Hill Hosp., Elkins Park, Pa.; chmn. gynpathology com. Albert Einstein Med. Ctr., Phila. Fellow Am. Coll. Obstetricians and Gynecologists, ACS; mem. Pa. Med. Soc., Phila. Colposcopy Soc. (pres.), Ex-Resident's Assn. (pres. Albert Einstein Med. Ctr. chpt.), Phila. County Med. Soc. (mem. com.), Phila. Bar Assn. (mem. com.), AMA. Jewish. Home: 1011 Valley Rd Melrose Park PA 19126

ROSEN, SHERRILL LYNN, lawyer; b. Denver, Jan. 26, 1955; d. Maynard Charles and Sandra Marilyn (Collinger) R. BS in Journalism, U. Colo., 1975; JD, U. Mo., 1978. Bar: Mo. 1979, U.S. Dist. Ct. (we. dist.) Mo. 1979. Pub. relations asst. Bicentennial Horizons of Am. Music, St. Louis, 1975-76; legal researcher Ctr. Research and Social Behavior, U. Mo.-Columbia, 1976-77; staff Ind. Legal Services Assn., Columbia, 1976-77, dir., 1977-78; atty. Legal Aid Western Mo., Kansas City, 1978-82; pvt. practice law, Kansas City, 1982—; lectr. Rockhurst Coll., 1982—, Sch. Law U. Mo., Kansas City, 1987, Penn Valley Community Coll., 1988—; cons. Adult Abuse Remedies Coalition, Columbia, 1978-80. Bd. dirs. Housing Assistance, Inc., Kansas City, 1984-86, sec., 1985; vice chmn. Jackson County Bd. Domestic Violence Shelters, 1984-85, sec., 1986-89, chmn. 1989-90. Recipient Vol. award Central Mo. Counties Human Devel. Corp., 1978; Criminal Justice award Rose Brooks Ctr., Inc., 1981; Margit Lasker award, 1982. Mem. ABA (exec. mem. family law sect., domestic violence com. 1984—, co-chmn. 1985-86, chmn. 86-87), Mo. Bar Assn. (family law com.), Kansas City Bar Assn. (adv. com. family law com. 1983—, chairperson 1989), Sigma Delta Chi, Kappa Tau Alpha. Office: 906 Grand Suite 600 Kansas City MO 64106

ROSENAU, BLANCHE GOTTARDO, educator; b. Chgo., Oct. 21, 1918; d. William James and Marie Josephine (Oplt) Hubeny; m. Paul Gottardo Jr., Oct. 24, 1942 (div. Aug. 1957); children: Laura Jane Gottardo Denault, Gail Ann Gottardo Fagan, Paul Gottardo III; m. Milton Joseph Rosenau, Dec. 27, 1967 (dec.). BS, Northwestern U., Evanston, Ill., 1940; MEd, U. fla., 1963. Cert. elem. and art edn. supervision, jr. coll. tchr., Fla. Instr. in art progressive edn. workshop Northwestern Ill., summer 1940, tchr. art lab. sch., 1940-41; tchr. elem., art coord. Fairlawn Sch., Ft. Pierce, Fla., 1958-68; tchr. elem. Chester A. Moore Sch., Ft. Pierce, 1968-69; tchr. art, dept. chmn. Ft. Pierce Cen. High Sch., 1970-81; reviser elem. art sect. curriculum guide St. Lucie County Schs., Ft. Pierce, 1976. Woman's chmn. St. Lucie County Farm Bur., Ft. Pierce, 1966; chmn. Ft. Pierce Opera Guild, 1980—; bd. dirs. St. Lucie County Humane Soc., Ft. Pierce, 1965; bd. dirs., sec. Treasure Coast Opera Soc., Ft. Pierce, 1979—. Mem. St. Lucie County Ret. Educators, AAUW (bd. dirs. 1983-84), Pelican Yacht Club Women's Aux. (bd. dirs. 1982—, pres. 1989-90), Woman's Club of Ft. Pierce (bd. dirs. 1984—, 1st v.p. 1989-90), Noble-ettes (1st v.p. 1988-89), Kappa Delta Pi. Democrat. Presbyterian. Home: 510 Hartman Rd Fort Pierce FL 34947 Office: Treasure Coast Opera Soc 1309 Indiana Ave Fort Pierce FL 34950

ROSENBAUM, ANN PHARMAKIS, portfolio manager; b. Taunton, Mass., Oct. 5, 1949; m. Richard C. Rosenbaum. PhB in Orgnl. Communications, Northwestern U., 1979; MBA, U. Chgo., 1983. Sr. mgr. Price Waterhouse, Chgo.; v.p. Elrick and Lavidge, Chgo.; fin. cons. Merrill Lynch, Chgo. Mem. Fin. Analysts Fedn., Corp. Mission, U. Chgo. Women's Bus. Group (bd. dirs. 1988—), Am. Inst. Banking (bd. regents Chicagoland 1984—), Northwestern Club (bd. dirs. 1989—). Home: 1915 Calvin Ct Riverwoods IL 60015 Office: Merrill Lynch Merchandise Mart Pla Ste 444 Chicago IL 60654

ROSENBAUM, ARLENE, direct marketing services executive; b. Bklyn., Feb. 17, 1944; d. Milton and Clara (Spector) Pollack; m. Steven Alan Rosenbaum, Apr. 5, 1964; children—Laura Ellen, Michelle Lynn. B.S., CCNY, 1964. Software programmer Gen. Foods, White Plains, N.Y., 1966-71; pres., cons. Starline Systems, Inc., New City, N.Y., 1972—; v.p. Magi, Elmsford, N.Y., 1983-85, pres., 1985-88, cons. 1988—. Mem. Direct Mktg. Assn. Office: Magi 3 Westchester Pla Elmsford NY 10523

ROSENBAUM, BARBARA AMDUR, management consultant; b. Balt., May 27, 1952; d. Carl Theodore and Frieda (London) Amdur; m. Henry M. Rosenbaum, Aug. 20, 1973; children: Ted Carl, Paulina Aliza. BA, U. Md., 1974; MBA, U. Rochester, 1976. Ops. rsch. analyst Eastman Kodak Co., Rochester, N.Y., 1976-80; supr. ops. rsch. and analysis Eastman Kodak Co., Rochester, 1980-81, supr. trans. systems, 1981-83, sr. analyst, ops. rsch., 1983-84; mgmt. cons. Cleve. Cons. Assocs., 1984—; treas. Balt. Roundtable of Coun. of Logistics Mgmt., 1989—. Author: (with others) Multi-Level Production/Inventory Control Systems: Theory and Practice, 1981, Service Level Relationships in a Multi-Echelon Inventory System, 1981. Alcoa Found. fellowship, 1975. Mem. Am. Prodn. and Inventory Control Soc., Inst. Mgmt. Sci. (past vice-chmn. Rochester chpt.), Beta Gamma Sigma. Home and Office: 7804 Seven Mile Ln Baltimore MD 21208

ROSENBAUM, BELLE SARA, personal property appraiser, interior designer, educator, museum director; b. N.Y.C., Apr. 1, 1922; d. Harry and Hinda (Sits) Heimowitz; m. Jacob H. Rosenbaum, Mar. 12, 1939; children: Linda Zelinger, Simmi Brodie, Martin, Arlene Levene. Cert. N.Y. Sch. Interior Design, 1945. Sr. mem. Am. Soc. Appraisers, Washington, 1979—; tchr./Judaica, Yeshiva U., 1984—; dir. Mus. Contemporary Judaica; pres. Jarvis Designs, Inc., Union City, N.J., 1955-75, Design Assocs., BLS., Monsey, N.Y., 1970-78; v.p. Lord & Lady Inc., Union City, 1955-70, Cardio-Bionic Scanning, Inc., Spring Valley, N.Y., 1975-78; v.p., treas. Rapitech Systems, Inc., 1985. Author of short stories, 1947-48; contbr. articles on interior design to profl. jours. Bd. dirs. Migdal Ohr Schs., 1971—. Named Woman of Valor State of Israel, 1960; ambulance driver North Hudson chpt. ARC during WWII. Mem. Internat. Soc. Artists (founding mem.), Yeshiva of North Jersey Women (hon. pres. 1955); bd. govs. Yeshiva Univ. mus.; mem. N.Y. State Coun. of Judaic Arts and Letters; mem. editorial bd. Light Found. Clubs: Amit Women (pres. 1955-57) (N.J.), AMI Women (treas. 1948-78), Community Synogogue-Monsey (v.p. 1982—). Avocations: collector of art, antiques, Judaica, artist, gardening, communal and charity work.

ROSENBAUM, JOAN HANNAH, museum director; b. Hartford, Conn., Nov. 24, 1942; d. Charles Leon and Lillian (Sharasheff) Grossman; m. Peter S. Rosenbaum, July 1962 (div. 1970). A.A., Hartford Coll. for Women, 1962; B.A., Boston U., 1964; student, Hunter Coll. Grad Sch., 1970-73; cert., Columbia U. Bus. Sch. Inst. Non Profit Mgmt., 1978. Curatorial asst. Mus. Modern Art, N.Y.C., 1966-72; dir. mus. program N.Y. Council on Arts, N.Y.C., 1972-79; cons. Michal Washburn & Assocs., N.Y.C., 1979-80; dir. Jewish Mus., N.Y.C., 1980—; mem. adv. bd. Pub. Ctr., N.Y.C. Bd. dirs. Artists Space, 1980—; officer Council Am. Jewish Mus., 1981—; mem. policy panel Nat. Endowment Arts, 1982-83. Knighted (Denmark) 1983; European travel grantee Internat. Council Mus., 1972. Mem. Am. Assn. Mus. (cons. 1979—), Assn. Art Mus. Dirs., N.Y. State Assn. Mus. (mem. council). Office: Jewish Mus 1109 Fifth Ave New York NY 10128

ROSENBAUM, LINDA JEAN, educator; b. Peoria, Ill., June 2, 1952; d. James Leo and Phyllis Jean (Sosamon) R. BS in Elem. Edn., Ill. State U., 1974, MS in Elem. Edn., 1984. Cert. tchr., Ill. Tchr. Dwight (Ill.) Elem. Sch., 1974—; presenter workshops on coop. edn., 1986—. Contbr. articles to edn. publs. Unit Leader, counselor-in-tng., asst. dir., then dir. Kickapoo coun. Girl Scouts U.S.A., 1975-82, leader, neighborhood chmn., mem. program com., bd. dirs., camp dir. Centrillio coun., 1975—. Mem. Nat. Coun. Tchrs. Math., Ill. Coun. Tchrs. Math., Nat. Sci. Tchrs. Assn., Dwight Edn. Assn. (pres. 1982, 86-87), NEA, Ill. Edn. Assn., Profl. and Bus. Women's Club, Delta Kappa Gamma. Republican. Home: 316 W Mazon 6 W Dwight IL 60420 Office: Dwight Elem Sch 807 Columbia St Dwight IL 60420

ROSENBERG, ALISON PODELL, government policy official; b. Miami, Fla., Sept. 5, 1945; d. Mortimer I. and Gail (Sklar) Podell; m. Jeffrey Alan Rosenberg, May 4, 1969; 1 child, Robert Aaron. BS in Econs., Smith Coll., 1967. Mng. officer Citibank, N.Y.C., 1967-69; legis. aide Senator Charles Percy, Washington, 1969-80; profl. staff mem. Senate Fgn. Rels. Com., Washington, 1981-85; assoc. asst. adminstr. Agy. for Internat. Devel., Washington, 1985-87; dir. African affairs Nat. Security Coun., Washington, 1987-88; dep. asst. sec. for Africa State Dept., Washington, 1988—. Office: Dept State African Affairs Bur 2201 C St NW Washington DC 20520

ROSENBERG, CAROLE, art dealer, real estate broker; b. Bklyn., Nov. 16, 1936; d. Hugo and Mildred (Wilinsky) Clemente; m. Jerome A. Halsband; children: Michael S. Halsband, Kenneth L. Halsband; m. Alex J. Rosenberg, May 15, 1977. Student, Hunter Coll., 1954-56; BA, Bklyn. Coll., 1956; postgrad., NYU, 1961-62, 64-65. Tchr. N.Y.C. Sch. System, 1958-59, 61-63, Fla. Sch. System, Miami Beach, 1959-61; gallery owner and dir. Original Graphics/Carole Halsband Gallery, N.Y.C., 1971-76; assoc. editor Transworld Art Inc., N.Y.C., 1974-78; exec. dir. Alex Rosenberg Gallery/Transworld Art Inc., N.Y.C., 1978-87; exec. dir., v.p. Ardmore Affiliates Ltd., N.Y.C., 1987—; real estate salesperson The Corcoran Group, N.Y.C., 1986—; curator Alex Rosenberg Gallery, N.Y.C., 1978-87, Artist Rights Today, N.Y.C., 1976-78; treas. 3/69 Owners Corp., N.Y.C., 1984-87, pres., 1987—. Editor: (art catalogs) Henry Moore, Howard Kanovitz, Mark Tobey, Lila Katzen, 1975; assoc. editor (portfolio) An American Portrait, 1976—. Com. mem. Friends of Upper East Side Hist. Dist., N.Y.C., 1983—; mem. art com. Lotos Club, N.Y.C., 1989—. Recipient Spl. Prize for Pub., 7th Internat. Triennial of Colored Prints, Grenchen, Switzerland, 1976, Mgmt. Achievement Award for Innovation, N.Y. Habitat Mag., N.Y.C., 1989. Mem. Real Estate Bd. N.Y.C., Parrish Art Mus. (patron, garden com.), Met. Mus. Art (N.Y.C., sustaining), Whitney Mus. (friend), Mus. Modern Art (contbg.), Nat. Arts Club, Watermill (N.Y.) Beach Club. Democrat. Jewish. Home: 3 E 69th St New York NY 10021

ROSENBERG, EDITH ESTHER, physiology educator, researcher; b. Berlin, Jan. 24, 1928; came to U.S., 1968; d. Theodor and Rela (Banet) Rosenberg; m. Leo Goldhammer, Jan. 1968 (div. 1972). BA, U. Toronto, 1950, MA, 1952; PhD, U. Pa., 1959. Asst. prof. U. Montreal Med. Sch., 1959-62, McGill U., Montreal, 1963-68; assoc. prof. physiology Howard U., Washington, 1968—. Contbr. articles to profl. jours. Recipient Percy Hermant Gen. Proficiency scholar, 1946-50, NRC Can. spl. scholar, 1957-59, 60-62, 63-68; Washington Heart Assn. grantee, 1970-71, NIH grantee, 1972-75. Mem. Am. Physiol. Soc. (physiol., respiration, comparative physiol. sects.), Can. Physiol. Soc., Biophys. Soc., Am. Thoracic Soc., N.Y. Acad. Scis. Jewish. Office: Howard U Coll Medicine Dept Physiology Washington DC 20059

ROSENBERG, ELLEN SMALL, clinical psychologist; b. Chgo., June 27, 1950; d. Raymond Leo and Rose (Small) Small; m. Marc L. Rosenberg, Aug. 30, 1970; children: Douglas Jeremy, Lauren Rebecca. BS magna cum laude, U. Ill., 1971; PhD, Northwestern U., 1975. Lic. clin. psychologist, Ill. Staff psychologist Inst. Psychiatry, Northwestern Meml. Hosp., Chgo., 1975-78; assoc. dept. psychiatry and behavioral scis. div. psychology Northwestern U. Med. Sch., Chgo., 1975—; pvt. practice clin. psychology Chgo., Evanston, Ill., 1976—; staff psychologist Northwestern U. Student Mental Health Svc., Evanston, 1983—; mem. med. staff, affiliated profl. staff Northwestern Meml. Hosp., Chgo., 1977—. Mentor Midwest talent search Northwestern U., Evanston, 1989—; mem. bd., membership chair McKenzie Sch. PTA, Wilmette, Ill., 1986—; benefit com. mental health profl. div. Jewish United Fund, Chgo., 1990. Ill. State scholar Ill. State Scholarship Com., 1968, James scholar U. Ill., 1968-71; Northwestern U. fellow, 1971-72; named Woodrow Wilson Fellowship finalist, 1971. Mem. Chgo. Assn. Psychoanalytic Psychology (founding mem., coun. 1988—, treas. 1985-88, pres.-elect 1990), Am. Psychol. Assn., Ill. Psychol. Assn., Am. Coll. Health Assn., Assn. for the Advancement of Psychology, Nat. Register for Health Svc. Providers in Psychology. Office: 333 N Michigan Ste 3400 Chicago IL 60601

ROSENBERG, GLENDA LERNER, psychotherapist, teacher; b. Houston, Dec. 12, 1939; d. Ben L. and Madeline (Nelkin) Lerner; m. Jack J. Rosenberg, Aug. 1, 1959 (div. 1979); children: Russell, Rene, Ilise. BS, U. Houston, 1962; MEd, Trinity U., San Antonio, 1976. Case worker, therapist Bexar County MHMR, San Antonio, Tex., 1975-76; head of outreach Dept. of Human Svcs., San Antonio, 1975-79; spl. edn. tchr. Northside Ind. Sch. Dist., San Antonio, 1979-84; exec. dir. Staff Tng. Ctr., San Antonio; counselor Edgewood Ind. Sch. Dist., San Antonio, 1976—; psychotherapist Inner Journey, San Antonio, 1987—; workshop presenter Northeast Ind. Sch. Dist., San Antonio, 1987—, Northside I.S.D., San Antonio, Mental Health Assn., San Antonio, Sta. KENS-TV spots on New Thought, 1990. Mem. edn. com., Northside C. of C., San Antonio, 1986-89; bd. dirs. San Antonio Women's Chamber, 1988-90, Ctr. for Peace Thru Culture, San Antonio, 1988-89. Mem. Am. Assn. for Counseling and Devel., Am. Mental Health Counselors Assn., Mind Sci. Found., Mental Health Assn., South Tex. Assn. for Counseling and Devel., Assn. for Parapsychology. Jewish.

ROSENBERG, IRENE VERA, writer; b. Phila., Feb. 8, 1936; d. Max and Fannie (Dwartzin) Cohen; m. Ronald Rosenberg, Aug. 3, 1958 (div. 1988); children: Ellen, David, Michael; m. Alan L. Wurtzel, Oct. 9, 1988. BS, U. Pa., 1958; MA, U. Md., 1973. Freelance playwright Washington; tchr. Writer's Ctr., Bethesda, 1988—; playwright in residence Tex. Women's U., Denton; free lance writer, playwright. Author numerous plays including Onward Victoria, 1978, Third Child, 1985, Stroke Three, 1979. Bd. dirs. Family Trust Va., Richmond, 1988—. Recipient Cine Golden Eagle award for documentary filmscript, 1987. Mem. Dramatists' Guild, ASCAP (award 1980), Women in Film and Video, Washington Ind. Writer, Playwrights Unit. Democrat. Jewish. Home: 1747 Corcoran St NW Washington DC 20009

ROSENBERG, JO, psychiatric social worker, psychoanalyst; b. Albany, N.Y., June 12, 1948; d. Irving H. and Madeline P. Rosenberg; B.A., Goucher Coll., Towson, Md., 1970; M.S., Columbia U., 1973; psychoanalysis cert. (fellow 1975-79), Postgrad. Center Mental Health, N.Y.C., 1979; postgrad. N.Y.U., 1981—. With maternal and child health dept. Bronx (N.Y.) Mcpl. Hosp. Center, 1973-76, coordinator emergency services children dept. child psychiatry, 1976-79; field work instr. N.Y.U. Sch. Social Work, 1977-79; sr. psychiat. social worker div. child and adolescent psychiatry N.Y. Hosp.-Cornell Med. Center, Westchester div., White Plains, N.Y., 1979-82, social work coordinator, 1982—; faculty Cornell U. Med. Sch., 1982—pvt. practice psychoanalysis and psychotherapy, N.Y.C. Fellow N.Y. State Soc. Clin. Social Work Psychotherapists; mem. Nat. Assn. Social Workers, Acad. Cert. Social Workers, Am. Orthopsychiat. Assn., Am. Group Psychotherapy Assn. Contbr. articles on group therapy to profl. jours. Home: 145 Woodland Ln White Plains NY 10607 Office: NY Hosp White Plains NY 10605

ROSENBERG, JUDITH M., brokerage executive; b. N.Y.C., Sept. 17, 1964. BS in Fin., Lehigh U., 1986. Trading asst. Morgan Stanley, N.Y.C., 1986; broker Bear Stearns & Co., N.Y.C., 1987, v.p., 1988, assoc. dir., 1989. Mem. Bklyn. Botanical Garden, The Met. Mus. of Art, The Mus. of Natural History; vol. United Jewish Appeals. Mem. NAFE, Lehigh Alumni. Republican. Office: Bear Stearns & Co 245 Park Ave 9th Fl New York NY 10167

ROSENBERG, LESLIE KAREN, media director; b. Camden, N.J., Mar. 3, 1949; d. Lorimer and Doris Selma (Kohn) R. BS in Radio, TV, Film, U. Tex., 1971. Continuity dir. WEAT-TV/AM/FM, West Palm Beach, Fla., 1971-74; media buyer Wm. F. Haselmire Advt., West Palm Beach, 1974-75, media dir., 1982-85; program and pub. svc. dir. WTBS-TV, Atlanta, 1975-78; nat. traffic coord. WXIA-TV, Atlanta, 1978-80; sr. sales asst. CBS Radio Spot Sales, Atlanta, 1980-82; acct. exec. WRMF-FM, West Palm Beach, 1985; media dir., acct. exec. Merlin Masters & Nomes Advt., West Palm Beach, 1985-88; pres., media dir. Media Magic Plus, Inc., West Palm Beach, 1988—; communications adv. bd. Palm Beach Jr. Coll., Lake Worth, 1972-74. Talent, author various radio commercials (Addy award 1973, 74), talent various TV commercials (Addy award 1974). Bd. dirs. and program co-chmn. Lake Worth (Fla.) Playhouse, 1989—. Mem. Advt. Club of the Palm Beaches (bd. dirs. 1983-85), NAFE, Nat. Acad. Arts & Sciences, Fireside Theatre, U.S. Racquetball Assn. (dir. tournament control 1976-80). Office: Media Magic Plus Inc PO Box 19962 West Palm Beach FL 33416-9962

ROSENBERG, LYNN STEPHANIE, sales executive; b. Paterson, N.J., Nov. 27, 1962; d. Spencer S. and Adele Patricia (Perkowski) R. BS, LIU, 1983. Account exec. Fin. Collection Agys., Paramus, N.J., 1986-87; asst. v.p. sales Kaplan & Kaplan, Neptune, N.J., 1988—. Home: 19 Jefferson St #C3 Hackensack NJ 07601

ROSENBERG, SANDRA, clinical social worker; b. N.Y., Aug. 18, 1942; d. Sydney A. and Rose B. (Kolisch) Weinstock, m. James Lee Rosenberg, Dec. 3, 1967; children: Jennifer, Matthew. BA, U. Miami, 1963; MA, U. Chgo., 1966. Social worker Dept. of Pub. Welfare, Miami, Fla., 1963-64; psychiatric social worker Psychiatry Dept. U. of Chgo. Hosp. and Clinic, Chgo., Ill., 1966-69; social worker Ill. Dept. of Children and Family Services, Chgo., 1970-71; psychiatric social worker Psychosomatic and Psychiatric Inst., Michael Reese Hosp., Chgo.; social worker New Trier Central Sch., Wilmette, Ill., 1979-88, Ill. Children's Home and Aid Society, 1970-71; pvt. practice Solopractice, Highland Park, Ill., 1977—. Lectr., presenter papers to workshops, 1983, 85. Sustaining mem. Art Inst. of Chgo. Mem. NOW, SANE, Nat. Assn. Social Workers, Ill. Soc. Clin. Social Work, Sierra Club. Home: 1126 Lincoln Ave S Highland Park IL 60035 Office: 480 Elm Pl #107 Highland Park IL 60035

ROSENBLATT, ELAINE ROCHELLE, nurse; b. Bronx, N.Y., Aug. 11, 1949; d. Morris and Sophie Beatrice (Katz) R. BA in Anthropology, SUNY, Binghampton, 1971; MS in Nursing with distinction, Lienhard Sch. of Nursing, 1976. Cert. family nurse practitioner. With pub. rels. dept. N.Y. Property Ins. Underwriting Assn., N.Y.C., 1971-73; pub. health advisor venereal disease control N.Y.C. Dept. of Health, 1973-74; nurse's aide Montefiore Hosp., Bronx, 1975; nurse practitioner, mgr. Univ. Hosp., Madison, Wis., 1976—; assoc. preceptor Sch. Nursing, Madison, 1989—. Contbr. articles to profl. jours. Vol. nurse Blue Bus Clinic, 1976-78; mem. adv. bd. United Health Care Project, 1980. Mem. Am. Nurses Assn., Coun.

Primary Health Care Nurse Practitioners, Wis. Nurses Assn. (treas. nurse practitioner coun. 1979-81), Sigma Theta Tau. Democrat. Jewish. Office: Univ Hosp 600 Highland Av Madison WI 53792

ROSENBLATT, JOAN RAUP, mathematical statistician; b. N.Y.C., Apr. 15, 1926; d. Robert Bruce and Clara (Eliot) Raup; m. David Rosenblatt, June 10, 1950. AB, Barnard Coll., 1946; PhD, U. N.C., 1956. Intern Nat. Inst. Pub. Affairs, Washington, 1946-47; statis. analyst U.S. Bur. of Budget, 1947-48; rsch. asst. U. N.C., 1953-54; mathematician Nat. Inst. Standards and Tech. (formerly Nat. Bur. Standards), Washington, 1955—, asst. chief statis. engring., 1963-68, chief statis. engring. lab., 1969-78, dep. dir. Ctr. for Applied Math., 1978-88, dep. dir. Ctr. for Computing and Applied Math., 1988—; mem. adv. com. on indsl. rels. Dept. Stats., Ohio State U., 1981—; mem. adv. com. in math. and stats. USDA Grad. Sch., 1971; mem. Com. Applied and Theoretical Stats., Nat. Rsch. Coun., 1985-88. Mem. editorial bd. Communications in Stats. 1971-79, Jour. of Soc. for Indsl. and Applied Math., 1965-75; contbr. articles to profl. jours. Chmn. Com. on Women in Sci., Joint Bd. on Sci. Edn., 1963-64. Rice fellow, 1946, Gen. Edn. Bd. fellow, 1948-50; recipient Fed. Woman's award, 1971, Gold medal Dept. Commerce, 1976, Presdl. Meritorious Exec. Rank award, 1982. Fellow AAAS (chmn. stats. sect. 1982, sec. 1987—), Inst. Math. Stats. (coun. 1975-77), Am. Statis. Assn. (v.p. 1981-83, dir. 1979-80), Washington Acad. Scis. (Achievement award in math. 1965); mem. AAUW, Am. Math. Soc., Royal Statis. Soc. London, Philos. Soc. Washington, Internat. Statis. Inst., Bernoulli Soc. for Probability and Math. Stats., Internat. Assn. Survey Statisticians, IEEE Reliability Soc., Caucus Women Stats. (pres. 1976), Assn. Women Math., Exec. Women Govt., Phi Beta Kappa, Sigma Xi (treas. Nat. Bur. Standards chpt. 1982-84). Home: 2939 Van Vess St NW Washington DC 20008 Office: Nat Inst Standards and Tech Bldg 101 Rm A438 Gaithersburg MD 20899

ROSENBLATT, LOUISE MICHEL, emerita educator; b. Atlantic City, Aug. 23, 1904; d. Samuel and Jennie (Berman) R.; BA with honors, Barnard Coll., 1925; certificat d'etudes francaises, U. Grenoble, France, 1926; D.Comparative Literature, U. Paris, 1931; postgrad. in Anthropology, Columbia U., 1932-34; m. Sidney Ratner, June 1932; 1 son, Jonathan. Instr., English, Barnard Coll., 1927-38; asst. prof. English Bklyn. Coll., 1938-48; asso. chief Western European sect., chief central reports sect. Bur. Overseas Intelligence, Office War Info., 1943-45; prof. English edn. N.Y. U., 1948-72, prof. emerita, 1972—; vis. prof. Rutgers U., 1972-75; mem. faculty insts. in English, Northwestern U., Mich. State U., U. Pa., U. Ala., U. Alta. (Can.), Auburn U., U. Mass., 1978—; participant Conf. on Methods in Philosophy and the Scis.; cons. in field. Franco-Am. Exchange fellow, 1925-26; Guggenheim fellow, 1942-43; recipient N.Y. U. Great Tchr. award, 1972; Nat. Council Tchr. English Disting. Service award, 1973; Russell award for disting. research, 1980; Leland Jacobs award for Lit., 1981; Disting. Alumna award Barnard Coll., 1990; named to the N.J. Literary Hall Fame, 1988. Mem. MLA, Am. Soc. Aesthetics, Nat. Council Tchrs. English, Nat. Conf. Research in English, Am. Comparative Literature, Internat. Comparative Lit. Assn., Phi Beta Kappa. Author: L'Idee de l'Art pour l'Art, 1931, reprinted, 1976; Literature as Exploration, 1938, 3d rev. edit., 1976, 4th edit., 1983; (with William S. Gray) Reading in an Age of Mass Communication, 1949; Research Development in the Teaching of English, 1963; The Reader, The Text, The Poem: The Transactional Theory of the Literary Work, 1978; (with Robert Parker) Developing Literacy, 1983; (with Charles Cooper) Researching Response to Literature, 1984; (with Patricia Demers) The Creating Word, 1985, Writing and Reading: The Transactional Theory, 1988; (with Jana Mason) Reading and Writing Connections, 1989; also articles on lit. theory, theory of composition, criticism, teaching of lit. Home: 11 Cleveland Ln Princeton NJ 08540

ROSENE, LINDA ROBERTS, organizational consultant, researcher; b. Miami, Fla., Nov. 1, 1938; d. Wilbur David and Dorothy Claire (Baker) Roberts; m. Ralph W. Rosene, Aug. 3, 1957; children: Leigh, Russ, Tim. MA, Fielding Inst., 1981, PhD in Clin. Psychology, 1983. Lic. clin. psychologist. Counselor Rapid City (S.D.) Regional Hosp., 1978-81, Luth. Social Services, Rapid City, 1978-83; v.p. Target Systems Inc., Dallas and Irving, Tex., 1983-85, cons., 1985—; cons. S.W. Home Furnishing Assn., Dallas, 1984, Northwestern Bell, Omaha, 1985; presenter, developer seminars gest-Accor Retail Assn. of Can., So. Home Furnishings Conventions, 1989, Am. Assn. Med. Assts. Pub. Profl. Furniture Merchants mag.; mem. nat. adv. group Nat. Assn. Convenience Stores; presenter Internat. Sheep Products Assocs., 1990, Proper Mgmt. Systems, 1990, S.E. Buying Assocs., 1990; developer copyrighted hiring system, 1985, rev., 1989, copyrighted recruitment tng. system for retail mgmt., 1988, rev., 1989. Bd. dirs. Assn. Children with Learning Disabilities, S.D., 1983-84, West River (S.D.) Alcoholism Services, 1983-84, Health Adv. Com. of Head Start, S.D., 1980-84, St. Martins Acad., S.D., 1971-75; mem. Rapid City Mayor's Commn. on Racial Conciliation, 1971-73, Nat. Trust for Hist. Preservation; charter mem. Nat. Mus. Women in the Arts. Research grantee Nat. Luth. Ch., 1981. Mem. Am. Psychol. Assn., N.C. Psychol. Assn., Aircraft Owners and Pilots Assn., S.W. Home Furnishing Assn., Internat. Platform Assn. Unitarian. Avocations: aviation, bicycling, racquetball, music, birdwatching. Home: 300 Shinoak Valley Irving TX 75063

ROSENFELD, IRENE KANTOR, editorial linguist; b. Boston, Aug. 8, 1919; d. Samuel and Alice (Katz) Kantor; m. Leonard S. Rosenfeld, June 7, 1942; 1 dau., Lynn. B.A., NYU, 1940, postgrad., 1940-42; M. Ed., Harvard U., 1956. Lic. tchr. Mass., Mich., N.Y. Performing pianist, singer, classical guitarist, 1940-55; elem., high sch., grad. sch. tchr., 1955-66; registrar, dir. admissions and student fins. Beth Israel Med. Ctr. Sch. Nursing, N.Y.C., 1966-70; asst. dir. dept. community medicine Hosp. for Joint Diseases and Med. Ctr., N.Y.C., 1971-73; asst. to gen. dir. N.C. Meml. Hosp., Chapel Hill, 1973, cons. ambulatory services, 1974-76; editor Internat. Fertility Research Program, Research Triangle, N.C., 1976-81; freelance multilingual editor, Chapel Hill, 1981—. Founding mem., mem. 1st bd. dirs. Am. Hosp. Assn. Soc. Patient Reps., 1st chmn. conf. and edn. com. Mem. Pi Lambda Theta, Mu Sigma. Author manuals, monographs and articles for profl. publs. Address: 1309 Arboretum Dr Chapel Hill NC 27514

ROSENFIELD, ANN BAKER, development executive; b. Cambridge, Mass., Mar. 7, 1961; d. Alan Robert and Margaret Ann (Young) R.; m. Peter Derrick Gress, Nov. 25, 1989. PhB, Miami U., Oxford, Ohio, 1983. Case adminstr. Hersh & Hersh, San Francisco, 1983-85; scheduler Gov. Richard F. Celeste, Columbus, Ohio, 1985-87; fgn. expert Hubei U., Wuhan, Peoples' Republic China, 1987-89; dir. devel. Planned Parenthood, San Rafael, Calif., 1989-90; dir. devel. and communications Goodwill Industries, San Francisco, 1990—; cons. Support Ctr./CTD, San Francisco, 1990; career adviser Alumnae Resources, San Francisco, 1989—. Mem. Nat. Soc. Fundraising Execs. (newsletter editor 1990), Devel. Execs. Roundtable, Amnesty Internat. (chair, treas. San Francisco group 1990), Phi Beta Kappa, Eta Sigma Phi, Phi Kappa Phi. Home: 673 9th Ave San Francisco CA 94118 Office: Goodwill Industries 2150 Army St San Francisco CA 94124

ROSENKRANTZ, BARBARA GUTMANN, history educator; b. N.Y.C., Jan. 11, 1923; d. James and Jeanette (Mack) G.; m. David P. Bennett, Sept. 5, 1942 (div.); 1 child, Louise; m. Paul Rosenkrantz, Apr. 19, 1950 (dec. 1986); children: Judith, Deborah; m. J. Nathaiel Marshall, 1988. A.B., Radcliffe Coll., 1944; Ph.D., Clark U., 1970. Research assoc. Harvard U., Cambridge, Mass., 1970-71, lectr., 1971-73, assoc. prof. history of sci., 1973-75, prof., 1975—, chmn. history of sci. dept., 1984-89, master Currier House, 1974-79. Author: Public Health and the State, 1972, (with William A. Koelsch) American Habitat, 1973; editor for history Am. Jour. Pub. Health, 1985-89. NIH research grantee, 1970-72; Rockefeller Found. fellow, 1979-80; Ctr. for Advanced Study in Behavioral Scis. fellow Stanford U., 1984, Inst. Medicine fellow; Sherman Fairchild Disting. Scholar, Calif. Inst. Tech., 1989. Fellow Am. Acad. Arts and Scis., Mass. Hist. Soc.; mem. Am. Hist. Assn., History of Sci. Soc., Am. Assn. for History of Medicine. Jewish. Office: Harvard U Dept History Sci Ctr 235 Cambridge MA 02138

ROSENSTEIN, DIANA SHIRLEY, psychologist; b. Chgo., June 9, 1953; d. Leonard Aaron and Elaine Doris (Markovitz) R.; m. Donald Russell Campbell, July 10, 1983; children: Nathaniel Rosenstein, Hannah Rosenstein. MA, U. Pa., 1981, postgrad., 1981—. Lic. psychologist, Pa. Fellow in evaluation psychiatry Inst. of Pa. Hosp., Phila., 1985-86, asst. dir. evaluation unit, 1986, staff psychologist, 1987—, research cons., 1986—; pvt. practice psychotherapy Phila., 1986—; research cons. Jefferson U., Phila., 1988. U. Pa. fellow, 1980, 82, Sigma Xi research grantee, 1981-83, U. Pa. research grantee, 1981-83, Sigmund Miller Found. grantee, 1987. Mem. Am. Psychol. Assn. (assoc.), Personality Assessment, Pa. Psychol. Assn., Phila. Soc. Psychoanalytic Psychology. Democrat. Jewish. Home: 505 Plymouth Rd Glenside PA 19038 Office: Inst Pa Hosp 111 N 49th St Philadelphia PA 19139

ROSEN-SUPNICK, ELAINE RENEE, physical therapist; b. N.Y.C., May 7, 1951; d. Oscar Arthur and Sydell (Zimmerman) R.;m. Jed Supnick. Apr. 21, 1985. BS, Hunter Coll., 1973; MS, L.I. U., Bklyn., 1977. Phys. therapy cons. Lenox Hill Hosp. Home Care, N.Y.C., 1977-83, GHI, Queens, N.Y., 1977-83; VNA UNA, Bklyn., 1977-83; sr. phys. therapist Bird S. Coler Hosp., Roosevelt Island, N.Y., 1973-77; assoc. prof. Hunter Coll. CUNY, 1977—; ptnr. Queens Phys. Therapy Assocs., Forest Hills, N.Y., 1982—. Mem. Am. Phys. Therapy Assn. (dist. dir. Greater N.Y. dist. 1984-88, merit award 1985, outstanding svc. award 1986, dist. svc. award 1988), N.Y. State Acad. Coordinators Clin. Edn. (treas. 1985-88). Democrat. Jewish. Office: Queens Phys Therapy Assocs 110-15 71st Rd Forest Hills NY 11375

ROSENTHAL, BOBBI, design director; b. Newark, Nov. 1, 1959; d. Myron and Anne Ida (Maranz) R. Student, U. Houston, 1977-78; BA in Visual Communications, Kean Coll. of N.J., 1981; postgrad., Sch. Visual Art, N.Y.C., 1982-84. Asst. art dir. Brodsky Graphics, Inc., N.Y.C., 1981-83; art dir. Taylor/Shain, Inc., N.Y.C., 1983-85; design dir., cons. Parent Guide Mag., N.Y.C., 1985-86; owner, pres. Balloonique, Inc., N.Y.&N.J., 1984-86; owner, art dir. Rosenthal Design Assocs., N.Y.C., 1986—; prodn. mgr. Adweek Portfolios, N.Y.C., 1986—. Book designer: Bagelmania, The "Hole" Story, 1987, Great Legs for Short Skirts, 1988, The Household Chart-A-Log, 1989. Mem. N.Y. Art Dirs. Club, Direct Mktg. Assn. (Echo award 1989). Democrat. Jewish. Home and Office: Rosenthal Design Assocs 151 Lexington Ave 5B New York NY 10016

ROSENTHAL, ELIZABETH ROBBINS, physician; b. Bklyn., Feb. 10, 1943; d. Marc and Ruth Jackson (Oginz) Robbins; m. Samuel Leonard Rosenthal, June 26, 1940; children: Thomas, Benjamin, Marc. AB, Smith Coll., 1963; MD, NYU, 1967. Diplomate Am. Bd. of Dermatology. Intern in pediatrics Upstate Med. Ctr., Syracuse, N.Y., 1967-68; resident in dermatology Henry Ford Hosp., Detroit, 1968-69, Roosevelt Hosp., N.Y.C., 1969-70, Boston U. Med. Ctr., 1972-74; pvt. practice Mamaroneck, N.Y., 1976—; asst. clin. prof. Albert Einstein Coll. Medicine, Bronx, 1978—. Bd. dirs. Community Counseling Ctr., Mamaroneck, N.Y., 1982—. Fellow Am. Acad. Dermatology; mem. N.Y. State Med. Soc., NOW, Westchester County Med. Soc., Am. Med. Women's Assn. Home: 444 E Boston Post Rd Mamaroneck NY 10543

ROSENTHAL, EVELYN DAOUD, advertising executive, property manager, lawyer; b. Bellaire, Ohio; d. Azeez Joseph and Nora (Yarbroudi) Tanous; m. Joseph Daoud, Feb. 6, 1932 (dec. Dec. 1963); children: Joseph A. III, Patricia, Alex; m. Milton Rosenthal, Dec. 5, 1975. Student, St. John's U., 1928-31; LLB, U. Miami, 1949. Bar: N.Y., 1932. Pvt. practice law Lawrence, N.Y., 1932; exec. sec. Joseph Daoud and Sons, Atlantic City, 1933-39; v.p. Joseph Daoud and Sons, Miami Beach, Fla., 1931-41; v.p., dir. Joseph Daoud Inc., Miami Beach, 1941-79; owner Rosenthal Outdoor Advt. Co., Miami Beach; pres. Almond Garden Apts., 1974—. Pres. St. Patrick's PTA, Miami Beach, 1955-56, bd. dirs. 1953-56, Barry Coll. Aux. 1954-56, 1952-57, Community Chest Dade County (Fla.) 1951-57, chief dir. fund drive, Miami Beach, 1950-60, Visiting Nurses Assn. Dade County, 1956, St. Francis Hosp. Aux., Miami Beach, 1954-57, Friends Bethany Home Dependent Teenage Girls, Miami, 1966-67, Miami Beach Libr., 1948—, also trustee; mem. endowment com. St. Jude's Research Children's Hosp., Memphis 1966—; sec. Miami Beach Pub. Library, 1956-60, bd. mem. adv. com. 1986, mem. adv. bd.; trustee, mem. Clients Council Legal Services Miami Beach, 1952-59, pres. Fedn. Med. Ctr., 1982-84. Named Woman Yr., Civic League, Miami Beach 1956. Mem. ABA, N.Y. Bar Assn., Am. Assn. Ret. Persons, Friends of Bass Mus., Patrician Club (bd. dirs. 1954-57), Syrian Lebanese Inst., Miami C. of C., Iota Tau Tau, Kappa Beta Pi. Home and Office: 1777 Michigan Ave #107 Miami Beach FL 33139

ROSENTHAL, HELEN NAGELBERG, county official, advocate; b. N.Y.C., June 6, 1926; d. Alfred and Esther (Teicholz) Nagelberg; m. Albert S. Rosenthal, Apr. 10, 1949; children: Lisa Rosenthal Michaels, Apryl Meredith Rosenthal Stuppler. BS, Bklyn. Coll., 1948; MA, NYU, 1950; postgrad., Adelphia U., L.I. U., Lehman Coll., 1975. Cert. early childhood and gifted edn. tchr., N.Y., N.J., elem. and secondary tchr., Fla. Tchr. gifted students Baldwin (N.Y.) Pub. Schs., 1977-79, N.Y. Bd Edn., Bklyn.; rep. community affairs County of Dade, Fla. Author: Criteria for Selection and Curriculum for the Gifted, 1977, Science Experiments for Young Children, 1982. Recipient Departmental award, 1948. Mem. CCEGT (officer), AGATE, AICR.

ROSENTHAL, MARTHA NEWMAN, ballet school director; b. N.Y.C., Oct. 8, 1956; d. Norman and Janice (Newman) R.; m. Adorno Sclano, Mar. 2, 1978 (div. 1986). B.A., Sarah Lawrence Coll., 1978. Jr. copywriter McCann-Erickson, Inc., N.Y.C., 1978-80; office mgr. Ed Libonati Prodns. Inc., N.Y.C., 1980-82; dir. spl. events and pub. relations Sch. Am. Ballet, N.Y.C., 1982-85; spl. cons., assoc. dir. of jr. council and new ballet audiences of Am. Ballet Theatre, N.Y.C., 1986, asst. dir., 1986-87; dir. Sch. Classical Ballet of Am. Ballet Theatre, N.Y.C., 1987—. Writer, editor, designer newsletters, 1982; writer, designer mailing pieces, 1982; editor, designer advt. jour., 1985. Club: Doubles. Avocations: travel, languages, cultural institutions. Office: American Ballet Theatre 890 Broadway New York NY 10003

ROSENTHAL, PAMELA SUSAN, copywriter; b. Newark, Mar. 23, 1959; d. Donald S. and Erika (Halpern) R. BA, Brandeis U., 1981; MBA, NYU, 1989. Promotion and advt. dept. mgr. Dell Pub. Co. at Bantam Doubleday, N.Y.C., 1981-88; promotion copywriter People Mag./Time, Inc., N.Y.C., 1988-89; product mgr. Scholastic, Inc., N.Y.C., 1989—. Mem. Brandeis U. Alumni Assn. Jewish. Office: Scholastic Inc 730 Broadway Rm 38-66 New York NY 10003

ROSER, ELENA MOSTEFERIS, school director; b. Pensacola, Fla., Mar. 21, 1952; d. Christy W. and Georgia (Sakellaris) Mosteferis; m. Jeffrey John Roser, July 16, 1976; children: Jasmin, Jade. AA, Okaloosa-Walton Community Coll., 1971; BA, Fla. State U., 1974; M in Edn., Xavier U., 1976. Cert. tchr. Fla., Am. Montessori tchr. Tchr. Okaloosa County (Fla.) pub. schs., 1976-80; owner, dir. Children's Day: The Montessori Sch., Niceville, Fla., 1980—. Edn. chair LWV, Okaloosa, 1989—; county chair Okaloosa County Dem. Pty., 1988-92; mem. Key Communicators, Okaloosa, 1988—, Okaloosa NOW, mem. rev. com. Red Carpet Schs. Mem. AAUW, NAACP, Nat. Assn. for Edn. of Young Children, Am. Montessori Soc., Okaloosa Assn. for Children Under Six, Phi Delta Kappa (chpt. pres. 1988—), Mardi Gras Club, Bay Area BPW. Greek Orthodox. Home: 916 47th St Niceville FL 32578 Office: Children's Day: The Montessori Sch 410 Fir Ave Niceville FL 32578

ROSETT, JACQUELINE BERLIN, financial executive; b. N.Y.C., Aug. 28, 1945; s. Marshall Hamilton and Lenore (Berlin) Rosett. BS in Physics, Columbia U., 1967. With George B. Buck Inc., N.Y.C., 1967-68; pres. Jacqueline Rosett Assocs., N.Y.C., 1968—; cons. in internat. investments. Photographer: The African Ark, 1974. Vol. counselor N.Y.C. Opera Guild, 1982—; mem. Diamond Club San Diego Zool. Soc., 1975—. Mem. Am. Soc. Profl. and Exec. Women, Nat. Assn. Female Execs., Bronx Zoological Soc. Democrat. Jewish. Club: Camerata (events chmn.). Office: Jacqueline Rosett Estate & Trust 300 E 74th St New York NY 10021

ROSHONG, DEE ANN DANIELS, educator; b. Kansas City, Mo., Nov. 22, 1936; d. Vernon Edmund and Doradell (Kellogg) Daniels; B.Mus.Ed., U. Kans., 1958; M.A. in Counseling and Guidance, Stanford U., 1960; postgrad. Fresno State U., U. Calif.; Ed.D., U. San Francisco, 1980; m. Richard Lee Roshong, Aug. 27, 1960 (div.). Counselor, psychometrist Fresno City Coll., 1961-65; counselor, instr. psychology Chabot Coll., Hayward, Calif., 1965-75; coord. counseling services Chabot Coll., Valley Campus, Livermore, Calif., 1975-81, asst. dir. student pers. svcs., 1981-89, Las Positas Coll., Livermore, Calif., 1989—; writer, coord. I, A Woman Symposium, 1974, Feeling Free to Be You and Me Symposium, 1975, All for the Family Symposium, 1976, I Celebrate Myself Symposium, 1977, Person to Person in Love and Work Symposium, 1978; The Healthy Person in Body, Mind and Spirit Symposium, 1979, Feelin' Good Symposium, 1980, Change Symposium, 1981, Sources of Strength Symposium, 1982, Love and Friendship Symposium, 1983, Self Esteem Symposium, 1984, Trust Symposium, 1985, Prime Time: Making the Most of This Time in Your Life Symposium, 1986, Symposium on Healing, 1987, How to Live in the World and Still Be Happy Symposium, 1988, Student Success is a Team Effort, Sound Mind, Sound Body Symposium, 1989, Creating Life's Best Symposium, 1990, others; mem. cast TV prodns. Eve and Co., Best of Our Times, Cowboy; chmn. Calif. Community Coll. Chancellor's Task Force on Counseling, Statewide Conf. on Emotionally Disturbed Students in Calif. Community Colls., 1982—, Conf. on the Under Represented Student in California Community Colleges, 1986, Conf. on High Risk Students, 1989. Mem. Assn. Humanistic Psychologists, Western Psychol. Assn., Nat. Assn. Women Deans and Counselors, Assn. for Counseling and Devel., Calif. Assn. Community Colls. (chmn. commn. on student services 1979-84), Calif. Community Colls. Counselors Assn. (Svs. award 1986, 87, award for Outstanding and Disting. Service, 1986, 87), Alpha Phi. Author: Counseling Needs of Community Coll. Students, 1980. Home: 808 Comet Dr Foster City CA 94404 Office: 3033 Collier Canyon Rd Livermore CA 94550

ROSKIND, SUSAN REIMER, health science association administrator; b. Rochester, N.Y., Feb. 19, 1951; d. Charles Blaisdell and Hester Louise (Ward) Reimer; m. Stanley C. Roskind, July 29, 1989. BS in Nursing, Vanderbilt U., 1973, MS in Nursing, 1975; MBA, Tulane U., 1985. Registered nurse, Tenn. Staff nurse VA Hosp., Nashville, 1973-74; psychiatric head nurse Hosp. Corp. Am., Nashville, 1975-76, dir. nursing, 1976-82, dir. in-patient adolescent, 1976-83, interim adminstr., 1982-83; asst. adminstr. Hosp. Corp. Am., New Orleans, 1983-84, interim hosp. exec. dir., 1984; adminstr. Psychiatric Insts. Am., New Orleans, 1984-89; chief oper. officer Ctrs. for Psychotherapy, New Orleans, 1989—; guest lectr. U. Tenn., Nashville, 1978-83. Bd. dirs., asst. sec. JoEllen Smith Governing Bd., New Orleans, 1984—; bd. dirs. Tulane Exec. Edn. Council, New Orleans, 1985—. Grantee NIMH, 1974. Fellow Ortho-Psychiatric Assn.; mem. NAFE, New Orleans Mental Health Assn., Am. Coun. Career Women (bd. dirs.), Harvey Canal Indsl. Assn., Menniger Found., Tulane U. Bus. Alumni Assn. (bd. dirs. 1985-88), New Orleans C. of C.. Democrat. Club: Krewe of Iris (New Orleans). Office: Ctrs for Psychotherapy Inc #1 Seine Ct Ste 400 New Orleans LA 70114

ROS-LEHTINEN, ILEANA, congresswoman; b. Havana, Cuba, July 15, 1952; d. Enrique Emilio and Amanda (Adato) Ros; m. Dexter Lehtinen. AA, Miami (Fla.) Dade Community Coll., 1972; BA, Fla. Internat. U., 1975, MS, 1987. Prin. Ea. Acad., from 1978; rep. State of Fla., 1982-86, senator, 1986-89; mem. 101st, 102nd Congresses from 18th Fla. Dist., Washington, 1989—. Roman Catholic. Office: US House Reps Offices of House Members Washington DC 20515*

ROSLEY-GRIFFIN, JOAN EVELYN, management consultant; b. Rio, Brazil, Dec. 22, 1958; came to U.S., 1962; d. Walter David and Marion J. (Mayer) Rosley; m. Peter J. Ryan, July 5, 1983 (div. Feb. 1986); m. Charles Griffin, Oct. 7, 1989. BS, U. Colo., 1980. From reporter to editor Tempe (Ariz.) Daily News, 1980-83; sales mgr. Prin. Fin. Group, Albuquerque, 1983-88; cons., co-owner Richard Baxter & Assocs., Albuquerque, 1988—; dir. seminar Werner Erhard & Assocs., Albuquerque. Fundraiser Joe Mercer for Gov., Albuquerque, 1986; presenation leader The Hunger Project. Mem. Albuquerque C. of C. (ambassador 1985-88), Civitan (pres. Albuquerque chpt. 1989-90), Leads Club (bd. dirs. 1984). Republican. Jewish. Home and Office: 2506 Thompson Loop NW Albuquerque NM 87104

ROSMAN-BAKEHOUSE, MARY PAT, physician; b. Harlan, Iowa, July 4, 1956; d. Louis G. and Irene (Kloewer) Rosman; m. James Richard Rosman-Bakehouse, Sept. 28, 1985; children: Amie Marie, Nathan J. BA in Chemistry, Biology, U. N. Iowa, 1978; DO, U. Osteo. Med. and Health Sci., Des Moines, 1983. Rotating intern Davenport (Iowa) Med. Ctr., 1983-84; family practice resident Des Moines Gen. Hosp., 1984-85; physician Rosman Clinic, Manilla, Iowa, 1985-88, Dyersville (Iowa) Family Practice, 1988-89, Rosman Clinic, Dyersville, 1989—; Cert. in family practice, Am. Coll. Gen. Practitioners, 1985. Recipient Symposium Scholarship, U. Northern Iowa, 1974-78. Mem. Am. Osteo. Assn., Am. Coll. of Gen. Practitioners, Iowa Osteo. Med. Assn., Am. Acad. Family Practice, Iowa Acad. Family Physicians. Republican. Roman Catholic. Home: 218 3rd St Dyersville IA 52040 Office: Rosman Clinic 337 1st Ave E Dyersville IA 52040

ROSNER, MARSHA RICH, biochemistry educator; b. Springfield, Mass., Nov. 8, 1950; d. David Abraham and Shirley Naomi (Becker) Rich; m. Robert Rosner, Sept. 5, 1971; children: Daniela K., Nicole E. AB, Harvard U., 1972; PhD, MIT, 1978. Postdoctoral fellow MIT, Cambridge, Mass., 1978-81, asst. prof. toxicology, 1982-85, assoc. prof. toxicology, 1986-87; assoc. prof. pharmacology and physiology U. Chgo., 1987—. Office: U Chgo Ben May Inst 5841 S Maryland Ave Chicago IL 60637

ROSNESS, BETTY JUNE, advertising and public relations company executive; b. Oklahoma City, Mar. 4, 1924; d. Thomas Harrison and Clara Marguerite (Stubblefield) Pyeatt; student Oklahoma City U., 1940-41; m. Joseph H. Rosness, Aug. 5, 1960; children: Melody L. Johnson (dec.), Michael C., Randall L., Melinda Rosness Mason, John C. Continuity dir. Sta. KFBI, Wichita, Kans., 1957-58; sales exec. Sta. KFH, Wichita, 1958-60; U.S. senatorial press sec., 1961-66; dir. advt. and public rels. Alaska State Bank, Anchorage, 1966-68; prin. Rosness Advt. Assocs., Goleta, Calif., 1968—; bd. dirs. Fin. Corp. Santa Barbara (Calif.). Pres., Goleta Valley Girls Club, 1972-75, Ret. Officers Womens Assn., 1970; v.p. Santa Barbara Symphony Assn., 1977-80; bd. dirs. Channel City Womens Forum, 1976—, Goleta Valley Community Hosp., 1989, elected treas.; chmn. U. Calif. at Santa Barbara Corp. Affiliates, 1989, Pvt. Industry Coun. Santa Barbara County, 1985-86; bd. dirs. Cancer Found., Santa Barbara, 1978-82, founding mem. Goleta Beautiful, Club West Track and Field; mem. allocations com., bd. dirs. United Way (Santa Barbara chpt.); founding mem., bd. dirs. Children's World of Hospice; elected chmn. corp. bd. U. Calif. San Barbara, 1989. Elected chmn. bd. U. Calif. Santa Barbara Affiliates, 1989-90. Named Woman of Yr. Santa Barbara County, 1978, Affiliate of Yr. U. Calif.-Santa Barbara, 1983-84, Woman of Distinction Soroptomist of Internat. Goleta. Mem. Greater Santa Barbara Advt. Club. (past v.p., hon. 1988), Goleta Valley C. of C. (past dir.), Santa Barbara C. of C. (bd. dirs. 1982-86), Goleta Valley C. of C. Home: 669 Larchmont Pl Goleta CA 93117

ROSOFF, AVIVA MARGOLIT, sales executive, educator; b. Eatontown, N.J., June 15, 1961; d. Jack M. and Barbara Lee (Ginsburg) R. BA, Rutgers U., 1983. Cert. elem. edn. tchr., N.Y. With Macy's, N.Y.C., 1983-86, asst. buyer, 1985-86; assoc. mdse. mgr. Macy's, L.I., N.Y., 1986; sales exec. Her Majesty Industries, N.Y.C., 1986-88, Crazy Horse, N.Y.C., 1988—. Fair Haven (N.J.) Bd. Edn. scholar, 1979-83, Voorhees scholar Douglass Coll., 1981-82. Mem. Am. Coll. Sports Medicine, Food and Nutrition Coun. Greater N.Y., Phi Beta Kappa. Jewish. Office: Crazy Horse 525 7th Ave New York NY 10018

ROSOFF, ELAINE BERNADETTE, producer; b. Washington, July 1, 1938; d. Dick Gee and Geneva Eileen (Beal) Lam; m. Royall Tyler, Mar. 5, 1961 (div. 1965); 1 child, Elizabeth. BFA, George Washington U., Washington, 1960; student, Corcoran Sch. Art, Washington, 1960, Art Students League, N.Y.C., 1965-68; MA, St. John's U., N.Y.C., 1989. Asst. Fulbright Found., Washington, 1960-61, Senator Proxmire, Washington, 1961-62; tchr. Convent of the Sacred Heart, Tokyo, 1962-64; co-founder, chief exec. officer Gilaine Enterprises, N.Y.C., 1968-89; chief exec. officer Gilaine Enterprises, Palm Beach County, Fla., 1989—. One-woman shows include Silvermine (Conn.) Gallery, 1970, Island-Country Gallery, Locust Valley, N.Y., 1983; exhibited in group shows at Corcoran Gallery, Washington, 1959; also pvt. collections. Commr. Landmarks Commn., Glen Cove, N.Y., 1976-88; vol. ARC, Walter Reed Hosp., Washington, 1972-73; advisor Riveria Beach Boys & Girls Club, Palm Beach County; dir. Lake Worth (Fla.) Art League, 1989-90. Recipient Scholarships, Corcoran Art Sch., Washington, 1957-60, Art Students League, N.Y.C., 1965-68, St. John's U., N.Y.C., 1987-89. Mem. AAUW (dir. 1978-82), Chinese Womens Club of China Inst., Panhellenic

Assn. (dir. 1972—), Four Arts Soc., Pi Beta Phi. Office: Gilaine Enterprises Inc 5540 N Ocean Dr Ste 12A Singer Island FL 33404

ROSS, BARBARA JEAN, educator; b. Waukegan, Ill., May 19, 1955; d. Earl Robert and Ann Elizabeth (Hogan) R. BS, William Woods Coll., Fulton, Mo., 1977; MEd, Nat. Coll., Evanston, Ill., 1984. Kindergarten tchr. Waukegan Pub. Schs., 1977-79, tchr. ESL, 1979—. Vol. Lake County Forest Preserve, 1989-90. Mem. Ill. Assn. for Multicultural Multilingual Edn., Lake County Assn. Children with Learning Disabilities, AAUW, Alpha Delta Kappa (past pres.). Roman Catholic. Home: 625 Dilger Ave Waukegan IL 60085

ROSS, BETTY GRACE, medical distributing company executive; b. N.Y.C., July 14, 1931; d. Philip and Nancy Anna (Meredith) Boccella; R.N., Presbyn. Hosp., 1952; student Ariz. State U., 1960-62; m. Robert W. Ross, Mar. 1, 1968 (div. July 1976). Sr. operating rm. nurse Roosevelt Hosp., N.Y.C., 1953-58, pvt. surg. nurse, neurosurgery group, 1958-59, orthopedic surgery group, 1960-64; sales assoc., ptnr. Zimmer-Ball Assocs., Phoenix, Ariz., 1964-71, owner, distbr. Zimmer Ross Assocs., Phoenix, 1971—, Zimmer-Ross Ltd., 1978—; instr. operating room nursing Englewood (N.J.) Hosp., 1960. Active on Taskforce for Homeless, Phoenix. Mem. Assn. Operating Room Nurses Phoenix (charter mem.), Bloomfield Coll. Alumni Assn. Republican. Club: Century. Home: 5713 Cattletrack Rd N Scottsdale AZ 85253 also: John Gardiner's Enchantment Sedona AZ 86336 Office: 1232 E Missouri St Phoenix AZ 85014 also: Z-R Assocs 6700 n Oracle Tucson AZ 85704 also: Z-R Ltd 457 Washington SE Albuquerque NM 87108 also: 497 N Resler Ste D El Paso TX 79912

ROSS, CHARLOTTE PACK, suicidologist; b. Oklahoma City, Oct. 21, 1932; d. Joseph and Rose P. (Traibich) Pack; m. Roland S. Ross, May 6, 1951 (div. July 1964); children: Beverly Jo, Sandra Gail. Student U. Okla., 1949-52; degree, New Sch. Social Research, 1953. Cert. tchr. Exec. dir. Suicide Prevention and Crisis Ctr. San Mateo County, Burlingame, Calif., 1966-88; pres., exec. dir. Youth Suicide Nat. Ctr., Washington, 1985—; pres. Calif. Senate Adv. Com. Youth Suicide Prevention, 1982-84; speaker Menninger Found., 1983, 84; instr. San Francisco State U., 1981-83; conf. coordinator U. Calif., San Francisco, 1971—; cons. univs. and health services throughout world. Contbg. author: Group Counseling for Suicidal Adolescents, 1984; Teaching Children the Facts of Life and Death, 1985. Mem. editorial bd. Suicide and Life Threatening Behavior, 1976—. Mem. regional selection panel Pres.'s Commn. on White House Fellows, 1975-78; mem. CIRCLON Service Club, 1979—, Com. on Child Abuse, 1981-85; founding mem. Women for Responsible Govt., co-chmn., 1974-79. Recipient Outstanding Exec. award San Mateo County Coordinating Com., 1971; Koshland award San Francisco Found., 1984. Fellow Wash. Acad. Scis.; mem. Internat. Assn. Suicide Prevention (v.p. 1985—), Am. Assn. Suicidology (sec. 1972-74), bd. govs. 1976-78, accreditation com. 1975—, chair region IX, 1975-82), Assn. United Way Agy. Execs. (pres. 1974), Assn. County Contract Agys. (pres. 1982). Club: Peninsula Press Club. Office: 1811 Trousdale Dr Burlingame CA 94010

ROSS, DEBRA ANN, sales manager; b. Chgo., Jan. 10, 1956; d. Frank James and Ann Barbara (Milos) R. BS in Mgmt. with honors, St. Joseph's Coll., Whiting, Ind., 1977. Opening mgr. Wendy City Corp., Chgo., 1977-80; sales, svcs. mgr. The Med. Team, Chgo., 1980-82, Docter Enterprises, South Holland, Ill., 1983—. Communications officer Finance Com. Holy Ghost Parish, South Holland, 1987—. Mem. Italian Cath. Fedn., Nat. Network of Women In Sales, Chgo. Council Fgn. Rels.

ROSS, DEBRA BENITA, marketing executive; b. Carbondale, Ill., May 1, 1956; d. Bernard Harris and Marian (Frager) R. BS, U. Ill., 1978; MS, U. Wis., 1979. Dir. mktg. Ambion Devel., Inc., Northbrook, Ill., 1983-89, Fitness Quest Internat., Inc., Northbrook, 1989—. Mem. Am. Mktg. Assn., Chgo. Advt. Club. Home: 1853 Mission Hills Ln Northbrook IL 60062 Office: Fitness Quest Internat Inc 5 Revere Dr Ste 200 Northbrook IL 60062

ROSS, DIANA, singer, actress, entertainer, fashion designer; b. Detroit, Mar. 26, 1944; d. Fred and Ernestine R.; m. Robert Ellis Silberstein, Jan. 1971 (div. 1976); children: Rhonda, Tracee, Chudney; m. Arne Naess, Oct. 23, 1985; 1 son: Ross Arne. Grad. high sch. Pres. Diana Ross Enterprises, Inc., fashion and merchandising, Anaid Film Prodns., Inc., RTC Mgmt. Corp., artists mgmt., Chondee Inc., Rosstown, Rossville, music pub. Lead singer until 1969, Diana Ross and the Supremes; solo artist, 1969—; albums include Diana Ross, 1970, 76, Everything Is Everything, 1971, I'm Still Waiting, 1971, Lady Sings The Blues, 1972, Touch Me In The Morning, 1973, Original Soundtrack of Mahogany, 1975, Baby It's Me, 1977, The Wiz, 1978, Ross, 1978, 83, The Boss, 1979, Diana, 1981, To Love Again, 1981, Why Do Fools Fall In Love?, 1981, Silk Electric, 1982, Swept Away, 1984, Eaten Alive, 1985, Chain Reaction, 1986, Workin' Overtime, 1989, Red Hot Rhythm and Blues, 1987, Surrender, 1989, Ain't No Mountain High Enough, 1989; films include Lady Sings the Blues, 1972, Mahogany, 1975, The Wiz, 1978; NBC-TV spl., An Evening With Diana Ross, 1977, Diana, 1981, numerous others. Recipient citation Vice Pres. Humphrey for efforts on behalf Pres. Johnson's Youth Opportunity Program, citation Mrs. Martin Luther King and Rev. Abernathy for contbn. to SCLC cause, awards Billboard, Cash Box and Record World as worlds outstanding singer, Grammy award, 1970, Female Entertainer of Year NAACP, 1970, Cue award as Entertainer of year, 1972, Golden Apple award, 1972, Gold medal award Photoplay, 1972, Antoinette Perry award, 1977, nominee as best actress of year for Lady Sings the Blues Motion Picture Acad. Arts and Scis., 1972, Golden Globe award, 1972; named to Rock and Roll Hall of Fame, 1988. Office: RTC Mgmt PO Box 1683 New York NY 10185 also: care Shelly Berger 6255 Sunset Blvd Los Angeles CA 90028*

ROSS, DOLORES ANNE, nurse; b. Bklyn., Apr. 4, 1952; d. John Joseph and Elizabeth Cecelia (Doonan) Ross. BS, BCNY, 1974; MA, NYU, 1982, postgrad., 1989—. Cert. rehab. registered nurse. Staff nurse Rusk Inst. NYU Med. Ctr., 1974-75, sr. staff nurse, 1975, team leader, 1975-76, asst. head nurse, 1976-77, head nurse, 1977-85, asst. dir., 1985-86, acting dir., 1986, asst. dir., 1986—. Mem. Assn. Rehab. Nurses, Am. Nurses' Assn., N.Y. State Nurses Assn. Roman Catholic.

ROSS, DORIS G., civic worker; b. Thompsonville, Conn.; d. Philip A. and Eva (Saffir) Sisitzky; student Barnard Coll., Max Reinhardt Drama Workshop, N.Y. U. Radio Workshop, Lee Strasberg Theatre Inst., Royal Acad. Dramatic Arts; m. Lewis H. Ross, Jan. 4, 1942; children—Phyllis, Allyne. Dir. New Eng. Zionist Youth Com., 1943-45; dir. theatre arts Manchester Inst. Arts and Scis., 1947-48; pres. Manchester Girls Clubs, 1950-51, dir., 1949-53, 54-58, 59-69, chmn. nat. adv. bd. Girls Clubs Am., 1955-57, v.p., 1956-57, pres., 1957-59, chmn. 15th Ann. Conf., 1960, first acting chmn. past pres. com., 1974, 1st pres. past pres. club, 1975-77, chmn. 15th ann. conf., 1960, chmn. silver jubilee com., 1969-70, chmn. directions and social concerns com., 1978-79, founder Children's Creative Theatre, 1978, chmn., 1979-81; hon. mem., 1981—; exec. com. Girls Clubs N.Y., 1970-73, bd. dirs., 1970-73, sustaining dir., 1973—, co-chmn. long range planning com., 1970-71; 1st pres. Theatre Art Players, Temple Emanuel, N.Y.C., 1970-71; trustee Actors Studio, 1978-82, 84, conceived Actors Studio Achievement awards celebration, 1981; dir. Manchester Settlement Assn., 1951-54, Manchester Vis. Nurses Assn., 1955-61; del. Nat. Soc. Welfare Assembly, 1957-59, White House Conf. on Children and Youth, 1960, voting del. nat. council state coms., 1960, mem. N.H. state exec. com., 1960, N.H. state sub-com. on Leisure Times Activities chmn., 1960; charter colleague Nat. Assembly Nat. Voluntary Health and Welfare Orgns., Inc., 1976—, mem. Nat. Juvenile Justice Program Collaboration, Mem. Pres.'s Citizens Adv. Com. on Fitness of Am. Youth, 1958-60; mem. exec. com. Gov.'s Com. on Children and Youth, 1961-63; Gov.'s rep. to Pres.'s Conf. on Youth Fitness, 1962; pres. Manchester Garden Club, 1963-64; dir. Opera League New Hampshire, Inc., 1964-69; trustee Actors Studio, 1978-82. Mem. Hadassah (pres. Manchester chpt. 1943-44, dir. Manchester chpt. 1942-49, New Eng. regional v.p. 1944-46). Address: 985 Fifth Ave New York NY 10021

ROSS, EUNICE LATSHAW, judge; b. Bellevue, Pa., Oct. 13, 1923; d. Richard Kelly and Eunice (Weidner) Latshaw; m. John Anthony Ross, May 29, 1943 (dec. Jan. 1978); 1 child, Geraldine Ross Coleman. BS, U. Pitts., 1945, LL.B., 1951. Bar: Pa. 1952. Atty., Pub. Health Law Research Project, Pitts., 1951-52; atty. jud. asst., law clk. Ct. Common Pleas, Pitts., 1952-70; adjunct law prof. U. Pitts., 1967-73; dir. family div. Ct. Common Pleas, Pitts., 1970-72; judge Ct. Common Pleas of Allegheny County, Pitts., 1972—; mem. Bd. Jud. Inquiry and Rev., Commonwealth of Pa., 1984-89, Gov's Justice Commn., 1972-78. Author: (with others) Survey of Pa. Public Health Laws, 1952. Contbr. articles to legal publs. Com. person for 14th ward, vice chmn. Democratic Com., Pitts., 1972; exec. com. bd. trustees U. Pitts., 1980-86, bd. dirs. law sch., 1985—; adv. bd. Animal Friends, Pitts., 1973—; bd. mem. The Program, Pitts., 1983-87, Pitts. History and Landmarks FDTN., West Pa. Hist. Soc., West Pa. Conservancy. Recipient Disting. Amumna award U. Pitts., 1973, Medal of Recognition, 1987; named Girl Scout Woman of Yr., Pitts. council Girl Scouts U.S., 1975; cert. of Achievement Pa. Fedn. Women's Clubs, 1975, 77. Mem. Allegheny County Bar Assn. (vice chmn., exec. com. young lawyers sect. 1956-59), Pitts. Bus. and Profl. Women's Club, Pa. State Trial Judges Conf. Home: 1204 Denniston Ave Pittsburgh PA 15217 Office: 1700 Frick Bldg Pittsburgh PA 15219

ROSS, FRANCINE HELEN, market research executive; b. N.Y.C., June 11, 1952; d. Benjamin and Esther (Coopersmith) R. BA, CUNY, 1974. Project dir. test mktg. Audits & Surveys, Inc., N.Y.C., 1973-75, project dir. survey research, 1975-77; mgr. test mktg. Paratest Mktg., Eastchester, N.Y., 1977-81; sr. research mgr. Whitehall Labs. div. Am. Home Products, N.Y.C., 1981-85; v.p. corp. communications Chase Manhattan Bank, N.Y.C., 1985-86; v.p., corp. mktg. rsch. dir. Combe Inc., White Plains, N.Y., 1986—. Mem. Am. Mktg. Assn., Assn. Nat. Advertisers (market rsch. com.), Am. Demographic Inst., Market Research Assn., Mktg. Advt. Rsch. Found., Non-Prescription Drug Mfs. Assn. (market rsch. com.). Democrat. Jewish. Home: 1 Bay Club Dr Bayside NY 11360 Office: Combe Inc 1101 Westchester Ave White Plains NY 10604

ROSS, GAIL SHARON, pediatric psychologist, educator; b. Paterson, N.J., Nov. 19, 1946; d. Samuel Michael and Matilda (Gershon) R.; B.A. magna cum laude with honors in Psychology, Barnard Coll., 1968; M.A., U. Chgo., 1969; Ph.D., Harvard U., 1978; m. Robert Jay Schwartz, Jr.; children—Matthew Alexander, Michael Benjamin, Alexandra Ross. Assoc. in research in psychology Yale U., New Haven, 1976-78; research assoc. in psychiatry and pediatrics Cornell U. Med. Coll., N.Y.C., 1978-80, instr. psychiatry and pediatrics, 1980, asst. prof. pediatrics, 1982—, staff psychologist Perinatology Center, N.Y. Hosp., N.Y.C., 1978—, research dir. perinatal follow-up program, 1986—; dir. Early Childhood Direction Center of Manhattan and Bronx, 1980-82. NDEA Title IV fellow, 1968-69; NIMH grantee, 1972-76; N.Y. State Developmental Disabilities grantee, 1979-82. Mem. Am. Psychol. Assn., Am. Acad. Scis., N.Y. Acad. Scis., Soc. Research in Child Devel., Am. Assn. Women in Psychology, Phi Beta Kappa, Phi Delta Kappa. Contbr. articles to profl. jours.; research in devel. of normal and highrisk infants. Office: Perinatology Ctr 525 E 68th St New York NY 10021

ROSS, HAZEL, health science association administrator; b. Bklyn., Oct. 29, 1934; d. Leo and Mae (Press) Leudesdorff; m. Harold B. Rosenthal (div. 1982); children: Donna Jean, Michael A., Robert F. Grad. high sch., Tilden. V.p. Recco Home Care Service, Inc., Massapequa, N.Y., 1977—, Recco HealthCare Services, Massapequa, 1984—, Cert. Mgmt. Corp., Massapequa, 1986—; mem. N.Y. State Health Adv. Commn., Albany, 1984-86. Organizer congl. campaign J. Halpern, Long Island, N.Y.; founder Laurelton Block Assn.. Long Island; pub. relations person Jackson Presdl. campaign, Long Island; pres. Marine Park Civic Assn., Bklyn. Mem. N.Y. State Assn. of Health Care Providers (legis. chair 1978-82), N.Y. State Assembly Com. on Home Care (Tallon com. 1982-84), Nat. Assn. for Health Care. Office: Recco Healthcare Assn 524 Hicksville Rd Massapequa NY 11758

ROSS, JUDITH PARIS, life insurance executive; b. Boston, Dec. 23, 1939; d. Max and Ruth Paris; ed. Boston U., 1961, UCLA, 1978; grad. Life Underwriting Tng. Council, 1978; 1 son, Adam Stuart. Producer, co-host Checkpoint TV show, Washington, 1967-71; hostess Judi Says TV show, Washington, 1969; brokerage supr., specialist impaired risk underwriting Beneficial Nat. Life Ins. Co. (now Nat. Benefit Life), Beverly Hills, Calif., 1973-82, dir. Salary Savs. program for West Coast, 1982-87; ins. and benefits specialist, cons. Alliance Assocs., 1987—; mktg. dir. Brougher Ins. Group, 1982-87; ins. and benefits specialist Alliance Assocs., Beverly Hills, 1987—; featured speaker ins. industry seminars. Active local PTA, Boy Scouts Am., Beverly Hills local politics; mem. early childhood edn. adv. com. Beverly Hills Unified Sch. Dist., 1977. Mem. Nat. Assn. Life Underwriters, Calif. Assn. Life Underwriters (dir. W. Los Angeles 1980—, v.p. chpt. 1982—, chmn. pub. relations), West Los Angeles Life Underwriters Assn. (v.p. fin. 1983-84). Office: Alliance Assocs 449 S Beverly Dr #210 Beverly Hills CA 90212

ROSS, JUNE ROSA PITT, biology educator; b. Taree, May 2, 1931; came to U.S., 1957; d. Bernard and Adeline (Nind) Phillips; m. Charles Alexander, June 27, 1959. BS with honors, U. Sydney, New S. Wales, Australia, 1953, PhD, 1959, DSc, 1974. Research assoc. Yale U., New Haven, 1959-60, U. Ill., Urbana, 1960-65; research assoc. Western Wash. U., Bellingham, 1965-67, assoc. prof., 1967-70, prof. biology, 1970—, chair dept. biology, 1989—; pres. Western Wash. U. Faculty Senate, Bellingham, 1984-85; conf. host Internat. Bryozoology Assn., 1986. Author: (with others) A Textbook of Entomology, 1982, Geology of Coal, 1984; editor (assoc.) Palaios, 1985-89; contbr. articles to profl. jours. Grantee NSF; recipient Western Wash. U. Outstanding Educator award, 1973, Western Wash. U. Research award, 1986. Mem. Am. Soc. Zoologists, The Paleontol. Soc. (councillor 1984-86, treas. 1987—), U.K. Marine Biol. Assn. (life), Electron Microscope Soc. Am. Office: Western Wash U Dept Biology Bellingham WA 98255

ROSS, KATHLEEN ANNE, college president; b. Palo Alto, Calif., July 1, 1941; d. William Andrew and Mary Alberta (Wilburn) R. B.A., Ft. Wright Coll., 1964; M.A., Georgetown U., 1971; Ph.D., Claremont Grad. Sch., 1979. Cert. tchr., Wash. Secondary tchr. Holy Names Acad., Spokane, Wash., 1964-70; dir. research and planning Province Holy Names, Wash. State, 1972-73; v.p. acads. Ft. Wright Coll., Spokane, 1973-81; research asst. to dean Claremont Grad. Sch., Calif., 1977-78; assoc. faculty mem. Harvard U., Cambridge, Mass., 1981; pres. Heritage Coll., Toppenish, Wash., 1981—; cons. Wash. State Holy Names Schs., 1971-73; coll. accrediting assn. evaluator N.W. Assn. Schs. and Colls., Seattle, 1975—; dir. Holy Names Coll., Oakland, Calif., 1979—; cons. Yakima Indian Nation, Toppenish, 1975—; speaker, cons. in field. Author: (with others) Multicultural Pre-School Curriculum, 1977, A Crucial Agenda: Improving Minority Student Success, 1989; Cultural Factors in Success of American Indian Students in Higher Education, 1978. Chmn. Internat. 5-Yr. Convocation of Sisters of Holy Names, Montreal, Que., Can., 1981; TV Talk show host Spokane Council of Chs., 1974-76. Recipient E.K. and Lillian F. Bishop Founds. Youth Leader of Yr. award, 1986, Golden Aztez award Washingotn Human Devel., 1989, Harold W. McGraw Edn. prize, 1989; Holy Names medal Ft. Wright Coll., 1981; Disting. Citizenship Alumna award Claremont Grad. Sch., 1986; named Yakima Herald Rep. Person of Yr. 1987; numerous grants for projects in multicultural higher edn., 1974—. Mem. Nat. Assn. Ind. Colls. and Univs. (bd. dirs.), Am. Assn. Higher Edn., Soc. Intercultural Edn., Tng. and Research, Sisters of Holy Names of Jesus and Mary. Roman Catholic. Office: Heritage Coll 3240 Fort Rd Toppenish WA 98948

ROSS, KATHLEEN B. HENRICH, marketing manager, dental hygienist, consultant; b. Providence, Dec. 25, 1947; d. Daniel Ernest Baker and Virginia Mary (Furey) Bidle; m. Clarence Dean Ross, Oct. 11, 1985. B.S. in Dental Hygiene, U. R.I., 1970. Dental hygienist various dental offices, Mass., Fla., Mo., Minn., Ga., 1970—; research cons. Forsyth Dental Research Ctr., Boston, 1970-72, Monsanto Co., St. Louis, 1973-79; instr. dental hygiene Forest Park Jr. Coll., St. Louis, 1975-76; ednl. cons. Dental Sci. Systems, Reston, Va., 1982-85; ednl. cons. Teledyne Water Pik, Ft. Collins, Colo., 1977-85, dir. continuing edn., 1985-86, dental profl. mktg. mgr., 1986—; pres. Candy Baker, Inc., Atlanta, 1981—. Mem. Am. Dental Hygiene Assn., Ga. Dental Hygiene Assn., Internat. Dental Health Found., Internat. Assn. for Dental Research, Internat. Platform Assn. Home and Office: 4322 Sprucebough Dr Marietta GA 30062

ROSS, LEABELLE I. (MRS. CHARLES R. ROSS), retired psychiatrist; b. Lorain, Ohio, Feb. 11, 1905; d. Charles E. and Harriet (Dobbie) Isaac; A.B., Western Res. U., 1927, M.D., 1930; m. Charles R. Ross, Sept. 23, 1941; children—Charles R., John Edwin. Surg. intern Lakeside Hosp., Cleve., 1931-32; resident obstetrics and gynecology Iowa State U. Hosp., 1932-33; resident obstetrics and surgery N.Y. Infirmary, N.Y.C., 1933-34; pvt. practice, Cleve., 1935-40; staff physician Cleve. State Hosp., 1938-42; dir. student health Bowling Green (Ohio) State U., 1942-45; psychiatrist Bur. Juvenile Research, Columbus, Ohio, 1946-47; psychiat. cons., 1948-51; psychiatrist Mental Hygiene Clinic, Columbus VA, 1951-55; dir. med. services Juvenile Diagnostic Center, 1955-59, acting supt., 1958, 61-62, dir. psychiat. services, 1959-62, clin. dir., 1962-70. Mem. Am. Psychiat. Assn., Ohio Psychiat. Assn., Am. Group Psychotherapy Assn., Tri-State Group Psychotherapy Soc., Neuropsychiat. Assn. Central Ohio, Assn. Physicians Div. Mental Hygiene and Correction (pres. 1963-64), Alpha Sigma Rho, Nu Sigma Phi. Club: Soroptimist. Home: 1289 Gold Ridge Rd Sebastopol CA 95472

ROSS, LESA MOORE, quality assurance engineer; b. New Orleans, Jan. 25, 1959; d. William Frank and Carolyn West Moore; m. Mark Neal Ross, Nov. 30, 1985; 1 child, Sarah Ann. BS in Engring., U. N.C., Charlotte, 1981; postgrad., U. North Tex., 1984—. Seismic qualification engr. Duke Power Co., Charlotte, N.C., 1981-82; quality assurance engr. Tex. Instruments Inc., Lewisville, Tex., 1982—. Recipient Nat. Sci. Found. Rsch. Grant, U. N.C., Charlotte, 1980. Mem. Am. Soc. for Quality Control (cert. quality engr., quality auditor), Zeta Tau Alpha (pres. 1984-85). Home: 4925 Wolf Creek Trail Flower Mound TX 75028

ROSS, LINDA ANNE, veterinarian, educator; b. Chgo., Jan. 22, 1951; d. Warren Robert and Ruth Bernice (Luebke) R. BS, U. Ill., 1972, DVM, 1974; MS, U. Ga., 1981. Diplomate Am. Coll. Vet. Internal Medicine. Intern South Shore VA, S. Weymouth, Mass., 1974-75; rsch. asst. Purdue U., W. Lafayette, Ind., 1975-76; resident U. Ga., Athens, 1977-80; pvt. practice Atlanta, 1976-77, Andover, Mass., 1980-81; assoc. prof. Sch. Vet. Medicine Tufts U., North Grafton, Mass., 1981—, chief-of-staff Foster Hosp. for Small Animals, 1989—; speaker numerous profl. meetings, 1983—. Editorial bd. Seminars in Veterinary Medicine and Surgery jour., 1989—; editor: (with others) Handbook of Small Animal Practice, 1987; contbr. articles to profl. jours. and books. Vol. Dem. candidates Barney Frank, Mike Dukakis and others, 1981—. Mem. AVMA, NOW, Am. Animal Hosp. Assn., Am. Soc. Nephrology (elected), Am. Coll. Vet. Internal Medicine (by exam, chair resident tng. com. 1987-88), Comparative Endocrinology Soc., Sierra Club. Office: Tufts U. Sch Vet Medicine 200 Westboro Rd North Grafton MA 01536

ROSS, LOIS INA, manufacturing and distributing company executive, new products marketing consultant; b. Boston, Nov. 5, 1947; d. Harry and Esther (Kashuck) Sadow; m. Paul M. Ross, Aug. 25, 1968; children—Gregory, Nicole. Student, Boston U. Asst. office mgr. Waldoroth Label Mfg., Mattapan, Mass., 1965-67; mem. union labor relations com., Stop & Shop, Hyde Park, Mass., 1967-68; office and personnel mgr. Friends Baked Beans, Malden, Mass., 1968-69; community relations rep. McDonalds Restaurant, Syracuse, N.Y., 1978-80; pres., owner Your Hats Desire, Inc., Manlius, N.Y., 1981—; speaker Syracuse U., 1984. Recipient Super Achiever award Admanco Mfg., 1984. Mem. Am. Camping Assn., Advt. Specialty Inst., Women Bus. Owners, Syracuse C. of C., Women's Am. Club. Jewish. Avocations: bridge, aerobics, tennis, theater. Office: Your Hats Desire Inc 116 Fayette St PO Box 434 Manlius NY 13104

ROSS, LORRAINE G., sales professional; b. Chgo., Mar. 23, 1935; d. Irving and Fannie (Brenner) Goldenberg; m. Aaron Ross, Sept. 3, 1954; children: Sheri Ellen Levine Mark Alan, Ronee Mae Dakin, Jay Randy. Student, Pierce Community Coll., Woodland Hills, Calif., Valley Jr. Coll., Van Nuys, Calif.; BA, Roosevelt U., Chgo., 1958. Co-owner Lorraine & Aaron Originals, Tarzana, Calif.; pres. Party Jester, Pasadena, Calif., Parties R Us, Studio City, Calif., Lorraine Ross & Assocs., Inc., Moorpark, Calif. Mem. NAFE, Western Toy and Hobby Rep. Assn., Women in Mfg. Network. Address: PO Box 2109 Moorpark CA 93020

ROSS, MADELYN ANN, newspaper editor; b. Pitts., June 26, 1949; d. Mario Charles and Rose Marie (Mangieri) R. B.A., Indiana U. of Pa., 1971; M.A., SUNY-Albany, 1972. Reporter Pitts. Press, 1972-78, asst. city editor, 1978-82, spl. assignment editor, 1982-83, mng. editor, 1983—; instr. Community Coll. Allegheny County, 1974-81; Pulitzer Prize juror, 1989, 90. Mem. Task Force Leadership Pitts., 1985—; v.p. Press Old Newsboys Charity Fund. Democrat. Roman Catholic. Clubs: Women's Press, Pitts. Press. Office: Pitts Press 34 Blvd of the Allies Pittsburgh PA 15230

ROSS, MARCIA J., human resources director; b. Springfield, Ill., Oct. 25, 1956; d. John Robert and Doris Darline (Anderson) Bartlett; m. Robert C. Ross, Nov. 5, 1983; 1 child, Megan Colleen. BBA, Ill. Wesleyan U., 1979; postgrad., Sangamon State U., 1989—. Community devel. officer City of Springfield, 1979-80, manpower cons., 1980, program operations specialist, 1980-81, mgr. div. manpower devel., 1980, community ombudsman, 1981-82; researcher So. Ill. U. Sch. Medicine, Springfield, 1982-84; personnel asst. Humana Hosp., Springfield, 1984-87, personnel dir., 1987-88; dir. human resources Doctors Hosp., Springfield, 1988—; cons. in field. Mem. Jr. League Springfield, 1987—; com. chmn. LincolnFest, Springfield, 1986. Mem. NAFE, Cen. Ill. Healthcare Personnel Mgrs. Assn., Personnel Assn. Cen. Ill., Soc. for Human Resource Mgmt. Home: 608 Old Tippecanoe Springfield IL 62707 Office: Doctors Hosp 5230 S 6th PO Box 19254 Springfield IL 62794-9254

ROSS, MARILYN JANE, insurance company executive; b. Fremont, Ohio, Dec. 11, 1944; d. Myron Elwood and Elvira Evelyn (Plagman) Magsig; m. John Francis Ross, III, Dec. 30, 1967 (div. Sept., 1974). BS in Edn., Capital U., Columbus, 1966; postgrad., U. Calif., Irvine, Fullerton, 1969-70. Tchr. pub. schs., Ohio, Calif., La., 1966-71; underwriter Tenn. Life Ins. Co., Houston, Tex., 1971-73; 2d v.p. Tenn. Life Ins. Co./Phila. Life Ins./Phila. Am. Life, Houston, 1971—; supr., mgr. contracts adminstrn. Phila. Life Ins. Co. (merger with Tenn. Life Ins. Co.), Houston, 1973-80; systems analyst Phila. Life Ins. Co., Houston, 1980-84; dir. market research/product devel. Phila. Am. Life Ins. Co. (merger Phila. Life Ins. Co.), Houston, 1984-87; 2d v.p. mktg. Phila. Am. Life Ins., Houston, 1987—. Vol. Spl. Olympics, Houston; tchr. Project Business, 1981. Recipient Outstanding Woman award, Houston YWCA, 1984. Mem. Am. Bus. Women's Assn., (chmn. edn. com. 1987-88), Soc. Group Contract Analysts (chmn. com. 1977-80). Republican. Lutheran. Office: Phila Am Life Ins 3121 Buffalo Speedway Houston TX 77098

ROSS, MARY COWELL (MRS. JOHN O. ROSS), lawyer; b. Oklahoma City, Okla., Oct. 1, 1910; d. Sears F. and Elizabeth (Van Zwaluwenburg) Riepma; A.B., Vassar Coll., 1932; LL.B., Memphis State U., 1938; LL.D., U. Nebr., 1973; m. Richard N. Cowell, Mar. 1, 1946 (dec. Jan. 1953); m. 2d, John O. Ross, Mar. 31, 1962 (dec. June 1966). Bar: Tenn. 1938, D.C. 1944, N.Y. 1947. Atty. U.S. Govt., Washington, 1940-44; pvt. practice Cromelin & Townsend, Washington, 1944-46. Royall, Koegel & Rogers and predecessors, N.Y.C., 1946-61; individual practice law, 1961—; treas., dir. 39 E. 79th St. Corp., 1966-73; treas., dir. 795 Fifth Ave. Corp., 1977—; mem. adv. com. N.Y. Commn. on Estates, 1965-67. Bd. dirs. Silver Cross Day Nursery, N.Y.C., 1963-70, Cunningham Dance Found., 1969-72, Central Park Community Fund, 1977-81, Sheldon Film Theater, 1988—; trustee U. Nebr. Found., 1966—, bd. dirs., 1974-79; hon. trustee Nebr. Art Assn. Mem. Am. Bar Assn., N.Y. Women's Bar Assn. (pres. 1955-57, dir. 1957-63, 74-80, adv. council 1963—), Bar Assn. City N.Y. (surrogate cts. com. 1961-65, library com. 1965-78, com. on profl. responsibility 1972-75), Nat. Assn. Women Lawyers (assembly del. 1962-64, 73-74, UN observer 1965-67, v.p. 1967, chmn. 1971 ann. conv., distinguished service award 1973), Vassar Coll. Alumnae Assn., Phi Alpha Delta, Delta Gamma, Dinner Dances, Inc. (bd. govs. 1979—). Address: 2 E 61st St Apt 2404 New York NY 10021

ROSS, MARY JANE, nuclear engineer; b. Bellefonte, Pa., July 13, 1961; d. Dean Franklin and Nadine Florence (Wasson) R. BS in Nuclear Engring., Penn State U., 1983; cert., Reactor Plant Sch., Groton, Conn., 1985. Asst test engr. Pearl Harbor (Hawaii) Shipyard, 1983-86, shift test engr., 1986-88, asst. chief test engr., 1988-89, chief test engr., 1989—. Mem. Honolulu County Com. on Status of Women, 1986-89. Mem. Bus. and Profl. Women. (Honolulu County com. 1988-89, Young Careerist 1988). Republican. Lutheran. Home: 94716 Paaona St Apt 5 Waipahu HI 96797 Office: Pearl Harbor Shipyard NED Code 2340 Box 400 Pearl Harbor HI 96797

ROSS, MIRIAM DEWEY, publishing executive; b. Cleve., Oct. 3, 1927; d. Kirk Martin and Grace Gray (Thomas) Dewey; m. James F. Ross, May 30, 1949; children: Deborah Jane, Steven Kirk, Rebekah Ruth. B.A., Doane Coll., 1949; M.A.T., George Washington U., 1972; M.S.L.S., Catholic U., 1976. Tchr. Riverside Ch. Nursery, N.Y.C., 1949-52, Short Hills Country Day, N.J., 1967-68; librarian Adv. & Learning Exchange, Washington, 1972-76; communications specialist D.C. Pub. Schs., Washington, 1978-81; owner Ross Book Service, Alexandria, Va., 1981-89; pres. Tools of the Trade: Books for Communicators, Alexandria, 1990—. Author numerous book revs. Active North Shore Hist. Soc., Pugwash, N.S., Can., 1975—; registrar joint archeol. expdn. Tell el-Hesi, Israel, 1979; bd. dirs. Am. Schs. Oriental Research, Phila., 1980-82, Albright Inst. Archeol. Research, Jerusalem, 1982-85. Mem. D.C. Library Assn., Am. Bookseller Assn., Soc. for Scholarly Pub., Women in COmmunications, Women's Nat. Book Assn., Network of Entrepreneurial Women, Direct Mktg. Assn. of Washington, D.C. Writers Ctr. Democrat. Mem. United Ch. of Christ. Avocations: travel, archaeology, textile arts. Home: 3718 Seminary Rd Alexandria VA 22304-0993 Office: Tools of the Trade Books for Communicators Box 12093 Seminary PO Alexandria VA 22304

ROSS, NANCY SCANDRETT, crossword puzzle constructor, editor; b. N.Y.C., May 8, 1932; d. Richard Brown Jr. and Mary (Landenberger) Scandrett; m. Robert Leonard Ross, Aug. 31, 1954; 1 child, Andrew. BA, Smith Coll., 1952. Staff writer, feature editor Scholastic Mags., N.Y.C., 1952-54; tchr. English Am. Sch., Manila, 1955-57; freelance writer, contbr. crossword puzzles to various publs., 1960—; events editor The Date Book, Pleasantville, N.Y., 1984—; Contbr. crossword puzzles to Games mag. tournaments, 1983, judge crossword puzzle tournament, 1984. Contbr. crossword puzzles to Games mag., 1983, 88, judge crossword puzzle tournaments, 1983, 84. Contbr. puzzles to N.Y. Times, USA Today, Dell Champion Crossword Puzzles, Simon & Schuster, Will Weng's Crossword Club, numerous others. Mem. AAUW (corr. sec. no. Westchester br. 1988—), Am. Crossword Puzzle Acad. (charter). Democrat. Home: Croton Ave Rte 4 Box 303 Peekskill NY 10566 Office: Date Book Publs 446 Bedford Rd Pleasantville NY 10570

ROSS, NELL TRIPLETT, financial consultant, educator, corporate secretary; b. Winterville, Miss., Feb. 14, 1922; d. Ethel Earl and Myrtie (Harrison) Triplett; m. William Dee Ross, Jr., July 25, 1944; 1 son, William Dee III. BA, Millsaps Coll., 1942. Tchr., Consol. Sch. of Chatham (Miss.), 1942-43, Glen Allan (Miss.) Consol. Sch., 1943-46; sec. econs. dept. Duke U., Durham, N.C., 1946; tchr. Durham High Sch., 1947, E.K. Powe Sch., Durham, 1947-48, Lakewood Elem. Sch., Durham, 1948-49; with purchasing dept. La. State U., Baton Rouge, 1949-50; enrollment officer La. Hosp. Service, Inc., Baton Rouge, 1950-51; owner Mentone Plantation, Erwin and Chatham, Miss., 1961—; owner, dir., corp. sec. Fin. Cons. Svcs., Inc., 1970—. Methodist. Clubs: Baton Rouge Country, Camelot. Home: 2738 McConnell Dr Baton Rouge LA 70809 also: 2763 Bocage Ct E Baton Rouge LA 70809

ROSS, PATRICIA ANN, educator; b. Knoxville, Tenn., July 23, 1935; d. James L. and Atha M. (Miller) Smith; m. Duane L. Ross, July 10, 1959; children: Mark, Glenn. BA, Western Mich. U., 1958, MA, 1978. Cert. tchr., Mich. Elem. tchr. Springfield Schs., Battle Creek, Mich., 1958-59, 63-67; elem. tchr. Portage Schs., Kalamazoo, Mich., 1959-60, Cherry Knoll Schs., Traverse City, Mich., 1961-63; elem. tchr. Pennfield Schs., Battle Creek, 1967-73, tchr. career edn., 1973-75, tchr. chpt. I, 1975-87, elem. librs. coord., 1987—. Editor: The Calhoun Collection, 1986; co-editor: Young Authors of Michigan, 1984. Nurture chairperson Birchwood Meth. Ch., Helmer at Gething, Battle Creek, 1987-88; drive chairperson Am. Cancer Soc., Battle Creek chpt., 1980—. Mem. AAUW, Mich. Assn. for Media in Edn., Calhoun County Reading Coun. (bd. dirs., pres., treas., MRA Literacy award 1989), Internat. Reading Assn. (Celebrate Literacy award 1986), Ben Franklin Philatelic Club (sponsor-leader 1976—). Home: 208 E Sunset Blvd Battle Creek MI 49017 Office: Pennfield Schools 8587 Q Dr North Battle Creek MI 49017

ROSS, PATTI JAYNE, physician; b. Sharon, Pa., Nov. 17, 1946; d. James J. and Mary N. Ross; B.S., DePauw U., 1968; M.D., Tulane, U., 1972; m. Allan Robert Katz, May 23, 1976. Asst. prof. U. Tex. Med. Sch., Houston, 1976-82, assoc. prof., 1982—, dir. adolescent obstetrics and gynecology, 1976—, also dir. phys. diagnosis; speaker in field. Bd. dirs. Am. Diabetes Assn., 1982—; mem. Rape Coun. Diplomate Am. Bd. Ob-Gyn. Mem. Tex. Med. Assn., Harris County Med. Soc. So. Perinatal Assn., Houston Obstetric and Gynecologic Soc., Assn. Profs. Obstetrics and Gynecology, Soc. Adolescent Medicine, AAAS, Am. Women's Med. Assn., Orgn. Women in Sci., Sigma Xi. Roman Catholic. Clubs: River Oak Breakfast, Profl. Women Execs. Contbr. articles to profl. jours. Office: 6431 Fannin St Houston TX 77030

ROSS, RHODA, artist; b. Boston, Dec. 24, 1941. Student, Carnegie Mellon U., 1960-62; BFA, RISD, 1964; MFA, Yale U., 1966. tchr. Hebrew Arts Sch., N.Y.C., 1987—; lectr. in field. One woman shows include Yale U., Pierson Coll., New Haven, , 1967, Convent of the Sacred Heart, N.Y.C., 1976, Mcpl. Art Soc., N.Y.C., 1978, L.I. U., N.Y.C., 1981, Dietal Gallery, Emma Willard Sch., Troy., N.Y., 1983, Marymount Manhattan Coll., N.Y.C. 1985; group shows include Paperwork Gallery, Larchmont, N.Y., 1983, Springfield Art Mus., 1983, Lehman Coll. Art Gallery, N.Y.C., 1985, Cape Mus. Fine Arts, Dennis, Mass., 1988, Kendal Gallery, Welfleet, Mass., 1988, 89, Lever Ho. N.Y.C., 1988, Gaumann-Cicchino Gallery, Ft. Lauderdale, Fla., 1989, S. Roper Gallery, Mind's Eye Gallery, Minot Art Gallery, Polk County Heritage Gallery, Wilkes Art Gallery, Kendal Gallery, 1989, The Poet Gallery, 1990, numerous others; commd. by Chem. Bank, N.Y.C., Burns & Levinson, Boston, Russian Tea Room, N.Y.C., Smith Barney Harris Upham & Co., N.Y.C., Waldorf Astoria, N.Y.C., Am. Hotel and Motel Assn., N.Y.C., Steelcase Inc., Indpls., numerous others; represented in permanent collections, The White House, The Honorable Edward I. Koch, Mus. of City of N.Y.C., St. Louis Conservatory Music., Chem. Bank National Hdqrs., L.I. U., The Juilliard Sch., Shiffer, Lichtfield & Assoc., The Waldorf Astoria Hotel, The Russian Tea Room, Rose Assoc., numerous others. Juror Nat. Assn. Women Artists, 1988-90. Skowhegan Sch. of Painting scholar, 1986; recipient 1st prize Madamoiselle mag. nat. competition, 1965, Grumbacher Gold medal Nat. Assn. Women Artists, 1985. Mem. RISD Alumni Assn. (treas. 1986, mem. alumni exec. com.), Phi Tau Gamma. Home and Studio: 473 West End Ave New York NY 10024

ROSS, ROBINETTE DAVIS, publisher; b. London, May 16, 1952; d. Raymond Lawrence and Pearl Agnes (Robinette) D.; m. William Bradford Ross III, Mar. 16, 1979; children: Nellie Tayloe, William IV, 1 stepchild, Aviza Tayloe. Student, Am. U., 1977-78. Asst. to editor The Chronicle of Higher Edn., Washington, 1978, advt. mgr., 1978-82, advt. dir., 1982-86, assoc. pub., 1986—; assoc. pub. The Chronicle of Philanthropy, 1988—. Mem. Am. Newspaper Pubs. Assn., Am. News Women's Club, City Tavern Club. Episcopalian. Home: 3908 Virgilia St Chevy Chase MD 20815 Office: The Chronicle of Higher Edn 1255 23d St NW Washington DC 20037

ROSS, SANDRA ELAINE POLK, advertising executive; b. Highsprings, Fla., Nov. 16, 1942; d. Jesse Lee and Verna (Minton) Polk; m. Robert Burl Ross, Jr. (dec. 1978); 1 child, Robert Kenneth. Student, Hillsborough County Sch. Practical Nursing, Tampa, Fla., 1983; Assoc. Sci. Nursing, SUNY, Albany, 1987, BS in Sociology, 1988. Cert. gerontol. nurse, nursing adminstr. Nursing asst. Oakwood Park Su Casa Nursing Ctr., Tampa, 1983; charge nurse Oakwood Park Sucasa Nursing Ctr., Tampa, 1983-87, supr., health care coord., 1987—; pres. Robert Ross Advt. Inc., Tampa, 1978—. Mem. NAFE, Am. Nurses Assn., Nat. League Nurses, Gerontol. Soc. Fla.

ROSS, SHEILA MAUREEN HOLMES, sales executive; b. San Jose, Calif., Nov. 1, 1951; d. Douglas F. and Mary A. (Zager) Murphy; B.A., San Jose State U., 1973; 1 child, Vanessa Katherine Ross. Exec. sec. J.M. Mfg., Santa Clara, Calif., 1972-74; mktg. coordinator Chick, Orthopedic/Hosmer-Dorrance, Campbell, Calif., 1974-75; mgr. mktg. adminstrn. Consol. Video Systems, Sunnyvale, Calif., 1975-83; regional mgr., Pacific dist. sales mgr. ADDA Corp., Los Gatos, Calif., 1977-84, N.W. regional mgr., 1983-84; broadcast sales mgr. Aurora Systems, San Francisco, 1984-86; dir. U.S. sales Vertigo Systems Internat., Inc., Vancouver, B.C., Can., 1986-87; sales mgr., Digital F/X, Inc., Santa Clara, Calif., 1987—. Soc. Motion Pictures and TV Engrs. Home: 28 Dartmouth Pl Danville CA 94526

ROSS, SUZANNE IRIS, fundraising executive; b. Chgo., Feb. 2, 1948; d. Irving and Rose (Stein) R. BA in Secondary Edn., Western Mich. U., 1971. Dir. youth employment Ill. Youth Svcs. Bur., Maywood, Ill., 1978-79; exec. dir. Edn. Resource Ctr., Chgo., 1979-82; asst. dir. devel. Art Inst. Chgo., 1982-83, mgr. govt. affairs, 1983-84, dir. govt. affairs, 1984-85; v.p. devel. Spertus Coll. Judaica, Chgo., 1985—; lectr. Sch. Art Inst., Chgo., 1982-85, Ill. Fire Inspectors Assn., Mt. Prospect, Ill., 1982-84, Episcopalian Archdiocese, Chgo., 1984, Nat. Soc. Fund Raising Execs. and Donor's Forum, Chgo., 1987; instr. DePaul U. Sch. for New Learning, 1987-88, Columbia Coll., Chgo., 1980—. Mem. adv. coun. Citizens Com. on Media, Chgo., 1978-80; adv. panelist Chgo. Office Fine Arts, 1981-82; mem. adv. coun. Greater Chgo. Food Depository, 1984-85; exec. com. Chgo. Coalition Arts in Edn., 1981-82; mem. info. svcs. com. Donors' Forum Chgo., 1986-88, mem. adv. bd. Chgo. Moving Co., 1987—. Mem. Nat. Soc. Fund Raising Execs., Am. Assn. Mus., Am. Coun. Arts, Ill. Arts Alliance. Democrat. Jewish. Avocation: attending cultural events. Home: 3709 N Janssen #2RB Chicago IL 60613 Office: Spertus Coll Judaica 618 S Michigan Ave Chicago IL 60605

ROSS, SUZANNE JEANNETTE, public relations executive; b. Royal Oak, Mich., Apr. 12, 1960; d. Thomas Jr. and Frances Laura (Harvey) R. Student, U. Mich., 1978-80; MusB, Ind. U., 1982. Coord. spl. events Detroit Renaissance Found., 1982-83; asst. dir. Am. O.R.T., Chgo., 1983-84; dir. pub. rels. and devel. Chiaravalle Montessori Sch., Evanston, Ill., 1984-85; sr. account exec. Connie Zonka & Assocs., Chgo., 1985-87; media dir. Mt. Sinai Med. Ctr., Chgo., 1987-88; dir. pub. rels. Columbus-Cabrini Med. Ctr., Chgo., 1988—; freelance musician. Bd. dirs. Chgo. String Ensemble, 1984-86, Chgo. House, AIDS, 1987—; mem. Chgo. Found. for Women, 1986—. Mem. Pub. Rels. Soc. Am., Am. Fedn. Musicians, Publicity Club Chgo. Episcopalian. Office: Columbus-Cabrini Med Ctr 467 W Deming Pl Chicago IL 60614

ROSS, VIRGINIA R., business executive; b. L.A.; d. Roy Renwick and Olivia Marie (Macbride) Wilson; B.S., U. Redlands; M.A., Calif. State U.; children: Will, Brian, Darrell, Leslie. Writer-editor, fiber artist, 1965-70; product mgr. A Stitch 'n' Time, San Marino, Calif., 1970-75; product mgr. research and devel. Hazel Pearson Handicrafts, Industry, Calif., 1976-81. Editor, REC, Inc., Arcadia, Calif., 1983-86; sr. tech. writer CSC, Pasadena, Calif., 1986-89. Mem. Am. Crafts Council, Surface Design Assn. Republican. Presbyterian.

ROSSBACHER, LISA ANN, geology educator, science writer, university administrator; b. Fredericksburg, Va., Oct. 10, 1952; d. Richard Irwin and Jean Mary (Dearing) R.; m. Dallas D. Rhodes, Aug. 4, 1978. BS, Dickinson Coll., 1975; MA, SUNY, Binghamton, 1978, Princeton U., 1979; PhD, Princeton U., 1983. Cons. Republic Geothermal, Santa Fe Springs, Calif., 1979-81; asst. prof. geology Whittier (Calif.) Coll., 1982-84; asst. prof. geology Calif. State Poly. U., Pomona, 1984-86, assoc. prof. geol. sci., 1986—, assoc. v.p. acad. affairs, 1987—; vis. researcher U. Uppsala, Sweden, 1984. Author: Career Opportunities in Geology and the Earth Sciences, 1983, Recent Revolutions in Geology, 1986; (with Rex Buchanan) Geomedia, 1988; columnist Geotimes, 1988—; contbr. articles to profl. jours. Recipient scholarship Ministry Edn. of Finland, Helsinki, 1984; grantee NASA, 1983—. Mem. AAAS (geol. nominating com. 1984-87), Assn. Earth Sci. Editors (assoc. editor 1985-87), Geol. Soc. Am., Sigma Xi (grantee 1976). Office: Calif State Poly U Office of Acad Affairs 3801 W Temple Ave Pomona CA 91768

ROSSER, WILLIE RUTH SEALS, county tax examiner; b. Lake Providence, La., May 14, 1935; d. Mabel (Anderson) Seals; m. Lewis R. Rosser, 1961 (div. 1979); divorced; 1 child, Rhonda Fay. Student, Pruitt Coll. Bus., L.A., 1953-54; student, Mercer County Community Coll., Trenton, N.J., Trenton State Coll., Rutgers U. Cert. tax assessor. Clk. typist N.J. State Dept. Civl Svcs., Trenton, 1956-59; sr. clk. typist Mercer County Bd. Taxation, Trenton, 1959-65, prin. clk., 1965-77, adminstrv. clk., 1977-87, sr. tax examiner, 1987—. Pres. LWV, Trenton, 1976, YWCA, Trenton, 1982-85; v.p. Greater Trenton Com. Mental Health Ctr., 1987—; coord. City Coun., Trenton, 1990; bd. dirs. LWV N.J., 1978; chairwoman Interfaith Orgn. for Community, Trenton, Rent Stabilization Bd., Trenton; mem. Mercer County Dem. Com. Mem. NAFE, Mercer County Assessors Assn., Mercer County Bd. Realtors. Baptist. Home: 777 W State St 10F Trenton NJ 08618 Office: Mercer County Bd Taxation 640 S Broad St Trenton NJ 08650

ROSSI, CYNTHIA ANN, advertising and public relations executive; b. Latrobe, Pa., Jan. 2, 1954; d. Gerald T. and Edith Mary (Condi) R. BA Cum Laude, Washington and Jefferson Coll., 1976. Coord. pub. rels. Washington (Pa.) Sch. Dist., 1976-77; account exec. Washington (Pa.) Broadcasting Co., 1978-79; dir. advt. pub. rels. Reed and Cameron Hardware, Inc., Washington, Pa., 1979-80; owner C.A. Rossi and Assocs., Washington, Pa., 1980—; lectr. mktg. and advt. various community and bus. groups, 1980—. Editor The Marginal Rev., 1978-80; author various poems, 1975-81; contbr. articles to profl jours. Bd. dirs. Washington and Jefferson Coll. Aux., 1986—, v.p., 1989—, many other community svcs. Recipient numerous graphic design awards. Mem. AAUW. Home and Office: 10 Thayer St Washington PA 15301

ROSSI, DIANA M., systems coordinator; b. Dover, N.J., Feb. 18, 1948; d. Joseph and Theresa (Knotz) Jautz. BA in Edn., Georgian Ct. Coll., 1970. Tchr. St. Ann's Sch., Raritan, N.J., 1971-86; mgr. bus. office Seacoast Publs., Inc., Toms River, N.J., 1974-86; gen. mgr. Rickart Collection Systems, Inc., North Brunswick, N.J., 1986-89; systems coord. Hughes-Plumer & Assocs., Somerville, N.J., 1990; ptnr. Cafe Italia, Princeton, N.J., 1990—. Mem. NAFE, MI Hummel Club (past pres. Raritan Valley chpt.). Address: 260 Sunnymeade Rd Somerville NJ 08876

ROSSI, LINDA ELAINE, management infosystems specialist; b. Bklyn., June 25, 1950; d. Vincent and Hazel Elaine (Long) R. Head bookkeeper Halden & Co., N.Y.C., 1968-73; adminstrv. officer A.G. Becker, Paribas, N.Y.C., 1973-84; mgr. client support, asst. v.p. Shearson Lehman Hutton, N.Y.C., 1984—. Republican. Roman Catholic.

ROSSI, LINDA JEAN, healthcare administrator; b. Sacramento, Nov. 2, 1956; d. Daniel Francis and Lillian Josephine (Snow) O'Brien; m. Randy Clayton Rossi, Sept. 29, 1979; children: Justin Franklin, Lauren Michelle. AA, Am. River Coll., 1976; BS in Nursing, U. Portland, 1979. R.N., Calif. Critical care nurse O'Connor Hosp., San Jose, Calif., 1979-81; mem. med. rev. team Calif. Dept. Health Svcs., San Jose, 1981-82; mgr. patient rev. svcs. Found. Med. Care, Campbell, Calif., 1982-83; coord. quality rev. svcs. Roseville (Calif.) Community Hosp., 1983-84; v.p. managed care Am. Gen. Group Ins./Am. Health Network, Sacramento, 1984—. Mem. Am. Med. Care Rev. Assn., Employee Benefits Coun., Tyrotoastmasters, C. of C. Republican. Roman Catholic.

ROSSI, ROSALIE CLARA, artist, consultant, educator, researcher; b. Newburgh, N.Y., Dec. 22, 1940; d. Joseph Emilio and Martha (Martinisi) R. BS in Art Edn., SUNY, New Paltz, 1963, MS in Art Edn., 1964; PhD in Art and Art Edn., NYU, 1978, postgrad., 1985-88. Cert. Neuro-Associative Conditioning Systems, 1985. Tchr. art Mamaroneck (N.Y.) Pub. Schs., 1963-66; tchr. N.Y.C. Bd. Edn., 1967-68; asst. prof. art Monmouth Coll., West Long Branch, N.J., 1968-73; pres. N.Y.C. Rose Prodns., 1974—; assoc. prof. art Cen. Mich. U., Mt. Pleasant, 1980-81; art cons. NCI East and RRI N.Y.C., 1984—; cert. staff artist Robbins Rsch. Internat., La Jolla, Calif., 1988—. Author: Contemporary British Sculpture, 1978, Art People, 1990; artist: Art in New York Rev. of Art, 1988; lectr. and exhibition Loeb Ctr., NYU, 1989, Ten Worlds Gallery, N.Y.C., 1988—, Marcoleo, Ltd., N.Y.C., 1988—. Vol. Hunger Project, N.Y.C., 1988. Mem. Alliance of Figurative Art, Artists Alliance, Toastmasters. Office: 41 Perry St New York NY 10014

ROSSINI, CARLOTTA, advertising executive; b. N.Y.C., Apr. 21, 1944; d. Luigi and Hulda (Lefridge) R. Student, Columbia U., 1963-64. Mgmt. trainee InterPub. Group of Cos., N.Y.C., 1966; media planner Wunderman, Ricotta & Kline Inc., N.Y.C., 1967; pres. Rossini/Steven Assocs., N.Y.C., 1967-70; v.p., supr. mgmt. Ogilvy & Mather Advt., N.Y.C., 1970-86; pres. Carlotta Rossini & Assocs., Inc., N.Y.C., 1986—. Recipient Addy award Am. Advt. Fedn., 1968, Effie award Am. Mktg. Assn., 1981; named to Outstanding Young Women Am., U.S. Jaycees, 1977. Mem. NOW, ACLU.

ROSS-JACOBS, RUTH ANN, investment company executive, retired golf and country club executive; b. Milw., Mar. 10, 1934; d. Arthur Theodore and Mary Marilyn (Digert) Kamman; m. Warren Ross, Aug. 9, 1957 (div. Sept. 1972); 1 child, Michael Edward; m. Albert Jacobs, June 28, 1973 (dec. Apr. 1978). BS, U. Miami, Coral Gables, Fla., 1958; MS, Wayne State U., 1961; postgrad. U. Wis., 1967-69. R.N., Fla., Wis., Mich. Staff nurse Lafayette Clinic, Detroit, 1958-59; instr. Milw. Inst. Tech., 1962-67; dir. inservice edn. St. Mary's Hosp., Milw., 1963-69; cons. Hearthside Rehab., Milw., 1968-69; owner Peddler Stores, Milw., 1969-72; pres. Jacobs & Densmore Ltd., Toronto, Ont., Can., 1978-83; v.p. Vaughn Ltd., Toronto, 1978-87; pres. Glen Road Leasing Ltd., Toronto, 1978-79, Evnor Apts. Ltd., Toronto, 1978-79, Norman Lathing Ltd., Toronto, 1978-79, Allied Capital Enterprises, Inc., 1989—; v.p. Elgin Mills Investments Ltd., Toronto, 1978-80. Author: Inservice Education, 1967; Nursing Procedures, 1969. Pres. PTO, Boca Raton, Fla., 1973-76; mem. Republican Nat. Com., Washington, 1984—; mem. Inner Circle, Washington, 1984—, Security and Intelligence Found, 1986—, Second Amendment Found., Washington, 1989—, Presdl. Roundtable, Washington, 1987—, Presdl. Task Force, Washington, 1986—, U.S. Com. for Battle of Normandy, Washington, 1987—, Heritage Found., 1990—, The Pres.'s Club. Recipient stipend NIH, Bethesda, Md., 1959. Mem. Pres. Club USO, Wayne State Univ. Deans Club, Internat. Platform Assn., NRA, Madisons Eagles, Boca Raton Club, Sigma Theta Tau. Republican. Lutheran. Avocations: real estate investments, travel, charity. Home: 2000 S Ocean Blvd Penthouse K Boca Raton FL 33432

ROSSMAN, TOBY GALE, genetic toxicologist educator, researcher; b. Weehawken, N.J., June 3, 1942; d. Norman N. and Sylvia Betty (May) Natowitz; m. Neil I. Rossman, Sept. 16, 1962 (div. Sept. 1980). AB, NYU, 1964, PhD, 1968; postgrad., Brandeis U., 1964-65. Instr. Polytech. Inst. of N.Y., N.Y.C., 1968-69; postdoctoral dept. pathology NYU, N.Y.C., 1969-71, from asst. to assoc. prof. Inst. for Environ. Medicine, 1974-85, prof. genetic toxicology Inst. for Environ. Medicine, 1985—. Mem. editorial bd. Molecular Toxicology, 1989—, Teratogenesis, Carcinogenesis, Mutagenesis, 1990—; contbr. numerous articles to profl. jours. EPA grantee, NIH grantee. Mem. AAAS, Assn. for Women in Sci., Am. Assn. for Cancer Rsch., Am. Soc. for Microbiology, Environ. Mutagen Soc. (councilor 1990—). Office: NYU Inst Environ Medicine Long Meadow Rd Tuxedo NY 10987

ROSSOTTI, BARBARA JILL MARGULIES, lawyer; b. Englewood, N.J., Feb. 28, 1940; d. Albert and Loretta (Jill) Margulies; m. Charles Ossola Rossotti; children: Allegra Jill, Edward Charles. BA magna cum laude, Mount Holyoke Coll., 1961; LLB, Harvard U., 1964. Bar: D.C. 1966. Assoc. Nutter McClennen & Fish, Boston, 1964-65, Covington & Burling, Washington, 1965-72; assoc. Shaw, Pittman, Potts & Trowbridge, Washington, 1972-73, ptnr., 1973—; mem., interim adv. com., adv. bd. Women's Nat. Bank, Washington, 1977-80. Trustee, Mt. Holyoke Coll., South Hadley, Mass., 1984—, vice chmn., 1989—, chmn. exec. com. Campaign for Mt. Holyoke Coll., 1986—; trustee Choral Arts Soc. Washington, 1989—; trustee Legal Aid Soc. D.C., 1979—, pres., 1985-89; founding chmn., mem. adv. bd. Sta. WAMU-FM, Am. U., 1979-83; bd. dirs. Washington Home, 1989—. Mem. ABA (com. on U.S. activities of foreigners and tax treaties, sect. on taxation 1978—, chmn., co-chmn. subcom. important devels. and publs. 1983-85, subcom. on tax treaties, U.S. source interests 1982-83, tax treaties 1981-82, non-resident, alien status and consequences 1979-80, taxation alien earnings 1978-79), Am. Soc. Internat. Law, Internat. Law Assn., D.C. Bar Assn., 1925 F Street Club. Office: Shaw Pittman Potts & Trowbridge 2300 N St NW Washington DC 20037

ROSSOW, RACHEL LEE WHEELER, mental health nursing consultant; b. Long Beach, Calif., Mar. 20, 1939; d. Robert Edward and Leila Palestine (Jacobsen) Wheeler; m. Carl Joseph Rossow, Dec. 27, 1964; children: Rachel Marie, Robert, Susan, Eddy, Ellen, Dina, Simone, David, Patrick, Charlie, Mary, Maria, Benjamin, Christa Lee, Roy, Jose Luis, Christopher, Michael, Aaron. BS, Salve Regina Coll., 1960, DHL, 1984; MS in Nursing, Cath. U. Am., 1973. Head nurse Medfield State Hosp., Harding, Mass., 1960-61; novice Discalced Carmelite Monastery, Barrington, R.I., 1961-63; nurse/therapist Edgemeade (Md.) Residential Sch., 1963-64, Extension Vols., Hanesville, Ky., 1965-66; pres. Alpha and Omega, Inc., Ellington, Conn., 1974—, Alpha and Omega/SimChris, Inc., Ellington, Conn., 1989—; pres. Alpha and Omega/SimChris, Inc., 1989—; cons. for children Conn. Dept. of Children and Youth Services, 1987—. Writer various booklets; contbr. articles to profl. jours. Mem. Conn. Gov.'s Com. on employment of Handicapped, 1983-85; sec. Conn. Commn. on Children and Youth, 1985—; bd. dirs., sec. Community Child Guidance Clinic, Manchester, Conn., 1974-79; chairperson Community Health Commn., Town of Ellington, 1974-81, mem. bd. fin., 1984-90, justice of peace, 1985-89, 90—; mem. Dem. Town Com., Ellington, 1972—, chairperson, 1988—. Recipient Spl. award Conn. Assn. Retarded Citizens, 1981, Family of Yr. award Greater Vernon (Conn.) Jaycees, 1981, Gt. Am. Family Community award, 1982, Humanitarian award Office of Human Devel. Svcs., 1989. Roman Catholic. Home: 15 1/2 Lanz Ln Ellington CT 06029

ROSS-RHOADES, VICKI ANN, accountant; b. St. Ansgar, Iowa, Apr. 27, 1957; d. Darwin Ross and Alice Josephine (Wirth) Rhoades; m. Steven James Ross, Sept. 18, 1982; children: Forrest Lee Ross, Axel Taylor Ross. BS, Mankato State U., 1979. CPA, Minn. Staff acct. Clapper, Kitchenmaster & Co., CPA's, Waseca, Minn., 1980, Goldfein, Silverman & Olson, CPA's, Mpls., 1980-81; prin. Krigbaum, Ross-Rhoades & Elliott, Ltd., CPA's, Bemidji, Minn., 1982—. Treas. Paul Bunyan Playhouse, Bemidji, 1982-89. Mem. Am. Inst. CPA's, Minn. Soc. CPA's, Jaycee Women (bd. dirs. Bemidji 1982), N.W. Minn. Woodland Owner's Assn. (treas. 1983-85). Lutheran. Home: Box 368 Pennington MN 56663 Office: Krigbaum Ross-Rhoades 315 5th St Bemidji MN 56601

ROTEMAN, CAROL BARBARA, critical care nurse; b. Bronx, N.Y., July 15, 1946; d. Jerome and Sylvia (Abramowitz) Saunders; m. Bradley Jay, Oct. 29, 1967; children: Ryan, Alexander. Student, Ga. State Coll., 1964-66; student, Crawford W. Long Sch. Nursing, Atlanta, 1964-66; diploma in nursing, Elizabeth (N.J.) Gen. Hosp., 1968; student, No. Va. Community Coll., 1984-85. Cert. primary nurse III. Office mgr. oral surgery Dr. Ben Marshall, Alexandria, Va., 1971-72; staff nurse Potomac Hosp., Woodbridge, Va., 1974-76; outpatient surgery and gen. OR staff Mt. Vernon Hosp., Alexandria, 1976—. Vol. coord. Potomac Mills Activity Ctr. for Muscular Dystrophy Assc., 1987-90; historian Dumfries (Va.) Magisterial Dist. Civic Assn., 1990—. Recipient award Muscular Dystrophy Assn., 1978, 79, 88, 89, 90; named One of Outstanding Young Women of Am. Woodbridge Jaycees, 1978, 79, 80, 81. Mem. Assn. Operating Rm. Nurses (nursing advisor world affairs confs. 1988-90). Office: 2501 Parker Ln Alexandria VA 22306

ROTERT, DENISE ANNE, occupational therapist, army officer; b. Sioux Falls, S.D., Nov. 18, 1949; d. Leonard Joseph and Irene Winnifred (Jennings) R. BS, U. Puget Sound, 1971; MA, U. No. Colo., 1975. Commd. 2d lt. Med. Specialist Corps, U.S. Army, 1970, advanced through grades to maj., 1983; staff occupational therapist Tripler Army Med. Center, Honolulu, 1973-76, officer in charge occupational therapy sect. Ireland Army Hosp., Fort Knox, Ky., 1976-77; clin. supr. occupational therapy sect. Letterman Army Med. Center, Presidio of San Francisco, 1977-79; chief instr. occupational therapy asst. course Acad. Health Scis., Ft. Sam Houston, Tex., 1979-84; chief occupational therapy Tri-Service Alcohol Recovery Dept., Naval Hosp., Bethesda, Md., 1984-89, Womack Army Hosp., Ft. Bragg, N.C., 1989—. Recipient Myra McDaniel Writer's award, 1989. Mem. Am. Occupational Therapy Assn., D.C. Occupational Therapy Assn., World Fedn. Occupational Therapists. Roman Catholic. Office: Womack Army Hosp Occupational Therapy Sect Fort Bragg NC 28307

ROTH, BARBARA, chemist, educator; b. Milw., June 9, 1916; d. John William Frederick III and Nellie May (Farr) R. BS, Beloit Coll., 1937; MS, Northwestern U., Evanston, Ill., 1939, PhD, 1941. Instr. Lake Forest (Ill.) Coll., 1940-41; rsch. chemist Am. Cyanamid Co., Bound Brook, N.J., 1941-

51; rsch. supr. Toni Div. The Gillette Co., Chgo., 1951-55; sr. rsch. chemist Burroughs Wellcome Co., Tuckahoe, N.Y., 1955-70; group leader, organic chemistry Burroughs Wellcome Co., Research Triangle Park, N.C., 1970-86; adj. prof. chemistry dept. U.N.C., Chapel Hill, 1986—; cons. Burroughs Wellcome Co., 1987-88; active rsch. grant study section, NIH, Washington, 1984-88. Inventor in field; contbr. author books in field; conbr. articles to profl. jours. Recipient Disting. Svc. award Beloit (Wis.) Coll., 1982. Fellow AAAS (chemistry com. 1980-83); mem. Am. Chem. Soc. (chmn. medicinal div. 1976-77), Nat. Audubon Soc. (editor, founding pres. New Hope chpt. 1975-77), The Sierra Club, N.Y. Acad. Scis. (life). Home: 7 Lone Pine Rd Chapel Hill NC 27514

ROTH, BARBARA EDESON, consultant, speech and language pathologist; b. Pitts., Dec. 29, 1955; d. Samuel and Anne Clare (Opachevsky) Edeson; m. James A. Roth, Jan. 15, 1984; 1 child, Sarah Ann. BS, Pa. State U., 1976; MA, Kent State U., 1978. Speech-lang. pathologist Youngstown (Ohio) Hearing and Speech Ctr., 1979, South Hills Health System, Home Health Agy., Pitts., 1980-83; pvt. practive, cons. Rye, N.Y., 1984—. Mem. Am. Speech, Lang. and Hearing Assn., N.Y. State Speech, Lang. and Hearing Assn., Westchester Speech, Lang. and Hearing Assn., Hadassah. Democrat. Jewish. Home: 11 Green Ave Rye NY 10580

ROTH, BATYA, lawyer; b. Newark, Oct. 27, 1954; d. Albert and Martha L. (Goldenberg) R.; children: Shana Elena, Michael Jaime, Matthew Daniel, Alissa Rachel. Student, Tel Aviv U., Israel, 1973-74; BA, Douglass Coll., 1976; MA, Columbia U., 1981; JD, Nova U., 1985. Bar: Fla. 1985, U.S. Ct. Appeals (D.C., 2d, 11th cirs.) 1986, (3d, 10th cirs.) 1987, U.S. Supreme Ct. 1989. Assoc. Britton, Cassel, Schantz & Schatzman, Miami, Fla., 1985; staff atty. SEC, Washington, 1985-89, U.S. C. of C., Washington, 1989—; adj. prof. Nat. Law Ctr., George Washington U., Washington, 1989—. Editor: Nova Law Jour., 1984-85. Vol. Rutgers Community Action, Piscataway, N.J., 1972-73, Cystic Fibrosis Found., Washington, 1986-88. Rsch. fellow dept. Middle East langs. and cultures, Columbia U., 1989, corps. and securities regulations, Nova U., 1983-84. Mem. ABA. Democrat. Jewish. Office: US Chamber of Commerce 1615 H St NW Washington DC 20062

ROTH, ELIZABETH ELAM, editor, publisher; b. Houston. BA, U. St. Thomas, 1983. Editorial asst. Houston City Mag., 1982-83; freelance dance critic Houston, 1982-85, Austin, Tex., 1985-89; copy editor Jour. Infectious Disease Baylor Coll. Medicine, Houston, 1984; owner Elam Roth Assocs., Austin, 1985—. Author over 50 works on dance history, criticism, and features, 1982-88. Vol. Austin Independent Sch. Dist., 1985—, Dance Umbrella, Inc., Austin, 1985—; panelist Austin Arts Commn. Peer Rev. Panel, Austin, 1986-87. Nat. Undergrad. Communication Conf. fellow DePauw U., 1982. Mem. Women in Communication Inc. (newsletter pub. Austin Profl. chpt.). Office: Elam Roth Assocs 2704 Cherry Ln Austin TX 78703

ROTH, JANE RICHARDS, federal judge; b. Phila., June 16, 1935; d. Robert Henry Jr. and Harriett (Kellond) Richards; m. William V. Roth Jr., Oct. 9, 1965; children: William V. III, Katharine K. BA, Smith Coll., 1956; LLB, Harvard U., 1965; LLD (hon.), Widener U., 1986. Bar: Del. 1965, U.S. Dist. Ct. Del. 1966, U.S. Ct. Appeals (3d cir.) 1974. Adminstrv. asst. various fgn. service posts U.S. State Dept., 1956-62; assoc. Richards, Layton & Finger, Wilmington, Del., 1965-73, ptnr., 1973-85; judge U.S. Dist. Ct. Del., Wilmington, 1985—. Trustee Hist. Soc. Del., Wilmington; mem. Chesapeake Bay coun. Girl Scouts U.S.A.; hon. chmn. Del. chpt. Arthritis Found., Wilmington; bd. overseers Widener U. Sch. Law. Recipient Nat. Vol. Service citation Athritis Found., 1982. Mem. Fed. Judges Assn., Del. State Bar Assn. Republican. Episcopalian. Office: US Dist Ct 844 King St Lockbox 12 Wilmington DE 19801

ROTH, SISTER M. AUGUSTINE, nun, educator; b. Mpls., Jan. 16, 1926; d. J.A., and Anne A. (Boies) R. BA, U. Minn., 1947, MA, 1948; PhD, Cath. U. Am., 1961. Joined Sisters of Mercy, Roman Catholic Ch., 1949. Faculty Mt. Mercy Coll., Cedar Rapids, Iowa, 1948-79, 80—, prof. dept. English and pub. rels.; v.p. bd. dirs. Mercy Hosp. Endowment Found., 1979—, exec. dir., 1987—, chmn. bd. trusees of hosp., 1987—. Author: Written in His Hands, 1976; With Mercy Toward All, 1979; Courage and Change, 1980, One Life, 1987. Home: 1125 Prairie Dr NE Cedar Rapids IA 52402

ROTH, MARIE MERCURY, retired chemistry educator; b. Boston, Apr. 30, 1926; d. Nicholas and Josephine (Borré) Mercury; m. Donald Alfred Roth, June 9, 1951; children: Catherine Roth Holcomb, Charles, Joanne Roth Wendelberger, Nancy. BA, Mt. Holyoke Coll., 1945, MA, 1947; PhD, U. Wis., Madison, 1952. Literature chemist PPG Industries, Milw., 1952; lectr. Carroll Coll., Waukesha, Wis., 1955, U. Wis. Ctr. System, West Bend and Milw., 1971-79, 86; adj. asst. prof. chemistry U. Wis., Milw., 1981; lectr. Marquette U., Milw., 1981-82; now ret.; judge Southeast Wis. Sci. Fair, Milw., 1982-90. Contbr. articles to sci. jour. Mem. Am. Chem. Soc. (chair Milw. sect. 1985), Sigma Xi, Phi Beta Kappa. Roman Catholic. Home: 1620 Revere Dr Brookfield WI 53045

ROTH, MARLEN DEANNE, state administrator, simultaneous translator; b. Havana, Cuba, Nov. 19, 1949; came to U.S., 1961, naturalized, 1971; d. Manuel Vilas and Gladys R. Diaz; m. Karl Paul Roth, Apr. 19, 1980. Grad. Cosmopolitan Prep. Sch., 1969. Free-lance translator, writer, 1966—; assoc. editor, art critic Dingo Hispano Newspaper, 1973-77; asst. producer, air personality La Cuba de Ayer radio show, 1975; dir. pub. relations, dancer Ballet Azteca, 1977-78; art critic, interviewer, air personality, news announcer, dir. spl. reports Sta. WOPA, 1978-83; office mgr., adminstrv. asst. to dir. Ill. Gov's Office Interagy. Coop., 1977-78, adminstrv. aide on women, 1977-84; asst. to dep. dir. for mktg. Ill. Dept. Commerce and Community Affairs, Chgo., 1984-87; exec. asst. to dir. Ill. State Lottery, 1987—; frequent guest on local TV and radio shows; frequent speaker for numerous civic, polit., bus. groups. Mem. Ill. Commn. on Status Women, 1981-83; active Minority Women's Employment Confs., 1981, 82; numerous Rep. activities, current ones being chmn. Hispanic Coun., Ill. Rep. State Com., 1981—, dep. committeeman for Hispanic Affairs, Proviso Twp., Ill., 1984-86. Mem. Pan Am. Coun. (life, bd. dirs. 1977-78, exec. v.p. 1978-84, pres. 1984-87), Am. Soc. Notaries (govt. relations com.), Spanish-Am. Pro Art and Culture Soc. (dir. pub. relations, bd. dirs.), Internat. Visitors Ctr., Nat. Assn. Cuban Journalists (exec. dir. Chgo. chpt. 1986—). Avocation: travel.

ROTH, REGINA SARAH, psychologist; b. Lake Forest, Ill., Mar. 6, 1950; d. Richard James and Shirley (White) R.; A.B. with honors, Conn. Coll., 1972; M.A., NYU, 1974, Ph.D. (NIMH trainee), 1976; postdoctoral student Northwestern U. Med. Hosp. Inst. Psychiatry, 1978-79 Staff cons. clin. div. Worthington Hurst & Assocs., Chgo., 1977-78; psychology postdoctoral trainee Hines (Ill.) VA Hosp., 1979; psychology postdoctoral trainee West Side VA Hosp., Chgo., 1979-80; pvt. practice clin. psychology, 1980—. Mem. Am. Psychol. Assn., Ill. Psychol. Assn., Nat. Register Mental Health Service Providers, Chgo. Assn. Psychoanalytic Psychology, Am. Group Psychotherapy Assn. Home: 3001 S King Dr Apt 508 Chicago IL 60616 Office: 1701 E Lake Ave Suite 445 Glenview IL 60025

ROTH, SALLY, information science specialist; b. Buffalo, Apr. 4, 1960; d. Charles Lawrence and Joan Frances (King) Scime; m. D. Allen Roth, Feb. 19, 1982. BA in Humanities, Medaille Coll., 1985; MLS, SUNY, Buffalo, 1986. Proposal analyst Utlas Internat., Kansas City, Mo., 1986-87; rsch. ctr. analyst United Telecom, Kansas City, 1987-89; competitor and industry analyst U.S. Sprint, Kansas City, 1989—. Bd. dirs. Longfellow Community Assn., Kansas City, 1988—. Mem. Spl. Libr. Assn. (bull. editor Heart of Am. chpt. 1988-90, bd. dirs. 1990—), Am. Soc. Info. Sci., Beta Phi Mu. Office: US Sprint 8140 Ward Pkwy PO Box 38 Kansas City MO 64114

ROTH, STACIA LYNN, sales executive; b. South Bend, Ind., Mar. 15, 1960; d. Perry Reese and Beverly C. (Carskadon) Taylor; m. David Richard Roth, Mar. 30, 1985. B of Communications, Ohio U., 1982. Sales rep. Procter and Gamble Distbg. Co., Cin., 1982-84; dist. field rep. Procter and Gamble Distbg. Co., Detroit, 1985-86, unit mgr.; chain unit mgr. Procter and Gamble Distbg. Co., Cin., 1989-90, Cen. div. corp. account area mgr., 1990—. Elder First Presbyn. Ch., Maumee, Ohio, 1988-90, nuture commn. chmn., 1988-90. Mem. Women in Communications, Inc., Ohio U. Alumni Assn. (trustee acad. 1988—), Pi Beta Phi Toledo Area Alumnae Club (pres. 1987-88, Evelyn Peters Kyle award 1988), Pi Beta Pi (Alumni of

Yr. Bowling Green State U. chpt. 1989-90). Republican. Home: 9613 St Andrews Rd Perrysburg OH 43551 Office: Procter/Gamble Distbg Co Patient Care Products PO Box 333 Cincinnati OH 45201

ROTH, SUSAN, psychologist, educator; b. N.Y.C., Apr. 16, 1948; m. Philip R. Costanzo, Mar. 10, 1979; 1 child, Anthony Roth. BA, Barnard Coll., 1970; MA, Northwestern U., 1972, PhD, 1973. Lic. psychologist, N.C. Dir. psychology clinic Duke U., Durham, N.C., 1979-81, dir. clin. tng. program, 1982-88, asst. prof. psychology, 1973-79, assoc. prof., 1979—. Mem. Am. Psychol. Assn., Soc. for Traumatic Stress Studies, Phi Beta Kappa. Researcher on psychol. recovery for rape and incest. Office: Duke U Dept Psychology Durham NC 27706

ROTHAUS, PAULA MONTGOMERY, nuclear medicine physician; b. Williamsport, Pa., Aug. 2, 1952; d. George L. and Pauline L. (Ritter) Montgomery; m. Kenneth O. Rothaus, Jan. 1, 1977; children: Alexander, Philip, Andrew. Student, U. Pa., 1970-71, Washington and Jefferson Coll., 1971-72; student pharmacy, Temple U., 1972-74; MD, Med. Coll. Pa., 1978. Diplomate Am. Bd. Nuclear Medicine. Intern, resident in internal medicine Abington Meml. Hosp., N.Y., 1978-81; fellow in nuclear medicine N.Y. Hosp.-Cornell U., 1981-83; pvt. practice nuclear medicine N.Y.C., 1983—; with HMO-Manhattan Med. Group, P.C., N.Y.C. Mem. Women's Polit. Caucus, N.Y.C. Named Outstanding Young Working Woman, Glamour mag., 1986. Mem. Soc. Nuclear Medicine, Am. Coll. Nuclear Physicians, Am. Women's Med. Assn. Democrat. Jewish. Office: Manhattan Med Group PC 172 Amsterdam Ave New York NY 10023

ROTHBEIN, SYLVIA, business executive; b. N.Y.C., June 27, 1951; d. Irving and Celia (Jacobson) Siegal; m. Howard Rothbein, Jan. 9, 1983; children: Paul, Ilana. Student, NYU, 1970-72. Mktg. dir. Revlon, Inc., N.Y.C., 1969-81; mktg. cons. Yanbal Internat., N.Y.C., 1981-83; pres. HR Industries, Inc., Ridgefield, N.J., 1983—. Mem. NAFE, Am. Women Entrepreneurs, Hadassah, N.J. Women Bus. Owners and Entreprenurial Club. Home: 816 Domm Ct Wyckoff NJ 07481 Office: HR Industries Inc 605 Broad Ave Ridgefield NJ 07657

ROTHBERG, JOAN O., advertising agency executive; b. Newark, Aug. 29, 1941; d. Abraham and Nettie (Rasnick) Oxman; m. Robert R. Rothberg, Sept. 1, 1963; 1 dau., Abra C. A.B., Vassar Coll., 1961; M.B.A., Harvard U., 1963. Asst. advt. media mgr. Scott Paper Co., 1963-65; v.p. SSC&B Advt. Inc., N.Y.C., 1965-72; sr. v.p., dir. Ted Bates C.A. Inc., N.Y.C., 1973-81; exec. v.p. Ted Bates/N.Y. Inc. (now Backer, Spielvogel, Bates, Inc.), from 1981; chmn. bd. Masterson Rothberg Advt., N.Y.C., 1988—. Recipient Tribute to Women in Internat. Industry award Nat. YWCA, 1981; Ford Found. fellow; Fulbright grantee Mex. *

ROTHBERG, KAREN PARKER, education educator; b. Detroit, Mich., Dec. 8, 1942; d. Walter Alton and Virginia Mae (Reitan) S.; m. Alan David Aug. 5, 1962 (div. 1974); children: Amy, Adam, Lauren. PhB, Wayne State U., 1964; MA, U. Denver, 1979, PhD, 1987. Rsch. cons. Community Coll. Denver, 1973-74; educator Cherry Creek Schs., Denver, 1974—, Cherry Creek High Sch., Englewood, Colo., 1975—. mem. Classical Assn. of Middle West/ South, Am. Classical League, Speech Communication Assn., Vergilian Soc. Home: 2900 S Quebec #17 Denver CO 80231

ROTHBERGER, SUE ELLEN, teacher; b. N.Y., Feb. 29, 1944; d. Irving Harry and Jean Dorothy (Seider) Weitz; m. Louis, June 30, 1972 (dec. Aug. 1976). BA, Bklyn. Coll., 1964, MA, 1968; Cert. in Bus. Adminstrn., L.I. U., 1980. Cert. tchr., N.Y. Tchr. N.Y.C. Bd. of Edn., 1964-70, Greenburgh Central #7, Hartsdale, N.Y., 1970—; pres. Greenburgh Tchrs. Fedn., Hartsdale, 1986—; policy bd. Westchester Tchr. Ctr., Hartsdale, 1986—; presenter Summer Inst. John Jay Coll., N.Y.C., 1988. Recipient Tchr. Incentive Project Westchester Tchr. Ctr., Hartsdale, 1987. Mem. N.Y. State Assn. of Fgn. Lang. Tchrs. (presenter 1988), Am. Assn. of Tchrs. of Spanish & Portuguese, N.Y. State United Tchrs., Kiwanis. Home: 5800 Arlington Ave Apt 16U New York NY 10471 Office: Woodlands High Sch Greenburg Cen Dist 7 475 W Hartsdale Ave Hartsdale NY 10530

ROTHBERG-SMOKE, F. DEE, insurance company executive; b. Phila., July 14, 1940; d. Samuel and Anne (Molotsky) Splaver; m. Sidney Smoke, May 4, 1978; children: Jay, Steve, Daniel. BS, Temple U., 1963, postgrad.; postgrad., Rutgers U. Lic. real estate agt.; cert. in real estate appraisal, abstracting and law. Mgr. South Jersey div. Chgo. Title Ins. Co., Cherry Hill, N.J.; mgr. Congress div. Meridian Title Ins. Co., Cherry Hill; assoc. bd. realtors Camden Co. Past pres. Cherry Hill chpt. Deborah Hosp.; exec. bd. Jewish Family Svc. South N.J. Office: Rte 70 PO Box 5479 Cherry Hill NJ 08034

ROTHENBERG, SAUNDRA HAMM, public relations executive; b. N.Y.C., May 30, 1943; d. Harold and Etta (Isaacs) Hamm; m. Max P. Rothenberg, Feb. 21, 1965; children: Dana, Jordan. BA, Bklyn. Coll., 1965; BRE, Tchrs. Inst. for Women, N.Y.C., 1964. Tchr., Ramaz Sch., N.Y.C., 1963-65, N.Y.C. Pub. Schs., 1965-67, Hebrew Acad., Miami Beach, Fla., 1967-68, Dade County Pub. Schs., North Miami Beach, Fla., 1968-70; prin., adminstr. Red and White Sch. House, Hollywood, Fla., 1972-87, Golden Glades Day Sch., Opa Locka, Fla., 1980—; regional field cons. For the State of Fla. for Am. Mizrachi Women, 1987—; lectr. in field. Bd. dirs. Hillel Day Sch., North Miami Beach, 1970-84, Hebrew Acad., Miami Beach, 1984-86 Cen. Agy. Jewish Edn., Dade County, 1985-87, Touro Coll., 1987-88; chmn. scholarship dinners Hillel Day Sch. and Hebrew Acad., chmn. jour. dinner Shaaray Tefilah; mem. adv. bd. Broward County 4-H, Fla., 1975-77, Broward Assn. Children Under Six, 1980-87, Broward County Kindergarten and Nursery Assn., 1980—; pres. S.W. Region Fla. Coun., 1983-87, pres. Galil chpt. Am. Mizrachi Women, North Miami Beach, 1969-72, pres. Vered chpt., North Miami Beach, 1972-83, pres. SEFLA Coun., 1983-87; del. So. Fla. Community Rels. Bd., 1984-85, 1987—; alt. del. Internat. Conf. on Women, Nairobi, Kenya, 1985. Recipient numerous awards including Am. Mizrachi Women, Builders award Hillel Community Day Sch., 1981, Community Svc. award Shaaray Tefliah, 1983, Key to City Miami Beach Svc. award, 1985, Mayor's Svc. award, 1985. Mem. South Broward Fedn., Women's Study Group North Miami Beach (chmn. 1980-84). Jewish. Avocations: travel, tennis, bowling, swimming, gourmet cooking. Home: 1320 NE 172d St North Miami Beach FL 33162

ROTHENBERG, SUSAN, artist; b. Buffalo, Jan. 20, 1945; d. Leonard M. and Adele (Cohen) R.; m. George Trakas, May 1, 1971-1976; 1 dau., Maggie. B.F.A., Cornell U., 1966. One-woman shows of paintings include Willard Gallery, N.Y.C., 1976, 77, 79, 81, 83, Univ. Art Mus., Berkeley, Calif., 1978, Walker Art Center, Mpls., 1978, Greenberg Gallery, St. Louis, 1978, Mayor Gallery, London, 1980, Akron (Ohio) Art Mus., 1981-82, Stedelijk Mus., Amsterdam, 1982, Los Angeles County Mus., 1983, San Francisco Mus. Art, 1983, Carnegie Inst. Mus. Art, Pitts., 1984; numerous group shows, 1974—, including Mus. of Modern Art, N.Y.C., 1980, Padiglione d'Arte Contemporanea di Milano, Italy, 1980, Clarke-Benton Gallery, Santa-Fe, 1980, Indpls. Mus. Art, 1980, Yarlow/Salzman Gallery, Toronto, 1980, Tex. Gallery, Houston, 1981, Young Hoffman Gallery, Chgo., 1981, Inst. Contemporary Art, Richmond, Va., 1981, Kunsthalle, Basel (Switzerland), 1981, Willard Gallery, N.Y., 1981, Los Angeles County Mus. Art, 1983, Inst. Contemporary Art, Boston, 1983, Barbara Krakow Gallery, Boston, 1984, Des Moines Art Ctr., 1985, A.P. Giannini Gallery, San Francisco; group exhbns. include A.M. Sachs Gallery, N.Y.C., 1974, Willard Gallery, 1975, 76, Inst. for Art and Urban Resources, Long Island City, N.Y., 1977, Mus. Modern Art, N.Y., 1977, Cleve. Mus. Art, 1978, Albright-Knox Art Gallery, N.Y., 1978, Whitney Mus. Am. Art, 1979, Renaissance Soc. of U. Chgo., 1979, Clarke-Benton Gallery, Santa Fe, 1980, Audrey Stohl Gallery, 1980, Tex. Gallery, Houston, 1981, Univ. Art Mus., Santa Barbara, 1981, Akron Art Mus., 1981, Art Inst. Chgo., 1982, Sidney Janis Gallery, 1982, Paula Cooper Gallery, N.Y., 1983, Fogg Art Mus., Harvard U., 1984, CDS Gallery, 1984, N.Y. Pub. Library, 1985, Seattle Art Mus., 1985, Daniel Weinberg Gallery, 1985,Barbara Mathes Gallery, 1986, Butlre Inst. Am. Art, Youngstown, Ohio, 1986, 1st Bank of Mpls., 1986-87, Mus. Fine Arts, Boston, 1986-87; represented in permanent collections, Mus. Modern Art. N.Y.C., Mus. Fine Arts, Houston, Whitney Mus. Am. Art, N.Y.C., Albright-Knox Art Gallery, Buffalo, Walker Art Center, Des Moines, Iowa., Akron Art Mus., Stedelijk Mus., Carnegie Inst. Mus. Art, Dallas Mus. Fine

Art. Guggenheim fellow, 1980. Office: care Sperone Westwater 142 Greene St New York NY 10012*

ROTHENSTREICH, MINDI CHERYL, nurse; b. Bkyln., Aug. 9, 1962; d. Jay and Carole (Goldstein) R. B in Nursing, U. Buffalo, 1983; M in Nursing, NYU, 1986. RN, N.Y. Nurse clinician NYU, N.Y.C., 1983—; chief embolization nurse NYU Med. Ctr. for Dr. Berenstein, 1985—; lectr. in field. Mem. Am. Radiology Nurses Assn., U. Buffalo Nursing Alumni, NYU Nursing Alumni, Sigma Theta Tau. Democrat. Jewish. Home: 7000 Bay Pkwy Brooklyn NY 11204 Office: NYU Med Ctr 560 First Ave New York NY 10016

ROTHERAM BORUS, MARY J., psychology educator; b. L.A., Dec. 7, 1949; d. Joseph Anthony and Rita Marie (Bacy) Rotheram; m. Michael Borus, Aug. 19, 1983 (widowed); 1 child, Erin Jill. Student, U. San Francisco, 1967-68; BA in Psychology, U. Calif., Irvine, 1968-71, postgrad., 1971-73; MA, PhD in Clin. Psychology, U. So. Calif., L.A., 1977. Asst. prof. psychology Ohio State U., Columbus, 1972-78; from asst. to assoc. prof. psychology Calif. State U., L.A., 1978-83; assoc. prof. psychology Columbia U., N.Y.C., 1983—; reviewer Adminstrn. for Children, Youth and Families, 1987-88; mem. ad hoc rev. panel NIMH, 1987-88, Nat. Inst. Child Health & Human Devel., 1989-90; mem. adv. bd. runaway risk reduction project Ctr. for Health, Promotion and Edn., 1989—. Mem. editorial bd. Health Psychology, 1988—, An Interdisciplinary Jour., 1988—; contbr. numerous articles to profl. jours.; author chpts. in books. Fulbright fellow to Nigeria, 1984, NIMH fellow U. So. Calif., 1973-75; W.T. Grant Found. scholar, 1988—. Mem. Am. Psychol. Assn., Soc. for Rsch. in Child Devel., Am. Assn. Orthopsychiatry (program com. 1984-88, inst. com. 1987-88), Internat. Ctr. for Integrative Studies (adv. bd. 1986—), Single Parents Resource Agy. (exec. bd. 1988—). Home: 2521 Palisade Ave #PHB Riverdale NY 10463 Office: Columbia U Div Psychiatry Coll Physicians & Surgeons New York NY 10032

ROTHERHAM, JEAN, biochemist, retired; b. Pompton Lakes, NJ, Jan. 4, 1922; d. Walter Scott and Elsie V. (Kirk) R. BA, Montclair State Coll., 1942; MS, PhD, U. N.C., 1954. Secondary education educator, scis. Freehold (N.J.) High Sch., 1942-44, Bordentown (N.J.) High Sch., 1947-49, Stuart Hall, Staunton, Va., 1950-52; rsch. chemist, biochemist NIH, Bethesda, Md., 1955-80. Contbr. articles to profl. jours. Lt. (j.g.) USN, 1944-46. Fellow Nat. Heart Inst., Nat. Cancer Inst.; mem. Sigma Xi. Democrat. Soc. of Friends.

ROTHERMUND, CATHY LOU, elementary educator; b. Wheeling, W.Va., Oct. 9, 1955; d. Richard L. and Martha L. (Vance) Ging; m. James E. Rothermund, Jr., July 26, 1980; 1 child, Derek James. BS in Edn., Ohio U., 1977; MA in Edn., W.Va. U., 1983. Cert. elem. tchr., W.Va. Elem. sch. tchr. Ohio County Schs., Wheeling, 1977—, also TESA instr. 1981-84, also bldg. chairperson, 1986—. Mem. W.Va. Edn. Assn., Ohio Valley Lang. Arts Council, AAUW (treas. 1989—), Jr. League of Wheeling (parliamentarian 1988—), Phi Kappa Phi. Presbyterian.

ROTHFIELD, NAOMI FOX, physician; b. Bklyn., Apr. 5, 1929; d. Morris and Violet (Bloomgarden) Fox; m. Lawrence Rothfield, Sept. 18, 1954; children—Susan, Lawrence, John, Jane. B.A., Bard Coll., 1950; M.D., N.Y. U., 1955. Intern Lenox Hill Hosp., N.Y.C., 1955-56; instr. N.Y. U. Sch. Medicine, 1956-62, asst. prof., 1962-68; assoc. prof. U. Conn. Sch. Medicine, Farmington, 1968-72; prof., chief div. rheumatic diseases U. Conn. Sch. Medicine, 1972—. Contbr. chpts. to books; contbr. articles to med. jours. Mem. Am. Soc. Clin. Investigation, Am. Rheumatism Assn., Assn. Am. Physics. Jewish. Home: 540 Deercliff Rd Avon CT 06001 Office: U Conn Health Ctr Farmington CT 06032

ROTHGARN, MILDRED, farmer, newspaper editor; b. Rugby, N.D., June 1, 1935; d. Arthur Thaddeus and Luella Sophia (Kjelbertson) R.; (ward) child, Ly Hun. BSBA, U. N.D., 1958; MA, Mich. State U., 1962; postgrad., U. R.I., 1963, Ohio State U., 1966. Acct. E.W. Brady & Co., Grand Forks, N.D., 1955-56; tchr. Willow City (N.D.) High Sch., 1958-60, Minnewaukan (N.D.) High Sch., 1960-6l; asst. prof., assoc. prof. U. S.D., Vermillion, 1962-66; asst. prof. Cen. Wash. State Coll., Ellensburg, 1967-69; farmer Willow City, N.D., 1969—; organizer, editor Centurian, Willow City, 1985—; vis. prof., workshop consult. Idaho State U., Pocatello, 1967, 69, Murray (Ky.) State U., 1970, La. State U., Baton Rouge, 1973; spl. instr. N.D. Coop. Extension Svc., Fargo, N.D., 197l; owner, mgr. Pin Pointers, Bottineau, N.D., 1971-81. Pres. Bottineau C. of C., 1979; chmn. bd. dirs. Good Samaritan Hosp. Assn., Rugby, 1985—; mem. fund mgmt. bd. Willow City Centennial, 1988; treas. Bottineau County Homemakers Coun., 1985-87, pres., 1987-89; mem. Willow City Community Club. Recipient Community Svc. award Willow City Jaycees, 1988, award Greater N.D. Assn.; named one of Outstanding Young Women of Am., 1971, N.D. Centennial Farm Owner, 1988, N.D. Centennial Women's Profile, 1989, N.D. Bus. and Prof. Women's Profile, 1989. Mem. AAUW (life), AAUP, Am. Home Econs. Assn., N.D. Newspaper Assn., N.D. Bus. and Profl. Women (treas. 1984-86), Bottineau Area Bus. & Profl. Women (charter pres. 1979-80, Pioneer Daus., Profl. Orgn. Investors (pres., ptnr. 1988-90), Order Ea. Star, Delta Kappa Gamma (life), Delta Delta Delta. Republican. Presbyterian.

ROTHMAN, DEANNA, electroplating company executive; b. Bklyn., Sept. 20, 1938; d. Frank Philip and Elsie (Goldstein) Dukofsky; m. Edward Rothman, Dec. 8, 1956 (div. July 1984); children: Jeffrey Scott, Michele Dawn, Robert Jay; m. Ronald Friedman, Aug. 17, 1986. B.A., Bklyn. Coll., 1968. Exec. Bronzemaster Co., Bklyn., 1969-80, Perma Plating Co. Inc., Bklyn., 1980-84; pres. Duratron Finishing Corp., Bklyn., 1984—. Sec. Tenants Assn., S.I., 1973-77; v.p. Orgn. Rehab. and Tng., Woodmere, N.Y., 1978-80; sponsor Spl. Olympics; mem. East N.Y. Local Devel. Corp. Mem. Masters Electroplating Assn., Am. Metal Finishers, NAFE, NOW. Republican. Jewish. Avocations: painting, collecing art deco, theatre. Home: 755 Flanders Dr North Woodmere NY 11581 Office: Duratron Finishing Corp PO Box 789 East NY Sta Brooklyn NY 11207

ROTHMAN, ESTHER POMERANZ, social agency executive, psychologist; b. N.Y.C., Nov. 25, 1919; d. Max and Anne (Reiner) Pomeranz; m. Arthur M. Rothman, Apr. 13, 1946; 1 dau., Amy. B.A., Hunter Coll., 1942; M.A., Columbia U., 1944; M.A., CCNY, 1946; Ph.D., NYU, 1958. Cert. psychologist, N.Y. Tchr., N.Y.C. Bd. Edn., 1944-57, prin., 1957-80; exec. dir. Glie Youth Program, N.Y.C., 1980-85; cons. Art. Correctional Edn. Consortium, 1985—; research psychologist Tchrs. Hot Line, N.Y.C., 1972-74. Author: Angel Inside Went Sour, 1972; Troubled Teachers, 1974; co-author: Disturbed Child, 1967. Mem. Citizens Com. for Children, N.Y.C., 1972—. Recipient Valley Forge Freedom award, 1976. Fellow Am. Assn. Orthopsychiatry (sec. 1976-79); mem. Am. Psychol. Assn. Home: 200 E 16 St New York NY 10003 Office: Correctional Edn Consortium 29-10 Thomson Ave Long Island NY 11101

ROTHMAN, JUDITH LEE, publisher; b. N.Y.C., Nov. 17, 1940; d. William and Beatrice (Schwartz) R. BA, CUNY, Queens, 1962; student, CBS Sch. Mgmt., N.Y.C. and Boston, 1979-80, Hennig/Jardim Mgmt. Sch. for Women, N.Y.C., 1979-81. Legal sec. Kaufman, Taylor & Kimmel, N.Y.C., 1962-64; editor Fairchild Publs., N.Y.C., 1964-71; prodn. asst. Paramount Pictures, N.Y.C., 1971; editor coll. div. Appleton Century Crofts, N.Y.C., 1971-73, Prentice-Hall, Inc., Englewood Cliffs, N.J., 1973-78; pub. humanities div., Holt Rinehart & Winston Publs., N.Y.C., 1978-80; editorial dir. CBS Edn. Pub., N.Y.C., 1980-81; sr. editor Random House, Inc., N.Y.C., 1981-84; editor in chief Harper & Row, Inc., N.Y.C., 1984-90; pub. Grolier Press, N.Y.C., 1990—; cons. Assn. Am. Publishers, N.Y.C., 1981-82. Mem. Nat. Women's Book Assn. (Women Who Make A Difference award 1987). Democrat. Jewish. Office: Grolier Press 387 Park Ave S New York NY 10016

ROTHMAN, PATRICIA MARY, educator; b. N.Y.C., May 30, 1946; d. Henry J. and Katherine (Enright) Parker; m. Neil F. Rothman, Aug. 30, 1945; children: Eric Parker, Craig Lawrence. BA, Mt. St. Mary Coll., Newburgh, N.Y., 1968; MA, Kean Coll., 1974; postgrad computer sci., Jersey City State Coll., 1984. Cert. elem. tchr., tchr. of handicapped, N.J. Learning disabilities tchr. Bd. Coop. Edn. Svcs., Westchester, N.Y., 1968-69; tchr. educable class Wanamassa Sch., Ocean, N.J., 1969-72; supplemental

tchr. Wall (N.J.) Cen. Sch., 1972-79; tchr. handicapped Brielle (N.J.) Elem. Sch., 1979—; tutor, Manasquan, N.J., summers 1968—. Mem. Manasquan Park Property Owners Assn., 1978—; team mother South Wall Little League, 1980-88. Mem. NEA, N.J. Edn. Assn., Brielle Edn. Assn. (sec. 1983-88), AAUW, Allaire Racquet Club (Wall). Democrat. Roman Catholic. Home: 1612 Holly Blvd Manasquan Park NJ 08736 Office: Brielle Elem Sch 605 Union Ln Brielle NJ 08730

ROTHMAN, SARA, research biochemist; b. Winthrop, Mass., July 29, 1929; d. George Saul and Rachel (Woolf) Weinstein; children—Stephen George Rothman, Richard Mark Rothman. B.S., Simmons Coll., 1965; M.A., Boston U., 1967, Ph.D., 1970. Postdoctoral fellow Tufts U. Sch. Medicine, Boston, 1970-73; rsch. assoc. Boston U. Sch. Medicine, 1973, rsch. asst. prof., 1973-77; rsch. assoc. Mallory Inst. Pathology, Boston City Hosp., 1975-77, spl. sci. staff, 1976-77; rsch. chemist Walter Reed Army Inst. Rsch., Washington, 1978—; faculty mem. FAES Grad. Sch., NIH, Bethesda, Md., 1982-83; vis. prof. Oreg. Health Scis. U., Portland, 1986-87. Contbr. articles to profl. jours. Fellow Am. Acad. Microbiology; mem. Am. Soc. Microbiology, Assn. for Women in Sci. (exec. bd.), Nat. Women's Polit. Caucus, Internat. Soc. on Toxicology, Sigma Xi. Avocation: photography. Office: Walter Reed Army Inst Rsch Washington DC 20307

ROTHMAN-DENES, LUCIA BEATRIZ, biology educator; b. Buenos Aires, Feb. 17, 1943; came to U.S., 1967; d. Boris and Carmen (Couto) Rothman; m. Pablo Denes, May 24, 1968; children: Christian Andrew, Anne Elizabeth. Lic. in Chemistry, Sch. Scis., U. Buenos Aires, 1964, PhD in Biochemistry, 1967. Vis. fellow NIH, Bethesda, Md., 1967-70; postdoctoral fellow biophysics U. Chgo., 1970-73, rsch. assoc., 1973-74, asst. prof., 1974-79, assoc. prof., 1980-83, prof. depts. molecular genetics, cell biology, biochemistry, 1983—; mem. microbial genetics study sect. NIH, 1980-83, genetic basis of disease study sect., 1985-89; mem. Damon Runyon and Walter Winchel Sci. Adv. Com., N.Y.C., 1989—. Contbr. numerous articles to profl. publs. Mem. AAAS, Am. Soc. Microbiology (div. chair 1985, div. group II rep. 1990—), Am. Soc. Virology (councilor 1987-90), Am. Soc. Biochemistry and Molecular Biology. Office: Univ Chgo 920 E 58th St Chicago IL 60637

ROTHROCK, CAROL SIMON, landscape artist; b. Augusta, Ga., Sept. 1, 1953; d. Henry Milton and Doris (Reynolds) Simon; m. Tony Frank Rothrock Jr., Nov. 28, 1976; children: Ashley Star, Christopher Henry. BFA, U. Ga., 1974. Cert. tchr., Tex. With White Oak (Tex.) Ind. Sch. System, 1977-78; ind. art tchr. Longview, Tex., 1976-78; freelance artist Tex., S.C., 1980-88; art tchr. Longview Arts Coun., 1987—. Group exhbns. include: Melrose Art Show, Dan Pauskie, S.C., 1986, Trinity Sch. Tex., Longview, 1988, Hilton Head (S.C.) Art League, 1987; represented in permanent collections Colorworks Gallery, Hilton Head, 1989, Moonshell Gallery, Hilton Head; juried exhbns. include Pastel Soc. of Am., 1989, S.E. Pastel Soc., Atlanta, 1987-88, Degas Pastel Soc., 1990, Pastel Soc. North Fla., 1990, Catharine Lorillard Wolfe Show, 1990. Brownie troop leader, Longview area Girl Scouts U.S., 1986-88; vol. art tchr., Willowbrook Manor Convalescent Ctr., Longview, 1987-88. Mem. Hilton Head Art League, Longview Mus. Art, San Francisco Mus. Art, Common Cause, Union of Concerned Scientists, LaLeche League, Sierra Club. Jewish. Home: 3 Gadwall Hilton Head SC 29928

ROTHROCK, JAN CAMPBELL, accountant; b. Duncan, Okla., Jan. 24, 1935; d. Robert E. and Mary Louise (Ingram) Campbell; m. Edward Strike Rothrock, Mar. 6, 1972; children: Faun, Ross, Strike III, Robin, Robert, Jon, Jan. Student, U. Houston, 1972, 75, 77, U. St. Thomas, summer 1975, spring 1977, Am. Coll. Advanced Ctr., 1980, Keele U., Eng., summer 1976. CPA, Tex.; cert. real estate broker. Sec.-treas. RES Leasing and Mgmt., Houston, 1967-72, pres., 1972—; pres. Jan C. Rothrock, Broker, Houston, 1973—; owner Jan Campbell, CPA, Houston, 1979—; bd. dirs. Sandy Reed & Assocs., Inc.; bd. dirs., treas. Total Life Care Ctr.; Maple Property Mgmt. Inc., 1988—, F & M Meat Processing, Inc., 1989—; lectr. in field. Bd. dirs. Lupus Found. Am., Houston, 1983, 88-90, hon. bd. dirs., 1986-88, chmn. fund raising, 1986—, mem. chmn. 1986; acctg. advisor S.W. Literacy Arts Coun., 1986—; trustee Big State Grass Farms, 1979—, AH & LB Wingate Charitable Trust, 1982—; acctg. adv. Tex. A&M Marine Mammal Standing Network, 1987, incorporator, bd. dirs., 1988—; bd. dirs., treas. Endangered Species Media Project. Mem. Tex. Assn. Realtors, Nat. Assn. Realtors, Houston Bd. Realtors, Am. Inst. CPA's, Tex. Soc. CPA's, Nat. Conf. CPA Practitioners, Internat. Platform Assn., Phi Eta Sigma, Alpha Lambda Delta. Home: 3257 Ella Lee Ln Houston TX 77019

ROTHSCHILD, AMALIE RANDOLPH, filmmaker, producer, director; b. Balt., June 3, 1945; d. Randolph Schamberg and Amalie Getta (Rosenfeld) R. BFA, R.I. Sch. Design, 1967; MFA in Motion Picture Production, NYU, 1969. Spl. effects staff in film and photography Joshua Light Show, Fillmore E. Theatre, NYC, 1969-71; still photographer TWA Airlines Pub. Relations Dept., Village Voice newspaper Rolling Stone magazine, Newsweek magazine, After Dark, N.Y. Daily News, numerous others, 1968-72; co-founder, partner New Day Films, distbn. coop., 1971—; owner, operator Anomaly Films Co., NYC, 1971—; mem., co-founder Assn. of Independent Video and Filmmakers, Inc., NYC, 1974, bd. dirs., 1974-78; instr. in film and TV, N.Y. U. Inst. of Film and TV, 1976-78; cons. in field to various organizations including Youthgrant Program of Nat. Endowment for Humanities, Washington, 1973-76; motion pictures include: Woo Who? May Wilson, 1969; It Happens to Us, 1972; Nana, Mom and Me, 1974; Radioimmunoassay of Renin, Radioimmunoassay of Aldosterone, 1973; Conversations with Willard Van Dyke, 1981; Richard Haas: Work in Progress, 1984; Painting the Town: The Illusionistic Murals of Richard Haas, 1989; editor: Doing It Yourself, Handbook on Independent Film Distribution, 1977. Mem. Community Planning Bd. 1, Borough of Manhattan, N.Y.C., 1974-86. Recipient spl. achievement award Mademoiselle mag., 1972; independent filmmaker grant, Am. Film Inst., 1973; film grantee N.Y. State Coun. on the Arts, 1977, 85, 87, Nat. Endowment Arts, 1978, 85, 87, Md. Arts Coun., 1977, Ohio Arts and Humanities Couns., 1985. Mem. Assn. Ind. Video Filmmakers (bd. dirs. 1974-78) Univ. Film and Video Assn., N.Y. Women in Film, Ind. Documentary Assn., Laboratorio Immagine Donna. Democrat. Address: 135 Hudson St New York NY 10013 also: Via delle Mantellate 19, Rome 00165, Italy

ROTHSCHILD, DIANE, advertising agency executive; b. Apr. 11, 1943; d. Morton Royce and Marjorie Jay (Simon) R.; 1 child, Alexandra Rothschild Spencer. B.A., Aldephi U., 1965. Copywriter Doyle Dane Bernbach Advt., Inc., N.Y.C., 1967-73, v.p., 1973-79, sr. v.p., assoc. creative dir., 1979-85, exec. v.p., creative dir., 1985-86; pres. Grace and Rothschild, N.Y.C., 1986—. Recipient maj. advt. awards. Mem. YWCA Acad. Women Achievers. Office: Grace & Rothschild 767 Third Ave New York NY 10017

ROTHSTEIN, BARBARA JACOBS, federal judge; b. Bklyn., Feb. 3, 1939; d. Solomon and Pauline Jacobs; m. Ted L. Rothstein, Dec. 28, 1968; 1 child, Daniel. B.A., Cornell U., 1960; LL.B., Harvard U., 1966. Bar: Mass. 1966, Wash. 1969, U.S. Ct. Appeals (9th cir.) 1977, U.S. Dist. Ct. (we. dist.) Wash. 1971, U.S. Supreme Ct. 1975. Pvt. practice law Boston, 1966-68; asst. atty. gen. State of Wash., 1968-77; judge Superior Ct., Seattle, 1977-80; judge Fed. Dist. Ct. Western Wash., Seattle, 1980-87, chief judge, 1987—; faculty Law Sch. U. Wash., 1975-77, Hastings Inst. Trial Advocacy, 1977, N.W. Inst. Trial Advocacy, 1979—. Recipient Matrix Table Woman of Yr. award, Women in Communications, 1980. Mem. ABA (jud. sect.), Am. Judicature Soc., Nat. Assn. Women Judges, Felloes of the Am. Bar, Wash. State Bar Assn., Phi Beta Kappa, Phi Kappa Phi. Office: US Dist Ct 705 US Courthouse 1010 5th Ave Rm 410 Seattle WA 98104-1187

ROTZIEN, MARY KATHRYN, therapist; b. La Porte, Ind., June 16, 1952; d. Dewey Sigsby and Irene Elizabeth (Garwood) R.; m. Brian French Buchanan, Sept. 18, 1982; 1 child, Keagan Dewey. BA in Psychology, Calif. State U., L.A., 1980; PhD in Psychology, Fuller Theol. Sem., Pasadena, Calif., 1989. Pvt. practice clin. psychotherapy, Pasadena, 1982—; founder, exec. dir. The Child S.H.A.R.E. Program, Inc., Van Nuys, Calif., 1984-86, program cons., 1986—. Stauffer fellow Fuller Theol. Sem., 1985. Mem. Am. Psychol. Assn. Presbyterian. Office: 510 S Marengo Ave Pasadena CA 91101

ROUBIK, SUSANNE EILEEN, architect; b. Milw., Dec. 1, 1959; d. Joseph Rudolph and Gertrude Mae (Brown) R. BS in Architecture, U. Wis., Milw., 1981, MArch, 1984; postgrad., Inst. of Architecture Studies, Paris, Barcelona, 1984. Archtl. designer Link & Assocs., Waukesha, Wis., 1983-84; archtl. photographer U. Wis., Milw., 1983-84, archtl. slide curator, 1983-84; sr. archtl. designer Skidmore, Owings & Merrill, Chgo., 1984—. Recipient award Nat. Inst. Archtl. Edn., 1984. Mem. AIA (program coord. Chgo. chpt. 1987-89, chmn. real estate com. 1989-91, bd. dirs. 1990-91, del. Young Architects Forum 1990, Chicago award 1984, Chgo. chpt.-Chgo. Bar Assn. Young Architect award 1987), Third Coast Women in Architecture (founder, pres. 1983), Third Coast Design Coop. (v.p. bd. dirs. 1981-84).

ROUDYBUSH, ALEXANDRA, novelist; b. Hyres, Cote d'Azur, France, Mar. 14, 1911; d. Constantine and Ethel (Wheeler) Brown; m. Franklin Roudybush, 1942. Student, St. Paul's Sch. for Girls, London, London Sch. Econs., 1930. Journalist London Eve. Standard, 1931, Time mag., 1933, French News Agy., 1935, CBS, 1936, MBS, 1940; White House corr. MBC Radio, 1940-48. Author: Before the Ball Was Over, 1965; Death of a Moral Person, 1967; Capital Crime, 1969; House of the Cat, 1970; A Sybaritic Death, 1972; Suddenly in Paris, 1975; The Female of the Species, 1977; Blood Ties, 1981. Mem. Crime Writers Am. and Brit., Am. Woman's Club (Paris), Miramar Golf Club (Porto, Portugal). Democrat. Episcopalian.

ROUILLARD JOHNSON, HOLLY, public relations specialist; b. Canton, Mass., Dec. 19, 1960; d. Lawrence Hadley Rouillard and Carol (Sreenan) Rouillard-Wolff. BS, U. Denver, 1983. Asst. pub. rels. dir. Colo. Ski Country USA, Denver, 1984-87; news bur. mgr. Colo. Tourism Bd., Denver, 1987-90; assoc. The Johnston Group, Denver, 1990—; mem. Colo. Bicycle Adv. Bd., Denver, 1990—, Denver '90 Com., Denver '89 Com., chmn. promotions com. 1990—. Mem. Rocky Mountain Ski Media (assoc.), U.S. Ski Journalists (assoc.). Democrat. Office: The Johnston Group 1512 Larimer St 7th Fl Denver CO 80202

ROUIN, CAROLE CHRISTINE, lawyer; b. L.A., Nov. 16, 1939; d. Orrie Mackey and Gene Margurite Nelson; m. Khahil Rouin, 1963 (div. 1970); 1 child, Christi Lynne Wilkins. BA, U. Oreg., 1963, MA, 1970; JD, U. of the Pacific, 1983. Bar: Calif. 1983, U.S. Dist. Ct. (ea. and cen. dist.) Calif. 1984, U.S. Ct. Appeals (9th cir.) 1984. Assoc. Ball, Hunt, Hart, Brown & Baerwitz, Long Beach, Calif., 1983-85, Spensley, Horn, Jubas & Lubitz, L.A., 1985-87; pvt. practice law L.A., 1988—; mem. adv. bd. paralegal cert. program Calif. State U., Long Beach, 1984-88. Mem., com. chmn. Task Force for Econ. Devel., Long Beach, 1986; bd. dirs. Vol. Ctr., Long Beach, 1984-87, Found Theater, Long Beach, 1983-87, Sarah Ctr., Long Beach, 1988. Mem. ABA, Calif. State Bar Assn. (state del. 1984-87, co-chmn. program com. labor and employment law sect. 1985-87), Long Beach Bar Assn. (mem. legis. com. 1984-86), Beverly Hills Bar Assn., L.A. County Bar Assn. (mem. jud. evaluation com. 1985-87, chmn. domestic violence com. 1986, chmn. large firm study com. 1984-86, chmn. community and media relations com. 1985-87). Office: 100 Oceangate Ave Ste 1010 Long Beach CA 90802

ROUKEMA, MARGARET SCAFATI, congresswoman; b. Newark, Sept. 19, 1929; d. Claude Thomas and Margaret (D'Alessio) Scafati; m. Richard W. Roukema, Aug. 23, 1951; children—Margaret, Todd (dec.), Gregory. B.A. with honors in History and Polit. Sci, Montclair State Coll., 1951, postgrad. in history and guidance, 1951-53; postgrad. program in city and regional planning, Rutgers U., 1975. Tchr. history, govt., public schs. Livingston and Ridgewood, N.J., 1951-55; mem. 97th-102nd Congresses from 5th N.J. dist., 1981—; vice pres. Ridgewood Bd. Edn., 1970-73; bd. dirs., co-founder Ridgewood Sr. Citizens Housing Corp. Trustee Spring House, Paramus, N.J.; trustee Leukemia Soc. No. N.J., Family Counseling Service for Ridgewood and Vicinity; mem. Bergen County (N.J.) Republican Com.; NW Bergen County campaign mgr. for gubernatorial candidate Tom Kean, 1977. Mem. Bus. and Profl. Women's Orgn. Clubs: Coll. of Ridgewood, Ridgewood Rep. Office: US Ho of Reps 303 Cannon House Office Bldg Washington DC 20515*

ROULEAU, CAROLYN FERNAN, computer systems executive; b. Miami, Fla., Jan. 1, 1950; d. Philip A. and Jeanne Fernan; m. Kenneth E. Rouleau, Mar. 3, 1973 (div. Feb. 1980); children: Tiffany Ann, Joseph Philippe. Student Fla. Atlantic U., 1969-71, Fla. Internat. U., 1972-73, U. Miami, 1985-89, Barry U., 1989—. Coordinator, Conservation Found. Air Quality Workshop, Miami, Fla., 1970-71, Ernst and Young, Miami, 1971—; dir. Colleen Mine, Balt., 1983—; owner, mgr. External Systems Service, 1986—. Patron, Greater Miami Opera. Mem. Nat. Assn. Female Execs., Bus. and Profl. Women's Club, LWV, Greater Miami Opera Guild, Dade County, Beta Gamma Sigma. Avocations: sailing, golfing, gardening.

ROUP, BRENDA JACOBS, nurse, army officer; b. Petersburg, Va., July 8, 1948; d. Eugene Thurman and Sarah Ann (Williams) Jacobs; m. Clarence James Roup, May 8, 1976. B.S.N., Med. Coll. Va., Richmond, 1970; M.S.N., Cath. U. Am., 1977; postgrad. U. Md., 1989—. Commd. 2d lt. U.S. Army, 1970, advanced through grades to lt. col., 1986; chief infection control Brooke Army MEDCEN, San Antonio, 1983-86; chief infection control Walter Reed MEDCEN, Washington, 1986—; nurse cons. in infection control to U.S. Army Surgeon Gen., 1986—. Mem. Assn. Practitioners in Infection Control, Assn. Mil. Surgeons, Sigma Theta Tau. Avocations: reading, swimming, cooking. Office: Walter Reed Army Med Ctr 16th St Washington DC 20307

ROURKE, ARLENE CAROL, publisher; b. N.Y.C., Feb. 1, 1944; d. Ralph and Adele (Rovegno) De Giso; m. Raymond Lawrence Rourke, Oct. 28, 1970; children: Elizabeth, Christopher. BA in English, Pace U., N.Y.C., 1966. Prodn. editor Fawcett Haynes, N.Y.C., 1966-67; prodn. asst., editor McGraw Hill, N.Y.C., 1967-70; owner, pres. Rourke Publs., Inc., Ft. Pierce, Fla., 1980—; v.p. Rourke Enterprises, Inc., Vero Beach, Fla., 1984—. Author: (Looking Good Series) Accessories, Clothing, Skin, Hands and Feet, Diet, Exercise, Hair, Decorating Your Room; (children's book) Things That Move; (bible stories) The Miracle on the Mountain, Elijah, Joseph, Man of Dreams, Martha and Mary, Isaac and Rebekah. Active Ctr. for Arts, Vero Beach, Fla., 1985—, Riverside Theatre, Vero Beach, 1985—; mem. ethics com. Turnabout Modeling Sch. and Agy., 1986.

ROUSE, TERRIE SUZITTE, museum director, consultant; b. Youngstown, Ohio, Dec. 2, 1952; d. Eurad R. and Florence (Wilcox) R.; 1 child, Malcolm Adam. BA, Trinity Coll., 1974; MS in Profl. Studies, Cornell U., 1977; certificate Internat. Affairs, Columbia U., 1979, MA, 1979. Mgr., curator Adam Clayton Powell St. Office Bldg., N.Y.C., 1979-81; sr. curator Studio Mus. Harlem, N.Y.C., 1981-86; dir. mus. N.Y. Transit Mus., Bklyn., 1986—; advisor Bellevue Hosp. Art Bd., 1981—. Contbr. articles to profl. jours. Mem. Conf. Mil. Transp. Ofcls. Named Outstanding Young Women Am., 1981-83. Mem. Am. Assn. Museums (assessor 1981—). Home: 409 Edgecombe Ave #7F New York NY 10032 Office: NYC Transit Authority 81 Willoughby St #802 Brooklyn NY 11201

ROUSH, ANN MARIE, teacher; b. E Palestine, Ohio, Oct. 11, 1937; d. J. Dale and Florence (Quilter) M.; m. Howard William, Dec. 28, 1957; children: Howard, William III, Amy, Valarie, Margaret and Benjamin (twins). BS, Ea. Mich. U., 1980; MA in Teaching, Oakland U., 1988. Office supr. U. Mich., Ann Arbor, 1980-84; tchr. Preservation Sch., Detroit, 1985-87, Transfiguration Sch., Detroit, 1988—. v.p. St. Vincent De Paul, Ann Arbor 1978-82. Mem. Internat. Reading Assn. Democrat. Catholic. Home: 8656 Tucson Warren MI 48093

ROUSON, VIVIAN REISSLAND, volunteer; b. New Orleans, July 18, 1929; d. Albert Isaac and Ophelia (Scott) Reissland; m. W. Ervin Rouson, June 22, 1953 (dec. May 1979); children: Lizette Hé'ène, Darryl Ervin, Brigette Maria, Janine Patrice, Damian William. BA, Xavier U., 1951; MS, Nova U., 1979; postgrad., U. Ky., 1965, U. South Fla., 1970. Tchr., cons. Gibbs Jr. Coll., St. Petersburg, Fla., 1958-60; tchr., cons. Pinellas County Schs., St. Petersburg,, Clearwater, Fla., 1960-78; freelance opinion editorial columnist U.S. newspaper, 1976-82; columnist Evening Independent, Pinellas County, Fla., 1976-78, Palm Beach (County, Fla.) Post, 1979-82; tchr., cons. Palm Beach County Sch., Lake Worth, W. Palm Beach, Fla., 1978-82; editorial writer St. Petersburg Times, 1979; program coord. Women's Resource Ctr., Normandale Community Coll., Bloomington, Minn., 1986-89, interim dir., 1989; vol., intern program coord. Inst. on Black Chem. Abuse, Mpls., 1989—; V.I.P. coord. Inst. on Black Chem. Abuse, Mpls., 1989-90; writing and fgn. lang. cons. Pinellas County and Palm Beach County, Fla., 1960-82. Author: The Hummingbird Within Us, 1980, Like a Mighty Banyau, 1982, Alcohol and Drug Abuse in Black America, 1988; editor conf. proceedings; editorial writer-columnist; editorial bd. St. Petersburg Times, 1979. Bd. dirs. St. Petersburg Cath. High Sch. Bd., 1976, Minn. div. Am. Cancer Soc., Mpls., 1983-90, Independent Sch. Dist. 191, Burnsville, Eagan, Savage, Minn., 1984-87, Minn. Valley YMCA, Dakota County, Minn., 1987-90. Named Outstanding Journalist south Atlantic region Alpha Kappa Alpha, 1978, 79, 80. Mem. Twin Cities Black Journalists (co-chair 1985-86, v.p. 1989-90), Minn. Polit. Congress Black Women (charter), Minn. Elected Women Officials, AAUW, Dakota County Soc. Black Women (founder, v.p. 1983-84), Pinellas County Fgn. Lang. Tchrs. (treas., pres.), The Links, Alpha Kappa Alpha (life). Roman Catholic. Home: 1871 Silver Bell Rd 308 Eagan MN 55122 Office: Inst on Black Chem Abuse 2616 Nicollet Ave Minneapolis MN 55408

ROUSSEAU, RITA ANN, adult day care center administrator; b. Waynesburgh, Pa., May 25, 1949; d. James William and Mary Lee (Clutter) Sturm; m. Charles H. Rousseau, Dec. 19, 1970; 1 child, Gretchen Ann. AS in Nursing Home Adminstrn., Providence Coll., 1983, BS in Health Svcs. Adminstrn., 1985. Activity leader Cresson (Pa.) State Sch. and Hosp., 1965-67; dir. cardiac testing/EEG St. Anne's Hosp., Fall River, Mass., 1971-86; self-employed cons. Assonet, Mass., 1983-86; exec. dir. Westerly (R.I.) Adult Day Care Ctr., Inc., 1987—. With U.S. Navy, 1967-70. Mem. R.I. Adult Day Care Assn. (pres. 1989—), NAFE, DAV. Democrat. Roman Catholic. Home: 7 Matawa Dr Assonet MA 02702 Office: Westerly Adult Day Care Ctr 65 Wells St Westerly RI 02891

ROUSSEL, BARBARA R., advertising professional; b. New Britain, Conn., May 1, 1937; d. Charles J. and Mary (Charney) Rund; m. Normand L. Roussel, Dec. 3, 1960; children: Dean Normand, Deena Marie. Student, Bryant Coll., Barbizon Sch. Modeling, N.Y.C. Office mgr. Challenge Advt., Inc., Providence. Mem. NAFE. Democrat. Roman Catholic. Address: 7 David Dr Johnston RI 02919

ROUSSELL, VANESSA LYNN, communications company adminstrator; b. New Orleans, Dec. 20, 1952; d. Dorothy Roussell. BS, Vanderbilt U., 1973. Asst. dial service adminstr. South Cen. Bell, New Orleans, 1974-75, adminstr. dial service, 1975-76; staff specialist Birmingham, Ala., 1976-81; mgr. New Orleans, 1981-83; product mgr. Bell South Services Co., Inc., Birmingham, 1983-87, group product mgr., 1987—; product mgr., cons. Dept. Def., Washington, 1987. Named one of Outstanding Young Women Am., 1977. Mem. Birmingham C. of C. (women's forum). Democrat. Baptist. Home: 3436 Loch Haven Dr Birmingham AL 35216

ROUT, KATHLEEN JOAN KINSELLA, educator; b. Syracuse, N.Y., July 16, 1942; d. Joseph John Kinsella and Elizabeth (Tindall) Halpin; m. Leslie Brennan, Nov. 27, 1969 (dec.); children: Deirdre Denise Rout, Leslie Brennan. BS, LeMoyne Coll., 1963; MA, Stanford U., 1966, PhD, 1975. Instr. Mich. State U., East Lansing, 1967-76, assoc. prof., 1976-90; prof. Mich. State U., 1990—. Author. Mem. Faculty Profl. Women's Assn., Soc. Study Midwestern Lit. Democrat. Office: Mich State U Dept Am Thought & Language Bessey Hall East Lansing MI 48824

ROUTSON, SUSAN HUTCHINS, educator, consultant, peer counseling specialist; b. Cin., May 13, 1943; d. Ralph Pearson and Sarah Minabelle (Abbott) Hutchins; m. Ronald Irving Routson, Oct. 7, 1967; children: Sarah Mary, David Patrick. BS in Math. and Biology, Purdue U., 1965; MS in Microbiology, Mich. State U., 1967. Cert. secondary maths. and biology tchr., Ind. Researcher Miami U., Oxford, Ohio, 1968; apt. mgr. Miami U. Student Housing, Oxford, 1969-74; substitute tchr. Richmond (Ind.) Community Schs., 1976—, coord. vol. tutors, 1978-80; bus. mgr. Richmond Cotillion, 1983-87; dir. Peer Info. Ctrs. for Teens Richmond YWCA, 1986—; trainer Planning Programs for Young Adolescents, 1989—; adult educator Treaty Line Girl Scouts U.S., Richmond, 1978—, svc. unit mgr., 1983-87; cons. YWCA, Richmond, 1987—; state bd. dirs. Ind. Youth Advocate Program, 1989—. Mem. Richmond Sch. Supt.'s Adv. Com., 1975-88; mem. exec. bd. Treaty Line Girl Scouts U.S., Richmond, 1976-88, pres., 1990—; mem., Greater Richmond Progress Com. Edn., Child Care, Teen Pregnancy and Substance Abuse Task Forces, 1986—. Named Vol. Leader of the Yr., Whitewater Valley United Way, 1986; recipient Thanks Badge, Treaty Line Girl Scouts U.S., 1984; honored as Exemplary Youth Orgn. Creator Lilly Endowment, 1988. Mem. Ind. Fedn. Communities for Drug Free Youth, Ind. Coun. on Adolescent Pregnancy, Children's Legal Found., AAUW (pres. elect 1989), Delta Kappa Gamma, Alpha Phi (pres. Richmond chpt. 1985—). Republican. Roman Catholic. Home: 4566 Smyrna Rd Richmond IN 47374 Office: Richmond YWCA 108 S 9th St Richmond IN 47374

ROUX, MILDRED ANNA, retired secondary educator; b. New Castle, Pa., June 1, 1914; d. Louis Henri and Frances Amanda (Gillespie) R. BA, Westminster Coll., 1936, MS in Edn., 1951. Tchr. Farrell (Pa.) Sch. Dist., 1939-55, New Castle (Pa.) Sch. Dist., 1956-76; ret., 1976; chmn. sr. high fgn. lang. dept. New Castle Area Sch. Dist., 1968-76, faculty sponsor sch. fgn. lang. newspapers, 1960-76, 1971-76, Jr. Classical League, 1958-76. Mem. Lawrence County Hist. Soc., AM. Classical League, 1958-76. Mem. AARP, AAUW, Nat. Ret. Tchrs. Assn., Lawrence County Br. Pa. Assn. Sch. Retirees (chmn. community participation com. 1978-81), Coll. Club of New Castle, Woman's Club of New Castle (chmn. pub. affairs com. 1988-90, internat. affairs com. 1990—, program com. 1990—). Republican. Roman Catholic.

ROVNER, ILANA KARA DIAMOND, federal judge; b. Aug. 21, 1938; came to U.S., 1939; d. Stanley and Ronny (Medalje) Diamond; m. Richard Nyles Rovner, Mar. 9, 1963; 1 child, Maxwell Rabson. AB, Bryn Mawr Coll., 1960; postgrad., U. London King's Coll., 1961, Georgetown U., 1961-63; JD, Ill. Inst. Tech., 1966; LittD (hon.), Rosary Coll., 1989, Mundelein Coll., 1989. Bar: Ill. 1972, U.S. Dist. Ct. (no. dist.) Ill. 1972, U.S. Ct. Appeals (7th cir.) 1977, U.S. Supreme Ct. 1982. Jud. clk. to chief judge U.S. Dist. Ct. (no. dist.) Ill., Chgo., 1972-73; chief pub. protection U.S. Atty.'s Office, Chgo., 1973-77; dep. gov., legal counsel Gov. James R. Thompson, Chgo., 1977-84; dist. judge U.S. Dist. Ct. (no. dist.) Ill., Chgo., 1984—. Trustee Bryn Mawr Coll., Pa., 1983-89; mem. bd. overseers Ill. Inst. Tech.-Kent Coll. Law, 1983-87; trustee Ill. Inst. Tech., 1989—. Recipient Spl. Commendation award U.S. Dept. Justice, 1975, 76, Ann. Nat. Law and Social Justice Leadership award The League to Improve the Community, 1975, Ann. Guardian Police award, 1977, Profl. Achievement award Ill. Inst. Tech. Chgo. Kent Coll. Law, 1986; named Today's Chgo. Woman of Yr., 1985, Woman of Yr., The Chgo. Woman's Club, 1986; honored by Midwest Women's Ctr., 1986, Judaica Svc. award Spertus Coll., 1987, Chgo. Found. for Women Ann. award, 1990. Mem. ABA, Ill. State Bar Assn., Chgo. Bar Assn. (Def. of Prisoners Com. Commendation 1987), Women's Bar Assn. Ill. (annual award 1989), Fed. Bar Assn. (following offices with Chgo. chpt. jud. selection com. 1977-80, treas. 1978-79, sec. 1979-80, 2d v.p. 1980-81, 1st v.p. 1981-82, pres. 1982-83, nat. 2d v.p. 7th cir. 1984, v.p. 7th cir. 1986), Chgo. Coun. Lawyers, The Decalogue Soc., Kappa Beta Pi. Republican. Jewish. Office: US Dist Ct 219 S Dearborn St Chicago IL 60604

ROW, LISA ANN, marine corps officer; b. Harrisburg, Pa., Aug. 4, 1959; d. James Clayton and Shirley Mae (Straub) R.; m. James Reid Gallagher, Sept. 7, 1985. BS in Psychology, U. Fla., 1983; grad., Marine Corps Inst., 1987, Navy Fighter Weapons Sch., 1987. Cert. Weapons and Tactics Inst. 1988. Staff sgt. USMC, 1977-83, commd. 2d lt., 1983; clk. supply adminstrn. USMC, Camp Pendleton, Calif., 1977-78; supply chief USMC, Okinawa, Japan; sgt. mil. police provost USMC, Arlington, Va., 1980-81; air def. control officer USMC, Beaufort, S.C., 1983-85, Cherry Point, N.C., 1985-89; adj. USMC, Parris Island, S.C., 1989—. Active Big Sisters, 1989—. Mem. NAFE, Marine Corps Assn., Marine Corps Res. Officer Assn., Naval ROTC Alumni Assn., Semper Fidelis Soc. (pres. 1982-83, author, editor, pub. newsletter 1982-83), Smithsonian Inst., Enlisted Club (chmn. adv. bd. 1979-80). Republican. Methodist. Home: 3 Alumni Rd Lady's Island SC 29902 Office: Recruit Tng Regt Parris Island SC 29905-5020

ROWAN, LYNNE ESTELLE, educator; b. Akron, Ohio, Apr. 22, 1947; d. Malcolm and June Estelle (Rummell) R. Student, Wittenberg U., 1964-66; BS, Kent State U., 1968; MA, U. Conn., 1972; PhD, Purdue U., 1982. Speech pathologist Cleve. Pub. Schs., 1968-70, State Svcs. for Crippled Children, Iowa City, 1972-73, St. Paul Pub. Schs., 1973-78; asst. prof. Ithaca (N.Y.) Coll., 1982-84, U. Ill., Champaign, 1984—. Contbr. articles to profl. jours. Mem. Jr. League, St. Paul, Champaign, 1975—. Mem. Am. Speech-Lang.-Hearing Assn. (cert. clin. competence), Soc. for Rsch. in Child Devel., Internat. Soc. Augmentative and Alternative Communication, Ill. Speech-Lang.-Hearing Assn., Linguistic Soc. Am. Mem. United Ch. of Christ. Office: U Ill 901 S Sixth St Champaign IL 61820

ROWE, DEBORAH LYNN, systems programmer; b. Ann Arbor, Mich., Feb. 18, 1953; d. Glenn Harley and Doris Jean (Noll) R. Student, Dale Carnegie Inst., summer 1982, Washtenaw Community Coll., 1982-86; BS in Computer Sci., Eastern Mich. U., 1989. Cashier Meijer Thrifty Acres, Ypsilanti, Mich., 1972-87; jr. rsch. scientist Environ. Rsch. Inst., Ann Arbor, 1987, programmer, 1988; assoc. systems programmer UNISYS Corp., Plymouth, Mich., 1989—; grad. asst. Dale Carnegie Inst., 1985. Mem. IEEE, ASsn. for Computing Machinery, Computer Soc. of IEEE. Mem. Unity Ch. Home: 44273 Duchess Canton MI 48187

ROWE, EVELYN KARLA, real estate broker; b. S.I., N.Y., Sept. 27, 1943; d. John Robert and Evelyn Karla (Christiansen) Conger; m. James G. Fitch, July 10, 1965 (div. June 1974); children: Elisabeth Ann Perez, Amy Elaine; m. Richard J. Rowe, Aug. 10, 1982. Grad., St. Petersburg Jr. Coll., 1965. Grad. Resdl. Inst. Ins. rater Allstate Ins. Co., St. Petersburg, Fla., 1961-72, Mut. Ins. Agy., St. Petersburg, 1973-76; sales person Area West Inc., Reno, 1977-78; br. mgr. Real Estate West, Sparks, Nev., 1978-80; sales person Palomino Valley Realty, Sparks, 1980-83; broker, owner E & R Realty, Sparks, 1983—; real estate cons., 1984-89. Rep. dep. registrar, Washoe County, Reno, 1987—. Mem. Reno/Sparks Bd. Realtors (mem. grievance com. 1985-89, chmn. edn. com. 1987, grievance com. 1989), Mensa (mem.-at-large 1985, 89), Pythian Sisters (past chief and grand mgr.), Order Eastern Star, Spanish Springs Trap Club, Women's Coun. of Realtors. Home: 2235 Capurro Way Sparks NV 89431 Office: E & R Realty 1205 N Rock Blvd Sparks NV 89431

ROWE, FANNY BICKART, artist, editor; b. N.Y.C., Sept. 21, 1927; d. Charles and Ida (Leventhal) Bickart; m. Gilbert Rowe, July 3, 1948; children: Charles Bickart, Toby Taft. Cert., Cooper Union, 1948. Editor Washington-Irving Times, N.Y.C., 1942-44; artist N.Y. World-Telegram & Sun, N.Y.C., 1944-53; freelance artist, 1953—; editor LWV, N.J., 1989—. Bd. dirs. Clark (N.J.) Adult Sch., 1952-54. Mem. LWV (pres. Linden, N.J. chpt. 1957-59, v.p. Morristown, N.J. chpt. 1986-90, state bd. dirs.). Home: 110 Hillcrest Ave Morristown NJ 07960 Office: LWV of NJ 204 W State St Trenton NJ 08608

ROWE, GENEVA LASSITER, psychotherapist, counseling center administrator, consultant; b. Atlanta, Aug. 11, 1927; d. Hoyt Cleveland and Tinie (Gresham) Lassiter; m. Fred Earnest Rowe, May 3, 1958; children: Carol, Vickie, Randall. BA, Oglethorpe U., 1968; MSW, U. Ga., 1970; PhD, Fla. State U., 1978. Accredited Acad. Cert. Social Workers; lic. marriage and family therapist, Ga.; approved AAMFT supr., 1986. Alcohol and drug counselor Georgian Clinic, Atlanta, 1968; outpatient counselor DeKalb Guidance Clinic, Atlanta, 1969; protective services supr. DeKalb Family and Children Services, Decatur, Ga., 1970-72; outpatient therapist Cen. DeKalb Mental Health Ctr., 1972-75; marriage and family therapist Fla. State U., 1977; lectr. sociology Oglethorpe U., 1978-81; psychotherapist, clin. supr., dir., owner N.E. Counseling Ctr., P.C., Atlanta and Lawrenceville, Ga., 1978—; clin. supr. master's students in practicum Ga. State U., 1980—; approved AAMFT supr., 1986—; allied health profl. CPC Parkwood Hosp., 1987—. Fellow Am. Orthopsychiat. Assn., Internat. Council Sex Edn. and Parenthood; mem. AAUW, Am. Assn. Marriage and Family Therapy (clin. mem., approved supr.), Nat. Speaker's Assn., Ga. Speaker's Assn., Ga. Assn. Marriage & Family Therapy (pub. relations chmn. 1984-86), Gwinnett County C. of C., Am. Soc. Tgn. & Devel., Atlanta C. of C., Young Women of Arts, Omicron Nu. Methodist. Home: 2005 Woodsdale Rd NE Atlanta GA 30324 Office: NE Counseling Ctr PC 2995 Lawrenceville Hwy Lawrenceville GA 30245

ROWE, LISA DAWN, computer programmer; b. Kenton, Ohio, Feb. 2, 1966; d. Daniel Lee and Frances Elaine (Johnson) Edelblute; m. Jeffrey Mark Rowe, Feb. 13, 1982; children: Anthony David, Samantha Paige Elizabeth. Student, Inst. of Lit., 1988-90, Acad. Ct. Reporting, 1988. Writer, model Newslife, Marion, Ohio, 1982-83; bookkeeper Nat. Ch. Residences, Columbus, Ohio, 1985, Insty-Prints, Columbus, 1985; asst. editor Columbus Entertainment, 1984-85; book reviewer, writer Columbus Dispatch, 1989—; writer Consumer News, Delaware, Ohio, 1989—; computer programmer, supr. Dyserv, Inc., Columbus, 1986-90; bookkeeper, acct., office mgr. Marion Music Ctr., Inc., 1990—. Editor newsletter Assn. for System Users, 1989—, articles; contbr. articles, revs. to profl. publs. Mem. NAFE, MADD, DAV (chaplain 1990). Republican. Mormon. Home: 1062 E Center St Marion OH 43302 Office: Marion Music Ctr Inc 143 E Center St Marion OH 43302

ROWE, MAE IRENE, investment company executive; b. Gardner, Mass., Dec. 6, 1927; d. Clifford Wesley and Mertie (Moore) Mann; m. Willard Chase Rowe, June 18, 1951 (div. 1979); children—Gail B. Rowe Simons, Bruce C. B.A. with high honor, Am. Internat. Coll., 1949. Cert. real property adminstr. Social worker City of Montague, Turners Falls, Mass., 1949-51; mgr. Park Investment Co., Cleve., 1979—. Pres., v.p., bd. dirs. Park Ridge Counseling Service, Ill., 1972-76; clk. Village of Kildeer, Ill., 1977; bd. dirs. Maine Township Mental Health Service, Park Ridge, 1975-76; trustee Heathermore Condominium Assn., 1987, pres. 1988, sec.-treas., 1989. Mem. Cleve. Bldg. Owners Mgrs. Assn. (mem. edn. com. 1983—), Bldg. Owners Mgrs. Assn. Internat., Soc. Real Property Adminstrs. (cert.), LWV (v.p., mem. city adv. com. 1973-76), Am. Mensa Soc. Republican. Unitarian. Club: Cleve. Racquet. Lodge: Kiwanis (bd. dirs.) Avocations: tennis. Home: 34108 Chagrin Blvd Apt 5103 Moreland Hills OH 44022 Office: Park Investment Co 907 Park Bldg Cleveland OH 44114

ROWE, MARIELI DOROTHY, media literacy education organization executive; b. Bonn, Fed. Republic of Germany, Aug. 13; came to U.S., 1939; m. John Westel Rowe; children: Peter Willoughby, William Westel, Michael Delano. BA, Swarthmore Coll.; postgrad., U. Colo., 1990; MA, Edgewood Coll., 1990. Interim exec. dir. Friends of Sta. WHA-TV, Madison, Wis., 1976; exec. dir. Nat. Telemedia Coun., Madison, 1978—; project assoc. Loyola U., Chgo., 1989—; bd. dirs. Sta. WYOU, Madison; cons. in field. Editor jour. Telemedium, 1980—; co-producer, author TV documentary Kids Meet Across Space, 1983. Vice-pres. bd. Nat. Friends of Pub. Broadcasting, N.Y. and Washington, 1970-76; pres., v.p. bd. Wis. Coun. and Am. Coun. for Better Broadcasts, Madison, 1963-75; commr. Gov.'s Blue Ribbon Commn. on Cable Communications, Wis., 1971-73; bd. dirs. Broadband Telecommunications Regulatory Bd., Madison, 1978-81. Recipient Spl. Recognition award, Am. Coun. Better Broadcasts, 1981. Mem. Soc. Satellite Profls. (charter), Internat. Visual Literacy Assn., Internat. Platform Assn., Zeta Phi Eta (Marguerite Garden Jones award 1989). Unitarian. Home: 1001 Tumalo Trail Madison WI 53711

ROWE, MARY SUE, accounting professional; b. Melrose, Kans., Aug. 31, 1940; d. Gene and Carmen (Glidewell) Woffard; m. Edward Rowe, Nov. 27, 1985; children from previous marriage: Denise, Dynell, Dalene, Denette. Student, MTI Bus. Coll., 1968, Calif. State U., Fullerton, 1969; cert. Sch. Bus. Mgmt., Calif. State U., San Bernardino, 1986. Variou bookkeeping and secretarial, 1968-76; asst. mgr., acct. RM Dean Contracting, Chenango Forks, N.Y., 1976-80; acctg. asst. Hemet (Calif.) Unified Sch. Dist., 1981-86; dir. acctg. Desert Sands Unified Sch. Dist., Indio, Calif., 1986—. Bd. dirs. Family Svcs. Assn., Hemet, 1982-83. Mem. NAFE, Riverside Assn. Chief Accts. (co-chmn. 1986-88), Calif. Assn. Sch. Bus. Ofcls. (acctg., R & D coms., vice chairperson 1988-90, chairperson 1990—, state acctg. adv. com. 1990—), Desert Schs. Mgmt. Assn. Republican. Home: 41080 Grand Teton Hemet CA 92344 Office: Desert Sand Unified Sch Dist 82-879 Hwy 111 Indio CA 92201

ROWE, RUTH WANDA, medical physics researcher, educator; b. Sedgefield, Eng., Jan. 5, 1954; came to U.S., 1981; d. David John Michel and Lily (Friedmann) R.; m. Jason Andrew Horwege, Aug. 15, 1987. BS (hons.) in Physics, U. Birmingham, Eng., 1975; MS in Med. Physics, U. Aberdeen, Scotland, 1976, PhD in Med. Physics, 1980. Rsch. fellow Sci. Ctr., IBM U.K., Winchester, Eng., 1980-81; rsch. assoc. Brookhaven Nat. Lab., Upton, N.Y., 1981-83, rsch. collaborator, 1983-86; rsch. assoc. North Shore U. Hosp., Manhasset, N.Y., 1983-86; asst. prof. med. physics Med. Coll. Cornell U., N.Y.C., 1985-86, adj. asst. prof., 1987—; asst. prof. Health Sci. Ctr., U. Tex., Houston, 1986—; cons. J&P Engring., Reading, Eng., 1978-80, SUNY, Stonybrook, 1983, KLD Assocs., Huntington, N.Y., 1984-85, North Shore U. Hosp., 1983—. Reviewer Am. Jour. Physiol. Imaging, 1985—. Bd. dirs. The Sound Symphony, Shoreham, N.Y., 1985-86. Co-recipient rsch. grant N.Y. Diabetes affiliate Am. Diabetes Assn., 1984-85; rsch. grantee NIH/North Shore U. Hosp., Manhasset, 1985-86, NIH/U. Tex., Houston, 1987-88, Tex. Higher Edn. Coord. Bd., Austin, 1988—. Mem. IEEE (occasional reviewer Transactions on Med. Imaging 1986—), NIH (spl. study sect. for biomedical computer rsch. resource, rsch. grantee 1985-86, 87-89), Nat. Assn. Female Execs., Soc. of Nuclear Medicine, Houston Soc. Engring. in Medicine and Biology, Houston Area League Personal Computer Users. Office: U Tex Health Sci Ctr 6431 Fannin St MSB CYCF102 Houston TX 77030

ROWE, SANDRA MIMS, newspaper executive editor; b. Charlotte, N.C., May 26, 1948; d. David Lathan and Shirley (Stovall) Mims; m. Gerard Paul Rowe, June 5, 1971; children—Mims Elizabeth, Sarah Stovall. B.A., E. Carolina U., Greenville, N.C., 1970. Reporter to asst. mng. editor The Ledger-Star, Norfolk, Va., 1971-80, mng. editor, 1980-82; mng. editor The Virginian-Pilot and The Ledger Star, Norfolk, Va., 1982-84, exec. editor, 1984-86, v.p., exec. editor, 1986—; mem. nominating jury for Pulitzer Prize in Journalism, 1986, 87; mem. Nieman Selection Com., 1987—. Bd. dirs. Hampton Rds. YMCA, 1987—. Named Woman of Yr. Outstanding Profl. Women of Hampton Rds., 1987. Mem. AP Mng. Editors, Am. Soc. Newspaper Editors, Va. Press Assn. (bd. dirs. 1985—), Am. Press Inst. (adv. bd. 1984—). Episcopalian. Home: 1020 Baldwin Ave Norfolk VA 23507 Office: Virginian-Pilot 150 W Brambleton Ave Norfolk VA 23510

ROWEN, ROSE LEE, mathematician; b. Chgo., Feb. 11, 1917; d. Benjamin and Sarah (Browdy) Greenberg; widowed; children: William Edward, Celia Rowen Barash. AA, Woodrow Wilson Coll., 1936; BA, NYU, 1945. Cert. med. tech. With Army Map Service, Washington, 1947-49, Bur. Standards, Washington, 1949-50, Joint Chief of Staff, Washington, 1950-52; with aircraft and space divs. Hughes Aircraft Co., Culver City, Calif., 1953-60; with Horton project Aero. Corp., Los Angeles, 1961-63; earthquake researcher UCLA, 1963-65; with space contracts Hughes Aircraft Co., Hawthorne, Calif., 1965-67; with Watkins-Johnson Co., Gaithersburg, Md., 1976—. Contbr. over 50 articles on math., physics, and computer sci. to profl. jours. Mem. Soc. Applied Math., Am. Math. Soc., Soc. Women Engrs., Pi Mu Epsilon, Sigma Pi Sigma. Democrat. Lutheran. Club: Cosmos. Home: 1060 Pipestem Pl Potomac MD 20854

ROWEN, RUTH HALLE, musicologist, educator; b. N.Y.C., Apr. 5, 1918; d. Louis and Ethel (Fried) Halle; m. Seymour M. Rowen, Oct. 13, 1940; children: Mary Helen Rowen, Louis Halle Rowen. B.A., Barnard Coll., 1939; M.A., Columbia U., 1941, Ph.D., 1948. Mgmt. ednl. dept. Carl Fischer, Inc., N.Y.C., 1954-63; assoc. prof. musicology CUNY, 1967-72, prof., 1972—, mem. doctoral faculty in musicology, 1967—. Author: Early Chamber Music, 1948, reprinted, 1974; (with Adele T. Katz) Hearing-Gateway to Music, 1959, (with William Simon) Jolly Come Sing and Play, 1956, Music Through Sources and Documents, 1979, (with Mary Rowen) Instant Piano, 1979, 80, 83; contbr. articles to profl. jours. Mem. ASCAP, Am. Musicol. Soc., Music Library Assn., Coll. Music Soc., Nat. Fedn. Music Clubs (nat. musicianship chmn. 1962-74, nat. young artist auditions com. 1964-74, N.Y. state chmn. Young Artist Auditions 1981, dist. coordinator 1983, mem. nat. bd. dirs. 1989—), N.Y. Fedn. Music Clubs (pres.), Phi Beta Kappa. Home: 115 Central Park W New York NY 10023

ROWLAND, DEBRAN MAXINEE, newspaper editor, writer; b. Jersey City, Feb. 28, 1963; d. Gregor Rowland and Carol Miller; m. Luke Hanley, Dec. 31, 1986. BA in English, Carleton Coll., 1985; MA in Anthropology, Columbia U., 1986. Tchr. N.Y.C. schs., 1986-87; reporter English edit. The Korea Times, N.Y.C., 1987-88; reporter, writer The New Pitts. Courier, Apr. to Sept., 1988, city editor, writer, 1988—. Cartographer maps (book) Aztec Warriors; free-lance writer, illustrator, graphic artist. Recipient Robert L. Vann award for best print series, Black Media Fedn., 1988. Mem. Squirrel Hill chpt. NOW. Democrat. Office: New Pitts Courier 315 E Carson St Pittsburgh PA 15219

ROWLAND, JAN BROWNSTEIN, marketing statistician; b. Phila., July 22, 1958; d. Martin and Sylvia (Cohen) Brownstein; m. James R. Rowland, Aug. 16, 1981. BS in Math., Psychology, U. Pitts., 1980, PhD in Epidemiology, 1984; postgrad. in mktg., NYU, 1989. Biostatistician Revlon Health Care Group, Tarrytown, N.Y., 1984-85; policy analyst Empire Blue Cross and Blue Shield, N.Y.C., 1985-86; v.p. mktg. statistics Citibank, N.A., N.Y.C., 1986—; appointed cons. U. S. Congress task force studying impact of office automation on quality of work life, 1984. NSF grantee, 1981-84. Mem. Am. Statistical Assn., Am. Mktg. Assn., Inst. Mgmt. Scis. Office: Citibank 330 Madison New York NY 10017

ROWLAND, JANET MILLER, lawyer; b. San Bernardino, Calif., Dec. 14, 1961; d. Joseph R. and Elizabeth (Leverett) Miller; m. Charles K. Rowland, Aug. 16, 1986. BS in Organizational Communications, U. Tex., Austin, 1984; JD, Tex. Tech. U., 1987. Bar: Tex. Assoc. Law Office of Clifford Bridwell, Wichita Falls, Tex., 1987-88, Barlow Garsek & Bowers, Ft. Worth, 1988, Hyatt Legal Svcs., Ft. Worth, 1988-89, Law Offices of Phillip Galyen, Ft. Worth, 1989—. Speaker, vol. Child Advocates of Tarraut County, Inc., Ft. Worth, 1988—; active Jr. League of Ft. Worth, 1988—; mem. Jr. League of Wichita Falls, 1987-88. Mem. Tarrant County Young Lawyers Assn., Tarrant County Faculty Bar Assn. Office: Law Office Phillip Galyen 1105 B Bedford Rd Fort Worth TX 76022

ROWLAND, LESLIE WIGGINS, congressional director; b. Rome, N.Y., Dec. 18, 1958; d. Dudley Ely Jr. and Virginia Ann (Packer) R.; m. Frederick Hill Hager, Aug. 19, 1989. BA, SUNY, Potsdam, 1981. Mgr. pub. rels. Empire Airlines, Inc., Utica, Rome, N.Y., 1981-86; mgr. pub. rels. Piedmont Airlines, Winston-Salem, N.C., 1986-87; mgr. pub. info. Air Transport Assn. Am., Washington, 1987-89; dir. U.S. Ho. of Reps., Utica, 1989—. Mem. pub. rels. com. United Way, Utica, 1989—, chairwoman, 1981-86; vol. Am. Cancer Soc., Utica, 1979-84. Mem. Nat. Press Club, Aviation Space Writers Assn. Nat. Aviation Assn., Aero Club Washington.

ROWLAND, PATRICIA BRITTINGHAM, accountant, real estate executive; b. Guyton, Ga., July 14, 1941; d. Kenneth L. and Faye (McClelland) Brittingham; student DeKalb Coll., U. Ga.; m. J.D. Rowland; children—Philip Charles, Debora Faye, Jeffrey Allan. Various corp. sec.-treas. and controller positions, 1970-78; pres. Charles S. Roberts & Co., Atlanta, 1978-82; corp. sec. Spalding & Co., Securities Brokers, Atlanta, 1980-81; acct., salesperson Adams Realty, Inc., Royston, Ga., 1982-84; assoc. broker Pinehurst Realty Co., Lavonia, Ga., 1984-86; broker, co-owner Watermark Realty Co., Lavonia, 1986—. Democrat. Episcopalian. Home: 155 Teepee Ln Lavonia GA 30553 Office: Watermark Realty Co PO Box 613 Lavonia GA 30553

ROWLANDS, GENA, actress; b. Cambria, Wis., June 19, 1936; d. Edwin Merwin and Mary Allen (Neal) R.; m. John Cassavetes (dec.); children: Nicholas, Alexandra, Zoe. Student, U. Wis., Am. Acad. Dramatic Art, N.Y.C. Theatrical appearance include The Middle of the Night, 1956; films include The High Cost of Loving, 1958, Lonely Are The Brave, 1962, A Child is Waiting, 1962, Spiral Road, 1962, Faces, 1968, At Any Price, 1970, Minnie and Moscowitz, 1971, Woman Under the Influence, 1973, Two Minute Warning, 1976, Opening Night, 1977, The Brinks Job, 1978, One Summer Night, 1979, Gloria, 1980, Tempest, 1982, Love Streams, 1983, Light of Day, 1987, Another Woman, 1988; TV movies A Question of Love, 1978, Strangers, 1979, Thurday's Child, 1983, Early Frost, 1986, The Betty Ford Story, 1987, Montana; numerous other TV appearances. Recipient Acad. award nomination. Mem. Actors Equity Assn., Screen Actors Guild, AFTRA, Am. Guild Variety Artists. Office: care Lou Pitt Internat Creative Mgmt 8899 Beverly Blvd Los Angeles CA 90048*

ROWLETTE, RONNA, social psychologist; b. Chickasha, Okla., July 26, 1942; d. Ivan Lee and Mona (Sims-Smith) Rowlette; m. Gilbert S. Santoscoy, Mar. 2, 1962; children: Susan Santoscoy Goldschmidt, Gilbert Gregory, Deirdre. BS, Friends U., Wichita, Kans., 1986; PhD, Union Grad. Sch., Cin., 1989. Research asst. Sch. Medicine, Emory U., Atlanta, 1962-63, Rochester (Minn.) Meth. Hosp., 1967-68; program dir. Epilepsy Kans., Inc., Wichita, 1986-87; cons. human resource devel. Wichita, 1987—; intern social policy Nat. Office Psychologists for Social Responsibility, Washington; lectr., cons. community devel. Baha'i Faith, 1977—. Mem. St. Francis Med. Aux., Wichita, 1969—, Mayor's Task Force on Drug Abuse, Wichita, 1976-77, Peace Links, 1985—; mem. adv. bd. Inst. Logopedics, Wichita, 1970-72; mem. aux. bd. Baha'i Faith, Wilmette, Ill., 1977—; bd. dirs. Inter-Faith Ministries, Wichita, 1985—; mem. organizing com. World Inst. Cooperation, Kans., 1986—. Office: PO Box 360154 Tampa FL 33673

ROWLEY, CAROL S., paralegal; b. St. Louis, Sept. 21, 1943; d. Robert lee and Alice C. (Ostermaver) Stubblefield; m. David H. Rowley, June 18, 1966; children: Christopher, Charles. BA, U. Tex., 1965. Cert. secondary tchr., Tex. Tchr. Spring Br. Ind. Sch. Dist., Houston, 1965-68, Lumberton (Tex.) Ind. Sch. Dist., 1968-69; paralegal Long, Aldridge & Norman, Atlanta, 1988—. Mem. AAUW (sec. br. 1977-79, pres. br. 1984-86, sec. div. 1984-86, treas. 1986-90), Ga. Assn. Legal Assts., Delta Gamma. Democrat. Episcopalian. Home: 115 S Shore Ct Roswell GA 30076

ROWLEY, JANET DAVISON, physician; b. N.Y.C., Apr. 5, 1925; d. Hurford Henry and Ethel Mary (Ballantyne) Davison; m. Donald A. Rowley, Dec. 18, 1948; children: Donald, David, Robert, Roger. PhB, U. Chgo., 1944, B.S., 1946, M.D., 1948; DSc (hon.), U. Ariz., 1989, U. Pa., 1989. Cert. Am. Bd. Med. Genetics. Rsch. asst. U. Chgo., 1949-50; intern Marine Hosp., USPHS, Chgo., 1950-51; attending physician Infant Welfare and Prenatal Clinics Dept. Pub. Health, Montgomery County, Md., 1953-54; rsch. fellow Levinson Found., Cook County Hosp., Chgo., 1955-61; clin. instr. neurology U. Ill., 1957-61; USPHS spl. trainee, Radiobiology Lab. The Churchill Hosp., Oxford, Eng., 1961-62; rsch. assoc. dept. medicine and Argonne Cancer Rsch. Hosp. U. Chgo., 1962-69, assoc. prof. dept. medicine and Argonne Cancer Rsch. Hosp., 1969-77, prof. dept. medicine and Franklin McLean Meml. Rsch. Inst., 1977-84, Blum-Riese Disting. Svc. prof., dept. medicine and dept. molecular genetics and cell biology, Franklin McLean Meml. Rsch. Inst., 1984—; mem. Nat. Cancer Adv. Bd., 1979-84. Co-founder, co-editor Genes, Chromosomes and Cancer; mem. editorial bds. Cancer Cells, Cancer Communications, Cancer Genetics and Cytogenetics, Cancer Surveys, Cytogenetics and Cell Genetics, Genomics, Internat. Jour. Cancer, Jour. Clin. Oncology, Leukemia; past mem. editorial bd. Blood, Cancer Rsch., Hematol. Oncology, Leukemia Rsch.; contbr. chpts. to books, articles to profl. jours. Mem. Bd. Sci. Counsellors, Nat. Inst. Dental Rsch., NIH, 1972-76, chmn. 1974-76, Nat. Cancer Adv. Bd. Nat. Cancer Inst., 1979-84, Frederick Cancer Rsch. Facility adv.com., 1983-85, med. adv. bd. Leukemia Soc. Am., 1979-84, MIT Corp. vis. com., Dept. Applied Biol. Scis., 1983-86, selection com., scholar awards in Biomed. Sci., Lucille P. Markey Charitable Trust, 1984-87; trustee Adler Planetarium, Chgo., 1978—; bd. dirs. Am. Bd. Med. Genetics, 1982-83, Am. Bd. Human Genetics, 1985-88; bd. sci. cons. Meml. Sloan-Kettering Cancer Ctr., 1988-90; nat. adv. com. McDonnell Found. Program for Molecular Medicine in Cancer Rsch., 1988—; adv. com. Ency. Britannica, U. Chgo., 1988—; adv. bd. Howard Hughes Med. Inst., 1989-91. Served with USPHS, 1950-51. Recipient First Kuwait Cancer prize, 1984, Esther Langer award Ann Langer Cancer Rsch. Found., 1983, A. Cressy Morrison award in natural scis. N.Y. Acad. Scis., 1985, Past State Pres.' award Tex. Fedn. Bus. and Profl. Women's Clubs, 1986, Karnofsky award and lecture Am. Soc. Clin. Oncology, 1987, prix Antoine Lacassagne Lique Nationale Francaise Contre le Cancer, 1987, King Faisal Internat. prize in medicine (co-recipient), 1988, Katherine Berkan Judd award Meml. Sloan-Kettering Cancer Ctr., 1989, (co-recipient) Charles Mott Prize Gen. Motors Cancer Rsch. Found., 1989. Mem. Am. Soc. Human Genetics, Genetical Soc. (Gt. Britain), Am. Soc. Hematology (Presdl. Symposium 1982, Dameshek prize, 1982), Am. Assn. Cancer Rsch. (G.H.A. Clowes Meml. award, 1989), Sigma Xi (William Proctor prize for sci. achievement, 1989). Episcopalian. Home: 5310 University Ave Chicago IL 60615 Office: U Chgo 5841 Maryland Ave Box 420 Chicago IL 60637

ROWLEY, RAE CAROL, advertising agency executive; b. Reinbeck, Iowa, Mar. 11, 1924; d. Raymond C. and Bertha Caroline (Rickert) Shoup; m. Harry John Rowley, Nov. 9, 1946 (dec. Apr. 1983); children: Cynthia C. Rowley Neville, Michael A., David R. A.S. in Bus., Am. Inst. Bus., Des Moines, 1942. Order clk. Peanut Products Co., Des Moines, 1943-44, office mgr., Indpls., 1944-48; pub. relations adminstrv. asst. Caldwell-Van Riper, Inc., Indpls., 1957-70, media planner, 1970-72, v.p., media dir., 1972-88, media cons., 1988—. Columnist Lawrence Jour., 1962-64. Co-founder Marshall Athletes Mothers Assn., John Marshall High Sch., Indpls., 1970; treas. N.E. Wood Club, Indpls., 1972. Recipient Lifetime Achievement award Am. Women in Radio and TV and Ind. Fedn. of Advt. Agys., 1989. Mem. Am. Women in Radio and TV, Exec. Women Internat. (publs. dir. Indpls. chpt. 1965-66, program dir. 1966-68, pres. 1969-70, adv. bd. 1970—), Am. Legion Aux. (officer 1977-78). Republican. Roman Catholic. Home: RR 2 Box 82 Fountaintown IN 46130

ROY, CATHERINE ELIZABETH, physical therapist; b. Tucson, Jan. 16, 1948; d. Francis Albert and Dorothy Orme (Thomas) R.; m. Richard M. Johnson, Aug. 31, 1968 (div. 1978); children: Kimberly Anne, Troy Michael. BA in Social Sci. magna cum laude, San Diego State U., 1980; MS in Phys. Therapy, U. So. Calif., 1984. Staff therapist Sharp Meml. Hosp., San Diego, 1984-89, chairperson patient and family edn. com., 1986-87, chairperson sex edn. and counselling com., 1987-89, chairperson adv. bd. for phys. therapy, asst. for edn. program, 1987-89; mem. rehab. phys. therapy San Diego Rehab. Inst., Alvarado Hosp., 1989—; lectr. patient edn., family edn., peer edn.; mem. curriculum rev. com. U. So. Calif. Phys. Therapy Dept., 1982; bd. dirs. Ctr. for Edn. in Health; writer, reviewer licensure examination items for phys. therapy Profl. Examination Services.. Tennis coach at clinics Rancho Penasquitos Swim and Tennis Club, San Diego, 1980-81; active Polit. Activities Network, 1985. Mem. Am. Phys. Therapy Assn. (research presenter nat. conf. 1985, del. nat. conf. 1986-89, rep. state conf. 1987-89, Mary McMillan student award 1984, mem. exec. bd. San Diego dist. 1985—), AAUW, NAFE, Am. Coll. Sports Medicine, Am. Congress Rehab. Medicine, Phi Beta Kappa, Phi Kappa Phi, Chi Omega. Home: 13133 Via del Valedor San Diego CA 92129 Office: San Diego Rehab Inst Alvarado Hosp San Diego CA 92120

ROY, DELLA MARTIN, materials science educator, researcher; b. Merrill, Oreg., Nov. 3, 1926; d. Harry L. and Anna (Cacka) Martin; m. Rustum Roy, June 8, 1948; children: Neill R., Ronnen A., Jeremy R. BS, U. Oreg., 1947; MS, Pa. State U., 1949, PhD, 1952. Various rsch. positions Pa. State U., University Park, part-time 1952-60, sr. rsch. assoc. geochem., 1960-62, sr. rsch. assoc. materials sci. engr., 1962-69, assoc. prof. materials sci. engr., 1969-75, prof. materials sci. engr., 1975—; cons. in field. Editor: Instructional Modules in Cement Science, 1985; editor jour. Cement & Concrete Research, 1971—; contbr. articles to profl. publs. Chmn. status of cement, concrete Materials adv. bd., Washington, 1977-80; spl. adv. concrete durability Nat. Rsch. Coun., 1985—; mem. coun. Materials Rsch. Soc., 1988—. Recipient award for outstanding slag rsch. Can. Ctr. Mineral and Energy Tech. Am. Concrete Inst., 1989. Fellow AAAS, Am. Ceramic Soc. (Jeppson Medal award 1982, Copeland award, 1987), Mineral. Soc. Am., Am. Concrete Inst. (keynote address 1980), Inst. Concrete Tech. (hon.); mem. Materials Rsch. Soc. (chmn. cement symposia 1980, 81, 86-88, trustee 1988-90), Nat. Acad. Engring. (elected mem. 1987, mem. acad. adv. bd. 1989—), Am. Ceramic Soc. (trustee 1990—). Democrat. Office: Pa State U 217 MRL University Park PA 16802

ROY, ELSIJANE TRIMBLE, federal judge; b. Lonoke, Ark., Apr. 2, 1916; d. Thomas Clark and Elsie Jane (Walls) Trimble; m. James M. Roy, Nov. 23, 1943; 1 son, James Morrison. JD, U. Ark., Fayetteville, 1939; LLD (hon.), U. Ark., Little Rock, 1978. Bar: Ark. 1939. Atty. Ark. Revenue Dept., Little Rock, 1939-44; mem. firm Reid, Evrard & Roy, Blytheville, Ark., 1945-54, Roy & Roy, Blytheville, 1954-63; law clk. Ark. Supreme Ct.,

Little Rock, 1963-65; assoc. justice Ark. Supreme Ct., 1975-77; U.S. dist. judge then sr. judge Ea. and We. Dists. Ark., Little Rock, 1977—; judge Pulaski County (Ark.) Cir. Ct., Little Rock, 1966; asst. atty. gen. Ark., Little Rock, 1967; sr. law clk. U.S. Dist. Ct., Little Rock and Ft. Smith, 1967-75; Mem. med. adv. com. U. Ark. Med. Center, 1952-54; Committeewoman Democratic Party 16th Jud. Dist., 1940-42; vice chmn. Ark. Dem. State Com., 1946-48; mem. chmn. com. Ark. Constnl. Commn., 1967-68. Recipient Disting. Alumna citation U. Ark., 1978, Gayle Pettus Pontz award, 1986; named Ark. Woman of Yr. Bus. and Profl. Women's Club, 1969, 76, Outstanding Appellate Judge Ark. Trial Lawyers Assn., 1976-77. Mem. ABA, Nat. Assn. Women Lawyers, Ark. Bar Assn., Ark. Women Lawyers (pres. 1940-41), Little Rock Women Lawyers (pres. 1939, 42), AAUW, Mortar Bd., P.E.O., Altrusa, Delta Theta Phi (Mem. of Yr. award 1989), Chi Omega. Club: Altrusa. Office: US Dist Ct PO Box 3255 Little Rock AR 72203

ROY, JEAN ZELLERS, counselor, educator; b. Washington Twp., N.J., Aug. 20, 1930; d. George Byran and Jessie (Cobb) Zellers; m. David Lantz Roy, Apr. 25, 1953; children: Sarah, D. Insley, Mary Jean, Daniel Seth, Jonathan Bruce. BA, Rutgers U., 1951, MEd, 1958. Tchr. North Hunterdon Regular High Sch., Clinton, N.J., 1951-53, Hackettstown (N.J.) High Sch., 1958-59; from tchr. to counselor Frankford Twp. (N.J.) Sch., 1965-68; counselor New Hartford (N.Y.) High Sch., 1968-85, ret., 1985. Mem. Sussex County Rep. Com., Newton, N.J., 1960-68; founder, bd. dirs., pres. Vis. Homemakers Assn., Sussex County, 1962-68; lay speaker United Meth. Ch., 1988—. Mem. Oneida County Counselors Assn. (sec. 1968-85, chair coll. night com. 1974-85), Nat. Assn. Cert. Counselors, AAUW, North Cen. N.Y. Conf. (sec. nominations com. 1989—), North Cen. N.Y. Conf. United Meth. Women (v.p. 1985-90, pres. 1990—), Delta Kappa Gamma. Methodist. Home: RD#2 Box 114 Cherry Valley NY 13320

ROY, KATHLEEN ANNE, technical sales specialist; b. Detroit, Apr. 9, 1964; d. Kenneth Alfred and Helene (Ruhana) R. BSChemE with honors, Mich. State U., 1985. Comml. assignments program engr. Dow Chem. Co., Midland, Mich., Pittsburg, Calif. and Atlanta, 1985-88; tech. sales specialist Dow Chem. Co., Walnut Creek, Calif., 1988—. Patentee sustained release microbiological control composition. Democrat. Roman Catholic.

ROY, PATRICIA JANE, osteopathic physician; b. Muskegon, Mich., Feb. 27, 1956; d. Frank J. and Mary Jo (Gores) Stariha; m. Paul E. Roy, Jr., July 2, 1977; 1 child, Jennifer Jo. Student U. Mich., 1974-75; BS magna cum laude, Aquinas Coll., 1978; DO, Mich. State U., 1981. Diplomate Am. Bd. Osteo. Gen. Practice, Nat. Bd. Osteo. Examiners. Intern, Muskegon (Mich.) Gen. Hosp., 1981-82, chief-of-staff elect, 1987, chmn. exec. staff com., 1987, chief of staff, 1988, trustee, 1987-89; practice family medicine and obstetrics, Muskegon, 1982—; mem. staff Muskegon Gen. Hosp., Muskegon Hackley Hosp. Mem. med. adv. panel Hospice, Inc.; mem. Mich. Osteo. Medicine Adv. Bd., 1989—; mem. profl. edn. com. Muskegon County unit Am. Cancer Soc.; del. City of Muskegon precinct, 1979-81; chmn. citizens adv. com. reproductive health Muskegon Pub. Schs., 1985-87. Named One of 5 Outstanding Young Women, Mich. Jaycees, 1984; named Bus. Woman of Yr., Quadrangle Bus. and Profl. Women, 1986. Mem. Am. Osteo. Assn., Am. Coll. Gen. Practitioners, Osteo. Gen. Practitioners Mich., Am. Acad. Family Practice, Am. Med. Women's Assn., West Mich. Osteo. Assn. (dir. 1984-86), Muskegon Area Women's Med. Assn. (founder, pres.), Fedn. Bus. and Profl. Women, Muskegon Area C. of C. (bd. dirs. 1985-88), Muskegon Quadrangle Club, Mich. Fedn. Bus. and Profl. Women (Young Career Woman Yr. 1983-84), Muskegon Econ. Growth Alliance (bd. dirs. 1988—). Office: 1864 Lakeshore Dr Muskegon MI 49441

ROYAL, JANICE MARIE, insurance professional; b. San Diego, Aug. 31, 1964; d. Delwin Edward and Marilyn Grace (Milke) Floodberg; m. Jonathan Rob Royal, Jan. 14, 1989. BA summa cum laude, U. Calif., Santa Cruz, 1983; BA, Calif. State U., Long Beach, 1987; MA, Claremont (Calif.) Grad. Sch., 1990. Scholarship asst. U. Calif., Santa Cruz, 1982-83; student asst. to v.p. Calif. State U., Long Beach, 1983-86; editorial asst. Orange Coast Mag., Costa Mesa, Calif., 1985-86; asst. to v.p. Gerald J. Sullivan and Assocs., Inc., L.A., 1986-90; asst. mktg. dir. of open market facility G.J. Sullivan Co. Inc.e, Pasadena, Calif., 1990—. Calif. grad. fellow in social scis., 1988-89. Mem. Am. Studies Student Assn., Calif. Scholarship Fedn. (life), Toastmasters (ednl. v.p. 1989-90), Nat. Assn. Ins. Women, Golden Key, Phi Beta Kappa. Democrat. Home: 1835-4 E J4 Lancaster CA 93535 Office: Gerald J Sullivan Co Inc 135 N Los Robles Pasadena CA 91101

ROYE, SHERRY RENEE, security administrator; b. Whitney, Tex., Sept. 3, 1960; d. James Richard Roye and Mary Lou (Martin) Rogers. BBA, Tex. Wesleyan Coll., 1983. Mgmt. intern Citran City Transit, Ft. Worth, Tex., 1982-83; receptionist, sec. Nat. Guardian Security Svcs. Corp., Ft. Worth, Tex., 1983-84; br. exec. sec. Nat. Guardian Security Svcs., Ft. Worth, Tex., 1984-86, regional exec. sec., 1986-88, regional dir. of adminstr., 1988—. Mem. Assn. Security Services and Investigators of State of Tex., Nat. Assn. Female Execs. Baptist. Office: Nat Guardian Security Svcs 7434 Tower St Fort Worth TX 76118

ROYER, KATHLEEN ROSE, airline pilot, flight engineer; b. Pitts., Nov. 4, 1949; d. Victor Cedric and Lisetta Emma (Smith) Salway; m. Michael Lee Royer, June 6, 1971 (div. Aug. 1975). Student, Newbold Coll., 1968-69; BS, Columbia Union Coll., 1971; MEd, Shippensburg U., 1974; student, Lehigh U., 1974-75. Cert. tchr. Pa. Music tchr. Harrisburg (Pa.) Sch. Dist., 1971-77; flight instr. Penn-Air, Inc., Altoona, Pa., 1977; capt., asst. chief pilot Air Atlantic Airlines, Centre Hall, Pa., 1977-80; capt., chief pilot Lycoming Air Svc., Williamsport, Pa., 1980-81; govs. pilot Commonwealth of Pa., Harrisburg, 1981-87; flight engr. Pan-Am., N.Y.C., 1987—; first woman pilot/engr. crew mem. on 747, 1989—; chief pilot, cons. Mem. Internat. Soc. Women Airline Pilots, Flight Engrs. Internat. Assn. (scheduling rep. 1989, scheduling dir. 1990, 1st vice chmn., mem. bd. adjustments 1989), 99's (local chairwoman Cen. Pa. chpt. 1987), Whirley-Girls (Washington). Republican. Home: 20470 Raleigh Rd Hummelstown PA 17036 Office: PanAm World Airways Inc PanAm Bldg New York NY 10166

ROYLANCE, LYNN MICHELLE, electrical engineer; b. San Francisco, Nov. 27, 1951; d. Jack Clifton and Alice Helen (Gordh) R.; m. Julian Payne Freret Jr., June 21, 1979; children: Morgan Elizabeth Freret, Taylor Susanne Freret. BSEE, BS in Physics, MIT, 1972; MSEE, Stanford U., 1973, PhD in Elec. Engring., 1978. Instr. Stanford U., Stanford, Calif., 1974; mem. tech. staff Hewlett-Packard Labs., Palo Alto, Calif., 1977-81; project mgr. Hewlett-Packard Labs., Calif., 1981-87, project mgr. Cir. Tech. Group R & D, 1987-89; sect. mgr. Cir. Tech. Group R & D, 1989—; Mem. program com. Internat. Symposium on Very Large Scale Integration Tech., 1982-85. Contbr. articles to profl. jours. NSF fellow, 1972-75. Mem. IEEE, Am. Mgmt. Assn., Phi Beta Kappa, Sigma Xi, Tau Beta Pi (program com., No. Calif. Electronic Material Symposium 1981, chmn. 1983-84, treas. No. Calif. section 1985-87). Home: 1160 Laureles Dr Los Altos CA 94022 Office: Hewlett-Packard 5301 Stevens Creek Blvd Santa Clara CA 95052

ROYSTER, CONSTANCE LAUREL, lawyer; b. New Haven, Feb. 7, 1949; d. Marshall Thomas and Eunice (Baker) R.; m. Laurence B. Liebowitz, May 4, 1979. Student, Wheaton Coll., 1968-69; BA cum laude, Yale Coll., 1972; JD, Rutgers U., 1977. Bar: N.Y. 1978, U.S. Dist. (so. dist.) N.Y. 1978, U.S. Ct. Appeals (6th cir.) 1978, U.S. Dist. Ct. (ea. dist.) N.Y. 1981. Letters corrs. Time Mag., N.Y.C., 1972-74; law clk. to judge U.S. Ct. Appeals (6th cir.), Detroit, 1977-78; asst. U.S. atty. U.S. Atty. Office of U.S. Atty. (so. dist.) N.Y., 1979-81; assoc. Paul Weiss Rifkind Wharton & Garrison, N.Y.C., 1978-79, 81-84; prin. Liebowitz, Villanova & Royster, P.C., Elmsford, N.Y., 1984-86, Liebowitz & Royster, P.C., Elmsford, 1986-88, Cooper, Liebowitz & Royster, P.C., Elmsford, 1988-90; ptnr. Cooper, Liebowitz, Royster & Wright, Elmsford, N.Y., 1990—. Notes and comments editor Rutgers Law Review. Trustee Wykeham Rise Sch., Washington, Conn., 1969-79, 84-88; bd. dirs. Chiropractic Edn. Found. of N.Y., Inc., 1986—. Leopold Schepp Found. fellowship, 1974-77, Bates fellowship 1971; English Speaking Union scholarship, 1967-68, scholarship Yale U., 1969-72,. Mem. ABA, Nat. Bar Assn., Westchester C. of C. Democrat. Epsicopalian. Office: Cooper Liebowitz Royster & Wright 3 W Main St Elmsford NY 10523

ROZANSKI, CYNTHIA LEANN, special education teacher; b. Camden, N.J., Sept. 12, 1965; d. Charles Lewis and Rosalie A. (DiPaola) Dunhour; m. Henry Edward Rozanski, Jan. 23, 1988. BS in Spl. Edn. and Elem. Edn., U. Del., 1987. Cert. tchr., N.J. Spl. educator Cinnaminson (N.J.) Twp. Bd. Edn., 1987-89, Mercer County Spl. Svcs. Sch. Dist., Trenton, N.J., 1989-90, Princeton (N.J.) Regional Schs., 1990—; participant Integration of Therapy in the Classroom, Trenton, 1987—, Whole-Lang. Reading Tchr. for minority, inner-city children; art cons. Jamison Galleries. Vol. in hispanic community, Trenton. Mem. N.J. Edn. Assn., Mercer County Edn. Assn. Republican. Roman Catholic. Home: 392 Andover Pl Robbinsville NJ 08691

ROZEBOOM, LORA LYN, college official; b. Benson, Minn., Jan. 20, 1956; d. Conrad A. and Vera June (Aukes) R. AA, Willmar (Minn.) Community Coll, 1976; BS, Winona State U., 1979; MEd in Adminstrn., Wichita State U., 1986, EdS, 1989. Occupational therapist Camp Winebago, Caledonia, Minn., 1978; ednl. therapist Chileda Inst., La Crosse, Wis., 1978-79; ednl. specialist Inst. Logopedics, Wichita, Kans., 1979-81; elem. learning disabilities specialist Unified Sch. Dist. 261, Haysville, Kans., 1981-84, high sch. learning disabilities specialist, 1984-89; coord. spl. needs, instr. Butler County Community Coll., El Dorado, Kans., 1989—; ednl. cons., 1978—; mem. evaluation team North Cen. Visitation Team, Wichita, 1987; front desk mgr. Days Inn East Inc., Wichita, 1988; ednl. counselor Nutri-System East, Wichita, 1989—. Instr. Bethany Ref. Ch., Clara City, Minn., 1972-79; leader Girl Scouts U.S.A., Winona, Minn., 1976-79; swimming aid instr. Minn. Crippled Children Program, Winona, 1977; den leader Cub Scouts for Handicapped, Wichita, 1980-81. Mem. Am. Coun. on Rural Spl. Edn., Haysville Edn. Assn. (pres. 1985-86, 88-89), Haysville C. of C. Home: 9400 E Lincoln Apt 621 Wichita KS 67207 Office: Butler County Community Coll El Dorado KS 67042

ROZMAN, SHERYL ANN, military officer; b. Aberdeen, Wash., July 13, 1956; d. Jack Ivan and Edit Louise (Greenstreet) Rozman; m. Gerald Lynn Hess, Nov. 30, 1985; 1 child, James John. BS in Social Sci., Portland (Oreg.) State U., 1988. Food svc. specialist, helicopter pilot, unit clk., recruiter U.S. Army N.G., 1974—; captain, instrument flight examiner U.S. Army N.G., Fort Indiantown Gap, Pa., 1986—. Mem. Assn. U.S. Army, N.G. Assn. U.S., Army Aviation Assn. Am., Nat. Assn. Female Execs., The Whirlygirls, Lebanon County C. of C. (mem. women in bus. com.). Democrat. Methodist. Home: 2008 Laurel Glen Dr Harrisburg PA 17110 Office: Ea Army Nat Guard Aviation Tng Site c/o DMA Fort Indiantown Gap Annville PA 17003-5004

ROZZI, SANTA CAPUTO, deputy county executive; b. Brklyn., Aug. 4, 1950; d. Frank Vincent and Mary (LaCava) Caputo; m. Samuel J. Rozzi, Mar. 7, 1981. BA, Marymount Coll., N.Y., 1971; JD, St. John U. Law Sch, Jamaica, N.Y., 1981. Admission Bar of N.Y., 1982. Sec. Office of Town Atty., Town of Oyster Bay, N.Y., 1972-73, Office of County Comptroller, County Nassau, Mineola, N.Y., 1973-81; insp. Office of Compt. County of Nassau, Mineola, N.Y., 1981-82, dep. county atty., 1982-84, deputy county treas., 1984-86; bur. chief BREI, Office of County Atty., County Nassau, N.Y., 1986-88; deputy county exec. County of Nassau, Mineola, N.Y., 1988-. Mem. Long Island Ctr. for Bus. and Profl. Women, N.Y., 1988. Mem. Bar Assn. of Nassau County, Nassau Suffolk Women's Bar Assn., Columbian Layers Assn. of N.C. Republican. Roman Catholic. Office: County Nassau 1 West St Mineola NY 11501

RUARK, DONNA MCLEOD, information systems consultant; b. Columbus, Ohio, Aug. 24, 1958; d. Ralph E. and Maribel (Moore) McLeod; m. Rodney Dale Ruark; children: Nicholas Glen, Kathleen Elizabeth. Assoc. in EDP Auditing, Columbus Tech., 1983. Info. system cons. Computer People, Columbus, Ohio, 1980-81; sr. programmer analysis R.G. Barry, Pickerington, Ohio, 1981-89; info. systems cons. Software Systems, Columbus, 1989-90; cons. Analysts Internat. Corp., Columbus, 1990—. Mem. Assn. System's Users, NAFE, Mensa. Home: 6387 Refugee Rd SW Pataskala OH 43062

RUARK-HEARST, MARGO LYNN, editor; b. Huron, S.D., June 4, 1956; d. Roger D. and Ardis L. (Lehfeldt) Ruark; m. James R. Hearst III, 1990; 1 child, Marshall Douglas. BA in Art History, U. Uppsala, Sweden, 1979, MA in Esthetics, 1981; MA in Phys. Edn. and Dance, U. Wis., 1983; postgrad., DePaul U., 1988—. Prof. dancer, choreographer, artistic dir. Margo Ruark & Dancers, Madison, Wis., 1983-86; guest artist in residence Black Horse Theatre, Copenhagen, Denmark, 1986-87; mktg. specialist Blue Cross and Blue Shield Assn., Chgo., 1987-88; sr. editor Joint Commn. on Accredition Healthcare Orgns., Chgo., 1988—. Author: History of Dance (Swedish) 1979. Mem. NAFE, Am. Mktg. Assn. Democrat. Office: Joint Commn on Accredition 1 Renaissance Blvd Oakbrook Terrace IL 60181

RUBACH, PEGGY, mayor; b. N.Y.C., July 7, 1947; children: Kristin, Jon, Matthew. BA in Psychology, SUNY, Buffalo; postgrad., Ariz. State U.; Diploma, Harvard U. Cost analyst, med. claims adminstr. Aetna Life and Casualty; project coordinator Mesa (Ariz.) community Coll.; dist. asst. Congressman John McCain; mayor City of Mesa, 1988—; mcpl. rep. Ariz. Consortium on Edn.; cons. Luth. Healthcare Network; adv. bd. U.S. Conf. Mayors, chair, subcom. on pub. transp. Adv. bd. U. Ariz. Cancer Ctr.; treas. Ariz. Women Mcpl. Govt.; gov's. task force Cactus League Baseball; chmn. math. basic goals com. Ariz. Bd. Edn.; mem. Sister City Assn. of Mesa, East Valley Partnership, policy com. Nat. league of Cities' and Econ. Devel.; bd. dirs. Regional Pub. Transp. Authority; assoc. mem. Urban Land Inst. Home: 2145 E Glencove Mesa AZ 85213 Office: Office of Mayor 55 N Center St PO Box 1466 Mesa AZ 85211-1466

RUBB, PEGGY-GRACE PLOURD, artistic director, dancer; b. Hartford, Conn., Sept. 27, 1931; d. Launcelot J. and Margaret (Feeney) Plourd; m. Milton Robert Rubb, June 6, 1953; children: Bonnie Leigh, Eric John, Michael Robert. Student, Hartt Conservatory of Music, Hartford, 1938-49; student, Shenandoah Conservatory, Winchester, Va., 1949-51, Froman Profl. Ballet Sch., New London, Conn., 1959-62, Hampton Acad. Ballet, Va., 1962-63, Nat. Ballet, Washington, 1963-66. Tchr. R.H. Lee Elem. Sch., Glen Burnie, Md., 1951-52; dancer Common Glory Jamestown Corp., Williamsburg, Va., 1963; accompanist Annapolis (Md.) Modern Dance Assn., 1973, Ballet Mistress Dance Studio, Crofton, Md., 1974-78; dance instr. gymnastics camp Washington Coll., Chestertown, Md., 1977; artistic dir. Crofton-Bowie (Md.) Sch. of Ballet and affiliated cos., 1978—; choreographer Tom Thumb Players, Annapolis, 1972, Nat. Assn. for Regional Ballet, Inc. Choreography Conf., 1987; dancer Hampton Roads Civic Ballet, Va., 1962-63; composer, lyricist in field; dance coach Glen Burnie (Md.) Artistic Skate Club, 1980-81. Bd. dirs. Annapolis Children's Theatre, 1977-78. Mem. NAFE, Md. Coun. for Dance, Internat. Platform Assn., U.S. Naval Acad. Class '53 Wives Club (pres. San Diego chpt. 1957, pres. New London chpt. 1959), Severn Town Club, Md. Club, Gen. Fedn. Women's Club (co-mem.), Phi Beta Sigma. Home: 1 Pennsylvania Ave Edgewater MD 21037 Office: 2411 Crofton Ln Chelsea House Ste 2 Crofton MD 21114

RUBEN, REGINA LANSING, biologist; b. Newark, Jan. 2, 1950; d. Harold Jason and Freda (Sperling) Lansing; m. Jeffrey Mark Ruben, June 22, 1975; children: Adam Jeremy, Rachel Aliza. BA, U. Rochester, 1972; MS, Ohio State U., 1974, PhD, 1975. Postdoctoral assoc. U. Ill., Chgo., 1975-78; sr. instr. Hahnemann U., Phila., 1978-79, asst. prof., 1979-82; rsch. scientist E. I. duPont de Nemours & Co., Inc., Glenolden, Pa., 1982-86, prin. scientist, 1986-88, product info. scientist, 1989-90, group leader, 1990—; cons. Rochester Alumni Career Exploration Referral Service, 1972—, Brandywine Sci. Alliance, 1988—. Contbr. Articles to profl. jours. U. Rochester hon. scholar, 1968. Mem. Tissue Culture Assn., Am. Assn. Anatomists, Women in Cancer Rsch., Am. Assn. for Cancer Research, Drug Info. Assn., Sigma Xi. Avocations: piano, bicycling, handicrafts. Home: 2317 Lighthouse Ln Wilmington DE 19810 Office: EI DuPont de Nemours & Co Inc Med Products Dept P26/2110 Wilmington DE 19880-0026

RUBENSTEIN, MARGO ANN, dentist; b. Paterson, N.J., May 1, 1955; d. Joseph L. and Doris R. (Rosenthal) R.; m. Peter Amil Winkler, May 9, 1982; children: Zachary Charles, Dylan Ross. BS, Rutgers U., 1976; DDS, Loyola U., Maywood, Ill., 1980. Dental assoc. Phoenix, 1980-84; pvt. practice Scottsdale, Ariz., 1984—. Mem. ADA, Ariz. State Dental Assn., Chgo. Dental Soc., Am. Assn. Women Dentists, Jewish Bus. and Profl. Women's Assn., Nature Conservancy, Soroptimists Internat., Alpha Omega (sec., treas. 1989—, v.p. 1990—). Home: 5833 N 70th Pl Paradise Valley AZ 85253 Office: 7110 E McDonald Dr C-2 Scottsdale AZ 85253

RUBENSTEIN, NANCY LEE, newspaper editor; b. Fall River, Mass.; d. R. Ralph and Rose (Edelstein) Horne; m. Edwin R. Rubenstein, Sept. 23, 1951; 1 child, David A. BA, Boston U., 1950. With various newspapers, 1951-71; editor Today Newspapers, Butler, N.J., 1972-86; editor Suburban Life, North Caldwell, N.J. Recipient over 65 journalistic awards. Mem. N.J. Press Assn., N.J. Press Women, PICA Club. Club: North Jersey Press. Home: 33 Meadowbrook Ln Cedar Grove NJ 07009 Office: Today Newspapers 10 Park Pl Butler NJ 07405

RUBIN, ARLINE BARBARA, nurse; b. Phila., Aug. 11, 1942; d. Samuel E. and Cecelia (Breitman) Rubin; children: Neil, Lynn, Ron. RN, St. Joe's Hosp., 1975; BS, Albright Coll., 1981; MS, U. Pa., 1985. Cert. Infection Control; Nursing Home Adminstr. Intensive care nurse Community Gen. Hosp., Reading, Pa., 1975-79; intravenous therapist Community Gen. Hosp., Reading, 1979-81, infection control nurse, 1981-85; nursing dir. Regina Nursing Ctr., Norristown, Pa., 1985-87; infection control practitioner VA Med. Ctr., Lebanon, Pa., 1987-89; asst. adminstrn. Leader II Nursing Ctr., Bethlehem, Pa., 1989-90; adminstr. Leader II Nursing Ctr., Norristown, Pa., 1990—; cons. and instr. in field; chair VA Dist. 4 AIDS Task Force, 1988; coord. Infection Control Practitioners, 1988; bd. dirs. AIDS Task Force Lebanon County, 1989. Contbr. articles to prof. jour. Recipient Ednl. Advancement award Assn. Practitioners in Infection Control, 1985. Mem. Assn. Practitioners Infection Control, Am. Contract Bridge League, Hosp. Assn. Pa. (Innovations in Cost Containment award), B'nai Brith Women (pres.). Democrat. Jewish. Home: 322A Willowbrook Dr Jeffersonville PA 19403 Office: Leader II Nursing Ctr 2004 Old Arch Rd Norristown PA 19401

RUBIN, BARBARA JEAN, real estate licensing program director; b. Ashtabula, Ohio, Aug. 30, 1945; d. Marvin Louis and Edith Louise (Stevenson) R. AB, Grove City Coll., 1967; MEd, Temple U., 1971; postgrad., U. Pa., 1978-79. Elem. tchr. Colonial Sch. Dist., Plymouth Meeting, Pa., 1967-79; bus. mgr. Lifespring, Phila., 1979-81; asst. dir. ops. Lifespring, San Rafael, Calif., 1981-82, asst. to v.p., 1982-83; program dir. Assessment Systems, Inc., Phila., 1983—. Trustee Presbyn. Ch. of Chestnut Hill, Phila., 1986-88, mem. Christian edn. com. 1986—, elder, 1990—. Mem. Real Estate Educators Assn., Phi Delta Kappa. Home: 8561 Trumbauer Dr Wyndmoor PA 19118 Office: Assessment Systems Inc 718 Arch St Philadelphia PA 19106

RUBIN, CATHY ANN, educator; b. Denver, July 17, 1948; d. Harry Phillip and Charlotte Ruth (Brinig) R. BA, Colo. State U., 1970; MA, U. No. Colo., 1971. Cert. tchr., Colo. Tchr. Adams County Dist. 50 Schs., Westminster, Colo., 1971-72; tchr. educationally handicapped Jefferson County Pub. Schs., Golden, Colo., 1972—; typist, bookkeeper Kenmark-Shaw's Jewelers, Denver, 1966—. Sec.-treas. Hillel Found., Denver, 1979-81; fundraiser Women's Am. ORT, Denver, 1979—; bookkeeper Religious Coalition for Abortion Rights, Denver, 1982-90; vol. TV PBS sta., Denver, 1985—; fundraiser Mus. Dystrophy Assn. Mem. Nat. Coun. Tchrs. English. Democrat. Jewish. Home: 3500 S Ivanhoe St Denver CO 80237-1123

RUBIN, DEBRA JILL, public relations company executive; b. Livingston, N.J., June 6, 1958; d. Seymour and Shirley (Ruff) R. BA magna cum laude, Washington U., St. Louis, 1980; MS in Journalism, Northwestern U., 1981. Asst., assoc. and mng. editor Toy and Hobby World mag., N.Y.C., 1981-83; assoc. publicist Crown Pub. Group, N.Y.C., 1983-84, publicist, 1984-85, publicity mgr., 1985-87, assoc. dir. publicity, 1988-89; account exec. Howard J. Rubenstein Assocs., N.Y.C., 1989-90, sr. account exec., 1990—; mem. publicity com. N.Y. Is Book Country, N.Y.C., 1985. Mem. Pubs. Publicity Assn. (planning com. 1986-89).

RUBIN, DIANE MARIE, accountant; b. Seattle, Oct. 26, 1951; d. Ellsworth Sydney and Betty Jane (Krause) Paulson; m. Asher Rubin, Dec. 4, 1982; children: Jacob, Shaina. BA, U. Wash., Seattle, 1973, MBA, 1975. CPA, Calif., Wash. Audit mgr. Price Waterhouse, N.Y.C. and San Francisco, 1975-81; mgr. fin. reporting Fireman's Fund Ins., Novato, Calif., 1981-84; controller Westnet Bank, San Francisco, 1984-85, Paribas Tech., San Francisco, 1985-86; v.p., controller Arthur J. Gallagher & Co., San Francisco, 1986-89; owner Diane M. Rubin, CPA, San Francisco, 1989—. Bd. dirs. Florence Crittendon Svcs., San Francisco, 1980-89. Mem. AICPAs, Calif. Soc. CPAs, Wash. Soc. CPAs, Soc. Chartered Property Casualty Underwriters, Jr. League of San Francisco, Profl. Women's Network. Office: 703 Market St 20th Fl San Francisco CA 94103

RUBIN, KAREN BETH, executive recruitment company executive; b. N.Y.C., Aug. 30, 1951; d. Samuel M. and Eleanor (Spiegel) Rubin; m. Neil Leiberman, Dec. 29, 1983; children: David, Eric. BA, SUNY, Binghamton, 1972. Sr. editor Travel Agt. mag., N.Y.C., 1973-86, Tour & Travel News, Manhasset, N.Y., 1986-89; pres. Travel Exec. Search Great Neck, N.Y., 1989—; founder, pub., editor Making It!, Great Neck, 1981—. Author: Flying High in Travel, 1986; contbr. thousands of articles to newspapers and profl. jours. Recipient Neal Cert. of Merit, Am. Bus. Press, 1984. Mem. Nat. Assn. Exec. Females. Office: Travel Exec Search 5 Rose Ave Great Neck NY 11021

RUBIN, NANCY RUTH ZIMMAN, journalist, author; b. Boston, Nov. 25, 1944; d. Stuart Wendell and Ethel Charlotte (Rabinovitz) Zimman; m. Peter H. Rubin, July 9, 1967; children: Elisabeth Kara, Jessica Ann. BA, Tufts U., 1966; MA in Teaching, Brown U., 1967. English tchr. Brighton High Sch., N.Y., 1967-68, N.Y. Schs., Pittsford, 1969-70; playwright, dir. Equity Library Theatre, Roundabout, Joseph Jefferson and St. Clement's theaters, N.Y.C., 1971-74; writer Westchester-Gannett newspapers and mags., 1975-77; free-lance reporter N.Y. Times, N.Y.C., 1977—; faculty affiliate Bush Ctr. in Child Devel., Yale U., New Haven, 1981—; mem. Westchester County Women's Adv. Bd., chair, 1988. Author: The New Suburban Women: Beyond Myth and Motherhood, 1982, The Mother Mirror: How A Generation of Women is Changing Motherhood in America, 1984; contbg. editor Parents Mag., 1987—; contbr. articles to nat. jours., mags., newspapers. Time, Inc.-Bread Loaf Writers' Colony scholar, 1979. Fellow McDowell Colony; mem. Author's Guild, Am. Soc. Journalists and Authors, PEN, NOW. Office: care Agnes Birnbaum Bleecker St Assocs 88 Bleecker St New York NY 10012

RUBIN, TILLIE EVA, social worker; b. Boston, May 12, 1919; d. Samuel and Fannie (Kallen) Feingold; m. Milton David Rubin, Sept. 9, 1944; children: Mark Jonathan, Lise Diane. BSW, Middlesex Coll., Bedford, Mass., 1973. Social worker Boston U. Child Guidance Clinic, 1973-74, Newton (Mass.) Guidance Clinic, 1974-76; foster care coord. Middlesex East II, Inc., Waltham, Mass., 1977-80; tng. coord. on adolescent sexuality Newton Multi-Svc. Ctr., 1978-79; dir. Cambridge (Mass.) Halfway House, 1978-79. Mem. Newton Dem. City Com., 1961—; chair fgn. econ. policy Newton LWV, 1960-62. Mem. Brandeis U. Nat. Women's Com.

RUBIN, VERA COOPER, research astronomer; b. Phila., July 23, 1928; d. Philip and Rose (Applebaum) Cooper; m. Robert J. Rubin, June 25, 1948; children: David M., Judith S. Young, Karl C., Allan M. BA, Vassar Coll., 1948; MA, Cornell U., 1951; PhD, Georgetown U., 1954; DSc (hon.), Creighton U., 1978, Harvard U., 1988, Yale U., 1990. Research assoc. to asst. prof. Georgetown U., Washington, 1955-65; physicist U. Calif.-LaJolla, 1963-64; astronomer Carnegie Instns., Washington, 1965—; Chancellor's Disting. prof. U. Calif, Berkeley, 1981; vis. com. Harvard Coll. Obs., Cambridge, Mass., 1976-82, Space Tel. Sci. Inst., 1990—; Beatrice Tinsley vis. prof. U. Tex., 1988. Assoc. editor: Astrophys. Jour. Letters, 1977-82; editorial bd.: Sci. Mag., 1979-87; contbr. numerous articles sci. jours.; assoc. editor: Astron. Jour., 1972-77. Pres.'s Disting. Visitor, Vassar Coll., 1987. Mem. Smithsonian Instn. Council, 1979-85; Phi Beta Kappa scholar, 1982-83. Mem. Am. Astron. Soc. (council 1977-80), Internat. Astron. Union (pres. Commn. on Galaxies 1982-85), Assn. Univs. Research in Astronomy (dir. 1973-76), Nat. Acad. Scis. (Space Sci. Bd. 1974-77, 81, 87—, com. on human rights), Am. Acad. Arts and Scis., Phi Beta Kappa. Democrat. Jewish.

RUBINI, EILEEN, fashion designer; b. Union City, N.J., June 2, 1948; d. Julius and Mary (Fitzgerald) R. Student, Iona Coll., Fashion Inst. Tech., N.Y.C.; studied design at Parsons Sch., N.Y.C. With pub. relations and advt. depts. Jaeger Co., N.Y.C., 1972-75; merchandiser Arthur Richards Woman, Inc., N.Y.C., 1975-78; v.p., merchandiser Jerry Silverman Sportswear, N.Y.C., 1978-79, Don Sayres Co., N.Y.C., 1979-81; v.p. design Yukiko Hanai, N.Y.C., 1981-83; v.p., designer Signatures Inc., N.Y.C., 1983-86; designer, owner Eileen Rubini Inc., N.Y.C., 1986—; freelance merchandiser, designer Kellwood Cos., N.Y.C., 1986—. Office: Kellwood Cos 214 W 39th St Ste 902 New York NY 10018

RUBINO, KATHY, fashion designer; b. Hackensack, N.J., Jan. 13, 1959; d. Alfonso and Irma (DeRosa) R. A.A.S., Fashion Inst. Technology, N.Y.C.; BA with honors Philosophy, Fordham U. Head designer, merchandiser P.J.'s Place Ltd., N.Y.C., 1982-87; head designer Tracy Evans Ltd., N.Y.C., 1988; owner Creative Design Options, Ft. Lee, N.J., 1989—. Mem. Am. Women Entrepreneurs, Nat. Assn. for Female Execs., Phi Kappa Phi, Alpha Sigma Lambda. Home: 1 Alfred Rd W Merrick NY 11566

RUBINO, MARY ANN, freelance writer; b. Chgo., Nov. 24, 1965; d. Paul Joseph and Ann Marie (Freborg) R. BA in Econs., Brown U., 1987. Freelance writer Chgo., 1988; ind. researcher Bari, Italy, 1989—. Author: The Girl Who Cried True Love, 1987-89. Mem. Brown U. Recent Alumni Group (founder, chmn. 1987-89). Roman Catholic.

RUBINSTEIN, SHIRLEY JOY, nursing service executive; b. Toronto, Ont., Can., Nov. 19, 1927; came to U.S., 1928, naturalized, 1948; d. Harry Hyman and Ida Ruth (Albert) Adel; m. Philip F. Rubinstein, Aug. 17, 1947; children: David Brian, Wendy Sue, Hope Terri. With Jewish Agy. for Palestine, Washington, 1947-49; coord. Nursing Staff, Inc., 1975-78; co-founder, pres. Nursing Svcs., Inc., Silver Spring, Md., 1978—; founder, pres. Fantasy Factory Inc., Pegasus Limosine Svcs.; founder, co-owner Caplans of Ellicott City Antiques, 1988—. Democrat. Jewish. Club: B'nai Brith. Office: 11161 New Hampshire Ave Ste 440 Silver Spring MD 20904

RUBLE, ANN, clergywoman; b. Seattle, Oct. 26, 1953; d. Monte Rahe and Stella (Terefinko) Ruble; m. Francis Michael Trotter, Aug. 29, 1984. Cert. sec., Met. Bus. Coll., Seattle, 1972. Ordained to ministry Ch. of Scientology, 1980. Minister Ch. of Scientology, Seattle, 1980—, dir. pub. affairs, 1983; pres. Ch. of Scientology of Wash. State, Seattle, 1984-88, dir., 1989—. Bur. chief Jour. Freedom News, 1984-88. Mem. Citizen's Commn. Human Rights, Seattle, 1984—, Com. on Religious Liberties, Seattle, 1985—, Wash. Environ. Coun., 1989—. Mem. Internat. Platform Assn. Office: Ch of Scientology of Washington State 2603 Third Ave Seattle WA 98121

RUCH, PEGGY ANN F., data processing executive; b. Phila., May 19, 1940; d. Sidney and Sonya (Auerbach) Friedenberg; m. Garry G. Ruch, Aug. 25, 1963; children: Stacy, Eric. AB, Albright Coll., 1962; EdM, Temple U., 1963; cert., Maxwell Inst., Norristown, Pa., 1981. Sch. counselor Nazareth (Pa.) Area Sch. Dist., 1963-67; homebound instr. Centennial Sch. Dist., Warminster, Pa., 1976-81; programmer trainee Henkels & McCoy, Inc., Blue Bell, Pa., 1981-82, programmer, 1982-84, programmer analyst, 1984, system adminstr., 1985-86, mgr. MIS support, 1986-89, data processing mgr., 1989—. Supr. big sisters Big Sisters of Bucks County, Doylestown, Pa., 1975-76, v.p. bd. dirs., 1976-77. Named Outstanding Vol., Big Sisters of Bucks County, 1977. Mem. Delaware Basin Unisys User Group (pres. 1987-89), Nat. Unisys User Group (sub-group officer 1985-90, publs. coordinator 1989-90), Neshaminy-Warwick Presbyn. Ch. Women's Assn. (pres. 1978-80). Home: 238 Beatrice Ave Hatboro PA 19040 Office: Henkels & McCoy Inc 985 Jolly Rd Blue Bell PA 19422

RUCHIN, CECILE ANN, communications executive; b. Bay Shore, N.Y., Sept. 30, 1936; d. Zan and Genvieve (Veshura) R.; m. John Quinn, Aug. 1957 (div.); children: Michael, Laurette, Craig. Student, Seton Hall Acad., 1954, New Sch. Social Research, N.Y.C., 1960, NYU, 1963. Prodn. asst. ABC-TV, Hollywood, Calif., 1959-60; account exec. Dirusso and Falborn Advt., N.Y.C., 1962-64; asst. producer Sta. BBDO-TV, N.Y.C., 1964-66; pres. Complete Newspaper Group, Inc., N.Y.C., 1966-69, Holographic Design/Devel. Corp., N.Y.C., 1969-70, Internat. Holographics Corp., N.Y.C., 1970-71, Holographic Communications Corp., N.Y.C., 1971—; mktg. cons. Conductron, Ann Arbor, Mich., 1969-70, cons. Metro-Goldwyn-Mayer, Hollywood, 1972, Simon and Schuster, N.Y.C., 1980; holography mktg. rep. McDonnell Douglas Electronics, St. Charles, Mo., 1970-73; hologram producer for Salvador Dali, N.Y.C. and Spain, 1971-72; founder N.Y. Sch. for Holography, Ctr. for Holography, Santa Monica, Calif. Author: Holographic Special Effects for Theatre, 1988, (video book) Holography and Lasers for Human Energy Studies, 1986; inventor electromagnetic camera Verograph, 1980; developed 1st multiplexed moving hologram. Pres. The Irving Tenants Assn., N.Y.C., 1978-81. Mem. Am. Mgmt. Assn., Women in Film, Laser Inst. Am., Internat. Soc. for Optical Engring., U.S. Psychotronics Assn. (founder N.Y. chpt., sec., treas.), Union of Concerned Scientists, Film and Video Arts. Republican. Roman Catholic. Office: Holographic Communications Corp 250 W 77th St New York NY 10024

RUCKERT, ANN JOHNS, musician, singer; b. N.Y.C., Mar. 12, 1945; d. G. Wallace and Elizabeth (Johns) R. Student, Julliard Sch., 1961-69, NYU, 1969-70, Royal Acad. Music, London, 1972; studies in composition with Nadia Boulanger, Paris, 1972-73; studies with Helen Hobbs Jordon, N.Y.C., 1973-75; studies with David Sdrin Collyer, 1975-78. Profl. musician over 3, 000 commercially released records, 1960—; owner, pres. Ann Ruckert Music, N.Y.C. and Los Angeles, 1980—; chairperson N.Y. Jazz Mus., N.Y.C. 1977-79; bd. dirs. Jazzmobile, N.Y.C., 1983-89; TV com. Grammy awards, 1985-87; creative staff Lifetime Achievement awards show, 1987; adv. Universal Jazz Coalition, N.Y.C., 1979-87; cons. rec. industry. musician, singer (recs.) Strawbs, Greatest Hits (Gold Record award, 1975). Commr. Deed, N.Y., 1986—, Schomberg Collection N.Y.C. Pub. Library; mem. county com. Westside Manhattan, 1980-89. Mem. Nat. Acad. Rec. Arts and Scis. (named Most Valuable Player 1982, 89, trustee, gov., v.p. N.Y. chpt., bd. trustees 1989—, bd. dirs. World Hunger Yr.), Soc. Singers (bd. dirs. N.Y.C. chpt.). Democrat. Episcopalian. Home and Office: 119 W 71st St New York NY 10023

RUCKI, ROBIN LYNN, marketing and operations executive; b. East Orange, N.J., Sept. 19, 1961; d. George William and Enid Joyce (Dupont) R. Student, County Coll. of Morris. Agt. IBM Corp., Compaq; reseller Novell; instr. word processing Parsippany (N.J.) Hills Adult Sch.; supr. Crum & Forster, Inc., 1979-83; sr. analyst U.S. Ins. Group, 1983-86; tech. support mgr. Gambal & Assocs., 1986-87; account exec. Microage Computer Stores, 1987-88; v.p. corp. mktg. and ops. 800 Spirits, Hackensack, N.J., 1988—. Office: 800 Spirits 2 University Pla Ste 308 Hackensack NJ 07601

RUDACILLE, SHARON VICTORIA, medical technologist; b. Ranson, W. Va., Sept. 11, 1950; d. Albert William and Roberta Mae (Anderson) R.; B.S. cum laude, Shepherd Coll., 1972. Med. technologist VA Center, Martinsburg, W. Va., 1972—, instr. Sch. Med. Tech., 1972-76, asso. coordinator edn., 1976-77, edn. coordinator, 1977-78, quality assurance officer clin. chemistry, 1978-80, lab. service quality assurance and edn. officer, 1980-84, clin. chemistry sect. leader, 1984—; adj. faculty mem. Shippensburg (Pa.) State Coll., 1977-78. Mem. Am. Soc. Med. Tech., Am. Soc. Clin. Pathologists, W.Va. Soc. Med. Technologists, Shepherd Coll. Alumni Assn., Sigma Pi Epsilon. Baptist. Home: PO Box 14 Ranson WV 25438

RUDAITIS, LORETTA GLORIA, microbiologist; b. Chgo., Dec. 15, 1956; d. John and Lydia Martha (Marasas) Rudaitis. BS in Biol. Scis., U. Ill., Chgo., 1980. Chem. technician Helen Curtis Industries, Inc., Chgo., 1980-81, microbiologist, 1981-86, sr. microbiologist, 1986—. Mem. Soc. Indsl. Microbiology, Am. Soc. Microbiology, Internat. Assn. Milk, Food & Environ. Sanitarians, U.S. Fedn. Culture Collections. Office: Helene Curtis Industries Inc 4401 W North Ave Chicago IL 60639

RUDD, CAROLYN ELAINE, sports management firm executive, consultant; b. Norfolk, Va., Aug. 12, 1949; d. Alvin R. and Margaret E. (McMannenn) R.; m. D.K. Ulrich, Oct. 10, 1978 (div. May 1981); children: Geoffrey Len, Bryan Ray. Student, Queens Coll. Pres. Rudd Racing, Chesapeake, Va., 1975-80; advt. dir. promotions Charlotte Motor Speedway, Harrisburg, N.C., 1980-84; cons. Jefferson Broadcasting, Charlotte, N.C., 1984-85; pres., co-owner Sports Mgmt. Group, Charlotte, 1985—. Fundraiser Multiple Sclerosis, Charlotte, 1984-85. Mem. Nat. Motorsports Press Assn., Nat. Assn. Sportscars, Am. Racing Writers Assn. Home: 21400 Rio Oro Dr Davidson NC 28036 Office: Sports Mgmt Group Inc PO Box 1857 Davidson NC 28036

RUDD, HYNDA L., city official; b. Salt Lake City, May 20, 1936; d. Morris and Irene (Feldman) Aronovich; m. Eugene B. Chernick, Nov. 26, 1954 (div. Aug. 1955); 1 child, Jeffrey Allen; m. Hyman Z. Rudd, Mar. 7, 1956 (div.); 1 child, Melinda Renee Rudd Feldman. BS, U. Utah, 1974, MS, 1978; MLS, U. So. Calif., L.A., 1981. Co-owner Salt Lake Sanitation Co., Salt Lake City, 1961-73; librarian Marriott Library, U. Utah, Salt Lake City, 1970-74; records mgmt. specialist U. Utah, Salt Lake City, 1974-78; archivist City of L.A., 1980-85, records mgmt. officer, 1985—; established Jewish archives U. Utah, 1976; speaker records program City of L.A., So. Calif., 1980—; cons. Info. Mgmt., Glendale, Calif., 1986—. Author: Mountain West Pioneer Jewry: An Historical and Genealogical Source Book, 1980. Pres. Homeowner's Assn., Glendale, 1983—; campaigner polit. offices, L.A. and Glendale, 1985—. Mem. L.A. City Hist. Soc. (bd. dirs. 1984—, pres. 1986-87), So. Calif. Hist. Soc. (bd. dirs. 1981—, v.p. 1985-87), Assn. Records Mgmt. and Adminstrs. (edn. chair 1988—), Soc. Am. Archivists, Soc. Calif. Archivists, Great Books and Reading Discussion Group. Home: 107 W Mountain Unit G Glendale CA 91202 Office: City of LA 555 Ramirez St Space 320 Los Angeles CA 90012

RUDDEN, EILEEN MARIE, software company executive; b. South Bend, Ind., Sept. 1, 1950; d. Francis Joseph and Georgette (Heinecke) R.; m. Joshua Charles Posner, May 29, 1976; children: Samuel, Joseph, Charles. BA, Brown U., 1972; MBA, Harvard U., 1976. Cons. Boston Consulting Group, 1976-79, mgr., 1979-83; dir. corp. planning Wang Labs., Lowell, Mass., 1983-85; dir. installed base mktg. Wang Labs., Lowell, 1985-86; gen. mgr. Lotus Devel. Corp., Cambridge, Mass., 1986-87; dir. strategic mktg. Lotus Devel. Corp., Cambridge, 1987-88, gen. mgr., 1989—. Democrat. Roman Catholic. Home: 32 Arlington St Cambridge MA 02140 Office: Lotus Devel Corp 55 Cambridge Pkwy Cambridge MA 02142

RUDEN, VIOLET HOWARD (MRS. CHARLES VAN KIRK RUDEN), religious educator, practitioner; b. Dallas; d. Millard Fillmore and Henrietta Frederika (Kurth) Howard; B.J., U. Tex., 1931; C.S.B., Mass. Metaphys. Coll., 1946; m. Charles Van Kirk Ruden, Nov. 24, 1932. Radio continuity writer Home Mgmt. Club broadcast Sta. WHO, Des Moines, 1934; joined First Ch. of Christ Scientist, Boston, 1929; C.S. practitioner, Des Moines, 1934—; C.S. minister WAC, Ft. Des Moines, 1942-45; 1st reader 2d Ch. of Christ Scientist, Des Moines, 1952, Sunday sch. tchr., 1934—; instr. primary class in Christian Sci., 1947—. Trustee Asher Student Found. Drake U., Des Moines, 1973. Mem. Women in Communications, Mortar Bd., Orchesis, Cap and Gown, Theta Sigma Phi (pres. 1931). Republican. Club: Des Moines Women's. Home: 5808 Walnut Hill Dr Des Moines IA 50312

RUDER, AVIMA MERISE, epidemiologist; b. Chgo., Sept. 29, 1941; d. Samuel Abraham and Miriam (Hochman) R. BA in English Lit., NYU, 1966; PhD in Biology, U. Oreg., 1982. Freelance editor, writer and indexer N.Y.C., 1970-77; biostatistician dept. epidemiology Chaim Sheba Med. Ctr., Tel Hashomer, Israel, 1983-85; vis. scientist dept. plant genetics Weizmann Inst., Rechovot, Israel, 1983-85; postdoctoral fellow dept. epidemiology Manitoba Cancer Found., Winnipeg, Can., 1985-86; biostatistician Westchester County Health Dept., White Plains, N.Y., 1986-89; epidemiologist NIOSH, Cin., 1989—. Author: monograph Wheat in the Tropics, 1985, (with others) Complete Guide to Editorial Freelancing, 1974; contbr. articles to profl. jours. Nat. Rsch. Svc. fellow, 1978-82. Mem. Am. Soc. for Human Genetics, Soc. for Epidemiologic Rsch., Am. Women in Sci., Am. Pub. Health Assn. Office: NIOSH Mail Stop R-6 4676 Columbia Pkwy Cincinnati OH 45226

RUDIE, EVELYN, actress, playwright; b. Los Angeles, Mar. 28; d. Emery and Edith Bernauer; m. Christie Oscar DeCarlo Jr. Student, UCLA, 1966-73. Child actress performed in over 60 films and TV shows, 20th Century Fox, Los Angeles, 1957, TV, 1956-63; artistic dir. Am. Youth Cultural Ambassadors, Santa Monica, Calif., 1989—, Actors Repertory Theater, Santa Monica, 1974—, Santa Monica Playhouse, 1973—; dir. Mobile Touring Project, 1977—; artist-in-residence Young Profl.'s Co., Santa Monica, 1979—. Author: (mus.) Author, Author, 1976, The Clown Prince, (Drama-Logue award 1979) Family Theater Matinee Series, 1977—. Recipient Key to City The U.S. Treasury, Washington, 1958, Patsy award, 1958, Emmy nomination Nat. Acad. TV Arts and Scis., 1957, star in Hollywood Blvd.'s walk of fame. Mem. Actors Equity Assn., Am. Fedn. TV and Radio Artists, Dramatists Guild, ASCAP. Office: Actors Repertory Theater at Santa Monica Playhouse 1211 Fourth St Santa Monica CA 90401

RUDIN, ANNE NOTO, mayor; b. Passaic, N.J., Jan. 27, 1924; m. Edward Rudin, June 6, 1948; 4 children. BS in Edn., Temple U., 1945, RN, 1946; MPA, U. So. Calif., 1983. R.N., Calif. Mem. faculty Temple U. Sch. Nursing, Phila., 1946-48; mem. nursing faculty Mt. Zion Hosp., San Francisco, 1948-49; mem. Sacramento City Council, 1971-83; mayor City of Sacramento, 1983—; mem. World Conf. of Mayors for Peace. Pres. LWV, Riverside, Sacramento, 1957, 61, Calif. Elected Women's Assn., 1973-89; bd. dirs. Sacramento Commerce and Trade Orgn., 1984-89; mem. U.S. Conf. of Mayors. Recipient Women in Govt. award U.S. Jaycee Women, 1984; Woman of Distinction award Sacramento Area Soroptimist Clubs, 1985, Civic Contbn. award LWV Sacramento, 1989; Woman of Courage award Sacramento History Ctr., 1989; named Girl Scouts Am. Role Model, 1989. Office: City of Sacramento Office of Mayor 915 I St Rm 205 Sacramento CA 95814

RUDKO, FRANCES HOWELL, lawyer; b. Elgin, Okla., Nov. 25, 1935; d. Paul Basil and Bertie Eleanor (Maggart) Howell; children: Michael, Stephen Craig, Peter Gregory. BA, So. Meth. U., 1959; JD, U. Ark., 1973, MA in History, 1983. Bar: Ark. 1973, U.S. Dist. Ct. (we. dist.) Ark. 1973. Tchr. English, Grand Prairie Schs. (Tex.), 1959-60; pvt. practice law, Fayetteville, 1973—; judge Prairie Grove Mcpl. Ct. (Ark.), 1976. Author: Truman's Court: A Study in Judicial Restraint, 1988. Bd. dirs. Arts Ctr. Ozarks, Springdale, 1976-77, North Ark. Symphony Soc., 1981—, Butterfield Trail Retirement Ctr., 1981—. Mem. ABA, AAUW, Washington County Bar Assn. (sec. treas. 1977), Ark. Bar Assn (chmn. family law sect. 1975-76), Fayetteville C. of C., Am. Assn. Women Lawyers, Phi Beta Kappa, Altrusa Club (treas. 1979-81), Washington County Med. Aux. Club (pres. 1980-81), Methodist. Home: 1410 Oakcliff St Fayetteville AR 72701 Office: 3000 Market St Ste B Fayetteville AR 72701

RUDKOFF, DOUGLASS MCFERRIN, English educator; b. Mt. Pleasant, Tenn., Dec. 28, 1925; d. James Abston and Annie Hall (Acuff) McFerrin; m. George Channing Rudkell III, Sept. 27, 1947; children: Virginia Ann, Julia, G. Channing IV, Elizabeth McFerrin; m. William Rudkoff, June 11, 1979. Student, Huntingdon Coll., Montgomery, Ala., 1943-45; BA, U. Tenn., Knoxville, 1947; MA, George Peabody Coll., 1964; postgrad., Middle Tenn. State U., Emory U. Cert. tchr., Mo. Tchr. Maury County Schs., Columbia, Tenn., 1960-62; tchr. English Franklin County Schs., Sullivan, Mo., 1962-65; instr. to prof., chmn. humanities div. Reinhardt Coll., Waleska, Ga., 1965-78; instr. Tri-County Community Coll., Murphy, N.C., 1978-81, chmn. dept. English, 1985—; dir. tchr. cert. class, N.C., 1980; dir. writing workshop for engrs., Emerson Electric Co., Murphy, 1989. Contbr. numerous articles to various publs. vice chmn. Dem. precinct, Murphy, 1990. Grantee NEH, 1974, 78. Mem. AAUW (program v.p. Cherokee br. 1988-90, chair pub. forums with county commrs., 1990), DAR (regent Murphy br. 1986-88), Southwestern N.C. Geneal. Soc., N.C. Geneal. Soc. Methodist. Home: Fern Hollow Rte 5 Box 100A Murphy NC 28906 Office: Dept English Tri County Community Coll Murphy NC 28906

RUDNICK, ELLEN AVA, health care company executive; b. New Haven; d. Harold and C. Vivian (Soybel) R.; children from previous marriage: Sarah, Noah. BA, Vassar Coll., 1972; MBA, U. Chgo., 1973. Sr. fin. analyst Quaker Oats, Chgo., 1973-75; various positions Baxter Internat., Deerfield, Ill., 1975-80, dir. planning, 1980-83, corp. v.p., 1985-1990; pres. Baxter Mgmt. Services, Deerfield, 1983-1990; pres., chief exec. officer Healthcare Knowledge Systems, Northbrook, Ill., 1990—. Chief crusader Met. Chgo. United Way, 1982-85; pres. council Nat. Coll. Edn., Evanston, Ill., 1983—; circle of friends Chgo. YWCA, 1985—. Mem. Chgo. Network. Club: Econs. Chgo. (officer, bd. dirs.). Office: Healthcare Knowledge System 255 Revere Dr Ste 101 Ste 101 Northbrook IL 60062

RUDNICK, IRENE KRUGMAN, lawyer, state legislator, educator; b. Columbia, S.C., Dec. 27, 1929; d. Jack and Jean (Getter) Krugman; A.B. cum laude, U. S.C., 1949, JD, 1952; m. Harold Rudnick, Nov. 7, 1954; children—Morris, Helen Gail. Admitted to S.C. bar, 1952; individual practice law, Aiken, S.C., 1952—, now ptnr. Rudnick & Rudnick; instr. bus. law, criminal law U. S.C., Aiken, 1962—; tchr. Warrenville Elem. Sch., 1965-70; supt. edn. Aiken County, 1970-72; mem. S.C. Ho. of Reps., 1972-78, 80-84, 86—; Active, Aiken County Democratic Party, S.C. Dem. Party. Recipient Citizen of Yr. award, 1976-77, Bus. and Profl. Women's Career Woman of Yr., 1978, Aiken County Friend of Edn. award. Mem. NEA, S.C. Tchrs. Assn., Aiken County Tchrs. Assn., Am. Bar Assn., Aiken County Bar Assn., Nat. Order Women Legislators, AAUW, Alpha Delta Kappa. Jewish. Clubs: Order Eastern Star, Hadassah, Am. Legion Aux., Lioness. Office: PO Box 544 224 Park Ave Aiken SC 29802

RUDNIK, SISTER MARY CHRYSANTHA, retired librarian; b. Winona, Minn., Dec. 2, 1929; d. Basil John and Sarah (Knopick) R. Student Loyola U., 1951-52, Felician Coll., 1952-54, Cardinal Stritch Coll., 1954-57, Coll. St. Francis, 1957; PhB, DePaul U., 1958; postgrad. Mundelein Coll., 1959-60, Northeastern Ill. State U., 1964; MA, Rosary Coll., 1962. Joined Congregation of Sisters of St. Felix of Cantalice, Roman Cath. Ch., 1948; cert. fund raising exec. Nat. Soc. Fund Raising Execs. Page, clk. Hill Reference Libr., St. Paul, 1946-48; tchr. Holy Innocents Sch., Chgo., 1948-49, 50-54, St. Bruno Sch., Chgo., 1954-55, Holy Family Sch., Cudahy, Wis., 1955-57, Good Counsel High Sch., Chgo., 1958-67; instr. Felician Coll., Chgo., 1963-86, head libr., 1957-82, dir. devel. and pub. rels., 1975-86. Organizer, coord. Felician Libr. Svc., 1966-74, Arts and Crafts Festival, 1972-86; coord. instl. self-study for accreditation North Cen. Assn.; mem. task force for study of instl. rsch. for Ill. Assn. Community and Jr. Colls., 1968; v.p., Coun. on Lubr. Tech., 1970, pres. 1971; libr. cons. St. Clement Sch., 1969. Rev. Cert. fund raising exec. Nat. Soc. Fund Raising Execs. Mem. Cath. Libr. Assn. (life, chmn. No. Ill. unit 1968-69, exec. bd. 1981-87, Andrew Bowhuis Meml. scholar 1960), Art Inst. Chgo. (life). Address: 3800 Peterson Ave Chicago IL 60659

RUDOLPH, DEBORAH ANN, manufacturing planner/buyer, author; b. San Antonio, Dec. 18, 1958; d. James Richard and Lola Mae (Muenchow) R. BS, Tex. A&M U., 1981. Operating rm. technician Sch. Vet. Medicine Tex. A&M U., College Station, 1978-81; cardio-pulmonary technician St. Joseph Hosp., Bryan, Tex., 1981-84; with Argon Med., Athens, Tex., 1985—, vendor devel. analyst, 1986, master scheduling supr., 1987-88, inventory control supr., 1988-89; buyer/planner Alcon Labs., Inc., Ft. Worth, 1990—. Mem. Nat. Audubon Soc., Nat. Wildlife Found. Mem. Am. Prodn. and Inventory Control Soc., Nat. Geographic Soc., NAFE. Office: Alcon Labs Inc 6201 S Freeway Fort Worth TX 76134

RUDOLPH, ELAINE TAYLOR, executive search and financial placement executive; b. Milw., Nov. 25, 1926; d. Harry Arthur and Florence Ann (Randall) Taylor; m. Gordon Edmund Rudolph, Aug. 9, 1947; 1 child, Nancy Jean Rudolph Wood. BA, U. Wis., 1950; postgrad. U. So. Calif., 1961. Registered employment cons. Personnel dir. Knee Action div. A.O. Smith, Milw., polit. candidate cons., greater Los Angeles area, 1964-72; gen. mgr., v.p., Bookkeepers Unltd., Los Angeles, 1972-79; pres. Accts. Plus and Bookkeepers Plus Agy., Los Angeles, 1979—; profl. devel. dir., pres. Los Angeles chpt. Nat. Assn. Accts., 1986-87; vice chmn. exhibitor rels. So. Calif. Bus. Show; congl. del. The White House Small Bus. Conf., 1986. Chmn. Crime Prevention Bd., Sierra Madra, Calif., 1982—; mayor, mem. city council, Sierra Madre, 1978-82; mem. pub. safety state com. League of Calif. Cities, 1978-82, Los Angeles County Sanitation Bd., 1981-82, del. So. Calif. Div. League of Calif. Cities, 1980-82; alt. del. San Gabriel Cities Assn., 1979-81; del. Ind. Cities, 1978-79; parks and recreation commr. Sierra Madre, 1977-78; del., alt., del. Rep. State Cen. Com., 1956—, mem. 61st Rep. County Cen. Com., 1974-83, alt. mem. 42d Rep. County Cen. Com., 1983—; chmn. job and econ. devel. com. State Rep. Party, 1988-90; mem. adv. coms. for Assemblyman Richard Mountjoy, Congressman John Rousselot, Senator Bill Richardson; town chmn. Sierra Madre Republicans; chmn. bd. dirs. Sierra Madre Hosp. Recipient SBA Dist. and Regional Acct. Adv. award, 1987. Mem. Nat. Assn. Accts. (past pres., various coms.), Century City C. of C. (speakers bur., membership com.), Western Los Angeles Regional C. of C. (fin. coun.), Town Hall, Nat. Assn. Female Execs. (network dir.), AAUW (pres. Arcadia br. 1971). Presbyterian. Author: So You Are Looking for a Job?, 1980, So You've Been Promoted?, 1981. Home: 1935 Liliano Dr Sierra Madre CA 91024 Office: Bookkeepers Accountants Plus 10061 Telbert Ave #200 Fountian Valley CA 92798 also: 10061 Talbert Ave Fountain Valley CA 92708

RUDOLPH, SONDRA, zoological society executive; b. Phila., Jan. 2, 1934; d. Irving S. and Nettie (Gruman) Bernstein; m. Howard Victor Rudolph, Oct. 3, 1954; children—Steven Paul, Andrew Lawrence. B.S., Temple U., 1955. Vice pres. mktg. U.S. Postal Service Fed. Credit Union, Washington, 1978-83; personnel dir. CMG Telemarketing (formerly Campaign Mktg. Group), Alexandria, Va., 1983-84; dir. dept. human resources Friends of Nat. Zoo, Nat. Zool. Park, Washington, 1985-88; mem. Credit Union Promotional Com. Greater D.C., 1981-82. Recipient Golden Mirror award Credit Union Exec. Soc. for newsletter, 1981, for handbook, 1981, for membership brochure, 1982, for splty. advt., 1982. Mem. Am. Mktg. Assn., Am. Soc. for Personnel Adminstrn. Republican. Jewish. Home: PO Box 1107 Bodega Bay CA 94923 Office: 1805 Seaway Bodega Bay CA 94923

RUDY, ANN LIZETTE, human resources professional; b. Marion, Ind., Dec. 1, 1957; d. Edmund Albert and Margaret Ann (Knight) Schulz; m. John Thomas Rudy, May 7, 1983. BSBA, Valparaiso U., 1980. Underwriting supr. Prudential Ins. Co., Merrillville, Ind., 1980-83; sr. staff specialist, underwriting cons. AllState Ins. Co., Deerfield, Ill., 1984-89; recruiting coord. Luth. Brotherhood, Naperville, Ill., 1990—. Fellow Life Mgmt. Inst. Lutheran. Home: 20 Indian Dr Clarendon Hills IL 60514 Office: Luth Brotherhood Naperville IL

RUDY, RUTH CORMAN, state legislator; b. Millheim, Pa., Jan. 3, 1938; d. Orvis E. and Mabel Jan (Stover) Corman; m. C. Guy Rudy, Nov. 21, 1956; children: Douglas G., Donita Rudy Koval, Dianna F. Degree in x-ray tech. Carnegie Inst., 1956; student Pa. State U., 1968-71. Clk. of cts. County of Centre (Pa.), Bellefonte, 1976-82; rep. Pa. Gen. Assembly, Harrisburg, 1982—. Mem. Dem. Nat. Com., 1980—, chair women's caucus, 1989—; past pres. Pa. Fedn. Dem. Women, Harrisburg; pres. Nat. Fedn. Dem. Women, 1987-89. Named Woman of Yr., Pa. Fedn. Dem. Women, 1982. Methodist. Office: Pa Ho Reps PO Box 115 Harrisburg PA 17120

RUEBE, BAMBI LYNN, interior/environmental designer; b. Huntington Park, Calif., Nov. 13, 1957; d. Leonard John Ruebe and Vaudis Marie Powell. BS, UCLA, 1988. Millwright asst. Kaiser Steel Corp., Fontana, Calif., 1976-79; electrician Fleetwood Enterprises, Riverside, Calif., 1977; fashion model internat., 1977-85; free-lance draftsman, 1982-83; project coord. Philip J. Sicola Inc., Culver City, Calif., 1982-83; prin. designer Ruebe Inclusive Design, Highland, Calif., 1983-89, Ventura, Calif., 1990—; cons. mfg. design Burlington Homes New Eng. Inc., Oxford, Maine, 1987—, DeRose Industries, Chambersburg, Pa., 1984, Skyline Corp., Redlands, Calif., 1982-84; cons. lighting Lightways Corp., L.A., 1984-87; mem. design rev. bd. San Bernadino (Calif.) Downtown Main St. Redevel. Com., 1987-89. Mem. World Affairs Coun., Inland So. Calif., 1986—; mem. citizens adv. com. Highland Calif. Gen. Plan, 1988—; co-chmn. civil rights com. AFL-CIO, Fontana, 1978-79. Recipient Cert. Merit Scholastic Art award Scholastic Mags. Inc., Southeastern Calif., 1974. Mem. Nat. Trust for Hist. Preservation. Democrat. Office: Ruebe Inclusive Design 50 N Oak St San Buena Ventura CA 93001

RUEHL, JEANETTE LOUISE, travel agency executive; b. Bronx, N.Y., Apr. 12, 1957; d. Theodore Charles and Dorothy (Errico) R. AAS in Fine and Graphic Arts, Rockland Community Coll., Suffern, N.Y., 1978; BA in Fine and Graphic Arts, Ramapo Coll., Mahwah, N.J., 1984. Asst. mgr.

McDonald's Corp., Bloomfield, N.J., 1974-87; reception and info. clk. Welcome Aboard Travel Specialists, Ramsey, N.J., 1987-90, acctg. asst., 1990—. Mem. Rockland Ctr. for Arts, Wesy Nyack, N.Y., 1990, The N.Y. Art Review, 1990; foster parent Foster Parents Plan, 1987—; head com. to choose design and approve posters Antrim Playhouse, 1985-87; active St. Labre Indian Sch., Ashland, Mont., 1985—. Mem. Rockland Ctr. for Arts, West Nyack, N.Y., 1990; foster parent Foster Parents Plan, 1987—; head com. to choose design and approve posters Antrim Playhouse, 1985-87; active St. Labre Indian Sch., Ashland, Mont., 1985—; head com. to choose, design and approve Antrim Playhouse, 1985-87. Mem. Nat. Wildlife Fedn., Nature Conservancy, Ramapo Coll. Alumni Assn. Office: Welcome Aboard Travel Specialists 29 Church St Ramsey NJ 07446-0368

RUEST, SUE ELLEN, computer specialist; b. Huntington, W.Va., Sept. 19, 1944; d. Ray Shirlon and Edith Abigail (Blood) Colburn; m. Richard G. Ruest, Oct. 3, 1970; children: Christopher Andrew, Peter Michael, Jeffrey Scott. BA, Centre Coll. Ky., 1966. Data analyst market research dept. Procter & Gamble Co., Cin., 1966-68; analyst, programmer Computer & Sci., Inc., Glenn Dale, Md., 1968-69; sr. programmer Apollo project UNIVAC, Glenn Dale, Md., 1969-72; programmer customer service Control Data Corp., Rockville, Md., 1980-81; systems mgr. 3-M Corp., Middleway, W.Va., 1981-83; sr. programmer, analyst Mack Trucks, Inc., Hagerstown, Md., 1983-88; sr. systems analyst Corning Glass Works, Martinsburg, W.Va., 1988—; tchr. adult edn. St. Maria Goretti High Sch., Hagerstown, 1983-85; instr. Hagerstown Jr. Coll., 1986-88. Bd. dirs., chmn. water safety, instr. swimming ARC, Martinsburg, W.Va., 1976-79. Democrat. Presbyterian. Home: 304 Greenbriar Rd Martinsburg WV 25401 Office: Corning Glass Works Rte 11 S Martinsburg WV 25401

RUETHER, ROSEMARY RADFORD, theologian; b. St. Paul, Nov. 2, 1936; d. Robert Armstrong and Rebecca Cresap (Ord) Radford; m. Herman J. Ruether, Aug. 31, 1957; children: Rebecca, David, Mimi. A.B., Scripps Coll., 1958; M.A., Claremont Grad. Sch., 1960, Ph.D., 1965. Assoc. prof. Howard U., Washington, 1966-76; Georgia Harkness prof. Garrett Sem., Evanston, Ill., 1976—; lectr. Princeton Theol. Sem., 1971, 73; prof. Roman Cath. studies Harvard U., Cambridge, Mass., 1972-73; lectr. Yale Div. Sch., 1973-74. Author: The Church Against Itself, 1967, Communion is Life Together, 1968, Gregory Nazianzus, Rhetor and Philosopher, 1969, The Radical Kingdom, 1970, Liberation Theology, 1972, Religion and Sexism: Images of Women in the Judeo-Christian Tradition, 1974, Faith and Fratricide, 1974, New Woman/New Earth, 1975, Mary, The Feminine Face of the Church, 1977, The Liberating Bond, 1978, Women of Spirit, 1979, (with Rosemary Keller) Women and Religion in America, 1981, To Change the World: Christology and Cultural Criticism, 1981, Disputed Questions: On Being a Christian, 1982, Sexism and God-talk, 1983, Women and Religion in America: The Colonial Period, 1983, Womanguides: Texts for Feminist Theology, 1985, Women and Religion in America, 1900-1968, 1986, Women-Church: Theology and Practice of Feminist Liturgical Communities, 1986, Contemporary Catholicism, 1987, The Wrath of Jonah: The Crisis of Religious Nationalism in the Israel-Palestinian Conflict, 1989; contbg. editor: The Ecumenist; contbr. articles to profl. jours. Kent fellow, 1962-65; Danforth fellow, 1960-61. Mem. Soc. Religion in Higher Edn., Am. Theol. Assn., Soc. Arts, Religion and Culture. Home: 1426 Hinman Ave Evanston IL 60201*

RUETSCHLIN, TRACEY MARIE, clothing executive; b. Phila., Jan. 21, 1961; d. James Henry and Kathryn Mary (Shaw) R. BA, Mount St. Mary's Coll., Emmittsburg, Md., 1982. Asst. designer Nite & Day Lingerie, N.Y.C., 1982-83; sales mgr. LRM Enterprises, West Paterson, N.J., 1983-84; sales supr. Tri-State Radio Corp., Ft. Lee, N.J., 1984-88; v.p. Night Star Lingerie Inc., N.Y.C., 1988—. Author numerous poems. Sponsor Christian Children's Internat., 1987—. Mem. Doris Day Animal League, Greenpeace, Nat. Wildlife Fedn. Republican. Roman Catholic. Office: Night Star, Inc. 4 Park Ave Ste 8H New York NY 10016

RUFENER, JAYNE MICHELLE, marketing specialist, model; b. Monroe, Wis., Jan. 18, 1964; d. Emil (Mike) and JoAnne (Jeremiason) R. Cert., Internat. Mktg. Symposium, West Germany, 1985; BS with highest honors, U. Wis., La Crosse, 1986; postgrad., U. Wis., Madison, 1988—. Lic. real estate broker. Corp. rels. mgr. Anchor Real Estate Svcs., Madison, Wis., 1986-87; customer svc. rep. Thomas Garraway Foods, Madison, 1987; mktg. specialist Wis. Dept. Agr., Trade and Consumer Protection, Madison, 1988—; comml. model, food stylist, grad. asst. Dale Carnegie Human Rels. Course, 1987. Mem. Wis. Bus. and Profl. Women (State Career Woman com., Wis. Outstanding Young Career Woman in Bus. 1987), Madison Bus. and Profl. Women (Outstanding Young Career Woman 1987). Roman Catholic. Office: Wis Dept Agr Trade and Consumer Protection 801 W Badger Rd PO Box 8911 Madison WI 53708

RUFF, KATHERYN LORENE, business owner; b. Ft. Monmonth, N.J., Oct. 4, 1954; d. Robert T. and Mary Ann (Halpin) R.; m. Stephen B. Lewis, May 10, 1980. BS, Ind. U., 1976. With Federated Dept. Stores, Indpls. and Columbus, Ohio, 1976-78; account exec. Burroughs Corp., Chgo. and Indpls., 1978-81, STC, Chgo., 1981-84; owner Tablescapes Ltd., Chgo., 1987—. Bd. dirs. Theatre Bldg., Chgo., 1983—, Aux. Bd. North Ave. Day Nursery, Chgo., 1983—. Mem. Internat. Spl. Event Soc., Jr. League of Chgo. Office: Tablescapes Ltd 345 N Canal #1005 Chicago IL 60610

RUFFALO, MARIA THERESE, mechanical engineer; b. Seattle, Feb. 26, 1963; d. Patrick and Helen (Eckhardt) R.; m. Joseph Patrick Otterbine, May 5, 1987. BS in Mech. Engring., U. Rochester, 1985. Proj. engr. Polycast Tech. Corp., Hackensack, N.J., 1985-86, sr. project engr., 1986-87; cons. Polycast Tech. Corp., Hackensack, 1987; project engr. ink div. J.M. Huber Corp., Edison, N.J., 1987-89; maintenance and project engr. Himont USA, Inc., East Brunswick, N.J., 1990—. Mem. ASME, Nat. Assn. Female Execs. Democrat. Roman Catholic. Home: 342 Woodbine Dr Aberdeen NJ 07735

RUFFIN, MARGARET ELAINE, education educator; b. Ocala, Fla., Jan. 26, 1936; d. Robert Edward Flagg and Mildred Elizabeth (Harris) Golson; m. George Ruffin, Sept. 6, 1959 (div. 1964); 1 child, Bonita Levette. BS, Bethune Cookman Coll., Daytona Bch., Fla., 1956; MA, The U. W. Fla., 1971. Elem. tchr. Escambia County Sch. Dist., Pensacola, Fla., 1956-68, tchr., 1968-76, adult educator, 1988—; adjunct instr. Pensacola (Fla.) Jr. Coll.; learning mgr. George Stone Vocat., Pensacola, Fla., 1976-85, individualized manpower tng. system coord., 1985-88; program coord. Literacy Vols. Am. Escambia, Pensacola, Fla., 1985—; asst. adminstr. Panhandle Area Literacy, (vol. project) Pensacola 1986-88. Recruiter votger registration Democratic Group, Pensacola 1984-88. Mem. Fla. Adult Edn. Assn., Literacy Volunteers Am. FL (treas. 1988--), Fla. Vocational Assn., Escambia Edn. Assn., Delta Sigma, (treas. 1976-77), Theta Sorority. Episcopalian. Home: PO Box 18130 Pensacola FL 32523-8130 Office: Escambia County Sch Dist 30 E Texar Dr Pensacola FL 32503

RUFFMAN, JILL VALERIE, psychologist; b. Englewood, N.J., May 28, 1958; d. Jack and Norma (Marks) Shipley; m. Mitchel Ruffman, Dec. 31, 1983; 1 child, Caitlin Nicole. BA with high honors, U. Calif., Santa Barbara, 1980; MA, Calif. Sch. Profl. Psychology, San Diego, 1982, PhD, 1985. Lic. psychologist, Calif., Mass. Counseling psychologist U.S. Army, Mannheim, West Germany, 1986-87; clin. psychologist U.S. Army, Heidelberg, West Germany, 1987-88; psychologist Bexar County Jail and Probation Dept., San Antonio, 1989; dir. Family Support Ctr., chief Family Matters br. USAF, Colorado Springs, Colo., 1989—. Mem. United Svc. Orgn. Coun.-Pikes Peak region, Colorado Springs, 1989—. Mem. Am. Psychol. Assn., Calif. Psychol. Assn., Assn. for Advancement of Behavior Therapy. Office: 1003d Mission Support/MSF Peterson AFB CO 80914-5000

RUGG, JANET VERA, home healthcare administrator, consultant; b. Holden, Mass., Nov. 29, 1949; d. Edgar Earle and Elizabeth Annie (Peoples) R.; m. Lonnie R. Harrington III, Jan. 1, 1976; children: Lonnie, Emmalia. BA, Boston U., 1971; MS in Edn., Wheelock Coll., 1974; postgrad., St. John's U., Jamaica, N.Y., 1988—. Dir. Fenway Day Care Ctr., Boston, 1971-73; social worker State of Mass., Boston, 1973-77; program mgr. City of N.Y. Dept. Human Resources, N.Y.C., 1977-80; exec. dir. Home Svc. Systems, Inc., Astoria, N.Y., 1980—. Trustee, officer Home Care Industry Union Health Fund, N.Y.C., 1988—. Mem. Home Care Coun. N.Y.C. (official-at-large 1983-85, Outstanding Svc. award 1984, 85, 86), N.Y. State Home Care Assn., Nat. Assn. Home Care, Hellenic Am. Neighborhood Action Com. (cons. N.Y.C. chpt. 1985-88).

RUGG, MARJORIE ALICE, educator; b. Charleston, W. Va., Nov. 4, 1916; d. Charles and Helen Pauline (Gurski) Listing; m. Charles Richard Rugg, June 18, 1938 (dec. Sept., 1989); children: Judith Ann Benson, Jennifer Helen Cantine. BS in Journalism, Northwestern U., 1938; MA in Edn., U. Northern Iowa, 1965. Cert. tchr., Iowa. Reporter Cedar Falls Gazette, Cedar Rapids, Iowa, 1940; tchr. Cedar Falls (Iowa) High Sch., 1965-81. Pres. Gladbrook, Iowa Sch. Bd., 1951-60; pres. Iowa Social Studies Coun., 1967-71; organizer, charter pres. Friends of Cedar Falls Pub. Libr., 1982, bd. dirs., 1982-91; bd. dirs., trustee Cedar Falls Pub. Libr., 1984—. Mem. AAUW, Iowa Libr. Assn., Iowa Artists, Waterloo Art Assn. Presbyterian. Home: 1421 W Ridgewood Dr Cedar Falls IA 50613

RUGGIERI, PAMELA JOY, psychologist; b. Chgo., Mar. 25, 1944; d. Armand Rudolph and Ruth Joy (Hildebrand) R. BS, Butler U., 1965; postgrad., L'Ecole des Beaus Arts, Aix-en-Provence, France, 1969-70; MA, U. Chgo., 1975, Calif. Sch. Profl. Psychology, San Diego, 1981; PhD, Calif. Sch. Profl. Psychology, San Diego, 1984. Lic. psychologist, Ind.; cert. tchr., Ill. Caseworker Luth. Child & Family Svcs., River Forest, Ill., 1966-69; tchr. Chgo. Bd. of Edn., 1970-71, Sch. Dist. 150, South Holland, Ill., 1971-74; rsch. asst. Ctr. for Ednl. Devel., Coll. of Medicine U. Ill., Chgo., 1975-76; social worker Oak Community Ctr., Oak Park, Ill., 1976-79; psychologist CMHS, Muncie, Ind., 1984-87; supr., psychologist Southlake Ctr. for Mental Health, Merrillville, Ind., 1987—. Mem. Nat. Wildlife Fedn., 1984—, Friends of the Ind. Dunes, 1988—. Mem. APA, Ind. Psychol. Assn., NOW, ACLU. Home: 7647 Hemlock Ave Gary IN 46403 Office: Southlake Ctr Mental Health 8555 Taft Merrillville IN 46410

RUGGIERO, LINDA SUE, secretarial/word processing service owner; b. Washington, May 3, 1952; d. Donald Hartley and Beverly Jane (Searle) Hasbrouck; m. Kenneth Richard Ruggiero, Sept. 23, 1972; children: Kristine Marie, Melissa Sue, Kenneth Richard, Jr., Kimberly Anne. Assoc. Sci., Quinnipiac Coll., 1972. Sec. Benedict Cos.-Realtors, Hamden, Conn., 1971-73; sec. buyer Am. Powdered Metals Co., Cheshire, Conn., 1973-79; owner Letter Perfect Secretarial Word Processing Svc., Cheshire, 1988—; active Conn. Down Syndrome Congress, Wethersfield, 1986—; dist. advisor La Leche League Conn., 1986-88, dist. coord., 1988-89, adminstrv. asst., 1990—; cert. leader, La Leche League Internat., Franklin Park, Ill., 1983—. Newsletter editor Conn. Down Syndrome Congress, Wethersfield, 1988—. Mem. Cheshire (Conn.) Jaycee Women, 1984, Spl. Edn. PTO, Cheshire. Named Jaycee of the Month, Outstanding Woman, Cheshire Jaycee Women, 1984. Mem. Nat. Assn. Secretarial Svcs. (sec. Conn. chpt. 1989—), Assn. for Retarded Citizens Greater New Haven Conn., Cheshire C. of C., Waterbury Area Mothers of Twins Club (newsletter editor 1988-89, outreach chmn. 1986-88). Republican. Methodist. Office: Letter Perfect 393 S Rolling Acres Rd Cheshire CT 06410

RUGGIERO, MARY TINA, physician, anesthesiologist; b. Bklyn., July 23, 1958; d. Raffaele and Carmela (Debenedetto) R. BS, Wagner Coll., 1979; MD, U. Autonoma de Guadalajara, 1983. Fifth pathway St. Vincent's Hosp., Staten Island, N.Y., 1984; intern in internal medicine L.I. Coll. Hosp., Bklyn., 1985-86; resident in anesthesiology Downstate Med. Ctr., Bklyn., 1985-87, fellow in obstetrical anesthesia, 1988; attending anesthesiologist Bayley Seton Hosp., Staten Island, 1989—. Mem. Am. Soc. Anesthesiology, N.Y. State Soc. Anesthesiologists, Internat. Anesthesia Rsch. Soc., AMA. Republican. Roman Catholic. Home: 1315 73 St Brooklyn NY 11228 Office: Baley Seton Hosp 75 Vanderbilt Ave Staten Island NY 10304

RUGGLES, CONNIE PATRICIA, marketing consultant; b. Ponca City, Okla., Oct. 15, 1940; d. Lawrence Sterling and Marion (Conn) Burke; m. Robert Mitchell Ruggles, June 11, 1961; 1 child, Kelly Elizabeth. BA in Journalism, U. Okla., 1962. Pub. info. officer, editor alumni publs., then asst. to v.p. U. Okla., Norman, 1965-74; asst. to dir. Fla. Press Assn., Tallahassee, 1974-76; pub. info. exec. staff Fla. Dept. Health and Rehab. Svcs., Tallahassee, 1976-85, dir. pub. info., 1985-87; prin., mktg. and communications cons. Connie Ruggles Consulting, Tallahassee, 1987—. Mem. Fla. Pub. Rels. Assn. (bd. dirs. Capital chpt. 1988—; Golden Image award 1986). Democrat. Episcopalian. Home and Office: Connie Ruggles Consulting 2318 Hampshire Way Tallahassee FL 32308 Home: 2318 Hampshire Way Tallahassee FL 32308

RUIZ-VALERA, PHOEBE LUCILE, librarian; b. Barranquilla, Colombia, Jan. 27, 1950; d. Ramon and Marion (Mehlman) Ruiz-Valera; m. Thomas Patrick Winkler, Mar. 27, 1981. BA cum laude, Westminster Coll., 1971; MLS, Rutgers U., 1974; MA, NYU, 1978. Libr. trainee Passaic (N.J.) Pub. Libr., 1973-74, reference libr., 1974; libr. assoc., cataloger NYU Law Libr., N.Y.C., 1974-79, asst. curator, cataloger, 1979-81; libr. III, cataloger Rutgers U. Library, New Brunswick, N.J., 1981-82; chief cataloger Assn. Bar City N.Y., 1982-85, head tech. svcs., 1985—. Mem. ALA, Am. Assn. Law Librs., Am. Translators Assn. (cert. translator English to Spanish), Law Libr. Assn. Greater N.Y., Reforma, Salalm. Democrat. Presbyterian. Office: Assn Bar City NY 42 W 44th St New York NY 10036

RUMBAUGH, MARGARET GUTJAHR, association professional, writer; b. Mount Holly, N.J., Sept. 26, 1961; d. Herbert Otto and Ingrid Ellie (Herbst) Gutjahr; m. James O. Rumbaugh III. BA cum laude, Susquehanna U., 1983; postgrad., U. Pa., 1983-84; cert. in procurement, U. Va., 1988; MBA, Fla. Inst. Tech., 1990. Cert. profl. contract mgr. Contract specialist ships parts control ctr. USN, Mechanicsburg, Pa., 1984; purchasing agt., analyst CACI, Inc., Arlington, Va., 1985; contract adminstr. TRW, Inc., Fairfax, Va., 1985-88, Unisys, Inc., McLean, Va., 1988-89; tech. writer, com. chmn. Nat. Contract Mgmt. Assn., Vienna, Va., 1989—; cons. Geraghty and Miller, Inc., Plainview, N.Y., 1989. Mem. NAFE, African Violet Soc. Am. Republican. Lutheran. Home: 2997 Emerald Chase Dr Herndon VA 22071 Office: Nat Contract Mgmt Assn 1912 Woodford Rd Vienna VA 22182

RUMBAUT, MICHELLE, hospital administrator; b. Albuquerque, July 29, 1963; d. Ruben Dario and Carmen (Riera) R.; m. Dugan Clinton Taylor, May 3, 1986. BS in Healthcare, S.W. Tex. State U., 1984; MS in Healthcare, Trinity U., 1986. Asst. adminstr. Guadalupe Valley Hosp., Seguin, Tex., 1986—. Mem. Tex. Hosp. Assn., Tex. Soc. for Quality Assurance. Office: Guadalupe Valley Hosp 1215 E Court Seguin TX 78155

RUMBERGER, REGINA, retired English educator; b. Pitts., Aug. 6, 1921; d. Edward T. and Margaret (Berry) Flynn; m. Wilson A. Rumberger, July 31, 1943 (div. 1974); children: Edward, Wilson J., Susan A., Gerard, Paul, Nancy, Joe. BEd, Duquesne U., 1942; MEd, U. Pitts., 1950; grad., State Office Div. Blind Svcs., Ft. Myers, Fla., 1984. Primary tchr. Allegheny County Pub. Sch., Pa., 1942-43, Sharpsburg (Pa.) Schs., 1943-50; instr. English, Edison Community Coll., Ft. Myers, 1964-78; ret., 1978; media cons., Lee County and Ft. Myers, 1956; cons., evaluator State of Fla. and Lee County, 1987-88; cons., evaluator Lee County Dept. Transp., Ft. Myers, 1988-90. Chmn. water safety ARC, Ft. Myers, 1960-65, first aid minstr., 1965-68; pres. Lee County Med. Aux., 1965-66; consumer rep. Lee County Dept. Transp.; bd. dirs. Met. Planning Orgn., Ft. Myers, 1990—; v.p. S.W. Fla Curia, 1988—; asst. tour guide to Fr. Stanislaw Pierog, tour dir. Andrew's Pilgrimages, Stockbridge, Mass., 1990—; mem. Lee County Med. Aux., 1956-65, pres., 1963-64. Recipient award Boy Scouts Am., Ft. Myers, 1967, State of Fla., 1984, Ft. Myers Care Ctr./Lee Convalesence, 1990. Mem. AAUW (pub. rels. com. Ft. Myers 1987-90). Roman Catholic. Home: 2140 Cottage St Apt 109 Fort Myers FL 33901

RUMPFF, BARBARA BRYANT, marketing executive, consultant; b. Orlando, Fla., Sept. 25, 1951; d. Allen Leroy Bryant and Trudy (Whittington) McGarity; m. Cornelis J. Rumpff, May 15, 1976. B.S., Fla. State U., 1972, M.B.A., 1974; student U. Valencia, Spain, 1971, U. Belgrade, Yugoslavia, 1973. Research asst. Chevron Petroleum, The Hague, Holland, 1974; field mgr. Procter & Gamble, Cin., 1975-77; sales promotion mgr. Internat. Playtex, Stamford, Conn., 1978; pres. European Am. Mktg. Corp., Atlanta, 1979—. Pres. Assn. Internat. Students in Econs. and Commerce, Tallahassee, Fla., 1970-74. Mem. Am. Mktg. Assn., Orlando C. of C., World Trade Club, Netherlands C. of C. in the U.S.

RUMYANTSEV, NELLY, management; b. Kirov, USSR, Dec. 20, 1963; came to the U.S., 1979; d. Yefim and Lyudmila Rumyantsev. BS in Mgmt. Sci., Case Western Reserve U., 1985, MS in Ops. Rsch., 1986. Bus. mgr. The Observer (CWRU Newspaper), Cleve., 1986; tech. staff The Analytic Scis. Corp., Reading, Mass., 1987—. Mem. Soc. for Advancement Mgmt., Ops. Rsch. Soc. Am. Republican. Home: 264 E Haverhill St #13 Lawrence MA 01841 Office: The Analytic Svcs Corp 55 Walkers Brook Dr Reading MA 01867

RUNAC, PAMELA JOAN, banker; b. Greensburg, Pa., Jan. 29, 1948; d. James George and Dolores Marion (Cantini) Minoski; m. Mark Paul Jr., Aug. 30, 1969, (div. Feb. 1985); children: Colin Gale, Justin Matthew. BA, Slippery Rock State Coll., 1970; postgrad., No. Ill. U., DeKalb, 1980; student, Va. Commonwealth U., Richmond, 1982. Mgmt. trainee Mich. Nat. Bank, Lansing, Mich., 1977-79; operations training specialist F&M Bank, Richmond, 1980-81; procedure analyst Central Fidelity Bank, Richmond, 1981-84; bank ops. analyst mgr. Crestar Bank, Richmond, asst. v.p. retail ops. support, 1984—. Treas. Duntreath Homeowners Assn., Richmond, 1984-85, pres., 1986. Mem. Fin. Women Internat. Home: 10213 Maremont Cir Richmond VA 23233

RUNDLE, JULIET WALKER, state legislator; b. Aug. 27, 1938; m. Richard G. Rundle; 1 child, Janet Marie. BS, Wayne State U.; JD, W.Va. U. Atty.; senator from dist. 9 W.Va. State Senate, 1989—. Mem. Assn. Trial Lawyers Am., W.Va. Trial Lawyers. Baptist. Democrat. Home: PO Box 469 Pineville WV 24874*

RUNKLE, ETHEL MONA, artist; b. Davenport, Iowa, Dec. 4, 1921; d. Louis and Agnes (Jungjohann) Behrens; m. Karl Ehresman Runkle, Jan. 25, 1947; children: Carol Ann, Richard Louis. Grad., Shimer Coll., Mt. Carroll, Ill., 1942; student, St. Ambrose Coll., Davenport, Iowa, 1943, Chgo. Art Inst., 1945, N.Y. Sch. Interior Design, 1955. Cert. Nat. Watercolor Soc. Illustrator Rock Island (Ill.) Arsenal, 1942-44; stewardess United Air Lines, Chgo., 1944-46; craft dir. Westbury (N.Y.) Country Club, 1967; owner, operator Polynesian Fashions, Huntington, N.Y., 1967-71, The Woodshed, Escondido, Calif., 1975-77; art dir. Holland-Am. Lines, Seattle, 1986-87; artist San Diego, 1983—; operator Hawaii Condo Rentals, San Diego, 1964—; art demonstrator San Marcos Art Assn., Calif., 1987, Escondido Art Assn., Calif., 1987, La Jolla Art Assn., La Jolla, Calif., 1986. illustration San Diego, 1987; executed mural, 1987; represented in pvt. collections; exhibited in group show of Nat. Watercolor Soc., L.A., 1987. Historian Clipped Wings, San Diego, 1985-86, Lloyd Harbor Hist. Assn., N.Y., 1966-71, Huntington Hist. Soc., N.Y., 1963-71, Soc. Preservation L.I. Antiquities, N.Y., 1967-70. Recipient Pres.'s Citation of Merit, Nat. Soc. Paint Casein & Acrylic, N.Y., 1988, second place award Escondido Art Assn., 1987. Mem. Am. Soc. Marine Artists, Internat. Soc. Women Marine Artists, Nat. Watercolor Soc. (rep. Alaska and Hawaii 1987-88), USCG Art Program, Clairmont Art Guild, San Diego Watercolor Soc. (pres. 1987-88, 3rd pl. award 1988), La Jolla Art Assn., Nat. Soc. of Painters in Casein and Acrylic. Republican. Lutheran. Home: 17772 Via Gracia San Diego CA 92128

RUNNELS, PAMALA DIANNE, service executive, entertainer, entrepreneur; b. Hattiesburg, Miss., Jan. 24, 1950; d. W. L. and Naomi Virginia (Brothers) R. MusB in Edn., U. So. Miss., 1972. Tchr. music pub. schs. of Miss., 1970-72; profl. entertainer Richard Kravit Mgmt., L.A., 1972-75; with parts mgmt. div. Mazda Motors-Gen. Motors, Baton Rouge, 1975-82; entrepreneur Critter Care, Inc., Baton Rouge, 1982—; music cons. Holiday Inns of Am., Miss., La. and Fla., 1973-75; music dir. Fairwood Country Club, Baton Rouge, 1983—. Assoc. Women in Politics, Baton Rouge, 1989—; bd. dirs. Vol. Pet Therapy Group, Baton Rouge, 1987. Recipient Cost Cutter award Western Petroleum Svcs., 1982. Mem. NOW, Women Bus. Owners Assn. (mem. chmn. 1989—), Am. Bus. Women's Assn., Capital Area Animal Welfare Soc. Republican. Home: 1825 Darren Dr Baton Rouge LA 70816 Office: Critter Care Inc 2900 W Fork Ste 200 Baton Rouge LA 70816

RUNTE, ROSEANN, college principal; b. Kingston, N.Y., Jan. 31, 1948; came to Can., 1971, naturalized, 1983; d. Robert B. and Anna Loretta (Schorkopf) O'Reilly; m. Hans-Rainer Runte, Aug. 9, 1969. BA summa cum laude, SUNY-New Paltz, 1968; MA, U. Kans., 1969, PhD, 1974, DLitt (hon.), Acadia U., 1989, Meml. U., 1990. Lectr. Bethany Coll., W.Va., 1970-71; lectr. adult studies St. Mary's U., Halifax, N.S., Can., 1971-72; from lectr. to assoc. prof. Dalhousie U., Halifax, 1972-83, asst. dean, 1980-82, chmn. dept. French, 1980-83; pres. Universite Sainte-Anne, Pointe-de-l'Eglise, N.S., Can., 1983-88; prin. Glendon Coll., Toronto, 1988—. Author: Brumes bleues, 1982; Faux-Soleils, 1984; editor: Studies in 18th Century Culture, vols. VII, VIII, IX, 1977, 78, 79; co-editor: Man and Nature, 1982, Le Développement régional, 1986, 87; rev. editor French Rev., 1988—; co-translator Local Development, 1987. Bd. dirs. Assn. Med. Svcs.; adv. bd. Nat. Library; chairwoman pubs. com. Hannah Found. Recipient Prix Fr. Coppée French Acad., 1988; regents scholar SUNY-New Paltz, 1965; NDEA Title IV grantee U. Kans., Lawrence, 1968; Acad. Palms, 1986. Mem. Internat. Soc. 18th Century Studies (assoc. treas. 1983-87), Internat. Assn. of Comparative Lit. (treas. 1985—), Can. Fedn. Humanities (pres. 1982-84), Atlantic Soc. 18th Century Studies (pres. 1972-76), Canadian Soc. 18th Century Studies (pres. 1975-76), Soc. for Study Higher Edn. (bd. dirs.). Roman Catholic. Home and Office: Glendon College, 2275 Bayview, Toronto, ON Canada M4N 3M6

RUNYON, GERRI LEWIS, banker; b. Sharon, Pa., June 18, 1949; d. Gerald T. and Mary Jean (Evans) Lewis; m Thomas E. Runyon, Aug. 3, 1969; 1 child, Deborah Lee. BS, Montclair State Coll., 1976; Applied Diploma in Retail Banking, Am. Inst. Banking, 1989. Customer svc. rep. First Nat. State Bank South Jersey, Basking Ridge, N.J., 1981-82; adminstrv. asst. First Nat. State Bank South Jersey, Bernardsville, N.J., 1982-84; asst. cashier, asst. br. mgr. First Fidelity Bank N.A., Basking Ridge, 1984-86, First Nat. Bank Cen. Jersey, Warren, N.J., 1986-87; br. mgr. First Nat. State Bank South Jersey, Bedminster, N.J., 1987-89; asst. treas., br. mgr. Somerset Trust Co., Bedminster, 1990—. Mem. Fin. Women Internat. (sec. RAritan Bay group 1987—), AAUW, Somerville Rotary (v.p. 1990—). Presbyterian. Home: 103 Lyons Rd Basking Ridge NJ 07920 Office: Somerset Trust Co Rt 202 and Lamington Rd Bedminster NJ 07921

RUNYON, MARY LUCILLE, banker; b. Mt. Sterling, Ky., Aug. 17, 1927; d. Jess and Mary (Martin) Gilbert; m. Troy H. Runyon, Dec. 23, 1949; children: joy Lynette Ramirez, Pamela Lea Perez, Dreama Carol. Student, U. Ky. Lic. in real estate. V.p. 1st Nat. Bank, Palm Beach, Fla., 1969-85, Bankers Trust of Fla., West Palm Beach, 1987—. Founder, v.p. Adopt-A-Family of Palm Beach, Inc., West Palm Beach, 1984—; bd. dirs. Vol. Ctr. of Palm Beach, 1983—, League of Charities, Palm Beach, 1987—; com. mem. Am. Heart Auction, West Palm Beach, 1985—; v.p. Good Samaritan Hosp. Aux., West Palm Beach, 1987—. Recipient Congrl. award for volunteerism Pres. Reagan, 1984, Jefferson award Channel 12, 1985-86, Vol. award Bankers Trust Co., 1988. Fellow Nat. Am. Bank Women. Republican. Baptist. Lodge: Shriners. Home: 12062 Basin St SW Palm Beach FL 33414

RUPP, GERALDLYNN SUE, public relations executive; b. Denver, Apr. 13, 1946; d. Gerald Monroe and Grace Isabel (Evans) R.; m. William S. Yurong, 1967 (div. 1983); children: Tamara Jene, William Anthony. BA, Calif. State U., Sacramento, 1978; postgrad., Calif. State U., 1980—. Asst. for alumni pub. relations McGeorge Sch. Law/U. of the Pacific, Stockton, Calif., 1979-81, dir. alumni pub. relations, 1981-83; asst. devel. dir. Sacramento Symphony, 1983-85; dir. communications and community rels. Sacramento Assn. Realtors, 1985—; cons., lectr. in field. Dir. communications Sacramento Realtor mag., 1985 (several awards). Bd. dirs. EnCorps/Symphony Assn., Sacramento, 1985-86, Am. Lung Assn., Sacramento, 1986, communications com. chmn. 1989—; div. chmn. United Way Campaign, 1985; bd. dirs. Calif. Christmas CanTree, 1985-1990, steering com. Sacramento Chamber Music Soc., 1987; friend Sta. KVIE-Channel 6 Pub. TV; panel mem. Weekend of the Stars Cerebral Palsy Telethon, 1985. Mem. Am. Soc. Assn. Execs. (Gold Circle trophy 1985), Sacramento Soc. Assn. Execs. (communications-publs. sect. chmn. 1987-88, chmn. com. mktg., pub. rels. 1988—), Internat. Assn. Bus. Communicators (Creativity award 1986,

Crystal award 1989), Sacramento Pub. Rels. Assn., Toastmasters, Comstock Club. Home: 4520 Ulysses Dr Sacramento CA 95864

RUPP, SHERON ADELINE, photographer, educator; b. Mansfield, Ohio, Jan. 14, 1943; d. Warren Edmund Rupp and Frances Adeline (Hanson) Christian. BA in Sociology and Psychology, Denison U., 1965; MFA in Photography, U. Mass., 1982. Teaching asst. in photography Hampshire Coll., Amherst, Mass., 1981; instr. photography Northfield (Mass.) Mt. Hermon Sch., 1982-83, U. Mass., Amherst, 1984, Holyoke (Mass.) Community Coll., 1986, 87-88; vis. asst. prof. photography Hampshire Coll., 1985, 87; guest artist, lectr. Boston Mus. Sch., Portland (Maine) Sch. Art, NYU, U. Mass., Deerfield (Mass.) Acad., others. Exhibited in one-person shows at Portland Sch. Art, 1989, Tisch Sch. Arts, NYU, 1987; exhibited in group shows at Zone Art Ctr., Springfield, Mass., 1986, Mus. Modern Art, N.Y.C., 1987; represented in collections at Mus. Modern Art, N.Y.C., Fogg Art Mus. at Harvard U., Rose Art Mus. at Brandeis U., Smith Coll. Mus. Art, U. Mass.; contbr. photographs and articles to jours. Bd. dirs., mem. artistic com. Zone Art Ctr., 1987—. Recipient Mass. Fellowship award in photography Artists Found., 1984, 87; visual arts fellow Nat. Endowment for Arts, 1986; Guggenheim fellow, 1990. Mem. Soc. Photog. Edn., Photog. Resource Ctr. Home and Office: 100 Chestnut St Florence MA 01060

RUPPERT, BARBARA LEE, research scientist, consultant; b. East Orange, N.J., Jan. 15, 1949; d. Cleldon Francis and Betty Caroline (Boudier) R. BS, Fla. State U., Tallahassee, 1971; MS, Baylor Coll. Medicine, 1974, PhD, 1979. Project investigator Anderson Hosp. and Tumor Inst., Houston, 1979-81; research fellow Baylor Coll. Medicine, Houston, 1981-82, mem. faculty, 1982—; cons. in field. Contbr. articles to profl. jours.; patentee in field. Mem. Am. Soc. for Cell Biology, Tissue Culture Assn., Internat. Soc. Appraisers (assoc.). Democrat. Presbyterian. Home: 5909 Darnell Houston TX 77074 Office: 5909 Darnell Houston TX 77074

RUPPERT, SUSAN DONNA, health science educator; b. LaSalle, Ill., Aug. 17, 1953; d. Joseph J. and Phyllis A. (Koontz) Stachowicz; m. Robert M. Ruppert; children: Sarah E., Michael R. AAS in Nursing, Ill. Valley Community Coll., Oglesby, 1974, AS in Sci., 1975; BS in Nursing, No. Ill. U., 1976; MS in Nursing, U. Tex., San Antonio, 1979; postdoctoral, Tex. Woman's U. Cert. critical care nurse. Evening supr. Met. Gen. Hosp., San Antonio, 1978-79; instr. U. Iowa Coll. Nursing, Iowa City, 1979-81; program coord. continuing edn. Meth. Hosp., Houston, 1981-89; asst. prof. U. Tex. Health Sci. Ctr., Houston, 1989—. Contbr. articles to profl. jours. Mem. NAFE, Am. Assn. Critical Care Nurses (bd. dirs.), Am. Nurses Assn., Tex. Nurses Assn., Am. Soc. Profl. and Exec. Women, Am. Bus. Women's Assn., N.Am. Nursing Dianosis Assn., Meeting Planners Internat., Sigma Theta Tau. Home: 2514 Chimneystone Circle Sugar Land TX 77479 Office: U Tex Health Sci Ctr at Houston Sch Nursing 1100 Holcombe Blvd 5.522 Houston TX 77030

RUPPRECHT, CAROL SCHREIER, comparative literature educator, dream researcher; b. Stafford Springs, Conn., June 30, 1939; d. William Joseph and Caroline Brown (Comstock) Schreier; divorced; children: Jody Francine, Whitney Glenn; m. Richard P. Suttmeier, May 8, 1987. BS, U. Va., 1962; MA, Yale U., 1963, M in Philosophy, 1973, PhD, 1977. Teaching fellow Yale U., 1973; asst. prof. Kirkland Coll., Clinton, N.Y., 1974-78; asst. prof. Hamilton, Coll., Clinton, 1978-81, assoc. dean, 1981-82, assoc. prof. comparative lit., 1982-89; prof., 1989—, chmn. dept., 1984-89; lectr. Switzerland, Israel, The Netherlands, Ireland, People's Republic China, Eng. Co-editor and author: Feminist Archetypal Theory, 1985. Contbr. articles to profl. jours., chpts. to books. NEH fellow Dartmouth Dante Inst., 1986. Founding mem. Assn. for Study Dreams, 1983, Conn. Assn. Jungian Psychology, 1981. Merrill fellow Bunting Inst., 1970-72. Mem. MLA, Am. Comparative Lit. Assn., Shakespeare Soc., Assn. Study of Dreams (pres., v.p. bd. dirs., mem. editorial bd.), Conn. Assn. for Jungian Psychology (bd. dirs.). Avocations: sports; wilderness activities. Office: Hamilton Coll Clinton NY 13323

RUPPRECHT, NANCY ELLEN, historian; b. Coeur d'Alene, Idaho, Sept. 23, 1948; d. George John and Nancy Berneeda (Baird) R. BA with honors, U. Mo., 1967, MA, 1969; PhD, U. Mich., 1982. Acad. dir. pilot program U. Mich., Ann Arbor, 1971-73, lectr. in women studies, 1973-75; vis. lectr. history U. Mo., St. Louis, 1976-77; vis. instr. of history Wash. U., St. Louis, 1977-79, Grinnell (Iowa) Coll., 1979-81; asst. prof. Oakland U., Rochester, Mich., 1981-83; asst. prof. of history Mid. Tenn. State U., Murfreesboro, 1985—; dir., women's studies program Middle Tenn. State U., 1989—, publicity dir. women's history month, 1988—. Contbr. articles to profl. jours. Mem. NOW. Mem. AAUP (chpt. pres. 1989—, v.p. 1988-89), Am. Hist. Assn., Middle Tenn. Women's Studies Assn., Women in Higher Edn. in Tenn., German Studies Assn., Phi Kappa Phi, Phi Alpha Theta (sponsor 1986-89), Tri-Penta. Home: 1619 Hanover M-3 Murfreesboro TN 37130 Office: Middle Tenn State U Box 23 History Dept Murfreesboro TN 37132

RUPRECHT, MARY MARGARET WYANT, office automation management consultant; b. O'Neill, Neb., Oct. 20, 1934; d. Charles Ellsworth and Mary Loretto (Cuddy) Wyant; m. Gregory Earl Ruprecht, Sept. 24, 1955; children: Mary Debra, Sharie Marie. Student Coll. St. Benedict, 1952-54; cert. Am. Inst. Banking, 1970. Cert. mgmt. cons. Dist. clk. U.S. Soil Conservation, Aitkin, Minn., 1956-68; comml. loan sec. No. City Nat. Bank, Duluth, Minn., 1965-71; office mgr. Fryberger, Buchanan Law Firm, Duluth, 1971-72; pvt. practice word processing and mgmt. cons., Duluth, 1972-76; v.p., prin. Altman & Weil, Inc., mgmt. cons., 1976-79; pres. Mary M. Ruprecht & Assoc., 1979—; tchr. Am. Inst. Banking; internat. lectr. Author: (with others) Managing Office Automation, Office Automation: Concepts and Principles, Office Automation: A Management Approach, Integrated Office Systems, 1987, Integrated Office Systems A Management Approach and Office Automation Technologies, 1988, Integrated Office Systems Automation Dictionary, 1987; contbr. editor Office Systems Jour.; also articles. Mem. adv. council Minn. State Bd. Edn., Duluth Office Edn. Assn., Coll. Applied Scis. at Miami U., Oxford, Ohio, Ball State U., Muncie, Coll. of St. Scholastic, Duluth, Minn., treas. Senator Sam Solon 1964—, Ind. Fin. dir. 8th Congressional Dist. Dem.-Farm Labor Party, 1972-73. Mem. Assn. Info. Systems Profl. (former internat. pres.), Internat. Word Processing Assn. (internat. pres. 1974-75), Am. Inst. Banking (nat. chmn. women's com. 1970-71), Adminstrv. Mgmt. Soc., Am. Mgmt. Assn., Office Systems Research Assn. (conf. chmn. 1985, 86), Bus. and Profl. Women's Assn., Internat. Platform Assn., Inst. Mgmt. Cons. of N.Y. Home: 140 W Myrtle St Duluth MN 55811

RUSAK, HALINA RODKO, librarian, artist; b. Navahradak, Byelorussian Soviet Socialist Republic; came to U.S., 1949; d. Filaret and Vera Rodko; m. Vasil Rusak, July 21, 1951; children: Ludmila Rusak Grant, Natalia. BA, Rutgers U., 1954, MLS, 1956, MA, 1976. Art bibliographer, reference librarian Douglass Coll. Rutgers U., New Brunswick, N.J., 1956-83, slide libr., 1970-83; art librarian Rutgers U., New Brunswick, 1983-85, dir. art libr., 1985—; art cons. Byelourussian Inst. Art and Sci., Rutherford, N.J., 1978—; mem. steering com. art and architecture program RLG, Mountain View, Calif., 1988—. Contbr. articles to profl. jours.; exhibited in group shows. Mem. planning bd. N.J. Dept. State Ethnic Ctr., Trenton, 1978-81; mem. heritage com. Garden State Arts Ctr., Holmdel, 1978-83. Rutgers U. grantee, 1981, 84, 85, N.J. Com. for Humanities grantee, 1983, NEH grantee, 1986. Mem. Art Libr. Soc. N.Am. (v.p. N.Y. chpt. 1984-85, pres. 1985-86, co-chmn. architecture sect. 1989-90), Coll. Art Assn., Women's Caucus for Art, Byelorussian-Am. Assn. (v.p. N.J. chpt. 1982—), Nature Conservancy, Nat. Resources Def. Coun., Sierra Club. Eastern Orthodox. Home: 40 Deerfield Rd Somerset NJ 08873 Office: Rutgers U Art Libr Voorhees Hall CAC New Brunswick NJ 08903

RUSCHE, SUE, drug abuse prevention administrator; b. Troy, Ohio, Mar. 8, 1938; d. William D. and Merle (Pierce) Boller; m. Harry Rusche, Mar. 23, 1963; children: Philip, Steven. Student, Miami U. of Ohio, 1956-58; cert., Cin. Acad. Graphic Design, 1960. Asst. art dir. Doyle Dane Bernbach, N.Y.C., 1960-62; rsch. asst. So. Regional Coun., Atlanta, 1963-65; vol. art tchr. Project Headstart, Atlanta, 1965-67; founder, owner The Graphics People, Atlanta, 1970-79; co-founder, exec. dir. Families in Action, Atlanta, 1977—; cons. Nat. Inst. Drug Abuse, Office for Substance Abuse Prevention, Dept. Edn., Drug Enforcement Adminstrn., ACTION, Surgeon Gen. Office, Nat. Hwy. Traffic Safety Adminstr., Washington, 1978—; adv. bd. Alcohol, Drug Abuse, Mental Health Adminstrn., Washington, 1985-88; founding bd. mem. Nat. Fedn. Parents, Drug Free Youth, Washington, 1980-84;, Ga. Task Force on Alcohol and Other Drugs, Atlanta, 1984-87. Columnist: Straight Talk on Drugs, King Features, N.Y.C., 1984-89; editor: Drug Abuse Update, Atlanta, 1982—; author: (manual) How to Form a Families in Action Group, 1979; contbr. articles to profl. publs. Bd. mem. Arts Festival Atlanta, 1972-79, Best Youth Clubs, Atlanta Pub. Housing Authority, 1989, Cascade Parent Group, Atlanta, 1988—; lifetime mem. Ga. PTA. Recipient Pacesetter award, Nat. Inst. Drug Abuse, Washington, 1980; Paul Harris fellow, Rotary Internat., 1989. Office: Nat Families in Action 2296 Henderson Mill Rd Ste 204 Atlanta GA 30345

RUSCH WALTON, SANDRA LEE, city administrator; b. Milw., Aug. 3, 1957; d. Leo John and Elinore Helen (Buk) Rusch; m. Joseph H. Walton, Oct. 28, 1989. BA in History, Theology, Carroll Coll., Waukesha, Wis., 1979. Teaching asst. Marquette U., Milw., 1980-81; loan officer U. Wis.-Milw., Fin. Aid Office, 1981-82; office mgr. Marquette U., 1982-85; legis. asst. City of Milw., Alderwoman, Lyon Common Coun., 1985-89; staff asst. spl. events City of Milw., 1989-90, spl. asst. to city controller, 1990—. Capaign worker various polit. campaigns, 1985—. Recipient Zachariah Davies award, Carroll Coll., 1979. Mem. Women in Communications (v.p. programming 1989-90, v.p. profl. devel. 1990—), Alpha Gamma Delta (pres. 1983-89, editor 1984—, altruistic chmn. 1987—). Lutheran. Home: 8227 W Lisbon Ave Milwaukee WI 53222 Office: City of Milwaukee 200 E Wells St #404 Milwaukee WI 53202

RUSCO, LINDA SUZANNE, electronics company analyst; b. Salem, Mass., Dec. 26, 1951; d. Gerald F. Collins and Dorothy (White) Collins Chrisinger; m. Gene E. Rusco, Mar. 4, 1989. Student, Mission Coll., 1989—. Advt. copywriter Rich's Dept. Stores, Salem, 1974-80; dir. advt. Interscapes, Inc., Norfolk, Va., 1980-83; mng. editor Nat. Energy Jour., Phoenix, 1983-85; software configuration analyst Kaiser Electronics, San Jose, Calif., 1985—. Mem. Al-Anon.

RUSH, CATHERINE PATRICIA, corporate professional; b. Montclair, N.J., May 29, 1944; d. Thomas Patrick and Helen (Howard) R. Corp. sec., office mgr. Beck's Montclair Moving & Storage, Inc., 1962-68; corp. sec., gen. mgr. Rimback Storage Co., Millburn, N.J., 1968—; mem. communications coordination com. UN; speaker UN World Environ. Day, 1989. Contbr. article to pubs. Mem. Friends of N.J. Opera. Mem. Internat. Health Network for Women and Children (past dir.), N.J. Fedn. Bus. and Profl. Women (bd. dirs.), World Info. Transfer, Allied Van Lines Profl. Sales Assn., Montclair Bus. and Profl. Women (Young Career Woman award 1966), Bus. and Profl. Women Millburn-Short Hills, Millburn-Short Hills C. of C. (bd. dirs.). Republican. Office: Rimback Storage Co 161 Spring St Millburn NJ 07041

RUSH, JULIANNE, editor; b. Ft. Rucker, Ala., Jan. 17, 1968; d. David Charles and Sandra Ann (Williams) R. BS in Psychology, Okla. State U., Stillwater, 1989, So. Meth. U., 1989. Fashion cons. Seifert's, Oklahoma City, Okla., 1985-87; staff writer Student Media Pub. Co., Inc., Dallas, 1986, sr. staff writer, 1988; arts and entertainment editor So. Meth. U., Dallas, 1989; features editor Yukon (Okla.) Rev., 1990; mgr. Joy of Ireland, Dallas, 1990—. Mem. Women in Communications, Inc., Pub. Rels. Student Soc. Am. Home: 6318 Gaston Ave Dallas TX 75214

RUSHFORD, ELOISE JOHNSON, land manager; b. Elmwood, Ill.; d. Albert Earl and Edna Merle (Dixon) Johnson; (div. June 1967); children: Gregory Gene, Barbara Merle Rushford Grimes. BA, Bradley U., 1936. Cert. tchr., Ill. Tchr. English Manual High Sch. Dist. 150, Peoria, 1955-56; ptnr. Johnson Devel. Co., 1956-76; v.p. Johnson's Men's Store, 1972-74; land mgr. Peoria, 1974—. Bd. dirs. Crippled Children's Found., Peoria, Women's Civic Fedn., Symphony Guild; mem. Women's Assn. First Federated Ch., pres. Mothers' Club; mem. Women's Adv. bd. Internat. Christian U., Tokyo. Mem. AAUW (pres. 1958-60, chmn. bd. dirs. Peoria br., award 1977), Lasertoma (pres. Peoria chpt. 1962-63), First Federated MOthers' Club and Women's Assn., Pi Beta Phi (pres. Peoria chpt. alumnae 1960-61). Republican. Congregationalist. Home: 220 Merle Ln Peoria IL 61604

RUSHING, DOROTHY MARIE, history educator; b. Bonham, Tex., Aug. 28, 1925; d. Van Bain and Ada Belle (Price) Hawkins; m. Jasper Eugene Rushing, Aug. 6, 1960 (dec. 1985); children: Charles Maret, Bill Maret, Bob Maret, Charles Rushing, Martha Rushing Sosebee. BA, Tex. Woman's U., Denton, 1972; MA, East Tex. State U., Commerce, 1974; PhD, U. North Tex., Denton, 1981. Cert. history, lang. arts. secondary tchr., Tex. Pub. sch. tchr. various schs., Garland, Tex., 1972-85; instr. asst. prof. East Tex. State U., Commerce, 1972-74, 1980-81; teaching fellow U. North Tex., Denton, 1975-76; from instr. to prof. Richland Coll., Dallas, 1975-89; instr. prof. Collin County Community Coll., Mckinney, Tex., 1985-88; lectr., Dallas, 1972—; counselor individualized instrn., Dallas, 1988—, tutor aliens Richland Coll., Dallas, 1975—; speaker pub. rels. N.E. Tex. Libr. System., Dallas, 1980—; statis. analyst Dallas County Community Coll. Dist.; historian archivist JCPenney, Inc., 1988—. Author: 500 Years of Ignorance, 1988, Texas: A World in Itself; editor and author: Texas: The Lone Star State, 1984; contbg. author: Beyond Sundown, Commercial Drama, 1975, Handbook of Texas, 1990. Chmn. Garland, Tex. Sesquicentennial com., 1985-86; chmn. bd. trustees Garland Libr., 1980-89; rep. N.E. Tex. Libr. System, 1984-89. Recipient 2 scholarships, 2 fellowships East Tex. State U. and North Tex. State U., 1972-75; NEH postdoctoral fellow Johns Hopkins U., 1985, U. Va., 1989; Dallas County Community Coll. Dist. grantee 1984; recipient Hon. Cross of Lorraine French Army, 1979. Mem. DAR, Tex. Hist. Soc., NEA (dir. Tex. Faculty Assn., 1984-88), Neoteric Study Garland, Tex. (pres. 1989-90), Phi Kappa Phi, Sigma Alpha Theta, Sigma Tau Delta. Home: 1214 Patricia Ln Garland TX 75042 Office: 12800 Abrams Rd Dallas TX 75243

RUSIECKI, WANDA A., mental health worker; b. Waterbury, Conn., May 3, 1954. AB, Mt. Holyoke Coll., 1976; MEd, Northeastern U., 1978. Cert. spl. edn. tchr., Mass. Sr. program analyst Mass. Dept. Mental Health, Boston, 1979-82; asst. dir. New Eng. Ctr. for Autism, Southborough, Mass., 1982-84; day treatment program dir. Young Adult Inst., N.Y.C., 1984-88, cons., 1988-89; program specilist, young adults Westchester County Dept. Community Mental Health, White Plains, 1989—; manuscript reviewer Hosp. and Community Psychiatry, Washington, 1988—. Vol. tchr. ESL, Internat. Inst. Boston, 1982-83. Fellow Am. Orthopsychiat. Assn. (chmn. conf. planning com. N.Y.C. 1989); mem. Assn. for Persons with Severe Handicaps, Am. Assn. on Mental Retardation, Assn. for Behavior Analysis, Assn. for Care Children's Health (chmn. local legis. com. 1981, treas. No. New Eng. affiliate 1984, chmn. conf. planning com. Boston 1984). Office: Westchester County Dept MH 112 E Post Rd White Plains NY 10601

RUSKAI, MARY BETH, mathematics researcher, educator; b. Cleve., Feb. 26, 1944; d. Michael J. and Evelyn (Gortz) R. BS, Notre Dame Coll., Cleve., 1965; MA, PhD, U. Wis., 1969. Battelle fellow in theoretical physics U. Geneva, 1969-71; research assoc. in math. MIT, Boston, 1971-72; rsch. assoc. in physics U. Alta., Edmonton, Can., 1972-73; asst. prof. math. U. Oreg., Eugene, 1973-76; asst. prof. U. Lowell, Mass., 1977-82, assoc. prof., 1982-86, prof. dept. math., 1986—; sci. scholar Bunting Inst., Cambridge, Mass., 1983-85; vis. prof. Rockefeller U., N.Y.C., 1980-81, U. Vienna, Austria, 1981; faculty rsch. assoc. Naval Surface Warefare Ctr., Silver Springs, Md., 1986; vis. mem. Courant Inst. Math. Sci., NYU, 1988-89; cons. Bell Labs., Murray Hill, N.J., 1972, 83, 88-89; conf. dir. NSF/CBMS Conf. on Wavelets, 1990; vis. prof. Rome, 1988. Contbr. articles to profl. jours.; editorial bd. Wavelets and Their Applications, 1990—. NSF predoctoral fellow, 1965-69; recipient NSF Career Advancement award, 1988-89. Mem. Internat. Assn. Math. Physicists, Am. Math. Soc. (reviewer, session chairperson, com. mem. 1987—), Math. Assn. Am., Am. Phys. Soc. (reviewer), Assn. Women in Math., Assn. Women in Sci. (pres. New Eng. chpt. 1986-87), Sigma Xi. Club: Appalachian Mountain (Boston) (winter leader 1979—). Office: U Lowell Dept Math 1 University Ave Lowell MA 01854

RUSONIS, ELISA JO SLATER, psychologist; b. Buffalo, Jan. 5, 1961; d. Phillip Harold and Roslyn Clara (Oberlander) Slater. BA magna cum laude, Tulane U., 1982; MS, U. Ga., 1984, PhD, 1986. Asst. prof. U. Md., Balt., 1986-89; clin. pychologist Annapolis (Md.) Pediatrics, 1989—; clin. dir. CMG Health, Owings Mills, Md., 1989—. Contbr. articles to profl. jours. Mem. Am. Psycholo. Assn., Planning Com. Adolescent Health Tng. Programs,. Home: 7822 Old Farm Ln Ellicott City MD 21043 Office: CMG Health 25 Crossroads Dr Ste 140 Owings Mills MD 21117

RUSS, HELENE GIZELLE, psychologist; b. N.Y.C., July 1, 1957; m. Laurence Brian Zuckerman, June 26, 1988. MA, Columbia U., 1981; PhD, Adelphi U., 1988. Psychologist Hall Health Clinic, U. Wash., Seattle, 1990—; Lic. psychologist, N.Y., Wash. Mem. Am. Psychol. Assn., Wash. State Psychol. Assn., Phi Beta Kappa. Home: 1127 Olympic Way W #107 Seattle WA 98119 Office: Hall Health Ctr U Wash G-10 Seattle WA 98119

RUSSAVAGE, JANET MARIE, optometrist; b. Pittston, Pa., Apr. 10, 1962; d. Clement Joseph and Elinor Ruth (Ostrowski) R. Student, Pa. State U., 1980-83; OD, Pa. Coll. Optometry, 1987. Resident optometrist The Eye Inst., Pa. Coll. Optometry, Phila., 1987-88; optometrist-ptnr. Drs. Levin & Russavage, Shiremanstown, Pa., 1988—; vis. clin. staff The Eye Inst., Pa. Coll. Optometry, Phila., 1988—. Tutor Cen. Pa. Literacy Coun., Harrisburg, 1990; supporter Planned Parenthood, Harrisburg, 1989—. Mem. Cen. Pa. Optometric Soc., Pa. Optometric Assn., Am. Optometric Assn., Am. Bus. Women's Assn. (treas. Harristowne, Pa. chpt. 1988—). Republican. Roman Catholic. Home: 819 Old Silver Spring Rd Mechanicsburg PA 17055 Office: Drs Levin & Russavage 5 E Main St Shiremanstown PA 17011

RUSSAW, JOYCE BELYNDA, automotive company executive; b. St. Augustine, Fla., July 31, 1952; d. James and Daisy Estelle (Selmore) Colbert. BA, Clark Atlanta U., 1974. Legis. aide Ga. Gen. Assembly State Capitol, Atlanta, 1975; sr. clk. GM, Atlanta, 1976-80, employee benefits rep., 1980-88, corp. recruiter, 1988-89, nat. instr. UAW, 1989-90; tng. instr. Buick-Oldsmobile-Cadillace Lansing Ednl. Devel. Gen. Motors, Lansing, Mich., 1990—. Advisor Jr. Achievement, Atlanta, 1981; tchr., counselor Am. Leadership Study Groups, Worchester, Mass., 1986—; mem. Allen Temple A.M.E., Atlanta, 1989. Mem. ASTM, NAFE, Smithsonian Assocs. Democrat. Office: 1001 Brookside #309 Lansing MI 48917

RUSSEL, MARJORIE ELLEN, genetics educator; b. N.Y.C., July 16, 1944; d. Alfred and Myra (Teicher) R.; m. Peter Henry Model, June 21, 1981; 1 child, Sascha. BA, Oberlin (Ohio) Coll., 1966; MS, U. Wis., 1968; PhD, U. Colo., 1977. Rsch. asst. genetics dept. U. Wash., Seattle, 1968-70, U. Geneva, 1970-72; postdoctoral fellow Rockefeller U., N.Y.C., 1977-78, rsch. assoc., 1978-87, asst. prof. microbial genetics, 1987—. Contbr. articles to profl. jours. Mem. Am. Soc. for Microbiology, Am. Soc. for Virology. Office: Rockefeller U 1230 York Ave New York NY 10021

RUSSELL, ATTIE YVONNE, academic administrator, dean, pediatrics educator; b. Washington, Aug. 10, 1923; d. George and Kathleen L. (Millimer) Werner; m. Rex Hillier, Apr. 19, 1954 (div.); m. Henry J. Russell, 1960 (div. 1971); children: Richard Russell, Margaret Jane Russell; m. Harry F. Camper, Sept. 2, 1984. BS, Am. U., 1944; PhD, State U. Iowa, 1952; MD, U. Chgo., 1958. Intern Phila. Gen. Hosp., 1958-59; resident in pediatrics Bronx (N.Y.) Mcpl. Hosp., 1960-61, Del. Hosp., Wilmington, 1962-63; dir. maternal and child health, crippled children's svcs. Del. State Bd. Health, Dover, 1963-68; asst. dean community health affairs, assoc. prof. pediatrics U. Cin. Coll. Medicine, 1968-71; clin. assoc. prof. pediatrics Med. Coll. Pa., Phila., 1966-68, 71-74; dep. dir. div. pub. health State of Del., Dover, 1971-74; dir. Santa Clara Valley Med. Ctr., San Jose, Calif., 1974-79; assoc. dean, clin. prof. pediatrics, family medicine Stanford (Calif.) U. Sch. Medicine, 1974-79; dir. USPHS Hosp., Boston, 1979-81, Balt. City Hosps., 1981-82; asst. v.p. community affairs, prof. pediatrics U. Tex. Med. Br., Galveston, 1982-88, asst. v.p. student affairs, dean students, prof. pediatrics, 1988—; reviewer Coun. for Internat. Exchange of Scholars, Washington, 1987—; dir. III Symposium on Health and Human Svcs. in the U.S.-Mex., Brownsville, 1988; mem. sci. coun. Am. Fedn. for Aging Rsch., Inc., 1983-86. Contbr. articles and abstracts to profl. jours. Mem. budget com. United Way, Galveston, 1982-84; mem. Mayor's Adv. Com. for Sr. Citizens and Handicapped Persons for the City of Galveston, 1983-85; bd. dirs. Galveston County Coordinated Community Clinics, 1983—; bd. advisors Galveston Hist. Found., 1983—; mem. Com. for Coop. Action Planning, 1983—, Houston-Galveston Health Promotion Consortium, 1983—, Injury Control Prevention (Houston), 1984—, aging programs adv. com. Houston-Galveston Area Coun., 1985—. Recipient Disting. Alumni award Am. U., 1984. Fellow Am. Acad. Pediatrics, Am. Pub. Health Assn.; mem. AMA, Am. Coll. Preventive Medicine, Soc. for Adolescent Medicine, Am. Physiol. Soc., Am. Fedn. for Aging Rsch., Am. Geriatrics Soc., Mass. State Med. Soc., Galveston Med. Soc., Tex. Med. Assn., Tex. Pediatric Soc., Galveston C. of C. (legis. com. 1983—), Order of Eastern Star, Sigma Xi, Alpha Omega Alpha. Office: U Tex Med Branch Rm 1.208 Ashbel Smith Bldg Galveston TX 77550

RUSSELL, BERNICE K., computer systems analyst; b. Lafollette, Tenn., Oct. 20, 1961; d. Bill Gillard and Nellie May (Osborne) Kentz; m. Barry L. Russell, Nov. 7, 1987. BA, Western Ky. U., 1983; postgrad., Nashville Tech. Inst. Lic. in ins., Tenn. Fin. advisor Penn Mut. Life, Nashville; ins. rep. Phoenix Mut. Life, Nashville; systems support analyst St. Thomas Hosp., Nashville. Mem. NAFE, Alpha Kappa Alpha. Baptist. Office: St Thomas Hosp Dept Info Systems 4220 Harding Rd Nashville TN 37208

RUSSELL, CAROL ANN, personnel service company executive; b. Detroit, Dec. 14, 1943; d. Billy and Iris (Driver) Koud; m. Victor Rojas (div.). Student, Hunter Coll., 1961-64. Registered employment cons. Positions in temp. help cos. N.Y.C., 1964-74; v.p. Wollborg-Michelson, San Francisco, 1974-82; co-owner, pres. Russell Personnel Svcs. Inc., San Francisco, 1983—. Named for Outstanding Advt., Calif. Assn. Personnel Consultants, 1984, named to the Inc. 500, 1989. Mem. No. Calif. Human Resources Coun., Calif. Assn. Temp. Svcs. (pres. 1984-85), Bay Area Personnel Assn. (pres. 1983-84). Office: Russell Personnel Svcs Inc 120 Montgomery St San Francisco CA 94104

RUSSELL, CATHERINE MARIE, retired clinical microbiologist, educator; b. Tuckahoe, N.Y., Nov. 20, 1910; d. Leslie Bloomer and Margaret (Farrell) R. BS, Coll. Mt. St. Vincent, 1932; MA, Columbia U., 1948; PhD, U. Va., 1951. Diplomate Am. Bd. Med. Microbiology. Technician rsch. and diagnostic labs State Health Dept., N.Y.C., 1939-41; technician N.Y. Med. Coll., N.Y.C., 1941-42, instr. bacteriology and parasitology, 1942-48; from instr. to asst. prof. microbiology U. Va. Sch. Medicine, Charlottesville, 1948-58, assoc. prof. microbiology and clin. pathology, 1958-74, prof. clin. pathology and microbiology, 1974-77; cons. Blue Ridge Sanitorium, Charlottesville, Va., 1960-75, Health Dept. and Martha Jefferson Hosp., Charlottesville, 1955-77. Contbr. articles to profl. jours. Dir. rite of Christian initiation for adults St. Thomas Aquinas Cath. Ch., 1979—. Mem. Am. Soc. Microbiology, Med. Mycol. Soc. of the Ams., Sigma Xi. Home: 511 N 1st St Apt 505 Charlottesville VA 22901

RUSSELL, CATHERINE STOUT, critical care nurse, vintner; b. Fort Leavenworth, Kans., Jan. 6, 1955; d. Morris Cowan and Marilyn Enize (Herrmann) Stout; m. Erich Lee Russell, Aug. 4, 1984. BS in Nursing, U. Utah, 1978. RN. Staff RN Cedars Sinai Med. Ctr., L.A., 1978-80; critical care relief staff nurse Nursing Svcs. Internat., Beverly Hills, Calif., 1980-82; office nurse, clin. trials coord. Cardiology Assocs. of Santa Rosa (Calif.), Inc., 1982—; co-owner Rabbit Ridge Vineyards and Winery, Healdsburg, Calif., 1984—; instr. basic cardiac life support, Am. Heart Assn., Santa Rosa, 1982—. Mem. AAUW (program dir. 1990), Delta Delta Delta Alumnae Chpt. Republican. Home: 3291 Westside Rd Healdsburg CA 95448 Office: Cardiology Assocs of Santa Rosa 1111 Sonoma Ave #316 Santa Rosa CA 95405

RUSSELL, CHARLOTTE SANANES, biochemistry educator, researcher; b. N.Y.C., Jan. 4, 1927; d. Joseph and Marguerite (Saltiel) Sananes; m. Joseph Brooke Russell, Dec. 20, 1947; children: James Robert, Joshua Sananes. BA, Bklyn. Coll., 1946; MA, Columbia U., 1947, PhD, 1951. Asst. prof. biochemistry CCNY, N.Y.C., 1958-68, assoc. prof., 1968-72, prof., 1972—. Ad hoc reviewer sci. jours. including Jour. Solid State Chemistry, Biochemistry jour.; contbr. rsch. articles to sci. publs. Mem. Am. Soc. Biochemistry and Molecular Biology, Am. Chem. Soc., Royal Chem. Soc. (London), AAAS, N.Y. Acad. Scis., AAUP, AAUW (internat.

fellowship panel 1986-89), NSF, NIH, Amnesty Internat., Urgent Action Network, Sigma Xi. Office: CCNY Dept Chemistry 138th St & Convent Ave New York NY 10031

RUSSELL, COLETTE MARIE, auto sales and leasing company executive; b. Detroit, Dec. 10, 1957; d. Nicholas John and Marie A. (Cooke) Taddia; m. Charles A. Russell, Jr., Aug. 19, 1977; children: Lauren M., Dante G. AA, Macomb Community Coll., Warren, Mich., 1987; student, Oakland U. Exec. sec. Mich. Nat. Bank, Warren, 1976-77; fin. analyst Chrysler Corp., Highland Park, Mich., 1977-80; v.p., owner Titan Excavating, Inc., Utica, Mich., 1980-87; bus. cons., 1987—; controller Barron Leasing, Inc., Utica, 1989—. Mem. Am. Inst. Banking (chpt. rep. 1976-77), Sterling Hts. C. of C. (rep. 1989—), Profl. Tiddly Wink Assn. (pres. 1985—). Republican. Roman Catholic. Home: 44293 Providence Mount Clemens MI 48044

RUSSELL, CRISTINE ELAINE, senior gas contract analyst; b. Ogallala, Nebr., Aug. 20, 1953; d. Donald Eugene and Elaine Marie (Geisert) R.; 1 child, Sanger Anne. BS in Edn., U. Colo., 1976; MBA in Mktg. with high honors, Oklahoma City U., 1989. Independent landman Bill Maddox Oil Properties, Denver, 1979, Baker Oil/Aeon Energy, Denver, 1980-82; field landman Exxon Co. U.S.A., Denver, 1980-81; cons. landman Phoenix Resources Co., Oklahoma City, 1982; staff asst. Anadarko Petroleum Corp., Oklahoma City, 1982-89; sr. gas contract analyst Anadarko Petroleum Corp., Houston, 1989—. Vol. for charity benefits Metro Denver March of Dimes Found., 1976-79, Children's Diabetes Found., Denver, 1976-79, Sickle Cell Anemia Found., Denver, 1976-79. Scholastic scholar Metro Denver March of Dimes, 1971; recipient Scholastic Achievement award Brith Benet Found., Denver, 1971. Mem. NAFE, Denver Assn. Petroleum Landmen, Rocky Mountain Inst. Petroleum Landmen, Colo. Bd. Realtors (assoc.), Okla. Bd. Realtors (assoc.), Natural Gas Assn. of Houston. Republican. Lutheran. Office: Anadarko Petroleum Corp 16855 Northchase PO Box 1330 Houston TX 77251-1330

RUSSELL, ELIZABETH ANN, graphics artist; b. Salisbury, N.C., Aug. 12, 1955; d. Garland Thomas and Mary Elizabeth (Wyatt) R. B Creative Arts, U. N.C., Charlotte, 1977. Tchr. art YMCA, Conover, N.C., 1978-79; picture framer The Finishing Touch, Hickory, N.C., 1982; sr. graphics technician Meredith-Burda Graphics, Hickory, 1982—. Mem. Newton-Conover Rescue Squad. Presbyterian. Home: 105 E Trace Dr Newton NC 28658 Office: Meredith-Burda Graphics Tate Blvd Newton NC 28658

RUSSELL, ELIZABETH G., defense and arms control researcher; b. Chgo., Apr. 15, 1958; d. Charles Wilbur and Patricia Ann (Lincoln) R. BA in Internat. Rels., Mount Holyoke Coll., 1980; postgrad., Dartmouth U., 1980-81, Harvard U., 1983-85, U. Md., 1987—. Aide Sen. Charles H. Percy, Washington, 1979-80; legal historian Nat. Vets. Law Ctr., Washington, 1980-83; researcher Resource Policy Ctr., Hanover, N.H., 1980-81; exec. interviewer Temple, Barker & Sloane, Lexington, Mass., 1987; MacArthur fellow Ctr. Internat. Security Studies U. Md., College Park, 1987-88; rsch. fellow in def. & arms control Ctr. Internat. Security MIT, 1989—. Fundraiser Mass. Abortion Coalition, Boston, 1986; legal aide Nat. Vets. Task Force on Agt. Orange, Washington, 1979-83. Thayer Sch. Engring fellow Dartmouth Coll., 1980-81. Democrat. Club: Yankee Rescue (Andover, Mass.). Home: 139 Weston Rd Wellesley MA 02181

RUSSELL, ELIZABETH IRENE, accountant; b. Commerce, Tex., Jan. 27, 1959; d. Billy Grant and Evelyn Irene (Adams) R. BBA, Stephen F. Austin State U., 1981. CPA, Tex. Staff auditor Touche Ross & Co., Dallas, 1981-82, semi-sr. auditor, 1982-83, sr. auditor, 1983-84; internal audit mgr. Great Am. Res. Ins. Co., Dallas, 1984-87, asst. v.p. audit/analysis, 1987—; bd. dirs., edn. rep. FLMI Soc. N. Tex., Dallas, 1988—. Fellow Life Mgmt. Inst.; mem. AICPA, Tex. Soc. CPA's. Home: 9523 Culberson Dallas TX 75227 Office: Great Am Res Ins Co 2020 Live Oak Dallas TX 75221

RUSSELL, FRANCIA, ballet director, educator; b. Los Angeles, Jan. 10, 1938; d. W. Frank and Marion (Whitney) R.; m. Kent Stowell, Nov. 19, 1965; children: Christopher, Darren, Ethan. Studies with, George Balanchine, Vera Volkova, Felia Doubrouska, Antonina Tumkovsky, Benjamin Harkarvy; student, NYU, Columbia U. Dancer, soloist N.Y.C. Ballet, 1956-62, ballet mistress, 1965-70; dancer Ballets USA/Jerome Robbins, N.Y.C., 1962; tchr. ballet Sch. Am. Ballet, N.Y.C., 1963-64; dir. staging over 90 George Balanchine ballet prodns. including Soviet Union and Peoples Republic of China for the first time., throughout N.Am., Europe and Asia, 1964—; co-dir. Frankfurt (Fed. Republic Germany) Opera Ballet, 1976-77; dir., co-artistic dir. Pacific N.W. Ballet, Seattle, 1977—; affiliate prof. of dance U. Wash. Named Woman of Achievement Matrix Table Women in Communications, Seattle, 1987. Mem. Dance/USA, Ballet Am. (v.p.). Home: 2833 Broadway E Seattle WA 98102 Office: Pacific NW Ballet 4649 Sunnyside Ave N Seattle WA 98103

RUSSELL, HARRIET SHAW, social worker; b. Detroit, Apr. 12, 1952; d. Louis Thomas and Lureleen (Hughes) Shaw; m. Donald Edward Russell, June 25, 1980; children: Lachante Tyree, Krystal Lanae. BS, Mich. State U., 1974; AB, Detroit Bus. Inst., 1976; BA in Pub. Adminstrn., Mercy Coll. Detroit, 1988. Cert. notary pub. Factory employee Gen. Motors Corp., Lansing, Mich., 1973; student supr. tour guides State of Mich., Lansing, 1974; mgr. Ky. Fried Chicken, Detroit, 1974-75; unemployment claims examiner State of Mich. Dept. Labor, Detroit, 1975-77, asst. payment worker, 1977-84, social services specialist, 1984—; moderator Michigan Opportunity Skills and Tng. Program, 1985-86. Vol. Mich. Cancer Soc., East Lansing, 1970-72, Big Sisters/Big Bros., Lansing, 1972-73; elected rep. Mich. Coun. Social Svcs. Workers; speaker Triumphant Bapt. Ch., Detroit, 1976-80; chief union steward Mich. Employees Assn., Lincoln Park, 1982-83; leader Girl Scouts U.S.A.; area capt. Life Worker Project Program. Recipient Outstanding Work Performance Merit award Mich. Dept. Social Services, 1979. Mem. NAFE, Am. Soc. Profl. and Exec. Women, Assn. Internat. Platform Speakers, Mich. Coun. Social Svcs. Workers, Nat. Fedn. Bus. and Profl. Women's Clubs, Inc. U.S.A. (elected del. to China), Delta Sigma Theta. Democrat. Baptist. Office: PO Box 361 Lincoln Park MI 48146

RUSSELL, HEATHER ANNE, management consultant; b. Hannibal, Mo., Dec. 6, 1965; d. Marvin Edward and Anne Sheridan (Volma) R. BSBA in Orgnl. Behavior, U. Ill., 1988. Cons. Andersen Consulting, Chgo., 1988—. Republican. Office: Andersen Consulting 33 W Monroe St Chicago IL 60603

RUSSELL, INEZ SNYDER, executive director non-profit organization; b. Highland Falls, N.Y., June 29, 1951; d. Charles and Catherine (Collins) Snyder; m. William Edward Russell, Mar. 31, 1984; children: Kenneth Shawn, Charles Daniel. Student, McLennan Community Coll., 1971-72, Baylor U., 1972, 79. Pvt. practice cons. Dallas, Austin, Waco and San Antonio, Tex., 1969-79; instr. Datapoint Corp., Waco, 1979-82; founder, pres. The Last Word, Waco, 1982-89; founder, exec. Friends for Life, Waco, 1989—; counselor U.S. Small Bus. Adminstrn. Small Bus. Devel. Ctr.; bd. dirs. The Internat. Women's Resource Ctr. Author: (manual) Control User Guide, 1980, Production Inventory Control User Guide, 1980, Integrated Electronic Office System Reference Manual, 1981, Work Order System, 1981; contbr. articles to profl. jours. Tchr. First Bapt. Ch., Hewitt, Tex., 1980—; mem. occupational adv. com. McLennan Community Coll., 1984—; chairperson Wheels For Life program St. Jude Children's Hosp., Waco, 1987. Mem. NAFE, Cen. Tex. Womens Network, Better Bus. Bur., Internat. Women's Resource Ctr., Nat. Fedn. Ind. Bus., Tex. Computer Industry Council, Greater Waco C. of C. Office: Friends for Life 3801 W Waco Dr Waco TX 76710

RUSSELL, JANE TERRILL, finance executive; b. St. Louis, Mar. 2, 1945; d. Grant Edwin and Stella Norton (Slater) R.; m. David G. Stern, June 27, 1970 (div. May 1978); m. Frederick J.E. Gorman, Feb. 11, 1984. BA, Coll. Wooster, 1967; MBA, Boston Coll., 1980. Asst. dir. pub. procedures course Radcliffe Coll., Cambridge, Mass., 1967-71; editorial asst. Harvard U., Cambridge, Mass., 1972-78; internship coord. Boston Coll., Chestnut Hill, Mass., 1979-80; real estate analyst The Boston Fin Croup Inc., Boston, Mass.; v.p. investor svcs. The Boston Fin. Group Inc., Boston, Mass., 1987-88; dir. Heritage Art, 1989—. Editor: The Charter of Harvard Coll., 1976. Mem. Beacon Hill Civic Assn., Boston, 1982—, the Bulfinch Soc., Boston, 1988—, mem. com. Hist. Neighborhoods Found., Boston, 1988—. Mem. Tennis and Racquet Club. Democrat. Presbyterian.

RUSSELL, KITTY ELIZABETH, legal services consultant; b. Washington, Sept. 26, 1953; d. Jack Keith and Alice Joan (Maphis) R. BA in Am. Govt., U. Va., 1975; paralegal cert., George Wash. U., 1976, MBA/Information Systems, 1983. Loan processor D.C. Nat. Bank, 1975-76; paralegal Howrey & Simon, Washington, 1976-78, Danzansky & Dickey, Washington, 1978-82, Finley, Kumble, Wagner, Heine, Underberg, Manley et al, Washington, 1982-87; paralegal coordinator King & Spalding, Atlanta, 1987-89; mgr. Price Waterhouse, Bethesda, Md., 1990—. Mem. Legal Assts. Mgmt. Assn. (chmn. Atlanta chpt. 1988-89). Home: 101 Skyhill Rd Unit 103 Alexandria VA 22314

RUSSELL, LAURA, psychotherapist; b. Louisville, Aug. 22, 1945; d. Leonard and Esther Bernice (Baker) Potash; m. Thomas Frances Cravens (div. 1970); 1 child, Thomas Lancaster; m. David George Russell, May 18, 1974; 1 child, George Aaron. BA, U. Louisville, 1967, MEd, 1969; MA, Internat. Coll./UWW, Santa Monica, Calif., 1982, PhD, 1985. Cert. counselor. Spl. edn. tchr. II St. Louis State Sch. & Hosp., 1969-70; spl. edn. tchr. Granite City (Ill.) Pub. Schs., 1970-71, L.A. County Supt. Schs., 1971-73; intake counselor Behavioral Health Svcs., Redondo Beach, Calif., 1975-76; drug counselor II UCLA Methadone Clinic, 1976; personnel officer Nat. Black Vets. Orgn., L.A., 1976-77; substitute spl. edn. tchr. L.A. County Supt., 1977; spl. edn. tchr. Lynwood (Calif.) Pub. Schs., 1977-78, Manhattan Beach (Calif.) City Schs., 1978-82; pvt. practice Gentle Support Counseling Svcs., Torrance, Calif., 1983—; spl. edn. tchr. Canyon Verde Sch., Hermosa Beach, Calif., 1982; career guidance tchr. Centinela Valley Union HIgh Sch. Dist., Lawndale, Calif., 1982; cons. South Bay Rape Hotline, Torrance, Calif., 1985-89; psychol. asst. Western Health Svcs., Harbor City, Calif., 1984-85. Author: Gentle Support Trauma Workshop, 1990. Mem. Am. Assn. Marriage and Family Therapy, Am. Assn. Counseling and Devel., Calif. Assn. Marriage and Family Therapists, Calif. State Psychol. Assn., L.A. County Psychol. Assn. Office: Gentle Support Counseling 24050 Madison St Ste 100R&Q Torrance CA 90505

RUSSELL, LOUISE, educator, folklorist; b. Stratford, Okla., Aug. 9, 1931; d. Virgel Wylie and Louise J. (Hayden) R. BA magna cum laude, Oklahoma City U., 1953; MA, Northwestern U., 1955; PhD, Ind. U., 1977. Tchr., Sterling, Colo., 1958-59, Washington-Lee High Sch., Arlington, Va., 1959-62, John Handley High Sch., Winchester, Va., 1962-63, Weld Sch. Dist. No. 6, Greeley, Colo., 1963-68, 72-87, Colegio Internacional, Valencia, Venezuela, 1968-69, Holmdel Schs., N.J., 1971-72; chmn. staff devel. team English and basic skills, subject specialist Northland Pioneer Coll., Holbrook, Ariz., 1987—. Author: Understanding Folklore, 1975, Understanding Folk Music, 1977; also articles. Named Tchr. of Yr. Masons. Mem. MLA, Am. Anthrop. Assn., Am. Folklore Soc., Nat. Coun. Tchrs. English, Apache County Hist. Soc. (mus. bd.), Phi Delta Kappa. Office: Northland Pioneer Coll Saint Johns AZ 85936

RUSSELL, REBECCA PALMER, financial analyst; b. Ankara, Turkey, May 1, 1965; came to U.S., 1965; d. Sargent and Elizabeth Wood (Goodell) R. BA in Linguistics, Cornell U., 1988. Acctg. clk. Logistix, Milpitas, Calif., 1984-85; account analyst Transformational Technologies, Sausalito, Calif., 1985; computer operator DMLL, Cornell U., Ithaca, N.Y., 1985-86; office systems designer Transformational Technologies, Sausalito, 1986; office asst. III DMLL, Cornell U., Ithaca, 1986-88; adminstrv. asst. The Holiday Project, San Francisco, 1987; fin. analyst Wells Fargo Investment Advisors, San Francisco, 1988—. Nat. Merit scholar, 1983; Acad. Yr. fellow, 1986-87, William Knox Holt Found. fellow, 1987-88 Cornell Tradition, Cornell U. Mem. Nat. Assn. Female Execs., Cornell Club. Democrat. Home: 1390 Market St 2212 San Francisco CA 94102

RUSSELL, VIRGINIA WILLIS, foundation administrator, researcher; b. Buffalo, Feb. 13, 1913; d. Jay Burroughs and Faith Lillian (Wright) Willis; m. James Washington Russell; children: James Willis, Brian Jay, Robert Alan, Gary Lloyd. B.A., SUNY-Buffalo, 1934, postgrad., 1934-47. Mem. staff Erie County Emergency Walfare Svcs., 1941-45; rsch. assoc. physics SUNY-Buffalo, 1959-65; tree farmer, Buffalo, 1952—; founder, bd. dir. Universal Field Found., Buffalo, 1958—. Contbr. articles to profl. jours.; editor Audubon Outlook; patentee in field. Mem. Erie County Bd. Suprs.; N.Y. State chmn. conservation Fedn. Women's Clubs' chmn. Women's Day 125th Anniversary Buffalo; bd. dirs. Erie County LWV. Recipient Civil Def. award, Rep. Woman of Yr. award. Mem. N.Y. Acad. Sci., AAAS, Am. Chem. Soc., Planetary Soc., History of Sci. U. Buffalo Alumni Assn. (treas, v.p.), Tesla Soc. (bd. dir.), AAUW, Buffalo Soc. Natural Sci. Republican. Presbyterian. Club: Sierra. Current work: Writing patents on control of Radiation emissions; researching Universal Field equations. Home and Office: Universal Field Found 435 Crescent Ave Buffalo NY 12414

RUSSO, IRMA HAYDEE ALVAREZ DE, pathologist; b. San Rafael, Mendoza, Argentina, Feb. 28, 1942; came to U. S., 1972; d. Jose Maria and Maria Carmen (Martinez) de Alvarez; m. Jose Russo, Feb. 8, 1969; 1 child, Patricia Alexandra. BA, Escuela Normal MTSM de Balcarce, 1959; MD, U. Nat. of Cuyo, Mendoza, 1970. Intern, Sch. of Medicine Hosps., Argentina, 1969-70; resident in pathology Wayne State U. Sch. Medicine, Detroit, 1976-80; rsch. asst. and instr. Inst. of Histology and Embryology Sch. Medicine U. Nat. of Cuyo, 1963-71, assoc. prof. histology Faculty of Phys., Chem. and Math. Scis., 1970-72; rsch. assoc. Inst. for Molecular and Cellular Evolution, U. Miami, Fla., 1972-73; rsch. assoc. exptl. pathology lab. div. biol. scis., Mich. Cancer Found., Detroit, 1973-75, rsch. scientist, 1975-76, vis. rsch. scientist, 1976-82, asst. mem., pathologist, 1982-89, assoc. rsch. mem., 1989—, co-dir. pathology reference lab., 1982-86, chief exptl. pathology lab., 1989—; co-dir. Mich. Cancer Found. Lab. Svcs., 1986—; chief resident physician dept. pathology Wayne State U. Sch. Medicine, 1978-80, asst. prof., 1980-82; mem. staff Harper-Grace Hosps., Detroit, 1980-82; Rockefeller grantee, 1972-73; Nat. Cancer Inst. grantee, 1978-81, 84-87; Am. Cancer Soc. grantee 1988-89; guest lectr. dept. obstetrics Sch. Medicine U. Nat. of Cuyo, 1965-71. Diplomate Am. Bd. Pathology. Mem. AAAS, Nat. Cancer Inst. (breast cancer working group, breast cancer program 1984-88), Nat. Alliance Breast Cancer Orgns. (med. adv. bd. N.Y.C. chpt. 1986—), Coll. Am. Pathologists, Am. Soc. Clin. Pathologists, Am. Assn. for Cancer Research, Mich. Soc. Pathologists, Am. Assn. Clin. Chemistry, Electron Microscopy Soc. Am., Mich. Electron Microscopy Forum, Sigma Xi. Roman Catholic. Contbr. numerous articles on pathology to profl. jours. Office: 110 E Warren Ave Detroit MI 48201

RUSSO, ROSEMARY, computer graphics specialist; b. Flushing, N.Y., Feb. 7, 1951; d. Joseph Leo Russo and Agnes Marie (Ancona) McGrellis. BA in Math., SUNY, Buffalo, 1973; MS, SUNY, Stony Brook, 1978. Permanent teaching cert., N.Y. Tchr. math. Longwood High Sch., Middle Island, N.Y., 1973-74; substitute tchr. Lindenhurst (N.Y.) High Sch., 1974; statis. analyst Grumman Aircraft Systems, Bethpage, N.Y., 1974-78, program bus. mgr., 1978-85; mgr. tng. group Grumman Engring. Mfg. System, Bethpage, N.Y., 1985-88; tng. mgr. CAD, McDonald's Corp., Oak Brook, Ill., 1988—. Mem. NAFE, CADAM Users Exchange (bd. dirs., sec. 1983-85), CADAM Users Exchange N.Am. (bd. dirs. 1985—, chief fin. officer 1985-87, pres. 1987—). Home: 2334 Sedgfield Ct Schaumburg IL 60194

RUSSO, SHARON KAY, psychologist; b. Paris, Tex., Oct. 4, 1948; d. Carthel R. and Murrell J. (Wortham) Green; m. William J. Russo, Apr. 1, 1972; 1 child, Jessica N. BA, East Tex. State U., 1970, MEd, 1973, EdD, 1979. Lic. psychologist; cert. provisional secondary tchr., profl. spl. edn. counselor. High sch. tchr. Kaufman (Tex.) Ind. Schs., 1970-71; mid. sch. tchr. Mesquite (Tex.) Ind. Sch. Dist., 1971-74; sch. counselor Garland (Tex.) Ind. Sch. Dist., 1974-79, sch. psychologist, 1979-85; prin. Sharon K. Russo, Ed.D., Garland, 1985—; cons. psychologist, practicum supr. Carrollton (Tex.)-Farmers Br. Ind. Sch. Dist., 1985—; contract staff Brookhaven Psychiat. Pavillion, Dallas, 1990—. Mem. Am. Psychol. Assn. Office: Sharon K Russo EdD 2301 Forest Ln Ste 101 Garland TX 75042

RUSSO, VIVIAN ALFONSINA, cosmetic company executive, creative consultant; b. Bklyn., Apr. 21, 1949; d. Louis Anthony and Iole Primetta (Barbaglia) R.; m. Robert Ferro, May 26, 1968 (div. 1975). Student Bernard Baurch Coll., 1966, Brooklyn Coll., 1967, Fashion Inst. Tech., 1971-77. Assoc. advt. mgr. Kayser-Roth Corp., N.Y.C., 1968-77; advt. and sales promotion mgr. GAF Corp., N.Y.C., 1977-80; sales promotion and merchandising mgr. Revlon, N.Y.C., 1980-82; dir. creative services Del Labs., Farmingdale, N.Y., 1982—; lectr. Briarcliff Bus. Coll., Hicksville, N.Y., 1985. Creative dir. (coop. program) Co-op Advt. Credit Card Program (Sales and Mktg. Mgmt. Mag. award), 1976, (sampling program) Excello Shirts-Fabric Swatch (Sales and Mktg. Mgmt. Mag. award), 1977, (product catalogue) View-Master Catalogue (Nat. Endowment Arts award), 1978, GAF Star-Vinyl Floors Catalogue (Nat. Endowment Arts award), 1980. Friend of Bd. Nat. Found. Ileitis and Colitis, Inc., N.Y.C., 1981. Recipient Mgmt. award Am. Mgmt. Assn., 1979. Mem. Cosmetic Exec. Women, Advt. Women N.Y., Inc., The Fashion Group, Theatre Guild Assn. Republican. Roman Catholic. Avocations: Tennis; painting; photography; fishing. Office: Del Labs 565 Broadhollow Rd Farmingdale NY 11735

RUST, PATRICIA JOAN, television production company executive, writer/producer; b. L.A., Sept. 24, 1958; d. William Evans Jr. and Jacquelyn (Knox) R.; m. Victor Frederic Phillips III, Mar. 29, 1986. BA, UCLA, 1978, postgrad., 1978-80, 87-89; student, Am. Film Inst. Internat. fashion model, 1972-78; writer, producer PBS, L.A., 1978-79; corr. ABC-TV, L.A., 1979-82; pres. Patricia Rust Prodns., L.A., Honolulu, 1982—; communications cons. U. Hawaii, Honolulu, 1983-84; founder Palisades Women's Surfing Assn., 1977; host, writer, creator, producer numerous syndicated spls., 1982-89; host, moderator local TV debates, Santa Monica, Calif., 1985—; writer, producer comedy shows and spls. Prime Time Network. Syndicated columnist The Rust Report, 1986—; film and TV writer including network comedy spls., TV movies, episodes including The Entertainment Report, The Rust Report, On Cue, On Location; contbr. articles to profl. publs. and mags. including monthly column for Beverly Hills: The Magazine; author Dewey, 1990; creator TV series Friends in the Sea, 1990. Mem. Fashionettes, Hollywood Presbyn. Hosp., 1988—. Recipient Golden Mike award Radio and TV News Assn., Hollywood, 1984, award Kiwanis Club, Honolulu, 1984; named Miss Flame, L.A. County Fire Dept., 1976, Miss Am. Health and Beauty, 1976; winner comedy writing competition Am. Film Inst., 1989. Mem. NATAS, Hollywood Radio and TV Soc., Nat. Cable TV Acad., Assn. Producers and Assoc. Producers, Women in Film, Assn. for Women in Entertainment, TV Acad. Writers Repetory Group, Malibu-Pacific Club, Masters Swim Team, Am. Film Inst. Office: Patricia Rust Prodns 616 San Vicente Blvd Ste A Santa Monica CA 90402

RUST, RACHEL LOUISE, family therapist; b. Wharton, Tex., Oct. 18, 1955; d. Lloyd Gates and Rose Marie (Dominy) R. B.Social Work, U. Tex.-Austin, 1978; M.S., U. Tex.-Dallas, 1981; M.S. in Social Work, U. Tex.-Arlington, 1983. Cert. social worker, Assn. Cert. Social Workers; advance clin. practitioner. Group counselor Salesmanship Club Youth Camps, Palestine, Tex., 1978-80; case mgr. Juliette Fowler Home, Inc., Dallas, 1981-82; family therapist Salesmanship Club Ctr., Dallas, 1983—. Mem. Nat. Assn. Social Workers, Mental Health Assn., Tex. Corrections Assn. Presbyterian. Club: 500 Inc (Dallas). Home: 5907 LaVista Dallas TX 75206 Office: Salesmanship Club Dallas Ctr 110 E 10th St Dallas TX 75203

RUTENBERG-ROSENBERG, SHARON LESLIE, journalist; b. Chgo., May 23, 1951; d. Arthur and Bernice (Berman) R.; m. Michael J. Rosenberg, Feb. 3, 1980; children—David Kaifel and Jonathan Reuben (twins). Student, Harvard U., 1972; B.A., Northwestern U., 1973, M.S.J., 1975; cert. student pilot. Reporter-photographer Lerner Home Newspapers, Chgo., 1973-74; corr. Medill News Service, Washington, 1975; reporter-newsperson, sci. writer UPI, Chgo., 1975—. Interviewer: exclusives White House chief of staff, nation's only mother and son on death row; others. Vol. Chgo.-Read Mental Health Ctr. Recipient Peter Lisagor award for exemplary journalism in features category, 1980, 81; Golden Key Nat. Adv. Bd. of Children's Oncology Service Inc., 1981; Media awards for wire service feature stories, 1983, 84, wire service news stories, 1983, 84, all from Chgo. Hosp. Pub. Relations Soc. Mem. Profl. Assn. Diving Instrs., Nat. Assn. Underwater Instrs., Hon. Order Ky. Cols., Hadassah, Sigma Delta Chi, Sigma Delta Tau. Home: 745 Marion Ave Highland Park IL 60035

RUTGERS, KATHARINE PHILLIPS (MRS. FREDERIK LODEWIJK RUTGERS), dancer; b. Butler, Pa., Sept. 2, 1910; d. Thomas Wharton and Alma (Sherman) Phillips; diploma Briarcliff Coll., 1928; student L'Hermiage, Versailles, France, 1929-30; pupil ballet Vera Trefilova, Paris, Carl Raimund, Vienna, Varga Troyanoff, Budapest; pupil modern dance with Iris Barbura, Bucharest Ballet, Vincenzo Celli, N.Y.C., Igor Schwezoff, N.Y.C., Jean Yazvinsky, N.Y.C.; m. Frederik Lodewijk Rutgers, Feb. 2, 1942; children—Alma, Corinne (Mrs. James Tolles). Performed dance concerts Bucharest, 1937-40, U.S., 1941—; repertoire includes patriotic, dramatic, poetical dances, religious interpretations; dance therapist St. Barnabas Hosp., N.Y.C., 1965-70. Chmn. ethnol. dance dept. Bruce Museum Assos., Greenwich, Conn., 1970—. Bd. dirs. Bruce Museum. Recipient citation for promoting culture with dance programs Nat. Fedn. Music Clubs, 1973. Mem. Conn. Fedn. Music Clubs (chmn. dance dept. 1965-66), Nat. League Am. Pen Women (local pres. 1973-78), Alliance Francaise, Mayflower Soc., Colonial Dames Am., DAR, Federated Music Club N.Y.C. (dir., dance chmn.). Clubs: Met. Farm and Garden (dir.) (N.Y.C.), Indian Harbor (Greenwich, Conn.). Author numerous pamphlets on the dance, also verses for choreographies. Home: La Cova Pecks Land Rd Greenwich CT 06830 Studio: 211 W 58th St New York NY 10023

RUTH, IRMA, executive; b. Amarillo, Tex., May 6, 1929; d. Lee McKamie and Gertrude B. (Griffin) McBride; children: Valene Ann Pollak, Marcia Jean Wilcox. BA in Bus. Admistrn., Nat. U., San Diego, 1979, M, 1980. Pub. relations rep. The Marquardt Corp., Ogden, Utah, 1961; salesperson mutual fund & ins. Mutual Fund Assoc., San Diego, 1963-67; exec. sec. Solar Turbines, San Diego, 1967-75, adminstrv. asst., specialist, sales rep., 1977-80; mgr. project Solar Turbines, 1980-84; mgr. equal employment opportunity Solar Turbines, San Diego, 1984-85; retired, 1985-87; v.p., adminstrn. Altresco, Inc., Denver, Colo., 1987-89; pres. Custon Land Cruises, 1989—.

RUTH, LOIS-JEAN, statistical analyst, business manager; b. Abbottstown, Pa., Aug. 24, 1931; d. Stewart Philip and Florence Kathryn (Mummert) Ruth. BA, Pa. State U., 1953. Engring. expeditor AMP Inc., Harrisburg, Pa., 1953-56, statis. analyst, 1956-59, head statis. analysis, 1959-73, systems procedures coord., 1957-73, mem. divisional cost improvement com., 1966-73, sales stats. tng. coord., 1963-73; v.p., asst. sec. Mobile Home Brokers Inc., Hanover, Pa., 1973-83; co-owner Suburban Developers, Gettysburg, Pa.; office mgr., loan processor Shelter Am. Corp, Aurora, Colo., 1984; v.p., treas. GTP Enterprises, Inc., Gettysburg; supr. caseworkers. Domestic Rels. Office Adams County, Pa., 1986-88; with Harry Ness & Co., 1988; v.p. fin. and adminstrn. Adams County United Way, 1988—. Chmn. legis. task force Pa. Mfg. Housing Assn., Harrisburg, Pa., 1979-80. Mem. Gov.'s Com. for Constl. Rev., State of Pa., 1963-66; chmn. Parks and Recreation Commn., 1966-72; sec. Zoning Hearing Bd., 1972-79; mem. Zoning Revision Com., Boro of New Cumberland, Pa., 1977-79; mem. exec. bd., chmn. personnel YWCA, Gettysburg, 1980-83; mem. Indoor Sports Complex Fund Commn., 1978-81; active Coll. Liberal Arts Endowment Fund; mem. alumni coun. Pa. State U., 1984—, bd. advisers, Mont Alto. Mem. AAUW (bd. dirs. 1954-56), Coll. of Liberal Arts Alumni Soc. (pres. 1982-88, Alumni award 1988), Dwight Eisenhower Soc., Pa. Fedn. Women's Clubs (pres., chmn. legis. com. New Cumberland, Pa. chpt.), Phi Mu. Republican. Methodist. Home: 841 Hancock Dr Lake Heritage Gettysburg PA 17325

RUTH, MARSHA DIANE, hospital chief financial officer; b. Lafe, Ark., Dec. 7, 1950; d. Bueford and Ellen Emmaline (Williams) Hendrix; m. Louis Michael Miller, Aug. 14, 1971 (div. Apr. 1981); m. Leslie Lee Ruth, Jr., Nov. 9, 1985. BS, U. Ark., Little Rock, 1975; MBA, U. Ark., 1981. CPA Ark. Asst. internal auditor U. Ark. Med. Scis., Little Rock, 1976-77; dir. internal audit U. Ark. Med. Scis., 1977-80; dir. patient accounts Univ. Hosp. Ark., Little Rock, 1980-81; fin. mgr. Univ. Hosp. Ark., 1981-82, asst. dir. clin. fin., 1982-83, dir. clin. fin., 1983—; chmn. cost and productivity monitoring com. Univ. Hosp. Consortium, Oakbrook Terrace, Ill., 1987-89. Mem. Healthcare Fin. Mgmt. Assn. (advanced), Ark. Soc. CPAs, Ark. Health Execs. Forum, Phi Kappa Phi, Beta Gamma Sigma. Democrat. Baptist. Office: Univ Hosp Ark 4301 W Markham Slot 726 Little Rock AR 72205

RUTHCHILD, GERALDINE QUIETLAKE, training and development consultant, writer, poet; d. Nathan and Ruth (Feldman) Stein. BA summa cum laude, Queens Coll., 1977; MA in Am. Lit., Johns Hopkins U., 1980, PhD in Am. Lit., 1983. Asst. prof. Albion (Mich.) Coll., 1982-84; assoc. Investor Access Corp., N.Y.C., 1984-85; program dir. Exec. Enterprises, Inc., N.Y.C., 1985-86; pres. Ruthchild Assocs., N.Y.C., 1987-90, Exemplar, N.Y.C., 1991—; cons. to Citibank N.A., Chase Manhattan Bank N.A., Nat. Westminster Bank, U.S.A., Robert Morris Assocs., Dean Witter Reynolds, Inc., others, 1987—. Contbr. articles, poems to profl. and lit. jours. Vol. handicapped children N.Y. Foundling Hosp., N.Y.C., 1988—, Fgn. Visitors Desk, Met. Mus. of Art, N.Y.C., 1989—. Hopkins fellow Johns Hopkins U., 1979-80, Andrew Mellon Found. fellow, 1980-81, 81-82. Mem. ASTD, Assn. Bank Trainers and Cons., Internat. Soc. Philos. Enquiry, Phi Beta Kappa. Office: Exemplar 501 E 87th St 12th Fl New York NY 10128

RUTKOVSKY, LISA ELLEN, pediatrician; b. Bklyn., Jan. 6, 1962; d. Charles and Frances (Shinehoft) Rosner; m. Edward Victor Rutkovsky, Jan. 13, 1985. BA in Chemistry, Queen's Coll., 1982; MD, NYU, 1986. Intern pediatrics Bellevue Hosp. NYU, N.Y.C., 1986-87; resident pediatrics North Shore U. Hosp., Manhasset, N.Y., 1987-89; pediatric cardiology fellow Bellevue Hosp. NYU, N.Y.C., 1989—. Fellow Am. Acad. Pediatrics; mem. Phi Beta Kappa. Office: Bellevue Hosp Pediatric Cardiology 1st Ave at 27th St New York NY 11016

RUTLEDGE, CAROL MARIE BRUNNER, writer, historian; b. Newton, Kans., Mar. 9, 1938; d. Daniel and Alice May (Anderson) Brunner; m. Donavon Roby Rutledge, July 13, 1957; children: Lance D., Daniel E., Doni Marie, Joel Roby. BA cum laude, Wichita (Kans.) State U., 1977. Rsch. asst. Wichita Unified Sch. Dist., 1978-80, rsch. technician, info. dissemination, 1980-86, asst. supr. test editing, 1986-88; exec. dir. Hist. Topeka, Kans., 1989; freelance writer Topeka, 1989—. Author: We Had Feelings, 1979, A Time to Remember, 1981, The Brothers of Ark Valley, 1985, The Story of Wichita, 1986, The Women of Hypatia, 1986; playwright: Threads of My Life, 1981, Trappers and Traders of Plains, 1983, Hidden on the Prairie, 1983, Come to Stay, 1986; contbg. writer ednl. cablevision programs. Mem. Wichita Libr. Bd., 1982-88; producer Summer-Shakespeare in the Park, Wichita, 1982-87; founder Midtown Citizens Assn. for restoration of hist. inner city; past bd. dirs. Work Options for Women, YWCA, Wichita Free U., Vol. Action Agy. Recipient Woman of Yr. Matrix award Women in Communications, 1976, Good Neighbor award Midtown Citizens' Assn., 1977, Liberty Bell award Wichita Bar Assn., 1981. Democrat. Mem. Christian Ch. (Disciples of Christ). Home and Office: 1500 SW Plass Ave Topeka KS 66604

RUTMAN, SUSAN H., visual artist, photographer, entrepreneur; b. Bklyn., Jan. 16, 1948; d. Hyman L. and Judy (Sontag) R. B.F.A., Boston U., 1969. Sculptor, art tchr. Pub. Schs., Watertown, Mass., 1969-72; owner, sculptor The Craft Arcade, St. Johnsbury, Vt., 1972-76; freelance photographer, N.Y.C., 1976—; pres. The Townhouse Collection, N.Y.C., 1981-86. Mem. Nat. Assn. Female Execs., Small Bus. Service Bur., Am. Woman's Econ. Devel. Corp., Am. Craft Council, NOW.

RUTTER, DEBORAH FRANCES, orchestra administrator; b. Pottstown, Pa., Sept. 30, 1956; d. Marshall Anthony and Winifred (Hitz) R. BA, Stanford U., 1978; MBA, U. So. Calif., 1985. Orch. mgr. L.A. Philharm., 1978-86; exec. dir. L.A. Chamber Orch., 1986—. Bd. dirs. AIDS project Los Angeles, 1985—, Assn. Calif. Symphony Orch., 1987—, pres. 1988—; active Jr. League Los Angeles, 1982—. Mem. Am. Symphony Orch. League, Assn. Calif. Symphony Orchs., Chamber Music Soc. L.A. (bd. dirs. 1987—), Ojai Festival (pres.'s coun.). Democrat. Episcopalian. Office: LA Chamber Orch 315 W 9th St Ste 300 Los Angeles CA 90015

RUTTER, ITALA T.C., Italian language educator; b. Trieste, Italy, Dec. 16, 1940; came to U.S., 1953; d. Royal Ross and Maria (Pieri) Coryell; m. George W. Rutter (div. 1968). BA, UCLA, 1970, MA, 1974, PhD, 1977. Asst. prof. Romance langs. U. Mich., Ann Arbor, 1977-78; asst. prof. comparative lit. U. Calif., San Diego, 1978-79; asst. prof., postdoctoral fellow in Italian UCLA, 1979-80; asst. prof. Italian U. Ill., Chgo., 1980-83, Wheaton Coll., Norton, Mass., 1983—. Contbr. articles to profl. jours. Mem. scholarship com. Pirandello Lyceum, Cambridge, Mass., 1989-90. Fulbright fellow, 1985, 89. Mem. Am. Assn. Italian Studies, Assn. Internazionale per le Studio della Lingua e Letteratura Italiana, MLA, Renaissance Soc. Am., Am. Boccaccio Assn. Home: One Hart St Providence RI 02906

RUTZ, KAREN ELISABETH, marketing executive; b. Chgo., July 29, 1954; d. Erwin August and Gertrud (Staack) R.; m. Daniel Raymond Porth, Sept. 3, 1977 (div. Mar. 1982). BA in Biology, William Woods Coll., 1975; BA in Nursing, Baylor U., 1977; MBA, U. Dallas, 1984. RN. Staff nurse Children's Med. Ctr., Dallas, 1977-78; operating room staff nurse Baylor Univ. Med. Ctr., Dallas, 1978-84; mktg. dir. Emergicenter Physician Care, Dallas, 1983-84; dir. mktg. Baylor Health Care System, Dallas, 1984-86; pres. MediMax Mgmt. Systems, Dallas, 1986-87; sales rep. Ender Assocs., Inc., Dallas, 1987-88; dir. research and devel. Roll-A-Sheet, Inc., Dallas, 1987-89; project mgr. dept. edn. programs Joint Commn. on Accreditation of Healthcare Orgns., Chgo., 1989—; office mgr. Northlake Family Clinic, Dallas; vol. Alumni Career Assistance Program U. Dallas. Author, programmer (software) Lintrax, 1986. Mem. Nat. Honor and Profl. Mgmt., Am. Mgmt. Assn., Nat. Assn. Female Execs., Dallas Women's Found., Health Services Grad. Assn. (pres. 1984-85), Sigma Iota Epsilon, Alpha Phi. Republican. Lutheran. Club: Evangelism and Singles (Dallas) (advisor 1985—). Home: 59 Norfolk Clarendon Hills IL 60514 Office: 871 N Michigan Ave Chicago IL 60611

RUYLE-HULLINGER, ELIZABETH SMITH (BETH RUYLE-HULLINGER), association executive; b. Atlanta, Oct. 26, 1946; d. Daniel Lester and Mae (Coley) Smith; BA, U. Fla., 1968; MPA, U. Ga., 1975; m. Craig Harlan Hullinger, Oct. 24, 1985; children: Clint, Bret, Leigh Ann. Health planner Met. Council for Health, Atlanta, 1970-72; govtl. relations coord. Atlanta Regional Commn., 1972-76, govtl. affairs coord., 1976-78; exec. dir. South Suburban Mayors' and Mgrs. Assn., Homewood, Ill., 1978—; exec. dir. South Towns Agy. Risk Mgmt., 1980—, South Towns Area Benefits Coop., 1983—, South Towns Bus. Growth Corp., 1983—; cons. Planning Devel. Svc., University Park, Ill., 1986—. Mem. World's Fair Adv. Com., Chgo., 1986, Met. Planning Coun., Cook County Housing Adv. Com., Cook County Tax Reform adv. council, South Suburban Arts Coun., Ill. Airport Adv. Coun., Coun. Urban Econ. Devel., 1986, adv. coun. Urban Innovations, Chgo., 1987, Chgo. Assembly Project; mem. The Regional Partnership; bd. dirs. South Suburban Hosp., Regional Econ. Devel. Coordinating Coun. of the So. Suburbs. Mem. Internat. City Mgmt. Assn., Ill. City Mgmt. Assn., Met. City Mgrs. Assn., Ill. Pub. Employer Labor Rels. Assn., Pub. Risk Ins. Mgmt. Assn., South Suburban Chiefs of Police Assn., South Suburban C. of C., Chgo. Assn. Commerce and Industry, Plank Rd. Trail Assn., Lambda Alpha (mem. land econ. soc. Ely Chpt.). Methodist. Contbr. articles to profl. and devel. mags. Home: 1415 Pinewoods Ct University Park IL 60466 Office: South Suburban Mayors/Mgrs Assn 1154 Ridge Rd Homewood IL 60430

RUZICKA, ANNETTE MARIE, communications administrator; b. Fond du Lac, Wis., June 18, 1960; d. Wayne Arthur and Elaine (Burkhardt) Borst; m. Bradley Robert Ruzicka, May 22, 1982. BS, U. Wis., Platteville, 1981; postgrad., Cardinal Stritch Coll., Milw., 1989—. Announcer Sta. WSWW-AM/FM, Platteville, 1981-82; pub. relations asst. Assn. for Retarded Citizens, Madison, Wis., 1982-83; admissions mgr. Capri Cosmetology Coll., Madison, 1983-84; communications asst. Greater Milw. Conv. Bur., 1984-85, communications mgr., 1985-87, communications/membership mgr., 1987-89; dir. communications Minn. Soc. CPAs, Mpls., 1989—. Editor monthly newsletter Footnote, 1989—; contbr. articles to profl. jours. Mem. Women in Communications (bd. dirs. 1990—, v.p. membership 1990—), Am. Soc. Assn. Execs., Internat. Assn. Bus. Communicators. Democrat. Roman Catholic. Home: 1759 Kirkwood Ln N Plymouth MN 55441 Office: Minn Soc CPAs 7900 Xerxes Ave S Suite 1230 Minneapolis MN 55341

RUZICKA, VICKI, marketing executive; b. Chgo., Apr. 30, 1945; d. Victor Hugo and Ellyn Marie (Doyle) Reid, stepdaughter John Reid. B.S., Northeastern Ill. U., Chgo., 1976. Prodn. mgr. Signature Direct Response Mktg., Evanston, Ill., 1981-82, purchasing mgr., 1983-84; credit promotions media mgr. Montgomery Ward, Chgo., 1982-83; fulfillment purchasing mgr. The Signature Group, Schaumburg, Ill., 1984-87; sr. credit analyst Citicorp Diners Club, Chgo., 1987-88; mgr. advt., prodn. Maginnis and Assocs., 1989—. Author: Trips: Head, Bod and Side, 1968; contbr. articles and poetry to mags. and profl. jours. including Am. Poetry Anthology, Poetry Mag., Lifestyle Lit. Jour. Served with USAF, 1979-83. Mem. Women's Direct Response Group, Feminist Writers Guild, Sierra Club, Wilderness Soc. Roman Catholic. Avocations: sailing, golf, classical piano, baseball.

RUZINSKY, ELLEN FERN, market research company executive; b. Paterson, N.J., June 4, 1961; d. Edwin Howard and Enid Gilda (Schnitzer) R.; m. Evan Jay Lerner, Dec. 20, 1986. BS, Ithaca Coll., 1983. Asst. project dir. Simmons Market Rsch. Bur., N.Y.C., 1983-84, project mgr., 1984-85, mgr., 1985-86, sales exec., 1986-88, v.p., 1988—. Mem. Media Rsch. Dirs. Assn., Bus. Advt. Rsch. Coun., Advt. Rsch. Found. Democrat. Jewish. Office: Simmons Market Rsch Bur 380 Madison Ave New York NY 10017

RYAN, CAROLINE MENSLAGE, insurance training executive; b. Quincy, Mass., Feb. 20, 1939; d. George C. Sr. and Eileen V. (Connors) Menslage; m. George E. Ryan, Sept. 24, 1966; children: Fredrick, DAvid, Carrie, Patricia, Colleen, Caitlin. BA, Regis Coll., 1960; MEd, Boston State Coll., 1980; postgrad., Am. Coll., Bryn Mawr, Pa. Registered rep. multi-line fin. svcs. Secondary sch. tchr. Hanover (Mass.) Pub. Schs.; account rep. Met. Life, Hingham, Mass.; field tng. instr. Met. Life, NEHO, Warwick, R.I. Mem. NAFE, Boston Life Underwriters Assn., Nat. Assn. LIfe Underwriters. Home: 163 Bulrush Farm Rd North Scituate MA 02066 Office: PO Box 459 Hingham MA 02043 Also: 25 Recreation Park Dr Hingham MA 02043

RYAN, CATHY KAMAN, lawyer; b. Rochester, N.Y., Feb. 27, 1953; d. Jack A. and Carol (Katzen) K.; m. James F. Ryan, May 16, 1981; children: Kerry Kaman, Kevin Connor. BS in Journalism, Northwestern U., Evanston, Ill., 1975; JD, SUNY, Buffalo, 1980. Bar: N.Y. 1981, U.S. Dist. Ct. (we. dist.) N.Y. 1981. Mng. editor Brighton-Pittsford (N.Y.) Post, 1976-77; law clk. to U.S. Atty. U.S. Dist. Ct. (we. dist.) N.Y., Buffalo, 1978; assoc. Nixon Hargrave Devans & Doyle, Rochester, 1980-89; spl. counsel Phillips, Lytle, Hitchcock, Blaine & Huber, Rochester, 1989—. Contbg. author: Problems in Law of Mass Communications, 1976. Active Perinton Rep. Town Com., Fairport, N.Y., 1981-85. Mem. N.Y. State Bar Assn. (mem. subcom. on condominiums 1983—), Monroe County Bar Assn. (mem. real estate coun. 1983-87). Jewish. Office: Phillips Lytle et al 1400 1st Federal Pla Rochester NY 14614

RYAN, ELEANORE A., clinical psychologist; b. Chgo.; BS with honors in Chemistry, Mundelein Coll.; PhD in Clin. Psychology, Northwestern U., 1978; children: Robert, James, Mark, John, Christopher, Marynel. Staff psychologist Porter-Starke Services, Valparaiso, Ind., 1978-80; psychol. cons. Gary (Ind.) Community Mental Health Center, 1980-81; pvt. practice clin. and cons. psychology, Clarendon Hills, Ill., 1981—; dir. Assocs. in Clin. Treatment, 1987—; psychologist Hines VA Hosp. (Ill.), 1983-88, Oak Park (Ill.) Vet. Ctr., 1988—. Cert. psychologist, Ill., Ind. Mem. Am. Psychol. Assn., Ill. Psychol. Assn., Midwest Psychol. Assn., Assn. DuPage Psychologists (pres. 1990), Nat. Register Health Service Providers in Psychology, Soc. for Clin. and Exptl. Hypnosis, Soc. for Traumatic Stress Studies, Health Services Adv. Bd., DuPage Assn. for Children with Learning Disabilities (mem. adv. bd.), Chgo. Psychologists in Addictive Behavior, Consortium Vietnam Vet. Service Providers. Roman Catholic. Home and Office: 215 Coe Rd Clarendon Hills IL 60514

RYAN, ELLIE LOUISE, cooperate training executive; b. Mansfield, Ohio, Mar. 9, 1945; d. Frank Philip and Florence Alice (Dunmire) Volz; m. Oct. 9, 1965 (div. 1984); children: Rebekah Gale, R. Philip, Heather Gwen. Student, Saddleback Coll., 1988—. Owner, pres. Psychodynamic Sucess Inst., Lake Forest, Calif., 1983—, Indoor Tng. Systems, Inc., Laguna Hills, Calif., 1987--; owner The Great Ropes, Lake Forest, Calif., 1986--. Author: Kinesic Engineering, 1985, inventor,The Great Ropes, 1986, P.A.C.E., 1986. Block parent Irvine Sch. Bd., 1980-83. Mem. Nordonia Hills Women's Club. Republican. Office: The Great Ropes 24412 Muirlands Blvd Lake Forest CA 92630

RYAN, HOLLY ANNE, nurse, civic worker; b. Oak Park, Ill., Dec. 25, 1945; d. Bernard Lawrence and Ethel Eleanor (Kropf) Daleske; m. Patrick Michael Ryan, Aug. 31, 1968; children: Rebecca, Brendan, Abigail, Lucas. Student, Coll. St. Teresa, 1963-65; diploma in nursing, Oak Park Hosp., 1968. R.N., Wis. Staff nurse Misericordia Hosp., Milw., 1968-69, Dean Clinic, Madison, Wis., 1969-70, Marina View Manor, Milw., 1970-76. Cochair gen. gifts, United Performing Arts Fund, Milw., 1976-77; panel mem., United Way Ozaukee County, Milw., 1978-84; pres., Cedarburg (Wis.) Presch., 1980-81; chair, Citizen Rev. Bd. Milwaukee County, 1981-84; bd. dirs., Cedarburg Youth Ctr., 1987—; mem., treas. Cedarburg Sch. Dist. Bd. Edn., 1988—; active Ctr. for Integrated Living, 1989—. Mem. Jr. League Milw. (chair 1981-84), Cedarburg Soccer Club (sec. 1987-89). Home: 363 Huntington Dr Cedarburg WI 53012

RYAN, IONE JEAN ALOHILANI, educator, counselor; b. Honolulu, Oct. 18, 1926; d. William Alexander and Lilia (Nainoa) Rathburn; m. Edward Parsons Ryan, June 23, 1962 (dec.); children: Ralph M., Lilia K. BEd, U. Hawaii, 1948; MS in Pub. Health, U. Minn., 1950; EdD, Stanford U., 1960. Lic. marital and family therapist. Tchr. W.R. Farrington High Sch., Honolulu, 1948; instr. to asst. prof. U. Hawaii, Honolulu, 1950-66; assoc. prof. to prof., counselor East Carolina U., Greenville, N.C., 1966—; adv. com. Eastern Regional Tng. Program, Greenville, N.C., 1975-80; cons. Title III Grant, Lenoir Community Coll., Kinston, N.C., 1981; adult svcs. adv. com. Pitt County Mental Health, Greenville, N.C., 1976-78. Contbr. articles to profl. publs. Recipient scholarship Honolulu C. of C., 1948-50. Mem. Am. Psychol. Assn., N.C. Coll. Personnel Assn., N.C. Assn. Counseling & Devel. Republican. Mormon. Office: East Carolina University Counseling Ctr Wright Bldg 315 Greenville NC 27858

RYAN, SISTER JANICE E., college administrator, nun. BA in English, Trinity Coll., 1965; MEd in Spl. Edn., Boston U., 1967; postgrad., U. Minn., 1968, U. Lund, Sweden, 1971, Harvard U., 1974-76, 80. Dir. pub. relations Trinity Coll., Burlington, Vt., 1967-71, asst. prof. spl. edn., 1967-74, pres., 1979—; mem. Am. Council on Edn.'s Govtl. Relations Commn. on Nat. Challenges in Higher Edn.; corporator, dir. Bank of Vt., trustee Vt. Law Sch.; task force on econ. devel. infrastructure, edn. and tng. NE-Midwest Leadership Council. Exec. com. Campus Compact, chair fed. initiatives task force; active Vt. Higher Edn. Council. Am. Assn. Higher Edn. (participant Spring Hill Conf. 1987). Office: Trinity Coll 208 Colchester Ave Burlington VT 05401*

RYAN, LORETTA ANN, pediatrician; b. Galesburg, Ill., Dec. 7, 1955; d. Joseph James and Rose Mary (Dages) Ryan; m. Eric John Tuegel, Apr. 23, 1983; 1 child, Thomas Ian. BS, St. Mary of the Woods Coll., 1978; MD, U. Ill., 1982. Diplomate Am. Bd. Pediatrics. Pvt. practice Alton, Ill., 1985—. Mem. AMA, Am. Acad. Pediatrics. Office: Pediatric/Adolescent Health 215 E Center Dr Ste E Alton IL 62002

RYAN, MARLEIGH GRAYER, Japanese language educator; b. N.Y.C., May 1, 1930; d. Harry and Betty (Hurwick) Grayer; m. Edward Ryan, June 4, 1950; 1 child, David Patrick. B.A., NYU, 1951; M.A., Columbia U., 1956, Ph.D., 1965; Cert., East Asian Inst., 1956; postgrad., Kyoto U., 1958-59. Research assoc. Columbia U., N.Y.C., 1960-61, lectr. Japanese, 1961-65, asst. prof., 1965-70, assoc. prof., 1970-72; vis. asst. prof. Yale U., New Haven, 1966-67; assoc. prof. U. Iowa, Iowa City, 1972-75, prof., 1975-81, chmn. dept., 1972-81; prof. Japanese SUNY, New Paltz, 1981—, dean liberal arts and scis., 1981-90; vice chair seminar on modern Japan, Columbia U., 1984-85, chair, 1985-86; co-chmn. N.Y. State Conf. on Asian Studies, 1986. Co-author: (with Herschel Webb) Research in Japanese Sources, 1965; author: Japan's First Modern Novel, 1967, The Development of Realism in the Fiction of Tsubouchi Shoyo, 1975; assoc. editor: Jour. Assn. Tchrs. Japanese, 1962-71, editor, 1971-75. East Asian Inst. fellow Columbia U., 1955; Ford Found. fellow, 1958-60; Japan Found. fellow, 1973, Woodrow Wilson Ctr. Internat. Scholars fellow, 1988-89; recipient Van. Am. Disting. Book award Columbia, 1968. Mem. MLA (sec. com. on teaching Japanese Lang. 1962-68, mem. del. assembly 1979-87, mem. exec. com. div. Asian lit. 1981-86), Assn. Tchrs. Japanese (exec. com. 1969-72, 74-77), Assn. Asian Studies (bd. dirs. 1975-78), Midwest Conf. Asian Studies (pres. 1980-81). Office: SUNY FT 414 New Paltz NY 12561

RYAN, MARY A., diplomat; b. New York, N.Y., Oct. 1, 1940. B.A., St. John's Univ., 1963, M.A., 1965. With Foreign Service, Dept. of State, 1966—; consular and adminstrv. officer Naples, Italy, 1966-69; personnel officer Am. Embassy, Tegucigalpa, Honduras, 1970-71; consular officer Am. Consulate Gen., Monterrey, Mexico, 1971-73; adminstrv. officer Bur. of African Affairs, Dept. of State, Washington, 1973-75, post mgmt. officer, 1975-77; career devel. officer Bur. of Personnel, Dept. of State, 1977-80; adminstrv. counselor Abidjan, Ivory Coast, 1980-81, Khartoum, Sudan, 1981-82; inspector, Office of Insp. Gen. Dept. of State, Washington, 1982-83, exec. dir. Bur. of European and Can. Affairs, 1983-85, exec. asst. to Under Sec. of State for Mgmt., 1985-88; ambassador to Swaziland, 1988-90; dep. asst. sec. Bur. of Consular Affairs, Washington, 1990—. Address: care Dept of State 2201 C St NW Washington DC 20520*

RYAN, NANCY MARIE, educator; b. Johnson City, N.Y., Mar. 13, 1938; d. Edward P. and Margie E. (Devine) R. BA, N.Y. State Coll. for Tchrs., 1960, MA, 1966. Cert. Spanish-English tchr., N.Y. Spanish-English tchr. Weedsport (N.Y.) Cen. High Sch., 1960-64; English tchr. Universidad de la Frontera, Temuco, Chile, 1964-65; Spanish-English tchr. Guilderland (N.Y.) Cen. High Sch., 1966—. Author: Shades of Green and Darkness, 1981, Islands in a Bay, 1989, Past Green Edges of Realities, 1990, numerous poems. Vol. Albany (N.Y.) Ronald McDonald House, 1984—; Papal vol. Roman Cath. Ch., Temuco, Chile, 1964-65. Recipient Vol. Svc. award Guilderland Elks Lodge, 1988. Home: 111 Beverwyck Dr Guilderland NY 12084

RYAN, SANDRA BELCHER, chemistry educator, realtor; b. Norfolk, Va., Jan. 19, 1943; d. William Alexander and Mabel Lee (Smith) Belcher; m. William Stanhope Jr., Dec. 30, 1963; children: James Christopher, Patricia Lynn, Jon Patrick. BS, Westhampton Coll., Richmond, Va., 1964; MS, Va. Commonwealth U., 1977. Clk. FCC, Norfolk, 1961-63; tchr. physics Hermitage High Sch., Richmond, Va., 1965-66; lab. specialist surgery dept. Med. Coll. Va., Richmond, 1966-74; instr. chemistry Va. Commonwealth U., Richmond, 1974-78, U. Richmond, 1975-79; tchr. chemistry J. Sargent Reynolds Community Coll., Richmond, 1979—; analytical chemist Consol. Lab., Richmond, 1979-80, James River Corp., Richmond, 1980-85; chmn. sci. dept. Steward Sch., Richmond, 1986-88; marketer Retail Groceries Inventory Specialists, Richmond, 1988—; wellness cons. Mary Kay Cosmetics, Richmond, 1985—; realtor Coldwell Banker, Hall and Buckingham. Singer Richmond Symphony. Mem. Am. Chem. Soc., Sigma Kappa Epsilon. Home: 2501 Swathmore Rd Richmond VA 23235

RYAN, SHERRY LYNN, executive administrator; b. South Bend, Ind., June 21, 1944; d. Charles Roscoe and Barbara Jeanne (Westfall) Jones; m. James J. Ryan, Dec. 18, 1971 (div. May 1984); children: Christopher Jeffrey, Jennifer Leigh, Cameron James. AA, Va. Intermont Coll., Bristol, Va., 1964. Med. sec. Drs. Montgomery, Greer & Howard, White Plains, N.Y., 1964; exec. sec. Mobil Oil Corp., N.Y.C., 1964-69; office mgr. Allen M. Ross, M.D., Darien, Conn., 1969; exec. sec. to pres. The Norwalk Co., Norwalk, Conn., 1969-70; exec. sec. Xerox Data Systems, Hackensack, N.J., 1971-73; from exec. asst. to asst. v.p. Capital Assocs., Inc., Redondo Beach, Calif., 1980—. Pres. mother's group Nat. Assn. for Retarded Children, 1976-77; vol. Torrance (Calif.) Meml. Med. Ctr. Mem. NAFE, Nat. Mothers of Twins Club. Methodist. Home: 5228 W 190th St Torrance CA 90503

RYAN, SUZANNE IRENE, nursing educator; b. Yonkers, N.Y., Mar. 13, 1939; d. Edward Vincent and Winifred E. (Goemann) R. BA in Biology, Mt. St. Agnes Coll., Balt., 1962; BSN, Columbia U., 1967, MA in Nursing Svc., 1973, MEd in Nursing Edn., 1975; MS in Oncology, San Jose (Calif.) State Coll. U., 1982. RN, N.Y. Prof. nursing Molloy Coll., Rockville Centre, N.Y., 1970—, co-dir. health svcs., dir. ednl. programs, 1987—; mem. N.Y. State AIDS Coun, 1987—, L.I. Alcohol Consortium, 1987—. Exhibited in group shows, 1963-87; photographer 2 books on Monteray Peninsula. USPHS fellow, 1962, Nat. Cancer Inst. fellow, 1981-82. Mem. Nat. Congress Oncology Nurses, AAUP, World Wildlife Orgn., Audubon Soc., Nature Conservancy, Sierra Club, Sigma Theta Tau (rsch. grantee 1985, 87). Roman Catholic. Home: 16 Walker St Malverne NY 11565

RYAN, THERESA ANN JULIA, accountant; b. N.Y.C., Mar. 1, 1962; d. John Patrick and Diane Elizabeth (Duggan) R. BA in Math. and Econs., Fordham U., 1984, MBA in Profl. Acctg., 1989. With sales dept. Abraham & Straus, White Plains, N.Y., 1980-84; adminstrv. asst. Companion of N.Y., Rye, 1984-86, asst. fin. analyst, 1986-87; with tech. ctr. Fordham U., N.Y.C., 1987-88; staff acct. Konigsberg Wolf & Co., N.Y.C., 1989—. Mem. N.Y. State Assn. CPA Candidates, Beta Gamma Sigma. Republican. Roman Catholic. Home: 5 Clare Terr Yonkers NY 10707 Office: Konigsberg Wolf & Co CPAs 440 Park Ave South New York NY 10016

RYAN, THERESE EILEEN, nursing administrator; b. Chgo., Mar. 22, 1952; d. William B. and Catherine T. (Fennell) R. BSN, Coll. of St. Theresa, Winona, Minn., 1974; MSN, Loyola U., 1979. RN, N.Y., Ill. Asst. head nurse Rush-Presbyn. St. Luke's Med. Ctr., Chgo., 1974-76; staff nurse Northwestern U. Hosp., Chgo., 1976-77; mem. faculty Wesley Passavant Sch. Nursing, Chgo., 1977-79; clin. nurse specialist U. Chgo. Med. Ctr., 1979-83; asst. dir. nursing Chgo. Lakeshore Hosp., 1983-87; assoc. adminstr. of nursing Hillside Hosp. L.I. Jewish Med. Ctr., Glen Oaks, N.Y., 1987—. Mem. Am. Pscyhiat. Nurses Assn., Nat. League Nursing. Democrat. Roman Catholic. Office: Hillside Hosp 75-59 263d St Glen Oaks NY 11004

RYAN, TULA FLESHMAN, health service consultant and nursing facility administrator; b. Rich Creek, Va., Feb. 5, 1927; d. John Elijah and Ophelia Kline (Cooper) Fleshman; m. James Joseph Ryan, May 1, 1948 (div. June 1973); children: John Keith, James Kenneth. Diploma in gen. nursing, Passaic (N.J.) Gen. Hosp., 1947; BS in Nursing, Ariz. State U., 1963; MA in Nursing Adminstrn., Columbia U., 1970; Cert. in Advanced Nursing Adminstrn., 1983, 88. Pub. health nurse City Health Dept, Newark, 1947-53; supr. nursing Vincent Pallotti Hosp., Morgantown, W.Va., 1953-55; instr. nursing Lewis-Gale Hosp., Roanoke, Va., 1955-60, Good Samaritan Hosp., Phoenix, 1963-67; asst. adminstr., dir. nursing services John C. Lincoln Hosp., Phoenix, 1970-76; adminstr. nursing Whittaker Corp. and Hosp. Corp. Internat., Al-Mutabighani Health Svc., Jeddah, Tabuk and Riyadh (Saudi Arabia), Al-Ain Abu Dhabi, United Arab Emirates, 1976-83; cons. Al-Mutabighani Health Svc., Jubail Industrial City, Saudi Arabia, 1984—; adminstr. Portamedic, Phoenix, 1985; nursing adminstrn. cons. Thunderbird Health Care Ctr. and Phoenix Jewish Care Ctr., Phoenix, 1986-87; cons. Manzanita Manor, Payson, Ariz., 1987; patient svcs. cons., nursing adminstr. Hinduja Nat. Hosp., Bombay, 1987-88; cons. Hinduja Nat. Hosp., Bombay; patient svcs. cons. and nursing adminstr., 1987-88. USPHS scholar, 1963. Mem. Am. Nurses Assn. (del. 1965), Ariz. Nurses Assn. (sec. 1963-64), Gerontol. Nursing Services (edn. coordinator). Republican. Lodge: Soroptimists (sec. Camelback chpt. 1974, v.p. 1975). Home: 518 E Boca Raton Rd Phoenix AZ 85022 Office: 2945 E Thomas Rd Phoenix AZ 85016

RYANT, MARY LOUISE, educator; b. Wichita, Kans., July 14, 1942; d. Dennis Alfonso and Valerie Zenona (Reichenberger) Neville; m. Carl George Ryant, Aug. 5, 1970; 1 child, Neville George. BA in Art Edn., Wichita State U., 1964; MA in Art Therapy, U. Louisville, 1972, postgrad., 1972-80. Cert. tchr., Ind. Vol. educator Papal Vols., Brownstown, Jamaica, 1964-66; tchr. visual arts Andale (Kans.) Sch. System, 1966-67, Lancashire Ednl. Authority, Ashton-under-Lyne, Eng., 1967-68, Bury (Lancashire, Eng.) Grammar Sch. for Girls, 1975-75, Greater Clark Schs., Charlestown, Ind., 1968—; head arts dept. Charlestown High Sch., 1970—. Exhibited in group shows. Vol. Am. Heart Assn., Louisville, 1978—, Am. Cancer Soc., Louisville, 1978—, Leukemia Soc., Louisville, 1978—. Mem. NEA, Nat. Art Edn. Assn., Am. Art Therapy Assn. (cert.), Visual Arts Assn., Ind. Edn. Assn., Greater Clark Edn. Assn. (faculty rep. 1970—), J.B. Speed Mus. Democrat. Roman Catholic. Home: 1839 Roanoke Ave Louisville KY 40205

RYAN-WHITE, JEWELL, public relations executive; b. Columbus, Miss., May 24, 1943; d. Larry A. and Martha (Williams) Ryan; 1 child, Donald

Andre White. Student, Alcorn A&M State U., 1961-63, Joliet (Ill.) Jr. Coll., 1976-79, 81-82, Olive Harvey Coll., 1979-82, Ill. State U., 1982-85. V.p., bd. dirs., chmn. EEOC and AA coms. Nat. Fedn. Local Cable Programmers, Washington, 1985-90; asst. mgr. recruiting Bur. of the Census U.S. Dept. Commer, Hollywood, Calif., 1989-90; producer, host, cable TV market researcher CBS-TV City, Robert Brilliant, Inc. Contbr. articles to profl. publ. Campaign mgr. Com. to Elect Andy Hinch, Joliet, 1985-87, Com. to Elect Mayor John Bourg, Joliet, 1985-86; chmn. bd. dirs. Joliet Will County Community Action Bd., 1982; chmn. labor div. Joliet chpt. Am. Cancer Soc., 1982; chmn. bd. dirs. United Way Will County, Joliet Cath. High Sch., 1983-85; bd. dirs. Big Bros., 1984; chmn. bd. Housing Authority Joliet, 1987; active Urban League, Operation PUSH, Guardian Angel Home, St. John Vianney Cath. Ch., So. Christian Leadership Conf., Nat. Campaign Human Devel., Beverly Hills & Hollywood NAACP, 1989—, L.A. Urban League, 1989—, Lit. Resource Task Force. Recipient Award of Appreciation Nat. Campaign Human Devel., 1987, Campaign Human Devel. Joliet Cath. Diocese, 1986, Am. Ambassador award Am. Cablesystems, 1986, Crusade award Am. Cancer Soc., 1980, Pace Setter award City of Hope, 1979, Appreciation award United Way Will County, 1977, Literacy award, 1987, Cable Excellence award, 1987; named Citizen of Month City of Joliet, 1982. Mem. Internat. Conv. for Communications Workers Am., Black Trade Unionists, Smithsonian Assn., Women in Cable, Ladies of Columbus (pres. Joliet chpt. 1976-87), Am. Film Inst. Home: 136 S Virgil Ave #213 Los Angeles CA 90040

RYBARCZYK, HEIDI MARY, accountant; b. Chgo., May 17, 1957; d. Iwan and Katharina (Frahammer) Paszko; m. Richard J. Rybarczyk, Aug. 29, 1981. AA in Fgn. Langs., Wright Jr. Coll., 1978; BS in Acctg., U. Ill., Chgo., 1981. CPA, Ill. Sr. staff acct. Arthur Andersen & Co., Chgo., 1981-85, Morrison & Morrison, Ltd., Chgo., 1985-89; staff acct. Temchuk and Co., Park Ridge, Ill., 1989—. Mem. Am. Inst. CPA's, Ill. CPA Soc. Home: 1731 Monmouth Pl Downers Grove IL 60516 Office: Temchuk & Co 1105 S Vine Park Ridge IL 60068

RYBURN, BETTY CORNETT, sociology educator; b. Northfork, W.Va., Jan. 12, 1935; d. Clyde Jefferson and Berthelda Alice (Northen) Cornett; 1 dau., Pam. AS, Marshall U., 1955, BA, 1957; MA, Ohio U., 1958; PhD, U. Santa Barbara, 1975. Mem. faculty Towson State Coll. (Md.), 1959-61, 67-68, U. Md.-Balt., 1967, George Mason U., 1970-75, Am. Tech. U., 1979-82; pvt. practice Family Counseling Service, Harker Heights, Tex., 1979-82; assoc. prof. sociology Mobile Coll. (Ala.), 1982-86, assoc. dean extended programs, 1984-86, assoc. prof. sociology and psychology, 1986—; cons., lectr. on human relations, leadership skills and mil. families; owner BlossomShop, Mobile. Author: The Relationship Between Certain Sociological Factors and Grade Achievement, 1958; Alienation: Generative Social Structural Conditions, Role Conflict/Strain, and Resulting Social Consequences, 1975; contbr. articles to profl. jours., papers to profl. confs. Chmn. Am. Heart Assn. Drive, Am. Cancer Soc. Drive; bd. advisers U. West Fla. Ctr. on Aging. Mem. Am. Sociol. Assn., Mid-South Sociol. Assn., So. Sociol. Soc., Ala.-Miss. Sociol. Assn., AAUP, AAUW, Alpha Lambda Delta, Alpha Kappa Delta. Baptist. Home: 25 Cobblestone Way W Mobile AL 36608 Office: Mobile Coll Dept Sociology College Pkwy Mobile AL 36613

RYCHECK, JAYNE BOGUS (MRS. ROY RICHARD RYCHECK), retired educational administrator; b. Schenectady; d. Peter and Sylvia (Cywinski) Bogus; M.A., N.Y. U., 1953; B.S. State U. N.Y., Albany, 1941; postgrad. Syracuse U., 1957-66; m. R. Richard Rycheck, July 26, 1942. Tchr. various schs., 1935-43; elementary sch. tchr. Schenectady (N.Y.) City Schs., 1943-51, leadership intern, 1951-52, elementary sch. prin., 1952-61, dir. spl. edn., 1961-72. Instr. Russell Sage Coll., 1955-58, State U. N.Y., Oneonta, 1956; cons. bur. handicapped children N.Y. Edn. Dept., 1966-76, mem. commrs. and hoc coms., 1964-72, State Planning Com. Insts. for In-Service Edn., 1964-67; rep. to Community Welfare Council Schenectady County, 1961-62; adv. council N.Y. State Joint Legislative Com. Mental and Phys. Handicapped, 1970-72; mem. adv. com. Schenectady County Office for Aging, 1976-81, vice chmn., 1977-78, chmn., 1978-81; advisory com. Older Ams. Act program N.Y. State Office of Aging, 1977-80. Trustee, chmn. edn. Schenectady Mus., 1974-77; mem. human services adv. com. Schenectady County Community Coll., 1977—. Recipient Humanitarian service awards United Cerebral Palsy Schenectady County, 1966, 67, Capital dist. Assn. for Brain-Injured Children, 1967, Today's Woman award Schenectady YWCA, 1987, various citations from N.Y. State Sen. and Assembly, Am. Assn. Ret. People, AAUW, Schenectady County Legis., N.Y. State Legis., 1986, and others; named Sr. Citizen of Yr. Schenectady County, 1986 ; recipient Meritorious Alumni award State U. N.Y. Coll. at Oneonta, 1972; Capitol Dist. Speech and Hearing award, 1972, Distinguished Service award N.Y. Fedn. chpts. Council for Exceptional Children, 1972, Joseph P. Kennedy, Jr. Found. award for outstanding activity for the mentally retarded, 1972, Achievement award for contbns. to quality of life for sr. citizens N.Y. State Legislature , 1979, Disting. Service award Council Adminstrs. Spl. Edn., 1980, N.Y. State Achievement award by Senate Com. on Aging and Assembly Standing Com. on Aging for outstanding dedication to task improving quality on N.Y. State sr. citizen, 1986, Schenectady YWCA Recognition award for to Today's Women, 1987; cert. of appreciation for community service by the City of Schenectady Coun. and Mayor Karen b. Johnson, 1986; cert. of merit for outstanding com. service N.Y. State Senator Huge T. Farley, 1986, cert. in recognition of valuable pub. service Schenectady County Bd. of Reps., 1986, citation N.Y. State Assembly, 1986. Mem. N.Y. State (sec. 1967-68), Nat. councils adminstrs. spl. edn., Assn. Childhood Edn. (sec. 1952-55, state exec. bd. 1951-59), Council Exceptional Children (mem. chpt. regional and state bds. 1966-78, state regional dir. 1966-68, state adv. bd. 1966-72, v.p. 1968-69, state pres. 1970), Schenectady County Assn. Childhood Edn. (treas. and v.p. 1952), N.Y. State Assn. Childhood Edn. Internat. (sec., v.p. 1962-65), Am. Assn. Mental Deficiency, N.Y. State Assn. Brain-Injured Children (state adv. bd. 1963-67, dist. adv. bd. 1966-72), Nat. Soc. Autistic Children, Assn. Retarded Children (adv. bd.), Gifted Children Soc. (adv. com.), Schenectady C. of C. (edn. com.), Schenectady County Ret. Tchrs. Assn. (v.p. 1973, pres. 1974-76), Am. Assn. Ret. People (program com. chpt. 1973-76, legis. chmn. 1981-84, cert. of appreciation for dedicated service 1986, 87), AAUW (topic chmn. 1977-79, chpt. Name Grant honoree 1981), N.Y. Assn. Elementary Prins. (hon. life), N.Y. State Ret. Tchrs. Assn. (county dir. Eastern zone, del. state conv. 1974-76), Schenectady County Hist. Soc. (rec. sec., dir. 1982-84, 1st v.p. 1986-87), Delta Kappa Gamma (chmn. chpt. profl. affairs com. 1972-76, del. state legis. forum 1974-79, mem. state com. profl. affairs 1974-75). Contbr. articles to pubs. Home: 1537 Kingston Ave Schenectady NY 12308

RYCHECKY, HELEN ROSE, educator; b. Ohiowa, Nebr., May 28, 1922; d. Cyril Methodias and Helen (Votipka) Bernasek;m. Leo Rychecky, Oct. 6, 1945 (dec. June 1988). BS, U. Nebr., 1960. Elem. tchr. rural schs. Fillmore County, Nebr., 1939-42; elem. tchr. Alliance (Nebr.) Pub. Schs., 1944-46, Ohiowa Pub. Schs., 1947; kindergarten tchr. Sunflower Rural Schs., Mitchell, Nebr., 1951-53; elem. tchr. Scottsbluff (Nebr.) Pub. Schs., 1953-72, jr. high counselor, 1972-73; co-mgr. Family Farms, Morrill, Kimball Counties, Nebr., 1973-88, mgr., 1988—; assoc. prof. U. Nebr. summer session, 1962. Mem. AAUW, Presbyn. Women Assn., Pi Lambda Theta. Republican. Home: 2406 3rd Ave Scottsbluff NE 69361

RYDELL, SHEILA VERONICA, cablevision company official, producer, editor; b. Spokane, Wash., July 12, 1964; d. William John and Adele Joan (Davenport) Rydell. BA in Communication, U. Hawaii, 1987. Clerical asst. East-West Ctr., Honolulu, 1984-85; data processor dept. oceanography U. Hawaii at Manoa, Honolulu, 1986; asst. prodn. coord. Oceanic Cablevision, Honolulu, 1986-88, traffic coord., 1988—; freelance dir. Afro-Am. Assn. Hawaii, Honolulu, 1987-88; freelance editor Visitor Cable Network, Honolulu, 1989—. Writer, producer, dir., editor video Road to Nowhere, 1987. Pell grantee, 1985-87; Hemenway scholar, 1987. Mem. Am. Film Inst., NAFE. Home: 350 Ward Ave Apt 106 Honolulu HI 96814 Office: Oceanic Cablevision 875 Waimanu St Ste 600 Honolulu HI 96813

RYDER, SANDRA SMITH, communications specialist, publicist; b. Great Lakes, Ill., July 6, 1949; d. Dennis Murrey and Olga (Grosheff) Smith. BS, Northwestern U., 1971; MA, Annenberg Sch. Communications at U. So. Calif., 1986. Columnist Camarillo Daily News (Calif.), 1971-76; editor Fillmore Herald (Calif.), 1976-78; pub. info. officer Oxnard Union High Sch. Dist. (Calif.), 1980-82; pub. info. officer Ventura County Community Coll.

Dist., 1982-83; pub. relations dir. Murphy Orgn., Oxnard, Calif., 1983-84; pub. affairs rep. Gen. Telephone Calif., Thousand Oaks, 1984-88; adminstr. regulated bus. communications GTE Telephone Ops., Irving, Tex., 1988—. Co-chmn. Ventura County Commn. for Women, 1981-88. Mem. Women in Communications, Soc. Profl. Journalists.

RYHERD, GERALDINE SCHNEIDER, retired educator; b. Lacona, Iowa, Mar. 17, 1929; d. Joseph Mathew and Margaret Dora (Miller) S.; widowed; children: Robert Jr., Billie Walker, Margaret Brown, Dan Ryherd, Tim Ryherd, Tony Ryherd. BA in Elem. Edn., U. No. Iowa, 1966, MA in Spl. Edn., 1976. Tchr. Iowa Schs., 1949-67; tchr. spl. edn. Waterloo (Iowa) Community Schs., 1967-73; tchr. learning disabilities Clayton County Schs., Elkader, Iowa, 1973-75, MFL Consolidated Schs., Monona, Iowa, 1975-77; curriculum cons. Keystone Area Edn. Agy., Elkader, 1977-81, work experience coord., 1981-86. Vol. Vols. for Youth, Oelwein, Iowa, 1984—, bd. dirs. 1987—; bd. chmn. Alternative Living Care Review, Oelwein, 1988—; vol. Parent Share and Support, Oelwein, 1989—; county com. Rep. County Orgn., Fayette Co., Iowa, 1984—; mission quilters Sacred Heart Mission Quilters, Oelwein, 1987—; instr. ARC, Oelwein, 1988—; bd. dirs. South Fayette County Red Cross, 1987—; chmn. Care Review Com., 1988—. Recipient Cert. Vols. for Youth, 1985. Mem. AAUW, Cath. Daugs. of the Ams. (pres. 1989—), Oelwein Area Retired Tchrs. (membership chmn. 1989—), Sacred Heart Rosary Soc. Republican. Roman Catholic. Home: 20 2nd St NW Oelwein IA 50662

RYMER, PAMELA ANN, federal judge; b. Knoxville, Tenn., Jan. 6, 1941. AB, Vassar Coll., 1961; LLB, Stanford U., 1964; LLD (hon.), Pepperdine U., 1988. Bar: Calif. 1966, U.S. Ct. Appeals (9th cir.) 1966, U.S. Ct. Appeals (10th cir.), U.S. Supreme Ct. Assoc. Lillick McHose & Charles, L.A., 1966-72, ptnr., 1973-75; ptnr. Toy and Rymer, L.A., 1975-83; judge U.S. Dist. Ct. (cen. dist.) Calif., L.A., 1983-89, U.S. Ct. Appeals (9th cir.) L.A., 1989—; faculty The Jud. Coll., 1984—. Mem. Calif. Postsecondary Edn. Commn., 1974—, chmn., 1980-84; mem. Los Angeles Olympic Citizens Adv. Commn.; bd. visitors Stanford U. Law Sch., 1986—, Pepperdine U. Law Sch., 1987; mem. Edn. Commn. of States Task Force on State Policy and Ind. Higher Edn., 1987; bd. dirs. Constl. Rights Found., 1985—. Mem. ABA, Los Angeles County Bar Assn. (chmn. antitrust sect. 1981-82), Assn. of Bus. Trial Lawyers, Stanford Alumni Assn., Stanford Law Soc. So. Calif., Vassar Club So. Calif. (past pres.). Office: US Dist Ct 312 N Spring St Los Angeles CA 90012

RYNDRESS, SHIRLEY ANN, retired nursery school administrator; b. Caro, Mich., July 31, 1929; d. Mark Roy and Doris Evelyn (Aldrich) Smith; m. Robert P. Ryndress, Aug. 11, 1951; children: Margo Ann, Jan Elizabeth, Kristyn Lynn. BS, Cen. Mich. U., 1951; Mich. permanent cert., Wayne State U., 1953; postgrad. Oakland U., Rochester, Mich., 1978. Tchr. Mt. Morris (Mich.) Pub. Schs., 1949-51, Royal Oak (Mich.) Pub. Schs., 1951-54, Royal Oak Coop. Nursery, 1958-59, Lathrup Coop. Nursery, Southfield, Mich., 1963-70; founder, dir. Northbrook Nursery Sch., Birmingham, Mich., 1970-83; ret., 1983. Dir. troop svcs. Girl Scouts U.S.A., Birmingham, 1964-74; crisis intervention counselor Manatee Glens, Bradenton, Fla., 1985—. Mem. Nat. Acad. Early Childhood Programs (validator 1985—), AAUW (mentor program Bradenton 1990—), Treasures Porcelain Artists (pres. 1989-90). Republican. Presbyterian. Home: 3440 Wild Oak Bay Blvd Apt 134 Bradenton FL 34210

RYON, MARGARET STEVENS, computer graphic artist; b. Schenectady, N.Y., Jan. 19, 1951; d. Walter Ghoring and Marie Patricia (Fitzgerald); m. George Diem Uibel, Jan. 20, 1973 (div. 1982); m. Peter James McCormick, May 25, 1986. BFA with honors, Pratt Inst., Bklyn., 1974; postgrad., Hunter Coll., N.Y.C., 1977; MA in Communications cum laude, N.Y. Inst. of Tech., 1986. Med. photographer Lenox Hill Hosp., N.Y.C., 1974-78; vis. instr. Pratt Inst. Photography Dept., Bklyn., 1981-82; chief med. photographer Meml. Hosp. Pathology Dept., N.Y.C., 1978-88; owner Pix Elation, N.Y.C., 1986-; yearbook designer N.Y. Microscopical Soc., 1978; bd. dirs. Biological Photographic Assn., N.Y.; vice chairperson Biological Photographic Assn., N.Y., 1980-81; judge Nikon Small World Contest, N.Y.C., 1986. Illustrator: Immunobiology for the Clinician, 1978; photographer Armed Forces Inst. of Pathology Fasicle, 1982. Recipient Cert. of Special Merit Printers Industry Met., N.Y., 1978. Mem. Graphic Artists Guild, Siggraph. Protestant.

RYPCZYK, CANDICE LEIGH, employee relations executive; b. Norman, Okla., Apr. 24, 1949; d. John Anthony and Lee (Brunswick) Wirth; m. Peter Charles Rypczyk, Nov. 27, 1976. BA, Kalamazoo Coll., 1971; cert. labor studies extension program, Cornell U., N.Y. Sch. Indsl., Labor Relations, Middletown, 1985. Personnel asst. PFW div. Hercules Inc., Middletown, N.Y., 1973-77, asst. personnel mgr., 1977-79, mgr. employee relations, 1979—. Mem. Am. Soc. for Pers. Adminstrn. (v.p. Mid-Hudson Valley chpt. 1985, pres. 1986, treas. N.Y. State coun. 1986, dist. bd. dirs. 1988-90, cert.), Orange County C. of C. (Vol. of the Yr. 1986, program com., treas., exec. com.). Office: PFW Div Hercules Inc 33 Sprague Ave Middletown NY 10940

RYTYCH, BARBARA ELIZABETH, accounting professor; b. Red Cloud, Nebr., May 11, 1949; d. LeRoy E. and S. Elizabeth (Maness) Mohler; m. Franklin J. Rytych, Jan. 3, 1970; children: Kathleen Lani, Germaine Cassandra, James Derrick. BSBA in Acctg., Ft. Hays (Kans.) State U., 1970, MSBA in Acctg., 1975. CPA, Kans. Acct. Peak Transport Svc., Inc., Chester, Nebr., 1971; clk. Arbuthot Drug Co., Belleville, Kans., 1971-72; teaching asst. Ft. Hays State U., 1973-75; acctg. prof. Kans. Wesleyan U., Salina, 1975-82, Bethany Coll., Lindsborg, 1982—; prin. Barbara E. Rytych, CPA, Falun, Kans., 1975—; div. and faculty chair Kans. Wesleyan U., 1975-82; chair faculty policy com. Bethany Coll., 1990—. Sunday sch. tchr. Falun Luth. Ch., 1982—; treas. Lindsborg Community Hosp., 1982—, also trustee. Mem. Nat. Assn. Accts., Am. Acctg. Assn. Republican. Office: Bethany Coll Presser Hall 421 N First Lindsborg KS 67456

RYZNAR, CAROLINE LUCILLE, producer, graphic designer; b. Berwyn, Ill., Jan. 31, 1950; d. John William and Eleanor Virginia Ryznar. BFA, Carnegie-Mellon U., 1968. Designer Hallmark Cards, Kansas City, Mo., 1968-70; art dir. N.W. Ayer Advt., Chgo., 1970-72; dir. design Jack O'Grady Studios, Chgo., 1972-73; corp. creative dir. Gen. Electric, Stamford, Conn., 1973-75; pres., creative dir. Master Prodns. Inc., Westport, Conn., 1975—; chief exec. officer, producer Abraxaz XXII, Inc., Los Angeles and Hong Kong, 1978—. Exec. producer (film) Initiations (TV pilot) Strange Reality. Republican. Office: Master Prodns Inc ABRAXAZ XXII Inc 11 Cedar Ln Weston CT 06883

RZEWNICKI, JANET C., state official; b. Akron, Ohio, May 21, 1953; d. Robert Myers; m. Victor Rzewnicki, June 3, 1972. B.S. in Acctg. and Fin. with distinction, U. Del. CPA. Sr. acct. Peat, Marwick Mitchell, Wilmington, Del., 1978-80; corp. acct. internat. sect. Hercules Inc., Wilmington, 1980-81; acctg. instr. U. Del., Newark, 1980-82; pvt. practice acctg., Wilmington, 1981-82; state treas. State of Del., Dover, 1983—; mem. Del. Econ. Adv. Coun. Leader People to People Del., People's Republic of China, 1985; v.p. Del. Children's Fire Safety Found.; treas., bd. dirs. March of Dimes, Newark, 1979—; bd. dirs. United Way of Del., Wilmington, 1980-82; active Gov.'s Coun. on Drug Free Del., 1982—. Mem. Nat. Assn. State Treas., AICPA, Del. Soc. CPAs, Pa. Inst. CPAs, Am. Soc. Women Accts. (bd. dirs. 1981), Beta Gamma Sigma. Republican. Office: Office of State Treas Thomas Collins Bldg PO Box 1401 Dover DE 19903•

SAAB, DEANNE KELTUM, real estate broker, shop owner; b. Allentown, Pa., Jan. 27, 1945; d. James A. and Agnes G. (Hanzlik) S. BA, Cedar Crest Coll. 1966; MS, U. Calif., Santa Barbara, 1973; realtors cert. Calif. State U. 1978. Tchr. Ojai (Calif.) Unified Sch. Dist., 1966-74; real estate broker/appraiser pvt. practice, Allentown, Pa., 1978—; pres./treas. DeAnne & Assoc., Inc., Allentown, Pa., 1987—; owner Heritage Gardens, Allentown, Pa., 1981—. Mem. AAUW (various offices), Nat. Assn. Realtors, Pa. Assn. Realtors, Allentown (Pa.) Lehigh County Bd. Realtors (various offices), Soc. of Real Estate Appraisers, Cedar Crest Coll. Alumnae Assn. (various offices), Lehigh Valley Guild Craftsmen (various offices). Home: 1360 Dorney Ave Allentown PA 18103

SAAD, JOYCE RAY, psychologist; b. Flushing, N.Y., Dec. 14, 1954; d. Jacques and Sarina (Moghrabi) S. BA magna cum laude, U. Pa., 1977; MA, Calif. Sch. Profl. Psychology, Berkeley, 1979; PhD, Calif. Sch. Profl. Psychology, 1983. Lic. psychologist, Calif. Predoctoral intern O.M.I. Family Ctr., San Francisco, 1981-82, Kaiser Hosp. & Med. Ctr., San Rafael, Calif., 1982-83; postdoctoral intern Kaiser Hosp. & Med. Ctr., South San Francisco, Calif., 1983-84, Garfield Geropsychiatric Hosp., Oakland, Calif., 1983-84; psychologist, supr. Family Svc. Agy., Livermore, Calif., 1984-85, Bayview-Hunter's Point Mental Health Svc., Children's Svc., San Francisco, 1985-87; sr. treatment specialist Dept. of Health, Concord, Calif., 1987-88; clin. psychologist AB3632 project Bayview-Hunter's Point Found., San Francisco, 1988—; pvt. practice San Fransico, 1984—; cons. in field. Mem. San Francisco Psychol. Assn., Am. Psychol. Assn., Phi Beta Kappa. Office: 1810 Divisadero St San Francisco CA 94115

SAAVEDRA, RO, communications director; b. Albuquerque, Sept. 20, 1952; d. Ben and Josephine (Martinel) S.; m. Gary D. Doll, Aug. 25, 1973 (div. 1979). B Univ. Studies, U. N.Mex., 1981, MA, 1983. Dir. communications KPMG Peat Marwick, Albuquerque, 1984—. Editor newsletter N.Mex. Enterpreneurs Assn., 1985-87. Bd. dirs. Sr. Citizen Aid Found., Albuquerque, 1986-87; diplomats com. Albuquerque C. of C., 1987-89. Mem. Women in Communications, Inc. (editor newsletter 1984-85, v.p 1985-86, pres. 1986-87), Pub. Rels. Soc. Am., N.Mex. Press Women, United Way Greater Albuquerque (account exec. 1990 campaign). Office: KPMG Peat Marwick 6565 Americas Pkwy NE 700 Albuquerque NM 87110

SABATELLA, ELIZABETH MARIA, physical education educator, author; b. Mineola, N.Y., Nov. 9, 1940; d. D. F. and Blanche M. (Schmetzle) S; 1 child, Kevin Woog. BS, SUNY, Brockport, 1961; MA, SUNY, Stony Brook, 1971, MSW, 1983. Lic. social worker, N.Y.; cert. tchr., N.Y. Tchr. physical edn. Comseqogue Sch. Dist., Port Jefferson, N.Y., 1968-73, 84-87, 88—; therapist adolescents, 1973-84; mem. family systems Network for Continuing Edn., Central Islip, Calif. and Colo., 1978-80; with biofeedback, meditation com. McLean Hosp. Tng., Boston, 1978, therapeutic touch team East and West Ctr., N.Y.C., 1980—. Contbr. poetry and children's story to various publs. Recipient Editor's Choice award and Best New Poet award Nat. Libr. Poetry, 1988. Mem. Writers Assn. Democrat. Home: 202 Foxhill Dr Baiting Hollow NY 11933

SABAU, CARMEN SYBILE, chemist; b. Cluj, Romania, Apr. 24, 1933; naturalized U.S. citizen; d. George and Antoinette Marie (Chiriac) Grigorescu; m. Mircea Nicolae Sabau, July 11, 1956; 1 child, Isabelle Carmen. MS in Inorganic and Analytical Chemistry, U. C.I. Parhon, Bucharest, Romania, 1955; PhD in Radiochemistry, U. Fridericiana, Karlsruhe, Fed. Republic of Germany., 1972. Chemist, Argonne (Ill.) Nat. Lab. 1976—. Internat. Atomic Energy Agy. fellow, 1967-68, Humboldt fellow, 1970-72. Mem. Am. Chem. Soc., Am. Nuclear Soc., Am. Romanian Acad. Arts and Sci., Assn. for Women in Sci., N.Y. Acad. Sci., Sigma Xi. Author: Ion-exchange Theory and Applications in Analytical Chemistry, 1967; contbr. articles to profl. jours. Home: 689 Banbury Way Bolingbrook IL 60439 Office: Argonne Nat Lab 9700 S Cass Ave Bldg 205 Argonne IL 60439

SABBAGH, SHERAINE KAY, textile designer; b. Springfield, Ill., Mar. 2, 1959; d. Russ B. and Beverly Jane (McCarthy) Dhondy; m. John Peter Sabbagh, July 26, 1986. BFA in Textile Design, Sophia Polytechnic, Bombay, India, 1981; AOS, Pratt Inst., N.Y.C., 1983. Trainee designer Laxmi-Vishnu Textile Mills, Ltd., Bombay, 1981; lectr. history of textiles Sophia Polytechnic, Bombay, 1981-82; textile designer Piramal Spinning and Weaving Mills, Ltd., Bombay, 1981-82; colorist Quaker Fabric Corp., N.Y.C., 1984; spl. assist. designer Spectrum Fabrics Corp., N.Y.C., 1984-85; pres., owner, designer Sheraine Kay Designs, 1983—; cons. The Master Weavers of India show, Smithsonian Instn., Washington, 1986; guest lectr., film producer Mus. Natural History, N.Y.C., 1988, 90, N.Y. Pub. Libr., Great Neck, 1987, 88. Producer, art dir. (documentary film) Journey to Arhikkal, 1988; set designer (play) The Elephant Man, 1981; exhibited textile designs at Sophia Poly., Bombay, India, 1979, 80, 81, Internat. House, N.Y.C., 1983, Pratt Inst., N.Y.C., 1983. Mem. Ea. Dem. Club of Queens (N.Y.), 1989—; activist Families and Friends of the Mentally Ill, Manhattan, N.Y., 1989—. Recipient 2d prize (Woven div.) 11th Ann. Competition, The Home Fashion Products Assn., N.Y.C., 1983, Best Student of Yr. award Sophia Polytechnic, 1980, 81, merit award for BFA (ranked third in India), Bombay U., 1981, art merit scholarship Maharashtra State Directorate, Bombay, 1979.

SABIN, JULIA LEIGH, quality control manager; b. Fairbanks, Alaska, Sept. 13, 1959; d. George Lincoln and Carolyn Jean (Farris) S.; m. Darryl George Stephens, Oct. 26, 1958. BS in Biochemistry, U. Calif., 1983. Food technologist R. W. Knudsen & Sons, Inc., Chico, Calif., 1983-87; quality control mgr., safety coordinator Chico, 1987—; tchr. Calif. State U., Chico, 1986. Mem. Inst. Food Technologists. Democrat. Home: 88 Grinding Rock Rd Chico CA 95969

SABLAN, SUZANNE BARBARA, educator; b. Plainview, N.Y., Aug. 25, 1962; d. Anthony and Elaine Florence (Freeth) Pellegrino; m. Joseph Andrew Sablan, Aug. 26, 1982. Student, NYU, 1981; AA, Valencia Community Coll., 1985; BA, Rollins Coll., 1987. Night auditor Days Inns Am., Orlando, Fla., 1981-82, Sheraton World Resort, Orlando, 1982-84; dividend processor Sun Banks, Inc., Orlando, 1984, supr. 1984-88; tchr. Dr. Phillips High Sch., Orlando, 1988—. Author: (poem) Slipping Away; contbg. poet On the Threshold of a Dream. Mem. Nat. Assn. Female Execs., Nat. Writers Club, Phi Theta Kappa. Democrat. Episcopalian. Office: Dr Phillips High Sch 6500 Turkey Lake Rd Orlando FL 32819

SABLE, BARBARA KINSEY, music educator; b. Astoria, L.I., N.Y., Oct. 6, 1927; d. Albert and Verna Rowe Kinsey; B.A., Coll. Wooster, 1949; M.A., Tchrs. Coll. Columbia U., N.Y.C., 1950; D.Mus., U. Ind., 1966; m. Arthur J. Sable, Nov. 3, 1973. Office mgr., music dir. sta. WCAX, Burlington, Vt., 1954; instr. Cottey Coll., 1959-60; asst. prof. N.E. Mo. State U., Kirksville, 1962-64; asst. prof. U. Calif., Santa Barbara, 1964-69; prof. music U. Colo., Boulder, 1969—. Author: The Vocal Sound, 1982. Mem. Nat. Assn. Tchrs. Singing (past state gov., asso. editor bull.). AAUP, Colo. State Music Tchrs. Assn. Democrat. Avocation: poetry. Home: 3430 Ash Ave Boulder CO 80303 Office: U Colo Coll Music Campus Box 301 Boulder CO 80309

SABOL, SUSAN ANN, clinical psychologist; b. Westfield, Mass., Jan. 2, 1957; d. William Joseph Sipitkowski and Loretta Ann (Stomsky) Grimaldi; m. John Joseph Beszczad, June 1, 1985. BS summa cum laude, U. Bridgeport, 1979, MS, 1981; D of Psychology, Forest Inst., Wheeling, Ill., 1987. Human rsch. engr. Dunlap & Assocs., Darien, Conn., summer 1980; psychologist intern Fed. Correctional Instn., Danbury, Conn., 1986-87; staff psychologist, sr. clinician chem. dependency unit Gaylord Hosp., Wallingford, Conn., 1988—; pvt. practice Opsahl & Assocs., Watertown, Conn., 1989—. Mem. Am. Psychol. Assn., Conn. Psychol. Assn. Home: 18 Woodbury Pl Woodbury CT 06798

SABOSIK, PATRICIA ELIZABETH, publisher, editor; b. Newark, Aug. 25, 1949; d. George Aloysius and Elizabeth Ann (Simko) S.; m. Kenneth Donald Gursky, Apr. 21, 1972 (div. 1980). BA in English, Kean Coll. N.J., 1976; MBA in Mktg., Seton Hall U., 1984; cert. advanced study in fin., Fairfield U., 1989. Proofreader Baker & Taylor, Somerville, N.J., 1969-71, database coordinator, 1971-74, prodn. editor, 1974-77, publs. mgr., editor, 1977-82; dir. mktg. services H.W. Wilson Pub. Co., Bronx, N.Y., 1982-84; editor, pub. Choice mag., Am. Library Assn., Middletown, Conn., 1984—; project dir. Books for Coll. Libraries, Middletown, 1985-88, Guide to Reference Books, 1988—. Contbr. articles to profl. jours. Party rep. Twp. Com. Cranford, N.J., 1977-79; hon. bd. advisors U. Conn. Women's Ctr., 1989—. Mem. ALA, AAUW, Soc. for Scholarly Pub. (membership com., editor newsletter 1988—, budget and fin. com. 1990—), Serials Industry Systems Adv. Com. (vice chmn. 1985-86, membership chmn. 1983-89, newsletter editor 1986-87). Republican. Roman Catholic. Club: Appalacian Mountain (Conn.); Women Outdoors (New Haven) (newsletter editor 1984-86, regional rep. 1986-87). Office: Choice Mag 100 Riverview Ctr Middletown CT 06457

SABOUNGI, MARIE-LOUISE JEAN, chemist, researcher; b. Tripoli, Lebanon, Jan. 1, 1948; came to U.S., 1973; d. Jean C. and Alice (Assaf) S.; children: Benjamin, Alice; m. David C. Long Price, Nov. 25, 1989. PhD in Physics, U. Marseille, France, 1973. Postdoctoral fellow Argonne (Ill.) Nat. Lab., 1973-75, chemist, 1975-86, sr. chemist, 1986—. Mem. editorial bd. CALPHAD. Fellow AAAS; mem. Am. Phys. Soc. Electrochem. Soc., Gordon Rsch. Conf. on Molten Salts and Liquid Metals (chmn. 1989). Roman Catholic. Office: Argonne Nat Lab 9700 S Cass Ave Argonne IL 60439

SACCA, HARRIET WANDS, music educator; b. Pittsfield, Mass; d. Harry J. and Anna F. (Mara) Wands; B.S., Coll. St. Rose, 1939, M.A., 1962; student SUNY, Albany, Oneonta. Tchr. pub. schs., Albany, N.Y., 1942-66; instr. Coll. St. Rose, 1962-63; dir. music edn. Albany (N.Y.) Bd. Edn. 1966—; bur. assoc. examiner personnel N.Y. State Dept. Edn. Past pres. Soroptimist Internat., 1969-70, City Club Albany, Inc., 1974-75; active Albany County Dem. Com., 1962—; jud. del. 19, 3d Jud. del. area N.Y. State. 1975-90; mem. Albany Local Devel. Corp.; bd. dirs. St. Joseph's Housing Corp., Albany Tulip Festival; mem. adv. bd. capital Region Ctr. Arts in Edn., 1983—, Albany County Aliteratives to Incarceration, 1985-90, chair sub com., 1985—; bd. dirs. Coop. Extension Community Resources Devel., 4 County Youth Symphony Orch., 1970-84; project dir. N.Y. Council on Arts; chair festival N.Y. Sch. Music, 1988; mem. com. of 5 appointed select name for 16,000 seat Civic Arena. Recipient Citizen of Yr. award Ford Motor Co., 1971; Women Helping Women award Soroptimist, 1975; Disting. Service award N.Y. State PTA, 1985. Fellow Harry Truman Library; mem. Music Educators Nat. Conf., N.Y. State Sch, Music Assn., Capitol Hill Choral Soc. (dir.), N.Y. St. Council Arts Award Childrens Opera (dir. project), Albany Adminstrs. Assn., Albany Civic Auditorium (dir.), Delta Kappa Gamma, Delta Epsilon. Democrat. Roman Catholic. Clubs: Bus. and Profl. Women's, Soroptimist, Club of Albany, Cath. Women's Service League, Coll. St. Rose Alumni, Pres.'s Soc. Home: 226 Morris St Albany NY 12208 Office: Albany Bd Edn Acad Park Albany NY 12207

SACCO, RACHEL ROGNRUD, chamber of commerce executive; b. Mpls., Dec. 29, 1956; d. John Thomas and Eugenie (Hunecker) Rognrud; m. Joseph Francis Sacco, Jr., May 25, 1984; children: Nicholas Joseph, Sarah Elizabeth. BA, Ariz. State U., 1979. Mgr. membership Phoenix Valley of Sun Visitors and Conv. Bur., 1979-81, mgr. tourism sales, 1981-83, nat. sales mgr., 1983-86; dir. conv. and tourism Scottsdale (Ariz.) C. of C., 1986—. Recipient Spirit of Excellence award Am. Airlines, 1990. Mem. Hotel Sales and Mktg. Assn. (pres. 1984-85, sec. 1985-86, v.p. 1986-87, Mem. of Yr. award 1985), Meeting Planners Internat. (v.p. Phoenix 1987-88), Am. Soc. Assn. Execs., Soc. Incentive Travel Execs., Greater Phoenix Hotel Sales and Mkktg. Assn. (pres. 1987-88, Mem. of Yr. award 1985). Office: Scottsdale C of C 7333 Scottsdale Mall Scottsdale AZ 85251

SACCOMAN, PATRICIA LINDEN, Arabian horse breeder, writer; b. Chgo., Mar. 27, 1933; d. John Wendell and Ruth (Blanchard) Linden; m. William John Saccoman, June 11, 1964; children—Melinda, Joseph, John, Mark. Student San Diego State U., U. Ariz. Founder, pres. Pied Pier Tours for Children, San Diego, 1967-71; owner, mgr., pres. Lazy Diamond Ranch, Jerome, Idaho, 1971-82; owner, mgr., pres. Stallion Oaks Arabians, El Cajon, Calif., 1975—, Stallion Oaks Enterprises, El Cajon, 1980—; chmn. bd. The Adventures of Studley, El Cajon, 1984—. Author: Studley Sets his Goal, 1984; The Runaways, 1985. Bd. dirs. Salvation Army, El Cajon, 1982—, YMCA HDD Dept., San Diego, 1970-73, 87. Recipient cert. of appreciation Salvation Army, 1983, YMCA, 1976, Purple Rag award. Mem. Internat. Arabian Horse Assn. (youth com.), Arabian Horse Registry, Arabian Horse Trust (regent 1975—), Arabian Riders and Breeders (del., bd. dirs. 1981—), Desert Arabian Horse Assn., Star World of Arabians, San Diego Med. Aux., Delta Gamma. Republican. Avocations: swimming; tennis; aerobics; music. Home: 5816 Stallion Oaks Rd El Cajon CA 92021 Office: Stallion Oaks Enterprises 505 N Mollison El Cajon CA 92021

SACHS, LORRAINE PHYLLIS, professional society administrator; b. Jersey City, Feb. 25, 1936; d. Abe and Ann (Beitel) S. BA, U. Mich., 1956; MA, Columbia U., 1958. Cert. assn. exec. Asst. dir. evaluation Nat. League for Nursing, N.Y.C., 1959-69, dir. evaluation, 1969-73, dir. test svc., 1973-83; dep. exec. dir. Nat. Assn. State Bds. Accountancy, N.Y.C., 1984—. Author: Measurement and Evaluation in Nursing Education, 1980; contrb. articles to Nursing Outlook, 1975-82. Scholar U. Mich. Alumni Assn., 1987-90. Mem. Am. Assn. for Counseling & Devel., Am. Psychol. Assn., Am. Psychol. Soc., Am. Soc. Assn. Execs., Nat. Coun. on Measurement in Edn. N.Y. Assn. for Applied Psychology, N.Y. Soc. Assn. Execs. Home: 420 E 55th St 6C New York NY 10022 Office: NASBA 545 Fifth Ave New York NY 10017

SACHSE, BARBARA KAY, home economist; b. Milw., May 18, 1961; d. Thomas Edward and Joyce (Heck) S. B.S., U. Wis.-Stout, 1983. Food svc. mgr. Szabo Foodsvc., Columbus, Ohio, 1983; unit mgr. Saga Corp., Racine, Wis., 1984; R & D home economist Croissant Etc. Corp., Milw., 1984-86; field support mgr. Alto-Shaam, Inc., Menomonee Falls, Wis., 1986-89; mgr. R & D Wis.-Pak Foods, Butler, 1989; merchandiser, sales rep. Trump Co., Inc., Milw., 1989—. Vol. Milw. Pub. Mus. Named One of Outstanding Young Women of Am., 1986. Mem. NAFE, Home Econs. Profl. Improvement Coun., Home Economist in Bus. (chmn., chmn. profl. devel. coll. and univ. rels., chmn.-elect membership com.), Am. Home Econs. Assn. (Wis. chpt.), Toastmasters (edn. v.p., dep. area gov.). Avocations: aerobics, outdoor activities, reading, sports. Office: Associated Speakers Inc 12700 Bluemound Rd Elm Grove WI 53122

SACHSE, ELINOR YUDIN, economist; b. N.Y.C., Sept. 10, 1940; d. Lazarus Simon and Genevive (Goldberg) Yudin; B.A. with honors in Econs., Barnard Coll., 1962; M.A., Columbia U., 1964, Ph.D., 1968; m. Harry R. Sachse, Nov. 30, 1975; children—Michael Judah, Marianna Victoria. Mem. faculty dept. econs. SUNY, N.Y.C., 1966-69; various positions World Bank, Washington, 1969-79, chief internat. economy div., 1974-78; sr. staff economist internat. trade Council Econ. Advs., White House, 1980-82; cons. EYS Assocs., Washington, 1982—, Office of Balance of Payments Analysis U.S. Treasury, 1988—. Ford Found. fellow, 1965-66; Internat. Econs. Workshop fellow, 1963-64, 64-65; Francis M. Dibblee scholar, 1962-63. Author: Human Capital Migration, Direct Investment and the Transfer of Technology, 1976; also articles. Mem. Am. Econs. Assn. Jewish. Home: 2934 Newark St NW Washington DC 20008

SACINO, SHERRY WHEATLEY, public relations executive; b. Wilmington, Del., July 14, 1959; d. Lawrence McClusky and Carolyn Aria (Alexander) W.; m. Ronald Anthony Sacino, Dec. 29, 1984. BA, Ariz. State U. 1980. Pub. rels. exec. Phoenix Pro Soccer, 1980-81; owner, pres. Wheatley Advt. and Pub. Rels., Phoenix 1981-83; owner, pres. Sherry Wheatley Sacino, Inc., 1983—; pub. rels. counselor Intermedia Communications of Fla., Inc., 1988—; dir. news KZZZ/KAAA radio, Kingman, Ariz., 1976-77; promotional dir. KUPD/KUKQ radio, Phoenix, 1979-80; acct. supr. Wood, Cohen, Leonard & Bush Advt. and Pub. Rels., Tampa, Fla., 1983-84; mem. exec. com. Super Task Force, Tampa; founder, exec. dir. Tampa Bay Council for Internat. Visitors, Inc., 1984-87; exec. dir. Internat. Culinary Festival, Tampa, 1984; owner Ariz. Coaching Acad., Phoenix, 1981-83; pub. rels. dir. Richard Simmons Concert, Phoenix, 1982, Phoenix Clean Community System, 1982-83, Larry's Ice Cream Exchange, USSR, 1987; nat. spokesperson McDonald's Restaurant, 1977. Creator Ruby Slippers Kit, 1983; internat. mktg. dir. TicoFrut, Costa Rica; internat. mktg. cons. Gulf Machinery Co. Vol. pub. rels. coord. Muscular Dystrophy Assn., Ariz. and Fla., 1974-84, Arthritis Assn., Ariz. and Fla., 1980-84; dir. pub. rels. Dan Fogelbert Concert for Ariz. Gov. Babbitt, Phoenix, 1982; mem. Ariz. Gov.'s Council on Health and Fitness, 1983; mem. Global Family Citizens Moscow Summit, 1988, Handshake Exchange Moscow Summit, 1988; bd. dirs. Pinellas County March of Dimes; mem. Tampa Bay Internat. Trade Council; internat. publicist Moscow Internat. Peace Marathon, 1988-89; mem. adv. bd. World Runners; presenter Goodwill Games Human Rights Conf., Seattle, 1990. Recipient award Phoenix Clean Community System, 1982; cons. Costa Rican Citrus Industry, 1988—; internat. marketer food processing plants, 1989—; internat. publicist Moscow Marathon Project, 1989. Mem. Phoenix AD2 Club (v.p. 1983), Sigma Delta Chi (sec. 1978-80). Republican. Roman Catholic. Avocations: developing cultural awareness,

---

aviation, running. Home: 2507 Pass-A-Grille Way Pass-A-Grille Beach FL 33706 Office: 235 Central Ave Saint Petersburg FL 33701

SACKETT, MARY LOU, chiropractor; b. Ann Arbor, Mich., May 12, 1949; d. Lester Walter and Helen Beeken (Miller) S.; children: Samantha Lou Smith, Terry Lee Knoll II. A.S., Monroe County Community Coll., 1975; D in Chiropractic, Palmer Coll. Chiropractic, Davenport, Iowa, 1979. Diplomate Am. Bd. Chiropractic Examiners. Chiropractor, Hillsdale (Mich.) Family Chiropractic Life Center, 1980—. Mem. Planetary Soc. Home and Office: 2806 Carleton Rd Hillsdale MI 49242

SACKETT, SUSAN DEANNA, film and television production associate, writer; b. N.Y.C., Dec. 18, 1943; d. Maxwell and Gertrude Selma (Kugel) S. B.A. in Edn., U. Fla., 1964, M.Ed., 1965. Tchr. Dade County Schs., Miami, Fla., 1966-68, L.A. City Schs., 1968-69; asst. publicist, comml. coordinator NBC-TV, Burbank, Calif., 1970-73; asst. to creator of Star Trek Gene Roddenberry, 1974—; prodn. assoc. Star Trek: The Next Generation TV Series, 1987—; writer Star Trek: the Next Generation, 1990—; lectr. and guest speaker STAR TREK convs. in U.S., Eng., Australia, 1974—. Author and editor: Letters to Star Trek, 1977; co-author: Star Trek Speaks, 1979; The Making of Star Trek-The Motion Picture, 1979; You Can Be a Game Show Contestant and Win, 1982, Say Good/Night Gracie, 1986, The Hollywood Reporter Book of Box Office Hits, 1990. Mem. ACLU, Acad. Television Arts & Scis., Acad. Sci. Fiction, Fantasy and Horror Films, Writers Guild Am., Am. Humanists Assn., Mensa, Sierra Club. Democrat. Office: Paramount Pictures 5555 Melrose Ave Hollywood CA 90038

SACKLOW, HARRIETTE LYNN, advertising agency executive; b. Bklyn., Apr. 12, 1944; d. Sidney and Mildred (Myers) Cooperman; m. Stewart Irwin, July 2, 1967; 1 child, Ian Marc. BA, SUNY, Albany, 1965, postgrad., 1967-69; postgrad., Union Coll., 1969-70, Telmar Media Sch., N.Y.C., 1981. Tchr. math. Guilderland (N.Y.) Cen. Schs., 1967-76; v.p. Wolkcas Advt., Inc., Albany, N.Y., 1975—; supr. internship programs Coll. St. Rose, Albany, 1981; lectr. to area colls., Albany, 1981-83. V.p. Sisterhood Congregation Ohav Sholom, Albany, 1983-84; mem. bd. Congregation Ohav Sholom, Albany, 1983—; bd. dirs. Northeastern N.Y. chpt. Arthritis Found.; advisor Ronald McDonald House. Mem. NAFE, Am. Women in Radio and TV (pres. 1982-84, chmn. task force for new mem. acquisition, v.p. N.E. area 1987-89, chmn. area conf. 1987, pres. 1982-84, speaker, dir. 2), Advt. of the Capital Dist., Albany (N.Y.) Yacht Club. Office: Wolkcas Advt Inc 435 New Karner Rd Albany NY 12205

SACRE, MARY ALICE, employee benefits executive; b. St. Louis, Apr. 8, 1933; d. Homer E. and Alice E. (Cameron) Klipstine; m. Byron Lee Sacre, Nov. 21, 1959. A.A., Harris Tchrs. Coll., 1953. Night supr. Merc. Trust Co., St. Louis, 1952-53; asst. to sales mgr. Shampaine Co., St. Louis, 1953; policy writer Pearl Assurance Co., L.A., 1953-54; pers. specialist, editor Honeywell, Inc., Gardena Calif., 1954-67; indsl. relations mgr. Interform Inc., 1967-73; pension adminstr. So. Calif. Rapid Transit, L.A., 1973-78; corp. benefits dir. Denny's Inc., La Mirada Calif., 1978-86; exec. dir. Wash. Counties Ins. Fund, Olympia, 1986—. Mem. Self Ins. Inst. Am. (dir. 1984-86), Am. Soc. Pers. Adminstrs. Office: Wash Counties Ins Fund 1211 E 4th Ave Olympia WA 98501

SADDLEMYER, ANN (ELEANOR SADDLEMYER), critic, theater historian, educator; b. Prince Albert, Sask., Can., Nov. 28, 1932; d. Orrin Angus and Elsie Sarah (Ellis) S. BA, U. Sask., 1953; MA, Queen's U., 1956, LLD, 1977; PhD, U. London, 1961; DLitt (hon.), U. Victoria, 1989, McGill U., 1989, Windsor U., 1990. Lectr. Victoria (B.C.) Coll., 1956-57, instr., 1960-62, asst. prof., 1962-65; assoc. prof. U. Victoria, 1965-68, prof. English, 1968-71; prof. English Victoria Coll. U. Toronto, 1971—, dir. Grad. Centre for Study of Drama Victoria Coll., 1972-77, 85-86; sr. fellow Massey Coll., 1975-88, master, 1988—; Berg prof. NYU, 1975. Dir. Theatre Plus, 1972-84; dir. Colin Smythe Pubs.; Author: The World of W.B. Yeats, 1965, In Defence of Lady Gregory, Playwright, 1966, Synge and Modern Comedy, 1968, J.M. Synge Plays Books One and Two, 1968, Lady Gregory Plays, 4 vols, 1970, Letters to Molly: Synge to Maire O'Neill, 1971, Letters from Synge to W.B. Yeats and Lady Gregory, 1971, Collected Letters of John Millington Synge, Vol. 1, 1983, vol. II, 1984, Theatre Business, The Correspondence of the First Abbey Theatre Director, 1982, (with Colin Smythe) Lady Gregory Fifty Years After, 1987, Early Stages: Theatre in Ontario, 1800-1914, 1990; co-editor Theatre History in Canada, 1980-86; editorial bds. Modern Drama, 1972-82, English Studies in Can., 1973-83, Themes in Drama, 1974, Shaw Rev, 1977—, Research in the Humanities, 1976—, Irish Univ. Rev. 1970—, Yeats Ann., 1982-86, Studies in Contemporary Irish Lit., 1986—, McGill Studies in Drama, 1988—; contrbr. articles to profl. jours. Can. Council scholar, 1958-59; fellow, 1968, Guggenheim fellow, 1968, 77, sr. research fellow Connaught, 1985; recipient Brit. Acad. Rose Mary Crawshay award, 1986, Disting. Service award Province of Ont., 1985. Fellow Royal Soc. Can., Royal Soc. Arts; mem. Internat. Assn. Study Anglo-Irish Lit. (chmn. 1973-76), Assn. Can. Theatre History (pres. 1976-77), Can. Assn. Irish Studies, Assn. Can. Univ. Tchrs. English, Can. Assn. Univ. Tchrs., Assn. Can. and Que. Lit. Home: 100 Lakeshore Rd E, Apt 803, Oakville, ON Canada L6J 6M9 Office: Massey Coll, 4 Devonshire Pl, Toronto, ON Canada M5S 2E1

SADER, CAROL HOPE, state representative, legal editor; b. Bklyn., July 19, 1935; d. Nathan and Mollie (Farkas) Shimkin; m. Harold M. Sader, June 9, 1957; children: Neil, Randi Sader Friedlander, Elisa. BA, Barnard Coll., Columbia U., 1957. Sch. tchr. Bd. Edn., Morris, Conn., 1957-58; legal editor W. H. Anderson Co., Cin., 1974-78; freelance legal editor Shawnee Mission, Kans., 1987—; mem. Ho. of Reps. 22d Kans. Dist., 1987—. Contrbr. articles to profl. jours. Chmn. bd. Johnson County Community Coll., Overland Park, Kans. 1984-86, trustee, 1981-86; bd. dirs. Ct. Aptd. Spl. Adv. Project County, Shawnee Mission, United Community Svcs. of Johnson County, Shawnee Mission, 1984—, Jewish Vocat. Svc. Bd., 1983—, Johnson County Community Coll. Found., Jewish Community Rels.; co-chmn. Johnson County Eldernet Coalition. Recipient Trustee award Assn. of Women in Jr. and Community Colls., 1985, award Kans. Pub. Transit Assn., 1990. Mem. Coun. Women Legislators, LWV (pres. Johnson County chpt. 1983-85, mem. state bd. 1986-87), Phi Delta Kappa. Democrat. Home: 8612 Linden Dr Prairie Village KS 66207 Office: Kans Ho Reps Rm 272-W Topeka KS 66612

SADICK, BARBARA ANN, publishing production manager; b. Bklyn., July 31, 1952; d. Richard L. and Marion (Weiss) S. B.A. cum laude, NYU, 1974. Asst. editor Bus. Research Pubs., N.Y.C., 1977-80; prodn. mgr., editor MacRae's Blue Book, 1980-84; prodn. mgr. Bus. Research Publs., N.Y.C., 1982-84, Media Horizons, N.Y.C., 1985-87, Aperture, N.Y.C., 1987; prodn. coordinator Am. Pizzi Offset Corp., N.Y.C., 1987—. Mem. Women in Prodn., NOW. Office: Am Pizzi Offset Corp 141 E 44th St New York NY 10017

SADLE, AMY ANN, watercolorist, printmaker; b. Council Bluffs, Iowa, Aug. 3, 1940; Student State U. Iowa, U. R.I.; studied with Fritz Eichenberg, Claude Croney, Virginia Cobb, Ed Whitney, Naoko Matsubara, and others. One woman shows U. N.D. 1986, San Diego Print Club, 1985, others; exhibited Tour of Spain, U. Kans., United Individualist, N.Y.C., Dartmouth Coll., N.H., St. Johns, Nfld., Haymarket Gallery, Lincoln, Nebr., 1989; represented in permanent collections Statue of Liberty, Tulsa Libr., Des Moines Art Ctr., Nebr. Hist. Commn., Nebr. Indian Commn.; corp. dir. (book and tour) Impact: The Art of Nebraska Women; author: Home of Wooden Men and Iron Men. Recipient Best of Show award San Diego Print Club, 1984; Daniel Smith grantee for rsch. art materials, 1987. Mem. Artists Equity, Phila. Print Club, N.J. Internat. Print Club, AWS Watercolor Assn.

SADLER, MARY KATHRYN, sales executive; b. Columbus, Ohio, Nov. 13, 1953; d. J.E. Jr. and Clara Rose (Thompson) S. BSN with honors, U. Ky., 1978; MBA, U. S.C., 1987. Primary nurse U. Ky. Med. Ctr., Lexington, 1978-79; charge nurse Richland Meml. Hosp., Columbia, S.C., 1980-83; clin. dir., nursing agt. Hematology & Oncology Assocs., Columbia, 1983-86; charge nurse Lexington Med. Ctr., West Columbia, S.C., 1986-89, leader svc. excellence workshop, 1988-89; surg. nurse St. Mary's Hosp., Huntington, W.Va., 1989; thrombolytic info. specialist pharm. sales dept. Genentech, Inc., Huntington, 1989—. Program dir. S.C. So. Heritage Celebration. Recipient Nat. Ladies Appreciation award SCV, 1988; Fed.

---

scholar Graduate Nursing Adminstrn, 1980-81. Mem. NAFE, Am. Mgmt. Assn., Nat. Coun. Jewish Women; vol. RN emergency dept. Raleigh Gen. Hosp.; counselor to abused children. Office: 634 Ridgewood Rd Huntington WV 25701

SADOFF, MICKY, organization administrator; b. Chgo., Apr. 30, 1944; m. Ronald B. Sadoff, June 12, 1965; children: Bryan D., Michael A. BA in Edn., Cardinal Stritch Coll., Milw., 1981. On-air producer, interviewer sta. WUWM-FM, Milw., 1977-82; founder, pres., southeastern Wis. chpt. MADD, Milw., 1982-87; nat. bd. MADD, 1984-88, pres., 1988—; mem. nat. MADD bd. fin., legis.; chmn. victim issues and exec. coms.; organized two state confs. with nat. speakers, 1983, 85; supervised and marketed all activities for MADD regarding pub. rels., media, speakers bur.'s, legislation, vol. tng., fund raising, edn. and monitoring justice system, 1982-87; apptd. Gov.'s ADv. Coun. Hwy. Safety, Wis., 1984-89, Nat. Safety Coun. Hwy. Safety Com., 1985—, Milw. County Safety Commn., 1986-89, Sta. WUWM-FM Community Adv. Bd., 1983-89; speaker in field. Mem. Harvard Alcohol Com., 1988; bd. dirs. Nat. Safety Coun., 1989. Recipient J.C. Penney Golden Rule award, 1983, Voluntary Action Ctr. award, 1985, Wis. Drivers Edn. Vol. award, 1986, Dept. Transp. Citizen Activist award, 1986, Nat. Hwy. Traffic Safety Adminstrn. Citizen award, 1986, Award of Excellence for Vol. Leadership Assn. for Vol. Adminstrs., 1987, Ione Quinby Griggs award Vis. Nurses Assn., 1987, Cardinal Stritch Coll. Alumni award, 1989. Office: MADD 669 Airport Frwy Ste 310 Hurst TX 76053

SADOWSKI, DENISE A., nursing consultant; b. Lorain, Ohio, Jan. 28, 1958; d. John A. and Theresa L. (Zator) S. BSN, Bowling Green State U., 1980; MS in Burn and Trauma Nursing, U. Cin., 1984. Cert. ATLS nurse, instr. in ACLS, BLS and advanced burn life support. Burn clin. nurse specialist Vanderbilt U. Med. Ctr., Nashville, 1984-85, Shriners Burns Inst., Cin., 1985-88; clin. nurse specialist, cons. Cin., 1988—; lectr. in field nationally and internationally. Contbr. numerous articles to profl. jours. and chpts. to books; guest appearances on radio and TV. Mem. vol. faculty U. Cin. Sch. Nursing, 1985-88; mem. adjunct faculty Vanderbilt U. Sch. Nursing, Nashville, 1984-85; active Updowntowners, Cin., 1989—. Recipient Clin. Rsch. award; named an Outstanding Grad. Student. Mem. ASPRSN, ACCH, AARC, AACN, Internat. Soc. for Burn Injuries, Am. Burn Assn. (nat. edn. com., com. for orgn. and delivery of burn care), Emergency Nursing Assn., Am. Cons. League, Sigma Theta Tau (hon.), Alpha Lambda Delta (hon.). Roman Catholic. Home and Office: 7312 Plainfield Rd Cincinnati OH 45236

SADOYAMA, NANCY ARTIS, administrative operations analyst; b. Oakland, Calif., June 12, 1947; d. Robert Lee and Norma Lee (Dyches) Artis; m. Edward T. Sadoyama, June 18, 1978. BA in Psychology, Calif. State U., Hayward, 1974, MPA with highest deptl. honors, 1987. Personnel rep. Mack Western, Hayward, 1970-73; with Calif. State U., Hayward, 1974-87, adminstrv. ops. analyst, 1987—; microcomputer cons. Milklejohn Hall, Calif. State U., Hayward, 1984—; treas., bd. dirs. Calif. State U. mem. presdl. selection adv. com., Hayward staff assembly, chmn. social sub-com., 1989-90. Recipient Vivian Cunniffe Outstanding Staff award Calif. State U., Hayward, 1986. Mem. Hayward MPA Alumni Assn., Faculty Club, Commonwealth San Francisco. Home: 24400 Armada Ctr Armada MI 48005 Office: Calif State U Liberal Studies Hayward CA 94542

SAEF, KAREN BAILIS, psychologist; b. St. Louis, Jan. 7, 1954; d. Seymour Elliot and Eunice Evelyn (Weinhaus) Bailis; m. Jerold Lawrence Saef, May 15, 1983; children: Joshua Michael, Benjamin Ari, Rachel Marie. BA cum laude, U. Colo., 1975; MA, U. Mo., 1978, PhD, 1981. Lic. psychologist, Fla., Mo., Mass. Asst. attending psychlogist Med. Sch. Harvard U., Boston, 1981-87; pvt. practice Boston, 1981-87, Stuart, Fla., 1987-88; supr. psychology dept. Washington U., St. Louis, 1988-90; pvt. practice St. Louis, 1988-89, Bradenton, Fla., 1990—. Mem. Am. Psychol. Assn., Fla. Psychol. Assn., Mass. Psychol. Assn.

SAELENS, DEBORAH LYNN, marketing executive; b. Summerville, Ga., June 25, 1955; d. Hubert Len and Joann Harriet (Stiles) Teems; m. Edward Robert Saelens, May 23, 1977; children: Brandon Edward, Brianne Amanda. BA in Psychology and Sociology, Oakland U., Rochester, Mich., 1976; MA in Bus. Mgmt., Cen. U., Mt. Pleasant, Mich., 1980. Prodn. supr. Chesterfield (Mich.) Trim, 1976-78; supr. prodn. control Ford Motor Co., Chesterfield, 1978; sr. prodn. contr. Vinyl Plant Ford Motor Co., Mt. Clemens, Mich., 1978-80; mgr. prodn. planning Centronics Line Printer div., Rochester, 1980-82, product specialist, 1982-83, product mgr., 1983-85; mktg. supr. TRW Vehicle Safety Systems Inc., Washington, Mich., 1985—. Vol. United Found. Mem. Am. Mktg. Assn., Nat. Fedn. Bus. Women, Lioness. Home: 24400 Armada Ctr Armada MI 48005 Office: TRW Vehicle Safety Systems 4505 W Twenty Six Mile Rd Washington MI 48094

SAENZ, CAROL JUNE, public relations executive, actress; b. Chgo., Feb. 25, 1944; d. Ernest Bernard and Gertrude Esther Larson; m. Ralph Arthur Saenz, Mar. 5, 1960 (div. July 1983); children: Jon, Ralph; m. William Patrick Olmstead, June 7, 1986. Student, Fenger Jr. Coll., Chgo., 1961-62, Actors Workshop, Chgo., 1990. Publicist Barbara Gardner & Assocs., Studio City, Calif., 1983-86; prin. Gardner & Saenz Pub. Rels., North Hollywood, Calif. 1986-87; prin. Carol Saenz Pub. Rels., North Hollywood, 1987-88; prin. Hollywood (Calif.) Live, 1988—; writer, narrator, promoter OK Video Prodns.; free-lance producer, writer. Appeared in films Terminal Velocity, The Psychic, Suicide Squeeze, The Monitors, in plays Goodnight Ladies, Play It Again Sam, The Odd Couple, Send Me No Flowers, The Guardsman, Beginners Luck, The Owl and the Pussycat, Mary Mary, Who's Happy Now, Chapter Two, others; host, co-host (TV programs) Mid Morning L.A., Success Story, A Spl. Child, Bd. and Care for the Aged, (videos) A Taste of L.A., A Spirited Visit; host and narrator other programs and videos; contbr. articles to mags. Bd. dirs. Jeffrey Found. for Handicapped, 1987, promoter pub. svc. announcements; pres., chair Women for Jeffrey. Recipient Appreciation award Cystic Fibrosis Found., 1985, Cert. of Merit Jeffrey Found. for Handicapped, 1988, Jeanne Golden Halo award So. Calif. Motion Picture Coun., 1989. Home: 12153 Lull St North Hollywood CA 91605

SAENZ, LYDIA, aircraft company administrator; b. L.A., Dec. 22, 1953; d. Celso Webb and Frances (Briones) Garcia; m. Ralph Saenz, Mar. 13, 1971; children: Ralph, Richard, Robby. Student, Coll. Transp., Boston, 1987. With Hughes Aircraft Co., Canoga Park, Calif., 1978—; now rate and traffic analyst Hughes Aircraft Co.

SAFA, CYNTHIA SHAKLEE, pediatrician; b. Cheverly, Md., June 13, 1960; d. William Eugene and Rose Marie (Miller) Shaklee; m. Jihad Abdulhalim Safa, Nov. 18, 1983; 1 child. Nashalla Jihad. BA, U. Okla., Norman, 1981; MD, U. Okla., Oklahoma City, 1985. Diplomate Am. Bd. Pediatrics. Resident in pediatrics Tulsa Med. Coll., 1985-88; pvt. practice, 1988—. Fellow Am. Acad. Pediatrics (candidate); mem. AMA, Okla. Med. Assn. Democrat. Moslem. Office: Young Peoples Clinic 3401 E 21st St Tulsa OK 74114

SAFARS, BERTA See FISZER-SZAFARZ, BERTA

SAFERITE, LINDA LEE, library director; b. Santa Barbara, Calif., Mar. 25, 1947; d. Elwyn C. and Polly (Frazer) S.; m. Andre Doyon, July 16, 1985. BA, Calif. State U., Chico, 1969; MS in Library Sci., U. So. Calif., 1970; cert. in indsl. Relations, UCLA, 1976; MBA, Pepperdine U., 1979. Librarian-in-charge, reference librarian Los Angeles County Pub. Library System, 1970-73, regional reference librarian, 1973-75, sr. librarian-in-charge, 1975-78, regional adminstr., 1978-80; library dir. Scottsdale (Ariz.) Pub. Library System, 1980—. Bd. dirs. Scottsdale-Paradise Valley YMCA, 1981-86. Recipient Cert. Recognition for efforts in civil rights Ariz. Atty. Gen.'s Office, 1985. Mem. ALA, Ariz. State Library Assn. (pres. 1987-88), Mountain Plains Library Assn. Republican. Clubs: Metropolitan Bus. and Profl. Women (Scottsdale pres. 1986-87). Lodge: Soroptimist (pres. 1981-83). Office: Scottsdale Pub Libr 3839 Civic Ctr Blvd Scottsdale AZ 85251

SAFFELL, VIRGINIA MARIE, writer, educator; b. Jan. 20, 1923; d. Estle Marvin Long and Sarah Adelaide Stephens; m. John A. Saffell, Dec. 25, 1942 (wid. 1983); children: Sandra, John Brian, Leslie. BA cum laude, Pacific

Lutheran U., 1978, MAH, 1980. Experiential learning asst. and instr. Fort Steilacoom Community Coll., Tacoma, Wash., 1978-80; tchr. City Univ., Tacoma, 1982; community editor Lakewood Press, Tacoma, 1983-86; creative writing instr. Clover Park Vo-Tech Sch., Tacoma, 1988—; swimming instr., 1943-57. Co-author: Creativity to Copywrite, 1968; cons. editor Schindler Creative Svcs., 1963-89; contbr. articles to newspapers. Vol. Girl Scouts, 1951-67, Wash. State Crime Prevention, 1988-89, Srs. Against Crime, Tacoma, 1987-89, Olympia (Wash.) Symphony Orch., 1989, various polit. campaigns, Tacoma, 1969-88. Named Miss Lakewood candidate, Lakewood Community, Tacoma, 1985. Mem. AAUW, United Singles Bridge Club, Phi Theta Kappa. Republican. Presbyterian.

SAFFLE, SHERRY WOOD, advertising executive; b. Corpus Christi, Tex., Mar. 9, 1959; d. Henry Franklin Wood and Mary Sue (Wagnon) Bolton; m. Douglas Karl Saffle, Jan. 13, 1990. BA, Tex. Tech. U., Lubbock, 1981. Advt. sales rep. Plano (Tex.) Daily Star Courier, 1981-82, Avalanche Jour., Lubbock, 1982-83; account exec. Cox Cable Rep., Lubbock, 1983—. vol. United Way of Lubbock, 1984-86; ways and means chair Ballet Lubbock Guild, 1988; v.p. Tex. Tech. U. Mass Communications Alumni Coun., Lubbock, 1988-90, pres., 1990—. Named Outstanding Venturist of Yr., Soroptomist Internat., Lubbock, 1989. Mem. Women in Communications (pres. elect 1990-91, Mem. of Yr. 1987, Silver award 1988, Pres.'s Award for Excellence 1990), Lubbock Advt. Fedn., Ex-Students Assn., Venture Club Lubbock (pres. 1988-89). Methodist. Home: 2410 89th St Lubbock TX 79423

SAFFO, MARY BETH, research biologist; b. Inglewood, Calif., Apr. 8, 1948; d. Paul Laurence and Joan (Wilson) S.; m. Erik Alfred Whitehorn, Sept. 2, 1978; one child, Nathan Alexander Whitehorn. BA, U. Calif., Santa Cruz., 1969; PhD, Stanford U., 1977. Miller research fellow U. Calif., Berkeley, 1976-78; asst. prof. Swarthmore (Pa.) Coll., 1978-85; ind. investigator Marine Biol. Lab., Woods Hole, Mass., 1979-84; assoc. research marine biologist U. Calif., Santa Cruz, 1985—, lectr., 1988—; vis. scholar U. Wash., Seattle, 1982. Grantee Research Corp., 1980, 84, Am. Philos. Soc., 1980, 83, NSF, 1981, 84, 85, Whitehall Found., 1984; Steps Toward Independence fellow, 1979; AAUW fellow U. Calif., Berkeley, 1981-82. Fellow AAAS (electorate nominating com. sect. G. 1989—); mem. Western Soc. Naturalists, Am. Soc. Zoologists (program officer div. Invertebrate Zoology 1985-87, mem. con. to ensure equal opportunity 1988-90), Mycological Soc. Am., Internat. Soc. Endocytobiology, Soc. Study of Evolution. Democrat. Office: U Calif Inst Marine Scis Santa Cruz CA 95064

SAFFRAN, JUDITH, toxicologist, educator; b. Montreal, Que., Can., Nov. 5, 1923; came to U.S., 1969; d. Philip and Pauline (Wigdor) Cohen; m. Murray Saffran, June 8, 1947; children: David, Wilma, Arthur, Richard. BSc, McGill U., Montreal, 1944, PhD, 1948. Registered in clin. chemistry. Clin. endocrinologist Jewish Gen. Hosp., Montreal, 1955-69; rsch. assoc. Instr. Med. Rsch., Toledo Hosp., 1969-74; assoc. prof. biochemistry, assoc. prof. ob-gyn. Med. Coll. Ohio, Toledo, 1974-79, asst. prof. pathology, 1990—; clin. chemist Med. Coll. of Pathology Med. Coll. Ohio Hosp., 1980-85, toxicologist, 1985—. Contbr. articles to sci. jours. Mem. Women's Am. Orgn. for Rehab. through Tng., 1985—. Home: 2331 Hempstead Rd Toledo OH 43606 Office: Med Coll Ohio Toledo OH 43699

SAFI, DEBORAH CAVAZOS, lawyer; b. Dallas, Feb. 8, 1953; d. Arnaldo Nelson and Ila Mae (Rinn) Cavazos; m. Hazim Jawad Safi, July 28, 1979; children: Jawad Joseph, Aminah Mae. BA, Baylor U., 1975, JD, 1977. Bar: Tex. 1977. Assoc. Andrews & Kurth, Houston, 1977-81; corp. atty. Transco Energy Co., Houston, 1981-83; of counsel Harman & Timby P.C. (formerly Anderson, Harrell & Timby P.C.), Houston, 1985-88, Bennett & Broocks, Houston, 1988-89; pvt. practice Houston, 1983-85, 89—. Mem. fund raising com. Children's Mus., Houston, 1986; co-leader Blue Bird/Camp Fire Girls, Waco, Tex., 1972-73, Tex. Bd. Legal Specialization, Real Estate Law Adv. Commn., 1988-89; vice chmn. combat hunger and homeless com. State Bar Tex. Named one of Outstanding Women of 1982, Transco Energy Co. and YWCA, Houston 1982. Fellow Tex. Bar Found., Houston Bar Found.; mem. ABA, Houston Bar Assn., Houston Young Lawyers Assn. (chmn. directory planning com. 1987-88, com. chair 1981-82, bd. dirs. 1982-84, treas. 1984-86, v.p. 1986-87, named Outstanding Com. Chmn. 1980-81, 87, 88), Tex. Young Lawyers Assn. (bd. dirs. 1986-88, co-editor newsletter 1986-87, treas. 1988-89, mktg. and pub. rels. com. chmn. 1987-88), Tex. Bar Assn., Fed. Energy Bar Assn., Houston Bar Assn. (editorial bd. Houston Lawyer 1988—), State Bar Tex. (vice chmn. Combat Hunger and Homeless com.), Delta Delta Delta, Phi Delta Phi.

SAFIAN, SHELLEY CAROLE, advertising agency executive; b. Bklyn., May 29, 1954; d. Jack Israel and Harriet Sara (Cohen) S. B.F.A., Parsons Sch. Design/New Sch. for Social Research, 1975. Asst. art dir. Axelrod and Assocs., N.Y.C., 1975-77; art dir. Sta. WDBO-TV-AM/FM, Orlando, Fla., 1978-80; owner, pres. Safian Communications Services, Inc., Orlando, 1981—; mem. adv. com. Career Edn., Orange County, Fla., 1981—, chmn., 1982-83; advt. cons. post-secondary vocat. and community edn. div. Orange County Pub. Schs., 1983-84. Exec. producer/dir. March of Dimes Telethon, Orlando, 1984; bd. dirs. Boy Scouts Am., 1987—; exec. dir. United Cerebral Palsy Telethon, Orlando, 1982-83; pub. relations Liaison-United Cerebral Palsy, Orlando, 1983-84; founder Career Dir. for the Deaf, Orlando, 1985. Recipient 1st pl. Addy awards Orlando Advt. Fedn., 1981, 87, 88, 1st pl. Addy award, 2d pl. awards, merit awards, 1982, 84, 85, 87, 88, Nat. Telly award Bronze Statue, 1988, Up and Coming award Price Waterhouse/Orlando Bus. Jour., 1988. Mem. Broadcast Promotion and Mktg. Execs. Assn. (Silver Medallion 1983, nat. finalist 2 Silver Microphone awards 1986, 87), Broadcast Designer's Assn. (bd. dirs. 1980-82), Am. Women in Radio and TV (bd. dirs. 1980-81). Republican. Avocation: horseback riding. Office: Safian Communications Svcs 2211 Lee Rd Ste 223 Winter Park FL 32789

SAGAL-MUTRYNOWSKI, LAURIE MAE, finance company administrator; b. Windsor, Ont., Can., Sept. 11, 1950; came to U.S., 1951; d. John and Virginia Marie (Webber) Sagal; m. Alan Joseph Mutrynowski, May 22, 1976. AA, Macomb Community Coll., 1968; BA, Oakland U., 1972, MBA, 1984. Clk. accounts payable Fruehauf Corp., Detroit, 1972-73; with Fruehauf Fin. Co., Detroit, 1973-87; mgr. fin. analysis Fruehauf Corp., Detroit, 1987-90; leasing contr. OCE Credit Corp., Chgo., 1990—. Mem. NAFE. Democrat. Methodist. Lodge: Masons. Home: 1427 Valley Lake Dr Apt 1146 Schaumburg IL 60195 Office: Fruehauf Fin Co 10900 Harper Detroit MI 48232

SAGAWA, SHIRLEY SACHI, lawyer; b. Rochester, N.Y., Aug. 25, 1961; d. Hidetaka H. and Patricia (Ford) S.; m. Gregory A. Baer. AB, Smith Coll., 1983; MSc, London Sch. Econs., 1984; JD, Harvard U., 1987. Bar: Md. 1988. Chief counsel youth policy, labor and human resources com. U.S. Senate, Washington, 1987—. Mem. exec. bd. Orgn. for Pan Asian Am. Women, Washington, 1987-89; mem. Women in Color Leadership Coun. Recipient cert. of recognition Nat. Coun. Jewish Women, 1989; Harry S. Truman scholar, 198l; Smith Coll. Alumnae Assn. fellow, 1983, AAUW fellow, 1986. Mem. Md. Bar Assn. Democrat. Episcopalian. Office: US Senate Com on Labor and Human Resources Washington DC 20510

SAGE, JEANETTE BONNER, nurse; b. Ponca City, Okla., Oct. 22, 1945; d. Eugene Roy and Betty Jean (Robinson) Bonner; m. Earl Edward Sage, Apr. 9, 1966; 1 child, Elizabeth Jean. Diploma in X-Ray Tech., Richland County Hosp., Columbia, S.C., 1965; AA in Nursing, St. Mary's Coll., 1975; BS in Nursing, Lindenwood Coll., 1983; MA, Webster U., 1988. Registered nurse, Mo., lic. nursing home adminstr., Mo. X-ray technologist Mallinckrodt Inst., St. Louis, 1965-66; nuclear med. x-ray technologist St. Joseph Hosp., Kirkwood, Mo., 1966-68; nuclear med. technologist Normandy (Mo.) Osteo. Hosp., 1968-70; staff nurse St. Lukes Hosp., Chesterfield, Mo., 1975, St. Joseph Health Ctr., St. Charles, Mo., 1975-79; supr. St. Joseph Health Ctr., St. Charles, 1979-83, asst. dir., 1983-90, patient care coord.in skilled nursing facility, 1990—. Mem. Mo. Orgn. Nurse Execs., Am. Nurses Assn., Mo. Nurses Assn., Am. Coll. Health Care Execs., Nat. League for Nursing, NAFE, Mo. League Nursing Home Adminstrs. Democrat. Home: 154 Cole Blvd Saint Charles MO 63301

SAGER, JO ANN, public relations executive; b. Ft. Lewis, Wash., May 1, 1956; d. Robert Alan and Virginia Henderson (Taylor) S.; m. Thomas D. Pickett, June 11, 1983 (div. 1988). Student, Universidad de los Andes, Bogota, Colombia, 1976; BA in Spanish, Wake-Forest U., 1978; postgrad., U. Tex., 1978-79. Imagery analyst CIA, Washington, 1979-82; account exec. Schneider, Parker, Jakuc Pub. Rels., Boston, 1982-84; sr. account exec. Ingalls Pub. Rels., Boston, 1984-85; pub. rels. mgr. to dir. mktg. communications Computer Corp. of Am., Cambridge, Mass., 1985-87, dir. mktg. communications, 1988; account supr. Miller Communications, Boston, 1988; mng. dir. Miller Communications, L.A., Calif., 1989; v.p. Miller Communications, Marina del Rey, Calif., 1990—. Inst. Latin Am. Studies fellow U. Tex., 1978. Mem. Pub. Rels. Soc. of Am., Women in Communications Inc., Software Pubs. Assn. (assoc.). Democrat. Mem. Covenant Ch. Office: Miller Communications 4640 Admiralty Way Marina del Rey CA 90292

SAGER, JOYCE TOSHIYE TANIMOTO, medical infosystems specialist; b. Gridley, Calif., Jan. 23, 1950; d. Masashi Mike and Satomi (Ishihara) Tanimoto; m. Richard A. Sager, Sept. 13, 1975. BS in Foods and Nutrition, U. Calif., Davis, 1968; MPH, U. Calif., Berkeley, 1973; postgrad., U. Utah, 1986—. Dietitian St. Alphonsus Regional Med. Ctr., Boise, Idaho, 1974-75; nutrition lectr. Boise State U., 1974; pub. health nutritionist SW Dist. Dept. Health, Caldwell, Idaho, 1975-76; state dir. women, infants and children nutrition program Idaho Dept. Health and Welfare, Boise, 1976-86; research asst. in med. informatics Latter Day Sts. Hosp., Salt Lake City, 1986—. Recipient Sci. and Math. Achievement award Bank Am., 1968, Certificate of Recognition, Gov. Idaho, 1986. Mem. Am. Dietetic Assn., Utah Dietetic Assn., Nat. Assn. Women, Infants and Children Dirs. (western region rep. 1980-81). Democrat. Home: PO Box 58341 Salt Lake City UT 84158

SAGER, RUTH, geneticist; b. Chgo., Feb. 7, 1918; married, 1973. BS, U. Chgo., 1938; MS, Rutgers U., 1944; PhD, Columbia U., 1948. Merck fellow Nat. Research Council, 1949-51; asst. in biochemistry Rockefeller Inst., 1951-55; research assoc. in zoology Columbia U., N.Y.C., 1955-60, sr. research assoc. in zoology, 1961-65; prof. biology Hunter Coll., CUNY, 1966-75; prof. cellular genetics Harvard Med. Sch., 1975-88, prof. emeritus, 1988—; chief genetics div. Dana-Farber Cancer Inst., from 1975. Author: (with F.J. Ryan) Cell Heredity, 1961, Cytoplasmic Genes and Organelles, 1972. Recipient Gilbert Morgan Smith medal Nat. Acad. Scis., 1988; Guggenheim fellow, 1972-73. Fellow AAAS; mem. Am. Acad. Arts and Sci., Nat. Acad. Scis., Am. Soc. Cell Biologists, Genetics Soc. Am., Am. Assn. Cancer Rsch., Am. Soc. Biol. Chem., Sigma Xi, Phi Beta Kappa. Office: Dana-Farber Cancer Inst 44 Binney St Boston MA 02115

SAGINAW, ROSE BLAS, advertising agency executive; b. Detroit, Jan. 10, 1926; d. Harry B. and Lillian (Sher) Blas; m. Sol L. Saginaw, Nov. 17, 1945; children: Harry J., Jane N. Student, Wayne U., 1944-46. Treas. Brake-O Brakes, Dallas, 1965-70; edn. dir. Temple Shalom, Dallas, 1972-76; pres. Rose Saginaw Advt., Dallas, 1976-78; sr. v.p. Anderson Fischel Thompson div. J. Walter Thompson, Dallas, 1978—; cons. Tex. Occupational Therapy Assn., 1987-88, Ctr. for NonProfit Mgmt., Dallas, 1983-84; guest lectr.; mem. adv. bd. Sch. Bus. U. Tex., Denton, 1988—. Book reviewer. Bd. advisers Baylor Hosp. Homecare, Dallas, 1987—. Recipient 1st Place Nat. Publicity award Jewish Fedn., 1958; award of merit Dallas Home for Jewish Aged, 1988, others. Home: 3831 Turtle Creek 6-B Dallas TX 75219 Office: Anderon Fischel Thompson 5151 Beltline Rd Ste 700 Dallas TX 75240

SAHANEK, TATANA, librarian, editor; b. Prague, Czechoslovakia, Nov. 2, 1922; d. Emanuel and Frances (Blovsky) S.; naturalized, 1969; JUDr., Masaryk U., Brno, Czechoslovakia, 1947; B.L.S., U. Toronto (Ont., Can.), 1953; Ph.D. (Higher Edn. Act fellow), U. Tex.-Austin, 1973. Cataloger, Toronto Pub. Library, 1953-55; law librarian, gen. reference librarian Ont. Legis. Library, Toronto, 1956-61; head catalog and classification div. Harvard Law Sch. Library, 1962-65; head catalog dept. Law Library, U. Mich., Ann Arbor, 1965-66; translator, interpreter Dow Chem. Internat., Midland, Mich., 1967-68; librarian-translator Dow Chem. Co., Tex. div., Freeport, 1968-70; asst. librarian Antioch Sch. Law, Washington, 1972-74; editor Index to Legal Priodicals, H.W. Wilson Co., Bronx, N.Y., 1974-78; coordinator Saginaw (Mich.) Med. Ctr., 1978-79; acquisitions librarian Exec. Office of Pres. Info. Ctr., Washington, 1980—. Recipient award U. Tex. Grad. Sch. Subvention Fund, 1972; spl. achievement award Exec. Office of Pres., 1981, Dir.'s award for Disting. Service Exec. Office of Pres., 1986. Mem. Assn. Am. Law Libraries, Spl. Libraries Assn., ALA, Canadian, Ont. library assns., Czechoslovak Soc. Arts and Scis. Club: Worldwide Sportmen's. Author: Entries for Provincial Publications, Province of Ontario, 1867-1960, 1960; editor Index to Legal Periodicals, 1973-79. Home: 205 Yoakum Pkwy #1602 Alexandria VA 22304 Office: New Exec Office Bldg Washington DC 20503

SAHLI, BRENDA PAYNE, toxicologist, consultant, educator; b. Richmond, Va., Sept. 28, 1942; d. Thomas Frederick and Nancy (Rhoades) Payne; m. Muhammad Saleh Sahli, Oct. 14, 1967; children—Andrea, Kevin, Heather. B.S. in Applied Sci. with honors, Richmond Profl. Inst. (Va.), 1964; M.S. in Pharm. Chemistry, Med. Coll. Va., Richmond, 1967; Ph.D., Va. Commonwealth U., 1974. Research asst. Am. Tobacco Co., Richmond, 1964-65; chemist Firestone Synthetic Fibers and Textiles Co., Hopewell, Va., 1967-69; research chemist E.I. duPont de Nemours & Co., Richmond, 1974-77; toxicologist Toxic Substances Info., Va. Dept. Health, Richmond, 1977-82, dir., 1983-84, voluntary compliance dir. Bur. Occupational Health, 1982-83; adj. prof. Va. Commonwealth U., 1975-77, U. Va.-Falls Church Regional Ctr., 1984-87; occupational health/environ. toxicology cons., 1984—; lectr. and speaker in field of occupational health, toxicology and related topics. Contbr. articles to profl. jours. Mem. Springhill-Gatewood Civic Assn., Richmond; corr. sec. Reams Road Elem. Sch. PTA, 1985-86; sec./treas. Cub Scout Pack, 1985-86; troop leader Girl Scouts U.S., 1985—, alt. del., 1989—, Jr. cons., 1987—; 1989—; discussion leader Jr. Great Books, 1984-89; mem. fin. com. Calvary United Meth. Ch., 1987—, dirs. conf. del., 1988; cultural arts chmn. Providence Elem. Sch. PTA, 1987-88; gubernatorial appointee Va. Pesticide Control Bd., 1989-91; chmn. Pesticide Control Bd. Budget Com., 1989—. Named outstanging Girl Scout Leader Providence Svc. Unit, 1989. Mem. Am. Conf. Govt. Indsl. Hygienists, Am. Coll. Toxicology, Soc. Occupatioanl and Environ. Health, Am. Pub. Health Assn., Audubon Soc., Sigma Xi, Rho Chi, Iota Sigma Pi. Methodist. Home: 2900 Wicklow Ln Richmond VA 23236

SAIIA, BARBARA ANN, health science association administrator, nurse; b. Milw., July 16, 1950; d. Richard Anthony and L. Audrey (Wieneke) Kraus; m. Joseph Michael Saiia, July 10, 1971; children: Andrew J., Matthew A., Brett T. RN, Milw. County Hosp., 1971; BSN, Alverno Coll., 1980; MEd in Psychology, Marquette U., 1983. RN. Staff nurse St. Mary's Hosp., Milw., 1971-76, Meml. Hosp., Oconomowoc, Wis., 1976-80; clin. rsch. coord. Wilkinson Clinic, Oconomowoc, 1980-82; assoc. dir. clin. rsch. Inst. for Biol. R & D, Newport Beach, Calif., 1982-83, dir. clin. rsch., 1983-87; sr. dir. clin. rsch. Inst. for Biol. R & D, Irvine, Calif., 1987—; freelance rsch. cons., Delafield, Wis., 1982. Mem. Citizens for a Better Environment, Milw.; supporting mem. Wis. Pub. Radio and TV, Milw.; active mem. Friends of the Arts, Milw.; mem. governing bd. Alverno Coll., 1989—. Mem. N.Y. Acad. Scis., Drug Info. Assn., U. of the Lake Sch. Parents Assn., Marquette U. Women, Green Peace. Home: S 10 W 31796 Gray Fox Run Delafield WI 53018-3433 Office: Inst for Biol R&D 2525 Campus Dr Irvine CA 92713-9759

SAIKI, LOREL KEIKO, art director, photographer; b. Chgo., May 8, 1954; d. Hiroshi and Jessie Keiko (Kawasuna) S. Student U. Colo., Colorado Springs, 1972-73, Art Ctr. Coll. Design, Los Angeles, 1973-76. Art dir. Robertson Co., Los Angeles, 1975-76, Bozell & Jacobs, Inc., Los Angeles, 1976-82; sr. art dir. Evans/Weinberg Advt., Inc., Los Angeles, 1982-84; freelance art dir., advt. cons., 1984—; freelance photographer, Los Angeles, 1987—; freelance writer, Los Angeles, 1988—. Recipient award Art Dirs. Club Los Angeles Advt. Show, 1978, cert. of merit Am. Advt. Fedn. Show, 1978, Lulu awards Los Angeles Advt. Women, 1978, Gold medal Indsl. TV Assn., Los Angeles, 1982, Graphics Gallery award Strathmore Paper Co., 1988. Mem. Am. Soc. Mag. Photographers, Los Angeles Advt. Industry Emergency Fund, U.S. Polo Assn.

SAIKI, PATRICIA (MRS. STANLEY MITSUO SAIKI), congresswoman; b. Hilo, Hawaii, May 28, 1930; d. Kazuo and Shizue (Inoue) Fukuda; m. Stanley Mitsuo Saiki, June 19, 1954; children: Stanley Mitsuo, Sandra Saiki Williams, Margaret C., Stuart K., Laura H. BA, U. Hawaii, 1952. Tchr. U.S. history Punahou Sch., Kaimuki Intermediate Sch., Kalani High Sch., Honolulu, 1952-64; sec. Rep. Party Hawaii, Honolulu, 1964-66, vice chmn., 1966-68, 82-83, chmn., 1983-85; rsch. asst. Hawaii State Senate, 1966-68; mem. Hawaii Ho. of Reps., 1968-74, Hawaii State Senate, 1974-82, 100th-101st Congresses from 1st Hawaii dist., Washington, 1987-91; mem. Pres.'s Adv. Coun. on Status of Women, 1969-76; mem. Nat. Commn. Internat. Women's Yr., 1969-70; commr. Western Interstate Commn. on Higher Edn.; fellow Eagleton Inst., Rutgers U., 1970. Mem. Kapiolani Hosp. Aux.; sec. Hawaii Rep. Com., 1964-66, vice chmn., 1966-68, chmn., 1983-85; del. Hawaii Constl. Conv., 1968; alt. del. Rep. Nat. Conv., 1968, del., 1984; Rep. nominee for lt. gov. Hawaii, 1982; mem. Fedn. Rep. Women.; trustee Hawaii Pacific Coll.; past bd. govs. Boys and Girls Clubs Hawaii; mem. adv. coun. ARC; bd. dirs. Nat. Fund for Improvement of Post-Secondary Edn., 1982-85; past bd. dirs. Straub Med. Rsch. Found., Honolulu, Hawaii's Visitors Bur., Honolulu, Edn. Commn. of States, Honolulu, Hawaii Visitors Bur., 1983-85; trustee U. Hawaii Found., 1984-86, Hawaii Pacific Coll., Honolulu. Episcopalian. Home: 784 Elepaio St Honolulu HI 96816 Office: US Ho of Reps 1609 Longworth Bldg Washington DC 20515

SAILER, LYNNE BARGER, health care consulting executive; b. Montgomery, Ala., Feb. 8, 1956; d. Richard Douglas and Mary (Philips) Barger; m. Robert Othmar Sailer. BS in Nursing magna cum laude, Seattle Pacific U., Wash., 1978, BS in Biology, Chemistry magna cum laude, 1983; postgrad., U. Wash., 1983-85. Nurse ICU, CCU NW Hosp., Seattle, 1978-79; nurse pediatric ICU Children's Hosp. Med. Ctr., Seattle, 1979-81; nurse pvt. duty Quality Care, Nurse Finders, Pediatric Homecare, Seattle, 1981-85; rsch. tech. U. Wash. Dept. Microbiology, 1984; clin. coord. Vis. Nurse Svcs., Seattle, 1985-86; Hospice clin. dir. Swedish Hosp., Seattle, 1986-88; quality assurance coord. Wash. Homecare, Seattle, 1988; pres. health care cons. LBS & Assocs., Inc., Redmond, 1988—. Author: (manual) Quality Assurance in Home Care, 1989; lectr. in field. Lectr. Jewish Family Svcs., Seattle, 1987, Joint Commn. for Accreditation of Healthcare Orgns., 1990, Quality Assurance in infusion therapy, 1990. Named Outstanding Clin. Practitioner Seattle Pacific U., 1978. Mem. NAFE, ANA, Wash. State Nurses Assn. (task force 1987), Wash. Homecare Assn., Nat. Homecare Assn., Nat. Assn. Quality Assurance Profls., Homecare Assn. N.Y., Am. Soc. Parenteral & Enteral Nutrition, Evergreen State Quality Mgmt. Profls., Nat. Assn. Vascular Acess Networks. Home and Office: 20425 NE 37th Way Redmond WA 98053

SAILORS, SUSANNE CREECH, retired elementary educator; b. Balboa, Calif., July 16, 1913; d. Irvin Woods and Elizabeth Ann (Horton) Creech; m. Delbert Glenn Sailors, Nov. 27, 1937 (dec. 1975); children: Mary-Jane Sailors Goodman, Delbert Irvin, Elizabeth Ann, Richard Glenn, Timothy Michael. BA in Spl. Secondary Art, Fresno (Calif.) State Coll., 1936; Posgrad. in Gen. Secondary Edn., U. Calif., Berkeley, 1936-37; postgrad. in standard elem. edn., Calif. State U., Fresno, 1970. Tchr. Shasta High Sch., Redding, Calif., 1938-39, St. Ann's Parochial Sch., Porterville, Calif., 1942-43, Cherry Ave. Jr. High Sch., Tulare, Calif., 1943-44, Woodville (Calif.) Elem., 1944, Pioneer Jr. High Sch., Porterville, 1963-64, Richgrove (Calif.) Elem., 1964-80; ret., 1980; sec. Porterville High Sch. PTA, 1955-56; pres. Bartlett Jr. High Sch. PTA, Porterville, 1954-56. Active Porterville area Cub Scouts, Brownie Scouts, 4-H Club; pres. St. John's Episc. Ch. Women, Porterville, 1984—. Named Honorary Life Mem. Bartlett PTA, 1955. Mem. AAUW (local v.p. 1954-55, pres. 1955-56), DAR (Alta Mira chpt., Lindsay, Calif., regent 1986-88, vice-regent 1988-90), Nat. Ret. Tchrs. Assn., Calif. Tchrs. Assn. (pres. Richgrove chpt. 1969-71, 75-80), InterSe (sec. Porterville chpt. 1985-89, pres. 1989-90), Emblem Club (recording sec. 1947-48). Republican.

ST. ANDREWS, BARBARA FITTERER (TROMBLEY ST. ANDREWS), clergywoman; m. John A. Fitterer, Dec. 23, 1977. A.B. in English, magna cum laude, U. Rochester, 1966, M.A. in English Lit., 1967; M.Div. magna cum laude, Wesley Theol. Sem., 1979; postgrad. Princeton Theol. Sem., 1983-84; PhD., Theol. Union, Berkeley, 1989. Ordained deacon Episcopal Ch., 1979, ordained priest, 1979. Tchr. English, Pittsford High Sch., N.Y., 1967-68; instr. English, U. Rochester, N.Y., 1967-68; editor, nat. cons. Houghton Mifflin Pub. Co., 1968-75, mgr. Washington office, 1976-79; Presidential fellow President's Exec. Exch. Program, Washington, 1975-76; assigned U.S. Travel Svc. Dept of Commerce; curate Parish of St. John the Evangelist, Hingham, Mass., 1979-80; with Bishop's staff Episcopal Diocese Calif., 1980-83; assoc. rector St. Stephen's Episcopal Ch., Belvedere, Calif., 1983-84, St. John's Episcopal Ch., Ross, Calif., 1984-86; host Mosaic program Sta. KPIX-CBS/TV, San Francisco, 1989; bd. dir. ecumenical ministry First Bapt. Ch. Washington, 1976-78; liturgist U.S. Naval Chapel, Washington, 1977-79; clin. pastoral Sibley Hosp., Washington, 1978; offered opening prayers U.S. Ho. of Reps. and U.S. Senate, 1982, 83, 85, 87, 88, 89 (first ordained woman to do so). Active coun. U. Rochester, 1975-85; elected to standing com. Diocese of Calif., 1983, 84. With Chaplain's Res. Corps, USN, 1978-80. Named to Outstanding Young Women Am.; Reading fellow Coll. Preachers, Washington, 1983. Mem. Am. Bus. Women's Assn. (hon.), Rockefeller Found. (Bellagio 1987). Office: St John's Episcopal Ch PO Box 5202 Larkspur Standing Sta Larkspur CA 94939-5202 Mailing Address: Box 534 Ross CA 94957

ST. CLAIR, CAROLYN SUE, lawyer, nurse; b. Ulysses, Kans., July 20, 1957; d. Harold Floyd and Betty Jane (Vincent) Schluntz. BS in Nursing, U. Tex., 1979; JD, South Tex. Coll. Law, 1986. Bar: Tex. 1987. Operating rm. nurse St. Luke's/Tex. Heart Inst., Houston, 1979-81, The Meth. Hosp., Houston, 1982-83; med. legal cons. Howard Nations Law Firm, Houston, 1983-87; briefing atty. Supreme Ct. of Tex., Austin, 1987-88. Tex. Trial Lawyers Assn., Assn. Trial Lawyers Am., State Bar Tex. (continuing legal edn. com.), Safari Club, Sigma Theta Tau. Baptist. Office: 12 Greenway Pla 11th Fl Houston TX 77046

ST. CLAIR, JANE ELIZABETH, management; b. Concord, Mass., Aug. 15, 1944; d. James F. and Mary E. (Clyne) Connell. BA, Salem State Coll., 1969; postgrad., Columbia U., N.Y.C., 1987. Field rep., safety program Am. Red Cross of Greater N.Y., 1971-72; program dir. Bronx Community Coll., N.Y., 1973-75; dir. edn. Council N.Y.C., Inc., 1975-77, asst. exec. dir., 1978; exec. dir. Regional Emergency Med. Services, N.Y., 1979--; adjunct asst. prof., Hunter Coll. N.Y., 1973--. Contbr. articles to profl. jours. Mem. Emergency Cardic Care Com. N.Y., Heart Assn., Am. Soc. Safety Engrs., Profl. Edn. Com., Am. Red Cross, First Aid Com. Office: Regional Emergency Med Svcs 475 Riverside Dr Rm 1370 New York NY 10029

ST. CYR, VIRGINIA C., real estate executive; b. Dover, N.H., Sept. 20, 1928; d. Ferdinand Vilbon and Myrtle Alice (Beede) Rheaume; m. Richard G. St. Cyr, Spt. 2, 1946; children: Jeanne, Judy, Joy, Jon, Daniele, Robert, Deanne, Nancy, Richard, Jayne. Student, Moore Sch., MDTA Bus. Coll., 1968; grad., Lee Inst. Real Estate, Manchester, N.H., 1969. Real estate broker, owner R.E. Firms- Family Tree Assn., Londonderry, N.H. Active 4-H Club; chairperson Londonderry Dem. Town Com. Mem. NAFE (dir.), Nat. Bd. Realtors (cert.), Londonderry C. of C. (plaque), N.H. Dept. Edn. Address: 3167 Akala Dr Kihei HI 96753

ST. GERMAIN, JEAN MARY, medical physicist; b. N.Y.C.; d. Herbert and Mary J. (Newman) S.; BS, Marymount Manhattan Coll., 1966; MS, Rutgers U., 1967. Diplomate Am. Bd. Med. Physics. Fellow radiol. health USPHS, Rutgers U., New Brunswick, N.J., 1967; fellow dept. med. physics Meml. Hosp., N.Y.C., Cornell U. Med. Coll., 1967-68, asst. physicist, 1968-71, instr. radiology (physics), 1971-78, clin. asst. prof., 1979—; asst. attending physicist Meml. Sloan-Kettering Cancer Ctr.; cons. in field. Diplomate Am. Bd. Health Physics. Fellow Am. Assn. Physicists in Medicine (sec., bd. dirs.); mem. Am. Inst. Physics (gov. bd.), Am. Endocuric Therapy Soc., Health Physics Soc., Radiol. Soc. N.Am., N.Y. Acad. Scis., Radiol. & Med. Physics Soc. N.Y. (past pres.), Nat. Soc. Arts and Letters (regional dir., pres. N.Y. chpt.). Iota Sigma Pi (treas., pres. V chpt.). Author: The Nurse and Radiotherapy, 1978; contbr. articles, chpts. to med. jours., texts. Office: 1275 York Ave New York NY 10021

ST. JAMES, LYN, business owner, professional race car driver; b. Cleve., Mar. 13, 1947; d. Alfred W. and Maxine W. (Rawson) Cornwall; m. John Raymond Carusso, Dec. 7, 1970 (div. 1979). Cert. in piano, St. Louis Inst. Music, 1967. Sec. Cleve. dist. sales office U.S. Steel Corp., 1967-69, Mike Roth Sales Corp., Euclid, Ohio, 1969-70; co-owner, v.p. Dynasales Fla., Hollywood, 1970-79; owner, pres. Autodyne, Ft. Lauderdale, Fla., 1974—,

Creative Images, Inc., 1979—; race car driver Ford Motor Co., Dearborn, Mich., 1981—, spokesperson, cons., 1981—; media spokesperson 3M Co., Mpls., 1987. Author: Lyn St. James Car Owner's Manual, 1989; contbg. editor automotive articles Seventeen mag., 1987—, Cosmopolitan mag., 1989-90. Bd. trustees Women's Sports Found., N.Y.C., 1988—. Recipient Woman of Yr. award McCalls mag., 1986, Leadership award Girl Scouts U.S., 1988. Mem. Internat. Motorsports Assn., Sports Car Club of Am. Republican. Office: Creative Images Inc 4011 SW 47th Ave Ste 1107 Fort Lauderdale FL 33314

ST. JEAN, CATHERINE AVERY, advertising executive; b. Dubuque, Iowa, Oct. 10, 1950; d. Harvey Dale and Mary Theresa (Heinz) Avery; m. Kenneth R. St. Jean, June 24, 1978 (div. May 1983); m. Paul J. Frahm, Mar. 7, 1987; children: Ian, Christian. BA in Communications, Loyola U., Chgo., 1977. Video editor Needham, Harper & Steers, Chgo., 1978, creative coord., 1979-80, presentations svcs. mgr. Needham, Harper & Steers/U.S.A., Chgo., 1980-82, v.p., corp. dir. communications svcs. Needham, HarperWorldwide, Inc., N.Y.C., 1982 v.p., 1983, v.p., asst. dir. creative svcs., 1985-86; v.p., dir. creative svcs. DDB Needham Worldwide, 1986—, sr. v.p., 1988—. Author, art dir. direct mail brochure: How to Keep the Heart in New York for Tri-State United Way (Merit award 1982, bronze medal N.Y. Internat. Film and TV Festival 1984), 1982. Recipient Crystal Prism award Am. Advt. Fedn., 1987. Mem. Advt. Women in N.Y. (chmn. 1984, bd. dirs 1985, 1986—, 2d v.p. 1987, chmn. U.S. Premier Cannes Film Festival Gala at Lincoln Ctr. 1986, 87). Avocation: photography. Office: DDB Needham Worldwide 437 Madison Ave New York NY 10022

ST. JOHN, MARGARET KAY, research coordinator; b. Clifton Forge, Va., Apr. 20, 1953; d. Clarence Robinson Jr. and Betty Jean (Miller) St.J. BS in Life Scis., Worcester Poly. Inst., 1975. Electron microscopy asst. St. Vincent Hosp., Worcester, Mass., 1974-80, med. and research technologist I, 1980-81; researcher U. Nebr. Med. Ctr., Omaha, 1981-85, research coordinator, 1985—. Contbr. articles to sci. jours. Counselor Personal Crisis Ctr., 1982-83; sec. Citizens Media Adv. Council, Omaha, 1983-85; mem. Episcopal Ch. Women, 1984—; sci. coach in biology, chemistry, physics NAACP-Afro-Am. Cultural Technol. Sci. Olympics Competition, 1985—; mem. Urban League, Omaha, 1987—. Mem. AAAS, New Eng. Soc. for Electron Microscopy, Electron Microscopy Soc. Am., Am. Assn. Profl. and Exec. Women, N.Y. Acad. Scis., Am. Mgmt. Assn. Democrat. Home: 423 N 40th St #3 Omaha NE 68131 Office: U Nebr Med Ctr Dept Pathology 42d and Dewey Ave Omaha NE 68105

ST. JOHN, MARY ANN, financial planner; b. Vlissingen, The Netherlands, Oct. 28, 1958; came to U.S., 1968; d. Johan Paskal and Willy (Blokkerus) van Grieken; m. Richard Edward St. John, June 6, 1981; 1 child, Brian Richard. BS in Acctg. with honors, Lehigh U., 1981; MS summa cum laude, N.J. Inst. Tech., 1989. Auditor, staff to sr. acct. Arthur Andersen & Co., Roseland, N.J., 1979-84; acctg. mgr. Pers. Computing Mag., Inc. (formerly Hayden Publ. Co.), Totowa, N.J., 1984-86; contr. Pers. Computing Mag., Inc. (formerly Hayden Publ. Co.), Hasbrouck Heights, N.J., 1986-87, dir. fin., chief fin. officer, 1988—. Mem. NAFE, Nat. Assn. Accts. Republican. Office: Pers Computing Mag Inc 999 Riverview Dr Totowa NJ 07512

ST. JOHN, NANCY MARIE, computer animation executive; b. Summerside, P.E.I., Can., Nov. 12, 1953; came to U.S., 1984; d. Ernest Patrick and Agnes C. (McKearney) St. J. BA, Carleton U., 1975. Paralegal McClaws & Co. Barristers & Solic., Calgary, Alta., Can., 1977-78; freelance writer, 1978-80; dir., v.p., producer Allen Jones Prodn., Vancouver, B.C., Can., 1980-84; producer, mgr. Vertigo Computer Imagery, Vancouver, 1984; producer Digital Prodns., L.A., 1985; exec. producer Abel Image Rsch., L.A., 1985-86; mgr. Nat. Ctr. for Supercomputing Applications, Champaign, Ill., 1986-88; mktg. dir., producer Pacific Data Images, Sunnyvale, Calif., 1988-89; exec. producer, gen. mgr. ILM Computer Graphics, San Rafael, Calif., 1989—. Home: 20 Big Pine Rd Woodside CA 94062

ST. JOHN SOMMER, MARY MARGARET, accountant; b. Long Beach, Calif., Jan. 5, 1940; d. James Stewart and Zenie Elizabeth (Walker) St. J.; m. Errol Dey Sommer, June 27, 1959 (div. Nov. 1962); 1 child, Robert Stewart. Grad. high sch., L.A. Pvt. practice L.A., 1955-78, 81-88, Oceanside, Calif., 1978-81, Sant Maria, Calif., 1988—. Presbyterian. Home: 330 E Enos Dr #151 Santa Maria CA 93454

ST. LOUIS, EILEEN MARIE, realtor; b. Ft. Ord, Calif., July 5, 1957; d. Norman Edward and Barbara June (Benson) St. L. BA in Econs., Coll. William and Mary, 1979. Asst. area br. mgr. Va. Nat. Bank, Alexandria, 1980-81; retail banking officer, mgr. Sovran Bank NA, Falls Church, Va., 1981-84; asst. v.p., mgr. Sovran Bank NA, McLean, Va., 1984-85; mktg. and bus. devel. officer Arlington (Va.) Bank, 1985-86, bus. devel. officer, 1986-87; v.p. Arlington Bank, Tysons Corner, Va., 1987-89; sales rep. Ryan Homes Inc., Springfield, Va., 1989—. Fin. advisor Jr. Achievement Am., Falls Church, 1983. Mem. Greater Rosslyn Bus. and Profl. Assn. (treas. 1986-88, 2d v.p. 1988), Seven Corners Mcht. Assn., Mason Dist. Jaycees, Nat. Assn. Bank Women, Nat. Assn. Female Execs., Am. Mgmt. Assn., Ballston Partnership, Arlington County C. of C., Fairfax County C. of C., McLean Bus. and Profl. Assn., Kappa Alpha Theta. Republican. Roman Catholic. Lodge: Jobs Daus. Office: Arlington Bank 7880 Backlick Rd Springfield VA 22152

ST. MARK, CAROLE F., business executive. Formerly v.p. corp. planning and devel. Pitney Bowes, Inc., pres. bus. supplies and svcs. unit, from 1988, now pres. logistics systems and bus. svcs. unit. Office: Pitney Bowes Inc 1 Elmcroft Rd Stamford CT 06926*

ST. PETER, LORI ANN, operations analyst; b. Pittsfield, Mass., Feb. 12, 1960; d. Robert N. and Josephine M. (DiConza) St. P. BSBA in Mktg., Western New Eng. Coll., 1982. Account exec. Holyoke Transcript Telegram, Springfield, Mass., 1982-83; asst. group rep. State Mut. Assurance Co., Boston, 1983-85; jr. acct. BCI Assocs., Pensacola, Fla., 1985-86; bus. adminstr. The Berkshire Mus., Pittsfield, 1986; office mgr., asst. to pres. Krupp Realty Co., Boston, 1986-88, ops. analyst, 1988—. Mem. NAFE, Nat. Inst. Bus. Mgmt. Roman Catholic. Home: 43 School St Charlestown MA 02129 Office: Krupp Realty Co 470 Atlantic Ave Boston MA 02210

ST. ROSE, EDWINA LOSEY, lawyer; b. Charlottesville, Va., Aug. 25, 1952; d. Edward Lee and Emma Jane (Brown) Losey; m. Dennis Anthony St. Rose, Oct. 6, 1979; 1 child, Dennis Anthony II. BA, Barnard Coll., 1973; JD, George Washington U., 1976. Bar: Pa. 1978, U.S. Ct. Appeals (D.C. cir.) 1984, U.S. Dist. Ct. (D.C.) 1988. Legal editor Bur. Nat. Affairs, Washington, 1977-80; atty., advisor Social Security Adminstrn., Arlington, Va., 1980-83; employee relations, devel. specialist Naval Intelligence Command, Washington, 1983-85; sole practice Ft. Washington, 1985—; investigator EEO, 1985-88; specialist Dept. Housing and Urban Devel., 1988-89; atty. EEO Commission, 1989—. Named One of Outstanding Young Women of America, 1984. Mem. ABA, Pa. Bar Assn., D.C. Bar Assn. Baptist. Home: 761 Gleneagles Dr Fort Washington MD 20744

ST. TAMARA (TAMARA KOLBA), painter, printmaker; b. Navahradak, Byelorussia; came to U.S., 1950, naturalized, 1956; d. Alexander and Maria (Borys) Stahanovich; m. Alexander Kolba. BA, Western Coll., Oxford, Ohio, 1954; MFA, Columbia U., 1956. Free-lance printmaker, artist, 1956—. One-woman shows include: Western Coll., 1955, Aenle Gallery, N.Y.C., 1956, Avanti Galleries, N.Y.C., 1968, Asbury Park (N.J.) Art Mus., 1973, Free Pub. Library of Woodbridge (N.J.), 1975, Guild of Creative Art, Shrewsbury, N.J., 1975, 77, West Long Branch (N.J.) Library, 1979; exhibited in group shows Young Printmakers traveling exhbn., 1967-69, Herron Sch. Art, Indpls., Nat. Print and Drawing Exhbn., DeKalb, Ill., 1968, UNICEF, N.Y.C., 1969, 74, 76, 79, Audubon Artists, N.Y.C., 1971, 79, Davidson (N.C.) Nat. Print and Drawing Competition, 1972, 73, First Miami (Fla.) Graphics Biennial, 1973, G.W.V. Smith Mus., Springfield, Mass., 1973, 74, 76, 77, 3d Hawaii Nat. Print. Exhbn., Honolulu, 1975, 65th Ann. Exhbn., Wadsworth Atheneum, Hartford, Conn., 1975, Va. Highlands Festival, Abington, Va., Salmagundi Club, N.Y.C., 1979, 11th Ann. Biennial Nat. Art Exhbn., Valley City, N.D., 1979, 81, Printmaking Council of N.J., Somerville, 1981, Charlotte (N.C.) Printmakers Soc., 1981, 1st Ann. Juried Show, Southport, N.C., 1981, Nat. Miniature Show, Cuyahoga Falls, Ohio, 1982, 14th Nat. Art Show, La Junta, Colo., 1982, Lever House, N.Y.C., 1982, N.Mex. Art League, Albuquerque, 1987, Audubon Artists, N.Y.C., 1987, 2d Crossing Gallery, Valley City, N.D., 1987, Castle Gallery, Billings, Mont., 1987, Del Bello Gallery, Toronto, 1987, Monmouth Mus., Lincroft, N.J., 1988. Illustrator: Biography of a Polar Bear, 1972; Come Visit a Prairie Dog Town, 1976; Animal Games, 1976; Save that Raccoon, 1978; author, illustrator: Asian Crafts, 1970; Chickaree—A Red Squirrel, 1980. Mem. Guild Creative Art, Byelorussian Inst. Arts and Scis., Catherine Lorillard Wolfe Art Club, Print Club of Albany. Home: 235 Hockhockson Rd Tinton Falls NJ 07724

SAITO, KIYOMI, investment banking executive; b. Tokyo, Japan, Dec. 1, 1950; d. Genichiro and Kimiko Saito; m. Tsuguo Tadakawa, Aug. 20, 1974 (div. Aug. 1975). B.A., Keio U., Tokyo, 1973; M.B.A., Harvard Bus. Sch., 1981. Staff Nihon Econ. Jour., Tokyo, 1973-74; asst. Sony Corp., Tokyo, 1975-79; account officer, product specialist Bank of Am., Tokyo, 1981-82; mktg. mgr. Elizabeth Arden, Tokyo, 1982-84; v.p. Morgan Stanley Internat., Tokyo, 1984-88, N.Y.C., 1988-89, Morgan Stanley Realty, 1989—. Author: A Woman's New Start, 1984. Home: 255 E 49th St Apt 31C New York NY 10017 Office: Morgan Stanley Realty Inc 1251 Ave of the Americas New York NY 10020

SAIZAN, PAULA THERESA, oil company executive; b. New Orleans, Sept. 12, 1947; d. Paul Morine and Hattie Mae (Hayes) Saizan; m. George H. Smith, May 26, 1973 (div. July 1976). BS in Acctg. summa cum laude, Xavier U., 1969. CPA, Tex.; notary pub. Systems engr. IBM, New Orleans, 1969-71; acct., then sr. acct. Shell Oil Co., Houston, Tex., 1971-76, sr. fin. analyst, 1976-77, fin. rep., 1977-79, corp. auditor, 1979-81, treasury rep., 1981-82, sr. treasury rep., 1982-86; asst. treas. Shell Credit Inc., Shell Leasing Co., Shell Fin. Co. 1986-88, sr. pub. affairs rep., 1988-89, sr. staff pub. affairs rep., 1990—. Bd. dir. Greater Houston Conv. and Visitors Bur.; mem. adv. coun. U.S. SBA region VI, Houston. Mem. AICPA, Tex. Soc. CPA's (chair pub. affairs and polit. action coms. Houston chpt.), Nat. Assn. Accts., Am. Petroleum Inst. (constituencies resources task force com.) Inwood Forest Improvement Assn., Houston Area Urban League, LWV of Houston, Xavier U. Alumni Assn. (membership dir.), Greater Houston C. of C. (mem. K-12 edn. com.), Phi Gamma Nu. Roman Catholic. Home: 5426 Long Creek Ln Houston TX 77088 Office: Shell Oil Co 1510 One Shell Plaza PO Box 2463 Houston TX 77252

SAKAI, HIROKO, trading company executive; b. Nishiharu, Aichi-ken, Japan, Jan. 9, 1939; came to U.S., 1956; d. Kichiya and Saki (Shiraishi) S. BA, Wellesley Coll., 1963; MA, Columbia U., 1967, PhD, 1972. Journalist Asahi Evening News, Tokyo, 1963-65; escort interpreter Dept. State, Washington, 1967-68; econ. analyst Port Authority N.Y. and N.J., N.Y.C., 1968-69; sr. cons. Harbridge House, Inc., Boston, 1970-84, Quantum Sci. Corp., White Plains, N.Y., 1984-87; corp. planner C. Itoh & Co. (Am.), Inc., N.Y.C., 1988—. Interpreter Govt. Mass., Boston, 1974. Fellow Wellesley Coll., 1960-63, Columbia U., 1965-68; grantee Columbia U., 1969. Mem. Regional Sci. Assn., Japan Soc. Buddhist. Buddhist. Home: 235 E 51st St Apt 5C New York NY 10022 Office: C Itoh & Co (Am) Inc 335 Madison Ave New York NY 10017

SAKELL, EDITH B., public relations consultant; b. Columbia, S.C., Oct. 7, 1939; d. Jule Daniel and Edith Mitchiner (Sherrod) Bullock; m. Nicholas Theodore Sakell, Aug. 2, 1958. BE, U. S.C., 1958. Cert. secondary educator. Pub. rels. dir. Fraunces Tavern Mus., N.Y.C., 1977-79, The N.Y. Hist. Soc., N.Y.C., 1979-83; cons. N.Y.C., 1984-87; dir. pub. rels. Caswell-Massey, N.Y.C., 1987-89; cons. N.Y.C., 1989—. Com. mem., vol. Internat. Hospitality Com. of Nat. Coun. Women, N.Y.C., 1984—. Mem. Women in Communications, Am. Assn. Mus. Democrat. Home: 156 W Clinton Ave Irvington-on-Hudson NY 10533

SAKS, JUDITH-ANN, artist; b. Anniston, Ala., Dec. 20, 1943; d. Julien David and Lucy-Jane (Watson) S.; student Tex. Acad. Art, 1957-58, Mus. Fine Arts, Houston, 1962, Rice U., 1962; BFA, Tulane U., 1966; postgrad. U. Houston, 1967; m. Haskell Irvin Rosenthal, Dec. 22, 1974; 1 child, Brian Julien. One-man shows include: Alley Gallery, Houston, 1969, 2131 Gallery, Houston, 1969; group shows include: Birmingham (Ala.) Mus., 1967, Meinhard Galleries, Houston, 1977; Galerie Barbizon, Houston, 1980, Park Crest Gallery, Austin, 1981; represented in permanent collections including: L.B. Johnson Manned Space Mus., Clear Lake City, Tex., Harris County Heritage Mus., Windsor Castle, London, Smithsonian Instn., Washington: comms. include: Pin Oak Charity Horse Show Assn., Roberts S.S. Agy., New Orleans, Cruiser Houston Meml. Rm., U. Houston; curator student art collection U. Houston, 1966-72; artist Am. Revolution Bicentennial project Port of Houston Authority, 1975-76. Recipient art awards including: 1st prize for water color Art League Houston, 1969, 1st prize for graphics, 1969, 1st prize for sculpture, 1968, 1st place award for original print, DAR, Am. Heritage Com., 1987. Mem. Art League Houston, Houston Mus. Fine Arts, DAR (curator 1983-85, contbr. Tex. sesquicentennial drawing for DAR mag.), Daus. Republic Tex. Home: PO Box 1793 Bellaire TX 77401

SALAFIA, LINDA MARY, municipal government official; b. Norwich, Conn., Oct. 16, 1946; d. James Washington and Albina (Bawza) Frederick; m. Philip Salafia Jr., Sept. 7, 1968 (div. 1984); children: Christopher, Angela. Grad. high sch., Norwich Free Acad., 1964. Legal sec. George Gilman, Atty., Norwich, 1964-72; ct. clk. Norwich Probate Ct., 1974-81, judge of probate, 1981—, region 7 coord., 1987; dir. Dime Savs. Bank, Norwich. Mem. editorial bd. Conn. Probate Law Jour., Bridgeport, 1987. Bd. dir. Vol. Action Ctr., Norwich, 1984-89, Am. Cancer Soc., Norwich, 1986-89, Widowed Persons Svc., Waterford, Conn., 1985-88, Norwich Free Acad., 1981—, Backus Found., 1987—; mem. Preston Community Chorus, 1989—; rec. sec. Conn. Probate Assembly, 1990—. Named Woman of Yr., Norwich Bus. and Profl. Women's Club, 1985. Mem. Nat. Coll. Probate Judges, Conn. Coun. Adoption. Democrat. Roman Catholic. Club: Norwich Federated Womens. Lodge: Rotary. Office: Norwich Probate Ct City Hall 100 Broadway Norwich CT 06360

SALAM, DEBERA JEAN, consulting firm executive, owner; b. Milw., Apr. 1, 1957; d. Leonard John Stadler and Joanne (Allen) Huberty; m. Robert Keith Ellington, Oct. 8, 1988; 1 child, Anthony Robert Ellington. Student, Marquette U., 1974-76, U. Houston, 1985-86. Cert. payroll profl. Payroll adminstr. Vetco Offshore, Houston, 1979-80; payroll mgr. Oncor Corp., Houston, 1980-83, Waukesha-Pearce Corp., Houston, 1983-87; mgmt. cons. Automatic Data Processing, Roseland, N.J., 1987-90; pres., owner Payroll Support Assocs., Houston, 1990—; mem. bd. advisors Bus. and Reference div. MacMillan Corp., Paramus, N.J., 1990—. Author Year-End Compliance, 2d edit., 1990, (home study course) Mastering Payroll, 2d edit., 1990; mng. editor Propub Publs., 1989—. Mem. NAFE, Am. Soc. Payroll Mgmt. (chairperson govt. affairs 1990—), Am. Payroll Assn. (pres. Houston chpt. 1986-87, spl. achievement award 1987, cert.), Am. Inst. Profl. Bookkeepers (mem. bd. advisors 1988—). Home and Office: 4638 Clydesdale Houston TX 77084 Office: Automatic Data Processing 1 ADP Blvd MS 487 Roseland NJ 07068

SALAMACHA, JUDY ANNE, marketing professional; b. Bakersfield, Calif., July 30, 1944; d. Charles Henry and Mary Patricia (Fitzsimmons) McKaye; m. Robert James Salamacha, June 22, 1972; children: Jeremy, Jody. AA, Bakersfield Coll., 1964; BA, UCLA, 1966. English tchr. Kern High Sch. Dist., Bakersfield, 1968-74; talk show host Sta. KNTB-AM subs. CBS, Bakersfield, 1982-83; mktg. mgr. Swenson's of Bakersfield and Lancaster, 1983-84; dir. promotion/pub. affairs Sta. KGET-TV subs. NBC, Bakersfield, 1984-88; adv. dir. Kern County Bd. of Trade, Bakersfield, 1984-89, pres., 1986-87; mktg. mgr. Oceanic Communities, Inc. subs. Castle & Cooke, Bakersfield, 1988—; cons. mktg. Kern High Sch. Dist., 1987. Bd. dirs. Kern Econ. Devel. Corp., 1986-87, United Way of Kern, 1989—, Sch. Liberal Arts and Scis. Calif. State U., Bakersfield; media advisor Larwood for Supr. campaign, 1982. Recipient Friend of Edn. award Calif. Tchrs. Assn., 1988. Mem. AAUW (chpt. pres. 1982-83, Calif. State div., AAUW state div. quar. newspaper), Broadcast Promotions Mktg. Execs., Bakersfield Advt. Club, Kern Press Club, Bakersfield C. of C. (career woman award nominee 1987). Republican. Roman Catholic. Office: Oceanic Communities Inc PO Box 11165 Bakersfield CA 93306

SALAMON, LINDA BRADLEY, university dean, English literature scholar; b. Elmira, N.Y., Nov. 20, 1941; d. Grant Ellsworth and Evelyn E. (Ward) Bradley; divorced; children: Michael Lawrence, Timothy Martin. B.A., Radcliffe Coll., 1963; M.A., Bryn Mawr Coll., 1964, Ph.D., 1971; Advanced Mgmt. Cert., Harvard U. Bus. Sch., 1978. Lectr., adj. asst. prof. Eng. Dartmouth Coll., Hanover, N.H., 1967-72; lectr. English Smith Coll., Northampton, Mass., 1972-73; mem. faculty lit. Bennington Coll., Vt., 1974-75; dean students Wells Coll., Aurora, N.Y., 1975-77; exec. asst. to pres. U. Pa., Phila., 1977-79; assoc. prof. English Washington U., St. Louis, 1979-88, prof., 1988—, dean Coll. Arts and Scis., 1979—; cons. Acad. Ednl. Devel., 1978-80; mem. faculty Bryn Mawr Summer Inst. Women, 1979—. Author, co-editor: Nicholas Hilliard's Art of Limning, 1983; co-author: Integrity in the College Curriculum, 1985; contbr. numerous articles to literary and ednl. jours. Bd. dirs. Assn. Am. Colls., vice chmn., 1985, chmn., 1986; bd. dirs. Greater St. Louis council Girl Scouts U.S.A.; trustee Coll. Bd., St. Louis Coll. Pharmacy. Fellow Radcliffe Coll. Bunting Inst., 1973-74; Am. Philos. Soc. Penrose grantee, 1974; fellow Folger Shakespeare Library, 1986, NEH Montaigne Inst., 1988. Mem. Renaissance Soc. Am., Modern Langs. Assn., Phi Beta Kappa. Office: Washington U Campus Box 1117 Saint Louis MO 63130

SALAMON, RENAY, real estate broker; b. N.Y.C., May 13, 1948; d. Solomon and Mollie (Friedman) Langman; m. Maier Salamon, Aug. 10, 1968; children: Mollie, Jean, Leah, Sharon, Eugene. BA, Hunter Coll., 1969. Licensed real estate borker, N.J. Mgr. office Customode Designs Inc., N.Y.C., 1966-68; co-owner Salamon Dairy Farms, Three Bridges, N.J., 1968-86; assoc. realtor Max. D. Shuman Realty Inc., Flemington, N.J., 1983-85; pres., chief exec. officer Liberty Hill Realty Inc., Flemington, N.J., 1985—; cons. Illva Saronna Inc. (Illva Group), Edison, N.J. 1985—; real estate devel. joint venture with M.R.F.S. Realty Inc. (Illva Group), 1986—. Environ. Commr. Readington Twp. Environ. Commn., Whitehouse Sta., N.J. 1978-87; fund-raiser Rutgers Prep. Sch., Somerset, N.J. 1984-87; mem. N.J. Assn. Environ. Commrs., Trenton, N.J. 1978-87. Named N.J. Broker Record, Forbes Inc., N.Y.C. 1987. Mem. Nat. Assn. Realtors, N.J. Assn. Realtors, Hunterdon County Bd. Realtors (mem. chair 1986), Realtor's Land Inst. Republican. Jewish. Office: Liberty Hill Realty Inc 415 Hwy 202 Flemington NJ 08822

SALAMONE, DEBBIE, newspaper reporter; b. S.I., N.Y., Oct. 21, 1965; d. Joseph John and Eileen Theresa (Parker) S. AA, Brevard Community Coll., Melbourne, Fla., 1985; BS in Journalism, U. Fla., 1987. Reporter The Orlando (Fla.) Sentinel, 1987—. Recipient 1st Place writing award for spot news coverage Soc. Profl. Journalists, 1987. Mem. Jaycees (bd. dirs., 1st place writing contest 1989), Cen. Fla. Dance Club (1st place award for ballroom dancing 1989). Roman Catholic. Home: 1120 Reflections Circle #305 Casselberry FL 32707 Office: The Orlando Sentinel 541 N Palmetto Ave Ste 105 Sanford FL 32771

SALAND, LINDA CAROL, anatomy educator, researcher; b. N.Y.C., Oct. 24, 1942; d. Charles and Esther (Weingarten) Gewirtz; m. Joel S. Saland, Aug. 16, 1964; children—Kenneth, Jeffrey. B.S., CCNY, 1963, Ph.D. in Biology, 1968; M.A. in Zoology, Columbia U., 1965. Research assoc. dept. anatomy Columbia U. Coll. Physicians and Surgeons, N.Y.C., 1968-69; sr. research assoc. dept. anatomy Sch. Medicine, U. N.Mex., Albuquerque, 1971-78, asst. prof., 1978-83, assoc. prof., 1983-89, prof., 1989—. Mem. editorial bd. Anat. Record, 1980—; contbr. articles to profl. jours. Predoctoral fellow NDEA, 1966-68; research grantee Nat. Inst. on Drug Abuse, 1979-83, NIH Minority Biomed. Research Support Program, 1980—; NIH research grantee, 1986—. Mem. Am. Assn. Anatomists, Soc. for Neurosci., Am. Soc. Cell Biology, Am. Soc. Zoologists, AAAS, Sigma Xi. Office: U NMex Sch Medicine Dept Anatomy Basic Med Sci Bldg Albuquerque NM 87131

SALANT, MINDI, assistant health facility administrator, nurse; b. Newark, N.J., July 12, 1956; d. Albert Aaron and Lenore (Weiner) S. BS in Nursing, Boston U., 1978; postgrad., Fairleigh Dickinson U., 1985—. RN, cert. occupational hearing conservationist, advanced cardiac life support system operator. Staff nurse Newark (N.J.) Beth Israel Med. Ctr., 1978-80; nursing supr. St. Joseph's Hosp. & Med. Ctr., Paterson, N.J., 1980-85; dir. Gen. Med-Care, East Rutherford, N.J., 1985-86; asst. adminstr. family practice, dir. indsl. health services John F. Kennedy Med. Ctr., Edison, N.J., 1986-87; trauma coordinator N.J. State Trauma Ctr. U. Hosp., Newark, 1987-88, instr. in hazardous material awareness and basic emergency svc., 1988—; instr. emergency med. technician Passaic County Coll., Paterson, 1982—; instr. basic cardiac life support, St. Joseph's Hosp. & Med. Ctr., Paterson, 1982—. Bd. dirs. Carolyn Dorfman Dance Co., Summit, N.J., 1985—, past treas. and sec. Mem. Emergency Nurses Assn., Aplastic Anemia Found. Am., Am. Trauma Soc. Office: NJ State Trauma Ct UMDNJ U Hosp 150 Bergen St Newark NJ 07103-2425

SALAS, MARILYN SUE, academic director; b. Sabetha, Kans., June 4, 1943; d. Lee R. and Agnes M. (McPeak) Cashman; m. Henry C. Salas, Aug. 1, 1970. Student, Kans. State U., 1961-62, Kans. U., 1962-64; BA in Bus. Adminstrn., Emporia State U., 1965. Cert. secondary bus. edn. and psychology tchr., Kans., Calif. High sch. tchr. Pacifica High Sch., Garden Grove, Calif., 1966-68; word processor Orange County, Calif., 1968-72; ednl. service rep. IBM, Anaheim, Calif., 1969-70; coll. instr. Cerritos Coll., Norwalk, Calif., 1970-74; adult edn. instr. Lincoln Edn. Tng., Garden Grove, 1972-78; coll. instr. Golden West Coll., Huntington Beach, Calif., 1973-80, Orange Coast Coll., Costa Mesa, Calif., 1976-79, Cypress (Calif.) Coll., 1977-79; freelance word processor Burlington Northern, Newport Beach, Calif., 1978-79; cons. in field, Orange County, 1979; coll. instr. Saddleback Coll., Mission Viejo, Calif., 1979; dir. The Word Processing and Computer Sch., Anaheim, 1980-87. Mem. Assn. Info. Systems Profls. (mem. ednl. task force), Am. Soc. Tng. and Devel., Calif. Bus. Educators Assn., Anaheim C. of C., Nat. Assn. Trade and Tech. Schs. Accrediting Agy. (accredited). Democrat. Methodist. Home: 41105 Valle Vista Murrieta CA 92362

SALAVERRIA, HELENA CLARA, Spanish educator; b. San Francisco, May 19, 1923; d. Blas Saturnino and Eugenia Irene (Loyarte) S.; AB, U. Calif., Berkeley, 1945, secondary teaching cert., 1946; MA, Stanford U., 1962. High sch. tchr., 1946-57; asst. prof. Luther Coll., Decorah, Iowa, 1959-60; prof. Spanish, Bakersfield (Calif.) Coll., 1961-84, chmn. dept., 1973-80. Vol., Hearst Castle; mem. srs. adv. group edn. Cuesta Coll. Community Services. Mem. Calif. (dir. 1976-77), Kern County (pres. 1975-77) fgn. lang. tchrs. assns., NEA, Union Concerned Scientists, Natural Resources Def. Council, Calif. Tchrs. Assn. (chpt. sec. 1951-52), AAUW (edn. com.), Yolo County Council Retarded, LWV of the U.S., RSVP, Amnesty Internat., Common Cause, Sierra Club, Prytanean Alumnae, U. Women of Cambria, U. Calif. Alumni Assn., Stanford U. Alumni Assn. Democrat. Presbyn. Address: PO Box 63 Cambria CA 93428

SALAY, CAROLYN JEANNE, advertising agency executive; b. Birmingham, Ala.; d. Augustus Alexander and Mary Elizabeth (White) S. BA, Birmingham So. Coll., 1966; postgrad., U. Ala., Tuscaloosa, 1966-68. Client liaison Unigrafix, Birmingham, 1970-71; traffic mgr. Luckie & Forney Advt., Inc., Birmingham, 1972-76; creative dir. Perry-Hoyle Advt., Inc., Birmingham, 1976-77; freelance copywriter Birmingham, 1977; copywriter Bentley Huggins Smith & Whittington, Inc., Birmingham, 1977-78, Bear Britton Black Advt., Montgomery, Ala., 1978-82; creative dir. Bear Advt., Montgomery, 1982-88, Salay St. Advt., Montgomery, 1988-90, Salay Advt., Montgomery, 1990—. Copywriter Bank Marketing Assn. (Best of Print Pub. award 1982); contbr. articles to advt. jours. Charter mem. Montgomery Mus.; active various local charities; campaign staff Folmar for Gov., Montgomery, 1982. Recipient Class of '86 award Ala. Bus. Rev., Montgomery, 1986, Best of Show award Huntsville (Ala.) Advt. Fedn., 1988, numerous Gold and Silver Addy awards. Mme. NAFE, Montgomery Advt. Fedn. (bd. dirs. 1979-80, pres. 1986-87, vice chmn. Pres.'s coun. 1986-87, 1st chmn. pres.'s coun., Copywriter of Yr. 1979, 84, 86, Best of Show 1982, 86, 88), Am. Advt. Fedn. (7th dist. club: vice-chmn. pres.'s coun. 1986-87, Advt. for Advt. award 1986-87; mem. nat. club achievement and awards com. 1987-89, nat. pub. svc. com. 1989—, Ad Club Pres. of Yr. 1986-87, Saatchi & Saatchi Compton Edn. award 1986-87), Community Rels. Soc. for Advancement of Mgmt. (v.p. Montgomery chpt. 1988-90), Capital City Club (bus. com. 1989—). Episcopalian. Office: Salay Advt PO Box 230422 Montgomery AL 36123-0422

SALAY, CINDY ROLSTON, systems consultant, nurse; b. Roanoke, Va., July 18, 1955; d. Gilbert Wilson and Elinor Patterson (Sandridge) Rolston; m. John Matthew, July 7, 1988. AAS, Va. Western Community Coll., 1976; AS, J. Sargeant Reynolds Community Coll., 1982; BS, Va. Commonwealth U., 1984. RN. Operating room RN Henrico Doctors Hosp., Richmond, Va., 1979-80; nursing supr. Johnston Willis Hosp., Richmond, 1980-87; systems analyst, coord. Health Corp Va., Richmond, 1983-87, sr. project leader, 1987-88; sr. systems analyst Hosp. Corp. Am., Nashville, 1987; sr. systems cons. Spectrum Healthcare Solutions (partnership of IBM and Baxter Healthcare Corp.), Reston, Va., 1988—. Presbyterian. Home: 1128 Arborhill Dr Woodstock GA 30188 Office: Spectrum Healthcare Solutions 12355 Sunrise Valley Dr Reston VA 22091

SALAZAR, DEBRA, human services administrator; b. Indpls., Aug. 21, 1952; d. Robert Allen and Sarah Jane (Fix) Pedigo; m. Mike A. Salazar, Mar. 27, 1986; children: Justin, Alicia. BA, Ball State U., 1974; MS, U. Ill., 1979. Tchr. Champaign (Ill.) Pub Schs., 1974-81; UniServ cons. NEA, Jefferson City, Mo., 1981-84; UniServ cons. NEA, Santa Fe, 1984—, coord. leadership tng., 1987—, staff mem. NEA Employee Intern Program, 1990-91; ea. coord. Project Teach, No. Ill. U., Dekalb, 1980-84. Materials coord. Muncie (Ind.) Pub. Schs., 1973-74; adult leader Girl Scouts U.S.A., Champaign, 1975-77, exec. counselor, program dir. Girl Scout Day Camp, Champaign, 1976-79; cons. Great Books Program, Champaign Pub. Libr., 1979-81; dep. registrar Champaign County, 1979-81; mem. Asbury Cafe Project for homeless, Albuquerque , 1985-90. Mem. NAFE, NOW (coord. Springfield chpt. 1983-84, pres. 1984), Nat. Staff Orgn. (region 4 dir., bd. dirs. western states div. 1988—), U. Ill. Alumni Assn., Ball State U. Alumni Assn., Kappa Delta Pi. Democrat. Methodist.

SALBER, EVA JULIET, medical educator, author; b. Capetown, South Africa, Jan. 5, 1916; came to U.S., 1956, naturalized, 1961; d. Moses and Fanny (Srolowitz) S.; m. Harry Tarley Phillips, Nov. 1, 1939; children: David, Mark, Rosalie, Philip. M.B., Ch.B., U. Capetown, 1938, D.P.H., 1945, M.D., 1955. Intern Provincial Hosp., Port Elizabeth, South Africa, Elliot Sir Henry Hosp., Umtata, South Africa; resident Capetown Free Dispensary and Queen Elizabeth Hosp. for Children, London, 1940-44; rsch. assoc. epidemiology Harvard Sch. Pub. Health, Boston, 1959-61; sr. rsch. assoc. Harvard Sch. Pub. Health, 1961-66; dir. Martha Eliot Family Health Center, Boston, 1967-69; sr. assoc. Harvard Center Community Health and Med. Care, Boston, 1969-70; prof. community and family medicine Duke U., Durham, N.C., 1971-82; prof. emeritus Duke U., 1982—; cons. in field.; Milton rsch. assoc. Harvard Sch. Pub. Health, Boston, 1957-58; lectr. Harvard Med. Sch., 1967-70, U. N.C., 1972-78. Author: Caring and Curing: Community Participation in Health Services, 1975, (with Connie Service) Community Health Education: The Lay Advisor Approach, 1977, Don't Send Me Flowers When I'm Dead: Voices of Rural Elderly, 1983, (with H.T. Phillips) Services to the Elderly in England, 1980, The Mind is Not the Heart: Recollections of a Woman Physician, 1989; contbr. numerous articles to profl. jours. Sr. bursar South Africa Coun. Indsl. and Sci. Rsch., 1950-55; bd. dirs. N.C. Student Rural Health Coalition, 1978—, N.C. Black Ch. Project, Raleigh, 1980—, Community Mental Health Ctr., Chapel Hill, N.C., 1981-83. Recipient Margaret Sanger award Planned Parenthood, Orange County, N.C., 1990; Radcliffe Inst. scholar, 1966-67; Sr. Internat. fellow NIH, London, 1980. Fellow Am. Pub. Health Assn.; mem. Internat. Epidemiology Assn., Am. Gerontol. Soc. Democrat. Jewish.

SALBERG, BATSHEVA, industrial psychologist, systems analyst; b. Tel Aviv, June 4, 1953; came to U.S., 1954; d. Philip and Sara Bock; m. David Salberg, Oct. 9, 1977; 1 child, Jodi. BS, Bklyn. Coll., 1975; MA, NYU, 1979, PhD, 1983. Teaching asst. NYU, N.Y.C., 1977; rsch. analyst Life Office Mgmt. Assn., N.Y.C., 1977-78; pers. rsch. intern IBM, Armonk, N.Y., 1978-79; pers. rsch. analyst Met. Life Ins. Co., N.Y.C., 1979-81; sr. evaluation assoc. Nat. Ctr. Pub. Productivity, N.Y.C., 1983; tests and measurement specialist N.Y.C. Dept. Pers., 1983-89; rsch. cons. Newark (N.J.) Bd. Edn., 1989-90; systems analyst AT&T, East Brunswick, N.J., 1990—. Mem. Hadassah (Marlboro (N.J.) chpt.), 1989-90, Women's Am. ORT, Staten Island, N.Y., 1987-88, Freehold, N.J., 1989-90. NYU fellow, 1971-73. Mem. Am. Psychol. Assn., Internat. Pers. Mgmt. Assn., Soc. Indsl./Organizational Psychology, Met. N.Y. Assn. Applied Psychology, Western Monmouth Newcomers Club, Psi Chi. Democrat. Jewish. Home: 17 Monterey Ln Manalapan NJ 07726

SALDAÑA, ELSA ANTONIA, advertising agency executive; b. Brownsville, Tex., Oct. 13, 1950; d. Juan Angel and Blasita (Garza) S.; m. Nasrat Arif Raouf. BS with spl. honors, U. Tex., 1973. Media planner Compton Advt., N.Y.C., 1977-78; sr. media planner Grey Advt., N.Y.C., 1978-79; supr. Young & Rubicam, N.Y.C., 1979-83; assoc. media dir. Young & Rubicam/Dentsu, L.A., 1983-85; assoc. media dir., v.p. McCann-Erickson, L.A., 1985-87; cons. media planning and buying cons., L.A., 1987-88; media planning supr., Hispanic specialist GSD&M, Inc., Austin, Tex., 1988-89; Hispanic media cons., L.A., 1989-90; media dir., v.p. Mendoza, Dillon & Asociados, Inc., Newport Beach, Calif., 1990—. Mem. Women in Communications, NAFE.

SALE, SARA LEE, history educator; b. Neosho, Mo., Feb. 27, 1954; d. Onal Carter and Margaret Lee (Hyde) Sale. BA, Mo. So. State Coll., 1977; MA, Cen. Mo. State U., 1979; postgrad., Okla. State U., 1988--. Cert. tchr., Mo. Acad. adv. Longview Community Coll., Lee's Summit, Mo., 1978-81; adjunct history lectr. Longview Community Coll., Lee's Summit, 1979-85, Rockhurst Coll., Kansas City, Mo., 1980-85; social sci. instr. Neosho (Mo.) High Sch., 1985-86; history instr. Okla. State U., Stillwater, Okla., 1986-88; asst. prof. history, geography Mo. So. State Coll., Joplin, Mo., 1989--. Co-author: Neosho: City of Springs, 1984; Show Me Missouri Women, 1989; contbr. articles profl. jours. Recipient rsch. grant Harry S. Truman Libr. Inst., Independence, Mo., 1988-89. Fellow Harry S. Truman Libr. Inst.; mem. AAUW, Am. Hist. Assn., Orgn. Am. Historians, State Hist. Soc. Mo., Phi Alpha Theta, Beta Sigma Phi. Democrat. Methodist. Office: Mo So State Coll Social Sci Dept Newman & Duquesne Rds Joplin MO 64801-1595

SALEM, DOROTHY CARLSON, historian, consultant; b. Dayton, Ohio, Jan. 29, 1946; d. Donald R. and Ethel (Carlson) Meyer; m. Thomas Coopland (dec. 1967); m. Thomas Gregory Salem, Oct. 21, 1932; children: Kelle Ann, Beth Marie, Jennifer Lynn. AS, Cuyahoga Community Coll., Cleve., 1969; BA, MA, Cleve. State U., 1971-72; PhD, Kent State U., 1985. Teaching asst. Cleve. State U., 1971-72, adj. prof., 1985—; lectr. Cuyahoga Community Coll., Cleve., 1972-75, from asst. prof. to prof. social sci. women's studies, 1975-85, prof. history, 1989—, dir. Inst. on Human Rels., 1985-89; cons. multicultural curriculum and women's studies Cleve. Pub. Schs., 1987—. Author: To Better Our World, 1990; contbr. articles to profl. jours. Adv. bd. Displaced Homemakers Networks, Cleve., 1987—. Recipient Besse award Teaching Excellence Cuyahoga Community Coll., 1985, Nat. Teaching Excellence award Nat. Inst. Staff and Orgn. Devel., 1989, Distinguished Alumnae award Cleve. State U., 1990. Mem. Am. Assn. Community and Jr. Colls. (Inst. for Leadership), AAUW (Am. fellow), Orgn. Am. Historians, Am. Hist. Assn., Nat. Women's Studies Assn., Assn. for Anthropology & Gerontology, Ohio Acad. History. Democrat. Lutheran. Office: Cuyahoga Community Coll 2900 Community College Ave Cleveland OH 44115

SALEMBIER, VALERIE BIRNBAUM, publishing executive; b. Teaneck, N.J., July 2, 1945; d. Jack and Sara (Gordon) Birnbaum; m. David J. Salembier, June 23, 1968 (div. 1980). Student, Fordham U., 1970-72; B.A., Coll. of New Rochelle, 1973. Merchandising mgr. Life Internat., Time, Inc., N.Y.C., 1964-69; merchandising copywriter Newsweek, Inc., N.Y.C., 1970; promotion prodn. mgr. Newsweek, Inc., 1971, adv. sales rep., 1972-76; advt. dir. Ms. Mag., N.Y.C., 1976-79, assoc. pub., 1979-81; pub. Inside Sports Mag., N.Y.C., 1982; v.p., pub. 13-30 Corp., N.Y.C., 1983; sr. v.p. advt. USA Today, 1983-88; pub. TV Guide, Radnor, PA, 1988-89; pres. N.Y. Post, N.Y.C., 1989-90; lectr. in field. Bd. trustees Coll. New Rochelle. Mem. United Jewish Appeal (exec. mktg. com.), Women's City Club, Supportive Children's Advocacy Network (bd. dirs.), Orgn. for Rehab. Through Tng. Home: 300 E 34th St New York NY 10016 Office: NY Post 210 South St New York NY 10002

SALENGER, LUCY LEE, television producer; b. St. Louis, Sept. 12, 1938; d. Leo and Lucille (Mier) Berner; m. Stephen Salenger, Aug. 10, 1961 (div. Sept. 1966); 1 child, Laura; m. Marvin Zonis, Jan. 4, 1976; children: Nadia, Leah. BA with honors, UCLA, 1961. Press asst. Kennedy for Pres., L.A., 1968; field producer, reporter, researcher 60 Minutes, CBS News, L.A., 1970-72; reporter, producer Sta. WLS-TV, Chgo., 1972-74; field producer CBS News, Chgo., 1974-75; dir. Ill. Film Office, Chgo., 1975-83; gen. ptnr. The Odeon Group, Chgo., 1986—; sr. cons. Harpo Studios, Chgo., 1988-89; assoc. producer Brewster Place, Chgo., 1989-90; cons. to gov. on culture State of Ill., Chgo., 1988. Bd. advisors Ill. State Fair, Chgo., 1980-83; bd. dirs. Chgo. Film Festival, 1978-82, Rehab. Inst. Chgo., 1981-83, Mus. Broadcasting, Chgo., 1984-89, Chgo. Coalition, 1980-83. Recipient 1st achievement award Facets Multimedia, 1980, ann. award Chgo. Coalition, 1983, Woman of Yr. award Sta. WBBM, Chgo., 1985; urban fellow Northeastern U., 1985. Mem. Chgo. Network (bd. dirs. 1989—), Women in Film (adv. bd. Chgo. 1990, 1st ann. achievement award 1987), Nat. Assn. Film Communicators (bd. dirs. 1984—). Jewish. Home: 4942 S Ellis Ave Chicago IL 60615

SALEWSKI, RUBY MARIE GRAF, nursing educator; b. Vernon, Tex., Feb. 22, 1932; d. Albert Carl and Olga Emma (Mertink) Graf; children: Stephen, Elizabeth, Matthew, Rebecca, Deborah. Diploma in nursing, Meth. Hosp. Sch. Nursing, Dallas, 1952; BSN, U. Tex., Galveston, 1956, postgrad.; postgrad., St. Louis U., 1960-61; MEd in Nursing, U. Minn., 1967, postgrad. Lic. nurse, Minn. Mem. nursing faculty U. Tex., Galveston, 1956-59, Luth. Hosp., St. Louis, 1959-60, Anoka-Ramsey Community Coll., Coon Rapids, Minn., 1968-69; mem. nursing faculty, pre-nursing advisor U. Minn., Mpls., 1970, 72, 73-74; mem. nursing faculty Austin (Minn.) Community Coll., 1975-76; nursing educator, course leader ADN program Rochester (Minn.) Community Coll., 1976—, coord. continuing edn. in nursing, 1981-82; staff nurse Rochester Meth. Hosp., 1988, St. John's Hosp., Springfield, Ill.; staff/charge nurse Dist. #1 Hosp., Faribault, Minn., U. Tex. Med. Br. Hosps., Galveston, Meth. Hosp., Dallas, Meml. Hosp., Springfield, Seton Hosp., Austin, Tex.; nurse orthopedic staff St. Mary's Hosp., Rochester; seminar leader in field. Bd. dirs., coord. Family Edn. Ctr., 1985; vol. crisis hotline Telephone Ministries, 1984—; mem. evangelism and stewardship com. Redeemer Luth. Ch., 1986; mem. organized caring and sharing ministry Good Shepherd Luth. Ch., 1990. Mem. ANA, LWV (bd. dirs. local chpt. 1985-88), MEA, NEA, Minn. Nurses Assn. (mem. approval com. 1987-88, govtl. affairs com. 1987—, chair dist. 13 1988), Nat. League for Nursing, Minn. League for Nursing (v.p. 1985-87, founding com. mem. educators coun.), Rochester Community Coll. Faculty Assn., Adlerian Soc., Sigma Theta Tau. Home: 540 15th St Owatonna MN 55060

SALGUEIRO, CARMEN ESCUDÉ, educator, concert pianist, accompanist; b. Santiago-de-Cuba, May 11, 1950; came to U.S., 1962; d. Juan and Maria del Carmen (Ramos) Escude; m. Robert Da Costa Salgueiro. MusB, Cath. U.; MusM, Manhattan Sch. Music; Degree in Theory & Solfege, Conservatory Music, Santiago, Cuba. Cert. ednl. supr., tchr. Vocal Music K-12, bilingual-bicultural edn., elem. edn., tchr. ESL, ednl. prin., N.J. Tchr. piano and theory Villa Walsh Acad., Morristown, N.J.; elem. vocal music tchr. Lafayette St. Sch., Newark, 1972-75, Hawkins St. Sch., Newark, 1975-76; elem. bilingual tchr. South St. Sch., Newark, 1980-84; elem. summer sch. tchr. Oliver St. Sch., Newark, 1984; tchr. ESL, Newark, 1984—; concert pianist (solo and orchestra), Cuba, U.S., Italy, 1955—; Organist Our Lady of Mercy Ch., Park Ridge, N.J., 1982; choir dir. Student Community Concerts, Newark, 1984—. Sec. Congress of Portuguese Speaking Peoples, Newark, 1974, Peter Francisco Meml. Commn., Newark, 1976; mem. Portuguese-Am. Scholarship Found., Newark, 1973—, scholarship com., 1984—. Scholar Villa Victoria Acad., 1962-67, Manhattan Sch. Music, 1971, Cath. U., 1967-71, Kean Coll., 1979-82, Seton Hall U., 1979-81; Master Tchr. Status Newark Bd. Edn., 1985. Mem. N.J. Tchrs. English to Speakers of Other Langs.-Bilingual Educators Assn. (ESL Tchr. Yr. 1988), Newark Tchrs. Union, Sigma Alpha Iota.

SALHANY, LUCILLE, broadcast executive. Pres. domestic TV div. Paramount TV Group, Hollywood, Calif. Office: Paramount TV Group Domestic TV Div 5555 Melrose Hollywood CA 90038*

SALICE, BARBARA FARENGA, educational administrator; b. N.Y.C., Aug. 16, 1944; d. Felix Anthony and Irene Dorothy (O'Keefe) Farenga; m. Ralph Ronald Salice, July 3, 1965; children: Nicole, Danielle. BA, U. Hawaii, 1966, MEd, 1970; EdD, U. So. Calif., 1990. Cert. sec. sch. tchr., counselor, Hawaii; trainer, Literacy Vols. Am. Tchr. Pub. Sch. 112, Bronx, N.Y., 1967, Windward Sch. Dist., Kailua and Kaneohe, Hawaii, 1968-74; head counselor Sacred Hearts Acad., Honolulu, 1980-82; adminstrv. asst. Honolulu Symphony, 1984; literacy coordinator Windward Sch. for Adults, Kailua, 1986—; instr. Hawaii Loa Coll., Kaneohe, 1988-89; lectr. Windward Community Coll., Kailua, 1989—; cons. Dept. Corrections, Waiawa, Hawaii, 1987-88, Dept. Labor, Honolulu, 1988. Contbr. articles to profl. jours. Vice chmn. Hawaii Gov.'s Coun. for Literacy, 1987-88, speaker's chmn. 1988-89; facilitator Project Literacy U.S., Honolulu, 1986-88; field worker Hawaii Dem. Com., Windward, Oahu, 1987. Named First Lady's Vol. of Yr., Honolulu, 1987; recipient outstanding literacy program award Windward Supt. Edn., 1987, 88, 89, Outstanding Community Edn. award, 1990. Mem. Literacy Vols. Am., Laubach Literacy Action, Am. Assn. for Adult and Continuing Edn., Hawaii Adult Edn. Assn., Nat. Women's Studies Assn., AAUW (exec. bd. 1970—), Hawaii Hist. Assn., Symphony Guild (pres. 1984-85), Daus. Hawaii. Roman Catholic. Home: 664 Old Mokapu Rd Kailua HI 96734 Office: Windward Sch for Adults 730 Iliaina St Kailua HI 96734

SALINAS, DORA, communications company public relations executive; b. Brownsville, Tex., Apr. 2, 1936; d. Alfonso E. and Virginia (Garza) Alonso; children: Ruth V., Stephen A. Student, San Antonio Jr. Coll., 1957-58. Operator Southwestern Bell Telephone Co., San Antonio, 1954-71, service rep. customer services, 1971-73, supr. bus. office, customer services, 1973-76, mgr. customer services, 1976-79, dist. mgr. customer services, 1979-84, dist. mgr. external affairs, 1984—. Chairperson Mcpl. CSC, Multiple Sclerosis Soc.; elected commr. Fiesta Commn.; planning com. San Antonio Women's Hall of Fame; ednl. com. and adv. council Upward Bound; bd. dirs. Centro Del Barrio, Inc., San Antonio Livestock Exposition, Inc., Target 90/Goals for San Antonio, Nat. League of United Latin Am. Citizens Edn. Service Ctr., Pvt. Industry Coun., Via Met. Transit Authority; chair Internat. Mex. Day com., collaborative task force, fin. com. Cumberland Presbyn. Ch., also past ruling elder; bd. contbrs. United Way, also chairperson allocation panel; active Alumni Leadership San Antonio-Greater C. of C., Mexican Am. Legal Def. and Edn. Fund; zoning commr. City of San Antonio, Market Sq. Commission; fund raising com. San Antonio Symphony; trustee United Way Tex., Market Square Commn. Recipient Sykes award Nat. Multiple Sclerosis Soc.; Award for Volunteerism San Antonio Coalition for Children, Youth and Families (S.A. CARES), Service to Mankind award Sertoma Club; named Gov.'s Yellow Rose of Tex.; honoree Women's Hall of Fame; inductee Hispanic Hall of Fame. Mem. Mexican C. of C. (past pres. San Antonio chpt., vol. of yr. award 2 yrs.). Office: Southwestern Bell Tel Co 1010 N St Mary's Rm 1319 San Antonio TX 78215

SALINGER, MARION CASTING, international studies educator, poet, consultant; b. Buffalo, May 22, 1917; d. George Alfred and Mary Helen (Knopf) C.; m. Herman Salinger, Nov. 29, 1941; children: Jill Hudson Salinger Winter, Wendy Lang, Jennifer Wilson Salinger Duffy. Student, U. Buffalo, 1936, U. Wis., 1938-40. Journalist Kenmore (N.Y.) Ind. Record, 1934; syndicated journalist Madison, Wis., 1937-39; pvt. sec. library Duke U., Durham, N.C., 1956-60, adminstrv. mgr. Ctr. for internat. Studies, 1966-85, adminstrv. coordinator Can. Studies Ctr., 1979-89; cons. on Canada Forest History Soc., Inc., 1989—. Poems published in mags. Kaleidoscope, N.Mex. Quar., Fantasy, Little Treasury of World Poetry, Dimension, Archive, Chronicle of Higher Edn.; editor, co-editor numerous articles and monographs; contbr. articles to profl. jours. Recipient Silver medal Women of Achievement, Durham, 1984. Mem. Assn. Can. Studies in U.S. (Donner award 1985), Soc. Internat. Devel. (pres. local chpt. 1985—), So. Atlantic States Assn. for Asian-African Studies (exec. dir. 1980-82), Nat. Coun. Social Studies, P.E.O. Sisterhood (state pres. 1960), Internat. Visitors Coun. (bd. dirs. 1988—). Democrat. Episcopalian. Home: 3444 Rugby Rd Durham NC 27707

SALINGER, RUTH ANGIER, international trade company executive, environmental administrator; b. Newton, Mass., July 21, 1931; d. Ralph Loveland and Elizabeth (Chase) Angier; m. Richard Burtis Salinger, June 26, 1954; children: Peter Dennison, Jennifer Angier. BS in Edn., Wheelock Coll., Boston, 1953. Cert. in elem. edn. Tchr. Claflin Sch., Newton, 1953-54; dir. religious edn. Eliot Ch. of Newton, 1955-60; dist. case worker Mass. Senate Ways and Means Com., Boston, 1983-85; dir. constituent svcs. Congressman Chester G. Atkins, Lowell, Mass., 1985; pres., founder Greeley Found., Concord, Mass., 1986-90; pres., co-founder The Salinger Group, Gloucester, Mass., 1990—; chief exec. officer, co-founder Global Initiatives, Inc., Gloucester, 1990—; co-founder Just-A-Start, Boston and Cambridge, 1964-67; founder, pres. Concord-Carlisle Human Rights Council, 1979-83, Mass. Women Sch. Com. Mems., Boston, 1974-79. Co-editor: Forward Through the Ages, 1986. Chmn. Concord Sch. Com., 1972-79; trustee METCO, 1979-83; co-chmn. U.S./USSR Citizen Summit, Moscow, 1990; mem., adviser Women for Mut. Security, 1986—. Recipient Peace Day award Nat. Peace Day Com., 1986. Mem. Wheelock Coll. Alumnae Assn. (trustee 1979-83, chmn./pres. social action com. 1979-83, Centennial Alumnae award 1989). Democrat. Unitarian. Home: 53 Laurel St Concord MA 01742 Office: The Salinger Group Inc 3 Crafts Rd Gloucester MA 01930

SALINSKY, CATHY JOAN, social worker; b. Manchester, Conn., Oct. 8, 1953; d. David Theodore and Lillian Mae (Richardson) Robbins; m. Terry Michael Salinsky, July 29, 1972; children: Adam Michael, Destiny Lynn. Student, Willimantic Cosmotology, Conn., 1974; BA in Psychology, Ea. Conn. State U., 1987. Hairdresser Glastonbury, Conn, 1974-75; mental retardation aide State of Conn., Mansfield, 1977-80; day care provider Coventry, Conn., 1980-84; recreation director Riverside Health Care, E. Hartford, Conn.; social worker Riverside Health Care Ctr., East Hartford, Conn., 1988; pres. Country Industries, Inc., 1986-87. Mem. Conn. Traumatic Brain Injury, Conn. Assn. Soc. Workers. Congregationalist. Office: Riverside Health Care Ctr 745 Main St East Hartford CT 06108

SALISBURY, ALICIA LAING, state senator; b. N.Y.C., Sept. 20, 1939; d. Herbert Farnsworth and Augusta Belle (Marshall) Laing; m. John Eagan Salisbury, June 23, 1962; children: John Eagan Jr., Margaret Laing. Student Sweet Briar Coll., 1957-60; BA, Kans. U., 1961. Mem. Kans. Senate, 1985—, chmn. labor, industry and small bus. com., vice chmn. fin. instns. and ins. com., mem. ways and means, econ. devel. com. , pub. health and welfare com., reapportionment com; mem. Kans. Supreme Ct. Task Force on Permanency Planning, 1987—. Elected mem. State Bd. Edn., Topeka, 1981-85; past pres. Jr. League of Topeka; trustee Leadership Kans., 1982-89; bd. dirs. Topeka Community Found., 1983—, Topeka Pub. Sch. Found., 1985-89, Capitol Area Pla. Authority, 1989—; mem. adv. commn. Juvenile Offenders Program, Kans., 1985-89; mem. adv. bd. Kans. Action for Children, 1982—, Kans. Ins. Edn. Found., 1984—, Youth Center at Topeka, 1987—; mem. Nat. Fedn. Rep. Women; former bd. dirs. Topeka C. of C., United Way Greater Topeka, ARC, Family Service and Guidance, Topeka, Shawnee County Mental Health Assn., Florence Crittenton Services, Topeka, Kans. Action for Children, Topeka City Commn. Govtl. Adv. Com. Mem. Nat. Conf. State Legislators (labor com., vice chmn.), Nat. Republican Legislators' Assn., Shawnee County Rep. Women, Kappa Kappa Gamma. Episcopalian. Avocations: tennis; downhill skiing; water sports; horseback riding; gardening. Office: Kans State Senate Topeka KS 66612

SALISBURY, JENNY OLIVIA, marketing company executive; b. Berea, Ohio, May 15, 1959; d. Donald Edward and Dorothy Olivia (Theurer) S. Student, Bowling Green U., 1977-81, Cleve. State U., 1981—. Collection supr., computer operator, sales rep. Preview Subscription TV, Cleve., 1981-83; account exec. US Sprint Communications, Independence, Ohio, 1983-87; real estate agt. Ohio Savs. Realty, North Olmstead, Ohio, 1987-88, Hunter Realty, 1987-88; pres., owner NorthCoast Telemktg., Cleve., 1987—; telemarketing tng. cons., Ohio. Mem. Sales and Mktg. Execs. Internat., Greater Cleve. Growth Assn. Republican. Episcopalian. Club: Sixth Day (pres. 1987—). Home and Office: 12900 Lake Ave #321 Cleveland OH 44107

SALISBURY, MARY ANN, sales professional; b. Euclid, Ohio; d. Geoffrey C. Salisbury. BS in Edn., Bowling Green State U., 1982. Sales supr. Telecheck Ohio, Cleve.; sales rep. Curtis 1000, Cleve. Mem. NAFE, Am. Bus. Woman's Assn., Grove Ct. Condominium Assn. (v.p./sec. 1988-89).

SALISBURY, PATRICIA DIANNE, printing company executive; b. North Kingstown, R.I., Oct. 6, 1951; d. John Edward and Noella Dianne (Choiniere) S.; m. Kenneth Richard Castle, Dec. 20, 1975. Student, R.I. Coll., 1976-81, Community Coll. R.I., 1981-83. Operator New England Telephone Co., Pawtucket, R.I., 1970-71; sales rep. Standard Wire and Cable Co., Attleboro, Mass., 1972-74; exec. sec. Gold Filled Mfrs. Assn., Attleboro, 1974-78; pvt. practice bookkeeping Pawtucket, 1978-80; asst. to owner Nautical Enterprises, Pawtucket, 1980-82; pres. Rapid Printing Inc., N. Providence, R.I., 1982—. Dir. adv. bd. Fund for Community Progress, Providence, 1986-89; mem. R.I. Coll. Graphics Arts Adv. Bd., Providence, 1984—; bd. dirs. Hist. Cen. Falls. Mem. Nat. Assn. Quick Printers, Providence Club of Printing House Craftsmen (bd. dirs.), NAFE, North Cen. C. of C. (bd. dirs., founding mem.). Office: Rapid Printing Inc 1361 Mineral Spring Ave North Providence RI 02904

SALITA, CHRISTINE THERESA, library administrator; b. Amityville, N.Y., Oct. 4, 1951; d. Stefan and Evelyn (Bogacki) S. BA, Adelphi U., 1973; MS, Long Island U., 1975. Pub. Librarianship. Reader's advisor Farmingdale Pub. Library, N.Y., 1975-77; head of reference dept. South Huntington Pub. Library, N.Y., 1977-86; asst. dir. Lindenhurst Memorial Lib., N.Y., 1986--. Mem. Am. Library Assn., Am. Soc. for Pub. Adminstr., N.Y. Library Assn. Office: Lindenhurst Meml Library 1 Lee Ave Lindenhurst NY 11757

SALITERMAN, LAURA SHRAGER, pediatrician; b. N.Y.C., June 26, 1946; d. Arthur M. and Ida (Wildman) Shrager; m. Richard Arlen Saliterman, June 15, 1975; 1 child, Robert Warren. AB magna cum laude, Brandeis U., 1967; MD, NYU, 1971. Intern Montefiore Hosp. and Med. Ctr., Bronx, N.Y., 1971-72, resident in pediatrics, 1972-74; pediatrician Morrisania Family Care Ctr., N.Y.C., 1974-75; pediatrician Share Health Plan, St. Paul, 1975-85, dir. pediatrics, 1976-82; pediatrician Aspen Med. Group, St. Paul, 1985—; clin. asst. prof. U. Minn. Med. Sch. Mem. Am. Acad. Pediatrics (chair accident prevention com. Minn. chpt. 1985-89), Phi Beta Kappa. Club: Oak Ridge. Home: 11911 Live Oak Dr Minnetonka MN 55343 Office: 1020 Bandana Blvd W Saint Paul MN 55108

SALLIN, SANDRA FRIEDMAN, artist, educator; b. Los Angeles, Nov. 13, 1940; d. Simon and Ann (Kibrick) Friedman; m. Robert S. Sallin; children: Susannah Leigh, Matthew David. BFA, UCLA, 1963. Guest lectr. Calif. State U., L.A., 1983, 87, Laguna Beach Mus. Art, 1984; guest lectr. UCLA, 1987, extension instr., 1982-89; represented by Koplin Gallery, Los Angeles. Exhbns. include Brea (Calif.) Civic Cultural Ctr. Gallery, 1980, 81, Jewish Community Art Gallery, San Diego, 1980, Chatauqua (N.Y.) Art Assn. Galleries, 1981, Butler Inst., Youngstown, Ohio, 1981, Orange County Ctr. Contemporary Art, Santa Ana, Calif., 1981, Conejo Valley Art Mus., Thousand Oaks, Calif., 1982, Calif. State U., Dominguez Hills, 1983, ARCO Ctr. Visual Art, Los Angeles, 1983, Calif. State U., Hayward, 1984, Fairbanks Art Assn. Civic Ctr. Gallery, 1985, Visual Arts Ctr. Alaska, 1985, Design Ctr. Los Angeles, 1986, Soho 20, N.Y.C., 1986, Alaska State Mus., Juneau, 1986, Los Angeles Conv. Ctr., 1986, Koplin Gallery, Los Angeles, 1986, 87, 90, Sun Valley (Idaho) Art Ctr., 1987; represented in numerous pvt. and corp. collections. Address: care Koplin Gallery 8225 1/2 Santa Monica Blvd Los Angeles CA 90046

SALMON, JOAN BERNADETTE, sales executive; b. Phila., July 19, 1957; d. Lawrence Ignatius and Lucy (Ann Walls) S. BS, Temple U., 1979; MS, Eastern Ill. U., 1980. Athletic trainer U. Pa., Phila., 1980-81, Temple U., Phila., 1981-87; area sales mgr. Thera-Kinetics, Mt. Laurel, N.J., 1987—. Home: 10703 Pelle Circle E Philadelphia PA 19154 Office: Thera Kinetics Mount Laurel NJ

SALMON, JOYCE MARTINE, nursing supervisor; b. Mendon, Mo., July 21, 1946; d. Oakie Floyd and Lois May (Ratcliff) Rank; m. Garnett A. Salmon, Aug. 26, 1967; children: Terry Scott, Travis Lee, Timothy Eric. Diploma, St. Luke's Sch. Nursing, Kansas City, Mo., 1967; student in nursing, Webster U., Kansas City, Mo., 1988—. Cert. in inpatient obstetric nursing, emergency med. technician. Staff nurse Johnson County Meml. Hosp., Warrensburg, Mo., 1967-68; staff nurse Wetzel Hosp., Clinton, Mo., 1968-69, Mary Washington Hosp., Fredricksburg, Mo., 1970-71, Wetzel Hosp., Clinton, 1971-72; community health nurse II Cass County Health Dept., Harrisonville, Mo., 1972-81; staff nurse Golden Valley Meml. Hosp., Clinton, 1981-87; maternal-child health nursing supr. Cass Med. Ctr., Harrisonville, 1987—; child-birth educator Golden Valley Hosp., Clinton, 1983-87, Cass Med. Ctr., Harrisonville, 1987-88; fetal-monitoring cons. Vernon County Area Vocat. Sch., Nevada, Mo., 1989. Dem. cen. committeewoman, Henry County, Mo., 1986-88; mem. Saturday Club, G.F.W.C., Creighton, Mo., 1976-80, Urich Baptist Ch., Urich, Mo., 1981-89; chmn. Creighton Bicentennial Youth Parade, 1976. Cert. in Advanced Fetal Monitoring, St. Luke's Hosp. Perinatal Ctr., Kansas City, 1988, Cert. in Advanced Cardiac Life Support, Am. Heart Assn., 1990. Mem. Nurses Assn. of Am. Coll. Obstetricians and Gynecologists. Democrat. Baptist. Home: Rte 1 Box 149 Creighton MO 64739 Office: Cass Med Ctr 1800 E Mechanic Harrisonville MO 64701

SALMON, PHYLLIS WARD, computer company executive; b. Dallas, Aug. 10, 1948; d. Clinton David and Reba (Gilbert) Ward; m. James Y. Barbo, Dec. 12, 1970 (div. Jan. 1975); m. William Wellington Salmon, Jan. 21, 1977; 1 child, Megan Alyssa. A. in Acctg., Richland Coll., 1977; B.S. in Edn., Stephen F. Austin U., 1971. Cert. tchr. secondary edn., Tex. Cost acct. Jackson-Shaw, Dallas, 1975-79, Dal-Mac Devel., Dallas, 1979-81; store mgr. Shepard & Vick, Dallas, 1983-84; mktg. coordinator Tex. Instruments, Dallas, 1984-85; pres. Computer Expertise, Richardson, Tex., 1985—; pres. TI's Only, 1986—, pres. TechnaServe, 1987— . Mem. Nat. Assn. Female Execs., Tex. Computer Dealers Assn. (organizing mem.), Dallas Needlework and Textile Guild. Republican. Episcopalian. Club: St. Clare's Guild (bd. dirs. 1980-81)(Dallas). Avocations: needlepoint; photography; travel. Office: Computer Expertise Inc 811 Alpha Dr Suite 359 Richardson TX 75081

SALMONS, JOANNA, nursing administrator; b. Smiths Grove, Ky., Nov. 7, 1931; d. Walter Scott and Birdie Wilma (Jackson) Parker; m. William L. Salmons, June 6, 1970; children by previous marriage: Robert B. Morrow, Scott Alan Morrow. RN, Fla. Hosp. Sch. Nursing, 1954; student, So. Missionary Coll., 1979; cert. in health systems mgmt. Harvard U., 1980, Yale U., 1985; BS in Nursing, SUNY, 1982; postgrad., Trinity Coll. Dir. nursing Larkin Gen. Hosp., Miami, Fla.; adminstr., Fort Walton Beach (Fla.) Hosp., 1974-75; dir. surg. nursing Fla. Hosp., Orlando, 1976-78; v.p. profl. standards Adventist Health Systems/Sunbelt Corp., Orlando, 1978-79, bd. dirs. 1986-87; sr. v.p. Fla Hosp. Med. Ctr., Orlando, 1979—; dir. Health Care Mgmt. Corp.; cons. in field. Mem. A Thousand Plus com. Am. Cancer Soc. Recipient Outstanding Achievement award, Larkin Gen. Hosp., Miami, 1969. Mem. NAFE, Fla. Nurses Assn. (bd. dirs. 1980-81, 83-84, Nurse of Yr. award dist. 8 1988, for Fla., 1988, Nursing Adminstr. of Yr. 1988), Am. Heart Assn., Retarded Children's Assn. Orange County, Fla. Hosp. Assn., Am. Nurses Assn. (cert. nurse adminstr.), Fla. Orgn. Nursing Execs., Am. Orgn. Nursing Execs., Assn. Seventh-Day Adventist Nursing Execs. (bd. dirs.), Adventist Health Care Execs. (bd. dirs. 1986-87), Am. Health Care Execs. Assn., Ventura Lakes Golf and Tennis Club, Summer Island Racquet Club, Rotary. Home: 1212 Waverly Way Longwood FL 32750 Office: 601 Rollins St Orlando FL 32803

SALOMON, MURIEL, real estate school executive; b. New Haven, Oct. 10, 1933; d. Daniel Joseph and Ceila (Chideckle) Kaufman; m. Raymond James St. Jacques (div.); 1 child, Michael Gene; m. Dietrich Wilhelm Salomon, May 30, 1973. Grad., Realtor Inst., New Haven. Cert. residential salesman, residential broker, Conn. Editor feminine topics column New Haven Register, 1952; mgr. Royal Plastics Co., R.I.; owner, mgr. Ft. Hale Realty (now ERA Ft. Hale Realty), New Haven, 1972—; founder, dir. Real Estate Inst. Learning, Inc., New Haven, 1985—. Author real estate courses. Mem. Profl. Women's Appraisal Orgn., Real Estate Educators Assn. (Conn. state prs. 1989-90, N.E. reg. v.p. 1987—, nat. bd. dirs.), Cert. Resdl. Specialists Conn. (pres.), Women's Coun. Realtors (pres. New Haven chpt. 1984, Conn. 1985), Conn. Assn. Realtors (award 1982), Greater New Haven Bd. Realtors (edn. com. 1982-83, chmn. polit. action com. 1988), East Haven C. of C. (bd. dirs.), Real Estate Edn. Assn. Democrat. Jewish. Office: Real Estate Inst Learning 451 George St New Haven CT 06511

SALOMON, NANCY KELLY, investment executive; b. Niagara Falls, N.Y., Aug. 17, 1958; d. John Edward and Elizabeth Ann (O'Connell) Kelly; m. Robert S. Salomon III, Aug. 2, 1980; children: Victoria Kelly, Timothy Robert. BA summa cum laude, Bucknell U., 1980. Credit tng. program Marine Midland Bank, Nat. Assn., N.Y.C., 1980-81, asst. corp. banking officer, 1980-82; jr. analyst Salomon Bros. Inc., N.Y.C., 1982; dir. equity investments GEICO Corp., Washington, 1983-89. Fellow Fin. Analysts Fedn.; mem. Wash. Soc. of Investment Analysts. Republican. Roman Catholic. Home: 7804 Mary Knoll Ave Bethesda MD 20817 Office: GEICO Corp GEICO Plaza Washington DC 20076

SALSBURY, GLENNA RUTH, communications executive; b. Peoria, Ill., Sept. 13, 1937; d. Glenn Albert and Helen Bethia (Lake) Arnold; BS, Northwestern U., 1959; MA, UCLA, 1961; MA, Fuller Theol. Sem., Pasadena, Calif., 1977; m. James W. Salsbury, Feb. 10, 1979; children by previous marriage: Monica, Melissa, Michelle. Pres. Salsbury Enterprises, Paradise Valely, Ariz., 1980—; mgmt. and sales tng. cons. Mem. Nat. Speakers Assn. Republican. Mem. Christian Ch. Avocations: reading, walking. Author: Reflections, 1977, The Bible: Fact or Fiction?, 1968, Can Humans Be Christians?, 1972, Have You Considered Job?, 1972. Home and Office: 9228 N 64th Pl Paradise Valley AZ 85253

SALTA, LINDA JEAN, psychologist; b. N.Y.C., Feb. 6, 1950; d. Charles Joseph and Mary (Suda) S.; m. Paul J. Roth, Mar. 4, 1978; children: Lauren, Eric. BA, SUNY, Stony Brook, 1972; EdM in Counseling Psychology, Boston U., 1974, EdD in Counseling Psychology, 1979. Lic. psychologist, sch. psychologist, N.J., sch. psychologist, N.Y. Intern Tufts-New Eng. Med. Ctr., Boston, 1975-76, Mass. Gen. Hosp. St. Youth Clinic, Boston, 1976-77; chief clinician Adolescent Day Treatment/North Cen. Mental Health Ctr., Fitchburg, Mass., 1977-78; dir. sch. consultation Community Ctrs. Mental Health, Dumont, N.J., 1978-88; sch. psychologist Northvale (N.J.) Pub. Schs., 1989—; pvt. practice, sr. assoc. Psychoednl. Assocs., Englewood, N.J., 1989—. Office: Psychoednl Assocs 163 Engle St Englewood NJ 07675

SALTA, WENDY ANN KEHL, public relations/fund raising executive; b. Akron, Ohio, Mar. 16, 1942; d. James Howard and Alice Jayne (Hilbish) Ake; B.A., Pacific Northwestern U., 1961, M.B.A., 1963; 1 son, John Thomas. Spl. survey technician Dept. Commerce, Bur. Census, N.Y.C., 1970-71; dir. devel. Queensboro Soc. Prevention Cruelty to Children, N.Y.C., 1971-73; regional coordinator Muscular Dystrophy Assn., N.Y.C., 1973-77; dir. mktg. Greater Jamaica Devel. Corp., N.Y.C., 1977-80; nat. dir. devel. Myasthenia Gravis Found., N.Y.C., 1980-82; cons. on fund raising and pub. relations, 1982—; founder, owner Service Bur. for Lawyers, N.Y.C., 1970; owner Posh Antigues and Collectibles, 1982—, Kress Travel Svc., Inc., 1989—. Campaign mgr. for state senator, 1967, state assemblyman, 1978. Mem. Am. Arbitration Assn., Nat. Soc. Fund Raising Execs., Archaeol. Soc. Presbyterian. Home: 35-20 Leverich St Jackson Heights NY 11372 Office: 33-13 30th Ave Long Island City NY 11103

SALTER, DIANA G., marketing executive; b. Evanston, Ill., Apr. 25, 1956; d. Douglas Cameron Salter and Angela Morrow (Brady) Ross. BS, Cornell U., 1979, BA, 1979; MBA, U. Chgo., 1982. Consultant Inland Steel Co., Chgo., 1979-81; brand asst. Procter & Gamble, Cincinnati, 1982-83, asst. brand mgr., 1983-85, brand mgr., 1985-89; dir. Space Design Internat., Cincinnati, 1989-90, v.p., 1990—. Trustee Cincinnati Ballet, 1987--, v.p. mktg. 1989--. Mem Am. Mktg. Assn., Queen City Dog Tng. Club, Gordon Setter Club of Am. Office: Space Design Internat 311 Elm St Cincinnati OH 45202

SALTER, MARGERY, psychologist; b. Boston, June 17, 1952; d. Gershon and Edythe (Falk); m. Henry B. Biller, Oct. 7, 1979; 1 child, Benjamin. BA, Sarah Lawrence Coll., 1974; MA, Loyola U., Chgo., 1981, PhD, 1982. Lic. psychologist, R.I., Mass. Tchr., therapist Michael Reese Hosp., Chgo., 1974-75; psychology intern Emma Pendleton Bradley Hosp., Riverside, R.I., 1977-78; psychologist, asst. dir. Taunton (Mass.) Area Assocs. for Human Svcs., 1982-83; psychologist, cons. Fuller Meml. Hosp., Attleboro, Mass., 1988-89; psychologist Counseling Ctr. R.I. Coll., Providence, 1990; pvt. practice Assocs. for Adolescent and Family Psychotherapy, Warwick, R.I., 1985—; rsch. assoc. Child Study Ctr., Boston U., Providence, 1979-81; researcher Ambulatory Pediatrics, R.I. Hosp., Providence, 1989—; presenter in field. Contbr. articles to profl. jours. Scholarship NIMH, 1976-77. Mem. Am. Psychol. Assn., R.I. Psychol. Assn. Home: 227 Crestwood Rd Warwick RI 02886 Office: Assocs Adol/Family Psycho 1087 Warwick Ave Warwick RI 02888

SALTIEL, NATALIE, accountant; b. Chicago, Mar. 19, 1927; d. Henry Carl and Dorothy (Maremont) S.; m. Sidney D. Levin, Oct. 13, 1963; 1 child, Erica Saltiel Levin. BBA with highest distinction, Northwestern U., 1948. CPA, Ill. Staff acct. firm, Chgo., 1948-52; practice acctg., Chgo., 1952—. Bd. dirs., mem. exec. com., com. chmn. United Way Chgo., 1979-85, United Way/Crusade of Mercy, 1980-88; mem. adv. council, chmn. com. Sta. WBEZ Chicagoland Pub. Radio, 1981—. Mem. AICPAs Ill. CPA Soc., Chgo. Women's Soc. CPAs, Chgo. Fin. Exchange (bd. dirs. 1987-90), Beta Gamma Sigma. Office: 105 W Madison St Chicago IL 60602

SALTMAN, ANNE BREGY, environmental consultant; b. Phila., Oct. 1, 1951; d. Philip Anderson and Emilie (Rivinus) B.; m. Roger Leslie Saltman, Aug. 7, 1977; children: Joshua, Adam, Jonathan. BS, Alfred U., 1977; MS, Syracuse U., 1987. Adminstrv. supr. N.Y. State Diagnostic Lab., Ithaca, N.Y., 1978-82; rsch. asst. Cornell U., Ithaca, 1983; cons. exec. Fedn. Lake Assns., Inc., Cazenovia, N.Y., 1987—, mem. Sci. Adv. Bd., 1989—. Co-author: Diet for a Small Lake, 1989; editor Waterworks newsletter, 1987—. Exec. bd. dirs. Cazenovia Children's Program, 1988—. Grantee Edna Baily Sussman Fund, 1986. Mem. N.Am. Lake Mgmt. Soc., Environ. Mgmt. Coun. (vice chmn. 1989—), Madison County Fedn. Lakes, Tuscarora Lake Assn., Freshwater Found., Nature Conservancy, Sierra Club. Home and Office: 2175 Ten Eyck Ave Cazenovia NY 13035

SALTURELLI, LYNN STRAWN, restaurant owner, magazine publisher; b. Cheyenne, Wyo., Apr. 15, 1943; d. John Charles and Margaret (Parman) Warner; 1 child, Christopher John. BA in Journalism, U. Mo., 1965. In residential real estate Mary Rae & Assocs., Denver, 1977-82; owner, operator Bay Wolf Restaurant, Denver, 1982—; pub. Cherry Creek mag. Horizons Mktg. & Promotions Inc., Denver, 1987—. Mem. Cherry Creek Commerce Assn., Denver, 1983—; bd. dirs. Cherry Creek North Inc., Denver, 1986-88, Cherry Creek Improvement Assn., Denver, 1983-89. Republican. Roman Catholic. Home: 4300 E Bayaud Denver CO 80222

SALTZ, CAROLE POGREBIN, publisher; b. N.Y.C., Feb. 23, 1949; d. Isidore Lee and Dorothy (Greene) Pogrebin; 1 child, Sam Isaiah. BA, Bard Coll., 1970. Editorial asst. Praeger Spl. Studies, N.Y.C., 1970-72; from asst. mng. editor to mng. editor Appleton-Century-Crofts, N.Y.C., 1972-74; editorial cons. Carole Saltz Pub., N.Y.C., 1974-76; v.p. Springer Pub., N.Y.C., 1976-84; pub. Tchrs. Coll. Press-Columbia U., N.Y.C., 1984—. Rep. New Lincoln Parents Assn., N.Y.C., 1986—. Mem. Book Industry Study Group (statistics com. 1986—), Assn. Am. Pub., Assn. Am. Univ. Presses, Women in Production, Women's Nat. Book Assn. Home: 175 W 79th St New York NY 10024 Office: Tchrs Coll Press Tchrs Coll Columbia U 1234 Amsterdam Ave New York NY 10027

SALTZMAN, IRENE CAMERON, perfume manufacturer, art gallery owner; b. Cocoa, Fla., Mar. 23, 1927; d. Argyle Bruce and Marie T. (Neel) Cameron; m. Herman Saltzman, Mar. 23, 1946 (dec. May 1986); children: Martin Howard (dec.), Arlene Norma Hanly. Owner Irene Perfume and Cosmetics Lab., Jacksonville, Fla., 1972—, Irene Gallery of Art, Jacksonville, 1973—. Mem. Cummer Gallery of Art, Jacksonville, 1972—; mem. Jacksonville Gallery of Art, 1972—; mem. The Nat. Mus. of Women in the Arts, Washington, 1972—. Mem. NAFE, Internat. Soc. Fine Arts Appraisers, Aircraft Owners and Pilots Assn., Internat. Platform Assn., Women Bus. Owner Jacksonville, Am. Soc. Profl. and Exec. Women, USAF Assn., Jacksonville C. of C., Ponte Vedra Club, Jackson Navy Flying Club. Democrat. Episcopalian. Club: Ponte Vedra. Home: 2701 Ocean Dr S Jacksonville Beach FL 32250

SALTZMAN, LINDA RENÉE, insurance executive; b. Phila., Dec. 2, 1951; d. Erwin and Mollie (Finkel) S. BBA in Mktg., Temple U., 1973. Pension sales mgr. Phoenix Mutual Life Ins. Agy., Phila., 1973-77; v.p. pension sales Retirement Plans of Am., Phila., 1977-79; assoc. dir. pension sales Ins. Co. of N. Am., Phila., 1979-81; investment mgr. Butcher & Singer, Inc., Phila., 1981; pension sales specialist Provident Mutual Life Ins. Co., Phila., 1981-82; regional pension mgr. CIGNA Corp., Phila., 1982-89; nat. leader, regional pension mgr. Life Ins. Co. N.Am. div. CIGNA Co., Phila., 1988—; v.p. sales and mktg. Trilog, Inc., Phila., 1989—. Mem. Nat. Assn. Female Execs., Phila. Assn. Life Underwriters. Democrat. Jewish. Office: Trilog Inc One Logan Sq Ste 1600 Philadelphia PA 19103

SALTZMAN, NANCY ELISE, critical care nurse; b. Miami Beach, Fla., Sept. 6, 1965; d. Philip Saltzman and Jurate Orantas. AS in Nursing, Broward Community Coll., 1986, AA, 1989. RN. Staff nurse Hollywood (Fla.) Med. Ctr.; nurse med. pers. pool Hi Tech Home Health Care, Hollywood; staff nurse Humana Hosp. Biscayne, Aventura, Fla.; instr. Boward Community Coll., 1990. Mem. AIDS oversight com. Broward Community Coll. Recipient numerous scholarships. Mem. AACCN, NAFE, Am. Heart Assn., Am. Diabetes Assn., Assn. Smithsonian Assocs., Phi Theta Kappa (chpt. officer). Address: 7791 NW 37th St Hollywood FL 33024

SALVADOR, DOROTHEA, association executive; b. Schenectady, Sept. 4, 1935; d. Nicholas and Stella (Grisanti) DeMartino; m. Ronald J. Salvador, Aug. 6, 1983. Exec. asst. N.Y. State Bar Assn., Albany, 1960—. Mem. Nat. Assn. Bar Execs., Soc. Assn. Execs. of Upstate N.Y., Am. Soc. Assn. Execs., Hemisphere Club. Republican. Roman Catholic. Home: 1423 Hawthorne St Schenectady NY 12303 Office: New York Bar Assn One Elk St Albany NY 12207

SALVANT, PATRICIA JEAN, business owner, interior designer; b. Richmond, Va., Mar. 10, 1939; d. Thomas Whitcomb and Mary Christine (Seay) Rosen; m. Jackson Boland Sr., Aug. 7, 1959; children: Jackson Boland Jr., Jeffrey N., Thomas A. Student, Coll. of William & Mary, 1957-59, Va. Commonwealth U., 1978-82; B in Interior Design, La. State U., Baton Rouge, 1985. Designer So. Decorating, Richmond, 1976-78; mgr., designer Decorating Shoppe @ Lipscomb Bros., Mechanicsville, Va., 1978-80; designer, dept. mgr. Capitol Decorating, Richmond, 1980-81; pres., designer By Design Inc., Richmond, 1981-83, Baton Rouge, 1983-85, Coral Springs, Fla., 1985—; judge pinnacle awards com. Fla. Atlantic Builders Assn., Boca Raton, Fla., 1990. Mem. ASID, Beta Sigma Phi (pres. city coun. 1970-71, chmn. Va. state conv. 1977, Silver Circle award 1984, Girl of the Yr. 1978). Methodist. Office: By Design Inc 9337 W Sample Rd #200 Coral Springs FL 33065

SALVATORE, DONNA ANN, advertising executive; b. Hartford, Conn., June 6, 1953; d. Dominick Joseph and Germaine Simone (Bougie) S; m. Matthew Michael Vaccaro Jr., Sept. 3, 1988; 1 child, Benjamin Salvatore Vaccaro. Student, Fairleigh Dickinson U., 1971-73; BA, SUNY, Stony Brook, 1976. Broadcast asst. N.W. Ayer, N.Y.C., 1978-80; broadcast supr. Needham, Harper & Steers, N.Y.C., 1980-81; asst. dir. nat. broadcast Benton & Bowles (now D'Arcy, Masius, Benton & Bowles), N.Y.C., 1981-84, assoc. dir. nat. broadcast, 1984-89; v.p. D'Arcy, Masius, Benton & Bowles, N.Y.C., 1985-86, sr. v.p., 1986—, group dir. nat. broadcast, 1990—. Mem. Advt. Club of N.Y. Office: D'Arcy Masius Benton & Bowles Inc 1675 Broadway New York NY 10019

SALVATORE, NANCY BARBARA, company executive; b. Holyoke, Mass., June 21, 1953; d. Robert E. and Barbara Jean (Skidmore) Johnson; m. Paul A. Salvatore,. BSBA, Western New England Coll., 1982. Site mgr. MacMillan & Son Inc., Springfield, Mass., 1982-84; sales trainee Marmon Keystone, Southampton, Mass., 1984; regional resident property mgr. Ln. Mgmt. Inc., Springfield, 1984-87; gen. mgr. Sage & Seaver, Inc., Amherst, Mass., 1987—; bd. dirs. Pioneer Valley Housing Assn., Amherst; chmn. bldg. maintenance. Bd. dirs. Florence Congl. Ch., 1986--. Mem. Rotary Internat., Northampton Club. Republican. Home: 125 Cross Path Rd Northampton MA 01060 Office: Sage & Seaver Inc 79 Ss Pleasant St Amherst MA 01002

SALVESEN, B(ONNIE) FORBES, artist; b. Elgin, Ill., Nov. 6, 1944; d. Donald Behan and Helen Elaine (Krajacik) Forbes; m. Bruce Michael Salvesen, Sept. 3, 1966. Pvt. edn., 1972-82; student, Am. Acad. Art, 1976, Sch. Art Inst. Chgo., 1980-82, Kulick-Stark, 1983. Asst. to purchasing agt. Harnischfeger, Crystal Lake, Ill., 1962-64; rec. sec. Electric Mfrs. Credit Bur., Cary, Ill., 1964-66; student and practicing artist, 1968—. illustrator: (book) There were Reasons, 1983. Recipient numerous awards of excellence in art, most recent being award for pho tography AAUW, Elgin, 1988, 1989, award for art, Randhurst (Ill.) Art Fair, 1988, J. Hindley hon. award Kenosha Pub. Mus., 1989, 1st place award Itasca Jr. Woman's Club, 1989, 1st place award Kenosha Lake Arts Coun., 1990, Award of Excellence, Barrington Area Arts Coun., 1990, Outstanding Fine Arts award Haymarket Guild of Artists, 1990, Arts Alliance of Ogle County award, 1990. Democratic. Roman Catholic. Home and Office: 1312 Whippoorwill Dr Crystal Lake IL 60014

SALVUCCI, SUZANNE MARY, nurse; b. Brighton, Mass., Nov. 28, 1962; d. Loreto and Theresa Lucy (Profetto) S. BS, Boston Coll., 1984. RN Boston City Hosp., Boston, 1985-88; permanent charge nurse Boston City Hosp., 1986-87; RN Newton (Mass.) Wellesley Hosp., Newton, 1988—. Mem. Mass. Nurses Assn. Democrat. Roman Catholic. Home: 24 Albert St Waltham MA 02154

SALZBERG, BETTY JOAN, computer science educator; b. Denver, Jan. 19, 1944; d. Theodore Herbert and Hilda (Herzel) S.; m. Harold Mead Stark, June 21, 1964 (div. 1977); 1 child, Pearl Stark; m. Lawrence Edward Morris, Sept. 2, 1978. BA in Math., UCLA, 1964; MA in Math., U. Mich., 1966, PhD in Math., 1971. Asst. prof. math. Northeastern U., Boston, 1971-77, assoc. prof. math., 1977-82, assoc. prof. Coll. Computer Sci., 1982-90, prof. Coll. Computer Sci., 1990—. Author: An Introduction to Database Design, 1986, File Structures: An Analytic Approach, 1988; contbr. articles to tech. publs. NSF rsch. grantee, 1988—. Mem. Assn. Computing Machinery, Spl. Interest Group Mgmt. of Data Assn. Computing Machinery, IEEE Computer Soc. Office: Northeastern U Coll Computer Sci Boston MA 02115

SALZMAN, ANNE MEYERSBURG, psychologist; b. N.Y.C., Feb. 25, 1928; d. Reuben and Dorothy (Steinberg) Meyersburg; m. Paul Salzman, Sept. 11, 1952; children: Harold, Richard. BA, U. N.Mex., 1949; MA, NYU, 1950. Lic. psychologist. Psychologist, field instr. UCLA Psychology Clinic Sch., L.A., 1952-55; psychologist Temple Beth Am, L.A., 1956-60; psychologist, co-dir. Acad. Guidance Svcs., L.A., 1960-76; psychologist, dir. The Guidance Ctr., Santa Monica, Calif., 1976—. Mem. Am. Psychol. Assn., Fedn. Am. Scientists, Calif. State Psychol. Assn., L.A. County Psychol. Assn., Greenpeace. Democrat. Jewish. Office: The Guidance Ctr 2116 Wilshire Blvd Ste 204 Santa Monica CA 90403

SALZMAN, MARILYN JEAN, lawyer; b. N.Y.C., Aug. 21, 1939; d. Benjamin S. and Betty (Isaacs) Bzura; m. Robert L. David, Apr. 28, 1962 (div. Nov. 1973); children: Jeffrey M., Steven B.; m. Stanley P. Salzman, Feb. 3, 1974; children: Ira J., Mark B., Debra G. BA, Queens Coll., 1961; JD, Hofstra U., 1984. Bar: N.Y. 1985, Fla. 1985, U.S. Dist. Ct. (so. and ea. dists.) N.Y. 1985, N.J. 1986, D.C. 1986, U.S. Ct. Appeals (2d cir.) 1986, U.S. Supreme Ct. 1988. Assoc. Friesner & Salzman, Great Neck, N.Y., 1984—; Bd. dirs. Jacques DuBois Inc., Ann Arbor, Mich. V.p. fundraising Cancer Care, Jericho, N.Y., 1968-69. Mem. ABA, N.Y. State Bar Assn., N.Y. County Lawyers Assn., Women's Bar Assn. State of N.Y., Nassau County Women's Bar Assn. Democrat. Jewish. Office: Friesner & Salzman 1000 Northern Blvd Great Neck NY 11022

SAMARA, BRENDA MARY, psychologist; b. Cambridge, Mass., Dec. 8, 1941; d. Edward and Helen (Malouf) S. BA, Bennington (Vt.) Coll., 1963; MA, U. N.H., 1965; PhD, Temple U., 1974. Staff psychologist Phila. State Hosp., 1965-67, Phila. Gen. Hosp., 1967-69, Jefferson Community Mental Health Ctr., Phila., 1969-70; pvt. practice Pa., 1970—; instr. in psychology Inst. of Awareness, Phila., 1970-76; group facilitator Dept. Mental Health State of N.J., Trenton, 1974-78; clin. supr. Antioch Coll., Phila., 1974; instr. U. Pa., Phila., 1974-78; instr. U. Pa., Phila., 1974-78; cons. YWCA of Phila., 1974, Villanova (Pa.)úU. Law Sch., 1975, Walden Prep. Sch., Merion, Pa., 1976. Instr. SYDA Found., Phila., 1980—. Home and Office: 539 Abington Ave Glenside PA 19038

SAMELA, LORRAINE ANN, educator; b. Waterbury, Conn., Oct. 18, 1947; d. Marco and Alda (Giusti) S. BS, So. Conn. State U., 1969; MS, Cen. Conn. State U., 1970. Cert. elem. tchr., Italian educator, Conn. Tchr. Webster Sch., Waterbury, 1970-78, Regan Elem. Sch., Waterbury, 1978—. Mem. Waterbury Symphony Orch., 1980-88, Waterbury Civic Theatre, 1973-80, Statue of Liberty-Ellis Island Found., N.Y., 1980—, Nat. PTA, Conn. PTA, 1978—. Mem. NEA, Conn. Edn. Assn., Waterbury Tchrs. Assn., Cen. Conn. State U. Alumni, So. Conn. State U. Alumni. Roman Catholic.

SAMFORD, JUDITH LEE, psychologist, consultant; b. Wayne County, Ill., Nov. 22, 1939; d. Ernest Lawrence and Mary Lutitia (Templeman) L.; m. Donald Francis, Dec. 23, 1967 (div. 1978); 1 child, Lance Adams. BS in Edn., So. Ill. U., 1960, MS, 1963; postgrad., Bradley U., 1965, U. Fla., 1966; PhD, Fla. Inst. Tech., 1981. Lic. psychologist, Ill, Hawaii. Psychologist Mo. Dept. Mental Health, St. Louis, 1962-64, Ill. Div. Alcoholism, Chgo., 1964-69; mental health adminstr. Ill. Dept. Mental Health, Chgo., 1969-84; chief of service-geriatrics Chgo. Read Mental Health Ctr., 1985-86; instr. U. Hawaii, Kauai, 1986-87; psychologist Waimano Tng. Sch. and Hosp., Hawaii, 1987-88, 89; program chief adult svcs. Hawaii State Hosp., Kaneohe, 1989—; behavior scientist William A. Howe Developmental Disabilities Ctr., Tinley Park, Ill., 1988—; cons. Forkosh Hosp., Chgo., 1981-86; organizer, leader Alateen Group, Carbondale, Ill.; faculty assoc. academic advisor learning resource cons. William Lyon U., San Diego, Calif., 1988—. Co-author: Illinois State Plan for Alcoholism, 1974. Bd. dirs. So. Ill. Com. on Alcoholic Concerns, Carbondale, 1965-67. Recipient I Dare You award Danforth Found., 1952-57. Mem. Am. Psychol. Assn., Am. Soc. Clin. Hypnosis, Chgo. Soc. Clin. Hypnosis, Internat. Soc. Hypnosis, Nat. Edn. Assn., VFW, Am. Legion Aux., Fraternal Order Eagles, N.Y. Acad. Scis., Alpha Lambda Delta, Kappa Omicron Phi. Democrat. Club: 4-H (Wayne County). Office: Hawaii State Hosp 45-710 Keaalala Kaneohe HI 96744

SAMII, MARY ALICE, secondary school educator; b. San Antonio, Nov. 10, 1951; d. Mario A. and Maria Luisa (Mu(ñ)oz) Garza; m. Abbas Monshizadeh Samii, Dec. 26, 1987. BA, St. Mary's U., 1973; MA, U. Tex., San Antonio, 1976; postgrad., Tex. A&M U., 1976, U. Tex., 1986-87, S.W. Tex. State U., 1987. Tchr. Edgewood Ind. Sch. Dist., San Antonio, 1973-78, Tech. Night Sch., San Antonio, 1978-79, San Antonio Ind. Sch. Dist., 1978-79; tchr./history chairperson Austin (Tex.) Ind. Sch. Dist., 1979-87; coord. fgn. lang. Lexington (Mass.) Pub. Schs., 1987—, E.S.L. supr., 1987—; E.I.S.D. curriculum writer Lexington Fgn. Exchange Coord. Mem. Chinese Parent Adv. Coun., Lexington, 1987—; chairperson Fgn. Lang. Citizens Adv. Com., Lexington, 1989—. Named Tchr. of Yr. Dobie Jr. High Sch., Austin, 1982-83, 1986-87; fellowship Free Enterprise. Mem. Tchrs. of English to Speakers of Other Langs., Mass. Fgn. Lang. Assn., Mass. Assn. of Tchrs. of English to Speakers of Other Langs., Nat. Educators Assn., Mass. Tchrs. Assn., Assn. of Supervision and Curriculum Devel. Roman Catholic. Home: 79 Central #6 Waltham MA 02154

SAMIIAN, BARAZANDEH, business owner, educator; b. Tehran, May 13, 1939; came to U.S., 1958. B.A., Woodbury U., Los Angeles, 1961; B.A., Immaculate Heart Coll., Los Angeles, 1979; M.A., Webster U., Geneva, 1981. 1 child, Mina P. Cullimore. Cons., Design & Architecture, Tehran, 1965-72; bus. cons. multinat. corps., Calif., 1970-77; co-owner Samiian and Solomon Assocs., Geneva, 1978-86; owner, B. Samiian Assocs., Jacksonville, Fla., 1987—; adj. prof. Webster U., Geneva, 1981—, U. North Fla.; cons. and lectr. human resources devel. Named Woman of Yr., 1983; recipient Gov's. citation State of Md., 1983. Mem. Internat. Alliance Exec. Women (bd. dirs. 1988—). Office: B Samiian Assocs PO Box 23825 Jacksonville FL 32241-3825

SAMMARTINO, SYLVIA, university co-founder; b. Boston, Dec. 5, 1903; d. Louis J. and Anna E. (Bianchi) Scaramelli; m. Peter Sammartino, Dec. 5, 1933. A.B., Smith Coll., 1925; M.A., Columbia U., 1926; LL.D. (hon.), Kyung Hee U., Korea, 1964; D.H.L. (hon.), Fairleigh Dickinson U., 1966. Tchr. public high sch. N.Y.C., 1927-28, 33-35; treas. Scaramelli & Co., Inc., N.Y.C., 1928-33; ednl. editor Atlantica, 1933-35; circulation mgr. La Voix de France, N.Y.C., 1935-37; registrar Fairleigh Dickinson U., Rutherford, N.J., 1942-50; dir. admissions Fairleigh Dickinson U., 1950-59, dean of admissions, 1959-67. Chmn. N.J. Commn. on Women, 1971; mem. bd. govs. N.Y. Cultural Ctr., 1968-73; mem. exec. com. Restore Ellis Island Commn., 1974-79; pres. Garden State Ballet Found., 1975-80; trustee Newark Symphony Hall, 1976-79, William Carlos Williams Ctr. for Performing Arts, Rutherford, N.J., 1980—; trustee, chmn. Integrity, Inc., 1980-89; trustee, sec.-treas. Williams Inst., 1981—. Decorated knight Order of Merit Italy; comdr. Order Star of Africa Liberia; officer Order Nat. Ivory Coast; recipient Amita award, 1960; Smith Coll. medal, 1967; President's medal Mercy Coll., 1980, Humanitarian award William Carlos Williams Ctr. for the Arts, 1988; named Woman of Yr., Rutherford C. of C. Home and Office: 140 Ridge Rd Rutherford NJ 07070

SAMMET, JEAN E., computer scientist; b. N.Y.C.; d. Harry and Ruth S. B.A., Mount Holyoke Coll., Sc.D. (hon.), 1978; M.A., U. Ill. Group leader programming Sperry Gyroscope, Great Neck, N.Y., 1955-58; sect. head, staff cons. programming Sylvania Electric Products, Needham, Mass., 1958-61; with IBM, 1961-88; adv. program mgr. Boston, 1961-65; program lang. tech. mgr. IBM, 1965-68; programming tech. planning mgr. Fed. Systems div., 1968-74, programming lang. tech. mgr., 1974-79, software tech. mgr., 1979-81, div. software tech. mgr., 1981-82, programming lang. tech. mgr., 1983-88; programming lang. cons. Bethesda, Md., 1989—; chmn. history of computing com. Am. Fedn. Info. Processing Socs., 1977-79. Author: Programming Languages: History and Fundamentals, 1969; editor-in-chief: Assn. Computing Machinery Computing Revs, 1979-87; contbr. articles to profl. jours. Mem. Assn. Computing Machinery (pres. 1974-76, Disting. Service award 1985), Nat. Acad. Engring., Upsilon Pi Epsilon. Office: PO Box 30038 Bethesda MD 20824

SAMMONS, DORELEENA ANN, state agency administrator; b. Okinawa, Japan, Oct. 6, 1954; d. Hearold Kingslar Sammons and Joanna Ann (Maultsby) Chatman. Student, MIT, 1974-75; BS in Pre Medicine, Bennett Coll., 1976; postgrad., Smith Coll., 1976-77; MS in Nutrition, Harvard U., 1979. Lic. dietitian. Pub. health nutritionist Person County Health Dept., Roxboro, N.C., 1980-82; program specialist D.C. Women, Infants and Children Program, Washington, 1982-86; dir. Ga. Spl. Supplemental Food Program for Women Infants & Child, Atlanta, 1986-89; div. dir. N.J. Div. of Aids Prevention and Control, Trenton, 1989—. Bd. dirs. Belmonte Hills Home Owners Assn., Atlanta, 1987-89. Mem. Am. Dietetic Assn., Ga. Dietetic Assn., Am. Pub. Health Assn., Ga. Pub. Health Assn. (sect. chmn. nutrition com. 1987-88), Nat. Assn. WIC Dirs. (sec.-treas. 1988—), Eastern Star, Delta Sigma Theta. Democrat. Baptist. Home: 3 Tyson Dr Ewing Twp Mercer County NJ 08638 Office: NJ Div of Aids 363 W State St CN363 Trenton NJ 08625

SAMPAS, DOROTHY M., government official; b. Washington, Aug. 24, 1933; d. Lawrence and Anna Cornelia (Henkel) Myers; m. James George Sampas, Dec. 8, 1962; children: George, Lawrence James. AB, U. Mich., 1955; postgrad., U. Paris, 1955-56; PhD, Georgetown U., 1970; cert., Nat. War Coll., Washington, 1987. With Bur. Pub. Affairs Dept. State, Washington, 1958-60, analyst, 1973-75, div. chief, dep. chief Office of Position and Pay Mgmt., 1979-83, div. chief Office of Mgmt., 1983-84, dir. Office of Mgmt., 1984-86; vice consul Am. Consulate Gen., Hamburg, Fed. Republic Germany, 1960-62; cons. Trans Century Corp., Washington, 1972; gen. svcs. officer Am. Embassy, Brussels, 1975-79; embassy minister, counselor Am. Embassy, Beijing, 1987-90. Presbyterian. Home: 4715 Trent Ct Chevy Chase MD 20815 Office: Dept of State 2101 C St NW Washington DC 20520

SAMPEL, PAMELA J., personnel director; b. Des Moines, Dec. 7, 1959; d. James Richard and Nelda Jean Sampel. BBA, U. Iowa, 1981; MPA, U. Wash., 1983. Specialist pers. mgmt., mgmt. analyst, mgr. profl. svcs. Pacific Health Assocs. Seattle, 1982-87; pers. dir. KCTS #9, Seattle, 1987—. Bd. dir. Chicken Soup Brigade. Edn. Svcs. fellow; State of Iowa scholar. Mem. Soc. for Human Resource Mgmt., Am. Mgmt. Assn., Women's Bus. Exch.

SAMPLE, BEVERLY A., real estate professional; b. Brown County, Ind., Oct. 17, 1944; d. Albert H. and Kathryn M. (Stogdill) Cross; widowed; children: Brian, Lynn, Jackie. Student, House of James Beauty Coll., 1961-62; grad. real estate course, Bloomington, Ind. Lic. real estate agent, Ind. Cosmetologist Bloomington, 1964-77, real estate professional, 1977—; sales mgr. Rod Figg Realtors, Bloomington, 1986-89; sales mgr. F.C. Tucker/Bloomington, 1989-90, dir. affiliate svcs., 1990—. Pres. Monroe County Plan Commn., Bloomington, 1989, v.p. Bd. Zoning Appeals, 1989; candidate for Monroe County Commn., 1990. Mem. Am. Bus. Women Assn. (treas., pres., recording sec., Woman of Yr. 1986), Bloomington Bd. Realtors (past treas., Realtor of Yr. 1985), Ind. Assn. Realtors (state pub. rels. chair), Nat. Assn. Realtors (pub. rels. com.). Republican. Home: 1489 W Lawson St Bloomington IN 47401 Office: FC Tucker Bloomington 2670 E 2d St Bloomington IN 47401

SAMPLE, CONSTANCE JEANNE, real estate broker, mortgage broker, land planner; b. Balt., June 11, 1950; d. Wayne E. and Albert (Maenner) Colburn; m. Richard Eaton Sample, Dec. 6, 1969;children: Barbara Dianne, Bonnie Kathleen. BS, Fla. State U., 1975. Lic. mortgage broker, realtor, Fla. Quality contr. Milton Roy Co., St. Petersburg, Fla., 1976-77; social worker Fla. Dept. Health and Rehab., Tampa, 1978-80; ops. mgr. First Southeastern Co., Tampa, 1981-85; adminstr., real estate broker Cape Sands, Inc., St. Petersburg, 1984—; v.p., real estate broker, adminstr. Profl. Devel. Enterprises, St. Petersburg, 1985—; ops. mgr. Cert. Capital Corp., St. Petersburg, 1986-87, Cert. Investments Corp., St. Petersburg, 1987; mortgage loan officer Gt. Western Bank, Tampa, 1987-88; v.p., owner Help-U-Sell of North Tampa, 1989-90; pres., owner Park Place Affiliates, Inc., Tampa, Fla., 1989—; v.p. Cert. Mortgage Corp., 1985-88; ind. mortgage broker, 1988—. Tchr. mem. fellowship com. and circle club Village Presbyn. Ch., Tampa, 1988, historian Presbyn. Women's Coun., 1989-90); mem. Berkely Prep. Parents Club, Tampa, 1977—, Countryside Parents Club, 1987-88; mem. bd. Tampa Christian Acad., 1989; sec. Parents of Tampa Christian Acad. Bd., 1989; vol. worker sport competitions. Named Leader of Yr., Ali Lassen's Leads Club, Tampa, 1988. Mem. Women's Coun. Realtors, Nat. Assn. Realtors, Fla. Assn. Realtors (realtor/builder com.), State U. Alumni Assn. (life), Carrollwood Area Bus. Assn., Leads Club (Leader of Yr. 1988). Home: 15813 Sapwood St Tampa FL 33624 Office: Park Place Affiliates Inc 11734 N Dale Mabry Tampa FL 33618

SAMPLE, JUDITH NEUER, utility company official; b. Rochester, N.Y., Dec. 4, 1943; d. Edward George and Elizabeth Grace (Specht) N.; m. Joseph Paul Sample, July 8, 1986. B.S. in Biology, Alfred U., 1965. Rsch. assoc. U. Rochester Med. Sch., 1965-68; computer systems analyst Rochester Inst. Tech., 1968-70, now lectr.; systems cons. Sybron Corp., 1970-72, mgr. order processing, 1973-75, distbn. and customer svc. mgr., 1975-76; mgr. stores and receiving Xerox Corp., Webster, N.Y., 1976-77, mgr. systems and ops. planning, 1977-79, mgr. mfg. ops., 1980-85; quality specialist Fla. Power and Light, Miami, 1985—. Program cons. women in bus. and career devel. Rochester YMCA; founding mem. steering com., bd. dirs. Women's Career Ctr. of Rochester; bd. mgrs. Lost Mountain Manor Condominium Complex. Mem. Am. Prodn. and Inventory Control Soc., AAUW. Republican. Presbyterian. Home: 3002 Cove Rd Tequesta FL 33469 Office: Fla Power & Light PO Box 14000 Juno Beach FL 33408

SAMPLE, KAREN ANN, educator, administrator; b. Poteau, Okla., July 12, 1949; d. Paul Leroy and Ruby Nell (Nummy) Coggins; children: John, Jeffrey. BS, U. Okla., 1975, postgrad., 1987-88; MEd, East Cen. U., 1978. Cert. secondary tchr., Okla. Instr. sci. Ada (Okla.) Sr. High Sch., 1977-81, instr. sci., chmn. sci. dept., 1981—; spl. cons., ind. study cons. U. Okla., Norman, 1983—. Mem. NEA, Nat. Sci. Tchrs. Assn., Okla. Edn. Assn., Okla. Sci. Tchrs. Assn., Noble Assn. Classroom Tchrs. (v.p. 1982-83), Beta Sigma Phi. Home: 212 Forest Hills Noble OK 73068 Office: Noble Sr High Sch 48th Ave SE & Etowah Rd Noble OK 73068

SAMPLE, WENDY ELIZABETH, school system administrator; b. Boston, Jan. 17, 1956; d. Wilbur Harry and Joanne Grace (Demaray) S. Student, U. Maine, 1974; BS in Recreation and Park Mgmt., U. Oreg, 1980. Profl. jazz dancer Bob Heath Co., Portland, Oreg., 1975-77; unit leader, counselor YMCA Camp, Otis, Oreg., 1976-77; mgr. VIP's Restaurant Lounge, Portland, 1977-78; dir. new student host program U. Oreg., Eugene, 1979; with front desk ops. Eugene Family YMCA, 1979-80; community sch. coordinator Oregon City (Oreg.) Sch. Dist., 1980-83, Portland Park Bur., 1983-89; assoc. dir. Concordia Coll., 1989—; dir., lectr. fitness workshops, Portland; publicist Bodyworks, Portland, 1986—. State rep. Hershey (Pa.) Nat. Track and Field Program, 1980-82; co-chair Am. Heart Assn., Portland, 1985-88; active Big Sister program S.E. Svc. Ctr., Portland, 1987—; mem. Portland YMCA, cert. phys. fitness leader. Recipient vol. research award N.W. Community Edn. Ctr., 1982, Outstanding Service award Atkinson Community Mems., Portland, 1986; named Vol. of Yr., Am. Heart Assn., 1986-87. Mem. Nat. Community Edn. Assn. (conv. liaison 1984-85), Oreg. Community Edn. Assn. (bd. dirs. 1984-85, pres. 1985-87, Contbr. award 1988), Nat. Assn. Women, NOW, Mastermind. Democrat. Office: Concordia Coll 2811 NE Holman Portland OR 97211

SAMPLES, MARTINA, nursing home administrator; b. Phila., Nov. 20, 1942; d. Martin Rulon and Mallette Mary (Holden) Sembach; m. Billy Irwin Samples, May 13, 1987; children: Lauren, Lynne, Michael, Andrew, Toni, Christopher, Roberta, John. AA, Daytona Beach Community Coll., 1978; student, Southwest Tex. Coll., 1986-88. Lic. practical nurse, lic. nursing home adminstr., Tex. Adminstr. Purple Hills Manor/Gray Enterprises, Bandera, Tex., 1985-86, Comanche View-Nat. Heritage, Ft. Stockton, Tex., 1986-87, Louis Pasteur Care Ctr./Camlu Care Ctrs., San Antonio, 1987-88, Castle Hills Manor/Campbell-White Assocs., San Antonio, 1988-89, Briarcliff Health Care Ctr., Greenville, Tex., 1989—. Mem. Tex. Health Care Assn., NAFE, Am. Legion, Greenville C. of C., Order Eastern Star, VFW. Republican. Methodist. Home: Rte 3 Box 94A1 Quinlan TX 75474

SAMPSON, BONNIE P., career and management consultant, speaker; b. Ogden, Utah, July 29, 1942; d. E. Lamar and Mary (Soffe) Parkin; m. Ralph R. Sampson, June 27, 1981; children: Trina, Tamra, Kent, Scott, Brent, Sharon. BS. Lic. real estate agt.; cert. med. sales mgr. Pharm. sales rep. Hoechst Rousell, Sommerville, N.J., 1974-75; mgr. N.W. region Mallinckrodt, Inc., St. Louis, 1975-83; sales rep. Berlex Imaging, Wayne, N.J., 1983-88; resident sales specialist Bob Miguel and Assocs. Real Estate, Danville, Calif., 1988-89; pres. Discovery-Advanced Devel. Programs, Danville, Calif., 1989—. Mem. NAFE, Assn. Calif. Soc. Radiologist Tech., Danville C. of C., Beta Sigma Phi. Address: 900 El Capitan Dr Danville CA 94526

SAMPSON, DEBORAH K., microcomputer consultant; b. Oklahoma City, Apr. 17, 1951; d. Nolan William and Marie M. (Seeliger) Schlobohm; m. Robert Jay Sampson, Aug. 7, 1982. BA in English Edn., Bethany Coll., 1973; postgrad., U. Kans., 1974-76. Tchr. Tipton (Kans.) High Sch., 1973-74; dir. pub. rels. Kans. Lung Assn., Topeka, 1976-77; dir. planning, pub. info. Shawnee County Community Action, Topeka, 1977-83; dir. pub. rels. Kaw Valley coun. Girl Scouts U.S., Topeka, 1983-84; mgr. learning ctr. Valcom, Topeka, 1985; systems cons. The Computer Patch, Topeka, 1985-86; owner, cons. Sampson & Assocs., Lawrence, Kans., 1987—; instr. continuing edn. program, Washburn U., Topeka, 1987—; trainer, U. Kans. Capitol Complex, Topeka, 1987-88; cons., Interactive Concepts, Inc., Lawrence, 1989. Editor newsletters, workbooks. Chair bd. dirs., Topeka Battered Women's Task Force, 1979-80; bd. dirs., Every Woman's Resource Ctr., Topeka, 1980-81, Topeka YWCA, 1981-82, Trinity Foster Home, Lawrence, 1984-85; sec., Douglas County Dem. party, Lawrence, 1988-90. Mem. Nat. Computer Graphics Assn. (co-editor Kansas City chpt. 1988-89), Ind. Computer Cons. Assn. Democrat. Lutheran.

SAMPSON, JUNE ELISABETH, historical museum administrator; b. Phila., May 31, 1946; d. William Herbert and Helen Elizabeth (Whitall) Stafford; B.A. in History, Earlham Coll., Richmond, Ind., 1968; M.A. in History Mus. Tng., SUNY, Oneonta, 1972; m. Earl Sampson, Jan. 22, 1972; stepchildren—Earl Brett, Daniel C., Shawn, Indira. Mus. curator S.D. State Hist. Soc., Pierre, 1969-72; asst. dir. W.H. Over Mus., U. S.D., Vermillion, 1972-73, dir., 1973-79; dir. Western Heritage Center, Billings, Mont., 1980-83; grant writer Powell County Mus. and Arts Found., Deer Lodge, Mont., 1983-84; dir. The Danish Immigrant Mus., Elk Horn, Iowa, 1984—; instr. dept. anthropology U. S.D., 1973-79. Mem. Landmarks, Inc., Billings, 1980-84. Mem. Am. Assn. Mus., Iowa Mus. Assn., Am. Assn. for State and Local History. Office: The Danish Immigrant Mus Box 178 Elk Horn IA 51531

SAMPSON, MIKKI LYNN, computer services coordinator; b. Harvey, Ill., July 4, 1950; d. Eugene Paul Cunningham and Shirley Mae (Stearman) Hildreth; m. John Eldridge Sampson, Apr. 18, 1969; children: Timothy John, Melanie Dawn. AAS in Office Support, Mohave Community Coll., Kingman, Ariz., 1987. Claims coord. Dynamic Health Svcs., Kingman, 1983-85; instrn. asst. Mohave Community Coll., Kingman, 1985; office mgr. Dermatology Care Ctr., Kingman, 1985-87; prosecution asst. Mohave County Atty.'s Office, Kingman, 1986-87; computer svcs. mgr. Mohave/La Paz JTPA Program, Kingman, 1987—; mem. Ariz. Mgmt. Info. Systems Task Force, 1990—, Ariz. Prosecuting Atty.'s Coun., 1986-87. Asst. leader Girl Scouts Am., Kingman, 1984-87; bd. dirs. Boy Scouts Am., Kingman, 1980-85. Mem. NAFE. Office: Mohave/La Paz JTPA Career Ctrs 412 E Oak St (PO Box 711) Kingman AZ 86401

SAMPSON, PATSY HALLOCK, college president; b. Picher, Okla., July 9, 1932; d. Daniel Webster and Mary Gladys (Whitehead) Hallock; children: Catherine, Jacquelyn, Rebecca. B.A. with spl. distinction, U. Okla., 1961; Ph.D. in Psychology, Cornell U., 1966. Asst. prof. SUNY, Binghamton, 1965-66; NIMH postdoctoral fellow Cornell U., 1966-67; asst. prof. Wellesley (Mass.) Coll., 1967-70; prof., chmn. dept. psychology Calif. State Coll., Bakersfield, 1970-73; adminstr. Nat. Inst. Child Health and Human Devel., Bethesda, Md., 1973-75; psychologist Nat. Inst. Alcohol Abuse and Alcoholism, Washington, 1975-77; dean faculty, prof. psychology Pitzer Coll., Claremont, Calif., 1977-80; dean Coll. Liberal Arts, Drake U., Des Moines, 1980-83; pres. Stephens Coll., Columbia, Mo., 1983—. Bd. dirs. Commn. on Women in Higher Edn., 1984-87, Council for Advancement of Experiential Learning, 1986—; mem. Pres.'s Commn. of Nat. Collegiate Athletic Assn., 1984-86; trustee The Fielding Inst., 1986—; mem. nat. adv. bd. Outward Bound U.S.A., 1987-90. Mem. Am. Council Edn. (bd. dirs. 1985-88), AAUP, North Cen. Assn. Colls. and Schs. (exec. commr. commn. on instns. of higher edn. 1988—), Phi Beta Kappa, Sigma Xi. Office: Stephens Coll Columbia MO 65215-0001

SAMPSON, THYRA ANN, mediator; b. Oakland, Calif., Apr. 22, 1948; d. Harold Joseph and Velma Louise (Robinson) S.; 1 child, Leon Broussard III. BA, U. Calif., 1970; JD, Hastings Coll of Law, 1978. Project dir. Univ. Calif. Medical Sch., L.A., 1980-81; legislative staff Calif. State Assembly, Sacramento, 1981-85; adminstr. support for dir. Toward Utility Rate Normalization, San Francisco, 1985-86; program devel. rep. Network Solutions Inc., Sacramento, 1988-89; mediator Sacramento Mediation Ctr., 1990—; staff cons. Calif. Legislative Black Caucus, Sacramento, 1982, Angel City Dental Soc., L.A., 1978-79. Campaign cons., precinct leader Jessie Jackson for Pres., 1988. Mem. Fannie Lou Hamer Dem. Club, Black Am. Polit. Assn. Calif.

SAMPSON-LANDERS, CAROLE, pharmaceutical company executive; b. Detroit, Aug. 10, 1946; d. Charles Harrie and Lucille (Harper) Sampson; m. Theodore Craig Landers Sr., Dec. 31, 1979; children: Theodore C. Jr., Terrence C. AB, Douglass Coll., 1969; M in Med. Sci., Rutgers U., 1972; MD, Temple U., 1976. Rsch. asst. Ortho Diagnostics, Raritan, N.J., 1969-72; resident physician Howard U. Hosp., Washington, 1976-77; with clin. rsch. Ortho Pharm. Corp. Johnson Pharm. Rsch. Inst., Raritan, 1979-88, dir. clin. rsch., 1988-90; exec. dir. clin. affairs Advanced Card Products-Rsch., Raritan, 1990—. Career counselor Douglass Alumni Assn., 1982—, YWCA, 1980—; sec. Twin Forum Mgmt. Bd., 1988-89; mem. adv. bd. Consortium Ednl. Equity, 1987—. Recipient Tribute to Woman in Industry award YWCA, 1980. Mem. Drug Info. Assn., AAAS, Nat. Med. Assn., Am. Coll. Clin. Pharm., Nat. Council Negro Women, Am. Fertility Soc. Home: 3 Deer Run Lebanon NJ 08833 Office: Advance Care Products-Rsch West Rte 202 Box 300 Raritan NJ 08869-0602

SAMRA, RISE JANE, communication educator; b. Green Bay, Wis., Mar. 19, 1952; d. Emile Abou and Ruth Elaine (Farha) S. BA, Western Mich. U., 1973; MA, U. Mich., 1975; PhD, U. Ariz., 1985. Cert. Am. Acad. Dramatic Arts. Asst. prof. Northwood Inst., Midland, Mich., 1975-79; profl. office salesperson Dow Chem. Co., Des Plaines, Ill., 1979-80; teaching assoc. U. Ariz., Tucson, 1980-84; communications cons. Tucson, 1985-86; assoc. prof. communication Barry U., Miami Shores, Fla., 1986—; cons. Metro-Dade Parks and Recreation Dept., Miami, Fla., 1989, Tucson Electric Power Co., 1985, U. Ariz., 1980-85; radio-TV performer, Tucson and Miami, 1982—. Author, performer in ednl. films; contbr. articles to profl. jours. Office mgr. U.S. Congl. Campaign, Tucson., 1982; media promotor Miss Tucson Ednl. Pageant, 1985; coord., performer South Fla. Unites, 1987; participant Miami Coalition for a Drug-Free Am., 1989. Mem. Speech Communication Assn., So. Speech Communication Assn., Fla. Communication Assn., Pub. Rels. Soc. Am. (ednl. com. 1987—), Women in Communications, Inc., Kappa Delta Pi. Episcopalian. Office: Barry U 11300 NE 2d Ave Miami Shores FL 33161

SAMS, DORIS LAVERNE, college counselor; b. Youngwood, Pa., Apr. 26; d. Benjamin F. and Lucinda (Myers) S.. BA, Seton Hill Coll., 1950; postgrad., U. Pitts., 1959. Lic. mental health counselor, Fla., nat. bd. cert. counselor Nat. Acad. Cert. Clin. Mental Health Counselors. Psychiat. aide Inst. of Living, Hartford, Conn., 1950-51; employment interviewer Conn. State Employment Service, Thompsonville, 1951-53; tchr. Hempfield Area Schs., Greensburg, Pa., 1953-58, sch. psychologist, 1958-66; sr. prof., counselor Broward Community Coll., Ft. Lauderdale, Fla., 1966—; human potential seminar leader Rational Behavior Therapist. Mem. Gov.'s Com. on Handicapped. Frick scholar. Mem. Am. Mental Health Counselors Assn., Am. Psychol. Assn. (assoc.), Nat. Assn. Cert. Clin. Mental Health Counselors, Am. Assn. Counseling and Devel., Humane Soc., Pet Rescue. Republican. Home: 1400 SW 19th St Fort Lauderdale FL 33315 Office: Broward Community Coll Hollywood FL 33024

SAMS, MARY ANN PACELLA, educational administrator, corporate executive; b. Chgo., Sept. 14, 1933; d. Carmen Harold and Helen Frances (Strauk) Pacella; A.B. cum laude, Mundelein Coll., 1958; M.Ed., U. Puget Sound, 1970; postgrad. U. San Francisco, 1977—; certificate San Francisco State U., 1973, Central Wash. State Coll., 1969, Am. Montessori Tchr. Tng. Inst., 1966, U. Kans., 1964, Chgo. Tchrs. Coll., 1960; m. Wendell M. Sams, Aug. 12, 1973; 1 son, Derek John. Spl. services tchr. Chgo. Pub. Schs., 1958-61; social and personal adjustment tchr. Vocat. Rehab. Div., Topeka, Kans., 1962-64; tchr. kindergarten, primary grades Chgo. Pub. Schs., 1964-66; master tchr., tchr.-trainer Park Ridge (Ill.) Montessori Sch., 1966-67, Spring Valley Montessori Sch., Federal Way, Wash., 1967-68; tchr. Annie Wright Sem., Tacoma, Wash., 1968-69; instr. U. Puget Sound, Tacoma, 1968-70; early childhood specialist Franklin Pierce Pub. Sch. Dist., Tacoma, 1969-70; project mgr. Project Learn, Behavioral Research Labs., Menlo Park, Calif., 1970-71; dir. Sullivan Presch. and Sullivan Sch. Redwood City, Calif., 1971, exec. dir. curriculum and personnel Sullivan Presch. and Sullivan Elem. Sch., Irving, Calif., 1971-73; coordinator reading and English as second lang. Dept. Def., Mil. Dependents Schs., Japan, 1973-74; program dir. Western Region, Mini-Skools Ltd., Irving, Calif., 1974-75; supr. personnel San Francisco Unified Sch. Dist., 1975-78, program mgr. Children's Centers Dept., 1978-79; dir. Children's Centers Dept., Oakland (Calif.) Unified Sch. Dist., 1979-80, adminstr. child devel. Piedmont Children's Center, 1981-86; prin. Piedmont Ave. Sch. and Child Devel. Ctr., 1986-89, Piedmont Ave. Sch., 1989—; grad. instr. early childhood edn. U. San Francisco; cons. in field; lectr. in field. Recipient Cert. of Appreciation, San Francisco Unified Sch. Dist. Bd. Edn., 1978; Tribute, Oakland Unified Sch. Dist. Bd. Edn., 1980; Appreciation award Oakland Dept. Children's Centers, 1980. Mem. Calif. Child Devel. Adminstrs. Assn. (state exec. bd. 1979-81, Cert. of Excellence 1980, Keeper of Dream award 1981), United Adminstrs. of Oakland Schs., Nat. Assn. for Edn. of Young Children, Council for Exceptional Children, Am. Assn. Sch. Personnel Adminstrs., Am. Soc. for Personnel Adminstrs. Bay Area Sch. Personnel Assn., Am. Montessori Soc., Nat. Black Child Devel. Inst., Assn. Montessori Internationale, Assn. Calif. Sch. Adminstrs., Phi Delta Kappa. Roman Catholic. Contbr. articles in field to profl. jours. Office: 4314 Piedmont Ave Oakland CA 94611

SAMUEL, CHARLENE, medical technologist, chemist; b. Now Roads, La., Feb. 2, 1956; d. Leonard Louis and Rose (Nelson) S. BS in Med. Tech., So. U., 1978. Clin. intern Charity Hosp. Sch. of Med. Tech., New Orleans, 1978, phelebotomist, 1978; med. technologist Baton Rouge Gen. Med. Ctr., Baton Rouge, 1979-83, Gen. Health Svcs., Baton Rouge, 1983-84; evening shift supr. Health Mgmt. Svcs., Baton Rouge, 1984-85; evening shift supr. La. Reference Labs., Baton Rouge, 1985-88, chemistry supr., 1988—. Big buddy Big Buddy Program, Baton Rouge, 1988—. Mem. Am. Soc. Clin. Pathologists (cert.), TCB Social Club (pres. Port Allen, La. chpt.). Democrat. Baptist. Home: 12151 Catalina Baton Rouge LA 70814

SAMUELS, BRENDA ELLIAN, federal official; b. Phila., July 21, 1948; d. Anthony J. and Ella C. (Miller) Snively, Jr.; divorced; children: Christina K., Malcolm P. Student, Howard U., 1966-69. Contract officer Nat. Tools Ctr. GSA, Washington, 1973-87; procurement analyst GSA, 1987—. Artist: dough sculpture Sun Face 1st runner up Fed. Workplace Art Competition, 1981; group exhibition Fed. Bldg. Washington, 4 water colors untitled, 1983. Mem. Neighborhood Adv. Com. Ward 4, Washington, 1979-80. Mem. Nat. Inst. Govtl. Purchasing (cert. profl. pub. buyer), Nat. Assn. Black Procurement Profls. (charter mem.). Episcopalian. Home: 8830 Piney Branch Rd #1012 Silver Spring MD 20903

SAMUELS, CYNTHIA KALISH, journalist, television news producer; b. Pitts., May 21, 1946; d. Emerson and Jeanne (Kalish) S.; m. Richard Norman Atkins, Sept. 12, 1971; children: Joshua Whitney Samuels Atkins, Daniel Jonathan Samuels Atkins. BA, Smith Coll., 1968. Press aide McCarthy for Pres. Campaign, Washington, 1968; assoc. producer Newsroom program Sta. KQED, San Francisco, 1972-73; with CBS News, 1973-80, researcher, Washington, 1969-71, documentary researcher, N.Y.C., 1973-74, asst. fgn. editor, 1974-76, asst. N.Y. bur. chief, 1976-80; writer, field producer Today program NBC News, N.Y.C., 1980-84, polit. producer Today program, 1984-89; planning producer, 1988-89; sr. producer Main Street program NBC News, N.Y.C., 1987; exec. producer Channel One program, 1989—; v.p. Whittle Communications, N.Y.C., 1989—. Author: It's A Free Country!: A Young Person's Guide to Politics and Elections, 1988; contbr. book revs. to N.Y. Times Book Rev., Washington Post Book World. Recipient local Emmy award No. Calif. Acad. TV Arts & Scis., 1974, Columbia DuPont citation, 1975. Office: Channel One 655 3d Ave #1500 New York NY 10017

SAMUELS, GLORIA, lawyer; b. N.Y.C., June 26, 1926; d. Joseph and Lena (Rinsler) Siegel; m. Robert Samuels, June 11, 1948; children: Deborah Samuels Freeman, Joel, Leslie Samuels Entsminger. BS, Bklyn. Coll., 1946; JD, Ind. U., 1977. Bar: Ind., Tenn. Lawyer Legal Svcs. Ind., Indpls., 1977-78, Legal Svcs. Upper East Tenn., Johnson City, 1979—; lawyer ABA grant to establish child advocacy orgn. in Washington County, Tenn., 1981-83; active class actions resulting in improved child support enforcement in Tenn., 1985-88, others. Mem. Female Attys. of the Mountain Empire. Home: 1908 Pleasant View Johnson City TN 37604 Office: Legal Svcs Upper East Tenn 311 W Walnut Johnson City TN 37604

SAMUELS, JANET LEE, lawyer; b. Pitts., July 18, 1953; d. Emerson and Jeanne (Kalish) S.; m. David Arthur Kalow, June 18, 1978; children—Margaret Emily Samuels-Kalow, Jacob Richard Samuels-Kalow. B.A. with honors, Beloit Coll., 1974; J.D., NYU, 1977. Bar: N.Y. 1978, D.C. 1980. Staff atty. SCM Corp., N.Y.C., 1977-80, corp. atty., 1980-83, sr. corp. atty., 1983-85, assoc. gen. counsel Allied Paper div., 1983-86, Holtzmann, Wise & Shepard, 1986—. Mem. ABA, Assn. Bar City N.Y., N.Y. State Bar Assn., Mortar Board, Phi Beta Kappa. Office: Holtzmann Wise & Shepard 745 Fifth Ave New York NY 10151

SAMUELS, KATHLEEN, property manager; b. Pitts., June 9, 1952; d. Frank and Leodakya Marie (Godzinski) Shonsky; widowed; children: Jonathan David, Michael Joseph. BA in English, Carnegie-Mellon U., Pitts.,

1974. Lic. in real estate, Pa. Editor Green Tab, Pitts., 1974-75; ptnr., mgr. Rental Info. Svcs., Inc., Pitts., 1977-79; sales/leasing mgr. ShaefferRealty Co., Pitts., 1979-84; leasing dir. Perr Mgmt. Co., Pitts., 1984-87; leasing mgr. Kossman Devel. Co., Pitts., 1987-89; property mgr. Union Real Estate Co., Pitts., 1989—. Mem. Nat. Assn. Female Execs., Internat. Council Shopping Ctrs., Greater Pitts. Bd. Realtors. Republican. Christian Ch. Home: 502 Arlington Dr Pittsburgh PA 15239 Office: Union Real Estate Co 300 Lawyers Bldg 428 Forbes Pittsburgh PA 15219

SAMUELS, MICHELE LAUREN, public relations executive; b. Ft. Bragg, N.C., Aug. 23, 1962; d. Irwin Mark Samuels and Rochelle S. (Weiss) Friedman; m. James Elliott Campbell, Aug. 13, 1989. BA in Communications, Oberlin Coll., 1984. Pvt. practice MSPR, Pitts., 1984-86, cons. pub. rels., 1988-89; acct. exec. Makovsky and Co., N.Y.C., 1986-88; asst. stage mgr. Alvin Ailey Repertory Ensemble, N.Y.C., 1989; dir. pub. rels. and audience devel. MidAm. Prodns., N.Y.C., 1989-90; cons. pub. rels. and mktg. N.Y.C., 1990—; cons. Shelly Friedman for Judge Com., Pitts., 1985, 89, Performing Arts Resources, N.Y.C., 1989-90, NuVision, 1990. Dir. publicity com., mem. steering com. Action Com. for Reasonable Real Estate Taxes, N.Y.C., 1990; participant N.Y. State Nat. Abortion Rights Action League, 1988—; bd. dirs. Catcendix Corp. Mem. NAFE. Office: 410 Central Park W Ste 7D New York NY 10025

SAMUELS, MYRA LEE, statistician, educator; b. Chgo., Mar. 23, 1940; d. Willis Kingsley and Shirley Pearl (Gorenstein) Jordan; m. Stephen Mitchell Samuels, Mar. 17, 1967; children: Jordan, Ellen. BS, Swarthmore Coll., 1961; PhD, U. Calif., Berkeley, 1969. Mathematician U.S. Naval Rsch. Lab., Washington, 1961-63; instr. dept. of stats. Purdue U., West Lafayette, Ind., 1968-69, vis. asst. prof. dept. of stats., 1970-76, lectr. dept. of stats., 1976-87, instr., asst. supr. stats. cons., dept. of stats., 1987—; vis. asst. prof. dept. of stats., Stanford (Calif.) U., 1978-79; stats. cons. U.S. FDA, Washington, 1980-87, Cancer Ctr., Purdue U., 1978, dept. of clin. pharmacology, Stanford U., 1978-79. Author: Statistics for the Life Sciences, 1989; contbr. articles to profl. jours. Rsch. grantee Cancer Ctr., Purdue U., 1979-80; nat. scholar Gen. Motors, 1957-61. Mem. Am. Stat. Assn., Biometric Soc., Soc. for Clin. Trials, Assn. for Women in Sci. Office: Dept Statistics/Purdue Univ West Lafayette IN 47907

SAMUELS, VALERIE BRYANT, nursing administrator; b. N.Y.C., Aug. 20, 1952; d. David and Lucy B. (Hairstone) Bryant; m. Emmanuel M. Samuels, July 1, 1971 (div. June 1986); children: Christopher D., Diantha L. Student, Sch. Performing Arts, 1970; AA, Eugenio Marie de Hostos Coll., 1972; BS, Herbert Lehmann Coll., 1974; postgrad., St. Joseph Coll., 1985. RN. RN Fordham Hosp., N.Y.C., 1972-76; charge RN Albert Einstein Coll. Medicine, N.Y.C., 1976-77, coordinator, 1977-80; coordinator Good Samaritan Hosp., N.Y.C., 1980-83; head nurse Booth Meml. Hosp., N.Y.C., 1983-86, nursing dir. renal services, 1986—, acting dir., 1987—; nurse cons. Harbor Nephrology, Fla., 1979-83, Good Samaritan Hosp., Bayshore, N.Y., 1983-85, South Shore Renal Hosp., Hempstead, N.Y., 1984-86; lectr. in field. Mem. NAACP, Nat. Assn. Patients on Hemodialysis and Transplantation (exec. bd.), Am. Assn. Nephrology Nurses, Texarkana Nat. Dialysis Assn. (exec. bd. patient and staffing issues), Nat. Assn. Female Execs. Republican. Lodge: Lions Internat. (Roosevelt, N.Y.), (sec. 1985-87, pres. 1987—, Lioness of yr. 1986, first female pres. 1987—). Home: 11 Longbeach Ave Roosevelt NY 11575 Office: Booth Meml Hosp 56-45 Main St Flushing NY 11355

SAMUELSON, MARIE GAYLE, publishing professional; b. Mpls., Mar. 25, 1956; d. Harry Merlin and Thelma Marie (Chandler) S. BS, U. Oreg., 1977. Editor Fricke-Parke Press, Fremont, Calif., 1977-80; nat. promotions dir. Arrowhead, Inc., San Rafael, Calif., 1980-83; asst. pub. Bay Area Bus. Mag., Emeryville, Calif., 1983-85; assoc. pub. Calif. Exec., San Francisco, 1985-86; dir. spl. publs. San Francisco Bus. Times, 1986-89; dir. publs. Practical Prodns., Inc., San Francisco, 1989—; sales cons. Toror Art Cons., San Francisco, 1990—; cons. Silicon Valley Engr. Mag., Menlo Park, Calif., 1989-90. Publs. dir. Mng. Ptnr., 1988, Inside Story I & II, 1989, Bus. Visitors Guide, 1989; pub. Used Auto Book, 1990. Recipient cert. of honor for literacy activities, City of Alameda, Calif., 1989, 90. Mem. Women in Communications Inc., Soc. Mktg. & Sales Adminstrs., Commonwealth Club, Ad Club, Sales Mgmt. Soc. Am. Unitarian. Office: Practical Prodns Ste 415 400 Oyster Point Blvd South San Francisco CA 94080

SAMZ, JANE DEDE, editor, writer; b. Closter, N.J., Jan. 2; d. Benjamin and Ruth (Burstein) S. A.B. in Math., Smith Coll., 1969; postgrad., U. Ky., 1969-70; M.A. in History of Sci., U. Wis.-Madison, 1971. Teaching asst. physics dept. U. Ky., Lexington, 1969-70; editorial asst. Sci. World mag., Scholastic Mags., Inc., N.Y.C., 1972-73, asst. editor, 1973-76, assoc. editor, 1976-79, editor, 1979-87, sr. editor, sci. cons., 1987-88; lectr. communications dept. Stanford U., Calif., 1979; freelance writer Grolier Ency. Yearbook, 1977-79, Funk & Wagnalls Ency. Yearbook, 1981-83, Prentice-Hall, Inc., 1986, Contemporary Ednl. Svcs., Inc., 1989, Parachute Press, 1989—; also freelance cons. Author: Drugs & Diet, 1988, Vision, 1990; creator, author: Matter--Science World Visuals 9, 1975; co-author: Voyage to Jupiter, 1980; freelance writer, editor Curriculum Concepts, Inc., N.Y.C., 1987; contbr. articles to Sci. World, World Book Science Year, 1988, World Book Health and Medical Annual, 1988, Futures, 1988, Creative Classroom, 1988-90, World Book Science Year Annual, 1988, Little People The Big Book About Dinosaurs, 1989. Camille and Henry Dreyfus Found. sci. writer's fellow Stanford U., 1978-79. Mem. AAAS, Am. Mus. Natural History, N.Y. Acad. Scis., Internat. Platform Assn. Home: 55-612 River Dr S Jersey City NJ 07310

SANBORN, ANNA LUCILLE, pension and insurance consultant; b. Bklyn., Mar. 29, 1924; d. Peter Francis and Matilda M. (Stumpp) Galligen; B.A., Bklyn. Coll., 1945; 1 son, Dean Sanborn. Head dept. benefit and estate planning Union Central Life Ins. Co., N.Y.C., 1949-51; adminstr. employee benefits Seaboard Oil Co., N.Y.C., 1952-56; with Frank J. Walters Assocs., Inc., N.Y.C., 1957—, pres., 1970—. Bd. dirs. Archdiocesan Service Corp. Mem. Am. Acad. Actuaries, Republican. Roman Catholic. Home: 58-11 Seabury St Elmhurst NY 11373 Office: Frank J Walters Assocs 509 Madison Ave New York NY 10022

SANBORN, DOREEN KAY, systems engineer manager; b. Sellersville, Pa., Feb. 5, 1948; d. Harold Wilson and Ruth Violet (Moore) Roberts; m. Richard Ronald Wolownik (div. Apr. 1976); m. Stephen Brock Sanborn, Jan. 4, 1986. Student, Am. Univ., 1979. Service rep. Bell Telephone Co. of Pa., Lansdale, 1966-68; statistician ITT Nesbitt, Phila., 1969; research asst. Ctr. for Naval Analyses, Arlington, Va., 1968, 70-74, Mitre Corp., McLean, Va., 1974-77; computer analyst Nat. Coal. Assn., Washington, 1977-79; tech. adv., systems engr. Motorola Computer Systems, Vienna, Va., 1979-87; tech. engr. mgr. Sun Microsystems, Vienna, 1987—. Mem. Nat. Assn. Female Execs. Home: 8732 Beechwood Dr Fairfax VA 22031 Office: Sun Microsystems 8219 Leesburg Pike Suite 700 Vienna VA 22180

SANBORN, DOROTHY CHAPPELL, librarian; b. Nashville, Apr. 26, 1920; d. William S. and Sammie Maude (Drake) Chappell. BA, U. Tex., 1941; MA, George Peabody Coll., 1947; MPA, Golden Gate U., 1982; m. Richard Donald Sanborn, Dec. 1, 1943; children: Richard Donald, William Chappell. Asst. cataloger El Paso (Tex.) Pub. Libr., 1947-52, Libr. of Hawaii, Honolulu, 1953; cataloger Redwood (Calif.) City Pub. Libr., 1954-55, 57-59, Stanford Rsch. Inst., Menlo Park, Calif., 1955-57; libr. Auburn (Calif.) Pub. Libr., 1959-62; cataloger Sierra Coll., Rocklin, Calif., 1962-64; reference libr. Sacramento City Libr., 1964-66; county libr. Placer County (Calif.), Auburn, 1966-89, ret., 1989; chmn. Mountain Valley Libr.System, 1970-71, 75-76, 1984-85; cons. county libr. Alpine County Libr., Markleeville, Calif., 1973-80. With WAVES, 1944-46. Mem. AAUW (pres. chpt. 1982-84), ALA, Calif. Libr. Assn., Soroptimists. Democrat. Mem. United Ch. Christ. Home: 125 Midway St Auburn CA 95603

SANBORN, SHEREE-MARIA, newspaper official; b. Chgo., Jan. 18, 1958; d. Lawrence J. and Ingrid Lief; m. Theodore John Sanborn, June 11, 1988. BA, Am. U., 1981, MA, 1988. Admissions asst. Am. U., Washington, 1980-81, admissions counselor, 1981-84, asst. dir. recruitment, 1984-87; personnel assoc. Conde Nast Publs., N.Y.C., 1987-88, Nanny Placement Svcs., Inc., Washington, 1988-89; personnel recuriter Washington Post, 1989—. Newspaper columnist, 1975-76; contbr. articles to newspapers. Tutor Literacy Coun. Washington, 1988—. Recipient staff award for outstanding svc. Am. U., 1985; Am. U. scholar, 1985, 87. Mem. Victorian Soc. Am., AAUW, Jr. League Washington. Republican. Presbyterian. Home: 1946 Kennedy Dr McLean VA 22102

SANCETTA, CONSTANCE ANTONINA, oceanographer; b. Richmond, Va., Apr. 17, 1949; d. Anthony Louis and Joyce Louise (Kellogg) S. BA, Brown U., 1971, MSc, 1973; PhD, Oreg. State U., 1976. Rsch. assoc. Stanford (Calif.) U., 1977-78; assoc. rsch. scientist Columbia U., N.Y.C., 1979-84, rsch. scientist, 1985-87, sr. rsch. scientist, 1988—; adv. com. ocean scis. NSF, Washington, 1981-86, 89—. Editorial bd. Marine Micropaleontology, 1983—; contbr. articles to profl. jours. Fellow Geol. Soc. Am., AAAS; councilor The Oceanograpy Soc., Am. Quaternary Soc.; mem. Am. Geophys. Union (sec. ocean sci. sect. 1988-90). Office: Lamont Doherty Geol Observ Palisades NY 10964

SANCHEZ, BEATRICE RIVAS, artist, art school administrator; b. San Antonio, June 17, 1941. MFA, U. Mass., 1975. Artist in residence Trinity U., San Antonio, 1976; coord. fine arts program Fla. Sch. Art, Palatka, 1976-78; acad. dean, assoc. dean Md. Coll. Art & Design, 1978-82; dean Cranbrook Acad. Art, from 1982; pres. Kansas City Art Inst., 1987—. Exhibited at Women's Nat. Exhbn., Washington, 1980. Trustee Native Am. and Alaskan Indian Culture Inst., Santa Fe; mem. citizen's stamp adv. com. U.S. Postal Svc. Mem. Nat. Assn. Schs. of Art and Design (com. on accreditation), Alliance Ind. Colls. of Art (bd. dirs.). Office: Kansas City Art Inst 4415 Warwick Blvd Kansas City MO 64111*

SANCHEZ, CAROL ASHTON-EVANS, artist; b. Ft. Oglethorpe, Ga., Aug. 2, 1943; d. Joseph Vance and Alberta Hannah (Ashton) Evans; m. Henry Wayne Sanchez, May 19, 1962; children: Leila Carol, Warren Reed. Student, Wesleyan Coll., Macon, Ga., 1961-62; pvt. study in fine and comml. art with Henrietta Joseph, John Korver, Iris Curry, BJ. McKee, Baton Rouge, 1954—. Founder Art Guild of Gonzales, La., 1971, v.p. 1971-72, pres. 1974. One-man shows exhibited at Gonzales Town Hall, 1970, Gonzales Pub. Library, 1971; exhibited in group shows at Jambalaya Festival of Art, Gonzales, 1968-74 (2d place oils, 1968, 1st and 2d place watercolors, 69, 1st place watercolors, 70, 2d place drawing, hon. mention watercolors, 71, 3d place profl. watercolors, 72, hon. mention watercolors, 73, hon. mention profl. watercolors, 74), La. Art and Artist's Guild Fall Show, Baton Rouge, 1968 (hon. mention), La. Art and Artist's Guild Gallery, 1971, La. Art and Artist's Guild Great River Road Show, 1972 (1st place), Art Guild of Gonzales' Fall Arts and Crafts Show, 1972 (2d place watercolors). Tchr. Faithful United Meth. Ch., St. Amant, La., 1972-86, treas., 1974-80, ch. sch. supt., 1983-85, bd. trustees, 1988—, ch. historian, 1989-90, tchr, bible study, 1990; pres. UMW, 1990. Democrat. Home: 13030 Li'l Tony Rd Saint Amant LA 70774

SANCHEZ, D. JEAN, lawyer; b. Lima, Ohio, Apr. 17, 1948; d. Lester Eugene and Betty Lou (Haley) McBeth; m. Jesse Antonio, May 22, 1977; children: Darcy Hempker, Nino. Postgrad., Ohio State U., Lima, Ohio, 1981; BS, Ohio No. U., Ada, 1983, JD, 1986. Staff atty. Lima Legal Aid, Lima, Ohio, 1987-88; pvt. practice DaPorer Assocs., Lima, Ohio, 1988—. Office: 130 W North St Lima OH 45802 also: 139 Oak Ottawa OH 45875

SANCHEZ, JANICE PATTERSON, psychotherapist, educator; b. Indpls., Nov. 5, 1948; d. Jack Downey and Elizabeth (Evard) Patterson; m. Adel Sanchez, Sept. 20, 1972; children: Christina, Alison. BS in Edn., Ind. U., 1970; MSW, Cath. U. Am., 1983. Lic. clin. social worker, Va. Tchr. Fairfax County Pub. Schs., McLean, Va., 1970-76; psychotherapist D.C. Inst. Mental Hygiene, Washington, 1984-89; pvt. practice Arlington, Va., 1989—; mem. advanced psychotherapy tng. program Washington Sch. Psychiatry, 1988—. Vol. tchr. jr. gt. books Taylor Elem. Sch., Arlington, Va., 1987-89. Mem. Nat. Assn. Social Workers, Greater Washington Soc. for Clin. Social Work, Jr. League No. Va. Office: 3801 N Fairfax Dr Arlington VA 22203

SANCHEZ, MARCIA ODALYS, communications company executive; b. Havana, Cuba, Apr. 29, 1962; came to U.S., 1968; d. Antonio Marino Sanchez and Gladys Dania (Thope) Khodor. AA in Computer Sci., Miami Dade Community Coll., 1983; BS in Computer Sci., Fla. Internat. U., 1986. Processing supr. Southeast Bank, Miami, Fla., 1978-83; collection supr. Pan Am. Bank, Miami, 1983-84; adminstrv. asst. NCNB Nat. Bank, Miami, 1984-86; processing mgr. Tel Plus Communications, Boca Raton, Fla., 1986—. Author manual in field. Mem. NAFE.

SANCHEZ, MARISABEL, public affairs director; b. Guayama, P.R., Mar. 15, 1964; d. Miguel Sanchez and Raquel Roque Sullivan. Student, U. P.R., 1980—; BA, U. Tex., 1986. Radio producer KTEP/NPR Radio, El Paso, Tex., 1980, KXCR/NPR Radio, El Paso, 1981; fellowship Congl. Hispanic Caucus, Washington, 1986; TV producer Univision TV Network, Washington, 1987, ZGS TV Prodns., Washington, 1987; acct. exec. Uniworld Group, Inc., N.Y.C., 1988; dir. pub. affairs, dept. mgr. Thomason Hosp., El Paso, 1989—. Mem. Hispanic Leadership Program, Washington, 1986—. Recipient Leadership Mark award Pub. Schs. Assn., 1980, Excellence award P.R. Higher Edn. Bd., 1980, Mark of Excellence award Soc. Profl. Journalist, 1983. Mem. Nat. Assn. Hispanic Journalist, Soc. Profl. Journalists, Hispanic Acad. Media Arts and Scis. Baptist. Office: 4815 Alameda Ave El Paso TX 79905

SANCHEZ, VICTORIA WAGNER, science educator; b. Milw., Apr. 11, 1934; d. Arthur William and Lorraine Marguerite (Kocovsky) Wagner; m. Rozier Edmond Sanchez, June 23, 1956; children: Mary Elizabeth, Carol Anne, Robert Edmond, Catherine Marie, Linda Therese. BS cum laude, Mt. Mary Coll., 1955; MS, Marquette U., 1957; postgrad., U. N.Mex., 1979-86. Cert. secondary tchr., N.Mex. Chemist Nat. Bur. Standards, Washington, 1958-60; tchr., chmn. sci. dept. Albuquerque Pub. Schs., 1979—; chmn. pub. info. area convention Nat. Sci. Tchrs. Assn., 1984, mem. sci. review com. Albuquerque Pub. Schs., 1985-86. Bd. dirs. Encino House, Albuquerque, 1976—, treas., 1977-79; leader Albuquerque troop Girl Scouts U.S., 1966-77. Named Outstanding Sci. Tchr. N.W. Regional Sci. Fair, Albuquerque, 1983, 1988; recipient St. George's award N.Mex. Cath. Scouting com., Albuquerque, 1978, Focus on Excellence award Assn. Supervision and Curriculum Devel., Albuquerque, 1985,89, Presdl. Awards for Excellence in Sci. and Math. Mem. AAUW (Albuquerque br. officer 1976-77, N.Mex. div. officer 1977-78), Nat. Sci. Tchrs. Assn., N.Mex. Sci. Tchrs. Assn. (treas. 1988-90), Albuquerque Sci. Tchrs. Assn. (treas. 1984-85, v.p. and pres.-elect, 1986-87, pres. 1987-88), N.Mex. Acad. Sci., Albuquerque Rose Soc. (sec. 1962-63). Democrat. Roman Catholic. Home: 7612 Palo Duro NE Albuquerque NM 87110 Office: Van Buren Sch 700 Louisiana SE Albuquerque NM 87108

SANCHIDRIAN, MARIA DEL CARMEN, architect, design consultant; b. Las Villas, Cuba, May 8, 1954; came to U.S., 1957; d. Miguel Angel and Fe Maria (Rosario) S. Student, Englewood Cliffs Coll., 1972-74, St. Peter's Coll., Jersey City, 1974-76; BS in Archtl. Tech., N.Y. Inst. Tech., 1986. Archtl. intern Kessler & Kalfas Assocs., Edgewater, N.J., 1983, Inc. Cons. Ltd., N.Y.C., 1984, CBS, N.Y.C., 1985; asst. architect N.Y.C. Transit Authority, Bklyn., 1986—. Scholar, 1972. Mem. Am. Mgmt. Assn., NAFE.

SANCHO, GLORIA PRECIOUS MANNEH, accountant; b. Monrovia, Liberia, Feb. 12, 1960; d. Theodore Josiah and Annie Roselyn (Burgess) S.; m. J. Napoleon Cassell, Aug. 8, 1981 (div. Jan. 1984); children: Ayofemi Crystal Yvette. BA, Detroit Inst. Tech., 1981; BSc, Dyke Coll., 1984. Bookkeeper Standard Oil Co. of Ohio, Cleve., 1981-84; acct. SDAC Home Care Services, Bklyn., 1984-86; supr., bookkeeper Home Attendant Vendor Agy., Bklyn., 1986-89; auditor N.Y. State Dept. Ins., N.Y.C., 1989—. Mem. Nat. Assn. MBA Execs., Nat. Assn. Female Execs. Episcopalian. Lodge: Order Eastern Star. Home: PO Box 4302 Danbury CT 06818-4302 Office: Gloria P Sancho & Co PO Box 4302 Danbury CT 06813-4302

SANCHO, ROSEMARIE, educational administrator; b. Weslaco, Tex., Jan. 14, 1949; d. Frank and Carmen (Gonzalez) S. AA, Reedley Jr. Coll., 1970; BA, Calif. State U., Fresno, 1972; MA in Edn. Adminstrn., Supervision with distinction, Calif. State U., 1983. Cert. tchr., adminstr., Calif. Elem. bilingual tchr. Sanger (Calif.) Unified Sch. Dist., 1972-75, tchr. Spanish, phys. edn. ESL, folk dance, 1975-78, dist. coordinator migrant edn., 1978-85; prin. Lincoln Sch., 1985—; coordinator adult sch. for family edn., 1982-85. Named Educator of Yr., Comite Civico Sanger, 1984. Mem. Assn. for Supervision and Curriculum Devel., Nat. Assn. for Edn. Young Children, Calif. Assn. for Edn. Young Children, Assn. Calif. Sch. Adminstrs., Calif. Assn. for Bilingual Edn. Democrat. Roman Catholic. Home: 2133 N Garden St Fresno CA 93703 Office: Lincoln Sch 1700 14th St Sanger CA 93657

SANDAGE, ELIZABETH ANTHEA, market research executive; b. Larned, Kans., Oct. 13, 1930; d. Curtis Carl and Beulah Pauline (Knupp) Smith; student Okla. State U., 1963-65; BS, U. Colo., 1967; MA, 1970; PhD in Communications U. Ill., 1983; m. Charles Harold Sandage, July 18, 1971; children by previous marriage: Diana Louise Danner White, David Alan Danner. Pub. rels. rep., editor Martin News, Martin Marietta Corp., Denver, 1960-63, 65-67; retail advt. salesperson Denver Post, 1967-70; instr. advt. U. Ill., 1970-71, vis. lectr. advt., 1977-84; v.p., corp. sec., dir. Farm Rsch. Inst., Urbana, 1984—. Exec. dir. Sandage Charitible Trust, 1986—. Mem. Kappa Tau Alpha. Republican. Presbyterian. Editor: Occasional Papers in Advertising, 1971; The Sandage Family Cookbook, 1976, 2d edit., 1986; The Inkling, Carle Hosp. Aux. Newsletter, 1975-76. Home: 106 The Meadows Urbana IL 61801

SANDAHL, BONNIE BEARDSLEY, pediatric nurse practitioner; b. Washington, Jan. 17, 1939; d. Erwin Leonard and Carol Myrtle (Collis) B.; m. Glen Emil Sandahl, Aug 17, 1963; children: Cara Lynne, Cory Glen. BSN, U. Wash., 1962, MN, 1974, cert. pediatric nurse practitioner, 1972. Dir. Wash. State Joint Practice Commn., Seattle, 1974-76; instr. pediatric nurse practitioner program U. Wash., Seattle, 1976, course coordinator quality assurance, 1977-78; pediatric nurse practitioner/health coordinator Snohomish County Head Start, Everett, Wash., 1975-77; clin. nurse educator (specialist) Harborview Med. Ctr., Seattle, 1978—, dir. child abuse prevention project, 1986—; speaker legis. focus on children, 1987; clin. assoc. Dept. of Pediatrics, U. Wash. Sch. medicine, 1987, clin. faculty Sch. Nursing. Mem. Task Force on Pharmacotherapeutic Courses, Wash. State Bd. Nursing, 1985-86; Puget Sound Health Systems Agy., 1975—. pres., 1980-82; mem. child devel. project adv. bd. Mukilteo Sch. Dist., 1984-85; mem. parenting adv. com. Edmonds Sch. Dist., 1985—; chmn. hospice-home health task force Snohomish County Hospice Program, Everett, 1984-85, bd. dirs. hospice, 1985-87, adv. com. 1986—; mem. Wash. State Health Coordinating, Council, 1977-82, 86—, chmn. nursing home bed projection methodology task force, 1986-87; mem., interim chair Nat. Council Health Planning and Devel., HHS, 1980-87; mem. adv. com. on uncompensated care Wash. State Legislature, 1983-84; mem. Joint Select Com., Tech. Adv. Com. on Managed Health Care Systems, 1984-85. Pres., Alderwood Manor Community Council, 1983-85; treas. Wash. St. Women's Polit. Caucus, 1983-84; mem. com. to examine changes in Wash. State Criminal Sex Law, 1987; appointee county needs assessment com. Snohomish County Govt. United Way, 1989. Named Nurse of Yr., King County Nurses Assn., 1985; recipient Golden Acorn award Seattle-King County PTA, 1973, Katherine Rickey Vol. Participation award, 1987. Mem. Am. Nurses Assn. (chmn. pediatric nurse practitioner subcom. Com. Examiners Maternal-Child Nursing Practice, 1986—, chair Com. Examiners Maternal-Child Nursing Practice 1988-90), Wash. State Nurses Assn. (hon. leadership award 1981), King County Nurses Assn., Wash. State Soc. Pediatrics, Sigma Theta Tau. Democrat. Methodist. Home: 1814 200th St SW Alderwood Manor WA 98036 Office: Harborview Med Ctr 325 9th Ave MS ZA-53 Seattle WA 98104

SANDBERG, SHARON KAY, retail executive; b. Anoka, Minn., Apr. 29, 1959; d. John Richard and Patricia Lucille (Jones) S.; m. Brahme Roopan Singh, Mar. 20, 1981 (div. Jan. 1984); 1 child, Annita. Cert. in fashion merchandising, Lowthian Fachion Merchandising Sch., Mpls., 1979. Mgr. Motherhood Maternity, Minnetonka, Minn., 1977-78; asst. mgr. Susie's Casuals, Edina, Minn., 1979-80; asst. buyer County Seat, Eden Prairie, Minn., 1980-82; mdse. technician Target Stores, Inc., Mpls., 1980-82, 82-84; asst. market rep. The May Co., N.Y.C., 1984-85; purchasing agt. Metal Masters, Plymouth, Minn., 1985-86; free-lance mktg. rep. Mpls., 1986—. Mem. NAFFE. Home: 19605 34th Ave N Apt 339 Plymouth MN 55441

SANDBORG, SHIRLEE J., health science facility professional; b. Williamson County, Ill., Aug. 4, 1934; d. Charles A.J. and Mabel M. (Koonce) Myers; m. C. Richard Sandborg; children: Jeffrey, Rebecca, Rex, Tara. Student, Knox Coll., U. Kans., Kansas City, Ctrs. Disease Control, Atlanta. Cert. Am. Med. Technologists, Internat. Soc. Clin. Lab. Tech., Nat. Cert. Agy. Clin. Lab. Pers. Med. tech., supr. lab. Galesburg (Ill.) Rsch. Hosp.; med. tech. St. Mary's Med. Ctr., Galesburg; med. tech., supr. Med. Arts Clinic, Galesburg; mgr. lab. svcs. Galesburg Clinic Assocs.; pres. Sandborg Specialities. Mem. Altar and Rosary Soc. Corpus Christi Cath. Ch., St. Mary's Med. Ctr. Aux., Galesburg Community Chorus. Recipient Outstanding Achievement award, Internat. Soc. Presdl. award. Mem. Clin. Lab. Mgrs. Assn. Address: 3315 N Seminary St Galesburg IL 61401

SANDE, BARBARA, interior decorating consultant; b. Twin Falls, Idaho, May 5, 1939; d. Einar and Pearl M. (Olson) Sande; m. Ernest Reinhardt Hohener, Sept. 3, 1961 (div. Sept. 1971); children: Heidi Catherine, Eric Christian; m. Peter H. Forsham, Apr. 1990. BA, U. Idaho, 1961. Asst. mgr., buyer Home Yardage Inc., Oakland, Calif., 1972-76; cons. in antiques and antique valuation, Lafayette, Calif., 1977-78; interior designer Neighborhood Antiques and Interiors, Oakland, Calif., 1978-86; owner, Claremont Antiques and Interiors, Berkeley, Calif., 1987—; cons., participant antique and art fair exhibits, Orinda and Piedmont, Calif., 1977—. Decorator Piedmont Christmas House Tour, 1983, 88, 89, Oakland Mus. Table Setting, 1984, 85, 86, Piedmont Showcase Family Room, 1986, Piedmont Showcase Music Room, 1986, Piedmont Kitchen House Tour, 1985, Santa Rosa Symphony Holiday Walk Benefit, 1986, Piedmont Benefit Guild Showcase Young Persons Room, 1987, Piedmont Showcase Library, 1988, Piedmont Showcase Solarium, 1989, Jr. League Table Setting, Oakland-East Bay, 1989, 90. Bd. dirs. San Leandro Coop. Nursery Sch., 1967; health coord. parent-faculty bd., Miramonte High Sch., Orinda, 1978, Acalanes Sch. Dist., Lafayette, Calif., 1978; bd. dirs. Orinda Community Ctr. Vols., 1979; originator Concerts in the Park, Orinda, 1979. Assoc. Am. Soc. Interior Design, Am. Soc. Appraisers; mem. Am. Decorative Arts Forum, De Young Mus., Nat. Trust Historic Preservation, San Francisco Opera Guild, San Francisco Symphony Guild. Democrat. Avocations: travel; hiking.

SANDEFER, NORMA STEELE, small business owner; b. Williamson, WVa., Mar. 16, 1958; d. Robert Everett and Phyllis Sue (Walls) Steele; m. Donald R. Sandefer, apr. 4, 1980 (div. 1985); 1 child, Sean Michael. Grad. high sch., Port Clinton, Ohio; student, Terra Tech. Coll., Fremont, Ohio, 1986-88. Adminstrv. asst. African Lion Safari, Port Clinton, Ohio, 1976; mgr. Fox Photo, Inc., Vicksburg, Miss., 1977-78; documentation asst. Grand Gulf Nuclear Power Sta., Port Gibson, Miss., 1978-82; night auditor Phil's Inn Motel, Port Clinton, Ohio, 1982-87; pres., owner S & L Enterprises, Inc., Port Clinton, Ohio, 1988--; cons. Port Clinton Ohio 1988--. Author: Poetry, Cornicopia 1977. Mem. PTO, Port Clinton, 1988--, Port Clinton Ohio 1988--; dist. dir. Ohio Jaycees, 1990—. Mem. Northcoast Jaycees (affiliation mem. 1989, pres. 1989), No. Ohio Landlord Assn., Put-In-Bay C. of C. Republican. Lutheran. Home: 615 E 3d St Port Clinton OH 43452 Office: S&L Enterprises Inc PO Box 528168 Port Clinton OH 43452

SANDER, DENISE OLIVIA, medical product sales and marketing specialist; b. Bellville, Tex., July 19, 1960; d. Charles Morris and Corinne Olive (Bakke) S. Assoc., S.W. Tex. State U., 1981, BS in Allied Health Mgmt., 1982. Cardiodiagnostician Katy Community Hosp., Katy, Tex., 1982-84; staff cardiodiagnostician Sharpstown Gen. Hosp., Houston, 1984-85; cardiodiagnostician, noninvasive lab. supr. W. Houston Med. Ctr., Houston, 1985-86; with Pro-Tech Med. Assocs., Houston, 1985-86; clinical applications specialist Hewlett-Packard Co., Houston, 1986-87; field application specialist Acuson, Houston, 1987—. Fellow Am. Registry Diagnostic Med. Sonographers, Am. Soc. Diagnostic Sonographers, Tex. Gulf Coast Ultrasound Soc., Am. Soc. Echocardiography, Bluebonnet Soc. Bellville, Alpha Delta Phi. Republican. Episcopalian. Office: Acuson 600 E John Carpenter Ste 300 Irving TX 75039

SANDER, LINDA DIAN, physiologist, educator; b. Harrisburg, Pa., Sept. 2, 1947; d. Wayne E. and Bonita (Lynn) Monn; m. William J. Sander, June 20, 1970; children: James, Joshua. BS, Ariz. State U., 1969; PhD, U. Okla.,

Oklahoma City, 1973. Asst. prof. La. State U., New Orleans, 1976-82; asst. prof. Meharry Med. Coll., Nashville, 1982-84, assoc. prof., 1984—. Contbr. articles to profl. jours. Ariz. State U. scholar, 1965-69; grantee Schlieder Found., 1980-82, NIH, 1982-85, 86-91; fellow NSF, 1971-73, PHS, 1974-76. Mem. APA. Baptist. Office: Meharry Med Coll Dept Dept Physiology 1005 D B Todd Blvd Nashville TN 37208

SANDERS, ANITA MARIE, computer infosystems engineer; b. Youngstown, Ohio, Jan. 19, 1953; d. Ralph Francis and Marie Thres (Strauch) S. BS, Case Western Reserve U., 1975; MSEE, Northeastern U., 1982. Sr. engr. Raytheon Co., Wayland, Mass., 1975-84, CNR, Inc., Needham, Mass., 1984—. Mem. Assn. for Computing Machinery, Soc. Women Engrs., Armed Forces Communications and Electronics Assn. Office: CNR Inc 220 Reservoir St Needham MA 02194

SANDERS, AUGUSTA SWANN, nurse; b. Alexandria, La., July 22, 1932; d. James and Elizabeth (Thompson) Swann; m. James Robert Sanders, Jan. 12, 1962 (div. 1969). Student, Morgan State U., 1956. Pub. health nurse USPHS, Washington, 1963-64; mental health counselor Los Angeles County Sheriff's Dept., 1972-79; program coordinator Los Angeles County Dept. Mental Health, 1979-88; program dir. L.A. County Dept. Health Svcs., 1989—. Mem. Assemblyman Mike Roo's Commn. on Women's Issues, 1981—, Senator Diane Watson's Commn. on Health Issues, 1979—; chmn. Commn. Sex. Equity Los Angeles Unified Sch. Dist., 1984-90. Mem. Los Angeles County Employees Assn. (v.p. 1971-72), So. Calif. Black Nurses Assn. (founding mem.), NAFE, Internat. Fedn. Bus. and Profl. Women (pres. Los Angeles Sunset dist. 1988-89, dist. officer 1982-89), Chi Eta Phi. Democrat. Methodist. Office: Augustus F Hawkins Mental Health Ctr 1720 E 120th St Los Angeles CA 90805

SANDERS, BARBARA JANE, social services administrator; b. Sioux City, Iowa, June 29, 1936; d. Glenn Berlin and Grace Goldie (Huffman) Sharp; m. Richard L. Sanders, Dec. 17, 1958; children: James, Michael. BA, Nat. U., 1984, MA, 1986; Lic. vocat. nurse, Good Samaritan Hosp. Sch. Nursing, Phoenix, 1955. Cert. alcoholism counselor. Nurse various hosps.; presentence investigation and evaluation mgr., info. specialist Nat. Coun. Alcoholism, San Diego, pres., 1978; pres. social svcs. union Met. Area Adv. Com., Chula Vista, Calif., 1984, v.p. social svcs. union, 1985-86, mgr. drinking driver program, 1986—; mem. Nat. Coun. on Alcohol, 1987; charter mem. San Diego Women's Alcohol Commn., 1976—; speaker on alcohol abuse. Mem. hospitality com. St. Charles Cath. Ch., 1988—; vol. instr. crisis intervention; vol. numerous ch. and community activities 1963—. Recipient 2 Leadership awards. Mem. NAFE, Drinking Driver Program (south area com.), Health Systems Agy. Democrat. Home: 545 Park Way #10 Chula Vista CA 92010-3646 Office: 45 Third Ave Ste 101 Chula Vista CA 92010

SANDERS, BETH MEHNE, psychologist; b. Indpls., July 20, 1960; d. Richard Gerald and Jacquelyn Jeanne (Barding) Mehne; m. Lee Eric Sanders, July 9, 1988. BA, DePauw U., 1982; MS, Ind. U., 1985. Cert. sch. psychologist. Sch. psychologist Grant Wood Area Ednl. Agy., Cedar Rapids, Iowa, 1985-86, Deer Valley Unified Sch. Dist., Phoenix, 1986—. Mem. Nat. Assn. Sch. Psychologists, Ariz. Assn. Sch. Psychologists, Delta Delta Delta, Order Ea. Star.

SANDERS, EVELYN BEATRICE, postmaster, business owner; b. Parkersburg, W.Va., Sept. 20, 1931; d. William Perley and Beatrice Elizabeth (Mahaffey) Huffman; m. Kenneth Everett Sanders, Aug. 7, 1950 (dec. Nov. 1981); children: Stephen Patrick, Michael Alan. Postmaster City of Torch, Ohio, 1971—; owner Sanders Gen. Store, Torch, 1981—. Mem. Nat. Assn. Postmasters, League of Postmasters, Alumni Singers, Unity Singers. Democrat. Methodist. Home and Office: 35 Torch St Torch OH 45781-9998

SANDERS, JACQUELYN SEEVAK, psychologist, educator; b. Boston, Apr. 26, 1931; d. Edward Ezral and Dora (Zoken) Seevak; 1 son, Seth. B.A., Radcliffe Coll., 1952; M.A., U. Chgo., 1964; Ph.D., UCLA, 1972. Counselor, asst. prin. Orthogenic Sch., Chgo., 1952-65; research assoc. UCLA, 1965-68; cons. Osawatomie State Hosp. (Kans.), 1965-68; asst. prof. Ctr. for Early Edn., Los Angeles, 1969-72; assoc. dir. Sonia Shankman Orthogenic Sch., U. Chgo., 1972-73, dir., 1973—; curriculum cons. day care ctrs. Los Angeles Dept. Social Welfare, 1970-72; instr. Calif. State Coll., Los Angeles, 1972; lectr. dept. edn. U. Chgo., 1972-80, sr. lectr., 1980—; instr. tchr. edn. program Inst. Psychoanalysis, Chgo., 1979-82. Author: Greenhouse for the Mind, 1989; editor: (with Barry L. Childress) Psychoanalytic Approaches to the Very Troubled Child: Therapeutic Practice Innovations in Residential & Educational Settings, 1989; contbr. articles to profl. jours. UCLA Univ. fellow, 1966-68; Radcliffe Coll. Scholar, 1948-52. Mem. Am. Assn. Children's Residential Ctrs. (program chair 1977-79, treas. 1979-81, 87—, pres. elect 1989), Am. Ednl. Research Assn., Am. Orthopsychiat. Soc., Am. Psychol. Assn., Nat. Soc. Study Edn., Am. Assn. Psychiat. Services for Children (sec.). Jewish. Clubs: Quadrangle, Raquet (Hyde Park, Ill.); Radcliffe of Chgo. (sec/treas. 1986-87, pres. 1987-89); Harvard of Chgo. (bd. dirs. 1986—). Home: 5842 S Stony Island Ave Apt 2G Chicago IL 60637 Office: Sonia Shankman Orthogenic Sch of U Chgo 1365 E 60th St Chicago IL 60637

SANDERS, JEAN MARIE, creativity consultant, pianist; b. Beloit, Kans., May 12, 1939; d. Donald Alfred and Martha Louise (Elfrink) S. MusB, U. Nebr., 1961, MusM, 1962. Owner Profl. Typing and Word Processing, Lincoln, Nebr., 1959-88; pvt. practice profl. pianist Lincoln, 1959—88, pvt. practice tchr. piano, 1961-85; arts critic Lincoln Star, 1980-84; pvt. practice cons., 1987—. Contbr. articles to profl. jours. Mem. Lancaster County Cen. Dem. Com., Lincoln, 1988—, Lincoln Arts Coun., 1980—; del. State Dem. Party Convs., 1984, 86, 88; pres. Nebr. Assn. Community Theatres, 1976-78, Lincoln Community Playhouse Guild, 1985-87, Nebr. Chamber Orch. Guild, Lincoln, 1986—, Lincoln Children's Zoo Aux., 1976-78. Recipient Vol. award Lincoln Community Playhouse, 1973, 84. Mem. Nat. Speakers Assn., Internat. Platform Assn., Internat. Tng. in Communication (pres. Peaks and Plains region 1988-89, Accreditation 1984, div. II v.p. 1989-90), C. of C., Quill (pres. Lincoln chpt. 1980-81), Lincoln Volksport, Nebr. Wander-Freunde. Office: Creative Cons 2828 Arlington Ave Lincoln NE 68502

SANDERS, JOANNE, small business owner; b. Trenton, N.J., Mar. 9, 1949; d. Sidney Sanders and Frieda Anna (Gramas) Crowe; m. Raymond Edward Sliva, Nov. 20, 1973. Grad. high sch., Metuchen, N.J., 1967. Recruiter Jean Arnone Assocs., Menlo Park, N.J., 1985-88; mng. dir. Joanne Sanders, Inc., Woodbridge, N.J., 1988—. Mem. NAFE, Nat. Assn. Pers. Cons., Mid Atlantic Assn. Pers. Cons., Nat. Assn. Profl. Saleswomen, Nat. Assn. Bank Women, Nat. Banking Network, N.J. Assn. Women Bus. Owners. Republican. Greek Orthodox. Office: PO Box 1290 Woodbridge NJ 07095-1290

SANDERS, JOYCE E., sales executive; b. Balt., Jan. 10, 1943; d. Albert Clinton and Catherine (Thomas) Greene; m. James Clifford Sanders, Nov. 5, 1978; children: Elizabeth, Staccato, Tyrock, Aaron, Eddie. Cert. notary pub. Clk., typist Suburban Trust Co., Balt.; sec. work incentive program Office of Mayor, Balt.; office supr. Dept. Pub. Safety and Corrections State of Md.; sales dir. Mary Kay Cosmetics, Dallas. Bd. dirs. entertainment USO, 1973-75. Mem. NAFE, Religious Conf. Mgmt. Assn., Nat. Quartette Assn. Interdenominational of Am. (sec. 1969—). Home: 3006 Glen Ave Baltimore MD 21215

SANDERS, LINDA, banker; b. Council Bluffs, Iowa, Jan. 25, 1950; d. Nolan Glen and Mary Lucille (Dunken) J.; m. Gary E. Sanders, Feb. 14, 1970. Grad., U. Wis., Am. Inst. Banking; student, U. Colo., U. Denver. Various positions First Nat. Bank Bear Valley (name changed to United Bank Bea, Colo., 1969-79; v.p. adminstrn. First Nat. Bancorp., 1979-83; pres., chief exec. officer Equitable Bank of Littleton, 1983 --; founder The Fin. Consortium; pres., chief exec. officer Young Ams. Bank, Denver, 1987 -- , also vice-chmn. bd. dirs.; chmn. bd., pres. Young Ams. Edn. Assn.; mem. faculty adv. com. Am. Inst. Banking. Contbr. articles to Time and Newsweek. Bd dirs. Cherry Creek Commerce Assn., Denver, 1987--, Cherry Creek Arts Festival, Denver, 1989--; pres. elect Nat. Camp Fire, bd dirs. PSP; chmn. adv. bd. Denver Area Campfire. Named hon. life mem. Denver Area CampFire, numerous other awards Camp Fire Inc. Mem. Am. Banker's Assn. (trustee Fund Teaching Econs.), Found. Teaching Econs. (trustee), Colo. Bankers Assn. (community rels. com., media response team), Denver Rotary Club. Republican. Office: Young Americans Bank 250 Steele St Denver CO 80206

SANDERS, MADELINE SANDY, city official; b. Chgo., Dec. 24, 1943; d. Elijah and Lucille Pauline (Hilliard) S.; 1 child, Cyril Alexander. BA, Northwestern U., 1973. Legal asst. Mendolsohn, Fastiff & Tichy, San Francisco, 1978-80, Browne & Kahn, San Francisco, 1980-82; program developer Citizens' Congress for Community Involvement, Chgo., 1982-84; pub. policy researcher Roosevelt Ctr. for Am. Policy Studies, Chgo., 1984-85; tng. and devel. cons. Coalition for Improved Edn. in South Shore, Chgo., 1985—; manpower planner City of Chgo., 1986—; cons. Human Resources Devel. Inst., Chgo., 1984-85. Bd. dirs. Citizens Schs. Com., Chgo., 1988—, League United Latin Am. Citizens, Chgo., 1988—; pres. local mgmt. bd. Rebecca K. Crown Ctr., Chgo., 1989-90; mem. Chgo. Coun. on Urban Affairs, 1989—; mem. steering com. Acad. for Math. & Sci. Tchrs. in Chgo. Recipient cert. Literacy Vols. Chgo., 1984, Outstanding Tutoring Svc. award Human Resources Devel. Inst., 1985; Woodrow Wilson fellow, 1973. Mem. ASCD, ASTD, AAAS, NAFE, CCASTD. Home: 7655 S Euclid Chicago IL 60649 Office: City of Chgo 510 N Peshtigo Chicago IL 60611

SANDERS, MARLENE, television correspondent; b. Cleve., Jan. 10, 1931; d. Mac Sanders and Evelyn (Menitoff) Fisher; m. Jerome Toobin, May 27, 1958 (dec. Jan. 1984); children: Jeff, Mark. Student, Ohio State U., 1948-49. Writer, producer Sta. WNEW-TV, N.Y.C., 1955-60, P.M. program Westinghouse Broadcasting Co., N.Y.C., 1961-62; asst. dir. news and public affairs Sta. WNEW, N.Y.C., 1962-64; anchor, news program ABC News, N.Y.C., 1964-68, corr., 1968-72, documentary producer, writer, anchor, 1972-76, v.p., dir. TV documentaries, 1976-78; corr. CBS News, N.Y.C., 1978-87; host Currents Sta. WNET-TV, N.Y.C., 1987-88; host Met. Week in Review, 1988—. Co-author: Waiting for Prime Time: The Women of Television News, 1988. Recipient award N.Y. State Broadcasters Assn., 1976, award Nat. Press Club, 1976, Emmy awards, 1980, 81, others. Mem. Am. Women in Radio and TV (Woman of Yr. award 1975, Silver Satellite award 1977), Women in Communications (past pres.), Women's Forum, Soc. Profl. Journalists. Office: Sta WNET-TV 356 W 58th St New York NY 10019

SANDERS, MARY LOUISE, psychologist; b. Chgo., July 23, 1977; d. Alexander and Mia Louise (Pearson) S.; m. Karl Wendell Jackson, July 23, 1977; children: Ashley Nicole, Morgan Alexis. AB in Psychology, Washington U., St. Louis, 1972; MA in Psychology, U. Calif., Riverside, 1975, PhD in Psychology, 1979. Lic. psychologist, Calif. Rsch. asst. counseling ctr. U. Nebr., Omaha, 1972-73; assoc. psychology U. Calif., Riverside, 1974-76; intern Child Guidance of Orange County, Huntington Beach, Calif., 1977-78, Loma Linda (Calif.) U. Med. Ctr., 1979-80; assoc. in psychology U. Calif., Riverside, 1975-77; pvt. practice Riverside, 1981-83; v.p., psychologist Riverside Psychol. Consultants, 1983-89; pvt. practice Santa Barbara, Calif., 1989—. Contbr. to profl. publs. Mem. Am. Psychol. Assn., Am. Ednl. Rsch. Assn., Calif. State Psychol. Assn. Office: PO Box 61356 Santa Barbara CA 93160

SANDERS, PHYLLIS ADEN, radio and television broadcaster; b. Buenos Aires, June 27, 1919; d. Fred and Anna Almeda (Pettit) Aden; BA, Occidental Coll., 1941; MA, Scarritt Coll., 1943; m. Olcutt Sanders, Apr. 8, 1947; children: Lynn Edwin, Marta Almeda, Jay Olcutt, Fred Aden, R. Elizabeth. Formerly tchr., lectr., workshop leader on changing roles of women, 1973-75; producer, host weekly radio interview show Changing World of Women, Sta. WNYC, N.Y.C., 1972-79; TV reporter, host, commentator on women's issues Sta. WNYC-TV, N.Y.C., 1975-78; regular weekly commentator Prime of Your Life, NBC-TV, N.Y.C., 1979-83; reporter Age Whys, AM Phila., Sta. WPVI-TV, 1981-83; producer, host weekly series Growing Older with Style, WCAU-TV, Phila., 1983-84, feature reporter Noonbreak, 1984, senior reporter NEWS, 1987—; producer, host series on aging WHYY-TV, 1984-85; reporter, interviewer Modern Maturity TV series on aging, nat. PBS-TV, 1986-88; host weekly talk show Over 50 Sta. WCAU-TV, 1989—. Community relations dir. Town of New Castle (N.Y.), 1972-73, originator, coordinator Community Day, New Castle, 1971; coordinator N.Y.C. women's adv. com. on meeting with network mgmt., 1976-77. Recipient award N.Y. chpt. NOW, 1973, N.J. Women, 1976; named to Phila. Mayor's Sr. Citizen Honor Roll, 1984. Mem. AFTRA, Nat. Acad. TV Arts and Scis., Women's Inst. for Freedom of Press, ACLU, Friends Com. on Nat. Legis., NOW, Older Women's League, Occidental Coll. Alumni (award 1985). Mem. Soc. of Friends. Home: 135 S 20th St #305 Philadelphia PA 19103

SANDERS, STEPHANIE ANN, psychologist; b. Somerville, N.J., Mar. 3, 1954; d. Curtis Francis and Eliedia Katherine (Mammi) S. BA in Chemistry, Rutgers U., 1976, MS in Psychology, 1979, PhD in Psychology, 1984. Family planning counselor dept. Ob-Gyn Hosp. of U. Pa., Phila., 1975, 77, 78; instr. dept. psychology Manhattanville Coll., Purchase, N.Y., summer 1982; rsch./teaching asst. dept. psychology Rutgers U., New Brunswick, N.J., 1976-82, instr. psychology dept., 1979-82; rsch. assoc. Ind. U., Bloomington, 1982-86, asst. scientist, 1986-90, assoc. scientist, 1990—; sci. asst. to the dir. The Kinsey Inst. for Rsch. in Sex, Gender, Reprodn./Ind.U., Bloomington, 1982-88, asst. dir., 1988—; asst. dir. Summer Inst., The Kinsey Inst., 1986; faculty Midwest AIDS Tng. and Edn. Ctr., Ind. U. Sch. Medicine, Indpls., 1988—; rsch. cons. 1987—; mgmt. cons. 1989—. Editor: Masculinity/Femininity: Basic Perspectives, 1987, Homosexuality/Heterosexuality, 1990; contbr. articles to profl. jours. Lectr. local civic and profl. orgsn. Named to Outstanding Young Women in Am., 1984; recipient Ortho Pharm. Scholarship, 1972, rsch. grants Nat. Inst. Drug Abuse, NIH, 1989-94, Fund for Human Dignity, 1986, Charles and Johanna Busch Meml. Fund, Rutgers U., 1980-81. Mem. Am. Psychol. Assn., Internat. Soc. Devel. Psychobiology, Internat. Acad. Sex Rsch. (assoc.) Am. Soc. Psychosomatic Ob-Gyn, Soc. for Menstrual Cycle Rsch., Soc. for Scientific Study of Sex, Sigma Xi. Home: 800 North Smith Rd Apt 2V Bloomington IN 47408 Office: The Kinsey Inst Morrison Hall/Ind Univ Bloomington IN 47405

SANDERSEN, ELAINE M., art director, graphic designer; b. Jersey City, Aug. 19, 1941; d. Alfred A. and Elizabeth Pastine; m. Robert Sandersen, May 19, 1963 (div. May 1978); children: Lynda, Eric. Student, Parsons Sch. Design, 1962. Assoc. art dir. Silver, Burdett & Ginn, Morristown, N.J., 1978—. Mem. Art Dirs. Club N.J. Office: Silver Burdette & Ginn 250 James St Ste CN 1918 Morristown NJ 07960

SANDERSON, SARA LEE, educational amdinistrator; b. Madison, Wis., Mar. 28, 1942; d. John Christopher and Rosetta (Powers) Mackin; m. P. Michael Sanderson, Mar. 28, 1981; 1 child, Christopher Michael. BS, Fla. State U., 1964; MEd, U. Miami, Coral Gables, Fla., 1969; EdD, Nova U., 1979. Tchr. Dade County Pub. Schs., Miami, 1964-69; counselor Miami Dade Community Coll., Miami, 1969-72, instr., 1972-77, adminstr., prof., 1977—, chmn. dept.; cons. in field. Contbr. articles, revs. to profl. pubs. Vol. For Kids Sake, Miami, 1988; team mother Howard-Palmetto Khoury League, Miami, 1989; vol. Pinecrest Elem. Sch., Miami, 1987—. Mem. Nat. Assn. Devel. Edn., Nat. Coun. Instnl. Adminstrs., Nat. Assn. Community and Jr. Colls., St. Louis Women's Club (bd. dirs. 1988-89). Home: 12330 Pine Needle Ln Miami FL 33156 Office: Miami Dade Community Coll 11011 SW 104 St Miami FL 33176

SANDIDGE, KANITA DURICE, communications company executive; b. Cleve., Dec. 2, 1947; d. John Robert Jr. and Virginia Louise (Caldwell) S. AB, Cornell U., 1970; MBA, Case Western Res. U., 1979. Supr. assignments service ctrs. and installation AT&T, Cleve., 1970-78, chief dept. data processing and acctg., 1979-80; adminstrn. mgr. exec. v.p. staff AT&T, N.Y.C., 1980-83; sales forecasting and analysis mgr. resources planning AT&T, Newark, 1983-86; planning and devel. mgr. material planning and mgmt. AT&T Network Systems, Morristown, N.J., 1986-87; dir. adminstrv. services AT&T Network Systems, Lisle, Ill., 1987—. Mem black exchange program Nat. Urban League, N.Y.C., 1986—. Named Black Achiever in Industry, Harlem YMCA, 1981; recipient Tribute to Women and Industry Achievement award YWCA, 1985. Mem. Nat. Black MBA's, Alliance Black AT&T Mgrs., Am. Mgmt. Assn., Nat. Assn. for Female Execs., NAACP, Beta Alpha Psi. Mem. African Meth. Episcopal Ch. Home: 820 Cardiff Rd Naperville IL 60565 Office: AT&T Network Systems 2600 Warrenville Rd Lisle IL 60532

SANDIFORD, KIMBERLY ELYSE, banker; b. Bklyn., July 20, 1965; d. Bernard E. and Una Joyce (Hector) S. Assoc., Nassau County Coll. Human resources rep. Melweitz Foodtown, East Meadow, N.Y., 1981-83; billing clk. Reuben H. Donnelley, Garden City, N.Y., 1982; sales rep. Hempstead China Shop, Westbury, N.Y., 1982-84; prodn. standard coordinator Global Computer Supplies, Plainview, N.Y., 1984-87; ops. supr. Global Computer Supplies, Norcross, Ga., 1987; help desk analyst E.F. Hutton, Manhattan, N.Y., 1987—; help desk mgr. Union Bank Switzerland, Manhatten, N.Y., 1988—; cons. and tutor in field. Fellow NAFE, Am. Networking Assn. (bd. dirs.). Home: 201 Oswego St North Bellmore NY 11710

SANDIN, A. BONNIE, small business owner; b. Norwalk, Conn., May 19, 1942; d. Stanley and Lilien (Goldman) Schiff; m. John R. Sandin, Oct. 27, 1962 (div. Nov. 1985); children: Amy Carla, Eric John. Student, Falls Ch. High Sch., 1960, George Mason U., 1960-62. Adjustor Aetna Life and Casualty Ins., Wash. D.C., 1960-62; adminstrv. office mgr. Hevener and Rice Ins. Agy., Alexandria, Va., 1962-63; adminstrv. asst. Denlingers Publishers, Centreville, Va., 1975-77; v.p., agy. Doncaster Ins., Centreville, Va.; owner, agt. State Farm Ins. Agy., McLean, Va., 1978--; v.p. Nat. Assn. State Farm Agts., College Park, 1986--, No. Va. Assn. State Farm Agts., Springfield, 1988--, cons. Va. Bur. Ins. Exam. Review Commn., Richmond 1987--. Editor: newsletter No. Va. State Farm Agts. Assn., 1985. Chairperson The League of Women Voters, Arlington 1963-65, charter pres. Clifton, Fairfax Lioness Club, 1978-79, speaker, cons., The Women's Ctr. No. Va., 1986--. Mem. Va. Assn. of Female Execs. (dir. 1988--), McLean Bus. and Profl. Assn., McLean Bus. and Profl. Women, The Tower Club. Home: 1650 Westwind Way McLean VA 22101 Office: Bonnie Sandin State Farm Insurance 6707 Old Dominion Dr McLean VA 22101

SANDIN, CAROLINE TOWLEY, county commissioner; b. St. Peter, Minn., Nov. 18, 1915; d. Gabriel Heiberg and Victoria Louise (Almen) Towley; m. Howard Victor Sandin, July 20, 1941; children: Caroline, Howard II, Sarah, Victoria, Catherine, Martha, Elizabeth. Student pub. schs. Comml. instr. S.W. Bell Telephone Co., East St. Louis, Ill., 1941-44; comml. rep. N.W. Bell Telephone Co., Shakopee, Minn., 1939-41; part-time clk. Windmill Art Gallery, Ashland, Wis., 1983—; county commr. Ashland County Bd., 1978—. Pres., founder LWV, Ashland, 1956-60; mem., pres. Bd. Edn., Ashland, 1961-83; mem. bd. regents U. Wis. system, Madison, 1968-77; mem. Ashland Common Coun., 1978-86, Econ. Devel. Coun., 1988—; mem. bd. visitors U. Wis.-Superior, 1978-86, pres., 1983-85; mem. Bay Area Rural Transit Commn., 1978—, v.p., 1978, sec., 1984-88; mem. Family Forum Bd., 1984—, pres. 1986—; chmn. Health and Social Services Com., 1988; mem. Unified Svcs. Bd., 1980—, pres., 1985—; chmn. Luth. Social Svcs. Adv. Coun., 1987—; bd. dirs. Attys. Profl. Responsibility Wis. Supreme Ct., 1982-88. Recipient Disting. Alumni award U. Wis.-Superior, 1977; named Woman of Yr., C. of C., 1979; Outstanding Citizen of Yr., Chequamegon VFW, 1984. Republican. Lutheran. Home: 703 W 7th St Ashland WI 54806

SANDLER, BERNICE RESNICK, education association executive; b. N.Y.C., Mar. 3, 1928; d. Abraham Hyman and Ivy (Ernst) Resnick; children: Deborah Jo, Emily Maud. BA cum laude, Bklyn. Coll., 1948; MA, CCNY, 1950; EdD, U. Md., 1969; LLD (hon.), Bloomfield Coll., 1973, Hood Coll., 1974, R.I. Coll., 1980, Colby-Sawyer Coll., 1984; LHD (hon.), Grand Valley State Coll., 1974; Dr. Pub. Service (hon.), North Adams State Coll., 1985. Research asst., nursery sch. tchr., employment counselor, adult edn. instr., sec.; psychologist HEW, 1970; tchr. psychology Mt. Vernon Coll., 1970; head Action Com. for Fed. Contract Compliance, Women's Equity Action League, 1970-71; edn. specialist U.S. Ho. Reps., Washington, 1970; dep. dir. Womens Action program, HEW, Washington, 1971; dir. project on status and edn. of women Assn. Am. Colls., Washington, 1971—; vis. lectr. U. Md., 1968-69; adv. bd. Women's Equity Action League Ednl. and Legal Def. Fund, 1980—, trustee, 1974-80, Women's Equity Action League, 1971-78; adv. com. Math/Sci. Network, 1979—, Wider Opportunities for Women, 1978-85, Women's Legal Def. Fund, 1978-84; adv. bd. N.J. project Inst. for Rsch. on Women Rutgers U., New Brunswick, 1987—, Nat. Coun. for Alternative Work Patterns Inc., 1978-85, Women's Hdqrs. State Nat. Bank for Women's Appointments, 1977-78, and others. Mem. adv. bd. Jour. Reprints Documents Affecting Women, 1976-78, Women's Rights Law Reporter, 1970-80; contbr. articles to profl. jours. Mem. bd. overseers Wellesley Coll. Ctr. for Research on Women, 1975-87; bd. dirs. Ctr. for Women's Policy Studies, 1972—; mem. exec. com. Inst. for Ednl. Leadership, 1982-87, mem. program adv. com., 1987—, chair bd. dirs., 1981, chair adv. com., 1975-81; mem. affirmative action com., task force on family, nat. affairs commn. Am. Jewish Com., 1978—, bd. dirs. D.C. chpt.; tech. adv. com. Nat. Jewish Family Ctr., 1980-89; adv. council Ednl. Devel. Ctr., 1980-85; adv. bd. Urban Inst., 1981-85, Women Employed Inst., 1981-84, Ex-New Yorkers for N.Y., 1978-79; mem. adv. com. Arthur and Elizabeth Schlesinger Library History of Women in Am., 1981-85, Ctr. for Women Scholars, 1979-83; nat. adv. com. Shelter Research Inst., Calif., 1980-82; chair adv. panel project on self-evaluation Am. Insts. for Research, 1980-82; bd. dirs. Equality Ctr., 1983—, Evaluation and Tng. Inst., Calif., 1980—, Inst. for Studies in Equality, 1975-77. Recipient Athena award Intercollegiate Assn. Women Students, 1974, Elizabeth Boyer award Women's Equity Action League, 1976, Rockefeller Pub. Svc. award Princeton U., 1976, Women Educators award for activism, 1987, Anna Roe award Harvard U., 1988, Readers Choice honors Washington Woman Magazine, 1987; named one of 100 Most Powerful Women Washingtonian Mag., 1982. Mem. Am. Psychol. Assn., Assn. for Women in Sci. Found. (bd. dirs. 1977—), Am. Soc. Profl. and Exec. Women (adv. bd. 1980—). Office: Assn Am Colls 1818 R St NW Washington DC 20009

SANDLER, DALE P., epidemiologist; b. Hartford, Conn., Jan. 24, 1951; d. Bernie and Jeanette (Glassman) Pearlman; m. Robert S. Sandler, Aug. 4, 1973; children: David, Michael. BA in Math. and Philosophy cum laude, Boston U., 1972; MPH in Chronic Disease Epidemiology, Yale U., 1975; PhD in Epidemiology, Johns Hopkins U., Balt., 1979. Data analyst dept. internal medicine Yale U. Sch. Medicine, New Haven, 1973-74, rsch. asst. dept. epidemiology and pub. health, 1974-75; health statistician, program specialist lipid metabolism br. Nat. Heart Lung and Blood Inst., NIH, Bethesda, Md., 1975-76; co-prin. investigator, project dir. Johns Hopkins U. Sch. Hygiene and Pub. Health, Balt., 1978-79; statistician epidemiology program, biometry br. Nat. Inst. Environ. Health Scis., Research Triangle Park, N.C., 1979-81, epidemiologist epidemiology br. div. biometry, 1981—; adj. asst. prof. dept. epidemiology Sch. Pub. Health, U. N.C., Chapel Hill, 1984-89, adj. assoc. prof., 1990—; trainee USPHS, 1974-75, 76-77; mem. interagy. coord. com. on kidney, urologic and hematologic diseases UPSHS, 1986—; mem. med. rev. bd. Southeastern Kidney Coun., 1988—; mem. renal community coun. U.S. Renal Data System, 1988—; chair Cancer and Leukemia Group B Core Workgroup on Epidemiology, 1989—. Reviewer jours. Am. Jour. Epidemiology, Am. Jour. Pub. Helath, Environ. Health Perspectives, Internat. Jour. Cancer, Internat. Jour. Epidemiology, Jour. Nat. Cancer Inst., Epidemiology; contbr. articles to profl. jours. Mem. Community Schs. Adv. Bd., Chapel Hill, N.C., 1986-90; v.p. Tudeu Reform Congregation, Durham, N.C., 1985-87. Fellow Am. Coll. Epidemiology; mem. Delta and Scarlet Key. Office: Nat Inst Environ Health Sci PO Box 12233 Research Triangle Park NC 27709

SANDLER, MARION OSHER, savings and loan association executive; b. Biddeford, Maine, Oct. 17, 1930; d. Samuel and Leah (Lowe) Osher; m. Herbert M. Sandler, Mar. 26, 1961. BA, Wellesley Coll., 1952; postgrad., Harvard U.-Radcliffe Coll., 1953; MBA, NYU, 1958; LLD (hon.), Golden Gate U., 1987. Asst. buyer Bloomingdale's (dept. store), N.Y.C., 1953-55; security analyst Dominick & Dominick, N.Y.C., 1955-61; sr. fin. analyst Oppenheimer & Co., N.Y.C., 1961-63; sr. v.p., dir. Golden West Fin. Corp. and World Savs. & Loan Assn., Oakland, Calif., 1963-75, vice chmn. bd., co-mng. officer, dir., mem. exec. com., 1975-80, pres., co- chief exec. officer, dir., mem. exec. com., 1980—; mem. Thrift Insts. Adv. Coun. to Fed. Res. Bd., 1989—. Vice-chmn. industry adv. com. Fed. Savs. and Loan Ins. Corp., 1987-88; bd. overseers NYU Schs. Bus., 1987-89; mem. capital formation task force White House Conf. on Small Bus., 1979; mem. Pres. Carter's Housing Task Force, 1980, Pres.'s Mgmt. Improvement Coun., 1980; mem.

policy adv. bd. Ctr. for Real Estate and Urban Econs. U. Calif., Berkeley, 1981—; mem. exec. com. Policy Adv. Bd., Ctr. for Real Estate and Urban Econs. U. Calif., Berkeley, 1985—; mem. ad hoc com. to rev. Schs. Bus. Adminstrn. U. Calif., Berkeley, 1984-85; mem. adv. coun. Fed. Nat. Mortgage Assn., 1983-84; v.p. Thrift Insts. Adv. Coun. to Fed. Res. Bd., 1990—. Mem. Phi Beta Kappa, Beta Gamma Sigma. Office: Golden W Fin Corp 1901 Harrison St Oakland CA 94612

SANDLES, ELLEN JOAN, sales professional; b. N.Y.C., May 15, 1960; d. Leonard Marion and Ina Gloria (Shapiro) S. BA magna cum laude, Columbia U., 1983. Asst. media buyer Dancer Fitzgerald Sample Advt., 1978-79; credit and collections Xerox Corp., 1982-84; pub. relations adminstrv. asst. Vogue mag., 1984-85; legal sales rep. Harris/Lanier Corp., 1985-87; acct. rep. Prentice Hall Info. Network, N.Y.C., 1987-89; acct. mgr. AT&T Paradyne, N.Y.C., 1989—. Project coordinator New York Cares, 1988-89. Mem. Barnard Bus. and Profl. Women's Club. Office: AT&T Paradyne 1 Exchange Plaza New York NY 10006

SANDLES, FAITH MEYER, social worker; b. Albany, N.Y., Apr. 9, 1942; d. Henry Marten and Anita Charlotte (Witte) Meyer; m. Albert Warren Sandles, Oct. 28, 1972; 1 child, Abigail Beth. BA in Psychology, Hartwick Coll., 1964; cert. in gerontology, U. Mich., 1971. Exec. dir., cons. Cohoes (N.Y.) Multi-Svc. Sr. Citizens Ctr., 1967-77; with various offices and depts. State of N.Y., Albany, 1970-84; interior decorator freelance, Albany, 1984—; coordinator sr. companion program OD Heck Devel. Ctr., Schenectady, N.Y., 1986—; bd. dirs., chair various coms. Voluntary Action Ctr., Albany, 1977-83; bd. dirs., officer, chair various com.s Troy-Cohoes YWCA, 1978-84; ofcl. del. White House Conf. Aging, 1971. Officer N.Y. Assn. Learning Disabled, Capital Dist., 1976—; co-founder Capital Dist. Parkinsons Support Group, Albany, 1986; bd. dirs., officer, chair various coms. Troy-Cohoes YWCA, 1978-84; vol. Internat. YWCA to Trinidad, Tobago, Barbados and Antigua, 1965. HEW fellow U.S. Dept. Health Edn. and Welfare, 1971. Mem. Nat. Assn. Female Execs. Lutheran. Office: OD Heck Devel Ctr Balltown and Consaul Rds Schenectady NY 12304

SANDORSE-LOVEY, DONNA IRENE, business systems analyst; b. Elizabeth, N.J., Apr. 21, 1957; d. Ronald Patrick and Barbara Irene (Keller) S.; m. Charles J. Lovey, June 14, 1986. BA, Rutgers u., 1979, cert. in teaching, 1982. Cert. French tchr., N.J. Tchr. French Benedictine Acad., Elizabeth, N.J., 1979-81; supr. escrow dept. Jersey Mortgage Co., Elizabeth, 1982-84; tchr. reading South Plainfield (N.J.) Bd. Edn., 1981-82; asst. v.p. Crestmont Fed. Savs. & Loan, Westfield, N.J., 1984-86, The Ramapo Bank, Wayne, N.J., 1986-87; bus. systems analyst Citicorp Mortgage Inc., Teaneck, N.J., 1987-88; appl. devel. mgr./asst. v.p. Citicorp Mortgage Inc., N.Y.C., 1988-89; systems analyst UJB Financial, Hackensack, N.J., 1989—. Tchr. sch. Elmora Presbyn. Ch., Elizabeth, 1973-81, youth advisor, 1975-81. Democrat. Office: UJB Financial 190 Moore St Hackensack NJ 07204

SANDQUIST, CAROL PATRICIA, dentist; b. N.Y.C., Oct. 3, 1957; d. James Patrick and Barbara (May) S.; m. Sheldon Roy Shulman, Sept. 4, 1983. BA, SUNY, Buffalo, N.Y., 1979; DMD, Tufts U., 1983. Assoc. dentist Group Practice, Great Neck, N.Y., 1983-85; dentist, owner solo practice, Rego Pk., N.Y., 1985—, Garden City, N.Y., 1986—; hostess Greater L.I. Dental Meeting, Uniondale, N.Y., 1986—. Bd. dirs. Stevenson Dem. Club, Flushing, N.Y., 1984—. Mem. Queens County Dental Soc., Am. Dental Soc., Dental Soc. State of N.Y.

SANDS, SHARON LOUISE, graphic design executive; b. Jacksonville, Fla., July 4, 1944; d. Clifford Harding Sands and Ruby May (Ray) MacDonald; m. Jonathan Michael Langford, Feb. 14, 1988. BFA, Cen. Washington U., 1968; postgrad, UCLA, 1968. Art dir. East and West Network, Inc., L.A., 1973-78, Daisy Pub., L.A., 1978; prodn. dir. L.A. mag., 1979-80; owner, creative dir. Carmel Graphic Design, Carmel Valley, Calif., 1981-85; creative dir., v.p. The Video Sch. House, Monterey, Calif., 1985-88; graphic designer ConAgra, ConAgra, Nebr., 1988; owner, creative dir. Esprit deFleurs, Ltd., Carmel, Calif., 1988—; lectr. Pub. Expo, L.A., 1979, panelist Women in Mgmt., L.A., 1979; redesign of local newspaper, Carmel, Calif., 1982. Contbr. articles to profl. mags. Designer corp. ID for Carmel Valley C. of C., 1981, 90; redesigner local newspaper, Carmel, Calif., 1982. Recipient 7 design awards Soc. Pub. Designers, 1977, 78, Maggie award, L.A., 1977, 5 design awards The Ad Club of Monterey Peninsula, 1983, 85, 87, Design awards Print Mag. N.Y., 1986, Desi awards, N.Y., 1986, 88. Mem. NAFE, Soc. for Prevention of Cruelty to Animals, Greenpeace. Democrat. Home: 37302 Tassajara Carmel Valley CA 93924

SANDS, VELMA AHDA, lawyer; d. John T. and Thelma Jane (Davis) Carlisle; m. Henry William Sands, Aug. 3, 1985; children: Jay, Clinton, Kenyatta, Tisa. BS, Calif. State U., Dominguez Hills, 1976; JD, Southwestern U., 1985. CPA. V.p. Security Pacific Bank, L.A., 1981-86; contr. L.A. Investors, 1986; mgr. IRC div. FN Realty Svcs., Pasadena, Calif., 1986-88; mgr. fin. reporting Luz Internat. Ltd., L.A., 1988-89; pvt. practice law L.A., 1990—; cons. Peat Marwick Main, L.A., 1980-81. Participant career day programs for local high schs. Lawyers scholar Nat. Assn. Black Women, 1982. Mem. NAFE, Nat. Assn. Bank Women (chair ways and means com. of scholarship fund 1986, scholar 1984), L.A. Bench and Bar Affiliates (mem. scholarship com., meeting host, scholar 1983), Phi Alpha Delta. Home: PO Box 38 Lawndale CA 90260

SANDSTROM, ALICE WILHELMINA, accountant; b. Seattle, Jan. 6, 1914; d. Andrew William and Agatha Mathilda (Sundius) S. BA, U. Wash., 1934. CPA, Wash. Mgr. office Star Machinery Co., Seattle, 1935-43, Howe & Co., Seattle, 1943-46; pvt. practice acctg., Seattle, 1945—; controller Children's Orthopedic Hosp. and Med. Ctr., Seattle, 1948-75, assoc. adminstr. fin., 1975-81; lectr. U. Wash., Seattle, 1957-72. Mem. Wash. State Title XIX Adv. Com., 1975-82, Wash. State Vendors Rate Adv. Com., 1980-87, Mayor's Task Force for Small Bus., 1981-83; bd. dirs. Seattle YWCA, 1981—, pres., 1986-88; bd. dirs. Sr. Services Seattle/King County, 1985, treas., 1986, pres. 1988—; bd. dirs. Children's Orthopedic Hosp. Found., 1982—. Fellow Hosp. Fin. Mgmt. Assn. (charter, state pres. 1956-57, nat. treas. 1963-65, Robert H. Reeves Merit award 1970, Frederick T. Muncie award 1985), Wash. State Hosp. Assn. (treas. 1956-70), Am. Soc. Women Accts. (pres. Seattle chpt. 1946-48), Am. Soc. Women CPAs, Women's Univ. Club (Seattle), City Club (Seattle, charter mem.). Home and Office: 5725 NE 77th St Seattle WA 98115

SANDT, SHERRY KAY, corporate executive; b. Williamsport, Pa., May 23, 1962; d. Wayne A. and Audrey Jane (Snyder) Newton; m. Gary L. Sandt, June 15, 1985. BS, Kutztown (Pa.) U., 1984; postgrad., U. Scranton, Pa., 1986-87. Cert. optometric vision therapy technician. Substitute tchr. Williamsport Sch. Dist., 1984; camp counselor Diller Vacation Home for Blind Children, Avalon, N.J., 1984; tchr. of blind B.L.a.S.T., Towanda, Pa., 1984-86; child care worker Friendship House, Scranton, 1986; vision therapist Binocular Vision Ctr., Scranton, 1986, lead vision therapist, 1986-87; asst. adminstrv. dir. Binocular Vision Ctr. and Personal Eye Care, King of Prussia, Pa., 1987-90; itinerant tchr. visually impaired Elwyn Inst., Phila., 1990—. Lutheran.

SANDWEISS, MARTHA A., museum curator, author; b. St. Louis, Mar. 29, 1954; d. Jerome Wesley and Marilyn Joy (Glik) S. BA magna cum laude, Radcliffe Coll., 1975; MA in History, Yale U., 1977, MPhil in History, 1981, PhD, 1985. Smithsonian-Nat. Endowment Humanities fellow, Nat. Portrait Gallery, Washington, 1975-76; curator photographs Amon Carter Mus., Ft. Worth, 1979-86, adj. curator photographs, 1987-89; dir. Mead Art Mus. Amherst Coll., 1989—, adj. assoc. prof. of fine arts and Am. studies, 1989—. Author: Carlotta Corpron: Designer with Light, 1980, Masterworks of American Photography, 1982, Laura Gilpin: An Enduring Grace, 1986, (catalogue) Pictures from an Expedition: Early Views of the American West, 1979; co-author: Eyewitness to War: Prints and Daguerreotypes of th Mexican War, 1989; editor: Historic Texas: A Photographic Portrait, 1986, Contemporary Texas: A Photographic Portrait, 1986, Denizens of the Desert, 1988. Fellow Ctr. for Am. Art and Material Culture, Yale U., 1977-79, Nat. Endowment for the Humanities, 1988. Office: Mead Art Mus Amherst Coll Amherst MA 01002

SANDY, CYNTHIA SUE, nursing administrator, researcher, nurse; b. Steubenville, Ohio, Nov. 1, 1959; d. Ronald Jerry and Judy May (LeMasters) Rice; m. Robert Mark Sandy. BSN cum laude, U. Akron, Ohio, 1982; postgrad., U. South Fla., 1987—, U. Sarasota, 1991—. RN. Staff nurse labor and delivery unit Akron City Hosp., 1982-83; clin. supr. Rapid Response North, Cuyahoga Falls, Ohio, 1983-86; office coord. Med. Care Mgmt. Systems, Bradenton, Fla., 1987; rsch. adminstr./rsch. coord. Memory Assessment Clinics, Inc., St. Petersburg, Fla., 1987-88; clinic dir. Memory Assessment Clinics, Inc., St. Petersburg & Sarasota, Fla., 1988-89; assoc. dir. clinic ops. Memory Assessment Clinics, Inc., Sarasota, 1989—. U. Akron scholar, 1978. Mem. NAFE, Sigma Theta Tau. Democrat. Home: 3802 31st Ave W Bradenton FL 34205 Office: Memory Assessment Clinics 1217 East Ave S Ste 209 Sarasota FL 34239

SANFILIPPO, MARIANNE, controller; b. Buffalo, May 29, 1944; d. Joseph A. and Angeline (D'Agostino) SanF. BA, SUNY, Buffalo, 1966, MBA, 1976. Tchr. social studies Bishop Colton High Sch., Buffalo, 1966-69; sr. ins. examiner N.Y. State Ins. Dept., N.Y.C., 1969-80; controller Exchange Ins. Co., Buffalo, 1980—. Mem. Soc. Fin. Examiners, NAFE. Republican. Roman Catholic. Home: 47 Lloyd Dr Cheektowaga NY 14225 Office: Exchange Ins Co 741 Delaware Ave Buffalo NY 14209

SANFORD, DIANE LYNN, psychologist, researcher; b. Balt., Dec. 22, 1956; d. Bernard and Frances (Kornfeld) Goldstein; . Stephen Allan, May 19, 1985; 1 child, Jessica Lauren. BA magna cum laude, U. Mich., 1977; MS, Syracuse (N.Y.) U., 1982, PhD, 1984. Lic. psychologist, Mo. Intern in psychologist VA Med. Ctr., Oklahoma City, 1983-84; asst. to exec. dir. Narcotics Svc. Coun., St. Louis, 1984-86; psychologist Four County Mental Health, Inc., St. Louis, 1984-87, Mental Health Group of St. Louis, 1987-90; pvt. practice psychologist St. Louis, 1990—. Author: (chpt. in book) Spouse Abuse, 1983. Bd. dirs. Jewish Children's Home, St. Louis, 1988—, Jewish Family & Children's Svcs., St. Louis, 1989-90; co-founder Gateway Postpartum Rsch. Collective, 1989—. Syracuse U. grantee, 1982-83, United Way grantee, 1985-87. Mem. Am. Psychol. Assn., Mo. Psychol. Assn., St. Louis Psychol. Assn., St. Louis Network Women Psychologists. Office: 7494 Ethel Saint Louis MO 63117

SANFORD, ISABEL GWENDOLYN, actress; b. N.Y.C.; d. James Edward and Josephine (Perry) S.; m. William Edward Richmond (dec.); children: Pamela (Mrs. Eddie Ruff), William Eric, Sanford Keith. Ed. pub. schs. Stage appearances in off-Broadway prodns., also in L.A.; Broadway appearance in Amen Corner; film appearances include Guess Who's Coming to Dinner, 1968, Pendulum, 1969, Stand Up and Be Counted, 1972, The New Centurions, 1972, Love at First Bite, 1979; appeared in TV film The Great Man's Whiskers, 1973, series All in the Family, numerous guest appearances various series, The Carol Burnett Show; co-star: TV series The Jeffersons, 1974-85. Mem. Kwanza Found. Address: care Harvey Gold & Assocs 12725 Ventura Blvd Ste E Studio City CA 91604*

SANFORD, KATHERINE KOONTZ, cancer researcher; b. Chgo., July 19, 1915; d. William James and Alta Rachel (Koontz) S.; m. Charles Fleming Richards Mifflin, Dec. 7, 1971. BA, Wellesley Coll., 1937; MA, Brown U., 1939, PhD, 1942; DSc (hon.), Med. Coll. Pa., 1974, Cath. U. Am., 1988. Teaching asst. Brown U., Providence, R.I., 1937-39; rsch. asst. Brown U., Providence, 1939-41; instr. biology Western coll., Oxford, Ohio, 1941-42, Allegheny Coll., Meadville, Pa., 1942-43; asst. dir. Johns Hopkins Nursing Sch., Balt., 1943-47; rsch. biologist Nat. Cancer Inst. NIH, Bethesda, Md., 1947-74; head cell physiology and oncogenesis sect. Lab. Biochemistry, Bethesda, 1974-77; chief in vitro carcinogenesis sect. Nat. Cancer Inst. NIH, Bethesda, 1979—. Contbr. 150 articles to profl. jours. Ross Harrison fellow, 1954. Mem. Phi Beta Kappa, Sigma Xi. Home: 101 Stuart Dr Dover DE 19901 Office: Nat Cancer Inst Vitro Carcinogenesis Sect Bethesda MD 20892

SANFORD, RUTH EILEEN, data processing company administrator; b. Two Harbors, Minn., Mar. 15, 1925; d. John Arvid and Helene (Lind) Bostrom; m. Keith N. Sanford, Sept. 21 1950 (div. Sept. 1960); m. Michael R. Notaro, Mar. 10, 1984. Degree in bus., Cable's Secretarial Coll., 1944; student, Northwestern U., 1966. Exec. sec. 1st Am. Nat. Bank, Duluth, Minn., 1944-48; pvt. sec. Adam Thomson, Duluth, Minn., 1948-52; exec. sec. and administrv. asst. Res. Mining Co., Silver Bay, Minn., 1952-62, United Calif. Bank, San Francisco, 1963-64; office mgr. Poly-Tech, Mpls., 1964-66; corp. sec. and administrv. asst. to pres. Statis. Tabulating Corp., Chgo., 1966-90. Mem. Chgo. Coun. Fgn. Rels. Mem. NAFE. Roman Catholic. Club: Butterfield Country (Hinsdale, Ill.). Lodge: Women of Moose. Home: 500 Linden Ave Oak Park IL 60302

SANFORD, SUSAN HASPEL, arts council administrator; b. Memphis, Nov. 14, 1944; d. Sam M. and Geraldine F. Haspel; m. Jeffry B. Sanford, Feb. 12, 1966 (div. 1990); children: Julie Ann, Jill Suzanne. BS, U. Wis., Madison, 1967. Sr. rsch. assoc. WHBQ-TV, Memphis, 1982-83; dir. devel. Memphis Brooks Mus. Art, 1983-87; v.p. Memphis Arts Coun., 1987—. Pres. Memphis sect. Nat. Coun. Jewish Women, 1978-80; trustee Day Found., Memphis, 1981-85; sec.-treas. Leadership Memphis, 1982-83; chair United Way Greater Memphis, 1988-89. Named Vol. of Yr., Vol. Ctr. Memphis, 1980. Mem. Nat. Soc. Fund Raising Execs. Democrat. Office: Memphis Arts Council 2714 Union Ave Extended Memphis TN 38112

SANFORD-HARRIS, JUDITH LESLIE, academic administrator; b. Boston, Feb. 22, 1953; d. Harvey Franklin and Alice Elizabeth (Taylor) Sanford; m. Joseph Edwin Harris Jr. AB, Brown U., 1974; MEd, Boston Coll., 1976, postgrad. Coordinator community outreach AID program Salem (Mass.) State Coll., 1976-79; counselor Mass. Bay Community Coll., Wellesley, 1979-80; asst. acad. dean Pine Manor Coll., Chestnut Hill, Mass., 1980-84, Bunker Hill Community Coll., Boston, 1984—. Trustee Commonwealth Sch. Alumna, 1983-85; mem. Garrison-Trotter Neighborhood Assn. Named one of Outstanding Young Women Am., 1981, 82, 84, 86. Mem. Nat. Acad. Advising Assn. (jour. editorial bd. 1984-, bd. dirs. 1981-83, 85-89), Assn. Black Women in Higher Edn., Nat. Assn. Women Deans, Adminstrs. and Counselors, Coll. Bd. Coun. on Acad. Affairs, Acad. Affairs Adminstrs., E. Alice Taylor Community Club (Boston), Delta Sigma Theta. Club: E. Alice Taylor Community (Boston). Office: Bunker Hill Community Coll New Rutherford Ave Boston MA 02129

SANGER, ELEANOR, television producer, director, writer; b. Hong Kong, Sept. 15, 1929; d. Richard and Lonni (Wernicke) S.; m. Robert Nelson Riger, June 10, 1950 (div. July 1981); children: Christopher Robin, Victoria Riger Phillips, Robert Paris, Charlotte Riger Hull; m. Peter Lersch Keys, Feb. 11, 1985. BA magna cum laude, Smith Coll., 1950; postgrad. Russian Inst., Columbia U., 1951-52. Mgr. pub. affairs Sta. WNBC-TV, N.Y.C., 1957-60; writer ABC News, N.Y.C., 1967; mgr. client rels., assoc. producer ABC Sports, N.Y.C., 1966-69, staff producer, writer, dir., 1973-86; producer Winter and Summer Olympics ABC Sports, 1968, 76, 84, 88, Winter Olympics, 1980; producer Bobsled and Luge Competition ABC Sports/Winter Olympics, Calgary, Can., 1987-88; producer equestrian events NBC Sports/Summer Olympics, Seoul, Republic of Korea, 1988; freelance producer, writer TV documentaries, 1969-70; producer, writer Tomorrow Entertainment, N.Y.C., 1971-73; adj. lectr. electronic journalism media arts dept. U. Ariz., 1990, media arts dept., 1990—, chmn. adv. bd. media dept., 1990. Producer The Open Mind, 1958-60 (Robert E. Sherwood award 1958), Winter and Summer Olympics, 1968, 76, 84, 88, Winter Olympics, 1980. Mem. adv. bd. Women's Sports Found. Recipient 7 Emmy awards for Winter and Summer Olympics, 1976, Summer Olympics Preview, 1976, Winter Olympics, 1980, Summer Olympics, 1984, 88, NCAA Football, 1981, Gold Video award for ABC Funfit with Mary Lou Retton, Rec. Industry Assn. Am., 1985, Vira award for best dir. home video, 1985, Smith Coll. medal, 1982; named ABC-YMCA Woman Achiever of Yr., 1983. Mem. Acad. TV Arts and Scis., Writers Guild Am. West, Am. Women in Radio and TV, Women in Communications, Dirs. Guild. Am., Phi Beta Kappa. Democrat. Episcopalian.

SANGIULIANO, IRIS AGATHA, psychotherapist; b. N.Y.C.; d. Vincent and Virginia (Capello) Sangiuliano; m. Leo Chalfen, Feb. 10, 1952; 1 child, Lucian. PhD, Fordham U., 1952. Rsch. asst. Fordham U., N.Y.C., 1945-47; intern Kings County Hosp., Bklyn., 1948-49; teaching assoc. in psychiatry SUNY Med. Ctr., Bklyn., 1950-51; staff psychologist Kings County Hosp., 1951-53; pvt. practice psychotherapy N.Y.C., 1953—; cons. N.Y. Alcoholism Vocat. Rehab., N.Y.C., 1960-62, Group Therapy Ctrs., Washington, 1969-70, Marathons for Groups in Impasse, Washington, 1972-75; conducted workshops New Sch. Social Rsch., 1969-75, 79-80; creative cons. Flight Level Video, N.Y.C., 1986—. Author: In Her Time, 1979; co-author: Psychotherapy - The Therapists Contribution, 1964, Alcoholism, 1966; contbr. articles to profl. jours.; short stories havee appeared in Quartet, Wis. Rev., Cimarron Rev.; TV appearances as "expert" on nat. shows, such as The Today Show. Feminist advocate Mayoral Election, candidate Rudy Giuliani, N.Y.C., 1989. Mem. Am. Psychol. Assn., N.Y. State Psychol. Assn., Cosmopolitan Club, Sigma Xi. Office: 223 E 66 St New York NY 10021

SAN JUAN, VIVIAN, service manager; b. Santa Lucia, Cuba, Sept. 2, 1957; d. Sabino and Clara Aurora (Alvarez) SanJ.; m. Jerry Bernard Hochberg, Sept. 20, 1980 (div. Jan. 1983); 1 child, Jeri Ana; m. Cameron L. Basden, Aug. 20, 1983. BA in Art Edn., Montclair (N.J.) State Coll., 1980. Asst. printing mailing Advertisers Print Mail Svc., Elizabeth, N.J., 1973-75; office asst. Montclair (N.J.) State Coll., 1975-79; art instr. Elizabeth (N.J.) Bd. Edn., 1980-81; customer svc. coord. Gaylin Buick Dealership, Union, N.J., 1982-83; mgr. internat. distbn. Khazindar Establishment, Hoboken, N.J., 1983-85; customer svc. rep. Mastercard Internat., N.Y.C., 1985-86, customer svc. supr., 1986-88, mgr. refund acctg., 1988-89, mgr. customer svcs., 1989—. Recipient state scholarship N.J. State Bd. Edn., Trenton, 1975, Jr. Achievement award, Elizabeth, 1974. Republican. Roman Catholic. Home: 7 East 14 St #309 New York NY 10003 Office: Mastercard Internat 888 7th Ave New York NY 10106

SANKPILL, LINDA LUCAS, investment broker; b. Rio de Janerio, Sept. 13, 1945; came to U.S., 1947; d. John T. and Marian (Schaffer) Lucas; m. J. Conrad Sankpill, July 30, 1969. BEd, U. Miami, Coral Gables, Fla., 1967. Customer svc. mgr. The Mailhouse, Mpls., 1970-72; prodn. control mgr. U.S. Caster, Lenexa, Kans., 1972-75; prodn. scheduler Yarbrough's Inc., Harlingen, Tex., 1976-78; officer mgr. A.O.C., Inc., Harlingen, 1978-80; investment broker A.G. Edwards & Sons, Inc., Harlingen, 1980—; assoc. v.p. A.G. Edwards & Sons, Inc., St. Louis, 1988—; bd. dirs., mem. adv. bd. Pan Am. U., Edinburg, Tex., 1989. Contbr. articles to newspapers. Bd. dirs. County Playhouse, Harlingen, 1982-85, Harlingen Proud Campaign, 1989; chmn. rules com. Tex. Rep. Com., Cameron County, 1987—, precinct chmn., 1986—; pres. Rep. Women, Harlingen. Mem. Inst. Cert. Fin. Planners, Cen. Tex. Soc. Inst. Cert. Fin. Planners, United Shareholders Assn., Zonta, Beta Sigma Phi (pres. 1979). Office: A G Edwards & Sons Inc 1313 E Washington Harlingen TX 78550

SANNA, LUCY JEAN, writer; b. Menomonie, Wis., Apr. 20, 1948; d. Charles Albert and Margaret Sheila (McGee) S.; m. Peter Lawrence Frisch, Jan. 2, 1971, 1 child, Katherine Sanna. BA., St. Norbert Coll., 1969; postgrad. U. Wis., Madison, 1970-74. Asst. editor Scott Foresman & Co., Glenview, Ill., 1970-73; freelance editor, Palo Alto, Calif., 1973-75; editor FMC Corp., San Jose, Calif., 1975-78; supr. corp. advt. Memorex Corp., Santa Clara, Calif., 1978-79, exec. presentations adminstr., 1979; mgr. communications svc. Electric Power Rsch. Inst., Palo Alto, 1980-87, exec. speech writer, 1988-89; mgr. exec. communications, 1989—. Office: Electric Power Rsch Inst PO Box 10412 Palo Alto CA 94303

SANNELLA, MARIA AMELIA, educator; b. Boston, May 6, 1942; d. Nicholas M. and Gloria L. (Mottola) S. BA, San Jose (Calif.) State Coll., 1964; MEd, Boston Coll., 1966, MBA, 1982, PhD, 1990. Tchr. elem. various pub. schs. Mass.; mktg. rep. Lawrence (Mass.) Gen. Hosp., 1980-82; tchr. 5th grade Arlington (Mass.) Pub., 1983—; instr. in mktg. Boston Coll., Chestnut Hill, Mass., 1988—; owner, dir. reading clinic Anthony Reading, Andover, Mass., 1980-87. Horace Mann grantee Arlington Pub. Schs., 1987. Mem. Nat. Tchrs. Assn., Mass. Tchrs. Assn., N.E. Coalition Ednl. Leaders, Arlington Edn. Assn. (v.p. 1980-81). Roman Catholic. Home: 8 Wethersfield Dr Andover MA 01810

SANQUIST, NANCY JEAN, facility management automation specialist, preservationist, architectural historian, educator; b. Muncie, Ind., Aug. 31, 1947; d. Charles Elof and Pauline Lydia (Murphy) S.; m. Jim Johnson, Dec. 1988. BA, UCLA, 1970; MA, Bryn Mawr Coll., 1973; MS, Columbia U., 1978. Instr. Lafayette Coll., Easton, Pa., 1973-74, Muhlenberg Coll., Bethlehem, Pa., 1974-75, Northampton Area Community Coll., Bethlehem, 1974-75; dir. Preservation Office City of Easton, 1977-78; cons. El Pueblo de Los Angeles State Historic Park, 1978-79; dir. restoration Bixby Ranch Co., Long Beach, Calif., 1979-82; mgr. computer applications Cannel-Heumann & Assoc., Los Angeles, 1982-84; asst. dir., account mktg. Computer-Aided Design Group, Marina del Ray, Calif., 1984—; adj. instr. UCLA, 1979-86, Grad Sch. Calif. State U., Dominguez Hills, 1981. Author numerous tech. manuals. Bd. dirs. Historic Easton, Inc., 1977-78, Simon Rodia's Towers in Watts, Los Angeles, 1979-81, Los Angeles Conservancy, 1982-86, Friends of Schindler House, West Hollywood, Calif., 1978—, pres., 1982-85. Recipient Outstanding Contbn. award Nat. Computer Graphics Assn., 1987. Mem. Internat. Facility Mgmt. Assn. (seminar leader 1987—). Home: 4 Jib St Marina del Rey CA 90292 Office: Computer-Aided Design Group 4215 Glencoe Ave Marina del Rey CA 90292

SANSONE, MARLEEN BARBARA, artist, municipal official; b. Chgo., Nov. 13, 1942; d. Douglas William and Mary (Zaloudek) Hoover; m. John R. Gabriel, Feb. 10, 1963 (div. June 1971); children: David Gabriel, Benjamin Gabriel (dec.), Naomi Gabriel; m. Joseph A. Sansone, Nov. 12, 1974 (div. Aug. 1989); 1 child, Eva Marie. Student, Sch. Art Inst. Chgo., 1960-62, Albertus Magnus Coll., 1978-80; BA, Charter Oak Coll., 1980; MA, Goddard Coll., 1982; Specialist in Creative Arts, Wesleyan U., 1984. Tchr. arts, crafts Wooster Sq. Creative Arts Workshop, New Haven, Conn., 1970-74; grantwriter United Way of Greater New Haven, 1974-79; exec. dir. Conn. Advs. for the Arts, Hartford, 1979-86, Cultural Arts Council East Haven, 1980—; tchr. art The Hammonasset Sch., Madison, Conn., 1987—; instr. art history U. New Haven. Exhibited in group shows at N.H. Colony Hist. Soc., 1985, Real Artways Artworks Gallery, Hartford, Randolph St. Gallery, Chgo.; executed murals Park City Hosp., Bridgeport, Conn., numerous other locations; contbr. articles to profl. jours. Cons. Arts Council Greater New Haven, 1980-83, New Haven Found., 1980-83. Recipient numerous prizes and awards at juried art shows in Conn. Mem. Women's Caucus for Art (pres. Conn. chpt. 1984-87), East Haven Arts Council (pres. 1977-82), Shoreline Alliance for the Arts (bd. dirs.). Democrat. Roman Catholic. Home: 43 Maltby Ave West Haven CT 06516 Office: Cultural Arts Council East Haven At the Trolley Trolley Sq East Haven CT 06512

SANT, JONI ROSE, pharmacist; b. Mckeesport, Pa., Feb. 22, 1963; d. Russell Jay and Ann Elizabeth (Wilcox) S. BS, U. Pitts., 1987. Lic. pharmacist, Pa. Pharmacist Lincoln Enterprises, Millvale, Pa., 1987; pharmacist Pharmor Inc., Pitts., 1987-89, pharmacy mgr., 1989—. Mem. Am. Pharm. Assn. Office: Pharmor #11 11685 Penn Hills Dr Pittsburgh PA 15235

SANTAELLA, IRMA VIDAL, N.Y. State supreme court justice; b. N.Y.C., Oct. 4, 1924; d. Rafael and Sixta (Thillet) Vidal; children: Anthony, Ivette. Acctg. degree, Modern Bus. Coll., 1942; BA, Hunter Coll., 1959; LLB, Bklyn. Law Sch., 1961, JD, 1967. Bar: N.Y. 1961. Sole practice N.Y.C., 1961-63, with ptnr., 1966-68; dep. commr. N.Y.C. Dept Correction, 1963-66; mem. N.Y. State Human Rights Appeal Bd., N.Y.C., 1968-83, chmn., 1975-83; justice N.Y. State Supreme Court, N.Y.C., 1983—; mem. N.Y.C. Adv. Council on Minority Affairs, 1982—, N.Y.C. Commn. on Status of Women, 1975-77. Founder, chmn. Legion of Voters, 1962-68; nat. del. Presdl. Democratic Convs., 1968, 72, 76, 80; vice chmn. N.Y. State del. 1976 Conv.; founder Nat. Assn. for Puerto Rican Civil Rights, 1962, Hispanic Community Chest Am., 1972; chmn. bd. dirs. Puerto Rican Parade, 1962-67; bd. dirs. Catholic Interracial Council, 1968-81; nat. co-chmn. Coalition Hispanic People, 1970; fund raiser Boy Scouts Am., 1962-63; chmn. Children's Camp, South Bronx (N.Y.) 41st Police Precinct, 1967; active City-Wide Steering Com. for Quality Edn., 1962-64, Community Service Soc., 1972-74, Talbott Perkins Children's Services, 1973-75, Planned Parenthood Assn., 1968-69, Puerto Rican Crippled Children's Fund, 1965-69; founder N.Y. chpt. Clinica Grillasca, P.R. Cancer Assn., 1974—. Recipient citations for civic work Gov. Rockefeller, 1972, Gov. Carey, 1982; citations for work on voting and human rights N.Y. State Assembly, 1982, P.R. Senate, 1982, others. Mem. Am. Judicature Soc. Roman Catholic. Home: 853 Seventh Ave New York City NY 10019 Office: Supreme Ct State NY 60 Centre St New York NY 10007

SANTANDREA, MARY FRANCES, lawyer; b. Melrose Park, Ill., Apr. 14, 1952; d. Francis Paul and Agnes Rose (Franch) S. BA, U. Ill., 1974, MA, 1976; JD cum laude, Santa Barbara Coll. Law, 1982. Bar: Calif. 1982, U.S. Dist. Ct. (cen. dist.) Calif. 1982, U.S. Dist. Ct. (no., so., ea. dists.) Calif., 1985, U.S. Ct. Appeals (9th cir.) 1982. Legal researcher Cavalletto, Webster, Mullen & McCaughey, Santa Barbara, Calif., 1979-80, M.J. Treman, Santa Barbara, 1980-81, Bargiel & Carlson, Santa Barbara, 1981-82; research atty. Halde, Thomas, Kallman & Hulse, Santa Barbara, 1982-83; litigation atty. Anderson & Geller, Santa Ana, Calif., 1983-85, Ambrosi & Lavoie 1985-86, Smith & Smith, Costa Mesa, Calif., 1986-88, Saxon, Alt, Dean, Mason, Brewer & Kincannon, Orange, Calif., 1988—. James scholar, 1974. Mem. ABA, Calif. Bar Assn., Los Angeles County Bar Assn., Orange County Bar Assn. Democrat. Roman Catholic. Office: Saxon Alt Dean Mason Brewer and Kincannon 333 City Blvd W Ste 1600 Orange CA 92668-2924

SANTELLO, VICKI, financial consultant; b. Rockville Centre, N.Y., Mar. 20, 1956; d. Paul F. and Estelle (Steinberg) Aden; m. John Joseph Santello. BA cum laude, Bryn Mawr Coll., 1977; MBA with honors, Boston U., 1980. Lic. commodity broker, stockbroker, ins. agt., N.Y. Trainee EEC, Brussels, 1978-79; trading asst. Dunn & Hargitt S.A., Brussels, 1979; account exec. ACLI Internat. Inc., White Plains, N.Y., 1981-84; v.p. Dean Witter Reynolds, Inc., N.Y.C., 1984-85, Drexel Burnham Lambert, N.Y.C., 1985-86; cons. CIGNA Inc., N.Y.C., 1986; v.p. Elders Futures Inc., N.Y.C., 1986-89; Shearson Lehman Hutton Inc., 1989—. Mem. LWV, NOW, Nat. Action Rights Abortion League, Princeton Club, Beta Gamma Sigma. Republican. Jewish. Home: 3703 SE 11th Pl Ocala FL 32671

SANTIAGO, RAMONA A., funeral director; b. Rochester, N.Y., Mar. 3, 1952; d. Joseph A. and Vivian E. (Nicholson) S.; children: Jessica Santiago Diaz, Gregory Santiago Diaz. BA, Kean Coll., 1985; student at law, Seton Hall U.; student, Am. Acad. McAllister, Inst. Funeral Svc., Manhattan, N.Y. Dir. Santiago Funeral Home, Newark; lectr. in field. Sponsor Newark Ironbound Little League. Recipient Cert. of Appreciation Am. Heart Assn., Boys Clubs Am., La Tribuna Newspaper. Mem. ABA (law sch. div.), Nat. Assn. Funeral Dirs., N.J. Assn. Funeral Dirs., Essex County Assn. Funeral Dirs., St. James Hosp. Aux., Mt. Carmel Soc., Crime Stoppers, Club Espana. Home and Office: 255 Lafayette St Newark NJ 07105

SANTILLO, ROSEMARY ROSS, sales executive; b. Youngstown, Ohio, Mar. 30, 1948; d. Frank and Mary Dorothy (Stanko) Ross; m. Joseph Cosimo Santillo, Feb. 5, 1972. Student, Youngstown State U., 1967-69, Sinclair Coll., Dayton, 1980-86, Wright State U., Dayton, 1982-84; BA in Sociology, Ohio State U., 1989. Lic. real estate agt. Asst. store mgr. Casual Corner, Green Bay, Wis., 1977-78; sales design cons. Vreeland Homes, Dayton, Ohio, 1986; sec. city planning comm. City of Springboro, Ohio, 1986-87; sales agt. HER Realtors Inc., Columbus, Ohio; medical sales agt. Merit Med. Systems, Inc., Salt Lake City. Artist drawing No Words Needed, 1986. Mem. Real Estate Pol. Action, Columbus Ohio, 1988, vol. Granville Hosp Aux., Dayton, 1985-86, Red Cross, Kaneohe, Hawaii, 1975-76,. Mem. Nat. Assn of Realtors, Ohio Assn. of Realtors, Columbus Bd. of Realtors, Dublin Area Realtors, Dublin Women in Bus. and Professions, Officer Wives Club. Home: 6896 Avery Rd Dublin OH 43017

SANTO, NANCY, banker; b. N.Y.C., Sept. 14, 1928; d. Ascenzio and Maria (Amodeo) S. Student, Am. Inst. Banking, N.Y.C., 1984. Typist Mfrs. Hanover Trust Co., N.Y.C., 1946-53, sec., 1953-60, asst. mgr., 1960-68, asst. sec., 1968-77, asst. v.p., 1977-84, v.p., 1984-89; ret., 1989. Mem. Nat. Assn. Bank Women (pres. 1984-85, adv. bd. 1985—), Mfrs. Hanover Trust Co. Quarter Century Club (pres. 1987—). Roman Catholic. Home: 3B Village Mall Jamesburg NJ 08831 Office: Mfrs Hanover Trust 270 Park Ave New York NY 10017

SANTOLI, JOAN MURPHY, railroad administrator; b. Boston, Jan. 5, 1961; d. Walter Francis and Margaret Ann (Utley) Murphy; m. Paul Santoli, May 7, 1988. BA in Social Scis., SUNY, Stony Brook, 1982; MS in Policy Analysis and Pub. Mgmt., Harriman Coll., Stony Brook, 1985. Assoc. staff analyst N.Y.C. Transit Authority, Bklyn., 1985-89; budget adminstr. L.I. R.R., Jamaica, N.Y., 1989—. Democrat. Roman Catholic. Office: LI Railroad 146-01 Archer Ave 1421 Jamaica NY 11435

SANTORO-PUTNAM, KAREN ANN, accounting executive; b. White Plains, N.Y., Nov. 21, 1954; d. Ernest Daniel and Dorothy Joyce (Wilson) Santoro; m. William G. Putnam, July 9, 1988; 1 child, William Bradford. Grad., Good Counsel Acad., White Plains, N.Y., 1972. Sec. Owens-Corning Fiberglas Corp., Scarsdale, N.Y., 1973-74; acctg. exec. Lawn Masters Inc., Hawthorne, N.Y., 1977-78; adminstrv. asst. to exec. v.p. Star Case Co. Inc., Pleasantville, N.Y., 1978-80; controller Frank Boufford Co. Inc., Bedford, N.Y., 1980-81; owner, pres. Santoro Office Service Inc., White Plains, N.Y., 1981—. Office: S O S Inc 200 Hamilton Ave White Plains NY 10601

SANTOS, JEAN ANNE, business consultant; b. Honolulu, May 23, 1959; d. Raymond Benjamin and Vivian Mae (Mattos) S.; m. Kenneth Mark Gilbert, May 22, 1982. BA, U. Hawaii, 1985, MA, 1989. Freelance model Honolulu, 1979-81; ptnr., sr. cons. Bus. Cons. Resources, Honolulu, 1983—. Bd. dirs. Hawaii Arthritis Found., Honolulu, 1986-88, Make A Wish Hawaii Found., 1989; bus. coord. Cec Heftel for gov. campaign, Honolulu, 1986. Mem. U.S. Assn. for Small Bus. and Entrepreneurship, Hawaii C. of C. Roman Catholic. Office: Bus Cons Resources 1164 Bishop St Honolulu HI 96813

SANTOS, LAURA MARIE, chemical engineer; b. Elizabeth, N.J., July 9, 1965; d. Anthony Manuel and Alcina (Silva) S. BSChemE, Rensselaer Poly. Inst., 1987; postgrad., U. New Haven, 1988—. Devel. engr. Olin Chems. Corp., New Haven, 1987-88, devel. engr. I, coll. recruiter, 1988—. Mem. Am. Inst. Chem. Engrs., Water Quality Assn., Olin Mgmt. Club (bd. dirs. 1989—). Republican. Roman Catholic. Office: Olin Chems Corp Hwy 933 Brandenburg KY 40108

SANTRY, BARBARA LEA, securities analyst and investment banker; b. Key West, Fla., Jan. 20, 1948; d. Jere Joseph and Frances Victoria (Appel) S. BS in Nursing, Georgetown U., 1969; MBA, Stanford U., 1978. Program analyst, br. chief U.S. Dept. HEW, Washington, 1973-76; mgr. cons. div. Arthur Andersen and Co., San Francisco, 1978-80; asst. v.p. Am. Med. Internat., Washington, 1980-83; v.p. Alex Brown and Sons, Inc., Balt., 1983-86; ptnr. Wessels, Arnold and Henderson, Mpls., 1986-88; v.p. Dain Bosworth Inc., Mpls., 1988—, sr. v.p., 1990—. Lt. (s.g.) USNR, 1967-72. Mem. Mpls. Athletic Club. Office: Dain Bosworth Inc 100 Dain Tower Minneapolis MN 55402

SAO, MARIA DA CONCEICAO, fashion designer; b. Evora, Portugal, Apr. 27, 1946; came to U.S., 1974; d. Manuel Mendes and Diamantina Maria (Sequeira) Ginja; 1 child Andre Gustav Sao; m. Georg Bo Andresen, June 11, 1964 (div. 1976); m. John Patrick Heininger, Aug. 24, 1976 (div. 1987); m. Björn Gustav Sao, Jan 1, 1989. Student, artist, designer, Aarhus, Denmark, 1964-71. Resident, Nairobi, Kenia, 1972-74; owner, designer Sao's Studio, Washington, 1975-84; pres. SAO Ltd., N.Y.C., 1983—; exhibitor, lectr. Corcoran Gallery, Washington, 1980, Smithsonian Inst., Washington, 1975-83, Textile Mus., Washington, 1979, R.I. Sch. Design, Providence, 1981, Am. Ctr. Arts, Paris, 1981. Author: Wearable Art, 1979; also articles and catalogues. Nat. Endowment Arts grantee, 1981; D.C. Commn. Arts fellow, 1981; recipient Design award Woman in Design Internat., 1981. Roman Catholic. Avocations: horseback riding, exercise. Office: SAO Ltd 202 W 40th St Suite 1201 New York NY 10018

SAPHIRE, NAOMI CARROL, banker; b. Cleve., Mar. 22, 1938; d. Ben F. and Marian (Lackritz) S.; m. Sanford M. Goldstein (div. 1979); children: Jodi Hayes, Jonathan Goldstein, Daniel Goldstein. BS, CSU, Fullerton, 1980. Tax svc. coord. ADP, LaPalma, Calif., 1980-87; conversion analyst Bank of Am., Anaheim, Calif., 1987—. Home: 707 W Santa Ana #192 Anaheim CA 92805

SAPIN, CORY ROBERTA, clinical psychologist; b. L.A., May 5, 1951; d. Abraham and Tinie Brill Sapin; m. John Reginald Forward, Mar. 21, 1981; children: Joseph Reginald, Rachel Melanie. BA, Northwestern U., 1972; PhD, U. Colo., 1979. Intern VA Outpatient Clin., Boston, 1977, VA Hosp., Bedford, Mass., 1978; tchr. MA Program Antioch Extension, Denver, 1980; psychotherapist Kaiser Permanente, Lakewood, Colo., 1981-84; pvt. practice psychotherapy Arvada, Colo., 1980-88; clin. psychologist Psychiat. Assocs., Wheat Ridge, Colo., 1988—; cons. City of Arvada, 1984—; staff assoc. West Pines Psychiat. Hosp., Wheat Ridge, 1988, Luth. Hosp., Wheat Ridge, 1989; expert witness Jefferson County (Colo.) Dist. Atty., 1987—. Recipient scholarship State of Calif., 1968, Northwestern U., Evanston, Ill., 1968-72; fellow NIMH, 1972-76. Mem. Am. Psychol. Assn., Colo. Psychol. Assn. (liaison 1988), Nat. Employee Assistance Org., Phi Beta Kappa. Home: 6650 Carr Arvada CO 80004 Office: Psychiat Assocs 10185 W 49th St Wheat Ridge CO 80033

SAPINSLEY, LILA MANFIELD, state official; b. Chgo., Sept. 9, 1922; d. Jacob and Doris (Silverman) Manfield; B.A., Wellesley Coll., 1944; D. Pub. Service, U. R.I., 1971; D.Pedagogy, R.I. Coll., 1973; m. John M. Sapinsley, Dec. 23, 1942; children—Jill Sapinsley Mooney, Carol Sapinsley Rubenstein, Joan Sapinsley Lewis, Patricia Sapinsley Levy. Mem. R.I. Senate, 1972-84, minority leader, 1974-84; dir. R.I. Dept. Community Affairs, 1985; chmn. R.I. Housing and Mortgage Fin. Corp., 1985-87; Commr. R.I. Pub. Utilities Commn., 1987—. Mem. R.I. Gov.'s Commn. on Women; commr. Edn. Commn. of States; pres. bd. trustees Butler Hosp., 1978-84; trustee R.I. State Colls., 1965-70, chmn., 1967-70; trustee U. R.I., R.I. Coll. Found.; bd. dirs. Miriam Hosp., Hamilton House, Trinity Repertory Co., Lincoln Sch., Wellesley Center for Research on Women, 1980. Recipient Alumnae Achievement award Wellesley Coll., 1974; Outstanding Legislator of Yr. award Republican Nat. Legislators Assn., 1984. Republican. Jewish. Home: 25 Cooke St Providence RI 02906

SAPORITO, RHENDA C., real estate broker, business owner; b. Dallas, Nov. 15, 1950; d. William Lee Cofer and Agnes (Chambless) Miller; m. Jerry L. Saporito, Apr. 4, 1981; children: Scott Andrew, Christopher Barrett. Student, La. State U., Baton Rouge; BS, La. Tech. U., 1974; diploma, Grad. Realtors Inst., 1979. Tchr. St. Bernard Parish, Chalmette, La., 1974-77; asst. mgr. Hyatt Regency Hotel, New Orleans, 1977-78; real estate agt. Stan Weber & Assocs., Metairie, La., 1978—; real estate broker, 1980—; owner Saporito Interiors, 1980—. Head com. Lark in the Park, New Orleans, 1988-89, Eye Ear Nose & Throat Hosp., New Orleans, 1990—; co-chmn. sugarplum ball Children's Hosp., New Orleans, 1989. Mem. La. Bar Aux., Jefferson Bar Aux., Am. Home Econs. Assn., Jefferson Bd. Realtors, La. Real Estate Commn., Kappa Delta Alumnae Assn. (sec. 1987, v.p. 1988), Tri P Investors (v.p. 1987, pres. 1988). Republican. Home: 4724 Hessmer Ave Metairie LA 70002

SAPOS, MARY ANN, advertising agency executive. Formerly with Al Paul Lefton, Inc.; gen. mgr., Yellow Pages advt. dir. Hutchins/Young & Rubicam, 1976—, from v.p. to exec. v.p. Office: Hutchins/Young & Rubicam 400 Midtown Tower Rochester NY 14604*

SAPP, KATHY CAMBRIDGE, naval officer; b. Live Oak, Fla., July 12, 1955; d. Herbert Virgil and Alma Dorothy (Livingston) Cambridge; m. Jeffrey Kendall Sapp, Mar. 5, 1978; 1 child, Jeffrey Kendall, II. BS, Fla. State U., 1977; MS, Naval Postgrad. Sch., 1983. Aviation tng. officer Naval Air Res. U., Alameda, Calif., 1977-78; div. officer Svc. Sch. Command, San Diego, 1978-81; student Naval Postgrad. Sch., Monterey, Calif., 1981-83; div. officer Naval Pers. R&D Ctr., San Diego, 1983-86; asst. chief of staff Naval Base, San Diego, 1986-89; exec. officer Pers. Support Activity Puget Sound (Bnagor), Silverdale, Wash., 1989—. Mentor Bremerton (Wash.) High Sch., 1990. Decorated Navy Commendation medal with one gold star; recipient Tribute to Womenand Industry Honor YWCA, 1988; named Navy Woman of Yr. Navy League (South Bay Cities coun.), 1984. Mem. Nat. Naval Officers Assn. (San Diego chpt., pres. 1986-87, cert. 1985). Democrat. Methodist.

SAPP, PEGGY BROTHERTON, non-profit organization administrator; b. Richlands, Va., June 27, 1942; d. Robert Burke and Ella (Payne) Brotherton; m. Neil Carleton Sapp, June 10, 1962; children: Erin Lynn Sapp Beldy, Kerrie Ellen. Student, U. Md., 1960-62; BS in Liberal Studies, Barry U., Miami, Fla., 1981. Pres. Coconut Grove (Fla.) After Sch. Ho., 1974-77; edn. coordinator Parent Resource Ctr., Miami, 1978-79; tng. dir. Jr. League Miami, Inc., Miami, 1979-80, community v.p., 1980-81, skills bank coordinator, 1981-82; founding v.p. Informed Families of Dade County, Miami, 1982, exec. dir., 1984—; pres. Transition Miami, Inc., 1981-83; mem. adv. com. Barry U. Sch. Social Work, 1988—; cons. Nat. Inst. on Drug Abuse, Washington, 1988—. Editor Informed Families Newsletter, 1985—; author, editor guide book: Miami A-Z, 1981. Bd. dirs. Nat. Fedn. Parents for Drug-Free Youth, Washington, 1988—; pres. PTSA, Coral Gables, Fla., 1981, 85; bd. dirs. Jr. League Miami, 1975-81, Urban League, Miami, 1981-82; mem. Gov.'s Challenge Program for Leadership Fla., 1981. Recipient Outstanding Edn. Project award Fedn. Jr. Women's Club, 1971. Mem. Fla. Informed Parents, Fla. Alcohol and Drug Abuse Assn., Greater Miami C. of C. (Leadership Miami 1982), NAFE, Riviera Country Club, Fisher Island Club, Kappa Delta, Delta Epsilon Sigma. Episcopalian. Home: 7201 SW 47th Ct Miami FL 33143 Office: Informed Families Dade Cty 9200 S Dadeland Blvd Ste 509 Miami FL 33156

SAPP, SHARON ANN, communications executive; b. Phila., May 26, 1952; d. Roland Robert and Nedra Lorena (Schleig) Cecconi; m. James Alfred Sapp Jr., Aug. 28, 1976. AS in Mktg., Mgmt., Montgomery County Community Coll., 1970-77. Gen. clk. Bell of Pa., Conshohocken, 1970-71; sr. clk. Bell of Pa., Conshahocken, 1971; service rep., analyst Bell of Pa., Norristown and Phila., 1971-75; dist. sec. Bell of Pa., Norristown, 1975-76; supr. Bell of Pa., King of Prussia, 1976-77; programmer, designer AT&T, Somerset (N.J.) and Phila., 1977-84; analyst, designer AT&T, Somerset, 1984-88, product mgr., 1988—. Mem. Nat. Assn. Female Execs. Democrat. Roman Catholic. Home: 26 Sunset Rd Limerick PA 19468 Office: AT&T 55 Corporate Dr Bridgewater NJ 08807

SAPPENFIELD, DIANE HASTINGS, real estate executive, civic worker; b. Marion, Ohio, Apr. 22, 1940; d. Edgar Dean and Marguerite Elizabeth (Alexander) Hastings; B.A. in Sociology and Econs., Mills Coll., 1962; tchr.'s cert. Calif. State U., Los Angeles, 1963; M.S. in Fin. and Real Estate, Am. U., 1986; m. Ronald Eugene Sappenfield, July 6, 1962; children—Derek Ronald, Ann Elizabeth. Tchr. elem. sch., El Segundo, Calif., 1963-66; asst. dir. admissions Mills Coll., 1972-74; v.p., dir. DDA Assocs., Inc., McLean, Va., 1978—; real estate investment cons., Shannon and Luchs, Washington, 1987—; asst. to chmn. bd. Watergate Complex, Washington, 1979-81; dir. corp. mktg. Watergate Devel. Inc., McLean, 1981-82; pres. Am. U. Real Estate Alumni Chpt.; Vol. tchr. Saugatuck Elem. Sch., Westport, Conn., 1976-79; active benefits for Corcoran Sch. Art, Nat. Symphony Orch., Women's Bd. Am. Heart Assn., Hope Ball, Meridian House, Washington; bd. dirs. Westport-Weston Arts Council, 1973-79, Young Concert Artists, 1984—; mem. Levitt Pavilion Governing Com., 1974-79; pres. Friends of Levitt Pavilion, 1977; trustee Stauffer-Westport Fund, 1976-79; mem. Westport Young Woman's League, 1969-79, pres., 1975-76, Jr. League of Washington D.C., 1980—; bd. dirs. Stamford-Norwalk br. Jr. League, 1977-78. Mem. Washington D.C. Bd. Realtors, Mills Coll. Club N.Y., Washington Jr. League. Home: 7612 Georgetown Pike McLean VA 22102

SAPPENFIELD, MARY FRANCES, director of university development; b. Washington, Apr. 16, 1937; d. Joseph Francis and Frances Genevieve (Oddi) McGowan; children: Charles Ross, Sarah Kathleen. BA, Trinity Coll., Washington, 1958; Cert. in Bus. Adminstrn., Harvard-Radcliff Program, 1959; student, Ball State U., 1984. Systems engr. IBM, Cambridge, Mass., 1959-61; editorial researcher Kiplinger Washington Editors, Washington, 1961-63; feature writer Ball State U., Muncie, Ind., 1983-85, editor, Coll. of Bus., 1985-86, coord. alumni and devel., 1986-88, dir. major gifts and donor rels., 1988-90; bd. dirs. Ball State U. Art Gallery, Can. Yr., Ball State U. Editor Mid-Am. Jour. of Bus., 1987; editor: Indiana's Investment Banker, 1985, Managing Change, 1986, Mexon Corporation . . . The First 70 Years, 1986; contbr. articles to profl. jours. Pres. Muncie Clean City, 1985, 86; bd. dirs. Muncie YMCA, 1985—, Muncie Children's Mus., 1981-84. Mem. CASE, Women in Communications, Art Students League (pres.), Ball State U. Women (pres. 1989-90), Art Gallery Alliance (pres. 1989-90), Jr. League of Indpls., Psi Iota Xi. Republican. Episcopalian. Office: Sweet Briar College Sweet Briar VA 24595

SAPPENFIELD, RITA CUMMINS, management consultant, educator; b. Utica, N.Y., Feb. 2, 1929; m. Robert C. Sappenfield, July 20, 1951 (div. 1986). BS, Cornell U., 1950. Ptnr., dir. profl. devel. Leadership Inst., Phila., 1955-85; mgmt. cons. Yardley, Pa., 1986—; asst. to chmn. bd. Gallup Group Cos., Princeton, N.J., 1962-72; rep. of trustees Gerard B. Lambert Awards in Healthcare, Princeton, 1970-75; sr. cons. Coun. for Continuing Edn., Richmond, Va., 1980-86; mem. adj. faculty Mercer County Community Coll., Trenton, N.J., 1987—; cons. U.S. C. of C. Insts. for Orgn. Mgmt., Washington, 1989—. Author: Things To Do until Company Arrives, 1970, Abigail Revel Cooks, 1971-74; contbr. articles to mag. Bd. dirs. YMCA Bucks County, Pa., 1977-83, 88—, YWCA Bucks County, 1978-82, Delaware Valley Symphony Orch., 1988—. Recipient vol. recognition award Children's Hosp. Phila., 1977, YWCA Bucks County, 1979, 85. Mem. NAFE, Lower Bucks County C. of C. (com. chmn., SITAWE award 1988), Am. Craft Coun., Pa. Guild Craftsmen, Friends Silver Lake Nature Ctr., Soroptimists. Republican. Presbyterian. Home and Office: 1782-A N Dove Rd Yardley PA 19067

SAPPINGTON, CHERYL ELIZABETH, government official, accountant; b. Decatur, Ill., Feb. 1, 1949; d. Milford Davis and Ruth Elizabeth (Speagle) Robb; children: Scott C., Christopher E.; m. Warren A. Sappington, Feb. 9, 1979. BS magna cum laude, Millikin U., 1984. CPA, Ill. Typist Boland Electric Supply Co., Decatur, 1967-70; ins. clk. Borg Warner Co., Decatur, 1973-74; legal sec. Record, Sappington, Healy and Wrigley, Decatur, 1974-77; agt. IRS, Decatur, 1984—. Millikin U. scholar, 1978-80, CX of CEO scholar, 1978. Mem. Nat. Acctg. Assn., Ill. CPA Soc. Republican. Lutheran. Office: IRS 306 W Eldorado St Decatur IL 62522

SAPRIEL, SHERYL-HOPE, textile executive; b. Boston, Oct. 13, 1957; d. Melvin Bernard and Anita-Claire (Goodman) Alperin; m. Jacques Sapriel, Aug. 4, 1985; children: Jeremy, Ari. AA, Fashion Inst. Tech., N.Y.C., 1977. Mgr. mdse. Halston V and VI, N.Y.C., 1977-79; buyer piece goods Calvin Klein Ltd., N.Y.C., 1979-81; owner, chief exec. officer Swatches Ltd., N.Y.C., 1981-85; buyer, mgr. sales Jo-Mar Textiles, Phila., 1985-87, F. London Textiles, Bensalem, Pa., 1987-88; owner, pres. The Fabric Stock Exch., Phila., 1988—; cons. Oleg Cassini, N.Y.C. 1981. Jewish. Home and Office: 88 Grant Dr Holland PA 18954

SARADA, THYAGARAJA, chemist; b. Madras, Tamilnadu, India, Apr. 19, 1929; d. Margam Thyagaraja and Srinivasa Ranganayaki. MA, Annamalai U., Madras, 1952; MS, Am. U., 1970, PhD, 1972. Head dept. of chemistry Padmavathi Coll., Tirupati, A.P., India, 1952-67; rsch. pool officers Cen. Leather Rsch. Inst., Madras, 1975-76; rsch. asst. Am. U., Washington, 1976-78, part-time prof., 1978-79; asst. prof., sr. chemist Celanese Rsch. Co., Summit, N.J., 1979-82; sr. chemist Pitney Bowes, Norwalk, Conn., 1982-85, mgr. applied chemistry, 1985—. Patentee in field; editor glossary of non impact printing terms, 1990. Fundraising vol. Mem. TAPPI (chmn. printing and imaging com. 1990—, chmn. task force 1990-91, session chmn. for internat. conf. 1988—), Am. Chem. Soc., Sigma Xi, Phi Kappa Phi. Democrat. Hindu. Office: Pitney Bowes 35 Waterview Dr Shelton CT 06484

SARALEGUI, CRISTINA MARIA, journalist; b. Havana, Cuba, Jan. 29, 1948; came to U.S., 1960; d. Francisco and Cristina (Santamarina) S.; m. Marcos Avila, June 9, 1984; children: Cristina Amalia, Jon Marcos. Student mass communications U. Miami. Features editor Vanidades Continental, Miami, Fla., 1970-73; editor Cosmpolitan Spanish, Miami, 1973-76, editor-in-chief, 1979-89; dir. entertainment Miami Herald, 1976-77; editor-in-chief Intimidades mag., Miami, 1977-79, TV y Novelas mag., 1986-89; hostess The Cristina Show Univision Network, 1989—. Featured in bestseller Latin Beauty, 1982; keynote speaker Union Am. Women, P.R., 1981, Lgendary Women of Miami. Mem. internat. jury Miss Venezueala Pagent, 1982, Miss Columbia Pagent, 1987. Recipient Keys to City Cartagena, Colombia, 1987. Mem. NAFE, Women in Communications (keynote speaker 1986), Am. Soc. Profl. and Exec. Women, Am. Mgmt. Assn., Nat. Network Hispanic Women (Corp. Leader award), Latin Bus. and Profl. Women's Club. Republican. Roman Catholic. Office: Editorial America SA 6355 NW 36th St Virginia Gardens FL 33166

SARANDON, SUSAN ABIGAIL, actress; b. N.Y.C., Oct. 4, 1946; d. Phillip Leslie and Lenora Marie (Criscione) Tomalin; m. Chris Sarandon, Sept. 16, 1967 (div.); children: Eva Maria Livia Amurri, Jack Henry Robbins. B.A. in Drama and English, Cath. U. Am., 1968. Actress (plays) including A Coupla White Chicks Sittin' Around Talkin', An Evening with Richard Nixon, A Stroll in the Air, Albert's Bridge, Private Ear, Public Eye, Extremities, (films) including Joe, 1970, Lady Liberty, 1971, The Rocky Horror Picture Show, 1974, Lovin' Molly, 1974, The Great Waldo Pepper, 1975, The Front Page, 1976, Dragon Fly, 1976, Walk Away Madden, The Other Side of Midnight, 1977, The Last of the Cowboys, 1977, Pretty Baby, 1978, King of the Gypsies, 1978, Loving Couples, 1980, Atlantic City, 1981, Tempest, 1982, The Hunger, 1983, Buddy System, 1984, Compromising Positions, 1985, The Witches of Eastwick, 1987, Bull Durham, 1988, Sweet Hearts Dance, 1988, A Dry White Season, 1989, The January Man, 1989, White Palace, 1990; TV appearances include The Last of the Belles, The Riders of Eldritch, June Moon, The Haunting of Rosalind, The Satan Murders, The Life of Ben Franklin, Owen Marshall, A World Apart, A.D. 1985, Mussolini and I, 1985, (serial) Search For Tomorrow. Mem. AFTRA, Screen Actors Guild, Actors Equity, Acad. Motion Picture Arts and Scis., NOW, MADRE, Amnesty Internat., ACLU. *

SARASON, ESTHER KROOP, clinical psychologist, consultant; b. N.Y.C., Dec. 14, 1918; d. Benjamin and Pauline (Gershfeld) Kroop; m. Seymour Sarason, May 22, 1943; 1 child, Julie. PhD, Clark U., 1950. Psychologist Southbury (Conn.) Tng. Sch., 1943-45; rsch. assoc. dept. psychology Yale U., New Haven, 1961-70, 88—, rssch. assoc. Inst. for Social and Policy Studies, 1970-88. Contbr. articles to profl. jours. Fellow Am. Orthopsychiat. Assn.; mem. Am. Psychol. Assn., Conn. Psychol. Assn. Home: 136 Hartley St North Haven CT 06473

SARCOPSKI, SHARON A. COLEMAN, health program quality assessment administrator; b. Wheeling, W.Va., Nov. 5, 1951; d. Raymond P. and Margaret K. (Hoffman) Coleman; children: David, Douglas. Diploma, Wheeling Hosp. Sch. Nursing, 1972; postgrad., W.Va. U., 1975-77, St. Joseph's Coll., Windham, Maine. RN, W.Va., Ohio. Pediatric staff nurse Wheeling Hosp., 1972-85; ambulatory claims coord. Health Plan Upper Ohio Valley, St. Clairsville, Ohio, 1985-89, dir. ambulatory rev. and provider rels., 1989-90, dir. quality assessment dept., 1990—. Active PTO Cen. Cath. High Sch. Boosters. Mem. NAFE, Wheeling Hosp. Alumnae. Democrat.

SARGENT, ANNEILA ISABEL, astrophysicist; b. Kirkcaldy, Fife, Scotland; came to U.S., 1964; d. Richard Anthony and Annie (Blaney) Cassells; m. Wallace Leslie William Sargent, Aug. 5, 1964; children: Lindsay Eleanor, Alison Clare. BSc, U.Edinburgh, 1963; MS, Calif. Inst. Tech., 1967, PhD, 1977. Postdoctoral rsch. fellow Calif. Inst. Tech., Pasadena, 1977-80, mem. profl. staff, 1980-88, sr. rsch. fellow, 1988-90, sr. rsch. assoc., 1990—. Contbr. articles to profl. jours. Grantee NASA, NSF. Fellow Royal Astron. Soc.; mem. Am. Astron. Soc., Internat. Astron. Union. Roman Catholic. Office: Calif Inst Tech 320-47 Downs Pasadena CA 91125

SARGENT, DIANA RHEA, corporate executive; b. Cheyenne, Wyo., Feb. 20, 1939; d. Clarence and Edith (de Castro) Hayes; grad. high sch.; m. Charles Sargent, Apr. 17, 1975; children: Rene A. Coburn, Rochelle A. Rollins, Clayton R. Weldy, Christopher J.; stepchildren: Laurie Branch, Leslie E. Sargent. IBM proof operator Bank Am., Stockton, Calif., 1956-58, gen. ledger bookkeeper, Modesto, Calif., 1963-66; office mgr., head bookkeeper Cen. Drug Store, Modesto, 1966-76; pres. Sargent & Sargent Inc., Modesto, 1976—; ptnr. R.C.D. Farms (almond ranch), Just a Little Something (antique dolls and miniatures). Mem. Stanislaus Women's Center,

Mem. NOW, San Francisco Mus. Soc., Nat. Soc. Public Accts. Office: 915 14th St Modesto CA 95353

SARGENT, PAMELA, writer; b. Ithaca, N.Y., Mar. 20, 1948. BA, SUNY, Binghamton, N.Y., 1968, MA, 1970. Am. Editor: The Bulletin of the Sci. Fiction Writers Am., Johnson City, N.Y., 1983—, mng. editor, Binghamton, 1970-73, asst. editor, 1973-75; editor (anthology) Women of Wonder, 1975, Bio-Futures, 1976, More Women of Wonder, 1976, The New Women of Wonder, 1978, (with Ian Watson) Afterlives, 1986; author Starshadows, 1977, The Best of Pamela Sargent, 1987, Cloned Lives, 1976, The Sudden Star, 1979, Watchstar, 1980, The Golden Space, 1982, The Alien Upstairs, 1983, Earthseed, 1983, Eye of the Comet, 1984, Homesmind, 1984, Venus of Dreams, 1986, The Shore of Women, 1986, Alien Child, 1988, Venus of Shadows, 1988. Office: PO Box 486 Johnson City NY 13790

SARICKS, JOYCE GOERING, librarian; b. Nov. 8, 1948; d. Joe W. and Lovella Goering; m. Christopher L. Saricks, Aug. 21, 1971; children: Brendan James, Margaret Katherine. BA with highest distinction in Eng.& Ger, U. Kans., 1970; MA in Comparative Lit., U. Wis., 1971; MA/MAT in Library Sci., U. Chgo., 1977. Reference librarian Downers Grove (Ill.) Pub. Library, 1977-80, head tech. svcs., 1980-83, coordinator lit. and AV svcs., 1983—; presenter workshops in field. Author: (with Nancy Brown) Readers' Advisory Service in the Public Library, 1989. Mem. Read Ill. adv. com., 1990. Woodrow Wilson fellow, 1970; recipient Allie Beth Martin award Pub. Library Assn., 1989. Mem. ALA, Ill. Library Assn., Adult Reading Round Table (founder), Phi Beta Kappa, Delta Phi Alpha, Pi Lambda Theta, Beta Phi Mu. Home: 1116 61st St Downers Grove IL 60516 Office: Downers Grove Pub Library 1050 Curtiss Downers Grove IL 60515

SARKISIAN, CHERILYN See CHER

SARNA, JEANNE ANNE NORMAN, home economist; b. Chgo., Apr. 10, 1952; d. Harold and Kathryn (Milivich) Norman; m. Michael T. Sarna. BS, Marygrove Coll., 1974. Cert. Home Economist. Freelancer Sarna & Assoc. Inc., Troy, Mich., 1975-86; home economist, dir. test kitchen, writer Detroit Free Press, 1989—. Cub scout leader pack 1709 Boy Scouts Am., Troy, 1985—. Mem. Mich. Home Econs. Assn. (pres. 1987-90), Detroit Metro Home Economists in Action, Home Economists in Bus., AAUW. Office: Detroit Free Press 321 W Lafayette Detroit MI 48231

SARNO, PATRICIA ANN, biology educator; b. Ashland, Pa.; d. John Thomas and Anna (Harvest) S.; B.S., Pa. State U., 1966, M.Ed., 1971; postgrad. Bucknell U., 1967, Bloomsburg U., 1970. Programmer planetarium, tchr. sci. Pottsville (Pa.) High Sch., 1967; tchr. biology Schuylkill Haven (Pa.) Area High Sch., 1967—, sci. chmn., coordinator dist., 1973—; cons. Pa. Edn. Dept., career program Pottsville Hosp. Dow Chem. Co. grantee, 1971. Mem. Pa. Edn. Assn. (exec. bd.), AAAS, Nat. Assn. Biology Tchrs., Nat. Tchrs. Assn., Pa. Tchrs. Assn., NEA, Am. Inst. Biol. Scis., Pa. Acad. Scis., Pa. State U. Alumni Assn., Schuylkill Haven Edn. Assn., Phi Sigma, Delta Kappa Gamma. Contbr. to profl. jours. Discoverer spider species Atypus snetzingeri, 1973. Home: 49 S Balliet St Frackville PA 17931 Office: Schuylkill Haven High Sch Schuylkill Haven PA 17972

SARNOFF, LILI-CHARLOTTE DREYFUS (LOLO SARNOFF), artist, business executive; b. Frankfurt, Germany (Swiss citizen), Jan. 9, 1916; d. Willy and Martha (Koch von Hirsch) Dreyfus; grad. Reimann Art Sch. (Germany), 1934, U. Berlin, 1935; student U. Florence (Italy), 1936-37; m. Stanley Jay Sarnoff, Sept. 11, 1948; children: Daniela Martha Bargezi, Robert B.L. Came to U.S., 1941, naturalized, 1944. Rsch. asst. Harvard Sch. Pub. Health, 1948-54; rsch. assoc. cardiac physiology Nat. Heart Inst., Bethesda, Md., 1954-59; pres. Rodana Rsch. Corp., Bethesda, 1958-61; v.p. Catrix Corp., Bethesda, 1958-61; inventor FloLite light sculptures under name Lolo Sarnoff, 1968; one-woman shows include Agra Gallery, Washington, 1969, Corning Glass Ctr. Mus., Corning, N.Y., 1970, Gallery Two, Woodstock, Vt., 1970, Gallery Marc, Washington, 1971, Hood Coll., Frederick, Md., 1972, Internat. Art Mart, Basel, Switzerland, 1972, Franz Bader Gallery, Washington, 1976, Gallery K, Washington, 1978, 81, Washington Project for Arts, 1980, Alwin Gallery, London, 1981, Galerie von Bartha, Basel, Switzerland, 1982, Gallery K, Washington, 1982, 83, 84, 85, 87, 88, 89, La Galerie L'Hotel de Ville, Geneva, Switzerland, 1982, Washington Women's Art Ctr., 1985, Ctr. Internat. d'Art Contemporain, Paris, 1985, Pfalzgalerie, Kaiserlautern, Fed. Republic of Germany, 1985, Gallery K, Washington, 1987, Garden Show McCrillis Gardens, Bethesda, Md., 1987, Rockville (Md.) Recreational Ctr. Garden Show, 1988, Galerie Les Hirondelles, Geneva, 1988, Rockville (Md.) Civic Ctr., 1988, Washington Square Sculpture Group, 1989, Internat. Sculpture Congress, Washington, 1990; represented in collections:Fed. Nat. Mortgage Assn., Washington, Corning Glass Ctr. Mus., Nat. Air and Space Museum, Washington, David Lloyd Kreeger Collection, Washington, Kennedy Ctr., Washington, Nat. Acad. Sci., Chase Manhattan Bank, N.Y.C., Israel Mus., Jerusalem, Nat. Mus. Women in the Arts, Washington, others. Past trustee Nat. Ballet, Mt. Vernon Coll.; pres., founder Art Barn; founder, pres. Arts for the Aging, Inc., Washington, 1988; bd. dirs. Fgn. Student Svc. Coun., Washington Performing Arts Soc. Mem. women's com., former trustee Corcoran Gallery of Art. Recipient Gold medal Accademia Italia delle Arti e del Lavoro, 1980. Club: City Tavern (Washington). Democrat. Co-inventor electrophrenic respirator; inventor flowmeter. Home: 7507 Hampden Ln Bethesda MD 20814

SAROS, CARMEN NYDIA, former educator; b. N.Y.C., Feb. 14, 1936; d. Ernesto Alejandro and Carmen Alejandra (Silva) Ruperti; m. William John Saros, July 18, 1959; children: Gregory, Lisa, Laura. BA, U. Conn., 1958; MS, Cen. State U., 1968; postgrad., St. Joseph's Coll., 1986-87. Tchr. Meriden (Conn.) Bd. Edn., 1961; chmn. math. dept. Hanover Elem. Sch., Meriden, 1981-83, chair social studies dept., 1983-84. Pres. Council Community Services, Meriden, 1985-86; bd. dirs. United Way Meriden and Wallingford, Conn., 1987-88. Recipient cert. recognition Meriden YWCA, 1986; Meriden Bd. Edn. grantee, 1986, 87. Mem. NEA, Delta Kappa Gamma. Republican. Lutheran. Home: 125 Amity St Meriden CT 06450

SARPEL, GÜNSELI, neurology educator; b. Hatay, Turkey, Sept. 9, 1945; came to U.S., 1973; d. Hüseyin Avni and Arife (Kecik) Rasa; m. C. Süleyman, Jan. 10, 1970; children: Umut, Dost. MD, Hacettepe U., Ankara, Turkey, 1969. Diplomate Am. Bd. Psychiatry and Neurology. Resident in neurology and psychiatry Hacettepe Hosps., 1969-73; resident in neurology U. Ill. Hosps., Chgo., 1973-76; rsch. asst. in neurology, asst. prof. U. Ill. Abraham Lincoln Sch. Medicine, Chgo., 1977-81; chief EMG Lab., VA West Side Med. Ctr., Chgo., 1978-81; assoc. prof. neurology, head dept. Cukurova U. Faculty Medicine, Adana, Turkey, 1981-83; asst. prof. neurology U. Health Scis.-Chgo. Med. Sch., North Chicago, Ill., 1983-85, assoc. prof., 1985—, assoc. prof. radiology, 1988—, assoc. radiology group, 1987—; attending neurologist VA Med. Ctr., North Chicago, 1983—. Contbr. articles to med. jours. Mem. Am. Acad. Neurology, Soc. Magnetic Resonance Imaging, Internat. Soc. Magnetic Resonance, Am. Soc. Neuroimaging, Chgo. Neurol. Soc. Office: U Health Scis Chgo Med Sch 3333 Greenbay Rd North Chicago IL 60064

SARRAF, ROBERTA JEAN, planning consultant; b. Pitts., Nov. 9, 1945; d. Walter H. and Margaret E. (Ondof) S. BA, U. Pitts., 1967, M in Urban & Regional Planning, 1969. Intern Rep. James G. Fulton, Washington, 1965; planner Pa. Dept. Community Affairs, Pitts., 1970-76; dir. community devel. Twp. of Upper St. Clair, Pitts., 1976-82; cons. planning Pitts., 1982—; instr. Pa. Dept. Community Affairs, 1976—; del. Environ. Planning to People's Republic of China. Creator and performer (musical program), History of Am. Popular Music. Sec., bd. dirs. Chartiers Mental Health Ctr., Bridgeville, Pa., 1986-90; vol. U. Pitts. Ann. Giving Fund, 1973—; Dem. comitteewoman, Mt. Lebanon, Pa., 1965-68, 82-88; speaker civic and svc. clubs; long range planning com. and choir Bower Hill Community Ch., elder, 1990—; mem. Presbyn. Ch. Mem. Am. Planning Assn. (pres. Pitts. chpt. 1982-83), Nat. Assn. Housing and Redevel. Ofcls. (v.p. Pitts. chpt. 1980-81), Pa. Planning Assn. (bd. dirs. 1975-76, state conf. chmn. 1981), Women in Community Devel. (charter mem.), Am. Fedn. Musicians, Grad. Sch. Alumni Assn. (chmn. com. 1987-88), Am. Inst. Cert. Planners, Three Rivers Corvette Club (activities com. 1987), Lions Club (pres. 1990-91). Democrat. Home and Office: 1316 Bowerhill Rd Pittsburgh PA 15243

SARTELLI, DEBORAH NELSON, music educator; b. Bridgeport, Conn., Mar. 9, 1953; m. Carlo Sartelli, Jan. 2, 1977; 1 child, Desiderio Nelson Sartelli. MusB in Edn., Fla. State U., 1975; postgrad., Fla. Atlantic U., 1984, Fla. Atlantic U., 1988, U. South Fla., 1986. Cert. music tchr., Fla. Tchr. music Palm Beach County Sch. Bd., West Palm Beach, Fla., 1975-80, 83—, Holy Name of Jesus Sch., West Palm Beach, 1982-83; coach, translator in Italian local opera and singers, W. Palm Beach, 1990—. Sunday sch. tchr. St. Juliana's Parish, West Palm Beach, 1988-90. Edn. Found. Palm Beach County grantee, 1985, Harriette Evans Schields Scholarship grantee, 1989. Mem. Am. Orff-Schulwerk Assn., South Fla. Orff Assn. (charter, co-pres.), Palm Beach County Classroom Tchrs. Assn., Fla. Teaching Assn., NEA. Home: 357 Churchill Rd West Palm Beach FL 33405

SARTEN, IRINE CHAMPION, educator; b. Mayfield, Ky., Jan. 10, 1943; d. Edwin Perry and Milta Malee (Henley) Champion; 1 child, Jeffery Todd. BS, Murray (Ky.) State U., 1967, MA, 1970. With Smith's Supermarket, 1963-67; tchr. bus. edn. Patoka High Sch., 1967-69; tchr. bus. edn. and math. Belleville High Sch., 1969-71; English tchr. Antelope Valley (Calif.) High Sch., 1971-72; tchr. bus. edn. and math. Mary McCloud Jr. High Sch., Washington, 1972-74; with clerical County of Graves, 1975-76; instr. McCracken Pub. Schs., Ky., 1976; with clerical Union Carbide corp., 1976-77, clk., 1977, dept. sec. project mgmt., 1972-83; sr. reports and data assoc. ops. planning Martin Marietta Energy Systems, Inc., 1983—. Bd. dirs. tng. United Way, Paducah, Ky., 1987, 88, communion program for the Homebound-Clinton United Meth. Ch.; tutor, bd. dirs. PLUS, Mayfield, 1989—; sponsor Alateen Group, Mayfield, 1989—; group rep. Alanon Group, Mayfield; mem. United Meth. Women Group; tutor Laubach Literacy Action. Mem. Nat. Inst. Bus. Mgmt., Ctr. for Creative Leadership, Profl. Bus. Women's Assn. Democrat. Methodist. Home: Rte 1 Box 123 Fulton KY 42041 Office: Martin Marietta Energy PO Box 1410 Paducah KY 42001

SARTON, MAY, author, poet; b. Wondelgem, Belgium, May 3, 1912; came to U.S., 1916, naturalized, 1924; d. George Alfred Leon and Eleanor Mabel (Elwes) Sarton; student Shady Hill Sch., Cambridge, Mass., Inst. Belge de Culture Francaise, Brussels, 1924-25; grad. Cambridge High and Latin Sch., 1929; Litt.D. (hon.), Russell Sage Coll., 1959, Clark U., 1975, U. N.H., 1976, Bates Coll., 1976, Colby Coll., 1976, Thomas Starr King Sch. Ministry, 1976, U. N.H., 1976, U. Maine, 1981, Bowdoin Coll., 1983, Bucknell U., 1985, Providence Coll., 1989, Centenary Coll., 1990. Lectr. poetry U. Chgo., Harvard U., U. Iowa, Colo. Coll., Wellesley Coll., Beloit Coll., U. Kans., Denison U., others; Briggs-Copeland instr. composition Harvard U., 1950-52. Recipient Golden Rose award for poetry, 1945, Edward Bland Meml. prize Poetry Mag., 1945, Alexandrine medal Coll. St. Catherine, 1975, Deborah Morton award, Westbrook, 1981, Ministry to Women award Unitarian Universalist Women's Fedn., 1982, Avon/COCOA Pioneer Woman award, 1983, Fund for Human Dignity award, 1984, Human Rights award, 1985, Am. Book award, 1985, Maryann Hartman award U. Maine, 1986, N.E. Author award N.E. Booksellers Assn., 1990; Bryn Mawr fellow in poetry, 1953-54, Guggenheim Found. fellow, 1954-55; Nat. Found. Arts and Humanities grantee, 1967. Fellow Am. Acad. Arts and Scis.; mem. N.E. Poetry Soc., Poetry Soc. Am. (Reynolds lyric award 1953). Author: Encounter in April (poems), 1937; The Single Hound, 1938; Inner Landscape (poems), 1939; The Bridge of Years, 1946, The Lion and The Rose (poems), 1948; Shadow of a Man, 1950; The Leaves of the Tree (poems), 1950; A Shower of Summer Days, 1952; The Land of Silence (poems), 1953; Faithful Are the Wounds, 1955; The Birth of a Grandfather, 1957; In Time Like Air (poems), 1957; The Fur Person (fiction), 1957; I Knew a Phoenix (autobiography), 1959; The Small Room, 1961; Cloud, Stone, Sun, Vine (poems), 1961; Joanna and Ulysses, 1963; Mrs. Stevens Hears the Mermaids Singing, 1965; A Private Mythology (poems), 1966; Miss Pickthorn and Mr. Hare, 1966; As Does New Hampshire (poems), 1967; Plant Dreaming Deep (autobiography), 1968; The Poet and the Donkey, 1969, Kinds of Love, 1970; A Grain of Mustard Seed (poems), 1971; A Durable Fire (poems), 1972; Journal of a Solitude, 1973; As We Are Now, 1973; Collected Poems, 1974; Punch's Secret, 1974; Crucial Conversations, 1975; A World of Light (autobiography), 1976; A Walk Through the Woods, 1976; The House by the Sea (journal), 1977; A Reckoning, 1978; Selected Poems of May Sarton, 1978; Halfway to Silence (poems), 1980; Recovering (journal), 1980; Writings on Writing (essays), 1981; A Winter Garland (poems), 1982; Anger, 1982; At Seventy, A Journal, 1984; Letters from Maine (poems), 1984; The Magnificent Spinster, 1985; May Sarton: a Self Portrait, 1986; editor: Letters to May, 1986, After the Stroke (jour.), 1988, The Phoenix Again (poems), 1988, The Silence Now (poems), 1988, Honey in the Hive (autobiography), 1988, The Education of Harriet Hatfield, 1989.

SARUBIN, MYRA NORMA, medical records administrator; b. Phila., Sept. 5, 1940; d. Abraham and Esther (Fine) Stein; m. Leonard Allen Heims, Mar. 8, 1959 (div. Jan. 1976); children: Howard Lee, Mandi Joy; m. Neil Dennis Sarubin, Sept. 17, 1976. AAS, Community Coll. Phila., 1973; BS in Health Adminstrn., Phila. Coll. Textiles and Sci., 1981; BA in Adminstrn. and Mgmt., Columbia Pacific U., 1990. Accredited record technician. Dir. med. records Oxford Hosp., Phila., 1970-74; dir. med. records and quality assurance St. Christopher's Hosp. for Children, Phila., 1974-77; dir. med. records Med. Coll. Pa., Phila., 1977-85; dir. med. records, instr. Sch. Health Scis. and Humanities Hahnemann U. Hosp., Phila., 1985—; instr. med. terminology N.E. Cath. Evening Sch., 1973-76, Community Coll. Phila., 1975-76; vis. prof. Med. Coll. Pa., 1978-85; instr. med. terminology dept. human resources, Sch. Health Scis. and Humanities Hahnemann U., 1989—. Mem. Am. Med. Record Assn., Am. Records Mgmt. Assn., Pa. Med. Record Assn., Southeastern Pa. Med. Record Assn. (pres. 1986-87, past pres. 1987-88). Jewish. Office: Hahnemann U Hosp Broad and Vine St Philadelphia PA 19102

SASEK, GLORIA BURNS, English language and literature educator; b. Springfield, Mass., Jan. 20, 1926; d. Frederick Charles and Minnie Delia (White) Burns; B.A., Mary Washington Coll. of U. Va., 1947; Ed.M., Springfield Coll., 1955; postgrad. Sorbonne, summer 1953; M.A., Radcliffe Coll., 1954; postgrad. Universita per Stranieri, Perugia, Italy, summer 1955; m. Lawrence Anton Sasek, Sept. 5, 1960. Tchr., head dept. jr. and sr. high sch. English, Somers, Conn., 1947-51, 52-59; tchr. English, Winchester (Mass.) pub. schs., 1959-60; faculty La. State U., Baton Rouge, 1961—, asst. prof. English, 1971—, chmn. freshman English, 1969-70. Recipient George H. Deer Disting. Tchr. award La. State U., 1977. Mem. MLA, South Central Modern Lang. Assn., South Central Renaissance Soc., AAUP (chpt. v.p. 1981-84). Address: 1458 Kenilworth Pkwy Baton Rouge LA 70808

SASEK, SUSAN KAYE, corporate cash manager; b. San Francisco, June 16, 1958; d. Harry Irvin and Lucille (Walker) Sheldon; m. Joseph Edward Sasek, May 12, 1984; children: Ryan Matthew, Andrew Jeremy, Kevin Timothy. Student, Golden Gate U., 1984-85. Acct. payable supr. Lane Pub., Menlo Pk., Calif., 1980-84; corp. cash mgr. Esprit de Corp, San Francisco, 1984-88. Mem. Friends of the Vineyards. Republican.

SASMOR, JEANNETTE LOUISE, educational consulting company executive; b. N.Y.C., May 17, 1943; d. Sol and Willmyra J. (Reilly) Fuchs; m. James C. Sasmor, May 30, 1965. BS, Columbia U., 1966, MEd, 1968, EdD, 1974; adult primary care nurse practitioner, U. Md., Balt., 1982; MBA, U. South Fla., 1990. Cert. adult primary care nurse practitioner, ob-gyn. nurse practitioner, risk mgr. Coord. MCH div. ANA, N.Y.C., 1972-73; MCH cons. test constrn. div. Nat. League for Nursing, N.Y.C., 1973; dir. continuing nursing edn. U. South Fla., Tampa, 1973-89; dir. edn. Continuing Edn. Cons., Inc., Sedona, Ariz., 1989—; dir. internat. study tours USSR, 1986, New Zealand/Australia, 1990. Author: What Every Husband Should Know About Having a Baby, 1972, Father's Labor Coaching Log and Review Book, 1972, 82, Childbirth Education: A Nursing Perspective, 1979. Del. White House Conf. on Families, 1980. Am. Acad. Nursing fellow, 1977, Robert Wood Johnson fellow Nurse Faculty in Primary Care, 1981-82. Mem. Internat. Coun. on Women's Health Issues (pres. 1986-90), Am. Soc. Childbirth Educators (pres.), Fla. Nurses Assn. (pres. dist. 4 1976-77), Lions (treas. Oak Creek Canyon club 1990—), Phi Theta Kappa, Pi Lambda Theta, Sigma Theta Tau, Kappa Delta Pi. Home: 235 Arrowhead Dr RR 4 Sedona AZ 86336

SASSO, ELEANOR CATHERINE, state senator; b. Fall River, Mass., Dec. 9, 1934; d. Robert Charles and Ellen (O'Hare) Ashworth; m. Louis Anthony Sasso, 1957; children—Ellen Marie, Ann Marie, Robert. B.S., Immaculata Coll., Pa., 1957. Mem. R.I. State Senate, 1979—; researcher Bur. Nat. Affairs, from 1978. Chmn. Cranston Recycling Commn., 1972-73; mem. Cranston Transvan Com., from 1973; mem. Spl. Gov.'s Commn. To Study Entire Election Process, 1977-78. Mem. LWV, Met. Nursing and Health Assn. (bd.), Common Cause, Save the Bay. Democrat. Roman Catholic. Office: R I State Senate Providence RI 02903 Other: 60 Glenmere Dr Cranston RI 02920*

SATCHEL, DORETHEA BROWNING, school administrator; b. Tallahassee, Oct. 5, 1942; d. John Arthur and Bertha (Eumar) Browning; m. Frank Richard Satchel, Mar. 27, 1966; children: Faedra Rhondelle, Roslyn Monise. BS, Fla. Agrl. and Mech. U., 1965; MEd, U. North Fla., 1977. R.N., Fla.; cert. tchr., Fla. Staff nurse Lakeland (Fla.) Gen. Hosp., 1966-68; tchr. health and sci. Mellon Elem. Sch., Palatka, Fla., 1969-71; tchr. sci., dept. head Eugene J. Butler 7th Grade Ctr., Jacksonville, Fla., 1971-82, Crestwood Middle Sch., West Palm Beach, Fla., 1982-84; asst. prin. Crestwood Middle Sch., 1985—; ind. tutor. Conf. 1st v.p., 11th Episc. Dist. Women's Missionary Soc., Fla. and Bahamas, 1973, 2d v.p., 1984-88; rep., West Palm Beach United Way, 1985-88; musician, Bethel AfricanMeth. Episc. Ch., Pompano Beach, Fla., 1987-88. Mem. Asst. Prin. Assn. Palm Beach County, Fla. A&M U. Alumni Assn., Alpha Kappa Alpha, Phi Delta Kappa. Democrat. Home: 4009 N Shelley Rd West Palm Beach FL 33407

SATELL, MARGARET COX, speech pathologist; b. Bklyn., Jan. 28, 1947; d. Jere Coleman Cox and Jane Dunseath (O'Neill) C.; m. Edward M. Satell, July 7, 1985; children: Matthew Jackson, Clifford Canan. Student Chatham Coll., 1965-67; B.A. cum laude and with distinction, Mt. Holyoke Coll., 1969; M.A., Northwestern U., 1971. Speech pathologist Berkshire Rehab. Center, Pittsfield, Mass., 1972-78, clin. supr., 1978; speech pathologist Hosp. U. Pa., Phila., 1979-86, chief speech pathology, 1985-86; instr. dept. otorhinolaryngology Med. Sch. U. Pa., 1979-86; cons. Ashmere Manor Nursing Home, Hinsdale, Mass., 1975-78, Bennington (Vt.) Convalescent Center, 1975-77. Rehab. Services Adminstrn. trainee, 1969-71. Vol. Meals-on-Wheels; bd. dirs. Tri-County Concert Assn. Recipient award for continuing edn., 1983, 86. Mem. Am. Speech Lang. and Hearing Assn. (cert. clin. competence 1973), Pa. Speech-Lang.-Hearing Assn., Southeastern Pa. Speech and Hearing Assn. Republican. Presbyterian. Clubs: Mendelssohn, Women's Faculty U. Pa., Mt. Holyoke Alumnae. Home: 1158 West Valley Rd Wayne PA 19087

SATER, GAIL BESETH, management; b. St. Cloud, Minn., Feb. 24, 1949; d. Marvin H. and Bernice (Lamb) Beseth; m. Gerald E. Klein (div. 1985) m. Robert A. Sater. BA, U. Minn., 1971; Assoc. in Risk Mgmt., Coll. Ins., N.Y.C., 1982. Underwriter Ins. Co. N. Am., Mpls., 1973; new bus. coordinator Alexander & Alexander, Mpls., 1974-76, account exec., 1976-79; casualty mgr. Control Data Corp., Mpls., 1979-82; risk mgr. Cenex, St. Paul, 1982-85, Super Valu Stores, Inc., 1985--; sec. Risk & Ins. Mgmt. Soc., Minn. Chap. 1982-83; v.p. Risk & Ins. Mgmt. Soc., Minn. Chap. 1983-84. Swimming Instr. Courage Ctr. Adaptive Aquatics, Golden Valley Minn. 1969-. Mem. Risk & Ins. Mgmt. Soc. Office: Super Valu Stores Inc 11840 Valley View Rd Eden Prairie MN 55344

SATERN, MIRIAM NELLA, physical education educator; b. Rock Rapids, Iowa, Mar. 27, 1951; d. Richard Warren and Vera Viola (Baumgarn) S. BS, Iowa State U., 1973; MS, U. Ariz., 1975; EdD, U. N.C., Greensboro, 1986. Instr. Tex. Wesleyan Coll., Ft. Worth, 1975-81, asst. prof., 1981-82; lectr. U. N.C., Greensboro, 1985-86; asst. prof. Kans. State U., Manhattan, 1986—; basketball coach Tex. Wesleyan Coll., Ft. Worth, 1975-82. Mem. Internat. Soc. Biomechanics, Internat. Soc. Biomechanics in Sports, Am. Coll. Sports Medicine, Am. Alliance for Health, Phys. Edn., Recreation & Dance, Kans. Assn. for Health, Phys. Edn., Recreation & Dance, Nat. Assn. for Phys. Edn. in Higher Edn., Nat. Strength & Conditioning Assn. Democrat. Lutheran. Home: 714 Humboldt 3 Manhattan KS 66502

SATINOVER, TERRY KLIEMAN, lawyer; b. Chgo., Apr. 25, 1936; d. Charles D. and Mary (Klieman) Satinover; student Shimer Coll., 1952-54; B.A. cum laude, U. Chgo., 1955, J.D. magna cum laude (Weymouth Kirkland scholar), 1958; m. Richard Rees Fagen, June 15, 1958 (div. June 1970); children—Sharon, Ruth, Elizabeth, Michael. Admitted to Ill. bar, 1970; practice in Chicago, 1971—; partner firm Pope, Ballard, Shepard & Fowle, Chgo., 1971—; mem. inquiry panel Ill. Atty. Registration and Disciplinary Commn., 1971-76. Bd. dirs. Congregation Rodfei Zedec, Charles Satinover Fund. Mem. Am. Friends Hebrew U. Order of Coif, Phi Beta Kappa. Jewish (v.p. congregation). Office: Pope Ballard Shepard & Fowle 69 W Washington St Ste 3200 Chicago IL 60602*

SATLOW, MARCIA FAITH ELAINE, neurologist, educator; b. Jamaica, May 1, 1949; d. Godfrey C. and Monica (Nicholson) Lawrence; m. Stephen J. Satlow, Apr. 2, 1974 (div.); 1 child, Aaron James; m. Philip Wyman Danforth, 1985. MB, BS U. W.I., 1973. Diplomate Am. Bd. Psychiatry and Neurology, diplomate Am. Bd. Electrodiagnostic Medicine. Intern Univ. Hosp. of the W.I., Jamaica, 1973-74; resident in Neurology Ottawa (Ont., Can.) Civic Hosp., 1975-77, Nassau (N.Y.) County Med. Ctr., 1977-79; asst. instr. dept. neurology SUNY-Stony Brook, N.Y., 1978-79, instr., fellow, 1979-81; vis. fellow Electromyography Neurol. Inst. of N.Y., N.Y.C., 1979-80, asst. prof., 1981-85; cons. neurologist Southbury (Conn.) Tng. Sch., 1985—, Conn. Bur. Disability Determination, Hartford, 1985—, cons. neurologist Dept. of Mental Retardation, Conn., med. dir. region 6, 1989-90, Waterford, Conn.; med. dir. United Cerebral Palsy Assn. Southeastern Conn., Inc., 1990; mem. exec. bd. Muscular Dystrophy Assn., L.I., N.Y., 1981-85. Mem. AMA, New Haven County Med. Assn., Conn. Med. Assn., N.Y. Acad. Scis, Am. Acad. Neurology, Am. Assn. Electromyography and Electrodiagnosis. Anglican.

SATO, MAKIKO, planetary scientist; b. Nishinomiya, Japan, May 29, 1947; came to U.S., 1970; d. Masakazu and Yone (Takeichi) Hayashi; m. Makoto Sato, Dec. 27, 1969; 1 child, Tomokazu Frederick. BS in Physics, Osaka U., Toyonaka, Japan, 1970; MA in Physics, Yeshiva U., 1972, PhD in Physics, 1978. Rsch. scientist Columbia U., N.Y.C., 1978; rsch. assoc. SUNY, Stony Brook, 1978-79; scientific analyst contractors to NASA, N.Y.C., 1980—; co-investigator of Voyager missions, NASA, 1980-89. Contbr. articles to profl. jours. Recipient group achievement awards NASA, Washington, 1982. Mem. Am. Astron. Soc. (div. planetary scis.). Home: 240 Anderson Ave Closter NJ 07624 Office: STX at NASA Goddard Inst for Space 2880 Broadway New York NY 10025

SATTERFIELD, MARY (YARBROUGH) MCADEN, retired educator, civic worker; b. Semora, N.C., Mar. 15, 1911; d. John H. and Ella T. (Yarbrough) McAden; A.B., Meredith Coll., 1931; postgrad. N.C. State U., 1965, U. Va. Extension, 1965, U. N.C., summer, 1963, Appalachian U., summer 1932; m. Lynn Banks Satterfield, Nov. 29, 1933; children: Lynn Banks, John De Berniere. Tchr. Caswell County (N.C.) elem. schs., 1931-34; tchr. sci. Caswell County high schs., 1934-36; postmaster U.S. Post Office, Milton, N.C., 1936-41; tchr. elem. grades Caswell County Pub. Schs., 1962-71. Clk., Town of Milton, 1959-61, sec. bd. of elections, 1976, registrar bd. of elections, 1979-81, registrar Town Bd. of Elections, 1987—; mem. Caswell County Transp. Efficiency Council, 1981-83. Named Caswell County Mother of Yr., 1980, Merit Mother of Yr. N.C. Mothers Assn., 1980. Mem. N.C., Caswell County (pres. 1962-64, sec. 1977-86) hist. assns., N.C. Assn. Educators, Nat. Ret. Tchrs. Assn., Semora Homemakers Extension, Mus. Assos. of N.C., UDC. Democrat. Baptist. Clubs: Milton Woman's (pres. 1961-62, v.p. 1962-64, sec. 1965—), Milton Community (sec. 1937-44, pres. 1965-67), Order Eastern Star.

SATTERTHWAITE, HELEN FOSTER, state legislator; b. Blawnox, Pa., July 8, 1928; d. Samuel J. and Lillian (Schreiber) Foster; B.S. in Chemistry, Duquesne U., 1949; m. Cameron B. Satterthwaite, Dec. 23, 1950 (div. July 1979); children—Mark Cameron, Tod Foster, Tracy Lynn, Keith Alan, Craig Evan. Biol. technician U.S. Dept. Agr., 1967-68; research asst. Iowa State U. Coll. Agr., 1971; lab. technician U. Ill. Coll. Agr., 1968-70; research chemist E.I. duPont de Nemours & Co., Wilmington, Del., 1951-53; research asst. Gulf Research and Devel., Harmarville, Pa., 1950; natural sci. lab. technician U. Ill. Coll. Vet. Medicine, 1971-74; rep. Gen. Assembly Ill., 1974—, chairperson House com. on higher edn., 1983—, vice-chairperson elem. and secondary edn.; mem. Commn. on Mental Health and Devel.

Disabilities, 1975-85, mem. exec. com., 1977-85, vice chairperson, 1979-85; mem. Commn. to Visit and Examine State Instns., 1977-85. Bd. dirs. East Central Ill. Health Systems Agy., 1977-79; bd. dirs. Champaign County (Ill.) United Way, 1970-74, mem. budget com., 1973-74, mem. joint rev. com. on funding Champaign County Mental Health Programs, 1973; co-chairperson Task Force on Mental Retardation for Champaign County Mental Health Bd., 1973; mem. Ill. Developmental Disability Advocacy Authority, 1977-85, vice chmn., 1979-80; chairperson Ill. House Democratic Study Group, 1979-81; mem. Edn. Commn. of the States, 1985—; mem. Nat. Conf. State Legis. Commn. on Labor and Edn., 1985—. Recipient Freshman Legislator of Yr. award Ill. Edn. Assn., 1975; commendation Ill. State's Attys. Assn., 1975; Best Legislator award Ind. Votors Ill., 1976, 78, 80, 82, 84, 86, 88, 90; cert. honor Assn. Students Govts., 1977; Disting. Service cert. Am. Vets. World War II, Korea and Viet Nam, 1977; Environ. Legis. of Yr. award Ill. Environ. Council, 1977, 79, 81, 83; Meritorious Svc. award Champaign County Council on Alcoholism, 1978, Ill. Community Coll. Trustees Assn., 1986; Perfect Voting Record award Ill. Credit Union League, 1979, Ill. Wildlife Fedn., 1979; cert. spl. recognition Ill. Women's Polit. Caucus, 1979, 80, Public Service award Izaak Walton League, 1980, Friend of Edn. award Ill. State Bd. Edn., 1985, Cert. of Appreciation Champaign County Urban League, 1987, Resolution of Honor Ill. Libr. Assn., 1987, 100 percent award Ill. State Coun. Sr. Citizens Orgns., 1989, Dare to be Great award Ill. Women Adminstrs., 1989; named Person of Yr., Champaign County Mental Health Assn., 1981, Pub. Citizen of Yr., Illini Dist. and Ill. chpt. Nat. Assn. Social Workers, 1981, Legislator of Yr., Ill. Assn. Sch. Social Workers, 1989. Mem. Ill. Conf. Women Legislators (co-convenor 1981-83), Nat. Order Women Legislators (dir. Region IV 1982, treas. 1983-84), Delta Kappa Gamma. Quaker. Office: 2031 Stratton Office Bldg Springfield IL 62706 Other: 118 E University AVe Champaign IL 61820

SATTERWHITE, DEBRA DAWN, data processing executive; b. Forest City, Iowa, Aug. 6, 1949; d. Gilbert and Nadine Hefti; m. Joseph Charles Satterwhite, III, June 20, 1971. Student Drake U., 1967-69; BS, Mankato State U., 1971; MBA, Fla. State U., 1982. Cert. mgmt. acct.; cert. data processor; cert. systems profl. Sr. programmer Mankato (Minn.) State U. Systems, 1971-74; sr. systems analyst Fla. Dept. Law Enforcement and Fla. Parole and Probation Commn., 1974-76; EDP project leader, data processing mgr. Burns Data Ctr., Fla. Dept. Transp., Tallahassee, 1976-81, dep. comptroller-systems, 1981-84, data processing mgr., 1984-89, asst. data ctr. dir. Fla. Dept. of Corrections, 1989—; mem. agencywide fin. task force, 1980. Recipient Citizenship award Hancock County (Iowa), 1967; State of Iowa scholar, 1967-69. Episcopalian. Office: Fla Dept of Corrections MIS 2601 Blairstone Towers Tallahassee FL 32399-0250

SATTLER, CAROL ANN, electron microscopist; b. DuBois, Pa., Sept. 23, 1946; d. James Lesile and Lucille Barbara (Erickson) Hinderliter; m. Gerald Leon Sattler, Aug. 8, 1971; children: Matthew Ryan, Andrew James. BA, Thiel Coll., 1968; PhD, U. Colo., Boulder, 1974. Rsch. assoc. dept. pathology U. Wis.-Madison, 1974-75, rsch. assoc. dept. oncology McArdle Lab. Cancer Rsch., 1975-77, asst. scientist dept. oncology McArdle Lab. Cancer Rsch., 1977-81, assoc. scientist dept. oncology McArdle Lab. Cancer Rsch., 1982—. Mem. AAAS, Am. Soc. Cell Biology, Midwest Soc. Electron Microscopists. Lutheran. Home: 446 Mineau Pkwy Madison WI 53711 Office: McArdle Lab Cancer Rsch 1400 University Ave Madison WI 53706

SATURDAY, KAREN RENÉE, insurance company executive; b. Wichita, Kans., June 19, 1961; d. Irving and Patricia (Hamilton) Bird; m. Shawn Bryant Saturday, Oct. 15, 1987. BA, Wichita State U., 1986. Claims rep. State Compensation Ins. Fund, San Bernardino, Riverside, Calif., 1986-89; sr. claims examiner, workers compensation claims supr. Alexsis Risk Mgmt., West Covina, Calif., 1989—; cons., speaker Med. Office Mgmt., Montclair, Calif., 1989-90; mng. dir. Intervention, San Bernardino, 1990—. Democrat. Office: Alexsis Risk Mgmt 1501 NW Cameron Ave Ste C300 West Covina CA 91790

SATYSHUR, ROSEMARIE FRANCES DIMAURO, nurse educator, researcher; b. Camden, N.J., Oct. 8, 1955; d. Valentino Raymond and Rosemaria Carole (Fulginiti) DiMauro; m. Michael Peter Satyshur, June 16, 1984; children: Matthew Valentino, Maria Francine. Diploma, Helene Fuld Sch. Nursing, 1976; BSN, Thomas Jefferson U., 1982; MSN, Cath. U. Am., 1984, DNSc, 1990. Primary nurse West Jersey Hosp., Voorhees Twp., N.J., 1976-77; infant care coord. Thomas Jefferson U. Hosp., Phila., 1977-80, advanced staff nurse transport and cardiac catheterizaton teams, 1980-82; clin. and theoretical instr., clin. assoc., rsch. assoc. Cath. U. Am. Sch. Nursing, Washington, 1984-86; nursing tutor Edward Klein Tutoring Svc., Washington, 1986; teaching asst. Cath. U. Am. Sch. Nursing, Washington, 1986-88; pvt. practice Pediatric Home Health Care, 1986—. Contbr. articles to profl. jours. Recipient various scholarships and grants. Mem. Am. Nurses Assn., Md. Nurses Assn., Assn. for Care of Children's Health, Coun. Maternal Child Nursing, Sigma Theta Tau. Republican. Roman Catholic. Home: 7030 Storch Ln Seabrook MD 20706

SATZ, PHYLLIS ROBYNE SDOIA, musician, educator; b. N.Y.C., Feb. 23, 1935; d. Candido and Helen (Borsody) Sdoia; m. Barry Satz, Feb. 16, 1957; children: Stephen Mark, Rana Bambi, Michael Eric, Martin Craig. AA summa cum laude, Miami Dade Community Coll., 1981; BA summa cum laude, Fla. Internat. U., 1983; postgrad., U. Miami, Fla., 1983-85. Classical concert pianist, 1952—; dir. Sdoia Satz Music Inst., Miami, Fla., 1983—; music dir., St. Paul's Meth. Ch., Miami, 1985—, Shores Sch., Miami, 1986—; instr. music, Miami Dade Community Coll., 1987—; presents seminars, master classes to music tchrs., orgns. Solo debut Carnegie Hall, N.Y.C., 1952; featured soloist, numerous orchestras, U.S., Can., Mex., Bermuda; author: The Acquired Art of Teaching Music: A Basic Text, 1990. Lt., Aux. Police Svcs., N.Y.C., 1965-78. Winner Naumberg Competition, N.Y.C., 1951, Young Am. Artist, 1952, Mus. Artists in the Schs., 1952, Levintritt Piano Competition, 1953. Mem. NAFE, ASCAP, Music Educators Nat. Conf., Music Tchrs. Nat. Assn., Nat. Guild Piano Tchrs., Am. Coll. Musicians, Bandmasters Assn., Trumpet Guild, Orangists Guild, Hillel, Phi Theta Kappa. Democrat. Jewish. Office: Sdoia Satz Music Inst 256 NE 85th St Miami FL 33138

SAUER, MARY JULIA, educator; b. Pitts., Oct. 10, 1949; d. Edward Henry and Julia Ann (Polkabla) S.; 1 child, Jason Michael Sauer. BS in Art Edn., Edinboro State Coll., 1971; MS in Spl. Edn., Clarion State Coll., 1980; postgrad, U. Pitts., 1988—. Cert. art tchr., spl. edn. tchr. for mentally retarded. Tchr. Polk (Pa.) State Sch. & Hosp., 1971-72; vol. VISTA, Bath, N.Y., 1972-73; tchr. Polk Ctr., 1973-80, program specialist, 1980—; lectr., speaker, video on local TV on history of Polk Ctr., 1987. Patentee beer bottle shaped cake pan, 1987; cakes displayed in various mags.; creator local history video. Mem. Internat. Cake Expn. Soc. Democrat. Roman Catholic. Home: PO Box 98 Stoneboro PA 16153

SAUERBREY, ELLEN ELAINE RICHMOND, state legislator; b. Balt., Sept. 9, 1937; d. Edgar Arthur and Ethel Frederika (Landgraf) Richmond, m. Wilmer John Emil Sauerbrey, June 27, 1959. AB summa cum laude in Biology and English, Western Md. Coll., 1959. Biology instr., chmn. sci. dept. Baltimore County Sch. System, 1959-64; dist. mgr. Baltimore County U.S. Census, 1970; mem. from 10th legis. dist. Md. Ho. of Dels., Annapolis, 1978—, minority leader, 1986—. Del. Rep. nat. convs., 1968, 76, 84, 88, mem. credentials com., 1984, mem. platform com., chmn. subcom. on the economy; vice chmn. Rep. State Cen. Com. of Balt. County, 1966-71; trustee Md. Coun. Econ. Edn., Franklin Sq. Hosp. Named Legislator of Yr., Md. Assn. Bldrs. and Contrs., 1982; recipient Pvt. Property award Greater Balt. Bd. Realtors, 1984; named Western Md. Coll. Alumni of the Yr., 1988. Mem. DAR, Md. Fedn. Rep. Women, Am. Legis. Exec. Coun. (nat. chmn., Legislator of Yr. 1986), Nat. Taxpayers Union, Md. Farm Bur., Women Legislators of Md., So. Legis. Conf. (econ. devel., trade and commerce com.), Md. Conservative Union, Beta Beta Beta. Presbyterian. Office: Md Ho of Dels Lowe House Office Bldg Annapolis MD 21401

SAUL, BARBARA ANN, educator; b. Vincennes, Ind., Feb. 20, 1940; d. Charles Dudley and Essie Faye (York) Green; children: Beth Suzanne, Becca Lynn, Brian William. BA with honors, So. Ill. U., Carbondale, 1961; MS, So. Ill. U., Edwardsville, 1988. Cert. Eng. elem. tchr., Mo., spl. reading K-12, Mo., lang. arts spl. K-12, Ill., Eng. 2-12, Ill. English tchr. James Island High Sch., Charleston, S.C., 1961-63, Waterloo (Ill.) High Sch., 1963-65; instr. rhetoric and composition Belleville Area Coll., 1966-67; homebound tchr. Belleville Twp. High Sch., 1966-73; Title I reading tchr. Freeburg (Ill.) Community High Sch., 1973-80; grad. asst. So. Ill. U., Edwardsville, 1986-87; reading specialist Hazelwood Schs., St. Louis, 1987—; instr. Lion's Quest, 1988—; team mem. Write-On project, Highland (Ill.) Community Schs., 1980-81; clinician Edwardsville Adult Literacy Prescription Project, 1986-88. Bd. dirs. preschool 1st Presbyn. Ch., Belleville, 1969-73; mem. coun., conf. del. Evang. United Ch. of Christ, Highland, 1979-85, mem. choir, 1985-87; del. St. Louis Assn. United Ch. of Christ, 1988—; mem. Jr. High Reading Curriculum Revision Com. Mem. NEA, Internat. Reading Assn., Mo. Reading Assn., St. Louis Suburban Reading Coun., Phi Kappa Phi, Kappa Delta Pi, Sigma Kappa. Home: 3017 Willow Creek Estates Florissant MO 63031 Office: Kirby Jr High Sch 1865 Dunn Rd Saint Louis MO 63138

SAUL, CONNIE CLINE, educator; b. Portsmouth, Va., Aug. 26, 1954; d. Barry Armstrong and Alice Grayson (Henderson) Cline; m. Robin Alan Saul, Apr. 28, 1979; 1 child, Bryan Geoffrey. BS in Edn., Old Dominion U., 1976, MS in Edn., 1982; Student, Coll. of William & Mary, 1989—. Instrl. specialist Chesapeake (Va.) Pub. Schs., 1976-85, tchr., 1985—; presenter, cons. workshops in field; mem. Supt.'s Planning Coun., Chesapeake. Mem., v.p. Polit. Action Com., CEA, Chesapeake, 1983-85. Recipient Disting. Svc. award Norfolk Highlands PTA, Chesapeake, 1983, Leadership Effectiveness award Va. Commonwealth Leadership, 1988; Hampton Rhoads Inst. for Advanced Study fellow, 1989. Mem. Assn. Supervision and Curriculum Devel., Salem Woods Civic Assn., Phi Delta Kappa, Alpha Delta Kappa (historian 1986-88, rec. sec. 1988-90, v.p. 1990-92), Delta Kappa Gamma (rec. sec. 1988-90, v.p. 1990—), Sigma Sigma Sigma. Democrat. Baptist. Home: 1412 Chartfield Ct Virginia Beach VA 23456 Office: Chesapeake Pub Schs 1420 Great Bridge Blvd Chesapeake VA 23320

SAUL, DEBORAH MANGUM, infosystems executive; b. New Orleans, Jan. 26, 1963; d. James Alfred and Barbara Elizabeth (Hopkins) Mangum; married, 1989. BS in Mgmt. Sci., So. Meth. U., 1985. Mgr. printing and distbn. Southwestern Bell Telephone Co., Dallas, 1985-86, mgr. computer ops., 1986-87, mgr. user adminstrn., disbursements and payroll processing, 1987-90, mgr. bus. computing support, 1990—. Small bus. solicitor for 1989 campaign United Way, 1988; vol. Suicide and Crisis Prevention Ctr., Dallas, 1990—. Mem. Toastmasters Internat. Republican. Presbyterian. Home: 18625 Midway Rd #1304 Dallas TX 75287

SAUL, NANCY GOODWINE, executive director cultural organization; b. Bellefontaine, Ohio, Oct. 20, 1952; d. Robert Samuel Jr. and Betty Jane (Baxley) Goodwine; m. Roger Allen Saul, Aug. 3, 1974; children: Justin, Kathryn, Amy. BA, Ohio State U., 1975. Unit sec. Ohio State Univ. Hosps., Columbus, 1972-74; dir. Child Care Program YMCA Camp Willson, Bellefontaine, Ohio, 1986-87; exec. dir. Internat. Friendship Ctr., Bellefontaine, 1988—. Advisor 4-H Club, Bellefontaine, Ohio, 1987—; pres. Sch. PTO, Bellefontaine, 1988; instr. Sat. Enrichment Acad., Bellefontaine, 1987—. Mem. AAUW, Ohio Tchrs. of ESL, The Art Club (v.p.), Theta Circle of King's Daughters (pres. 1985). Methodist. Home: 862 E Sandusky Ave Bellefontaine OH 43311 Office: Internat Friendship Ctr 117 E Columbus Bellefontaine OH 43311

SAULNESS, FIONA, real estate executive; b. Manchester, Eng., Jan. 15, 1956; came to U.S., 1956; d. Douglas Munro Masters and Joan Elina (Gerrard) Hall; m. Robert Paul Saulness, July 11, 1981. Grad. high sch., Seattle. Legal sec. Foster, Pepper and Riviera, Seattle, 1974-78; salesperson, mgr. West Coast Homes Real Estate Co., Seattle, 1978-84; salesperson, trainer Home Realty, Inc., Seattle, 1984-88, Windermere Real Estate, Seattle, 1988—. Episcopalian. Office: Windermere Real Estate 10004 Aurora Ave N Ste 10 Seattle WA 98133

SAUM, ELIZABETH PAPE, community volunteer; b. Evanston, Ill., Aug. 7, 1930; d. Karl James and Catherine (Schwall) Pape; m. William Joseph Saum, Dec. 31, 1960; children: JeanMarie, Katherine Anne, Mary Elizabeth. BA in English cum laude, Fontbonne Coll., 1952; MA in English, Northwestern U., 1958. Cert. tchr., Ill. Tchr. Our Lady of Perpetual Help, Glenview, Ill., 1952-55, Wilmette (Ill.) Jr. High Sch., 1955-61; dir. religion edn. St. Paul's Ch., Valparaiso, Ind., 1972-76; activities dir. Heritage Manor Nursing Home, Plano, Tex., 1982-84; exec. dir. Jessamine County Assn. Exceptional Citizens, Nicholasville, Ky., 1985-89; ret., 1989. Pres. bd. dirs. Women's Neighborly Orgn., Lexington, 1977-81, Bluegrass Long-Term Ombudsman, Lexington, 1984-89, pres., 1986-88; bd. dirs. Women's History Coalition of Ky., Midway, 1985-90; creator, pres. Ky. Women's Heritage Mus., Lexington, 1986-90. Mem. AAUW (bd. dirs. 1977-81, 84-90, named gift Ky. div. 1988-90, Gift honoree Lexington br. 1987, pres. Lexington br. 1984-86, 88-90, editor newsletter Louisville br. 1990-91), Bluegrass Assn. for Retarded Citizens, Newcomers (newsletter editor 1976-78). Democrat. Roman Catholic. Home: 7004 Fox Valley Ct Prospect KY 40059

SAUNDERS, ANTOINETTE MERCIER, psychologist, educator; b. Detroit, Sept. 30, 1947; d. Frank Breckenridge and Barbara (Shuell) S.; m. Terrence Joseph, Nov. 26, 1986; 1 child, Annie. BS, St. Louis U., 1969; MEd, U. Tex., El Paso, 1970; PhD, St. Andrews U., Dundee, Scotland, 1972. Lic. psychologist, Ill. Postdoctoral fellow Loyola U., Chgo., 1972-74; asst. prof. psychology U. Ill. Med. Sch., Chgo., 1974-80; dir., founder Stress Edn. Ctr. (now Capable Kid Ctr.), Evanston, Ill., 1980—; faculty family studies, Northwestern U., Evanston, 1978—. Author: Stress Proof Child, 1984, (curriculum) Capable Kid Program, 1980—. Mem. Am. Psychol. Assn., Ill. Psychol. Assn., Nat. Coun. on Self Esteem. Office: Capable Kid Orgn 1615 Orrington Ave Evanston IL 60201

SAUNDERS, BEATRICE NAIR (MRS. DERO AMES SAUNDERS), editor, association executive; b. New Britain, Conn., Dec. 26, 1915; d. Frank and Sophie (Adler) Nair. B.A., Smith Coll., 1936; m. Dero Ames Saunders, May 23, 1936; children: David Nair, Richard Ames. Tchr. pub. schs., New Britain, 1936; editorial asst. Cordon Co., N.Y.C., 1937-39, Family Welfare Assn. Am., N.Y.C., 1939-42; supr. editorial div. publs. div. ARC, Washington, 1943-46; free-lance editor various publs. N.Y.C., 1946-50; editor-in-chief, publs. dept. Girl Scouts U.S., N.Y.C., 1950-55; dir. publs. dept., editor Social Work, Nat. Assn. Social Workers, N.Y.C., 1955-82, publs. cons., 1982—; mem. adj. faculty, editor-in-residence Grad. Sch. Social Svcs., Fordham U., Lincoln Ctr., N.Y.C., 1982—; cons. Sch. of Social Work, Rutgers U., New Brunswick, N.J., 1985—. Founding editor Affilia, Jour. Women and Social Work, 1986—. Vol. ARC, Freeport, L.I., 1946-47, Child Care Ctr., Freeport, 1946-47; chmn. parents assn. Downtown Community Sch., 1948-50; chmn. 22d-21st St. Community Coun., 1954-58, 62-63; chmn. com. on existing housing Chelsea Community Coun., 1957-60; vice chmn. Chelsea Com. for Neighborhood Devel., 1960-63, chmn., 1963-65; sec. West 400 Block Assn., 1987—. Clubs: Smith Coll., Heights Casino. Home: 446 W 22d St New York NY 10011

SAUNDERS, CAROL SILVER, healthcare administrator; b. Rochester, N.Y., May 21, 1953; d. Lester and L. Beulah (Gossin) Silver; m. Jerome Lewis Saunders, Aug. 18, 1974; children: Jason Matthew, Benjamin Stephen, Charles Andrew. BS, Ithaca (N.Y.) Coll., 1974; postgrad., Cornell U., 1974-75; MA, Cen. Mich. U., 1984. Dir. community rels. Beloit (Wis.) Meml. Hosp., 1979-84; dir. pub. rels. Rockford (Ill.) Meml. Hosp., 1984-87; v.p. The Stamford (Conn.) Hosp., 1987—; instr. Blackhawk Tech. Inst., Janesville, Wis., 1980-83. Chmn. pub. svc. United Way, Stamford, Conn., 1988, Stateline United Way, Beloit, 1980-84, gen. campaign chmn., 1983-84. Mem. Am. Soc. Hosp. Mktg. and Pub. Rels. (cert.), Fairfield County Pub. Rels. Assn., Women in Communications, N. England Hosp. Pub. Rels. Assembly. Office: The Stamford Hosp PO Box 9317 Stamford CT 06904

SAUNDERS, JOYCE CAROL, commercial interior designer; b. Winchester, Mass., Feb. 16, 1938; d. Richard Oswald and Rosalie Alda (Blaisdell) Skane; 1 child, Diane Carol. MA, Boston U., 1955-56, New England Sch. of Art and De, Boston, 1969. Designer, space planner John Hancock Mutual Life Ins. Co., Boston, 1969-72, from sr. project mgr. to mgr., 1974-87; v.p. Jordan A. Berman Assocs., Boston, 1972-74; dir. Boston Coll., 1987—; mem. adv. bd. Boston Design Ctr., 1982—, CADD FM Conf., N.Y.C., 1986, Workplace Environment, Edison, N.J., 1986—, Wentworth Inst. Tech., Boston, 1988—. Mem. Inst. of Bus. Designers (nat. dir. 1983-85, pres. New England chpt. 1981-83), Internat. Facility Mgmt. Assn. Office: Boston Coll Brock House 78 Coll Rd Chestnut Hill MA 02167

SAUNDERS, KAREN ESTELLE, educator; b. San Carlos, Ariz., June 13, 1941; d. Walter Carl and Irma Marie (Gallmeyer) Sorgatz; m. John Richard Saunders, Dec. 27, 1962 (div. Nov. 1981). BA, Ariz. State U., 1964, MA, 1968, postgrad., 1982—. Tchr., chair art dept. Corona del Sol High Sch., Tempe, Ariz., 1977—, chair fine arts dept., 1987—; tchr., chair art dept. McClintock High Sch., Tempe, 1964-77; coord. artists-in-schs. program Tempe Union High Sch., 1975-80, program adminstr. travel/study program, 1976-78, 80; program chair Four Corners Art Educators Conf., Scottsdale, Ariz., 1982; co-chair S.W. Indian Art Collectibles Exhbn., Carefree, Ariz., 1982, also editor, designer catalogue; mem. adv. editorial bd. Sch. Arts Mag., 1989—. Mem. State Art Guide Com., Tempe, 1975-77; mem. planning com. Sheldon Lab. Systems Facilities, 1980-83; chmn. Tempe Sculpture Competition, Fine Arts Ctr., 1983; bd. dirs. Ariz. Scholastic Art Adv. Bd., Phoenix, 1983-87; judge Mill Avenue Arts Festival, Tempe, 1989. Recipient Vincent Van Gogh award Colo. Alliance for Arts Edn., 1978, Ariz. Art Educator of Yr. award Ariz. Art Edn. Assn., 1979, award Four Corners Art Educators Conf., 1982, Lehrer Mel. award Ariz. State U. Sch. Art, 1986; Ariz. State U. fellow, 1967-68. Mem. NEA, Nat. Art Edn. Assn. (v.p., bd. dirs. 1980-82, editorial bd. 1982-85, Secondary Art Educator of Yr. Pacific region 1985), Ariz. Alliance for Arts Edn. (bd. dirs. 1976-81, co-chair western regional conf. 1978), Tempe Secondary Edn. Assn., Ariz. Art Edn. Assn. (pres. 1976-78), Mortar Bd., Phi Delta Kappa, Alpha Phi. Club: Women's Image Now (Tempe). Home: 930 S Dobson Rd #22 Mesa AZ 85202 Office: Corona del Sol High Sch 1001 E Knox Rd Tempe AZ 85284

SAUNDERS, KATHRYN A., retired data processing administrator; b. Elgin, Minn., Apr. 12, 1920; d. William P. and Mathilda M. (Mielke) Hagner; m. James L. Saunders, June 14, 1952; children: Gary, Wade, Brian. BA, U. Calif., Berkeley, 1941; cert., Coll. of Marin, Kentfield, Calif., 1948. Mem. gen. staff Fed. Res. Bank, San Francisco; with civilian pers./payroll dept. USAF, Hamilton AFB, Calif.; coord. data processing Sir Francis Drake High Sch., San Anselmo, Calif. Sec. program resource United Meth. Women, 1988—; active First United Meth. Ch. Mem. AAUW, Calif. Sch. Employees Assn., Calif. Scholarship Fedn. (life), Nat. Assn. Ret. Fed. Employees, Calif. Alumni Assn., Delta Zeta. Address: 118 Tamal Vista Dr San Rafael CA 94901

SAUNDERS, LAUREL BARNES, librarian; b. Ainsworth, Nebr., Aug. 17, 1926; d. Howard Enos and Flossie Agnes (Marr) Barnes; married; 1 child, Kelvin Edwin Saunders. BA, U. S.D., 1948; MA, U. Mich., 1950. Librarian pub. schs. Howell, Mich., 1950-51; asst. librarian, U.S. Army post Ft. Bliss, Tex., 1951-53; base librarian Biggs Army Airfield Was Biggs AFB, Ft. Bliss, Tex., 1953-62; supervisory librarian U.S. Air Def. Sch., Ft. Bliss, Tex., 1962-64; chief cataloguing and acquistions U.S. Army Tech. Library, White Sands (N.Mex.) Missile Range, N.Mex., 1964-74; chief librarian U.S. Army Tech. Library, White Sands (N.Mex.) Missile Range, 1975—. Pres. Quaestors Sunday Sch. class, Trinity First Meth. Ch., 1985-89, adminstrv. bd., 1986-87. Mem. Fed. Mgrs. Assn. (2d v.p. 1982-83, 1st v.p. 1989, pres. 1984-87, 90, bd. dirs., Mgr. of Yr. award 1985, sec. 1988), N.Mex. Libr. Assn. (vice-chmn. Documents Roundtable 1984-85, chmn. 1985-86), Border Regional Libr. Assn., U.S. Army Libr. Inst. (active procurement working group 1980-84), Past Matrons Club, Order of Eastern Star (Worthy Matron 1970, treas. 1982-90).

SAUNDERS, LUCY LEATHERBEE, writer; b. Birmingham, Mich., Oct. 21, 1957. AB, Hamilton Coll., Clinton, N.Y., 1981. Communications assoc. Arthur Andersen & Co., Chgo., 1981-83, SPSS Inc., Chgo., 1983-85; communications mgr. Heidrick and Struggles, Chgo., 1985-87; assoc. editor Fancy Food Mag., Chgo., 1988-89; freelance food writer Chgo., 1989—p. Co-author: Heartland Cuisine, 1989; contbr. articles to profl. jours. and newspapers. Mem. Am. Inst. Wine and Food, Internat. Foodsvc. Editorial Coun., Chgo. Culinary Guild (bd. dirs. 1988-90), Culinary Historians, Phi Beta Kappa. Office: 2250 N Lincoln Ave Ste 131 Chicago IL 60614-2389

SAUNDERS, PATRICIA GENE, computer consultant; b. Tulsa, Okla., Nov. 29, 1946; d. Eugene Merritt and Patricia May (Hough) Knight; m. George Wesley Person, Jr., Aug. 29, 1971 (div. 1974); m. Kenneth Deward Vincent, Dec. 29, 1975 (div. 1985); m. Joseph Eugene Saunders, June 24, 1989. BA, Baylor U., 1969. Tchr. Arlington (Tex.) Ind. Sch. Dist., 1971-77, Garland (Tex.) Ind. Sch. Dist., 1977-79; spl. projects assoc. Electronic Data Systems, Dallas, 1979-81; adminstrv. asst. Diversifield Innovators, Dallas, 1981-82; system ops. mgr. Span Instruments, Plano, Tex., 1982-86; data processing mgr. Claire Mfg., Addison, Ill., 1986-87, Everpure, Inc., Westment, Ill., 1987-88; software cons. Software Alternatives, Inc., Downers Grove, Ill., 1988-89; data processing asst., cons. J&J Maintenance, Inc., Austin, Tex., 1989-90; pres. Cardinal Software Solutions, Inc., Austin, 1990—. Active IBM Bus. Ptnr. Program. Mem. Mapics User Group Ill., Morton Arboretum, Smithsonian Instn., Dallas Mus. Fine Arts, Greater Austin C. of C., Austin Assn. Women in Computing. Republican. Baptist. Home: 12524 Taylor Rd Buda TX 78610 Office: Cardinal Software Solutions Inc PO Box 19400 Ste 466 Austin TX 78760-9400

SAUNDERS, PHYLLIS S., financial and business consultant; b. N.Y.C., May 2, 1932; d. Jack and Bella (Bader) Bloom; widowed; children: Todd B., Dean B. Student, U. Miami, 1950—. Pres. P.S. Export Co., buying service, bus. cons., fin. cons., money mgmt. for Cen. and S.Am., Bahamas, Caribbean, 1971—; cons., investor since 1961. Mem. Am. Bus. Women's Assn., Nat. Assn. Women Bus. Owners, Am. Liver Found., Am. Jewish Com., Nat. Home Asthmatic Children, Hope Ctr. Mentally Retarded, U. Miami Booster Club, U. Miami Ctr. for Liver Diseases, U. Miami AIDS Research Ctr., Fla. Feminist Bank. Republican. Avocations: golf, tennis, aerobics, fishing, boating. Home: 2 Grove Isle Apt #205 Coconut Grove FL 33133

SAUNDERS, REBECCA ANN, educator; b. Charlotte, N.C., Apr. 12, 1949; d. John Marshall Saunders and Barbara (Williams) Polk. BA in English, Music, U. Mass., 1978; MA, Tufts U., 1982, PhD, 1990. Tchr. Bay State Jr. Coll., Boston, 1979-81, U. Mass., Boston, 1976-79, 82; teaching asst. Tufts U., Medford, Mass., 1981-82, tchr.; cons., editorial asst. Bedford Books, Boston, 1985-87; rhetoric assoc. Boston U., 1986; lectr. in English, U. Mass., 1982--, seminar leader Syntax the Word Co., Milton, Mass., 1984--. Mem. Modern Language Assn., New England Modern Language Assn., Canadian Assn. Asian Studies, Am. Assn. Asian Studies, Southeastern Nineteenth Century Studies. Democrat. Home: 71 Jay St Cambridge MA 02139

SAUNDERS, RUTH LYNCH, psychoanalyst, psychotherapist; b. Longview, Wash., Nov. 4, 1927; d. Harry Hudson and Marion Lucille (Gibson) Lynch; BS, UCLA, 1949; MSW, Columbia U., 1976; cert. Psychoanalytic Tng., Inst. for Contemporary Psychotherapy, 1979; m. Frank A. Saunders, May 24, 1958 (dec. Oct. 1989); 1 child, Anthony David. Projects editor The Sat. Rev. of Lit., N.Y.C., 1960-65; asst. med. editor McCall's, N.Y.C., 1965-67; editor Warner Bros., N.Y.C., 1967-69, Roche Med. Image, 1969-73; tng. analyst, supr., Inst. for Contemporary Psychotherapy, N.Y.C., 1976—; supr. staff Ctr. for the Study of Anorexia and Bulimia, N.Y.C., N.Y., 1979—; pvt. practice, N.Y.C. Mem. Manhattan adv. bd. N.Y. Urban League, 1962-74, pres. Lucy Stone League, 1972-74. Diplomate Nat. Assn. Social Workers (cert.); mem. Phi Beta Kappa, Alpha Mu Gammaa. Clubs: Sankaty Head Golf, Siasconset Casino (Nantucket, Mass.). Home: 680 West End Ave 9B New York NY 10025 Other: Box 248 Siasconset MA 02564 Office: 940 Park Ave New York NY 10028

SAUNDERS, SALLY LOVE, poet, educator; b. Bryn Mawr, Pa., Jan. 15, 1940; d. Lawrence and Dorothy (Love) S. Student, Sophia U., Tokyo, Japan, 1963, U. Pa., Columbia; B.S., George Williams Coll., 1965. Tchr. Shipley Sch., Bryn Mawr, 1962-65, Agnes Irwin Sch., Wynnewood, Pa., 1964-65, Montgomery County Day Sch., Wynnewood, 1962, Miquon (Pa.) Sch., Waldron Acad., Merion, Pa., 1965-66, Phelps Sch., Malvern, Pa., 1965-70, Frankford Friends Sch. Phila., 1965-66, Haverford (Pa.) Sch., 1965-66, Friends Sem. Sch., N.Y.C., 1966-68, Ballard Sch., N.Y.C., 1966-67, Lower Merion Sch., Ardmore, Pa., nights 1967-71, Univ. Settlement House, Phila., 1961-63, Navajo Indian Reservation, Fort Defiance, Ariz., 1963, Young Men's Jewish Youth Center, Chgo., 1964-65, Margaret Fuller Settlement House, Cambridge, Mass., 1958-61; poetry therapist Pa. Hosp. Inst., 1969-

74; also drug rehab. house Pa. Hosp. Inst., Phila.; poet in residence Tyrone Guthrie Ctr., Newbliss, Ireland, Aug. 1988; poetry workshop leader Pendle Hill Quaker Ctr., Wallingford, Pa., Apr. 1988; poetry week leader Ferry Beach, Saco, Maine, summer 1988; pioneer in poetry therapy. Poet, 1946—; poems pub. in periodicals including others; Author: Pauses, 1978, Fresh Bread, 1982; Contbr. poems to newspapers. Mem. Acad. Am. Poets, Nat. Fedn. State Poetry Socs., Am. Poetry League, Nat. League Am. Pen Women, Poetry Therapy Assn. (v.p.), Avalon Orgn., Authors Guild, Nat. Writers Club, Pen and Brush Club, N.H., Pa. poetry socs., Cath. Poetry Soc. (asso.), Fla. State Poetry Soc. (asso.). Episcopalian. Home: 1420 Locust St #36C Philadelphia PA 19102 Office: 617 Williamson Rd Bryn Mawr PA 19010 also: 1177 California St #1122 San Francisco CA 94108

SAUNDERS, SUSAN PRESLEY, real estate executive; b. South Bend, Ind., Feb. 27, 1956; d. William Presley Jr. and Anne Summers (Winburn) S. Student, Converse Coll., 1974-77, Sandhills Community Coll., Southern Pines, N.C., 1978-86. With Gouger, O'Neal & Saunders, Southern Pines, 1973-74, 75, Ceralon Mfg., Aberdeen, N.C., 1976; bank teller The Carolina Bank, Aberdeen, 1977-78; from clk. to v.p. fin. G.O.S., Inc., Southern Pines, 1978—. Mem. Am. Soc. Profl. and Exec. Women, Am. Inst. Profl. Bookkeepers, NAFE, Sandhills Area C. of C. (membership com. Southern Pines chpt. 1989—). Democrat. Presbyterian. Home: 130 Pebble Beach Pl Southern Pines NC 28387 Office: GOS Inc 216 Commerce Ave Southern Pines NC 28387

SAUNDERS, TONI LYNNE, construction company executive; b. Columbus, Ohio, Aug. 19, 1949; d. Larry Brook Wells and Mildred Carole (Talbott) Cozart; m. William Kenneth Riley, May 13, 1969 (div. Mar. 1971); m. Albert Eugene Saunders, Sept. 28, 1971; 1 child, Randy Lee Saunders. Grad. high sch., Xenia, Ohio, 1967. Corp. sec. Ind. Horizontal Boring, Inc., Indpls., 1981-82; pres., chmn. bd. Ind. Horizontal Boring, Inc., New Palestine, Ind., 1982—; also bd. dirs. Ind. Horizontal Boring, Inc., Indpls.; founder Pride Cons., New Palestine, Ind., 1986—. Mem. adv. com. Nontraditional Role Model Linkages Project/Ind. Region Eight Taskforce, 1988. Mem. NAFE, Nat. Assn. Women in Constrn. (v.p. Indpls. chpt. 1988-89, fundraiser 1984, 85, 86, chmn. women's bus. enterprise com. 1984-86, mem. long range planning com. 1988-89, profl. edn. com. 1988-89, chmn. ways and means com. 1988-89, pres. elect 1989-90, pres. 1990—), Nat. Assn. Self-Employed, Nat. Fedn. Ind. Businesses, Associated Builders and Contractors, Nat. Women's Bus. Enterprise Assn. (rep. to Ind. women's bus. devel. ctr. adv. counsel), Ind. Women's Bus. Enterprise Assn., Inc. (chpt. sec. 1988-90), Am. Subcontractors Assn. (co-chair minority and women bus. enterprise, editor newsletter). Office: Ind Horizontal Boring Inc PO Box 197 New Palestine IN 46163

SAUNDERS-SPENCER, BRENDA DEE, public relations executive; b. Columbus, Ohio, Feb. 1, 1962; d. Billy and Virginia G. (Hunter) Sanders; m. Timothy R. Spencer Jr., Apr. 12, 1986; 1 child, Brea Nicole Spencer. BS in Communications, Ohio U., 1984. Asst. to exec. producer, intern Warner Amex Cable Communications, Columbus, 1984; sec. I State of Ohio-Communications, Columbus, 1984-85; asst. dir. community svcs. Sta. WCMH-TV, Channel 4, Columbus, 1985-86; community rels. dir. Jr. Achievement of Cen. Ohio, Columbus, 1986—. Freelance writer The Martin L. King Ctr., Columbus, 1986—; co-author: (brochures) Building a Dream, 1986, If You Want TV Air Time, 1986. Hostess State of Ohio-Gov.'s Awards, Columbus, 1985; mem. Martin L. King Jr. Ctr. for Cultural and Performing Arts, 1986—, pub. rels. com., 1986-90, mktg. task force com., 1987-88; mem. Columbus Clean Community, 1986-89, Scioto Superfest Publicity Com., 1987-88, Just Say No Parade Planning, 1986-87, Kidspeak Exec. Adv. Coun., 1987-88. Named for Best Spl. Prodn., Ft. Hayes Career Ctr., Columbus, 19890, for a Record Performance, Nat. Jr. Achievement, 1987-88, Outstanding Young Woman, Outstanding Young Women Am., 1987. Women in Communications Inc. (bd. dirs. Columbus chpt. 1988-89, membership recruitment com. 1987-88, chairperson matrix table publicity com. 1988), NAFE. Democrat. Baptist. Office: Jr Achievement Cen Ohio Inc 538 D East Town St Columbus OH 43215

SAUNTRY, SUSAN SCHAEFER, lawyer; b. Bangor, Maine, May 7, 1943; d. William Joseph and Emily Joan (Guenter) Schaefer; m. John Philip Sauntry, Jr., Aug. 18, 1968; 1 child, Mary Katherine. BS in Foreign Service, Georgetown U., 1965, JD, 1975. Bar: D.C. 1975, U.S. Dist. Ct. D.C. 1975, U.S. Ct. Appeals (D.C. cir.) 1975, (4th cir.) 1977, (6th cir.) 1978, (10th cir.) 1983, U.S. Supreme Ct. 1983. Congl. relations asst. OEO, Washington, 1966-68; program analyst EEO Com., Washington, 1968-70, U.S. Dept. Army, Okinawa, 1970-72; assoc. Morgan, Lewis & Bockius, Washington, 1975-83, ptnr., 1983—. Co-author: Employee Dismissal Law: Forms and Procedures, 1986; contbr. articles to profl. jours. Mem. ABA, D.C. Bar Assn., D.C. Women's Bar Assn., Am. Assn. Univ. Women, USA, Phi Beta Kappa, Pi Sigma Alpha. Democrat. Office: Morgan Lewis & Bockius 1800 M St NW Washington DC 20036

SAUSEDO, ANN ELIZABETH, newspaper librarian; b. Douglas, Ariz., Nov. 19, 1929; d. Eugene Ephraim and Bertha Evelyn (Kimpton) Bertram; m. Richard Edward Sausedo, July 22, 1952 (div. 1966); 1 dau., Robin Marie. Student Calif. schs. Asst. librarian Stockton Record (Calif.), 1948-51, head librarian, 1955-67; stewardess Calif. Central Airlines, 1951; library dir. Washington Star, 1967-76; free-lance organizer file systems, Palo Alto, Calif., 1976-78; library dir. Los Angeles Herald Examiner, 1978—. Contbr. chpt. to book in field. Mem. Spl. Libraries Assn., Nat. Assn. Female Execs. Office: LA Herald Examiner 1111 S Broadway Los Angeles CA 90015

SAUVE, JACQUELINE ANNMARY, management consultant; b. Toledo, Dec. 21, 1943; d. Elwood Jack and Marie Anna (Mikesell) Erwin; m. Daniel Theodore Raymond Sauve, May 19, 1984 (wid. July 1986). BS in Edn., U. Toledo, 1964, MS in Labor Rels. and Humanities, 1980. Bookkeeper Toledo Automobile Club, 1965-69; compensation specialist Questor Corp., Toledo, 1976-79; personnel dir. People's Jewelry Co., Toledo, 1976-79; asst. dir. tng. Toledo Trust Co., 1979-82; owner, cons. Comprehensive Profl. Svcs., Toledo, 1982—; facilitator U. Toledo seminars. Contbr. articles to profl. jours. Bd. govs. Rescue-Crises Svcs. Mem. Internat. Assn. Pers. Women (past nat. dir., past pres. Toledo chpt.), Am. Soc. Tng. and Devel., Am. Soc. Pers. Adminstrn., Am. Compensation Assn., Toledo Indsl. Recreation and Employee Svcs. Coun. (past pres., exec. dir.), Toledo Pers. Mgmt. Assn. (dir.), N.W. Ohio Hotel & Motel Assn. (exec. dir.) The Profl. Network (exec. dir.). Republican. Lutheran. Office: 800 Washington Toledo OH 43624 Home: 3165 River Rd Toledo OH 43614

SAUVÉ, JEANNE, former governor general of Canada; b. Prud'homme, Sask., Can., Apr. 26, 1922; d. Charles Albert and Anna (Vaillant) Benoît; m. Maurice Sauvé, Sept. 24, 1948; 1 son, Jean-François. Grad., U. Ottawa, D (hon.); diploma in French Civilization, U. Paris, 1952; several hon. doctorate degrees. Nat. pres. Jeunese etudiante catholique, Montreal, 1942-47; tchr. French London County Council, 1948-50; asst. to dir. youth sect. UNESCO, Paris, 1951; journalist, broadcaster, 1952-72; bd. dirs. Union des Artistes, Montreal, 1961, v.p., 1968-70; v.p. Canadian Inst. on Pub. Affairs, 1962-64, pres., 1964; mem. Can. Centennial Commn., 1967; gen. sec. Fedn. des Auteurs et des Artistes du Can., 1966-72; mem. Parliament for Ahuntsic, Montreal, 1972-79, Parliament for Laval-des-Rapides, 1980; advisor external affairs Sec. of State, 1978; minister sci. and tech., environment and communications, speaker House of Commons Govt. of Canada, Ottawa, Ont., 1979-84, gov. gen., comdr. in chief of armed forces, 1984-90. Founder, hon. chmn. Jeanne Sauvé Youth Found., 1990. Decorated comdr. Order of Mil. Merit, companion of Order of Can.; named Privy Councillor; recipient La Médaille de la Chancellerie des U. de Paris, Sorbonne U.; first woman to hold position of gov. gen. of Can. Hon. fellow Royal Archtl. Inst. Can.; founding mem. Inst. Polit. Research. Mem. Liberal Party of Can. Roman Catholic. Home: 2474, rue de la Montagne, Montréal, PQ Canada H3G 2A6

SAVAGE, DONNA MARIE, nursing educator and manager, consultant; b. Chgo., May 9, 1953; d. Elwin James and Virginia (Dzorbray) Savage. LPN, Kankakee Community Coll., 1975, ADN, 1978; BSN, Governors State U., 1984, MSN, 1985. RN, Ill. Nurse St. Mary's Med. Ctr., Kankakee, Ill., 1975-79; nurse mgr. Fontanbleu Nursing Ctr., Kankakee, 1979-80; primary care nurse Carle Found. Hosp., Urbana, Ill., 1980-81, Mercy Hosp., Urbana, 1981-82; charge nure mgr. Kankakee Terrace Nursing Ctr., Bourbonnais, Ill., 1982-86; assoc. registered nurse James A. Haley VA Med. Ctr., Tampa, Fla., 1986-87; asst. dir. nurses Kankakee Royale Nursing Ctr., Inc., 1987-88; clin. nurse specialist Olympia Fields (Ill.) Osteo. Med. Ctr., 1988—; career cons., Kankakee, 1984—. Mem. Women in Mgmt., Ill. Nurses Assn., Sigma Theta Tau. Roman Catholic. Home: 3611 W 214th Pl Apt 104 Matteson IL 60443 Office: Olympia Fields Osteo Ctr 20201 S Crawford Olympia Fields IL 60461

SAVAGE, GALE ELEANOR, public health physician, epidemiologist; b. Schenectady, N.Y.; d. Otis Wesley Clements and Eleanor Alice (Wagner) Springfels; m. Marcal Jose Barros, July 5, 1969 (div. 1981); 1 child, Tev Marcal; m. Maury Jack Savage, Jr., July 23, 1984. AA, Green Mountain Coll., 1960; postgrad., CUNY, 1966-68; MD, Souza Marques Med. Sch., Rio de Janeiro, 1981; MPH, Uniformed Svcs. U. Health Sci., Bethesda, Md., 1986. Resident ob-gyn Catholic U., Rio de Janeiro, 1982-84; dir. edn. The British Coun., Rio de Janeiro, 1973-76; adminstr. of vols. Rio Health Collective, Rio de Janeiro, 1981-84; staff physician CPAIMC-US AID/WHO Family Planning, Rio de Janeiro, 1982-84; pvt. practice ob-gyn Meneschal Clinic, Rio de Janeiro, 1981-84; cons. human toxic substance exposure Karch & Assocs., Washington, 1987—; project dir. EPITECH US AID-Statistica, Inc., Rosslyn, Va., 1987-89; cons. epidemiology Am. Inst. Biol. Scis., Rosslyn, Va., 1989—; med. officer Ctrs. for Disease Control/Agy. for Toxic Substances Registry, Atlanta, 1989—; team leader, evaluator U.S. AID-DIATECH Coop. Agreement, Seattle, 1988, U.S. AID-WIHTC grante, Zimbabwe, Malawi, 1988, U.S. AID-Morehouse Project, Liberia, Burkina, 1988; dir., adminstr. U.S. AID-Malaria Field Trials, Papua, New Guinea, 1988; vol. faculty occupational medicine Mercer Sch. Medicine, Macon; asst. prof. environ. health/epidemiology Emory Sch. Medicine, Dept. Pub. Health, Atlanta; assoc. prof. envirom. health Emory U. Sch. of Medicine and Sch. of Pub. Health, Atlanta, 1990. Author: (monograph) Menstrual Problems, 1984; co-author: (project paper) EPITECH Project, 1987. Com. mem. Internat. Soc. Hypertension in Blacks, Atlanta, 1988—; guest lectr. Rio Health Collective, Brazil, 1982—; vol. physician Cath. Ch. health clinic, Brazil, 1982; vol. faculty Dept. of Internal Medicine Mercer U. Sch. of Medicine, Mason, Ga., 1990. Recipient scholarship Columbia Presbyn. Hosp., N.Y., 1961, Green Mountain Coll., Poultney, Vt. Fellow Am. Assn. Pub. Health Physicians; mem. Internat. Epidemiol. Assn. (com. mem. 1989—), Am. Soc. Tropical Med. Hygiene, Am. Soc. Parasitology, Am. Coll. Occupational Medicine, Nat. Coun. Internat. Health, Am. Pub. Health Assn. Presbyterian. Home: 2101 Thomas View Rd Reston VA 22091 Office: Ctrs for Disease Control 1600 Clifton Atlanta GA 30324

SAVAGE, MARCIA A., academic administrator. BA, Clark U., 1961, MA, 1962, PhD in Edn., 1966. Asst. prof. edn. community colls., summer 1967; assoc. dean studies Clark U., 1967-69, asst. prof. edn., 1968-69, dean undergrad. student affairs, 1969-70, dean studies, 1970-72, exec. asst. to pres., affirmative action officer, 1973-74, assoc. dean acad. affairs, then dean, from 1974; Am. Coun. Edn. intern, spl. asst. to pres. Haverford U., 1972-73; pres. Hartford (Conn.) Coll. for Women, Manhattanville Coll., Purchase, N.Y., 1985—. Office: Manhattanville Coll Office of Pres Purchase NY 10577*

SAVAGE, MARY HELEN, environmental consultant; b. Cleve., Aug. 29, 1956; d. George Roland and Helen Jeanne (Riley) S.; m. Robert Lee Riemer, May 31, 1980. BA in Microbiology, Kans. U., Lawrence, 1978, MS in Environ. Health Sci., 1979, BA in Biochemistry, 1980. Rsch. technician Kans. Geol. Survey, Lawrence, 1979-81, Exxon Prodn. Rsch., Houston, 1984-85; cons. Peer Consultants, Inc., Rockville, Md., 1985-86; sr. environ. engr. The Earth Tech. Corp., Alexandria, Va., 1986—. Mem. Hazardous Materials Control Rsch. Inst., Water Pollution Control Fedn. Office: Earth Tech Corp Ste 700 300 N Washington St Alexandria VA 22314

SAVAGE, PATRICIA WERNER, health care and human service executive, consultant; b. Reading, Pa., Nov. 17, 1949; d. Carl Clenroy and Margaret Eveline (Harris) Werner; m. John William Savage, Jr. BA, Alvernia Coll., Reading, 1971; MSW, Marywood Coll., Scranton, Pa., 1976; MS in Adminstrn., U. Scranton, 1988. Lic. social worker, Pa.; lic. nursing home adminstr., Pa. Dir. sr. companion program Telespond Sr. Svcs., Scranton, 1975-78; coord. aftercare and geriatrics N.E. Tri-County Mental Health-Mental Retardation, Carbondale, Pa., 1978-85; dir. Hospice St. John, Luth. Welfare Svc. N.E. Pa., Kingston, 1985-88; v.p. for adminstrn. Luth. Welfare Svc. N.E. Pa., Hazleton, 1988—; social work cons. Devereux Found., Devon, Pa., 1984—. Pres. Women's Resource Ctr., Scranton, 1982-85; pres., bd. dirs. Breadbasket N.E. Pa., Scranton, 1988, Victims Resource Ctr., Wilkes-Barre, Pa., 1989—; bd. dirs. ELCA div. Soc. Ministry Orgns., 1989—. Recipient P.E.A.R.L. award YWCA, Hazleton, Pa., 1989, Athena award Greater Hazleton C. of C., 1990. Mem. NOW, AAUW, Nat. Assn. Social Workers, Acad. Cert. Social Workers, Am. Coll. Healthcare Execs. Lutheran. Home: RR 2 Box 1014 Cresco PA 18326 Office: Luth Welfare Svc NE Pa 901 Stacie Dr Hazleton PA 18201

SAVARY-OGDEN, GERALDINE, computer company and landscaping company executive, researcher and developer, inventor; b. Brooksville, Fla., Sept. 22, 1929; d. Norman Pinckney and Maude (Bullard) Savary; m. Robert Thomas Ogden, Aug. 12, 1950; children: Robert Thomas, Jr., Donna Lee Bonomi. Profl. tng. in horticulture, research and writing, nursing. Pres. Sign of the Time, Selden, N.Y., 1970-74, B.G. Micro-Purchasing, Inc., Scottsdale, Ariz., 1979—; owner, author, pub. Ogden Advt. & Research, Floral City, Fla., 1975-78; owner, mgr. Ogden Nursery Products, Inverness, Fla., 1974-79, Dove Systems, Scottsdale, 1980—, Lady Am. Women Ins. Co., Scottsdale, 1985—; owner Dove Landscaping and Citrus Nursery, Floral City, Fla., 1986—; v.p. sales Computer Clinic, Mesa, Ariz., 1982-84; researcher Geri-Health of Fla., 1984-85; owner Dove Med. Systems, Dove Med. Limo and Taxi Svc., Dove Airways Courier Express, Dove Tour 'De South Dinner Bus Tour, Dove Citrus Landscaping and Lawn Care, Dove Fla. Home and Bus. Sitting Svc. Author: Inverness and Citrus County Mapping Guide; What Florida Residents Should Know About Taxes; A Touch of Soul, 1983; (poetry) From A Liberated Mind, 1972; Favorite Recipes of 40 U.S. Presidents, 1985. Contbr. articles to profl. jours. and popular mags.; designer white dove symbol for women's Internat. movement, 1970, Gerihealth VA Med. Ctr. and Nursing Home, Floral City, Fla., Fla. Deep Sping Water Cannery, Fla. Air Port Water Bars; inventor numerous devices. Democrat. Home: PO Box 854 Floral City FL 32636

SAVILLE, LYNN ADELE, freelance photographer; b. Durham, N.C., July 6, 1950; d. Lloyd Blackstone and Eugenia Turk (Curtis) S.; m. Philip Henry Fried, Oct. 5, 1985. BFA, Duke U., 1971; MFA, Pratt Inst., 1976. Photographer/author: (children's book) Horses in the Circus Ring, 1989; portfolio published in Photographie Mag., Switzerland, 1989; one-woman shows include Lincoln Ctr., N.Y., 1984, U. Tex., 89, U. Colo., 1987, Duke U., 1987, U. Ark., 1988, Bertha Urdang Gallery, 1987, 89, 90, Bennett & Siegel Ltd., N.Y.C., 1990, Chevron Corp. Art Gallery, San Francisco, 1990; exhibited in group shows at UN, 1983, Foto Gallery, 1983, Coos Art Mus., Oreg., 1984, AAUP, 1984, Mus. of City of N.Y., 1985, NYU, 1989, Focal Point Gallery, City Island, N.Y. 1990; represented in collections at Bklyn. Mus., N.Y. Pub. Libr., Columbia U., Goldman Sachs, others. Photography fellow N.Y. Found. for the Arts, 1987; recipient Lee Witkin award Perkins Art Ctr., 1982. Mem. Am. Soc. Mag. Photographers, Found. for the Community of Artists. Democrat. Home: 440 Riverside Dr #45 New York NY 10027

SAVINO, EVELYN GOLDSTEIN BUHLER, retired lawyer, insurance broker; b. N.Y.C., Aug. 11, 1916; d. Max and Rachel Leah (Goldstein) Goldstein; m. David George Buhler, Oct. 6, 1940 (dec. 1970); children: Alan S., Barry R., Robert L., Gwen B. Dreilinger; m. Peter John Savino, Dec. 18, 1971. BA, Hunter Coll., 1936; LLB, Bklyn. Law Sch., St. Lawrence U., 1940. Bar: N.Y., 1943. Practicing atty. Buhler & Buhler, Esqs., N.Y.C., 1943-70. Del., Dem. Nat. Conv., Atlantic City, 1964. Mem. Women's Am. ORT (chmn. capital funds South Palm Beach County region 1983—, pres. Boca Glades chpt. 1982-84), Golden Circle, Bklyn. Law Sch. Alumni Assn., U. Miami Sch. Medicine Friends For Life, Brandeis Women, Hadassah. Avocations: golf, music, public charity. Home: 10390 Camelback Ln Boca Raton FL 33498

SAVINO-JONES, MARIE DAUPHINE, writer, promotion assistant; b. Bridgeport, Conn., Oct. 12, 1961; d. John Michael and Millicent Marie (LaConte) Savino; m. Ronald Douglas Jones, Aug. 6, 1988. Student, San Diego State U., 1979-81; degree, Inst. Children's Lit., 1984; student, UCLA, 1987—. Asst. mgr. Size 5-7-9 Shops, San Diego, 1977-79; mgr. Size 5-7-9 Shops, L.A. and San Diego, 1979-82; sales demonstrator Marche Cosmetics Co., San Diego, 1982-84; asst. tchr. Spreckels Elem. Sch., San Diego, 1983-87; script reader United Artists Assn. Film Group, L.A., 1987-88, Omega Films, L.A., 1988-89; prodn. asst. Cinema Preview Entertainment, L.A., 1988-89; chief writer Sweetalk Prodns., L.A., 1987—; promotion asst. Warners Bros. Records, L.A., 1988—; movie reviewer Tuned in Mag., San Diego, 1980-86, Video Update, San Francisco, 1982-86; voice-over scripter Lip Svc. Prodns., L.A., 1987—. Author short stories; editorial writer San Diego Union/Tribune, 1980-87. Mem. Planetary Soc., Pasadena, Calif., 1987—, Calif. Abortion Rights Com., L.A., 1989—; v.p. People for the Ethical Treatment of Animals, San Diego, 1984-86; pres. Animal Rights Coalition, San Diego, 1980-86. Winner Screenwriter Contest, Writer's Digest mag., 1987. Fellow Mut. UFO Network (assoc., field investigator 1988-90), Ctr. for UFO Studies (assoc., field investigator), Orion (assoc., field investigator), Found. for Shamanic Studies. Democrat. Home and Office: 230 N Valley St #101 Burbank CA 91505

SAVITZ, MAXINE LAZARUS, aerospace company executive; b. Balt., Feb. 13, 1937; d. Samuel and Harriette (Miller) Lazarus; m. Sumner Alan Savitz, Jan. 1, 1961; children: Adam Jonathan, Alison Carrie. BA in Chemistry summa cum laude, Bryn Mawr, 1958; PhD in Organic Chemistry, MIT, 1961. Instr. chemistry Hunter Coll., N.Y.C., 1962-63; sr. electrochemist Mobility Equipment Rsch. and Devel. Ctr., Ft. Belvoir, Va., 1963-68; prof. chemistry Federal City Coll., Washington, 1968-72; program mgr. NSF, Washington, 1972-74; dir. FEA Office Bldgs. Policy Rshc. U.S. Dept. Energy, Washington, 1974-75, dir. div. indsl. conservation, 1975-76, from dir. div. bldgs. and community systems to dep asst sec., 1975-83; pres. Lighting Rsch. Inst., 1983-85; asst. to v.p. engring. The Garrett Corp., 1985-87; dir. Garrett Ceramic Components div. Allied-Signal Aerospace Co., Torrance, Calif., 1987—; lectr. in field; bd. dirs. Am. Coun. for Energy Efficient Economy, 1984—, Internat. Inst. for Energy Conservation, 1984—; cons. State Mich., Dept. of Commerce, 1983, N.C. Alternative Energy Corp., 1983, Garrett Corp., 1983, Energy Engring Bd., Nat. Rsch. Bd., 1986-92, Office Tech. Assessment, U.S. Congress Energy Demand Panel, 1987-89, Nat. Materials Adv. Bd., Nat. Rsch. Coun., 1989-91; bd. dirs. U.S. Advanced Ceramic Assn., 1989—, pres.-elect, 1990. Editor Energy & Bldgs.; bd. editors The Energy Jour.; contbr. articles to profl. jours. NSF postdoctoral fellow, 1961, 62, NIH predoctoral fellow, 1960, 61. Office: Garrett Ceramic Components 19800 Van Ness Ave Torrance CA 90509

SAVOLT, LOUANN SUE, retailer; b. Ft. Wayne, Ind., Sept. 28, 1942; d. Harold Edwin and Norma Esther (Mertz) Hartman; m. Larry Gene Savolt, Sept. 6, 1980; children: Neil Reith, Sheila Reith. AD in Nursing, Garden City Community Coll., 1977. RN, Kans. Health nurse Garden City Community Coll., Kans., 1977-80; staff nurse St. Catherine Hosp., Garden City, 1983; owner, mgr. Personally Yours Lingerie, Garden City, 1984—. Hot line vol. Family Crisis Services, Finney County, Kans., 1982-84; pub. edn. chmn. Am. Cancer Soc., Finney County, 1978-84; co-chmn. Coalition for Prevention of Child Abuse and Neglect, Finney County, 1978-79, chmn., 1979-80. Recipient Service award Finney County Am. Cancer Soc., 1981, Family Crisis Services, 1984. Mem. Women's C. of C., Nat. Retail Mchts. Assn., NAFE, Fedn. of Ind. Businesses. Lutheran. Avocations: reading, snowmobiling, traveling. Home: Rte 2 Box 51 Holcomb KS 67851 Office: Personally Yours Lingerie 503 N Main Garden City KS 67846

SAVOY, JACQUELINE SANDRA, investment executive; b. Phila., Aug. 19, 1951; d. Maurice M. and Beatrice (Medoff) S. BS in Health Edn. magna cum laude, Temple U., 1973, postgrad. in bus., 1980, 85; MA in Secondary Sch. Counseling with honors, Villanova (Pa.) U., 1977; JD (hon.), Del. Law Sch. of Widener U., 1986. Cert. in health edn. and secondary sch. counseling; registered rep. N.Y. Stock Exchange. Tchr. health edn. Phila. Sch. System, 1974-75; advisor curriculum and bus. programs Temple U., Phila., 1975-76, advisor acad. and prelaw programs, 1976-83; rep. Roth & Co., Bala Cynwyd, Pa., 1981-83; investment broker Butcher & Singer, Inc., Phila., 1983-89; asst. v.p. investments Tucker Anthony Inc., Phila., 1989—. Mem. Am. Coll. Personnel Assn., Am. Personnel and Guidance Assn., Stockbrokers Soc., Phila. Women's Network, Phila. C. of C. (ambassador), Sweet Adelines (Valley Forge chpt.), Kappa Delta Pi. Republican. Jewish. Office: Tucker Anthony Inc 14th Fl 1760 Market St Philadelphia PA 19103

SAWICKI, HOLLY, electronics executive; b. Atlantic City, Sept. 26, 1954; d. Hollis and Mary T. (Parks) Livingston; m. Maximo Sawicki, Sept. 24, 1977; 1 child, Steven. BS, Internat. Fine Arts Coll., Miami, Fla., 1976. Cert. security dealer bus. mgr. V.p. VCC Techs. Corp., Hollywood, Fla.; pres., owner Security Maintenance Corp., Miami, Am. Alarms Inc. Active Dynamics Personal Leadership, 1984, Leadership for Women, 1987. Mem. NAFE, NOW. Home: 11500 Taft St Hollywood FL 33026 Office: 99 NW 183 St #207 Miami FL 33169

SAWICKI, KATHERINE RIVAS, retired educator; b. Monticello, N.Y., Jan. 11, 1929; d. Anthony Rivas and Anna (Rapp) Coy; m. Francis A. Sawicki, Dec. 18, 1954. BS, SUNY, Plattsburg, 1950; MA, Columbia U., 1955. Permanent cert. home econs. tchr., N.Y. Elem. tchr. home econs. Uniondale (N.Y.) Pub. Schs., 1950-54, high sch. tchr., chmn. dept., 1954-74, dist. chmn. home econs., tchr., 1974-80; cons. Nassau County Home Econs. Tchrs. Assn., 1964-66. Author courses on child devel., family rels., consumer edn., foods and nutrition. Mem. sch. bd. Epiphany Luth. Sch., Hempstead, N.Y., 1960-68. Mem. AAUW (corr. sec. Garden City br. 1983-85, chair pub. info. com. 1986-89, v.p. membership com. 1989—), Am. Home Econs. Assn. (pres. L.I. dist. 1964-65). Republican. Home: 59 Poplar St Garden City NY 11530

SAWYER, BLANCHE MELTON, real estate company executive; b. Waynesboro, Tenn., May 23, 1932; d. James Clarence and Edna (Hampton) Melton; m. David W. Sawyer Sr., Nov. 24, 1956 (div. July 1987); children: David W. Sawyer Jr., Kerri S. Norman. BS, Union U., 1953; postgrad., Tenn. Tech., 1954, Southwestern U., 1955. Acct. Jackson-Madison County (Tenn.) Gen. Hosp., 1953-54; tchr. Hamburg (Ark.) High Sch., 1954-55, Caney (Kans.) High Sch., 1955-56; realtor Fleming Realty, Ft. Smith, Ark., 1972-74, Phillips-Foltz, Ft. Smith, 1974-76; owner Sawyer Realty, Ft. Smith, 1976—. Copyright "Splatter-Platter), 1973. Pres. Jr. Civic League, Ft. Smith, 1977; co-chmn. Ft. Smith United Way, 1978; bd. dirs. ARC, Ft. Smith. Named Realtor of Yr., Ft. Smith Bd. Realtors, 1983. Mem. Ft. Smith Bd. Realtors (sec. 1979, bd. dirs. 1980-83, Realtor of Yr. 1983), Ark. Chpt. Cert. Residential Specialists (charter), Ft. Smith C. of C. (bd. dirs. 1984—), Realtors Nat. Mktg. Inst., Town Club, Hardscrabble Country Club, Fianna Hills Country Club. Democrat. Baptist. Home: 9711 Kingsley Pl Fort Smith AR 72903 Office: Sawyer Realty 104 N 13th Ste 205 Fort Smith AR 72901

SAWYER, CELIA MAE, educational administrator; b. San Pedro, Calif., June 14, 1946; d. Walter Herman and Dorothy Elaine (Torgerson) S. BA, Calif. Luth. U., Thousand Oaks, 1969; MA, Calif. Luth. U., 1980; postgrad., Pepperdine U., Malibu, Calif. Aquatics dir. Camp Mozumdar Met. YMCA, Cedar Pines Park, Calif., 1965-68 summers; dir. deaf camp Camp Big Pines, summer 1969; clk. Camping Svcs. Met. YMCA, L.A., 1969-71 summers; tchr. Carson (Calif.) High Sch., 1969-76; cons. Student Aux. Svcs., L.A. Unified Sch. Dist., 1976-80; field coordiantor South Youth Svcs., L.A. Unified Sch. Dist., Gardena, Calif., 1980—; active various phys. edn. activies, L.A. Unified Sch. Dist.; cons. in field. Drill team coord. opening ceremonies 1984 Olympics, logistics coord. closing ceremonies, Liberty Weekend, 1986; asst. choreographer Pope's visit, Dodger Stadium, 1987, Brit. Airways comml., 1989; mem. San Pedro Reclamation Com., 1989, Commn. for South Gate Youth, 1989, San Pedro and Peninsula YMCA, 1979—. Recipient Mayor's Cert. of Apprecation, Mayor of L.A., 1988, Inspiration award, Nat. Assn. Sport and Phys. Edn., 1985, Award of Excellence, City of L.A., 1989, others. Mem. AAHPER,Calif. Assn. health, Phys. Edn., Recreation and Dance (v.p. recreation 1987-88), Orgn. Mgmt. Adminstrs., Calif. Luth. U. Booster Club. Home: 23115 Van Deene Torrance CA 90502 Office: South Youth Svcs 2060 W 156th St Gardena CA 90249

SAWYER, CONSTANCE BRAGDON, astrophysicist, oceanographer; b. Lewiston, Maine, June 3, 1926; d. William Hayes and Beatrice Goulding (Burr) S.; children: Joel Howar McCulloch, Sarah Charlock, David Warwick,

Rachel Warwick. AB, Smith Coll., 1947; AM, Radcliffe Coll., 1948, PhD, 1952. Astronomer Sacramento Peak Obs., Sunspot, N.Mex., 1953-55, High Altitude Obs., Boulder, Colo., 1955-58; physicist, astronomer NOAA, Boulder, 1958-82; rsch. staff Radiophysics, Inc., Boulder, 1983—; cons. D-Peek, Boulder, 1983. Co-author: Solar Flare Prediction, 1986. Mem. Am. Astron. Soc. (sec. 1982-85), Am. Geophys. Union, Internat. Astron. Union, Sigma Xi, Phi Beta Kappa. Democrat. Mem. Soc. of Friends. Home: 850 20th St Apt 705 Boulder CO 80302 Office: Radiophysics Inc 5475 Western Ave Boulder CO 80301

SAWYER, (L.) DIANE, journalist; b. Glasgow, Ky., Dec. 22, 1945; d. E.P. and Jean W. (Dunagan) S.; m. Mike Nichols, Apr. 29, 1988. B.A., Wellesley Coll., 1967. Reporter Sta. WLKY-TV, Louisville, 1967-70; adminstr. press office White House, 1970-74; researcher Richard Nixon's memoirs, 1974-78; gen. assignment reporter, then Dept. State corr. CBS News, 1978-81; co-anchor Morning News CBS, from 1981, co-anchor Early Morning News, 1982-84; corr., co-editor 60 Minutes CBS-TV, 1984-89; co-anchor Prime Time Live ABC News, 1989—. Recipient Peabody award for pub. svc., 1988. Mem. Council Fgn. Relations. Office: ABC News 1330 Ave of the Americas New York NY 10019*

SAWYER, DOROTHY STRAKER, social services administrator; b. Hammond, Ind., Jan. 12, 1924; d. Joseph and Veronica (Gyorgyi) Straker; m. Baldwin Sawyer, Sept. 6, 1947; children: Dorothy Carol, Ann Sawyer Williams, Charles Baldwin, Elizabeth Rood. BMus, Am. Conservatory Music, Chgo., 1947; MA in Human Svcs., John Carroll U., 1982. Instr. Carnegie Inst. Tech., Pitts., 1947-51, Moravian Coll. for Women, Bethlehem, Pa., 1953-54, Cleve. Inst. Music, 1957-60, Laurel Sch. for Girls, Shaker Heights, Ohio, 1960-65; founder, dir. Inst. for Personal Health Skills (formerly Cancer Project), Cleve., 1978—, exec. dir., 1978—; lectr., writer in field; instr. continuing edn. U. Hawaii, Honolulu, 1989. Contbg. author: Anthology of Imagery Techniques, 1985. Mem. exec. com. Adv. Coun. Western Res. Hist. Soc., Cleve., 1969-73; mem. Women's Coun. Cleve. Mus. Art, 1972—; pres. women's com. Cleve. Inst. Music, 1968-70. Mem. Am. Guild Organists (assoc.), Am. Assn. Self-Regulation and Biofeedback, Assn. Applied Psychophysiology and Biofeedback. Office: Inst Personal Health Skills 11501 Shaker Blvd #315W Cleveland OH 44040

SAWYER, GENE, retired journalist; b. Danvers, Mass., Sept. 9, 1910; d. Morse Leon and Harriet Elizabeth (Adams) Lewis; grad. Cushing Acad., Ashburnham, Mass., 1928; student Syracuse U., 1928-30; m. W.P. Sawyer, Sept. 9, 1930. Radio announcer, writer, producer, Honolulu, N.Y.C., China, 1937-49; officer U.S. Fgn. Service, Burma, Cambodia, Indonesia, Washington, 1950-65; corr. in Honolulu, Voice of Am., Washington, 1966-71; student interviewer manuscripts Hawaii Pacific Coll. and East West Center, Honolulu, 1972-79; editor original material on Burma and Cambodia, U. Hawaii, 1980-81. Vice-pres., Hawaii div. U.N. Assn., 1971-73, bd. dirs., 1975—. Recipient cert. of Merit, Sr. Achievement, 1980, First Lady's award for Outstanding Vol. of Yr., East West Ctr., 1985. Mem. Women in Communications (Headliner award Hawaii chpt. 1986), Honolulu Acad. Arts, Fgn. Service Assocs., Friends of East-West Ctr. (life), Theta Sigma Phi. Author: Celebrations, Asia and the Pacific, 1978. Home: 1465 Aala St Apt 802 Honolulu HI 96817

SAWYER, HELEN ALTON, painter; b. Washington; d. Wells Moses and Kathleen Alton (Bailey) S.; m. Jerry Farnsworth, Aug. 26, 1925. Student, Master's Sch., Dobbs Ferry, 1914-18; studied art with Johansen and Hawthorne. Painter, artist in oil and water color, lithographer; exhibited at principal galleries and museums of U.S.; represented permanent collections numerous museums,including Whitney Mus. Am. Art, Pa. Acad., Toledo Mus., Syracuse U. Mus., John Herron Mus., Indpls., Atlanta Mus., Amherst Coll. Mus., Williams Coll. Mus. Art, Chrysler Mus., U. Fla. Mus. Collection, others; IBM collection, Libr. of Congress, C. & O. R.R. collections, Norfolk Mus., Samuel P. Harm Mus. of Art, Gainesville, Fla., Holyoke Pub. Mus.; contbr. articles and verse to jours. Recipient numerous awards, honors. Mem. N.A.D., Nat. Arts Club, Provincetown, Yonkers, Sarasota art assns., Audubon Artists, Nat. Assn. Women Artists. Home: 3482 Flamingo Sarasota FL 34242

SAWYER, JANE ORROCK, engineer; b. Richmond, Va., June 15, 1944; d. Harry Wayland and Grace (Hale) Orrock; m. Calmet Marston Sawyer, Sept. 17, 1965; (div. 1979); children: Curtis Marton, Tracy Lauren. BS, V.P.I., Blacksburg, 1966, MS, 1968; PhD, V.P.I., S.U., Blacksburg, 1975. Instr. mathematics Mary Baldwin Coll., Staunton, Va., 1969-72; asst. profr. Mary Baldwin Coll., Staunton, 1972-78, assoc. profr., 1978-81; supr. Am. Safety Razor Co., Verona, Va.; quality engr. Am. Safety Razor Co., Verona, 1982-84; project engr. Am. Safety Razor Co., 1984-89, mgr. data processing, 1989—; tchr. Gov. Sch. for the gifted, Staunton, 1974-75; dir. NASA Fellowship NASA Langley Rsch. Ctr., Hampton, Va., 1975-77. Co-author: Glasnik Mathematika - on Mathematics, 1968, Proceedings Am. Math Soc., 1988. Recipient NASA Fellowship NASA, 1966-69, Outstanding Math Grad., VPI, Blacksburg, 1966; named Outstanding Young Women Am., 1979. Mem. Soc. Mfg. Engrs. (sr., chmn. elect 1989). Democratic. Presbyterian. Home: HCR33 Box 6 Churchville VA 24421 Office: Am Safety Razor Co PO Box 500 Staunton VA 24401

SAWYER, KATHERINE H. (MRS. CHARLES BALDWIN SAWYER), librarian; b. Cleve., July 11, 1908; d. Willard and Martha (Beaumont) Hirsh; AB, Smith Coll., 1930; MS in Libr. Sci., Case Western Res. U., 1956; m. Charles Baldwin Sawyer, Aug. 19, 1933; children: Samuel Prentiss, Charles Brush, William Beaumont. With Cleve. Pub. Libr., profl. libr. hosps., instns. dept., 1956-61; med. libr. St. Luke's Hosp., Pittsfield, Mass., 1965-66; libr. cons. Ministry of Health, Guyana, S. Am., 1966-68; curator Sophia Smith Collection, 1969-70; counselor Friends of Smith Coll. Libr.; chmn. Friends of Western Res. Hist. Libr., 1973-78, hon. trustee, 1980—; dir., trustee Friends of Pima-Green Valley Libr.; trustee Episcopal Ch. Home, 1965— ; bd. govs. Case Western Res. U., 1957-66, bd. visitors Sch. Libr. Sci., 1958-68, 69-72; trustee Friends of Cleve. Pub. Libr., 1962-67, Christian Residences Found., 1976-82, WRHS, 1979—; counselor Friends of Smith Coll. Libr. , 1962-68. Mem. Ariz. State Libr. Assn., Case Western Res. Hist. Soc., Archeol. Inst., Spl. Librs. Assn., Nat. League Am. Pen Women. Episcopalian (vestryman 1974-77). Clubs: Union, Allience Française; Green Valley Country; Intown. Co-author (talking books for blind) Gardening for Blind Persons, 1962; Beauty, Glamour and Style, 1963. Home: 525 Paseo del Mundo Green Valley AZ 85614

SAWYER, NANCY ELIZABETH (WRIGHT), sales executive, consultant; b. L.A., Sept. 6, 1961; d. Phillip Webster and Jane Ann (Twomey) W.; m. Michael Sawyer. BA in Phys. Edn., U. Calif., Santa Barbara, 1983; MA in Phys. Edn. and Applied Physiology, San Diego State U., 1988. Asst. dir. program devel. Pres.' Coun. on Phys. Fitness and Sports, Washington, 1983; phys. edn. instr. San Diego State U., 1985-86; physiologist St. John's Hosp., Santa Monica, Calif., 1987-88; adminstrv. mgmt. cons. The Sports Med. Centre, L.A., 1987-88; pvt. practice L.A. and Orange County, Calif., 1988—; profl. sales rep. Quinton Instrument Co., Seattle, 1989—; cons. Nat. Inst. of Cardiovascular Tech., Newport Beach, Calif., 1986, Nat Athletic Inst., L.A., 1986. Mem. Kappa Alpha Theta. Republican. Home: 1005 Mar Vista Ave Seal Beach CA 90740 Office: Quinton Instrument Co 2121 Terry Ave Seattle WA 98121

SAWYER, PHYLLIS ROSE, county government official; b. Pitts., June 7, 1923; d. Ralph and Mary (Langone) Tullio; m. Robert Sawyer, 1947 (dec. Aug. 1975); children: Robert R. Jr., Virginia Ann Burkitt, Tom, Frank. Student, Ill. Bus. Coll., 1942. Sec. U.S. Post Office, Chgo., 1941-43, Q.M.C., Washington, 1943-45, Nurenburg Trials, Fed. Republic of Germany, 1945-47; mgr. DOC Sawyer's Marina at Charles Mill Lake, 1959-71; clk. bd. elections Richland County, Mansfield, Ohio, 1975-77, dep. dir. bd. elections, 1978-80, dir. bd. elections, 1980—; clk. Mansfield City Coun., 1977-78. Mem. Dem. Women's Fedn., 1976—, Legis. Agt. and Trustee, Columbus, Ohio, 1981—; sec. Dem. Exec. Com., Mansfield, 1976—. Mem. Mem. Bd. of Elections (sec. Mansfield chpt. 1980—), Westbrook Country Club. Roman Catholic. Home: 266 S Main St Mansfield OH 44903 Office: Bd of Elections 7 S Diamond St Mansfield OH 44902

SAWYER, SYDNEY WHITE, physical therapist, educator; b. Camden, Maine, Aug. 29, 1960; d. Frank White and Elizabeth (O'Brien) S. BS, Northeastern U., 1983. Registered phys. therapist, Nev., Va. Staff therapist Las Vegas (Nev.) Inst. for Phys. Therapy and Sports Medicine, 1983-86, The Phys. Therapy Ctr., Springfield, Va., 1980-89; dir. The Phys. Therapy and Sports Assessment Ctr., Woodbridge, Va., 1989—, coord. clin. edn. for No. Va., 1988—, clin. coord., 1986—. Alumni recruiter Northeastern U., Boston, 1986—. Mem. Am. Phys. Therapy Assn. (bd. dirs. Va. chpt. 1988-90, chmn. legis. com. 1987-88, 90—). Home: 11907 Henderson Ct Clifton VA 22024 Office: Phys Therapy & Sports Assessment Ctr 13562 Jefferson Davis Hwy Woodbridge VA 22191

SAWYERS, ELIZABETH JOAN, librarian, administrator; b. San Diego, Dec. 2, 1936; d. William Henry and Elizabeth Georgiana (Price) S. A.A., Glendale Jr. Coll., 1957; B.A. in Bacteriology, UCLA, 1959, M.L.S., 1961. Asst. head acquisition sect. Nat. Library Medicine, Bethesda, Md., 1962-63, head acquisition sect., 1963-66, spl. asst. to chief tech. services div., 1966-69, spl. asst. to assoc. dir. for library ops., 1969-73; asst. dir. libraries for tech. services SUNY-Stony Brook, 1973-75; dir. Health Scis. Library Ohio State U., Columbus, 1975-90, spl. asst. to dir. Univ. librs., 1990—. Mem. Assn. Acad. Health Scis. Library Dirs. (sec./treas. 1981-83, pres. 1983-84), Med. Library Assn., Am. Soc. for Info. Sci., Spl. Libraries Assn., ALA. Office: Ohio State U State Univ Librs 1858 Neil Ave Columbus OH 43210

SAX, MARY RANDOLPH, speech pathologist; b. Pontiac, Mich., July 13, 1925; d. Bernard Angus and Ada Lucile (Thurman) TePoorten; m. William Martin Sax, Feb. 7, 1948. BA magna cum laude, Mich. State U., 1947; MA, U. Mich., 1949. Supr. speech correction dept. Waterford Twp. Schs., Pontiac, 1949-69; lectr. Marygrove Coll., Detroit, 1971-72; pvt. practice speech and lang. rehab., Wayne, Oakland Counties, Mich., 1973—; adj. speech pathologist Southfield, Mich., Farmington, Mich.; pub. speaking coach, 1989—; adj. faculty SS. Cyril and Methodius Sem., Orchard Lake, Mich., 1989—. Mem. sci. coun. stroke Am. Heart Assn. Grantee Inst. Articulation and Learning, 1969, project choices and funding Meadow Lake Community Coun., Birmingham, Mich., 1989; christian svc. commn. St. Owen, Birmingham, others. Mem. AAUW, Am. Speech-Lang.-Hearing Assn. (clin. competence cert.), Mich. Speech-Lang.-Hearing Assn. (com. community and hosp. svcs.), Am. Heart Assn. of Mich. (mem. stroke awareness seminar, planning and operation ednl.), Stroke Com. of Am., Internat. Assn. Logopedics and Phoniatrics (Switzerland), Founders Soc. of Detroit Inst. Arts, Mich. Humane Soc., Theta Alpha Phi, Phi Kappa Phi, Kappa Delta Pi. Contbr. articles to profl. jours. Home and Office: 31320 Woodside Franklin MI 48025

SAXE, ELIZABETH LEE, commodities executive, marketing consultant; b. N.Y.C., June 10, 1934; d. Hugo and Katherine Knowles (McMunn) Steiner; m. John Brooke Saxe, Feb. 25, 1956 (dec. Mar. 1970); children: John M., Charles C., Andrew F. AB, Radcliffe Coll., 1955; MA, Richmond Coll., S.I., N.Y., 1972; PhD, Yale U., 1979. Research analyst Mocatta Metals Co., N.Y.C., 1979-80; regulatory analyst N.Y. Stock Exchange, 1980-82; communications analyst Merrill Lynch Futures, N.Y.C., 1982-84; mktg. specialist N.Y. Mercantile Exchange, N.Y.C., 1984-86; mgr. pub. info. and metals mktg. N.Y. Mercantile Exchange, 1986-88; dir. market rsch. & devel. Mchts. Exch. St. Louis, 1988—. Contbr. articles to profl. jours. Profiled in documentary film By Themselves, 1974. Mem. St. Louis Agri-Bus. Club, Nat. Assn. Bus. Economists, Yale Club N.Y.C. Home: 12111 Vivacite Walk Saint Louis MO 63146 Office: Mchts Exch St Louis 5100 Oakland Ave Saint Louis MO 63110

SAXMAN, ANNA ESTHER, lawyer; b. Latrobe, Pa., May 14, 1949; d. Harry Suydam and Eleanor Ruth S.; m. Robert Halpert, Feb. 18, 1989. BS magna cum laude, U. Vt., 1978, JD magna cum laude, 1985. Clk. to presiding justice Vt. Supreme Ct., Montpelier, 1985-86; assoc. Langrock, Sperry, Parker & Wool, Burlington, Vt., 1986—; mem. Task Force on Gender Bias in the Legal System, Montpelier, 1988—. Editor U. Vt. Law Rev. Pres., bd. trustees Vt. Assn. for Mental Health, Montpelier, 1989—. Mem. ABA, Vt. Bar Assn. (chmn. women's sect. 1989—, chmn. com. on rights of the mentally and physically handicapped, 1988-89), Assn. Trial Lawyers Am. Office: Langrock Sperry et al PO Box 721 Burlington VT 05402

SAXON, FRANCES SHIVER, retired social services administrator, counselor; b. Walhalla, S.C., Jan. 12, 1928; d. Noble Calhoun and Caroline (Ansel) Shiver; m. James Hendricks Saxon, Sept. 3, 1949; children: James Hendricks, Frank, Scott, Suzanne, Carol, Andrew, Dorothy, David. Student, U. N.C., Greensboro, 1946-49; BA in Psychology with honors, U. N.C., Charlotte, 1975, MEd, 1981. Commuter life coordinator U. N.C., Charlotte, 1974-77; founder, exec. dir. Women's Ctr., Charlotte, 1977-89; cons. Handicapped Organized Women, Charlotte, 1983-84, Women's Concerns program Mecklenburg Presbytery, Charlotte, 1985. Recipient Outstanding Svc. award U. N.C., Charlotte, 1975. Mem. Nat. Assn. Counseling and Devel., N.C. Assn. Counseling and Devel., Southeastern Women's Studies Assn., Nat. Assn. Bus. and Profl. Women, Nat. Assn. Group Work, Nat. Assn. Female Execs., Nat. Assn. Women's Centers. Home: 3120 Libeth St Charlotte NC 28205

SAXTON, CAROLYN VIRGINIA, health facilities administrator; b. Charleston, W.Va., June 24, 1948; d. Robert Everett and Jo Ann (Rader) S.; m. Jon H. Rickey, June 20, 1970 (div. 1988); children: Jon Hamilton Jr., Leigh Ann; m. Harlow William Gregory, Jr., May 27, 1989. BA, W.Va. Wesleyan Coll., 1971; postgrad., Loma Linda U., 1989—. Counselor Open Door, Annapolis, Md., 1971-73; social worker Salvation Army, Charleston, 1977-79; patient educator Womens Health Ctr., Charleston, 1979-83; community edn. specialist Shawnee Hills Mental Health, Charleston, 1983; exec. dir. W.Va. Nat. Abortion Rights Action League, Charleston, 1983-86; lobbyist Charleston, 1986; exec. dir. Community Hospice, Ashland, Ky., 1986-89; dir. home hospice VNANorth, Evanston, Ill., 1989-90; exec. dir. Community Chest Oak Park/River Forest, Ill., 1990—. Active Ky. Cancer Program Network, Ashland, 1986—, Ky. Religious Coalition for Abortion Rights, Frankfort, 1987-88; mem. W.Va. Task Force on Adolescent Residential Treatment Ctr./Drug Abuse, 1983; mem. Nat. Abortions Rights Task Force on Minor's Access, 1986-87; mem. com. on minor's access W.Va. Dept. Health, 1986-87; mem. Jr. League Charleston, 1982-86; chmn. usher com. Paramount Womens Assn., Ashland, 1988-89; mem. choir lst Presbyn. Ch., Ashland, 1986-89, Sunday sch. tchr., 1988-89; choir mem. Fair Oaks Presbyn. Ch., 1990—. Mem. Nat. Hospice Orgn. (award of excellence 1988), Ky. Assn. Hospice (bd. dirs., mem.-at-large, 1989, nominating com. chmn. 1988-89), Coun. for Non-Profits (vol. action com. 1988-89, co-chmn. community support com. 1989), Oak Park/River Forest Women's Assn. for Chgo. Art Inst., Zonta, Rotary. Democrat. Home: 851 N Fair Oaks Oak Park IL 60302 Office: Community Chest Oak Park/ River Forest 1042 Pleasant St Oak Park IL 60302

SAXTORPH, GERTRUDE MARGRETA, retired teacher; b. Golden, Colo., Dec. 2, 1902; d. Francis Klein and Laura Agnes (Kock) Klein-Sandstrom; m. Henrik Andreas Saxtorph, June 16, 1927; 1 child, Margot Saxtorph Conway. AB, Colo. Coll., 1923; student, Peoples Coll., 1952, U. Innsbrock, 1952, Inst. San Miquel, 1963. Classroom tchr. Lewistown (Mont.) Jr. High Sch., 1923-26, Great Falls (Mont.) High Sch., 1926-27; substitute tchr. various schs., 1927-44; jr. high and sr. high sch. tchr., 1948-63, ret., 1963; Officer Mont. Ednl. Assn., Lewistown, 1947-52. Chmn. Dem. Women, Lewistown, 1952-58. Mem. AAUW, Am. Wildlife Found., World Wildlife Found., Am. Legion Auxiliary, Worl War I Auxiliary, Eagles Auxiliary (various coms.). Democrat. Roman Catholic. Home: 4300 Vrain St #403 Denver CO 80212

SAY, MARLYS MORTENSEN (MRS. JOHN THEODORE SAY), superintendent; b. Yankton, S.D., Mar. 11, 1924; d. Melvin A. and Edith L. (Fargo) Mortensen; B.A., U. Colo., 1949, M.Ed., 1953; adminstrv. specialist U. Nebr., 1973; m. John Theodore Say, June 21, 1951; children—Mary Louise, James Kenneth, John Melvin, Margaret Ann. Tchr. Huron (S.D.) Jr. High Sch., 1944-48, Lamar (Colo.) Jr. High Sch., 1950-52, Norfolk Pub. Sch., 1962-63; Madison County supt., Madison, Nebr., 1963— . Mem. NEA (life), AAUW, Am. Assn. Sch. Adminstrs., Dept. Rural Edn., Nebr. Assn. County Supts., Nebr. Elementary Prins. Assn., N.E. Nebr. County Supts. Assn., Assn. Sch. Bus. Ofcls., Nat. Orgn. Legal Problems in Edn., Assn. Supervision and Curriculum Devel., Nebr. Edn. Assn., Nebr. Sch. Adminstrs. Assn. Republican. Methodist. Home: 4805 S 13th St Rte 2 Norfolk NE 68701 Office: Courthouse Madison NE 68748

SAYER, JANE M., chemist; b. Keene, N.H., Mar. 7, 1942; d. Winthrop and Laura (McKinley) S. BA, Middlebury Coll., 1963; PhD, Yale U., 1967. Postdoctoral fellow Brandeis U., Waltham, Mass., 1967-69, sr. rsch. assoc., 1969-74; asst. prof. chemistry U. Vt., Burlington, 1974-79; guest worker NIH, Bethesda, Md., 1979-83, spl. expert, 1983-85, rsch. chemist, 1985—. Contbr. articles to profl. jours. Mem. Am. Chem. Soc., N.Y. Acad. Scis., Sigma Xi. Office: NIH Bldg 8 Rm 1A-11 Bethesda MD 20892

SAYERS, CHERA LEE, economist, educator; b. Lansing, Mich., Apr. 14, 1959; d. Vernon L. and Shirley Ann (Armour) S.; m. S. Nuri Erbas, May 19, 1990. BA, Mich. State U., 1981; MS, U. Wis., 1984, PhD, 1986. Vis. asst. prof. U. N.C., Chapel Hill, 1987-88; asst. prof. Haverford (Pa.) Coll., 1986-87, U. Houston, 1988—; rsch. economist div. econ. analysis Commodity Futures Trading Commn., Washington, 1988—; article referee various journals in economic field. Bd. editors Order and Chaos. Recipient Bd. of Trustees scholarship Mich. State U. 1981, Harry Bullis scholarship U. Wis. 1985. Mem. Econometric Soc., Am. Econ. Assn., AAUW, Univ. Houston Women's Assn., Com. on the Status of Women in the Econs. Profession, U. Wis. Alumni Assn., Mich. State U. Alumni Assn., Phi Kappa Phi. Office: U Houston Dept Econs 4800 Calhoun Houston TX 77204-5882

SAYERS, HAZEL JEAN, nurse, researcher; b. Nappanee, Ind., Nov. 18, 1927; d. Chauncey Arthur and Freda Irene (Neumann) Neff; m. Rastislav Boris Sayers, July 3, 1953. Cert. in nursing, Ind. U. Tng. Sch. for Nurses, Indpls., 1948; cert. advancement, City Hosp. of St. Louis U., 1951. Staff nurse operatig rm. Ind. U. Med. Ctr., Indpls., 1948-51; operating rm. supr. Kauikiolani Children's Hosp., Honolulu, 1951-53; head nurse Rehab. Ctr. Hawaii, Honolulu, 1954-56; head nurse recovery rm. UCLA Med. Ctr., 1956-63; head nurse rsch. lab. Harbor Gen. Hosp., Torrance, Calif., 1964-67; rsch. program specialist U. Calif., San Diego, 1967-85, coord. postgrad. surgery assembly Sch. of Medicine, 1982; coord., mem. faculty Microsurgery Edn. & Rsch. Found.'s Microsurg. Tng. Workshops, 1982-85; transplant coord. Transplant Organ Found. of Am., 1983-85; rsch. assoc. dept. surgery Coll. of Medicine U. Cin., 1985-90. Contbg. author: The Gray Whale, 1984; contbr. numerous articles to profl. jours. Mem. Am. Cetacean Soc. (editorial advisor Jour., Woman of Yr. award 1981), Internat. Microsurg. Soc. (treas. 1976-89, sec.-gen. 1989—), Soc. Microsurg. Specialists (chartered), Soc. for Marine Mammalogy (assoc.), Sierra Club, Nature Conservancy. Democrat. Home: 2785 Little Dry Run Rd Cincinnati OH 45244 Office: U Cin Med Ctr Coll Medicine Dept of Surgery-558 Cincinnati OH 45267-0558

SAZAMA, KATHLEEN, pathologist; b. Sutherland, Nebr., May 8, 1941; d. Roger William and Esther Mary (Reitz) Paulman; m. Franklin Jed Sazama, Aug. 26, 1962; children: Clare Ann, Jill Patrice. BS, U. Nebr., 1962; MS, Am. U., 1969; MD, Georgetown U., 1976; JD, Cath. U. Am., 1990. Diplomate Am. Bd. Pathology; lic. pathologist Mich., Va., Md., D.C., Calif. Chief lab. of blood bank products FDA Ctr. for Biologics Evaluation and Rsch., Bethesda, Md., 1986-89; cons. Ober, Kaler, Grimes & Shriver, Balt., 1989-90; assoc. med. dir. Sacramento (Calif.) Med. Found. Blood Ctr., 1990—; intern and resident Georgetown U. Med. Ctr., Washington, 1976-78; resident NIH, Bethesda, Md., 1978-79; asst. clin. prof. pathology U. Calif., Davis, 1990—; adj. asst. prof. patholgy U. Calif., Davis; clin. asst. prof. pathology Uniformed Svcs. U. of Health Scis., Bethesda, 1981-89; clin. affiliate Ferris State Coll., Big Rapids, 1985-86; v.p. Bd. Met. Washington Blood Banks, Inc., 1981-84; speaker in field. Author: (with others) Stat: The Laboratory's Role, 1986; contbr. numerous articles to profl. jours. Comdr. USPHS, 1986-89. Fellow Coll. Am. Pathologists, Am. Soc. Clin. Pathologists; mem. AMA, ABA, Montgomery County Med. Soc., Med. and Chirurgical Faculty of Md., Am. Assn. Blood Banks, Sacremento-El Dorado Counties Med. Soc., Calif. Blood Bank Soc., Nat. Health Lawyers Assn., Coll. Legal Medicine, Phi Kappa Phi, Beta Beta Beta. Office: Sacramento Med Found Blood Ctr 1625 Stockon Blvd Sacramento CA 95816-7089

SCAFFIDI, JUDITH ANN, school volunteer program administrator; b. Bklyn., Aug. 2, 1950; d. Anthony William and Rose Virginia (Nocera) S. BA, SUNY, Plattsburg, 1972, MS, 1973; postgrad. Kennedy Learning Ctr., Einstein Coll. Medicine, 1983. Cert. secondary edn. English. VISTA mem. ACTION, N.Y.C., 1976-77; coord. cultural resources N.Y.C. Sch. Vol. Program, N.Y.C., 1977-80; dist. coord. in Bklyn. N.Y.C. Sch. Vol. Program, 1980—; field supr., adj. faculty Coll. for Human Svcs., N.Y.C., 1984-86; adv. coun. chairperson Retired Sr. Vol. Program in Bklyn, 1983-86, adv. bd., 1986—; adv. bd. Retired Sr. Vol. Program in N.Y.C., 1983-86. Named for Svcs. in the Promotion of Literacy, Internat. Reading Assn. and the Bklyn. Reading Coun., 1986, for Outstanding Leadership as Adv. Coun. Chairperson, Retired Sr. Vol. Program, 1986. Mem. Nat. Sch. Vol. Program, Ptnrs. in Edn., NAFE, Cath. Tchrs. Assn. Bklyn. (del. sch. dist. 18, 1982—), Am. Mus. Natural History, Cath. Alumni Club N.Y. Roman Catholic. Home: 2330 Ocean Ave Apt 3H Brooklyn NY 11229 Office: NYC Sch Vol Program 443 Park Ave South 9th Fl New York NY 10016

SCAIA, MARY JULIE, special education educator; b. Torrington, Conn., May 7, 1953; d. Geno William and Mollie Rose (Silano) S. BS, So. Conn. State U., 1975; MEd, Northeastern U., 1985. Cert. elem., secondary spl. edn. tchr., Conn. Spl. edn. resource room tchr. Ledyard Pub. Sch. System, Gales Ferry Sch., Gales Ferry, Conn., 1975-76; spl. edn. tchr., team coordinator Torrington Pub. Sch. System, Vogel Jr. High Sch., Torrington, Conn., 1976—; communications cons. deaf/blind group homes; mem. profl. sign lang., dance and mime troupe Cridders; area coordinator Northwestern Conn. Spl. Olympics, Torrington, 1979-80; mem. sch. adv. panel Conn. Pub. TV, Hartford, 1978-79, Litchfield County Hike for the Handicapped Campaign, Torrington, 1981—, Handicapped Task Force on Learning Disabilities, Boston, 1984-85; instituted sign lang. program.; taught and designed courses for talented and gifted students. Contbr. to Conn. Pub. TV newsletter, 1978. bd. dirs. Litchfield County Assn. for Retarded Citizens, Torrington, 1980-82, Friendship Plus! - An Ind. Citizen Advocacy Network, Torrington, 1987—; master of ceremonies Telethons for local cable, Torrington, 1985-86. Recipient Teacher of the Yr. award Probus Club of Torrington, 1987-89; finalist, runner-up Conn. Teacher of the Yr., 1988-89. Mem. NEA, Conn. Edn. Assn. (del. to Washington NEA program), Torrington Edn. Assn. (v.p. 1980-82), Conn. Registry of Interpreters for the Deaf, Assn. for Children and Adults with Learning Disabilities, Zeta Delta Epsilon, Alpha Delta Kappa (v.p. 1982-84). Democrat. Roman Catholic.

SCALES, DIANN ROYLETTE, librarian; b. Birmingham, Ala., Aug. 15, 1945; d. Alphonso Monroe and Ella (Allen) Scales. BA in Am. History, Miles Coll., Birmingham, Ala., 1966; MA in European History, Atlanta U., 1969, MSLS, 1973. Substitute tchr. C.W. Hayes High Sch., Birmingham, 1967-68; reserve librarian Atlanta U., 1969-73, ref. librarian, 1973-81; ref. librarian Miles Coll., Birmingham, 1981-82, U. Montevallo, Ala., 1984—. Mem. Coalition of 100 Black Women, Birmingham, 1990—. Mem. Nat. Librs. Assn., Ala. Libr. Assn., Assn. Social and Behavioral Scientists, So. Hist. Assn., Delta Sigma Theta Sorority, Inc. (corres. sec. 1987-89). Democrat. Baptist. Home: 616 6th St N Birmingham AL 35203 Office: University of Montevallo Station 6109 Montevallo AL 35115

SCANDARY, E. JANE, special education educator, consultant; b. Saginaw, Mich., Sept. 12, 1923; d. Leonard William and Reva Charlotte (Smith) Leipprandt; m. Theodore John Scandary, Sept. 1, 1950; children: John S., Robert G. BA, Mich. State U., East Lansing, 1945, EdS, 1963, PhD, 1968; MEd, Wayne State U., 1951. Cert. secondary and spl. edn. tchr., Mich. Tchr. cons. Ingham Intermediate Schs., Mason, Mich., 1961-68, coord. tchr. cons. svcs., 1968-72, supr. programs for phys., hearing and visually impaired, 1972-78; spl. edn. cons. Mich. Dept. of Edn., Lansing, 1978-87; contractual spl. edn. cons. Livingston Intermediate Schs., Howell, Mich., 1987—; rsch. assoc. Mich. State U., East Lansing, 1965-66, adj. prof., 1969-75, 81-82; field editor Coun. for Exceptional Children, Washington, 1976-86, pres. div. for physically handicapped, 1982-83; guest lectr. in field. Contbr. articles to profl. jours. Vol. PAM Assistance Ctr., Lansing, 1987-89. Mem. Nat. Coun. for Exceptional Children (pres. 1982-83), Internat. Coun. for the Edn. of Visually Handicapped.

SCANDURA, TERESA ANNE, management educator; b. Cin., Aug. 22, 1960; d. Alfred Joseph and Nevilyn Mae (Zobjeck) S. BBA, U. Cin., 1982,

PhD, 1988. Data processing asst. U.S. EPA, Cin., 1980-82; orgn. devel. Gen. Electric Aircraft Engines, Cin., 1982-83; research, teaching asst. dept. mgmt. U. Cin., 1983-88; research asst. Nagoya (Japan) U., 1983-88; asst. prof. mgmt. dept. mgmt. U. Miami, Coral Gables, Fla., 1990—; asst. prof. U. Miami, Coral Gables, 1990—; cons. Frito-Lay, Dallas, 1984-85, PEDCO Engring., Cin., 1985-86, Mayor's Office Tng. and Devel., Lexington, 1989—. Contbr. articles to profl. jours., chpts. to books. Big Sister vol. Big Bros./Big Sisters Greater Cin., Inc., 1987-88. Dissertation fellowship Am. Assembly Collegiate Schs., Bus., St. Louis, 1988, univ. dean. U. Cin., 1988, rsch. com. grantee U. Ky., 1989; U.S. Dept. Labor rsch. grantee. Mem. Nat. Acad. Mgmt. (reviewer, jr. mem. nominating com. 1983—), Am. Psychol. Assn., Decision Scis. Inst., Beta Gamma Sigma. Democrat. Roman Catholic. Office: U Miami Coll Bus Adminstrn Dept of Mgmt 345C BE Bldg Coral Gables FL 33124

SCANLAN, KATHERINE ANN, editor; b. Parma, Ohio, Oct. 8, 1940; d. Lyle Wesley and Doris Katherine (Hart) Schaef; m. William H. Scanlan, May 11, 1968 (div. 1976). Student, Hamot Hosp., 1960; BA, SUNY, 1965. Med. reporter The Telegram, Worcester, Mass., 1967-68; asst. editor The Overseas Family, Frankfurt, Fed. Republic Germany, 1968-70; feature writer, copy editor Stars and Stripes, Darmstadt, Fed. Republic Germany, 1970-72; dir. info. Eastern Ski Assn., Brattleboro, Vt., 1973-75; editor U. Mass., Amherst, 1976—. Recipient Silver award for tabloid pub., 1986, Bronze award for excellence in writing, Coun. for the Advancement of Edn., 1987. Mem. Phi Beta Kappa. Democrat. Lutheran.

SCANLAN, SHARON ANN, retail executive; b. Madison, Wis., Feb. 1, 1948; d. William Emmett and Mary Jane (Murrish) Brewer; m. Stephen Robert Scanlan, Oct. 22, 1974; children: Karen Lynn, Christopher Robert. Student Hamline U., St. Paul, 1966-67; BS, U. Wis., 1970. Group mdse. mgr., Alhambra, Calif., 1978-80, territorial mdse. mgr., 1980, store mgr., San Luis Obispo, Calif., 1981-84, group operating mgr., Phoenix, 1984-87, regional gen. mdse. mgr., Honolulu, 1987-88; gen. mgr. Hawaii region, 1988-89; mgr. Seattle region, 1989—. Bd. dirs. Pvt. Industry Council, San Luis Obispo, 1981-84, San Luis Obispo County Symphony, 1981-84, Crossroads Meth. Ch., Phoenix, 1986-87; pres. San Luis Obispo C. of C., 1984. Mem. Honolulu C. of C. (bd. dirs.), Hawaii Retail Mcht. Assn. (bd. dirs.), Toastmistress Club, Rotary. Republican. Avocations: golf, sewing. Office: Sears Roebuck & Co Seattle Region Office PO Box 97026 Redmond WA 98073-9726

SCANLON, DOROTHY THERESE, history educator; b. Bridgeport, Conn., Oct. 7, 1928; d. George F. and Mazie (Reardon) S.; A.B., U. Pa., 1948, M.A., 1949; M.A., Boston Coll., 1953; Ph.D., Boston U., 1956; postdoctoral scholar Harvard U., 1962-64, 72. Tchr. history and Latin Marycliff Acad., Winchester, Mass., 1950-52; tchr. history Girls Latin Sch., Boston, 1952-57; prof. Boston State Coll., 1957-82, Mass. Coll. Art, 1982—. Recipient Disting. Service award Boston State Coll., 1979, Faculty Award of Excellence, Mass. Coll. Art, 1985, Faculty Disting. Service award, Mass. Coll. Art, 1987. Mem. Pan-Am. Soc., Latin Am. Studies Assn., Am. Hist. Assn., Orgn. Am. Historians, Am. Studies Assn., Am. Assn. History of Medicine, History of Sci. Soc., AAUP, AAUW, Phi Alpha Theta, Delta Kappa Gamma. Author: Instructor's Manual to Accompany Lewis Hanke, Latin America: A Historical Reader, 1974; contbr. Biographical Dictionary of Social Welfare, 1986. Home: 140 Thornton Rd Chestnut Hill MA 02167 Office: Mass Coll Art Dept History 621 Huntington Ave Boston MA 02115

SCANTLEBURY, VELMA PATRICIA, surgeon; b. Barbados, West Indies, Oct. 6, 1955; came to U.S., 1970; d. Delacey Whitstanley and Kathleen (Jordan) S. BS, L.I. U., 1977; MD, Columbia U., 1981. Intern in surgery Harlem Hosp. Ctr., N.Y.C., 1981-82, resident in surgery, 1982-86; fellow in transplantation U. Pitts., 1988, instr. in surgery, 1988; asst. prof. dept. surgery U. Pitts. 1989—. Vol. King County Hosp., Bklyn., 1972. Recipient Martin Luther King Sch. award, 1973-74, Am. Fedn. Tchrs. Sch. award, 1973-75, Nat. Med. Found. award 1977-78, Joseph Collins Found. Sch. award 1978; named Outstanding Young Women of Am. 1988. Mem. AMA, ACS, P&S Alumni Assn., Black and Latin Students Orgn. (treas. N.Y.C. 1979-80), Slpha Epsilon Delta, Phi Sigma Soc. (sec. Bklyn. chpt. 1976-77). Democrat. Home: 625 Copeland St Pittsburgh PA 15232

SCARBOROUGH, RUTH ELLEN, library director; b. Scranton, Pa., Mar. 31, 1917; d. Charles Bishop and Reba May (Joslyn) S. BS in Edn., Marywood Coll., 1939; BS in Libr. Sci, Syracuse U., 1940; MLS, Rutgers U., 1972. Cert. librarian. Libr. dir. Monmouth Jr. Coll., Long Branch, N.J., 1940-43; reference libr. Post Libr., Fort Monmouth, N.J., 1943-46; libr. dir. Centenary Coll., Hackettstown, N.J., 1946-82. Mem. Hackettstown (N.J.) Community Hosp. Auxiliary, 1982—; co-archivist Hackettstown Hist. Soc., 1989—, co-treas., 1990-91. AAUW (co-treas. local br. 1990-92), Am. Libr. Assn., N.J. Libr. Assn. Presbyterian. Home: 504 E Valley View Ave Hackettstown NJ 07840

SCARBROUGH, DAWN DENISE, gift service executive; b. Atlanta, Nov. 11, 1962; d. Donald E. and Diana Dawn (Swann) S. BA in Communications, U. Ala., Tuscaloosa, 1984. Passenger svc. rep. Delta Air Lines, Inc., Atlanta, 1984-86; recruiter Phillips Coll., Atlanta, 1986-88; pres. Giftsource Unltd., Atlanta, 1988—. U. Ala. athletic scholar, 1980-82. Mem. Atlanta C. of C. Republican. Home: 5716 Woodvalley Trace Norcross GA 30071 Office: Giftsource Unltd PO Box 7597 Atlanta GA 30357

SCARNE, STEFFI NORMA, English educator, games company executive; b. Englewood, N.J., Jan. 18, 1925; d. Leo Patrick and Marie Elizabeth (Duffy) Kearney; m. John Scarne, 1956 (dec. 1985); 1 child, John Teeko. B.S. magna cum laude, Seton Hall U., 1971, M.A., 1973; Ph.D., Pacific Western U., 1986. Vice pres., editor, cons. John Scarne Games Inc., North Bergen, N.J., 1950—; exec. sales rep. Hamilton Shoe Co., N.Y.C., 1954-68, Grove Co., N.Y.C., 1968-71; English tchr. North Bergen High Sch., 1971-88. Recipient Dean's Gold Medal for Acad. Excellence, Seton Hall U., 1971. Mem. NEA, Am. Fedn. Tchrs., Nat. Assn. Female Execs. Office: John Scarne Games Inc 4319 Meadowview Ave North Bergen NJ 07047

SCARROW, PAMELA KAY, health care manager; b. Washington, Nov. 4, 1949; d. Edward Charles and Elsie Lorine (Kay) Scarrow; m. Antonio Joseph Franz, Sept. 4, 1979; 1 child, Vanessa Motil Franz. AA, Navarro Coll., Tex., 1981; BS, Golden Gate U., 1983. Cert. med. staff coordinator, 1986. Adminstrv. asst. Trust Ter. of the Pacific Islands, Saipan, Mariana Islands, 1976-79; adminstrv. asst. Navarro Coll., Corsicana, Tex., 1979-81; staff asst. San Francisco Symphony, 1981-82; med. staff liaison Calif. Med. Assn., San Francisco, 1982-87; provider, practitioner cons. Calif. Med. Rev., Inc., San Francisco, 1987—; mem. Patient Care Assessment. Editor: Contracting Resource and Assistance Dept., Inc., Economic Resource Guide, 1986, Medical Staff Resources Manual, 1987. Mem. Nat. Assn. Med. Staff Services. Democrat. Roman Catholic. Office: Calif Med Rev Inc 60 Spear St Ste 500 San Francisco CA 94105

SCATENA, LORRAINE BORBA, rancher, women's rights advocate; b. San Rafael, Calif., Feb. 18, 1924; d. Joseph and Eugenia (Simas) de Borba; m. Louis Giovanni, Feb. 14, 1960; children: Louis Vincent, Eugenia Gayle. BA, Dominican Coll., San Rafael, 1945; postgrad., Calif. Sch. Fine Arts, 1948, U. Calif., Berkeley, 1956-57. Cert. elem. tchr., Calif. Tchr. Dominican Coll., 1946, San Anselmo (Calif.) Sch. Dist., 1946, Fairfax (Calif.) Pub. Elem. Sch., 1946-53; asst. to mayor Fairfax City Recreation, 1948-53; tchr., libr. U.S. Dependent Schs., Mainz am Rhine, Fed. Republic Germany, 1953-56; translator Portugal Travel Tours, Lisbon, 1954; bonding sec. Am. Fore Ins. Group, San Francisco, 1956-60; rancher, farmer Yerington, Nev., 1960—; hostess com. Caldecott and Newbury Authors' Awards, San Francisco, 1959; adv. com. Fleischmann Coll. Agr. U. Nev., 1977-80, 81-84; speaker Choices for Tomorrow's Women, Fallon, Nev., 1989. Mem. Lyon County Friends of Libr., Yerington, 1971—, Lyon County Mus. Soc., 1978, Lyon County Rep. Cen. Com., 1973-74, Nev. State Legis. Commn. Sex Discrimination in Nev. Law, 1975; trustee Wassuk Coll., Hawthorne, Nev. 1984-87; sec., pub. info. chmn. Lyon County Rep. Women, 1968-73, v.p. programs, 1973-75; coord. Nevadans for ERA, 1975-78, rural areas rep., 1976-78; lobbyist for Equal Rights Amendment, 1975; Nev. rep. to 1st White House Conf. for Rural Am. Women, Washington, 1980; mem. Marin County Soc. of Artists, San Anselmo, Calif., 1948-53; participant internat. reception for rural visitors from 34 countries, Washington, 1980. Recipient Soroptimist Internat. Women Helping Women award 1983, invitation to first all-women delegation to U.S.A. from People's Republic China, U.S. House Reps., 1979. Mem. Lyon County Ret. Tchrs. Assn. (unit pres. 1979-80, 84-86, v.p. 1986-88, Nev. div. Outstanding Svc. award 1981, state conv. gen. chmn. 1985), Rural Am. Women Inc., AAUW (br. pres. 1972-74, 74-76, edn. found. programs, 1983-90, state convention gen. chmn. 1976, 87, state div. sec. 1970-72, state div. legis. program chmn. 1976-77, state div. chmn. internat. rels. 1979-81, travelship, Div. Humanities award 1975, Future Fund award 1983), Mason Valley Country Club, Italian Cath. Fedn. Club (pres. 1986-88), Uniao Portuguesa Estado da Calif. Roman Catholic. Home: 1275 Hwy 208 Yerington NV 89447

SCATES, ALICE YEOMANS, former government official, consultant; b. Pitts., Jan. 21, 1915; d. William E. and Georgiana L. (Lloyd) Yeomans; BS, State Tchrs. Coll., Glassboro, N.J., 1936; MEd, Duke U., 1949; EdD, George Washington U., 1963. Tchr. elem. sch., Haddon Heights, N.J., 1937-43; civilian personnel officer Sedalia Army Airfield, Mo., Greenville Army Air Field, S.C., 1944-46; tng. officer VA Center, Dayton, Ohio, 1947-48; rsch. assoc., dir. Am. Coun. on Edn. Staff for Office Naval Rsch. Projects, 1949-53; asst. dir. Nat. Home Study Coun., 1954; editor, rsch. asst. Office of Edn., HEW, 1955, rsch. analyst and coord. coop. research program, 1956-64, program planning officer occupational rsch. program, 1965-66, dir. basic rsch. br. secondary edn., 1967-69, program planning and eval. officer Nat. Ctr. Ednl. Rsch. and Devel., 1969-71, eval. specialist Office Program Eval., 1971-80; eval. officer Office of Mgmt., U.S. Dept. Edn., 1980-82; cons., 1982—. Served to capt. U.S. Army, 1943-46. Fellow AAAS; mem. Am. Sociol. Assn., Am. Anthrop. Assn., Am. Acad. Polit. and Social Sci., Am. Ednl. Rsch. Assn. Adult Edn. Assn., Kappa Delta Pi, Phi Delta Gamma. Author research reports, articles in field. Home: 560 N St SW Washington DC 20024 Office: Box N-501 560 N St SW Washington DC 20024

SCEMONS, DONNA J., home health and hospice administrator; b. Chgo.; d. Harold M. and June E. (Sellers) Strange. AA in Nursing, L.A. Trade Tech., 1974; BSN in Nursing, Calif. State U., L.A., 1977, MA in Health, 1986. Cert. enterostomal therapist. Inservice dir. Van Nuys Community Hosp., Van Nuys, Calif., 1974-78; dir. Ednl. Devel. Svcs., Van Nuys, 1977-80; patient care coord. Vis. Nurse Assn. L.A., Van Nuys, 1980-81; dir. home health Med. Ctr. Tarzana, Tarzana, Calif., 1981-82; staff nurse critical care Valley Hosp. Med. Ctr., Van Nuys, 1982; home care specialist Shield health Care Ctr., Van Nuys, 1982-83; dir. home health NSI Home Health Care, Inc., Beverly Hills, Calif., 1983-84; corp. dir. NSI Svcs., Inc., Beverly Hills, 1984-87; exec. dir. home health/home hospice St. Joseph Med. Ctr., Burbank, Calif., 1987—; pres. Healthcare Devel. Systems, 1989; cons., Calif., 1987—; lectr. various orgns., 1977—. Editor on articles, Williams and Wilkins Pubs.; contbr. articles to profl. jours. Mem. Calif. Assn. Health Svc. at Home, So. Calif. Pub. Health Assn., Nat. Hospice Orgn., Am. Heart Assn., Internat. Assn. Enterstomal Therapists. Office: St Joseph Med Ctr Home Health Hospice Svcs 2101 W Alameda Burbank CA 91506

SCERBO, FRANCES CAROLYN GARROTT, architectural technician; b. Bowling Green, Ky., Mar. 10, 1932; d. Irby Reid and Carrie Mae (Stahl) Cameron; m. Leslie Othello Garrott, Oct. 12, 1951 (dec. Feb. 1978); children—Dennis Leslie, Alan Reid; adopted children—Carolyn Maria, Karen Roxana; m. Raymond William Scerbo, May 31, 1978. Student Fla. State U., 1951, St. Petersburg Jr. Coll., 1962-74; grad. Pinellas Vocat. Tech. Inst., 1975. With Sears, Roebuck and Co., Rapid City, S.D., 1951-52, St. Petersburg, Fla., 1961-62; bookkeeper Ohio Nat. Bank, Columbus, 1953-54, Sunbeam Bakery, Lakeland, Fla., 1955-56; with Christies Toy Sales, Pennsauken, N.J., 1958-60; exec. sec. Gulf Coast Automotive Warehouse, Inc., Tampa, Fla., 1970-73, office mgr., 1975-78; sec., treas., chief pilot, co-owner Tech. Devel. Corp., St. Petersburg, Fla., 1970-78; freelance archtl. draftsman and designer, archtl. cons., constrn. materials estimator, 1975—, Fla. state judge Vocat. Indsl. Clubs of Am. Skills Olympics, 1986. Nat. Assn. Women in Constrn. scholar, 1974. Mem. Nat. Assn. Women in Constrn., Alpha Chi Omega. Democrat. Home and Office: 11298 53d Ave N Saint Petersburg FL 33708

SCHAAF, BARBARA CAROL, writer, consultant, educator; b. Chgo.; d. William and Mary (Krutilla) S. BS cum laude, Roosevelt U., 1971; MBA, U. Chgo. Exec. Program, 1976. Free-lance writer, Harvey, Ill., 1977—; cons. health care delivery systems, transp., housing, taxation, labor and econs.; cons. Continental Air Transport,, Cook County treas., Chgo. HMO; lectr. urban, labor, mil. and ethnic history, English medieval history, writing; lectr. on urban and ethnic history USIA, 1978; mem. adv. com. Artists in Residence Program, Chgo. Coun. Fine Arts, 1979-83; bd. dirs. Chgo. Ctr. Hosp., 1982-87; treas., bd. dirs. Chgo. Ctr. Health System, 1985-87; instr. Richard J. Dale Coll., 1988—. Author: Mr. Dooley's Chicago, 1977 (Carl Sandburg award 1978, also nominee Am. Hist. Assn. Gershoy award and Pulitzer prize), Mr. Dooley, We Need Him Now, 1988, Shattered Vows, 1991; contbr. articles to newspapers, mags. Press sec. Eleanor McGovern, 1971-72, Richard M. Daley, 1979-80J. F. and Robert F. Kennedy presdl. campaigns and other polit. campaigns; treas. Harvey Pub. Libr. Bd. Trustees, 1977—. Nat. Found. for Humanities fellow Writing in Chgo. Program, 1978; Ind. scholar urban history and mil. history. Mem. ALA, Nat. Book Critics Circle, PEN, Soc. Midland Authors, Mystery Writers of Am., Ill. Libr. Assn., Richard III Soc., South Downers, Jane Austen Soc. Home and Office: 400 Streamside Dr Harvey IL 60426

SCHAAF, KATHRYN ANN, psychologist; b. South Bend, Ind., Apr. 20, 1954; d. Robert William and Joanne (Anderson) S. BS with highest honors, Wayne State U., 1979, MA, 1983. Ltd. lic. psychologist, Mich. Psychologist Blue Care Network, Saginaw, Mich., 1983-90, Green Road Counseling Ctr., Ann Arbor, Mich., 1990—. Wayne State U. merit scholar, 1973-79, grad. profl. scholar, 1981-83. Mem. Am. Psychol. Assn. (assoc.), Mich. Psychol. Assn. (assoc.). Office: Green Road Counseling Ctr 2000 Green RdSte 250 Ann Arbor MI 48105

SCHAAR, VICTORIA LYNN, airline executive; b. Brookfield, Ill., Oct. 21, 1959; d. Ronald H. and Virginia Diane (Prillwitz) S. Student, Western Ill. U., 1977-80; BA, Nat. Coll., 1988. Cert. CPR, ARC, First Aid. Recreation office mgr. Oak Lawn (Ill.) Park Dist., 1983-84, recreation coord., 1984-86, athletic coord., 1986-88, community pavilion mgr., 1988; sales agt. Midway Airlines, Chgo., 1988, mgr. crew, 1989—; counselor, Oak Lawn High Sch. Job Fair, 1984-87. Vol. spl. events, Oak Lawn C. of C., 1984, K.C. Help for Retarded Children, Chgo., 1985-86, tornado disaster relief for Plainfield, Ill., 1990; spl. events coord. Oak Lawn Park Dist., 1985, mem. safety com. athletic div., 1987-88; mem. Anti-Cruelty Soc., 1989, PTA, 1987—. Mem. U.S. Slo-Pitch Softball Assn. (bd. dirs. 1985—), South Suburban Parks and Recreation Assn., Walt Disney's Magic Kingdom Club. Republican. Roman Catholic.

SCHABOT, CATHERINE MARY, nurse; b. Mitchell, S.D., Dec. 31, 1938; d. Lawrence Nichols and Mary Muriel (Samp) S. Diploma, Presentation Sch. of Nursing, 1959; BS, Coll. of St. Francis, Joliet, Ill., 1972, MS, 1986. Staff nurse St. Joseph's Hosp., Mitchell, 1959-60; staff nurse Menorah Med. Ctr., Kansas City, Mo., 1960-64, head nurse, 1964-66; staff nurse Mt. Sinai Hosp., Mpls., 1966-68; from head nurse St. Mary's Hosp., Mpls., 1968—; clin. supr., asst. dir. nursing dept., dir. Rehab Ctr., Mpls., 1968—; cons. Chemquest, Mpls., 1987—. Author: chpt. Women in Health and Wellness, 1986. Mem. Nat. Nurses Soc. on Addictions, Twin Cities Orgn. of Nurse Execs. Democrat. Roman Catholic. Office: St Marys Chem Dependency Riverside at 25th Minneapolis MN 55423

SCHACHTEL, BARBARA HARRIET LEVIN, epidemiologist, educator; b. Rochester, N.Y., May 27, 1921; d. Lester and Ethel (Neiman) Levin; m. Hyman Judah Schachtel, Oct. 15, 1941; children: Bernard, Ann. Student Wellesley Coll., 1939-41; BS, U. Houston, 1951, MA in Psychology, 1967; PhD, U. Tex.-Houston, 1979. Psychol. examiner Meyer Ctr. for Devel. Pediatrics, Tex. Children's Hosp., Houston, 1967-81; instr. dept. pediatrics Baylor Coll. Medicine, Houston, 1967-81, asst. prof. dept. medicine, 1982—; asst. dir. biometry and epidemiology Sid W. Richardson Inst. for Preventive Medicine, Houston, 1981-88, dir. quality assurance, 1988—; mem. instl. rev. bd. for human rsch. Baylor Coll. Medicine, Houston, 1981-87; mem. devel. bd. U. Tex. Health Sci. Ctr., Houston, 1987—; mem. dean's adv. bd. Sch. Architecture U. Houston, 1987. Contbr. articles to profl. jours. Vice pres., bd. dirs. Houston-Harris County Mental Health Assn., 1966-67; vice-chmn. bd. mgrs. Harris County Hosp. Dist., Houston, 1974-90, chmn. 1990—, bd. dirs., 1970—; trustee Inst. Religion in Tex. Med. Ctr., 1990—. Named Great Texan of Yr., Nat. Found. for Ilietis and Colitis, Houston, 1982, Outstanding Citizen, Houston-Harris County Mental Health Assn., 1985; recipient Good Heart award B'nai B'rith Women, 1984. Mem. Am. Psychol. Assn., Am. Pub. Health Assn., S.W. Psychol. Assn., Tex. Psychol. Assn., Houston Psychol. Assn. (psychol. assoc. rep. 1974). Avocations: golf, tennis, books. Home: 2527 Glenhaven Blvd Houston TX 77030 Office: Sid W Richardson Inst for Preventive Medicine Meth Hosp Ste 400 6565 Fannin St Houston TX 77030

SCHACHTER, ESTHER RODITTI, lawyer, author, publisher; b. Los Angeles, Feb. 7, 1933; d. David and Lucy Roditti; m. Oscar H. Schachter, Aug. 8, 1957; children—Charles David, Susan Dayana. B.A., UCLA, 1954; J.D., Harvard U., 1957. Bar: N.Y. 1959. Assoc. Stickles, Hayden and Kennedy, N.Y.C., 1957-62; asst. dir. Legis. Drafting Fund Columbia U., N.Y.C., 1962-65, cons., 1965-67; cons. N.Y.C. Air Pollution Control Dept., 1965-67; instr. and cons. New Sch. for Social Research, N.Y.C., 1968-70; cons. Internat. League for Rights of Man, N.Y.C., 1969, Rand Inst., N.Y.C., 1969, U.S.-Soviet Environ. Studies Program, UN Assn., N.Y.C., 1969; sr. research assoc. Ctr. for Policy Research Columbia U., 1970-73; sr. program officer Ford Found., N.Y.C., 1972-78; pres. Esther Roditti Schachter, P.C., N.Y.C., 1978-83; ptnr. Schachter & Froling, N.Y.C., 1983-85, Schachter, Courter, Purcell & Kobert, N.Y.C., 1985—; speaker, lectr., panelist profl. assn. confs., forums, workshops, U.S., Can., Tokyo, London. Author: N.Y.C. Air Pollution Control Code Annotated, 1965; Enforcing Air Pollution Controls, 1979; Financial Support of Women's Programs in the 1970's, 1979; Computer Contracts Reference Directory, 1979-83; co-author: Charities and Charitable Foundations, 1974; author, co-author articles in field; legal editor: Computer Economics, 1983—; editor Computer Law & Tax Report, 1984-86, pub., editor, 1986—. Nat. governing bd. Common Cause, 1979-82, mem. state governing bd., N.Y., 1982-84; mem. com. on urban environ. Citizens Union, N.Y.C., 1969-73; mem. West Side Democratic Club, 1958-63. Ford Found. grantee, 1970; NSF grantee, 1971; recipient Award for Outstanding Service Brandeis U., Nat. Women's Com., 1973. Mem. ABA (lectr. 1987), Assn. Bar City N.Y. (founder, chmn. com. on computer law 1980—), N.Y. State Bar Assn., Computer Law Assn. (lectr. 1985), Am. Arbitration Assn. (chair com. for computer disputes 1985—), Phi Beta Kappa. Club: Panther (Alamuchy, N.J.).

SCHACTER, BERNICE ZELDIN, researcher; b. Phila., June 20, 1943; d. Aaron and Jean (Beckman) Zeldin; m. Lee Phillip Schacter, Aug. 23; children: Elizabeth, Sara. AB, Bryn Mawr (Pa.) Coll., 1965; PhD, Brandeis U., Waltham, Mass., 1970. Instr. U. Miami (Fla.), 1971-72, Johns Hopkins U., Balt., 1974-76; mem. staff Cleve. Clinic, 1976-77; asst. prof. pathology Case Western Res. U., 1977-82, assoc. prof. pathology, 1982-84; sr. scientist Bristol-Myers, Wallingford, Conn., 1984-86; assoc. dir. Bristol-Myers Squibb Pharm. Rsch. Inst., Wallingford, 1986—; vis. prof. Wesleyan U., Middletown, Conn., 1988—; mem. Nat. Inst. Allergy and Infectious Disease Transplantation Biol. Adv. Com., Bethesda, Md., 1977-82; mem. U. Conn. Environ. Health Adv. Com., Storrs, 1986—. Contbr. articles to profl. jours. Mem. Am. Assn. Immunologists, Am. Soc. Histocompatibility and Immunogenetics (v.p. 1983-84), Am. Soc. Human Genetics, Am. Soc. Cancer Rsch. Home: 748 Durham Rd Madison CT 06443 Office: Bristol Myers Squibb 5 Research Pkwy Wallingford CT 06492

SCHADE, ARDITH ANN, federal adminstrative contracting official; b. Pueblo, Colo., Oct. 22, 1945; d. Robert Melvin and Henrietta Grace (Morgan) S. AA, U. So. Colo., 1965; BS, Colo. State U., 1973; MA, Webster U., Colorado Springs, 1981; attended, Air Force Inst. Tech., 1989-90. Profl. designation in contract mgmt. Sec. 2nd Weather Wing, Wiesbaden, Fed. Republic Germany, 1968-70; home econs./bus. tchr. Cheraw Consolidated Sch., Cheraw, Colo., 1973-75, Dept. Defense Schs. Europe, Fulda, Fed. Republic Germany, 1975-78; clk.-stenographer pub. affairs USAF Acad., Colo., 1978-79; clerical asst., civilian liaison officer USAF Acad. Hosp., Colo., 1979-80; mgmt. asst. 46th Aerospace Defense Wing, Peterson Air Force Base, Colo., 1980-81; contract price analyst Hdqrs. Air Force Space Command, Peterson Air Force Base, 1981-83; contract negotiator/specialist, officer Hdqrs. Air Force Space Command, 1983-87; adminstrv. contracting officer 1st Space Wing, 1987—. Del. People to People Citizen Ambassador Group, People's Republic China, 1988. Mem. Nat. Contract Mgmt. Assn. (treas. 1984-85, nat. bd. dirs. 1987-89, professions devel. chair Colorado Springs/So. chpt. 1985-86, pres. Colo. chpt. 1986-87, v.p programs 1990—). Home: 1020 McArthur Ave Colorado Springs CO 80909 Office: 1st Space Wing/LKD Peterson AFB CO 80914-5000

SCHADE, CHARLENE JOANNE, teacher; b. San Bernardino, Calif., June 26, 1935; d. Clarence George Linde and Helen Anita (Sunny) Hardesty; m. William Joseph Jr., Apr. 12, 1958 (div., 1978); children: Sabrina, Eric, Camela, Cynthia; m. Thomas Byron Killens, Sept. 25, 1983. BS, UCLA, 1959. Tchr. dance & pe L.A. Unified Secondary Schs., Calif., 1959-63; dir., instr. (Kindergym) La Jolla YMCA, Calif., 1972-76; instr. older adult San Diego Community Colls., 1977—; artist in residence Wolf Trap/Headstart, 1984-85; workshop leader Southwest Dance, Movement & Acro-Sports Workshop (SWDM&A), Am. Alliance for Health, Physical Edn., Recreation & Dance (AAHPERD), Calif. Assn. for Health, Physical Edn., Recreation & Dance (CAHPERD), Head Start, San Diego Assn. for the Edn.of the Young Child (SDAEYC), San Diego Community Colls. (SDCC), Internat. Dance Exercise Assn. (IDEA), Am. Soc. on Aging (ASA), 1977—; featured guest KFMB & KPBS TV Shows, San Diego, 1980—; prime time adult activities coord., SWDM&A, Riverside. Author: Move With Me From A to Z, 1982, Move With Me, One, Two, Three, 1988; co-author: Prime Time Aerobics, 1982, Muevete Conmigo, uno, dos, tres, 1990. Dir. We Care Found., San Diego, 1977-79, Meet the Author programs San Diego County Schs., 1988—; founder SOLO, San Diego, 1981-83; adminstr., v.p. ODEM chpt. Toastmasters, San Diego, 1982. dir. We Care Foundn., San Diego, 1977-79; founder SOLO, San Diego, 1981-83; adminstr. v.p. ODEM chptr. Toastmasters, San Diego, 1982. Office: Exer Fun/Prime Time Aerobic 3098C Clairemont Dr Ste 130 San Diego CA 92117

SCHADLER, MARGARET HORSFALL, biologist, educator; b. Geneva, N.Y., Aug. 31, 1931; d. James G. and Sue Belle (Overton) Horsfall; m. Harvey Walter Schadler, Aug. 28, 1954; children: Janet, Edward, Linda Sue. AB, Cornell U., 1953; MS, Union Coll., 1971, PhD, 1977. Rsch. asst. Sloan-Kettering Inst., N.Y.C., 1953-54, Purdue U., West Lafayette, Ind., 1954-57; vis. instr. Union Coll., Schenectady, N.Y., 1969-77; vis. asst. prof. Union Coll., Schenectady, 1977-81, rsch. asst. prof., 1981-88, rsch. assoc. prof., 1988—; dir. Affirmative Action Union Coll., 1981-87, assoc. dean undergrad. programs, 1988—. Editor: The Lake George Ecosystem, 1982; contbr. articles to jours. Trustee Ea. N.Y. Chpt. Nature Conservancy, 1970-79; pres. Jr. League, Schenectady, 1971-72; bd. dirs. Environ. Clearinghouse Schenectady, 1971-75, Orgn. for Action on the Riverfront, Schenectady, 1978—; v.p. Lake George (N.Y.) Assn., 1980-82; pres. bd. dirs. GE Realty Plot, 1990—. Recipient grant N.Y. State Sci. and Tech. Found., 1980, NSF, 1981-82, 86-89. Mem. AAAS, Am. Soc. Mammalogists (com. chair 1986—), Soc. Study of Reprodn., Am. Assn. for Higher Edn., Sigma Xi (chpt. pres. 1989—). Home: 1333 Lowell Rd Schenectady NY 12308 Office: Union Coll Sci & Engring Deans Office Sci and Engr Schenectady NY 12308

SCHAEFER, CARLA JO, communications executive; b. Alice, Tex., Dec. 23, 1952; d. Walter Carl and JoBeth (Fannett) S.; div.; children: Sarah Beth Stew, Samuel Schaefer Stew. BA in Govt. and English, U. Tex., 1977. Cert. secondary sch. tchr., Tex. Tchr. Austin (Tex.) Ind. Sch. Dist., 1978-81; adminstrv. asst. Tex. Classroom Tchrs. Assn., Austin, 1981-82; editor Women in Communications, Austin, 1983-84; coord. grad. med. edn. Tex. Med. Assn., Austin, 1984-87; dir. communications, editor Internat. Assn. Hospitality Accts., Austin, 1987—. Editor: The Bottomline, 1987—. Bd. dirs. Travis County Adult Lit. Coun., Austin, 1987—, co-chair long-range planning, 1988, chair communications com., 1985—; bd. dirs. Joslin PTA, Austin, 1989-90, bd. mem. PTA, 1989-90. Recipient awards of excellence in edn. Am. Soc. Assn. Execs., Washington, 1985, Gold Circle, 1989. Mem. Women in Communications. Presbyterian. Home: 2805 Sissinghurst Austin TX 78745 Office: Internat Assn Hosp Accts 3636 Executive Center Dr Austin TX 78731

SCHAEFER, HELEN SCHWARZ, community volunteer; b. Evanston, Ill., Apr. 26, 1933; d. Irving J. and Marie L. Schwarz; m. John P. Schaefer, May 18, 1958; children: Ann, Susan Schaefer Kliman. BS, U. Mich., 1955; MS, U. Ill., 1957, PhD, 1978; postgrad., Calif. Inst. Tech., 1958-59, U. Ariz., 1967-71. Teaching asst., rsch. asst. U. Ill., Urbana, 1955-60; rsch. asst. U. Calif., Berkeley, 1959-60; teaching asst. U. Ariz., Tucson, 1960-61, 62-63; sec. Carondelet Mgmt. Corp., Tucson, 1985—; chmn. Catalina Bank of Commerce, 1987-88; bd. dirs. U. Ariz. Women's Studies Adv. Coun., U. Ariz. Women Sci. and Engring. Adv. Bd. Pres., bd. dirs. Tucson Symphony, 1984-85, Ariz. for Cultural Devel., Phoenix, 1987-88; treas., bd. dirs. YWCA of Tucson, 1985-89; bd. dirs. Ariz. Acad., Phoenix, 1985-89; chmn. St. Mary's Hospice Devel. Bd., 1987—; bd. mgrs. Ott YMCA; bd. dirs. Ariz. Repertory Singers; vice chmn. Pima Coun. Aging, 1987—. Named Woman of Yr. Tucson Advt. Club, 1977; recipient Spirit of Life award City of Hope, Duarte, Calif., 1990. Mem. AAAS, AAUW, Am. Chem. Soc., Assn. Women in Sci., Grad. Women in Sci., League Women Voters Tucson, Sigma Xi, Iota Sigma Pi, Sigma Delta Epsilon.

SCHAEFER, MARILYN LOUISE, art educator; b. Cedar Rapids, Iowa, Apr. 22, 1933; d. Henry Richard and Maria Augusta (Dickel) S. AA, Monticello Coll. for Women, 1953; BFA, Cranbrook Acad. Art, 1956, MFA, 1960; MA cum laude, U. Chgo., 1958; MA, St. John's Coll., Santa Fe, 1979. Rsch. asst. editor Encyclopaedia Britannica, Chgo., 1960-63; humanities editor Encyclopedia Americana, N.Y., 1964-68; acquisitions editor Litton Ednl. Pub., N.Y., 1968-70; from instr. to prof. art and advt. design dept. N.Y.C. Tech. Coll., CUNY, 1970—; contbg. editor Encyclopedia Americana, 1979—, Coll. Teaching jour., 1979. Contbr. articles to profl. publs. including Art and Auction mag., Art and Antiques mag., Am. Artist mag., Encyclopedia Americana, 1970—. Luce Found. postgrad. study fellow St. John's Coll., 1976-79; Ingram Merrill Found. grantee, 1983-84. Mem. Advt. Women of N.Y., CUNY Acad. Arts and Scis. Home: 306 W 76th St New York NY 10023 Office: NYC Tech Coll CUNY 300 Jay St Brooklyn NY 11201

SCHAEFER, MARY ANN, health facility administrator; b. Chgo., May 18, 1942; d. Joseph and Mary A. (Kozyra) Strosnik; m. Robert Earl Schaefer, May 18, 1963; children: Debra Ann, Robert Joseph. Diploma in nursing, St. Francis Hosp. Sch. Nursing, Evanston, Ill., 1962; BA, Nat. Coll. Edn., Evanston, 1980; MBA in Health Svc. Mgmt., Webster U., 1990. Med. and surg. nurse Resurrection Med. Ctr., Chgo., 1963-67, charge nurse labor and delivery, 1978-79; coord. maternal child care Humana, Hoffman Estates, Ill., 1979-81; nurse mgr. labor and delivery Resurrection Med. Ctr., Chgo., 1981—, mgr. labor and delivery; seminar leader on childbirth edn. Contbr. to Motor Facilitation Handbook. Mem. NAACOG (cert. in inpatient obstetric nursing), NAFE, Nat. Perinatal Assn., Perinatal Assn. Ill. (mem. exec. bd.), Am. Orgn. Nurse Execs. Home: 23370 Juniper Ln Barrington IL 60010

SCHAEFER, MARY B., business education instructor; b. Flint, Mich., Apr. 17, 1932; d. William Thomas and Isabelle Mathilda (Todd) Bulger; m. Robert William Schaefer, July 12, 1958; children: Michael Paul, Mark Gerard, Paddy Elizabeth, Bridget Mary, Thomas William. BS, Cen. Mich. U., 1954; MEd, U. Minn., 1985. Tchr. Grant Jr. High Sch., East Detroit, Mich., 1954-56, 1958, Am. High Sch., Kaiserlautern, Fed. Rep. of Germany, 1956-57, St. Paul Acad., St. Paul, 1977-79, South St. Paul High Sch., 1979-83; instr. Inver Hills Community Coll., Inver Grove Heights, 1975--; tchr. intern Coll. of St. Thomas, St. Paul, summer 1986. Mem. Minn. Bus. Edn. Inc., Minn. Community Coll. Faculty Assn., NEA, AAUW, Delta Pi Epsilon. Home: 7750 Boyd Ave E Inver Grove Heights MN 55076 Office: Inver Hills Community Coll 8445 Coll Trail Inver Grove Heights MN 55076

SCHAEFER, MARY JESSE, research associate; b. Norwalk, Conn., Oct. 1, 1963; d. Lawrence Vincent and Patricia Ann (Scallen) S. BA in Sociology, U. Wis., 1985, MA in Rehab. Psychology, 1988. Cert. in rehab. counseling. Chief work adjustment specialist Devel. Svcs., Inc., Columbus, Ind., 1988-89; rsch. assoc., project coord. Inst. for the Study Devel. Disabilities, Ind. U., Bloomington, 1989—; vol. Winant-Clayton Found., Heml Hempstead, England, 1986. Co-author: Interviewer's Handbook, 1989. Bd. dirs. Madison (Wis.) Sustaining Fund & Found., 1987-88, Zoe Bayliss Coop., Madison, 1987-88. Mem. Am. Rehab. Counseling Assn., NAFE, Phi Beta Kappa, Phi Kappa Phi, Rho Chi Sigma, Alpha Kappa Delta. Democrat. Roman Catholic. Home: 1630 W Skillman Ave Roseville MN 55113

SCHAEFER, PAMELA JOY, health care planner; b. Valley City, N.D., June 30, 1949; d. Ralph Calvin and Adlaine Jeanette (Kroke) Bailey; m. Richard Ray Schaefer, Dec. 23, 1973 (div. Oct. 1979); 1 child, Eric Bailey. BA in Nursing, Jamestown Coll., 1974; MS in Nursing, U. Minn., 1985; postgrad., Moorhead State U., 1987—. Camp nurse Camp Grassik, Dawson, N.D., 1970; psychiat. nurse St. Luke's Hosps., Fargo, N.D., 1970-72; nurse supr. N.D. State Hosp., Jamestown, 1972-73; nurse clinician N.D. State Hosp., 1975-76; clin. instr. nursing Jamestown Coll., 1976; coronary care nurse St. Luke's Hosps., Fargo, 1976-77; cons. Profl. Assocs. for Continuing Edn., Mpls., 1977-80; asst. coord. patient edn. St. Luke's Hosps., Fargo, 1977-82; dir. corp. planning and research St. Luke's Hosps.-Merit-Care, Fargo, 1983—; cons. strategic planning, Fargo, 1986—. Bd. dirs. parish fellowship Olivet Luth Ch., Fargo, 1987-89, coord. bd. lay ministry, 1989—; com. mem. United Way, Fargo, 1987—. Mem. N.D. Nurses Assn. (bd. dirs. 1979-81, chmn. bylaws com. 1983-87, various bds. and coms.), Am. Hosp. Assn., Soc. for Healthcare Planning and Mktg., Am. Mgmt. Assn. Democrat. Home: 1439 25th Ave S 101 Fargo ND 58103 Office: St Lukes Hosps MeritCare 720 N 4th St Fargo ND 58122

SCHAEFER, PATRICIA, librarian; b. Ft. Wayne, Ind., Apr. 23, 1930; d. Edward John and Hildegarde Hartman (Hormel) S. MusB, Northwestern U., 1951; MusM, U. Ill., 1958; MLS, U. Mich., 1963. With U.S. Rubber Co., Ft. Wayne, 1951-52; sec. to promotion mgr. Sta. WOWO, Ft. Wayne, Ind., 1952, sec. to program mgr., 1953-55; coord. publicity and promotion Home Telephone Co., Ft. Wayne, 1955-56; sec. Fine Arts Found., Ft. Wayne, 1956-57; libr. asst. Columbus (Ohio) Pub. Libr., 1958-59; audio-visual librarian Muncie (Ind.) Pub. Libr., 1959-86, asst. libr. dir., 1981-86; libr. dir., 1986—; chmn. Ind. Libr. Film Cir., 1962-63; treas. Ind. Libr. Film Svc. 1969-70, 83-85; mem. trustee adv. coun. Milton S. Eisenhower Libr., Johns Hopkins U.; cons. in field. Weekly columnist Libr. Lines, Muncie Evening Press, 1981-83; Contbr. articles to profl. jours. Dir. Franklin Electric Co., Inc. Bd. dirs. Muncie Symphony Assn., 1964-74, 85—; trustees Masterworks Chorale; bd. dirs. Cen. City Bus. Assn. Mem. adv. com., bookshop dir. Midwest Writers Workshop, 1976-77; sec. Del. County Coun. for the Arts, 1978-79, pres., 1979-81, bd. dirs., 1985-86; mem. pres.'s coun. Berea Coll.; bd. dirs. Muncie YWCA, 1977-82, 85—, treas., 1981-82, 88-89; gen. chmn. Ind. Renaissance Fair, 1978-79; pres. Muncie Matinee Musicale, 1965-67; past pres. Ind. Film and Video Coun.; bd. dirs. Wapehani coun. Girl Scouts U.S., 1989—. Named Woman Achievement Pub. Svcs., 1986. Mem. ALA, Ind. Libr. Assn. (pres. 1987-88), Nat. League Am. Pen Women (pres. Muncie br. 1974-78), Am. Recorder Soc., Northeastern Ind. Recorder Soc., Altrusa (pres. 1986-87), Riley-Jones Club, Delta Zeta, Mu Phi Epsilon. Republican. Roman Catholic. Home: 405 S Tara Ln Muncie IN 47304 Office: 301 E Jackson St Muncie IN 47305

SCHAEFER, SUSAN MARIE, psychologist; b. New Ulm, Minn., Jan. 31, 1952; d. Henry Roland and Marjorie Lillian (Gilbertson) S. BA in Psychology summa cum laude, U. Minn., 1974, MA in Psychology, 1978. Lic. psychologist, Minn.; cert. chem. dependency counselor. Counselor, program mgr. Chrysalis Ctr. Women, Mpls., 1975-80; instr. U. Minn., Mpls., 1975-78; counselor Relate Counseling Ctr., Minnetonka, Minn., 1981-83; pvt. practice psychology Mpls., 1983—; adj. prof. St. Mary's Coll., Mpls., 1984-86; co-chmn. tng. insts. com. State Task Force Sexual Exploitation by Counselors and Therapists, 1985-86; bd. dirs. Sojourner Shelter, Hokins, Minn., 1982-85; trainer, cons. Program in Human Sexuality, U. Minn. Med. Sch., 1979-85. Contbr. articles to profl. jours. and books. Recipient Rsch. award Am. Psychol. Assn., 1988. Mem. Minn. Women Psychologists, Minn. Assn. Lic. Psychologists, Inst. Chem. Dependency Profls. Minn., Minn. Psychol. Assn. Democrat. Roman Catholic. Office: 2400 Blaisdell Ave S Minneapolis MN 55404

SCHAEFFER, BARBARA HAMILTON, company executive, travel consultant; b. Newton, Mass., Apr. 26, 1926; d. Peter Davidson Gunn and Harriet Bennett (Thompson) Hamilton; m. John Schaeffer, Sept. 7, 1946; children—Laurie, John, Peter. Student, Skidmore Coll., 1943-46; AB in English, Bucknell U., 1948; postgrad. Montclair State U., 1950-51, Bank St. Coll. Edn., 1959-61, Yeshiva U., 1961-62; student Daytona Beach Coll., 1984. Cert. primary, secondary tchr., N.J. Dir. Pompton Plains Sch., N.J., 1959-62; adviser Episcopal Sch., Towaco, N.J., 1968-70; v.p. Deltona-De-Land Trolley, Orange City, Fla., 1980-81; pres. Monroe Heavy Equipment Rentals, Inc., Orange City, 1981—, also Magic Carpet Travel, 1985-88 cons. TLC Travel Club, Orange City, 1981-88; lectr. on children's art, 1959-70. Contbr. articles to profl. publs. Mem. Internat. Platform Assn., Am. Soc. Travel Agts., Orange City C. of C., Small Bus. Devel. Regional Ctr. (Stetson U. chpt.), DeLand Area C. of C. (transp. com. 1981-85). Episcopalian. Avocations: restoring old homes, oil painting, piano. Home: 400 Foothill Farms Rd Orange City FL 32763 Mailing Address: PO Box 668 De Bary FL 32713

SCHAEFFER, KARREN TELFORD, legal educator, lawyer; b. San Bernardino, Calif., May 19, 1952; d. O. Lynn and Gladys E. (Martin) Telford; m. James Parker, Jr., Aug. 17, 1968; m. William Anthony Schaeffer, Jan. 26, 1975; 1 child, Tray James. BLS, Western State U., Fullerton, Calif., 1982, JD, 1984. Bar: Calif. 1984, U.S. Ct. Appeals (9th cir.) 1985. In mktg. Hancock Labs., Johnson & Johnson, Anaheim, Calif., 1972-78; in mgmt. Delta Med. Industries, Costa Mesa, Calif., 1978-84; atty. Law Offices of K.T. Schaeffer, Santa Ana, Calif., 1984-89; prof. law So. Calif. Coll. Law, Brea, 1985-89, asst. dean, 1989—, dir. paralegal studies, 1987-88; dean So. Calif. Coll. Bus. and Law, Brea, 1989—; bd. dirs. Luth. Social Svcs. So. Calif., L.A., 1989—. Vol., Casita de San Jose, Santa Ana, 1988—. Mem. NAFE, AAUW, Am. Bar Assn., Orange County Bar Assn., So. Calif. Assn. Law Librs., Packards Internat., Buick Club Am. (treas. 1986-88), Classic Car Club Am., Delta Theta Phi. Republican. Lutheran. Office: Southern Calif Coll Bus 595 W Lambert Rd Brea CA 92621

SCHAEFFER, SUSAN FROMBERG, author, educator; b. Bklyn., Mar. 25, 1941; d. Irving and Edith (Levine) Fromberg; B.A., U. Chgo., 1961, M.A. with honors, 1963, Ph.D. with honors, 1966; m. Neil J. Schaeffer, Oct. 11, 1970; children—Benjamin Adam, May Anna. Instr. English, Wright Jr. Coll., Chgo., 1964-65; asst. prof. Ill. Inst. Tech., Chgo., 1965-67; successively asst. prof., asso. prof., prof. Bklyn. Coll., 1967—; guest lectr. U. Chgo., Cornell U., U. Ariz., U. Maine, Yale U., U. Tex., U. Mass. John Simon Guggenheim fellow; recipient E.L. Wallant award, Friends of Lit. award.; Prairie Schooner's Lawrence award; O. Henry award; Poetry award Centennial Rev. Mem. PEN, Authors Guild, Poetry Soc. Am. Democrat. Jewish. Author novels: Falling, 1973; Anya, 1974; Time In Its Flight, 1978; Love, 1981; The Madness of a Seduced Woman, 1983; Mainland, 1984, The Injured Party, 1986, Buffalo Afternoon, 1989; poetry: The Witch and the Weather Report, 1972; Alphabet For the Lost Years, 1976; Granite Lady (nominee Nat. Book award), 1974; Rhymes and Runes of the Toad, 1975; The Bible of the Beasts of the Little Field, 1980; short stories: The Queen of Egypt and Other Stories, 1980; children's novel: The Dragons of North Chittendon, 1986, The Four Hoods and Great Dog, 1988. Address: 783 E 21st St Brooklyn NY 11210*

SCHAFER, CAROLYN MARIE GROUND, accountant, controller; b. Decatur, Ill., Oct. 29, 1955; d. Harry L. and Carol J. (Riggins) Ground; m. C. Crane Schafer, May 28, 1977; children: Michael Benson, Jordan Leigh, Matthew Lynn. Student, So. Ill. U., 1973-76; BS, Ill. State U., 1977. Cost acct. Stewart Warner-Hobbs, Spring Valley, Ill., 1977-78; assessment clk. Bureau County, Princeton, Ill., 1978-79; acctg. asst. Conco, Inc. div. H.D. Conkey & Co., Mendota, Ill., 1979-80, head acct., 1980-81, chief acct., 1981-88; corp. contr. H.D. Conkey & Co., Mendota, 1988—; sec.-treas. Riverport Inc., Mendota, 1989—. Ill. State scholar, 1973, Pres.'s scholar So. Ill. U., 1973-76. Mem. Jr. Woman's League (pres. Princeton chpt. 1989—), Alpha Gamma Delta. Democrat. Methodist. Office: HD Conkey & Co 1304 Division Mendota IL 61342

SCHAFF, PAULA KAY, industrial company executive; b. Cape Girardeau, Mo., Oct. 10, 1945; d. Charles Henry Sr. and Elnora Pauline (Ridge) Canine; m. Fred Jon Schaff; 1 child, Kevin Jon. Student, Washtenaw Community Coll., U. Ill., Dana U. Successively records clk. PTO div., accounts payable clk., sec., sales specialist, exec. sec., customer svc. specialist Dana Corp., Chelsea, Mich., 1967-78, supr. customer svc., 1978-79, supr. customer svc., shipping and assembly PTO div., 1979-81; distbn. mgr. Dana Corp., Athens, Ga., 1981-85, Maumee, Ohio, 1985-88; gen. mgr. warehouse ops. div. Dana Corp., 1989—. Mem. NAFE, Toledo Women in Industry. Republican. Methodist. Office: Dana Corp Warehouse Ops Div PO Box 455 Toledo OH 43692

SCHAFFER, BONNIE LYNN, psychologist; b. N.Y.C., Mar. 25, 1957; d. Leonard Harry and Lillian Clara (Simon) Grossflam; m. Neil Leonard Schaffer, May 15, 1988; 1 child, Beth Erin. BA, U. Rochester, 1978; MS, Kans. State U., 1981, PhD, 1983. Psychologist Ruston (La.) State Sch., 1983-85; psychologist Rome (N.Y.) Devel. Ctr., 1985-87, O.D. Heck Devel. Ctr., Schenectady, N.Y., 1987—. Mem. Am. Psychol. Assn. Nat. Assn. Sch. Psychologists, N.Y. Assn. Sch. Psychologists. Democrat. Jewish.

SCHAFFER, DIANE MAXIMOFF, social work educator; b. Chgo., Mar. 11, 1946; d. Lyle Edward and Betty Alice (Maximoff) S. BA in Psychology, Stanford U., 1968, MA in Sociology of Edn., 1970, PhD in Edn. and Psychology, 1977. Asst. prof. Sch. Social Work San Jose (Calif.) State U., 1977-82, assoc. prof., 1982-88, prof., 1988—; vis. scholar Ctr. for Rsch. on Women, Stanford U., 1984; curriculum cons., faculty mem. Internat. Women's Studies Inst., San Francisco, 1984-86; coord. women's studies program San Jose State U., 1985-89. Contbr. chpt. International Feminization of Poverty, 1988. Co-chair Women's Coun. of State Univs., Calif. Rsch. grantee NIMH, 1979, 82. Mem. Am. Psychol. Assn., Nat. Women's Studies Assn., Assn. for Women in Devel., Soc. for Psychol. Study of Social Issues, Phi Kappa Phi. Home: 253 Aptos Beach Dr Aptos CA 95003 Office: San Jose State U Sch Social Work San Jose CA 95192

SCHAFFER, MIRIAM ELLEN, publicist; b. Providence, Jan. 15, 1955; d. Joseph Jess and Eva (Levine) S.; m. Jeffrey Louis Idelson, Apr. 14, 1984; 1 child, Laiah Jo Idelson. BA, Skidmore Coll., 1977. Producer Sta. WCPX-TV, Orlando, Fla., 1977-79, Sta. WNEP-TV, Wilkes-Barre, Pa., 1979-80, Sta. KRON-TV, San Francisco, 1981-86; publicist All Star Promotions, Walnut Creek, Calif., 1986—. Mem. NAFE.

SCHAFFNER, VALERIE LYNN, mechanical engineer, retired military officer; b. St. Charles, Mo., Aug. 22, 1959; d. Jack Alfred Jr. and Marcia Ann (Flesch) S. BSME, U. Mo., 1984. Engr. in tng., Mo. Engring. intern Superior Oil Co., Bakersfield, Calif., summer 1982, AMF Wyott, Inc., Cheyenne, Wyo., summer 1983; asst. resident officer in charge of constrn. Clark AFB (Philippines), Pampanga, 1985-87; dir. facilities maintenance engring. dept. U.S. Naval Air Sta., Sicily, Italy, 1987-89; mech. engr. Nolte and Assocs., San Jose, Calif., 1989—; ballet dancer St. Charles Ballet Co., 1971-77. Fundraiser USN, Clark Air Base, 1987. With USN, 1984-89. Mem. ASME, Soc. Am. Mil. Engrs. Home: 5275 Camden Ave #218 San Jose CA 95124

SCHAITEL, JEANNE MARIE, portrait photographer; b. Sparta, Wis., July 17, 1952; d. Hugh Kenneth and Mildred Emma (Leonhardt) Hesselberg; m. Leonard J. Schnaitel, July 22, 1972 (div. 1986); children: Matthew L., Jacob J., Kristin R. Student, U. LaCrosse, 1978-85, Viterbo Coll., 1987—. Bookkeeper, clerk Leon Supply Co., Sparta, Wis., 1972-75; income tax preparation Sparta, 1978-, portrait photographer, 1981-. Home: Rte 5 #29 Oak Meadows Sparta WI 54656 Office: Jeanne's Photography 109 S Water St Sparta WI 54656

SCHALK, BARBARA ANN, strategic planner; b. Detroit. AS, Henry Ford Community Coll., Dearborn, 1968; BS, U. Mich., 1981. With Gen. Motors Corp., 1977—; staff asst. Gen. Motors Corp., Warren, Mich., 1987-88; sr. strategic planner Gen. Motors Corp., Detroit, 1988—. Mem. AAUW, Lake Orion, Mich., 1986-88; counselor, advisor Jr. Achievement, Royal Oak, Mich., 1982; chmn. archtl. control com. Keatington Homeowner's Assn., Lake Orion, 1987, 88; bd. dirs. U. Mich.-Dearborn Alumni Soc., 1981-83. Named Alumni of the Yr., U. Mich., 1985. Office: Gen Motors Corp 3044 W Grand Blvd #12-222 Detroit MI 48202-3091

SCHALK, BEVERLY VANDYKE, nurse, educator; b. Hillsboro, Oreg., Aug. 13, 1959; d. Ervin Aloysius and Jane Margaret (Bernards) Van Dyke; m. David Charles Schalk, Aug. 20, 1983; children: Laura Beverly, Christopher David (dec.), Katelyn Ann. B.S., Oreg. State U., 1982, MEd in Adult Edn., 1988; A.S. in Nursing, Chemeketa Community Coll., 1984. Coordinator vols. escape field studies program U. Oreg., Eugene, 1979-80; fetal alcohol syndrome directory coordinator Benton-Linn Council on Alcohol, Corvallis, Oreg., 1982; early pregnancy instr. March of Dimes, Salem, Oreg., 1982-84; staff nurse Salem Hosp., 1983-84, nurse perinatal educator, 1984-88; edn. coordinator Health Resource Ctr. St. Vincent and Med. Ctr., Portland, Oreg., 1987—; stress mgmt. workshop designer/facilitator U. Oreg., 1982, Salem Sr. Ctr., 1983, Village Retirement Ctr., Dallas, Oreg., 1986; early pregnancy instr. March of Dimes, Salem, 1982-84, pub. health edn. com., 1982-84. Mem. Nurses Assn. of Am. Coll. Obstetricians and Gynecologists, Oreg. Council Healthcare Educators, Oreg. Gerontol. Assn., Salem Childbirth Edn. Assn., Eta Sigma Gamma (pres. chpt. 1980-82). Democrat. Roman Catholic. Home: 28400 SW Canyon Creek Rd Wilsonville OR 97070 Office: Health Resource Ctr St Vincent Hosp & Med Ctr 9205 SW Barnes Rd Portland OR 97225

SCHALL, AMY ELIZABETH, controller; b. Kingston, Pa., May 9, 1964; d. George Russell and Judith (Ruggere) S. BS summa cum laude, Boston Coll., 1986. CPA, Va. Sr. acct. Laventahal & Horwath, Washington, 1986-89; asst. contr. Kaempfer Co. Investment Builders, Washington, 1989—; fin. com. mem. Sutton Towers Fin. Com., Washington, 1988, 89, 90. Tutor Higher Achievement Program, Washington, 1987, 88; vol. George Bush for Pres. Campaign, Washington, 1988, Presdl. Inaugural Com., Washington, 1988, 89; fundraiser Hospice Care of D.C., Washington, 1989, 90. Mem. Jr. League Washington, Beta Gamma Sigma. Republican. Home: 3101 New Mexico Ave NW #228 Washington DC 20016

SCHALLER, JANE GREEN, pediatrician; b. Cleve., June 26, 1934; d. George and May Alice (Wing) Green; children: Robert Thomas, George Charles, Margaret May. A.B., Hiram (Ohio) Coll., 1956; M.D. cum laude, Harvard U., 1960. Diplomate Am. Bd. Pediatrics, Am. Bd. Med. Examiners. Resident in pediatrics Children's Hosp.-U. Wash., Seattle, 1960-63; fellow immunology and arthritis Children's Hosp.-U. Wash., 1963-65; mem. faculty U. Wash. Med. Sch., 1965-83, prof. pediatrics, 1975-83; head div. rheumatic diseases Children's Hosp., Seattle, 1968-83; prof., chmn. dept. pediatrics Tufts U. Sch. Medicine/New Eng. Med. Ctr., 1983—; pediatrician-in-chief Boston Floating Hosp., 1983—; vis. physician Med. Research Council, Taplow, Eng., 1971-72; bd. visitors Sch. of Medicine U. Pitts., 1989—. Author articles in field.; Editorial bds. profl. jours. Bd. dirs. Seattle Chamber Music Festival, 1982-85; trustee Boston Chamber Music Soc., 1985—. Mem. Soc. Pediatric Research, Am. Pediatric Soc., Am. Acad. Pediatrics (chmn. subcom. on children and human rights 1989—, com. on internat. child health 1990—), Am. Rheumatism Assn., New Eng. Pediatric Soc. (councillor 1984—), Brazilian Congress Rheumatology, N.Z. Rheumatism Soc., Chilean Soc. Rheumatology, Australian Rheumatism Assn., Assn. Med. Sch. Pediatric Chmn. (exec. com. 1986-89, rep. to council on govt. affairs and council of acad. socs.), Com. Health in So. Africa (exec. com. 1986—), Physicians for Human Rights (exec. com. 1986—, pres. 1986-89) Aesculapian Club (pres. 1988-89), Harvard U. Med. Sch. Alumni Council (v.p. 1977-80, pres. 1982-83), Saturday Club. Office: Tufts U Sch Medicine New Eng Med Ctr/Floating Hosp 750 Washington St Boston MA 02111

SCHALOW, GAYLE JEAN, small business owner; b. Marshfield, Wis., May 27, 1951; d. Milton Gustave and Darlene Beverly (Hendrickson) Dommer; m. Russell Ray Schalow, Sept. 20, 1975; children; Tanya Lynn, Ashley Ann. Student, P.J. Jacobs High Sch., Steven Point, Wis., 1969, NCTI, Wausau, Wis., 1974; Postgrad., MSTI, Marshfield, Wis., 1988--. Laborer Land O' Lakes, Spencer, Wis., 1971-73; cert. surgical tech. St. Joseph Hosp., Marshfield, Wis., 1974-86; real estate broker McNeely Real Estate, Spencer, Wis., 1984-86. Leader coun. Girl Scouts U.S., 1985. Recipient Elsie Daggett award Wis. Jaycees 1987, Co-owner, Bookkeeper awards G&D Spencer Wis. 1986--. Mem. Trophy Dealers & Mfrs., Spencer Area C. of C. Lutheran.

SCHAMEL, CHERYL, education educator; b. Waverly, N.Y., Dec. 6, 1947; d. Max Elliott and Frances (Henton) Coleman; children: Mark Elliott, Kendra Anne. BS, SUNY, Geneseo, 1969; MS, SUNY, Buffalo, 1975. Cert. permanent tchr., N.Y. Tchr. Penfield (N.Y.) Cen. Schs., 1969-71, Akron (N.Y.) Cen. Schs., 1971-73, Williamsville (N.Y.) Cen. Schs., 1976-84; instr. edn. Johnson County Community Coll., Overland Park, Kans., 1987-89; tchr. Union Endicott Schs., N.Y., 1989—. Republican. Methodist. Home: 2 Carol Court Endwell NY 13760

SCHANSTRA, CARLA ROSS, technical writer; b. Berwyn, Ill., Sept. 4, 1954; d. Caroles Schanstra and Heather Millar (Thomson) Alonso. BA, Western Ill. U., 1976; postgrad., U. Ill. Circle, Chgo., 1980-81. Assoc. editor Hitchock Pub., Wheaton, Ill., 1976-80; assoc. product mgr. Advanced Systems, Inc., Elk Grove Village, Ill., 1980-81; tech. writer Profl. Computer Resources, Oak Brook, Ill., 1982; sr. tech. writer AT&T Bell Labs., Naperville, Ill., 1982—; freelance writer, 1980-85. Author: (stage plays) A Little Bit of Both, The Reversible Play, Survivors, Snakes and Apple Pie, It Should Be Obvious, Pastiche; contbr. articles to profl. jours. Violist Du Page Symphony, Glen Ellyn, Ill., 1984-87, 90—, Elgin Symphonette, Elgin, Ill., 1985-87. Mem. So. Tech. Communication Assn. (Awd. of Excellence 1985), Dramatists Guild, Feminist Writers Western Suburbs (founder 1988), Feminist Writers Guild Chgo. (adv. panel), Internat. Soc. Dramatists, Feminist Writer's Guild (adv. panel), Ill. Theatre Assn., Writers Workshop (co-founder 1980—) (Warrenville, Ill.). Office: AT&T Bell Labs IH-6R-209 Wheaton-Naperville Rd Naperville IL 60566

SCHANZLIN, PATRICIA ROBERTS, mortgage banking company executive; b. York, Pa., Apr. 15, 1944; d. Thomas William and Mary Elizabeth (Christine) Roberts; m. Donald Nelson Schanzlin, Feb. 19, 1966; children: Todd Byron, Lauren Leigh. BS, Beaver Coll., 1966. Asst. v.p. City Fed. Savs. & Loan, Somerset, N.J., 1978-81; sr. v.p. adminstrn. City Mortgage, Somerset, 1981-82; sr. v.p. loan adminstrn. City Fed. Mortgage, Somerset, 1982-86; sr. v.p. systems and ops. Meritor Mortgage Group/Meritor Fin., Phila., 1986-88; sr. v.p. loan adminstrn. Cenlar Fed. Savs. Bank, Princeton, N.J., 1988—. Bd. dirs. jr. bd. Florence Crittenden Home, Trenton, N.J., 1973-76, chair, 1975-76. Mem. Mortgage Bankers of Am. (chmn. automation com. 1985-87, vice chmn. loan adminstrn. com. 1986-90, chmn. 1990-91, chmn. FHA/VA liaison com. 1988-90, gov. 1989—), Computer Power Inc. User's Group (steering com. 1985—, chairperson 1989-91). Republican. Office: Cenlar Fed Savs Bank 101 Carnegie Ctr Princeton NJ 08543

SCHAPIRO, RUTH GOLDMAN, lawyer; b. N.Y.C., Oct. 31, 1926; d. Louis Albert and Sarah (Shapiro) Goldman; m. Donald Schapiro, June 29, 1952; children: Jane Goldman, Robert Andrew. A.B., Wellesley Coll., 1947; LL.B., Columbia U., 1950. Bar: N.Y. 1950, D.C. 1978. Asst. to reporters Am. Law Inst. Fed. Income Tax Statute, N.Y.C., 1950-51; assoc., then ptnr. Proskauer Rose Goetz & Mendelsohn, N.Y.C., 1955—; mem. nominating commn. U.S. Tax Ct., 1978-81. Notes editor: Columbia Law Rev., 1949-50; editor: Tax Shelters, Practising Law Inst., 1983; contbr. articles to legal jours. Vice-chmn. adv. com. NYU Inst. Fed. Taxation, 1979-85; mem. adv. com. NYU-IRS Continuing Legal Edn. Project. Fellow Am. Bar Found., N.Y. Bar Found.; mem. ABA, N.Y. State Bar Assn. (chmn. tax sect. 1981-82, exec. com. 1982-84, ho. of dels., 1981-84, 89—, chmn. fin. com. 1984-87, chmn. spl. com on Women in the Crts. 1986-89), Assn. Bar City N.Y. (taxation com. 1972-75, 78-79, chair personal income tax com. 1990—), N.Y. County Lawyers Assn., Am. Coll. Tax Counsel, Am. Judicature Soc., N.Y. Wellesley Club. Jewish. Club: N.Y. Wellesley (N.Y.C.). Home: 1035 Fifth Ave New York NY 10028 Office: Proskauer Rose Goetz & Mendelsohn 1585 Broadway New York NY 10036

SCHARETT, ANN ELIZABETH, rehabilitation center executive; b. Corning, N.Y., Aug. 17, 1941; d. Theodore LeRoy Reed and Elizabeth Almira (Guernsey) Schoonover; m. David Leonard Scharett, Aug. 10, 1962; children: Donna Leigh, David Thomas. BS, St. Joseph's Coll., North

Windham, Maine, 1984. Cert. nursing adminstr. ANA. From staff nurse to organizer alcoholic treatment program Willard (N.Y.) Psychiatric Ctr. (formerly Willard State Hosp.), 1962-81; nurse adminstr., alcoholism rehab. coordinator Dick Van Dyke Clinic, Willard, 1981-86; asst. dir. John L. Norris Treatment Ctr., Rochester, N.Y., 1986—; guest lectr. Tompkins-Cortland Community Coll., Ithaca, N.Y., 1984-86; chairperson Region 2 Alcoholism Service Providers Group, Rochester, 1980; bd. dirs. Finger Lakes Alcoholism Counsel and Referral Agy., Clifton Springs, N.Y., 1975-77. Vol. United Way, Willard, 1983-85, ARC Seneca County, 1983-87; bd. dirs. Interlaken (N.Y.) Christian Sch., 1977-78, 84-87; youth advisor First Bapt. Ch. Interlaken, 1985-86, Sunday sch. tchr., 1962—. Recipient Cert. for 25 Yrs. Service N.Y. State Div. Alcoholism, 1985. Mem. NAFE, Nat. Soc. RN's, N.Y. Fedn. Alcoholism Counselors. Republican. Baptist. Office: John L Norris Treatment Ctr 1600 South Ave Rochester NY 14620

SCHAROLD, MARY LOUISE, psychoanalyst, educator; b. Wichita Falls, Tex., Mar. 3, 1943; d. Walter John and Louise Helen (Hartman) Baumgartner; m. William Ballew McCollum, Aug. 23, 1964 (div. 1981); m. Harry Karl Scharold, June 19, 1982; children: Margaret Louise, Walter Ballew. BA with highest distinction, U. Kans., 1964; MD, Baylor Coll. Med., 1968; postgrad. Topeka Inst. for Psychoanalysis, 1981. Diplomate Am. Bd. Psychiatry and Neurology. Intern Meml. Baptist. Hosp., Houston, 1968-69; resident in psychiatry Baylor Coll. Med., Houston, 1969-72, chief resident, 1971-72; practice of medicine specializing in psychoanalysis, Houston, 1972—; asst. prof. Baylor Coll. Med., Houston, 1973-76, asst. clin. prof., 1981-84, assoc. clin. prof., 1984—; dir. Baylor Psychiat. Clinic, Houston, 1973-76; co-dir. Rice U. Psychiat. Service, Houston, 1981-82; asst. clin. prof. U. Kans. Sch. Medicine, Kansas City, 1977-81; teaching assoc. Topeka Inst. Psychoanalysis, 1980-81; instr. Houston-Galveston Psychoanalytic Inst., 1984-86, teaching analyst, 1986—; Adv. bd. Leavenworth Mental Health Assn., Kans., 1977-81. Watkins scholar U. Kans., 1961-64. Fellow Am. Psychiatric Assn. (chmn. Tex. peer review 1984-88); mem. Am. Psychoanalytic Assn. (cert. 1982, peer rev. com. 1985—, prof. ins. commn. 1986—), Am. Group Psychotherapy Assn., Houston Psychiatric Soc. (v.p. 1984-85, pres. elect 1985-86, pres. 1986-87), Houston-Galveston Psychoanalytic Soc. (sec.-treas. 1984-86, pres.-elect 1986-88, pres. 1988-90), Am. Psychiat. Assn. (quality assurance com. 1986-87), Houston Group Psychotherapy Soc. (adv. bd. 1984-85), Mortar Bd., Phi Beta Kappa, Delta Phi Alpha, Alpha Omega Alpha, Hilltopper, Pi Beta Phi Alumni Assn. Republican. Lutheran. Office: 4101 Greenbriar Dr Suite 240 Houston TX 77098

SCHARRER, BERTA VOGEL, anatomy and neuroscience educator; b. Munich, Fed. Republic Germany, Dec. 1, 1906; d. Karl and Johanna V.; widowed. PhD in Zoology, U. Munich, 1930; MD (hon.), U. Giessen, Fed. Republic Germany, 1976; DSc (hon.), Northwestern U., 1977, U. N.C., 1978, Smith Coll., 1980, Harvard U., 1982, Yeshiva U., 1983, Mt. Holyoke Coll., 1984, SUNY, 1985; LLD, U. Calgary, Alta., Can., 1982. Research assoc. Research Inst. for Psychiatry, Munich, 1931-34, Neurol. Inst., Frankfurt-am-Main, 1934-37, U. Chgo. Dept. Anatomy, 1937-38, Rockefeller Inst., N.Y.C., 1938-40; instr., fellow Western Res. U. Dept. Anatomy, Cleve., 1940-46; John Guggenheim fellow U. Colo. Dept. Anatomy, Denver, 1947-48, spl. USPHS research fellow, 1948-50; asst. prof. (research) dept. anatomy U. Colo. Sch. Medicine, Denver, 1950-55; prof. anatomy Albert Einstein Coll. Medicine, 1955-77, acting chmn., 1965-67, 76-77, prof. emeritus anatomy and neurosci., 1978—; mem. com. on brain scis. NRC; researcher in comparative neuroendocrinology, neurosecretion, neuropeptides. Recipient Kraepelin Gold medal, 1978, F.C. Koch award Endocrine Soc., 1980, Nat. Medal Sci., 1983. Mem. Nat. Acad. Scis., Am. Acad. Arts & Scis., Deutsche Acad. Naturforscher Leopoldina (Schleiden medal 1983), Am. Assn. Anatomists (pres. 1978-79, Henry Gray award 1982), Am. Soc. Zoologists (hon. mem.), Soc. Neurosci., Endocrine Soc. (F.C. Koch award 1980), Internat. Brain Research Orgn. Home: 1240 Neill Ave Bronx NY 10461 Office: Albert Einstein Coll Medicine/Dept Anatomy 1300 Morris Park Ave Bronx NY 10461

SCHATTINGER, JOAN MYERS, history writer; b. Cleve., Sept. 6, 1936; d. Walter Edward Myers and Janet Louise (Shelhart) Myers-Clayton; m. James Henry Schattinger, July 28, 1961; children: Elisabeth Myers, James Douglas. BA, Wellesley Coll., 1957; postgrad., Harvard U., 1958; MA, Case Western Res. U., 1965. Cer. tchr., Mass., Ohio. Editorial asst. Harvard Law Sch., Cambridge, Mass., 1957-58; tchr. English Orange Bd. Edn., Cleve., 1958-61, Brookline (Mass.) bd. Edn., 1961-63; free-lance writer, editor Cleve., 1963—; vis. artist We Clevelanders Program, Cleve., 1984-86; cons. in field, Cleve., 1979—. Author: Cleveland's Flats: The Incredible City Under the Hill, 1979, Cleveland's Flats on Tour, 1987; author study guides. Bd. dirs. Cleve. Wellesley, 1978—, Shaker Lakes Regional Nature Ctr. Women's Bd., Cleve., 1986-87. Mem. Internat. Soc. British Genealogy and Family History (trustee), Cotillion Soc. Club: Cleve. Skating.

SCHATZ, PAULINE, dietitian; b. Sioux City, Iowa, Sept. 25, 1923; d. Isaac and Haya (Kaplan) Epstein; m. Hyman Schatz, Sept. 2, 1951; children: Barbara, Larry. BS, UCLA, 1945, MS, 1950, MS in Public Health, 1963; EdD, U. So. Calif., 1984. Head dietitian VA, 1946-54; asso. prof. Los Angeles City Coll., 1958-68; prof. home econs. Calif. State U., Los Angeles, 1968-83, prof. emeritus, 1983—, dir. center dietetic edn., 1979—, Calif. State U., Northridge, 1988—. Grantee VA, Kellogg Found., HEW. Mem. Am. Dietetic Assn. (Disting. Service award 1986), Am. Home Econs. Assn., Calif. Dietetic Assn. (Zellmer grantee 1966-69, Disting. Service award 1986), Los Angeles Dietetic Assn., Omicron Nu. Author: Manual for Clinical Dietetics, 1978, 3d edit., 1983; also articles to profl. jours. Office: Calif State U Dept Home Econs Los Angeles CA 90032

SCHAUB, MARILYN MCNAMARA, religion educator; b. Chgo., Mar. 24, 1928; d. Bernard Francis and Helen Katherine (Skehan) McNamara; m. R. Thomas Schaub, Oct. 25, 1969; 1 dau., Helen Ann. B.A., Rosary Coll., 1953; Ph.D., U. Fribourg, Switzerland, 1957; diploma, Ecole Biblique, Jerusalem, 1967. Asst. prof. classics and Bibl. studies Rosary Coll., River Forest, Ill., 1957-69; prof. Bibl. studies Duquesne U., Pitts., 1969-70, 73—; participant 8 archeol. excavations, Middle East.; adminstrv dir. expedition to the Southeast Dead Sea Plains, Jordan, 1989—; hon. assoc. Am. Schs. Oriental Rsch., 1966-67, trustee, 1986—; Danforth assoc., 1972-80. Author: Friends and Friendship for St. Augustine, 1964; translator: (with H. Richter) Agape in the New Testament, 3 vols, 1963-65. Mem. Soc. Bibl. Lit., Catholic Bibl. Assn., Am. Acad. Religion. Democrat. Home: 25 McKelvey Ave Pittsburgh PA 15218 Office: Duquesne U Theology Dept Pittsburgh PA 15282

SCHAUENBERG, SUSAN KAY, educator, counselor; b. Rock Island, Ill., Oct. 23, 1945; d. Albert George and Elizabeth (Stedman) Grill; m. Robert Dale Schauenberg Jr.; 1 child, Trevor Alan. BA, Marycrest Coll., 1967; MA, U. Iowa, 1968. Counselor, assoc. prof. Black Hawk Coll., Moline, Ill., 1971—; bus. cons., Rock Island, 1984—; v.p. faculty senate Black Hawk Coll., 1980-82. Planning com. United Way Orgn., Quad-Cities, Ill., 1981-84, agy. relations com., 1981-82, allocations com., 1980-82; den mother Rock Island chpt. Boy Scouts Am., 1978-79. Named one of Most Admired Women of the Quad-Cities, 1975. Mem. Assn. of Psychol. Type, Friends of Jung, Am. Fedn. Tchrs., Ill. Guidance and Personnel Assn. (Black Hawk chpt.), U. Iowa Alumni Assn., Phi Gamma Delta (mem. Parents Assn.). Home: 1327 46th Ave Rock Island IL 61201 Office: Black Hawk Coll 6600 34th Ave Moline IL 61265

SCHAUER, CATHARINE GUBERMAN, public affairs specialist; b. Woodbury, N.J., Sept. 24, 1945; d. Jack and Anna Ruth (Felipe) Guberman; m. Irwin Jay Schauer, July 4, 1968; children: Cheryl Anne, Marc Cawin. AB, Miami-Dade Jr. Coll., 1965; BEd, U. Miami, 1967; postgrad. Mercer U., 1968, Old Dominion U., 1990. Writer, Miami (Fla.) News, 1962-63; tchr. Dade County Schs., Miami, Fla., 1967-68; coordinator pub. info. Macon Jr. Coll. (Ga.), 1968-69; writer Atlanta Jour., 1969-72; editor Ridgerunner newspaper, Woodbridge, Va., 1973-75; pub. info. specialist Dept. Interior, Washington, 1980-82; writer Dept. Army, Ft. Belvoir, Va., 1982-84, chief prodn., design and editorial, publs. div., 1984-85; head writer-editor SE region U.S. Naval Audit Service, Virginia Beach, Va., 1986; pub. affairs specialist, tech. rep. for vis. ctr. ops. NASA Langley Rsch. Ctr., Hampton, Va., 1987-89, acting head Office Pub. Svcs., 1989; columnist, writer Potomac News, Woodbridge, 1972-85. Contbr. articles to profl. jours. Historian, publicity chmn. PTO, Woodbridge, 1974; publicity chmn. Boy Scouts Am., Woodbridge, 1974-83, Girl Scouts U.S., Woodbridge, 1974-79; bd. dirs. Congregation Ner Tamid, Woodbridge, 1984-85. Recipient Outstanding Tng. Devel. Support award U.S. Army, 1983; 1st place news writing award and 1st place for advt. design Fla. Jr. Coll. Press Assn., 1964, 1st place feature writing award, 1964, 1st place news writing award Sigma Delta Chi, 1965, 70th anniversary team NASA, 1988. Mem. Va. Press Women, Women in Communications, Nat. Fedn. Press Women. Democrat. Jewish. Home: 120 Tide's Run Yorktown VA 23692-4333 Office: NASA Langley Rsch Ctr Mail Code 154 Hampton VA 23665-5225

SCHAUF, VICTORIA, pediatrician, educator, researcher, consultant; b. N.Y.C., Feb. 17, 1943; d. Maurice J. and Ruth H. (Baker) Bisson; 1 child by previous marriage: Christine A. Schauf; m. Michael W. Delaney; 1 child, Michael T. Delaney. BS with honors in Microbiology, U. Chgo., 1965, MD with honors, 1969. Chief resident pediatrics Children's Hosp. Nat. Med. Ctr., Washington, 1971-72; rsch. trainee NIH, Bethesda, Md., 1972; asst. prof. microbiology Rush Med. Coll., Chgo., 1972-74; prof. pediatrics, head pediatric infectious diseases U. Ill., Chgo., 1974-84; med. officer FDA, Rockville, Md., 1984-86; chmn. dept. pediatrics Nassau County Med. Ctr., East Meadow, N.Y., 1986—; prof. pediatrics SUNY, Stony Brook, 1987—; mem. vis. faculty Chiang Mai (Thailand) U., 1978; mem. ad hoc com. study sects. NIH, Bethesda, 1981-82; bd. dirs. Pearl Stetler Rsch. Found., Chgo., 1982-84; cons. FDA, 1987-88, Can. Bur. Human Prescription Drugs, Ottawa, 1990—. Producer TV programs in field; contbr. articles to profl. jours., chpts. to books. Vol. physician Cook County Hosp., Chgo., 1974-84; mem. adv. com. Nat. Hansen's Disease Ctr., La., 1977, Nassau County Day Care Coun., N.Y., 1988—; mem. adv. bd. Surg. Aid to Children of World, N.Y., 1986—. Am. Lung Assn. grantee U. Ill., 1977; recipient contract NIH, U. Ill., 1978-81, grantee, 1979-84. Fellow Infectious Diseases Soc. Am.; mem. Pediatric Infectious Diseases Soc. (exec. bd.), Soc. Pediatric Rsch., Am. Pediatric Soc., AAAS, Am. Soc. Microbiology, Am. Acad. Pediatrics, NOW, Phi Beta Kappa, Alpha Omega Alpha. Home: 11 Jeanette Dr Port Washington NY 11050 Office: Nassau County Med Ctr 2201 Hempstead Turnpike East Meadow NY 11554

SCHAUFLER, ROBIN GORDON, software engineer; b. Glen Cove, N.Y., May 1, 1957; d. Jack and Florence (Peyser) Gordon; m. Casey Bruce Schaufler, July. BS in Computer Sci., Rensselaer Polytechnic Inst., 1979. Systems programmer Amdahl Corp., Sunnyvale, Calif., 1979-83; software engr. Qubix Graphics Systems, San Jose, Calif., 1983-85, Sun Microsystems Inc., Mountain View, Calif., 1985--. Contbr. articles to profl. jours. Mem. Assn. Computing Machinery, ACM, SIGGRAPH, IEEE. Office: Sun Microsystems Inc 2550 Garcia Ave 14-40 Mountain View CA 94043

SCHAUTZ, CAROL A., advertising agency executive. Former v.p. and treas., now sr. v.p. and treas. Wunderman Worldwide, N.Y.C. Office: Wunderman Worldwide 675 Ave of the Americas New York NY 10010*

SCHAUWECKER, MARGARET LIDDIE, construction company executive; b. Louisa, Ky., July 28, 1934; d. Mitchell and Mary Lou (Thompson) McKinster; m. Norman Walter Schauwecker, Aug. 30, 1953 (div. Oct. 1968); children: Johanna L., Mitchell Walter, Shawna Ann. Student, Bliss Coll., 1952-54, El Segundo Coll., 1957-59. Sec. N. Am. Aviation, Columbus, Ohio, 1952-1955, Gilfillan Electronics, Los Angeles, 1956-62; adminstrv. asst. Columbus Wood Preserving Co., 1970-78; pres. Ohio State Tie and Timber Inc., Louisa, Ky., 1978—. Named to Honorable Order Ky. Cols. Commonwealth Ky., 1984; recipient Outstanding Achievement in Sales Vol. award Ohio Dept. Econ. Devel., 1980, 81, 82; recipient Top 100 Small Bus's. in Ohio award Ohio House Reps., 1983. Mem. Am. Wood Preservers Assn., Railway Tie Assn., Bus. and Profl. Women in Constrn. Baptist. Club: Louisa Woman's. Lodges: Order Eastern Star, Rebekah. Home: Rte 1 Box 2360 Louisa KY 41230 Office: Ohio State Tie and Timber Rte 1 Box 2360 Louisa KY 41230

SCHECHTER, GERALDINE POPPA, hematologist; b. N.Y.C., Jan. 16, 1938; d. Josif and Victoria (Nosi) P.; m. Alan Neil Schechter, Feb. 6, 1965; children: Daniele Malka, Andrew M.R. AB, Vassar Coll., Poughkeepsie, N.Y., 1959; MD, Columbia U., 1963. Diplomate Am. Bd. Internal Medicine, Am. Bd. Hematology. Intern, resident Presbyn. Hosp., N.Y.C., 1963-65; resident, fellow, rsch. assoc. VA Med. Ctr., Washington, 1965-70, staff physician, 1970-74, chief hematology, 1974—; asst., assoc. prof. medicine George Washington U., Washington, 1971-81, prof. medicine, 1981—; mem. hematology com. Am. Bd. Internal Medicine, Phila., 1985-91, bd. govs., 1990—. Mem. editorial bd. Blood, 1985-89. Contbr. articles to hematologic jours. Office: VA Med Ctr 50 Irving St NW Washington DC 20422

SCHECTER, PEGGY SMOLER, sales executive; b. N.Y., May 5, 1958; d. Avrum David and Helene Marilyn (Morris) Smoler; m. Scott Michael Schecter, Mar. 21, 1987. BA, Lehigh U., 1980; postgrad, NYU, 1986-89. Sr. underwriter Chubb Group of Ins., N.Y.C., 1980-85; regional sales mgr. Computers Ins Banking, N.Y.C., 1986-87; sales mgr. Bank Adminstrn. Inst., N.Y.C., 1987-90; account exec. Hanson Pub., Stamford, Conn., 1990—. Home: 1675 York Ave New York NY 10128

SCHEETZ, SISTER MARY JOELLEN, college president; b. Lafayette, Ind., May 20, 1926; d. Joseph Albert and Ellen Isabelle (Fitzgerald) S. A.B., St. Francis Coll., 1956; M.A., U. Notre Dame, 1964; Ph.D., U. Mich., 1970. Tchr. English, Bishop Luers High Sch., Fort Wayne, Ind., 1965-67; acad. dean St. Francis Coll., Fort Wayne, 1967-68; pres. St. Francis Coll., 1970—. Mem. Delta Epsilon Sigma. Office: St Francis Coll 2701 Spring St Fort Wayne IN 46808

SCHEFFLER, LINDA W., psychologist, educator; b. N.Y.C., Feb. 15, 1936; d. Robert Lee and Helen (Sonnenstrahl) Weingarten; m. Fred Shure, June 14, 1955 (div. 1962); m. Philip B. Scheffler, July 1, 1966. BA, U. Mich., 1957, MA, 1958, PhD, 1963. From asst. prof. to assoc. prof. psychology Hunter Coll. CUNY, N.Y.C., 1969—; pvt. practice psychology, N.Y.C., 1972—. Author: Help Thy Neighbor-How Counseling Works and When It Doesn't, 1984. Pres. Met. Coll. Mental Health Assn., N.Y.C., 1983-84. Office: 1430 2d Ave Ste 109 New York NY 10021

SCHEID-RAYMOND, LINDA ANNE, company executive; b. Rochester, N.Y., Aug. 13, 1953; d. Arthur F. and Anna M. Scheid; m. Dan Raymond, June 27, 1987. BFA, U. Colo., 1975. Leasing agt. Richard E. Rudolph, Boulder, Colo., 1975-77; adminstrv. asst. for Denver area Harsh Investment Corp., Denver, 1977-83; property mgr. A.G. Spanos Mgmt., Colorado Springs, Colo., 1984-85, Carmel Devel. and Mgmt., Denver, 1985-88; dist. property mgr. Property Asset Mgmt., Denver, 1989—. Contbr. photographs to profl. mags.

SCHEIDT, LOIS ANN, government official; b. Columbus, Ind., Apr. 11, 1959; d. Norval Lee and Harriet Jane (Klipsch) S. BS, Ball State U., 1983; MPA, Ind. U., Indpls., 1989. Program liaison person for exec. edn. Ind. U., 1988-89; personnel mgmt. specialist Naval Weapons Support Ctr., Crane, Ind., 1989—; fis. planning cons. Town of Hope (Ind.), 1987. Coord. DeClue for Judge, Perkins for Prosecutor, Columbus, 1986; mem., vice chmn. Columbus Human Rights Commn., 1985-86; tester Ind. Civil Rights Commn., Indpls., 1987; vice chmn. Perkins for State Rep., Columbus, 1987-88; publicity chmn. Ind. Young Reps., 1987-88, parliamentarian, 1988-89; treas. Bartholomew County Young Reps., 1986-87. Mem. Am. Soc. for Pub. Adminstrn., Am. Soc. for Tng. and Devel., Internat. Personnel Mgmt. Assn., AAUW (div. membership v.p. 1988—), Pi Alpha Alpha. Office: Naval Weapons Support Ctr Crane IN 47522

SCHEIMER, JANICE SCHAEFER, financial consultant, planner; b. Alva, Okla., Sept. 21, 1948; d. Andrew August and Ruth Ida (Boyce) Schaefer; m. Gary Lee Scheimer, Aug. 10, 1968; children: Scott Allen, Eric Lee. BS, Ariz. State U., 1971, MBA, 1972. Cert. fin. planner. Rate analyst Northwest Pipeline, Salt Lake City, 1976-78; mktg. mgr. Western Fed. Savs., Colorado Springs, 1979-82; fin. cons. Shearson, Lehamn, Hutton/Am. Express, Gimsbach, Fed. Republic Germany, 1982-83, Colorado Springs, Fed. Republic Germany, 1982-83, 1985—; fin. cons. Integrated Resources, Gimsbach, Fed. Republic Germany, 1983-85; v.p., treas. Golden Horizons, Inc., Cheyenne Wells, Colo., Fed. Republic Germany, 1979—; sec., treas. Schaefer Farms, Inc., Cheyenne Wells, Colo., Fed. Republic Germany, 1985—; v.p. S.S. & N., Inc., Cheyenne Wells, Colo., Fed. Republic Germany, 1985—; instr. U. Md., Fed. Republic Germany, 1984-85; lectr. Meml. Hosp. Women's Ctr.; cons. Pro-Trac, 1984; v.p., treas. S.S. & N. Inc., Cheyenne Wells, 1984—; mem. econ. devel. com. City Colorado Springs. Soccer team mother Am. Youth Assn., Ramstein, Fed. Republic Germany, 1982-85; mem. Homebuilders Assn., Colorado Springs, 1985—; mem. econ. devel. com. City of Colorado Springs. Mem. Inst. Cert. Fin. Planners, Nat. Assn. Female Execs., Speakers' Bur. Networking Assn. Republican. Clubs: Officers Wives (Ramstein) (treas. 1984-85). Home: 365 Allegheny Pl Colorado Springs CO 80919 Office: Linsco/Pvt Ledger 630 Southpointe Ct# 101 Colorado Springs CO 80906

SCHEIN, SALLY JOY, social services and learning disabilities consultant, marriage and family counselor; b. Chgo., July 6, 1930; d. Rudolph James and Lillian (Cohen) Good; m. Michael Schein, Apr. 9, 1955; children: Jack Edward, David Lee. BA, U. Chgo., 1950, Columbia U., 1952; MS, CCNY, 1953; EdS, Seton Hall U., 1982, also doctoral coursework; EdD. Nova U., 1986. Occupational therapist Monmouth Meml. Hosp., Longbranch, N.J., 1953-54; tchr. nursery kindergarten N.Y. Dept. Welfare, N.Y.C., 1954-55; tchr. kindergarten Yonkers Pub. Sch., N.Y., 1955, Dumont Pub. Sch., N.J., 1955-56; learning disabilities teaching cons. Haworth, N.J., 1968-72, Caldwell, N.J., 1972-79, Cranford Pub. Sch., N.J., 1979-90; psychologist extern North Caldwell, Closter, N.J., 1976-77; counselor Community Mental Health Ctr., Dumont, 1981-82. Author: Welcome to Danish International Studies, 1979; (with E. Riley et al) Sparking Divergent Ability, 1985, Reducing Children's Vulnerability After Divorce, 1987. Founding mem. bd. Community Mental Health Ctr., Dumont, 1958-60. Mem. Am. Assn. Marriage and Family Therapists, Nat. Assn. Sch. Psychologists, Assn. Learning Cons., Council Exceptional Children, Orton Soc. Avocations: Sculpting; art; jogging; travel. Home: 4 Harding Ave Dumont NJ 07628

SCHEIN, VIRGINIA ELLEN, psychologist; b. Rahway, N.J., June 23, 1943; d. Jacob Charles and Anne S.; BA cum laude, Cornell U., 1965; PhD, N.Y.U., 1969; 1 child, Alexander Nikos. Sr. research assoc. Am. Mgmt. Assn., N.Y.C., 1969-70; mgr. personnel research Life Office Mgmt. Assn., N.Y.C., 1970-72; dir. personnel research Met. Life Ins. Co. N.Y.C., 1972-75; asso. prof. Sch. Mgmt. Case Western Res. U., Cleve., 1975-76; vis. asso. prof. Sch. Orgn. and Mgmt., Yale U., New Haven, 1976-77; asso. prof. mgmt. Wharton Sch. U. Pa., Phila., 1977-80; mgmt. cons. Virginia E. Schein, Ph.D., P.C., 1975—; assoc. prof. psychology Bernard M. Baruch Coll., City U. N.Y., 1982-85; prof. mgmt. Gettysburg Coll., Pa., 1986—. Author : (with others) Power and Organization Development, 1988; contbr. articles to profl. jours., Bd. dirs. Family Planning Ctr. Mem. Am. Psychol. Assn. (council reps. 1978-80, com. on women 1980-83), Met. Assn. Applied Psychology (pres. 1973-74), Acad. Mgmt., (rep. orgn. devel. div. 1979-81), Internat. Assn. Applied Psychology, Psi Chi. Office: Gettysburg Coll Dept Mgmt Gettysburg PA 17325

SCHELAR, VIRGINIA M., chemistry educator; b. Kenosha, Wis., Nov. 26, 1924; d. William and Blanche M. (Williams) S. BS, U. Wis., 1947, MS, 1953; MEd, Harvard U., 1962; PhD, U. Wis., 1969. Instr. U. Wis., Milw., 1947-51; info. specialist Abbott Labs., North Chgo., Ill., 1953-56; instr. Wright Jr. Coll., Chgo., 1957-58; asst. prof. No. Ill. U., DeKalb, 1958-63; prof. St. Petersburg (Fla.) Jr. Coll., 1965-67; asst. prof. Chgo. State Coll., 1967-68; prof. Grossmont Coll., El Cajon, Calif., 1968-80; cons. Calif., 1981—. Author: Kekule Centennial, 1965; contbr. articles to profl. jours. Active citizens adv. coun. DeKalb Consol. Sch. Bd.; voters svc. chair League Women Voters, del. to state and nat. convs., judicial chair, election laws chair. Standard Oil fellow, NSF grantee; recipient Lewis prize U. Wis. Fellow Am. Inst. Chemists; mem. Am. Chem. Soc. (membership affairs com., chmn. western councilor's caucus, exec. com., councilor, legis. counselor, chmn. edn. com., editor state and local bulletins). Office: 5702 Baltimore Dr #282 La Mesa CA 92042

SCHELDT, JUDI WINSOME, registered nurse; b. Stubenville, Ohio, May 23, 1946; d. John Everett and Wilma Lois (Tope) Longsworth; m. Robert Frederick Scheldt, Dec. 16, 1972 (div. 1977); 1 child, Jason Frederick. Grad. nursing sch., Washington Hosp. Ctr., 1967. RN. Staff nurse U. Calif. Med. Ctr., San Francisco, 1967-68, Washington Hosp. Ctr., 1968-70; pvt. practice, 1970-77; staff nurse Ohio State U. Hosps., Columbus, 1977—; Author: (pamphlets) Supraglottic Eating Technique, 1979, Home Care for Supraglottic Laryngectomy, 1980, Home Care for the Tracheostomy Patient, 1987. Mem. Ohio Nurses Assn., Am. Nurses Assn., Nat. Nursing Soc. on Addictions, Soc. Otorhinolaryngology and Head-Neck Nurses (nat. sec. 1981-82). Jewish. Home: 657 Garrett Dr Columbus OH 43214

SCHELL, ANNE MCCALL, psychologist; b. Waco, Tex., Apr. 23, 1942; d. Abner Vernon and Frances Laura (Bortle) McCall; m. George A. Schell, June 20, 1960, (div. 1974); 1 child, Michael A.; m. Allen Stuart Chroman, Sept. 7, 1980; 1 child, Lauren. BS, Baylor U., 1963; MA, U. So. Calif., 1968, PhD, 1970. Asst. prof. U. So. Calif., L.A., 1970-71; asst. prof. Occidental Coll., L.A., 1971-78, assoc. prof., 1978-85, prof., 1985—; cons. Nat. Ctr. for Hyperactive Children, Encino, Calif., 1980. Contbr. articles to profl. jours. Grantee Fragrance Found., N.Y., 1987. Mem. Greenpeace, Am. Psychophysiol. Assn., Soc. Psychophysiol. Rsch. Home: 870 Old Mill Rd Pasadena CA 91107 Office: Occidental Coll Dept Psychology 1600 Campus Rd Los Angeles CA 90041

SCHELLHOUS, NANCY SHICK, outplacement executive; b. Youngstown, Ohio, Feb. 15, 1940; d. Robert C. and Nell Louise (Redman) Shick; m. James H. Reed. Apr. 21, 1960 (div. May. 1972); children: Bradley, Tobin, Steven; m. Edward A. Schellhous, Oct. 4, 1974. AA, U. Cin., 1975, BS, 1979, postgrad., 1979-84. Mgr. office H. Derringer Co., Cin., 1970-72; researcher Promark Co., Cin., 1972-73; asst. to treas. Frederick Rauh & Co., Cin., 1973-75; v.p. adminstrn. Promark Co., Cin., 1975-78, pres., 1978—; pres. Outplacement Internat., Phoenix, 1990—. Chmn. Pvt. Industry Coun., 1989—; vice chmn. Cin. chpt. ARC, 1989—; past chmn. adv. bd. Great Oaks Career Resource Ctr., 1985-89; sec. Leadershpi Cin. Alumni Bd., 1989—; trustee Cin. Tech. Sch., 1990—. Recipient ann. achiever award Greater Cin. C. of C., 1980-85, Career Woman of Achievement award YWCA, 1989. Mem. Internat. Assn. Personnel Women (pres. cin. 1985-86), Employment Mgmt. Assn., Soc. Human Resource Mgrs. Republican. Home: 6296 Glade Ave Cincinnati OH 45230 Office: Promark Co 3814 West St Cincinnati OH 45227

SCHELLIE, CORALEE ANN, librarian; b. Topeka, Kans., Oct. 22, 1931; d. Harry LeRoy and Anna Mary (Thorson) Rice; m. Donald Robert Schellie, Aug. 15, 1953; children: Leslie Ann, Kendall Sue Ingrid, Kristina Lee. BA, Baker U., Baldwin City, Kans., 1952; MEd, U. Ariz., Tucson, 1972. Tchr. history Olathe (Kans.) High Sch., 1952-53; tchr. Champaign (Ill.) Jr. High Sch., 1954-55, Tucson Doolen Jr. High Sch., 1955-58; libr. Amphitheater Jr. High Sch., Tucson, 1969-81; head libr. Canyon del Oro High Sch., Tucson, 1981—; exec. bd. Sch. Libr. Media Div., 1986—. Mem. NEA, Ariz. Edn. Assn., Amphitheater Edn. Assn., Ariz. State Libr. Assn., Nature Conservancy, Jr. League, Phi Delta Kappa, Phi Mu. Democrat. Congregationalist. Home: 5641 N Bonita Dr Tucson AZ 85704 Office: 25 W Calle Concordia Tucson AZ 85737-7599

SCHELLING, JOYCE ELAINE, account executive; b. Fort Wayne, Ind., Oct. 14, 1937; d. George Martin and Lucille Alice (Schuckel) Schmeling. BA, St. Francis Coll., 1962; MA, Catholic U., 1968; PhD, NYU, 1987. Lic. tchr., Ind., N.J. Dir. drama St. Francis Coll., Ft. Wayne, 1966-70; instr. South Plainfield (N.J.) High Sch., 1970-80, NYU, N.Y.C., 1980-82; account exec. On-Line Software, Fort Lee, N.J., 1982-86, SDI, Hackensack, N.J., 1986-88, Microbank Software, Inc., N.Y.C., 1988—. Mem. N.J. Network Bus. and Profl. Women, Nat. Assn. Female Execs., NOW. Democrat. Home: 2100 Linwood Ave I5R Fort Lee NJ 07024

SCHELZEL, SHARON SULLIVAN, child care consultant; b. Rochester, N.H., June 18, 1949; d. Arthur and Eleanor (Raab) Sullivan; m. Curtis B. Schelzel, Aug. 22, 1970; 1 child, Katie. RN, Sacred Heart Hosp., 1970; AA, Notre Dame Coll., Manchester, N.H., 1987, BA in Behavioral Sci., 1988; postgrad. in adminstrn., Wheelock Coll. Supr. Manchester Pediatric Group, 1975-81; co-dir., co-owner Butterflies are Free Infant/Toddler Ctr.,

Manchester, 1981-83; asst. dir. Greater Manchester Child Care Assn., 1984-87; cons. Work/Family Directions, Boston, 1987-88; cons., owner New England Child Care Cons. Svc., Manchester, 1987—; exec. dir. St. Francis of Assisi Child Care Ctr., Manchester, 1987—; bd. dirs. Child Care Craft Skill Ctr., Manchester, 1987—; mem. Mayor's Child Care Adv. Com. Mem. Nat. Assn. for Edn. Young Children, Zonta (v.p.), Alpha Sigma Lambda. Roman Catholic. Office: New Eng Child Care Cons Svc 299 Stark Ln Manchester NH 03102

SCHEMAN, BLANCHE, reading specialist; b. N.Y.C., Oct. 17, 1917; d. Adolf and Rose (Bistrong) Kirsch; m. Paul Scheman, June 29, 1941 (dec. Dec. 1987); children: Naomi, Carol, Judith. BA, Bklyn. Coll., 1939; MA, Columbia U., 1941. Guidance counselor U.S. Employment Svc., N.Y.C., 1942-46; reading therapist Reading and Learning Clinic Reading and Learning Ctr. Adelphi U., Garden City, N.Y., 1957-66; reading specialist Cold Spring Harbor (N.Y.) Sch. Dist., 1958-85; vol. reading specialist English as Second Lang. and Lit. Vol., Huntington, N.Y., 1988—. Named Woman of Yr. Anti-Defamation League, B'nai B'rith, Freeport, L.I., N.Y., 1953. Mem. AAUW (edn. chair, exec. com. 1988—), Harbor Tchr. Assn. (chair retiree chpt. exec. com. 1987—). Democrat. Jewish. Home: 5 Shore Dr Huntington NY 11743

SCHEMAN, RITA SUSAN, publishing executive; b. Brooklyn, N.Y., Mar. 20, 1950; d. Max Meyer and Mary (Goldberg) S. BA in English, Brooklyn Coll., Brooklyn, 1971; MA in English Lang. and Lit., U. Mich., Ann Arbor, 1973; advanced profl. cert., NYU Bus. Sch., N. Y., 1986. Editor/rsch. Inst. for Burn Medicine, Ann Arbor, 1973-74; asst. editor Arco Pub. Co., N.Y.C., 1974-76; prodn. editor Raven Press Ltd., N.Y.C., 1976-79; asst. v.p./mng. editor Raven Press Ltd., 1980-83, v.p./mng. editor, 1983-85, v.p./gen. mgr., 1986-; writing tchr., CUNY, N.Y., 1976-77. Vol. Spl. Olympics, Bklyn., 1989; mem. Bklyn. Philharmonia Chorus, 1979-83; bd. dirs. Prospect Park West Owners Corp., Bklyn. Mem. Soc. for Scholarly Pub., Assn. of Am. Pubs. Jours. Com., Wome's Nat. Book Assn. Democrat. Office: Raven Press Limited 1185 Avenue of the Americas New York NY 10036

SCHENCK, JANE E., human resources specialist; b. Zanesville, Ohio, Oct. 2, 1949; d. John R. and Mary E. (Ellis) McGreevy; children: Michael, Christopher. BA, Seton Hill Coll., 1971; MEd, U. Pitts., 1979, ABD, 1980. Cert. tchr. of gifted and talented. Pres., owner Homing Instinct, Catalyst Systems; mgr. tng. and devel. Consol. Natural Gas Co., Inc., Pitts.; mem. adj. faculty mgmt. devel. svcs. Pa. State U., Pitts. Bd. dirs. Greater Pitts. Lit. Coun., 1989—; vol. Make-a-Wish Found., 1990. Mem. Human Resources Planning Soc. (pres. Pitts. chpt.). Home: 1442 Navahoe Dr Pittsburgh PA 15228

SCHEND, VALERIE A., pharmacist; b. Kenosha, Wis., July 13, 1957; d. Eugene K. and Arlene M. (Amo) S. Student, U. Wis., 1982. Staff pharmacist Evansville (Wis.) Rx, 1987—, Corner Drug Store, Dodgeville, Wis., 1983-87, Belleville (Wis.) Pharmacy, 1989—; cons. pharmacist Bloomfield Manor, Dodgeville, 1983-87. Mem. Phi Delta Chi. Home: 4913 Paul Ave Madison WI 53711 Office: Evansville Pharmacy 26 W Main Evansville WI 53536

SCHENGRUND, CARA-LYNNE, biochemist, educator; b. N.Y.C., Feb. 18, 1941; d. George Ruben and Georgette (Arnold) Elder; m. David Michael Schengrund, Sept. 2, 1961; children: Kevin Michael, Karin-Ann. BS, Upsala Coll., 1962; MS, Seton Hall U., 1965, PhD, 1966. Instr. Upsala Coll., East Orange, N.J., 1967; postdoctorate rsch. assoc. Columbia U. Coll. Physicians and Surgeons, N.Y.C., 1967-69; rsch. assoc. Milton S. Hershey Med. Ctr. Pa. State U., Hershey, 1969-72, asst. prof., 1972-79, assoc. prof., 1979—, acting dept. chmn., 1986-87. Contbr. articles to profl. publs. Vice chmn. adv. bd. Dauphin County (Pa.) Parks and Recreation, 1986—; chmn. Dauphin County Open Space Study Group, 1990. Mem. Am. Soc. Neurochemistry (parliamentarian 1977—), Am. Chem. Soc., Am. Soc. Biochemistry and Molecular Biology, AAAS. Home: 1483 Deerfield Dr Hummelstown PA 17036 Office: Milton S Hershey Med Ctr Pa State U. Hershey PA 17033

SCHENKEL, SUSAN, psychologist, lecturer, author; b. Wroclaw, Poland, Apr. 21, 1946; came to U.S., 1949; d. Leon and Siddi (Fiedleholz) S.; m. Alvin Helfeld, Apr. 8, 1984. BA, U. Wis., 1967; MA in Clin. Psychology, SUNY, Buffalo, 1970, PhD in Clin. Psychology, 1973. Lic. psychologist, Mass. Psychologist Fitchburg (Mass.) State Coll., 1972-75, instr. in psychology, 1973-74; staff psychologist div. of alcoholism Boston City Hosp., 1975-76; chief psychologist Cambridge (Mass.) Ct. Clinic, 1976-80; instr. in psychology dept. psychiatry Med. Sch. Harvard U., 1976-80; pvt. practice psychology Cambridge, 1976—; instr. in psychology U. Mass., Boston, 1978; speaker in field. Author: Giving Away Success, 1984, German edit. 1986, Brazilian edit. 1988, rev. edit. 1990; contbr. articles to profl. jours. USPHS fellow, 1967-70; N.Y. State Regents scholar, 1968-70; SUNY Rsch. Found. grantee, 1971-72. Mem. Am. Psychol. Assn., Mass. Psychol. Assn., Am. Soc. Tng. and Devel., Assn. for Advancement of Behavior Therapy.

SCHENK-ZIEBELMAN, CYNTHIA MARIAN, import executive; b. Fort Worth, Jan. 18, 1954; d. Eugene F. and Florence (Klein) S.; m. Peter H. Ziebelman, Sept. 1, 1985. BS, Tex. Christian U., 1976. Asst. mgr. Foxmoor Casuals, Livingston, N.J., 1972-75; mgr. Klein Signs, Fort Worth, 1975-76; asst. mdse. mgr. Pier 1 Imports, Fort Worth, 1976-77, mdse. mgr., 1977-81; v.p. Intercontinental Art, Inc., Gardena, Calif., 1981-85; pres. Designer Ideas Inc., Palo Alto, Calif., 1985—. Mem. Nat. Assn. Female Execs.

SCHEPIS, DIANE JO, television studio manager; b. Libertyville, Ill., Dec. 15, 1962; d. Joseph Paul and Stella (Borenzweig) S. BS in Communications, No. Ill. U., 1985. News producer US Cable Lake County, Waukegan, Ill., 1985-87, local programming mgr., 1987—; mem. adv. com. Cable Lake County, Grayslake, Ill., 1987—. Mem. pub. relations com. Lakefrontfest, City of Waukegan, 1987. Recipient 1st Place local programming, 1985, 3rd Place pub. affairs, 1986 Women in Cable, Am. Dental Assn. award, 1986, Community Spirit award United Way Lake County, 1988, 1989 Women of the Year for Pub. Svc. award YWCA of Lake County. Office: US Cable Lake County 3233 W Grand Ave Waukegan IL 60085

SCHER, ANN I., computer consultant; b. Balt., Feb. 25, 1956; d. Herbert I. and Marilyn E. (Garte) S.; m. Michael O. Shneier, May 25, 1980. BA, U. Rochester, N.Y., 1978; MS, U. Md., 1981. Computer scientist Children's Hosp., Wash., 1981-83; computer graphics programmer Videomagic Lab., Rockville, Md., 1983-85; project leader IBM, Bethesda, Md., 1985-87; pvt. practice Wilton, Conn. Contbr. articles to profl. jours., 1978-82. Mem. Inst. Electrical & Electronic Engrs., Assn. for Computing Machinery.

SCHER, ELLEN JUDITH, locomotive engineer; b. Balt., Mar. 24, 1953; d. Sheldon and Etta (Wacke) S. AA with highest honors, Catonsville Community Coll., Balt., 1980. Cert. and qualified locomotive engr. Locomotive engr. CSX Transp., Balt., 1979-86; locomotive engr. Amtrak, Washington, 1986-88, Harrisburg, Pa., 1988—. Meeting facilitator 12 Step Recovery Group, Balt., 1987—; active lst and Franklin Street Ch., Balt., 1987—; team capt. Operation Red Block, Harrisburg, 1989—. Mem. Brotherhood Locomotive Engrs. (pres. local #459 May 1990). Democrat. Jewish. Office: 50 Massachusetts Ave Washington DC 20002

SCHERBA, ELAINE LOUISE, investment banker, financial analyst; b. Milw., Mar. 24, 1949; d. Raymond Arthur and Isabelle (Benson) Podolske; m. Stephen Scherba Jr., June 19, 1971. BA, Carroll Coll., 1971; MBA, U. Wash., 1977. Fin. analyst Rainier Nat. Bank, Seattle, 1977-78; officer fin. analysis Seattle-1st Nat. Bank, 1978-79, asst. v.p., mgr. capital investment analysis, 1979-80, v.p., mgr. fin. analysis and cons., 1980-81, v.p., mgr. asset-liability div., 1982-83, sr. v.p., mgr. fin. planning and reporting div., 1983-84, sr. v.p., mgr. retail delivery systems div., 1985-86, sr. v.p., mgr. fin. adv. services, 1986-89; treas. Egghead Discount Software, Issaquah, Wash., 1989—. Pres., bd. trustees Univ. Prep. Acad., Seattle, 1987-89; bd. dirs. Friends of Youth, Seattle, 1987-89. Republican. Episcopalian. Clubs: Rainier, Wash. Athletic (Seattle). Home: 509 Crockett St Seattle WA 98109 Office: Egghead Discount Software 22011 SE 51st St PO Box 7004 Issaquah WA 98027

SCHERER, ANITA (ANITA STROCK), advertising executive; b. Cleve., Sep. 20, 1938; d. William John Stock and Gertrud Clara (Kaufmann) Bacher; m. Richard Phillip Scherer, Nov. 25, 1961; children: William Richard, Christopher Howard. Student U. Cin., 1956-57. AB Jones Bus. Coll., 1958. Account sec. Northlich, Stolley Inc., Cin., 1978-79, account asst., 1979-80, asst. account mgr., 1980-81, account mgr., 1981-84, mktg. svc. assoc., 1984-89, mgr., 1989—; lectr. local schs., univs., Cin. 1980—. Co-editor: monthly newsletter Badge, 1967-72; designer assorted notepads, 1986. Lector, Our Lady of Victory Roman Cath. Ch., Cin., 1972—; corr. sec. Delhi Police Assn. Inc., Ohio, 1967-72; pres. Delhi Hills Community Coun., Ohio, 1974-75; adv. bd. mem. Coll. Mount St. Joseph, Ohio, 1974-80; v.p. adminstr. Stagecrafters, Cin., 1983-85, publicity chmn., 1984-89; mktg. bd. mem. Contemp. Arts Ctr., 1985—, chmn. Advt./Graphic Arts div. Fine Arts Fund Campaign, 1988; trustee Arts and Humanities Resource Ctr. for Elderly, 1990—. Winner nat. competition Am. Assn. Advt. Agys., 1980; recipient Outstanding Performance award Assn. Community Theatres, Cin., 1983, Excellence in Acting award Ohio Community Theatres Assn., 1984. Mem. NAFE, Cin. Direct Mktg. Assn., Am. Mktg. Assn., Acad. Health Services Mktg. (adv. bd. dirs. 1989), Am. Coll. Healthcare Mktg., Cin. C. of C. (lectr. 1984-86). Avocations: travel, reading, medieval/renaissance history, community theater. Home: 5511 Palomino Dr Cincinnati OH 45238 Office: Northlich Stolley LaWarre Inc 200 W 4th St Cincinnati OH 45202

SCHERER, CAROL LOUISE, investment manager; b. Horton, Kans., Nov. 21, 1945; d. Allan Dean and Gertrude Katherine (Olson) Erdley; m. Timothy James Scherer; children: Bruce Derek LaCava, Jeffrey Brian LaCava. BS with honors, U. Oreg., 1978. Acct. exec. Smith, Barney, Harris, Upham, Eugene, Oreg., 1980-84; sole proprietor Scherer Asset Mgmt., Eugene, 1984—. Study group mem. Oreg. Dept. Water Resources, Salem, 1989. Mem. Profl. Women's Network, Beta Gamma Sigma, Alpha Kappa Psi. Office: Scherer Asset Mgmt 84984 Appletree Dr Eugene OR 97405-9727

SCHERER, JEANNE CATHERINE, nurse, author; b. Buffalo, Apr. 8, 1928; d. Albert and Florence Rose (Steinman) Scherer. R.N., Buffalo Gen. Hosp. Sch. Nursing, 1954; B.S. in Nursing, D'Youville Coll., 1966; M.S., Canisius Coll., 1972. Staff nurse various hosps., 1954-66; clin. instr. Sisters Hosp. Sch. Nursing, Buffalo, 1966-68, 78-86 , asst. dir., med. surg. nursing coordinator, 1968-78, cons., 1986—. Author: Introductory Clinical Pharmacology, 1975, 3d edit., 1987; Introductory Medical-Surgical Nursing, 1977, 4th edit., 1986; Student Work Manual for Introductory Medical-Surgical Nursing, 1977, 4th edit., 1986; Student Work Manual for Introductory Clinical Pharmacology, 1982, 3d edit., 1987; Lippincott's Nurses' Drug Manual, 1985. Mem. Western N.Y. League for Nursing. Republican. Roman Catholic. Office: PO Box 763 West Seneca NY 14224

SCHERER, KARLA, foundation executive, venture capitalist; b. Detroit, Jan. 13, 1937; d. Robert Pauli and Margaret (Lindsey) S.; m. Peter R. Fink, Sept. 14, 1957 (div. July 1989); children: Christina Lammert, Hadley Anne Fink McKenzie, Allison Scherer. Student, Wellesley Coll., 1954-55; BA, U. Mich., 1957. Bd. dirs. R.P. Scherer Corp., Troy, Mich., 1984-89; chmn. Karla Scherer Found., Detroit, 1989—; adv. shareholders' rights; speaker on corp. governance to various univs., profl. assns.; condr. workshops; led only successful proxy contest of major U.S. publicly held corporation, 1988. Trustee Eton Acad., Birmingham, Mich., 1989—; mem. vis. com. Fordham U. Grad. Sch. Bus. Adminstrn.; former mem. bd. dirs. Cottage Hosp., Univ. Liggett Sch., Music Hall, Detroit League for Handicapped; former mem. adv. bd. Wellesley Coll.; former mem. Rep. Dennis M. Hertel's Candidate Selection Com. for Armed Svcs. Acads. Named Outstanding Woman Leader of Yr., Oakland U., 1990. Mem. Women's Forum Mich., Econ. Club Detroit, Women's Econ. Club Detroit, Detroit Club, Detroit Athletic Club, Country Club Detroit, Grosse Pointe Club, Renaissance Club. Office: 400 Renaissance Ctr Ste 500 Detroit MI 48243

SCHERER, MARCIA JOSLYN, psychotherapy educator; b. Buffalo, June 9, 1948; d. Alfred John and Marjorie (Greene) J.; m. John Vincent Scherer Jr., Jan. 2, 1976. BS, Syracuse U., 1970; MS, SUNY, Buffalo, 1977; MPH, PhD, U. Rochester, 1986. Diplomate Am. Bd. Med. Psychotherapy; cert. rehabilitation counselor. Editor Mental Health Assn., Buffalo, 1973-80; psychotherapist Erie County Dept. Mental Health, Buffalo, 1980-82; asst. prof. Nat. Tech. Inst. for Deaf, Rochester, N.Y., 1986—; instr. Eastman Sch. Music, Rochester, 1989—; researcher Internat. Ctr. Rsch. on Hearing and Speech, Rochester, 1989—. Author: Communication in the Human Services: A Guide to Therapeutic Journalism, 1980; (assessment instruments) Assistive Technology Device Predisposition Assessment, 1989, Technology Overload Assessment, 1989, Educational Technology Predisposition Assessment, 1990; contbr. articles to profl. jours. Dissertation grantee NSF, 1985; recipient Literary award Rho Chi Sigma, 1984. Mem. AAUW (life, grantee 1983), Nat. Rehab. Assn., Am. Assn. for Counseling & Devel., Am. Ednl. Rsch. Assn., Chi Sigma Iota (life). Democrat. Methodist. Home: 486 Lake Rd Webster NY 14580 Office: Nat Tech Inst for Deaf 1 Lomb Memorial Dr Rochester NY 14623

SCHERGENS, BECKY LOU, university administrator; b. Tell City, Ind., May 25, 1940. BA, So. Meth. U., 1962, tchr. cert., 1963; cert. mgmt., U. Denver, 1982, MPA, 1982. Cert. mediator. Tchr. Dallas Independent Sch. Dist., 1964-65; policy analyst Sorin-Hall, Inc., Washington, 1965-67; asst. dir. CUNY, Washington, 1967-68; dir. advt. and pub. relations Am. Assn. of Mus., Washington, 1968-69; staff asst. to sec. to spl. asst. to dep. asst. sec. for edn Dept. Health, Edn. and Welfare, Washington, 1969-76; exec. dir. Nat. Congress of Parents and Tchrs., Chgo., 1977-80; v.p. and dir. Hansen and Assocs. Inc., Denver, 1981-83; from dir. pub./pvt. initiatives to exec. dir. for instnl. advancement to v.p. instnl. advancement U. Houston-Clear Lake, 1983—; instr. pub. policy U. Houston-Clear Lake. Active Clear Lake Area Econ. Devel. Found., Coun. for Advancement and Support of Edn.; bd. dirs. Clear Lake Area Symphony. Mem. Am. Acad. of Polit. Sci., Am. Assn. of Higher Edn., Am. Assn. for Policy Analysis and Mgmt., Am. Soc. for Pub. Adminstn., Assn. of Bus. and Profl. Women, Clear Lake C. of C. (bd. dirs., v.p., mem. exec. com. 1987-90), Forum Club of Houston, Houston C. of C. (econ. diversification planning com. 1984-86, internat. com.), Nat. Soc. of Fund Raising Execs., South Western Aerospace Profl. Reps. Assn. (exec. com., v.p.), Space Found., Tex. Indsl. Devel. Coun., Beta Gamma Sigma, Phi Delta Kappa, Pi Alpha Alpha. Office: U Houston Clear Lake Houston TX 77058

SCHERGER, MOZELLE SPAINHOUR, librarian; b. Forsyth County, N.C., Dec. 17, 1916; d. Earnest Sidney and Mertie Blanche (Hauser) Spainhour. B.S., Appalachian State Tchrs. Coll., Boone, N.C., 1937; B.S. in L.S., U. N.C., 1943; m. George Richard Scherger, Feb. 23, 1946; children: Teresa Ann Scherger Martin, George Richard, Joseph John, Daniel M. Tchr. English and French, sch. libr. Cramerton (N.C.) High Sch., 1937-42; libr. Laurinburg-Maxton AFB, 1943, Piedmont Jr. High Sch., 1944, Pope Field AFB, 1945-46, Charlotte (N.C.) Coll., 1957-64; documents and serials libr. U. N.C. at Charlotte, 1965-69, asst. reference libr., 1969-78, reference libr., 1979-80. Home: 701 St Julien St Charlotte NC 28205

SCHERMER, JUDITH KAHN, lawyer; b. N.Y.C., Feb. 28, 1949; d. Robert and Barbara Kahn; m. Daniel Woodrough Schermer; 1 child, Sarah Nicole. BA, U. Chgo., 1971; JD, William Mitchell Coll. Law, 1987. Bar: Minn. 1987, U.S. Dist. Ct. Minn. 1987. Advt. and promotion specialist U. Chgo. Press, 1971-75; systems analyst Allstate Ins. Co., Northbrook, Ill., 1975-78, Lutheran Brotherhood, Mpls., 1980-83; polit. aide Mpls. City Coun., 1986-87; ptnr. Schermer, Altman & Izek, Mpls., 1987—. Chmn. 62nd Dist. DFL, Mpls., 1988—; del. DFL State Cen. Com., Minn., 1988—; mem. Minn. Women's Polit. Caucus, 1990. Mem. Minn. Trial Lawyers Assn., Minn. State Bar Assn., Minn. Women Lawyers. Home: 4624 Washburn Ave S Minneapolis MN 55410 Office: Schermer Altman & Izek 1600 Foshay Twr 821 Marquette Ave Minneapolis MN 55402

SCHERMERHORN, DEBRA CAROL, pharmacist, consultant; b. Woodbury, N.J., Oct. 5, 1961; d. Thurman Mills and Frances Carrie (Jones) Drabold; m. Stuart William Schermerhorn, Nov. 5, 1988. BS, Phila. Coll. Pharmacy & Sci., 1985. With Kelly's Deli, Pennsville, N.J., summer 1978; cashier, clk. Marriotts-N.J. Turnpike, Penns Grove, N.J., 1978-82; intern, then resident in pharmacy Neede & Boonin Pharmacy, Phila., 1982-87; pharmacist cons. Comp-U-Dose Pharmacy, Phila., 1985—; pharmacist mgr. Pennsport Pharmacy, Phila., 1987—; intern Syntex Pharms., Palo Alto, Calif., 1984; cons. Comp-U-Dose Pharmacy, Wilmington, Del., 1985—, Amherst Pharmacy, Burlington, N.J., 1986. Fellow Am. Soc. Cons. Pharmacists, Am. Pharm. Assn., Del. Pharm. Soc., Pa. Pharm. Assn. Baptist. Home: 10 Meadow Rd Pennsville NJ 08070

SCHEROKMAN, BARBARA JEANNE, neurologist, educator; b. Memphis, Apr. 28, 1949; d. Edward and Jeanne (Hooper) S. BS in Chemistry, Furman U., 1971; MD, Med. Coll. of Ga., 1975. Diplomate Nat. Bd. Med. Examiners, Am. Bd. Psychiatry and Neurology. Med. intern Duke U. Med. Ctr., Durham, N.C., 1975-76, med. resident, 1976-78, resident in neurology, 1978-80, dir. clin. neurology div., 1986—; assoc. prof. neurology Uniformed Svcs. U. of the Health Scis., Bethesda, Md., 1981—; chief neurology cons. svc. Walter Reed Army Med. Ctr., Washington, 1986—; clin. asst. prof. dept. neurology Georgetown U. Med. Ctr., Washington, 1989—. Author: Diagnostic Tests in Neurology: A Photographic Guide to Bedside Techniques, 1985. Mem. Nat. Adult Children of Alcoholics, 1984—. Comdr. USNR, 1981—. Recipient Scholarship Book award Mosby Publs., 1975, Physicians Recognition award AMA, 1984; decorated Def. Meritorious Svc. medal, 1985. Fellow Am. Acad. Neurology (seminar dir. 1988—); mem. Uniformed Svcs. Orgn. of Neurologists, Alpha Omega Alpha, Alpha Epsilon Delta. Office: Uniformed Svcs U Health Sci 4301 Jones Bridge Rd Bethesda MD 20889

SCHETLIN, ELEANOR M., retired university official; b. N.Y.C., July 15, 1920; d. Henry Frank and Elsie (Chew) Schetlin; B.A., Hunter Coll., 1940; M.A., Tchrs. Coll., Columbia U., 1942, Ed.D., 1967. Playground dir. Dept. of Parks, N.Y.C., 1940-42; librarian Met. Hosp. Sch. Nursing, N.Y.C., 1943-44, dir. recreation, 1944-48, dir. recreation and guidance, 1948-59; coordinator student activities SUNY, Plattsburgh, 1959-63, asst. dean students, 1963-64; asst. prof., coordinator student personnel services CUNY, Hunter Coll., 1967-68; asst. dir. student personnel Columbia U., Coll. Pharm. Scis., N.Y.C., 1968-69, dir. student personnel, 1969-71; assoc. dean for students Health Scis. Center, SUNY, Stony Brook, 1971-73, asst. v.p. for student services, 1973-74, assoc. dean of students, dir. student services, 1974-85. Mem. Nat. Assn. Women Deans, Adminstrs. and Counselors. Contbr. articles to profl. jours. Home: 20 Barberry Ln Sea Cliff NY 11579

SCHEUERMAN, LOLA KATHRYN, educator; b. Oklahoma City, July 1, 1939; d. William A. and Gladys O. (Rogers) Murrison. BS, U. Kans., 1961; ME, Wichita State U., 1969; EdS, Emporia State U., 1975. Elem. tchr. Wichita (Kans.) Pub. Schs., 1961-70, Shawnee Heights Pub. Schs., Topeka, Kans., 1970-72; elem. reading specialist Shawnee Heights Pub. Schs., Tecumseh, Kans., 1972-89; elem. learning ctr. specialist Shawnee Mission (Kans.) Pub. Schs., 1989—; realtor assoc. Lewis-Cobb and Co., 1976-79; presenter and trainer in field. Contbr. articles to profl. jours. Tutor Topeka Literacy Coun.; receptionist Arthritis Found.; vol. Stormont-Vail Hosp.; vol. Topeka Civic Theater; block and telethon worker Muscular Dystropy Assn.; block worker Am. Heart Assn., Am. Lung Assn.; sch. dist. campaign coord. United Way, 1982; mem. designer showcase com. Every Woman Resource Ctr. Mem. NEA (life, del. nat. conv. Topeka area 1981), Internat. Reading Assn. (pres. Topeka coun. 1984-85, del. internat. conv. 1985, coord. for Kans. 1985—), Kans. Edn. Assn. (assembly del. 1980-89), Kans. Reading Assn. (bd. dirs. 1982—, exec. bd. 1985—), Shawnee Heights Edn. Assn. (pres. 1981-82), AAUW, U. Kans. Alumni Assn. (life), Emporia State U. Alumni Assn., PTA (hon. life), Beta Sigma Phi, Phi Delta Kappa, Delta Kappa Gamma (exec. bd., sec. 1982-84). Republican. Home: 6852 W 125th Overland Park KS 66209

SCHEUERMANN, MONA, English educator; b. N.Y.C., June 6, 1946; d. Philip and Irene Rifkin; B.A., Queens Coll., 1967; M.A., Hunter Coll., 1969; Ph.D., SUNY-Stony Brook, 1974; m. Peter Scheuermann, Dec. 28, 1973. Asst. prof. English, York Coll., 1974-75; asst. prof. J.S. Reynolds Community Coll. 1974-76; asst. prof. Oakton Community Coll., Des Plaines, Ill., 1976-79, assoc. prof. 1979-84, prof., 1984; guest prof. U. Hamburg, 1985; vis. prof. U. Utrecht. NDEA fellow. Mem. MLA, Am. Assn. Eighteenth-Century Studies, Keats-Shelley Assn., Wordsworth Soc., Phi Beta Kappa. Author: The Novels of William Godwin, 1980; Social Protest in the Eighteenth-Century English Novel, 1985; contbr. articles to profl. jours. Office: 1600 E Golf Rd Des Plaines IL 60016

SCHEURENBRAND, KIM RENE, savings and loan association executive; b. Aberdeen, S.D., Oct. 11, 1960; d. James P. and Dorothy L. (Schroeder) S. BSBA, U. Fla., 1982. Chartered fin. analyst. Sales asst. Smith Barney Harris Upham & Co., Inc., Atlanta, 1982-83; asst. nat. bank examiner Office of the Comptroller of the Currency, Atlanta, 1983-84; asst. v.p., supervisory agt. Fed. Home Loan Bank of Atlanta, 1984-89; v.p. regulatory rels. div. Southeastern Savs. Bank, Inc., Charlotte, N.C., 1989-90, chartered fin. analyst, 1990—. Mem. Assn. for Investment Mgmt. and Rsch. Republican. Roman Catholic. Home: 4622-T Colony Rd Charlotte NC 28226 Office: Southeastern Savs Bank Inc 112 S Tryon St Charlotte NC 28284

SCHEURER, ELIZABETH JEANNE, nurse; b. Grand Rapids, July 3, 1930; d. Andrew William and Daisy Alice (Pew) Newberg; m. Frederick Constans Scheurer, Sept. 29, 1950 (dec. Sept. 1971); children: Karl Anton, Frederick Constans Jr., Constance Lee, Elizabeth Scheurer Swamhild. Grad., Northwestern Hosp. Sch. Nursin, Mpls., 1951. RN, Minn. Staff nurse Northwestern Hosp., Mpls., 1951-52; pvt. duty nurse U. Minn., 1953-64, Minn. Thoracic Group, Mpls.; staff nurse Abbott Northwestern Hosp., Mpls., 1972—. Mem. AACCN (sec., pres. Greater Twin Cities chpt. 1978-81, nat. bd. dirs. 1982-85, regional cons. for clin. practice 1990—, Nurse of Yr. award 1988), Am. Nurses Assn., Minn. Nurses Assn., Women's Aux. Met. Musicians Assn. Republican. Lutheran. Home: 4941 Aldrich Ave S Minneapolis MN 55409

SCHEURING, HELEN, real estate company executive, developer, consultant; b. Greene, Ohio, Apr. 12, 1940; d. Donald and Wilma (Harvey) Gibbs; m. Bob Gunther, 1960 (dec. 1967); children: Arthur, Alvin; m. Tim Scheuring, Apr. 8, 1969. Student real estate devel., Lakeland Coll., 1982, Ohio U., 1984. Salesperson Old Reserve Realty, Jeferson, Ohio, 1982-84, Lin-Con Inc., Columbus, Ohio, 1984-86; saleswoman, comml. and indsl. specialist Delores Knowlton Realtors, Chardon, Ohio; pres. Global Mktg., Exporting and Importing Co., New Bloomington, Ohio, 1984; comml., indsl. specialist CREDO, Inc., Columbus, 1989—. Mem. Ohio Council Vocat. Edn., Westerville, Chardon Realty Bd. Mem. Ohio Planning Dirs. (treas.), Ohio Devel. Assn., Future Farmers Am. Republican. Office: CREDO Inc 6480 Busch Blvd Ste 221 Columbus OH 43229

SCHEUTZOW, MONET DOROTHY, traveling executive; b. Berea, Ohio, May 12, 1953; d. Raymond Joseph and Florine Tyrone (Sage) Mahoney; m. Richard Niles Scheutzow, May 20, 1972; children: Glenn Arthur, Benjamin Russell. Grad. high sch., Parma Hts., Ohio, 1971. Travel expense mgr. Matrix Essentials, Inc., Solon, Ohio, 1984--. Home: 11141 Ronald Dr Parma OH 44130

SCHEWEL, ROSEL HOFFBERGER, educator; b. Balt., Mar. 1, 1928; d. Samuel Herman and Gertrude (Miller) Hoffberger; m. Elliot Sidney Schewel, June 12, 1949; children—Stephen, Michael, Susan. A.B., Hood Coll., 1949; M.Ed., Lynchburg Coll., 1974; Ed.S., 1982. Reading resource tchr. Lynchburg Pub. Schs., Va., 1967-75; adj. prof. edn. Lynchburg Coll., 1973-79; cons., seminar leader Woman's Resource Ctr., Lynchburg, 1980—; assoc. prof. edn. Lynchburg Coll., 1980—. Trustee, exec. com. Lynchburg Coll., Va., 1985; chair Va. Found. for Humanities and Pub. Policy, 1985; chair New Vistas Sch.; trustee Va. Mus. of Fine Arts, 1985; appointed Commn. on Edn. for All Virginians, 1990. Recipient Disting. Service award NCCJ, 1973, Outstanding Woman in Edn. award YWCA, 1988. Mem. Assn. of Children with Learning Disabilities (dir.), Internat. Reading Assn., Lynchburg Area Counselors Assn. Democrat. Jewish. Address: 4316 Gorman Dr Lynchburg VA 24503

SCHIAPPA, JANICE MILLER, nutrition consultant; b. Bridgeport, Conn., Sept. 13, 1950; d. Carl J. Jr. and Hilda (Collins) Miller; m. Gary Frederick Schiappa, Aug. 31, 1975; children: Joseph, Natalie, Lauren. BS, U. Conn., 1972; MBA, U. New Haven, 1989. Cons. nutrition So. New Eng. Telephone Co., New Haven; dietitian Hosp. of St. Raphael, New Haven, 1975-77; office mgr. fin. ops. Schiappa Janitorial Svc., Shelton, Conn., 1977—; cons., organizer weight mgmt. and nutrition edn. programs for small groups, Sheldon, The Barden Corp., Danbury, Conn., 1990—, Mrs. Glover's Nursery Sch., 1987—. Nutrition workshop coord. Housatonic Community Coll., Stop and Shop Supermarkets Inc., 1984, Schoolwide nutrition fair, 1989; cons. Long Hill Sch., 1990.; coord. Elizabeth S. Shelton Sch. PTA (bd. dirs., co-chairperson health and safety com. 1987—); initiated, chaired Dial-a-Dietitian program S. Cen. Conn. chpt. Am. Heart Assn., 1975-78 (bd. dirs. 1977-78). Mem. Am. Dietetic Assn. (registered dietitian), Conn. Dietetic Assn. (chmn. Nat. Nutrition Month 1980-84, co-chmn. pub.rels. 1982-84, chmn. membership com. 1977-80, treas. 1984-86), Soc. for Nutrition Edn. Home: 116 Soundview Ave Shelton CT 06484

SCHIAPPACASSE, DEEANN LYNN, nurse, private pilot; b. Detroit, Feb. 8, 1951; d. George John and Helen Louise (Dorosevich) Houdek; m. Richard Henry Schiappacasse, Dec. 1, 1973; children: Michael, Angela. BSN, Wayne State U., 1973, postgrad., 1979-82. RN; lic. pvt. pilot. Coronary care nurse St. John Hosp., Detroit, 1973-75; pub. health nurse Macomb County Health Dept., Mt. Clemens, Mich., 1975-77, supr. infectious disease clinic, 1977-79; staff nurse St. Joseph Hosp., Mt. Clemens, Mich., 1979-82. Merit scholar, 1969-73. Mem. Macomb County Med. Soc. (v.p., treas., pres. 1980-85), St. Joseph Hosp. Aux. (treas. 1989-90), Women in Aviation (hospitality chmn. 1989-90), Families for Children (chmn. 1986-88), Airplane Owners and Pilots Assn., Sigma Theta Tau. Republican. Roman Catholic. Home: 12916 Easton Ct Shelby Township MI 48315

SCHIAVI, ROSEMARY FILOMENA, educator; b. Syracuse, N.Y., Feb. 20, 1947; d. Stefano and Rose (Falso) Schiavi; AA, Maria Regina Coll., 1967; BA, Brescia Coll., 1969; MS, Syracuse U., 1973, EdD U. S.C., 1989; cert. advanced studies tchr. edn. and curriculum devel., Syracuse U., 1987. Tchr., Syracuse City Sch. Dist., 1969-83, tchr. Meachem Sch., 1973-83, acting prin., 1979; adminstrv. intern Syracuse U./West Genesee Teaching Ctr., 1985-86; rsch. asst. U. S.C., 1986-89; asst. office of profl. devel. and field programs Syracuse U., 1984-85; rsch. asst. U. S.C., 1986-89; asst. prof. edn., U. Evansville, Ind., 1989—; adminstrv. intern West Genesee/Syracuse U. Teaching Ctr., 1985, Bus. Ednl. Exchange Com. Mem. exec. bd. Maria Regina Coll., pres. exec. alumni assn. Mem. S.C. Assn. for Supervision and Curriculum Devel., Am. Fedn. Tchrs., N.Y. United Tchrs. Assn., Syracuse Tchrs. Assn., N.Y. State Assn. Tchr. Educators, Brescia Coll. Alumni Assn., Syracuse U. Alumni Assn., S.C. Alumni Assn., Ind. Assn. Tchr. Educators, Am. Edn. Rsch. Assn., Assn. Tchr. Educators, Assoc. Photographers Internat., NAFE, Audubon Soc., U. Evansville Women's Club, Phi Delta Kappa, Pi Lambda Theta.

SCHIER, MARY JANE, science writer; b. Houston, Mar. 10, 1939; d. James F. and Jerry Mae (Crisp) McDonald; B.S. in Journalism, Tex. Woman's U., 1961; m. John Christian Schier, Aug. 26, 1961; children—John Christian, II, Mark Edward. Reporter, San Antonio Express and News, 1962-64; med. writer Daily Oklahoman, also Oklahoma City Times, 1965-66; reporter, med. writer Houston Post, 1966-84; sci. writer, univ. editor U. Tex. M.D. Anderson Cancer Ctr., 1984—. Recipient award Tex. Headliners Club, 1969, Tex. Med. Assn., 1972-74, 76, 78, 79, 80, 82 Tex. Hosp. Assn., 1974, 82, Tex. Public Health Assn., 1976, 77, 78, others. Lutheran. Club: Houston Press (pres. 1974-75). Home: 9742 Tappenbeck St Houston TX 77055 Office: 1515 Holcombe Blvd Houston TX 77030

SCHIEROW, LINDA-JO, research associate, consultant; b. Milw., Aug. 17, 1947; d. Joseph August Schierow and Ruth Eleanore (Beyersdorff) Heuer. BS in Edn. with honors, U. Wis., 1969, MS in Land Resources, 1980, PhD in Land Resources, 1983. Cert. tchr., Wis. Tchr. elem. Cedarburg (Wis.) Pub. Schs., 1972-78; lectr. environ. studies U. Wis., Madison, 1984, project assoc. Water Resources Ctr., 1985; asst. prof. U. Okla., Oklahoma City, 1985-88; rsch. fellow U. Okla., Norman, 1988; rsch. assoc. MIT, Cambridge, 1989-90; ind. cons., 1990—; cons. U.S.-Can. Internat. Joint Commn., Windsor, Ont., Can., 1985; mem. editorial bd. Risk: Issues in Health and Safety. Mem. Okla. State Groundwater Protection Strategy Com., Oklahoma City, 1985-88; bd. dirs. Ctr. for Community Tech., Madison, 1983-84. Mem. AAAS, APHA (liaison 1989—), Soc. for Risk Analysis (liaison 1989—), New Eng. Soc. for Risk Analysis, Sigma Xi. Democrat. Home: 24 Payson Rd Belmont MA 02178

SCHIESS, BETTY BONE, priest; b. Cin., Apr. 2, 1923; d. Evan Paul and Leah (Mitchell) Bone; m. William A. Schiess, Aug. 28, 1947; children: William A. (dec.), Richard Corwine, Sarah. B.A., U. Cin., 1945; M.A., Syracuse U., 1947; M.Div., Rochester Ctr. for Theol. Studies, 1972. Ordained priest Episcopal Ch., 1974; priest assoc. Grace Episc. Ch., Syracuse, N.Y., 1975; mem. Gov.'s Task Force on Life and Law, 1985—; chaplain Syracuse U., 1976-78, Cornell U., Ithaca, N.Y., 1978-79; rector Grace Episc. Ch., Mexico, N.Y., 1984—; instnl. rev. bds. Crouse-Irving Hosp. and Upstate Med. Ctr., Syracuse, 1986—; cons. Women's Issues Network Episc. Ch. in U.S., 1987—; writer, lectr., cons. religion and feminism, 1979—. Author: Take Back the Church, Indeed The Witness, 1982, Creativity and Procreativity: Some Thoughts on Eve and the Opposition and How Episcopalians Make Ethical Decisions, Plumline, 1988. Bd. dirs. People for Pub. TV in N.Y., 1978, Religious Coalition for Abortion Rights; mem. infant care rev. com. Crouse-Meml. Hosp.; trustee Elizabeth Cady Stanton Found., 1979; mem. policy com. Coun. Adolescent Pregnancy. Recipient Gov.'s award Women of Merit in Religion, 1984, Ralph E. Kharas award ACLU Cen. N.Y., 1986 Goodall disting. alumna award & Hills Sch., 1988, Human Rightes award Human Rights Commn. of Syracuse and Orange County, N.Y., 1989; hon. life membership Na'amat U.S., 1987. Mem. NOW (Syracuse), Internat. Assn. Women Ministers (dir. 1978, pres. 1984-87), Am. Soc. Law and Medicine, Clergy Assn. Diocese of Cen. N.Y. (v.p. 1985—), Mortar Bd., Theta Chi Beta. Democrat. Home: 107 Bradford Ln Syracuse NY 13224

SCHIESSWOHL, CYNTHIA RAE SCHLEGEL, lawyer; b. Colorado Springs, July 7, 1955; d. Leslie H. and Maime (Kascak) Schlegel; m. Scott Jay Schiesswohl, Aug. 6, 1977; children: Leslie Michelle, Kristen Elizabeth. BA cum laude, So. Meth. U., 1976; JD, U. Colo., 1978; postgrad. U. Denver, 1984. Bar: Colo. 1979, U.S. Dist. Ct. (Colo.) 1979, U.S. Ct. Appeals (10th cir.) 1984, Wyo. 1986, Ind. 1988. Rsch. clk. City Atty.'s Office, Colorado Springs, 1976; investigator Pub. Defender's Office, Colorado Springs, 1976; dep. dist. atty., 4th Jud. Dist. Colo., 1979-81; pvt. practice law, Grand Junction, Colo., 1981-82, Denver, 1983-84; assoc. Law Offices of John G. Salmon P.C., 1984-85; pvt. practice, Laramie, Wyo., 1985-88, Indpls., 1988-90; of counsel Abbott, Rund, Small & Goerges, 1990—; guest lectr. Pikes Peak Community Coll., 1980. Staff U. Colo. Law Rev., 1977. Advisor, Explorer Law Post, Boy Scouts Am., 1980-81; ex officio mem. ch. devel. com. Cen. Rocky Mt. region Christian Ch. (Disciples of Christ), 1986-88; mem. evangelism commn. United Meth Ch., 1987-88, fin. com. youth and music depts., 1979-81, lay del. Rocky Mountain Ann. Conf., 1986-87, academic tutor youth program, 1989—; mem. Meridian St. United Meth. Ch., 1988—, ch. and soc. com., 1989—; hearing officer Wyo. Dept. Edn., 1987-88; vol. Project Motivation, Dallas, 1974; chairperson Wyo. Med. Rev. Panel, 1987; panelist Ind. Pastor's Conf., Rethinking Prisons Conf., 1990. Named U. Scholar So. Meth. U., 1973. Mem. ABA (internat. law com.), Ind. State Bar Assn., Wyo. State Bar, Colo. Bar Assn. (ethics com. 1984-85, long range planning com. 1985-88, chairperson 1986-87), Am. Immigration Lawyers Assn., Indpls. Bar Assn. (internat. law sect. 1990—), Pi Sigma Alpha, Alpha Lambda Delta, Alpha Delta Pi. Republican.

SCHIFF, JAYNE NEMEROW, underwriter; b. N.Y.C., Aug. 8, 1945; d. Milton E. Nemerow and Shirley (Kaplan) Wachtel; m. Albert John Schiff, Mar. 7, 1971; children: Matthew Evan, Kara Anne. BS in Bus., Marymount Coll., 1981. Corporate sec., treas. Albert J. Schiff Assocs., Inc., N.Y.C., 1970-78; field underwriter MONY Fin. Svcs., Greenwich, Conn., 1973—; freelance employee benefit cons. Greenwich, 1979—; regional dir. mktg., MONY Fin. Services, N.Y.C., 1978-79. Bd. dirs. N.Y. League Bus. and Profl. Women, 1976-78, Temple Sinai, Stamford, Conn., 1979-84, N.Y. Ctr. Fin. Studies; leader Webelos Cub Scouts, 1977-78; treas. Ann. Mother's Bd. Benefit Greenwich Acad., 1988, upper sch. acquisitions chmn., 1989, chmn. spl. acquisitions Greenwich Acad. Benefit, 1990—. Named Ct.'s Outstanding Young Woman, 1979. Mem. Am. Soc. Chartered Life Underwriters, N.Y. Ctr. Fin. Studies, N.Y.C. Life Underwriters Assn. (bd. dirs. 1977-78), League Women Voters. Jewish. Office: 30 Stanwich Rd Greenwich CT 06830

SCHIFF, LAURIE, lawyer; b. Newark, Apr. 24, 1960; d. Norman Nathan and Claire Jane (Schott) S. BS in Law, We. State U., Fullerton, Calif., 1987, JD, 1988. Bar: Calif. 1989. Ptnr. Schiff Mgmt., Newport Beach, Calif., 1983-89; pvt. practice law Irvine, Calif., 1989—. Producer: (record album) Boys Just Want to Have Sex, 1984. Mem. ABA, Orange County Bar Assn., Am. Mensa, Am. Polocrosse Assn., Saddlebrook Polocrosse. Democrat. Jewish. Home: 2 Riptide Ct Newport Beach CA 92663 Office: 18300 Von Karman Ave Ste 800 Irvine CA 92715

SCHIFF, MARLENE SANDLER, entrepreneur; b. Great Barrington, Mass.; d. Jack and Lena Yetta (Klein) Sandler; m. Haskel Schiff (dec. Feb. 1967), 1 child, Melissa Robin. BA, U. Mass., 1960; OPM, Harvard U., 1985. Founder, chief exec. officer, chmn. Transceiver East inc., N.Y.C., 1971-88. Mem. eye adv. com. N.Y. Hosp. Cornell Med. Ctr., 1988—; bd. dirs., Sol C. Schneider Entrepreneurial Center at Wharton Sch., Phila., 1989—, chairperson, 1990—. Mem. Commn. of 200 (bd. dirs. 1990—, regional chmn. N.E. chpt. 1989—), Am. Fedn. of Arts (membership and spl. events com. 1990—). Home: 950 Fifth Ave New York NY 10021

SCHIFFEL, SUZANNE DRISCOLL, musician, real estate associate; b. Ossining, N.Y., Nov. 6, 1946; d. Edwin Taylor and Marion (Burdick) Driscoll; m. Jeffrey Allen Schiffel, Aug. 28, 1971; children: Jonathan, Matthew. MusB, Lawrence U., 1968; MusM, Ohio U., 1971. Violinist Charleston (W.Va.) Symphony, 1968-71; violinist Columbus (Ohio) Symphony Orch., 1971-85, asst. pers. mgr., 1978-84; freelance musician, tchr. music Topeka, 1985-87; pers. mgr., libr., violinist Topeka Symphony Orch., 1985-87; violinist Wichita Symphony Orch., 1988—; hostess Landmark Communities, Wichita, Kans., 1988-89; real estate assoc. Landmark Communities, Wichita, 1989—; 1988—. Active Grace Episcopal Cathedral, Topeka, 1986-87, St. John's Episcopal Ch., Wichita, 1989—; bd. dirs. Topeka Festival Singers, Topeka, 1986-87. Mem. Am. String Tchrs. Assn., Wichita Musicians Union. Democrat. Home: 3129 N Governeour Wichita KS 67226 Office: Landmark Communities Inc 3500 N Rock Rd #100 Wichita KS 67226

SCHIFFER, JEAN MARIE, bank professional; b. Bklyn., Oct. 11, 1962; d. Robert George and Cecelia Patricia (Carney) S. AA, Nassau Community Coll., Uniondale, N.Y., 1982; BS, L.I. U., 1984; postgrad., Am. Inst. Banking, 1988—. Various positions Children's Place, Garden City, N.Y., 1980-87; sales asst. Telerep, N.Y.C., 1987; customer svc. rep. Bank of N.Y., Freeport, 1987—.

SCHIFFMAN, MIA HELEN, marketing professional, musician; b. Lorain, Ohio, Nov. 7, 1953; d. Martin and Elizabeth Rose (Danzig) S. BA, U. Cin., 1977; MBA, Northeastern U., Boston, 1985. Reporter, theater reviewer Chronicle-Telegram, Elyria, Ohio, 1976-77; various temporary assignments Boston and Cambridge, Mass., 1978-80; asst. to mktg. dir. Warner-Eddison Assocs./Inmagic, Inc., Cambridge, 1980-81; exec. asst. to pres., telmktg. supr. Imero Fiorentino Assocs., Inc., N.Y.C., 1981-83; cons. Investment Mgmt. Info., Inc., Cambridge, 1985; from sales support analyst to systems mktg. program mgr. Prime Computer, Inc., Natick, Mass., 1984-89; mktg. prof. Univ. Coll. at Northeastern U., Boston, 1990—. Contbr. articles to profl. jours. Northeastern U. scholar; recipient Excellence award Sec. Assn. Execs., 1986. Mem. Actor's Equity Assn., Am. Mktg. Assn., AFTRA, Greater Boston Real Estate Bd. Office: Univ Coll at Northeastern U 260 Huntington Ave Boston MA

SCHIFFMAN, NANCY ELIZABETH, consultant; b. Everett, Mass., May 6, 1937; d. Joseph Coelho and Helen (Buchanan) Perry; m. Yale M. Schiffman, June 23, 1974; children: Daivd, Steven. BA cum laude, Boston U., 1973, MS in Urban Affairs, 1976; m. Yale M. Schiffman, June 23, 1974. Community rels. specialist YWCA, Natick, Mass., 1975-76; regional transp. planner Cen. Mass. Regional Planning Commn., Worcester, 1977-79; Congl. rsch. staff Rockwell Internat., Arlington, Va., 1980-82; v.p. SES, Inc., Springfield, Va., 1982-84, chief exec. officer, 1984-86; pres., 1982-86; cons., 1986—. Editor profl. publs. for NASA, NOAA, 1982—; contbr. articles to profl. jours. Mem. women's and minority com. Area Manpower Planning Bd., Marlboro, Mass., 1976; mem. subcom. Sudbury Housing Authority, 1977; pres., Conf. Connection, Inc., 1987—; chairperson bd. dirs. Offender Aid and Restoration of Arlington, Va., 1980; pres. Orange Hunt Sq. Homeowners Assn., 1987—; chmn. Springfield Coun. Civic Assns., 1986—; mem. Rep. County Com., Fairfax, Va., 1982-86, chmn. Springfield dist. Coryell for 8th Congl. Dist. and Kemp for Pres., 1986, trea. 8th Congl. Dist.; treas. 8th Congl. Dist.; mem. exec. com. Fairfax Rep. Com.; candidate for Va. Senate, 1983; vice chmn. Springfield Coun. Civic Assns., 1985; pres. Orange Hunt Sq. Homeowners Assn., 1986, 87, 88; mem. Citizens' Adv. Coun. on Pub. Safety, Fairfax County, 1986. Mem. Am. Pub. Transit Assn. (coun. on preserving urban motility), Am. Meteorol. Soc. (editor publs.), Am. Assn. Geographers (editor publs.), Nat. Fedn. Rep. Women (patron). Home: 7406 Forest Hunt Ct Springfield VA 22153

SCHIFFMAN, SHIRLEE, environmental protection administrator; b. Bklyn., Mar. 14, 1942; d. Phil and Mary (Rubin) Schwartz; m. Arnold Schiffman, Feb. 9, 1963; children: Erica, Robyn. BS in Geology, CCNY, 1963. Cert. pub. mgr.; cert. seconary sci. tchr. Tchr. sci. Anne Arundel County Pub. Schs., Annapolis, Md., 1975-79; environ. specialist N.J. Dept. Environ. Protection, Trenton, 1979-84, bur. chief (mgr.), 1984—. Mem. Cert. Pub. Mgr. Soc., Water Pollution Control Assn. (co-chmn. hazardous waste regulations 1988-90), cert. of appreciation 1990). Jewish. Home: 20 Aqueton Ln West Treton NJ 08628 Office: NJ Dept Environ Protection Div Hazardous Waste Mgmt 401 E State St Trenton NJ 08625

SCHIFFMAN, SUSAN STOLTE, medical psychologist, educator; b. Chgo., Aug. 24, 1940; d. Paul R. and Mildred (Glicksman) Stolte; m. Harold Schiffman (div.); 1 child, Amy Lise; m. H. Troy Nagle, July 22, 1989. BA, Syracuse U., 1965; PhD, Duke U., 1970. Lic. psychologist, N.C. Postdoctoral fellow Duke U., Durham, N.C., 1970-72, asst. prof., 1972-77, assoc. prof., 1978-83, full prof., 1983—; cons., mem. adv. bd. Nutrasweet, Chgo., 1978—, Nestle, Vevey, Switzerland, 1990, Fragrance Rsch. Fund, N.Y.C., 1986—, and others. Author: Introduction to Multidimensional Sealing: Theory, Methods and Applications, 1981, Flavor Set-Point Weight Loss Cookbook, 1990. Nat. Inst. Aging grantee, 1972—. Mem. Assn. Chemoreception Scis., European Chemoreception Rsch. Orgn., Soc. for Neurosci. Office: Duke U Dept Psychology Durham NC 27706

SCHIFLETT, MARY FLETCHER CAVENDER, researcher, educator; b. El Paso, Tex., Sept. 23, 1925; d. John F. and Mary M. (Humphries) Cavender; 1 son, Joseph Raymond. BA in Econs. with honors, So. Meth. U., 1946, BS in Journalism with honors, 1947; MA in English, U. Houston, 1971. Writer, historian Office Price Adminstrn., Dallas, 1946-47; asst. editor C. of C. Publs., Dallas, 1947-48; bus. writer Houston Oil, 1948-49; market analyst Cravens-Dargan, Ins., Houston, 1949-52; bus. writer Bus. Week and McGraw-Hill Pub. Co., Houston, 1952-56; freelance writer in bus. econs., banking and ins., 1956-68; spl. projects coordinator Center for Human Resources, Houston, 1969-73; dir. publs. Energy Inst., U. Houston, 1974-78; sr. research assoc. Inst. Labor and Indsl. Relations, 1973-80, adj. faculty Coll. Architecture, 1976-85, dir. Ctr. for Health Mgmt., Coll. Bus. Adminstrn., 1980-83; assoc. dir. research and planning Tex. Med. Ctr., Inc., Houston, 1984; dir. spl. projects and pub. affairs Tex. Med. Ctr., 1985—. Bd. dirs. Houston Acad. Motion Pictures, Houston World Trade Assn., Performing Arts Council for Tex. Med. Ctr. Pres., Houston Ct. Humanities, 1978-80; project dir. Houston Meets Its Authors I-IV, 1980-84; pub. program dir. Houston: Internat. City, 1980-83. Mem. Internat. Council Indsl. Editors, World Future Soc., Tex. Folklore Soc., Friends of the Library, Houston C. of C. (future studies com. 1975-84, small bus. council 1981-83), Nat. Assn. Bus. Economists, AIA (profl. affiliate), Mortar Bd., Theta Sigma Phi, Alpha Theta Phi, Delta Delta Delta. Methodist. Club: Downtown (pres. 1987-89). Lodge: Rotary. Author: (with others) Dynamics of Growth, 1977, Applied Systems and Cybernetics, 1981, The Ethnic Groups of Houston, 1984, Names and Nicknames of Places and Things, 1986. Office: Tex Med Ctr 406 Jesse H Jones Library Bldg Houston TX 77030

SCHIFTER, CATHERINE CRUTCHFIELD, academic administrator; b. Abilene, Tex., Sept. 24, 1950; d. James Willard and Josephine (Palmer) Crutchfield; m. Stephan Clay Schifter, Aug. 17, 1974. BS, Baylor U., 1972; MEd, U. Houston, 1973; PhD, U. Pa., 1986. Rsch. asst. Baylor Coll. Med., Houston, 1972-73; dental hygienist Phila., 1975-78; assoc. Sch. Dental Medicine U. Pa., Phila., 1973-74, asst. prof., 1978-85, dir. residency, 1985-86; asst. dean The Annenberg Sch. Communications, U. Pa., Phila., 1986—. Contbr. articles to dental jours., 1978-86. Active Am. Heart Assn., 1978—, Phila. Orchestra Assn., 1981—. Recipient Acad. Effort award, Pa. Dental Hygiene Assn., 1981, Earl Banks Hoyt Award, Sch. Dental Medicine, U. Pa., 1982. Mem. AAUP, Am. Assn. Dental Schs., Am. Ednl. Research Assn., Alpha Phi, Sigma Phi Alpha. Methodist. Office: Annenberg Sch Communication 3620 Walnut St Philadelphia PA 19104-6220

SCHILD, JOYCE ANNA, otolaryngologist, surgeon; b. Chgo., May 26, 1931; d. William Paul and Helen (Kammer) S.; m. John A. Hegber, Dec. 15, 1973. BS, U. Ill., Chgo., 1954, MD, 1956. Diplomate Am. Bd. Otolaryngology. Intern St Francis Hosp, Peoria, Ill., 1956-57; residency in otolaryngology U. Ill., 1958-61, fellow in bronchoesophagology, 1961-62, clin. instr. to assoc. prof. otolaryngology, 1958-82, interim acting head dept. otolarygology, 1978-79; prof. otolaryngology head and neck surgery Coll. Medicine U. Ill., 1982—; mem. staff U. Ill. Hosp.; otolaryngologist, surgeon Ill. Eye and Ear Infirmary, Chgo.; from adj. to assoc. attending otolaryngologist Presby. St. Luke's Hosp., Chgo., 1964-76; acting head bronchoesophagology dept. Children's Meml. Hosp., Chgo., 1972-76, cons. staff, 1976—; courtesy staff dept. surgery sect. otolaryngology St. Joseph's Hosp., Chgo., 1961-74; numerous presentations and lectrs. in field. Mem. AMA, Ill. State Med. Soc., Chgo. Med. Soc., Am. Laryngol. Assn., Soc. Univ. Otolaryngologists, Am. Laryngol., Rhinol. and Otol. Soc., Am. Soc. Pediatric Otolaryngolgy, Chgo. Laryngol. and Otol. Soc. (pres. elect 1983-84, pres. 1984-85, council mem. 1985-86), Am. Broncho-Esophagological Assn. (v.p. 1976-77, pres. elect 1978-79, pres. 1979-80, thesis com. 1981-82), Am. Council Otolaryngology, Soc. Ear, Nose and Throat Advances in Children, Am. Acad. Pediatrics (com. on accident and poison prevention 1982-85), Pan-Am. Assn. Oto-Rhino-Laryngology, Head and Neck Surgery, Am. Laryngol. Assn. Office: Ill Eye and Ear Infirmary 1855 W Taylor St Ste 2 42 Chicago IL 60612

SCHILDE, BARBARA D., transportation safety specialist; b. Baton Rouge, Aug. 21, 1933; d. Alvin and Delilah (Hobgood) S. BS, La. Tech. U., 1955; MS, La. State U., 1963, postgrad. Asst. home economist LA Cooperative Ext. Service, New Roads, La., 1955-56; asst., assoc. home economist LA Cooperative Ext. Service, Donaldsonville, La., 1956-58; home economist LA Cooperative Ext. Service, Hahnville, La., 1958-70; assoc. specialist LA Cooperative Ext. Service, Baton Rouge, specialist. Contbr. articles to profl. jours. Mem. La. Lung Assn., 1984-88, La. chpt. Am. heart Assn., Destrehan, 1985. Mem. AAUW, Nat. Assn. Extension Home Economists (Disting. Svc. award 1970), Am. Home Economists. Assn., United Fedn. of Doll Collectors, Inc. (judge 1984), Nat. Assn. Minature Collectors, La. Extension Home Economists Assn., La. Home Economists Assn., La. Safety Coun., Pilot Club of Baton Rouge, Around the Clock Garden Club, Epsilon Sigma Phi, Gamma Sigma Delta (pres. 1974-82, 84-86), Sigma Kappa. Democrat. Baptist. Home: 1913 Glenmore Ave Baton Rouge LA 70808 Office: LA Cooperative Ext Knapp Hall LSC Baton Rouge LA 70803

SCHILLER, ALICE ANN, cleaning service executive; b. N.Y.C., May 6, 1950; d. Seymour and Shirley (Lander) Yanofski; m. Leonard J. Schiller, Mar. 4, 1971; children: Ilana Beth, Felicia Jill. BA, Lehman Coll., 1972, MS, 1978. Cert. tchr., N.Y., N.Y.C., N.J. Tchr. N.Y.C., 1972-76, Orange (N.J.) Bd. Edn., 1980-81, Union (N.J.) Bd. Edn., 1982-85; v.p. Dimensional Bldg. Svcs., Avenel, N.J., 1985—; exec. com. Bldg. Svc. Contractors, Fairfax, Va., 1987-89; mem. indsl. com. Real Estate Women, Woodbridge, N.J., 1988-89. Vice pres. program, Hadassah, Maplewood, N.J., 1987, v.p. mem., 1986, sec., 1985; leader Girl Scouts U.S., South Orange, N.J. Mem. Nat. Assn. Profl. Saleswomen, N.J. Assn. Women Bus. Owners Essex County. Office: Dimensional Bldg Svcs 225 Avenel St Avenel NJ 07001

SCHILLER, GABRIELLE ANTONIA, banker; b. Toronto, Ontario, Canada, Aug. 10, 1962; came to U.S., 1964; d. Richard Lee and Jutta (Wolters) Zwayer; m. Dean C. Schiller, 1982. BS in Bus. and Mktg., Ohio State U., 1989. Clerical positions BancOhio Nat. Bank, Columbus, Ohio, 1981-88; supr. asst. to v.p. BancOhio Nat. Bank, Columbus, 1988-90; market rsch. analyst BancOhio Nat Bank, Columbus, 1990—; floral designer pvt. practice, Galloway, Ohio, 1986—. Dep. asst. coord. United Way of Franklin County, Columbus, 1987-89. Mem. NAFE, Am. Inst. Banking. Republican. Lutheran. Home: 6395 Cabin Craft Dr Galloway OH 43119 Office: BancOhio Nat Bank Mktg Dept 155 E Broad St 9th Fl Columbus OH 43251

SCHILLER, JO ANNE, publishing executive; b. Chgo., Feb. 18, 1938; d. Joseph Gideon and Lurlene Gertrude (McAuliff) Jolicoeur; m. Stephen Alfred Schiller, Dec. 12, 1971. BBA, Northwestern U., 1971, MBA, 1976. Various positions Sci. Rsch. Assocs. subs. IBM, Chgo., 1962-86; v.p. Deltak subs. Nat. Edn., Naperville, Ill., 1986-88; pres. Jolicoeur and Assocs., Chgo., 1988-89; pres., chief exec. officer Everyday MathTools Pub. Co., Evanston, Ill., 1989—; bd. dirs. Allegiance Corp., Naperville. Bd. dirs. Alliance Française de Chgo., 1989—, New City YMCA, Chgo., 1985-88. Mem. Econ. Club Chgo. Home: 210 E Pearson St Chicago IL 60611 Office: Everyday MathTools Pub Co 1007 Church St Evanston IL 60201

SCHILLER, LYNNE ANN, computer engineer; b. Pitts., June 20, 1966; d. Frank James and Anastasia (Duran) S. BS in Computer Engring., Lehigh U., Bethlehem, Pa., 1988. Computer systems engr. Gen. Dynamics, Ft. Worth, 1988—. Mem. NAFE. Office: Gen Dynamics Box 748 Fort Worth TX 76132

SCHILLING, DEBORAH JAN, tour coach operator, public relations specialist; b. Summit, N.J., Nov. 22, 1951; d. Herbert Harold and Genevieve (Ellicks) Schilling. Diploma, Berkeley Secretatial Sch., East Orange, N.J., 1970. Pvt. sec. Sandoz-Wander, Inc., East Hanover, N.J., 1970-73; driver, dispatcher, safety officer Barkman Buses/Kent Bus Co., Berkeley Hts., N.J., 1973-83; sr. operator mgmt. and customer rels., R&D Passaic Valley Coaches, Summit, N.J., 1983—. Recipient 2d place award for ann. bus. rodeo N.J. Dept. Transp. , 1979, 2d place, 1980, 5th place, 1981. Mem. NAFE. Office: Passaic Valley Coaches 179 Division Ave Summit NJ 07901

SCHILLING, JANET NAOMI, dietitian; b. North Platte, Neb., Mar. 1, 1939; d. Jens Harold and Naomi Frances (Meyer) Hansen; m. Allan Edward Schilling Jr., June 1, 1969; children: Allan Edward III, Karl Jens. BS, U. Neb., 1961; MS, Ohio State U., 1965. Registered dietitian. Tchr. home econs. Peace Corps., Dimbokro, Ivory Coast, 1962-64; cons. nutrition Wis. Div. Health, La Crosse, 1966-67, 69; dietary cons. Cozad (Neb.) Community Hosp., 1968; instr. Viterbo Coll., La Crosse, 1974-81; lectr. U. Wis., La Crosse, 1982-84; teaching asst. ESL Sch. Dist. La Crosse, 1984-87; nutrition educator WIC Program, 1988—; nutrition cons. LaCrosse, 1987—. Author: Life in the Nutrition Community, 1980, Life on the Nutrition Cycle II, 1980; co-author: Nutrition Activities, 1984, Recipe Book of Nutritious Snacks, 1985. Mem. La Crosse Sch. Dist. Nutrition Task Force, 1976—; sunday sch. tchr., supr. Our Saviors Luth. Ch., 1976-86, chmn., Mobile Meals, 1982-86; v.p. membership booster club Cen. High Sch., La Crosse, 1985-87, pres. 1987-88; bd. dirs. YMCA, La Crosse, 1982-88. Mem. AAUW (pres. 1978-80, Name Grant scholar 1981), La Crosse Area Dietetic Assn. (1st pres. 1968-69, Outstanding Dietitian Yr. 1985), Wis. Dietetic Assn. (chmn. educators 1983-85), No. Wis. Dietetic Assn. (pres. 1982), Am. Dietetic Assn. (educators practice group 1978—), La Crosse Jaycees (Carol award 1973), French Discussion Group. Democrat. Home: 3465 Carlson Blvd Apt 5 El Cerrito CA 94530

SCHILLING, STACEY LYNN, management consultant; b. Bklyn., Feb. 12, 1964; d. Donald L. and Annette (Garber) S. AB, Columbia U., 1986; postgrad., Baruch Coll. Computer specialist, treas., v.p. Re Assocs., Inc., N.Y.C., 1980—. Author tng. manuals in mgmt. communications. Mem. NAFE, ASTD, Order of Ea. Star. Republican. Jewish. Home: 101 W 12th St #6S New York NY 10011

SCHILTZ, JANE ANN, lawyer, insurance company executive; b. Denton, Tex., Oct. 20, 1955; d. James Henry and Teresa Loretta (Ungs) S. BBA, St. Mary's Coll., Notre Dame, Ind., 1977; JD, U. Iowa, 1980. CLU, fin. cons. Atty., asst. mgr. advanced mktg., officer Northwestern Mut. Life Ins. Co.,

Milw., 1980—. Author: The Unfunded Irrevocable Life Insurance Trust, 1984, rev. edit., 1987; contbr. articles to profl. jours. Mem. charitable giving task force Million Dollar Round Table, Chgo., 1985, deferred giving com., trust and estate adv. com. Marquette U., Milw., 1987—, devel. com. Wis. affiliate Am. Heart Assn., 1986-87; chmn. planned giving com. Mem. ABA, Wis. Bar Assn., Am. Soc. CLU, Am. Soc. Chartered Fin. Cons., St. Mary's Coll. Alumnae Assn. (nat. bd. dirs. 1981-86), Phi Delta Phi. Office: Northwestern Mut Life Ins Co 720 E Wisconsin St Milwaukee WI 53202

SCHINDEL, RONNIE SUSAN LEVINE, advertising executive, writer; b. N.Y.C., Oct. 14, 1939; d. Harold and Ada (Simon) Levine; m. Samuel M. Schindel, July 2, 1960; children—Robert Harold, Shari Jill. B.S. magna cum laude, NYU, 1960; M.A., Columbia U., 1962. Tchr. Pub. Sch. 125, Manhattan, N.Y.C., 1960-62, Walker AFB Elem. Sch., Roswell, N.Mex., 1962-64; freelance writer, Huntington, N.Y., 1964—; movie reviewer Radio Sta. WGSM, Huntington, 1977—, Women's Record, Roslyn, N.Y., 1985—; creative dir. Ray Adell Media Enterprises, Inc., Greenlawn, N.Y., 1977—, v.p., 1982—, v.p., sec., 1983—, also bd. dirs. Author: (children's books) I Am Jungle Soup, 1967, Hermit Crab, 1967; also programmed reading instruction materials, radio commls., movie revs. Pres., Woodhull Sch. PTA, Huntington, 1975-76, Kehillath Shalom Synagogue, Cold Spring Harbor, N.Y., 1976-77; vol. Sta. WGSM Call for Action, Huntington, 1975-77. Recipient Founders Day award NYU, 1960; grantee Columbia U., 1960-62. Mem. Nat. Assn. Women Bus. Owners, Delegation L.I. Bus. and Profl. Women (bd. dirs. 1986—, co-chair publicity 1985—), L.I. Ctr. for Bus. and Profl. Women, Nat. Assn. for Female Execs., L.I. Communicators Assn., Advancement for Commerce and Industry, L.I. Assocs., Press Club of L.I., Sigma Delta Chi. Office: Ray Adell Media Enterprises Inc 103 Broadway Greenlawn NY 11740

SCHINDLER, GAYLE ANN, data communications specialist; b. Bay Village, Ohio, May 4, 1950; d. Clayton Aloysius and Marcella Belle (Stockard) Smith; m. David Stanley Schindler, Feb. 16, 1980. Grad. high sch., Rocky River, Ohio. Keypunch operator Sherwin-Williams Paint Co., Cleve., 1970-74, tape librarian, 1974-77, remote ops. controller, 1977-80; hardware specialist Informatics, Inc., Columbus, Ohio, 1980-81; network specialist BancOhio Nat. Bank, Columbus, 1981-85, sr. network specialist, 1985-88, datacommunications specialist II, 1988-89, supr. datacommunications, 1990—. Democrat. Lutheran. Office: BancOhio Nat Bank 770 W Broad St Columbus OH 43251

SCHINDLER, JUDITH KAY (JUDI SCHINDLER), public relations, marketing consultant; b. Chgo., Nov. 23, 1941; d. Gilbert G. and Rosalie (Karlin) Cone; m. Jack Joel Schindler, Nov. 1, 1964; 1 child, Adam Jason. BS in Journalism, U. Ill., 1964. Assoc. editor Irving Cloud Publs., Lincolnwood, Ill., 1963-64; asst. dir. publicity Israel Bond Campaign, Chgo., 1965-69; v.p. pub. relations Realty Co. of Am., Chgo., 1969-70; dir. pub. relations Pvt. Telecommunications, Chgo., 1970-78; pres. Schindler Communications, Chgo., 1978—; del. White House Conf. on Small Bus., Washington, 1980, 86; mem. adv. bd. Continental Air Transport Suburban Service, 1987-89, Entrepreneurship Inst., Chgo., 1988—. Bd. dirs. Friends of Chgo. Pub. Libr., 1985-88; leader luncheon coun. YWCA, Chgo., 1987, 89-90; appointee small bus. com. Ill. Devel. Bd., 1988-89. Named Nat. Women in Bus. Adv. SBA, 1986, Chgo. Woman Bus. Owner of Yr., Continental Bank, 1989. Mem. Nat. Assn. Women Bus. Owners (pres. Chgo. chpt. 1980-81, nat. v.p. membership, 1988-89, Chgo. Woman Bus. Owner of Yr. 1989), Forum for Real Estate Discussion and Analysis, Ind. Bus. Assn. of Ill., Publicity Club of Chgo., Alpha Epsilon Phi. Office: Schindler Communications 869 N Dearborn St Chicago IL 60610

SCHIRCH, CAROL ANN, educator; b. Wadsworth, Ohio, Jan. 4, 1937; d. Wilmer Schantz and Emma (Good) Shelly; m. LaVerne Gene Schirch, Aug. 9, 1936; children: Douglas Michael, Michelle Schirch Shelly, Lisa Lynn. BS in Edn., Bluffton Coll., 1958; MA in Reading, Va. Commonwealth U., 1984. Cert. devel. reading elem. sch., elem. edn., reading specialist, Va. Elem. tchr. Huron Valley Schs., Milford, Mich., 1958-60; substitute tchr. Ann Arbor (Mich.) Schs., 1960-62; substitute tchr. Bluffton (Ohio) Exempted Village Schs., 1965-74, title I reading tchr., 1974-78; reading resource tchr. Henrico County Schs., Richmond, Va., 1978—, chmn. English/reading dept., 1986—; mem. vis. self study team Va. State Dept. Edn., Richmond, 1986. Violinist Richmond Community Orch., 1978—. Mem. Internat. Reading Assn., Va. State Reading Assn., Richmond Area Reading Assn., Henrico Edn. Assn. Democrat. Mennonite. Home: 5815 Rinker Dr Mechanicsville VA 23111

SCHIRO-GEIST, CHRISANN, rehabilitation counselor; b. Chgo., Dec. 31, 1946; d. Joseph Frank and Ethel (Fortunato) Schiro; m. John J. Conway Sr., Oct. 26, 1985; children: Jennifer, Daniel; stepchildren: Patricia, Nicole, John Jr., Denise, Christine. BS, Loyola U., Chgo., 1967, MEd, 1970; PhD, Northwestern U., 1974. Registered psychologist, Ill.; cert. sex edn. cons. Tchr. sci. Northbrook (Ill.) Jr. High Sch., 1967-70; dir. career counseling and placement Mundelein Coll., Chgo., 1972-74; counselor human devel. Regional Service Agy., Skokie, Ill., 1975-87; assoc. prof. psychology, rehab. counselor Ill. Inst. Tech., Chgo., 1975-87; assoc. prof. rehab. and counseling psychology U. Ill., Champagne-Urbana, 1987—. Co-author: Placement Handbook for Counseling Disabled Persons, 1982; author, editor: Vocational Counseling with Special Populations, 1990. Research grantee Northwestern U., 1974; Region V Short-Term Tng. grantee Rehab. Services Adminstrn., 1978-79, Long-Term Tng. grantee, 1983-86, 86-87, 88—; Mary E. Switzer fellow NIDRR, 1989-90. Mem. Am. Psychol. Assn., Am. Assn. Counseling and Development, Nat. Rehab. Assn., Nat. Council Rehab. Edn. (named Educator of Yr. 1987), Ill. Rehab. Counseling Assn. (pres. 1979-80), Council on Rehab. Edn. (pres. 1982-85), Kappa Beta Gamma Alumni Assn. (nat. officer). Office: U Ill Div Rehab Edn 1207 S Oak Champaign IL 61820

SCHLACKS, DEBORAH DAVIS, English educator; b. Sherman, Tex., Jan. 8, 1956; d. Ralph Wayne and Bettye Joyce (Avery) Davis; m. Eric Lee Schlacks, June 18, 1988. BA in Psychology, Baylor U., 1978; postgrad., Trinity U., San Antonio, 1978; MA in English, Tex. Woman's U., 1982; PhD in English, Tex. Women's U., 1986. Grad. asst. tchr. Tex. Woman's U., Denton, 1980-86; lectr. U. Nev., Las Vegas, 1986-89. Author: short stories, 1987-88; contbr. abstracts to profl. publs. Judge speech contest VFW, Las Vegas, 1988, Univ. Interscholastic League Denton, 1980-86. Mem. Far West Popular Culture Assn., Nat. Coun. of English Tchrs., Popular Coun. Assn., S. Cen. Modern Lang. Assn., Modern Lang. Assn., Nev. Coun. English. Tchrs., Real Orators, Toastmasters (sec. 1987). Democrat. Presbyterian. Home: 4392 Boca Lago Circle Las Vegas NV 89117

SCHLAERTH, SALLY ANNE GALLAGHER, newspaper librarian; b. Erie, Pa., May 23, 1928; d. Raymond Aloyisius and Eleanor (Curriden) Gallagher; m. Joseph Donald Schlaerth, Nov. 27, 1954; children—Kathi, Sharon, Sally Jo, Joseph Donald. B.A. cum laude, D'Youville Coll., 1950; postgrad. Canisius Coll., 1950-51; M.L.S., SUNY-Buffalo, 1969. Tchr. English, McMahon High Sch., Buffalo, 1950-51; service rep. N.Y. Telephone Co., Buffalo, 1951-55; librarian Kaegebein Sch., Grand Island, N.Y., 1968-73; chief librarian Buffalo News, 1973—. Mem. Spl. Library Assn., Kappa Gamma Pi, Sigma Delta Chi. Roman Catholic. Home: 47 Milton St Williamsville NY 14221 Office: Buffalo News One News Plaza Buffalo NY 14240

SCHLAFLY, PHYLLIS STEWART, author; b. St. Louis, Aug. 15, 1924; d. John Bruce and Odile (Dodge) Stewart; m. Fred Schlafly, Oct. 20, 1949; children: John F., Bruce S., Roger S., Phyllis Liza Forshaw, Andrew L., Anne V. BA, Washington U., St. Louis, 1944, JD, 1978; MA, Harvard U., 1945; LLD, Niagara U., 1976. Bar: Ill. 1979, D.C. 1984, Mo. 1985, U.S. Supreme Ct. 1987. Syndicated columnist Copley News Svc., 1976—; pres. Eagle Forum, 1975—. Author, pub.: Phyllis Schlafly Report, 1967—; broadcaster, Spectrum, CBS Radio Network, 1973-78, commentator, Cable TV News Network, 1980-83, Matters of Opinion, radio sta. WBBM, Chgo., 1973-75; author: A Choice Not an Echo, 1964, The Gravediggers, 1964, Strike From Space, 1965, Safe Not Sorry, 1967, The Betrayers, 1968, Mindszenty The Man, 1972, Kissinger on the Couch, 1975, Ambush at Vladivostok, 1976, The Power of the Positive Woman, 1977; editor: Child Abuse in the Classroom, 1984, Pornography's Victims, 1987, Equal Pay for Unequal Work, 1984, Who Will Rock the Cradle, 1989, Stronger Families or Bigger Government, 1990. Del. Rep. Nat. Conv., 1956, 64, 68, 84, 88, alt., 1960, 80; pres. Ill. Fedn. Rep. Women, 1960-64; 1st v.p. Nat. Fedn. Rep. Women, 1964-67; mem. Ill. Commn. on Status of Women, 1975-85; nat. chmn. Stop ERA, 1972—; mem. Ronald Reagan's Def. Policy Adv. Group, 1980; mem. Commn. on Bicentennial of U.S. Constn., 1985—; mem. Adminstrv. Conf. U.S., 1983-86. Recipient 10 Honor awards Freedoms Found.; Brotherhood award NCCJ, 1975; named Woman of Achievement in Pub. Affairs St. Louis Globe-Democrat, 1963, one of ten most admired woman in world Good Housekeeping poll, 1977—. Mem. ABA, DAR (nat. chmn. Am. history 1965-68, nat. chmn. bicentennial com. 1967-70, nat. chmn. nat. def. 1977-80, 83—), Ill. Bar Assn., Phi Beta Kappa, Pi Sigma Alpha. Office: 68 Fairmount Alton IL 62002

SCHLAGENHAFT-EDWARDS, PAM LYNN, veterinarian; b. Beloit, Wis., Sept. 1, 1960; d. William August and Mary Ellen (Marten) Schlagenhaft; m. Steven Mark Edwards, June 21, 1980; 1 child, Ashlie Lynn. BS, U. Wis., Platteville, 1982; DVM, U. Wis., 1989. Lic. veterinarian, Wis. Veterinarian Prairie Animal Hosp., Beloit, 1989—, Geiger Vet. Clin., Delavan, Wis., 1990—; speaker in field. Leader, Daisy Girl Scouts Am., Beloit, 1989-90; mem. Bro. Dutton Sch. Bd., Beloit, 1990. Mem. NAFE, Am. Profl. Bus. Womens Assn., Am. Vet. Medicine Assn., Wis. Vet. Medicine Assn., Rock Valley Vet. Medicine Assn., Nat. Wildlife Fedn., Greenpeace, Purina Profl. Breeders Club. Republican. Roman Catholic. Home: 801 Portland Ave Beloit WI 53511 Office: Prairie Animal Hosp 2770 Prairie Ave Beloit WI 53511

SCHLAIN, BARBARA ELLEN, lawyer; b. N.Y.C., May 28, 1948; d. William and Evelyn (Youdelman) S.; B.A., Wellesley Coll., 1969; M.A., Columbia U., 1970; J.D., Yale U., 1973. Bar: N.Y. 1974, U.S. Dist. Ct. (so. dist.) N.Y. 1974, U.S. Ct. Appeals (2d cir.) 1975, U.S. Dist. Ct. (ea. dist.) N.Y. 1977. Assoc. firm Donovan Leisure Newton & Irvine, N.Y.C., 1973-76, Graubard Moskovitz McGoldrick Dannett & Horowitz, N.Y.C., 1976-79; atty. McGraw-Hill, Inc., N.Y.C., 1979-80, asst. gen. counsel, 1980-86, v.p., assoc. gen. counsel, asst. sec., 1986—. sec. proprietary rights com. Info. Industry Assn., 1982-83. Author outlines Practicing Law Inst., 1983, 84, 85, 86, 88; contbr. numerous articles to profl. jours. Bd. dirs., v.p., sec. Dance Research Found., N.Y.C., 1983-86, chmn. 1986—. Phi Beta Kappa scholar, Durant scholar Wellesley Coll., 1967-69. Mem. Assn. Am. Pubs. (lawyers com. 1979—), Assn. Bar City N.Y. (communications law com. 1985-88), N.Y. State Bar Assn. Office: McGraw-Hill Inc 1221 Ave of the Americas New York NY 10020

SCHLEGEL, BEVERLY FAYE, private clubs administrator; b. San Diego, May 15, 1950; d. Frederick Hugh and Fern (Bailey) Einhaus; m. Heinz Dieter Schlegel, Oct. 27, 1976; 1 child, Kailo Heinz. Mgr. The Town Club of Salem, Mass., 1976-84, The Shenendoah Club, Roanoke, Va., 1984—. Mem. Club Mgrs. Am. Assn., Balt., Va. Restaurant Assn. Baptist. Home: Rte 1 Box 55 Montvale VA 24122 Office: The Shenandoah Club Inc 24 Franklin Rd Roanoke VA 24122

SCHLEGELMILCH, MARGARET ELIZABETH, retired librarian; b. Montrose, Minn., Aug. 26, 1918; d. Clarence Cole and Lillian Sarah (Redman) Roberts; m. Reuben Orville Schlegelmilch, Aug. 22, 1943; children: Janet, Raymond, Joan, Margaret Ann. BA, Cornell Coll., Mt. Vernon, Iowa, 1940; BS in LS, U. Ill., 1942. Asst. libr. SE Mo. State Coll., Cape Girardeau, 1942-43; libr. Endwell (N.Y.) Jr. High Sch., 1964-67. Vol. libr. Annandale (Va.) United Meth. Ch., 1972—, pres. United Meth. Women, 1979-80, chmn. coun. on ministries, 1981-84. Mem. AAUW (rec. sec. Springfield-Annandale br., legis. chmn.), DAR (libr. 1986-90, vice-regent descendants of '76 chpt. 1990—), Phi Beta Kappa, Beta Phi Mu.

SCHLEICHER, NORA ELIZABETH, banker, treasurer, accountant; b. Balt., Aug. 10, 1952; d. Irvin William and Eleanor Edna S.; m. Ray Leonard Settle Jr., July 27, 1985. AA cum laude, Anne Arundel Community Coll., 1972; BS summa cum laude, U. Balt., 1975. CPA, Md. Staff auditor Md. Nat. Bank, Balt., 1975-76, sr. staff auditor, 1976-77, supr. auditing dept., 1977-78; full charge acct. Wooden & Benson, CPA's, Balt., 1978-81; asst. to treas. First Fed. Savs. & Loan Assn., Annapolis, Md., 1981, asst. treas., 1982-83, v.p., 1984; v.p., treas. First Fed. Savs. & Loan Assn. (now First Annapolis Bank), 1984—. Bd. dirs., treas. Coll. Manor Community Assn. Mem. AICPA, Md. Assn. CPA's, Fin. Mgrs. Soc., Coll. Manor Community Assn. (bd. dirs., treas.). Methodist. Office: First Annapolis Savs Bank 2024 West St Annapolis MD 21401

SCHLEIN, MIRIAM, author; b. N.Y.C.; d. William and Sophie (Bigleisen) S.; children—Elizabeth Weiss, John Weiss. B.A. in Psychology, Bklyn. Coll., 1947. Author over 60 books for children, natural sci. books, concept books, story books, picture books, including: Shapes, 1952, It's About Time, 1955, The Way Mothers Are, 1963, I, Tut: The Boy Who Became Pharaoh, 1978, Antarctica, the Great White Continent, 1980, Project Panda Watch, 1984 (Children's Sci. Book award N.Y. Acad. Scis. 1985), Giraffe, The Silent Giant (Children's Book of Yr. Child Study Assn. 1976), What the Elephant Was, 1986, Pigeons, 1989, Pandas, 1989, Hippos, 1989; author adult fiction and non-fiction in publs. including Redbook, McCall's, Ladies Home Jour., Good Housekeeping, Univ. Rev., Creative Living, Colorado Quar.; included in anthologies; transl. into Danish, Swedish, Italian, French, Dutch, Norwegian, German, Braille. Awards include: Outstanding Sci. Trade Book for Children, Nat. Sci. Tchrs. Assn./Children's Book Council Joint Com. for: Snake Fights, Rabbit Fights, and More, 1979, Lucky Porcupine, 1980; Billions of Bats, 1982; The Dangerous Life of the Sea Horse, 1986, Virginia Kirkus 100 Best Books and Westchester Library Best Children's Books 1974-75 for What's Wrong with Being a Skunk?, 1974; Children's Book Showcase Title/Children's Book Council for Giraffe, The Silent Giant, 1976; Jr. Lit. Guild selections include: The Four Little Foxes, 1952, Elephant Herd, 1954, City Boy, Country Boy, 1955, The Big Cheese, 1957, The Pile of Junk, 1962; Herald Tribune Honor Book award for Elephant Herd, 1954; Boys' Clubs Am. Jr. Book Award for Fast Is Not a Ladybug, 1953; Children's Books of Yr. award Child Study Assn. for Giraffe, The Silent Giant, 1976; honor book N.Y. Acad. Scis. for Project Panda Watch, 1985. Mem. Authors Guild, PEN Am. Center, Forum of Writers for Young People (pres. 1975-76). Author filmstrip materials Guidance Assocs.; textbook editor Harcourt Brace Jovanovich, 1980; editor Scribner Ednl. Pubs., 1985. Home and Office: 19 E 95th St New York NY 10128*

SCHLESINGER, JUDITH SUSAN, psychologist; b. Bronx, N.Y., Aug. 30, 1950; d. Joseph and Bertha (Levitt) S.; m. (div. 1981). BA, Syracuse U., 1971; MA, NYU, 1976, PhD, 1985. Psychologist Psychiatric Crisis Team, Valhalla, N.Y., 1981-83, The Masters Sch., Dobbs Ferry, N.Y., 1985-89; adj. prof. Coll. of New Rochelle, N.Y., 1984—. Editor The Behavioral Counselor, 1980-81; cons., reviewer The Am. Psychologist, 1980-82; contbr. articles to profl. jours. Mem. Am. Psychol. Assn., N.Y. Acad. Scis., N.Y. Neuropsychol. Group, Psi Chi, Kappa Delta Pi, Phi Beta Kappa. Home: 300 Broadway Dobbs Ferry NY 10522

SCHLESINGER, LORA, art consultant; b. Newark, May 3, 1937; d. Alex and Eva (Bogin)ûGrabow; m. Barry Schlesinger (div. 1973). Student, Douglass Coll., 1955-57, NYU, 1957-59. Ptnr. Hunsaker/Schlesinger Assocs., Los Angeles, 1975—. Mem. Museum Contemporary Art Los Angeles (founding mem.), Modern and Contemporary Art Council, Curators Council of Museum of Contemporary Art. Democrat. Home: 1617 S Beverly Glen Los Angeles CA 90024 Office: Hunsaker/Schlesinger Assocs 812 N La Cienega Los Angeles CA 90069

SCHLESINGER, REGINE, radio news reporter; b. Lyon, France, Oct. 29, 1951; came to U.S., 1953; d. Charles and Marie (Wind) S.; m. Stuart Meisel, Oct. 16, 1983; children: Jeremy Jacob, Rachel Sara, Ariella Danit. BS in Journalism, Northwestern U., 1973. Writer, producer CBS, Inc., Chgo., 1973-79, radio news reporter, anchor, 1979—. Recipient cert. of recognition Chgo. Dental Soc., 1985. Jewish. Office: CBS 630 N McClurg Ct Chicago IL 60611

SCHLETTE, SHARON ELIZABETH, utility company executive; b. Bklyn., May 25, 1945; d. Albert Valentine and Dorothy Lee (Jacobs) Kunz; m. Arthur F. Schlette, Oct. 12, 1985. Student, St. Johns U., 1978-82. With Consol. Edison Co., 1963-89; acctg. clk., 1963-67, dist. office teller, 1967-69; customer service rep. Consol. Edison Co., 1969-72, asst. supr. Manhattan customer service, 1972-78; unit mgr. Br. III-Westside, Manhattan customer service, 1978-81, Lincoln Center Br., 1981-82; unit mgr. Yorkville Br., 1982-87, unit mgr. final accounts/collections dept., 1987-89; adjustor bankcard svcs. Barnett Bank of Fla., Jacksonville, 1990—. Mem. Nat. Rifle Assn., NAFE, Aircraft Owners and Pilots Assn. (lic. pilot). Republican. Home: 1257 Willow Oaks Dr W Jacksonville Beach FL 32250

SCHLEUSSNER, MRS. ROBERT, JR. See **STEVENS, ELISABETH GOSS**

SCHLIEMAN, MABLE STORIE, community worker, religious educator; b. Gouverneur, N.Y., Dec. 12, 1932; d. Theron William and Edith May (Clark) Storie; m. Donald B. Miller, Apr. 6, 1956 (div. Apr. 1976); children: Alan D., Kenneth B.; m. Robert Francis Schlieman, Apr. 24, 1976. BS in Early Childhood Edn., State U. Tchrs. Coll., Potsdam, N.Y., 1954; MA in Teaching of Speech, Columbia U., 1955. Assoc. Christian educator Reformed Ch. in Am., 1981. Elem. tchr. Niskayuna Pub. Schs., Schenectady, N.Y., 1957-60, Ballston Spa (N.Y.) Pub. Schs., 1955-56; dir. religious edn. Niskayuna Reformed Ch., Schenectady, 1974—; Meals on Wheels driver and intake worker Cath. Family and Community Svcs., Schenectady, 1977-80, Meals on Wheels coordinator, 1980—; program assoc. cons. Albany Synod Reformed Ch. in Am., Schenectady, 1976—, TV awareness trainer, 1978—, tchr. Friendship Program for retarded adults, 1984-86; Stephen ministry leader Niskayuna Reformed Ch., 1986—. Treas., Birchwood PTA, 1967. Mem. AAUW, Christian Educators of Reformed Ch. in Am., Nat. Assn. Meal Programs. Home: 4 Tamarack Ln Schenectady NY 12309 Office: Nutrition Program/Elderly Glendale Home Hetcheltown Rd Scotia NY 12302

SCHLIPF, BETTY JEAN, administrative assistant; b. Long Beach, Calif., Dec. 22, 1943; d. Wayne Simon and Rena Evelyn (Swiderski) Stieneke; m. Ronald, Apr. 24, 1965 (div. Aug. 1985); children: Sandra M., Laura A. BS, Ill. State U., Normal, 1965, MS, 1968. Tchr. Fairbury (Ill.) Cropsey Unit #3, 1965-69; office adminstr. Ind. Ins. Agent, Fairbury, 1976-78; employee benefits co-ordinator IAA Trust Co., Bloomington, Ill., 1978-84, securities processing adminstr.; adminstrv. asst. Fidelity Mgmt. Trust Co., Boston, 1989—; com. mem. MSTC User Steering Com., Chgo., 1985-87. Named Employee of the Year IAA Trust Co., 1983. Mem. NAFE. Home: 149 Oakland St Apt 17 Mansfield MA 02048

SCHLOSS, CAROLYN DINA, investment analyst; b. Evanston, Ill., May 14, 1963; d. Nathan and Rosita (Montalvo) S. BS in Fin., Miami U., Oxford, Ohio, 1985; postgrad., U. Chgo., 1989. Assoc. analyst Kemper Fin. Svcs., Chgo., 1985-88, investment analyst, 1988—. Wish granter Make-A-Wish Found., Chgo., 1989—. Mem. Chgo. Sci. Analysts (treas. 1987—). Jewish. Office: Kemper Fin Svcs 120 S LaSalle St Chicago IL 60603

SCHLOSS, JO ANN BOCK, entrepreneur; b. Denver, Aug. 9, 1932; d. Samuel and Rose Bock; B.A. in Communications, U. Colo., 1972, M.A. in Orgnl. Behavior and Communications, 1975; m. Charles M. Schloss Jr., Dec. 19, 1948; children: Charles M., III, Sindi Jo, Kristy Anne. Community rels. cons. Denver Commn. Community Rels., 1972-73, project dir. comm. youth, 1973-75; with Cen. Bank of Denver, 1976-82, v.p. staff rels. and devel., 1979-81, v.p. human resources planning and devel., 1981-82; chief operating officer Schloss & Shubart, Inc., 1983-84; pres., chief exec. officer Profitable Decisions, Inc., Englewood, Colo., 1985—; adj. faculty Met. State and Regis Coll. Masters Program. Chair Arap. County Pvt. Industry Coun.; Rockies Venture Club. Named to hon. faculty dept. communication U. Colo., Regis Coll.; Grad. fellow U. Colo., 1975. Mem. Am. Soc. Tng. and Devel., Internat. Assn. Bus. Communicators, Human Resources Planning Soc., Soc. Human Resources Mgmt., Leadership Denver, Women's Forum Colo., World Future Soc., Nat. Assn. Women Bus. Owners, Denver C. of C., Phi Beta Kappa.

SCHLOSSER, ANNE GRIFFIN, librarian; b. N.Y.C., Dec. 28, 1939; d. C. Russell and Gertrude (Taylor) Griffin; m. Gary J. Schlosser, Dec. 28, 1965. BA in History, Wheaton Coll., Norton, Mass., 1962; MLS, Simmons Coll., 1964; cert. archives adminstrn. Nat. Archives and Records Service, Am. U., 1970. Head UCLA Theater Arts Library, 1964-69; dir. Louis B. Mayer Libr., Am. Film Inst., L.A., 1969-88, dir. film/TV documentation workshop, 1977-87; head Cinema-TV Libr. and Archives of the Performing Arts, U. So. Calif., L.A., 1988—. Project dir.: Motion Pictures, Television, Radio: A Union Catalogue of Manuscript and Special Collections in the Western United States, 1977. Active Hollywood Dog Obedience Club, Calif. Numerous grants for script indexing, manuscript cataloging, library automation. Mem. Soc. Am. Archivists, Soc. Calif. Archivists (pres. 1982-83), Theater Library Assn. (exec. bd. 1983-86), Assn. Entertainment Industry Computer Profls. (bd. dirs. 1986—). Democrat. Episcopalian. Avocations: running, swimming, reading, dog obedience training. Office: U So Calif Cinema-TV Library Univ Library Los Angeles CA 90089-0182

SCHLOSSER, ELEANOR FLORENCE, realtor, broker; b. Frederick, Md., Jan. 4; m. Leonard W. Schlosser, Sept. 19, 1959; children: Karen A. Johnston, Timothy M. Grad. hairdressing sch., Bladensburg, Md., 1959; student, Nike Real Estate sch., Vienna, Va., 1979. Hairdresser Vincent Salon, Md., 1959-62; hairdresser Sherries Salon, Md., 1962-70; hairdresser, owner Greenbert, Greenbelt, Md., 1970-75; hairdresser Town Ctr. Salon, Va., 1978-82; realtor The Thomas Co., Leesburg, Va., 1979—; part-time hairdress Adam & Eve Salon, Va., 1983—. Mem. Rpact Com., Leesburg, 1980-82. Mem. Hairdresser of Am., Loudon Bd. Realtors (awards com. 1987—, million dollar club 1987-89), PWP-Woman Club of Va. Home: Rte 1 Box 570 Waterford VA 22190 Office: The Thomas Co 114 Edwards Ferry Rd Leesburg VA 22075

SCHLOSSER, MARY ANN, clinical psychologist, consultant; b. Washington, Dec. 8, 1960; d. Wilbur Martin and Susan (Shapiro) S. BS, Syracuse U., 1982; MA, Calif. Sch. Profl. Psychology, 1985, PhD, 1987. Lic. psychologist, Mass., N.H. Intern Astor Home for Children, Rhinebeck, N.Y., 1986-87; staff psychologist Judge Baker Children's Ctr., Boston, 1987—; pvt. practice Seacoast Resource Assocs., Portsmouth, N.H., 1989—; cons., supr. Judge Baker Children's Ctr., Boston, 1988—. Mem. Am. Psychol. Assn., Nat. Register Health Providers, Soc. Pediatric Psychology, Play Therapy Assn. Office: Seacoast Resource Assocs 875 Greenland Rd Ste B3 Portsmouth NH 03801

SCHLOTFELDT, ROZELLA MAY, nursing educator; b. DeWitt, Iowa, June 29, 1914; d. John W. and Clara C. (Doering) S. BS, State U. Iowa, 1935; MS, U. Chgo., 1947, PhD, 1956; DSc (hon.), Georgetown U., 1972, Adelphi U., 1979, Wayne State U., 1983, U. Ill.-Chgo., 1985, U. Cin., 1989; LHD (hon.), Med. U. S.C., 1976; DSc, Kent State U., 1987. Staff nurse State U. Iowa, VA Hosp., 1935-39; instr., supr. maternity nursing (State U. Iowa), 1939-44; asst. prof. U. Colo. Sch. Nursing, 1947-48; asst., then assoc. prof. Wayne State U. Coll. Nursing, 1948-55; prof., assoc. dean Wayne State U. Coll. Nursing (Coll. Nursing), 1957-60; dean Frances Payne Bolton Sch. Nursing, Case Western Res. U., 1960-72, prof., 1960-82, prof., dean emeritus, 1982—; Spl. cons. Surgeon Gen.'s Adv. Group on Nursing, 1961-63; mem. nursing research study sect. USPHS, 1962-66; mem. Nat. League for Nursing-USPHS Com. on Nursing Edn. Facilities, 1962-64; mem. com. on health goals Cleve. Health Council, 1961-66; mem. Cleve. Health Planning and Devel. Commn., 1969-72; adv. com. div. nursing W.K. Kellog Found., 1959-67; v.p. Ohio Bd. Nursing Edn. and Nurse Registration, 1970-71, pres., 1971-72; mem. Nat. Health Services Research Tng. Com., 1970-71; mem. supply and edn. panel Health Manpower Com., 1966-67; rev. com. Nurse Tng. Act, 1967-68; bd. visitors Duke U. Med. Center, 1968-70; mem. council, exec. com. Inst. Medicine of Nat. Acad. Scis., 1971-75; mem. nat. adv. health services council Health Services and Mental Health Adminstrn., 1971-75; mem. def. adv. com. on women in services Dept. Def., 1972-75; bd. mem., treas. Nursing Home Adv. and Research Council, 1975—; mem. adv. panel Health Services Research Commn. on Human Resources, Nat. Acad. Sci., 1977-85; cons. Walter Reed Army Inst.; adv. council on nursing, U.S. VA, 1965-69, chmn., 1966-69; mem. Yale U.; Council Com. on Med. Affairs, 1981-86; mem. adv. bd. Scholarly Inquiry for Nursing Practice, 1987—. Mem. editorial bd.: Advances in Nursing Sci, Inquiry, 1982-85, Jour. Nursing Edn., 1982; contbr. numerous articles to profl. jours. Served to 1st lt. Army Nurse Corps, 1944-46. Recipient Distinguished Service award U. Iowa, 1973. Fellow Am. Acad. Nursing (v.p. 1975-77), Nat. League Nursing; mem. Am. Nurses Assn. (chmn. commn. on nurse edn. 1967-70, mem. com. for studying credentialling 1976-79, adv. com. W. K. Kellogg Nat. Fellowship program 1981-85), Pi Lambda Theta, Sigma Theta Tau (nat. v.p. 1948-50, selection com., disting. lectr. program 1986-87, Founders award for creativity 1985). Home: 1111 Carver Rd Cleveland Heights OH 44112 Office: 2121 Abington Rd Cleveland OH 44106

SCHLOTT, MARY CAMILLE, lawyer; b. Keokuk, Iowa, Sept. 29, 1932; d. Roy A. and Marjorie Louise (Dadant) Grout; m. Richard J. Schlott, Aug. 23, 1953 (div. May 1977); children: David, Susan, Nicholas; m. Harry A. Repenning, Oct. 21, 1977. BS, Iowa State U., 1955; MS, Purdue U., 1959; JD, John Marshall Law Sch., 1974. Bar: Ill. 1974, U.S. Dist. Ct. (no. dist.) Ill. 1974, U.S. Supreme Ct. 1979. Asst. atty. gen. State of Ill., Chgo., 1974-76; pvt. practice Arlington Heights, Ill., 1976-78, 1982—; ptnr. Schlott & Wolf, Ltd., Arlington Heights, 1978-82; gen. counsel Wheeling Twp. Rep. Orgn., Arlington Heights, 1983—; bd. dirs. Cook County Legal Assistance Found., Chgo., 1983-85. Commr. Arlington Heights Environ. Control Commn., 1971-74, Arlington Heights Planning Commn., 1982—; parliamentarian Community and Econ. Devel. Assn. of Cook County, Chgo., 1984-87; pres. LWV, Arlington Heights, 1968-69, Friends Arlington Heights Library, 1968-69. Recipient Outstanding Service award Vol. Service Bur., 1983, Disting. Service award Community and Econ. Devel. Assn. Cook County, 1984. Mem. ABA, Ill. Bar Assn., Chgo. Bar Assn., Women's Bar Assn. Ill., Northwest Suburban Bar Assn., Nat. Assn. Social Security Claimants' Reps. (sustaining), Rotary. Republican. Presbyterian. Office: 750 W Northwest Hwy Arlington Heights IL 60004

SCHLUTTER, LOIS COCHRANE, psychologist; b. Indpls., Oct. 18, 1953; d. Roy and Mavis (Wolfe) Cochrane; m. Dennis James Schlutter, Oct. 30, 1976; 1 child, Nathan Paul. BS, U. S.D., 1974, MA, 1975, PhD, 1978. Licensed cons. psychologist, Minn. Psychologist, asst. Neurol. Inst. and Pain Ctr., Sioux City, Iowa, 1975-77; staff Mpls. Psychotherapy Inst., St. Louis Park, Minn., 1978-80; pvt. practice psychology, St. Louis Park, 1980-87; with strategic planning Vail Place, Mpls. and Hopkins (Minn.), 1988—; bd. dirs. Vail Pl.; allied health staff, cons. Meth. Hosp., St. Louis Park., 1978—, mem. hospice adv. com., 1984—, child abuse consortium, 1985—; staff psychologist, Sister Kenny Inst., Mpls., 1980-81; cons. Dept. Vocat. Rehab., St. Paul. 1984—; supr. Pastoral Care/AAPC, St. Louis Park, 1984—; lectr. St. Mary's Hosp. and Coll., Mpls., 1984—; psychologist, dir. Family Dynamics, St. Louis Park., 1980—. Co-author: (play) The Extrapolator, 1968; contbr. articles to profl. jours. Mem. task force Vinland Nat. Ctr.; chmn. adult edn., Hopkins United Meth. Ch., 1988—. Recipient rsch. grant Lederle Pharms., 1979. Mem. Am. Psychol. Assn., Minn. Psychol. Assn., Am. Assn. Pastoral Counselors (profl. affiliate), Brookside Condominium Assn., Boulevard Condominium Assn., Internat. Platford Assn., Phi Beta Kappa, Kappa Alpha Theta, Alpha Lambda Delta, Psi Chi. Office: Family Dynamics 4039 Brookside Ave S Saint Louis Park MN 55416

SCHMALTZ, KATHLEEN MARY (KATHLEEN MARY REARDON), television news anchor, writer; b. Detroit, Apr. 7, 1958; d. Donald Edward and Gwendolyn Rita (Strotz) S. BA in Communication Arts, Mich. State U., 1980. Promotion asst., coordinator tour guides Sta. WJBK-TV2, Detroit, 1974-76; news, sports, pub. affairs Mich. State Radio Network, East Lansing, Mich., 1976-79; news reporter, announcer Sta. WKAR-AM-FM, East Lansing, 1978-79, Sta. WITL-AM-FM, Lansing, Mich., 1979—; news anchor, writer Sta. WILX-TV, Lansing and Jackson, Mich., 1979—; ascertainment study researcher Mich. State Radio Network, East Lansing, 1978—; host Easter Seal Telethon, 1984-89, Children's Miracle Network Telethon, 1989; guest speaker various orgns. Mem. Mich. State U. Student Adv. Group, 1977-79, Mid-Mich. Easter Seal Soc. Recipient Recognition award USAF, 1983, Disting. Service award Royal Oak Beaumont Hosp., 1983, Outstanding Community Service award for Crime Prevention in City of Lansing, 1984, Outstanding Mich. Media award Crime Prevention Assn. Mich., 1984, Tri-County Recognition award for Outstanding Vol. Service, 1987, Spl. award for Outstanding Service Big Bros./Big Sisters, 1987; named Vol. of Yr., 1989. Mem. Women in Communications. Office: WILX-TV 10 PO Box 30380 Lansing MI 48909

SCHMEER, ARLINE CATHERINE, cancer research executive, chemotherapy scientist; b. Rochester, N.Y., Nov. 14, 1929; d. Edward Jacob and Medeline Margaret (Haines) S. BA, Coll. St. Mary of the Springs, Columbus, Ohio, 1951; MS in Biology, Notre Dame U., 1961; PhD in Biomedicine, U. Colo., 1969; DSc (hon.), Albertus Magnus Coll., SUNY, Potsdam, 1974, 90. Chmn. sci. dept. Watterson High Sch./Diocese of Columbus, 1954-59, St. Vincent Ferrer High Sch./Archdiocese of N.Y., N.Y.C., 1959-62; chmn. dept. biology Ohio Dominican Coll., Columbus, 1963-72; chmn. dept. anti-cancer agents of marine origin Am. Cancer Rsch. Ctr., Denver, 1972-82; dir. Mercenene Cancer Rsch. Inst. Hosp. St. Raphael, New Haven, 1982—; sr. prin. investigator Marine Biol. Lab., Woods Hole, Mass., 1962-72, corp. mem., mem. libr. com., 1964—; rsch. prof. Med. Sch., U. Wüzburg, Fed. Republic Gemany, 1969-70; pres., chief exec. officer Med. Rsch. Found., 1972—. Contbr. articles to biol. publs. Grantee Am. Cancer Soc., 1965; NSF fellow, 1957-62, NIH fellow, 1966-69. Fellow Royal Microscopical Soc. Eng. (life); mem. N.Y. Acad. Sci. (life), Am. Soc. Cell Biology. Roman Catholic. Office: Mercenene Cancer Rsch Inst Office of Dir Hosp St Raphael New Haven CT 06511

SCHMELZ, BRENDA LEA, legal assistant; b. Washington, Mo., June 13, 1958; d. Edward G. and Wilma D. (Hektor) R.; m. Jan M. Schmelz, Oct. 7, 1978; children: Edward L., Brent T. Secretarial sci. cert. with honors, East Cen. Coll., Union, Mo., 1977. Sec., paralegal Mittendorf & Mittendorf, Union, 1976-83, Eckelkamp, Eckelkamp, Wood & Kuenzel, Washington, 1983—; mem. legal secretarial adv. bd. East Cen. Coll., 1978, chmn., 1987. Nat. Assn. Legal Assts. (cert.), Nat. Assn. Legal Secs. (cert., Mo. Assn. Legal Secs. (sec. 1984-86, 89-91, v.p. 1986, dir. pub. rels. 1987-89, Legal Sec. of Yr. award 1987), Franklin County Legal Secs. Assn. (sec. 1979, 81-84, gov. 1982-84, v.p. 1985-88, Legal Sec. of Yr. award 1987, pres. 1989), Union Women of Today, Phi Beta Kappa. Republican. Roman Catholic. Home: 142 Highland Dr Union MO 63084 Office: Eckelkamp Eckelkamp Wood & Kuenzel Bank of Washington Bldg Main & Oak Washington MO 63084

SCHMID, PATRICIA ANN, librarian; b. Erie, Pa., Nov. 18, 1948; d. Daniel Francis and Helen Irene (Sullivan) S. BS, Edinboro (Pa.) U., 1970; MLS, U. Pitts., 1978; cert., Katharine Gibbs, Boston, 1970. Asst. law libr. sch. law U. Pitts., 1978-83, libr. semester at sea program, 1983; reference libr. Morgan, Lewis & Bockius, Washington, 1984-85; asst. libr. MPR Assocs., Washington, 1985-86; staff asst. Dem. Policy Com., U.S. Senate, Washington, 1986-88; govt. publs. cataloguer U.S. Senate Libr., Washington, 1988—. Pres. Western Pa. Law Libr. Assn., Pitts., 1983-84; mem. George Washington Birthday Celebration Com., Alexandria, 1986-88, Dem. Com., Alexandria, 1985-87. Mem. AAUW (v.p. membership Alexandria br. 1986-87), Woman's Nat. Dem. Club, Kappa Delta Pi, Beta Phi Mu. Roman Catholic. Office: US Senate Libr US Capitol Washington DC 20510

SCHMIDT, BARBARA ELLYN, nuclear medicine technologist; b. Evanston, Ill., Apr. 13, 1954; d. William Ferdinand and Dorothy Marie (Wagner) S.; m. Kurt F. Werner, June 2, 1989. AAS, Oakton Community Coll., 1975. Cert. nuclear medicine technologist, radiologic technologist. Radiol. technologist Skokie (Ill.) Valley Hosp., 1974-76, nuclear medicine technologist, 1976-80; nuclear medicine technologist Christ Hosp., Oak Lawn, Ill., 1980-81; chief technologist Imaging Ctr., Oak Lawn, 1983—; nuclear cardiology technologist Holy Cross Hosp., Chgo., 1981-89; nuclear medicine specialist Mica, Inc., Buffalo Grove, Ill., 1989—. Mem. children's com. Starlight Found., Chgo., 1989—. Mem. Soc. Nuclear Medicine Technologists (sec. 1986-88, nominating com., financing com. Cen. chpt., technologist sect. 1985-86, assocs. and tech. affiliates Chgo. adv. bd. 1979-87, assocs. & tech. affiliates Chgo. chmn. nominating com. 1986, assocs. & tech. affiliates Chgo. chpt. 1982, assocs. & tech. affiliates Chgo. chpt. pres. 1984-85), Am. Soc. Clin. Pathologists, Nuclear Medicine Technologists, Am Registry Radiologic Technologists. Lutheran. Office: Mica Inc 801 Asbury Dr Buffalo Grove IL 60089

SCHMIDT, BETTY J., motel and trailer court executive, accountant; b. Kearney, Nebr., Sept. 3, 1938; d. LaVerne Ivan and Vivian Jane (Johnson) Banks; married Aug. 25, 1954; children: LaVerne, Dennis, Linda. Student U. Wyo.; BBA in Acctg., U. San Diego, 1982; MBA, U. Phoenix. Owner, mgr. Blue Ribbon Cafe & Lounge, Meeteetse, Wyo., 1976-78; mgr. Schmidt Ranch and Limousin Cattle Co., Meeteetse, 1965-78, Don Neet Limousin Cattle Co., Meeteetse, 1970-76; head bookkeeper First State Bank, Cody, Wyo., 1968-71; bookkeeper Barling Constrn. Co., Meeteetse, 1971-73; owner, mgr. Sagebrush Motel and Trailer Ct., Wamsutter, Wyo., 1978—; fin. dir., treas. City of Imperial Beach., Calif., 1987-88; chief fiscal officer Legal Aid Soc. San Diego, 1984-87; dir. adminstrv. svcs. Town of Kingman, Ariz., 1989—. Custodian of the fund Marine Corps Recreation Depot, San Diego, 1982-84; chairwoman Mohava/LaPaz Procurement Com.; fin. chair Kingman Airport Authority. Mem. Govt. Fin. Officers' Assn., Ariz. Fin. Officers' Assn., Wyo. Limousin Assn., Nat. Assn. Limousin Breeders, Wyo. Stockgrowers Assn., Mcpl. Treas.'s Assn., City Mcpl. Officers Assn., Soroptimists, Beta Alpha Psi. Republican. Lutheran. Home and Office: 1975 Pacific Ave Kingman AZ 86401

SCHMIDT, CAROL SUZANNE, hospital administrator; b. River Rouge, Mich., Aug. 8, 1936; d. J. T. Grant Vaden and Virginia Jean (Senker) Vaden Webster; m. Ronald Lee Schmidt, Aug. 18, 1957; children: Karen Suzanne Corsilius, Linda Martin, Ronald Lee. RN diploma Hinsdale Hosp. Sch. Nursing, Ill., 1958; BS in Nursing cum laude, Met. State Coll., Denver, 1981; M.A. cum laude, Webster U.-Denver, 1984. RN, Colo. Operating room nurse Porter Meml. Hosp., Denver, 1961-69, charge relief nurse, 1975-76, adminstrv. supr., 1976-77, head nurse ortho/neuro unit, 1977-82; disease control nurse Vis. Nurse Assn., Denver, 1961-63; nurse Denver Gen. Hosp., 1966-67; office mgr., bookkeeper Timber Ridge Constrn., Evergreen, Colo., 1967-79; asst. dir. nursing Boulder Meml. Hosp., Colo., 1982-83, dir. nursing, 1983-84; v.p. Avista Hosp., 1984—. Tchr. Seventh Day Adventist Ch., Boulder and Denver, 1958-85; vol. Colo. Health Fair, Denver, 1979, 80; tchr. basic life support Am. Heart Assn., Denver, 1980-82. Recipient Dist. Nurse of Yr. award Colo. Nurse Assn., 1975. Mem. Am. Coll. Hosp. Execs. of Am. Hosp. Assn., Am. Orgn. Nurse Execs., Assn. Seventh Day Adventist Nurses (bd. dirs. 1984-86), Colo. Soc. Nurse Execs. (active image of nursing 1985), Bus. and Profl. Women (legis. com. 1985). Avocations: needlework; travel. Office: Avista Hosp 100 Health Park Dr Louisville CO 80027

SCHMIDT, DEBRA PODRAZA, financial services executive; b. Hampton, Va., Oct. 19, 1957; d. Joseph Ronald Sr. and Beda Marie (Morehouse) Podraza; m. Erwin Rudolph Schmidt III, July 16, 1983; 1 child, Erwin Rudolph Schmidt IV. AAS, Erie Community Coll., 1977. Accounts receivable cons. GC Svcs., Phila., 1978-85; regional mktg. specialist Norwest Fin. Leasing, L.A., 1985-89; nat. sales recruiter Norwest Fin. Leasing, Denver, 1989—. Vol. San Antonio Cath. Ch., Anaheim Hills, Calif., 1986-88, Goodson Recreation Ctr., Littleton, Colo., 1989-90; mem. Consumer Credit Assn., Pa., N.J., Del., 1981-84, Internat. Consumer Credit Assn., Phila., 1984-86, Hosp. Fin. Mgmt. Assn., Phila., 1983-84. Mem. Buffalo Models Guild (pres. 1977-78), Ridgeview Tennis-Swim Club (sec. 1988-89), Shar-Pei Club N. Am. Republican.

SCHMIDT, GLENDA BOTTOMS, science teacher; b. Marianna, Fla., June 19, 1949; d. Hill and Evelyn (Wachob) Bottoms; m. James David Schmidt, Dec. 16, 1972; children: Christopher Ian, Robert Aaron. AA, Chipola Jr. Coll., Marianna, 1969; BS in Chemistry, U. West Fla., 1971; postgrad., U. Fla., 1971-73; MEd, Southeastern La. U., 1982. Cert. tchr., S.C., La. Tchr. St. Helena Jr. High Sch., Beaufort, S.C., 1973-74, East Jefferson High Sch., Metairie, La., 1974-75; tchr., chmn. sci. dept. Salmen High Sch., Slidell, La., 1975—; camp counselor John C. Stennis Space Ctr., Miss., 1988—; cons., speaker in field. Co-author booklet, ednl. materials. Participant NEWMAST program NASA, Huntsville, Ala., 1987; mem. World Wildlife Fund, 1989—. Mem. La. Sci. Tchrs. Assn. (award 1988), Nat. Sci. Tchrs. Assn., Am. Assn. Physics Tchrs., Am. Chem. Soc. (George Drake award La. sect. 1989), Assn. Supervision and Curriculum Devel., Nat. Sci. Supervisors Assn., Lacombe C. of C., Phi Kappa Phi. Roman Catholic. Office: Salmen High Sch 4040 Berkley St Slidell LA 70458

SCHMIDT, JANET MARIE, system engineer; b. Louisville, Apr. 22, 1963; d. Richard John and Gloria Rose (Mikuta) S. BSEE, Ohio State U., 1987. Engr.-in-tng. IBM, Manassas, Va., 1987-88, assoc. engr./scientist, 1988-89; assoc. programmer IBM, Gaithersburg, Md., 1990—. Mem. Computer Programmers for Social Responsibility. Republican. Roman Catholic. Office: IBM 708 Quince Orchard Rd Gaithersburg MD 20878

SCHMIDT, JEAN MARIE, microbiology educator; b. Waterloo, Iowa, June 5, 1938; d. John Frederick and Opal Marie (Lowe) S. BA, U. Iowa, 1959, MS, 1961; PhD, U. Calif., Berkeley, 1965. NIH postdoctoral fellow U. Edinburgh, Scotland, 1965-66; asst. prof. Ariz. State U., Tempe, 1966-71, assoc. prof., 1971-79, prof. microbiology, 1979—, asst. dir. for biology Cancer Research Inst., 1982—, acting chair dept. microbiology, 1988-89. Author: (with others) Bergey's Manual of Systematic Bacteriology, 1989; contbr. articles to jours. NSF grantee, 1981. Fellow AAAS; mem. Am. Soc. Microbiology (div. chmn. 1979-80), Soc. Gen. Microbiology, Phi Beta Kappa, Sigma Xi. Democrat. Methodist.

SCHMIDT, JOANNE HARPER, real estate broker and realtor; b. Tullahoma, Tenn., June 20, 1938; d. J. W. and Dortha Mae (Poe) Harper; m. Murray Ray Schmidt, Apr. 12, 1958; children: Karen Denise, Lamar Richard. Student, U. Fla., 1962-65, U. Cen. Fla., 1977-79. Sec. Shands Teaching Hosp., Gainesville, Fla., 1961-65; with real estate sales Windover Farms, Titusville, Fla., 1978-83; city councilwoman City of Titusville, 1979-85; independent real estate broker Titusville, 1983—. Vice mayor City of Titusville, 1979-85; dir., sec., v.p. and pres. Brevard League of Cities, Brevard County, Fla., 1979-83; bd. dirs. Fla. League of Cities, Tallahassee, 1981-85, Fla. Downtown Devel. Assn., Tallahassee, 1981-85, Fla. Future Quality Cities, Fla., League of Cities, Tallahassee, 1981-85; mem. exec. bd. Task Force on Future Fla. League of Cities, Tallahassee, 1984-85; bd. dirs. adv. bd. Salvation Army, Titusville, 1983-88, chmn. bd. dirs., 1985-88. Mem. Titusville Bd. Realtors (key contact 1974—), Space Coast Devel. Comn. (bd. dirs. 1986-88), Titusville C. of C. (bd. dirs. 1987-88, better bus. div. 1978, Outstanding Community Svc./Govt. Leadership award 1982), Young Rep. Club (pres. 1970-73), Keep Brevard Beautiful Club (pres. 1985-86), Keep Brevard Beautiful County Wide (pres. 1987-88), Pilot Club. Republican. Home: 449 N Dixie Ave Titusville FL 32796 Office: 4401 S Hopkins Ave Box 112 Ste 103 Titusville FL 32780

SCHMIDT, KARYN BETH, department assistant; b. Youngstown, Ohio, June 1, 1951; d. Karl John and Margaret Elizabeth (Foisel) S. BS in English, Bowling Green State U., 1973. Lic. tchr., Ohio. Substitute tchr. South Euclid/Lyndhurst (Ohio) Schs., 1973-75, Mayfield Sch. System, Mayfield Heights, Ohio, 1973-75; med. claims approver John Hancock Ins., Cleve., 1975-76; dept. asst. Case Western Res. U., Cleve., 1976—. Ch. sch. tchr. Messiah Luth. Ch., Lyndhurst, 1973—, parish edn. com., 1980—. Mem. AAUW (bd. dirs. 1985—, newsletter editor Cleve. chpt. 1987—, publicity chair 1987—, named Gift Honoree to the Margaret F. Bolton Fellowship Endowment 1989), Saxon Fraternal Lodge. Office: Case Western Res U Dept Family Medicine 2119 Abington Rd Cleveland OH 44106

SCHMIDT, KATHRYN ANN, dietitian; b. Cedar Rapids, Iowa, Nov. 13, 1958; d. James Edward and Virginia Agnes (McDonnell) Regan; m. Herbert Ernst Schmidt, Apr. 22, 1989. BS in Dietetics, Iowa State U., 1984. Clin. dietitian Jane Lamb Health Ctr. (ARA Svcs.), Clinton, Iowa, 1984-86, Burlington (Iowa) Med. Ctr., 1986—; cons. nutrition, Iowa and Ill., 1987—; nutrition advisor Cardiac Support Group, Burlington, 1987—, Cancer Support Group, 1988—; instr. Burlington Med. Ctr., 1986—, guest speaker, 1987—, mem. nutrition support com., 1987—, mem. pharmacy and therapeutic com., 1990—. Author: (series) Ask A Dietitian, 1989; developed ednl. pamphlets; guest speaker radio and TV. Bd. dirs. Am. Heart Assn., Burlington, 1989—. Scholarship Am. Legion, 1977-79, Internat. Ednl. Exchange, 1978. Mem. AAUW (program v.p., chair), Am. Dietetic Assn. (sponsor), Misssissippi Valley Dietetic Assn., Iowa Dietetic Assn. (coord. nat. nutrition month 1990). Roman Catholic.

SCHMIDT, LYNN ANNE, accountant; b. Passaic, N.J., July 31, 1958; d. William W. and Barbara M. (Urban) Butler; m. Donald A. Schmidt, June 28, 1980; children: Kristine, Andrea, Steven. BS, N.H. Coll., 1980; cert., NAt. Tax Tng. Sch., 1986. Bookkeeper Cogan-Zeitlin CPA, Paramus, N.J., 1976, United Parcel Service, Manchester, N.H., 1977; acctg. asst. Unified Data Products, Paramus, 1978; comptroller Lamont Labs. Inc, Londonderry, N.H., 1978-79; acct. World Relief Refugee Services, Nyack, N.Y., 1980, Modafferi, Ritter & Furfaro, CPA's, Nanuet, N.Y., 1980-81; pvt. practice acctg. Sloatsburg, N.Y., 1983—; acct., mgr. office Marvin Nyman, CPA, Bardonia, N.Y., 1985—; speaker in field. Mem. Nat. Alliance Homebased Bus. Women, Nanuet, 1968-88. Mem. N.Y. Soc. Pub. Accts., Nat. Soc. Pub. Accts. Episcopalian. Home and Office: Eagle Valley Rd Tuxedo Sloatsburg NY 10974

SCHMIDT, MARY MAY, English educator, consultant, bookkeeper; b. Batavia, N.Y., June 3, 1949; d. Ralph Ellis and Mary Frances (Watson) Swenson; m. Gary Charles Schmidt, July 3, 1971; children: Daniel Glenn, Christopher Gregory. BS in English, SUNY, Potsdam, 1971; MS in English Edn., SUNY, New Paltz, 1983; postgrad., Marist Coll., 1988—. Cert. English tchr., N.Y. Instr. in humanities Sullivan County Community Coll., Loch Sheldrake, N.Y., 1981-85; instr. English Pace U., N.Y.C., 1986—; adj. instr. speech and Am. humanities div., adminstr. satellite program Pace U., Swan Lake, N.Y., 1988—; acad. adviser, Am. humanics adj. prof. Pace U., 1988—. Author poetry. Vol. Ambulance Corp., 1972-86; multiple offices PTA, Monticello, 1981-84; v.p., bd. dirs. United Way, Sullivan County, Monticello, 1984-86, chmn. 1986-88; bd. dirs. Sullivan County Arts Coun., 1989—; mem. Citizen's Adv. Panel, Town of Thompson. Recipient Leadership award United Way of Sullivan County, 1989. Mem. AAUW (com. chmn. 1982-85), Catskill Art Soc., Nat. Assn. Women Deans, Adminstrs. and Counselors, Nat. Assn. Academic Affairs Adminstrs. (N.E. Region). Republican. Methodist. Home: 55 Jefferson St Monticello NY 12701 Office: Pace Univ Swan Lake NY 12783

SCHMIDT, MARY MORRIS, art librarian; b. Mpls., June 28, 1926; d. Arthur Marvin and Clara Gladys (Cronk) Morris; m. Philip Fred Schmidt, Mar. 17, 1950 (dec. Nov. 1977); children: Eric Morris, Aaron McCagg; m. John Steuart Wilson, Oct. 18, 1983. BA, U. Minn., 1949, MS in LS, 1955, MA in Art History, 1956. Art libr. U. Minn., Mpls., 1954-55; editor art index H.W. Wilson Co., Bronx, N.Y., 1958-68; fine arts libr. Columbia U., N.Y.C., 1968-77; libr. Marquand Libr., Princeton (N.J.) U., 1977-89, spl. projects libr., 1989—. Mem. Art Librs. Soc. N.Am., Art Librs. Soc. N.J., Art Libr. Soc. N.Y. (chmn. 1975-76), Coll. Art Assn., Soc. Archtl. Historians. Home: 425 Alexander St Princeton NJ 08540 Office: Princeton U Libr Princeton NJ 08544

SCHMIDT, RUTH ANN, college president; b. Mountain Lake, Minn., Sept. 16, 1930; d. Jacob A. and Anna A. (Ewert) S. B.A., Augsburg Coll., Mpls., 1952; M.A., U. Mo., 1955; Ph.D., U. Ill., 1962; LLD, Gordon Coll., 1987. Asst. prof. Spanish Mary Baldwin Coll., Staunton, Va., 1955-58; asst. prof. Spanish SUNY-Albany, 1962-67, assoc. prof., 1967-78, dean of humanities, 1971-76; provost Wheaton Coll., Norton, Mass., 1978-82; pres. Agnes Scott Coll., Decatur, Ga., 1982—; chair Women's Coll. Coalition, 1986-88. Author: Ortega Munilla y sus novelas, 1973, Cartas entre dos amigos del teatro, 1969. Trustee Gordon Coll., Wenham, Mass., 1980-86; dir. DeKalb C. of C., 1982-85; mem. exec. com. Women's Coll. Coalition, 1983-88; bd. dirs. Atlanta Coll. Art, 1987—. Named Disting. Alumna Augsburg Coll., 1973. Mem. Assn. Am. Colls. (dir. 1979-82, treas. 1982-83), Soc. Values in Higher Edn., Am. Council Edn. (commn. on women in higher edn. 1985-88), AAUW, Assn. Pvt. Colls. and Univs. Ga. (pres. 1987-89). Democrat. Presbyterian. Office: Agnes Scott Coll Decatur GA 30030

SCHMIDT, RUTH CAROLINE, civic worker; b. Appleton, Wis., Apr. 2, 1922; d. William Gustavus and Gladys (Emily) Richter Gust; m. Robert Walter Schmidt, Nov. 14, 1941; 1 child, David Robert. Student Appleton Bus. Coll., 1940-41. Contbr. articles to ednl. jours. and newspapers. Pres. Elkhart Lake Sch. Bd., Wis., 1964-82; pres. Wis. Assn. Sch. Bds., Madison, 1978; del., mem. steering com. White House Conf. on Libraries, 1978-83; pres. Wis. PTA, Madison, 1983-85; chmn. Council of Library and Network Devel., Madison, 1981—; bd. dirs. Nat. PTA, Chgo., 1983-85; organizer student assistance program Drug and Alcohol Abuse Program, Elkhart Lake, 1983—; founder Am. Field Service Program, Elkhart Lake; bd. dirs. Wis. Assn. Sch. Bds. Edn. Found., 1989; mem. task force on Sch. Libr. Media Issues, 1989. Recipient Recognition of Service award Wis. Sch. Library Assn., 1978, Reading for Excellence award Sch. Bd., Elkhart Lake, Wis., 1984, Citation, Wis. Legislature, 1982, Dedicated Service to Edn. award Wis. Assn. Sch. Adminstrs., 1986. Mem. Nat. PTA (hon. life), Wis. PTA (hon. life), Wis. Assn. Sch. Bds. (life). Republican. Mem. United Ch. of Christ. Clubs: Elkhart Lake Study (pres.), Quit Quie Golf (Elkhart Lake) (pres.). Lodge: Order Eastern Star. Avocations: golf; swimming; bridge; reading. Home: 220 Crystal Lake Dr Plymouth WI 53073

SCHMIDT, SANDRA KAY, financial aid director; b. Franklin, Nebr., Nov. 12, 1941; d. Floyd Nelson and Leola Fern (Boyce) Meade; m. Gene LeRoy Schmidt, Nov. 1, 1941. Grad., Cen. Comm. Coll., 1976; student, Kearney State Coll., 1988. Sec., bookkeeper Franklin Pub. Schs., 1963-69; office mgr. George Risk Industries, Columbus, Nebr., 1969-71; VA certifying official Cen. Community Coll.-Platte, Columbus, 1971-83, fin. aid officer, 1983-86; fin. aid coordinator Cen. Comm. Coll.-Platte, Columbus, 1986-89, fin. aid dir., 1989—; ptnr. Images Unlimited Photography. Mem. Am. Bus. Women (Bus. Woman of the Yr. 1986), NAFE, Nebr. Assn. Student Fin. Aid Adminstrs., Nat. Assn. Student Fin. Aid Adminstrs., Adult Continuing Edn. Assn. Office: Cen Community Coll-Platte 4500 63d Columbus NE 68601-1027

SCHMIDT, STEPHANIE ELIZABETH, healthcare administrator; b. Detroit, Oct. 11, 1954; d. Chris William and Pauline Ann (Pavlis) Charouhis; m. John David Schmidt, Nov. 29, 1980; children: Suzanne Nicole, Christopher, William. BSN, Barry U., 1977; M in Health Mgmt., St. Thomas U., 1988. Cert. nursing adminstr., healthcare risk mgr. Staff nurse Miami (Fla.) Children's Hosp., 1975-76; with Victoria Hosp., Miami, 1976-90, dir. nursing, 1984-89, v.p. patient svcs., 1989-90; adminstr. SPI Managed Care Inc., Miami, 1990—. Mem. edn. com. Am. Heart Assn., Miami, 1981-84; mem. Marian Ctr. for the Mentally Retarded, Miami, 1984—; bd. dirs. Ransom Everglades Sch., Miami, 1987, 88. Mem. Am. Nurses Assn., Fla. Nurses Assn., Fla. Orgn. Nurse Execs., South Fla. Orgn. Nurse Execs. Home: 7385 SW 123d Terr Miami FL 33156 Office: 11701 Mills Dr Miami FL 33183

SCHMIDT, WENDY S(UE), financial executive; b. Neenah, Wis., May 6, 1959; d. Allan Gilbert and Marlene Jean (Beimborn) Wohlers; m. Charles Donald Schmidt, Oct. 17, 1981. Grad., pvt. schs. Cert. profl. sec., fin. paraplanner. Cert. clk. AAL/Life Issue Svcs., Appleton, Wis., 1977-79, cert. verifier, 1979; corr. AAL/Premium Svcs., Appleton, 1979-81; investment analysis clk./mortgages and real estate AAL/Investment Div., Appleton, 1981-87; exec. asst. to pres. AAL Distbrs. Inc., AAL Advisors Inc., Appleton, 1987—. Vol. ICT (vol. orgn.) of AAL, Appleton, 1980—. Mem. Nat. Assn. Securities Dealers, Profl. Secs. Internat. (pres. 1988—). Office: AAL Mut Fund Cos 222 W College Ave Appleton WI 54919-0007

SCHMIDTMANN, LUCIE ANN, systems/software engineer; b. Jamaica, N.Y., Oct. 22, 1963; d. Otto Stanislaus and Nancy Dorothy (Koonmen) S. BS in Computer Sci., Siena Coll., Loudonville, N.Y., 1985; MS in Computer Sci., Stevens Inst. Tech., Hoboken, N.J., 1989; student, U.S. Coast Guard Acad., New London, Conn., 1981-82, St. John's U., 1980-81, 83. Computer cons. dept. computer sci. Siena Coll., Loudonville, N.Y., 1984-85; figure clk. King Kullen Grocery Co., Westbury, N.Y., 1983-85; project mgr. AT&T Bell Labs., Whippany, N.J., 1985-88; asst. to rsch. and devel. mgr. AT&T Bell Labs., 1988-89, system/software engr., 1990—; source selection cons. Highpoint Condominium Assn., Stanhope, N.J., 1989—; computer cons. Champcare, Inc., Davenport, Iowa, 1989—. Vol. N.J. Spl. Olympics, Area 3, Flanders, N.J., 1985—, vol. coord., 1985—, design/graphic artist, 1989—. With USCG, 1981-82. Recipient Vol. award, N.J. Spl. Olympics Area 3, 1989. Mem. ACM (vice chmn. 1984-85, capt. programming team 1984-85), Performance Mgmt. Assn. (mem. north Jersey chpt. planning com. 1990), IEEE Computer Soc., Math. Assn. Am. Republican. Roman Catholic. Home: 10-186 Dell Pl Stanhope NJ 07874 Office: AT&T Bell Labs 1 Whippany Rd Whippany NJ 07981

SCHMILOVICI, INA, health facility administrator. BA cum laude, U.S. Internat. U., San Diego, 1983, MA, 1984, PhD, 1989. Dir. La Jolla (Calif.) Inst. for Psychotherapy. Author: On the Relationship Between Bulimia and Food Addictions. Mem. APA, NAFE, San Diego Acad. Psychologists. Address: 1150 Silverado St La Jolla CA 92037

SCHMITMEYER, DEBRA A., fundraising executive, consultant; b. Sidney, Ohio, Feb. 24, 1951; d. Alfred J. and Rosalia A. (Klikovits) S. BA, Columbus (Ohio) U., 1975. Adminstrv. coord. Piqua (Ohio) Meml. Hosp., 1976-84; exec. dir. Piqua Meml. Hosp. Found., 1978-84; dir. devel. Barberton (Ohio) Citizens Hosp., 1984-88; exec. dir. Meml. Found., Inc., Belleville, Ill., 1988—; cons. Summit Montessori Sch., Barberton, 1984-86, Wooster (Ohio) Community Hosp., 1988—. Mem. Piqua Meml. Aux., 1979-84. Named to Outstanding Young Women of Am., 1981. Mem. Nat. Soc. Fundraising Execs. (chpt. bd. dirs. 1988), Nat. Assn. for Hosp. Devel. (cert., accredited, chmn. region VI career devel. com. 1985-88), Ohio Assn. for Hosp. Devel. (v.p. N.W. chpt. 1979-80, v.p. membership 1980-81, v.p. N.E. chpt. 1985-86, v.p. membership 1986-87, asst. v.p. program 1987-88, v.p. program 1988), Altrusa Club, Optimists. Office: Meml Found Inc 4501 N Park Dr Belleville IL 62223

SCHMITT, BARB, manufacturing executive; b. Denver; d. William Frank and Eulalia Florence (Steinbach) Hafdell; children: Brian, Jennifer, Kelly. Ed., S.W. Mo. State U. Acct. Kemp Shoe Co., Denver; advt. liaison ABC network Sta. KBTV, Denver; owner, pres. Bar-Tech Industries, Brookline, Mo. Contbr. articles to profl. newsletters. Bd. dirs. tornado relief com. Springield Area Coun. of Chs. Mem. NAFE, Vietnam Vets. Am., Golden Key Nat. Honor Soc. Address: Rte 1 Box 72-D Brookline MO 65619

SCHMITT, LISA MARIE, sales professional; b. Neptune, N.J., Oct. 31, 1963; d. James Alfred and Charlene Mary (Marty) S. BSChemE, U. Ariz., 1986. Prodn. supr. Pepsi-Cola West, Phoenix, 1986-87; prodn. supr. Pepsi-Cola West, Torrance, Calif., 1987-88, warehouse supr., 1988; tech. sales rep. Union Carbide Indsl. Svc. Co., Fontana, Calif., 1988—. Mem. Am. Inst. Chem. Engrs., Soc. Women Engrs., Pacific Energy Assn., NAFE. Republican. Roman Catholic. Office: Union Carbide Indsl Svcs Co 10829 Etiwanda Ave Fontana CA 92335

SCHMITT, MADELINE HUBBARD, nursing educator, sociologist; b. Rochester, N.Y., July 1, 1943; d. Lloyd Bertrand and Mae Thelma (Ketchum) Hubbard; m. Albert Thomas Schmitt, Oct. 18, 1963 (div. Oct. 1972); m. Michael Patrick Farrell, Aug. 7, 1976. BS, U. Rochester, 1965, MA, 1970; PhD, SUNY, Buffalo, 1976. RN, N.Y. Pub. health nurse Monroe County Health Dept., Rochester, 1965-67; asst. prof. nursing and sociology U. Rochester Sch. Nursing, 1972-78, assoc. prof. sociology, 1978-87, assoc. prof. nursing, 1978—, asst. dean grad. studies, 1972-74, dir. rsch. office, 1977-80, Univ. mentor, 1983-84; tng. cons. VA Med. Ctr., Buffalo, 1983—, also numerous others; Helen Denne Schulte vis. assoc. prof. U. Wis. Sch. Nursing, Madison, 1988. Co-author, editor: Behavioral Science and Nursing Theory, 1983 (Book of Yr. award Am. Jour. Nursing 1984); mem. editorial bd. Advances in Nursing Sci., 1982—, Rsch. in Nursing and Health, 1989—; contbr. numerous articles and revs. to nursing and social sci. jours., also chpts. to books. Group leadership trainer and facilitator Cancer Action, Inc., Rochester, 1979—. Recipient vol. award United Way Greater Rochester, 1985; Dean's award for excellence in teaching U. Rochester Sch. Nursing, 1986, Disting. Faculty Colleague award, 1987; Disting. Nurse Researcher award N.Y. State Nurses Assn. Found., 1988; USPHS spl nurse rsch. fellow, 1967-69, 70-72, NEH fellow, 1979, U. Rochester faculty bridging fellow, 1980-8l; HEW grantee, 1977, 80, U. Rochester grantee, 1983-87. Fellow Am. Acad. Nursing; mem. Am. Nurses Assn. (coun. nurse researchers 1982—), Am. Sociol. Assn., Oncology Nursing Soc. (rsch. com. 1984-86, faculty 1986-88), Sigma Theta Tau. Democrat. Mem. Soc. of Friends. Home: 99 Bastian Rd Rochester NY 14623 Office: U Rochester Sch Nursing 60l Elmwood Ave Box HWH Rochester NY 14642

SCHMITT, MARIE, computer company executive; b. Milw., Apr. 14, 1947; d. Carl A. and Kathryn Mae (Sturm) S. BA, Marquette U., Milw., 1969; postgrad., U. Wis., Milw. Educator Wauwatosa (Wis.) Pub. Sch.; account exec. Xerox Corp., Dallas and Houston; exec. programs mgr. Apple Computer, Cupertino, Calif., now mgr. exec. programs; mem. rsch. expedition program U. Calif. Mem. Mus. Soc., Commonwealth Club. Home: 2250 Homestead Ct #104 Los Altos CA 94024

SCHMITZ, DOLORES JEAN, teacher; b. River Falls, Wis., Dec. 27, 1931; d. Otto and Helen Olive (Webster) Kreuziger; m. Karl Matthias Schmitz Jr., Aug. 18, 1956; children: Victoria Jane, Karl III. BS, U. Wis., River Falls, 1953; MS, Nat. Coll. Edn., 1982; postgrad., U. Melbourne, Australia, 1989, Cardinal Stritch Coll., Milw., 1990. Cert. tchr., Wis. Tchr. Manitowoc (Wis.) Pub. Schs., 1953-56, West Allis (Wis.) Pub. Schs., 1956-59, Lowell Sch., Milw., 1960-63, Victory Sch., Milw., 1964; tchr. Palmer Sch., Milw., 1966-84, 86—, unit leader, 1984-86; co-organizer Headstart Teaching Staff Assn., Milw., 1968; insvc. organizer Headstart and Early Childhood, Milw., 1969—. Author: (curriculum) Writing to Read, 1987, Cooperation and Young Children (ERIC award 1982). Supporter Milw. Art Mus., Milw. Pub. Mus., Milwaukee County Zoo, Whitefish Bay Pub. Libr.; vol. fgn. visitor program Milw. Internat. Inst., 1966—, vol. holiday folk fair, 1976—; vol. Earthwatch, 1989; lobbyist Milw. Pub. Sch. Bd. and State of Wis., 1986—. Grantee Greater Milw. Ednl. Trust, 1989. Mem. Nat. Assn. for Edn. of Young Children, Tchrs. Applying Whole Lang., Wis. Early Childhood Assn., Milw. Tchrs. Ednl. Assn. (co-chmn. com. early childhood 1984-86), Milw. Kindergarten Assn. (corr. sec. 1986-90), Assn. for Childhood Edn. (charter pres. 1955-56). Roman Catholic. Home: 4754 N Sheffield Ave Milwaukee WI 53211 Office: Palmer Sch 1900 N 1st St Milwaukee WI 53212

SCHMOLL, BETTY LEE, healthcare administrator, educator; b. Cin., Apr. 13, 1936; d. Ezekiel Lee Begley and Bertha Irene (Burroughs) Pepper; m. Walter Charles Schmoll, Jan. 5, 1957; children: Karen, W. John, Susan, Robert, Linda. AD, Kettering Coll. Med. Arts, 1970; BS, Wright State U., 1975; MS, Ohio State U., 1978. RN, Ohio. Nurse Kettering Med. Ctr., Dayton, Ohio, 1970-75, VA Med. Ctr., Dayton, 1975-77; asst. prof. sch. medicine Wright State U., 1976—, adj. faculty sch. nursing; exec. dir., pres., chief exec. officer Hospice of Dayton, Inc., 1978—; paidela coord. Skyview Elem.Sch., Thornton, 1990—; bd. dirs., pres., v.p., treas. Ohio Hospice Orgn., Columbus, 1978-88; bd. dirs. Nat. Hospice Orgn., Arlington, Va., 1988—, treas. 1990; cons., speaker various hospice groups, 1978—. Contbr. articles to profl. jours. Rep. exec. div. United Way Dayton, 1985; chmn. bd. Ohio Cancer Consortium Long Range Planning, Columbus, 1986-87; bd. dirs. AIDS Found., Dayton, 1988—. Mem. Ohio Nurses Assn. (bd. dirs. dist. ten 1987-89), Wright State U. Alumni Assn. (bd. dirs. Dayton chpt. 1980-86), Kettering Coll. Alumni Assn., Zeta Phi Chpt., Sigma Theta Tau)pres. 1982-84), Dayton Community Oncology Program (bd. dirs. 1989—). Office: Hospice Dayton Inc 1040 S Smithville Rd Dayton OH 45403

SCHMUCKER, RUBY ELVY LADRACH, nurse, educator; b. Sugarcreek, Ohio, Nov. 17, 1923; d. Walter F. and Carrie M. (Mizer) Ladrach; R.N., Aultman Hosp., Canton, Ohio, 1945; B.S. in Nursing, U. Akron, 1970, M.S. in Edn., 1973; children—Gary, David, Barbara, Steven. Gen. duty nurse, head nurse Aultman Hosp., 1945-47, part-time, 1950-62, instr. nursing, 1962-64, 69-74; instr. nursing Coll. Nursing, U. Akron (Ohio), 1974-76; instr. div. nursing edn. Children's Hosp., Akron, 1976-78; psychiat. nurse and supr. Massillon (Ohio) State Hosp., 1978-80, cons. to nursing dept., 1980-81 , dir. nursing edn., 1981-84; supr. Molly Stark Hosp., 1984-88; charge nurse, individual and group therapist Cuyahoga Falls Gen. Hosp., 1984—; cons. Stark-Tuscarawas Counties Student Nurses Assn., 1973-74. Health chmn. Avondale Sch. PTA, Canton, 1956, mem. coms., 1954-70; vol. instr. home nursing courses ARC, 1959-62, instr. CPR, 1979-83. Cert. psychiat. nurse. Mem. Aultman Hosp. Sch. Nursing Alumni Assn., Am. Nurses' Assn., Nat. League Nursing, Am. Personnel and Guidance Assn., Am. Coll. Personnel Assn., U. Akron Alumni Assn., Alpha Sigma Lambda. Mem. Ch. of Christ. Office: 4214 Bellwood Dr NW Canton OH 44708

SCHMUDE, JUDY GAIL, health care administrator; b. Kenosha, Wis., Mar. 2, 1939; d. Howard D. and Joycelyn V. (Correll) Ohlgart; divorced; children: Frederick E., Randall H. BS, U. Wis., Whitewater, 1962, MS, 1971; MT, Kenosha Mem. Hosp., 1971; PhD, Marquette U., 1983. Cert. tchr. Tchr. gen. sch. Kenosha Unified Schs., 1962-67; instr. sci. Gateway Tech. Inst., Kenosha, 1967-75; edn. coordinator Kenosha Mem. Hosp., 1975-80, dir., 1980-86; v.p. women's care St. Joseph's Hosp. and Med. Ctr., Phoenix, 1986—, v.p. maternal and child health, 1989-90, v.p. ambulatory svcs., 1990—; adj. faculty U. Phoenix, 1986—; faculty Cardinal Stritch Coll., Milw., 1985-86; cons. Kenosha Mem. Hosp., 1983-86. Author: Quality Assurance Nursing Schools, 1985, Politics in Health Care Administration, 1988; contbr. articles to profl. jours. Pres. Wish. Health Edn., 1986, Am. Cancer Soc., Kenosha, 1985; elected mem. Ariz. Women's Town Hall, 1987, 88, 89, panel chair, 1989; state chair Ariz. Prenatal Care Coalition, 1988-89. Mem. Am. Coll. of Hosp. Execs., Ariz. Hosp. Assn., Phi Delta Kappa. Democrat. Lutheran. Clubs: Squaw Peak Hiking (Phoenix). Office: St Josephs Hosp Med Ctr 350 W Thomas Rd Phoenix AZ 85013

SCHMUTZ, DANA MAY, accountant; b. St. George, Utah, Nov. 17, 1938; d. David Marshall and Verna (Burgess) S.; m. Joseph Case, Mar. 30, 1965 (div. Aug. 1974); children: David June, Douglas LeRoy, Jan Marie, John Whitney; m. Spencer Lars Stephens, Mar. 25, 1989. Student, Calif. State U., Northridge, 1974-76; BS, Southern Utah State Coll., 1977. CPA, Utah. Staff acct. Huskinson & Savage, CPAs, St. George, 1977-81; ptnr. Savage, Schmutz & Esplin, CPAs, St. George, 1981-86; pvt. practice St. George, 1986—. Chmn. Utah Gov.'s Task Force on Miscellaneous Taxes, 1985—; treas. Utah Bus. and Profl. Women, Salt Lake City, 1986-88; bd. dirs. S.W. Symphony, St. George, 1987—, Five County Displaced Homemaker-Single Parent Program, 1988—. Recipient Woman of Achievement award Utah State Bus. and Profl. Women, 1989-90, So. Dist. Woman of Achievement award, 1989. Mem. AICPA, Utah Assn. CPAs, AAUW (pres. Saint George chpt. 1986-87), Saint George Bus. and Profl. Women (pres. 1984-85, Woman of the Yr. award 1985, Woman of Achievement award 1989), Saint George C. of C. (bd. dirs., v.p. fin. 1988—), Garden Tour Scholarships (treas. 1985—). Republican. Mormon. Home: 1725 E 800 N Saint George UT 84770 Office: 530 E Tabernacle Saint George UT 84770

SCHNACK, GAYLE HEMINGWAY JEPSON (MRS. HAROLD CLIFFORD SCHNACK), corporate executive; b. Mpls., Aug. 14, 1926; d. Jasper Jay and Ursula (Hemingway) Jepson; student U. Hawaii, 1946; m. Harold Clifford Schnack, Mar. 22, 1947; children: Jerrald Jay, Georgina, Roberta, Michael Clifford. Skater, Shipstead & Johnson Ice Follies, 1944-46; v.p. Harcliff Corp., Honolulu, 1964—, Schnack Indsl. Corp., Honolulu, 1969—, Nutmeg Corp., Cedar Corp.; ltd. ptnr. Koa Corp. Mem. Internat. Platform Soc., Beta Sigma Phi (chpt. pres. 1955-56, pres. city council 1956-57). Established Ursula Hemingway Jepson art award, Carlton Coll., Ernest Hemingway creative writing award, U. Hawaii. Office: PO Box 3077 Honolulu HI 96802 also: 1200 Riverside Dr Reno NV 89503

SCHNEBLY, DIANE DEE, broadcast executive; b. Spokane, Wash., Nov. 14, 1961; d. Carl Orval and Margaret Anne (Lemon) S. BA in Pub. Relations and Advt., U. Idaho, 1983. Radio, TV traffic computer operator Sta. KHQ-TV, Spokane, 1984-85, TV promotions exec., 1985-86; TV production mgr. Cox Cable Spokane, 1987—; freelance still photography, Spokane, 1989—. Producer, dir. (documentaries) Great Citizen, 1988, L'Arche Spokane, 1990; also commls. Mem. NAFE, Advt. Club of Spokane, Nat. Acad. Cable Programming. Office: Cox Cable Spokane E 1717 Buckeye Spokane WA 99207

SCHNECKENBURGER, KAREN LYNNE, finance executive; b. Peoria, Ill., Sept. 12, 1949; d. Walter Carl and Judith Jane (Grimshaw) S. BS in Acctg., Bradley U., 1971. CPA, Ill. Auditor Ernst & Whinney, Chgo., 1971-76; controller C.A. Roberts Co., Franklin Park, Ill., 1976-78; mgr. fin. and investments Gould Inc., Rolling Meadows, Ill., 1978-86; treas. Fairchild Industries, Inc., Chantilly, Va., 1986—. adviser Jr. Achievement, Chgo., 1979-83. Mem. Am. Inst. CPA's, Ill. CPA Soc., Chgo. Fin. Exchange. Home: 2249 Cedar Cove Ct Reston VA 22091-4108 Office: Fairchild Industries Inc PO Box 10803 Chantilly VA 22021-9998

SCHNEE, AMANDA MERYL MACNAB, physician; b. North Berwick, Scotland, Dec. 3, 1945; came to U.S., 1975; d. Hamish Stuart Duncan and Marjorie Daphne Croal (McDonald) M.; M.B., Ch.B., St. Andrews U., Scotland, 1968; m. Mark Schnee, Oct. 21, 1967; children—Samantha Joanne, Jicky Miranda, Pippa Meryl, Briony Amanda. Intern, Ballochmyle Hosp., Mauchline, Ayrshire, Scotland, 1968-69; resident in family practice Ayrshire Central Hosp., Irvine, Ayrshire, 1969-71; gen. practice medicine, Glasgow, Scotland, 1971-75; physician USAF, Omaha, 1975-77; mem. faculty U. Tex. Med. Sch., Houston, 1977-81. asst. prof. dept. family practice, 1979-81; dir. Student Health Center, Rice U., Houston, 1981—. Diplomate Am. Bd. Family Practice. Mem. Am. Acad. Family Practice, Am. Med. Women's Assn. Home: 2318 Underwood Blvd Houston TX 77030 Office: Rice U Student Health Ctr PO Box 1892 Houston TX 77251

SCHNEEBERG, HELEN BASSEN, retired educator; b. Phila., Apr. 5, 1920; d. Carl and Minnie (Aion) Bassen; m. Norman Grahn Schneeberg, Nov. 3, 1940; children—Susan, Karen. B.A., U. Pa., 1941, Cert. of Advanced Studies, 1984; M.L.S., Drexel U., Phila., 1966. Cert. librarian. Bacteriologist, Mount Sinai Hosp., Phila., 1941-43; librarian West Phila., High Sch., 1966-67, Temple U., Phila., 1967-68; research asst. Franklin Inst. Research Lab., Phila., 1968-69; teaching assoc. Temple U., Phila., 1970-71; dir., listen-read project Sch. Dist., Phila., 1971-76. Contbr. articles to research reports. Bd. dirs. Please Touch Mus., Phila., 1979-81; steering com. Physicians for Social Responsibility, Phila., 1982-84; area legis. coordinator Women's Agenda, Phila., 1984—; mem. steering com., Sch.-age Child Care Coalition, Phila., 1988—. Mem. N.Y. Acad. Scis., Soc. Research in Child Devel., Infant Mental Health of De. Valley. Democrat. Avocations: travel, reading, music, theatre, sailing, swimming. Home: 2010 Rittenhouse Sq Philadelphia PA 19103

SCHNEIDER, ADELE GOLDBERG, librarian, educator; b. N.Y.C., May 13, 1924; d. Abraham and Anna (Levy) Goldberg; B.A., Bklyn. Coll., 1945; M.L.S., Pratt Inst., 1965; M.A., L.I.U., 1971; m. Noel Schneider, Jan. 1, 1950; children—Adam Matthew, Tracy Lynn. Field interviewer Gallup Poll, N.Y.C., 1941-48; social worker N.Y.C. Dept. Social Services, 1949-52; editor Bklyn. Coll. Alumni Quarterly, 1961-65; instr. Kingsborough Community Coll. CUNY, 1965-70, asst. prof. dept. library, 1970-72, assoc. prof., 1972-88, prof., 1988—. Contbr. articles to profl. jours. Mem. ALA, Library Assn. City U. N.Y., N.Y. Tech. Services Librarians, Beta Phi Mu. Home: 124 Oxford St Brooklyn NY 11235 Office: 2001 Oriental Blvd Brooklyn NY 11235

SCHNEIDER, BARBARA JEAN, radiologic technologist; b. Bloomington, Ill., Oct. 4, 1962; d. William Benjamin Schneider and Margaret Diane (Graff) Bennett. AS, Ill. Cen. Coll., East Peoria, 1982. Radiologic technol., ultrasound tech. Iroguois Meml. Hosp., Watseka, Ill., 1982-86, St. Joseph's Hosp., Bloomington, 1986-87; ultrasound technologist Fla. Keys Meml. Hosp., Key West, 1987—. Recipient Outstanding Student award Pekin Meml. Hosp., Ill. 1982. Mem. Am. Registry of Radiology Technol., Soc. Diagnostic Med. Sonographers. Home: Rte 6 Box 451-P Summerland Key FL 33042

SCHNEIDER, BARBARA S., pediatric nurse practitioner; b. San Francisco, Calif., Oct. 25, 1933; d. Samuel George and Miriam (Wasserman) H.; m. Allan M. Schneider, Mar. 22, 1958. M Nursing, Vassar Coll., Poughkeepie, 1954; MA, Yale U., New Haven, 1957. Certified Pediatric Nurse Practitioner, Am. Nurses Assn., 1979. Pub. health nurse Seattle-King County Health Dept., Seattle, Wa., 1957-58; instr. in family life edn. Seattle Community Coll., Seattle, 1959-60,62-67, Columbia Basin Coll., 1967-75; pediatric nurse practitioner Ednl Inst. Rural Families and Individualized Bilingual Instr, Pasco, Wa., 1975-85; curriculum coordinator & instr. City U., Bellevue, Wa., 1986--; pvt. practice pediatric nurse practitioner Child Health Ctr. PS, Bellevue, 1986--; nurse cons. 30 day care ctr., King County, Wash., 1986—; health provider Nisqually (Wash.) Indian Tribe, 1987—; sch. nurse, Bethlehem Luth. Sch., 1976-82. Author: Handicapped Children, 1956, Health Care; contbr. articles to profl. jours.; developed network for health care for migrant children within Wash. State and Tex. Troop leader, cons. Girl Scouts Am. Recipient Award of Appreciation, migrant Edn., Pasco, Wash., 1984. Mem. Com. for Nurse Practitioners (exec.), Nurse Entrepreneur Spl. Interest Group (sec. 1987—), Altrusa Internat. Republican Jewish.

SCHNEIDER, CAROL, computer maintenance technician; b. Washington, Dec. 10, 1964; d. Thomas Allen and Ana Gloria (Esobar) Mann; m. Hans Peter Schner, Jan. 21, 1984. AAS in Data Processing, Itawamba Jr. Coll., 1985. Sales clk. Backstage Dance Co., Occoquan, Va., 1983-84; sec. Itawamba Jr. Coll., Tupelo, Miss., 1984-85; asst. mgr. Computer Ctr., Spangdahlem, Fed. Republic Germany, 1986-87; substitute tchr. Bitbnurg (Fed. Republic Germany) Am. Elem. Sch., 1986-87; computer maintenance technician USAF, Ellsworth AFB, SD, 1988—; enlisted USAF, 1988.

SCHNEIDER, CHERYL JUDITH, investor relations executive; b. Bronx, N.Y., Feb. 25, 1954; d. Sol and Irene J. (Pechenik) Weinberg; m. Daniel Schneider, Oct. 22, 1983; children: Gabrielle, Rebecca. BA, SUNY, Binghamton, 1976; MBA, NYU, 1978. Mgr. fin. rsch. Burson Marsteller, N.Y.C., 1982-84; midwest mgr. Am. Stock Exch., N.Y.C., 1978-82, dir. investor rels., 1984-85, asst. v.p. investor rels., 1985—. Mem. Nat. Investor Relations Inst. Democrat. Jewish. Home: 301 E 22nd St 3F New York NY 10010 Office: Am Stock Exch 86 Trinity Pl New York NY 10006

SCHNEIDER, CHRISTINE LYNN, customs inspector; b. Staten Island, N.Y., Feb. 3, 1960; d. Howard Thomas and Ina Elise (Beyer) S. BS, SUNY, Bronx, 1984. Lic. 3d mate, U.S. Mcht. Marine. Inspector U.S. Customs Svc., San Diego, 1989—. Lt. USNR, 1984-87. Democrat. Lutheran. Home: 2950 Alta View Dr Apt H 104 San Diego CA 92139 Office: US Customs Svc 720 E San Ysidro Blvd San Ysidro CA 92073

SCHNEIDER, CLAUDINE CMARADA, congresswoman; b. Clairton, Pa., Mar. 25, 1947. Student, U. Barcelona, Spain, Rosemont Coll.; BA, Windham Coll., 1969. Exec. adminstr. Concern, Inc., 1969; founder R.I. Com. on Energy, 1973; exec. dir. Conservation Law Found., 1974; fed. coord. R.I. Coastal Zone Mgmt. Program, 1978; producer, hostess public affairs program Sta. WJAR-TV, Providence, 1978-79; U.S. rep. from R.I., 1981—; mem. Merchant Marine and Fisheries Com., Sci. Space and Tech. Com. Author: The Global Warning Prevention Act of 1989. State chmn. spl. events Am. Cancer Soc., 1979. Named Woman of Year R.I., Women's Polit. Caucus, 1978. Republican. Roman Catholic. Office: US Ho of Reps 1512 Longworth House Office Bldg Washington DC 20515*

SCHNEIDER, DEBRA ANN, restaurant executive; b. Cherry Point, N.C., Apr. 26, 1963; d. Roger James and Aida (Marini) S. BA, U. Calif., Riverside, 1985; MBA, San Diego State U., 1990. Shift supr. Marie Callender's Restaurants, San Diego, 1985-88; tng. instr. Marie Callender's Restaurants, Orange, Calif., 1987-88; human resource mgr. Marie Callender's Restaurants, Chgo., 1989-90; human resources cons. Marie Callender's Restaurants, Orange, Calif., 1990—; bus. communications grad. asst. San Diego State U., 1987-89. Mem. Toastmasters Internat. (Best Speaker award 1988—). Republican. Roman Catholic. Office: Marie Callender's Restrts 1100 Town & Cntry Ste 1300 Orange CA 92668

SCHNEIDER, ELOISE COVELL, legal assistant; b. Casale, Italy, Feb. 1, 1923; came to U.S., 1924; naturalized, 1944; d. Joseph and Rosina (Malchiodi) Malchiodi; m. Robert E. Covell, Oct. 20, 1944 (div. Apr. 1947); 1 child, Margaret Rose Covell; m. Ludwig Schneider, Sept. 16, 1967 (dec. Feb. 1968). Grad. high sch., Amityville, N.Y. Legal asst. various attys., L.I. area, N.Y., 1942—, Law Office Joseph Cardino Jr., Copiague, N.Y., 1987—; real estate agt. L.I. area, 1950—; speaker in field. Author numerous poems; contbr. articles to profl. jours. Chmn. Bicentennial for Babylon (N.Y.) Village, 1975-76; worked on various polit. campaigns, 1961-78. Lodge: Sons of Italy (historian 1970-78, past bd. dirs.). Office: Law Office Joseph Cardino Jr 1475 Great Neck Rd Copiague NY 11726

SCHNEIDER, JANICE LINNEA, manufacturing executive; b. Bessemer, Mich., June 26, 1938; d. Edward John and Ina Ingeborg (Nyman) Johnson; m. Lester Joseph Schneider, July 1, 1960 (div. 1967); children: Jay, Sherry. BS with honors, Elmhurst (Ill.) Coll., 1985. CPA. From chief bookkeeper to programmer Chgo. Blower Corp., Glendale Heights, Ill., 1969-77, cost mgr., 1978—. Republican. Lutheran. Home: 1570 Glen Ellyn Rd Glendale Heights IL 60139

SCHNEIDER, JEAN MARIE, finance administrator; b. Belleville, Ill., June 26, 1929; d. Lawrence Maximillian and Gladys Louise (Snow) S. Cert. Higher Accountancy, La Salle Extension U., 1959. Acctg. clk. St. Elizabeth's Hosp., Belleville, 1947-48; acctg. supr. St. Elizabeth's Hosp., 1948-66, controller, 1966-75, dir. fiscal svc., 1975-78, asst. adminstr. fin., 1978—. Mem. Healthcare Fin. Mgmt. Assn. (charter mem., pres. 1978-79, pres.-elect 1977-78, chmn. bd. dirs. 1979-80, sec., treas., Founders award 1973, 79, 81, J. Edmondson award 1985, So. Ill. chpt.). Roman Catholic. Office: St Elizabeths Hosp 211 S 3rd St Belleville IL 62222

SCHNEIDER, JUDITH ANN, marketing executive; b. Toledo, Oct. 12, 1944; d. James Macolm Stults and Laura Margret (LaValley) Stepelton; m. John Jacob Schneider, Aug. 6, 1966; children: Jeffery J., Laura A. BS, BFA, Bowling Green State U., 1966. Traveling art tchr. Toledo Bd. Edn., 1966-68; tchr. Bedford (Mich.) Pub. Schs., 1968-70, Monroe (Mich.) Pub. Schs., 1968-74; supr. adult edn., academic supr. Bedford (Mich.) Pub. Schs., 1974-79; supr. advt. edn. Mason (Mich.) Consol. Schs., 1979-87; dir. spl. projects Mich. Gerontec, Ptnr., Monroe, 1987-90; rental and mktg. cons. Health Care Retirement Corp. Am., Toledo, 1988-89, regional mktg. mgr., 1989—; pub. rels. coord. Monroe County Adult Edn. Consortium, 1974-87. Contbr. articles to profl. manuals. Mem. Nat. Abortion Rights Action League; vol. Crosby Gardens. Mem. Interconnection (assoc.), Ohio Health Care Assn., Nat. Womens Polit. Caucus, Green Peace, Rainbow Ctr., Kiwanis. Democrat. Episcopalian. Home: 1808 Brim Dr Toledo OH 43613 Office: Health Care Ret Corp Am One Seagate Toledo OH 43666

SCHNEIDER, LEILA MARIE, graphic designer. BA in Psychology, U. Calif., Riverside, 1986; cert. in graphic design, Calif. State U., L.A., 1989. Temp. prodn. mgr. Inland Cath. newspaper, San Bernardino, 1987-88; employment devel. asst. Calif. State U., L.A., 1987-88; prodn. artist F.C. Enterprises, L.A., 1988-90; freelance graphic designer Alhambra, Calif., 1987—; prodn. mgr. Morava Oliver Berté, Santa Monica, Calif., 1990—. Mem. U. Calif.-Riverside Alumni Assn., Los Angeles County Mus. Art, Sierra Club, Psi Chi, Kappa Kappa Gamma. Roman Catholic.

SCHNEIDER, LINDA ANN (LYNN SCHNEIDER), human resources executive; b. N.Y.C., Dec. 2, 1945; d. Arthur William and Helen G. (Iuen) S. AA in Gen. Studies, Montgomery Coll., Rockville, Md., 1988; BS in Psychology, Columbia Union Coll., Takoma Park, Md., 1990; accredited in pers. and human resources, Personnel Accreditation Inst., 1985—. Legal sec. Kilroy and Sullivan, Washington, 1964-67; adminstrv. asst. Exec. Inst., Washington, 1967-69; accredited profl. in human resources Tri/Valley Growers, San Francisco, 1969-72; office adminstr. Jewish Community Ctr., Oakland, Calif., 1972-75; area adminstr. Calif. Computer Products, Rockville, 1975-78; sr. human resources rep. Libra Tech., Rockville, 1978-80, mgr. human resources, 1980-83; mgr. human resources Nat. Data Corp., Rockville, 1983-89, dir. human resources, 1989—. Democrat. Unitarian. Home: 15405 Pin Cherry Ln Gaithersburg MD 20878

SCHNEIDER, LORI BETH, neurologist; b. N.Y.C., Mar. 8, 1960; d. Allan Joel and Arlene (Schulman) S. BS in Biology, Rensselaer Poly. Inst., 1982; MD, Albany Med. Coll., 1984. Diplomate Nat. Bd. Med. Examiners, Am. Bd. Psychiatry and Neurology. Intern in medicine Cleve. Clinic Found., 1984-85, resident in neurology, 1985-88, fellow electromyography, 1988; sr. staff neurologist Henry Ford Hosp., Detroit, 1988—. Fellow Am. Bd. Electrodiagnostic Medicine; mem. AMA, Am. Acad. Neurology, Stroke Coun. Am. Heart Assn., Am. Assn. Electromyography and Electrodiagnosis, Mich. State Med. Soc., Ariz. State Med. Soc. Office: Henry Ford Hosp 2799 W Grand Blvd Detroit MI 48202

SCHNEIDER, MICHELLE (SHELLY SCHNEIDER), software engineer; b. N.Y.C., Dec. 27, 1952; d. Louis and Sylvia (Fischler) Goldstein; m. David Schneider, July 21, 1973. BSEE, MIT, 1973; MS, Harvard U., 1975. Sr. engr. Instrumentation Engring., Franklin, N.J., 1975-78; sr. engr., cons. Giordano Assoc., Sparta, N.J., 1978-81; v.p. Softest, Inc., Ridgewood, N.J., 1981-85; project dir. JJ Kenny, N.Y.C., 1985-86; sr. staff engr. Allied Signal, Teterboro, N.J., 1986-87; cons. Woodland Hills, Calif., 1987—. Fundraiser Woodlake Ave Sch., 1987—. Mem. IEEE. Home and Office: 5338 Hinton Ave Woodland Hills CA 91367

SCHNEIDER, PENNY LOIS, assistant district attorney; b. Chgo., Jan. 26, 1954; d. Seymour and Geraldine (Weintraub) S. BA, Northwestern U., 1976; JD, DePaul U., Chgo., 1981. Bar: Ill. 1981, Calif. 1983. Pvt. practice Chgo., 1981-84; asst. dist. atty. L.A. Dist. Atty.'s Office, 1984—; mem. teaching faculty Calif. Dist. Atty.'s Assn., Sacramento, 1985—. Author handbook on prosecution of child physical and sexual abuse offenders, 1987-89. Mem. Anti-Defamation League B'nai Brith, L.A., 1986—. Mem. ABA, Calif. Dist. Atty.'s Assn., Interagency Coun. on Child Abuse and Neglect Calif. Dept. Justice, L.A. County Bar Assn. Office: Office of LA Dist Atty 210 W Temple St Los Angeles CA 90012

SCHNEIDER, PHYLLIS LEAH, writer, editor; b. Seattle, Apr. 19, 1947; d. Edward Lee Booth and Harriet Phyllis (Ebbinghaus) Russell; m. Clifford Donald Schneider, June 14, 1969; 1 child, Pearl Brooke. B.A., Pacific Luth. U., 1969; M.A., U. Wash., 1972. Fiction, features editor Seventeen Mag., N.Y.C., 1975-80; mng. editor Weight Watchers Mag., N.Y.C., 1980-81; editor Young Miss mag., N.Y.C., 1981-86. Author: Parents Book of Infant Colic, 1989; contbr. articles and fiction to mags. Recipient Centennial Recognition award Pacific Luth. U. Democrat. Episcopalian.

SCHNEIDER, SANDRA LEE, immunology educator, scientist; b. Pueblo, Colo., July 10, 1944; d. Joseph A. and Evelyn (Strovas) S.; m. Raymond M. Costello, 1972. BS, U. So. Colo., 1966; M.T., U. Colo., Denver, 1966; MPH, U. Tex., Houston, 1988, DrPH, 1990. Med. technologist Belle Bonfils Blood Bank, Denver, 1966-67; med. technologist, supr. East Tenn. Bapt. Hosp. Blood Bank, Knoxville, 1968-69; med. technologist II U. Kans. Med. Ctr. Dept. Pathology, Kansas City, 1969-70; med. technologist, rsch. asst. Knoxville Blood Ctr., 1970-71; rsch. asst. L.A. Red Cross, 1971-72; rsch. scientist Southwest Found. Rsch./Edn., San Antonio, 1973-81, U. Tex. Health Sci. Ctr. Dept. Pediatrics, San Antonio, 1981-85; rsch. instr. medicine tech. cell and hybridoma lab. U. Tex. Health Sci. Ctr./Medicine, San Antonio, 1985-87; rsch. instr. immunology tech. dir. lab. U. Tex. Health Sci. Ctr./Periodontics, San Antonio, 1987—. Contbr. articles to profl. jours.; reviewer sci. jours. Mem. Coun. City of Grey Forest, Tex., 1978-80; co-dir. It's Me Child Life Program, San Antonio, 1987—; panelist Mayor's Commn. on the Status of Women, San Antonio, 1983; exec. com. Woman's Faculty Assn., U. Tex. Health Sci. Ctr., San Antonio, 1989—. Belle Bonfile Meml. scholar, Denver, 1965, Red Cross Blood Bank scholar, L.A., 1971. Mem. Am. Soc. Clin. Pathology, Am. Assn. Blood Banks, Am. Soc. Microbiology (judge Alamo Region Sci. Fair 1981-89), Am. Soc. Primatologist, Tissue Culture Assn. (lab. material and biosafety com. 1987—, devel. com. 1989—), Am. Pub. Health Assn., Nat. Assn. Pub. Health Policy, AAS, Air and Waste Mgmt. Assn., Sigma Xi. Office: U Tex Health Sci Ctr 7703 Floyd Curl Dr San Antonio TX 78284

SCHNEIDER, SUSAN LEE, social worker; b. Buffalo, Jan. 29, 1957; d. Thomas Ernest and Nicolina J. (Mogavero) S. BA in Sociology, SUNY, Albany, 1979; MSW, SUNY, Buffalo, 1985. Cert. social worker, N.Y. Counselor Transitional Svcs., Inc., Buffalo, 1979-84; mental health aide Buffalo, Psychiat. Ctr., 1985; psychiat. social worker Erie County Med. Ctr., Buffalo, 1985-88, treatment team coord., 1988—. Mem. Nat. Assn. Social Workers. Office: Erie County Med Ctr 462 Grider St Buffalo NY 14215

SCHNEIDER, TAMARA ROMAN, company executive; b. Oak Park, Ill., Jan. 5, 1952; d. John Raymond and Darlyn Joy (Lenartson) Roman; m. Paul Fredrick Schneider, Apr. 19, 1950. BS in Biology/Chemistry, No. Ill. U., 1975. Cert. lighting cons. With Delnor Hosp., St. Charles, Ill., 1975-76; customer rep. McCaffery Co., South Bend, Ind., 1976-80; ptnr. McCaffery Lighting, South Bend, 1980-84; pres. McCaffery Inc., South Bend, 1984—. Bd. dirs., devel. chmn. Jr. League, South Bend, 1988-89. Mem. Am. Lighting Assn., Women Bus. Owners Assn., Elkhart County Home Bldrs. Assn., St. Joseph County Home Bldrs. Assn., AaUW (bd. dirs., pub. relations chmn. 1988-89). Lutheran. Office: McCaffery Inc 1628 N Ironwood Dr South Bend IN 46635

SCHNEIDER, VALERIE LOIS, speech educator; b. Chgo., Feb. 12, 1941; d. Ralph Joseph and Gertrude Blanche (Gaffron) S. BA, Carroll Coll., 1963; MA, U. Wis., 1966; PhD, U. Fla., 1969; cert. advanced study Appalachian State U., 1981. Tchr. English and history Montello High Sch. (Wis.), 1963-64; dir. forensics and drama Montello High Sch., 1963-64; instr. speech U. Fla., Gainesville, 1966-68, asst. prof. speech, 1969-70; asst. prof. speech Edinboro (Pa.) State Coll., 1970-71; assoc. prof. speech East Tenn. State U., Johnson City, 1971-76, prof. speech, 1976—; instr. newspaper course Johnson City Press Chronicle, 1979, Elizabethton Star, Erwin Record, Mountain City Tomahawk, Jonesboro Herald and Tribune, 1980. Editor East Tenn. State Univ. evening and off-campus newsletter, 1984—. Chmn. AAUW Mass Media Study Group Com., Johnson City, 1973-74. Recipient Creative Writing award Va. Highlands Arts Festival, 1973; award Kingsport (Tenn.) Times News, 1984, 85, Tri-Cities Met. Advt. Fedn., 1983, 84; Danforth assoc., 1977. Mem. Speech Communication Assn. (Tenn. rep. to states adv. council 1974-75), So., Tenn. (exec. bd. 1974-77, publs. bd. 1974-78, pres. 1977-78), Religious Speech Communication Assn. (Best article award 1976), Tenn. Basic Skills Council (exec. bd. 1979-80, v.p. 1980-81, pres. 1981-82), AAUW (v.p. chpt. 1974-75, pres. 1975-76, corp. rep. for East Tenn. State U. 1974-76), Am. Assn. Continuing Higher Edn., Bus. and Profl. Women's Club (chpt. exec. bd. 1972-73, v.p. 1976-77), Nat. Assn. Remedial Developmental Studies in Post Secondary Edn., Mensa, Delta Sigma Rho-Tau Kappa Alpha, Phi Delta Kappa, Delta Kappa Gamma, Pi Gamma Mu. Presbyterian. Assoc. editor: Homiletic, 1974-76; columnist Video Visions, Kingsport Times-News (Tenn.), 1984-86; book reviewer Pulpit Digest, 1986-90; contbr. articles on speech to profl. jours., newspapers. Home: 3201 Buckingham Rd Johnson City TN 37604 Office: East Tenn State U Box 24429 Johnson City TN 37614

SCHNEIDER-CRIEZIS, SUSAN MARIE, architect; b. St. Louis, Aug. 1, 1953; d. William Alfred and Rosemary Elizabeth (Fischer) Schneider; m. Demetrios Anthony Criezis, Nov. 24, 1978; children: Anthony, John and Andrew. BArch, U. Notre Dame, 1976; MArch, MIT, 1978. Registered architect, Wis. Project designer Eichstaedt Architects, Roselle, Ill., 1978-80, Solomon, Cordwell, Buenz & Assocs., Chgo., 1980-82; project architect Gelick, Foran Assocs., Chgo., 1982-83; asst. prof. Sch. Architecture U. Ill., Chgo., 1980-86; prin. Criezis Architects, Evanston, Ill., 1986—. Graham Found. grantee MIT, 1977, MIT scholar, 1976-78; Prestressed Concrete Inst. rsch. grantee, 1981. Mem. AIA, Chgo. Archtl. Club, Chgo. Women in Architecture, Am. Solar Energy Soc., NAFE, Jr. League Evanston, Evanston C. of C. Roman Catholic. Office: Shand Morahan Pla 1007 Church St Ste 101 Evanston IL 60201

SCHNEIDERS, ANNE ELIZABETH, social work and academic administrator, consultant; b. Evanston, Ill., May 3, 1938; d. Alexander Aloysius and Glen Elizabeth (Ogle) S. BA, St. Joseph Coll., Emmitsburg, Md., 1962; MSW in Adminstrn., Fordham U., 1973; postgrad., Cath. U. Law Sch., 1988—. Lic. social worker, N.Y., Mass., Md., D.C. Elem. tchr. Our Lady of Peace Sch., Canton, Ohio, 1959-62, Our Lady Queen of Peace Sch., Washington, 1962-65, St. Mary's Sch., Troy, N.Y., 1965-67, St. Joseph Sch., Holbrook, Mass., 1967-69, St. Ambrose Sch., Endicott, N.Y., 1969-70; social worker Cath. Home Bur., N.Y.C., 1970-71; asst. exec. dir. The Astor Home for Children, Bronx, N.Y., 1973-77; exec. dir. The Kennedy Child Study Ctr., N.Y.C., 1977-79, The Astor Home for Children, Rhinebeck, N.Y., 1979-86; dir. of admissions Cath. U. Am. Nat. Cath. Sch. Social Svc., Washington, 1986—; cons. Cath. Charities U.S.A., Washington, 1986—, St. Christopher-Ottilie Svcs. for Children and Families, Sea Cliff, N.Y., 1986—. Bd. dirs. St. Mary's Hosp., Troy, 1979-86. Mem. ABA, Nat. Assn. Social Workers, Acad. Cert. Social Workers. Office: Nat Cath Sch Social Svc Cath U Am Shahan Hall Washington DC 20064

SCHNEIDER TOWN, JANIS ELMA, nurse; b. Ocean City, N.J., Jan. 23, 1950; d. Henry George and Ethel Louise (Hedelt) Schneider; m. Charles Edward Town, May 24, 1969 (div. Apr. 1986; children: Teresa L., Brian E. AS in Nursing, Atlantic Com. Coll., 1980; BS in Nursing, Stockton State Coll., 1985; MS in Nursing, Widener U., 1990. RN, N.J. Instr. Childbirth Edn. Assn., Somers Point, N.J., 1973-81; RN Surgical Neurology, Somers Point, 1979-84; staff, charge nurse surgical unit Burdette Tomlin Meml. Hosp., Cape May Court House, N.J., 1980-81, staff, charge nurse emergency dept., 1981-90, acting mgmt. staff nurse emergency dept., 1989; clin. nurse specialist critical care units/med.-surg. units Shore Meml. Hosp., Somers Point, N.J., 1989—; organizer, group leader Cape/Atl. Head Injury Group, Linwood, N.J., 1985-88. Author: Information Guide for Families of Head Injured, 1985. Committeewoman Rep. Club, Upper Township, N.J., 1979-81. Lt. USAR, 1987—. Mem. Am. Nurses Assn., Emergency Nurses Assn., Am. Assn. Neurosci. Nurses, Sigma Theta Tau. Roman Catholic. Home: 211 Tennyson Pl Oceanview NJ 08230

SCHNELL, GERTRUDE HELEN, educator; b. Olean, N.Y., July 29, 1934; d. Edwin J. and Grace (Mallory) S. BS in Edn., Mansfield (Pa.) State Coll., 1955; MS in Edn., St. Bonaventure (N.Y.) U., 1973. Tchr. elem. Franklinville (N.Y.) Cen. Sch., 1955—. Vice pres. Ischua Valley Hist. Soc., Franklinville, 1989—. Mem. N.Y. State United Tchrs. Republican. Roman Catholic. Home: 25 Second Ave Franklinville NY 14737

SCHNEPFE, MARIAN MOELLER, research chemist; b. St. Pedro de Macoris, Dominican Republic, Nov. 15, 1923; came to U.S., 1924; d. Benjamin Andrin Moeller and Marguerite (Maude) Moeller Stickley; m. August William Jr. Schnepfe, Sept. 17, 1954. RN, Biltmore Hosp. Sch. Nursing, N.C., 1945; BS, George Washington U., 1953, MS, 1960, PhD, 1966. RN, N.C. Chemist U.S. Geol. Survey, Washington and Reston, Va., 1954-80; cons. U.S. Geol. Survey, Bandung, Indonesia, 1981-82. Contbr. articles to profl. jours. Pres. Toastmasters Internat., Reston, 1970's. 1st lt. AUS Nurse Corps, 1945-50. Fellow NSF, 1962-63, NASA, 1963-66. Fellow Washington Acad. Sci., Sigma Xi; mem. Am. Chem. Soc., Phi Delta Gamma (program chmn. 1960's), Iota Sigma Pi.

SCHNETZLER, ANNE-MARIE FRACASSI, hospital administrator; b. Casablanca, Morocco, Morocco, Aug. 8, 1940; came to U.S., 1968; d. Henry Albert and Caroline (Fracassi) S. MS in Nutrition, Sch. of Dietetics U. Medicine, Marseilles, France, 1964; MA magna cum laude in Fr., U. So. Calif., 1972; MS in Mgmt., U. of Redlands, 1982. Registered dietitian, Cert. tchr. secondary, lifetime French, Calif. Clin. dietitian La Durante Hosp., Marseilles, France, 1964-65; lab. technician, rsch. Givaudan Hoffmann LaRoche, Geneva, Switzerland, 1966-68; clin. dietitian Rancho Los Amigos Los Angeles County Hosp., Downey, Calif., 1969-71; supr. dietitian Rancho Los Amigos Los Angeles County Hosp., Downey, 1973-79; clin. dietitian Fairview State Hosp., Costa Mesa, Calif., 1979-80; asst. dir. dietetics Fairview State Hosp., Costa Mesa, 1980-82; dir. dietetics Fairview Devel. Ctr., Costa Mesa, 1982-85, hosp. adminstr. resident, 1985-86, hosp adminstr., 1986—; tchr. French, Torrance (Calif.) Sch. Dist. 1970-74. Mem. Am. Dietetics Assn., French Honorary Soc. Pi Delta Phi. Democrat. Mem. French Reformed Ch. Office: Fairview Devel Ctr 2501 Harbor Blvd Costa Mesa CA 92626

SCHNEYER, CHARLOTTE ALPER, physiologist, researcher, educator; b. St. Louis, Nov. 21, 1923; d. Nathan and Anna (Schoenfeld) Alper; m. Leon H. Schneyer, June 11, 1945 (dec. Oct. 1976). A.B. with final honors, Washington U., St. Louis, 1945; M.S., NYU, 1947, Ph.D., 1952. Research asst. Marine Biology Lab, Woods Hole, Mass, 1944; grad. teaching fellow NYU, 1945-52; rsch. assoc. U. Ala., Birmingham, 1952-55, asst. prof. dentistry, 1955-59, assoc. prof. dentistry, 1959-64, prof. dentistry, 1964—, asst. prof. physiology, 1962-65, assoc. prof. physiology, 1965-67, prof., 1967—, dir. Lab. Exocrine Physiology, 1977—, sr. scientist Cystic Fibrosis Rsch. Ctr., 1981—; grant reviewer NSF; mem. spl. grants rev. com. Nat. Inst. Dental Research, 1979-82; mem. nat. adv. gen. med. scis. council Nat. Inst. Health and Gen. Med. Scis., 1972-76; honored invitee to numerous internat. symposia. Co-editor: Secretory Mechanisms of Salivary Glands, 1967; contbr. chpts. to numerous books; manuscript reviewer Am. Jour. Physiology, Jour. Autonomic Nervous System, Archives Oral Biology, Jour. Oral Pathology, Jour. Dental Rsch., Proc. Soc. Exptl. Biology and Medicine (mem. editorial bd. 1980-86), Clin. Investigation, others. adj. curator art glass Birmingham Mus. Art, 1985—. Nat. Inst. Dental Research research grantee, 1958—. Mem. Am. Physiol. Soc., Soc. for Exptl. Biology and Medicine, Hungarian Dental Assn. (hon.), Sigma Xi, Omicron Kappa Upsilon (hon.), Alpha Lambda Delta. Office: U Ala at Birmingham Lab Exocrine Physiology University Sta Birmingham AL 35294

SCHNITMAN, HARRIET, dentist; b. New Haven, Aug. 17, 1957; d. Joseph Irving and Jane (Asheim) S.; m. Lee Phillip Crockett, Sept. 7, 1986. BA, Skidmore Coll., 1979; DMD, Boston U., 1986. Pvt. practice, New Haven, 1986—; mem. faculty dept. implant dentistry Harvard U. Dental Sch., Boston, 1986; lectr. on maintenance dental implants N.Y. Dental Conv., New Eng. Dental meeting, Yankee Dental Congress, New Haven Dental Soc., 1987-88. Mem. ADA, Acad. Gen. Dentistry, Mass. Women's Dental Assn., New Haven Dental Assn. Office: 291 Whitney Ave New Haven CT 06511

SCHNITZER, ARLENE DIRECTOR, art dealer; b. Salem, Oreg., Jan. 10, 1929; d. Simon M. and Helen (Holtzman) Director; m. Harold J. Schnitzer, Sept. 11, 1949; 1 child, Jordan. Student, U. Wash., 1947-48; BFA (hon.) Pacific NW Coll. Art, 1988. Founder, pres. Fountain Gallery of Art, Portland, Oreg., 1951-86; sr. v.p. Harsch Investment Corp., 1951—. Apptd. to Oreg. State Bd. Higher Edn., 1987-88; former bd. dirs. Oreg. Symphony Assn., v.p. Oreg. Symphony; bd. dirs., exec. v.p., exec. com. U.S. Dist. Ct. Hist. Soc.; bd. dirs. Boys and Girls Club, 1988—; mem. Gov.'s Expo '86 Commn., Oreg.; mem. exec. com., former bd. dirs. Artquake; mem. adv. bd. Our New Beginnings; bd. dirs. Artists Initiative for a Contemporary Art Collection. Recipient Aubrey Watzek award Lewis and Clark Coll., 1981, Pioneer award U. Oreg., 1985, Met. Arts Commn. award, 1985, White Rose award March of Dimes, 1987, Disting. Svc. award Western Oreg. State Coll. 1988, Oreg. Urban League Equal Opportunity award 1988, Gov's. award for Arts, 1987, Woman of Achievement award YWCA, 1987; honored by Portland Art Assn., 1979, Oreg. Art Inst., 1979. Mem. Univ. Club, Multnomah Athletic Club, Portland Golf Club. Office: Harsch Investment Corp 1121 SW Salmon St Portland OR 97205

SCHNITZER, IRIS TAYMORE, financial management executive; b. Cambridge, Mass., Aug. 3, 1943; d. Joseph David and Edith (Cooper) Taymore; m. Stephen Mark Schnitzer, Sept. 10, 1966. BA in Econs., Boston U., 1967; CLU, Am. Coll., Bryn Mawr, Pa., 1973, grad. cert. in fin. counseling, 1975, grad. cert. in advanced pension planning, 1978; cert. fin. planner, Coll. for Fin. Planning, Denver, 1981. Lic. real estate broker, life ins. advisor, life ins. and health ins. broker; NASD registered rep. Real estate broker Woods Real Estate, Braintree, Mass., 1968; real estate broker, property mgr. Village Gate Realty, Brockton, Mass., 1969; agt. Prudential Ins., Boston, 1970-73; supr. edn. and advanced underwriting, agt. Northwestern Mutual Life, Boston, 1973-78; fin. planning cons. Iris Taymore Schnitzer Assocs., Boston, Mass., 1973-79; trainer fin. planners Gerstenblatt Co., Newton, Mass., 1978-79; founder, pres. The Fin. Forum, Inc., Boston, 1979—, TFF, Inc. at the Chase Exchange, N.Y.C., 1980-83; bd. dirs., clk. Mister Tire, Inc., Abington, Mass.; bd. dirs., chmn., pres., treas. The Fin. Forum, Inc., Boston. Contbr. articles to profl. jours. Chmn. credit com., bd. dirs., Mass. Feminist Fed. Credit Union, Boston, 1975-77; bd. dirs. Ledgewood, Brookline, Mass., 1967-70, LWV, Brockton, Mass., 1968-70, NOW, Boston, 1972-73; gov. Women's City Club, Boston, 1976-80; pres. Mass. div. Women's Equity Action League, 1977-79; mem. Navy League U.S., Boston, 1985—. Named One of the Best Fin. Planners in the U.S., Money Mag., 1987, to Mutual Funds Panel, Sylvia Porter's Personal Fin. Mag., 1988, 89. Mem. Am. Assn. Individual Investors (pres. Boston chpt. 1987-89), Boston Estate Planning Coun., Women in World Trade, Internat. Assn. for Fin. Planning (bd. dirs. Boston chpt. 1977-81), Down Town Club, Boston Club. Republican. Jewish. Office: The Fin Forum Inc 50 Milk St Boston MA 02109

SCHNORRENBERG, BARBARA BRANDON, historian; b. Concord, N.C., Mar. 17, 1931; d. William Pew and Katherine McKean (Wolff) Brandon; m. John Martin Schnorrenberg, July 8, 1962; children: David Martin, Katherine Laura. BA, Wellesley Coll., 1951; MA, U. N.C., 1953; PhD, Duke U., 1958. Tchr. Rosemary Hall, Greenwich, Conn., 1951-52; asst. prof. Women's Coll., U. N.C., Greensboro, 1956-62; lectr. U. N.C., Chapel Hill, 1962-76; ind. scholar Birmingham, Ala., 1976—. Author: (chpt.) The Women of England, 1979; contbr. articles to profl. jours. Recipient Fulbright scholarship, U.S. Govt., West Germany, 1955-56. Mem. Am. Soc. 18th Century Studies (bd. mem. 1986-88, treas. 1989—), So. Hist. Assn. (bd. mem. 1987-89), So. Conf. British Studies (bd. mem. 1979-83, pres. 1987-89), So. Assn. Women Hist. (sec., treas. 1972-85). Democrat. Episcopalian. Home: 3824 11th Ave Birmingham AL 35222

SCHOBER, DOROTHY FLORENCE, consultant; b. Green Bay, Wis., Sept. 19, 1910; d. Max William and Addie (Stone) S.; B.A., U. Wis., 1932; M.P.H., Yale U., 1948; m. Ralph E. Hoffmeyer, Sept. 3, 1982. Visitor, dist. supr., dist. dir. Fla. Welfare Bd., Jacksonville, 1932-37; dir. Pub. Welfare Dept., Green Bay, Wis., 1937-42; cons. Div. Pub. Assistance, Wis. Dept. Pub. Welfare, Madison, 1942-44; counselor USPHS, 1944-45; health edn. cons. Council Social Agys., New Haven, 1946-49; heart work cons. State Com. on Tb and Pub. Health, N.Y., 1949-52; program cons., exec. asst. Am. Heart Assn., 1952-64, asst. dir. affiliate relations and services, 1964-65, asst. dir. dept. councils and internat. program, 1965-70, assoc. dir., 1970-73, assoc. dir. div. sci. affairs, chief sci. councils, 1973-75. Recipient Gold Heart Bracelet in appreciation 10 year service Staff Conf. Heart Assn., 1962. Fellow Am. Pub. Health Assn.; mem. Phi Kappa Phi, Alpha Kappa Delta. Home: 58-B Calle Cadiz Laguna Hills CA 92653 Home: 1114 11th Ave Albany GA 31707

SCHOCH, BERNADETTE HELEN, accountant; b. Phila., Apr. 16, 1930; d. Stephen and Pauline Susannah (Kirner) Novak; m. John Patrick Glennon, July 14, 1951 (div. 1983); children: Robert J., Patricia B. Glennon Nichols, Alan David; m. Robert Hamilton Schoch, Dec. 19, 1983; stepchildren: Randi Van Bemmel, Diana Allegretto, Carol Finger. AA, Bucks County Community Coll., 1977; BS, LaSalle U., 1983. Legal sec. Sears, Roebuck and Co., Phila., 1948-54; bookkeeper, acct. Artcraft Machine Co., Langhorne, Pa., 1959-83; computer acct. Charles Biderman Co., Jackson, N.J., 1987-88; ind. office svcs. provider Toms River, N.J., 1983—. Mem. AAUW (recording sec. Toms River chpt. 1988-89, co-pres. 1989-91), Ladies of Conwell (pres. 1971-72), Nat. Assn. Ret. Fed. Employees. Republican. Roman Catholic. Home and Office: 816 Bartlett Circle Toms River NJ 08753

SCHOCH, CLARISSA ANTHONY, singer, educator, executive assistant; b. Redmond, Oreg., Jan. 17, 1935; d. John Henry and Eleanor (Edwards) Berning; m. Jack Williams Anthony, Jr., June 26, 1960 (dec. 1982); m. Albert E. Schoch, Mar. 22, 1986; children: Rebecca Ellen, Julia Kathleen. BA, U. Oreg., 1957, MMus, 1959. Voice instr. William Paterson Coll., Wayne, N.J., 1979-84, Fairleigh Dickinson U., Rutherford, N.J., 1983-89; pvt. practice voice and flute tchr., Upper Montclair, N.J., 1971—; exec. sec. Nat. Westminster Bancorp N.J., 1985—; owner garden ctr. Jack and the Preacher's, Holmdel, N.J., 1972-83; profl. singer, 1959—; soprano soloist Montclair State Coll., 1981-85, William Paterson Coll., 1981-82, Temple Emanu-EL, N.Y.C., 1962-79, Union Congl. Ch., Montclair, 1973—. Chmn. youth com. Union Congl. Ch., 1983-87, mem. parish life, 1985—, mem. music com., 1983-85. Winner voice and oratorio N.J. Young Artists, Nat. Fedn. Music Clubs, N.J., 1966. Mem. Nat. Assn. Tchrs. of Singing (treas. N.J. 1984—), N.Y. Singing Tchrs. Assn. (chairperson young artists auditions 1980-86), Internat. Bach Soc. (performing fellow 1969), AAUW, Phi Beta (nat. grad. grantee 1964), Montclair Music Club (Young Artists Audition chairperson 1982—), Rehearsal Club. Democrat. Home: 8 Waterbury Rd Upper Montclair NJ 07043

SCHOCH, JACQUELINE LOUISE, university official; b. DuBois, Pa., July 17, 1929; d. Horace Gordon and Cora (Wineberg) S.; B.Sc. in Health and Phys. Edn., Pa. State U., 1951, M.Ed. in Counseling and Psychology, 1960, D.Ed. in Counseling and Psychology, 1965; cert. Inst. Ednl. Mgmt., Harvard U., 1979. Tchr. girls' phys. edn. Jr.-Sr. High Sch., Ford City, Pa., 1951-52; tchr. girl's phys. edn., acad. U.S. history DuBois Area Sr. High Sch., 1952-56, girls' guidance counselor, 1956-65; dir. guidance DuBois Area Sch. Dist., 1965-67, dir. instrn., 1967-70; asst. dir. for resident instrn. DuBois campus Pa. State U., 1970-76, assoc. dir. acad. affairs, 1976-78, dir. DuBois campus, 1978—, campus exec. officer, also mem., chmn. univ. coms., faculty senate. Instr. polit. action courses local C. of C., 1963; instr. adult swimming classes local YMCA, 1953-55; instr. continuing edn. program Pa. State U., 1967-70, also asst. prof. edn., 1970—. Cons. Appalachia project, W.Va., 1967-68; mem. evaluating teams for evaluating secondary schs. Middle States Evaluation Com., 1960-62; chair Penelec Consumer Adv. Com.; mem. Penelec Ednl. Com.; mem. commn. for women Pa. State U.; mem. adv. com. Pa. State U. Alumni Assn. Bd. dirs. DuBois area United Fund, co-chmn. fund raising campaign, 1967-68, 2d v.p., 1970—; bd. dirs. DuBois council Girl Scouts, 1954-56, Family Life Center-Luth. Services, 1972-76; treas. DuBois Ednl. Found., 1981—; bd. dirs. DuBois Area YMCA; v.p. bd. dirs. Clearfield County Area Agy. on Aging; elder St. Peters United Ch. of Christ. Named Boss of Yr., Internat. Secs. Assn., 1977; recipient Disting. Citizens award Jaycees, 1990. Mem. Delta Mu Sigma, Delta Psi Omega, Iota Alpha Delta, Delta Kappa Gamma, Pi Lambda Theta, Phi Delta Kappa. Lodge: Rotary (Paul Harris fellow 1989). Office: DuBois Campus Pa State U DuBois PA 15801

SCHOCK, ELAINE IRENE See PURCELL, ELAINE IRENE

SCHOCK, JACQUI VIRGINIA, counselor, data operations specialist; b. Atlanta, Nov. 24, 1938; d. Herman Lee and Martha Jane (Hunsecker) Turner; m. Raymond J. Torres, Oct. 20, 1990. AA in Human Svcs., Bucks County Community Coll., 1986; BA in Human Svcs., Antioch U., 1987; MS in Addictions, Chestnut Hill Coll., 1988; MA in Applied Psychology, U. Santa Monica, Calif., 1990. Counselor Bucks County Rehab. Ctr., Doylestown, Pa., 1983-88; addictions counselor Clearbrook Friendship Ctr., Phila., 1988-89; in-patient counselor Penn Found., Sellersville, Pa., 1988-89; pvt. practice Warminster, Pa., 1989—; data entry operator SPS Techs., Jenkintown, Pa., 1963-65, data entry supr., 1965-70, data mgr., 1970—. Mem. exec. bd. Counseling Assn. Greater Phila., 1988—, W. Phila. Fund for Human Devel., Phila., 1989—. Mem. NAFE, Am. Psychol. Assn., Am. Assn. Counseling and Devel., Pa. Counselors Assn., Data Engry Mgrs. Assn., Fraternal Order of Police, Phi Theta Kappa Alumni Assn. Office: SPS Techs Highland Ave Jenkintown PA 19046

SCHOCKAERT, BARBARA ANN, marketing executive; b. Queens, N.Y., Dec. 13, 1938; d. Lawrence Henry and Eleanor Veronica (Tollner) Grob; children: Donna Ann, Don. Student, Ocean County Coll., Toms River, N.J., 1987. Cert. notary pub. Assoc. Ocean County Realty, Toms River; v.p. ops. Am. Vitamin Products, Inc., Freehold, N.J. Past pres. mayor's adv. coun., past pres. of help line Town of Jackson, N.J.; past bd. dirs. Big Bros. of Ocean County; speaker community svc. orgns. Named Woman of Yr. Jaycees, 1974. Mem. N.J. Realtors Assn. Address: 977 Fairview Dr Toms River NJ 08753

SCHOELD, CONSTANCE JERRINE, financial planner; b. Wichita, Kans., July 20, 1935; d. Joe Delos and Volna May (Liston) Lumbert; m. Edmund Allan Schoeld, Oct. 4, 1953 (div. Dec. 1974); children: Nancy Ann., Elsa Charlene, Jennie Marie, Brian Shelton, Richard Zweibruck. Student, St. Olaf Coll., 1953-54, Lindenwood Coll., 1960-62, U. Mich., 1967-68, Harper Jr. Coll., 1970. Cert. fin. planner. Mgr. Walden Books, Schaumburg, Ill., 1972-74; owner Books, Etc., Mt. Prospect, Ill., 1974-77; sales rep. Fawcett Books/CBS, N.Y.C., 1977-78, Lawyers Cooperative Pub., Rochester, N.Y., 1978-83; owner Associated Lawyers Svc., Palatine, Ill., 1982-86; broker investments A.G. Edwards & Sons, Aurora and Roselle, Ill., 1983—. Sec. Northwest Mental Health/Retardation Ctr., Arlington Hts., Ill., 1971, Mental Health Ctr. Elk Grove/Schaumburg Twp., Ill., 1970-72, vice chmn., bd. dirs.; v.p. PTA, St. Charles Girl Scouts Am., 1965-66; mem. com. Dist. 54 Bd. Edn., Schaumburg, 1969-72; bd. dirs. Mental Health Ctr. St. Charles, 1963-66, Mental Health Ctr. Schaumburg Twp., chmn. 1969-72. Named one of Outstanding Young Women Am., 1964. Mem. Internat. Bd. Cert. Fin. Planners, LWV (bd. dirs. St. Charles 1964-66, Hoffman Estates-Schaumburg 1969-71), DAR (Outstanding Mem. award 1964), Greater O'Hare Assn. (bd. dirs., amb., co-chmn. 1989), Nat. Assn. Women in Careers, NAFE, NW Bus. and Profl. Women (rec. sec. 1988-89, asst. treas. 1989—), Epsilon Sigma Alpha. Republican. Episcopalian. Office: AG Edwards & Sons 1350 W Lake St Roselle IL 60172

SCHOEN, DELORES CHRISTINA, nurse educator; b. Wentworth, Mo., May 8, 1938; d. Mason Oliver and Opal Margaret (Priest) Harmon; m. Robert Schoen, Mar. 25, 1967. BSN, Drury Coll., 1967; MS, San Francisco State U., 1974; MSN, U. Ind., 1989; PhD, U. Ill., 1980. RN. Operating rm. supr. Burge Protestant Hosp., Springfield, Mo., 1966-67; evening supr. 861st

Med. Group Hosp., Glasgow AFB, Mont., 1967-68; instr., chair jr. yr. curriculum St. Joseph Sch. of Nursing, San Francisco, 1968-73; instr., curriculum coord. Sch. of Nursing Ravenswood Hosp. Med. Ctr., Chgo., 1973-74; mem. nursing faculty Parkland Coll., Champaign, Ill., 1974-89; assoc. prof. Sch. of Nursing U. Md., Balt., 1989—. Author: The Nursing Process in Orthopaedics, 1986; contbg. editor: OPCARE Vol. 1 Musculoskeletal Structure and Function, 1987, OPCARE Vol. 2 Reconstructive Joint Procedures, 1987, OPCARE Vol. 3 Trauma/Functional Management, 1987; contbr. articles to profl. jours.; mem. editorial bd. Jour. Orthopaedic Nursing, 1982-89. Coord. cardio-pulmonary resuscitation for community mems., Champaign, 1975; mem. adv. bd. Home and Health Care Profls. Inc., Thomasboro, Ill., 1983-89; pres. Higland Condominium Assn., Champaign, 1988-89; bd. dirs. Champaign County Br. Arthritis Found., Champaign, 1975-85, chair bd. dirs., 1981-83, NSF Field Ctr., Champaign, 1980-84. Am. Cancer Soc. scholar, 1956-59; recipient Nat. Vol. Svc. award Arthritis Found., 1983, Book of the Yr. award Am. Jour. Nursing, 1986. Mem. Am. Nurses Assn., Nat. Assn. Orthopaedic Nurses (task force on grad. and undergrad. curriculum 1986-89, chair rsch. com. 1987-89), Ill. Nurses Assn. (commn. on nursing rsch. 1987-89), Nat. League for Nursing, Population Assn. Am. Office: U Md Sch of Nursing 655 W Lombard St #502C Baltimore MD 21201

SCHOEN, LINDA ALLEN, public affairs administrator; b. Lynch, Ky., July 9, 1936; d. Wert Harvey and Mary Mabel (Ramsey) Allen; m. Stanly M. Schoen, Apr. 8, 1972 (div. 1980). BA, Northwestern U., 1958. Rsch. technician G.D. Searle & Co., Chgo., 1958-60; rsch. assoc., asst. sec. com. cutaneous health and cosmetics AMA, Chgo., 1960-75; dir. mktg. svcs. Neutrogena Corp., L.A. 1975-83, dir. mktg. svcs., 1983-87, v.p. pub. affairs, 1987—. Mem. IABC, PRSA, Soc. Cosmetic Chemists, The Fashion Group. Episcopalian. Club: Opera Assn. (Northwestern U. Alumni). Editor The Look You Like column Today's Health mag., 1962-74; The AMA Book of Skin and Hair Care, 1976, The Look You Like Book, 1989; contbr. articles to Harper's Bazaar, Vogue, Redbook, Beauty Handbook. Mem. Soc. Cosmetic Chemists, Internat. Assn. Bus. Communicators. Episcopalian. Avocations: cross country skiing, travel, opera. Office: Neutrogena Corp 5755 W 96th St Los Angeles CA 90045

SCHOEN, REGINA NEIMAN, psychotherapist; b. Bronx, N.Y., Feb. 21, 1949; d. Louis and Bertha (Hoffman) Neiman; m. Dennis Leo Schoen, Dec. 2, 1979; 1 child, Leah F. B, Hunter Coll., N.Y.C., 1969; M, Columbia U., N.Y.C., 1971; M (social work), Hunter Coll., N.Y.C., 1977. Cert. Psychoanalytic Psychotherapist, Wash. Square Inst. N.Y.C., 1983, Family Therapist, Postgrad. Ctr. for Mental Health N.Y.C., 1986. Tchr., advisor Brandeis High Sch., N.Y.C., 1972-75; family service counselor N.Y. Assn. for New Am., N.Y.C., 1978-82; psychiatric social worker Lutheran Med. Ctr., Bklyn., 1982-84; mental health practitioner Montefiore Med. Ctr., Riker's Island, N.Y.; ptnr. Counseling & Psychotherapy Assoc., N.Y.C., 1987—; moderator & speaker Nat. Assn. Social Workers Alcoholism Inst. N.Y.C., 1989; presenter Young Women's Christian Assn. N.Y.C., 1987—; speaker Greater N.Y. Hosp. Assn., 1983; commentator WNYC Radio Women & Rape N.Y.C., 1982; co-dir. Strategies for Change; mem. faculty Postgrad. Ctr. Mental Health, 1990; speaker Empire Blue Cross/Blue Shield, N.Y., 1990. Mem. Nat. Assn. Social Workers. Office: Regina Schoen CSW 488 Seventh Ave Suite 9A New York NY 10018

SCHOENBERGER, NANCY JANE, poet, educator, arts administrator; b. Oakland, Calif., Dec. 3, 1950; d. Sigmund Bernard and Betty Ellen (Beydler) S.; m. Sam Kashner, Aug. 8, 1989. B.A., La. State U., 1972, M.A., 1974; M.F.A., Columbia U., 1981. Instr. U. Mont., Missoula, 1975-78; editor Columbia, A Mag. of Poetry & Prose, Columbia U., N.Y.C., 1980-81; assoc. producer N.Y. Ctr. for Visual History, N.Y.C., 1981-82; program dir. Acad. Am. Poets, N.Y.C., 1982-88, exec. dir., 1988-89; writer-in-residence Coll. William and Mary, Williamsburg, Va., 1989-90; cons. Mont. Com. for Humanities, 1976-78; vis. artist Poetry in the Schs., Missoula, 1978-79; instr. creative writing workshop Acad. Am. Poets, 1983—, assoc. prof., adjunct poetry workshop, Columbia U., 1988—; presenter poetry readings; resident Centrum, Port Townsend, Wash., 1984, Rockefeller Found.'s Bellagio Study and Conf. Ctr., 1985. Author: The Taxidermist's Daughter, 1979; Girl on a White Porch (Devins award), 1987; contbr. poems to various jours. Nat. Endowment for Arts poetry fellow, 1984; recipient N.Y. Found. for the Arts award, 1988. Mem. Poetry Soc. Am. (Mary Carolyn Davies Meml. award 1984). Office: Coll William & Mary English Dept Williamsburg VA 23185

SCHOENBRUNN, GAIL MARIE, advertising executive; b. Sewickley, Pa., July 12, 1950; d. Alfred George and Lydia Jane (Morse) S. Student, Simmons Coll., 1968-71, Harvard U., 1979—. Sales rep. Boston Phoenix Newspaper, 1975-77; traffic mgr. Marvin & Leonard Advt., Boston, 1977-79; copywriter Ingalls Assoc. Advt., Boston, 1986-87; assoc. creative dir. Ingalls Quinn & Johnson, Boston, 1986-87, v.p. group creative dir., 1987—; tchr. Art Inst. Of Boston, 1980-81. Recipient Clio awards Clio Com., 1984, 85, 88, Hatch awards Hatch Com., 1978, 79, 83, 84, 86. Unitarian. Home: 135 Appleton St Boston MA 02116 Office: Ingalls Quinn & Johnson 855 Boylston St Boston MA 02116*

SCHOENE, KATHLEEN SNYDER, lawyer; b. Glen Ridge, N.J., July 24, 1953; d. John Kent and Margaret Ann (Bronder) Snyder; m. Charles Alan Schoene, Aug. 16, 1974. BA, Grinnell (Iowa) Coll., 1974; MS, So. Conn. State Coll., 1976; JD, Washington U., St. Louis, 1982. Bar: Mo. 1982, U.S. Dist. Ct. (we. and ea. dist. cts.) Mo. 1982, Ill. 1983. Head librarian Mo. Hist. Soc., St. Louis, 1976-79; assoc. Peper, Martin, Jensen, Maichel & Hetlage, St. Louis, 1982-88, ptnr., 1989—. Author: (with others) Missouri Corporation Law and Practice, 1985; contbr. articles to profl. jours. Mem. ABA, Nat. Health Lawyers Assn., Nat. Assn. Bond Lawyers, Mo. Bar Assn., Ill. Bar Assn., Bar Assn. Met. St. Louis (exec. com. 1988—, chair small bus. com. 1987-88, chair bus. law sect. 1988-89, exec. com. young lawyers sect. 1988-90), Grinnell Coll. Alumni Assn. (bd. dirs. 1987—, v.p. 1990—). Home: 7824 Cornell Ave Saint Louis MO 63130 Office: Peper Martin Jensen Maichel & Hetlage 720 Olive St 24th Fl Saint Louis MO 63101

SCHOENEMAN, MARCELLE ANN, federal agency administrator; b. Wausau, Wis., June 4, 1921. BA in Applied Behavioral Sci., Nat. Coll. Edn., 1981, MS in Mgmt. and Devel. of Human Resources, 1983. Supr. clerical processing U.S. Govt., Milw., 1956-66, loan asst., 1966-71, loan specialist, 1971-76, chief loan mgmt. br., 1976—. Lay reader St. Thomas of Canterbury Episcopal Ch., Greendale, Wis., 1980—. Mem. Fed. Mgrs. Assn., Nat. League Am. Penwomen, Fed. Execs. Assn., Milwaukee County Geneal. Soc., AAUW. Lodge: Rosicrucians (AMORC). Home: 3174 S 57th St Milwaukee WI 53219 Office: US Dept Housing and Urban Devel 310 W Wisconsin Ave Suite 1380 Milwaukee WI 53203

SCHOENFISCH, SANDRA ANN, public health administrator; b. Troy, N.Y., June 24, 1942; d. Edward Hubert and Virginia Margaret (Millett) Willa; m. Warren Henry Schoenfisch, Sept. 27, 1962; children: Elizabeth, Karin. BS in Nursing, The Am. U., 1974; MS, U. Md., Balt., 1976; PhD, Fla. State U., 1983. Primary care nurse Georgetown U. Med. Ctr., Washington, 1973-76; asst. prof. nursing George Mason U., Fairfax, Va., 1976-79, Fla. State U., Tallahassee, 1979-83; nursing cons. health and rehab. svcs. HRS State Fla. State Health Office, Tallahassee, 1983-88, program adminstr., 1988—; cons. HMO Am., Tallahassee, 1985-87, Upjohn Health Care, Tallahassee, 1983-86, Sr. Soc. Planning Coun., Tallahassee, 1982-86. Mem. Am. Cancer Soc. (sec. 1989—), Am. Heart Assn., Am. Pub. Health Assn. Office: Fla Dept Health and Rehab Svcs AIDS Program 1317 Winewood Blvd Tallahassee FL 32301

SCHOETTLER, GAIL SINTON, state treasurer; b. Los Angeles, Oct. 21, 1943; d. James and Norma (McLellan) Sinton; children: Lee, Thomas, James; m. Donald L. Stevens, June 23, 1990. BA in Econs., Stanford U., 1965; MA in History, U. Calif., Santa Barbara, 1969, PhD in History, 1975. Businesswoman Denver, 1975-83; exec. dir. Colo. Dept. of Personnel, Denver, 1983-86; treas. State of Colo., Denver, 1987—; bd. dirs. Pub. Employees Retirement Assn., Denver; past bd. dirs. Women's Bank, Denver, Equitable Bankshares of Colo., Littleton. Mem. Douglas County Bd. Edn., Colo., 1979-87, pres., 1983-87; trustee U. No. Colo., Greeley, 1981-87; pres. Denver Children's Mus., 1975-85. Recipient Disting. Alumna award U. Calif. at Santa Barbara, 1987. Mem. Nat. Women's Forum (bd. dirs., pres. 1983-85), Women Execs. in State Govt. (bd. dirs. 1981-87, chmn. 1988), Leadership Denver Assn. (bd. dirs. 1987, named Outstanding Alumna 1985), Nat. Assn. State Treas., Stanford Alumni Assn. Democrat.

SCHOFIELD, SUSAN MCMULLIN, middle school educator; b. Norristown, Pa., Aug. 12, 1947; d. J. Robert and Jean Irma (Schwartz) McMullin; m. James Dobson Schofield III, Nov. 17, 1973; 1 child, Joshua Derek. BS in Edn., Temple U., 1969; postgrad., West Chester State U., 1973. Cert. in elem. edn. Tchr. Methacton Sch. Dist., Fairview Village, Pa., 1969, now tchr. 6th grade social studies and English; chmn. Methacton Assistance Program for Students, Eagleville, Pa., 1986, 88—; coach field hockey Arcola Intermediate Sch., 1990; speaker in field. Deacon, Trinity United Ch. of Christ, Norristown, 1970, youth dir., 1969; den mother Boy Scouts Am., Evansburg, Pa., 1986; mem. crisis Intervention Task Force, Fairview Village, 1984. Recipient Community Svc. award Methacton Area Com., 1989; Am. Field Svc. exchange student Germany, 1964. Mem. AAUW (co-pres. 1989—), Methacton Fedn Tchrs. Home: 175 Level Rd Collegeville PA 19426 Office: Methacton Sch Dist Kriebel Mill Rd Fairview PA 19403

SCHOLER, SUE WYANT, county official; b. Topeka, Oct. 20, 1936; d. Zint Elwin and Virginia Louise (Achenbach) Wyant; m. Charles Frey Scholer, Jan. 27, 1957; children: Elizabeth Scholer Truelove, Charles W., Virginia M. Scholer McCal. Student, Kans. State U., 1954-56. Draftsman The Farm Clinic, West Lafayette, Ind., 1978-79; assessor Wabash Twp., West Lafayette, 1979-84; commr. Tippecanoe County, Lafayette, Ind., 1984—; mem. Tippecanoe County Area Plan Commn., 1984—. Bd. dirs. Crisis Ctr., Lafayette, 1984-89, Tippecanoe Arts Fedn., 1990, United Way, Lafayette, 1990; mem. Lafayette Conv. and Visitors Bur., 1988—. Recipient Salute to Women award, 1986. Mem. Ind. Assn. County Commrs. (treas. 1990), Assn. Ind. Counties (legis. com. 1988—), Greater Lafayette C. of C. (ex-officio bd. 1984—), Sagamore Bus. and Profl. Women, LWV, P.E.O., Purdue Women's Club (past treas.), Kappa Kappa Kappa (past pres. Epsilon chpt.), Delta Delta Delta (past pres. alumnae). Republican. Presbyterian. Home: 807 Essex St West Lafayette IN 47906 Office: Tippecanoe County Bd Commrs 20 N 3d St Lafayette IN 47901

SCHOLL, DEBRA LYNN, sales executive; b. Myrtle Point, Oreg., Sept. 29, 1956; d. Elsworth Leroy Nelson and Sandra Jean (Roberson) Nelson Elbert; m. Douglas Kent Scholl, Aug. 25, 1984. Student Chapman Coll., 1976-77, Saddleback Coll., 1980; teaching cert. J.R. Powers Trade Sch., 1978. Personnel asst. Chapman Coll., Orange, Calif., 1976-78; personnel asst. Kimstock, Inc., Santa Ana, Calif., 1978-79, sales rep., 1979-84, sales mgr. for So. Calif., 1984-87; owner, founder D & D Sales, Mission Viejo, Calif., 1987—. Active fund raising for City of Hope, Los Angeles, 1983—. Mem. The Exec. Female, NOW, Republican Nat. Com. Avocations: sewing, reading. Home: 21605 Fernbrook Mission Viejo CA 92692 Office: D&D Sales 25108 Marguerite Pkwy Ste B-249 Mission Viejo CA 92692

SCHOLL, IDAMAE, bank administration executive; b. St. Paul; d. Louis Gotlieb and Isabelle Mae (Campbell) Reeck; m. Lloyd Leonard Scholl; children: Thomas, Steven, Jerome. BA, U. Mo., Carthage, 1954; postgrad. bus. mgmt., Mgmt. Ctr., 1970; postgrad. mgmt. sci., Mpls. Tech. Inst., 1971; postgrad. telecommunications, Drake U., 1984. Savs. supr. First Nat. Bank, St. Paul, 1963-69; with Norwest Bank, St. Paul, 1969—, adminstrv. services mgr., 1982—. Pres., bd. dirs. Capitol Community Services, St. Paul, 1983—; bd. dirs. Nat. Coll. Bd., St. Paul, 1982—; vol. Battered Women's Shelter, St. Paul, 1983-86; float chmn. St. Paul Winter Carnival Assn., 1983, 85; solicitor St. Paul United Way,1985-86, mem. steering com. 1987—; solicitor ARC, 1983-86, Am. Cancer Soc., 1985-86. Recipient Theme awards, St. Paul Winter Carnival Assn., 1983, 86, 87, YWCA Leadership award, Norwest Corp., 1984, 86, Leadership award Pres. Ronald Reagan, 1988, Vol. award Gov. Rudy Perpich, 1989. Mem. Internat. Women in Telecommunications (charter), Nat. Fedn. Bus. and Profl. Women (nat. task force 1985-86, Minn. 2d v.p. 1986-87, Minn. 1st v.p. 1989-90, pres. 1989, Bus. Woman of the Yr. 1983, Minn. Woman of Achievement award 1987, pres. elect 1988, state pres. 1989), Nat. Assn. Bank Women, Am. Inst. Banking, Minn. Women's Consortium, Minn. Econ. Devel. Assn., Female Execs. Minn., Minn. Minority Purchasing Coun., Minn. Women's Candidate Coalition, N.W. Corp. Vol. Coun. (Svc. award 1987). Home: 6301 Oak Knoll Pla Woodbury MN 55125

SCHOLL, PRISCILLA IRENE, nursing administrator; b. Amherst, Wis., Mar. 17, 1925; d. Charles Gerald and Lydia Francis (Schrader) Shanklin; grad. Deaconess Hosp. Sch. Nursing, 1946; student Milw. Tech. Coll., 1957-58, U. Wis., Milw., 1958-71; B.S. in Health Arts, Coll. of St. Francis, 1981; m. Robert Philip Scholl, May 22, 1948; children—Judith Ann, Susan. Staff nurse Deaconess Hosp., Milw., 1946-49, staff nurse circulating evenings, 1956-57, asst. clin. instr. and nursing service supr., 1957-64, inservice supr., 1964-67, supr. and instr. of renal program, 1966-87, Good Samaritan Med. Ctr., 1987; with Renal Clinic, 1987-90; instr. Milw. Area Tech. Coll., 1989; ret.; cons. Dialysis Mgmt. and Nephrology Nursing. guest lectr. on renal failure to various nursing orgns. and lay orgns., 1970-78. Bd. dirs. Kidney Found. of Wis., 1973-89, mem. med. and sci. com., 1973-89, patient services com., 1971-75, chmn., 1974-75. Mem. Am. Nurses Assn., Am. Assn. Nephrology Nurses and Technicians (organizer Wis. chpt. 1978, pres. 1985-86) Am. Nephrology Nurses Assn. (pres. 1987-88), Network 13 (sec.-treas. exec. com. 1984-86). Pioneer in nephrology nursing.

SCHOLL, SARAH RODERICK, teacher; b. Detroit, Feb. 19, 1938; d. Howard Franklin and Emily (Olmsted) Roderick; m. Robert Allan, Aug. 17, 1963; children: Jennifer Legate, Andrew Minter. BS, U. Mich., 1960; MA, Calif. State U., Hayward, 1981. Calif. Tchrs. Life Credential. Tchr. Springfield Twp. Sch. Dist., Springfield, Pa., 1960-62, Mpls. Sch. Dist., 1962-63, Fargo (N.D.) Unified Sch. Dist., 1963-64, San Ramon Valley Unified Sch. Dist., Danville, Calif., 1977—; mentor tchr. San Ramon Valley Unified Sch. Dist., Danville, 1984-86; tchr. Children and Youth in Am. History, Berkeley, Calif., 1986-88. Campaign co-mgr. San Ramon City Council, 1983, 87; vol. U. Rsch. Expedition Program, Berkeley, 1988. Named Woman of Distinction San Ramon Sorptimists, 1988; recipient Reading Incentive/Authors Prog. award San Ramon Valley Edn. Found., 1986, Author's Prog. to Sch. Tri-Valley Community Fund award, 1985; named Dist. Tchr. of the Yr., 1988. Mem. Oakland Mus. Assn. (docent 1976-90), Calif. Reading Assn., Red Barn Assn. (pres. 1985-88), San Ramon Arts Coun. (v.p. 1988, pres. 1990), San Ramon Valley Community Concerts Assn. (sec. 1985-88, pres. 1989-90), AAUW. Home: 30 Broadmoor Ct San Ramon CA 94583 Office: San Ramon Valley Unified Sch Dist 699 Old Orchard Rd Danville CA 94526

SCHOLL, WENDY ZONENBLIK, personnel manager; b. Chgo., Mar. 1, 1955; d. Louis David and Barbara Lois (Stone) Zonenblik; m. Gary Lee Scholl, Aug. 24, 1975 (div. Apr. 1985); children: Stacy, Holly, Jaclyn. Student, Bradley U., 1973-74. Bur. mgr. Pinellas County Tampa (Fla.) Bay Mag., 1980-82; pub. rels., lobbyist Dissatisfied Parents Together, Vienna, Va., 1983; pres. state chpt. Dissatisfied Parents Together, St. Petersburg, Fla., 1983-86; br. mgr. Personnel Pool Am., Inc., Pinellas Park, Fla., 1985-90; mktg. mgr. employment svcs. Abilities of Fla. Inc., 1990—. Contbr. articles to Tampa Bay Mag., 1981-82; producer, writer, director video tape on vaccine injured children. Mgr., fundraiser Abilities Rehab. Ctr., Pinellas county bur. Chi-Chi Rodriegez Youth Found., 1981; with pub. rels. for Pinellas county Vietnam MIAs, 1982; with outreach program United Jewish Appeal, 1983-84 (award of merit 1983-84); media coord. Jewish Media Rels.; proposed and had imput on U.S. gov. reporting systems for adverse reaction to vaccines. Jewish. Home: 9085 109th Ave N #408 Largo FL 34647 Office: 7907 Sailboat Key Blvd South Pasadena FL 33707

SCHOLTZ, ELIZABETH, botanical garden administrator; b. Pretoria, South Africa, Apr. 29, 1921; came to U.S., 1960, naturalized, 1978; d. Tielman Johannes and Vera Vogel (Roux) Roos-Scholtz. B.Sc., Witwatersrand U., 1941; D.H.L., Pace U., 1974; D.Sc., L.I. U., 1982. Technician South African Inst. Med. Research, Johannesburg, 1942-44; technician dept. medicine Johannesburg and Pretoria gen. hosps., 1944-46; with Groote Schuur Hosp., Capetown; as technician charge student labs. Groote Schuur Hosp., 1948-52, technician charge hematology lab., 1952-60; mem. staff Bklyn. Bot. Garden, 1960—, asso. curator instrn., 1964-71, acting dir., 1972-73, dir., 1973-80, v.p., 1980-87, dir. emeritus, 1987—; trustee Independence Savs. Bank. Recipient Arthur Hoyt Scott Garden and Horticulture award, 1981. Mem. Am. Hort. Soc. (Liberty Hyde Bailey medal 1984), Am. Assn. Bot. Gardens and Arboreta (dir. 1976-79), Royal Hort. Soc. (Veitch Gold medal 1990), Hort. Soc. N.Y. (bd. dirs. 1988—), Garden Club Am. (Medal of Honor 1990), Bklyn. Heights Casino Club, Cosmopolitan Club. Home: 111 Hicks St Brooklyn NY 11201 Office: Bklyn Bot Garden 1000 Washington Ave Brooklyn NY 11225

SCHOLZ, JANE, newspaper publisher; b. St. Louis, July 31, 1948; d. Robert Louis and Mildred Virginia (Hudgins) S.; m. Jay W. Johnson, June 1979 (div. Dec. 1981); m. Douglas C. Balz, Jan. 1, 1983. B.A., Mich. State U., 1970; M.B.A., U. Miami, 1981. Reporter Jour.-Gazette, Fort Wayne, Ind., 1970-73; reporter The Miami Herald, Fla., 1973-77, asst. city editor, 1977-80; advanced mgmt. devel. participant Knight-Ridder Inc., Miami, Fla., 1980-85; pres., pub. Post-Tribune, Gary, Ind., 1985—. Bd. dirs. United Way of Lake county, Ind., Gary chpt. Urban League, Ind., NW Ind. Forum. Mem. Am. Newspaper Pubs. Assn., Ind. C. of C. (bd. dirs.), Inland Press Assn. (bd. dirs.), Sigma Delta Chi. Home: 7118 Forest Ave Hammond IN 46324 Office: Post-Tribune Post-Tribune Pub Inc 1065 Broadway Gary IN 46402*

SCHOLZ, MARKIE LOUISE, business owner, consultant; b. Ft. Collins, Colo., May 8, 1947; d. Kenneth Carl and Phyllis Ann (McFarland) S.; m. Richard Alan Termes, Jan. 27, 1979; children: Lang, Kabe. BS in Eng. Edn., U. S.D., 1969. With law enforcement div. U.S. Park Svc., Bandelier, N.Mex., 1969; tour guide U.S. Park Svc., S.D. and, N.Mex., 1970; tri-county dir. Head Start Marshal Day and Roberts County, S.D., 1970-71; owner Dragons are Too Seldom Puppet Prodns., Spearfish, S.D., 1971—. Mem. AAUW (v.p. Spearfish chpt. 1990—). Home and Office: Rt 2 Box 435B Spearfish SD 57783

SCHONTHALER, JOAN ANN, psychotherapist; b. Providence, Nov. 7, 1948; d. Kurt William and Mildred Emily (Lutz); m. James Anthony Charles, Aug. 14, 1976; children: Justin Joseph, Lauren Elizabeth. BA in English and Psychology, Mercy Coll., Detroit, 1976; MS in Clin. Psychology, Ea. Mich. U., 1980. Cert. forensic examiner, profl. counselor, Ga.; lic. social worker, Mich. Regional youth coordinator Fla. Drug Abuse Program, West Palm Beach, 1972-74; therapist Boniface Community Action Corp., Detroit, 1974-76; sr. women's therapist Rubicon-Odyssey House, Detroit, 1975-76; chief clinician Ctr. Forensic Psychiatry, Ann Arbor, Mich., 1976-80; dir. adult services Dekalb County Mental Health, Decatur, Ga., 1980-82; profl. devel. cons. So. Co. Services, Atlanta and Birmingham, Ala., 1984-85; pres. The Counseling Coop., Atlanta, 1985—; dir. psychol. svcs. Nat. Med. Systems, Inc., Atlanta, 1987-89; regional dir. Preffered Health Care, Ltd., Atlanta, 1989; cons. in field. Contbr. articles to profl. jpurs. Bd. dirs. Open City/CREATE, Atlanta, 1985-88. Mem. Ga. Psychol. Assn., Am. Assn. Counseling and Devel. Democrat. Home: 519 Saint Charles Ave NE Atlanta GA 30308 Office: Counseling Coop PO Box 8391 Atlanta GA 30306

SCHOOLEY, CAROLINE NAUS, laboratory administrator; b. San Francisco, Feb. 15, 1932; d. George Mortimer and Ruth Raymond (Lange) Naus; m. John Campbell Schooley, Aug. 8, 1953; children: Diana, Karen, Peter. BA, U. Calif., Berkeley, 1954, MA, 1958. Rsch. asst. zoology dept. U. Calif., Berkeley, 1953-54, 56-59, staff rsch. assoc. R.D. Ogg Electron Microscope Lab., 1967-83, facility supr., 1983—; rsch. asst. Oak Ridge Inst. Nuclear Studies, 1955. Fellow Royal Micros. Soc.; mem. Electron Microscopy Soc. Am. (coun. 1985-88), Am. Soc. Cell Biology, No. Calif. Soc. Electron Microscopy (sec. 1974-77). Home: 3036 Hillegass Ave Berkeley CA 94705 Office: U Calif Electron Microscope Lab 26 Giannini Hall Berkeley CA 94720

SCHOOLEY, CONSTANCE ELAINE, nurse, insurance professional; b. N.Y.C., Jan. 6, 1945; d. James Francis and Elsie A. (Grote) Magurno; m. Thomas Burton Schooley, Dec. 17, 1966; children: Tammy Marie, Brian Scott. Diploma, Jackson Meml. Hosp. Sch. Nursing, 1966; cert. advanced cardiac life support, Miami-Dade Jr. Coll., 1981; BPS, Barry U., 1988, MS, 1990. R.N., Fla. Head nurse emergency dept. AMI Kendall Regional Med. Ctr., Miami, Fla., 1973-81; head nurse, quality assurance coord. U. Miami Pub. Health Trust, 1981-85, claims adjuster, 1985-86, med. malpractice claims adminstr., 1986-89; v.p. risk mgmt. and adjusting svc., 1989-90; dir. risk mgmt. dept. St. Francis Hosp., 1990—; expert witness, Fla., 1985-89; instr., trainer Am. Heart Assn., Miami, 1975-85; with Dade County Civil Def., Miami, 1976-84. Patentee in field; contbr. to med. publs. Asst. den leader, pack nurse, Miami area Boy Scouts Am., 1976-78; vol., Dade County Schs., 1978-84. Mem. So. Fla. Soc. Hosp. Risk Mgmt. Republican. Presbyterian. Home: 13324 SE 110 Terr Miami FL 33186

SCHOOLEY, DOLORES HARTER, entertainment administrator; b. Nora Springs, Iowa, May 2, 1905; d. Amil A. and Elizabeth (Sefert) Zemke; m. Leslie J. Harter, June 5, 1934 (dec. 1963); m. Charles Earl Schooley, Apr. 1, 1966. BE, BA, U. Colo., 1927; MA, Northwestern U., 1931. Tchr. high sch. Consol. Schs., Johnstown, Colo., 1927-28, Byers, Colo., 1928-29, Clayton, Mo., 1931-34; theatrical makeup, 1937-86; instr. theatrical makeup, dramatic clubs, N.J. Theatre League; lectr., demonstrator theatrical makeup, dramatic and women's clubs, high schs., N.J. and N.Y. area, 1937-53; dir., entertainer mil. posts First Army, 1951-53; cons. radio broadcast series Sta. WNYC, 1962-65; dir. community rels. Wingspread Summer Theatre, Colon, Mich., 1955; co-chmn. Valley Shore Community Concerts, Conn., 1958-61; artist mgr., 1959—; chmn. benefit ball Sharon Hosp., 1970; founder, pres. Berkshire Hills Music and Dance Assn., 1970-78; mem. Music Mountain Corp., Falls Village, Conn., 1975-81. Trustee Sharon Creative Arts Found., 1970-73; hon. trustee Bar Harbor Festival, 1968—; founder, pres. Wingspread Found., 1977—. Mem. Montclair Dramatic Club (chmn. and instr. makeup), Rehearsal Club (program chmn.), Women's Club (dir. plays, chmn. drama dept.), Sharon Women's Club, Sharon Rep. Women's Club (pres. 1982-85), Sharon Country Club, Hendersonville Country Club, Alpha Omicron Pi, Phi Beta (dir. nat. project for mil. 1951-61, nat. officer, Nat. Coun. 1956-61). Congregationalist. Address: PO Box 746 Hendersonville NC 28793

SCHOOLEY, VIRGINIA GEIST, insurance brokerage firm executive, lawyer; b. Chgo., Nov. 12, 1946; d. Leslie George and Helen Angela (Van Wormer) Geist; m. James Ervin Schooley, May 1, 1982. B.A., U. Ill., 1968; J.D., Ill. Inst. Tech., 1980. Asst. corp. sec. Rollins Burdick Hunter Co., Chgo., 1973-80, v.p., corp. sec., 1980—. Mem. ABA, Chgo. Bar Assn. Home: 3017 W Edgemont Ln Park Ridge IL 60068 Office: Rollins Burdick Hunter Co 123 N Wacker Dr Chicago IL 60606

SCHOONOVER, JEAN WAY, public relations executive; b. Richfield Springs, N.Y.. AB, Cornell U., 1941. With D-A-Y Pub. Rels., Ogilvy & Mather Co., N.Y.C., 1949—, D-A-Y Pub. Rels. Inc. and predecessor, N.Y.C., 1949—; owner, pres. Dudley-Anderson-Yutzy Pub. Rels. Inc. and predecessor, N.Y.C., 1970—; chmn. Dudley-Anderson-Yutzy Pub. Relations Inc. and predecessor, 1984-88; merger with Ogilvy & Mather, 1983; sr. v.p. Ogilvy & Mather U.S., 1984—; vice chmn. Ogilvy Pub. Relations Group, 1986—; mem., historian, Pub. Relations Seminar; mem. U.S. Dept. Agriculture Agribusiness Promotion Council, 1985—. Trustee Cornell U., 1975-80; mem. Def. Adv. Com. on Women in Svcs., 1987-89. Named Advt. Woman of Yr. Am. Advt. Fedn., 1972, one of Outstanding Women in Bus. & Labor, Women's Equity Action League, 1985.; recipient Matrix award, 1976, Nat. Headliner award, 1984, N.Y. Women in Communications, 1976, leadership award Internat. Orgn. Women Bus. Owners, 1980, Entreprenurial Woman award Women Bus. Owners N.Y., 1981. Mem. Women Execs. in Pub. Rels. N.Y.C. (pres. 1979-80), Pub. Rels. Soc. Am., Pub. Rels. Soc. N.Y. (pres. 1979). Home: 25 Stuyvesant St New York NY 10003 Office: Ogilvy Pub Rels Group 708 3d Ave New York NY 10017

SCHOR, MARY ANN MCCARTHY (MRS. WARREN SCHOR), public relations executive; b. Washington; d. Jeremiah John and Ann (Horstkamp) McCarthy; grad. George Washington U., 1962, grad. publ. specialist program, 1977; EPS Program, Trinity Coll., 1982; m. Warren Schor, May 2, 1964; 1 dau., Elizabeth Ann. Public relations, various accounts, Washington, 1962-66; dir. public relations program Met. Police Dept., Washington, 1966-69; public relations D.C. Dept. Public Health, Washington, 1979-70, D.C. Police Dept., Washington, 1970-75; public relations cons., 1976—. Mem. public relations com. D.C. Tb and Respiratory Disease Assn., 1969—. Mem. Am. Newspaper Women's Club (bd. dirs 1988), Advt. Club Washington, Zonta. Roman Catholic. Editor: Rambling thru Georgetown, 1978-80;

Rambling thru Alexandria, 1978-80. Home: 6206 Wedgewood Rd Bethesda MD 20817

SCHOR, OLGA SEEMANN, mental health counselor, real estate broker; b. Havana, Cuba, Mar. 2, 1951; came to U.S., 1961; d. Olga del Carmen (Hernandez) S.; m. David Michael Schor, Apr. 22, 1979; 1 child, Andrew. A.A., Miami Dade Community Coll., 1971; B.A., U. Fla.-Gainesville, 1973; M.Edn., U. Miami, Fla., 1976; Psy.D., Nova U., 1981; cert. Bert Rodgers Sch. Real Estate, Miami, 1981, Gold Coast Sch. Real Estate, 1988; lic. real estate broker. Teaching asst. U. Fla., Gainesville, 1972-73; counselor U. Miami, Fla., 1974-79; assoc. psychotherapist Linda H. Jamrozy & Assocs., Miami, 1976-78, Interactive Systems, Miami, 1978-79; psychometrist Jackson Meml. Hosp., Miami, 1978-79; assoc. psychotherapist Behavioral Medicine Inst., Miami, 1979-85, Tony Ciminero & Assocs., Miami, 1985-86; lectr. U. Miami, 1976-78, Jackson Meml. Hosp. Sch. Nursing, Miami, 1976; real estate broker The Keyes Co. Realtor, Coral Gables, 1981-88, Keyes Exec. Mgmt., Miami, 1988—; sec./treas. bd. dirs. BODS Inc., Miami. Recipient Assoc. of Quarter award Keyes Co. Realtors, 1986. Mem. Am. Psychol. and Guidance Assn., Keyes Comml. Roundtable, Keyes Inner Circle, Coral Gables Bd. Realtors, Dade County Mental Health Assn., Million Dollar Sales Club. Club: South Fla. Sailing Assn. (Miami). Avocations: sailing; diving; reading; running; theater; acting; tennis. Office: 100 N Biscayne Blvd Ste 1302 Miami FL 33132

SCHORR, LISBETH BAMBERGER, child and family policy analyst, author, educator; b. Munich, Germany, Jan. 20, 1931; d. Fred S. and Lotte (Krafft) Bamberger; m. Daniel L. Schorr, Jan. 8, 1967; children—Jonathan, Lisa. B.A. with highest honors, U. Calif., Berkeley, 1952. Med. care cons. U.A.W. and Community Health Assn., Detroit, 1956-58; asst. dir. Dept. Social Security AFL-CIO, Washington, 1958-65; acting chief CAP Health Services, OEO, 1965-66; chief program planning Office for Health Affairs, OEO, Washington, 1967; cons. Children's Def. Fund, Washington, 1973-79; scholar-in-residence Inst. of Medicine, 1979-80; chmn. Select Panel on Promotion Child Health, 1979-80; adj. prof. maternal and child health U. N.C., Chapel Hill, 1981-85; lectr. social medicine and health policy Harvard U. Med. Sch., 1984—; mem. working group early life and adolescent health policy Harvard U. Div. Health Policy Research and Edn., 1982—; nat. council Alan Gutmacher Inst., 1974-79, 82-85; pub. mem. Am. Bd. Pediatrics, 1978-84; vice chmn. Found. for Child Devel., 1978-84, bd. dirs. 1976-84, 86—; mem. council Nat. Resource Ctr. for Children in Poverty, 1987—; mem. children's program adv. com. Edna McConnell Clark Found., 1987—; mem. steering com. Nat. Forum on the Future of Children and Families, 1988—. Author: Within Our Reach: Breaking the Cycle of Disadvantage, 1988. Mem. Inst. Medicine, Nat. Acad. Scis., Phi Beta Kappa. Home: 3113 Woodley Rd NW Washington DC 20008

SCHORR, THELMA M., publishing company executive, nurse; b. New Haven, Dec. 15, 1924; d. Simon and Rebecca (Katz) Mermelstein; m. Norman A. Schorr, Mar 6, 1955; children—Susan, Marjorie, Elizabeth. Diploma, Bellevue Sch. Nursing, 1945; B.S., Columbia U., N.Y.C., 1952; D.Sc. in Nursing (hon.), U. Pa., 1985; D Nursing (hon.), Vt. Coll., Norwich U.; D.Sc. (hon.), Curry Coll., 1988. Head Nurse Bellevue Hosp., N.Y.C., 1945-50; asst. editor Am. Jour. of Nursing, N.Y.C., 1950-53, assoc. editor, 1953-63, sr. editor, 1963-70, editor-in-chief, 1970-81; pres., pub. Am. Jour. of Nursing Co., N.Y.C., 1981—; mem. bd. dirs. Nurses Ednl. Funds, N.Y.C., 1981—, Community Family Planning Council, N.Y.C., 1984—, Palliative Care Project, Calvary Hosp., Bronx, N.Y., 1984—; cons. pub. relations com. Sigma Theta Tau, Indpls., 1984—, Kimberly Quality Care, Boston, 1989—;. Co-author Making Choices, Taking Chances, 1988; contbr. articles to profl. jours. Recipient Disting. Svc. award Boston U., 1975, Leadership award Tchrs. Coll., 1983; Hon. Recognition award N.Y. County Registered Nurses Assn. Mem. Am. Nurses' Assn., Am Soc. Mag. Editors, Mag. Pubs. Assn., Sigma Theta Tau, Soc. Profl. Journalists. Democrat. Jewish. Home: 32 E 64th St New York NY 10021 Office: Am Jour of Nursing 555 W 57th St New York NY 10019

SCHOTT, MARGE, professional sports team owner; b. 1928; d. Edward and Charlotte Unnewehr; m. Charles J. Schott, 1952 (dec. 1968). Owner Schottco, Cin.; ltd. ptnr. Cin. Reds, 1981-84, gen. ptnr., 1984-85, owner, pres., 1985—, chief exec. officer. Office: Cin Reds 100 Riverfront Stadium Cincinnati OH 45202*

SCHOWE, SHERAL LEE SPEAKS, not-for-profit organization executive; b. San Francisco, June 14, 1953; d. Veral John and Myrtle Lee (Hunter) Speaks; m. Derryll Boyd Schowe, Aug. 7, 1982; 1 child, Devin. B degree, Brigham Young U., 1977, M degree, 1979; AA, Ricks Coll., Rexburg, Idaho, 1974; fellow, Gallaudet Coll., 1978. Lic. therapeutic recreation specialist. Asst. Calif. Jud. Edn. and Rsch., Berkeley; coord. Cottonwood Elem. Sch., Holladay, Utah; coord. handicap svcs. Granite Community Edn., Salt Lake City; area dir., exec. dir. Utah Spl. Olympics, Sandy. Contbr. numerous articles to profl. jours. Mem. archtl. barriers com. Salt Lake 504 Coun., 1978-80; mem. Salt Lake County Community Devel. Citizens Adv. Coun., 1981, vice chair, 1982, chair, 1983; mem. panel Salt Lake County Title XX Adv. Coun., 1984-87. Named Edn. of Handicapped of Yr. Mental Retardation Assn., 1982, Woman of Yr. Salt Lake City JayCees, 1982; recipient Outstanding Contribution to Fitness award Utah Gov's. Coun. on Health & Physical Fitness, 1990. Mem. Utah Community Edn. Assn. named Profl. Community Educator of Yr. 1987), Nat. Assn. Spl. Olympics Profls., Nat. Fund Raising Execs., Am. Soc. Assn. Execs., Sandy C. of C., Zonta (svc. com. chair 1987, bd. dirs. 1988, pub. rels. chair 1990). Democrat. Presbyterian. Home: 11454 High Mountain Dr Sandy UT 84092 Office: Utah Spl Olympics 9192 S 300 West Ste 3 Sandy UT 84092

SCHRADE, ROLANDE MAXWELL YOUNG, composer, pianist, educator; b. Washington, Sept. 13; d. Harry Robert and Isabelle Martha (Maxwell) Young; m. Robert Warren Schrade, Dec. 21, 1949; children: Robelyn, Rhonda Lee, Rolisa, Randolph, Rorianne. Pupil Harold Bauer, N.Y.C., Vittorio Giannini; student, Manhattan Sch. Music, Juilliard Sch. Music.. Debut as concert pianist Town Hall, N.Y.C., 1953, Nat. Gallery, Washington, 1954; founder, dir. ann. performances Sevenars Concerts, Inc., Worthington, Mass., 1968—, music dir., 1975—, also broadcasts, 1984, 85; recitalist radio Sta. WGMS-FM, Washington; mem. music faculty Allen-Stevenson Sch., N.Y.C., 1968-89; v.p., treas. Sevenars Music House, Inc., N.Y.C., 1968—. Concerts include Lincoln Ctr., Alice Tully Hall, 1980, Sevenars Concerts, Inc., ann. music festival, Worthington, Mass., 1968—, tour, N.Z., 1982, 84; appearances PM Mag., TV, 1980, 81; composer, pub. and recorded over 100 songs; albums include American 76, Original and Traditional Songs for Special Days, 1988; editor: songs of Carrie Jacobs Bond, Boston Music Co. Mem. ASCAP, DAR (Bicentennial award 1972), Mut. Artists Mgmt. Alliance (founder, bd. dirs.). Episcopalian. Home and Office: 30 E End Ave New York NY 10028 also: Sevenars Worthington MA 01098

SCHRAER, ROSEMARY S. J., university chancellor; b. Ilion, N.Y., Aug. 1, 1924; d. Ulysses Sidney and Rose Katherine (Ortner) Schmidt; m. Allan Gramlick Jenkins, May 3, 1946 (dec. Aug. 13, 1947); 1 child, David; m. Harald Schraer, June 12, 1952. AB, Syracuse U., 1946, MS, 1949, PhD, 1953. Vis. research assoc. Harvard Med. Sch., Boston, Mass., 1967-68; vis. scientist Radcliffe Inst. Ind. Study, Cambridge, Mass., 1967-68; acting head dept. computer sci. Pa. State U., University Park, 1973-74, assoc. dean for research, 1973-78, prof. biochemistry, 1975-86, assoc. provost, 1981-85; exec. vice chancellor U. Calif., Riverside, 1986-87, chancellor, 1987—; fellow Cavendish Coll., Cambridge (Eng.) U., 1987—; bd. dirs. Am. Coun. on Pharm. Edn., Chgo., 1983-88, Accrediting Commn. for Sr. Colls. and Univs., Oakland, Calif., 1988—, Presley Inst. of Corrections Rsch. and Trng., Sacramento, 1988—; bd. visitors Southwestern U. Sch. Law, L.A., 1988—. Mem. Monday Morning Group, Riverside, 1987—, Coun. on Competitiveness, Washington, 1988, adv. bd. dirs. Nat. Prepaid Tuition Plan, Overland Park, Kans., 1988—; bd. dirs. Inst. for Evaluating Health Risks, San Francisco, 1988—, Community Health Corp., 1988—, Riverside Land Conservancy, 1988—; co-chair United Way Indland Valleys, 1990. Univ. fellow Syracuse U., 1951-52. Mem. AAAS, Am. Chem. Soc., Am. Inst. Chemists, Am. Soc. for Cell Biology, Am. Soc. Biol. Chemists, Am. Physiol. Soc., Phi Beta Kappa. Office: U Calif-Riverside 900 University Ave Riverside CA 92521-4009

SCHRAG, CRYSTAL BLYTHE, retail executive; b. Moundridge, Kans., Nov. 12, 1965; d. John Milford and Judy Carlene (Stucky) S. Student, Wichita State U., 1984-87; BS in Journalism, U. Kans., 1989. Dispatcher, sec. Digital Computing Ctr., Wichita, Kans., 1985-86; production asst. Stephan Advt. Agy., Wichita, 1986-87; asst. to exec. sec. Kans. Scholastic Press Assn., Lawrence, 1987-89; recreation leader Boston Recreation Ctr., Wichita, 1987; profl. intern The Clay Ctr. Dispatch, Clay Center, Kans., 1988; photography stringer AP, 1988; exec. trainee Dillard Dept. Stores, Inc., Wichita, 1989-90, area sales mgr., 1990—. Recipient U.S. Nat. Leadership Merit award, 1984; Frances E. Taylor scholar, U. Kans., 1988. Mem. Women in Communications, Inc., Order of Omega, Alpha Phi (promotions chmn. and philantropy chmn. Gamma Xi chpt. 1987—). Home: RR 1 Box 52 McPherson KS 67212 Office: Dillard Dept Stores 4600 W Kellogg Wichita KS 67209

SCHRAGE, ROSE, educational administrator; b. Montelimar, France, Apr. 15, 1942; came to U.S., 1947; d. Abraham and Celia (Silbiger) Levine; m. Samuel Schrage, Dec. 12, 1935 (dec. 1976); children: Abraham, Leon. BRE, Beth Rivkah Tchrs. Sem., Bklyn., 1968; Paralegal, Manpower Career Devel. Agy., Bklyn., 1973; MS, L.I. U., 1975; Advanced Cert. Ednl. Adminstrn., Bklyn. Coll., 1983. Cert. sch. dist. adminstr., guidance counselor, tchr., asst. prin. Sec. N.Y.C., 1964-68; police adminstrv. aide N.Y.C. Police Dept., 1974-75; coordinator state reading aid program Sch. Dist. 14, Bklyn., 1977-78, project dir. Title VII, 1978-81, asst. dir. reimbursable fed. and state programs, 1981-85, dist. bus. mgr., 1985—; chmn. N.Y.C. Bd. Edn. IMPACT Com., Bklyn., 1986—. Author: poem Never Again, 1983. Del. Republican. Jud. Conf., 1968; founder, pres Concerned Parents, Bklyn., 1977; radio co-host Israeli War Heroes Fund-Radiothon, Bklyn.; family counselor local social agys., Bklyn. Mem. NAFE, Am. Assn. Sch. Adminstrs., Am. Assn. Sch. Adminstrs., Assn. Orthodox Jewish Tchrs., N.Y. State Assn. Sch. Bus. Ofcls., N.Y.C. Assn. Sch. Bus. Ofcls.

SCHRAGER, MINDY RAE, corporate executive; b. Paterson, N.J., Jan. 18, 1958; d. Julius Maxwell and Miriam (Max) S. BA, Dickinson Coll., 1979; MBA, Babson Coll., 1981. Cons., Nolan Norton & Co., Lexington, Mass., 1981-86; mgr. sales support Logos Corp., Dedham, Mass., 1986-87; mgr. customer satisfaction Codex Corp., Mansfield, Mass., 1987—.Co-author: Non Product Quality: The Cornerstone for Sucess. Mem. NAFE, Am. Soc. Quality Control, Assn. for Rsch. and Enlightenment, Women in Mgmt., Internat. Customer Svc. Assn., Assn. Quality and Participation. Avocation: ballroom dance. Home: 80 Walnut St Canton MA 02021

SCHRAMEK, LYNN BETH, communications executive; b. Cin., Mar. 19, 1956; d. Lloyd George and LaVerne (Wolf) Shone. BA in Journalism, Ohio State U., 1978. Supr. Ohio State U. Music Rm., Columbus, 1976-78; customer svc. rep. Warner Qube, Columbus, 1978; sales rep. Stewart Sandwiches & Coffee Inc., Columbus, 1979; corp. pub. rels. coordinator Copco Papers, Inc., Columbus, 1979-83; assoc. dir. communications Ohio Sch. Bds. Assn., Westerville, 1983-84; assoc. communications coord. J.C. Penney Casualty Is. Co., Westerville, 1985-87; customer communications coord. J.C. Penney Casualty Ins. Co., Westerville, 1987-89; dir. pub. rels. Fekete & Co., Columbus, Ohio, 1989; pub. info. officer Ohio Dept. Edn., Columbus, 1990—; pub. rels. vol. Youth for Understanding Internat. Exchange, Columbus, 1989. Mem. Internat. Assn. Bus. Communicators (community rels. dir. 1988-89, pres. 1984-85, Disting. Communicator of Yr. Columbus chpt. 1989), Pub. Rels. Soc. Am. Jewish. Home: 5477 Sharon Park Ave Columbus OH 43214 Office: Ohio Dept Edn 65 S Front St Columbus OH 43215

SCHRAMM, JANE MARIE, youth organization adminstrator; b. Clintonville, Wis., Oct. 6, 1960; d. Leonard F. and Grace A. (Lorbeck) Jacoboski; m. Timothy E. Schramm, Sept. 26, 1987. BS, U. Wis., 1986. Asst. aquatics dir. Metro. YMCA, Madison, Wis., 1982-84; clin. researcher U. Wis., Madison, 1983-85; legis. asst. State of Wis., Madison, 1986; aquatics dir. Albany YMCA, Albany, N.Y., 1986-87; membership & mktg. dir. Albany YMCA, 1987—. Pub. speaking United Way, Albany, 1988—. Mem. Assn. Profl. Dirs., Nat. Water Safety Com. North East, Kiwanis (promotion dir. Albany chpt. 1988—). Roman Catholic. Office: Albany YMCA 274 Washington Ave Albany NY 12203

SCHRAMM, MARILYN JEAN, lawyer; b. Chgo., Nov. 14, 1951; d. Robert and Dorothy (Wood) S. BA, DePaul U., 1977; MA, Northwestern U., 1981, JD, 1981. Bar: Ill. 1981, U.S. Dist. Ct. (no. dist.) Ill. 1981. Assoc. Sidley & Austin, Chgo., 1981-85; atty. Quaker Oats Co., Chgo., 1985—. Mem. ABA, Chgo. Bar Assn., Women's Bar Assn. Ill., Pi Gamma Mu. Home: 6166 N Sheridan Rd #2K Chicago IL 60660 Office: The Quaker Oats Co 321 N Clark St Chicago IL 60610

SCHRAM-MCRAE, NORMA, management and educational consultant; b. Houston, Apr. 5, 1957; d. Albert Julius and Betty Laverne (Deskin) S. Student, Tex. Tech U., 1978; BSED in Guidance Counseling, North Tex. State U., 1980; MEd in Ednl. Adminstrn., Tex. Christian U., 1985. Admissions counselor Richland Community Coll., Dallas, 1978-80; interim youth dir. Park Cities Bapt. Ch., Dallas, 1980-81, asst. to single adult ministers, 1980-81; admissions counselor Dallas Bapt. U., 1981-83, dir. admissions, dir. student affairs; Youth Program Specialist City of Dallas, 1983; dir. residential living-learning program Tex. Christian U., Ft. Worth, 1983-86; tng. specialist City of Dallas Housing Authority, 1986—; owner, cons. Norma Schram and Assocs., Dallas, 1986—; youth counselor, Dallas, Ft. Worth, 1978—; cons. Pregnancy Lifeline, Ft. Worth, 1985-86; instr. CPR, first aid, ARC, Dallas, instr. defensive driving Greater Dallas Safety Assn., 1987, Dallas County Community Coll., 1986-87; seminar leader for oncology patients, Presbyn. Hosp., 1989—; keynote speaker Dallas So. Bapt. Conv., 1980—. Cons. City of Dallas, Inner City Task Force, 1983; vol. Leukemia Soc., 1989—; v.p., bd. dirs. Life-Link. Named one of Notable Women of Tex., 1985, Outstanding Student Devel. Profl., 1981, DHD and Assocs., Admissions Assoc. of Yr., Nat. Assn. Coll. Registrars and Admissions Officers, 1980. Mem. Assoc. Women Entrepreneurs Dallas, Dallas C. of C., Nat. Assn. Female Executives, Am. Soc. Tng. and Devel., Nat. Assn. Housing and Redevel. Officials. Republican. Home and Office: 704 Versailles Mesquite TX 75149

SCHRANK, HOLLY L., education educator; b. Hinsdale, Ill., Dec. 24, 1941; d. Robert H. and Alice L. (Knoblauch) S. BS, U. Wis., 1964, MS, 1965; PhD, Ohio State U., 1970; student, Purdue U., 1989—. High sch. tchr. Joliet (Ill.) Twp. High Schs., 1965-66; instr. Heidelberg Coll., Tiffin, Ohio, 1966-68; asst. to assoc. prof. Mich. State U., East Lansing, 1970-75; assoc. prof. to dept. head Oreg. State U., Corvallis, Oreg., 1975-80; prof. U. Ky., Lexington, 1980-82; prof., dept. head Purdue U., West Lafayette, Ind., 1982-88, prof., 1988—. Author: Teacher's Manual for The Visible Self, 1973; contbg. author 1990 Conf. Book of Cen. States Conf. on Teaching of Fgn. Langs.; editor Purdue Retailer, 1989—; contbr. articles to profl. jours. Deacon Cen. Presbyn. Ch., Lafayette, Ind., 1989—. Recipient acad. adminstrn. internship Mich. State U., 1973-74. Mem. Soc. Consumer Affairs Profls., Community Devel. Soc., Am. Collegiate Retailers Assn., Greater Lafayette C. of C. (com. chmn. 1986-88), PEO Sisterhood (various offices 1965—), Omicron Nu, Phi Upsilon Omicron, Phi Kappa Delta. Democrat. Office: Consumer Scis/Retailing Purdue Univ Matthews Hall West Lafayette IN 47907

SCHREIBER, ALICE MILDRED, research engineer; b. Havertown, Pa., Nov. 26, 1927; d. Augustus Darnell and Florence Charlotte (Richter) S.; m. Miles Jamison Willard Jr., June 22, 1950 (div. June 1970); children: Nancy E., Janice M., David A.; m. John Campbell Williamson, June 27, 1981. BSChemE, Drexel U., 1950; MEd in Guidance and Counseling, U. Idaho, 1975; MS in Chem. Engring., Washington State U., Pullman, 1978. Sales engr. Brown Instrument, Phila., 1950-51; adminstrv. asst. Miles Willard, Food Processing Cons., Idaho Falls, 1964-70; substitute tchr. Latah County and Whitman County Sch. Dists., Idaho and Wash., 1974-76; engr. Rockwell Hanford Ops., Richland, Wash., 1977-80; rsch. engr. Battelle N.W. Lab., Richland, Wash., 1980—. Moderator bd. and congregation N.W. United Protestant Ch., Richland, 1988, 89. Mem. AAUW, NAFE, NOW, Soc. Women Engrs., Am. Inst. Chem. Engrs., Am. Nuclear Soc., Phi Kappa Phi, Tau Beta Pi, Pi Nu Epsilon. Democrat. Home: 1509 Cimarron Ave Richland WA 99352 Office: Battelle NW Labs PO Box 999 Richland WA 99352

SCHREIBER, EILEEN SHER, artist; b. Denver; d. Michael Herschel and Sarah Deborah (Tannenbaum) Sher; student U. Utah, 1942-45, N.Y.U. extension, 1966-68, Montclair (N.J.) State Coll., 1975-79; also pvt. art study; m. Jonas Schreiber, Mar. 27, 1945; children—Jeffrey, Barbara, Michael. Exhibited Morris Mus. Arts and Scis., Morristown, N.J., 1965-73, N.J. State Mus., 1969, Lever House, N.Y.C., 1971, Paramus (N.J.) Mus., 1973, Newark Mus., 1978, Am. Water Color Soc., Audubon Artists, N.A.D. Gallery, N.Y.C., Pallazzo Vecchio Florence (Italy), Art Expo 1987, 1988; represented in permanent collections Morris Mus., Seton Hall U., Bloomfield (N.J.) Coll., Barclay Bank of Eng., N.J., Somerset Coll., NYU, Morris County State Coll., Broad Nat. Bank, Newark, IBM, Am. Telephone Co., RCA, Johnson & Johnson, Champion Internat. Paper Co., SONY, Mitsubishi, Celanese Co., Squibb Corp., Nabisco, Nat. Bank Phila., NYU, Data Control, Sperry Univac, Ga. Pacific Co., Public Service Co. N.J., others; also pvt. collections. Recipient awards N.J. Watercolor Soc., 1969, 72, Nat. Assn. Women Artists, 1970; 1st award in watercolor Hunterdon Art Center, 1972, Best in Show award Short Hills State Show, 1976, Tri-State Purchase award Somerset Coll., 1977, Art Expo, N.Y.C. 1987, 88; numerous others. Mem. Nat. Assn. Women Artists (chmn. watercolor jury; Collage award 1983), Nat., N.J. artists equity, Nat. Painter and Sculptors Assn., Hunterdon Art Center. Home: 22 Powell Dr West Orange NJ 07052 Office: Art Forms Red Bank NJ Zenith Galleries 4137th NW Washington DC Other: CS Schulte Gallery Broadway NY 10021

SCHREIBER, MAXINE ELLEN, psychotherapist; b. Newark, Mar. 14, 1945; d. Herman Joseph and Anne (Kraemer) S. BA, Newark State Coll., 1969; MEd, Lesley Coll., 1977. Lic. mental health counselor, Fla. Alcoholism coord. Cambridge (Mass.) Hosp., 1974-76, milieu therapist, 1976; coord. alcoholism Harvard Community Health Plan, Boston, 1977-80, project coord. Research Dept., 1980-81; therapist outpatient The Women's Alcoholism Program, Cambridge, 1981-83; dir. program Palm Beach Retreat of Comprehensive Alcoholism Rehab. Prog., West Palm Beach, Fla., 1983-84; therapist The Ctr. for Family Svcs., West Palm Beach, 1985-87, clin. dir., 1987-89; pvt. practice psychotherapy West Palm Beach, 1989—; mem. part-time faculty Lesley Coll., Cambridge, 1977. Active in Palm Beach County Dem. campaign, 1988; bd. dirs. Big Bros./Big Sisters of Palm Beach County, 1989—. Mem. Am. Assn. Counseling and Human Devel., Am. Mental Health Counselors Assn., Mental Health Assn. Palm Beach County. Office: 4623 Forest Hill Blvd Ste 109-1 West Palm Beach FL 33415

SCHREIBER, SELMA EMDIN, office products company owner; b. Bklyn., Aug. 9, 1918; d. Jacob and Mary (Lickumovitz) Emdin; m. Sol J. Schreiber, Sept. 10, 1939; children: Gloria Chekanow, Marjorie Karvonen, Roberta Morrison. BA, Bklyn. Coll., 1941. Co-owner Gables Stationers, Coral Gables, Fla., 1952-80; owner Barnett Office Supply, Miami, Fla., 1980—. Mem. Group Against Smokers Pollution, Miami, 1979—. Mem. Am. Soc. Technion (life), NOW, Women's Am. Organ. for Rehabilitive Tng. (pres. 1976-80), Mental Health Assn. Dade County, Assn. Retarded Persons Dade County, Nat. Office Products Assn., Bklyn. Coll. Alumni Assn. (life), B'nai B'rith Women, Hadassah (life). Democrat. Jewish. Home: 7001 SW 77th Pl Miami FL 33143

SCHREINER, BEVERLY ETHEL, medical transcriptionist; b. Spokane, Wash., Dec. 7, 1931; d. Charlie P. and M. Jerrine (Cannon) Nolasco; m. George J. Schreiner, Feb. 4, 1951 (div. Feb. 1961); children: Michael, David, Judy. Student, Franklin Hosp. Sch. Nursing, 1951, San Francisco City Coll., 1953, Am. Inst. Banking, San Francisco. Certified med. transcriptionist. Sec. Darrell Kammer, M.D., Nampa, Idaho, 1967-73; supr. med. records Idaho State Sch. and Hosp., Nampa, 1966-75; pvt. med. transcriptionist, Nampa, 1984—; med. transcriptionist Caldwell Internal Medicine, Idaho, 1976—; supr. evening shift med. records office Mercy Med. Ctr., Nampa, 1967-87. Mem. Nat. Assn. Med. Transcriptionists, Idaho Assn. Med. Transcriptionists. Avocations: reading, sewing, crafts. Home: 102 W Willowbrook Dr Meridian ID 83642 Other: Caldwell Internal Medicine 222 E Elm St Caldwell ID 83605

SCHREINER, JOAN MAU, accountant; b. Appleton, Wis., July 12, 1944; d. John F. and Agnes M. (Hartzheim) Mau; m. Edwin A. Schreiner, June 17, 1967; children: Teri Lee, Douglas Edwin, Catherine Anne. BBA, U. Wis., Madison, 1966, MS, 1968. CPA, N.Y. Staff acct. Price Waterhouse & Co., Milw., 1968-69; sr. tax acct. Price Waterhouse & Co., Seattle, 1969-72; pvt. practice acct. Rochester, N.Y., 1973-80; tax analyst GTE Corp., Stamford, Conn., 1981-83; tax mgr. U.S. Tobacco Co., Greenwich, Conn., 1983-84; dir. tax acctg. UST Inc., Greenwich, 1984—. Mem. AICPA, Tax Execs. Inst. Home: 529 Nod Hill Rd Wilton CT 06897 Office: UST Inc 100 W Putnam Ave Greenwich CT 06830

SCHRERO, RUTH LIEBERMAN, artist; b. N.Y.; m. Elliot Mitchell. bd. dir. N.Y. Soc. of Women Artists. Commissioned portrait bust of the Hon. Edward Weinfeld, NYU Law Sch., 1977. Recipient Bronze Works award CLWAC, Anna Hyatt Huntington Bronze Medal for Sculpture, 1984, Catharine Lorillard Wolfe award, 1972, Bronze Medal for Sculpture, 1989.

SCHREYER, NANCY KRAFT, medical science researcher; b. Chelsea, Mass., Apr. 18, 1952; d. Meyer Louis and Eileen Marguerite (McCauley) Kraft; m. Raymond Scott Schreyer, Aug. 22, 1976; children: Kraftin Ellice, Evan Kraft. BS, Simmons Coll., 1974; PhD, Hahnemann Med. Coll., 1979. Instr. Hahnemann Med. Coll., Coll. Allied Health Professions, Phila., 1977-79, sr. instr., 1979-80; asst. instr. Hahnemann Med. Coll., Phila., 1977-79, instr., 1979-80, sr. instr., 1980-81; asst. prof. Hahnemann U., Sch. Allied Health Professions, Phila., 1980-88, Hahnemann U. Sch. Medicine, Phila., 1981-88, Hahnemann U. Grad. Sch., Phila., 1983—; non-affiliated mem. Instl. Animal Care and Use Com., E.R. Squibb & Sons, Princeton, N.J., 1988—. Contbr. articles to profl. jours. Recipient rsch. grants, Am. Heart Assn., Phila., 1986, Hahnemann U., 1983. Mem. Am. Soc. Hypertension, N.Y. Acad. Scis., Am. Soc. Primatologists, Physiol. Soc. Phila., Am. Assn. Lab. Animal Sci.

SCHREYER-THOMSON, CAMELLA JOY, artist, editor, corporate executive; b. Lawrence, Kans., July 17, 1949; d. George Maurice and Camella Inez (Burnette) Schreyer; BA cum laude, Pfeiffer Coll., 1971; MA, East Carolina U., 1974; research studies Europe and Gt. Britain; m. Douglas Arthur Thomson, May 6, 1973. One-woman shows: Allas Art Galleries, Charlotte, N.C., 1971, Pfeiffer Coll. Gallery, 1975, 79; group shows include: Durham (N.C.) Art Guild, Fayetteville (N.C.) Mus. Art, Shooren's, Rockport, Mass., East Carolina U.; represented in permanent collection Pfeiffer Coll., also pvt. collections; editor-in-chief Am. Biog. Inst., Raleigh, N.C., 1973—; class agt. Pfeiffer Coll. Alumni Assn., 1976—. Mem. citizens adv. council Am. Inst. Cancer Research. Cert. tchr. kindergarten through 9th grades, N.C. Mem. Am. Fedn. Arts, Nat. League Am. Pen Women, Stanly County Art Guild, Durham Arts Council, Nat. Wildlife Assn., Raleigh C. of C., Raleigh Bus. and Profl. Women, Soc. Suisse de Phaleristique (hon.), Order Sundial, Phi Delta Sigma. Methodist. Contbr. poems to lit. jours.; art editor The Phoenix of Pfeiffer Coll., also various annuals. Address: 5436 Pine Top Circle Raleigh NC 27612

SCHRICKER, JOANIE MARIE, financial management professional; b. Frederick, Md., July 17, 1962; d. Robert Lee and Helen Marie (Harwood) S. BA, Va. Intermont Coll., 1983. Mktg. rep. Health Physics Svcs., Rockville, Md., 1986-89; devel. staff Gettysburg (Pa.) Area Health Care, 1989-90; fin. mgr. Dr. Cleveland Null, DDS, Gettysburg, 1990—. Mem. NAFE. Home: 349 Buchanan Valley Rd Orrtanna PA 17353

SCHRIFT, SHIRLEY See WINTERS, SHELLEY

SCHROCK, ROSALIND, small business owner; b. Toowoomba, Queensland, Australia, May 26, 1937; d. Francis Smedley-Seagrave and Evelyn Mary (Stewart) MacFarlane; m. Lyle Eugene Schrock, Dec. 20, 1975. Diploma, Nat. Inst. Dramatic Art, U. New South Wales, Australia, 1962; ATCL in Speech, Trinity Coll., London/Brisbane, Queensland, Australia, 1955; postgrad. in directing, Barat Coll., Lake Forest, Ill., 1983-84, Lake Forest Coll. Profl. actress, radio, TV, theatre various theatre companies, radio and TV programs, New Zealand and Australia, 1959-71; internat beauty cons. Dorothy Gray Skin Care House, Sydney, Australia, 1971-73, Coty Cosmetics, New Zealand, 1973-75; ptnr. Radiant Attractions Enterprises, Lake Forest, 1984—; owner English Garden Enterprises, Lake Forest, 1986—. Organizing mem. Touchstone Theatre, Lake Forest, 1985—; mem. Chicago Botanic Garden, Glencoe, Ill., 1977—, Jr. Garden Club of Lake Forest, 1986—. Republican.

SCHROEDEL, HUBERTA GOWEN WOLF, non-profit foundation administrator; b. Phila., Oct. 8, 1943; d. Richard O'Shea and Huberta Horan (Gowen) Wolf; m. Serafettin Ugur; 1 child, Kemal. BS in Sociology, Daemen Coll., 1967; MS in Counseling, U. Ariz., 1969. Lic. notary pub.; cert. infant massage educator. Rehab. counselor Fountain House, Inc., Rockland State Hosp., N.Y.C., 1969-72; tchr. of the deaf N.Y.C. Bd. of Edn., Hearing Edn. Svcs., 1974—; exec. dir. N.Y. Ctr. for Law and the Deaf, N.Y.C., 1980—; cons. St. Joseph Sch. for the Deaf, Bronx, N.Y., 1978-82; mem. nat. adv. com. The Captions Ctr., 1987—. Exec. producer TV video series, New York Connection, 1987—. Chairperson N.Y. Deaf Women, 1981; adv. bd. N.Y.C. Mayor's Office for Handicapped, 1984—. Recipient Durfee award for enhancing human dignity Durfee Found., 1987. Mem. Nat. Assn. Female Execs., Lexington Mental Health Ctr. for the Deaf (adv. bd.). Democrat. Roman Catholic. Office: NY Ctr for Law and the Deaf 275 Seventh Ave New York NY 10001

SCHROEDER, BETTY LOUISE, bookkeeper; b. Aldrich, Mo., Apr. 20, 1937; d. Raymond Fenton and Josie Margaret (Redman) Slagle; m. Earl Freddie Schroeder, Mar. 8, 1958 (div. 1981); children—Kathryn, David, Robert. Student pub. schs., Pleasant Hope, Mo. Head sec. Jackson Extension Ctr., Independence, Mo., 1964; typist MWM Colorpress, Aurora, Mo., 1965; income tax preparer, H&R Block, Aurora, 1969-77, preparer, owner, 1977-83, preparer, owner, West Plains, Mo., 1984—. Fund raiser Houn Dawg Band, Aurora, 1975-85. Baptist. Avocation: handcrafts. Office: H&R Block-Schroeder Bookkeeping 1406 Kentucky St West Plains MO 65775

SCHROEDER, CAROLE GIBSON, computer company executive; b. Bloomington, Ind., Mar. 20, 1943; d. Melburne Evert and Neva Mae (Bechtel) G.; m. Richard D. White, Aug. 31, 1962 (div. 1972); 1 child, Kenneth Donald; m. Charles R. Schroeder, Apr. 7, 1973 (div. 1983). BS in Pharmacy, Wayne State U., 1972; postgrad., Va. Commonwealth U., 1980-83. Registered pharmacist, Mich. Va. Staff pharmacist St. Joseph Hosp., Pontiac, Mich., 1972-73; dir. pharmacy St. Mary Hosp., Livonia, Mich., 1974-76; resident Detroit Receiving Hosp., 1977-78; clin. faculty pharmacy Med. Coll. of Va., Richmond, 1978-83; dir. pharmacy ops. Med. Coll. Va. Hosps., Richmond, 1978-83; mktg. mgr. TDS Healthcare Systems Corp., Atlanta, 1983-86; sr. cons. Gerber Alley, Norcross, Ga., 1986; dir. product mgmt. Baxter Healthcare Systems, Reston, Va., 1986-89; program dir. Integrated Systems Tech. Inc., Reston, 1989—. Mem. Am. Soc. of Hosp. Pharmacists, Am. Pharm. Assn., Rho Chi.

SCHROEDER, CYNTHIA R., controller; b. Wichita, Kans., May 27, 1949; d. Charles R. and Marjorie M. (Scott) Crawley; m. Steve Schroeder, Nov. 14, 1987; children: Jennifer, Amie. Student, Wichita State U. Chief exec. officer Farmstead, Inc., Wichita; owner, operator Exec. Extension, Inc., Wichita; controller, officer Master Innovations, Inc., Wichita. Mem. NAFE, Wichita Ski Club. Home: 914 S Holyoke Wichita KS 67218

SCHROEDER, DANA J., health facility administrator; b. Urbana, Ill., Sept. 8, 1956; d. Ralph Richard and Thelma Sharon (Romine) Crowder; m. Howard F. Cue, Mar. 21, 1976 (div. 1979); m. Theodore L. Schroeder, Aug. 29, 1981; children: Timothy Edward, Allison Leigh. AA, Onlone Coll., 1976, AA in Nursing, 1978; BS in Nursing, San Jose State U., 1983; postgrad., U. San Francisco. R.N., Calif. Staff nurse, then charge nurse San Jose (Calif.) Health Ctr., 1978-79, Kaiser Hayward, Calif., 1979-82; relief charge nurse, then relief house supr. Santa Teresa Hosp., San Jose, 1982-87; mgr. recovery area Sereno Surgery Ctr., Los Gatos, Calif., 1987—; owner, adminstr. Argus Residential Care for Elderly, San Jose, 1988—. Vol., Beyond War, San Jose, 1988. Mem. Am. Nurses Assn. Democrat. Mormon. Office: Argus Residential Care 5307 Meridian Ave San Jose CA 95119

SCHROEDER, DEBORAH M., English educator; b. Oak Park, Ill., Apr. 29, 1952; d. Abraham Moglin and Madeline Anna (Ungari) Felsten; m. William Francis Schroeder, July 15, 1973 (div. Dec. 1980). BA, U. Ill., 1972. Tchr. Harlan High Sch., Chgo. Bd. Edn., 1972—, chairperson English dept., 1989—. Office: Harlan High Sch 9652 S Michigan Ave Chicago IL 60628

SCHROEDER, KAREN RUTH, publisher; b. Albany, N.Y., June 28, 1946; d. Kenneth Rockwell Gordon and Ruth Eleanor (Fleahman) Kirk; m. Gary Alan Schroeder; children: Scott, Mark, Michael, Kevin. BS, Ithaca Coll., 1967; MS, SUNY, 1969. Cert. elem. tchr. Music tchr. N.Y. State Sch., Rochester, 1967-72; dir. basic texts Prentice-Hall Appleton Century Crofts, N.Y.C., 1972-80; editor in chief F.A. Davis Med. Pub., Phila., 1980-81; assoc. pub. CBS Dryden Press, Hinsdale, Ill., 1981-83; v.p. Schroeder Assoc., Clearwater, Fla., 1983-. Trustee, pres., bd. dirs. YWCA Greater Clearwater, 1986-89, mem. Tribute to Women of Pinellas County com., 1988—; mem. lower sch. com., St. Paul's Sch., 1988—. Mem. Tiger Bay Club. Democrat. Episcopalian. Home and Office: 3120 Masters Dr Clearwater FL 34621

SCHROEDER, MARY ESTHER, wood products executive; b. Dayton, Ohio, July 29, 1947; d. James Walter and Mary Agnes (Danzig) McIver; m. Reinhard Schroeder, Sept. 10, 1966 (div. Mar. 1989). BS in Forest Industries Mgmt., Ohio State U., 1978. Fiber supply supr. Crown Zellerbach, Inc., Port Townsend, Wash., 1978-83; fiber supply and transp. mgr. Port Townsend Paper Corp., Bainbridge Island, Wash., 1983-87; dir. Pacific Wood Fuels, Redding, Calif., 1987-90; fuel mgr. Wheelabrator Shasta Energy, Anderson, CA, 1990—; bd. dirs. Peninsula Devel. Assn., Port Angeles, Wash., 1985—. Screenwriter: As the Chips Fall, 1988. Precinct committeeman Kitsap County Reps., Poulsbo, Wash., 1984-86; active Rep. Presdl. Task Force. Mem. Soc. Am. Foresters, Shasta Alliance for Resources and Environment, Am. Pulpwood Assn., Timber Assn. Calif., Writers' Forum, Am. Film Inst. Home: 2710 Summerbreeze Pl Redding CA 96001 Office: Wheelabrator Shasta Energy 20811 Industry Rd Anderson CA 96007

SCHROEDER, MARY MURPHY, federal judge; b. Boulder, Colo., Dec. 4, 1940; d. Richard and Theresa (Kahn) Murphy; m. Milton R. Schroeder, Oct. 15, 1965; children: Caroline Theresa, Katherine Emily. B.A., Swarthmore Coll., 1962; J.D., U. Chgo., 1965. Bar: Ill. 1966, D.C. 1966, Ariz. 1970. Trial atty. Dept. Justice, Washington, 1965-69; law clk. Hon. Jesse Udall, Ariz. Supreme Ct., 1970; mem. firm Lewis and Roca, Phoenix, 1971-75; judge Ariz. Ct. Appeals, Phoenix, 1975-79, U.S. Ct. Appeals (9th Cir.), Phoenix, 1979—; vis. instr. Ariz. State U. Coll. Law, 1976, 77, 78. Contbr. articles to profl. jours. Mem. Am. Bar Assn., Ariz. Bar Assn., Fed. Bar Assn., Am. Law Inst., Am. Judicature Soc. Democrat. Club: Soroptimists. Office: US Ct Appeals 9th Cir 6421 Courthouse & Fed Bldg 230 N 1st Ave Phoenix AZ 85025

SCHROEDER, PATRICIA, nursing consultant; b. Milw., Oct. 6, 1953; m. Steven Ruhig, 1980; 1 child, Amy Ruhig. BS in Nursing, Marquette U., 1975, MS in Nursing, 1978. RN, Wis. Staff nurse Milw., 1975-78; clin. nurse specialist St. Luke's Hosp., Milw., 1978-79, St. Michael Hosp., Milw., 1979-84; quality assurance coord. St. Michael's Hosp., 1984-86, nursing quality assurance coord./rsch. facilitator, 1986-88; pres. Quality Care Concepts, Inc., Thiensville, Wis., 1986—; jour. editor Aspen Pubs., Inc., Rockville, Md., 1985—; cons. on nursing nationwide, mem. editorial bd. of quality progress Am. Soc. of Quality Control, editorial bd. several nursing publs. Co-editor, co-author: Nursing Quality Assurance, 1984, Commitment to Excellence, 1988; editor, co-author: 3 vol. Encyclopedia of Nursing Quality Assurance, 1990; editor: Journal of Nursing Quality Assurance, 1985—; lectr. in field. Recipient feature article award, Sigma Theta Tau, 1988; named Outstanding Nurse Scholar, Sigma Theta Tau-Delta Gamma chpt., Milw., 1988; namesake for Patricia Schroeder Award for Excellence, Resource Applications, Hanover, Md., 1989—. Mem. Am. Nurses Assn., Am. Soc. for Quality Control, Sigma Theta Tau. Home: 524 BelAire Dr Thiensville WI 53092

SCHROEDER, PATRICIA ELAINE, banker; b. Manhasset, N.Y., July 2, 1954; d. William Rowe and Louise Virginia (Prem) Collins; m. Michael George Schroeder. BA in Psychology, Geneseo State U., 1976, BA in Sociology. Social worker Lighthouse for the Blind, Lake Worth, Fla., 1976-78; teller to asst. mgr. First Am. Bank and Trust, Palm Beach Gardens, Fla., 1981-83; br. mgr. Glendale Fed. Bank, North Palm Beach, Fla., 1983—. Bd. dirs., cons. Jr. Achievement Palm Beach, 1988; bd. dirs. Pvt. Inidustry Coun., West Palm Beach; mem. Palm Beach County Commn. on Status of Women. Mem. Palm Beach C. of C. (chmn. edn. com.), Nat. Women's Bus. Network (pres. Palm Beach Gardens 1989—). Office: Glendale Fed Bank 800 US Highway One North Palm Beach FL 33408

SCHROEDER, PATRICIA SCOTT (MRS. JAMES WHITE SCHROEDER), congresswoman; b. Portland, Oreg., July 30, 1940; d. Lee Combs and Bernice (Lemoin) Scott; m. James White Schroeder, Aug. 18, 1962; children: Scott William, Jamie Christine. B.A. magna cum laude, U. Minn., 1961; J.D., Harvard U., 1964. Bar: Colo. 1964. Field atty. NLRB, Denver, 1964-66; practiced in Denver, 1966-72; hearing officer Colo. Dept. Personnel, 1971-72; mem. faculty U. Colo., 1969-72, Community Coll., Denver, 1969-70, Regis Coll., Denver, 1970-72; mem. 93d-102nd Congresses from 1st Colo. dist., 1973—; co-chmn. Congl. Caucus for Women's Issues, 1976—; mem. Ho. of Reps. armed services com., chair subcom. mil. installations and facilities, judiciary com., post office and civil service com.; mem. select com. on children, youth and families. Congregationalist. Office: 2208 Rayburn House Office Bldg Washington DC 20515

SCHROEDER, RITA MOLTHEN, chiropractor; b. Savanna, Ill., Oct. 25, 1922; d. Frank J. and Ruth J. (McKenzie) Molthen; m. Richard H. Schroeder, Apr. 23, 1948 (div.); children—Richard, Andrew, Barbara, Thomas, Paul, Madeline. Student, Chem. Engring., Immaculate Heart Coll., 1940-41, UCLA, 1941, Palmer Sch. of Chiropractic, 1947-49; D. Chiropractic, Cleve. Coll. of Chiropractic, 1961. Engring.-tooling design data coordinator Douglas Aircraft Co., El Segundo, Santa Monica and Long Beach, Calif., 1941-47; pres. Schroeder Chiropractic, Inc., 1982—; dir. Pacific States Chiropractic Coll., 1978-80, pres. 1980-81. Recipient Palmer Coll. Ambassador award, 1973. Parker Chiropractic Research Found. Ambassador award, 1976, Coll. Ambassador award Life West Chiropractic Coll. Mem. Internat. Chiropractic Assn., Calif. Chiropractic Assn., Internat. Chiropractic Assn. Calif., Assn. Am. Chiropractic Coll. Presidents, Council Chiropractic Edn. (Pacific State Coll. rep.), Am. Pub. Health Assn., Royal Chiropractic Knights of the Round Table. Home: 9870 N Millbrook Ave Fresno CA 93710 Office: Schroeder Chiropractic Inc 2535 N Fresno Ave Fresno CA 93703

SCHROEDER, TERRI LEA, consulting firm executive; b. Elgin, Ill. Mar. 11, 1955; d. Earl and Caroline Louise Christensen. Student William Rainey Harper Coll., summers, 1973-77; BS in Edn., No. Ill. U., 1977, MPA, 1979; postgrad. Triton Coll., River Forest, Ill., William Rainey Harper Coll., Palatine, Ill. Lic. pub. water supply operator Ill. EPA Class C; cert. water treatment plant operator Iowa Dept. Environ. Quality Grade I. Tchr., English, Sch. Dist. 202, Plainfield, Ill., 1977-78; adminstrv. asst. to village mgr. Village of Deerfield (Ill.), 1978-79; asst. village mgr. Village of Lincolnshire (Ill.), 1979-81, village mgr., 1981-82; city mgr. City of Iowa Falls (Iowa), 1982-88; pres., chief exec. officer Lighthouse Assocs., Ackley, Iowa, 1988—; bd. dirs. Iowa River Greenbelt Trust; cons. exec. dir. Lake County Youth Svc. Bur., Lake Villa, Ill., 1979-80, Iowa Natural Heritage Found.; communications and pub. rels. coord. Univ. Health Ctr., DeKalb, Ill., 1977-78; legal asst. Winnebago County Legal Aid, Rockford, Ill., spring 1979. Former trustee, mem. budget com., bd. dirs. Iowa conf. 1st Congl. Ch., Iowa Falls, 1982-87; bd. dirs., mem. leadership com. Com. of 80's Iowa Falls, 1982-88; mem. DeKalb Human Rels. Commn., 1977-79; lobbyist for Student Assn. on Higher Edn. Appropriations, 79th Gen. Assembly, Washington; chairperson for polit. awareness week, DeKalb, 1977; mem. Gov.'s Com. on Future of Econ. Growth of Iowa, 1984; mem. Gov.'s Ptnrship Econ. Progress, 1985-87; mem. Iowa Electric's Indsl. Adv. Panel, 1986; mem. direct dialonge Northwestern Bell Telephone, 1984-86; founder Iowa Falls 2000, 1985, Iowa Falls Area Arts Coun., 1985. Named Iowa's Young Career Woman of 1982-83, Iowa Fedn. Bus. Profl. Women, 1983; named Outstanding Young Working Woman, Glamour Mag., 1984; Esper A. Peterson Found. scholar, 1976-79; Gen. Assembly scholar. Mem. Bus. Profl. Women (Young Career Woman, chmn. dist. IV northwest Iowa 1983-84), Internat. City Mgmt. Assn. (assoc.), Iowa City Mgmt. Assn., North Cen. Iowa City Mgmt. Assn. (founder, exec. bd. dirs.), Am. Econ. Devel. Coun., Iowa Profl. Developers, Iowa Assn. Bus. and Industry Keeper, U.S. Lighthouse Soc., Lighthouse Preservation Soc., Community Devel. Soc. Iowa, Pinelake Wildlife Club, Iowa River Conservation and Improvement Club (bd. dirs.), Rotary (bd. dirs. Ackley chpt.), numerous others. Office: Lighthouse Assocs 907 Sherman Ave Ackley IA 50601-1651

SCHROER, BARBARA CLAIRE, optometry executive; b. Sidney, Mont., Dec. 8, 1958; d. Bernard John and Helen Catherine (Schrader) S. BS, San Diego State U., 1981; grad., Dale Carnegie, 1989. Exec. adminstr. Associated Vision Care, San Diego, 1981—. Chairperson, mem. Soroptimist Internat. of Lemon Grove, Lemon Grove, Calif., 1985—. Mem. NAFE, Am. Mktg. Assn., Lemon Grove C. of C. Republican. Roman Catholic. Home: 6104 DeCena #14 San Diego CA 92120 Office: Associated Vision Care 7860 Golden Ave Lemon Grove CA 92045

SCHROLLER, CHRISTINE MARIE, mortgage consulting company executive; b. Orange, N.J., Aug. 12, 1950; d. Theodore John and Marie Renee (Topolski) Mazur; m. Gary Robert Schroller, July 20, 1974 (dec. Aug. 1980). Student, Bloomfield (N.J.) Coll., 1968-69; basic, standard and Essex County certs., Am. Inst. Banking, Caldwell, N.J., 1975-78. Lic. real estate saleswoman, N.J. Mortgage adminstr. Howard Savs. Bank, Livingston, N.J., 1969-83; asst. v.p. BBS Mortgage Svcs., Inc., Livingston, 1983-85; supr. Salomon Bros., Inc., N.Y.C., 1985-87; asst. v.p. Dean Witter Reynolds, Inc., N.Y.C., 1987-88; pres., owner C.M.S. Mortgage Svcs., Inc., Wyckoff, N.J., 1988—, Petite Feasts, Inc., catering, Wyckoff, 1989—. Mem. Nat. Assn. Realtors, Mortgage Bankers Assn. N.J. (ltd., secondary mortgage markets com. 1989-90), Morris County Bd. Relators, NAFE, N.J. Fedn. Bus. and Profl. Women. Roman Catholic. Home and Office: 100 Edison St Wyckoff NJ 07481

SCHROM, ELIZABETH ANN, educator; b. Princeton, Minn., June 7, 1941; d. Raymond Alois and Grace Eleanor (Hayes) S. Student, U. Minn., 1960; BA, St. Scholastica Coll., Duluth, Minn., 1963; postgrad., Princeton U., 1965; MEd, Temple U., 1972; MLS, Drexel U., 1974; postgrad., New York U., 1981, Russian Temple U., 1983. Tchr. Strandquist High Sch., Strandquist, Minn., 1963-64, Hutchinson High Sch., Hutchinson, Minn., 1964-65, Peace Corps, Ankara, Turkey, 1965-67, Phila. Sch. Dist., 1968-80; children's libr. Laurel (Del.) Pub. Libr., 1983—. Author: (poem) American Haiku, 1962. Mem. Jewish Com. on Middle East, Washington, 1988-89, Nat. Coun. Returned Peace Corps Vols., Washington, 1989-90, Nat. Taxpayers Union, Washington, 1988-90; bd. policy Liberty Lobby, Washington, 1989-90; Emergency Com. Stop Immigration, Marietta, Ga., 1989, English Now, Washington, 1989, Common Cause, Washington, 1989-90. Populist. Roman Catholic. Home: Box 224 Rte 2 Ontonville MN 56278

SCHROPP, MARY LOU, public relations executive; b. Havre-de-Grace, Md., Aug. 13, 1947; d. Howard James and Maude Elizabeth (Parker) S.; 1 child, Matthew Austin. Student, George Washington U., 1965-68. Vice pres. Snyder Assoc., Inc., Washington, 1969-76; pres. Health Communications, Inc., Washington, 1976-80; creative services project mgr. U.S. Catholic Conf., Washington, 1980-81; pres., owner MLS Creative Services, Falls Church, Va., 1981—. Editor: Electronic Media, Popular Culture and Family Values, 1985; Rehabilitation Facilities Sourcebook, 1984, 85; periodicals, textbooks. Exec. producer videotapes, 1982. Coord. World Communications Day, Washington, 1982—; cons. Cath. Communication Campaign, Washington, 1982-84; fund raising cons. Nat. 4-H Coun., Chevy Chase, Md., 1985-86; v.p. devel. Aviation Rsch. and Edn. Found., Herndon, Va., 1985—. Mem. Pub. Relations Soc. Am., Washington Independent Writers, Religious Pub. Rels. Coun. (v.p. local chpt. 1981-82, DeRose-Hinkhouse Communications award 1981, 82, 80), Nat. Soc. Fund Raising Execs. Democrat. Office: MLS Creative Svcs 7711 Trevino Ln Falls Church VA 22043

SCHROTBERGER, GLORIA MAE, school system administrator; b. Long Beach, Calif., May 21, 1929; d. William Hartford Schmidt and Viola Analea (Barcus) Schmidt-Musser; m. Francis Aaron Schrotberger, Feb. 27, 1946; children: Francis Aaron, Marsha, Michael, Richard, Jon. Grad., high sch.; cert. in dietary mgmt., North Platte Vocat.-Tech., 1984. Supr. Bethesda Care Ctr., Sutherland, Nebr., 1975-78; cook, mgr. North Platte (Nebr.) Sr. Ctr., 1978-80; dietary supt. North Platte Pub. Schs., 1980—, also mem. nutrition bd., 1988—; mem. bd. for food and commodities Bd. Edn., Lincoln, Nebr., 1987—. Mem. Nebr. Sch. Food Assn., Nat. Sch. Food Assn., Dietary Mgrs. Assn., Dist. VIII Sch. Food Assn. (pres. 1987-88). Home: 615 S Oak St North Platte NE 69101

SCHROTH, EVELYN MARY, retired language educator; b. Ellington, Wis., Aug. 5, 1919; d. Henry A. and Clara M. (Komp) Schroth. BS, U. Wis., 1940; MS, U. Ill., 1948, AM, 1955; PhD, Pacific Western U., 1979. Tchr. Rhinelander (Wis.) High Sch., 1940-42; chmn. English dept. Waupun (Wis.) High Sch., 1942-44; tchr. Chgo. pub. schs., 1953-63, chmn. dept. English Lindblom High Sch., 1956-62; instr. dept. English U. Ill., Urbana, 1948-50; lectr. Northeastern U., Chgo., 1962-63; assoc. prof., then prof. English, Western Ill. U., Macomb, 1963-87. Program dir. U.S.O., 1946-48. John Hay fellow, 1961. Mem. Linguistic Soc. Am., Nat. Council Tchrs. English, Ill. Tchrs. English, AAUP, Phi Beta, Phi Kappa Phi. Home: 139 Kurlene Dr Macomb IL 61455

SCHRUMPF, ROBYN LYNN, dentist; b. San Francisco, July 15, 1959; d. Walter Fred and Donna De Ella (Rogelstad) S. BS, U. Calif., Davis, 1981; DDS, Creighton U., 1985; cert. gen. practice residency, VA Med. Ctr., Palo Alto, Calif., 1986. With dental staff VA Med. Ctr., Palo Alto, 1985-86; with dental staff VA Med. Ctr., Menlo Park, Calif., 1985-86, respite team cons. dentist, 1986; assoc. Milpitas (Calif.) Dental Ctr., 1987—, Sunnyvale (Calif.) Dental Group, 1987-89; pvt. practice Sunnyvale, 1989—; dentist Macy (Nebr.) Indian Reservation, 1984, Spinal Cord Injury Ctr., Palo Alto, 1985-86, Blind Rehab. Ctr., Palo Alto, 1985-86; instr. preventive dental care Girl Scouts U.S., Sunnyvale, 1987. Regents scholar U. Calif., Davis, 1977-78, Albert Bijou Meml. scholar U. Calif., Davis, 1978-79; Lonney White scholar Creighton U., 1984. Mem. ADA, Am. Soc. Dentistry for Children (pres. Creighton U. chpt. 1982-85, merit award 1985), Calif. Dental Assn., Calif. Soc. Dentistry for Children, Calif. Scholarship Fedn. (pres. 1977), U.S. Gymnastics Fedn., Omicron Kappa Upsilon. Lutheran.

SCHUBERT, HELEN C., public relations executive; b. Washington City, Wis.; d. Paul H. and Edna (Schmidt) S. BS, U. Wis., Madison. Dir. consumer div. Philip Lesly Co., Chgo., 1956-61; pub. relations dir. United Cerebral Palsy, Chgo., 1961; adminstrv. dir. Nat. Design Ctr., Chgo., 1962-67; owner Schubert Pub. Relations, Chgo., 1967—; bd. dirs. Fashion Group, Chgo., 1989-90. Mem. women's bd. Am. Cancer Soc., Chgo., 1988-90, Art Resources in Teaching, Chgo., 1988-90. Recipient Communications award, Am. So. Internat. Designers, Chgo., 1979, 83, 88. Fellow Nat. Home Fashion League; mem. Women's Ad Club of Chgo. (pres. 1981-83, Woman of Yr. award 1987), Women in Communications (pres. 1969-70), Am. Advt. Fedn. (lt. gov. 1983-85). Lutheran. Home: 1360 Lake Shore Dr Chicago IL 60610

SCHUBERT, KATHRYN ILYNE, retail executive; b. Oct. 10, 1941; d. Louis Isaac and Mae Mary (Solomon) Schubert; m. Ron Frith, Sept. 26, 1986 (div. 1988). BA in Psychology, Northwestern U., Evanston, Ill., 1962. Advt. sec. Ogilvy & Mather, N.Y.C., London, 1965; prodn. sec. Channel 11 WTTW, Chgo., 1966, Wilding Studio, Chgo., 1967; film conformer Film Fair, Chgo., 1968-69, Editor's Choice, Chgo., 1970-71; film editor My Sister's Cutting Room, Chgo., 1972—; owner Kangaroo Connection, Australia-New Zealand Gen. Store, Chgo., 1986—; dir. running-walking events promotion various bus., 1980—. Contbr. articles to profl. jours. Mem. Chgo. Women in Film (pres. 1974-75), Chgo. Area Runners Assn. (bd. dirs. 1980-81), Lincoln Park Pacers (ppres. 1986), Evanston Running Club (bd. dirs. 1984). Home: 1113 W Webster Ave Chicago IL 60614 Office: Kangaroo Connection 1113 W Webster Ave Chicago IL 60614

SCHUBERT, LISA LYNN, physical therapist; b. Mendota, Ill., Mar. 2, 1961; d. Stephen Edward and Joan Eleanor (Olson) S. Student, La Crosse, 1979-81; BS, U. Ill., 1983; MHS, U. Indpls., 1989. Staff phys. therapist Phys. Therapy Svcs., Inc., Des Plaines, Ill., 1983-85, Santa Fe (N.Mex.) Phys. Therapy, 1985; ctr. mgr. Baxter Phys. Therapy Div., Austin, Tex., 1985—. Mem. Am. Phys. Therapy Assn. Methodist. Office: Baxter Physical Therapy Div 630 W 34th St #301 Austin TX 78705

SCHUBERT, NANCY ELLEN, service executive, management consultant, franchise director; b. Chgo., June 25, 1945; d. Raymond James and Kathleen Mary (Gibbons) Nugent; m. Emil Joseph Schubert, Jan. 14, 1967; children: James Bryant, Erin Heather, Shannon Kathleen. BFA, Mundelein Coll., 1968. Freelance artist, Chgo., 1968; tchr. St. Pius X Sch., Lombard, Ill., 1975-76; pres., treas., dir. Super Style, Inc., Hoffman Estates, Ill., 1981—, Super Six, Inc., Glendale Heights, Ill., 1983—, N.E.S. Mgmt. Inc., Schaumburg, Ill., 1985—, Super Style III, Inc., Berwyn, Ill., 1985—; created and developed Super Style concept and system of operation; created Super-Style logo and design trademarked in 1983. Mem. Cermak Pla. Mcht. Assn. (pres. 1989, 90—). Republican. Roman Catholic. Avocations: downhill skiing, private pilot. Office: Super Style Inc 707 W Golf Rd Hoffman Estates IL 60194

SCHUBERT, RUTH CAROL HICKOK, artist; b. Janesville, Wis., Dec. 24, 1927; d. Fay Andrew and Mildred Willmette (Street) Hickok; m. Robert Francis Schubert, Oct. 20, 1946; children: Stephen Robert, Michelle Carol. Student DeAnza Coll., 1972-73; AA, Monterey Peninsula Coll., 1974; BA with honors, Calif. State U.-San Jose, 1979. Owner, mgr. Casa De Artes Gallery, Monterey, Calif., 1977-86; dir. Monterey Peninsula Mus. Art Council, 1975-76. One woman show include Aarhof Gallery, Aarau, Switzerland, 1977, Degli Agostiniani Recolletti, Rome, 1977, Wells Fargo Bank, Monterey, 1975, 78, 79, Seaside (Calif.) City Hall Gallery, 1979, 89, Sierra Nev. Mus. Art, Reno, 1980, Bard Hall Gallery, San Diego, 1980, San Diego Nat. Watercolor Show, Mid-West Nat. Watercolor Show, Rahr-West Mus, Manitowoc, Wis., 1980, Rosicrucian Mus., San Jose, 1981, 84, Village Gallery, Lahaina, Hawaii, 1983, 86, 89, Portola Valley Gallery, 1984, 85, Rose Rock Gallery, Carmel, 1984-86, Calif. State Agri-Images, Sacramento, 1984; XVII Watercolor West, Brea Civic Cultural Ctr., 1985, Nat. Pen Women at Marjorie Evans Gallery, Carmel, Calif., 1986, Monterey County Juried Expo, Monterey Peninsula Mus. Art, Monterey, Calif., 1986, 87, Taupo (N.Z.) Arts Soc., 1988, Geyserland Art Mus., Rotorua, N.Z., 1988, Wanganui (N.Z.) Art Soc., 1988, Rogue Gallery, Medford, Oreg., 1989, Hallie Brown Ford Gallery, Roseburg, Oreg., 1991; nat. shows include Internat. Art Show for End of World Hunger, Ashland, Oreg., 1990; represented in permanent collections: Monterey Calif. Peninsula Mus. Art, Nat. Biscuit Co. subs. RJR Nabisco, San Jose, Waikato Mus. Art, Hamilton, N.Z., Muscular Dystrophy Assn., San Francisco, Nanoose Bay, Old Sch. House Mus., Qualicum Bay, Vancouver Island Brit. Columbia, also numerous pvt. collections. Recipient 1st prize Monterey County Fair, 1979, Jade Fon Watercolor award Hall of Flowers, San Francisco, 1980, 1st Nat. Art Show N.Y. Am. Artist mag., 1980 Nat. Art Appreciation, 1984, Norcal State Art Fair, 1985, Watercolor award 25 Ann. Aquedus Media Show, Salem, Oreg., 1990; numerous other awards for watercolor paintings. Mem. Artists Equity Assn., Am. Watercolor Soc. (assoc.), Nat. Watercolor Soc. (assoc.), Soc. Western Artists, Watercolor Soc. Oreg., LaHaina Arts Soc., Rogue Valley Art Gallery, Monterey Peninsula Watercolor Soc., N.W. Watercolor Soc. (assoc.), Arts coun. So. Oreg., Mid-West Watercolor Soc., Cen. Coast Art Assn. (pres. 1977-78), Nat. League Am. Penwomen (pres. 1983-84, 86-87), Art Alumni San Jose State U. Club: Eastern Star (Milw.). Contbr. to profl. publs. Home: 2462 Senate Way Medford OR 97504

SCHUCH, DIANE JEAN, non-profit organization administrator; b. St. Louis, Dec. 28, 1942; d. Bernard and Dora (Shaikewitz) Goldenhersh; m. Phillip Schuch, May 28, 1968 (dec. Sept. 1975); 1 child, Gretchen Nicole. BA, Nat.-Louis U., 1987. Mgr. fund raising Haney Assocs., Concord, Mass., 1971-73; juvenile probation officer Yavapai County Probation Dept., Prescott, Ariz., 1973-75; freelance writer St. Louis, 1982-84; coord. spl. events Temple Shaare Emeth, St. Louis, 1984-85; adminstrv. asst. The Family Ctr. Clayton Sch. Dist., St. Louis, 1985-86; dir. programs and adminstrn. Ethical Soc. St. Louis, 1986—; cons. pub. rels. various orgns., St.

Louis, 1984-86; cons. non-profit organizational devel. various orgns. Mem. strategic planning action com. Spl. Sch. Dist. of St. Louis, 1989—. Recipient Women in Leadership award CORO Found., 1989. Mem. Am. Soc. Tng. and Devel. (position referral com.), Gateway Assn. Ch. and Synagogue Adminstrs., Assn. Children and Adults with Learning Disabilities (adv. com.). Democrat. Jewish. Office: Ethical Soc St Louis 9001 Clayton Rd Saint Louis MO 63117

SCHUCK, VICTORIA, political science educator; b. Oklahoma City, Mar. 16, 1909; d. Anthony B. and Anna (Priebe) S. A.B. with great distinction, Stanford U., 1930, M.A., 1931, Ph.D., 1937; L.H.D. (hon.), Mt. Vernon Coll., 1980. Univ. fellow Stanford U., 1931-33, teaching asst., 1934-35, acting instr., 1935-36, instr., 1936-37; asst. prof. Fla. State Coll. Women, 1937-40; mem. faculty Mt. Holyoke Coll., 1940-77, prof. polit. sci., 1950-77; pres. Mt. Vernon Coll., Washington, 1977-80, ret.; vis. lectr. Smith Coll., 1948-49; vis. prof. Stanford U., summer 1952, vis. scholar polit. sci., 1982—; guest scholar Brookings Instn., 1967-68, summers 68, 70, Woodrow Wilson Ctr. Internat. Scholars, 1980; Prin. program analyst, planning for local bds. OPA, 1942-44; rep. Am. Polit. Sci. Assn. UN World Conf. of UN Decade for Women, Nairobi, Kenya, 1985; sponsor Women's Fgn. Policy Council, N.Y., 1986; cons. Office Temporary Controls, 1945-47; mem. internat. secretariat UN Conf. San Francisco, 1945; mem. Mass. Commn. Interstate Coop., 1957-60, U. Mass. Bldg. Authority, 1960-68; Mass. adv. com. U.S. Commn. Civil Rights, 1962-78; cons. GAO, 1980-82; non-govtl. rep. UN Commn. on Status of Women, Vienna, Austria, 1988. Regional editor: Ency. Brit., 1958-61; co-editor and contbr.: Women Organizing: An Anthology, 1979, New England Politics, 1981; contbr. articles to profl. jours. Mem. Pres.'s Commn. Registration and Voting Participation, 1963; mem. Berkshire Community Coll. Planning Com., 1964-68, Greenfield Community Coll. Planning Com., 1965-68, Mass. Bd. Higher Edn., 1976-77; mem. Town of South Hadley Planning Bd., 1959-67, chmn., 1961-67; trustee U. Mass., 1958-65. Grantee Haynes Found., 1951-52; Grantee Asia Soc., 1971-72. Mem. Am. Polit. Sci. Assn. (sec. 1959-60, v.p. 1970-71), New Eng. Polit. Sci. Assn. (pres. 1950-51), Northeastern Polit. Sci. Assn. (pres. 1972-73), AAUW (pres. Mass. 1946-50, nat. chmn. legis. prog. com., bd. dirs. 1965-69), Am. Soc. Pub. Adminstrn., AAUP (pres. Mt. Holyoke 1962-64), Internat. Polit. Sci. Assn., Acad. Coun. on UN System, Supreme Ct. Hist. Soc., Mortar Bd. (hon.), Phi Beta Kappa, Chi Omega. Club: Cosmopolitan (N.Y.C.), Cosmos (Washington). Home: 4000 Cathedral Ave NW Washington DC 20016

SCHUCKMAN, NANCY LEE, educational adminstrator; b. Bklyn., June 3, 1939; d. Abraham Benjamin and Sophie (Kalefsky) S. B.A., Bklyn. Coll., 1961, M.S., 1964, postgrad., 1965-69; postgrad. Hofstra U., 1970-72, Columbia U., 1979-80. Tchr. N.Y.C. Bd. Edn., 1961-69, adminstr., Bklyn., 1969-77, prin., 1977—; ednl. journalist East New Yorker, East N.Y. Devel. Corp., Bklyn., 1974-76, Starrett City Sun, Bklyn., 1975-76; co-owner Lanah Ednl. Toys, Bklyn., 1975-76. Mem. Thomas Jefferson Democratic Club, Bklyn., 1978—, Kings County Democratic. Com., 1981-87; polit. campaign coordinator John F. Kennedy Democratic Club, Bklyn., 1974-76; mem. exec. bd. John F. Kennedy Democratic Club, Bklyn., 1974-75. Mem. Council Suprs. and Adminstrs. (conv. registration chmn.), Adminstrv. Women in Edn., Am. Assn. Sch. Adminstrs., N.Y.C. Elementary Prins. Assn. (exec. bd. 1984—), Bklyn. Reading Council. Democrat. Jewish. Avocations: edn. law; journalism; oil painting; photography; traveling; sports. Office: PS 202 982 Hegeman Ave Brooklyn NY 11208

SCHUESSLER, MARY ANN PETERY, executive recruiter; b. Portland, Oreg., June 1, 1936; d. Walter Henry and Ida May (Harzell) Bauer; children: Melinda, Lorri. Degree in mgmt., Harvard U., 1977. With Selma Pressure Treating Co., Calif., 1965—; sec./treas. Selma Leasing Co., 1971-77; pres. Selma Leasing Co., Calif., 1978-85; recruiter exec. ITT Employer Services, West Los Angeles, 1985-86; pres. Drake & Assocs., Beverly Hills, Calif., 1986—; cons. SBA; mem. adv. council to chancellor forest products dept. U. Calif.; mem. adv. council Sch. Bus., Calif. State U., Fresno; del. White House Conf. Small Bus.,; del 1980 White House Conf. om Small Bus. Mem. Town Hall, Los Angeles, 1986, Friends Hollywood Bowl, Los Angeles, 1988. Mem. Am. Wood Preservers Assn., Harvard Bus. Sch. Assn., Better Bus. Bur. (dir.), Fresno County Hist. Soc., DAR, Fresno Geaneal. Soc., Am. His. Soc. Germans from Russia, New Eng. Geaneal. Soc. Office: Drake & Assocs 9454 Wilshire Blvd Ste 650 Beverly Hills CA 90212

SCHUESSLER, SUZANNE WRIGHT, pediatrician; b. Dayton, Ohio, Dec. 25, 1959; d. John Major and Suzanne (Ussery) S. BS, Samford U., 1981; MD, U. Ala., 1985. Intern The Children's Hosp., Birmingham, Ala., 1985-86, resident, 1986-88; pediatrician The Children's Clinic, P.A., La Grange, Ga., 1988—; mem. bd. Troup County Coun. on Child Abuse, La Grange, 1988-89. Fellow Am. Acad. Pediatrics; mem. AMA, Med. Assn. Ga., Troup County Med. Assn., Phi Kappa Phi. Republican. Episcopalian. Home: 110 Waverly Way La Grange GA 30240 Office: The Childrens Clinic PA 606 S Greenwood St La Grange GA 30240

SCHUESSLER FIORENZA, ELISABETH, theology educator; b. Tschanad, Romania, Apr. 17, 1938; came to U.S., 1970; d. Peter and Magdalena Schuessler; m. Francis Fiorenza, Dec. 17, 1967; 1 child, Christina. MDiv., U. Wuerzburg, Federal Republic of Germany, 1962; ThD, U. Muenster, Federal Republic of Germany, 1970; Lic.Theol, U. Wuerzburg, 1963. Asst. prof. theology U. Notre Dame, South Bend, Ind., 1970-75, assoc. prof., 1975-80, prof., 1980-84; instr. U. Muenster, 1966-67; Talbot prof. New Testament Episcopal Div. Sch., Cambridge, Mass., 1984-88; Krister Stendahl prof. div. in New Testament studies Harvard U., Cambridge, Mass., 1988—; Harry Emerson Fosdick vis. prof. Union Theol. Sem., N.Y.C., 1974-75; guest prof. U. Tuebingen, Federal Republic of Germany, 1987. Author: Der Vergessene Partner, 1964, Priester für Gott, 1972, The Apocalypse, 1976, Invitation to the Book of Revelation, 1981, In Memory of Her, 1983, Bread not Stone, 1984, Judgement of Justice, 1985; founding editor Jour. Feminist Studies in Religion; also editor other works. Mem. Am. Acad. Religion, Soc. Bibl. Lit. (past pres.). Office: Harvard Div Sch 45 Francis St Cambridge MA 02138

SCHUK, LINDA LEE, legal assistant; b. Scott Field, Ill., July 19, 1946; d. Frank A. Schuk and Jessie (Bumpass) Stearns; divorced; 1 child, Earl Wade. BBA, U. Tex., El Paso, 1968. Lic. life and health ins. agt., Tex. Acct., traffic mgr. Farah Mfg. Co., El Paso, 1970-71; adminstrv. asst. Horizon Corp., El Paso, 1971-76; adminstrv. asst. in charge office ops. Foster-Scwartz Devel. Corp., El Paso, 1976-78; legal sec. Howell and Fields, El Paso, 1978-80; supr. Southland Corp., San Antonio, Waco, ElPaso, 1980-83; sales mgr. Southland Corp., San Antonio, 1983-84, dist. mgr., 1984-87; dist. supr. E-Z Mart Conveniance Stores, San Antonio, 1987-89; legal asst. Watkins & Brock, San Antonio, 1989—; instr. San Antonio Community Coll., 1989—. Mem. NAFE. Democrat. Baptist. Home: 5822 Burkely Springs San Antonio TX 78233 Office: Watkins & Brock 803 E Mistletoe San Antonio TX 78212

SCHUK, ROSALIND, small business owner; b. Ellenville, N.Y., Jan. 5, 1949; d. Max and Edith (Rubnitz) Blut; married; 1 child, Dawn. Mgr., buyer Sample Nook Stores, Blkyn., 1968-73; owner Quality and Prestige, Rockville Ctr., N.Y., 1977—; cons. fashion, displays, merchandiser Conspiquous, Rockville Ctr., 1977—. Bd. dirs. City of Long Beach Disasters Com., 1987—, bd. dirs. City of Long Beach St. Fund rebuild com. 1983-85, beautify com. 1983-85. Mem. Nat. Edwards Mchts. Assn. (pres. 1982-86). Democrat. Jewish. Office: Conspicuous 313 Sunrise Hwy Rockville Centre NY 11570

SCHULER, ALISON KAY, lawyer; b. West Point, N.Y., Oct. 1, 1948; d. Richard Hamilton and Irma (Sanken) S.; m. Lyman Gage Sandy, Mar. 30, 1974; 1 child, Theodore. AB cum laude, Radcliffe Coll., 1969; JD Harvard U., 1972. Bar: Va. 1973, D.C. 1974, N.Mex. 1975. Assoc. Hunton & Williams, Richmond, Va., 1972-75; asst. U.S. atty. U.S. Atty's. Office, Albuquerque, 1975-78; adj. prof. law U. N.Mex., 1983-85, 90; ptnr. Sutin, Thayer & Browne, Albuquerque, 1978-85, Montgomery & Andrews, P.A., Albuquerque, 1985-88; sole practice, Albuquerque, 1988—. Bd. dirs. Am. Diabetes Assn., Albuquerque, 1980-85, chmn. bd. dirs., 1984-85; bd. dirs. June Music Festival, 1980—, pres., 1983-85; bd. dirs. Albuquerque Conservation Trust, 1986—; chairperson Albuquerque Com. Fgn. Rels., 1984-85; mem. N.Mex. Internat. Trade and Investment Coun., Inc., 1986—. Mem. Fed. Bar Assn. (coord.), ABA, Va. Bar Assn., N.Mex. State Bar Assn. (chmn. corp., banking and bus. law 1982-83, bd. dirs. internat. and immigration law sect. 1987—), Harvard U. Alumni Assn. (mem. fund campaign, regional dir. 1984-86, v.p. 1986, chmn. clubs com. 1985-88, chmn. communications com. 1988—), Radcliffe Coll. Alumnae Assn. Bd. Mgmt. (regional dir. 1984—, chmn. communications com. 1988—), Harvard-Radcliffe Club (pres. 1980-84). Home: 632 Cougar Loop NE Albuquerque NM 87122 Office: 5700 Harper NE Ste 430 Albuquerque NM 87109

SCHULER, CARLA EGLY, psychologist; b. Ft. Wayne, Ind., May 26, 1959; d. Verlin Keith and Janice Kay (Burroughs) Egly; m. Richard Andrew Schuler, Aug. 16, 1980. BA in Sociology, Wheaton Coll., 1981; MA in Theology, Fuller Sem., 1988, PhD in Clin. Psychology, 1989. Psychol. asst. Nancy R. Rhodes PhD, Pasadena, Calif., 1987—; psychologist Kaiser Permanente, L.A., 1989—; adj. asst. prof. psychology Fuller Sem., Pasadena, 1989—. Author: Dictionary of Pastoral Care and Counseling, 1989. Ill. State scholar, 1977-81, Gene Pfrimmer Meml. scholar Fuller Sem., 1986, Coll. Women's Club scholar, 1987. Mem. Am. Psychol. Assn., Assn. for Women Psychologists. Office: Kaiser Mental Health Ctr 765 W Coll Los Angeles CA 90012

SCHULER, MAUREEN PATRICIA, psychologist; b. Cin., Jan. 7, 1932; d. Francis Jerome and Mary Catherine (Kessing) S. BS in Edn., U. Dayton, 1967; MEd, Xavier U., 1969; PhD in Psychology, Wright State U., Dayton, Ohio, 1987. Lic. psychologist. Tchr. various schs. Ohio, Ind., Va. and Calif., 1956-67, St. Charles Borromeo Sch., Kettering, Ohio, 1967-81; psychology trainee various practicum sites Dayton, 1983-87; psychology intern Ft. Meade (S.D.) Black Hills Psychology Consortium, 1986-87, Hamilton County Mental Health Ctr., Cin., 1987-88; psychologist House of Affirmation, Whitinsville, Mass., 1988-90; asst. dir. Berea (Ohio) Children's Home, 1990—. Mem. Am. Psychol. Assn., Am. Soc. Clin. Hypnosis, Ohio Psychol. Assn., Nat. Register of Health Svc. Providers in Psychology.

SCHULMAN, SANDRA JEAN, marketing professional; b. Burbank, Calif., July 12, 1954; d. Harold L. and June M. (Ringnell) Bryan; m. Robert E. Schulman, Jan. 27, 1974; 1 child, Aaron Daniel. BS, Calif. State U., L.A., 1984; MBA, Whittier Coll., 1987. Mktg. analyst Van de Kamp's Frozen Foods, L.A., 1977-81; assoc. prodn. mgr. Knudsen, L.A., 1984-85; product mgr. Beatrice/Hunt-Wesson, Fullerton, Calif., 1985-87; group mktg. mgr. Knudsen Div. Kraft, L.A., 1987-90; v.p. mktg. Weider Health and Fitness, Woodland Hills, Calif., 1990—. Mem. L.A. County Mus. of Art, 1985, Greater L.A. Zoo Assn., 1984. Recipient cert. appreciation L.A. City Coun., 1989, Red Cross, 1987. Mem. NAFE. Office: Weider Health and Fitness 21100 Erwin St Woodland Hills CA 91367

SCHULMAN, TAMMY BETH, communications executive; b. Queens, N.Y., Sept. 1, 1960; d. David Abraham and Diane Lois (Herman) Schulman; m. Kurt James Anderson, Sept. 14, 1986 (div. 1990); m. Kenneth Steven Peterson, 1990; stepchildren: Tanya, Kathleen, Amanda. Degree in comml. art, Hennepin County Vocat.-Tech., Eden Prairie, Minn., 1978; postgrad., Coll. St. Catherine, St. Paul, 1985—. Corr. sec. Ross Investment Co., Edina, Minn., 1980; quality control rep. Hubbard Milling Co., Minnetonka, Minn., 1980-81; ins. insp. Underwriters Svc. Co., Hopkins, Minn., 1982-83; dir. publs., communications mgr. Lifetouch Nat. Sch. Studios, Mpls., 1984—. Author, editor: Versatile Beans, 1978, Exposure mag., 1986—. Tutor Glenwood-Lyndale Community Ctr., Mpls., 1982; women's advocate Sojourner Shelter, Minnetonka, 1984—; active Sta. KFAI-Radio, Mpls., Simon Weisenthal Ctr., Mpls., 1985-86. Mem. NAFE, Women in Communications Inc., Upper Miss. Blues Soc. Democrat. Jewish. Office: Lifetouch Nat Sch Studios 7800 Picture Dr Minneapolis MN 55435

SCHULTE, MARY ANN, finance executive; b. Phoenix, Feb. 6, 1953; d. Walter Barry and Norma Gladys (Caffey) S. BSBA, U. So. Calif., 1975, MBA, 1989. Mgr. acctg. Coldwell Banker, Los Angeles, 1975-78; controller Adams, Ray and Rosenberg, Inc. (now Triad Artists), Century City, Calif., 1978-81; co-owner Marwal, Inc., Los Angeles, 1976-82; controller, chief fin. officer DNA Group, Inc., Pasadena, Calif., 1982-86; chief fin. officer Sukut Constrn., Inc., Santa Ana, Calif., 1986—; cons. Mikeselle DeKorff, Los Angeles, 1981-82, Hollywood (Calif.) High Sch., 1986-87; cons., bd. dirs. Inner Ear Prodns., Los Angeles, 1983-85. Assoc. producer (documentary film) Echoes of The Ozarks, 1989; speaker in field. Staff leader drop out prevention program Hollywood High Sch., 1986. Mem. Nat. Assn. Accts. (past bd. dirs.), Am. Soc. Women Accts. (speaker), U. So. Calif. Commerce Assocs., Alpha Chi Omega. Republican. Roman Catholic. Office: Sukut Constrn Inc 4010 W Chandler Santa Ana CA 92704

SCHULTS, CAROL ANNE, portfolio manager; b. Englewood, N.J., Apr. 11, 1961; d. John Edward and Carol S. (Saums) S. BA in Polit. Sci., Am. U., 1983. Intern Herrick & Smith, Boston, 1981, Ernst & Whinney, Boston, 1981, Senator Bill Bradley, Washington, 1981; rsch. asst. Am. U., Washington; asst. portfolio mgr. Oppenheimer Mgmt. Corp., N.Y.C., 1985—. Assoc. Spl. Olympics Wash. 1982-84, Bill Bradley Re-Election Campaign N.J. 1984. Mem. NAFE, Am. Mgmt. Assn., Am. U. Alumni Assn., St. Barts Club, Phi Mu. Episcopalian. Office: Oppenheimer Mgmt Corp 2 World Trade Ctr 34th Fl New York NY 10048

SCHULTZ, AMY TOMBLINSON, diaper service executive; b. Flint, Mich., Apr. 8, 1962; d. James Edmund and Betsy Hannah (Kinley) Tomblinson; m. Frank Carl William Schultz II, May 23, 1987. Grad., U. Mich., 1980-84; postgrad., Coll. of Charleston, 1990—. Problem communication coord. Troy Design, Lansing, Mich., 1985-86; account coord. Campbell Ewald Co., Detroit, 1986-87; exec. asst. Norwest Bank, Rochester, Minn., 1987-88; membership rep. Minn. Pub. Radio, Rochester, 1989; owner A Little Bird Told Me, Rochester and Charleston, S.C., 1988-90; sales cons. Waterford Wedgwood, Inc., Charleston, 1989-90; v.p., mgr. Baby's Best Diaper Svc., Inc., Charleston, S.C., 1990—. Founding mem. Jr. Svc. League of Rochester, 1988-89; mem. budget and planning coms. United Way of Olmsted County, Rochester, 1988. Mem. U. Mich. Alumni Club, Assn. Jr. Leagues, Pi Beta Phi Alumni Club. Republican. Presbyterian. Home and Office: Baby's Best Diaper Svc Inc 1445 Pine Island View Mount Pleasant SC 29464

SCHULTZ, DEBORAH ANN, small business owner; b. St. Paul, Sept. 30, 1949; d. Harley J. and Patricia E. (Schluter) Beers; children: Ashley, Jason, Dain. Student, U. Minn. Cert. CPR instr., emergency med. tech. Nurses aide Cedarview Nursing Home, Owatonna, Minn.; riding instr. Owatonna; pres. Deb's Saddles and Such, Owatonna. Mem. Am. Quarter Horse Assn., Minn. Quarter Horse Assn., Palomino Horse Breeders Am., Owatonna Saddle Club. Home: Rt 4 Box 62 Owatonna MN 55060 Office: 1430 E Main Owatonna MN 55060

SCHULTZ, DOROTHY TERESA, home economist. BS, U. Louisville, 1981; MA in Mktg., Webster U., St. Louis, 1989. Tchr. Sec. tchr. Ninth & O Christian Sch., Louisville, 1981-83, Pine Hills Christian Acad., Orlando, 1983-86; home economist GE Appliances, Louisville, 1987--; educator, specialist GE Appliances Asst. A Sch. Program, Louisville, 1988-89. Author: Science Projects Guidelines, 1984, Human Factors Product Reviews, 1988, CITL Promotional Information, 1988; editor: 1.0 Microwave Turntable GE Cookbook, 1988. Interpeter Ch., Louisville, 1981; Woman's Tchr. Ch., Louisville, 1988; Participator Woman's C. of C., Louisville, 1988. Recipient High Honors U. Louisville, 1981. Mem. Home Economist in Bus., Am. Home Econ. Assn., Nat. Assn. for Female Execs., Phi Kappa Phi Honor Soc., Kappa Delta Pi Honor Soc. in Edn. The Woodcock Honor Soc. of U. Louisville. Home: 1202 Rudgate Cove Louisville KY 40214

SCHULTZ, EMILY CELESTIA, medical researcher; b. Mankato, Minn., May 30, 1907; d. Walter Wyman and Kathryn Alice (Savage) Smith; m. Clarence H. Schultz, Nov. 20, 1946 (dec. Aug. 1971); children: Martha Kathryn, Carl Wyman, John Albert. AA Pre-Med., Rochester (Minn.) Jr. Coll., 1926; BA, U. Minn., 1944; BS in Exptl. Path./Hematology, Mayo Found., Rochester, 1947; postgrad., Mo. State So. Coll., 1974; MS in Exptl. Pathology, Mayo Found. Worker bacteriology, hematology, gastric labs. Mayo Clin., Rochester, 1926-47; worker hormone labs. Inst. Exptl. Medicine, Rochester, 1935-36; streptomycin therapist Mineral Springs TB Sanatorium, Cannon Falls, Minn., 1937-41; researcher on animal trials Anderson Inst. for Biol. Rsch., Red Wing, Minn., 1942; rsch. fellow on TB-Antibiotics Mayo Found., Rochester, 1944-46; geriatric cardiology study in nursing home Neosho, Mo., 1982—; mem., sec., treas. County Health Bd., Newton County, Mo., 1967-71; state health bd., Mo. Federated Women's Club, 1965-66. Contbg. author Book on Pioneer American Gardening, 1951. Curator Newton County Hist. Soc., 1970-80; contbr. art to Spiva Art Ctr., Joplin., Mo. State Coll., 1973—; tchr. lab. tech. classes Michael Reese Hosp., Chgo., 1932; treas. Carver Birthplace Assn., Carver Nat. Monument, 1971-80. Mem. DAR (registrar, treas.), AAUW, Assn. Ret. Fedl. Workers, Neosho (Mo.) Travel Club, Neosho Meth. Circle, Alpha Epsilon Iota. Unitarian. Home and Office: Neosho Sr Ctr 330 S Wood St Neosho MO 64850

SCHULTZ, ESTELLE PETERSON, music teacher; b. Kansas City, Mo., July 16, 1935; d. Theodore Magnus and Margaret Laura (Miller) Peterson; m. Richard L. Schultz, June 7, 1958; children: Lori Schultz Simpson, Dana Schultz Schmitt, Mark R. BM, Bethany Coll., 1957. Elem. vocal and instrumental tchr. Cunningham, Kans., 1957-58; elem. and secondary vocal and instrumental tchr. Carbondale, Kans., 1958-59; pvt. flute and piano tchr. Amarillo, Tex., 1962, Miami, Fla., 1963-64, Topeka, 1965-70, Springfield, Va., 1970-90, Moneta, Va., 1990—. Mem. Nat. Flute Soc., Wash. Flute Soc., Music Tchrs. Nat. Assn., Va. Fedn. Music Clubs, Nat. Fedn. Music Clubs, Springfield Music Club, Sigma Alpha Iota.

SCHULTZ, JANET DARLENE, credit union executive; b. Oakland, Calif., July 22, 1942; d. Charles Emile and Viola Iva (Ogden) Ranvier; m. Orville Carl Schultz Sr., Apr. 7, 1971; children: Carol Marie, Donald Courtland. BSBA, U. Wis., 1978. Cert. credit union mgmt. Loan officer Sierra Schs. Fed. Credit Union, Reno, 1974-79; mgr. Nev. Realtors Credit Union, Reno, 1979-81; pres., chief exec. officer Reno Fed. Credit Union, 1979-85; cons. Union Credit Union, Sparks, Nev., 1986; mgr., chief exec. officer Union Credit Union, Sparks, 1986-88; gen. mgr. Colt Svcs. Ctr., Battle Mountain, Nev., 1988-89; pres., chief exec. officer Gallup Santa Fe Fed. Credit Union, Belen, N.Mex., 1989—; vice chmn. Nev. Cen. Credit Union, Las Vegas, 1980-83; treas. Western Nev. Chpt. Nev. CLU, Reno, 1980-84. Tng. chmn. Boy Scouts Am., 1980, Pow Wow chmn., 1978; treas. Pop Warner Football League, Sparks, 1981, pres. 1987. Recipient Dist. Award of Merit, Boy Scouts Am., 1978. Mem. Nat. Assn. Female Execs., Reno Women Bus. Network, Nat. Notary Assn., Cuna Mktg. Inst., Cuna Fin. Inst., Cuna Alumni Assn., Inc. Democrat. Roman Catholic. Home: 914 Glen Martin Dr Sparks NV 89431 Office: Union Credit Union 1110 Greg St Sparks NV 89431

SCHULTZ, KAREN LEE, fire and water restoration company executive; b. Hempstead, N.Y., June 24, 1953; d. Odd Andre and Irene Mae (Cortez) Solbakken; 1 child, Miakoda Li. Sr. recreation therapist Posada del Sol, Tucson, 1977-81; pres., owner Intimate Luxury, Tucson, 1981-85; gen. mgr. Global Restoration, Tucson, 1985-86; pres., owner A&D Restoration, Tucson, 1986—; owner, sec., treas. Ariz. Quality Refinishing, Inc., 1988-89. Pres. Activities Dirs. Assn. Tucson, 1979-80; mem. candidate evaluation com. C. of C., Tucson, 1984-86; asst. leader Girl Scouts U.S.A., 1984-85. Mem. Tucson Bus. and Profl. Women, (pres., chmn. Trade Fair 1985-86), Tucson Women's Symposium, So. Ariz. Claims Adjusters, NAFE. Democrat. Office: A&D Restoration Inc 1665 E 18th Ste #108 Tucson AZ 85706

SCHULTZ, LESLIE BROWN, management executive; b. Fresno, Calif., Dec. 9, 1936; d. Albert Brown and Marion Jean (Riese) Brown-Propp; married, Jan. 20, 1957 (div. 1972); children: Susan, Steven, David, Thomas. BS, U. So. Calif., 1958. Office mgr. pvt. practice physician, Long Beach, Calif., 1971-73; cost acct. Panavision, Inc., Tarzana, Calif., 1974-76; exec. sec. Hartman Galleries, Beverly Hills, Calif., 1976-78; adminstrv. asst. Galanos Originals, L.A., 1978—. Mem. Alpha Epsilon Phi Found. Inc. (nat. pres. 1985-89, sec. 1990—). Republican. Jewish. Home: 1745 Bentley Ave #1 Los Angeles CA 90025 Office: Galanos Originals 2254 Sepulveda Blvd Los Angeles CA 90064

SCHULTZ, LINDA KATHRYN, property adjuster; b. Queens, N.Y., Dec. 9, 1961; d. Frank Giacalone and Janet Rose (Somma) Biondo; m. Carl William Schultz, Dec. 6, 1986. BS in Social Work, SUNY, Brockport, 1983. Property adjuster GAB Bus. Svc., Rochester, N.Y., 1987-88, Travelers Ins., Rochester, 1988—. Com. chmn. Parkminster Presbyn. Ch., Rochester, 1989—. Scholar SUNY-Brockport Alumni, 1980, 83, Alt. Coll. at Brockport, 1983.

SCHULTZ, LINDA MICHELLE, retail manager; b. Chgo., Nov. 18, 1960; d. Raymond J. and Frances M. (Zibert) S. BA, Northern Ill. U., 1981; MBA, Keller Grad. Sch. Mgmt., 1988. Mgr. B. Dalton, Chgo., 1982-87; asst. buyer Claires Boutiques, Wooddale, Ill., 1987-89; bus. mgr. Janis, Chgo., 1989—. Mem. Women in Bus., Ill. Dressage & Combined Tng. Assn. Republican. Roman Catholic. Home: 415 W Fullerton Chicago IL 60610 Office: Janis 200 W Superior St Chicago IL 60610

SCHULTZ, LUCY J., bank officer; b. Burke, S.D., July 3, 1962; d. Lewis Rudie and Jeanne Donna (Manthey) S. BA, Westmar Coll., LeMars, Iowa, 1984. Loss prevention specialist Jasa and Assocs., Inc., Omaha; with IRS, Aurora, Ill.; accounts receivable field examiner Metrobank, Gardena, Calif. Mem. NAFE.

SCHULTZ, MARCY LYNN, foundation executive; b. Theresa, Wis., Nov. 15, 1957; d. Robert Julius and Irene Laura (Wecker) Schultz. BS in Natural Scis., U. Wis., 1979. Exec. asst. Wis. Phys.Therapy Svcs., Madison, 1975-80; dir. pub. relations Wis. DHI Coop., Madison, 1980-83; dir. devel. U. Wis. Found., Madison, 1983—; cons. Marks Entertainment and Pub. Relations, 1985—; bd. dirs. Dane County Dairy Promotions Bd., 1986—. Vol., United Way of Dane County, 1987. Mem. Nat. Agrl. Mktg. Assn., Pub. Relations Soc. Am., Assn. Women in Agr., Wis. Women for Agr., Wis. Women's Bus. Coalition (bd. dirs. 1988-89), Women in Communications (pres. Madison 1988-89), Downtown Madison Kiwanis, Alpha Zeta. Republican. Lutheran. Home: 434 Rushmore Ln Madison WI 53711 Office: U Wis Found 150 E Gilman St Madison WI 53703

SCHULTZ, MARY ELIZABETH, lawyer; b. Seattle, June 12, 1958; d. Peter James and Lillian (Parma) S. BA with honors, U. Tex., 1980; JD, Gonzaga U., 1983. Bar: Wash. 1984, U.S. Dist. Ct. (we. and ea. dists.) Wash. 1984, U.S. Ct. Appeals (10th cir.) 1986, U.S. Ct. Appeals (9th cir.) 1989. From intern to dep. prosecutor City of Spokane Legal Dept., Wash., 1983-84; dep. prosecutor Spokane County Prosecutor's Office, 1984-85; solo practice Spokane, 1985—. Poetry included in Am. Poetry Anthology, 1986. Mem. Assn. Trial Lawyers Am., Wash. State Trial Lawyers Assn., Spokane Bar Assn., Wash. Criminal Def. Lawyers, Profl. Karate League (3rd in region 1 1988 overall women's black belt fighting, 19th 1988 overall combined men's/women's black belt forms). Roman Catholic. Office: Rockpoint Corp Ctr N 1212 Washington Ste 116 Spokane WA 99201

SCHULTZ, PAMELA BUSCH, musician, composer; b. Parkersburg, W.Va., Sept. 20, 1951; d. William Harold and Mary Kathryn (Weaver) Busch; m. Robert M. Schultz, May 3, 1975. MusB, W.Va. U., 1973, MusM, 1975; MusD, U. Miami, Coral Gables, Fla., 1988. Instr. piano preparatory dept. W.Va. U., Morgantown, 1971-78; piano tchr. W.Va.,Fla., 1975-86; piano instr., faculty accompanist Salem (W.Va.) Coll., 1977-78; piano instr. Miami (Fl.) Dade Community Coll., 1979-82; writer, arranger and editor keyboard staff CPP/Belwin, Inc., Miami, 1982-89; workshop clinician CPP/Belwin, Inc., U.S., Can., 1985—; ednl. piano writer and arranger CPP/Belwin, Inc., 1989—; piano adjudicator, 1980—. Author, editor: (supplementary materials) Schultz Piano Library, 1982—; Coauthor: Schultz Piano Course, 1986. Mem. NAFE, Nat. Fedn. Music Clubs, Nat. Guild Piano Tchrs., Miami Music Tchrs. Assn., Fl. State Music Tchrs. Assn., Music Tchrs. Nat. Assn., Cousteau Soc., Nat. Wildlife Fedn., Environ. Def. Fund, World Wildlife Fund, Wilderness Soc., 1000 Friends Fla. Home: 9925 S W 82d Ave Miami FL 33156

SCHULTZ, PAMELA KAY, real estate broker, supermarket executive; b. Madison, Wis., Oct. 21, 1947; d. Charles Floyd and Delores Marie (Rector) Duane; student Madison Area Tech. Coll., 1975; m. James Mallory Schultz, Jan. 22, 1966; children: Julie Katherine, Jennifer Kay, Karen Elizabeth. Sec.

to v.p. Nat. Mut. Benefit Life Ins. Co., Madison, 1965-66; sec., bookkeeper Family Market Enterprises, Inc., DeForest, Wis., 1966—, v.p., sec. 1986—; real estate broker, DeForest; bd. dirs. customer adv. coun.Madison Gas and Electric Utility Co.; founder Win-Fore Women's Investment Club. Leader, Blackhawk council Girl Scouts U.S.A., 1974, 75, 77, 79-80; founder DeForest Area Hist. Soc., 1975, active membership dr., 1975-79, sec.-treas., 1975-79, bd. dirs., 1975-81; treas. DeForest Moravian Ch., 1977-83, bd. elders, 1986—, mem. Christian edn. com., 1986-88. Recipient Small Bus. award U. Wis., 1986. Mem. DeForest C. of C. (dir. 1984-85, pres. 1986, chmn. retail revitalization com. 1987-88). Home: 305 Meadow Ln DeForest WI 53532 Office: 302 N Main St DeForest WI 53532

SCHULTZ, PHYLLIS MAY, financial property manager; b. Knox County, Ill., Dec. 17, 1933; d. Clarence Cleo and Mildred Ruth (Hultberg) Cooper; m. Wayne Willard Mohr, Apr. 23, 1955 (div. Sept. 1965); Jeffery Lee Mohr, Kelly Marie Mohr (dec.); m. Robert William Schultz, Sept. 14, 1968. Student, L.A. Valley Coll., 1979-82. Fire and casualty ins. lic., Calif. Keypunch operator Gale Products Outboard Marine Corp., Galesburg, Ill., 1952-55; office mgr. movie and video distbn. Rainbow Distbrs., Inc., 1965-89; fin. property mgr. and acctg. John Lamb, L.A., 1989—; co-owner Real Estate Investments, Ill., Calif., 1980-89. Mem. Lutheran Social Svcs., L.A., 1989. Mem. Women's Am. Bowling Congress Assn. Republican. Home: 6309 Morella Ave North Hollywood CA 91606

SCHULTZ, RUBY ETHEL, educator; b. Bklyn., Feb. 26, 1934; d. Joseph and Celia (Friedman) Warshaw; m. Bernard M. Schultz, Nov. 1, 1959 (div. 1971); children: Stacy, Susan (twins). BA, Bklyn. Coll., 1956, MS in Edn., 1958; postgrad., Kingsboro Coll., Bklyn., 1985. Cert. elem. tchr., N.Y. Tchr. Pub. Sch. 9, Bklyn., 1956-61; elem. tchr. Pub. Sch. 253, Bklyn., 1970-90. Vol. Cerebral Palsy, N.Y.C., 1980—, Muscular Dystrophy Assn., N.Y.C., 1980.

SCHULTZ, RUTH ANNE, home economics educator, parenting consultant; b. Oneida, N.Y., Jan. 27, 1953; d. Herman Lyon and Anna Marie (Jarvis) S. BS, Cornell U., 1975; MS, Syracuse U., 1982; postgrad., Plattsburgh State U., 1986, 89. Cert. tchr., N.Y.; cert. home economist. Tchr. home econs. Phelps-Clifton Springs (N.Y.) Cen. Schs., 1975-77, adult educator, 1976-77; home econs. tchr. Fabius (N.Y.)-Pompey Cen. Schs., 1977-82; home econs. tchr. Chittenango (N.Y.) Cen. Schs., 1982—, adviser Future Homemakers Am. club, 1986—; parenting educator Cornell Coop. Extension, Madison County, Morrisville, N.Y., 1985—; cons. N.Y. Dept. Edn., 1988—, Reelizations, Woodstock, N.Y., 1990. Primary author curriculum materials. Community rep. Madison County Head Start Policy Coun., Morrisville, 1985-88. Mem. Home Econs. Edn. Assn. (v.p. 1988-90, pres. elect 1990-91), N.Y. State Home Econs. Tchrs. Assn. (pres. 1986-88, state conv. chair 1989-90, legislation co-chair 1989-90), N.Y. State Home Econs. Assn. (elem., secondary, adult chair 1989-90, New Achiever award 1988, Tchr. of Yr. 1989), Am. Home Econs. Assn. (nat. leadership com. 1989-91), Cen. N.Y. Home Econs. Tchrs. Assn. (Tchr. of Yr. 1985). Democrat. Roman Catholic. Home: RD 3 Cazenovia NY 13035 Office: Chittenango High Sch West Genesee St Chittenango NY 13035

SCHULTZ, SHELLY IRENE, business entrepreneur; b. Oak Park, IL, June 9, 1953; d. Davis William and Irene Francis (Rock) Shaw; m. Robert V. Schultz, Feb. 12, 1971; children: Robert G., Trina Reneé, Cherie Anne. Student, Moody Bible Inst., Chgo., 1972-73; artistry master workshops tng., Grand Rapids, Mich., 1978, 80, 82, 84, 86, 88. Exec. sec. H.C. Prange & Co., Rockford, Ill., 1978-80; asst. mgr. Nat. Car Rental, Rockford, 1980-81, Budget Rent-A-Car, Rockford, 1981-82; mgr. Bonanza Restaurant, Rockford, 1982-83; ptnr., owner Diamond Pubs., Inc., Aurora, Ill., 1987—; owner, mgr. TrendSetters, Aurora, 1971—. Vol. Rep. Party, Ill., 1980-84; organizer Awana Youth Club, Polo, Ill., 1977-78. Mem. Internat. Diamond Bldrs. (sec. 1980-88), Ambassadors Internat. (award of appreciation 1988), NAFE. Office: TrendSetters PO Box 475 Sterling IL 61081

SCHULTZE, SHARON EDEL, municipal official; b. LeMars, Iowa, Sept. 14, 1939; d. Alvin M. and Edel (Jensen) Petersen; children: Blair, David, Carol. BA, Wesleyan U., Lincoln, Nebr., 1960; postgrad., Kans. State U., San Diego State U. Adminstrv. asst. Bd. Edn., San Diego; asst. dir. Community Mediation Program San Diego; city coun. rep. San Diego City Coun.; lectr. in field. Author: Urban and Community Politics, American Government Today. Mem. Soc. Profls. Dispute Resolution, Phi Kappa Phi. Home: 3559 Albatross St San Diego CA 92103 Office: 202 C St 10th Fl San Diego CA 92101

SCHULZ, BARBARA, academic administrator; b. South Weymouth, Mass., Sept. 18, 1954; d. Albert Raymond and Mary Louise (Jacob) Petrell; m. George Louis Schulz, May 6, 1955; 1 child, Jonathan Louis. MB, Boston U., 1976; MSAM, Lesley Coll., 1988. Cert elem., high sch. tchr., Mass. Staff asst. Harvard U., Cambridge, Mass., 1976-79; collection officer Boston U., 1979-81; asst. collection mgr. Lesley Coll., Cambridge, Mass., 1981-83; collection mgr. Lesley Coll., Cambridge, 1983-85; bursar Cambridge, 1985-88; dir. bus. svc. and purchasing Lesley Coll., Cambridge, 1988—. Mem. NAFE, Nat. Assn. of Ednl. Buyers (v.p. NE region 1990-91), Nat. Assn. Coll. and Univ. Bus. Officers. Office: Lesley Coll 29 Everett St Cambridge MA 02138

SCHULZ, BONNIE LOU, real estate broker, business owner; b. Oelwein, Iowa, Nov. 21, 1951; d. Clarence and Philomena (Kass) Phillips; m. Roger Albert Schulz, Jan. 16, 1971; 1 child, Vicki Lynn. Diploma, Grad. Realtors Inst., 1978. Store auditor Montgomery Ward's & Co., Oelwein, 1970-74; real estate agt. Darwin Rueber Realtors, Oelwein, 1974-79; real estate broker, owner Schulz & Assocs. Realtors, Oelwein, 1979—; co-owner Schulz Constrn. Co., Inc., Oelwein, 1979—; property mgr. various investor clients, Oelwein, 1979—. Mem. Landlords of Iowa (v.p. Iowa chpt.), Pvt. Industry Coun. of Iowa (1st vice chairperson SDA-1), Iowa Assn. Realtors (various coms.), Oelwein Indsl. Devel. Corp., Backbone Bd. Realtors, Oelwein C. of C. Roman Catholic. Home: PO Box 528 Oelwein IA 50662 Office: Schulz & Assocs 1101 S Frederick Oelwein IA 50662

SCHULZ, CAROL DORIS, clinical nurse specialist; b. Aurora, Ill., Feb. 4, 1953; d. Ralph David and Doris Ann (Carlson) Ginger; m. John F. Schulz, Oct. 25, 1975; children: David Andrew, Marcus John, Kelly Nicole. Diploma, Wesley-Passavant Sch. Nursing, Chgo., 1974; BSN, Aurora Coll., 1983; MS in Nursing, No. Ill. U., 1986. RN, Ill. Staff nurse ICU, Mercy Ctr. for Health Care Svcs., Aurora, 1974-78, staff nurse emergency room, 1978-87, clin. nurse specialist, 1987-88, 89—, trauma coord., 1987-88; trauma nurse coord. emergency med. svcs. Cen. DuPage Hosp., Winfield, Ill., 1988-89. Mem. AACCN (Ill. Critical Care Nurse of Yr. award 1985), Emergency Nurses Assn., Sigma Theta Tau (treas. Lambda Upsilon at-large chpt. 1989—). Home: 10717 Legion Rd Yorkville IL 60560 Office: Mercy Ctr for Health Care Svcs Emergency Dept 1325 N Highland Ave Aurora IL 60506

SCHULZ, KAREN GAYLE, financial planner; b. Wessington Springs, S.D., Nov. 16, 1959; d. Walter William and Lois Augusta (Thomas) S. BS, S.D. State U., 1982. Asst. mgr. Lerner Shops, Rapid City, S.D., 1982-84, mgr., Denver, 1984-85; fin. planner IDS/Am. Express, Northglenn, Colo., 1985—. Mem. Internat. Assn. for Fin. Planning, Inst. Cert. Fin. Planners (cert. fin. planner), Bus. and Profl. Women's Orgn. (treas., chair young careerist com. Colo. chpt. 1987-88, 2d and 1st v.p.). Lutheran. Avocation: skiing. Home: 13467 N Osage St Northglenn CO 80234 Office: IDS/Am Express 1385 S Colorado Blvd Ste 620 Denver CO 80222

SCHULZ, PATRICIA LYNN, human resources generalist; b. Buffalo, Nov. 18, 1957; d. Edward F. and Janice C. (Repman) Couche; m. Brian L. Schulz, June 5, 1982; children: Lauren Ashley, Robert Michael. BSBA, SUNY, Buffalo, 1979, MBA, 1985. Supr. employee rels., pers. specialist Carborundum Abrasives Co., Niagara Falls, N.Y.; human resources supr. Graphic Controls Corp., Buffalo; dir. human resources C.J. Tower Inc., Buffalo. Mem. Soc. for Human Resources Mgmt., Am. Soc. for Tng. and Devel., Orgnl. Devel. Network. Home: 5420 Thompson Rd Clarence NY 14031 Office: 128 Dearborn St Buffalo NY 14207

SCHULZE, TASCHA JON, cellist, educator; b. Oct. 5, 1950; d. John Henry and Mary LaVonne (Foster) S. Student, Ind. U., 1970-71; MusB, U. Iowa, 1981; MusM, Ariz. State U., 1985, postgrad., 1988. Pvt. tchr. cello Iowa City, from 1967, Phoenix and Tempe, Ariz., 1982—; instr. cello Grand Canyon U., Phoenix, 1985—; cellist Orquesta Sinfonica, Xalapa, Mex., 1973-76, Quartetto Brunello, Xalapa, 1978-80, TOS Performing Arts Ensemble, 1982-88, Phoenix Quartet, Tempe, 1983—, Los Cellistas, Tempe, 1988—; asst. prin. cellist Orquesta Camera, U. Veracruzana, Xalapa, 1978-80; assoc. prin. cellist Orquesta Sinfonica Veracruz (Mex.), 1980-81; prin. cellist Nouveau West Chamber Orch., Tempe, 1983-88, bd. dirs., 1985-88; organizer prep. music sch. for string players Inst. Mus. Arts, Phoenix, 1986. Composer: Tasseled Juncture, 1984 (award performance Scottsdale Ctr. for Arts 1984, invitational performance Cervantino Festival Internat. 1986), Waves for cello, saxaphone and piano (performed Kerr Cultural Ctr., Scottsdale 1987); rec. artist Orion Master Rec. Mem. Am. Musicians Union, Am. String Tchrs. Assn., Chamber Music Am., Ariz. Cello Soc. (scholar), Sigma Alpha Iota. Home: 3402 N 43d Pl Phoenix AZ 85018 Office: Grand Canyon U Phoenix AZ 85017

SCHUMACHER, CYNTHIA JO, secondary education educator, retired; b. Sebring, Fla., Sept. 24, 1928; d. Floyd Melvin and Espage Love (Rogers) S. BA, Fla. State U., 1950, MA, 1951; MS, Nova U., 1978; postgrad., Fla. State U., 1968-69. Cert. elem. and secondary sch. tchr., ednl. adminstr. and supr., Ga., Fla. English tchr. Grady County Sch. System, Cairo, Ga., 1951-53; elem. tchr. Brevard County Sch. System, Melbourne, Fla., 1953-55; elem. tchr., curriculum generalist, secondary tchr. Lake County Schs., Tavares, Fla. area, 1955-85; retired, 1985; mem. Edn. Standards Commn., Fla., 1980-85, Quality Instrn. Incentives Coun., Fla., 1983-84. Author: (poetry) Seeds from Wild Grasses, 1988. Pres. League of Women Voters of Lake County, 1989-91; mem. Lake Conservation Coun., The Nature Conservancy, Habitat for Humanity of Lake County. Named Fla. Tch. of Yr., Fla. Fedn. Women's Clubs, 1966, Lake County Tchr. of Yr., Lake County Sch. Systems, 1986, East Cen. Fla. Tchr. of Yr., finalist State of Fla., 1986. Mem. Lake County Edn. Assn. (pres. 1971-72, cons. 1985—). Democrat. Roman Catholic. Office: Lake County Edn Assn PO Box 490816 Leesburg FL 34749

SCHUMACHER, KATHLEEN MILES, innkeeper; b. Rochester, N.Y., June 5, 1954; d. Laverne Franklin and Jean Elizabeth (Kostelnik) Miles; m. John Arthur Schumacher, Feb. 16, 1986; stepchildren: Brandi Jansson, Carlton John. BS in Food & Nutrition, U. Conn., 1978; MS in Nutrition, Case Western Res. U., 1979. Clin. dietitian Cleve. Met. Gen./Highland View Hosps., Cleve., 1979; chief clin. nutritionist Cleve. Met. Gen./Highland View Hosps., 1979-84; innkeeper/co-mgr. Schumacher's New Prague Hotel, Inc., New Prague, Minn., 1984—; proprietor/mgr. Schumacher Gifts, Inc., New Prague, 1988—; bus. cons. Schumacher's Travel, New Prague, 1988—. Mem. Ind. Innkeepers Assn., AAUW, Am. Dietetic Assn., Minn. Dietetic Assn., Nat. Restaurant Assn., Minn. Restaurant Assn., New Prague C. of C. (bd. dirs. 1988—). Home and Office: Schumacher's Hotel 212 W Main St New Prague MN 56071

SCHUMACHER, LYNN INGRAHAM, oncology specialist; b. McAllen, Tex., May 16, 1956; d. Clyde T. and Delores Marie (Taflan) Ingraham; m. David G. Schumacher, Jr., June 7, 1980. BS in Agr. summa cum laude, U. Mo., 1978; postgrad., Temple U., 1978-79. Med. rep. Syntex Labs., Inc., various locations, 1979-86; lab. specialist Boehringer Mannheim Diagnostics, East Coast territory, 1986-88; diagnostic specialist Boehringer Mannheim Diagnostics, Washington, 1988; sr. oncology specialist Bristol-Myers-Squibb/Mead Johnson, Md. and Washington, 1988—; mem. nat. sales adv. bd., oncology div. Bristol-Myers, 1989, nat. sales trainer and counselor, 1990. Vol., Arthritis Found., 1990. Mem. Humane Soc. U.S., Animal Protection Inst. Am., Herrington Harbor Sailing ASsn., Pi Beta Phi (pres. 1984-85), Gamma Sigma Delta. Presbyterian. Home and office: 1042 Windrush Ln Sandy Spring MD 20860

SCHUMACK, JOAN MARIA, poet, journalist; b. Methoni, Greece, Nov. 4, 1953; came to U.S., 1958; d. Eugene John and Lydia Mary (Stellpflug) S. BA, Marquette U., 1976, MA in Mass Communications and Journalism, 1984. Editor Post Newspapers, West Allis, Wis., 1975-79; with employee communications dept. Allis-Chalmers Corp., 1979; freelance writer Wauwatosa, Wis., 1979-81; info. officer Common Council, Milw., 1981-84; founder, editor, publisher ETHNOS mag., Wauwatosa, 1985-88; polit. writer Community Newspapers, Wauwatosa, 1988—; community programmer Viacom Cablevision, Glendale, Wis., 1983—. Author of poetry appearing in various jours.; assoc. editor: Bicycling Mag., 1980; polit. writer for local newspapers, 1989—. Active Adoption Info. and Direction, Milw., 1982—; Friend of Milw. Symphony, 1985—, Milw. Art Museum, 1984—; sponsor Cyprus Childrens' Fund, N.Y.C., 1985—; established (with Mrs. Lydia M. Schumack) Eugene J. Schumack Meml. Journalism Fund in the Coll. of Journalism at Marquette U. for grad. study, 1986. Recipient Spl. Award Nat. Council Tchrs. of English, 1972. Mem. Soc. Profl. Jours. (Mark of Excellence award 1975), Milw. Press Club, Women in Communication, Inc., Nat. Assn. Female Execs., Marquette Journalism Alumni Assn. (bd. dirs. 1976-78, 1980-82), Nat. Fedn. Local Cable Programmers, Phil-Hellenic Greek Profl. Soc., Alpha Sigma Nu, Kappa Tau Alpha. Democrat. Eastern Orthodox. Club: Florentine Opera (Milw.). Office: Community Newspapers 11063 W Bluemound Rd Wauwatosa WI 53226

SCHUMAN, PATRICIA GLASS, publishing company executive, educator; b. N.Y.C., Mar. 15, 1943; d. Milton and Shirley Rhoda (Goodman) Glass; m. Alan Bruce Schuman, Aug. 30, 1964 (div. 1973). AB, U. Cin., 1963; MS, Columbia U., 1966. Libr. trainee Bklyn. Pub. Libr., 1963-65; tchr. libr. Brandeis High Sch., N.Y.C., 1966; asst. prof. libr. N.Y. Tech. Coll., Bklyn., 1966-71; assoc. editor Sch. Libr. Jour., N.Y.C., 1970-73; sr. editor R.R. Bowker Co., N.Y.C., 1973-76; pres. Neal-Schuman Pubs., N.Y.C., 1976—; vis. prof. St. John's U., Queens, N.Y., 1977-79, Columbia U., N.Y.C., 1981—; adj. prof. Rutgers U., New Brunswick, N.J., 1981; cons. N.Y. State Coun. on Arts, 1987, Office Tech. Assessment, U.S. Congress, 1982, 84, Coordinating Coun. Libr. Mags., N.Y.C., 1987, NEH, 1980, Temple U., 1978-80; bd. visitors Sch. Libr. and Computer Studies, Pratt Inst., 1987; juror Best of Libr. Lit., 1988; mem. adv. bd. Sch. Libr. and Info. Studies, Queens Coll., 1989. Author: Materials for Occupational Edn., 1973, 2d edit., 1983 (Best Edn. Book award 1973), Library Users and Personnel Needs, 1980; editor: Social Responsibilities and Libraries, 1976; mem. editorial bd. Urban Acad. Libr., 1987-89; contbr. articles to profl. jours. Bd. dirs. Women's Studies Abstracts, Albany, N.Y., 1970-74; mem. Com. To Elect Major Owens to U.S. Congress, 1983, N.Y.C. Major's Com. for N.Y. Pub. Ctr., 1984-85. Recipient Fannie Simon award Spl. Librs. Assn., 1984; U.S. Office Edn. fellow, 1969. Mem. ALA (councillor 1971-79, 84-88, exec. bd. 1984-88, 90—, treas. 1984-88, chmn. legis. com. 1989—, v.p., pres.-elect 1990—, Disting. Coun. Svc. award 1979, 88), Am. Soc. for Info. Sci., Assn. for Libr. and Info. Sci. Edn., N.Y. Libr. Assn. Office: Neal-Schuman Pubs Inc 23 Leonard St New York NY 10013

SCHUMANN, KAREN LYNN, purchasing executive; b. Chgo., Dec. 2, 1941; d. Richard J. and Corinne A. (Johnson) S. BA, DePaul U., Chgo., 1984, MA, 1988. Lic. real estate broker, Ill. Buyer Clybourn Machine Co., Skokie, Ill., Adams Elevator, Skokie; internat. buyer Cole Parmer Instrument Co., Niles, Ill. Mem. Women in Internat. Trade, NAFE. Home: 7620 N Osceola Ave Niles IL 60648

SCHUMITZ, ELIZABETH DOROTHY, mathematics educator, tutor; b. Newark, N.J., Dec. 29, 1935; d. Lester Herbert Sr. and Elizabeth (Snowden) Erickson; m. Rudolph William Schumitz Jr., Aug. 31, 1957 (dec. Sept. 1971); children: Robert Wayne, William Richard. BA, Montclair State Coll., 1957; postgrad., Rutgers U., 1959, N.J. Inst. Tech., 1959-60; MA, Fairleigh Dickinson U., 1977; postgrad., Kean Coll., Jersey City State Coll. Tchr., N.J.; prin./supr. cert., N.J. Coordinator math. dept., tchr. math. and computers Thompson Middle Sch., Middletown, 1986—; tchr. math. various high schs., N.J., 1957-86; coord. math. dept. Thompson Jr. High, Middletown, N.J., 1979-86; mem. curriculum devel. com. Middletown Twp. Bd. Edn., 1969—; external tchr. Marlboro (N.J.) State Hosp., 1966-67; tchr. math. summer sch. Red Bank (N.J.) Regional Bd. Edn., 1985—. Author: Eric and the Red Beard, 1977. Election challenger, Middletown Rep. Com., 1976, 80; com. chmn., treas., merit badge counselor, Boy Scouts. Am., Middletown, 1971—; elder, choir, bell choir Westminster Presbyn Ch., Middletown, 1963—. Recipient award of Merit Boy Scouts Am., 1990; scholarship Horace A. Moses Found., 1953, Newark Tchrs. Assn., 1953, N.J. State scholarship, 1953-57, and others; grantee Rutgers U., 1959. Mem. NEA, Middletown Twp. Edn. Assn., Monmouth County Edn. Assn., N.J. Edn. Assn., Nat. Coun. Tchrs. Math (ref. to editorial panel 1988—), Nat. Middle Schs. Assn., Assn. Math. Tchrs. N.J. (Recognition award 1989), Assn. Supervision and Curriculum Devel., Order Rainbow, Math. Assn. Am., Kappa Mu Epsilon, Kappa Delta Pi. Home: 1 Lakewood Pl Port Monmouth NJ 07758 Office: Thompson Middle Sch Middletown Lincroft Rd Middletown NJ 07748

SCHUMM, CHRISTINE LYNN, management consultant; b. Joliet, Ill., Oct. 30, 1960; d. Edward Daniel and Brunhild Helga (Weimann) Kafka; m. Theodore John, Sept. 12, 1981. BS in Med. Tech., No. Ill. U., Dekalb, 1983; MBA, Westminster Coll., Salt Lake City, 1989. Med. technologist microbiology Christ Hosp., Oak Lawn, Ill., 1983-84; virology research technologist Gull Labs., Salt Lake City, 1984-85; med. technologist microbiology Primary Children's Med. Ctr., Salt Lake City, 1985-87; med. sales rep. Organon Teknika Corp., Durham, N.C., 1987; med. technologist microbiology, product mgmt. specialist Assoc. Regional & U., Salt Lake City, 1987--. Mem. Am. Soc. of Clinical Pathologists, Am. Soc. for Microbiology. Republican. Roman Catholic. Home: 1823 Shaleh Meadows Rd Salt Lake City UT 84117 Office: Associated Regional & U Pat 390 Wakara Way Salt Lake City UT 84108

SCHUR, SUSAN DORFMAN, state legislator; b. Newark, Feb. 27, 1940; d. Norman and Jeanette (Handelman) Dorfman; B.A., Goucher Coll., 1961; children—Diana Elisabeth, Erica Marlene. Adminstr. fed. housing, fgn. aid, anti-poverty programs, 1961-67; mem. Mass. Housing Appeals Com., 1977-81; mem., v.p. Bd. of Alderman, Newton, Mass., 1974-81; mem. Mass. Ho. of Reps., 1981—; mem. Spl. Commn. on Divorce. Bd. dirs. Mass. chpt. Ams. for Dem. Action. Mem. Newton Dem. City Com., 1970—. Office: State House Boston MA 02133

SCHURE, TERI, publishing executive. Pub. World Press Rev., N.Y.C. Office: World Press Rev 200 Madison Ave New York NY 10016*

SCHURRER, SUZANNE BARBARA, systems analyst, paralegal; b. Elkhorn, Wis., Oct. 14, 1945; d. Maurice George and Thelma (Rendall) McDowell; m. Ronald Herman Schurrer, Oct. 27, 1974; children: MaryBeth, Rachael, Sherry, Erin, Brenda, Esther. A in Paralegal, So. Career Inst., 1974; BS, U. Wis., 1978; A in Automation Mgmt., Ins. Coll. Am., 1990. Cert. profl. legal sec. Law office adminstr. Toman Law Offices, Madison, Wis., 1964-79; relief adminstr. Fond du Lac (Wis.) County, 1979-83; cons. Relief Cons. Svcs., Fond du Lac, 1983-88; entrepreneur Rosey Dawn Entertainment, Wheaton, Ill., 1980-90, Relief Cons. Svcs., Fond du Lac, 1983-88; systems analyst AXIA Inc., Oak Brook, Ill., 1988—; systems cons. Town of Ashford, Wis., 1983-88, Town of Eden, Wis., 1983-88, Town of Friendship, Wis., 1983-88. Author: Relief Administration, 1985; creator, writer Rosey Dawn on-line computer entertainment systems, 1978—. Lobbyist Wis. Welfare Assn., Fond du Lac, 1987-88, Welfare Adminstr. of Yr., 1986. Mem. Nat. Assn. Legal Assts., Nat. Assn. Legal Secs. Republican. Congregationalist. Office: AXIA Inc 122 W 22nd St Oak Brook IL 60521

SCHUSTER, EULA ELAINE, lawyer; b. Oklahoma City, June 8, 1936; d. John Otto and Eula Delone (Campbell) Schuster; AB, Sweet Briar Coll., 1958; MA in Econs. and Fin., U. Okla., 1961, JD, 1968. Bar: Okla. 1968, U.S. Dist. Ct. (we. dist.) Okla. 1969, U.S. Ct. Appeals (10th cir.) 1976, U.S. Dist. Ct. (no. dist.) Okla. 1981. Prof. econs. Southeastern State U., Durant, Okla., 1961-65; assoc. Whitten & Whitten, Oklahoma City, 1968-71; asst. dist. atty. Oklahoma County, 7th Dist., 1972-78; ptnr. Jones, Schuster & Flaugher, Oklahoma City, 1978-82; pvt. practice E. Elaine Schuster, P.C., 1982—; lectr. in field. Mem. Oklahoma County Bd. Adjustment, 1978—, chmn., 1984-86, citizen mem. profl. liaison com. City of Oklahoma City, 1980-90; mem. Bd. Edn., Oklahoma City Area Vocat. Tech. Sch., Dist. 22, 1982—, pres., 1984-85; mem. ch. bd. University Pl. Christian Ch., 1982-86, 89—, elder, 1989—; bd. overseers Sweet Briar Coll., 1986—. GE grantee, 1963; named Outstanding Bus. Woman. of Okla. Town Club of Bus. and Profl. Women, 1986 . Mem. ABA, Okla. Bar Assn., Okla. County Bar Assn., Okla. Trial Lawyers Assn., AAUW (br. pres. 1978-80, Okla. div. bd. 1969-75, 81-83, 85-87, Polished Diamond award S.W. cen. region 1987), Kappa Beta Pi, Delta Kappa Gamma (hon. mem.). Avocations: hiking, photography, travel. Office: Heritage Law Ctr 515 NW 13th St Oklahoma City OK 73103

SCHUSTER, INGEBORG IDA, chemistry educator; b. Frankfurt, W. Ger., Oct. 30, 1937; came to U.S. 1947; d. Ludwig Karl and Mariluise (Kautetzky) S. BA, U. Pa., 1960; MS, Carnegie Inst. Tech., Pitts., 1963; PhD, Carnegie Inst. Tech., 1965. Postdoctoral fellow Bryn Mawr (Pa.) Coll., 1965-67; asst. prof. chemistry Pa. State U., Abington, 1967-73; assoc. prof. chemistry Pa. State U., 1973-83, prof. chemistry, 1983—. Contbr. articles to profl. jours. Huff fellow, 1966; E. Gerry fellow, 1982. Mem. Am. Chem. Soc. Republican. Roman Catholic. Office: Pa State Univ 1600 Woodland Rd Abington PA 19001

SCHUSTER, SHARON LEE, professional association administrator; b. Beech Grove, Ind., Aug. 26, 1939; d. Morris and Dorothy (Galinsky) Fox; m. Sheldon Herbert Schuster, June 29, 1958; children: Jacqueline Beth, Donald Jeffrey. BA, Calif. State U., San Jose, 1959. Cert. elem. tchr., exceptional children tchr. Tchr. Livermore (Calif.) Sch. Dist., 1959-60, L.A. Unified Sch. Dist., 1970-76; chief dep. Councilwoman Joy Picus, L.A., 1977-89. Mem. L.A. Women's Leadership Network, 1982-84, Women in Pub. Affairs, 1980—; bd. dirs. Haven Hills Shelter for Battered Women, 1978-89; v.p. Haven Hills, 1985-89; founding mem. City Hall Exec. Women, 1988; mem. membership com. Town Hall, 1986-88. Recipient Cert. of Appreciation, L.A. County, 1989, Women Honoring Women award Nat. Women's Polit. Caucus, 1986, Women Helping Women award Soroptomists Internat., 1984. Mem. AAUW (pres. 1989—, chairperson ednl. found. 1989—, pres. advocacy fund 1985-89, del. to internat. fedn. univ. women conf. 1983, 86, coord. exec. dir. search com. 1985-86, ednl. found. named endowment 1984). Democrat. Jewish. Home: 24458 Eilat St Woodland Hills CA 91367 Office: AAUW 2401 Virginia Ave NW Washington DC 20037

SCHUTH, MARY MCDOUGLE, interior designer, educator; b. Kansas City, Mo., Jan. 19, 1942; d. William Darnall and Marie DeArmond (Meiser) McDougle; m. Howard Wayne Schuth, Sept. 4, 1965; 1 child, Andrew Wayne. BS in Interior Design, Communications, Northwestern U., 1964; Cert. Basic Mgmt., U. Mo., 1966. Lic. interior designer, La. Interior designer Cottington's Interiors, Glen Ellyn, Ill., 1964-65, Robnett-Putman Interiors, Columbia, Mo., 1966-67, Nu-Idea Furniture Co., New Orleans, 1973, Maison Blanche, New Orleans, 1974-75, Mary M. Schuth Interior Design, Metairie, La., 1977—; instr. interior design U. New Orleans div. Continuing Edn., 1973—; judge model homes U.S. Homes, Mandeville, La., 1978, 80; bd. dirs. Interior Design Adv. Com. Delgado Coll., New Orleans, 1981—; speaker in field. Co-author: cookbook From the Privateers' Galley, 1980; design work featured in profl. jours. Recipient 3rd place Batik Design Juried Art Show Columbia (Mo.) Art League, 1969. Mem. Am. Soc. Interior Designers (allied), AIA (profl. affiliate), La. Landmarks, Alpha Chi Omega. Club: Alumnae (New Orleans).

SCHUTTE, PAULA MARION, information systems strategist, consultant; b. St. Paul, Oct. 29, 1941; d. Paul Maurice and Marion (McAllister) S. BA in Chemistry, Rosary Coll., River Forest, Ill., 1963; MBA, NYU, 1985. Med. research chemist Geigy Chem. Corp., Ardsley, N.Y., 1964-70; group leader, sci. systems CIBA-Geigy Corp., Ardsley, N.Y., 1970-77, mgr. sci. info., 1980-83, sr. research fellow, 1985-86, dir. end user services, 1986-87; dir. info. techs. CIBA-Geigy Corp., Ardsley, 1987—; dir. med. systems pharm. div. CIBA-Geigy Corp., Summit, N.J., 1977-80; dir. sci. info. systems pharm. div. CIBA-Geigy Corp., Summit, 1983-85; research coordinator Prism, Cambridge, Mass., 1985—; info. systems cons. St. Jude's, Thornwood, N.Y., 1985-86; adv. Pace U. Computer Sci. and Info. Systems Bd. Patentee in field. Mem. Am. Mgmt. Assn., Assn. Computing Machinery. Office: CIBA-Geigy Corp 444 Saw Mill River Rd Ardsley NY 10502

SCHUTZENHOFER, KAREN KELLY, registered nurse, administrator; b. Granite City, Ill., Mar. 6, 1950; d. Walter Howard and Dorothy (McCroskey) Kelly; m. Ben Schutzenhofer, June 18, 1971; children: Eric, Katie. BSN, So. Ill. U., 1972, MSN, 1977, EdD, 1983. Staff nurse Centreville Twp. Hosp., East St. Louis, Ill., 1972-74; instr. Luth. Med. Ctr., St. Louis, 1974-75; instr. nursing Lewis and Clark Community Coll., Godfrey, Ill., 1976-81; asst. inst. U. Mo., St. Louis, 1981-83, asst. prof., 1983-88, asst. dean, 1985-88; dir. Ctr. of Nursing Excellence St. Louis Children's Hosp., 1988—. Mem. editorial adv. bd. Jour. Nursing Adminstrn., 1989—, Image: Jour. Nursing Scholarship, 1990—; reviewer, mem. editorial adv. bd. Nursing Outlook, 1990—; contbr. chpt. to book, articles to profl. jours. Recipient Disting. Alumna award Sch. Nursing, So. Ill. U., 1987; Sigma Theta Tau grantee, 1989. Mem. Ill. Nurses Assn. (pres. 10th dist. 1987-89, bd. dirs. 10th dist., bd. dirs. state-level 1989-91), Nat. League for Nursing, Midwest Nursing Rsch. Soc., Midwest Alliance in Nursing (assoc.), Am. Nurses Assn. (coun. of nurse researchers), Sigma Theta Tau. Home: 4575 D'Lynn Dr Granite City IL 62040

SCHUUR, DIANE, vocalist; d. Dave Schuur; stepmother: Carrie S. Schuur. Albums include Pilot of My Destiny, 1983, Deedles, Schuur Thing, 1986, Timeless (Grammy award for female jazz vocal 1986), Diane Schuur and the Count Basie Orchestra (Grammy award for female jazz vocal 1987), Talkin' 'Bout You, 1988; performed at the White House, Monterey Jazz Festival, Hollywood Bowl; toured Japan, Europe. Office: care Paul Cantor Ents Ltd 14332 Dickens St Ste 1 Sherman Oaks CA 91423*

SCHUYLER, JANE, fine arts educator; b. Flushing, N.Y., Nov. 2, 1943; d. Frank James and Helen (Oberhofer) S.; BA, Queens Coll., 1965; MA, Hunter Coll., 1967; PhD, Columbia U., 1972. Asst. prof. art history Montclair State Coll., Upper Montclair, N.J., 1970; coord. fine arts, asst. prof. York Coll., CUNY, Jamaica, 1973-77, 78-87, assoc. prof., 1988— , C.W. Post Coll., LIU, Greenvale, N.Y., 1971-73, adj. assoc. prof., 1977-78. Mem. Fine Arts Com. Internat. Women's Arts Festival, 1974-76; pres. United Community Democrats of Jackson Heights, 1987-89. N.Y. Columbia U. Summer Travel and Research grantee, 1969; recipient PSC-CUNY Rsch. award, 1990-91. Mem. Coll. Art Assn. Am., Women's Caucus for Art, AAUP, Nat. Trust Hist. Preservation, Renaissance Soc. Am. Roman Catholic. Contbr. articles on occult and art to Cakes and Ale, 1978, Italian Quar., 1982, Secac Jour. on Italian Renaissance art, 1983, 85, Source, 1986-90, Studies in Iconography, 1987. Author: Florentine Busts: Sculpted Portraiture in the Fifteenth Century, 1976. Home: 35 37 78th St Jackson Heights NY 11372

SCHWAB, CAROL ANN, lawyer; b. Washington, Mo., Mar. 2, 1953; d. Calvin George and Edith Emma (Starke) Schermann; m. Steven Joseph Schwab, May 31, 1975. BA, Southeast Mo. State U., 1975; JD, U. Mo., 1978; LLM, Washington U., St. Louis, 1985. Bar: Mo. 1979, N.C. 1986. Law clk. to presiding justice U.S. Dist. Ct. (we. dist.), Kansas City, Mo., 1979-82; assoc. Bryan, Cave, McPheeters & Roberts, St. Louis, 1982-84, Smith, Anderson, Blount, Dorsett, Mitchell & Jernigan, Raleigh, N.C., 1985-87; asst. prof., resource mgmt. specialist N.C. Agrl. Extension Svc., Raleigh, 1988—; instr. legal writing St. Louis U. Sch. Law, 1984. Contbr. articles to profl. jours. Bd. dirs., co-chair fin. com., N.C. chpt. Nat. Com. for Prevention Child Abuse, 1988-90, pres.-elect, 1990. Recipient John S. Divilbiss award U. Mo., 1977. Mem. ABA, N.C. Bar Assn. (editor The Will and the Way quarterly publ. 1990—, chair estate planning and fiduciary law sect. 1990—), Mo. Bar Assn. Republican. Roman Catholic. Office: NC State U Box 7605 Raleigh NC 27695-7605

SCHWAEBER, MARLENE ROBIN, ; b. N.Y.C., Feb. 12, 1966; d. Henry T. and Lois (Lipschitz) S. BA, Johns Hopkins U., 1988; postgrad., Columbia U. Assoc./analyst The Fuji Bank, Ltd., N.Y.C., 1988-90. Active Nat. Found. for Ileitis and Colitis. Mem. NAFE, Phi Beta Kappa. Jewish. Home: 190 Harbor Ln Roslyn Harbor NY 11576

SCHWAN, JUDITH ALECIA, photographic researcher; b. Middleport, N.Y., Apr. 16, 1925; d. James William and Mary Alecia (Wythers) S. BSChemE, U. Cin., 1948; MS, Cornell U., 1950. Research scientist Eastman Kodak Co., Rochester, N.Y., 1950-65, lab. head, 1965-68, asst. div. dir. emulsion research div., 1968-71, div. dir. emulsion research div., 1971-75, asst. dir. research labs., 1975-86, dir. photographic research labs., photographic products group, 1986-87, ret., 1987; bd. trustees Eastman Savs. & Loan Assn., Rochester, 1977-87. Patentee in field. Trustee St. John Fisher Coll., Rochester, 1975—; active Meml. Art Gallery, Rochester, Rochester Philharm. Orch., Rochester Mus. and Sci. Ctr., George Eastman House, Rochester; mem. task force Women in Ch. of Rochester Cath. Diocese; mem. econ. pastoral steering com. Rochester Cath. Diocese; mem. parish coun. St. Stephen's Ch., Middleport, N.Y.; mem. Diocesan Pastoral Coun., Buffalo. Recipient Disting. Alumnus award U. Cin. Coll. of Engring., 1976. Fellow Soc. Motion Picture and TV Engrs. (Herbert T. Kalmus Meml award for Outstanding Contbn. in Color Films, 1979); mem. Am. Chem. Soc., Nat. Acad. Engring. Soc. Photographic Scientists and Engrs. Clubs: Shelridge Country (Medina, N.Y.). Home: 45 Park Ave Middleport NY 14105

SCHWARCZ, SUSAN KOLODNY, lawyer; b. N.Y.C., Feb. 4, 1954; d. Armand and Elaine (Witkin) Kolodny; m. Steven L. Schwarcz, Aug. 24, 1975; children: Daniel, Rebekah. BA cum laude, Barnard Coll., 1975; postgrad. in social work, Columbia U., 1975-76; JD, Yeshiva U., 1979. Bar: N.Y. 1980. Pleadings atty. U.S. Fidelity & Guaranty Co., N.Y.C., 1980-81; pvt. practice Great Neck, N.Y., 1981-85, Scarsdale, N.Y., 1985—. Mem. Friends Eldridge Street Synagogue, N.Y.C., 1982—; mem. polit. action com. Jewish Action Com., N.Y.C., 1986—. Mem. Westchester County Bar Assn. (family law com. 1985—), Westchester Law Guardians Assn., Sierra Club. Democrat. Office: 30 Ogden Rd Scarsdale NY 10583

SCHWARDT, SUSAN KELLY, civic organization executive; b. Corning, N.Y., Dec. 26, 1936; d. Merle John and Marcia Phillips (Smith) Kelly; m. David Noel Schwardt, June 6, 1956; children: Ellen Schwardt Popp, Judith Schwardt Bray, Jeffrey David, Kevin John. BA in Psychology, U. Rochester, 1960. Officer LWV, Rochester, N.Y., 1971-84; dir. election law and govt. LWV of N.Y. State, Albany, 1985-87, v.p., 1987-89, pres., 1989—. Mem. curriculum adv. com. Webster (N.Y.) Cen. Sch. Dist., 1970s; pres. of congregation First Unitarian Ch., Rochester, 1973-75; mem. Town of Webster/State of N.Y. Waterfront Revitalization Com., 1985-86. Office: LWV NY State 35 Maiden Ln Albany NY 12207-2712

SCHWARTING, ANNE ANGEVINE, energy consultant; b. Rochester, N.Y., Nov. 19, 1945; d. Oliver Lawrence and Helene Ruth (Berman) Angevine; m. Robert H. Schwarting, June 7, 1969; children: Katrina H., Christopher R. BS in Home Econs., Cornell U., 1967; MS in Textiles, Pa. State U., 1968. Cert. secondary tchr., N.Y. Home econs. agt. Coop. Extension, Oswego, N.Y., 1968-69; cafeteria mgr. Spencer (N.Y.)-Van Ettan Schs., Spencer, 1969-70; tchr. Bd. Coop. Ednl. Svcs., Cortland, N.Y., 1970-71; acct. Officers Clubs, U.S. Army, Nürnberg, Fed. Republic Germany, 1972-74; asst. dir. info. and referral Cornell U., Ithaca, N.Y., 1979-81; energy specialist Ithaca Neighborhood Housing Svcs., 1981-89; energy cons. Keuka Housing Coun., Penn Yan, N.Y., 1987—; cons. Corning (N.Y.) Community Found., 1988—, N.Y. State Electric and Gas Corp., Geneva, 1987—. Bd. dirs. Human Svcs. Coalition, Ithaca, 1980-85; mem. Energy-Housing Com., Ithaca, 1981-85; pres. Coop. Extension Program Com., Ithaca, 1984-85; pres. Yates County Hist. Soc., Penn Yan, 1989—. Mem. AAUW. Office: Keuka Housing Coun 160 Main St Penn Yan NY 14527

SCHWARTZ, ALYSE BETT, systems analyst; b. Bronx, N.Y., Aug. 8, 1960; d. Irwin Aaron and Beryl (Leff) S. AAS, SUNY, Farmingdale, 1980; BBA, Hofstra U., 1987. Programmer trainee State Ins. Fund, N.Y.C., 1980; programmer analyst cons. Bradford Nat. Corp., N.Y.C., 1981-83; programmer E.F. Hutton, N.Y.C., 1983; programmer analyst Chase Manhattan Bank, N.Y.C., 1983-87; sr. systems analyst Met. Life Ins. Co., N.Y.C., 1987-89; sr. programmer, analyst Orion Pictures Corp., N.Y.C., 1989—. Mem. Bayshore Skating Club, Commack Skating Club, Massapequa Road Runners Club, N.Y. Road Runners Club. Republican. Jewish. Home: 367 Atlantic Ave Massapequa Park NY 11762

SCHWARTZ, CAROL A., optometrist, editor, consultant; b. Alton, Ill., Dec. 19, 1953; d. Andrew C. and Joyce L. (Barnes) S.; m. Robert Standish Billups, June 14, 1980. Student, Ill. State U., 1972-74; OD, Ill. Coll. Optometry, Chgo., 1978; MBA, U. Chgo., 1985. Cons. Wesley-Jessen, Chgo., 1978-79, mgr. clin. svcs., 1980-83; pres. On Call, Ltd., Chgo., 1983-85; editor Contact Lens Forum, Gralla Publs., N.Y.C., 1985—; internat. lectr. in field. Contbr. numerous articles to sci. jours. Office: Gralla Publs 1515 Broadway New York NY 10036

SCHWARTZ, CAROL LEVITT, former government official; b. Greenville, Miss., Jan. 20, 1944; d. Stanley and Hilda (Simmons) Levitt; m. David H. Schwartz (dec.); children: Stephanie, Hilary, Douglas. BS in Spl. and Elem. Edn., U. Tex., 1965. Mem. transiton team Office of Pres. Elect, 1980-81; con. office presdl. personnel The White House, Washington, 1981; cons. U.S. Dept. Edn., Washington, 1982; pres. sec. U.S. Ho. Reps., Washington, 1982-83; mem. Coun. of D.C., Washington, 1985-89; vice chmn. Nat. Adv. Coun. on Edn. Disadvantaged Children, 1974-79; mem. D.C. Bd. Edn., 1974-82; lectr. in field; radio commentator, 1990—. Asst. treas. Met. Police Boys and Girls Club, 1983, asst. sec., 1984, sec., 1985-89, lst v.p., 1989—, chmn. membership program, 1984—, bd. dirs., 1981—; mem. adv. coun. Am. Coun. Young Polit. Leaders, 1982—; mem. nat. coun. Friends of Kennedy Ctr., 1984—; bd. dirs. Whitman-Walker Clinic, 1988—, St. John's Child Devel. Ctr., 1989—; mem. adv. bd. AAA, 1988—; active numerous other civic, cultural and ednl. orgns. Mem. Cosmos Club. Republican. Jewish.

SCHWARTZ, CORINNE O'HARE, business owner; b. Lebanon, N.H., Mar. 28, 1929; d. Robert Joseph and Catherine (Forest) O'Hare; m. Fred Jerome Schwartz, Aug. 11, 1949; children: Theresa O'Hare Schwartz, Abby Roberta Burke. Grad. high sch., Keene Valley, N.Y. Pres. la Femme Interiors, Lake Placid, N.Y., 1968-74; stylist Carillon Fashions, N.Y.C., 1975-77; sales dir. Kay Kipps Fashions, N.Y.C., 1977-80; dir. Robert Cappelo div. Carillon, N.Y.C., 1980-83; pres. Corinne O'Hare Inc., N.Y.C., 1985—. Roman Catholic.

SCHWARTZ, DORIS RUHBEL, nursing educator, consultant; b. Bklyn., May 30, 1915; d. Henry and Florence Marie (Shuttleworth) S. B.S., NYU, 1953, M.S., 1955. RN, N.Y. Staff nurse Methodist Hosp., Bklyn., 1942-43; pub. health nurse Vis. Nurse Assn., Bklyn., 1947-51; pub. health nurse Cornell U. Med. Coll., Cornell-N.Y. Hosp. Sch. Nursing, N.Y.C., 1951-61, tchr. pub. health nursing, geriatric nursing, 1961-80; sr. fellow U. Pa. Sch. Nursing, Phila., 1981-90. Contbr. articles to profl. jours. Served to capt., N.C., U.S. Army, 1943-47, PTO. NSF fellow, 1975-76; recipient Diamond Jubilee Nursing award N.Y. County Registered Nurses Assn., 1979. Fellow Am. Pub. Health Assn. (disting. career award nursing sect. 1979) mem. Am. Nurses Assn. (Pearl McIver award 1979), Am. Acad. Nursing (governing council 1973-74), Inst. Medicine, Sigma Theta Tau (recipient founders award 1979). Democrat. Mem. Soc. of Friends. Club: Soroptimist Internat. (N.Y.C.) (v.p. 1974-75).

SCHWARTZ, ELEANOR BRANTLEY, academic administrator; b. Kite, Ga., Jan. 1, 1937; d. Jesse Melvin and Hazel (Hill) Brantley; children: John, Cynthia. Student Mercer U., Ga. So. Coll., 1956-57; BBA, Ga. State U., 1961, MBA, 1963, DBA, 1969. Adminstrv. asst. Fin. Agy., 1954, Fed. Govt., Va., Pa., Ga., 1959-61; asst. dean admissions Ga. State U., Atlanta, 1961-65, asst. prof., 1965-70; assoc. prof. Cleve. State U., 1970-80, assoc. dean, 1975-80; dean, Harzfeld prof. U. Mo., Kansas City, 1980-87, vice chancellor acad. affairs, 1987—; disting. vis. prof. Berry Coll., Rome, Ga., N.Y. State U. Coll., Fredonia, Mons U., Belgium; cons. pvt. industry, U.S., Europe, Can.; bd. dirs. Sentinel Consumer Products, Inc., Am. Carriers, Inc. Am. Bank and Trust Co. of Kansas City. Author: Sex Barriers in Business, 1971, Contemporary Readings in Marketing, 1974; (with Muczyk and Smith) Principles of Supervision, 1984. Chmn., Mayor's Task Force in Govt. Efficiency, Kansas City, Mo., 1984; mem. community planning and research council United Way Kansas City, 1975-78; bd. dirs. Jr. Achievement, 1982—, Greater Kansas City ARC. Recipient Disting. Faculty award Cleve. State U., 1974, Cleve. Community Career Achievement award YMCA, 1980, 60 Women of Achievement Girls Scouts Council Mid Continent, 1983; named Career Woman of Yr. Kansas City, Mo., 1989. Mem. Am. Mkt. Assn., Acad. Internat. Bus., Am. Mgmt. Assn., Am. Case Research Assn., Internat. Soc. Study Behavioral Devel., Phi Kappa Phi, Golden Key, Alpha Iota Delta, Beta Gamma Sigma (bd. govs.). Office: Univ Mo Sch Acad Affairs Kansas City MO 64110

SCHWARTZ, ESTAR ALMA, lawyer; b. Bklyn., June 29, 1950; d. Henry Israel and Elaine Florence (Scheiner) Sutel; m. Lawrence Gerald Schwartz, June 28, 1976 (div. Dec. 1977); 1 child, Joshua. JD, N.Y.U., 1980. Mgr., ptnr. Scheiner, Scheiner, DeVito & Wytte, N.Y.C., 1966-81; fed. govt., social security fraud specialist DHHS, OI, OIG, SSFIS, N.Y.C., 1982-83; pensions Todtman, Epstein, et al, N.Y.C., 1983-85; office mgr., sec. Sills, Beck, Cummis, N.Y.C., 1985-86; office mgr., bookkeeper Philip, Birnbaum & Assocs., N.Y.C., 1986-87. Democrat. Jewish. Home and Office: 67-20 Parsons Blvd 2A Flushing NY 11365

SCHWARTZ, ESTHER LATTERMAN, educator; b. Pitts., Feb. 23, 1938; d. Harry W. and Helen (Sherman) Latterman; m. David L. Schwartz, June 19, 1966; children: Paul M., Howard D. AB, U. Pitts., 1959; cert. edn., Mich. State U., 1960; MA, Pa. State U., 1962. Cert. secondary tchr., Pa. Tchr. W. Mifflin (Pa.) Area Schs., 1962-66; tchr. Pitts. Pub. Schs., 1966-69, homebound and ESL tchr., 1969-72; homebound and ESL tchr. Gateway Sch. Dist., Monroeville, Pa., 1970-84; tchr. Seton LaSalle High Sch., Pitts., 1984; instr. Allegheny County Community Coll., Pitts., 1985—; tutor Allegheny County Community Coll., Pitts., 1985—, writing workshop founder, 1987; newspaper sponsor W. Mifflin Area Schs., 1962-66. Editor: Hadassah-Pgh, 1972-75. Pres. Medina Na'Amat, Pitts., 1970-74, sec. Pitts. Coun. Na'Amat; vol. Ladies Hosp. Aid Montefiore Hosp., 1966—. Mem. Women in Communications, Inc. (founder Pitts. chpt. 1969, v.p. 1963-65), Pi Delta Epsilon. Home: 2012 Hampstead Dr Pittsburgh PA 15235 Office: Allegheny Community Coll 412 Milton Hall 808 Ridge Ave Pittsburgh PA 15212

SCHWARTZ, FELICE N., public sector administrator; b. N.Y.C., Jan. 16, 1925; d. Albert and Rose (Kaplan) Nierenberg; m. Irving L. Schwartz, Jan. 12, 1946; children: Cornelia Ann, Tony, James Oliver. BA, Smith Coll., 1945, LHD, 1981; LHD, Pace U., 1980. Founder, exec. dir. Nat. Scholarship Svc. and Fund for Negro Students, N.Y.C., 1945-51, now mem. adv. bd.; v.p. prodn. Etched Products Corp., N.Y.C., 1951-54; founder, pres. Catalyst, N.Y.C., 1962—. Author numerous books and articles. Mem. adv. bd. Nat. Women's Polit. Caucus; bd. visitors CUNY Grad. Ctr.; bd. dirs. Bus. Coun. N.Y. State; adv. com. Kellogg Nat. Fellowship Program. Recipient Mademoiselle medal for singular achievement in edn., 1949, Disting. Alumnae medal Smith Coll., 1976, Susan B. Anthony award NOW, 1981; named Human Resource Profl. of Yr., Internat. Assn. Pers. Women, 1983. Mem. Am. Mgmt. Assn., Women's Forum, Inc. Office: Catalyst 250 Park Ave S New York NY 10003*

SCHWARTZ, GERRI E., psychologist, psychopharmacologist, clinician; b. N.Y.C.; d. Marcus Schwartz and Diana Shuster. BA, CCNY, 1970; PhD, CUNY, 1974. Lic. psychologist, N.Y. Asst. prof., chairperson SUNY, Old Westbury, 1975-81; asst. dir. Sandoz Rsch. Inst., N.J., 1981-84, Lorex Pharmaceuticals, Chgo., 1985-88; assoc. dir. Janssen Rsch. Found., Piscataway, N.J., 1988—; lectr. dept. of psychiatry Columbia U., N.Y.C., Coll. of Physicians and Surgeons, N.Y.C. Author: Family Member Rating Scale For Drug Research, 1983; editor: Readings in Personality and Adjustment, 1976, 77, 78, 79; contbr. articles to profl. jours. Mem.. Am. Coll. Neuropsychopharmacology (liaison mem. to industry, academia and govt. 1987-89), Am. Soc. Clin. Pharmacology and Therapeutics, AAAS, Am. Psychol. Assn., The Gerontol. Soc. Am., N.Y. Acad. Scis., Psi Chi, Sigma Xi. Office: Janssen Rsch Found 40 Kingsbridge Rd Piscataway NJ 08855

SCHWARTZ, ILENE, psychotherapist, educator; b. Phila., June 19, 1942; d. Israel Gerson and Jean (Soloway) Schiffman; m. Victor Louis Schwartz, Jan. 6, 1970 (div. 1980); 1 child, Amy Jill. B.S., Temple U., 1970; postgrad. U. Pa., 1981-82, Antioch U., 1990—. Instr. psychology Pratt Inst., Bklyn., 1969-70; psychotherapist Phila. Mental Health Clinic, 1972-74, Phila. Consultation Ctr., 1974-80, Help, Inc., Phila., 1974-80; pvt. practice psychologist, Phila., 1980—; instr. Community Coll. Phila., 1974-80; crisis counselor Women In Transition, 1988-89; cons. in field. Mem. Am. Psychol. Assn.

SCHWARTZ, ILSA ROSLOW, neuroscientist; b. Bklyn., Aug. 20, 1941; d. David and Lottie (Warshall) Roslow; m. Alan Gordon Schwartz, July 19, 1964; children: Leah Ellen, Seth Roslow. AB magna cum laude, Vassar Coll., 1962; MS, Yale U., 1964, PhD, 1968. Postdoctoral fellow Albert Einstein Coll. Medicine, Bronx, N.Y., 1968-69; rsch. assoc. ctr. for neural scis. Ind. U., Bloomington, 1970-73, asst. prof. anatomy and physiology, 1973-75; asst. prof. med. scis. Ind. U. Sch. Medicine, Bloomington, 1976-77; vis. rsch. anatomist UCLA Sch. Medicine, 1976-77, asst. prof. in- residence head and neck surgery, 1977-81, assoc. prof., 1981-87; assoc. prof. Yale U. Sch. Medicine, New Haven, 1987-89, prof. surgery otolaryngology and neuroanatomy, 1899—; mem. communicative disorders review com. Nat. Inst. Neurol. Communicative Disorders and Stroke, Bethesda, 1981-83, chair, 1983-85; sci. adv. coun. House Ear Inst., L.A., 1989. Recipient Jacob Javits Neurosci. Investigator award Nat. Inst. Neurol. Communicative Disorders and Stroke, 1988-95; grantee NIH, 1973—; fellow Vassar Coll., 1962-63, NIH, 1962-68, 68-69. Mem. Assn. for Rsch. in Otolaryngology (coun. mem. 1986-89), Nat. Inst. on Deafness and Other Communication Disorders (bd. dirs.), Soc. for Neurosci. (chair Bloomington Ind. chpt. 1975-76), Am. Assn. Anatomists, Women in Neurosci., AAAS. Jewish. Office: Yale U Sch Medicine 333 Cedar St New Haven CT 06510

SCHWARTZ, JANE SUSAN, nurse; b. Fall River, Mass., May 28, 1955; d. William and Sylvia Evelyn (Hillman) S. MusB, Hartt Coll. Music, 1976; Diploma in Nursing, Peter Bent Brigham Sch., Boston, 1983; MS in Nursing, Yale U., 1988. RN, Mass., Conn.; cert. specialist in psychiatric nursing, 1989. Psychiat. nurse McLean Hosp., Belmont, Mass., 1983-86, Yale Psychiat. Inst., New Haven, 1982-88; nurse mgr. psychiatry Leonard Morse Hosp., Natick, Mass., 1988-90; clin. nurse adminstr. Yale Psychiatric Inst., New Haven, 1990—; harpsichordist, various performances, 1976—. Mem. Mass. Orgn. Nurse Execs., Nurses United for Responsible Svc. Home: 24 Greenway St Hamden CT 06517 Office: Yale Psychiat Inst Box 12A Yale Sta New Haven CT 06520

SCHWARTZ, JOYCE GENSBERG, pathologist; b. San Antonio, July 24, 1950; d. Frank and Sara Gensberg; B.A., U. Tex.-Austin, 1971, M.A., 1972; M.D., U. Tex.-San Antonio, 1980; m. Alan R. Schwartz, July 17, 1977. Speech pathologist Northeast Ind. Sch. Dist., San Antonio, 1971-73; vet. asst., 1973-74; resident in pathology Audie Murphy VA Hosp., San Antonio; pathology Faculty U. Tex. Health Sci. Ctr. at San Antonio, 1984. Mem. AMA, Coll. Am. Pathologists, Bexar County Med. Assn., Women's Faculty Assn. (pres. 1988-89), San Antonio Soc. Pathologists (pres. 1988-89), Phi Kappa Phi. Jewish.

SCHWARTZ, JUDY ELLEN, navy cardiothoracic surgeon; b. Mason City, Iowa, Oct. 5, 1946; d. Walter Carl and Alice Nevada (Moore) Schwartz. B.S., U. Iowa, 1968, M.D., 1971. Diplomate Am. Bd. Surgery, Am. Bd. Thoracic Surgery. Intern, Nat. Naval Med. Center, Bethesda, Md., 1971-72, gen. surgery resident, 1972-76, thoracic surgery resident, 1976-78, staff cardiothoracic surgeon, 1979-82, chief cardiothoracic surgeon, 1982-83; chmn. cardiothoracic surg. dept. Naval Hosp., San Diego, 1983-85, quality assurance program dir., 1985—, exec. officer Rapidly Deployable Med. Facility Four, 1986—; asst. prof. surgery Uniformed Services Univ. Health Scis., Bethesda, from 1983; cardiothoracic speciality cons. to naval med. command U.S. Navy, Washington, 1983-84. Contbr. articles to various publs. Fellow Am. Coll. Cardiology, Am. Coll. Surgeons; mem. Am. Thoracic Soc., Am. Med. Women's Assn., AMA, Uniformed Services Univ. Surg. Assocs., Am. Mgmt. Assn., Am. Acad. of Med. Dirs. Lutheran. Office: Naval Hosp Quality Assurance Unit San Diego CA 92134*

SCHWARTZ, LAURIE KOLLER, association executive, development consultant; b. Munich, Germany, Oct. 19, 1947; came to U.S., 1949, naturalized, 1954; d. Felix and Sally (Wiernik) Koller; m. Michael Louis Schwartz, Aug. 20, 1967; children: Jonas David, Adam Avi, Samara Beth. Diploma in radiol. tech. Mercy Hosp., Balt., 1967; BA, U. Balt., 1988. Lic. real estate agt., Md. Radiol. technologist Central Med. Ctr., Balt., 1967-68, Greenstein, Baitch & Friedman, Balt., 1968-70; ptnr. Creme de la Creme, Balt., 1976-78; bd. dirs., coordinator Mid-Atlantic region Internat. Assn. Near Death Studies, U. Conn., Storrs, 1982—; pres. Koller Cons.; cons. Mgmt. Tng. Systems, Inc., Springfield, Va., 1985—. Active various polit. campaigns, Balt.; chmn. study group Hadassah Med. Orgn., Balt., 1975-76. Mem. Am. Soc. Tng. and Devel., Assn. Transpersonal Psychology, Inst. Noetic Scis., Am. Register Radiol. Technologists, Exec. Women's Network, Nat. Alliance Female Execs., Second Generation-Children of Survivors of the Holocaust, Inst. Noetic Scis., Assn. Transpersonal Psychology. Democrat. Jewish. Club: Mercantile (Balt.) Avocations: jazz and aerobic dancing, theatre, reading, French cooking. Home: 7041 Concord Rd Baltimore MD 21208

SCHWARTZ, LILLIAN FELDMAN, artist, filmmaker, art historian, author; b. Cin., July 13, 1927; d. Jacob and Katie (Green) Feldman; m. Jack James Schwartz, Dec. 22, 1946; children: Jeffrey Hugh, Laurens Robert. RN, U. Cin., 1947; Dr. honoris causa, Kean Coll., 1988. Nurse Cin. Gen. Hosp., 1947; head supr. premature nursery St. Louis Maternity Hosp., 1947-48; cons. AT&T Bell Labs., Murray Hill, N.J., 1968—; pres. Computer Creations Corp., Watchung, N.J., 1989—; cons. Bell Communications Research, Morristown, N.J., 1984—; artist-in-residence Sta. WNET, N.Y.C., 1972-74; cons. T.J. Watson Rsch. Lab. IBM Corp., Yorktown, N.Y., 1975, 82-84; vis. mem. computer sci. dept. U. Md., College Park, 1974-80; adj. prof. fine arts Kean Coll., New Brunswick, N.J., 1980-82, Rutgers U., New Brunswick, N.J., 1982-83; adj. prof. dept. psychology NYU, N.Y.C., 1985-86, assoc. prof. computer sci.; guest lectr. Princeton U., Columbia U., Yale U., Rockefeller U. Co-author: THE Computer Art Book; contbr. chpts. to books, also Trans. Am. Philos. Soc., vol. 75, Part 6, 1985; one-woman shows of sculpture and paintings include Columbia U., 1967, 68, Rabin and Krueger Gallery, Newark, 1968; films shown at Met. Mus., N.Y.C., Franklin Inst., Phila., 1972, U. Toronto, 1972, Am. Embassy, London, 1972, L.A. County Mus., Corcoran Gallery, Washington 1972, Whitney Mus., N.Y.C., 1973, Grand Palais, Paris, Musee Nat. d'Art Moderne, Paris, IBM, and others. Recipient numerous art and film awards, Emmy award Mus. Modern Art, 1984; named Outstanding Alumnus, U. Cin., 1987; grantee Nat. Endowment for Arts, 1977, 81, Corp. Pub. Broadcasting, 1979, Nat. Endowment Composers/Librettists, 1981. Mem. Nat. Acad. TV Arts and Scis., Am. Film Inst., Info. Film Producers Am., Soc. Motion Picture and TV Engrs., Internat. Sculptors Assn., Centro Studi Pierfrancescani (Sansepolero, Italy, founding mem.).

SCHWARTZ, MARY KAY, psychologist; b. Millersburg, Ohio, Feb. 12, 1941; d. John M. and Susan (Schlabach) Kaufman; m. Murray Walter Stein, Aug. 3, 1968 (div. 1975); 1 child, Charles Christopher; m. Larry Richard Schwartz, Nov. 8, 1987. BA in Edn., Goshen (Ind.) Coll., 1963; postgrad., C.G. Jung Inst., Zurich, 1970-72; ME in Counseling, U. Houston, 1975; PhD in Counseling Psychology, Kent (Ohio) State U., 1982. Lic. psychologist. Coord. gerontology Cuyahoga Valley Community Mental Health Ctr., Cuyahoga Falls, Ohio, 1977-83; supr. counseling svcs. HMD Health Ohio, Akron, Ohio, 1983—; pvt. practice Akron (Ohio) Family Inst., 1990—. Co-author videotape: A Psychodrama: Widowhood, 1983. Precinct committeeperson Dem. party, Akron, 1989-90. Mem. Am. Psychol. Assn., Psychologists for Social Responsibility, Ohio Psychol. Assn., Akron Area Profl. Psychologists. Presbyterian. Home: 1951 Wiltshire Akron OH 44313 Office: Akron Family Inst 3451 S Arlington Rd Akron OH 44312

SCHWARTZ, MODEST EUPHEMIA, real estate company executive; b. Chgo., Dec. 14, 1915; d. Giles E. and Evelyn (Tomczak) Ratkowski; m. Edward Joseph Schwartz, Feb. 9, 1946 (dec. July 1979); children: Kathryn Ann, Edward Thomas. BA, UCLA, 1936, MA, 1938; libr. credential, Immaculate Heart Coll., L.A., 1958. Cert. tchr., libr., Calif. Tchr. Alhambra (Calif.) City Schs., 1938-58, libr., 1958-72; v.p. Fremont Svc., Alhambra, 1959-83, pres., 1983-86; v.p. Moulding Supply Co., Alhambra, 1967-83, pres., 1983-85; v.p., bd. dirs. Sequoia Mgmt. Co., Alhambra, 1969-86; mng. ptnr. SRSH Realty Ptnrs., Alhambra, 1986-89. Bd. dirs. Found. for Cardiovascular Rsch., Pasadena, Calif., 1973-85, Progressive Savs., Alhambra, 1979-85; mem. Ret. Sr. Vol. Program, Alhambra, 1979—, Alhambra Community Hosps. Aux., 1987—, Friends Alhambra Pub. Libr., 1981—; pres. bd. trustees Alhambra Pub. Libr., 1981-83, 89—; L.A. County Art Mus., Met. Mus., N.Y. Mem. ALA, NEA, Calif. Ret. Tchrs. Assn., AAUW (life, Edn. Found. grant in her name 1988, br. treas. 1986-88, 89—), UCLA Alumni Assn., Friends of Alhambra Libr., Alhambra Community Hosp. Aux., Women's City Club. Home: 1117 N Stoneman Apt K Alhambra CA 91801

SCHWARTZ, MONA, toy company sales executive; b. N.Y.C., Jan. 30, 1953; d. Harry and Annette (Ressler) S. BA, Bklyn. Coll., 1974. High sch. tchr. biology N.Y.C. Sch. System, 1974-76; sales inventory person Eden Toys Inc., N.Y.C., 1976-77, salesperson, 1977-80, sales mgr., 1980-87; nat. sales mgr., 1988; nat. sales mgr., 1989-90, v.p. sales, 1990—. Mem. NAFE, Childrenswear Mfrs. Assn. Democrat. Jewish. Avocations: racquetball, boating, reading, scuba diving. Home: 1123 Sussex Rd Teaneck NJ 07666

SCHWARTZ, ROSALYE ANN, education educator; b. Detroit, Mar. 9, 1936; d. Oscar and Goldie (Rubin) Klaper; m. Sy E. Schwartz (div. Jan. 1976); children: Todd, Loren. BS, Wayne State U., 1967; MS, Western Wash. U., 1975. Tchr. Thurston High Sch., Detroit, 1957-62; instr. edn. R.I. Coll., Providence, 1965, Cen. Wash. U., Ellensburg, 1966, Whatcom Community Coll., Bellingham, Wash., 1975-84; instr. edn. Western Wash. U., Bellingham, 1984—, supr. student teaching edn. dept., 1987—; curriculum devel. tng. specialist Bellingham Pub. Schs., 1984—; disciplinary hearing officer Seattle Pub. Schs., 1988—. Bd. dirs. Planned Parenthood, Bellingham, 1982-86; mem. Wash. Women United, Olympia, 1985—. Am. Soc. for Tng. and Devel. Home: 13446 Greenwood Ave N Seattle WA 98133

SCHWARTZ, ROSELIND SHIRLEY GRANT, podiatrist; b. N.Y.C., Apr. 23, 1922; d. Joseph and Amy (Jacobs) Grant; m. Herman Schwartz, Dec. 19, 1943 (dec. Sept., 1980); children: Arthur Zachary, Raymond Dana. BA, NYU, 1943; D Podiatry cum laude, L.I. U., 1947; DPM, Long Island U., 1970; student, L.A. Trade Technical Coll., 1973-75. Notary pub., Calif. Pvt. practice Podiatry N.Y.C., 1947-73; cons. L.A., 1973-76, travel cons., 1974—. Bd. dirs. Welfare League for Retarded Children, 1955-73, chmn. Annual Souvenir Jour., 1955-65, Annual Luncheon, 25th anniversary, 1968, pres., 1969-70; pres. Sisterhood of Community Ctr. of Israel, N.Y., 1966-67; Cub den mother Boy Scouts Am., N.Y., 1960-63; class mother Pub. Schs., N.Y., 1960-66, pres. Parents' Assn. Jr. High Sch., N.Y., 1966-69; bd. dirs., pres. Barrington-Terryhill Condominium Assn., 1981—; vol. UCLA, 1981—; mem. Adv. Coms., Nurse Anesthesists, Infant & Child Care, 1981—. Recipient testimonial Community Ctr. Israel, Bronx, N.Y., 197l, award for devoted leadership Welfare League, 1963, 65. Mem. Assn. Wives of Physicians, Podiatry Soc. N.Y. State, Bus. and Profl. Women. Home: 612 S Barrington Ave #410 Los Angeles CA 90049

SCHWARTZ, RUTH WAINER, physician; b. New London, Wis.; d. Louis M. and Kathryn Ann (Schwall) W.; m. Seymour I. Schwartz, June 18, 1949; children: Richard, Kenneth, David. BS, U. Wis., 1947, MD, 1950. Diplomate Am. Bd. Ob-Gyn. Intern Genesee Hosp., Rochester, N.Y., 1950; resident Strong Meml. Hosp., Rochester, N.Y., 1951-54; pvt. practice ob-gyn. Rochester, 1954—; examiner Am. Bd. Obstetrics and Gynecology, 1976—, bd. dirs., 1981-89; dir. colposcopy, dysplasia and DES Clinic, colposcopy and laser tutor Genesee Hosp.; clin. prof. ob/gyn U. Rochester Sch. Medicine and Dentistry; pres. med. staff Genesee Hosp., 1972-74; bd. dirs. Genesee Health Svc., 1972-75, ARC, med. adv. com.; trustee Rochester Acad. Medicine, 1975-78; vis. prof. U. Kuwait Med. Sch., 1984, U. Toledo Sch. Medicine, 1985, U. N.Mex. Sch. Medicine, 1989. Contbr. numerous articles to med. jours. and chpts. to med. textbooks; cons. editor and contbr. to The Merck Manual, 15th edit, 1983, 16th edit., 1987. Mem. med. adv. bd. N.Y. State Task Force on Child Abuse. Named one of Best Women Doctors in Am., Harper's Bazaar mag., Nov., 1985. Mem. Am. Coll. Surgeons, Am. Coll. Obstetricians and Gynecologists (health care commn., Women in Ob/Gyn task force, patient edn. com. 1879-83, task force on hysterectomy 1987-89, adv. bd. Dist. II 1982, task force on aging 1989-91), Am. Soc. of Colposcopy and Colpomicroscopy, Gynecologic Laser Soc. (bd. dirs.), Am. Fertility Soc., AMA (accreditation council on continuing med. edn. 1987-91), N.Y. State Med. Assn., Monroe County Med. Soc. (maternal mortality com., pub. health com.), Am. Bd. Med. Specialties (fin. com.). Home: 18 Lake Lacoma Dr Pittsford NY 14534

SCHWARTZ, (ELLEN) SHIRLEY ECKWALL, chemist; b. Detroit, Aug. 26, 1935; d. Emil Victor and Jessie Grace (Galbraith) Eckwall; m. Ronald Elmer Schwartz, Aug. 25, 1957; children: Steven Dennis, Bradley Allen, George Byron. B.S., U. Mich., 1957; M.S., Wayne State U., 1962, Ph.D., 1970; B.S., Detroit Inst. Tech., 1978. Asst. prof. Detroit Inst. Tech., 1973-78, head div. math. sci., 1976-78; research staff mem. BASF Wyandotte Corp., Wyandotte, Mich., 1978-81, head sect. functional fluids, 1981; staff research scientist Gen. Motors Corp., Warren, Mich., 1981—. Contbr. articles to profl. jours.; patentee in field. Corr. sec. Childbirth Without Pain Edn. Assn., 1962; corr. sec. Warren-Centerline Human Rels. Coun., 1968. Recipient McCuen award Gen. Motors Rsch., 1988, Kettering award Gen. Motors Corp., 1988, Gold award Engring. Soc. Detroit, 1989. Mem. Soc. Tribologists and Lubrication Engrs. (treas. Detroit sect. 1981, vice chmn. 1982, chmn. 1982-83, chmn. Wear Tech. com. 1987-88, dir. 1985—, assoc. editor 1988-90, Wilbur Deutsch award 1987), Am. Chem. Soc., Tissue Culture Assn., Soc. Automotive Engrs. (Excellence in Oral Presentation award 1988), Mensa, Sigma Xi. Lutheran. Club: Classic Guitar Soc. Mich., U.S. Power Squadrons, Detroit Navigators. Office: GM Rsch Labs Warren MI 48090

SCHWARTZ, VALERIE BREUER, interior designer; b. Senica, Czechoslovakia, May 13, 1912; came to U.S., 1928, naturalized, 1928; d. Jacob and Ethel (Weiss) Breuer; m. Leo Schwartz, Feb. 5, 1939; children—Catherine, Robert, William. Student States Real Gymnazium, Prague, 1925-28; Parsons N.Y. Sch. of Fine and Applied Arts, 1930-32. Cert. Am. Soc. Interior Designers. Self-employed interior designer, N.J., 1932—. Contbr. to various mags. including N.Y. Times, House & Garden, Cue Mag., Confort, Argentina; guest radio talk shows. Mem. Hadassah (life). Designed Holocaust Room, Kean Coll., N.J.

SCHWARTZ, VICKI ANNE, physician; b. N.Y.C., Jan. 12, 1954; d. Leon and Sylvia Lillian (Orling) S.; m. David Nahum Gale, Nov. 8, 1981. Student, Brown U., 1972-75; MD, Harvard U., 1979. Diplomate Am. Bd. INternat. Medicine, Am. Bd. Rheumatology. Intern, then resident Bronx Mcpl. Hosp. Ctr., N.Y.C., 1979-82; emergency rm. physician Harrington Meml. Hosp., Southbridge, Mass., 1982-83; fellow in rheumatology Mass. Gen. Hosp., Boston, 1983-86; staff rheumatologist Milford (Mass.) Whitinsville Regional Hosp., 1986—. Fellow Am. Coll. Rheumatology, Mass. Med. Soc. Office: Pastorello Health Ctr 355 E Central St Franklin MA 02038

SCHWARTZBERG, LINDA KAY, accountant, financial executive; b. San Antonio, Apr. 15, 1949; d. Jerry Joseph and Dolores Mae (McCurry) Rasmussen; m. Steven Alan Schwartzberg, Apr. 19, 1970; 1 child, Laurie Rachelle. BS, Lindenwood Coll., 1987. CPA, Mo. Office mgr. Coopers & Lybrand, St. Louis, 1982-84; controller The Type House, Inc., St. Louis, 1984-86; cons. Arthur Young & Co., St. Louis, 1986-87; v.p. fin. Amedco Health Care, Inc., Wright City, Mo., 1987—. Pres. bd. trustees Congregation B'nai Torah, St. Charles, Mo., 1989-90. Mem. Wright City C. of C., Beta Sigma Phi (v.p. St. Peters, Mo. chpt. 1988-89, Woman of Yr. 1988-89). Home: 44 Heather Dr Saint Peters MO 63376 Office: Amedco Health Care Inc 401 S Outer Service Rd Wright City MO 63390

SCHWARZ, BARBARA RUTH BALLOU, elementary school teacher; b. East Orange, N.J., Aug. 8, 1930; d. Robert Ingram Ballou and Ruth Edna Sweeney; m. Eugene A. Schwarz Jr., Dec. 24, 1954 (div. 1977); children: Ruth Ellen Schwarz Caraher, Eugene A. BS, Trenton State Coll., 1952. Tchr. West Orange N.J. Schs., 1952-54, Franklin Sch., Ft. Wayne, Ind., 1955-56, Parliament Place Sch., North Babylon, N.Y., 1965—; trustee welfare trust fund North Babylon Tchrs. Orgn., N.Y., 1988—. Vol. Safe Home, L.I. Womens Coalition, Bay Shore, N.Y., 1979—; sec. Victims Info. Bur., Suffolk, 1987-88, v.p., 1989-90, pres. 1990—, rep. to Women's Equal Rights Coalition, Suffolk County Human Rights Commn., 1989—. Mem. AAUW (membership v.p. Islip area br. 1982-84, pres. 1984-88, legis. chair 1988—, chair of promoting individual liberties Nassau-Suffolk dist. 1989—, rep. to Women on Job task force 1986—, pro-choice coord. N.Y. State div., chair-elect dist. VI interbr., named honoree 1988), Phi Delta Kappa. Republican. Methodist. Home: 23 Wyandanch Ave Babylon NY 11702 Office: Parliament Place Sch Parliament Pl North Babylon NY 11703

SCHWARZ, PATRICIA TZUANOS, real estate company executive; b. New Orleans, Oct. 1, 1948; d. John Angelo Tzuanos and Marion Gertrude (Johnson) Rodriquez; m. Kenneth W. Zylicz Nov. 1, 1965 (div. May 1969); 1 child, Sheryl Anne; m. Erik B. Schwarz, June 1, 1970 (div. Oct. 1982); 1 child, Erika Rachael; m. Barney Leroy Core, Dec. 31, 1982. BA, U. New Orleans, 197l. Cert. real estate instr., La. Mgr., v.p. Wagner Truax Realtors, Metairie, La., 1975-77; owner, mgr. Patricia Schwarz, Inc./Realtors, Folsom, La., 1977—; sec.-treas. Folsom Thoroughbred Tng. Ctr., 1980—; mem. profl. standards com. St. Tammany Bd., Slidell, La., 1983-87, chmn. real estate fair, 1988; dir. Miss Covington (La.) Beauty Pageant, 1988-90, Miss La. Am. Pageant, 1989—; judge for Miss America Preteen, Coed Pageants, Little Miss La., and Master La. Pageants. Chmn. fair St. John's Ch., Folsom, 1987-89; treas. Village of Folsom Fairs and Festivals, 1988-89; bd. dirs. St. Tammany Econ. and Devel. Found., 1989-90. Mem. Realtors Nat. Mktg. Inst. (cert. residential specialist, cert. residential broker), Nat. Assn. Realtors (life), La. Bd. Realtors (grad. realtors Inst., trustee polit. action com. 1987-88), La. Realtors Assn. (bd. dirs. 1989-90, bd. dirs. econ. and devel. com. 1990, mem. legis. com. 1990), St. Tammany Bd. Realtors (bd. dirs. 1988-90, life mem. Million Dollar Club, Honor Soc. award 1988-89), Jefferson Bd. Realtors (life mem. Million Dollar Club), Krewe of Iris (New Orleans). Democrat. Roman Catholic. Home: 44 Park Ln Folsom LA 70437 Office: PO Box 837 Folsom LA 70437

SCHWARZ, SHIRLEY JEAN, fine arts professor; b. Upper Darby, Pa., Sept. 27, 1935; d. Herman Joe and Francis Ella (Stoneback) Schick; m. George Carl Schwarz, Oct. 23, 1967 (div.); children: Elyse, Christopher, Peter. BA, St. Olaf Coll., 1957; MFA, U. Fla., 1963; MA, U. Md., 1970, PhD, 1974. Grad. asst. U. Fla., Gainesville, 1958-63; lectr. Towson (Md.) State Coll., 1967; instr. George Mason U., Fairfax, Va., 1972-75; asst. prof. George Mason U., Fairfax, 1975-76, Ohio State U., Columbus, 1976-84, Castleton (Vt.) State Coll., 1985-86; dept. head U. Evansville, Ind., 1986-87, assoc. rof., 1985—; rsch. cons. Smithsonian Instn., Washington, 1975—. Author: HERACLES: The Twelve, 1984; contbr. articles to numerous profl. jours. Bd. dirs. New Harmony (Ind.) Gallery of Contemporary Art, 1987-90, Friends of Art, Evansville, 1986—. Recipient Fellowship NEH, 1990, U. Evansville, 1990, 88, 86-87; grantee Am. Coun. Edn., 1985. Fellow Am. Sch. Classical Studies; mem. U. Evansville Senate, Am. Acad. in Rome, Archeol. Inst. Am., Assn. Ancient Historians, New Harmony Gallery Contemporary Art, Soc. women Geographers. Home: 2415 Bayard Pk Dr Evansville IN 47714

SCHWARZMUELLER, LYNNE MARIE, computer infosystem engineer; b. Buffalo, N.Y., Apr. 23, 1953; d. Harry and Helen Elizabeth (Schmitz) Schwarzmueller. BS in Edn., SUNY, Geneseo, N.Y., 1975; M Edn., U. Ariz., 1983. Special edn. tchr. VisionQuest, Tucson, 1976-77, Amphitheater Pub. Sch., Tucson, 1977-82; mgr. of tng. ComputerLand, Tucson, 1983--; Editor: Microsoft Works Training Guide. Mem. Ariz. Soc. Tng. and Devel., U. Ariz. Alumni Club. Republican. Roman Catholic. Office: Computerland Learning Ctr 3655 N Oracle Rd Tucson AZ 85715

SCHWARZROCK, SHIRLEY PRATT, author, lecturer, educator; b. Mpls., Feb. 27, 1914; d. Theodore Ray and Myrtle Pearl (Westphal) Pratt; BS, U. Minn., 1935, MA, 1942, PhD, 1974; m. Loren H. Schwarzrock, Oct. 19, 1945 (dec. 1966); children: Kay Linda, Ted Kenneth, Lorraine V. Sec. to chmn. speech dept., U. Minn., Mpls., 1935, instr. in speech, 1946, team tchr. in creative arts workshops for tchrs., 1955-56, guest lectr. Dental Sch., 1967-72, asst. prof. (part-time) of practice adminstrn. Sch. Dentistry, 1972-80; tchr. speech, drama and English, Preston (Minn.) High Sch., 1935-37; tchr. speech, drama and English, Owatonna (Minn.) High Sch., 1937-39, also dir. dramatics, 1937-39; tchr. creative dramatics and English, tchr.-counselor Webster Groves (Mo.) Jr. High Sch., 1939-40; dir. dramatics and tchr.-counselor Webster Groves Sr. High Sch., 1940-43; exec. sec. bus. and profl. dept. YWCA, Mpls., 1943-45; tchr. speech and drama Covent of the Visitation, St. Paul, 1958; editor pro-tem Am. Acad. Dental Practice Adminstrn., 1966-68; guest tchr. Coll. St. Catherine, St. Paul, 1969; vol. mgr. Gift Shop, Eitel Hosp., Mpls., 1981-83; cons. for dental med. programs Normandale Community Coll., Bloomington, Minn., 1968; cons. on pub. relations to dentists, 1954—; guest lectr. to various dental groups, 1966—; lectr. Internat. Congress on Arts and Communication, 1980, Am. Inst. Banking, 1981; condr. tutorials in speaking and profl. office mgmt., 1985—; owner Shirley Schwarzrock's Exec. Support Svc., 1989—. Author books (series): Coping with Personal Identity, Coping with Human Relationships, Coping with Facts and Fantasies, Coping with Teenage Problems, 1984; individual book titles include: Do I Know the "Me" Others See?, My Life-What Shall I Do With It?, Living with Loneliness, Learning to Make Better Decisions, Grades, What's So Important About Them, Anyway?, Facts and Fantasies About Alcohol, Facts and Fantasies About Drugs, Facts and Fantasies About Smoking, Food as a Crutch, Facts and Fantasies About the Roles of Men and Women, You Always Communicate Something, Appreciating People-Their Likenesses and Differences, Fitting In, To Like and Be Liked, Can You Talk With Someone Else? Coping with Emotional Pain, Some Common Crutches, Parents Can Be a Problem, Coping with Cliques, (with L.H. Schwarzrock) Crises Youth Face Today; Effective Dental Assisting, 1954, 59, 67, (with J.R. Jensen), 1978, 82, (with J.R. Jensen, Kay Schwarzrock, Lorraine Schwarzrock), 1990, Effective Dental Assisting, (with L.H. Schwarzrock) 1954, 59, 67, (with J.R. Jensen) 1973, 78, 82, (with J.R. Jensen, Kay Schwarzrock, Lorraine Schwarzrock) 1990, Workbook for Effective Dental Assisting, 1960, 68, 73, (with Lorraine Schwarzrock), 1978, 82, 90, Manual for Effective Dental Assisting, 1968, 73, 78, 82, 90, (with Donovan F. Ward), Effective Medical Assisting, 1969, 76, Wookbook for Effective Medical Assisting, 1969, 76, Manual for Effective Assisting, 1969, 76; author: (with C.G. Wrenn) The Coping with Series of Books for High School Students, 1970, 73, The Coping With Manual, 1973, Contemporary Concerns, of Youth, 1980. Pres. University Elem. Sch. PTA, 1955-56. Fellow Internat. Biog. Assn.; mem. Minn. Acad. Dental Practice Adminstrn. (hon.), Internat. Platform Assn., Zeta Phi Eta (pres. 1948-49), Eta Sigma Upsilon.

SCHWEIG, MARGARET BERRIS, meeting and special events company executive; b. Detroit, Mar. 23, 1928; d. Jacob Meyer and Anne Lucille (Schiller) Berris; m. Eugene Schweig Jr., Nov. 24, 1951 (dec.); children: Eugene III, John A., Suzanne. Student, U. Mich., 1945-47. Pres., owner St. Louis Scene, Inc., 1975—. Mem. St. Louis Conv. and Visitors Commn., St. Louis Forum. Mem. Meeting Planners Internat., Am. Soc. Assn. Execs., Profl. Conv. Mgmt. Assn., Meeting Cons. Network, Nat. Assn. Exposition Mgrs., Internat. Spl. Events Soc., Hotel Sales Mgmt. Assn. (bd. dirs. 1977-80), Regional Commerce and Growth Assn., The Network (pres. 1980-81). Office: St Louis Inc 711 N 11th St Saint Louis MO 63101

SCHWEIGER, DEBRA JEAN, small business owner; b. Urbana, Ill., Apr. 17, 1953; d. Jean Burtch Wright; m. Wesley Schweiger, Aug. 6, 1977. BA in Polit. Sci. with high distinction, U. Ill., 1975, MPA, 1979. Congressional intern Washington, 1974; intern IRS, Washington, 1975; legis. intern Ill. Senate Appropriations Com., Springfield, 1975; budget analyst Ill. Senate Appropriations Com., 1975-77, Ky. Legis. Rsch. Commn., Frankfort, 1977-80; rsch. analyst Minn. Legislature Audit Commn., St. Paul, 1980-81; fin. analyst Group Health, Inc., Mpls., 1981-85; pres., owner Internat. Bus. Assocs. (U.S., Mex., Korea), Shoreview, Minn., 1985—; speaker in field. Charles Merriam scholar. Mem. Women Entrepreneur's Network, NAFE, Nat. Assn. Women Bus. Owners, Nat. Polit. Sci. (hon.), Pi Sigma Alpha. Republican. Home and Office: 4308 Brigadoon Dr Shoreview MN 55126

SCHWEINHAUT, MARGARET COLLINS, state senator; b. Washington; ed. George Washington U., Nat. U. Law Sch.; LL.D., St. Joseph Coll. Mem. Md. Ho. of Dels., 1955-61; mem. Md. Senate, 1961-63, 67—. Chmn. Md. Commn. on Aging, 1959-82. Bd. dirs. Nat. Council of Aging. Recipient Certificate of Merit, Nat. Council of Sr. Citizens; Margaret Schweinhaut Sr. Ctr. named in her honor, 1982. Mem. Internat. Gerontological Soc., Montgomery Retarded Children's Assn. Office: Md State Senate Annapolis MD 21401

SCHWEINLE, FRIEDA E., customs broker; b. Houston, July 22, 1952; d. William E. and Elfrieda (Grunwald) S. AA, Alvin Jr. Coll., 1974; BBA, U. Houston, Clear Lake City, 1975. Lic. customs broker. Contract adminstr., trader Armada Petroleum Corp., Houston, 1978-81; oil trader Tricentrol Oil Trading Inc., Houston, 1981-84; customs broker J.F. Moran Co., Inc., Houston, 1985—; owner, officer W.J.M.F. Investments, Rosharon, Tex., 1986—; bd. dirs. Brazosand, Inc., Rosharon, Brazosand Supply Co. Inc. Mem. Phi Theta Kappa, Phi Kappa Phi. Office: J F Moran Co Inc 602 Sawyer St Ste 430 Houston TX 77007

SCHWEITZER, N. TINA, photojournalist, television producer, director, writer, international consultant public relations, media relations and government relations; b. Hartford, Conn., Apr. 7, 1941; d. Abraham Aaron Morris and Ruth Blanche (Shifreen) S. BS, Emerson Coll., 1964. Freelance writer Boston and Washington, 1965-67; editor, chief prodn. maj. feature publ., mem. press-info. staff Embassy of Republic of Indonesia, Washington, 1967-68; researcher, writer Congl. Quar., Inc., Washington, 1969-70; owner Schweitzer Assocs., Hartford, Conn. and Washington, 1970-78, 79—; dir. community and govtl. rels. Advocacy Svcs. for the Deaf, West Hartford, Conn., 1978-79; del. White House Conf. Small Bus., 1986; profl. model. Corr. The Farmington (Conn.) Valley Herald, 1984; first bus. columnist Hartford Woman newspaper, 1984; contbr. articles to numerous govtl. and comml. publs.; author: Media Kit, 1978, Women's Job Hunting Guide, 1983, You Can Do It! A Practical Guide for Job Hunting and Career-Changing, 1987; writer, designer, producer series of TV videotape pub. svc. announcements on employment deaf or hard-of-hearing, 1983-84; contbr. editorials to TV Stas. WFSB, 1977, 84, 86, WVIT, 1983; writer, ind. producer, dir., talk-show host Sta. WVIT-TV, 1987. Mem. State-wide Health Coordinating Coun., a U.S. Govt./Conn. Health Dept. project, 1978-80; adviser Conn. Office Advocacy to Handicapped; mem. legis. task force State of Conn., 1978-80, 1978-79; del. first Conn. Gov.'s Conf. on Libr. and Info. Svcs., 1978; candidate Conn. Ho. of Reps., 1982; aux. police officer Hartford Police Dept., 1976-77; acting chmn. communications com. Unitarian Meeting House, West Hartford; dir. pub. rels. Greater Hartford Com. UNICEF, 1984-86; affiliated Rep. Town Com., Hartford., 1989; apptd. to Nat. Pub. Rels./Advt. Adv. Coun. Am. Mensa Ltd., 1989; press rep. Mensa Internat. 1st Joint Conf. Am. Coun. Edn. and Conf. European Rectors, 1989. Fellow John F. Kennedy Presdl. Libr. Mus. Found. Mem. Nat. Press Photographers Assn., Mensa, Sigma Delta Chi. Office: Schweitzer Assocs 30 Woodland St Ste 9P Hartford CT 06105

SCHWENK, WENDY ANN, government analyst; b. Darien, Conn., Aug. 7, 1962; d. William Charles and Mary Louise (Van Aernam) S. AB in History and German, Mount Holyoke Coll., 1984; MS in Fgn. Svc., Georgetown U., 1987. Intern West German Bundestag, Bonn, 1984, U.S. Mission, West Berlin, 1986; govt. analyst Washington, 1988—. Contbr. chpts. to Foreign Policy Choices for Americans, 1984. Mem. German Lang. Soc., Phi Beta Kappa.

SCHWENK-BERMAN, LAURA LEACOCK, dancer; b. Evanston, Ill., Aug. 7, 1956; d. Henry Carl and Carol Gay (Godwin) Schwenk; m. Scott Cary Berman, May 29, 1988. BS in Dance, Skidmore Coll., 1978; postgrad., Northwestern U., 1989—. Contemporary dancer Joan Lombardi Dance Co., N.Y.C., 1978-79; ballet dancer-soloist Garden State Ballet, Newark, 1979-81; ballet dancer Boston Repertory Ballet, 1981, Pacific Northwest Ballet, Seattle, 1981-87; instr. Columbia Coll., Chgo., 1987-88, Northwestern U., Evanston, Ill., 1989-90; contemporary dancer, choreographer Chgo. Repertory Dance Ensemble, 1988-90; tchr., choreographer Acad. Movement & Music, Oak Park, Ill., 1987-90; tchr. Summerfest Sch., Grand Rapids, Mich., 1990—; dancer, actor "Nutcracker The Movie" Seattle, 1986; dancer, tchr. Young Audiences, Chgo., 1987-88. Bd. mem. Northwest Dance Coalition, Seattle, 1985. Fellow: Tidmarsh Arts Orgn., Chgo. Dance Artists Coaliton. Home: 8826 Crooked Crow NE Grand Rapids MI 49301 Office: Summerfest Sch 233 E Fulton Grand Rapids MI 49503

SCHWERTNER, MARJORIE FRANK, health science facility administrator; b. Holland, Tex., Sept. 11, 1924; d. George Henry and Linnie Bell (Latham) Frank; m. Darwin Ray Schwertner, Jan. 8, 1945 (div. Sept. 1978); children: Kay Schwertner Psencik, Darwin Ray Jr., Cynthia Schwertner Kirby. Student, U. Mary Hardin-Baylor, 1942-44. Med. sec. McCloskey Gen. Hosp., Temple, Tex., 1944-45; sec. to comdt. llth Naval Dist. Shore Patrol, 1945-46; hostess YMCA, College Station, Tex., 1946-47; med. sec. Scott and White Clinic, Temple, 1956-66, clerical supr., 1966-76, assoc. adminstrv. clerical support svcs., 1976-82, assoc. dir. projects, 1982—. Mem. Med. Group Mgmt. Assn. Democrat. Home: 2450 Canyon Creek Dr Temple TX 76502 Office: Scott and White Clinic 2401 S 31st St Temple TX 76508

SCHWIER, PRISCILLA LAMB GUYTON, television broadcasting company executive; b. Toledo, Ohio, May 8, 1939; d. Edward Oliver and Prudence (Hutchinson) L.; m. Robert T. Guyton, June 21, 1963 (dec. Sept. 1976); children—Melissa, Margaret, Robert; m. Frederick W. Schwier, May 11, 1984. B.A., Smith Coll., 1961; M.A., U. Toledo, 1972. Pres. Gt. Lakes Communications, Inc., 1982—; vice chmn. Seilon, Inc., Toledo, 1981-83, also dir.; pres. Lamb Enterprises, Inc., Toledo, 1983—; dir. Lamb Enterprises, Inc., Toledo, 1976—. Contbr. articles to profl. jours. Trustee Wilberforce U., Ohio, 1983—, Planned Parenthood, Toledo, 1979-83; trustee Maumee Valley Country Day Sch., Toledo. Episcopal Ch., Maumee, Ohio, 1983—; bd. trustees Toledo Hosp. Democrat. Episcopalian. Home: 345 E Front St Perrysburg OH 43551 Office: 129 W Wayne St Maumee OH 43537

SCHWOPE, MARY KATHRYN, state legislator; b. Rock Springs, Wyo., July 21, 1917; d. Charles Alfred and Mary Frances (Moriarty) Viox. Student pub. schs., Green River, Wyo., 1923-35; m. Eldridge Lawson Schwope, July 15, 1940; children: Michael Lawson, Fachon J. Schwope Wilson, Patricia K. Schwope Murphy Perry, Madalaine M. Schwope Connolly. With Union Pacific R.R., 1936-46; mem. Wyo. Ho. of Reps., 1975-76, 79—. Mem. Dem. Precinct Com., Cheyenne, 1957-67; vice chmn., dist. capt. County Dem. Com.; sec. City-County CD Coun., 1962-63, Laramie County Fair Bd., 1966-76; mem. State Adv. Coun. Vocat. Edn., 1976-81; mem. Silver-Haired Legis. Adv. Com., 1982-83, Wyo. Gov.'s Task Force for Employment Older Ams., 1981-86; apptd. to Nat. Coun. State Legislature Labor Com., 1989-90. Recipient Nat. Merit cert. Am. Revolutionary Bicentennial Adminstrn., 1976, cert. Nat. Disabled Am. Vets. Orgn. for Legis. Action, 1987; Four Chaplains Legion of Honor, 1979. Mem. Am. Legion Aux. (state pres. 1968-69, nat. exec. com. 1969-70), Am. Assn. Ret. Persons, Wyo. Hist. Soc. (sr. citizens adv. coun. 1989), Wyo. Wildlife Fedn., Cheyenne Sr. Citizens, Wyo. Pioneer Assn. Roman Catholic. Clubs: Zonta, Cheyenne Women's.

SCIBA, JOANN, social worker; b. Manistee, Mich., Oct. 19, 1946; d. Raymond Peter and Bernardine Alice (Wroblewski) Sciba. Student, Muskegon Bus. Coll., 1964-66; BS, Ferris State U., 1969; MSW, Western Mich. U., 1982. Tchr. North Muskegon (Mich.) High Sch., 1969-70; caseworker Muskegon County Dept. Social Svcs., Muskegon, 1970-76, child welfare specialist, 1976-88; med. social work cons. Muskegon Dept. Social Svcs., 1988—. Vol., United Way, Muskegon, 1985-86; H-PAC mem. March of Dimes, Grand Rapids, Mich., 1988—; program chmn. Friends of Norton Shores Library, Muskegon, 1990. Recipient Cert. of Recognition Nat. Assn. Social Workers, 1986. Mem. Mich. Coun. Social Svcs. Workers. Democrat. Roman Catholic. Home: 665 Lake Forest Ln R-12 Muskegon MI 49441

SCIBILIA, LAURIE JEAN, accountant; b. Lynn, Mass., June 10, 1960; d. John Peter and Carol Ann (Jachowicz) S. AS in Acctg., Middlesex Community Coll., Bedford, Mass., 1980; BSBA, Bentley Coll., 1987. Assoc. acct. Adage, Inc., Billerica, Mass., 1980-84; acctg. technician Cobb, Inc. div. Upjohn Co., Littleton, Mass., 1984-86; acctg. supr. Mech. & Energy Systems, Woburn, Mass., 1986-87, Kaye Instruments, Inc., Bedford, Mass., 1987—; acctg. tutor Middlesex Community Coll., 1978-80. Nat. Assn. Accts., NAFE. Roman Catholic. Office: Kaye Instruments Inc 15 DeAngelo Dr Bedford MA 01730

SCIOLINO, SUSAN FRANCES, division training coordinator; b. Buffalo, Oct. 4, 1957; d. Joseph Francis and Louisa Frances (Zelazny) S. BA in Edn., CUNY, Buffalo, 1979. Trng. skills coordinator TGI Friday's Inc., Dallas, 1984; mgr. new restaurant openings, 1985-86, mgr. tng. program devel., 1986; dir. tng. and devel. Champions Sports, Inc., Washington, 1986-87; div. tng. coordinator TGI Friday's Inc., Dallas, 1987—. Mem. Am. Soc. Tng. & Devel. Democrat. Roman Catholic. Home: 3961 Meadowview Dr N Jacksonville FL 32225 Office: TGI Fridays 2102 Park Pl Ponte Vedra Beach FL 32082

SCIPIO, BEVERLY YVETTE, public relations and marketing company executive; b. Cleve., Nov. 15, 1951; d. Clifford Edward and Gladys (Beverly) S. BA, Mt. Holyoke Coll., 1974; MPA, Atlanta U., 1976; cert. achievement, Inst. Fin. Edn., Chgo., 1979. Devel. dir. United Negro Coll. Fund, Inc., N.Y.C., 1977-79; mktg. officer Ill./Svc. Fed. Savs. & Loan, Chgo., 1979-81;

mgmt. trainee Harris Trust and Savs. Bank, Chgo., 1981-82; spl. asst. to pres. St. Augustine's Coll., Raleigh, N.C., 1982-84; fin. devel. dir. YWCA Cleve., 1986-88; pres., bd. dirs. Beverly Bur. Corp., Cleve., 1987—. Mem. fin. com. Episcopal Diocese, Cleve., 1987-89, mem. Commn. on World and Nat. Missions, 1990—; vestrywoman St. Andrew's Episcopal Ch., Cleve., 1990—; rep. area alumnae admissions Mt. Holyoke Coll., 1989—. Recipient Kizzy award Kizzy Award Assn., 1980. Mem. NEA, Fla. Fgn. Lang. Assn., AAUW, Am. Assn. Tchrs. of Spanish and Portuguese. Republican. Home: 1501 E 191st St Apt 407 Cleveland OH 44117 Office: Beverly Bur Corp 19436 Scottsdale Blvd Cleveland OH 44122

SCITOVSKY, ANNE AICKELIN, economist; b. Ludwigshafen, Germany, Apr. 17, 1915; came to U.S., 1931, naturalized, 1938; d. Hans W. and Gertrude Margarete Aickelin; 1 dau., Catherine Margaret. Student, Smith Coll., 1933-35; B.A., Barnard Coll., 1937; postgrad., London Sch. Econs., 1937-39; M.A. in Econs., Columbia U., 1941. Mem. staff legis. reference svc. Libr. of Congress, 1941-44; mem. staff Social Security Bd., 1944-46; with Palo Alto (Calif.) Med. Rsch. Found., 1963—, chief health econs. div., 1973—; lectr. Inst. Health Policy Studies, U. Calif., San Francisco, 1975—; mem. Inst. Medicine of NAS, Pres.'s Commn. for Study of Ethical Problems in Medicine and Biomed. and Behavioral Rsch., U.S. Nat. Com. on Vital and Health Stats., 1975-78, Health Resources and Svcs. Adminstrn., AIDS adv. com., 1990—; cons. HHS, Inst. Medicine Coun. on Health Care Tech. Assessment. Mem. Am. Econ. Assn., Am. Public Health Assn. Home: 161 Erica Way Menlo Park CA 94025 Office: Palo Alto Med Found Rsch Inst 860 Bryant St Palo Alto CA 94301

SCLAFANI, FRANCES ANN, federal agency executive; b. N.Y.C., Aug. 25, 1949; d. Joseph John and Clementina Theresa (Polite) S. BA (hon.), St. John's U., 1971, JD, 1974. Bar: N.Y. 1975, U.S. Dist. Ct. (ea. and so. dists.) N.Y., 1975, U.S. Ct. Appeals (2d cir.) 1975, U.S. Supreme Ct. 1978, U.S. Dist. Ct. D.C. 1987, U.S. Ct. Appeals (D.C. cir.) 1987. Spl. congl. asst. U.S. Congress, Washington, 1971; asst. dist. atty. County of Suffolk (N.Y.), Riverhead, 1974-86; assoc. dir. U.S Office Personnel Mgmt., Washington, 1986—; head of Office Fed. Investigations, Washington, 1986—; bd. fgn. svc. Dept. State, Washington, 1986-90; bd. dirs. Fed. Law Enforcement Tng. Ctr., Glynco, Ga., 1986—; dep. chief Felony Trial Bur., 1981-82, Major Offense Bur., 1982-83. Rep. candidate for N.Y. state atty. gen., 1982; commr. President's Commn. on Organized Crime, Washington, 1983-86, mem. com. on narcotics control and interdiction, 1984-86; rep. to Western Hemisphere Conf. on Narcotics Control, Washington, 1985—; faculty U.S. Dept. of Justice Ann. Internat. Drug Traffickers Prosecution Conf., 1983. Recipient award for svc.to victims rights Decision for Women in Commerce and Professions, 1984. Mem. ABA (asst. sec. criminal justice sect. 1980-82), Nat. Dist. Attys. Assn. (assoc. dir. 1980-86), D.C Bar Assn., N.Y. Bar Assn. Roman Catholic. Office: Office of Pers Mgmt Tng & Investig Group 1900 E St NW Washington DC 20415

SCLAROW, BARBARA HARRIET, database publishing director; b. Phila., June 11, 1946; d. Samuel and May (Finkelman) Greenberg; m. Edward Thomas Sclarow; 1 child, David. BA, Beaver Coll., 1968; postgrad., Villanova U., 1968-72. Cert. secondary educator, Pa. French/English tchr. Springfield Twp. Secondary Sch., Erdenheim, Pa., 1968-74; publ. systems specialist Inst. for Sci. Info., Phila., 1979-82, publ. systems supr., 1982-83, asst. mgr., 1983-84, sr. mgr. database operations, 1984-88, asst. dir. product operations, 1988—. Mem. Soc. for Scholarly Pub. Home: 351 W Waverly Rd Glenside PA 19038 Office: Inst For Sci Info 3501 Market St Philadelphia PA 19104

SCOFIELD, SANDRA KAY, state legislator; b. Chadron, Nebr., June 16, 1947; d. Maurice William and Mildred Elizabeth (Connell) S. BS, U. Nebr., 1969, MA, 1974. Tchr. Westside High Sch., Omaha, 1969-71; tech. writer, coord. Kentron Hawaii, Honolulu, 1971-73; script writer Nebr. Dept. Edn., Lincoln, 1974-75, U. Mid-Am., Lincoln, 1975, Nebr. Ednl. TV Consortium for Higher Edn., Lincoln, 1975-79, Nebr. Ednl. TV, Lincoln, 1975-79; dir. planning Chadron State Coll., 1979-81, career counselor, 1979, 82-83, dir. career devel. ctr., 1983; mem. Nebr. Legislature, Lincoln, 1983—; vice chair com. on agr., food policy and rural devel. Nat. Conf. State Legislators; chmn. Nebr. Legis. Select Com. on Children and Families, 1987-89. Mem. appropriations com., bd. dirs. Nebr. Preservation Coun., Nebr. Groundwater Found., Nebr. 4-H Devel. Found.; mem. Environ. Control Coun., Lincoln, 1983; pres. Dawes County Hist. Soc., Chadron, 1981-83. Mem. Bus. and Profl. Women, AAUW, Soroptomists, Delta Kappa Gamma. Democrat. Lodge: Eagles. Office: Nebr State Legis State Capitol Bldg Lincoln NE 68509

SCOLLARD, CYNTHIA MCNUTT, mechanical engineer, author, publisher; b. Compton, Calif., Jan. 13, 1954; d. Benjamin Harrison Jr. and Doris Mae (Smith) McN.; m. Rodrick Ward Scollard, Apr. 6, 1985. Student, U. Calif., Irvine, 1977; AA, Golden West Coll., 1979; BSME, Calif. State Poly. U., 1983. Adminstrv. asst. med. ctr. U. Calif. Irvine, Orange, 1973-77; intern McDonnell-Douglas Aircraft Co., Long Beach, Calif., 1981-82; mech. engr. Ford Aerospace and Communications, Inc., Newport Beach, Calif., 1984; engr. mfg. rsch. and devel. Boeing Comml. Airplanes, Seattle, 1984-88; owner Scollard Industries and Miralta Press, Kent, Wash., 1988—; aerospace project engr. Heath Tecna Aerospace Co., Kent, Wash., 1989—. Author: Muffins: From Healthfood to Junkfood, 1988. Recipient scholarship ALCOA Aluminum Co., 1980. Mem. Pi Tau Sigma, Tau Beta Pi.

SCOLLARD, DIANE LOUISE, educator; b. Seattle, Mar. 12, 1945; d. James Martin and Viola Gladys (Williams) S. BA in Edn., Wash. State U., 1967; 5th yr. cert. in edn., U. Wash., 1970; cert. edn., Oakland U., 1977. Tchr. Battle Ground (Wash.) Sch. Dist., 1967-70, Lapeer (Mich.) Community Schs., 1970—. Mem. NEA, Am. Bus. Women's Assn., Mich. Edn. Assn., Lapeer Edn. Assn. (bldg. rep. 1985, 89), AAUW, Beta Sigma Phi. Democrat. Episcopalian. Office: Elba Elem Sch 300 N Elba Rd Lapeer MI 48446

SCOPELIANOS, MARGARET ANTHOU, bank executive; b. Canonsburg, Pa., Dec. 15, 1959; d. Sam. and Maria (Sahinis) Anthou; m. Angelo G. Scopelianos, May 29, 1983; children: Georgie, Samuel. BA in Russian and Econs., Pa. State U., 1981. Pa. real estate sales license, 1981. Mgmt. trainee Mellon Bank, Pitts., 1981-83; corp. lender Chem. Bank Del., Wilmington, Del., 1983-85; credit officer Chem. Bank Del., Wilmington, 1986-88; v.p., comml. lender Chem. Bank N.J., Roseland, N.J., 1989; v.p., unit mgr. First Fidelity Bank, Newark, 1989-90; mem., assoc. Robert Morris Assocs., Phila., 1986-88. Treas. Hellenic U. Club, Wilmington, 1983-89; mem. Krikos Scholarship Soc., New Brunswick, N.J., 1989-90. Phi Beta Kappa scholar. Greek Orthodox. Office: First Fidelity Bank 550 Broad St Newark NJ 07102

SCOPINICH-BUHLER, JILL LORIE, editor, writer; b. Seattle, Dec. 7, 1945; d. Oscar John and Marcella Jane (Hearing) Younce; m. John Buhler, June 10, 1990; 1 child, Lori Jill. AA in Gen. Edn., Am. River Coll., 1969; BA in Journalism with honors, Sacramento State U., 1973. Reporter Carmichael (Calif.) Courier, 1968-70; mng. editor Quarter Horse of the Pacific Coast, Sacramento, 1970-75, editor, 1975-84; editor Golden State Program Jour., 1978, Nat. Reined Cow Horse Assn. News, Sacramento, 1983-88, Pacific Coast Jour., Sacramento, 1984-88, Nat. Snaffle Bit Assn. News, Sacramento, 1988; pres., chief exec. officer Communications Plus, Port Townsend, Wash., 1988—; mag. cons., 1975—. Interviewer Pres. Ronald Reagan, Washington, 1983; mng. editor: Wash. Thoroughbred, 1989-90. Mem. 1st profl. communicators mission to the USSR, 1988; bd. dirs. Carmichael, Winding Way, Pasadena Homeowners Assn., Carmichael, 1985-87. Recipient 1st pl. feature award, 1970, 1st pl. editorial award Jour. Assn. Jr. Colls., 1971, 1st pl. design award WCHB Yuba-Sutter Counties, Marysville, Calif., 1985. Mem. Am. River Jaycees (Speaking award 1982), Am. Horse Publs. (1st Pl. Editorial award 1983, 86), Mensa (bd. dirs., asst. local sec., activities dir. 1987-88, membership chair 1988-90), Thoroughbred Horse Racing's United Scholarship Trust (scholarship com.). Republican. Roman Catholic. Club: 5th Wheel Touring Soc. (Sacramento) (v.p. 1970). Home: 440 Adelma Beach Rd Port Townsend WA 98368

SCOTT, ALICE H., librarian; b. Jefferson, Ga.; d. Frank D. and Annie D. (Colbert) Holly; m. Alphonso Scott, Mar. 1, 1959; children—Christopher, Alison. A.B., Spelman Coll., Atlanta, 1957; M.L.S., Atlanta U., 1958; Ph.D., U. Chgo., 1983. Librarian Bklyn. Pub. Library, 1958-59; br. librarian Chgo. Pub. Library, 1959-72, dir. Woodson Regional Library, 1974-77, dir. community relations, 1977-82, dep. commr., 1982-87, asst. commr., 1987—. Doctoral fellow, 1973. Mem. ALA (councilor 1982-85), Ill. Library Assn., Chgo. Library Club, Chgo. Spelman Club, Chgo. Art Inst., DuSable Mus., Chgo. Urban League. Democrat. Baptist. Office: Chgo Pub Library 1224 W Van Buren Chicago IL 60607

SCOTT, AMY ANNETTE HOLLOWAY, nurse educator; b. St. Albans, W.Va., Apr. 10, 1916; d. Oliver and Mary (Lee) Holloway; m. William M. Jefferson, June 22, 1932, (div. Oct. 1933); 1 child, William M. Jefferson, m. Vann Hyland Scott, Mar. 15, 1952, (dec. Dec. 1972). BS in Nursing Edn., Cath. U., Washington, 1948; cert., Sorbonne, Paris, 1959. Indsl. nurse Curtiss Wright St. Louis Lambert Air Field, 1939-44; faculty U. Santa Thomas, Manila, Philippines Island, 1951-52; pub. health nurse Mcpl. Nurses, St Louis, 1952-56; capt. USAF Nursing Corps, Paris, 1956-60; resigned as maj. USAF (M.C.), 1960; faculty St. Louis State Hosp., 1960-66; dept. head St. Vincents Hosp., St. Louis, 1966-67; faculty registered nurse Jewish Hosp., 1967-72; adminstrv. nurse St. Louis State Hosp., 1972-84. Author: Storms, 1987. Past bd. dirs. county bd. Mo. U., 1984-88. Mem. AAUW, Internat. Fedn. Univ. Women, Internat. Soc. Quality Assurance in Health Care, Am. Biog. Inst. (life, governing bd.), Cambridge Centre Eng. Roman Catholic.

SCOTT, AMY HOLLOWAY, health facility administrator; b. St. Albans, W.Va., Apr. 10, 1922; d. Oliver W. and Mayme I. (Lee) Holloway; m. Vann Hylon Scott, 1952; 1 child, William Jefferson Jr. BS in Nursing Edn., Cath. U., Washington, 1948; diploma in nursing, City Hosp., St. Louis, 1936; cert. psychiat. nursing, Sorbonne, France, 1959. Lic. psychiat. nurse, indsl. nurse. Indsrl. nurse Curtiss Wright Hosp., St. Louis, 1939-44; tchr. U. St. Thomas, Manila, Philippines; comml. capt. N.C. USAF, Paris, 1956; faculty St. Louis State Hosp., 1960-67; faculty, psychiat. nurse coord. Jewish Hosp., St. Louis, 1968-72; adminstrv. nurse St. Louis State Hosp., 1972-84. Author: Storms, 1987, The Burn Patient, Trends in Living. Major USAF, 1956-59. Mem. AAUW, ANA, ARC, YWCC (bd. dirs.), Air Force Hist. Found., Amvets, Disabled Am. Veterans, Union Concerned Scientists, Sci. Ctr., Glennon Soc., Internat. Soc. for Quality Assurance in Health Care, Mo. Exec. Coun., Commanderes Club (bd. dirs.), Folio Soc. Roman Catholic. Home: 1526 Laclede Station Rd Saint Louis MO 63117

SCOTT, ANDREA KAY, academic administrator; b. Grand Rapids, Mich., Jan. 25, 1948; d. John Andrew and Maretha Lavera (Hutcheson) Larsen; m. David James, June 19, 1971. BA, U. Mich., 1970, MA, 1974. Admissions specialist U. Minn., Mpls., 1971-73, asst. to dean grad. sch., 1973—. Mem. Met. coun. emergency Med. Svcs. Adv. Bd., St. Paul, 1977-81; adv. bd. Colleagues of the U. Minn. Art Mus., 1984—; bd. dirs. Big Bros./Big Sisters of Greater Mpls., 1984—, pres., 1990. mem. AAUW (v.p. 1982-84, named gift honoree 1986), Am. Assn. Collegiate Registrars and Admission Officers, Leadership Mpls., U. Mich. Club of Twin Cities. Home: 4374 Vernon Ave S Minneapolis MN 55436 Office: U Minn Grad Sch 322 Johnston Hall 101 Pleasant St SE Minneapolis MN 55455

SCOTT, ANDREA LYNNÉ, entrepreneur; b. Rochester, N.Y., Oct. 21, 1962; d. Eleanore Jeanne (Vinci) S. BA, U. Rochester, 1985; Student, NYU, 1985-87. Sr. acct. rep. Siemens Info. Systems, N.Y.C., 1986-89; prin., pres. To The Nines Formal Rentals for Women, Washington, 1990—. Mem. NAFE, Nat. Retail Fedn.

SCOTT, ANITA IRMA, insurance executive, trade association executive; b. Lewiston, Maine, July 1, 1949; d. Leo Ferdinand and Therese Bernadette (Pelletier) Morin; m. William Charles Scott, Oct. 11, 1980. Grad. high sch., Lewiston, Maine. Group leader stats. Liberty Mutual Ins. Co., Lewiston, Maine, 1971-73; supr. stats Liberty Mutual Ins. Co., Lewiston, 1973-76; under analyst Liberty Mutual Ins. Co., Weston, Mass., 1976-77; sr. under analyst Liberty Mutual Ins. Co., Weston, 1977-78; under asst. to dir fiel ops. Liberty Mutual Ins. Co., Boston, 1978-80, analyst computer system, 1980-84, sr. analyst computer system, 1984-86; sr. analyst Nat. Coun. on Compensation Ins., Boca Raton, Fla., 1986-87; mgr. Nat. Coun. on Compensation Ins., Boca Raton, 1987—. Mem. NAFE. Office: Nat Coun on Compensation Insur 750 Park of Commerce Dr Boca Raton FL 33487

SCOTT, ANN BESSER, musicologist, educator; b. Newark, June 8, 1933; d. Hyman and Fannie (Bear) Besser; A.B., Radcliffe Coll., 1955; M.F.A., Brandeis U., 1957; Ph.D., U. Chgo., 1969; m. Gordon H.S. Scott, May 3, 1958; children—Ellen, Melinda. Instr., then asst. prof. music U. Chgo., 1968-73; mem. faculty Bates Coll., Auburn, Maine, 1973—, prof. music, 1979—, chmn. dept., 1974—, chmn. div. humanities, 1976-80; mem. music panel Maine Commn. Arts and Humanities, 1975-81; mem. Maine Humanities Council, 1981—, vice chmn., 1985-87, chmn., 1987—. Editor book review ; editor: College Music Symposium, 1986-88. Fellow Nat. Endowment Humanities, 1981. Mem. Am. Musicol. Soc. (sec. council 1974-79, editorial bd. jour. 1975-80, bd. dirs. 1985-87), Coll. Music Soc., Phi Beta Kappa. Jewish. Author articles in field. Office: Box 1218 RFD 3 Winthrop ME 04364*

SCOTT, ANN HARVEY, community volunteer; b. Raleigh, N.C., Mar. 28, 1939; d. Paul Henry and Ethel Marie (Larson) Harvey; m. Herbert Pearce Scott, Apr. 6, 1939; children: H. Pearce, A. Paige. BA, U. N.C., 1961; BS, U. N.C., Wilmington, 1987. Office mgr. Herbert P. Scott, atty.-at-law, Wilmington, N.C., 1983-89. Pres. Historic Wilmington Found., 1989—; treas. Friends of U. N.C.-Wilmington, 1987-88; treas., pres. YMCA Swim Team Parents, 1988-89. Democrat. Presbyterian. Address: 1917 Ashbrook Dr Wilmington NC 28403

SCOTT, ANNE BYRD FIROR, history educator; b. Montezuma, Ga., Apr. 24, 1921; d. John William and Mary Valentine (Moss) Firor; m. Andrew Mackay Scott, June 2, 1947; children: Rebecca, David MacKay, Donald MacKay. AB, U. Ga., 1940; MA, Northwestern U., 1944; PhD, Radcliffe Coll., 1958; LHD (hon.), Lindenwood Coll., 1968, Queens Coll., 1985, Northwestern U., 1989, Radcliffe Coll., 1990, U. of the South, 1990. Congressional rep., editor LWV of U.S., 1944-53; lectr. history Haverford Coll., 1957-58, U. N.C., Chapel Hill, 1959-60; asst. prof. history Duke U., Durham, N.C., 1961-67; assoc. prof. Duke U., 1968-70, prof., 1971-80, W.K. Boyd prof., 1980—, chmn. dept., 1981-85; vis. prof. Johns Hopkins U., 1972-73, Stanford U., 1974, Harvard U., 1984; bd. dirs. Carnegie Corp. N.Y., 1977-85, Woodrow Wilson Internat. Ctr., 1980-85, Nat. Humanities Ctr., 1987—; adv. com. Schlesinger Library. Author: The Southern Lady, 1970, (with Andrew MacKay Scott) One Half the People, 1974, Making the Invisible Woman Visible, 1984; editor: Jane Addams, Democracy and Social Ethics, 1964, The American Woman, 1970, Women in American Life, 1970, Women and Men in American Life, 1976; editorial bd.: Revs. in Am. History, 1976-81, Am. Quar., 1974-78, Jour. So. History, 1978-84; contbr. articles to profl. jours. Chmn. Gov.'s Commn. on Status of Women, 1963-64; mem. Citizens Adv. Council on Status of Women U.S., 1964-68. AAUW fellow, 1956-57; grantee Nat. Endowment for Humanities, 1967-68, 76-77; grantee Nat. Humanities Center, 1980-81; fellow Ctr. Advanced Study in Behavioral Sci., 1986-87. Mem. Am. Antiquarian Soc., Orgn. Am. Historians (exec. bd. 1973-76, pres. 1983), So. Hist. Assn. (exec bd. 1976-79, pres. 1989). Democrat. Office: Duke Univ Dept History Durham NC 27706

SCOTT, BARBARA ANN, sociology educator, feminist, peace activist; b. N.Y.C., Jan. 3, 1937; d. Richard W. and Lia (Varell) Scott; m. Josiah Bartlett Page, June 8, 1958 (div. 1975); children: Evan Bartlett, Eric Scott. BA magna cum laude, Pembroke Coll., Brown U., 1958; MA in Sociology, Grad. Faculty New Sch. for Social Rsch., 1972, PhD in Sociology, 1979. Elem. tchr. The Harley Sch., Rochester, N.Y., 1958-61, Poughkeepsie Day Sch., N.Y., 1968; instr. sociology SUNY-New Paltz, 1973-79, asst. prof., 1979-84, assoc. prof., 1984—, co-organizer, co-chmn. intercollegiate conf. Liberal Arts in a Time of Crisis; mem. bd. panelists NEH, 1980—; panelist 1st Internat. Conf. on Comparative, Hist. and Critical Analysis of Bureaucracy, Gottlieb Duttweiler Inst., Zurich, Switzerland, 1982; vis. scholar Ctr. Def. Info., Washington, 1986-87 (cons., mem. adv. bd.); mem. bd. adv. editors Social. Inquiry, 1990—. Author: Crisis Management in American Higher Edn., 1983 (Albert Salomon Meml. award 1980). Editor: The Liberal Arts in a Time of Crisis, 1990. Contbr. articles in profl. jours. Founder, coord. Mid-Hudson chpt. Educators for Social Responsibility, 1983-87; trustee Shoreline Found. for Folk Lit. and Art, Branford, Conn., 1983—; alumni speaker Grad. Faculty New Sch. for Social Rsch., 1977; del. Salvadoran/U.S. women-to-women dialogue sponsored by Found. for Compasionate Soc., Curnwaca, Mex., 1989, del. conf. on Media in a Time of Crisis, 1989. Recipient 2nd prize Quest for Peace Essay contest Citizen Edn. for Peace Project, 1988; rsch. grantee Am. Coun. Learned Socs., 1990—. Mem. AAUW (Issue Focus grant 1988-89), NOW, SANE/FREEZE, Internat. Peace Rsch. Assn. (chair N.Am. sect., women and peace commn. 1990—, del. to 25th Ann. Conf., 1990), War Resisters League, World Federalist. Assn., Soc. Study Social Problems, Am. Sociol. Assn., Assn. for Humanist Sociology, N.Y. State Sociol. Assn. (bd. dirs. 1974-75), Mid-Atlantic Radical Historians Orgn. (regional assoc. 1979—), Eastern Sociol. Soc. (com. undergrad. teaching 1974-76), Women's Internat. League for Peace and Freedom, Union Concerned Scientists, Women's Action for Nuclear Disarmament, Mothers Embracing Nuclear Disarmament, Women Strike for Peace, Greenpeace, Women for a Meaningful Summit, Phi Beta Kappa. Home: Box 313 Rural Route 1 Hurley Rd Salt Point NY 12578 Office: Sociology Dept SUNY New Paltz NY 12561

SCOTT, BARBARA ANN HEIM, educator; b. Tampa, Fla., May 15, 1959; d. Orville Edward and Rosalie Marie (Rodrigue) Heim; m. Thomas Ward Scott, July 30, 1983. BA, U. Fla., 1981, MEd, 1982, EdS, 1988. Cert. tchr., Fla. Tchr. preschool physically impaired children Metcalfe Elem. Sch., Gainesville, 1981-88, tchr. kindergarten physically impaired children, 1988-89; tchr. preschool mentally handicapped children Stephen Foster Elem. Sch., Gainesville, 1989—; com. chmn. Our Own Games, Gainesville, 1987-89, Very Spl. Arts Festival, Gainesville, 1985-86; guest speaker Nova U., Gainesville, 1987-89; speaker Preschool Inst., U. South Fla., Tampa, Fla., summer 1988. Reviewer: (jour.) Teaching Exceptional Children, 1989. Team capt. March of Dimes, Gainesville, 1988-89. Recipient Ednl. Improvement award, Alachua County Sch. Bd., Gainesville, 1989; rsch. assistantship U. Fla., Gainesville, 1981. Mem. Coun. for Exceptional Children (chpt. advisor 1985-87, v.p. 1983-84, pres. 1984-85), Alachua County Edn. Assn. Democrat. Roman Catholic. Home: 527 NW 35th Terr Gainesville FL 32607

SCOTT, BETH O'BRIANT, computer consultant manager; b. Easton, Md., Feb. 13, 1960; d. Thomas Lester and Margaret O'Briant; m. Theodore M. Scott. BS, Shepherd Coll., 1982. Programmer analyst Planning Rsch. Corp., McLean, Va., 1982-84; task leader Vanguard Technologies Inc., Fairfax, Va., 1984-87; mgr. Maxima Corp., Rockville, Md., 1987—. Tutor No. Va. Literacy Coun., Annandale, 1987—. Mem. Nat. Assn. for Female Execs., Phi Gamma Nu (life mem., regional dir. 1983-85). Democrat. Presbyterian.

SCOTT, CAROL SEELEY, retired librarian, researcher; b. Phila., Aug. 10, 1921; d. Walter James and Emetta Susan (Weed) Seeley; m. Harley Augustus Scott, Jr., Feb. 2, 1943; children: Michael H., Elisabeth, Sally, David W., John S. BA, Duke U., 1941; BS in Libr. Sci., U. N.C., 1942; MA in Teaching, Winthrop Coll., Rock Hill, S.C., 1957. Cert. in Libr. Sci. Libr. Pittsylvania County Pub. Libr., Chatham, Va., 1942-43; jr. profl. asst. D.C. Pub. Libr., Washington, 1943-44; libr. Winthrop Tng. Sch., Rock Hill, 1956-57, Rock Hill High Sch., 1959-70, 73-84, Castle Heights Jr. High, Rock Hill, 1970-73; part-time libr. Winthrop Coll. Libr., Rock Hill, 1984-85. Author: William Scott 1732-33 to 1800 of Cabarrus County, North Carolina and Some of His Descendants, 1987. Pres. Guild of Mus. of York County, S.C., 1988-89. Mem. S.C. Libr. Assn. (pres. 1966-70, also v.p.), S.C. Assn. Sch. Librs. (bd. dirs., regional network 1980-81), AAUW, AARP, Sierra Club, Phi Beta Kappa. Democrat.

SCOTT, CATHERINE DOROTHY, librarian, consultant; b. Washington, June 21, 1927; d. Leroy Stearns Scott and Agnes Frances (Meade) Scott Schellenberg. AB in English, Cath. U. Am., 1950, MS in Library Sci., 1955. Asst. Librarian Export-Import Bank U.S.A., Washington, 1951-55; asst. librarian Nat. Assn. Home Builders, 1955-62, reference librarian, 1956-62; chief tech. librarian, Bellcomm, Inc., subs. AT&T, Washington, 1962-72; chief librarian Nat. Air and Space Mus., Smithsonian Instn., Washington, 1972-82, chief librarian Mus. Reference Ctr., 1982—; bd. visitors Cath. U. Am. Library Sci. Sch. and Libraries, 1984—; mem. Nat. Commn. Libraries and Info. Sci., 1971-76. Editor International Handbook of Aerospace Awards and Trophies, 1980, 81, Directory of Aerospace Resources, 1984; guest editor Spl. Collections in Aeronautics and Space Flight Collections, 1985. Vice-chmn. D.C. Rep. Com., 1960-68; mem. platform com. Rep. Nat. Com., 1964, sec., 1968; del. Rep. Nat. Conv., San Francisco, 1964, Miami, Fla., 1968. Recipient Sec.'s Disting. Service award Smithsonian Instn., 1976, Alumni Achievement award Cath. U. Am., 1977. Mem. Spl. Libraries Assn. (pres. Washington chpt. 1973-74, cons. 1976—, chmn. aerospace div. 1980-81, Disting. Service award 1982, nat. dir. 1986-89), Am. Soc. Info. Scis. (com. chmn.), Internat. Fedn. Library Assns. (del. 1976, 83, 85, 88, 89), Friends of Cath. U. Libraries (founder, pres. 1984-88, bd. dirs. 1984—), Nat. Fedn. Rep. Women, Rep. Women's Fed. Forum. Roman Catholic. Club: Capital Yacht (assoc. mem.) (Washington). Office: Smithsonian Instn Cen Ref and Loan SI Librs NHB 27 Washington DC 20560

SCOTT, DOLORES H., psychiatrist; b. Newark, Aug. 24, 1927; d. Albert Emory and Rosetta Louise (Hill) Scott; m. David Bridgeford III, 1960 (div. 1972); 1 child, Denise C. Bridgeford. BA, Fisk U., 1953; MD, Meharry U., 1960. With Phila. Dept. Health, 1947-49; social worker Phila. Dept. Social Svcs., 1950-56; intern Homer C. Phillips Hosp., St. Louis, 1961; psychiatric resident Washington U., St. Louis, 1961-62, King Drew-UCLA Med. Ctr., 1978-81; staff physician State of Calif. Mental Health, Costa Mesa, 1962-63, Pomona, 1963-64; pub. health physician Los Angeles County, L.A., 1964-67; pvt. practice family practice West Covina, Calif., 1967-78; mental health psychiatrist Los Angeles County, 1978—; cons. in field. Mem. Physician's Adv. Bd., State Assemblyman, L.A., 1988—. NIH grantee, 1953. Mem. Black Psychiatrists of Am., Nat. Med. Assn., Assn. Black Women M.D.'s, Meharry Med. Coll. Alumni Assn., UCLA Alumnae Assn., Fisk U. Alumnae Assn., NAACP, Alpha Kappa Alpha, Phi Beta Kappa, Beta Kappa Chi. Republican. Episcopalian. Office: Los Angeles Mental Health 5850 S Main Los Angeles CA 90008

SCOTT, DOROTHY MARIE, retired educator, civic worker; b. Mineral Wells, Tex., Jan. 31, 1921; d. Theophilus J. and Vesta Rebecca (Howson) S. BA, Tex. Woman's U., 1942, MA, 1946; EdD, U. North Tex., 1965. Cert. tchr., supr., adminstr., Tex. High sch. tchr Brownsville (Tex.) High Sch., 1942-45, Corsicana (Tex.) Ind. Sch. Dist., 1945-46; high sch. tchr Tyler (Tex.) Ind. Sch. Dist., 1946-63, dir. secondary instrn., 1963-79; instr. Sch. Edn. and Psychology, U. Tex., Tyler, 1979-83; ret., 1983; instr. jr. colls., Brownsville, 1942-45, Tyler, 1946-48; bd. dirs. Smith County Tchrs. Credit Union, Tyler, 1953-63; mem. exec. bd. East Tex. Study Coun., Commerce, 1966-68; bd. dirs. East Tex. Rsch. and Devel. Ctr., Nacogdoches, 1989—. Contbr. articles to ednl. publs. Vol. Mental Health Assn. Tyler, 1983—; chmn. bd. dirs. Neighborhood Crime Watch, Tyler, 1988—; bd. dirs. East Tex. Coun. on World Affairs, 1988—; mem. selection com. C. of C. Leadership Tyler, 1985; community coord. Gt. Decisions 1989, Tyler. Named Educator of Month, Tex. Sch. Bus. mag., 1967, Woman of Yr., Tyler City Women's Commn., 1989, Woman of Yr. East Tex. Coun. on World Affairs, 1989. Mem. Assn. for Supervision and Curriculum Devel. (pres. Tex. chpt. 1968-68), AAUW (pres. Tyler br. 1985-86, bd. dirs., Dorothy Scott scholarship named in her honor 1985), Tex. Assn. Univ. Women (bd. dirs. 1984-86), M M Investment Club (pres. 1988—), Zonta (pres. Tyler 1976-78, Woman of Yr. award 1985, 89), Phi Delta Kappa (pres. Rose City chpt. 1979-81), Delta Kappa Gamma (pres. Theta Nu chpt. 1957-58). Democrat. Baptist. Home: 933 E 8th St Tyler TX 75701

SCOTT, EILEEN DIANE, human resources professional; b. Lackawana, N.Y., Mar. 28, 1953; d. Joseph P. and Gladys (Lejeune) Wilkinson Tsuji; m. James P.F. Scott, Sept. 11, 1981; 1 child, Alexander G.M. BA in Econs., U. Pitts., 1978. Staff acct. Joseph Horne Co., Pitts., 1978-80; payroll mgr. Joseph Horne Co., 1980-82, benefits mgr., 1982-86, benefits and compensation dir., 1986-88; asst. dir. human resources Gen. Nutrition, Inc., Pitts., 1988-89, dir. human resources, 1989—. Pacesetter chmn. United Way, 1985-87. Mem. NAFE, Am. Soc. Personnel Adminstrs., Pitts. Personnel Assn. Office: Gen Nutrition Inc 921 Penn Ave Pittsburgh PA 15222

SCOTT, ELEANOR MEYER, educator; b. Houston, Mar. 10, 1933; d. Gustav Jackson and Lillian Elizabeth (Piehl) M.; m. Henry Lee Scott, June

2, 1956 (dec. June 1967); children: Stephen Lee, Stuart Henry. BS in Home Economics, U. Tex., 1956; MEd, U. Houston-Park, 1976. Cert. elem. tchr., Tex. With Clear Creek Schs., 1958—; elem. tchr. Clear Creek Schs., League City, Tex., 1958-64, tchr. gifted/talented program, 1985—; elem. tchr. Stewart Elem., Kemah, Tex., 1964-66, White Elem. Sch., Seabrook, Tex., 1969-72, Clear Lake City Sch., Houston, 1976-85. Author: (with others) Math Manipulatives in Elem., 1986; contbr. articles to profl. jours. Pres. Seabrook (Tex.) Civic Club, 1975-76, Seascape Property Owners Assn., Seabrook Tex. 1973-74; mem. Bi-Centennial Com., Seabrook, 1976; chmn. Lunar Rendezvous Festival Children's Fair, Houston, 1977. Endorsement in Gifted Talented U. St. Thomas, 1989. Mem. Nat. Edn. Assn., Clear Creek Educators Assn. (conv. del. 1961-62, sec. 1962-63, scholar 1988), Tex. State Tchrs. Assn. (scholar 1986-87), Tex. Classroom Tchrs. Assn., Tex. Assn. Gifted and Talented, Bay Area Panhellenic Assn. (Most Outstanding Mem. award 1975-76, Golden Egg award 1972, 73, 74), Delta Kappa Gamma Soc. Internat., Theta Zeta (pres., Achievement award 1989, scholarship 1989). Republican. Methodist. Home: 625 Bay Club Dr Seabrook TX 77586 Office: Clear Creek Schs Gifted Programs 1506 Anders St Seabrook TX 77586

SCOTT, GAIL ELIZABETH, purchasing agent; b. Taunton, Mass., Sept. 30, 1954; d. Alfred and Alice Jane (Ouellette) Henricks; m. Neil Adams Scott, Aug. 2, 1986; 1 child, Troy. Student, Bristol Community Coll., Fall River, Mass.; cert. purchase and materials mgmt., UCLA, 1982. Purchasing supr., office mgr. Sequoia Container, Brea, Calif., 1983-86; sr. engring. buyer, sheet metal and fab buyer Philips Ultrasound, Inc., Santa Ana, Calif., 1989—, Medstone Internat., Irvine, Calif.; purchasing supr. Medstone Internat. Mem. NAFE, Am. Mgmt. Assn., Purchasing Mgmt. Assn. Office: Medstone Internat 9975 Toledo Irvine CA 92718

SCOTT, GLORIA DEAN RANDLE, academic administrator; b. Apr. 14, 1938; d. Freeman and Juanita (Bell) Randle; m. Will Braxton Scott. AB, Ind. U., 1959, MA, 1960, PhD, 1965, LLD, 1977; DHL, Fairleigh Dickinson U., 1978. Rsch. assoc. in genetics Inst. Psychiat. Rsch. Ind. U. Med. Ctr., Indpls., 1961-63; instr. biology Marian Coll., Indpls., 1961-65; dean students Knoxville (Tenn.) Coll., 1965-67; asst. to pres. N.C. Agrl. and Tech. State U., 1967-68, prof., 1967-76, dir. planning Inst. Rsch., 1973-76; prof. Tex. So. U., 1976-78; v.p., prof. Clark Coll., 1978-86; prof. Grambling State U., 1987; now pres. Bennett Coll., Greensboro, N.C. Del. head UN Decade for Women Internat. Forum, Nairobi, Kenya, 1985; chmn. bd. Nat. Scholarship Fund for Negro Students, 1984-85; 1st v.p. Girl Scouts U.S., 1972-75, pres., 1975-78. Office: Bennett Coll 900 E Washington St Greensboro NC 27401-3239*

SCOTT, JANICE MARIE, insurance executive; b. Loreauville, La., Mar. 29, 1955; d. Hurley Davis and Lovenia (Willis) Williams; m. Johnny Lee Scott, Nov. 17, 1979 (div. 1981). BS in Criminal Justice, Sam Houston State U., 1976. Adjuster Allstate Ins. Co., Houston, 1977-83, supr., 1983-84, mgr., 1984—. Mem. Job Plus, Houston, 1986—, Houston Proud, 1987—, Urban League. Recipient Vol. Recognition Houston Proud, 1987. Mem. NAACP, Nat. Assn. Female Execs., Delta Sigma Theta (Civic award 1988). Club: Ski Jammers. Home: 15902 Jersey Dr Houston TX 77040

SCOTT, JANICE VERONICA, oil company professional; b. Jacksonville, Fla., June 7, 1958; d. Willie C. Scott and Henrietta Marie (Thurmond) Jones. AB, Dartmouth Coll., 1980; MS in Indsl. Adminstrn., Carnegie Mellon U., 1988. Ops. planning analyst BP Chems., Cleve., 1988-89; planning assoc. in strategic planning BP Oil Co., Cleve., 1989—. Mem. Nat. Black MBA Assn. (dir. corp. com. Cleve. chpt. 1989). Office: BP Oil Co 200 Public Square Cleveland OH 44147

SCOTT, JENNIFER N. S., managing editor, consultant; b. Phila., Aug. 31, 1960; d. Arthur Gilbert and Annetta (Yoffee) Segal; m. Erin William Scott, Oct. 31, 1982. BA in Communications, Goucher Coll., 1982; postgrad., Nova U., 1986—. Dir. mktg. and new bus. devel. Gainesville (Fla.) State Bank, 1987-88; mng. editor, chief exec. officer Today Mags., Gainesville, 1988—; producer, dir. WGCB-TV, Red Lion, Pa., 1981-82; pub. rels. dir. Harbor Health Care Ctr., Balt., 1981-82; travel coord. Peat, Marwick, Mitchell Corp., Phila., 1982; pub. rels. dir. The Reliable Stores Corp., Columbia, Md., 1982-83; pub. rels. and spl. events coord. The Fla. State Mus., 1983-85; pres. Simply Elegant Chocolates, 1984-86; dir. mktg. and community rels. HCA Grant Ctr. Hosp. of North Fla., Citra, 1985-87; pres. Scott Communications Group, 1985—; mktg. and spl. events cons. RAX Restaurants, 1985-86; bd. dirs. Altrusa Internat. Mem. Leadership Gainesville, Jr. League of Gainesville; cons., bd. dirs. Jr. Achievement; mem. exec. bd. Alachua County Med. Auxiliary; former bd. dirs. County Child Abuse Coun., Fla. State Mus.; bd. dirs. Cris Collinsworth Golf Classic; former pres. Mental Health Assn., DANCE ALIVE!; 1st v.p. Mental Health Svcs. Found.; pres. elect Thomas Ctr. Assocs.; 2nd v.p., past 3rd v.p. Gainesville Jr. Women's Club. Recipient 1st Place award Am. Advt. Assn., 1985, 86, 87, Gen. Excellence award Fla. Mag. Assn., 1989; named Outstanding Young Woman in Am., 1983, 84, 86. Mem. Fla. Mag. Assn. (com. chmn., Gen. Excellence award, 1989), Fla. Pub. Rels. Assn. (Regional Golden Image award Best of Show, 1984, 1st Place, 1984, 85, State Golden Image award 1st Place, 1984, Judges award, 1984), Nat. Assn. Banking Women, Gainesville Women's Forum, Fla. Women's Alliance, Ocala Women's Forum (former bd. dirs.), Gainesville Area C. of C. (bd. dirs., com. chmn.), Partnership for Progress (founder), Com. of 100 (trustee). Republican. Episcopalian. Office: Today Mags 2770 NW 43rd St Gainesville FL 32606

SCOTT, JOAN WALLACH, historian; b. Bklyn., Dec. 18, 1941; d. Samuel and Lottie (Tanenbaum) Wallach; m. Donald M. Scott, Jan. 30, 1965; children: Anthony Oliver, Elizabeth Rose. BA, Brandeis U., 1962; MA, U. Wis., 1964, PhD, 1969. Asst. prof. history U. Ill., Chgo., 1970-72; asst. prof. Northwestern U., 1972-74; assoc. prof. U. N.C., Chapel Hill, 1974-77, prof., 1977-80; Nancy Duke Lewis prof., prof. history Brown U., Providence, 1980-85, now adj. prof.; dir. Pembroke Ctr. for Teaching and Rsch. on Women, 1981-85; now prof. Sch. Social Sci., Inst. for Advanced Study, Princeton, N.J.; dir. Summer Seminar for Coll. Tchrs., NEH, 1977, dir. Seminar for Coll. Tchrs., 1980-81; mem. Inst. for Advanced Study, Princeton, 1978-79. Social Sci. Rsch. Coun. rsch. tng. fellow, 1966-68, NEH fellow, 1975-76; Am. Council Learned Socs. grantee, 1978. Mem. Am. Hist. Assn. (chmn. com. on women historians 1978-80, Joan Kelly prize 1989), Berkshire Conf. Women Historians, Soc. French Hist. Studies. Author: The Glassworkers of Carmaux, 1974 (Am. Hist. Assn. Herbert Baxter Adams prize 1974), (with Louise Tilly) Women Work and Family, 1978, rev. edit., 1987, Gender and the Politics of History, 1988. Office: Inst for Advanced Study Olden Ln Princeton NJ 08540

SCOTT, KAREN ANN, dentist; b. Gary, Ind., Jan. 7, 1957; d. Jay R. and Bernadette (Hogan) S. BS, U. Notre Dame, 1979; BSD, U. Ill., Chgo., 1983, DDS, 1985. Pvt. practice dentistry Chgo., 1985—. Active Grant Park Concert Soc. Notre Dame scholar, 1975-79; recipient Achievement award Internat coll. Dentists, 1985. Mem. ADA, Ill. Dental Soc. (sci. presenter 1987), Chgo. Dental Soc., Internat. Vis. Ctr., Alpha Epsilon Delta, Omicron Kappa Upsilon. Clubs: Young Variety (Chgo.), Young Internat. Home: 1400 N State Pkwy Chicago IL 60610 Office: 55 E Washington St Ste 3102 Chicago IL 60602

SCOTT, KATHLEEN ANNETTE, management executive; b. Ora, Ind., Mar. 31, 1943; d. Harold Hophis and Louise Maxine (Strevey) Scott; m. Anton William Cihak, Dec. 15, 1962 (div. June 1976); children: Anton William II, Elizabeth Annette. BS in Sociology, U. Md., 1981, BS in Tech. Mgmt., 1986, postgrad. Adminstrv. specialist U.S. Army, Ft. Meade, Md., 1976-81; home health care coord. Quality Care, Inc., Silver Spring, Md., 1980; supr. ID svcs. U. Md., College Park, 1980-81, veteran's coord., 1981-82, mgr. payroll svcs. Dept. Phys. Plant, 1982—; cons. automated payroll system, Dept. Phys. Plant, U. Md., 1988-90. Pub. speaker women in the mil., Laurel, Md., Washington, 1986-89; poll judge Dem. Com., College Park, Laurel, 1988. Mem. Am. Payroll Assn., Assn. Phys. Plant Adminstrs., Nat. Assn. Exec. Women, Non-Commissioned Officers Assn. Democrat. Office: Univ Md Dept Physical Plant College Park MD 20742

SCOTT, LENORE DORSEN, import executive; b. N.Y.C., June 17, 1940; d. Alfred Jan and Mary Louise (Campanile) Dorsen; m. Allan Scott, Feb. 27, 1965; children: Tammy Lee, Robert Allan. Degree in restaurant mgmt., UCLA, 1983. Rsch. coord.and various positions CBS, Inc., L.A., N.Y.; importer Lee's Asian Treasures, Thousand Oaks, Calif. Mem. NAFE, Women in Internat. Trade, Asia Soc., Fgn. Trade Assn., Hong Kong Assn. So. Calif. Home: 511 E Gainsborough Rd Thousand Oaks CA 91360 Office: 511 E Gainsborough Rd Thousand Oaks CA 91360

SCOTT, LOIS ALISON, investment banker; b. Phila., Dec. 8, 1960; d. John Richard and Doris Rita (Brooks) S.; m. David Raphael May, June 30, 1984. BS, Cornell U., 1982, MBA, 1983. Registered rep., Ill. Comml. banking officer First Nat. Bank Chgo., 1983-85; v.p. L.F. Rothschild, Chgo., 1985-87, Donaldson, Lufkin & Jenrette, Chgo., 1987—. Bd. dirs. City Lit Theater, Chgo., 1986—, North Avenue Day Nursery, Chgo., 1987—; fund raiser Nat. Abortion Rights Action League, Washington, 1986; fellow Leadership Greater Chgo., 1989-90. Mem. Assn. Mcpl. Women, Chgo. Mcpl. Analysts Soc., AAUW (life), Mcpl. Bond Club. Clubs: Mcpl. Bond, Bond (Chgo.). Office: Donaldson Lufkin & Jenrette 115 S LaSalle St #2700 Chicago IL 60603

SCOTT, MALORA COURTNEY, financial company executive; b. Cin., Mar. 1, 1949; d. Court and Mildred Catherine (Neeley) C. Student So. Ohio Coll., 1983-84. Computer operator, invoice supr. Parke Davis div. Warner Lambert, Blue Ash, Ohio, 1967-83; mgr. data processing Micro Med, Inc., Fairfield, Ohio, 1983-85; credit mgr. Bobcat of Atlanta, Conley, Ga., 1985-86, Ogden Materials, Handling Systems, Inc., Atlanta, 1986-87; March Constrn., Inc., Atlanta, 1987—; owner, pres. Scott & Scott Enterprises, Inc., Marietta, 1987—. Den. Leader Campfire Girls Southwestern Ohio, Cin., 1972-1974; vol. Muscular Dystrophy Assn., Cin., 1972-74, ARC, Cin., 1968-70; sponsor GOP Victory Fund, 1984-86, Greenpeace, 1989—. Mem. NRA, NAFE (N. Atlanta pres.). Republican. Avocations: camping, music, needlework, swimming. Office: Scott & Scott Enterprises Inc 1825 Walter Rd NE Marietta GA 30066

SCOTT, MARGARET LOUISE, aerospace company executive; b. Santa Monica, Calif., June 21, 1925; d. Earl Joseph and Stella May (Miller) Scott; student Los Angeles City Coll., 1947-51, El Camino Coll., 1973. Flight test analyst N.Am. Aviation, Los Angeles, 1943-51; graphics artist N.Am. Rockwell, Los Angeles, 1951-74; illustrations project coordinator Rockwell Internat., Los Angeles, 1974-75, dept. head graphics art dept., Los Angeles div., El Segundo, Calif., 1975-89; project mgr. L.A. Basin Data Svcs. Ctr. Rockwell Internat., 1989—. Mem trade advisory com. El Camino Coll., Glendale Community Coll., West Los Angeles Coll., 1975—. Home: 1601 Sunset Plaza Dr Los Angeles CA 90069 Office: 827 N Douglas St Los Angeles CA 90009

SCOTT, MARGARET SIMON, mortgage broker; b. Boston, May 12, 1934; d. Frank A. and Margaret Alice (Gotham) Simon; m. Walter Neil Scott, Nov. 21, 1959; children: Walter David Kimbley, Benjamin Bray. BA in Physics, Wellesley Coll., 1956; MA in Polit. Sci., Boston U., 1965; MS Human Resources Mgmt., U. Utah, 1974. Registered mortgage broker, N.Y. Rsch. asst. Bell Tel. Labs., Whippany, N.J., 1956-58; rsch. asst. med. sch. U. Louisville, 1959-60, Harvard U., Boston, 1960-64; instr. polit. sci. Trinity U., San Antonio, 1966-67; cons. info. systems U.S. Dept. Labor, Washington, 1968; dir. manpower planning N.Y.C. Human Resources Adminstrn., 1968-71; asst. v.p. First Nat. City Bank, N.Y.C., 1972-77; v.p. Citibank, N.A., N.Y.C., 1978-86, AMEV Asset Mgmt., Inc., N.Y.C., 1986-88; pres. Mortgage Adv. Svcs., Inc., N.Y.C., 1988—. Vol. Jr. League, Louisville, N.Y.C., 1957-74; sec. 1095 Park Ave Corp., N.Y.C., 1976-86; bd. mgr. N.Y. Jr. League, N.Y.C., 1972-74; bd. dirs. N.Y.C. YWCA, 1980-85. Mem. N.Y. Assn. Mortgage Brokers, Nat. Assn. Mortgage Brokers, N.Y. C. of C. and Industry, Empire State Mortgage Bankers Assn., Fin. Management Assn., Real Estate Bd. N.Y., Inc., Fin. Women's Assn., Spinsters' Cotillion Club, Wellesley Club. Democrat. Presbyterian. Home: 441 W 24th St New York NY 10011

SCOTT, MARIANNE FLORENCE, librarian, educator; b. Toronto, Ont., Can., Dec. 4, 1928; d. Merle Redvers and Florence Ethel (Hutton) S. BA, McGill U., Montreal, Que., Can., 1949, BLS, 1952; LLD, York U., 1985. Asst. librarian Bank of Montreal, 1952-55; law librarian McGill U., 1955-73, law area librarian, 1973-75, dir. libraries, 1975-84, lectr. legal bibliography faculty of law, 1964-75; nat. librarian Nat. Library of Can., Ottawa, Ont., 1984—. Co-founder, editor: Index to Can. Legal Periodical Lit, 1963—; contbr. articles to profl. jours. Mem. Internat. Assn. Law Libraries (dir. 1974-77), Am. Assn. Law Libraries, Can. Assn. Law Libraries (pres. 1963-69, exec. bd. 1973-75, honored mem. 1980—), Can. Library Assn. (council and dir. 1980-82, 1st v.p. 1980-81, pres. 1981-82), Corp. Profl. Librarians of Que. (v.p. 1975-76), Can. Assn. Research Libraries (pres. 1978-79, past pres. 1979-80, exec. com. 1980-81, sec.-treas. 1983-84), Ctr. for Research Libraries (dir. 1980-83), Internat. Fedn. Library Assns. (honor com. for 1982 conf. 1979-82), Council of Dirs. of Nat. Libraries (chmn. 1988—). Home: 2084 Chalmers Rd, Ottawa, ON Canada K1H 6K6 Office: Nat Libr Can, 395 Wellington St, Ottawa, ON Canada K1A ON4*

SCOTT, MARTHA SUE, food company executive; b. San Antonio, Aug. 10, 1961; d. Charles and Susie (Lara) S. Student, U. Tex., San Antonio, 1979-82. Crew mem. McDonald's Corp., San Antonio, 1979-80; asst. mgr. McDonald's Corp., 1980-84, store mgr., 1984-88, area supr., 1988—. Recipient Archie award, McDonald's, 1981, named Outstanding Store Mgr., 1987, 88. Mem. Nat. Assn. Female Execs. Democrat. Roman Catholic. Home: 170 De Chantle #304C San Antonio TX 78201 Office: McDonalds 7663 Guilbeau Rd San Antonio TX 78250

SCOTT, MARY DAVIES, federal judge; b. 1944. BA, Trinity U., San Antonio; JD, U. Ark., Little Rock. Admitted to bar, 1979. Bankruptcy judge U.S. Dist. Ct. Ark., Little Rock. Office: US Dist Ct PO Box 2381 Little Rock AR 72203*

SCOTT, MARY ELIZABETH, management consultant; b. Hartford, Conn., June 14, 1951; d. William J. and Ruth E. (Giannettino) S. BA, St. Joseph Coll., West Hartford, Conn., 1974; MBA, U. Conn., 1983. Asst. dir. admissions St. Joseph Coll.; dir. Aetna Life and Casualty, Hartford; pres. M.E. Scott and Co., Hartford. Editorial adv. bd.: Recruiting Mag. Bd. dirs. Urban League Greater Hartford, 1986-89. Mem. Employment Mgmt. Assn., Am. Soc. for Tng. and Devel., Coll. Placement Coun. Office: 8 N Main St Ste 365 West Hartford CT 06107

SCOTT, MARY SHY, music consultant; b. Atlanta, July 19, 1929; d. Robert and Flora Shy; m. Alfred Scott, Feb. 11, 1951; children: Alfredene Cheely, Arthur Robert, Alfred Jr. AB, Spelman Coll., Atlanta, 1950; MA, N.Y.U., 1969. Life Cert. Edn. State Ga. Elem. music specialist Atlanta Pub. Sch., Atlanta, 1950-87; music cons. Atlanta, 1987—; first nat. v.p, nat. pres. elect Alpha Kappa Alpha Sorority, Inc., 1990-94. Contbr. Articles to Profl. Jours. Bd. mem. SCLC Nat., 1986; Mem. Steward Athen Temple AME Ch., Atlanta, 1989. Recipient Plaque Meritorious Svc. Award - Eta Omega Chpt. Omega Psi Phi Fraternity, 1987, Plaque Peachtree Suburban Chpt. for leadership and dedicated svc, 1988, Plaque for Outstanding Contbn. in the Advancement of the Arts Top Ladies of Distinction, Inc., 1988. Home and Office: 2781 Baker Ridge Dr NW Atlanta GA 30318

SCOTT, NANCY ELLEN, psychological counselor; b. El Paso, Tex., Nov. 1, 1960; d. Robert Churchill and Annie Jo (Schmidt) S. BS, U. Tex., El Paso, 1982; MS, Springfield Coll., 1985; MA, Columbia U., 1987, EdM, 1989. Cert. tchr., Tex. Assoc. Occupational Health Consulting Inc., W. Nyack, N.Y., 1985-88; psychiat. rehab. counselor Met. Hosp., N.Y.C., 1988—. Contbr. articles to profl. jours. Mem. Am. Psychol. Assn. (student affiliate group div. 17, affiliate), Am. Assn. Counseling and Devel. Office: Metropolitan Hosp Ctr 1901 1st Ave at 97th St New York NY 10029

SCOTT, NELLIE CHAVARRIA, corporate professional; b. Juárez, Chihuahúa, Mex., Nov. 20, 1956; d. Saul Chavarria and Justina (Gonzales) Rubio. Cert. mgmt., U. So. Calif., 1987. Adminstrv. asst. Wall-Pride, Inc., Van Nuys, Calif., 1979-81; exec. asst. Larry Flynt, Century City, Calif., 1981-82; dir. client relations Martin, Algaze-CPA's, Santa Monica, Calif., 1982-86; mgr. corp. devel. Windsor Publs., Inc., Northridge, Calif., 1986-90, product ngr., 1990—. Mem. Los Angeles Advt. Club. Republican. Roman Catholic. Office: Windsor Publs Inc 9121 Oakdale Ave PO Box 2500 Chatsnorth CA 91313

SCOTT, SHERRY LEE, insurance agency executive; b. Zanesville, Ohio, Apr. 5, 1950; d. Richard and Kate (Dickerson) S.; m. Charles H. Drake, Nov. 25, 1988. V.p. Columbia Nat. Gen. Ins. Agy., Columbus, Ohio, 1979-83; pres., co-founder Safeware, Ins. Agy., Inc., Columbus, 1983—. Mem. Nat. Assn. Ins. Women. Office: Safeware Ins Agy Inc 2929 N High St Columbus OH 43202

SCOTT, SUSAN ELLEN, systems analyst; b. Sanford, Maine, Jan. 11, 1964; d. Jack William and Gloria Ann (Caron) S. BA in Math., Wells Coll., Aurora, N.Y., 1986. Programmer CBORD Group, Ithaca, N.Y., 1986-87; systems analyst Digicomp Rsch. Corp., Ithaca, 1987—. Mem. IEEE, Assn. Old Crows. Home: 285 Breed Rd Locke NY 13092 Office: Digicomp Rsch Corp Terrace Hill Ithaca NY 14850

SCOTT, SUSAN JANE BOYLE, educational organization administrator; b. Terre Haute, Ind., July 17, 1947; d. James Robert and Barbara Jane (Rinehart) Boyle; m. Bradley R. Rutledge, June 17, 1972 (div. 1980); m. Max D. Scott, Nov. 7, 1981; 1 child, Kevin Andrew. AB in English, Ind. U., 1969; MA in English, Ind. State U., 1971. Asst. prof. English Vincennes (Ind.) U., 1971-72; assoc. faculty in English Ind. U.-Purude U., Indpls., 1972-73; coord. adminstrv. svcs. Ind. Higher Edn. Telecommunications System, Indpls., 1974-81, asst. dir. communications, 1981-83, dir. communications svcs., 1983-85, dir. program svcs., 1985—; mem. dean's adv. coun. on continuing edn. Ball State U., Muncie, Ind., 1988—. Contbr. articles to ednl. jours. Mem. Nat. Univ. Continuing Edn. Assn., Women in Communications (poast officer local chpt., nat. fin. adv. com. 1988—, Kleinhenz Svc. award 1990). Episcopalian. Office: Ind Higher Edn Telecommunications System 975 W Michigan St Indianapolis IN 46202-5184

SCOTT, SUSAN RICE, educator; b. Brownsville, Tenn., Aug. 11, 1942; d. Moreau Estes and E. Estelle (Walker) Rice; m. Charles E. Scott, Feb. 28, 1969 (div. July 1985); children: Tamera W., David W. BS, U. Tenn., Martin, 1964; EdM, Memphis State U., 1979, EdD, 1989. Cert. master tchr., Tenn. Elem. tchr. Lauderdale County Bd. Edn., Ripley, Tenn., 1964-65; exchange tchr. USIA, Washington, Netherlands, 1986-87; chmn. English dept. Am. Sch. of The Hague, Netherlands, 1987-88; secondary tchr. Haywood County Bd. Edn., Brownsville, Tenn., 1974-86, tchr. vocat. English, 1989-90, dir. adult basic edn., 1990—; mem. curriculum task force Tenn. Dept. Edn., Nashville, 1985-86, mem. collaorative task force, 1989—. Local elector Tenn. President's Trust, Knoxville, 1989-90; mem. Sister Cities Commn., Brownsville, 1990. Named Outstanding Tchr. by students U. Chgo., 1989. Mem. NEA, Nat. Coun. Tchrs. English (regional composition judge 1984-86), Tenn. Edn. Assn., Tenn. Tchrs. Study Coun. (state steering com. 1984-86), Sigma Tau Delta, Phi Delta Kappa, Kappa Delta Pi. Methodist. Home: 321 N Washington Ave Brownsville TN 38012 Office: Haywood County Bd Edn 900 E Main St Brownsville TN 38012

SCOTT, SYLVIA RACHEL JEANNE, fashion marketing professional; b. June 19, 1949; d. Roger Lewis and Betty Jo (Ives) S. Student, Okla. State U., 1967-69; BSBA in Mktg., U. Tulsa, 1969-71; cert., Tobe-Coburn Sch., 1976; postgrad., San Francisco State U., 1985—. Owner High Country Designs, Breckenridge, Colo., 1980-85; exec. dir. San Francisco Design Network, 1985-88; mktg. dir. David Polizzi for Santa Fe Nouveau, 1988-89; owner The Fashion Liaisons, San Francisco, 1989—; bd. dirs. The Fashion Group Internat., San Francisco. Editor, pub.: The Who's of Fashion Journalism, 1989. Vol. coord. San Francisco Clothing Bank Sale, 1988. Mem. NAFE, San Francisco Fashion Industries Assn. (community rels. and events coms. 1989—), Delta Delta Delta Alumnae chpt. (bd. dirs. 1985-88). Office: Fashion Liaisons Ste 180 370 Turk St San Francisco CA 94102 Other Office: 1204 Third Ave Ste 240 New York NY 10021

SCOTT, TERRI RENAE, corporate professional; b. Denver, May 11, 1959; d. James Alvin Sumey and Maxine May (Meyer) Inman. Student, Colo. State U., 1977-78; BEd in Music, U. No. Colo., 1982; cert. profl. supr., Colo. U., 1985. Cert. total quality trainer. Electronic test technician Inex Inc., Denver, 1981-83; electronic test technician Fischer Imaging Corp., Thornton, Colo., 1983-84, prodn. supr., 1984-86, electronic engring. technician, 1986-88, corp. quality specialist, product acct. mgr., 1988—. Colo. State U. scholar, 1977, Fluke Meml. scholar, 1981. Mem. NAFE, Am. Soc. Quality Control, IEEE (student chpt.), Denver Musician's Assn., Network Colo., Internat. Trumpet Guild (sec. Colo. chpt. 1980-81). Office: Fischer Imaging Corp 12300 N Grant St Thornton CO 80241

SCOTT, VALERIE DON, counseling psychologist, educator; b. Grand Rapids, Mich., June 30, 1949; d. Robert Vernon and Phyllis June (Skinner) S.; m. Elliott Maddox, Oct. 27, 1969 (div. Mar. 1977); 1 child, Donielle; m. Ernest Wyman Garrett, June 7, 1981; children: Kellye, Ernest Wyman Jr. BA, U. Mich., Dearborn, 1971; MS, Upsala Coll., East Orange, N.J., 1978; EdD, Rutgers U., 1983. Dir. ednl. opportunity fund program Upsala Coll., 1975-78; asst. prof. Upsala Coll., E Orange, N.J., 1987—; therapist Upsala Coll., 1987—; psychologist pvt. practice, Newark; cons. Ednl. Testing Svc., Princeton, N.J., 1981, VA Hosp., Orange, N.J., 1987—. Mem. Nat. Assn. Black Psychologists, N.J. Assn. Black Psychologists (v.p. 1987—), Am. Psychol. Assn., N.J. Psychol. Assn., Jack and Jill. Democrat. Methodist. Office: Upsala Coll Prospect Ave East Orange NJ 07019

SCOTT FERNANDEZ, M. CRISTINA, aging specialist, consultant; b. Maracaibo, Venezuela, Nov. 1, 1952; d. Jesus S. and Elsa L. (Moran) Fernandez; m. Jesse P. Scott, Mar. 14, 1983; children: Veronica C. Pizzorni, Stephanie Scott. Le Mesnil, Montreaux, Switzerland; student, Oxford, Eng.; A.A. in Psychiatry, cert. in human svc., Miami-Dade Community Coll., Miami, Fla.; BA in Psychiatry, Fla. Internat. U., Miami. Social worker supr. Miami Beach (Fla.) Community Ctr., 1985-88; v.p. Samedin Internat. Corp., Miami, 1986-88; mgr. Straight Nat. Drug Treatment, Miramar, Fla., 1989; specialist, mgr. Area Agy. on Aging, Miami, 1989—. Creator programs for hispanic elderly and outreach for juvenile drug abuse; mem. adv. coun. Broward Community Coll. Recipient recognition awards United Way, HRS. Mem. Nat. Profl. Womens Assn., Bridge Against Drugs, Greater Miami C. of C., Camacol, Alliance for Aging, Safe Space, Informed Families. Roman Catholic. Home: 1640 NE 104th St Miami Shores FL 33138 Office: Area Agy on Aging 50 NE 109th St Miami FL 33161

SCOTT-FINAN, NANCY ISABELLA, government administrator; b. Canton, Ohio, June 13, 1949; d. Milton Kenneth and Gertrude (Baker) Scott; m. Robert James Finan II, Aug. 23, 1986. Student, Malone Coll., 1970-73; BA magna cum laude, U. Akron, 1976, postgrad., 1976; postgrad., Kent State U., 1977. Cert. tchr. Ohio. Legal sec. Krugliak, Wilkins, Griffiths & Dougherty, Canton, 1969, Amerman, Burt & Jones, Canton, 1970-77; legal sec., paralegal Black, McCuskey, Souers & Arbaugh, 1977-81; adminstrv. staff mem. com. on judiciary U.S. Senate, Washington, 1981-86; adminstrv. asst. to counsel to Pres., The White House, Washington, 1986-89; adminstrv. asst. to former counsel to pres. O'Melveny & Myers, Washington, 1989—; asst. dir. congl. relations Office Legis. Affairs, U.S. Dept. Justice, Washington, 1989—; substitute tchr. North Canton City Sch. System, 1979-80; dance, excercise instr. Siffrin Home for the Developmentally Disabled, Canton, 1980; residential tutor Canton City Sch. System, 1980-81, Fairfax (Va.) County Sch. System, 1983. East coast regional v.p. for spl. projects Childhelp USA, Washington, 1988—; mem. Rep. Women of Capitol Hill, Washington, 1984—. Mem. Am. Assn. of U. Women. Presbyterian. Home: 2056 Hopewood Dr Falls Church VA 22043

SCOTTI, DIANA S., telecommunications executive; b. Denver, Sept. 8, 1962; d. Alfred J. and Gretel (Luparello) S. Contract adminstr. Contel/Executone, Gaithersburg, Md.; program support specialist Nat. Telecommunications Network, Gaithersburg; mktg., installation coord. Suranet, College Park, Md. Mem. NAFE, Capitol Women and Men in Telecommunications. Home: 7402 Garland Ave Takoma Park MD 20912 Office: Suranet 8400 Baltimore Blvd College Park MD 20740

SCOTT-JOHNSON, BARBARA ANN, principal; b. Boise, Idaho, July 3, 1949; d. Doyle Leonard and Ruth Elizabeth (McCown) Scott; m. Gene Evaun Alder Johnson, June 21, 1980; children: Elizabeth Ann, Matthew

Scott. BA, Boise State U., 1970; MA, Oreg. State U., Corvallis, 1972. Classroom tchr. Vancouver (Wash.) Sch. Dist. 37, 1970-78, gifted program facilitator, 1978-80, elementary prin., 1980—; mem. gifted edn. leadership team State of Wash., Olympia, 1978-80. Area capt. United Way, Vancouver, 1984-86, bldg. coord., 1980-90. Recipient Golden Acorn award Salmon Creek PTA, Vancouver, 1984. Mem. Assn. Vancouver Adminstrs. (pres. 1984-86, vice-chair 1987-90), Nat. Assn. Elem. Sch. Prins., Assn. Sch. Curriculum Devel. Home: 6106 Riverside Dr Vancouver WA 98661 Office: Vancouver Sch Dist 37 PO Box 8937 Vancouver WA 98668-8937

SCOTTO, LAURA FRANCES, computer programmer, microcomputer consultant; b. Bklyn., May 31, 1962; d. Thomas and Vancenza Carole (Restucci) S. Student, St. Joseph's Coll., Bklyn., 1979-80; BS, St. John's U., S.I., N.Y., 1984. Computer cons. Dr. Lee Salk, N.Y.C., 1984-85; sr. tech. support specialist Integrated Resources, N.Y.C., 1985-87; microcomputer specialist Cresap, McCormick & Paget, N.Y.C., 1987-88; programmer, analyst Brown Bros. Harriman & Co., N.Y.C., 1988—; cons. CFC, Inc., N.Y.C., 1987—. N.Y. State Regents scholar, 1980. Mem. N.Y. Personal Computing Assn. Office: Brown Bros Harriman & Co 63 Wall St New York NY 10005

SCRIBER, BETTY PRATT, medical record administrator; b. Jan. 4, 1953; d. James Cason and Eloise (Nelson) Pratt; m. Glenn A. Scriber, Oct. 11, 1952; children: Ashley Dawn, Erin Elizabeth. BS Med. Record Adminstrn., La. Tech. U., 1975, MA in Human Relations, 1989. Registered record adminstr. Asst. dir. med. records Schumpert Med. Ctr., Shreveport, La., 1975-76; dir. med. records Minden Med. Ctr., Minden, La., 1976-79, Lincoln Gen. Hosp., Ruston, La., 1979-88; dir. profl. svcs. Lincoln Gen. Hosp., 1988-89; dir. med. records Hendrick Med. Ctr., Abilene, Tex., 1989—; clin. instr. La. Tech. U., Ruston, 1976-84; med. record cons. numerous nursing home facilities in several La. cities, 1979—. Mem. Ruston Jaycee Women, 1983-84, Lincoln Parish Red Cross, Ruston, 1989, Am. Bus. Women's Assn., Ruston, 1989. Named for Outstanding New Project, Ruston Jaycee Women, 1984. Mem. NAFE, Am. Med. Record Assn. (house of dels. 1981-82), La. Med. Record Assn. (pres. 1981-83, pres.-elect 1980-81, chmn. continuing edn. 1977-78, chmn. nominating com. 1984-85, chmn. data quality com. 1986-87, chmn. PRO liaison/alliance com. 1988-89, exec. com. 1978-84), S.E. Hosp. Conf. (bd. dirs. 1981-83), N.E. La. Med. Record Assn., N.W. La. Med. Record Assn. (pres.-elect 1978-79, chmn. nominating com. 1977-78, chmn. program com. 1976-77), La. Hosp. Assn. (peer rev. adv. coun. 1987-89), Tex. Med. Record Assn., Big Country Med. Record Assn. Republican. Baptist. Home: Rte 3 Box 5820 Dubach LA 71235

SCRIBNER, BOBETTE GILPATRIC, insurance agent; b. Littleton, N.H., Apr. 22, 1947; d. Robert E. and Maybelle R. (Foster) Gilpatric; m. Roy N. Scribner, May 15, 1971; children: Edward, Andrew, Aaron. BS, Trinity Coll., Burlington, Vt., 1989. CLU, ChFC, FLMI. Gen. agt. Berkshire Life Ins. Co., Burlington, Vt. Bd. dirs. Parents Anonymous, 1988—. Mem. CLUChFCs (pres.) Vermont Assn. Life Underwriters, Nat. Assn. Life Underwriters, LUPAC, GAMA (v.p.), Internat. Assn. Fin. Profls., Rotary Club. Republican. Office: Berkshire Life Ins Co Burlington VT 05401

SCRIVNER, BARBARA E., piano educator; b. Oreg., May 25, 1931; student (piano student of Lawrence Morton), Bob Jones U., 1962-66; corr. student Inst. Children's Lit., Redding Ridge, Conn., 1974-76; children—R. Dick, Lawrence C., Barbara Ann, Betty Jo. Part time sec., Oreg., 1948-50, 60-62, S.C. 74-76, 80-86, Census Bur., S.C., 1980-82; piano tchr., Greenville, S.C., 1963—; instr. more than 90 student/tchr. recitals; freelance pianist, local chs. and restaurants. Active Rep. Nat. Com., Nat. Rep. Senatorial Com., Nat. Rep. Congressional Com., S.C. Rep. Party. Mem. S.C. Music Assn., Music Tchrs. Nat. Assn., Liberty Found. Contbr. articles, letters to newspapers and columns; editor, pub. Golden Nuggets of Truth, 1982—. Office: PO Box 2444 Greenville SC 29602

SCROGGIE, LUCY ETHELYN, analytical chemist; b. Knoxville, Tenn., May 29, 1935; d. Everett and Ethelyn (Powell) S. BS in Chemistry, U. Tenn., Knoxville, 1957, MS in Chemistry, 1959; PhD in Chemistry, U. Tex., 1961. Analytical chemist Oak Ridge (Tenn.) Nat. Lab., 1961-66, Union Carbide Corp., South Charleston, W.Va., 1966-69, U.S. TVA, Muscle Shoals, Ala., 1970-75; rsch. chemist U.S. TVA, Chattanooga, Tenn., 1975-80; mgmt. trainee U.S. TVA, Norris, Tenn., 1980-81; project mgr. U.S. TVA, Knoxville, 1981—. Contbr. articles to profl. jours. Mem. Am. Chem. Soc., Am. Conf. Govtl. Indsl. Hygienists, Pilot Club Internat., Phi Beta Kappa, Sigma Xi, Phi Kappa Phi. Methodist.

SCROGGINS, NANCY E.J., entrepreneur, financial manager; b. Mason, Tex., Apr. 25, 1950; d. J.D. and Joyce Jordan; m. Jerry Scroggins, Dec. 8, 1972. Cert. payroll profl. Acctg. and fin. mgr. Circle S. Co., Gillette, Wyo.; corp. officer Fox Hill Corp., Rozet, Wyo. Mem. NAFE. Office: PO Box 2306 13970 E Hwy 51 Gillette WY 82717

SCRUGGS, JENNIFER JULIETTE, scriptwriter; b. Nashville, July 25, 1966; d. Julius Richard and Francina (Bannister) S. BA, U. Montevallo, Ala., 1988. Radio announcer Sta. WNDA, Huntsville, Ala., 1983-84, 1988-9; switcher, camera operator Sta. WHNT-TV, Huntsville, 1987-88, camera operator, 1989; consumer affairs specialist Ala. Power Co., Birmingham, 1988; prodn. asst. Ala. A&M U., Normal, 1989, scriptwriter, producer, 1989—. Mem. sanctuary choir First Bapt. Ch., Huntsville, 1977—, mem. singles ministry, 1990—. Mem. NAFE, Delta Sigma Theta (spl. projects com. 1989-90). Democrat. Home: 2701 Farriss Dr NW Huntsville AL 35810 Office: Ala A&M U Telecommunications Ctr PO Box 174 Normal AL 35762

SCRUGGS, MOLLIE SUE, transportation executive; b. Tampa, Fla., Aug. 4, 1957; d. Paul Beckley Scruggs and Lucy Margarite Proctor. BS in Psychology, U. South Fla., 1976. Asst. mgr. Hotel Mutiny, Miami, Fla., 1978-82; mgr. Dolo Corp., Miami, 1983-85; ops. mgr. Hampton Hackney, Ltd., East Hampton, N.Y., 1985-87; owner Leisure Limousine, Sag Harbor, N.Y., 1987-88; co-ptnr. Clause Limousine, Southampton, N.Y., 1988—. Vol. Southampton (N.Y.) Hosp.; mem. Southampton Women's Softball League. Mem. East Hampton C. of C. (cons. 1986—), Southampton C. of C. Democrat. Club: Fleet (Miami) (pres. 1982-83). Home: 47 Lewis St Southampton NY 11968 Office: Clause Limo Ltd Clause Commons 801 Montauk Clause Commons Southampton NY 11968

SCRUGHAM, NANCY LEE, pharmacist; b. Welch, W. Va., Dec. 17, 1954; d. Hal Miller and Irma Elizabeth (Middleton) S. BS in Pharmacy, Auburn (Ala.) U., 1976, MBA, 1985; student, U. Montevallo, Ala., 1972-73; postgrad., Ga. So. Coll., 1983-84. Reg. pharmacist, La., Tex., Ga., Ala. Pharmacy extern VA Hosp., Montgomery, Ala., 1975; intern Northside Hosp., Atlanta, 1976-77; clin. pharmacist U. Ala. Hosps. & Clinics, Birmingham, Ala., 1976, 77-81; pharmacist Lakeshore Hosp., Birmingham, 1981-82; asst. dir. pharmacy Lifemark Pharmacy Mgmt., Wetumpka, Ala., 1982-83; dir. pharmacy Lifemark/AMI Pharmacy Mgmt. Svcs., Reidsville, Ga., 1983-85, AMI Riverview Med. Ctr., Gonzales, La., 1986-87, EPIC/Doctor's Hosp. of Opelousas, La., 1987—; adminstr. Skilled Nursing Facility, Doctor's Hosp, 1987—. Lectr. Arthritis Found. Help Group, Opelousas, 1987, 88; mem., founder Parents Against Drug Dealers, Opelousas, 1988-89. Mem. Am. Soc. Hosp. Pharmacists, Am. Bus. Women's Assn. (edn. chmn. Bon Ami chpt.), La.-So. Cen. La. Soc. Hosp. Pharmacists, Optimists Club, Kappa Epsilon, Rho Chi, Phi Kappa Phi. Republican. Baptist.

SCUCCI, MARY KAY, controller; b. Pitts., May 28, 1958; d. Michael and Lucy (Schott) Crossey; m. Rick Scucci, July 3, 1982. BA in Polit. Sci., Duquesne U., 1980; BA in Acctg., William Paterson, 1986; postgrad., Wharton Sch. Bus., 1989—. CPA. Fin. rep. Assoc. Consumer Finance Co., Monroeville, Pa., 1980-81; asst. branch mgr. Assoc. Consumer Finance Co., Monroeville, 1981-82; acctg. clk. Shasta Beverages Inc., Elizabeth, N.J., 1982-83; regional fin. analyst Shasta Beverages Inc., Emwood Park, N.J., 1983; cost analyst Essex Splty. Products, Inc., Clifton, N.J., 1983-86; sr. bus. analyst Essex Splty. Products, Inc., Clifton, 1986-87, div. finance mgr., 1987; controller Berlex Labs., Wayne, N.J., 1987—; cons. in field; adj. prof. County Coll. Morris, Randolph, N.J., 1988. Coach St. Cecelia's Ch., Rockaway, N.J., 1984-85. Mem. Nat. Acctg. Assn. Republican. Roman Catholic. Home: 103 Toner Rd Boonton NJ 07005 Office: 300 Fairfield Rd Wayne NJ 07470

SCUDERI, FILOMENA PERONE, retired physical education educator, consultant; b. Elizabeth, N.J., Dec. 22, 1930; d. Fred and Jennie Perone; m. Joseph E. Scuderi, 1958; children: Joseph E. Jr., Mary-Jo, Michael. BS, Panzer Coll., 1953; MA, NYU, 1958; postgrad., Seton Hall U., 1983. Cert. health and phys. edn. educator, prin., supr. driver edn. tchr. Tchr. health and phys. edn. New Market Sch., Piscataway, N.J., 1953-54; tchr., dir. phys. edn. East Orange (N.J.) High Sch., 1954-65; prof. phys. edn. Kean Coll. N.J., Union, 1965-88, basketball coach, 1965-75, field hockey coach, 1969-79, women's athletic dir., 1959-72; ret., 1988; coord. student taching program phys. edn. Kean Coll., Union, 1970-88, coord. phys. edn. major program, 1983-88, prof. phys. edn., 1965-88; cons. Westfield (N.J.) Pub. Schs., 1988—; cons., expert witness Archdiocese of Newark, 1981-88; expert witness various legal firms, N.J.; mem. N.J. Bd. Women's Basketball Ofcls., 1950-75; basketball ofcl., field hockey ofcl. N.J. State Interscholastic Athletic Assn., 1975—. Recipient outstanding achievement award N.J. Assn. Basketball Ofcls., 1980. Mem. AAHPER and Dance, AAUP, N.J. Assn. Health, Phys. Edn. Recreation and Dance, AAUW. Republican. Home: 1491 Deer Path Mountainside NJ 07092

SCUDIERI, LORRAINE ALBERTO, mathematician, educator; b. Montclair, N.J., Apr. 25, 1940; d. Harry and Evelyn C. (Palmerie) Alberto; m. Bart Scudieri, Aug. 14, 1965; children: Laura, Matt, Chris, Tim, Patrick. B.A., Montclair State Coll., 1962; M.A., Rutgers U., 1966, M.S. in Statistics, 1987; postgrad. in mgmt., Rutgers U., Newark, 1988—. Tchr., Pascack Valley High Sch., Hillsdale, N.J., 1962-65, Pascack Hills High Sch., Montvale, N.J., 1976-77, Montclair State Coll., Upper Montclair, N.J., 1966-68, 69-70, 71, 74, 79-83, 85-87; stat. studies analyst bus. research div., Bell Atlantic Corp., Newark, 1987—; instr. Fairleigh Dickinson U., 1969-72, 79-81, William Paterson Coll., Wayne, N.J., 1974-76, 82-83, Wyckoff (N.J.) Community Learning Center, 1979, Upsala Coll., East Orange, N.J., 1979-81; instr. decision scis. Rider Coll., Lawrenceville, N.J., 1983-85. Den mother Boy Scouts Am. NSF grantee, 1962-66. Mem. Ops. Research Soc. Am., Soc. Indsl. and Applied Math.

SCULL, DOROTHY MAE, insurance agent; b. Dorris, Calif., Feb. 18, 1948; d. James Melvin and Freeda Marie (Durham) Flowers; m. Martin Dale Scull, July 13, 1968; children: Suzy Lynette, Sheila Charlene. Sec. Federal Crop Ins., Klamath Falls, Ore., 1969, Klamath County Farm Bur., Ore., 1970-74, 80-87; office asst. Dr. E. Mayeans, Coos Bay, Ore., 1976-79; sec. Ore. Doctors Union, Coos Bay, Ore., 1975-79; farmer Scull Farms, Midland, Ore., 1979—; bookkeeper Flowers Bros., Inc., Ore., 1980—; ins. agent Dorothy Scull Ins. Agy., Klamath Falls, Ore., 1987--. Com. Mem. Keno Elem. Sch. Bd., Oreg., 1985-90; Area Rep. Youth For Understanding, Klamath Falls Ore. 1988—. Mem. Oreg. Grange Ins. Agents Coun. (sec. 1989—), EVAC Club (Klamath Falls), Midland Grange Lodge (lady asst. 1987-88). Office: Dorothy Scull Ins Agy 18122 Keno Worden Rd Klamath Falls OR 97601

SCULLION, ANNETTE MURPHY, lawyer, educator; b. Chgo., Apr. 6, 1926; d. Edmund Patrick and Anna (Nugent) Murphy; 1 son, Kevin. B.Ed., Chgo. Tchrs. Coll., 1960; J.D., DePaul U., 1964, M.Ed., 1966; M.Ed., Loyola U., Chgo., 1970; Ed.D., No. Ill. U., 1974. Bar: Ill. 1964, U.S. Dist. Ct. (no. dist.) Ill. 1965, U.S. Ct. Appeals (D.C. cir.) 1978. Lectr. Chgo. Community Coll., 1964-68; pvt. practice law, Chgo., 1964—; asst. prof. bus. edn. Chgo. State U., 1966-69, assoc. prof., 1970-73, prof., 1974—. Club founder, adviser Bus. Edn. Students Assn., Chgo. State U., 1976—; sch. law workshop coordinator Ill. Div. Vocat. and Tech. Edn., 1981. Mem. Nat. Bus. Edn. Assn., Women's Bar Assn. Ill., ABA, Am. Tchr. Edn., Beta Gamma Sigma Home: 386 Muskegon Ave Calumet City IL 60409 Office: Chgo State U 95th and King Dr ED 203 Chicago IL 60409

SCULLY, TAMARA ANNALORA, lawyer; b. Miles City, Mont., Oct. 14, 1957; d. Anthony James and Louise K. Annalora. BS in Bus. with honors, Mont. State U., 1981; JD with high honors, U. Mont., 1986. Bar: Mont. 1986. Assoc. Moulton, Bellingham, Longo & Mather, P.C., Billings, Mont., 1986—. Mem. ABA, Assn. Trial Lawyers Am., Mont. Bar Assn., Mont. Trial Lawyers Assn. Office: Moulton Bellingham et al PO Box 2559 Billings MT 59103

SCULLYWEST, ELIZABETH MARY, geologist; b. Bklyn., Dec. 10, 1953; d. Michael R. and Mary L. (McQueeney) Scully; m. Edward Stember Scullywest, May 19, 1979; children: Michael Charles, Mark David. B.A. with honors, Skidmore Coll., 1976; M.S., U. Kans., 1978. Geologist, ArCo Exploration Co., Denver, 1978-80, sr. geologist, Lafayette, La., 1980-84, Midland, Tex., 1984-85; geologist U.S. Army C.E., Seattle, 1985-86. Vol. Weicker for Senator, Conn., 1970. Mem. Geol. Soc. Am., Am. Assn. Petroleum Geologists, Sierra Club, Nat. Assn. Female Execs., Sigma Gamma Epsilon. Home: 19529 2d Dr SE Bothell WA 98012

SEABRA-VEIGA, LISA RUTH, dentist, convalescent home dental consultant; b. Waterbury, Conn., Sept. 25, 1956; d. Adriano and Rita Seabra-Veiga; m. Jack Zazzaro; 1 child Adriana Adele. BA, Vassar Coll., 1978; DMD, U. Conn., Farmington, 1984. Gen. practice dental resident Waterbury (Conn.) Hosp., 1984-85; gen. practice dentistry Waterbury, 1985—; assoc. dir. Security Savs. and Loan Bank, Waterbury, 1987—. Bd. dirs. Waterbury Symphony Orch., Am. Cancer Soc. Mem. ADA, Conn. State Dental Assn., Acad. Gen. Dentistry, Dental Soc. Greater Waterbury, Acad. Cosmetic Dentistry, U. Conn. Health Ctr. Alumni Assn. (exec. com.). Democrat. Roman Catholic. Office: 1389 W Main St Suite 202 Waterbury CT 06708

SEABROOKS, NETTIE HARRIS, automobile company executive; b. Mt. Clemens, Mich., Feb. 22, 1934; d. Ivan Joseph and Katherine Marshall (Davis) Harris; m. Aug. 23, 1958 (div. 1986); children: Victoria D., Franklyn E. BS in Chemistry, Marygrove Coll., Detroit, 1955; AM in Library Sci., U. Mich., 1957. Librarian Detroit Pub. Library, 1956-58; instr. Tenn. State U., Nashville, 1958-62; librarian Gen. Motors Corp., Detroit, 1962-72; mgr. pub. rels. staff libr. Gen. Motors Corp., 1972-84, dir. pub. affairs info. svcs., 1985; dir. gove. and civic affairs Chevrolet/Pontiac/Can. Grp. Gen. Motors Corp., Warren, Mich., 1985—. Bd. trustees Marygrove Coll., Detroit, 1986—, Leukemia Soc. Am., Detroit, 1985-87; bd. dirs. Detroit Inst. Commerce, 1988-90. Mem. Links Inc. Office: Chevrolet-Pontiac Canada Group Hdqrs Warren MI 48090

SEABURG, LISA S., graphic designer; b. Stamford, Conn., July 13, 1956; d. William Eugene and Beverly Lois (Bishop) S.; m. Gregory R. Stone, Jan. 14, 1984 (div. June 1989); 1 child, Eric Daniel. Grad. high sch., Darien, Conn. Legal sec. John H. Imhoff, Jr., Norwalk, Conn., 1979-81, Edward Kweskin, Stamford, 1981-84; prin. Seastone Graphics, Bethel, Conn., 1984—; designer MC Graphics, Bethel, 1989—. Mem. Conn. Horse Coun., Hartford, 1986—. Mem. Westchester/Fairfield Dressage Assn. (bd. dirs. 1987—), Entreprenuers Women's Network. Democrat. Congregationalist. Home: 30 Midway Dr Bethel CT 06801

SEABURY, CANDI PYNES, counselor; b. Texarkana, Tex., Dec. 21, 1947; d. Marvin and Pauline (Murphy) Pynes. BA, U. Houston, 1969; MEd, U. Mo., 1980. Lic. counselor, Mo. Counselor careers for homemakers St. Louis Community Coll. at Florissant Valley, 1981-83, coord. career info. ctr., 1983-87; counselor St. Louis Community Coll., Meramec, 1987—. Mem. Mo. Career Devel. Assn. (pres. 1983-84), Mo. Assn. for Counseling and Devel., St. Louis Assn. for Counseling and Devel. Office: St Louis Community Coll 11333 Big Bend Rd Saint Louis MO 63122

SEAGRAVES, MARILYN KAYE, assistant treasurer; b. Martin, Tenn., Oct. 1, 1951; d. A.G. and Hilda Kathryn (Pritchett) Campbell; m. Jesse F. Seagraves, Aug. 29, 1976; 1 child, Amy Rebecca. BS in Bus. Adminstrn., U. Tenn., 1976. Cash mgr. Ingram Industries, Inc., Nashville, Tenn., 1981-83; asst. to the treas. Ingram Industries, Inc., Nashville, 1983-85, dir. fin., 1985-87, asst. treas., 1987—. Mem. Fin. Mgrs. Assn. (program co-chmn. 1986-87, v.p. 1987-88, pres. 1988-89, bd. mem. Nashville 1989—), NCCMA (regional pres. 1988-89). Office: Ingram Industries Inc One Belle Meade Pl PO Box 23049 Nashville TN 37202

SEAL, ARLENE B., academic, social welfare administrator; b. Cambridge, Mass., May 27, 1946; children: Bethany, David, Randall. BS magna cum laude, U. Pitts., 1980, MEd with honors, 1981, PhD counselor in Psychology, Edn., 1984. Cons. to provost U. Pitts., asst. dir. honors program, asst. dean U. Hons. Coll.; founder, pres. Campuses Without Drugs, Inc.; 1st former acad. adminstr. to form a nat. drug prevention orgn. that combines all sectors. Contbr. papers and articles to seminars and profl. jours. Conferee White House Conf. for a Drug-Free Am; mem. Nat. Fed. of Parents for Drug Free Youth, Parent Rsch. Inst. for Drug Edn; exec. bd. Allegany Trails Explorers Boy Scouts of Am. Recipient Alumni Grad. Rsch award, U. Pitt, Rsch. fellowship, U. Pitt, Owens fellowship, Provost grad. fellowship, U. Pitt; grantee Office of the Atty Gen., Pa., Aware, Inc. Mem. AAAS, AAUW, Amer. Assn. Counseling and Devel., Am. Soc. for Tng. and Devel., Coms. of Correspondence Inc. (bd. dirs.). Office: 2530 Holly Dr Pittsburgh PA 15235

SEALS, BETTY, federal agency administrator; b. Hamlet, N.C., Jan. 10, 1944; d. Tommye Clarence and Winnell (Collins) S. Student, Troy State U., 1964-68, Enterprise State Jr. Coll., 1969-70, Delta State U., 1976-77. Instr. air traffic control U.S. Army, Ft. Rucker, Ala., 1969-74; air traffic control specialist FAA, Greenville, Miss., 1974-75, Mobile, Ala., 1977—. With U.S. Army, 1962-68. Mem. Nat. Assn. Air Traffic Specialists, Air Traffic Control Assn., Federally Employed Women (newsletter editor 1978-80, pres. Mobile chpt. 1980-81), Profl. Women Controllers, Greater Mobile Fed. Safety and Health Coun. (sec. 1989-91). Roman Catholic.

SEALS, LINDA, graphic designer; b. Dallas, May 26, 1951; d. Fred Clifford and Dorothy (Hardy) S. BA, Colo. State U., Ft. Collins, 1973. Co-founder B. Vader Phototypesetting, Ft. Collins, ptnr., 1975-77, pres., gen. mgr., 1977-84, designer, owner, 1985—; mng. ptnr. The CLS Co., Ft. Collins, 1980-87; co-founder Salt Cedar mag., art. dir., 1977-80; judge bus. graphics competition Colo. Future Bus. Leaders Am., 1984; bd. dirs. Crossroads Safehouse, 1988—. Designer poster in permanent collection Auschwitz Mus., Poland, 1985; group shows include: Auschwitz Mus., 1985. Sponsor Ft. Collins Parks and Recreation teams, 1979-80; mem. Task Force on Alt. Trolley Routes, 1984-85, Pkwy. Preservation Soc., 1983—. Recipient Design award Rocky Mountain Book Pubs. Assn., 1986, 88. Mem. Typographers Internat. Assn. (typographic excellence awards), Nat. Composition Assn. (awards), U.S. Tennis Assn., Ft. Collins Tennis Assn., Rocky Mountain Book Pub. Assn. Democrat. Avocations: tennis, gardening, reading. Office: B Vader Design Prodn 1331 W Mountain Ave Fort Collins CO 80521

SEAPKER, JANET KAY, museum director; b. Pitts., Nov. 2, 1947; d. Charles Henry and Kathryn Elizabeth (Dany) S.; m. Edward F. Turberg, May 24, 1975. BA, U. Pitts., 1969; MA, SUNY, Cooperstown, 1975. Park ranger Nat. Park Svc., summers 1967-69; archtl. historian N.C. Archives and History, Raleigh, 1971-76, hist. preservation adminstr., 1976-77, grant-in-aid adminstr., 1977-78; dir. New Hanover County Mus., Wilmington, N.C., 1978—; bd. dirs. Bellamy Mansion Found., Wilmington, 1986-89, Lower Cape Fear Hist. Soc., Wilmington, 1985-88; N.C. rep. SE Mus. Conf., 1986-90; field reviewer Inst. Mus. Svcs., 1982—. Contbr. articles to profl. jours. Bd. dirs. Downtown Area Revitalization Effort, Wilmington, 1979-81, Hist. Wilmington Found., 1979-84, pres., 1980-81; mem. Community Appearance Commn., Wilmington, 1984-88, 250 Ann. Commn., Wilmington, 1986-90. Grad. program fellow SUNY, Cooperstown, 1969-70. Mem. N.C. Mus. Council (sec.-treas. 1978-84, pres. 1984-86), Am. Assn. Mus. (mem. accreditation vis. com. 1983—, mus. assessment program reviewer 1982—), Nat. Trust Hist. Preservation, Hist. Preservation Found. of N.C. (sec. 1976-78). Democrat. Presbyterian. Home: 307 N 15th St Wilmington NC 28401 Office: New Hanover County Mus Lower Cape Fear 814 Market St Wilmington NC 28401

SEARIGHT, PATRICIA ADELAIDE, retired radio and television executive; b. Rochester, N.Y.; d. William Hammond and Irma (Winters) S. BA, Ohio State U. Program dir. Radio Sta. WTOP, Washington, 1952-63, gen. mgr. info., 1964; radio and TV cons., 1964-84; ret., 1984; producer, dir. many radio and TV programs; spl. fgn. news corr. French Govt., 1956; v.p. Micro Beads, Inc., 1955-59; sec., dir. Dennis-Inches, Corp., 1955-59; exec. dir. Am. Women in Radio and TV, 1969-74; fgn. service officer U.S. Dept. State, AEC, ret. Mem. pres.'s coun. Toledo Mus. Art. Recipient Kappa Kappa Gamma Alumna achievement award. Mem. Am. Women in Radio and TV (program chmn.; corrs. sec.; dir. Washington chpt.; pres. 1958-60, nat. membership chmn. 1962-63, nat. chmn. Industry Info. Digest 1963-64, Mid-Eastern v.p. 1964-66), Soc. Am. Travel Writers (treas. 1957-58, v.p. 1958-59), Nat. Acad. TV Arts and Scis., Women's Advt. Club (Washington, pres. 1959-60), Nat. Press Club, Soroptimist, Kappa Kappa Gamma. Episcopalian. Home: 10549 E Desert Cove Ave Scottsdale AZ 85259

SEARING, SUSAN ELLIS, women's studies librarian; b. Lockport, N.Y., Aug. 5, 1950; d. Samuel Richard and Dorothy Jean (Meeks) S. BA, SUNY, Binghamton, 1972; AMLS, U. Mich., 1976. Reference librarian Yale U., New Haven, Conn., 1976-82; women's studies librarian U. Wis., Madison, 1982--; lectr. U. Wis. Sch. of Libr. & Info. Studies, Madison, 1988. Author; Introduction to Library Research in Women's Studies, 1985;. Recipient: Phi Beta Kappa, 1972. Mem. ALA (co-chair 1986-87), Women' Studies Section.

SEARL, JACALYN JOY, special education consultant; b. Sioux Falls, S.D., Mar. 16, 1953; d. Robert Edwin and Myrna Mae (Groeneveld) D. BS in Spl. and Elem. Edn., U. S.D., 1976, MA in Spl. and Early Childhood Edn., 1986. Cert. elem. tchr., spl. edn. tchr., S.D., elem. tchr., early childhood for the handicapped, generic spl. edn. tchr., Tex. Tchr. spl. edn. Emerson Sch., Sioux Falls, 1976-84; tchr. early childhood Hawthorne Elem. Sch., Sioux Falls, 1985-86; cons. early childhood for handicapped Region 18 Edn. Service Ctr., Midland, Tex., 1986—. Sec. Emerson Sch. PTA, 1976-83; chaperone S.D. Spl. Oympics, 1976-84; chaperone/coach Internat. Spl. Olympics, Baton Rouge, summer 1983; mem. pub. relations staff Sioux Falls Republican. Com. 1983. Mem. Council Exceptional Children, Assn. Sch. and Community Devel., Nat. Assn. Female Execs., Am. Legion Aux., Phi Delta Kappa, Phi Beta Pi. Lutheran. Home: 1606 Tennessee Odessa TX 79764 Office: Region 18 Edn Service Ctr PO Box 60580 Midland TX 79711

SEARLE, MARGARET ANN, computer company executive; b. Buffalo Center, Iowa, Mar. 4, 1944; d. James Harrison and Margaret Cecilia (Hayes) Sowers; m. Leroy Frank Searle, Feb. 15, 1969; children: James Harrison Sowers, Cassandra Searle-Ewer, Sabrina Searle-Porter. BA in English, U. Iowa, 1966, MA in Brit. and Am. Lit., 1968. Promotion dir. WXXI Channel 21, Rochester, N.Y., 1971-74; pub. relations coordinator Visual Studies Workshop, Rochester, 1974-77; pub. relations officer Seattle Art Mus., 1977-78, pub. relations, grants mgr., 1978-86, pub. affairs officer, 1980-85; exec. officer Delphi Computers & Peripherals, Seattle, 1985—; cons. in field. Editor: In Public: Art of Public Relations, 1985, manual, 1988. Bd. dirs. Planned Parenthood, Rochester, 1976-77; mem. Rochester Arts Adv. Com., 1975-77; bd. dirs. Arts Resource Svc., Seattle, 1977-79; mem. Mayor's of Seattle Task Force on Arts, 1981. Recipient Excellence in Promotion award Corp. for Pub. Broadcasting, 1973. Mem. Women Bus. Exchange, Wash. Tech. Assn., Nat. Women in Visual Art, Women Bus. Owners, City Club. Democrat. Home: 6273 19th Ave NE Seattle WA 98115 Office: Delphi Computers 510 NE 65th St Seattle WA 98115

SEARLE, NORMA DORIS, polymer photochemist; b. N.Y.C., Jan. 26, 1925; d. David and Sylvia (Goodman) Zizmer; m. Bernard George Searle, Aug. 7, 1949. BA in Chemistry, Hunter Coll., 1946; PhD in Phys. Chemistry, NYU, 1959. Rsch. chemist Am. Cyanamid Co., Stamford, Conn., 1957-69, sr. rsch. chemist, 1969-74; group leader Am. Cyanamid Co., Bound Brook, N.J., 1974-82; cons. polymer photochemist Searle Assocs., Bridgewater, N.J., 1982—; cons. in field. Contbr. chpts. to books, articles to sci. jours. Rsch. fellow Tex. Co., NYU, 1956-57. Mem. Am. Chem. Soc., Am. Soc. Testing Materials, Am. Assn. Textile Chemists and Colorists, N.J. Computer Club, Somerset Naturalists (pres. 1983-85, publicity chmn. 1986—). Home and Office: Searle Assocs 106 D Finderne Ave Bridgewater NJ 08807

SEARLES, ANNA MAE HOWARD, educator, civic worker; b. Osage Nation Indian Terr., Okla., Nov. 22, 1906; d. Frank David and Clara (Bowman) Howard; A.A., Odessa (Tex.) Coll., 1961; B.A., U. Ark., 1964; M.Ed., 1970; postgrad. (Herman L. Donovan fellow), U. Ky., 1972—; m. Isaac Adams

Searles, May 26, 1933; 1 dau., Mary Ann Rogers (Mrs. Herman Lloyd Hoppe). Compiler news, broadcaster sta. KJBC, 1950-60; corr. Tulsa Daily World, 1961-64; tchr. Rogers (Ark.) High Sch., 1964-72; tchr. adult class rapid reading, 1965, 80; tchr. adult edn. Learning Center Benton County (Ark.), Bentonville, 1973-77, supr. adult edn., 1977-79; tchr. North Ark. Community Coll., Rogers, 1979-90, CETA, Bentonville, 1979-82; tchr. Joint Tng. Partnership Act, 1984-85; coordinator adult edn. Rogers C. of C. and Rogers Sch. System, 1984—. Sec. Tulsa Safety Council, 1935-37; leader, bd. dirs. Girl Scouts U.S.A., Kilgore, Tex., 1941-44, leader, Midland, Tex., 1944-52, counselor, 1950-61; exec. sec. Midland Community Chest, 1955-60; gray lady Midland A.R.C., 1958-59; organizer Midland YMCA, Salvation Army; dir. women's div. Savings Bond Program, Midland; mem. citizens com. Rogers Hough Meml. Library, women's aux. Rogers Meml. Hosp.; vol. tutor Laubach literacy orgn., 1973—; sec. Beaver Lake Literacy Council, Rogers, 1973-83, Little Flock Planning Commn., 1975-77, Benton County Hist. Soc., 1981—; pub. relations chmn. South Central region Nat. Affiliation for Literacy Advance, 1977-79; bd. dirs. Globe Theatre, Odessa, Tex., Midland Community Theatre, Tri-County Foster Home, Guadalupe, Midland youth centers, DeZavala Day Nursery, PTA, Adult Devel. Center, Rogers CETA, 1979-81; vol. recorder Ark. Hist. Preservation Program, 1984—; docent Rogers Hist. Mus., 1988—. Recipient Nice People award Rogers C. of C., 1987, Thanks badge Midland Girl Scout Assn., 1948, Appreciation Plaque award Ark. Natural Heritage Commn., 1988; Cert. of recognition, Rogers Pub. Schs., 1986; Instr. of Yr. award North Ark. Community Coll. West Campus Mem. NEA (del. conv. 1965), Ark. Assn. Public Continuing and Adult Edn. (pres. 1979-80), South Central Assn. for Lifelong Learning (sec. 1980-84), PTA (life), Future Homemakers Am. (life; sec. 1980—), Delta Kappa Gamma. Episcopalian. Clubs: Altrusa (pres. 1979—), Apple Spur Community (Rogers). Home: Rte 2 Rogers AR 72756

SEARLS, EILEEN HAUGHEY, lawyer, librarian, educator; b. Madison, Wis., Apr. 27, 1925; d. Edward M. and Anna Mary (Haughey) S.; B.A., U. Wis., 1948, J.D., 1950, M.S. in L.S., 1951. Admitted to Wis. bar, 1950; cataloger Yale U., 1951-52; instr. law St. Louis U., 1952-52, asst. prof., 1953-56, asso. prof., 1956-64, prof., 1964—, law librarian, 1952—. Mem. Wis. Bar Assn., Bar Assn. Met. St. Louis, Am. Assn. Law Librarians, Mid-Am. Assn. Law Libraries, Council Law Library Consortium (chmn.), Southwestern Assn. Law Libraries. Club: Altrusa. Office: 3700 Lindell Blvd Saint Louis MO 63108

SEASHOLTZ, JOANNE MARIE, nursing administrator, consultant, nurse; b. West Reading, Pa., Apr. 25, 1953; d. Earl Carl and Betty Marie (Moyer) S. Student, Elizabethtown (Pa.) Coll., 1971-73; BSN, Widener U., 1975; MSN, U. Pa., 1978; PhD, U. Pitts., 1985. RN, Pa. Critical care staff nurse Reading Hosp. and Med. Ctr., West Reading, 1975-77; cardiovascular clin. specialist Rolling Hill Hosp., Elkins Park, Pa., 1978-79; critical care instr. Albert Einstein Med. Ctr.-Daroff, Phila., 1979-81; cardiovascular clin. specialist North Hills Passavant Hosp., Phila., 1981-82, asst. dir. nursing, 1982-89; preceptor Genetech, San Francisco, 1982-89; dir. critical care div. W.Va. U. Hosps., 1989—; cons. in field; preceptor for students LaRoche Coll., 1987-89. Chaperone GRAIL, Reading, 1976; active telethon YMCA, Pitts., 1986; mem. Audubon Soc. Western Pa., 1987—; fraternal communicator Luth. Brotherhood, Pitts., 1986—; mem. alumni legis. com. Widener U., Chester, Pa., 1988-89; mem. Am. Heart Assn. Mem. Nat. Am. Assn. Critical Care Nurses, Three Rivers chpt. Am. Assn. Critical Care Nurses (pres. elect 1985-86, pres. 1986-87, past pres. 1987-88), Am. Orgn. Nurse Execs. Home: 4003 Morningside Way Morgantown WV 26505 Office: W Va U Hosps Med Ctr Dr Morgantown WV 26505

SEATS, PEGGY CHISOLM, marketing executive; b. Lisman, Ala., Oct. 12, 1951; d. William H. and Bernice (Berry) Chisolm; m. Melvin Seats (div.). BA in Communications cum laude, Lewis U., 1974. Account exec. Globe Broadcasting, Chgo., 1976-78, Merrill Lynch, Chgo., 1978-79, Transp. Displays, Inc., Chgo., 1979-81; nat. accounts mgr. Soft Sheen Products Co., Chgo., 1981-83; mktg. cons. Reverie, Inc., Chgo., 1983-85, Atlanta, 1987—; pub. rels., mktg. mgr. Proctor & Gardner Advt., Chgo., 1985-86; dir. pub. rels., mktg. Morris Brown Coll., Atlanta, 1986-87; mgr. mktg. Howard U. Press, Washington, 1989—; founder Black Pub. Rels. Soc., Atlanta, 1987. Contbr. numerous articles to newspapers and mags. Bd. dirs Lewis U. Alumni, Ill., 1979; state advisor U.S. Congl. Adv. Bd., Ill. 1982. Recipient Kizzie award Black Women Hall of Fame, Chgo., 1981, Svc. award Nat. Assn. Women in Media, Chgo., 1982; inductee Outstanding Women of Am., 1975, 87. Mem. Internat. Assn. Bus. Communicators, Pub. Rels. Soc. Am., Bus. and Pub. Rels. Specialists (pres. emeritus), Nat. Assn. Market Developers. Republican. Baptist. Home: 2020 Pennsylvania Ave Ste 225 Washington DC 20006

SEAVEY, AVA BETH, TV production executive; b. Elizabeth, N.J., July 20, 1954; d. Harold M. and Billie Jean (Holt) Tulchin; m. John P. Seavey Jr., June 7, 1987. BA, Columbia U., 1978. V.p. sales and mktg. Tulchin Studios, N.Y.C., 1982—. Office: Tulchin Studios 240 E 45th St New York NY 10017

SEAVY, MARY ETHEL INGLE, art educator; b. Alpena, S.D., Mar. 23, 1910; d. James Albert and Mollie (Ceny) Ingle; m. Donald Lee Seavy, Mar. 19, 1940; 1 child, Judith Ann. BS, No. State Tchrs. Coll., Aberdeen, S.D., 1934; MA inArt, U. Iowa, 1937, postgrad., 1949-53; postgrad., Columbia U., 1940. Cert. permanent profl. tchr., Iowa. Art coord. pub. schs., Decorah, Iowa, 1937-38, Waterloo, Iowa, 1938-40, Whiting, Ind., 1940-41; instr. art Luther Coll., Decorah, 1942-43, U. Iowa, Iowa City, 1945-47; tchr. Solon (Iowa) Elem. Sch., 1949-53; art coord. Mil. Sch., Aschaffenburg, Fed. Republic Germany, 1962-64; tchr. Iowa City Pub. Schs., 1965-75; artist, tchr. Stauffenburg Studio, Marengo, Iowa, 1987-90; One-woman show Hawkeye State Bank, 1987; exhibited in group shows, 1986, State Fair, Des Moines, 1989, community theatre, 1990. Recipient award for short story State Federated Women's Club, 1987, 90, award for essay, 1987, 90. Mem. Iowa Watercolor Soc., AAUW, DAR (past regent Iowa City), Iowa City Women's Club, Order Ea. Star, Order White Shrine of Jerusalem (past worthy high priestess), Order of Amaranth, Delta Kappa Gamma, Zeta Tau Alpha (v.p. Alpha Omicron chpt. 1970-71). Christian Scientist. Home and Studio: 534 Clark St Iowa City IA 52240

SEAY, AUDREY BOSCHEN, medical association administrator; b. Richmond, Nov. 30, 1930; d. Henry Chisholm and Gladys Ercelle (Morrissett) Boschen; m. Perry Seay, Sept. 12, 1951; children: Perry Christopher, Jefferson Taylor, Pamella, Ann Marie. BS, Eastern Mich. U., 1973; MHA, U. Mich., 1975. Nurse Swedish Hosp., Seattle, Wash., 1951-52, Seaway Hosp., Trenton, Mich., 1962-65, Chrysler Corp., Trenton, 1965-69, Ford Motor Co., Woodhaven, Mich., 1969-74; research asst. Oakwood Hosp., Dearborn, Mich., 1974-75; asst. dir. Oakwood Hosp., Dearborn, 1975-79; emergency med. svcs. coord. Emergency Med. Svcs., Detroit, 1979--; exec. dir. Health Emergency Med. Services, Westland, Mich., 1980--. Mayor City of Trenton, councilman City of Trenton, Mich., bd. dirs. Recipient Svc. award Down River Rep. Club, 1984. Mem. Am. Coll. Healthcare Exec., Am. Hosp. Assn., Soroptimist Internat. Roman Catholic. Home: 2717 Riverside Dr Apt 12 Trenton MI 48183 Office: Health Emergency Med Svcs Svcs 2345 Merriman Westland MI 48185

SEAY, LELLA DELORES, computer specialist; b. Ringgold, Ga., Sept. 27, 1946; d. Calvin Conard Sr. and Eva Lucille (Dean) Fugatt; m. Michael Seay, June 21, 1979; children: Steven Michael, Aaron Daniel. Student, Edmondson Bus. Coll., Chattanooga, 1966. Med. clk. Provident Life Ins. Co., Chattanooga, 1966-67; sec. Title Guaranty and Trust Co., Chattanooga, 1967-68; southeast customer rep. Duracell Products Co., Chattanooga, 1968-75; paralegal trainee Brown, Harriss, Hartman, Rossville, Ga., 1975-77; info. systems specialist Tenn. Valley Authority, Chattanooga, 1977—. Office: Tennessee Valley Authority 1101 Market St Chattanooga TN 37402

SEAY, MARY BURT, psychology educator; b. Lancaster, Pa., June 27, 1953; d. Arthur A. and Miriam (Hoar) Burt; m. Thomas A. Seay, Mar. 4, 1978; children: Michael A., Brian A., Kaitlyn A. BS, Albright Coll., Reading, Pa., 1976; MS, Lehigh U., 1979, PhD, 1985. Vis. asst. prof. Muhlenberg Coll., Allentown, Pa., 1985-86, Lehigh U., Bethlehem, Pa., 1986-88; asst. prof. Kutztown (Pa.) U., 1988-89; asst. prof. psychology Allentown Coll., Center Valley, Pa., 1990—; cons. Community Psychol. Svcs. Cons., Allentown, 1988—. Contbr. articles to profl. publs. Mediator, Common Ground, Allentown, 1990. Mem. Am. Psychol. Soc., Ea. Psychol. Assn. Home: 1420 Walnut St Allentown PA 18102 Office: Allentown Coll Dept Psychology Center Valley PA 18034

SEBASTIANI, SUSAN MARIE, title insurance company executive; b. Trenton, N.J., Jan. 16, 1954; d. Louis Peter and Emma (Rendemonti) Carlucci; m. Anthony E. Sebastiani, Sept. 17, 1977; 1 child, Alexandra Ellen. Student, Mercer County Community Coll., 1972. Sec. Eastern Abstract Co., Trenton, 1973-75; sec., title examiner Commonwealth Land Co., Trenton, 1975-77; asst. v.p. Continental Title Ins. Co., Trenton, 1977-84; pres. Mercer Title Services Agy., Inc., Trenton, 1984—. Mem. Mercer County Bd. Realtors, Mercer County Bar Assn. (affiliate), U.S. C. of C., N.J. Land Title Assn., Am. Land Title Assn. Home: 14 Cheryl Ln Clarksburg NJ 08510 Office: Mercer Title Services Agy Inc 5 Stults Ave PO Box 3710 Trenton NJ 08629

SEBASTIANI-CUNEO, MARY ANN, property manager; b. Sonoma, Calif., July 1, 1947; d. August David and Sylvia Emily (Scarafoni) Sebastiani; m. Richard Angelo Cuneo, Feb. 1, 1940; children: Angelo, Marc, Josef. BA, U. Santa Clara (Calif.), 1969; student, U. Calif., Davis, 1970, Anthony Schs., 1985. Elem. tchr. West Davis Elem., Davis, Calif., 1971-72; tchr. Northwood Elem., Napa, Calif., 1972-74; pub. relations person Sebastiani Vineyards, Sonoma, Calif., 1974—; founder, chief exec. officer, pres. Plaza Properties, Inc., Sonoma, 1980-84; real property mgr. Triple C Investments, Sonoma, 1978—; v.p. Sebastiani Vineyards-Real Estate, Sonoma, 1987—. Chairperson Sonoma County Boy Scouts Am., 1987. Mem. Sonoma County Winegrowers. Republican. Roman Catholic. Office: PO Box 4 Vineburg CA 95487

SEBECK, KAREN PLEASY, retail executive; b. Steubenville, Ohio, Jan. 24, 1946; d. Burr Eugene and Ethel May (Jones) McKnight; m. Robert Brown Sebeck, Aug. 19, 1967; children: Amy LeeAnne, Derek Creighton. Degree in Nursing, Montifiore Hosp., U. Pitts., 1967; degree in nurse anesthesiology, Ohio Valley Hosp., 1976. RN, 1967; cert. RN anesthetist. RN Purdue U. Health Ctr., West Lafayette, Ind., 1967-68, Children's Hosp., Columbus, Ohio, 1968-69, Lutheran Gen. Hosp., Park Ridge, Ill., 1971-72, St. John Med. Ctr., Steubenville, Ohio, 1972-74; pvt. duty Chgo., 1970-71; cert. RN anesthetist Ohio Valley Hosp., Steubenville, 1976-77, St. John Med. Ctr., Steubenville, 1977-80, Ohio Valley Hosp., Steubenville, 1982-86; sec. of corp. Borden Office Equipment Co., Steubenville, 1983—. Treas. Hemlock Twig, Steubenville; bd. dirs. YWCA, Steubenville, Friends of Alive, Steubenville, A.L.I.V.E. Steubenville. Mem. Am. Assn. Nurse Anesthetist. Democrat. Methodist. Home: 4407 Fairway Dr Steubenville OH 43952 Officce: Borden Office Equipment Co 141 N Fifth St Steubenville OH 43952

SEBELA, VICKI DAWN, association executive; b. Des Plaines, Ill., Mar. 7, 1964; d. James Edward and Mary Nell (Davis) S.; m. Julius Michael Colangelo, Oct. 8, 1988. AA, AS, Harper Coll., 1984; BS, Roosevelt U., 1986. Adminstrv. asst. McDonald's Corp., Rolling Meadows, Ill., 1979-83; info. specialist William Rainey Harper Coll., Palatine, Ill., 1983-84; teller Arlington Fed. Savs. and Loan, Arlington Heights, Ill., 1984-85; asst. to the pres. Ill. Women's Agenda, Chgo., 1984-85; student outreach coord. William Rainey Harper Coll., Palatine, 1985-86; adminstrv. asst. women's affairs Office of the Gov., Chgo., 1986-88; exec. adminstr. Social Engring. Assocs., Inc., Chgo., 1988-89; exec. dir. Greater Wheaton (Ill.) C. of C., 1989—. Contbr. articles to Ency. Britanica. Cert. paraprofl. Talk Line/Kids Line Crisis Hot Line, Elk Grove Village, Ill., 1983. Harper Coll. scholar, 1982, Roosevelt U. scholar, 1984. Mem. Chgo. Women in Govt. Rels. (membership chair, bd. dirs. 1988-89), NAFE, Roosevelt U. Alumni Assn., Am. Psychol. Assn., Women Employed, Lions, Phi Theta Kappa. Republican. Office: Greater Wheaton C of C 331 W Wesley Wheaton IL 60187

SEBESTYEN, OUIDA GLENN, author; b. Vernon, Tex., Feb. 13, 1924; d. James Ethridge and Byrd (Lantrip) Dockery; m. Adam Sebestyen, Dec. 21, 1960 (div. 1966); 1 child, Corbin. Student, U. Colo. speaker, leader workshops at pub. schs. and ednl. orgns. Author: Words by Heart, 1979 (Internat. Reading Assn. award 1979, Am. Book award 1982), Far from Home, 1980 (Silver Pencil award 1984), IOU's, 1982 (Tex. Inst. Letters award 1983), On Fire, 1985, The Girl in the Box, 1988; author short stories in 3 anthologies. Home and Office: 115 S 36th St Boulder CO 80303

SEBREN, LUCILLE GRIGGS, teacher; b. Chesterfield, S.C., May 21, 1922; d. Manley Oscar and Clara Blanche (Rivers) Griggs; m. Herbert Lee Sebren, Dec. 19, 1943; children: Herbert Lee Jr., George Hall, Samuel Robert Franklin. BA, Flora Macdonald Coll., Red Springs, N.C., 1942; MEd, Coll. of William and Mary, 1966. Cert. tchr., Va., N.C., S.C. Tchr. Cheraw (S.C.) Elem. Sch., 1942-44; tchr. kindergarten Larchmont Meth. Ch., Norfolk, Va., 1951-53; tchr. Norfolk Acad., 1953—, supr., cons., adminstr. primary dept., 1970-82, master tchr., cons. elem. grades, 1987—. Contbr. articles to profl. jours. Mem. Va. Symphony and Symphony Aux., Norfolk, 1946—, Norfolk Soc. of the Arts, 1970—, Chrysler Mus., Norfolk, 1965—, Va. Opera Assn, Norfolk, 1974—. Mem. AAUW (sec. exec. bd. 1974-76), Alpha Delta Kappa (pres. Va. chpt. 1978-80, pres. S.E. region 1981-83, grand chaplain 1983-85, grand pres.-elect 1985-87, grand pres. 1987-89), Kappa Delta Pi. Republican. Baptist. Office: Norfolk Acad 1585 Wesleyan Dr Norfolk VA 23502

SEBRING, MARJORIE MARIE ALLISON, home furnishings company executive; Burnsville, N.C., Oct. 8, 1926; d. James William and Mary Will (Ramsey) Allison Shockey; student Mars Hill Coll., 1943, Home Decorators Sch. Design, N.Y.C., 1948, Wayne State U., 1953; cert. home furnishings rep. U. Va., 1982; 1 child, Patricia Louise Banner Krohn. Dir. decorating div. Robinson Furniture, Detroit, 1949-57; head buyer Tyner Hi-Way House, Ypsilanti, Mich., 1957-63; head buyer Town and Country, Dearborn, Mich., 1963-66; instr. Nat. Carpet Inst., 1963-65; owner Adams House, Inc., Plymouth, Mich., 1966-72; exec. v.p. mktg. and sales, regional sales and mktg. mgr. Triangle Industries, L.A., 1972-89; co-owner Markham-Sebring, Inc., St. Petersburg, Fla., 1983-89; dir. contract div. Kane Furniture, 1984-85; co-owner Accessories, Etc., 1985-89; rep.-at-large Heritage Lakes, U.S. Home. Charter mem. Presdl. Task Force. Recipient nat. sales awards, recognition for work with youth and aged. Mem. Internat. Home Furnishings Assn., Fla. Home Furnishings Rep. Assn. (officer), Am. Security Coun., Williamsburg Found., USCG Aux., Nat. Audubon Soc., Internat. Platform Assn. Republican. Contbr. creative display to Better Homes and Gardens, 1957-64. Home: 2601-3 Grist Mill Circle New Port Richey FL 34655-1311

SECKEL, CAROL ANN, church conference superintendent; b. Bklyn., Oct. 28, 1949; d. Leonard Immanuel and Anna Beth (Eggleston) Klotz; m. Richard Kevin Seckel, June 27, 1970; children: Joshua Allen, Jason Andrew, Jeremy Jacob. B in Edn., U. Toledo, 1971; MDiv, MA in Christian Edn, Meth. Theol. Sch. Ohio, 1978. With Stouffer's Restaurant, Toledo, 1971-72; pre-sch. tchr. Liberty Community Ctr., Delaware, Ohio, 1972-73; co-dir. work study program Early Childhood Ctr., Methesco, Delaware, 1977-78; co-pastor numerous chs., Middleburg, Ohio, 1975-78, Chiloquin, Oreg., 1978-82; pastor Sitka (Alaska) United Meth. Ch., 1982-86; dist. supt. Oreg. Idaho Conf. United Meth. Ch., Salem, Oreg., 1986-88; conf. supt. Alaska Missionary Conf. United Meth. ch., Anchorage, 1988—; co-presenter United Meth. Bishops Com. on Faithful Disciples-Vital Congregation, Nashville, 1987. Mem., pres. bd. dirs. Klamath County Women's Crisis Ctr., Klamath Falls, Oreg., 1979-82, Sitkans Against Family Violence, Sitka, 1983-86; trustee Willamette U., Salem, 1986-88, Alaska Pacific U., Anchorage, 1988—; mem. Community Choir, Sitka, 1983-85; v.p. Tongass coun. Girl Scouts U.S., 1984-86. Fellowship United Meths. in Worship, Music and Other Arts. Democrat. Office: 3402 Wesleyan Dr Anchorage AK 99508

SEDDON, MARGARET RHEA, physician, astronaut; b. Murfreesboro, Tenn., Sept. 8, 1947; d. Edward C. Seddon; m. Robert L. Gibson; children: Paul Seddon Gibson, Edward Dann Gibson. B in Physiology, U. Calif., Berkeley, 1970; MD, U. Tenn., 1973. Intern, resident Memphis; astronaut NASA Lyndon B. Johnson Space Ctr., Houston, 1979—, participant shuttle flight STS-51D, 1985. Mem. Am. Coll. Emergency Physicians, Am. Med. Women's Assn., Tex. Med. Assn., Harris County Med. Soc., 99's. Address: NASA Johnson Space Ctr Astronaut Office Houston TX 77058*

SEDERGREN, MURIEL DWYER, banker; b. Barnet, Vt., July 14, 1942; d. Dale Stuessel and Elizabeth Julia (Champany) Dwyer; m. Rodney Doane Sedergren, Aug. 6, 1960 (dec.); 1 child, Anita Marie Hughes. AA, Williams Coll., 1976; cert., Am. Inst. of Banking, 1986; MS in Banking with honors, Fairfield U., 1982; student, N.Eng. Sch. Banking. Asst. treas., br. mgr. Proctor (Vt.) Bank, 1962-79; v.p. ops. Marble Bank, Rutland, Vt., 1979-84; v.p., cashier Woodstock (Vt.) Nat. Bank, 1984—. Incorporator Ottauquechee Health Ctr., 1987; dir. ARC, Rutland, 1980-84; mem. Pentangle Coun. of Arts; v.p., fundraiser Vt. and N.H. Easter Seals. Mem. Am. Inst. Banking (v.p., edn. chmn. Vt. chpt. 1973-75, Woman of Yr. 1975), Vt. Bankers Assn. (ednl. chmn. mortgage com. 1987), Bank Adminstrn. Inst. (pres. Vt. chpt. 1985-86, state bd. dirs. 1979-80), Ottauquechee Bus. and Prof. Women (pres. 1985-86, Woman of Achievement 1988), Nat. Assn. Banking Women, NAFE, Woodstock Area C. of C. (bd. dirs. 1986-89), Woodstock Hist. Soc., Billings Farm and Mus., Woodstock Vis. Nurse Assn. Republican. Episcopalian. Address: PO Box 761 Woodstock VT 05091 Office: Woodstock Nat Bank 21 Elm St Woodstock VT 05091

SEDGWICK, RAE, psychologist, lawyer; b. Kansas City, Kans., Apr. 7, 1944; d. Charles and Helen (Timmons) Sedgwick. RN, Bethany Sch. Nursing, 1965; BS, U. Iowa, 1967; MA, U. Kans., 1970, PhD, 1972, JD, 1986. Cert. psychologist, Kans.; bar: Kans. 1986. Med./surg., orthopedic and obstet. nurse, Iowa City, Iowa, 1965-67; with Community Mental Health Nursing, Kansas City, Kans., 1967-68; specialist Lab. Edn., Washington, 1971-72; adj. clin. staff community psychiatry, 1975-76; coordinator Health C.A.R.E. Clinic, Pa. State U., 1974-76; head grad. program in community mental health nursing and family therapy, Pa. State U., 1974-76, asst. prof., 1972-76; pvt. practice psychology, Bonner Springs, Kans., 1976—; cons. in field.; staff Bethany Med. Ctr., Kansas City, Kans., Cushing's Meml. Hosp., Leavenworth, Kans., St. John's Hosp., Leavenworth; del. Internat. Council Nurses, Frankfurt, Germany, People for People, People's Republic of China, 1982, Internat. Congress Psychology, Sydney, Australia, 1988. Active Am. Heart Assn.; city councilwoman Bonner Springs, 1981-89, pres. pro tem, 1983-87, mayoral candidate, 1989; mem. Kans. Internat. Women's Yr. Commn. Recipient Outstanding Young Woman award, U. Kans., Bus. and Profl. Women's Club scholar; elected to Kans. U. Women's Hall of Fame, 1987. Fellow Am. Orthopsychiat. Assn.; mem. AAAS, ABA, Kansas Bar Assn., Am. Assn. Psychiatric Services for Children, Am. Group Psychotherapy Assn. (dir.), Am. Nurses Assn., Am. Psychol. Assn., Anthrop. Assn. for Study of Play, Council of Advanced Practitioners in Psychiat. Mental Health Nursing, Kans. Psychol. Assn., Council Nurse Researchers, Sigma Theta Tau. Republican. Methodist. Club: Pilot. Author: Family Mental Health, 1980; The White Frame House, 1980; contbr. articles to profl. jours.

SEDGWICK-HIRSCH, CAROL ELIZABETH, financial executive; b. Cin., Apr. 16, 1922; d. Howard Malcolm Sedgwick and Lucile Alleen (Willard) Sedgwick-Schenk; m. Donald Sebastian Freeman, Nov. 25, 1944 (div. July 1968); children: Elizabeth P. Freeman Closson, Lucy S. Freeman Kyle; m. William Christian Hirsch, June 16, 1983. BS, U. Cin., 1944, postgrad., 1972; postgrad., Art Acad. of Cin., 1953-56; MEd, Xavier U., 1966. Dir., head tchr. Sacred Heart Acad. PreSch., Cin., 1952-53; caseworker dependent children Hamilton County Welfare Dept., Cin., 1959-62; instr. ednl. psychology and child devel. Wright State U., Fairborn, Ohio, 1970-71, 71-72; pres., chief exec. officer Joseph England Hutton Enterprises, Cin., 1979—. Vol., ct. apptd. spl. advocate Victim/Witness Reconcilliation Program, Petoskey, Mich., Office Prosecuting Atty. Emmet County, Petoskey. Mem. Cin. Womans Club (philanthropic com. 1985-87), Cin. Club of Cin. Home: PO Box 118557 Cincinnati OH 45211 Home: PO Box 72 Conway MI 49722-0072 Office: Joseph England Hutton Enterprises 605 E Epworth Ave Cincinnati OH 45223 also: PO Box 118557 Cincinnati OH 46211-8557

SEDLACEK, EVELYN ANN, library developer; b. Mpls., Sept. 18, 1919; d. Guy Galen and Eleanor Rose (Stein) Harper; m. James Arthur Sedlacek, June 6, 1945; children: Judith, Joan, Karen. BS, U. Nebr., Omaha, 1973, MS, 1985. Rsch. libr. Joslyn Art Mus., Omaha, 1974-75; law libr. Smith, Peterson Law Firm, Council Bluffs, Iowa, 1977-84; libr. developer Papio Natural Resources Devel., Omaha, 1977-81; pres. BHS and Assocs., Omaha, 1982—. Bd. dirs. Camp Fire Girls, Omaha, 1955-76; mem. Omaha Opera; mem. coms. Omaha Symphony Guild, 1946-69; sewing com. Omaha Home for Girls, 1958-66. Mem. AAUW, Nebr. Libr. Assn., Mountain Plains Libr. Assn., Spl. Instl. Libr. Assn., Phi Alpha Theta, Kappa Delta Pi, Phi Delta Gamma. Home: 8628 Broadmoor Dr Omaha NE 68114

SEDLAK, VALERIE FRANCES, educator, university administrator; b. Balt., Mar. 11, 1934; d. Julian Joseph and Eleanor Eva (Pilot) Sedlak; 1 child, Barry. AB in English, Coll. Notre Dame, Balt., 1955; MA, U. Hawaii, 1962; postgrad., U. Pa., 1982. Tchr. Sacred Heart Sch., Pensacola, Fla., 1955-56; grad. teaching fellow East-West Cultural Ctr. U. Hawaii, 1959-60; adminstrv. asst. Korean Consul Gen., 1959-60; tchr. Boyertown (Pa.) Sr. High Sch., 1961-63; asst. prof. English U. Balt., 1963-69; asst. prof. Morgan State U., Balt., 1970—, sec. to faculty, 1981-83, faculty research scholar, 1982-83, communications officer, 1989—. Author poetry and lit. criticism. Coord. Young Reps., Berks County, Pa., 1962-63; chmn. Md. Young Reps., 1964; election judge Baltimore County, Md., 1964-66; regional capt. Am. Cancer Soc., 1978-79; mem. adv. bd. Md. Our Md. Anniversary, 1984, The Living Constitution: Bicentennial of the Fed. Constitution, 1987. Fellow Morgan-Penn Faculty, 1977-79, Nat. Endowment Humanities, 1984; named Outstanding Teaching Prof., U. Balt. Coll. Liberal Arts, 1965, Outstanding Teaching Prof. English, Morgan State U., 1987. Mem. MLA, AAUW South Atlantic MLA, Coll. Lang. Assn., Coll. English Assn. (v.p. Mid.-Atlantic Group 1987-90, pres. 1990—), Women's Caucus for Modern Langs., Md. Council Tchrs. English, Md. Poetry and Literary Soc., Mid. Atlantic Writers' Assn. (founding 1981), Delta Epsilon Sigma, U. Auburn Club. Roman Catholic. Home: 102 Gorsuch Rd Lutherville-Timonium MD 21093 Office: Morgan State U Office Instl Advancement Baltimore MD 21239

SEDLOCK, JOY, psychiatric social worker; b. Memphis, Jan. 23, 1958; d. George Rudolph Sedlock and Mary Robson; m. Thomas Robert Jones, Aug. 8, 1983. AA, Ventura (Calif.) Jr. Coll., 1978; BS in Psychology, Calif. Luth. U., 1980; MS in Counseling and Psychology, U. LaVerne, 1983; MSW, Calif. State U., Sacramento, 1986. Research asst. Camarillo (Calif.) State Hosp., 1981, tchr.'s aide, 1982; sub. tchr. asst. Vertura County Sch. Dist., 1981; teaching asst. Ventura Jr. Coll., 1980-82, tchr. adult edn., 1980-84; psychiatric social worker Yolo County Day Treatment Ctr., Broderick, Calif., 1986, Napa (Calif.) State Hosp., 1986—. Mem. People for the Ethical Treatment of Animals; active vol. Napa County Humane Soc. Mem. NOW. Home: PO Box 1095 Yountville CA 94599 Office: Napa State Hosp Napa/Vallejo Hgwy Napa CA 49558

SEDUSKI, MARYANN, advertising executive; b. Glen Cove, N.Y., Mar. 2, 1950; d. Henry Walter and Anna Lucia (Ladyzinski) S.; m. David Alan Stuteville, May 11, 1980; 1 child, Royce David. AB in Maths., Mt. Holyoke Coll., South Hadley, Mass., 1972; MBA in Fin., NYU, 1982. Mktg. rep. IBM Corp., N.Y.C., 1972-79; with AT&T, 1979—; mgr. pub. rels. dept. AT&T, N.Y.C., 1986-87, media mgr. corp. advt. dept., 1987—. Mem. Advt. Women of N.Y., 722 Owner's Corp. Bd. Dirs. (treas. 1986-88, pres. 1988-89), Mt. Holyoke Club N.Y. (bd. dirs.). Office: AT&T 550 Madison Ave New York NY 10022

SEE, KAREN MASON, federal judge; b. Springfield, Mo., Jan. 31, 1952; d. Robert Wayne and Mildred Lucille (Stockstill) Mason; m. Andrew B. See, Nov. 24, 1979. BS in Edn. cum laude, SW Mo. State U., 1973; JD, U. Mo., 1978. Bar: Mo. 1978. Tchr. Springfield (Mo.) Dist., 1973-75; law clk. Judge William E. Turnage, Mo. Ct. of Appeals, Kansas City, 1978-79; assoc. atty. Slagle & Bernard, Kansas City, 1979-84, ptnr., 1984-86; judge U.S. Bankruptcy Ct., Kansas City, 1986-89; adj. instr. U. Mo. Law Sch., Kansas City; mem. adv. bd. Greater Mo. Focus on Leadership. Active Mo. Bicentennial Commn., Jefferson City, 1987—, Kansas City Bicentennial Commn., 1987—; bd. dirs. Mo Found Women's Resources, Inc. Named an Outstanding Young Alumnus S.W. Mo. State U., 1988. Mem. ABA, Mo. Bar Assn. (vice chmn. comml. law com., bd. editors Mo Bar Jour.), Kansas City Met. Bar Assn., Kansas City Lawyers Assn., Nat. Conf. of Bankruptcy Judges, Am. Judicature Soc. Office: US Bankruptcy Ct 811 Grand Ave Rm 905 Kansas City MO 64106

SEE, SARAH GAVIN, communications consultant; b. Taunton, Mass., July 27, 1922; d. Philip Ambrose and Helen (Whitaker) G.; m. Charles Milton See, May 23, 1943 (dec.); children—Sarah H., Ellen H., Pamela H., Randolph B. B.A., Smith Coll., 1943; M.Ed., U. Va., 1966. Tng. dir. Monmouth council Girl Scouts U.S.A., N.J., 1963-65; dir. writing lab. Norfolk State U., Va., 1965-67; dir. inst. programming Human Research and Resources Orgn., Alexandria, Va., 1967-69; devel. mgr. Westinghouse Learning Press, Palo Alto, Calif., 1969-77; asst. provost Evergreen Valley Coll., San Jose, Calif., 1977-87; communications cons., 1987—. Del. CICEC, People's Republic of China, 1990. Contbr. articles to profl. jours. Home: 1064 Laureles Dr Los Altos CA 94022

SEEBERT, KATHLEEN ANNE, international marketing consultant; b. Chgo.; d. Harold Earl and Marie Anne (Lowery) S.; BS U. Dayton, 1971, M.A., U. Notre Dame, 1976; M.M., Northwestern U., 1983. Publs. editor ContiCommodity Services, Inc., Chgo., 1977-79, supr. mktg., 1979-82; dir. mktg. MidAm. Commodity Exchange, 1982-85; internat. trade cons. to Govt. of Ont., Can., 1985-90; dir. mktg. and bus. devel. Internat. Orientation Resources. 1990—; guest lectr. U. Notre Dame. Registered commodity rep. Mem. Futures Industry Assn. Am. (treas.). Republican. Roman Catholic. Clubs: Notre Dame of Chgo., Kellogg Mgmt. of Chgo. Office: 707 Skokie Blvd Ste 350 Northbrook IL 60062

SEEGER, MELINDA WAYNE, realtor; b. Albert Lea, Minn., Dec. 31, 1940; d. Oscar Earnest and Evelyn Josephine (Pihl) Wayne; BS, U. Minn., 1963; m. Robert Charles Seeger, Mar. 16, 1964; 1 child, Jeffrey Wayne. Chief occupational therapy Rehab. Inst. Oreg., Portland, 1964-66; supr. phys. disabilities and gen. medicine and surgery occupational therapy Mpls. VA Hosp., 1966-68; supr. phys. disabilities occupational therapy Nat. Naval Med. Ctr., Bethesda, Md., 1968-71; assoc. chief rehab. svcs., dir. occupational therapy UCLA Med. Center, 1974-85, cons., prin. investigator rheumatology div. dept. medicine, 1985-86; realtor Merrill Lynch Realty, Los Angeles, 1987—. Mem. utilization rev. com. Vis. Nurse Assn. Los Angeles, 1975-85, mem. profl. adv. com., 1979-80; mem. exec. com. Allied Health Professions sect. Arthritis Found., 1980-85, chmn. edn. com., 1982-85, mem. profl. edn. com.; bd. dirs. Calif. Occupational Therapy Found., 1984-85, Westwood-Holmby Hills Homeowners Assn., Los Angeles. Recipient Spl. Achievement award Nat. Naval Med. Ctr., 1971, Outstanding Performance award, 1971; Spl. Performance award UCLA, 1980, 84; Addie Thomas Service award for outstanding service to rheumatology community Arthritis Found., 1986, Cert. of Appreciation award, 1989; mem. Million Dollar Club. Mem. Am. Occupational Therapy Assn., Occupational Therapy Assn. Calif., Allied Health Professions Assn. (chmn. edn. com. 1982—), Los Angeles Bd. Realtors, San Fernando Valley Bd. Realtors, West Los Angeles C. of C., Blue Diamond Club. Author, editor articles in field. Office: 1401 Westwood Blvd Los Angeles CA 90024

SEEGRETC, CAROLE RUTH, clinical psychologist; b. Cleve., Apr. 20, 1947; d. Richard John Edward and Ruth Dorothy (Petch) S.; m. Peter W. Salomonson, Feb. 6, 1967 (div. Nov. 1973); children: Holly Ann, Matthew Wertheim. BA, Conn. Coll., 1975; MS, U. Ky., 1980, PhD, 1984. Lic. psychologist, Wash. Staff psychologist Womack Army Community Hosp., Ft. Bragg, N.C., 1982-84; psychologist Human Resource Cons., Chapel Hill and Lafayette, N.C., 1984-85; grad. sch. instr. Pembroke (N.C.) State U., 1984-85; staff psychologist Western State Hosp., Ft. Stellacoom, Wash., 1985-89; psychologist Traywick, Green and Assocs., Tacoma, Wash., 1988—. Mem. Puget Sound Coalition Mental Health Profls., Wash., 1990, Deacon Mercer Island United Ch. Christ, Seattle, 1986-88. Capt. U.S. Army, 1981-84. Grantee NIMH, 1976-77. Mem. APA (div. psychology of women), Wash. State Sex Offence Specialists Assn. (bd. dirs. 1990—), Wash. State Psychol. Assn., Seattle Forensic Inst. Home: 20321 92d Ave W Edmonds WA 98020 Office: Traywick Green & Assocs 6314 19th St W Tacoma WA 98466

SEEKINGS, SARA MARGARET, industrial chemist; b. Mt. Vernon, N.Y., Jan. 22, 1953; d. John Kenneth and Irene Clare (Conner) S. BS, Framingham State Coll., 1974; MBA, Simmons Coll., 1987. Rsch. asst. Worcester Found. of Exptl. Biology, Shrewsbury, Mass., 1974-76; rsch. technician GTE Labs., Waltham, Mass., 1976-77; rsch. chemist Barnstead Co., W. Roxbury, Mass., 1977-78; assoc. scientist Polaroid Corp., Waltham, Mass., 1978-85, scientist, 1985-89, vice chmn. affirmative action com. chem. ops. div., 1978-80, 85—, tech. tanm coord., 1989—. Patentee in field. Mem. Am. Chem. Soc., AAAS, NAFE, Support Women in Mgmt. Roman Catholic. Avocations: reading, music, guitar, tennis. Home: 39 Walcott Valley Dr Hopkinton MA 01748 Office: Polaroid Corp 1265 Main St W6 Waltham MA 02154

SEEKINS, ANNA MARIE, manufacturing executive; b. Lexington, Nebr., Oct. 22, 1948; d. Frederick Reo and Doris Louise (Hollibaugh) Green; m. James Lee Seekins, Jan. 3, 1969; children: Heidi Anne, Amy Marie. Grad. Westminster High Sch., Colo., 1966. With Forsythe & Dowis Carnival, 1950-64, Green's Amusements, 1964-68; collator, Jeppesen Time-Mirror, Denver, 1967-73; typesetter AAA Marking, Colorado Springs, Colo., 1975-78; seamstress Camp 7, Longmont, Colo., 1978-80; co-owner AMS Products, Inc., Longmont, 1980—; order clk. Staydynamics, Longmont, 1982-84. Vol., Army Community Service Ctr., Colorado Springs. Republican. Baptist. Home: 2242 Sherman St Longmont CO 80501 Office: AMS Products 824 S Lincoln PO Box 1842 Longmont CO 80502

SEELEY, JEANE MCWORKMAN, medical librarian; b. Indpls., June 7, 1916; d. Delamar and Harriet (Orcutt) McWorkman; m. John Cooley Seeley, May 6, 1967 (dec. 1986); children: Martha Federico, Carol Jeane Lotze Atkins. BS, U. Mich., 1937. Lit. searcher E.I. du Pont de Nemours & Co., Wilmington, Del., 1938-40; translator, lit. searcher Tech. Lib. Research Service, Ann Arbor, Mich., 1946-65; research librarian Warner - Lambert, Ann Arbor, Mich., 1958-74; hosp. chaplain U. Mich. Med. Ctr., Ann Arbor. Mem. Phi Beta Kappa, Phi Kappa Phi, Kappa Kappa Gamma. Presbyterian. Home: 815 Greenhills Ann Arbor MI 48105

SEELEY, KIMBERLEY ANN, protection services official; b. Urbana, Ill., Oct. 21, 1960; d. William Edward and Patricia Ann (Philbeck) Tarte; m. Ronald Eugene Seeley, Jan. 21, 1985; 1 child, Edward Raymond. AS, Parkland Coll., 1981; BS, U. Ill., 1982. Sec., bookkeeper Tarte's TV and Marine, Rantoul, Ill., 1972-78; police dispatcher City of Champaign, Ill., 1978-82, police officer, 1982—, mem. tactical unit, 1985-86; realtor, Coldwell Banker Hallmark Realtor, Inc., 1987-88. Recipient Merit award Champaign Police Dept., 1984, 86. Mem. Police Protective and Benevolent Assn., N AFE, Fraternal Order of Police, Ill. Police Assn., Nat. Assn. Realtors, Ill. Assn. Realtors, Champaign County Bd. Realtors. Republican. Lutheran. Avocations: downhill snow skiing, target shooting. Office: Champaign Police Dept 82 E University Champaign IL 61820

SEELEY, MARYANN DEL VISCO, communications and marketing executive; b. Newark, Oct. 14, 1948; d. James and Vincenzina (Cimirro) Del Visco; m. Timothy Allen Seeley, May 30, 1981; children—Vanessa Christina, Timothy Allen Jr. BA in English, Rutgers U., 1970; MA in Communications Arts, William Paterson Coll., 1974; MS in Ednl. Adminstrn. SUNY, 1989. Mgr. communications, asst. cashier Midlantic Nat. Bank div. Midlantic Banks, Inc., Newark, 1970-74; supr. info. N.J. Bell Telephone Co., Newark, 1974-75; exec. printing sales Newark Printing Co., 1975-76; sales rep. Xerox Corp., 1976-78, mgr. shareholder relations, 1978-81; co-owner T.A. Seeley Office Systems Co., Glens Falls, N.Y., 1981-88; secondary sch. tchr. French and Spanish Salem (N.Y.) Ctr. Sch., 1988-89, Hudson Falls Sch. Dist., 1989—. Assoc. editor N.J. Bell and Communication Mags., 1974-75; innovator in design of magapaper publs. Active communications group N.J. Bicentennial Celebrations Com. Recipient awards Publ. Design Writing, Soc. Publ. Designers, 1974, Financial World, 1974, N.Y. Bus. Communicators, 1974. Mem. Communicators Assn. N.J. (pres. 1973-75, dir. 1976-78, Publ. Design Writing award 1974), Internat. Assn. Bus. Communicators (Pub. Design Writing award 1974, speaker creative supervision ann. conf.), Art Dirs. Club N.J., Lake George Bus. and Profl. Women's Club (co-chair pub. relations 1985-87), N.Y. State Assn. Fgn. Lang. Tchrs. Office: RR Box 3023 Lake George NY 12845

SEELEY, REBECCA ZAHM, publishing exective; b. Johnstown, Pa., Apr. 2, 1935; d. Daniel Jones and Anne (Hindman) Z.; m. Earl Edwin Seely, June 22, 1957; children: Laura Rothe, Daniel Zahm, Elizabeth Anne. BA, Pa. State U., 1957; BA in Bus., George Washington U., 1978. Corp. advt. mgr. Washington Post, Washington, 1970-81; mktg. dir. Washington Bus. Jour., McLean, Va., 1982-83; pub. Washington Woman, 1983-84; cons. Mid-Atlantic Country, Alexandria, Va., 1984-87; mgr. No. Va. Va. Bus., Richmond, 1987-88; pub. Washington Flyer Mag., Alexandria, 1989—. Author: Tidewater Dynasty, 1981. Republican. Presbyterian. Home: 6609 Tina Ln McLean VA 22101 Office: Washington Flyer Mag 11 Canal Centre Pla Alexandria VA 22314

SEELHAMMER, CYNTHIA MAE, public adminstrator; b. Fargo, N.D., Oct. 29, 1957; d. John Robert and Betty Jane (Brausen) S.; m. Barry Minett Robinson, May 31, 1980 (div. 1983); m. Douglas Lynn Myrland, Oct. 19, 1984. Student Kerevan Yhteskoulu, Kerava, Finland, 1975-76; BA in English, St. Cloud State U., 1976-80; MPub. Adminstrn. Golden Gate U., 1987; postgrad. Hamline U., 1989—. Editor Sherburne County Hist. Soc., Becker, Minn., 1978-80; assoc. editor SCS Chronicle, St. Cloud, Minn., 1979-80; reporter Chandler Arizonan, Ariz, 1980-81; coord. pub. rels. Bashas' Markets, Inc., Chandler, 1981-84; owner, mgr. Seelhammer Pub. Rels., 1984—; pub. info. specialist City Mesa, Ariz., 1984-88; asst. to Library dir. for fiscal and personnel mgmt., City of Mesa, 1988-89; asst. to mayor City of St. Paul, 1989—. Author feature stories for papers, mags., 1980—. Editor: The Growth of Sherburne County, 1980, The St. Paul Experiment: Initiatives of the Latimer Adminstrn., 1989. Dept. registrar Pinal County Dems., Florence, Ariz., 1983-85; chmn. Chandler Neighborhood Coun., 1981-82; exec. bd. dirs. Chandler Boys and Girls Club of the East Valley, 1985; judge for Ariz. Tchr. Yr. awards, 1984, 85. Recipient Best Editorial award Minn. Newspaper Assn., 1980; MECCA fellow U. Denver, 1980. Mem. LVW, Internat. Assn. Bus. Communicators, Soc. Profl. Journalists (Best Editorial award Region 6 1980), Ariz. Press Women (v.p. pub. rels. 1981-82, Best Feature award 1980), Internat. City Mgrs. Assn. (scholarship to Montreal conf.1987), Ariz. Fed. Credit Union (mem. supr. com.), Minn. Assn. Urban Mgmt. Assts. (chair bylaws com. 1990), Internat. Assn. City Mgmt., Toastmasters (CTM 1989), Soroptimists (officer Mesa chpt. 1985, 86, 87, pres. 1988, Minn. Internat. Ctr.). Avocations: gourmet cooking, gardening, travel, horseback riding. Home: 2660 Highwood Ave Saint Paul MN 55119 Office: St Paul Mayor's Office 347 City Hall Saint Paul MN 55102

SEELY, ANNE LOFGREN, investment executive, consultant; b. Corning, N.Y., Aug. 6, 1947; d. Harry Gustav and Marie Arlene (Ford) Lofgren; m. H. Marvin Hosier Jr., Dec. 10, 1966 (div. July 1973); m. John Conor Seely, Feb. 24, 1983. BS, Elmira Coll., 1975. Asst. instr. media specialist Corning Community Coll., 1974-76; retail buyer B. Forman Co., Rochester, N.Y., 1976-79; v.p. ops. Real Equity Diversification, Inc., Denver, 1979-80; v.p., sec. Resort Accommodations, Inc., 1980-84; exec. v.p. Real Equity Investment, Inc., 1984-85, v.p., sec., 1985—; cons. Real Equity Diversification, Inc., Denver, 1980—; bd. dirs. Resort Accommodations, Inc., Real Equity Investment Fund Inc. Republican. Office: The Seely Group 4600 S Ulster St Suite 700 Denver CO 80237

SEELY, KAREN ANN, medical laboratory administrator; b. Dimmitt, Tex., Dec. 24, 1955; d. Gene C. and Cleo (Flenniken) S. AAS, Amarillo (Tex.) Coll., 1976; BS, Lubbock (Tex.) Christian Coll., 1985. Lic. med. technologist, X-ray technician, Tex. Staff technician Union County Gen. Hosp., Clayton, N.Mex., 1976-77; staff technologist Hosp. Corp. Am., Levelland, Tex., 1977-78, 79-82, acting dir. lab., 1978-79, 81, dir. lab., 1982; dir. lab. Summit Health Ltd., Levelland, 1982-88; dir. lab. and infection control Meth. Hosp., Levelland, 1988—; instr. Interaction Mgmt., Levelland, 1985—. Mem. Am. Soc. Med. Technologists, Tex. Soc. Med. Technologists, Med. Lab. Technician Club (pres. 1975-76). Mem. Church of Christ. Office: Meth Hosp Levelland 1900 S College Ave Levelland TX 79336

SEELY, MARTHA ANN, designer manager; b. Syracuse, N.Y., July 18, 1952; d. Samuel and Helen (Anderson) S.; m. Jon Robert Quillard. BA, Connecticut Coll., 1974; MFA, Carnegie Mellon, 1977. Wardrode mistress Pitts. Pub. Theatre, 1977-78; asst. costume designer Trinity Square Theatre, Providence, 1978-80; costume designer, instr. Brown Univ., Providence, 1978-80; asst. art dir. Revolver Inc., Boston; traffic mgr., pub. rels. specialist Provandie and Chirurg, Boston, 1982-83; art dir., pub. rels. specialist Cambridge (Mass.) Communications, 1983-86; creative dir. N.E.C.S.A., Newton, Mass., 1985—; pres. Artistic License, Somerville, Mass., 1986—; prodn. designer The Imported Bridgeroom, Cambridge, 1988, Start-Up, Cable TV Program, Boston, 1988-89, Workin' the System, Boston, 1990; costume designer drama dept. Tuft U., Boston, 1985-88, Missionery Man, N.Y., 1990. Mem. Bus. Entertainment Network (steering com. 1988-89), Women in Film and Video (Golden Slate award 1989), NEPA. Democrat. Home: 22 Sycamore St Somerville MA 02143

SEEWALD, CAROL SANDRA, administrative director; b. Bklyn., Feb. 9, 1947; d. Jack and Irene (Lippman) Gross; m. Jeffrey Seewald, Oct. 9, 1965; 1 child, Jay. Student, Coll. of S.I., 1972-74; BS, Barry U., 1986; MBA, Nova U., 1988. Exec. sec. Michael G. Cohen, Inc., N.Y.C., 1964-65, Level Export Corp., N.Y.C., 1965-67; adminstrv. asst. YWCA, S.I., N.Y., 1969-72; adminstrv. sec. Superior Confections, Inc., S.I., 1973, Pompano Fence Co., Pompano Beach, Fla., 1974; adminstrv. asst. YMCA, Boca Raton, Fla., 1974-77, ops. dir., 1977-80, exec. dir., pres., 1980-89, mem. cluster steering com., 1984-85, mktg. cons., 1986-89. Bd. dirs. Boca Del Mar Improvement Assn., Boca Raton, 1985-86, YMCA of Palm Beaches, 1990. Mem. NOW, YMCA Assn. Profl. Dirs. (bd. dirs. 1985-87), Nat. Soc. Fund Raising Execs. (charter), Coun. Human Svc. Execs. (treas. 1984-85), West Boca C. of C., WOmen's Forum, Soroptimists (treas. Boca Raton 1983-84, v.p. 1984-85, pres. 1985-86), Kiwanis (bd. dirs. 1988-89, v.p. 1990—), Alpha Chi. Democrat. Jewish. Home: 22860 Ponderosa Dr Boca Raton FL 33428

SEFRNA, ANN BARNETT, small business owner, librarian; b. Corpus Christi, Tex., Sept. 8, 1949; d. Browning Owen and Mary Allene (Mizzell) Barnett; m. Ronald Brian Sefrna, May 22, 1971; children: Katharine Faye, Benjamin Browning. BA, U. Tex., 1971, MLS, 1974. Libr. Austin (Tex.) Pub. Libr., 1973-74, Harris County Pub. Libr., Houston, 1974-75, Houston Pub. Libr., 1975-77; owner, mgr. Under the Hill Books, Tyler, Tex., 1978-86, Times Sq Books, Tyler, 1985-86, Mus. Bookshop, Tyler, 1986—; Bd. dirs. Tyler Pub. Libr. (chairperson) 1984--. Vol. Meals on Wheels, 1980—; mem. br. advocacy coun. Planned Parenthood, 1985-86; bd. dirs. Camp Fire Inc., 1989—; co-founder East Texans for Choice, 1989, also pres. 1990. Mem. AAUW, LWV. Democrat. Home and Office: 226 E 1st St Tyler TX 75701

SEGAL, ARLENE ESTA, radiologist; b. N.Y.C., Nov. 12, 1937; d. Moe and Fanny (Schlussel) S.; m. Richard Thomas Logan, Aug. 14, 1969. BA, Duke U., 1958; MD, Albert Einstein Coll. Medicine, 1962. Diplomate Am. Bd. Radiology, Am. Bd. Nuclear Medicine. Intern Bronx Mcpl. Hosp. Ctr., N.Y.C., 1962-63, resident in radiology, 1963-66; instr. radiology Albert Einstein Coll. Medicine, N.Y.C., 1966-68, asst. prof., 1968-71; practice medicine specializing in gen. diagnostic radiology Rye, Nanuet and Hornell, N.Y., 1971-82; assoc. prof. U. Mo. Sch. Medicine, Kansas City, 1982—; staff radiologist Children's Mercy Hosp., Kansas City, 1982-83, radiologist-in-chief, 1983-90. Mem. Soc. for Pediatric Radiology, Radiol. Soc. N.Am., Am. Coll. Radiology, Am. Assn. Women Radiologists. Office: Children's Mercy Hosp 24th & Gillham Kansas City MO 64108

SEGAL, GERALDINE ROSENBAUM, sociologist; b. Phila., Aug. 26, 1908; d. Harry and Mena (Hamburg) Rosenbaum; m. Bernard Gerard Segal, Oct. 22, 1933; children: Loretta Joan, Richard Murry. BS in Edn., U. Pa., 1930, MA in Human Rels., 1963, PhD in Sociology, 1978; MS in Libr. Sci., Drexel U., 1968. Social worker County Relief Bd., Phila., 1931-35; sociologist, Phila., 1935—; cons. and lectr. in field. Author: In Any Fight Some Fall, 1975; Blacks in the Law, 1983. Bd. dirs. NCCJ, 1937-47, 82—, sec., 1983—; bd. overseers U. Pa. Sch. Social Work, 1983—; bd. dirs., Juvenile Law Ctr., 1984—; chair Phila. Tutorial Project, 1966-68. Co-recipient Nat. Neighbors Disting. Leadership in Civil Rights award, 1988; recipient Nonviolence Drum Major award PHila. Martin Luther King, Jr. Assn., 1990. Democrat. Jewish. Home: 2401 Pennsylvania Ave Apt 19-C-44 Philadelphia PA 19130

SEGAL, KATHLEEN RITA, advertising executive; b. Chgo., May 26, 1952; d. Harry L. and Margaret (Casey) S.; m. Craig S. Baron, Oct. 16, 1982; 1 child. BA in English, No. Ill. U., 1974. Broadcast buyer Lee King & Ptnrs., Inc., Chgo., 1974-77; media/research supr. Campbell Mithun, Inc., Chgo., 1977-79; dir. media planning, v.p. BBDO Chgo., 1979—. Mem. NOW, Women's Advt. Club Chgo., Broadcast Advt. Club, Media Rsch. Club. Office: BBDO Chgo 410 N Michigan Ave Chicago IL 60611

SEGAL, LINDA GALE, insurance executive; b. Panama City, Fla., Dec. 14, 1947; d. Homer Ford Jr. and Mary Virginia (Phillmon) F. m. Howard Arthur Segal, Dec. 29, 1970; 1 child, David Samuel. Student, Orlando (Fla.) Jr. Coll., 1966-69, Rollins Coll., 1972. Sales asst. Sta. WESH-TV, Orlando, Fla., 1973-76; mktg. coordinator Sta. WFBC-TV, Grenneville, S.C., 1976-77; traffic mgr. STa. WRDW-TV, Augusta, Ga., 1978-80; field underwriter Liberty Life Ins. Co., Greenville, 1980-81; agt. benefits dept. J. Rolfe Davis Ins. Agy., Orlando, 1981-84; sr. market sales rep. Humana, Inc., Orlando, 1984-86; dir. mktg. Nat. Med. Mgmt., Orlando, 1986-87; sr. account exec. Physicians Health Plan Fla., Inc., Tampa, 1987-88, N.E. Fin. Services, Orlando, 1988-89; mktg. mgr. Ins. Mgmt. Svcs., Inc., Greenville, S.C., 1989—; pvt. practice ins. cons., Tampa and Orlando, Fla., 1986-89. Mem. Am. Bus. Women's Assn., Nat. Assn. Profl. Saleswomen, Nat. Assn. Health Underwriters, Assn. Life Underwriters, Women Life Underwriters Confedn., Nat. Assn. Securities Dealers (registered rep.). Republican. Methodist. Club: Commerce.

SEGAL, VALERIE JUDITH, handwriting examiner; b. N.Y.C., Aug. 26, 1950; d. Martin Quentin and Jean Leandra (DeSale) Wittner; m. Joshua Leon Segal, July 4, 1971; children: Julie Snow, Jay Nathan. BS, Russell Sage Coll., Troy, 1972. Cert. master graphoanalyst. Tchr. New Hampshire Tech. Inst., Concord, 1987—, Nashua (N.H.) Adult Learning Ctr., 1986—, Rivier Coll., Nashua, 1989—; lectr. New Hampshire and Mass., Provide personnel screening for bus., provide document examination svc. legal and other offices, Provide Jury screening svc for legal offices, Provide a variety of Individual handwriting analyses for pvt. clients. Author: Intermediate Workships in Handwriting Analysis, 1988, Introduction to Handwriting Analysis, 1989, Dateline New Hampshire, The 1590 Broadcaster. Mem. Am. Assn. Handwriting Analysts, Am. Handwriting Analysis Found., Internat. Graphoanalysis Soc. Nat., Internat. Graphoanalysis Soc. New Hampshire Chpt., World Assn. Document Examiners. Democrat. Jewish. Home and Office: 12 Briarwood Dr Nashua NH 03063

SEGALL, LAURA JEANNE, public relations executive; b. Boston, Mar. 26, 1958; d. Robert Emmett and Shirley Jean Fredricks; m. Jeffre Norman Segall, July 27, 1953. BA cum laude, Occidental Coll., L.A., 1980; MA, U. Ill., Champaign, 1981; postgrad., U. Minn., 1981-82. Asst. account exec. Hill & Knowlton Inc., L.A., 1982-84; mgr. media rels. L.A. C. of C., 1984-86; v.p. Rogers & Assocs., L.A., 1986—. Mem. Soc. Automotive Analysts, Internat. Motor Press Assn., So. Calif. Assn. Philanthropy, Radio and TV News Assn., Publicity Club L.A. (dir. 1987-88), Occidental Coll. Alumni (bd. govs. 1986-88), L.A. Jr. C. of C. (dir., charity found. pres. 1988—), L.A. Athletic Club, Porter Valley Country Club. Roman Catholic. Office: Rogers & Assocs 2029 Century Prk E Ste 1010 Los Angeles CA 90067

SEGAR, MARY LOU, office management educator; b. Alden, Mich., Mar. 26, 1936; d. Wilbur and Mary Elizabeth (Hutchinson) Claypool; m. James Henry Segar, Dec. 28, 1958; children: Jamie Segar Daum, Laurie. BS, Atlantic Union Coll., South Lancaster, Mass., 1984. Lectr. in secretarial sci. Middle East Coll., Beirut, 1968-70, sec. to pres., 1971-74; sec. Gen. Conf. of Seventh-day Adventists, Takoma Park, Md., 1975-77, So. New Eng. Conf. Seventh-day Adventists, South Lancaster, 1977-78; with Atlantic Union Coll., South Lancaster, 1979—, asst. to pres., 1988-89, asst. prof. office mgmt., 1989—. Recipient Sec. of the Yr. award Clinton (Mass.) Area C. of C., 1988. Mem. NAFE. Office: Atlantic Union Coll 338 Main St South Lancaster MA 01561

SEGER, MARTHA ROMAYNE, government official, economist; b. Adrian, Mich., 1932. BBA, U. Mich., 1954, MBA, 1955, PhD, 1971. Began career in econs. dept. GM; later with Fed. Res. Bank Chgo., 3 yrs.; chief economist Detroit Bank & Trust Co., 1967-74 ; v.p. in charge of econs. and investment Bank of Commonwealth, Detroit, 1971-74; assoc. prof. bus. econs. U. Mich., 1976-79; assoc. prof. econs. and fins. Oakland U., 1980; commr. fin instns. State of Mich., 1981-82; prof. fin. Cen. Mich. U., 1983-84; mem. bd. govs. Fed. Res. System, 1984—. Office: FRS Bd of Govs 20th & Constitution Ave NW Washington DC 20551

SEGGERMAN, MARIANNE GURNEY CATHARINE, programmer analyst; b. N.Y.C., June 24, 1954; d. Harry Gurney Atha and Anne Sarah (Crellin) Seggerman. BA in Math. and Theater, Denison U., 1976. Computer operator Dura Plastics, Westport, Conn., 1976; programmer trainee Systems Mgmt., South Norwalk, Conn., 1976-77; contract programmer Software Designs, Norwalk, Conn., 1977-85; programmer/analyst Fisher Camuto, Stamford, Conn., 1985—, Act-Up, N.Y.C., 1988—. Seamstress, designer 2 quilt panels The Names Project, 1988, 89. Active Act-Up, N.Y., 1988—. Mem. steering com. Conn. Coalition for Lesbian and Gay Civil Rights, Norwalk, 1989—. Republican. Roman Catholic. Home: 105 Saugatuck Ave #2B Westport CT 06880 Office: Fisher Camuto 9 W Broad St Stamford CT 06902

SEGIL, LARRAINE DIANE, materials company executive; b. Johannesburg, South Africa, July 15, 1948; came to U.S., 1974; d. Jack and Norma Estelle (Cohen) Wolfowitz; m. Clive Melwyn Segil, Mar. 9, 1969; 1 child, James Harris. BA, U. Witwatersrand, South Africa, 1967, BA with honours, 1969; JD, Southwestern U., Los Angeles, 1979; MBA, Pepperdine U., 1985. Bar: Calif. 1979, U.S. Supreme Ct. 1982. Cons. in internat. transactions, Los Angeles, 1976-79; atty. Long & Levit, Los Angeles, 1979-81; chmn., pres. Marina Credit Corp., Los Angeles, 1981-85; pres., chief exec. officer Electronic Space Products Internat., Los Angeles, 1985-87; mng. ptnr. The Lared Group, Los Angeles, 1987—. Bd. govs. Cedars Sinai Med. Ctr., Los Angeles, 1984—; bd. dirs. So. Calif. Tech. Execs. Network. Mem. ABA (chmn. internat. law com. young lawyers div. 1980-84), Internat. Assn. Young Lawyers (exec. council 1979—, council internat. law and practice 1983-84), Word Tech. Execs. Network (chmn.). Club: Regency (Los Angeles) (house com.). Avocations: piano, horseriding. Office: 1901 Avenue of the Stars Ste 280 Los Angeles CA 90067

SEGO, TRINA ANN, communications educator; b. Louisville, June 29, 1965; d. Donald Ray and Loretta J. (Sanders) S. BA, U. Louisville, 1987; postgrad., U. Ky., 1989-90; MA, Purdue U., 1990. Instr. dept. communications Purdue U., West Lafayette, Ind., 1987-89; instr. dept. journalism U. Ky., Lexington, 1989-90; instr. dept. advt. U. Tex., Austin, 1990—. Mem. So. States Communication Assn., Speech Communication Assn. Home: 2407 Dulworth Ave Louisville KY 40216 Office: Dept Advt Univ Texas Austin TX 78713

SEGOVIS, ELIZABETH WILSON, lawyer; b. Pasadena, Calif., Aug. 10, 1948; d. Frank Stedman and Jeannette Frances (MacKenzie) Wilson; m. James Courtney Segovis, Dec. 22, 1971; children—Colin Michael, Ian Patrick, Courtney Michelle. B.A., Cornell U., 1970; M.A., SUNY-Albany, 1973; J.D., So. Meth. U., 1978. Bar: Tex. 1978, U.S. Dist. Ct. (no. dist.1979, ea. dist. 1987) Tex. 1979; cert. Family Law, 1985. Social worker George Jr. Republic, Freeville, N.Y., 1970-72; felony probation officer Supreme Ct. N.Y., Bklyn., 1973-74; family ct. counselor Dallas County Juvenile Dept., Dallas, 1974-75; assoc. Johannes Robertson & Wilkinson, Dallas, 1976-79; asst. county atty. County Atty.'s Office, Sherman, Tex., 1979-84; assoc. Thompson, Green, Shaffer, Redwine, Denison, Tex., 1984-85; staff atty. North Tex. Cen. Legal Svcs., McKinney, Tex., 1985-89, mng. atty, 1989—; bd. dirs. Legal Services Found., Dallas, 1978-79, Crisis Ctr. of Grayson County, 1984-88. Adv. bd. Grayson County Guidance Clinic, Sherman, Tex., 1984; trustee Grace United Meth. Ch. 1982-83. Mem. Grayson County Bar Assn. (v.p. 1980-81, 84-85), State Bar Tex., Collin County Bar Assn., Dallas County Bar Assn. Home: 707 Concord Ln Allen TX 75002 Office: Legal Svcs of No Tex 114 W Louisiana St McKinney TX 75069

SEGRE, MARIANGELA BERTANI, microbiologist/immunologist; b. Milan, Oct. 4, 1927; came to U.S., 1952; d. Carlo and Armida (Seveso) Bertani; m. Diego R. Segre, June 22, 1952; children: Carlo, Alberto. Maturita Classica, Liceo Beccaria, Milan, Italy, 1945; DSc in Biology, U. Milan, 1949. Postdoctoral fellow Coll. Vet. Medicine U. Milan, 1949-51; bacteriologist Montecatini Corp., Milan, 1951-52, Nebr. State Dept. Health,

Lincoln, 1953-54; rsch. assoc. dept. pathobiology Coll. Vet. Medicine U. Ill., Urbana, 1963-73, asst. prof. dept. pathobiology, 1973-85, assoc. prof. dept. pathobiology, 1985—; vis. investigator, Nat. Animal Disease Rsch. Inst., Weybridge, Eng., 1951, Lab. of Immunology NIH, Bethesda, Md., 1989. Contbr. numerous articles to profl. jours. Office: Univ Ill 2001 S Lincoln Ave Urbana IL 61801

SEIB, ELIZABETH JUNE, advertising executive; b. St. Louis, Oct. 23, 1936; d. Vincent John and Mary Elizabeth (Harper) S. Cert. bus. adminstrn., Washington U., 1978. Various clk. positions to acctg. clk. D'Arcy Advt. Co., St. Louis, 1962-63, supr. broadcast dept., 1963-68, radio-TV buyer, 1966-70, buying supr., 1970-75; media planner D'Arcy MacManus & Masius, St. Louis, 1969-75, media supr., assoc. media dir., 1975-79, v.p., assoc. media dir., 1979—. Mem. St. Louis Advt. Club, Town and Country Racquet Club. Republican. Baptist. Office: D'Arcy Masius Benton & Bowles One Memorial Dr Saint Louis MO 63102

SEIBEL, MARY ANN, music educator, musician; b. Pitts., Apr. 18, 1950; d. Herman Joseph and Florence Justine (Dunsavage) S. BS in Music Edn., Bowling Green State U., 1972; M Music Edn., Duquesne U., 1976. Cert. tchr., Pa. Tchr. vocal music Pitts. Bd. Pub. Edn., 1972-73, Baldwin Whitehall Sch. Dist., Pitts., 1973—; cantor, Kane Hosp. Allegheny County, Pitts., 1973-79; music dir. for musical prodns., Canevin High Sch., Pitts., 1974-75; music dir., Brentwood Borough Day Camp, Pitts., 1980; vocal music tchr. and supr. Fulbright Tchr. Exch., Fife Region, Scotland, 1980-81; cantor, St. Mary of the Mount Parish, Pitts., 1981-87; tchr. vocal technique, Community Coll. Allegheny County, Pitts., 1988; cons. internat. div., Fulbright Tchr. Exch., U.S. Dept. Edn., 1981-83. Mem., soloist, Mendelssohn Choir Pitts., 1972-80; mem. Choeur de Paris, France, 1985; singer, actress various community and community coll. operas, operettas, musicals, Pitts., Chautauqua, N.Y., and Europe, 1972-85. Vol., Kane Hosp. Allegheny County Home, Pitts., 1973-80. Scholarship, Pa. Opera Festival, Pitts., 1975, Chautauqua Opera Workshop, 1976. Mem. Music Educators Nat. Conf., Kodaly Educators Am., NEA, Pitts. Ski Club, Sigma Alpha Iota. Republican. Roman Catholic. Office: Baldwin Whitehall Sch Dist McAnnulty Sch 5151 McAnnulty Rd Pittsburgh PA 15236

SEIBEL, MARY ANN, national guard officer; b. St. Louis, May 9, 1945; d. Erwin Joseph and Mary Agnes (Speckman) Huller; m. Conrad William Seibel, July 27, 1979. BA, Columbia Coll., 1975; grad., Air War Coll., 1989. Commd. 1st lt. Air N.G., 1976, advanced through grades to maj., 1983; adminstrv. officer 157th Tactical Control Group, Mo. Air N.G., St. Louis, 1979-86, exec. officer 131st Mission Support Squadron, 1986-87, comdr. 131st mission support flight, 1987-89, dir. pers. 131st Tactical Fighter Wing, 1989—; mem. adv. com. Parks Coll. of St. Louis U., Cahokia, Ill., 1986—. Participant Leadership St. Louis Program, 1986-87; mem. Confluence St. Louis, 1988-89. Mem. NAFE, Air Force Assn. (life, pres. St. Louis chpt. 1981-83, nat. bd. dirs. 1985—), Aerospace Edn. Found. (charter sustaining life), World Affairs Coun. Greater St. Louis, Jr. Womens C. of C. Greater St. Louis. Roman Catholic. Home: 2012 Trailcrest Kirkwood MO 63122 Office: Mo Air NG 131st TFW 10800 Natural Bridge Rd Bridgeton MO 63044-2371

SEID, EVA, graphic designer; b. N.Y.C., July 29, 1950; d. Allen and Yee Duc (Chang) S.; m. Paul Stuart Gruberg, May 25, 1984. BFA magna cum laude, Parsons Sch. Design, N.Y.C., 1971. Asst. art dir. Lord, Geller, Federico, N.Y.C., 1971-72; freelance graphic design cons. N.Y.C., 1972-77; graphic designer Brecker and Merryman, N.Y.C., 1977-83; pres. Eva Seid Design, N.Y.C., 1983-90; owner Sleepy Bear Antiques, Fremont Center, N.Y., 1990—. Active Basket Creek Hist. Soc., Long Eddy, N.Y., 1989. CAPS fellow N.Y. State Coun. on Arts, 1975. Mem. Am. Inst. Graphic Arts, Graphic Artists Guild (graphics chmn. profl. practices com. 1986—), Internat. Assn. Bus. Communicators, Wayne Sullivan Pike Counties Antique Dealers Assn. Office: 85 South St New York NY 10038

SEIDEL, DIANNE MARIE, management executive; b. Reading, Pa., Feb. 1, 1959; d. Frederick Jacob and Claire Marie (Paskey) S. ASBA, Pa. State U., 1986; BA, Alvernia Coll., Reading, Pa., 1988. Office asst. Berks-Lehigh Valley Farm Credit Service, Fogelsville, Pa., 1977-80, sr. office asst., 1980, office supr., 1980-83, office mgr., 1983-86; v.p. fin. and adminstrv. services, chief fin. officer Berks-Lehigh Valley Farm Credit Service, Fogelsville, 1986-88; exec. v.p. Keystone Farm Credit ACA, 1989—. Tutor Literacy Coun. of Reading-Berks. Mem. Nat. Assn. Female Execs., Pa. State U. Alumni Assn. Home: 720 Girard Ave Hamburg PA 19526

SEIDEL, GLENDA LEE, newspaper publisher; b. Pitts., Feb. 21, 1936; d. Howard Arthur and Elizabeth Jean (Peters) Jackson; m. Frederick Rex Seidel, Jan. 19, 1963; children: Paula Jean, Carol Ann. Grad. high sch., Ft. Myers, Fla., 1976. Editorial asst. Success Unltd. Mag., Chgo., 1953-54; sec. various cos., Chgo. and Skokie, Ill., 1955-68; editorial asst. Popular Sci. mag., Chgo., 1959-68; reporter, columnist, photographer weekly Suburban Reporter, Ft. Myers, 1975-76; editor Lehigh (Fla.) News, 1977-78, mng. editor, 1979-84, publisher, 1984—, also columnist, 1977—; v.p. Lehigh Corp., Lehigh Pub. Co., 1985—. Past sec. Lehigh Players; past mem. Lehigh Acres Community Council. Named Best Actress of Yr. Lehigh Players, 1970, Best Supporting Actress, 1975. Mem. Nat. League Am. Pen Women, Fla. Press Assn., Nat. Newspaper Assn., Lehigh C. of C. (Community Service award). Republican. Office: Lehigh News PO Box 908 Lehigh Acres FL 33970-0908

SEIDELMAN, MARSHA JOYCE, internist; b. N.Y.C., Apr. 20, 1957; d. Marvin S. and Lillian (Litofsky) S.; m. Gerald M. Scheinman, Sept. 21, 1986. BS in Econs. and Math., SUNY, Albany, 1978; MD, Yeshiva U., 1983. Diplomate Am. Bd. Internal Medicine. Inter, resident in internal medicine Albert Einstein-Jacobi Hosps.; fellow in pulmonary medicine Montefiore Hosp.; pvt. practice, Silver Spring, Md., 1988—. Recipient award for teaching Albert Einstein Med. Coll., 1986. Mem. ACP, AMA, Am. Coll. Chest Physicians. Home: PO Box 9279 Silver Spring MD 20906 Office: 10301 Georgia Ave Ste 304 Silver Spring MD 20902

SEIDELMAN, SUSAN, film director; b. Pa., Dec. 11, 1952. Student, Drexel U., NYU. Dir. films Smithereens, 1982, Desperately Seeking Susan, 1985, She-Devil, 1989, Cookie, 1989; dir., co-exec. producer Making Mr. Right, 1987; dir. debut with short film and You Act Like One, Too (Student film award Acad. Motion Picture Arts and Scis.). Address: c/o ICM 40 W 57th St New York NY 10019

SEIDEMAN, RUTH EVELYN YOUNG, nurse educator; b. Okeene, Okla., July 7, 1934; d. Ewald Julius and Alma Alexander (Smith) Kramer; m. Jack Lee Young, Nov. 27, 1954 (div. Mar. 1986); children: Stanley Daryl, Steven Glenn, Roger Neil; m. Walter Elmer Seideman, May 21, 1988. BS, Tex. Woman's U., 1958; MA, U. Okla., 1970, MS, 1975, PhD, 1987. RN, Okla. Staff nurse, supr. U. Hosp., Oklahoma City, Okla., 1955-57; sch. nurse Dallas Pub. Schs., 1958-60; staff nurse St. Francis Hosp., Tulsa, 1963-65, Cen. State Hosp., Norman, Okla., 1966-68; supr. Cen. State Hosp., Norman, 1970-71; instr. Oklahoma City U., 1971-72, Sch. Nursing St. Anthony Hosp., Oklahoma City, 1972-75; asst. prof. Coll. Nursing U. Okla., 1975-82, assoc. prof., 1982—. Author: Community Nursing Workbook:Family as Client, 1983; contbr. articles to profl. jours. Mem. Am. Nurses Assn. (del. 1985—), Midwest Nursing Research Soc., Sigma Theta Tau, Sigma Xi. Home: 10812 Quail Cir Oklahoma City OK 73120 Office: Coll Nursing PO Box 26901 Oklahoma City OK 73190

SEIDERS, LORI ANN, human resources administrator; b. Carlisle, Pa., June 19, 1955; d. William Frederick and Harriet Levan (McKee) Lightner; m. Michael Lee Musser, Aug. 11, 1978 (div. 1981); m. Terry Lee Seiders, Sept. 15, 1984; 1 child, Courtney Ann. BS, Shippensburg U., 1977, MS in Psychology, 1985. Site protection officer Metropolitan Edison Co., Middletown, Pa., 1978; p.i. investigator Investigative Cons. Inc., Harrisburg, Pa., 1978-80; site protection officer GPU Nuclear Corp., Middletown, Pa., 1981-83, scheduling coord. trng., 1983-85, adminstr. human resources, 1985—; co-owner Picture Perfect Lawn Care, Middletown, 1989—; sec. Liberty Fire Co., 1987-89. Republican. Seventh Day Adventist. Office: GPU Nuclear Corp RT 441 S Middletown PA 17057

SEIDLER, M. BONNIE, marketing executive; b. Bronx, Oct. 4, 1942; d. Norman and Florann (Sacher) F.; children: Jessica Kay, Alyson Kay, Mikelle Kay; m. Arie Z. Seidler, Jan. 18, 1987; stepchildren: Daniel, Michael. BS, Hofstra U., 1978; MS, L.I. U., 1979. Tchr. bus. Berkeley-Claremont Sch., Hicksville, N.Y., 1977-78; tchr. various subjects Bellmore-Merrick (N.Y.) Cen. High Sch. Dist., 1978-81; mktg. mgr. The Wheatley Group, Ltd., Melville, N.Y., 1983-85, dir. mktg., 1985-87, v.p. mktg. sales, 1988—. Mem. Ins. Mktg. Communications Assn., Nat. Assocs. Ins. Women. Republican. Jewish. Office: The Wheatley Group Ltd 1 Huntington Quadrangle Melville NY 11747

SEIDMAN, ELLEN SHAPIRO, lawyer, government official; b. N.Y.C., Mar. 12, 1948; d. Benjamin Harry Shapiro and Edna (Eysen) Stern; m. Walter Becker Slocombe, June 14, 1981; 1 child, Benjamin William. AB, Radcliffe Coll., 1969; JD, Georgetown U., 1974. Bar: D.C., 1975. Law clk. U.S. Ct. of Claims, Washington, 1974-75; assoc. Caplin & Drysdale, Washington, 1975-78; atty., advisor U.S. Dept. of Transportation, Washington, 1978-79, dep. asst. gen. counsel, 1979-81; assoc. gen. counsel Chrysler Corp Loan Guaranty Bd., Washington, 1981-84; atty., advisor U.S. Dept. of Treasury, Washington, 1981-86, spl. asst. to the Under Sec. Fin., from 1986; now v.p., asst. to chmn. Fed. Nat. Mortgage Assn., Washington. Mem. Women's Bar Assn., Women's Transportation Seminar. Office: Fed Nat Mortgage Assn 3900 Wisconsin Ave NW Washington DC 20016

SEIDNER-EDELSON, SUELLEN, data processing executive; b. Bklyn., Dec. 26, 1952; d. Morris Irwin and Joan Hariett (Salit) Naham; m. Mark Seth Edelson, Dec. 8, 1985. AAS, Kingsborough Coll., Bklyn., 1971; student, Bklyn. Coll., 1971-73. Assoc. analyst City of N.Y., 1972-82; sr. systems analyst First Jersey Nat. Bank, Jersey City, 1982-84; data processing cons. NYSE/AMEX, N.Y.C., 1984-86; ind. data processing cons. N.Y.C., 1986-87; v.p. Bear Stearns & Co. Inc., N.Y.C., 1987-88; dir. mktg. Comprehensive Computer Solutions, Inc., N.Y.C., 1988-89; ind. cons., N.Y.C., 1989-90; artificial intellegence sr. knowledge engr. Automatic Data Processing Inc., Roseland, N.J., 1990—. Campaigner mayoral election, N.Y.C., 1977, coordinator, 1981; campaigner Congl. election, N.Y.C., 1980. Recipient award for community service Kingsborough Coll., Bklyn., 1971. Mem. NAFE, Am. Assn. Systems Mgmt.

SEIF, SUE SOLOMON, medical illustrator; b. Balt., Dec. 7, 1946; d. Frank Stanley and Leah (Toney) Solomon; m. Thomas Franklin Seif, Aug. 25, 1968; (div. 1980); 1 child, Alix Eden; m. Stuart Crossett Kirkland, Oct. 6, 1983. Student, Clark U., 1964-66; BA, Goucher Coll., Towson, 1968; postgrad., U. Iowa, 1969; MA, Johns Hopkins U., 1977. Dental illustrator U. Iowa Sch. Dentistry, Iowa City, 1968-69; illustrator Ga. Consumer Svc. Agy., Atlanta, 1969-70; biology tchr. Balt. City Sch. System, Balt., 1970-72; asst. dir. pub. info. Johns Hopkins U., Balt.; asst. profr. med. illustrator Med. Coll. Va., Richmond, 1977-82; assoc. profr. dir. Med. Coll. Va., 1982-83; principle med. illustrator The Graphics Projects, Richmond, 1983-86; v.p. litigation svcs. Medivisuals, Inc., Richmond, 1986—; cons. Dept. Family Practice MCV Richmond, 1983-85, Dept. Surgery Howard U., Wash., 1986, Va. Military Inst., Lexington, Va., 1983; lectr. many legal profl. socs., 1985—, many univs. and profl. groups, 1979—. Illustrator: Sensory Innervation of Hand, 1979, also others; editor Jour. Biocommunication, 1981-86. Instr., bd. dirs. Childbirth Edn. Assn. Balt., 1972-77; contbr. design Congregation Beth Ahabah Archive Trust, Richmond, 1987—. Recipient Outstanding Svc. Award Assn. Med. Illustrators, 1987, Best Illustration Tone Assn. Med. Illustrators, 1986, Best Designed Jour. Sandoz Pharm., 1982, Svc. Award Health Sciences Communication Assn., 1984. Mem. Assn. Med. Illustrators (pres.), Health Sciences Communications Assn. (bd. dirs. 1982-84). Democrat. Jewish. Office: Medivisuals Inc 1024 W Broad St Glen Allen VA 23060

SEIFERT, CHERYL ETTA, management; b. Glendale, Calif., Sept. 26, 1952; d. Lester Eugene and Bernadette (Corriveau) Roy; m. William Henry Seifert, Dec. 17, 1983. Student, Calif. State Poly U., 1983. Asst. mgr. Palomar Transport, Inc., Upland, Calif., 1979-81; div. mgr. Palomar Transport, Inc., Upland, 1981-84, dist. mgr., 1984-85; ops. supr. Laidlaw Transit, Inc., Upland, 1985-87, div. mgr., 1987--.

SEIGLER, RUTH QUEEN, state agency administrator, consultant, nurse; b. Conway, S.C., July 31, 1942; d. Charles Isaac and Berneta Mae (Weaks) Queen; m. Rallie Marshall Seigler, Sept. 1, 1963; children: Rallie Marshall Jr., Scot Monroe. ADN, Lander Coll., 1962; BSN, U. S.C., 1964, MSN, 1980. Pub. health nurse Richland County Health Dept., Columbia, S.C., 1964-66; dir. nurses Columbia Area Mental Health Ctr., 1966-69; program nurse specialist Midlands Health Dist., 1969-72; discharge planner Richland Meml. Hosp., 1972-73, clin. dir., 1973-75; exec. dir. S.C. State Bd. Nursing, 1976-83; v.p. nursing dept. Self Meml. Hosp., Greenwood, S.C., 1983-86; exec. dir. S.C. Commn. on Aging, Columbia, 1986—; bd. dirs. Queen Gas Co., Barnwell, S.C.; nurse cons. Creative Nursing Mgmt., Mpls., 1984—. Advisor: The Role of County Mental Health Nurse, 1971. Recipient Disting. Alumni award Lander Coll., 1978, Career Woman Recognition award Columbia YWCA, 1980, William S. Hall award S.C. Assn. Residential Care Homes, 1988; named one of Ten Women of Achievement, S.C. March of Dimes, 1987. Mem. Am. Nurses Assn., S.C. Nurses Assn. (sec. 1965-68, bd. dirs. 1986-88, Excellence award 1984, Recognition award 1984), S.C. Hosp. Assn., S.C. Gerontol. Soc., Am. Pub. Health Assn., Columbia Luncheon Club, S.C. Fedn. Older Ams., Evening Mission Action Group, Bd. Nursing Home Examiners, Pilot Club, Inc. (pres. 1988-89), Rotary Internat., Sigma Theta Tau. Baptist. Home: 2220 Bermuda Hills Rd Columbia SC 29223 Office: SC Commn on Aging 400 Arbor Lake Dr Ste 8500 Columbia SC 29223

SEIKUS, PATTI RAE, publishing consultant; b. San Francisco, Calif., Oct. 11, 1953; d. Raymond Bruce and Erma Johanna (Giebel) Rajski; m. Edward George Seikus, June 18, 1977. BS, Ill. State U., 1975. Cert. tchr., Ill. Tchr. Sch. Dist. 98, Berwyn, Ill., 1975-80; editor Scott, Foresman & Co., Glenview, Ill., 1980-84; assoc. pub. Communication Channels, Inc., Atlanta, 1985-88; project dir. Marmac Pub. Co., Atlanta, 1989-90; pub. cons. Atlanta, 1990—. Mem. Women in Communications, Inc. (v.p. communications 1990—), Alpha Lambda Delta. Republican. Home and Office: 3722 Peachtree Rd NE Atlanta GA 30319

SEILER, CHARLOTTE WOODY, retired educator; b. Thorntown, Ind., Jan. 20, 1915; d. Clark and Lois Merle (Long) Woody; m. Wallace Urban Seiler, Oct. 10, 1942; children: Patricia Anne Seiler Bootzin, Janet Alice Seiler Sawyer. AA, Ind. State U., 1933; AB, U. Mich., 1941; MA, Central Mich. U., 1968. Tchr. elem. schs., Whitestown, Ind., 1933-34, Thorntown, Ind., 1934-37, Kokomo, Ind., 1937-40, Ann Arbor, Mich., 1941-44, Willow Run, Mich., 1944-46; instr. English div. Delta Coll., University Center, Mich., 1964-69, asst. prof., 1969-77, ret., 1977; organizer, dir. Delta Coll. Puppeteers, 1972-77. Mem. Friends of Grace A. Dow Meml. Library, 1974—, treas. 1974-75, 77-79, corr. sec., 1975-77; mem. Midland Art Assn.; adv. bd. Salvation Army, 1980—, sec., 1984-87; leader Sr. Ctr. Humanities program Midland Sr. Ctr., 1978—. Mem. AAUW (fellowship honoree 1979), Mich. Libr. Assn., Midland Symphony League, Tuesday Rev. Club (pres. 1979-80), Seed and Sod Garden Club (v.p. 1986-87, pres. 1987-88), Pi Lambda Theta, Chi Omega. Presbyterian. Home: 5002 Sturgeon Creek Pkwy Midland MI 48640

SEILER, ELAINE ANN, foundation administrator; b. N.Y.C., Feb. 8, 1940; d. Jacob Martin and Florence Seiler; m. Stephen H. Gross, July 21, 1963 (div. 1976); children: Elizabeth, Richard, Barbara, Patti. BA, Barnard Coll., 1963. Tchr. English Japanese Jr. High Sch., Nagano, Japan, 1962-63; social worker Jewish Child Care Assn., N.Y.C., 1963-64; asst. to Margaret Mead, N.Y.C., 1971-72; co-dir. New Concepts, Westport, Conn., 1972-73; dir. Future Options Workshop, Westport, 1973-86; tchr., group leader Ctr. of the Light, Gt. Barrington, Mass., 1982-85; pres. Resource Mgmt. Ltd., Gt. Barrington, 1984—; exec. dir. Found. for Advancement World Peace, Gt. Barrington, 1985—; co-mgr. Crystal Coun. Inc., Mt. Ida, Ark., 1983-85, chmn. bd., 1988; bd. dirs. Equity Inst., Amherst, Mass. Co-author: Quartz Crystal: A Gift From the Earth, 1985; creator (gift package) The Peace Crystal, 1987. Bd. dirs. Children of War, 1987—, mem. adv. bd., 1988; bd. dirs. Shadow Box Theatre, N.Y.C., 1988—. Mem. Threshold Found. (circle of advisors 1985-86). Office: Resource Mgmt Ltd Box 799 Great Barrington MA 01230

SEILER, JANE F., office manager; b. Antigo, Wis., Apr. 28, 1959; d. Herbert James and Anna Mary (Wild) Fleischman; m. Joseph Ferris Seiler, Sept. 17, 1983. AA, N.E. Wis. Tech. Coll., Green Bay, 1980; student, U. Wis., Stevens Point, 1977-78, U. Wis., Green Bay, 1989—. Customer svc. rep. W.A. Vorpahl, Inc., Green Bay, Wis., 1982-85; mktg. coord. Temployment, Inc., Green Bay, 1985; supr. to office mgr. Kelly Temp. Svcs., Inc., Green Bay, 1985—. Youth advisor Interfaith Fellowship, Green Bay, 1988—; activities com. OAKE Nat. Conf., Manitowoc, Wis., 1989-90; mem. Basic Skills/Fed. Projects Adv. com., 1988—. Mem. Mgmt. Women (membersip, strategic planning com. 1988—, chmn. tech. com. 1990—), N.E. Wis. Personnel Assn., NAFE. Republican. Home: 2626 Forestville Dr Green Bay WI 54304 Office: Kelly Temporary Services 1551 Park Pl Green Bay WI 54304

SEILER, ROSLYN LILA, educator; b. Bklyn., Feb. 13, 1930; d. Irving and Anna (Pickenik) Lipson; m. Theodore Valentine Seiler, Aug. 30, 1981. BA in English, Hunter Coll., 1973, MA in Speech and Theatre, 1976; postgrad., Fordham U., 1977-78. Legal sec. Otterbourg, Steindler, Houston and Rosen, N.Y.C., 1958-60, office mgr., 1960-62; personal sec. Strasser, Spiegelberg, Fried and Frank, N.Y.C., 1962-66, Dunnington, Bartholow and Miller, N.Y.C., 1966-70; sec. Lasky and Singer, N.Y.C., 1970-71; English tchr. Bd. of Edn., Bklyn., 1973—, South Shore High Sch., Bklyn., 1985—; co-dir., drama coach Martin Luther King, Jr. High Sch., N.Y.C., 1978-79; drama coach Enrico Fermi Jr. High Sch., Bklyn., 1974-75; test coord. Stuyvesant High Sch., N.Y.C., 1979-80; lectr. various reading/writing confs., Marymount Coll. Vol. Infants' Home of Bklyn., 1949-50, Jewish Hosp., Bklyn., 1951-52, Bellevue Neuro Ward, Bellevue Hosp., N.Y.C., 1959-60; advisor Tenants Coms., N.Y.C., 1974-76; local equal opportunity coord. Wash. Irving High Sch., N.Y.C., 1981-82. Mem. Hunter Alumni Assn., United Fedn. Tchrs., Phi Beta Kappa. Office: 6565 Flatlands Ave Brooklyn NY 11236

SEKOWSKI, CYNTHIA JEAN, corporate executive, contact lens specialist; b. Chgo., Feb. 14, 1953; d. John L. and Celia L. (Matusiak) S. PhD in Health Svcs. Adminstrn., Columbia Pacific U., 1984. Chief contact lens dept. Lieberman & Kraff, Chgo., 1974-87; pres., chief exec. officer Seko Eye Care, Inc., Chgo., 1988—; researcher, technologist U. Ill., Chgo., 1976-78. Mem. Chgo. Zool. Soc., 1984—; sponsor Save the Children Orgn., 1983—; asst. to campaign mgr. Rep. State Senatorial candidate, Chgo., 1972. Fellow Contact Lens Soc. Am.; mem. Ill. Soc. Opticianry, Opticians Assn. Am., Better Vision Inst., Nat. Contact Lens Examiners, Nat. Geog. Soc., Columbia Pacific U. Alumnae Assn. Roman Catholic. Office: Seko Eye Care Inc 4200 N Central Ste 107 Chicago IL 60634

SELANDER, LUCY MAE, librarian; b. Mpls., June 26, 1946; d. Gustav Martinus and Marion (Aagaard) Svang; m. Dennis Duane Selander, June 9, 1973; children: Andrea Marie, Adrian Francis (dec.), Christina Louise, Elizabeth Mae. BA, U. Minn., 1969. Libr. aide I history dept. Mpls. Pub. Libr., 1969-70; libr. asst. adult sect. Mpls. Pub. Libr.-East Lake br., 1970-73; libr. asst. children's sect. Mpls. Pub. Libr.-Roosevelt br., 1973-82, Mpls. Pub. Libr.- Nokomis br., 1982—. Mem. ALA, Minn. Libr. Assn. Home: 3921 27th Ave S Minneapolis MN 55406 Office: Mpls Pub Libr Nokomis 5100 34th Ave S Minneapolis MN 55417

SELBY, CECILY CANNAN, educator, scientist; b. London, Feb. 4, 1927; d. Keith and Catherine Anne Cannan; m. Henry M. Selby, Aug. 11, 1951 (div. 1979); children: Norman, William, Russell; m. James Stacy Coles, Feb. 21, 1981. A.B. cum laude, Radcliffe Coll., 1946; Ph.D. in Phys. Biology, MIT, 1950. Teaching asst. in biology MIT, 1948-49; adminstrv. head virus study sect. Sloan-Kettering Inst., N.Y.C., 1949-50; asst. mem. inst. Sloan-Kettering Inst., 1950-55; research assoc. Sloan-Kettering div. Cornell U. Med. Coll., N.Y.C., 1953-55; instr. microscopic anatomy Cornell U. Med. Coll., 1955-57; tchr. sci. Lenox Sch., N.Y.C., 1957-58; headmistress Lenox Sch., 1959-72; nat. exec. dir. Girl Scouts U.S.A., N.Y.C., 1972-75; adv. com. Simmons Coll. Grad. Mgmt. Program, 1977-78; mem. Com. Corp. Support of Pvt. Univs., 1977-83; spl. asst. acad. planning N.C. Sch. Sci. and Math., 1979-80, dean acad. affairs, 1980-81, chmn. bd. advisors, 1981-84; cons. U.S. Dept. Commerce, 1976-77; dir. Avon Products Inc., RCA, NBC, Loehmanns Inc., Nat. Edn. Corp. pres. Am. Energy Ind., 1976; co-chmn. commn. pre-coll. math. and sci. Nat. Sci. Bd., 1982-83; adj. prof. NYU, 1984-86, prof. sci. edn., 1986—; mem. policy steering com. Gov. Cuomo's Conf. on Sci. and Engring., 1989-90. Contbr. articles to profl. jours., chpt. to book. Founder, chmn. N.Y. Ind. Schs. Opportunity Project, 1968-72; mem. invitational workshops Aspen Inst., 1973, 75, 77, 79; trustee MIT, Bklyn. Law Sch., Radcliffe Coll., Woods Hole Oceanographic Instn., Women's Forum N.Y., Skin Disease Found., N.Y. Hall of Sci., 1982—, vice chmn., 1989—; mem. Yale U. Peabody Mus. Adv. Coun., 1981-89. Mem. Headmistresses of East (hon., pres. 1970-72), Sigma Xi, Phi Beta Kappa. Clubs: Cosmopolitan (N.Y.C.). Office: 45 Sutton Pl S New York NY 10022 also: 100 Ransom Rd Falmouth MA 02540

SELBY, NANCY CHIZEK, educator; b. South Bend, Ind., Sept. 15, 1935; d. Cletus and Mildred (Mauck) Chizek; m. David K. Selby, June 22, 1957; children: Pamela, Katherine, Susan, Elizabeth. BS, Miami U., Oxford, Ohio, 1957. Instr., v.p. Verbal Communications, Dallas, 1972-79; founder, dir. Spine Edn. Ctr., Dallas, 1979—; mem. adv. bd. Dallas Safety Coun., 1985—. Author: Care for Your Back, 1983, Back Injury Prevention Resource Handbook, 1984, My Aching Back, 1988; author videotape Backache Blues, 1983. Tel. recruiter Rep. Party, Dallas, 1976—; active Friends of the Libr., Team Coalition Exec. Com. Mem. Am. Soc. Tng. and Devel., Tex. Safety Assn. (dir., chmn. bd.), Am. Soc. Safety Engrs. (S.W. chpt., chmn. safety coun. Greater Dallas, citizens safety adv. com., past pres.), Dallas County Med. Aux., Pi Beta Phi. Avocations: golf, sailing, running, reading. Office: Spine Edn Ctr 6161 Harry Hines Blvd Dallas TX 75225

SELCO, JODYE I., chemistry educator; b. L.A., June 12, 1957; d. Marlow I. Selco and Letty Jo (Baron) Randell. BS, U. Calif., Irvine, 1979; PhD, Rice U., 1984. Postdoctoral fellow Ind. U., Bloomington, 1983-85; asst. prof. Miss. State U., Mississippi State, 1985-87; asst. prof. chemistry U. Redlands, Calif., 1987—; cons. Battelle/U.S. Army, Redstone Arsonal, Ala., 1986, 87, Universal Energy Systems, USAF, Edwards AFB, Calif., 1988. Contbr. articles to profl. publs. Grantee Parson's Found., 1988, U. Redlands, 1988, 89. Mem. AAUP, AAUW, Am. Chem. Soc., Am. Phys. Soc., Iota Sigma Pi. Office: Dept Chemistry Univ Redlands PO Box 3080 Redlands CA 92373

SELDEN, ANNIE ALEXANDER, mathematics educator; b. Torrington, Conn., Feb. 1, 1938; d. Adolf Laurer and Annie (Wopperer) Anderson; m. Herbert Lloyd Alexander Jr., Oct. 7, 1961 (div. July 1970); children: Neil Brooks, Kim Anne; m. John Selden, May 24, 1974. BA, Oberlin Coll., 1959; MA, Yale U., 1962; PhD, Clarkson U., 1974. Instr. SUNY, Potsdam, 1969-71; sr. lectr. Bayero U., Kano, Nigeria, 1978-85; asst. prof. Hampden Sydney (Va.) Coll., 1973-74, Bosphorus U., Istanbul, Turkey, 1974-78; asst. prof. Tenn. Tech. U., Cookeville, 1985-90, assoc. prof., 1990—; external examiner Fed. Advanced Tchrs. Coll., Katsina, Nigeria, 1979-82, Gumel, Nigeria, 1981-82. Dept. editor UME Trends: News and Reports on Undergrad. Math. Edn., 1989—; contbr. articles to profl. jours. NSF grad. trainee Clarkson U., 1972-73; NSF grantee SUNY, Binghamton, 1971. Mem. AAUP, Am. Math. Soc., Math. Assn. Am. (dept. rep. 1986—), Assn. Women in Math., Nat. Assn. Math., Assn. for Computing Machinery, Nigerian Math. Soc. (organizer 5th ann. conf. 1984), Internat. Group for Psychology of Math. Edn., Nat. Coun. Tchrs. Math., Tenn. Acad. Sci., Women in Higher Edn. in Tenn. (Tenn. Tech. chpt. pres. 1990—), Phi Beta Kappa, Sigma Xi, Pi Mu Epsilon, Kappa Mu Epsilon. Office: Tenn Tech U Math Dept Box 5054 Cookeville TN 38505

SELESNICK, ROSE GOODMAN, nursery school director; b. Gary, Ind., July 16, 1926; d. Hyman and Ray (Kleinman) Goodman; m. Sheldon Selesnick, Apr. 27, 1953 (dec. Dec. 1967); children: Albie, Tony. B., U. Mich., 1948; spl. cert., Sch. for Nursery Years, L.A., 1951; M., Calif. State U., Northridge, 1976. Dir. Compton (Calif.) Coop. Nursery Sch., 1951-58; instr. child devel. Compton Coll., 1951-58; dir. Crestwood Hills Coop. Nursery Sch., L.A., 1967—; instr. child devel. Santa Monica (Calif.) Coll., 1978-79; early childhood coord. Kenter Canyon Elem. Sch., L.A., 1978-80; bd. dirs., cons. Westside Children's Ctr., Santa Monica, 1988—. Author: Parent Development in a Co-op, 1976. Mem. ACLU, L.A., 1955—, Westside

Coalition for the Homeless, Santa Monica, 1988—. Mem. Nat. Assn. for the Edn. Young Children, Assn. Child Devel. Specialists. Democrat. Jewish. Home: 4507 Alla Rd 6 Marina Del Rey CA 90292 Office: Crestwood Hills Nursery Sch 986 Hanley Ave Los Angeles CA 90049

SELFON, ROSANNE NANCY, business executive, educator; b. Lancaster, Pa., Oct. 6, 1948; d. Lester Robert and Madaline (Cremer) Miller; m. David J Selfon, Feb. 28, 1970; children: Lysa, Amanda. BS, Boston U., 1970. Cert. tchr., Pa. Tchr. Baltimore County Schs., Balt., 1970-72; bus. owner Rosanne Selfon, Stationer, Lancaster, Pa., 1974—, SRS, Lancaster, 1989—; pres. Samuel Miller & Son, Inc., Lancaster, 1974—; tchr. Hempfield Sch. Dist., Landisville, Pa., 1985—. Dist. 5 pres., nat. bd. dirs. Nat. Fedn. Temple Sisterhoods (mem. exec. nominating com. Named Woman of Valor, 1980), 1988—; pres., trustee Congregation Shaarai Shomayim (Named Woman of Yr.), 1987—; trustee Jewish Community Ctr., 1981-84;editor Jewish Ctr. News, 1975-80. Republican. Jewish. Home: 3232 Grande Oak Pl Lancaster PA 17601 Office: Samuel Miller & Son Inc PO Box 881 37 W Clay St Lancaster PA 17604

SELIGMAN, MURIEL, editor; b. N.Y.C., Nov. 7, 1922; d. Nathan S. and Sylvia (Feldman) Bienstock; m. Selig Seligman (dec.); children: Joel, Brad, Dale Wendel, Lucy Kanazawa, Adam Ward. BA, Queens Coll., 1944; MA, Columbia U., 1946. Pers. dir. Reuben Donelly Corp., N.Y.C., 1945—, Darling Shops Corp., N.Y.C., 1947; lic. underwriter Mut. Benefit Life, N.Y.C., 1947-50. Mem. Nat. Tourette Syndrome Assn. (chmn. communications com., bd. dirs., story editor, 1970—), Calif. Tourette Syndrome Assn. (so. Calif. chpt.). Home and Office: 10501 Wilshire Blvd Los Angeles CA 90024

SELK, ELEANOR HUTTON, artist; b. Duboise, Nebr., Oct. 21, 1918; d. Anderson Henry and Florence (Young) Hutton; R.N., St. Elizabeth Hosp., Lincoln, Nebr., 1938; m. Harold Frederick Selk, Aug. 3, 1940; children: Honey Lou, Katherine Florence. Nurse, Lincoln, 1938-40, Denver, 1940-50; with Colo. Bd. Realtors, 1956-66; owner, mgr. The Pen Point, graphic art studio, Colorado Springs, 1974—; one-woman shows: Colo. Coll., 1970, 72, Nazarene Bible Coll., 1973, 1st Meth. Ch., 1971 (all Colorado Springs); exhibited in group shows: U. So. Colo., 1969, 70, 71, 72, Colorado Springs Art Guild, 1969-72, Pike's Peak Artists Assn., 1969-73, Mozart Art Festival, Pueblo, Colo., 1969-74, numerous others; represented in permanent collection U.S. Postal Service, Pen-Arts Bldg., Washington, Medic Alert Found. Internat. Hdqrs., Turlock, Calif. Rec. sec. Colo. chpt. Medic Alert Found. Internat., 1980—, chairperson El Paso County and Colorado Springs chpt., 1980—, Colo. bd. dirs., 1980-89, rec. sec., 1980-89. Recipient 3d pl. award Nat. Tb and Respiratory Disease and Christmas Seal Art Competition, 1969, finalist award Benedictine Art competition Hanover Trust Bank, N.Y.C., 1970; numerous awards and certs. for pub. service and art . Mem. Nat. League Am. Pen Women (rec. sec. 1972-74, travelling art slide collection 1974—, designer jewelry, awards for book cover art, numerous Gold Bangle awards). Contbr. med. articles, short stories, poetry to newspapers. Home: 518 Warren Ave Colorado Springs CO 80906 Office: 333 N Tejon St Agora Mall Colorado Springs CO 80903

SELK, GAIL BARBARA, publisher; b. Rice Lake, Wis., Jan. 16, 1937; d. Robert John and Eleanor Irene (Massoni) Volck; m. Bruce Reynolds, Apr. 11, 1957 (div. 1959); 1 child, Michelle Elizabeth; m. James D. Selk, June 21, 1969. BA, Macalester Coll., 1958; student U. Wis., 1980, 85. Account rep. Madison Newspapers, Inc., Wis., 1961-76; dir. advt. Consumer Publs., Madison, 1976-77; pub., advt. dir. Madison Mag., Wis., 1977—. Dir. Take I Civic Center, 1982; chmn. Advt. Fedn., Madison, 1982, Downtown Madison Advt., 1985; dir. Connection, Madison, 1982-85; sec. Tempo, Madison, 1983-84. Chair Wis. Winter Carnival, 1987; active fund raising Employment Options, Hospicecare, Festival of the Lakes, Madison Civic Ctr.; sponsor Concerts on the Square. Recipient Woman of Distinction award YWCA, 1987. Mem. Madison Bd. Realtors (chmn. advt. 1970-72), Madison Symphony Orch. Assn., Madison Art Ctr., Madison Reporttory Theatre, Children's Theatre of Madison, Madison Club, Wisconsin Club (dir. 1985). Advocations: windsurfing; swimming; boating; skiing. Home: 414 N Livingston St Madison WI 53703 Office: Madison Mag 123 E Doty St Madison WI 53703

SELKE, ELOISE WILDENTHAL, language educator; b. Cotulla, Tex., Feb. 18, 1924; d. John and Lois (Pearce) Wildenthal; m. Harold E. Selke, Sept. 1, 1946 (div. July 1966); children—Harold Edward, Kenneth Wayne. BS in Edn., U. Tex., Austin, 1945; M in Elem. Edn., Tex. A&M U., 1974. Trust dept. clk.-typist Frost Bank, San Antonio, 1945-46; clk.-typist R.R. Commn., Austin, 1946-47, Exxon Co., Corpus Christi, 1947-49; elem. tchr. Spanish and English, Houston Ind. Sch. Dist., 1966-84; tchr. Spanish, Richmond Pla. Bapt. Sch., Houston, 1986—, Gesthemane Sch. for Little Children, 1988—. Mem. Congress Houston Tchrs. (life), Tex. State Tchrs. Assn. (life), Sigma Delta Pi, Pi Lambda Theta. Democrat. Methodist. Home: 5010 Carew St Houston TX 77096

SELKE-KERN, BARBARA ELLEN, university official, writer; b. Houston, Dec. 14, 1950; d. Oscar Otto Jr. and Edith Hicks (Hardey) Selke; m. Homer Dale Kern, May 31, 1985. BS, U. Colo., 1973; MA, U. Tex., 1981, PhD, 1986. Cert. elem. and secondary tchr., Tex. Co-owner Colo. Sound, Denver, 1972-76; tchr. Jefferson County Schs., Lakewood, Colo., 1974-76; dir. Harvest Time Day Care Ctr., Austin, 1976-77; mgr. TourService, Inc., Austin, 1977-82; curriculum specialist U. Tex., Austin, 1982-87, matl. devel. coord., 1987-88, matl. devel. dir., 1988—. Author (books): Retail Travel Marketing, 1983, Communication Skills, 1984, Orientation to Cosmetology Instructor Training, 1984, Resumes and Interviews, 1984, Competency in Teaching, 1985, Guidelines for the Texas Cosmetology Commission Instructor Licensing Examination, 1985, Effective Communication, 1986, Effective Teaching, 1986, Balancing the Curriculum for Marketing Education, 1987, Bulletin Board Designs for Marketing Education, 1987, Marketing Education I, 1988, Flashcards for Marketing Education, 1988, Glossary for Marketing Education, 1988; co-author: Higher Level Thinking in Marketing Education, 1990; author (computer software): Emergency Aid, 1986, 2nd edit., 1989, Measuring Employee Productivity, 1986, Retail Pricing in Action, 1987, Marketing Fibers and Fabrics, 1989; editor: Training Plans for Marketing Education, 1987, Correspondence, 1988, Instructional Planning, 1988; contbr. articles to profl. jours. Recipient scholarship Am. Bus. Women's Ass., 1985. Mem. Nat. Univ. Continuing Edn. Assn., Phi Delta Kappa, Kappa Delta Phi, Phi Kappa Phi. Home: 6518-B Hart Ln Austin TX 78731 Office: U Tex PO Box 7218 Austin TX 78713-7218

SELL, JOAN ISOBEL, mobile home company owner; b. Johnson City, Tenn., May 5, 1936; d. Earl Walter and Jeanne Mason (Lyle) S.; m. Dale L. Moss, Jan. 15, 1956 (div. Nov. 1977); children: Carol Anne, John D.; m. Edward Eugene Biddix, Nov. 2, 1978 (div. Dec. 1988). BS, East Tenn. State U., Johnson City, 1961. Cert. tchr., Tenn., Ga. Tchr. Asbury Sch., Johnson City, 1961-62, Richard Arnold High Sch., Savannah, Ga., 1964-66, Windsor Forest High Sch., Savannah, 1966-67, Boones Creek High Sch., Jonesborough, Tenn., 1967-68; co-owner Moss-Sell Mobile Homes, Johnson City, 1968-77; co-owner Biddix Budget Homes, Inc. (formerly Budget Mobile Homes), Johnson City, 1978-87, v.p., sec., 1987—; pres., treas. Budget Homes, Inc. (formerly Biddix Budget Homes), Johnson City, 1988—. Mem. Washington County Rep. Exec. Com. Mem. Tenn. Manufactured Housing Assn., Upper East Tenn. Manufactured Housing Assn., DAR, United Daus. of Confederacy, Order Ea. Star. Mem. Brethren Ch. Home: Knob Creek Rd Rte 3 PO Box 9 Johnson City TN 37604 Office: Budget Homes Inc 3301 N Roan St Johnson City TN 37601

SELLERS, BARBARA JACKSON, judge; b. Richmond, Va., Oct. 3, 1940; m. Richard F. Sellers; children: Elizabeth M., Anne W., Catherine A. Student, Baldwin-Wallace Coll., 1958-60; BA cum laude, Ohio State U., 1962; JD magna cum laude, Capital U. Law Sch., Columbus, Ohio, 1979. Bar: Ohio 1979, U.S. Dist. Ct. (so. dist.) Ohio 1981, U.S. Ct. Appeals (6th cir.), 1986. Jud. law clk. Hon. Robert J. Sidman, U.S. Bankruptcy Judge, Columbus, Ohio, 1979-81; assoc. Lasky & Semons, Columbus, 1981-82; jud. law clk. Hon. Thomas M. Herbert, U.S. Bankruptcy Judge, Columbus, 1982-84; assoc. Baker & Hostetler, Columbus, 1984-86; U.S. Bankruptcy Judge So. Dist. Ohio, Columbus, 1986—; lectr. on bankruptcy univs., insts., assns. Recipient Am. Jurisprudence prize contracts and criminal law, 1975-76, evidence and property, 1976-77, Corpus Juris Secundum awards, 1975-76, 76-77. Mem. ABA (corp., litigation sect. 1986—, banking and bus. law sect., 1981—, jud. adminstrv. sect. 1983-84), Ohio Bar Assn. (banking, comml. and bankruptcy law com. 1985—), Comml. Law League of Am., Am. Bankruptcy Inst., Nat. Conf. Bankruptcy Judges, Order of the Curia, Phi Beta Kappa. Home: 241 S Cassady Rd Bexley OH 43209 Office: US Bankruptcy Ct 147 US Courthouse 85 Marconi Blvd Columbus OH 43215-2889

SELLERS, MARLENE, artist, educator; b. Phila., Aug. 8, 1933; d. Frank and Rose (Goldberg) S. BS, Temple U., 1955; MFA, U. Pa., 1965; MEd, Temple U., 1971. Tchr. art Sch. Dist. City of Phila., 1966—. Out-of-Town scholar Art Students League N.Y., 1958. Fellow MacDowell Colony, "Yaddo" Artists Colony; mem. Pa. Acad. Fine Arts (fellowship), Phila. Art Alliance, Abington Art Ctr. Home: Benson Manor 803 Jenkintown PA 19046

SELLERS, SHIRLEY NESBIT, director, teacher; b. Norfolk, Va., Feb. 3, 1926; d. Palmer Lilburn and Harriet Kirby SMith; m. John Franklin Nesbit, May 31, 1947 (div.); children: John Franklin III, Craig Emerson, Blair Kirby; m. Paul Howard Sellers, Feb. 3, 1979. Student, Rollins Coll., 1966-67; BS, Old Dominion Coll., 1970, MS, 1974. Cert. secondary tchr., Va. Dispatcher Marine Engrs. Benefit Assn. #11, Norfolk, 1944-52; tchr., permanent substitute Norfolk Pub. Schs., 1955-63, 68-70; bookkeeper Hall-Hodges County, Norfolk, Fla., 1954-55, 63-65; reading instr. Orange County Schs., Orlando, Fla., 1965-66; OEO tchr. Head Start, 1966-67; dir. presch. Windermere (Fla.) Union Ch., Norfolk, 1967-68; tchr. Norfolk pub. schs., 1968-83; dir. presch. Larchmont United Meth. Ch., Norfolk, 1986—; mem. edn. com. Willowwood Presbyn. Ch., Norfolk, 1968—, tchr., 1968—; storyteller, storyteller workshop presenter Norfolk Story League, 1970—. Author poems. Elder, mem. choir, tchr. Willowwood Presbyn. Ch., 1949—; usher, vol. Va. Opera Assn., Norfolk, 1980—; vol. chair candidacy Hailey for House of Dels., Norfolk, 1983; chmn. bd. ecumenical hunger ministry Lafayette Shores Ministry, Norfolk, 1985-88. Mem. Poetry Soc. Va., Tidewater Writers' Conf., AAUW (pres. Norfolk br. 1980-82, 84-86, grantee 1988), Friends of Women's Studies (bd. dirs. 1988—), NEA (life mem.), Acad. Am. Poets, Friends of Norfolk Pub. Library, Friends of Chrysler Mus., Friends of Fred Huette Ctr. Democrat. Home: 6240 Rolfe Ave Norfolk VA 23508

SELMAN, HELEN COLLINS, state legislator; b. Douglasville, Ga., Aug. 5; d. Vivion and Sadie (Wood) Collins; m. James Spencer Bomar Jr. (dec. Mar. 1946); children: James Spencer III, Collins, Harriet; m. William A. Selmen, Dec. 22, 1959 (dec. Dec. 1972). BS in Edn., U. Ga., 1951; MA, Vanderbilt U., 1970. Cert. elem. sch. adminstr., Ga. Tchr. Fulton County Bd. Edn., Atlanta, 1946-56, prin., 1956-79; mem. Ga. Ho. of Reps., Atlanta, 1982—; chmn. justice and consumer affairs com. So. Legis. Conf., 1990—. Contbr. articles to profl. jours. Publicity chmn. Christian City, Inc., College Park, Ga., 1983-87; mem. exec. bd. Cochran Mill Nature Ctr. and Arboretum, Fairburn, Ga., 1986; bd. advisors State Bot. Gardens, 1989—. Recipient Good Citizens award Atlanta Jour. & Constn. Newspapers, 1986. Mem. Ga. Edn. Assn. (legis. com.), Fulton County Elem. Prins. (chmn.), South Fulton C. of C. Democrat. Methodist. Home: 12525 Jones Ferry Rd Box 315 Palmetto GA 30268 Office: Ga Legislature 18 Capitol Sq Ste 604 Atlanta GA 30334

SELMAN, KELLY, biology educator and researcher; b. Cleve.; d. Morton I. and Evelyn (Critchfield) S.; m. Robin A. Wallace. Student, Skidmore Coll., 1960-62; BA, U. Mich., 1964; PhD, Harvard U., 1972. Instr. Simmons Coll., Boston, 1966-67, U. Va., Charlottesville, 1971-72; postdoctoral assoc. Harvard U., Boston, 1972-74; asst. prof. dept. anatomy and cell biology Coll. of Medicine U. Fla., Gainesville, 1974-79, assoc. prof. dept. anatomy and cell biology Coll. Medicine, 1979—. Mem. Am. Soc. for Cell Biology, Am. Assn. Zoologists, Marine Biol. Labs. Jewish. Office: U Fla Coll Medicine Dept Anatomy and Cell Biology Gainesville FL 32611

SELMONSKY, JILL SHARON, marketing professional; b. Bklyn., Mar. 16, 1964; d. Richard William and Joyce Sandra (Mann) S. BS, SUNY, Albany, 1985. Sales asst. Merrill Lynch, N.Y.C., 1985-86; fgn. currency trader Manfra Tordella & Brookes, N.Y.C., 1986-88; account mgr. Crest Uniforms, N.Y.C., 1988—. Mem. NAFE, Albany Alumni Assn., Advt. Club N.Y. Republican. Jewish. Office: Crest Uniforms 1115 Broadway New York NY 10010

SELTZER, ELLEN, financial planner, educator; b. N.Y.C., June 24, 1958; d. Jerome and Jeannette (Korn) S. BBA, Pace U., 1982; MBA, Northeastern U., 1984. Contr. Andrews Assocs., Boston, 1984-85; gen. acct. Digital Equipment Corp., Boston, 1986-88, fin. cons., 1988-89, fin. planner, analysis mgr., 1989—; lectr. Northeastern U., Boston, 1989—. Democrat. Jewish. Home: 43 Braddock Pk Boston MA 02116

SELTZER, VICKI LYNN, obstetrician, gynecologist; b. N.Y.C., June 2, 1949; d. Herbert Melvin and Marian Elaine (Willinger) S.; m. Richard Stephen Brach, Sept. 2, 1973; children: Jessica Lillian, Eric Robert. BS, Rensselaer Poly. Inst., 1969; MD, NYU, 1973. Diplomate Am. Bd. Ob-Gyn. Intern Bellevue Hosp., N.Y.C., 1973-74, resident in ob-gyn, 1974-77; fellow gynecol. cancer Am. Cancer Soc., N.Y.C., 1977-78, Meml. Sloan Kettering Cancer Ctr., N.Y.C., 1978-79; assoc. dir. gynecol. cancer Albert Einstein Coll. Medicine, N.Y.C., 1979-83; assoc. prof. ob-gyn., SUNY, Stony Brook, N.Y.C., 1983—; prof. ob-gyn. Albert Einstein Coll. Medicine, 1989—; dir. ob-gyn., Queens Hosp. Ctr., Jamaica, N.Y., 1983—, pres. med. bd., 1986—. Author: Every Woman's Guide to Breast Cancer, 1987; mem. editorial bd. Women's Life mag., 1980-82; mem. editorial bd. Jour. of the Jacobs Inst. Women's Health, 1990—; contbr. over 60 articles to profl. jours.; host Weekly Ob-Gyn. TV Program, Lifetime Med. TV. Chmn. health com. Nat. Coun. Women, N.Y.C., 1979—; mem. Mayor Beame's Task Force on Rape, N.Y.C., 1974-76; bd. govs. Regional Coun. Women in Medicine, 1985—; chmn. Coun. on Resident Edn. in Ob-Gyn., 1987—. Galloway Fund fellow 1975; recipient citation Am. Med. Women's Assn., 1973, Nat. Safety Coun., 1978, Achiever award Nat. coun. Women, 1985, Achiever award L.I. Ctr. Bus. and Profl. Women, 1987. Fellow N.Y. Obstet. Soc., Am. Coll. Ob-Gyn (gynecol. practice com. 1981); mem. Women's Med. Assn. (v.p. N.Y. 1974-79, editorial bd. jour. 1985—), Am. Med. Women's Assn. (com. chmn. 1975-77, 78-79, editorial bd. jour. 1986—), N.Y. Cancer Soc., NYU Med. Alumni Assn. (bd. govs. 1979—, v.p. 1987—), Alpha Omega Alpha. Office: Ob-Gyn Queens Hosp Ctr 82-68 164th St Jamaica NY 11432

SELVY, BARBARA, dance instructor; b. Little Rock, Jan. 20, 1938; d. James Oliver and Irene Balmat Banks; m. Franklin Delano Selvy, Apr. 15, 1959; children: Lisa Selvy Yeargin, Valerie Selvy Miros, Lauren, Franklin Michael. Student, Central U. Of Ark., 1955-57. Founder, dir. Carolina Ballet Theater, Greenville, S.C., 1973—; Advisory bd. dirs. Met. Arts Council and S.C. Governors Sch. Appeared in numerous TV commls., on Goodson-Toddman game show Play Your Hunch, 1958-59; toured Far East with TV show Hit Parade, 1958; named Miss Ark., 1956, Mrs. S.C., 1981; dir. and staged Mrs. Va., Mrs. N.C., Mrs. S.C. pageants; choreographed Little Theater prodns., Furman U. Opera. Mem. So. Assn. Dance Masters (ballet adviser, regional dir.), Dance Educators Am., Dance Masters of Am., Profl. Dance Tchrs. Office: Carolina Ballet Theatre 872 Woodruff Rd Woodruff Rd Rte 6 Greenville SC 29607 Home: 206 Honey Horn Dr Simpsonville SC 29681

SELWYN, BEATRICE JOSEPHINE, epidemiologist, educator, researcher; b. San Antonio, July 29, 1942; d. Robert Edward and Beatrice Eleanor (DeHart) S. BS, Vanderbilt U., 1964; MS in Hygiene, Tulane U., 1970; ScD, SPH-Tropical Medicine, 1974. Rsch. assoc. Internat. Ctr. Med. Rsch., Cali, Colombia, 1971-74; rsch. coord. Program Rsch. Comprehensive Health Planning Pan Am. Health, Cali, 1973-74; asst. prof. Sch. Pub. Health U. Tex., Houston, 1974-86; rsch. assoc. prof. U. Tex., 1986-87, assoc. prof., 1987—; cons. WHO, Geneva, 1973—; tech. assistance cons., NRC, Washington, 1985—. Author: Principles of Epidemiology, 1982; contbr. articles to profl. jours. Recipient Traineeship USPHS, 1970-72; U.S. EPA grantee, 1980, WHO grantee, 1982; named sr. vis. scholar NRC, NAS, 1988. Mem. AAAS, Am. Pub. Health Assn. (sec. 1981-83), Nat. Council Internat. Health, Soc. Epidemiologic Rsch., Soc. Pediatric Epidemiologic Rsch. Roman Catholic. Office: U Tex Sch Pub Health PO Box 20186 Houston TX 77225

SEMPLE, MURIEL VIRGINIA, retired educator, civic worker; b. Bklyn., Aug. 22, 1915; d. Michael James and Jennie Anne (Maguire) Campion; m. Robert L. Semple, Apr. 19, 1944 (dec. 1977); children: Edmund Campion, Susan Jane, Robert Louis, Michael James. BA, St. Joseph's Coll., Bklyn., 1937; MDH, Columbia U., 1939; MS in Edn., New Paltz State Coll., N.Y., 1961. Cert. tchr. N.Y., Fla., dental hygienist N.Y. Dental hygienist Raymond M. Bristol, DDS, N.Y.C., 1939-42; tchr. dental hygiene Elwood Schs., N.Y., 1957; elem. tchr. Huntington, Port Jefferson, Copiague Schs., N.Y., 1957-80; vol. Citizens Crime Watch, Boca Raton, Fla., 1983-90, Covenant House, Fort Lauderdale, Fla., 1985-90; vol., resource person, sec. Maidstone Park Springs Civic Assn., East Hampton, N.Y., 1970-72; recording sec. Boca Towne Centre Owners Assn., 1982-83; mem. St. Joan of Arc Ch., commd. edcharistic min., 1989—, St. Joan of Arc Guild, 1984-90; mem. Migrant and Homebound Ministries, 1989-90; mem. South Huntington PTA. Recipient Tchr. of Yr. South Huntington PTA, 1980. Mem. Columbia U. Sch. Dentistry Alumni Assn., NEA, N.Y. State Tchrs. Assn.; mem. AAUW, S. Huntington PTA (Tchr. of Yr. 1980), Royale Woman's Club (apptd. chaplain 1990—, corr. sec. 1988-90, editor newsletter 1985, rec. sec. 1986—, chmn. Irish sweepstakes Irish Country Fair, 1988, Boca Raton), Boca Raton Garden Club, Boca Raton Hist. Soc. Republican. Roman Catholic.

SEN, COLLEEN TAYLOR, public relations executive; b. Toronto, Ontario, Canada, Mar. 17, 1944; came to U.S., 1966; d. Leonard Samuel and Kathleen Sarah (Gilbert) Taylor; m. Ashish K. Sen, Apr. 7, 1972. BA with honours, U. Toronto, 1965, MA, 1966; PhD, Columbia U., 1972. Vis. prof. Modern Langs. Roosevelt U., Chgo., 1973-75; editor IGT Highlights Inst. Gas Tech., Chgo., 1975-78, sr. energy policy analyst, 1978-83, mgr. external rels., 1983-87, asst. dir. external rels., 1987—, assoc. dir. external rels., 1990—. Translator: (Russian book) Let History Judge, 1970; contbr. articles to mags., profl. jours. Decorated Chevalier, Ordre des Palmes Academiques, Govt. of France, 1985. Mem. Internat. Assn. Energy Economists (exec. v.p., sec. 1985-87), Publicity Club of Chgo., Am. Inst. Food and Wine, Can. Club of Chgo. (bd. dirs. 1983—, pres. 1984-85). Home: 2557 W Farwell Chicago IL 60645 Office: Inst Gas Tech 3424 S State St Chicago IL 60616

SENACK, MARSHA MARIAM, entrepreneur; b. Paterson, N.J., Feb. 19, 1949. BS, NYU, 1970; MBA, UCLA, 1974. Project adminstr. Brown U., Providence, 1974-75; adminstv. dir., bus. mgr. McCarter Theatre Co., Princeton, N.J., 1975-78; mgmt. rep. Am. Automobile Assn., Falls Ch., Va., 1979-80; mgmt. analyst Bus. Resources Unltd., Burke, Va., 1980-82; gen. mgr. Miami Beach (Fla.) Devel. Corp., 1983-84; prin., chief exec. officer Ad-centive Mktg., Burke, 1984—; lectr. U. Md., Coll. Md., 1981-82; trustee Coalition for Arts and Humanities in N.J., 1976-78; commr. City of Providence Celebration, 1975. Com. mem. Internat. Children's Festival, 1985. Fellow Nat. Endowment for the Arts, 1978. Mem. Nat. Assn. for Profl. Saleswomen (com. mem., com. chair), Reston Bd. Commerce, Tysons Corner Bus. Club (pres.), Phi Chi Theta. Office: Ad-centive Mktg 6124 Rockwell Ct Burke VA 22015

SENATOR, ROCHELLE B. (SHELLY SENATOR), library media specialist; b. N.Y.C., Aug. 16, 1939; d. Paul and Esther (Wolfson) Adelman; m. Melvin Senator, Jan. 25, 1958; children: Laura Julie, Susan Linda. BA, Bklyn. Coll., 1960; MLS, So. Conn. State U., 1969; cert. intermediate supr., Fairfield U., 1982. Cert. K-12 library media specialist, intermediate supr. K-8 tchr. Librarian Center Sch., New Canaan, Conn., 1969-83; librarian, media specialist Saxe Mid. Sch., New Canaan, 1983—; K-12 library dept. chmn., New Canaan, 1974—; cons. workshops on local, state and nat. levels, 1984—. Contbr. articles to profl. publs. Grantee State Telecommunications, State of Conn., New Canaan, 1989, Interlibrary Cooperation, State of Conn., New Canaan, 1983. Mem. ALA, Nat. Coun. Tchrs. English (workshop leader 1989), Conn. Ednl. Media Assn. (bd. mem., program devel. chmn. 1987-89), Am. Assn. Sch. Libraries, Conn. Assn. for Supervision and Curriculum Devel., Assn. for Supervision and Curriculum Devel., Phi Beta Kappa, Delta Kappa Gamma. Office: Saxe Mid Sch 468 S Ave New Canaan CT 06840

SENATORE, ROSEMARY, municipal official; b. Belleville, N.J., Nov. 6, 1949; d. Emil and Mary (Vuono) S.; 1 child, Jason Emil. BS, Seton Hall U., 1975; MPA, Kean Coll., 1990; grad., Am. Sch. of Real Estate, Verona, N.J., 1986. Cert. tchr. K-8, N.J., pub. mgmt. cert., real estate lic. Tchr. Belleville (N.J.) Bd. of Edn.; dir. div. of housing and community devel. County of Essex, Cedar Grove, N.J. Author: (handbook) New Parents Handbook for Private Academy. Recipient Cert. Achievment, Dun and Bradstreet, Outstanding Community Svc. award WERC radio. Mem. NAHRO, NACCED, Nat. Assn. Counties, Urban County Community Devel. Assn. Home: 68 Berkeley Ave Belleville NJ 07109

SENDGRAFF, MARY LOU, corporate professional; b. Dodge, Nebr., Oct. 14, 1935; d. Pete and Theresa (GrosseRhode) Sellhorst; m. Raymond John Sendgraff, Aug. 18, 1955; children: Joan, James, Marla, Mike, Paul. Student, Metro Community Coll., 1989—. V.p. Allied Appliance Inc., Fremont, Nebr., 1961—; dir. Mech. Examining Bd., Fremont, 1987—. Coord. Meals on Wheels. Mem. Fremont C. of C., Rotary. Republican. Roman Catholic.

SENG, ANN FRANCES, civic organization executive; b. Chgo., Jan. 5, 1936; d. William John and Helen Christine (Steger) S. BA, Alverno Coll., Milw., 1957; MA, Loyola U., Chgo., 1970. Tchr. Alvernia High Sch., Chgo., 1958-65; exec. dir. Community House Cath. Charities, Chgo., 1965-67; adminstr. Sch. Sisters St. Francis, Chgo., 1967-69; dir. uptown advocacy program Chgo. Cath. Interracial Coun., 1970-71; community devel. dir. Uptown Ctr. Hull House, Chgo., 1971-81; dir. rsch. and pub. policy Hull House Assn., Chgo., 1981-88; pres., chief exec. officer Chgo. Coun. Urban Affairs, 1988—; bd. dirs. Jane Addams Conf., Chgo., 1987—, Chgo. Capital Fund, 1988—, Women Employed Inst., Chgo., 1988—. Mem. Pvt. Industry Coun., Chgo., 1988—; vice-chair Chgo. Com. Urban Opportunity, 1988—. Mem. LWV, NOW, Ill. Women's Agenda (chair 1983-84),. Office: Chgo Coun Urban Affairs 6 N Michigan Ave Ste 1308 Chicago IL 60602

SENK, MARCYANNE ROSE, telecommunications analyst; b. New Britain, Conn., July 17, 1941; d. Stanley S. and Mildred (Koscieniak) S.; children: William, Todd, Christopher, Kerilee, Alyssa, Derrick. BA in Math., St. Joseph Coll., West Hartford, Conn., 1963; MS in Computer Sci., Rensselaer Poly. Inst. Tchr. math. St. Paul High Sch., Bristol, Conn., 1980-81; analyst telecommunications Hartford (Conn.) Ins. Group, 1981—. V.p. PTO, Burlington, Conn., 1975. Republican. Roman Catholic. Home: 3 Summit Dr Burlington CT 06013 Office: Hartford Ins Group Hartford Pla NP-5 Hartford CT 06105

SENKEVITCH, JUDITH ANNE JAMISON, information studies researcher, educator; b. Ft. Worth, Nov. 11, 1943; d. John Milton and Louise (Littlepage) Jamison; m. Anatole Senkevitch, Jr., Dec. 4, 1965; children: Anna A., Alexander A. BA with high honors, U. Tex., 1965; MA, Tex. Tech U., 1967; MSLS, Cath. U. Am., 1975; PhD, Rutgers U., 1989. Cert. tchr., N.Y., Tex., Va. Tchr. French and Spanish univ. and secondary schs., 1966-72; grad. rsch. asst. Cath. U. Am., Washington, 1973-74; rsch. assoc. George Washington U., Washington, 1974-76; dir. Nat. Rehab. Info. Ctr., Washington, 1977-80; project dir. Finger Lakes Libr. System, Ithaca, N.Y., 1981-83; head instrnl. and learning resources Tompkins Cortland Community Coll., Dryden, N.Y., 1983-84; teaching asst. Sch. Communication, Info. and Libr. Studies, Rutgers U., New Brunswick, N.J., 1984-87; vis. scholar, adj. lectr. info. studies U. Mich., Ann Arbor, 1989; asst. prof. info. sci. U. Wis., Milw., 1990—; cons. on info. systems planning to state and fed. agys., Washington, N.Y., Calif., Oreg., Wash., 1975—. Contbr. articles to profl. publs., chpts. to books. Mem. ALA, Am. Soc. for Info. Sci. (co-chmn. doctoral rsch. conf. East Coast region 1987), Phi Beta Kappa, Phi Kappa Phi, Phi Beta Mu. Home: 2240 Mershon Dr Ann Arbor MI 48103 Office: U Wis Milw Enderis Hall Milwaukee WI 53201

SENN, GLENDA EDNA NICHOLS, small business owner; b. Montgomery, Ala., Mar. 9, 1950; d. Glenn Thomas and Louise Anna (Powers) Nichols; m. Frank James Senn, Apr. 14, 1979; children: Jonathan Ashley, Christopher Patrick, Frank James II. Cert. in gen. bus., So. Nazarene U., 1971. Legal sec. Piel & Lynn, Attys. at Law, Montgomery, 1979-80; dept. sec. social work services Bapt. Med. Ctr., Montgomery, 1981-

86; co-owner, corp. sec. All Pest Exterminators, Inc., Montgomery, 1980—. Mem. Frazer Meml. United Meth. Ch., Montgomery, 1980—. Mem. Montgomery Mental Health Assn., Nat. Alliance for the Mentally Ill. Home: 616 Fieldbrook Ct Montgomery AL 36117 Office: All Pest Exterminators Inc 1813 W Third St Montgomery AL 36106

SENN, MARILYN HELENE, health science association administrator; b. Belden, Nebr., Jan. 16, 1939; d. Frederick Glen and Helena Sophia (Beuck) Boysen; m. George A. Senn, June 30, 1957 (div. Oct. 1968); children: Julie Senn Muszynski, Kelly Dean, John Jay. AA, Augustana Coll., Sioux Falls, S.D., 1973; BA, U. Phoenix, 1985, MBA, 1988. From staff therapist to shift supr. Mesa Luth. Hosp., Mesa, Ariz., 1973-1976; staff therapist to supr. tech. dir. cardiopulmonary svc. Desert Samaritan Hosp., Mesa, Ariz., 1976-85, adminstrv. dir. cardio-pulmonary services, 1985-90; adminstrv. dir. Cardio-Pulmonary Svcs. Mesa Luth. Hosp., 1990—; chairperson for adv. bd. Crestwood Career Acad., Tempe, Ariz., 1987-88; kinetic therapy mgr. Kinetic Concepts Inc. Mem. Nat. and State Assn. for Respiratory Care, Ariz. Soc. Cardiac Rehabilitation. Mem. Toastmasters. Democrat. Lutheran. Office: Desert Samaritan Hosp 1400 S Dobson Rd Mesa AZ 85202

SENS, GLORIA JANE, educator; b. Kansas City, Mo., June 12, 1936; d. Ulysses Button and Jane (Faye) Squier; m. James Frederick Sens, June 15, 1958 (div. 1978); 1 child, Philip Marion II. BS, Ohio U., 1963; MS, U. Wis., Platteville, 1978. Title investigator Dwyer-Curlett, Inc., L.A., 1956-59; tchr. Jefferson (Wis.) Jr. High Sch., 1963-68; legal sec. Harris Intertype Corp., Cleve., 1959-60; tchr. Lancaster (Wis.) Mid. Sch., 1970—, coord. Title IX, 1976, dept. chmn., 1983-85; instr. U. Wis., Platteville, 1984; participant task force Wis. Dept. Pub. Instrn., Madison, 1982. Pres. Platteville (Wis.) Arts Bd., 1987-88; sec. Graham Fund Com., Platteville, 1987-89; mem. performing arts com. U. Wis., Platteville, 1988—. Fellow NEH, 1984, 89. Mem. NEA, Wis. Edn. Assn. (coun. 1963-68, 70—), Lancaster Edn. Assn. (negotiating team 1989—). Office: Lancaster Mid Sch 925 W Maple St Lancaster WI 53813

SENS, LORETTA SUSAN, ultrasound consultant, educator; b. Sandusky, Ohio, Jan. 24, 1956; d. Harold Eugene and Rita Dorothy (Saccaro) S.; m. Patrick James Sweeney, June 4, 1988. Cert. in x-ray, St. Luke's Hosp., Cleve., 1978; cert. in ultrasound, Hillsboro Community Coll., Tampa, Fla., 1983. Asst. chief radiology Hubert Rutland Hosp., St. Petersburg, Fla., 1977-78; trauma x-ray technician Stateline (Nev.) Emergency, 1980-82, Gateway Hosp., St. Petersburg, 1982-83; staff ultrasonographer Bayfront Med. Ctr., St. Petersburg, 1983-84; ultrasound cons. Preferred Diagnostic Svcs., Seminole, Fla., 1984-85; ultrasound cons., dir. Sensible Sonographic Svcs., St. Petersburg, 1985—; tchr., co-dir. Golfcoast Ultrasound Inst., St. Petersburg, 1985—. Co-producer videos Introduction to Carotid Ultrasound, 1988, Introduction to Duplex Vascular Exam, 1989; contbr. articles on ultrasound continuing edn. to profl. publs. Mem. Am. Registry Diagnostic Sonographers, Am. Registry Radiologic Technologists, Am. Registry Cardiac Sonographers, Am. Registry Vascular Technologists, Phi Theta Kappa. Republican. Roman Catholic. Home and Office: 7766 Bristol Ct Saint Petersburg FL 33709

SENSABAUGH, MARY ELIZABETH, financial consultant; b. Eastland, Tex., Aug. 15, 1939; d. Johnnie and L.G. (Tucker) Roberts; m. Dwight Lee Sensabaugh, Dec. 22, 1956; children: Robert Lee, Mark Jay. Student, Odessa Jr. Coll., 1959-63, North Tex. State U., 1963-67. Sr. acct. Braniff Internat. Airlines, Dallas, 1967-68; acct. Computer Bus. Services, Dallas, 1968-72; sec.-treas. Robert D. Carpenter, Inc., Dallas, 1972-76; controller Broadway Warehouses, Dallas, 1976-78; asst. controller S.W. Offset, Dallas, 1978-79; sec.-treas., cons. Carpenter, Carruth & Hover, Inc., Dallas, 1979—. Mem. Nat. Assn. Women in Constrn. (bd. dirs. Dallas chpt. 1983-84), Internat. Platform Assn., Beta Sigma (pres. Irving, Tex. chpt. 1973-74), NAFE. Home: 702 Hughes Irving TX 75062 Office: Carpenter Carruth & Hover Inc 1210 River Bend Dr Ste 200 Dallas TX 75247

SENSENICH, ILA JEANNE, lawyer, magistrate; b. Pitts., Mar. 6, 1939; d. Louis E. and Evelyn Margaret (Harbourt) S.; BA, Westminster Coll., 1961; JD, Dickinson Sch. Law, 1964. Bar: Pa., 1964. Assoc. Stewart, Belden, Sensenich and Herrington, Greensburg, Pa., 1964-70; asst. public defender Westmoreland (Pa.) County, 1970-71; U.S. magistrate for Western Dist. Pa., Pitts., 1971—; adj. prof. law Duquesne U., 1982-87; mem. magistrate's com. Judicial Conf. of U.S.; liason 3d Cir. Jud. Coun. Mem. Nat. Coun. U.S. Magistrates (sec. 1979-81, rec. sec. 1988-89, treas. 1989-90), ABA, Pa. Bar Assn., Allegheny County Bar Assn., Nat. Assn. Women Judges, Westmoreland County Bar Assn., Allegheny County Bar Assn. (fed. ct. sect.), Allegheny Bar Assn. (civil litigation sect., com. women in law). Democrat. Presbyterian. Avocations: skiing, sailing, bicycling, classical music, cooking. Author: Compendium of the Law of Prisoner's Rights, 1979; contbr. articles in field. Office: 518B US PO and Courthouse Pittsburgh PA 15219

SENSOR, MARY DELORES, hospital official, consultant; b. Erie, Pa., July 20, 1930; d. Sergie Pavl Malinowski and Leocadia Mary Francis (Machalinski) Harner; m. Robert Louis Charles Sensor, Apr. 21, 1945; children—Robert Louis Paul, Stephen Maxmillian Augustus, Therese Blaze, Katryn Anne. Student in Pre-Medicine, Gannon U., 1968-72, M.S. in Health Care Adminstrn., 1986; B.S. in Hosp. Adminstrn., Daemon Coll., 1972. Intern in hosp. adminstrn. Harvard U., Boston, 1972; dir. med. records St. Mary Hosp., Langhorne, Pa., 1972-74, Moses Taylor Hosp., Scranton, Pa., 1975-77, Erie County Geriatric Ctr., Fairview, Pa., 1977-82; dir. utilization rev. Millcreek Community Hosp., Erie, Pa., 1983-90, mgr. med. records, 1990—; bd. dirs. Christian Health Care Ctr., Erie, 1983-84; cons. prof. in-hosp. adminstrn. and med. records U. Pitts. and Temple U., 1972-74; contbr. paper 6th World Congress Automated Med. Data, Washington; presenter paper, Computer Adaption of SNOMed to DRG Assignment, to 12th Annual Symposium on Computer Application in Med. Care, Washington., Bd. dirs St. John Kanty Prep. Sch., Erie, 1970-71, pres. Ladies Aux., 1970-71. Mem. Am. Med. Rec. Assn., Pa. Med. Record Assn., NW Pa. Med. Record Assn. (sec. treas. 1982-84), Nat. Assn. Quality Assurance Profls., Pa. Assn. Quality Assurance Profls. Roman Catholic. Club: Siebenburger Singing Soc. Avocations: Profl. classical dancing; researcher early man's migration patterns; gourmet cooking; collecting jazz. Home: 3203 Regis Dr Erie PA 16510

SENTENNE, JUSTINE, public relation executive; b. Montreal, Que., Can., Mar. 22, 1936; d. Paul Emile and Irene Genevieve (Laliberte) S. Postgrad., McGill U., U. Que., Montreal, 1990—, Ecole Nationale d'Administration Publique. Fin. analyst, assoc. mgr. portfolio Bush Assocs., Montreal, 1970-82; city councillor, mem. exec. com. City of Montreal and Montreal Urban Com., 1978-82; adminstrv. asst. Palais des Congres, Montreal Conv. Ctr., 1983; dir. sponsorship Cen. Com. for Montreal Papal Visit, 1984; dir. pub. rels. Coopers & Lybrand, Montreal, 1985-87; exec. dir. Que. Heart Found., 1987-89; v.p. pub. rels. Chouinard, Gasse & Assocs., 1990—; v.p., bd. dirs. Armand Frappier Found., Laval, Can., Chateau Dufresne Mus. Decorative Arts, Montreal, 1985-90; chmn. bd. Wilfrid Pelletier Found., Montreal, 1986—; bd. dirs. St. Joseph's Oratory, 1979—; mem. jury John Labatt Ltd., London, Ont., 1982-86. Adminstr. Caisse Populaire Desjardins Notre Dame de Grace, Montreal, 1980—; mem. bd. govs. Youth and Music Can., Montreal, 1981-86; chmn. bd. The Women's Ctr., Montreal, 1986-88, Vol. Bur. Montreal, 1986-87; bd. dirs. Palais des Congres de Montreal, 1981-89, Port of Montreal, 1983-84, Can. Ctr. for Ecumenism, Montreal, 1968-85, Villa Notre-Dame de Grace, Montreal, 1979-87, Montreal Diet Dispensary, 1989—, Montreal Diet Dispensary, 1989—. Named Career Woman of Yr., Sullivan Bus. Coll., 1979; recipient Silver medal Ville de Paris, 1981, Women's Kansas City Assn. for Internat. Rels. and Trade medal, 1982. Fellow Fin. Analysts Fedn. N.Y., Inst. Fin. Analysts, Montreal Soc. Investment Analysts; mem. Cercle Fin. et Placement, Corporation Professionelle des adminstrs. agrées. Roman Catholic.

SENTER, MERILYN P(ATRICIA), state legislator, retired freelance reporter; b. Haverhill, Mass., Mar. 17, 1935; d. Paul Barton and Mary Etta (Herrin) Staples; m. Donald Neil Senter, Apr. 23, 1960; children: Karen Anne Hussey, Brian Neil. Grad., McIntosh Bus. Coll., 1955. Sec. F.S. Hamlin Ins. Agy., Haverhill, Mass., 1955-60; free lance reporter Plaistow-Hampstead News, Rockingham county newspapers, Exeter and Stratham, N.H., 1970-89; state legislator N.H. Gen. Ct., Rockingham Dist. 9, 1989-90. Sec. Hwy. Safety Com., Plaistow, N.H., 1971—' state rep. N.H. Gen. Ct., Rockingham Dist. 9, 1989-90, Sec., bd. dirs. Region 10 Community Support Svcs. Inc., Atkinson, N.H., 1982-88. Named Woman of Yr., N.H. Bus. and Profl. Women, 1983. Mem. Lionesses. Republican. Home and Office: 11 Maple Ave Plaistow NH 03865

SENTER, MICHELLE FAYE, nutritionist; b. Emporia, Kans., Aug. 5, 1959; d. James J. and Laurretta Faye (Howard) Williams; m. Bill Scott Senter, Aug. 27, 1983; 1 child, Brandon Shay. BS Dietetics Mgmt., Abilene Christian U., 1981, BEd in Phys. Edn., Health, 1982; student, Cisco Jr. Coll., Abilene, Tex., 1984. Registered dietetic technician. Dietetic technician W. Tex. Med. Ctr. Humana, Abilene, 1981-83; asst. mgr., nutritionist The Fitness Racquet, Inc. & Health Ctr., Abilene, 1983-85; nutritionist Abilene Independent Sch. Dist., 1985—; menu planner Serenity House, Abilene, 1985-88; task force mem. Am. Heart Assn., Abilene, 1986—, Project Comply. Active Leadership Abilene Class, Taylor County Young Reps., Abilene Philharm. Guild, Patron 200, Friends Abilene Pub. Library, Abilene Preservation League, Abilene Fine Arts Mus., Abilene Zool. Soc; mem. budget com. United Way, 1989—, Jr. League, Abilene, 1989; bd. dirs, sec. Abilene Food Bank, 1989—. Mem. Abilene Sch. Food Service Assn., Tex. Sch. Food Service Assn., Am. Sch. Food Service Assn., Tex. Dietetics Assn., Am. Dietitcs Assn., Abilene Bd. Realtors, Tex. Assn. Realtors, Nat. Assn. Realtors, Jaycees (assoc. 1985—, numerous coms. 1983-84, Miss Taylor County 1981), Sigma Theta Chi, Sigma Tau Alpha. Mem. Church of Christ. Home: 2901 S 1st Abilene TX 79605

SENTZ, CATHERINE JEANNE, prospect researcher; b. Oakland, Calif., May 4, 1947; d. Melvin Benjamin and Helen Margaret Lilly Lindquist; m. Ronald Mellott Sentz, Apr. 16, 1971; children: Kristy Anne, Nathan Tait. AA, York (Pa.) Jr. Coll., 1968; BS, Elizabethtown (Pa.) Coll., 1970; postgrad., Western Conn. State Coll., Danbury, 1971-73. Vocal music tchr. Dover Union Free Sch. Dist. No.2, Dover Plains, N.Y., 1970-73; research asst. Gettysburg (Pa.) Coll, 1981-82, campaign asst., 1981-84; dir. prospect research Mt. St. Mary's Coll., Emmitsburg, Md., 1984—; cons. Thompson & Pendel Assoc. Arlington Va., 1985-86, Jeffery R. Shy Assoc., Inc. Williamsburg Va., 1985--. Sec. Save the Endless Mountains, Inc. Wyalusing Pa., 1975-76; mem. Grantham Oratoria Soc. Grantham Pa., 1982; coordinator Gettysburg Am. Youth Soccer Orgn. Girls' Div. Gettysburg, 1986-87. Mem. Council for Advancement and Support Edn., Nat. Assn. Women Deans, Administr. and Counselors, Am. Prospect Research Assn. Democrat. Protestant. Home: 670 Weikert Rd Gettysburg PA 17325 Office: Mt St Mary's Coll Emmitsburg MD 21727

SEPAHPUR, HAYEDEH C(HRISTINA), investment banker; b. Lincoln, Nebr., Dec. 8, 1958; d. Bahman and Marylin Lou (Duffy) S. BS, Lehigh U., 1983. V.p. Drexel Burnham Lambert Inc., N.Y.C., 1982—. Sponsor Jr. Statesmen of Am. Found., Washington, 1976—; charter mem. Nat. Mus. Women in the Arts, Washington, 1985—; active Friends of Library; literacy vol.; bd. dirs. Coll. Express Project, Bronx, N.Y., 1987—. Mem. Am. Film Inst., Mensa, Nat. Trust Hist. Preservation, The Asia Soc., N.Y. Hist. Soc., Japan Soc., Mcpl. Art Soc., French Inst., Gamma Phi Beta. Club: Downtown Athletic (N.Y.C.). Home: 46 St Marks Pl New York NY 10003 Office: Drexel Burnham Lambert Inc 55 Broad St 2d Fl New York NY 10004

SEPPALA, KATHERINE SEAMAN (MRS. LESLIE W. SEPPALA), retail executive, clubwoman, b. Detroit, Aug. 22, 1919; d. Willard D. and Elizabeth (Miller) Seaman; B.A., Wayne State U., 1941; m. Leslie W. Seppala, Aug. 15, 1941; children—Sandra Kay, William Leslie. Mgr. women's bldg. and student activities adviser Wayne State U., 1941-43; pres. Harper Sports Shops, Inc., 1947-85, chmn. bd., treas., sec., v.p. 1985—; ptnr. Seppala Bldg. Co., 1971—. Mich. service chmn. women grads. Wayne State U., 1962—, 1st v.p., fund bd., Girl and Cub Scouts; mem. Citizen's adv. com. on sch. needs Detroit Bd. Edn., 1957—, mem. high sch. study com., 1966—; chmn., mem. loan fund bd. Denby High Sch. Parents Scholarship; bd. dirs., v.p. Wayne State U. Fund; precinct del. Rep. Party, 14th dist., 1956—, del. convs.; mem. com. Myasthenia Gravis Support Assn. Recipient Ann. Women's Service award Wayne State U., 1963. Recipient Disting. Alumni award Wayne State U., 1971. Mem. Intercollegiate Assn. Women Students (regional rep. 1941-45), Women Wayne State U. Alumni (past pres.), Wayne State U. Alumni Assn. (dir., past v.p.), AAUW (dir. past officer), Council Women as Public Policy Makers (editor High lights) Denby Community Ednl. Orgn. (sec.), Met. Detroit Program Planning Inst. (pres.), Internat. Platform Assn., Detroit Met. Book and Author Soc. (treas.), Mortar Bd. (past pres.), Karyatides (past pres.), Anthony Wayne Soc., Alpha Chi Alpha, Alpha Kappa Delta, Delta Gamma Chi, Kappa Delta (chmn. chpt. alumnae adv. bd.). Baptist. Clubs: Zonta (v.p., dir.); Les Cheneaux. Home: 22771 Worthington Saint Clair Shores MI 48081 Office: Harper Sporting Goods Corp 17157 Harper Ave Detroit MI 48224

SEPRODI, JUDITH CATHERINE, accounting administrator; b. Terre Haute, Ind., June 16, 1955; d. Ferris Lee and Mary Ann (Tully) Roberson; m. Donald Matthew Seprodi, Aug. 1, 1972; children: Antoinette, Autumn, Jacob, Brooklyn. AA, Ivy Tech., 1990. Lic. property/casualty ins. agt.; notary public. Sec. Equifax, Oklahoma City, 1975-76; ins. clk. Northside Family Medicine, Del City, Okla., 1976; office mgr. Dick Clark Ins., Terre Haute, 1981, Simrell's, Terre Haute, 1981-85; ADC acctg. clk./typist V Vigo County Welfare, Terre Haute, 1985-86, head ADC acctg., clk./typist IV, 1986-87; purchasing agt. Bruce Fox, Inc., New Albany, Ind., 1987-88; acctg. mgr. Terre Haute Coke and Carbon, 1988—, acting sec. bd. dirs., 1989; cons. Seprodi Constrn., Terre Haute, 1989—. Author employee manuals. Coach, Terre Haute Youth Soccer Assn., 1979-82, bd. dirs., 1979-82; player North Tex. Women's Soccer Assn., Plano, 1977-78. Mem. Vigo County Taxpayers Assn., Exec. Females Assn. Democrat. Roman Catholic. Home: 1805 S 25th St Terre Haute IN 47802 Office: Terre Haute Coke & Carbon 1341 Hulman St Terre Haute IN 47802

SERAFINI, ANGELA, retired microbiologist; b. Sassoferrato, Italy, July 27, 1913; came to U.S., 1919; d. Aurelio and Anna (Mencotti) S. Student, Grace Hosp. Med. Tech. Sch., Detroit, 1931-32; BA, Wayne State U., 1950; MS, U. Mich., 1956. Technologist, tchr., lab. adminstr. Grace Hosp., Detroit, 1935-44; mem. lab. staff Wayne County Gen. Hosp., Eloise, Mich., 1933-35; sr. microbiologist, instr. med. tech. students Parke Davis Y Co., Detroit, 1944-56; assoc. rsch. virologist Sch. Medicine Wayne State U., Detroit, 1956-71, instr. med. tech. dept. microbiology, 1970-72, researcher dept. pathology, 1972-75; part time instr. dept. allied health Wayne County Community Coll., Detroit, 1974-75. Author virological rsch. papers. Mem. Am. Soc. Microbiology (emeritus), Mich. Br. Soc. Microbiology (emeritus), Grosse Pointe chpt. AAUW, Am.-Italian Profl. and Bus. Women Club. Roman Catholic. Home: 1255 Woodbridge Dr Saint Clair Shores MI 48080

SERATTE, ANDREA RAE, financial executive; b. Phila., June 20, 1954; d. Harold E. and Margaret (Thomas) Parshall; m. David B. Johnson, Aug. 8, 1977 (div. 1986); m. Joe Seratte, Oct. 21, 1989. AS, U. Mass., 1974, BS, 1977; student, U. Nev., 1976-77; postgrad., Fla. Atlantic U., 1979-80. CPA, Ariz. Tchr. Clark County Sch. Dist., Las Vegas, Nev., 1977-79; bus. mgr./owner Designwear, Inc., Phoenix, 1981-85; internal auditor Cyclops Corp., Phoenix, 1985-86, Bapt. Healthcare Sys., Phoenix, 1986-87; acctg. mgr. Phoenix Bapt. Hosp., 1987; corp. controller Phoenix Gen. healthcare Sys., 1987-88; reg. chief fin. officer Rehab. Sys. Co., 1988—. Mem. healthcare Fin. Mgmt. Assn., Ariz. Soc. CPA's, AICPA's. Republican. Office: Valley of Sun Rehab Hosp 13469 N 67th Ave Glendale AZ 85304

SERBUS, PEARL SARAH DIECK, free-lance writer, former editor; b. Riverdale, Ill.; d. Emil Edwin and Pearl (Kaiser) Dieck; m. Gerald Serbus, Jan. 26, 1946 (dec. Aug. 1969); children—Allan Lester, Bruce Alan, Curt Lyle. Mem. home econs. staff, writer Chgo. Herald Examiner, 1934-39; operator test kitchen Household Sci. Inst., Mdse. Mart, Chgo., 1940-45; free-lance writer grocery chains, Chgo., 1945-49; Riv.-Dolton corr. Calumet Index, Chgo., 1953-58, editorial asst., 1958-60, asst. editor, 1960-68, editor, 1968-72; with Suburban Index, Chgo., 1959-72, editor, 1960-72; mng. editor Index Publs., 1972-74; free lance writer, 1974—. Public relations vol. New Hope Sch., 1959-67; bd. dirs. United Fund of Riverdale, Roseland Mental Health Assn., Thornton chpt. Am. Field Service. Recipient Disting. Service Meml. scroll PTA, 1959, Sch. Bell award Ill. Edn. Assn., 1965, Outstanding Citizen award Chgo. South C. of C., 1972. Named Outstanding Civic Leader Am. Mem. Ill. Woman's Press Assn. (past pres. Woman of Distinction 1968, recipient 46 state awards, 3 nat. awards), Ark. Press Women, Nat. Fedn. Press Women (past pres. parley past presidents 1981, dir. protocol), Riverdale (v.p. 1966-68), Chgo. South (v.p., dir.) chambers commerce. Home: 1421 N University Apt N-215 Little Rock AR 72207

SEREDA, SHERYL LOUISE, healthcare executive; b. Cleve., Dec. 3, 1946; d. Murray Eugene and Marion Louise (Vassar) Garnett; m. Johnny L. Hutton, Sept. 7, 1968 (div. 1978); 1 child, Brian; m. Peter Sereda, Dec. 8, 1984. BS, U. Nebr., Lincoln, 1970. Prodn. asst., assoc. prodn. WKYC-TV NBC, Cleve., 1971-78; sales rep. Chase Bag Co., Chagrin Falls, Ohio, 1978-79; dir. pub. rels. City of Cleveland Heights, Ohio, 1979-83; dir. communications Greater Cleve. Hosp. Assn., 1983-87; exec. asst. to pres. MetroHealth Med. Ctr., Cleve., 1987—. Bd. trustees MetroHealth System Found., 1987—; bd. dirs. Art Studio, 1987—; mem. Cuyahoga County Fin. Issues Task Force, 1989; mem. pub. affairs com. Greater Cleve. Growth Assn., 1988—; mem. allocation panel United Way Svcs., 1988—; bd. mgrs. Cleve. Edn. Ptnrs., 1988—, Cleve. Bd. Edn., 1988. Recipient Gavel award ABA, 1976, Gold Medal award Film and TV Festival N.Y., 1977, Award of Excellence, French Paper Co., 1981, Mgmt. Innovation award Am. Coll. Healthcare Execs., 1986. Mem. Pub. Rels. Soc. Am. (bd. dirs. 1987—), Am. Coll. Healthcare Mktg., Soc. Bank (adv. bd. 1989). Office: MetroHealth System 3395 Scranton Rd Cleveland OH 44109

SERIO, KATHRYN BETH, pianist, educator, choral director, organist; b. Buffalo, Aug. 14, 1957; d. Daniel Walter and Carole Ann (Rosenbach) Kayne; m. Michael Thomas Serio, June 25, 1982; 1 child, Anthony Michael. BFA magna cum laude, SUNY, Buffalo, 1979, MFA, 1987; postgrad., Eastman Sch. Music, 1982-86; artist diploma, Accademia Musicale di Chigiana, Siena, Italy, 1984. Choir dir., organist Stephen's-Bethlehem United Ch. Christ, Williamsville, N.Y., 1978-80, North Presbyn. Ch., North Tonawanda, N.Y., 1981-83, Leroy (N.Y.) Bapt. Ch., 1983-85, 1st Congl. Ch., Stoughton, Mass., 1988—; lectr. piano Genesee Community Coll., Batavia, N.Y., 1985-86; instr. piano SUNY, Buffalo, 1978-80, Community Music Sch., Buffalo, 1981-83; music dir. Community Choir Sharon, Mass., 1988-90; mem. faculty Longy Sch. Music, Cambridge, Mass., 1989—. Composer (choral works) Gloria Alleluia, 1978, A Christmas Medley, 1981. Eastman Sch. Music grantee, Italy, 1984. Mem. MTNA.

SERMOS, SYBIL FALK, artist; b. Boston, June 8, 1938; d. Edward I. and Etta (Goldman) Falk; m. Kemon A. Sermos, Apr. 4, 1968; children: Evan, Holly. BFA, Mass. Coll. Art, 1960. Tchr. Art Inst. Boston, 1962-69; pres. Holly Dolls by Sybil, Somerville, Mass., 1972-82; free-lance artist Harvard U. Med. Sch. News Office, Boston, 1981-89, Larkin Publs., Chestnut Hill, Mass., 1981—. Group shows include Art Inst. Boston, 1967, Boston City Hall, 1977, Marlborough House Boston, 1978; works include Family of Dolls quilt (pub. in The National Bicentennial Quilt Exposition, 1976, and The Big Book of Applique, 1978). Mem., past chairperson Somerville Arts Lottery Coun., 1980-86; mem. Mass. Coun. on Arts and Humanities, 1984-87, Mass. Cultural Coun., 1990—, Mass. Arts Lottery Coun., 1985-90, vice chmn., 1988—. Recipient Richard R. Mitton award Jordan Marsh, 1960; 2d Place Crafts award Am. Mothers Com. Mass., 1976, 78; Best of Show Craft award Marblehead Art Festival, 1977, 1st prize Mixed Media award Winthrop Art Festival, 1978, 80, 82, 84, 90, 3d prize, 1989, 2nd prize Craft award, 1989, Spl. award for excellence in watercolor, 1984, 85, 86, 90. Mem. Winthrop Art Assn. (pres. 1981-83), Mass. Cultural Alliance, Boston Women's Caucus for Art. Democrat. Jewish.

SEROTA, SUSAN PERLSTADT, lawyer; b. Chgo., Sept. 10, 1945; d. Sidney Morris and Mildred (Penn) Perlstadt; m. James Ian Serota, May 7, 1972; children: Daniel Louis, Jonathan Mark. AB, U. Mich., 1967; JD, NYU, 1971. Bar: Ill. 1971, D.C. 1972, N.Y. 1981, U.S. Dist. Ct. (no. dist.) Ill. 1971, U.S. Dist. Ct. (so. dist.) N.Y. 1981, U.S. Dist. Ct. (ea. dist.) N.Y. 1985, U.S. Ct. Claims 1972, U.S. Tax Ct. 1972, U.S. Ct. Appeals (D.C. cir.) 1972. Assoc. Gottlieb & Schwartz, Chgo., 1971-72, Silverstein & Mullens, Washington, 1972-75, Cahill Gordon & Reindel, N.Y.C., 1975-82; assoc. Winthrop, Stimson, Putnam & Roberts, N.Y.C., 1982, ptnr., 1983—; adj. prof. Sch. Law, Georgetown U., Washington, 1974-75; mem. faculty Practicing Law Inst., N.Y.C., 1983—. Assoc. editor Exec. Compensation Jour., 1973-75; dep. editor Tax Mgmt., Estate and Gift Taxation and Exec. Compensation, 1972-75; mem. editorial adv. bd. Benefits Law Jour., 1988—; contbr. articles to legal jours. Mem. ABA (chmn. joint com. employee benefits 1988-89, vice-chmn. com. employee benefits taxation sect. 1988—), N.Y. State Bar Assn. (exec. com. tax sect. 1988—). Democrat. Office: Winthrop Stimson Putnam & Roberts One Battery Park Pla New York NY 10004-1490

SEROWKA, JUANITA DOMICELLA, health science facility administrator; b. Chgo., Dec. 17, 1946; d. Edward Roman and Felicia Rosalie (Pachucka) S. BS in Nursing, U. Ill., Chgo., 1968; MS in Nursing, Ind. U., Inpls., 1980; student, Kennedy-We. U., 1988—. RN, Ind. Staff nurse Wesley Meml. Hosp., Chgo., 1968-69, Loyola U. Med. Ctr., Maywood, Ill., 1969-70; unit coordinator Loyola U. Med. Ctr., 1970-71, nursing supr., 1971-73; unit dir. Ind. U. Hosp., Indpls., 1973-76; mgmt. engr. St. Vincent Hosp., Indpls., 1976-79; unit mgr. Meth. Hosp., Indpls., 1979-80; dir. nursing Winona Meml. Hosp., Indpls., 1980-86; v.p. nursing Margaret Mary Community Hosp., Batesville, Ind., 1986—. Author: The First Step, 1974. Campaign worker Rep. Com., Indpls., 1982-84. Mem. Ind. Orgn. Nurse Execs. (sec.-treas. 1985), Greater Cin. Hosp. Coun., Soc. Nursing Profls., NAFE, Hilcrest Country Club. Republican. Roman Catholic. Home: 347 Whirppoorwill Dr Batesville IN 47006 Office: Mary Margaret Comm Hosp 321 Mitchell Ave Batesville IN 47006

SERR, BARBARA JEAN, employment services specialist; b. Grand Forks, N.D., Dec. 7, 1943; d. Lyle Luther Raymond and Zona Luciel (Neumann) Swanson; 1 child, Kim. BA, U. N.D., 1965. Sec., bookeeper Capitol Aviation Corp., Bismarck, N.D., 1966-69; placement interviewer Job Svc. N.D., Bismarck, 1969-84, dislocated workers unit specialist, 1989—; supr. tchr. placement, lead coord., editor newsletter Quality Circles Job Svc., Bismarck, 1984-89. Mem. Cen. Dakota Human Resources Assn. (treas., Mem. of Yr. 1986-87), Assn. of Quality Participation, Highnooners Toastmasters (Adm. v.p., sec., Competent Toastmaster 1989), Internat. Assn. Pers. in Employment Security (pres. honor roll 1988-89). Home: 207 Ave C E Bismarck ND 58501

SERRA, PATRICIA JANET, social services administrator; b. St. Louis, Mo., Aug. 9, 1933; d. Lewis John and Constance Loyola (Egan) Protheroe; m. Mauricio Tadeo, Sept. 3, 1960; children: Mauricio Antonio, Patricia Suzanne, Mark Lewis. BS, St. Louis U., 1955; MSW, San Jose (Calif.) State U., 1974. Social worker Associated Catholic Charities, New Orleans, 1956-61; med. social worker Charity Hosp., New Orleans, 1961-63; counselor City of New Orleans, 1963-64; child welfare worker City of San Francisco; social worker Cath. Social Svc., San Francisco, 1970-74; counselor Golden Gate Regional Ctr., 1974-76; case mgr. San Andreas Regional Ctr., San Jose, 1976-84; program dir. United Cerebral Palsy Assn. Santa Clara, Mountainview, Calif., 1984—; faculty field instr., San Jose State U., San Jose, 1985. Mem. San Jose Disability Adv. Com.. Recipient awards of Recognition United Cerebral Palsy Assn. Santa Clara, San Mateo Counties, 1989, Bd. Suprs. County San Mateo, Calif., 1989. Mem. Parents Helping Parents, San Mateo County Coordinating Coun. Devel. Disabilities, Nat. Assn. Wocial Workers. Democrat. Roman Catholic. Home: 4556 Bald Eagle Way San Jose CA 95118

SERRANO, MYRNA, materials scientist, chemical engineer; b. San Sebastian, P.R., Aug. 21, 1954; d. Francisco Serrano and Obdulia Méndez. B Chem. Engring., U. P.R., 1977; M Chem. Engring., U. Del., 1980; PhD in Chem. Engring., U. Mass., 1986. Chem. engr. Hercules Inc., Wilmington, Del., 1980-82; sr. rsch. engr. Dow Chem. Co., Midland, Mich., 1986-87; sr. rsch. engr. western div. Dow Chem. Co., Walnut Creek, Calif., 1987-89; project leader cen. rsch. Dow Chem. Co., Midland, 1990—. Contbr. articles to profl. jours. Mem. Am. Inst. Chem. Engrs., Material Rsch. Soc., Soc. for Advanced Material Plastics Engrs. Office: Dow Chemical Company Bldg 1702 Advanced Composites Lab Midland MI 48640

SERRANO, ROSE ARLENE, educator; b. Bklyn., Sept. 1, 1950; d. Anibal Lorenzo and Connie (Millet) S. BA in Elem. Edn., U. P.R., 1975; BS in Spl. Edn., Nazareth Coll., Rochester, N.Y., 1983; postgrad., SUNY, Brockport,

1986—. Cert. sch. adminstr., N.Y. Tchr. P.R. Sch. Dist., San Juan, 1975-79, Sch. 41, City Sch. Dist., Rochester, 1979—; adj. prof. P.R. Jr. Coll., San Juan, 1978-79. Leader Girl Scouts U.S.A., Rochester, 1984-88; vol. usher Rochester Philharm. Orch., 1988—; edn. chmn. Genesee Valley PTA, Monroe County, N.Y., 1989—, sec. 1990. Recipient Ernest DuBois-Educator of Yr. award Genesee Valley PTA, 1988. Roman Catholic. Home: 686 Seward St Rochester NY 14611-3822 Office: Sch 41 279 Ridge Rd W Rochester NY 14615

SERRILL, PATRICIA WHITFIELD, newspaper publishing executive; b. Walhalla, S.C., Feb. 26, 1941; d. C. and O. Gladys (McMurry) Whitfield; m. Theodore A. Serrill, Feb. 21, 1987; children: Mark Schaffer, Eric Schaffer, Jill Goss. AA, Wingate (N.C.) Coll., 1975; student, Cen. Fla. Tech. Coll., Valencia Community Coll., Orlando, Fla. Lic. real estate sales, Fla. Mem. circulation staff Orlando (Fla.) Sentinel; real estate agt. Park Place Assocs., Winter Park, Fla.; bus. mgr. Pinllas Review, Inc., St. Petersburg, Fla. Asst. editor: Counterpoint, Wingate Coll. 1975. Treas. Clearwater Rep. Club, 1987-88. Mem. ABWA, FALs, NALs, NAFE, Clearwater Bar Assn. (aux.-hon.), Clearwater Legal Secs. Assn. Home: 1413 Embassy Dr Clearwater FL 34624 Office: PO Box 14446 Saint Petersburg FL 33733 also: 14100 US 19 S Clearwater FL 34624

SERSTOCK, DORIS SHAY, microbiologist, educator, civic worker; b. Mitchell, S.D., June 13, 1926; d. Elmer Howard and Hattie (Christopher) Shay; B.A., Augustana Coll., 1947; postgrad. U. Minn., 1966-67, Duke U., summer 1969, Communicable Disease Center, Atlanta, 1972; m. Ellsworth I. Serstock, Aug. 30, 1952; children—Barbara Anne, Robert Ellsworth, Mark Douglas. Bacteriologist, Civil Service, S.D., Colo., Mo., 1947-52; research bacteriologist U. Minn., 1952-53; clin. bacteriologist Dr. Lufkin's Lab., 1954-55; chief technologist St. Paul Blood Bank of ARC, 1959-65; microbiologist in charge mycology lab. VA Hosp., Mpls., 1968—; instr. Coll. Med. Scis., U. Minn., 1970-79, asst. prof. Coll. Lab. Medicine and Pathology, 1979—. Mem. Richfield Planning Commn., 1965-71, sec., 1968-71. Fellow Augusta Coll.; named to Exec. and Profl. Hall of Fame; recipient Alumni Achievement award Augustana Coll., 1977; Superior Performance award VA Hosp., 1978, 82, Cert. of Recognition, 1988; Golden Spore awards Mycology Observer, 1985, 87. Mem. Am. Soc. Microbiology, N.Y. Acad. Scis., Minn. Planning Assn. Republican. Lutheran. Clubs: Richfield Women's Garden (pres. 1959), Wild Flower Garden (chmn. 1961). Author articles in field. Home: 7201 Portland Ave Richfield MN 55423 Office: VA Hosp Minneapolis MN 55417

SERVAAS, MARGARET ANN, real estate agent; b. Clearfield, Pa., Sept. 11, 1952; d. Robert Leonard and Dorothy Ann (Harter) Smeal; m. Thomas Michael SerVaas, Mar. 10, 1978 (div. July 1981). BA in Polit. Sci., Juniata Coll., Huntingdon, Pa., 1974; MS in Mgmt., Purdue U., 1976. Mktg. rep. IBM, Idpls., 1977-78, Lanier Bus. Products, Denver, 1978-80; real estate sales Realty World, Castle Rock, Colo., 1980-85, Re/Max Town and Country, Castle Rock, 1985—. Patron, mem. Douglas County (Colo.) Econ. Devel. Council, 1986—; planning commr., Town of Castle Rock, 1984—; mem. LWV, 1984—, Douglas County Arts and Humanities Council, 1984—. Mem. Colo. Assn. Realtors, Nat. Assn. Realtors, Douglas/Elbert Bd. Realtors (Community Svc. award 1984), AAUW (exec. bd. dirs. 1981—, past pres., state bd. dirs. 1987—, named honoree for ednl. found. program 1987). Republican. Methodist. Home: 1280 South St Castle Rock CO 80104 Office: Re/Max Town and Country 719 Wilcox St Castle Rock CO 80104

SESEN, HARRIET ROBERTA, art consultant; b. Boston, June 10, 1940; d. Samuel Benjamin and Eva Rebecca (Golden) Cutler; m. Peter Alan Sesen (div. 1972); children: Michael, Scott, Jennifer. Student, U. Mass., 1962. Account exec. R.E. Fleming Advt., Framingham, Mass., 1973-74; reporter, interviewer WKOX Radio, Framingham, 1973-75; adminstrv. asst. Bicentennial celebration We The People, Boston and Washington, 1974-75; adminstrv. asst. Moment mag., Newton, Mass., 1975-76; founder Hang Ups Inc., Framingham, 1969-76, Creiger Sesen Assocs. Inc., Boston, 1976-85, Harriet Sesen Assocs. Ltd., Brookline, Mass., 1985—; producer, host, (TV show) Collage, 1986—. Trustee Pub. Action Arts Endowment, Boston, 1987—; mem. council Mus. Fine Arts, Boston, 1985—, Inst. Contemporary Art, Boston, 1985—; bd. dirs. Civic Symphony Orch., Boston, 1989—; mem. com. Archives of Am. Art, 1990. Home: 25 Gardner Rd Brookline MA 02146 Office: Harriet Sesen Assocs Ltd 25 Gardner Rd Brookline MA 02146

SESSION, WILLIE MAE, nurse, clinical instructor; b. Daytona Beach, Fla., Jan. 1, 1943; d. Willie Lee and Mamie (Jones) Edwards; m. Johnny Van Session, Jan. 27, 1975; children: Tyrone, Theressa, Vanessa. AA, Volusia County Community Coll., Daytona Beach, 1962, Advanced degree in nursing, 1975; BS, Bethune-Cookman Coll., 1983; MS in Nursing, U. Fla., 1987. Nurse Am. Heart Assn., Daytona Beach, 1984-86; with Halifax Med. Ctr., Daytona Beach, 1975—, clin. instr. ednl. services dept., 1987-90; asst. prof. nursing Bethune Cookman Coll., Daytona Beach, 1990—; CPR instr. ARC, Daytona Beach, 1985—; adj. asst. prof. of nursing Bethune Cookman Coll. Mem. Fla. Nurses Assn., Fla. Assn. Health and Social Services, Sigma Theta Tau. Democrat. Baptist. Home: 1108 Lakewood Park Dr Daytona Beach FL 32017

SESSOMS, STEPHANIE THOMPSON, accountant; b. Norton, Va., June 17, 1963; d. Lowell Prentice and Elizabeth Claudine (Steffey) Thompson; m. Wesley Ray Sessoms, Dec. 18, 1988. BS in Bus. and Pub. Adminstrn., Va. Commonwealth U., 1983; postgrad., U. Va., Wise, 1983-85. Account clk. Sterchi Bros. Stores, Inc., Lexington, Ky., 1985-86; asst. office mgr. Ky.-Ind. Lumber, Inc., Lexington, 1986-87; acct. Kennedy's Piggly Wiggly Stores, Coeburn, Va., 1987-88, Davis Mining & Mfg., Inc., Coeburn, 1988; programs asst. Mountain Empire Older Citizens, Wise, 1988—. Researcher (handbook) Guide for Increasing Sales, 1985. Mem. Clinch Valley Coll. of the U. Va. Alumni, the Red & Gray Soc., Wise, 1990. Mem. NAFE, AAUW. Baptist. Home: 705 Laurel Ln Norton VA 24273

SESTILE, CYNTHIA JEANNE, financial analyst, management consultant; b. Ambridge, Pa., May 24, 1956; d. Joseph John and Elise May (Blackford) S. AA, U. South Fla., 1977, BA in Polit. Sci., 1979; postgrad., So. Meth. U., 1980-81; MBA, U. Tex., Arlington, 1987. Acct. NDC, Dallas, 1984-87; cons. fin. and acctg. Dallas, 1987-88; mgr. fin. services Cathey Hutton & Assocs., Dallas, 1988—. Mem. Nat. Assn. Female Execs., MBA Assn., Beta Gamma Sigma, Pi Sigma Alpha. Republican. Methodist.

SETLICH-DROZDA, KIMBERLY KAY, public relations executive; b. Bainbridge, Md., Apr. 26, 1956; d. Janet G. (Vernon) Hepner; 1 child, Scott R. Student, Ohio State U., 1975-76; BA, Am. Inst. Banking, Chgo., 1980; postgrad, LaRoche Coll., Pitts., 1982-83; postgrad., Fairfield (Conn.) U., 1984-85. Owner, operator The Best Cellar Shoppe, Dover, Ohio, 1977-81; actress N.Y., Calif., 1972—; cons. pub. relations, advt. various corps., Conn., N.Y., N.J., Calif., 1984—; pres., chief exec. officer Silverscreen Prodns., Mansfield, Ohio, 1985—; cons., dir. Madison Comprehensive High Sch., Mansfield, Ohio, 1987-88; cons. Advt. Area Media, Los Angeles, 1985-88; dir. Software Interface Internat., Independence, Ohio, 1988—. Author: (news digest Class In Style, 1988, Receptionist/Secretary's Handbook, 1988; (newsletter) Computing of Public and Private Security, 1988. Chairperson Mansfield Symphony, 1986-87; buyer, trustee Mansfield Art Ctr., 1986-87; com. chair person Downtown Mchts. Assn., Dover, 1978-83, Downtown Growth Assn., 1978-83. Mem. Screen Talent Ltd. (Extrodinary Workmanship award 1987), Nat. Orgn. Women, Profl. Bus. women Assn. (com. chmn. 1978-81). Methodist. Mktg. (Columbus, Ohio) (pres. 1987-88), Advt. Unltd. (St. Louis) (chairperson 1988-89). Office: Silverscreen Prodns 540 Biscayne Dr Mansfield OH 44903

SETSER, CAROLE SUE, food science educator; b. Warrenton, Mo., Aug. 26, 1940; d. Wesley August and Mary Elizabeth (Meine) Schulze; m. Donald Wayne Setser, June 2, 1969; children: Bradley Wayne, Kirk Wesley, Brett Donald. BS, U. Mo., 1962; MS, Cornell U., 1964; PhD, Kans. State U., 1971. Grad. asst. Cornell U., Ithaca, N.Y., 1962-64; instr. Kans. State U., Manhattan, 1964-72, asst. prof., 1974-81, assoc. prof., 1981-86, prof., 1986—. Recipient Rsch. Excellence award Coll. of Human Ecology, Manhattan, 1990. Mem. Am. Assn. Cereal Chemists (assoc. editor 1989—), Inst. Food Techs. (chmn. sensory evaluation div. edn. com. 1989—, other offices), Omicron Nu (Excellence for Rsch. award 1987), Sigma Xi, Phi Upsilon Omicron, Gamma Sigma Delta. Office: Dept Foods and Nutrition Kansas State U/Justin Hall Manhattan KS 66506

SETTLE, MARY LEE, author; b. Charleston, W.Va., July 29, 1918; d. Joseph Edward and Rachel (Tompkins) S.; student Sweet Briar Coll., 1936-38; m. William Littleton Tazewell, Sept. 2, 1978; 1 son, Christopher Weathersbee. Assoc. prof. Bard Coll., Annandale-on-Hudson, N.Y., 1965-76; vis. lectr. U. Va., 1978, U. Iowa, 1976. Served with Womens Aux., RAF, 1942-43. Recipient Merrill Found. award, 1974, Nat. Book award, 1978, Janet Heidinger Kafka Prize for fiction, 1983. John Simon Guggenheim fellow, 1958, 60. Democrat. Author: The Love Eaters, 1954; The Kiss of Kin, 1955; O Beulah Land, 1956; Know Nothing, 1960; Fight Night on a Sweet Saturday, 1964; All The Brave Promises, 1966; The Clam Shell, 1971; Prisons, 1973; Blood Tie, 1977; The Scapegoat, 1981; The Killing Ground, 1982; Celebration, 1986; Charley Bland, 1989. Office: care Farrar Straus & Giroux 2027 Minor Rd Charlottesville VA 22903

SETZER, DORIS WILLS, fashion, retail management lecturer and consultant; b. Portland, Oreg., Mar. 15, 1917; d. Ralph Edward and Maude (Anderson) Wills; m. James Dallas Setzer, Mar. 15, 1946; 1 child, Suzan Wendy Setzer Berry. Student, Portland Bus. Sch., 1935-36. With Charles F. Berg Inc., Portland, 1936-76, v.p., exec. officer, 1956-75, chief exec. officer, 1975-76; cons. fashion retail mgmt. Portland, 1976—; fashion cons. travel wardrobe planning Ellis-Ranian Travel Inc.; bd. dirs. Contemporary Crafts Gallery, 1988—. Mktg. advisor Jr. League Portland, 1980-83; vol. researcher Oreg. Hist. Soc.; 2d v.p. Portland YWCA, 1980, bd. dirs., 1978-81; adv. bd. Portland Community Coll.; guest curator 100 Years Oreg. Fashion Oreg. Hist. Soc., 1987-89; chmn. com. Nordstrom Portland Remodeling Celebration Benefit, 1989. Mem. Fashion Group Inc. (charter Portland chpt., 2d regional dir. 1950-52), DAR. Republican. Episcopalian.

SEURKAMP, MARY PAT, education educator; b. Pitts., Sept. 6, 1946; d. Frank H. and Loretta (Husic) Reuwer; m. Robert W. Seurkamp, Aug. 6, 1983; children: Kris, Robert, Brooke. BA, Webster U., 1968; MA, Washington U., 1969; PhD, SUNY, Buffalo. Counselor to dir. student living Gannon U., Erie, Pa., 1969-76; assoc. v.p. St. John Fisher Coll., Rochester, N.Y., 1976—; cons. Women's Career Ctr., Rochester, N.Y., 1987—. Com. mem. various parish coms., Pittsford, N.Y., 1983—, Diocesan Com. Devel. of Ministers and Employees, Rochester, 1986-89; mentor Career Beginnings Program. Mem. AAUP, Am. Assn. High Edn., Nat. U. Continuing Edn. Assn. Republican. Roman Catholic. Home: 29 Brickston Dr Pittsford NY 14534 Office: St John Fisher Coll 3690 East Ave Rochester NY 14618

SEVER, DOLORES L., special education educator; b. Cleve., Jan. 26, 1936; d. Louis and Anna (Lechko) S. BS in Edn., St. John's Coll., Cleve., 1964; MS in Edn., Delta State U., Cleve., Miss., 1972; postgrad. Edn. Specialist, Delta State U., 1974. Cert. elem. edn., elem. adminstrn. reading, supervision, spl. subject supervision. Tchr. Our Lady of Fatima, Oak Park, Mich.; lead tchr. Greenwood (Miss.) Pub. Schs., instructional supr. Mem. TOSF, Sisters of St. Joseph. Named Tchr. of Yr., Woman of Distinction. Mem. Assn. Supervision and Curriculum, Nat. Coun. Tchrs. Math., Miss. Reading Assn. Miss. Coun. Tchrs. Math., Internat. Reading Assn., Delta Kappa Gamma (sec./treas.). Home: 504 W Market PO Box 1442 Greenwood MS 38930

SEVER, JANA SUE, therapist; b. Ft. Worth, Tex., Feb. 28, 1963; d. Robert and Dorothy Louise (Swenson) Jonas; m. Nuri Rashid Sever, June 22, 1985. AA, San Jacinto Community Coll., Houston, 1983; BS cum laude, U. Houston, 1985, MA, 1987. Lic. profl. counselor, Tex. Sales and check-out supr. K-Mart, Pearland, Tex., 1980-88; biofeedback intern West Oaks Hosp., Houston, 1987; caseworker II Mental Health and Mental Retardation Clinic, Houston, 1988; biofeedback specialist West Oaks Hosp., Houston, 1988-90; pvt. practice Houston, 1990—; biofeedback therapist Meml. City Rehab. Hosp., Houston, 1990—. Mem. Am. Psychol. Assn. (assoc.), Biofeedback Soc. Harris County, Biofeedback Soc. Tex. (affiliate), Psi Chi.

SEVERANCE, MARTHA ELAINE, pharmacist; b. Worcester, Mass., Apr. 1, 1957; d. Thomas Francis and Margaret May (Moore) S.; m. Charles Joseph LaTendresse, May 22, 1984; children: Thomas Lee, Kimberly Ann. BS in Pharmacy, Drake U., 1980. Pharmacist Manly Drug Store, Inc., Grundy Center, Iowa, 1980—; cons. pharmacist Grundy County Meml. Hosp.-LTC, Grundy Care Ctr. Mem. Bd. Edn. Mem. AAUW (pres. 1983-85, v.p. 1986-88), Iowa Pharm. Assn., Am. Pharm. Assn. Republican. Presbyterian. Office: Manly Drug Store Inc 621-623 G Ave Grundy Center IA 50638

SEVERINO, ELIZABETH FORREST, consulting company executive; b. Bryn Mawr, Pa., Dec. 29, 1945; d. John Joseph and Elizabeth (Patton) Girard-diCarlo; m. Joseph Domenic Severino, Oct. 20, 1973 (div. Oct. 1983); 1 child, Nicole Marie. AB, Vassar Coll., 1967; MS in Computer Sci., Syracuse U., 1969. Systems programmer IBM Corp., Poughkeepsie, N.Y., 1967-71; competitive analyst IBM Corp., Phila., 1977-79; systems analyst Fidelity Bank, Phila., 1971-72; mng. editor Auerbach Pubs., Phila., 1972-77; v.p. editorial and technology McGraw-Hill Pubs., Delran, N.J., 1979-81; v.p. Symcro Systems, Pennsauken, N.J., 1981-82; pres. The PC Group, Inc., Cherry Hill, N.J., 1982—, also bd. dirs.; bd. dirs. CompCar Leasing, Cherry Hill, Life Mgmt. Systems, Inc., Cherry Hill. Author over 125 articles on computers. Mem. Assn. of Personal Computers Cons. (bd. dirs. Phila. chpt., pres. 1987-90), NAFE, Phila. Area Computer Soc. Republican. Episcopalian. Office: The PC Group Inc 715 Kings Croft Cherry Hill NJ 08034

SEVERNS, PENNY L., state legislator; b. Decatur, Ill., Jan. 21, 1952. BS in Polit. Sci. and Internat. Relations, So. Ill. U., 1974. Spl. asst. to adminstr. AID, Washington, 1977-79; city councilwoman Decatur, from 1983; Ill. Dem. state senator, 1987—. Address: State Senate Springfield IL 62706*

SEVERO, LEANNE, social services administrator; b. Meadville, Pa., July 10, 1959; d. Richard Joseph and Katherine Ann (Piccirillo) S.; m. Timothy Wynn Hunter, Sept. 27, 1986. BS, Edinboro U., 1983. Residential program aide United Cerebral Palsy, Meadville, Pa., 1984, dir. ind. living rehab. program for Crawford, Venengo and Clarion Counties, 1984-87, asst. administr., 1987—; camp counselor Easter Seals, Conneact Lake, Pa., summers 1975, 76, 77, 81, Assn. Retarded Citizens, Meadville, summer 1984. Active Meadville Community Council, 1986-87. Mem. Nat. Assn. Female Execs., Speech and Hearing Soc. (bd. dirs. Meadville 1986—). Roman Catholic. Home: RD #6 Stauffer Rd Meadville PA 16335 Office: United Cerebral Palsy 405 Finley Ave Meadville PA 16335

SEVERSON, PATRICIA LOU, education educator; b. Mason City, Iowa, Sept. 18, 1937; Herbert Elmer and Eleanor Madeline (Sobieski) Christensen; m. LaVerne Glenn Severson, June 24, 1956; children: Becky Sue Hanssen, Vicki Lynn. AA, Mason City Jr. Coll., 1966; BS, Mankato State U., 1967, MS, 1972. Media specialist Clear Lake (Iowa) Community Sch., 1968—. Mem. Assn. of Ednl. Communication and Tech., Iowa Ednl. Media Assn., Phi Delta Kappa (north Iowa chpt).

SEVERY, LINDA ANDREA, social worker; b. N.Y.C., June 15, 1945; d. Frithjof Ole and Gudrun (Eriksen) Anstensen; m. Lawrence James Severy, Aug. 20, 1966; children: Beth Andrea, Lisa Ellen. Diploma, Henry Ford Hosp. Sch. Nursing, Detroit, 1966; AA, Santa Fe Community Coll., Gainesville, Fla., 1978; BS in Journalism with high honors, U. Fla., 1982. RN, Mich., Colo. Nurse Henry Ford Hosp., 1966, Boulder (Colo.) Meml. Hosp., 1967-70; sec. specialist U. Fla. Coll. Dentistry, Gainesville, 1986-87; sec., aide coord. Alachua County Older Ams. Coun., Gainesville, 1983-85, 88-89, case mgr., 1989-90, aide supr., 1990—; mem. health adv. com. Alachua County Sch. Bd., 1982-85; sec. Spl. Projects-Interagy. Coun. for Elderly, Gainesville, 1989—; v.p. Upjohn Homehealth Care Adv. Com., 1990—. Mem. Gold Key. Democrat. Methodist. Home: 1600 NW 68th Terr Gainesville FL 32605 Office: Alachua County Older Ams Coun 1024 NE 14th St Gainesville FL 32601

SEVILLE, LINDA JONES, hotel executive; b. Atlanta, May 12, 1954; d. Nathan Blanton and Alma Elizabeth (Pitchford) Jones. Cert. hotel, restaurant mgmt., Internat. Correspondence Sch. Cert. sales negotiator. Group sales rep. Sabena Belgian World Airlines, Atlanta; co-owner Mt. Health Enterprise, Stowe, Vt.; dir. sales Topnotch at Stowe Resort & Spa, exec. asst. mgr.; dir. mktg. and sales The Inn at Essex, Essex Jct., Vt., Hawk Resorts; adj. lectr., sales person. Chmn. Burlington Conv. and Visitors Bur., 1990—. Mem. Vt. Lodging and Restaurant Assn. (exec. bd. dir., co-chmn. mktg. com.) Hotel Sales and Mktg. Assn. (sec. 1987-88, treas. 1988-89, v.p. 1989-90, pres. 1990—), Hotel Sales and Mktg. Internat. (cert.), Greater Burlington Hospitality Assn. (sec. 1989-90, pres. 1990—), Meeting Planners Internat., Lake Chaplain Regional C. of C. (bd. dirs. 1990—). Office: PO Box 1458 Stowe VT 05672

SEVILLE, MARY ALICE, accountant, educator; b. Sandwich, Ill., July 25, 1942; d. Harold Thornton and Margaret Raed (Miller) S. BA, So. Meth. U., 1964; BBA, U. Alaska, 1975; MA, U. Ill., 1968, PhD in Accountancy, 1983. CPA, Oreg. Tchr. Byron (Ill.) Community Schs., 1964-65; asst. dir. Head Start Rural Alaska Community Action, Anchorage, 1968-70; tchr. Quality Edn. Devel., Anchorage, 1970-71; child devel. specialist State Operated Schs., Anchorage, 1971-73; staff acct. Va. Cutshall, CPAs, Anchorage, 1973-75, Johnson and Morgan, CPAs, Anchorage, 1975-77; asst. prof. U. Alaska, Anchorage, 1977-79; controller Alaska Legal Services, Anchorage, 1979-80; assoc. prof. Oreg. State U., Corvallis, 1983—. Contbr. articles to profl. jours. U. Ill. fellow, 1980-82. Mem. Oreg. Soc. CPAs (discussion leader 1986), Alaska Soc. CPAs (discussion leader 1987), Am. Soc. Women Accts. (chpt. pres. 1984-87, v.p. edn. found.), Am. Acctg. Assn., Am. Inst. CPAs, Am. Women's Soc. CPA's (v.p. edn. found.), Assn. Gov. Accts., Govt. Fin. Officers Assn. (spl. rev. com.). Office: Oreg State U Coll of Bus 200 B Bexell Hall Corvallis OR 97331

SEWARD, KATHRYN ELLEN, county official; b. Flint, Mich., May 2, 1926; d. Benjamin Franklin Sharp and Edna Vigor (Davis) Sharp Smith; m. Orville Herbert Seward, June 28, 1947; children—Duane Orville, Keith Brian, Gayle Rene Seward Gibbs. Student Owosso Bus. Coll., 1943-44, Lansing Community Coll., 1973-77, Mich. State U., 1980, U. Mich. 1981. Clk. planning dept. Redmond Co., Mich., 1943-44, sec. methods dept., 1944-48, with operation and routing dept., 1948-52; assignment clk., clk. of cir. ct. Shiawassee County, Mich., 1966-76, register of deeds, 1976-89; cabinet officer preservation com. Shiawassee County Courthouse, 1986—. Cubscout denmother, 1956-65; bd dirs. United Way, Owosso (Mich.), 1985—; v.p. Shiawassee County Republicans, 1979-80, Shiawassee County coordinator of Mich. Mem. com. Ellen M. Tower Meml. Celebration, 1988-89. 150 First Lady award, 1987. Mem. Internat. Assn. Clks. (ret. mem.), Recorders, Election Ofcls. and Treasurers, Mich. Assn. Registers of Deeds (ret. mem.), United County Officers Assn. (ret. mem.), Shiawassee County Geneology Assn., Shiawassee County Hist. Soc. (mem. bd. dirs.). Methodist. Lodge: Zonta (sec. 1982-83) Avocation: genealogy and history of the county. Home: 4601 Simpson Rd Owosso MI 48867 Office: Shiawassee County Register Deeds 208 N Shiawassee St Corunna MI 48817

SEWELL, BEVERLY JEAN, financial executive; b. Oklahoma City, July 10, 1942; d. Benjamin B. Bainbridge and Faith Marie (Mosier) Allision; m. Ralph Byron Sewell, Jan. 23, 1962; children: M. Timothy, Pamela J. Student, U. Okla., 1960-61, Jackson Community Coll., 1973-77; BA in Bus., Mesa Coll., 1982; cert., Coll. Fin. Planning, 1984. Sole practice fin. planning Grand Junction, Colo., 1985-87; fin. planner, broker Interpacific Investors Services, Grand Junction, 1987-88; investment broker A.G. Edwards & Sons, Inc., Grand Junction, 1988—. Alt. del. Rep. Party, Grand Junction, 1986, del., 1988, precinct capt., Grand Junction, 1988; commr. Grand Junction Planning Commn., 1987—. Mem. Inst. Cert. Fin. Planners, Internat. Assn. Fin. Planning. Home: 717 Wedge Dr Grand Junction CO 81506 Office: A G Edwards & Sons Inc 501 Main St Grand Junction CO 81501

SEWELL, ELIZABETH, author, English educator; b. Coonoor, India, Mar. 9, 1919; came to U.S., 1949; d. Robert Beresford Seymour and Dorothy (Dean) S. BA, Cambridge U., Eng., 1942, MA, 1945, PhD, 1949; LittD (hon.), Fordham U., N.Y.C., 1968, U. Notre Dame, 1984. Lectr. English Vassar Coll., Poughkeepsie, N.Y., 1951-52; vis. prof. Fordham U., 1954-55, 58-59, chair Bensalem Experimental Coll., 1967-69; lectr. Christian Gauss sem. Princeton U., N.J., 1957; vis. prof. English Bennett Coll., Greensboro, N.C., 1960-61, Tougaloo Coll., Miss., 1963-64; prof. English, Hunter Coll. CUNY, 1971-74; Rosenthal prof. humanities U. N.C., Greensboro, 1974-77. Author 3 novels, 1952, 1955, 1962, 3 poetry collections, 1962, 1968, 1984 (Nat. award AAAL 1981). Recipient Zoe Brockman Kincaid award N.C. Poetry Soc., 1985; fellow Howald Rsch., 1949-50, Sr. Simon, 1955-57, Ashley, 1979. Mem. Nat. Writers Union, Lewis Carroll Soc. N.Am., PEN Am. Ctr. Home: 854 W Bessemer Ave Greensboro NC 27408

SEWELL, PHYLLIS SHAPIRO, retail chain executive; b. Cin., Dec. 26, 1930; d. Louis and Mollye (Mark) Shapiro; m. Martin Sewell, Apr. 5, 1959; 1 child, Charles Steven. B.S. in Econs. with honors, Wellesley Coll., 1952. With Federated Dept. Stores, Inc., Cin., 1952-88, research dir. store ops., 1961-65, sr. research dir., 1965-70, operating v.p., research, 1970-75, corp. v.p., 1975-79, sr. v.p., research and planning, 1979-88; dir., mem. exec. compensation com. and audit com. Lee Enterprises, Inc., Davenport, Iowa; dir., mem. nominating and exec. compensation coms. Huffy, Inc., Dayton, Ohio; bd. dirs. Pitney Bowes Inc. Bd. dirs. Nat. Cystic Fibrosis Found., Cin., 1963—; chmn. div. United Appeal, Cin., 1982; mem. bus. adv. council Sch. Bus. Adminstrn., Miami U., Oxford, Ohio, 1982-84; bd. trustees Cin. Community Chest, 1984—. Named One of 100 Top Corp. Women Bus. Week mag., 1976; named Career Woman of Achievement YWCA, 1983; recipient Alumnae Achievement award Wellesley Coll., 1979, Disting. Cin. Bus. and Profl. Woman award, 1981; named to Ohio Women's Hall of Fame, 1982. Office: Federated Dept Stores Inc 7 W 7th St Cincinnati OH 45202

SEWELL, VALERIE ROESCH, training program analyst; b. Burlington, N.C., June 30, 1954; d. Alfred and Helen Louise (Blankenship) Roesch; m. Stuart Jeb Sewell, Apr. 25, 1981; children: Scott Bigelow, Amanda Lynn. AA in English, Auburn (N.Y.) Community Coll., 1974; BA in English, Colgate U., 1976; MA in Community Svc. Adminstrn., Alfred U., 1988. Rsch. libr. asst. Syracuse U., 1976-78, sr. acct. clk., 1978-79; claims examiner N.Y. Dept. of Labor, Jamestown, 1979-88; E&T program analyst N.Y. Dept. of Labor, Albany, 1988—; pub. mgmt. intern N.Y. State Governor's Office of Employee Relations, Albany,1988-90. Mem. Internat. Assn. of Personnel in Employment Security, Am. Soc. of Pub. Adminstrs. Office: NY State Dept Labor Bldg 12 Rm 223 Albany NY 12240

SEXTON, CAROL BURKE, financial institution executive; b. Chgo., Apr. 20, 1939; d. William Patrick and Katharine Marie (Nolan) Burke; m. Thomas W. Sexton Jr., June 30, 1962 (div. June 1976); children: Thomas W., J. Patrick, M. Elizabeth. BA, Barat Coll., 1961; cert. legal, Mallinckrodt Coll., 1974. Tchr. Roosevelt High Sch., Chgo., 1961-63, St. Joseph's Sch., Wilmette, Ill., 1975-80; dir. Jane Byrne Polit. Com., Chgo., 1980-81; mgr. Chgo. Merc. Exch., 1981-84, sr. dir. govt. and civic affairs, 1984-87, v.p. pub. affairs, 1987—; mem. internat. trade an investment subcom. Chgo. Econ. Devel. Commn. Mem. exec. com. Boy Scouts Am., Chgo., 1984—, mem. civic com., 1987—; bd. dirs. Ditka Found., 1989—. Mem. Exec.'s Club of Chgo., Econs. Club, Chgo. Conv. and Tourism Bur. (sec. 1989—, exec. com. 1987—, chmn. elect 1990, chmn. 1991, mem. risk mgmt. subcom.), Internat. Visitor's Ctr. Roman Catholic. Office: Chgo Merc Exch 30 S Wacker Chicago IL 60606

SEXTON, JO ANN, nursing educator; b. Covington, Ky., July 15, 1933; d. Edward Joseph and Annabel Butler S. BSN, Coll. Mt. St. Joseph, Ohio, 1955; postgrad., Xavier U., 1958-65. Cert. CPR instr. Clin. teaching resident Good Samaritan Hosp., Cin., 1955-56, instr. nursing, 1958-73, instr. ednl. svcs. dept., 1973-89, project coord. ednl. svcs. dept., 1989—; instr. nursing St. Elizabeth Hosp., Covington, Ky., 1956-58. Active ARC, Am. Heart Assn. Mem. ANA, Am. Assn. Critical Care Nurses, Nat. League for Nursing. Home: 2891 Robers Ave Cincinnati OH 45239

SEYBERT, JANET ROSE, lawyer, military officer; b. Cin., Feb. 7, 1944; d. Peter Robert and Helen Rose (Young) S. BA in Classics, BS in Edn., U. Cin., 1966; MA in Classics, U. Iowa, 1968; JD, Chase Coll. Law, 1975; ML, Army JAG Sch., 1984. Bar: Ohio 1975, U.S. Ct. Mil. Appeals 1975, Colo. 1981, U.S. Ct. Claims 1985. Instr. Latin, ancient history Salem Coll., Winston-Salem, N.C., 1968-70; instr. N.C. Gov.'s Sch., Winston-Salem, N.C., 1969; instr. phys. edn., Latin Kemper Hall, Kenosha, Wis., 1970-71; instr. in Latin Carthage Coll., Kenosha, Wis., 1970-71; commd. 2d lt. USMC, 1972;

completed interservice transfer to USAF, 1978, advanced through grades to maj., 1982; lawyer USAF Acad. USAF, Colorado Springs, Colo., 1978-81; chief civil law Sheppard AFB, Tex., 1981-84; dep. staff judge adv., chief mil. justice Homestead AFB, Fla., 1984-88; chief civil law Lowry AFB, Colo., 1988—; legal advisor Armed Forces Disciplinary Control Bd., Child and Family Advocacy Council USAF, Homestead AFB, 1984-88. Vol. Muscular Dystrophy Assn., Colorado Springs, 1978-81; contbr. Ellis Island Resoration Program, Homestead AFB, 1985-88; active Nat. Mus. Women in Arts, Nat. Air and Space Mus.; officer in charge Lowry Silver and Blue Choir. Mem. ABA, Judge Adv. Assn., Edn. Profl. Assn., Ohio Bar Assn., Fed. Bar Assn., Colo. Bar Assn., Am. Bus. Women's Assn. (chmn. audit com. Homestead charter chpt., hist. com. 1987, pres. Visions charter chpt. 1990-91, Top 10 Bus. Women 1987, Woman of Yr. 1987), Phi Beta Kappa, Kappa Delta Pi. Home: 378 Florence Aurora CO 80010 Office: USAF LTTC/JA Lowry AFB CO 80230-5000

SEYBOLD, ADELE NEELY, former Democratic national committeewoman, civic worker; b. Comanche, Tex., Nov. 11, 1919; d. Eugene Gentry and Nell (Orand) Neely; B.A., U. Tex., 1940; tchrs. certificate U. Tex., 1940; m. Eugene Murphy Locke, Oct. 27, 1941; children—Aimee Locke Jacoble, John, Tom; m. 2d, William Dempsey Seybold, 1977. State chmn. women's activities Tex. gov.'s primary campaign, 1964; mem. Democratic Nat. Com., 1964-66, exec. com., 1964-66. Mem. hospitality bd. Met. Opera, Dallas, 1962-66, 69-70; mem. exec. com. Greater Dallas Council Chs., 1964-66; area chmn. Dallas Mental Health Assn., 1964; bd. dirs. women's group Dallas Council of World Affairs, 1970—, Bishop Mason Retreat and Conf. Center; hon. chmn. pub. edn. Tex. div. Am. Cancer Soc., also bd. dirs.; bd. dirs., sec. to bd. visitors U. Tex. System Cancer Center, M.D. Anderson Hosp. and Tumor Inst.; mem. found. adv. council Coll. Liberal Arts, U. Tex., Austin; mem. exec. com. chancellor's council U. Tex. Timberlawn Found.; mem. Fine Arts Commn., U.S. Dept. State. Mem. Daus. Republic Tex. (asso.), Ashbel Lit. Soc., Jr. League, Mus. Fine Arts, Young Women of the Arts, Dallas County Heritage Soc. (dir.), Dallas Jr. Assembly (dir. 1961-64). Soc. for Abandoned and Neglected Children, Mortar Bd., Phi Beta Kappa, Alpha Lambda Delta, Sigma Delta Pi, Phi Eta Sigma, Pi Lambda Theta, Pi Beta Phi. Episcopalian (edn. guild leader). Clubs: Dallas Country, Dallas Woman's; River Oaks Country; Houston, Houston City. Home: 3805 McFarlin Blvd Dallas TX 75205

SEYFERT, THERESA, information systems executive; b. Balt., Dec. 17, 1956; d. Lawrence and Mary R. (Walton) Ingiosi Sr.; m. William L. Seyfert, Nov. 23, 1985; children: Jennifer P. Albertson, William A. Albertson. Certificate data processing, County Vocat. Tech. Sch., Aston, Pa., 1973. Head teller, asst. proof supr. 1st Nat. Bank of Wilmington, Del.; data processing mgr. First Fed. Savings Bank; computer systems mgr. PUMH. Named Outstanding Student County Vocat. Tech., 1973; recipient Tech. Achievment Burroughs award, Alton Tng. Edn. Ctrs. Mem. NAFE, Nat. Assn. Bus. Women, AIB. Home: 901 Philadelphia Pike Wilmington DE 19809

SEYFFARTH, LINDA JEAN WILCOX, corporate executive, controller; b. Montour Falls, N.Y., May 10, 1948; d. Maurice Roscoe and Theodora (Van Tassell) Wilcox; m. Richard Seyffarth, May 8, 1971 (div. Apr. 1987); 1 child, Kristin. BA magna cum laude, Syracuse (N.Y.) U., 1970; MBA with honors, NYU, 1977. Programmer Prudential Ins. Co., Newark, 1970-73; with Hoffmann-La Roche Inc., Nutley, N.J., 1973—, corp. controller, 1985-88, v.p., controller, 1989—. Bd. dirs., treas. St. Barnabas Burn Found., West Orange, N.J. Mem. Fin. Execs. Inst., Nat. Assn. Accts., Phi Beta Kappa, Beta Gamma Sigma. Office: Hoffmann-LaRoche Inc 340 Kingsland St Nutley NJ 07110

SEYMOUR, JANE, actress; b. Hillingdon, Middlesex, Eng., Feb. 15, 1951; came to U.S., 1976; d. John Benjamin and Mieke Frankenberg; m. David Flynn, July 18, 1981; 2 children. Student, Arts Ednl. Sch., London. Appeared in films Oh What A Lovely War, 1968, The Only Way, 1968, Young Winston, 1969, Live and Let Die, 1971, Sinbad and the Eye of the Tiger, 1973, Somewhere in Time, 1979, Oh Heavenly Dog, 1979, Lassiter, 1984, Head Office, Scarlet Pimpernel, Haunting Passion, Dark Mirror, Obsessed with a Married Woman, Killer on Board, The Tunnel, 1988, The French Revolution; TV films include Frankenstein, The True Story, 1972, Captains and The Kings, 1976 (Emmy nomination), 7th Avenue, 1976, The Awakening Land, 1977, The Four Feathers, 1977, Battlestar Galactica, Dallas Cowboy Cheerleaders, 1979, Our Mutual Friend, PBS, Eng., 1975, Jamaica Inn, 1982, Sun Also Rises, 1984, Crossings, 1986, Keys to Freedom, Angel of Death, 1990; Broadway appearances include Amadeus, 1980-81; TV mini-series include East of Eden, 1980, The Richest Man in the World, 1988 (Emmy award), The Woman He Loved, 1988, Jack the Ripper, 1988, War and Remembrance, 1988, 89; host PBS documentary, Japan, 1988. Named Hon. Citizen of Ill., Gov. Thompson, 1977. Mem. Screen Actors Guild, AFTRA, Actors Equity, Brit. Equity. Office: Barrett Benson McCartt & Weston 10390 Santa Monica Blvd Ste 310 Los Angeles CA 90025*

SEYMOUR, JOSEPHINE EVANS, retired music educator, church musician; b. Carthage, Mo., Jan. 22, 1912; d. Walter Mitchell and Genevieve (Clark) Evans; m. Otto Cleveland Seymour, Nov. 15, 1938 (dec. 1971); children: Thomas Ewans, Elizabeth Jayne Seymour. BA, Mo. Valley Coll., 1933, MusB, 1933. Music tchr. R-8 Schs., Joplin, Mo., 1960-76; sec., educator Christian studies Presbyn. Ch. U.S.A., Joplin, 1933-39, dir. choirs, 1950-60; organist Presbyn. Ch. U.S.A., Carthage, 1976—. Pres. bd. dirs. YWCA, Joplin, 1942-44; active Carver Nursery Bd., Joplin, 1950; recording sec. adv. bd. Salvation Army, Joplin, 1979-80; sec. Carthage Pub. Libr. Bd., 1983-89. Mem. AAUW (pres. Joplin chpt. 1946-49, pres. Mo. State div. 1957-59, woman of distinction 1988), Mo. State Tchrs. Assn., Mo. Ret. Tchrs. Assn., PEO Sisterhood (pres. 1944-46. 81-83), Cheretė Study Club (pres. 1957-58, 78-79), Delta Kappa Gamma (Gamma chpt. pres. 1972-74). Republican.

SEYMOUR, MARY FRANCES, lawyer; b. Durand, Wis., Oct. 20, 1948; d. Marshall Willard and Alice Roberta (Smith) Thompson; m. Marshall Warren Seymour, June 6, 1970; 1 foster child, Nghia Pham. BS, U. Wis., LaCrosse, 1970; JD, William Mitchell Coll., 1979. Bar: Minn. 1979, U.S. Dist. Ct. Minn. 1979, U.S. Ct. Appeals (8th cir.) 1979, U.S. Supreme Ct. 1986. With Cochrane and Bresnahan, P.A., St. Paul, 1979—. Mem. Assn. Trial Lawyers Am., Minn. Bar Assn., Ramsey County Bar Assn., Minn. Trial Lawyers Assn. Office: Cochrane & Bresnahan PA 24 E Fourth St Saint Paul MN 55101

SEYMOUR, MARY POWELL, state senator; b. Raleigh, N.C., Apr. 12, 1922; d. Robert C. and Annie (Seymour) Powell; m. Hubert Elmo Seymour, Feb. 3, 1945; children: Hubert Seymour III, Robert John. AA, Peace Coll., Raleigh, 1941; postgrad., Harvard U., 1946-47, U. Mich., 1949-50. Lic. real estate broker. Legal sec., ct. reporter; sec. to dean Harvard U. Grad. Sch. Bus.; adminstnr. med. supply ORD, Greensboro; sec., claims adjustor Social Security; rep. N.C. Gen. Assembly, 1976-84, senator, 1987-88, re-elected 1990; govtl. cons., lobbyist N.C. R.R. Assn., N.C. Bankers Assn., 1985-86; mayor pro tempore City of Greensboro, N.C., 1973-75; mem. Greensboro City Council, 1967-75. Active Tar Heel Triad Girls Scout Council Inc., Hayes Taylor YMCA, N.C. Arts Council, N.C. Parks and Recreation Council, United Arts Council; bd. visitors Peace Coll.; mem. N.C. Inst. Medicine, N.C. Task Force Pub Radio Interconnection, N.C. Bd. Nat. Conf. Ins. Legis., Nat. Conf. State Legis. Telecommunications Com., transp. adv. council, N.C. law-related edn. bd., women and econ. devel. bd. Named Disting. Alumna, Peace Coll., Woman of Yr., Quota Club; recipient Disting. Service award YWCA, Legis. award N.C. Bar Assn., Disting. Service award N.C. Pub. Health, Good Sam award for Legislation for Hearing Impaired, Community Service award Bennett Coll., Legis. award N.C. Recreation and Parks, 1984, Eleanor Roosevelt award, Bryant Citizenship award, Dolley Madison award. Mem. Carolina Soc. Assn. Execs., Women's Profl. Forum, Nat. Order Women Legislators, U.S. Power Squadron. Clubs: O. Henry Womans, Greensboro Council of Garden, Dem. Women, Belews Creek Sailing. Address: 1105 Pender Ln Greensboro NC 27408*

SEYMOUR, PEARL M., retired psychologist; b. St. Louis, Oct. 22, 1929; d. Carl S. and Leland Pearl (Disbrow) S. AB, Hunter Coll., 1969; MS, George Williams Coll., 1972. Psychologist III Elgin Mental Health Ctr., Elgin, Ill., 1971-89; ret., 1989. Mem. Am. Orthopsychiat. Assn., Phi Beta Kappa. Republican. Epsicopalian.

SEYMOUR, STEPHANIE KULP, federal judge; b. Battle Creek, Mich., Oct. 16, 1940; d. Francis Bruce and Frances Cecelia (Bria) Kulp; m. R. Thomas Seymour, June 10, 1972; children: Bart, Bria, Sara, Anna. B.A. magna cum laude, Smith Coll., 1962; J.D., Harvard U., 1965. Bar: Okla. 1965. Practiced in Boston, 1965-66, practiced in Tulsa, 1966-67, 71-79, practiced in Houston, 1968-69; assoc. firm Doerner, Stuart, Saunders, Daniel & Anderson, Tulsa, 1971-75; ptnr. firm Doerner, Stuart, Saunders, Daniel & Anderson, 1975-79; judge U.S. Ct. Appeals 10th Circuit, Tulsa, 1979—; assoc. bar examiner Okla. Bar Assn., 1973-79; trustee Tulsa County Law Library, 1977-78; mem. U.S. Jud. Conf. Com. Defender Svcs., 1985—, chmn., 1987—. Mem. various task forces Tulsa Human Rights Commn., 1972-76, legal adv. panel Tulsa Task Force Battered Women, 1971-77. Mem. Am. Bar Assn., Okla. Bar Assn., Tulsa County Bar Assn., Phi Beta Kappa. Office: US Ct Appeals 4562 US Courthouse 333 W 4th St Tulsa OK 74103

SGAMBATI, CATHERINE JANE, owner, corporate officer; b. Fayetteville, Tenn., Aug. 24, 1959; d. Amos Lionel and JoAnne (Owen) White; m. Richard C. Sgambati, Apr. 17, 1982; 1 child, Brooke Elizabeth. BS, Mid. Tenn. State U., 1981. Sales exec. Cumberland Mag., Nashville, 1978-79; owner Atlantis Pools & Spas, Nashville, 1979—. Contbr. articles to mags. and newspapers. Mem. Bravo/Tenn. Performing Arts, Nashville, 1990, Nashville Symphony Supporters, 1990. Mem. Nat. Spa & Pool Inst. (cons. 1990), Better Bus. Bur., Home Builders Assn., C. of C. Office: Atlantis Pools & Spas 2700 Murfreesboro Rd Antioch TN 37013

SHABBIR, MAHNAZ MEHDI, healthcare marketing manager; b. Phila., Apr. 6, 1959; d. Mir Inayeth and Meher (Mehdi) Ali Khan; m. S. Farrukh Shabbir, June 29,1979; children: S. Ali, S. Adil. BBA, U. Mo., 1982, MBA, 1984. Resident administrv. Bapt. Med. Ctr., Kansas City, 1983-84; with gerontology practicum Mid-Am. Regional Coun., Kansas City, 1984; mkt. rsch. analyst St. Joseph Health Ctr., Kansas City, 1984-87; dir. mktg. and planning support svcs. Carondelet Health Corp., Kansas City, 1987—; mentor U. Mo., 1987. Fund raiser United Way, 1986-87. Mem. Am. Coll. Health Execs. (adv. council 1986—), Kansas City Regional Soc. Healthcare Planning and Mktg. (pres. 1986-87), Am. Mktg. Assn., Soc. Healthcare Planning and Mktg. Home: 13009 St Andrew Dr Kansas City MO 64145 Office: Carondelet Health Corp 1310 Carondelet St Ste 230 Kansas City MO 64114

SHABEL, KAREN LIND, printing company executive; b. East Chicago, Ind., Oct. 3, 1948; d. Earl R. Lind; m. Dennis Shabel. A.B., Ind. U., 1970. Tchr. Gen. Edn. Devel. program OEO, 1970-72; dir. consumer div. Better Bus. Bur., Chgo., 1972-77; pres. Communicate, Inc., Westchester, Ill., 1977—; mem. faculty adult continuing edn. dept. Moraine Valley Community Coll., 1974-76; speaker various colls. and univs., civic and community orgns.; arbitrator constrn. panel Am. Arbitration Assn.; editor The Oak Leaf and The InnerView newsletters. Past bd. dirs., past sec. to bd. N.Am. Family and Ednl. Resources Found.; v.p. Oakwood Homeowners Assn.; past trustee Ill. Council on Econ. Edn.; apptd. commr. Village of Westmont Recycling Commn.; v.p. Oakwood Homeowners Assn.; consumer div., adv. council Better Bus. Bur., Chgo.; past bd. dirs., v.p. local PTO Manning Sch. Dist. 201, local Luth. ch. women, DAR, La Grange, Ill.; past bd. dirs. Family Fin. Counseling Svc. Greater Chgo.; past mem. nursing and health programs com. Mid-West chpt. ARC. Mem. AAUW (sec. Oak Brook, Ill. chpt.), Soc. Consumer Affairs Profls. (founding and charter mem.), DAR (corr. sec. La Grange, Ill. chpt.). Office: Communicate Inc 10407 W Cermak Rd Westchester IL 60154

SHABLIN, LISABETH TERESA, marketing executive; b. Worcester, Mass., June 8, 1964; d. Vitte William and Teresa Veronica (Kotomski) S. BSEE summa cum laude, Worcester Poly. Inst., 1986. Market planner AT&T Network Systems, Holmdel, N.J., 1986-89; mktg. mgr. AT&T Network Systems, Purchase, N.Y., 1989—. Mem. IEEE, NAFE, Am. Mgmt. Assn., Tau Beta Pi. Democrat. Roman Catholic. Office: AT&T Network Systems 2 Manhattanville Rd Purchase NY 10577

SHACKELFORD, LAUREL, editor, writer; b. New Brunswick, N.J., Nov. 19, 1946; d. James Murdoch and Laura (Stevens) S.; m. Donald R. Anderson, June 18, 1971. Student Rutgers U., 1964, Upsala Coll., 1964-66; A.B., U. N.C., 1968. Writer Civil Rights Digest, Washington, 1968-69; reporter Louisville Times, 1969-73, 76-79, city editor, 1982-86; editorial writer Courier Jour., 1986—; editor Appalachian Oral History, Pippa Passes, Ky., 1973-75; asst. city editor Courier Jour., Louisville, 1979-82. Contbr. articles to various publs.; editor: Our Appalachia: An Oral History (Weatherford award 1972), 1971. Nieman fellow Harvard U., 1981. Office: Louisville Courier-Jour 525 W Broadway Louisville KY 40202

SHACKELFORD, LOTTIE HOLT, civic worker, former mayor; b. Pulaski County, Ark., Apr. 30, 1941; d. Curtis and Bernice Linzy Holt; m. Calvin H. Shackelford Jr. (div.); children: Russell, Karla, Karen. BS, Philander Smith Coll., 1979, LHD (hon.), 1988; student, Harvard U., 1983, U. Ark., Little Rock; LHD (hon.), Shorter Coll., 1987. City dir. City of Little Rock, 1978—, mayor, 1987-89; del. Italian Econ. Trade Mission, 1987, U.S.-Soviet Women's Wilderness Dialogue, USSR, 1987; panelist Harvard U. Inst. Polits. Pub. Affairs Forum, 1987; bd. dirs. Little Rock Advt. and Promotion, Econ. Opportunity Agy., Little Rock Job Corps, Elizabeth Mitchell's Children Ctr., Links, Inc.; adv. com. Ark. Vocat. and Tech. Edn., Sta. KARK-TV; speaker in field. Del., mem. platform com. Dem. Nat. Conv., 1984; vice chmn. Dem. Nat. Com.; mem. Dem. Policy Commn.; bd. dirs. Nat. League Cities, Ark. Mcpl. League, Ark. Women's Polit. Coun., Urban League, ARC, Ark. PTA, YWCA; bd. dirs. So. Regional Coun., pres., 1988-90; regional bd. dirs. Nat. Black Caucus Local Elected Ofcls., 1979—; youth dir. St. Peter's Bapt. Ch., 1969-73; pres. Little Rock PTA Coun., 1973; coord. human and civil rights workshops, 1975-77, also others. Recipient Women of Style award Pulaski County Council, 1987. Mem. Nat. Assn. State Dem. Chairmen (sec.), Links, Delta Sigma Theta, Gamma Phi Delta, Alpha Kappa Mu. Office: 500 W Markham St Little Rock AR 72201*

SHACKELFORD, MARY JO, personnel executive; b. Zanesville, Ohio, Mar. 7, 1949; d. Moneer and Nellie Rita Hatem; m. Douglas A. Shackelford, Dec. 14, 1968; 1 child, Joseph. BA, Ohio Dominican Coll., 1977. Sales coordinator Roach, Inc., Columbus. Ohio, 1977-78; instr. Milw. Stratten Coll., 1978-81; franchise owner Norrell Corp., Atlanta, 1981-84, dist. mgr., 1984-87; regional mgr. Word Processors Personnel Inc., Palo Alto, Calif., 1987—; mem. franchise adv. bd. Norrell Services, Inc., Atlanta, 1983-84, ops. task force, 1984—, mem. Pres.'s Club, 1985-86. Bd. dirs women's aux. St. Francis CAAC, Milw., 1978-81, v.p. 1980-81; bd. dirs. St. Vincent's Children's Ctr., Columbus, Ohio, 1976-78; vol. Spl. Olympics, West Chester, Pa.; mem. adv. bd. Lima Tech. Ohio State U., 1982-84. Mem. Bus. and Profl. Women, Nat. Assn. Female Execs., Nat. Mgmt. Assn. (chair arrangements 1981-84). Democrat. Roman Catholic. Home: 886 Westtown Rd West Chester PA 19382 Office: Word Processors Personnel 490 S California Ave Palo Alto CA 94306

SHACKLETON, SUZANNE M., librarian; b. Quincy, Ill., Sept. 5, 1950; d. Alvin Louis and Marie Caroline (Juette) S. Student, Quincy Coll., Ill., 1970; BA, Ill. State U., Normal, 1972; MLS, U. Ill., Champaign, 1973. Teaching Cert. Libr. Notre Dame High Sch., Quincy, Ill., 1973-74, Ill. Environ. Protection Agy., Springfield, 1974-76, Ill. Vocational Curriculum Center, Springfield, 1976--. Mem. Ill. Libr. Assn., Spl. Librs. Assn., Phi Alpha Theta. Office: Illinois Vocat Curriculum Sangamon State U Springfield IL 62794-9243

SHADEROWFSKY, EVA MARIA, photographer, writer; b. Prague, Czechoslovakia, May 20, 1938; came to U.S., 1940; d. Felix Resek and Gertrude (Telatko) Frank; children: Tom, Paul. Student, Oberlin Coll., 1955-56; BA, Barnard Coll., 1960. Exhibited in one-person shows at The Photo Show Internat, N.Y., 1974-86, The Left Bank Gallery, Wellfleet, Mass., 1974, Art Ctr. No. N.J., Tenafly, 1975, The Colorfax Galleries, Washington, Bethesda, Balt., 1978, Soho Photo, N.Y., 1974, 80, Esta Robinson Gallery, 1982, Fairleigh Dickinson U., 1983, Donnell Libr., N.Y.C., 1985, Piermont (N.Y.) Libr., 1987, The Turning Point, Piermont, N.Y., 1988, Hopper House, Nyack, N.Y., 1989; group shows include Soho Photo Gallery, N.Y., 1974, Fashion Inst. Tech., N.Y.C., 1975, Portland (Maine) Mus. Art, 1977, Maine Photog. Workshop, Rockport, 1978, Marcuse Pfeifer, N.Y., 1977, 78, Chrysler Mus., Norfol,, Va., 1978, Exposure Gallery Wellfleet, 1978, 79, The Art Ctr. No. N.J., Tenafly, 1980, Neuberger Mus., Purchase, N.Y., 1982, Hudson River Mus., 1982, Foto, N.Y., 1982, Barnard Coll., N.Y.C., 1983, Rockland Ctr. for Arts, 1978, 89, Print Club, Phila., 1988; represented in collections at Bklyn. Mus., Portland (Maine) Mus. Art, Met. Mus. Art, N.Y.C.; author and photographer (book) Suburban Portraits, 1977; photographer Women in Transition, 1975; contbr. story to anthology Touching Fire, 1989; contbr. photography to Camera 35 mag. Recipient Photography award Rockland Ctr. for Arts, 1978, Gt. Am. Photo Contest, 1981, Demarais Press, 1982, Harrison Art Coun., SUNY-Purchase, 1982, The Cape Codder, 1976, 79-82. Mem. NOW, Greenpeace, Am. Assn. Ret. Persons. Home and Office: 284 Maple Rd Valley Cottage NY 10989

SHADID, NANAY LAPORTE, dentist, educator; b. Enid, Okla., May 29, 1959; d. W. Dale and Jeannine (Puyear) L.; m. Scot R. Shadid, Aug. 6, 1983; children: Alex T., Natalie Anne. BS, Okla. State U., 1982; DDS, U. Okla., Oklahoma City, 1985. Pvt. practice, Shawnee, Okla., 1985—; instr. dentistry U. Okla., 1985—. Mem. ADA, Okla. Dental Assn. (ho. of dels. 1987-90), Pottowatomie County Dental Assn. (pres. 1988-90). Methodist. Home: 4310 N Aydelotte Shawnee OK 74801 Office: 400 W MacArthur St Shawnee OK 74801

SHADLE, SUSAN BETH, security company executive; b. Pottsville, Pa., July 6, 1957; d. Irvin Elias and Louise Hilman (Reise) S. B.S., Pa. State U.-Middletown, 1979. Security supr. Marriott Hotel, Harrisburg, Pa., 1980-81; officer Paxtang Police Dept., Harrisburg, 1980-81; press attendant AMP Inc., Tower City, Pa., 1981; officer U.S. Secret Service, Washington, 1981-82; ops. supr. MVM Inc, Washington, 1982-86; mgr. in charge Boston br., Guardsmark, Inc., Memphis, 1987-89; resident mgr. mass dept. pub. safety, 1984-89; pres. Intelligent Woman Esquire, Randolph, Mass., 1989—; security specialist Bank of Boston, 1990—. Mem. NAFE, Am. Soc. Indsl. Security. Republican. Home: 26 Chestnut W Randolph MA 02368 Office: 28 S Main St Ste 176 Randolph MA 02368

SHADLEY, MERI LOUISE, family therapist, organizational consultant; b. Kansas City, Mo., Feb. 1, 1948; d. George Albert and Virginia Rose (Hawkins) Little S. B.S. in Sociology, S.W. Mo. U., 1970; M.A. in Psychology, U. Nev., 1972; postgrad. Saybrook Inst., 1980—. Cert. marriage and family therapist, Nev.; cert. substance abuse counselor/adminstr., Nev. Grad. asst. to student union and psychology dept. U. Nev.-Las Vegas, 1970-72; asst. dir., counselor Operation Bridge/Crisis Hotline, Las Vegas, 1972-73; dir., counselor Nike House, Las Vegas, 1973-76; dir. family support services Nev. Mental Health Inst., Reno, 1976-79, dir. clin. support services, 1979-80, chmn. human rights com., 1978-80; pvt. practice marriage and family therapy, Reno, 1980—; founder, pres. bd. Oikos Inc., Reno, 1977-81; chmn. bd. New Employment Opportunities Nev., Reno, 1979-81; cons., trainer Com. to Aid Abused Women, Reno, 1980-84, mem. adv. bd., 1981-86. Co-author: Substance Abuse Confidentiality Course, 1978; A Kalaidoscope of Family Systems, 1981. Mem. Am. Assn. Marriage and Family Therapy, Am. Psychol. Assn., Family Mediators Assn., Women's Polit. Caucus. Democrat. Co-developer, trainer family therapy tng. program for community service workers, 1979. Office: 1005 Forest St Reno NV 89509

SHADOAN, SHELLEY ANN, broadcasting executive; b. Sheridan, Wyo., June 9, 1964; d. George Gary Shadoan and Lynn Anne (Sugden) Lieder. AA in Interior Design, Brooks Coll., 1987; BS, U. Redlands, 1989; MBA, Pepperdine U., 1990. Art dir. intern NBC, Burbank, Calif., 1987; adminstrv. asst. CBS, L.A., 1987-88, broadcast supr., 1988-89, program coord., 1989—. Assoc. Big Sisters of Am., L.A., 1990. Named to Alpha Beta Gamma, 1987. Mem. NAFE, Women in Film. Republican. Office: CBS 7800 Beverly Blvd Los Angeles CA 90036

SHAER, PATRICIA ANN BLACHA, freelance reporter, writer; b. Hartford, Conn., Sept. 12, 1941; d. Antoni and Mary (Tricka) Blacha; m. Robert Noel Shaer, Aug. 10, 1963; children: Kathryn Ann, Deborah Marie. BA, Albertus Magnus Coll., 1963; postgrad., Syracuse U., 1972, Middletown (Ohio) Fine Arts Ctr., 1974-79, Rice U., 1986. Asst. underwriter Travelers Ins. Co., Hartford, 1963-64; tchr. various schs., Conn. and Ohio, 1963-75; reporter, photographer Monroe (Ohio) Jour., 1976-77; arts reporter WGUC-FM, Cin., 1982-83; news dir. WPFB-AM/FM, Middletown, 1983-85; news anchor, reporter WRMZ-FM/WMNI-AM, Columbus, Ohio, 1985; arts reporter KUHF-FM, Houston, 1987-90; freelance reporter, writer Houston, 1990—; cons. La. State U. Communications Dept., Baton Rouge, 1989; active S.W. Ohio Speakers Bur.; pub. rels. coord. Very Spl. Arts, Houston, 1990—. Pres. Lemon-Monroe High Sch. Booster Assn., 1979-83; dir. art show Apple Butter Festival, Monroe, 1979-80; dir., newsletter editor Sand Creek Community Assn., 1987—. Mem. AAUW (v.p. programs 1990—), Internat. Assn. Bus. Communicators, Women in Communications (Houston chpt. v.p. membership 1990—, co-chmn. MATRIX competition 1990, sec. 1989), Soc. Profl. Journalists, Beta Sigma Phi (numerous offices N.Y., Ohio). Home: 2723 Cedarville Dr Kingwood TX 77345

SHAEVITZ, MARJORIE HANSEN, psychotherapist; b. Fresno, Calif., May 22, 1943; d. Robert and Evelyn (Beck) Hansen; m. Morton H. Shaevitz, Mar. 11, 1972; children: Geoffrey, Marejka. BA, Fresno State Coll., 1964; MA, Stanford U., 1967. Resident asst Lagunita Ct., Stanford U., Stanford, Calif., 1965-67; Orientation Officer East-West Ctr., Honolulu, Hawaii, 1967-68; dean student's staff mem. Stanford U., Stanford, Calif., 1968-70; instr. Disadvantaged Employee Devel. Program, U. Calif., San Diego, 1970; coord. Adult Counseling Svcs., U. Calif., San Diego, 1971-78; dir. Inst. Family and Work Rels., La Jolla, Calif., 1977—; dir. Programs for Mental Health Profls., La Jolla, Calif., 1973-78; cons. Coll. Hosp. Women's Ctr., Costa Mesa, Calif., 1990. Bd. dirs. La Jolla (Calif.) Chamber Orchestra; bd. trustees Charter 100, La Jolla, Calif., La Jolla (Calif.) Country Day School, adv. com. Pete Wilson for Gov. Campaign; Gov. appointee Calif. Com. on Status Women, Sacramento, 1983—. Named Woman of Tribute Calif. Women in Govt., 1989. Mem. The Ireland Report (editorial bd.), La Jolla, Calif., Scripps Meml. Hosp. (editorial bd., newsletter), La Jolla, Calif., Am. Psychol. Assn., Calif. Assn. Marriage and Family Counselors. Republican. Office: Inst Family and Work Rels 1020 Prospect Ste 400 La Jolla CA 92037

SHAFER, JOHANNA MARIE, social worker, consultant; b. Bridgeport, Conn., July 6, 1945; d. Leo Charles and Astrid (Lindgren) Bauby; m. Michael Gales Shafer, June 17, 1967; children: Reuben, Gail. BA, Bard Coll., 1967; cert. in counseling, Found. for Religion & Mental Health, 1983; MSW, SUNY, Albany, 1988. Lic. social worker, N.Y. Tchr. Martin Luther King Sch., New Haven, 1967-69; founder, dir. St. John's Pre-Sch., South Salem, N.Y., 1975-85; co-dir. Vista House Transitional Residence, Lewisboro, N.Y., 1973-85; coord. teen suicide prevention program Albany County Dept. Mental Health, 1988—; presenter Parsons Sage Inst., Albany, 1989; guest lectr. SUNY, Albany, 1989, Coll. of St. Rose, Albany, 1989, Russell Sage, Troy, N.Y., 1989. Mem. Lewisboro Hist. Soc., South Salem, 1975-81, Watervliet (N.Y.) Community Coun., 1990—, AIDS Coun. of Northeastern N.Y., Albany, 1986-89. Mem. NASW. Office: Albany County Dept Mental Health 845 Central Ave Albany NY 12206-1504

SHAFER, LINDA ANN, real estate sales executive; b. Berwyn, Ill., Sept. 6, 1947; d. Frank and Irene (Smid) Java; m. Warren C. Shafer, Aug. 27, 1947; children: Darrick C., Tiana M. BS, U. Ill., 1969. Media buyer Davis, Kirby and Gray Advt., Chgo., 1969-71; media dir. Vollbrecht Caver Advt., Chgo., 1971-74; franchising Omnicon Cable, Lake Forest, Ill., 1979-81; sales assoc., dir. human resources Century 21 Pride Realty, New Lenox, Ill., 1985-89; sales exec., mgr. corp. relocation Am. Better Homes and Gardens, New Lenox, 1989—. V.p., Parent Tchr. Orgn., New Lenox Dist. 122, 1984-86, bd. mem., 1982-83. Recipient Presidents Club award Will County Bd.of Realtors, 1986, 1987, 1988. Mem. Will County Bd. Realtors, Southwest Suburban Bd. Realtors, New Lenox Lioness Club (sec. 1989—), Alpha Gamma Delta, Alpha Gamma Delta Northwest Suburban Alumnae Club. Office: Am Better Homes and Gardens 205 W Maple New Lenox IL 60451

SHAFER, LORRAINE PAT, title company executive, director; b. Shreveport, La., May 19, 1958; d. Lawrence T. Walker and Catherine E. (Marksberry) Michael. Student, Ariz. State U., Tempe, 1982-84. From receptionist to asst. underwriter Marlar, Johnson & Allen Ins. Agy., Phoenix, 1977-81; ins. agt. Ins. West, Inc., Phoenix, 1981-83, Alliance Ins. Agy., Phoenix, 1983-84, Anderson, Reeve & Assocs., Scottsdale, Ariz., 1984-86;

employee benefits adminstr. Fidelity Nat. Title Ins. Co., Scottsdale, 1986-89; v.p., dir. human resources South Coast Title Co., Santa Ana, Calif., 1989—; arbitrator Maricopa County Arbitration Bd., Phoenix, 1988-89; health ins. advisor Discovery Rsch., Irvine, Calif., 1989—. Vol. Maricopa County Crisis Nursery, Phoenix, 1988-89, Coaltion Against Illiteracy, Phoenix, 1989. Democrat.

SHAFER, ROBERTA W. CROW, human resources executive, venture capital consultant; b. Long View, Tex., Oct. 31, 1950; d. George Clifford and Marie (Mitchell) C.; m. Gary Stuart Shafer, July 23, 1988. Student U. Ala., 1968-70; A.A.S. in Fine Arts-Drama, Music, Am. Musical & Dramatic Acad., N.Y.C., 1972. Cert. personnel cons., Nat. Assn. Personnel Cons. Exec. trainee/retail merchandising and mgmt. Bergdorf-Goodman, N.Y.C.; account exec., cons. Lawrence Agy., N.Y.C., 1974-77; store mgr., dist. sales mgr. Career House, Bensalem, Pa. and N.Y.C., 1977-82; dir. research and recruting Retail Recruiters, Internat., N.Y.C., 1982-83; dir. exec. search/retail and mfg. Lloyd Cons., Inc., N.Y.C. and Chgo., 1983-85; dir. human resources R.P. McCoy Apparel, Ltd. dba Labels for Less, N.Y.C., 1985-87; pvt. practice venture capital and human resources consulting, N.Y.C., 1985—; ind. cons. Donaldson, Lufkin & Jenrette, N.Y.C., 1985; guest lectr. Lab. Inst. Tech., N.Y.C., 1985—; v.p. Ann H. Tanners Co., N.Y.C., 1988—; pres. Crow-Shafer Assocs., N.Y.C., 1990—. Mem. Nat. Assn. Female Execs., Nat. Assn. Personnel Cons., Am. Mgmt. Assn. Democrat. Episcopalian. Avocations: attending theatre and concerts, internat. traveling, study of foreign cultures and languages, collecting antiques, vintage collectibles. Home: 1365 York Ave Apt 26G New York NY 10021 Office: Ann H Tanners Inc 30 E 42d St New York NY 10017

SHAFF, BEVERLY GERARD, educational administrator; b. Oak Park, Ill., Aug. 16, 1925; d. Carl Tanner and Mary Frances (Gerard) Wilson; m. Maurice A. Shaff, Jr., Dec. 20, 1951 (dec. July 1967); children: Carol Maureen, David Gerard, Mark Albert. MA, U. Ill., 1951; postgrad., Colo. Coll., Lewis and Clark Coll., Portland State U. Tchr. Haley Sch., Berwyn, Ill., 1948-51; assoc. prof. English, Huntingdon Coll., Montgomery, Ala., 1961-62; tchr. English, William Palmer High Sch., Colorado Springs, Colo., 1964-67, 72-76, dir., 1967-72; tchr. English, Burns (Oreg.) High Sch., 1976-78; tchr. English as 2d lang. Multnomah County Ednl. Svc. Dist., Portland, Oreg., 1979-85; coord. gen. studies Portland Jewish Acad., 1984—. Del. Colorado Springs Dem. Com., 1968, 72; active Rainbow Coalition, Portland. Mem. Nat. Assn. Admnstrs., Nat. Assn. Schs. and Colls., Nat. Coun. Tchrs. Math., Nat. Coun. Tchrs. English. Home: 4676 SW Comus Pl Portland OR 97219 Office: Portland Jewish Acad 6651 SW Capitol Hwy Portland OR 97219

SHAFFER, ANITA MOHRLAND, educator, counselor; b. Racine, Wis., Apr. 5, 1939; d. Milton Arthur and Gudrun Amanda (Sundvoll) Stoffel; m. Ronald Dean Williams, June 24, 1987. BS magna cum laude, U. Wis.-Madison, 1961; MEd, U. Wash., 1966; postgrad. Ariz. State U., 1971-76. Cert. in elem. edn., social sci. secondary edn., spl edn., Tex., Ariz.; lic. profl. counselor, Tex.; diplomate Internat. Acad. Behavioral Medicine, Counseling and Psychotherapy. Tchr. Racine Unified Dist. 1, 1961-63, Edmonds Sch. Dist. 15, Alderwood Manor, Wash., 1963-70; tchr. Ariz. Dept. Corrections, Phoenix, 1971-77; tchr. spl. edn. Pasadena Ind. Sch. Dist. (Tex.); 1977-78, spl. edn. counselor, 1978—. Mem. Am. Assn. Counseling and Devel., Am. Mental Health Counselors Assn., Am. Sch. Counselor Assn., Tex. Assn. Counseling and Devel., AAUW, NAFE, Mus. Fine Arts Houston (patron), Beta Sigma Phi, Pi Lambda Theta. Home: 260 El Dorado Blvd H 801 Webster TX 77598 Office: Pasadena Ind Sch Dist Spl Svcs 1515 Cherrybrook Pasadena TX 77502

SHAFFER, AUDREY JEANNE, medical records administrator, educator; b. Hutchinson, Minn., Nov. 24, 1929; d. Floyd R. and Edna C. (Seppman) Kleiman; m. Frank L. Shaffer, July 15, 1948; 1 child, Cynthia Louise Shaffer Wilkinson. BS, Loma Linda U., 1973; MA, Central Mich. U., 1982. Registered records adminstr. Med. records clk. San Bernardino County Hosp., Calif., 1948-50; radiology receptionist White Meml. Med. Ctr., Los Angeles, 1950-52; med. records clk. Portland Adventist Hosp., Oreg., 1952-53; med. record mgr. Tempe Community Hosp., Ariz., 1953-54; clin. faculty Loma Linda U., Calif., 1975—; dir. med. info. services Corona Community Hosp., Calif., 1973-89; med. records cons. Calif., Utah, Fla. and Philippines Pilot, 1981—, med. asst. Liga Internat., Mex., 1964-68; chmn. Corona Blood Bank, 1957-68; chmn. vols. Corona Community Hosp. Aux., 1965-68; archaeology supr. Caesarea Expdn., Am. Schs. Oriental Research, Israel, summers 1974—. Recipient Vol. Service award Corona Community Hosp., 1968; Congeniality award Caesarea Archeol. Expdn., 1975. Mem. Loma Linda U. Med. Record Alumni (pres. 1979-81), Am. Med. Record Assn., Calif. Med. Record Assn. (mem. quality assurance com. 1980-81, pub. rels. com. 1988-89), Nat. Assn. Quality Assurance Profls., Archeol. Inst. Am., Inland Quality Assurance Network (pres. 1988). Clubs: Women's Improvement (program chmn. 1960-61), Corona Flying (sec. 1960-68) (Corona). Home: 880 Encanto Dr Corona CA 91719 Office: Corona Community Hosp 800 S Main St Corona CA 91720

SHAFFER, DOROTHY BROWNE, educator, mathematician; b. Vienna, Austria, Feb. 12, 1923; d. Hermann and Steffy (Hermann) Browne; arrived U.S., 1940; m. Lloyd Hamilton Shaffer, July 25, 1943 (dec. 1978); children: Deborah Lee, Diana Louise, Dorothy Leslie. AB, Bryn Mawr Coll., 1943; MA, Harvard U., 1945, PhD, 1962. Mathematician, MIT, Cambridge, 1945-47; tchg. fellow, research asso., Harvard U., Cambridge, 1947-48; asso. mathematician Cornell Aeronautical Lab, Buffalo, N.Y., 1952-56; mathematician Dunlap & Assoc., Stamford, Conn., 1958-60; lectr. grad. engrng. U. of Conn. at Stamford, 1962; prof. math Fairfield (Conn.) U., 1963—; vis. prof. Imperial Coll. Sci. and Tech., London, fall 1978, U. Md., College Park, spring 1981; vis. prof. U. Calif.-San Diego, summer 1981; vis. scholar, 1986; NSF faculty fellow IBM-T.J. Watson Research Center, Yorktown Heights, N.Y., 1979. Contbr. numerous papers in math. analysis. Mem. Am. Math. Soc., Math. Assn. of Am., Assn. for Women in Math., London Math. Soc. Home: 156 Intervale Rd Stamford CT 06905 Office: Fairfield U Dept of Math & Computer Sci Fairfield CT 06430

SHAFFER, ETHEL ARMSTRONG, volunteer speaker; b. Gloversville, N.Y., Feb. 12, 1914; d. Clarence Edwin and Edith May (Collins) Armstrong; m. Rollin Gregory Shaffer, May 31, 1941; children: Nancy Elizabeth, Gregory John. BS in Edn., Syracuse U., 1935, MS in Edn., 1938. Exec. sec. Syracuse-in-China, Syracuse, N.Y., 1935-42; women's chapel counselor Syracuse U., 1938-42, chapel adviser oriental students, social svc. coms., 1938-42; vol. speaker Luth. World Fedn., 1952—. Contbr. book revs., daily devotionals to ch. publs. Vice pres. Nutley (N.J.) Bd. Edn., 1959-68; bd. dirs. ARC, Nutley, 1968-84, pres., 1981-84; bd. dirs. social missions Luth. Synod, N.J., 1954-60, campus ministry, 1962-65; del. Nat. Luth. Ch. Conv., 1964-66; treas. residents coun. S.W. Fla. Retirement Ctr., 1990—. Mem. AAUW (pres. Nutley chpt. 1955-57, hon. life mem., fellowship named in her honor 1973), Friday Afternoon Club (pres. 1967-69), P.E.O. Democrat. Home: 900 S Tamiami Trail Apt 514 Venice FL 34285

SHAFFER, FRANCES ANNETTE, minister; b. Mauk, Ga., Sept. 22, 1946; d. Sam and Myrtice (McCrary) Jenkins; m. Thomas Shaffer, Apr. 26, 1976. Lic. practical nurse, Columbus (Ga.) Vocat. Tech., 1971; certificate, Wash. Bible Coll., Lanham, Md., 1975, Patricia Stevens Coll., Washington, 1976; BA in Rehab. Counseling, Faith Coll., 1978. Ordained Elder African Meth. Episcopal Ch., 1977. Resource specialist Taylor County Bd. of Edn., Butler, Ga., 1969-73; family svc. counselor Atlanta Housing Authority, 1973-75; records supr. Assn. of Am. Med. Colls., Washington, 1975; dir. Middle Flint Coun. on Aging, Albany, Ga., 1977-78, Eviron. Protection Program, Albany, 1978-83; pastor African Meth. Episc. Ch., Atlanta, 1980—; coord. first Internat. Women in Ministry Seminar of African Meth. Episcopal Ch., Turner Theol. Seminary, Atlanta; first female to deliver annual sermon in the Atlanta N. Georgia Annual Conf. of African Meth. Episcopal Ch. Leader Nat. Girl Scouts of U.S., Macon, Ga., 1964-66; bd. dirs. Sr. Citizen Bd., Butler, Ga., 1977—; mem. adv. coun. Atlanta Recreation Assn., 1989—. Mem. NAFE, NAACP, African Meth. Episcopal Ministers Alliance, Thomasville Ministers Community Rels. Alliance (sec. 1986), Smithsonian Inst., Les Jeun Bon Temps (pres. Atlanta 1979-84), Order of Eastern Star. Democrat. Home: 2723 Penwood Pl Lithonia GA 30058 Office: Mt Carmel African Meth Episcopal Ch 1140 Henry Thomas Dr SE Atlanta GA 30315

SHAFFER, GAIL S., state government official; b. Kingston, N.Y., Aug. 1, 1948; d. Robert E. and Marion (Gallagher) S. BA summa cum laude, Elmira Coll., 1970; student, U. Paris, 1968-69. Editor Sam Har Press, 1972-76; legal asst. Rahmas Law Firm, 1973-76; spl. asst. to commr. N.Y. State Environ. Conservation, 1977-79; exec. dir. N.Y. State Rural Affairs Council, 1979-80; mem. N.Y. State Assembly, 1981-83; sec. state State of N.Y., Albany, 1983—. Mem. N.Y. State Dem. Com., 1976—; chair Yonkers Emergency Fin. Control Bd., 1985—. Mem. Women Execs. in State Govt., N.Y. State Assn. Women Officeholders (pres.). Presbyterian. Office: Sec of State NY 162 Washington Ave Albany NY 12231

SHAFFER, JUDY ANN, educator, data processing professional; b. Boone, Iowa, Dec. 24, 1942; d. Vernon Sherwood and Josephine (Bean) Peterson; m. James Nelson Shaffer, Jr., Feb. 28, 1970. BS, Morningside Coll., 1965; MS, Iowa State U., 1969. Cert. tchr., Va. Tchr. math. Plaza Jr. High Sch., Virginia Beach, 1971; instr. Ivy Ind. Vocat. Tech. Coll., Ft. Wayne, Ind., 1973-74, Ind. Purdue U., Fort Wayne, 1974-76; programmer Bowmar, Fort Wayne, 1976-77; programmer analyst GTE Data Service, Fort Wayne, 1977-79, sr. programmer analyst, supr. ops. Med. Mgmt. Systems Inc., Fort Wayne, 1979-87, instr. Dept. Math. Scis., Ind., Purdue, Ft. Wayne, 1987-89; data processing mgr. Drees Perugini & Co., 1989—; instr. Star II, Purdue U., Layfayette, Ind.; mem. assoc. faculty IPFW, Fort Wayne, 1984-85. Charter mem. Ft. Wayne Area Community Band, 1979—, personnel mgr., 1979-84; mem. Ft. Wayne Women's Bur., 1977—, Career Planners, Ft. Wayne, 1985—. Mem. PEO (treas. 1973-75), Kappa Mu Epsilon. Avocations: music; model railroading; gardening.

SHAFFER, JULIET POPPER, statistics educator; b. N.Y.C., May 23, 1932; d. Abraham Louis and Harriet Estelle (Marcus) Popper; m. Harry George Shaffer, Aug. 11, 1960 (div. May 1975); children: Ronald Eric, Leonard Joseph, Tanya Elaine; m. Erich Leo Lehmann, Feb. 24, 1977. BA, Swarthmore Coll., 1953; PhD, Stanford U., 1957. Postdoctoral fellow Ind. U., Bloomington, 1957-58; SSRC research tng. fellow U. Calif., Berkeley, 1973-74, lectr. dept. stats., 1977-81, sr. lectr. dept. stats., 1981—; from. asst. prof. to prof. dept. psychology U. Kans., Lawrence, 1958-77. Stats. editor: Computer Studies in the Humanities and Verbal Behavior, 1970-74, (assoc.) Psychometrika, 1983-85; assoc. editor Jour. Ednl. Stats., 1983-85, 1990—, editor, 1986-89; contbr. articles to profl. jours. Fellow Am. Statis. Assn. (bd. dirs. 1984-86); mem. Psychometric Soc. (bd. trustees 1982-84). Office: U Calif Dept Stats Berkeley CA 94720

SHAFFER, ROBERTA IVY, law librarian; b. Oceanside, N.Y., Nov. 27, 1953; d. Joseph Ceicel and Gladys (Dellerson) Shaffer. AB in Econs., Vassar Coll., 1973; M of Librarianship, Emory U., 1975; JD, Tulane U., 1980; cert. in arts mgmt., Am. U., 1987. Bar: Tex. 1982, U.S. Dist. Ct. (so. dist.) Tex., U.S. Ct. Appeals (5th cir.), U.S. Supreme Ct. Dir. legal communications U. Houston Law Ctr., 1980-84, assoc. dir. law and tech., 1982-84; spl. asst. to law libr. Libr. of Congress, Washington, 1984-87; Fulbright sr. researcher Tel Aviv Faculty Law, 1987-88; pvt. practice cons. Washington, 1988-89; dir. devel. Washington Project for the Arts, 1989; acting libr. dir. George Washington U. Law Ctr., Washington, 1990; cons. Coca-Cola Co., Atlanta, 1975-76, Research Info. Service, Houston, 1982-84; edn. rep. Westlaw, St. Paul, 1982-83. Mem. ABA, Am. Soc. Assn. Execs., Am. Assn. Museums, Nat. Soc. Fund Raising Execs. Home: 4242 East West Hwy #1009 Chevy Chase MD 20815

SHAFFER, SARA ALENE, assistant food service director; b. Ridgway, Pa., Mar. 7, 1913; d. Mark Bennet and Clara Anna (Scott) S. BA, Allegheny Coll., 1934. Staff mem. Pa. Dept. of Pub. Assistance, Erie, 1935-42; asst. food svc. dir. Allegheny Coll., Meadville, Pa., 1942-72; food svc. dir. Centenary Jr. Coll., Hackettstown, N.J., 1944-46, Student Union DePauw U., Greencastle, 1953-55. Vol. mgr. gift shop at Wesbury United Meth. Community, 1973—. Recipient Nat. Vol. of Yr. award United Meth. Assn. Health and Welfare Ministries, Phila., 1977. Republican. Methodist. Home: 31 Park Ave Meadville PA 16335

SHAFFER, SUSAN E., insurance company executive; b. Nashville, Apr. 14, 1947; d. James G. and Esther W. Shaffer; m. Robert Gallinari, June 30, 1982. B.A. in English, Elmhurst (Ill.) Coll., 1969; postgrad. Rutgers U., 1987—. Mem. claim dept. Allstate Ins. Co., 1971-76, unit mgr., Springfield, Pa., 1976-77, regional life claim mgr., Basking Ridge, N.J., 1977-79, dist. claim mgr., Latham, N.Y., 1979-87. Mem. Albany Claim Mgrs. Council, Colonie C. of C., Life Office Mgmt. Assn., Ins. Inst. Am. (asso. in mgmt.). Office: 700 Troy Schenectady Rd Latham NY 12110

SHAFIR, GRACE CHASTAIN, sales and marketing executive, publisher; b. Anderson, S.C., May 5, 1948; d. David Ramsey and Margaret Caroline (Littlejohn) Chastain; m. Jere Adam Shafir, Dec. 15, 1972 (dec.); children: Nicole, Melody, Jereann, Georgeanna; m. Robert Sidney Reiss, Apr. 30, 1988. BA in journalism, U. S.C., 1970. Treas. Kingshead Corp., Hackensack, N.J., 1972-84; v.p. sales and advt. Kingshead Corp., Hackensack, 1979-81, pres., 1981-89; pres. Kingshead Kids, Englewood Cliffs, N.J., 1989—, Grace Shafir Publs., Inc., Englewood Cliffs, 1989—. Mem. Com. of 200, Nat. Assn. Chain Drug Stores, Nat. Sch. Supply & Equipment Assn., Mortar Bd., Nat. Assn. Women Bus. Owners, Pvt. Label Mfrs. Assn. (1st woman bd. mem.), Am. Pubs. Assn., Am. Booksellers Assn., Phi Beta Kappa, Kappa Tau Alpha. Republican. Presbyterian. Clubs: Coral Ridge Country, Ft. Lauderale, Englewood Field. Office: Kingshead Kids Inc 600 Sylvan Ave Englewood Cliffs NJ 07632

SHAHID, AIDA MESHKI, insurance executive; b. Tehran, Iran, May 25, 1959; came to U.S., 1981; d. Labib and Esmat (Meshkat) S.; m. Cyrus Meshki, Oct. 24, 1977 (div. 1985); 1 child, Hamed. M Econs., Farah Pahavi U., Tehran, 1981. Office mgr. Barnes Ins. Svc., Santa Monica, Calif., 1981-82; asst. to life specialist E.F. Hutton, Santa Monica, 1982-84; ins. agt. Mut. of Omaha, L.A., 1984-86, Met. Life Ins. Co., Woodland Hills, Calif., 1986-88; ind. ins. agt., security rep. Woodland Hills, 1988—. Mem. Nat. Assn. Life Underwriters, Nat. Assn. Securities Dealers, Sherman Oaks C. of C. Office: Aida Shahid Ins Svc Ste 213 6351 Owensmouth St Woodland Hills CA 91365

SHAHZADE, ANN MARY, retired speech and language pathologist; b. Arlington, Mass., Jan. 25, 1928; d. Nazar Michael and Mary (Israelian) Skenian; m. Herbert Sarkis Shahzade, Aug. 28, 1955 (div.); children: Joyce, John, David, Edward. AB, Emerson Coll., 1949, MA, 1950; postgrad., Boston U., 1952-72. Speech pathologist Lynn (Mass.) Pub. Schs., 1949-56, Somerville (Mass.) Sch. Dept., 1957-58, Cambridge (Mass.) Sch. Dept., 1969-74; co-founder speech clinic Children's Hosp., Boston, 1952-57; asst. dir. Inst. for Speech Correction, Boston, 1949-59; dir. speech and lang. dept. Cambridge Pub. Schs., 1974-89, ret., 1989; instr. pub. speaking John Roberts Powers Sch., Boston, 1950-55; speech pathology cons. to pediatricians, Arlington, 1949-60; pvt. practice, Boston, 1957-69. Author: Oral Language Development, 1982, also kindergarten screening test. Mem. NEA, Mass. Tchrs. Assn., Cambridge Tchrs. Assn. (Disting. Svc. award 1989). Democrat. Mem. Armenian Apostolic Ch. Home: 35 Temple St Arlington MA 02174

SHALALA, DONNA EDNA, political scientist, educator; b. Cleve., Feb. 14, 1941; d. James Abraham and Edna (Smith) S. AB, Western Coll., 1962; MSSC, Syracuse U., 1968, PhD, 1970; 14 hon. degrees, 1981-89. Vol. Peace Corps, Iran, 1962-64; asst. to dir. met. studies program Syracuse U., 1965-69; instr. asst. to dean Syracuse U. (Maxwell Grad. Sch.), 1969-70; asst. prof. polit. sci. Bernard M. Baruch Coll., U. City N.Y., 1970-72; assoc. prof. politics and edn. Tchrs. Coll. Columbia U., 1972-79; asst. sec. for policy devel. and research HUD, Washington, 1977-80; prof. polit. sci., pres. Hunter Coll., CUNY, 1980-88; prof. polit. sci., chancellor U. Wis., Madison, 1988—. Author: Neighborhood Governance, 1971, The City and the Constitution, 1972, The Property Tax and the Voters, 1973, The Decentralization Approach, 1974. Bd. govs. Am. Stock Exchange, 1981-87; trustee TIAA, 1985--89, Com. Econ. Devel., 1981—; bd. dirs. Inst. Internat. Econs., 1981—, Children's Def. Fund, 1980—, Am. Ditchely Found., 1981—, Spencer Found., 1988—; mem. Trilateral Commn., 1988—; mem. Knight Commn. on intercollegiate sports, 1990—; trustee The Brookings Inst., 1989—. Ohio Newspaper Women's scholar, 1958, Western Coll. Trustee scholar, 1958-62; Carnegie fellow, 1966-68; Nat. Acad. Edn. Spencer fellow, 1972-73; Guggenheim fellow, 1975-76; recipient Disting. Svc. medal Columbia U. Tchrs. Coll., 1989. Mem. Am. Polit. Sci. Assn., Am. Soc. Pub. Adminstrn., Nat. Acad. Pub. Adminstrn., Coun. Fgn. Rels., Nat. Acad. Edn. Office: U Wis-Madison 158 Bascom Hall 500 Lincoln Dr Madison WI 53706

SHALLBERG, MARY ANN HARRIS, university administrator; b. Baton Rouge, Sept. 4, 1942; d. Carl Houston and Johnnie Chloe (Sylvest) Harris; m. William Leslie, May 28, 1977. BS, La. Coll., Pineville, 1964. Sec. & exec. sec. U. Houston, 1964-76, special asst. to pres., 1976-78; asst. to pres. U. Houston System, 1978-80; asst. to pres. U. Houston-Clear Lake, exec. asst. to pres., 1985—. Chmn. Ballet San Jacinto Houston Tex. 1986-89. Chmn. Clear Lake Met. Ballet, Houston, 1990—. Mem. AAUW, Am. Coun. Edn. (steering com. presdl. assts. in higher edn.), Tex. Orgn. Presdl. Assts., U. Houston-Clear Lake Women's Assn., Lunar Rendezvous Festival, Cultural Arts Coun., Clear Lake Area C of C, Bay Area Mus. Guild, South Shore Harbour Country Club. Republican. Baptist. Avocation: running. Home: 18220 Lakeside Ln Nassau Bay Houston TX 77058 Office: U Houston Clear Lake 2700 Bay Area Blvd Houston TX 77058-1050

SHALOM, LILIANE WINN, investment company executive; b. Casablanca, Morocco, May 28, 1940; d. Joseph and Madeleine (Corcos) Levy; 1 child, Dominique Winn; m. Stephen Shalom, Jan. 18, 1983. Brevet Etudes Premier Cycle, Alliance Israelite, Casablanca, 1956; cert. proficiency in English, U. Mich., 1960. English tchr. U.S. Info. Agy., Casablanca, 1959-61; multilingual guide, interpreter for VIPs, heads of state UN, N.Y.C., 1962-65; designer-ptnr., v.p. I.Q. Originals, Inc., N.Y.C., 1977-82; pres. EON Holdings, Inc., N.Y.C., 1981—. Editor, pub., contbr. The Sephardi World quar. mag., 1975-82. Fin. com. Carter for Pres., N.Y.C., 1975-76, Moynihan for Senate, N.Y.C., 1976, Dukakis for Pres., N.Y.C., 1987-88; chmn. fundraising Congl. Fgn. Rels. Com., N.Y.C., 1986. Recipient Louise Waterman Wise award Am. Jewish Congress, 1984, Stanley Isaacs Human Rels. award Am. Jewish Com., N.Y., 1986; named Comdr. of Ouissam Alaouite, King of Morocco, 1987. Mem. Am. Sephardi Fedn. (pres. 1975-82), World Zionist Congress (presidium 1971—), Moroccan Jewish Orgn. (founder, chmn. 1978), United Jewish Appeal (bd. dirs.), Hebrew Immigration Aid Soc. (v.p. 1990—), World Jewish Congress (econ. and social commn.). Democrat. Office: 645 Fifth Ave Ste 710 New York NY 10022

SHAMBERG, BARBARA A(NN), psychologist; b. Atlantic City, July 22, 1953; d. Martin and Margaret (Fox) Shamberg; m. Allan Weisberg, Aug. 29, 1987. BA, New Coll., 1975; MA, Hofstra U., 1979, PhD, 1984. Lic. psychologist, N.Y. Mem. faculty Fairleigh Dickinson U., Madison, N.Y., 1977; psychologist Hofstra U., Hempstead, N.Y., 1978-84, SUNY, Farmingdale, 1981-82, Bd. of Coop. Ednl. Svcs., Yorktown, N.Y., 1982-83, N.Y.C. (N.Y.) Bd. Edn., 1983-88; supervising psychologist Childrens' Village, Dobbs Ferry, N.Y., 1989—; pvt. practice clin. psychology N.Y.C. and Scarsdale, N.Y., 1984—; sr. clin. cons. psychologist Ctr. for Behavior Therapy, Scarsdale, 1989—; lectr., workshop leader in field; expert interviewee ABC News, N.Y.C., Sta. WMID, Atlantic City. Author: Wives' Marital Satisfaction, 1984. Bd. dirs. 218 E. 29th St. Owners' Corp., 1984-89. Mem. Am. Psychol. Assn. Home: 4 Hidden Glen Rd Scarsdale NY 10583 Office: Ctr for Behavior Therapy 1495 Weaver St Scarsdale NY 10583

SHAMLIN, ROSE, university administrator; b. Lima, Ohio, Mar. 11, 1918; d. Senekerim Hagop and Arax (Yapujian) Arkelian; m. Henry Shamlin, July 4, 1941; children: Dianne Joy Shamlin Kassabian, George Henry. BA, Fresno State U., 1938; postgrad., UCLA, 1938-39. Psychometrist Fresno County Supt. of Schs., Fresno, 1939-41, 43-47; substitute tchr. Fresno City and County Schs., 1953-54, 59-60, Sacramento City Schs., 1941-42, Fresno State Coll., 1955; adminstrv. asst. Calif. State U., Fresno, 1948-79; mem. pres.'s adv. bd. Calif. State U., 1981—. Asst. editor catalog: California State University, Fresno General Catalog, 1955-64; mng. editor cookbook: Dorcas Guild Cookbook, 1985. Trustee Pilgrim Armenian Congl. Ch., Fresno, 1978-81; vol. tchrs. aid Temperance-Kutner Elem. Sch., Fresno, 1983—; active various fund raising activities. Mem. Calif. State Employees Assn. (v.p. 1963-64), AAUW, Ret. Pub. Employees Assn., Henry Madden Library Assocs., Dorcas Guild, Calif. State U. Alumni Assn., Calif. State U. Pres.'s Club. Democrat. Congregationalist.

SHANABROOK, LINDA, oncological nurse; b. N.J., May 7, 1956; d. James G. and Jean T. (Lunde) Jensen; m. Jed Shanabrook, June 17, 1978; children: Erik, Denise. AAS, Middlesex County Coll., Edison, N.J., 197 , student, St. Joseph's Coll., Windham, Maine. Cert. oncology, CPR ins.r./trainer, IV therapy, physical assessment, audiometric technician, spirometry. Supr. Planned Parenthood, New Brunswick, N.J., 1981-86; nurse Live for Life Profile J&J Health Mgmt., New Brunswick, 1987-89; field supr., oncology prog. coord. Staff Builders, North Brunswick, N.J., 1988—. Mem. Intravenous Nurses Soc., Hospice Nurses Assn., Oncology Nurses Soc., Am. Nurses Assn.

SHANAHAN, EILEEN, editor; b. Washington, Feb. 29, 1924; d. Thomas Francis and Vena (Karpeles) S.; m. John Virgil Waits, Jr., Sept. 16, 1944; children: Mary Beth, Kathleen. AB, George Washington U., 1944. Reporter UPI, Washington, 1944-47, Cronkite Radio News Bur., Washington, 1949-50, Rsch. Inst. Am., Washington, 1951-61, Jour. Commerce, Washington, 1956-61, N.Y. Times, Washington, 1962-77; spl. asst. to asst. sec. U.S. Dept. Treasury, Washington, 1961-62; asst. sec. pub. affairs U.S. Dept. Health, Edn. and Welfare, Washington, 1977-79; asst. mng. editor Washington Star, 1979-81, Pitts. Post-Gazette, 1981-84; assoc. prof. Medill Sch. Journalism, Evanston, Ill., 1984-85; reporter Congl. Quar., Washington, 1986; co-founder, exec. editor Governing mag., Washington, 1987—; mem. exec. com. Reporters Com. for Freedom of Press, Washington, 1972-76, Oral History Project, Washington Press Club, 1987—; mem. adv. com. Nieman Found., Cambridge, Mass., 1975-76, 79-82; vis. faculty summer program for minority journalists U. Calif., Berkeley, 1976—; bd. dirs. Washington Journalism Ctr. Mem. Pub.-Pvt. Partnership Coun., D.C. Pub. Schs. Communications Program, Washington, 1984—. Recipient Bus. Journalism award U. Mo., 1966, Alumni Achievement award George Washington U., 1982; named Newspaper Woman of Yr., N.Y. Women in Communications, 1975. Fellow Nat. Acad. Pub. Adminstrn. Home: 3608 Van Ness St NW Washington DC 20008 Office: Governing 1414 22d St NW Washington DC 20037

SHANAHAN, MARIE JULIE, lawyer; b. St. Louis, Apr. 22, 1958; d. John Joseph and Marie Jocelyn (Gerecke) S. BA, Quincy Coll., 1980; JD, St. Mary's U., 1983. Bar: Mo. 1983. Assoc. Kell, Kell, Custer, Weller & Crowe, St. Louis, 1983-85; ptnr. Crowe & Shanahan, St. Louis, 1985—. Mem. ABA, Bar Assn. Met. St. Louis, Nat. Orgn. Social Security Claimant's Reps. Roman Catholic. Home: 12823 Tammy Kay Dr Saint Louis MO 63128 Office: Crowe & Shanahan 915 Olive Ste 1001C Saint Louis MO 63101

SHANAS, ETHEL, sociology educator; b. Chgo., Sept. 6, 1914; d. Alex and Rebecca (Rich) S.; m. Lester J. Perlman, May 17, 1940; 1 child, Michael Stephen. A.B., U. Chgo., 1935, A.M., 1937, Ph.D., 1949; L.H.D. (hon.), Hunter Coll., N.Y.C., 1985. Instr. human devel. U. Chgo., 1947-52, research assoc. prof., 1961-65; sr. research analyst City of Chgo., 1952-53; sr. study dir. Nat. Opinion Research Ctr., Chgo., 1956-61; prof. sociology U. Ill.-Chgo., 1965-82, prof. emerita, 1982—; vice chmn. expert com. on aging UN, 1974; mem. com. on aging NRC, Washington, 1978-82, panel on statistics for an aging population, 1984-86; mem. U.S. Com. on Vital and Health Stats., Washington, 1976-79. Author: The Health of Older People, 1962; (with others) Old People in Three Industrial Societies, 1968; editor: (with others) Handbook of Aging and the Social Sciences, 1976, 2d edit., 1985. Bd. govs. Chgo. Heart Assn., 1972-80; mem. adv. council on aging City of Chgo., 1972-78. Keston lectr. U. So. Calif., 1975; recipient Burgess award Nat. Council on Family Relations, 1978; Disting. Chgo. Gerontologist award Assn. for Gerontology in Higher Edn., 1988. Fellow Gerontol. Soc. Am. (pres. 1974-75, Kleemeier award 1977, Brookdale award 1981), Am. Sociol. Assn. (chmn. sect. on aging 1985-86 Disting. Scholar award, 1987); mem. Midwest Sociol. Soc. (pres. 1980-81), Inst. Medicine of Nat. Acad. Scis. (sr. mem.). Home: 222 Main St Evanston IL 60202 Office: U Ill-Chgo Dept Sociology PO Box 4348 Chicago IL 60680

SHANDLER, BARBARA ROCHELLE, orthodontist; b. N.Y.C., Aug. 2, 1955; d. Philip and rose (Pines) S.; Joseph Allen Tucher, Aug. 3, 1980. BA,

NYU, 1976, DDS, 1979, orthodontic cert., 1984. Dentist various dental offices N.Y., N.J., 1980-82; gen. practice dental resident Albert Einstein, Bronx Mcpl. Hosp., Bronx, N.Y., 1979-80; pvt. practice orthodontist Forest Hills, N.Y., 1985—, N.Y.C., 1988—; clin. asst. prof. faculty postgrad. dept. orthodontics NYU Dental Sch., N.Y.C., 1984; attending orthodontics Gouveneur Hosp., N.Y.C., 1985—. Scholar Knights of Pythias, N.Y.C., 1972. Mem. ADA, Am. Assn. Orthodontics, Mid-Queen Treatment Conf. (sec. 1987—). Office: 107-05 70th Ave Forest Hills NY 11375 also: 304 Grand St Apt M-3 New York NY 10002

SHANK, CLARE BROWN WILLIAMS, political leader; b. Syracuse, N.Y., Sept. 19, 1909; d. Curtiss Crofoot and Clara Irene (Shoudy) Brown; m. Frank E. Williams, Feb. 18, 1940 (dec. Feb. 1957); m. Seth Carl Shank, Dec. 28, 1963 (dec. Jan. 1977). B.Oral English, Syracuse U., 1931. Tchr., 1931-33, merchandising exec., 1933-42; Pinellas County mem. Rep. State Com., 1954-58; life mem. Pinellas County Rep. Exec. Com.; exec. com. Fla. Rep. Com., 1954-64; Fla. committeewoman Rep. Nat. Com., 1956-64, mem. exec. com., 1956-64, asst. chmn. and dir. women's activities, 1958-64; alt., mem. exec. arrangements com., major speaker Rep. Nat. Conv., Chgo., 1960; alt., program and arrangement coms. Rep. Nat. Conv., 1964. Pres. St. Petersburg Women's Rep. Club, 1955-57; Mem. Def. Adv. Com. on Women in Services, 1959-65; trustee St. Petersburg Housing Authority, 1976-81. Recipient George Arents medal Syracuse U., 1959; citation for patriotic civilian service 5th U.S. Army and Dept. Def.; 1st woman to preside over any part of nat. polit. conv., Rep. Nat. Conv., Chgo., 1960. Mem. AAUW, Gen. Fedn. Women's Clubs, DAR, Colonial Dames 17th Century, Fla. Fedn. Women's Clubs (dist. pres. 1976-78), Zeta Phi Eta, Pi Beta Phi (nat. officer 1945-48). Methodist. Clubs: Woman's (St. Petersburg) (pres. 1974-76), Yacht (St. Petersburg). Home: 1200 North Shore Dr NE Apt 408 Saint Petersburg FL 33701

SHANKMAN, CHERYL ANN, business development manager; b. Chgo., July 21, 1952; d. Louis and Agnes C. Niemiec; m. Brian Jay Shankman, May 23, 1982. Student, U. Kyoto, Japan, 1973; AA, Parkland Coll., Champaign, Ill., 1976; BA, U. Ill., 1980; MA, U. Dallas, 1988. Copywriter McCann-Erickson Advt., Dallas, 1981-82; instructional designer Seville Tng. Systems, Irving, Tex., 1982-86; sr. instructional designer Singer-Link, Irving, 1986-87; bus. devel. mgr. Hughes Tng. System, Arlington, Tex., 1987—. Mem. Assn. for Devel. Computer-Based Instruction, Computer-Based Tng. Group (chmn. 1980—), Am. Soc. Tng. and Devel., Nat. Soc. for Performance and Instrn. (newsletter writer), Human Factors Soc. Home: 3701 Windomere Dr Bedford TX 76021 Office: Hughes Tng Systems 2116 Arlington Downs Rd Arlington TX 76011

SHANKS, ANN ZANE, filmmaker, photographer, writer; b. N.Y.C.; d. Louis and Sadye (Rosenthal) Kushner; m. Ira Zane (dec.); children—Jennifer, Anthony; m. Robert Horton Shanks, Sept. 25, 1959; 1 child, John. Student, Carnegie-Mellon U., Columbia U. tchr., moderator spl. symposiums Mus. Modern Art, N.Y.C.; tchr. New Sch. for Social Research. Filmmaker, photographer, writer for numerous mags. and newspapers; producer, dir.: (movie shorts) Central Park, 1969 (U.S. entry Edinburgh Film Festival, Cine Golden Eagle award, Cambodia Film Festival award), Denmark... A Loving Embrace (Cine Golden Eagle award 1973), Tivoli, 1972-79 (San Francisco Film Festival award, Am. Film Festival award), (TV series) American Life Style (Silver award, 5 Gold medal awards Internat. TV and Film Festival N.Y., 2 Cine Golden Eagle awards), "He's Fired, She's Hired"; producer CBS TV "Drop-Out Mother"; producer, writer (TV short) Mousie Baby; dir. (TV movie) Friendships, Secrets and Lies, NBC; producer: (TV movie) Drop-out Father, CBS, (video spl.) The Avant-Garde in Russia 1910-1930, Arts and Entertainment channel, ABC Morning Show, Good Afternoon Detroit; producer, dir. (TV spl.) A Day in the Country, PBS, (Emmy award nomination); producer, dir. play S.J. Perelman in Person; producer Broadway play Lillian; exhibited photographs Mus. Modern Art, Mus. City N.Y., Met. Mus. Art, Jewish Mus.; author: (photographs and text) The Name's the Game, New Jewish Ency; contbr.: (photographs) Old Is What You Get, Busted Lives...Dialogues with Kids in Jail, 1983; writer, photographer Juvenile Garbage and Stuff. Recipient 4 awards from internat. competitions. Mem. Am. Soc. Mag. Photographers (bd. govs.), Overseas Press Club Am., Women in Film (v.p.), Dirs. Guild Am.

SHANKS, GENEVIEVE MADELINE, company executive; b. Clearmont, Mo., May 25, 1923; d. Lewis Albert and Faye Jayne (Johnston) Teuscher; m. Dewey Dawson Shanks, Dec. 23, 1940; children: Camille Genevieve, Joseph Craig. LPN, Chgo. Sch. Nursing, 1955. Tchr. Sch. Dist. Pierce #2, Villisca, Iowa, 1941-42, Sch. Dist. Red Oak, Iowa, 1942, Consolidated Sch., Vine Grove, Ky., 1944-45; post engr. U.S. Civil Svc., Ft. Knox, Ky., 1945; ptnr. Lake Estes Drive-In Theatre & Circle S Ford-Merc., Estes Park, Colo., 1953-60, Dry Gulch Ford-Merc.-Lincoln/Lone Pine Subdiv., Estes Park, 1965-74; office/pvt. duty nurse Dr. Henry Reid, Estes Park/Palm Springs, 1954-55; ptnr. E-Z Homes, Inc., Estes Park, 1971—, E-Z Lift, Ltd., Internat., Estes Park, 1977—. Vol. ARC, Vine Grove, Ky., 1944-45. Mem. Def. Mfrs. & Suppliers Assn., Am. Legion Aux., Order Eastern Star. Methodist. Home: 1760 High Pine Dr Estes Park CO 80517 Office: E-Z Lift Ltd Internat Box 1499 Estes Park CO 80517

SHANKS, JUDITH WEIL, editor; b. Montgomery, Ala., Nov. 2, 1941; d. Roman Lee and Charlotte (Alexander) Weil; m. Hershel Shanks, Feb. 20, 1966; children: Elizabeth Jeannette, Julia Emily. BA in Econs., Wellesley Coll., 1963; MBA, Trinity Coll., 1980. Econs. asst. Export-Import Bank, Washington, 1963-68; cons. econs. and social sci., 1968-76; researcher Time-Life Books, Alexandria, Va., 1976-80, prin. researcher, 1980-83, illustrations editor, 1983, editorial adminstr., 1984—. Mem. Garden Writers Am., Internat. Alliance, Washington Alliance Bus. Women, Leadership Greater Washington, Washington Wellesley Club (career caucus). Democrat. Jewish. Home: 5208 38th St NW Washington DC 20015

SHANKS, KATHRYN MARY, health care administrator; b. Glens Falls, N.Y., Aug. 4, 1950; d. John Anthony and Lenita (Combs) S. B.S. summa cum laude, Spring Hill Coll., 1972; M.P.A., Auburn U., 1976. Program evaluator Mobile Mental Health, Ala., 1972-73; dir. spl. projects Ala. Dept. Mental Health, Montgomery, 1973-76; dir. adminstrn. S.W. Ala. Mental Health/Mental Retardation, Andulusia, Ala., 1976-78; adminstr. Mobile County Health Dept., 1978-82; exec. dir. Coastal Family Health Ctr., Biloxi, Miss., 1982—; ptnr. Shanks & Allen, Mobile, 1979—; cons. S.W. Health Agy., Tylertown, Miss., 1984-86; preceptor Sch. Nursing, U. So. Miss., Hattiesburg, 1983, 84; advisor Headstart Program, Gulfport, Miss., 1984—, LPN Program, Gulf Coast Community Coll., 1984—; lectr. Auburn U., Montgomery, 1977-78. Bd. dirs. Mobile Community Action Agy., 1979-81; mem. S.W. Ala. Regional Goals Forum, Mobile, 1971-72, Cardiac Rehab. Study Com., Biloxi, Miss., 1983-84, Mothers and Babies Coalition, Jackson, Miss., 1983—, Gulf Coast Coalition Human Services, Biloxi, Miss., 1983—. Spring Hill Coll. Pres.'s scholar, 1972. Mem. Miss. Primary Health Care Assn. (pres.), Med. Group Mgmt. Assn., Biloxi C. of C., ACLU, Soc. for Advancement of Ambulatory Care, Spring Hills Alumni Assn. Avocations: tennis; home restoration. Office: Coastal Family Health Ctr PO Box 475 300 E Division St Biloxi MS 39530

SHANKS, MARGARET MCCLOSKEY, lawyer; b. Chgo., Nov. 19, 1953; d. Robert Eugene and Kathryn (O'Neill) McCloskey; m. Robert B. Shanks, Sept. 15, 1984; children: Bruce, Grace. BS, DePaul U., 1975; JD, Loyola U., Chgo., 1978. Bar: Ill. 1978, D.c. 1980, Md. 1986. Law clk. to presiding jusitce Fed. Dist. Ct. V.I., 1978-79; assoc. Baker & McKenzie, Washington, 1979-81; trial atty. Dept. of Justice, 1981-84; assoc. Bryan, Cave, McPheeters & McRoberts, Washington, 1984-88, ptnr., 1989—. Assoc. editor Loyola Law Jour., 1977-78. Mem. ABA, Ill. Bar Assn., Md. Bar Assn., D.C. Bar Assn., Womens Bar Assn. (co-chmn. jud. endorsement com.), City Tavern Club. Home: 3615 Edmunds St NW Washington DC 20007 Office: Bryan Cave McPheeters & McRoberts 1015 15th St NW Ste 1000 Washington DC 20000

SHANNON, IRIS REED, educational administrator; b. Chgo.; d. Ira Paul and Iola Sophia (Williams) S.; m. Robert Alwood Shannon, Aug. 21, 1953. B.S. in Nursing, Fisk U.-Meharry Med. Coll., 1948; M.A., U. Chgo., 1954; Ph.D., U. Ill., Chgo., 1987. Staff nurse Chgo. Bd. Health, 1948-50; instr. pub. health nursing Meharry Med. Coll., Nashville, 1951-56; tchr.-nurse, health coordinator child devel. Head Start, Chgo. Bd. Edn., 1957-66; dir. community nursing Mile Sq. Neighborhood Health Center, Presbyn.-St. Luke's Hosp., Chgo., 1966-69; co-dir. nurse assoc. programs Rush Presbyn.-St. Luke's Hosp., 1971-76; chairperson community nursing Rush U., Chgo., 1972-77; acting chairperson Rush U., 1988-90; asst. prof. pub. health nursing U. Ill., 1971-74; assoc. prof. community nursing Rush U., 1974—; adj. faculty Sch. Public Health, U. N.C., 1977-85; mem. profl. adv. bd. Vis. Nurse Assn. Chgo., 1973-75; cons. Video Nursing, Inc.; mem. profl. adv. com. Mile Sq. Home Health Unit, Chgo., 1975-77; mem. Nat. Adv. Council on Nurse Tng., HEW, 1978-81; Mem. Nat. Task Force on Credentialing in Nursing, 1979-82; mem. Chgo. regional com. Ill. White House Conf. on Children, 1979-80. Recipient award of merit Ill. Public Health Assn., 1979, Outstanding Achievement award YWCA of Met. Chgo., 1988, Disting. Svc. award Chgo. chpt. Meharry Alumni, 1989H; Rockefeller fellow, 1953-54. Fellow Am. Pub. Health Assn. (chmn. pub. health nursing sect. 1977-79, governing coun. 1980-82, exec. bd. 1985-87, pres. 1988-89), Royal Soc. Health (hon. 1989), Am. Acad. Nursing; mem. Am. Nurses Assn., Inst. Medicine of Nat. Acad. Scis., Delta Sigma Theta, Sigma Theta Tau.

SHANNON, MARGARET SHERRY, employee benefits specialist; b. Buffalo, N.Y., Oct. 24, 1954; d. John Patrick and Elizabeth Amelia (Kieffer) S. BS, SUNY, Buffalo, 1976; BA, SUNY, 1979. Acct. Mobil Oil Corp., Buffalo, 1976-78; acct. personnel dept. Pyramid Constrn. Co., Syracuse, N.Y., 1980-81; benefits adminstr. HBH Co., Arlington, VA., 1981-83, Nat. Railway Labor Conf., Washington, 1983—. Advisor Jr. Achievment, Buffalo, 1978; career counselor Displaced Homemakers, Buffalo, 1979. Mem. SUNY Alumni Assn. (steering com. 1986-87). Roman Catholic. Office: Nat Railway Labor Conf 1901 L St NW Suite 500 Washington DC 20036

SHANNON, MARTHA ALBERTER, field underwriter; b. Johnstown, Pa., Oct. 9, 1958; d. Rodman Russell and Eleanor Ruth (Christner) S. BA in Econs., U. Pitts., Johnstown, Pa., 1980; MBA magna cum laude, U. Alaska, 1987. Area mgr. Fed. Gold Exchange, Inc., Denver, 1980-81; dept. mgr. Time Service, Inc., Aurora, Colo., 1981-82; exec. dir. John E. Randall II, Investments, Anchorage, 1982-85; portfolio mgr. M.B.A. Co., Anchorage, 1986-87; v.p. portfolio mgmt., corp. sec./treas. Security Portfolio Mgrs., Inc., Anchorage, 1987-88, also bd. dirs.; agt. N.Y. Life Ins. Co., Anchorage, 1988—; registered rep. Mony Fin. Svcs., Anchorage, 1989—; agt. Retirement Planning Assocs., Anchorage, 1988—; adj. prof. fin. U. Alaska., 1988—; bd. dirs. Matrax, Inc. Mem. Am. Mktg. Assn., Fin. Analysts Fedn., Internat. Chartered Fin. Analysts Fedn., Women Life Underwriters Confederation (bd. dirs. local chpt., asst. regional dir.), Nat. Assn. Life Underwriters. Office: MONY Fin Svcs 301 W Nothern Lights Blvd Ste 400 Anchorage AK 99503

SHANNON MCCONAGHY, MARILYN, lawyer; b. Providence, Jan. 3, 1953; d. William Joseph and Ellen Agnes (Fay) S.; m. Raymond Joseph McConaghy Jr., June 23, 1984. BA, U. R.I., 1975; JD cum laude, Boston Coll., 1978. Bar: R.I. 1978, Mass. 1978, U.S. Dist. Ct. 1978. Law clk. to chief judge U.S. Dist. Ct. R.I., Providence, 1978-79; assoc. Tillinghast Collins & Graham, Providence, 1979-84, ptnr., 1984—; senator R.I. Senate, Providence, 1981-83; bd. dirs. R.I. Supreme Ct. Disciplinary Bd., 1989—. Bd. dirs. YMCA of Pawtucket (R.I.), 1988—, bd. dirs. R.I. Coll. Found., Providence, 1987—, Meeting St. Sch., 1987—, Boys and Girls Club of Pawtucket, 1988, Insight; v.p., bd. dirs. Community Counseling Ctr. of Pawtucket, 1983—. Mem. R.I. Assn. for Blind and Visually Impaired (past pres.). Democrat. Roman Catholic. Office: Tillinghast Collin & Graham Old Stone Sq Providence RI 02903

SHANNON-SPALDING, LOUISE MAY, real estate investment company executive; b. Frankfort, Fed. Republic Germany, Mar. 15, 1961; d. William J. and Sietske Louise (Linnartz) Shannon; m. Charles Joseph Spalding, Aug. 6, 1988; children: Cameron Ross, Chelsea Louisa. BA in Gen. Biology, Armstrong State Coll., 1986. Cert. elem. tchr. Freelance photographer Savannah, Ga., 1980—; restaurant bar mgr. various businesses Savannah, Atlanta, 1980-86; educator Castle Heights Acad., Savannah, 1986-89, extracurricular cons., 1986-88; v.p. No. Sun Inc., Savannah, 1987—; owner, exec., cons. Chatham County Bur. Legal Recovery, Savannah, 1989—; cons. Chatham County Legal, Savannah, 1989—; sec. Tri-Beta Biol. Soc., Savannah, 1984-86; mem. Student Govt. Assn. Edn., Savannah, 1984-86; extracurricular cons. Castle Height Acad., Savannah, 1986-88; pres. Ga. Bur. Legal Recovery, Inc., Northern Sun, Inc., real estate investment co. Campaign cons. Terrence Shannon for Rep., Savannah and Atlanta, 1987. Mem. Armstrong State Coll. Alumni Assn., Beta Beta Beta. Republican. Roman Catholic. Home: 730 E 48th Savannah GA 31405

SHAPIRO, AMY ROSEMARIE, film studio executive; b. Stamford, Conn., Dec. 31, 1949; d. Salem Seeley and Edith Geraldine (Herwitz) S. BA, Goucher Coll., Towson, Md., 1971. Asst. to dir. Manpower Adminstrn. U.S. Dept. Labor, Washington, 1971-73; editorial asst. Distbn. Codes, Inc., Washington, 1973-75; asst. to v.p. Pay-TV dept. Universal Pictures, Inc., N.Y.C., 1976-80; adminstr. Pay-TV div. Universal Pictures, Inc., Los Angeles, 1980-82; dir. sales Pay-TV div. Universal Pictures Inc., Los Angeles, 1983-84; v.p. sales Pay-TV div. MCA Home Entertainment Group, Los Angeles, 1985-87, v.p. adminstrn. and new mktg. devel., 1988—. Coordinator Udall Presdl. Campaign, Weston, Conn., 1976; mem. Dem. Town Com., Weston, Conn., 1976-77; vol. coordinator Gary Hart Presdl. Campaign, Los Angeles, 1984. Recipient Case Study award Cable TV Adminstrn. and Mktg. Soc., 1988. Democrat. Jewish. Home: 4401 Sepulveda Blvd Sherman Oaks CA 91403 Office: Universal Pay TV 70 Universal City Plaza Universal City CA 91608

SHAPIRO, ANN R., English educator; b. Bklyn., Feb. 28, 1937; d. Murray and Jeanette Rabinowitz; children: Rona Gail, Wendy Lynn, Edward Ira. AB cum laude, Radcliff Coll., 1958; MA in Teaching, Harvard U., 1960; PhD, NYU, 1985. Instr. English Rider Coll., 1962-65, Suffolk County (N.Y.) Community Coll., 1966-67; prof. SUNY, Farmingdale, 1974—; speaker in field. Author: Unlikely Heroines: Nineteenth-Century American Women Writers and the Woman Question; Introduction (with Joy Gould Boyum), A Country Doctor (Sarah Orne Jewett); contbg. author: Smashing the Idols; contbr. articles to profl. jours. Fellow Nat. Inst. for Leadership Devel., 1987, Salzburg seminars, 1988, NEH Summer seminar, 1990. Mem. MLA, Women's Caucus in the Modern Langs., Nat. Council Tchrs. Club: Harvard (N.Y.C.). Home: 1148 Fifth Ave New York NY 10128 Office: SUNY Dept English Farmingdale NY 11735

SHAPIRO, CAREN KNIGHT, microbiology educator; b. Berkeley, Calif., Apr. 19, 1945; d. Allen Lewis and Ruby Marie (Hatfield) Knight; m. Stuart Charles Shapiro, July 16, 1972. AB, U. Calif., 1967; MS, U. Wis., 1971, PhD, 1972. NIH trainee U. Wis., Madison, 1967-71, teaching asst., 1971-72; rsch. assoc. Ind. U., Bloomington, Ind., 1973-74, Ind. U. Med. Sch., Indpls., 1975-76; rsch. affiliate Roswell Park Meml. Inst., Buffalo, N.Y., 1977; asst. prof. D'Youville Coll., Buffalo, 1977-82, assoc. prof., 1982—. Mem. AAUW (bd. dirs. 1978-80, 81-83, 85-87), Assn. Women in Sci. (sec. local chpt. 1982-84), AAAS, Am. Soc. for Microbiology, N.Y. Acad. Scis., Sigma Xi. Home: 142 Viscount Dr Williamsville NY 14221 Office: D Youville Coll 320 Porter Ave Buffalo NY 14201

SHAPIRO, CAROL SADIE, plastic and reconstructive surgeon; b. Pitts., Sept. 24, 1939; d. Leo I. and Charlotte H. (Heller) S.; m. Donald E. Morgan, May 19, 1974; children: Donald E., Leslie Marie. BS, U. Pitts., 1961; MD, Med. Coll. Pa., 1965. Diplomate Am. Soc. Plastic and Reconstructive Surgery. Intern Phila. Gen. Hosp., 1965-66; resident gen. surgery Georgetown U. Hosp., Washington, 1966-69; practice medicine specalizing in plastic surgery Woodbridge, Manassas, Va., 1972—; pres. med. staff Prince William Hosp., Manassas, Va.; dir. Potomac Home Health Care, Woodbridge, Va. Bd. trustees Potomac Hosp., Woodbridge, 1983, 84, 86; pres. Potomac Profl. Village Unit Owners Assn., Woodbridge, 1989. Recipient Outstanding Achievement award, Prince Willian County Com. for Disabled, 1988. Mem. AMA (physician's recongnition award 1972, 76, 80, 85) Med. Soc. Va. (chmn. hwy. safety com. 1984—, physician's health and effectiveness com. 1989—), Na. Capital Soc. Plastic Surgeons (exec. com. 1988, sec./treas. 1989-90), ASPRS (bd. cert. 1986—), ASAPS, Ea. Prince William County C. of C. Home: 7822 Gingerbread Ln Fairfax Station VA 22039 Office: 1940 Opitz Blvd Woodbridge VA 22191

SHAPIRO, CHARLOTTE HELLER, psychologist, educator; d. Morris E. and Sadie Clara (Rosenfeld) Heller; m. Leo I. Shapiro, June 4, 1931; children: Carol S. Shapiro-Morgan, Ilene L. Shapiro-Heyison, Donna Lu Shapiro-Brandstein. BA, U. Pitts., 1932, MA, 1933, PhD, 1955; postgrad. studies, numerous univs., worldwide, 1936-63. Cert. tchr., prin., elem. and secondary schs., sch. psychologist, spl. edn., physically and orthopedically handicapped, mentally retarded, socially and emotionally disturbed. Supr. Allegheny County Emergency Relief Bd., Pitts.; med. and psychiatric case worker and supr. Allegheny Gen. Hosp., Pitts.; prin. Pitts. Bd. Edn.; cons. Allegheny Intermediate Unit, Pitts. Author: History and Organization of Jewish Family Welfare of Pittsburgh, Personal and Social Problems of Junior High Mentally Retarded Students. Trustee Mayview State Hosp., Slippery Rock U.; del. to Presidential meetings Women in the War on Poverty. Recipient George Washington Carver Achievment award, 1972. Mem. NEA, APA, Pa. Assn. of Coun. of Trustees (treas. 1984—), Pa. Psychol. Assn., numerous others.

SHAPIRO, CYNTHIA ROSE, dentist; b. Cape Town, South Africa, Aug. 19, 1946; d. Morris Joseph Zion and Annette Goldwater; m. Douglas Alan Shapiro,. Student, Cape Town U., 1962, Forsyth Sch. for Hygienists, 1971; DMD, Tufts Dental Sch., 1983. Gen. dentist Private Practice, Chestnut Hill, Mass., 1983--. Author:Dental Anatomy, 1972. Mem. ADA, Greater Boston Dental Soc., Am. Acad. Cosmetic Dentistry, Sigma Phi Alpha. Republican. Office: 200 Boylston St Chestnut Hill MA 02167

SHAPIRO, DEBBIE LYNN (LYNN SHAPIRO), singer, actress, dancer; b. Santa Monica, Calif., Sept. 29; d. Morton Harold and Anne (Lipsman) S.; m. Beau Gravitte, Sept. 21, 1986. Appeared in Broadway shows including Jerome Robbins' (Tony award 1989, N.Y. Women Stopper award 1989), Zorba, Blues in the Night, Perfectly Frank, (Broadway debut) They're Playing our Song, Annie get your Gun, Spotlight, Swing, King's Tapestry, Berlin to Broadway, Gentleman Prefer Blonds, Mack and Mabel; TV shows include Broadway Plays Washington, CBS Cable Songwriters Series, Trial and Error; TV appearances Pat Sajak, Merv Griffin Show; recs. include Mack and Mabel in Concert, (with Anthony Quinn) Zorba, The Songs of Stephen Sondheim, The Songs of N.Y., Jerome Robbins Broadway, They're Playing Song, The first Nudie Musical; nightclubs acts include Sands Hotel, Atlantic City, Harrah's, Atlantic City, Freddy's Supper Club, N.Y.C., Rainbow and Stars, Rockefellar Ctr., N.Y.C., Les Mouches, N.Y.C., The St. Regis Hotel, N.Y.C., others.

SHAPIRO, ELLEN LOUISE, environmental policy analyst; b. Boston, Oct. 25, 1950; d. Thelma (Novick) S. BS in Math. cum laude, U. Mass., 1972; MS in Chem. Engring., N.C. State U., 1978. Lab. technician dept. microbiology U. Colo., Boulder, 1972-73; research asst. Appalachian Research and Def. Fund, Inc., Charleston, W.Va., 1973-75; programmer Union Carbide Corp., South Charleston, W.Va., 1976; engr. W.Va. Air Pollution Control Commn., Charleston, 1978-83; policy analyst Jellinek, Schwartz, Connolly and Freshman, Inc., Washington, 1983-85; div. dir. Pub. Health Found., Washington, 1985-89; policy analyst U.S. EPA Office of Toxic Substances, Washington, 1989—. Author, editor: Resource Guide for Environmental Health Risk Assessment, 1986; (newsletter) Environ. Health Bull., 1985—. Bd. dirs. W.Va. chpt. Nat. Abortion Rights Action League, Charleston, 1982-83. Mem. Amnesty Internat., World Affairs Council, Am. Pub. Health Assn., Air Pollution Control Assn., Nat. Environ. Health Assn., Soc. Risk Analysis, Met. Washington Environ. Profls. (bd. dirs., v.p. 1987—), Folklore Soc. of Greater Washington, Alpha Lambda Delta. Democrat. Jewish. Office: Pub Health Found 1220 L St NW Suite 350 Washington DC 20005

SHAPIRO, ELLEN MARIE, graphic design company executive; b. L.A., June 26, 1948; d. Leon e. and Elizabeth (Nussbaum) S.; m. Jerry Miller, Oct. 10, 1980 (div. 1986); 1 child, Alex Miller. BA, UCLA, 1970. Art dir. UCLA Alumni and Devel. Ctr., 1970-72; sr. designer Lubalin Smith Carnase, Inc., N.Y.C., 1972-74; art dir. Barton-Gillet Co., N.Y.C., 1974-76; ptnr. Design Concern, N.Y.C., 1976-78; pres. Shapiro Design Assocs., Inc., N.Y.C., 1978—; mem. faculty dept. communication design, Parsons Sch. Design, N.Y.C., 1986—; judge design and advt. shows, U.S. and Can. Art dir., Upper & Lower Case, 1988; author: Clients and Designers, 1989. Recipient over 60 awards from profl. orgns. Mem. Am. Inst. Graphic Arts (v.p. N.Y. chpt. 1987-89), N.Y. Art Dirs. Club (Gold and Silver awards), N.Y. Type Dirs. Club. Office: Shapiro Design Assocs Inc 141 Fifth Ave New York NY 10010

SHAPIRO, JAN A., jazz educator, vocalist, writer; b. St. Louis, May 10, 1949; d. Earl and Virginia (Roth) S.; children: Aaron, Adam. ASN, Maryville Coll., 1969; B in Music Edn., Howard U., 1969; postgrad., New Eng. Conservatory, 1986-87; MEd, Cambridge (Mass.) Coll., 1988. Clinician Howard U., Washington, 1981-85; instr. Fontbonne Coll., St. Louis, 1981-85, So. Ill. U., Edwardsville, 1983-85; adjucator Mass. chpt. U. N.H., Durham, 1990—; asst. prof. Berklee Coll., Boston, 1985-89; assoc. prof. Berklee Coll., 1989—; featured vocalist Boston Globe Jazz Festival, 1987, 90; vocalist in jazz/pop field. Dir. devel. com., adv. bd. Boswell Mus.; mem. Berklee High Sch. Jazz Festival, 1990, Univ. N.H., 1990. Nat. Endowment for the Arts grantee, 1989-90. Mem. Internat. Assn. Jazz Educators (Cert. of Appreciation 1988, 89, 90). Home: 111 Auburndale Ave West Newton MA 02165

SHAPIRO, JOAN ISABELLE, laboratory administrator, nurse; b. Fulton, Ill., Aug. 26, 1943; d. Macy James and Frieda Lockhart; m. Ivan Lee Shapiro, Dec. 28, 1968; children: Audrey, Michael. RN, Peoria Methodist Sch. Nursing, Ill., 1964. Nurse, Grant Hosp., Columbus, Ohio, 1975-76; nurse Cardiac Thoracic and Vascular Surgeons Ltd., Geneva, Ill., 1977—, mgr. non-invasive lab., 1979—; owner, operator Shapiro's Mastiff's 1976-82; sec.-treas. Sounds Svcs., 1976—, Mainstream Sounds Inc., 1980-84; co-founder Cardio-Phone Inc., 1982—, Edgewater Vascular Inst., 1987-89, Associated Profls., 1989—; v.p., bd. dir. Computer Specialists Inc., 1986-89. Mem. Soc. Non-invasive Technologists, Soc. Peripheral Vascular Nursing (community awareness com. 1984—), Kane County Med. Soc. Aux. (pres. 1983-84, adviser, 1984-85). Lutheran. Office: Cardiac Thoracic and Vascular Surgeons Ltd PO Box 564 Geneva IL 60134

SHAPIRO, JUDITH R., anthropology educator, university official; b. N.Y.C., Jan. 24, 1942. B.A., Brandeis U., 1963; postgrad. Ecole des Haute Etudes Institut d'Etudes Politiques, Paris, 1961-62; Ph.D., Columbia U., 1972. Asst. prof. U. Chgo., 1970-75; postdoctoral fellow U. Calif.-Berkeley, 1974-75; Rosalyn R. Schwartz lectr., asst. prof. anthropology Bryn Mawr Coll., Pa., 1975-78, assoc. prof., 1978-85, prof., 1985—, chmn. dept., 1982-85, acting dean undergrad coll., 1985-86, provost, 1986—; contbr. articles to profl. jours., chpts. to books. Fellow Woodrow Wilson Found., 1963-64, Columbia U., 1964-65, NEH Younger Humanist, 1974-75, Am. Council Learned Socs., 1981-82; grantee NSF summer field tng., 1965, Ford Found. 1966, NIMH, 1974-75, Social Sci. Research Council, 1974-75; Mem. Phila. Anthrop. Soc. (pres. 1983), Am. Ethnol. Soc. (nominations com . 1983-84, pres. elect 1984-85, pres. 1985-86), Am. Anthrop. Assn. (ethics com. 1976-79, bd. dirs. 1984-86, exec. com. 1985-86), Social Sci. Research Council (com. social sci personnel 1977-80), Royal Anthrop. Inst., Phi Beta Kappa, Sigma Xi. Office: Bryn Mawr Coll Office of Provost Bryn Mawr PA 19010*

SHAPIRO, MARIAN KAPLUN, psychologist; b. Lexington, Mass., July 13, 1939; d. David and Bertha Rebecca (Pearlman) Kaplun; m. Irwin Ira Shapiro, Dec. 20, 1959; children: Steven, Nancy. BA, Queens Coll., 1959; MA in Teaching, Harvard U., 1961, EdD, 1978. Cert. psychologist. Tchr. North Quincy High Sch., Quincy, Mass., 1962-64; instr. Carnegie Inst., Boston, 1968-74; staff psychologist South Shore Counselling Assn., Hanover, Mass., 1978-80; pvt. practice psychologist Lexington, Mass., 1980—; adj. instr. Mass. Sch. Profl. Psychology, Dedham, 1985—. Author: 2nd Childhood: Hypnoplay Therapy with Age--Regressed Adults, 1989; contbr. articles on hypnotherapy and teaching reading to profl. jours. Fellow Am. Orthopsychiat. Assn.; mem. Am. Psychol. Assn., Mass. Psychol. Assn., Northeast Soc. Group Psychotherapy, Am. Soc. Group Psychotherapy, Am. Soc. Clin. Hypnosis, New Eng. Soc. for the Study Multiple Personality Disorders, Internat. Soc. for the Study Multiple Personality Disorders, New Eng. Soc. Clin. Hypnosis, Sigma Alpha, Pi Lambda Theta. Jewish. Home and office: 17 Lantern Ln Lexington MA 02173

SHAPIRO, MARILLYN IRENE, artist, special educator; b. Washington, Dec. 20, 1925; d. Aaron Samuel and Yetta B. (Schooler) Lesser; m. Leon Shapiro, Jan. 18, 1948; children: David, Paula, Jeanie. Cert., Corcoran Sch. of Art, Washington, 1948; AA, Villa Julie Coll., Lutherville, Md., 1985. Cert. activity coord., Md. Ptnr. Paul Shapiro & Sons Real Estate Mgmt., Balt., 1950—; tchr. Art for Children Studio Place, Balt., 1966-81; instr. in drawing, painting, crafts, mktg. various adult day care ctrs. for disabled, 1981-85; art unit specialist Prologue, Inc., Owings Mills, Md., 1985-88; community living counselor Howard County Assn. for Retarded Citizens (sect. ARC), Columbia, Md., 1988—; instr. art, Catonsville Community Coll., Balt. Paintings exhibited Artist's Equity of Md., Peale Mus., Balt., Corcoran Gallery of Art, Washington. Sec. Alliance for Mentally Ill of Howard County, 1985-86; instr. Day Treatment Ctrs. Catonsville Community Coll. Human Svcs. Dept., 1981—; bd. dirs. Artists Equity of Md., 1973, 85; PTA pres. Pikesville (Md.) Sch., 1961, 62; bd. dirs. Prologue, Inc., 1982; pres. Alliance for Mentally Ill of Balt. Area, 1982, 83. Named Best in Show, Milbrook Sch. Exhibits, Balt.; cited in La Revue Moderne (Paris mag.). Democrat. Jewish. Home: 12126 Red Streamway Columbia MD 21044

SHAPIRO, MYRA STEIN, poet; b. Bronx, N.Y., May 21, 1932; d. David M. and Ida Betty (Leader) Stein; m. Harold M. Shapiro, Feb. 15, 1953; children: Karen S., Judith M. BA, U. Tenn., 1968; MA in English, Middlebury Coll., 1973. reader, Internat. Women's Day, Jefferson Market Libr., N.Y.C., 1989; reading performance Midday Muse Series, Folger Shakespeare Libr., Washington, 1983, NEA Hunter Mus., Chattanooga, 1985, Bower's Mus., Santa Ana, Calif., 1986, 88. Author: (poems) The Ohio Review, 1989, Education For Peace, 1988, Kalliope, 1988, Ailanthus, 1988. Recipient Dylan Thomas Poetry award, The New Sch., N.Y.C., 1981, The MacDowell Colony Fellowship, The MacDowell Colony, Peterborough, N.H., 1985, 87. Mem. Poetry Soc. Am. Office: 111 4th Ave 12I New York NY 10003

SHAPIRO, NORMA SONDRA LEVY, federal judge; b. Phila., July 27, 1928; d. Bert and Jane (Kotkin) Levy; m. Bernard Shapiro, Aug. 21, 1949; children: Finley, Neil, Aaron. B.A. in Polit. Theory with honors, U. Mich., 1948; J.D. magna cum laude, U. Pa., 1951. Bar: Pa. 1952, U.S. Supreme Ct. 1978. Law clk. to presiding justice Pa. Supreme Ct., 1951-52; instr. U. Pa. Law Sch., 1951-52, 55-56; assoc. Dechert Price & Rhoads, Phila., 1956-58, 67-73; ptnr. Dechert Price & Rhoads, 1973-78; judge U.S. Dist. Ct. (ea. dist.) Pa., 1978—; assso. trustee U. Pa. Law Sch., 1978—; trustee Women's Law Project, 1978—, Albert Einstein Med. Center, 1979—, Fedn. Jewish Agys., 1980—, Jewish Publ. Soc., 1980—; mem. lawyer's adv. panel Pa. Gov.'s Commn. on Status of Women, 1974; legal adv. Regional Council Child Psychiatry. Guest editor: Shingle, 1972. Mem. Lower Merion County (Pa.) Bd. Sch. Dirs., 1968-77, pres., 1977, v.p., 1976; v.p. Jewish Community Relations Council of Greater Phila., 1975-77; chmn. legal affairs com., 1978; pres. Belmont Hills Home and Sch. Assn., Lower Merion Twp.; legis. chmn. Lower Merion Sch. Dist. Intersch. Council; mem. Task Force on Mental Health of Children and Youth of Pa.; treas., chmn. edn. com. Human Relations Council, Lower Merion; v.p., parliamentarian Nes Ami Penn Valley Congregation, Lower Merion Twp. Named Woman of Yr., Oxford Circle Jewish Community Center, 1979, Woman of Distinction, Golden Slipper Club, 1979; Gowen fellow, 1954-55. Mem. Am. Law Inst., Am. Bar Found., ABA (vice chmn. com. law and mental health sect. family law), Pa. Bar Assn. (ho. of dels. 1979—), Phila. Bar Assn. (chmn. com. women's rights 1972, 74-75, chmn. bd. govs. 1977—, chmn. public relations com. 1978), Fed. Bar Assn., Nat. Assn. Women Lawyers, Phila. Trial Lawyers Assn., Am. Judicature Soc., Phila. Fellowship Commn., Order of Coif (chpt. pres. 1973-75), Tau Epsilon Rho. Office: US Dist Courthouse Rm 10614 US Courthouse Independence Mall W Philadelphia PA 19106*

SHAPIRO, SANDRA, lawyer; b. Providence, Oct. 17, 1944; d. Emil and Sarah (Cohen) S. AB magna cum laude, Bryn Mawr Coll., Pa., 1966; LLB magna cum laude, U. Pa., 1969. Bar: Mass. 1970, U.S. Dist. Ct. Mass. 1971, U.S. Ct. Appeals (1st cir.) 1972, U.S. Supreme Ct. 1980. Law clk. U.S. Ct. Appeals for First Cir., Boston, 1969-70; assoc. Foley, Hoag & Eliot, Boston, 1970-75; ptnr. Foley, Hoag & Eliot, 1976—; Mem. Bd. Bar)verseers Mass. Supreme Judicial Ct., 1988—, Gender Bias Study Com., 1986-89. Contbr. articles to profl. jours. Woodrow Wilson fellow 1966. Mem. Women's Bar Assn. of Mass. (pres. 1985-86), New Eng. Women in Real Estate, Nat. Women's Law Ctr. Network, ABA, Mass. Bar Assn. (chmn. real property sect. coun.), Boston Bar Assn. (coun. mem.), U. Pa. Law Sch. Alumni Assn. (bd. mgrs. 1990—), Order of the Coif. The Boston Club. Office: Foley Hoag & Eliot One Post Office Sq Boston MA 02109

SHARBAUGH, KATHRYN KENNEDY, artist; b. Norwich, Conn., June 28, 1948; d. Theodore and Mary (Waters) Kennedy; m. Charles Carroll Sharbaugh, June 21, 1975. BFA, Kans. City Art Inst., 1967-71; MFA, Cranbrook Acad. of Art, Bloomfield Hills, Mich., 1974. Freelance pattern designer Corning (N.Y.) Glass Works, 1974, Mikasa, N.Y., 1975, Lauffer, N.Y., 1975; instr. Flint (Mich.) Inst. of Arts. Maker: dinnerware, teapots exhibited in pub. collections including Cranbrook Mus. Art, Flint Inst. Arts, Mus. R.I. Sch. Design, Cooper-Hewitt Decorative Arts Mus. of Smithsonian Inst., Slater Mus., Mus. Het Kruithuis/Netherlands. Nat. Endowment of Arts fellow, 1980, Mich. Coun. of Arts fellow, 1985. Mem. Pewabic Soc., Detroit Inst. Arts, Audubon Soc. Home: 4304 Grange Hall Rd Holly MI 48442 Office: Flint Inst of Arts E Kearsley Flint MI 48503

SHARBEL, JEAN M., editor; b. Lansford, Pa.; d. Joseph and Star (Nemir) Sharbel. BA in Journalism, Hunter Coll., N.Y.C. Editorial dir., v.p. Dauntless Books, N.Y.C., 1962-75; editor romance mags., Macfadden Holdings Inc., N.Y.C., 1976—. Office: True Romance Macfadden Holdings Inc 233 Park Ave South New York NY 10003

SHAREFF, KAREN RAE, interior design company executive; b. N.Y.C., Sept. 1, 1945; d. Harold and Miriam (Gofrener) Friedlander; m. Ira Shareff, Nov. 1, 1975. BS, Pratt Inst., 1968; student, U. Cin., 1963-66. Project designer Samson Contract Furniture Co., Inc., N.Y.C., 1968-73; dir. design Wendover Devel. Corp., Irvington, N.Y., 1973-76, Sci. Environs., Inc., N.Y.C., 1980-83; co-ptnr. Shareff Designs, N.Y.C., 1976-80; sr. project mgr. Belmuth Design Group, Ltd., N.Y.C., 1983-84; dir. design Am. Contract Designers, N.Y.C., 1984-88; pres. Shareff Creative Concepts, Inc., N.Y.C., 1988—; cons. Integrated Svcs. Corp., N.Y.C., 1988—, Eeco Devel. Corp., Virginia Beach, Va., 1988—. Mem. Am. Soc. Interior Designers (cert., profl.), Am. Crafts Coun. Home and Office: 81 Irving Pl New York NY 10003

SHARFMAN, CAROLINE SHARP, commercial paper credit analyst; b. Ann Arbor, Mich., Aug. 27, 1942; d. Mahlon Samuel and Mary Patricia (Potter) Sharp; m. William Lee Sharfman, Sept. 5, 1964 (div. 1985); m. James Edmund Bacon, Nov. 4, 1989. BA with distinction, U. Mich., 1964; MBA, Columbia U., 1975. Assoc. Goldman, Sachs & Co., N.Y.C., 1975-80, v.p., 1980-83; v.p. Goldman Sachs Money Markets Inc., N.Y.C., from 1983. Chmn. fin. com., vestry mem. Christ & St. Stephens Ch. Mem. Phi Beta Kappa, Phi Sigma Iota, Beta Gamma Sigma. Episcopalian.

SHARMA, SANTOSH DEVRAJ, obstetrician and gynecologist, educator; b. Kenya, Feb. 24, 1934; came to U.S., Jan. 1972; d. Devraj Chananram and Lakshmi (Devi) S. BS, MB, B.J. Medical Sch., Pune, India, 1960. Resident in ob-gyn. various hospitals, England, 1961-67; lectr., sr. lectr. in ob-gyn. Makerere Med. Sch., Kampala, Uganda, 1967-72; asst. prof. ob-gyn. Howard U. Med. Sch., Washington, 1972-74; assoc. prof. John A. Burns Sch. Med., Honolulu, 1974-78, prof., 1978 --. Fellow Royal Coll. Ob-Gyn., Am. Coll. Ob-Gyn.

SHARP, ANNE CATHERINE, artist, educator; b. Red Bank, N.J., Nov. 1, 1943; d. Elmer Eugene and Ethel Violet (Hunter) S. BFA, Pratt Inst., 1965; MFA (teaching fellow 1972), Bklyn. Coll., 1973. Tchr. art Sch. Visual Arts, 1978-89, NYU, 1978, SUNY-Purchase, 1983, Pratt Manhattan Ctr., N.Y.C., 1982-84, Parsons Sch. Design, N.Y.C., 1984—. One-person shows Pace Editions, N.Y.C., Ten/Downtown, N.Y.C., Katonah (N.Y.) Gallery, 1974, Contemporary Gallery, Dallas, 1975, Art in a Public Space, N.Y.C., 1979, Eatontown Hist. Mus., N.J., 1980, N.Y. Pub. Library Epiphany Br., 1988, Books and Co., N.Y., 1989; group shows include Arnot Art Mus., Elmira, N.Y., 1975, Bronx Mus., 1975, Mus. Modern Art, N.Y.C., 1975-76, Nat. Arts Club, N.Y.C., 1979, Calif. Mus. Photography, Riverside, 1983-89, Jack Tilton Gallery, N.Y.C., 1983, Lincoln Center, N.Y.C., 1983, Cabo Frio Print Biennale, Brazil, 1983, Pratt Graphic Ctr., N.Y.C., 1984, State Mus. N.Y., Albany, 1984, Kenkeleba Gallery, N.Y.C., 1985, Hempstead Harbor Art Assn., Glen Cove, N.Y., 1985, Mus. Modern Art, Weddel, Fed. Republic of Germany, 1985, Kenkeleba Gallery, N.Y.C., 1985, Paper Art Exhbn. Internat. Mus. Contemporary Art, Bahia, Brazil, 1986, Mus. Salon-de-Provence, France, 1987, Mus. Contemporary Art, Sao Paulo, Brazil, 1985-86, Salon de Provence, France, 1987, Adirondack Lakes Ctr. for Arts, Blue Mountain Lake, N.Y., 1987, Kendall Gallery, N.Y.C., 1988, Exhibition Ctr. Parsons Sch. Design, N.Y.C., 1989, F.M.K. Gallery, Budapest, Hungary, 1989, Galerie des Kulturbundes Schwarzenberg, German Dem. Republic, Q 1989, Sen Do Gallery, Kobe, Japan, 1989, Davidson Galleries, Seattle, 1989, Anchorage (Alaska) Mus. History and Art, 1990-91; represented in permanent collections Smithsonian Instn., Nat. Air and Space Mus., Washington, Albright Knox Gallery, Buffalo, St. Vincent's Hosp, N.Y.C., N.Y. Pub. Libr., N.Y.C., White House (Reagan, Bush adminstrns.), others; Moon Shot series to commemorate moon landing, 1970-76, Cloud Structures of the Universe Painting series, 1980-86, Am. Landscape series, 1987-89, Thoughtlines, fall 1986, Swimming in the Mainstream with Her, U. Va., Charlottesville; author: Artist's Book - Travel Dreams U.S.A., 1989. Artist-in-residence grantee Va. Center for Creative Arts, 1974, Artpark, Lewiston, N.Y., 1980, Vt. Studio Colony, 1989; recipient Pippin award Our Town, N.Y.C., 1984. Mem. Coll. Art Assn. Am., Nat. Space Soc., Found. for Community Artists, Pratt Alumni Assn., Artists Equity.

SHARP, JANE ELLYN, deputy operations director; b. Chgo., Jan. 5, 1934; d. Truman V. and Mildred L. (Sweitzer) Lasswell; m. David H. Sharp, July 24, 1965 (div. Aug. 1979); children: Michelle Lynn, Lisa Elizabeth. BBA, Coll. Santa Fe, 1985, MBA, 1988. Adminstrv. asst. San Diego State U., 1956-58; dir. classified personnel Grossmont (Calif.) Union High Sch. and Jr. Coll. Dist., 1959-62; legal asst. Stockly & Boone, Attys., Los Alamos, N.Mex., 1974-75; with adminstrn. Los Alamos (N.Mex.) Nat. Lab., 1976-78, pub. rels. specialist, 1978-81, asst. group leader, 1981-82, dep. group leader, 1982-83, asst. div. leader, 1983-84, office dir. protocol, 1984-89, dep. assoc. dir. for ops., 1989—. Mem. adv. bd. Youth Working for Youth, Los Alamos, 1985—; mem. Adults Working for Youth, Los Alamos, Santa Fe Rail Link Task Force, 1987—, Los Alamos Community Devel. Com., 1989—; bd. dirs. Los Alamos Econ. Devel. Corp., 1989—. Recipient Woman at Work award Coun. on Working Women, 1984. Mem. Tri Area Assn. for Econ. Devel., Los Alamos Nat. Lab. Community Coun. (rep. exec. bd. 1986—). Democrat. Office: Los Alamos Nat Lab PO Box 1663 MS P368 Los Alamos NM 87544

SHARP, JERRILYN SUE, medical technologist; b. Kalamazoo, Mich., July 15, 1957; d. James Cleveland and Jacqueline Jean (Corradini) VanAtta; m. Larry Lee Sharp, Apr. 25, 1981 (div. 1989); 1 child, Courtney Maline. Cert. in med. technology, Lakeland Med. Acad., Mpls., 1976. Intern VA Hosp., Sturgis, S.D., 1976; med. technologist Pinal Gen. Hosp., Florence, Ariz., 1976-79, Bronson Vicksburg (Mich.) Hosp., 1979-88, Family Health Ctr., Kalamazoo, 1989-90, War Meml. Hosp., Sault Ste. Marie, Mich., 1990—. Mem. Internat. Soc. Clin. Lab. Technologists. Home: 207 E Ann St Sault Sainte Marie MI 49783 Office: War Meml Hosp 500 E Osborn Sault Sainte Marie MI 49783

SHARP, LINDA ELIZABETH, engineering company administrator, consultant; b. Leesville, S.C., Feb. 7, 1948; d. Vivian Jacob and Mabel Elizabeth (Bouknight) Eargle; m. Darden Edward Sharp, Aug. 31, 1968; 1 child, Laura. BA in Psychology, Chaminade U., Honolulu, 1976; MBA, Cen. Mich. U., 1977. V.p. Fairway Golf Sales, Honolulu, 1975-77; asst. purchasing agt. McDonnell Douglas, St. Louis, 1978; mfr.'s rep. Western Electric, St. Louis, 1978-80; sales mgr. Southwestern Bell, Houston, 1980-82; tech. rep. AT&T, Houston, 1982-84; pres., owner Sharp Svcs., Inc., Houston, 1984-89; supervising engr. communications Cygna Group, Houston, 1989—. Mem. Assn. for Women in Computing. Repubican. Lutheran. Home: 1310 Plantation Dr Richmond TX 77469 Office: Cygna Group 5353 W Alabama Suite 555 Houston TX 77056

SHARP, MARY LUCILLE, sales representative publishing company; b. Chattanooga, Nov. 24, 1938; d. James Floyd and Margaret Lucile (Moore) S. BS, U. Tenn., 1961; MA in Teaching, U. Chattanooga, 1969. Airline stewardess Delta Air Line, Atlanta, 1961-62; legal sec. Witt Gaither Abernathy Caldwell & Wilson, Chattanooga, 1962-64; sec. IBM, Huntsville, Ala., 1964-65, Chattanooga; welfare worker Tenn. Dept. Pub. Welfare, Chattanooga, 1966-67; sch. social worker Chattanooga Pub. Schs., 1967-69; supr. liaison tchr. counsellor Moccasin Bend Mental Health Ctr., Chattanooga, 1969-75; dist. sales mgr. Jos Schlitz Brewing Co., Milw., 1977—; sales rep. Matthew Bender, N.Y.C., 1977—. Advocate of Youth Chattanooga C. of C. Neighborhood Council, 1973-75; bd. dirs. Mental Health Assn., Chattanooga, 1973-75. Mem. Alpha Delta Pi. Methodist. Home: PO Box 24376 Nashville TN 37202

SHARP, MICHIKO MAEZAWA, translator; b. Iida, Japan, Mar. 10, 1957; came to U.S., 1978; d. Kiyoshi and Naomi (Suzuki) Maezawa; m. Robert W. Sharp, Jan. 21, 1987. AA, San Diego Mesa Coll., 1980; BA, San Diego State U., 1982, MA, 1986. Exec. adminstrv. asst. Sanyo Calif. Corp., San Diego and Tijuana, Mex., 1984-87; internat. specialist Sharp HealthCare, San Diego, 1987-89; prin., translator, interpreter Sharp Japanese Translations & Svcs., San Diego, 1989—. Home: 5705 Friars Rd Unit 42 San Diego CA 92110

SHARPE, KATHLEEN CONKLIN, accountant; b. Suffern, N.Y., Sept. 29, 1955; d. Robert Charles and Shirley Ann (Oakley) Conklin; m. Joseph Darius Causey, Nov. 17, 1976 (div. 1981); 1 child, Angela Diane; m. Leland J. Sharpe Jr., Sept. 26, 1986; 1 child, Leland J. Sharpe, III. BS in Acctg., U. S.C., 1986. Asst. to mdse. mgr. Western Big Wheel, North Bergen, N.J., 1974-75; telecom supr. Dept. of Army, Fort Jackson, S.C., 1977-82; tax acct., Columbia, S.C., 1977-88; asst. to dir. S.C. Sentencing Guidelines Commn., Columbia, 1982-86; probation and parole pub. svc. employment coord. Parole and Community Corrections, Columbia, 1986-88; staff acct. Levitan and Yegidis, CPA's, Middletown, N.Y., 1988—; data analysis staff S.C. Jail Commn., 1982-83, Gov.'s JJ Coun., 1982-83, Sentencing Guidelines, 1982-83. Guardian-ad Litem Guardian-Ad-Litem Project, 1983-88; choir dir. children's choir Incarnation Lutheran Ch., 1984-86; co-chmn. fin. ocm. Community Ch. of Bloomingburg, N.Y., 1989—; co-leader Girl Scout U.S., Bloomburg; bd. dirs. Sarah Wells Girl Scouts Coun., Middletown; parents' adv. coun. Richland Sch. Dist. 1, 1984-85. With U.S. Army, 1975-77. Recipient Sustained Superior Performance award Dept. Army, 1981. Mem. Am. Correctional Assn., S.C. Correctional Assn., S.C. Victim Assistance Network, NAFE, Am. Soc. Notaries, Am. Philatelic Soc., Golden Key. Republican. Avocation: professional singer. Home: RD #1 Box 2 Bloomingburg NY 12721 Office: Levitan and Yegidis CPA's 40 Dunning Rd Middletown NY 10940

SHARPE, KATHRYN MOYE, psychologist; b. Barnesville, Ga., Nov. 27, 1922; d. Herbert Johnston and Henri Lucile (Winter) Moye; m. William Herschel Sharpe, Mar. 2, 1946; children: William Herschel Jr., Mark Stephens. AB, Piedmont Coll., Demorest, Ga., 1942; MA, U. N.C., 1947; PhD, U. S.C., 1975. Tchr., guidance counselor Charleston (S.C.) Pub. Schs., 1947-66; prof. sociology, chmn. dept. Bapt. Coll. at Charleston, 1966-88, prof. emeritus, 1988—; pvt. practice psychology, Charleston, 1975—. Kathryn Moye Sharpe scholarship given in her honor Bapt. Coll. at Charleston, 1988. Fellow Am. Assn. for Marriage and Family Therapy (approved supr., pres. S.C. div. 1975-77). Mem. Ch. of Christ. Home and Office: 6 Cavalier Ave Charleston SC 29407

SHARPE, MARTHA HAYES, small business owner; b. Calhoun, Ga., Feb. 5, 1942; d. George Marion and Avaleen (Hogan) Hayes; m. James A. Sharpe Jr., Mar. 10, 1963; children: Gregory Brian, Stacey Lynn. BA, Tex. Western U., 1964; M Libr. Sci. Media, Ga. State U., 1976. Cert. records mgr. Tchr. English Rome (Ga.) City Sch. System, 1967; head librarian Berkmar High Sch., Gwinnett County Sch. System, Lilburn, Ga., 1976-77; adminstrv. asst. Jordan, Jones & Goulding, Atlanta, 1977-84; founder, pres. The File Cabinet, Atlanta, 1984—. Mem. Assn. of Records Mgrs. and Adminstrs. (pres. 1988, chmn. bd. dirs. 1989, mem. of yr. 1987). Republican. Methodist. Office: The File Cabinet 3625 Zip Industrial Blvd Atlanta GA 30354

SHARPLES, VIRGINIA MITCHELL, engineering writing consultant; b. Indpls., July 3, 1942; d. James S. and Ruth K. Mitchell; BA (Operation Outstanding award 1974), Butler U., Indpls., 1964, MS, 1970; m. Richard J. Sharples, Dec. 24, 1973; children: Allison Virginia, Scott Brydson, Gregory Mitchell, Glen Ryan. High sch. tchr., Phoenix, 1971-74, Tucson, 1974-75, Houston, 1977-78, Rockwall, Tex., 1987; customer services rep. Advanced Computer Techniques, Tucson, 1976-77; tech. services engr. SWACO div. Dresser Industries, 1978-81, engring. writer Atlas div., Houston, 1981-82; copywriter Ogilvy & Mather, 1982-83; reservation sales agent Delta Air Lines, 1988—; nat. editor U.S. Woman Engr. Mag. seminar leader, engring. writing cons. Mem. Soc. Women Engrs. Dallas (v.p. 1987-88, producer slide show 1985, mem. nat. editorial bd. 1986-89), Soc. Petroleum Engrs. Episcopalian. Club: Dresser Toastmasters (pres. 1981, area gov. 1983-84). Author papers in field. Home and Office: 321 Yacht Club Dr Rockwall TX 75087

SHARRAR, VICTORIA ANNE, publishing company executive; b. San Jose, Calif., June 2, 1958; d. Hans Christian Gunnar and Dolores Valerie (Barton) Sorensen; m. Kenneth Andrew Sharrar, Aug. 6, 1983. BS, U. So. Calif., 1981. Office adminstv. mgr. nat. radio div. CBS, Inc., Los Angeles, 1982-84; account exec. Orange (Calif.) Broadcasting Corp., 1984-85; account exec. Dun and Bradstreet/Donnelley Info. Pub., Garden Grove, Calif., 1985-86, gen. tng. mgr., 1986, dist. sales mgr., 1986-89, regional area mgr., 1989—. Mem. NAFE, Broadcast Music Inc. (writer), Long Beach C. of C. Republican. Office: Donnelley Info Pub 300 Plaza Alicante Garden Grove CA 92640

SHARROW, MARILYN JANE, library administrator; bd. Oakland, Calif.; d. Charles L. and H. Evelyn S.; m. Lawrence J. Davis. BS in Design, U. Mich., 1967, MALS, 1969. Librarian Detroit Pub. Library, 1968-70; head fine arts dept. Syracuse (N.Y.) U. Libraries, 1970-73; dir. library Roseville (Mich.) Pub. Library, 1973-75; asst. dir. libraries U. Wash., 1975-77, assoc. dir. libraries, 1978-79; dir. libraries U. Man., Winnipeg, Can., 1979-82; chief librarian U. Toronto, Can., 1982-85; univ. librarian U. Calif., Davis, 1985—. Mem. program com. Ctr. for Research Libraries. Recipient Woman of Yr. in Mgmt. award Winnipeg YWCA, 1982; named Woman of Distinction, U. Calif. Faculty Women's Research Group, 1985. Mem. ALA, Research Libraries Group (bd. dirs.), Assn. Research Libraries (bd. dirs., v.p., pres-elect 1989—), Internat. Fedn. Library Assns. (univ. libraries sect.). Office: U Calif-Davis 108 Shields Library Davis CA 95616

SHATTO, GLORIA MCDERMITH, college president, economist; b. Houston, Oct. 11, 1931; d. Ken E. and Gertrude (Osborne) McDermith; m. Robert J. Shatto, Mar. 19, 1953; children: David Paul, Donald Patrick. B.A. with honors in Econs., Rice U., 1954, Ph.D. (fellow), 1966. Mkt. rsch. Humble Oil & Refining Co., Houston, 1954-55; tchr. pub. sch. C.Z., 1955-56; tchr. Houston Ind. Sch. Dist., 1956-58; asst. prof. econs. U. Houston, 1965-69, assoc. prof., 1969-72; prof. econs., assoc. dean Coll. Indsl. Mgmt., Ga. Inst. Tech., Atlanta, 1973-77; George R. Brown prof. bus. Trinity U., San Antonio, 1977-79; pres. Berry Coll., Mt. Berry, Ga., 1980—; small bus. adv. com. U.S. Treasury, 1977-81; trustee Joint Council Econ. Edn., 1985-88; dir. Ga. Power Co., K-Mart Corp., So. Co., Becton Dickinson and Co., Citizens and So. Ga. Corp., The Citizens and So. Nat. Bank. Contbr. articles to profl. jours.; Editor: Employment of the Middle-Aged, 1972; mem. editorial bd.: Ednl. Record, 1980-82. Mem. Tex. Gov.'s Commn. on Status of Women, 1970-72; trustee Ga. Tech. Research Inst., 1975-77, Berry Coll., Ga., 1975-79, Ga. Forestry Commn., 1987—; mem. Ga. Gov.'s Commn. on Status of Women, 1975; mem. commn. on women in higher edn. Am. Council on Edn., 1980-82, chmn., 1982; mem. Ga. Study Com. on Public Higher Edn. Fin., 1981-82; v.p. Ga. Fund Ind. Colls., 1981, pres., 1982; mem. adv. bd. to Sch. Bus. Adminstrn., Temple U., Phila., 1981-83; mem. Study Com. on Ednl. Processes, So. Assn. Colls. and Schs., 1981-82, Ga. United Meth. Commn. on Higher Edn. and Campus Ministry, 1981—; bd. trustees Redmond Park Hosp., Rome, Ga., 1981-87. Recipient Disting. Alumni award Rice Univ., 1987; OAS fellow, summer 1968. Mem. Royal Econ. Assn., Am. Econ. Assn., So. Econ. Assn., Southwestern Econ. Assn. (pres. 1976-77), Am. Fin. Assn. (nominating com. 1976), Southwestern Social Scis. Assn., Fin. Execs. Inst. (chmn. Atlanta edn. com. 1976-77, mem. com. on profl. devel. 1981), AAUW (area rep. 1967-68, Tex. chmn. legis. program 1970-71, mem. internat. fellowships and awards com. 1970-76, chmn. 1974-76), Phi Beta Kappa, Phi Kappa Phi, Omicron Delta Epsilon. Office: Berry Coll 39 Mount Berry Sta Rome GA 30149

SHATTO, MAYME W., federal agency administrator; b. Russellville, Ky., Apr. 26, 1936; d. Phillip Eddie and Rose Maidson (Bond) Williams; m. Harry William Shatto, June 5, 1956; children: Harry, Christian. Cert., Nashville Bus. Coll., 1956, Watkins Inst., 1956; student, Sinclair Coll., 1963, Trident Tech. Coll., 1976. With Govt. of Guam, 1961-62; adminstr. City of Dayton, Ohio, 1962-63; adminstr. air force logistics command Wright-Patterson AFB, Ohio, 1964-74; adminstr. Naval Facilities Engring. Command, Charleston, S.C., 1974-75; contract specialist Naval Electronic Systems Engring. Command, Charleston, 1976-78; with Procurement Adminstrn. Def. Fuel Supply Ctr., Alexandria, Va., 1978-80; contract adminstr. Naval Facilities Engring. Command, Washington, 1980-82, Naval Telecommunications Command, Washington, 1982-84; adminstr. USN ADP Selection Office, Washington, 1984-85; contract adminstr. U.S. Army Info. Systems Selection/Acquisition Activity, Alexadria, 1985-88; supr. contract specialist dept. treasury Bur. Engraving and Printing, Washington, 1988—. Adult leader Boy Scouts Am. Mem. Nat. Contract Mgmt. Assn.

SHATTUCK, BARBARA ZACCHEO, investment banker; b. New Rochelle, N.Y., Dec. 25, 1950; d. John Nicholas and Mary-Jane (Haller) Zaccheo; m. John Garrett Shattuck (div.); m. Arthur M. Dubow. AB, Conn. Coll., 1972; postgrad. NYU Sch. Bus., 1974-75. Bond analyst Standard & Poor's, N.Y.C., 1972-76; assoc. Blyth, Eastman Dillon & Co., N.Y.C., 1976; v.p. Goldman, Sachs, N.Y.C., 1976-82; ptnr. Cain Bros, Shattuck & Co., N.Y.C., 1982—; speaker Practicing Law Inst., Am. Hosp. Assn. Fundraiser Mondale for Pres., N.Y.C., 1983-84, mem. nat. fin. com. Dukakis for Pres.; bd. dirs. Seltzer Found.; mem. friends of collection com. Parrish Art Mus., Southampton, N.Y. Mem. Women's Econ. Round Table. Democrat. Episcopalian. Club: India House (N.Y.C.).

SHATTUCK, CATHIE ANN, lawyer, government official; b. Salt Lake City, July 18, 1945; d. Robert Ashley S. and Lillian Culp (Shattuck). B.A., U. Nebr., 1967, J.D., 1970. Bar: Nebr. 1970, U.S. Dist. Ct. Nebr. 1970, Colo. 1971, U.S. Dist. Ct. Colo. 1971, U.S. Supreme Ct. 1974, U.S. Ct. Appeals (10th cir.) 1977, U.S. Dist. Ct. D.C. 1984, U.S. Ct. Appeals (D.C. cir.) 1984. V.p., gen. mgr. Shattuck Farms, Hastings, Nebr., 1967-70; asst. project dir. atty. Colo. Civil Rights Commn., Denver, 1970-72; trial atty. Equal Employment Opportunity Commn., Denver, 1973-77; vice chmn. Equal Employment Opportunity Commn., Washington, 1982-84; pvt. practice law Denver, 1977-81; mem. Fgn. Svc. Bd., Washington, 1982-84, Presdl. Personnel Task Force, Washington, 1982-84; ptnr. Epstein, Becker & Green, L.A. and Washington, 1984—; lectr. Colo. Continuing Legal Edn. Mem. editorial bd. The Practical Litigator, 1988—. Mem. Met. Opera Guild, N.Y.C.; bd. dirs. KGNU Pub. Radio, Boulder, Colo., 1979, Denver Exchange, 1980-81, YWCA Met. Denver, 1979-81. Recipient Nebr. Young Career Woman Bus. and Profl. Women, 1967; recipient Outstanding Nebraskan Daily Nebraskan, Lincoln, 1967. Mem. ABA (mgmt. chair labor and employment law sect. com. on immigration law 1988-90, mgmt. chair com. on legis. devels. 1990—), Nebr. Bar Assn., Colo. Bar Assn., Colo. Women's Bar Assn., D.C. Bar Assn., Nat. Womens Coalition, Delta Sigma Rho, Tau Kappa Alpha, Pi Sigma Alpha, Alpha Xi Delta. Club: Denver.

SHAUGHNESSY, APRIL MARIE, pharmacist; b. Chgo., May 12, 1957; d. John Clyde and Frances Pauline (Gucciardi) S. BS in Pharmacy, Creighton U., Omaha, 1981. Pharmacist U. Chgo. Hosps., Chgo., 1982-84, Walgreens Pharmacy, Chgo., 1982-88; exec. resident Am. Pharmaceutical Assn., Wash., 1987-88; profl. affairs assoc. Am. Pharm. Assn., Wash., 1988—. Named Outstanding Young Women of Am., 1987; recipient Upjohn Achievement award Creighton U., Omaha, 1981. Mem. Am. Pharmaceutical Assn., Am. Assn. Colls. of Pharmacy. Office: Am Pharm Assn 2215 Constitution Ave NW Washington DC 20037

SHAUGHNESSY, MARIE KANEKO, artist, business executive; b. Detroit, Sept. 14, 1924; d. Eishiro and Kiyo (Yoshida) Kaneko; m. John Thomas Shaughnessy, Sept. 23, 1959. Assocs. in Liberal Arts, Keisen Women's

Coll., Tokyo, 1944. Ops. mgr. Webco Alaska, Inc., Anchorage, 1970-88; ptnr. Webco Partnership, Anchorage, 1983—, also bd. dirs. Paintings include Lilacs, 1984, Blooms, 1985, The Fence, 1986 (Purchase award 1986), Red and Green Tomatoes, 1989 (award), Grapes, 1989 (award), Dancing Daisies, 1989 (award), Yellow Lilies, 1990 (award, Vermillion Mum, 1990 (award). Bd. dirs. Alaska Artists Guild, 1971-87; commr. Mcpl. Anchorage Fine Arts Commn., 1983-87; organizing com. Japanese Soc. Alaska, 1987. Recipient Arts Affiliates award, Anchorage Community Coll., 1975, 1978, 1984; named Univ. Artist, Alaska Pacific U., 1986, Red and Green Tomatoes award, 1989, Grapes award, 1989, Dancing Daisies award, 1989, Yellow Lilies award, 1990, Vermillion Mum award, 1990. Mem. Potomac Valley Watercolorists (bd. dirs.), Va. Watercolor Soc., Art League, Sumi-E Soc. of Am. (bd. dirs., pres. Washington area chpt.), San Diego Watercolor Soc., Alaska Watercolor Soc. (life). Republican. Episcopalian. Home: 1200 Allendale Rd McLean VA 22101

SHAUGHNESSY, MARY ROSE, English educator; b. Kansas City, Mo., Apr. 28, 1931; d. Joseph Bernard and Frances (Shepherd) S. BA, St. Mary's Coll., Notre Dame, Ind., 1952; MA, U. Notre Dame, 1960; PhD, U. Chgo., 1973. Prof. English, Chgo. State U., 1968—. Author: Women, Success and Society in Works of Edna Ferber, 1977, Fannie Hurst, 1981; contbr. articles to profl. jours. Bd. dirs. Hyde Park Art Ctr., Chgo., 1987—. Fulbright prof. Nanjing (People's Republic China) U., 1985-86. Mem. MLA, George Eliot Fellowship, U. Chgo. Alumni Assn., Jackson Park Yacht Club (bd. dirs. 1988-89). Roman Catholic. Home: 4940 East End Ave Chicago IL 60615 Office: Chgo State U 95th and King Dr Chicago IL 60628

SHAVER, TAMI LEE, rehabilitation center administrator; b. Liberty, N.Y., May 7, 1958; d. Larry Fredrick and Betty Lou (Hornbeck) S. BS in Phys. Edn., SUNY, Brockport, 1981; postgrad., Marist Coll., Poughkeepsie, N.Y., 1988—. Outdoor educator Frost Valley Environ. Ctr., Oliverea, N.Y., 1982-83; substitute tchr. Sullivan County Pub. Schs., South Fallsburg, N.Y., 1983-84; remedial educator Sullivan County Assn. for Retarded Citizens, South Fallsburg, 1984-87; spl. instr. Sullivan County Community Coll., Loch Sheldrake, N.Y., 1985-87; program dir., team leader Crystal Run Village, Inc., Middletown, N.Y, 1987-89; program coordinator Children's Rehab. Ctr., Kingston, N.Y., 1989—; summer recreation supr. Yankee Lake, Wurtsboro, N.Y., 1984-85. Mem. NAFE, SUNY-Brockport Alumni Assn. Democrat. Methodist. Home: 14 Grand St Poughkeepsie NY 12601

SHAVERS, LISA, social worker; b. L.A., Sept. 15, 1963; d. Harry and Beverly (Ambrester) S. BA in Psychology, Antioch U., 1985; MA in Psychology, Pacific So. U., 1987. Clin. asst. Venice (Calif.) Family Clinic, 1984; program supr., project counselor Exceptional Children's Found., L.A., 1985-88; client program coord., resource devel. specialist, social worker So. Central L.A. Regional Ctr. for Devel. Disabled Persons, L.A., 1988—; social worker, cons. Care Visions, Anaheim, Calif., 1989; dir. spl. projects Bryant Group, Beverly Hills, Calif., 1989. Mentor Fulfillment Fund, Beverly Hills, Calif., 1990. Regalettes Inc. scholar, 1983-84. Mem. NAACP, Assn. Black Psychologists, Alpha Kappa Alpha (undergrad. advisor). Democrat. Methodist. Office: South Central LA Reg Ctr 2160 W Adams Blvd Los Angeles CA 90018

SHAW, CAROL JEAN, insurance company executive; b. Joliet, Ill., July 27, 1952; d. Henry and Ethel Virginia (Klipfel) S.; m. Daniel Wilson Hopkins, Aug. 17, 1974 (div. Sept. 1978). BA cum laude, No. Ill. U., 1974. CPCU. Collection dept. Sears, Roebuck & Co., Schaumburg, Ill., 1974-76; sec. City of Bloomington, Ill., 1976-79; supr. State Farm Ins. Co., Bloomington, 1979-81, tng. analyst, 1981-84. Panel mem. McLean County (Ill.) United Way, McLean County, 1985-89; fundraiser McLean County Humane Soc., 1988-90. Mem. Soc. CPCUs (new designee rep. 1986-87, chmn. candidate devel. 1988-89). Democrat. Methodist. Office: State Farm Ins Co 1 State Farm Pla Bloomington IL 61710

SHAW, CAROLE, editor, publisher; b. Bklyn., Jan. 22, 1936; d. Sam and Betty (Neckin) Bergenthal; m. Ray Shaw, Dec. 27, 1957; children: Lori Eve Cohen, Victoria Lynn. BA, Hunter Coll., 1962. Singer Capitol Records, Hilton Records, Rama Records, Verve Records, 1952-65; TV appearances Ed Sullivan, Steve Allen, Jack Paar, George Gobel Show, 1957; owner The People's Choice, L.A., 1975-79; founder, editor-in-chief BBW mag., Beverly Hills, Calif., 1979—; creator BBW label clothing line. Author: Come Out, Come Out Wherever You Are, 1982. Office: BBW: Big Beautiful Woman 9171 Wilshire Blvd #300 Beverly Hills CA 90210

SHAW, CATHLEEN MALIN, sales executive; b. Seattle, July 28, 1958; d. Wilfred H. and Ethelann (Malin) S. Mgr. Osceola Lake Inn, Hendersonville, N.C., 1977-86; mgr. Seacoast Towers Suite Hotel, Miami Beach, Fla., 1986-89, v.p. sales, 1989—. Mem. Dade County Women's Polit. Caucus, Miami, 1990—, Miami Beach C. of C., 1987, The Miami Forum, 1990—. Mem. Soc. Incentive Travel Execs., Fla. Soc. Assn. Execs., Meeting Planners Internat., NAFE, Assn. Corp. Travel Execs., Fla. Hotel and Motel Assn., Greater Miami Conf. and Visitors Bur. (corp. adv. bd. 1990). Republican. Presbyterian. Office: Seacoast Towers Suite Hotel 5151 Collins Ave Miami Beach FL 33140

SHAW, ELEANOR JANE, newspaper editor; b. Columbus, Ohio, Mar. 23, 1949; d. Joseph Cannon and Wanda Jane (Campbell) S. BA, U. Del., 1971. With News-Jour. newspapers, Wilmington, Del., 1970-82, acting bus. editor, 1976-77, editor HEW desk, asst. met. editor, 1977-80, bus. editor, 1980-82; topics editor USA Today, 1982-83; asst. city editor The Miami Herald, 1983-85; projects editor The Sacramento Bee, 1985-87, news editor, 1987—. Bd. dirs. Del. 4-H Found., 1978-83. Mem. No. Calif. Wine Soc. (bd. dirs.). Office: The Sacramento Bee PO Box 15779 Sacramento CA 95852

SHAW, GRACE GOODFRIEND (MRS. HERBERT FRANKLIN SHAW), publisher, editor; b. N.Y.C.; d. Henry Bernheim and Jane Elizabeth (Stone) Goodfriend; m. Herbert Franklin Shaw; 1 son, Brandon Hibbs. Student, Bennington Coll.; BA magna cum laude, Fordham U., 1976. Reporter Port Chester (N.Y.) Daily Item; editorial coordinator World Scope Ency., N.Y.C.; assoc. editor Clarence L. Barnhart, Inc., Bronxville, N.Y.; freelance-writer for reference books; editing supr. World Pub. Co., mng. editor, sr. editor; mng. editor Peter H. Wyden Co., N.Y.C., 1969-70; assoc. editor Dial Press, N.Y.C., 1971-72; sr. editor Dial Press, 1972, David McKay Co., N.Y.C., 1972-75, Grosset & Dunlap, 1975-79; chief editor Today Press (Grosset), 1977-79; sr. editor, coll. dept. Bobbs-Merrill, N.Y.C., mng. editor, exec. editor trade div., 1979-80; pub. Bobbs-Merrill, 1980-84; mng. editor Rawson Assocs. div. Macmillan Pub., 1985—. Club: Overseas Press (bd. dirs. 1984-88, chmn. fgn. policy book awards 1983-87). Home: 85 Lee Rd Scarsdale NY 10583 Office: 866 3d Ave New York NY 10022

SHAW, HELEN LESTER ANDERSON, nutrition educator; b. Lexington, Ky., Oct. 18, 1936; d. Walter Southall and Elizabeth (Guyn) Anderson; m. Charles Van Shaw, Mar. 14, 1988. BS, U. Ky., 1958; MS, U. Wis., 1965, PhD, 1969. Registered dietitian. Dietitian Roanoke (Va.) Meml. Hosp., 1959-60, Santa Barbara (Calif.) Cottage Hosp., 1960-61; dietitian, unit mgr. U. Calif., Santa Barbara, 1961-63; rsch. asst., NIH fellow U. Wis., Madison, 1963-68; from asst. prof. to prof. U. Mo., Columbia, 1969-88, assoc. dean, prof., 1977-84; prof., chair dept. food and nutrition U. N.C., Greensboro, 1989—; cluster leader Food for 21st Century rsch. program U. Mo., 1985-88. Contbr. articles to rsch. publs. Elder 1st Presbyn. Ch., Columbia, 1975-89. Recipient Teaching award Home Econ. Alumni Assn., 1981, Gamma Sigma Delta, 1984; rsch. grantee Nutrition Found., 1971-73, NIH, 1972-75, NSF, 1980-83. Mem. Am. Inst. Nutrition, Am. Bd. Nutrition, Am. Soc. for Clin. Nutrition, Am. Dietetic Assn., Am. Home Econs. Assn., Soc. for Nutrition Edn., Sigma Xi, Phi Upsilon Omicron, Omicron Nu. Democrat. Office: U NC Dept Food and Nutrition A4 Park Bldg Greensboro NC 27401-5001

SHAW, HELEN LOUISE HAITH, educational administrator; b. Glen Raven, N.C., Oct. 6, 1931; d. Samuel and Robie (Summers) Haith; m. Benjamin Franklin Shaw, Apr. 9, 1954; children: Ronald Elliott, Roland Eric. BS, N.C. Agrl. and Tech. State U., Greensboro, 1953; postgrad., D.C. Tchrs. Coll., 1962-64, Monterey Peninsula Coll., 1966, 86, LaVerne Coll., 1975-77, Gavilan Coll., 1985-87. Cert. child devel. tchr., Calif. Elem. tchr. Lynchburg (Va.) City Schs., 1953-54, D.C. Pub. Schs., Washington, 1960-65; receptionist, dental asst. Dr. Benjamin Franklin Shaw, Seaside, Calif., 1970-85; from office pers. to adminstrv. asst. Infant Care Ctr., Inc., Seaside, 1984—. Life mem. NAACP. Mem. Black Am. Polit. Assn. Calif., Monterey Bay Dental Wives Group, Am. Legion Aux., Marina Women's Club, Howard U. Dental Student Wives Club, Fort Ord Officers Wives Club, Nat., Coun. Negro Women, Bus. and Profl. Women, Lions Wives Group, Citizens League for Progress, Ea. Stars, Heroines of Jericho, Quettes, Alpha Kappa Alpha (Kappa Gamma Omega chpt.). Democrat. Methodist.

SHAW, JANINE ANN, psychologist; b. Lamar, Mo., Feb. 21, 1955; d. Gerald Joseph and Lena (Caldwell) S. BA, Centenary Coll., Shreveport, La., 1977; PhD, Tex. Tech. U., Lubbock, 1984. Lic. psychologist. Psychologist Houston Police Dept., 1984-87, VA Med. Ctr., Houston, 1987—; mem. faculty Baylor Coll. Medicine, Houston, 1987—; cons. depts. ob-gyn. and dermatology Baylor Coll. Medicine, Houston, 1987—; pvt. practice, Houston, 1984—. Contbr. articles to profl. jours. Recipient Superior Performance award VA Med. Ctr., Houston, 1989, 90. Mem. Am. Psychol. Assn., Tex. Psychol. Assn. (publicity chair 1989), Houston Psychol. Assn. (ethics chair 1989—, pres. elect 1990-91, bd. trustees 1990, sec.-treas. 1988-89). Democrat. Roman Catholic. Office: VA Med Ctr Psychology Svc 2002 Holcombe Houston TX 77030

SHAW, LOIS WILLIAMS, inrerior designer, salesperson; b. Camden, S.C., Nov. 25, 1942; d. John Thomas Ray and Alberta (Branham) Williams; children: John Scott, Jennifer Leah. AB, Midland Tech. Coll., 1964; student, N.Y. Sch. Design, 1965, Furman U., 1970-75. Civil svs. USN, 1966-70; adminstrv. officer U.S. Dept. Interior, Clemson, S.C., 1971-82; interior designer Belk Dept. Store, Seneca, S.C., 1982-83; owner Interior Expressions, Inc., Seneca, S.C., 1983-84; contract officer Sherwin-Williams Co., North Myrtle Beach, S.C., 1984-86; contract mgr. Sands Contract Source, Myrtle Beach, S.C., 1986-88; owner, pres. Lois Shaw & Assocs., Inc., Myrtle Beach, S.C., 1988—. Sec. Nat. Cancer Soc., Seneca, 1981, pres., 1982;. Mem. NAFE, Nat. Builders Orgn. (assoc.), Hotel-Motel Orgn., Nat. Bus. and Profl. Women's Orgn. (sec. 1980-81), Nat. Assn. Women in Construction, Constrn. Specifications Inst. Republican. Lutheran. Home: 3307 Palm St North Myrtle Beach SC 29582 Office: Lois Shaw & Assocs Inc 4705B Oleander Dr Myrtle Beach SC 29577

SHAW, MARTHA LOUISE, physical therapist; b. Springfield, Mass., Sept. 11, 1959; d. Lewis Albert and Carol (Roper) S. BS, Springfield Coll., 1981; cert. in phys. therapy, Mayo Sch. Health Related Scis., Rochester, Minn., 1983. Staff phys. therapist Manchester Phys. Therapy, Bedford, N.H., 1983-88; sr. staff phys. therapist, facility mgr. Affiliated Phys. Therapists, Ltd., Phoenix, 1988—. Mem. Am. Phys. Therapy Assn. (chairperson membership N.H. chpt. 1986-88, pub. rels., 1985-88, orthopedic sect. 1988—).

SHAW, MARY ANN, psychologist; b. Dallas, July 5, 1937; d. Leon V. and Mabel (Bartlett) S.; B.S., U. Tex., 1959; M.Ed., U. Houston, 1966, Ed.D., 1973. Tchr. educable mentally retarded Spring Branch, Tex., 1959-64; vocat. counselor, Houston, 1964-66; psychometrist pvt. psychol. clinic, Houston, 1966-70; coordinator research Tex. Edn. Agency grant project, 1970-72; dir. psychol. services Tex. Scottish Rite Hosp. for Crippled Children, Dallas, 1972-82; dir. Dean Evaluation Ctr., Dallas, 1982-84; pvt. practice, 1982—; mem. clin. staff U. Tex. Health Sci. Center; cons. pvt. and public schs. Mem. Am. Psychol. Assn., Dallas Psychol. Assn., Assn. Pediatric Psychologists. Author: What Do I Do When; contbr. article to profl. jour.; research in field.

SHAW, SUSAN COULTER, school psychologist; b. Niagara Falls, N.Y., Mar. 25, 1943; d. John Alvah and Elizabeth (Heller) S. BA, Mt. Holyoke Coll., 1965; MS, Calif. State U., Hayward, 1974. Lic. ednl. psychologist, Calif. Teaching asst. Fulbright Teaching Assistantship, Biella, Italy, 1965-66; elem. tchr. Oakland (Calif.) Sch. Dist., 1968-71; sch. psychologist Castro Valley (Calif.) Sch. Dist., 1974-75, classroom aide, summer 1975; sch. psychologist Brisbane (Calif.) Sch. DIst., 1974-78, Millbrae (Calif.) Sch. Dist., 1977-78, Laguna Salada Sch. Dist., Pacifica, Calif., 1978-85, San Mateo County Office Edn., Redwood City, Calif., 1984—; cons. Ravenswood Sch. Dist., E. Palo Alto, Calif., 1990—, Diagnostic Sch.-No. Calif., San Francisco, 1989—, mem. adv. com. drug-exposed presch. project, 1989—. NDEA fellow, 1966-67. Mem. Nat. Assn. Sch. Psychologists, Calif. Tchrs. Assn., Sch. Psychologist Assn. San Mateo County (pres. 1987-88). Home: 319A Clipper St San Francisco CA 94114 Office: ECE Program 65 Tower Rd San Mateo CA 94402

SHAW, VIRGINIA RUTH, clinical psychologist; b. Salina, Kans., Dec. 10, 1952; d. Lawrence Eugene and Gladys (Wilbur) S. BA magna cum laude, Kans. Wesleyan U., 1973; MA, Wichita State U., 1975; PhD, U. Southern Miss., 1984. Rsch. fellow Wichita (Kans.) State U., 1973-75; rsch. fellow, teaching fellow U. So. Miss., 1978-79, 80-81; staff psychologist Big Spring (Tex.) State Hosp., 1976-78; predoctoral clin. psychology intern U. Okla. Health Scis. Ctr., Oklahoma City, 1981-82; postdoctoral fellow in neuropsychology Neuropsychiat. Inst., UCLA, 1982-83; rsch. psychologist, neuropsychologist L.A. VA Med. Ctr. Wadsworth Div., 1983-84; clin. neuropsychologist Patton (Calif.) State Hosp., 1984-85; clin. neuropsychologist Brentwood div. LA VA Med. Ctr., 1985; clinical, neuropsychologist Timberlawn Psychiatric Hosp., Dallas, 1985-87, Dallas Rehab. Inst., 1987—; cons. clin. neuropsychology Dallas area hosps., Willowbrook Hosp., Waxahachie, Tex., Cedars Hosp., Waxahachie; presenter profl. meetings, 1975—. Contbr. articles to profl. jours. Mem. Dallas Mayor's Com. for Employment of the Disabled, 1987, 500 Inc., Dallas, 1988—. Remiatte Meml. scholar Kans. Wesleyan U., 1970-73; recipient Nat. Disting. Svc. Registry award in rehab., 1989. Mem. Am. Psychol. Assn., Internat. Neuropsychol. Soc., Nat. Head Injury Found., Tex. Head Injury Found., Dallas Head Injury Found., Am. Congress Rehab. Medicine, Nat. Rehab. Assn., Nat. Acad. Neuropsychologists. Office: Dallas Rehab Inst 9713 Harry Hines Blvd Dallas TX 75220-5441

SHAW-GALLANT, CATHARINE, marriage and family therapist, writer; b. Washington, Feb. 13, 1944; d. Earl Wilbur and Catharine Estelle (Bishop) Shaw; children: Shannon, Jason. BFA, Md. Inst. Art, Balt., 1975; MEd, Lynchburg (Va.) Coll., 1980; MD, Johns Hopkins U., 1986. Cert. art, English and counseling tchr. Head art dept., counselor Chatham (Va.) Hall; counselor Bedford Schs., Forest, Va.; specialist fine arts and antiques Mayhill Publs., Knightsville, Ind.; pvt. practice therapy, free-lance writer, counselor Lynch Station, Va. Mem. DAR. Address: Mount Herman Farm Lynch Station VA 24571

SHAWHAN, DOROTHY SAMPLE, English educator, writer; b. Tupelo, Miss., July 16, 1942; d. George Vay and Jessie Mable (Talley) Sample; m. Ralph Thompson Shawhan, Sept. 16, 1969 (div.); 1 child, George Thompson. BA, Miss. U. for Women, 1964; MA, La. State U., 1966; MFA, George Mason U., Fairfax, Va., 1990. Instr. La. State U., Baton Rouge, 1966-69; editor Ind. U. Pubs., Bloomington, 1970-74; writer/editor Agy. for Instructional TV, Bloomington, 1975-81; prof. English Delta State U., Cleveland, Miss., 1981—. Editor Jour. of Miss. Council Tchrs. English, 1984-90; contbr. articles, short stories to profl. jours. Sec. Habitat for Humanity, Cleveland, Miss., 1987-89; bd. dirs. Crosstie Arts Council, Cleveland, 1987-89. Grantee, Radcliffe Coll. of Harvard U., 1985, AAUW, 1986, 89, Nat. Archives, 1987, Ford Found., 1988, Miss. Arts Commn., 1990. Mem. Miss. Council Tchrs. English, Nat. Council Tchrs. English, Assn. Tchrs. of Tech. Writing, AAUW (v.p. 1986-89). Methodist. Home: 217 S Leflore Cleveland MS 38832

SHAYEVITZ, JESSIE REBECCA, veterinarian; b. Dallas, Apr. 24, 1960; d. Berton Robert and Myra (Baker) S.; m. Robert Kellman, Sept. 3, 1989. BA with honors, Conn. Coll., 1982; DVM, Tufts U., 1986. Veterinarian Nashoba Valley Vet. Hosp., Westford, Mass., 1986-88, Mattydale Animal Hosp., Syracuse, N.Y., 1989-90, Greater Lowell (Mass.) Kennel Club, 1990—. Lectr. on vet. medicine to local schs. and Girl Scouts U.S.A. Vera B. Snowe fellow, 1982; Johnson scholar, 1983. Mem. AVMA. Jewish. Home: 100 Mountain View Dr Holyoke MA 01040

SHAYNE, JANE HIRSCH, advertising executive, director; b. Chgo., Nov. 7, 1946; d. Samuel Hirsch and Cecile Sylvia (Franks) Shayne Daskal; m. Carroll Joseph Clapp Jr., Feb. 11, 1971 (div. 1976). Student, Roosevelt U., 1964-65, Parsons Coll., 1965-67, Santa Monica (Calif.) Coll., 1968-69. Dir. coop. advt. New World Pictures, Inc., L.A., 1977-82; dir. advt. Landmark Theatres, Inc., L.A., 1982-83; nat. dir. coop. advt. and promotion spl. projects Samuel Goldwyn Co., L.A., 1983; promotion dir. Sta. KROQ-FM/KLAC, L.A., 1984; announcer Sta. KSRF-FM/KNJO-FM, Santa Monica, 1984-85; dir. creative svcs. Sta. WPIX-FM, N.Y.C., 1985-87; dir. advt., mktg. and promotion, announcer Sta. KTWV-FM, L.A., 1987-89; creative svcs. dir. and airstaff WQCD FM, Tribune Broadcasting, N.Y.C., 1989—; mktg. cons. Satellite Music Network, Dallas, 1988. Author poems, singer-songwriter. Mem. ASCAP, Broadcast Music, Inc. (writer), Broadcast Promotion Mktg. Execs., AFTRA. Democrat. Jewish. Office: WQCD FM 220 E 42nd St #2812 New York NY 10017

SHEA, ANNE JOAN, fashion editor; b. Beacon, N.Y., Dec. 29, 1907; d. Patrick Henry and Mary Loretta (Walsh) S. AB in Liberal Arts, Syracuse (N.Y.) U., 1929. Fashion editor The Bride's Mag., N.Y.C., 1952-63; dir. fashion promotion Angelo Bridals, N.Y.C., 1964-65; asst. to N.Y. mgr. Nat. Home Fashions League, 1965; freelance sec. to mgr. Union League Club of N.Y., 1963, 65; fashion cons. to pub. rels. dir. French Lace Inst., Paris, 1965-67; freelance fashion cons., stylist, 1966-70. Bd. dirs. Dag Hammerskjold Fund; mem. mobile blood bank unit ARC; vol. Svcs. for Children, Bide-A-Wee Home, Fairchild Tropical Gardens, Miami Heart Inst. Aux., Am. Mus. Natural History. Mem. Women in Communications, Fashion Group (bd. dirs. Fashion Critics award), Syracuse U. Alumni Assn., AAUW, Am. Assn. Ret. Persons, English Speaking Union, Internat. Platform Assn., Lucy Stone League, Smithsonian Assocs., Theta Phi Alpha. Home: 948 Bay Dr Miami Beach FL 33141

SHEA, DIANE SULLIVAN, county and municipal lawyer; b. Springfield, Mass.; d. Thomas C. and Mary J. (Buiso) Sullivan; 1 child, David A. BS, Ind. U., Purdue U., Indpls., 1979; JD, Ind. U., Indpls., 1989. Bar: Ind. Rsch. assoc. Ind. Assn. Cities & Towns, Indpls., 1980-82, rsch. dir., 1982-83, asst. legis. dir., 1983-84; asst. dir. Assn. Ind. Counties, Indpls., 1984—. V.p. LWV Indpls., 1976, chmn. juvenile justiceInd., 1984; pres. Marion county Juvenile Justice Task Force, Indpls., 1982; mem. Ind. Recycling Coalition; bd. dirs. Ind. Community Devel. Soc., 1986—. Mem. Ind. Bar Assn., Ind. Planning Assn. (Earle H. Franke award 1984, bd. dirs. 1984—), Ind. Soc. for Pub. Adminstrn. (v.p. 1983-85). Office: Ice Miller Donadio & Ryan One Amer Square Box 82001 Indianapolis IN 46282

SHEAHAN, MELODY ANN, transportation executive; b. Cin., Aug. 5, 1959; d. Earl Sterling and Willie Catherine (Stonestreet) McCoy. AA in Mech. Engrng. Tech., U. Cin., 1979; student, Marshall U., 1980-86, U. N. Fla., 1987—, Fla. Community Coll., 1988—. Engrng. tech. Chessie System R.R., Huntington, W.Va., 1979-81, asst. supr. motor vehicles, 1981-86; staff asst. CSX Transp., Jacksonville, Fla., 1986, engr. system material, 1986—. Named Outstanding Young Women Am., 1985. Mem. Am. Coun. R.R. Women (sec. 1984-86, 1st v.p. 1986-88, pres. 1988-90), Am. R.R. Engrng. Assn., U. Cin. Alumni Assn., First Coast Bus. and Profl. Women's Club (Jacksonville, Fla. chpt.), Order of Eastern Star. Home: 5321 Buggy Whip Dr Jacksonville FL 32257 Office: CSX Transp 500 Water St Jacksonville FL 32202

SHEAHEN, MARY CAROL, psychotherapist, social worker, pastoral counselor; b. Plainfield, N.J., Jan. 12, 1944; d. Elwood Cameron and Antoinette (Franklin) Conaway; m. Thomas Patrick Sheahen, May 27, 1967; children: Laura, Allan, Andrew. MSW, Rutgers U., 1970; MS, Loyola U., Columbia, Md., 1984. Diplomate Am. Bd. Clin. Social Work. Probation officer Probation Dept., N.Y.C., 1966-67; social worker Bur. Children's Svcs., Morristown, N.J., 1967-68; clin. social worker VA Hosp., Lyons, N.J., 1970-72; group therapist Waiden Resources, Silver Spring, Md., 1982-83; pastoral counselor NIH, Bethesda, Md., 1982-84; therapist United Parish Counseling Svc., Lantham, Md., 1984-87; adminstrv. dir. Affiliated Community Counselors, Rockville, Md., 1985, assoc. dir., 1985-89; pvt. practice psychotherapist Rockville, 1985—, Germantown, Md., 1989—; field instr., supr. U. Md., 1986-89, adj. prof., 1989; field liaison sch. social work Cath. U., Washington, 1989-90. Mem. Nat. Assn. Social Workers, Clin. Soc. Greater Washington, NAFE, Women's Bus. Orgn. Roman Catholic. Home: 18708 Woodway Dr Derwood MD 20855 Office: 13216 Executive Park Terr Germantown MD 20874

SHEAR, IONE MYLONAS, archaeologist; b. St. Louis, Feb. 19, 1936; d. George Emmanuel and Lella (Papazouglou) Mylonas; B.A., Wellesley Coll., 1958; M.A., Bryn Mawr Coll., 1960, Ph.D., 1968; m. Theodore Leslie Shear, June 24, 1959; children—Julia Louise, Alexandra. Research asst. Inst. for Advanced Study, Princeton, N.J., 1963-65; mem. Agora Excavation, Athens, 1967, 72—; lectr. art and archaeology Princeton U., 1983-84; also excavator various other sites in Greece and Italy. Mem. Archaeol. Inst. Am., Greek Archaeol. Soc. (hon.). Author: The Panagia Houses at Mycenae, 1987; contbr. articles to profl. jours. Address: 87 Library Pl Princeton NJ 08540

SHEAR, NANCY J., broadcaster; b. Phila., July 1, 1946; d. Leonard and Mildred (Goldstein) S. MusB, Temple U., 1972. Orchestra librarian Phila. Orchestra, 1964-69, Curtis Inst. Music, Phila., 1972-78, Internat. Festival Youth Orchestras, Eng., Scotland, Wales, summers 1974-76; broadcaster, producer Sta. WHYY-FM, Phila., 1978-80, Sta. WNYC-FM, N.Y.C., 1980—; free-lance writer, 1978—; speaker in field. Bd. dirs. Eleanor Roosevelt Ctr. at Val-Kill, Hyde Park, N.Y., 1986—; mem. exec. com. Eleanor Roosevelt Meml. Fund, N.Y.C., 1987—; coordinator pub. relations Musicians Against Nuclear Arms, N.Y.C., 1985—, Van Cliburn Internat. Piano Competition, 1988—, Steinway & Sons Piano Co., 1989—, Nat. Task Force on Performing Arts, 1989—. Mem. Am. Women in Radio and TV, Classical Music Assn., Am. Symph. Orchestra League, Assn. Inds. in Radio, Assn. Performing Arts Presenters. Home and Office: 180 West End Ave New York NY 10023

SHEARD, NORMA FAE VOORHEES, poet; b. Somerville, N.J., Apr. 15, 1936; d. Norman Hughes and Helene Patricia (Vielock) Vorhees; m. Eric A. Sheard, Oct. 12, 1957; children: Beth Eileen, Jeff Voorhees. Grad. high sch., Princeton, N.J. Owner, mgr. Postings, sending svc., Ringoes, N.J., 1988—; v.p., treas. Lescon, Inc., Flemington, N.J., 1975—; speaker on creativity and writing Federated Women's Clubs, N.J., 1988—; participant Bread Loaf Writers Conf., Middlebury, Vt., 1989. Author: (poetry) (with Robert Mahon) Tracks, 1988; contbr. poetry to various publs. Elder Flemington Presbyn. Ch. Poetry fellow N.J. Coun. on Arts, 1988-89. Mem. U.S. 1 Poets' Coop., Haiku Soc. Am., Nat. League Am. Pen Women, Acad. Am. Poets, Nat. Writers' Union, N.J. Poetry Soc., Princeton Arts Coun., Flemington Woman's Club (trustee). Republican. Home: 14 Fawn Dr Flemington NJ 08822

SHEARER, CAROLYN JUANITA, teacher; b. Heber Springs, Ark., May 20, 1944; d. James A. and Juanita Ruth (Wallace) S. BS, U. Colo., Boulder, 1966, MA, 1972. Cert. tchr., Colo. Tchr. Aurora (Colo.) Pub. Schs., reading resource tchr.; presenter writing process workshops. Author curriculum materials. Active local PTA, Neighbors Making a Difference--Rebuilding A Drug-Free Neighborhood; chairperson United Way, 1985-90; rep. ARC, 1980-84. Mem. NEA, Colo. Edn. Assn., Aurora Edn. Assn. (negotiations team, bd. dirs.), Internat. Reading Assn., Colo. Reading Assn., Aurora Reading Assn., Assn. Supervision and Curriculum Devel., Order Ea. Star, Pi Lambda Theta. Democrat. Methodist. Office: West Middle Sch 10100 E 13th Ave Aurora CO 80010

SHEARER, CYNTHIA LOUISE, executive; b. Cin., June 19, 1957; d. Robert Bruce and Cynthia Pearl (Castle) S.; m. William Thomas Mahood Jr., Nov. 26, 1986. BA, Wright State U., 1978; MA, Antioch U., London, 1979; DA, SUNY, Albany, 1982. Supr. writing lab. Wright State U., Dayton, Ohio, 1981-82; asst. prof. Rollins Coll., Winter Park, Fla., 1982-84, Mankato (Minn.) State U., 1984-87; pres. Wells & Bridges, Inc., Dayton, 1987—; adj. faculty Wittenberg U., Springfield, Ohio, 1980-81, Wright State U., Dayton, 1980-82, U. So. Maine, Portland, 1987-88, Antioch Coll., Yellow Springs, Ohio, 1989. Producer TV videos including Who Do We Think We Are: Images of Ourselves in Public Access TV, 1987; editorial bd. Newsmonthly Mankato State U., 1986-87. Faculty grantee Mankato U., 1985-86. Mem. NAFE, Coll. English Assn., Midwest Modern Language Assn., Popular Culture Assn., Dramatists Guild. Office: Wells & Bridges Inc 5585 Brandt Pike Dayton OH 45424

SHEARER, MARCIA CATHRINE, microbiologist, taxonomist; b. Akron, Ohio, Oct. 27, 1933; d. William Peter and Kathleen Dorthea (Leifheit) Epple; m. Charles Moyer Shearer, June 7, 1958. BS, Ohio State U., 1956; MS, Wayne State U., 1963. Assoc. microbiologist Parke, Davis & Co., Detroit, 1956-61, microbiologist, 1962-68; microbiologist Smith Kline & French Labs., Phila., 1968-72, sr. microbiologist, 1972-75, assoc. sr. investigator, 1975-85, cons. in taxonomy, 1985-86; sr. scientist Schering-Plough Corp., Bloomfield, N.J., 1986-89, prin. investigator, 1990—; presenter in field. Contbr. articles to profl. jours.; patentee antibiotics field. Mem. Am. Soc. for Microbiology, Soc. for Indsl. Microbiology, U.S. Fedn. for Culture Collections (sec.-treas. 1980-84, bd. dirs. 1989—), Sigma Xi. Home: 210 Green Hollow Dr Iselin NJ 08830 Office: Schering-Plough Corp 60 Orange St Bloomfield NJ 07003

SHEARIN, BETTY SPURLOCK, educational institution administrator; b. Salem, Va., Nov. 7, 1931; d. Thomas Shirley and Willie Ann (Borden) Spurlock; m. Alexander Moore Shearin Jr., June 1, 1957; 1 child, Victoria Louise. BS, Va. State U., 1954. Mem. staff Benedict Coll., Columbia, S.C., 1957—; acting pres. Benedict Coll., 1984-85, v.p. adminstrn., 1986-87, coord. archives, telecommunications, 1987-88, spl. asst. to v.p. bus. affairs, 1988—. Bd. dirs., Benedict Coll. Fed. Credit Union, 1974-79, 84—; asst. sec. bd. trustees, Benedict Coll., 1976-85, sec., 1985-86; sec. Colonial Park Community Home Assn., Columbia, 1988—. Mem. Assn. Records Mgrs. and Adminstrs. (sec. bd. dirs. 1983-85), Soc. Am. Archivists, NAFE, Columbia Personnel Assn., Am. Bus. Women's Assn., Alpha Kappa Alpha. Democrat. Episcopalian. Home: 4116 Grand St Columbia SC 29203 Office: Benedict Coll Harden and Blanding Streets Columbia SC 29204

SHEDD, REBECCA LYNN, wholesale distribution company manager, literacy trainer; b. Toledo, Nov. 24, 1954; d. Richard George and Marjorie Ann (Lunn) S. BA in Edn., DePauw U., 1976; postgrad. U. Minn. Purchasing agt. Water Products Co., Eden Prairie, Minn., 1977—, mgr. data processing, 1984-90, mgr. tng.purchasing, 1990—; tutor, trainer Laubach Literacy, Mpls., 1979—. Tutor, trainer, bd. dirs. Minn. Literacy Coun., Roseville, 1979—; lead trainer Mpls. Literacy Project, 1979—; v.p. program Minn. Literacy Coun.; corp. purchasing coord. Water Products Co. Recipient Gold award Minn. Literacy Coun., 1984 Mem. Nat. Assn. Purchasing Mgrs., Laubach Literacy Action (nat. tng. and cert. com. 1989—), DePauw U. Alumni Assn., Am. Soc. Tng. and Devel. Methodist. Avocations: skiing, biking, swimming, reading, traveling. Home: 4554 Wentworth Ave S Minneapolis MN 55409 Office: Water Products Co Corp Hdqrs 7887 Fuller Rd Eden Prairie MN 55344

SHEDRICK, GENEVIEVE MITCHELL, retired educator; b. Pittsburg, Kans.; d. Henry Levi and Emily Jane (Fonchoser) Mitchell; m. Wilbur Lawrence Shedrick, Aug. 19, 1942. BS, Savannah State U., Ga.; postgrad., Pittsburg (Kans.) Tchrs. Coll., 1941. Tchr. Terrell County Bd. Edn., Dawson, Ga., 1938-76; instr. Terrell County Adult Edn. Prog., Dawson, 1976—. Participant Vacation Bible Sch., Dawson, 1957-89; fin. sec. Sardis Bapt. Ch., Dawson, 1984; judge Terrell County Sch.'s Spelling Bee, Dawson, 1984—; vol. Terrell County Girls Club, 1986. Named Terrell County Tchr. of the Yr., 1957-58, Vol. award, Gov. Ga., 1988, Community Svc. award, Ga. Ret. Tchrs. Assn., 1989. Mem. Ga. Ret. Tchrs. Assn., Terrell/Lee Ret. Tchrs. Assn. (pres. 1984-88), Decemetts Social Club (sec.), Darcas Ch. Club (sec.), Am. Legion (pres. 1986-90). Democrat. Baptist. Home: 745 Center St NE Dawson GA 31742

SHEDRICK, MARY BERNICE, state legislator; b. Chickasha, Okla., Aug. 9, 1940; m. R. Mike Shedrick, 1957; children: Crystal Dawn, Michael Scott (dec.), Steven Link. BS, Okla. State U., 1969, MS, 1972; JD, Okla. City U. Law Sch., 1983. Educator, 1969-80, atty., mem. Okla. State Senate. Mem. Stillwater Okla. C. of C., Stillwater Arts and Humanities Council, Okla. State U. Alumni Found., Delta Kappa Gamma, Kappa Kappa Iota. Democrat. Baptist. Office: PO Box 843 Stillwater OK 74076*

SHEEDY, ALLY (ALEXANDRA ELIZABETH SHEEDY), actress; b. June 13, 1962; d. John and Charlotte (Baum) S. Student, U. So. Calif. Former model. Film debut in Bad Boys, 1983; other films include Wargames, 1983, Oxford Blues, 1984, The Breakfast Club, 1985, St. Elmo's Fire, 1985, Twice in a Lifetime, 1985, Short Circuit, 1986, Blue City, 1986, Maid to Order, 1987, Heart of Dixie, 1989; TV films include The Day the Loving Stopped, 1981, The Violation of Sarah McDavid, 1981, Deadly Lessons, 1983; author: (children's book) She Was Nice to Mice, 1975; contbr. articles to jours. Office: care Internat Creative Mgmt 8899 Beverly Blvd Los Angeles CA 90048*

SHEEHAN, DEBORAH ANN, radio station and theater executive; b. Paterson, N.J., Mar. 29, 1953; d. John J. and Ruth (Badertschier) S.; m. Emidio S. Quattrocchi, Mar. 15, 1985. B.A., William Patterson Coll., 1975. With radio Sta. WWDJ, Hackensack, N.J., 1980-83, Shadow Traffic, N.Y.C., 1981-83; dir. news, community affairs WPAT-AM/FM, N.Y.C., 1979—. Actress-tchr. Paterson Arts Ctr., 1975-79; host radio show Bus. Jour. N.J., 1984; host, producer radio show Debbie Sheehan mag., 1983; host FDU Focus, Cable Network N.J.; writer plays. Exec. dir., actress Learning Theater Co., Paterson, 1975—; sec. bd. dirs. YMCA Passaic Valley, Paterson, 1983—; mem. N.J. Legal Bd., Montclair, N.J., 1984—; mem. Paterson Edn. Found., 1984—; bd. dirs. United Way Passaic Valley, Conn., 1985. Recipient Edward R. Murrow Gold medal B'nai B'rith, 1983, finalist 1984-85; Gold medal Internat. Radio Festival, 1983; Best Reporter award Sigma Delta Chi, 1985-87, Personality Profile award local chpt., 1987, Best Pub. Service award, 1987; Best Feature award AP, 1985, 87; Angel Excellence award, Los Angeles, 1985, 87; Internat. Press Assn. fellow, Japan, 1985. Club: Zonta. Avocations: weaving; travel; acting. Office: WPAT-AM-FM 1396 Broad St Clifton NJ 07013

SHEEHAN, ELIZABETH ELLEN, social service organization executive; b. East Williston, N.Y., Jan. 15, 1940; d. Robert Vaughan and Evelyn Elizabeth (Horton) Jones; m. Robert Thomas Sheehan, Sept. 12, 1964 (dec. Mar. 1987); children: Kerith Leah, Robert Vaughan, Jonathan Lindsey. AB in Econs., Chatham Coll., 1961; postgrad. in social scis., U. Chgo., 1962. Teaching asst. Harvard U. Grad. Sch. Bus., Cambridge, Mass., 1962-63; mktg. rsch. analyst N.Y. Telephone Co., N.Y.C., 1963-64, writer, editor, 1964-65; v.p., treas. Focus Strategy Group, Inc., Princeton, N.J., 1984-87; v.p. mktg. Ctr. for Pub. Resources, N.Y.C., 1988—. Trainer, facilitator, cons. Jr. League Delaware Valley, Princeton, 1977-80; fund raiser Harvard-Radcliffe Parents Assn., N.Y.C., 1983-84; trustee McCarter Theatre Assocs., Princeton, 1985-88, Princeton Regional Scholarship Fund, 1985-87. Mem. Am. Mktg. Assn., N.Y. Jr. League, N.Y. Athletic Club. Republican. Episcopalian. Office: Ctr for Pub Resources 366 Madison Ave New York NY 10017

SHEEHAN, PATRICIA QUEENAN, pharmaceutical company specialist; b. Newark, Feb. 22, 1934; d. Michael and Sarah (McAfee) Queenan; m. Daniel M. Sheehan, June 25, 1957 (dec. Dec. 1961); children: Elizabeth, Daniel Jr., Michael. AB in History and Govt., Trinity Coll., Washington, 1955; LLD (hon.), St. Elizabeth Coll., Convent Sta., N.J., 1974, Rider Coll., 1975, St. Peter's Coll., Jersey City, 1977. Compensation and benefits analyst Johnson & Johnson, New Brunswick, N.J., 1963-72; corp. rels. adminstr. Johnson & Johnson, N.J., 1972-74; commr. State of N.J. Dept. Community Affairs, 1974-78; exec. dir. Hackensack (N.J.) Meadowlands Devel. Commn., 1978-80; mgr. corp. rels. Johnson & Johnson, New Brunswick, 1980—; mem. exec. com. Middlesex (N.J.) County Commn. on the Status Women, New Brunswick, 1985-89; mem. Middlesex County Regional C. of C., New Brunswick, 1982-88. Mem. adv. commn. Liberty State Pk., Jersey City, 1980-87; mayor City of New Brunswick, 1967-74; co-chair human resources com. U.S. Conf. Mayors, 1973; bd. trustees St. Peter's Med. Ctr., New Brunswick, 1989—, Trinity Coll., Washington, 1987—. Named Woman of the Yr., Archdiocese of Newark, 1975, Woman of the Yr., Iron Bound Mfg. Assn., 1980; recipient Achievement award YWCA of Cen. Jersey, 1989. Mem. Mil. Order of Malta, N.J. BIA (vice chair edn. com. Trenton, N.J. area 1985—), Bus. and Profl. Women's Assn. Democrat. Roman Catholic. Office: Johnson & Johnson 1 Johnson & Johnson Pla New Brunswick NJ 08933

SHEEHAN, RUTH CONROY, communications educator; b. Boston, May 5, 1954; d. Joseph Francis and Mary Martha (Hannon) Conroy; m. Joseph Paul Sheehan, Jr., Apr. 20, 1985; 1 child, Michael Bond. BS, Emerson Coll., Boston, 1977, MA, 1989. Tng. specialist Lechmere Sales Co., Cambridge, Mass., 1977-79; press coord. Student Competitions on Relevant Engring., Cambridge, 1979; energy analyst Tech. Rsch. Analysis Co., Falls Church, Va., 1980-81; project mgr. Exec. Forum, Boston, 1981-82; reg. rep. First Investors Corp., Boston, 1983-84; staff asst. Lasell Jr. Coll., Newton, Mass., 1984-88; instr. Framingham (Mass.) State Coll., 1988—, Northeastern U., Boston, 1989—, Endicott Coll., Beverly, Mass., 1989—. Mem. Weston (Mass.) Community Children's Assn., 1988—. Mem. Am. Soc. Tng. and Devel., Longwood Cricket Club. Roman Catholic. Home and Office: 484 Concord Rd Weston MA 02193

SHEEHAN, SUSAN, writer; b. Vienna, Austria, Aug. 24, 1937; came to U.S., 1941, naturalized, 1946; d. Charles and Kitty C. (Herrmann) Sachsel; m. Neil Sheehan, Mar. 30, 1965; children—Maria Gregory, Catherine Fair. B.A. (Durant scholar), Wellesley Coll., 1958. Editorial researcher Esquire-Coronet, N.Y.C., 1959-60; free-lance writer N.Y.C., 1960-61; staff writer New Yorker mag., N.Y.C., 1961—. Author: Ten Vietnamese, 1967, A Welfare Mother, 1976, A Prison and a Prisoner, 1978, Is There No Place on Earth for Me?, 1982, Kate Quinton's Days, 1984, A Missing Plane, 1986; contbr. articles to various mags., including N.Y. Times Sunday Mag., Washington Post Sunday Mag., Harper's, Atlantic, New Republic, McCall's, Holiday, Boston Globe Sunday Mag. Judge Robert F. Kennedy Journalism Awards, 1980, 84; mem. lit. panel D.C. Commn. on Arts and Humanities, 1979-84; mem. pub. info. and edn. com. Nat. Mental Health Assn., 1982-83; mem. adv. com. on employment and crime Vera Inst. Justice, 1978-86; chair Pulitzer Prize nominating jury in gen. non-fiction for 1988. Recipient Sidney Hillman Found. award, 1976, Gavel award ABA, 1978, Individual Reporting award Nat. Mental Health Assn., 1981, Pulitzer prize for gen. non-fiction, 1983, feature writing award N.Y. Press Club, 1984, Alumnae Assn. Achievement award Wellesley Coll., 1984; Guggenheim fellow, 1975-76; Woodrow Wilson Ctr. for Internat. Scholars fellow, 1981. Mem. Phi Beta Kappa. Home: 4505 Klingle St NW Washington DC 20016 Office: New Yorker Mag 20 W 43rd St New York NY 10036

SHEEHAN, VIRGINIA MARY, educator; b. New Bedford, Mass., Sept. 14, 1945; d. Timothy Joseph and Ellen (Murray) Lawlor; m. Robert Francis Sheehan, Sept. 28, 1963 (div. 1988); children: Elizabeth, Deborah, Timothy. BA in English, Southeastern Mass. U., 1982. Cert. tchr., Mass. Tchr. English New Bedford (Mass.) City Schs., 1985—; tutor New Bedford Sch. Dept., 1985—. Mem. sch. improvement coun. C.S. Ashley Sch., New Bedford, 1985-86, New Bedford High Sch., 1986-88. Mem. NEA, Mass. Tchrs. Assn., New Bedford Educators Assn., Nat. Coun. Social Workers. Democrat. Roman Catholic. Home: 427 Prescott St New Bedford MA 02745 Office: Roosevelt Jr High Sch 120 Dennis St New Bedford MA 02742

SHEEHY, MARYANN C., English educator; b. Greenwich, Conn., June 7, 1954; d. Joseph William and Mary Carol (Modugno) Gagon; m. Joseph John Sheehy, July 25, 1981. BS in English Edn., Western Conn. State U., 1976, MS, 1983, postgrad. Inst. on Thinking and Learning, Bard Coll., 1986-87. Cert. tchr., Conn. Tchr. English, New Milford High Sch., Conn., 1978—. Mem. Nat. Council Tchrs. English, Conn. Edn. Assn., NEA. Democrat. Roman Catholic. Avocations: writing, music, guitar, historic restoration, travel.

SHEELEY, RACHEL EVELYN, reporter; b. Richmond, Ind., Nov. 22, 1966; d. Lysle Leavitt and Alecia Eilene (Hindsley) S. BA, Franklin Coll. of Ind., 1989. Intern, writer weekend dept. Indpls. Star, 1988; intern, writer Brandon (Man., Can.) Sun, 1989; intern, writer Palladium-Item, Richmond, 1986-89, reporter, 1989—. Mem. YMCA. Winner first prize Bulwer-Lytton Fiction Contest, San Jose State U., 1988. Mem. Women in Communications, Phi Alpha Theta. Home: PO Box 38 6282 High St Williamsburg IN 47393 Office: Palladium-Item 1175 N A St Richmond IN 47374

SHEETS, MARTHA LOUISE, civic activist; b. Toledo, Mar. 25, 1923; d. Ira Elmo and Nellie Gertrude Merrill; m. Ted Charles Sheets, Dec. 21, 1946; children: Thomas Merrill, Susan Ruth, Laura Louise, Charles Ira. B in Edn., U. Toledo, 1945. Charter mem., trustee, sec.-treas., v.p., pres. Citizens for Metroparks, Inc.; commr. Met. Park Dist. Bd., 1976; mem. Gov.'s Commn. Restoration of State Capitol Bldg., Nashville, 1986; appointee City Commn. to Greenway Adv. Bd., 1989; active numerous civic orgns. including garden clubs, ch. groups. Mem. AAUW (chmn. 75th Birthday luncheon 1982, grantee Ednl. Found. program), ASME (chmn., pres. Northwest Ohio sect. women's aux.), Jr. Coterie Club (founding pres.), Zonta Internat. Svc. Club, Little Theatre Assocs. (past pres.), Murray Hills Garden Club, Tenn. Fedn. Garden Clubs (dist. historic preservation chmn. 1981-85, state historic preservation chmn. 1987-89), Chattanooga Coun. Carden Clubs (awards chmn.).

SHEETS, SUE LAURA, newspaper editor; b. Dayton, Ohio, Nov. 15, 1929; d. Charles LeRoy and Dorothy Ethel (Leis) Schaaf; student Ohio State U., 1947-48, hon. degree Nat. Cash Register Posting Sch., Denver, 1952; student YMCA Coll. of Commerce, Newark, Ohio, 1968; grad. Inst. Children's Lit., Redding Ridge, Conn., 1982; m. R.E. Walters; children—Steven Mitchell, Douglas Charles, Gregg Joseph; m. 2d, Ralph D. Sheets, June 21, 1969. Sec. with Ohio Fin. Co., Dayton, 1948-50, Goulds Pumps, Seneca Falls, N.Y., 1950-52, 53-54; poster, Colo. Nat. Bank, Denver, 1952-53; reporter Ace News, Heath, Ohio, 1966-68; founding dir. LEADS, Buckeye Lake, Ohio, 1968-72; sec. with Garwood Industries, Heath, 1973-74; columnist, editor, editor bus. and farm page, The Advocate, Newark, Ohio, 1978-82, entertainment and TV editor, 1982—; tchr. painting oils and acrylics, owner, operator arts and crafts shop, Hebron, Ohio, 1968-77. Organizer sr. citizens group, Buckeye Lake, 1968. Mem. Licking County Art Assn., Friends of Daweswood, NRA. Democrat. Methodist. Clubs: Order Eastern Star (Hebron)., Land of Legend Rifle and Pistol. Home: 180 S 5th St Newark OH 43055 Office: 25 W Main St Newark OH 43055

SHEETZ, CHRISTINE NINFA, food service director; b. Hilongos, Leyte, Phillipines, Nov. 10, 1940; d. Heracleo and Elena (Urgel) Suarez; m. Donald Lester Sheetz, May 9, 1981. BS in Home Econs. magna cum laude, U. San Carlos, Cebu City, Phillipines, 1962; MA in Edn. with high honors, U. San Carlos, 1974; postgrad., Lebanon Valley Coll., Annville, Pa., 1979. Cert. tchr. Pa. Elem. sch. tchr. Phillipine Pub. Schs., 1962-65; high sch. tchr. Franciscan Coll., Phillipines, 1965-70, instr., 1970-73; secondary prin. Santo Nino Acad., Phillipines, 1973-76, St. Christopher Acad., Phillipines, 1976-79; resident advisor Threshold Rehab. Services, Reading, Pa., 1981-82; food services supr. Fleetwood (Pa.) Area Sch. Dist., 1983-86, Exeter Twp. Sch. Dist., Reading, 1986—. Mem. Pa. Sch. Food Service Assn. (pres. ea. chpt. 1986-87). Republican. Roman Catholic. Home: Rte 4 Box 4355A Fleetwood PA 19522 Office: Exeter Twp Sch Dist 3650 Perkiomen Ave Reading PA 19606

SHEFF, HONEY A., clinical psychologist, educator; b. Bklyn., Nov. 24, 1954; d. Herbert Jack and Helene Ida (Sussman) Mendelson; m. Michael Robert Sheff, May 30, 1976. BA summa cum laude, Queens Coll., CUNY, 1975; MA, SUNY, Stony Brook, 1978, PhD, 1981. Lic. clin. psychologist. Psychologist Callier Ctr. for Communication Disorders, U. Tex., Dallas, 1981-83; pvt. practice clin. psychology cons., Dallas, 1983—, TV and radio appearances, Dallas, 1983—; lectr. U. Tex., Dallas, 1982—, clin. instr. psychology, dept. psychiatry Southwestern Med. Sch., 1983-86, clin. asst. prof. in psychology, 1986—, guest lectr. dept. emergency med. svcs. Health Sci., Southwestern Med. Sch., 1985—, also cons. rsch. project dept. psychiatry; oral examiner state cert. and licensing exam Tex. State Bd. of Examiners of Psychologists, 1989; cons. psychologist McKinney Job Corps Ctr., Tex., 1984-86; mem. Allied Health Profls.; staff mem. Green Oaks Hosp., Dallas, 1988—; presenter, workshop leader, tng. on family violence, Tex., N.Y. and N.H., 1977—; liaison com. Mental Health Assn. Dallas County and Mental Health Assn. Collin County; mem. profl. adv. bd. Dallas Ind. Sch. Dist. Psychol. Svcs., 1988—. Chmn. Dallas County Mental Health-Mental Retardation Ctr. task force to rev. svcs. to children and adolescents, 1985; chmn. Profl. Adv. Com. on Child and Adolescent Svcs., Dallas County Mental Health-Mental Retardation Ctr., 1986-89, vice chair, 1989—; founding mem. Parents Helping Parents Task Force, 1982-85; project designer Adolescent Mental Health Needs Dallas County, 1984; apptd. Mayor's Task Force on Child Abuse, Dallas, 1988—, also mem. task force tng., chair 2 subcoms.; facilitator Dallas County Child Protective Svcs. Community Forum, 1989, mem. assessment ctr. task force, 1989—; co-author jour. article, paper for profl. conf. (now chpt. in book). Charter mem. Parker Vol. Fire Dept., Tex., 1982—, sec.-treas., 1983-85. Recipient Robert S. Woodworth medal for excellence in psychology, Queens Coll., CUNY, 1975; commendation dept. psychology SUNY-Stony Brook, 1977, spl. recognition and award Dallas County Rape Crisis and Child Sexual Abuse Ctr. for Svc. to Community, 1985. Mem. Am. Psychol. Assn., Tex. Psychol. Assn. (regional rep. membership com.), Dallas Psychol. Assn. (pub. forum 1984), Nat. Register of Health Svc. Providers in Psychology, Mental Health Assn. Dallas County (mem., chmn. coms., award 1985, community svc. mental health award 1989, elected to bd. dirs.), Collin County Mental Health Assn. (charter 1988—), Nat. Council Family Relations, Tex. Council Family Violence, Internat. Soc. Prevention Child Abuse and Neglect, Phi Beta Kappa. Democrat. Jewish. Avocations: horseback riding, knitting and needlepoint, reading. Office: 13760 Noel Rd Ste 805 Dallas TX 75240

SHEI, JULIANA C., management specialist; b. Tokyo, Aug. 27, 1948; d. Wellington J. and Yoshiko (Araki) Chiang; m. Shen-Ann Shei; children: Irene, Ryan. BS, Nat. Cheng Kung U., Taiwan, 1971; MS, Southeastern Mass. U., 1975; MBA, Rensselaer Poly. Inst., 1987. Tech. interpreter Shionogi Pharm. Co., Taiwan, 1971-73; gen. mgr. Enterpreneurial Pub. Co., Los Alamitos, Calif., 1975-77; asst. chemist Ames lab. Iowa State U., 1977-81; rsch. scientist Tech. Ctr. U.S. Steel Corp., Monroeville, Pa., 1982-85; group coord. Sterling Drug Co., Rensselaer, N.Y., 1986—. Contbr. to tech. pubs. Mem. NAFE (sec.-treas. Pitts. sect. 1983-84, treas.-elect 1985), Assn. Women in Sci., Am. Chem. Soc., Am. Mgmt. Assn., Profl. Women's Network (pres. Capital dist. N.Y.).

SHEID, IRMA ELIZABETH, finance executive, accountant; b. Willmar, Minn., July 29, 1943; d. John E. and Elizabeth (Scheltens) Buss; m. John Rodney Veurink, Aug. 5, 1965 (div. 1971); 1 child, Chadwick Lynn; m. William Horace Sheid, Mar. 1, 1973 (dec. Feb. 1990). Grad. high sch., Everett, Wash. Office clk. Meth. Hosp., Mitchell, S.D., 1966-69; receptionist, bookkeeper Robert Radcliff, M.D., Modesto, Calif., 1969-71; orthodontic asst. R.A. Gaard, DDS, Modesto, Calif., 1971-73; bookkeeper Sheppard Trading Co., Mountain Village, Alaska, 1973-75; owner Melady Lanes, Arlington, Wash., 1976-78; controller Omni Enterprises, Bothell, Wash., 1979-88; v.p. fin. Nelson Marine & Equipment, Inc., Monroe, Wash., 1988—. Home: 13910 Spruce Ln Arlington WA 98223

SHEINGOLD, ROBIN, sales professional; b. N.Y.C., Apr. 12, 1952; d. Jack and Shirley (Bornstein) S. BA magna cum laude, Boston U., 1973. Mng. editor VIVA mag., N.Y.C., 1975-78; prodn. mgr. Working Woman mag., N.Y.C., 1978-80, N.Y. Times U.S. Mag., N.Y.C., 1980-84; account exec. Temp Connection, N.Y.C., 1984-86, sales mgr., 1986—. mem. N.Y. Assn. Temporary Svcs., Assn. Publ. Prodn. Mgrs. Home: 401 E 34th St New York NY 10016 Office: Temp Connection 16 E 40th St New York NY 10016

SHEININ, ROSE, biochemist, educator; b. Toronto, Ont., Can., May 18, 1930; d. Harry and Anne (Szyber) Shuber; BA, U. Toronto, 1951, MA (scholar), 1953, PhD in Biochemistry, 1956, L.H.D., 1985; DHL (hon.), Mt. St. Vincent U., 1985; DSc (hon.) Acadia U., 1987; m. Joseph Sheinin, July 15, 1951; children—David Matthew Khazanov, Lisa Basya Judith, Rachel Sarah Rebecca. Demonstrator in biochemistry U. Toronto (Ont., Can.), 1951-53, asst. prof. microbiology, 1964-75, asst. prof. med. biophysics, 1967-75, prof. microbiology, 1975-90, prof. med. biophysics, 1978-90, assoc. prof. med. biophysics, 1975-78, chmn. microbiology and parasitology, 1975-82, vice dean Sch. Grad. Studies, 1984-89; vice-rector acad., prof. dept. biology, Concordia U., Montreal, Que., Can., 1989—; mem. Health Scis. Com.; vis. rsch. assoc. chem. microbiology, Cambridge U., 1956-57, Nat. Inst. Med. Research, London, 1957-58; rsch. assoc. fellow div. biol. research Ont. Cancer Inst., 1958-67; sci. officer cancer grants panel Med. Research Council Can.; mem. Can. Sci. Del. to People's Republic of China, 1973; mem. adv. com. Provincial Lottery Health Research Awards; mem. adv. com. on biotech. NRC Can., 1984-87; mem. Sci. Council Can., 1984-87; adv. com. on sci. and tech. CBC, 1980-85; vis. prof. biochemistry U. Alta., 1971. Nat. Cancer Inst. Can. fellow, 1953-56, 58-61; Brit. Empire Cancer Campaign fellow, 1956-58; Recipient Queen's Silver Jubilee medal, 1978, Woman of Distinction award Health and Edn., YWCA, 1988; Josiah Macy Jr. Faculty scholar, 1981-82; fellow Ligue Contre le Cancer, France, 1981-82. Fellow Am. Acad. Microbiology, Royal Soc. Can. (chair women in scholarship com. 1990—); mem. Can. Biochem. Soc. (pres. 1974-75), Can. Soc. Cell Biology (pres. 1975-76), Am. Soc. Virology, Am. Soc. Microbiologists, Canadian Assn. Women in Sci., Scitech, Soc. Complex Carbohydrates, Toronto Biochem. and Biophys. Soc. (pres. 1960-70, council 1970-74). Assoc. editor Can. Jour. Biochemistry, 1968-71, Virology, 1969-72, Intervirology, 1974-85; editorial bd. Microbiol. Revs., 1977-80; author, co-author various publs. Office: Concordia U, 7141 Sherbrooke St W, Montreal, PQ Canada H4B 1R6

SHEINKMAN, BETTY FRANCES, employee benefits consultant, executive; b. Sherman, Tex., Aug. 9, 1931; d. Fred Adair and Grace Violet (League) Johnson; m. Jacob Sheinkman, May 31, 1954; children: Michael Adair, Joshua Louis, Mark Robert. BA in History, U. Okla., 1952; MA in English, Manhattanville Coll., 1971. Cert. English tchr., N.Y. Asst. libr. CIA, Washington, 1952-54; adminstrv. asst. Martin E. Segal Co., N.Y.C., 1954-57; tchr. English Scarsdale (N.Y.) Jr. High Sch., 1971-72, Hebrew Acad. High Sch., Yonkers, N.Y., 1973-74; v.p. Martin E. Segal Co., N.Y.C., 1975—; mem. cons. com. Internat. Found. Employee Benefit Funds, Brookfield, Wis., 1979-80, mem. edn. com., 1980-81, chmn. intern com., 1980-81. Democrat. Jewish. Home: 52 W 76th St Apt 3 New York NY 10023

SHELBY, CAROLYN JUNE, writer; b. Long Beach, Calif., June 17, 1949; d. Eugene Forrest and Barbara May (Magruder) S.; m. Christopher Ames, Feb. 11, 1973; 1 child, Samantha Shelby Ames. BA in Theatre Arts, UCLA, 1972. Writer feature and TV shows various prodns., 1980-90; writer Growing Pains Warner Bros. TV, Burbank, 1986-88; story editor, writer The Charmings Embassy Communications, Hollywood, 1987; exec. story cons., writer Once A Hero New World TV, Los Angeles, 1987; exec. story cons., writer TV series based on movie Dirty Dancing, 1988; feature writer film Interscope Communications Westwood and Twentieth Century Fox., L.A., 1985-90. Mem. Women's Com. Writers Guild Am., Women in Film. Unitarian.

SHELDON, BROOKE EARLE, librarian, educator; b. Lawrence, Mass., Aug. 29, 1931; d. Leonard Hadley and Elsie Ann (Southerl) Earle; m. George Duffield Sheldon, Mar. 28, 1955 (dec.); children: L. Scott, G. Stephen. B.A., Acadia U., 1952, D.C.L. (hon.), 1985; M.L.S., Simmons Coll., 1954; Ph.D., U. Pitts., 1977. Youth librarian Detroit Public Library, 1954-55; base librarian Ent AFB, Colorado Springs, Colo., 1955-57, U.S. Army, Germany, 1956-57; br. librarian Albuquerque Public Library, 1959-61; coordinator adult services Santa Fe Public Library, 1965-67; head library devel. N.Mex. State Library, Santa Fe, 1967-72; asst. dir. leadership tng. inst. U.S. Office Edn., Washington, 1971-73; head tech. services and tng. Alaska State Library, Juneau, 1973-75; dean Sch. Library Info. Studies, Tex. Woman's U., Denton, 1977—, provost, 1979-80. Recipient Alumni Achievement award Simmons Coll., 1983; Disting. Alumni award Sch. Library Info. Sci., U. Pitts., 1986. Mem. ALA (pres. 1983-84), Tex. Library Assn., S.W. Library Assn., Beta Phi Mu. Democrat. Episcopalian. Office: Tex Woman's U Sch Library & Info Studies PO Box 22905 Denton TX 76204

SHELDON, ELEANOR HARRIET BERNERT, sociologist; b. Hartford, Conn., Mar. 19, 1920; d. M.G. and Fannie (Myers) Bernert; m. James Sheldon, Mar. 19, 1950 (div. 1960); children: James, John Anthony. A.A., Colby Jr. Coll., 1940; A.B., U. N.C., 1942; Ph.D., U. Chgo., 1949. Asst. demographer Office Population Research, Washington, 1942-43; social scientist U.S. Dept Agr., Washington, 1943-45; asso. dir. Chgo. Community Inventory, U. Chgo., 1947-50; social scientist Social Sci. Research Council, N.Y.C., 1950-51; research grantee Social Sci. Research Council, 1953-55, pres., 1972-79; research asso. Bur. Applied Social Research, Columbia, 1950-51; social scientist UN, N.Y.C., 1951-52; lectr. sociology Columbia U., 1951-52, vis. prof., 1969-71; research assoc., lectr. sociology UCLA, 1955-61; assoc. research sociologist, lectr. Sch. Nursing U. Calif., 1957-61; sociologist, exec. assoc. Russell Sage Found., N.Y.C., 1961-72; vis. prof. U. Calif. at Santa Barbara, 1971; dir. Equitable Life Assurance Soc., Mobil Corp., H.J. Heinz Co. Author: (with L. Wirth) Chicago Community Fact Book, 1949, America's Children, 1958, (with R.A. Glazier) Pupils and Schools in N.Y.C,

1965; Editor: (with W.E. Moore) Indicators of Social Change; Concepts and Measurements, 1968, Family Economic Behavior, 1973; Contbr. (with W.E. Moore) articles to profl. jours. Bd. dirs. Colby-Sawyer Coll., 1979-85, UN Research Inst. for Social Devel., 1973-79; trustee Rockefeller Found., 1978-85, Nat. Opinion Research Ctr., 1980-87, Inst. East-West Security Studies, 1984-88. William Rainey Harper fellow U. Chgo., 1945-47. Fellow Am. Acad. Arts and Scis., Am. Sociol. Assn., Am. Statis. Assn.; mem. U. Chgo. Alumni Assn. (Profl. Achievement award), Sociol. Research Assn. (pres. 1971-72), Council on Fgn. Relations, AAAS, Am. Assn. Pub. Opinion Research, Eastern Sociol. Soc., Internat. Sociol. Assn., Internat. Union Sci. Study of Population, Population Assn. Am. (2d v.p. 1970-71), Inst. of Medicine (chmn. program com. 1976-77). Club: Cosmopolitan. Home and Office: 630 Park Ave New York NY 10021

SHELDON, GEORGIANA HORTENSE, consultant; b. Lawrenceville, Pa., Dec. 2, 1923; d. William Franklin and Georgiana (Root) S.; m. James R. Sharp, May 18, 1979. B.A., Keuka Coll., 1945; M.S., Cornell U., 1949. Dir. admissions Stetson U. Coll. Law, 1954-56; exec. asst. Republican Nat. Com., 1956-61; exec. sec. Hon. Rogers Morton (rep., Md.), 1962-69; dep. dir. Def. Civil Preparedness Agy., Washington, 1969-75; dir. Office Fgn. Disaster Assistance, dep. dir. internat. disaster assistance AID, 1975-76; vice chmn. CSC, 1976-77; mem. Fed. Power Commn., 1977—; mem. Fed. Energy Regulatory Commn., 1977-85. Recipient Alumni award for profl. advancement Keuka Coll., 1966. Republican. Presbyn. Home: 1200 N Nash St Arlington VA 22209

SHELDON, INGRID KRISTINA, city councilmember; b. Ann Arbor, Mich., Jan. 30, 1945; d. Henry Ragnvald and Virginia Schmidt (Clark) Blom; m. Clifford George Sheldon, June 18, 1966; children: Amy Elizabeth, William David. BS, Eastern Mich. U., 1966; MA, U. Mich., 1970. Cert. tchr., Mich. Tchr. Livonia (Mich.) Pub. Schs., 1966-67, Ann Arbor Pub. Schs., 1967-68; bookkeeper Huron Valley Tennis Club, Ann Arbor, 1978—; acct. F.A. Black Co., Ann Arbor, 1984-88; coun. mem. Ward II City of Ann Arbor, 1988—; chair Housing Bd. Appeals, Ann Arbor, 1988—; del. S.E. Mich. Coun. of Govts., 1989. Mem. Ann Arbor Planning Commn., 1988—, Parks Adv. Commn., 1987—, Ann Arbor Hist. Found., 1985—, Huron Valley Child Guidance Clinic, Ann Arbor, 1984—, excellence com. Ann Arbor Publ Schs. reorgn., 1985; treas. SOS Community Crisis Ctr., Ypsilanti, Mich., 1987—; precinct ward city vice-chair Ann Arbor Rep. City Com., 1978—. Recipient Community Svc. award Ann Arbor Jaycees, 1980; AAUW fellowship, 1982. Mem. Mich. Mcpl. League (delegate 1989—), Mich. Recreation and Park Assn., Women's City Club (chair endowment com. 1989—, fin. com. 1987—). Republican. Methodist. Home: 1416 Folkstone Ct Ann Arbor MI 48105

SHELDON, JOAN REDDEN, writer, social worker; b. Birmingham, Ala., Apr. 7, 1928; d. Richard Frederick and Janice Louise (Felts) Reoden; m. George Morgan Sheldon, June 15, 1948; children: Jennifer, David. AA in Social Sci., San Jose State Coll., 1947; BS in Sociology, U. Utah, 1964; cert. (3 yr.), Sch. of Theology, Diocese of Olympia, Wash., 1982. Social worker Dept. of Social Welfare, Ventura, Calif., 1965-68; supr. social workers Dept. Social and Health Svcs., Jacksonville, Fla., 1969-70; social worker Dept. Social and Health Svcs. Wash. State, Olympia, 1971-73, welfare program specialist, 1973-75; missionary S. Am. Missionary Soc. Episcopalian Ch., Ecuador, 1982-84; case mgr. Area Agy. on Aging, Olympia, Wash., 1987-88. Author: Yeshua: The Hidden Years, 1988. Vol. chaplain St. Peter Hosp., Olympia, Wash., 1981-82, 1985; bd. dirs. Children's Home Soc., Tacoma, Wash., 1975-80. Recipient of AAUW grant, Olympia, Wash., 1979.

SHELDON, NANCY WAY, management consultant; b. Bryn Mawr, Pa., Nov. 10, 1944; d. John Harold and Elizabeth Semple (Hoff) W.; m. Robert Charles Sheldon, June 15, 1968. BA, Wellesley Coll., 1966; MA, Columbia U., 1968, M in Philosphy, 1972. Mgmt. cons. ABT Assocs., Cambridge, Mass., 1969-70; mgmt. cons. Harbridge House, Inc., 1970-79, Los Angeles, 1977-79, v.p., 1977-79; mgmt. cons., pres. Resource Assessment Inc., 1979—; ptnr., real estate developer Resource Devel. Assocs., 1980—; ptnr. Anubis Group, Ltd., 1980—. Author: Social and Economic Benefits of Public Transit, 1973. Contbr. articles to profl. jours. Columbia U. fellow, 1966-68; recipient Nat. Achievement award Nat. Assn. Women Geographers, 1966. Mem. Nat. Environ. Health Assn., Am. Mining Congress, Am. Inst. Mining, Metall. and Petroleum Engrs., Nat. Wildlife Fedn., Nat. Audubon Soc., Nature Conservancy, World Wildlife Fund (charter mem.), Grad. Faculties Alumni Assn. Columbia U., DAR, Air Pollution Control Assn. Office: Resource Assessment Inc 1431 Washington Blvd Ste 2817 Detroit MI 48226

SHELDON, SUSAN FRANCES, data administration manager; b. Portland, Oreg., Dec. 3, 1948; d. Arthur John and Mary Frances (Blake) Tonsing; m. Donald L. Sheldon, July 4, 1976 (div. 1984); 1 child, Stephanie Koren. BS in Edn. with honors, U. Oreg., 1970; postgrad., Portland Community Coll., 1973-75, 74-76. Bus. analyst Fred Meyer Inc., Portland, 1970-76; supr. payroll services Am. Data Services, Portland, 1976-77; systems analyst Meier & Frank subs. May Co., Portland, 1977-79; systems analyst Nike Inc., Beaverton, Oreg., 1979-83, data adminstr., 1983-88; data administration manager SAIF Corp., Salem, Oreg., 1988—. Group leader and sponsor Beaverton Alcoholics Anonymous programs, 1985-87; mem. Info. Tech. Commn., City of Salem, 1989—. Mem. Data Adminstrn. Mgmt. Assn. (founder, sec. Portland chpt. 1984-86), Nat. Assn. Female Execs. Republican. Episcopalian. Home: 1846 Kamela Dr S Salem OR 97306 Office: SAIF Corp 400 High St SE Salem OR 97306

SHELLABERGER, DONNA JEAN, lawyer; b. DeKalb, Ill., May 9, 1920; d. Alva Edison Shellaberger and Margaret Ruth (White) Daw. BE, No. Ill. U., 1940; JD, U. Pa., 1949. Bar: Mass., Pa. From instr. to rsch. assoc. Law Sch. & Am. Law Inst. U. Pa., Phila., 1953-59; asst. prof. lit. and drama Coll. Art Am. Law Inst., Phila., 1959-62, asst. dir. com. on continuing legal edn., 1964-68; pvt. practice Reading, Pa., 1980-85, Orleans, Mass., 1985—; commr. Long Beach Twp., N.J., 1971; instr. Inst. for Paralegal Tng., Phila., 1975. Author: play There Came a Stick, 1963, Huey!, 1964 (2d Pl.); author: Manual CLE Lecturers, 1969; author poetry. Bd. dirs. theatre, writing workshop Long Beach Island Found. of Arts and Sci., 1962-64. Capt. WAC, 1942-46. Gowen fellow U. Pa., 1958. Mem. Mass. Bar Assn., Barnstable (Mass.) County Bar Assn. (family law com., supplemental lawyers referral plan 1988-90), Women's Bar Assn. Mass., Orleans Acad. Performing Arts, Cape Mus. Fine Arts, Pa. Poetry Soc. Democrat. Home: 56 Locust Rd PO Box 1566 Orleans MA 02653

SHELLENBARGER, MELANIE T., management consultant; b. Pitts., Aug. 25, 1953; m. Mark Shellenbarger. BA, St. Mary's Coll., Notre Dame, Ind., 1975; MBA, John Carroll U., 1981. Mgr. mktg., health care consulting, mktg. analyst Ernst & Whinney, Cleve.; sr. mgr. health care consulting Ernst & Whinney, Dallas; sr. mgr. internat. planning Ernst & Young, N.Y.C.; v.p. Mktg. & Rsch. Ptnrs., Denver. Contbr. to profl. publs. Mem. Am. Mktg. Assn. (v.p.), Am. Mgmt. Assn., Alliance Profl. Women, Planning Forum.

SHELLEY, CAROLE AUGUSTA, actress; b. London, Aug. 16, 1939; came to U.S., 1964; d. Curtis and Deborah (Bloomstein) S.; m. Albert G. Woods, July 26, 1967 (dec.). Student, Arts Ednl. Sch., 1943-56, Prepatory Acad. Royal Acad. Dramatic Art, 1956-57; studies with Iris Warren. Trustee Am. Shakespeare Theatre., 1974-82. Appeared in revues, films, West End comedies, including Mary Mary at the Globe Theatre; appeared as Gwendolyn Pigeon in stage, film and TV versions of The Odd Couple; The Norman Conquests (Los Angeles Drama Critics Circle award 1975); appeared as Rosalind in As You Like It, as Regan in King Lear, as Neville in She Stoops to Conquer, Stratford, Ont., Can., 1972, as Mrs. Margery Pinchwife in The Country Wife, Am. Shakespeare Festival, Stratford, Conn., 1973, as Nora in A Doll's House, Goodman Theatre, Chgo., as Ann in Man and Superman, as Lena in Misalliance, Zita in Grand Hunt; appeared at Shaw Festival, 1977, 80, Steppin Out, 1986 (Tony nomination 1986), Broadway Bound, 1987-88; appeared in: The Play's the Thing, Bklyn. Acad. Music, 1978; played Eleanore in stage prodn. Lion in Winter, 1987; other stage appearances include Nat. Co. of The Royal Family (L.A. Drama Citics Circle award 1977), The Elephant Man (Outer Critics Circle award 1978-79 season, Tony award for best actress 1978-79 season); appeared inaugural season, Robin Phillips Grand Theatre Co. (Tony award nomination 1986-87), London, Ont., Can., 1983-84, Broadway and Nat. Co. of Noises Off, 1985, Waltz of the Toreadors, 1986, Oh Coward, 1986-87; co-dir. Lion in Winter, 1987; appeared as Kate in Broadway Bound by Neil Simon The Nat. Co. and L.A. Premiere, 1987-88; played Lettice in Lettice and Lovage Globe Theatre, London, 1989-90; appeared in films The Boston Strangler, The Odd Couple; created: voice characters in Walt Disney films Robin Hood, The Aristocats. Recipient Obie Award for Twelve Dreams N.Y. Shakespeare Festival, 1982. Jewish. Office: Gersh Agy 130 W 42nd St New York NY 10036

SHELLEY, DONNA LOUISE, developer historic properties, consultant; b. New London, Conn., May 27, 1945; d. Carlye Dart and Louise (Dodge) S.; m. H. Donald Fisher III, (div. Aug. 1976); children: Stephen Jon Fisher, Faith Louise Shelley. Student, Conn. Coll., 1962-64; BFA, RISD, 1968; MA, U. of R.I., 1972; MS, U. Calif., San Diego, 1974. Pediatric therapist U. Ariz., Tucson, 1974-78; assoc. N.E. Real Estate Devel., Kingston, N.Y., 1978-82; exec. asst. John F. Saladino, Inc., N.Y.C., 1982-86; assoc. Stephen P. Mack Assocs., Westerly, R.I., 1986-87; pres. Bard Ltd., Norwich, Conn., 1987—; cons. Merchant's Sq., Norwich, 1988—, The Pla. of Norwich, 1988—. Author: (game) Norwich the Game, 1988. Participant Washington Task Force on Women in Unusual Occupations; bd. dirs. N.Y. State Coun. for Arts, 1982-86. Facade grantee City of Norwich, 1988. Mem. Nat. Trust for Hist. Preservation, Trout Unltd., Preservation Soc. Newport, Morris Club Am. Republican. Episcopalian. Office: Bard Ltd 60 Main St Norwich IL 06360

SHELLEY, MARY MICHAEL, artist; b. Doylestown, Pa., Feb. 19, 1950; d. Frederick Morris and Virginia Louise (Shaw) S.; children: Evan, Zia Anger. BA, Cornell U., 1972. Artist Ithaca, N.Y., 1974—. Represented in permanent collections Am. Mus., Bath, Eng., Mus. Am. Folk Art, N.Y.C., N.Y. State Hist. Soc., Cooperstown, N.Y., Smithsonian Instn., Washington. Grantee N.Y. State Coun. on Arts, 1989.

SHELLEY, NANCY KAY, educational coordinator; b. Amarillo, Tex., Apr. 12, 1946; d. J.B. and Madge Elizabeth (Neal) Scott; m. Larry Andrew Shelley, June 7, 1970; children: Andrea, Jason, Eric. AA, Lubbock Christian Coll., 1965; BA, Harding Coll., 1967; MEd, Memphis State U., 1969. Cert. tchr., Okla., Tenn. Phys. edn. instr. Harding acad., Memphis, 1967-72; realtor Jennings, Rogers & Capron ERA, Inc., Las Cruces, N.Mex., 1976-79; edn. coord. Great Plains Psychiatric Hosp., Lawton, Okla., 1985—. Probation officer Juvenile Ct., Memphis, 1969-73. Home: 7622 NW Folkstone Way Lawton OK 73505 Office: Great Plains Hosp 1602 SW 82nd St Lawton OK 73505

SHELLOW, JILL RACHEL, lawyer; b. Milw., June 24, 1956; d. James M. and Gilda (Bloom) S. BA, Johns Hopkins U., 1982; JD, Georgetown U., 1989. Prin. TNTA Assocs., Washington D.C., 1976-82; dir. devel., corp. sec. Urban Inst., Washington D.C., 1982-85; dir. issues devel. People for Am. Way, Washington D.C., 1986; law clk. Caplin & Drysdale, Chartered, Washington D.C., 1986-89, assoc., 1989—. Editor: The Grant Seekers Guide (1st edn. 1981, 2nd edn. 1985, 3rd edn. 1989). Bd. mem. Nat. Immigration, Refugee & Citizenship Forum, 1985--, founding com. Jewish Fund for Justice, 1982-84, Washington D.C. Mem. Nat. Assn. Criminal Defense Lawyers, ABA, Charles Fahy American Inn of Court. Office: Caplin & Drysdale Chartered One Thomas Cir NW Washington DC 20005

SHELQUIST, VIVIAN RAMPY, educator; b. Monroe County, Iowa, Sept. 22, 1917; d. Thomas Newman and May (Lewis) Forsyth; m. Marion DeWayne Rampy, Dec. 5, 1941 (dec. Dec. 1951); children: Thomas Marion, Richard DeWayne; m. Carl A. Shelquest, July 23, 1970. BA, Drake U., 1962, MA, 1964. Tchr. Monroe County, Iowa, 1936-56; elem. tchr. Chillicothe (Iowa) Schs., 1956-58, Eddyville (Iowa) Schs., 1958-62, Ottumwa (Iowa) Community Schs., 1962-80. V.P. Christian Social Svc. Regional Bapt. Bd., 1989—; del. conv. Rep. party, 1984, 86, 88, 90; fin. officer Monroe County Rep. Cen. Com., 1988—; Sunday Sch. tchr. Bapt. Ch., Albia, Iowa, 1982—; missions chair Bapt. Ch., Pleasant Corners, Iowa. Recipient Soil Conservation award Monroe County Soil Conservation Svc., 1958. Mem. AAUW (historian Ottumwa chpt.), Am. Assn. Ret. Persons (coord. Iowa), Environ. Protection Agy., Wilderness Soc., Sierra Club, Ret. Tchrs. Assn. (pres. Monroe County unit 1982-90, sec. Ottumwa unit 1985—), Monroe County Geneal. Soc. (editor 1983—, treas. 1987—). Home: Rte 3 Albia IA 52531

SHELTON, ANNE ELIZABETH, public relations, marketing consultant; b. Bluefield, W.Va., Mar. 2, 1948; d. Randolph Edison and Jean Permelia (Tomlinson) S. BA, Marshall U., 1970. Tchr. English Danville (Va.) Pub. Schs., 1970-77; mng. editor Specialized Agr. Publs., Raleigh, N.C., 1977-81; editor Tobacco Reporter, 1981-89; owner, consultant Wordcraft, Inc., Raleigh, 1987—. Bd. dirs. WestWood Homeowners Assn., Raleigh, 1988—. Mem. N.C. Farm Writers and Broadcasters (pres. 1981-82). Republican. Presbyterian. Office: Wordcraft Inc 512 Brookfield Rd Raleigh NC 27615

SHELTON, DOROTHY AUBINOE, interior designer; b. Washington, Feb. 19, 1927; d. Alvin Love and Dorothy (Barron) Aubinoe; m. William Ray Shelton, 1985; children: June, Paul, Tod, Holly. A.B., Rollins Coll., 1948; grad. teaching cert. U. Md., 1949; diploma Internat. Inst. Interior Design, 1958. Owner, interior designer Griffith Assos., Inc., Bethesda, Md., 1958-78; owner, dir. Griffith Gallery, Miami, Fla., 1978-84; owner, pres. Griffith Investments. Mem. alumni council Rollins Coll., 1983—, trustee, 1983-86, nat. dir. Coll. Fund, 1985-87. Recipient Disting. Service award Rollins Coll. Alumni Assn., 1988. Mem. Am. Soc. Interior Designers. Home: 322 Toll Gate Shores Dr Islamorada FL 33036 also: Rte 1 Box 142-7 Walnut Cove NC 27052

SHELTON, JAMMI M., municipal official; b. Frankfort, Fed. Republic of Germany, May 1, 1947; came to U.S., 1952; d. Fredrick George and Magda (von Tiermann) S. BA, U. Ky., 1969, MA, 1974, BS, 1977. Planning technician Dept. Long Range Planning, Lexington, Ky., 1977-80; environ. planner Dept. Planning/Zoning, Harrisburg, Pa., 1980-81; landscape supr. Am. Nurseries, Lexington, 1981-83; planning/zoning dir. Bourbon County Planning/Zoning, Paris, Ky., 1983-84; landscape supr. Lexington County Club, 1984-85; planner II Beaufort (S.C.) County Joint Planning Commn., 1985-87; sr. landscape architect T.J. Scangarello Assocs., Medford, 1987; planner III City of St. Petersburg, Fla., 1987—. Recipient grad. assistantship U. Ky., Lexington, 1972-74. Mem. Am. Planning Assn. Democrat. Office: St Petersburg Planning Dept 475 Central Ave Saint Petersburg FL 33701

SHELTON, JUDY MCLELLAND, wildlife center official; b. Ft. Worth, July 31, 1958; d. Charles Edward and Phillip Irene (Van Dyke) McLelland; m. Dennis Dean Ross, Feb. 19, 1977 (div. 1981); m. William H. Shelton, Aug. 22, 1987. Student, Tarrant County Jr. Coll., 1977-81. Adminstrv. coordinator Fox and Jacobs, Inc., Ft. Worth, 1977-79; sec. Rotan Mosle, Inc., Ft. Worth, 1979-80; adminstrv. asst. Am. Quasar Petroleum Co., Ft. Worth, 1980-82; exec. adminstr., dir. visitor svcs. Fossil Rim Wildlife Ranch, Inc., Ft. Worth, 1982—; wardrobe and fashion cons., Ft. Worth, 1986—. Vol. Big Bro.-Big Sisters Ft. Worth. Mem. Nat. Assn. Female Execs., Ft. Worth Civic Leaders Assn. Republican. Baptist. Home: 9820 Ravensway Benbrook TX 76126 Office: Fossil Rim Wildlife Ctr RR 1 Box 210 Glen Rose TX 76043

SHELTON, KATHERINE W., songwriter, lyricist, poet; b. Guilford County, N.C., July 13, 1943; d. George Monroe and Flossie Mae (Ramey) Weiss; 1 child, Jewel V. Songwriter; lyricist; poet. Historian Kernersville Mayor's Coun. for Handicapped, 1988—. Recipient Golden Poet award, 1989, 90. Mem. Songwriter's Recording Club.

SHELTON, LUCY, soprano; B.A., Pomona Coll.; Mus. M. in Voice, New Eng. Conservatory Music, 1968. Asst. prof. voice Eastman Sch. Music, U. Rochester, 1979; vis. prof. Cleve. Inst. Music, 1986; appeared at Chamber Music N.W., Bethlehem Bach and Aspen music festivals, Casals Festival with Baroque ensemble; appeared as soloist with orchs., including Chgo., Boston, Denver, Houston, Balt., St. Louis symphonies, Los Angeles Chamber Orch., St. Paul Chamber Orch., Minn. Orch., BBC Proms in London, performance world premiere of Schwantner work with St. Louis Symphony, and nationwide tour as soloist with Helmuth Rilling and Los Angeles Chamber Orch.; also recitals, guest appearances with various groups, including Calliope and Twentieth Century Consort; recs. with Nonesuch Records, Vox, Vanguard, Grenadilla, Sonory, and Smithsonian Instn.; winner Walter W. Naumburg prize, 1977 (with Jubal trio) and 1980 (solo). Office: care Sheldon Soffer Mgmt Inc 130 W 56th St New York NY 10019*

SHELTON, M. LINDA GALE, insurance company executive, consultant; b. Newport News, Va., Aug. 27, 1952; d. Josiah and Zillie (Page) Hall; m. Thomas Allan Phillips Jr., June 13, 1970 (div. Apr. 1976); children: Thomas Allan III and Tamara Alyna (twins). AA in Bus. Mgmt., Community Coll. Balt., 1979; BS in Mgmt. Sci., Coppin State U., Balt., 1989. Acctg. clk. T. Rowe Price Assocs., Balt., 1975-78; salesperson men's sportswear dept. Hutzler's Dept. Store, Towson, Md., 1977-78; jewelry salesperson direct sales dept. N.Y. Celebrity Fashion Jewels, Pikesville, Md., 1978-80; acctg. Social Security Adminstrn., Woodlawn, Md., 1978-80; collection rep. holiday spa Great Am. Fin., Towson, 1980-82; med. accounts rep. Collection Investigation Bur. of Am., Balt., 1982-84; sr. collector North campus John's Hopkins Homewood Hosp., Balt., 1984-88; team leader collection dept. Md. Gen. Hosp., Balt., 1988-90; head comml. ins. dept. Shock Trauma Assocs., A.A., Balt., 1990—; cons. B.S. & L.S. Assocs., Balt., 1987—; bus. mgr. Alpha & Omega Video, Balt., 1988—. Sec. NAACP, Balt., 1980. Mem. Balt. Pastor's Aid Soc. (sec. 1986—), U.S. Bapt. Congress, Balt. Bapt. Mass Choir, Balt. Bapt. Women's Alliance (pres. 1982-84, Leadership award 1984). Democrat. Home: 5330 Cordelia Ave Baltimore MD 21215 Office: Shock Trauma Assocs PA 11 S Paca St Ste 500 Baltimore MD 21201

SHELTON, SALLY ANGELA, political scientist, writer, educator, editor; b. San Antonio, Aug. 29, 1944; d. Harlan Bryan and Edith Angela (Pratka) S.; m. William Eagan Colby, Nov. 20, 1984. BA, U. Mo., 1966; student, Institut des Scis. Politiques, Paris, 1968; MA, John Hopkins U., 1968; PhD (hon.), Mt. St. Mary's Coll., Emmitsburg, Md., 1986. Legis. asst. Sen. Lloyd Bentsen, Washington, 1971-77; deputy asst. Sec. of State Dept. of State, Washington, 1977-79; U.S. Ambassador Eastern Caribbean U.S. Govt., Barbados, 1979-81; fellow Harvard U., Cambridge, Mass., 1981-82; v.p. Internat. Bus. Govt. Couns., Washington, 1982-84, Baultens Trust Co., Washington, 1984-86; Multinati, Banks & Corps. Multinati, Baults & Corps, Washington, 1986—; co-editor Global Assessment, Washington, 1988—; adj. prof. Georgetown U., Washington, 1989—; dir. Nat. Endowment for Democracy, Washington, Ctr. for Internat. Bus. Studies, Texas A & M U.; v.p. bd. dirs. Coun. of Am. Ambassadors, Washington; mem. Coun. Overseas Devel. Coun., Washington. Author: several articles including N.Y. Times, Washington Post, Los Angeles Times, and Jour. of Commerce. Dir. U.S. Com. of the U.N. Fund for Women, Washington, Atlantic Coun. of the U.S., Washington, 1989, Internat. Planned Parenthood Fedn./Western Hemisphere Region,. Recipient Fulbright fellowship John Hopkins U., 1968. Mem. Washington Inst. for Fgn. Affairs, Coun. on Fgn. Rels., NOW, Nat. Women's Pol. Coun., Fulbright Alumni Assn. Democrat. Roman Catholic. Home: 3028 Dent Pl NW Washington DC 20007

SHELTON, SANDRA LEE, teacher; b. East Cleve., Jan. 12, 1952; d. Kermit Blair and Bonnie Irene (Buschagen) S. BS in Edn., Bowling Green State U., 1974; MS in Edn., U. Dayton, 1985. Cert. tchr. Tchr. Northmont City Schs., Englewood, Ohio, 1975—; advisor High Sch. newspaper, Englewood, 1975—, Future Tchrs. of Am., 1987-89, Mock Trial Team, 1985-90; mem. Ohio Network: Tng. and Assistance for Schs. and Communities Northmont Sch. Dist., 1989-90, Bldg. and Dist. Faculty Coun., Green Pride com., Morale com., co-chairperson Back to Sch. Day, 1985-90. Contbr. articles to newspapers. Mem. NEA (rep. to Nat. Rep. Assembly), Ohio Edn. Assn. (rep. to State Rep. Assembly), Western Ohio Edn. Assn. (rep. to Rep. Assembly), Northmont Dist. Edn. Assn. (social chairperson 1985-90, communications chair 1985-90, bldg. rep.). Office: Northmont High Sch 4916 W National Rd Clayton OH 45315

SHELTON, WANDA CAROL, nurse; b. Riverside, Calif., Jan. 2, 1956; d. Wallace Campbell and Erma Frances (Elliott) Wendelstadt; m. Rodney Jay Shelton, Feb. 16, 1980; 1 child from previous marriage, Wendy Mae Cox. Cert. in voc. nursing, United Health Careers, 1982; AS, San Bernardino Valley Coll., 1987. RN, Calif. Tchr. piano Fontana, Calif., 1969-75; underwriter Prudential Ins. Co., San Bernardino, Calif., 1977; newspaper editor Allied Constrn. Ind., San Bernardino, 1979-82; nursing asst. San Bernardino County Med. Ctr., 1982-83; voc. nurse Remedy Health Svcs., San Bernadino, 1983; voc. nurse Kaiser Permanente, Fontana, 1983-87, RN, 1987—. Mem. choir Calvary Bapt. Ch. Mem. NAFE, United Nurses Assn. Calif., Grange Club, Order of Rainbow for Girls, Alpha Gamma Sigma.

SHEMER, MARTHA EVVARD, investment company executive; b. Ames, Iowa, Apr. 19, 1919; d. John Marcus and Martha (Cooper) Evvard; m. Jack Corvin Shemer, June 24, 1937 (dec. 1967); children: Jack Evvard, William Barry; m. Andrew Bobby, July 11, 1987. Pioneer of properties, Phoenix, Scottsdale, Ariz., LaJolla, Calif. and Del Mar, Calif., 1941-75; pres. Shemer Enterprises, Phoenix, 1975-83, Shemer Investment Co., Phoenix, 1975—. History columnist Paradise Valley Ind. newspaper, 1987. Benefactor Shemer Art Ctr. and Mus. to City of Phoenix, 1984. Recipient Quill and Scroll nat. contest award, 1936. Republican. Avocations: helping humanity, bridge, poker, spite malice card games, reading, writing, travel, horses, inventing, needlepoint.

SHEMORRY, CORINNE JOYNES, marketing executive; b. Rolla, N.D., Jan. 24, 1920; d. William H. and Edna Ruth (Conn) Joynes; children: Gay, Jan. Publisher, Williston (N.D.) Plains Reporter, 1953-78; mktg. dir. Williston Credit Union, 1979—; journalist, lectr., cons., author, reporter. Recipient numerous awards in journalism on state and nat. level, including Outstanding Woman in Journalism in N.D., 1987, 1st Place Golden Mirror award Credit Union Nat. Assn. Mem. N.D. Press Assn., N.D. Press Women (past pres.), Nat. Press Women, Williston C. of C., NAFE, Fin. Mktg. Assn. (charter), Sigma Delta Chi. Club: Bus. and Profl. Women's (past pres.). Home: 210 E 14th St PO Box 1030 Williston ND 58801

SHEN, CATHERINE, newspaper publisher; b. Boston, Oct. 31, 1947; d. Shu Chu and Helena (Wong) S.; m. Peter L.D. Hendley, Apr. 10, 1971 (div. Apr. 1976). BA, Wellesley Coll., 1969; MA, Claremont Grad. Sch., 1970. Art editor Harcourt Brace Jovanovich, Inc., San Francisco, 1970-73; reporter Brunswick (Maine) Times-Record, 1973-74; copy editor San Francisco Chronicle, 1974-80, Sunday mag. editor, 1980-81, features editor, 1981-85; dep. mng. editor Life sect. USA Today, Arlington, Va., 1985-86; pub. Honolulu Star-Bulletin, 1986-89; assoc. pub. Marin Ind. Jour., San Rafael, Calif., 1989—. Bd. dirs. Aloha United Way, Honolulu, 1987, Rehab. Hosp. Pacific, Honolulu, 1987, Nature Conservancy, Honolulu, 1987, Aloha Cou.il Boy Scouts Am., Honolulu, 1987, Girl Scout Coun. of the Pacific, Honolulu, 1988, ARC, Honolulu, 1988. Named Fellow of Pacific, Hawaii Pacific Coll., 1987. Mem. Asian-Am. Journalists Assn. (adv. com. 1986—), Hawaii Pubs. Assn., Nat. Women's Forum. Club: Pacific (Honolulu). Office: Marin Ind Jour PO Box 330 San Rafael CA 94915

SHEN, GRACE CHI-MEI, business systems specialist; b. St. Louis, Nov. 23, 1950; d. Kwan-ting and Nai-hsuan (Chang) S. BA magna cum laude, Georgian Court Coll., Lakewood, N.J., 1977. Sr. tech. assoc. Bell Labs., Holmdel, N.J., 1977-79; mem. adminstrv. group Bell Labs., Murray Hill, N.J., 1979-80; sr. tech. assoc. Bell Labs., South Plainfield, N.J., 1980-82; systems analyst Sea-Land Corp., Elizabeth, N.J., 1982-85; bus. systems specialist CIGNA Systems, Phila., 1985—. Mem. Data Processing Mgmt. Assn., Assn. for Women in Computing (convener N.J. 1980-81), AAUW, Lower Camden County Bus. and Profl. Women (2d v.p. 1988-89, 1st v.p. 1989-90, corr. sec. 1990-91), Pacific Asian Coalition. Home: 5910 Society Hill Estates Lindenwold NJ 08021 Office: CIGNA Systems 1600 Arch St 7 Tower Philadelphia PA 19192

SHENTON, MARTHA ELIZABETH, research psychologist; b. Concord, N.H., Nov. 11, 1952; d. Enoch and Loretta Marie (Halle) S., m. George Santiccioli; 1 child, Jessica. AB, Wellesley Coll., 1973; MS, Tufts U., Medford, Mass., 1976; MA, Harvard U., 1981, PhD, 1984. Research fellow Mclean Hosp. Mailman Research Ctr., Belmont, Mass., 1979-84; lecturer Brandis U., Walton, Mass., 1984-85; post doctoral research fellow Harvard Med. Sch., Mass. Mental Health Ctr., Boston, 1984-86; research assoc. Harvard Med. Sch., Veterans Adminstv. Med. Ctr., Boston; asst. prof.

psychology, dept. psychiatry Med. Sch. Harvard U. Contbr. articles to profl. jours. Mem. Am. Psychol. Assn., Mass. Psychol. Assn., Phi Beta Kappa. Office: Veterans Adminstv Med Ctr Dept Psychiatry 940 Belmont St Brockton MA 02140

SHEON, SARAH LYNN, city manager; b. St. Louis, Nov. 19, 1958. AB, Princeton U., 1980; JD, Harvard Law Sch., 1984. Staff analyst Dept. Housing & Urban Devel., Washington, 1977, 1978; atty. Paul, Weiss, Rifkind, Wharton, Garrison, N.Y.C., 1984-86; asst. to dept. mayor N.Y.C., 1986-89; Author: Lincoln Inst. for Land Use Policy, 1983. Author: Lincoln Inst. for Landise Policy, 1983. Mem. Women in Housing Fin., Mcpl. Arts Soc.

SHEPARD, CONNIE CHRISTINE, nurse anesthetist; b. Ft. Lauderdale, Fla., July 19, 1947; d. Cyrus Robert and Betty Jane (Burcham) Christensen. Nursing diploma, Petersburg (Va.) Gen. Hosp. Sch. Nursing, 1968; diploma, Richland Meml. Hosp. Sch. Nurse Anesthesia, Columbia, S.C., 1975; postgrad., Stephens Coll., 1975-78. RN, Fla.; cert. anesthetist. Enlisted Army Student Nurse Program WAC, 1967-68; oper. rm. nurse U.S. Army Nursing Corps, Med. Field Svc. Sch., Ft. Sam Houston, Walson Army Hosp., Fort Dix, N., J., Patterson Army Hosp., Ft. Monmouth, N.J., Republic Vietnam, 1968-72; asst. supr. U.S. Army Hosp., Ft. Stewart, Ga., 1968-72; lt. col. USAR Nurse Corps, 1972—; staff nurse Med. Coll. S.C., Charleston, 1968; pediatric nurse Scripps Meml. Hosp., La Jolla, Calif., 1972; oper. rm. staff nurse Richland Meml. Hosp., Columbia, S.C., 1973, nurse anesthetist, clin. instr., 1975-76; staff nurse anesthetist Hialeah (Fla.) Hosp., 1978-82; pvt. practice, 1980—; assoc. traveling staff Worldwide Anesthesia Assocs. Inc., Ukiah, Calif., 1984; staff nurse anesthetist Hialeah Anesthesia Group Inc., 1985-89; sec.-treas. Office Anesthesia Specialists, P.A., Hollywood, Fla., 1986—. Mem. Am. Assn. Nurse Anesthetists Inc., Fla. Assn. Nurse Anesthetists Inc. (sec.-treas. Edn. Dist. II 1976-77, nominating com. 1976-77, chmn. edn. workshop program 1981, trustee 1980-83), Res. Officers Assn. (life), Disabled Am. Vets. (life), Am. Soc. Mil. Surgeons of U.S., VFW, Am. Legion, Viet Nam Vets. Am. Inc., Vets. of Viet Nam War Inc., Harley Owners Group. Republican. Presbyterian. Home and Office: 1141 SW 8th Terr Fort Lauderdale FL 33315

SHEPARD, JANIE RAY (J. R. SHEPARD), software development executive; b. Montebello, Calif., Feb. 23, 1954; d. George Allen and Ada Janette (Barrow) Ray; 1 child, April Lynn. Grad. high sch., Albany, Ga. Adminstrv. asst. to pres. FRC Office Products, Jacksonville, Fla., 1979-82; adminstrv. asst. to v.p. comml. lending Stockton Savs., Dallas, 1983-84; exec. sec. to v.p. ops. Metromedia Long Distance, Ft. Lauderdale, Fla., 1985-87; owner, pres. RaceCom, Inc., Ormond Beach, Fla., 1986—. Developer computer text file editing system and computer artificial intelligence. Active Jacksonville and Dallas area Girl Scouts U.S., 1980-86. Democrat. Methodist. Home: 6 Sea Raven Terr Ormond Beach FL 32176 Office: RaceCom Inc 555 W Granada Blvd Ste E-10 Ormond Beach FL 32174

SHEPARD, LINDA MARY, real estate management company executive; b. Rochester, N.Y., Feb. 23, 1949; d. Angelo Anthony and Mary M. (Steiner) Costanza; m. Theodore L. Shepard, Jr., July 8, 1972; 1 son, Theodore James. A.A., Green Mountain Coll., 1969; B.A., U. Rochester, 1971. Vice pres. Glenbrook Manor Assocs., Rochester, 1972-83; pres. Shepard Signal, Inc., Canandaigua, N.Y., 1980-83, Costanza Enterprises, Rochester, 1983—; bd. dirs. Costanza Constrn. Co., Rochester, Shepard Bros., Inc., Canandaigua. Mem. Inst. Real Estate Mgmt., Bldg. Owners and Mgrs. Assn., Phi Theta Kappa. Office: Costanza Enterprises 14 Franklin St Rochester NY 14604

SHEPARD, MIKKI MAUREEN ALLISON, real estate broker; b. Queens, N.Y., May 12, 1951; d. George William and June Rita (Ferrary) S.; m. Tom C. Blankenheim, July 2, 1983; 1 child, Jeffrey Thomas. BA, U. Colo., 1982. Cert. real estate brokerage mgr. Employment counselor Centennial Personnel, Colorado Springs, Colo., 1977-78; ins. auditor Associated Ins. Utah, Colorado Springs, 1978-79; broker, co-owner TCB Realty and Investment Co., Inc., Colorado Springs, 1979—; speaker Nat. Assn. Realtors, Chgo., 1985—. Contbr. articles to Real Estate Today, Colo. Realtor News Communiqué, Gazette Telegraph. Pres. Christmas Unlimited, Colorado Springs, 1988, 89; campaign worker El Paso County Reps., Colorado Springs, 1977-78; mem. Realtors Polit. Action Com., Chgo., 1979—; mem. Profl. Women's Rep. Club, Colorado Springs, 1987. Served with USAF, 1970-74. Mem. Colo. Assn. Realtors (dir. 1986—), Colorado Springs Bd. Realtors (bd. dirs. 1981, 84, treas. 1985-86, sec. 1987-88, pres.-elect 1988-89, pres. 1989-90), Realtors Nat. Mktg. Inst., Women's Council Realtors (Colo. chpt. pres.-elect 1988, pres. 1989—, gov. 1990, Pikes Peak chpt. treas. 1984-85, pres. 1986-87, Woman of Yr. Pikes Peak chpt. 1986), Nat. Women's Council Realtors (leadership tng. grad. 1987, edn. chmn. 1987-88), Nu Skin Internat. Exec. Methodist. Office: TCB Realty and Investment Co Inc PO Box 241 Manitou Springs CO 80829

SHEPHERD, MARY ANNE, educator; b. Washington, Jan. 26, 1950; d. Edwin Joseph and Louise Therese (McKay) Zabel; m. Robert A. Shepherd, June 25, 1988. BS, U. Md., 1972; MEd, George Mason U., 1976. Tchr. elem. schs. Montgomery County Public Schs., Rockville, Md., 1972-74, Fauquier County Pub. Schs., Warrenton, Va., 1974-76, Wooster (Ohio) Pub. Schs., 1976—. Advisor 4-H Club, Apple Creek, Ohio, 1982-87; vestrywoman St. James Episcopal Ch., Wooster, 1984-86, 88—. Mem. Wooster Edn. Assn. (treas. 1984—). Republican. Home: 4872 Medina Rd Akron OH 44321 Office: Wooster City Schs 144 N Market St Wooster OH 44691

SHEPPERSON, GERALDINE STISH, school district administrator; b. Hazleton, Pa., Sept. 21, 1940; d. Wesley G. and Marie (Gallagher) Stish; m. Thomas E. Shepperson, Apr. 23, 1962; 1 child, Lisa Shepperson Capece. Diploma in nursing, Hazleton State Hosp., 1961; BS in Edn., Bloomsburg U., 1977; MS in Counselor Edn., U. Scranton, 1980; PhD in Edn. Leadership, U. Pa., 1985. Cert. secondary sch. counselor, sex educator, supr. sch. health svcs, supr. pupil svcs., supt. Staff nurse St. Joseph's Hosp., Hazleton, 1961; med. office mgr. W.G. Stish, M.D., Hazleton, 1962-80; mgmt. cons. Luth. Welfare Svcs., Hazleton, 1982—, counselor, 1985—; consultation/edn. specialist Hazleton-Nanticoke (Pa) Mental Health/Mental Retardation Svcs.; supr. sch. health svcs. Hazleton Area Sch. Dist., 1980-81; drug and alcohol coord., home bound instruction coord. Hazleton Area Sch. Dist., 1989—; presenter in field. Author curriculum in field. Campaign mgr. Com. to Elect Stish State Rep., Hazleton, 1988, 90; chair Community Adv. Coun. for Drug and Alcohol, Hazleton, 1989—; bd. dirs. Hazleton City Health Authority, 1989—; mem. Task Force to Provide Prenatal Care to Area Poor, Hazleton, 1987; v.p., bd. dirs. Am. Cancer Soc., Hazelton, Hazelton Nanticoke Mental Health-Mental Retardation Ctr., Victim's Resource Ctr.; sec. bd. dirs. Eckley Mus. Assocs.; pres. N.E. Region Dept. Pupil Svcs. Pa. State Edn. Assn. Recipient Pearl award YWCA, Hazleton, 1985; named Pa. Sch. Nurse of Yr., 1989, Nat. Sch. Nurse, 1990-91. Mem. AAUW, Women's Coalition, Nat. Assn. Sch. Nurses, Nat. Assn. Sch. Prins. Assn., Phi Delta Kappa. Democrat. Roman Catholic. Home: 210 W 12th St Hazleton PA 18201 Office: Hazleton Area Sch Dist 101 S Church St Hazleton PA 18201

SHEPPERSON, JACQUELINE R., biology educator, researcher; b. Hopewell, Va., Feb. 10, 1935; d. Weaver Augustus and Ruth (Jones) S. BS in Biology, Va. State U., 1954; MS in Biology, N.C. Central U., Durham, 1956; PhD in Zoology, Howard U., Washington, 1964. Instr. biology Fort Valley (Ga.) State U., 1955-59; asst. prof. zoology Howard U., 1964-65; prof. biology Winston-Salem (N.C.) State U., 1965—. Author: Parasitology-Lab Exercises, 1985; contbr. articles to sci. rsch. jours. Mem. N.C. Acad. Sci., Helminthological Soc. Washington. Office: Winston-Salem State U PO Box 13145 Winston-Salem NC 27110

SHER, JOANNA RUTH HOLLENBERG, physician; b. Winnipeg, Man., Can., May 23, 1933; came to U.S., 1949, naturalized, 1958; d. Joseph and Dorothy Hollenberg; m. Norman Sher, Dec. 28, 1955; children: Jonathan Aaron, Katherine Amy. AB, U. Chgo., 1952, BS, 1956, MD, 1956. Rotating intern Kings County Hosp., Bklyn., 1956-57, resident pathology, 1957-58; fellow pathology Kings County Hosp., SUNY Downstate Med. Center, Bklyn., 1960-62; Nat. Inst. Neurol. Diseases spl. fellow in neuropath. SUNY Downstate Med. Center, 1962-64; asst. neuropathologist Kings County Hosp., Bklyn., 1964-70, dir. neuropath. lab., 1970—; prof. clin. pathology, SUNY Health Sci. Ctr., Bklyn., 1977-87, asst. dean, 1977-83, disting. service prof., 1987—; cons. depts. pathology Brookdale Hosp. and Med. Center, Bklyn., Maimonides Hosp. and Med. Center, Bklyn., Bklyn. Hosp., L.I. Coll. Hosp. Diplomate Am. Bd. Pathology. Fellow Am. Soc. Clin. Pathologists, Coll. Am. Pathologists; mem. Internat. Acad. Pathology, Am. Acad. Neurology, Am. Assn. Neuropathologists, Phi Beta Kappa, Sigma Xi, Alpha Omega Alpha. Editor: (with D. Ford) Primary Intracranial Neoplasms, 1979; author: (with R. Lechtenberg) Aids in the Nervous System, 1988; contbr. articles in fieldld to profl. jours. Home: 2347 E 63d St Brooklyn NY 11234 Office: SUNY Health Sci Ctr 450 Clarkson Ave Box 25 Brooklyn NY 11203

SHER, LINDA ROSENBERG, lawyer; b. Chgo., May 16, 1938; d. Sidney and Rebecca Rosenberg; B.A., U. Chgo., 1959; LL.B., Yale U., 1962; m. Stanley O. Sher, Aug. 11, 1963; children—Jeremy Jay, Hellyn Sue. Admitted to D.C. bar, 1962; counsel constl. rights subcom. Senate Judiciary Com., 1962-64; atty. NLRB, 1964-77, asst. gen. counsel supreme ct. br., 1977—. Office: NLRB 1717 Pennsylvania Ave NW Washington DC 20570*

SHER, MARGERY LEVEEN, child care consultant; b. Paterson, N.J., Oct. 8, 1947; d. A. Alan and Bella Betsy (Smith) Leveen; m. Gerson S. Sher, June 29, 1969; children: Jeremy Daniel, Adam Leveen. BA, Goucher Coll., Towson, Md., 1969; MEd, Rutgers U., 1973. Tchr. South Brunswick (N.J.) Sch. System, 1969-74; dir. Falls Church-McLean (Va.) Children's Ctr., 1974-86; pres. Fried & Sher, Inc., Herndon, Va., 1985—. Co-author: (booklet) Dick & Jane as Victims, 1973. Mem. Va. Day Care Coun., Richmond, 1985-89; fgn. lang. chmn. Kent Garden's Sch. PTA, McLean, 1983-86; mem. nat. adv. bd. Child Care Action Campaign, 1989—. Named Child Care Profl. of Yr., 1984, Fairfax County Bd. Suprs. Mem. No. Va. Assn. for Edn. Young Children (bd. dirs. 1975-77, 84-86), Bus. and Profl. Women McLean (legis. chmn. 1988). Democrat. Jewish. Home: 7015 Sea Cliff Rd McLean VA 22101 Office: Fried & Sher Inc 465 Carlisle Dr Herndon VA 22070

SHER, PATRICIA RYAN, health care executive, insurance consultant; b. Rutland, Vt., June 22, 1947; d. Joseph Thomas and Jane Frances (Stebbins) Ryan; m. Harvey B. Sher, Sept. 5, 1970; children: Rachel, Danice, Alyssa. BS in Nursing, U. Fla., 1969, MA in Polit. Sci., 1980; BA in Polit. Sci., U. North Fla., 1975. Cons. on cost containment Blue Cross-Blue Shield Fla., Jacksonville, 1982-83; v.p. cost containment Am. Gen. Group Ins. Co., Jacksonville, 1983-87; regional exec. dir. Managed Health Care Svcs. Inc., Jacksonville, 1987—. Contbg. author: The New Healthcare Market, 1985. Bd. dirs. YMCA, Jacksonville, 1985-87; mem. 4th Jud. Cir. Grievance Com., Jacksonville, 1986-89, Jacksonville Mayor's Econ. Devel. Coun., 1987—. Lt. Nurse Corp, USN, 1969-73. Mem. Am. Assn. Preferred Provider Orgns., Jacksonville C. of C. (health care coalition 1985-89), Jacksonville Track Club (pres. 1982-83). Democrat. Roman Catholic. Office: Managed Health Care Svcs 111 Riverside Ave Jacksonville FL 32202

SHERA, JOYCE ANN, financial consultant; b. San Antonio, May 29, 1944; d. Edwin Alfred and Clara Mildred (Weyenberg) Copp; children: Joseph Michael Bond, Pamela Catherine Bond; m. Daniel Carey Shera, Feb. 28, 1981. Student, U. Dayton, 1962-68. Registered rep. N.Y. Stock Exchange, N.Y. Futures Exchange, Chgo. Bd. Trade, Chgo. Merc. Exchange; lic. fin. cons., ins. agt. Tchr. Archdiocese of Cin., Dayton, Ohio, 1965-67; dir., founder Hollywood Child Devel. Ctr., Franklin, Ohio, 1965-70, Warren County Head Start Program, Franklin, 1970-71; area social svc. dir. Palm Beach County, West Palm Beach, Fla., 1971-74; dir. med. rehab. svcs. Orange County, Orlando, Fla., 1974-77; dir. social svc. Gulfcoast Oncology Ctr., St. Petersburg, Fla., 1978-79; mcpl. bond underwriter M.G. Lewis Investment Bankers, Winter Park, Fla., 1979-81; account exec. Thomson McKinnon Securities, Orlando, 1981-82; fin. cons. Shearson Lehman Hutton, Inc., Winter Park, 1981-90, coord. fin. planning, 1989-90; assoc. v.p. investments Prudential Bache Securities, Winter Park, Fla., 1990—; lectr. fin. Expert Lecturers, Inc., Miami, Fla., 1984—; radio and TV panel appearances, 1979—; fin. lectr. on cruise ships, 1989—. Bd. dirs. Found. for Enrichment Emotionally Disturbed Children, Orlando, 1989—, The Dogwood Ridge Found., Camden, Ohio, 1990—. Mem. Nat. Assn. Securities Dealers, Fin. Planning Coun. (Top 5 award 1989), Rollins Coll. Friends of Cornell, Maitland Arts Ctr., Cornell Fine Arts Mus., Univ. Club. Office: Prudential Bache Securities 206 Park Ave S Winter Park FL 32789

SHERBELL, RHODA, painter, sculptor; b. Bklyn.; d. Alexander and Syd (Steinberg) S.; m. Mervin Honig, Apr. 28, 1956; 1 dau., Susan. Student, Art Students League, 1950-53, Bklyn. Mus. Art Sch., 1959-61; also; pvt. study art, Italy, France, Eng., 1956. Cons., council mem. Emily Lowe Gallery, Hofstra U., Hempstead, N.Y., 1978, pres., 1980-81, life mem. bd. friends, pres. bd. trustees; tchr. Mus. Modern Art, Nat. Acad. Design, Art Students League, N.Y.C.; instr. Mus. Modern Art, N.Y.C., 1959, Art Students League, N.Y.C., 1988-89, Nat. Acad. Design Art Sch., N.Y.C., 1985-90. Exhibited one-woman shows Country Art Gallery, Locust Valley, N.Y., Bklyn. Mus. Art Sch., 1961, Adelphi Coll., A.C.A. Galleries, N.Y.C., 1967, Capricorn Galleries, Rehn Gallery, Washington, 1968, Gallery Modern Art, N.Y.C., 1969, Morris (N.J.) Mus. Arts and Scis., 1980, Bergen Mus. Arts and Scis., N.J., 1984, William Benton Mus., Conn., 1985, Palace Theatre of the Arts, Stamford, Conn., Bronx Mus. Arts, 1986, Hofstra Mus. Art, L.I., N.Y., 1989, 90; one-woman retrospective at N.Y. Cultural Ctr., 1970, Nat. Arts Collection, Washington, 1970, Montclair Mus. of Art, 1976, Nat. Art Mus. of Sport, 1977, Jewish Mus. of N.Y.C., 1980, Black History Mus., 1981, Queens Mus., 1981, 82, Nat. Portrait Gallery, Washington, 1981, 82, Bronx Mus., N.Y., Bklyn. Mus., Mus. Modern Art, N.Y.C., Country Art Gallery, 1990, Port Washington Library, Nat. Mus. Am. Art, The Smithsonian Instn., 1982, Nat. Acad. Design, N.Y.C., 1984, 89, Castle Gallery Mus., N.Y.C., 1987, Emily Lowe Mus., N.Y.C., 1987, Heckshire Mus., N.Y.C., 1989, Islip Art Mus., N.Y.C., 1989; exhibited group shows Heckscher Mus, 1989, Islip Mus., 1989, Nassau Dept. Recreation and Parks, 1989, Downtown Gallery, N.Y.C., Maynard Walker Gallery, N.Y.C., F.A.R. Gallery, N.Y.C., Provincetown Art Assn., Detroit Inst. Art, Pa. Acad. Fine Arts, Bklyn. and L.I. Artists Show, Old Westbury Gardens Small Sculpture Show, Audubon Artists, NAD, Allied Artists, Heckscher Mus., Nat. Art Mus. Sports, Mus. Arts and Scis., L.A., Am. Mus. Natural History, Post of History Mus., 1987, 88, Caslte Gallery Mus., N.Y.C., 1987, Emiloy Lowe Mus., N.Y., 1987, Bronx Mus. Arts, 1987, Chgo. Hist. Soc., Mus. of Modern Art, N.Y.C., 1988, Sands Point Mus., L.I., NAD, Hofstea Mus, 1990, others; represented permanent collections, Stony Brook Hall of Fame, William Benton Mus. Art, Colby Coll. Mus., Oklahoma City Mus., Montclair (N.J.) Mus., Schonberg Library Black Studies, N.Y.C., Albany State Mus., Hofstra U., Bklyn. Mus., Colby Coll. Mus., Nat. Arts Collection, Nat. Portrait Gallery, Smithsonian Instn., Baseball Hall of Fame Cooperstown, N.Y., Nassau Community Coll., Hofstra U. Emily Lowe Gallery, Art Students League, Jewish Mus., Queens Mus., Black History Mus., Nassau County Mus., Stamford Mus. Art and Nature Ctr., Jericho Pub. Library, N.Y., African-Am. Mus., Hempstead, N.Y., 1988, Stamford (Conn.) Mus. Art and Scis., Silvermine Artists North East exhibition, 1989; also pvt. collections, TV shows, ABC, 1968, 81; ednl. TV spl. Rhoda Sherbell-Woman in Bronze, 1977; important works include Seated Ballerina, portraits of Aaron Copland (Bruce Stevenson Meml. Best Portrait award Nat. Arts Club 1989), Eleanor Roosevelt, Variations on a Theme (36 works of collaged sculpture), 1982-86; appeared several TV shows; guest various radio programs; contbr. articles to newspapers, popular mags. and art jours. Council mem. Nassau County Mus., 1978, trustee, 1st v.p. council; asso. trustee Nat. Art Mus. of Sports, Inc., 1975—; cons., community liaison WNET Channel 13, cultural coordinator, 1975-83; host radio show Not for Artists Only, 1978-79; trustee Women's Boxing Fedn., 1978. Recipient Am. Acad. Arts, Letters and Nat. Inst. Arts and Letters grant, 1960, Gold medal Allied Artists of Am., 1989; Louis Comfort Tiffany Found. grant, 1962; Alfred G. B. Steel Meml. award Pa. Acad. Fine Arts, 1963-64; Helen F. Barnett prize NAD, 1965; Jersey City Mus. prize for sculpture, 1961; 1st prize sulpture Locust Valley Art Show, 1966, 67; Ann. Sculpture prize Jersey City Mus.; Bank for Savs. 1st prize in sculpture, 1950; Ford Found. purchase award, 1964; MacDowell Colony fellow, 1976; 2 top sculpture awards Mainstreams 77; Cert. of Merit Salmagundi Club, 1978; prize for sculpture, 1980, 81; award for sculpture Knickerbocker Artists, 1980, 81; top prize for sculpture Hudson Valley Art Assn., 1981; Sawyer award NAD, 1985; Gold medal of honor Audubon Artists, 1985, 39th Ann. Silvermine Exhbn. award, Gold medal Allied Artists Am., 1990; Ford Found. grantee, 1964, 67, aslo award. Fellow Nat. Sculpture Soc.; mem. Sculpture Guild (dir.), Nat. Assn. Women Artists (Jeffery Childs Willis Meml. prize 1978), Allied Artists Soc. (dir., Gold medal 1990), Audubon Artists (Greta Kempton Walker prize 1965, Chaim Gross award, award for disting. contbr. to orgn. 1979, 80, Louis Weskeem award; dir.), Woman's Caucus for Art, Coll. Art Assn., Am. Inst. Conservation Historic and Artistic Works, N.Y. Soc. Women Artists, Artists Equity Assn. N.Y., Nat. Sculpture Soc. (E.N. Richard Meml. prize 1989), Internat. Platform Assn., Profl. Artists Guild L.I., Painters and Sculptors Soc. N.J. (Bertram R. Hulmes Meml. award), Am. Watercolor Soc. (award for disting. contbn. to orgn.), Catharine Lorillard Wolfe Club (hon. mention 1968), Nat. Arts Club (N.Y.C., Stevenson Meml. award 1989), Nat. Acad. Design (Leila Gordon Sawyer prize 1989). Home: 64 Jane Ct Westbury NY 11590

SHERBLOM, ANNE PARTRIDGE, grants associate; b. New Haven, July 31, 1949; d. Edward L. and Dorothy A. (Hutchison) Partridge; m. John C. Sherblom, May 25, 1974 (div. Nov. 1984); m. David Clark, Mar. 3, 1990. BS, Bates Coll., 1971; PhD, Dartmouth Coll., 1975. Vis. asst. prof. Dartmouth Coll., Hanover, N.H., 1975-76; rsch. assoc. Bowdoin Coll., Brunswick, Maine, 1976-77, Okla. State U., Stillwater, 1977-80; asst. prof. U. Maine, Orono, 1980-86, assoc. prof., 1986-90, prof., 1990; grants assoc. office of dir., office extramural rsch. NIH, Bethesda, Md., 1990—; vis. sci. NIH, Nat. Cancer Inst., Bethesda, 1986-87; mem. rsch. com. Am. Heart Assn. Maine affiliate, 1982-85, chair 1985-86; ad hoc reviewer Pathobiochemistry Study sect. NIH, 1988. Contbr. articles to profl. jours. mem. Am. Chem. Soc., Am. Soc. for Biochemistry and Molecular biology, Soc. for Complex Carbohydrates, Sigma Xi.

SHERBURNE, MARY LELA, commercial real estate broker-advisor; b. Spruce Pine, N.C., June 21, 1926; d. Galen and Abbigail (Blalock) Sparks; m. Edward Gill Sherburne, Mar. 1, 1958; 1 child, Edward Gill III. BS, U. N.C., 1950; MS, Am. U., 1985. Cert. internat. property specialist. Talent producer Discovery-Sta. WGBH-TV, Boston, 1955-58; dir. Edn. Devel. Ctr., Watertown, Mass., 1960-68; project mgr. Nat. Ctr. Housing Devel., Washington, 1969-72; investment broker Smithy Bradeon Co., Washington, 1972-85; mgr. comml. sales Long & Foster Real Estate, Washington, 1985-89; mgr. investment real estate svcs., sr. v.p. Barrueta & Assocs., Washington, 1989—. Mem. Washington Assn. Realtors, D.C. Bldg. Industry Assn., Comml. Real Estate Women, Asian Real Estate Assn., Fedn. Internat. Real Estate (pres. 1988-89). Office: Barrueta & Assocs One Thomas Circle NW Ste 1000 Washington DC 20005

SHERF, SANDEE CROFT, real estate corporation executive; b. Okmulgee, Okla., Feb. 24, 1950; d. C. Don and Joyce Marie (Harris) Croft; m. Paul P. DiGeronimo, Nov. 4, 1970 (div. 1980); children: Shawn Dale, Aimee Vanessa; m. E.W. Sherf, May 15, 1983; 1 child, Summer Ashley. Student Maryville Coll., 1969. Flight attendant Piedmont Airlines, Salem, N.C., 1969-70; credit card mgr. Blount Nat. Bank, Maryville, Tenn., 1970-72; travel agt. AAA of Va., Lynchburg, 1972-76; real estate agt. Century 21, Houston, 1979-81; real estate developer E.W. Sherf Interests, Humble, Tex., 1981-84; comml. property mgr. SCS Mgmt. Co., Inc., Spring, 1984—; real estate acquisitions MRR, Inc., 1987—; pres. Reid Rd. Mcpl. Utility Dist., Houston, 1983—. Leader San Jacinto coun. Girl Scouts U.S., 1983; mem. Champion Forest Civic Club, Houston, 1983, Mus. Fine Arts, Houston, Smithsonian Inst., Washington. Recipient Managerial Acctg. and Fin. Concepts award Bldg. Owners and Mgrs. Inst., 1983. Mem. Tex. Assn. Realtors, Nat. Assn. Realtors, Houston Bd. Realtors, Real Estate Securities and Syndications, Realtors Nat. Mktg. Inst., Inst. Real Estate Mgmt., Houston Apt. Assn., Internat. Coun. Shopping Ctrs., Writer's Guild. Republican. Baptist. Avocations: skiing, swimming, race car driving, dancing, writing. Office: SCS Mgmt Co Inc 3845 FM 1960 West Ste 230 Houston TX 77068

SHERFEY, GERALDINE RICHARDS, educational administrator; b. Pontiac, Mich., Dec. 11, 1929; d. William and Ethel (Spurr) Richards; m. William E. Sherfey, Aug. 4, 1950 (div.); children: Emily J., Laura A., Susan E., William E. B.S., Ind. State U., 1963, M.S., 1965; Ed.S., U. Ga., 1973, Ed.D., 1978. Biology and gen. sci. instr. Hammond (Ind.) Tech.-Vocat. High Sch., 1963-65; advanced biology instr. Griffith (Ind.) Sr. High Sch., 1965-70, dept. chmn. grades K-12, acting sci. cons., 1968-70; mgr. sch. programs (asst. supt. for curriculum and instrn.) Greenville (S.C.) Pub. Schs., 1972-73; instr. edn. Purdue U., Calumet Campus, Hammond, Ind., 1973-75; guest lectr. Purdue U. Calumet Campus and Ind. U. N.W., Gary, 1975-78; sci. instr. grades 7 and 8, Spohn Middle Sch., Hammond, 1975-78, prin. A.L. Spohn Elem./Middle Sch., 1978-80, adminstrv. asst. for curriculum and instruction Hammond Schs., 1980-82, coord. vocat. program devel. and extended programs 1982-85, dir. curriculum/ops. area career ctr., 1985—; dir. curriculum and plan mgmt., 1985-87; pres. Sherfey-Chirinos Corp., 1986—; biology instr. Gavit MS/HS, 1987-89; coord./mentor Program Reaching Indiviual Middle Sch. Student. Co-editor Ind. State newsletter for adult and continuing edn., 1985; contbr. articles to profl. jours. Ind. State U. teaching fellow, 1964-65; U. Ga. grad. asst., 1970-72. Mem. World Coun. for Curriculum and Instruction, Assn. for Supervision and Curriculum Devel., Nat. Sci. Tchrs. Assn., Nat. Middle Schs. Assn., Ind. Middle Schs. Assn., Ind. Assn. Adult and Continuing Edn. (recipient Outstanding Contbn. award 1986. Democrat. Roman Catholic. Home: 540 W 56th Ave Merrillville IN 46410 Office: 5727 Sohl Ave Hammond IN 46320

SHERIDAN, HELEN MARIE, health care executive; b. Providence, Apr. 4, 1953; d. Edward William and Edith Alice (Ryan) S.; m. Thomas Peter Marsden, July 11, 1987. Diploma in respiratory therapy, R.I. Hosp., 1973; student in bus. adminstrn., We. Conn. State U., 1982—. Cert. respiratory therapy technician. Staff respiratory therapist R.I. Hosp., Providence, 1974-75; respiratory therapist Pulmonary Assocs., Providence, 1975-79; contract respiratory therapist Linde Homecare Med. Systems, Inc., Warwick, R.I., 1979-80, sales rep., 1980-81; sales mgr. Linde Homecare Med. Systems, Inc., Wilton, Conn., 1981-83, dist. mgr., 1983-85; region mgr. Linde Homecare Med. Systems, Inc., Brookfield, Conn., 1985-89, Lincare Inc. (formerly Linde Homecare Med. Systems), 1989—; vice chmn. pub. affairs com. Union Carbide Corp., 1986-87. Mem. NAFE, Am. Assn. Respiratory Care, Am. Lung Assn. of Conn., Conn. Thoracic Soc., Conn. Assn. Med. Equipment Dealers (bd. dirs. 1986-88), New Eng. Med. Equipment Dealers (bd. dirs. 1988—, program chmn. 1988—), Danbury Area Women's Network. Office: Lincare Inc 61 Commerce Dr Brookfield CT 06804

SHERIDAN, LINDA MARY, insurance professional; b. Bristol, Conn., Oct. 15, 1953; d. Joseph Francis and Eleanor (Farrell) Newpeck; m. James William Schepker, Aug. 13, 1975 (div. 1978); m. Albert John Sheridan, Aug. 15, 1980; 1 stepson, Kevin. BA, U. Conn., 1975; MBA, U. Hartford, 1985. Rsch. analyst Life Ins. Market Rsch. Assn., Farmington, Conn., 1976-78; sr. rsch. analyst Aetna Life and Casualty, Farmington, 1978-80; analyst infosystems, then mgr. bus. systems Hartford (Conn.) Steam Boiler Inspection and Ins. Co., 1980-86, dir. bus. systems, 1987-89, asst. v.p. infosystems, 1989-90, asst. v.p. new products, 1990—. Mem. Planning and Zoning Bd., Granby, Conn., 1989—. Mem. Chartered Property Casualty Underwriters, Hartford Area Trainers (treas. 1984-87), Data Processing Mgrs. Assn. Democrat. Roman Catholic. Office: Hartford Steam Boiler InsCo 1 State St Hartford CT 06102

SHERIDAN, TERESA WEAVE, nurse; b. Blytheville, Ark., Nov. 11, 1959; d. William Royce and Mary Alice (Nichols) Weaver; m. Rickey Leah Sheridan, May 7, 1983; 1 child, Keaghlan Marie. AS in Nursing, Union U., Jackson, Tenn., 1980. RN, Tenn. Operating room nurse Jackson-Madison County Gen. Hosp., 1980-82; operating room nurse Meth. Hosp.-Cen., Memphis, 1982-83, critical care nurse, 1983-85; dialysis nurse Dialysis Clinic Inc., Humboldt, Tenn., 1985-87; head nurse in dialysis Dialysis Clinic Inc., Brownsville, Tenn., 1987—. Republican. Evangelical. Home: 185 E University Pkwy Jackson TN 38305 Office: Dialysis Clinic Inc 1214 Anderson Brownsville TN 38012

SHERIFF, LINDA LEPPER, real estate property manager; b. Cin., May 31, 1954; d. Milton Webster and Marie Hinz (Becker) Lepper; m. Richard William Briggs, June 30, 1981 (div. Mar. 1983); m. Warren Calvin Sheriff, July 10, 1987 (div. 1990). BA in History, Stephens Coll., 1977. Cert. apartment mgr. Property supr. Chelsea Moore Corp., Cin., 1980-85; regional property mgr. The Mayerson Co., Cin., 1987—. Mem. Young Reps., Columbia, Mo., 1975-76. Mem. No. Ky. Apt. Assn. (v.p. 1989, gov. 1989—), Greater Cin. Apt. Assn. (bd. dirs. 1989—, Cert. Apt. Mgr. of Yr.

award 1989). Presbyterian. Home: 7670-3 Catawba Ln Florence KY 41042 Office: The Mayerson Co 105 E Fourth St Ste 1900 Cincinnati OH 45202

SHERMAN, ARLENE, television producer; b. Washington, Sept. 12, 1947; d. Burton H. and Ann M. (Butt) S. BFA, NYU, 1970. Free lance film editor U.S., France, Eng., 1970-78; prodn. coordinator Children's TV Workshop, N.Y.C., 1978-81, assoc. producer, 1981-85, producer, 1985—; assoc. dir. TV programs, 1985—. Producer TV series Sesame St., 1988 (Emmy award); dir. film The Machine, 1970 (Cannes Film Festival award 1970). Mem. Am. Film Inst., Nat. Acad. TV Arts and Scis., Dirs. Guild Am. Office: Children's TV Workshop 1 Lincoln Plaza New York NY 10023

SHERMAN, BEATRICE ETTINGER, business executive; b. N.Y.C., May 29, 1919; d. Max and Stella (Schrager) Ettinger; m. Herbert Jacob Howard, Feb. 15, 1942 (dec. 1971); children: Robert David Howard, Carolyn Howard Smith; m. Ernest John Sherman, Dec. 29, 1974. Student, Gulf Park Jr. Coll., Gulfport, Miss., 1934-35, Shimer Jr. Coll., Mt. Carroll, Ill., 1936-38; B.A., U. Miami, Fla., 1940; postgrad. Harvard U., 1940, Paris-Am. Acad., Paris, 1972, Alliance Française, Paris, 1973. Corp. sec., dir. Save Electric Corp., Toledo, 1940-67, Verd-A-Ray Corp., Toledo, 1944-67, Penetray Corp., Toledo, 1962-67; ptnr. Stella Assocs., Newark, 1960-80, BHS Ptnrs., Miami, 1983—; pres. Besman Inc., Coral Gables, Fla., 1975—, All Am. Mobile Tel. Co., Coral Gables, 1986—. Vol. worker Jewish Welfare Fedn., Toledo, 1942-69; nat. speaker United Jewish Appeal; mem. womens div. Greater Miami Jewish Fedn., 1969—, trustee, 1986; active Miami advertiser adv. bd. Bell South Advt. and Pub. Co. Recipient Lion of Judah award Greater Miami Jewish Fedn., 1986. Mem. Assn. Telemessaging Svcs. Internat., Telocator Network Am., Pioneers of Miami Beach, Biltmore Club (Coral Gables, Fla.). Home: 5108 SW 72d Ave Miami FL 33155 Office: Besman Inc 141 Aragon Ave Coral Gables FL 33134

SHERMAN, ELAINE C., gourmet foods company executive, educator; b. Chgo., Aug. 1, 1938; d. Arthur E. and Sylvia (Miller) Friedman; m. Arthur J. Spiegel, Jan. 1989; children: Steven J., David P., Jaime A. Student, Northwestern U., 1956-58; diploma in cake decorating, Wilton Sch. Profl. Cake Decorating, 1973; diploma, Dumas Pere, L'école de la Cuisine Française. Tchr. cooking and adult edn. Maine, Oakton, Niles Adult and Continuing Edn. Program, Park Ridge, Ill., 1972-82; corp. officer The Complete Cook, Glenview, Ill., 1976-82, Madame Chocolate, Glenview, 1983-87; food columnist Chgo. Sun Times, 1985-87; dir. mktg. Sue Ling Gin, Chgo., 1987-88; co-owner Critical Eye, Chgo., 1988—; v.p., gen. mgr. Foodstuffs, Inc., Evanston, Ill., 1990—. Author: Madame Chocolate's Book of Divine Indulgences, 1984 (nominated Tastemaker award 1984). Bd. dirs. Chgo. Fund on Aging and Disability, 1989—; co-chmn. Meals on Wheels, 1989-90. Mem. Les Dames D'Escoffier (founding pres.), Women's Foodservice Network (pres.), Confrerie de la Chaine Des Rotisseurs (vice conselliere gastronomique), Am. Inst. Wine and Food (bd. dirs.). Home and Office: 1728 D Wildberry Dr Glenview IL 60025 Office: Foodstuffs 2106 Central St Evanston IL 60201

SHERMAN, GRETA GAIL, advertising executive; b. Louisville, Oct. 11, 1951; d. James O. and Georgia (Jackson) Gibson; m. Daniel P. Sherman, July 10, 1977 (div. Apr. 1980); 1 child, Jacob A. Sherman. BS in Journalism, U. Ky., 1973. Owner/editor Tri-City Times, Hardinsburg, Ky., 1977-82; mng. editor Streator (Ill.) Times-Press, 1982-84; exec. editor Painesville (Ohio) Telegraph, 1984-86; market devel. mgr. David Advt., Cleve., 1987-88; v.p./br. mgr. Bernard Hodes Advt., Chgo., 1988—; bd. dirs. UPI, Chgo., 1982-84, AP, Cleve., 1984-86. Author: children's book Sugar Bears and Elephants, 1974. Bd. dirs. YMCA, Willoughby, Ohio, 1987-88, Unity Ch.-Communications, Chesterland, Ohio, 1987-88. Winner 1st place Addy Award Am. Assn. Advt. Agys. 1974, gold award and merit award Health Care Recruitment and Retention, 1990, Women of Achievement award Greater Cleve. YMCA, 1986. Mem. Gifted Children's Parents' Coun. (pres. 1988-89), Cleve. Advt. Club, Internat. Assn. Bus. Communicators, Nat. Assn. Health Care Recruiters, Am. Mgmt. Assn., U. Chgo. Lab Schs. Parents Group. Mem. Unity Ch. Home: 5345 Hyde Park Blvd Chicago IL 60615 Office: Bernard Hodes Advt 205 Wacker Dr Chicago IL 60606

SHERMAN, HENRIETTA MARIE, educator; b. Chestertown, Md., May 30, 1940; d. John George and Irene Elizabeth (Hinkel) Schauber; m. Joseph Thomas Randow, Jan. 2, 1960 (div. 1976); children: Joseph, Colleen, Teri, Joan, Michael; m. Sidney Wayne Sherman, Aug. 10, 1978. AA, Coastal Carolina Community Coll., Jacksonville, N.C., 1976; BS, Nova U., 1986, MBA, 1988. Stenographer Civil Svc., Jacksonville, 1970-79; adminstrv. asst. Digital Equipment Corp., Charlotte, N.C., 1979-81; quality engr. GE, Daytona Beach, Fla., 1981-89; instr. Univ. Research Corp., Palm Coast, Fla., 1989—; v.p. Introspect, Daytona Beach, Fla., 1988-89. With USMC, 1958-60. Mem. Christian Profl. Women's Assn. (spl. projects chmn. 1988-89). Home: 55 Wedgewood Ln Palm Coast FL 32137 Office: Univ Rsch Corp 4500 Palm Coast Pkwy E Palm Coast FL 32037

SHERMAN, JOYCE CHESTANG, quality assurance specialist; b. Mobile, Ala., Oct. 16, 1946; d. Morris and Dorothy (Brazile) Chestang; m. Thomas Oscar Sherman, May 12, 1973; children: Alfred, Morris, Katherine. AA, DeAnza Coll., Cupertino, Calif., Am. River Coll., Sacramento; student, Calif. State U., Bakersfield. Logistics specialist China Lake (Calif.) NWC, 1984-85, quality assurance specialist, 1982—. Sunday sch. tchr., 1989—; youth counselor Union Missionary Bapt. Ch., Ridgecrest, Calif. Mem. NAFE, Soc. Logistics Engrs. Democrat. Home: 813 W Howell St Ridgecrest CA 93555

SHERMAN, LORETTA SUE, elementary school educator; b. Springfield, Mass., Apr. 1, 1946; d. Edward and Rose (Davis) Kempner; m. Richard Mark Sherman, June 26, 1965; children: Debra Lynn Sherman Newman, Tammra Joy. AA with honors, Mercer County Community Coll., 1977; BA, Thomas Edison State Coll., 1981; student, Trenton State Coll., 1985-86. Cert. elem. sch. tchr. Instr. Helikon, Princeton, N.J., 1981; sec. music dept. Mercer County Community Coll., Trenton, N.J., 1982-83; instr. Sylvan Learning Ctr., Hamilton, N.J., 1988-89; tchr. Hamilton Day Sch., Mercerville, N.J., 1988 --; del. Conf. Women Returning to Work, Thomas A. Edison State Coll., 1979; instr. creative writing workshop Mercer County Conf. Gifted and Talented Edn., 1982; adj. instr. Mercer County Community Coll. Div. External Svcs. Summer Camp, Trenton, 1983-85, 1989-90. Contbr. articles to newspapers, poems to lit. mags. Democrat. Jewish.

SHERMAN, MARY ANGUS, public library administrator; b. Lawton, Okla., Jan. 3, 1937; d. Donald Adelbert and Mabel (Felkner) Angus; m. Donald Neil Sherman, Feb. 8, 1958; children: Elizabeth Sherman Cunningham, Donald Neil II. BS in Home Econs., U. Okla., 1958, MLS, 1969. Br. head Pioneer Libr. System, Purcell, Okla., 1966-76; regional libr. Pioneer Libr. System, Norman, Okla., 1976-78, asst. dir., 1978-80, dir., 1987—. Named one of Distinguished Alumni Sch. Home Econs., U. Okla., 1980. Mem. ALA (councilor Okla. chpt. 1988—, planning and budget assembly 1990—), AAUW (pres. Okla. chpt. 1975-77, nat. bd. dirs. 1983-87, S.W. cen. region dir. 1983-85, v.p. nat. membership 1985-87, Woman of the Yr. Purcell chpt. 1982), Okla. Library Assn. (pres. 1982-83, Disting. Service award 1986), Norman C. of C. (bd. dirs. 1988—), Altrusa Internat., Rotary, Norman Assistance League Club, Delta Gamma Mothers (pres. 1978-79), Kappa Alpha Theta (pres. Alpha Omicron House Corp. 1984-87, nat. dir. house corps. 1987-88), Beta Phi Mu, Phi Beta Kappa. Democrat. Methodist. Office: Pioneer Libr System 225 N Webster Norman OK 73069

SHERMAN, PATSY O'CONNELL, technical development administrator, chemist; b. Mpls., Sept. 15, 1930; d. James Patrick and Edna Fern (Stitzel) O'Connell m. Hubert Townsend Sherman, Aug. 15, 1953; children: Sharilyn Kay Sherman Loushin, Wendy Jane Sherman Heil. BA, Gustavus Adolphus Coll., 1952. Chemist 3M, St. Paul, 1952-67, rsch. specialist, 1967-73, tech. mgr., 1973-82, mgr. tech. devel., 1982—; trustee GMI Engring. and Mgmt. Inst., Flint, Mich., 1986—; bd. dirs. Advanced Optics Inc., Mpls. Contbr. numerous articles to profl. jours.; patentee in field. Trustee Gustavus Adolphus Coll., 1989—. Recipient Disting. Alumni award Gustavus Adolphus Coll., 1975, Spurgeon award Boy Scouts Am., 1980; named to Minn. Inventors Hall of Fame Minn. Inventors Congress, 1989. Mem. Am. Chem. Soc., Am. Soc. Tng. and Devel., Am. Soc. Engring. Edn. (dir. continuing prof. devel. div. 1986-89, chair 1989-90). Home: 9300 11th Ave S Bloomington MN 55420 Office: 3M 3M Ctr Bldg 225-1N-10 Saint Paul MN 55144

SHERMAN-APPEL, LORI RAE, nurse; b. Newark, Oct. 16, 1955; d. Albert Paul and Janice E. (Waldholz) S.; m. Carl A. Appel, June 25, 1989. BS cum laude in Nursing, Adelphi U., 1977; postgrad., Internat. Diabetes Ctr., Mpls., 1987, Joslin Clin., Boston, 1987. RN, N.J.; cert. diabetes educator. Discharge planner, home health nurse Middlesex Gen. Univ. Hosp., New Brunswick, N.J., 1982-84; acting dir., supr. A-Round the Clock Health Care Svcs., Inc., Chatham, N.J., 1984-85; mgmt. cons. Home Health Assocs., Totowa, N.J., 1985-86; pvt. practice diabetics edn. cons. Union, N.J., 1986-88; program dir., diabetes nurse educator Internat. Diabetes Ctr., East Hanover, N.J., 1987-88; coord. diabetic edn. St. Mary's Hosp., Orange, N.J., 1988-90; diabetes edn. specialist Diabetes Ctr. N.J., Edison, 1990—. Author: (with others) Home Health Administration, 1988. Mem. Am. Assn. Diabetes Educators (cert. 1987), Garden State Assn. Diabetes Educators, Am. Nurses Assn., N.J. State Nurses Assn., Am. Diabetes Assn. (pres. Union County chpt. 1986-88, com. patient edn. N.J. affiliate), Juvenile Diabetes Found. (bd. dirs. Essex County), Sigma Theta Tau. Home: 702-6 Pinehurst Ct Union NJ 07083

SHERN, STEPHANIE MARIE, accountant; b. Taylor, Pa., Jan. 7, 1948; d. Joseph and Stephanie (Malodovitch) Andrews; m. George Emil Shern, Sept. 25, 1971. AA, Keystone Jr. Coll., 1967; BS, Pa. State U., 1969. CPA, N.Y. Staff accountant to ptnr., nat. dir. retail svcs. Ernst & Young, N.Y.C., 1969—; dir. Met. Retail Fin. Execs., N.Y.C. Contbr. articles to profl. jours. Named Keystonian of Yr., Keystone Jr. Coll., 1984. Mem. N.Y. State Soc. CPAs (bd. dirs. 1985—), Am. Inst. CPAs, Women's Econ. Round Table, Beta Alpha Psi (mem. adv. forum 1984—). Republican. Ukrainian Orthodox. Club: Panther Valley Golf (Allamuchy, N.J.). Home: 113 Prospect St Little Falls NJ 07424 Office: Ernst & Young 277 Park Ave New York NY 10172

SHEROWITZ-SHENY, PHYLLIS J., graphics design company executive, consultant; b. N.Y.C., Feb. 24, 1953; d. Jerome and Rita Lillian (Schainuck) Sherowitz; m. Moshe Sheny, Sept. 25, 1983. Cert., Parsons Sch. Design, 1973; BFA, New Sch. for Social Rsch., 1974. Artist Norman, Craig & Kummel, N.Y.C., 1973-76; asst. art dir. Smith, Greenland, N.Y.C., 1976-77; jr. art dir. Laddin & Co., N.Y.C., 1977-79; art dir. Saffer Cravit, Freedman, N.Y.C., 1979-80; pres., art dir. Phyllis Sherowitz Sheny Design, N.Y.C., 1980—; instr. ballroom dancing Dancing Oasis, N.Y.C., 1978-79; fin. officer Datanamics Inc., N.Y.C., 1985—, producer Dianetics: The Talk Show, cable TV, 1986—, desk top pub. cons., 1987—. Exec. dir. Happiness Project N.Y.C., 1981-82; counselor, vol., Celebrity Ctr. N.Y., 1985-88; rsch. coord. Citizens Commn. on Human Rights, N.Y.C., 1985-86; pub. rels. vol. Religious Freedom Crusade, L.A., 1986. Recipient citation for typog. excellence N.Y. Type Dirs. Club, 1983, cert. of achievement Celebrity Ctr. N.Y., 1985. Mem. Graphic Artists Guild, NAFE. Republican. Jewish. Home and Office: 310 E 46th St New York NY 10017

SHERREN, ANNE TERRY, chemistry educator; b. Atlanta, July 1, 1936; d. Edward Allison and Annie Ayres (Lewis) Terry; m. William Samuel Sherren, Aug. 13, 1966. BA, Agnes Scott Coll., 1957; PhD, U. Fla.-Gainesville, 1961. Grad. teaching asst. U. Fla., Gainesville, 1957-61; instr. Tex. Woman's U., Denton, 1961-63, asst. prof., 1963-66; rsch. participant Argonne Nat. Lab., 1973-80; assoc. prof. chemistry N. Cen. Coll., Naperville, Ill., 1966-76, prof., 1976—. Clk. of session Knox Presbyn. Ch., 1976—, ruling elder, 1971—. Mem. Am. Chem. Soc., Am. Inst. Chemists, AAAS, AAUP, Ill. Acad. Sci., Sigma Xi, Delta Kappa Gamma, Iota Sigma Pi (nat. pres. 1978-81, nat. dir. 1972-78, nat. historian 1989—). Presbyterian. Contbr. articles in field to profl. jours. Office: N Cen Coll Box Naperville IL 60566

SHERROD, DONNA LOUISE, mechanical engineer; b. Forest, Miss., Jan. 8, 1962; d. Donald Earl and Barbara (Jackson) S. BSME, Tufts U., 1984. Prodn. engr. Delco Moraine div. GM, Dayton, Ohio, 1984-87; product ops. engr. aircraft engines group GE, Evendale, Ohio, 1987-89, turbine design engr., 1989—. Vol. Big Sisters-Big Bros., Boston, 1983, Dayton, 1984; mentor Project Continued Success, Cin., 1987—; mentor engr. program GE-U. Cin., 1989. Mem. NAFE, Soc. Women Engrs., Delta Sigma Delta. Democrat. Roman Catholic. Office: GE Aircraft Engine Group 1 Neumann Way Evendale OH 45215

SHERRY, KATHLEEN SUSAN, state developmental disabilities consultant; b. Chgo., May 17, 1954. BA in Philosophy, Ariz. State U., 1988, BA in Psychology, 1988, postgrad. Cert. emergency med. technician. Behavioral and devel. skills trainer Muskegon (Mich.) Regional Ctr. for Devel. Disabilities, 1973-77; proprietor, portrait photographer, sales, pub. rels. Tempe, Ariz., 1977-82; cons. Dept. Econ. Security, Div. Devel. Disabilities State of Ariz., Tempe, 1979—. Mem. Ariz. Country Dancers Assn., Golden Key Nat. Honor Soc., Alpha Kappa Psi (historian Ariz. State U. 1989—). Home and Office: 937 S Acorn Tempe AZ 85281

SHERRY, SUSAN THERESA, social worker; b. Jersey City, Nov. 6, 1952; d. Edward Joseph and Theresa Marie (Krajewski) S. BA, U. Mass., 1974; MA, Goddard Coll., 1978; doctoral work, Brandeis U., 1989. Licensed social worker. Placement coord., family therapist Ctr. for Human Devel., Springfield, Mass., 1974-78; area supr. Office for Children, Westfield, Mass., 1978; exec. dir. Sojourn, Inc., Northampton, Mass., 1978-80; regional dir. The Key Program, Cambridge, Mass., 1980-82; exec. dir. Jamaica Plain Neighborhood, Boston, 1982-83, Health Care For All, Boston, 1984-89; dir. state affaris Nat. Health Care Campaign, Washington, 1989—; gov.'s study com. on health ins. Commonwealth Mass., Boston, 1988-89, on health care, 1986-87, hosp. conversion bd., 1988-89. Bd. dirs. Mass. Human Svcs. Coalition, Boston, 1985-89; mem. Boston AIDS Consortium, 1988-89; trustee North Shore Health Planning Counsel, Peabody, Mass., 1985-87; treas. North Shore Gay & Lesbian Alliance, Marblehead, Mass., 1983-89. Recipient Contbn. to Social Change award Midwest Acad., 1988, Annual Health Care award Mass. Am. for Dem. Action, 1988, Annual award Mass. Rainbow Coalition, 1988. Mem. Takaoma Pk. Lesbian & Gay Coalition. Office: Nat Health Care Campaign 1334 G St NW Washington DC 20005

SHERWOOD, MIDGE, author; b. Ironton, Ohio; d. Roy and Addie (Brace) Winters; m. Jack E. Sherwood, Jan. 19, 1946; children: Margaret Sherwood Simms, Melanie Winters. BJ, U. Mo., 1938. Women's editor Ironton Daily Tribune, 1933-38; city editor Ironton Daily News, 1938-40; asst. mgr. West coast news bur. TWA, Los Angeles, 1940-42; pub. relations dir. Western Air Lines, 1942-45; aviation columnist, corr. Skyways, So. Flight, 1945-48; owner, operator Midge Winters Agy., 1945-48; assoc. editor Matrix Mag., Women in Communications, 1950-55; book reviewer Los Angeles Times, 1963, Western Hist. Quarterly; free-lance writer, 1958—; columnist Pasadena (Calif.) Star-News, 1987. Author: And How it Grew, 1965; San Marino Ranch to City, 1977; Days of Vintage, Years of Vision, Vol. 1, 1982, Vol. II, 1987. Chmn. Hertrich Meml., 1967; mem. Soc. Fellows of Huntington Library, 1967; founder, archivist San Marino Hist. Soc. Recipient double award Conf. Calif. Hist. Socs., 1987; named Outstanding Citzen of San Marino, 1988. Mem. Western Writers of Am., Women in Communication, PEO, Huntington Westerners (founder), Westerners Internat. (bd. dirs.), Phi Mu. Home: 1867 Windsor Rd San Marino CA 91108

SHETTEL, PATRICIA FRANCES, research facility administrator; b. McKees Rocks, Pa., Nov. 11, 1934; d. John William and Marcella (Sokolowski) Rogansky; m. Anthony Vitale, Feb. 16, 1954 (div. 1974); children: Deborah Jean, Craig Douglas; m. Harris Harlan Shettel, Mar. 20, 1984. Student, U. Pitts., 1964-65, Montgomery Coll., Rockville, Md., 1975-82, George Washington U., 1987. Clk., sec. Alcoa Co., Pitts., 1952-54, Equitable Life Assurance Soc., Denver, 1954-55; exec. sec. W. Craig Chambers Advt., Pitts., 1958-60, Sta. WQED-TV, Pitts., 1961-64, U. Pitts., 1964-65, Miller-Thomas-Gyekis, Inc., Pitts., 1965-71; adminstrv. assoc. Am. Inst. for Rsch., Pitts., 1971-80; adminstrv. officer Washington, 1980-88, dir. rsch. support svc., 1988—. Author: Serialized Bibliography, 2 vols., 1979, Sponsor Index, 1978, 80, 82, 84,88, Staff Reference Book, 1980, 1981, 1982, 1984, Serialized Bibliography, 3 vols., 1987, Sponsor Index, 1988, Serialized Bibliography, Vol. III, 1989, Abbreviations and Acronyms, 1989. Active Nat. Mus. for Women in Arts, Washington, 1987, 88, 89, 90, Rockville Little Theatre, 1988. Mem. NAFE. Democrat. Roman Catholic. Office: Am Inst for Rsch 3333 K St NW Washington DC 20007

SHETTY, YOLAN LEE, educator; b. Valparaiso, Ind., Nov. 8, 1948; d. Arthur LeRoy and Florence Ruth (Tomlinson) Cole; m. Ratnakar S. Shetty, Mar. 20, 1976; children: Kiran Craig, Nathan Sunil. BAE magna cum laude, Wayne (Nebr.) State Coll., 1969; MA, Marquette U., 1972; postgrad., U. Pitts. Cert. tchr. English and Spanish, N.Y. Instr. English Marquette U., Milw., 1971-72; tchr. English and Spanish Burr's Lane Jr. High Sch., Dix Hills, N.Y., 1973-76; instr. gen. writing and basic writing U. Pitts., 1984-86, instr. lit., 1986-87, computer asst. dept. English composition project, 1987-88; lectr. dept. English Pa. State U., Beaver, 1988—. Bibliographer; columnist; contbr. poetry and articles to jours. Mem. exec. planning bd. Beaver County United Way, 1990—, v.p. allocations, 1983-84; mem. Beaver County Children and Youth Svcs. Adv. Bd., 1981-85, chmn., 1983-84; mem. women's council Merrick Art Gallery, 1988-89; mem. adv. bd. Mt. Gallitzin Acad., 1984-86, v.p., 1990—. Mem. MLA, AAUW (v.p. membership 1981-83, legis. chmn. 1983-84), Nat. Council Tchrs. English, Outlook Club Beaver Falls (edn. chmn. 1985-86, publicity chmn. 1989—), Ladies Reading Club, Sigma Tau Delta, Kappa Delta Pi, Cardinal Key.

SHEVELL, NANCY ELLEN, pediatrician; b. Bklyn., Sept. 2, 1930; d. Max and Catherine (Barrett) S.; m. William John Sciales, June 9, 1956; children: Mary, Bridget, John, Christopher, Monica, James. BA, Manhattanville Coll., 1952; MD, SUNY, Bklyn., 1956. Pvt. practice, Flushing, N.Y., 1960—. Mem. AMA, N.Y. State Med. Soc., Queens Med. Soc. (pres. 1976). Republican. Roman Catholic. Office: 163-03 Oak Ave Flushing NY 11358

SHEW, ANITA KRAMER, law librarian; b. Tiffin, Ohio, Apr. 15, 1944; m. James C. Shew; children: Jonathan, Paul, Kelley. BA, Coll. of Wooster, 1966; MSLS, Western Res. U., 1967. Asst. law libr. U. Akron (Ohio) Sch. of Law, 1967-71; dir. Butler County Law Libr., Hamilton, Ohio, 1978—. Editor: Ohio Legal Resources-Annotated Bibliography and Guide, 1982; contbr. articles to profl. jours. Mem. Am. Assn. Law Librs. (editor section newsletter), Ohio Regional Assn. Law Librs. (pres. 1985-86, editor newsletter 1990—, Disting. Law Libr. award 1983), Kiwanis. Office: Butler County Law Libr Assn 141 Court St Hamilton OH 45011

SHEY, JANE ELIZABETH, trade association executive, real estate agent; b. Algona, Iowa, Dec. 2, 1956; d. Daniel Jeremiah and Jean Lois (Balgeman) S. BA, Briar Cliff Coll., 1979. Caseworker Congressman Berkley Bedell, Sioux City, 1979-81; pastoral minister St. Cecelia's Ch., Algona, 1981-84; chaplain Washington Hosp. Ctr., 1984-86; congl. candidate 6th Congl. Dist. of Iowa, Algona, 1986; legis. asst. congressman Berkley Bedell, Washington, 1986, Tim Penny, Washington, 1986-88; dir. govt. affairs Corn Refiners Assn., Washington, 1988—. Mem. Women in Govt. Rels. (co-chair agrl. task force Washington chpt. 1988-89, 90-91), Women in Internat. Trade, Jaycees. Democrat. Roman Catholic. Office: Corn Refiners Assn 1100 Connecticut Ave NW Washington DC 20036

SHIELDS, ALISON R., lawyer; b. Rockville, N.Y., Apr. 2, 1964; d. Joseph Howard Jr. and Rosemary (O'Connor) S. BA, NYU, 1985; JD, Bklyn. Law Sch., 1989. Bar: N.Y. Atty. Bower and Gardner, N.Y.C. Active recording for the blind, Christian Children's Fund. Recipient various scholarships. Mem. Am. Bar Assn., N.Y. State Bar Assn. Home: 75 California St Long Beach NY 11561 Office: 110 E 59th St New York NY 10022

SHIELDS, JANIS DARLENE, public relations company executive, communications professional; b. Balt., Aug. 5, 1957; d. Richard Thomas and Mayme (Molock) S.; 1 child, Bryan Darnell. BS in Edn., U. Del., 1980, BA and Sci. in Mass Communications, 1981. Mktg. rep. Ctr. for Community Edn., Newark, Del., 1978-81; mktg. asst. Marchand Inc., Wilmington, Del., 1981-82; prodn. asst. Sta. KYW-TV, Phila., 1982-83; tchr. asst. Christina Sch. Dist., Newark, 1983-84; program dir., producer, news reporter Rollins Cablevision, Wilmington, 1984-88; pub. info. officer Del. Coun. on Crime and Justice, Wilmington, 1988-89; pres. The Media Works, Wilmington, 1990—; communications assoc. United Way Del.. Wilmington, 1989—, news asst. Sta. WHYY-TV, Wilmington, 1979-80; producer, announcer Sta. WILM, Wilmington, 1989—; pub. rels., media rels. and organizational promotions cons. Henrietta Johnson Med. Ctr., Wilmington, 1990—. Cons. Wilmington Cable Adv. Com., 1988; cons. Com. to Elect Rourke Moore, Wilmington, 1990. Recipient 1st place media award Del. Edn. Assn., 1987.; scholar SICO Found., 1975. Mem. Women in Communications, Pub. Rels. Soc. Am., Nat. Fedn. Local Cable Programmers (Hometown award 1988, 89), Del. Media Assn., Brandywine Profl. Assn., Quill and Scroll. Methodist. Avocations: photography, sewing, poetry, championship dogs. Home: 512 W 3d St Wilmington DE 19801 Office: The Media Works PO Box 26208 Wilmington DE 19899 also: United Way Del 625 Orange St 3d Fl Wilmington DE 19801

SHIELDS, LAURA AULL, public relations counselor; b. Taylorville, Ill., Oct. 24; d. Frank and Gladys (Montgomery) Aull; m. Roger V. Shields, Nov. 20, 1940 (div.); children: Deborah, Beth, Roger, Clark, Constance. Student Ill. State U., 1935-37. Owner Shields Communications, Santa Monica, Calif., 1974—; speaker in field. Mem. Pub. Rels. Soc. Am. and Counselors Acad., Women in Communications, Women in Bus., Santa Monica Bay Area C. of C. Office: 159 Wadsworth Ave Santa Monica CA 90405

SHIELDS, MARY, service executive; b. Pitts., May 20, 1955; d. Robert Gerard and Helen Marie (Stein) S.; m. Scott A. Leibold, May 7, 1977. BS, U. Pitts., 1977, MEd, 1979. Clk. U.S. Postal Service, Pitts., 1974-81, customer service rep., 1981-86, sr. account rep., 1986—. Historian Ea. States Women's Traffic Conf., 1988-89; vol. Friends of the Murrysville Community Library, 1989. Mem. NOW (treas. East Hills chpt. 1987-89, 90—, treas. Pa. chpt. 1990—), Women's Traffic Club Pitts. (pres. 1986-87, v.p. 1985-86, chmn. 1987-88, chmn. nominating com. Ea. States Conf. 1987-89, chmn. membership com. 1989—, bd. dirs. 1989-90), NAFE, Nat. Assn. Postal Suprs., Greater Pitts. Postal Customer Coun., Foothills Area Postal Customer Coun., Zonta Internat. Roman Catholic. Home: 4755 Nob Hill Dr Murrysville PA 15668 Office: US Postal Service 1001 California Ave Pittsburgh PA 15290

SHIELDS, MOLLY T., lawyer; b. Milw., Apr. 15, 1961; d. Richard F. and Charleen (Fagan) S. BA, U. Minn., 1983; JD cum laude, Hamline U., 1986. Bar: Minn. 1986. Assoc. Doherty, Rumble & Butler, St. Paul, Minn., 1986—; trustee Chpt. 7 Panel of the U.S. Trustee's Office, Dept. Justice, St. Paul, 1987—. Mem. Minn. State Bar Assn. (bankruptcy bulletin, bankruptcy section, acting chmn. legis. com. bankruptcy section 1988-89), Silver Gavel Honor Soc. Office: Doherty Rumble & Butler 7th St 30E Saint Paul MN 55101

SHIELDS, NANCY CLAIRE, educator; b. Taunton, Somerset, Eng., Feb. 21, 1925; came to U.S., 1946; d. Reginald Stanley and Frances Claire (Moore) Dollins; m. Arthur Waterman Shields, June 24, 1944; children: Jonh (dec.), Carolyn Sue, James Arthur, Deborah Kay. BS, Tenn. Tech., 1972, MA, 1975; postgrad., Middle Tenn. State U., 1976-81. With Genesco, McMinnville, Tenn., 1956-66; tchr. Warren County Schs., McMinnville, Tenn., 1966—; tchr. (part-time) Tenn. Tech. U., Cookville, 1972—. Mem. Tenn. Fgn. Lang. Tchrs. Assn., Tenn. Edn. Assn., NEA, Warren County Edn. Assn., Phi Kappa Phi, Kappa Delta Pi. Home: Rt 10 Box 233 McMinnville TN 37110

SHIELDS, TAMARA WEST-O'KELLEY, accountant; b. Lewiston, Idaho, Oct. 23, 1948; d. Brooks E. and Dona J. (Rogers) O'Kelley; m. Thomas J. Hanson Jr., 1 son Stewart Alan. BBA cum laude, North Tex. State U., 1976; Staff acct. James C. Beach CPA, Carrollton, Tex., 1972-76, Deloitte, Haskins & Sells, CPA, 1976-77; chief fin. officer Communications Systems, Inc. (name changed to Scott Cable Communications 1983), Irving, Tex., 1977-84; pvt. practice acctg., Dallas, 1984—. lectr. in field. Bd. trustees local charity; active St. Andrews United Meth. Ch. Mem. AICPA, Tex. Soc. CPAs (Dallas chpt. ethics com.), Beta Alpha Psi.

SHIERK, CATHERINE KIM, lawyer; b. St. Joseph, Mich., July 30, 1956; d. Theodore Taft and Virginia Ann (O'Connell) S.; m. James David Robb, Aug. 8, 1981; children: Christopher James, Kathryn Ann. BA, Mich. State U., 1978; JD, U. Detroit, 1984. Bar: Mich. 1985; cert. paralegal, Mich. Paralegal Dykema Gossett, Detroit, 1978-84; assoc. Dykema Gossett, Bloomfield Hills, Mich., 1985—; advisor Prep. Ctr., Warren (Mich.) Consol.

Schs., 1988—. Bd. dirs. Mich. chpt. Scoliosis Assn., 1986-87. Mem. ABA, Mich. Bar Assn., Oakland County Bar Assn. Office: Dykema Gossett 505 N Woodward Ave Ste 3000 Bloomfield Hills MI 48013

SHIH, HELEN, floral shop franchise founder; b. Taipei, Taiwan, Mar. 31, 1953; came to U.S., 1975; d. Shiaw-Shan and Hsian-Yann (Pai) S.; m. Peter A. Callihan, May 3, 1980. MS, Occidental Coll., 1978. Gen. ptnr. She's Florists, L.A., 1979—; pres., chief exec. officer She's Flowers, Inc., L.A., 1986—; cons. Constrnl. Rights Found., L.A., 1987-88; bd. dirs. Teleflora, Inc., Calif. region. Mem. Town Hall Calif., 1988-89. Mem. L.A. C. of C., Floral Transnat. Delivery Assoc., Women in Franchising. Home: 21 S Venice Blvd #6 Venice CA 90291 Office: She's Flowers Inc 604 Monterey Pass Rd Monterey Park CA 91754

SHIH, JOAN FAI, artist, educator; b. Guangdong, China, Sept. 4, 1932; came to U.S., 1953; d. Henry Ken-Wai and Laura Suk-Wee (Chen) S. Student, Art Students' League, N.Y.C., 1953; BFA, Kansas City Art Inst., 1956, MFA, 1961; postgrad., Pa. Acad. Fine Arts, 1957-59, 61-63. Instr. art Kansas City (Mo.) Art Inst., 1959-61, Converse Coll., Spartanburg, S.C., 1966-67; lectr. painting Rosemont (Pa.) Coll., 1969-88. One woman shows include Brit. Council, Gloucer Bldg., Hong Kong, 1956, Cedar Crest Coll., Allentown, Pa., 1969, Danville (Va.) Mus. Fine Arts, 1986; exhibited in group shows including Nelson and Atkins Mus. Art, Kansas City, Mo., 1954, Pa. Acad. Fine Arts, 1963, 69-70, 72, 74, 76, 81, 83, Phila. Civic Ctr. Mus., 1970, 74, 79-80, 82, Woodmere Art Mus., Phila., 1987, Art Inst. Phila., 1987, John Geiszel All Transparency Watercolor Show., Phila, 1988, 89, Plastic Club Ann. Art Exhbn., Phila., 1988, 89 (Marion Cohee Meml. award 1989); traveling exhbn. Nat. Assn. Women Artists, 1978-80, 80-82, 83-85, 85-87, Huntington Mus., N.Y.C., 1981, Bergen Mus., Paramus, N.J., 1983; represented in permanent collections including D.W. Newcomer's Sons Gallery, Kansas City, Mo. (Ann. Show award 1960), Meth. Hosp., Phila. Kansas City Art Inst. scholar, 1953-56; Kansas City Art Inst. grantee, 1959-61. Mem. Nat. Assn. Women Artists (Elizabeth Erlanger Meml. prize 1980), Fellowship of Pa. Acad. Fine Arts, Coalition of Women's Art Orgns., Phila. Watercolor Club, Hong Kong Art Club. Episcopalian. Home: 2013 Locust St Philadelphia PA 19103

SHIH CARDUCCI, JOAN CHIA-MO, cooking educator, biochemist, medical technologist; b. Rukuan, Chunghua, Republic of China, Dec. 21, 1933; came to U.S., 1955; d. Luke Chiang-hsi and Lien-chin (Chang) S.; m. Kenneth M. Carducci, Sept. 30, 1960 (dec. July 1988); children: Suzanne R., Elizabeth M. BS in Chemistry, St. Mary Coll., Xavier, Kans., 1959; intern in med. tech., St. Mary's Hosp., Rochester, N.Y., 1960. Med. researcher Strong Meml. Hosp. (U. Rochester), 1960-61; pharm. chemist quality control Strasenburgh Labs., Rochester, 1961-62; cooking tchr. adult edn. Montgomery County Pub. Schs., Rockville, Md., 1973-79; cooking tchr. The Chinese Cookery Inc., Rockville, 1975-86; cooking tchr. The Chinese Cookery Inc., Silver Spring, Md., 1986—, pres., bd. dirs., 1975—; chemist NIH, Bethesda, 1987—. Author: The Chinese Cookery, 1981, Hunan Cuisine, 1984. Mem. Internat. Assn. Cooking Profls. Democrat. Roman Catholic. Home and Office: The Chinese Cookery Inc 14209 Sturtevant Rd Silver Spring MD 20905

SHILDNECK, BARBARA JEAN, accounting magazine editor; b. Waynesboro, Pa., Apr. 1, 1937; d. Barry Price and Helen Matilda (Armstrong) S. B.A. in English Lit., Wilson Coll., Chambersburg, Pa., 1959. With AICPA, N.Y.C., 1959—, jr. prodn. asst., 1959-62, sr. prodn. asst., 1962-66, editor The CPA, 1969-73, asst. editor to manuscript editor Jour. of Accountancy, 1966-79, from mng. editor to exec. editor, 1979—; editor Centennial issue AICPA, May, 1987; panelist edn. program video tapes Dunwoody & Co., Chartered Accts., Toronto, Ont., Can., 1977, AICPA, 1980; lectr. in field. Contbr. articles to profl. jours. Recipient Gold Circle award Am. Soc. Assn. Execs., 1986, Bronze Ozzie for spl. issue Mag. Design and Prodn., May 1987, Soc. Nat. Assn. Publs. award, 1987, award of distinction Soc. Tech. Communication, 1987. Mem. NAFE, Am. Soc. Bus. Press Editors, Am. Acctg. Assn. Democrat. Office: AICPA 1211 Ave of the Americas New York NY 10036

SHILINIS, NATASHA V., librarian; b. Leningrad, USSR, Oct. 1, 1926; came to U.S., 1982; d. Vladimir Y. and Nina V. (Petrova) Shiperovitch; m. Julius A. Shilinis; 1 child, Vlado; m. Espylee E.L. Sanders Jr., Aug. 12, 1949. MD in Linguistics, Leningrad U., USSR, 1949; diploma, Sch. Bus. Machines, Jersey City, 1984; MLS, Rutgers U., 1985. Sr. libr. Libr. of Acad. Sci. USSR, Leningrad, 1949-51; head dept. lit. in fgn. langs. Regional Libr., Pskov, USSR, 1953-54; prof. Inst. Tech., Leningrad, 1953-54; sr. translator Rsch. Inst. Telecommunications, Leningrad, 1954-81; tchr.'s aide Jersey City Pub. Sch. System, 1982-84; prof.'s aide journalism faculty Rutgers U., New Brunswick, N.J., 1984-85; reference libr. Jersey City Pub. Libr., 1985—; cons. Grigory Gurevich Arts Ctr., Jersey City, 1987—. Translator: The Frescoes of Tassili, 1957, Structural Anthropology, 1960, Henry Matisse, 1972. Recipient Participation in World War II medal USSR, 1943, medal of Honor USSR, 1965. Home: 700 Newark Ave #808 Jersey City NJ 07306 Office: Jersey City Pub Libr 472 Jersey Ave Jersey City NJ 07302

SHILLADEY, ANN, video post production company administrator; b. Omaha, June 4, 1933; d. Louis W. and Louise E. (FitzSimmons) S.; children: Charles Ferguson, Elizabeth A. Ferguson, Timothy S. Ferguson. BS, U. Ill., 1955. Assoc. dir. Sheil Ctr./Northwestern Univ., Evanston, Ill.; dir. ops. HCM/Marsteller, Chgo.; supr. exec. svcs. Andersen Cons. Arthur Andersen & Co., S.C., Chgo.; adminstrv. mgr. Editel Inc., Chgo. Pres. PTA, Skokie, Ill., 1971-73, exec. v.p., 1970-71, treas., 1969-70; commr. consumer affairs commn. Village of Skokie, 1970-71; chmn. All Star Salute to Secs. Luncheon for Assoc. Com. Arthritis Found., 1989-90. Mem. NAFE, Lakeview Tenants Orgn., Pi Beta Phi. Roman Catholic. Home: 668 W Roscoe 2W Chicago IL 60657 Office: Editel 301 E Erie Chicago IL 60611

SHILLING, KAY MARLENE, psychiatrist; b. Scottsbluff, Nebr., July 1, 1952; d. Harrison Gene and Rose Marie (Allen) Herber; m. Mark Randall Shilling, July 2, 1977. B.S., U. Nebr.-Lincoln, 1976; M.D., U. Nebr.-Omaha, 1980. Diplomate Nat. Bd. Med. Examiners. Resident in psychiatry Nebr. Psychiat. Inst., Omaha, 1981-84; practice medicine specializing in psychiatry, Omaha, 1984—; cons. Meth. Childrens Hosp. Family Life Ctr., Omaha, 1985—; bd. dirs. Indian-Chicano Health Ctr., Omaha. Mem. AMA, Am. Med. Women's Assn. (pres. Omaha br. 1986-88, dir. Nebr. State chpt. 1988—, book reviewer for JAMWA, Outstanding Physician award 1989), Am. Psychiat. Assn., Met. Omaha Med. Soc., Nebr. Med. Assn., Alpha Xi Delta. Avocations: gourmet cooking, interior decorating, house renovation. Home: 1103 S 80th St Omaha NE 68124 Office: 7602 Pacific St Suite 302 Omaha NE 68114

SHILLINGBURG, PATRICIA MOSER, brokerage firm development specialist; b. Summit, N.J., Jan. 10, 1943; d. Richard Goodwin and Alice (House) Moser; m. James Edward Shillingburg, May 13, 1967; children: Lillian, Donald, Emily. BA, Wheaton Coll., Norton, Mass., 1965. Cons. on pvt. investment housing United Cerebral Palsy Assns. N.J., 1988-89; editor Pvt. Investment Housing Report, South Orange, N.J., 1988—; project devel. mgr. Personal Control Fin. Network Pub. div. Donaldson, Lufkin & Jenrette, Jersey City, 1989—. Author: Kids Can Touch Computers, 1983, Adults Can Touch Computers, 1983, Lotus Made As Easy As 1-2-3, 1983, The IBM PC--A Beginner's Guide, 1983, IBM PCjr: First Steps in BASIC Programming, 1984, The Best of the North Fork, 1987, The Teacher's Computer Book, 1987. Vice chmn., mem. numerous coms. N.J. Bd. Human Svcs., 1977-85; Union County rep. parent adv. coun. for handicapped N.J. Dept. Edn., 1985-87; founder, mem. adv. bd. Our House, Inc., 1979—; mem. Parents' Assn. bd., co-chmn. No. N.J. antiques show and sale, Newark Acad., 1989; trustee, chmn. govtl. affairs com. ARC, Essex, N.J., 1988—; mem. residential svcs. com. Assn. for Retarded Citizens N.J., 1983—; chmn. bd My Home, Inc., 1989—. Home: 228 Conway Ct South Orange NJ 07079

SHILLINGSBURG, MIRIAM JONES, educator; b. Balt., Oct. 5, 1943; d. W. Elvin and Miriam (Reeves) Jones; BA, Mars Hill Coll., 1964; MA, U. S.C., 1966, PhD, 1969; m. Peter L. Shillingsburg, Nov. 21, 1967; children: Robert, George, John, Alice, Anne Carol. Asst. prof. Limestone Coll., Gaffney, S.C., 1969; asst. prof. Mississippi State (Miss.) U., 1970-75, assoc. prof., 1975-80, prof. English, 1980—, asst. to provost, 1987-88, assoc. v.p. for acad. affairs, 1988—; vis. fellow Australian Def. Force Acad., 1989; lectr. Fulbright U. New South Wales, Duntroon, Australia, 1984-85. Nat. Endowment Humanities fellow in residence, Columbia U., 1976-77. Mem. Soc. Study So. Lit., Southeastern Soc. Eighteenth Century Studies, Nat. Acad. Advising Assn., South Atlantic Modern Lang. Assn., Australia-New Zealand Am. Studies Assn., Phi Kappa Phi. Author: Mark Twain in Australasia, 1988; editor: Conquest of Granada, 1988; mem. editorial bd. Works of W.M. Thackeray; assoc. editor Miss. Quarterly; contbr. articles to profl. jours. and mags.

SHILSTONE, SANDRA SCIACCA, journalist; b. New Orleans, Dec. 23, 1956; d. Frank Henry and Teddy L. (Liuzza) Sciacca; m. Cecil M. Shilstone II, Apr. 19, 1980; 1 child, Scott Maxwell. BA in Journalism, Loyola U., 1978, postgrad., 1983. News producer WDSU-TV NBC, New Orleans, 1976-80; writer, producer Syndistar Prodn., New Orleans, 1980-81; pub. info. officer Mayor's Office City Hall, New Orleans, 1981-83; editor-in-chief Sunbelt Exec. Mag., Regional, La.; editor-in-chief, assoc. pub. New Orleans Mag., 1984-86; contbg. sports reporter Jim Mora Show-WGNO-TV, 1987; pub. relations cons. Shilstone & Assoc., New Orleans, 1987-89; TV news assignment editor WWL-TV CBS, New Orleans, 1989—; instr. Tulane Univ., New Orleans, 1981. Fellow, Met. Area Com. Tulane Univ., New Orleans, 1985-86, Bd. dirs. Jr. League New Orleans. Mem. League Women Voters. Democrat. Roman Catholic. Home: 1527 4th St New Orleans LA 70130

SHIM, EUNSHIL, nutrition consultant, educator; b. Pusan, Kyungsang, Republic of Korea, July 10, 1952; came to U.S., 1969; d. Myungwon and Haeran (Kim) Shim; m. W.E. Gene Holder, Aug.l 16, 1986; children: Michael-Saejong, Michelle. B in Dietetics, Mich. State U., 1975; M in Advanced Human Nutrition, U. Fla., 1979. Lic. dietitian, Fla. Dietary interviewer U. Fla., Gainesville, 1979; sr. dietitian Sunland Ctr., Gainesville, 1979-82; asst. prof. U. Fla., 1983-87; dietitian cons. Nutrition Assocs. of Jacksonville, Fla., 1987—; adj. instr. U. Fla., 1981-82; vol. dietitian VA Med. Ctr., Gainesville, 1979; acting project dir. NIH Rsch. Grant, Gainesville, 1985-87; gov. apptd. mem. Long Term Care Ombudsmen Com., 1987-89; instr. Fla. Community Coll. at Jacksonville, 1990—; cons. in field. Named one of Outstanding Young Women Am., 1986; Fla. Dietetic Assn. scholar, 1979. Mem. Am Assn. Mental Deficiency, Am. Dietetic Assn. (exhibit chair gerontological nutritionists group 1989-90, area coord. 1990—), Fla. Dietetic Assn. (chmn. dist. pres. 1986-87, awards com. 1987-88, chmn. scholarship com. 1988-89, chair bylaws com. 1990—), Jacksonville Dietetic Assn. (bylaws com. chmn. 1987-88, 89-90, 90—), Gainesville Dist. Dietetic Assn. (edn. com. chmn. 1982-83, sec. 1983-84, mem. com. chmn. 1984-85, pres. elect 1984-85, pres. 1985-86, ex-officio and nominating com. chmn. 1986-87), Mandarin Jr. Women's Club (newsletter editor, pub. rels. com. chair 1989—). Presbyterian. Home: 9967 Larkdale Ct Jacksonville FL 32257 Office: 9428 Baymeadows Rd Suite 129 Jacksonville FL 32216

SHIMADA, LINDA MICHI, financial consultant; b. Honolulu, Oct. 22, 1963; d. Glenn Atsuo Shimada and Amy Ayako (Takeda) Shimada Wong. BBA, U. Hawaii, 1985. Lic. life ins. solicitor, registered issuer of securities, Hawaii. Salesperson McInerny, Honolulu, 1982-83; clk. U. Hawaii Bd. Regents, Honolulu, 1982-84; sales rep. A.L. Williams, Honolulu, 1984, sales mgr., 1984-85, dist. mgr., 1985, div. mgr., 1986; traffic prodn. mgr., account exec. DiCarlo Advt. Agy., Honolulu, 1986-87; asst. account exec. Pearlman/Wohl/Olshever/Marchese, L.A., 1987-88; fin. cons. Merrill Lynch, Pierce, Fenner & Smith, Inc., Santa Ana, Calif., 1988—. Mem. NAFE, Am. Entrepreneurs Assn., Nat. Assn. Securities Dealers (cert.), Asian Pacific Women's Network, Advt. Club L.A., Alpha Beta Chi (chpt. sec. 1983-84, chpt. pres. 1984-85). Democrat. Office: Merrill Lynch Pierce Fenner Smith 2670 N Main St Santa Ana CA 92701

SHIMADA, TOMIKO, company executive; b. Tokyo, Oct. 12, 1932; came to U.S., 1966, naturalized, 1976; d. Fumio and Fukue (Kobayashi) S. BS in Chemistry, Tokyo Coll. Sci., 1964; MS in Microbiology, U. Mich., 1968, PhD in Environ Microbiol., 1975. Postdoctoral intern U. Mich., Ann Arbor, 1975-76; postdoctoral fellow The Wistar Inst., Phila., 1976-78; research assoc. Am. Health Found., Valhalla, N.Y., 1978-79; head in vitro sys. facility Am. Health Found., 1979-83; IPA spl. expert Nat. Cancer Inst., Frederick, Md., 1983-86; sr. scientist Biol. Research Faculty & Facility, Jamesville, Md., 1983-88; dir. U.S.A. rep. office Shin Nippon Biomed. labs., Ltd., Frederick, Md., 1988—; adj. faculty NYU, Plattsburg, 1982—; cons. in field. Contbr. articles to profl. jours. Mem. Am. Soc. Microbiology, Tissue Culture Assn., Environ. Mutagen Soc., Soc. Toxicology, Genetic Toxicology Soc., AAAS.

SHIMMIN, KATHLEEN GRACE, environmental agency executive; b. Santa Rosa, Calif., Mar. 7, 1939; d. Melvin Raleigh and Helen Marguerite (Grace) S.; m. Louis John Lenertz, Feb. 14, 1973 (div. 1980); m. Donald Phillip Harvey, June 27, 1980. BS in Sanitary Sci., U. Calif., Berkeley, 1960, MA in Bacteriology, 1963, postgrad. in environ. health scis., 1963-69; postgrad. in counseling psychology, U. San Francisco, 1986—. Research, tchr. Sch. Pub. Health U. Calif., Berkeley, 1963-64, 66-69; chief microbiology sect. EPA, Alameda, Calif., 1969-73, co-chair women's com., 1972-74, chief regional lab., 1974-78; chief water enforcement EPA, San Francisco, 1978-81, chief compliance and response, 1981-83, chief field ops. br., 1983-86, chief Office of Health and Emergency Planning, 1986—; instr. John F. Kennedy U., Martinez, Calif., 1969. Vol. counselor alcoholism outpatient clinic VA Hosp., Martinez, 1987—. Republican. Club: Women's Faculty (Berkeley), Presidio Officers (San Francisco). Office: EPA 215 Fremont St San Francisco CA 94105

SHIMP, KAREN ANN, accountant, transportation company administrator; b. Atlantic, Iowa, July 17, 1959; d. Emerson Arnold and Verna Louise (Schmeling) Fett; m. Philip Kenneth Shimp, Jan. 30, 1988; 1 child, Keith Emerson. BSBA, Drake U., 1981. Acct. Midwest Mut. Ins. Co., West Des Moines, Iowa, 1981-84; staff acct. Deborah J. Kent, CPA, Palm Desert, Calif., 1985; fin. analyst Massey Sand & Rock Co., Indio, Calif., 1986-88; supr. interline Greyhound Lines, Inc., West Des Moines, 1989—; coordinator Drake U. Bus. Aid Soc., 1980. Treas. Luth. Women's Missionary League, Indio, 1986-88, sec., 1988-89; v.p. Aid Assn. for Lutherans, Indio, 1988-89. State of Iowa scholar, 1977. Mem. Inland Soc. Tax Cons., Nat. Assn. Accts. Democrat. Home: 1182 11th St Apt 13 West Des Moines IA 50265 Office: Greyhound Lines Inc 4900 University Ave West Des Moines IA 50265

SHIN, YONG AE IM, chemist; b. Seoul, Korea, Aug. 2, 1932; came to U.S., 1953; d. Duk Ho and Hung Ye (Song) Im; m. Bong Ju Shin, June 11, 1961; children: Hyun Ja, Hyun Joe, Sue-Joe. BS, Mercer U., Macon, Ga., 1956; MSc, Ohio State U., Columbus, 1958, PhD, 1960. Rsch. assoc. U. Ill., Urbana, 1961-63; rsch. chemist gerontology rsch. ctr. NIH, Balt., 1965-89; health sci. adminstr. Nat. Inst. Gen. Med. Scis. NIH, Bethesda, Md., 1990—. Contbr. articles to sci. jours. Fellow Am. Inst. Chemists; mem. Am. Soc. Biochemistry and Molecular Biology, Korean Scientists and Engrs. Am. (chpt. pres. 1983-85), Am. Biophys. Soc. Home: 13710 Princess Anne Way Phoenix MD 21131 Office: Gerontology Rsch Ctr Baltimore MD 21224

SHINDLER, ELAINE ROSALIE G., publisher; b. Bklyn., May 16, 1934; d. Harry and Anna (Fader) Goldstein; m. Kurt Shindler, June 14, 1953; children: Steven, David. Student, U. Vt., 1951-53. Promotion dir. New York mag., 1981-84, mktg. dir., 1984-85, assoc. pub., 1986-87; pub. Star mag., N.Y.C., 1987-90, Soap Opera Digest/Soap Opera Weekly, N.Y.C., 1990—. Mem. Proprietary Assn., Advt. Women N.Y., Cosmetic, Toiletry & Fragrances Assn., Fashion Group N.Y. Office: Soap Opera Digest New York NY

SHINGLEDECKER, JANE ANN, accountant; b. Shaldon, Devon, Eng., Nov. 10, 1963; came to U.S. 1987; d. Raymond Edward and Eileen (Renfree) George; m. David Anthony Shingledecker, Feb. 12, 1988; stepchildren: Walther A., Lorraine E. A in English and Math., Swindon Coll. Higher Edn., Eng., 1984; postgrad. in mgmt. and fin., Ctr. for Degree Studies, Scranton, Pa. Data controller Gardner Merchants, Eng., 1980-81; computer programmer Blick Internat. Sys., Ltd., Eng., 1981-83; acct. B.J. Golding Constrn., Eng., 1983-87, Smarts Group Ltd., Eng., 1987; project mgr. McCallie Assocs., Inc., Bellevue, Nebr., 1988—. Mem. Brit. Inst. Mgmt. Ch. of England. Home: 28 Jackson Keeseville NY 12944 Office: McCallie Associates Inc 1620 Wilshire #222 Bellevue NE 68005

SHINN, FRANCES MILLER, financial executive; b. Oakwood, Tex., Aug. 20, 1942; d. Warren Philip and Helen Ophelia (Tinsley) Miller; m. Albert Wayne, Aug. 30, 1964, (div. Nov. 1973); 1 child, Stanley Wayne. Grad. high sch. Property mgr. Fin. Packaging Corp., Houston, 1973-74, The Oaks of Woodlake Apts. and Townhomes, Houston, 1972-74; escrow sec. Transamerica Title Ins., Houston, 1974-75, So. Title Co., Houston; escrow assoc. Stewart Title Co., Houston, 1977-79; escrow officer Capital Title Ins. Co., 1979-84; escrow officer Ticor Title Ins. Co., Houston, 1984-88, Coppell, Tex., 1989—. Republican. Home: 215 N Moore Rd #7025 Coppell TX 75019 Office: 102 Meadowcreek #106 Coppell TX 75019

SHINN, LINDA J., nurse, association executive; b. Ft. Wayne, Ind., Jan. 10, 1948; d. Richard Kenneth and Dorothy Elaine (Carrier) S. Nursing degree, Meml. Hosp., South Bend, Ind., 1965-68; B, Ind. U., Indpls., 1977; M, Ind. Cen. U., 1983. Staff nurse Meml. Hosp., South Bend, 1968, Robert Long Hosp, Indpls., 1969-70; dir. legisl. and labor relations program Ind. State Nurses Assn., Indpls., 1969-71, asst. exec. dir., 1971-73, assoc. exec. dir., 1973-80, exec. dir., 1980-83; div. dir. Am. Nurses' Assn., Kansas City, Mo., 1983-87, dep. exec. dir., 1987—; adj. lectr. Ind. U., 1980-83; adj. instr. U. Kans., Kansas City, 1986—. Contbg. author Networking for Nurses, 1983. Mem. Gov.'s Commn. on Status of Women, Indpls., 1975, Gov.'s Council on Sports Medicine, Indpls., 1980-82; mentor Purdue U., Lafayette, Ind., 1974-83, Avila Coll., Kansas City, Mo., 1986; 2d v.p. Spay-Neuter Services, Inc., Indpls.; mem. adv. group Nat. Disaster Med. System, Washington, 1985. Mem. Am. Nurses' Assn., Am. Mgmt. Assn., Am. Soc. Assn. Execs. (cert. 1989), Sigma Theta Tau, Epsilon Sigma Alpha. Office: Am Nurses' Assn 2420 Pershing Rd Kansas City MO 64108

SHINN, SUSA JANE, operating room nurse; b. Marion, Ind., Apr. 9, 1940; d. Frederick Maurice and Marguerite (White) S. Diploma, Parkview Meth. Sch. Nursing, Ft. Wayne, Ind., 1961; BS, Tex. Woman's U., 1983. Cert. operating rm. nurse, cardiovascular nurse specialist. Physicians asst. Ft. Wayne; supr. operating rm. and recovery room Med. Ctr. Del Oro Hosp., Houston; supr., asst. Meth. Hosp., Houston, mgr. operating rm. Mem. ANA, NAFE, Tex. Nurses Assn., Assn. Operating Rm. Nurses, Houston Orgn. Nurse Execs., Fedn. Houston Profl. Women, Parkview Meth. Sch. Nursing Alumni Assn., Tex. Woman's U. Alumni Assn., Smithsonian Instn., Zool. Soc. Houston. Methodist. Home: 3211 Elmridge St Houston TX 77025

SHINPOCH, JAN WILLA, international human rights consultant; b. Washington, Oct. 26, 1953; d. Albert Neil and Barbara Yolande (Bliss) S. BA in Polit. Philosophy, Fairhaven Coll., 1973. Mgmt. analyst Wash. Dept. Social and Health Svcs., Olympia, 1975-76, chief planning and devel. Bur. Juvenile Rehab., 1976-78; govt. rels. analyst Seattle Metro, 1978-79; legis. dir. to Congressman Mike Lowry, U.S. Ho. of Reps., Washington, 1979-82, staff dir. subcom. on internat. devel. instns., 1982-85; cons. on internat. devel. fin., Washington, 1985-87; chief staff to Congressman Mike Lowry, Washington, 1987-89; dir. adminstrv. ops. Nat. Security Archive, Washington, 1989; project dir. human rights handbook series Ctr. for Internat. Policy, Washington, 1989—; lectr. Seattle U. Sch. Pub. Svcs., 1989—; cons. svc. com. Unitarian Universalist Ch., Boston, 1989-90; cons. Georgetown U., Washington, 1990; mem. faculty Washington Sch. Inst. for Policy Studies, 1984—. Co-founder Seattle Mcpl. Elections Com., 1977; sec. Human Rights Polit. Action Com., Washington, 1985—. Democrat. Roman Catholic. Home: 1725 17th St NW Apt 104 Washington DC 20009 Office: Ctr for Internat Policy 1755 Massachusetts Ave NW Washington DC 20036

SHIPLEY, ALICE MILDRED, civics and American history educator, civic worker; b. Westminster, Md., Feb. 16, 1927; d. Paul and Marea (Royer) Shipley. BA cum laude, Western Md. Coll., Westminster, 1948; MA, U. Md., 1966. Cert. advanced profl., Md. Tchr. Harford County Pub. Schs., Jarrettsville, Md., 1948-50; tchr. Carroll County Bd. Edn., Westminster, 1950-86, social studies coordinator East Middle Sch., 1983-86. Co-author: The First 150 Years, 1987. Rec. sec. adminstrv. bd. Westminster Meth. Ch., 1964, coord. adult ministries, 1986-89, chmn. communications, 1990—; mem. mus. com. United Meth. Hist. Soc., 1989—; mem. Hist. Soc. Carroll County, 1954—; mem. Sesquicentennial Com. of Carroll County, 1987; project coord. Bd. Edn. and Hist. Soc. of Westminster, 1988-89; active Girl Scouts U.S., 1950-53. Recipient Gov.'s citation State of Md., 1986; letter of appreciation Pres. Reagan, 1986, others. Mem. AAUW (rec. sec. 1954-56), DAR (co-chmn. jr. Am. citizens William Winchester chpt. 1988-89), Ret. Tchrs. Assns.. Republican. Home: 74 W Green St Westminster MD 21157

SHIPLEY, JOYCE DEBORAH, psychologist; b. Boston, Sept. 6, 1956; d. Kenneth Saul and Elinor Miriam (Godes) Wolfson; m. Anthony Alfred Shipley, Sept. 1, 1985; 1 child, Justin John. BA, U. So. Calif., L.A., 1978; PhD, Calif. Sch. Profl. Psychology, 1984. Psychiat. aide North Hollywood Community Hosp., Hollywood, Calif., 1979-80; psychol. asst. Arroyo Counseling Svcs., Pasadena, Calif., 1983-84; program dir. The Psychol. Ctr., Lawrence, Mass., 1984-85; clin. psychologist Chelmsford (Mass.) Med. Assocs., 1984-86; co-dir. Chelmsford Family Counseling Ctr., 1986—; tutor Elmira (N.Y.) Correctional Facility, 1974-75; community cons. Lowell High Sch., 1988—; supr. Boston Coll. Interns, Chelmsford, 1986—; co-dir., cofounder Chelmsford Family Counseling Ctr., 1987—. Mem. Am. Psychol. Assn., Mass. Psychol. Assn., Amnesty Internat. Democrat. Jewish. Home: 267 Wellman Ave North Chelmsford MA 01863 Office: Chelmsford Family Ctr 15 Tyngsboro Rd North Chelmsford MA 01863

SHIPLEY, NANCY LOUISE, health science association executive; b. Wilkinsburg, Pa., June 26, 1950; d. Oran G. and Catherine P. (Soisson) S. BS, Slippery Rock (Pa.) State Coll., 1972, MEd, 1974. Tchr. phys. edn. Monroeville (Pa.) Jr. High Sch., 1972-77; rep. sales Knoll Pharms., Whippany, N.J., 1978-80; regional rep. med. sales Surgidev Corp., Morristown, N.J., 1980-82, Ioptex, Morristown, 1982-84; pres. surg. custom trays Surg. Services and Supplies, Inc., Montvale, N.J., 1984-85; sales med. instruments Allergan Humphrey Corp., New Eng., 1985-87; exec. adminstr. Eye Inst. Essex, Belleville, N.J., 1987-89; sr. sales exec. Allergan Med. Optics, Detroit, 1989-90; N.Y. regional sales mgr. Allergan Med. Optics, Scotch Plains, N.J., 1990—; cons. for pvt. outpatient eye surg. ctrs., 1980-90. Contbr. articles to profl. jours. Republican. Home: PO Box 484 Fanwood NJ 07023 Office: 2137 Jersey Ave Scotch Plains NJ 07076

SHIPLEY, SHIRLEY DAHL, oil company executive; b. Orange, N.J., Oct. 17, 1932; d. Conrad George and Sylvia Marion (Gronquist) D.; m. William Stewart Shipley II, July 2, 1955; children: William Stewart III, Linda Ann, Elizabeth Marion. BS, Cedar Crest Coll., 1954. Tchr., Radnor Twp. (Pa.) Schs., 1954-55, Sarasota County (Fla.) Schs., 1955-56; v.p. adminstrn. Shipley Oil Co., Inc., York, Pa., 1977—. Pres., York Suburban Sch. Dist. Bd., 1973-79; bd. dirs., co-chmn. York Country Day Sch., York County Library System, York County Mental Health Center, Greater York, Inc., United Community Services, York County Literacy Council, ARC, Women's Assn. York Symphony Orch., York Found.; pres. Childrens Home; trustee, mem. exec. com. York Coll. of Pa., 1972—; mem. York, Franklin and Adams County Intermediate Unit Sch. Bd. pres. Jr. League York, 1967-69; nat. bd. dirs. Assn. Jr. Leagues, 1970-72; mem. Pa. adv. council U.S. Commn. Civil Rights; trustee York Coll. Pa. Mem. Pa. Petroleum Assn., Petroleum Marketers Assn. Am. Republican. Presbyterian. Home: 1000 Clubhouse Rd York PA 17403 Office: 550 E King St PO Box 946 York PA 17405

SHIPLEY, V. FERN WILSON, personnel recruiting company executive; b. Manchester, Okla., Sept. 29, 1921; d. Charles C. and Oma (Ready) Wilson; m. David McNalley Shipley, Jan. 21, 1943 (div. Nov. 1968); children—Davon David, Sondra Fern Busch. Student U. Colo., 1961-62. Cons., Cartwright Employment Agy., Boulder, 1969-71, head cons., 1973-77; mgr. Western Permanent Services, Boulder, 1972; owner, mgr. Shipley Personnel Recruiting, Boulder, 1978—. Currently doing exec. recruiting book research. Fund raiser Mountain View Methodist Ch., 1960; tchr. Sunday Sch., Meth. Ch., 1954-56, chmn. Bible Sch., 1954; leader, Colo. Muscular Dystrophy Research Fund Drive, 1955; mgr. telethon drive, Boulder, 1955. Republican. Avocations: Travel; sewing; oil painting; interior design; swimming. Home: 7205 Ballygar Way Elk Grove CA 95758 Office: 1300 Canyon Blvd Ste 1 Boulder CO 80302

SHIPMAN, JEAN PUGH, medical librarian; b. Chambersburg, Pa., Aug. 6, 1957; d. Andrew Richard and Sara Elizabeth (Bert) Pugh; m. Mark James Shipman, Oct. 8, 1988. BA, Gettysburg Coll., 1979; MSLS, Case Western Res. U., 1980. Reference libr. Johns Hopkins Sch. Medicine, Balt., 1980-81, sr. reference libr., 1981-82, access libr., 1982-84, psychiatry-neuroscis. librarian, 1984-88; mgr. libr. and audiovisual svcs. Greater Balt. Med. Ctr., 1988—. Contbr. articles to profl. jours. Mem. Med. Libr. Assn. (program com. Mid-Atlantic chpt. 1989), Md. Assn. Health Scis. Librs. (v.p. 1989—), Adventures Club Towson (Md.), Balt. Bike Club, Beta Phi Mu, Beta Beta Beta. Republican. Lutheran. Office: U Md at Balt RMLS 111 S Greene St Baltimore MD 21201

SHIPMAN, WANDA PALMER, librarian; b. Mobile, Ala., Aug. 7, 1950; d. William Harold Palmer and Lora (Davidson) Griffith; m. Jimmy Ray Shipman, June 12, 1988. BA, Winthrop Coll., 1972; MEd, U. S.C., 1978. Cert. spl. edn. tchr., S.C. Libr. S.C. Sch. for the Deaf, Blind and Multi-Handicapped, Spartanburg, 1972-88, assoc. libr. of reference and rsch., 1988—; mem. adv. coun. S.C. State Libr. for the Blind and Physically Handicapped, Columbia, 1980-89. Mem. adv. com. Spartanburg Tech. Coll., 1986-88. Mem. NEA, S.C. Edn. Assn., S.C. Libr. Assn., Assn. Edn. and the Visually Impaired, Spartanburg chpt. Handicapped Organized Women, AAUW. Home: 2939 Hwy 215 Roebuck SC 29376 Office: SC Sch for the Deaf Blind and Multihandicapped Cedar Spring Sta Spartanburg SC 29302

SHIPP, MAURINE SARAH HARSTON (MRS. LEVI ARNOLD SHIPP), realtor; b. Holiday, Mo., Mar. 6, 1913; d. Paul Edward and Sarah Isabel (Mitchell) Harston; grad. Ill. Bus. Coll., 1945; student real estate Springfield Jr. Coll., 1962; student law LaSalle Extension U., 1959-62; m. Levi Arnold Shipp, Jan. 30, 1941; children—Jerome Reynolds, Patricia (Mrs. Rodney W. England). With Ill. Dept. Agr., Springfield, 1941-65, supr. livestock industry Brucellosis sect.; saleswoman Morgan-Hamilton Real Estate Co., Springfield, 1962-64; owner, mgr. Shipp Real Estate Agy., Springfield, 1965—. Prin. appraiser urban renewal HUD, 1971-72; mem. Public Bldg. Commn. Springfield. Bd. dirs. Springfield Travelers Aid, 1971—. Mem. NAACP, Urban League, Iota Phi Lambda. Episcopalian. Mem. Order Eastern Star. Club: Bridge. Home: 335 Bellerive Rd Springfield IL 62704

SHIPPE, MARY LOU, instructional designer and developer; b. Kansas City, Mo., Nov. 25, 1942; d. Hiram Arthur and Clio (Robinson) Cooley; m. Donald Louis Shippe, Aug. 13, 1966; children—Kenneth Louis, Angela Lou. B.A., Kans. U., 1964; M.P.A., Okla. U., 1979; D.P.A. candidate Nova U., 1983—. Research technician Dept. Def., Md., 1964-66, analyst, 1970-71; substitute tchr. Howard County Schs., Md., 1972-76; instr. Los Angeles Community Coll. Overseas, Japan, 1976-79; asst. Pub. Today News Service, Washington, 1979; village mgr. Town Ctr. Community Assn., Md., 1980-83; instructional designer, developer computer based tng. Ford Aerospace Corp., Hanover, Md., 1983—; People to People technology del. to Australia and New Zealand, 1988. Mem. Columbia Forum, Md., 1980—, Housing and Human Services Task Force, Columbia, 1980-82. Mem. Am. Soc. Pub. Adminstrn., Am. Bus. Womens Assn. (v.p. 1985-86, pres. 1986-88, named Woman of the Yr. 1987, 88, 89), Assn. Ednl. Communications and Tech., LWV Howard County, 1982-83. Club: Zonta (dir. 1982-83, v.p. 1986-88, pres. 1989—). Avocations: travel, theatre, boating. Home: 9573 Long Look Ln Columbia MD 21045 Office: Ford Aerospace Corp 7100 Standard Dr Hanover MD 21076

SHIRK, ANNADORA VESPER, English educator; b. Altoona, Pa., Aug. 9, 1918; d. Harry M. and Jessie (Birchfield) Spengler; m. Albert R. Vesper (dec.); m. Eugene L. Shirk, 1949; children: Albert, Thea. PhD in Rhetoric, Temple U., 1977. Instr. English, Albright Coll., Reading, Pa., 1946, asst. prof., 1949-66, assoc. prof., 1966-76, prof., 1976—, chmn. dept., 1978-82, faculty chmn., 1980-82; speaker, 1955—. Mem. Reading Sch. Bd., 1955-61. Named Coll. Prof. of Yr., Reading C. of C., 1980; Lindback fellow, 1978. Mem. AAUW (pres. Reading, 1976-78). Republican. Methodist. Home: 1503 N 12th St Reading PA 19604 Office: Albright Coll English Dept 13th St Reading PA 19604

SHIRK, EVELYN URBAN, philosophy educator; b. Flushing, N.Y., Sept. 12, 1918; d. Amos Urban and Mary Jane (Welchans) S.; m. Justus Buchler, Feb. 20, 1943; 1 child, Katherine Urban. B.A., Wilson Coll., 1940; M.A., Columbia U., 1942, Ph.D., 1949. Instr. Bklyn Coll., 1942-48; asst. prof. Hofstra Coll., Hempstead, N.Y., 1949-53, assoc. prof., 1953-63; prof. Hofstra U. (formerly Hofstra Coll.), 1963—, dept. chmn., 1980-89. Contbg. editor: Readings in Philosophy, 1946; Adventurous Idealism: The Philosophy of Alfred Lloyd, 1952; The Ethical Dimension, 1965; In Pursuit of Awareness, 1967. Mem. Am. Philos. Assn., Soc. Advancement Am. Philosophy (program chmn. 1976, exec. com 1977-79), L.I. Philos. Soc. (exec. com.), AAUP, Phi Beta Kappa. Home: 3 Homestead Ave Garden City NY 11530

SHIRLEY, BARBARA ANNE, zoology educator; b. Muskogee, Okla., Oct. 15, 1936; d. Harvey Burton and Nona Leone (Smith) S. BA, Okla. Bapt. U., 1956; MS, U. Okla., 1961, PhD, 1964. Asst. prof. biology U. Tulsa, 1964-70, assoc. prof., 1970-79, prof., 1979-; cons. Hillcrest Infertility Ctr., Tulsa, 1982-88, In Vitro Lab Systems of Okla.,Tulsa, 1985-86. Author: Lab. Manual of Mammalian Physiology, 1975, 2d edition, 1982; contbr. articles to profl. jours. Mem. Okla. Acad. Sci. (fellow 1970, pres. 1975), AAUP (pres. Tulsa chpt. 1978-79), Okla. Soc. Physiologists (pres. 1990-91), Sigma Xi (pres. Tulsa chpt. 1972-73). Presbyterian. Office: Univ Tulsa Dept Biol Sci 600 S College Tulsa OK 74104

SHIRLEY, ELEANOR, social service agency executive; b. Adams, Mass., May 9, 1937; d. Joseph Lucian and Elsie (Barschdorf) Freeman; m. Edward Salmond Shirley, Aug. 10, 1963; 1 child, Rebecca Salmond. BA, Wheaton Coll., Mass., 1959; MA, Hartford (Conn.) Sem. Found., 1961; MBA, Tulane U., 1985. Dir. edn. St. Peter's Ch., Beverly, Mass., 1961-63; dir. coll. work Mt. Holyoke Coll., South Hadley, Mass., 1965-68; staff La. State U. Episcopal Chapel, Baton Rouge, 1969; dir. Women and Employment Program, Baton Rouge, 1977-80; dir. program devel. Office of Women's Services, Baton Rouge, 1980—. Pres. LWV, Baton Rouge, 1972-75; mem. alumni admissions com. Tulane U., Baton Rouge, 1987-88; mem. exec. com., bd. dirs. local YWCA, 1989—. Named Outstanding Woman, Links Inc. of Baton Rouge, 1975. Mem. Baton Rouge C. of C. (pres. alpha adv. bd. to Northdale Magnet Sch. 1987—, mem. edn. com. 1987—, mem. Leadership program 1987-88). Democrat. Club: Episcopalian Ch. Women (Baton Rouge) (pres. 1985-86). Home: 10203 Winterhue Dr Baton Rouge LA 70810 Office: Women's Services 150 Riverside Mall Baton Rouge LA 70802

SHIRLEY, JULIA LINN, editor; b. San Pedro, Calif., June 27, 1956; d. Johannes Harrison and Barbara Ann (Barton) Shirley. B.A., Calif. State U.-Long Beach, 1979. Asst news editor Anaheim Bull. (Calif.), 1979-81, tempo editor, 1981-86, mng. editor, from 1986, now editor. Mem. Orange County Press Club, Sigma Delta Chi. Office: Anaheim Bull PO Box 70004 Anaheim CA 92825*

SHIRLEY, NORMA, librarian, bibliographer; b. Chatham, N.Y., Mar. 22, 1935; d. George and Bertha (Shattuck) Shirley. B.A., Russell Sage Coll., 1962; M.L.S., SUNY-Albany, 1963, M.S. in Ednl. Adminstrn., 1980. Asst. reference librarian Jr. Coll. Albany, 1963-65; librarian Hudson Area Library (N.Y.), 1966-67; reference librarian Russell Sage Coll., Troy, N.Y., 1967-69; librarian Poughkeepsie High Sch. (N.Y.), 1970-71; library media specialist Spl. Edn. Ctr., Dutchess County BOCES, Poughkeepsie, 1971—. Co-author: Checklist of Serials in Psychology and Allied Fields, 1969; Serials in Psychology and Allied Fields, 1976. Mem. Dutchess County Library Assn. (past pres.), Sch. Library Media Specialists Southeastern N.Y. (past pres.), ALA, N.Y. Library Assn., NEA, Dutchess County Mental Health Assn., N.Y. State Tchrs. Handicapped. Home: PO Box 2401 Poughkeepsie NY 12603

SHIVERS, JANE, corporate executive, director; b. Georgetown, Tex., June 29, 1943; d. Marvin Bishop and Jewell (Petrey) Edwards; m. Harold E. Shivers; children: Clay Houston, Will Davis; m. Don Evans Hutcheson. BA, U. Md., 1965. Reseacher Amex Broadcasting Co., San Francisco, 1965-67; pub. info. officer Semester at Sea, Orange, Calif., 1967-69; dir. pub. rels. Atlanta Arts Alliance, 1974-78, RSVT, Atlanta, 1978-82; pres. Shivers Communications, Atlanta, 1982-84; exec. v.p., dirs. Ketchum Pub. Rels., Atlanta, 1985—; v.p. Midtown Bus. Assocs., Atlanta, 1987-89. Trustee Alliance Theatre Co., Atlanta, 1980-89, Care, Internat., Atlanta, 1988-89. Recipient Mgmt. Woman Achievement award Women in Communication, Atlanta, 1984. Mem. Pub. Rels. Soc. Am., Cen. Atlanta Progress Club, Commerce Club, Peachtree Club. Episcopalian. Home: 238 15th St Atlanta GA 30309 Office: Ketchum Pub Rels 2 Midtown Pla 1360 Peachtree St SE Atlanta GA 30309

SHIVNAN, JANE CAROLINE, nurse; b. Redhill, Surrey, Eng., Jan. 16, 1955; came to U.S., 1984; d. Martin Patrick and Barbara Anne (Brown) S.; m. Timothy J. Marks, July 28, 1979 (div. 1988); 1 child, Martin Patrick. BSc, U. Sussex, Brighton, Eng., 1975; diploma in nursing, Princess Alexandra Sch., London, 1981; postgrad., Johns Hopkins U., 1988. RN, Md. Nursing asst. St. Christophers Hosp., London, 1977-78; staff nurse London Hosp., 1981-82, Reed Nurse, London, 1982-83; practice nurse Covent Garden Med. Ctr., London, 1983-84; clin. nurse Johns Hopkins Oncology Ctr., Balt., 1984-86, sr. clin. nurse, 1986-87, shift coord., 1987, head nurse, 1987—. Contbr. articles to profl. jours. Treas., trustee Stephen and Matilda Tenants Coop., London, 1981-84; speaker regional workshops Am. Leukemia Soc., 1988. Mem. Oncology Nursing Soc., AACCN (cert.), Johns Hopkins U. Sch. Nursing Honor Soc. Office: Johns Hopkins Oncology Ctr 600 N Wolfe St Baltimore MD 21205

SHKURKIN, EKATERINA VLADIMIROVNA (KATIA SHKURKIN), social worker; b. Berkeley, Calif., Nov. 20, 1955; d. Vladimir Vladimirovich and Olga Ivanovna (Lisenko) S. Student, U. San Francisco, 1972-73; BA, U. Calif., Berkeley, 1974-77; MSW, Columbia U., 1977-79; postgrad., Union Grad. Sch., 1986. Cert. police instr. domestic violence, Alaska. Social worker Tolstoy Found., N.Y.C., 1978-79, adminstr., 1979-80; program supr. Rehab. Mental Health Ctr., San Jose, Calif., 1980-81; dir. service counselor Kodiak (Alaska) Crisis Ctr., 1981-82; domestic violence counselor Abused Women's Aid in Crisis, Anchorage, 1982-85; pvt. practice social work specializing in feminist therapy Susitna Therapy Ctr., Anchorage, 1985—; field instr. Abused Women's Aid in Crisis, Anchorage, 1983-88; expert witness Anchorage Mcpl. Cts., 1982—; interim faculty U. Alaska, Anchorage, summer 1985, fall 1988—, LaVerne U., Anchorage, spring 1986, fall, 1987, summer 1988, winter 1988—. Coordinator Orthodox Christian Fellowship, San Francisco, 1972-76; pub. speaker Abused Women's Aid in Crisis, Anchorage, 1982—; active nat. and local election campaigns, 1968—. Mem. Nat. Assn. Social Workers (cert.). Democrat. Russian Orthodox. Home: 3605 Arctic Blvd #768 Anchorage AK 99503-5704

SHMAVONIAN, NADYA KAY, administrative services administrator; b. Durham, N.C., Jan. 20, 1960; d. Barry M. and Verna M. (Andersen) S.; m. David Edwin Loder, Mar. 12, 1988. BA in U.S. History, U. Chgo., 1981; MBA Health Care Adminstrn, U. Pa., 1986. Intern Soc. for Health & Human Values, Phila., 1981-82; rsch. asst. Temple U. Hosp., Phila., 1982-83; vol. Internat. Rescue Com., Thailand, 1984; cons. Pa. Hosp., Phila., 1985; intern, cons. Prospective Payment Assessment Commn., Washington, 1985-86; cons. N.J. Dept. Health, Trenton, 1986; program officer health & human svcs. Pew Charitable Trusts, Phila., 1986-88; acting dir. health & human svcs. Pew Charitable Trusts, 1988-89, dir. admistrv. svcs., 1989—. Mem. Am. Pub. Health Assn., Pa. Pub. Health Assn. Democrat. Office: The Pew Charitable Trusts 3 Parkway Ste 501 Philadelphia PA 19102-1305

SHNELL-HOBBS, SHARON LYNN, nurse; b. Santa Ana, Calif., July 8, 1958; d. Jack Elmer and Audrey Patricia (Marston) Shnell; m. Vergil Allen Hobbs, Nov. 1, 1986. BSN, U. Nev., Reno, 1982; MSN, U. Calif., San Francisco, 1986. Staff nurse I Washoe Med. Ctr., Reno, Nev., 1982-83; staff nurse II Community Hosp., Santa Rosa, Calif., 1983-85; research asst. U. Calif., San Francisco, 1985-86; clin. instr. Santa Rosa Jr. Coll., 1985-86; pulmonary rehab. coordinator Sequoia Hosp., Redwood City, Calif., 1986-87; supr. cardiopulmonary rehab. Sequoia Hosp., 1987-89; adminstrv. nurse chest and allergy-immunology faculty practices San Francisco Med. Ctr., U. Calif., 1989-90; svc. unit mgr. internal medicine Kaiser Permanente, Santa Rosa, Calif., 1990—. Contbr. articles to profl. jours. Mem. fund devel. com. Am. Lung Assn., San Mateo County, 1986-88, bd. dirs., 1987-89, chmn. prog. com. 1988-89; adv. com. Dept. Pub. Health, San Mateo County, 1986-88. Mem. Am. Nurses Assn., Calif. Thoracic Soc., Pulmonary Rehab. Network (sec. 1988-89), Am. Assn. Cardiovascular and Pulmonary Rehab., Am. Thoracic Soc. Republican. Episcopalian. Home: 7350 Rasmussen Way Rohnert Park CA 94928 Office: Kaiser Permanente 401 Bicentennial Way Santa Rosa CA 95403

SHNIDER, RUTH WOLKOW, retired nuclear physicist; b. Louisville, June 15, 1915; d. I. Leo and Sarah Estelle (Tick) Wolkow; m. Jack Carl Shnider, Dec. 21, 1947. AB, Wellesley (Mass.) Coll., 1934; SM, U. Chgo., 1937, postgrad., 1942. Instr. U. Chgo., U.S. Army Signal Corps Program, 1942-43; instr. physics dept. U. Ind., Bloomington, 1943-44; radio engr. USN Radiol. Rsch. Lab., Washington, 1944-47, physicist, 1947-52; physicist, sr. investigator USN Radiol. Rsch. Lab., San Francisco, 1952-64; rsch. physicist, sr. investigator USN Radiol. Rsch. Lab, San Francisco, 1964-69; prin. rsch. physicist URS Rsch. Co., URS Corp., Burlingame and San Mateo, Calif., 1969-76; prin. rsch. physicis, sr. systems analyst Ctr. for Planning and Rsch., Palo Alto, Calif., 1976-81; cons. weapons effects Ctr. for Planning and Rsch., Palo Alto, 1981-83, ret., 1983. Author numerous reports, 1947-83. Docent San Francisco Zoo, 1990—; bd. dirs. adv. panel Exploratorium, San Francisco, 1986—. em. AAAS, Am. Strategic Def. Soc., Acad. Scis. (disting. friend 1984—). Home: 2745 Summit Dr Burlingame CA 94010

SHOBE, JANET WAYNE, nurse; b. Louisville, Apr. 2, 1952; d. Zack and Maude M. (Rhea) S. Assoc. degree in nursing, Ea. Ky. U., Richmond, 1975; BSN, U. Louisville, 1981. Cert. Advanced Cardiac Life Support, 1989. Charge nurse Louisville Gen. Hosp., 1975-79, staff nurse, 1980-81; staff nurse, preceptor CCU Humana Hosp. of U. Louisville, 1982-89, utilization rev. coord., 1989—; lectr. in field; mem. Ky. Nurse Day Com., 1989. Vol. Ky. Ctr. for the Arts; past vol. Kidney Found. Recipient recognition award Ky. Nurse Day, 1989. Mem. Kyana Black Nurses Assn., NAFE (exec. com. 1989—), U. Louisville Sch. Nursing Alumni Assn. (bd. dirs. 1987-89, pres. 1989), U. Louisville Alumni Assn. (bd. dirs. 1988—), Nat. Coun. Negro Women. Democrat. Baptist. Home: 1812 S 22d St Louisville KY 40210 Office: Humana Hosp of U Louisville 530 S Jackson Louisville KY 40210

SHOCK, KATHY BETH, data processing professional; b. Ponca City, Okla., July 10, 1956; d. D'Arcy Adriance and Barbara Beth (Lounsbury) S. BA, Okla. State U., Stillwater, 1978. Programmer Cities Service Oil and Gas Corp., Tulsa, 1978-79, programmer/ analyst, 1979-81, systems analyst, 1981-82, 1982-83; programmer/analyst Hilti Inc., Tulsa, 1982; systems analyst, project leader Citgo Petroleum Corp., Tulsa, 1983—. Vol. Reagan Presdl. Campaign, Tulsa, 1980. Mem. Nat. Assn. Female Execs. Republican. Club: Swing Dance.

SHOCKLEY, ANN ALLEN, librarian; b. Louisville, June 21, 1927; d. Henry and Bessie (Lucas) Allen; children: W. Leslie Shockley Jr., Tamara Ann Shockley. BA, Fisk U., 1948; M.S.L.S., Case Western Reserve U., 1959. Asst. librarian Del. State Coll., Dover, 1959-60; asst. librarian U. Md. Eastern Shore, Princess Anne, 1960-66; assoc. librarian U. Md. Eastern Shore, 1966-69, Fisk U., Nashville, 1969—. Author: (novels) Loving Her, 1974, Say Jesus and Come to Me, 1982, (short stories) The Black & White of It, 1980, (with E. J. Josey) Handbook of Black Librarianship, 1977, (with Sue P. Chandler) Living Black American Authors, 1973; editor: (anthology) Afro-American Women Writers 1746-1933, 1988 (Susan Koppelman Award 1988). Recipient Hatshepsut Award for Lit., N.Y., 1981, Martin Luther King Jr. Black Author award, Nashville, 1982. Mem. The Authors Guild, ALA (Black Caucus, Black Caucus award for editing caucus newsletter 1975), Nat. Women's Studies Assn., Coll. Lang. Assn., Assn. Black Women Historians, Soc. Am. Archivists. Home: 5975 Post Rd Nashville TN 37205-3232 Office: Fisk Univ Library Nashville TN 37203

SHOCKLEY, CYNTHIA WARING, computer systems executive; b. Fresno, Calif., Mar. 23, 1950; d. Marion Kent Shockley and Elizabeth Eleanor (Scharf) Sitzman. BA, The George Wash. U., 1972; MLS in Library Sci., U. Md., 1981. Sr. systems analyst Online Computer Systems, Inc., Gaithersburg, Md., 1978-81; asst. dir. Nat. Ctr. for Epilepsy Info. Epilepsy Foundn. of Am., Landover, Md., 1981-83; sr. mgr. Price Waterhouse, Bethesda, Md., 1983-86; research fellow Logistics Mgmt. Inst., Bethesda, 1986—; bd. mem. U. Md. Alumni Assn. Internat., Coll. Park, Md., 1984—, Coll. of Library and Info. Svcs. Alumni council-U. Md., Coll. Park, 1984—. Author: report, Design of NATO Scientific and Technical Information System, 1987, Capitalizing on Intelligent Gateway Software, 1988, Acquisition and Logistics Automated Information Systems Architecture, 1990. Mem. Am. Soc. for Info. Sci. Democrat. Episcopalian. Office: Logistics Mgmt Inst 6400 Goldsboro Rd Bethesda MD 20817

SHOEMAKER, CLARA BRINK, chemistry educator, retired; b. Rolde, Drenthe, The Netherlands, June 20, 1921; came to U.S., 1953; d. Hendrik Gerard and Hendrikje (Smilde) Brink; m. David Powell Shoemaker, Aug. 5, 1955; 1 child, Robert Brink. PhD, Leiden U., The Netherlands, 1950. Instr. in inorganic chemistry Leiden U., 1946-50, 51-53; postdoctoral fellow Oxford (Eng.) U., 1950-51; rsch. assoc. dept. chemistry MIT, Cambridge, 1953-55, 58-70; rsch. assoc. biochemistry Harvard Med. Sch., Boston, 1955-56; project supr. Boston U., 1963-64; rsch. assoc. dept. chemistry Oreg. State U, Corvallis, 1970-75, rsch. assoc. prof. dept. chemistry, 1975-82, sr. rsch. prof. dept. chemistry, 1982-84, prof. emerita, 1984—. Sect. editor: Structure Reports of International Union of Crystallography, 1967, 68, 69; co-author chpts. in books; author numerous sci. papers. Bd. dirs. LWV, Corvallis, 1980-82, bd. dirs., sec., Salem, Oreg., 1985-87. Recipient fellowship Internat. Fedn. Univ. Women, Oxford U., 1950-51. Mem. Metall. Soc. (com. on alloy phases 1969-79), Internat. Union of Crystallography (commn. on structure reports 1970-90), Am. Crystallographic Assn. (crystallographic data com. 1975-78, Fankuchen award com. 1976), Sigma Xi, Iota Sigma Pi (faculty adv. Oreg. State U. chpt. 1975-84), Phi Lambda Upsilon. Office: Dept Chemistry Oreg State U Corvallis OR 97331

SHOEMAKER, DIANE MARIE, medical technology consultant; b. Parkers Prairie, Minn., Mar. 9, 1952; d. Darrel Lawrence and Marlys Mary (Kuhne) Pexsa. div.; 1 child, Wendy Ann Shoemaker. BS, U. Minn., 1979, MS in Genetics, 1985, MD, 1985. Fellow computer sci. U. Minn., Mpls., 1985; resident internal medicine Abbott NW Hosp., Mpls., 1985; dir. med. communications Minn. Laser, St. Paul, 1986-87; mktg. specialist Medtronic, Mpls., 1987-88; pres. D. Shoemaker & Assocs., Mpls., 1988—; with med. communications Schneider U.S.A. Recipient Scholarship U. Minn., 1974-79, Scholarship Am. Bus. Women's Assn., 1981, Scholarship Am. Med. Assn. Mpls., 1982. Mem. AMA, Am. Coll. Physicians, Am. Assn. Med. Informatics, Minn. Med. Assn., Minn. Entrepreneur Club. Home: 4270 Larch Pl Plymouth MN 55442

SHOEMAKER, ELEANOR BOGGS, television production company executive; b. Gulfport, Miss., Jan. 20, 1935; d. William Robertson and Bessie Eleanor (Ware) Boggs; m. D. Shoemaker, April 9, 1955 (div. 1987); children: Daniel W., William Boggs. Student in protocol, Southeastern U., 1952-53; student, George Washington U., Washington, 1953-56; BA in Communications and Polit. Sci. with honrs, Goucher Coll., 1981; postgrad., Villanova U., 1989—. Feature writer Washington Times Herald, 1951-54; dir. Patricia Stevens Modeling Agy., Washington, 1955-56; free-lance model Julius Garfinkel, Woodward & Lothrop, Washington, 1951-56; research analyst Balt. County Council, Towson, Md., 1980-81; feature news reporter Sta. WGCB-TV, Red Lion, Pa., 1980—; pub. speaker, protocol The Reliable Corp., Columbia, Md., 1982-86; media cons. The Enterprise Found., Columbia, Md., 1985-86; faculty, TV prodn. and communication St. Francis Prep Sch., Spring Grove, Pa., 1985-88; owner Windswept Prodns. Co., Felton, Pa., 1989—; mem. conservation bd. Pa. Parks and Recreation Soc., 1984—; producer The Pa. County TV Prodn., 1981; producer, host Westar 4 Channel 9 half hour weekly news program Keystone Report. Producer: The Pa. County TV prodn., 1981, documentary Human Rights: A Special Report, Sta. WGCB-TV, 1989; producer, host, weekly news program Keystone Report, 1990. Bd. dirs. York (Pa.) County Parks and Recreation, 1972-87, YWCA, York, 1957-82, Hist. York, 1990—; mem. exec. com. York County Reps., 1972-82; accreditation adv. com. York Coll. of Pa.; instr. YWCA Women in Politics, founder; founder, mem. Child Abuse Taskforce, York, 1983—; mem. select com. Pa. Agrl. Zoning, 1988; mem. steering com. York Forum, 1989—; co-chmn. Cross Mill Restoration, 1987—; mem. Displaced Homemaker's Bd., 1989—; bd. dirs. Hist. York, 1990—; founder, host Old Rose Tree Pony Club, 1967—; chair Spring Valley County Pk. Task Force, 1972; master of fox hounds Mrs. Showmaker's Hounds, 1969—; master of beagles Mrs. Showmaker's Weybright Beagles, 1988—. Recipient pro bono child legal representation grant Pa. Bar Assn., 1983, Pa. Tree Farmer of Yr., 1987; selected journalist for Novosti Press USSR-U.S. Press Exch. program, 1989; recipient Lay Person of Yr. award, Pa. Recreation and Parks Assn. and Gov. Thornburg, 1982. Mem. Am. Polled Hereford Assn., York Area C. of C., York County C. of C. (publicity com. 1985—, agri. bus. com.), Masters of Foxhounds Assn. Episcopalian. Home and Office: PO Box 167 Felton PA 17322

SHOEMAKER, LINDA F., client support representative; b. Hagerstown, Md., June 28, 1952; d. George Emanuel Jr. and Betty Jane (Cooper) Ashbaugh; m. Mark W. Shoemaker, Apr. 21, 1973. AA in Data Processing, Hagerstown Jr. Coll. Bookkeeper, computer system adminstr. Morgan-Keller, Inc., Frederick, Md., 1979-90; ind. software cons. Timberline Software, 1987—; client support rep. Automation Counselors, Inc., 1990—. Mem. NAFE, Phi Theta Kappa. Home: Rte 5 Box 382 Hagerstown MD 21740

SHOEMAKER, MELINDA ANNE, director of counseling, educator, psychotherapist; b. Fairmont, W.Va., Nov. 19; d. Lawrence E. and Kathleen (Pitrolo) S. AA in Liberal Arts, Broward Community Coll., Ft. Lauderdale, Fla., 1982; BS in Community Psychology, Nova Coll., 1984; MS in Counseling, Nova U., 1987, cert. in substance abuse, 1988. Physician's asst. Fla. Med. Ctr., Lauderdale Lakes, 1982-86; adminstr. asst. dept. psychology Nova U., Ft. Lauderdale, 1980-86; counseling intern Nova U. Community Mental Health Clinic, Ft. Lauderdale, 1985-87; guidance intern Nova Coll., Ft. Lauderdale, 1986-87; clin. assoc. Ctr. for Psychol. Svcs., Boca Raton, Fla., 1988—; dir. counseling svcs. Coll. of Boca Raton, 1987—, asst. prof., 1988—. Mem. Am. Psychol. Assn., Am. Assn. Counseling and Devel. (Outstanding Mem. award 1987), Nat. Assn. for Alcohol and Drug Abuse Counselors, Am. Mental Health Counselors Assn., Am. Sch. Counselor Assn. Lutheran. Office: Coll of Boca Raton 3601 N Military Trail Boca Raton FL 33431

SHOEN, TERRI LYNN, gas company executive; b. Idaho Falls, ID, May 27, 1948; d. Bob J. and Pat Flora Bybee; m. Greg R. Shoen, July 1, 1968; children: Zac B., Joe C. Student, Idaho State U., 1966-67. With Intermountain Gas Co., Boise, Idaho, 1971—, div. office mgr., 1974-79, adminstrv. mgr., 1979-84, regional adminstrv. mgr., 1984-86, systems evaluation program adminstr., 1986-88, mgr. customer svc., 1988—. Vol. United Way, Bannock County, 1974, 83; advisor Jr. Achievement, 1974; mem. job svc. improvement program com. Dept. Employment; mem. Idaho Comm. on Women's Programs, 1983-86; panel mem. Idaho State Bd. Medicine, 1983—; chair Families in Crisis, 1984; mem. adv. Career Ctr., YWCA, 1989—. Named Bus. Woman of the Yr., 1987. Mem. Greater Pocatello C. of C. (chair leadership 1984—, bd. dirs. 1984—, mem. various coms.), NAFE, Am. Bicycle Assn. (bd. dirs. Boise chpt.), Zonta (bd. dirs. Pocatello area chpt. 1983, Outstanding Zontian of Yr. 1982, pres. 1982). Office: Intermountain Gas Co 555 S Cole Rd Boise ID 83707

SHOENFELT, CATHERINE RUTH, marketing executive; b. Dallas, Dec. 9, 1954; d. Marion Justus and Nell (Harden) S. B of Music Edn., U. Tex., San Antonio, 1980. Tchr. music Viva Musica, San Antonio, 1980-81, Northside Ind. Sch. Dist., San Antonio, 1981-84; mktg. mgr. Austin Pathology Assocs., Tex., 1984-86; dir. mktg. Nat. Lab. Svcs., Inc., Austin, 1987; clin. sales rep. Roche Biomed. Labs., Inc., 1987-88; sales rep. Milex So., 1989—. Singer Chamber Choralet Symphony, San Antonio, 1982; vol. Symphony Designer Showplace, Austin, 1986-87, Healthfest-Pathology Booth, Austin, 1986. Mem. NAFE, Blair County Genealogy Soc. Club. (Altoona, Pa.). Republican. Lutheran. Avocations: music, tennis, reading, needlework, swimming. Home: 3600 Greystone Dr #706 Austin TX 78731 Office: Milex So PO Drawer M Weatherford TX 76086

SHOENIGHT, PAULINE ALOISE SOUERS (ALOISE TRACY), author; b. Bridgeport, Ill., Nov. 20, 1914; d. William Fitch and Carrie (Milhouse) Souers; m. James Richard Tracy, Sept. 18, 1946 (dec. Aug. 1972); m. 2nd,

Hurley F. Shoenight, June 25, 1976. BEd, Eastern Ill. U., 1937 . Mem. hon. bd. advs. Am. Biog. Inst; active Nat. Arbor Day Found. Mem. Nat. Ret. Tchrs. Assn., Eastern Ill. Alumni Assn. (life), PEO Sisterhood, The Causteau Soc., Am. Bible Soc., Am. Poets Fellowship Soc. (hon. life mem.), The Pensters, Pleasure Island Sr. Citizens Club (charter), Ill. Poetry Soc. (charter), Ala. State Poetry Soc., Acad. Am. Poets, Baldwin Heritage Mus. Assn. (charter life), Friends of U. Mo. Libraries (life), Friends of Foley Library. Republican. Baptist. Clubs: Baldwin Sr. Travelers, Bible-A-Month Club. Author: His Handiwork, 1954, Memory is a Poet, 1964, The Silken Web, 1965, A Merry Heart, 1966, In Two or Three Tomorrows, 1968, All Flesh Is Grass, 1971, Beyond The Edge, 1973. Address: 7425 Riverwood Dr W Foley AL 36535

SHOHEN, SAUNDRA ANNE, health care communications and public relations executive; b. Washington, Aug. 22, 1934; d. Aaron Kohn and Malvina (Kleiman) Kohn Blinder; children: Susan, Brian. BS, Columbia Pacific U., 1979, MS in Health Svcs. Adminstrn., 1981. Adminstr. social work dept. Roosevelt Hosp., N.Y.C., 1978-79; adminstr. emergency dept. St. Luke's-Roosevelt Hosp. Ctr., N.Y.C., 1979-83, assoc. dir. pub. rels., 1983-87; pres. Saundra Shohen Assocs., Ltd., N.Y.C., 1987—; v.p. program devel. and media rels. Pub. Rels. Sci. and Medicine Internat., N.Y.C., 1988—; cons. Tureck Bach Inst., N.Y.C., 1985—, also bd. dir.; panelist ann. Emmy awards NATAS, N.Y.C., 1983, 84. Author: (health scripts for radio) Voice of America, 1983 (Presdl. Recognition award 1984), (with others) AIDS: A Health Care Management Response, 1987, EMERGENCY!, 1989. Mem. NATAS, Internat. Hosp. Fedn., Am. Soc. Hosp. Mktg. and Pub. Rels., Vols. in Tech. Assistance. Democrat. Jewish. Home: 240 Central Park S New York NY 10019 Office: 488 Madison Ave New York NY 10022

SHOJI, JUNE MIDORI, import/export trading executive; b. Long Beach, Calif., June 21, 1957; d. Sam Masatsugu and Tomiyo (Kinoshita) S. BA in Psychology and Econs., UCLA, 1975-79; cert. Japanese, Waseda U., Tokyo, 1980-82; Grad. Gemologist, Gemol. Inst., Santa Monica, Calif., 1984. Mktg. rep. IBM Corp., L.A., 1982-84, Xerox Corp., El Monte, Calif., 1984-86; adminstrv. drilling analyst Arco Internat. Oil & Gas, L.A., 1986-89; logistics analyst Honda Internat. Trading, Torrance, Calif., 1989—. Home: 1865 W 166th St Gardena CA 90247

SHOMAKER, SHARON DIANE, nurse; b. Radford, Va., July 16, 1966; d. Edwin Baker and Wanda Lou (Quesenberry) S. AAS, Wytheville (Va.) Community Col, 1986. Staff nurse Pulaski (Va.) Community Hosp., 1986-87; charge nurse Radford (Va.) Community Hosp., 1987—. Mem. Jaycees. Republican. Home: 700 Randolph St Radford VA 24141 Office: Radford Community Hosp PO Box 3527 FSS Radford VA 24143

SHONTZ, PATRICIA JANE, restaurateur; b. Mercer, Pa., Mar. 29, 1933; d. Thomas Cloyd and Glaydes Evelyn (Pease) Buckley; student pub. schools, Grove City, Pa.; m. George Edward Shontz, July 22, 1962; 1 dau. by previous marriage, Sandra Lee McCandless. Clerical asst. Am. News Co., Washington, 1950-51; acct., office mgr. Mundt Motors Chevrolet & Buick, Grove City, 1953-62; sec.-treas. Cajun Corp., Madeira Beach, Fla., 1972—; pres. John's Pass Seafood Festival Corp., 1981—. Madeira Beach City commr., 1973-79, vice mayor, 1977-79, co-chmn. planning bd., 1979-82, city commr., 1983-87; chmn. Bicentennial Com., Madeira Beach, 1975-76; mem. John's Pass Village Assn., 1970—, Pinellas County Tourist Devel. Council, 1978-79, Madeira Beach Taxpayers Assn., 1964—; mem. Republican Nat. Com. Named Madeira Beach Citizen of Yr., 1974, 79. Mem. Nat. Restaurant Assn., Fla. Restaurant Assn., Madeira Beach C. of C. (dir. 1965, 81-82, 87-90, pres. 1967-69, 83). Presbyterian. Clubs: Bus. and Profl. Women, Soroptimist, Order Eastern Star, Order White Shrine, Rotary (1st woman Rotarian in Fla., Gulf Beaches). Office: 100 Medeira Way Medeira Beach FL 33708

SHOOKS, MARI-CAROLE, nurse; b. Manitowoc, Wis., June 23, 1949; d. Bernard Joseph and Marie Francis (Pritzl) Schermetzler; m. Charles A. Shooks, May 10, 1975 (div. Oct. 1988); children: Amy Jane, Adam Charles, Dominic Joseph. Diploma, Mt. Sinai Hosp. Sch. Nursing, Milw., 1970. RN, Wis., Conn. Staff nurse Mt. Sinai Hosp., Milw., 1970-72, asst. head nurse, 1972-73; staff nurse Mt. Sinai Hosp., Hartford, Conn., 1973-75; nurse Windham Ctr. (Conn.) Sch., 1984—; staff nurse Windham Adult Day Ctr., North Windham, Conn., 1987-89; office nurse to pvt. practice physician, Willimantic, Conn., 1989, 90. Columnist for local newspaper, 1986-89. History nurse ARC, Willimantic, 1978—; vol. Am. Cancer Soc., Willimantic, 1978; bd. dirs. Windham Free Libr. Assn., 1988—, pres. bd., 1989—. Recipient Vol. Recognition award Am. Cancer Soc., 1986, 88. Mem. Windham Fedn. Sch. Nurses (head nurse 1988—), Assn. Sch. Nurses Conn., St. Joseph's Women's Club. Democrat. Roman Catholic. Home: 20 Windham Ctr Rd Windham Center CT 06280 Office: Windham Pub Schs Rt 14 Windham Center CT 06280

SHORE, CINDY BROCKMAN, financial executive, accounting administrator; b. Phila., Nov. 4, 1956; d. Samuel and Sylvia Ellen (Neigut) Brockman; m. Joseph Lloyd Shore, June 18, 1978; children: Michael Stephen, Perry Mason. BBA, Temple U., 1978, MBA, 1980. Staff acct. Bandel, Lazerow & Co., Jenkintown, Pa., 1977-78; sr. acct. Lionel Corp., Phila., 1978-80; acctg. supr. GE, Phila., 1980-82; mgr. system support GE, Mt. Laurel, N.J., 1983-85, mgr. fin. systems project, 1985-87; mgr. acctg. svcs, Nutri/System Inc., Willow Grove, Pa., 1987-88, mgr. acctg. ops., 1988-89, dir. acctg. ops., 1989—; mem. user exec. com. Ross Systems, Inc., Palo Alto, Calif., 1988-90. Contbr. articles to profl. jours. Active Dem. Com., Bensalem, Pa., 1987-88; mem. fin. com. Beth Chaim Synagogue, Feasterville, Pa., 1989. Mem. NAFE, Am. Acctg. Assn., Am. Payroll Assn., Beta Alpha Psi (alumnus treas. 1977-78). Home: 70 Redwood Dr Richboro PA 18954 Office: Nutri/System Inc 3901 Commerce Ave Willow Grove PA 19090

SHORES, JANIE LEDLOW, state justice; b. Georgiana, Ala., Apr. 30, 1932; d. John Wesley and Willie (Scott) Ledlow; m. James L. Shores, Jr., May 12, 1962; 1 dau., Laura Scott. J.D., U. Ala., Tuscaloosa, 1959. Bar: Ala. 1959. Pvt. practice Selma, 1959; mem. legal dept. Liberty Nat. Life Ins. Co., Birmingham, Ala., 1962-66; asso. prof. law Cumberland Sch. Law, Samford U., Birmingham, 1)66-74; asso. justice Supreme Ct. Ala., 1974—; legal adviser Ala. Constn. Revision Commn., 1973; mem. Nat. Adv. Council State Ct. Planning, 1976—. Contbr. articles to legal jours. Mem. Am. Bar Assn., Am. Judicature Soc., Farrah Order Jurisprudence. Democrat. Episcopalian. Office: Ala Supreme Ct PO Box 218 Montgomery AL 36101

SHORES, PEARL MARIE, health care company executive; b. Warsaw, N.Y., Aug. 29, 1946; d. Lawrence Dean and Mary Ellen (Sly) Arnold; m. Bruce Reid Dedrick, May 9, 1964 (div. 1966); 1 child, Dawn Aileen; m. James Lee Shores, Sept. 13, 1981. BBA cum laude, Nat. U., San Diego, 1979; MBA, Nat. U., 1981. Chief lab. technician Schoenfield Clin. Lab., Albuquerque, 1970-76, Allergy Med. Group, San Diego, 1976-78; chemstrip specialist BioDynamics/BMC, San Diego, 1978-80; sr. ter. mgr. Hollister, Inc., San Diego, 1980-84; dist. mgr. Hollister, Inc., New Eng. dist., 1984-86; sales rep. E.R. Squibb/CONVATEC, San Diego, 1986-87; br. mgr. HOMEDCO, San Diego, 1987-89; dir. infusion therapy Spl. Solutions, 1989—. Office: Spl Solutions 9285 Chesapeake Dr Ste H Suite H San Diego CA 92123

SHORR, MIRIAM KRONFELDT, artist; b. N.Y.C.; m. Eli Yale Shorr, 1931. Student, Hunter Coll.; Exhibited in ann. shows Audubon Artists, City Ctr. Gallery, N.Y.C., Nat. Soc. Painters in Casein; Knickerbocker, Whitney, Bklyn. and Norfolk Mus.; one man shows Brandeis U., Bklyn. Coll., U. Maine, Rutgers U., LaSalle Coll., Hillside U., Gettysburg Coll., U. Tampa, Miami, R.I., Albany, Ga. and Colby U. One-man shows throughout U.S.; one-man showing of tapestries Cen. Libr., St. Petersburg, Fla., 1982, Plymouth Harbor Gallery, Sarasota, 1990; one-man show paintings Ctr. Libr., Bradenton, Fla., 1988; numerous group shows. Recipient 1st prize for drawing Nat. Assn. Women Artists, 1962, Lena Newcastle award, 1961, 65, Aileen O. Webb prize, 1974, 1st prize Fibres and Fabrics, Longboat Key Art Assn., 1979, 1st prize enamels Venice (Fla.) Art Assn., 1982, 2d prize for painting Sarasota Art Assn., 1983, 1st prize Venice Art League, 1985, Ann. Parade of Prize Winners, 1982-88, Longboat Key Art Assn., 1982-88. Mem. Artists Equity Assn. (bd. dir. 1958-64), Nat. Assn. Women Artists (bd. dir. 1970-72), Sarasota Art Assn. (chmn. exhbns. 1976-78, editor The Bull. 1979-81), Art League Manatee County, Fla. Artists Group, Longboat Key Art Assn., Venice Art League. Home: 888 Blvd of the Arts Unit 1607 Sarasota FL 34236

SHORS, SUSAN DEBRA, lawyer; b. Detroit, Nov. 23, 1954; d. Clayton Marion and Arlene Lois (Towle) S.; m. Brian F. Connors; 1 child, Ian Shors Connors. BA, Pitzer Coll., 1976; JD, Golden Gate U., 1984. Bar: Calif. Extern, Calif. Supreme Ct., San Francisco, 1983; research atty. Calif. Ct. Appeal, San Francisco, 1984-85; appellate atty., San Francisco, 1985—; staff atty. 6th dist. Appellate Program, 1988-89; cons. Nob Hill Neighbors, San Francisco, 1982-86. Sr. editor Golden Gate Law Rev. Notes and Comments, 1985; mem. editorial bd. Barrister's Club Mag., 1986-89. Atty. Lawyers Com. for Urban Affairs/Asylum Project, San Francisco, 1986. Mem. ABA, ACLU, Calif. Bar Assn., Calif. Women Lawyers, Bar Assn. San Francisco (mem. appellate com. 1986—), Nat. Assn. Criminal Def. Lawyers. Democrat. Office: Law Offices 2500 Clay St San Francisco CA 94115

SHORT, AGNES E., banker; b. Binghamton, N.Y., Feb. 5, 1930; d. Frank J. and Elizabeth M. (Scharch) S. Asst. v.p. Chase Lincoln First Bank, N.A., Binghamton. Bd. dirs. Am. Cancer Soc. Broome County chpt., 1986-90; mem. Broome Community Coll. Found. Mem. Fin. Women Internat. (pres. south cen. chpt.). Republican. Roman Catholic. Home: 6 Curran Ave Binghamton NY 13903 Office: Chase Lincoln First Bank NA Main Office PO Box 700 Binghamton NY 13902

SHORT, CAROL NOVATNAK, teacher, researcher; b. Tuscaloosa, Ala., Dec. 9, 1945; d. George Jacob and Doris (McCray) Novatnak; m. William Amos Short Jr., Sept. 11, 1968 (div. Aug. 1983); children: William Amos III, Jonathan Jacob, Christopher Nathaniel. BS in Elem. Edn., U. Ala., 1968, MS in Elem. Edn., 1988. Cert. elem. edn. tchr., Ala. Tchr. Tuscaloosa City Bd. Edn., 1968-69, Cumberland County Bd. Edn., Fayetteville, N.C., 1969-72, Sylacauga (Ala.) City Bd. Edn., 1972-73; pvt. practice photography, Bessemer, Ala., 1976-86; tchr. Tuscaloosa County Bd. Edn., Duncanville, Ala.; mem. in-svc. devel. program Tuscaloosa County Bd. Edn., 1989—; chmn. in-svc. com. Maxwell Elem. Sch., Duncanville, 1990—. Social chmn. Bessemer Bar Aux., 1976-77; vol. photographer 1st Presbyn. Ch, Bessemer, 1979-83, Civitans, Tuscaloosa, 1985. Recipient Portrait Photography award Birmingham Malls, 1981. Mem. NEA, Ala. Edn. Assn., Tuscaloosa County Edn. Assn. (local rep. 1989—), Assn. for Supervision and Curriculum Devel., Cooperative Learning Network, Learning/Tchrs. Styles and Brain Behavior Network, Phi Delta Kappa, Kappa Delta Pi. Democrat. Home: 22 Southmont Dr Tuscaloosa AL 35405 Office: Maxwell Elem Sch Rt 1 Box 231 Duncanville AL 35456

SHORT, MARGARET ANN, utility professional; b. Berkeley, Calif., Aug. 26, 1947; d. John Archie Jr. AA, Merritt Coll., Oakland, Calif., 1968. With Pacific Gas & Electric Co., Oakland, 1968-81, pers. and labor rels., 1978-81; corp. indsl. rels. rep. Pacific Gas & Electric Co., San FranciscoOakland, 1981-87, sr. indsl. rels. rep., 1987-88, cons. indsl. rels., 1988—. Mem. reunion com. Berkeley High Sch. Class of 1965; bd. dirs. Homeowners Assn., Pinole, Calif., 1989-90. Mem. NAFE, Pacific Gas and Electric Women's Network, Pacific Gas and Electric Black Employees Assn. Office: Pacific Gas and Electric Co 215 Market St San Francisco CA 94106

SHORT, PAULA MYRICK, educational administration educator; b. Pinehurst, N.C., Feb. 25, 1945; d. John Howard and Ruby Pauline (Fields) Myrick; m. Rick Jay Short, Feb. 2, 1980; children: Jeffrey Brent, John Ryan, Rick Jay Jr. BA, U. N.C.-Greensboro, 1967, MEd, 1970; PhD, U. N.C., Chapel Hill, 1983. Tchr., Greensboro City Schs., N.C., 1967-68, Orange County Schs., Hillsborough, N.C., 1968-69; media coord. Alamance County Schs., Mebane, N.C., 1970-71; tchr. Neal Jr. High Sch., Durham, N.C., 1971-74, Chewing Jr. High Sch., Durham, 1977-79; system level dir. Chapel Hill-Carboro City Schs., 1979-80, vice-prin.; ednl. cons. div. ednl. N.C. Dept. Pub. Instrn., Raleigh, 1980-82; asst. prof. ednl. adminstrn. Coll. Edn., Tex. Woman's U., Denton, 1984-85, Centenary Coll., Shreveport, La., 1985-86, U. Nebr. at Omaha, 1986-87, Auburn (Ala.) U., 1987—; cons. Ga. Dept. Edn. Mem. editorial bd. Rural Educator; contbr. articles to profl. jours. Chmn. day care com. Chapel Hill Service League, 1977-78; mem. Danforth Found. Program for Profs. of Ednl. Adminstrn., 1986—. Delta Kappa Gamma state scholar 1982; Danforth Found. fellow, 1986—. Mem. Nat. Assn. Secondary Sch. Prins. (nat. assessor trainer), Am. Ednl. Rsch. Assn. (presentor in field), Nat. Coun. Profs. Ednl. Adminstrn. (chair-elect), S.W. Ednl. Research Assn., La. Assn. Sch. Execs., Tex. Assn. Supervision and Curriculum Devel., Nebr. Assn. Sch. Adminstrs., Nebr. Assn. for Supervision and Curriculum Devel., Nebr. Assn. Student Councils (asst. exec. dir.), Soc. Sch. Librarians Internat. (bd. dirs. 1985-86), Assn. Supervision and Curriculum Devel., N.C. Media Council (pres. 1982), Delta Kappa Gamma, Phi Delta Kappa (pres.), Pi Lambda Theta. Methodist. Home: 536 Shelton Ln Auburn AL 36830

SHORT, PEGGY CARMACK, publishing company executive; b. Granite City, Ill., May 27, 1945; d. William Howard and Juita (Bigham) Carmack; m. Robert Gray Short, Mar. 27, 1965; children: Christopher, Jennifer, Michelle. Mng. editor, assoc. pub. Gear Tech., Elk Grove Village, Ill.; editor-in-chief, founder Confetti mag., Elk Grove Village; v.p., chief operating officer Randall Pub. Inc., Elk Grove Village. Recipient Maggie awards, Ozzie awards, Raddie award, Printing Industries Am. award, others. Mem. Chgo. Women in Pub., Western Publs. Assn., Alpha Phi Omega. Address: 310 Cornell Lane Algonquin IL 60102

SHORTAL, HELEN MARY, editor; b. Hartford, Conn., July 10, 1961; d. James Patrick and Helen Mary (Daly) S. BA in Film Studies, Yale U., 1986. Asst. producer Holiday Parade Series Md. Pub. TV, Owings Mills, 1986-87, fl. dir. A.M. Weather, 1987-88; editorial asst. In Motion, Annapolis, 1988-89, staff reporter, assoc. editor, 1989-90, mng. editor, 1990—; co-founder Impossible Indsl. Action Theater Co., Balt., 1987-88; writer, critic Md. Art Place Vis. Critics Residency Program, Balt., 1988. Contbr. articles, revs. to various publs. Mem. Washington Ind. Writers. Office: In Motion Mag 1203 West St Annapolis MD 21401

SHORTLEY, JEAN NEMEC, infosystems specialist; b. Chgo., May 3, 1960; d. Joseph Edward and Genevieve Lauren (Barglik) Nemec; m. Timothy Grant Shortley, Oct. 6, 1979; 1 child, Timothy Grant Jr. BS in Edn., Fla. Atlantic U., 1982, MEd, 1986. Bus. edn. instr. Palm Beach County Sch. Bd., W. Palm Beach, Fla., 1982-85; programmer, analyst City of Boynton Beach (Fla.), 1985-86; communications network specialist Palm Beach County Automated Info. Mgmt., W. Palm Beach, 1986-88; assoc. programmer IBM Corp., Boca Raton, Fla., 1988—. Mem. NEA, Fla. Vocat. Assn. Democrat. Roman Catholic. Home: 8365 Theresa Rd Boynton Beach FL 33437 Office: IBM Corp PO Box 1328 Boca Raton FL 33429-1328

SHORT-MAYFIELD, PATRICIA AHLENE, business owner; b. Fort Benning, Ga., Oct. 12, 1955; d. William Pressley and Ilse Marie (Hofmann) Short; m. Thomas Hicks Fort, June 2, 1973 (div. Jan. 1981); m. Michael Patrick Mayfield, Aug. 11, 1984; 1 child, William Zachary. Grad. high sch., Butler, Ga., 1973. Staff mem. Fairyland Day Care, Canton, Ga., 1973-74, Small World Child Care, Thomaston, Ga., 1974-77; nurses aide Kenneston Hosp., Marietta, Ga., 1978-80; staff worker Mental Health Ctr., Smyrna, Ga., 1980-81; dir. Kiddie Kollege, Marietta, 1981-85; bus. owner, mgr. Spiffy Clean by Mayfield, Marietta, 1985—. Choir staff Eastside Bapt. Ch., Marietta, 1988-89; vol. East Valley Elem. Sch., 1989—; active Nat. Congress Parents and Tchrs. Mem. NAFE, Cobb County C. of C., Atlanta High Mus. of Art. Republican. Baptist. Home: 2791 Georgian Terrace Marietta GA 30068 Office: Spiffy Clean By Mayfield 194 Powers Ferry Rd Marietta GA 30067

SHOSS, CYNTHIA RENÉE, lawyer; b. Cape Girardeau, Mo., Nov. 29, 1950; d. Milton and Carroll Jane (Duncan) S.; m. David Goodwin Watson, Apr. 13, 1986. BA, Newcomb Coll., 1971; JD, Tulane U., 1974; LLM in Taxation, NYU, 1980. Bar: La. 1974, Mo. 1977, Ill. 1978, N.Y. 1990. Law clk. to presiding justice La. Supreme Ct., New Orleans, 1974-76; assoc. Stone, Pigman et al, New Orleans, 1976-77, Lewis & Rice, St. Louis, 1977-79, Curtis, Mallet-Prevost, N.Y.C., 1980-82; ptnr. LeBoeuf, Lamb, Leiby & MacRae, N.Y.C., 1982—, London, 1987-89. Contbr. articles to profl. jours. Mem. ABA, NAFE, NACD, Internat. Fiscal Assn., Internat. Tax Planning Assn. Office: LeBoeuf Lamb Leiby & MacRae 520 Madison Ave New York NY 10022

SHOTZ, LINDA FLEISCHMAN, marriage and family therapist, artist; b. Asbury Park, N.J., Aug. 16, 1949; d. Erwin Lewis and Ruth (Koegel) Fleischman; m. Frederick A. Shotz, Sept. 18, 1973. AA Miami Dade Jr. Coll., 1969; BA cum laude U. Fla., 1971; MS summa cum laude Nova U., 1975; Ph.D. Calif. Coast U., 1985; licensed marriage and family therapist, lic. mental health counselor. Social worker Div. Family Services, Miami, 1971-73; clin. psychotherapist Counseling Assocs., Hollywood, Fla., 1974—; exec. dir. Intimacy Disorders Found., Inc., Davie, 1983—; registered art therapist, 1975—, expressive therapist, 1975—; fellow in sex therapy, fellow in med. psychotherapy; faculty mem. life drawing, painting Broward Art Guild, Ft. Lauderdale, Fla.; artist, co-dir., cons. in field; sculptor Bakehouse Art Complex, Inc., Miami. Author: (with others) Training Crisis Counselors; (book of erotic art & poetry) Breathmarks in the Wind, 1988, Better Sex Video Series. Fellow Menninger Found., 1983, Am. Bd. Med. Psychotherapists, Am. U., Washington, 1985. Fellow Internat. Council Sex Edn. and Counseling; mem. Am. Assn. Sex Educators, Counselors, and Therapists, Soc. for Sci. Study of Sex, Am. Assn. Counseling and Devel., Am. Expressive Therapy Assn., Am. Art Therapy Assn. Avocations: reading, video art, travel. Office: Counseling Assocs 4000 Hollywood Blvd Hollywood FL 33021

SHOUP, JANET BLOM, children's bookstore owner; b. Chgo., Mar. 6, 1943; d. John E. and Renzine (Holman) Blom; m. David L. Shoup, June 22, 1968; children: Heather, Heidi (twins), Jeffrey. BA, Hope Coll., 1964; MLS, Rosary Coll., 1972. Tchr. Palos Heights (Ill.) Sch. Dist., 1964-66, 68-70; organizer, tchr. Stavanger Am. Sch., Norway, 1966-67; children's libr. Franklin Park (Ill.) Pub Libr., 1972-81; media specialist Oak Park (Ill.) Sch. Dist., 1982-84; owner, mgr. The Magic Tree Bookstore, Oak Park, 1985—; story teller librs. and schs. throughout Ill., 1972—; instr. Triton Coll., River Grove, Ill., 1978-89; cons., speaker Reading Prescription, Oak Park, 1984—. Dir. Christian edn. Fair Oaks Presbyn. Ch., Oak Park, Ill., 1990—. Mem. AAUW (pres. local chpt. 1978-80, many other offices), ILA (pres. state children's libr. 1981-82), Prairie State Story League (pres.). Home: 511 Ridgeland Ave Oak Park IL 60302 Office: Magic Tree Bookstore 141 N Oak Park Ave Oak Park IL 60302

SHOWALTER, MADELEINE JULIET, librarian; b. McKinney, Tex., June 29, 1958; d. Ray Thomas and Madeleine (Caldwell) Anderson; m. Michael Eugene Showalter, June 18, 1988. BS, Abilene Christian U., 1980; M Libr. and Info. Sci., U. Tex., 1986. Libr. periodicals Abilene (Tex.) Christian U., 1987—; founder, pres. InfoSearch, 1990—. Muse scholar U. Tex., 1985. Mem. ALA, NAFE, Tex. Lib. Assn., Tex. Assn. for Ednl. Tech. (speaker 1989). Mem. Ch. of Christ. Office: Abilene Christian Univ ACU Sta Box 8177 Abilene TX 79699-8177

SHOWALTER-KEEFE, JEAN, data processing executive; b. Louisville, Mar. 11, 1938; d. William Joseph and Phyllis Rose (Reis) Showalter; m. James Washburn Keefe, Dec. 6, 1980. BA, Spalding U., 1963, MS in Edn. Adminstrn., 1969. Cert. tchr., Ky. Tchr., asst. prin. Louisville Cath. Schs., 1958-71; cons. and various editorial positions Harcourt Brace Jovanovich Co., Chgo. and N.Y.C., 1972-82; dir. editorial Ednl. Challenges, Alexandria, Va., 1982-83; mgr. project to cons. Xerox Corp., Leesburg, Va., 1983-88, mgr. systems edn., 1988-89; curriculum devel. mgr. corp. edn. and tng. Xerox Corp.Hdqrs., Stamford, Conn., 1989—; instr. Sales Exec. Club N.Y., 1974-79; cons. Houston, 1980-82. Moderator Jr. Achievement, Louisville, 1968-70; cons. Future Bus. Leaders Am., Dade County, Fla. 1983. Named Outstanding Young Educator Louisville Jaycees, 1968. Mem. Nat. Assn. Female Execs., Am. Soc. Tng. and Devel., Am. Mgmt. Assn. Home: 12766 Flat Meadow Ln Herndon VA 22071 Office: Xerox Corp PO Box 2000 Leesburg VA 22075

SHRAUNER, BARBARA WAYNE ABRAHAM, electrical engineering educator; b. Morristown, N.J., June 21, 1934; d. Leonard Gladstone and Ruth Elizabeth (Thrasher) Abraham; m. James Ely Shrauner, 1965; children: Elizabeth Ann, Jay Arthur. BA cum laude, U. Colo., 1956; AM, Harvard U., 1957, PhD, 1962. Postdoctoral researcher U. Libre de Bruxelles, Brussels, 1962-64; postdoctoral researcher NASA-Ames Rsch. Ctr., Moffett Field, Calif., 1964-65; asst. prof. Washington U., St. Louis, 1966-69, assoc. prof., 1969-77, prof., 1977—; sabbatical Los Alamos (N.Mex.) Sci. Lab., 1975-76, Lawrence Berkeley Lab., Berkeley, Calif., 1985-86; cons. Los Alamos Nat. Lab., 1979, 84, NASA, Washington, 1980, Naval Surface Weapons Lab., Silver Spring, Md., 1984. Contbr. articles on transport in semiconductors plasma physics to profl. jours. Mem. Am. Phys. Soc. (div. plasma physics, exec. com. 1980-82), Am. Geophys. Union, AAUP (local sec.-treas. 1980-82), Phi Beta Kappa, Eta Kappa Nu, Sigma Xi, Sigma Pi Sigma. Home: 7452 Stratford Saint Louis MO 63130 Office: Washington U Dept Elec Engring 1 Brookings Dr Saint Louis MO 63130

SHREVE, MARGARET LINN, not-for-profit organization executive; b. Cin., Mar. 27, 1950; d. Robert Linn and Frances M. (Thomson) S.; m. Paul Franklin Hines, Aug. 18, 1971 (div. Dec. 1972). BA with honors, U. Cin., 1972; postgrad., Ind. U. Law Sch., 1975-76, U. Mass., 1979-80. Exec. sec. Conn. Gen. Life Ins. Co., Cin., 1973; claims interviewer Ind. Employment Security, Indpls., 1974; adminstrn. sec. Health and Hosp. Corp. Marion County, Ind., Indpls., 1974-75; asst. dir. field activities Alsac-St. Jude Children's Rsch. Hosp., Indpls., 1975-76; Dir. Community Svcs. United Cerebral Palsy, Cin., 1976-78; Dir. Svcs. Stavros Ctr. Ind. Living, Amherst, Mass., 1978-80; exec. dir. The Whole Person, Inc., Kansas City, Mo., 1980-86; dir. devel. and adminstrn. Nat. Coun. Ind. Living, Chgo., 1986-89; cons. pvt. practice, Chgo., 1989—; Mem. speakers bur. Edgewater Community Coun.. Presenter numerous presentations in field, editor articles in field. Mem. Chicagoland Assn. Signed Theater, Art Inst. Chgo., Chgo. Symphony Orchestra subscriber, Lyric Opera Chgo. subscriber, Goodman Theater Chgo. subscriber, Chgo. Deml. Scoialists Am.; leader Great Rivers Girl Scouts U.S. Coun., Cin., 1976-78. Recipient Pres. awd. Nat. Coun. Ind. Living, Outstanding Svc. Mo. Easter Seal, Human Rels. Cin. Coun. Jewish Women. Mem. Nat. Coun. Ind. Living, Am. Disabled for Accessible Pub. Transit, Disability Rights and Edn. Defense Fund, Ind. Sector, Access Living, The Whole Person,Inc., Assn. Ind. Living Ctrs. N.Y., The Smithsonian Institution, WTTW, Channel ll, WBEZ-FM subscriber. Democrat. Office: Maggie Shreve Cons 1523 W Edgewater 1 Chicago IL 60660-4210

SHREVE, PEG, educator; b. Spencer, Va., July 23, 1927; d. Hubert Smith and Pearl (Looney) Adams; m. Don Franklin Shreve, June 17, 1950 (dec. Sept. 1970); children: Donna, Jennifer, John, Don. BA, Glenville State U., 1948. Cert. elem. tchr., Va., Wyo. Reading tchr. Wood County Bd., Parkersburg, W.Va., 1948-50; elem. tchr. Mt. Solon, Va., 1950-52, Bridgewater, Va., 1952-53, Cody, Wyo., 1970-86. Pres. PEO AO, Cody, 1981-82; dir. Walden Cancer Found., Cheyenne, Wyo., 1985—; mem. scout council Girl Scouts Am., White Sulphur Springs, W.Va., 1962-65; chair com. Travel, Recreation and Wildlife State House of Reps., Wyo., 1983—; co-chair Legis. Exec. Conf., Wyo., 1987; mem. Nat. Con. State Legislatures, 1982—, Nat. Women Legislators, 1984—, Rep. Women, 1975—. Mem. AAUW (exec. bd.), Beta Sigma Phi (Lady of Yr. award 1986). Presbyterian. Lodge: Soroptimist (Women Helping Women award 1985). Home: PO Box 2257 Cody WY 82414

SHREVE, SUSAN RICHARDS, author, English literature educator; b. Toledo, May 2, 1939; d. Robert Kenneth and Helen (Greene) Richards; children—Porter, Elizabeth, Caleb, Kate. BA, U. Pa., 1961; MA, U. Va., 1969. Prof. English lit. George Mason U., Fairfax, Va., 1976—; vis. prof. Columbia U., N.Y.C., 1982—. Author: (novels) A Fortunate Madness, 1974, A Woman Like That, 1977, Children of Power, 1979, Miracle Play, 1981, Dreaming of Heroes, 1984, Queen of Hearts, 1986, A Country of Strangers, 1989; (children's books) The Nightmares of Geranium Street, 1977, Family Secrets, 1979, Loveletters, 1979, The Masquerade, 1980, The Bad Dreams of a Good Girl, 1981, The Revolution of Mary Leary, 1982, The Flunking of Joshua T. Bates, 1984, How I Saved the World on Purpose, 1985, Lucy Forever and Miss Rosetree, Shrinks, Inc., 1985, Joshua T. Bates In Charge, 1990, Daughters of the New World, 1990. Recipient Jenny Moore award George Washington U., 1978; John Simon Guggenheim award in fiction, 1980; Nat. Endowment Arts fiction award, 1982. Pres. PEN/Faulkner Found. Mem. Phi Beta Kappa.

SHRIVER, EUNICE MARY KENNEDY (MRS. ROBERT SARGENT SHRIVER, JR.), civic worker; b. Brookline, Mass.; m. Robert Sargent Shriver, Jr., May 23, 1953; children: Robert Sargent III, Maria Owings, Timothy Perry, Mark Kennedy, Anthony Paul Kennedy. BS in Sociology, Stanford U., 1943; student, Manhattanville Coll. of Sacred Heart, LHD, 1963; LittD, U. Santa Clara, 1962; LHD, D'Youville Coll., 1962; LLD, Regis Coll., 1963; LHD, Newton Coll., 1973, Brescia Coll., 1974, Holy Cross Coll., 1979, Princeton U., 1979, Boston Coll., 1990; also hon. degrees, U. Vt., Albertus Magnus Coll., St. Mary's Coll. With spl. war problems div. State Dept. Washington, 1943-45; sec. Nat. Conf. on Prevention and Control juvenile Delinquency, Dept. of Justice, Washington, 1947-48; social worker Fed. Penitentiary for Women, Alderson, W.Va., 1950; exec. v.p. Joseph P. Kennedy, Jr. Found., 1950—; founder (1968) Spl. Olympics Internat.; social worker House of Good Shepherd, Chgo., also Juvenile Ct., Chgo., 1951-54; regional chmn. women's div. Community Fund-Red Cross Joint Appeal, Chgo., 1958; mem. Chgo. Commn. on Youth Welfare, 1959-62; cons. to Pres. John F. Kennedy's Panel on Mental Retardation, 1961; founder Community & Caring, Inc., 1986. Editor: "A Community of Caring", 1982, 85, "Growing Up Caring, 1990. co-chmn. women's com. Democratic Nat. Conv., Chgo., 1956. Decorated Legion of Honor; recipient Lasker award, Humanitarian award A.A.M.D., 1973, Nat. Vol. Service award, 1973, Phila. Civic Ballet award, 1973, Prix de la Couronne Française, 1974, Presdl. Medal of Freedom, 1974, 84, others. Address: care Joseph P Kennedy Jr Found 1350 New York Ave Ste 500 Washington DC 20005

SHRIVER, JOYCE ELIZABETH, anatomy educator; b. Quincy, Ill., Sept. 14, 1937; d. Victor Henry and Alma Freida (Henerhoff) S. BA magna cum laude, William Jewell Coll., Liberty, Mo., 1959; PhD, U. Kans., 1965. Fellow coll. physicians and surgeons Columbia U., N.Y.C., 1964-67, spl. fellow, 1967-68; asst. prof. Mount Sinai Sch. Medicine, N.Y.C., 1968-71, assoc. prof., 1971—, asst. dean for student affairs, 1976-81, assoc. dean for student affairs, 1981—. Contbr. articles to profl. jours.; author of numerous videorecordings. Vol. Community Soup Kitchen, N.Y.C., 1986—. Nat. Inst. Neurol. Disorders grantee, 1969-72. Mem. Soc. for Neuroscience, Am. Assn. Anatomists, Am. Soc. Zoologists, Assn. for Rsch. in Nervous and Mental Disease, N.Y. Acad. Sci., Harvey Soc., CCNY Acad. for Humanities and Scis. (bd. dirs. 1988—), Sigma Xi. Mem. Christian Ch. Home: 711 West End Ave New York NY 10025 Office: Mount Sinai Sch Medicine PO Box 1007 One Gustave Levy Pl New York NY 10029

SHROKA, JOYCE ANN, steel company manager; b. Gary, Ind., Mar. 8, 1955; d. Albert Andrew and Patricia Ann (Kennedy) Krieter; m. Steven Paul Shroka, May 24, 1980; children: Adrienne Lea, Gregory Charles. AAS, Purdue U., 1976, AAS in Computer Programming, BS in Computer Sci., 1977. Programmer Standard Oil of Ind., Chgo., 1977-79; cons. WD Farlow & Assoc., South Holland, Ill., 1979-82, account mgr., 1982-86; supr. systems payroll maintenance Inland Steel, East Chicago, Ind., 1983-87, supr. order processing systems, 1987-90; supr. planning and scheduling systems Inland Steel, 1990, sect. mgr. mfg. systems, 1990—. Mem. NAFE, Am. Prodn. and Inventory Control Soc. Roman Catholic. Home: 13521 Schneider Court Cedar Lake IN 46303 Office: Inland Steel 3210 Watling St East Chicago IN 46312

SHUEY, JUDITH LEWIS, counselor; b. Atlanta, Oct. 2, 1946; d. Oliver McCutchen and Hazel Kyle (Jones) Lewis; m. Theodore G. Jr. Shuey, June 21, 1969 (div. 1986); children: Ellen Lewis, Theodore G. III. BA in Econ., Bridgewater Coll., 1968; student, U. Va., 1969-71; MEd, James Madison U., 1990. Cert. fin. planner. Tchr. Augusta County Schs., Staunton, Va., 1968-70; sec.-treas. Cabinet Craft Va., Inc., Richmond, 1977-80; choir master Christ Luth. Ch., Staunton, 1982-88; career counselor Staunton City Schs., 1987—; Co-creator PULSAR (award winning substance abuse prevention project), Staunton, 1989, cons. on PULSAR to gov. Va., 1990—; creator Student Assistance Program (winner state and local awards). Bd. dirs. Christ Luth. Ch., Staunton, 1985-88, 90—, Staunton CADRE, 1988—. Recipient Citation for substance abuse prevention, Va. Atty. Gen. Mary Sue Terry, Richmond, 1990. Mem. NEA, Va. Edn. Assn. (presenter state instrnl. conf. 1990), Slaunton Mental Health Assn. (bd. dirs. 1989—). Democrat. Home: 504 Rainbow Dr Staunton VA 24401

SHUGART, DONNA LEA, cultural organization administrator, vocalist; b. Denver, July 7, 1948; d. Harold E. and Vivian C. (Wickham) Wilson; m. Steven R. Shugart, July 25, 1980; children: Jay, Jessica, Kelly. BA, Aquinas Coll., 1980; postgrad., Cen. Mich. U., 1983, Lake Superior State U., 1990—. Exec. dir. Grand Rapids (Mich.) Folklore Soc., 1974-78; freelance vocalist Grand Rapids, 1975-80; dir. spl. events Interlochen (Mich.) Ctr. for the Arts, 1980—. Planner Garfield Twp. Planning and Zoning Commn., Traverse City, Mich., 1988—. Democrat. Methodist. Office: Interlochen Ctr for the Art PO Box 199 Interlochen MI 49643

SHUGART, ELIZABETH LANCASTER, economic adviser; b. Doylestown, Pa., Nov. 6, 1963; d. George Graham and Amy Priestly (Sadler) Lancaster; m. David Adams Shugart, Apr. 23, 1988. BA in Econs., Randolph-Macon Woman's Coll., 1986. Jr. claims examiner The Prudential, Ft. Washington, Pa., 1985; fin. adviser Pa. Equities, Florham Park, N.J., 1986-87; accounts payable specialist McCallion Temporaries, Montgomeryville, Pa., 1987-88; Army learning ctr. operator Cen. Tex. Coll., Babenhausen, Fed. Republic Germany, 1989—. Mem. Bn. Wives Club (treas. Babenhausen br. 1989-90). Republican. Episcopalian. Home: 137 Lafayette St Doylestown PA 18901 Office: US Army Edn Ctr Learning Resource Ctr APO New York NY 09455

SHULER, SALLY ANN SMITH, computer services and software company executive; b. Mt. Olive, N.C., June 11, 1934; d. Leon Joseph and Ludia Irene (Montague) Simmons; m. Henry Ralph Smith Jr., Mar. 1, 1957 (div. Jan. 1976); children: Molly Montague, Barbara Ellen, Sara Ann, Mary Kathryn; m. Harold Robert Shuler, Aug. 2, 1987. BA in Math., Duke U., 1956; spl. studies, U. Liège, Belgium, 1956-57; postgrad. in bus. econs., Claremont Grad Sch., 1970-72. Mgr. fed. systems Gen. Electric Info. Services Co., Washington, 1976-78; mgr. mktg. support Gen. Electric Info. Services Co., Rockville, Md., 1978-81; dir. bus. devel. info. tech. group div. Electronic Data Systems, Bethesda, Md., 1981-82; v.p. mktg. optimum systems div. Electronic Data Systems, Rockville, 1982-83; v.p. planning and communications Electronic Data Systems, Dallas, 1983-84; exec. dir. comml. devel. U.S. West Inc., Englewood, Colo., 1984-90; v.p. mkt. and devel. Cin. Bell Info. Systems Inc., 1990—. Recipient Gen. Electric Centennial award, Rockville, 1978. Fellow Rotary Internat. Found.; mem. Phi Beta Kappa, Tau Psi Omega, Pi Mu Epsilon. Democrat. Presbyterian. Home: 1626 S Syracuse St Denver CO 80231 Office: Cin Bell Info Systems Inc 600 Vine St PO Box 1638 Cincinnati OH 45201

SHULKO, PATSY LEE, nutrition consultant, realtor; b. Indpls., Sept. 24, 1934; B.S., Mich. State U., 1956, M.A., 1970; m. Richard M. Shulko, Aug. 4, 1973; 1 child, Gregory. Asst. prof. Med. Coll. Ga., Augusta, 1972-82; nutrition cons., 1982—; assoc. Meybohm Realty, Inc., Augusta, 1987—. Mem. Am. Dietetic Assn., Ga. Dietetic Assn., Augusta Dietetic Assn., Am. Home Econ. Assn., Ga. Heart Assn., Ga. Nutrition Coun., Soc. Nutrition Edn., Nutrition Today Soc. (charter), Nutritionists in Nursing Edn. (nat. chmn. 1983-84), AAUP, AAUW, GRI, Houndslake Country Club, Racquet Club, Million Dollar Club, Omicron Nu, Pi Beta Phi. Home: 425 Waverly Dr Augusta GA 30909

SHULTZ, LEILA MCREYNOLDS, botanical curator, educator; b. Bartlesville, Okla., Apr. 20, 1946; d. Leo Allen and Odie (Thompson) McReynolds; 1 child, Kirsten Ann. BS, U. Tulsa, 1969; MA, U. Colo., 1975; PhD, Claremont Grad. Sch., 1983. Secondary tchr. Kans., 1969-70; rsch. asst. U. Colo. Mus., Boulder, 1971-73; curator Intermountain Herbarium Utah State U., 1973—; cons. U.S. Forest Svc., 1978—, EPA, 1987, U.S. Fish and Wildlife Svc., 1980—; co-prin. investigator NSF, 1989-93. Co-author: The Atlas of the Vascular Plants of Utah, 1988; taxon editor: (12 vols.) Flora of North America, 1987—. Tchr. Nat. Wildlife Fedn. Faculty fellow UCLA, 1989; vis. scholar Harvard U., 1988-89. Mem. Am. Bot. Soc. (systematics rep. 1988-90), Am. Soc. Plant Taxonomists (coun. 1990—). Office: Utah State U Dept Biology Logan UT 84322-5500

SHULTZ, MARTHA JANE See DIETRICH, MARTHA JANE

SHUMAN, DEANNE, dental hygienist, educator; b. Manhattan, Kans., June 7, 1953; d. Donald Gene and Sharlene (Cochran) S. BS in Dental Hygiene, Old Dominion U., 1974, MS, 1976, PhD in Urban Svcs., 1984—. With Old Dominion U., Norfolk, Va., 1975—; assoc. prof. Old Dominion U., Norfolk, 1983-89, prof., chairperson, 1989—. Contbr. articles to profl. jours. Team mem. Operation Smile, Norfolk, 1987. Mem. Am. Dental Hygienists Assn. (contbg. editor Chgo. 1986-90), Am. Assn. Dental Schs. (del. Chgo. 1987—), Internat. Assn. Dental Rsch., Profl. and Organizational Devel. Network in Higher Edn., Old Dominion U. Alumni Assn. (faculty liaison Norfolk chpt. 1987), Sigma Phi Alpha (sec. 1981—). Presbyterian. Office: Old Dominion U Sch Dental Hygiene Norfolk VA 23529-0499

SHUMATE, GLORIA JONES, retired educational administrator; b. Meridian, Miss., Jan. 8, 1927; d. Thomas Marvin and Flora E. (Suggs) Jones; m. Jack B. Shumate, Nov. 19, 1946; children: Jack B. Jr., Thomas Edward. BS, Miss. State U., 1960; MA, U. South Fla., 1969, postgrad. in vocat. edn., 1970-72. Cert. guidance counselor, psychology and social studies specialist, Fla. High sch. tchr. Lauderdale County Schs., Meridian, 1952-56; tchr. vocat. edn. Manpower Devel. and Tng., St. Petersburg, Fla., 1964-69; counselor City Ctr. for Learning St. Petersburg Vocat.-Tech. Inst., 1969-70, registrar, 1970-72, asst. dir., 1972-80, exec. dir., 1980-85; dir. vocat.-tech., adult edn. ops. Pinellas County Schs., Largo, Fla., 1985-89; chmn. Fla. Equity Council, 1980-81; mem. Fla. Adv. Council on Vocat. Edn., 1980-85, Fla. Job Tng. Coordinating Council, 1983-84. Named Outstanding Educator Pinellas Suncoast C. of C., 1980. Mem. Nat. Council Local Adminstrs., Am. Vocat. Assn., Fla. Vocat. Assn., So. Assn. Colls. and Schs. (standards com. 1975-81), Phi Delta Kappa, Kappa Delta Pi. Democrat. Baptist. Home: 900 63d St S Saint Petersburg FL 33707

SHURE, MYRNA BETH, psychologist, educator; b. Chgo., Sept. 11, 1937; d. Sidney Natkin and Frances (Laufman) S.; student U. Colo., 1955; BS, U. Ill., 1959; MS, Cornell U., 1961, PhD, 1966. Asst. prof. U. R.I., head tchr. Nursery Sch., Kingston, 1961-62; asst. prof. Temple U., Phila., 1966-67, assoc. prof., 1967-68; instr. Hahneman Med. Coll., Phila., 1968-69, sr. instr. psychology, 1969-70, asst. prof., 1970-73, assoc. prof., 1973-80, prof., 1980—. NIMH research grantee, 1971-75, 77-79, 82-85, 87, 88—. Recipient Lela Rowland Prevention award Nat. Mental Health Assn., 1982; . lic. psychologist, Pa. Fellow Am. Psychol. Assn. (Disting. Contbn. award div. community psychology 1984); mem. Am. Psychol. Assn. (Task Force on Prevention award 1987), Eastern Psychol. Assn., Soc. Research in Child Devel., Phila. Soc. Clin. Psychologists. Author: (with George Spivack) Social Adjustment of Young Children, 1974; (with George Spivack and Jerome Platt) The Problem Solving Approach to Adjustment, 1976; (with George Spivack) Problem Solving Techniques in Childrearing, 1978. Editorial bd. Jour. Applied Developmental Psychology.

SHURLING, ANNE MARLOWE, psychology educator, consultant; b. Lexington, Ky., Jan. 25, 1947; d. Charles Franklin and Margaret Helen (Crossfield) Marlowe; m. Thomas Lennard Shurling, June 25, 1982; 1 child, Jayne-Margaret. B.M., U. Ky., 1969, Ph.D., 1979; M.S., Fla. State U., 1970. Lic. counseling psychologist, Ky. Asst. dir. student activities Eastern Ky. U., Richmond, 1971-73; mental health specialist Ky. Dept. for Human Resources, Frankfort, 1973-76; personnel research analyst IBM, Lexington, Ky., 1976-79, sr. assoc. instr., 1979-81; asst. v.p. C & S Georgia Corp., Atlanta, 1981-82; prof. psychology Transylvania U., Lexington, 1982—, psychologist Ea. State Hosp., 1989—; staff psychologist Anxiety Mgmt. Ctr., Lexington, 1984-85; cons. and guest presenter to various groups. Author: Greek Membership: Its Impact on the Value Orientations and Moral Development of College Freshmen, 1979. Contbr. articles in field of psychology to profl. jours. Bd. dirs. Inst. for Social Change, Lexington, 1979-86. Mem. Am. Psychol. Assn., Ky. Psychol. Assn., Phi Delta Kappa. Republican. Mem. Christian Ch. (Disciples of Christ). Avocations: gardening; music; cooking. Home: 326 Curtin Dr Lexington KY 40503 Office: Transylvania U 300 N Broadway Lexington KY 40508

SHUTTS, SHARON E., psychologist; b. Macon, Mo., July 11, 1940; d. Clarence Miller and Margaret Jane (Burke) Cox; m. William Allen Bowlin, June 12, 1960 (div. 1973); children: Lori Christine, William Alan; m. Ellis Lynn Shutts, Sept. 3, 1976 (dec. 1978). BS Psychology, Mo. W. State Coll., 1975; MA Psychology, U. Mo., 1977, Ednl. Spl., 1989. Mental health coord. Greater St. Joseph Area Head Start, St. Joseph, Mo., 1973-79; profl. counselor Clin. Counseling and Cons. Svc., St. Joseph, Mo., 1975—; psychologist I Woodson Children's Psychiatric Hosp., St. Joseph, Mo., 1979—; bd. dirs. Mental Health Assn., St. Joseph, Mo. Mem. Task Force on Sexual Assault and Interpersonal Violence, St. Joseph, Mo., Head Start Adv. Coun., Am. Assn. Counseling and Devel., Am. Psychol. Assn., Mo. Psychol. Assn., Assn. Applied Psychophysiology and Biofeedback. Office: Clin Counseling 322 Kirkpatrick Bldg Saint Joseph MO 64501

SHWAYDER, ELIZABETH YANISH, sculptor; b. St. Louis; d. Sam and Fannie May (Weil) Yaffe; m. Nathan Yanish, July 5, 1944 (dec.); children: Ronald, Marilyn Ginsburg, Mindy. Student, Washington U., 1941, Denver U., 1960; pvt. studies. One-woman shows include Woodstock Gallery, London, 1973, Internat. House, Denver, 1963, Colo. Women's Coll., Denver, 1975, Contemporaries Gallery, Santa Fe, 1963, So. Colo. State Coll. Pueblo, 1967, others; exhibited in group shows: Salt Lake City Mus., 1964, 71, Denver Art Mus., 1961-75, Oklahoma City Mus., 1969, Joslyn Mus., Omaha, 1964-68, Lucca (Italy) Invitational, 1971, others; represented in permanent collections include Colo. State Bank, Bmh Synagogue, Denver, Colo. Women's Coll., Har Ha Shem Congregation, Boulder, Colo., Faith Bible Chapel, Denver, others. Chmn. visual arts Colo. Centennial-Bicentennial, 1974-75; pres. Denver Council Arts and Humanities, 1973-75; mem. Mayor's Com. on Child Abuse, 1974-75; co-chmn. visual arts spree Denver Pub. Schs., 1975; trustee Denver Center for the Performing Arts, 1973-75; chmn. Concerned Citizens for Arts, 1976; pres. Beth Israel Hosp. Aux., 1985-87; organizer Coat Drive for the Needy, Denver and N.Y.C., 1982-87; bd. dirs. Mizel Mus., Srs., Inc.; mem. Mayor's Com. on Cultural Affairs, Nat. Mus., Women in the Art Mus. Recipient McCormick award Ball State U., Muncie, Ind., 1964, Purchase award Colo. Women's Coll., Denver, 1963, Tyler (Tex.) Mus., 1963, 1st prize in sculpture 1st Nat. Space Art Show, 1971; Humanities scholar Auraria Libraries, U. Colo., Denver. Mem. Artists Equity Assn., Rocky Mountain Liturgical Arts, Allied Sculptors Colo., Allied Arts Inc. Hist. Denver, Symphony Guild, Parks People, Beth Israel Aux. Home: 131 Fairfax St Denver CO 80220

SHYMANSKI, CATHERINE MARY, psychiatric clinical nurse specialist; b. Omaha, Jan. 23, 1954; d. Leo Michael and Mildred Mary (Swank) Shymanski. A.A.S. in Nursing, Iowa Western Community Coll., 1977; B.S.N., Buena Vista Coll., 1978; B.F.A., Drake U., 1980; M.S.N., Columbia Pacific U., 1984. Charge nurse Nebr. Psychiat. Inst., Omaha, 1977-78; staff nurse Menninger Found., Topeka, 1978-79; staff devel. instr., clin. coord. Stormont Vail Regional Med. Ctr., Topeka, 1979-80; charge nurse Allen County Hosp., Iola, Kans., 1980-81; asst. dir. nursing Arkhaven at Erie, Kans., 1980; dir. shift ops. Truman Med. Ctr., Kansas City, Mo., 1983; nursing supr. Osawatomie (Kans.) State Hosp., 1981—. Mem. River City Players, Osawatomie, 1984—. Mem. AAUW, Bus. & Profl. Women (pres. Osawatomie chpt. 1985-86, 88-89, dist. dir. 1987-88, Young Career Woman award 1982, 84, Woman of Yr., 1982-83), Kans. State Nursing Assn. (pres. dist. 1985-86), Am. Cat Fanciers Assn. Lutheran. Avocations: raise and show cats, gardening, reading. Office: Osawatomie State Hosp PO Box 500 Osawatomie KS 66064

SIAHPOOSH, FARIDEH TAMADDON, librarian; b. Eshghabad, Turkestan, Russia, Nov. 15, 1928; came to U.S., 1964; d. Hosane and Ghamar (Ramzi) Tamaddon; m. Ismail Siahpoosh, Nov. 30, 1958. BA, Tehran U., Iran, 1962; postgrad., Columbia U., 1967; MLS, Queens Coll., Flushing, N.Y., 1972. Cert. librarian, N.Y. Reference libr. Queens Borough-Pub. Libr. Brs., N.Y.C., 1974-85, asst. br. mgr., 1985—. Mem. ALA. Mem. Baha'i Faith. Home: 19 Ridge Dr E Roslyn NY 11576

SIANTZ, MARY LOU DELEON, nursing educator; b. Hollywood, Calif., June 26, 1947; d. Santiago and Teresa (Farfan) deLeon; m. James Edward Siantz, Dec. 22, 1973; children: Elena Victoria, Elizabeth Julia. BS, Mt. St. Mary's Coll., 1969; M in Nursing, UCLA, 1971; PhD, U. Md., 1984. Dir. tng. in nursing. U. So. Calif., L.A., 1971-73; asst. prof. dept. psychat. nursing U. Mich., Ann Arbor, 1974-75; dir. tng. in nursing Georgetown U., Washington, 1975-78; coord. Migrant Headstart Program, 1978-82; asst. prof. dept. psychiat. mental health nursing Ind. U., Bloomington, 1984—; adj. faculty UCLA, Georgetown U., Washington, D.C., sch. of nursing Children's Hosp., L.A.; with program for child devel. U. of Am. Sch. of Nursing; mem. nat. adv. com. Hispanic Health Care Utilization Rsch. Project, 1990—, infant mortality tech. rev. group office for minority health HHS, 1990. Contbr. artilces to various med. jours. Mem. Boys Club Aux., Bloomington, 1985—. Joseph P. Kennedy fellow in bioethics, 1977-79; recipient Disting. Citizen award Georgetown U. Latin Am. Family Edn. Program, 1989. Mem. Nat. Assn. Hispanic Nurses (chair awards com. 1980—, Ildaura Murrillo Rohde award for Ednl. Excellence 1986), Soc. for Rsch. in Child Devel. (mem. social policy com. 1989—), Advocates for Child Psychiat. Nursing (nat. co-chair, chair advocacy com. 1985-89), Am. Nurses Assn., Soc. for Rsch. and Edn. in Psychiat. Nursing (chair advocacy com. 1989—), Coalition of Spanish Speaking Mental Health and Human Svcs. Orgn. (sr. rsch. fellow 1987-90), Sigma Theta Tau (award in rsch.1988). Office: Ind Univ Sch of Nursing 610 Barnhill Dr Indianapolis IN 46202-5107

SIAS, MARCIA, college secretary; b. Holyoke, Mass., Apr. 14, 1947; d. John Fenton and Adeline Rose (Banas) Ayers; m. Richard Paul Marshall, Mar. 6, 1971 (div. Dec. 1981); 1 child, J. A. Marshall; m. Dean Sias, Oct. 26, 1985. Student, Southeastern Mass. U., 1965-68; BA, Westfield Coll., 1989. Cert. profl. sec., 1987. Adminstrv. asst. Ames Hill Ctr. Gifted, Springfield, Mass., 1980-81; exec. sec. WGGB Channel 40 TV, Springfield, 1981-87, adminstrv. asst., 1987-88; sec. Westfield State Coll., 1988—. Troop Leader Girls Scouts U.S., 1972, vol. 1978; treas. Cub Scouts Boy Scouts Am., 1980. Recipient Sr. Prize award Mus. Fine Arts, 1965. Fellow Cert. Profl. Secs. Acad.; mem. Profl. Secs. Internat. (v.p. 1986, bd. dirs. 1985-87, Springfield chpt.). Democrat. Roman Catholic. Home: 64 Old Farm Rd Westfield MA 01085 Office: Westfield State Coll Western Ave Westfield MA 01086

SIBILIA, RHONDA VICTOR, public information officer; b. Miami, Fla., Jan. 20, 1957; d. Jacques and Francine E. (Cohen) Victor; m. James Sibilia, Mar. 14, 1981; children: Kari Lee, Wendi Ann. AA, U. Fla., 1975, BS, 1977. Reporter WJXT-TV, Jacksonville, Fla., 1977-78; producer, reporter WNWS-AM, Miami, 1978-79; newscaster, host WWOK-AM, Miami, 1980; news dir., anchor WKAT-AM, Miami Beach, Fla., 1980-83; corr. CBS Radio, AP, UPI, Fla. Network, Miami, 1980-87; anchor, reporter WINZ-AM, Miami, 1983-87; communications coord. Metro-Dade County Communications Dept., Miami, 1987—; creator edn. campaign Don't Drink This, 1989-90, Solid Waste Recycling, 1989-90; host pub. affairs TV Metropolis, 1987-90. Editor Inside Metro, 1989. Mem. Kappa Tau Alpha. Office: Metro-Dade Communications 111 NW 1st St Ste 2510 Miami FL 33128-1986

SIBLESZ, ISABEL MARIA, educator; b. Miami, Fla., May 17, 1962; d. Rodolfo Maximo and Isabel Elvira (Fernandez) S. AA, Miami-Dade Community Coll., 1981; BS, Fla. Internat. U., 1983, MS, 1986. Sec. Miami Beach Sr. High Sch., Fla., 1979-81; bus. edn. instr. Miami-Dade Community Coll., Miami, Fla., 1982-83; instr. Charron Williams Coll., Miami, Fla., 1983, Miami-Dade Community Coll., Miami, 1983-85; supr. word processing Miami Herald Pub. Co., 1983-88; office tech. chairperson, instr. CompuTech Inst., Miami, 1986-88; tchr. bus. edn. Dade County Pub. Schs., Miami, 1988—; researcher on word processing equipment and its ednl. value Fla. Internat. U., 1986. Named Beginning Tchr. of Yr., Dade County Pub. Schs., 1989. Mem. Corona Coll. Edn. Alumni Assn., Fla. Vocat. Assn., Dade Vocat. Assn., U.S. Assn. for Supervision and Curriculum Devel., Am. Soc. Notaries, NAFE, Nat. Bus. Edn. Assn., Fla. Bus. Edn. Assn., Dade County Bus. Edn. Assn. Republican. Roman Catholic. Office: Miami Edison Mid Sch 6101 NW 2d Ave Miami FL 33127

SIBLEY, CAROL MORSE, communications executive; b. San Antonio, Jan. 11, 1944; d. Edison Spencer and Cecile (Bernard) Morse; student U. Del., 1962-64; B.S., Hahnemann Med. Coll., 1966; m. Frederick Drake Sibley, Mar. 15, 1975; 1 child, Janet Bernard. Med. writer internat. div. Bristol-Myers, N.Y.C., 1968-72; assoc. biomed. communications Turner Assocs., Greenwich, Conn., 1972-73; clin. rsch. assoc. Pfizer Pharms., N.Y.C., 1974-76, mgr. sci. communications, 1976; cons. pharm. industry, Montclair, N.J., 1976-89; assoc. biomed. communications J.L. Shapiro Assocs., Metuchen, N.J., 1979-82; dir. sci. affairs Audio Visual Med. Mktg., N.Y.C., 1982-83, pres. Med.-Sci. Communications, Inc., Montclair, 1989—. Committeeman Rep. Party, Phila., 1965-66, Twp. of Montclair, 1989-90. Mem. Am. Soc. Microbiology, N.Y. Acad. Scis., Am. Soc. Clin. Pathologists, NAFE. Episcopalian. Home and Office: 50 Pine St Ste 312 Montclair NJ 07042

SIBLEY, CHARLOTTE ELAINE, pharmaceutical industry executive; b. Holliston, Mass., June 11, 1946; s. C. Edward and Jane Forbes (Kelly) S. ; m. Leif Magnusson, Oct. 1, 1988. A.B., Middlebury Coll., 1968, M.B.A., U. Chgo., 1970. Market research mgr. Pfizer Inc., N.Y.C., 1970-73; security analyst Donaldson, Lufkin & Jenrette, N.Y.C., 1973-76; cons., N.Y.C., 1976-78; mktg. research mgr. Lipton Co., Englewood Cliffs, N.J., 1978-80; market research mgr. Johnson & Johnson Products Inc., New Brunswick, N.J., 1980-84; research dir. Med. Econs. Co., Inc., Oradell, N.J., 1984-87; dir. worldwide mktg. rsch. Bristol-Myers Squibb Corp., Princeton, N.J., 1987-88. Cons., Vol. Urban Cons. Group, N.Y.C., 1974-78. V.p., treas. St. Cecilia Chorus, N.Y.C., 1974-88. Republican. Home: 15 Eggert Ave Metuchen NJ 08840 Office: Bristol Myers Squibb Corp PO Box 4000 Princeton NJ 08543-4000

SIBLEY, DAWN BUNNELL, advertising executive; b. Jersey City, Nov. 14, 1939; d. Milton Joseph and Dorothy (Nicoll) Bunnell; m. John Winthrop Sibley, Mar. 5, 1962 (div. 1975). BA, Wellesley Coll., 1960. Planner to sr. v.p., media dir. Ted Bates & Co., N.Y.C., 1967-76; sr. v.p., media dir. Compton Advt., N.Y.C., 1977-82; exec. v.p., media dir. Ally & Gargano, N.Y.C., 1982—; exec. bd. Leading Ind. Agy. Network. Media dir. Gerald Ford Election Campaign, Washington, 1976. Named one of Women Achievers of Yr., YWCA, 1983. Mem. 4A's Media (chmn., policy com., bd. dirs.). Home: 29 Craw Ave Rowayton CT 06853 Office: Ally & Gargano Inc 805 Third Ave New York NY 10022

SICHENZE, CELESTE MARIE, business educator; b. Bklyn., Aug. 28, 1937; d. Louis R. and Carmela M. (Esposito) Costagliola; m. John Anthony Sichenze, July 4, 1959; children: John A. II, Louis D., Andrea C. BS in Gen. Bus. cum laude, L.I. U., 1959, MS in Bus. Adminstrn. cum laude, 1965; PhD, George Washington U., 1988. Adminstrv. asst. to v.p., provost L.I. U., 1959-61; tchr. adult edn. Manchester (Mass.) Schs., 1965-68; tchr. Pingree Sch., Hamilton, Mass., 1968-71; substitute tchr. Fairfax City (Va.) Pub. Schs., 1972-74; from lectr. to prof. bus. mgmt. No. Va. Community Coll., Annandale, 1974—. Contbr. articles to profl. jours. Mem. Fairfax County Fedn. Citizens Assn., bus. mgmt. curriculum adv. com. No. Va. Community Coll.; pres. Carriage Hill Civic Assn., Vienna, Va., 1975-76, 88—, v.p. 1985-86, Oakton High Sch. PTA, Vienna, 1977-79; chmn. ways and means com. Oakton High Sch. Band Boosters, Vienna, 1980-83. Named an Outstanding Young Woman of Am., Chgo., 1969. Mem. Am. Mgmt. Assn., Indsl. Relations Research Assn., Va. Community Coll. Assn. (chmn. research and publs. commn. 1984-86). Roman Catholic. Home: 2020 Post Rd Vienna VA 22181 Office: No Va Community Coll 8333 Little River Turnpike Annandale VA 22003

SICKERMAN HOFFMAN, CAROL WENDY, publishing company executive; b. Bklyn., Nov. 2, 1956; m. Irwin Hoffman. Student, C.W. Post Coll., 1974-76; AAS, NYU, 1983. Mem. fin. staff Amalgamated Textile Workers Am., N.Y.C., 1978-81; cons. N.Y.C., 1981-83; office mgr. Superior Oil and Belting Co., Bklyn., 1982-84; account exec. Sterling's Mags., Inc., N.Y.C., 1984-89; managerial cons. Sterling's Mags., Inc., 1989—. Mem. NAFE, Am. Women Entrepreneurs, Met. Mus. Art, Gamma Psi Delta. Home: 103-11 68th Dr Forest Hills NY 11375 Office: Sterling Mags Inc 355 Lexington Ave New York NY 10017

SICKINGER LINS, DEBRA ROSE, loan officer; b. New London, Wis., Aug. 7, 1958; d. Jerome John and Audrey Mae (O'Connell) Sickinger; m. Kendall Steven Lins, May 28, 1988. BA, Lakeland Coll., 1979; MBA, U. Wis., 1984. Tax asst. Lakeshore Farm Mgmt. Assn., Valders, Wis., 1978-79; agrl. loan officer Fed. Land Bank Assn. of Baraboo, Wis., 1979-83; v.p., sr. loan officer Valley Bank Sauk Prairie, Sauk City, Wis., 1983—; instr. Am.

Inst. Banking. Mem. Nat. Dairy Shrine, Madison, Wis., State Wis. Dept. Agrl. Trade and Consumer Protection Task Force on Plant Security, 1988. Named Farm Bur. Queen, Manitowoc (Wis.) County, 1976-77. Mem. Am. Agr. Women, Sauk County Bankers Assn. (pres., v.p., sec. 1987-90), Wis. Bankers Assn. (bd. dirs. agr. sect. 1988-91), Eagle Bluff Wis. Women for Agr. (pres. Sauk Prairie chpt. 1983-85), U. Wis. Alumni Assn., Future Farmers Am. Alumni. Roman Catholic. Office: Valley Bank Sauk Prairie 726 Water St Sauk City WI 53583

SICKLESMITH, DONNA LOU, art director; b. Uniontown, Pa., Oct. 13, 1953; d. James V. Sicklesmith and Mary E. (Kriner) Honsaker. Student, Georgetown U., 1972-74; BA in Polit. Sci., Purdue U., 1975; cert. publ. specialist, George Washington U., 1981. Designer Ice House Graphics, Washington, 1981-82; art. dir., owner Donna Sicklesmith Graphic Design, Washington, 1982-83; designer Wickham & Assocs., Washington, 1983-84; art dir., ptnr. Sicklesmith & Egly, Washington, 1984-86; art dir., owner Sicklesmith Design, Washington, 1986—; instr. in publ. specialist program continuing edn. George Washington U., 1982-83. Mem. Art Dirs. Club Met. Washington (7 Certs. Merit 1985-89, sec. 1985-86, 2d v.p. 1986-87), Internat. Design by Electronics Assn. Unitarian. Home and Office: 1368 G St SE Washington DC 20003

SIDAWAY, HAZEL KIDWELL, teacher; b. Canton, Ohio, Nov. 9, 1943; d. Earl Johns and Hilda Isabella (Cowley) Donovan; m. Richard Wilson Kidwell, June 3, 1962 (div. May, 1975); children: Mary Kidwell Roshong, Amy Esther; m. Theodore Sidaway, Dec. 23, 1989. BS, Malone Coll., 1970; MEd, U. Akron, 1978; workshop on money mgmt., Wharton Sch. Bus., 1987. Dir. religious edn. Faith United Meth. Ch., North Canton, Ohio, 1970-71; elem. tchr. Canton (Ohio) City Schs., 1971-87, resource for parent involvement, 1987-89, elem. tchr., 1989—; bd. dirs. State Tchrs. Retirement System of Ohio, Columbus. Recipient Grant, Canton City Schs., 1983. Mem. NEA, Ohio Edn. Assn., E. Cen. Ohio Edn. Assn. (pres. 1985-86), Delta Kappa Gamma. Democrat. Mem. Ch. of the Brethren. Home: 463 Roxbury Ave NW Massillon OH 44646

SIDEL, ENID RUTH, educator; b. N.Y.C., Apr. 15, 1936; d. Jerome and Mae (Sklaroff) Lipskin; m. H. David Sidel (div. May 1970). AB, Hunter Coll., 1958; MEd, U. Buffalo, 1961; postgrad., Rutgers U., 1978-. Grad. asst. U. Buffalo (N.Y.), 1958-59; English tchr. Buffalo City Bd. Edn., 1959-60; tchr. Matawan (N.J.) Bd. Edn., 1969-70; coll. prof. Brookdale Community Coll., Lincroft, N.J., 1970-; field faculty Goddard Coll., Plainfield, Vt., 1977-78; freelance cons. Matawan, 1970—; speaker Am. Assn. Higher Edn. Author, editor Bayshore Community Hosp. Newsletter, Holmdel, 1968-70. Mem. Nat. Council Tchrs. English, Pi Lambda Theta. Democrat. Hebrew. Office: Brookdale Community Coll 765 Newman Springs Rd Lincroft NJ 07738

SIDRAN, MIRIAM, retired physics educator, researcher; b. Washington, May 25, 1920; d. Morris Samson and Theresa Rena (Gottlieb) S. BA, Bklyn. Coll., 1942; MA, Columbia U., N.Y.C., 1949; PhD, NYU, 1956. Rsch. assoc. dept. physics NYU, N.Y.C., 1950-55, postdoctoral fellow, 1955-57; asst. prof. Staten Island Community Coll., Richmond, N.Y., 1957-59; rsch. scientist Grumman Aerospace Corp., Bethpage, N.Y., 1959-67; prof. N.Y. Inst. Tech., N.Y.C., 1967-72; NSF rsch. fellow Nat. Marine Fisheries Svc., Miami, Fla., 1971-72; assoc. prof. then prof. physics Baruch Coll., N.Y.C., 1972-89, chmn. dept. natural scis., 1983-89, prof. emerita, 1990—; v.p. Baruch chpt. Profl. Staff Congress, 1983-89. Contbr. numerous articles to profl. and govtl. publs., chpts. to books. N.Y. State Regents scholar, 1937-41; NSF summer fellow, Miami, 1970. Mem. N.Y. Acad. Scis., Am. Assn. Physics Tchrs. Home: 210 W 19th St #5G New York NY 10011

SIDUN, NANCY MARIE, clinical psychologist, art therapist; b. Newark, July 9, 1955; d. Albert and Mae (Clement) S. BA, Colo. Womens Coll., 1976; MS, Emporia State U., 1978; PsyD, Ill. Sch. Profl. Psychology, 1986. Art therapy intern The Menninger Found., Topeka, 1978-79; art psycholotherapist Childrens Med. Ctr., Tulsa, 1979-82; clin. psychologist, pvt. practice Chgo., 1983—, Ill. State Psychiat. Inst., Chgo., 1987—; adj. asst. prof., U. Ill., Chgo., 1982-84, clin. dir., Young Expressions, Chgo., 1985-87, vis. lectr., Sch. Art Inst., Chgo., 1984—, psychologist, Henry Horner Childrens Ctr., Chgo., 1986-87, cons. The Touchstone Group, Chgo., 1987, Creative Devel. Ctr., Chgo., 1985-88, psychologist, Weight Mgmt. Svcs., Chgo., 1988-89. Contbr. articles to profl. jours. Mem. Am. Psychol. Assn., Am. Art Therapy Assn., Ill. Psychol. Assn., Ill. Art Therapy Assn., Symbolic Lang. Sexually Abused Individuals, Diagnostic Drawing Series Network. Office: Ill State Psychiat Inst 1601 W Taylor St Chicago IL 60612

SIEBENMANN, NANCYLEE ARBUTUS, hospital administrator, nurse; b. Ladysmith, Wis., Oct. 12, 1933; d. Herbert O. and Arbutus H. (Ruckdashel) Hartig; m. John F. Siebenmann, Apr. 13, 1957; children: John Hart, Lori Jean. Diploma St. Luke's Sch. Nursing, Duluth, Minn., 1954; BS in Nursing Adminstrn., U. Minn., 1957; MA in Nursing Adminstrn., U. Iowa, 1971; grad. Ohio State U., 1988. RN, Iowa. Staff nurse St. Luke's Hosp., 1954, U. Minn., Mpls., 1955-57, Iowa Meth. Hosp., Des Moines, 1957; head nurse pre/post surg. unit St. Luke's Hosp., Cedar Rapids, Iowa, 1957-59, instr., asst. dir. St. Luke's Sch. Nursing, 1960-71; founding chmn. and dir. nursing program Coe Coll., Cedar Rapids, 1972-74; assoc. adminstr. St. Luke's Hosp., 1974-80, v.p. corp. devel. adminstrn., 1980-82, staff asst. to pres., 1983-87; v.p. St. Luke's Health Resources, 1982-87; v.p. patient care svcs. Allen Meml. Hosp., Waterloo, Iowa, 1989; lectr. in field. Mem. Small Bus. Adv. Council; commr., sec. Iowa Environ. Protection Commn., 1986—; bd. dirs. local chpt. ARC, 1986-89. USPHS grantee, 1956, 57, 71. Mem. Am. Coll. Hosp. Adminstrs., Am. Hosp. Assn. (del.-at-large 1979-82, mem. council on nursing 1980-83), Sigma Theta Tau. Republican. Lutheran. Contbr. articles to profl. publs.

SIEBERT, MURIEL, business executive, former state banking official; b. Cleve.; d. Irwin J. and Margaret Eunice (Roseman) Siebert; student Western Res. U., 1949-52; D.C.S. (hon.), St. John's U., St. Bonaventure U., Molloy Coll., Adelphi St. Francis Coll., Mercy Coll., Coll. New Rochelle. Security analyst Bache & Co., 1954-57; analyst Utilities & Industries Mgmt. Corp., 1958, Shields & Co., 1959-60; partner Stearns & Co., 1961, Finkle & Co., 1962-65, Brimberg & Co., N.Y.C., 1965-67; individual mem. (first woman mem.) N.Y. Stock Exchange, 1967; chmn., pres. Muriel Siebert & Co., Inc., 1969-77; trustee Manhattan Savs. Bank, 1975-77; supt. banks, dept. banking State of N.Y., 1977-82; dir. Urban Devel. Corp., N.Y.C., 1977-82, Job Devel. Authority, N.Y.C., 1977-82, State of N.Y. Mortgage Agy., 1977-82; chmn., pres. Muriel Siebert & Co., Inc., 1983—; assoc. in mgmt. Simmons Coll.; mem. adv. com. Fin. Acctg. Standards Bd., 1981; guest lectr. numerous colls. Mem. women's adv. com. Econ. Devel. Adminstrn., N.Y.C.; trustee Manhattan Coll.; v.p., mem. exec. com. Greater N.Y. Area council Boy Scouts Am.; mem. N.Y. State Econ. Devel. Bd., N.Y. Council Economy; bd. overseers NYU Sch. Bus., 1984-88; bd. dirs. United Way of N.Y.C.; trustee Citizens Budget Commn.; mem. bus. com. Met. Mus. Recipient Spirit of Achievement award Albert Einstein Coll. Medicine, 1977; Women's Equity Action League award, 1978; Outstanding Contbns. to Equal Opportunity for Women award Bus. Council of UN Decade for Women, 1979; Silver Beaver award Boy Scouts Am., 1981; Elizabeth Cutter Morrow award YWCA, 1983; Emily Roebling award Nat. Women's Hall of Fame, 1984; NOW Legal Def. and Edn. Fund award, 1981, Brotherhood award Nat. Conf. of Christians and Jews, 1989, Women on the Move award Anti-Defamayion League, 1990. Mem. River Club, Doubles Club, Nat. Arts Club. Home: 435 E 52nd St New York NY 10022 Office: Muriel Siebert & Co Inc 444 Madison Ave New York NY 10022

SIEBERT, STEPHANIE RAY, video production company executive; b. Phoenix, Sept. 17, 1949; d. Richard and Jacquelyn (Schmunk) S. AA, Yavapai Community Coll., 1967; BS, U. Minn., 1970. Acctg. mgr. Ski Mart of Newport Beach, Calif.; contr. Brown Jay Prodns., L.A.; gen. mgr. Video Tape Libr., Ltd., L.A.; pres. Film/Video Stock, Inc., L.A. Bd. dirs., officer Buddhist orgn. Mem. NAFE (past pres. Laguna Beach), Women in Film, Am. Film Inst., NOW, Am.Mgmt. Assn., Am. Assn. Female Execs., Am. Soc. Exec. Women, Hollywood C. of C., Bus. and Profl. Women's Assn., Women in Show Bus. Republican. Office: 10700 Ventura Blvd Ste E Studio City CA 91604

SIEFERT, TINA GILBERT, public relations professional; b. Kokomo, Ind., July 6, 1965; d. Byron David and Carolyn Sue (Catron) Gilbert; m. John Daniel Siefert, May 16, 1987. BS, Ind. State U., 1987. Merchandising intern L.S. Ayres and Co., Indpls., 1987; asst. mgr. Payless ShoeSource, Indpls., 1987, Melons subs. Fashion Concepts, Indpls., 1987-88; pub. rels. asst. Am. Legion Dept. of Ind., Indpls., 1988-89, editor, pub. rels. rep., 1989—. Student co-chairperson United Way of Wabash Valley, Terre Haute, Ind., 1985. Acad. scholar Ind. State U., 1983-87. Mem. NAFE, Nat. Am. Legion Press Assn. (mem. newspaper staff), Hoosier Am. Legion Press Assn. (editor Hoosier Legionnaire 1989-90). Republican. Office: Am Legion Dept of Ind 777 N Meridian St Indianapolis IN 46204

SIEFERT-KAZANJIAN, DONNA, corporate librarian; b. N.Y.C.; d. Merrill Emil and Esther (Levins) S.; m. George John Kazanjian, June 15, 1974; 1 child, Merrill George. BA, NYU, 1969; MSLS, Columbia U., 1973; MBA, Fordham U., 1977. Asst. librarian Dun & Bradstreet, N.Y.C., 1969-73; research assoc. William E. Hill & Co., N.Y.C., 1973-76; sr. info. analyst Info. for Bus., N.Y.C., 1976-77; librarian Handy Assocs., N.Y.C., 1979—. Mem. Spl. Librs. Assn., Rsch. Roundtable, Am. Mensa Ltd. Roman Catholic. Office: Handy Assocs 250 Park Ave New York NY 10177

SIEGEL, BARBARA Z(ENZ), biology research scientist, educator; b. Detroit, July 22, 1931; d. Joseph and Barbara (Justh) Zenz; m. Sanford Marvin Siegel, June 24, 1950; children: Stephanie Siegel Morgan, Andrea, Peter Marc, David Nathaniel. AB in Philosophy, U. Chgo., 1960; MA in Zoology, Columbia U., 1963; PhD in Biology, Yale U., 1966. Postdoctoral fellow Yale U., New Haven, 1966-67; dir. biology program U. Hawaii, Honolulu, 1967-72, sr. researcher Pacific Biomed. Research Ctr., 1975-87, interim dir. research adminstrn., dean grad. sch., 1979-82, dir. pesticide hazard assessment project, 1983-87, prof. microbiology and botany grad. dept. pub. health, 1986-89, assoc. dean sch. pub. health, 1989—; co-chmn. radiation sub-com. Com. Space Research Hdqrs., Paris, 1975-82; vis. prof. Heidelberg (Fed. Republic of Germany), 1973, Weizmann Inst., Rehovot, Israel, 1986, vis. prof. Geology, Botany, U. Brit. Columbia, 1982; vis. scholar People's Republic of China, 1985; vis. colleague Nat. Research Council of Italy, Pisa, 1987—; sr. lectr. Fulbrights-Hays, Finland, 1988. Editor: Hawaii Energy Resource Overviews: Geothermal Development, 1980; contbr. numerous articles to profl. jours. Chmn. Govs. Panel on Pesticides, Honolulu, 1985; nominated by gov. to Commn. on Pesticides, Honolulu, 1986-88; mem. Peace Inst., Honolulu, 1985, univ. commn. status of women Hawaii Assn. Women in Sci. and Faculty Women's Caucus, 1986; co-investigator U.S./Israel Bionational, 1988—. Fulbright-Hays scholar Yugoslavia, 1972; Fulbright Research fellow U.S. Info. Services, Yugoslavia and Fed. Republic of Germany, 1972-73, scholar to Finland, 1988—. Mem. Am. Chem. Soc., Internat. Chem. Ecology Assn., Sigma Xi. Home: 3119 Beaumont Woods Pl Honolulu HI 96822 Office: U Hawaii Sch Pub Health Biomed D104M Honolulu HI 96822*

SIEGEL, BETTY LENTZ, college president; b. Cumberland, Ky., Jan. 24, 1931; d. Carl N. and Vera (Hogg) Lentz; m. Joel H. Siegel, June 6; children: David Jonathan, Michael Jeremy. B.A., Wake Forest Coll., 1952; M.Ed., U. N.C., 1953; Ph.D., Fla. State U., 1961; postgrad., Ind. U., 1964-66; hon. doctorate, Miami U., 1985, Cumberland Coll., 1985. Asst. prof. Lenoir Rhyne Coll., Hickory, N.C., 1956-59; assoc. prof., 1961-64; asst. prof. U. Fla., Gainesville, 1967-70; assoc. prof. U. Fla., 1970-72, prof., 1973-76, dean acad. affairs for continuing edn., 1972-76; dean Sch. Edn. and Psychology Western Carolina U., Cullowhee, N.C., 1976-81; pres. Kennesaw State Coll., Marietta, Ga., 1981—; bd. dirs. Atlanta Gas Light Co., Equifax Inc., Nat. Services Industries; cons. numerous sch. systems. Author: Problem Situations in Teaching, 1971; contbr. articles to profl. jours. Mem. Metro Atlanta Community Found.; bd. dirs. Operation SMART. Recipient Outstanding Tchr. award U. Fla., 1969; Mortar Bd. Woman of Yr. award U. Fla., 1973, Mortar Bd. Educator of Yr., Ga. State U., 1983, CASE award, 1986; named One of 100 Most Influential People in State of Ga., Ga. Trend Mag. Mem. Am. Psychol. Assn., Assn. Supervision and Curriculum Devel., Am. Assn. Colls. Tchr. Edn., Nat. Univ. Extension Assn., Adult Edn. Assn., Nat. Assn. of Intercollegiate Athletics (nat. exec. com.), Nat. Assn. State Univs. and Land Grant Colls., Am. Assn. State Colls. (bd. dirs., chmn. 1990), Am. Coun. Edn. (bd. dirs., bd. advisors), Atlanta C. of C. (bd. dirs.), Internat. Alliance for Invitational Edn. (cofounder, co-dir.), Cobb C. of C., Phi Alpha Theta, Pi Kappa Delta, Alpha Psi Omega, Kappa Delta Pi, Pi Lambda Theta, Phi Delta Kappa, Delta Kappa Gamma, Kiwanis (Atlanta chpt.). Baptist. Office: Kennesaw State Coll PO Box 444 Marietta GA 30061

SIEGEL, CAROLE, mathematician; b. N.Y., Sept. 29, 1936; d. David and Helen (Mayer) Schore; m. Bertram Siegel, Aug. 18, 1957; children: Sharon, David. BA in Math., NYU, 1957, MS in Math., 1959, PhD in Math., 1963. With computer dept. Atomic Energy Commn., 1957-59; rsch. asst. Courant Inst. of Math. Sci., 1959-63; rsch. scientist dept. of engring. NYU, N.Y.C., 1963-64; rsch. math. Info. Scis. Div. Rockland Rsch. Inst., Orangeburg, N.Y., 1965-74; head Epidemiology and Health Svcs. Rsch. Lab Stat. Scis., Epidemiology Div./Nathan S. Kline Inst. Rsch., Orangeburg, N.Y., 1974—; rsch. prof. dept. of psychiatry, NYU, 1987—; grant reviewer NIHM, 1988-92. Editor: (with S. Fischer) Psychiatric Records in Mental Health Care, 1981; contbr. articles to profl. jours. Recipient grants NIMH, 1988-91, Nat. Ctr. for Health Svcs. Rsch., 1979-82, Nat. Inst. Alcohol Abuse, 1978-82. Mem. Assn. for Health Svcs. Rsch., Am. Soc. Clin. Pharmacology and Therapeutics, Assn. Women in Math., Am. Statis. Assn. Office: Nathan S Kline Inst Orangeburg NY 10962

SIEGEL, CYNTHIA ALLISON, marketing executive; b. Miami Beach, Fla., Aug. 17, 1964; d. David Alan and Gerry Marcia (Torme) S.; m. Stanley Glenn Einhorn, Sept. 3, 1989. BS in Econs., U. Pa., 1986. Asst. product mgr. Lea & Perrins, Inc., Fairlawn, N.J., 1986-88; brand asst. Clorox Co., Oakland, Calif., 1990—; mgr., cons. Cen. Hardware Co., Miami Beach, 1989. Artist functional and decorative ceramics, Am. quilting. Mem. Am. Mktg. Assn., Wharton Alumni Assn., Am. Youth Hostels, U.S. Servas. Home: 801 Stannage Ave #6 Albany CA 94706

SIEGEL, EVA STERN, social services administrator; b. Budapest, Feb. 8, 1956; d. Bill and Gizella (Deszberg) S.; m. Lee M., Aug. 10, 1980; children: Michael Robert, Traci Lauren. BA, Queens Coll., N.Y., 1977; MSW, Columbia U., N.Y., 1979. Cert. Social Worker. Caseworker N. Y. Assn. for New Am., N.Y.C., 1979-80; instr. sociology dept. Gettsburg (Pa.) Coll., 1981-83; social worker Jewish Family Svc., Harrisburg, Pa., 1980—. Pres. Kesher Israel Sisterhood, Harrisburg, 1987-90, AMIT Women, Harrisburg, 1983. Mem. Nat. Assn. of Social Workers. Democrat. Jewish. Office: 3332 N 2d St Harrisburg PA 17110

SIEGEL, GLENDA JUNE, social services specialist; b. Birmingham, Mo., Oct. 3, 1934; d. Oscar Arthur and Geraldine Lenore (Mosby) Runge; m. Aaron Howard Siegel, Feb. 9, 1963; children: Angela Dawn, Anthony David. BA, Calif. State U., L.A., 1960; postgrad., U. So. Calif., L.A., 1963. Child welfare worker L.A. Bur. of Pub. Welfare, 1960-64; with County of Ventura (Calif.) Pub. Social Svcs. Assn., 1964—, tng. supr., 1968-70; dist. mgr. County of Ventura (Calif.) Pub. Social Svcs. Agy., Simi Valley, Calif., 1970—. Fellow NOW, NAFE; mem. Soroptimist Internat. (v.p.). Democrat. Home: 1530 Stoddard Thousand Oaks CA 91360 Office: County of Ventura Pub Svcs 2003 Royal Ave Simi Valley CA 93065

SIEGEL, LEAH ROTHSTEIN, psychotherapist, artist; b. N.Y.C., Jan. 22, 1919; d. Louis and Anita (Levine) Rothstein; m. George T. Siegel, Nov. 14, 1944; children: Laurence F., Roger M., Amy Siegel Feldman. BA magna cum laude, Bklyn. Coll., 1971; MSSW, Columbia U., 1973; postgrad., New Hope Guild, 1973-75. Cert. clin. social worker, N.Y. Secretarial worker various firms N.Y.C., Bklyn., 1937-50; learning disability tutor Coney Island Hosp., Bklyn., 1969-71; social worker Maimonides Hosp., Bklyn., 1970-71; social worker develmentally disabled children Kings County Hosp., Bklyn., 1973-74; social worker adult psychiatry Coney Island Hosp., Bklyn., 1974-76; psychotherapist Bklyn., 1976-86; pvt. practice artist Ft. Pierce, Fla., 1986—; adj. prof. Kingsborough Community Coll., 1981-86. Mem. Nat. Assn. Social Workers, AAUW. Democrat. Jewish. Home: 17 Ecuador Ct Fort Pierce FL 34951

SIEGEL, LUCILLE PAMELA, state official; b. San Rafael, Calif., Jan. 28, 1956; d. Earl and Gladys Ruth (Concors) S.; m. Edward Anthony Wesolowski, Jr., Aug. 20, 1988. BA, Guilford Coll., 1978; MPH, U. N.C., 1984. Maternal child health specialist, tech. cord. Peace Corps, Kathmandu, Nepal, 1978-81; program asst. Ctr. for Early Adolescence, Chapel Hill, N.C., 1982; evaluator Adolescent Pregnancy Prevention Project, Snow Hill, N.C., 1983; trainer U. N.C., Chapel Hill, 1983; dir. Office Adolescent Health, Del. Div. Pub. Health, Dover, 1984-89; coord. AIDS activities Del. Dept. Health and Social Svcs., Wilmington, 1989—; mem. adv. bd. People With AIDS Housing Settlement Program, Wilmington, 1990—, Middle Atlantic AIDS Regional Ednl. Tng. Ctr. Contbr. articles to profl. jours. Mem. needs, initiatives and planning com. United Way of Del., Wilmington, 1985-90, Gov.'s Adolescent Pregnancy Task Force.; bd. dirs. career exploration program, 1987—. Recipient Leadership Del. award United Way Del., 1985. Mem. APHA, Del. Pub. Health Assn. (pres. 1988-90, bd. dirs. 1988—), Del. Perinatal Assn., Am.-Nepal Soc. Office: Dept Health and Social Svcs 3000 Newport Gap Pike Bldg B Wilmington DE 19808

SIEGEL, LUCY BOSWELL, public relations executive; b. N.Y.C., July 5, 1950; d. Werner Leiser and Carol (Fleischer) Boswell; m. Henry Winter Siegel, Nov. 11, 1979; children: David Alan, Joshua Adam. BA, Conn. Coll., 1972. Assoc. editor Conn. Western, Litchfield, Conn., 1972-73; assoc. editor, editor United Bus. Publ., N.Y.C., 1974-78; mgr. communications Equitable Life Assurance Soc., N.Y.C., 1978-86; mgr. internat. affairs Cosmo Pub. Relations Corp., Tokyo, Japan, 1986; dir. internat. affairs Cosmo Pub. Relations Corp., Tokyo, 1987-88; mng. dir. Cosmo Pub. Rels. Corp., N.Y.C., 1988—, also bd. dirs.; cons. in field; bd. dirs. Cosmo Pub. Rels. Corp., Tokyo. Contbr. articles to jours. and mags. Mem. Internat. Assn. Bus. Communicators, Pub. Rels. Soc. Am., Women Execs. in Pub. Rels. Democrat. Jewish. Home: 41 W 96th St Apt 12B New York NY 10025 Office: Cosmo Pub Rels Corp 500 Fifth Ave Ste 300 New York NY 10110

SIEGEL, LYNNE ELISE MOORE, lawyer; b. Sterling, Colo., Sept. 28, 1957; d. James Hamilton and Mabel Louise (White) Moore. B.A. in Liberal Arts, Colo. Coll., 1979; J.D., U. Denver, 1983. Bar: Colo. 1983. Law clk. Dailey, Goodwin et al, Aurora, Colo., 1980-81; asst. to prof. U. Denver, 1981; law clk. Gorsuch, Kirgis et al, Denver, 1982; assoc. Kirkland & Ellis, Denver, 1982; intern to presiding justice Denver Dist. Ct., 1983; assoc. Montgomery, Little, Young, Campbell & McGrew, Denver, 1983-88; law clk. to presiding judge, Colo. Ct. Appeals, 1988; pvt. practice, 1988—. Past bd. dirs. Colo. Women's Employment and Edn., Inc.; past bd. dirs. Colo. Spl. Olympics, Jr. League of Denver, Inc. Contbr. articles to profl. jours, chpts. to book. Denver Panhellenic scholar, 1977. Mem. ABA, Colo. Bar Assn., Kappa Alpha Theta (Founders' Meml. scholar). Home and Office: 765 Lafayette St Denver CO 80218

SIEGEL, NAOMI ANNE, writer, producer, photo-journalist; b. Council Bluffs, Iowa, May 15, 1926; d. Morris Mendelson and Rose (Bleicher) Samuelson; m. Sidney Irving Siegel, Apr. 20, 1944; children: Judith Siegel Pearson (dec.), Eve-Lynn Siegel Novick, David Bruce. BA in English Edn. and Pub. Speaking, Wayne State U., Detroit, 1964, MA in Mass Communication, 1973. Ptnr. Telespot Prodns., Detroit, 1955-69; dir. pub. rels. Mich. Cancer Found., Detroit, 1969-72; pub. info. dir. Oakland County Helath Dept., Southfield, Mich., 1971-73; regional dir. advt. and pub. rels. Dayton-Hudson Shopping Ctrs., Southfield and Mpls., 1973-74; account exec. creative svcs., pub. rels., mktg., writer Chrysler Inst. and Wayne County Office Manpower, 1977-78; contract photojournalist Mich. Bell Telephone Employee Newsletter, Detroit, 1979; copywriter to sr. writer/editor AAA, Mich. Advt., T&D, Dearborn, Mich., 1980-83; communications coord. tng. and devel. Blue Cross/Blue Shield, Detroit, 1983-86; pres. Making It Happen/Telespot Prodns., Birmingham, Mich., 1975—; cons. Amy Devon's Rehab. Program, pub. health fairs, Dept. Social Svc., others. Originator, writer, cinematographer, producer: Halloween, 1967, The Ghost You Save May Be Your Own; photo-journalist Six-Day War Aftermath, 1968, Retailing/Shopping Centers are Big Business, 1979; scriptwriter First Offenders "I'm Somebody, You're Somebody, 1988. Pub. rels. advisor Am. Cancer Soc., Oakland County, Mich., 1986-88; pub. rels./mktg. advisor AIDS Clinic, Wayne County, Mich., 1987-89, environ. planning clean-up, Oakland County, 1990; staff pub. rels./info. dir. Pub. Health, Mich. Cancer Found., Detroit, 1969-71, Oakland County Health Dept., Southfield, Mich., 1971-73. Recipient First Prize environ. filmscript Mich. Outdoor Writers Assn., 1979, award City of Detroit, 1973, Headliners award Wayne State U., 1973, Silver Circle award NATAS. Mem. Am. Women in Radio and TV (past pres. Detroit chpt.), Pub. Rels. Soc. Am., Women in Communications, Inc., Met. Detroit Press Photographers Assn., Writers Info. Network. Jewish. Home and Office: 6360 Dakota Circle Birmingham MI 48010

SIEGELMAN, LOIS SUSAN DASHEF, hospital administrator; b. Boston, May 1, 1945; d. Jacob and Helen (Levine) Dashef; m. Raymond Siegelman, Aug. 5, 1973; 1 child, Jodi. BS, Boston U., 1967, MS, 1971. Staff phys. therapist Lemuel Shattuck Hosp., Boston, 1967-69; dir. phys. therapy Mass. Rehab. Hosp., Boston, 1970-73; chief phys. therapy Univ. Hosp., Boston, 1973-76, adminstrv. coord. rehab. medicine, 1975-80, asst. adminstr. clin. support svcs., 1978-80, clin. adminstr., 1980-86; v.p. adminstr. New England Rehab. Hosp., Woburn, Mass., 1986-88, chief exec. officer, 1988—; lectr. Boston U. Sargent Coll., Boston U. Sch. Medicine, Simmons Coll., Boston. Choreographer Children's Dance Theatre of Concord, Mass. Mem. Am. Coll. Healthcare Execs., Healthcare Mgmt. Assn. Mass. (bylaws com., program com.), Women Healthcare Execs. Jewish. Office: NE Rehab Hosp 2 Rehabilitation Way Woburn MA 01801

SIEGERT, BARBARA MARIE, health care administrator; b. Boston, May 22, 1935; d. Salvatore Mario and Mary Kathleen (Wagner) Tartaglia; m. Herbert C. Siegert (dec. Apr. 1974); children: Carolyn Marie, Herbert Christian Jr. Diploma, Newton-Wellesley (Mass.) Hosp. Sch. Nursing, 1956; MEd, Antioch U., 1980. Diplomate Am. Bd. Med. Psychotherapists. Supr. nursing Hogan Regional Ctr., Hathorne, Mass., 1974-78; community mental health nursing advisor Cape Ann area office Dept. Mental Health, Beverly, Mass., 1978-79; dir. case mgmt. Dept. Mental Health, Beverly, 1979-87, dir. case mgmt. north shore area office, 1988—; mem. interdisciplinary faculty, profl. cons. com., lecture staff clin. pastoral counseling program Danvers State Hosp./Hoganberry Regional Ctrs., Hathorne, Mass., 1982-86; nursing edn. adv. com. North Shore Community Coll., Beverly, Mass., 1983—; tng. staff Balter Inst., Ipswich, Mass., 1987-88. Mem. Internat. Cultural Diploma Honor, 1989—. Recipient Spl. Recognition award Lexington (Mass.) Pub. Schs., 1973, Peter Torci award Lexington Friends of Children in Spl. Edn., 1974; named Internat. Biog. Roll of Honor, 1989—; life fellow Am. Biog. Inst., 1989—. Mem. Am. Nurses Assn., Mass. Nurses Assn., World Inst. Achievement. Home: 63 B Willow Rd Boxford MA 01921 Office: Dept Mental Health Greater North Shore Area Office 180 Cabot St 2nd Fl Beverly MA 01915

SIEGMAN, MARION JOYCE, physiology educator; b. Bklyn., Sept. 7, 1933; d. C. Joseph and Helen (Wasserman) S. BA, Tulane U., 1954; PhD, SUNY, Bklyn., 1966. Instr. physiology Thomas Jefferson U. Jefferson Med. Coll., Phila., 1967-68, asst. prof., 1968-74, assoc. prof., 1974-77, prof., 1977—; mem. physiology study sect. NIH. Editor: Regulation and Contraction of Smooth Muscle, 1987. Recipient award for excellence in rsch. and teaching Burlington No. Found., 1986, award for excellence in teaching Lindback Found., 1987; grantee NIH, 1967—. Mem. Am. Physiol. Soc., Soc. Gen. Physiologists, Physiol. Soc. Phila. (pres. 1972-73). Office: Jefferson Med Coll 1020 Locust St Philadelphia PA 19107

SIEGRIST, MICHELE ANNE, financial analyst; b. Pitts., Apr. 18, 1961; d. Max H. and Anna (Hentschel) Greeff; m. Donald Lacelle Siegrist, Jr. BA in Econs. and Internat. Rels., U. Calif., 1983. Fin. analyst Sierra Capital Cos., San Francisco, 1984-86; sr. fin. analyst Am. Savs. & Loan, Stockton, Calif., 1986-88. Mem. AAUW (treas. 1988--).

SIEH, MAURINE KAY, nurse; b. Leon, Iowa, Sept. 28, 1950; d. Vernon Charles and Dorothy Maxine (Akes) Dobson; B.S. in Nursing, N.E. Mo. State U., 1972; M.S. in Nursing, U. Miss.; m. Robert Hans Sieh, Nov. 18, 1972; children—Robert Carter, Jennifer Clarissa. Charge nurse psychiat. unit St. John's Hosp., Springfield, Mo., 1972-74; public health nurse Will County Health Dept., Joliet, Ill., 1974-75; unit nurse Mental Health Inst. (Elizabeth Ludeman Ctr.) Mentally Retarded Children, Park Forest, Ill., 1977-79; instr. Lamaze method childbirth, Park Forest, 1977-81; psychiat. nurse, chmn. nurse practice and standards com. Menninger Found., Topeka, 1981; nurse neuro-neurosurg. unit Univ. Med. Center, Jackson, Miss., 1981-82; prenatal nurse ob/gyn clinic U. Miss. Med. Ctr., 1982-86; with nursing faculty U. So. Miss., 1986—; instr. Lamaze method; cons. Women's Health Issues. Mem. Nat. League Nursing, Am. Soc. Psychoprophylaxis in Obstetrics, Internat. Childbirth Edn. Assn., Smithsonian Inst., Hastings Ctr., Sigma Theta Tau. Mem. Brethren Ch. Home: 4953 Oak Leaf Dr Jackson MS 39212

SIEKIERSKI, KAMILLA MALGORZATA, dental laboratory technician; b. Warsaw, Poland, Aug. 4, 1938; came to U.S., 1963, naturalized, 1970; d. Tomasz and Janina W. (Sendzimir) Piotrowski; cert. dental technician Sch. Dental Technicians, Krakow, Poland, 1957; m. Kazimierz Siekierski, Nov. 25, 1959; children—Marzanna, Eva. Owner, operator Kama's Dental Lab., Krakow, 1963; dental technician Dan's Dental Lab., Waterbury, Conn., 1963-65, Wilcox Dental Lab., Wethersfield, Conn., 1965-68; pres. Dentek, Inc., Milford, Conn., 1980—. Mem. Conn. Dental Lab. Assn. (pres. 1977-79), Nat. Assn. Dental Labs., Conf. Dental Labs. Home: 350 Gulf St Milford CT 06460 Office: 158 Cherry St Milford CT 06460

SIEKMAN, LULA BEATRICE, educator; b. Bradford, Ill., Sept. 22, 1912; d. Burless Truit and Mary Margaret (Harding) Sturm; 1 child, Richard. BA, U. S. Fla., St. Petersburg, 1977, MA in Adult Edn., 1986. Cert. adult edn. tchr., Fla. Owner Seaire Motel, Treasure Island, Fla., 1952-70; office mgr. No. Propane Gas Co., Pinellas Park, Fla., 1970-75; tchr. dept. lifelong learning St. Petersburg (Fla.) Jr. Coll., 1962-72; bus. tchr. Tomlinson Adult Learning Ctr., St. Petersburg, 1986-89. Author: Handbook of Florida Shells, 1964, The Book of Shells, 1965, The Shell Game, 1953; contbr. articles to Profl. Jours. Mem. Maxima Moorings Civic Assn., St. Petersburg, 1987-90; v.p. Maxima Moorings Women's Club, 1987-90. Named Outstanding VTAE Part Time Tchr., 1989-90. Mem. Pinellas Adult Vocat. Edn., Fla. Bus. Edn. Assn., Am. Malacological Union, St. Petersburg Shell Club (life, pres. 1958, 63), Blue Angels Choir. Republican. Methodist. Home: 5031 41st St S Saint Petersburg FL 33711

SIEL, SUSAN MICHELLE, educator; b. Port Huron, Mich., Dec. 20, 1961; d. Clayton Charles William and Joyce (Swank) Beach; m. William John Siel, June 16, 1984. BA in Communication, U. Wis., Parkside, 1985. Tchr. Kenosha (Wis.) Unified Sch. Dist. 1, 1989—. Vice pres. Kinship of Kenosha, 1989. Mem. Wis. Edn. Assn., NEA, Kappa Delta Pi. Home: 5953 5th Ave Kenosha WI 53140

SIELSKI, JOANN ELIZABETH, product manager; b. Marlette, Mich., Sept. 13, 1955; d. Gerald Joseph and Elizabeth (Moore) S. BS, Western Mich. U., 1976; MS, Rensselaer Poly. U., 1989. Sr. buyer Cadillac Electric Supply Co., Oak park, Mich., 1977-82; br. mgr. Cadillac Electric Supply Co., Riverview, Mich., 1982-84; field sales rep. Hubbell, Inc., Detroit; product mgr. Hubbell, Inc., Stonington, Conn., 1986—. Co-inventor Basetrak-Wall-trak Raceways. Recipient B/PAA Silver Target--Product/Packaging/Pop Displays Hartford, Conn. chpt. B/PAA, 1988, Hubbell Century Club award, 1990.

SIERRA, DEBRA LYNN, insurance company executive; b. San Antonio, June 1, 1962; d. Manuel Sierra and Delfina Catherine (Canales) Estrada. Grad. high sch., San Antonio; student, Richland Coll., 1989—. Lic. casualty ins. adjustor, Tex., Okla., N.Mex. Claims asst. and processor Lindsey & Newsom Ins. Adjusters, Inc., San Antonio, 1981-83, clerical supr., 1983-85, casualty claims adjuster, 1985-86; total theft examiner II, total loss negotiator Govt. Employees Ins. Co., Dallas, 1986-89; with N.Am. Claims Mgmt. Co., Dallas, 1989—. Vol. Nat. Kidney Found. Tex., Dallas, 1987—. Recipient spl. events vol. of yr. award Nat. Kidney Found. Tex., 1989. Mem. Ins. Women San Antonio, San Antonio Claims Assn. Office: North Am Claims Mgmt Co 7929 Brookriver Dr Ste 350 Dallas TX 75247

SIERZANT, PATRICIA LUCY, legal administrator; b. Mpls., July 23, 1948; d. Lawrence Albert and Lucy Katherine (Godlewski) S. BA, U. Minn., 1970. Legal asst. Dorsey & Whitney, Mpls., 1970-74, Maslon, Edelman, Borman & Brand, Mpls., 1974-76; legal adminstr. Lentz, Cantor, Kilgore & Massey Ltd., Paoli, Pa., 1977—; speaker in field. Mem. Assn. Legal Adminstrs. (pres. Phila. chpt. 1988-89, pres. -elect 1987-88), Nat. Assn. Legal Assts., Phila. Assn. Paralegals, Paoli Bus. & Profl. Assn. (treas., dir. 1983—). Home: One Muirfield Ct Newton Square PA 19073 Office: Lentz Cantor Kilgore Massey 30 Darby Rd Box 987 Paoli PA 19301

SIESS, JUDITH ANN, librarian; b. Urbana, Ill., Sept. 28, 1947; d. Chester Paul and Helen (Kranson) S.; m. Stephen Paul Bremseth, Aug. 27, 1983. BA cum laude, Beloit Coll., 1969; MA, Ea. N.Mex. U., 1973; MLS, U. Ill., 1982. Asst. extension agrl. economist dept. agrl. econs. U. Ill., Urbana, 1976-83; librarian Enzyme Tech. Corp., Ashland, Ohio, 1983-86, North Coast Biotechnology, Warrensville Heights, Ohio, 1986-87, NASA Lewis Rsch. Ctr., Cleve., 1987-88; engring. librarian Bailey Controls Co., Wickliffe, Ohio, 1988—. Editor: Price Forecasting and Sales Management, 1978. Mem. Am. Soc. Info. Sci., Spl. Librs. Assn. Home: 477 Harris Rd Richmond Heights OH 44143

SIEWERT, ROBIN NOELLE, chemical engineer; b. Heidelberg, Fed. Republic Germany, Dec. 14, 1956; (parents Am. citizens); d. Orville Ray and Norma Idella (Sprink) S. BS in Chem. Engring., U. Tex., 1979. Registered profl. engr. Start-up engr. Cen. Power and Light Co., Fannin, Tex., 1979-81; chem. engr. Cen. Power and Light Co., Corpus Christi, Tex., 1981-85, performance analysis engr., 1985-87, performance analysis supr., 1987—. Mem. NSPE, ASME, Soc. Women Engrs., Alpha Chi Sigma (pres. 1975). Republican. Baptist. Home: 4005 C Acushnet Corpus Christi TX 78413 Office: Cen Power & Light Co PO Box 2121 Corpus Christi TX 78403

SIEWICKI, BRENDA JOYCE, healthcare executive; b. Mt. Airy, Md., Aug. 21, 1949; d. Rudolph M. and Olga M. (Sofinowski) S. BS in Nursing, U. Md., 1971; M in Nursing, U. Wash., 1975. Clin. specialist United Gen. Hosp., Sedro Wolley, Wash., 1975-76; tchr., practitioner Rush-Presbyn. St. Luke's Med. Ctr., Chgo., 1976-79; v.p. Medicus Systems Corp., Evanston, Ill., 1978-79; healthcare cons. IBM Corp., Atlanta, 1989—. Contbr. chpt. to books and articles to profl. jours. Chmn. teen support group St. Philips Luth. Ch., Glenview, Ill., 1987-88; bd. dirs. Oak Park Townhome Assn., Atlanta, 1989. Mem. Am. Nurses Assn., Chgo. Coun. Fgn. Relations, Sigma Theta Tau. Office: IBM Corp Atlanta GA 30306

SIFF, MARLENE IDA, artist; b. N.Y.C., Sept. 20, 1936; d. Irving Louis and Dorothy Gertrude (Lahn) Marmer; m. Elliott Justin Siff, July 11, 1959; children: Bradford Evan, Brian Douglas. BA, Hunter Coll., 1957. Cert. elem. tchr., N.Y., N.J. Tchr. Stewart Manor (N.Y.) Sch. System, 1957-59, Teaneck (N.J.) Sch. System, 1959-60; free-lance interior designer Westport, Conn., 1966-70; designer indsl. plant Varo Inertial Products, Trumbull, Conn., 1970; corp. sec., treas. Belmar Corp., Westport, 1972—, also bd. dirs.; chmn. bd. Marlene Designs Inc., Westport, 1973-77; owner Marlene Siff Design Studio, Westport, 1978—; designer Signature Collections, J.P. Stevens & Co., Inc., 1974-78, J.C. Penney Co., N.Y.C., 1978, C.R. Gibson Co., Norwalk, Conn., 1980; aesthetic cons. ALCIDE Corp., Norwalk, 1980-88. One-woman shows include David Segal Gallery, N.Y.C., 1987, Conn. Pub. TV Gallery 24, Hartford, 1987, Paul Mellon Art Ctr. at Choate Rosemary Hall, Wallingford, Conn., 1989, Conn. Nat. Bank Hdqrs., Norwalk, 1990. Decorator ann. charity ball Easter Seal Home Svc., 1976; bd. dirs. United Jewish Appeal, Westport, 1982-86; mem. com. Levitt Pavillion Performing Arts, Westport, 1982-89. Recipient award Lower Conn. Mfrs. Assn., 1970. Mem. Kappa Pi. Home: 15 Broadview Rd Westport CT 06880

SIFFORD, MARILYN OAKLEY, human resources director; b. Roxboro, N.C., May 18, 1948; d. Osborne Hanley Jr. and Remell (Tingen) Oakley; m. C. Darrell Sifford, June 16, 1977; stepchildren: Jay, Grant. Student, Mars Hill Coll., 1966-67; BA In Psychol., E. Carolina U., 1970; MS, Am. U., 1983. Truant officer Raleigh City Schs., 1970-72; analyst test rsch. and devel. N.C. Employment Security Commn., Raleigh, 1972-74; personnel generalist Charlotte Observer and News, 1974-75, mgr. mkt. promotion, 1975-76; specialist tng. Colonial Penn. Ins. Co., Phila., 1976-77, supr. tng., 1977-80; cons. mgmt. Sun Co. Inc., Radnor, Pa., 1980-84; dir. human resource devel. Hosp. U. Penn., Phila., 1984-87; v.p., cons. CoreStates Fin. Corp., Phila., 1987-88; v.p. human resources and orgn. devel. IDS Fin. Svcs., Inc., Mpls., 1988—. Bd. dirs. Acad. House Condominium Coun., Phila. 1985-88. Mem. Human Resources Planning Group (sr. practitioner planning com. 1987-88), Orgn. Devel. Network. Home: 110 Bank St SE #202 Minneapolis MN 55414 Office: IDS Tower Human Resources & Orgn Devel Minneapolis MN 55440

SIGDA, MARY ELIZABETH, management consultant; b. Manchester, Conn., Jan. 1, 1960; d. Raymond R. and Evelyn Ann (Haber) S. AB, Smith Coll., 1981; MS in Pub. Policy, Harvard U., 1986. Caseworker Internat. Rescue Com., Bangkok, Thailand, 1981-83, sect. coordinator, 1983-84; cons. Arthur Young and Co., Washington, 1986-88; mgr. Ernst & Young, N.Y.C., 1988—. Mem. Am. Soc. for Pub. Adminstrn., Smith Coll. Alumnae Assn. Office: Ernst & Young 787 7th Ave New York NY 10019

SIGERSON, MARJORIE LORRAINE, librarian; b. Pitts., June 11, 1923; d. Roy Allen and Myrtle Mae (Bering) Parke; student Carnegie Inst. Tech., 1941-42, U. Pitts., 1942-43; m. David Kinley Sigerson, Apr. 9, 1943 (div. Dec. 1985); children—Diane Parke, David Kinley. Librarian, Mus. Arts and Scis., Daytona Beach, Fla., 1963—, trustee, 1978—, pres. Guild, 1978-79. Mem. com. Halifax Art Festival, 1963—; mem. council Garden Clubs of Halifax Dist., 1965-67; charter mem. Ormond Beach (Fla.) Meml. Hosp. Aux., 1967-76; pres. Street Sch. P.T.A., New City, N.Y., 1958-59; leader Girl Scouts U.S.A., 1956-58. Recipient award for disting. service, Mus. Arts and Scis., 1977, 79, 80, 81, 82. Presbyterian. Clubs: Harvard Dames (sec. 1946-47), Cherry Laurel Garden (pres. 1966-67), Oceanside Country (v.p. 9-Hole Golf Group). Home: 410 John Anderson Dr Ormond Beach FL 32176 Office: Mus Arts & Scis 1040 Museum Blvd Daytona Beach FL 32114

SIGLER, CHARLOTTE LEE LLEWEL, English and reading specialist; b. Frostburg, Md., Jan. 29, 1926; d. Thomas Price and Buelah (Willison) Llewellyn; m. Charles Harry Sigler, Oct. 12, 1947; children: Larry Allan, Dennis Wayne. BS, Frostburg State U., 1961, MEd, 1967; postgrad., W.Va. U., 1978-81. Cert. English and reading tchr., Md. Tchr. English, math., social studies and typing Allegany County Bd. Edn., Flintstone, Md., 1961-80; tchr. Alleghany County Bd. Edn., Mt. Savage, Md., 1981-83; English and secondary reading supr. Allegheny County Bd. Edn., Cumberland, Md., 1983—; tchr. English Mt. Savage High Sch., 1970-80; univ. supr., grad. asst. W.Va. U., Morgantown, 1980-81; supr. writing English curricula Allegany County Bd.Edn., Cumberland, 1983-88. Mem. network Women in Ednl. Leadership for Md. State Dept. Edn.; mem. Md. Vocat. Equity Program Network. Mem. AAUW (pres. 1976-80, editor newsletter 1978-80), Nat. Coun. Tchrs. of English, Assn. for Supervision and Curriculum Devel., Federated Garden Club (pres. 1977-79), Youghiogheny Mountain Lake Club, Phi Delta Kappa, Delta Kappa Gamma (prfes. 1982-84), Kappa Pi (life, pres. 1960-61). Home: 171 Washington St Frostburg MD 21532 Office: Allegany County Bd Edn 108 Washington St Cumberland MD 21502

SIGLER, KATHERINE, social planning professional; b. Fernandina Beach, Fla., Mar. 7, 1948; d. George J. and Elizabeth Wye (Pearson) Arfaras; m. Richard E. Sigler, Sept. 19, 1970; children: Richard E. Jr., Faith Elizabeth. Student, Fla. State U. Mem. catalog staff Sears Roebuck & Co., Tallahassee; mem. svc. staff Diner's Club, Miami, Fla.; dept. mgr. rsch. IRS, Atlanta; prin. Sigler Enterprises/Anchor Rental Party Prodns., Ft. Pierce, Fla. Mem. St. Lucie Rep. Exec. Com.; mem. County Arts Appropriation Com.; chmn. various civic groups. Mem. Advt. Fedn., St. Lucie Coun. Arts, Am. Bus. Women's Assn. (past pres.). Anglican. Office: 2835 S US #1 Fort Pierce FL 34982

SIGMAN, HELENE HANNAH, corporate communications executive; b. Chgo., Dec. 22, 1946; d. Edward Sigman and Helen Amanda (Hebert) Sigman Weil. AAS, Monticello Coll., 1967; BFA, U. Denver, 1969. Graphic designer Morgen Press, Hastings-on Hudson, N.Y., 1972, Murphey Printing Co., White Plains, N.Y., 1972-73; art dir. Cliggott Pub. Co., Greenwich, Conn., 1973-86; supr. corp. identity and visual communications Ameritech, Chgo., 1987—. Recipient award Soc. Illustrators, 1986; Silver and Gold awards Advt. Club of Westchester, 1985. Jewish. Office: Ameritech 30 S Wacker Chicago IL 60606

SIGMAN, JILL KAREN, Russian language specialist; b. Phila., Sept. 3, 1955; d. Lawrence and Jan (Morris) Rappaport; m. Lawrence M. Sigman, May 12, 1978; children: Robert Michael, Rachel Elise. BA, Brown U., 1977, MA, 1978, postgrad. in Slavic langs., 1987—. Social worker HIAS Coun., Phila., 1979-82, 86-87. Vol. Children's Theater, Montgomery County, Pa., 1988-89; counselor Intensive Care Unltd., Erdenheim, Pa., 1989-90. Solomon grantee Brown U., 1977-78, Univ. fellow, 1976-77. Mem. MLA, Parents Resource Assn., AAUW (program v.p. Montgomery County 1989-90, project dir. Career Shadowing Jenkintown, Pa. 1988-89), Phi Beta Kappa. Home: 1199 George Rd Meadowbrook PA 19046

SIGMON, ANNE ELIZABETH, marketing professional; b. Roanoke, Va., May 12, 1953; d. William E. and Betty (Hale) S. ABJ magna cum laude, U. Ga., 1974; MBA, Golden Gate U., 1984. Writer Publs. South, Atlanta, 1973-74, Univ. System Ga., Atlanta, 1974-75; with pub. relations dept. Bechtel Group, Inc., San Francisco, 1975-79, editor, 1979-81, mgr. employee communications, 1981-84, mgr. communications, 1985-87; mgr. pub. relations Bechtel Petroleum, Inc., Houston, 1984-85; mgr. mktg. Bechtel Nat., Inc., San Francisco, 1987-89; mgr. mktg. and bus. devel. Bechtel Environ., Inc., San Francisco, 1989—; instr. profl. seminars, 1980—. Recipient profl. achievement awards Internat. Assn. Bus. Communicators, profl. achievement awards Film and TV Festival N.Y.C. Mem. Am. Mktg. Assn., Pub. Relations Soc. Am. (accredited), The Planning Forum, Phi Beta Kappa, Kappa Tau Alpha. Office: Bechtel Nat Inc PO Box 3965 San Francisco CA 94119

SIGNOR, SHARON SMITH, educator; b. Kinderhook, N.Y., Mar. 17, 1943; d. Lyman Theodore and Eva May (Wormwood) Smith; m. Gene Daniel Signor, July 20, 1968; children: Aaron Gene, Jason Earl (twins). AAS, SUNY, Farmingdale, 1963; BS, SUNY, Cortland, 1983, MS in Edn., 1988. Cert. dental hygiene, nursery, and k-6 tchr., N.Y. Dental hygienist Dr. Raymond Ripp, DDS, Garden City, N.Y., 1963-65; tchr. dental hygiene Brentwood Pub. Schs., 1965-68; dental hygienist Drs. A. Scholnik and A. Hirschman, Brentwood, 1967-68; pub. health dental hygienist, supr. dental hygiene Onondaga County Health Dept., Syracuse, N.Y., 1968-70; dental hygienist Opportunities for Cortland County (N.Y.), Inc., 1970, Joseph J. Speicher, DDS, Cortland, 1970-71; substitute tchr. Cortland Madison Bd. of Coop. Ednl. Svcs., 1978; computer aide SUNY, Cortland, 1981-82; substitute tchr. various schs., N.Y., 1983-84; reading tchr. asst. Groton (N.Y.) Elem. Sch., 1984-85, kindergarten tchr., 1985—. Sunday sch. tchr. United Presbyn. Ch., Cortland, deacon, 1976-78; active Com. on Spl. Edn., Homer Cen. Schs., N.Y., 1976-78; mem. Homer-Scool Community Assn., Homer, 1975-78; active Seven Valley Reading Coun. Mem. Groton Faculty Assn. (negotiation com. 1987—), NEA, NEA of N.Y., Twins Mothers Club (chmn. 1972-73), Music Boosters (chmn. membership 1988—). Republican. Home: 3835 Highland Rd Cortland NY 13045 Office: Groton Elem Sch Elm St Groton NY 13073

SIGNORELLI, SUZANN MARIE, publications executive, director; b. Union City, N.J., Sept. 3, 1960; d. Frank Thomas and Rosemary R. (Fabiano) S. Student, Rutgers U., 1978-80; BA in English cum laude, Montclair State Coll., 1983. Editor Bowker Pub. Co., N.Y.C., 1978-80; freelance designer Fords, N.J., 1979-82; graphic designer Montclair State Coll., Upper Montclair, N.J., 1980-82; art dir. AT&T Ctr. for Systems Edn., Piscataway, N.J., 1982-83, instructional designer, 1983-85; sr. project mgr. edn. dept. IEEE, Piscataway, 1985-87; sr. tech. mgr. AGS, N.J. Techs., Clark, 1987-88; br. mgr. AGS Publs. Devel. Group, Ft. Lee, N.J., 1988; dir. AGS Publs. and Tng. Group, N.Y.C., 1988—. Mem. Am. Soc. Engring. Edn., Soc. Applied Learning Technology, IEEE, ASTD, Montclair State Coll. Alumni Assn. Office: AGS Pub and Tng Group 71 Fifth Ave New York NY 10003

SIH, GRACE JENNY, fashion designer; b. Bethlehem, Pa., July 2, 1963; d. George Charles and Jennice (Jen) Sih. BA in Mgmt., Moravian Coll., Bethlehem, 1985; postgrad., Lehigh U., 1985-86; AS in Fashion Design, Fashion Inst. Tech., N.Y.C., 1988; postgrad., Parsons Sch. Design, N.Y.C., 1989—. Head tennis profl. Camp Lindenmere, Henryville, Pa., 1982; with pers. dept. 1st Valley Bank, Bethlehem, 1983-84; tennis instr. Moravian Greyhound Tennis Camp, Bethlehem, 1986; asst. mgr. Plumm's, Bethlehem, 1986-87; office mgr. Comptek Corp., Allentown, Pa., 1983-87; visual merchandiser Hess's, Allentown, 1987; asst. designer Texwood Internat., N.Y.C., 1988; sales asst. Giorgio Armani, N.Y.C., 1988-89; assoc. designer Liz Claiborne Inc., N.Y.C., 1989—; with CAD dept. Microdynamics, Dallas, 1989. Republican. Roman Catholic. Home: 330 E 38th St Apt 40M New York NY 10016 Office: Liz Claiborne Dresses 1441 Broadway 16th Fl New York NY 10018

SIKORSKI, BARBARA, utilization review professional; b. Norwich, N.Y., Mar. 13, 1955; d. Harrison R. and Marie E. (Davis) Troxell; m. David Joel Sikorski, Aug. 30, 1986; children: Robert, Heather. Cert. in mgmt., Broome Community Coll., 1989. Grantsman So. Tier Found Med. Care, Binghamton, N.Y.; utilization rev. coord. Broome County Med. Soc., Binghamton; utilization rev. adminstr. Hinchliff Internat., Ithaca, N.Y.; presenter workshops. Mem. Oxford Revitalization Project, Inc. Mem. NAFE, Mensa, Am. Assn. Med. Assts.

SIKORSKI, LORENA LOUISE, educator; b. Sarasota, Fla., Nov. 28, 1951; d.Raymond J. and M. Louise (Fatjo) S. BA, Calif. State U., Fullerton, 1973, MS, 1984. Cert. educator. Tchr. pub. schs., Garden Grove, Calif., 1974—; adminstr., dir. Gay and Lesbian Educators So. Calif., Inc., Orange County, 1985—; propr. Sikorski Music Studio, Huntington Beach, Calif., 1974—. Composer: Just to Know Him, 1975, Happiest Christmas Ever, 1975. co-author: Invisible Minority, 1988. Conductor Oriental Chamber Orchestra, Bellflower, Calif., 1988; dir. Pacific Coast Freedom Band, Long Beach, Calif., 1990. Recipient Musicianship award Gt. Am. Yankee Freedom Band L.A., 1986, Gold Starr award, Gay and Lesbian Educators So. Calif., 1989, Community Svc. award Calif. Assembly, 1989. NEA. Democrat. Office: PO Box 6266 Garden Grove CA 92645

SILAGI, BARBARA WEIBLER, corporate secretary-treasurer; b. Chgo., June 26, 1930; d. Carleton Thomas and Catherine Josephine (Wolph) Weibler; m. Joseph Edward Sturgulewski (Sturgus), Feb. 12, 1953 (div. Aug. 1954); 1 child, Mariann Catherine; m. John Louis Silagi, Jr., July 2, 1960 (div. July 1968). BM in Edn., Northwestern U., 1958; MS in Edn., No. Ill. U., 1965. Cert. K-14 supervisory teaching, spl. edn. tchr., airline transport pilot, FAA dispatcher. Elem. sch. tchr. St. Mary's Sch., Chgo., 1947-49, Kingman, Ariz., 1949-52; legal sec. Judge Edward J. Mahoney, Quincy, Ill., 1954-55; elem. sch. tchr. C.M. Bardwell Sch., Aurora, Ill., 1955-76; flight instr. flight schs. Chgo., Aurora and Frankfort, Ill., Clinton, Iowa, 1960-77; aircraft dispatcher Transcontinental Airlines, Zantop Internat. Airlines, Ypsilanti, Mich., 1977-81; airline pilot Mannion Air Charter, Ypsilanti, 1977-80; head night auditor Howard Johnson, Quality Inn, Travelodge, BestWestern, others, Ocala, Fla., Silver Springs, Fla., 1983-87; sec.-treas. Diamond Design Svcs., Inc., Ocklawaha, Fla., 1985—. Author: Dispatch Training, 1989; editor tng. manuals, 1977-85. Violist Chgo. Suburban Symphony, Naperville, Ill., 1956-60; contralto Palestrina A cappella Choir, Aurora, Ill., 1956-60; life mem. Ill. PTA, Aurora, 1974—. Recipient 1st place Suburban Aviation Assn., Chgo., 1975, 5th place Illi-Nines Air Derby, Chgo., Moline, Ill., 1973, 2d place Leg prize Powder Puff Derby, McLean to Lincoln, Nebr., 1971; Eckstein scholar Northwestern U., 1952. Mem. AAUW (life), NEA (life), Ill. Edn. Assn., Ninety-Nines Internat., Illi-Nines Air Derby (handicap chmn. 1972-76, air marking chmn. Chgo. chpt. 1972-76, corr. sec. Chgo. chpt. 1976-77, 1st place 1972-78, 5th place 1973), Aircraft Owners and Pilots Assn., Model Engine Collectors Assn., Am. Orchid Soc., Ocala Orchid Soc. (sec.), Suburban Aviation Assn., Fla. Aero Club (v.p., sec.-treas. Ocala chpt. 1989—), Pi Lambda Theta (charter, life, rsch. chmn. Beta Delta chpt. DeKalb, Ill. 1962-63). Roman Catholic. Home: Rte 2 Box 1837-A Ocklawaha FL 32179-8757 Office: Diamond Design Svcs Inc PO Box 186 Ocklawaha FL 32179-0186

SILBERBERG-PEIRCE, SUSAN R., art history educator; b. Santa Monica, Calif., Aug. 1, 1949; d. Alfred and Ruth Hanna (Zingelbach) Silberberg; m. Roger Jameson Peirce. BA, U. Calif., 1971, MA, 1976, PhD., 1980. Cert. Art Historian, Calif. Lectr. L.A. County Mus. Art, 1977; lectr. art history Calif. State U., Northridge, 1979-81, U. Calif., Irvine, 1980-81; asst. prof. art history No. Ariz. U., Flagstaff, 1981-86; cons. The Getty Ctr. for History of Art and the Humanities Photo Archive, Santa Monica, Calif., 1987-88; lectr. Colo. State U., Ft. Collins, 1987, asst. prof. art history, 1988—; cons. reader Jour. Rocky Mountain Medieval and Renaissance Assn., 1982-86; organizer, moderator Politics of Art: A Women's Perspective—Colloquium, Flagstaff, 1984; vis. asst. prof. U. Calif., 1988; lectr. in field. Photographer: Photograph Annual, Acoma Stairs (finalist), Phantom Ranch Sunrise 1988 (finalist), Women in Photography Internat. Exhbn., Mountain West Biennial Photography Exhbn.; contbr. articles to profl. jours. Mem. adv. bd. Ariz. Ctr. for Medieval and Renaissance Studies, Tempe, 1983-86. Recipient NEH stipend, 1982; Dickson fellow UCLA, 1977-80; Regents grantee UCLA, 1977, numerous other grants and fellowships. Mem. Coll. Art Assn., Women in Photography, Archaeol. Inst. Am., Art Historians of So. Calif. Home: Box 2740 South Star Rte Lyons CO 80540

SILBERSTEIN, LYNN, rehabilitation company executive; b. N.Y.C., Feb. 26, 1951; d. Jesse Silberstein and Nancy (Cohen) Sawyer. BA, Antioch Coll., 1973. Saleswoman Dunhill Greater Phila., 1974-76, Meloy Labs., Phila., 1976-79, Physio Control, Phila., 1979-80, Datamedix, Phila., 1980-83; sr. v.p. C.P. Rehab. Corp. Midlantic, Phila., 1983-86; sr. v.p. sales and mktg., pres. C.P. Rehab. Corp., N.Y.C., 1986-87; pres. The Cardiac Rehab. Co., Phila., 1987—. Mem. Am. Assn. Cardiovascular and Pulmonary Rehab., Med. Group Mgmt. Assn., Am. Assn. Healthcare Cons. Jewish. Office: The Cardiac Rehab Co 38 Cabot Dr Wayne PA 19087

SILBERT, JACQUELINE, service company executive, accountant; b. Bklyn., Dec. 15, 1921; d. Leon and Mary Gittell; children—Laurence, Amy Silbert Block. B.A. in Edn. with honors, Hunter Coll., 1942. Co-founder MacClean Service Co. Inc., Bellerose, N.Y., 1953, pres., chief exec. officer, 1982—; dir. Liberty Nat. Bank, Conn. Editor: Hunter Coll. Alumni Newspaper, 1970-72. Contbr. articles to real estate publications. Mem. R.I. State Bd. Edn., 1950-52; bd. dirs., v.p. The Lighthouse, Queens, N.Y., 1970-74, chmn. fund raising, 1971-72; pres., bd. dirs. St. John's U. Aux., 1970—, co-chmn. fund raising, 1976—; bd. dirs. Walter Kaner's Childrens Fund, 1982—, Forest Hills Jewish Ctr. Aux., 1972-74. Named Woman of Yr., Nat. Conf. Christians & Jews, 1975; Pres. medal St. John's U., 1978. Mem. Bldg. Service Contractor's Assn., Internat. Sanitary Supply Assn., Service Employer's Assn. Club: Old Westbury Hebrew Congregation Bridge. Avocation: growing trees. Office: MacClean Service Co Inc PO Box 78 Bellerose NY 11426

SILBURN, ELAINE GWENDOLYN, banker; b. Denver, June 3, 1937; d. Russell Edwin and Genevieve (Johnson) Seay; m. David L. Silburn, June 16, 1957; children: Carla Anne, James Russell. A in Bus. Adminstrn., U. Denver, 1957; student Northwestern U., 1960, U. Okla., 1981. Trust officer United Bank of Denver, 1957-65; personal banker, personal banking officer, asst. v.p., v.p. United Bank of Skyline, Denver, 1978-83, sr. v.p., 1983-89, dir., 1984-89; v.p. exec. banking United Bank of Denver, 1989—; treas. Historic Denver, Inc., bd. dirs., 1988—. Vol. Denver Pub. Schs., alumni fund campaign U. Denver, Channel 6 Pub. TV Auction, Am. Cancer Soc., mem. major gifts fund com. Denver Symphony Orch., 1984-87; adv. bd. Mile High United Way, 1985; del. Rep. county and state assemblies. Recipient Women of Achievement award YWCA, 1985, 87. Mem. Nat. Assn. Bank Women, Mental Health Assn. Colo. (fin. devel. com.), Leadership Denver Assn., Denver C. of C., Cultural Affairs Task Force, Gamma Phi Beta, Sweet Adelines Club (High Country chpt., pres. 1977). Episcopalian. Home: 3119 S Akron Ct Denver CO 80231 Office: United Bank of Denver Exec Banking Dept 1700 Broadway Denver CO 80274

SILEO, ANN PFEIFFER, early intervention specialist; b. Woodbridge, N.J., June 16, 1937; d. Edward Lockwood and Irene Ann (Beatty) Pfeiffer; m. Thomas William Sileo, June 21, 1964; children: Nancy, Jane, Carrie. BA, Ladycliff Coll., 1961; MA, U. No. Colo., 1982. Tchr. Woodbridge Twp. Bd. Edn., 1961-64, Jefferson County Community Ctr. Found., Arvada, Colo., 1983-84, Anchorage Sch. Dist., 1984-85; early intervention specialist Programs for Infants and Children, Anchorage, 1985—. mem. Coun. for Exceptional Children (treas. Anchorage chpt. 1985—, div. for early childhood), Kappa Delta Pi. Home: 4230 C Woronzof Dr Anchorage AK 99517

SILINS, ASTRIDA I., anesthesiologist; b. Talsi, Latvia, July 9, 1928; came to U.S. 1951; d. Wilhelm and Zigrida (Skrebers) Grikmanis; m. V. Raymond Silins, Mar. 26, 1926; 1 child, Karen Ingrid. Cand.med., Baltic U., Hamburg, W. Ger., 1949; MD, U. Kiel, W. Ger., 1955. Diplomate Am. Bd. Anesthesiology. Resident in anesthesiology Presbyn.-St. Luke's Hosp., Chgo., 1960-61; asst. attending anesthesiologist Presbyn.-St. Luke's Hosp., 1962-67; assoc. attending anesthesiology Highland Park (Ill.) Hosp., 1967-75, Presbyn. St. Luke's Hosp., 1975—; asst. prof. anesthesiology Rush Med. Coll., Chgo., 1975—. Mem. Am. Cardiovascular Anesthesiologists Soc. Republican. Lutheran. Home: 277 Hibbard Rd Winnetka IL 60093 Office: Univ Anesthesiologists 1753 W Congress Chicago IL 60612

SILINSH, JOAN, publishing executive; b. Mexico City, Nov. 13, 1937; came to U.S., 1948, naturalized; d. Alson Byron and Carmen Elena (Ramos) Keeler; m. John Silinsh, May 15, 1958 (div. 1979). Student U. Houston, 1955-58; BA, Pace U., 1969. Asst. promotion mgr. Chem. Engring. Mag., N.Y.C., 1967-69, sales services mgr., 1969-76; assoc. mgr. communications McGraw-Hill Publs. Co., N.Y.C., 1976-79, mgr. communications, 1979-80, dir. mktg. communications, 1984-87, exec. dir. mktg. svcs. McGraw-Hill Info. Svcs., 1987—; dist. mgr. Internat. Mgmt. Mag., N.Y.C., 1980-84; guest lectr. internat. advt. and promotion Pace U., N.Y.C., 1981-82. Contbr. articles to profl. jours. Mem. N.Y. Bus. Press Editors (2d v.p. 1978-79, 1st v.p. 1980-81), Bus./Profl. Advt. Assn. (dir. 1985-88, v.p. 1988-89, pres., 1989—, editor N.Y. chpt. Intelligencer newsletter 1985-86), Am. Mktg. Assn., N.Y. Women Communications, Assn. Bus. Publs. (vice chmn. promotion). Avocations: photography, gourmet cooking, travel. Office: McGraw-Hill Info Svcs Co 1221 Sixth Ave 18th Fl New York NY 10020

SILLIMAN, ELAINE JOYCE RUBENSTEIN, speech and language pathologist, educator; b. Buffalo, June 16, 1938; d. Joseph and Dorothy Fineberg Rubenstein; m. Paul Harris Silliman, Jan. 28, 1961; children: Scott L., Dawn R. BS, Syracuse U., 1960; PhD (NDEA fellow), CUNY, 1976.Speech-lang. clinician Bronx Mcpl. Hosp. Ctr., 1960-62; supr. speech-lang. svcs. USPHS community health project Albert Einstein Coll. Medicine, Bronx, 1966-68; clin. supr. Ctr. for Communication Disorders, Hunter Coll., CUNY, 1973-76, prof. Sch. Health Scis., 1976-87, dir. communication scis. program, 1981-84, 85-87, acting dean, 1984-85; doctoral faculty CUNY program speech and hearing scis., 1984-87; prof., chair Dept. Communication Scis. & Disorders U. South Fla., 1987—. Mem. editorial bd. Lang., Speech and Hearing Svcs. in Schs., 1983—; contbr. articles to profl. jours and books. Fellow Am. Speech-Lang.-Hearing Assn. (cert. clin. competence); mem. N.Y. Acad. Scis., N.Y. State Speech-Lang.-Hearing Assn. (pres. 1982-84), Fla. Speech-Lang.-Hearing Assn., Soc. Research in Child Devel., Orton Dyslexia Soc. Office: U South Fla Dept Communication Scis & Disorders BEH 255 Tampa FL 33620

SILLS, BEVERLY (MRS. PETER B. GREENOUGH), opera company director, coloratura soprano; b. Bklyn., May 25, 1929; d. Morris and Sonia (Bahn) Silverman; m. Peter B. Greenough, 1956; children: Meredith, Peter B.; stepchildren: Lindley, Nancy, Diana. Grad. pub. schs.; student voice, Estelle Leibling; student piano, Paolo Gallico; student stagecraft, Desire Defrere; hon. doctorates, Harvard U., NYU, New Eng. Conservatory, Temple U. Gen. dir. N.Y.C. Opera, 1979-1989; pres. N.Y.C. Opera Bd., 1989—. Radio debut as Bubbles Silverman on Uncle Bob'sRainbow House, 1932; appeared on Major Bowes Capitol Family Hour, 1934-41, on Our Gal Sunday; toured with Shubert Tours, Charles Wagner Opera Co., 1950, 51; operatic debut Phila. Civic Opera, 1947; debut, N.Y.C. Opera Co. as Rosalinda in Die Fledermaus, 1955; debut San Francisco Opera, 1953; debut La Scala, Milan as Pamira in Siege of Corinth, 1969, Royal Opera, Covent Garden in Lucia di Lammermoor, London, 1971, Met. Opera, N.Y.C., 1975, Vienna State Opera, 1967, Teatro Fenice in La Traviata, Venice; appeared Teatro Colon, Buenos Aires; recital debut Paris, 1971, London Symphony Orch., 1971; appeared throughout U.S., Europe, S. Am. including Boston Symphony, Tanglewood Festival, 1968, 69, Robin Hood Dell, Phila., 1969; title roles in: Don Pasquale, Norma, Manon, Louise, Tales of Hoffmann, Daughter of the Regiment, The Magic Flute; ret. from opera and concert stage, 1980; numerous TV spls; author: Bubbles-A Self-Portrait, 1976, autobiography Beverly, 1987. Nat. chmn. March of Dimes' Mothers' March on Birth Defects; chmn. bd. Nat. Opera Inst.; cons. to council Nat. Endowment for the Arts; bd. dirs. N.Y.C. Opera. Recipient Handel medallion, 1973, Pearl S. Buck Women's award, 1979, Emmy award for Profiles in Music, 1976, Emmy award for Lifestyles with Beverly Sills, 1978, Medal of Freedom, 1980. Office: NYC Opera NY State Theater Lincoln Ctr New York NY 10023*

SILLS, SALLIE ALEXANDER, elementary educator; b. Ocala, Fla., Feb. 16, 1916; d. Joe and Marie (Jefferson) Alexander; m. Mell Sills, Sept. 16, 1936 (dec. 1980). AA, Bethune Cookman Coll., 1936, BS, 1948. Elem. tchr. Marion County Sch. Systems, 1936-46, elem. prin., 1938-47; tchr. 1st grade Gadsden County Schs., Quincy, Fla., 26 years. Contbr. poetry to anthologies. Mem. Vol. Tchrs. Group, Ocala, Fla., 1977—; tchr. 1st aid Am. Red. Cross, Quincy, 1964-66; dir. St. John Rhythm Band, Quincy, 1959-77; chmn. program com. St. John Bapt. Ch., Ocala, 1978-79, Mt. Moriah Bapt. Ch., Quincy, 1977-79; chmn. welfare and health Sojourner Truth Club, Ocala, 1988—. Mem. Marion County Ret. Tchrs. Assn. (Area 3 leader 1977—), Am. Assn. Ret. Persons, Nat. Ret. Tchrs. Assn., Nat. Assn. for Female Execs., Am. Legion. Democrat. Baptist. Home: 815 W Silver Springs Pl Ocala FL 32675

SILOS, IRENE M., raw material planner; b. Montclair, N.J., June 20, 1963; d. George J. and Clementina (Lluria) S. Student, Rutgers Coll. Engring., 1981-83, Univ. Coll. Rutgers, 1985—. Mgr. Elm-Tre Pool & Tennis Club, West Caldwell, N.J., 1980-82; draftsperson Gambal & Assocs., West Caldwell, 1982; purchasing sec. Cosmair Inc., Piscataway, N.J., 1984; receiving coordinator Cosmair Inc., Piscataway, 1984-85; systems coordinator Cosmair Inc. (L'Oreal Div.), Somerset, N.J., 1985-87; personal computer trainer Cosmair Inc. (L'Oreal Div.), Somerset, 1987, accts. payable coordinator, 1987-88, raw material planner, 1988-89, warehouse supr., 1989—. Assoc. mem. Nat. Wildlife Fedn., 1984—, Stony Brook-Millstone Watershed Assn., 1988—. Mem. NAFE, Am. Prodn. & Inventory Control Soc. Home: 904 Renate Dr #4 Somerville NJ 08876 Office: L'Oreal Hair Care Div 222 Terminal Ave Clark NJ 07066

SILSBY, LUCILLE LINDA, infosystems specialist; b. Saco, Maine, Aug. 22, 1953; d. Joseph Ronald and Doris Yvonne (Geoffroy) Boucher; m. Michael Joseph Silsby, Mar. 18, 1972; 1 child, Joseph Michael. Rater, coder Liberty Mut. Ins. Co., Portsmouth, N.H., 1972-73, tech. asst., 1973-80, programmer, 1980-85, systems analyst, 1985-89, systems mgr., 1989—; systems mgr. CB Meadowbrook, York, Maine, 1989—. Mem. choir St. Christopher's Ch., York. Mem. Million Dollar Club. Democrat. Roman Catholic. Office: CB Meadowbrook Rt 1 York ME 03909

SILVA, DONNA STEEDLE, publishing executive; b. Riverside, N.J., Dec. 12, 1957; d. William Edward and Shirley Elaine (Klingler) Steedle; m. Eldon Joseph Silva, Nov. 25, 1988. Student, Rider Coll., 1975-77. Cashier and office clerk Pantry-Pride Grocery Stores, Inc., Delran, N.J., 1975-79; account rep. P.F. Collier, Inc., Delran, N.J., 1979-81, customer svc. supr., 1981, asst. v.p. of ops., nat. sales svc. ctr., 1982-83, payroll dept. mgr., nat. sales svc. ctr., 1983-85, regional sales mgr., ednl. svcs. div., 1985-86, dir. adminstrn., ednl. svcs. div., 1986-88, v.p. adminstrn., ednl. svcs. div., 1988—; dir. ops. The New Grolier Interstate, Inc., White Plains, N.Y., 1981-82. Vol. Contemporary Arts Ctr., New Orleans, 1985—. Mem. NAFE. Republican. Roman Catholic. Office: PF Collier Inc 4741 Sanford Metairie LA 70006

SILVA, ELIZABETH TALBOT, librarian; b. Frankfurt, Germany, Nov. 25, 1947; came to U.S., 1948; d. Max Verne and Minerva Eugenia (Mann) Talbot; m. George C. Tomlinson, Dec. 23, 1969 (div. Jan. 1973); m. Richard Alwyn Silva, May 2, 1987; 1 stepchild, Kelly Silva; 1 child, Aimee Elizabeth. BA/Psychology, Sociology, San Diego State U., 1969; M in Libr. Information, U. Calif., Berkeley, 1974. Young adult libr. specialist Richmond (Calif.) Pub. Libr., 1973-76, Dublin (Calif.) Libr., Alameda County, 1976-78, Fremont (Calif.) Main Libr., 1978-79; branch mgr. Newark (Calif.) Libr., 1979-85; local support project dir. Alameda County Libr., Hawyward, Calif., 1985-87; community rels. coordinator Alameda County Libr., Fremont, 1987—; co-founder Coalition to Restore Quality Libr. Svc., Oakland, Calif., 1978-83. Compiler Sr. Citizen Discount Directory, 1979. Active pub. affairs leadership tng. for women, Coro Found., Oakland, 1982. Nominee for Vol. of Yr., City of Newark, 1983. Mem. Am. Libr. Assn. (council mem. 1979-83, John Cotton Dana award 1987), Calif. Libr. Assn. (co-chmn. fundraising chpt.), Toastmasters Internat. (v.p. 1980-83) Jaycees (v.p. 1981-82), Newark C. of C. Democrat. Home: 2125 Oak Creek Pl Hayward CA 94541 Office: Alameda County Libr Community Relations 2450 Stevenson Blvd Fremont CA 94538-2326

SILVA, OMEGA LOGAN, physician; b. Washington, Dec. 14, 1936; d. Louis Jasper and Ruth (Dickerson) Logan; m. C. Francis A. Silva, Oct. 25, 1958 (div. 1981); 1 child, Frances Cecile; m. Harold Bryant Webb, Nov. 28, 1982. Grad., Howard U., Washington, 1958, MD, 1967. Bio-chemist NIH, Bethesda, Md., 1958-63; asst. chief endocrinology Vets. Affairs Med. Ctr., Washington, 1967—; assoc. prof. George Washington U., Washington, 1975—; prof. Howard U., Washington, 1977—. Author: (with others) Endocrinology, 1990; contbr. articles to profl. jours. Charter mem. Nat. Mus. of Women in the Arts, Washington, 1986; health cons. River Pk. Mutual Homes, Inc., Washington, 1987; vol. Career Day, Chillum Elem. Sch., Career Week, George Washington Univ., Washington, 1988. Fellow ACP (Best Sci. Presentation award 1974); mem. Am. Chem. Soc., Am. Med. Women's Assn. (Br. I v.p. 1986-87, pres. 1987-88, legis. chair anti-smoking task force 1989—), Howard U. Med. Alumni (pres. 1983-88), Omega Alpha. Office: Veterans Affairs Med Ctr 50 Irving St N W Washington DC 20422

SILVAS, SHARON JUDY, magazine publisher, editor; b. Portland, Oreg., Mar. 21, 1944; d. Milton Frank and Sylvia June (Rosencrantz) Harbush; divorced; children: Geoffrey Leventhal, Jonathan Leventhal, Daniel Leventhal. Student, UCLA, 1964-67, Santa Monica City Coll., 1968; BA in Communications, U. Colo., 1977. Staff asst. U.S. Congressman Timothy E. Wirth, Lakewood, Colo., 1975-78; exec. dir., founder Colo. Ctr. for Women and Work, Denver, 1979-83; v.p., owner Cuarón, Silvas & Assocs., Denver, 1983-85; pres., owner SS Promotions, Inc., Denver, 1986-87; assoc. dir. Passages, Inc., Denver, 1987-88; pub., editor Colo. Woman News, Denver, 1988—; cons. mktg. stategy, publ. rels., advt., women's issues, promotion campaigns to women and minority-owned small bus.; speaker, trainer orgns., major agys., corps.; former staff mem. Community Coll. Denver in Aurora; mem. Gov.'s procurement com. Women's Econ. Devel. Commn., 1988—. Editor mag. sect. Col. Womanscene, 1970-80 ; producer Nat. Hispanic Speakers Directory, Hispanic Yellow Pages; author: (poems) Metamorphosis, 1983; contbr. articles to local and nat. publs. Participant Golda Meir House Project. Recipient Salute! award Big Sisters Colo., Denver, 1986. Mem. Colo. Women's C. of C. (founder, v.p. 1988—), Coun. on Working Women (exec. dir. 1979-83, Women at Work awards 1983, 85), Women in Communications (Matrix Byliner award). Democrat. Jewish. Office: Colo Woman News PO Box 16763 Denver CO 80216

SILVER, ADELE ZEIDMAN, museum editor; b. Birmingham, Ala., Feb. 16, 1932; d. Eugene Morris and Ida L. (Fisher) Zeidman; m. Daniel Jeremy Silver, July 19, 1956; children: Jonathan M., Michael L., Sarah J. BA, Goucher Coll., 1953. Editorial asst. Sunday dept. N.Y. Times, 1954-56; freelance editor, book reviewer, 1963-70; columnist editorial pages The Plain Dealer, Cleve., 1968-74, book reviewer, 1968—; dep. project dir., editor Council on Museums and Edn. in the Visual Arts, N.Y.C., Cleve., 1972-76; arts editor, critic Sta. WKYC-TV, Cleve., 1975-79; editor edn. publs. Cleve. Mus. Art, 1971-82, head pub. info. dept., 1982—; mem. Artable, N.Y.C., 1980; cons. Albright-Knox Art Gallery, Buffalo, 1978-79, Mpls. Inst. Arts, 1981. co-author, co-editor: The Art Museum As An Educator, 1978. Trustee Cleve. Opera, 1974-86, Cleve. Internat. Film Festival, 1975—. Mem. Am. Assn. Mus. Internat. Council. Mus., Arttable. Democrat. Jewish. Office: Cleveland Mus Art 11150 East Blvd Cleveland OH 44106

SILVER, BELLA WOLFSON, day care center executive; b. N.Y.C., Mar. 10, 1937; d. David Michael and Edith (Bienenstock) Wolfson; BS, Adelphi U., 1958; postgrad. Bank St. Coll., 1958-59, Nova U.; m. Kenneth A. Silver, Oct. 19, 1958; children: James, Daniel. Kindergarten tchr., N.Y.C., 1958, Madison (Wis.) Pub. Schs., 1959-61, White Fish Bay (Wis.) Public Schs., 1961-65; nursery sch. tchr., Deerfield, Ill., 1975-77; substitute tchr. Deerfield Pub. Schs., 1975-77; founder., dir., pres. Deerfield Day Care Ctr., 1978—; corp. cons. Day Care/Child Care Svcs., 1983—; pub. speaker on child care to North Shore high schs., 1984. Mem. Deerfield Caucus; active Cub Scouts, Deerfield, Outstanding Service award 1973-77; mem. exec. bd. Jewish United Fund; sec. Parents-Tchrs. Orgn. Recipient award Bahais of Deerfield, 1981; teaching cert., Wis., Ill.; lic. tchr., N.Y.C. Mem. AAUW, Assn. Childhood Edn. Internat., Nat. Assn. Edn. Young Children, Chgo. Assn. Edn. Young Children, Nat. Assn. Female Execs., Deerfield C. of C., Phi Sigma Sigma (Pyramid award 1965). Jewish. Home: 309 Willow Ave Deerfield IL 60015 Office: 445 Pine St Deerfield IL 60015

SILVER, HELENE MARCIA, health educator, speaker, author; b. Oakland, Calif., Apr. 2, 1947; d. Sam and Shirley Betty (Kerns) S. BA, UCLA, 1968; postgrad., San Francisco State Coll., 1970-72, Holistic Life U., 1978-79, Antioch U., 1979-80. Tchr. pub. schs. Oakland, 1968-76; nutritional counselor Mill Valley, Calif., 1976—; creator Women's Health Intensive, Mill Valley, 1977-79; project dir. nutrition edn. project Calif. Dept. Edn., San Rafael, Calif., 1979-80; founder, dir. Inner Beauty Inst., Sausalito, Calif., 1980—; health edn. cons., 1976—; founder Inner Beauty Mountain Retreat, 1987—; mem. Health Task Force in Marin County, 1978-80. Author: Inner Beauty/Outer Beauty, The Body Smart System, Creator of Body Smart System Nutritional Kit. Mem. AAUW, Soc. Nutrition Edn., Nat. Health Fedn. Office: 3A Gate 5 Rd Sausalito CA 94965

SILVER, IDORA, risk management consultant, environmentalist; b. Oakland, Calif., Nov. 19, 1948; d. Sam and Sylvia Kronick; m. John J. Silver, July 11, 1971 (div. June 1980); 1 child, John J. Jr. BA, U. Nev., 1970, MA, 1987. CPCU. Comml. casualty underwriter Fireman's Fund Ins. Co., Reno, 1975-77; mgr. Surplus Lines Assocs. Nev., Reno, 1977-78; dir. adminstrn. NML Ins. Co., Reno, 1978-85; owner, profl. liability cons. Idora Silver & Assocs, Reno, 1985—; exec. dir. Western Nev. Clean Communities, Inc., Reno, 1989—; mem. advisory com. Washoe County Dist. Health Dept. Solid Waste, Reno. Contbr. articles to profl. jours. Mem. Am. Soc. Tng. and Devel., Nat. Speakers Assn., Sierra Nev. chpt. CPCU (pres. 1984-86), Greenbelt Preservation Com., Leadership Reno Alumni Assn. Office: Profl Liability Cons Inc 1135 Terminal Way Ste 107 Reno NV 89502

SILVER, JACQUELINE, advertising agency executive. Formerly sr. v.p. and dir. strategic planning & rsch. Needham Harper & Steers; with Backer Spielvogel Bates, N.Y.C., 1980-90, exec. v.p., dir. rsch. svcs. & strategic planning. Office: Backer Spielvogel Bates Worldwide Inc 405 Lexington Ave New York NY 10174*

SILVER, JEAN, state legislator, accountant; b. Spokane, Wash., July 25, 1926; d. Harlow Eugene and Helen Grace (Merten) Merrill; m. Charles Wesley Silver; children: Douglas W., Mitchell C., Kipp E. BBA, Eastern Wash. U., 1975; postgrad., U. Wash., 1980-87. CPA, Wash. Prin. Jean Silver Acctg. Svc., Spokane, 1950—; acct. Coopers & Lybrand, Spokane, 1976-80; state legislator State of Wash., Olympia, 1983—; cons. econ. devel. financing City and County of Spokane, 1980-86; bd. dirs. Wash. Water Power Co.; chmn. govt. ops. and pension com. Nat. Conf. State Legislators, 1989—. Bd. dirs. Greater Spokane Bus. Devel. Assn., 1984—, Holy Names Ft. George Wright, Spokane, 1984—, Displaced Homemakers, Spokane, 1985-87; trustee Holy Family Hosp., Spokane, 1986--87, Jr. League, 1987—; mem. adv. bd. Spokane Incubator Assn., 1987-89. Named Legislator of Yr., Assn. Builders and Contractors, 1985, Outstanding Govt. Woman of Yr., YWCA, 1988, Hosp. and Health Care award 1989. Mem. WWash. CPA's Soc. Republican. Office: Wash State Legislature HOB #413 Olympia WA 98504

SILVER, MARY WILCOX, oceanography educator; b. San Francisco, July 13, 1941; d. Philip E. and Mary C. (Kartes) Wilcox; m. Eli A. Silver (div. 1984); children: Monica, Joel. BA in Zoology, U. Calif., Berkeley, 1963; PhD in Oceanography, U. Calif., La Jolla, 1971. Asst. prof. biology San Francisco State U., 1971-72; prof. marine sci. U. Calif., Santa Cruz, 1972—, chmn. dept., 1983-89. Contbr. numerous articles on biol. oceanography to profl. jours. Grantee NSF, 1979—. Mem. AAAS, Am. Soc. Limnology and Oceanography, Am. Phycological Soc. Office: U Calif Marine Sci Dept Santa Cruz CA 95064

SILVERFINE, BETSY SUSAN, organization executive; b. N.Y.C., Feb. 7, 1960; d. Edward and Ethel (Sussman) S. BS, Cornell U., 1981. Asst. buyer Abraham and Straus Dept. Store, Bklyn., 1981-82; product mgmt. analyst Securities Industry Automation Corp., N.Y.C., 1983-84; dir. alumni affairs Fiorello H. La Guardia Community Coll., Long Island City, N.Y., 1985-88; nat. dir. alumni affairs Am. Friends of Hebrew U., N.Y.C., 1988-89. Student advisor, liaison fund raiser Am. Field Svc., N.Y.C., 1986—. Mem. NAFE, Am. Mktg. Assn., Nat. Coun. Jewish Women, Children's Hope Found., Cornell U. Alumni Assn. (bd. govs. 1986-90). Home: 1601 3d Ave Apt 4E New York NY 10128

SILVERMAN, ANNA MAE, nurse; b. Phila., July 5, 1928; d. Charles Girth and Maude Yoast; m. Edward Silverman, Sept. 1, 1955 (div. Oct. 1978); children: Gail, Debra, Jeffrey. Diploma, Meth. Hosp., 1953. RN; cert. psychiatric nurse. Mem. RN staff Meth. Hosp., Phila., 1953-55, Wernesville (Pa.) State Hosp., 1968-70, St. Joseph Hosp., Reading, Pa., 1974—. Contbr. article to Nursing World Jour., 1986. Home: RD3 Box 3786 Mohnton PA 19540-9231

SILVERMAN, BARBARA GAIL, librarian; b. St. Louis, Apr. 2, 1937; d. William and Clara (Chaskelson) Simpkins; m. Jerome L. Silverman, Sept. 7, 1958; children: Charles, Gregg. AB, Washington U., St. Louis, 1960; MLS, Tex. Women's U., 1982; MS, Corpus Christi State U., 1989. Tchr. Get Set federally funded program, Phila., 1964-67; libr. Corpus Christi (Tex.) Pub. Libr., 1976-84, Tulaso-Midway Ind. Sch. Dist., Corpus Christi, Tex., 1984—; tchr. Corpus Christi (Tex.) State U., 1985-86. Author: papers and articles in field. Bd. dirs. Corpus Christi (Tex.) Literacy Coun., Mcpl. Arts. Com., Corpus Christi, Tex. Named Outstanding Teacher of Year Alpha Delta Kappa, Dist. IV, 1984. Mem. ALA, Internat. Reading Assn., Nat. Coun. Tchrs. English, Tex. Libr. Assn.(Children's Round Table), Tex. Assn. Sch. Librs., Beta Phi Mu. Jewish. Home: 1400 Ocean Dr 1201A Corpus Christi TX 78404

SILVERMAN, CHARLOTTE, federal agency administrator, epidemiologist; b. N.Y.C., May 21, 1913; d. Harry and Gussie (Goldman) S. BA, Bklyn. Coll., 1933; MD, U. Pa., 1938; MPH, Johns Hopkins U., 1942, PhD, 1948. Dir. Bur. Tuberculosis Balt. City Health Dept., 1946-56; chief epidemiology, planning and rsch. Md. State Dept. Health, Balt., 1956-62; med. officer NIMH, Bethesda, Md., 1962-68; dep. dir. div. biol. effects and other positions Bur. Health USDA/USPHS, Rockville, Md., 1968-83; assoc. dir. for human studies USDA, Rockville, 1983—; mem. faculty dept. epidemiology Johns Hopkins U. Sch. Hygiene and Pub. Health, Balt., 1950—. Author: Epidemiology of Depression, 1968; contbr. articles to profl. jours. With USPHS, 1944-45. Recipient Mary Pemberton Nourse Meml. award AAUW, 1941-42. Fellow Am. Coll. Preventive Medicine, Am. Pub. Health Assn., Am. Orthopsychiat. Assn., Am. Coll. Epidemiology, Am. Bd. Preventive Medicine (diplomate). Home: 4977 Battery Ln Bethesda MD 20814 Office: FDA 5600 Fishers Ln Rockville MD 20857

SILVERMAN, ELAINE ROSLYN, educator; b. Washington, Aug. 28, 1941; d. Mark and Rebecca (Leopold) S. B.S. in Edn., Temple U., 1963; Ed.M., George Mason U., 1977. Cert. tchr., Va. Group leader Dixon House, Phila., 1962; tchr. Hammond High Sch., Alexandria, Va., 1963-65, T.C. Williams High Sch., Alexandria, 1965—. Participant Alexandria City Democratic Mass Meeting for Presdl. Nomination, 1984. Mem. Va. Edn. Assn., Alexandria Edn. Assn., NEA, Nat. Council for Social Studies, Va. Council for Social Studies. Jewish. Avocation: reading in area of history of English monarchy. Office: TC Williams High Sch 3330 King St Alexandria VA 22311

SILVERMAN, ELLEN, speech-language pathologist; b. Milw., Oct. 12, 1942; d. Roy and Bettie (Schlaeger) Loebel; m. Feb. 5, 1967 (div.); 1 child, Catherine Bette. BS, U. Wis., Milw., 1964; MA, U. Iowa, 1967, PhD, 1970. Rsch. assoc. U. Ill., Urbana, 1969-71; asst. prof. speech pathology Marquette U., Milw., 1973-79; assoc. prof. speech pathology Marquette U., 1979-85; pvt. practice speech/lang. pathology Milw., 1985—; spl. reader Am. Speech/Hearing/Lang. Assn., Rockville, Md., 1989—. Contbr. articles to profl. jours., chpts. to books. Marquette U. grantee, 1982. Fellow Am. Speech, Hearing, Lang. Assn.; mem. Wis. Speech, Hearing, Lang. Assn., Sigma Xi.

SILVERMAN, MARY DELSON, cable television executive; b. N.Y.C.; d. Max and Dorothy (Haupt) Delson; children: Sarah, Benjamin. BA, Sarah Lawrence Coll., 1960. Exec. producer Lenox (Mass.) Arts Ctr., Music Theatre Performing Group, 1972-78; dir. acquisitions Phoenix Films, N.Y.C., 1978-81; v.p. program acquisitions Lifetime Cable TV, Astoria, N.Y., 1986—. Producer theater: The Club, Dr. Selavy's (Obie award 1977), Magic Theater, Nightclub (Obie award 1972), Cantata; asst. producer movie Mandy's Grandmother; producer movie What Do Children Think of When They Think of the Bomb?. Bd. dirs. Women in Need, N.Y.C. Mem. Women in Film, Women's Forum. Office: Lifetime Cable TV 36-12 35th Ave Astoria NY 11106

SILVERMAN, STACY M., consumer protection company executive; b. L.A., Mar. 1, 1962; d. Seymour and Marilyn M. (Zimmerman) S. Pres. AMSO, Santa Monica, Calif. Co-instr. Navi/Pari, Santa Monica, 1987-90; v.p. Alliance for Wildlife Awareness & Edn., 1988—. Recipient Honorable Svc. award l.A. Unified Sch. Dist., 1985. Mem. nat. Assn. Underwater Instrs., Profl. Assn. Diving Instrs. Democrat.

SILVERNAIL, LISA ANNE PHIPPS, insurance company executive; b. Conway, S.C., Sept. 19, 1958; d. Robert Colon Phipps Jr. and H. Grey (Cartrette) Walklin; m. Chris Reed Davis, Sept. 19, 1976 (div. Sept. 1982); 1 child, Alexis Grey; m. Errol-lynn Silvernail, Oct. 13, 1983 (div. July 1989). BA, U. S.C., 1980. Adjuster United Ins. Co. Am., Myrtle Beach, S.C., 1980-84, Atlanta, 1980-84; mgr. claims Sun Life Group, U.S.A., Atlanta, 1984-90, First Colony Life Ins. Co., Lynchburg, Va., 1990—. Contbr. articles to profl. publs. Vol. Am. Cancer Soc., Atlanta, 1989—, Homeless Vietnam Vets., Atlanta, 1989—. Mem. Internat. Claims Assn. (life com. 1987—, S.E. regional liaison person 1988—), So. Claims Assn. (chmn. life workshop 1987-89), Ga. Claims Assn. (sec.-treas. 1988, vice chmn. 1989, chairperson 1990). Democrat. Home: 221 Countryplace Ln Lynchburg VA 24501 Office: First Colony 700 Main St Lynchburg VA 24505

SILVERNALE, LAURA GASPARINI, personnel specialist; b. Port Chester, N.Y., July 10, 1962; d. Andreas and Barbara Ann (Storino) Gasparini; m. Mark David Silvernale, July 18, 1981. BA in Psychology magna cum laude, Western Conn. State U., 1983, postgrad., 1988—. Pers. clk. Fed. Correctional Inst., Danbury, Conn., 1983-84; office coord. Aeromail, Inc., Westport, Conn., 1984; label/insert quality control coord. Danbury Pharm. Inc., 1985; prodn. planner, expediter Eaton Pressure Sensors Div., Danbury, 1985-89; pers. supr., office automation specialist Olsten Temp. Svcs., Danbury, 1990—. Author: (info. guide) Guidelines for Basic Cat Care, 1989. Sponsor Christian Christian's Fund, Richmond, Va., 1987; docent Conn. Zool. Soc., Bridgeport, Conn., 1989; mem. Danbury Animal Welfare Soc., 1989, World Wildlife Fund, Washington, 1988, Digit Fund, Inverness, Colo., 1989. Mem. NAFE, Psi Chi. Republican. Office: Olsten Temp Svcs 182 White St Danbury CT 06810

SILVERSTEIN, CAROL LYNN, educator; b. Bay Shore, N.Y., Feb. 11, 1952; d. William Antonin and Mary Josephine (Bartik) Schovanec; m. Roy Silverstein, June 25, 1981. BS cum laude, SUNY, Buffalo, 1974; MALS, SUNY, Stony Brook, 1976. Educator Sachem Sch. Dist., Lake Ronkonkoma, N.Y., 1974—. Mem. Suffolk County Bus. Tchrs. Assn. Episcopalian. Home: 12 Scott Ave North Selden NY 11784

SILVERSTEIN, HELMA, psychologist; b. Phila., Jan. 28, 1937; d. Alex and Sylvia (Gart) Gardner; m. Raphael Silverstein, June 15, 1957 (div. 1962); children: Paula Lynn Silverstein Fry, Mitchell Scott. BS, Temple U., 1958, MEd, 1969, EdD, 1981. Lic. psychologist, Pa. Home and sch. visitor Phila. Sch. Dist., 1966-71, sch. counselor, 1969-71; sch. counselor Lower Merion Sch. Dist., Ardmore, Pa., 1971-77, sch. social worker, 1977-84; psychologist Bryn Mawr (Pa.) Child Study Inst., 1984-86; cons., supr. Lincoln Ctr. for Family and Youth, Bridgeport, Pa., 1986-90; clin. cons. Hill Top Prep. Sch., Rosemont, Pa., 1984-90; pvt. practice Wynnewood, Pa., 1984-90; asst. clin. prof. Hahnemann U., Phila., 1984-90, Widener U., Chester, Pa., 1989-90.

Vol. Neighbors for Ellen Fisher, Havertown, Pa., 1990. Grantee Pa. Dept. Edn., 1976. Mem. Am. Psycol. Assn., Del. Valley Group Psychotherapy Soc., Am. Assn. Counseling and Devel., Pa. Edn. Assn., Assn. Against Client Exploitation by Profls. (v.p. 1986-89). Democrat. Jewish. Home: 418 E Wynnewood Rd Wynnewood PA 19096

SILVERTON, LEIGH, psychologist; b. Beverly Hills, Calif., Nov. 11, 1956; d. Ron and Fanya (Carter) Silverton. AB magna cum laude, U. Southern Calif., 1976, PhD, 1985. Lic. psychologist, Calif. Predoctoral fellow Harvard Med. Sch., 1985; intern psychology McLean and Harvard Med. Sch., Boston, 1984-85; asst. prof. U. Nev., Reno, 1985-88; co-dir. outpatient svcs. Gateways Hosp., L.A., 1988-89; psychologist Western Psychol. Svcs., L.A., 1989—; rsch. asst. prof. U. So. Calif., L.A., 1988—; prof. Calif. Grad. Inst., L.A., 1988—; active devel. computerized assessment systems; author assessment systems; cons. in field. Contbg. co-author: Handbook of Schizophrenia, vol. 3, 1988, Psychiatry: Biological and Interpersonal Processes, vol. 52, 1988; creator tests and expert systems; contbr. articles to profl. jours. Grantee faculty U. Nev., Reno, 1986, 87. Mem. Soc. Psychopathology Rsch., Am. Psychol. Assn., Western Psychol. Assn., Calif. Psychol. Assn., AAAS, Life History Soc., Mus. Contemporary Art, Sigma Xi. Office: Western Psychol Svcs 12031 Wilshire Los Angeles CA 90025

SILVESTRIS, ELAINE JOY, employee relations administrator, notary public; b. Worcester, Mass., Jan. 8, 1943; d. Roland Joseph and Margaret Ann (Arnieri) Gustafson; m. Maurice Richard Silvestris, Nov. 6, 1965. Cert. in Human Resources, Moravian Coll., Bethlehem, Pa., 1985; student, Allentown Coll. of St. Francis de Sales, Center Valley, Pa., 1988—. Legal sec. Mirick, O'Connell, DeMallie and Lougee, Worcester, 1961-65, Edward J. Brady, Camden, N.J., 1966-69; legal sec. to ptnr. Sigmon, Briody, Littner and Ross, Bethlehem, 1969-70; legal sec. to sr. ptnr. Weaver and Weaver, Catasauqua, Pa., 1970-76; adminstrv. sec. to pres. and v.p. sales Lehigh Sales and Products, Allentown, Pa., 1976-78; sr. stenographer U.S. Postal Service, Lehigh Valley, Pa., 1978-82, injury compensation supr., 1982-85, employee relations mgr., 1985—; account rep. DialAmerica Mktg., Inc., 1988; notary pub., Lehigh County, Pa., 1974—. Recipient Cert. Appreciation for Outstanding Efforts in Hiring Visually Disabled People, Commonwealth Pa., 1987. Mem. Nat. Assn. Profl. Saleswomen (Lehigh Valley chpt.), Pa. Assn. Notaries, Pa. Soc. Profl. Engrs. (aux. group chmn. 1983-84, sec. 1978-80, v.p. 1978-79, 2nd v.p. and Pa. del. 1976-77), Nat. Assn. for Female Execs. Inc. Republican. Methodist. Office: US Postal Svce 1000 Postal Rd Lehigh Valley PA 18001

SILVESTRY, LYDIA MERCEDES, fashion design professional; b. San Juan, Puerto Rico, Dec. 25, 1946; d. Ivan and Lydia Chacon (Baco) S.; children: Abilio, Jorge. Student, Inst. Adminstrn., San Juan, 1964; EG, CPM, London Coll. Fashion, 1978. Editor, gen. mgr. Temas Mag., N.Y.C.; mng. dir. Whitbread Nolan Real Estate, London; editor El Nuevo Dia, San Juan; pres. Lydia Designs, Inc., Miami, Fla. Vol. Insight Transformational Seminars, 1988—. Mem. Inst. Dirs. (London), Inst. Adminstrn., Journalism and Pub. Rels. Mem. Unity Ch.

SILVIA, KATHLEEN FORD, insurance executive; b. Bronxville, N.Y., Dec. 29, 1954; d. James William and Evelyn (Gates) Moriarty; m. Ronald Joseph Silvia, May 1, 1982; children: Ronald Ford, Jennifer Ann. Cert., Ins. Inst. Am., 1976. CPCU, lic. ins. advisor, Mass. Claim service rep. Allstate Ins. Co., Weston, Mass., 1973; claim service rep. Fair & Yeager Agy., Inc., Natick, Mass., 1974, claim mgr., 1974-78, personal lines mgr., 1979-80, edn. mgr., 1978-82, comml. account exec., 1980-82; br. mgr. Centerville, Mass., 1982-87; owner, ptnr. The Fair Ins. Agy., Centerville, 1987—. Contbr. articles to newspapers. Mem. pastor parish rels. com. United Meth. Ch., Osterville, Mass., 1982-88, mem. choir, 1982-84, chairperson worship com., 1986-88, mem. spiritual growth com., 1989—; bd. dirs. Cape Counseling Ctr., 1990—. Mem. Nat. Assn. Ins. Women Internat. (recipient awards), Mass. Assn. Ins. Women (Ins. Woman Yr. 1984, v.p. 1982-83, pres. 1985, chair various coms., bd. dirs. 1987-88), Soc. CPCU's, Profl. Ins. Agts., Ind. Ins. Agts. Mass., Profl. Ins. Agts. N.E. (bd. dirs. 1988—, chmn. edn. com. 1988—, mem. tech. com., CIC com., and Mass. steering com. 1988—, errors and ommissions com. 1990), Rotary (bd. dirs. Osterville chpt.). Home: 190 Great Marsh Rd Centerville MA 02632 Office: The Fair Ins Agy Inc 619 Main St Centerville MA 02632

SIMCOX, GLENDA BEALL, company executive; b. Coleman, Tex., Jan. 4, 1939; d. Cecil A. and Betty (Wooten) Beall; m. H. Burton Simcox, Jr., Aug. 18, 1961 (div. Jan. 1978; children: E. Burton, Bradley Beall. Student, Tex. Christian U., 1960-61. Exec. sec. Gen. Dynamics, Fort Worth, 1959-60; adminstrv. asst., recruiter law Snakard & Gambill, Fort Worth, 1978-80; exec. asst. Nat. Fin. Credit Corp., Fort Worth, 1980-82; owner, mgr. Exec. Specialists, Fort Worth, 1983—, Simcox & Assocs., Fort Worth. Mem. allocations com. United Way, Fort Worth, 1981-82, sect. chmn., 1986; sect. chmn. Am. Heart Assn., Fort Worth, 1987; v.p. Jr. Woman's Club of Ft. Worth, 1976-77; bd. dirs. Woman's Club of Ft. Worth, 1977-78. Mem. Am. Soc. Assn. Execs., Bldg. Owners and Mgrs. Assn. (exec. dir. 1987—), Dallas/Fort Worth Assn. Execs., C. of C. Republican. Presbyterian. Home: 4217 Westmont Ct Fort Worth TX 76109 Office: Simcox & Assocs 777 Main St Ste 890 Fort Worth TX 76102

SIMECKA, BETTY JEAN, convention executive; b. Topeka, Apr. 15, 1935; d. William Bryan and Regina Marie (Rezac) S.; m. Alex Pappas, Jan. 15, 1956 (div. Apr. 1983); 1 child, Alex William. Student, Butler County Community Coll., 1983-85. Freelance writer and photographer L.A. and Kans., 1969-77; co-owner Creative Enterprises, El Dorado, Kans., 1977-83; coord. excursions into history Butler County Community Coll., El Dorado, 1983-84; dir. Hutchinson (Kans.) Conv. & Visitors Bur., 1984-85; dir. mktg. div. Exec. Mgmt., Inc., Topeka, 1985-87; exec. dir. Topeka Conv. & Visitors Bur., 1987—; dir. promotion El Dorado Thunderboat Races, 1977-78. Pres. El Dorado Art Assn., 1984; chmn. Santa Fe Trail Bike Assn., Topeka, 1988-90; co-dir. St. Mary's Summer Track Festival, 1973-81. Named Outstanding Female Athlete AAU. Mem. Nat. Tour Assn., Sales and Mktg. Execs., Internat. Assn. Conv. and Visitors Burs., Am. Soc. Assn. Execs., Travel Industry Kans. (membership chmn. 1988-89), St. Marys C. of C. (pres. 1975), I-70 (v.p. 1989—), Optimists (social sec. Topeka chpt. 1988-89). Republican. Methodist.

SIMER, CHERYL, marketing professional; b. Greenbay, Wis., Dec. 5, 1948; d. Harold Leslie Albert and Helen June Augusta (Delzer) Black; m. Harvey Josef Simer. BA in Math., Beloit Coll., 1971. Research asst. Nat. Consumer Fin. Assn., Washington, 1971; project dir. Pillsbury Co., Mpls., 1972-74, research analyst, 1975-77, research mgr., 1978-79; dir. mktg. research Munsingwear, Inc., Mpls., 1980-82; v.p., dir. mktg. research BBDO, Mpls., 1983—. Mem. Am. Mktg. Assn. *

SIMMONS, ADELE SMITH, foundation president, former educator; b. Lake Forest, Ill., June 21, 1941; d. Hermon Dunlap and Ellen T. (Thorne) Smith; m. John L. Simmons; children—Ian, Erica, Kevin. B.A., Radcliffe Coll., 1963; Ph.D., Oxford U., Eng., 1969; L.H.D. (hon.), Lake Forest Coll., 1976, Amherst Coll., 1977, Franklin Pierce Coll., 1978, U. Mass., 1982, Alverno Coll., 1986, Marlboro Coll., 1987; postgrad., Smith Coll., Northampton, Mass., 1989, Holyoke Coll., 1989. Dean Jackson Coll., Tufts U., Medford, Mass., 1970-72; asst. prof. history, dean student affairs Princeton U., N.J., 1972-77; pres. Hampshire Coll., Amherst, Mass., 1977-89, MacArthur Found., Chgo., 1989—; dir. Affil. Publs., Boston, Marsh & McLennan, N.Y.C., Boston Globe. Author: Modern Mauritius, 1980. Contbr. articles to profl. jours. Commr. Pres.'s Commn. on World Hunger, Washington, 1978-80; trustee Carnegie Found. for Advancement Teaching, 1978-86; trustee Union Concerned Scientists; dir. Synergos; bd. overseers Harvard U., 1972-79. Mem. Coun. Fgn. Rels., Synergos Assn. (bd. dirs.), Cosmopolitan Club, Phi Beta Kappa. Office: MacArthur Found 140 S Dearborn St Chicago IL 60603

SIMMONS, BARBARA J., human resources director; b. Detroit, Oct. 28, 1938; d. Jessie Stanley and Bernice Olivia (Abrams) Stanley; m. William Clark Estes, Dec. 26, 1959 (div. 1977); children: Brian Keith, Brenda Kay; m. David Louis Simmons, Dec. 6, 1980. BS, Wayne State U., 1969, MS in Bus., 1971. Tchr., coordinator Detroit Pub. Schs., 1969-72; project coordinator Wayne State U., Detroit, 1972-73; with indsl. relations dept. Ford Motor Credit Co., Rouge, Mich., 1973-74; personnel officer Mfgrs. Nat. Bank, Detroit, 1974-75; dir. employee relations The Bendix Corp., South Bend, Ind., Utica, N.Y., Troy, Mich., 1975-81; v.p., dir. personnel Advance Mortgage Corp., Southfield, Mich., 1981-83; dir. employment Fed. Nat. Mortgage Co., Washington, 1983-85; 1st v.p. human resources Mich. Nat. Corp., Farmington Hills, 1985-89; corp. v.p. human resources Henry Ford Health Care Corp., Detroit, 1989—; bd. dirs. Am. Inst. Banking, Detroit, 1985—, Blue Cross/Blue Shield, Detroit, 1985—. Mem. Detroit Urban League, 1985—, NAACP, Detroit, 1985—; mem. bd. ASPA Found., 1989—. Mem. Am. Soc. Personnel Adminstrs., Internat. Assn. Personnel Women, Am. Inst. Banking (bd. regents, bd. dirs. 1985—), Am. Banking Assn. (mem. adv. council), Blue Cross/Blue Shield (bd. dirs. 1985—), Southeastern Mich. Health Execs. Forum, Detroit Econ. Club. Episcopalian. Home: 38694 Northfarm Dr Northville MI 48167 Office: Mich Nat Bank Corp 30665 Northwestern Hwy Farmington Hills MI 48333-9065

SIMMONS, BARBARA JEAN, psychiatric social worker; b. Jefferson, Ala., Dec. 2, 1946; d. Hanibal and Juanita (Dale) S.; children: Darryl Deon Malden, Mark Anthony Simmons. BA in Sociology, Urban Social Svcs., U. Mass., Boston, 1976; MSW, Simmons Coll., 1978; postgrad., New Eng. Sch. of Law, 1987-88. Cert. psychiat. social worker. Staff social worker Brockton (Mass.) Multi-Svcs. Ctr., 1978-79; child therapist Putnam Childrens Ctr., Roxbury, Mass., 1978-80; dir. of alcohol treatment Roxbury Ct. Clinic, 1980-83; staff supr. Dept. of Social Svcs., Dorchester, Mass., 1983-86; dir. of advocacy healthy baby program Boston City Hosp., 1986-90; pvt. cons. and trainer Dorchester, 1990—; vis. prof. Met. Coll. boston U.; cons. employee assistance Moore and Fravenhofer, Brookline, Mass., 1987—, Psychol. Assocs. Chmn. Fairlawn Tenants Assn., Boston, 1988—; officer Charles St. AME Ch. Grantee Nat. Assn. of Alcoholism and Alcohol Abuse, 1978. Mem. Am. Pub. Health Assn., ABA, Nat. Bar Assn., Nat. Assn. Black Social Workers (past pres. Boston chpt., chmn. publicity 1987). Democrat. Methodist. Home: PO Box 674 Dorchester MA 02124

SIMMONS, BETTY JO, facilities operations executive; b. Caddo, Okla., Dec. 13, 1936; d. Robert Lee and Beatrice (Alexander) S.; m. Doanld Sherrill Stauffer, Jan. 3, 1959 (div. 1963); m. Daniel Oliver Amos, Oct. 20, 1972 (div. 1975). BA, City Coll.; student, U. Calif. Drafting clk. PacBell, 1956-59, jr. civil engr. draftsperson, 1959-61, sr. civil engr. draftsperson, 1961-62, civil engr. draftsperson, 1962-82, EEO counselor, 1973-77, supr., civil engr. draftsperson, 1982-83, liaison cons. civil rights, 1983-87; project adminstr. pre-apprenticeship tng. program Caltran, Compton, Calif., 1987-89; coord. govtl. affairs Caltran, L.A., 1989, chief facilities ops., 1989—; facilitator Govs. Commn. on the Status of Women, Fresno, Calif., 1980. Producer: Building a Future, 1988 (bronze Cindy award Assn. Visual Communicators). Bd. dirs. Morgan Canyon Inst. of Higher Learning, Fresno, 1978-82; fund raiser Hunger Project, L.A., Fresno, 1980—, Youth at Risk, L.A., 1986—. Office: Caltrans 120 S Spring St Los Angeles CA 90012

SIMMONS, CAROLINE THOMPSON, civic worker; b. Denver, Aug. 22, 1910; d. Huston and Caroline Margaret (Cordes) Thompson; m. John Farr Simmons, Nov. 11, 1936; children: John Farr (dec.), Huston T., Malcolm M. AB, Bryn Mawr Coll., 1931; MA (hon.), Amherst Coll. Chmn. women's com. Corcoran Gallery Art, 1965-66; vice chmn. women's com. Smithsonian Assos., 1969-71; pres. Decatur House Council, 1963-71; mem. bd. Nat. Theatre, 1979-80; trustee Washington Opera, 1955-65; bd. dirs. Fgn. Student Svc. Coun., 1956-79; mem. Washington Home Bd., 1955-60; bd. dirs. Smithsonian Friends of Music, 1977-79; commr. Nat. Mus. Am. Art, 1979-89; mem. Folger com. Folger Shakespeare Libr., 1979-86, trustee emeritus, 1986—; mem. Washington bd. Am. Mus. in Britain, 1970—; bd. dirs. Found. Preservation of Historic Georgetown, 1975-89; trustee Marpat Found., 1987—, Amherst Coll., 1979-81, Dacor-Bacon House Found., Phillips Collection, 1990—, Georgetown Presbyn. Ch., 1989—; v.p. internat. coun. Mus. Modern Art, N.Y.C., 1978—; bd. dirs. Alliance Francaise. Recipient award for eminent svc. Folger Shakespeare Libr., 1986. Mem. Soc. Women Geographers, Sulgrave Club, Chevy Chase Club. Address: 1508 Dumbarton Rock Ct Washington DC 20007

SIMMONS, CATHERINE CONSTANCE, human services administrator; b. Columbia, Mo., Feb. 27, 1956; d. Robert Eugene Webb and Betty Joan (Perrin) Cruz; m. Oscar Harold Simmons Jr., June 21, 1980. B of Music Therapy, Loyola U., New Orleans, 1978. Salesperson U.S. C. of C. Graphic Svc., El Paso, Tex., 1978-80, Computer Tech. Assoc., El Paso, 1980; behavior specialist Victory Villas Group Home Mentally Retarded Adults, Ft. Lauderdale, Fla., 1980-81; activity dir. Manor Pines Convalescence Ctr., Ft. Lauderdale, 1981-82; mental health tech. educator Coral Ridge Psychiat. Hosp., Ft. Lauderdale, 1982-87; leasing dir. Wyndham Park Retirement Community, Huntsville, Ala., 1988—. Producer, actress TV commls.; actress dinnertheater prodns., 1979—. Mem. NAFE, Huntsville C. of C., Smithsonian Assocs., Harmony Internat., Phi Beta. Home: 126 Morning View Dr Harvest AL 35749 Office: Wyndham Park 2004 Max Luther Dr Huntsville AL 35810

SIMMONS, CYNTHIA J., office management professional; b. Apple Valley, Calif., Nov. 18, 1957; d. David E. and W. Jean (Walters) Scroggins; children: Anthony D. Lane, Jonathan L. Simmons. Cert., Ind. Vocat. Tech. Coll., 1976. Exec. sec. Shasta Industries, Goshen, Ind., 1976-79; dist. stenographer No. Ind. Pub. Svc. Co., Goshen, 1979-80; exec. sec. Riverside (Calif.) Community Hosp. Found., 1980-87; office mgr. Price Waterhouse, Riverside, 1987-90. Active community theater. Mem. NAFE, Profl. Secs. Internat. (v.p. programs Lado del Rio chptr. 1983), Alpha Beta Gamma.

SIMMONS, DONNA MARIE, histotechnologist, neurobiology researcher; b. Hartford, Conn., Oct. 13, 1943; d. John Henry and Ellen Louise (Meehl) Strayer; m. Corvin Gale Simmons, Sept. 17, 1964. Student, U. Wash., Western Wash. State U. Histologic technician, instr. Tacoma Gen. Hosp. Sch. Med. Tech. Lab. U. Wash., 1963; technician Med. Sch. U. Wash., 1964; histologic technician Northgate Med. Lab., Seattle, 1964-67; rsch. technologist in neuroanatomy Regional Primate Rsch. Ctr., U. Wash., 1967-82; rsch. asst. Devel. Neurobiology Lab. Salk Inst., La Jolla, Calif., 1982-85; sr. technician, lab. mgr. Neural Systems Lab. Howard Hughes Med. Inst. at Salk Inst., 1985-90; rsch. assoc. dept. of biology Hedco Neurosci. Inst., U. So. Calif., L.A., 1990—; cons., lectr. in field.; judge Greater San Diego Sci. and Engring. Fair, 1987-89; leader sci. del. to People's Rep. of China, 1986; chair China Scientist Exchange Fund, 1986-87; mem. Swiss Histology Meeting Exch., 1990. Author tech. articles, revs. in field; mem. editorial bd. Jour. histotech. Recipient various svc. awards; best non-clin. pub. in field, 1985. Mem. AAAS, Am. Soc. Clin. Pathologists (affiliate), Wash. State Histology Soc. (past pres., histology liaison Am. Soc. Med. Tech.), Nat. Soc. Histotech. (charter mem., regional dir. 1980-82, jud. chair 1983-86), Calif. Soc. Histotech. (San Diego dir. protem 1985-86), Assn. Women in Sci. (San Diego charter mem., bd. dir. 1985-89), Soc. for Neurosci., Swiss Soc. for Histotech., Women in Neurosci., N.Y. Acad. Sci., NOW, Am. Alpine Club. Office: U So Calif Hedco Neurosci Inst Los Angeles CA 90089

SIMMONS, DORIS JEANETTE, chiropractic clinic administrator; b. Tuscaloosa, Ala., May 22, 1949; d. Earnest Joseph and Elma Ree (Simpson) Watkins; m. William Van Simmons, May 8, 1971; children: Susan, Tricia, Doris, Ashley. Grad. phys. therapy asst. Tex. Chiropractic Coll., Padadena, Tex., 1975; grad. chiropractic asst. Parker Chiropractic Research, Ft. Worth, 1977; student U. Ala.-Tuscaloosa, 1976-77, Internat. Acad. of Neuro-Vascular Disease, Atlanta, 1980, Nat. Coll. Chiropractic, Lombard, Ill., 1982. Fashion model, 1968—; telephone operator S. Central Bell, Tuscaloosa, 1966-69, service analyst, 1969-71; exec. dir. Simmons' Chiropractic Clinic, Tuscaloosa, 1980-89, adminstr., 1989—; tchr. 4th grade Christ Episc. Ch., also mem. Christian edn. com. Appeared in TV commls. Leader Tombigbee council Girl Scouts U.S.A., Tuscaloosa, 1976—. Named Chiropractic Wife of Yr., Ala. State Chiropractic Assn., 1983. Mem. Am. Chiropractic Aux., Nat. Rep. Senatorial Inner Circle, Ala. State Chiropractic Aux. (1st v.p. 1978-80, pres., 1980-82, parliamentarian 1982-84, raffle chmn. 1985—, bd. dirs.), Internat. Chiropractic Research Exchange, Nat. Assn. Female Execs. Episcopalian. Club: Soc. Fine Arts (Tuscaloosa). Avocations: modeling, river rafting, canoeing. Home: 17-709 Northwood Lake Northport AL 35476 Office: Simmons Chiropractic Clinic 2602 7th St Tuscaloosa AL 35401

SIMMONS, DORIS YVONNE, surveyor; b. Jennings, Fla., Oct. 13, 1939; d. John Otto and Viola (Burgess) Simmons. Grad. high sch. Rep. Nat. Com. mem., Washington, 1985—. Mem. NAFE, Mayan. Home: 1304 E 24th St Bradenton FL 34208

SIMMONS, GENEEN MARSHETT, electronics executive; b. Havana, Fla., July 15, 1966; d. Elijah Simmons and Betty Jean (Bush) Clayton. Student in data processing, Lively Vocat., Tallahassee, 1985-87. With First Nat. Bank, Tallahassee, 1986-87; computer operator II Dept. Banking and Fin., Tallahassee, 1987-88; computer programmer Dept. Revenue, Tallahassee, 1988-89; tech. cons. Datronics, Inc., N.Y.C., 1989—. Author: (poem) Black Butterfly, 1989 (honorable mention award 1989), (poetry) World of Poetry. Named to Outstanding Young Women of Am., 1988. Mem. NAFE. Democrat. Baptist. Home: 3804 Citation Ln Knoxville TN 37912

SIMMONS, HEATHER JANE EDITH, law librarian; b. Concord, Mass., Mar. 4, 1960; d. John Geden North and Dorothy (Gargate) Braithwaite; m. James Thomas Simmons, Aug. 19, 1989. BA, U. Mich., 1981; JD, Wayne State U., 1985; MLS, U. Mich., 1986. Bar: Mich. 1985. Internship U. Mich. Law Libr., Ann Arbor, 1985-86; reference librarian Wayne State U. Law Libr., Detroit, 1986-88; adj. faculty sci. program Wayne State U. Libr., Detroit, 1987—; asst. dir. Wayne State U. Law Libr., Detroit, 1988—; part-time librarian Wayne State U. Law Libr., Detroit, 1986; lectr. A.J. Seminars, Rockville, Md., 1988—. Named Outstanding Young Woman of Am. Outstanding Am., 1989. Mem. Librarians Using Computers (chair-elect 1988-89, chair 1989—), Mich. Assn. Law Librs. (sec. 1987-89), Am. Assn. Law Librs. (Matthew Bender Scholarship award 1988), ABA, Mich. Bar Assn. Office: Wayne State Univ Arthur Neef Law Library 468 W Ferry Mall Detroit MI 48202

SIMMONS, ILENE WHITE, investment security analyst; b. Burlington, N.C., Sept. 6, 1948; d. James W. and Sara (Roberts) White; m. K. Gary Simmons (div. 1980). BS in Bus., U. N.C., 1970, MBA, 1973. Securities analyst NCNB, Charlotte, N.C., 1973-80; v.p., sr. securities analyst Citizen & So. Nat. Bank, Atlanta, 1980-84, First Chgo. Investment Advisors (name now Brinson Ptnrs.), Chgo., 1984—. Mem. Chgo. Fin. Analyst Soc. Republican. Home: 155 N Harbor Dr #5007 Chicago IL 60601 Office: Brinson Ptnrs, 3 First Nat Pla, 70 W Madison St Chicago IL 60602-4298

SIMMONS, JEAN, actress; b. London, Jan. 31, 1929; d. Charles and Winifred Ada (Lovel) S.; m. Stewart Granger, Dec. 20, 1950 (div. June 1960); 1 dau., Tracy; m. Richard Brooks, Nov. 1, 1960; 1 dau., Kate. Ed., Orange Hill Sch., Burnt Oak, London. Motion picture actress, appearing in English and Am. films including Great Expectations, 1946, Black Narcissus, 1947, Hamlet, 1948 (Acad. award nomination), Adam and Evelyn, 1949, The Actress, 1953, Young Bess, 1953, Guys and Dolls, 1956, The Big Country, 1958, Home Before Dark, 1958, Spartacus, 1960, Elmer Gantry, 1960, The Grass Is Greener, 1960, All the Way Home, 1963, Rough Night in Jericho, 1967, Divorce American Style, 1967, The Happy Ending, 1969 (Acad. award nomination), The Dawning, 1989; also theatre appearance A Little Night Music, Phila. and on tour, 1974; appeared in: TV mini-series The Dain Curse, 1978, A Small Killing, 1981, Valley of the Dolls, 1981, The Thornbirds, 1983 (Emmy award), North and South, 1985, North and South Book II, 1986; TV film: December Flower, 1987, The Legend of Lost Loves, 1988, Great Expectations, 1989; TV series Murder She Wrote, 1989. Office: care Geoffrey Barr 9400 Readcrest Dr Beverly Hills CA 90210

SIMMONS, KAREN ANN, director of human resources; b. N.Y.C., Nov. 6, 1948; d. Arthur Magnus and Dorothy Ann (Myers) S. BA in Spanish, U. Bridgeport, 1970. Social worker St. Elizabeth Ch., Boone, N.C., 1972-73; adminstrv. asst. Glenmary Missioners, Fairfield, Conn., 1973-74; dir. human resources and adminstrn. Technoserve, Inc., Norwalk, Conn., 1974—; founding mem. Personnel Co-op, N.Y.C., 1979—. Sec. Appalachian Vols., Inc., Darien, Conn., 1984—; pres. Rowayton (Conn.) Ambulance Corps, 1985-86; vol. emergency med. technician Norwalk Hosp., 1984—, Stamford (Conn.) Ambulance Corps, 1987—; lector St. Thomas Aquinas Parish, Fairfield, 1977—, youth minister, 1980-84. Democrat. Roman Catholic. Home: 855 Old Stratfield Rd Fairfield CT 06430

SIMMONS, MARGUERITE SAFFOLD, pharmaceutical sales professional; b. Montgomery, Ala., Oct. 21, 1954; d. Arthur Edward and Gwendolyn Jane (Saffold) S. BS in Communications, U. Tenn., 1976. Press sec. Met. Mayor's Office, Nashville, 1976-77; advt. copywriter United Meth. Pub. House, Nashville, 1977-78; sales rep. No Nonsense Pantyhose, Houston, 1978-81, Breon Labs., Houston, 1981-82; profl. sales rep. Janssen Pharmaceutica, Inc., Houston, 1982-88, sr. sales rep., 1988—. Vol. Dem. Nat. Conv., Atlanta, 1988. Mem. NAFE, U. Tenn. Alumni Assn. (bd. dirs. Atlanta chpt. 1989-90), U. Tenn. Black Alumni Assn. (bd. dirs. 1989-91), Ga. Trust Hist. Soc., Ala. Geneal. Soc., Ga. Geneal. Soc., Nat. Trust Hist. Preservation, Delta Sigma Theta. Baptist. Office: PO Box 16934 Atlanta GA 30321

SIMMONS, MIRIAM QUINN, state legislator; b. Jackson, Miss., Mar. 28, 1928; d. Charles Buford and Viola (Hamill) Quinn; m. Willie Wronal Simmons, July 10, 1952; children: Dick, Sue, Wronal. BS, Miss. U. for Women, 1949. Tchr. Columbia (Miss.) City Schs., 1949-51, 53-54, literacy coord., 1986-87; home demonstration agt. Coop. Extension Svc., Bay Springs, Miss., 1951-52; tchr. Marion County Schs., Columbia, 1952-53, 54-55, Columbia Tng. Sch., 1961-63, Columbia Acad., 1970-73; rep. Miss. Ho. of Reps., Jackson, 1988—; adv. bd. Magnolia Fed. Bank for Savs; trustee State Inst. Higher Learning, Jackson, 1972-84; dir. Miss. Authority for Ednl. TV, Jackson, 1976-88. Named Marion County Outstanding Citizen Columbia Jr. Aux., 1981. Mem. Women's Culture Club, Hilltop Garden Club, Delta Kappa Gamma. Democrat. Methodist. Home: Rte 6 Box 348 Columbia MS 39429

SIMMONS, SADIE VEE, retired school administrator; b. Jackson, Miss., Oct. 19, 1929; d. Herbie Lewis Simmons and Sadie Vee (Watkins) Lewis. BA, U. Colo., 1951; MEd, Emory U., 1958; EdD, U. Ga., 1971, Ed.S., 1971. Cert. sch. adminstrn., elem. tchr., high sch. social sci. tchr. Elem. tchr. Trion City Schs., Trion, Ga., 1951-55, City Schs. Decatur, Decatur, Ga., 1955-56; elem. prin. City Schs. Decatur, 1956-64, 65-66, dir. research and fed. programs, 1966-68, elem. prin., 1968-72, from asst. prin. to assoc. prin., 1972-75, supt., 1975-86; mem. Profl. Practices Commn., Atlanta, 1984-86; pres. Assn. for Childhood Edn., Atlanta, 1968-70; chmn. Metro Supts., Atlanta, 1983-84; cons. Profl. Assn. Ga. Educators, Clarkston, 1986-89; presenter seminar Ednl. Adminstrn. Ga. State U., Adminstrv. Acad. Contbr. articles to Elem. Sch. Jour., Ga. Assn. Edn. Bd. dirs. YMCA, Decatur, Ga., 1974-86, Sam Jones Boys Club, Decatur, 1983-89; cons. Decatur Cooperative Ministry, 1969-73; vol. Decatur Emergency Assistance Ministry, 1986-89. Kellogg scholar Emory U., 1957, State of Ga. scholar, 1964; named Pub. Servant of Yr. Atlanta Jour., 1980, Woman of the Week, DeKalb News Sun, 1982, for City of Decatur Vee Simmons Day, Decatur City Commn., 1981. Mem. Am. Assn. Sch. Adminstrs., Delta Kappa Gamma (pres. 1962-64), Kappa Delta Pi, Phi Kappa Phi, Kappa Delta Epsilon, Westchester Garden Club (community rep. 1987-89), Decatur Adminstrs. Club. Democrat. Methodist.

SIMMONS, SYLVIA JEANNE QUARLES (MRS. HERBERT G. SIMMONS, JR.), university administrator, educator; b. Boston, May 8, 1935; d. Lorenzo Christopher and Margaret Mary (Thomas) Quarles; B.A., Manhattanville Coll., 1957; M.Ed., Boston Coll., 1962; m. Herbert G. Simmons, Jr., Oct. 26, 1957; children—Stephen, Alison, Lisa. Montessori tchr. Charles River Park Nursery Sch., Boston, 1965-66; registrar Boston Coll. Sch. Mgmt., Chestnut Hill, Mass., 1966-70; dir. fin. aid Radcliffe Coll., Cambridge, Mass., 1970-75, assoc. dean admissions and fin. aid, 1972-75, assoc. dean admissions, fin. aid and women's edn., 1975; assoc. dean admissions and fin. aid Harvard and Radcliffe, from 1975; assoc. v.p. for acad. affairs, central adminstrn. U. Mass., Boston, 1976—, spl. asst. to chancellor, 1979—; v.p. field services Mass. Higher Edn. Assistance Corp., 1982-84, sr. v.p., 1984—; mem. faculty Harvard U.; cons. Mass. Bd. Higher Edn., 1973-77. Bd. dirs. Rivers Country Day Sch., Weston, Mass., Simon's Rock Coll., Great Barrington, Mass., Wayland (Mass.) Fair Housing, Cambridge Mental Health Assn., Family Service Greater Boston, Concerts in Black and White, Mass. Higher Edn. Assistance Corp.; chmn. bd. dirs. North Shore Community Coll., 1986-88, mem. bd. dirs., 1985—; trustee and alumnae bd. dirs. Manhattanville Coll. Mem. adv. com. Upward Bound, Chestnut Hill Boston

Coll., 1972-74; Camp Chimvey Corners, Becket, Mass., 1971-77; bd. dirs. Mass. Am. Cancer Soc., 1987—. Named One of Ten Outstanding Young Leaders, Boston Jr. C. of C., 1971; recipient Bicentennial medal Boston Coll., 1976; Achievement award Greater Boston YMCA, 1977, Human Rights award Mass. Tchrs. Assn., 1988, Pres'. award Mass Ednl. Opportunity Assn., 1988. Mem. Women in Politics, Nat. (exec. council 1973-75), Eastern (1st v.p. 1973) assns. financial aid officers, Coll. Scholarship Service Council, Links, (pres. local chpt. 1967-69), Nat. Inst. Fin. Aid Adminstrs. (dir. 1975-77), Jack and Jill Am. (pres. Newton chpt. 1972-74, Delta Sigma Theta, Delta Kappa Gamma. Club: Manhattanville (pres. Boston 1966-68). Home: 3 Dean Rd Wayland MA 01778 Office: 330 Stuart St Boston MA 02116

SIMMONS, VIRGINIA RUTH MCCONNELL, writer; b. Nashua, Iowa, Jan. 27, 1928; d. Joseph Lyle and Ruth Eleanor (Mink) McCorison; children: Thomas Creston McConnell, Susan McConnell Sakys. BA, Oberlin Coll., 1949; MA, Adams State Coll., Alamosa, Colo., 1981. Instr. English U. Colo., Colorado Springs, 1965-68; assoc. editor Swallow Press, Denver, 1966; editor in chief Pruett Pub. Co., Boulder, Colo., 1968-70; assoc. editor, acting editor State Hist. Soc. Colo., Denver, 1970-72; columnist, feature writer various newspapers, Jiddah, Saudi Arabia and Alamosa, 1978—; owner Rabbitbrush Enterprises, Alamosa, 1986—. Author: Bayou Salado: The Story of the South Park (2d honor award Nat. Fedn. Press Women 1967), 1966, The San Luis Valley: Land of the Six-Armed Cross, 1980; co-author: Valley of the Cranes, 1988, The Upper Arkansas, 1990; contbr. articles, book revs. to profl. jours., mags. Recipient 1st honor award Nat. Fedn. Press Women, 1967. Mem. San Luis Valley Hist. Soc. (editor 1984-86, cert. recognition 1980, 87), Manitou Springs Hist. Soc. (hon. life), Western Writers of Am. Office: Rabbitbrush Enterprises 719 2d St Alamosa CO 81101

SIMMONS-DOUGLAS, (LA) RITA, media director; b. Goodson, Mo., Aug. 3, 1933; d. Benjamin A. and Floy E. (Patterson) Simmons; div.; children: Elvin Sidney Douglas III, Scott Simmons Douglas, Stephanie Douglas. Student, S.W. Bapt. Univ., 1951-52, Southwest Mo. State U., 1952-54; BSE, Cen. State U., Warrensburg, Mo., 1973, postgrad., 1974-86. Cert. tchr., Mo. Tchr. Judy Sch. Dist., Columbia, Mo., 1954-55; asst. personnel dir. M.F.A. Ins. Co., Columbia, 1955-57; media dir. Raymore-Peculiar (Mo.) Sch. Dist., 1976—; grant coord. Raymore-Peculiar Sch. Dist., 1976-77, 77-78, 1978-79; contact person Incentive for Sch. Excellence programs, 1985-86. Pres. Pre-sch. PTA, Harrisonville, Mo., 1962-64; sec. Harrisonville PTA, 1964-65. Mem. NEA (sec. Mo. unit 1988-90), Mo. Assn. Sch. Librs., Mo. State Tchrs. Assn. (sec. 1977-79), PEO (pres. 1970-72). Episcopalian. Home: 508 Arena Dr PO Box 546 Peculiar MO 64078 Office: Raymore-Peculiar Sch Dist Rte 211 at School Rd Peculiar MO 64078

SIMMONS-SIXTO, CAMILLE ANN, management services company executive; b. Newtown Kitty, Guyana, Sept. 12, 1953; came to U.S., 1973; d. Seidel Joseph Simmons and Lucille Norma Hinds; m. Alfredo Sixto; 1 child, Francesca Lucille. AA, Queensborough Community Coll., 1979; BBA, Bernard M. Baruch Coll., 1982. Lic. real estate broker, N.Y. Sec. C.I.T. Fin. Corp., N.Y.C., 1973-77; adminstrv. asst. Community Service Soc., N.Y.C., 1977-84; asst. to chief exec. officer Bramson Ort Tech. Inst., N.Y.C., 1984-85; instr. data processing Comml. Programming Unltd., N.Y.C., 1985; mgr. adminstrn. Metro-North Commuter R.R., N.Y.C., 1985-89; mgr. Chas P. Young Mgmt. Svcs., N.Y.C., 1990—. Mem. NAACP, Nat. Assn. Female Execs., Bernard M. Baruch Coll. Alumni Assn. Home: 6 Cohill Rd Valley Stream Long Island NY 11580

SIMMS, MARIA ESTER, health services administrator; b. Bahia Blanca, Argentina, Nov. 19, 1938; came to U.S., 1963; d. Jose and Esther (Guays) Barberio Esandi; m. Michael Simms, July 15, 1973; children: Michelle Bonnie Lee Carla, Michael London Valentine. Degree medicine, Facultad del Centenario, Rosario, Argentina, 1962; Physician Asst. Cert. (hon.), U. So. Calif., 1977. Medical diplomate. V.p. Midtown Svcs. Inc., Los Angeles, 1973—, AAA Med. Clinics Inc., Los Angeles, 1980—; sec.-treas. Han-Sim Corp., Los Angeles. V.P., editor The Ebell of L.A., 1985-88; chmn. bd. Neighborhoods for Peace, Inc., L.A. Fellow Am. Acad. Physicians' Assts.; mem. Bus. for Law Enforcement (northeast div.), Physicians for Soc. Responsibility, Mercy Crusade Inc., Internat. Found. for Survival Research, Supreme Emblem Club of U.S., Order of the Eastern Star, Flying Samaritans, Shriners.

SIMON, CARLY, singer, composer; b. N.Y.C., June 25, 1945; d. Richard S.; m. James Taylor, 1972 (div. 1983); children: Sarah Maria, Benjamin Simon; m. James Hart, Dec. 23, 1987. Studied with Pete Seeger. Singer, composer, rec. artist, 1971—. Appeared in film No Nukes, 1980; albums include Carly Simon, 1971, Anticipation, 1972, No Secrets, 1973, Hotcakes, 1974, Playing Possum, 1975, The Best of Carly Simon, 1975, Another Passenger, 1976, Boys in the Trees, 1978, Spy, 1979, Come Upstairs, 1980, Torch, 1981, Hello Big Man, 1983, Spoiled Girl, 1985, Coming Around Again, 1987, Greatest Hits Live, 1988, My Romance, 1990, Have You Seen Me Lately?, 1990; single records: Nobody Does It Better, 1977, Let the River Run, 1988 (Academy award best original song, 1989); recipient Grammy award as best new artist 1971; TV appearance: Carly in Concert: My Romance, 1990. Office: care Champion Entertainment 130 W 57th St New York NY 10019*

SIMON, CAROLINE K(LEIN), lawyer; b. N.Y.C.; d. Julia (Feist) and David Klein; m. Leopold King Simon (dec. 1952); children: Lee, Cathy Simon Silver (Mrs. Sidney Prince); m. Irving W. Halpern, 1953 (dec.). Student Columbia U.; LL.B., NYU; LL.D. (hon.), Jewish Inst. Religion, Hebrew Union Coll., 1966. Bar: N.Y., U.S. Dist. Ct. (so. dist.) N.Y., U.S. Supreme Ct. Gen. practice, N.Y.C.; of counsel Kaplan Kilsheimer; sec. of state State of N.Y., 1959-63; judge N.Y. State Ct. Claims, 1963-71. Mem. spl. legis. com. on ct. reorgn. N.Y. State Senate; formerly chmn. subcom. on the jury N.Y. Appellate Divs. 1st and 2d Depts.; mem. com. on discrimination in employment N.Y. State War Coun., 1943-45; commr. State Workmen's Compensation Bd., 1944-45, State Commn. Against Discrimination, 1945-55, State Youth Commn., 1956-59; legal adviser U.S. del. UN Human Rights Commn., 1958; mem. White House Confs. on Children, 1950, 60; bd. dirs., exec. com. Com. on Modern Cts., Fund for Modern Cts.; mem. med. malpractice mediation panel 1st Jud. Dept.; adv. coun. Nat. Ctr. for State Cts.; past chmn. bd. trustees, past mem. exec. com. Nat. Coun. on Crime and Delinquency, also mem. nat. adv. coun.; hon. bd. trustees, past chmn. com. on social affairs and pub. responsibility Jewish Bd. Family and Children's Svcs.; life mem. exec. bd., mem. adminstrv. com. and bd. govs. Am. Jewish Com.; mem. Nat. Jewish Welfare Bd.; chmn., trustee, former pres. Fedn. Employment and Guidance Svc.; bd. dirs., former v.p. Willkie House; bd. dirs. USO of N.Y.; former bd. dirs., asst. treas. Freedom House, also exec. com. and counsel to bd.; trustee N.Y. County Lawyers Found.; hon. bd. dirs. Manhattan chpt. Brandeis U. Nat. Women's Com.; hon. v.p. Nat. Assn. Women Artists, Inc.; trustee, exec. com. W.J.A., Fedn. Jewish Philanthropies; former chmn. Legacy com. Temple Emanu-El; candidate of Republican Party for pres. City Coun. of N.Y., 1957; Contbr. to books; contbr. articles on govt., law, social problems to publs. including N.Y. Times Mag., Jour. of Living, legal jours. Recipient Presdl. citation NYU, 1962. Outstanding Citizenship award Am. Heritage Found., 1961, citation and testimonial, Mass. Com. on Caths. Protestants and Jews, 1960. Bond Between Us Award for outstanding svc. to Israel, 1960, citation and testimonial dinner Assn. for Help of Retarded Children, 1960, Ann. Brotherhood award Temple Emanu-El, N.Y.C. 1961, Woman of Achievement award Fedn. Jewish Women's Orgns., Salute to Women award, 1962; named Woman of Achievement, Women's Internat. Exposition, 1957, Woman of Yr., Beth Israel Hosp. Sch. Nursing, 1960, Woman of History N.Y. State, 1980; named to Hall of Fame Mt. Vernon High Sch. (N.Y.), 1981. Mem. ABA (sect. jud. adminstrn., alt. del. to Internat. Bar Assn. 1966), N.Y. State Bar Assn. (sec. jud. adminstrn., former chmn. adminstrv. law com., currently mem. cts. and community com., com. on profl. issues and standards, com. on election law), N.Y. County Lawyers Assn. (coms. judiciary, forum, spl. com. profl. ethics, former mem. bd. dirs.), Assn. Bar City N.Y. (com. on profl. responsibility, joint com. on fee concilliation, sr. vol. lawyers com.), World Habeus Corpus (exec. com.), Nat. Assn. Spl. Ct. Judges, Nat. Ctr. for State Cts. (adv. coun.), Am. Arbitration Assn. (comml. law com. sect.), Delta Kappa Gamma (internat. hon.). Home: 200 E 66th St New York NY 10021 Office: 685 3d Ave 26th Fl New York NY 10017

SIMON, DEBRA WAGNER, accountant; b. Phila., July 24, 1959; d. Joseph and Annette (Schmerling) Wagner; m. Paul Stephen Simon, Sept. 5, 1982; 1 child, Jessica M. BSBA, Drexel U., 1982. CPA, Pa. Jr. acct. Mann Judd Landau, Phila., 1983-84, staff acct., 1984, sr. acct., 1985-88, BDO Seidman, Phila., 1989—. Mem. Surrey Pl. Civic Assn., Cherry Hill, N.J., 1985-86. Mem. AICPA, Pa.Inst. CPA's, Am. Women's Soc. CPA's, Am. Soc. Women Accts., Beta Alpha Psi. Avocations: tennis, computers. Office: BDO Seidman 1601 Market St Philadelphia PA 19103

SIMON, DORIS MARIE, nurse; b. Akron, Ohio, Jan. 24, 1932; d. Gabriel James and Nannie Eliza (Harris) Tyler; m. Matthew Hamilton Simon, Apr. 20, 1952; children: Matthew Derek, Denise Nanette, Gayle Machele, Doris Elizabeth. AA, El Paso (Tex.) Community Coll., 1976; student, St. Joseph's Coll., North Windham, Maine, 1985—. Med. asst. Dr. Melvin Farris, Akron, 1962-63, Dr. Samuel Watt, Akron, 1967-68, Drs. May, Fox and Buchwald, El Paso, 1972-76; nurse mgr. Providence Meml. Hosp., El Paso, 1977-87, nurse mgr., transplant coord., 1987—; head nurse dialysis and transplant Hotel Dieu Med. Ctr., El Paso, 1987—; head nurse transplant coordinator Providence Meml. Hosp., El Paso, 1987—; med. asst. instr. Bryman Sch. Med. Assts., El Paso, 1970-72. Med. Assts., El Paso, 1970-72, Leader children's choirs, Ft. Sill, Okla., 1964-67; choir dir. Ft. Sill area and Ft. Bliss, Tex., area, 1964-74; instr. piano and music theory, Ft. Sill, 1974—; youth choir dir., 1989; leader Ft. Sill Coun. Girl Scouts U.S., 1965-67; instr. Sch. for Handicapped, Lawton, Okla., 1965-67; del. to Peoples Republic China citizen ambassador program People to People Internat., 1988. Recipient Molly Pitcher award U.S. Army, 1966-67. Mem. Am. Nurses Assn., Am. Med. Assts. Assn., Am. Nephrology Nurses Assn. Baptist. Clubs: Les Charmantes (Akron) (pres./sec. 1950-52), Links. Home: 8909 Parkland Dr El Paso TX 79925 Office: Providence Meml Hosp 2001 N Oregon St El Paso TX 79902

SIMON, DOROTHY ELAINE, educator, retired; b. Madison, Wis., Nov. 17, 1931; d. William Rees and Beatrice Helena (Reque) Beckett; m. William Henry Simon, Oct. 1, 1955; children: Stephen Eric, William Edward. BS, So. Conn. State U., 1954. Cert. elem. tchr., Conn. Tchr. grade 1 Ctr. St. Sch., North Haven, Conn., 1954-57; tchr. grades 3-4 Clover St. Sch., Windsor, Conn., 1968-87; cooperating tchr. Internship Program, U. Hartford and Cen. Conn. State U., 1973-85; unit leader Multi Unit Sch., Windsor, 1972-87, ret., 1987. Corr. sec. Women's Aux. of Hartford Symphony, 1966-70; v.p. PTO, Windsor, 1965-68; co-chmn. Windsor ARC Drive, 1969. Recipient honorarium So. New Eng. Tel. Mem. NEA, Conn. Edn. Assn., Windsor Edn. Assn., Nat. Assn. Individually Guided Edn., Green Mountain Club (Vt.), Millbrook Golf Club (Windsor). Episcopalian. Avocations: sketching, writing, hiking, camping, bicycling. Home: 17 Priscilla Rd Windsor CT 06095

SIMON, ELIZABETH MARIE, public relations executive; b. Oak Park, Ill., July 8, 1947; d. Albert Joseph and Catherine J. (Schmidt) Fieldhouse; m. Jan H. Simon. Student, Loyola U., 1965-68. Accredited in pub. relations. Pub. relations assoc. Kaiser Aluminum & Chem. Corp., Oakland, Calif., 1983-85; pub. relations rep. Kaiser Aluminum & Chem. Corp., 1985-88, supr. pub. relations, 1988—. Author: 4 Degrees North: A Guide to Ghana, 1988. Bd. dirs., v.p. Project Artaud Corp., San Francisco, 1986-88, Theater Artaud, San Francisco, 1987-88, Univ. Rsch. Expdns. Program, Berkeley, Calif., 1989. Mem. Pub. Rels. Soc. Am. (bd. dirs. Oakland chpt. 1986-87). Office: Kaiser Aluminum & Chem Corp 300 Lakeside Rm 2349 Oakland CA 94643

SIMON, JACQUELINE ALBERT, political scientist, journalist; b. N.Y.C.; d. Louis and Rose (Axelroad) Albert; B.A. cum laude, NYU, M.A., 1972, Ph.D., 1977; m. Pierre Simon; children: Lisette, Orville. Adj. asst. prof. Southampton Coll., 1977, 79—; mng. editor Point of Contact, N.Y.C., 1975-76; assoc. editor, U.S. bur. chief Politique Internationale, Paris, 1979—; rsch. assoc. Inst. French Studies, N.Y. U., N.Y.C., 1980—, asst. prof. govt., 1982-83; assoc. Inst. on the Media for War and Peace; frequent appearances French TV and radio. Contbg. editor Harper's, 1984—; contbr. numerous articles to French mags., revs., books on internat. affairs. Bd. dirs. Fresh Air Fund. 1984—. Mem. Ams. for Democratic Action, Nat. Acad. Sci., Am. Polit. Sci. Assn., French-Am. Soc., Phi Beta Kappa. Home: 988 Fifth Ave New York NY 10021

SIMON, LORENA COTTS, music educator, composer, poet; b. Sherman, Tex., Jan. 16, 1897; d. George Godfrey and Willie (Jones) Cotts; student Am. Conservatory, summer 1938, Juilliard Music Sch., summer 1939; diploma Sherwood Music Sch., 1941; LittD (hon.), Internat. Acad. Leadership, Quezon City, Philippines; LHD (hon.), No. Pontificial Acad., Malmo, Sweden, 1969; MusD (hon.), St. Olav's Acad., Sweden, 1969; m. Samuel C. Simon, Nov. 6, 1918 (dec.). Tchr. violin, piano, theory and harmony, Port Arthur, Tex., 1919—. Organizer, dir. Schubert's Violin Choir, Port Arthur, 1919-55. Named Poet Laureate of Tex. 1961; Poet Laureate of Magnolia Dist., 1962-64; Poet Laureate of Port Arthur, 1962—; recipient gold plaque Tex. Fedn. Women's Club, 1962, spl. award 1st place in poetry and music Tex. heritage dept., 1963; medal of merit and diploma of merit Centro Studi Scambi Internat., Rome, Italy, 1965; Gold medal award, and hon. poet laureate-musician United Poets Laureate Internat., 1966, named Cath. Lady of Humanity, 1977; decorated Equestrian Order of Holy Sepulchre, 1981; inducted into Knights and Ladies of the Holy Sepulchre, Pope John II, 1982, Nat. Guild of Piano Tchrs.' Hall of Fame, 1986, Southeast Tex. Women's Hall of Fame, 1987; recipient Greatness and Leadership award U. Manila, 1967; Silver medal, Gold medal, Diploma Centro Studi E Scambi—Internazionali, 1967; Gold Laurel Wreath, Gold medal, Karte of Award, 1966; named to International Poets' Hall of Fame, 1969, named most outstanding woman internationally Congress of Doctors, Quezon City, Philippines, 1969; named Cath. Poet Laureate of World, 1967. Mem. Nat., Tex. press women's assns., Nat. Council Cath. Women, Nat. Guild Piano Tchrs. (charter mem.; adjudicator), Am. Coll. Musicians (adjudicator), Internat. Guild Library, Am. Poetry League, Poets Soc. Tex. (critic judge), Am. Poets Fellowship Soc. Corp., UN Assn. U.S.A., Alpha Delta Kappa. Clubs: Writers' (pres. 1963-64), Symphony. Author: The Golden Keys, 1958; From My Heart (1st place award Ann. Poetry Writers Contest of Tex. Press Women's Assn. 1961), 1959; Children's Story Hour (1st place award Nat. Fedn. Press Women's Ann. Writers' Contest 1962), 1960. Songs pub. include: Live Expectantly, 1962, In Search for Growth, 1963, Freedom's Light, 1963, What Can I Do for Jesus, 1963, I Was a Star, I Was a Lamb, I Was a Donkey; organ piece Mediation, 1967. Chmn. spl. editorial com. World Poets Laureate Anthology, 1969-70. Donor funds for constrn. of 9 churches in Africa. Home: 411 5th Ave Port Arthur TX 77642

SIMON, MARILYN, lawyer; b. N.Y.C., Dec. 22, 1941; d. Murray and Ray (Perlowitz) S. BA, Bklyn. Coll., 1963; JD, Seton Hall U., 1971. Bar: N.Y. 1971, U.S. Dist. Ct. (so. dist.) N.Y. 1975, (ea. dist.) N.Y. 1976, U.S. Ct. Appeals (2nd cir.) 1978. Asst. advt. mgr. Elizabeth Arden, N.Y.C., 1963-64; exec. sec. Buonacorsi & Murray, San Francisco, 1964-65; ofc. mgr. Joseph E. Murray and Assocs., San Francisco, 1965-67; v.p., sales mgr. Battani Ltd., Norwood, N.Y., 1967-75; law clk. to chief judge U.S. Bankruptcy Ct. (so. dist.) N.Y., N.Y.C., 1975; assoc. Leinwand, Maron, Hendler & Krause, N.Y.C., 1975-77, Phillips, Nizer, Benjamin, Krim & Ballor, N.Y.C., 1977; assoc., then ptnr. Levin, Weintraub & Crames, N.Y.C., 1977-85; pvt. practice N.Y.C., 1986—. Mem. ABA. N.Y. Bar Assn. (com. bankruptcy 1981), N.Y. County Lawyers Assn., N.Y. Bankruptcy Lawyers Assn. (bd. trustees). Democrat. Jewish. Office: 200 Park Ave S New York NY 10003-1503

SIMON, MARILYN W., art educator, sculptor; b. Chgo., Aug. 25, 1927; d. William and Caroline Mabel (Bergman) Weintraub; m. Walter E. Simon, Mar. 19, 1950; children: Nina Fay, Jacob Aaron, Maurine Joy Simon Rubinstein, Linda Gay Simon Shapiro. PhB, U. Chgo., 1947; MEd, Temple U., 1969. Cert. tchr., Pa. Bd. sec. Delaware Valley Smelting Corp., Bristol, Pa., 1957-89; art tchr. Calumet Sch. Dist., Ill., 1951-53; art tchr., chmn. elem. art program Cheltenham (Pa.) Sch. Dist., 1969—; real estate agt., Tullytown, Pa.; speaker in field. One woman show include Hohn Gallery, Phila., 1985; also represented in med. offices, pvt. colls.; author publs. on using art reproductions in edn. chmn. Phila. chpt. U. Chgo. Alumni Fund Assn., 1978-84. Recipient numerous art awards including 1st prize Doylestown Art League, 1986-87, Best Sculpture award Mummers's Mus. Phila., 1987, Juror's award Cheltenham Art Ctr., 1987-88, 3d prize Abington Art Ctr., 1988, 1st prize for sculpture Art Assn. of Harrisburg, 1989. Mem. Nat. Art Edn. Assn., Pa. Art Educators Assn. (regional rep. 1988-89, Outstanding Art Educator of Yr. award 1987), Oil Pastel Assn. N.Y.C. (invited mem.). Democrat. Jewish. Office: PO Box 29722 Elkins Park PA 19117

SIMON, NANCY SMITH, health education consultant; b. Bowling Green, Ky., Mar. 20, 1938; d. Edgar Buchanan and Irene Frances (Brock) Smith; m. James F. Simon, Aug. 9, 1959; 1 child, Sarah. BS in Health-Phys. Edn., Ind. U., 1959, MS in Health-Safety Edn., 1960. Cert. health edn. specialist, Ind. Tchr. Monroe County Community Schs., Bloomington, Ind., 1959-62, Univ. Schs., Bloomington, 1963-66, 68-69; substitute tchr. Beech Grove (Ind.) City Schs., 1969-73; dir. edn. Social Health Assn. Cen. Ind., Indpls., 1973-80; health edn. cons. Ind. Bd. Health, Indpls., 1980—, editor MCH Connection newsletter, 1985-87. Co-author: Modern Sex Education, 1980, 3d edit. pub. as Family Life and Human Sexuality, 1988. Deacon, leader Bible study Presbyn. Ch., Indpls. Mem. Ind. Assn. Health Educators, Ind. Pub. Health Assn., Ind. Coun. on Adolescent Pregnancy, Ind. Coun. on Family Rels. (bd. dirs. 1984-87, chmn. ann. meeting 1990), Ind. Congress Parents and Tchrs. (hon. life, bd. dirs., comprehensive health coord. 1978-84). Republican. Office: Ind Bd Health 1330 W Michigan St Indianapolis IN 46206-1964

SIMON, NANCY SUE, insurance executive; b. Royal Oak, Mich., Mar. 2, 1943; d. William and Evelyn (Thompson) S.; m. John Hawkins (div. June 1975); children: Thomas Hawkins, L.L.B. Bell, Boyd, Floyd. Dir. ops. INSTA-OFFICE, Southfield, Mich., 1980-84; exec. dir. Greater Detroit Assn. Life Underwriters, Detroit, 1984—; bd. dirs. Qualified Plans, Troy, Mich. Bd. dirs. Young Reps., Detroit, 1978-84. Mem. Met. Area Underwriters Assn. (bd. dirs. 1986—), Royal Oak Women's Club (pres. 1981-83). Office: Greater Detroit Assn 3331 W Big Beaver Ste 104 Troy MI 48084

SIMON, NORMA BERNICE, author; b. N.Y., Dec. 24, 1927; d. Nathan Philip and Winnie Bertha (Lepselter) Feldstein; m. Gerald Fromberg, June 6, 1948 (div. 1949); m. Edward Simon, June 7, 1951; children: Stephanie, Wendy (dec.), Jonathan. BA, Brklyn. Coll., 1947; MS in Edn., Bank St Coll, N.Y., 1968. Founder, dir., tchr. Community Coop. Nusery Sch., Rowayton, Conn., 1953-54; tchr. Norwalk (Conn.) Pub. Sch., 1962-63; cons. Stamford (Conn.) Pre-Sch. Program, 1965-69; special tchr. Mid-Fairfield Child Guidance Ctr., Norwalk, Conn.; cons. MacMillan Pub. Co., N.Y., 1968-70, Davidson Films, 1969-74, Bank St Coll. of Edn., N.Y., 1967-74, Aesop Films, San Francisco, 1975-79, Fisher-Price Toys, East Aurora, N.Y., 1978; cons. Dancer-Fitzgerald-Sample, Inc., N.Y.C., 1969-79; included in deGrummond Collection, U. So. Miss., Kerlan Collection, U. Mich. Author over 40 childrens books, 1954—, latest being Nobody's Perfect, Not Even My Mother, 1981, Where Does My Cat Sleep?, 1982, I Wish I Had My Father, 1983, Oh, That Cat!, 1986, The Saddest Time, 1986, Cats Do, Dogs Don't, 1987, Wedding Days, 1987, I Am Not a Crybaby, 1989; contbr. author: Dimensions of Language Experience, 1975. Pres. Westport Coop. Nursery Sch. Bd., 1957-58; mem. town com. Mid-Fairfield Child Guidance; mem. Oak Hill Coop. Nursery Sch. Bd., 1958-59; vol. pre-sch. com. program Nathaniel Ely Sch., Norwalk, 1963-64; program chmn. Princess Anne Elem. Sch. Home-Sch. Assn., Riverside, Ont., Can., 1959-60; mem. Wellfleet Elem. Sch. Com., 1974-79, mem. bldg. com., 1979—. Recipient Jeremiah Cahir Friend of Edn. award, 1987. Mem. Author's Guild, Soc. Children's Book Writers, Nat. Assn. for Edn. Young Children, Bank Street Coll. Edn. Alumni Assn. Democrat. Jewish. Home: PO Box 428 South Wellfleet MA 02663

SIMON, NORMA PLAVNICK, psychologist; b. Washington, Sept. 20, 1930; d. Mark and Mary (Ogus) Plavnick; m. Robert G. Simon, Dec. 18, 1949; children: Mark Allan, Susan. BA, NYU, 1952, cert. in psychoanalysis, 1977; MA, Columbia U., 1953, EdD, 1968. Diplomate Am. Bd. Profl. Psychology, 1988. Psychologist Queens Coll. Counseling Ctr., Flushing, N.Y., 1968-70, asst. dir., 1970-76, dir., 1976; gen. practice psychology N.Y.C., 1976—; faculty, supr. New Hope Guild, Bklyn., 1976—, dir. child and adolescent tng. prog., 1988—; adj. prof. clin. psychology Columbia U., N.Y.C., 1986—; supr. NYU Postdoctoral Prog. in Psychoanalysis, 1988—. Author: (with Robert G. Simon): Choosing a College Major: Social Science, 1981; mem. editorial bd. The Counseling Psychologist jour., 1986-89. Vice chairperson N.Y. State Bd. for Psychology State Edn. Dept., Albany, 1978-82, chairperson 1982-88; bd. dirs. Pelham (N.Y.) Guidance Coun., 1980-83. Fellow Am. Psychol. Assn. (bd. profl. affairs 1987-89). Office: 500A E 87th St #5A New York NY 10128

SIMON, OLGA, lawyer; b. N.Y.C., May 2, 1965; d. Jean and Cleomie Simon. BA, CUNY, 1984; JD, NYU, 1987. Asst. corp. counsel N.Y.C. Law Dept., 1987—. English instr. Têtes Ensembles, N.Y.C., 1988-89. Mem. ABA, N.Y. State Bar Assn., N.Y. City Bar Assn. Democrat. Roman Catholic. Office: NYC Law Dept 100 Church St New York NY 10007

SIMONDS, MARIE CELESTE, architect; b. Miami, Fla., Mar. 30, 1947; d. Hinton Joseph and Frances Olivia (Burnett) Baker; m. Clayton Richard Struse, July 27, 1968 (div. Sept. 1974); m. Albert Rhett Simonds, Jr., Oct. 9, 1974; children: Caroline Lamar, Frances Rhett. BA, U. Pa., 1968; BArch, U. Md., 1973. Registered architect, Va. Architect Harry Weese & Assocs., Washington, 1973-75; pvt. practice Alexandria, Va., 1976—. Com. chmn. Jr. Friends Alexandria YWCA, 1974-78; mem. Jr. League Washington, 1978—. NSF grantee, 1972. Mem. AIA (scholar 1971), Va. Soc. of AIA, West River Sailing Club (Galesville, Md.), Sierra Club. Episcopalian. Home and Office: 624 S Lee St Alexandria VA 22314

SIMONE, ANN MARIE, computer systems analyst; b. Bklyn., Mar. 3, 1958; d. Anthony Jr. and Marie (Caputo) S. Cert., Briarcliff Coll. for Bus., Hicksville, N.Y., 1977; student, Nassau Community Coll., Garden City, N.Y. Telex operator Ebasco, Jericho, N.Y., 1977-82; exec. sec. systems support dept. Chase Manhattan Bank, Lake Success, N.Y., 1982-86; with Sim I Computer Svcs., Floral Park, N.Y., 1987—; systems area coord. Profl. Fin. Analysts, Lake Success, 1986—. Mem. L.I. Computer Assn. (reviewer computer hardware and software 1989—). Home: 22 Whitney Ave Floral Park NY 11001 Office: Profl Fin Analysts Inc 2001 Marcus Ave Ste 265 Lake Success NY 11042

SIMONE, GAIL ELISABETH, research analyst; b. Boston, Dec. 3, 1944; d. Hugh Nelson and Louise Amelia (Shedrick) Saunders; m. Edburnne R. Hare, Sept. 7, 1968 (div. 1974); m. Joseph R. Simone, June 27, 1987. BA, The King's Coll., 1966; postgrad., Harvard U., 1976-77. Placement dir. Boston Bar Assn., 1966-67; pub. relations Emerson Coll., Boston, 1967-69; asst. to v.p. Vance, Sanders, Inc., Boston, 1969-70; office mgr. Trans. Displays, Inc., Boston, 1970-71; seminar coordinator Assn. Trial Lawyers Am., Cambridge, Mass., 1971-74; writer, researcher Ednl. Expeditions Internat., Belmont, Mass., 1975-76; analyst United Brands Co., N.Y.C., 1976-80; analyst Mil. Sealift Commd., USN, Washington, 1980-84, legis. affairs officer, 1984-88; rsch. analyst Bath Iron Works, Shipbuilders, Bath, Maine, 1988—; free-lance writer, editor, Boston, 1970-73. Vol. McCarthy Presdl. Campaign, Boston, 1968, Mass. Pax, Boston; foster parent Warwick, R.I., 1986—; mem. Amnesty Internat., N.Y.C., 1987—, various other orgns. Mem. Nat. Assn. Female Execs., Women's Trans. Seminar. Office: Bath Iron Works 700 Washington St Bath ME 04530

SIMONE, JOHANNA FRANCINE, accountant; b. Southington, Conn., June 9, 1963; d. Joseph F. and Lillian (Grande) S. BS in Acctg., Cen. Conn. State U., 1984; postgrad., U. Hartford, 1988—. CPA, Conn. Acct. Spitz, Sullivan, Wachel & Falcetta, Hartford, Conn., 1985-86, Deloitte, Haskins & Sells, Hartford, 1986-88, Standadyne, Inc., Windsor, Conn., 1988-89; pvt. practice acctg. Southington, 1989—. Office: 1006 S Main St Plantsville CT 06479

SIMONS, ELIZABETH R(EIMAN), biochemist, educator; b. Vienna, Austria, Sept. 1, 1929; came to U.S., 1941, naturalized, 1948; d. William and Erna Engle (Weisselberg) Reiman; B.Ch.E., Cooper Union, N.Y.C., 1950; M.S., Yale U., 1951, Ph.D., 1954; m. Harold Lee Simons, Aug. 12, 1951; children—Leslie Ann Mulert, Robert David. Research chemist Tech. Operations, Arlington, Mass., 1953-54; instr. chemistry Wellesley (Mass.) Coll., 1954-57; rsch. asst. Children's Hosp. Med. Center and Cancer Rsch. Found., Boston, 1957-59, rsch. assoc. pathology, 1959-62; research assoc. Harvard Med. Sch., 1962-66, lectr. biol. chemistry, 1966-72; tutor biochemical scis. Harvard Coll., 1971—; assoc. prof. biochemistry Boston U., 1972-78, prof., 1978—. Contbr. articles to profl. jours. Grantee in field. Mem. AAAS, Am.

Chem. Soc., Am. Heart Assn., Am. Soc. Biol. Chemists, Am. Soc. Cell Biology, Am. Soc. Hematology, Am. Fedn. Clin. Rsch., Assn. Women in Sci., Biophys. Soc., Internat. Soc. Thrombosis and Hemostasis, N.Y. Acad. Sci., Sigma Xi. Office: Boston U Sch Medicine 80 E Concord St Boston MA 02118

SIMONS, LOIS ANNE, retired university program director; b. Marshall, Minn., Oct. 31, 1917; d. Harry Stanley Simons and Lela May (Maxwell) Simons-Evans. BE with honors, Winona State U., 1939; MS, Wellesley Coll., 1941. Cert. tchr. Jr. and sr. high sch. tchr. Lakefield (Minn.) Pub Schs., 1939-40; instr. women's phys. edn. Morningside Coll., Sioux City, Iowa, 1941-42, U. Minn., Duluth, 1942-43; admissions counselor U. Wis., Madison, 1946-49; instr. women's phys. edn. U. Wis., LaCrosse, 1949-51; dir. student activities Northwest Mo. State U., Maryville, 1954-57; registrar Winona (Minn.) State U., 1957-68, dir. instl. rsch., 1968-79. Lt. comdr. USN, 1943-46, 51-54. Mem. AAUW (treas. 1975-76), Self Help for Hard of Hearing People Inc., DAR (treas. 1989—), Delta Kappa Gamma (treas. 1987-88, state directory rep. 1980-88). Republican. Methodist. Home: 514 Glenview Ct Winona MN 55987

SIMONS, LYNN OSBORN, state education official; b. Havre, Mont., June 1, 1934; d. Robert Blair and Dorothy (Briggs) Osborn; BA, U. Colo., 1956; postgrad. U. Wyo., 1958-60; m. John Powell Simons, Jan. 19, 1957; children: Clayton Osborn, William Blair. Tchr., Midvale (Utah) Jr. High Sch., 1956-57, Sweetwater County Sch. Dist. 1, Rock Springs, Wyo., 1957-58, U. Wyo., Laramie, 1959-61, Natrona County Sch. Dist. 1, Casper, Wyo., 1963-64; credit mgr. Gallery 323, Casper, 1972-77; Wyo. state supt. public instrn., Cheyenne, 1979—; mem. State Bds. Charities and Reform, Land Commrs., Farm Loan, 1979—; mem. State Commns. Capitol Bldg., Liquor, 1979—; Ex-officio mem. bd. trustees U. Wyo.; ex-officio mem. Wyo. Community Coll. Commn.; mem. steering com. Edn. Commn. of the States; mem. State Bd. Edn., 1971-77, chmn., 1976-77; advisor Nat. Trust for Hist. Preservation, 1980-86. Mem. LWV (pres. 1970-71), Am. Assn. Sch. Adminstrs., Coun. of Chief State Sch. Officers (bd. dirs.), Wyo. Assn. Sch. Adminstrs. Democrat. Episcopalian. Home: Box 185 Cheyenne WY 82002 Office: Edn Dept Hathaway Bldg 2nd Fl Cheyenne WY 82001

SIMONS, MELISSA JANE, office furniture company executive; b. Boston, Aug. 5, 1961; d. William M. Simons and Constance (Vernon) Simons Lappin. BA, Marietta Coll., 1983. Sec. Offices Unltd., Inc., Boston, 1983; sales rep. M. Brown, Inc., Boston, 1983-85; sales mgr. Osborne Office Furniture, Milton, Mass., 1985—. Editor-in-chief newspaper Portfolio, 1985—; contbg. editor newspaper IBD News, 1989—. Mem. Boston Soc. Architects (affiliate mem.), Inst. Bus.Designers (mem. industry council 1988—), Design Industries Found. for AIDS. Home: 54 Crescent Ave Apt 15B Boston MA 02125 Office: Osborne Office Furniture Co 360 Granite Ave Milton MA 02186

SIMONS, SHIRLEY ANN, educator; b. Des Moines, Apr. 19, 1937; d. Ernest Clinton and Lela (Trusler) Clark; m. Kenneth Kay Simons, Aug. 28, 1960; children: Deborah, DeAnn, Lorie. BS, Colo. U., 1973; MS, U. No. Colo., 1986. Tchr. Adams County Sch. #50, Westminster, Colo., 1973—. Asst. capt. Neighborhood Watch, Arvada, Colo., 1989; active Arvada United Meth. Ch., 1989. Mem. AAUW, Westminster Edn. Assn., Rocky Mountain Roadrunners Club, Elks, Order Eastern Star, Pi Lambda Theta. Republican. Home: 12033 W 67th Pl Arvada CO 80004

SIMONS, VICKI ANN, blood center director; b. Omaha, Nov. 30, 1950; d. Kenneth John and Alvina Mae (Wilson) Mumm; m. James F. Simons, Apr. 17, 1971; children: Jeffrey, Michael, Lucas. Student, U. Nebr., 1982-87; grad. med. technician, Med. Inst. Minn., 1970. Staff technician ARC Blood Svcs., Omaha, 1971-74, distbn. coord., 1974-78, dir. product mgmt., 1978-87, dir. hosp. svcs., 1987—, developer midwest tissue svcs., 1985—; mem. 1st Product Mgmt. Adv. Com., Washington, 1979-81; mem. nat. plasma adv. group ARC, Washington, 1986-87; originator, mem. Organ and Tissue Agys. Nebr., Omaha, 1987—; rep., officer Organ and Tissue Donor Task Force Nebr., Omaha, 1986—. Mem. choir, pianist Bethlehem Luth. Ch., Wahoo, Nebr., 1979—; loaned exec. United Way Midlands, Omaha, 1981. Recipient Mgr.'s Tiffany award ARC, 1987. Mem. Am. Soc. Clin. Pathologists (cert. lab. asst.), Am. Assn. Tissue Banks, P.E.O. (chaplain Nebr. Chpt. I, 1986-88, sec. 1988-90, v.p. 1990—). Republican. Office: ARC 3838 Dewey Ave Omaha NE 68105

SIMONSON, DONNA JEANNE, accountant; b. Malden, Mass., Sept. 6, 1947; d. George Francis and Dorothy Josephine (Bridges) Yost; m. Scott N. Simonson, June 30, 1967 (div. Feb. 1989); children: Stephanie Louise Burke, Kelly Lynn. AA Bus. Adminstrn., Corning Community Coll., 1979; BS in Mgmt., Keuka Coll., 1981. Bus. office supr. Steuben Allegany B.O.C.E.S., Bath, N.Y., 1969-75; staff acct. David L. Snyderwine & Co. CPA's, Bath, 1979-82; dir. bus. svcs. Steuben Assoc. for Retarded Children, Inc., Bath, 1982—; owner Donna J. Simonson, Taxes, & Acctg., Bath, 1982--. Pres. Pulteney Vol. Firemen's Auxiliary, 1973. Mem. Am. Assn. Univ. Women, Bath Area Humane Soc., Pulteney Free Library Assn., Fiscal Mgrs. Assn. Democrat. Presbyterian. Home: 1 Ellis Ave Bath NY 14810 Office: Steuben Arc RD 2 Box 149-1 Bath NY 14810

SIMONSON, SUSAN KAY, hospital administrator; b. LaPorte, Ind., Dec. 5, 1946; d. George Randolph and Myrtle Lucille (Opfel) Menkes; m. Richard Bruce Simonson, Aug. 25, 1973. BA with honors, Ind. U., 1969; MA, Washington U., St. Louis, 1972. Perinatal social worker Yakima Valley Meml. Hosp., Yakima, Wash., 1979-81, dir. patient support and hospice program, 1981—, dir. social svc., 1982—; Spanish instr. Yakima Valley Coll., Yakima, Wash., 1981—; pres. Yakima Child Abuse Council, 1983-85; developer nat. patient support program, 1981. Contbr. articles to profl. jours. Mem. Jr. League, Yakima; mem. adv. council Robert Wood Johnson Found. Rural Infant Health Care Project, Yakima, 1980, Pregnancy Loss and Compassionate Friends Support Groups, Yakima, 1982—, Teen Outreach Program, Yakima, 1984—. Recipient NSF award, 1967, discharge planning program of yr. regional award Nat. Glasrock Home Health Care Discharge Planning Program, 1987; research grantee Ind. U., 1968, Fulbright grantee U.S. Dept. State, 1969-70; Nat. Def. Edn. Act fellowship, 1970-73. Mem. AAUW, Soc. Med. Anthropology, Soc. Hosp. Social Work Dirs. of Am. Hosp. Assn. (regional award 1989), Nat. Assn. Perinatal Social Workers, Nat. Assn. Social Workers, Phi Beta Kappa. Office: Yakima Valley Meml Hosp 2811 Tieton Dr Yakima WA 98902

SIMONSON, TERESA M., financial executive; b. Torrance, Calif., Nov. 10, 1960; d. Frederick Anthony and Florence Katherine (Kramer) Tachovsky. BS, Calif. State U., Fresno, 1985. Cashier, bookkeeper Orville and Wilbur's Restaurant, Manhattan Beach, Calif.; accounts receivable clk. Mobil Oil Co., L.A.; gen. ptnr. Bentley/Simonson Partnership, Ojai, Calif.; chief fin. officer D and S Indsl. Svcs., Inc., Ojai. Mem. Ojai ValleyC. of C. (mem. of yr.), Toastmasters Internat., Ventura County Taxpayers Assn., Phi Kappa Psi, Alpha Kappa Psi.

SIMPKINS, ANNE EDDLEMAN, interior designer; b. Charlotte, N.C., July 9, 1950; d. Alton B. and Melba (Ketner) Eddleman; m. Jesse E. Simpkins, June 23, 1973. BA in Home Econs., Appalachian State U., Boone, N.C., 1972; postgrad., U. Tenn., 1982. Decorating cons. J.C. Penney's, Knoxville, Tenn., 1972-76, Decorating Den, Knoxville, 1976-80; interior designer Vaughan Furniture, Knoxville, 1981-85; pres., interior designer Living Interiors, Inc., Knoxville, 1985—. Contbr. articles to profl. publs. Com. mem., showhouse designer Symphony League, Knoxville, 1989. Recipient Designer's Choice award Mar. of Dimes, 1989, 2d Place People's Choice award Mar. of Dimes, 1989. Mem. Interior Design Soc. (nat. pres. 1990—), East Tenn. Interior Design Soc. (pres. 1986-88, bd. dirs.), Toastmasters (pres. 1988, award 1989). Office: Living Interiors Inc 6326 Papermill Rd 6B Knoxville TN 37919

SIMPSON, ADELE, costume designer; b. N.Y.C., Dec. 8, 1908; d. Jacob and Ella (Bloch) Smithline; m. Wesley William Simpson, Oct. 8, 1930; children: Jeffrey R., Joan Ellen. Grad., Pratt Inst., Bklyn. With Ben Gershel, N.Y.C., 1922-23, head dress designer, 1923; chief designer William Bass, N.Y.C., 1927-28; designer (own label) Mary Lee Fashions (named changed to Adele Simpson, Inc. 1949), N.Y.C., 1928-49, pres., dir., from 1949, now chmn. bd. Work displayed in Met. Costume Inst., Bklyn. Mus., Dallas Library. Recipient Neiman-Marcus Fashion award, 1946, Coty Fashion award, 1947, First Nat. Cotton Council award, 1953. Mem. Fashion Group, N.Y. Couture Group. Office: Adele Simpson Inc 530 7th Ave New York NY 10018*

SIMPSON, ANDREA LYNN, energy communication executive; b. Altadena, Calif., Feb. 10, 1948; d. Kenneth James and Barbara Faries Simpson; m. John R. Myrdal, Dec. 13, 1986; 1 child, Christopher Ryan Myrdal. BA, U. So. Calif., 1969, MS, 1983; postgrad. U. Colo., Boulder, 1977. Asst. cashier United Calif. Bank, L.A., 1969-73; asst. v.p. mktg. 1st Hawaiian Bank, Honolulu, 1973-78; v.p. corp. communications Pacific Resources, Inc., Honolulu, 1978—. Bd. dirs. Kapiolani Women's and Children's Hosp., 1988—, Hawaii Heart Assn., 1978-83, Child and Family Svcs., 1984-86, Coun. of Pacific, Girl Scouts U.S., 1982-85, Arts Coun. Hawaii, 1977-81, Hawaii Pub. Radio, 1989—; trustee Hawaii Loa Coll., 1984-86; commr. Hawaii State Commn. on Status of Women, 1985-87. Trustee Hawaii sch. for girls at LaPietra, 1989—; Bd. dirs. Honolulu Symphony Soc., 1985—, Sta. KHPR Hawaii Pub. Radio, 1988—. Named Panhellenic Woman of Yr. Hawaii, 1979, Outstanding Woman in Bus. Hawaii YWCA, 1980, Outstanding Young Woman of Hawaii Girl Scouts Coun. of the Pacific, 1985, 86, Hawaii Legis., 1980. Mem. Am. Mktg. Assn., Pub. Rels. Soc. Am. (bd. dirs. Honolulu chpt. 1984-86, Silver Anvil award 1984), Pub. Utilities Communicators Assn. (Communicator of Yr. 1984), Honolulu Advt. Fedn. (Advt. Woman of Yr. 1984), U. So. Calif. Alumni Assn. (bd. dirs. Hawaii 1981-83), Outrigger Canoe Club, Pacific Club, Kaneohe Yacht Club, Rotary (state pub. rels. chmn. 1988—, Honolulu chpt.), Alpha Phi (dir. Hawaii), Hawaii Jaycees (Outstanding Young Person of Hawaii 1978). Office: Pacific Resources Inc 733 Bishop St Ste 3100 Honolulu HI 96813

SIMPSON, BARBARA L., library director; b. Cleve., Apr. 6, 1947; d. Curley and Cora (Chambliss) Brown; children: Michelle, Crystal, Twilla. BS, Ohio State U., 1967; MS in Ednl. Media, Kent. State U. (Ohio), 1971, MLS, 1971. Adminstrv. supr. Cleve. pub. schs., 1968-72; libr. Cuyahoga Community Coll., Cleve., 1972-75, coord., 1975-77, interim dir., 1977-78, asst. dean, 1978-80, dir., 1980-84; dir. libr. Kean Coll., Union, N.J., 1984—; cons. Dembsy Assocs., Boston, 1967-81; editorial cons. Max Pub. Co., N.Y.C., 1967-81; cons. reader U.S. Office Edn., Washington, 1979-80; editorial cons. Jossey-Bass Pub. Co., 1979. Cons. editor Probe, 1975, Sch. Media Ctr., 1968, Booklist, 1969; contbr. articles to profl. jours. Bd. dirs. N.J. Adv. Bd. on the Status of Women, 1988, Africana Studies, 1988, N.J. State Libr. Adv. Bd., 1987; chairperson N.J. Acad. Libr. Network, N.J. Ednl. Activities Task Force Libr. Com. Recipient Phillips award Kent State U., 1970. Mem. ALA, Higher Edn. Reps., N.J. Acad. Libr. Network (chmn. 1987), Council N.J. Coll. Librs. (pres. 1987—), N.J. Libr. Assn., Oral History Soc., N.J. Hist. Soc., Jr. League (Cleve. vice chmn. 1981, 83), Concerned Parents Club (pres. 1984), Women's City Club. Avocations: music, reading. Office: Kean Coll Libr Morris Ave Union NJ 07083

SIMPSON, CAROL LOUISE, investment advisory company executive; b. Phila., Jan. 30, 1937; d. William Huffington and Hilda Agnes (Johnston) S. Student, Community Coll., 1985, 86, 87, U. Minn., 1986, 87, 88. Cert. Nat. Assn. Securities Dealers, Inc., Washington; registered options, mcpl. securities, gen. securities, fin. and ops. prin.; lic. life, accident, health ins. Exec. asst. Germantown Fed. Savs., Phila., 1954-67; asst. sec. Am. Med. Investment Co., Inc. (formerly Cannon and Co., Inc.), Blue Bell, Pa., 1967—; also bd. dirs. Cannon & Co., Inc., 1986; v.p., sec. AMA Investment Advisers, Inc. (formerly Pro Svcs., Inc.), Blue Bell, Pa., 1967—; also bd. dirs. AMA Investment Advisers, Inc. (formerly PRO Svcs., Inc.), Blue Bell, Pa., 1984-86. Mem. World Affairs Coun., Investment Co. Inst. (fed. legis. com. 1984—, investment advisers com. 1988—, compliance com. 1990), Internat. Assn. Fin. Planners, Investment Women's Club, Nat. Notary Assn., Pa. Assn. Notaries, Whitemarsh Valley Country Club. Republican. Home: 7701 Lawnton St Philadelphia PA 19128 Office: AMA Investment Advisers Inc 5 Sentry Pkwy W Ste 120 PO Box 1111 Blue Bell PA 19422

SIMPSON, CATHY ANN, land title company executive, real estate broker; b. Ripley, Miss., Aug. 6, 1953; d. Booth Obed and Annette Grace (Tapp) Simpson. m. Thomas Earl Jones, July 21, 1973 (div. Dec. 1981). B.A. with honors, Harding U., 1975. Real estate broker Houston Bd. Realtors, 1976—; mktg. broker cons. Capital Title Co., Houston, 1979-81; founder, owner The Settlers, 1979—, asst. v.p. Commerce Title Co., Houston, 1981-85; mktg. broker Capital Title Co., 1985—; faculty The Real Estate Sch. Mem. Tex. Real Estate Polit. Action Com. Mem. Nat. Assn. Realtors, Houston Bd. Realtors. Republican. Mem. Ch. of Christ. Home: 7723 W Bellfort #173 Houston TX 77071 Office: Capital Title Co 2929 Allen Pkwy Ste 200 Houston TX 77019

SIMPSON, CYNTHIA KAY, small business owner; b. Portland, Oreg., Feb. 24, 1953; d. Philip Justin and Beverly Ann (Keesey) Cleary; m. Larry Alan Simpson, June 2, 1979; children: Matthew, Andrew, Kristin. BA in Music, Whitman Coll., Walla Walla, Wash., 1975; postgrad., Portland State U., 1977. Cert. elem. tchr., Oreg. Sr. counselor Multnomah Edn. Service Dist., Portland, 1975; tng. dir. Meier and Frank Retail Store, Portland, 1975-85; owner, operator Neptune's Gift Shop, Seaside, Oreg., 1985-89, Cindy's Day Care, Portland, 1988—; owner, operator The Prom Corp., Seaside, 1985-87, Heritage Square Shopping Mall, Seaside, 1985—. Vol. Eastmoreland Aux. Oreg. Symphony, Portland, 1982—, Parry Ctr., Portland, 1983—, Jr. League, Portland, 1985-88, Holy Family Cath. Ch., Portland, 1987—, Azumano Homestay Program, Portland, 1988, Whitman Coll. Alumni Fund, 1982—. Mem. Portland Rose Soc., Delta Delta Delta (chaplain 1974-75), Mu Phi Epsilon (v.p. 1974-75). Democrat. Home and Office: 6705 SE 32 Portland OR 97202

SIMPSON, DEANNA LYNN, Christian education director; b. Amarillo, Tex., May 26, 1956; d. Carl V. and Audean (Gray) S. BS in Interior Design, Stepen F. Austin State U., 1978; MA in Christian Edn., Asbury Theol. Sem., Wilmore, Ky., 1989. Salesperson Gabberts Furniture, Dallas, 1979-86; salesperson, asst. mgr. Wood Works Plus, Carrollton, Tex., 1986-87; Christian edn. dir. Washington Crossing (Pa.) United Meth. Ch., 1989—. Republican. Office: Washington Crossing UMC 1895 Wrightstown Rd Washington Crossing PA 18977

SIMPSON, DEBORAH LYNNE, writer; b. Jacksonville, Fla., May 21, 1962. BS, U. Fla., 1986. Asst. producer Image Prodns. & Svcs., Miami, Fla., 1986-87; asst. producer/writer Multi-Media Prodns., Jacksonville, Fla., 1987; writer pvt. practice, Jacksonville, Fla., 1987—. Author, producer numerous projects. Recipient Crystal Reel awds, Fla. Motion Picture and TV, 1989. Home: 720 Trinidad Rd Jacksonville FL 32216

SIMPSON, DIANE JEANNETTE, social worker; b. Denver, Sept. 20, 1952; d. Arthur Henry and Irma Virginia (Jordan) S. BS, Nebr. Wesleyan U., 1974; MSW, U. Denver, 1977. Asst. Mile Hi coun. Girl Scouts U.S.A., Denver, 1971-77; social worker asst. Denver Pub. Schs., 1974-75, social worker, 1977—; field instr. Grad. Sch. of Soc. Work, U. Denver, 1974—. Tour leader Kenyan Safari to Kenya, East Africa, 1988. Vice pres. United Meth. Women, Christ United Meth. Ch., Denver, 1989, chmn. Christian action com., 1985-88; active Girl Scouts U.S.A., 1959—. Mem. NEA, Colo. Edn. Assn., Denver Classroom Tchrs. Assn., Colo. and Nat. Assns. Black Social Workers, Sister Cities Internat., Sippers and Sliders Ski Club Denver. Democrat. Home: 6865 E Arizona Ave #D Denver CO 80224 Office: Denver Pub Schs 900 Grant St Denver CO 80204

SIMPSON, ELIZABETH ANN, pharmacist, educator; b. Steubenville, Ohio, Nov. 11, 1941; d. Robert Thompson and Elizabeth Ann (Rogers) Lucas; m. James Lewis Simpson, Nov. 8, 1963; children: James L., Mary Elizabeth. BS in Pharmacy, W.Va. U., 1963; postgrad., U. Tex., 1986. Staff pharmacist, Mich., Pa., N.J.; staff pharmacist Mass., W.Va., 1964-80; staff pharmacist St. John Hosp. and Med. Ctr., Detroit, 1980-83, dir. pharmacy svcs. St. John Outpatient Corp., 1983—; adj. clin. instr. dept. pharmacy practice Coll. Pharmacy and Allied Health Professions, Wayne State U., Detroit, 1982—; presenter in field, 1986—; mem. pharmacy and therapeutics com. Georgian East Nursing Home, 1987-89. Contbr. articles to profl. jours. Pres. bd. dirs. Meml. Co-Op Nursery Sch., 1973-75; mem. various PTO coms. and bds. Grosse Pointe (Mich.) Sch. System, 1975-89; chmn. pub. affairs com. Jr. League Detroit, 1975-76, mem. exec. com., 1978-80; chmn. pub. affairs com. Jr. Leagues Mich., 1976-78. Recipient Vol. of Yr. award Jr. League Detroit, 1976, Torch Drive Communication award United Found., 1985. Fellow Am. Coll. Cons. Pharmacists; mem. Am. Soc. Hosp. Pharmacists, Am. Pharm. Assn. (ho. of dels. 1987—, William S. Apple program fellow 1986), Acad. Pharmacy Practice and Mgmt. (policy com. 1987, chmn. instnl. practice sect. 1990—, mem. edn. com. 1988-89), Mich. Pharmacists Assn. (physician dispensing adv. com. 1988—, chmn. profl. and pub. affairs com. 1987-90), Mich. Soc. Hosp. Pharmacists (profl. and legal affairs com. 1987—), Southeastern Mich. Soc. Hosp. Pharmacists, Lambda Kappa Sigma. Republican. Presbyterian. Home: 569 Fisher Rd Grosse Pointe MI 48230 Office: St John Hosp and Med Ctr 22151 Moross Rd Detroit MI 48236

SIMPSON, JEAN MARIE, retired nurse; b. Putnam, Okla., Jan. 31, 1927; d. George Britain Fry and Audrey Dean (Fruit) Hamby; m. Charley Burns Foster, June 29, 1947 (div. Nov. 1962); children: D. Ellen, Stephen Lee, Stanley Mark; m. Rufus Harold Eubanks, June 29, 1963 (dec. Mar. 1988); m. Harold Denton Simpson, Mar. 31, 1990. Student, Southwestern State U., 1945-47; RN, Western Okla. State Hosp. Sch., 1945-48; student, West Tex. State U., 1960-62, Bacone Coll., 1963-65. Office nurse Cunningham Clin., Clinton, Okla., 1949; staff nurse Western Okla. State Hosp., Clinton, 1950-56, U.S. Govt. Indian Hosp., Clinton, 1956-60; private duty nurse Canyon Meml. Hosp., 1960-61; staff nurse Vets. Adminstrn. Hosp., Amarillo, Tex., 1961-62, VA Hosp., Okla., 1962-67; med. floor supr. Muskogee Regional Med. Ctr., 1967-68, maternity supr., 1968-69, house supr., 1969—; ret., 1990; nurse of the day Okla. State Legis., 1981-83. coordinator of drug and alcohol program Muskogee Regional Med. Ctr., 1971-80. Author: Transplantation Manual, 1987, Manual of Patient Classification, 1988. Mem. ARC (nurses transplant com.), Am. Nurses Assn. (cert. nursing adminstr.), Am. Heart Assn., W.B. Kellogg Found., Okla. State Nurses Assn., Okla. Dist. #3 Nurses Assn., Western Okla. State Hosp. Alumni Assn. (pres. 1955). Democrat. Methodist. Home: 3416 S 27th St Muskogee OK 74401 Office: Muskogee Regional Med Ctr 300 Rockefeller Dr Muskogee OK 74401

SIMPSON, JOANNE MALKUS, meteorologist; b. Boston, Mar. 23, 1923; d. Russell and Virginia (Vaughan) Gerould; m. Robert H. Simpson, Jan. 6, 1965; children by previous marriage—David Starr Malkus, Steven Willem Malkus, Karen Elizabeth Malkus. B.S., U. Chgo., 1943, M.S., 1945, Ph.D., 1949. Instr. physics and meteorology Ill. Inst. Tech., 1946-49, asst. prof., 1949-51; meteorologist Woods Hole Oceanographic Instn., 1951-61; prof. meteorology UCLA, 1961-65; dir. exptl. meteorology lab. NOAA, Dept. Commerce, Washington, 1965-74; prof. environ. scis. U. Va., Charlottesville, 1974-76; W.W. Corcoran prof. environ. scis. U. Va., 1976-81; head Severe Storms br. Goddard Lab. Atmospheres, NASA, Greenbelt, Md., 1981-88, chief scientist for meteorology, 1988—; Goddard Sr. fellow Severe Storms br. Goddard Lab. Atmospheres, NASA, 1988-93; bd. dirs. Earth Scis. Author: (with Herbert Riehl) Cloud Structure and Distributions Over the Tropical Pacific Ocean; assoc. editor: Revs. Geophysics and Space Physics, 1964-72, 75-77; contbr. articles to profl. jours. Mem. Fla. Gov.'s Environ. Coordinating Council, 1971-74. Recipient Disting. Authorship award NOAA, 1969; Silver medal, 1967, Gold medal, 1972 both from Dept. Commerce; Vincent J. Schaefer award Weather Modification Assn., 1979; Community Headliner award Women in Communications, 1973; Profl. Achievement award U. Chgo. Alumni Assn., 1975, Lifetime Achievement award Women in Sci. engring, 1990; Elected Nat. Acad. Engring., 1988; Exceptional Sci. Achievement award NASA, 1982; named Woman of Yr. Los Angeles Times, 1963; Guggenheim fellow, 1954-55, Goddard Sr. fellow, 1988—. Fellow Am. Meteorol. Soc. (Meisinger award 1962, Rossby Research medal 1983, council 1975-77, 79-81, exec. com. 1977, 79-81, commr. sci. and tech. activities 1982-88, pres.-elect 1988, pres. 1989); mem. Am. Geophys. Union, Oceanography Soc., Cosmos Club, Phi Beta Kappa, Sigma Xi. Home: Harbour Sq Apt S-803 540 N St SW Washington DC 20024 Office: NASA Goddard Space Flight Ctr Lab Atmospheres Greenbelt MD 20771

SIMPSON, KATHRYN JACQUIN, retired publishing company executive; b. Peoria, Ill., June 22, 1924; d. Wentworth Cory and Kathryn Mathilda (Niehaus) Jacquin; m. Howard M. Simpson, Nov. 25, 1948; children: John N., Cory Simpson Christian, Michael H., David M., Dana Simpson Lyddon. AB with honors, Bradley U., 1946. With Charles A. Bennett Co. (name changed to Bennett Publ. Co. 1975-76), 1946-83, also dir.; sec. Cabco, Inc., 1970-76. Bd. dirs. Heart of Ill. United Fund, 1961-66, sec. 1962-66; bd. dirs. YWCA, Peoria, 1966-86, treas. 1970-71, vice pres. 1974-79, 83-85, chmn. planned giving 1984—, chmn. fin. development 1980-83, mem. adv. bd. 1986—; mem. ch. coun. St. Philomena Cath. Ch., 1981-85, sec. parish coun., 1983. Mem. Nat. Council Boy Scouts Am., East Cen. Region Com. Boy Scouts Am., Fin. Com. Boy Scouts Am., mem. W.D. Boyce coun. Boy Scouts Am., 1970—, exec. bd. W.D. Boyce Coun., 1972—, v.p., 1974-79, mem. planned giving com., 1986—, capital campaign advance gifts com., steering com., 1988-89; mem. Diocese of Peoria Cath. Com. Scouting, 1974—. Co-author: The United Way and the Local Coun., 1979, rev. 1981. Recipient Silver Beaver award W.D. Boyce Coun. Boy Scouts Am., 1971, St. George Emblem award Nat. Council Boy Scouts Am., 1974. Mem. Jr. League Peoria, Women's Civic Fedn., Lakeview Ctr. for Arts and Scis., Crystal Lakeshore Assn. (Benzie County, Mich. bd. dirs. 1986—, treas. 1986—, exec. com. 1986—, designing editor ann. membership brochure), Willow Knolls Country Club, Theta Alpha Phi, Pi Beta Phi. Republican.

SIMPSON, LAURA EVELYN, accountant; b. Herrin, Ill., July 19, 1917; d. Roy and Mary (Trout) Wilson; student public schs., Ill.; diploma acctg., income tax and C.P.A. coaching LaSalle Extension U., 1952; m. Levi C. Simpson, Oct. 16, 1936; children—Doris I. Simpson Hill, Suzanne Simpson Barnett, Troy E., Joy. Bookkeeper, Atlas Powder Co., 1932-48; self-employed, 1934-41; with acctg. div. Sherwin Williams Def. Corp., 1942-45, Roy Barger Acctg. Service, Marion, Ill., 1945-52; propr. acctg. service, Marion and Harrisburg, Ill., 1953-79; part-time practice acctg., New Port Richey, Fla., 1980—. Treas., Sunday sch. tchr. Cedar Grove United Meth. Ch., Marion, 1946-79; pres. women's div. Holiday United Meth. Ch., New Port Richey, Fla., until 1984, chmn. missions commn., 1984—, also ch. treas., nominating com. United Meth. Women; leader 4-H Club, 1951, 52; treas. United Meth. Ch. of Holiday; mem. nominating com. United Meth. Ch., St. Petersburg Dist. Card holder IRS. Mem. Nat. Fedn. Ind. Bus. (chmn. Saline and Williamson County 1966, nat. adv. council 1971), Nat. Soc. Public Accts., Internat. Platform Assn. Republican. Home: 3846 Claremont New Port Richey FL 34652

SIMPSON, LORA ELAINE, business administration educator; b. Springfield, Mo., Mar. 18, 1933; d. Grant Dearon and Lora Elmira (Clingings) S. BS, BS in Edn., S.W. Mo. State U., 1954; MS in Edn., Ind. U., 1957. Cert. life secondary tchr., Mo. Prof. bus. S.W. Bapt. U., Bolivar, Mo., 1957-63; prof. bus. adminstrn. St. Louis Community Coll. at Florissant Valley, 1964—; teaching assoc. Ind. U., Bloomington, 1957; free-lance organist numerous chs., 1954—. Booksale chmn. Friends of Ferguson (Mo.) Libr., 1986. Mem. AAUW (membership chmn. Ferguson-Florissant br. 1986-88), Am. Guild Organists (placement chmn. St. Louis chpt. 1982-85), Women's Symphony Assn. Baptist. Office: St Louis Community Coll 3400 Pershall St Saint Louis MO 63135

SIMPSON, LUCY PICCO, publisher; b. Berwyn, Ill., Sept. 11, 1940; d. John and Mary Rose (Vignocchi) Picco; m. Barry Darwood Simpson, Aug. 14, 1965; 1 child, Shelley Powell. BA, Park Coll., 1962; MA in Teaching, cert. further study, Wesleyan U., Middletown, Conn., 1964. Cert. secondary tchr., Mass. Tchr. social studies Duxbury (Mass.) High Sch., 1964-65; editorial asst. Columbia U. Grad. Sch. Journalism, N.Y.C., 1965-66; copy editor Praeger Pubs., N.Y.C., 1966-73; data coord. N.Y. Coun. on Adoptable Children, N.Y.C., 1973-77; editor, cons. McGraw-Hill Book Co., N.Y.C., 1977-81; founder, exec. dir. Orgn. for Equal Edn. of Sexes, Inc., Bklyn., 1977—; freelance copy editor, proofreader various pubs., N.Y.C., 1968-75; cons. H.W. Wilson Co., Bronx, N.Y., 1976, Ednl. Testing Svc., Princeton, N.J., 1981-82, The Feminist Press, Old Westbury, N.Y., 1982, Nat. Sex Equity Demonstration Project, Coral Gables, Fla., 1983. Founder, editor TABS: Aids for Ending Sexism in Sch., 1977-84; contbr. articles to various publs.; folk music performer various festivals, coffeehouses and recs. Mem. Park Slope Civic Coun., Bklyn., 1985—, Bklyn. Hist. Soc., Bklyn. Mus., Prospect Park Environ. Ctr.; mem. adv. commn. N.Y.C. Bd. Edn. Coun. on Occupational Edn., 1985-88; mem. N.Y.C. Sex Equity Network, 1983-86; founding mem. Nat. Mus. Women in Arts, Washington, 1987. Grantee U.S. Dept. Edn., Women's Ednl. Equity Act Program, 1982-85, 87,

89. Mem. AAUW, Nature Conservancy, N.Y. Pub. Interest Rsch. Group, Nat. Women's Studies Assn., Nat. Coalition for Sex Equity in Edn., NOW (founder, chmn. textbook com. 1972-75), Folk Music Soc. N.Y. (bd. dirs. 1976-82). Democrat. Home: 744 Carroll St Brooklyn NY 11215 Office: Orgn for Equal Edn Sexes 808 Union St Brooklyn NY 11215

SIMPSON, MARY ELIZABETH, personnel and benefits administrator; b. Newport News, Va., Dec. 13, 1946; d. Carl Edward and Edith Marie (Johnston) Routten; m. William Hugh Simpson Jr., Nov. 26, 1966 (div.); 1 child, William Charles. Student, Columbia (S.C.) Coll., 1985—. Clk. Allied Corp., Columbia, 1965-70, sec., 1970-78, adminstr. benefits, 1978—, asst. adminstr. personnel, 1979—; emergency med. technician Allied Corp., 1977—. cons. Jr. Achievement, Columbia, 1985-86; instr. ARC, 1980—; mem. Irmo Mid. Sch. Adv. council, 1986-87. Mem. Midlands Employer Health Council (sec. 1984-85). Republican. Methodist. Home: 2015 Cedarbrook Ct Columbia SC 29212 Office: Allied Corp 4402 St Andrews Rd Columbia SC 29210

SIMPSON, MARY MICHAEL, priest, psychotherapist; b. Evansville, Ind., Dec. 1; d. Link Wilson and Mary Garrett (Price) S. B.A., B.S., Tex. Women's U., 1946; grad. N.Y. Tng. Sch. for Deaconesses, 1949; grad., Westchester Inst. Tng. in Psychoanalysis and Psychotherapy, 1976; S.T.M., Gen. Theol. Sem., 1982. Missionary Holy Cross Mission, Bolahun, Liberia, 1950-52; acad. head Margaret Hall Sch., Versailles, Ky., 1958-61; pastoral counselor on staff Cathedral St. John the Divine, N.Y.C., 1974-87, canon residentiary, canon counselor, 1977-87, hon. canon, 1988—; ordained priest Episcopal Ch., 1977; cons. psychotherapist Union Theol. Sem., 1980-83; dir. Cathedral Counseling Service, 1975-87; priest-in-charge St. John's Ch. Wilmot, New Rochelle, N.Y., 1987-88; pvt. practice psycholanalyst, 1974—; Bd. dirs. Westchester Inst. Tng. in Psychoanalysis and Psychotherapy, 1982-84; trustee Council on Internat. and Pub. Affairs, 1983-87. Mem. Nat. Assn. Advancement of Psychoanalysis, N.Y. State Assn. Practicing Psychotherapists, N.Y. Soc. Clin. Psychologists. Author: The Ordination of Women in the American Episcopal Church: the Present Situation, 1981; contbg. author: Yes to Women Priests, 1978. Home and Office: 215 E 95th St #3J New York NY 10128

SIMPSON, PEGGY ANN, reporter, educator; b. San Antonio, Dec. 26, 1938; d. Robert H. and Mazie (Houston) S. BA, U. North Tex., 1960. News editor Hondo (Tex.) Anvil Herald, 1960-62; reporter, editor AP, Dallas, 1962, Austin, Tex., Washington, 1979; Washington corr. Boston Herald, 1979-82; econ. corr. Hearst Newspapers, Washington, 1982-88; bur. chief MS Mag., Washington, 1988-90; vis. prof. Sch. Journalism Ind. U., Bloomington, 1990—, journalist in residence, 1990—; founder, bd. dirs. Journalism and Women Symposium, 1989—; Washington corr. Working Woman, 1982-86. Co-author: Women, a Yearbook, 1980, rev. edit., 1984. Pres. Uplift House Community Ctr., Washington, 1973-74; v.p. Fund for Investigative Journalism, 1988—. Recipient Consumer award Nat. Press Club, 1982, Exceptional Merit Media award Nat. Women's Polit. Caucus, 1988, Emma Merit Media award, 1989; Nieman fellow, Harvard U., 1978-79. Mem. Washington Press Club (pres. 1975-76, founding bd. mem. Washington Press Club Found., 1985—, chmn. adv. com. 1986—). Methodist. Home: 1719 Swann St NW Washington DC 20009

SIMPSON, RUBY LAIRD, company president; b. Tempe, Ariz., May 16, 1910; d. Hugh Edward and Edna Viola (Hackett) Laird; m. Clayborn Edward Simpson, Aug. 14, 1933 (dec. 1956); children: Elna Rae, Laird Edward. BA, Arizona State U., 1932, MA, 1964. Elem., Sec. Sch. Adminstr. Tchr., Rural Sch., Tempe, 1931-32, Prescott High Sch., Tempe, 1932-33; social worker WPA, Phoenix, 1933-34; merchant, ptnr. Simpson's Market, Tempe, Ariz., 1934-56; tchr. Tempe Elem. Sch., Ariz., 1956-76; pres. Simpson Enterprises Ltd., Ariz., 1976--. Narrator, Video Tape, Temple Oral History, 1987. Mem. Temple Hist. Soc., 1976—. Mem. Jr. Woman's Club, Sr. Woman's Club, Order of Amaranth, Order Ea. Star, Daughter of the Nile, Kappa Delta. Democrat. Home: 819 Elna Rae St Tempe AZ 85281 Office: 819 Elna Rae St Tempe AZ 85281

SIMPSON, SUSAN GRACE, hospital purchasing executive; b. Riverside, Calif., Dec. 27, 1940; d. George Pritchard and Jewel Covert (Blomquist) Fraley; m. Marcus Leslie Pentoney, Dec. 30, 1961 (div. 1984); children: Stephen James (dec.); m. Kenneth Edwan Simpson, July 21, 1984; 1 child, kensey Chantelle. AA, Riverside City Coll., Calif., 1961. Dental asst./office mgr. Warrens S. Lavezo, DDS, El Centro, Calif., 1962-72, Keith Carlsgaard, DDS, El Centro, 1973-78; purchasing clk./supr. El Centro Community Hosp., 1978-84; dir. purchasing/central supply Pioneers Meml. Hosp., Brawley, Calif., 1984—. Editor hosp. newsletter PEN, 1989; forms layout cons. PMH, 1984—; contbr. articles to profl. jours. Leader Girl Scouts U.S.A., Imperial, Calif., 1987-89. Mem. Am. Soc. Hosp. Material Mgrs., Am. Bus. Women's Assn. (v.p. 1988-89, pres. 1989—, editor Bull. 1987). Republican. Office: Pioneers Meml Hosp 207 W Legion Rd Brawley CA 92227

SIMPSON, VI, state senator; b. Los Angeles, Mar. 18, 1946; d. Lloyd M. and Helen (Chacon) Sentman; m. Kenneth N. Simpson; children—Jason, Kristina. B.A. in Bus., Calif. State U.-Hayward, 1968. Asst. to chmn. Com. on Status of Women, Calif., 1974-75; dir. pub. affairs Calif. Parks and Recreation Soc., Sacramento, 1975-77; county auditor Monroe County, Ind., 1980-84; mem. Ind. Senate, 1984—; pres. Vi Simpson and Co., Inc., Bloomington, Ind., 1983—. Editor: Equal Rights Monitor mag., 1974-76. Syndicated newspaper columnist Know Your Rights, 1975-76. Named Freshman Democrat Senator of Yr., Ind. broadcasters Assn., 1985, Legis. of Yr., Ind. State Employees Assn., 1985. Bd. dirs. Ind. Am. Lung Assn. Mem. Ind. Constructo Inc., NAACP, AAUW. Methodist. Avocations: jogging; skiing; camping; hiking. Office: Vi Simpson & Co Inc 5185 W State Rd 46 Bloomington IN 47401*

SIMPSON, VIRGINIA WHITE, financial institution administrator; b. N.Y.C., Nov. 6, 1907; d. Arthur Elliott and Edith Mae (Lowe) White; m. Edward Barrington Sisley, Sept. 26, 1931 (dec. 1937); 1 child, Linda White (dec.); m. John Carman Simpson, Dec. 14, 1939 (dec.). Student, Leland Powers Sch., Boston, 1924-27. Coding and commn. officer Franklin Funds, San Mateo, Calif., 1974—. Vol., Mission Hospice, Burlingame, Calif. Republican. Episcopalian. Office: Franklin Funds 777 Mariners Island San Mateo CA 94404

SIMRALL, DOROTHY VAN WINKLE, psychologist; b. Morris, Ill., Dec. 20, 1917; d. Lapsley Ewing and Madge (Van Winkle) Simrall. BA, Grinnell (Iowa) Coll., 1940; MA, U. N.C., 1942; PhD, U. Ill., 1945. Instr. Mt. Holyoke Coll., S. Hadley, Mass., 1945-48; asst. prof. Tulane U., New Orleans, 1948-51, Albion (Mich.) Coll., 1951-57, Drake U., Des Moines, 1957-62; assoc. prof. psychology St. Bonaventure U., Olean, N.Y., 1965-70; dir. and psychologist Cresson Ctr., Cresson, Pa., 1972-84, Polk (Pa.) Ctr., 1972-84; cons. in field; lectr. in field. Contbr. articles to profl. jours. Mem. Am. Psychol. Assn., S.C. Psychol. Assn., Sigma Xi. Home: 706 Pelzer Hwy Box 168 Easley SC 29640

SIMS, CAROL S., editor; b. N.Y.C., June 17, 1937; d. Charles Franklyn and Zelda (Weiss) S. BA cum laude, Barnard Coll., 1958; MA, Columbia U., 1960. Art dir., designer Vogue-Butterick Inc., N.Y.C., 1963-70; freelance writer, designer N.Y.C., 1970-72; coordinator publs. CUNY, 1972-76, publs. cons., 1976-77; assoc. dir. communications, assoc. editor Clarion subs. Profl. Staff Congress, N.Y.C., 1977-84, assoc. dir., editor, 1984—. Vol. Montefiore Hosp., Bronx, N.Y., 1972-74. Recipient award of merit Council for Advancement and Support of Edn., 1975, 76. Mem. Women in Communications, Ednl. Press Assn., Metro Labor Press Assn., Phi Beta Kappa. Office: Profl Staff Congress/Clarion 25 W 43d St New York NY 10036

SIMS, CAROLYN DENISE, lawyer; b. Snowhill, N.C., Sept. 29, 1960; d. James Henry and Elnora (Jackson) Sims. BA, U. N.C., 1981; JD, N.C. Cen. U., 1984; LLM in Labor Law, Georgetown U., 1988. Bar: D.C. 1985, U.S. Dist. Ct. D.C. 1985, U.S. Dist. Ct. Nebr. 1985, U.S. Dist. Ct. Hawaii 1985, U.S. Tax Ct. 1985, U.S. Claims Ct. 1985, U.S. Mil. Appeals 1985, U.S. Army Ct. Mil. Rev. 1985, U.S. Ct. Appeals (D.C., 3d, 4th, 5th, 6th, 7th, 8th, 9th, 10th, 11th, fed. and D.C. cirs.) 1985, Va. 1986. Legal rsch. asst., law libr. asst. N.C. Cen. U., Durham, 1982-84; civil litigation intern City of Greensboro, N.C., 1983; criminal pros. litigation intern City of Durham, 1984; gen. atty. Office of the Solicitor U.S. Dept. Labor, Washington, 1984-88; asst. corp. counsel Office Corp. Counsel, Washington, 1988—. Contbr. articles to profl. jours. Mem. ABA, Nat. Bar Assn., Fed. Bar Assn., Bar Assn. of D.C., Nat. Assn. Black Women Attys., Delta Sigma Theta. Democrat. A.M.E. Home: 2801 Quebec St NW #110 Washington DC 20008

SIMS, ELIZABETH BALLARD, court reporter; b. Gastonia, N.C., Aug. 17, 1944; d. Fred Wilson and Mabel Elizabeth (Allen) Ballard; m. Robert Vincent Sims, Sept. 4, 1964; 1 dau., Candace Elizabeth Barkley. Student Gaston Meml. Hosp. Sch. Nursing, 1962-63, Gaston Coll. Dep. registrar deeds Gaston County, 1964-69; ofcl. ct. reporter, N.C., 1969-74; free-lance reporter, Dallas, N.C., 1974-86; ofcl. ct. reporter 26th Jud. Dist., State of N.C., 1986—; ofcl. ct. reporter U.S. Bankruptcy Ct. Western dist. N.C., Charlotte div., 1983-84; reporter jud. div. 26th Jud. Dist. Superior Ct., State N.C., 1986-90. Mem. com. Adminstrv. Office of Cts., 1977-78, N.C. Gov.'s Council on Status of Women, 1978—. Active Gaston County Democratic Women; Dem. precinct judge, 1973, youth rep. to area precinct meeting; chmn. Gaston County Mother's March of Dimes campaign, 1980-81. Mem. Nat. Shorthand Reporters Assn., N.C. Shorthand Reporters Assn. (legis. com., treas. 1987-88). Methodist. Home: 402 Sunset Circle Dallas NC 28034

SIMS, KAREN JACKSON, planning and zoning director; b. Springfield, Ohio, July 20, 1954; d. Harris Jay Jackson and E. Joanne (Davenport) Mumford; m. Leroy Sims, July 10, 1985; children: Glenda, Bridget, Tommy, Royan, Keith. BA, Mt. Holyoke Coll., South Hadley, Mass., 1976; M of City Planning, MIT, Cambridge, Mass., 1978. Dir. housing and community devel. Capitol Regional Coun. of Govts., Hartford, Conn., 1976-83; dir. Plan B Mgmt., St. Petersburg, Fla., 1983-88; prin. planner, planning and zoning dir. Manatee County Govt., Bradenton, Fla., 1988—; Author: From Public Housing to Homeownership, 1979. Bd. dirs. Newtown Little League, Sarasota, Fla., 1989—; dir. Black Polit. Women, St. Petersburg, 1987—; steward, dir. youth div. Payne Chapel AME Ch. Named Vol. of Yr. Newtown Little League, 1989. Mem. Am. Planning Assn., Fla. Planning and Zoning Assn, NAACP. Home: 6379 Ravenwood Way Sarasota FL 34235 Office: Manatee County Planning & Zoning 1112 Manatee Ave W Box 1000 Bradenton FL 34206

SIMS, KATHY LOU BUSEY, police officer; b. Pensacola, Fla., Oct. 11, 1954; d. Nick and Bessie Lois (Allen) Busey; m. Thomas Clyde Sims, Feb. 10, 1971 (div. 1976). Cert. in automobile mechanics, Falkner State Coll., Fayetteville, N.C., 1977; student, Troy State U., Pensacola, 1981-82, Pensacola Jr. Coll., 1987-88. Cashier Winn-Dixie Supermarket, Pensacola, 1971-72; mgr. Taco House Restaurant, Pensacola, 1972-73; bartender Bros. and Sisters, Pensacola, 1973-75, Stop & Shop, Pensacola, 1974-76; carpenter Waylon Constrn. Co., Fayetteville, N.C., 1978-79; officer Dept. Def. Police, Naval Air Sta. Pensacola, Fla., 1980-88, asst. chief police, 1989—, mentor, 1989-90; equal employment cons., Naval Air Sta. Pensacola, 1989—. Vol. Allie Yniestra Elem. Sch., 1989—. With U.S. Army, 1976-79. Recipient livesaving award ARC, Pensacola, 1985. Mem. NAFE, MADD. Democrat. Baptist. Office: Dept Def Police Bldg 1534 Naval Air Sta Pensacola FL 32508-5000

SIMS, LORETTA JAMES, employment counselor; b. Holly Springs, Miss., Feb. 7, 1948; d. Sylvester and Elmer (Greer) James; 1 child, Chyreese Tawana. BS in Bus. Edn. cum laude, Miss. Indsl. Coll., 1971. Pers. mgmt. specialist, then pers. staffing specialist U.S. CSC, Jackson, Miss., 1971-78; equal opportunity specialist Office Fed. Contract Compliance Programs, Kansas City, Mo., 1978-87; asst. dist. dir. Office Fed. Contact Compliance Programs, Birmingham, Ala., 1987—. Mem. ACLU, NAACP, So. Poverty Law Ctr., Common Cause, Urban League. Baptist. Home: 1720-A 14th Ave South Birmingham AL 35205 Office: DOL/OFCCP 2015 2nd Ave North Suite 202 Birmingham AL 35203

SIMS, MARGARET CHURCH, educator; b. London, May 26, 1949; d. Albert William and Miriam Edith (Rogers) Church; m. Daws Howard Sims; children: Daws Howard Jr., Vanessa Karen. BA, Delta State U., 1987, MEd, 1989. Cert. secondary edn. tchr. English tchr. Ruleville Jr. High Sch., Ruleville, Miss., 1987-90; English instr. Miss. Delta Community Coll., Moorhead, 1990—; part time instr. Delta State U., Cleveland, Miss.; tchr.-cons. Nat. Writing Project, Miss. area, 1987—. Contbr. articles to profl. jours. Named 1988 IMPACT Tchr., 1989 IMPACT Tchr., Miss. Effective Schs. Consortium; Nat. Writing Project fellow, 1987. Mem. Nat. Coun. Tchrs. English, Miss. Coun. Tchrs. English (co-editor jour. 1990—), Lambda Iota Tau (sec. 1986-87), Alpha Lambda Delta, Phi Kappa Phi, Phi Delta Kappa. Office: Miss Delta Community Coll MS 38761 Box 105 Ruleville MS 38771

SIMS, SHERYE LYNN, accountant; b. Lebanon, Tenn., Sept. 13, 1959; d. John Donald and Betty Jean (Payne) Smith; m. Richard Michael Sims; children: Craig, Joshua, Lauren, Jon. Student, Cumberland U., Lebanon, Inc. Acct. Marriott Corp., Nashville, 1982-85, Dana Corp., Gordonsville, Tenn., 1985-87, Humana, Inc., Lebanon, 1987—. Mem. Hosp. Fin. Mgmt. Assn. Office: Humana McFarland 500 Park Ave Lebanon IN 37087

SIMUNICH, MARY ELIZABETH HEDRICK (MRS. WILLIAM A. SIMUNICH), public relations executive; b. Chgo.; d. Tubman Keene and Mary (McCamish) Hedrick; student Phoenix Coll., 1967-69, Met. Bus. Coll., 1938-40; m. William A. Simunich, Dec. 6, 1941. Exec. sec. sales mgr. KPHO radio, 1950-53; exec. sec. mgr. KPHO-TV, 1953-54; account exec. Tom Rippey & Assos., 1955-56; pub. rels. dir. Phoenix Symphony, 1956-62; co-founder, v.p. Paul J. Hughes Pub. Rels., Inc., 1960-65; owner Mary Simunich Pub. Rels., Phoenix, 1966-77; pub. rels. dir. Walter O. Boswell Meml. Hosp., Sun City, Ariz., 1969-85; pub. rels. cons., 1985—; instr. pub. rels. Phoenix Coll. Evening Sch., 1973-78. Bd. dirs. Anytown, Ariz., 1969-72; founder, sec. Friends Am. Geriatrics, 1977-86. Named Phoenix Advt. Woman of Year, Phoenix Jr. Advt. Club, 1962; recipient award Blue Cross, 1963; 1st Pl. award Ariz. Press Women, 1966. Mem. NAFE, Women in Communications, Internat. Assn. Bus. Communicators (pres. Ariz. chpt. 1970-71, dir.), Pub. Rels. Soc. Am. (sec. dir. 1976-78), Am. Soc. Hosp. Pub. Rels. (dir. Ariz. chpt. 1976-78), Nat., Ariz. Press Women. Club: Phoenix Press. Home: 4133 N 34th Pl Phoenix AZ 85018

SINARD, ANTOINETTE KARABIN, education educator; b. Chgo., Nov. 6, 1909; d. Andrew and Antionette (Buland) Karabin; m. Charles Sinard, July 14, 1940. BA, Nat. Coll., Evanston, Ill., 1937; MA, Northwestern U., Evanston, Ill., 1941. Primary tchr. Cleve. Sch., Skokie, Ill., primary supr.; coll. instr. Nat. Coll., Evanston, Ill., 1947-77; reading cons. State of Ill., 1972-77; curriculum cons. Worth, Ill. 1976-77, Clinton Ill., 1976-77; lectr. PTA and Tchrs. Inst. 1976-77. Author: Unit Reader MacMillan, Brownie 1940, New Math for Silver Bardett, Beginners 1964. Mem. Rep. Party, Chgo. 1946—, ARC, Chgo. 1946—; lectr. PTA & Tchr's. Inst., 1947-77. Recipient Personalities of Midwest award Am. Biographical Soc., Raleigh 1973, Outstanding Educator award 1972. Mem. Oak Brook Civic Club, Ill. Republican. Roman Catholic. Home: 4 Oak Brook Club Apt F306 Oak Brook IL 60521

SINCLAIR, ANNE VAN NUYS (ANNE VAN NUYS DEICHERT), elementary educator, librarian; b. Belle Mead, N.J., June 18, 1924; d. Peter P. and Mary Servis (Martin) Van Nuys; m. Robert William Deichert, May 22, 1960 (div. Feb. 1971); 1 child, Wendy Carol Deichert Tyra; m. John C. Sinclair, Oct. 7, 1978 (div. Oct. 1987). AB, Wilson Coll., 1946; postgrad., McCormick Seminary, Chgo., 1947-48; MA in Early Childhood Edn, Columbia U., 1951. Cert. elem. tchr. nursery sch. and 3rd grade, N.J., Tenn. Ky. Social worker N.J. State Bd. Child Welfare, Morristown, N.J., 1946-47; sec. bur. alumni records Princeton (N.J.) U., N.J., 1948-49; 1st grade tchr. Lincoln Pub. Sch., Kingsport, Tenn., 1951-53; tchr., 1st-7th grades Leslie County Pub. Schs., Cinda, Ky., 1953-54; 4th grade tchr. Nishuane Pub. Sch., Montclair, N.J., 1954-55; 1st grade tchr. Brooklake Pub. Sch., Florham Park, N.J., 1955-60; dir., owner, head tchr. Five Oaks Country Day Sch., Belle Mead, 1963-83, dir. day camp, summers 1976-83; temporary employee Olsten Temps, Lawrenceville, N.J., 1983-84, J&J Temps, Princeton, N.J., 1984-85; asst. law libr. N.J. Dept. Pub. Adv., Trenton, 1985—; adj. tchr., Somerset (N.J.) County Community Coll., 1977. Vol. tchr. Thresholds, Mercer County Low Security Prison, Jones Farm, 1979-84, English as a second lang., 1987-89; singles task force chmn. New Brunswick Presbyterial, 1974-77; lay commr., Gen. Assembly of United Presbyn. Ch., U.S.A., Omaha, 1973; dean women's assn. Hillsborough Presbyn. Ch., Belle Mead, 1965-68, elder, 1968-84, pres.,1972; mem. Nassau Presbyn. Ch., Princeton, N.J., 1978—, mem. adult choir, 1979—, dean, 1981-84. Mem. Wilson Coll. Club (treas. 1982-88, v.p. 1988—). Republican. Home: 658B Rose Hollow Dr Yardley PA 19067 Office: NJ Dept Pub Advocates RJ Hughes Justice Complex Trenton NJ 08625

SINCLAIR, CAROL ANN, human resources executive; b. Lansing, Mich., June 30, 1949; d. Hart Elliott and Marion Delores (Steinle) S. AS, Lansing Community Coll., 1971, AS in Nursing, 1973; BS, Pace U., 1984; postgrad. in orgnl. psychology, Columbia U., 1990—. RN, Mich., N.Y. Nurse various hosps., Mich., N.Y, 1973-79; dir. health svcs. Equitable Fin. Cos., N.Y.C., 1979-83, pers. mgr., 1983-85, asst. v.p., 1985-86, v.p. human resources, 1986—. Adv. bd. Esteem. Mem. Internat. Assn. Pers. Women, Soc. for Human Resource Mgmt., Human Resource Planning Soc., N.Y. Pers. Mgmt. Assn. Office: Equitable Life Assurance Soc 40 Rector St 3A New York NY 10006

SINCLAIR, CAROLE, publisher, editor; b. Haddonfield, N.J., May 13, 1942; d. Earl Walter and Ruth (Sinclair) Dunham; 1 child, Wendy Sinclair Gross. Student, U. Florence, Italy, 1963; BA in Polit. Sci., Bucknell U, 1964. Advt. copywriter BBD&O Advertising, N.Y.C., 1966-67; sales promotion mgr. Macmillan Pub. Co., N.Y.C., 1967-71; mktg. mgr. Doubleday & Co., Inc., N.Y.C., 1972-74, promotion dir., 1974-76, advt. mgr., sales and promotion, chmn. mktg. com., 1976-80; v.p. mktg., editorial dir. Davis Pubs., N.Y.C., 1980-83; founder, pub., editorial dir., sr. v.p. Sylvia Porter's Personal Fin. Mag., N.Y.C., 1983-89; pres. The Sylvia Porter Orgn., Inc., N.Y.C., 1989—; mktg. dir. Denver Pub. Inst., summers 1975-78; lectr. Columbia U. Bus. Sch. and Sch. of Journalism, 1976; host nationally syndicated TV show, Sylvia Porter's Money Tips, syndicated daily radio show, Sylvia Porter's Personal Fin. Report, audio cassette series on fin. topics. contbg. editor Pushcart Prize, 1977; contbr. The Business of Publishing, 1980. Renaissance Art Program fellow, Florence, Italy, 1963; White House intern, 1962. Mem. Women's Forum, Intercorp. Communications Group, Mag. Pubs.' Assn., Advt. Women in N.Y., Spence Sch. Parent's League. Presbyterian. Club: Pubs. Lunch. Office: The Sylvia Porter Orgn Inc 650 Fifth Ave New York NY 10019

SINCLAIR, MARGARET KATHERINE (DAISY SINCLAIR), advertising executive; b. Perth Amboy, N.J., Mar. 22, 1941; d. James Patrick and Margaret (McAniff) Nieland; m. James Pratt Sinclair, May 25, 1978; children—Duncan, Gibbons. BA, Caldwell Coll., 1962. Jr. copywriter Young & Rubicam, N.Y.C., 1962-64; casting asst. Ogilvy & Mather, N.Y.C., 1964-68, casting dir., 1968-76, v.p., head casting, 1976-90, sr. v.p., 1990—. Mem. Am. Assn. Advt. Agy. (talent sub com. 1977), Drama League N.Y. (3d v.p. 1984—), Nat. Women's Republican Club, Edgartown Yacht Club, The Tuxedo Club (N.Y.C.). Republican. Episcopalian. Home: 4 E 95th St New York NY 10128 Office: Oglivy & Mather 309 W 49th St New York NY 10019

SINCLAIR, SUSAN JO, automotive parts wholesale company executive; b. Des Moines, Aug. 6, 1949; d. Joseph Edward and Elga Faye (Goddard) Davis. BA in Journalism, U. Minn., 1971. Merchandising mgr. Farm Progress Publs., Des Moines, 1973-78; v.p. Auto Parts Warehouse Co., Des Moines, 1974-85, exec. vp., 1985-87, pres., chief operating officer, 1987—, also bd. dirs., 1973-78; v.p., bd. dirs. Davis Investment Co., Des Moines, Porter Auto Parts, Altoona, Iowa, Midwest Motor Bearing Co., Waterloo, Iowa, Iowa Falls (Iowa) Motor Supply , City Automotive Supply, Chariton, Oelwein, Hampton, Cedar Rapids and Des Moines. Mem. Automotive Svc. Industry Assn., Automotive Warehouse Distbrs. Assn., Iowa Automotive Wholesalers Assn., Young Pres. Orgn., Bus. for Peace. Office: Auto Parts Warehouse Co 1658 E Euclid Ave Des Moines IA 50316

SINDEROFF, RITA JOYCE, property management company executive, real estate broker, mortgage broker; b. Bklyn., June 22, 1932; d. Joseph George and Mary (Cohen) Rothkopf; m. Arthur B. Schneider, Oct. 18, 1953 (div. Sept. 1973); children: Linda Ellen, Debra Carol. Degree in comml. art Pratt Inst., 1953; BA in Acctg., Bklyn. Coll., 1954. Controller Central Funding Co., Bklyn., 1973-80; owner, controller, realtor Riteway Mgmt. Inc., Coral Springs, Fla., 1980-86, Riteway Internat. Realty Corp., Coral Springs, 1986-87, realtor Regal Internat. Realty Inc.; mortgage broker Cam Regal Fin. Services and Regal Assn. Services, Coral Springs, Fla., 1987—; cons. in field; notary pub. Active Cancer Soc., Bklyn., 1954-73, March of Dimes, Bklyn., 1960-70. Recipient 1st art award City of N.Y., 1950. Mem. Nat. Bd. Realtors, Pompany Beach-North Broward Bd. Realtors, Fla. Assn. Mortgage Brokers (lic. community assn. mgr.), Nat. Real Estate Assn., Fla. Assn. Community Mgrs. (lic.) Democrat. Jewish. Avocations: reading, dancing, swimming. Office: Regal Assn Svcs 1515 University Dr Ste 104 Coral Springs FL 33071

SINDT, CAROL WOLD, telecommunications administrator, city official; b. Mpls., Nov. 26, 1949; d. Melvin Theodore and Mary Clare (Dalton) Wold; m. Michael Alan Sindt, June 27, 1981; 1 child, Matthew G.; stepchildren: Nathan, Zachary. BS, U. Minn., 1971. Aide to majority leader Mpls. City Council, 1974-78, pub. affairs cons., 1978-80; dir. community relations Storer Broadcasting, Mpls., 1981-83; bd. dirs. Met. Council, St. Paul, 1983-85; aide to pres. Mpls. City Council, 1984-85; asst. dir. telecommunications City of Mpls., 1985-87, dir. telecommunications, 1987—. Mem. Dem. Nat. Com., 1976-80; bd. dirs. State Med. Examiners, St. Paul, 1976-80. Mem. Mpls. TV Network, Nat. Assn. Telecommunications Officers and Adminstrs. Roman Catholic. Office: Office of Telecommunication City Hall Room 123 Minneapolis MN 55415

SING, MARGO, data processing company executive; b. Warsaw, Ind., Mar. 17, 1945; d. Adam Ernest and Erna Margaret (Wokeck) S. BA, Western Mich. U., 1967; postgrad., Washington State U. Mgr. prodn. and inventory control Gillette, Westlake Village, Calif., Revlon, Phoenix; mfg. mgr. Johnson and Johnson, Park Forest, Ill.; dir. ops. and support svcs. Western Data Systems, McLean, Va. Mem. APICS, NOW.

SINGER, CECILE D., state legislator. BA, Queens Coll. Past rep. Spl. Svcs. for Children, N.Y.C.; past exec. dir. N.Y. State Assembly Social Svcs. and Judiciary Coms., Joint Legis. Com. on Corps., Authorities and Commns.; past pub. rep. Yonkers (N.Y.) Emergency Control Bd.; past coord. Westchester County Assembly Dels.; past chief of staff for dep. minority leader; mem. N.Y. State Assembly, Albany, 1988—, mem. various coms.; past rep. Temp. Commn. to Revise Social Svcs. Law; mem. Presdl. Commn. on Privacy Conf., N.Y. State Senate Transp. Conf.; chair woman Rep. Freshman Conf.; mem. task force on substance abuse Am. Legis. Exch. Coun. Mem. adv. bd. Legal Awareness Women; mem. task force on certioraris Westchester County Sch. Bds. Assn.; sch. and community chairwoman Yonkers PTA; bd. dirs. Yonkers Gen. Hosp., Yonkers chpt. United Jewish Appeal. Recipient Jenkins Meml. award. Mem. Mental Health Assn. (mem. nominating and pub. affairs coms. Westchester County chpt.), Rotary. Home: 117 Cliffside Dr Yonkers NY 10710 Office: NY State Assembly Rm 827-LOB Albany NY 12248

SINGER, ELIZABETH WELLS, college dean; b. Winston-Salem, N.C., Dec. 11, 1933; d. James Royal and Louise (Gilbert) Higgins; m. John Carson Wells, Aug. 17, 1953 (div. Feb. 1974); 1 child, Renee Louise Doster; m. John Walter Singer, Dec. 18, 1976. BA, Wake Forest U., 1956; MA, Rollins Coll., 1970. Instr. East Bend (N.C.) Sch., 1956-57, Eau Gallie Jr. High Sch., Melbourne, Fla., 1957-59, U. Park, Melbourne, 1960-61; history instr. Melbourne High Sch., 1961-67; dir. instrn. Brevard Sch. Bd., Melbourne, 1967-68, master tchr. Am. history, 1968-74, curriculum coord., 1974-76; adminstv. adult edn., fed. projects Brevard Sch. Bd., Cocoa, Fla., 1976-82; dean adult and continuing edn. Brevard Community Coll., Cocoa, 1982—; coop. grouping Am. Hist. team spl. projects Ctr. for Orgn. Change the John Hopkins U., 1971-73. Author: Let's Work It Out-Skills for Parents, 1990. Named to Fla. Adminstrs. of Adult Edn. Hall of Fame, 1989, Bus. Assoc. of Yr., Am. Bus. Womens Assn., 1984; recipient Chmns. award Fla. Adminstrs. of Adult Edn., 1981, 83. Mem. Fla. Adult Edn. Assn. (pres. 1985-86, bd. dirs. 1982-88), Am. Assn. of Adult and Continuing Edn. (Nat. Competency

Unit award 1987). Republican. Baptist. Office: Brevard Community Coll 1519 Clearlake Rd Cocoa FL 32922

SINGER, GLADYS MONTGOMERY See MONTGOMERY, GLADYS

SINGER, HEDY KAREN, psychologist; b. Phila., Apr. 15, 1954; d. Aaron Norman and Lillian Sarah (Goldman) S. BS, Temple U., 1975, PhD, 1988; MA, Villanova U., 1977. Lic. psychologist, Pa. Tchr. Sch. Dist. Phila., 1975-77; counselor Montgomery County Intermediate U., Bluebell, Pa., 1978-80; intake supv., counselor Jewish Employment and Vocat. Svc., Phila., 1979-84; grad. asst. counseling ctr. Temple U., Phila., 1984-85; psychology intern Friends Hosp., Phila., 1985-86; staff psychologist Hall-Mercer Community MHMR Pa. Hosp., Phila., 1986-87, Abington (Pa.) Psychol. Assocs., 1987-88; sr. instr., staff psychologist div. adolescent psychiatry Hahnemann U., Phila., 1988-89; asst. prof. psychiatry Med. Coll. Pa., Phila., 1989—; cons. Hahnemann Adolescent Suicide Prevention, 1988-89; coord. psychology Chestnut Hill Rehab. Hosp., 1989—; trainer, suicide instrn. specialist, cons. substance abuse program Sch. Dist. Phila., 1990—. Mem. Am. Jewish Congress, 1988—, Jewish Community Rels. Coun., 1990—, Urban Coalition, Interfaith Coun., 1990—. Presdl. scholar, 1974; Temple U. fellow, 1984; Rsch. grantee Phila. Geriatric Ctr., 1990. Mem. APA, Nat. Assn. Counseling and Devel., Phila. Soc. Clin. Psychologists, Delaware Valley Group Psychotherapy Soc., Soc. Personality Assessment, Kappa Delta Phi. Office: Med Coll Pa 3200 Henry Ave Philadelphia PA 19129

SINGER, JANICE GAIL, psychotherapist, consultant; b. Chgo., Aug. 14, 1947; d. Harold and Dorothy (Kagen) S.; 1 child, Rachael Jacqueline. BA, U. Toledo, 1969; MSW, U. Wis., Milw., 1977; postgrad., Gestalt Inst., Cleve., 1982, Dreikers Relationship Ctr., Boulder, Colo., 1985; Reiki II, Nancy Retzlaff R.M., Milw., 1986. Program evaluator, project cons. Mental health Planning Council of Milw., 1976-78; counselor abortion WomanCare-West, Milw., 1978; treatment foster care worker Children's Service Soc. of Wis., Milw., 1978-81; mental health coordinator, primary psychotherapist Bread and Roses Women's Health Ctr., Inc., Milw., 1981-84; originator Friends' Psychotherapy Collective, Milw., 1984—; group facilitator People to People, Waukesha, Wis., 1976-80; mem. coalition sexual misconduct by psychotherapists, Wis., 1984-86, 88—; cons. Woman to Woman, Inc., Milw., 1981—. Co-author: (consumer guide) Making Therapy Work for You, 1986; creator therapy mode Action Oriented Therapy, 1983; co-creator: (workshops) Living Your Godness Enhancing Self-Esteem Thru Action, 1988, Living in Balance-Integrating Male & Female Energy, 1987, Grieving: The Benefits of Being a Cry Baby, 1988, Seeking the Self-A Shamanic Tradition, 1989, Working With Abusive, Noncompliant, Obnoxious Patients, What Your Body's Saying Whether Your Lips are Moving or Not, 1989, Codependency: When Your Drug of Choice is Anyone But You, 1989, Discovering Your E/Sensual Body-Being Sensual is Essential to Life, 1989, Celebration in Living!, 1984, Living Beyond AIDS, 1987, Transforming Body Image, 1987, Finding Peace in Your Body, others. Workshop leader Milw. AIDS Project, 1987; co-creator workshops Celebration in Living, 1984, Living Beyond AIDS, 1987, Transforming Body Image, 1987; active Maple Dale Sch. Human Sexuality, Milw., 1983-86; cirriculum com. Nicolet High Sch. Human Sexuality, 1987. Mem. Feminist Therapy Network (pres. 1984-87), Nat. Assn. Social Workers, Assn. for Human Animal Bonding, Wis. Assn. Outpatient Mental Health Facilities (mem. ethics com. 1981-86). Democrat. Home: 8428 N Regent Rd Milwaukee WI 53217 also: 3749 Mariana Way #B Santa Barbara CA 93109 Office: Friends Psychotherapy Collective 8426 N Regent Rd Milwaukee WI 53217

SINGER, JEANNE (JEANNE WALSH), composer, concert pianist; b. N.Y.C., Aug. 4, 1924; d. Harold Vandervoort and Helen (Loucks) Walsh; B.A. magna cum laude, Barnard Coll., 1944; artist diploma Nat. Guild Piano Tchrs., 1956; student in piano Nadia Reisenberg, 1945-60, composition, Douglas Moore, 1942-44, Ph.D. (hon.) in Music World U., 1984; m. Richard G. Singer, Feb. 24, 1945, dec.; 1 son, Richard V. Composer, concert pianist solo chamber ensembles N.Y., 1947—; tchr. piano Manhasset, N.Y., 1960—; lectr. in field. Recipient spl. award merit Nat. Fedn. Music Clubs, 1st prize in nat. competition Composers Guild, 1979, Grand prize Composers Guild, 1982, 1st prize Composers and Songwriters Internat., 1985, also various nat. awards; honored at all-Singer concert, Bogotá, Colombia, 1980; N.Y. Council Arts grantee. Fellow Internat. Biog. Assn.; mem. ASCAP (awards 1978-88), Am. Music Center, Internat. League Women Composers, Nat. League Am. Pen Women (nat. music chmn.), Composers, Authors and Artists Am. (v.p N.Y.C., music mag. editor 1972-80, nat. award 1981), Am. Women Composers, Phi Beta Kappa. Clubs: Barnard Coll. of L.I., Tuesday Morning Music Douglaston; Bohemians (N.Y.C.). Composed numerous instrumental, vocal works including: Summons (baritone), 1975, A Cycle of Love (4 songs with piano), 1976, Suite in Harpsichord Style, 1976, From The Green Mountains (trio), 1977, (choral work) Composers' Prayer, Nocturne for Clarinet, 1980, Suite for Horn and Harp, 1980, From Petrarch (voice, horn, piano), 1981, Quartet for Flute, Oboe, Violin, Cello, 1982, Trio for Viola, Oboe, Piano, 1984, Come Greet the Spring (choral), 1981, An American Vision (song cycle), 1985, Wry Rimes (voice and Bassoon), 1986, The Lost Garden (voice, paino, cello); 1988; performed Lincoln Center, radio, TV. Home and Office: 64 Stuart Place Manhasset NY 11030

SINGER, MARILYN JEAN, lawyer; b. San Francisco, Mar. 7, 1955; d. Isadore Milton and Sara Sue (Spitalny) S. BA, Bryn Mawr Coll., 1976; JD, Case Western Res. U., 1979. Bar: Ohio, 1979. Litigator Buckeye Union/ Continental Ins. Co., Cleve., 1980—. Mem. Ohio Bar Assn., Bryn Mawr Coll. Alumnae Assn. (treas. dist. VI, 1984—), Bryn Mawr Club Cleve. Democrat. Jewish. Office: 55 Public Sq Cleveland OH 44113

SINGER, MAXINE FRANK, biochemist; b. N.Y.C., Feb. 15, 1931; d. Hyman S. and Henrietta (Perlowitz) Frank; m. Daniel Morris Singer, June 15, 1952; children: Amy Elizabeth, Ellen Ruth, David Byrd, Stephanie Frank. AB, Swarthmore Coll., 1952, DSc (hon.), 1978; PhD, Yale U., 1957; DSc (hon.), Wesleyan U., 1977, U.Md.-Baltimore County, 1985, Cedar Crest Coll., 1986, CUNY, 1988, Brandeis U., 1988, Radcliffe Coll., 1990, Williams Coll., 1990. USPHS postdoctoral fellow NIH, Bethesda, Md., 1956-58; research chemist (biochemistry) NIH, 1958-74; head sect. on nucleic acid enzymology Nat. Cancer Inst., 1974-79; chief Lab. of Biochemistry, Nat. Cancer Inst., 1979-87, research chemist, 1987-88; pres. Carnegie Inst. Washington, 1988—; Regents vis. lectr. U. Calif., Berkeley, 1981; bd. dirs. Found. for Advanced Edn. in Scis., 1972-78, 85-86; mem. sci. council Internat. Inst. Genetics and Biophysics, Naples, Italy, 1982-86. Mem. editorial bd. Jour. Biol. Chemistry, 1968-74, Sci. mag, 1972-82; chmn. editorial bd. Procs. of Nat. Acad. Scis., 1988-92, 85; contbr. articles to scholarly jours. Trustee Wesleyan U., Middletown, Conn., 1972-75, Yale Corp., New Haven, 1975-90; bd. govs. Weizmann Inst. Sci., Rehovot, Israel, 1978—; bd. dirs. Whitehead Inst, 1985—. Recipient award for achievement in biol. sci. Washington Acad. Scis., 1969, award for research in biol. scis. Yale Sci. and Engring. Assn., 1974, Superior Service Honor award HEW, 1975, Dirs. award NIH, 1977, Disting. Service medal HHS, 1983, Presdl. Disting. Exec. Rank award, 1987, U.S. Disting. Exec. Rank award, 1987. Fellow Am. Acad. Arts and Scis.; mem. NAS (coun. 1982-85), AAAS (Sci. Freedom and Responsibility award 1982), Am. Soc. Biol. Chemists, Am. Soc. Microbiologists, Am. Chem. Soc., Am. Philos. Soc., Inst. Medicine of NAS, Pontifical Acad. of Scis. Home: 5410 39th St NW Washington DC 20015 Office: Carnegie Inst Washington 1530 P St NW Washington DC 20015

SINGER, NIECEE, genetic counselor; b. N.Y.C.; d. A. Nathan and Doris (Tenzer) Levy; children: Mark, Patricia, Nancy. BA magna cum laude, Wheaton Coll., 1950; MS, Sarah Lawrence Coll., 1976. Cert. in genetic counseling Am. Bd. Med. Genetics. Supr. genetics unit Westchester County Med. Ctr., Valhalla, N.Y., 1976-82; asst. dir. Morristown (N.J.) Meml. Hosp., 1982—; Contbr articles to profl. jours. Mem. Gov.'s Coun. on Prevention of Mental Retardation, 1988—. Mem. Am. Soc. Human Genetics, Human Genetics Assn. N.J. (pres. 1985-87), chairperson edn. com. 1984-85, co-chairperson legis. com. 1987—), Nat. Soc. Genetic Counselors (founding, treas. 1978-81), Mid-Atlantic Regional Human Genetics Network (mem. steering com. 1985-89), Phi Beta Kappa. Democrat. Office: Morristown Meml Hosp Genetics Birth Defects Ctr Morristown NJ 07960

SINGER, PHYLLIS, editor; b. Newark, May 22, 1947; d. Carl N. and Marion (Heller) S., m. Edward J. Lowe, Jr., Aug. 11, 1979; children—James, Daniel. B.S., Boston U., 1969. Mgr. print and broadcast traffic F. William

Free & Co., advt., N.Y.C., 1969-70; researcher, reporter, editor L.I. Comml. Rev., Syosset, N.Y., 1970-72; with Newsday, L.I., 1972—, asst. editor, then sr. editor viewpoints, now asst. mng. editor features; mem. bd. Newspaper Features Council. Mem. Am. Assn. Sunday and Feature Editors (v.p.). Office: Newsday Inc 235 Pinelawn Rd Melville NY 11747*

SINGER, SUSAN JENNIFER RUNDELL, biology educator; b. Schenectady, N.Y., July 1, 1959; d. Jeremiah Alston and Jean Ellen (Nielsen) Rundell; m. Gary Michael Singer, June 21, 1981; children: Jessica, Peter. BS, Rensselaer Inst., 1981, MS, 1982, PhD, 1985. Asst. prof. Carleton Coll., Northfield, Minn., 1986—. Contbr. articles to profl. jours. Pres. parents' bd. Northfield Day Care Ctr., 1987-89; leader La Leche League, 1990—. Recipient rsch. grant USDA, 1987-90, Rsch. Corp., 1987-89, NSF, 1988-91. Mem. Soc. Devel. Biology (edn. com.), Am. Soc. Plant Physiology, Plant Devel. Biology Group (edn. editor), Flowering Working Group, Botanical Soc., Sigma Xi. Office: Dept Biology Carleton Coll One North College St Northfield MN 55057

SINGER, SUZANNE FRIED, editor; b. N.Y.C., July 9, 1935; d. Maurice Aaron and Augusta G. (Ginsberg) Fried; m. Max Singer, Feb. 12, 1959; children: Saul, Alexander, Daniel, Benjamin. BA with honors, Swarthmore Coll., 1956; MA, Columbia U., 1958. Program asst. NSF, Washington, 1958-60; assoc. editor Bibl. Archaeology Rev., Washington, 1979-84, mng. editor, 1984—; mng. editor Bibl. Rev., Washington, 1985—; exec. editor Moment, Washington, 1987—. Mem. Am. Schs. Oriental Research. Jewish. Office: Bibl Archaeology Soc 3000 Connecticut Ave NW Suite 300 Washington DC 20008

SINGER, SYDNEE ROBIN, lawyer; b. Chgo., Apr. 3, 1955; d. Alvin Maynard and Ruth Helene (Bromberg) S. MusB, U. Miami, 1977, MusM, 1979, MBA, 1979; JD, Ind. U., 1984. Bar: Calif. 1988. Claims adminstr. Carl Warren & Co., San Diego, 1986-89; assoc. Howarth & Smith, L.A., 1989—. Bd. editors Ind. U. Law Jour., 1983-84. Bd. dirs. East Bluff Homeowners Assn., Del Mar, Calif., 1988-89, Del Mar Highlands Homeowners Assn., 1988-89. Mem. Calif. Bar Assn., Calif. Trial Lawyers Assn., L.A. County Bar Assn. Home: 415 S Broadway #A Redondo Beach CA 90277 Office: Howarth & Smith 700 S Flower St Ste 2900 Los Angeles CA 90017

SINGER-LEONE, MALLORY ANN, sales executive; b. N.Y.C., Jan. 14, 1950; d. George G. and Evelyn (Braver) S.; m. Dino J. Leone, May 1, 1983. BS, C.W. Post Coll., Greenvale, N.Y., 1972. Lic. tchr., N.Y. Asst. buyer J.C. Penney Co., N.Y.C., 1973-76; sales rep. Graphicenter, N.Y.C., 1976-78, Pellon Sales Corp., N.Y.C., 1978—; English tchr. Internat. Ctr., N.Y.C., 1984-88. Mem. Internat. Fund for Animal Welfare, Mass., 1989, Fashion Group. Mem. N.Y. State Horticultural Soc. Democrat. Jewish. Home: 245 E 25th St New York NY 10010 Office: Pellon Sales Corp 119 W 40th St New York NY 10018

SINGG, SANGEETA, psychology educator, counselor; b. Patiala, Punjab, India, Mar. 10, 1950; came to U.S., 1967; d. Jaswant Singh and Yashwant Kaur (Joshi) Modgil; m. Raghu N. Singh, Feb. 25, 1988 (div. Oct. 1979); 1 child, Raj K.; m. Charles Harris Williams, Nov. 24, 1985. BA in Sociology, Punjab U., 1967; MA in Sociology, Miss. State U., 1970; MS in Psychology, East Tex. State U., 1979, PhD in Psychology, 1981. Rsch. asst. Social Sci. Rsch. Ctr. U. Miss., Starkville, 1968-70; rsch. asst. Social Sci. Rsch. Ctr. East Tex. State U., Commerce, 1976, rsch. asst. dept. sociology, 1977, asst. instr. dept. psychology, 1977-80; asst. prof. dept. psychology and sociology Angelo State U., San Angelo, Tex., 1981—; pvt. practice psychology San Angelo, 1984—; program evaluator family life demonstration project, communicating sex respect USHHS, San Angelo, 1987-88; researcher, dir. Community Needs Assessment Survey of Del Rio-GTE S.W., San Angelo, 1988; dir., researcher effects of career cou. Contbr. articles to profl. jours. Group facilitator Families of AIDS Patients, San Angelo, 1987; mem. bd. truste. Mem. Am. Psychol. Assn., Southwestern Psychol. Assn., Tex. Faculty Assn., Tex. Acad. Sci., India Assn. (sec. Starkville chpt. 1969-70), Dames Club. Home: 3318 Grandview Dr San Angelo TX 76904 Office: Angelo State U San Angelo TX 76909

SINGH, SWAYAM PRABHA, food service executive; b. Bangalore, Mysore, India, Aug. 26, 1945; came to U.S., 1968; d. Kripal Ananda and Sharada (Bai) Singh Chauhan; m. Balaram K. Singh, June 29, 1967; children: Jyothi Kiran, Naveen Raj. BA, St. Philominás, India, 1967. Cert. comml. real estate loan broker. Sub. tchr. Good Shephard Convent, Mysore, 1964; pub. Singh Seven Seas' Publs., Lansing, Mich., 1979—; founder, pres., chief exec. officer Unique Foods of India, Inc., Lansing, 1984—; founder Joveen Mgmt., Lansing, 1985—, comml. real estate developer, 1988-90; lectr., instr. Lansing Community Coll., 1979-80. Author: Learn to Cook without Preservative, 1980, Unique Universal Gourmet Club, 1984, Swayam's Authentic Cookbook of India, 1987. Area rep. Edn. Found. for Fgn. Study, 1983; mem. Am. Film Inst., Wildlife Fedn., Sesquicentennial Com. for Ethnic Festival, 1987; elected del. Gov. Blanchard's Small Bus. Confs.; founder UFI Humna Devel. Ctr., 1987; founder Prestigious Once awards; founder campaign for better decent movies. Mem. Lansing Regional C. of C. (Excellence in Edn. cert. 1989, 90), Toastmasters, Mich. Pubs. Assn. (bd. dirs.). Democrat. Hindu. Office: Singh Seven Seas' Ctr 224 S Clippert St Box 22205 Box 22205 Lansing MI 48909

SINGLETARY, PATRICIA ANN, minister; b. N.Y.C., Mar. 3, 1948; d. George and Minnie Juanita (Williams) Nickens; m. Edward Franklin Singletary, Feb. 5, 1966 (div. Apr. 1973); children: Erik Franklin, Don Andre. BTh, New World Bible Inst. and Sem., 1984, MRE, 1986; postgrad., SUNY, Empire State Coll., 1985—; MDiv, Va. Sem. and Coll., 1988, DD, Tenn. Bapt. Sch. of Religion, 1989. Sr. reorgn. underwriter Depository Trust Co., N.Y.C., 1968-90, account coord. 1990—; former nat. corr. sec. Nat. Baptist Conv. U.S.A. Inc., 1984-87; vice chmn. Spiritual Life Commn. of Clergywomen, 1987—; assoc. minister Morning Star Missionary Bapt. Ch. of Jamaica, N.Y. Nat. editor: Ekklesia, 1986. Recipient Vol. Services award City of N.Y., 1980. Mem. Nat. Assn. Negro Bus. and Profl. Women, NAFE, Interdenominational Bd. Clergywomen (gen. sec. 1985—), Nat. Bapt. Women Ministers Conv. (bd. mgrs. 1983—), Ea. Bapt. Assn. (instr. 1981-83, v.p. evangelistic unit 1982-83, gen. dir. women's aux. 1988—), Nat. Coun. Women U.S., Internat. Platform Assn., Bronx Bapt. Ministers Evening Conf. Greater N.Y. and Vicinity. Office: Morning Star Missionary Bapt Ch 114-44 Merrick Blvd Jamaica NY 11434

SINGLETON, BARBARA ANN, social worker; b. St. Augustine, Fla., Nov. 13, 1949; d. Otis and Henrietta S. BS, Fla. Meml. Coll., 1971; MSW, Fla. State U., 1976. Lic. clin. social worker, Fla. Social worker HRS State of Fla., Palatka, 1972-74; ex-POW adminstrv. coord., clin. social worker VA Med. Ctr., Miami, Fla., 1983—, clin. social worker; clin. social worker Fla. Alcoholism Treatment Ctr., Avon Park, 1976-79; clin. social worker, geriatrics coord. Tri-County Mental Health Svcs., St. Augustine, 1979-83. Mem. Miami Assn. Black Social Workers (sec. 1986-90). Baptist.

SINGLETON, DONNA MARIE, travel agency manager; b. Dowagiac, Mich., Sept. 14, 1960; d. Lester Allen and Betty Lorella (Fryman) Stover; m. Mark Steven Singleton, Sept. 1, 1979; children: Christina Marie, Christopher Michael. Student, Assoc. Travel Sch., Miami, 1979. Cert. travel cons. Travel cons. Signal Travel & Tours, Inc., Niles, Mich., 1979-80; mgr. Signal Travel & Tours, Inc., Niles, 1980—, Dowagiac & Niles, Mich., 1985—; key coordinator Am. Airlines, Signal Travel, Niles, 1988—; coordinator Cert. Travel Cons., Niles, 1989—; sabre master local level Am. Airlines, 1983-86. Vol. United Way, Dowagiac, 1988. Mem. Dowagiac C. of C. (dir. 1987—), Bus. and Profl. Women (chair young careerists 1988—), Bd. Christian Edn. Federated Ch. (sec. 1988-). Office: Signal Travel & Tours Inc 227 E Main St Niles MI 49120

SINGLETON, LINDA GAIL, nurse, home healthcare company executive; b. Greenwood, Miss., Apr. 29, 1950; d. Willie Park and Jimmie Lee (Visor) Newman; m. Elmer E. Singleton (div.); children: Katryna L., Patricia Deneem. Diploma, Kennedy-King Coll., Chgo., 1978. RN, Ill. Staff nurse Jackson Park Hosp., Chgo., 1978-87; assoc. adminstr. Beverly Hills Home Health Agy., P.C., Chgo., 1987—; dir. fin. Med. Acad. Tech., Chgo., 1987-88. Active Roseland Hosp. Aux., Chgo., 1988—; mem. adv. bd. Kennedy-King

Coll., 1987—. Mem. Am. Nurses Assn., Chgo. Black Nurses Assn., Profl. Entrepreneur Network, Female Execs. Am., Kennedy-King Coll. Alumni Assn. Office: Beverly Hills Home Health 10540 S Western Ave Chicago IL 60643

SINGLETON, SARA, banker; b. Reading, Pa., Feb. 19, 1940; d. Walter S. and Sarah (Hain) Shearer; m. John H. Singleton, Nov. 9, 1957; children: Joanne Reagan, Suzanne Oliver. Student, Ursinus Coll., 1979-86. Teller, customer svc. rep. S.E. Nat. Bank, Phoenixville, Pa., 1972-81; mgmt. trainee Red Hill (Pa.) Savs. and Loan Assn., 1981, asst. mgr. ops., 1982-84; mgr. deposit acctg. Penn Savs. Bank, Wyomissing, 1984; asst. v.p. deposit svcs. Pa. Savs. Bank, Wyomissing, 1984-86, v.p. deposit svcs., 1987—; mem. check product adv. group Phila. Res. Bank, 1988—. Pres. Mont Clare (Pa.) Home and Sch. Assn., 1973-75; officer, bd. dirs. Holy Ghost Ch., Phoenixville, 1974-84; cons. Greater Valley Coun. Girls Scouts U.S., Reading, 1988—. Mem. Nat. Assn. Banking Women (treas. Reading 1988—), Berks County C. of C. (amb. com. 1986-88, edn. com. 1988—), Fin. Women Internat. (co-chair Berk County job fair 1990). Home: 310 Woodlyn Dr Collegeville PA 19426 Office: Penn Savs Bank 1130 Berkshire Blvd Wyomissing PA 19610

SINICKI, MAUREEN T., property management; b. Johnson City, N.Y., Mar. 29, 1952; d. Anthony and Mary (Solak) S. BA, SUNY, Buffalo, 1973; postgrad., N.Y. U. Ptnr. The Property Mgmt. Co., Alexandria, Va.; chief evaluation and review staff Office Rsch. and Devel. U.S. EPA, Washington; chief, program and info. mgmt. staff U.S. EPA, Washington, chief, facilities engring. and real estate br.; owner Property Mgmt. Assoc., Inc., Alexandria. Recipient Distinguished Svc. award Fedn. of the Handicapped, N.Y.C. Mem. Alexandria Ctr. for Employment, Inc. (past pres.). Home: 1600 Prince St #512 Alexandria VA 22314

SINICKI, SHEILA JEANNE, data processing executive; b. Queens, N.Y., June 3, 1952. BS, Hofstra U., 1974, MA, 1976; MBA, Adelphi U. Acct. mgr. Gen. Electric Consulting, N.Y.C.; project leader, analyst Doubleday & Co., Garden City, N.Y.; sr. programmer, analyst European Am. Bank, Merrick, N.Y.; project mgr. CSC Ptnrs., N.Y.C.; bd. dirs. Rough Riders Landing.

SINITZKY, MIRIAM MALKA, chief financial officer; b. Fed. Republic of Germany, Feb. 15, 1949; came to U.S., 1952; d. Moses and Sima (Rosenzweig) Meller; m. Stanley Sinitzky, Aug. 5, 1979; 1 child, Danielle. BS, Bklyn. Coll., 1972; MBA, L.I. U., 1983. CPA, N.Y. Jr. acct. Foote, Cone & Belding, N.Y.C., 1972-74; controller Neuville-Mobil Sox, Inc., N.Y.C., 1974-79; sr. Weiss & Stern, CPAs, N.Y.C., 1983-85; chief fin. officer Total Patient Care, Upjohn Healthcare Svcs., L.I., 1985-89, Choices Women's Med. Ctr., Inc., Queens, N.Y., 1989—; fin. cons. tax preparation and planning, L.I., 1983—. Mem. N.Y. State Soc. CPAs. Republican. Jewish. Home: 37 Oxford Rd East Rockaway NY 11518 Office: Choices Women's Med Ctr 97-77 Queens Blvd Queens NY 11374

SINK, ALVA GORDON (MRS. CHARLES A. SINK), clubwoman; b. Rose Twp., Mich.; d. Nathaniel J. and Ella M. (Highfield) Gordon; student Eastern Mich. U., summers 1914, 18; A.B., U. Mich., 1923; m. Charles A. Sink, June 18, 1923 (dec.). Tchr. pub. schs., Rose Center, Mich., 1914-17, Hickory Ridge, Mich., 1917-18, Holly, Mich., 1918-19, Canfield Pvt. Sch., Ann Arbor, Mich., 1919-22. Mem. Women's Republican Club, Ann Arbor. Dir. Washtenaw County chpt. ARC, 1943-48, 53-59, in charge First Aid and Accident Prevention, 1941-61; pres. Mich. House and Senate Club, 1929-30, U. Mich. Alumnae Club, 1931-33, Sara Browne Smith Group Alumnae Club, 1957-59, Women's Soc. Congl. Ch., 1946-48; regent Sarah Caswell Angell chpt. DAR, 1955-57. Recipient Red Cross citation, 1959, Alumnae Council award U. Mich., 1971, Disting. Alumni Service award U. Mich., 1978; Alva Gordon Sink Group of U. Mich. Alumnae named in her honor. Mem. Hist. Soc. Mich., Alumni Assn. U. Mich., French Huguenots, AAUW, Ann Arbor Art Assn., Henry P. Tappan Soc., P.E.O. Clubs: Art Study, Garden, Faculty Women, Presidents of U. Mich. (pres. emeritus 1975-76), Ann Arbor Women's City. Home: 1325 Olivia Ave Ann Arbor MI 48104

SINK, CLAIRE HUSCHKA, waste management/environmental services branch chief; b. Viroqua, Wis., Aug. 7, 1943; d. Clyde Groves and Helen (Kafer) Huschka; m. J.D. Sink (div. 1987); children: Kara, Karl. BS, U. Wis., 1965; MA, Pa. State U., 1968. Project assoc. Pa. State U., 1967-79; tech. writer Dynamac Corp., Rockville, Md., 1979-80; rsch assoc. Geomet Techs., Inc., Rockville, 1980-81; sect. leader EG&G, WASC, Inc., Morgantown, W.Va., 1981-83; tech. communication mgr. Morgantown Energy Tech. Ctr., 1983-87; lab. tech. transfer program mgr. U.S. Dept. Energy, 1987-90; chief tech. integration br. Office Environ. Restoration and Waste Mgmt. U.S. Dept. Energy, Germantown, Md., 1990—. Editor: Tech. 87, 88; contbr. articles to profl. jours. Review panel Research & Projects Panel, 1981-85. Named One of Outstanding Young Women of Am. 1972. Mem. U. Wis. Alumni Assn., Pa. State U. Alumni Assn., AAUW, Am. Assn. for the Advancement of Sci., Tech. Transfer Soc. Office: US Dept Energy Environ Restoration Waste Mgmt 12800 Middlebrook Rd Germantown MD 20874

SINK, NIGRA LEA (NIGRA LEA ROBERTS), employment specialist; b. Elberfeld, Ind., June 5, 1935; d. Jerrell Wilson and Nigeal Elaine (Besing) Roberts; m. J. Darhl Sink, Aug. 8, 1959 (div. Aug. 1978); 1 child, Karlin Roberts Sink. BS in Edn., Oakland City (Ind.) Coll., 1957; postgrad., Purdue U., 1959, Ball State U., 1961; MS in Edn., Ind. U., 1963. Cert. tchr., Ind., Ill.; lic. counselor, Ind. Ill. teacher-tng. sch., 1957-66, Wis., 1966-67; tchr. Huntley Mid. Sch., DeKalb, Ill., 1967-70; mgr. McDonald's, Jacksonville, Ill., 1972-84; project specialist Lewis & Clark Community Coll., Godfrey, Ill., 1985-90; employment specialist Lincoln Land Community Coll., 1990—; instr. part-time MacMurray Coll., Jacksonville, 1985—. Mem. Morgan County Rep. Women, Jacksonville. Gen. Electric Corp. fellow, 1959. Mem. Ill. Adult and Continuing Educators Assn., Ill. Employment and Tng. Assn., Rebeccas (noble grand 1990—), Order of Eastern Star (worthy matron 1979, sec. 1984—), White Shrine of Jerusalem (worthy high priestess 1987, 89, supreme instr. 1988, worthy scribe 1990). Methodist. Home: 514 N Diamond St Jacksonville IL 62650 Office: Lewis and Clark Coll 300-A E Walnut St Jacksonville IL 62650

SINKFORD, JEANNE CRAIG, dentist, educator; b. Washington, Jan. 30, 1933; d. Richard E. and Geneva (Jefferson) Craig; m. Stanley M. Sinkford, Dec. 8, 1951; children: Dianne Sylvia, Janet Lynn, Stanley M. III. B.S., Howard U., 1953, M.S., 1962, D.D.S. 1958, Ph.D., 1963; D.Sc. (hon.), Georgetown U., 1978. Instr. prosthodontics dentistry Howard U., Washington, 1958-60, mem. faculty dentistry, 1964—, assoc. dean rsch. coord., co-chmn. dept. restorative dentistry, 1968-75, dean Coll. Dentistry, 1975—, prof. prosthodontics grad. sch., 1977—; instr. research and crown and bridge Northwestern U. Sch. Dentistry, 1963-64; cons. prosthodontics and research VA Hosp., Washington, 1965—; resident Children's Hosp. Nat. Med. Ctr., 1974-75; cons. St. Elizabeth's Hosp.; mem. attending staff Freedman's Hosp., Washington, 1964—; adv. bd. D.C. Gen. Hosp., 1975—; mem. Nat. Adv. Dental Research Council, Nat. Bd. Dental Examiners; mem. ad hoc adv. panel Tuskegee Syphilis Study for HEW; sponsor D.C. Pub. Health Apprentice Program; mem. adv. council to dir. NIH; adv. com. NIH/NIDR/NIA Aging Research Council; mem. dental devices classification panel FDA; mem. select panel for promotion child health, 1979-80; mem. spl. med. adv. group VA; bd. overseers U. Pa. Dental Sch., Boston U. Dental Sch.; bd. advs. U. Pitts. Dental Sch. Mem. editorial rev. bd. Jour. Am. Coll. Dentists, 1988. Contbr. Nat. Symphony Orch.; adv. bd. United Negro Coll. Fund. Robert Wood Johnson Health Policy Fellowships; mem. Mayor's Block Grant Adv. Com., 1982; mem. parents coun. Sidwell Friends, 1983; mem. adv. bd. Jr. Citizens Corps, anat. rev. bd. D.C.; mem. spl. med. adv. group VA. Louise C. Ball fellow grad. tng., 1960-63. Fellow Am. Coll. Dentists, Internat. Coll. Dentists (award of merit); mem. ADA (chmn. appeal bd. coun. on dental edn. 1975-82), Am. Soc. for Geriatric Dentistry (bd. dirs.), Internat. Assn. Dental Research, Dist. Dental Soc., Am. Inst. Oral Biology, North Portal Civic League, Inst. Grad. Dentists (trustee), So. Conf. Dental Deans (chmn.), Wash. Coun. Adminstrv. Women, Assn. Am. Women Dentists, Am. Assn. Dentistry for Children (chmn. coun. deans), Am. Pedodontic Soc., Am. Prosthodontic Soc., Fed. Prosthodontic Orgn., Nat. Dental Assn. Inst. Medicine (coun.), Am. Soc. Dentistry for Children, N.Y. Acad. Scis., Smithsonian Assocs., Dean's Coun., Proctor and Gamble, Golden Key Honor Soc., Links Inc., Sigma Xi, Phi Beta Kappa, Omicron Kappa Upsilon,

Psi Chi, Beta Kappa Chi. Address: 1765 Verbena St NW Washington DC 20012

SINKHORN, MARY JEAN, real estate executive; b. Athens, Ga., May 19, 1941; d. Howard J. and Helen (Fields) Pickelsimer; m. Michael J. Gordon, Aug. 21, 1965 (div. 1985); children: Michael J. Jr., Mitzi J.; m. Walt P. Sinkhorn, Mar. 28, 1986. Degree, Lakeland Bus. Coll., 1960. Lic. realtor, Pa., Fla. Legal sec. C.A. Boswell, Sr., et al., Attys., Bartow, Fla., 1960-69; owner, operator Gordon and Whitaker Interiors, Phila., 1977-1978; assoc. realtor Fox al Luz, Haverford, Pa., 1979-83; dir. real estate services The Polo Group, Inc., Tampa, Fla., 1984—. V.p. Tampa Jr. Woman's Club, 1971; treas. Bartow Jr. Woman's Club, 1966; sec. Bartow Jayceettes, 1967; vol. Fla. Soc. for Prevention of Blindness, 1971. Mem. Women's Council Realtors (civic project chmn. 1986), Tampa Bd. Realtors, Edn. and Realtor Assn. (com. main line bd. realtors 1979-83). Office: The Polo Group Inc 12966 N Dale Mabry Tampa FL 33618

SINNEMAKI, ULLA ULPUKKA, nurse, educator; b. Antrea, Finland, Sept. 11, 1928; d. Otto William and Kaisa Viola (Jappinen) Spjut; m. Maunu Matti J. Sinnemaki, June 12, 1949 (div. Feb. 1968); children—Markku Taneli, Sirkka Astrid. B.A., NYU, 1972; B.S., SUNY-Stony Brook, 1976; M.Ed., McNeese State U., 1978, Ed.S., 1979, M.Ed., 1981. R.N., N.Y., La., Tex. Field interviewer Bur. Census, N.Y.C., 1973-75; Operating room asst. St. Charles Meml. Hosp., N.Y.C., 1965-72; staff nurse Lake Charles Meml. Hosp., La., 1976-77; head nurse South Cameron Hosp., Cameron, La., 1977-80, dir. nursing, 1983-84; staff nurse Humana Hosp., Oakdale, La., 1984, Lake Charles, La., 1987—. Translator books, articles from English to Finnish, 1961—; designer rya rugs. Mem. Com. 1000 Baton Rouge, 1983. Mem. Nat. League Nursing, Am. Nurses Assn., Assn. Ednl. Communications and Tech., Assn. Supervision and Curriculum Devel., Nat. Assn. Female Execs. Democrat. Lutheran. Avocations: gardening; music; photography. Address: 332 W State St Lake Charles LA 70605

SIPES, LORRI DEAN, architect; b. Omaha, Nov. 11, 1950; d. Lorey Burdette and Margaret Dean (Powell) S. B in Environ. Design, Kans. U., 1972; MArch, U. Mich., 1978. Registered architect, Mich. Pvt. practice drafter Kansas City, Mo., 1973-75; drafter Colvin Robinson, Ann Arbor, Mich., 1975-76; draftsman Hobbs & Black, Ann Arbor, 1976-78; architect William Kessler Assocs., Detroit, 1978-81, Fry-Peters Assocs., Ann Arbor, 1981-82; prin. Pokempner Sipes Assocs., Ann Arbor, 1982-84, Architects Four, Inc., Ann Arbor, 1984—; instr. Ea. Mich. U., Ypsilanti, 1986-87; adj. prof. U. Mich. Coll. of Architecture, Ann Arbor, 1988-89. Mem. AIA, Huron Valley chpt. AIA (bd. dirs.), Mich. Soc. Architects. Democrat. Office: Architects Four Inc 208 W Liberty Ann Arbor MI 48104

SIPKOFF, SUSAN STONE, marketing educator; b. Coronado, Calif., Oct. 30, 1950; d. Lester Jay and Marguerite Ridgaway (King) Stone; m. Martin Zachary Sipkoff, Oct. 27, 1984; 1 child, Benjamin. AB, Wilson Coll., 1977; MBA, Shippensburg U., 1980; Student, George Washington, U., 1987—. Asst. prof. mgmt. and mktg. Shippensburg (Pa.) U., 1983—, 1983—; dir. mktg. VSP Wastewater Tech., Gettysburg, Pa., 1982; mktg. cons. Svcs. Unltd., Gettysburg, 1975—; lectr. in field. Author (with Stephen J. Holoviak) Managing Human Productivity: People are Your Best Investment, 1987; contbr. articles to profl. jours.; asst. editor mag. USN Acad. Alumni Assn., 1973-74. Former land use chair League of Women Voters, Gettysburg; mem. fund raising com. for local candidates. Am. Mktg. Assn. fellow, 1986. Mem. Am. Mktg. Assn., Mensa, NAFE, Beta Gamma Sigma, Kappa Kappa Gamma. Republican. Episcopalian. Office: Shippensburg Univ Mgmt and Mktg Dept Shippensburg PA 17257

SIPPLE, CONSTANCE S., association executive; b. Binghamton, N.Y., Sept. 12, 1962; d. Conrad Robert and Winifred Mary (Zola) Sipple. BA in Psychology, U. Dayton, 1984. Adminstrv. asst. United Cerebral Palsy Assn. Greater Cleve., 1985-87, dir. devel., 1987—; lectr. in field. Trustee Beaumont Sch. for Girls, 1989—; vol. Cuyahoga County Rep. Com., 1988—, Womankind. Mem. Ohio Coun. Fundraising Execs., Beaumont Sch. for Girls Alumni Assn. (bd. dirs. 1982—), Friends Christ Child Soc. Republican. Roman Catholic. Office: United Cerebral Palsy 2141 Overlook Rd Cleveland OH 44106

SIRI, DENA SHAW, real estate assessment executive; b. Washington, Mar. 11, 1952; d. Benjamin C. and Edna Hope (Lites) Shaw. BSBA, U. Md., 1979; postgrad., U. Va., U.N.C. Real estate appraiser State Dept. Assessment and Taxation, Rockville, Md., 1979-84; appraisal supr. County of Arlington, Va., 1984; asst. dir. real estate assessments City of Arlington, Va., 1986; now dir. real estate assessments County of Fairfax, Va., 1990—. Mem. Internat. Assn. Assessing Officers (cert. assessment evaluator), Va. Assn. of Assessing Officers, Washington Metro Area Assessors Assn., Md. Quarter Horse Assn. (v.p.). Democrat. Methodist. Office: 4100 Chain Bridge Rd Fairfax VA 22030

SIROWER, BONNIE FOX, fundraising executive; b. Bklyn., Jan. 9, 1949; d. Stanley S. and Harriet (Fischer) Fox; m. Martin Alan Sirower, Sept. 20, 1970; children: Kenneth, Daniel. AB, Barnard Coll., 1970; MA, Columbia U., 1971. Tchr. United Cerebral Palsy, N.Y.C., 1970-73, Bergen County Bd. Spl. Svcs., Paramus, N.J., 1973-76; spl. events coord. Am. Heart Assn., Glen Ridge, N.J., 1979-81; dir. devel. Goodwill Industries, Astoria, N.Y., 1981-83; pres. Access Unltd., 1984-85; dir. devel. Cheshire Home, Inc., 1986-89, Barnert Meml. Hosp. Ctr., Paterson, N.J., 1989—; cons. New Concepts for Living, Hillsdale, N.J., 1983. Pres. Sisterhood Temple Beth Haverim, Mahwah, 1976-77; co-chmn. Glen Rock Independence Day Assn., 1983. Mem. N.J. Soc. Fund Raising Execs. (bd. dirs. 1989, chair mentoring com.), Women In Fin. Devel., Assn. Fund Raisers for Disabled (pres. 1981-83), N.J. Puzzlers' League (pres.), Phi Beta Kappa. Jewish. Home: 69 Godfrey Terr Glen Rock NJ 07452

SISCO, MARY ELIZABETH, lawyer, consultant; b. Ft. Worth, Nov. 16, 1937; d. Daniel Louis and Mary Elizabeth (Blanton) Creson; m. William Theodore Sisco, Aug. 7, 1959; children—Christopher Theodore, Gregory Samuel, Lois Danine. B.A., Tex. Christian U., 1959; J.D., Tex. Tech U., 1979. Bar: Tex. 1979. Provisional secondary teaching cert., Tex. Tchr., Fort Worth Ind. Sch. Dist., 1959-61, Memphis Ind. Sch. Dist., 1961-65; ind. market researcher, Rochester, Minn., 1968-72; pvt. practice, Lubbock, Tex., 1979—; owner Ctr. Mediated Solutions, Lubbock, 1989—; treas., bd. dirs. Y-Not Better Papers, Dallas, 1975-86. Trustee, Lubbock Ind. Sch. Dist., 1980-86; bd. dirs. Caprock council Girl Scouts U.S.A., Lubbock, 1980-88; mem. Tex. Legis. Cabinet, Girl Scouts U.S.A., Dallas, 1981-87, chmn., 1988—; bd. dirs. Lubbock Civic Ballet, 1983-85; co-chmn. Lubbock Assn. Concerned with Teenage Sexuality, 1984, pres., 1985; mem. adv. bd. Tex. Assn. Sch. Age Parents, 1987—, State Council of Vols., March of Dimes, 1987-88; bd. dirs. Found. for Excellence, Lubbock, 1987—; life mem. Lubbock PTA, Tex. PTA. Mem. ABA, Order of Coif, Alpha Chi, Delta Delta Delta. Methodist. Clubs: Lubbock Women's, Classic Toastmasters. Office: 3607 22d St Lubbock TX 79410

SISEMORE, CLAUDIA, producer-director educational films and videos; b. Salt Lake City, Sept. 16, 1937; d. Darrell Daniel and Alice Larril (Barton) S. BS in English, Brigham Young U., 1959; MFA in Filmmaking, U. Utah, 1976. Cert. secondary tchr., Utah. Tchr. English, drama and writing Salt Lake Sch. Dist., Salt Lake City, 1959-66; tchr. English Davis Sch. Dist., Bountiful, Utah, 1966-68; ind. filmmaker Salt Lake City, 1972—; filmmaker-in-residence Wyo. Coun. for Arts and Nat. Endowment for Arts, Dubois, Wyo., 1977-78; producer, dir. ednl. films Utah Office Edn., Salt Lake City, 1979—. Producer, dir. Beginning of Wisdom, 1984 (film festival award 1984), Dancing through the Magic Eye, 1986, Se Habla Espanol, 1986-87; writer, dir.-editor Building on a Legacy, 1988, An Early Winter (film), 1989; artist (abstract acrylic) exhibited Phillips Gallery, numerous pvt. and pub. collections. Juror Park City (Utah) Arts Festival, 1982, Utah Arts Festival, Salt Lake City, 1982. Am. Film Festival, 1985-86, Best of West Film Festival, 1985-86; bd. dirs. Utah Media Ctr., Salt Lake City, 198l-87; mem. multidisciplinary program Utah Arts Coun., Salt Lake City, 1983-87. Recipient award Utah Media Ctr., 1984, 85; Nat. Endowment for Arts grantee, 1978, Utah Arts Coun. grantee, 1980. Mormon. Office: Utah Office Edn 250 East 500 South Salt Lake City UT 84111

SISKO, MARIE FERRARIS, fund raising executive; b. N.Y.C., Feb. 3, 1938; d. Joseph and Jean (Boaro) F. B.A., Queens Coll., 1975; postgrad. Adelphi U., 1976; divorced; children—Warren Joseph, Robert Edward. Pers. dir. Daypac Inc., 1969-70; sales asst. Ponder & Best, 1971-73; sales adminstr. Ampacet Corp., 1973-75; mktg. rep. Better Bus. Bur., 1975-77; ast. dir. Leukemia Soc. Am., 1978-82; campaign dir. Ketchum, Inc., 1982-85; dir. maj. gifts Seton Hall U., 1985-88; program dir. Brakeley, John Price Jones, 1988—; v.p. Sisko Enterprises N.Y. World's Fair, 1963-65; editor Malba (N.Y.) News & Views Newspaper, 1969-80. Del. White House Conf. on Small Bus., N.Y.C., 1978. Mem. Nat. Soc. Fund Raising Execs., AAUW, Queens Coll. Alumni Assn. (trustee 1976—), pres. Ace chpt. 1977-79). Lutheran. Home: 32 Center Dr Malba NY 11357

SISKO, WENDY LEE, fashion designer; b. Silvercreek, N.Y., July 10, 1957; d. Kenneth Francis and Ruth Ensign (White) Pope; m. Ronald S. Sisko, Jan. ll, 1974 (div. Apr. 1979); children: Kerry A., Jennifer R., Christopher K. Nickl, Michelle A. Nickl. Student, Felician Coll., Lodi, N.J., 1978-79, Bergen Community Coll., Paramus, N.J., 1984-85, Hillcrest Coll., Paramus, 1986. Asst. mgr. G&G Shop, Passaic, N.J., 1972-75; food and beverage mgr. Best Always Restaurant, Passaic, 1976-80; sales mgr. Johnathons, Hasbrouck Heights, N.J., 1980-85; pres. Grandma's Sewing Room, Oradell, N.J., 1986—. Mem. U.S.C. of C., Oradell C of C., N.J. Assn. Women Bus. Owners. Republican. Home: 812 Midland Rd Oradell NJ 07649 Office: Grandma's Sewing Room Inc 812 Midland Rd Oradell NJ 07649

SISLEY, BECKY LYNN, physical education educator; b. Seattle, May 10, 1939; d. Leslie James and Blanche (Howe) S. BA, U. Wash., 1961; MSPE, U. N.C., 1964, EdD, 1973. Tchr. Lake Washington High Sch., Kirkland, Wash., 1961-62; instr. U. Wis., Madison, 1963-65, U. Oreg., Eugene, 1965-68; prof. phys. edn. U. Oreg., 1968—, women's athletic dir., 1973-79, head undergrad. studies in phys. edn., 1985—. Co-author: Softball for Girls, 1971; contbr. articles to profl. jours. Admitted to Hall of Fame, N.W. Women's Sports Found., Seattle, 1981, Honor Awad, N.W. Dist. Assn. for Health, Phys. Edn., Recreation and Dance, 1988. Mem. Nat. Interscholastic Athletic Adminstrs. Assn., N. Am. Soc. Sport Mgmt., AAHPERD, Oreg. Alliance for Health, Phys. Edn., Recreation and Dance, We. Soc. for Phys. Edn. of Coll. Women (exec. bd. 1982-85), Oreg. High Sch. Coaches Assn., Nat. Softball Coaches Acad., N.W. Coll. Womens Sport's Assn. (pres. 1977-78), Oreg. Women's Sports Leadership Network (dir. 1987—), Phi Epsilon Kappa and others. Office: Univ of Oreg Dept Phys Edn Eugene OR 97403

SISSON, BETTY, real estate broker; b. Burbank, Calif., Apr. 21, 1934; d. Harvey Orville and Isabel Marion (Melville) Angermeir; children: James Harvey, William Frank. Student pub. schs., Burbank. Sales assoc. Rich Port Realtors, Oak Brook, Ill., 1971-76, sales mgr., 1976-78, v.p., 1978-83; exec. v.p. Am. Growth Real Estate Corp., Oak Brook, 1979-80, The Midwest Club, Oak Brook, 1980-83, Selected Properties, Inc., Oak Brook, 1983-85, Pringle & Booth, Inc., Chgo., 1985-88, Ambriance! Inc., Burr Ridge, Ill., 1987—; dir., exec. v.p. Am. Growth Group, Burr Ridge, Ill., 1983—. Mem. Birchwood Golf and Country Club, The DuPage Club (Oakbrook), Internat. Club. Republican. Home: 15 Ambriance! Burr Ridge IL 60521

SISSON, JAMIE CLIFTON, real estate developer; b. Jacksonville, Fla., Nov. 12, 1960; d. James Carlton and Joan Dee (Betts) Clifton. Student, Edison Community Coll., Ft. Myers, Fla., 1979-80. Legal sec. Alderman and Taminosian, P.A., Ft. Myers, Fla., 1978-79; fin. mgr. Bill Branch Chevrolet, Inc., Ft. Myers, Fla., 1979-81, Sam Galloway Ford, Inc., Ft. Myers, Fla., 1981; project mgr. Williams and Assocs., Inc., Ft. Myers, Fla.; exec. sec. Black Diamond Potato Farm, Ft. Myers, Fla., 1982—; real estate broker Diamond Preferred Properties, Fla., 1985—; sec.-treas. Diamond Plumbing, Inc.; owner, mgr. Wave Lengths Hair Salons of Fla., Inc. Mem. Lee County Humane Soc., Ft. Myers, 1987, Doris Day Animal League, Wash., 1989, North Shore Animal League, Port Wash., 1987. Republican. Baptist. Office: Diamond Preferred Properties 17412 Ingram Rd SE Fort Myers FL 33912

SISTERSON, JANET MARGOT, physicist, educator; b. Edinburgh, Scotland, July 7, 1940; came to U.S. 1968, naturalized, 1985; d. Thomas James and Lucy Margaret (Smith) Brownlee; m. L. Keith Sisterson, Oct. 23, 1965; children: James, Mark. BS, U. Durham, 1961; PhD, Imperial Coll. Sci. and Tech., U. London, 1965; Cert. in Advanced Mgmt. Studies Radcliffe Coll., 1989. Basic grade physicist London Hosp., 1964-66; sr. physicist Chelsea Hosp. for Women, London, 1966-68; rsch. fellow Cambridge (Mass.) Electron Accelerator, 1968-73; rsch. assoc. Harvard Cyclotron Lab., 1973—. Contbr. articles to profl. jours. Mem. exec. bd. Harrington Sch. PTA 1977-83. Mem. Am. Phys. Soc., Am. Assn. Physicists in Medicine, Am. Nuclear Soc., Am. Women in Sci. Office: 44 Oxford St Cambridge MA 02138

SISTRUNK, CATHERINE EILEEN, nurse; b. Norfolk, Va., Dec. 5, 1958; d. Frank Carlton and Joyce Mable (Toop) Johnson; m. Derek Francis Carroll, May 26, 1977 (div. Sept. 1982); 1 child, Derek E.; m. Robert Fred Sistrunk, June 12, 1983; 1 child, Robert Douglas. AD in Nursing, U. Ark., Fayetteville, 1979. RN. Cert. critical care. Registered nurse U. Miss. Med. Ctr., Jackson, Ms., 1980-82, Miss. Bapt. Med. Ctr., Jackson, 1982-83, Duke U. Med Ctr., Durham, N.C., 1983-84, Terrebonne Gen. Med Ctr., Houma, La., 1984-86; v.p. Tri Mktg., Inc., Jackson, 1986-88; pres., owner Tri Mktg., Inc., 1988—. Instr. ARC, Jackson, 1988—, community health edn. classes, River Oaks Hosp., Jackson, 1987—. Capt. U.S. Army Nurse Corps Res., 1981—. Mem. Nat. Fedn. of Ind. Bus., Assn. of Critical Care Nurses, Assn. of Am. Businesswomen. Republican. Episcopalian. Office: Tri Mktg Inc 1563 E County Line Rd Ste 301 Jackson MS 39211

SITARZ, ANNELIESE LOTTE, pediatrics educator, physician; b. Medellin, Colombia, Aug. 31, 1928; came to U.S., 1935; d. Hans and Elisabeth (Noll) S. BA cum laude, Bryn Mawr (Pa.) Coll.; 1950; MD, Columbia U., 1954. Diplomate Nat. Bd. Med. Examiners, Am. Bd. Pediatrics., Am. Bd. Pediatric Hematology and Oncology. With Columbia U., N.Y.C., 1957—, assoc. prof. clin. pediatrics, 1974-83, prof. clin. pediatrics, 1983—; cons. pediatrics, hematology and oncology Harlem Hosp., N.Y.C., 1967-72, Overlook Hosp., Summit, N.J., 1975—. Contbr. numerous articles to profl. jours. Pres. Mt. Prospect Assn., Summit, 1987—. Fellow Am. Acad. Pediatrics; mem. Am. Assn. Cancer Rsch., Am. Soc. Clin. Oncology, Am. Soc. Hematology, Internat. Soc. Hematology, Harvey Soc. Republican. Episcopalian. Office: Babies Hosp 3959 Broadway New York NY 10032

SITARZ, PAULA GAJ, writer; b. New Bedford, Mass., May 25, 1955; d. Stanley Mitchell and Pauline (Rocha) Gaj; m. Michael James Sitarz, Aug. 26, 1978; children: Andrew Michael, Kate Elizabeth. BA, Smith Coll., 1977; MLS, Simmons Coll., 1978. Children's libr. Thomas Crane Pub. Libr., Quincy, Mass., 1978-84; dir. Reader's Theatre Workshop Thomas Crane Pub. Library, Quincy Mass., 1985. Author: Book, Picture Book Story Hours: From Birthdays to Bears, 1986, More Picture Book Story Hours 1989. Mem. New Eng. Libr. Assn., Libr. Sci. Honor Soc., Smith Club of Southeastern Mass. (v.p. 1987-89, pres. 1989—), Beta Phi Mu. Roman Catholic. Home and Office: 26 Swanson Dr South Dartmouth MA 02748

SITTERLY, CONNIE SUE, management training specialist, author, consultant; b. Fairfax, Okla., Oct. 9, 1953; d. Claude O. and Virda (Smith) S. AA, Frank Phillips Coll., 1973; BS, West Tex. State U., 1975, MA, 1978; postgrad., Tex. A&M U., 1990. Instr. Frank Phillips Coll., Borger, Tex., 1978-80; asst. prof. Amarillo (Tex.) Coll., 1980-85; owner Mgmt. Tng. Specialists, Ft. Worth, 1982—; adj. assoc. prof. Tex.'s Woman's U., Denton, 1986-90. Author: A Woman's Place: Management, 1988; contbr. over 30 articles to profl. jours. Mem. Am. Soc. Quality Control, Am. Bus. Women's Assn., ASTD. Republican. Home: 2808 5th Ave Fort Worth TX 76110 Office: 1201 W Presidio Ste 204 Fort Worth TX 76102

SIZEMORE, DEBORAH LIGHTFOOT, writer, editor; b. Lamesa, Tex., Mar. 18, 1956; d. Glenn Billy and Francis Earlene (Cable) Lightfoot; m. O.E. Gene Sizemore, June 19, 1981. BS in Agrl. Journalism summa cum laude, Tex. A&M U., 1977. Writer, Tex. Agrl. Extension, College Station, 1977; copy editor Abilene Reporter-News (Tex.), 1978; customer svc. rep. Motheral Printing Co., Ft. Worth, 1978-79; prodn. coord. Graphic Arts, Inc., Ft. Worth, 1980-81; writer, editor, Crowley, Tex., 1981—; freelance writer, editor Boy Scouts Am., Irving, Tex., 1981—; contbg. editor

Dairymen's Digest, Arlington, Tex., 1981-89. Longhorn Scene, Ft. Worth, 1982-84; writer, photographer Harvest Times, Dallas, 1983-84; Simbrah World, Ft. Worth, 1985-87; author: Your Future With The BSA, 1989; contbg. editor Lone Star Horse Report, Ft. Worth, 1985-86; contbr. photographs to mags.; contbr. articles mags. Women's issues chmn., v.p. membership, info. officer, newsletter editor AAUW of Tarrant County, 1981-86, 90-91; organizer nat. security pub. debate, Ft. Worth, 1983. Recipient Sr. Merit award in Agrl. Journalism, Tex. A&M U., 1978, Thomas S. Gathright Acad. Excellence award, 1976, Cert. of Merit, Livestock Publs Coun., 1984, 86, 2d place Nonfiction Book award Tex.-Wide Writers' Competition, 1988, 89, 2d Place Feature Story Dairy Communications Competition Nat. Milk Producers Fedn., 1989. Mem. Nat. Writers Club, Soc. Children's Book Writers, Tex. Freelance Writers Assn., Western Writers Am., Am. Agri-Women, Phi Kappa Phi, Gamma Sigma Delta. Club: Ft. Worth A&M. Office: 19 Frazier Ln Crowley TX 76036

SJOGREN, DEBORAH MARY, accountant; b. Ely, Minn., Aug. 1, 1953; d. Stanley Joseph and Justine Pauline (Korent) Boldine; m. Mark Robert Sjogren, Aug. 21, 1976. A.A., Vermillion Community Coll., 1973; B.S., St. Cloud State U., Minn., 1975. Br. acct. Montgomery Ward, St. Paul, 1975-77; fin. processing cons. region III Mgmt. Info. Service/Elem., Secondary, Vocat., St. Cloud, Minn., 1977-78; acctg. supr. Vision Ease Corp., St. Cloud, 1978-83; controller Franciscan Sisters of Little Falls, Little Falls, Minn., 1983-88, dir. finance, 1988—. Yugoslav Nat. Home scholar, 1971. Mem. Profl. Women's Orgn. (founder), Conf. Religious Treasures (vice chair Region XI), Cen. Minn. Nat. Assn. Accts. (bd. dirs.), Phi Chi Theta (charter). Avocations: horseback riding, reading. Office: Franciscan Sisters Little Falls 116 8th Ave SE Little Falls MN 56345

SKAFTE, MARJORIE DORIS, retired publisher and editor; b. Osseo, Wis., Aug. 1, 1921; d. Nels and Regine (Severson) Westegard; m. Lloyd Albert Skafte, Feb. 14, 1942 (div. Feb. 1979); children: Merilee Skafte Main, Patricia Skafte Pearman, Linwood, Robert. Student, St. Olaf Coll., Northfield, Minn., 1939-41, U. Minn., Duluth, 1965-66. Editorial asst. Ojibway Press (later Harcourt Brace Jovanovich Publs.), Duluth, 1964-67, mng. editor, 1967-68; editor Edgell Communications (formerly Harcourt Brace Jovanovich), Duluth, 1968-89, pub., editor Hearing Instruments, 1971-89; ret., 1989; cons., lectr., writer in field, 1989—; mem. adv. bd. Better Hearing Found., Washington, 1988—, Sertoma Internat. Found., Kansas City, Kans., 1988—, Eddy Found., Duluth, 1987—. Author: 50 Years of Hearing Health Care, 1990; contbr. numerous articles to profl. publs. Membership sec.-treas., v.p. Univ. for Srs., U. Minn., Duluth, 1990. Recipient Internat. Achievement award Better Hearing Inst., 1985, Golden Ear award Hearing Aid Assn. Calif., 1985, lifetime achievement award Acad. Dispensing Audiologists, 1989, cert. of appreciation and recognition Am. Speech, Lang. and Hearing Assn., 1989; hon. fellow Nat. Hearing Aid Soc., 1984. Mem. Hearing Industries Assn. (life), Am. Assn. Ret. Persons, Sons of Norway, Zonta (bd. dirs. Duluth 1990), Order Ea. Star (worthy matron 1960). Republican. Lutheran. Home: 4311 Tioga St Duluth MN 55804

SKAKLE, SYBIL AUSTIN, pharmacist; b. Hatteras, N.C., Jan. 10, 1926; d. Andrew Shanklin and Inez Lynn (Daniels) Austin; m. Donald Edmund Skakle, Feb. 7, 1947 (dec. Apr. 1980); children: Donald Edmund, Stanley Andrew, Clifford Dwight; m. Charles Andre Fetterroll, May 21, 1983 (div. July 1990). BS in Pharmacy, U. N.C., 1949. Lic. pharmacist. Staff pharmacist Durham County Hosp. Corp., Durham, N.C., 1967-85, 87—; drug screener Blue Cross/Blue Shield, Durham, 1985-86; staff pharmacist Durham County Gen. Hosp, Durham, 1987; researcher Shearing Archbell, Attys., Kitty Hawk, N.C., 1986-87; on call pharmacist Eckerds Drug Stores, 1986-87. Author: Hatteras Merchant, 1986; Traveling Sands of Hatteras, 1990; (poetry) Giant, 1990, Forgiveness, 1990. Fellow N.C. Pharm. Assn.; mem. Durham-Orange Pharm. Assn.; mem. Republican Woman's Club, Univ. Woman's Club, Disciplined Order of Christ, Kappa Epsilon. Methodist. Home: 269 Severin St Chapel Hill NC 27516

SKALSKI, JOANNE DOROTHY, healthcare executive, educator, consultant; b. Stevens Point, Wis., May 9, 1934; d. Stanley Sylvester and Johanna Barbara (Borchardt) S. BS in Bus., Alverno Coll., 1959; MA in Adminstrn., Marquette U., 1965. Tchr. Archdiocesan Cath. Schs., Milw., 1955-62, 71-72; from bus. tchr. to asst. prin. Pacelli High Sch., Stevens Point, 1962-70; secretarial instr. Patricia Stevens Career Coll., Milw., 1970-71; vicar provincial Sisters of St. Joseph, Stevens Point, 1972-75; dir. for sponsorship Sisters of St. Joseph, Chgo., 1985—; adminstr. The Social Svcs. Ctr., New Orleans, 1975-77; bus. tchr., counselor Alternative Schs.-Prologue, Chgo., 1977-81; adminstrv. asst. DePaul U., Chgo., 1981-85; mem. resource strategic planning for edn. Archdiocese of Chgo., 1989—; mem. adminstrv. team Sisters of St. Joseph, South Bend, Ind., 1989—; chairperson bd. dirs. Marymount Healthcare Systems, Garfield Heights, Ohio, 1986—; pres. bd. membership corps., Ill. Mich. and Ohio, 1986—. Mediator Neighborhood Justice Ctr., Chgo., 1980-82; bd. dirs. Alternative Schs. Network Bd., Chgo., 1981; trustee Neighborhood Justice Ctr. Bd., Chgo., 1981. Mem. Cath. Health Assn., Nat. Health Lawyers Assn., Acad. for Healthcare Leadership. Roman Catholic. Home: 4878 N Magnolia #A3 Chicago IL 60640 Office: Instnl Sponsorship Bd PO Box 408517 Chicago IL 60640

SKEEL, JUDY ANN, civil engineer; b. Phila., Oct. 5, 1957; d. David Arthur Skeel and Betty Lou (Gardner) Williamson. BCE, Ga. Tech. U., 1979. Registered profl. engr., Ga. Staff engr. Law Engring. Co., Atlanta, 1980-82; project engr. Atec Assocs., Inc., Marietta, Ga., 1983-84; site devel. coord. City of Atlanta, 1984-89; ops. mgr. solid waste dept. County of Cobb, Marietta, 1989-90, interim mgr. solid waste dept., 1990—. Mem. NAFE, Am. Pub. Works Assn., High Mus., Atlanta Hist. Soc., Cumberland Jaycees. Republican. Presbyterian. Office: Cobb County Solid Waste Dept 1897 County Farm Rd Marietta GA 30060

SKELLY, JUNE AVON, university administrator; b. Erie, Pa., June 3, 1946; d. Henrick Christian and Esther Berniece (Struchen) Pihl; m. Alton Joseph Skelly, Apr. 26, 1968; children: Janice Alynn, Alan Joseph, Andrew Jason. AB in Sociology, Thiel Coll., Greenville, Pa., 1968. Elem. tchr. Harborcreek (Pa.) Sch. Dist., 1968-70; liaison to com. on handicapped Averill Park (N.Y.) Sch. Dist., 1983-84; enumerator, field rep. Bur. Census, Erie, Pa., 1988-90, supr. field ops., 1990—; sec. aide Office of the Pres. Gannon U., Erie, Pa., 1990—. Leader Girl Scouts U.S.A., Wilmington, Del., 1977-78, leader, chmn. svc. unit, Averill Park, 1978-84, Pottstown, Pa., 1986-87; vol. Family Svcs. Mother to Mother Program, 1990. Mem. AAUW (chmn. Edn. Found. 1987, rept. internat. rels. area 1989, program chmn. 1990, Outstanding Woman award 1987), Zeta Tau Alpha (v.p. alumnae chpt. 1989-90). Lutheran. Home: 5701 Footemill Rd Erie PA 16509 Office: Office of the Pres Gannon U Univ Square Erie PA 16541

SKELTON, DOROTHY GENEVA SIMMONS (MRS. JOHN WILLIAM SKELTON), educator; b. Woodland, Calif.; d. Jack Elijah and Helen Anna (Siebe) Simmons; B.A., U. Calif., 1940, M.A., 1943; m. John William Skelton, July 16, 1941. Sr. research analyst War Dept., Gen. Staff, M.I. Div. G-2, Pentagon, Washington, 1944-45; vol. researcher, monuments, fine arts and archives sect. Restitution Br., Office Mil. Govt. for Hesse, Wiesbaden, German, 1947-48; vol. art tchr. German children in Bad Nauheim, Germany, 1947-48; art educator, lectr. Dayton (Ohio) Art Inst., 1955; art educator Lincoln Sch., Dayton, 1956-60; instr. art and art ed. U. Va. Sch. Continuing Edn., Charlottesville, 1962-75; researcher genealogy, exhibited in group shows, Calif., Colo., Ohio, Washington and Va.; represented in permanent collections Madison Hall, Charlottesville, Madison (Va.) Center. Mem. Nat. League Am. Pen Women, AAUW, Am. Assn. Museums, Coll. Art Assn. Am., Inst. for Study of Art in Edn. Dayton Soc. Painters and Sculptors, Nat. Soc. Arts and Letters (life), Va. Mus. Fine Arts, Cal. Alumni Assn., Air Force Officers Wives Club. Republican. Methodist. Clubs: Army Navy Country, Lake of the Woods (Va.) Golf and Country. Chief collaborator: John Skelton of Georgia, 1969; author: The Squire Simmons Family, 1746-1986, 1986. Address: Lotos Lakes Brightwood VA 22715

SKELTON, GLENDA CAROL, banker, accountant; b. Birmingham, Ala., Apr. 25, 1950; d. Robert McKinley and Jewel (Wingo) S. BSBA, U. Ala., Birmingham, 1972, MBA, 1983. Flexowriter Norpac/Falconer Check Printers, Birmingham, 1968-73; various positions Fed. Res. Bank, Birmingham, 1973-74; acctg. officer Nat. Bank Commerce, Birmingham, 1984-88; asst. v.p. South Trust Bank Ala., Birmingham, 1988—; tchr.

Unit award 1987). Republican. Baptist. Office: Brevard Community Coll 1519 Clearlake Rd Cocoa FL 32922

SINGER, GLADYS MONTGOMERY See MONTGOMERY, GLADYS

SINGER, HEDY KAREN, psychologist; b. Phila., Apr. 15, 1954; d. Aaron Norman and Lillian Sarah (Goldman) S. BS, Temple U., 1975, PhD, 1988; MA, Villanova U., 1977. Lic. psychologist, Pa. Tchr. Sch. Dist. Phila., 1975-77; counselor Montgomery County Intermediate U., Bluebell, Pa., 1978-80; intake supv., counselor Jewish Employment and Vocat. Svc., Phila., 1979-84; grad. asst. counseling ctr. Temple U., Phila.-1984-85; psychology intern Friends Hosp., Phila., 1985-86; staff psychologist Hall-Mercer Community MHMR Pa. Hosp., Phila., 1986-87, Abington (Pa.) Psychol. Assocs., 1987-88; sr. instr., staff psychologist div. adolescent psychiatry Hahnemann U., Phila., 1988-89; asst. prof. psychiatry Med. Coll. Pa., Phila., 1989—; cons. Hahnemann Adolescent Suicide Prevention, 1988-89; coord. psychology Chestnut Hill Rehab. Hosp., 1989—; trainer, suicide instrn. specialist, cons. substance abuse program Sch. Dist. Phila., 1990—. Mem. Am. Jewish Congress, 1988—, Jewish Community Rels. Coun., 1990—, Urban Coalition, Interfaith Coun., 1990—. Presdl. scholar, 1974; Temple U. fellow, 1984; Rsch. grantee Phila. Geriatric Ctr., 1990. Mem. APA, Nat. Assn. Counseling and Devel., Phila. Soc. Clin. Psychologists, Delaware Valley Group Psychotherapy Soc., Soc. Personality Assessment, Kappa Delta Phi. Office: Med Coll Pa 3200 Henry Ave Philadelphia PA 19129

SINGER, JANICE GAIL, psychotherapist, consultant; b. Chgo., Aug. 14, 1947; d. Harold and Dorothy (Kagen) S.; 1 child, Rachael Jacqueline. BA, U. Toledo, 1969; MSW, U. Wis., Milw., 1977; postgrad., Gestalt Inst., Cleve., 1982, Dreikers Relationship Ctr., Boulder, Colo., 1985; Reiki II, Nancy Retzlaff R.M., Milw., 1986. Program evaluator, project cons. Mental health Planning Council of Milw., 1976-78; counselor abortion WomanCare-West, Milw., 1978; treatment foster care worker Children's Service Soc. of Wis., Milw., 1978-81; mental health coordinator, primary psychotherapist Bread and Roses Women's Health Ctr., Inc., Milw., 1981-84; originator Friends' Psychotherapy Collective, Milw., 1984—; group facilitator People to People, Waukesha, Wis., 1976-80; mem. coalition sexual misconduct by psychotherapists, Wis., 1984-86, 88—; cons. Woman to Woman, Inc., Milw., 1981—. Co-author: (consumer guide) Making Therapy Work for You, 1986; creator therapy mode Action Oriented Therapy, 1983; co-creator: (workshops) Living Your Godness Enhancing Self-Esteem Thru Action, 1988, Living in Balance-Integrating Male & Female Energy, 1987, Grieving: The Benefits of Being a Cry Baby, 1988, Seeking the Self-A Shamanic Tradition, 1989, Working With Abusive, Noncompliant, Obnoxious Patients, What Your Body's Saying Whether Your Lips are Moving or Not, 1989, Codependency: When Your Drug of Choice is Anyone But You, 1989, Discovering Your E/Sensual Body-Being Sensual is Essential to Life, 1989, Celebration in Living!, 1984, Living Beyond AIDS, 1987, Transforming Body Image, 1987, Finding Peace in Your Body, others. Workshop leader Milw. AIDS Project, 1987; co-creator workshops Celebration in Living, 1984, Living Beyond AIDS, 1987, Transforming Body Image, 1987; active Maple Dale Sch. Human Sexuality, Milw., 1983-86; cirriculum cons. Nicolet High Sch. Human Sexuality, 1987. Mem. Feminist Therapy Network (pres. 1984-87), Nat. Assn. Social Workers, Assn. for Human Animal Bonding, Wis. Assn. Outpatient Mental Health Facilities (mem. ethics com. 1981-86). Democrat. Home: 8428 N Regent Rd Milwaukee WI 53217 also: 3749 Mariana Way #B Santa Barbara CA 93109 Office: Friends Psychotherapy Collective 8426 N Regent Rd Milwaukee WI 53217

SINGER, JEANNE (JEANNE WALSH), composer, concert pianist; b. N.Y.C., Aug. 4, 1924; d. Harold Vandervoort and Helen (Loucks) Walsh; B.A. magna cum laude, Barnard Coll., 1944; artist diploma Nat. Guild Piano Tchrs., 1954; student in piano Nadia Reisenberg, 1945-60, composition, Douglas Moore, 1942-44, Ph.D. (hon.) in Music World U., 1984; m. Richard G. Singer, Feb. 24, 1945, dec.; 1 son, Richard V. Composer, concert pianist solo chamber ensembles N.Y., 1947—; tchr. piano Manhasset, N.Y., 1960—; lectr. in field. Recipient spl. award merit Nat. Fedn. Music Clubs, 1st prize in nat. competition Composers Guild, 1979, Grand prize Composers Guild, 1982, 1st prize Composers and Songwriters Internat., 1985, also various nat. awards; honored at all-Singer concert, Bogotá, Colombia, 1980; N.Y. Council Arts grantee. Fellow Internat. Biog. Assoc.; mem. ASCAP (awards 1978-88), Am. Music Center, Internat. League Women Composers, Nat. League Am. Pen Women (nat. music chmn.), Composers, Authors and Artists Am. (v.p. N.Y.C., music mag. editor 1972-80, nat. award 1981), Am. Women Composers, Phi Beta Kappa. Clubs: Barnard Coll. of L.I., Tuesday Morning Music Douglaston; Bohemians (N.Y.C.). Composed numerous instrumental, vocal works including: Summons (baritone), 1975, A Cycle of Love (4 songs with piano), 1976, Suite in Harpsichord Style, 1976, From The Green Mountains (trio), 1977, (choral work) Composers' Prayer, Nocturne for Clarinet, 1980, Suite for Horn and Harp, 1980, From Petrarch (voice, horn, piano), 1981, Quartet for Flute, Oboe, Violin, Cello, 1982, Trio for Viola, Oboe, Piano, 1984, Come Greet the Spring (choral), 1981, An American Vision (song cycle), 1985, Wry Rimes (voice and Bassoon), 1986, The Lost Garden (voice, paino, cello), 1988; performed Lincoln Center, radio, TV. Home and Office: 64 Stuart Place Manhasset NY 11030

SINGER, MARILYN JEAN, lawyer; b. San Francisco, Mar. 7, 1955; d. Isadore Milton and Sara Sue (Spitalny) S. BA, Bryn Mawr Coll., 1976; JD, Case Western Res. U., 1979. Bar: Ohio, 1979. Litigator Buckeye Union/Continental Ins. Co., Cleve., 1980—. Mem. Ohio Bar Assn., Bryn Mawr Coll. Alumnae Assn. (treas. dist. VI, 1984—), Bryn Mawr Club Cleve. Democrat. Jewish. Office: 55 Public Sq Cleveland OH 44113

SINGER, MAXINE FRANK, biochemist; b. N.Y.C., Feb. 15, 1931; d. Hyman S. and Henrietta (Perlowitz) Frank; m. Daniel Morris Singer, June 15, 1952; children: Amy Elizabeth, Ellen Ruth, David Byrd, Stephanie Frank. AB, Swarthmore Coll., 1952, DSc (hon.), 1978; PhD, Yale U., 1957; DSc (hon.), Wesleyan U., 1977, U.Md.-Baltimore County, 1985, Cedar Crest Coll., 1986, CUNY, 1988, Brandeis U., 1988, Radcliffe Coll., 1990, Williams Coll., 1990. USPHS postdoctoral fellow NIH, Bethesda, Md., 1956-58; research chemist (biochemistry) NIH, 1958-74; head sect. on nucleic acid enzymology Nat. Cancer Inst., 1974-79; chief Lab. of Biochemistry, Nat. Cancer Inst., 1979-87, research chemist, 1987-88; pres. Carnegie Inst. Washington, 1988—; Regents vis. lectr. U. Calif., Berkeley, 1981; bd. dirs. Found. for Advanced Edn. in Scis., 1972-78, 85-86; mem. sci. council Internat. Inst. Genetics and Biophysics, Naples, Italy, 1982-86. Mem. editorial bd. Jour. Biol. Chemistry, 1968-74, Sci. mag, 1972-82; chmn. editorial bd. Procs. of Nat. Acad. Scis., 1985-88; contrb. articles to scholarly jours. Trustee Wesleyan U., Middletown, Conn., 1972-75, Yale Corp., New Haven, 1975-90; bd. govs. Weizmann Inst. Sci., Rehovot, Israel, 1978—; bd. dirs. Whitehead Inst, 1985—. Recipient award for achievement in biol. scis. Washington Acad. Scis., 1969, award for research in biol. scis. Yale Sci. and Engring. Assn., 1974, Superior Service Honor award HEW, 1975, Dirs. award NIH, 1977, Disting. Service medal HHS, 1983, Presdl. Disting. Exec. Rank award, 1987, U.S. Disting. Exec. Rank award, 1988. Fellow Am. Acad. Arts and Scis.; mem. NAS (coun. 1982-85), AAAS (Sci. Freedom and Responsibility award 1982), Am. Soc. Biol. Chemists, Am. Soc. Microbiologists, Am. Chem. Soc., Am. Philos. Soc., Inst. Medicine of NAS, Pontifical Acad. of Scis. Home: 5410 39th St NW Washington DC 20015 Office: Carnegie Inst Washington 1530 P St NW Washington DC 20015

SINGER, NIECEE, genetic counselor; b. N.Y.C.; d. A. Nathan and Doris (Tenzer) Levy; children: Mark, Patricia, Nancy. BA magna cum laude, Wheaton Coll., 1950; MS, Sarah Lawrence Coll., 1976. Cert. in genetic counseling Am. Bd. Med. Genetics. Supr. genetics unit Westchester County Med. Ctr., Valhalla, N.Y., 1976-82; asst. dir. Morristown (N.J.) Meml. Hosp., 1982—. Contbr articles to profl. jours. Mem. Gov.'s Coun. on Prevention of Mental Retardation, 1988—. Mem. Am. Soc. Human Genetics, Human Genetics Assn. N.J. (pres. 1985-87, chairperson edn. com. 1984-85, co-chairperson legis. com. 1987—), Nat. Soc. Genetic Counselors (founding, treas. 1978-81), Mid-Atlantic Regional Human Genetics Network (mem. steering com. 1985-89), Phi Kappa Phi. Democrat. Office: Morristown Meml Hosp Genetics Birth Defects Ctr Morristown NJ 07960

SINGER, PHYLLIS, editor; b. Newark, May 22, 1947; d. Carl N. and Marion (Heller) S.; m. Edward J. Lowe, Jr., Aug. 11, 1979; children—James, Daniel. B.S., Boston U., 1969. Mgr. print and broadcast traffic F. William

Free & Co., advt., N.Y.C., 1969-70; researcher, reporter, editor L.I. Comml. Rev., Syosset, N.Y., 1970-72; with Newsday, L.I., 1972—, asst. editor, then sr. editor viewpoints, now asst. mng. editor features; mem. bd. Newspaper Features Council. Mem. Am. Assn. Sunday and Feature Editors (v.p.). Office: Newsday Inc 235 Pinelawn Rd Melville NY 11747*

SINGER, SUSAN JENNIFER RUNDELL, biology educator; b. Schenectady, N.Y., July 1, 1959; d. Jeremiah Alston and Jean Ellen (Nielsen) Rundell; m. Gary Michael Singer, June 21, 1981; children: Jessica, Peter. BS, Rensselaer Inst., 1981, MS, 1982, PhD, 1985. Asst. prof. Carleton Coll., Northfield, Minn., 1986—. Contbr. articles to profl. jours. Pres. parents' bd. Northfield Day Care Ctr., 1987-89; leader La Leche League, 1990—. Recipient rsch. grant USDA, 1987-90, Rsch. Corp., 1987-89, NSF, 1988-91. Mem. Soc. Devel. Biology (edn. com.), Am. Soc. Plant Physiology, Plant Devel. Biology Group (edn. editor), Flowering Working Group, Botanical Soc., Sigma Xi. Office: Dept Biology Carleton Coll One North College St Northfield MN 55057

SINGER, SUZANNE FRIED, editor; b. N.Y.C., July 9, 1935; d. Maurice Aaron and Augusta G. (Ginsberg) Fried; m. Max Singer, Feb. 12, 1959; children: Saul, Alexander, Daniel, Benjamin. BA with honors, Swarthmore Coll., 1956; MA, Columbia U., 1958. Program asst. NSF, Washington, 1958-60; assoc. editor Bibl. Archaeology Rev., Washington, 1979-84, mng. editor, 1984—; mng. editor Bibl. Rev., Washington, 1985—; exec. editor Moment, Washington, 1987—. Mem. Am. Schs. Oriental Research. Jewish. Office: Bibl Archaeology Soc 3000 Connecticut Ave NW Suite 300 Washington DC 20008

SINGER, SYDNEE ROBIN, lawyer; b. Chgo., Apr. 3, 1955; d. Alvin Maynard and Ruth Helene (Bromberg) S. MusB, U. Miami, 1977, MusM, 1979, MBA, 1979; JD, Ind. U., 1984. Bar: Calif. 1988. Claims adminstr. Carl Warren & Co., San Diego, 1986-89; assoc. Howarth & Smith, L.A., 1989—. Bd. editors Ind. U. Law Jour., 1983-84. Bd. dirs. East Bluff Homeowners Assn., Del Mar, Calif., 1988-89, Del Mar Highlands Homeowners Assn., 1988-89. Mem. Calif. Bar Assn., Calif. Trial Lawyers Assn., L.A. County Bar Assn. Home: 415 S Broadway #A Redondo Beach CA 90277 Office: Howarth & Smith 700 S Flower St Ste 2900 Los Angeles CA 90017

SINGER-LEONE, MALLORY ANN, sales executive; b. N.Y.C., Jan. 14, 1950; d. George G. and Evelyn (Braver) S.; m. Dino J. Leone, May 1, 1983. BS, C.W. Post Coll., Greenvale, N.Y., 1972. Lic. tchr., N.Y. Asst. buyer J.C. Penney Co., N.Y.C., 1973-76; sales rep. Graphicenter, N.Y.C., 1976-78, Pellon Sales Corp., N.Y.C., 1978—; English tchr. Internat. Ctr., N.Y.C. 1984-88. Mem. Internat. Fund for Animal Welfare, Mass., 1989, Fashion Group. Mem. N.Y. State Horticultural Soc. Democrat. Jewish. Home: 245 E 25th St New York NY 10010 Office: Pellon Sales Corp 119 W 40th St New York NY 10018

SINGG, SANGEETA, psychology educator, counselor; b. Patiala, Punjab, India, Mar. 10, 1950; came to U.S., 1967; d. Jaswant Singh and Yashwant Kaur (Joshi) Modgil; m. Raghu N. Singh, Feb. 25, 1967 (div. Oct. 1979); 1 child, Raj K.; m. Charles Harris Williams, Nov. 24, 1985. BA in Sociology, Punjab U., 1967; MA in Sociology, Miss. State U., 1970; MS in Psychology, East Tex. State U., 1979, PhD in Psychology, 1981. Rsch. asst. Social Sci. Rsch. Ctr. U. Miss. Starkville, 1968-70; rsch. asst. Social Sci. Rsch. Ctr. East Tex. State U., Commerce, 1976, rsch. asst. dept. sociology, 1977, asst. instr. dept. psychology, 1977-80; asst. prof. dept. psychology and sociology Angelo State U., San Angelo, Tex., 1981—; pvt. practice psychology San Angelo, 1984—; program evaluator family life demonstration project, communicating sex respect USHHS, San Angelo, 1987-88; researcher, dir. Community Needs Assessment Survey of Del Rio-GTE S.W., San Angelo, 1988; dir., researcher effects of career cou. Contbr. articles to profl. jours. Group faciliator Families of AIDS Patients, San Angelo, 1987; mem. bd. truste. Mem. Am. Psychol. Assn., Southwestern Psychol. Assn., Tex. Faculty Assn., Tex. Acad. Sci., India Assn. (sec. Starkville chpt. 1969-70), Dames Club. Home: 3318 Grandview Dr San Angelo TX 76904 Office: Angelo State U San Angelo TX 76909

SINGH, SWAYAM PRABHA, food service executive; b. Bangalore, Mysore, India, Aug. 26, 1945; came to U.S., 1968; d. Kripal Ananda and Sharada (Bai) Singh Chauhan; m. Balaram K. Singh, Juen 29, 1967; children: Jyothi Kiran, Naveen Raj. BA, St. Philomina's, India, 1967. Cert. comml. real estate loan broker. Sub. tchr. Good Shephard Convent, Mysore, 1964; pub. Singh Seven Seas' Publs., Lansing, Mich., 1979—; founder, pres., chief exec. officer Unique Foods of India, Inc., Lansing, 1984—; founder Joveen Mgmt., Lansing, 1985—, comml. real estate developer, 1988-90; lectr., instr. Lansing Community Coll., 1979-80. Author: Learn to Cook without Preservative, 1980, Unique Universal Gourmet Club, 1984, Swayam's Authentic Cookbook of India, 1987. Area rep. Edn. Found. for Fgn. Study, 1983; mem. Am. Film Inst., Wildlife Fedn., Sesquicentennial Com. for Ethnic Festival, 1987; elected del. Gov. Blanchard's Small Bus. Confs.; founder UFI Humna Devel. Ctr., 1987; founder Prestigious Once awards; founder campaign for better decent movies. Mem. Lansing Regional C. of C. (Excellence in Edn. cert. 1989, 90), Toastmasters, Mich. Pubs. Assn. (bd. dirs.). Democrat. Hindu. Office: Singh Seven Seas' Ctr 224 S Clippert St Box 22205 Box 22205 Lansing MI 48909

SINGLETARY, PATRICIA ANN, minister; b. N.Y.C., Mar. 3, 1948; d. George and Minnie Juanita (Williams) Nickens; m. Edward Franklin Singletary, Feb. 5, 1966 (div. Apr. 1973); children: Erik Franklin, Don Andre. BTh, New World Bible Inst. and Sem., 1984, MRE, 1988; postgrad., SUNY, Empire State Coll., 1985—; MDiv, Va. Sem. and Coll., 1988, DD, Tenn. Bapt. Sch. of Religion, 1989. Sr. reorgn. underwriter Depository Trust Co., N.Y.C., 1968-90, account coord. 1990—; former nat. corr. sec. Nat. Baptist Conv. U.S.A. Inc., 1984-87; vice chmn. Spiritual Life Commn. of Clergywomen, 1987—; assoc. minister Morning Star Missionary Bapt. Ch. of Jamaica, N.Y. Nat. editor: Ekklesia, 1986. Recipient Vol. Services award City of N.Y., 1980. Mem. Nat. Assn. Negro Bus. and Profl. Women, NAFE, Interdenominational Bd. Clergywomen (gen. sec. 1985—), Nat. Bapt. Women Ministers Conv. (bd. mgrs. 1983—), Ea. Bapt. Assn. (instr. 1981-83, v.p. evangelistic unit 1982-83, gen. dir. women's aux. 1988—), Nat. Coun. Women U.S., Internat. Platform Assn., Bronx Bapt. Ministers Evening Conf. Greater N.Y. and Vicinity. Office: Morning Star Missionary Bapt Ch 114-44 Merrick Blvd Jamaica NY 11434

SINGLETON, BARBARA ANN, social worker; b. St. Augustine, Fla., Nov. 13, 1949; d. Otis and Henrietta S. BS, Fla. Meml. Coll., 1971; MSW, Fla. State U., 1976. Lic. clin. social worker, Fla. Social worker HRS State of Fla., Palatka, 1972-74; ex-POW adminstrv. coord., clin. social worker VA Med. Ctr., Miami, Fla., 1981—; clin. social worker, admry.; clin. social worker Fla. Alcoholism Treatment Ctr., Avon Park, 1976-79; clin. social worker, geriatrics coord. Tri-County Mental Health Svcs., St. Augustine, 1979-83. Mem. Miami Assn. Black Social Workers (sec. 1986-90). Baptist.

SINGLETON, DONNA MARIE, travel agency manager; b. Dowagiac, Mich., Sept. 14, 1960; d. Lester Allen and Betty Lorella (Fryman) Stover; m. Mark Steven Singleton, Sept. 1, 1979; children: Christina Marie, Christopher Michael. Student, Assoc. Travel Sch., Miami, 1979. Cert. travel cons. Travel cons. Signal Travel & Tours, Inc., Niles, Mich., 1979-80; mgr. Signal Travel & Tours, Inc., Niles, 1980—, Dowagiac & Niles, Mich., 1985—; key coordinator Am. Airlines, Signal Travel, Niles, 1988—; coordinator Cert. Travel Cons., Niles, 1989—; sabre master local level Am. Airlines, 1983-86. Vol. United Way, Dowagiac, 1988. Mem. Dowagiac C. of C. (dir. 1987—), Bus. and Profl. Women (chair young careerists 1988—), Bd. Christian Edn. Federated Ch. (sec. 1988—). Office: Signal Travel & Tours Inc 227 E Main St Niles MI 49120

SINGLETON, LINDA GAIL, nurse, home healthcare company executive; b. Greenwood, Miss., Apr. 29, 1950; d. Willie Park and Jimmie Lee (Visor) Newman; m. Elmer E. Singleton (div.); children: Katryna L., Patricia Deneem. Diploma, Kennedy-King Coll., Chgo., 1978. RN, Ill. Staff nurse Jackson Park Hosp., Chgo., 1978-87; assoc. adminstr. Beverly Hills Home Health Agy., P.C., Chgo., 1987—; dir. fin. Med. Acad. Tech., Chgo., 1987-88. Active Roseland Hosp. Aux., Chgo., 1988—; mem. adv. bd. Kennedy-King

Coll., 1987—. Mem. Am. Nurses Assn., Chgo. Black Nurses Assn., Profl. Entrepreneur Network, Female Execs. Am., Kennedy-King Coll. Alumni Assn. Office: Beverly Hills Home Health 10540 S Western Ave Chicago IL 60643

SINGLETON, SARA, banker; b. Reading, Pa., Feb. 19, 1940; d. Walter S. and Sarah (Hain) Shearer; m. John H. Singleton, Nov. 9, 1957; children: Joanne Reagan, Suzanne Oliver. Student, Ursinus Coll., 1979-86. Teller, customer svc. rep. S.E. Nat. Bank, Phoenixville, Pa., 1972-81; mgmt. trainee Red Hill (Pa.) Savs. and Loan Assn., 1981, asst. mgr. ops., 1982-84; mgr. deposit acctg. Penn Savs. Bank, Wyomissing, 1984; asst. v.p. deposit svcs. Pa. Savs. Bank, Wyomissing, 1984-86, v.p. deposit svcs., 1987—; mem. check product adv. group Phila. Res. Bank, 1988—. Pres. Mont Clare (Pa.) Home Sch. Assn., 1973-75; officer, bd. dirs. Holy Ghost Ch., Phoenixville, 1974-84; cons. Greater Valley Coun. Girls Scouts U.S., Reading, 1988—. Mem. Nat. Assn. Banking Women (treas. Reading 1988—), Berks County C. of C. (amb. com. 1986-88, edn. com. 1988—), Fin. Women Internat. (co-chair Berk County job fair 1990). Home: 310 Woodlyn Dr Collegeville PA 19426 Office: Penn Savs Bank 1130 Berkshire Blvd Wyomissing PA 19610

SINICKI, MAUREEN T., property management; b. Johnson City, N.Y., Mar. 29, 1952; d. Anthony and Mary (Solak) S. BA, SUNY, Buffalo, 1973; postgrad., N.Y. U. Ptnr. The Property Mgmt. Co., Alexandria, Va.; chief, evaluation and review staff Office Rsch. and Devel. U.S. EPA, Washington; chief, program and info. mgmt. staff U.S. EPA, Washington, chief, facilities engring. and real estate br.; owner Property Mgmt. Assoc., Inc., Alexandria. Recipient Distinguished Svc. award Fedn. of the Handicapped, N.Y.C. Mem. Alexandria Ctr. for Employment, Inc. (past pres.). Home: 1600 Prince St #512 Alexandria VA 22314

SINICKI, SHEILA JEANNE, data processing executive; b. Queens, N.Y., June 3, 1952. BS, Hofstra U., 1974, MA, 1976; MBA, Adelphi U. Acct. mgr. Gen. Electric Consulting, N.Y.C.; project leader, analyst Doubleday & Co., Garden City, N.Y.; sr. programmer, analyst European Am. Bank, Merrick, N.Y.; project mgr. CSC Ptnrs., N.Y.C.; bd. dirs. Rough Riders Landing.

SINITZKY, MIRIAM MALKA, chief financial officer; b. Fed. Republic of Germany, Feb. 15, 1949; came to U.S., 1952; d. Moses and Sima (Rosenzweig) Meller; m. Stanley Sinitzky, Aug. 5, 1979; 1 child, Danielle. BS, Bklyn. Coll., 1972; MBA, L.I. U., 1983. CPA, N.Y. Jr. acct. Foote, Cone & Belding, N.Y.C., 1972-74; controller Neuville-Mobil Sox, Inc., N.Y.C., 1974-79; sr. Weiss & Stern, CPAs, N.Y.C., 1983-85; chief fin. officer Total Patient Care, Upjohn Healthcare Svcs., L.I., 1985-89, Choices Women's Med. Ctr., Inc., Queens, N.Y., 1989—; fin. cons. tax preparation and planning, L.I., 1983—. Mem. N.Y. State Soc. CPAs. Republican. Jewish. Home: 37 Oxford Rd East Rockaway NY 11518 Office: Choices Women's Med Ctr 97-77 Queens Blvd Queens NY 11374

SINK, ALVA GORDON (MRS. CHARLES A. SINK), clubwoman; b. Rose Twp., Mich.; d. Nathaniel J. and Ella M. (Highfield) Gordon; student Eastern Mich. U., summers 1914, 18; A.B., U. Mich., 1923; m. Charles A. Sink, June 18, 1923 (dec.). Tchr. pub. schs., Rose Center, Mich., 1914-17, Hickory Ridge, Mich., 1917-18, Holly, Mich., 1918-19, Canfield Pvt. Sch., Ann Arbor, Mich., 1919-22. Mem. Women's Republican Club, Ann Arbor. Dir. Washtenaw County chpt. ARC, 1943-48, 53-59, in charge First Aid and Accident Prevention, 1941-61; pres. Mich. House and Senate Club, 1929-30, U. Mich. Alumnae Club, 1931-33, Sara Browne Smith Group Alumnae Club, 1957-59, Women's Soc. Congl. Ch., 1946-48; regent Sarah Caswell Angell chpt. DAR, 1955-57. Recipient Red Cross citation, 1959, Alumnae Council award U. Mich., 1971, Disting. Alumni Service award U. Mich., 1978; Alva Gordon Sink Group of U. Mich. Alumnae named in her honor. Mem. Hist. Soc. Mich., Alumni Assn. U. Mich., French Huguenots, AAUW, Ann Arbor Art Assn., Henry P. Tappan Soc., P.E.O. Clubs: Art Study, Garden, Faculty Women, Presidents of U. Mich. (pres. emeritus 1975-76), Ann Arbor Women's City. Home: 1325 Olivia Ave Ann Arbor MI 48104

SINK, CLAIRE HUSCHKA, waste management/environmental services branch chief; b. Viroqua, Wis., Aug. 7, 1943; d. Clyde Groves and Helen (Kafer) Huschka; m. J.D. Sink (div. 1987); children: Kara, Karl. BS, U. Wis., 1965; MA, Pa. State U., 1968. Project assoc. Pa. State U., 1967-79; tech. writer Dynamac Corp., Rockville, Md., 1979-80; rsch assoc. Geomet Techs., Inc., Rockville, 1980-81; sect. leader EG&G, WASC, Inc., Morgantown, W.Va., 1981-83; tech. communication mgr. Morgantown Energy Tech. Ctr., 1983-87; lab. tech. transfer program mgr. U.S. Dept. Energy, 1987-90; chief tech. integration br. Office Environ. Restoration and Waste Mgmt. U.S. Dept. Energy, Germantown, Md., 1990—. Editor: Tech. 87, 88; contbr. articles to profl. jours. Review panel Research & Projects Panel, 1981-85. Named One of Outstanding Young Women of Am., 1972. Mem. U. Wis. Alumni Assn., Pa. State U. Alumni Assn., AAUW, Am. Assn. for the Advancement of Sci., Tech. Transfer Soc. Office: US Dept Energy Environ Restoration Waste Mgmt 12800 Middlebrook Rd Germantown MD 20874

SINK, NIGRA LEA (NIGRA LEA ROBERTS), employment specialist; b. Elberfeld, Ind., June 5, 1935; d. Jerrell Wilson and Nigeal Elaine (Besing) Roberts; m. J. Darhl Sink, Aug. 8, 1959 (div. Aug. 1978); 1 child, Karlin Roberts Sink. BS in Edn., Oakland City (Ind.) Coll., 1957; postgrad., Purdue U., 1959, Ball State U., 1961; MS in Edn., Ind. U., 1963. Cert. tchr., Ind., Ill.; lic. counselor, Ind. Ill., Tchr. pub. schs. Ind., 1957-66, Wis., 1966-67; tchr. Huntley Mid. Sch., DeKalb, Ill., 1967-70; mgr. McDonald's, Jacksonville, Ill., 1972-84; project specialist Lewis & Clark Community Coll., Godfrey, Ill., 1985-90; employment specialist Lincoln Land Community Coll., 1990—; instr. part-time MacMurray Coll., Jacksonville, 1985—. Mem. Morgan County Rep. Women, Jacksonville. Gen. Electric Corp. fellow, 1959. Mem. Ill. Adult and Continuing Educators Assn., Ill. Employment and Tng. Assn., Rebeccas (noble grand 1990—), Order of Eastern Star (worthy matron 1979, sec. 1984—), White Shrine of Jerusalem (worthy high priestess 1987, 89, supreme instr. 1988, worthy scribe 1990). Methodist. Home: 514 N Diamond St Jacksonville IL 62650 Office: Lewis and Clark Coll 300-A E Walnut St Jacksonville IL 62650

SINKFORD, JEANNE CRAIG, dentist, educator; b. Washington, Jan. 30, 1933; d. Richard E. and Geneva (Jefferson) Craig; m. Stanley M. Sinkford, Dec. 8, 1951; children: Dianne Sylvia, Janet Lynn, Stanley M. III. B.S., Howard U., 1953, M.S., 1962, D.D.S., 1958, Ph.D., 1963; D.Sc. (hon.), Georgetown U., 1978. Instr. prosthodontics dentistry Howard U., Washington, 1958-60, mem. faculty dentistry, 1964—, assoc. dean rsch. coord., co-chmn. dept. restorative dentistry, 1968-75, dean Coll. Dentistry, 1975—, prof. prosthodontics grad. schs., 1977—; instr. research and crown and bridge Northwestern U. Sch. Dentistry, 1963-64; cons. prosthodontics and research VA Hosp., Washington, 1965—; resident Children's Hosp. Nat. Med. Ctr., 1974-75; cons. St. Elizabeth's Hosp.; mem. attending staff Freedman's Hosp., Washington, 1964—; adv. bd. D.C. Gen. Hosp., 1975—; mem. Nat. Adv. Dental Research Council, Nat. Bd. Dental Examiners; mem. ad hoc adv. panel Tuskegee Syphilis Study for HEW; sponsor D.C. Pub. Health Apprentice Program; mem. adv. council to dir. NIH; adv. com. NIH/NIDR/NIA Aging Research Council; mem. dental devices classification panel FDA; mem. select panel for promotion child health, 1979-80; mem. spl. med. adv. group VA; bd. overseers U. Pa. Dental Sch., Boston U. Dental Sch.; bd. advs. U. Pitts. Dental Sch. Mem. editorial rev. bd. Jour. Am. Coll. Dentists, 1988. Contbr. Nat. Symphony Orch.; adv. bd. United Negro Coll. Fund, Robert Wood Johnson Health Policy Fellowships; mem. Mayor's Block Grant Adv. Com., 1982; mem. parents coun. Sidwell Friends, 1983; mem. adv. bd. Jr. Citizens Corps, asst. reg. bd. D.C.; mem. spl. med. adv. group VA. Louise C. Ball fellow grad. tng., 1960-63. Fellow Am. Coll. Dentists, Internat. Coll. Dentists (award of merit); mem. ADA (chmn. appeal bd. coun. on dental edn. 1975-82), Am. Soc. for Geriatric Dentistry (bd. dirs.), Internat. Assn. Dental Research, Dist. Dental Soc., Am. Inst. Oral Biology, North Portal Civic League, Inst. Grad. Dentists (trustee), So. Conf. Dental Deans (chmn.), Wash. Coun. Adminstrv. Women, Assn. Am. Women Dentists, Am. Assn. Dental Schs. (chmn. coun. deans), Am. Pedodontic Soc., Am. Prosthodontic Soc., Fed. Prosthodontic Orgn., Nat. Dental Assn. Inst. Medicine (coun.), Am. Soc. Dentistry for Children, N.Y. Acad. Scis. Smithsonian Assocs., Dean's Coun., Proctor and Gamble, Golden Key Honor Soc., Links Inc., Sigma Xi, Phi Beta Kappa, Omicron Kappa Upsilon,

Psi Chi, Beta Kappa Chi. Address: 1765 Verbena St NW Washington DC 20012

SINKHORN, MARY JEAN, real estate executive; b. Athens, Ga., May 19, 1941; d. Howard J. and Helen (Fields) Pickelsimer; m. Michael J. Gordon, Aug. 21, 1965 (div. 1985); children: Michael J. Jr., Mitzi J.; m. Walt P. Sinkhorn, Mar. 28, 1986. Degree, Lakeland Bus. Coll., 1960. Lic. realtor, Pa., Fla. Legal sec. C.A. Boswell, Sr., et al., Attys., Bartow, Fla., 1960-69; owner, operator Gordon and Whitaker Interiors, Phila., 1977-1978; assoc. realtor Fox and Lazo, Haverford, Pa., 1979-83; dir. real estate services The Polo Group, Inc., Tampa, Fla., 1984—. V.p. Tampa Jr. Woman's Club, 1971; treas. Bartow Jr. Woman's Club, 1966; sec. Bartow Jayceettes, 1967; vol. Fla. Soc. for Prevention of Blindness, 1971. Mem. Women's Council Realtors (civic project chmn. 1986), Tampa Bd. Realtors, Edn. and Realtor Assn. (com. main line bd. realtors 1979-83). Office: The Polo Group Inc 12966 N Dale Mabry Tampa FL 33618

SINNEMAKI, ULLA ULPUKKA, nurse, educator; b. Antrea, Finland, Sept. 11, 1928; d. Otto William and Kaisa Viola (Jappinen) Spjut; m. Maunu Matti J. Sinnemaki, June 12, 1949 (div. Feb. 1968); children—Markku Taneli, Sirkka Astrid. B.A., NYU, 1972; B.S., SUNY-Stony Brook, 1976; M.Ed., McNeese State U., 1978, Ed.S., 1979, M.Ed., 1981. R.N., N.Y., La., Tex. Field interviewer Bur. Census, N.Y.C., 1973-75; Operating room asst. St. Charles Meml. Hosp., N.Y.C., 1965-72; staff nurse Lake Charles Meml. Hosp., La., 1976-77; head nurse South Cameron Hosp., Cameron, La., 1977-80. dir. nursing, 1983-84; staff nurse Humana Hosp., Oakdale, La., 1984, Lake Charles, La., 1987—. Translator books, articles from English to Finnish, 1981—; designer rya rugs. Mem. Com. 1000 Baton Rouge, 1983. Mem. Nat. League Nursing, Am. Nurses Assn., Assn. Ednl. Communications and Tech., Assn. Supervision and Curriculum Devel., Nat. Assn. Female Execs. Democrat. Lutheran. Avocations: gardening; music; photography. Address: 332 W State St Lake Charles LA 70605

SIPES, LORRI DEAN, architect; b. Omaha, Nov. 11, 1950; d. Lorey Burdette and Margaret Dean (Powell) S. B in Environ. Design, Kans. U., 1972; MArch, U. Mich., 1978. Registered architect, Mich. Pvt. practice drafter Kansas City, Mo., 1973-75; drafter Colvin Robinson, Ann Arbor, Mich., 1975-76; draftsman Hobbs & Black, Ann Arbor, 1976-78; architect William Kessler Assocs., Detroit, 1978-81, Fry-Peters Assocs., Ann Arbor, 1981-82; prin. Pokempner Sipes Assocs., Ann Arbor, 1982-84, Architects Four, Inc., Ann Arbor, 1984—; instr. Ea. Mich. U., Ypsilanti, 1987; adj. prof. U. Mich. Coll. of Architecture, Ann Arbor, 1988-89. Mem. AIA, Huron Valley chpt. AIA (bd. dirs.), Mich. Soc. Architects. Democrat. Office: Architects Four Inc 208 W Liberty Ann Arbor MI 48104

SIPKOFF, SUSAN STONE, marketing educator; b. Coronado, Calif., Oct. 30, 1950; d. Lester Jay and Marguerite Ridgaway (King) Stone; m. Martin Zachary Sipkoff, Oct. 27, 1984; 1 child, Benjamin. AB, Wilson Coll., 1977; MBA, Shippensburg U., 1980; Student, George Washington, U., 1987—. Asst. prof. mgmt. and mktg. Shippensburg (Pa.) U., 1983—, 1983—; dir. mktg. VSP Wastewater Tech., Gettysburg, Pa., 1982; mktg. cons. Svcs. Unltd., Gettysburg, 1975—; lectr. in field. Author (with Stephen J. Holoviak) Managing Human Productivity: People are Your Best Investment, 1987; contbr. articles to profl. jours.; asst. editor mag. USN Acad. Alumni Assn., 1973-74. Former land use chair League of Women Voters, Gettysburg; mem. fund raising com. for local candidates. Am. Mktg. Assn. fellow, 1986. Mem. Am. Mktg. Assn., Mensa, NAFE, Beta Gamma Sigma, Kappa Kappa Gamma. Republican. Episcopalian. Office: Shippensburg Univ Mgmt and Mktg Dept Shippensburg PA 17257

SIPPLE, CONSTANCE S., association executive; b. Binghamton, N.Y., Sept. 12, 1962; d. Conrad Robert and Winifred Mary (Zola) Sipple. BA in Psychology, U. Dayton, Ohio, 1984. Adminstrv. asst. United Cerebral Palsy Assn. Greater Cleve., 1985-87, dir. devel., 1987—; lectr. in field. Trustee Beaumont Sch. for Girls, 1989—; vol. Cuyahoga County Rep. Com., 1988—, Womankind. Mem. Ohio Coun. Fundraising Execs., Beaumont Sch. for Girls Alumni Assn. (bd. dirs. 1982—), Friends Christ Child Soc. Republican. Roman Catholic. Office: United Cerebral Palsy 2141 Overlook Rd Cleveland OH 44106

SIRI, DENA SHAW, real estate assessment executive; b. Washington, Mar. 11, 1952; d. Benjamin C. and Edna Hope (Lutes) Shaw. BSBA, U. Md., 1979; postgrad., U. Va., U. N.C. Real estate appraiser State Dept. Assessment and Taxation, Rockville, Md., 1979-84; appraisal supr. County of Arlington, Va., 1984; asst. dir. real estate assessments City of Arlington, Va., 1986; now dir. real estate assessments County of Fairfax, Va., 1990—. Mem. Internat. Assn. Assessing Officers (cert. assessment evaluator), Va. Assn. of Assessing Officers, Washington Metro Area Assessors Assn., Md. Quarter Horse Assn. (v.p.). Democrat. Methodist. Office: 4100 Chain Bridge Rd Fairfax VA 22030

SIROWER, BONNIE FOX, fundraising executive; b. Bklyn., Jan. 9, 1949; d. Stanley S. and Harriet (Fischer) Fox; m. Martin Alan Sirower, Sept. 20, 1970; children: Kenneth, Daniel. AB, Barnard Coll., 1970; MA, Columbia U., 1971. Tchr. United Cerebral Palsy, N.Y.C., 1970-73, Bergen County Bd. Spl. Svcs., Paramus, N.J., 1973-76; spl. events coord. Am. Heart Assn., Glen Ridge, N.J., 1979-81; dir. devel. Goodwill Industries, Astoria, N.Y., 1981-83; pres. Access Unltd., 1984-85; dir. devel. Cheshire Home, Inc., 1986-89, Barnert Meml. Hosp. Ctr., Paterson, N.J., 1989—; cons. New Concepts for Living, Hillsdale, N.J., 1983. Pres. Sisterhood Temple Beth Haverim, Mahwah, 1976-77; co-chmn. Glen Rock Independence Day Assn., 1983. Mem. N.J. Soc. Fund Raising Execs. (bd. dirs. 1989, chair mentoring com.), Women In Fin. Devel., Assn. Fund Raisers for Disabled (pres. 1981-83), N.J. Puzzlers' League (pres.), Phi Beta Kappa. Jewish. Home: 69 Godfrey Terr Glen Rock NJ 07452

SISCO, MARY ELIZABETH, lawyer, consultant; b. Ft. Worth. Nov. 16, 1937; d. Daniel Louis and Mary Elizabeth (Blanton) Creson; m. William Theodore Sisco, Aug. 7, 1959; children—Christopher Theodore, Gregory Samuel, Lois Danine. B.A., Tex. Christian U., 1959; J.D., Tex. Tech U., 1979. Bar: Tex. 1979. Provisional secondary teaching cert., Tex. Tchr., Fort Worth Ind. Sch. Dist., 1959-61, Memphis Ind. Sch. Dist., 1961-65; ind. market researcher, Rochester, Minn., 1968-72; pvt. practice, Lubbock, Tex., 1979—; owner Ctr. Mediated Solutions, Lubbock, 1989—; treas. bd. dirs. Y-Not Better Papers, Dallas, 1975-86. Trustee, Lubbock Ind. Sch. Dist., 1980-86; bd. dirs. Caprock council Girl Scouts U.S.A., Lubbock, 1980-88; mem. Tex. Legis. Cabinet, Girl Scouts U.S.A., Dallas, 1981-87, chmn., 1988—; bd. dirs. Lubbock Civic Ballet, 1983-85; co-chmn. Lubbock Assn. Concerned with Teenage Sexuality, 1988-89, pres., 1985; mem. adv. bd. Tex. Assn. Sch. Age Parents, 1987—, State Council of Vols., March of Dimes, 1987-88; bd. dirs. Found. for Excellence, Lubbock, 1987—; life mem. Lubbock PTA, Tex. PTA. Mem. ABA, Order of Coif, Alpha Chi, Delta Delta Delta. Methodist. Clubs: Lubbock Women's, Classic Toastmasters. Office: 3607 22d St Lubbock TX 79410

SISEMORE, CLAUDIA, producer-director educational films and videos; b. Salt Lake City, Sept. 16, 1937; d. Darrell Daniel and Alice Larril (Barton) S. BS in English, Brigham Young U., 1959; MFA in Filmmaking, U. Utah, 1976. Cert. secondary tchr., Utah. Tchr. English, drama and writing Salt Lake Sch. Dist., Salt Lake City, 1959-66; tchr. English Davis Sch. Dist., Bountiful, Utah, 1966-68; ind. filmmaker Salt Lake City, 1972—; filmmaker-in-residence Wyo. Coun. for Arts and Nat. Endowment for Arts, Dubois, Wyo., 1977-78; producer, dir. ednl. films Utah Office Edn., Salt Lake City, 1979—. Producer, dir. Beginning of Winning, 1984 (film festival award 1984), Dancing through the Magic Eye, 1986, Se Habla Espanol, 1986-87; writer, dir., editor Building on a Legacy, 1988, An Early Winter (film), 1989; artist (abstract acrylic) exhibited Phillips Gallery, numerous pvt. and pub. collections. Juror Park City (Utah) Arts Festival, 1982, Utah Arts Festival, Salt Lake City, 1982, Am. Film Festival, 1985-86, Best of West Film Festival, 1985-86; bd. dirs. Utah Media Ctr., Salt Lake City, 1981-87; mem. multi-disciplinary program Utah Arts Coun., Salt Lake City, 1983-87. Recipient award Utah Media Ctr., 1984, 85; Nat. Endowment for Arts grantee, 1978, Utah Arts Coun. grantee, 1980. Mormon. Office: Utah Office Edn 250 East 500 South Salt Lake City UT 84111

SISKO, MARIE FERRARIS, fund raising executive; b. N.Y.C., Feb. 3, 1938; d. Joseph and Jean (Boaro) F. B.A., Queens Coll., 1975; postgrad. Adelphi U., 1976; divorced; children—Warren Joseph, Robert Edward. Pers. dir. Daypac Inc., 1969-70; sales asst. Ponder & Best, 1971-73; sales adminstr. Ampacet Corp., 1973-75; mktg. rep. Better Bus. Bur., 1975-77; ast. dir. Leukemia Soc. Am., 1978-82; campaign dir. Ketchum, Inc., 1982-85; dir. maj. gifts Seton Hall U., 1985-88; program dir. Brakeley, John Price Jones, 1988—; v.p. Sisko Enterprises N.Y. World's Fair, 1963-65; editor Malba (N.Y.) News & Views Newspaper, 1969-80. Del. White House Conf. on Small Bus., N.Y.C., 1978. Mem. Nat. Soc. Fund Raising Execs., AAUW, Queens Coll. Alumni Assn. (trustee 1976—, pres. Ace chpt. 1977-79). Lutheran. Home: 32 Center Dr Malba NY 11357

SISKO, WENDY LEE, fashion designer; b. Silvercreek, N.Y., July 10, 1957; d. Kenneth Francis and Ruth Ensign (White) Pope; m. Ronald S. Sisko, Jan. 11, 1974 (div. Apr. 1979); children: Kerry A., Jennifer R., Christopher K. Nickl, Michelle A. Nickl. Student, Felician Coll., Lodi, N.J., 1978-79, Bergen Community Coll., Paramus, N.J., 1984-85, Hillcrest Coll., Paramus, 1986. Asst. mgr. G&G Shop, Passaic, N.J., 1972-75; food and beverage mgr. Best Always Restaurant, Passaic, 1976-80; sales mgr. Johnathons, Hasbrouck Heights, N.J., 1980-85; pres. Grandma's Sewing Room, Oradell, N.J., 1986—. Mem. U.S.C. of C., Oradell C. of C., N.J. Assn. Women Bus. Owners. Republican. Home: 812 Midland Rd Oradell NJ 07649 Office: Grandma's Sewing Room Inc 812 Midland Rd Oradell NJ 07649

SISLEY, BECKY LYNN, physical education educator; b. Seattle, May 10, 1939; d. Leslie James and Blanche (Howe) S. BA, U. Wash., 1961; MSPE, U. N.C., 1964, EdD, 1973. Tchr. Lake Washington High Sch., Kirkland, Wash., 1961-62; instr. U. Wis., Madison, 1963-65, U. Oreg., Eugene, 1965-68; prof. phys. edn. U. Oreg., 1968—, women's athletic dir., 1973-79, head undergrad. studies in phys. edn., 1985—. Co-author: Softball for Girls, 1971; contbr. articles to profl. jours. Admitted to Hall of Fame, N.W. Women's Sports Found., Seattle, 1981, Honor Awad, N.W. Dist. Assn. for Health, Phys. Edn., Recreation and Dance, 1988. Mem. Nat. Interscholastic Athletic Adminstrs. Assn., N. Am. Soc. Sport Mgmt., AAHPERD, Oreg. Alliance for Health, Phys. Edn., Recreation and Dance, We. Soc. for Phys. Edn. of Coll. Women (exec. bd. 1982-85), Oreg. High Sch. Coaches Assn., Nat. Softball Coaches Acad., N.W. Coll. Womens Sport's Assn. (pres. 1977-78), Oreg. Women's Sports Leadership Network (dir. 1987—), Phi Epsilon Kappa and others. Office: Univ of Oreg Dept Phys Edn Eugene OR 97403

SISSON, BETTY, real estate broker; b. Burbank, Calif., Apr. 21, 1934; d. Harvey Orville and Isabel Marion (Melville) Angermeir; children: James Harvey, William Frank. Student pub. schs., Burbank. Sales assoc. Rich Port Realtors, Oak Brook, Ill., 1971-76, sales mgr., 1976-78, v.p., 1978-83; exec. v.p. Am. Growth Real Estate Corp., Oak Brook, 1979-80, The Midwest Club, Oak Brook, 1980-83, Selected Properties, Inc., Oak Brook, 1983-85, Pringle & Booth, Inc., Chgo., 1985-88, Ambriance! Inc., Burr Ridge, Ill., 1987—; dir., exec. v.p. Am. Growth Group, Burr Ridge, Ill., 1983—. Mem. Birchwood Golf and Country Club, The DuPage Club (Oakbrook), Internat. Club. Republican. Home: 15 Ambriance! Burr Ridge IL 60521

SISSON, JAMIE CLIFTON, real estate developer; b. Jacksonville, Fla., Nov. 12, 1960; d. James Carlton and Joan Dee (Betts) Clifton. Student, Edison Community Coll., Ft. Myers, Fla., 1979-80. Legal sec. Alderman and Taminosian, P.A., Ft. Myers, Fla., 1978-79; fin. mgr. Bill Branch Chevrolet, Inc., Ft. Myers, Fla., 1979-81, Sam Galloway Ford, Inc., Ft. Myers, Fla., 1981; project mgr. Williams and Assocs., Inc., Ft. Myers, Fla.; exec. sec. Black Diamond Potato Farm, Ft. Myers, Fla., 1982—; real estate broker Diamond Preferred Properties, Fla., 1985—; sec.-treas. Diamond Plumbing, Inc.; owner, mgr. Wave Lengths Hair Salons of Fla., Inc. Mem. Lee County Humane Soc., Ft. Myers, 1987, Doris Day Animal League, Wash., 1989, North Shore Animal League, Port Wash., 1987. Republican. Baptist. Office: Diamond Preferred Properties 17412 Ingram Rd SE Fort Myers FL 33912

SISTERSON, JANET MARGOT, physicist, educator; b. Edinburgh, Scotland, July 7, 1940; came to U.S. 1968, naturalized, 1985; d. Thomas James and Lucy Margaret (Smith) Brownlee; m. L. Keith Sisterson, Oct. 23, 1965; children: James, Mark. BS, U. Durham, 1961; PhD, Imperial Coll. Sci. and Tech., U. London, 1965; Cert. in Advanced Mgmt. Studies Radcliffe Coll., 1989. Basic grade physicist London Hosp., 1964-66; sr. physicist Chelsea Hosp. for Women, London, 1966-68; rsch. fellow Cambridge (Mass.) Electron Accelerator, 1968-73; rsch. assoc. Harvard Cyclotron Lab., 1973—. Contbr. articles to profl. jours. Mem. exec. bd. Harrington Sch. PTA 1977-83. Mem. Am. Phys. Soc., Am. Assn. Physicists in Medicine, Am. Nuclear Soc., Am. Women in Sci. Office: 44 Oxford St Cambridge MA 02138

SISTRUNK, CATHERINE EILEEN, nurse; b. Norfolk, Va., Dec. 5, 1958; d. Frank Carlton and Joyce Mable (Toop) Johnson; m. Derek Francis Carroll, May 26, 1977 (div. Sept. 1982); 1 child, Derek E.; m. Robert Fred Sistrunk, June 12, 1983; 1 child, Robert Douglas. AD in Nursing, U. Ark., Fayetteville, 1979. RN. Cert. critical care. Registered nurse U. Miss. Med. Ctr., Jackson, Ms., 1980-82, Miss. Bapt. Med. Ctr., Jackson, 1982-83, Duke U. Med Ctr., Durham, N.C., 1983-84, Terrebonne Gen. Med Ctr., Houma, La., 1984-86; v.p. Tri Mktg., Inc., Jackson, 1986-88; pres., owner Tri Mktg., Inc., 1988—. Instr. ARC, Jackson, 1988—, community health edn. classes, River Oaks Hosp., Jackson, 1987—. Capt. U.S. Army Nurse Corps Res., 1981—. Mem. Nat. Fedn. of Ind. Bus., Am. Assn. of Critical Care Nurses, Assn. of Am. Businesswomen. Republican. Episcopalian. Office: Tri Mktg Inc 1563 E County Line Rd Ste 301 Jackson MS 39211

SITARZ, ANNELIESE LOTTE, pediatrics educator, physician; b. Medellin, Colombia, Aug. 31, 1928; came to U.S., 1955; d. Hans and Elisabeth (Noll) S. BA cum laude, Bryn Mawr (Pa.) Coll., 1950; MD, Columbia U., 1954. Diplomate Nat. Bd. Med. Examiners, Am. Bd. Pediatrics, Am. Bd. Pediatric Hematology and Oncology. With Columbia U., N.Y.C., 1957—, assoc. prof. clin. pediatrics, 1974-83, prof. clin. pediatrics, 1983—; cons. pediatrics, hematology and oncology Harlem Hosp., N.Y.C., 1967-72, Overlook Hosp., Summit, N.J., 1975—. Contbr. numerous articles to profl. jours. Pres. Mt. Prospect Assn. Summit, 1987—. Fellow Am. Acad. Pediatrics; mem. Am. Assn. Cancer Rsch., Am. Soc. Clin. Oncology, Am. Soc. Hematology, Cancer Soc. Hematology, Harvey Soc. Republican. Episcopalian. Office: Babies Hosp 3959 Broadway New York NY 10032

SITARZ, PAULA GAJ, writer; b. New Bedford, Mass., May 25, 1955; d. Stanley Mitchell and Pauline (Rocha) Gaj; m. Michael James Sitarz, Aug. 26, 1978; children: Andrew Michael, Kate Elizabeth. BA, Smith Coll., 1977; MLS, Simmons Coll., 1978. Children's libr. Thomas Crane Pub. Libr., Quincy, Mass., 1978-84; dir. Reader's Theatre Workshop Thomas Crane Pub. Library, Quincy Mass. 1985. Author: Book, Picture Book Story Hours: From Birthdays to Bears, 1986, More Picture Book Story Hours 1989. Mem. New Eng. Libr. Assn., Libr. Sci. Honor Soc., Smith Club of Southeastern Mass. (v.p. 1987-89, pres. 1989—), Beta Phi Mu. Roman Catholic. Home and Office: 26 Swanson Dr South Dartmouth MA 02748

SITTERLY, CONNIE SUE, management training specialist, author, consultant; b. Fairfax, Okla., Oct. 9, 1953; d. Claude O. and Virda (Smith) S. AA, Frank Phillips Coll., 1973; BS, West Tex. State U., 1975, MA, 1978; postgrad., Tex. Woman's U., 1992-75; food and beverage mgr. Instr. Frank Phillips Coll., Borger, Tex., 1978-80; asst. prof. Amarillo (Tex.) Coll., 1980-85; owner Mgmt. Tng. Specialists, Ft. Worth, 1982—; adj. assoc. prof. Tex.'s Woman's U., Denton, 1986-90. Author: A Woman's Place: Management, 1988; contbr. over 30 articles to profl. jours. Mem. Am. Soc. Quality Control, Am. Bus. Women's Assn., ASTD. Republican. Home: 2808 5th Ave Fort Worth TX 76110 Office: 1201 W Presidio Ste 204 Fort Worth TX 76102

SIZEMORE, DEBORAH LIGHTFOOT, writer, editor; b. Lamesa, Tex., Mar. 18, 1956; d. Glenn Billy and Francis Earlene (Cable) Lightfoot; m. O.E. Gene Sizemore, June 19, 1981. BS in Agrl. Journalism summa cum laude, Tex. A&M U., 1977. Writer, Tex. Agrl. Extension, College Station, 1976-78; copy editor Abilene Reporter-News (Tex.), 1978; customer svc. rep. Motheral Printing Co., Ft. Worth, 1978-79; prodn. coord. Graphic Arts, Inc., Ft. Worth, 1980-81; writer, editor, Crowley, Tex., 1981—; freelance writer, editor Boy Scouts Am., Irving, Tex., 1981—; contbg. editor

Dairymen's Digest, Arlington, Tex., 1981-89. Longhorn Scene, Ft. Worth, 1982-84; writer, photographer Harvest Times, Dallas, 1983-84; Simbrah World, Ft. Worth, 1985-87; author: Your Future With The BSA, 1989; contbg. editor Lone Star Horse Report, Ft. Worth, 1985-86; contbr. photographs to mags.; contbr. articles mags. Women's issues chmn., v.p. membership, pub. info. officer, newsletter editor AAUW of Tarrant County, 1981-86, 90-91; organizer nat. security pub. debate, Ft. Worth, 1983. Recipient Sr. Merit award in Agrl. Journalism, Tex. A&M U., 1978, Thomas S. Gathright Acad. Excellence award, 1976, Cert. of Merit, Livestock Publs Coun., 1984, 86, 2d place Nonfiction Book award Tex.-Wide Writers' Competition, 1988, 89, 2d Place Feature Story Dairy Communications Competition Nat. Milk Producers Fedn. 1989. Mem. Nat. Writers Club, Soc. Children's Book Writers, Tex. Freelance Writers Assn., Western Writers Am., Am. Agri-Women, Phi Kappa Phi, Gamma Sigma Delta. Club: Ft. Worth A&M. Office: 19 Frazier Ln Crowley TX 76036

SJOGREN, DEBORAH MARY, accountant; b. Ely, Minn., Aug. 1, 1953; d. Stanley Joseph and Justine Pauline (Korent) Boldine; m. Mark Robert Sjogren, Aug. 21, 1976. B.A., Vermillion Community Coll., 1973; B.S., St. Cloud State U., Minn., 1975. Br. acct. Montgomery Ward, St. Paul, 1975-77; fin. processing cons. region III Mgmt. Info. Service/Elem., Secondary, Vocat., St. Cloud, Minn., 1977-78; acctg. supr. Vision Ease Corp., St. Cloud, 1978-83; controller Franciscan Sisters of Little Falls, Little Falls, Minn., 1983-88, dir. finance, 1988—. Yugoslav Nat. Home scholar, 1971. Mem. Profl. Women's Orgn. (founder), Conf. Religious Treasures (vice chair Region XI), Cen. Minn. Nat. Assn. Accts. (bd. dirs.), Phi Chi Theta (charter). Avocations: horseback riding, reading. Office: Franciscan Sisters Little Falls 116 8th Ave SE Little Falls MN 56345

SKAFTE, MARJORIE DORIS, retired publisher and editor; b. Osseo, Wis., Aug. 1, 1921; d. Nels and Regine (Severson) Westegard; m. Lloyd Albert Skafte, Feb. 14, 1942 (div. Feb. 1979); children: Merilee Skafte Main, Patricia Skafte Pearman, Linwood, Robert. Student, St. Olaf Coll., Northfield, Minn., 1939-41, U. Minn., Duluth, 1965-66. Editorial asst. Ojibway Press (later Harcourt Brace Jovanovich Publs.), Duluth, 1964-67, mng. editor, 1967-68; editor Edgell Communications (formerly Harcourt Brace Jovanovich), Duluth, 1968-89, pub., editor Hearing Instruments, 1971-89; ret., 1989; cons., lectr., writer in field, 1989—; mem. adv. bd. Better Hearing Found., Washington, 1988—, Sertoma Internat. Found., Kansas City, Kans., 1988—, Eddy Found., Duluth, 1987—. Author: 50 Years of Hearing Health Care, 1990; contbr. numerous articles to profl. publs. Membership sec.-treas., v.p. Univ. for Srs., U. Minn., Duluth, 1990. Recipient Internat. Achievement award Better Hearing Inst., 1985, Golden Ear award Hearing Aid Assn. Calif., 1985, lifetime achievement award Acad. Dispensing Audiologists, 1989, cert. of appreciation and recognition Am. Speech, Lang. and Hearing Assn., 1989; hon. fellow Nat. Hearing Aid Soc., 1984. Mem. Hearing Industries Assn. (life), Am. Assn. Ret. Persons, Sons of Norway, Zonta (bd. dirs. Duluth 1990), Order Ea. Star (worthy matron 1960). Republican. Lutheran. Home: 4311 Tioga St Duluth MN 55804

SKAKLE, SYBIL AUSTIN, pharmacist; b. Hatteras, N.C., Jan. 10, 1926; d. Andrew Shanklin and Inez Lynn (Daniels) Austin; m. Donald Edmund Skakle, Feb. 7, 1947 (dec. Apr. 1980); children: Donald Edmund, Stanley Andrew, Clifford Dwight; m. Charles Andre Fetterroll, May 21, 1983 (div. July 1990). BS in Pharmacy, U. N.C., 1949. Lic. pharmacist. Staff pharmacist Durham County Hosp. Corp., Durham, N.C., 1967-85, 87—; drug screener Blue Cross/Blue Shield, Durham, 1985-86; staff pharmacist Durham County Gen. Hosp, Durham, 1987; researcher Shearing Archbell, Attys., Kitty Hawk, N.C., 1986-87; on call pharmacist Eckerds Drug Stores, 1986-87. Author: Hatteras Merchant, 1986; Traveling Sands of Hatteras, 1990; (poetry) Giant, 1990, Forgiveness, 1990. Fellow N.C. Pharm. Assn., Durham-Orange Pharm. Assn.; mem. Republican Woman's Club, Univ. Woman's Club, Disciplined Order of Christ, Kappa Epsilon. Methodist. Home: 269 Severin St Chapel Hill NC 27516

SKALSKI, JOANNE DOROTHY, healthcare executive, educator, consultant; b. Stevens Point, Wis., May 9, 1934; d. Stanley Sylvester and Johanna Barbara (Borchardt) S. BS in Bus., Alverno Coll., 1959; MA in Adminstrn., Marquette U., 1965. Tchr. Archdiocesan Cath. Schs., Milw., 1955-62, 71-72; from bus. tchr. to asst. prin. Pacelli High Sch., Stevens Point, 1962-70; secretarial instr. Patricia Stevens Career Coll., Milw., 1970-71; vicar provincial Sisters of St. Joseph, Stevens Point, 1972-75; dir. for sponsorship Sisters of St. Joseph, Chgo., 1985—; adminstr. The Social Svcs. Ctr., New Orleans, 1975-77; bus. tchr., counselor Alternative Schs.-Prologue, Chgo., 1977-81; adminstrv. asst. DePaul U., Chgo., 1981-85; mem. resource strategic planning for edn. Archdiocese of Chgo., 1989—; mem. adminstrv. team Sisters of St. Joseph, South Bend, Ind., 1989—; chairperson bd. dirs. Marymount Healthcare Systems, Garfield Heights, Ohio, 1986—; pres. bd. membership corps., Ill., Mich. and Ohio, 1986—. Mediator Neighborhood Justice Ctr., Chgo., 1980-82; bd. dirs. Alternative Schs. Network Bd., Chgo., 1981; trustee Neighborhood Justice Ctr. Bd., Chgo., 1981. Mem. Cath. Health Assn., Nat. Health Lawyers Assn., Acad. for Healthcare Leadership. Roman Catholic. Office: 4878 N Magnolia #A3 Chicago IL 60640 Office: Instnl Sponsorship Bd PO Box 408517 Chicago IL 60640

SKEEL, JUDY ANN, civil engineer; b. Phila., Oct. 5, 1957; d. David Arthur Skeel and Betty Lou (Gardner) Williamson. BCE, Ga. Tech. U., 1979. Registered profl. engr.; Ga. Staff engr. Law Engring. Co., Atlanta, 1980-82; project engr. Atec Assocs., Inc., Marietta, Ga., 1983-84; site devel. coord. City of Atlanta, 1984-89; ops. mgr. solid waste dept. County of Cobb, Marietta, 1989-90, interim mgr. solid waste dept., 1990—. Mem. NAFE, Am. Pub. Works Assn., High Mus., Atlanta Hist. Soc., Cumberland Jaycees. Republican. Presbyterian. Office: Cobb County Solid Waste Dept 1897 County Farm Rd Marietta GA 30060

SKELLY, JUNE AVON, university administrator; b. Erie, Pa., June 3, 1946; d. Henrick Christian and Esther Berniece (Struchen) Pihl; m. Alton Joseph Skelly, Apr. 26, 1968; children: Janice Alynn, Alan Joseph, Andrew Jason. AB in Sociology, Thiel Coll., Greenville, Pa., 1968. Elem. tchr. Harborcreek (Pa.) Sch. Dist., 1968-70; liaison to com. on handicapped Averill Park (N.Y.) Sch. Dist., 1983-84; enumerator, field rep. Bur. Census, Erie, Pa., 1988-90, supr. field ops., 1990—; sec./aide Office of the Pres. Gannon U., Erie, Pa., 1990—. Leader Girl Scouts U.S.A., Wilmington, Del., 1977-78, leader, chmn. svc. unit, Averill Park, 1978-84, Pottstown, Pa., 1986-87; vol. Family Svcs. Mother to Mother Program, 1990. Mem. AAUW (chmn. Edn. Found. 1987, rep. internat. rels. area 1989, program chmn. 1990, Outstanding Woman award 1987), Zeta Tau Alpha (v.p. alumnae chpt. 1989-90). Lutheran. Home: 5701 Footemill Rd Erie PA 16509 Office: Office of the Pres Gannon U Univ Square Erie PA 16541

SKELTON, DOROTHY GENEVA SIMMONS (MRS. JOHN WILLIAM SKELTON), educator; b. Woodland, Calif.; d. Jack Elijah and Helen Anna (Siebe) Simmons; B.A., U. Calif., 1940, M.A., 1943; m. John William Skelton, July 16, 1941. Sr. research analyst War Dept., Gen. Staff, M.I. Div. G-2, Pentagon, 1944-45; vol. researcher, monuments, fine arts and archives sect. Restitution Br., Office Mil. Govt. for Hesse, Wiesbaden, German, 1947-48; vol. art tchr. German children in Bad Nauheim, Germany, 1947-48; art educator, lectr. Dayton (Ohio) Art Inst., 1955; art educator Lincoln Sch., Dayton, 1956-60; instr. art and edn. U. Va. Sch. Continuing Edn., Charlottesville, 1962-75; researcher genealogy, exhibited in group shows, Calif., Colo., Ohio, Washington and Va.; represented in permanent collections Madison Hall, Charlottesville, Madison (Va.) Center. Mem. Nat. League Am. Pen Women, AAUW, Am. Assn. Museums, Coll. Art Assn. Am., Inst. for Study of Art in Edn., Dayton Soc. Painters and Sculptors, Nat. Soc. Arts and Letters (life), Va. Mus. Fine Arts, Cal. Alumni Assn., Air Force Officers Wives Club. Republican. Methodist. Clubs: Army Navy Country, Lake of the Woods (Va.) Golf and Country. Chief collaborator: John Skelton of Georgia, 1969; author: The Squire Simmons Family, 1746-1986, 1986. Address: Lotos Lakes Brightwood VA 22715

SKELTON, GLENDA CAROL, banker, accountant; b. Birmingham, Ala., Apr. 25, 1950; d. Robert McKinley and Jewel (Wingo) S. BSBA, U. Ala. Birmingham, 1972, MBA, 1983. Flexowriter Norpac/Falconer Check Printers, Birmingham, 1968-73; various positions Fed. Res. Bank, Birmingham, 1973-74; acctg. officer Nat. Bank Commerce, Birmingham, 1984-88; asst. v.p. South Trust Bank Ala., Birmingham, 1988—; tchr.

in English cum laude, U. San Francisco, 1980. Editorial asst. Wadsworth Pub. Co., Belmont, Calif., 1983-84; pension plan coord. Profl. Retirement Svcs., Burlingame, Calif., 1984-86; worker's compensation claims supr. CNA Ins. Cos., San Bruno, Calif., 1986—. Home: 2000 Crystal Springs Rd Apt 1410 San Bruno CA 94066 Office: CNA Ins Cos 801 Traeger Ave San Bruno CA 94066 also: CNA Ins Co PO Box 7430 San Francisco CA 94120-7430

SLATON, BRENDA DALE, mechanical engineer; b. Anderson, S.C., Sept. 28, 1962; d. Thomas Jerry and Brenda Joyce (Charping) S. BSME, Clemson U., 1984. Project engr. Celanese Fibers Op., Charlotte, N.C., 1984-85; drafting cons. Nat. Coun. Engring. Examiners, Seneca, S.C., 1985-86; quotations analyst I.T.E. Elec. Products div. Siemens Energy and Automation Inc., Tucker, Ga., 1986-88; sales control specialist Siemens Energy and Automation Inc., Charlotte, 1988-89; sales engr. Siemens Energy and Automation Inc., Virginia Beach, Va., 1989—. Mem. ASME, NSPE, Nat. Assn. Investment Clubs, High Mus. Assn. Young Careers Club. Republican. Baptist. Home: 2722-2C Waterford Way Midlothian VA 23112 Office: Siemens Energy and Automation 1604 Santa Rosa Rd #239 Richmond VA 23229

SLAUGHTER, JANE MUNDY, author; b. Buchanan, Va., Oct. 2, 1905; d. Luther Thomas and Pearl Carnce (Karnes) Mundy; R.N., Jefferson Hosp., Roanoke, Va., 1926; m. Frank G. Slaughter, June 10, 1933; children—Frank G., Randolph M. Operating Room supr. Jefferson Hosp., 1923-24; pvt. duty nurse, 1924-33; freelance author, 1970—; author: Espy and the Catnappers, 1975; also 1st history of Fla. Med. Assn. Aux. Bd. dirs. Jacksonville (Fla.) YWCA, 1960-65. Mem. Fla. Hist. Soc., Jacksonville Hist. Soc., Fla. Fedn. Garden Clubs (life mem. Jacksonville), Fla. Med. Assn. Aux. (historian 1950). Democrat. Presbyterian. Club: Timuquana Country. Address: 5051 Yacht Club Rd Jacksonville FL 32210

SLAUGHTER, LOUISE MCINTOSH, congresswoman; b. Harlan County, Ky., Aug. 14, 1929; d. Oscar Lewis and Grace (Byers) McIntosh; m. Robert Slaughter, 1956; children: Megan Rae, Amy Louise, Emily Robin. BS, U. Ky., 1951, MS, 1953. Bacteriologist Ky. Dept. Health, Louisville, 1951-52, U. Ky., 1952-53; market researcher Procter & Gamble, Cin., 1953-56; mem. staff Office of the Lt. Gov. N.Y., Albany, 1978-82; state rep. N.Y. Gen. Assembly, Albany, 1983-86; U.S. congresswoman from 30th Dist. N.Y., Washington, 1987—; del. Dem. Nat. Conv., 1972, 76, 80, 88. Mem. Monroe County Pure Water Adminstrn. Bd., Ho. Rules Com., Nat. Ctr. for Policy alternatives Adv. Bd., Common Cause, League of Women Voters, Nat. Women's Polit. Caucus. Office: US Ho of Reps Office of House Mems 1313 Longworth Office Bldg Washington DC 20515*

SLAUGHTER, LURLINE EDDY, artist; b. Heidelberg, Miss., June 19, 1919; d. Gilbert Emmings and Lurline Elizabeth (Heidelberg) Eddy; B.S., Miss. U. for Women, 1939; m. James Fant Slaughter, Jan. 27, 1946; children—Beverly Lowery, Anne Towles. Tchr. high sch., Silver City, Miss., 1939-41; clk. VA, Washington, 1941-42; bd. dirs. Miss. Art Colony. One-woman shows Ahda Artzt Gallery, N.Y.C., 1967, Nat. Design Center, N.Y.C., 1967, 68, Delta State U., Cleveland, Miss., 1973, 84, Gulf States Gallery, Greenville, Miss., 1973, 76, 80, 84, Southeastern La. U., Hammond, 1977, Cheekwood Fine Arts Center, Nashville, 1978, Byars Gallery, Little Rock, 1984, San Pedro Theatre, San Antonio, 1981, Cottonlandia Mus., Greenwood, Miss., 1984 exhibited in group shows U. Fla., 1969, Brooks Art Mus., Memphis, 1970, Miss. State U., 1970, 85, Delta State U., 1971, 84; represented in permanent collection Miss. U. for Women, Miss. State U., Delta State U., Pine Bluff (Ark.) Art Ctr., Southeastern La. U., U. of South, Sewanee, Tenn., Eudora Welty Mepl. Library, Jackson, Miss.; represented in pvt. collections, Acapulco, Guadalajara, Mex., San Francisco, N.Y.C., so. states. Lt. (j.g.) USNR, 1942-45. Recipient Best in Show award Acapulco Ann., Hilton Hotel, 1979, Best in Show award Cottonlandia Mus., Greenwood, Miss., 1987. Tchr. Sunday Sch., Meth. Ch., 1953-67; pres. PTA; bd. dirs. Miss. Art Colony, 1965-85. Served as lt. (j.g.) USNR, 1942-45. Address: Seldom Seen Plantation Silver City MS 39166

SLAUGHTER, MARGO ANN, clinical social worker, consultant; b. Olean, N.Y., Jan. 8, 1951; d. Edward James and Mary E. (Kime) Fitzgerald; m. John Sim Slaughter, May 26, 1973; children: Jamie Kime, Carly Ann. BA, SUNY, Fredonia, 1973; MSW, SUNY, Buffalo, 1975. Cert. social worker, N.Y. Caseworker Cath. Charities, Dunkirk, N.Y., 1973-74; psychiat. social worker Chautauqua County Mental Health Dept., Jamestown, N.Y., 1974-79; adoption caseworker New Beginnings Children and Family Svcs., Fredonia, 1980—; instr. sociology and psychology SUNY, Fredonia, 1974, 87; cons. social work dept. Brooks Meml. Hosp., Dunkirk, 1980—, Lakeshore Nursing Home, Silver Creek, N.Y., 1981-85, Tri County Hosp., Gowanda, N.Y., 1981-85, Heritage Village Nursing Home, Gerry, N.Y., 1981-85, Presbyn. Nursing Home, Faloner, N.Y., 1981-85; pvt. practice, Fredonia, 1980—. Bd. dirs. S.T.E.P., alternative edn. program for high sch., Fredonia, 1989—. Mem. Nat. Assn. Social Workers, AAUW (sec. 1988-90, v.p. 1990-92). Home: 38 Middlesex Dr Fredonia NY 14063

SLAVESKI, ELIZABETH ANN, physical education educator; b. West Chester, Pa., Apr. 7, 1937; m. Michael W. Slaveski, May 30, 1959; children: Robyn Kimball, Susan Brice. BS, West Chester U., 1959; postgrad., Glassboro (N.J.) State U., 1970. Cert. phys. edn. and gen. sci. tchr., N.J., N.Y. Tchr., coach Lenape Regional High Sch., Medford, N.J., 1959-64, Garden City (N.Y.) High Sch., L.I., 1967-68; tchr. Northfield (N.J.) Pub. Schs., 1972—. Mem. NEA, N.J. Health, Physical Education, Recreation and Dance, Am. Assn. Health, Physical Education, Recreation, and Dance, N.J. Edn. Assn., Northfield Edn. Assn. (past pres). Republican. Roman Catholic. Home: 2301 Simpson Ave Ocean City NJ 08226

SLAVIN, ALEXANDRA NADAL, artistic director, educator; b. Port-au-Prince, Haiti, Oct. 26, 1943; came to U.S., 1946; d. Pierre E. and Marie Therese (Clerié) Nadal; m. Eugene Slavin, Dec. 24, 1967; 1 child, Nicholas V. Grad. high sch., Chgo. Dancer Ballet Russe de Monte Carlo, N.Y.C., 1960-61, Chgo. Opera Ballet and N.Y.C. Opera Ballet, 1961-64, Am. Ballet Theatre, N.Y.C., 1965-66, Ballet de Monte Carlo, 1966-67, The Royal Winnipeg (Can.) Ballet, 1967-72; artistic dir. Ballet Austin, Tex., 1972-89; owner, dir. The Slavin Nadal Sch. Ballet, Austin, 1989—. Recipient Achievement in the Arts award Austin chpt. YWCA, 1987. Roman Catholic. Office: Slavin-Nadal Sch Ballet 5521 Burnet Rd Austin TX 78756

SLAVIN, ROBERTA LANDAU, health facility administrator, psychotherapist; b. Bronx, N.Y., Dec. 10, 1929; d. Henry and Celia (Eisenberg) Landau; m. Alvin Theodore Slavin, Mar. 25, 1951; children: Martin Jay, Cheryl Anne, Jeri Beth. BA, Humter Coll., 1951; MA, CCNY, 1954; profl. diploma, Fordham U., 1974; postgrad., Internat. U. Psychologist East Islip (N.Y.) Pub. Schs., 1964-66, Clarkstown Pub. Schs., N.Y.C., 1966-67, N.Y.C. Pub. Schs., 1967-88; psychotherapist Washington Sq. Inst., 1980—; founder, dir. Midlife Ctr., Inc., Spring Valley, N.Y., 1985—. Contbr. articles to profl. jours. Supr. Vol. Counseling Svc., New City, 1983—. Fellow Am. Ortho Psychiat. Assn.; mem. Nat. Assn. Sch. Psychologists, Am. Psychol. Assn., Am. Group Psychotherapists Assn. Home: 21 Pleasant Ridge Rd Spring Valley NY 10977 Office: Midlife Ctr Inc Box 76 Pomona NY 10970

SLAVUTIN, DEBRA CLAIRE, insurance agency executive; b. Oceanside, N.Y., May 25, 1951; d. Herbert Nathanial Schwartz and Gloria Alice (Cressy) Levy; m. Lee J. Slavutin, Nov. 11, 1979; children: Aaron, Lydia. BA magna cum laude, SUNY, 1973; MA, McGill U., Montreal, 1975; MBA, Fordham U., 1983. Dir. Institional Investor, N.Y.C., 1978-85; exec. v.p. Stern, Slavutin & Slavutin, N.Y.C., 1985—; speaker Million Dollar Round Table, 1990. Contbr. articles to profl. jours. Mem. Nat. Assn. of Life Underwriters, Nat. Organ. of Women, Am. Soc. of Pension Activities, Nat. Assn. of Women Life Underwriters (speaker Top of the Table ann. meeting, 1989), Internat. Assn. Fin. Planners. Home: 321 W 78th St #5A New York NY 10024 Office: Stern Slavutin & Slavutin 645 Madison Ave New York NY 10022

SLAWEK, KIMBERLY ANN, investment banker; b. Lansdale, Pa., Sept. 20, 1961; d. Joseph Eugene and Diane Patricia (Kane) S. BA in Engring. Sci., Lafayette Coll., 1983; MBA in Fin., U. Pa., 1989. Sales engr. Tex. Instruments, Inc., Santa Clara, Calif., 1983-86; nat. accounts mgr. Siliconix, Inc., Santa Clara, 1986-87; assoc. Sumitomo Trust, Tokyo, 1988; with instnl. fixed income sales Bear Stearns & Co., Inc., N.Y.C., 1989—; cons. export devel., bd. advisors Very Spl. Arts Internat., Barbados and Africa, 1988—. Vol. Big Brother/Big Sister, Pa. and Calif., 1980-86. Mem. Lafayette Coll. Alumni Assn. (admissions com. Easton, Pa. chpt. 1984—), Maroon Key, Sigma Kappa (chairperson 1980-82). Republican. Roman Catholic. Office: Bear Stearns & Co Inc 245 Park Ave 4th Floor New York NY 10167

SLAYDON, KATHLEEN AMELIA, lawyer; b. Ft. Worth, June 1, 1951; d. A. Glynn and E. Jeanne (Miller) S.; m. John Mayer. BA, Rice U., 1973; JD, U. Tex., 1976. Bar: Tex. 1977, U.S. Dist. Ct. (so. dist.) Tex. 1978, U.S. Ct. Appeals (5th cir.) 1978, U.S. Ct. Appeals (11th cir.) 1981, U.S. Dist. Ct. (we. dist.) Tex. 1984, U.S. Supreme Ct. 1989. Assoc. Reynolds, Allen Cook, Houston, 1977-78; assoc. Ross, Banks, May Cron & Cavin, Houston, 1978-83, ptnr., 1983-89; comml. atty. liquidation div. FDIC, Houston, 1989—; speaker continuing legal edn. State Bar Tex., 1983-89. Mem. Tex. Assn. Bank Counsel, State Bar Assn. Tex., Houston Bar Assn., Rice Alumni Assn. (chairperson fund drive 1973, 78). Home: 725 E Creekside Dr Houston TX 77024 Office: FDIC Div Liquidation 7324 SW Fwy Ste 1600 Houston TX 77074

SLEEMAN, MARY (MRS. JOHN PAUL SLEEMAN), librarian; b. Cleve., June 28, 1928; d. John and Mary Lillian (Jakub) Gerba; B.S., Kent State U., 1965, also M.L.S.; m. John Paul Sleeman, Apr. 27, 1946; children—Sandra Sleeman Swyrydenko, Robert, Gary, Linda. Supervising librarian middle schs. Nordonia Hills Bd. Edn., Northfield, Ohio, 1965—; children's librarian Twinsburg (Ohio) Pub. Library, 1965-66. Mem. ALA, Ohio Sch. Librarians Assn., NEA, Summit County Librarians Assn., Storytellers Assn., North Eastern Ohio Tchrs. Assn. Methodist. Home: 18171 Logan Dr Walton Hills OH 44146 Office: 72 Leonard Ave Northfield OH 44067

SLESAR, PAULA JEAN, communications company official; b. Milw., Feb. 8, 1955; d. Daniel L. and Louise J. (Moresco) S. BA, Marquette U., 1977; MBA, Cardinal Sritch Coll., 1989. Claims rep. Social Security Adminstrn., HEW, Waukegan, Ill., 1978-79; market adminstr. Wis. Telephone Co., Milw., 1979-80, account exec., 1980-84; sr. account exec. Wis. Bell Communications, Milw., 1984—. Vol., Italian Community Ctr. Festa Italiana, Milw., 1978-89; participant Lake Front Festival, 1986-89. Mem. Am. Mktg. Assn. (chpt. sec. 1983-85, v.p. student rels. 1986), Internat. Orgn. Women in Telecommunications, Telecommunications Profls. of Wis., Marquette U. Coll. Speech Alumni Assn. (pres. 1984, bd. dirs. 1979-85), Marquette U. Alumni Assn. (bd. dirs. 1985—). Roman Catholic. Home: 2414 N 86th St Wauwatosa WI 53226 Office: Wis Bell Communications 17950 W Corporate Dr Brookfield WI 53005

SLETTO, VERONA GWENDOLYN, adult coordinator, educator; b. Slope County, N.D., Sept. 4, 1909; d. Peter Wilhelm and Mabel Julia (Urevig) Strom; m. Kenneth Sletto, June 27, 1937 (dec. Mar. 1972); children: Linda Rae Porten, Donald Alfred Sletto. BS, Dickinson (N.D.) U., 1966. Tchr. grade sch. Rhame (N.D.) Dist., 1949-59; libr. Dickinson Sch. Dist., 1968-75, tchr. English, 1975-82, tchr. ESL, 1977-78; coord. literacy program dept. pub. instruction Literacy Vols. for Illiteracy, Bismarck, N.D., 1986—; media specialist Dept. Pub. Instruction 3, Bismarck, 1969-75. Sec. citizens adv. bd. St. Joseph's Hosp., 1984-87. Mem. Alpha Omicron (parliamentarian 1984-86, 2d v.p. 1986-88). Home: 234 E 12th St Dickinson ND 58601

SLEWITZKE, CONNIE LEE, retired chief army nurse corps, academic director; b. Mosinee, Wis., Apr. 15, 1931; d. Leo Thomas and Amelia Marie (Hoffman) S. B.S.N., U. Md., Balt., 1971; M.A. in Counseling and Guidance, St. Mary's U., San Antonio, 1976. Staff nurse Sacred Heart Hosp., Eau Claire, Wis., 1952-53; staff nurse Los Angeles County Hosp., 1953-54, U. Ill. Research Hosp., Chicago, 1954-56, George Washington Hosp., Washington, 1956-57; enlisted U.S. Army, Fort Sam Houston., Tex., 1957; staff nurse Brooke Army Med. Ctr., Fort Sam Houston, Tex., 1957-59, Tripler Army Med. Ctr., Honolulu, Hawaii, 1959-61; asst. head nurse Kimbrough Army Hosp., Fort George G. Meade, Md., 1962-63, head nurse, 1963-64; med., surg. nurse 44th Surg. Hosp., Korea, 1964-65; asst. chief nurse U.S. Army Hosp., Albuquerque, 1965-67, 36th Evacuation Hosp., Vietnam, 1967-68; chief nurse 6th Convalescent Ctr., Vietnam, 1968; nurse supr. Walk-In Clinic, Fort Myer, Va., 1968-69; with Nursing Adminstrn. Br., 7th MEDCOMEUR, 1971-73; nurse, officer Hdqrs. Health Services Command, Fort Sam Houston, Tex., 1974-75, nursing cons., 1975-76; chief nurse U.S. Army Hosp., Seoul, Korea, 1977-78; chief dept. nursing Letterman Army Med. Ctr., Presidio of San Francisco, Calif., 1978-80; asst. chief Army nurse corps Office Surgeon Gen., Washington, 1980-83, chief Army nurse corps, 1983-87; ret. U.S. Army, 1987; dir. devel. Sch. Nursing, U. Md., Balt., 1988—. Contbr. articles to profl. jours. Decorated D.S.M., Legion of Merit, Bronze Star medal, Meritorious Service Medal with 2 oak leaf clusters, Joint Services Commendation medal, Army Commendation Medal, Nat. Def. Service medal, Vietnam Service medal with 4 devices, Overseas Service ribbon with 4 devices, Republic of Vietnam Campaign medal. Mem. Am. Nurses Assn., Va. State Nurses Assn., Alumni Assn. U.S.A. War Coll., Nat. Orgn. Nurse Execs., Assn. U.S. Army, Sigma Theta Tau. Office: U Md Sch Nursing Baltimore MD

SLEZAK, JANE ANN, chemistry educator; b. Amsterdam, N.Y., Nov. 12, 1935; d. Stephen Samuel and Celia Josephine (Karp) S. BS, SUNY, Albany, 1956; MS, SUNY, 1957; PhD, Rensselaer Polytechnic Inst., 1964. Cert. secondary tchr., N.Y.; cert. emergency med. technician, N.Y. Postdoctoral fellow Rensselaer Polytechnic Inst., 1979-87; asst. prof. chemistry Fulton Montgomery Community Coll., Johnstown, N.Y., 1987—; lectr. SUNY, Albany, 1982-87; cons. recycling Montgomery County Solid Waste Div., Fonda, N.Y. Contbr. articles to profl. jours. Ambulance attendant Greater Amsterdam (N.Y.) Vol. Ambulance Corps, past pres.; bd. dirs. Am. Heart Assn., Fulton-Montgomery br.; chief radiol. officer Montgomery County Office Emergency Preperation. Fellow NIH, Gen. Electric Co., AEC, NSF. Fellow Sigma Xi.

SLEZAK, KAREN PATRICIA, credit company executive; b. Paterson, N.J., July 20, 1950; d. Stephen and Florence (Scarmazzo) Messineo; m. Norman M. Slezak, May 29, 1971 (div. Oct. 1988); 1 child, Kimberly Ann. BA, William Paterson Coll. Bookkeeper J.L. Prescott Co., Passaic, N.J., 1969-70; acctg. clk. Drakes Bakeries, Wayne, N.J., 1970-72; mgr. Retailers Comml. Agy., Paterson, 1972-81; salesperson Equifax Svcs., Lyndhurst, N.J., 1982-83; pres. Credit Resources, Inc., West Paterson, N.J., 1983—. V.p. Park West Meadows Condominium Assn., 1986—. Mem. NAFE, Women Entrepreneurs of N.J., Internat. Credit Assn., Mortgage Bankers Assn. N.J (membership chmn. young mortgage bankers com. 1982-83), Mortgage Bankers Assn. N.Y. Republican. Roman Catholic. Office: Credit Resources Inc 999 McBride Ave PO Box 540 West Paterson NJ 07424

SLIM, ELIZABETH MIDDLETON, teacher; b. Camden, N.J., Dec. 29, 1931; d. Newell Melbourne and Myra (Munyan) Middleton; m. William Slim Jr., Aug. 22, 1953; children: Robin, Deborah, Wendy, Bonny. BA, Dickinson Coll., 1953; BSE, Ohio State U., 1977. Tchr. Southampton (Pa.) Pub. Schs., 1953-54, Lower Merion Pub. Schs., Ardmore, Pa., 1954-55; pub. rels. Worthington (Ohio) City Schs., 1966-71, tchr's. aide, 1971-77, tchr., 1977-78; tchr. Cen. Bucks Dist., Doylestown, Pa., 1979-83, Buckingham Friends Sch., Lahaska, Pa., 1983-89; fgn. and domestic travel coord., Buckingham Friends, Lahaska, 1986--. Author: 6 part series of historic fiction pub. in Worthington newspaper, 1973. Com. mem. Friends Hosp., Phila., 1981--; com. mem. Buckingham Friends Meeting, Lahaska, 1987--; pres. Peace Valley Nature Ctr., Doylestown, 1981-83. Mem. AAUW. Republican. Mem. Soc. of Friends. Home: 50 S Woods Doylestown PA 18901 Office: Buckingham Friends Sch Rte 202 Lahaska PA 18931

SLINGSBY, ANN MARY, art director; b. Bronx, N.Y., Aug. 10, 1930; d. Charles Angelo and Sarah (Smeraldi) Cimitile; m. Harry Stafford Slingsby, June 7, 1953; children: Robert, Keith, Tara. Degree in Art, Indsl. Arts Coll., N.Y.C., 1948; student Hunter Coll., N.Y.C., 1952-54. Head file dept. South African Govt., N.Y.C., 1950; salesperson, model Lord & Taylor, N.Y.C., 1950-53; art tchr. Bklyn. Archdiocese Schs., 1953-55, Archdiocese of N.Y. Schs., 1955-71; art dir. Clarkstown Recreation, New City, N.Y., 1973—; writer, producer, dir. sr. citizen annual show Town of Clarkstown, 1976—, other sr. citizen shows via cable TV, 1983-88. Author: Arts and Crafts Teaching Experiences, 1975. Den mother Rockland County council Boy Scouts Am., 1962-63; vol. dir. Clarkstown Sr. Citizen Show, 1984; mem. Elmwood Playhouse, 1983—; assoc. Hudson Valley Leisure Svcs., 1980—. Recipient Cert. Appreciation Summit Park Hosp. Vol. Svcs., 1984, N.Y. State Achievement award, 1984, cert. for 10 yrs. of dedicated svc. Town of Clarkston and County of Rockland, 1987. Roman Catholic. Avocations: sculpture; painting; crafts; drama; dance. Home: 46 Briarwood Dr New City NY 10956

SLINTAK, GRECIA ELCILIA, freelance artist; b. Hato Rey, P.R., Oct. 29, 1937; d. Eduard Andre and Justina (Garcia) Ló; m. Rudolph John Slintak, Sept. 3, 1958; children: Rudolf Ivan, Michael Sean, André Evan. Student, Fashion Inst. of Tech., 1956-58. Sewing instruction illustrator McCall Pattern Co., N.Y.C., 1959-66; freelance artist N.Y.C., 1966—; mgr. North Shore Equipment, Bloomingburg, N.Y., 1987—. Illustrator (booklet) Crafts, 1971. Vol. Mamakating First Aid Squad, Wurstboro, N.Y., 1983-85. Art Student's League scholar, 1956; recipient Bronze metal for harmonious inspiration Met. Mus. Art, N.Y.C., by Youths, Friends Assn. Inc., 1956. Mem. Bloomingburg Restoration Found. (v.p. 1986-88, trustee 1988-90). Home: RD2 Box 152 Grandview Dr Bloomingburg NY 12721-9520

SLIVE, HARRIET WEINMANN, lawyer; b. N.Y.C., Dec. 1, 1951; d. Richard A. and Bertha M. (Landes) Weinmann; m. Steven H. Slive, Sept. 3, 1982; 1 child, Lauren E. BA, Case Western Res. U., 1973, MA, 1974; JD, Cleve. State U., 1983. Adminstrv. dir. Free Med. Clinic Greater Cleve., 1973-84; ptnr. Slive & Slive, Cleve., 1985—. Mem. Divorce Equity Adv. Com., Cleve., 1985-87, Amnesty Internat., 1985—; guardian ad litem Cuyahoga County Juvenile Ct., Cleve., 1985—; panel mem. United Way, Cleve., 1984-87; legal vol. Free Med. Clinic Greater Cleve., 1984—. Office: Slive & Slive 526 Superior Ave Ste 740 Cleveland OH 44114

SLIVINSKY, SANDRA HARRIET, physicist; b. Bklyn., Sept. 26, 1940; d. Morris and Mathilda (Kosberg) Feldman; 1 child, Barry Keith Slivinsky. BA, Alfred (N.Y.) U., 1962; MS, Pa. State U., 1966, U. Calif., Davis, 1973; PhD, Stanford U., 1983. Ops. rsch. Dikewood Corp., Albuquerque, 1966-68; physicist Lawrence Livermore (Calif.) Lab., 1968-73; sr. rsch. engr. Lockheed Missiles & Space, Sunnyvale, Calif., 1973-76; tech. project engr. G.E., San Jose, 1976-85; sr. scientist United Technologies, San Jose, 1986-90; prin. investigator, sr. phys. scientist U. Dayton Rsch. Inst. at Edwards AFB, 1990—; scientist by mail Sci. by Mail, Boston, 1989-90. Contbr. articles to profl. jours.; patentee on laser skiving process. Mem. Am. Phys. Soc., Am. Ceramic Soc., IEEE, Soc. Matls. and Process Engrs. (scholarship chmn. 1987-90), Sigma Xi, Sigma Delta Epsilon. Office: Astronautics Lab AL(AFSC)/RKPL Edwards AFB CA 93523

SLOAN, BESSIE BERNICE, accountant; b. Middletown, Ohio, Apr. 17, 1949; d. Jessie and Pearlie Mae (Riley) Jemison; m. Ronald E. Sloan, Sr., Aug. 27, 1966; children—Ronald E., Natasha L. Student acctg., Miami U., Oxford, Ohio, 1978-82. Operator, Ohio Bell Telephone, Dayton, 1968-76; receptionist City of Middletown, 1976-77, account clk. I, 1977-78, account clk. II, 1978-81, city acct., 1981—. Sec. Middletown City Employees Assn., 1977—; com. chair Middfest, 1980—, Elk Creek Festival, 1983—. Mem. Nat. Assn. Female Execs., Nat. Assn. Accts., Profls. in Action (sec.-treas. 1984—), Am. Payroll Assn., NAACP. Democrat. Mem. African Methodist Episcopal Ch. Club: Ebone Inc (officer 1972—) (Middletown). Avocations: golfing; reading; gardening; reupholstering furniture. Office: City of Middletown One City Ctr Plaza Middletown OH 45042

SLOAN, JODY BETH, real estate executive; b. Atlanta, July 16, 1953; d. Myer and Beryl (Cowan) S.; Student, U. Tenn., 1970-71; B.A., Ga. State U., 1976; M. in City Planning, Ga. Inst. Tech., 1979. Office mgr. Exec. Chairs, Atlanta, 1972-76; researcher Ga. Inst. Tech., Atlanta, 1977-79; planning cons. CMCA Cons., Atlanta, 1976-78; urban planner Jefferson County, Ala., 1978-79; transp. planner, rep. U.S. Dept. Transp.-Urban Mass. Transp. Adminstrn., Ft. Worth and Atlanta, 1979-85; cons. The Real Estate Consortium Atlanta, 1985-86 ; real estate specialist U.S. Postal Service, Atlanta, 1986—; co-owner The Bare Walls, Atlanta, 1981—; owner Say CHEESE-cake, 1987—. Contbr. articles to profl. jours.; contbr. restaurant reviews. Mem. conservation com. Sierra Club, Atlanta, 1977—; mem. fundraising com. City of Hope Hosp. and Med. Ctr., Atlanta, 1983—; v.p., bd. dirs. Westover Plantation, 1984-86. Mem. Arthritis Found., Am. Planning Assn., Women in Transp., Nat. Assn. Female Execs. (assoc. 1982—), Nat. Assn. Corp. Real Estate Execs., Corp. Real Estate Women, High Mus. Art. Democrat. Home: 8 Newport Pl NW Atlanta GA 30318 Office: US Postal Service 4000 DeKalb Tech Pkwy Bldg 500 Suite 550 Atlanta GA 30340

SLOAN, PAMELA BRINK, nurse, administrative supervisor; b. Harrisburg, Pa., Mar. 21, 1946; d. Cornelius Persen Brink and Nathalie Harrison (Lewis) Emery; m. Francis Edwin Sloan, Oct. 14, 1967; children: John David, Sandra Gayle. Diploma, Presbyn. Sch. of Nursing, Phila., 1967; BS, Barry U., 1987; MA, MBA, Calif. Pacific U., 1990, postgrad. CCRN, cert. nursing adminstr. Critical care nurse various Tenn. hosps., 1971-78; physician's asst. Pulmonary And Allergy Assocs., Nashville, 1978-82; ICU head nurse Hendersonville (Tenn.) Hosp.; adminstrv. supr. Hosp. Corp. Am. Med. Ctr. of Port St. Lucie, Fla., 1983-84; prog. care dept. dir. HCA Med. Ctr. of Port St. Lucie, 1984-88, adminstrv. supr., coord., 1988—. Active Tenn. Lung Assn., 1979-82; sec. Sumner County chpt. Am. Heart Assn., 1982-83. Mem. Am. Assn. of Critical CAre, Fla. Orgn. Of Nurse Execs. Republican. Mem. Ch. of Christ. Home: 1586 SE Manth Ln Port Saint Lucie FL 34983 Office: HCA Med Ctr 1800 SE Tiffany Ave Port Saint Lucie FL 34952

SLOAN, SONIA SCHORR, organization executive, fundraising consultant; b. Wilmington, Del., Apr. 1, 1928; d. Sigmund and Rosalia (Hillersohn) Schorr; m. Gilbert Jacob Sloan, May 30, 1957; children: Victor S., Jonathan L. BS, Syracuse U., 1949; MS, Jefferson Med. Coll., 1950. Instr. Temple U. Med. Sch., Phila., 1950-52; mem. rsch. staff E.I. Du Pont de Nemours & Co., Wilmington, Del., 1952-59; office mgr., cons. coord. Fund for Neighborhood Devel., Wilmington, 1972; dir. fin. devel. YWCA New Castle County, Wilmington, 1987—; fundraising cons. various orgns., Wilmington, 1986—. Treas. ACLU, Wilmington, 1978—; pres. Planned Parenthood Del., 1980-84, mem. adv. bd., 1986—; v.p. North Atlantic region Planned Parenthood Fedn. Am., 1981-84. Recipient Hannah Solomon award Nat. Coun. Jewish Women, Wilmington, 1981, Community Builder award NCCJ, Wilmington, 1984. Mem. Nat. Soc. Fund Raising Execs. (pres. Brandywine chpt. 1989—), Phi Beta Kappa. Democrat. Home: 25 Indian Field Rd Wilmington DE 19810

SLOAN, SUSAN V., mutual fund manager; b. Budapest, Hungary, Jan. 7, 1945; came to U.S., 1949; d. Ernest and Seren (Kasser) Czin; m. Philip R. Sloan; children: Lisa, Michael. BA, Douglass Coll., 1966; postgrad., Pace U., 1980. V.p., portfolio mgr. Merrill Lynch Asset Mgmt., Princeton, N.J., 1966—; cons. in field. Mem. N.J. Women Bus. Owners, N.Y. Soc. Security Analysts. Republican. Home: 51 Hidden Lake Dr N Brunswick NJ 08902 Office: Merrill Lynch Asset Mgmt 800 Scudders Mill Rd Plainsboro NJ 08536

SLOAN, SUZANNE BARKIN, marketing and sales director; b. N.Y.C., Aug. 20, 1959; d. Stephen Samuel and Nanette Ruth (Barkin) Sloan; m. Gary Gittelsohn. B.A., U. Rochester, 1981; M.S., Columbia U., 1983; Cert. Sign Lang., Nat. Tech. Inst. for Deaf, 1980. Cert. social worker, N.Y. Dir. mktg. Anchorage Yacht Club, Lindenhurst, N.Y., 1983—; rep. alumni affairs Horace Mann-Barnard Sch., Bronx, 1985—; mem. Assoc. Humane Soc., 1980—, Am. Soc. Prevention of Cruelty to Animals, 1979—; exec. v.p. Sloan Marine Assocs . Bd. dirs Children of Bellevue Inc., 1988. Mem. Nat. Assn. Social Workers, Nat. Marine Mfrs. Assn., Nat. Maritime Assn. Home: 44 W 62d St New York NY 10023 Office: Sloan Marine Assocs 230 Park Ave New York NY 10169

SLOANE, BEVERLY LEBOV, writer, consultant; b. N.Y.C., May 26, 1936; d. Benjamin S. and Anne (Weinberg) LeBov; m. Robert Malcolm Sloane, Sept. 27, 1959; 1 child, Alison Lori. AB, Vassar Coll., 1958; MA, Claremont Grad. Sch., 1975; grad. exec. program., UCLA Grad. Sch. Mgmt., 1982; grad. profl. pub. course, Stanford U., 1982; grad. intensive bioethics course Kennedy Inst. Ethics, Georgetown U., 1987, advanced bioethics course, 1988; grad. sem.in Health Care Ethics, U. Wash. Sch. Medicine, Seattle, summer 1988, 89, 90; grad. Summer Bioethics Inst. Loyola

Marymount U., summer, 1990; grad. Annual Summer Inst. on Teaching of Writing, Columbia U. Tchrs. Coll., summer, 1990; ethics fellow Loma Linda U. Med. Ctr., 1989; cert. clin. intensive biomedical ethics, Loma Linda U., 1989. Circulation librarian Harvard Med. Library, Boston, 1958-59; social worker Conn. State Welfare, New Haven, 1960-61; tchr. English, Hebrew Day Sch., New Haven, 1961-64; instr. creative writing and English lit. Monmouth Coll., West Long Branch, N.J., 1967-69; freelance writer, Arcadia, Calif., 1970—; v.p. council grad. students, Claremont Grad. sch., 1971-72; mem. adv. council tech. and profl. writing Dept. English, Calif. State U., Long Beach, 1980-82; mem. adv. bd. Calif. Health Rev., 1982-83; mem. Foothill Health Dist. Adv. Council, L.A. County Dept. Health Svcs., 1987—, pres., 1989—, Ann. Key Mem. award, 1990. Author: From Vassar to Kitchen, 1967, A Guide to Health Facilities: Personnel and Management, 1971, 2d rel, 2d edit., 1977. Mem. pub. relations bd. Monmouth County Mental Health Assn., 1968-69; mem. task force edn. and cultural activities, City of Duarte, 1987-88, strategic planning task force com., campaign com. for pre-eminence, Claremont Grad. Sch., 1986-87; Vassar Coll. Class rep. to Alumnae Assn. Fall Coun. Meeting, 1989; mem. exec. program network UCLA Grad. Sch. Mgmt., 1987—; trustee Ctr. for Improvement of Child Caring, 1981-83; mem. League Crippled Children, 1982—, treas. for gen. meetings, 1989—, chair hostesses com., 1988-89, pub. rels. com., 1989—; bd. dirs. L.A. Commn. on Assaults Against Women, 1983-84; v.p. Temple Beth David, 1983-86; mem. community relations com. Jewish Fedn. Council Greater Los Angeles, 1985-87; del. Task Force on Minorities in Newspaper Bus., 1987-89. Recipient cert. of appreciation City of Duarte, 1988, County of L.A., 1988; Coro Found. fellow, 1979. Fellow Am. Med. Writers Assn. (dir. 1980—, Pacific S.W. del. to nat. bd. 1980-87, 89—, chmn. various cov. coms., chmn. nat. book awards trade category 1982-83, chmn. Nat. Conv. Networking Luncheon 1983, 84, chmn. freelance and pub. relations coms. Nat. Midyr. Conf. 1983-84, workshop leader ann. conf. 1984-87, nat. chmn. freelance sect. 1984-85, gen. chmn. 1985, Asilomar Western Regional Conf., gen. chmn. 1985, workshop leader 1985, program co-chmn. 1987, speaker 1985, 88-89, program co-chmn. 1989 nat. exec. bd. dirs. 1985-86, nat. adminstr. sects. 1985-86, pres.-elect Pacific S.W. chpt. 1985-87, pres. 1987-89, immediate past pres. 1989—, moderator gen. session nat. conf. 1987, chair gen. session nat. conf., 1986-87, chair Walter C. Alvarez Meml. Found. award 1986-87, Appreciation award for outstanding leadership 1989); mem. Women in Communications (dir. 1980—, v.p. community affairs 1981-82, N.E. area rep. 1980-81, chmn. awards banquet 1982, sem. leader ann. nat. profl. conf., 1985, program adv. com. Los Angeles chpt. 1987, v.p. activities 1989-90, chmn. Los Angeles chpt. 1st ann. Agnes Underwood Freedom of Info. Awards Banquet 1982, recognition award 1983, nominating com. 1982, 83, com. Women of the Press Awards luncheon 1988, Women in Communications awards luncheon 1988), Am. Assn. for Higher Edn., AAUW (legis. chmn. Arcadia br. 1976-77, books and plays chmn. Arcadia br. 1973-74, creative writing chmn. 1969-70, 1st v.p. 1975-76, networking chmn. 1981-82, chmn. task force promoting individual liberties 1987-88, Woman of Achievement award 1986, cert. of appreciation 1987), Ch Assn., Am. Pub. Health Assn., Calif. Press Women (v.p. programs Los Angeles chpt. 1982-85, pres. 1985-87, state pres. 1987-89, immediate past state pres. 1989—, chmn. state speakers bur. 1989—, del nat. bd. 1989—, moderator annual spring conv., 1990, chmn. onimating com. 1990—), AAUP, Internat. Communication Assn., N.Y. Acad. Scis., Ind. Writers So. Calif. (bd. dirs. 1989-90, dir. specialized group 1989-90, dir. at large 1989-90, bd. dirs. corp. 1988-89), Hastings Inst., AAAS, Am. Med. Writers Assn. (pres. 1987-89, nat. adminstr. sects. 1985-86, nat. exec. bd. dirs. 1985-86, chmn. nominating com. Pacific S.W. chpt., 1987-89, workshop leader annual conf. 1984-87, 90, steering com. seminar on med. writing 1988, program planning com. for daylong program on med. writing in collaboration with Ind. Writers So. Calif., 1988-89, topic leader Nat. Conf. Networking Breakfast 1988, del. nat. bd. 1989—, Appreciation award Outstanding Leadership, 1989, Presdl. award Pacific S.W. chpt. 1990), Nat. Fedn. Press Women, (bd. dirs. 1987-89, nat. co-chmn. task force recruitment of minorities 1987-89, del. 1987-89, nat. bd. dirs. 1989—, Plenary of Past Pres. state 1989—, speaker annual Nat. Conf. 1990, chair state women of achievement com. 1986-87, nat. dir. speaker's bur. 1989—), AAUW (chpt. Woman of Achievement award 1986, chmn. task force promoting individual liberties 1987-88, speaker 1987, recipient cert. of appreciation 1987), Soc. for Tech. Communication (workshop leader, 1985, 86), Kennedy Inst. Ethics, Soc. Health and Human Values, Assoc. Writing Programs. Clubs: Women's City (Pasadena), Vassar of So. Calif., Claremont Colls. Faculty House, Petroleum (L.A.), Pasadena Athletic, Town Hall of Calif. (vice chair community affairs sect. 1982—, speaker 1986, instr. Exec. Breakfast Inst. 1985-86, mem. study sect. council 1986—). Lodge: Rotary (chair Duarte Rotary mag. 1988-89, mem. dist. friendship exch. com. 1988-89, mem. internat. svc. com. 1989—). Home and Office: 1301 N Santa Anita Ave Arcadia CA 91006

SLOAT, BARBARA FURIN, cell biologist; b. Youngstown, Ohio, Jan. 20, 1942; d. Walter and Mary Helen (Maceyko) Furin; m. John Barry Sloat, Nov. 2, 1968; children: John Andrew, Eric Daniel. BS, Denison U., 1963; MS, U. Mich., 1966, PhD, 1968. Lab. asst. U. Ghent, Belgium, 1964; teaching fellow, lectr. U. Mich., Ann Arbor, 1964-66, 68-70, asst. rsch. biologist Mental Health Rsch. Inst., 1972-74; vis. asst. prof., lectr. U. Mich., Ann Arbor and Dearborn, 1974-76; dir. women in sci. U. Mich., Ann Arbor, 1980-84, assoc. dir. honors, 1986-87, rsch. scientist, 1976—, lectr. Residential Coll., 1984—. Author: Laboratory Guide for Zoology, 1979, Summer Internships in the Sciences for High School Women (CASE Silver medal), 1985; contbr. articles to profl. jours. Recipient Acad. Women's Caucus award, U. Mich., 1984, Grace Lyon Alumnae Award, Denison U., 1988; grantee NSF, U.S. Dept. Edcn., Warner Lambert Found., others. Mem. AAAS, Am. Soc. Cell Biology, N.Y. Acad. Scis., Nat. Assn. Women Deans, Adminstrs. and Counselors, Assn. for Women in Sci. (councilor 1988-90), pres.-elect 1990), Phi Beta Kappa, Sigma Xi. Home: 2010 Hall Ave Ann Arbor MI 48104 Office: U Mich Residential Coll 216 Tyler East Quad Ann Arbor MI 48109-1245

SLOCHOWER, JOYCE ANNE, psychologist, psychoanalyst, educator; b. N.Y.C., May 6, 1950; d. Harry and Muriel (Zimmerman) S.; m. Bruce Rodin, July 20, 1975; children: Jesse, Alison, Avi. Student, Clark U., 1968-70; BA, NYU, 1970-72; PhD, Columbia U., 1975. Cert. psychoanalyst, N.Y. Asst. prof. psychology Hunter Coll. CUNY, 1975-82, assoc. prof. Hunter Coll., 1982—; pvt. practice N.Y.C., 1976—. Author: Excessive Eating, 1983; contbr. numerous articles to profl. jours. NIMH grantee, 1980-82, CUNY grantee, 1981-83. Mem. Am. Psychol. Assn., Ea. Psychol. Assn., N.Y. Psychol. Assn., Phi Beta Kappa, Psi Chi. Jewish. Home and Office: 15 W 75th St New York NY 10023

SLOCUM, ROSEMARIE RACCARD, physician practice management search consultant; b. Port Arthur, Tex., Dec. 19, 1948; d. Edly and Ella (McNeely) Raccard; m. Audra Jerry Slocum, Jan. 28, 1967 (div. June 1969); 1 child, Blair Ashton. Student, La. State U., Alexandria, 1966-68; BS, La. State U., Baton Rouge, 1971. Cert. tchr., La. Edn. specialist La. Dept. Occupational Standards, Baton Rouge, 1971-74; account exec. Uarco, Inc., Baton Rouge, 1974-77; owner, broker Rosemarie Slocum Real Estate, Baton Rouge, 1977—; physician recruiter MSI, New Orleans, 1985-86; assoc. dir. physician recruitment Physician Search, Inc., Fairfax, Va., 1986-88; spl. cons. Caswell/Winters Physician Search Cons., Milw., 1988-89; v.p. U.S. Med. Search, Inc. subs. of Caswell/Winters, Milw., 1988-89; dir. physician recruitment/mktg. East Range Clinics, Ltd., Virginia, Minn., 1989—. Home: 602 N 13th St Virginia MN 55792 Office: E Range Clinics Ltd 910 N 6th St Virginia MN 55792

SLOCUMB, MARGARET ELIZABETH, retired teacher; b. Macon, Ga., July 22, 1908; d. Benjamin Franklin and Mattie Kathrine (Walker) S. BA, Wesleyan Coll., Macon, 1929; MEd, Mercer U., 1954; degree in math. edn., U. Ga., 1971; postgrad., Emory U., U. Mich. Cert. tchr., Ga. Tchr. math., sci. Steward County High Sch., Lumplin, Ga., 1929-30; elem. sch. tchr. Bibb County Bd. Edn., Ga., 1930-33; tchr. math. and choral music Bibb County Bd. Edn., 1934-75; now ret.; math. tutor Hephzibah Children's Home, 1976-83, math. tchr., 1984-88; tchr. piano Meth. Home for Children and Youth, 1984—. Past head jr. dept. Sunday sch., 1st Bapt. Ch. Macon, chancel choir alto, organizer jr. choir, mem. Keenagers Club; founder, charter mem. Macon Civic Chorale, 1975—. Mem. NEA (life), Ga. Edn. Assn., Bibb Assn. Educators, Nat. Assn. Ret. Tchrs., Ga. Ret. Tchrs. Assn., Bibb Ret. Tchrs. Assn., Nat. Fedn. Music Clubs, Ga. Fedn. Music Clubs, Macon Fedn. Music Clubs, Ga. Music Educators Assn., Music Tchrs. Nat. Assn., Music Tchrs. Ga. Assn., Macon Music Tchrs. Assn., Music Educators Nat. Conf., United Daus. of Confederacy, DAR (past treas.), AAUW, Delta Kappa Gamma. Democrat. Home: 359 Buford Pl Macon GA 31204

SLONE, SANDI, artist; b. Boston, Oct. 1, 1939; d. Louis and Ida (Spindiak) Sudikoff; children—Eric Solomon, Jon Solomon. Student Wheaton Coll., 1957-59, Boston Mus. Fine Arts Sch., 1970-73; B.A., Wellesley Coll., 1974. Instr. painting Boston Mus. Fine Arts Sch., 1970—, Brandeis U., Waltham, Mass., 1976, Harvard U., Cambridge, Mass., 1982. One person shows include: Harcus Krakow Gallery, Boston, 1978, 79, 80, 82, 84, Acquavella Contemporary Art, N.Y., 1977, 79, 80, 82, 84; group shows include Mus. Fine Arts, Boston, 1977, Corcoran Gallery of Art, Washington, 1977, Hayden Gallery, MIT, 1978, New Generation Andre Emmerich Gallery, N.Y., 1980-81, Am. Ctr., Paris, 1980-81, Amerika Haus, Berlin, 1980-81, Carpenter Ctr., Harvard U., 1983, Edmonton Art Gallery, 1977, 85, Gallery One, Toronto, Ont., Can., 1981; represented in permanent collections including Mus. Modern Art, N.Y.C., Albright-Knox, Buffalo, Mus. Fine Arts, Boston, Hirshhorn Mus., Washington, Mus. Fine Arts Boston fellow, 1977, 81; Ford Found. grantee, 1979. Address: care Harcus Gallery 210 South St Boston MA 02111*

SLOSHBERG, LEAH PHYFER, museum director; b. New Albany, Miss., Feb. 21, 1937; d. Sisco Knox and Mary Rachel (Sandlin) Phyfer; m. Willard Sloshberg, Dec. 8, 1961; 1 son, Simeon. B.F.A., Miss. State Coll., 1959; M.A. (Woodrow Wilson fellow), Tulane U., 1961. Arts curator N.J. State Mus., Trenton, 1968-69, asst. dir., 1969-71, dir., 1971—. Home: Box 190 RD #2 Stockton NJ 08559 Office: NJ State Mus 205 W State St CN 530 Trenton NJ 08625

SLOVER, GAIL PENNIMAN TURNER, biologist; b. Bradford, Pa., Mar. 14, 1938; d. Prescott Kingsbury Turner and Priscilla (Clark) Baker; m. William P. Slover, June 18, 1960 (div. July 1984); children: Cheryl Nordbeck, Gregory Lincoln, David William. BA, Conn. Coll., 1960; MEd, U. Hartford, 1978. Trainee med. technologist Harbor Gen. Hosp., Torrance, Calif., 1960-61; research asst. biochemistry Inst. of Living, Hartford, Conn., 1961-64; pvt. practice Parent Effectiveness Tng., Glastonbury, Conn., 1978-80; tchr., researcher Talcott Mountain Sci. Ctr., Avon, Conn., 1983-87; dir. chronobiology, cons. Body Time Tech., Glastonbury, 1986-90, Manchester, Conn., 1990—; cons. Newington (Conn.) VA Hosp., 1987, United Techs. Corp., Hartford, 1987; rsch. bd. dirs. Am. Biog. Inst., 1989—, dep. gov., 1989—. Bd. dirs. Montessori Sch. Hartford, West Hartford, Conn., 1968-69; pres., v.p. Hebron Ave Sch. PTO, Glastonbury, 1971-74; rep. task force for gifted/talented, Conn., 1977-78; diaconate Covenant Ch., 1985-86. Mem. DAR, Internat. Platform Assn., Internat. Soc. for Chronobiology, European Soc. for Chronobiology, Toastmasters (adminstrv. v.p. 1989). Home and Office: 20-C Esquire Dr Manchester CT 06040-2450

SLOVITER, DOLORES KORMAN, federal judge; b. Phila., Sept. 5, 1932; d. David and Tillie Korman; m. Henry A. Sloviter, Apr. 3, 1969; 1 dau., Vikki Amanda. A.B. in Econs. with distinction, Temple U., Phila., 1953, L.H.D. (hon.), 1986; LL.B. magna cum laude, U. Pa., 1956; LL.D. (hon.), The Dickinson Sch. Law, 1984. Bar: Pa. 1957. Assoc., then partner Dilworth, Paxson, Kalish, Kohn & Levy, Phila., 1956-69; mem. firm Harold E. Kohn (P.A.), Phila., 1969-72; assoc. prof, then prof. law Temple U. Law Sch., 1972-79; judge U.S. Ct. Appeals 3d Circuit, Phila., 1979—; mem. hearing panel Disciplinary Bd. Supreme Ct. Pa., 1978-79. Mem. SE region Pa. Gov.'s Coun. on Aging, 1976-79; mem. Com. of 70, 1976-79; trustee Jewish Publ. Soc. Am., 1983-89. Disting. Fulbright scholar, Chile, 1990; recipient Juliette Low medal Girl Scouts Greater Phila., Inc., 1990. Mem. ABA, Am. Law Inst., Fed. Bar Assn., Fed. Judges Assn., Phila. Bar Assn. (gov. 1976-78), Am. Judicature Soc. (bd. dirs.), Jud. Conf. U.S. Com. Bicentennial Constn., Phi Beta Kappa, Order of Coif (pres. U. Pa. chpt. 1975-77). Office: US Ct Appeals 18614 US Courthouse 601 Market St Philadelphia PA 19106

SLOWIK, BARBARA, interior designer; b. Worcester, Mass., Sept. 5, 1954; d. Francis Stanley and Antonina (Cieciura) S. BA, U. Mass., 1976; Assoc., Art Inst. Fla., 1978. Interior designer Design Group Assocs., Boston, 1979-82; mktg. rep. Koch & Lowy, Inc.a, L.I. City, N.Y., 1982-85, Kinder Harris/Dara, Stuttgart, Ark., 1985-87; mktg. exec. Decorating Den New Eng., Quincy, Mass., 1987-88; mktg. dir. Decorating Den New Eng., 1988—. Designer kitchen design Designers Showcase, 1978. Office: Decorating Den New Eng Inc 1266 Furnace Brook Pkwy Quincy MA 02169

SLOYAN, SISTER STEPHANIE, mathematics educator; b. N.Y.C., Apr. 18, 1918; d. Jerome James and Marie Virginia (Kelley) S. BA, Georgian Ct. Coll., 1945; MA in Math., Cath. U. Am., 1950, PhD, 1952. Asst. prof. math. Georgian Ct. Coll., Lakewood, N.J., 1952-56, assoc. prof., 1956-59, prof., 1959—, coll. pres., 1968-74; lectr. Grad. Sch. Arts and Scis., Cath. U. Am., Washington, 1960-82. Mem. Math. Assn. Am. (bd. govs. 1988—), Am. Math. Soc., Sigma Xi. Democrat. Roman Catholic. Office: Georgian Ct Coll Dept Math Lakewood NJ 08701

SLUDER, CHERYL LYNN, military officer; b. Maberzell, Hessen, Fed. Republic of Germany, July 17, 1960; came to U.S., 1961; d. Olen Vance and Irmtraud (Zittlau) S. BS in Animal Sci., Tarleton State U., 1981. Commd. 2d lt. U.S. Army, 1981, advanced through grades to capt., 1985; platoon leader 2d Ops. Bn. USAFSA, Augsburg, Fed. Republic of Germany, 1982-83; tng. standards officer U.S. Army Field Station, Augsburg, Fed. Republic of Germany, 1983-84; adj. Support Bn. USAFSA, Augsburg, Fed. Republic of Germany, 1984-85; chief collection mgmt. G2 101st Abn div. Air Assault, Ft. Campbell, Ky., 1986-87; chief all source prodn. section G2 101st Abn div. U.S. Army, Ft. Campbell, Ky., 1987-88; staff intelligence officer 101st Corp. Support Group, Ft. Campbell, 1988-89; dir. plans, tng. and security USAFS, Siuop, Turkey, 1989—. Mem. Assn. U.S. Army, NAFE, Assn. Old Crows, Tarleton Alumni Assn., Alpha Zeta. Lutheran. Club: Officer's (Ft. Campbell). Office: HMC USAFS Siuop PO Box 217 New York APO NY 09133

SLUSHER, RUTH VARNER, banking administrator; b. Harrison County, Ky., June 11, 1945; d. James Edgar and Myrtle Mae (Whitaker) Varner; m. Edward C. Slusher, Dec. 17, 1984; children: Vonda K. Birch Hall, Kevin W. Birch. Ed., Ky. Sch. Bus., Louisville, 1988. Cert. in mgmt. devel., gen. banking, prins. of banking, money and banking. Security officer, br. mgr., teller First Security of Clark County, Winchester, Ky., ops. officer, teller mgr. Mem. Lionesses (2d v.p. 1989, Lioness Tamer 1990). Office: 24 W Lexington Ave Winchester KY 40392-0097 also: PO Box 97 Winchester KY 40397-0097

SLUTSKY, LORIE ANN, foundation executive; b. N.Y.C., Jan. 5, 1953; d. Edward and Adele (Moskowitz) S. BA, Colgate U., 1975; MA in Urban Policy and Analysis, New Sch. for Social Rsch., N.Y.C., 1977. Program officer N.Y. Community Trust, N.Y.C., 1977-83, v.p., 1983-87, exec. v.p., 1987-89, pres., chief exec. officer, 1990—; bd. trustees Coun. on Founds., Inc., Washington, 1986—, Colgate U., Hamilton, N.Y., 1989—; bd. dirs. Found. Ctr., Inc., N.Y.C., Non-Profit Coordinating Com., N.Y.C. Office: NY Community Trust Two Park Ave New York NY 10016

SMAISTRLA, JEAN ANN, family therapist; b. South Gate, Calif., Oct. 12, 1936; d. Benjamin J. and Janet (Pollock) Craig; m. Charles J. Smaistrla, July 12, 1958; children: Amy Jean, Ben, John. BBA in Mktg., Lamar U., 1958; elec. edn. cert. Tex. Wesleyan Coll., 1963; MEd in Counseling, Tex. Christian U., 1975. Tchr. Houston Ind. Schs., 1958-61, Arlington Ind. Schs., Tex., 1961-72; counselor, therapist Arlington Counseling and Cons. Ctr., 1983-85; family therapist Willow Creek Adolescent Ctr., Arlington, 1985-86, dir. edn., 1986—; therapist, Bob Caprenter PhD and Assoc., 1987-89; pvt. practice, 1989—; owner, founder Adolescent Services Arlington, 1981—, founder, owner Mindtime, 1988—; cons. Charles J. Smaistrla, D.D.S., Arlington, 1978-85. Vice chmn. bd. Arlington Community Hosp., 1981-85, Willow Creek Adolescent Ctr., 1984-90. Active mem. PTA; bd. dirs. Arlington Art Assn., 1981-85, bd. S. Arlington Med. Ctr., 1987, Ctr. for Well-Being, 1985. Mem. Am. Assn. Marriage and Family Therapy (assoc.), Tarrant County Assn. Marriage and Family Therapy, North Central Tex. Assn. Counseling and Devel., Am. Assn. Counseling and Devel., Alpha Delta Pi. Republican. Roman Catholic. Clubs: Jr. League Arlington, Arlington Women's. Avocations: Sailing; sewing; doll collecting.

SMALL, ELISABETH CHAN, psychiatrist, obstetrician, gynecologist, educator; b. Beijing, July 11, 1934; came to U.S., 1937; d. Stanley Hong and Lily Luella (Lum) Chan; m. Donald M. Small, July 8, 1957 (div. 1980); children Geoffrey Brooks, Philip Willard Stanley. Student, Immaculate Heart Coll., Los Angeles, 1951-52; BA in Polit. Sci., UCLA, 1955, MD, 1960. Intern Newton-Wellesley Hosp., Mass., 1960-61; asst. dir. for venereal diseases Mass. Dept. Pub. Health, 1961-63; resident in psychiatry Boston State Hosp., Mattapan, Mass., 1965-66; resident in psychiatry Tufts New Eng. Med. Ctr. Hosps., 1966-69, psychiat. cons. dept. gynecology, 1973-75; asst. clin. prof. psychiatry Sch. Medicine Tufts U., 1973-75, assoc. clin. prof., 1975-82, asst. clin. prof. ob-gyn, 1977-80, assoc. clin. prof. ob-gyn, 1980-82; assoc. prof. psychiatry, ob-gyn U. Nev. Sch. Med., Reno, 1982-85; practice psychiatry specializing in psychological effects of bodily changes on women, 1969—; clin. prof. psychiatry U. Nev. Sch. Medicine, Reno, 1985-86, prof. psychiatry, 1986—, clin. assoc. prof. ob-gyn, 1985—; mem. staff Tufts New Eng. Med. Ctr. Hosps., 1977-82, St. Margaret's Hosps., Boston, 1977-82, Washoe Med. Ctr., Reno, Sparks (Nev.) Family Hosp., Truckee Meadows Hosp., Reno, St. Mary's Hosp., Reno; chief psychiatry svc. Reno VA Med. Ctr., 1989—; lectr. various univs., 1961—; cons. in psychiatry; mem. psychiatry adv. panel Hosp. Satellite Network; mem. office external peer rev. NIMH, HEW; psychiat. cons. to Boston Redevelopment Authority on Relocation of Chinese Families of South Cove Area, 1968-70; mem. New Eng. Med. Ctr. Hosps. Cancer Ctr. Com., 1979-80, Pain Control Com., 1981-82, Tufts Univ. Sch. Medicine Reproductive System Curriculum Com., 1975-82. Mem. editorial bd. Psychiat. Update Am. (Psychiat. Assn. ann. rev.), 1983-85; reviewer Psychosomatics and Hosp. Community Psychiatry, New Eng. Jour. of Medicine, Am. Jour. of Psychiatry Psychosomatic Medicine; contbr. articles to profl. jours. Immaculate Heart Coll. scholar, 1951-52; Mira Hershey scholar UCLA, 1955; fellow Radcliffe Inst., 1967-70. Mem. AMA, Am. Psychiat. Assn. (rep. to sect. com. AAAS, chmn. ad hoc com. Asian-Am. Psychiatrists 1975, task force 1975-77, task force cost effectiveness in consultation 1984—, caucus chmn. 1981-82, sci. program com. 1982—, courses subcom. chmn. sci. program com., 1986-88), Mass. Med. Soc., Am. Coll. Sports Medicine, Am. Geriatrics Soc., Am. Soc. Psychomatic Ob-Gyn (mem.-at-large 1982), Acad. Psychiatry (fellowship com. 1982—), Nev. Psychiat. Assn., Washoe County Med. Assn., Nev. Med. Soc., Am. Coll. Psychiatrists, Eastern Profl. Ski Instrs. Assn. Home: 2105 Chicory Way Reno NV 89509 Office: 1000 Locust St Reno NV 89520

SMALL, ELIZABETH ANNE, dermatologist; b. Streator, Ill., Jan. 9, 1951; d. John Davis and Mary Elizabeth (Gleim) S. BA, Wellesley (Mass.) Coll., 1973; MD, John Hopkins U., 1977. Intern Northwestern Meml. Hosp., Chgo., 1977-78; resident Johns Hopkins Hosp., Balt., 1978-81; dermatologist Zachary, La., 1981-86, Springfield, Ill., 1986-88; dermatologist Assoc. Dermatologists, Ltd., Springfield, 1989—; cons. Meml. Med. Ctr., Springfield, 1986—, St. John's Hosp., Springfield, 1986—. Durant scholar Wellesley Coll., 1973. Fellow Am. Acad. Dermatology; mem. AMA, Ill. Dermatology Soc., Am. Soc. Dermatol. Surgery, Chgo. Dermatology Soc., Phi Beta Kappa, Sigma Xi. Presbyterian. Office: Associated Dermatologists 301 N 8th Springfield IL 62701

SMALL, JOYCE GRAHAM, psychiatrist, educator; b. Edmonton, Alberta, Can., June 12, 1931; came to U.S., 1956; d. John Earl and Rachel C. (Redmond) Graham; m. Iver Francis Small, May 26, 1954; children: Michael, Jeffrey. BA, U. Saskatchewan, Can., 1951; MD, U. Manitoba, Can., 1956; MS, U. Mich., 1959. Diplomat Am. Bd. Psychiatry and Neurology, Am. Bd. Electroencephalography. Instr. in psychiatry Neuropsychiat. Inst. U. Mich., Ann Arbor, 1959-60; instr. in psychiatry med. sch. U. Oreg., Portland, 1960-61, asst. prof. in psychiatry med. sch., 1961-62; asst. prof. in psychiatry sch. of medicine Washington U., St. Louis, 1962-65; assoc. prof. in psychiatry sch. of medicine Ind. U., Indpls., 1965-69, prof. psychiatry sch. of medicine, 1969—; mem. initial rev. groups NIMH, Washington, 1972-76, 79-82, 87-91; assoc. mem. Inst. Psychiat. Rsch., Indpls., 1974—. Editorial bd: Quarterly Journal of Convulsive Therapy, 1984, and more than 150 publs. in field; contbr. articles to profl. jours. Rsch. grantee NIMH, Portland, Oreg., 1961-62, St. Louis, 1962-64, Indpls., 1967—, Epilepsy Found., Indpls., 1965; recipient merit award NIHM, Indpls., 1990. Fellow Am. Psychiat. Assn., Am. Electroencephalographic Soc. (councillor 1972-75, 1982); mem. Soc. Biol. Psychiatry, Cen. Assn. Electroencephalographers (sec., treas. 1967-68, pres. 1970, councillor 1971-72), Sigma Xi. Office: Larue D Carter Meml Hosp 1315 W 10th St Indianapolis IN 46202

SMALL, KATHY JEAN, economic development executive; b. Pocatello, Idaho, July 26, 1958; d. Leo A. and Barbara Jean (Pitts) Brill; m. Joseph Avery Small, Mar. 28, 1981 (div. Apr. 1983). Grad. high sch., Ponca, Nebr. Sec. Simpco, Sioux City, Iowa, 1976-77, planner trainee, 1977-79, adminstrv. asst., 1979-84, dir. mem. svcs., 1984-85; bookkeeper Heyl Truck Lines, Inc., Akron, Iowa, 1981-82; community devel. cir. rider West Cen. Nebr. Devel. Dist., Ogallala, 1985-86, exec. dir., 1986-88; exec. dir. Nebr. Futures Inc., Lincoln, 1988—; sec., treas. Dawson County Econ. Coun., Cozad, Nebr., 1988; exec. dir. W. Cen. Nebr. Housing Authority, Ogallala, 1987-88. Forum advisor New Horizons Project of Nebr. Legislature, 1988—; chmn. pre-White Ho. conf. com. Nebr. Libr. Commn., 1989—; adv. com. Nebr. Tech. Assistance Ctr., 1990—. Recipient Innovative Program award Nat. Assn. Devel. Orgn., 1987, 89. Mem. NAFE, Nebr. Indsl. Devels. Assn., Jaycees (pres. Ogallala chpt. 1988, v.p. Lincoln chpt. 1989-90, bd. dirs. Lincoln Jaycees Found. 1990—, v.p. Nebr. soc. 1990—), Nat. Assn. Towns and Twps. (spl. project adv. com. 1988—). Office: Nebr Futures Inc 206 S 13th St Ste 1122 Lincoln NE 68508

SMALL, NATALIE SETTIMELLI, pediatric counselor; b. Quincy, Mass., June 2, 1933; d. Joseph Peter and Edmea Natalie (Bagnaschi) Settimelli; m. Parker Adams Small, Jr., Aug. 26, 1956; children: Parker Adams III, Peter McMichael, Carla Edmea. BA, Tufts U., 1955; MA, EdS, U. Fla., 1976; PhD, 1987. Cert. Nat. Bd. Cert. Counselors, cert. child life specialist. Pediatric counselor U. Fla. Coll. Medicine, Gainesville, 1976-80; pediatric counselor, supr. child life dept. social work svcs Shands Hosp.-U. Fla., Gainesville, 1980—; mem. faculty Ctr. for Coop. Learning for Health and Sci. Edn., Gainesville, 1988—. Author: Mothers Know Best, 1987. Bd. dirs. Ronald McDonald House, Gainesville, 1980—; mem. health profl. adv. com. March of Dimes, Gainesville, 1986—. Scholar Boston Stewart Club, Florence, Italy, 1955; grantee Jessie Ball Du Pont Fund, 1978. Mem. Am. Psychol. Assn., Am. Assn. Counseling and Devel., Assn. for the Care of Children's Health, Child Life Coun. Roman Catholic. Home: 3454 NW 12th Ave Gainesville FL 32605 Office: Shands Hosp Dept Social Work Svcs J-306 Gainesville FL 32610

SMALL, REBECCA ELAINE, accountant; b. Meridian, Tex., Apr. 5, 1946; d. James Milford and Rosa Lee Elaine (Berry) Allen; m. Jay Austin Small, Sept. 16, 1964 (div.); children: Lashawn Renee, Jay Austin Jr.; m. Jerry Leon Cooper, Dec. 10, 1983 (div. Sept. 1985). Student Okla. Sch. Bus. and Banking, 1972; BS in Acctg. magna cum laude, Cen. State U., Edmond, Okla., 1977, MA in Exptl. Psychology summa cum laude, 1989. Staff acct. Robert A. Mosley, CPA, Moore, Okla., 1972-74, Robert Stewart, CPA, Edmond, 1974-75, Lowder & Co., Oklahoma City, 1975-81; pvt. practice acctg., Oklahoma City, 1981—. Recipient Rsch. award Dept. Psychology Cent. State U., 1988. Mem. Okla. Woman's Bus. Orgn. (chmn. 1982), Okla. Soc. CPA's, Am. Inst. CPA's, Am. Woman's Soc. CPA's, Nat. Assn. Accts. (hon.), Alpha Lambda Delta, Alpha Chi, Psi Chi. Democrat. Avocations: writing poetry, interior decorating, horticulture, bicycling.

SMALL, SARAH MAE, volunteer; b. Salisbury, N.C., Nov. 16, 1923; d. Clint and Lillie Mae (Wilbourn) Evans; m. Jesse Small Sr., May 4, 1941; children: Jesse Jr., Jean Carol Small Bell. Cert., Cortez Bus. Sch., 1948. File clk. gen. acctg. office Fed. Govt., Washington, 1941-47; sec., stenographer CIA, Washington, 1948-52; adminstrv. asst. CIA, McLean, Va., 1952-65; ret. CIA, 1965. Pres. Youth Triumph Ch., Washington, Md., S.C. and Ga., 1965-76; bd. dirs. ARC, Washington, 1986-87; mem. adv. bd. D.C. Gen. Hosp., 1985-86; bd. dirs. Children's Edn. Found., Inc., 1989—. Recipient Outstanding and Dedicated Vol. Svc. award Kiwanis Club of Capital Centre, 1985, Appreciation award Jr. Citizens Corp., Inc., 1990. Mem. Jr. Citizens Corps (life, pres. 1985—, Dedicated Community Svc. award 1983, Bus. and Community Svc. award 1986), Bus. and Profl. Women's League (treas. 1982-86), Women in Arts (chartered, pres. 1984—), Nat. Coun. Negro Women, World Affairs Coun. Washington, Agrl. Coun. Am., Exec. Travel Club

Riverdale. Democrat. Baptist. Home: 2010 Upshur St NE Washington DC 20018

SMALL, TAKITA DARNISE, newspaper official; b. Martinsville, Va., May 27, 1959; d. Thomas Lee and Dorothy Lamour (France) S. BS in Advt. Design, Austin Peay State U., 1983; postgrad., Va. Commonwealth U., 1989—. Cashier Ricks Cost Plus IGA, Clarksville, Tenn., 1980-83; advt. production clk. Richmond (Va.) Newspapers, Inc., 1983-84, photoengraving apprentice, 1984-87, journeyman engraver, 1987 (summer), asst. night supr., 1988—; part time paste up artist Mechanicsville (Va.) Local Newspaper, 1986 (summer). Vol. Nat. Coun. Artists' Last Stop Gallery, Richmond, 1987-88. Recipient Mayor's Cert. City of Clarksville, Tenn., 1983. Mem. Am. Bus. Women's Assn. (winner Spring Conf. Theme Contest 1988, pub. chmn. 1988-89), Delta Sigma Theta. Democrat. Baptist. Office: Richmond Newspapers Inc 333 E Grace St Richmond VA 23219

SMALLEY, EDITH RENEE, restaurant professional; b. West Union, Ohio, Sept. 13, 1960; d. Donald Eugene and Mabel Mildred (Gustin) S. BBA, Morehead State U., 1984. Youth counselor Adams County Youth Services, West Union, Ohio, 1984; clk. front desk Breckenridge (Colo.) Inn, 1984-85; asst. mgr. trainee Red Lobster Inns Am., Cin., 1985; asst. mgr. Red Lobster Inns Am., Huntington, W.Va., 1986, Lexington, Ky., 1986-87; asst. mgr. Red Lobster Can., Kitchner, Ont., 1987, St. Catherine, Ont., 1987; asst. mgr. Red Lobster Inns Am., Lexington, 1987; assoc. mgr. Red Lobster Inns Am., Owensboro, Ky., 1987-88, Cin., 1988—. Mem. Nat. Assn. Female Execs., Grange (fellow). Republican. Presbyterian. Home: 155 Glen Gustin Rd Peebles OH 45660 Office: Red Lobster Inns Am 6186 Glenway Ave Cincinnati OH 45211

SMALLEY, PENNY JUDITH, nursing consultant; b. Chgo., Feb. 20, 1947; d. Ernest Rich and Muriel L. (Touff) Brown; m. Ivan H. Smalley, Jan. 11, 1972; children: Cherie Ann, Michael John, Geoffry Paul. Grad., Evanston Hosp. Sch. Nursing, Ill., 1980. Cert. Am. Bd. Laser Surgery, 1989. Staff nurse Evanston Hosp., 1979-81, laser coord., 1981-83; office mgr. Women's Health Group, 1981; laser nurse specialist Cooper Lasersonics, various, 1983-86; ind. cons. Laser Resources and Cons. Svcs., Chgo., 1986—; mem. medicine/biology com. Laser Inst. Am., 1990; lectr., writer Sino Fgn. Laser Conf., People's Republic of China, 1987; trustee Midwest Bio Laser Inst., 1983-86. Contbg. author: Nursing Clinics of North America, 1990; editorial bd. Clin. Laser Monthly, 1990, Laser Nursing mag. 1989-90; contbr. articles to profl. jours. Leader Girl Scouts U.S., Chgo.; den mother Boy Scouts Am., Chgo; active PTA, Kilmer Elem. Sch., Chgo. Mem. Am. Soc. Laser Medicine and Surgery (chmn. edn. com. 1987-90, chmn. standards of practice 1990), British Med. Laser Assn. (course dir. first laser nursing conf. in United Kingdom 1990), Assn. Operating Room Nurses, Internat. Soc. Laser Surgery and Medicine (co-chmn. nursing 1989-90). Democrat. Home and Office: 1444 W Farwell Chicago IL 60626

SMALL-WEIL, SUSAN B., psychologist; b. Bklyn., Sept. 28, 1954; d. Arthur and Rita (Langholtz) Small.; m. Scott Weil, Dec. 28, 1974; 1 child, Cameron B. BS, Bklyn. Coll., 1975; MS, Tufts U., 1977, PhD, 1980. Teaching asst. Tufts U., Medford, Mass., 1976-77, rsch. asst., 1977-79; v.p. McCann Erickson, N.Y.C., 1979-84; exec. v.p. Warwick, Baker & Fiore, N.Y.C., 1984—; cons. Am. Mental Health Fund, Washington, D.C., 1986—. Contbr. articles to various advt. jours. Mem. Residents For A More Beautiful Pt. Washington, Pt. Washington, N.Y., 1987-90, Beacon Hill Assn., Pt. Washington, 1986-90. NSF fellow, 1976-77; recipient Research Assistantship NIMH, 1978-79. Mem. AMA, NAFE. Office: Warwick Baker & Fiore 100 Ave of Americas New York NY 10013

SMALLWOOD, CAROL, librarian, writer; b. Cheboygan, Mich., May 3, 1939; d. Lloyd Gouine and Lucy Drust; m. T.M. Smallwood, 1963 (div. 1976); 2 children. BS, Ea. Mich. U., 1961, M in History, 1963; MLS, We. Mich. U., 1976. Tchr. Redford Union High Sch., Livonia, Mich., 1961-62, Flat Rock (Mich.) Jr. High Sch., 1963-64; grad. asst. Western Mich. U., Kalamazoo, 1975-76; title 1 library cons. Northland (Mich.), Grand Traverse (Mich.) Library Systems, 1976-77; librarian Pellston (Mich.) Pub. Schs., 1977—; asst. dir. Northland Library System, Alpena, Mich., 1977; developer, operator ednl. materials clearinghouse, 1981-83; columnist Detroit News, 1983-85; adult edn. tchr. Cheboygan Area Schs., 1985—. Author: Free Mich. Materials for Educators, 1980, Exceptional Free Library Resource Materials, 1984, Librarians' and Teachers' Free Resource Builder, 1985, A Guide to Selected Federal Agency Programs and Publications for Librarians and Teachers, 1986, Health Resource Builder, 1988, An Educational Guide to the National Park System, 1989, Current Issues Builder, 1989, Puzzles/Wordgames for Librarians and Teachers, 1990, Crosswords for Reference, 1990; columnist Catch: The Entertainment News, 1988—, Sunshine Classroom, 1988—, Gannett News Svcs., 1989—, Michigan Woman, 1990; contbr. articles to mags, profl. jours.; author software. Charter bd. mem. Cheboygan Area Arts Coun., publicity chmn.; founder, pres. Cheboygan County Humane Soc., others. Mem. NEA, (people for the ethical treatment of animals), Humane Soc. U.S., Pellston Edn. Assn., Internat. Soc. Animal Rights, Mich. Edn. Assn. (columnist 1989—), Nat. Women Studies Assn., Nat. Humane Edn. Com., Mich. Assn. Media Edn., No. Mich. Edn. Assn., others. Home: 1359 Michigami Dr Cheboygan MI 49721 Office: Pellston High Sch Libr 172 N Park Ave Pellston MI 49769

SMART, ASHLYNN M., executive assistant; b. Ind., Nov. 14, 1950; d. Donald and Dorothy Schwartz; children: Rodney, Amy. Student, Husson Coll., Bangor, Maine, I.V.T.C., Lafayette, Ind., 1985. Cert. pvt. and legal sec., notary pub., Maine. Legal sec. Morris Pilot, Esq., Bangor; office mgr. Homecrafters, Inc., Hampden, Maine, exec. asst. Mem. NAFE, Am. Inst. Profl. Bookkeepers, Nat. Notaries Assn., Nat. Legal Secs. Assn., Penobscot Legal Secs. Assn. Address: PO Box 2095 Bangor ME 04401

SMART, DOROTHY CAROLINE, retired social worker; b. Osborn, Mo.; d. Allen A. and Caroline (Totzke) S. Student, U. Mo., 1929-30; AB, U. Kans., 1937, MSW, 1950; postgrad., U. Chgo., 1963, 65. Advt. copy writer Emery Bird Thayer, Kansas City, Mo., 1937-38; case worker Dept. Pub. Welfare, Kansas City, 1938-44, Jackson County chpt. ARC, Kansas City, 1944-49; disaster rep. Am. Nat. Red Cross, St. Louis, 1950-59, home service rep. area office, 1959-65, regional dir. svc. mil. families, 1965-70, asst. area dir. svc. to mil. families, 1970-76. Mem. Group Action Coun.; bd. dirs. Barnes Hosp. Aux. Mem. Nat. Assn. Social Workers, Nat. Conf. Social Welfare, Acad. Cert. Social Workers, Women in Communications (pres. Kansas City alumni chpt. 1943), Am. Assn. Ret. Persons (pres. 1989, bd. dirs. 1989-90), Pilot Club (St. Louis, pres. 1975-77, Lucy B. Allen Nat. award 1988, Gold medal. Home: 4475 W Pine Blvd Apt 905 Saint Louis MO 63108

SMART, MARRIOTT WIECKHOFF, geologist, information manager; b. Memphis, Aug. 26, 1935; d. Gerhard Emil and Beatrice (Flanegan) Wieckhoff; m. John A. Smart, May 9, 1959; children: Denise, Holly. B.S. in Geology, U. Tex.-Austin, 1957; M.L.S., U. Pitts., 1976. Geophysicist Mobil Corp., New Orleans, 1957-59; geologist Hanson Oil Co., Roswell, N.Mex., 1959-62; info. specialist Gulf Corp., Pitts., 1977-79, library mgr., Denver, 1979-84, library cons. team, Pitts., 1984; supr. Library-Info. Ctr., Amoco Minerals Co., Englewood, Colo., 1984; dir. Library-Info. Ctr., Cyprus Minerals Co., 1985—. Dist. chmn. Am. Cancer Soc., Arapahoe County, Colo., 1981-84; mem. choir Grace Presbyn. Ch., Littleton, Colo., 1979—; block worker Republican party, Arapahoe County, 1981—. Mem. Spl. Libraries Assn. (bull. bus. mgr. 1982, treas. petroleum and energy div. 1984-86, chmn. petroleum and energy div. 1987-88), Geosci. Info. Soc., Alpha Chi Omega (career network coord. 1984—). Home: 3337 E Easter Pl Littleton CO 80122 Office: Cyprus Minerals Co 9100 E Mineral Circle Englewood CO 80112

SMART, MARY-LEIGH CALL (MRS. J. SCOTT SMART), civic worker; b. Springfield, Ill., Feb. 27, 1917; d. S(amuel) Leigh and Mary (Bradish) Call; m. J. Scott Smart, Sept. 11, 1951 (dec. 1960). Diploma, Monticello Coll., 1934; student, Oxford U., 1935; B.A., Wellesley Coll., 1937; M.A., Columbia U., 1939, postgrad., 1940-41; postgrad., N.Y. U., 1940-41; painting student, with Bernard Karfiol, 1937-38. Dir. mgmt. Cen. Ill. Grain Farms, Logan County, 1939—; owner Lowtrek Kennel, Ogunquit, Maine, 1957-73, Cove Studio Art Gallery, Ogunquit, 1961-68; art collector, patron, publicist, 1954—, cons., 1970—. Editor: Hamilton Easter Field Art Found. Collection Catalog, 1966; originator, dir. show, compiler of catalog Art: Ogunquit, 1967; Peggy Bacon-A Celebration, Barn Gallery, Ogunquit, 1979. Program dir., sec. bd. Barn Gallery Assocs., Inc., 1958-69, pres., 1969-70, 82-87, asst. treas., 1987—, hon. dir., 1970-78; curator Hamilton Easter Field Art Found. Collection, 1978-79, curator exhbns., 1979-86; mem. acquisition com. DeCordova Mus., Lincoln, Mass., 1966-78; mem. chancellor's coun. U. Tex., 1972—, U. N.H., 1978—; bd. dirs. Ogunquit C. of C., 1966, treas. 1966-67, hon. life mem., 1968—; bd. overseers Strawbery Banke, Inc., Portsmouth, N.H., 1972-75, 3d vice chmn., 1973, 2d vice chmn., 1974; bd. advisors Univ. Art Galleries, U. N.H., 1973-89, v.p., bd. overseers, 1974-81, pres., 1981-89; bd. dirs. Old York Hist. and Improvement Soc., York, Maine, 1979-81, v.p., 1981-82; mem. adv. com. Bowdoin Coll. Mus. Art Invitational Exhibit, 1975, '76 Maine Artists Invitational Exhbn., Maine State Mus., Maine Coast Artists, Rockport, 1975-78, All Maine Biennial '79, Bowdoin Coll. Mus. Art juried exhbn.; mem. jury for scholarship awards Maine Com. for the Skowhegan Sch. Painting and Sculpture, 1982-84; mem. nat. com. Wellesley Coll. Friends of Art, 1983—; adv. trustee Portland Mus. Art, 1983-85, fellow, 1985—; mem. mus. panel Maine State Commn. on Arts and Humanities, 1983-86; mem. adv. com. Maine Biennial, Colby Coll. Mus. Art, 1983; mem. coun. advisors Farnsworth Libr. and Art Mus., Rockland, Maine, 1986—; mem. collections com. Payson Gallery, Westbrook Coll., Portland, Maine, 1987—; mem. corp. Mus. of Art Ogunquit, 1988-90. Served to lt. jg. WAVES, 1942-45. Recipient Deborah Morton award Westbrook Coll., 1988. Mem. Am. Fedn. Arts, Am. Coun. for Arts, Mus. Modern Art, Springfield Art Assn., Boston Mus. Fine Arts, Solomon R. Guggenheim Mus., Whitney Mus. Am. Art., Jr. League of Springfield, Western Maine Wellesley Club. Republican. Episcopalian. Address: 30 Surf Point Rd York ME 03909

SMART, MELISSA BEDOR, environmental consultant company executive; b. St. Johnsbury, Vt., Mar. 5, 1953; d. Leslie Oscar and Helen Catherine (Kenney) Bedor; m. Glenn Robin Smart, Oct. 1, 1983; children: Catherine Jean, Jenny Laura. BS in Ecology and Environ. Conservation, U. N.H., 1975; MS in Water and Land Use Planning, SUNY, Syracuse, 1981. Environ. instr. NSF, Hooksett, N.H., 1975; environ. scientist, planner Parsons Brinckerhoff Quade & Douglas, Inc., Boston, 1976-78, sr. environ. scientist, planner, 1981-82; research asst. SUNY Coll. Environ. Sci. and Forestry, Syracuse, 1978-79; environ. planner St. Lawrence Eastern Ontario Commn., Watertown, N.Y., 1979; sr. environ. scientist, mktg. dir. VTN Consolidated, Inc., Boston, 1982-83; pres. The Smart Assocs., Inc., Contoocook, N.H., 1984-90, Concord, N.H., 1990—; water resource cons. Soc. Protection N.H. Forests, Concord, 1984—; water resource lectr. Harris Ctr. Conservation Edn., Hancock, N.H., 1985; mem. steering com. N.H. Rivers Campaign, Concord, 1986. Author: Directory of Water Testing Expertise in New Hampshire, 1985. Pastor's aide So. Congl. Ch., Concord, 1988—; mem. N.H. Gov.'s Task Force on Wetlands. Am. Field Service scholar, Australia, 1970. Mem. Am. Water Resources Assn., Assn. State Wetlands Mgrs. (govs. task force), N.H. Water Works, N.H. Assn. of Wetland Scientists (pres.). Democrat. Congregationalist. Home: Rte 2 Box 14 Contoocook NH 03229 Office: The Smart Assocs Inc 72 N Main St Concord NH 03301

SMAYLING, LYDA MOZELLA, speech pathologist; b. Britton, Okla., Apr. 19, 1923; d. Miles and Evelyn (King) Maxwell; m. George F. Smayling, Sept. 12, 1944 (dec. 1985); children: Sally, Michael, Miles. BA magna cum laude, U. Wichita, Wichita, Kans., 1944; MA summa cum laude, U. Wichita, 1947. Dir., cons., assoc. U. Kans. Med. Ctr., Kans. City, 1947-56; cons. Westchester County Cerebral Palsy Assn., Bedford Village, N.Y., 1947-54; asst. dir. Inst. Logopedics, Wichita, 1957-68; instr. Wichita (Kans.) State U., 1957-68; cons. Wichita, 1957-68; pvt. practice Mpls., 1968—. Contbr. articles to profl. jours. V.p. PTA, Wichita, 1957-64, tchr. Unitarian Ch., Wichita, 1959-64;. Mem. Am. Speech-Language Hearing Assn., Minn. Speech Language Hearing. Unitarian. Home and Office: 3145 Dean Ct #I-903 Minneapolis MN 55416

SMEAL, ELEANOR CUTRI, organization executive; b. Ashtabula, Ohio, July 30, 1939; d. Peter Anthony and Josephine E. (Agresti) Cutri; m. Charles R. Smeal, Apr. 27, 1963; children: Tod, Lori. B.A., Duke U., 1961; M.A., U. Fla., 1963. Mem. bd. Upper St. Clair (Pa.) chpt. LWV, 1968-72, sec.-treas. Allegheny County Council, 1971-72; mem. NOW, 1971—; convenor, 1st pres. S. Hills (Pa.) chpt. NOW, 1971-73, 1st pres., state coordinator, 1972-75; nat. bd. dirs. NOW, 1973-75, chairwoman bd., 1975-77, pres., 1977-82, 85-87, mem. bd. Legal Def. and Edn. Fund, 1975—, chairwoman ERA Strike Force, 1977—; pres. Fund for Feminist Majority, Arlington, Va., 1987—; mem. 1st nominating com., founding conf. Nat. Women's Polit. Caucus, 1971; bd. dirs. Allegheny County Women's Polit. Caucus, 1971-72; co-founder, bd. dirs. S. Hills NOW Day Nursery Sch., 1972—; mem. Nat. Commn., Observance of Internat. Women's Year, 1977; mem. exec. com. Leadership Conf. on Civil Rights, 1979—; mem. Nat. Adv. Com. on Women, 1978. Named One of 25 Most Influential Women in U.S. World Almanac, 1978. Office: Fund For The Feminist Majority 1600 Wilson Blvd #704 Arlington VA 22209

SMEDRESMAN, INGEBORG FREUNDLICH, artist; b. Germany; came to U.S., 1937, naturalized, 1943; d. Paul and Erna Betty (Simon) Freundlich; B.S., U. Frankfurt, Germany, 1934; postgrad. in chemistry U. Zurich, Switzerland, 1934-37, art edn. Nat. Acad. Art Students League, Queens Coll; m. Sidney Smedresman, Aug. 10, 1937; children—Ingrid Braslow, Leonard C., Paulette Mehta, Suzanne van Oers. Art lectr. Forest Hills Jewish Center, 1966-68, Guggenheim Mus., 1973-76; art tchr. Queensboro Art Soc., 1969; art dir. Temple Beth El, Great Neck, L.I., 1969-75, YM-YWHA, Little Neck, 1975; art instr. Queens Coll. CUNY, 1988-90. One woman shows at Fine Arts Gallery, N.Y.C., 1970, Queens Coll., N.Y.C., summer 1975, 78, 81, 85, Harrison (N.Y.) Library, 1979, 80, Vleigh Place Library, 1984, Alley Pond Gallery, 1986, Alley Pond Environ. Ctr., 1986, Queens Coll. CUNY, 1990; exhibited in group shows at ACA Gallery, 1959, Contemporary Art Gallery, 1965-66, Raymond Duncan Gallery, Paris, France, 1965-66, Ahda Arzt Gallery, N.Y.C., 1970, Ten Voorde Gallery, Amsterdam, 1973, Carrol Condit Gallery, White Plains N.Y., 1973, Westchester Art Soc., 1970-75; represented in permanent collections Godwin-Ternbach Mus. of Queens Coll., Pfizer Inc. Internat. Hdqrs., N.Y.C., City Hall, Moncton, N.B., Can., Israel Mus., Jerusalem; art instr. YM-YWHA, Flushing; lectr. Cooper-Hewitt Mus. Recipient art awards Paris Water Colors, 1965, 66, Suffolk County Artists, 1966, Queensboro Art Soc., 1975, 1st prize Westchester Art Soc., 1975. Mem. Art Students League N.Y. (life), Artists Equity Assn., Am. Chem. Soc. Home: 147-43 77th Rd Kew Garden Hills NY 11367

SMELKINSON, LYNN MARIE, lawyer; b. Washington, May 4, 1955; d. Reuben and Klaire (Rosenthal) S.; m. Laurence Windham Brown, Apr. 18, 1987. BS, George Washington U., 1978; JD, U. San Francisco, 1981. Bar: Calif. 1982, N.Y. 1983, D.C. 1985, U.S. Ct. Appeals 1985, U.S. Supreme Ct. 1985. Research assoc. EPA, Washington, 1979; law clk. U.S. Atty's Office, San Francisco, 1980, Santa Rosa (Calif.) Mcpl. Ct., 1981; assoc. Roth & Ishida, Oakland, Calif., 1982; atty. Legal Facilities Mgmt., N.Y.C., 1983—; asst. gen. counsel U.S. C. of C., Washington, 1985—; sr. counsel Nat. Chamber Litigation Ctr.; legis. analyst Queen's Bench, San Francisco, 1982; legal advisor Washington Counsel for Progressive Radio, 1983. Mediator community bds., San Francisco, 1982; arbitrator Better Bus. Bur., San Francisco, 1982; publicist Bay Area Lawyers for Arts, San Francisco, 1982; vol. Washington Humane Soc. Mem. ABA, N.Y. State Bar Assn., Calif. Bar Assn., D.C. Bar Assn. (co-chmn. computer contract com.), Am. Corp. Counsel Assn. (co-chmn. intellectual property com.). Club: Toastmasters (adminstrv. v.p., Washington br.). Office: US C of C 1615 H St NW Washington DC 20062

SMELSER, REBECCA FORMAN, publisher, editor; b. Ville Platte, La., July 24, 1961; d. Garland Ray and Velma Janet (Keopp) Forman; m. Steven S. Smelser, July 27, 1987; 1 child, Samuel. Student, Baton Rouge Sch. Computers, 1988-89. Salesperson People's Shoe Store, Alexandria, La., 1979-85; office mgr. Res. Nat. Ins. Co., Oklahoma City, 1986-87; office mgr., co-owner United Health Svc., Baton Rouge, 1987—; pub. editor, co-owner Ins. World Publ., Alexandria, La., 1989—. Mem. Nat. Assn. Female Execs. Methodist. Home: 6012 Mil Mar Blvd Alexandria LA 71302

SMERLAS, DONNA, museum and library administrator; b. Boston, July 14, 1949; d. Constantine and Betty (Makris) S. BA, Smith Coll., 1971; MA, Boston U., 1977. Tech. writer, editor Raytheon Svc. Co., Burlington, Mass., 1971-72; editor, archivist JFK Presdl. Library & Mus., Boston, 1972-76; meeting and event planner JFK Presdl. Library & Mus., 1976-87; dir. adminstrn. and fin. JFK Presdl. Library & Mus., Boston, 1987—; ptnr., owner Triangle Assocs., Ltd., Boston, 1989. Editor: Massachusetts Soldiers in the Lexington Alarm, 1976. Dir., Smith Coll. Students for Kennedy for Senate, Northampton, 1970; organizer Paul Tsongas for U.S. Senate, 1978; dir. Mass. local programs Close Up Found., 1982-87; spl. events dir. Greek Orthodox Ch., Watertown, Mass., 1978-84; cons. Mass. Coun. Arts and Humanities, Boston, 1986-88. Nat. Historical Publs. and Records Commn. fellow, 1975. Mem. Nat. Orgn. for Women, Helicon Club (bd. dirs. 1986-88, v.p. 1988—), Axion Club, Smith Coll. Alumnae Assn. Democratic. Greek Orthodox. Home: 22 Stoneleigh Cir Watertown MA 02172 Office: JFK Presidential Libr & Mus Columbia Point Boston MA 02125

SMILEY, JANE TOWLER, retail promotion executive; b. Syracuse, N.Y., Mar. 18, 1925; d. Eugene Davis and Lucile (Hagen) Towler; m. Richard Henry Smiley, Sept. 19, 1964. BA, Smith Coll., 1947. Asst. buyer R.H. Macy, N.Y.C., 1947-49, Lord & Taylor, N.Y.C.; statis. researcher Hooperating, Norwalk, Conn.; office mgr. Pubs. Info. Bu., N.Y.C.; retail advt. cons. The New Yorker Mag., N.Y.C., 1953-74; nat. sales mgr. WestPoint Pepperell, Inc., 1974-76; v.p. spl. events and pub. Burdines, Miami, Fla., 1976—; bd. dirs. The Fashion Group, Miami. Sustaining cons. Jr. League, Miami, 1974-88; past chmn. Hispanic Heritage Coun., Miami, 1986, bd. dirs. 1976—; mem. Fla. Women's Alliance, 1988—. Named Woman of Yr. YWCA, 1982, Theatre Arts League, 1985. Mem. The Fashion Group (bd. dirs. 1986-89), Smith Coll. Club. Office: Burdines 22 E Flagler St Miami FL 33131

SMILEY, KAREN JANE, computer software engineer; b. New Kensington, Pa., Jan. 25, 1961; d. Paul Cornelius and Maureen Frances (Gross) S. BS in Indsl. Engring. and Ops. Research summa cum laude, U. Pitts., 1982; MS in Computer Sci., Stevens Inst. Tech., 1987. Engring. intern Armco Inc., Butler, Pa., 1980; research asst. Health Ops. Research Group, U. Pitts., 1981-82; computer software engr. Kearfott Guidance & Navigation Corp subs. Astronautics Corp. Am., Little Falls, N.J., 1982-88, sr. engr., 1988-90, engring specialist, 1990. Richard King Mellon Found. scholar, 1979-82, Armco, Inc. scholar, 1979-82. Mem. NAFE, Assn. for Computing Machinery, Mountainview Manor Condominium Assn. (mem. bd. trustees, 2d v.p. 1989-90, pres. 1990), Tau Beta Pi (pres. chpt. 1982). Avocations: reading, knitting, photography, cooking, bicycling. Office: Kearfott Guidance & Navigation Corp Mail Code 1DA73 1150 McBride Ave Little Falls NJ 07424

SMILIE, MOLLIE KAY WILLIAMS, accountant, educator; b. Bradford, Pa., Aug. 11, 1949; d. Albert Franklin and Martha Rae (Moore) Williams; m. Christopher Stephen Arthur, Sept. 11, 1969 (div. Apr. 1976); 1 child, Erik Ian; m. Michael Steven Smilie, May 9, 1980. BS, Colo. State U., 1979. CPA, Colo. Staff acct. Cady & Co., Fort Collins, Colo., 1979-80, Colo. State U., Fort Collins, 1980-81, asst. to controller, 1981-83, controller, 1983—; lectr. in field; mem. Colo. Quality Mgmt. Adv. Coun. Dem. Precinct Chmn. Larimer County, Fort Collins, 1978; bd. dirs. Larimer County Boy Scouts Am., Fort Collins, 1979, bd. dirs. Colo. Com. on Acctg. Standards for Higher Edn., Denver, 1983—, Amigos de las Americas, 1987—, Open Stage Inc., 1986-88. Mem. AICPA, Colo. Soc. CPAs, Nat. Assn. Coll. and Univ. Bus. Officers, Coun. on Govtl. Relations, Screen Actors Guild, Am. Fedn. TV and Radio Artists, Nat. Coun. Univ. Rsch. Adminstrs., Beta Alpha Psi. Republican. Unitarian. Avocations: acting; writing; horseback riding; skiing; travel. Home: PO Box 736 LaPorte CO 80535 Office: Colo State U 202E Johnson Hall Fort Collins CO 80523

SMIRL, MITZI LOU, purchasing analysis executive; b. Kansas City, Mo., June 6, 1961; d. Charles Claxton and Martha Jane (Hughes) S. BS in Home Econs., Tex. Christian U., Ft. Worth, 1983; MBA, U. Dallas, 1988. Cert. purchasing mgr. Purchasing agt. Zale Corp., Dallas, 1983-84; sec. Am. Airlines, Ft. Worth, 1985-86, asst. purchasing agt., 1986-87, purchasing agt., 1987-89, product display analyst, yield mgr., 1989—. Purchasing Assn. Dallas scholar, 1987, Rotary scholar, 1979, others. Mem. NAFE, Purchasing Mgmt. Assn. Dallas, Quality of Work Life Assn., Beta Sigma Phi. Baptist. Christian Ch. Home: 1524 Forest Park Cir #224 Bedford TX 76021 Office: Am Airlines 4333 Amon Carter Blvd MD 5281 Fort Worth TX 76155

SMITH, ADA L., state legislator; b. Va., Apr. 18, 1945; d. Thomas and Lilian Smith. Grad., CUNY, Baruch Coll. Dep. clk. N.Y.C.; state senator N.Y. Legislature, Albany; ranking minority mem. Mental Health com.; mem. Alcoholism and Substance Abuse com., Health com., Social Svcs. com., Child Care com., Elections com. Bd. visitors Bklyn. Ctr. for the Mentally Retarded and the Developmentally Disabled, 1981, 85; trustee, life dir. Coll. Fund Baruch Coll.; mem. Community I Bd. (chair social svcs. com.); chair. N.Y. Community Scvs. Coalition, Bklyn. Coalition Area Policy Bds.; treas. Bklyn. Pla. Med. Ctr., Friends Lindsay Park Anti-Crime Com., 67 Manhattan Ave. Block Assn.; bd. mgrs. Eastern Dist. YNCA; officer Williamsburg Tenats Assn.; mem. Community Action Bd.; exec. mem. Ctr. for Community Orgns.; mem. adv. bd. Woodhull Hosp.; mem. Area Policy Bd. 4; past pres. Williamsburg/Greenpoint Coalition Community Orgns.; past chair Area Policy Bd. 1; past bd. dirs., pres. Lindsay Park Housing Corp. Recipient numerous community svc. awards. Home: 67 Manhattan Ave Brooklyn NY 11206 Office: NY State Senate State Capitol Bldg 444 S 5th St Brooklyn NY 11211*

SMITH, AGNES MONROE, educator of history; b. Hiram, Ohio, Aug. 8, 1920; d. Bernie Alfred and Joyce (Messenger) Monroe; m. Stanley Blair Smith; children: David, Doris, Darl, Diane. AB, Hiram Coll., 1940; MA, W.Va. U., 1945; PhD, Western Res. U., 1966. Social sci. tchr. Freedom (Ohio) High Sch., 1940-44; instr. of history W.Va. U., Morgantown, 1945; instr. of social sci. Hiram Coll., 1946; inst. history and social sci. Youngstown (Ohio) State U., 1964-66, asst. prof. to prof. of history, 1966-84, prof. history emeritus, 1984—; vis. prof. history Hiram Coll., 1988-90. Co-editor: Bourgeois, San Culottes and other Frenchmen, 1981; contbr. articles to profl. jours. Mem. Ohio Acad. History, Delta Kappa Gamma, Phi Alpha Theta, Pi Gamma Mu. Mem. Christian Ch. (Disciples of Christ). Home: 16759 Main Market West Farmington OH 44491

SMITH, ALICE ELIZABETH SWILLEY, hospital services executive, consultant, clinical educator; b. Coral Gables, Fla., Sept. 24, 1948; d. Thomas and Alva (Zebendon) Swilley; m. Philip Edward Smith, June 26, 1971, 1 child, Eve Elizabeth. Cert. elementaire Le Cordon Bleu, Paris, 1969; B.A. in Home Econs., The Western Coll., 1970; postgrad. U. Dayton, 1972-73; dietetic intern Miami Valley Hosp., Dayton, Ohio, 1973-74; M.S. in Nutrition, No. Ill. U., 1978. Tchr. Miami Dade Jr. High, Opa Locka, Fla., 1970-71; food service coordinator Mercy Med. Ctr., Springfield, Ohio 1972-73; pub. health nutritionist Chgo. Bd. Health, 1974-78; assoc. dir. clin. dietetics Children's Meml. Hosp., Chgo., 1980-84, asst. clin. prof. U. Ill., Chgo., 1983—; dir. clin. dietetics Children's Meml. Hosp., Chgo., 1985-88, dir. clin. dietetics , food svc., 1988—; liaison rep. Am. Acad. Pediatrics Com. on Nutrition, Am. Dietetic Assn., Chgo., 1981—. Co-author: Superior Nutritional Care Cuts Hospital Cost, 1988; contbr. articles to profl. jours. Vol. 8th Day Ctr. for Justice, Chgo., 1976-77. Vol. Werner Erhard and Assocs., Chgo., 1985—. Grantee Mead Johnson Nutritional Co., 1983-88, Ross Labs, 1987-88. Mem. Am. Dietetic Assn., AAAS, Clin. Nutrition Mgmt. Practice Group (newsletter editor, 1983-84), Chgo. Dietetic Assn., Am. Soc. Parenteral and Enteral Nutrition, Dietitians in Pediatric Practice (nominating com. 1989-90). Avocations: Creative cookery, indoor gardening.

SMITH, ALISON J(ANN) DOCOS, management consultant; b. Syracuse, N.Y., Apr. 27, 1950; d. Andre S. Docos and Aurise P. (Coté) Fey. BA, Skidmore Coll., 1972; MBA, Coll. William and Mary, 1978. Corp. banking account mgr. Swiss Bank Corp., N.Y.C., 1979-81; asst. product mgr. Colgate-Palmolive Co., N.Y.C., 1981-83; mktg. dir. Schwab & Twitty Architects, Palm Beach, Fla., 1984-85; pres. Crown Cons. Group, Inc., Palm Beach, 1986—, 1986—. Pub. William and Mary Bus. Rev., 1978. Mem. Fla. Trust and Nat. Trust for Hist. Preservation, Jr. League; trustee Hist. Palm Beach County Preservation Bd., Boca Raton, Fla., 1984-88; bd. dirs. Preservation Collaborative. Mem. Exec. Women of the Palm Beaches, French-Am. C. of C., English Speaking Union., Jr. League. Office: Crown Cons Group Inc 139 N Country Rd Ste 23 Palm Beach FL 33480

SMITH, ANDREA PEDERSEN, interior designer; b. Milford, Mass., July 3, 1944; d. Alfred Edwin and Blanche (Jones) Pinkul; m. David Layton Smith, July. BA, U. Mass. at Amherst, 1966. Cert. interior designer Am. Soc. Interior Designers. Educator Secondary Level, Bourne, Mass., 1966-69; environ. education coord. Soc. Protection N.H. Forests, 1969-70; cons. Controlled Environ. Corp. and Hanslin Assn., Grantham, N.H., 1970-73; importer English, French Antiques, Furnishings, Grantham, 1973-80; proprietor Interior Design Bus., Mashpee, Mass., 1981—; owner Fabrication Bus., Cape Cod, 1982--; cons. Interior Design Profl., Cape Cod, 1987--; bd. dirs. DSA Systems Computer Software Developers, Mashpee; cons. Bd. mem. New Seabury Heart Fund, 1981-87. Mem. Bus. Profl. Women's Assn. Newport, League Women Voters, Women's Club. Home: 184 Walton Heath Way New Seabury MA 02649 Office: Andrea P Smith Interior Design 105 Summerfield Pk Mashpee MA 02649

SMITH, ANITA TORRES, language educator, educational consultant; b. Uvalde, Tex., May 1, 1928; d. Telésforo Flores and Praxedis Rodríguez (Mata) T.; m. Louis C. Castro, Apr. 13, 1953 (div. 1971); children: Fátima Yvón Cruz, Federico N., Celso A.; m. Donald Earl Smith, June 5, 1975. AA, SW Tex. Jr. Coll., Uvalde, 1949; BS, Sul Ross U., Alpine, 1961, EdM, 1975; EdD, Tex. A&I U., 1981. Cert. tchr., counselor, reading specialist, bilingual edn. Tchr. Uvalde Consolidated Ind. Sch. Dist., 1955-88; lectr. Sul Ross U., Alpine, Tex. and Uvalde, 1983—; visiting prof. Our Lady of the Lake U., San Antonio, 1983; cons. Robstown (Tex.) Ind. Sch. Dist., 1980; presentor at bilingual edn. conferences, 1983, 84, 85, 87; speaker Am. Legion Aux., Uvalde, 1986; writer County of Uvalde Historians, 1971. Author: (game) Developing Language Through Indian Symbols, 1983, The Relationship Between the Acquisition of Conservation and Language Proficiency of Mexican-American Children, 1981. Contbr. Time Capsule Historians, Uvalde, 1986; mem. symposia planning com. Columbian Quincentenary, 1988—; mem. Uvalde Tree Bd., 1989—; co-organizer Srs.' Crafts Group, 1989—. Named Diez y Seis Grand Parade Marshal, 1987. Mem. Tex. Assn. Bilingual Educators, Christian Counselors of Tex. (cofounder 1981, sec.-elect 1990—), Tex. State Tchrs. Assn. (local tchr. relations 1983-85, Tchr. of Yr. 1983), Am. Assn. Univ. Women (local chair Women's Issues 1983-85, presentor 1986), Delta Kappa Gamma (local chair ceremonials 1984-86). Democrat. Roman Catholic. Home: 217 S Crisp St Uvalde TX 78801

SMITH, ANN ELIZABETH, management and personnel consultant; b. Brockton, Mass., Feb. 19, 1957; d. Carl Victor and Elizabeth Pearson (Locke) S. AS in Fine Arts, Greenfield (Mass.) Coll., 1977; student, Mass. Coll. of Art, 1977-79. Bus. broker, asst. mgr. VR Bus. Brokers, Revere, Mass., 1982-83; personnel cons., mgr. Barclay Prsonnel Systems, Lynn, Mass., 1983—. Active, donor Greenpeace, 1985—, North Shore Animal League, 1985—, Peta, 1985—, Earth Island, Calif., 1986; donor Home for Little Wanderers, 1985—. Episcopalian. Office: Barclay Personnel Systems 30 State St Lynn MA 01901

SMITH, ANN MARIE, catering company executive; b. Phila., Nov. 3, 1960; d. Fred Nelson and Anna Marie (Garson) S. Student, Gettysburg Coll., 1978-79, Eastern Coll., 1981-83, W. Chester U., 1983-85. Registered rep. Shearson, Lehman and Hutton, Strafford, Pa., 1987-89; owner, mgr. Suburban Food Svc., Havertown, Pa., 1989—. Mem. Nat. Assn. Female Execs. Democrat.

SMITH, ANNE BOWMAN, academic administrator, editor; b. Craigsville, Va., Dec. 17, 1934; d. Joseph Benjamin and Louise Frances (Smith) Bowman; m. William Jerry Smith, June 29, 1957; children: Stacey Anne, Joan Elizabeth. Student, James Madison U., 1951-54, Old Dominion U., 1979-82; BA, Cath. U. Am. Reporter The Richmond (Va.) Times-Dispatch, 1955-56, The Miami (Fla.) Herald, 1965-68, 70-72, The Virginian-Pilot, Norfolk, 1968-70, 72-78; Portsmouth-Chesapeake city editor The Virginian-Pilot, 1978, govt. editor, 1978-80, asst. met. editor, 1980-82; dir. pub. info. Cath. U. Am., Washington, 1982-84, exec. dir. pub. affairs, 1984—; lectr. journalism Cath. U. Am., Washington, 1988—. Editor: Century Ended, Century Begun, 1990. Bd. dirs. Summer Opera Theatre Co., Washington, 1990—. Recipient numerous journalism awards including Va. Press Assn., Va. Press Women, Nat. Fedn. Press Women. Mem. Soc. Profl. Journalists. Office: Cath U Am Washington DC 20064

SMITH, ANNE MARIE, finance consultant; b. McMinnville, Oreg., Oct. 5, 1934; d. Emmanuel John and Sarah Christina (Kneale) Linke; m. Leon Smith, May 10, 1968; children: James David, Beverly Anne, Susan Marie, Patricia Joan.' Grad. high sch., McMinnville, Oreg., 1949-52. Bookkeeper Recreation Lares, The Dalles, Oreg., 1962-63; stable owner, Arabian horse trainer, 1968—. Leader, Brownie Scouts. Mem. Friends Columbia Gorge Coll., Oreg. Hist. Soc., Blazer Booster Club. Democrat. Home: 1501 E 19th St The Dalles OR 97058

SMITH, ANNE MOLLEGEN, editor; b. Meridian, Miss., July 28, 1940; d. Albert Theodore and Ione (Rush) Mollegen; m. David Fay Smith, Nov. 3, 1962; 1 dau., Amanda Wetherbee. B.A. (Smith Coll. Club of Washington scholar), Smith Coll., 1961. Asst. editor Ladies' Home Jour., Phila., 1961-62; advt. copywriter Hutzler's Dept. Store, Balt., 1962-64; feature editor China Post, Taipei, Taiwan, 1965; staff writer house organ J. C. Penney Co., N.Y.C., 1966; assoc. editor Redbook, N.Y.C., 1967-73, fiction editor, 1973-77; mng. editor Your Place mag. McCall Pub. Co., 1977-78, Redbook, N.Y.C., 1978-81; editor-in-chief Redbook, 1981-82; exec. editor Glamour Mag., N.Y.C., 1983-84; editor-in-chief Working Woman mag., N.Y.C., 1984-89, McCall's mag., N.Y.C., 1989—. Recipient 2d prize I Speak for Democracy contest Alexandria, Va., 1955, Karig Writing prize, 1957. Mem. Am. Soc. Mag. Editors (Redbook received Nat. Mag. award for fiction 1975), Women's Media Group (pres. 1978), Editors Organizing Com. (pres. 1982-87), Nuclear Times (bd. dirs., co-chmn. 1986-87). Club: Smith Coll. of N.Y. Home: 451 W 24th St New York NY 10011 Office: McCall's 230 Park Ave New York NY 10169*

SMITH, BARBARA ANGELA, management consultant; b. Mpls., Sept. 18, 1938. Chief exec. officer, chief fin. officer Barbara Smith & Assocs., Mpls., 1988—. Mem. NAFE (Twin Cities chpt.), Nat. Assn. Credit Mgrs., Mpls. C. of C., Nat. Assn. of Credit Mgmt. (north cen. div.), Calhoun Beach Club, Walker Art, Mpls. Art Inst. Office: Barbara Smith & Assocs Inc 3208 W Lake St #38 Minneapolis MN 55416

SMITH, BARBARA ANN, accountant, management consultant; b. Dallas, May 6, 1935; d. George Jefferson and Ina Pearl (Nowlin) Gardner; Asso. Mid. Mgmt., Mountain View Jr. Coll., 1975; 1 dau., Cynthia Marie Dixon. Asst. cashier U.S. Rubber Co., Dallas, 1954-57; sec.-treas. Am. Graphics Co., Dallas, 1974-79; pres. Am. Way Credit Union, Dallas, 1974-76; sec.-treas. Am. Legal Printing Co., Dallas, 1964-79, Abco Inc., Dallas, 1964-79, Am. Poster & Printing Co., Dallas, 1964-79; asst. sec.-treas. Am. Equity Press Inc., Dallas, 1974-79; prin. MS Svcs., Dallas, 1979—; v.p. Brainstorm, Inc., Dallas, 1984-86; pres. Body Telesis, Inc., 1987-88; v.p. Staffelbach Designs Inc., 1988—. Republican. Home: 3515 Brown St Apt 109 Dallas TX 75219 Office: 2525 Carlisle Dallas TX 75201

SMITH, BARBARA ANNE, corporate administrator; b. N.Y.C., Oct. 10, 1941; d. John Allen and Lelia Maria (De Silva) Santoro; m. Joseph Newton Smith, Feb. 5, 1961 (div. Sept. 1984); children: J. Michael, Robert Lawrence. Student, Oceanside/Carlsbad Coll. Real estate agt. Routh Robbins, Inc., Washington, 1973-75; gen. mgr. Mall Shops, Inc., Kansas City, Kans., 1975-80; regional mgr. FAO Schwarz, N.Y.C., 1980-84; clin. adminstr. North Denver Med. Ctr., Thornton, Colo., 1984-88; adminstrv. dir. Country Side Ambulatory Surgery Ctr., Leesburg, Va., 1989—; bd. dirs. Franz Carl Weber Internat., Geneva, 1982-84. Pres. Am. Women Chile, 1968; v.p. Oak Park Assn., Kansas City, 1977-78, pres., 1978-79. Mem. NAFE, Network Colo., Profl. Bus. Women Assn., Med. Group Mgmt. Assn., Federated Ambulatory Surgery Assn.

SMITH, BARBARA D., biochemistry educator; b. Boston, Mar. 17, 1943; d. Saul and Marcia (Rosen) Davis; m. J. David Smith, Sept. 5, 1964 (div. Mar. 1981); children: Steven Douglas, Sharon Elise; m. Laurence Krager Koff, Nov. 5, 1983; 1 child, Daniel Solomon. BS, Simmons Coll., 1964; MA, Boston U., 1966, PhD, 1970. Postdoctoral fellow Washington U., St. Louis, 1967-68, Retina Found., Boston, 1969-70; instr. Lasell Jr. Coll., Auburndale, Mass., 1970-71; rsch. chemist NIDR, NIH, Bethesda, Md., 1971-76; asst. prof. Boston U. Sch. of Medicine, 1976-84; rsch. biochemist VA Outpatient Clinic, Boston, 1976—; assoc. prof. Boston U. Sch. of Medicine, 1984—. Contbr. articles to profl. jours. Recipient grants NIH-NCI, 1978—, NIH-NIBLI, 1988—, others. Mem. Am. Soc. Biology and Molecular Biology, Am. Soc. Cell Biology, Am. Chem. Soc., AAAS, N.Y. Acad. Sci., Sigma Xi. Office: Boston Univ Sch Medicine 80 E Concord St Boston MA 02118

SMITH, BARBARA GAIL, economist; b. Phoenix, June 6, 1957; d. Loren Leonard Smith and Geneva May (Gabbert) Hewlett. BS in Environ. Sci., Grand Canyon Coll., 1979; postgrad., Ariz. State U. Power supply analyst Ariz. Pub. Service, Phoenix, 1981-84, rate devel. analyst, 1984-86, regulatory economist, 1986—; team supr. RGIS Inventory Services, 1981-83, Phoenix, tng. cons., 1982-85; profl. pianist, Phoenix, 1976—; free lance arranger, Phoenix, 1981—. Vol. Nat. Cancer Soc., Nat. Red Cross. Named Girl of the Yr. Ariz. Red Cross, 1974, one of Outstanding Young Women Am., 1979. Mem. Nat. Assn. Female Execs., Ariz. Bus. Women's Assn., Alpha Chi. Republican. Baptist. Home: 1449 E Highland #2 Phoenix AZ 85014 Office: 400 N 5th St Phoenix AZ 85004

SMITH, BARBARA GALLAER, nutritionist; b. Staten Island, N.Y., Feb. 22, 1961; d. George A. and Joan (Lyons) G.; m. David B. Smith, Mar. 17, 1990. BS in Clin. Nutrition, Syracuse (N.Y.) U., 1983. Clin. dietitian Nassau County Med. Ctr., East Meadow, N.Y., 1983-86; clin. dietitian NYU Med. Ctr., N.Y.C., 1986-87, sr. nutritionist, 1987—; nutritionist South Shore Diabetes Cons., Massapequa, N.Y., 1989—; guest speaker Sta. WCBS, N.Y.C., 1989—; speaker Cen. Gen. Hosp., Plainview, N.Y., 1990, Banker's Trust, N.Y.C., 1990. Mem. Am. Dietetic Assn., Am. Assn. Diabetes Educators, Greater N.Y. Dietetic Assn. (chairperson pub. rels. com. 1989). Home: 875 Blvd E Apt #39 Weehawken NJ 07087

SMITH, BARBARA JEANNE, library administrator; b. Jersey Shore, Pa., Apr. 14, 1939; d. Moyer Emerson and Mary Kathryn (Ebner) S. BS, Pa. State U., 1961; MS, SUNY, Oswego, 1967; MLS, U. Pitts., 1970; DEd, Pa. State U., 1981. Cert. secondary sch. tchr. Tchr. Binghamton (N.Y.) Sch. Dist., 1961-62, North Syracuse (N.Y.) Cen. Schs., 1962-69; reference librarian Pa. State Libraries, University Park, 1970-75, dept. head, 1975-82, asst. dean., 1982-89; grad. faculty prof. edn. Pa. State U., University Park, 1984-89; regional dir. U.S. Newspaper Project/NEH, University Park, 1985-87; dir. Smithsonian Instn. Libraries, 1989—. Contbr. articles to profl. jours. Life mem. Centre County Hist. Soc., State College, Pa., 1975—; mem. Friends of the Mus., State College, 1975—; bd. dirs. Georgetown Homeowner's Assn., State College, 1975-82; trustee Pitts. Regional Library Ctr., 1978-89. UCLA sr. fellow, 1982. Mem. ALA (coun. mem. 1988—), Assn. Coll. and Rsch. Libraries (chair com. on standards and accreditation 1984-86), Pa. Library Assn. (various offices 1976-89), AAUW, D.C. Library Assn., Phi Delta Kappa. Republican. Office: Smithsonian Instn Librs NHB22 Washington DC 20560

SMITH, BARBARA JOYCE, quality assurance professional, consultant; b. Pasadena, Calif., Feb. 25, 1954; d. Philip L. and Barbar J. (Douglass) S. BS in Med. Records Adminstrn., York Coll. of Pa., 1977. Cert. profl. in quality assurance; registered records adminstr. Quality assurance mgr. The Consortium, Phila., 1980-86; pres. Quality Assurance Resources, Phila., 1984—, coord. quality mgmt. program; coord. quality mgmt. program Sacred Heart Med. Ctr. Mem. Nat. Assn. Female Execs., Nat. Assn. Quality Assurance Profls., Southeastern Pa. Assn. Quality Assurance Profls. Home: 332 S 17th St Apt 3-A Philadelphia PA 19103

SMITH, BARBARA RODERICK, health and social services administrator; b. Peoria, Ill., Mar. 5, 1948; d. Fremont August and Jessie May (Burdess) Roderick; m. Ronald Nelson Smith, June 18, 1976; children: Yvette, Roderick, Jennifer. Student, Peoria Sch. Practical Nursing, 1967-68; assoc., Ill. Cen. Coll. Registered Nursing, 1971; BS, Coll. St. Francis, Joliet, 1981; postgrad., U. Ill., 1985-90, U. Iowa, LaSalle U., 1990—. Cert. sch. nurse; lic. social worker. Med. coord. Covenant Children's Home, Princeton, Ill.; cons. Donna Home Care, Bartonville, Ill.; nursing cons. Rose Shelter, Peoria; adminstr. health svc. Cath. Social Svc., Peoria; guest speaker St. Francis Coll. Nursing, Ill. State U. Mem. subcom. on nursing Forward Peoria; adv. com. Dept. Children and Family Svc. Home: 4913 S Alaska Bartonville IL 61607

SMITH, BERNICE DRISKELL, educator, writer; b. Fort Gaine, Ga., Feb. 27, 1916; d. Joseph A. Stanford and Mary (Agusta) Mount-Stanford; m. Abner Guy Smith (dec. 1934); 1 child, Marline Virginia Smith (dec.); m. William J. Smith, Apr. 19, 1947. BS, Fla. A&M U., 1970; cert., Oxford U., Eng., 1985. Cert. reading specialist, Tallahassee Bd. Edn. Magnetflux inspector USAF, Middletown, Pa., 1943-44; tchr. typing and shorthand Phila. Bus. Sch., 1945-50; asst. to dean of men Del. State Coll., Dover, 1960; girls counselor Morgan U., Balt., 1962, Bowie (Md.) State Coll., 1963; tchr. Phila. Bd. Edn., 1970-83; creative writing tchr. Bartlett Elem. Sch., 1978-79; lectr. poetry writing various schs. Author: (children's books) Pink Satin, 1963 (Writer of Yr. 1963), Company for thanksgiving, 1967, Bonny Squirrel and Mrs. Boyette, 1980, Shellbby Rumford, The Happy Rabbit, 1984, (poems) Shadopa, 1989. Named Writer of Yr. WWRL Radio and Sashstones, 1963, Community Hall of Fame WWRL Radio, 1963; recipient 2 awards for community svc. Chapel of Four Chaplains, 1963, 2 awards for svc. to children and schs. Belmount and Pallumbo Schs. Bds. of Edn., 1973. Mem. AAUW, Internat. Platform Assn. (book on display 1985), Nat. Profl. Writer's Club, Women's Way, Eastern Star Lodge, Zeta Phi Beta (sec., Woman of Yr. 1988), Kappa Omega Zeta (sec.). Republican. Baptist. Home: 6003 W Columbia Ave Philadelphia PA 19151

SMITH, BERT KRUGER, mental health services professional, consultant; b. Wichita Falls, Tex., Nov. 18, 1915; d. Sam and Fania (Feldman) Kruger; m. Sidney Stewart Smith, Jan. 19, 1936; children: Sheldon Stuart, Jared Burt (dec.), Randy Smith Huke. BJ, U. Mo., 1936; MA, U. Tex., 1949, DHL (hon.), 1985. Soc. and entertainment editor Wichita Falls Post, 1936-37; freelance writer Juneau, Alaska, 1937; assoc. editor Jr. Coll. Jour., Austin, Tex., 1952-55; spl. cons., exec. Hogg Found. for Mental Health, Austin, 1952—; chmn. bd. Austin Groups for the Elderly, 1985—. Author: No Language But A Cry, 1964, Your Non-Learning Child, 1968, A Teaspoon of Honey, 1970, Insights for Uptights, 1970, Aging in America, 1973, Looking Forward, 1983; contbr. numerous articles to profl. jours. Recipient Disting. Svc. award City of Austin, 1988, Cert. of Appreciation, Tex. Dept. Human Svcs., 1989, Ann. Bert Smith award Sr.'s Respite Svc., 1989; named to Tex. Women's Hall of Fame, 1988. Mem. Am. Fedn. for Aging Rshc., Adult Svc. Coun. (bd. dirs. 1970—), Family Eldercare (bd. dirs. 1979—), Author's Guild, Women in Communications, Inc., NAt. Assn. for Sci. Writers, Delta Kappa Gamma Soc. (hon.). Jewish. Home: 5818 Westslope Dr Austin TX 78731 Office: Hogg Found Mental Health PO Box 7998 Austin TX 78713-7998

SMITH, BETH ROBERTA, public safety media and public information officer; b. Detroit, Apr. 28, 1959; d. Richard Norton and Agnes Nancy Aitchison (Young) Chapman; 1 child, Stephanie Logan. Assoc. in Law Enforcement, Schoolcraft Community Coll., Livonia, Mich., 1979; BA in Criminal Justice, Mich. State U., 1981. Police dispatcher dept. pub. safety Mich. State U., East Lansing, 1981-87; media & pub. info. officer dept. pub. safety Mich. State U., 1987—; labor rep. Fraternal Order of Police, Lansing, Mich., 1983-85, 87—; advisor, v.p. fin., personnel and ops. Mich. State U. Women's Adv. Com., 1987—. Mem. Mich. State U. Bus. Women's Assn., Mich. State U. Coalition Labor Orgns., Fraternal Order of Police (exec. bd. 1987—). Republican. Roman Catholic. Office: Mich State Univ Dept Pub Safety Red Cedar Rd East Lansing MI 48823-1219

SMITH, BETSEY CLARK, occupational therapist; b. Gloucester, Mass., Apr. 17, 1957; d. Roland Henry and Virginia Hubbard (Parsons) Smith. BS in Occupational Ther., Quinnipiac Coll., Hamden, Conn., 1979; MS, U. Conn., 1986. Staff occupational therapist Ipswich (Mass.) Pub. Schs., 1979-81; cons. Cape Ann Nursing Home, Gloucester, 1979-81; occupational therapist coordinator Inst. of Living, Hartford, Conn., 1981-90; acting dir. occupational therapy program U. Hartford, West Hartford, Conn., 1988—, asst. prof., dir. occupational therapy program, 1990—; cons. Bristol Hosp., 1990—; cons., speaker, presenter workshops in field. Mem. editorial bd. Occupational Therapy Practice, 1989. Bd. dirs. single's program 1st Ch. of Christ, Wethersfield, Conn., 1984. Mem. Am. Occupational Therapy Assn. (regional faculty mem. 1986, panel of experts 1987), Conn. Occupational Therapy Assn. (mental health liaison 1984-86, pres. 1986—, com. state assn. pres. 1986—). Office: U Hartford Bloomfield Ave West Hartford CT 06117

SMITH, BETTY LORETTA, artist; b. Tulare, Calif., Feb. 2, 1937; d. Arthur L. and Mary Alice (Etier) Thweatt; m. Harry T. Webb (div. 1968); 1 child, Margo V. Tackett; m. Maurice J. Smith (dec.); 1 child, Betty Josephine Alexandra. Pink lady Fallbrook (Calif.) Hosp. Aux., 1980—; leader Girl Scouts, Fallbrook, 1985—; trustee, dir. M.J. Smith Trust, San Diego, 1980—; vol. Presdl. Task Force, Washington, 1983-86, lifetime mem. Mem. Nat. Orgn. Female Execs. (charter), Nat. Parks and Conservation Assn., AARP, Green Peace. Republican.

SMITH, BILLIE NELL BRYSON, nurse; b. Linden, Tenn., May 29, 1933; d. Barney Lee and Julia Mae (Hufstedler) Bryson; grad. St. Thomas Sch. Nursing, Nashville, 1955; m. Lee Garry Smith, Aug. 20, 1960; children—Lee Garry. Office nurse for Drs. G.H. Turner and B.L. Holladay, Linden, Tenn., 1955-56; dir. nursing Perry County Hosp., Linden, 1956-80, inservice dir., 1956-80; staff nurse, charge nurse Perry Meml. Hosp., Linden, Tenn., 1980—. Vol. nurse for mass polio vaccination Pub. Health Dept., 1963, 64; vol. nurse Am. Nat. Red Cross, 1955—. Licensed Tenn. Bd. Nursing. Mem. Tenn. Hosp. Assn., Tenn. Assn. Nursing Service Dirs., St. Thomas Sch. of Nursing Alumni Assn. Home: Route 4 Box 232 Linden TN 37096 Office: Perry Meml Hosp Squirrel Hollow Dr Linden TN 37096

SMITH, BONNIE BEATRICE, utilities executive; b. Dayton, Ohio, July 22, 1948; d. Joseph Edward and Phyllis Jean (Shook) S. BS in Journalism, Ohio U., 1970. Accredited bus. communicator. Reporter Piqua (Ohio) Daily Call, 1970-71; asst. dir. pub. rels. Bethesda Hosps., Cin., 1971-76; dir. communication St. Joseph's Hosp., Ft. Wayne, Ind., 1976-81; publs. editor E. Ohio Gas Co., Cleve., 1981-88, coord. customer communications, 1988-90; mgr. employee communications and wellness programs Picker Internat., Highland Heights, 1990—; speaker, seminar leader various hosps., bus. and profl. orgns., 1975—. Outreach vol. Cleve. Children's Mus., 1986-88, cochmn. outreach program, mem. speaker's bur., 1988-89, mem. pub. rels. task force, 1989—. Recipient numerous awards Ohio Hosp. Assn., Ohio Press Women, Acad. Hosp. Pub. Rels., Cin. Editors Assn., also others. Mem. Internat. Assn. Bus. Communicators (dir. mem. svcs. internal communications coun. 1985-88, chmn. directory mktg. coun. 1988—, dir. examiners accreditation bd. 1986-88), numerous awards 1975—). Home: 1700 E 13th St Apt 22S Cleveland OH 44114 Office: Picker Internat Inc 595 Miner Rd Highland Heights OH 44143

SMITH, CAROL ANN, lawyer; b. Birmingham, Ala., Apr. 23, 1949; d. James William and Mildred Viola (Ferguson) S. B.A., Birmingham So. Coll., 1971; J.D., U. Ala.-Tuscaloosa, 1975; LL.M., NYU, 1977. Bar: Ala. 1975, U.S. Dist. Ct. (no. dist.) Ala. 1977, U.S. Dist. Ct. (mid. dist.) Ala. 1976, U.S. Ct. Appeals (11th cir.) 1981, U.S. Ct. Appeals (5th cir.) 1979. Law clk. Ala. Supreme Ct., Montgomery, 1975-76; assoc. Lange, Simpson, Robinson & Somerville, Birmingham, 1977-81; assoc. Starnes & Atchison, Birmingham, 1981-83, ptnr., 1983—. Editorial bd. Ala. Law Rev., 1973-75. Mem. bd. mgmt. Metro YMCA, Birmingham, 1984—, exec. com., 1989. Mem. Birmingham Bar Assn. (pres. young lawyers sect. 1984), Ala. Bar Inst. for Continuing Legal Edn. (exec. com. 1979—), Ala. Def. Lawyers Assn. (bd. dirs. 1988—), Ala. Bar Assn. (editorial bd. The Ala. Lawyer 1979-88, assoc. editor 1984-88, exec. com. young lawyers sect. 1983-84, chmn. continuing legal edn. com. of young lawyers sect. 1984, mem. pres.'s adv. task foce 1984-85), 11th Cir. Jud. Conf. (alt. del. 1985-87), Phi Beta Kappa. Methodist. Club: Birmingham Jr. Music Bd. Home: 1511 Ridge Rd Homewood AL 35209 Office: Starnes & atchison 4 Metroplex Dr 7th Fl PO Box 598512 Birmingham AL 35259-8512

SMITH, CAROL ANN, music therapist, psychologist; b. Montgomery County, Tenn., Apr. 19, 1951; d. Carl and Ruth (Gettinger) S.; B.M.E. in Music Therapy, U. Kans., 1974; M.A. in Clin. Psychology, Mid. Tenn. State U., 1977; Ed.S. in Human Service Mgmt.; Vanderbilt U., 1979. Gen. therapeutic recreation specialist VA Med. Ctr., Murfreesboro, Tenn., 1973-79; music therapist VA Med. Ctr., Marion, Ind., 1979; chief, recreation therapy service VA Med. Ctr., Tucson, 1979-84; chief recreation therapy VA Med. Ctr., Northport, N.Y., 1984-87 ; Health Systems Specialist, Dir.'s Office, VA Med. Ctr., Cleve., 1987-88, adminstrv. asst. to assoc. dir., 1988—; adj. instr. Mid. Tenn. State U., part-time 1978—; guest speaker, 1975—; Mem. Am. Psychol. Assn. (assoc.), Nat. Assn. Music Therapy (cert.), NAFE, Am. Mgmt. Assn., Pi Lambda Theta. Democrat. Methodist. Contbr. articles to profl. jours. Home: 5800 Laurent Dr Apt 322 Parma OH 44129 Office: VA Med Ctr 10701 E Blvd Cleveland OH 44106

SMITH, CAROL TAYLOR, advertising agency executive; b. Benham, Ky., Oct. 6, 1935; d. John Milburn and Acsa Margaret (Hart) Taylor; m. Win Chester Smith, June 27, 1959; children: Brad Taylor, Lee Smith Rouda. Student, Edinburgh U., 1955-56; BMus., De Pauw U., 1957. Owner, prin. Carol Smith Assocs., Danville, Ill., 1982—. Author: Danville Lifestyle, 1984, Champaign-Urbana Lifestyle, 1988. Pres., bd. dirs. Danville Symphony Orch., 1978-82; chmn. Danville Civic Ctr. Authority, 1978-82; organizer Balloon Classic Ill., 1988—; mem. exec. com. Ill. Arts Coun., 1980-84; bd. dirs. Am. Symphony Orch. League, 1978-82, Vermilion Heritage Found., 1988—. Recipient 1st dist. award Coll. Sports Info. Dirs. Am., 1985, 3d nat. award, 1985; named Woman of the Yr. for 1989, Danville Bus. and Profl. Women's Club. Mem. Am. Soc. Advt. and Promotion, Advt. Club Champaign (bd. dirs. 1987), Ill. Devel. Council, Danville C. of C. (bd. dirs. 1989—), Champaign-Urbana C. of C. Republican. Lodge: Rotary. Office: 406 N Sheridan St Danville IL 61832

SMITH, CAROLE JEAN, banker; b. Russellville, Ark., Aug. 23, 1949; d. Garland Dee and Elmo (Williamson) Nichols. BSBA in Mktg., U. Ark., 1971, MBA, 1972; cert., Am. Inst. Banking, 1976; M in Banking, So. Meth. U., 1980. Mgmt. auditor U.S. GAO, St. Louis, 1972-73; asst. v.p. First Nat. Bank, Little Rock, 1973-80; v.p. Republic Bank and Trust, Tulsa, 1980-83; sr. v.p. Worthen Bank and Trust Co., Little Rock, 1983—; instr. banking Systematics, Inc., Little Rock, 1980—; mng. dir. Worthen Profl. Women's Adv. Bd., Little Rock, 1986—; dir., gen. mgr. Worthen Fin. and Investment, Inc., Little Rock, 1986—; bd. dirs. mid-south chpt., cen. Ark. chpt. Robert Morris Assocs., 1986—; mem. edn. standards com. Ark. State Bd. Accountancy,, 1986—. Bd. dirs. Ballet of Ark., 1986, Leadership Inst., 1986, Multiple Schlerosis, 1987, Ark. chpt. March of Dimes, 1990; mem. com. Fair and Rep. Govt., Little Rock, 1987. Recipient Pres.'s award Civitan Internat., 1977; named Ark. Outstanding Young Career Women, 1977, one of Outstanding Young Women Am., 1979. Mem. Assn. Female Execs., Little Rock C. of C. (com. chair 1987), Kappa Kappa Gamma Alumni Assn. Democrat. Methodist. Club: Pleasant Valley Country. Home: 4712 Kavanaugh Blvd Little Rock AR 72207 Office: Worthen Bank & Trust Co 200 W Capitol Little Rock AR 72201

SMITH, CAROLYN JEAN, educator; b. Glendale, Calif., Apr. 6, 1950; d. Martin Harry and Aleta Dorothy Smith. BA with honors, U. Calif., Riverside, 1972. Tchr. Rowland Unified, Rowland Heights, Calif., 1973-75, St. Marks Luth. Sch., Hacienda Heights, Calif., 1975-77, Calvary Christian Sch., Ontario, 1977-78, Victory Christian Sch., Pasadena, Calif., 1978-79, Pla-Skool in the Pines, La Habra, Calif., 1980-81, Montesssori Sch., Rowland Heights, 1981-83, Los Angeles Unified, 1983--. Composer (song) Songs of Praise and Worship, 1988. Pres. Miss Softball Am., Covina Hills League, 1971-72. Mem. Nat. Educators Assn., Coun. for Exceptional Children. Office: LA Unified Sch 1626 S Orchard St Los Angeles CA 90006

SMITH, CAROLYN JEAN, chemistry educator; b. Fitzgerald, Ga.; d. Thomas V. and Mildred (Ray) S.; m. James F. Weiher, Oct. 26, 1975. AB, Mercer U., 1959; PhD, Emory U., 1962. Rsch. chemist El du Pont de Nemours, Wilmington, Del., 1962-70; asst. prof. Lincoln (Pa.) U., 1972-73; assoc. prof. Cheyney (Pa.) State Coll., 1976-83; prof. Delaware County Community Coll., Media, Pa., 1984—. Contbg. author: World Book Ency., 1983—; author: Lab Experiences for Chemistry of the Environment, 1985; co-author: Lab Manual-General Chemistry I, 1986, Lab Manual for Introduction to Chemistry, 1987. Bd. dirs. Pinecrest Maintainence Corp.,

Wilmington, 1984—. Office: Delaware County Community Coll Media PA 19063

SMITH, CAROLYN LOUISE, retail manager, writer; b. Detroit, June 20, 1960; d. Charles Dominic and Helen Cecelia (Barsack) S. BS, Mich. State U., 1983. Mgr. Winkelman's, Canton, Mich., 1983—; caregiver Hospice, Naugatuck, Conn., 1986-88; tchr. Head Start, Lansing, 1982-83. Mem. AAUW (legis. chmn. 1985-88, program v.p. 1989—). Republican. Roman Catholic. Home: 1100 N Denwood Dearborn MI 48128 Office: Winkelman's 44540 Ford Rd Canton MI 48170

SMITH, CAROLYN SUE, oil company executive; b. Doeran, Ga., Feb. 17, 1944; d. James Washington and Corrie Irene (Hufstetler) Gunn; m. Jack Samuel Smith Sr., Apr. 3, 1942; children: Jack, Jill, Jody, John. Grad., Worth County High Sch., 1962. Lic. real estate. Program asst. USDA-ASCS Office, Moultrie, Ga., 1973-76; exec. Lubrico, Inc., Albany, Ga., 1977-83; owner, chief exec. officer S.E. Oil & Grease Co., Inc., Albany, 1983—. Mem. Women Bus. Owners, Nat. Lubricating Grease Inst., Am. Soc. Lubrication Engrs., Women In Constrn. Republican. Baptist. Lodge: Elks. Home: PO Box 4340 Albany GA 31706 Office: SE Oil & Grease Co Inc PO Box 4897 Albany GA 31706

SMITH, CAROLYN SUE, program executive; b. Houston, July 8, 1943; d. Alfred Lafayette and Fauvette Vivian (Thorne) Kemper; m. Harold Lee Smith, Mar. 5, 1966; children: Dana Suzanne, Keisha Fauvette. BS, Tuskegee Inst., 1965. Research chemist Baylor Coll. Medicine, Houston, 1965-71; sales rep. Nat. Cosmetics Co., Houston, 1971-78; dir. Harris County Voter Registration Group, Houston, 1978; sr. staff asst. U.S. House Reps., Houston, 1979-87; council coordinator City of Houston, 1987-89; mng. dir. Inroads/Houston, Inc., 1989—; coord. Tex. R.R. Commr., Houston, 1988; staff coord. Econ. Redevel. Revitalization Com., Houston, 1987-89. Vol. Congl. Black Caucas Found., Washington, 1987, Melody Ellis Sch. Bd. Campaign, Houston, 1987, Harold Washington for Mayor Campaign, Chgo., 1989; liaison YMCA Bd., Houston, 1989, mem. bd. , 1990. Recipient Outstanding Community Svc. award Gulf Coast Community Svc., 1988. Mem. NAFE, Leland Kibbutz Bd., Gulf Coast Community Svc. Bd., Jack & Jill of Am., Black Polit. Women's Congress (fin. sec. 1986-87). Democrat. Home: 5103 Knotty Oaks Trail Houston TX 77045 Office: Inroads/Houston Inc 1331 Lamar Ste 570 Houston TX 77010

SMITH, CASSANDRA LYNN, geneticist, educator; b. N.Y.C., May 25, 1947; d. Walter Smith and Natalie (Bluestone) Smith Nolan; m. Walter Klemperer (div. 1978). BS in Biology, W.Va. U., 1967, MS in Med. Microbiology, 1970; PhD in Genetics, Tex. A&M U., 1974. Postdoctoral fellow NIH, 1974; rsch. assoc. Columbia U., N.Y.C., 1978-87, asst. prof., 1987-89; assoc. prof. U. Calif., Berkeley, 1988—; sr. scientist Lawrence Berkeley Lab., 1989—; cons. FMC Corp., Phila., 1986—, Pharmacia-LKB, Stockholm, 1986—, Boehringer-Mannheim Gmb, Penzberg, Fed. Republic of Germany, 1990—. Editor: Genomics; Genetic Analysis: Techniques and Applications; Human Genome Abstracts; author numerous sci. articles. NIH grantee, 1978. Mem. Am. Soc. for Microbiology, Genetics Soc. Am., Am. Soc. Biochemistry and Molecular Biology, Am. Soc. Human Genetics, Internat. Human Genome Orgn., Harvey Soc. Office: Human Genome Ctr Lawrence Berkeley Lab Berkeley CA 94720

SMITH, CATHERINE HAMILTON, magazine editor; b. London, May 6, 1953; came to U.S., 1957; d. Howard Kingsbury and Benedicte (Traberg) S.; m. Dennis Roland Jolicoeur, Aug. 27, 1983. BA, Wesleyan U., 1975. Reporter The Argus Champion, Newport, N.H., 1975, Salem (Mass.) Evening News, 1976; writer Sta. WJLA-TV, Washington, 1977; news dir., reporter Sta. WNOR-AM-FM, Norfolk, Va., 1977-78; reporter Sta. WBAY-TV, Green Bay, Wis., 1978-79, Sta. WJAR-TV, Providence, 1979-80, Sta. WJXT-TV, Jacksonville, Fla., 1980-83; editor Bus. N.H. mag., Manchester, 1984-88, editor-in-chief, 1988—; editor Original New Eng. Guide, Manchester, 1988—, New Eng. Living mag., Manchester, 1989—. Office: New Eng Lifestyle Publs Inc 177 E Industrial Dr Manchester NH 03103

SMITH, CELIA MARIE, sales executive; b. Joplin, Mo., Nov. 25, 1944; d. Cecil Alonza and Thelma Leon (McIntosh) Thornhill; m. Kimball Trent Smith, Feb. 26, 1965 (div. 1976); children: Tobin Marie, Brett Kimball. Student, U. Kans., 1962-65. Mgr. Life Uniforms, Omaha, Nebr., 1973-75; dir. sales Uniform Shoppe, Tulsa, Okla., 1975-78; sales assoc. Am. Family Life, Tulsa, 1978-79; dist. mgr. sales Am. Family Life, 1979-81; sales assoc. Am. Family Life, Houston, 1981-83, San Deigo, 1983-86; sr. account exec. Health Plan Am., San Diego, 1986—. Ticket mgr. collesium L.A. Olympic Organizing Com., 1984; pres. New Neighbors League, Omaha, 1974. Mem. San Diego Women in Ins. Assn., San Diego C. of C., Ind. Ins. Agts. and Brokers Assn., Convention and Visitors Bur., Bus. Women's Assn., Entrepreneur Club. Home: 455 G Ave Coronado CA 92118

SMITH, CELIANNE MARIE, sports medicine professional; b. New Bedford, Mass., Aug. 5, 1953; d. Richard Gerrard and Cecile Pauline (Charbonneau) S. BS, Springfield Coll., 1975, MEd, 1976; postgrad., Northwestern U., 1986. Head athletic trainer Clark U., Worcester, Mass., 1976-79; sports medicine coord. SUNY, Oneonta, N.Y., 1979—; SUNY cons. Otsego Orthopedics, Oneonta, 1982—; bd. dirs. Irish Intersession, Oneonta, N.Y., 1982—. Bd. dirs. Otsego Found., Oneonta N.Y. Mem. Nat. Athletic Trainers Assn., Am. Coll. of Sports, Medicine, Am. Bd. of Cert. in Orthotics, Eastern Athletic Trainers Assn. Roman Catholic. Office: SUNY Oneonta Health and Phys Edn Bld Oneonta NY 13820

SMITH, CHARLOTTE DUNCAN, insurance holding company executive; b. Bogalusa, La., July 31, 1938; d. Prather Wesley Duncan and Cleo Louise (Scroggs) Sticker; m. Melvin Ray Smith, Apr. 23, 1956 (div. 1960); children: Wanda Louise Kelly, Melvin Wade. Student, Elizabeth Sullivan Meml., 1959-61, La. State U., 1964. Office mgr. Cutrer Ins. Agy., Bogalusa, La., 1958-63; office mgr. R.M. Cochran Co., Ltd., Baton Rouge, 1964-79, also bd. dirs.; casualty underwriter Hearin-Collins Ins. Agy., Baton Rouge, 1963-64; sr. exec. v.p. Protective Holding Corp., Baton Rouge, 1979—, Protective Casualty Ins. Co., Baton Rouge, 1979—, Protective Mgmt. Corp., Baton Rouge, 1979—, Protective Adjustment Co., Baton Rouge, 1979—; first v.p. Nat. Risk Retention Assn., 1989—; bd. dirs. Protective Holding Corp. and all subs. Author ins. policies and fidelity bonds; contbr. articles to profl. jours. Mem. fin. com. Richard Baker for Congress, Baton Rouge, 1986-87. Named Boss of Yr., Denham Springs Coop. Office Edn., 1978. Mem. La. Assn. Fire and Casualty Cos. (bd. dirs. 1984—), Nat. Council on Compensation Ins. (LA rating and classification com.), Nat. Risk Retention Assn. (founding dir., treas.). Democrat. Baptist. Home: 13011 Dorset Ave Baton Rouge LA 70818 Office: Protective Casualty Ins Co PO Box 80293 Baton Rouge LA 70898

SMITH, CHARLOTTE REED, educator; b. Eubank, Ky., Sept. 15, 1921; d. Joseph Lumpkin and Cornelia Elizabeth (Spenser) Reed; m. Walter Lindsay Smith, Aug. 24, 1949; children—Walter Lindsay IV, Elizabeth Reed. B.A. in Music, Tift Coll., 1941; M.A. in Mus. Theory, Eastman Sch. of Music, 1946; postgrad. Juilliard Sch., 1949. Asst. prof. theory Okla. Bapt. U., 1944-45, Washburn U., 1946-48; prof. music Furman U., Greenville, S.C., 1948—; chmn. dept. music, 1987— . Editor: Seven Penitential Psalms with Two Laudate Psalms, 1983; author: Manual of Sixteenth-Century Contrapuntal Style, 1989. Mem. Internat. Musicological Soc., Am. Musicological Soc., Soc. for Music Theory, AAUP (sec.-treas. Furman chpt. 1984-85), Nat. Fedn. Music Clubs, Pi Kappa Lambda. Republican. Baptist. Office: Furman U Poinsett Hwy Greenville SC 29613

SMITH, CHARLOTTE THERESE WERTZ, legal research director; b. Springfield, Ill., July 11, 1959. BS in Music Edn., Duquesne U., 1980, JD, 1987. Cert. paralegal. Tchr. Resurrection Sch., Pitts., 1980-81; paralegal Dickie, McCamey & Chilcote, P.C., Pitts., 1981-87; dir. legal rsch. Assn. Trial Lawyers Am., Washington, 1988—; instr. paralegal program U. Md., 1988—, faculty paralegal program. Author: (pamphlet) So You Want to be a Paralegal, 1983; editor Nat. Paralegal Reporter, 1984-85. Mem. Pitts. Paralegal Assn. (pres. 1985-86, treas. 1983-85), Law Librs. Soc. Washington, Am. Soc. Notaries, Am. Assn. Paralegal Edn. Office: Assn Trial Lawyers Am 1050 31st St NW Washington DC 20007

SMITH, CHERYL LYNN, copy editor, writer, reporter; b. Newark, June 20, 1958; d. Joseph and Earline Elizabeth (Gadson) S. BS in Journalism, Fla. A&M U., 1980; MS in Human Rels. and Bus., Amber U., 1986, postgrad. 1987-88. Exec. editor Capital Outlook News, Tallahassee, 1980-81; nat. prodn. coord. TV Watch of Scripps Howard, Dallas, 1981-82; mktg. compliance assoc. J.C. Penney Ins. Co., Dallas, 1983-84; prodn. asst. Am. Equity Press, Dallas, 1984-86; copy editor Jaggars Chiles Stovall, Dallas, 1986-88; editor Dallas Weekly, 1988—; author play: Sizzlin Red and the Seven Dudes, 1981; editor newsletter Dallas Pan Hellenic Coun., 1986—. Mem. Nat. Coun. Negro Women, Dallas, 1982; active, sec. Just Friends: Pregnant Teenagers Support Group; rep. Dallas chpt. Nat. Pan Hellenic Coun., 1985—, sec. 1986-88. Named one of Outstanding Young Women in Am., 1983-88. Mem. NAACP, Dallas/Ft. Worth Assn. Black Communicators (sec.), Fla. Black Pubs. (rep. 1980-81), Fla. A&M U. Alumni Assn. (pres. local chpt. 1985—), Soc. Profl. Journalists, NAFE, Dallas Metroplex Council Black Alumni Assns. (media specialist 1987-88, pres.), Nat. Polit. Congress Black Women, Delta Sigma Theta (rep. local chpt. 1981—, Svc. award 1981, 85, one of Outstanding Young Women 1987-88). Democrat. Baptist. Avocations: reading, working with children, writing, dancing. Home: Box 45331 Dallas TX 75245

SMITH, CHRISTINE GAY, criminalist; b. Boise, Idaho, Sept. 6, 1963; d. Richard Eugene and Joan Betty (Miller) S. BA in Chemistry, BA in Gen. Studies, East Oreg. State Coll., 1986. Criminalist Oreg. State Police Crime Lab., Portland, 1987—. Mem. AAUW, Northwest Assn. Forensic Scientists, Internat. Assn. Arson Investigators, Calif. Assn. Toxicologists, Am. Chem. Soc. Republican. Methodist. Office: Oreg. State Police Crime Lab 1111 SW 2nd Ave 12th Fl Portland OR 97204

SMITH, CLARA F., retired elementary school educator; b. Flushing, Mich., Aug. 28, 1912; d. Arthur Milton and Anna Bell (Rush) Freeman; m. Russell Frederick Smith, Dec. 21, 1952; stepchildren: Margaret Ann, Adelaide Smith Harris, James Edward. BS, Ea. Mich. U., 1939; MA, Northwestern U., 1942; postgrad., Mich. State U., 1943; PhD, U. Mich., 1962. Instr. Nat. Coll. Edn., Evanston, Ill., 1943-45; asst. prof. Ea. Mich. U., Ypsilanti, 1946-63, Auburn (Ala.) U., 1965, Kent (Ohio) U., 1966-67, NE Mo. State Coll., Kirksville, 1969; elem. tchr. Lansing (Mich.) Pub. Schs., now ret. Author: A History of Lincoln Consolidated Schools and Its Contributions to Improvement of Rural Education, 1961-62. Bd. advisors ABIRA; internat. dir. Disting. Leadership; chmn. and treas. social svc. Thrift Shop Ypsilanti; mem. Habitat for Humanity, First Bapt. Ch., Ypsilanti; charter mem. Ronald Reagan Presdsl. Found.; mem. adv. bd. Am. Biog. Inst.; tchr. class-adult Sunday Sch.; vol. various civic orgns. Mem. MEA, NEA, Am. Assn. Ret. People, Washtenaw Area Ret. Pers., Mus. Women in Arts. Home: 1003 Pearl St Ypsilanti MI 48197-2705

SMITH, CONSTANCE CROUCH, corporate image consultant; b. Port Arthur, Tex., Aug. 30, 1946; d. John Larkin Crouch Jr. and Kathryn Alealia (Chambers) Beilharz; m. Hal Hardeman McAfee, June 11, 1966 (div. 1970); m. Edgar Robert Smith, July 22, 1972 (div. 1990); children: Megan Kathleen, Shannon Marie. Cert., Longbotham Bus. Coll., 1966, Kennesaw State Coll., 1987, Profl. Image Inst., 1988. Adminstrv. asst. MID Svcs. Corp., Houston, 1967-69, Bank of Southwest, Houston, 1969-71, Mazda Motors Tex., Houston, 1971-72, Am. Capital Corp., Houston, 1972-73; owner, pres. Smith Image Assocs., Marietta, 1987—. Tutor, Marietta City Schs., 1985-87. Mem. Am. Soc. Tng. and Devel., Sales and Mktg. Execs. Atlanta (dir. mem. meetings 1990, pub. edn. com. 1989, secretarial seminar chair 1989), Sales and Mktg. Execs. Internat., Ga. Assn. Image Cons. (v.p. pub. rels. 1987-89), Nat. Speakers Assn., Ga. Speakers Assn. Republican. Episcopalian. Office: Smith Image Assocs 878 Park Creek Ct Marietta GA 30064

SMITH, CYNTHIA LAFRENIERE, lawyer; b. Chgo., May 3, 1958; d. Lewellyn and Dolores Regina (Gagota) LaFreniere; m. Christopher Douglas Smith, Mar. 19, 1959. BA, Northeastern Ill. U., Chgo., 1980; JD, Pace U., 1987. Bars: N.Y. 1988, Conn. 1988. Atty. Whitman & Ransom, Greenwich, Conn., 1988—. Mem. ABA, N.Y. Bar Assn., Westchester County Bar Assn., Greenwich Bar Assn. Republican. Roman Catholic. Home: 2101 Regent Dr Mount Kisco NY 10549 Office: Whitman & Ransom 2 Greenwich Pla Greenwich CT 06830

SMITH, CYNTHIA LYNN, sales executive; b. Atlanta, Nov. 28, 1958; d. James Rayford and Patricia Anne (Adams) S. BS in Psychology, Ga. Southwestern Coll., 1980; postgrad., Mercer U., Atlanta, 1985-86, U. S. Fla., 1987—. Cashier The Kroger Co., Atlanta, 1975-80; staff supr. The Kroger Co., 1980-81; sales rep. Nestle Foods Corp., Atlanta, 1981-83, account mgr., 1983-85, unit mgr., 1985-86; confections mgr. Nestle Foods Corp., Tampa, 1987-88, nat. account mgr., 1989—. Vol. Child Abuse Coun., Tampa. Mem. NAFE, Tampa C. of C. Office: Nestle Foods 14497 N Dale Mabry Hwy #211 Tampa FL 33618

SMITH, DANA KAY, geophysicist; b. Lubbock, Tex., Nov. 2, 1959; d. Cletus Carroll and Ruby Joan (Myrick) Lewis; m. Mark Alan Smith, Jan. 1, 1984; 1 child, Nolan. BS in Geophys. Engring., Colo. Sch. Mines, 1982; MS in Applied Geophysics, So. Meth. U., 1987. Geophysicist Mobil Exploration and Producing Svcs., Inc., Dallas, 1982-89. Mem. Soc. Exploration Geophysicists (assoc.). Republican. Methodist.

SMITH, DARLENE, special education educator; b. Hackensack, N.J., Sept. 3, 1949; d. Sam and Elizabeth (Failla) DePiano; m. Thomas John Smith, Feb. 14, 1990. BA, Jersey City State Coll., 1971; MEd, Boston Coll., 1972; supr. cert., Montclair State Coll., 1984. Cert. tchr. of blind or partially sighted, tchr. of handicapped, elem. sch. tchr., peripatologist. Peripatologist Mt. Carmel Guild, Newark, 1972-73; peripatologist N.J. Commn. for Blind and Visually Impaired, Newark, 1974-83, Paterson, 1983-89; edn. supr. Meyer Ctr. N.J. Commn. for Blind and Visually Impaired, Newark, 1989—; chmn. mobility com. Travelaids for Blind, Paoli, Pa., 1980-87. Mem. Assn. Edn. and Rehab. Office: NJ Commn for Blind 232 Freling Auysen Ave Newark NJ 07114

SMITH, DEBORAH BAILEY, home economics educator; b. Rutherfordton, N.C., Feb. 13, 1959; d. Palmer Dean and Frances Ruth (Gettys) Bailey; m. Ricky Warren Smith, Apr. 9, 1983. BS in Home Econs., Western Carolina U., 1981. Tchr. math. Rutherford County Schs., Forest City, N.C., 1981-84; tchr. home econs. Rutherford County Schs., East Rutherford High Sch., 1984—; advisor Interclub Coun., Forest City, 1984—, Future Homemakers Am., Forest City, 1984—, Project Graduation, Forest City, 1987—; advisor student govt. East Rutherford High Sch., 1984—. Pianist Bethel Bapt. Ch., Ellenboro, N.C., 1984—; singer Withrow Singers, Ellenboro, 1984—. Mem. N.C. Vocat. Assn., Am. Home Econs. Assn. Democrat. Home: PO Box 636 Ellenboro NC 28040 Office: East Rutherford High Sch Cavalier Dr Forest City NC 28043

SMITH, DEBORAH RUTH, lawyer; b. Burnett, Tex., Nov. 19, 1961; d. Hal Ray and Aletta Earlene (Smith) S. BA, Tex. A&M, 1984; JD, St. Mary's U., San Antonio, 1988. Bar: Tex. 1988, U.S. Dist. Ct. (no. dist.) Tex. 1989. Assoc. Ragir & Assocs., Dallas, 1988-89; assoc. Jones, Day, Reavis & Pogue, Dallas, 1989—. Contbr. articles to CAI Bull., 1988, 89. Vol. Dallas Ctr. for Independent Living, 1988—, Greater Dallas C. of C., 1990—; textbook reader North Tex. Taping for the Blind, Dallas, 1988—. Mem. ABA, Tex. State Bar Assn. Republican. Mem. Ch. of Christ. Office: Jones Day Reavis & Pogue 2001 Ross Ave Dallas TX 75201

SMITH, DENISE BREWER, financial analyst; b. Chgo., May 28, 1959; d. Carl Rouzie and Janet Rosa (Brewer) Smith. BS magna cum laude, Purdue U., 1981; MBA, Harvard U., 1985. CPA, Ill. Auditor Ernst & Whinney, Chgo., 1981-83; sr. fin. analyst Amoco Corp., Chgo., 1985-86; pres. Brewer-Smith, Ltd. CPA's, Chgo., 1986—; instr. Loop Coll., Chgo., 1986-87. Creator (bd. game) Entrepreneurs and Raiders, 1987. Vol. tutor Ill. Literacy Council, Chgo., 1986—. Mem. Am. Inst. CPA's, Cosmopolitan C. of C. Office: Brewer-Smith Ltd 180 N Michigan Ave #407 Chicago IL 60601

SMITH, DENISE GROLEAU, data processing professional; b. Worcester, Mass., Feb. 7, 1951; d. Edmond Laurence and Audrey Mildred (Paquin) Groleau; m. Wayne Marshall Smith, Apr. 17, 1976; 1 child, Andrew. BSBA, Fitchburg State U., 1983. Bindery worker Atlantic Bus. Forms, Hudson, Mass., 1969-73; proofreader New Eng. Bus., Townsend, Mass., 1974-75; computer operator New Eng. Bus., Groton, Mass., 1975-80, adminstrv. asst. bus. systems, 1980-82, adminstrv. asst. info. ctr., 1982-85; info. ctr. analyst Wright Line Inc., Worcester, 1985-88; personal computer coord. Thom McAn Shoe Co., Worcester, 1988—; cons. personal computer Buckingham Transp., Groton, 1987-90. Mem. Nat. Assn. Female Execs. Home: 14 Cedar Circle Townsend MA 01469 Office: Thom McAn Shoe Co 67 Millbrook St Worcester MA 01606

SMITH, DENISE MILLER, screen printing company executive; b. Independence, La., Mar. 2, 1959; d. Charles Alton and Agnese (Vickers) Miller; m. Hobert W. Smith III, June 25, 1982; children: Cassie, Hobert IV, Addie. Student, Southeastern La. U., 1976-79. Sec., clk. Whites Auto Sales, Amite, La., 1976-81; cashier Winn Dixie Store, Amite, 1981; sec. Farm Bur. Ins. Co., Greensburg, La., 1981-83; owner, airbrush artist The T-Shirt Shop, Amite, 1984—. Youth leader Hillsdale Bapt. Ch., 1988. Mem. Cen. Bus. Dist. Amite. Republican. Home: Rte 3 Box 417S Amite LA 70422 Office: The T Shirt Shop 119 W Oak St Amite LA 70422

SMITH, DIANA, radiology technician; b. Winchester, Va., June 10, 1955; d. Richard Beverly and Dolores (Miller) Knight; children: Tiffany Michele, Jason Todd. Student, Handley high sch., Winchester, Va., 1973, Winchester Med. Ctr., Va., 1975. Cert. Am. Registry, Va. Cashier Red Barn, Winchester, Va., 1972-73; registered radiology Wytheville Med. Assn., Va., 1975; cat. scan tech. Winchester Med. Ctr., Va., 1976-85; registered radiological technol. Va. Med. Ctr., Martinsburg, WVa., cat scan tech, 1988--; chief tech. trainer for cat scan Va. Med. Ctr., Martinsburg, Va., 1988—; inser vice lectr. Cat Scan Va. Med. Ctr., Martinsburg, VA. Recipient Outstanding Performance award Winchester Med. Ctr., Va. 1975, Va. Med. Ctr. Martinsburg 1988, Incentive award for Highly Satisfactory Performance Va. Med. Ctr. Martinsburg 1987; Named Employee of the Month Martinsburg Va. 1988. Mem. Am. Registry of Radiologic Technol., Beta Sigma Phi Winchester Va. (V.P. 1987--), Epsilon BSP Winchester Va. (Pres. 1988--), Beta Sigma Phi Internat. Winchester Va. Methodist. Home: 225 Brunswick Rd Stephens City VA 22655

SMITH, DONNA KWALL, psychologist, educator; b. New Castle, Pa., Nov. 17, 1944; d. Saul A. and Clara (Sigal) Kwall; m. John T. Smith, Jr., Aug. 22, 1968; 1 child, Lauren Shana. AB, Chatham Coll., Pitts., 1966; MEd, U. Pitts., 1967, PhD, 1971. Nat. cert. sch. psychologist; cert. elem. tchr., in elem. guidance, sch. psychologist, Pa.; lic. psychologist, Pa. Assoc. dir. univ. residences U. Pitts., 1968-70; sch. psychologist Pitts. Pub. Schs., 1970-72; clin. psychologist ARIN Intermediate Unit 28, Shelocta, Pa., 1972-76, supr. psychol. svcs., 1976—; mem. faculty dept. ednl. psychology and psychology U. Pitts., St. Francis Coll., Loretto Coll., Indiana (Pa.) U. Pa., 1969—; pvt. practice, Indiana, 1974—; cons., spl. edn. auditor Pa. Dept. Edn., Harrisburg; presenter nat. profl. confs. Fellow Pa. Psychol. Assn.; mem. Am. Psychol. Assn., Nat. Assn. Sch. Psychologists, Assn. Sch. Psychologists Pa., Western Pa. Sch. Psychologists Assn., Pa. Suprs. Psychol. Svcs. (chmn. 1986—), Zonta, Delta Kappa Gamma. Home: 120 Cambridge St Indiana PA 15701 Office: ARIN Intermediate Unit Box 175 Shelocta PA 15774

SMITH, DONNA S., lawyer; b. Columbus, Miss., June 26, 1957; d. Newmon A. and Doris V. (Smith) S. BS, Miss. State U. for Women, 1983; JD, Miss. Coll., 1986. Bar: Miss. 1986, Ga. 1986. Assoc. Colom & Colom Law Firm, Columbus, 1986-87; prin. Donna S. Smith Law Firm, Columbus, 1987—. Mem. adv. bd. Lowndes County (Miss.) Youth Ct., 1987—. Named Outstanding Young Women Am., 1988. Mem. ABA, Miss. Bar Assn., Ga. Bar Assn., Assn. Trial Lawyers Am., Miss. Trial Lawyers Assn., Miss. Women Lawyers Assn. Democrat. Methodist. Office: 112 3rd St S Columbus MS 39701

SMITH, DONNIE LOUISE, nurse; b. Mountain Home, Idaho, Aug. 14, 1952; d. Bernard Armour and Lillian Doris (Lazzari) S.; children: Daniel Taylor, Drew Thomas. AA in Nursing, Solano Community Coll., 1973. RN, Calif. Staff nurse Woodland (Calif.) Clinic Med. Group, 1973-74, 79; office nurse Gaing W. Chan, MD, West Sacramento, Calif., 1974-76; staff nurse med.-surg. and critical care unit Woodland Meml. Hosp., 1976-79; staff nurse coronary care unit Santa Barbara (Calif.) Cottage Hosp., 1979-80; charge nurse critical care unit Northbay Med. Ctr., Fairfield, Calif., 1981-83, endoscopy nurse specialist, 1983-87; dir. svcs. Sacramento Autologous Svc. Inc., Sacramento, 1987-90; endoscopy charge nurse North Bay Med. Ctr., Fairfield, Calif., 1989—, continuity care coord., 1990—; staff nurse Nurse Focus, Napa, Calif., 1989—. Mem. Rescue Now, Sacramento, 1985—. Recipient appreciation award Northbay Med. Ctr., 1987. Mem. Soc. Gastrointestinal Assts., Solano Community Coll. Profl. Registered Nurse Alumni (sec. 1986—). Democrat. Roman Catholic. Office: North Bay Med Ctr 1800 Pennsylvania Ave Fairfield CA 94533

SMITH, SISTER DORIS HELEN, college president; b. Cleve., June 1, 1930; d. Harold Peter and Ellen Mary (Keane) S. B.S., Coll. of Mt. St. Vincent, 1952; M.A., NYU, 1957; postgrad. Fordham U., 1960-65; L.H.D., (hon.), Manhattan Coll., 1979. Joined Sisters of Charity (N.Y.), 1952. Mem. faculty Coll. of Mount St. Vincent, Bronx, N.Y., 1955-71, adminstrv. asst. to pres., 1971-72, exec. v.p., 1972-73, pres., 1973—; spl. asst. to pres. Chatham Coll., Pitts., 1970-71; dir. Hudson River Trust of Equitable Variable Life Ins., N.Y.C.; trustee Higher Edn. Service Corp., Albany, N.Y., 1980-85, Com. on Independent Colls. and Univs., Albany, 1980-83. Recipient Higher Edn. Leadership award Com. on Independent Colls. and Corning Glass Works, 1983, several interfaith and brotherhood awards; named Riverdalian of Yr. Riverdale Community Council, 1978; Am. Council Edn. fellow, 1970-71. Mem. Assn. Colls. and Univs. of State of N.Y. (trustee 1989—), Bronx C. of C. Roman Catholic. Home and Office: Coll Mt St Vincent Office of Pres Riverdale Ave Bronx NY 10471

SMITH, DORIS KEMP, retired nurse; b. Bogalusa, La., Nov. 22, 1919; d. Milton Jones and Maude Maria (Fortenberry) Kemp; m. Joseph William Smith, Oct. 13, 1940 (dec.). BS in Nursing, U. Colo., 1957, MS in Nursing Adminstrn., 1958. RN, Colo. Head nurse Chgo. Bridge & Iron Co., Morgan City, La., 1941-45, Shannon Hosp., San Angelo, Tex., 1945-50; dir. nursing Yoakum County Hosp., Denver City, Tex., 1951-52; hosp. supr. Med. Arts Hosp., Odessa, Tex., 1952-55; dir. insvc. edn. St. Anthony Hosp., Denver, 1961-66; coord. Sch. Vocat. Nursing, Kiamichi Area Vocat.-Tech. Nursing Sch., Wilburton, Okla., 1969-77; supr. non-ambulatory unit Lubbock (Tex.) State Sch., 1978-85, ret., 1985; Mem. steering com. Western Interstate Commn. on Higher Edn. for Nurses, Denver, 1963-65; mem. curriculum and materials com. Okla. Bd. Vocat.-Tech. Edn., Stillwater, 1971-76; mem. Invitational Conf. To Plan Nursing for Future, Oklahoma City, 1976-77. Contbr. numerous articles to profl. jours. Recipient citation of merit Okla. State U., 1976. Mem. AAAS, Nat. League for Nursing, Tex. League for Nursing, Am. Nurses Assn., Tex. Nurses Assn., Dist. 18 Nurses Assn., Tex. Employees Assn. (v.p. 1984-85), AAUW (life), U. Colo. Alumni Assn., Am. Bus. Women's Assn. (pres. Lubbock 1986-87), Bus. and Profl. Women's Club, Pi Lambda Theta. Republican. Home: 2103 55th St Lubbock TX 79412

SMITH, DOROTHY JORDAN, social service organization administrator; b. Rockwood, Tenn., Aug. 29, 1940; d. Bishop and Corine (Peagler) Jordan; m. Jimor Smith, June 29, 1958; children: L'Tonia, Jimor Jr., Bishop LeRoy. BA in Edn., Chgo. State U., 1982; MA in Pub. Adminstrn., Governors State U., University Park, Ill., 1988. Bus. machines clk. Continental Ill. Nat. Bank, Chgo., 1963-69; libr. cons. Field Enterprises Ednl. Co., Chgo., 1972-79; rsch. analyst U.S. Dept. Commerce, Chgo., 1979-82; founder, tchr. Smith Tutoring Program, Chgo., 1982-86; instr. Chgo. City Coll., 1986-88; founder, exec. dir. Unwed Mothers Ill., Inc., 1987—. Mem. Trans-Africa, Washington, 1983; bd. dirs. NACAP, Oak Park, Ill., 1987; v.p. Washington Heights region Am. Cancer Soc., Chgo., 1982; mem. South Area Planning Bd., Chgo., 1989—. Bd. Govs. State Colls. and Univs. Fellow, 1986-87; Ill. Dept. Children and Family grantee, 1988. Mem. NAFE, Am. Soc. Notaries, Ill. Soc. Notaries, Chgo. Urban League, Sigma Iota Lambda. Democrat. Baptist. Office: Messiah Temple Devel Inst 10420 S Halsted St Chicago IL 60628

SMITH, ELAINE CECILE THOMPSON, artistic director; b. New Orleans, Mar. 20, 1947; d. James Jr. and Dorothy (Richard) Thompson; m. Frank Bernard Smith III, July 20, 1969; children: Frank Bernard IV, Hashimolu Bernard. BA, Dillard U., 1969; Health Cert., Hunter Coll., 1973; MA, Columbia U., 1977; degree in Cosmetology, Wilfred Beauty Sch. and Acad., 1987. Dance tchr. I. S. 136M, N.Y.C., 1970-85; dance tchr. I. S. 10M, N.Y.C., 1985—, dir. B-D-R dance troop, 1985—; liaison to Dance Theatre Harlem, N.Y.C., 1970—; dance instr. local YWCA, Garner Ctr. Daycamp, N.Y.C., 1980-84; pageant choreographer Hal Jackson Talented Teens Internat., N.Y.C., 1984—; participant opening ceremonies Australia Worlds Fair, 1988, N.Y. State Fair, 1987. Appeared in video Inside Your Schools, 1984; staged, choreographed and costumed dance concerts for New Orleans Pub. Schs., 1978, 79, 84, United Fedn. Tchrs. Spring Confs., 1978, 79, 80, 81, Borough Pres. Andrew Steins Manhattan Day Celebrations, 1980, 81, 82, N.Y. Bus. and Profl. Women's Black History Celebration, Riverside Ch., 1985, 86, Bahamas Musicians and Entertainers Union, 1980, Dist. Five Together Showcase, 1986, 87, 88, 89, Elaine Smith Dancer of I.S. 136M, 1970-85, Uptown Saturday Afternoon, 1990; choreographed and staged 20th Anniversary Hal Jackson Talented Teen Internat. N.Y. State Pageant, 1990; hosted Dancing in Streets, with Douglass Dancers, N.Y.C. Dance Festival, 1990; liaison for Dancing in the Streets Night of Tap, Apollo Theatre, 1990; others. Dance troupe rep. from N.Y.C, New Orleans World's Fair, 1984; mem. Com. for Positive Youth, N.Y.C., 1984—; dance group Manhattan Day Celebration, 1981-83. Recipient Proclamation Borough Pres. Andrew Stein, 1984, with Douglass Dancers 2d Place N.Y. State Holiday Commn. 3d Ann. Dr. Martin Luther King, Jr.'s Arts and Sci. Contest, 1988, recognition plaque for outstanding choreography and work with Positive Youth from Hal Jackson, 1988, 89, cert. of achievement and honor award I.S. 10M, 1990, medal of exellence ABI, 1990; named Dep. Gov. for Life, ABI. Fellow Internat. Biog. Assn.; mem. NEA, N.Y. State Union Tchrs., N.Y. State Dance Assn., Nat. Dance Assn., Am. Assn. Leisure Recreation, Nat. Am. Alliance for Health, Phys. Edn., Recreation and Dance, United Fedn. Tchrs., Am. Biog. Rsch. (dep. gov. 1989—), Phi Delta Kappa. Roman Catholic. Office: IS 10M Ednl Park Complex 2581 Adam Clayton Powell Jr Blvd New York NY 10039

SMITH, ELAINE JANET, social worker; b. Albert Lea, Minn., Nov. 25, 1939; d. Manville Arthur Frederick and Laura Bertha Louise (Hintz) Pestorius; m. John Vernon Smith, Nov. 27, 1968; stepchildren: E. Michelle, John M., Thomas M., James M. BA, U. Minn., 1960; MSW, U. Denver, 1965. Lic. social worker II, Colo. Social worker Rochester (Minn.) State Hosp., 1961-63, Denver pub. schs., 1965-67, Denver Gen. Hosp., 1967-78; real estate agt. Century 21, Denver, 1978-80; social worker Adams County Social Services, Commerce City, Colo., 1980-85, Children's Hosp., Denver, 1985-87, Adult Care Mgmt., Denver, 1987-88; with property mgmt. A-Action Realty, Denver, 1988-89, The Charlton Co., Aurora, Colo., 1989—; field instr. Community Coll. Denver, 1980-84. Organist United Ch. Montbello, Denver, 1978—. Recipient Outstanding Achievement Merit Increase award Denver Gen. Hosp., 1974. Mem. Nat. Assn. Social Workers, Alliance for Mentally Ill (asst. sec. local chpt. 1985—). Democrat. Home: 4986 Worchester St Denver CO 80239 Office: The Charlton Co 1350 Chambers Rd #207C Aurora CO 80011

SMITH, ELEANOR BUCZYNSKI, service executive; b. Sewickley, Pa., May 10, 1941; d. Stanley and Cecilia Frances (Wachowski) Buczynski; m. Edward Smith; children: Gregory, Jeffrey. Student, U. Pitts., 1987, Community Coll. Allegheny Cty., 1987—, Ga. State U., 1989. Clk. typist St. Francis Hosp., Pitts., 1958-62; pvt. sec. Buffalo Scale Co., Pitts., 1959-63; sec. Pitts. Plate Glass Co., 1965-66; front desk supr. Edgeworth, Sewickley, 1980-84, adminstrv. asst., 1984-86, asst. mgr., 1986—. Active Diocesan Coun. Cath. Women, 1965—, chmn. internat. affairs, 1981-82, co-chmn. convention, 1988-89, chmn. convention book, 1990; pres. Holy Family Inst. Women's Auxiliary, 1970-72; mem. adv. bd. Holy Family Inst., 1970-85; pres. Pitts. Diocesan Coun. Cath. Women, 1982-84; bd. dirs. Mission Awareness, 1982-85, Christian Assocs., 1982-85; active Nat. Coun. Cath. Women, World Union Coun. Cath. Women Orgn.; bd. dirs. Ecumenical Commn., 1990. Recipient Woman of Yr. award Women's Auxiliary Holy Family Inst., 1978, John Cardinal Wright award Diocesan Coun. Cath. Women, 1987. Mem. Club Mgrs. Assn., Harmony Twp. Civic Club (bd. dirs. 1978-80). Home: 574 Virginia Ave Ambridge PA 15003

SMITH, ELIZABETH ANN, medical records administrator, dancer; b. Niagara Falls, N.Y., Mar. 25, 1958; d. Alan Bateman Smith and Elizabeth (Latko) Sullivan. BS, Daemen Coll., 1980. Tutor computers Daemen Coll., Buffalo, 1979-80; with med. records coding Mt. St. Mary's Hosp., Lewiston, N.Y., 1980-82; clk. med. records, staff technician Niagara Falls Meml. Med. Ctr., 1982-85, asst. dir., analyst, 1986-88, dir. med. records, 1988—; adminstr. studio Debonaire Dance Studio, Buffalo, 1985—. Fellow Am. Med. Record Assn., NAFE, Nat. Scoliosis Assn., Scoliosis Assn. Western N.Y. Home: 235 State St Apt 424 Springfield MA 01103 Office: Baystate Med Ctr 759 Chestnut St Springfield MA 01199

SMITH, ELIZABETH BETH, small business owner; b. Nuremburg, Fed. Republic Germany, Apr. 4, 1956; d. James Wells and Margaret Sue (Lewis) Hull; m. Keith Scott, Aug. 27, 1983. BS in Therapeutic Recreat, U. Mo., Columbia, 1978; postgrad., U. Mo., 1981; BSN, U. Colo., 1990. Recreational therapist Crittenton Ctr., Kans. City, 1979-81; med. auditor Claim Cons., Inc., Massapequa, N.Y., 1983-88; recreation socialization planner Sussex County Welfare Bd., Sussex, 1983-87; owner, pres., med. auditor Med. Audit, Inc., Parker, Colo.; charter mem. Douglas County Bus. & Profl. Women. Recipient U. Colo. Health Services Ctr., Denver, 1988-89, Merit scholar Colo., 1989, Rose Med. Ctr. Nursing scholar, 1989. Mem. DAR, Jr. League of Denver, Pi Beta Phi Alumni. Protestant. Home: 9605 E Coronado Ct Parker CO 80134

SMITH, ELIZABETH MACKEY, financial planner, consultant; b. Phila., Mar. 23, 1941; d. William Norman Mackey and Celeste Parvin Barley; m. George Van Riper Smith, Aug. 15, 1964; children: Douglas George, Todd Mackey. BA, Gettysburg Coll., 1963; MA in Teaching, Ga. State U., 1978. Tchr. fgn. lang. Haverford (Pa.) High Sch., 1963-65; registered rep. IDS Fin. Svcs., Inc., Macon and Savannah, Ga., 1979—. Reader Alanta Svcs. for the Blind, 1968; hostess Atlanta Coun. for Internat. Visitors, 1972-74; pres. Forest Hills Elem. Sch. PTA, Decatur, Ga., 1975, fgn. exchange student coord. Loisirs Culturels a l'Etranger, 1990—. Mem. Phi Sigma Iota, Delta Phi Alpha, Delta Gamma. Home: 59 Fiddler's Ct Savannah GA 31419 Office: IDS Fin Svcs Inc 6606 Abercorn St Ste 205 Abercorn Profl Bldg Savannah GA 31405

SMITH, ELOUISE BEARD, restaurant owner; b. Richmond, Tex., Jan. 8, 1920; d. Lee Roy and Ruby Myrtle (Foy) Beard; m. Omar Smith, Nov. 27, 1940 (dec. July 1981); children: Mary Jean Smith Cherry, Terry Omar, Don Alan. Student, Tex. Womens U., 1937-39. Sec. First Nat. Bank, Rosenberg, Tex., 1939-41; owner Smith Dairy Queens, Bryan, Tex., 1947—. Author: The Haunted House, 1986; editor The College Widow, 1986. Omar and Elouise Beard Smith chair named in her honor Tex. A&M U., College Station, 1983, Elouise Beard Smith Human Performance Labs. named in her honor Tex. A&M U., 1984. Mem. AAUW. Republican. Baptist. Home: 411 Crescent Dr Bryan TX 77801 Office: Metro Ctr 3833 S Texas Ave Bryan TX 77802

SMITH, ELSKE VAN PANHUYS, university administrator; b. Monte Carlo, Monaco, Nov. 9, 1929; came to U.S., 1943; d. Abraham A.E. and Vera (Craven) Van P.; m. Henry J. Smith, Sept. 10, 1950 (dec. June 1983); children: Ralph A., Kenneth A. BA, Radcliffe U., 1950, MS, 1951, PhD, 1956. Rsch. assoc. Sacramento Peak Observatory, Sunspot, N.Mex., 1955-62; rsch. fellow Joint Inst. for Lab. Astrophysics, Boulder, Colo., 1962-63; assoc. to prof. U. Md., College Park, 1963-80, asst. provost, 1973-78, asst. vice chancellor, 1978-80; dean, coll. humanities and scis. Va. Commonwealth U., Richmond, 1980—; cons. NASA, Greenbelt, Md., 1964-76, reviewer, Washington, 1970's, NSF, Washington, 1970's, 86; vis. com. Assn. of Univ.'s for Rsch. in Astronomy, Tucson, 1975-78. Author: (with others) Solar Flares, 1963, Introductory Astronomy & Astrophysics, 1973; contbr. numerous articles to profl. jours. Mem. various environ. orgns. Rsch. grantee, Rsch. Corp., 1956-57, NSF, 1966-69, NIH, 1981—, NASA, 1964-78; program grantee Va. Found. for Humanities, 1985, Assn. Am. Colls., 1987. Fellow AAAS; mem. Am. Astron. Soc. (counselor 1977-80, vis. prof. 1975-78), Internat. Astron. Union (chief U.S. del. 1979, U.S. Nat. com.), Coun. Colls. of Arts and Scis. (bd. dirs. 1989), Phi Beta Kappa. Democrat. Home: 1816 Park Ave Richmond VA 23220 Office: Va Commonwealth U PO Box 2019 Richmond VA 23284-2019

SMITH, EMILY FOLLIN, automotive executive; b. Greenville, Miss., Nov. 14, 1959; d. Robert Russell Smith and Emily (Finlay) Wesley; m. John Robert Gerdy, Dec. 23, 1989. BA, Davidson Coll., 1981; MBA, U. Va., 1985. Asst. spl. events coord. Ivey's, Charlotte, N.C., 1981-82; asst. fashion coord. Belk Stores, Charlotte, 1982-83; sr. analyst exec. compensation GM, N.Y.C., 1985-86, sr. analyst new bus. devel., 1986-87, head trader investment portfolio, 1987-88, mgr. capital markets, 1988-89, dir. worldwide banking and U.S. cash mgmt., 1989-90; dir. corp. GM, 1909—. Treas. 79th St. Residence Corp., N.Y.C., 1986-89. Office: GM 767 Fifth Ave New York NY 10153

SMITH, EUGENIA SEWELL, funeral home executive; b. Albany, Ky., Oct. 24, 1922; d. Leo Matheny and Marjorie (Warinner) Sewell; m. James Frederick Smith, June 25, 1948; 1 child, Bryson Sewell. Student Berea Coll., 1937-41, Bowling Green Coll. Commerce, 1944-45. Owner, operator Sewell Funeral Home, Albany, 1977—; bd. dir. Citizens Bank of Albany, Ky, 1989—. Sec. Albany Woman's Club, 1950-54; den mother Cub Scouts, Boy Scouts Am., 1958-62; pres. Clinton County Homemakers, Albany, 1968-70; mission action chmn. Missionary Baptist Ch., 1965-82. Democrat. Lodge: Demolay Mother's (pres. Albany club 1966-67), Order Eastern Star (former assoc. conductress, former Martha and Esther). Home: RR 4 Burkesville Rd Albany KY 42602 Office: Sewell Funeral Home 115 Cross St Albany KY 42602

SMITH, EVA JOYCE, nurse; b. New Eagle, Pa., Mar. 16, 1932; d. Harold Elwood John and Vera Lena (Herd) Schlosser; m. Lyell G. Smith (div. 1980); children: Stephen Mark, Stephanie Anne, Shari Linne. Student, Marshall Coll., 1949-50; diploma, Wheeling Hosp. Sch. Nursing, W.Va., 1953; BS, Coll. St. Francis, Joliet, Ill., 1982, MS, 1986. R.N., Ill. Staff nurse Didsbury (Alta.) Hosp., Can., 1957-60, Annapolis Hosp., Wayne, Mich., 1963-64, Stagg Clinic, Hartford, Mich., 1969-72, Hinsdale (Ill.) Sanitorium and Hosp., 1972-76; staff nurse, instr., then clin. edn. coord. St. Luke's Med. Ctr., Phoenix, Ill., 1977-85; asst. dir. health arts program Coll. St. Francis, Joliet, 1985-87; clinic dir. Memory Assessment Clinics, Inc., Scottsdale, Ariz., 1988—. Mem. NAFE, Profl. Assn. Gerontology Educators and Svcs. (sec. 1985). Republican. Baptist. Home: 1015 E Villa Rita Dr Phoenix AZ 85022

SMITH, EVELYN, association executive; b. Statesboro, Ga., Jan. 13, 1949; d. Ollie and Ruthie Mae (Williams) S. BS in Biology, Chemistry, Albany (Ga.) State Coll., 1971, cert. in teaching, 1975. Cert. tchr., Ga. Mgr. domestics Zayres, Decatur, Ga., 1971-72, area mgr. trainee, 1972; instr. Candler County Sch. System, Metter, Ga., 1972-77; dir. UniServ S.E. region Ga. Assn. Educators, Metter, 1977-84; dir. field services Ga. Assn. Educators, Decatur, 1984-86, Atlanta, 1986-87; dir. membership organ./field services South Ga. Assn. Educators, Decatur, 1987-90, dir. membership and spl. svcs., 1990—; advisor NEA Human Immuno-deficiency virus edn. and tng. panel. Mem. textbook adoption com. first dist. Ga. Dept. Edn., Metter, 1980; vol. Nat. Coun. Negro Women, Inc., 1987, Elks Aidmore Children's Ctr., Conyers, Ga.; radio ministry announcer Fairfield Bapt. Ch., Redan, Ga.; nat. judge Thats What Friends are For, Dionne Warwick Found., 1989. Mem. NAFE, Swarovski Collectors Soc., NAACP (edn. com. 1987-89), Jackpot Birthday Club (pres. Atlanta chpt. 1986—). Democrat. Office: Ga Assn Educators 3951 Snapfinger Pkwy Decatur GA 30035

SMITH, EVELYN A., bank executive; b. Idaho Falls, Idaho, June 2, 1947; d. Joseph Paul and Doris Mae (Christensen) Mais; m. Bill D. Smith, Aug. 1, 1970. Grad, Idaho State U.; grad. with honors, Pacific Coast Banking Sch., Seattle, 1981. Cashier First Security Bank Havre, Mont.; comml. loan officer Farmers and Mchts. Bank, Spokane, Wash.; pres., chief exec. officer Pend Oreille Bank, Newport, Wash. Bd. trustees, sec. Newport Community Hosp.; mem. Pro-Pend Oreille Econ. Devel. Coun. Mem. Exec. Women's Network, Soroptimists (past treas.). Address: PO Box 1530 Newport WA 99156

SMITH, EVELYN JOYCE, family nurse practitioner; b. Elkhart, Ind., Nov. 15, 1938; d. Mary I (Hastings) Snearly; children: Rebecca J. and Amelia D. Diploma, Union Hosp. Sch. Nursing, 1959; BS in Nursing, St. Mary of the Plains Coll., 1979; cert., Wichita State U., 1976, M in Nursing, 1982. RN, Kans. Staff nurse Elkhart Gen. Hosp., Elkhart, 1959-61, Lawrence Mem. Hosp., Lawrence, Kans., 1961-72; interim prog. coordinator WSU Nurse Clin. Prog., Wichita, 1976-84; nurse practitioner Platte Med. Clinic, Platte City, Mo.; coord. Adult Medicine Prime Health, Kansas City, Mo., 1986—; editorial bd. Mem. Nurse Practitioner Jour., 1984--. Author: Nurse Practitioner Jour., 1980, The Kans. Nurse, 1982. Nominee for Syntex NP of the Year Award, 1988. Mem. Am. Nurses Assn. (cert. family nurse practitioner), Am. Acad. Nurse Practitioners.

SMITH, FRANCES ELIZABETH, tumor registrar; b. Danbury, Conn., Aug. 19, 1928; d. Burton Hawley and Rosanna Frances (Logan) S.; m. Roger L. Ferris, June 5, 1948 (div.); 1 child, Marguerite; m. Malcolm L. Smith, June 18, 1955 (dec. 1985); 1 child, Malcolm Jr. Student, Oakwood Sch., 1944-46, Edgewood Park Jr. Coll., 1947-48. Certified tumor registrar, 1983. Cancer coordinator Putnam Comm. Hosp., Carmel, N.Y., 1966-74, Holmes Reg. Med. Ctr., Melbourne, Fla., 1974-82, Orlando Reg. Med. Ctr., Orlando, Fla., 1980-82, Lawnwood Reg. Med. Ctr., Ft. Pierce, Fla., 1983-89, Jupiter (Fla.) Hosp., Lakeland, Fla., 1989—; cons. Fla. Tumor Registrar Assn., 1982. Contbr. articles to profl. mags. Mem. Fla. Tumor Registrar Assn., Nat. Tumor Register Assn., Hospice Treasure Coast, Hospice of Melbourne and Ft. Pierce. Protestant. Home: 922D Savannahs Point Dr Fort Pierce FL 33809 Office: Jupiter Hosp 1210 S Old Dixie Hwy PO Box 95448 Jupiter FL 33458

SMITH, GAIL HUNTER, artist; b. Nashville, Mar. 18, 1948; d. Walter Gray Smith and Eleanor Theresa (Cregar) Egan. Student, Memphis State U., 1966-67; BFA in Advt. Design, Memphis Acad. Arts, 1971. Prodn. asst. Visual Studios, Phila., 1970; asst. art dir. Eric Ericson and Assocs. and Ken White Design, Inc., Nashville, 1971-72; art dir. Contemporary Mktg., Inc., Ivan Stiles Advt., Bala Cynwyd (Pa.), Phila., 1972-74; specialist publs. design Temple U., Phila., 1974-75; represented by Mystic (Conn.) Maritime Gallery, Capricorn Gallery, Bethesda, Md., Cumberland Gallery, Nashville, 1982-83, The Studio L'Atelier, Nashville, 1983-85, Ambiance Fine Arts, Nashville, 1985, Alice Bingham Gallery, Memphis, 1985-87; judge Haddonfield (N.J.) Artists Exhbn., 1976; tchr. in field. Editor: Artists USA, 7th edit., Yacht Portraits, 1987; one-woman show Dow Jones & Co., Inc., Princeton, N.J., 1987, Johnson & Johnson, Inc., New Brunswick, N.Y., 1990; exhibited in group shows at 12th and 17th Tenn. All-State Artist Exhbn., Nashville, 1972, 77, Arnold Art Gallery, Newport, R.I., 1986, 87, 88, 89, 90, Wildfowl Festival, Easton, Md., 1987, Mystic Maritime Gallery, 1984, 85, 86, 88, 89, 90, Capricorn Gallery, 1987. Mem. Morgan Libr., Met. Mus. Recipient awards Nashville Ad Fedn., 1973. Mem. NAFE, Artists Equity Assn., Am. Inst. Graphic Arts, Am. Soc. Marine Artists, Am. Coun. of Arts, Soc. of Illustrators, Soc. of Scribes, Mus. of Women in Arts, Nat. Audubon Soc., Wilderness Soc., Sierra Club. Office: PO Box 217 Barnegat Light NJ 08006

SMITH, GRACE DONALDSON, social science educator; b. Statesboro, Ga., Oct. 11, 1930; d. George and Gussie (Lanier) Donaldson; m. Willie Albert Smith, Sr., June 5, 1951; children: Willie Albert Jr., Eric George. BA, Paine Coll., 1951; MEd, Ga. So. Coll., 1976. Social sci. tchr. Statesboro (Ga.) High Sch., 1969—, dept. head, 1973—. Sec. Ga. Fedn. of Dem. Women, Statesboro, 1976-78; chairperson Ga. Council for Social Studies, Statesboro, 1976; mem. adv. bd. Ogeeche Home Health Agy., Statesboro, 1980—; treas. Bulloch County Bi-centennial Commn., 1987—. Named Sch.'s Tchr. Yr. Bullock County Bd. Edn., Statesboro, 1982. Mem. AAUW (Stateboro chpt. v.p., chmn. program 1984-86, chmn. individual liberties), NEA, Ga. Assn. Educators, Bullock County Assn. Edn. (treas. 1975, sec. 1987), Negro Bus. and Profl. Women, Kappa Delta Pi (treas. Eta Gamma Pi chpt. 1987). Democrat. Methodist. Club: Stabucettes (Statesboro) (pres. 1976-78, 89, Deer Day Smith Svc. to Mankind award, 1989). Home: 18 James St Statesboro GA 30458

SMITH, GRACIE BERNON, dress designer, tailor; b. Hyden, Ky., Aug. 1, 1932; d. Joe and Eva Lee (Howard) Maggard; m. William Robert Smith, June 10, 1972; children by previous marriage: Donald Eugene Turpin, Jr., Daniel Edwin Turpin; stepchildren: Steven Carson Smith, Vicki Lynn Booth. Student Nat. Sch. Dress Design-Chgo., 1955-58; student in real estate Purdue U., 1973. Tailor Sovern Tailors, Lafayette, Ind., 1965-68; mgr. Millers Sportswear, Lafayette, 1968-70; with Benker Realty, Lafayette, 1973-75; service contract dept. head Montgomery Ward, Lafayette, 1975-77; alteration dept. head Montgomery Ward, 1977-80; owner, operator Bernon Custom Fashions, Lafayette, 1955—; cons. local 4-H Clubs, 1983—; local sales rep. Leiters Designer Fabrics, Kansas City, Mo., 1982-87; local sales mgr. House of Laird Fabrics, Lexington, Ky., 1985—. Com. mem. Tippecanoe County Fair, Lafayette, 1983-85. Fellow The Custom Tailors and Designers Assn. Am., Am. Bus. Womens Assn., mem. Nat. Assn. Female Execs. Baptist. Avocations: bowling; gardening; knitting; cooking; crocheting. Home and Office: 2350 N 23d St Lafayette IN 47904

SMITH, GWENDOLYN DELOIS MCEWEN, vocational educator; b. Memphis, Nov. 26, 1930; d. A. B. and Joanna (Wells) McEwen; m. Thomas Hoffman Smith, Sept. 29, 1962 (div. Nov. 1965); 1 child, Eric Lemuel. BS, Tenn. State U., 1952; MEd, Memphis State U., 1970, postgrad., 1971-86, 88. Cert. secondary sch. tchr.; cert. office mgmt., bus. edn., vocat. office tech. edn. tchr. Substitute tchr. Memphis City Schs., 1952; office mgr. Memphis Mortgage Guaranty Co., Memphis, 1952-63, Law Offices of Hooks, Willis, and Sugarmon, Memphis, 1953-68; tchr. Cortez W. Peters Bus. Coll., Chgo., 1963; bookkeeper, v.p. Supreme Mortgage & Realty Co., Memphis, 1966-68; tchr. vocat. office edn. Melrose High Sch., Memphis, 1969-70, Memphis Tech. High Sch., 1970-87, Comprehensive Pupil Svcs. Ednl. Ctr., Memphis, 1987—; bd. advisors Mut. Fed. Savs. & Loan, Memphis, 1958-68; incorporator Prog. Constrn. Co., Memphis, 1966-68. Author: (monograph) The Shorthand Dilemma, 1972, (play) Find Your Future in America's Schools, 1988. Recipient Tchr. Excellence award Rotary Club Internat., 1987, Outstanding Achievement award State of Tenn., 1987, Award of Merit City of Memphis, 1987, cert. of appreciation Shelby County Sheriff's Dept., Memphis, 1987. Fellow Assn. for Supervision and Curriculum Devel., United Tchrs. Profession, Am. Vocat. Assn., Nat. Bus. Assn., Memphis Bus. Edn. Tchrs. Assn. (pres., various offices 1969—), Memphis State U. Century Club, Delta Sigma Theta; mem. NAACP (life); Delta Pi Epsilon (charter mem., various offices Beta Xi chpt. 1970—, Disting. Leadership award 1974).

SMITH, HARRIET GWENDOLYN GURLEY, educator, writer; b. Goldsboro, N.C., Nov. 14, 1927; d. Charles Harvey and Sadye Reid (Morris) Gurley; m. Albert Goodin Smith, Aug. 29, 1953; children: Susan Reid Smith Erba, Alan English Smith. Grad., St. Mary's Coll., Raleigh, N.C., 1946; BA, U. N.C., 1948; MEd, La. State U., Shreveport, 1982. Cert. tchr., N.C., La. Tchr. English, Journalism, Social Studies Goldsboro City Schs., 1948-49, Rocky Mount (N.C.) City Schs., 1949-51, Durham (N.C.) City Schs., 1951-53, Durham County Schs., 1954-56; realtor assoc. Sam Fullilore and Assocs., Shreveport, 1984-87; contbg. editor, columnist The New Front Gallery Mag., Shreveport, 1988; bridge tchr. Caddo Magnet High Sch., La. State U., private groups, 1978—. Pres. Shreveport Med. Soc. Aux., 1985-86, chmn. various coms., 1970—; pres. Faculty Women's Club La. State U. Med. Ctr., 1990; mem. women's bd. dirs. Centenary Coll.; active United Meth. Women, Symphony Guild, Opera Guild, Rep. Women. Mem. Am. Contract Bridge League (life master, cert. tchr.), Am. Bridge Tchrs. Assn., La. Real Estate Commn., Bull and Bear Stock Club (sec. 1973-74, pres. 1975-76), Kappa Delta Pi. Home: 8502 Rampart Pl Shreveport LA 71106

SMITH, HELEN CATHARINE, writer; b. Chgo., June 7, 1903; m. H.C. Smith, June 7, 1932 (dec. 1972); children: Glen Dean, DeEtta Ellen (Mrs. Gerald L. Amdahl), George Dale. BA, Calif. State Coll., L.A., 1926; U. Wis. Extension Studies, 1954-56; MS, Christian Coll., 1962, PhD, 1965, D of Psychology, 1966; PhD (hon.) Free U., hon. doctorate Gt. China Arts Coll., 1969, St. Olav's Acad., Sweden, 1969, Internat. Acad. Sovereign Order Alfred Gt., Eng., 1969; JD, Ohio Christian Coll., 1969; PhD, U. Reno (Nigeria), 1975. Tchr. 2d grade Maple Lawn Sch., Clinton, Wis.; legal sec., Janesville, Wis., Office of City Atty., Evansville, Wis., 1933—; v.p., dir. Blue Moon poetry mag., 1952-57. Recipient 1st pl. award for article Herdman Meml. Competition Brit. Press, 1957; John Francis Sims Meml. award for poetry, 1955; award of honor UN Day, Philippines, 1967; laurel wreath, gold medal Pres. Philippines, 1967; cert. recognition Nat. Poetry Day Com., 1972; Disting. Svc. award Wis. Jaycees, 1975, cert. Am. Bicentennial Rsch. Inst., 1975, Hall of Honor award U. Wis., 1988; named Hon. Poet Laureate (Am.-Visayan), 1967; Internat. Woman of 1975 with laureate honors by Imelda R. Marcos; inducted into Wis. Rock County Cultural Ctr. Hall of Honor, 1988. Fellow Intercontinental Biog. Assn.; mem. AAUW (awards poetry, short stories 1972), Wis. Regional Writers Assn. (sec. 1949-55, 61—, hon. life dir., leadership citation 1956, Jade Ring winner for short story 1957), Nat. League Am. Pen Women, Am. Poetry League, Wis. Fellowship Poets, Wis. Acad. Scis. Arts and Letters, Brit. Press Assn., United Poets Laureate Internat. (Karta award), Wis. Council for Writers (life, 2d pl. award for short story 1980), Centro Studie Scambi Internazionali Roma (medal of honor 1966-67, internat. exec. bd.), Wis. Edn. Assn., Wis. Regional Artists, State Hist. Soc. Wis., Accademia Internazionale Leonardo Da Vinci (Rome; Gold medallion 1972), Accademia Internazionale Di Pontzen, Am. Lit. Assn. (life), World Poetry Soc. (hon. life), UN Assn., Phi Beta Kappa (sustaining), Alpha Psi Omega, Sigma Iota XI. Author: Laughing Child, books I, II, III, 1945, 46, 47; Off the Record, 1949; From the Countryside, 1952; Stars in My Eyes, 1954; Wind-Falls, 1955; Chiaroscura, 1964; But Not Yet, 1973; You Can't Cry All the Time, 1975. Editor: Evansville Anthology of Verse, 1952, No. Spring, anthology, 1956; Chiaroscura, 1964; Helen's Sketch Book, 1978; contbr. articles, stories to numerous mags., newspapers, anthologies. Home: 455 S 1st St Apt 19 Evansville WI 53536

SMITH, HELEN ELIZABETH, military officer; b. San Rafael, Calif., Aug. 11, 1946; d. Jack Dillard and Marian Elizabeth (Miller) S. BA in Geography, Calif. State U., Northridge, 1968; MA in Internat. Rels., Salve Regina, Newport, R.I., 1983; MS in Tech. Communications, Rensselaer Poly. Inst., 1988. Commd. ensign USN, 1968, advanced through grades to capt., 1989; adminstrv. asst. USN Fighter Squadron 101, Key West, Fla., 1969-70; adminstrv. officer Fleet Operational Tng. Group, Mountain View, Calif., 1970-72; leader human resource team Human Resource Ctr., Rota, Spain, 1977-79; adminstrv. officer Pearl Harbor (Hawaii) Naval Sta., 1979-80; dir. Family Svc. Ctr., Pearl Harbor, 1980-82; officer-in-charge R&D lab. Naval Ocean Systems Ctr., Kaneohe, Hawaii, 1983-85; exec. officer Naval ROTC, assoc. prof. Rensselaer Poly. Inst., Troy, N.Y., 1985-88; comdg. officer Navy Alcohol Rehab. Ctr., Norfolk, Va., 1988-90; faculty mem., commanding officer Naval Adminstrv. Command, dean adminstrv. support, comptr. Armed Forces Staff Coll., Norfolk, Va., 1990—. Author: (walking tour) Albany's Historic Pastures, 1987; composer (cantata) Night of Wonder, 1983. Chmn. Hawaii State Childcare Com., Honolulu, 1981-82; coun. mem. Hist. Pastures Neighborhood Assn., Albany, N.Y., 1985-88; mem. working group Mayor's Task Force on Drugs, Norfolk, 1989-90; bd. dirs. Va. Coun. on Alcoholism, 1989-90. Republican. Presbyterian. Club: Naval Inst. (Annapolis, Md.).

SMITH, HELEN HARDIE, retired office systems manager; b. São Paulo, Brazil, Oct. 11, 1918; came to U.S., 1936; d. Alva and Katherine (Hall) Hardie; m. William Harrison Smith Jr., Feb. 13, 1943; children: Peter, Stuart, David. BA, Agnes Scott, 1941. Sec. Pan Am. World Airways, Miami, Fla., 1941-42; office systems mgr. Fla. Filters, Inc., Miami, 1962-83. Br. pres. AAUW, Miami, 1979-81; bd. dirs., sec. Children's Home Soc., Miami, 1981—; bd. dirs. Presbyn. Homes Fla., Orlando, 1970s. Lt. (j.g.) USN, 1942-44. Mem. Thornhill Found. (bd. dirs.), Biscayne Study Club. Democrat. Presbyterian.

SMITH, ILEENE ANDREA, book editor; b. N.Y.C., Jan. 21, 1953; d. Norman and Jeanne (Jaffe) S.; m. Howard A. Sobel, June 3, 1979; 1 child, Nathaniel Jacob. BA, Brandeis U., Waltham, Mass., 1975; MA, Columbia U., 1978. Editorial asst. Atheneum Publishers, N.Y.C., 1979-82; sr. editor Summit Books, N.Y.C., 1982—; cons. editor Paris Review, N.Y., 1987—. Author introductory scripts for Met. Opera Telecasts, 1987—. Recipient Tony Godwin Meml. award, 1982, PEN/Roger Klein award, 1988 for editorial excellence. Mem. The Coffee House. Office: Summit Books 1230 6th Ave New York NY 10020

SMITH, IRIS FRANCINE, health maintenance organization director; b. N.Y.C., July 6, 1945; d. Peter and Belle (Nitzberg) S. BS, U. Bridgeport, 1967; teaching credential, San Francisco State U., 1972. Cert. tchr., Calif. Supr. computer room Pacific Tel. Co., San Francisco, 1970-71; pers. adminstr., intake social worker City and County of San Francisco, 1971-73; fin. coord., admitting dept. supr. Presbyn. Hosp., San Francisco, 1973-77; regional quality assurance dir. Quality Care Nursing Svcs., San Francisco, 1977-80; mktg. rep. Heals Health Plan, Emeryville, Calif., 1981-83; regional sales mgr. Health Plan of Am., Emeryville, 1983-85; dir. mktg. Westworld Community Health Plans, El Toro, Calif., 1985; dir. provider services Health Plan of America, Orange, Calif., 1985-88; dir. IPA ops. St. Jude Hosp. and Rehab. Ctr., Fullerton, Calif., 1988—. Fellow NAFE. Democrat. Jewish. Club: 20/30 (Orange) (1st v.p. 1986-88). Home: 57 Laurel Creek Ln Laguna Hills CA 92653 Office: N Orange County St Jude Med Group IPA Inc 100 W Valencia Mesa Dr Ste 210 Fullerton CA 92635

SMITH, JACKLYN J., state legislator; b. Campbell, Nebr., Nov. 12, 1934; m. Ramon G. Smith, 1952; children: Robb, Jeff, Kurt, Jon. BA, Kearney (Nebr.) State Coll. Asst. dir. Midland Area Agy. on Aging; mem. Nebr. State Legislature. Mem. Nebr. Bicentennial Commn.; bd. dirs. Adams County 4-H. Republican. Home: 528 Madden Rd Hastings NE 68901 Office: State Legislature Lincoln NE 68509 Other: Rte 3 Box 21 Hastings NE 68901*

SMITH, JAMESETTA DELORISE, author; b. Chgo., Jan. 26, 1942; d. James Gilbert and Ora Mae (Roberts) Howell; m. Leroy Smith, June 2, 1962; children: Leroy, Darryll Keith. Student, Tolleston high sch., Gary, Ind., 1960, Oxford Bus. Coll., Chgo., 1961-62. Office clerk Justice of the Peace, Gary, Ind., 1966-69; bookkeeper, office mgr. Jones Electric, Gary, Ind., 1971-85. Author: How Strong is Strong 1988; contbr. articles to profl. jours. 1988. Treas., bd. dirs. Lupus Found., Gary Ind. 1988—. Mem. Jones Electric Gary Ind. (Sec. 1986). Democratic. Baptist.

SMITH, JANE SCHNEBERGER, city clerk; b. Chgo., Aug. 9, 1928; d. Frank R. and Marion (Durante) Schneberger; m. Z. Erol Smith, Jr., Oct. 28, 1950 (div. 1974); children: Suzan McCue Kuester, Tracy Smith Cawley, Cameron Farley, Z. Erol III, Kimberly, Scott. B.A. in Chemistry, U. Colo., 1950; M.A. in Communication, Mich. State U., 1978, PhD in ednl. adminstrn. Mich. State U., 1987. Chemist, Kellogg Switchboard, Chgo., 1950-51; tchr. Crab Orchard Sch., Palos Heights, Ill., 1969-70; v.p. South Cook County Girl Scouts, Harvey, Ill., 1967-69, (Thanks badge 1972), staff advisor, 1970-72; program and tng. dir. Mich. Capitol coun. Girl Scouts U.S., Lansing, 1972-75; dir. svc. learning ctr. Mich. State U., East Lansing, 1975-81; city clk. City of Ashland, Wis., 1981-89; interim city adminstr., 1989—; cons. vol. adminstrn., Mich., Wis., 1975—. Co-editor Looking Backward Moving Forward; Contbr. articles to profl. jours. v.p. Mich. Capitol Girl Scout Council, Lansing, 1976-78 (cert. appreciation 1975); bd. dirs. Lansing RSVP, 1976-81, Ashland Mus., 1985-87, Ptnrs. in Recovery, 1985-87, New Horizons, 1985—. Mem. Internat. Assn. Mcpl. Clks., Wis. Mcpl. Clks. Assn. (dist. dir. 1984-86). Roman Catholic. Club: Am. Bus. Women's Assn. (scholarship chmn. 1985) (Ashland). Lodge: Zonta (pres. 1979-81). Avocations: stained glass, gardening. Home: 700 MacArthur St Ashland WI 54806 Office: City of Ashland 601 W 2nd St Ashland WI 54806

SMITH, JANE WARDELL, historian, philanthropist, entrepreneur; b. Detroit, Aug. 9, 1943; d. John Slater and Lucille Maude (Hoskins) Beck; m. marshall Smith, Oct. 31, 1964 (div. 1972); children: Aaron Wardell, Gerald Allen. Student, Detroit Bus. Coll., Cass Sch. Tech. Exec. sec. Wayne County Cir. Ct. 7th Dist., 1968-72, Wayne County Friend of Ct., Salem, W.Va., 1968-72; with exec. mgmt. City Detroit Pers. Dept., 1972-79; fin. analyst City of Detroit, 1979-82; salesperson Mason Soe Co., Chippewa Falls, 1968-72; fin. analyst A. J. Valenci, Salem, W.Va., 1968-72; examiner Mich. State Dept., Detroit, 1972-79. Critic various consumer groups. Vol. Richard Austin polit. campaign, Grand River, Mich., 1975, John Conters polit. campaign, Livernois, Mich., 1980; active local drama and theater clubs, Detroit, 1980—, local Bapt. Ch., 1984—. Recipient numerous awards, honors and achievements. Democrat.

SMITH, JANET MARIE, real estate executive; b. Jackson, Miss., Dec. 13, 1957; d. Thomas Henry and Nellie Brown (Smith) S. BArch, Miss. State U., 1981; MA in Urban Planning, CCNY, 1984. Draftsman Thomas H. Smith and Assocs. Architects, Jackson, 1979; mktg. coord. The Eggers Group, P.C. Architects and Planners, N.Y.C., 1980; program assoc. Ptnrs. for Livable Places, Washington, 1980-82; coord. asst. Lance Jay Brown, Architect and Urban Planner, N.Y.C., 1983-84; coord. architecture and design Battery Park City Authority, N.Y.C., 1982-84; pres., chief ops. officer Pershing Sq. Mgmt. Assn., L.A., 1985-89; v.p. stadium planning and devel. Balt. Orioles Meml. Stadium, 1989—; bd. dirs. Syska & Hennessy Inc., Engrs., N.Y.C., 1984—, Assn. Collegiate Schs. Architecture, Washington, 1979-82, Assn. Student Chpts. AIA, Washington, 1979-82. Guest editor: Urban Design Internat., 1985; assoc. editor: Crit, 1979-82; contbr. articles to profl. jours. Named Disting. Grad., Nat. Assn. State Univs. and Land Grant Colls., 1988, One of Outstanding Young Women of Am., 1982; recipient Spirit of Miss. award, Sta. WLBT, Jackson, 1987. Mem. AIA (assoc.), Urban Land Inst., Urban Design Adv. Coalition, So. Calif. Chpt. Soc. Archtl. Historians, L.A. Conservancy (docent), Toastmasters. Democrat. Episcopalian. Office: Balt Orioles Meml Stadium Baltimore MD 21218

SMITH, JANET SUE, systems specialist; b. Chgo., Jan. 15, 1945; d. Curtis Edwin and Margaret Louise (Yost) Smith; B.A., Ind. U., 1967. Sales mgr. Marshall Field & Co., Chgo., 1968-70, programmer, 1970-72; sr. programmer, analyst Trailer Train Co., Chgo., 1972-75; mgr. data base and systems devel. RAILINC-Assn. Am. R.R., Washington, 1975-85, asst. v.p. bus. services, corp. sec., 1985—. Nat. student v.p. YWCA, 1966-67; bd. dirs., v.p. planning and fin. Guide Internat., Friends of the Nat. Zoo; advisor Jr. Achievement. Mem. Am. Council R.R. Women, Ind. U. Alumni Assn. (life), Women's Transp. Seminar. Home: 2000 N St NW Washington DC 20036 Office: 50 F St NW Washington DC 20001

SMITH, JANICE FAYE (JAN SMITH), software engineer; b. Oneonta, Ala., July 11, 1945; d. Robert Conrad and Jeanette (Bailey) Hays; m. Fred Almon Smith, Oct. 19, 1974 (div. Dec. 1984); 1 child, Lance Almon. BS in Edn., Jacksonville State U., 1967, BS in Math., 1989. Assoc. engr. Boeing, Huntsville, Ala., 1967-69; mem. tech. staff Computer Sci. Corp., Huntsville, 1969-77, 79; engr. McDonnell-Douglas Automation Co., St. Louis, 1977-79; v.p. computer applications Nichols Rsch. Corp., Huntsville, 1979—. Rep. for industry State of Ala. Super Computer com., Huntsville, 1985-86. Republican. Methodist. Office: Nichols Rsch Corp 4040 S Memorial Pkwy Huntsville AL 35802

SMITH, JEAN HOLTHOUSE, guidance counselor; b. Lawrenceburg, Tenn., Nov. 13, 1929; d. Bernard Godfrey and Nelle (Williams) Holthouse; m. Lawrence J. Jr. Smith, Mar. 31, 1951; children: Beverly, Emily Smith Waverka, Melaine, Gregory, Kimberly. Student, St. Mary of the Woods Coll., 1947-49, SUNY, Buffalo, 1967-68; BS, St. Louis U., 1951; MEd, Shippensburg U., 1972. Cert. profl. counselor, Pa. Counselor career pvt. industry coun. Susqwhanna Employment & Tng., Harrisburg, Pa., summers, 80-82; counselor Central Dauphin Sch. Dist., Harrisburg, Pa., 1971—. Mem. editorial bd. Pa. Personnel and Guidance jour., 1978-79. Adv. com. Harrisburg Libr., 1969-71, Dept. Edn. State of Pa., Harrisburg, 1977-79, Dauphin County Task Force on Teenage Depression and Suicide, Harrisburg, 1986-87; bd. dirs. League Women Voters, Harrisburg, 1969-71. Harrisburg br. AAUW grantee, 1989. Mem. AAUW (bd. dirs. 1988-89), Pa. Sch. Counselors, Keystone Counselors Assn. (treas. 1976=86), Phi Delta Kappa, Delta Kappa Gamma (bd. dirs. 1988-89). Roman Catholic. Home: 990 Galion St Harrisburg PA 17111

SMITH, JEAN WEBB (MRS. WILLIAM FRENCH SMITH), civic worker; b. L.A.; d. James Ellwood and Violet (Hughes) Webb; B.A. summa cum laude, Stanford U., 1940; m. George William Vaughan, Mar. 14, 1942 (dec. Sept. 1963); children: George William, Merry; m. 2d, William French Smith, Nov. 6, 1964. Mem. Nat. Vol. Service Adv. Coun. (ACTION), 1973-76, vice chmn., 1974-76; dir. Beneficial Standard Corp., 1976-85. Vol. Community TV So. Calif. (KCET); mem. Calif. Arts Commn., 1971-74, vice chmn., 1973-74; bd. dirs. The Founders, Music Center, L.A., 1971-74; bd. dirs. costume coun. L.A. County Mus. Art, 1971-73; bd. dirs. United Way, Inc., 1973-80; bd. fellows Claremont Univ. Ctr. and Grad. Sch., 1987—; bd. dirs. Hosp. Good Samaritan, 1973-80; mem. exec. com., 1975-80; mem. nat. bd. dirs. Boys' Clubs Am., 1977-80; bd. dirs. L.A. chpt. NCCJ, 1977-80, Nat. Symphony Orch., 1980-85; mem. adv. bd. Salvation Army, 1979—; mem. bd. overseers The Hoover Instn. on War, Revolution and Peace; mem. President's Commn. on White House Fellowships, 1980—, Nat. Coun. on the Humanities, 1987—. Named Woman of Yr. for community service L.A. Times, 1958; recipient Citizens of Yr. award Boys Clubs Greater L.A., 1982, Life Achievement award Boy Scouts Am., L.A. coun., 1985. Mem. Jr. League of L.A. (pres. 1954-55), Assn. Jr. Leagues of Am. (dir. Region XII, 1956-58, pres. 1958-60), Phi Beta Kappa, Kappa Kappa Gamma. Home: 1256 Oak Grove Ave San Marino CA 91108

SMITH, JO ANNE, journalist, retired educator; b. Mpls., Mar. 18, 1930; d. Robert Bradburn and Virginia Mae S. BA, U. Minn., 1951, MA, 1957. Wire and sports editor Rhinelander (Wis.) Daily News, 1951-52; staff corr., night mgr. UPI, Mpls., 1952-56; interim instr. U. N.C., Chapel Hill, 1957-58; instr. U. Fla., Gainesville, 1959-65; asst. prof. journalism, communications U. Fla., 1965-68, assoc. prof., 1968-76, prof., 1976-88, ret., 1988, disting. lectr., 1977. Author: JM409 Casebook and Study Guide, 1976, Mass Communications Law Casebook, 1979, 3d edit., 1985. Active, Friends of Libr., Alachua County Humane Soc. Recipient outstanding Prof. award Fla. Blue Key, 1976; Danforth assoc., 1976-85. Mem. Women in Communications, Soc. Profl. Journalists, Assn. Edn. in Journalism, Phi Beta Kappa, Kappa Tau Alpha. Democrat. Unitarian. Home: 208 NW 21 Terr Gainesville FL 32603

SMITH, JO ANNE, mortgage company analyst; b. Sledge, Miss., Feb. 5, 1956; d. Tom Henry and Estelle (Young) S.; m. Raymond R. Garth, July 9, 1987 (div. Mar. 1989). AA, Forest Park Coll., St. Louis, 1977; student, U. Mo., St. Louis, 1978-80; BA, Nat. Coll. Edn., St. Louis, 1986; postgrad., Webster U., St. Louis, 1989. Sec. III Human Devel. Corp., St. Louis, 1974-79; stenographer Gen. Motors Corp., Pontiac div., St. Louis, 1979-80; word processing operator II Citicorp Homeowners, Inc., St. Louis, 1980-81; word processing coord. Citicorp Person-to-Person, Inc., St. Louis, 1981-84, system support specialist, 1984-85; product info. analyst Citicorp Mortgage, Inc., St. Louis, 1985—. Vol. Holiday Caring, St. Louis, 1985—, United Way, St. Louis, 1988, Parenting Fair, 1988—, Mathews-Dickey Boys' Club, St. Louis. Mem. Nat. Assn. Female Execs., Hogan User's Group. Democrat. Methodist. Home: 4236 W Pine Blvd Apt 208 Saint Louis MO 63108 Office: Citicorp Mortgage Inc 12855 N 40 Outer Rd Saint Louis MO 63141

SMITH, JOANNE J., retired publicity writer; b. Bklyn., Apr. 29, 1939; d. Lewis J. and Pauline (Dietz) Blackburn; m. Charles E. Smith, Oct. 19, 91985; children: Mark, Janet Ellis, Jana havers, Jackie Blair, Mike. AB in English Lit., Bucknell U., 1961. Cert. quality engr. Publicist Ins. Co. N.Am., Phila.; sales promotion coord. Nat. Assn. Accts., N.Y.C.; mgr. materials engring. Compaq Computer, Houston. Vol. cons. South Palm Beach County Mental Health, U.S. Fish and Wildlife Svc., Everglades Nat. Pk. Mem. Am. Soc. for Quality Control, Nat. Conf. of Standard Lab., Am. Businesswomen's Assn. Home: 6135 La Vida Terr Boca Raton FL 33433

SMITH, JOSEPHINE CARROLL, school system administrator; b. Washington, 1884; d. Dennis and Alice (Morgan) Carroll; m. William H. Smith, June 14, 1918 (dec. Feb. 1963). AB, Howard U., 1930; MA, Columbia U., 1937. Tchr. pub. schs., Washington, 1916-30, prin., 1930-31, adminstrv. prin., 1931-41, demonstration sch. prin., 1941-46, 46-55, divisional dir. div. 10, dir. elem. edn. in charge adminstrn., 1955—, ret., 1955-63; ret. v.p. Northwest Boundary Civic Assn., 1961—; mem. program com. Girl Scouts D.C. Mem. LWV D.C., Nat., D.C. edn. assns., D.C. Coun. Adminstrv. Women, Am. Assn. Sch. Adminstrs., Washington Planning and Housing Assn., Zeta Phi Beta (regional dir.). Baptist. Home: The Charter House 1316 Fenwick Ln Apt. 1013 Silver Spring MD 20910

SMITH, JOSEPHINE WOOLLEY, advertising agency executive; b. Findlay, Ohio, Mar. 15, 1934; d. Walton Douglas and Charlotte Josephine (Bente) Woolley; m. Lawrence Sophian, June 22, 1954; children—Celia, Catherine. B.A., Sarah Lawrence Coll., 1954. Advt. copywriter Batten, Barton, Durstine & Osborn, 1954-62; copy supr. Ogilvy & Mather, N.Y.C., 1962-70; v.p. Ogilvy & Mather, 1970-73, creative dir., 1973, sr. v.p., 1974—. Office: Ogilvy & Mather Worldwide Pla 309 E 49th St New York NY 10019

SMITH, JUANITA RANKIN, accountant; b. Bridgeton, N.J., Nov. 1, 1949; d. Andrew Jackson and Jessie Lee (Bryant) Rankin; m. Ronald Delaneo Smith, Mar. 23, 1968 (div. Nov. 1978); 1 child, LaJuana. BS, Glassboro State Coll., 1982. Operating acct. Communications-Electronics Command U.S. Army, Ft. Monmouth, N.J., 1984—; part-time instr. Union Tech. Inst., Neptune, 1989—. Bd. dirs. Bridgeton Housing Devel. Corp., 1984-85; pres. Bridgeton High Sch. PTA, 1982; trustee Macedonia Bapt. Ch., Neptune, N.J., 1986. Mem. Am. Soc. Mil. Compts., Nat. Assn. Negro Bus. and Profl. Women (fin. sec. Cen. Jersey Club 1988—), Assn. Govt. Accts. (dir. edn. Cen. N.J. chpt.). Democrat. Baptist. Home: 2130 Aldrin Rd Apt #6-A Ocean NJ 07712 Office: US Army Communications and Electronics Command AMSEL-CP-FA-GAB Fort Monmouth NJ 07703-5009

SMITH, JUDITH ANN, hospital services executive; b. Lakeland, Fla., Jan. 15, 1957; d. Clifford Charles and Mary Ellen (Keske) S. BS in Med. Records Adminstrn., U. Cen. Fla., 1979, MPH, 1985. Registered record adminstr. Utilization rev. coord., audit asst. Cape Canaveral Hosp., Cocoa Beach, Fla., 1979-80, asst. dir. med. records, 1980, dir. med. records, 1980-84; dir. med. record svcs. Winter Park (Fla.) Meml. Hosp., 1984—; nursing home cons. Courtenay Springs Health Care Ctr., Merrit Island, Fla., 1984, Orlando (Fla.) Luth. Towers, 1984-86; mem. med. record adminstrn. adv. bd., guest speaker med. record adminstrn. program U. Cen. Fla., Orlando, 1984—, mem. clin. faculty, 1985—, mem. health adv. bd., 1988—, chmn. med. record. adv. bd. 1989-90; mem. med. transcription program adv. com. Seminole Community Coll., Orlando, 1988-89; instr. quality edn. system Winter Park Meml. Hosp., 1989—. Eucharistic minister Good Shepherd Cath. Ch., Orlando, 1984—. Named one of Outstanding Young Women in Am., 1981. Mem. Am. Med. Record Assn. (hospitality task force 1988-89, del. 1990—), Fla. Med. Record Assn. (pres.-elect 1990—, mem. mid-yr. ednl. conf. com., mid-yr. ednl. conf. speaker 1986, bd. dirs. 1988-89, recruitment task force 1988-89, edn. com. 1984-88, program com. 1987-89), Cen. Fla. Med. Record Assn. (del. 1987-88, nominating com. 1984-89, release of info. com. 1986-87), Fla. Utilization Rev. Assn., Kappa Delta. Republican. Office: Winter Park Meml Hosp 200 N Lakemont Ave Winter Park FL 32792

SMITH, JUDITH ANN, microbiologist, dancer; b. Inglewood, Calif., Feb. 6, 1943; d. John L. and Maxine B. (Manges) Chadd; m. Roger James Smith, Dec. 16, 1967; children: Chadd D., Erik A. BS in Biology, Portland State Coll., 1966; PhD in Microbiology, Oreg. Health Scis. U., 1982. Rsch. asst. U. Oreg. Med. Sch., Portland, 1962-66, Reed Coll., Portland, 1966-67; instr. microbiology and ceramics Kuskoquim Community Coll., Bethel, Alaska, 1974-75; instr., dir. Aishalazar Dancers, Ronan, Mont., 1981-86; instr. biology and chemistry Salish-Kootenai Coll., Pablo, Mont., 1982-86; prin. investigator biol. rsch. Salish-Kootenai Coll., Paldo, Mont., 1982-86; instr., dir. Desert Rose Dance Ensemble, Gallup, N.M., 1986-90; cons. grant writing, 1982—; choreographer. Chmn., Red Cross Blood Drawing, Ronan, 1980-85. Mem. AAUW, Union Concerned Scientists.

SMITH, JUDITH WILSON, real estate broker; b. Harrisburg, Pa., Mar. 2, 1941; d. William Dengler and Dorothy (Thatcher) Wilson; m. Richard Evans Smith, Aug. 11, 1962; children: Amy Blaire, Matthew Thatcher, Ashley Jane. BS, Pa. State U., 1962. Lic. real estate broker, N.Y. Advisor home svc. Pub. Svc. Electric & Gas Co., Plainfield, N.J., 1962-66, Phila. Electric, 1964-65; broker Prudential Richard Albert, Realtors, Croton-on-Hudson, N.Y., 1973—. Bd. dirs. Community Adv. Bd. Harlem, Peeksill, N.Y., 1977—, pres., 1980-81; elder Peekskill Presbyn. Ch., 1983—, clk. session, 1988-90. Mem. AAUW (bd. dirs. 1984—), Nat. Assn. Realtors, N.Y. Assn. Realtors, Westchester County bd. Realtors (sec.-treas. 1986-88, v.p. 1989, pres. 1990, bd. dirs. 1985—). Office: Prudential Richard Albert 2 Croton Point Ave Croton-on-Hudson NY 10520-0308

SMITH, JULIA AMELIA, English educator; b. San Antonio, Tex., Dec. 25, 1935; d. George Leon and Julia E. (Garcia) S. BA, Our Lady of the Lake, San Antonio, Tex., 1956; MA, U. Tex., 1958; postgrad., Harvard U., 1961; PhD, U. Tex, 1969. Elem. tchr. San Antonio (Tex.) Sch. Dist., 1956-57; instr. Laredo (Tex.) Jr. Coll., 1959-68; prof. asst. Tex. A&I, Kingsville, 1969-72, assoc. prof., chmn. English dept., 1978—; dept. chair Tex. Art English Dept. Kingsville, 1977-83. contbr. articles to profl. jours. Organist St. Gertrude's Ch., Kingsville, Tex. Mem. Modern Language Assn., Nat. Council of Tchrs of English, Conf. of Coll. Tchrs. of English, Tex. Coll English Assn., Music Club of Kingsville, Audubon Soc., Delta Kappa Gamma, Kappa Nu. Democrat. Roman Catholic. Office: Texas A&I Box 162 Kingsville TX 78363

SMITH, JULIANN JOCELYN, lawyer; b. Hazleton, Pa., Nov. 30, 1953; d. Stanley John and Elsie Antoinette (Matusick) S.; m. Jeffrey T. Smith, Aug. 2, 1987. BS in Community Devel. with high distinction, Pa. State U.-University Park, 1975; postgrad. Boston U., 1978-79; JD, U. Denver, 1981. Bar: Colo. 1983, U.S. Dist. Ct. Colo. 1983. Assoc. Kutak Rock & Campbell, Denver, 1981-85, Gorsuch, Kirgis, Campbell, Walker and Grover, 1985-87; lawyer Colo. Housing and Fin. Authority, 1987—. Articles editor U. Denver Law Jour., 1980-81; contbr. articles to profl. jours. Recipient scholar, 1972-74. Vol. Spl. Olympics Boulder, 1988. Mem. ABA, Colo. Bar Assn., Denver Bar Assn. Office: Colo Housing & Fin Authority 1981 Blake St Denver CO 80202-1272

SMITH, JUNE BURLINGAME, educator; b. Barrington, N.J., June 1, 1935; d. Leslie Grant and Esther (Bellini) Burlingame; m. Gregory Lloyd Smith, July 6, 1963; children: Gilia Cobb Burlingame Smith, Cyrus Comstock. BA, Reed Coll., 1956; MS, Ind. U., 1959; MA, Calif. State U., Dominquez Hills, 1986. Sec. to dean Reed Coll., 1956-57; residence hall supr. Ind. U., 1957-59; buyer Macy's Calif., 1959-63; residence hall supr. U. Wash., 1963, interviewer Tchr. Placement Bur., 1964; music tchr. Chinook Jr. High Sch., Bellevue, Wash., 1964-68; pvt. practice music tchr., 1971-83; gifted grant coord. South Shores/CSUDH Magnet Sch., 1981; tchr. cons. L.A. Unified Sch. Dist., 1981-82; tchr. English composition L.A. Community Coll., 1988—. Chair Sex Equity Commn., LA Unified Sch. Dist. Mem. Am. Acad. Poets, AAUW (pres. San Pedro, Calif. br. 1989—), Phi Kappa Phi. Democrat. Home: 3915 Carolina St San Pedro CA 90731 Office: LA Community Coll Harbor 1111 Fiqueroa Pl Wilmington CA 90744

SMITH, KAREN C., advertising executive; b. Hartsville, S.C., Oct. 15, 1954; d. K.C. Smith and Mary Jane (Sylvestre) Hill; m. J. Gary Kroc, Sept. 28, 1974 (div. May 1978); 1 child, Dana Anne. Student, Moravian Coll., Bethlehem, Pa., 1985—. Sec. West Chester (Pa.) State Coll., 1972; receptionist SHS Employment Agy., Easton, Pa., 1972-73; sec. keypunch processing Northampton County Community Coll., Bethlehem, 1973-75; data ops. control Equitable Data Ctr., Easton, 1975-77; mgr. sales svcs. Rodale Press, Inc., Emmaus, Pa., 1977-83; gen. mgr. Fields Assocs., Allentown, Pa., 1983-86; prin. KCS Communications, Bethlehem, 1986—. Active Allentown Music Club, 1980—, Masterworks Chorale, 1982-89. Democrat. Roman Catholic. Home and Office: 213 Swarthmore Dr Lititz PA 17543

SMITH, KAREN GAIL, reading specialist; b. Tampa, Fla., Oct. 18, 1944; d. John Thomas and Dixie Lancaster (Duffy) Johnson; m. Glenn Nils Smith, June 19, 1971; children: Stephanie, Jennifer, Kristen. BS in Edn., Muskingum Coll., 1966; MEd in Reading, Loyola Coll., 1977; counseling cert., U. Tex., San Antonio, 1989; postgrad., U. Pa., 1990—. Cert. reading specialist, sch. counselor. Tchr. Columbus (Ohio) Pub. Schs., 1966-71, West Point (N.Y.) Elem. Sch., 1971-72, Westerville (Ohio) Pub. schs., 1972-74, Anne Arundel County Pub. Schs., Annapolis, Md., 1974-77; reading specialist Dept. Def. Schs., Karlsruhe, Fed. Republic of Germany, 1977-79, tchr. Dept. Def. Schs., Giessen, Fed. Republic of Germany, 1980-81; reading specialist Balt. County Pub. Schs., 1982-84, Haverford Twp. Pub. Schs., Havertown, Pa., 1989—; pres., owner Lollipops & Gingerbread, Columbia, Md., 1984—. Leader, Girl Scouts of Am., Ft. Sam Houston, Tex. and Columbia, Md., 1985-89; v.p. Ft. Sam Houston Sch. Bd., 1988-89. Recipient Outstanding Leadership award YWCA, San Antonio, 1988, San Antonio coun. Girl Scouts Am., 1988. Mem. Internat. Reading Assn., Nat. Coun. Tchrs. English, ASCD, Alpha Upsilon Alpha. Republican. Presbyterian. Home: 277 Upper Gulph Rd Radnor PA 19087 Office: Haverford Twp Schs Darby Rd Havertown PA 19083

SMITH, KATHLEEN MARIE, lawyer; b. Providence, Jan. 19, 1957; d. George Wesley and Grace (Huntoon) S. BA, Coll. of Holy Cross, 1979; JD, Antioch Sch. Law, Washington, 1986. Bar: Pa., N.J., U.S. Dist. Ct. (ea. dist.) Pa., U.S. Dist. Ct. N.J. Law clk. NLRB, Washington, 1985-86; atty. Phillips and Phelson, Phila., 1987-88; atty. firm Blackburn, Michelman & Tyndall, Phila., 1988—; instr. Careers Inst. Mem. Phi Alpha Theta. Office: Blackburn Michelman Tyndall 1520 Locust St Philadelphia PA 19102

SMITH, KATHLEEN MARIE, health facility administrator; b. Grand Rapids, Mich., Oct. 17, 1940; d. Albert Edward and Ila Melissa (Thorp) Andrews; m. John J. Smith, June 5, 1965; children: Lisa, Debra, Richard. BS, Aquinas Coll., 1965; postgrad., Mich. State U., 1969-70. Med. technologist St. Mary's Hosp., Grand Rapids, 1960-61, Holy Family Hosp., Des Plaines, Ill., 1962-64, Blodgett Meml. Hosp., Grand Rapids, 1964-65, St. Joseph's Hosp., Denver, 1965-66, Porter Meml. Hosp., Englewood, Colo., 1966-67, Ionia County Meml. Hosp., Ionia, Mich., 1967-73; med. technologist, sect. chief Clinton Meml. Hosp., St. Johns, Mich., 1974-80; lab. dir. Clinton County Med. Ctr., St. Johns, 1980—; tchr. Cath. edn., 1969-74, 88-90. Mem. singing group Me and My Friends, 1974-84. Mem. NAFE, Am. Soc. Clin. Pathologists (cert.), Am. Soc. Med. Technologists, Mich. Soc. Med. Technologists. Home: 600 Circle Dr Saint Johns MI 48879

SMITH, KATHRYN ANN, advertising executive; b. Harvey, Ill., Mar. 30, 1955; d. Kenneth Charles and Barbara Joan (Wise) S.; m. Donald Eugene Stonerock, Jr., Oct. 27, 1973 (div. Apr. 1977); m. Charles David Okoren, Oct. 31, 1980; 1 stepchild, Gwynne Marie. Student Art Inst. Chgo., 1973. Advt. salesperson Calumet Index, Inc., Riverdale, Ill., 1974-77, Towne & Country Ind., Hammond, 1977-78; owner, sales person Ad-Com, Merrillville, Ind., 1978—; pres., Crown Point, Ind., 1978—. Dir., producer cable TV comml., 1982; dir., producer TV comml., 1987-88. Mem. Advt. Agy. Owners Assn. (chair 1985-88). Avocations: painting, flying, outdoor activities.

SMITH, KATHRYN BAKER, educational administrator, economist; b. Atlanta, Feb. 8, 1946; d. William Martin Ross and Mildred (Walker) Ross Eatmon; m. William Hugh Baker, III, June 10, 1965 (div.); 1 child, William Hugh IV; m. R.C. Smith, Nov. 23, 1979. Student, Lubbock Christian Coll., 1963-64, U. N.Mex., 1964-65, Fla. State U., 1968; BA, U. Tex., Austin, 1974, MA, 1978. Rsch. assoc. Ctr. for Study of Human Resources, Austin, 1975-76; field researcher MDC, Inc., Chapel Hill, N.C., 1976-78; rsch. assoc. Nat. Rural Ctr., Austin, 1976-79; statewide coord. policy, planning and programs N.C. Dept. Nat. Resources and Community Devel., Employment and Tng., 1979-82; asst. to state pres. for policy Dept. of Community Colls., Raleigh, N.C., 1982-86, dir. planning, 1986-89, assoc. v.p. planning and rsch., 1989—; adv. bd. Small Bus. and Tech. Devel. Ctr., 1985-90, U. N.C. Govt. Execs. Inst., 1983, N.C. Edn. Policy Seminars, 1984-85, Rural Edn. for Action Learning, 1985—; v.p. Communications Women in Mgmt. Triangle chpt., 1989—. Co-author: Rural Jobs from Rural Public Works, 1979; contbr. articles to profl. jours. Bd. dirs., sec. Tex. Housing Devel. Corp., 1977-79; affirmative action com. Dem. Party of Tex., 1974; exec. sec. Young Dems. of Tex., 1973-75; Univ. fellow, 1974-75. Mem. Women in Mgmt. (pres. elect Triangle chpt. 1990—), N.C. Women's Forum (bd. dirs. 1984-87), Women in N.C. Higher Edn. (bd. dirs. 1985—). Office: Dept Community Colls 200 W Jones St Raleigh NC 27603

SMITH, KATHY ANN, teacher, senator; b. Muncie, Ind., Apr. 10, 1944; d. John Francis and H. Emily (Walter) Wallace; m. George Frederick Smith, June 22, 1979; 1 child, Alison Marie Smith. BS in Edn., Ind. U., 1966; postgrad., Ball State U., 1973. Cert. secondary lang. arts tchr., Ind. English tchr. New Albany (Ind.) Floyd Co. Sch. Corp., 1966—; adj. faculty Ind. U. S.E., New Albany, 1977-84. Ind. State senator Ind. Gen. Assembly, Indpls., 1986—; del. Dem. Nat. Conv., N.Y., 1976-80, San Francisco, 1984, Atlanta, 1988, Ind. Dem. State Conv., Indpls., 1980, 82, 84, 86, 88, 90; mem., del. Dem. Nat. Platform Com., Washington, 1984. Mem. New Albany Floyd

County Edn. Assn. (legis. chair 1977-86, exec. com. 1979-86), Ind. State Tchrs. Assn. (chair polit. action com. 1978-81, 83-86), NEA (NEA polit. action com. 1978-81, 83-84), Nat. Coun. Tchrs. of English, Pi Lambda Theta (hon., pres. 1986-88), Psi Iota Xi. Democrat. Home: 1214 Beechwood Ave New Albany IN 47150 Office: Ind State Senate Indianapolis IN 46204

SMITH, KIM O'QUINN, publications administrator; b. Lakeland, Fla., May 10, 1955; d. Ashley Warren and Lois Anne (Hock) O'Quinn. BFA in Advt./Art Studio, U. S.C., 1976. Graphic artist, illustrator S.C. Dept. Health and Environ. Control, Columbia, 1977-80, art dir., 1980-84, dir. div. printing, graphics and photography, 1984-88; dir. publs., art dir. Nat. Assn. for Campus Activities, Columbia, 1988-90; publs. mgr. NUSZ Corp., Aiken, S.C., 1990—. Recipient 1st place award for design competition Howard Paper Co., 1987; Internat. Minerals and Chems. scholar, 1973-77. Methodist. Home: 126 Woodbridge Dr Aiken SC 29801 Office: NUS Corp 900 Trail Ridge Rd Ste 200 Aiken SC 29801

SMITH, KRALEEN STANFIELD, information specialist, librarian; b. Swindon, Eng., June 5, 1958; came to U.S. 1958; d. James Krahe and Marjorie Janette (King) Stanfield; m. Tolby Lynn Smith, Jan. 5, 1985. B.A. cum laude, Tex. Woman's U., 1980, M.L.S., 1981. Info. specialist Price Waterhouse, Dallas, 1981—. Mem. Spl. Libraries Assn. (editor bull. Tex. chpt. 1988—), Dallas Soc. Acctg. Librarians (pres. 1983-85), Dallas Assn. Law Librarians (2d v.p. 1985), Beta Phi Mu. Baptist. Home: 6902 Buckhorn Rowlett TX 75088 Office: Price Waterhouse 1700 Pacific Ave Ste 1400 Dallas TX 75201

SMITH, LAURA LEE WHITELY WEISBRODT, nutritionist, consultant, educator; b. Georgetown, Ohio, July 16, 1903; d. Ferdinand and Addie (Marklay) Weisbrodt; m. Ora Smith; children: James, Sarah Jane Burton. BS, Miami (Ohio) U., 1925; MS, Iowa State U., 1927; PhD, U. Calif., 1930. Instr. Chem. Iowa State, Ames, 1925-27; instr. Nutrition U. Calif., Berkeley, Calif., 1927-30; instr. Cornell U., Ithaca, N.Y., 1936-42; prof. Cornell U., Ithaca, 1956-73, Culinary Inst. of Am., N.Y., 1972; prof. emeritus Cornell U., Ithaca, 1973—; nutrition cons. Inter Am. Inst. of Agr., Sci. in Costa Rica, 1946-48; Adult Edn. instr. Ithaca Pub. Schs., 1942-46; 1948-50; cons. Inst. Mgmt., Ithaca, 1939-44. Author: (book) Food Service Science, 1974; contbr. several articles to profl. jours, 1928—. Mem. Red Cross, Ithaca (chmn., nutritionist, 1935-70); sec. and leader, Girl Scouts U.S., Ithaca, 1931-39; treas. Ithaca Civic Ballet Co. 1960-70; charter mem. Finger Lakes Kennel Club Sch. Bd., Ithaca (pres. and sec.). Fellow Am. Inst. of Chem., Sigma Xi, Kappa Phi; mem. Am. Chem. Soc., N.Y. Acad. of Sci., AAUW, N.Y. Red Cross Nutrition Com. Home: 1707 Slaterville Rd Ithaca NY 14850 Office: Sch of Hotel Adminstrn Statler Ithaca NY 14850

SMITH, LAURIE MACMILLAN, aerospace company executive, financial analyst; b. L.A., Nov. 28, 1960; d. Donald Bather and Olaug Margrethe (Myhr) M. Student, U. Calif.-San Diego, 1978-80; B.B.A., Calif. State U.-Chico, 1982; M.B.A., U. So. Calif., L.A., 1988. Sr. project control adminstr. Hughes Aircraft Co., Torrance, Calif., 1983-88, fin. planning specialist, El Segundo, Calif., 1988—; aerobics instr., 1984-85; cons. Macola Record Co., Hollywood, Calif., 1984, Baby'O Recorders, Hollywood, 1985-86; Pres., co-founder Palos Verdes (Calif.) Girl's Club, 1971-75; participant L.A. Olympics Opening Ceremony Internat. Parade. Mem. Phi Chi Theta (v.p. 1982), Phi Kappa Phi, Beta Gamma Sigma, Sigma Iota Epsilon. Avocations: skiing, reading, sky diving, jogging, yoga. Home: 162 Hermosa Ave Hermosa Beach CA 90254 Office: Hughes Aircraft Co 505 Sepulveda Blvd El Segundo CA 90245

SMITH, LEILA HENTZEN, artist; b. Milw., May 20, 1932; d. Erwin Albert and Marian Leila (Austin) Hentzen; m. Richard Howard Smith, Sept. 12, 1959; 1 child, Jennie. BFA, Miami U., 1955; cert., Famous Artists Schs., 1959. Quilting tchr. Milw. Pub. Schs., 1975-79. Exhibited in two man shows West Bend (Wis.) Gallery of Fine Arts, 1963, George Watts Gallery, Milw., 1965, Mapledale Sch. Gallery, Bayside, Wis., 1981; group shows Milw. Art Ctr., 1961, Wustum Mus. Art, Racine, Wis., 1966, 77, John Michael Kohler Arts Ctr., Sheboygan, Wis., 1984, 87, 89, Ozaukee Art Ctr., Cedarburg, Wis., 1982, 83, 84, 85, 86, Artists' World Galle y, Cedarburg, 1975, Cedarburg 0ultural Ctr., 1988, 89; represented in permanent collections Milw. County Art. Commn., West Bend Gallery Fine Arts, Wheaton Franciscan Svcs. Women's aux. vol. Salvation Army, Milw. Recipient Honorable Mention for painting Bayshore Merchants Assn, 1969, Delta Gamma Art Fair, 1981, Best of Show for painting John Michael Kohler Arts Ctr., 1988. Mem. AAUW, Cedarburg Artists Guild, Seven Arts Soc. of Milw. (pres. 1967-68, painters group chmn. 1962-63), DAR (Milw. chpt., Holiday Folk Fair chmn. 1965-76, libr. historian 1974-77, corr. sec. 1977-80, dir. 1983-86, Outstanding Jr. mem. 1966), Wis. Soc. Daus. of Founders and Patriots of Am. (pres. 1964-66, 2nd v.p. 1966-68, 70-73, councillor 1970-76, corr. sec. 1976-79), Wis. Ct. Assts. Nat. Soc. Women Descendants Ancient and Honorable Artillery Co. of Boston, Wis. Soc. Mayflower Descendents, Delta Zeta. Congregationalist. Home: 9966 Corey Ln Mequon WI 53092

SMITH, LINDA A., state legislator; d. Vern Smith; children: Sheri, Robi. Office mgr.; former mem. Wash. State Ho. of Reps.; now mem. Wash. State Senate. Republican. Home: 10009 NW Ridgecrest Ave Vancouver WA 98685*

SMITH, LINDA ANN, public relations executive; b. Queens, N.Y., June 1, 1951; d. Edwin Joseph and Elaine A. (Gallo) S. BA, CUNY, 1987. Sec. rsch. Merrill Lynch, N.Y.C., 1965-69; adminstrv. mgr. Doremus Pub. Rels., N.Y.C., 1969-85. Bd. dirs. Make-A-Wish Found. of Met. N.Y. Mem. Publicity Club N.Y., PROMA, NAFE, Am. Mgmt. Assn. Office: Gavin Anderson Doremus & Co 11 W 42 St New York NY 10036

SMITH, LINDA LORRAINE, city and county official; b. Burbank, Calif., Oct. 14, 1947; d. Homer Austin and Lorraine Vanda (Grabowski) Hesselrode; m. Paul Evans Smith, Apr. 22, 1972. BA, Occidental Coll., 1969; MPA, Syracuse U., 1970; cert. Kennedy Sch. Govt., Harvard U., 1978. Budget analyst U.S. Office Mgmt. and Budget, Washington, 1970-73, asst. dir. for adminstrn., 1979-82; staff asst. House dist. com. U.S. Ho. of Reps., Washington, 1973-74, spl. asst. to chmn. budget com., 1974-75; dir. Exec. Secretariat, U.S. Dept. Transp., Washington, 1976-79; dir. MIS, U.S. Navy, Pearl Harbor, Hawaii, 1982-87; dir. fin. City and County of Honolulu, 1987—; bd. dirs. Pacific Allied Products, Ltd., Honolulu; mem. Honolulu Mayor's Task Force on Fin. Ctr., 1988—; mem. Reorgn. Commn. Honolulu, 1989—. Editor The Bureaucrat mag., 1979-82; contbr. articles to profl. publs. Deacon Community Ch. Honolulu, 1986-89; bd. dirs. Hawaii Humane Soc., 1989. Recipient achievement award U.S. Dept. Transp., 1977, 78, cert. of excellence USN, 1983; HUD fellow, 1970. Mem. Soc. Plastics Industries (co-chmn. solid waste task force 1988—), Am. Soc. for Pub. Adminstrn. (bd. dirs. 1974-82), C. of C. Hawaii, Phi Beta Kappa. Republican. Congregationalist. Office: City and County of Honolulu Honolulu HI 96813

SMITH, LINDY RAE, nurse; b. Portland, Oreg., Nov. 18, 1957; d. Byron Clifford and Janice Rae (Mattson) Horstman; m. Thomas Clifton Smith, Mar. 15, 1980; 1 child, Gabriel Matthew. Diploma in nursing, Good Samaritan Hosp., 1980; student, Oreg. Coll. of Edn., 1976-77. RN, Oreg. Staff nurse Good Samaritan Hosp. & Med. Weight Loss Clinic, Portland, 1980-81, counselor, nurse, 1981-82; analyst, claims processor Aetna Life and Casualty, Portland, 1982-83; medicare rev. analyst Blue Cross/Blue Shield of Oreg., Portland, 1983-84, precertification coord., 1984-85, mem. utilization and med. rev. com., 1985-88; utilization rev. coord. St. Vincent Hosp., Portland, 1988—; nurse cons. Profl. Orgn. for Wash., Seattle, 1990; mktg. rep., community liaison Synergos Neurol. Ctr., 1990—; with magnetic resonance imaging com. Blue Cross/Blue Shield, Portland, 1985-88. Fellow NAFE. Democrat. Home: 4026 162d Ave SE Bellevue WA 98006

SMITH, LORI KROMIS, newspaper official; b. Balt., Oct. 10, 1950; d. George Frederick and Anna (Crocamo) Kromis; m. Woodrow Wayne Smith, Aug. 11, 1973; children: Eric W., Kristen J. Sec. H.K. Porter Co., Riverside, N.J., 1968-71; sec., pers. asst. United Aero Products, Burlington, N.J., 1971-73; exec. sec. Burlington County Times, Willingboro, N.J., 1973-85, promotion mgr., 1985—. Mem. adv. com. Burlington County unit March of Dimes, 1985—; mem. Burlington County Literacy Com., 1988—; mem. exec. bd. Twin Hills PTA, Willingboro, 1989-90; mem. Muscular Dystrophy Assn. Mem. Internat. Newspaper Mktg. Assn. (4 promotion awards 1987-90), N.J. Press Assn. (6 promotion awards 1988-90), Rotary (treas. Marlton, N.J. 1990-91). Democrat. Roman Catholic. Home: 22 Nevada Ln Willingboro NJ 08046 Office: Burlington County Times Rte 130 Willingboro NJ 08046

SMITH, LORRIE LYNN, sales professional; b. Abilene, Tex., Oct. 4, 1963; d. Larry Martin and Pamela Lee (Allen) S. Student, Richland Coll. With inside supply sales staff Hester's Office Ctr., Lubbock, Tex.; gen. mgr. Rockwall (Tex.) Office Supply; sales svc. coord. Printing Resources Mgmt., Dallas. Literacy instr. for Tex., LIFT, 1988—. Named Woman of Yr., 1987, Young Career Woman of Yr., 1986, 87, 88; Thelma Blair scholar. Mem. Rockwall Bus. and Profl. Women (past pres., 1st v.p.), Rockwall County Humane Soc. (sec. 1986-88). Republican. Presbyterian. Home: 8515 Park Ln #403 Dallas TX 75231 Office: 6700 Denton Dr Dallas TX 75235

SMITH, LYNDA KAYE, air force officer, registered nurse; b. Ft. Riley, Kans., Sept. 2, 1952; d. John William and Minna M. (Blake) Stoner. BSN, U. Wash., 1974; MS in Nursing, Wright State U., 1983. Cert. critical care registered nurse; cert. emergency nurse; cert. trauma nurse. Staff nurse intensive care unit U.S. Navy, Portsmouth, Va., 1974-77, USPHS Hosp., Seattle, 1977-79; commd. 2d lt. USAF, 1979, advanced through grades to maj.; charge nurse spl. care unit USAF Hosp., Wright-Patterson AFB, Ohio, 1979-83, Clark Air Base, Philippines, 1983-85; officer in charge emergency svcs. USAF Hosp., Luke AFB, Tex., 1985-89; instr. nursing svc. mgmt. USAF Hosp., Sheppard AFB, Tex., 1989—; cons. emergency nursing Surgeon Gen. USAF, 1988—; cons. intensive care Pacific Air Force Surgeon Gen., 1983-85; instr. cardiopulmonary resuscitation, advanced cardiac life support, 1981—. Vol., Ctr. against Sexual Assaults, Phoenix, 1985-89, Humane Soc. Wichita County. Decorated Commendation medal 1983, Meritorious Svc. medals 1985, 1989, Achievement medal 1985, USAF. Mem. Am. Assn. Critical Care Nurses (chpt. pres.-elect 1984-85), Am. Assn. Nurses, Air Force Assn., Emergency Nurses Assn., Sigma Theta Tau. Office: 3790 MSTW/MSNOM Sheppard AFB TX 76311

SMITH, MARA A., small business owner, artist; b. Houston, July 31, 1945; d. Charles Parker and Mary Lee (Langford) S. BS, Tex. Woman's U., 1969, MFA, 1980. Owner, pres. Archtl. Murals in Brick, Seattle; lectr. in field. Executed murals in brick Loew's Anatole Hotel, Dallas, 1978, 83, Am. Bank and Trust Co. Bldg., Reading, Pa., 1982, Pacific N.W. Bell Ctr., Seattle, 1985, One Bethesda Ctr., Bethesda, Md., 1986, Dragon Hill Hotel, U.S. Army, Seoul, Republic of Korea, 1989, and others; contbr. articles to profl. jours. Mem. NOW (co-director). Named one of Outstanding Young Women of Am., 1978, Disting. Alumna, Tex. Woman's U. Mem. Internat. Sculpture Ctr., Artist Trust. Office: 339 NW 82 Seattle WA 98117

SMITH, MARCIA JEAN, accountant, tax specialist, financial consultant; b. Kansas City, Mo., Oct. 19, 1947; d. Eugene Hubert and Marcella Juanita (Greene) S.; student U. Nebr., 1965-67; BA (Coll. Ednl. Opportunity grantee), Jersey City State Coll., 1971; MBA in Taxation, Golden Gate U., 1976, postgrad., 1976-77; MS in Acctg., Pace U., 1982; Cert. of completion Cours Commerciaux de Geneve, 1985-86; Legal intern Port Authority N.Y., N.J., N.Y.C., 1972; legis. aide to Harrison A. Williams, U.S. Senator, Washington, 1973; tax accountant Bechtel Corp., San Francisco, 1974-77; sr. tax accountant Equitable Life Assurance Soc. U.S., N.Y.C., 1977; asst. sec. Equitable Life Holding Corp., N.Y.C., 1977-79, Equico Lessors, Inc., Mpls., 1978-79, Equitable Gen. Ins. Group, Ft. Worth, 1977-79, Heritage Life Assurance Co., Toronto, Ont., Can., 1978-79, Informatics, Inc., Los Angeles, 1978-79; sec. Equico Capital Corp., N.Y.C., 1977-79, Equico Personal Credit, Inc., Colorado Springs, Colo., 1978-79, Equico Securities, Inc., N.Y.C., 1977-79, Equitable Environ. Health, Inc., Woodbury, N.Y., 1977-79; tax sr. Arthur Andersen & Co., N.Y.C., 1979-82; pres. M.J. Smith Co., N.Y.C., 1983-85, prin. owner MJS Cons. Svcs. Internat. Tax Cons., Boston, Mass., 1988—; cons. U.N., specialized agys., Geneva, 1985-87; tax cons.; real estate salesperson. Spl. advisor U.S. Congl. Adv. Bd.; human rights chmn. YWCA, Lincoln, Nebr., 1966-67. Recipient Certificate of Recognition, Central Mo. State Coll., 1965, Unicameral award State Neb., 1967, Mary McLeod Bethune award Jersey City State Coll., 1971. Mem. AAAS, AAUW, NAA (Swiss Romande chpt.), Am. Mgmt. Assn., Nat. Soc. Pub. Accts., Nat. Assn. Accts., Am. Acctg. Assn., Internat. Assn. Fin. Planners, Internat. Fin. Mgmt. Assn., Am. Women's Club of Geneva, Nat. Assn. Women Bus. Owners, Am. Assn. Individual Investors, Inst. Internal Auditors, N.Y. Acad. Scis., Nat. Hist. Soc., Nat. Assn. Tax Practitioners, Assn. Managerial Economists, Postal Commemorative Soc., Am. Mus. Natural History, Nat. Trust Historic Preservation, Internat. Tax Inst., Am. Econs. Assn., Internat. Platform Assn., Inst. Internal Auditors, U.S. Senatorial Club. Office: MJS Cons Svcs Internat Tax Cons PO Box 3438 Boston MA 02101-3438

SMITH, MARCIA JEANNE, secondary educator; b. Carthage, N.Y., Apr. 27, 1935; d. Herman Leon and Vera Magdelena (Weir) Zahn; div.; 1 child, Patrick Brian. BA, Syracuse U., 1958; MA, Middlebury Coll., 1962. Cert. in secondary edn./English. Tchr. English South Jefferson Cen. High Sch., Adams, N.Y., 1958—; asst. prof. extension and evening div. Jefferson Community Coll., Watertown, N.Y., 1967-69. Mem. N.Y. State English Council (named High Sch. Tchr. of Excellence 1989), Nat. Council Tchrs. English, AAUW, Coll. Women's Club of Jefferson County (corr. sec. 1989-90), Pi Lambda Theta, Alpha Delta Kappa. Home: Ridge Rd Route 5 Watertown NY 13601

SMITH, MARGARET, state legislator; b. Chgo.; m. Fred J. Smith; 2 sons, (dec.). Student, Tenn. State U. Mem. Ill. Ho. of Reps., 1981-83; mem. Ill. Senate, dist. 12, 1983—. Trustee Chgo. Bapt. Inst. Democrat. Office: State Senate Springfield IL 62706 also: 130 E Garfield Blvd Chicago IL 60615*

SMITH, MARGARET ELEANOR JONES, teachers association coordinator; b. Beaver County, Okla., June 28, 1921; d. Gordon Sylvester and Anna Asenath (Miller) Jones; m. John W.V. Smith, June 8, 1942 (dec. Nov. 1984); children: Vernon Kent, David Gordon, Robert LeRoy. BS in Home Econs. and Edn., Northwestern State Coll., Alva, Okla., 1942; MA in Home Econs. and Social Studies, Ball State U., 1959. Cert. secondary sch. counselor. With religion edn. L.A. Ch. Fedn., 1947-49; freshman English tchr. Warner Pacific Bible Coll., Portland, Oreg., 1950-52; home econs. tchr. Anderson (Ind.) Community Schs., 1957-76; secondary sch. counselor Anderson High Sch., 1976-81; tchr. Asian Mission Sch., Ch. of God Mission Bd., 1981-82, West Indies Theol. Coll., Trinidad, 1983; editor Missions mag. Missions Edn., Anderson, 1986-87; state coord. Ind. Retired Tchrs., Indpls., 1988—. Editor, co-author (family genealogy) Jones, Miller, Smith, 1976—; editor: Called to Minister, 1988; contbr. newsletter for Ind. Retired Tchrs., 1988—. Ct. Appointed Spl. Advocate, Madison County, Ind., 1987-89; mem. Literacy Coalition, Madison County, 1986-88; mem., interviewer Women's History Coalition, Madison County, 1988-90; mem. Madison County Extension Adv. Com., 1989-90, LWV, Madison County, 1965-81. Named for community svc. Kiwanis Clubs of Anderson, Ind., 1989. Mem. AAUW (program chmn. 1990-92). Democrat. Ch. of God.

SMITH, MARGARET MARY, retired high school teacher; b. Denver, Oct. 11, 1912; d. Michael Joseph and Anna Mary S. (Lynch) S. AB, U. Colo., Boulder, 1934, MA, 1939; postgrad., U. Denver, 1960, U. Colo., 1961. Cert. tchr., 1942. Tchr. Latin, music, English Otis High Sch., Colo., 1934-36; tchr. Denver Pub. Schs., 1936-41; tchr. English, speech, drama, jour. Smiley Jr. High Sch., Denver, 1941-47; tchr. Latin East Denver High Sch., 1941-42, tchr. Latin, English, drama, 1947-51, tchr. Latin, English, Italian, 1952-77; chmn. Assy. Com., East High, Denver, 1960-66, chmn. fgn. lang. dept., East High Denver, 1966, 70, 74, 77, chmn. acad. award evening, sponsor drama club, thespian group, 1947-51; bd. dirs. Denver Tchr.'s Club. Reader, monitor recording for the blind, 1977—; Dem. supply judge elections, 1977-89, active Sen. John Carroll's hdqrs., 1958, 62, 66; vol. Bella Vita Nursing Home, 1977—, USO, 1941-43; mem. Bot. Gardens, Denver Art Mus., Friends of Denver Libr., Com. for 50th Reunion U. Colo. Fulbright scholar, 1961; named Colo. Tchr. of Yr., 1967. Mem. Am. Fedn. Tchrs., Colo. Fedn. Tchrs., Denver Fedn. Tchrs., Am. Classical League, Sch. Dames, Denver Pub. Schs. Ret. Employees (pres. 1982-83), Il Cicolo Italiano, English Speaking Union, St. Thomas Sem. Aux., Delta Kappa Gamma. Roman Catholic.

SMITH, MARGARET MARY, management consultant; b. N.Y.C., July 3, 1949; d. Joseph Leo and Caroline Dolores (Monahan) S. Sec. Western Electric, N.Y.C., 1966-71; product mgr. Citibank, N.Y.C., 1971-75; asst. v.p. European-Am. Bank, N.Y.C., 1975-80; sr. v.p. Mark Ponton Corp., N.Y.C., 1980—. Home: 531 Main St New York NY 10044 Office: The Mark Ponton Corp 7 High St Huntington NY 11743

SMITH, MARGARET PHYLLIS, editor, consultant; b. Plymouth, Pa., Aug. 24, 1925; d. Harold Dewitt and Mae Elmira (Bittenbender) S. AB magna cum laude, Bucknell U., 1946, AM, 1947; postgrad., U. Pa., summer 1951-54. Instr. English Bucknell U., Lewisburg, Pa., 1947-52, asst. prof., 1952-55; personnel asst. RCA Labs., Princeton, N.J., 1955-58, staff writer pub. affairs dept., 1958-76, adminstr. communications, 1976-87; editor spl. projects David Sarnoff Rsch. Ctr. (formerly RCA Labs.), Princeton, 1987—; mng. editor Vision mag. David Sarnoff Rsch. Ctr., 1987—, editor UPDATE newsletter, 1969—. Editor: 1942-67 Twenty-five Years at RCA Laboratories, 1968. Mem. corp. communications com. United Way, Princeton, 1976—. Mem. AAUW, N.J. Press Women (publicity dir. 1985-86), Internat. Assn. Bus. Communicators. Episcopalian. Office: David Sarnoff Rsch Ctr 201 Washington Rd Princeton NJ 08543-5300

SMITH, MARGHERITA, writer, editor; b. Chgo., May 24, 1922; d. Henry Christian and Alicia (Koke) Steinhoff; m. Rufus Zartman Smith, June 26, 1943; children: Matthew Benjamin, Timothy Rufus. AB, Ill. Coll., 1943. Proofreader Editorial Experts, Inc., Alexandria, Va., 1974; mgr. proofreading div. Editorial Experts, Inc., Alexandria, 1978-79, mgr. publs. div., 1979-81, asst. to pres., 1980-81; freelance editor, cons. Annandale, Va., 1981—; instr. proofreading and copy editing, George Washington U., Washington, 1978-82; presenter workshops on proofreading for various profl. orgns., 1981—; cons., TechEdit, Burke, Va., 1987—, ITA Distbrs., Inc., Dover, Del., 1989. Author: (as Peggy Smith) Simplified Proofreading, 1980, Proofreading Manual and Reference Guide, 1981, Proofreading Workbook, 1981, The Proof Is in the Reading: A Comprehensive Guide to Staffing and Management of Typographic Proofreading, 1986, Mark My Words: Instructions and Practice in Proofreading, 1987; newsletter editor Editorial Eye, 1979-81; contbr. articles and revs. to various publs. Recipient Best Instrnl. Reporting award, Newsletter Assn. Am., 1980, Disting. Achievement award for Excellence in Ednl. Journalism, Ednl. Press Assn. Am., 1981. Mem. Nat. Writers Union, Nat. Writers Club. Home and Office: 4560 King Edward Ct Annandale VA 22003

SMITH, MARGIE STOY, orchestra executive; b. Des Moines, Apr. 16, 1938; d. Earl G. Stoy and Azell Anderson; m. G. Morgan Smith, Oct. 23, 1988; children: Mark, Lisa, Anne, Jonathan Boylan. BA, U. Ariz., 1960; MA, U. Iowa, 1971; student, U. Md. Cert. tchr. German. Tchr. various instns. Iowa, Colo., Mont. Idaho; instructional TV cons. Idaho State Dept. Edn., Boise; dir. mktg. Idaho Pub. TV, Boise; gen. mgr. Boise Philharm. Active Arts for Idaho, Idaho Alliance for Arts Edn., Boise Arts Group, Boise Arts Commn.; apptd. by gov. to regional ITV and Pub. Broadcasting Commn., Drought Commn.; Idaho rep. Regional Energy Conf., Title IX Study. Office: Boise Philharm Assn 205 N 10th St Ste 617 Boise ID 83702

SMITH, MARIE EDMONDS, property manager, broker, contractor; b. Quapaw, Okla., Oct. 5, 1927; d. Thomas Joseph and Maud Ethel (Douglas) Edmonds; m. Robert Lee Smith, Aug. 14, 1966 (dec. 1983). Grad. vocat. nurse, Hoag Hosp., Costa Mesa, Calif., 1953; BA, So. Calif. Coll., 1955; MS, U. Alaska, 1963. Lic. vocat. nurse, Calif.; cert. sci. tchr., Alaska. Nurse Calif. Dept. Nurses, Costa Mesa, 1952-60; tchr. Alaska Dept. Edn., Aniak and Anchorage, 1955-60; tchr. sci. Garden Grove (Calif.) Sch. Dist., 1960-87; property mgr. Huntington Beach, Calif., 1970—; agt. Prodential Ins. Co., Fountain Valley, Calif., 1988—; broker Prudential Sterling Realtors, Huntington Beach, 1988—. Author: Ocean Biology, 1969. Bd. dirs., tchr. Harbor Christian Fellowship, Costa Mesa, 1966-83; com. chmn. Garden Grove Unified Sch. Dist. PTA, 1977. NSF grantee, 1960-62. Mem. Nat. Assn. Realtors, Calif. Realtors, AAUW, So. Calif. Coll. Alumnae Assn. Republican. Home: 8311 Reilly Dr Huntington Beach CA 92646 Office: 18153 Brookhurst St Fountain Valley CA 92708

SMITH, MARILYN MILLER, nursing educator; b. Pawtucket, R.I., July 17, 1941; d. Walter Earl and Irene Blanche (Miller) Smith; m. Jack Robert Smith, Aug. 16, 1987. BSN, Boston U., 1966, MSN, 1967; MBA, Northeastern U., Boston, 1974. RN, Mass. Instr. Boston U., 1967-69; with coll. nursing faculty Northeastern U., 1969—; cons. in career devel. Contbr. articles to profl. jours. Mem. ANA, Nat. League for Nursing, Mass. Pub. Health Assn., Sigma Theta Tau. Home: 27 Pearl St Randolph MA 02368 Office: Northeastern U 360 Huntington Ave Boston MA 02115

SMITH, MARILYN RUEDEANE, microbiologist; b. Americus, Ga., Jan. 12, 1950; d. Eddie Frank and Charlie Bell (Small) S. BS, Fla. A&M U., 1972; postgrad., Long Island U., 1988; cert., Women's Mgmt. Tng. Initiative, 1985. Microbiologist FDA, Bklyn., 1976-85; supervisory microbiologist FDA, Los Angeles, 1985—; mgr. womens's program FDA, Bklyn., 1984-85. Conbr. articles to profl. jours. Trainer Literacy Vols. of Am., N.Y.C., 1978-79; literacy vol. L.A. County; mem. NAACP, Englewood, N.J. and Hollywood, Calif. Mem. So. Calif. Soc. Microbiology, Nat. Orgn. Black Chemists and Chem. Engrs., NAFE, Nat. Coun. Negro Women, Internat. Training in Communication Assn. (sec. 1985, v.p., 1986), Federally Employed Women, Toastmasters, Am. Soc. Microbiology (N.Y. chpt.), Delta Sigma Theta. Democrat. Mem. African Methodist Episcopalian Ch. Home: 833 S Plymouth Blvd Los Angeles CA 90005 Address: 11 Chamin Pla Englewood NJ 07631

SMITH, MARILYNN ANN, systems engineer; b. Kewanee, Ill., Oct. 2, 1950; d. Kenneth Glen and Hazel Marie (Lasagna) S.; m. Harold James Martin, June 6, 1970 (div. July 1979); m. John P. Wrubleuski III, June 17, 1989. Student, Ariz. State U., Tempe, 1979. Supr. mktg. ITT Courier, Tempe, Ariz., 1974-79; programmer Blue Cross, Allentown, Pa., 1979-81; programmer analyst Saxon Industries, Miami, 1981-82; project leader Jartran Truck Rentals, Miami, 1982-85; cons. Self Employed, Miami, 1986-87; systems engr. Diamond Star Motors, Ill., 1988-89; systems analyst GTE Data Svcs., Tampa, Fla., 1989—. Mem. NAFE.

SMITH, MARTA MEDARIS, hospital administrator; b. Cin., Dec. 26, 1933; d. John Bruce and Virginia Rose (Smith) Medaris; m. Charles Kenyon Woody, June 8, 1957 (div. 1967); children: Lisa, Bruce, Faith, Christopher; m. Charles G. Smith, Sept. 29, 1967. BS, Coll. St. Francis, Joliet, Ill., 1982; MBA, U. N.Mex., Albuquerque, 1985. RN. Staff nurse, supr. Kula Hosp., Maui, Hawaii, 1967-68, Presbyn. Hosp., Albuquerque, 1968-69; tech. svcs. mgr. Cardiology Assocs. N.Mex., Albuquerque, 1969-80; dept. mgr. Presbyn. Healthcare Svcs., Albuquerque, 1980-83, assoc. planner, 1983-86, asst. adminstr., exec. dir., 1986-88; hosp. dir. U. Conn. Health Ctr., Norwich, 1988—; cons., lectr. U. Ariz., Tucson, 1986—; asst. prof. U. Conn. Sch. Medicine, Farmington, 1988—; lectr. U. N.Mex., Albuquerque, 1986-87. Contbr. articles to mgmt. jours. Chmn. bd. Health Care for the Homeless, Albuquerque, 1986-87; bd. dirs. Exec. Women Internat., Albuquerque, 1984-87; bd. mem., chmn. elect Martin House, Inc., Norwich, 1988—; mem. Nat. Coun. on Aging. Mem. Am. Coll. Healthcare Execs., Rotary Internat., Pautipaug Country Club (Baltic, Conn.). Democrat. Episcopalian. Office: Uncas on Thames Hosp 401 W Thames St Nowich CT 06360

SMITH, MARY ALICE See ALICE, MARY

SMITH, MARY HOWARD HARDING, civil service career executive; b. Washington, Jan. 24, 1944; d. John Edward Harding and Sonja (Karlow) Harding Mulroney; m. Douglas Sydney Smith, Oct. 4, 1969; stepchildren: Michael D., Martha, Thomas, Sue-Ellen, Brian, Stephen. AB, Duke U., 1965; MPA, Cen. Mich. U., 1975. With U.S. Army, 1968—; dir. program mgmt. systems devel. agy. U.S. Army, Washington, 1987—, dep. dir. program analysis and evaluation, 1987—. Contbr. numerous articles to profl. jours. Bd. dirs. Army Family Action Symposiu, Washington, 1982. Mem. Am. Soc. Mil. Comptrollers, NAFE. Home: 1805 S 24th St Arlington VA 22202-1534 Office: US Army Hdqrs ATTN: DACS-DPP Pentagon Rm 2A690 Washington DC 20310-0200

SMITH, MARY JOHN, lawyer; b. Andulusia, Ala., Feb. 20, 1943; d. John D. and Claudie L. (Bryan) S. AB, U. Ala., 1965, MA, 1967; PhD, U. Tex., 1975; JD, U. Va., 1988. Bar: Va. 1988. Instr. U. Ala., Tuscaloosa, 1965-70; teaching asst. U. Tex., Austin, 1971-75; asst. prof. U. Va., Charlottesville, 1975-82; assoc. prof. U. Wyo., Laramie, 1982-85; assoc. Robert M. Musselman & Assocs., Charlottesville, 1988-90; pvt. practice Charlottesville, 1990—. Author: Persuasion and Human Action, 1982, Contemporary Communication Research Methods, 1988; contbr. articles to publs. Mem. ABA, Internat. Communication Assn., Va. State Bar Assn.

SMITH, MARY LOUISE, real estate broker; b. Eldorado, Ill., May 29, 1935; d. Joseph Henry Smith and Opal Marie (Shelton) Hungerford; m. David Lee Smith, June 18, 1961; children: Ricky Eugene, Brenda Sue Smith Millsap. Student, So. Ill. U., 1954-56, 57-58. Cert. tchr., Mo.; cert. real estate broker/salesperson, Mo. With acctg. dept. Cen. Hardware Co., St. Louis, 1958-61; mgr. income tax office Tax Teller Inc., St. Louis, 1967-69, H&R Block Co., St. Louis, 1970-76; with acctg. dept. Weis Neumann Co., St. Louis, 1976-79; sales assoc. Century 21 Neubauer Realty, Inc., St. Louis, 1981-83, 88—, John R. Green Realtor, Inc., St. Louis, 1983-85; sales assoc. Century 21 Action Properties, St. Louis, 1985-86, real estate broker/salesperson, 1986-88; real estate broker/salesperson Century 21 Neubauer Realty, St. Louis, 1988—; substitute tchr., St. Louis Bd. Edn., 1967—. Childrens dir. Lafayette Park Bapt. Ch., St. Louis, 1981—, mem. Mem. Internat. Platform Assn., Am. Fedn. of Tchrs. Home and Office: 2627 Nebraska Saint Louis MO 63118

SMITH, MARY-ANN TIRONE, writer; b. Hartford, Conn., Feb. 6, 1944; d. Maurice Paul and Florence Marie (Deslauriers) Tirone; m. Jere Patrick Smith, Sept. 2, 1968; children: Jene Maria, Jere Paul. BA, Cen. Conn. State U., 1965. Vol. Peace Corps, Cameroon, 1965-67; librarian Stamford (Conn.) Pub. Libraries, 1968-69; tchr. Norwalk (Conn.) pub. schs., 1968-72; instr. Fairfield (Conn.) U., 1986—. Author (novels): The Book of Phoebe, 1985, Lament for a Silver-Eyed Woman, 1987, The Port of Missing Men, 1989; editor: Long Ridge Writers Group, 1990—; book critic N.Y. Times Book Rev., 1986—, Readers Digest Books, 1986-88. Active Nat. Abortion Rights, N.Y.C., 1989—, MADD, N.Y.C., 1987—, PTA, Ridgefield, Conn., 1977—; officer Ridgefield Little League, 1981—. Mem. PEN, The Authors Guild. Democrat. Home: 35 Virginia Court Ridgefield CT 06877 Office: Fairfield Univ North Benson Rd Fairfield CT 06430

SMITH, MAUREEN JACQUELENE, production designer; b. Chgo., Jan. 1, 1967; d. Robert William and Josephine Anne (Trusner) S. BS, Butler U., 1989. Public rels. intern Ind. Health Care Assn., Indpls., 1988, Melvin Simon & Assocs., Inc., Indpls., 1988; prodn. designer Inst. Real Estate Mgmt., Chgo., 1989—; sales clk. part-time Casual Corner, Lombard, Ill., 1989—; freelance graphic artist, Chgo., 1989—. Vol. Lyons (Ill.) Police and Fire Commn., 1990. Mem. Women in Communications, Inc. Democrat. Roman Catholic. Home: 4004 Anna Ave Lyons IL 60534

SMITH, MAURINE SLEEPER, English educator; b. Fort Gibson, Okla., Feb. 18, 1913; d. Louis Girtley and Cricket Nan (French) Sleeper; m. Noble Clay Smith (dec.); children: David Sleeper (dec.), James Clay (dec.), Robert Allen. BA, Northeastern State U., Tahlequah, Okla., 1934, MA in Teaching, 1962; MA, U. Ark., 1970. Sec. Nat. Park Service, Santa Fe, N.Mex., 1949-51; sec. to pres. Northeastern State U., 1951-64, asst. prof. English, 1964-78, lectr., 1978-85. Author: (play) Papa's Children, 1982, numerous works of fiction and poetry, 1982—. Vol. Tahlequah Hosp. Aux., 1982—. Mem. Okla. Edn. Assn., AARP, Northeastern State U. Alumni Assn. (Alumnus of Yr. 1968), AAUW, P.E.O. (pres. 1985-86). Democrat. Presbyterian. Home and Office: 406 E Jamestown Tahlequah OK 74464

SMITH, NANCY DUVERGNE, editor, writer, educator; b. Meridian, Miss., Mar. 22, 1951; d. Frank Gordin and Edna Henley (Brogan) S.; m. Mark Michael Sirdevan, Oct. 25, 1980. BFA, Tulane U., 1973; M in Liberal Arts, Harvard U., 1989. Newspaper reporter The Meridian (Miss.) Star, 1975-77, 81-82; mng. editor New Age mag., Brookline, Mass., 1978-80; English tchr. Am. Cultural Inst., Alexandria, Egypt, 1981; editorial dir. pub. affairs office Wellesley (Mass.) Coll., 1983—, lectr. writing program, 1989—. Paintings exhibited at Musee des Beaux Arts, 1981; editor NWU Databook, 1988; contbr. articles to mags. Mem. Radical Caucus of Faculty and Staff, Wellesley, 1986-88; mem. adv. bd. Boston Writers Rm., 1990—. Mem. Women in Communications, Nat. Writers Union (sec.-treas. 1985-89, nat. bd. mem.), Coun. for Advancement of Edn. and Support (conf. speaker 1988, 89). Democrat. Home: 11 Berry St Framingham MA 01701 Office: Wellesley Coll 230 Green Hall Wellesley MA 02181

SMITH, NANCY HOHENDORF, sales and marketing executive; b. Detroit, Jan. 30, 1943; d. Donald Gerald and Lucille Marie (Kopp) Hohendorf; m. Richard Harold Smith, Aug. 21, 1978 (div. Jan. 1984). BA, U. Detroit, 1965; MA, Wayne State U., 1969. Customer rep. Xerox Corp., Detroit, 1965-67; major account mktg. exec. Xerox Corp., Hartford, Conn., 1978-79; major account mktg. exec. Xerox Corp., N.Y.C., 1979-80, account exec. State of N.Y., 1981; N.Y. region mgr. customer support Xerox Corp., New Haven, 1982; N.Y. region sales ops. mgr. Xerox Corp., Greenwich, Conn., 1982; Ohio account exec. Xerox Corp., Columbus, 1983; new bus. sales mgr. Xerox Corp., Dayton, Ohio, 1983, major accounts sales mgr., 1984; info. systems sales and support mgr., quality specialist Xerox Corp., Detroit, 1985-87, new product launch mgr., ops. quality mgr., 1988, dist. quality mgr., 1989-90, dist. mktg. mgr., 1990—; mktg. rep. Univ. Microfilms subs. Xerox Corp., Ann Arbor, Mich., 1967-73, mktg. coord., 1973-74, mgr. dir. mktg., 1975-76; mgr. mktg. Xerox Corp., Can., 1976-77. Named to Outstanding Young Women of Am., 1968, Outstanding Bus. Woman, Dayton C. of C., 1984. Mem. NAFE, Am. Mgmt. Assn., Women's Econ. Club of Detroit, Detroit Inst. Arts Founders' Soc. Republican. Roman Catholic. Home: 23308 Reynard Dr Southfield MI 48034 Office: Xerox Corp Galleria Offcentre Bldg 300 Southfield MI 48034

SMITH, NANCY L., academic administrator; b. Coleman, Tex., Dec. 20, 1956; d. Louis Grady and Eugenia Hartsfield (Pauley) Pittard; m. Rodney Glenn Smith, Dec. 7, 1985; 1 child, Matthew. BS, McMurry Coll., 1979; MEd, North Tex. State U., 1982; cert. in real estate, Cisco Jr. Coll., 1986. Cert. tchr., Tex.; lic. real estate salesman, Tex. Tchr. Pilot Point (Tex.) Ind. Sch. Dist., 1980-82; advt. sales rep. Penny Wise, Denton, Tex., 1982; asst. dir. admissions McMurry Coll., Abilene, Tex., 1983-84, assoc. dir. admissions, 1984-87, assoc. dean students, 1987—, tchr., cons. remedial reading program, 1990—. Mem. planning and allocations com. United Way, Abilene, 1988—, bd. dirs. 1990—; chmn. bd. dirs. Abilene March of Dimes, 1989—; vol. Am. Heart Assn., Abilene, 1986-89; mem. Eating Disorders Task Force; inreach dir. Pioneer Dr. Bapt. Ch., 1988—; bd. dirs. Jr. Achievement, 1990—. Mem. Am. Bus. Womens Assn. (pres. 1986-87, v.p. 1989-90; Woman of Yr. 1987-88), Tex. Assn. Coll. and U. Student Personnel Adminstrs., Abilene C. of C., Leadership Abilene (loaned exec., steering com. 1990—). Home: 3110 Chim Rock St Abilene TX 79606 Office: McMurry Coll S 14th St and Sayles St Abilene TX 79697

SMITH, NANCY LYNNE, journalist; b. San Antonio, July 31, 1947; d. Tillman Louis and Enid Maxine (Woolverton) Brown; m. Allan Roy Jones, Nov. 28, 1969 (div. 1975); 1 dau., Christina Elizabeth Woolverton Jones. BA, So. Meth. U., 1968; postgrad. So. Meth. U., 1969-70, Vanderbilt U., 1964, Ecole Nouvelle de la Suisse Romande, Lausanne, Switzerland, 1962. Tchr. spl. edn. Hot Springs Sch. Dist. (Ark.), 1970-72; reporter, soc. editor Dallas Morning News, 1974-82; soc./celebrity columnist Dallas Times Herald, 1982—; stringer Washington Post, 1978; contbg. editor Ultra mag., Houston, 1981-82, Tex. Woman mag., Dallas, 1979-80, Profl. Woman mag., Dallas, 1979-80; mem. bd. advisors Ultra Mag., 1985—; appeared on TV series Jocelyn's Weekend, Sta. KDFI-TV, 1985. Bd. dirs. TACA arts support orgn., Dallas, 1980—, asst. chmn. custom auction, 1978-83; judge Miss Tex. USA Contest, 1984; mem. adv. bd. Cattle Baron's Ball Com., Dallas Symphony Debutante presentations; hon. mem. Dallas Opera Women's Bd., Northwood Inst. Women's Bd., Dallas Symphony League; mem. Friends of Winston Churchill Meml. and Library, Dallas Theatre Ctr. Women's Guild, Childrens' Med. Ctr. Auxiliary; hon. mem. Crystal Charity Ball Com.; mem. Community Council Greater Dallas Community Awareness Goals Com. Impact '88, 1985—. Mem. Soc. Profl. Journalists (v.p. communications 1978-79), Nat. Press Club, Dallas Press Club, DAR, Daus. of Republic of Tex. (registrar 1972), Dallas So. Memorial Assn., Dallas County Heritage Soc., Dallas Mus. Art League, Dallas Opera Guild. Club: Argyle (sec. 1983-84), The 500 (Dallas). Home: 6324-D Bandera Ave Dallas TX 75225 Office: Dallas Times Herald 1101 Pacific Ave Dallas TX 75202

SMITH, NANCY WEITMAN, advertising executive; b. Bklyn., Feb. 4, 1950; d. Warren Pershing Weitman and Esther (Lichterman) Sahn; m. Sidney James Smith, July 25, 1970 (div. July 1979); m. William Jackson Green, Mar. 21, 1987. BA in English, U. Pa., 1970. Purchase service asst. Young, Rubicam N.Y., N.Y.C., 1970-71, media planner, 1971-74, media supr., 1974-78, media group supr., 1978-79, v.p., 1979-84, group supr., 1984-86, sr. v.p., 1984—, media dir. for U.S. Army, 1987-88, dir. media svcs., 1988—. Mem. Assn. U.S. Army, YWCA Acad. Women Achievers. Office: Young & Rubicam Army Group 285 Madison Ave New York NY 10017*

SMITH, NELL WHITLEY, state senator; b. Washington, N.C., Nov. 12, 1929; d. Arthur H. and Alice (Whitley) S.; m. Harris Page Smith, Apr. 18, 1952 (dec.); children: Sam, Susan, Hugh, Phyllis. Student Salem Coll., 1947-48; BS, U. N.C., 1951; Doctorate (hon.) Central (S.C.) Wesleyan Coll., 1987. Owner, mgr. The House Antiques and Gifts; tchr. sci. Easley Pub. Schs., 6 yrs.; mem. S.C. Senate, 1981—. Mem. Pickens County Art Com. Bd., 1976-80, bd. dirs. Pickens County Library, 1975-78, Home Health Care, 1977-79; pres. Palmetto Cabinet, 1977-78. Recipient Phi Delta Kappa Edn. award Clemson U., 1986, Disting. Alumni award U. N.C., Greensboro, 1987; named Woman of Yr., Easley Bus. and Profl. Women's Club, 1984, Legislator of Yr., S.C. Coun. for Exceptional Children, 1986. Mem. Easley Book Club. Democrat. Presbyterian. Office: 512 Gressette Bldg Columbia SC 29202*

SMITH, OLIVE IRENE PERRY, realty company executive; b. nr. Shelbyville, Ill., Dec. 13; d. Joseph Luther and Pearl (Bushart) Perry; grad. Sparks Coll., 1928; student Milligan U., 1929, Northwestern U., 1934-36, UCLA, 1959-60; m. William Smith, May 11, 1942. Hosp. librarian, registrar Chgo. State Hosp., Cook County, 1929-40; dep. assessor San Diego County, Calif., 1951-52; real estate broker O.I. Smith, Hemet, Calif., 1953—; real estate investment and loan counselor. Local rep. Nat. Inst. Real Estate Bds. Active Southland Water Com., 1960-68. Mem. adv. bd. San Jacinto (Calif.) Jr. Coll., 1967-68. Mem. Nat. Inst. Real Estate Brokers, Nat. Traders, Comml., and Investment Brokers Div. (pres. 1961), Hemet-San Jacinto Bd. Realtors (sec. 1960), Calif. Real Estate Assn. (regional v.p. 1964-65), Riverside Art Assn. Republican. Club: Soroptimist (San Jacinto-Hemet, Calif.). Home: 3701 Fillmore St #180 Rancho Riverside Park Riverside CA 92505

SMITH, PAIGE ELAINE, retailer; b. Cin., Apr. 7, 1963; d. Paul Edward and Marlene (Polder) S. BS in Bus. and Mktg., Miami U., 1985. Asst. mgr. Cedar Closet, Oxford, Ohio, 1985-86; owner Alpha House, Oxford, 1986—. Tchr., United Meth. Ch., Oxford, 1987-89. Mem. NAFE, Miami Alumni, Tri Sigma. Republican. Methodist. Home: 707 W Chestnut 5 Oxford OH 45056 Office: 11 S Main St Oxford OH 45056

SMITH, PAMELA KAY, industrial equipment company official; b. Traverse City, Mich., July 9, 1962; d. Duane Arthur and Katherine C. (Davis) S. Student, Northwestern Mich. Coll., 1981-83, 88. Sec. Morrison Indsl. Equipment, Traverse City, 1982-84, parts clk., 1984-85, parts mgr., 1985-89; adminstrv. mgr. Morrison Indsl. Equipment, Grand Rapids, Mich., 1989—. Mem. Profl. Womens Network. Home: PO Box 280 Interlochen MI 49643 Office: Morrison Indsl Equipment 1940 Turner Ave NW Grand Rapids MI 49504

SMITH, PAMELA KAYE, management consultant; b. Omaha, Mar. 19, 1959; d. Stanley W. and Lucille E. (Moyer) S.; m. Paul Lombardo, Aug. 14, 1982 (div. Jan. 1985). BSBA, Washington U., St. Louis, 1981, MHA, 1983. Adminstr. Rep. Health Corp./Raleigh Hills Hosp., Jefferson City, Mo., 1983-85, St. Louis, 1984-85; adminstr. Rep. Health Corp./Shiloh Pk. Hosp., Garland, Tex., 1985; asst. adminstr. Rep. Health Corp./Garland Community Hosp., 1985; adminstr. Rep. Health Corp./Lakewood Gen. Hosp., Dallas, 1985-86; assoc. adminstr. Psychiat. Inst. Am./Baywood Hosp., Webster, Tex., 1986-87; asst. adminstr. Psychiat. Inst. Washington, 1987-88; pres. Pamela K. Smith & Assoc., Inc., Great Falls, Va., 1988—; adminstr. Washington Pain and Rehab. Ctr., Washington, 1989—. Mem. Am. Coll. Healthcare Execs., Am. Hosp. Assn., Assn. Health Care Adminstrs., Va. Assn. Female Execs. Republican. Unitarian. Office: 1272 Kenmore Dr Ste 100 Great Falls VA 22066-2224

SMITH, PATRICIA, Canadian provincial official. Mem. Province of Sask. Legis. Assembly; former minister of edn., former minister energy and mines; now dep. premier and minister urban affairs. Office: Sask Legis Assembly, Legislative Bldg, Regina, SK Canada S4S 0B3

SMITH, PATRICIA GRACE, government official; b. Tuskegee, Ala., Nov. 10, 1947; d. Douglas and Wilhelmina (Griffin) Jones; m. J. Clay Smith, Jr., June 25, 1983; children—Eugene Douglas, Stager Clay, Michelle L., Michael L. B.A. in English, Tuskegee Inst., 1968; postgrad. Auburn U., 1969-71, Harvard U., 1974, George Washington U., 1983; cert. sr. exec. service 1987; exec. mgmt. tng. devel. assignments Dept. Def., 1986, U.S. Senate Commerce Com., 1987. Instr. Tuskegee Institute, Ala., 1969-71; program mgr. Curber Assocs., Washington, 1971-73; dir. placement Nat. Assn. Broadcasters, Washington, 1973-74, dir. pub. affairs, 1974-77; assoc. producer Group W Broadcasting, Balt., 1977, producer, 1977-78; dir. affiliate relations and programming Sheridan Broadcasting Network, Crystal City, Va., 1978-80; chief consumer assistance and small bus. Office Pub. Affairs, FCC, Washington, 1980—; vice chmn. Nat. Conf. Black Lawyers Task Force on Communications, Washington, 1975-87. Mem. D.C. Donor Project, Nat. Kidney Found., Washington, 1984—; trustee, mem. exec. com., nominating com., youth adv. com. Nat. Urban League, 1976-81; mem. communications com. Cancer Coordinating Council, 1977-84; mem. Braintrust Subcom. on Children's Programming, Congl. Black Caucus, 1976—; mem. adv. bd. Black Arts Celebration, 1978-83; mem. NAACP; mem. journalism and communications adv. council Auburn U., 1976-78; mem. Washington Urban League, 1985—;bd. dirs. Black Film Rev., 1989—; mem D.C. Commn. on Human Rights, 1986-88, chmn. 1988—. Named Outstanding Young Woman of Yr., Washington, 1975, 78; recipient Sustained Superior Performance award FCC, Washington, 1982-89. Mem. Women in Communications, Inc. (mem. nat. adv. com.), Lambda Iota Tau. Club: Broadcasters (bd. dirs. 1976-77). Democrat. Baptist. Avocations: writing, swimming. Home: 4010 16th St NW Washington DC 20011 Office: FCC 1919 M St NW Suite 254 Washington DC 20554

SMITH, PATRICIA JACQULINE, marketing executive; b. Orange, N.J., June 13, 1944; d. Michael Joseph and Helen Francis (Costello) S. BS, U. Md., 1967. Field dir. Colgate Palmolive Co., N.Y.C., 1967-71; account exec. Foote Cone & Belding, N.Y.C., 1971-72; dir. regional sales ARA Services, Inc., Phila., 1973-76; dir. federally funded programs Ogden Food Service, Boston, 1976-79; v.p. Smith Tool Co., Manesquan, N.J., 1979-84; chmn., chief exec. officer Hygolet Metro, Inc., New Canaan, Conn., 1984-87; mktg. cons. Smith Mktg. Services, LaJolla, Calif., 1987—; bd. dirs. Smith Tool Co., Manesquan, N.J., Shore Precision, Inc., Manesquan, P.J. Smith Interiors, N.Y.C. Mem. Women in Sales, Nat. Assn. Profl. Saleswomen, Bus. and Profl. Women's Club N.Y. State. Republican. Home: 425 E 63d St New York NY 10021

SMITH, PATRICIA K., educator; b. East Stroudsburg, Pa., Mar. 8, 1934; d. Joseph George and Mabel Lorraine (Repsher) Kuchinski; m. Edwin Raymond Smith, Aug. 18, 1956; children: Timothy E., Steven M., Marianne F. BS in Edn., East Stroudsburg State Coll., 1955; MA, W.Va. U., 1969, DEdn, 1975. Elem. tchr. Pleasantdale Elem. Sch., West Orange, N.J., 1955-56, Tuscarora Sch. Dist., Mercersburg, Pa., 1956-59; reading specialist Robert F. Kennedy Ctr., Morgantown, W.Va., 1970-72; asst. prof. W.Va. U., Morgantown, 1975-79, assoc. prof. reading and lang. arts, 1979-86, prof., 1986—; mem. rev. bd. Prentice-Hall, Inc., Englewood Cliffs, N.J., 1979—; cons. Chpt. 1, Monongalia Pub. Schs., Morgantown, W.Va., 1983-84. Co-author: Keeping Yourself Out of Federal Court, 1980, 2d revision, 1986; mem. editorial bd. Reading Improvement, Chula Vista, Calif., 1983—. Postdoctoral teaching fellow Lilly Endowment, Inc., 1975-76; recipient Outstanding Tchr. award Coll. Human Resources and Edn., Morgantown, W.Va., 1978. Mem. W.Va. State Reading Council (pres. 1979-80), Human Resources and Edn. Alumni Assn. (pres. 1979-80, exec. dir. 1981-85), Kappa Delta Pi, Phi Delta Kappa. Democrat. Roman Catholic. Avocations: traveling, reading. Home: 1456 Dogwood Ave Morgantown WV 26505 Office: W Va U 607 Allen Hall Morgantown WV 26506

SMITH, PATRICIA LYNN, marketing professional; b. Elmhurst, Ill., Nov. 4, 1965; d. James A. Sr. and Myrna A. (Kraegel) S. AAS, Robert Morris Coll., 1984. Cashier Millie's Pancake House, Addison, Ill., 1981-84; media sec. Foote, Cone and Belding, Chgo., 1984-86; adminstrv. asst. account mgmt. J. Walter Thompson, Chgo., 1986; exec. asst. mktg. and promo Schal Assocs., Inc., Chgo., 1988-89; cast mem. Disney Store Disney Co., 1989—; compensation asst. No. Trust Corp., 1989—. Active Art Inst. Chgo., Elmhurst Community Theatre, Brookfield Zoo. Mem. Am. Film Soc., NATAS, Nat. Assn. Female Execs., Internat. Thespian Soc., Delta Zeta.

SMITH, PATSY JANE, hospital official; b. Rochester, Ind., Apr. 29, 1949; d. Leon Reynolds and Bertha (Wilson) Crippen; children: Jamie Lynn Shotts, Jodi Lynn Shotts; m. Timothy C. Smith, Dec. 15, 1988; stepchildren: Lyndee Ann, Jacob Timothy, Joshua James. Grad. high sch., Fulton, Ind. News reporter Pharos-Tribune, Logansport, Ind., 1967-69; advt. and editorial writer Chester White Swine Record Assn., Rochester, 1970-72; dir. community rels. Pulaski Meml. Hosp., Winamac, Ind., 1988—. Mem. pub. rels. com. Am. Cancer Soc., Pulaski County, 1988—, pres., 1990-91; mem. pub. edn. com. Am. Heart Assn., Pulaski County, 1990-91. Mem. Ind. Soc. for Healthcare Pub. Rels. and Mktg. Republican. Mem. Pentesostal Ch. Home: Rte 2 Box 157 Kewanna IN 46939 Office: Pulaski Meml Hosp 616 E 13th St Winamac IN 46996

SMITH, PAULA MARIE, accountant; b. Osceola, Nebr., Apr. 17, 1960; d. Everette W. and Rose Elizabeth Gaspers. BSBA, Creighton U., 1982; postgrad., U. Houston, 1988—. CPA, Nebr. Policy loan corr. United of Omaha, 1982; staff auditor Quick & McFarlin, Omaha, 1982-85; internal auditor Enron Corp., Omaha and Houston, 1985-86; sr. acct., supr. Enron Corp., Houston, 1987—. Mem. AICPAs, Tex. Soc. CPAs, Nebr. Soc. CPAs. Home: 5000 Milwee #56 Houston TX 77092

SMITH, PHYLLIS JOY, music educator; b. Kingston, Pa., June 22, 1944; d. Willard Joseph and Hazel (Forbes) Dreistadt; m. James Donald Smith, July 3, 1963; children: Steven, Sheri, Scott. Student, Met. State Coll., 1962-65, Cerritos (Calif.) Jr. Coll., 1964-66, Fullerton (Calif.) Coll., 1967-69. Owner, tchr. music Sunstyle Music Studio, Anaheim, Calif., 1963-75; office mgmt. Whittier (Calif.) Christian High Sch., 1979-85, mem. faculty, 1976-79; adminstr. Leffingwell Christian High Sch., Norwalk, Calif., 1985-87; prin. Sunstyle Gifts and Decorator Items, Mfr. and Sales, 1984—. Author, composer gospel music. Dir. music Grace Bretheren Ch., Anaheim, 1973-75; organist Anaheim Community Ch., 1975-79, Children's Edn. Dept. Republican. Baptist. Office: Sunstyle 16309 Landmark Dr Whittier CA 90604

SMITH, PHYLLIS MAE, health care consultant, educator; b. Coeur d'Alene, Idaho, May 2, 1935; d. Elmer Lee Smith and Kathryn Alice (Newell) Wilson. Diploma, Lutheran Bible Inst., Seattle, 1956, Emanuel Hosp. Sch. Nursing, Portland, Oreg., 1959; student Coll. San Mateo, Calif., 1971. Staff nurse in surgery Emanuel Hosp., Portland, 1959-61, St. Vincent's Hosp., Portland, 1962-63; head nurse central service Sacred Heart Hosp., Eugene, Oreg., 1964-69; dir. central services Peninsula Hosp., Burlingame, Calif., 1969-74; pres. Phyllis Smith Assocs., Inc., Lewiston, Idaho, 1975-88; sr. tech. advisor, dir. ednl. programs, Parkside Material Mgmt. Services, Park Ridge, Ill., 1988-90; AIDS coord. Asotin County Health Dist., 1989—; lectr., cons. in field in over 10 countries. Contbr. to manuals, profl. jours. Mem. Internat. Assn. Hosp. Central Service Mgmt. (dir. edn. 1973-88, chmn. technician edn. and affairs com. 1978-88, John Perkins award, 1977, Chesire award 1977), Assn. for Advancement Med. Instrumentation, Nat. Assn. Female Execs. Episcopalian. Lodge: Eagles Aux. Avocations: fishing, walking, photography, chess, reading. Home and Office: 3730 11th St Lewiston ID 83501

SMITH, RACHEL HUDSON, librarian; b. Jackson, Miss., Jan. 20, 1937; d. Henry Gurves and Winnie Mae (Buckley) Hudson; m. Ted Elwyn Smith, Sept. 2, 1962; children: Robin Smith Butts, Gregory N., Dale E. BS, Miss. Coll., 1960; MLS, U. Miss., Oxford, 1978, Advanced MLS, 1981. Tech. asst. Miss. Coll. Libr., Clinton, 1971-78, cataloger, 1978-87, asst. libr., 1987—; bus. mgr. Miss. Librs., Jackson, 1983—. Mem. ALA, Southeastern Libr. Assn., Miss. Libr. Assn. (treas. 1982), Miss. Assn. Women in Higher Edn., AAUW (sec. Clinton br. 1988-90), Beta Phi Mu. Baptist. Office: Miss Coll Libr Box 127 Clinton MS 39060

SMITH, RÄNDI SIGMUND, industrial psychologist, consultant; b. Washington, Mar. 18, 1942; d. Frederick William and Marie Rändi (Ensrud) Sigmund; m. Richard Peter Smith, Feb. 13, 1965; children: Robin Lynne, Rändi Marie. BA in Sociology, Coll. William and Mary, 1963; MA in Indsl. Psychology, Norwich U., 1985; EdD Columbia U., 1988. Info. ctr. staff mem. Nat. Assn. Food Chains, Washington, 1963-65; asst. corp. librarian Combustion Engring., Windsor, Conn., 1965-66; telephone usage counselor So. New Eng. Telephone, Hartford, Conn., 1966; quality assurance/systems analyst Aetna Life & Casualty, Hartford, 1966-67; pres. Smith and Assocs., Inc., West Hartford, Conn., 1968—; cons. interpersonal skills, corp. edn. Aetna Life & Casualty, Hartford, 1969-84, IBM Corp., White Plains, N.Y., 1975—, Xerox Corp., Webster, N.Y., 1975-85; workforce transition project cons. Pitney-Bowes, 1988—. Author: Written Communication for Data Processing, 1976-81; also profl. articles, children's story. Active Jr. League Hartford, 1976—, Lupus Found. Am.; pres. parent council, trustee Kingswood-Oxford Sch., West Hartford, 1985-86; eucharistic min. Roman Catholic Archdiocese of Hartford, 1972. Mem. Am. Soc. Tng. and Devel., Am. Mgmt. Assn., Internat. Assn. Airline Passengers, NAFE, Nat. Assn. for Performance and Instruction. Club: Hartford Golf. Avocations: scuba diving, bridge. Home and Office: 87 Westmont West Hartford CT 06117

SMITH, REBECCA MCCULLOCH, educator; b. Greensboro, N.C., Feb. 29, 1928; d. David Martin and Virginia Pearl (Woodburn) McCulloch; m. George Clarence Smith Jr., Mar. 30, 1945; 1 child, John Randolph. BS, Woman's Coll., U. N.C., 1947, MS, 1952; PhD, U. N.C., Greensboro, 1967; postgrad., Harvard U., 1989. Tchr. pub. schs., N.C. and S.C., 1947-57; instr. U. N.C., Greensboro, 1958-66, asst. prof. to prof. child devel. and family relations, 1967—, dir. grad. program, 1975-82; ednl. cons. depts. edn. N.C., S.C., Ind., Ont., Man.; vis. prof. N.W. La. State U., 1965, 67, U. Wash., 1970, Hood Coll., 1976, 86. Named Outstanding Alumna Sch. Home Econs., 1976; recipient Sperry award for service to families N.C. Family Life Council, 1979. Mem. Am. Home Econs. Assn., Nat. Council Family Relations (exec. com. 1974-76, treas. 1987-89, Osborne award 1973), Omicron Nu. Author: Teaching About Family Relationships, 1975, Klemer's Marriage and Family Relationships, 2d edit., 1975, Resources for Teaching About Family Life Education, 1976, Family Matters: Concepts in Marriage and Personal Relationships, 1982, assoc. editor Family Relations (Jour. Applied Family and Child Studies), 1980—; ednl. cons. Current Life Studies, 1977-84. Home: 1212 E Ritters Lake Rd Greensboro NC 27406 Office: U NC Dept Child Devel Sch Human Environ Scis Greensboro NC 27412

SMITH, REBECCA VIRTUE, state agency administrator; b. Oklahoma City, July 9, 1953; d. Richard Linn Cowan and Suzanne (Starr) Virtue; m. Dale R. Smith, Dec. 30, 1983; 1 child, Suzanne Starr. BS in Elem. Edn. magna cum laude, Lewis and Clark Coll., 1976; MA in Secondary Edn., U. Colo., Colorado Springs, 1983; postgrad., U. Colo., Denver, 1987. Cert. tchr., Colo. Tchr. kindergarten Fossil (Oreg.) Sch. Dist., 1976-78; tchr. remedial reading Cripple Creek (Colo.)-Victor Sch. Dist., 1978-80; coordinator newspaper in edn. Gazette Telegraph, Colorado Springs, 1980-83, Denver Post, 1983-85; coordinator pub. edn. Colo. Jud. Dept., Denver, 1985—, coordinator info., 1986-88; mem. task force social studies Colo. State Bd. Edn., Denver, chair statewide newspaper in edn. task force; adj. prof. Regis Coll., Denver, summer 1990. Author, creator, editor Colorado Kids' Corner. Mem. Bicentennial of U.S. Constn. Com. of Colo. Bar Assn., 1986; mem. sch. improvement planning team Teller Elem. Sch., Denver pub. schs., 1989—. Recipient award Mesa County Valley Sch. Dist. Bd. Edn., 1986; named a Dynamite Denverite Denver Mag., 1987. Mem. NAFE, Am. Judicature Soc., Nat. Coun. for Social Studies, Colo. Coun. for Social Studies, Colo. Assn. Ct. Employees, Assn. for Supervision and Curriculum Devel.,

Colo. Hist. Soc., Colo. Coun. Govt.Communicators, Colo. Press Assn. (assoc.), Women in Communications. Home: 1026 Steele St Denver CO 80206

SMITH, RETTA, rehabilitation services professional, nurse; b. Ashland, Ky., Mar. 7, 1960; d. Raymond and Peggy (Yates) Manning; m. Thomas L. Smith, May 22, 1982. BS, Berea Coll., 1982. RN, Ky. Staff nurse St. Luke Hosp., Ft. Thomas, Ky., 1982-85; benefits analyst Humana Inc., Louisville, 1985-87, case mgmt. specialist, 1987-89; clin. evaluator, assoc. New Medico Head Injury System, Lynn, Mass., 1989—. Mem. Nat. Assn. Rehab. Profls. in Pvt. Sector, Ky. Head Injury Assn. Baptist.

SMITH, ROBERTA E., television station executive; b. Boston, Aug. 19, 1946; d. Milton and Tillie (Gorewitz) Snyder; children: Gregory, Bret. Sales rep. Avon Corrugated, Canton, Mass., 1976-77; office mgr., then treas. Friends of Avi Nelson U.S. Senate campaign, Boston, 1987-82; spl. advisor pub. rels. to gov. Commonwealth of Mass., Boston; office mgr. MFP Inc., Lawrence, Mass., 1981-83, bus. mgr., 1983-87, asst. treas., 1983-90; founder, gen. mgr. WMFP-TV, Lawrence, Mass., 1981-90. Mem. Needham (Mass.) PTA, exec. com. Parent Assn.; numerous leadership roles civic and cultural orgns. Mem. NAFE, Nat. Assn. of TV Program Execs., Am. Women in Radio and TV, New Eng. Broadcasting Assn., Advt. Club of Greater Boston. Home: 41 Centre St #402 Brookline MA 02146

SMITH, ROBERTA HAWKINS, plant physiologist; b. Tulare, Calif., May 3, 1945; d. William Brevard and Freda Lois (Kessler) Hawkins; m. James Willie Smith, Jr., Aug. 21, 1968; children: James Willie, III, Cristine Lois. BS, U. Calif., Riverside, 1967, MS, 1968, PhD, 1970. Postdoctoral fellow dept. plant sci. Tex. A&M U., College Station, 1972-73, asst. prof. dept. plant sci., 1974-79, assoc. prof. dept. plant sci., 1979-85, prof. dept. soil and crop sci., 1985—; asst. prof. Sam Huston State U., Huntsville, Tex., 1973-74. Editorial bd. Biotech. Advances, 1986—, Plant Physiology, 1984—. Trustee Allen Acad., College Station, 1990. Mem. Crop Sci. Soc. Am. (chmn.-elect C-7 div. 1989—), Internat. Crops Rsch. Inst. Semi-Arid Tropics (bd. govs. 1989—), Faculty of Plant Physiology (chmn. 1987-89), Tissue Culture Assn. (chmn. plant div. 1983-86). Republican. Methodist. Home: Rt 1 PO Box 701 Hearne TX 77859 Office: Tex A&M Univ Dept Soil and Crop Sci College Station TX 77843

SMITH, ROSALIE HAIBLUM, adult educator; b. Bklyn., Nov. 3, 1933; d. Benjamin David and Sadie (Meyer) Haiblum; m. Jay Donald Smith, June 13, 1953; children: Andria, Eric, Ira. BA, Bklyn. Coll., 1954, MA, 1956; MA, Columbia U., 1985, EdD, 1986. Cert. Speech language clin. competency, 1968. Tchr. N.Y.C. High Schs., Bklyn., 1954-56; speech instr. Bklyn. Coll., 1959-60; asst. prof. speech U. Hartford (Conn.), 1963-71; speech cons. Town of West Hartford (Conn.); communication cons. Hartford Graduate Ctr., Hartford, Conn., 1976-87; pres. Dynamic Communication Tng., Conn., 1976--; adj. instr. U. CT Health Ctr., Farmington, Conn., 1984--. Author: How To Talk Your Way To A Better Job, 1981. Chair Women's Div. Israel Bonds, 1974-75; chair restoration com. Charter Oak Temple Cultural Ctr., 1987-89; bd. dirs. Info. Line, 1974-76; pres. Jewish Children's Svc. Orgn., 1976-78; com. chair Co. One Theater, 1987—; bd. dirs. Charter Oak Temple Cultural Ctr., Hartford, Conn., 1987, pres., 1990—; chair Matrix Award Dinner. Recipient Woman of Valor award State of Israel Bonds, 1978. Mem. ASTD, Women in Communication, Inc., Am. SP Hearing Lang. Assn., Speech Communication Assn., B'nai B'rith (pres. Hartford women chpt. 1971-73). Democrat.

SMITH, RUBY LUCILLE, librarian; b. Nobob, Ky., Sept. 19, 1917; d. James Ira and Myrtie Olive (Crabtree) Jones; A.B., Western Ky. State Tchrs. Coll., 1943, M.A., 1966; m. Kenneth Cornelius Smith, Dec. 25, 1946; children: Kenneth Cornelius, Corma Ann. Tchr. rural schs., Barren County, Ky., 1941-42; tchr. secondary sch. English, libr. Temple Hill Consol. Sch., Glasgow, Ky., 1943-47, 49-51, 53-56, sch. libr., 1956-83. Sec. Barren County Cancer Soc., 1968-70, Barren County Fair Bd., 1969-70; leader 4-H Club, 1957-72, mem. council Barren County; coord. AARP tax-aide program, 1985—, assoc. dist. dir., 1988—. Trustee Mary Wood Weldon Meml. Library, 1964—; trustee Barren County Pub. Libr., 1969—, sec., 1969—. Mem. NEA (life), Ky. Edn. Assn., Ky. Assn. Sch. Libr. (sec. 1970-71), 3d Dist. Libr. Assn. (pres. 1944, 66), Barren County Edn. Assn. (pres. 1960-62, treas. 1979-80), Ky. Audio Visual Assn., Ret. Tchrs. Assn. (pres. 1984-86, sec. 1989—), Ky. Libr. Trustee Assn. (bd. dirs. 1985—, pres. 1986-88, dir. Barren River region 1985—), Barren County Republican Women's Club, Monroe Assn. Woman's Missionary Union (dir. 1968-72, 79-83 Monroe Assn. Baptists (library dir. 1972-88, sec. 1985—), Ky. Library Assn., Delta Kappa Gamma. Home: 54 E Nobob Rd Summer Shade KY 42166

SMITH, RUTH ANN (RUSTY SMITH), educational administrator; b. Gowanda, N.Y., May 11, 1943; d. Nicholas Victor and Hallie Mae (Klapper) Smith; children: Dean Hunter, Allan Michael. BS, Buffalo State U., 1969; MS in Edn., SUNY, New Paltz, 1977; Cert., Victor Comptometer Sch., Buffalo, 1962. Cert. tchr., supr./adminstr. Supervising tchr. Assn. for Retarded Citizens Niagara County, Niagara Falls, N.Y., 1969-72; staff devel. specialist I-IV N.Y. State Office of Mental Retardation and Developmental Disabilities, Wassaic, 1972-76; staff devel. specialist IV N.Y. State Office of Mental Retardation and Developmental Disabilities, Newark, N.Y., 1977-78; dir. edn. and tng. N.Y. State Office of Mental Retardation and Developmental Disabilities, Rochester, 1978—; Fieldwork supr. Dutchess Community Coll., Poughkeepsie, N.Y., 1976. Editor video tapes. NSF grantee, 1960. Mem. Am. Assn. Mental Retardation, Antique Auto Club (bd. dirs. 1989—), Aster Terr. Homeowners Assn. (bd. dirs. 1988—), Corvair Club of Am. Republican. Roman Catholic. Office: NYSOMRDD 1160A Pittsford-Victor Rd Pittsford NY 14534

SMITH, SANDRA JANE, insurance company administrator; b. Worcester, Mass., Apr. 24, 1963; d. Robert Arthur and Ella Frances (Stapley) S. AS with honors, Becker Jr. Coll., Worcester, 1983. Bank teller Peoples Savs. Bank, Worcester, 1981-83; customer svc. rep. New England Telephone, Worcester, 1983-84; word processor activity coord.'s office Cen. New England Coll., Worcester, 1984-85; policy issue asst. State Mut. Cos., Worcester, 1985-87, policy issue specialist, 1987-89, med. claims examiner, 1989; with reins. support dept. Hanover Ins. Co., Worcester, 1989—. Editor, author: Central New England College Dialogue, 1984-85. Active St. George's Ch., Worcester, 1988—. Mem. Royal Scottish Country Dance Soc., Spanish Nat. Honor Soc. Roman Catholic. Home: 15 Hawthorne Rd Holden MA 01520 Office: Hanover Ins Co 100 N Parkway Worcester MA 01605

SMITH, SANDRA KAY, accommodations coordinator; b. Lebanon, Pa., Nov. 26, 1954; d. Walter H. and Esther M. (Kettering) Nye; m. Kevin L. Smith, Oct. 12, 1974; 1 child, Nicolle D. Diploma, Annville-Cleona High Sch., 1972. Small appliance sales mgr. S.E. Nichols, Annville, 1972-74; mem. clerical staff engring. dept. Hauck Mfg. Co., Cleona, Pa., 1974-77; sec., mgr. Messiah Luth. Ch., Lebanon, 1977-81; exec. sec. mktg. dept. Cornwall (Pa.) Manor, 1983-84, pub. rels. coord., 1984-85, accommodations coord., 1985—. Bd. dirs., chmn. com. Cornwall Children's Ctr., 1983—. Mem. NAFE, Friends of Spang Crest Auxiliary, Lebanon Opti-Mrs. Club (Merit award 1979-80). Democrat. Lutheran. Office: Cornwall Manor PO Box 125 Boyd St Cornwall PA 17016

SMITH, SANDRA LOUISE, small business owner; b. Clarksburg, W.Va., July 24, 1950; d. Raymond Junior and Dicie Chloe (Simmons) Hoover; 1 child, Amanda Rae Snider. Student, Three Rivers Tree Community Coll., 1972-73; cert., Dale Carnegie Course, Polar Bluff, Mo., 1975, Britt Corp. Sales Seminar, 1985. Endorsement underwriter GEICO, Bethesda, Md., 1969-71; collections mgr. Snider's IGA Foods, Poplar Bluff, 1971-82; owner, operator Tower Restaurant, Poplar Bluff, 1979-82, Brandy's Restaurant, Cabot, Ark., 1984-86; owner, sec. S & J Enterprises Inc., Cabot, 1984—; owner, pres. Cabot Conoco #2 Inc., 1984—; owner Smith's Feed Store, 1987—, Popcorn, Etc., 1986—. Mem. Mo. Restaurant Assn., Am. Barhman Assn., Jaycees Wives (Poplar Bluff) (pres. 1975-76), Cabot C. of C. Democrat. Methodist. Home: PO Box 133 Cabot AR 72023 Office: PO Box 133 Cabot AR 72023

SMITH, SHARON BENNETT, systems analyst, programmer; b. Staunton, Va., Apr. 29, 1953; d. James Paul and Ella (Callison) Bennett; m. Jack Wayne Smith, Nov. 20, 1973; children: David Allen, Jonathan Edward. BS in math., Longwood Coll., Farmville, Va., 1975; MBA, Nat. U., San Diego, 1989; cert. in computer sci., Cen. Tex. Coll., 1984; diploma in microcomputer programming, 1985. Acct./buyer N.O.W.C. Bazaar, Agana, Guam, 1982; nat. test examiner Navy Campus, Agana, 1982-83; math./biology tchr. St. John's Sch., Tumon Bay, Guam, 1983-84; configuration/data mgmt. engr. Martin Marietta Aerospace, Orlando, Fla., 1985-87; sys. analyst/programmer Meth. Hosp. of Memphis, 1989—, microcomputer cons., 1989. Recipient Letter of Appreciation, U.S. Army, 1987, Col. "Black Jack" Pershing medal, Martin Marietta, 1986. Mem. NAFE, Naval Officers Wives Club (v.p., treas. 1988-89). Republican. Methodist. Office: Meth Hosp of Memphis Info Systems Ste 400 MPE 1265 Union Ave Memphis TN 38104-3499

SMITH, SHARON LEE CHESNUTT, advertising executive; b. Corpus Christi, Tex., Aug. 18, 1947; d. James Horace and Harriet Leona (McCune) Chesnutt; m. Roger John Barry, Sept. 20, 1970 (div. 1975); m. Jerry Clark Smith, Oct. 14, 1975; 1 child, Wesley Chesnutt. Student Western Wash. State U., 1965-69, Bklyn. Mus. Art Sch., 1971, Pratt Inst., 1972, Sch. Visual Arts, N.Y.C., 1973. Reservation agt. United Air Lines, N.Y.C., 1969-70; art dir. Folwell Assocs., N.Y.C., 1970-71; ptnr. Folwell & Barry Advt., N.Y.C., 1971-73; freelance graphic artist, advt. cons. Cornwallville, N.Y., 1973-75; ptnr. Hudson River Graphics, Catskill, N.Y., 1976-77; ptnr. Chesnutt & Smith, Catskill, 1977—; instr. advt. Coxsackie Corr Inst., N.Y., 1974-75. Pres., Fedn. Block Assns., Bklyn., 1972. Mem. Catskill Mountain Kennel Club (pres. 1986-87), Albany Schenectady Golden Retriever Club (pres. 1980-82), Bernese Mountain Dog Club Am., Golden Retreiver Club Am. (Outstanding DAM award 1979, Dog Show Hall of Fame 1979, Best in Show 1988, 89), Mohawk Kennel Club, Mid-Hudson Kennel Club, Provisional Am. Kennel Club (judge for golden retrievers and bernese mount dogs). Republican. Lutheran. Office: Chesnutt & Smith 22 Spring St Catskill NY 12414

SMITH, SHARRON WILLIAMS, chemistry educator; b. Ashland, Ky., Apr. 3, 1941; d. James Archie and May (Waggoner) Williams; m. William Owen Smith, Jr., Aug. 16, 1964; children: Leslie Dyan, Kevin Andrew. BA, Transylvania U., 1963; PhD, U. Ky., 1975. Chemist, Procter & Gamble, Cin., 1963-64; tchr. sci. Lexington pub. schs., Ky., 1964-67; chemist NIH, Bethesda, Md., 1974-75; asst. prof. chemistry Hood Coll., Frederick, Md., 1975-81, assoc. prof., 1981-87, prof. 1987—; chair dept. chemistry, physics and astronomy, 1982-86, acting dean grad. sch. 1989—. NDEA fellow, 1967-70, Dissertation Yr. fellow U. Ky., Lexington, 1970-71; grantee Hood Coll. Bd. Assocs., 1981, 85, Beneficial-Hodson faculty fellow Hood Coll., 1984; grantee NSF, 1986. Mem. AAAS, AAUP, AAUW, Am. Chem. Soc., Am. Assn. Higher Edn., , Middle Atlantic Assn. Liberal Arts Chemistry Tchrs. (pres. 1984-85). Democrat. Office: Hood Coll Frederick MD 21701

SMITH, SHEILA BOWMAN, health care facility executive; b. Spartanburg, S.C., Sept. 1, 1953; d. Harold Jr. and Alstyne Brinkley (Glover) Bowman; m. Hugh Richard Smith, Sept. 30, 1973; children: Adam Weston, Leigh Anne. AS, Spartanburg Tech. Coll., 1973. Lab. technician B.J. Workman Meml. Hosp., Woodruff, S.C., 1973-86, lab. dir., 1987—; mem. Blood Utilization Rev. Com., Spartanburg, 1987—, Employee Recognition Com., Spartanburg, 1988—, Infection Control Com., Woodruff, 1989—. Mem. South Spartanburg Youth Athletic Assn., 1983—, March of Dimes, Spartanburg, 1987—. Mem. Am. Soc. Clin. Pathologists, Clin. Lab. Mgmt. Assn., Am. Assn. Blood Banks, Coll. Am. Pathologists. Republican. Baptist.

SMITH, SHIRLEY D., publisher; b. Morgan County, Ill., Mar. 20, 1942; d. Fred C. and Katherine L. (Nordsiek) Dotzert; m. Terry D. Smith, Oct. 14, 1962; children: D. Denoy, Sonya Smith Stowers. Program specialist, counter clk. ASCS, U.S. Dept. Agr., Jacksonville, Ill., 1960-63, 69-78; owner, operator Smith Pub., 1988—; pub. Shirley's Communique Monthly Magazet, 1989—; receptionist, bookkeeper Internat. Eyecare Ctr., Jacksonville, 1989-90; cons. Mary Kay Beauty, 1985—. Author: At Grandma's Knee, Shirley's Soapbox, Through the Kitchen Window, Hannah the Housewife; also articles; writer weekly column. Telethon coord. March of Dimes, Springfield, 1985-86; mem. Faith Luth. Ch. Address: Smith Rd R 1 Box 146 Virginia IL 62691

SMITH, SUE ANN, educational case manager, educator; b. Manchester, Iowa, May 14, 1944; d. Wilfrid F. and Shirley D. (Carner) Macheak; 1 child, Jennifer J. Student, Coll. of St. Teresa, 1962-63; BS, Mankato (Minn.) State U., 1965, MS, 1979, postgrad., 1985-86; postgrad., Adler Inst., Mpls., 1989. Cert. learning disabilities and English tchr., Iowa, Minn. Tchr. English Prairie Community Schs., Gowrie, Iowa, 1965-67, Richmond County Bd. Edn., Augusta, Ga., 1967-70, Storm Lake (Iowa) Community Schs., 1970-71; registration supr. Mankato State U., 1972-75, personnal acct., 1975-78; tchr. multi-disability Grant Alternative Sch., Mason City, Iowa, 1978-84; tchr. mentally handicapped John Adams Middle Sch., Mason City, 1984-85; tchr. emotional and behavior disorders Learning Ctr., St. Peter, Minn., 1985-86, Intermediate Dist. 287, Mpls., 1986-89; ednl. case mgr. Hennepin Tech. Coll., Mpls., 1989—; resource counselor mentally ill and mentall retarded adults Boston Health Care, St. Paul, 1989. Participant Parish Community of St. Joseph, New Hope, Minn., 1988—. Named Outstanding Tchr., Grant Alternative High Sch., 1984. Mem. Am. Fedn. Tchrs., Minn. Fedn. Tchrs., Minn. Educators of Emotional and Behavior Disordered, NAFE. Office: West Metro Edn Ctr 6800 Cedar Lake Rd Minneapolis MN 55426

SMITH, SUELLEN FANDT, marketing professional; b. Newton, N.J., June 9, 1943; d. Edward Lloyd and Mary (Boitano) Fandt; B.Mus., Westminster Coll., New Wilmington, Pa., 1965; postgrad. Trenton (N.J.) State Coll., Pace U.; m. Gary Thomas Smith, Aug. 3, 1968 (div. Sept. 1983). Tchr. elem. sch. music and reading, N.J., 1965-81; with E-Systems Co., Tampa, Fla., 1981; ops. clk. RAC Ctr. and Dart Ctr., GTE Co., Tampa, 1982—, Bus. Phone Systems div., 1984—, GTE Communications Corp., 1985—, system ops. instr., communications service advisor, 1986—; adminstr. proposal support, 1989—; lectr., Workshop presenter; cons. in field. Vol. counselor Hillsborough County Suicide and Crisis Center, 1984-86. Recipient John Phillip Sousa award, 1961. Mem. NEA, Music Educators Nat. Conf., N.J. Edn. Assn., Mu Phi Epsilon. Author curriculum materials. Office: GTE Communications Corp 1907 US Hwy 301 N Tampa FL 33619

SMITH, SUSAN CONVERSE, executive assistant; b. Concord, Mass., May 30, 1956; d. Harry Franklin and Phyllis Herndon (Goudey) Smith, Jr. AA, Pine Manor Coll., 1976; BA, U. Mass., 1984; postgrad., U. So. Calif., L.A., 1984-85. Asst. to dir. HBM/PR, Boston, 1982; from spl. events dir. to exec. asst. to chmn. various production cos. and films, L.A., 1985-90. Bd. dirs. Cushing Acad., Ashburnham, Mass., pub. rels. chmn. French Libr. Boston, co-founder I'Nouvi (Young Friends of the Boston Opera Co.). Mem. Am. Film Mktg. Assn. Office: Image Orgn Inc 9000 Sunset Blvd Ste 915 Los Angeles CA 90069

SMITH, SUSAN E., association executive; b. Phila., May 5, 1954; d. John M. and Helen (Krimmel) S. BA in Classics, Juniata Coll., 1976; MA, Wright State U., 1979. Cert. in effective speaking and human rels. Aviation history specialist Wright State U., Dayton, Ohio, 1977-79; dir. edn. and pub. rels. Pa. Assn. Mut. Ins. Cos., Harrisburg, 1979-85; dir. chamber svcs. Pa. Chamber Bus. and Industry, Harrisburg, 1985—; lectr. in field. Contbr. articles to profl. jours. Solicitor capitol region United Way, 1987-90; mem. workplace safety com. Dauphin County Cancer Unit, 1990—. Recipient citation Pa. Ho. of Reps., 1985, Outstanding Achievement award Pa. Chamber Bus. and Industry. Mem. AAUW (pres.-elect), Pa. Soc. Assn. Execs. (chmn. edn. com.), Assn. Membership Execs., Non-Dues Roundtable for State Chambers (founder). Republican. Presbyterian. Home: 46 Ringneck Dr Harrisburg PA 17112 Office: Pa Chamber Bus and Industry 222 N 3d St Harrisburg PA 17101

SMITH, SUSAN LOUISE, nurse, educator; b. Norfolk, Va., Nov. 15, 1959; d. William Lewis and Rebecca Louise (Jernigan) S. ADN, Norfolk State U., 1982; BSN, Hampton Inst., 1984, MSN, 1987; postgrad., Old Dominion U., 1989—. RN, Va. Staff nurse DePaul Hosp., Norfolk, 1982—; critical care nurse Richmond (Va.) Community Hosp., 1984-85; clin. instr. Norfolk State U., 1986—, instr. nursing, 1987—; asst. prof. Frederick campus Tidewater Com. Coll., 1989—; instr. Tidewater Heart Assn., 1988—. Kindergarten nurse Mt. Gilead Bapt. Ch., Norfolk, 1983. HEW grantee, 1986. Mem. Va. Nurses Assn., Critical Care Nurses Assn., Nat. Assn. Female Execs., Sigma Theta Tau. Democrat. Home: 1059 Johnston Rd Norfolk VA 23513 Office: Norfolk State U 2401 Corprew Ave Norfolk VA 23504

SMITH, SUSAN SAXTON, paralegal, small business owner; b. Jan. 18, 1959; d. Robert Hibberd and Jane (Morse) Saxton; m. Dudley Crawford Smith, June 9, 1984; 1 child, Elisabeth Saxton. BA, Baylor U., 1981; cert., Nat. Ctr. Paralegal Tng., Atlanta, 1983. Paralegal Storey, Armstrong, Steger & Martin, Dallas, 1983-84, Small, Craig & Werkenthin, Austin, 1984-85, Jenkens & Gilchrist, Austin, 1985-87; pvt. practice Austin, 1987—. Mem. Capitol Area Paralegal Assn., Jr. League of Austin, Symphony Sq. Com., Kappa Alpha Theta. Republican. Methodist. Home: 8604 Primrose Ln Austin TX 78758

SMITH, SYLVIA JO, arts association administrator; b. Tulsa, June 2, 1950; d. James Louis and Aleta Jo (Houston) Grotjan; m. E. Robert Lannon, Mar. 28, 1970 (div. Apr. 1976); m. Ronald Lynn Smith, Dec. 31, 1982; 1 child, Russell Lynn; stepchildren: Sheri Rene, Gregory Mark, Brenton Alan. Student, Tex. Christian U., 1969-70, 77, 80, Real Estate Tng. Inst., Ft. Worth, 1982. Lic. realtor. V.p. Ft. Worth Ventures, Inc., 1984-90. Bd. dirs. Ft. Worth Ballet, 1980-85, exec. com. 1980-85, 90—; exec. com. Ballet Guild of Ft. Worth, 1990—. Mem. Ft. Worth Garden Club (bd. dirs. 1987—). Methodist. Home: 4628 El Campo Fort Worth TX 76107

SMITH, TAGGART, management educator; b. Bloomfield, Ind., Mar. 15, 1939; d. Erwin and Hulda (Hash) Ramsey; children: Tanner Underwood, Travis Epes. BS, Ind. State U., 1961; MA, U. So. Fla., 1970; EdS, Ind. U., 1978, EdD, 1986. Cert. tchr., Ind. English tchr. jr. high and high sch. Ind. and Fla., 1961-75; coord. libr. media elem. and jr. high schs. Ind., 1978-81; libr. technician mil. svcs. Cub Naval Air Sta., Republic of Philippines, 1981-84; libr., tchr. dept. corrections State of Ind., 1984-87; prof. Purdue U., West Lafayette, Ind., 1987—; assoc. faculty Ind. U., Purdue U., Indpls.; flight attendant Am. Trans Air; instr. Bur. Motor Vehicles, Ind. Chair task force for correctional libr. standards Ind. State Libr., 1988-89; researcher Gov's. Task Force on Drunk Driving, Ind., 1989-90; mem. police policy and practices com. Purdue U., 1990; competition swimmer White River State Park Games, 1988; participant Walk Am., 1989; elder Presbyn. Ch. Mem. NAFE, Assn. for Ednl. Communications and Tech., Assn. for Bus. Communications, Orgn. Behavior Teaching Soc., Masters Swim Club, Lafayette Sailing Club, Phi Delta Kappa. Office: Purdue U Sch Tech West Lafayette IN 47907

SMITH, TAMMIE LOUISE, advertising executive; b. Mpls., June 7, 1959; d. Dwight Duane and Gloria Jean (Leonhardt) S. BS, Ariz. State U., 1981. Media asst. M.R. Bolin Advt., Mpls., 1981-82; media buyer Cuneo & Assocs. Advt., Burnsville, Minn., 1983-84, BBDO, Mpls., 1984-86; network, spot broadcast buyer Fallon McElligott, Inc., Mpls., 1986—. Office: Fallon McElligott Inc 701 4th Ave S Minneapolis MN 55415

SMITH, TERESA ANN, applications programmer; b. Seattle, Sept. 7, 1963; d. Michael and Dianne (Barnell) Martin. BA in Math., U. Wash., 1987. Applications programmer Computers N.W., Inc., Bellevue, Wash., 1987—. Mem. Nat. Women's Polit. Caucas, Seattle, 1988. Mem. U. Wash. Alumni Assn., Assn. for Women in Computing. Democrat. Roman Catholic. Home: 8851 166th St NE A203 Redmond WA 98052

SMITH, THELMA MARIE, mathematics educator; b. Jamaica, N.Y., May 21, 1936; d. Parlett Longsworth and Thelma (Crawford) Moore; m. Oliver A. Smith, Apr. 30, 1960; children: Oliver Alexander Jr., Monica Renée. BS, Morgan State U., 1958; MEd, Howard U., 1974; postgrad., Cath. U. With U.S. Dept. Commerce, Suitland, Md., 1961-68, 90—; asst. prof. math. U. D.C., Washington, 1969-77; sr. programmer analyst Computer Sci. Corp., Silver Spring, Md., 1977-79; bus. owner R & D, Pikesville, Md., 1981—; mem. faculty Prince George's Community Coll., Largo, Md., 1989; resource person Balt. City Schs.; adj. assoc. prof. U. D.C., Washington, 1985; enumerator U.S. Census Bur., Towson, Md., 1990. Active in community svc. Recipient Cert. of Appreciation, Rep. Nat. Com., 1986, Bronze medal for svc. Md. Sci. Ctr., 1985, Medal of Merit, Rep. Presdl. Task Force, 1990. Mem. IEEE (computer soc. tech. com. on operating systems), Assn. for Computing Machinery. Methodist. Home and Office: 7410 Rockridge Rd Pikesville MD 21208

SMITH, THELMA TINA HARRIETTE, artist, gallery owner; b. Folkston, Ga., May 5, 1938; d. Harry Charles and Malinda Estelle (Kennison) Causey; m. Billy Wayne Smith, July 23, 1955; children: Sherry Yvonne, Susan Marie, Dennis Wayne, Chris Michael. Student, U. Tex., Arlington, 1968-70; studies with various art instrs. Gen. office worker Superior Ins. Corp., Dallas, 1956-57, Zanes-Ewalt Warehouse, Dallas, 1957-67; bookkeeper Atlas Match Co., Arlington, 1967-68; sr. acct. Automated Refrigerated Air Conditioner Mfg. Corp., Arlington, 1968-70; acct. Conn. Gen. Life Ins. Corp., Dallas, 1972-74; freelance artist Denton, Tex., 1974—; gallery owner, custom framer Tina Smith Studio-Gallery, Mabank, Tex., 1983—. Editor Cedar Creek Art Soc. Yearbook, 1983—. Treas. Cedar Creek Art Soc., 1987-88, 89—, yearbook editor, 1989—. Recipient numerous watercolor and pastel awards Henderson County Art League, Cedar Creek Art Soc. Mem. Southwestern Watercolor Soc., Pastel Soc. of the S.W., Cedar Creek Art Soc. (v.p. 1983-86, treas.). Baptist. Office: Tina Smith Studio-Gallery 701 S 3d St Mabank TX 75147

SMITH, THOMASINA DENISE, computer programmer analyst; b. Columbia, S.C., Mar. 20, 1954; d. Thomas Smith and Tecora Claratine (Shaw) Drake; m. Jerry Williams, Mar. 15, 1982 (div. Jan. 1983). BS, Winthrop Coll., Rock Hill, S.C., 1974. Computer programmer trainee Blue Cross/Blue Shield, Columbia, S.C., 1974-75; computer operator Kline Iron & Steel Co., Columbia, 1976-78; jr. computer programmer NCR Corp., Dayton, Ohio, 1978-80; systems analyst Bank One, Dayton, 1980-83; programmer analyst Elder Beerman, Dayton, 1984-85, Def. Contract Adminstrn., Columbus, Ohio, 1985-86, U.S. Army, Atlanta, 1986—; owner, operator TDS Enterprises, Atlanta, 1988—. Vol. Adopt a Sister/Adopt a Brother, Atlanta, 1989, Ben Hill United Meth. Ch. Missionary Soc., Atlanta. Mem. Data Processing Mgmt. Assn., The Phoenix Soc. for Burn Survivors, Endometriosis Assn., Nat. Found. of Ileitis and Colitis. Zeta Phi Beta. Democrat. Home: 1693 Melrose Dr SW Atlanta GA 30310 Office: US Hdqrs Forscom FCJ6-PDB Atlanta GA 30330

SMITH, TONI COLETTE, human services administrator, social worker; b. Columbus, Ohio, Oct. 31, 1952. BA, Ohio State U., Columbus, 1974, postgrad., 1975-76; postgrad., Ohio State U., Columbus, 1978-90. Lic. social worker, Ohio. Cons. Ohio Dept. Human Svc., Columbus, 1974-75; mgr. Fisher Body Div., Columbus, 1977-78; with Franklin County Human Svc., Columbus, 1975—, supr., 1979-86, adminstr., 1986—; pub. speaker human svcs. program Franklin County Human Svc., 1988—; instr., trainer human svc. suprs. Columbus State Community Coll., 1990—. Mem. adv. bd. Columbus City Comprehensive Plan, 1989—, Syntaxis Group Home, Columbus, 1989—; Informed Neighbors Com., 1989—; v.p. Berwick Civic Assn., Columbus, 1990—. Mem. AAUW (corr. sec. Columbus chpt. 1988—), NAFE, Columbus Women's Network, LWV. Democrat. Roman Catholic. Home: 2665 Mitzi Dr Columbus OH 43209 Office: Franklin County Dept Human 80 E Fulton St Columbus OH 43215

SMITH, TRACEY LEE, corporate communication specialist; b. Scranton, Pa., Jan. 31, 1963; d. Peter Slocomb and Rosella Faye (Reinhold) S. BA in Journalism and Pub. Rels., Ga. State U., Atlanta, 1985. Copy editor McGraw Hill Publs., Atlanta, 1985-87; depts. editor Miller Freeman Publs., Atlanta, 1987-88; asst. editor Miller Freeman Prodns., Atlanta, 1988-89, assoc. editor, 1989; communication specialist Alumax Internat., Inc., Atlanta, 1989—. Mem. Internat. Assn. Bus. Communicators, Women in Communications, Inc. (v.p. membership 1990—, staff writer newsletter Ga. chpt. 1989-90, Communication Excellence award, Hon. Mention 1990), Atlanta Lawn and Tennis Assn. (capt. 1990), U.S. Lawn and Tennis Assn. Episcopalian. Home: 2105 Summerlake Dr Atlanta GA 30350 Office: Alumax Inc 5655 Peachtree Pkwy Norcross GA 30092

SMITH, VANGY EDITH, accountant, consultant, writer, artist; b. Saskatoon, Sask., Can., Dec. 17, 1937; d. Wilhelm and Anne Ellen (Hartshorne)

Gogel; m. Clifford Wilson, May 12, 1958 (de. Dec. 1978); children: Kenneth, Koral, Kevin, Korey, Kyle; m. Terrence Raymond Smith, Dec. 14, 1979. Student, Saskatoon Tech. Collegiate Inst., 1956, BBA, 1958, MBA, 1987, PhD in English with honors, 1988. Accounts payable clk. Maxwell Labs., Inc., San Diego, 1978; invoice clk. Davies Electric, Saskatoon, 1980-81; office mgr. Ladee Bug Ceramics, Saskatoon, 1981-87, Lazars Investments Corp., Eugene, Oreg., 1987; bookkeeper accounts payable Pop Geer, Eugene, Oreg., 1987; office mgr., bookkeeper Willamette Sports Ctr., Inc., Eugene, Oreg., 1987—. Contbr. articles to scholarly jours. (recipient doctoral award 1987). Counselor Drug & Rehab. Ctr., Eugene, 1970-88; trustee Children's Farm Home, Corvallis, Oreg., 1989—; 3d v.p. Lane County Coun. Orgn., 1988-89, 2d v.p., 1989—; mem. Found. Christian Living; pres. Oreg. State Christian Temperance Union, 1989—; mem. pub. safety adv. com. City of Eugene, 1989—; co-pres. Lane County UN Assn., 1989-90; appointed nat. pres. Nat. Bd. Edn., 1989; mem. adv. com. Dept. Pub. Safety for City of Eugene, Oreg., 1990; co-chmn. UN Assn. Lane County, 1990—. Recipient 3d and 4th place artists' awards Lane County Fair, 1987, 1st and 2d place awards Nat. Writing Contest, 1987, 88, 89. Mem. Am. Soc. Writers, Women's Christian Temperance Union (life, pres., state bd. dirs. projection methods circulation 1987—, Appreciation award 1982, Presdl. award 1985, Mgr. of the Yr. 1990). Democrat. Home and Office: 1730 Chicago Ave Evanston IL 60201

SMITH, VICKI LYN, psychology educator; b. Mexico, Mo., Apr. 2, 1961; d. R. Thomas and Carole A. (Wiese) S. BA, U. Calif., San Diego, 1983; PhD, Stanford U., 1987. Asst. prof. dept. psychology Northwestern U., Evanston, Ill., 1987—. Contbr. articles to profl. jours. Grad. fellow NSF, 1983-86, Stanford U., 1986-87; grantee Am. Psychol. Assn., Soc. for Psychol. Study of Social Issues, 1987, Northwestern U., 1989-90, Kellogg Grad. Sch. Mgmt., 1989-90. Mem. Am. Psychol. Assn., Am. Psychology-Law Soc., Law and Soc. Assn., Midwestern Psychol. Assn. Lutheran. Office: Dept Psychology Northwestern U Evanston IL 60208

SMITH, VIRGINIA DODD (MRS. HAVEN SMITH), congresswoman; b. Randolph, Iowa, June 30, 1911; d. Clifton Clark and Erville (Reeves) Dodd; m. Haven N. Smith, Aug. 27, 1931. A.B., U. Nebr., 1936; hon. degree, Nebr. U., 1987. Nat. pres. Am. Country Life Assn., 1951-54; nat. chmn. Am. Farm Bur. Women, 1954-74; dir. Am. Farm Bur. Fedn., 1954-74, Country Women's Council; world dep. pres. Asso. Country Women of World, 1962-68; mem. Dept. Agr. Nat. Home Econs. Research Adv. Com., 1960-65. Mem. Crusade for Freedom European inspection tour, 1958; del. Republican Nat. Conv., 1956, 72; bd. govs. Agrl. Hall of Fame, 1959—; mem. Nat. Livestock and Meat Bd., 1955-58, Nat. Commn. Community Health Services, 1963-66; adv. mem. Nebr. Sch. Bds. Assns., 1949; mem. Nebr. Territorial Centennial Commn., 1953, Gov.'s Commn. Status of Women, 1964-66; chmn. Presdl. Task Force on Rural Devel., 1969-70; mem. appropriations com., ranking minority mem. agrl. appropriations subcom., appropriations subcom. on energy and water devel. 94th-101st Congresses from 3d dist. Nebr.; v.p. Farm Film Found., 1964-74, Good Will ambassador to Switzerland, 1950. Apptd. adm. Nebr. Navy. Recipient award of Merit, DAR, 1956; Disting. Service award U. Nebr., 1956, 60; award for best pub. address on freedom Freedom Found., 1966; Eyes on Nebr. award Nebr. Optometric Assn., 1970; Internat. Service award Midwest Conf. World Affairs, 1970; Woman of Achievement award Nebr. Bus. and Profl. Women, 1971; selected as 1 of 6 U.S. women Govt. France for 3 week goodwill mission to France, 1969; Outstanding 4H Alumni award Iowa State U., 1973, 74; Watchdog of Treasury award, 1976, 78, 80, 82, 83, 84, 86, 88; Guardian of Small Bus. award, 1976, 78, 80, 82, 84, 86, 88; Nebr. Ak-Sar-Ben award, 1983, Agrl. Achievement, Nebr. U., 1987. Mem. AAUW, Delta Kappa Gamma (state hon. mem.), Beta Sigma Phi (internat. hon. mem.), Chi Omega, PEO (past pres.), Eastern Star. Methodist. Club: Business and Professional Women. Office: US Ho of Reps 2202 Rayburn Washington DC 20515*

SMITH, VME (VERNA MAE EDOM SMITH), sociology educator, freelance writer, photographer; b. Marshfield, Wis., June 19, 1929; d. Clifton Cedric and Vilia Clarissa (Patefield) Edom; children: Teri Freas, Anthony Thomas. AB in Sociology, U. Mo., 1951; MA in Sociology, George Washington, 1965; PhD in Human Devel., U. Md., 1981. Tchr. Alcohol Safety Action Program Fairfax County, Va., 1973-75; instr. sociology No. Va. Community Coll., Manassas, 1975-77, asst. prof., 1977-81, assoc. prof., 1981-84, prof., 1984—, coord. coop. edn., 1983-89; freelance writer, editor and photographer, 1965—; asst. producer history of photography program Sta. WETA-TV, Washington, 1965; rsch. and prodn. asst., photographer, publs. editor No. Va. Ednl. TV, Sta. WNVT, 1970-71; cons. migrant div. Md. Dept. Edn., Balt., summer 1977; researcher, photographer Roundabout presch. high sch. series on Am. Values Sta. WNVT, 1970-71. Author, photographer: Middleburg and Nearby, 1986; contbr. photography to various works including Visual Impact in Print (Hurley and McDougall), 1971, Looking Forward to a Career in Education (Moses), 1976, Child Growth and Development (Terry, Sorrentino and Flatter), 1979; photojournalism Migrant Child Welfare, 1977, (Cavenaugh), Caring For Children, 1973 (5 publications by L.B. Murphy), Department of Health, Education and Welfare, National Geographic, 1961, Head Start Newsletter, 1973-74; photographs exhibited by Mo. Hist. Soc., Wis. Hist. Soc., Nat. Press Photographer's Assn., Nat. Fedn. Press Women, Family Svc. Washington, others; contbr. articles to profl. publs. Mem. ednl. adv. com. Head Start, Warrenton, Va. Recipient Emmy Ohio State Children's Programming award. Mem. Va. Assn. Coop. Edn. (com. mem.). Democrat. Mem. Unitarian Ch. Office: No Va Community Coll 6901 Sudley Rd Manassas VA 22110

SMITH, WANDA JEAN, insurance professional; b. Atmore, Ala., July 25, 1949; d. Lloyd and Edith (DuBois) Scott; m. James A. Smith, Jr., May 29, 1970; children—Joyce A., Jeffrey A. B.A., St. Mary's U., 1970. Registered securities rep. Sec., So. Regional Edn. Bd., Atlanta, 1976-78; adminstrv. asst. Discovery Learning, Atlanta, 1978-79; sales sec. Mobay Chems., Atlanta, 1979-80; sales assoc. Lincoln Nat. Ins. Co., Atlanta, 1980-81, Am. Nat. Ins. Co., Atlanta, 1981-87 , Century 21 Grand South, College Park, Ga., 1984—, N.Y. Life Ins. Co., 1987—. Pub. relations vol. East Point Track Club, 1985; mem. parents orgn. Clayton County Athletic Assn., 1986. Mem. Nat. Assn. Female Execs., Nat. Assn. Life Underwriters. Avocations: bowling; crafts. Home: 2250 Sandgate Circle College Park GA 30349 Office: NY Life Ins Co 2 Peachtree St Ste 2000 Atlanta GA 30383

SMITH, YVONNE CAROLYN, therapist; b. Lockport, N.Y., June 12, 1923; d. William Louis and Bertha (Zoss) S. BA, Valparaiso U., 1948; M in Social Sci. Adminstrn., Case-Western Res. U., Cleve., 1955. Cert. social worker. Caseworker Niagara County Welfare Dept., Lockport, 1950-53, Luth. Children's Aid, Cleve., 1954, Luth. Family Svc., Chgo., 1955-56, Family Svc. Soc., Buffalo, 1956-62; therapist, dir. Child & Family Svcs., Buffalo, 1962-88; ret. Child & Family Svcs., Cheetowaga, N.Y., 1988; field instr. social work SUNY, 1962-80; cons. Genesee County Social Svcs., Batavia, 1975-85, cons. Seneca County Social Svcs. Waterloo, 1988. Bd. dirs. Luth. Svcs. Soc., Buffalo, 1979-85, 88—; speaker United Way of Buffalo, 1956-88. Sgt. WAC, 1944-46. Mem. Internat. Human Learning Resources Nwtwork. Republican. Home: 401 Englewood Apt 3 Buffalo NY 14223

SMITH-ALEXANDER, MELANIE SUE, physical therapist, consultant; b. Seattle, May 26, 1959; d. L. Henry Smith and Carol Sue (Gotwals) Skomp; m. Norman Lee Alexander, May 14, 1988. BA in French, Purdue U., 1981; MS in Phys. Therapy, U. Indpls., 1983. Lic. phys. therapist, Ind. Staff therapist Union Hosp., Terre Haute, Ind., 1984-85; chief phys. therapist Outpatient Phys. Therapy Clinics, Inc., Lexington, Ky., 1985-87; staff therapist Comprehensive Med. Rehab. Ctr. of Lexington, 1987-88; indsl. rehab. mgr. St. Mary's Comprehensive Indsl. Rehab. Ctr., Knoxville, Tenn., 1988-90; mgr. Back to Work Ctr. St. Elizabeth Hosp., Lafayette, Ind., 1990—; indsl. cons. St. Elizabeth Hosp. Health Promotion Svcs., Lafayette, 1990—. Mem. Am. Phys. Therapy Assn. (orthopedic sect. 1982—). Mem. Ch. of Christ. Home: RR 1 Box 328A Brookston IN 47923 Office: St Elizabeth Hosp PO Box 7501 Lafayette IN 47903

SMITHBURTON, CYNTHIA, chiropractor; b. Kansas City, Mo., May 3, 1959; d. Donald and Velta (Borner) Wright. Ed., Columbia (Mo.) Coll.; grad., Cleveland Chiropractic Coll., Kansas City, Mo., 1984. Lic. chiropractor, Ill., Mo. Chiropractic asst., ind. contractor; chiropractic physician Sandman Clinic, Chgo. Recipient Disting. Young Leadership award, George T. O'Donahue Achievement award. Mem. Internat. Chiropractic Assn., Mo. C. of C. Address: 600 E 8th St Kansas City MO 64106

SMITH-DORNAN, MAGGIE JO, marketing educator, academic administrator; b. Ft. Worth, Apr. 6, 1945; d. John Walter and Maggie Thelma (French) Williams; m. Paul Joseph Smith, Nov. 28, 1963 (div. Sept. 1974); 1 child, Stephen Christopher Smith; m. Randall Everett Dornan, July 10, 1982. BS in Bus., Northeastern U., Boston, 1976; MBA, U. Miami, 1977; PhD in Bus., U. Okla., 1980. Lic. real estate broker. Research asst. dept. mktg. U. Miami, Coral Gables, Fla., 1976-77; instr. mktg. U. Okla., Norman, 1977-80; asst. prof. Northeastern U., 1980-83; lectr. dept. mktg. Coll. Bus. Adminstrn. U. Fla., Gainesville, 1985—, assoc. dir. Ctr. for Retail Research and Edn., 1986—, mem. undergrad. program com., 1986; MIS mgr. Blue Cross Blue Shield Fla., 1989—; lectr. U. North Fla.; cons. retail, Fla., 1985—. Contbr. articles to profl. jours. Named Mktg. Tchr. of Yr., Coll. Bus. Adminstrn., U. Fla., 1985-90; Mass. State scholar, 1973-76. Mem. Am. Mktg. Assn. (advisor 1982-83, 89-90), Jacksonville Bd. Realtors, Sigma Epsilon Rho, Delta Sigma Pi (advisor 1985—). Republican. Home: 8112 Sarcee Tr Jacksonville FL 32244 Office: Blue Cross Blue Shield Fla Jacksonville FL 32203

SMITHERMAN, RUTH ROTHMEYER, retired educator; b. DePere, Wis., June 2, 1912; d. Elroy Ellis and Elizabeth Christine (Beuthien) Brown; m. Charles Otto Rothmeyer, Nov. 25, 1942 (dec. 1950); 1 child, Ruth Anne; m. William Henry Smitherman, Dec. 31, 1952. BA, No. Mich. U., 1935; MA, U. Mich., 1938; postgrad., U. Calif., Berkeley, San Francisco State U. Tchr. Beaverton (Mich.) Pub. Schs., 1935-37, Detroit Pub. Schs., 1937-39, Oak Park (Ill.) Pub. Schs., 1939-41, Elmhurst (Ill.) Pub. Schs., 1941-43, Hinsdale (Ill.) Pub. Schs., 1950-52, Burlingame (Calif.) Pub. Schs., 1955-75; now ret.; mgr. comml. property, Burlingame, 1981-89. Nominating com. 3d Mut., Leisure World, Laguna Hills, Calif., 1986, 89; women's organizer Laguna Hills Cityhood Com., 1989; vol. reading programs and story telling, local schs. Mem. DAR (regent, gold award 1980-82), Ebell Club Calif. (pres. 1983-84), Aliso Club at Leisure World (pres. 1986-87), Woman's Club Leisure World (pres. 1987-89), Treasure Seekers Guild (pres. 1985-87), Hist. Soc. Laguna Hills (2d v.p. 1987—). Republican. Episcopalian. Home: 5437 Via Carrizo Laguna Hills CA 92653

SMITHERS, JANE BRAITMAYER, manufacturing company executive; b. Washington, May 25, 1915; d. Otto Ernest and Kathleen (Ketcham) Braitmayer; B.A., Vassar Coll., 1937; m. William Henry Howell, Aug. 7, 1937 (dec. 1961); children: Kathleen, William David, Marian Braitmayer; m. John Abram Smithers, June 13, 1964; stepchildren: Margaret Smithers Koeniger, John A., Eleanor Smithers Blahnik, James P. Rec. sec. Children's Home, Inc., Poughkeepsie, N.Y., 1942, Dutchess County Planned Parenthood, 1941; corp. sec., dir. Smithers Tools and Machine Products, Inc., Rhinebeck, N.Y., 1965-88; former dir. Bankers Trust Hudson Valley, N.A. Chmn. com. on detention Dutchess County Social Planning Council, 1949; pres. Dutchess County Soc. Mental Health, 1958-59; mem. Dutchess County Youth Bd., 1968-70; founder, pres. No. Dutchess Community Svcs., 1969; founder, pres. No. Dutchess Day Care Ctr., Inc., 1971-73, mem. adv. bd.; bd. dirs. No. Dutchess Hosp. Clubs: Beverly Yacht (Marion, Mass.); Jr. League of Poughkeepsie-Vassar. Republican. Episcopalian. Home: RD 2 Box 116 Red Hook NY 12571

SMITH-EVERNDEN, ROBERTA KATHERINE, geological consultant; b. L.A., Dec. 17, 1931; d. Elmer-Harrison and Mary Katherine (Tilley) Smith; m. Mark Newell Christensen, July 14, 1956 (div. 1961); m. Jack Foord Evernden, Dec. 31, 1965. AA, L.A. Valley Coll., 1952; BA, U. Alaska, 1957; MA, U. Calif., Berkeley, 1960; PhD, U. B.C., Vancouver, B.C., Can., 1966. Registered geologist, Calif. Geologist Smithsonian Inst., Washington, 1965-73; asst prof. geology Howard U., George Washington U., Washington, 1966-70; geologist, prin. Smith-Evernden Assocs., Davenport, Calif., 1974—; rsch. assoc., lectr. U. Calif., Santa Cruz, 1974—; bd. dirs., pres. Santa Cruz County Resource Conservation Dist., Santa Cruz, 1980—; profl. affairs com. Calif. Bd. Registered Geologists & Geophysicists, Sacramento, 1982-86; tech. adv. com. Calif. Bd. of Forestry, Sacramento, 1987—; adv. com. Monterey Bay United Air Pollution Control Dist., Salinas, Calif., 1986—; soil conservation com. State of Calif. Dept. Conservation, Sacramento, 1990—. Contbr. sic. papers to profl. jours. mem. Assn. Engring. Geologists, Soc. for Sedimentary Geology, Soc. Woman Geographers, North Am. Micropaleontological Soc., Calif. Forest Soils Coun., Sigma Xi. Office: Smith Evernden Assocs PO Box 174 Davenport CA 95017

SMITH-HOLLAND, ELIZABETH EUGENIA, registered nurse; b. Richmond, Va., Aug. 10, 1960; d. Robert Graham and Mary Anne (von Gemmingen) Smith; m. Jerry Michael Holland. BSN, U. Va., 1982. RN. Staff RN gen. surgery/ICU Med. Coll. Va., RIchmond, 1982-84; contract staff nurse Med. Recruiters Am., Tampa, 1984-86; clin. mgr. ICU Roseville (Calif.) Community Hosp., 1986-90; high-risk infant specialist Valley Mountain Regional Ctr., Stockton, Calif., 1990—. Republican. Episcopalian. Office: Valley Mountain Regional 7210 Murray Dr Stockton CA 95210

SMITH-REARDON, JANET LINDA, management consultant; b. Morristown, N.J., Oct. 30, 1962; d. Walter Bruning and Mary Ann (King) Smith; m. Michael John Reardon, Feb. 25, 1989; 1 child, Sean Walter Reardon. BS summa cum laude, Montclair State Coll., 1984. Promotional inventory analyst Cosmair Inc., Piscataway, N.J., 1984-85; promotional planner Cosmair Inc., Piscataway, 1985-86; promotional merchandising mgr. Cosmair Inc., N.Y.C., 1986-87; regional sales mgr. United Jersey Bank, Hackensack, N.J., 1987-88; retail sales adminstr. and officer Morris Savs. Bank, Morristown, 1988-89; pres. Smith-Reardon Consulting, 1989—; mem. Cosmetic Industry Bd., N.Y.C., 1985—. Author: United Jersey Bank Sales Newsletter, 1987-88. Membership chmn. Boy Scouts of Bergen County, Hackensack, 1987-88; chmn. fund drive Charity Drive for Leukemia Victim, Morristown, 1988-89; chairperson United Way Campaign, United Jersey Bank, Hackensack, 1987-88; bd. dirs. County Coll. of Morris Alumni, Randolph, N.J., 1986-88. Mem. Bank Mktg. Assn., Bank Pricing Com. Republican. Presbyterian. Home: 553 New Vernon Rd Gillette NJ 07933 Office: Morris Savings Bank 21 South St Morristown NJ 07960

SMITH-WADE-EL, RITA RORATE, psychology educator; b. Washington, Oct. 1, 1948; d. James Edward and Eva (Stephens) Smith; m. Sherwood Wade-El, May 17, 1987; children: Ayodele Nsilo Smith-Jackson, Ismail Muhammed Smith-Wade-El. BA, Barnard Coll., 1970; MA, U. Pa., 197l, PhD, 1979. Asst. prof., minority affairs counselor East Stroudsburg (Pa.) U., 1972-73; asst. prof. Pan African studies dept. Temple U., Phila., 1974-83; asst. prof. psychology Millersville (Pa.) U., 1984—, assoc. prof., asst. chmn. dept., 1984—; reviewer NSF, 198l. Editor: State of Black Lancaster, 1986; contbr. articles to profl. jours. and newspapers. Active numerous civic orgns.; mem. govtl. rels. com. United Way Lancaster (Pa.), 1985—; vol. Big Bros.-Big Sisters Lancaster County, 1985—; mem. brain trust Pa. Black Legis. Caucus, 1987—; bd. dirs. Afcom Learning Ctr., Phila., 1976-84, John F. Kennedy Community Health Ctr., Phila., 198l-84, Delaware Valley Assn. for Infant Mental Health, Phila., 1982-84, Lancaster Guidance Clinic, 1987—, Lancaster-Lebanon Literacy Coun., 1986-87; mem. exec. coun. NAACP, Lancaster, 1984—. Recipient community svc. award A.M.E. Ch., Phila., 1980; Social Learning Lab. Ednl. Testing Svc. fellow, 1979; Pa. Legis. Office for Rsch. Liaison grantee, 1985, Pa. Dept. Edn. grantee, 1985, Pa. Coun. Arts grantee, 1986, Pa. Humanities Coun. grantee, 1986. Mem. Am. Psychol. Assn., Nat. Assn. Black Psychologists (bd. dirs. 1981-84, outstanding svc. award 1981), Delaware Valley Assn. Black Psychologists (past v.p., pres., mem. exec. coun., chmn. various coms.), Phi Kappa Phi (pres. Mu chpt. 1986—), Psi Chi. Democrat. Roman Catholic. Home: 947 Virginia Ave Lancaster PA 17603 Office: Millersville U Psychology Dept 1l9 Byerly Millersville PA 17551

SMITH-YOUNG, ANNE VICTORIA, health services professional; b. Long Beach, Calif., Aug. 25, 1947; d. James Warren and Jeanne Anne (Cooney) Wright; m. Lynn Walker Smith, Aug. 11, 1968 (div. Feb. 1980); children: Amy Lyanne and Caroline Walker (twins); m. Stephen Nicholas Young, May 29, 1982. AS, Long Beach City Coll., 1967; BS, Marymount Coll., 1984. Mgr. office Williams-Brinton Med. Corp., Huntington Beach, Calif., 1975-80; adminstr. Westchester Urol. Assocs., White Plains, N.Y., 1980-82; adminstr. Pediatric Urol. Assocs. Westchester County Med. Ctr., Valhalla, N.Y., 1982-86; clin. coord. urodynamics lab. cystocopy ste. dept. urology Westchester County Med. Ctr., Valhalla, 1986—, chairperson exec. com. employee adv. coun., 1987—; cons. Office Career Svcs., Marymount (N.Y.) Coll., 1984—; cons. to mfrs., individuals and healthcare providers on urinary incontinence. Mem. editorial bd. Sex Over Forty; contbr. articles to profl. jours. Mem. NAFE, Am. Urol. Assn. (allied, nat. fundraiser 1980-86, bd. dirs. N.Y. chpt. 1988—, recognition award 1985), Assn. Urinary Continence Control (bd. dirs. 1988—), Am. Assn. Med. Assts., Nat. Hist. Preservation Trust, Internat. Platform Assn., Mothers of Twins Club (Long Beach, pres. 1974-75), Lions (bd. dirs. White Plains 1989—, editor newsletter, recognition award 1990). Mem. Am. Urol. Assn. Allied (nat. fundraiser 1980-86, bd. dirs. N.Y. chpt. 1988—, Recogainition award 1985, diplomate, cons., Stamford, Conn., 1984-87, adminstrv. sec., 1987—), Assn. Urinary Continence Control (bd. dirs. 1988—), Am. Assn. Med. Assts., NAFE, Nat. Hist. Preservation Trust, Internat. Platform Assn., Lions (White Plains, N.Y., bd. dirs. 1989—, editor Lions Roar newsletter, Lion of the Month, Jan. 1990, 1st v.p.), Mothers of Twins Club (Long Beach, pres. 1974-75). Democrat. Home: 407 Strawberry Hill Ave Stamford CT 06902 Office: Westchester County Med Ctr Dept Urology Valhalla NY 10595

SMITLEY, BARBARA ANNE, accountant; b. Tell City, Ind., Aug. 4, 1956; d. James Heber and Regina Doris (Rogier) Lasher; m. Randy Allen Smitley, Aug. 3, 1974; children: Joshua, Leslie, Jefferey, Nicole, Jeremy. BS with high distinction, Ind. U., 1982. CPA, Ind. Acctg. clk. Brown & Williamson Tobacco Corp., Louisville, 1977; acctg. clk. BATUS, Inc., Louisville, 1977-80, assoc. fin. analyst, 1980-83, fin. analyst, 1984-85, acct., 1985-88, sr. acct., 1988—. Mem. Am. Soc. Women Accts. Roman Catholic.

SMITS, HELEN LIDA, hospital executive, physician, educator; b. Long Beach, Calif., Dec. 3, 1936; d. Theodore Richard Smits and Anna Mary Wells; m. Roger LeCompte, Aug. 28, 1976; 1 child, Theodore. BA with honors, Swarthmore Coll., 1958; MA, Yale U., 1961, MD cum laude, 1967. Intern, asst. resident Hosp. U. Pa., 1967-68; fellow Beth Israel Hosp., Boston, 1969-70; chief resident Hosp. U. Pa., 1970-71; chief med. clinic U. Pa., 1971-75; assoc. adminstr. for patient care svcs. U. Pa. Hosp., 1975-77; v.p. med. affairs Community Health Plan Georgetown U., Washington, 1977; dir. health standards and quality bur. Health Care Financing Adminstrn., HHS, Washington, 1977-80; sr. rsch. assoc. The Urban Inst., Washington, 1980-81; assoc. prof. Yale U. Med. Sch., New Haven, 1981-85; assoc. v.p. for health affairs U. Conn. Health Ctr., Farmington, 1985-87; prof. community medicine U. Conn. Sch. Medicine, Farmington, 1985—; hosp. dir. John Dempsey Hosp., Farmington, 1987—; adv. panel Pew Charitable Trusts, Phila., 1986—; corporator St. Francis Hosp. and Med. Ctr., Hartford, Conn., 1988—; commr. Joint Com. on Accreditation Hosps., Chgo., 1989—. Contbr. numerous articles to profl. jours. Bd. dirs. The Children's House, Essex, Conn., 1987-88, The Ivoryton, Playhouse Fedn., Inc., 1990—; mem. Dem. Town Com., Essex, 1982-89. Recipient Superior Svc. award HHS, Washington, 1982; Royal Soc. Medicine Found. fellow, London, 1973; Fulbright scholar, 1959-60. Fellow Am. Coll. Phsyicians (regent 1984-90); mem. Phi Beta Kappa, Alpha Omega Alpha. Episcopalian. Home: 81 Main St Ivoryton CT 06442 Office: U Conn Health Ctr John Dempsey Hosp Office of Dir Farmington CT 06032

SMIZINSKI, LINDA SUZANNE, county government official, realtor; b. Chgo., July 7, 1947; d. Bruno Albert and Wanda Casmira (Tarkowski) S. BA, Loyola U., 1969, MS in Indsl. Relations, 1976. Grad. Realtors Inst. Index clk. City Chgo., 1969-70; job analyst technician Bureau Adminstrn. Cook County Govt., Chgo., 1970-73, job analyst II, 1973-81, job analyst III supr., 1981-86, labor relations officer, 1986—; job analyst Hay Mgmt. Cons., Chgo., 1978-82. Recipient award Nat. Assn. Counties, Chgo., 1986. Mem. Nat. Assn Female Execs., Chgo. Met. Chpt. Intergovtl. Personnel Mgmt. Assn., Nat. Assn. Realtors, Ill. Assn. Realtors, Chgo. Bd. Realtors, Northwest Real Estate Bd., North Side Real Estate Bd. Democrat. Roman Catholic. Club: Chgo. Health. Office: Cook County Govt County Bldg Room 818 118 N Clark St Chicago IL 60602 also: Am Title Realty Co Inc 6253 N Milwaukee Ave Chicago IL 60646

SMOCK, CONNIE SUE, physical therapist; b. Omaha, Aug. 18, 1960; d. Raymon Ira and Mary Jean (McCarroll) S. Student, U. Nebr., 1978-81; BS in Phys. Therapy, U. Kans., Kansas City, 1983. Registered phys. therapist. Phys. therapist Phys. Therapy and Hand Rehab., North Kansas City, Mo., 1983-85; adminstrv. asst. Phys. Therapy and Hand Rehab., North Kansas City, Kans., 1985-86; phys. therapist St. John Hosp., Leavenworth, Kans., 1986-87, sr. phys. therapist, 1987; phys. therapist Profl. Rehabilitative Svcs., Kansas City, Kans., 1987-90, indsl. rehab. specialist, 1990—; phsy. therapist Wx: Work Capacities, Independence, Mo., 1990—. Mem. Kansas City Orthopedic Study Group, Greater Kansas City Dog Tng. Club. Home: 5523 N Troost Kansas City MO 64118

SMOCK, JERALDINE (JERRI), psychologist; b. Albany, Calif., May 19, 1943; d. James William Curry and Virginia Charlotte (Williams) Durrie; m. Jon D. Smock, Mar. 16, 1978 (div. 1989); 1 child, Kathleen Louise Camacho. AA in Communications, Chabot Community Coll., Hayward, Calif., 1978; BA in Pub. Adminstrn., U. San Francisco, 1980, MA in Counseling, 1982; PhD, Calif. Sch. Family Psychology, 1987. Lic. marriage and family counselor, child counselor. Cons. gov.'s office State of Calif., Sacramento, 1975-76; cons. WIN Systems, Inc., Sacramento, 1976—; pvt. practice Fairfield, Calif., 1985—; cons. Dem. Nat. Com., Washington; campaign cons. various local, state, and nat. campaigns; cons. U.S. Dept. Justice, 1989—, Nat. Sch. Safety Ctr., 1988-89; bd. mem. Atty. Gen.'s Adv. Bd. on Missing and Exploited Children, 1989—. Author: Missing Children: The Effects of a Prevention Program on Children and Their Families, 1987, A Storybook for Adults and Other Children: The Swan, 1988. Mem. Nat. Orgn. for Victims Assistance, Soc. for Study of Traumatic Stress, Calif. Assn. Marriage and Family Therapists, Calif. State Psychol. Assn., Calif. Assn. Profls. Against Child Abuse, Am. Assn. Profls. Against Child Abuse, Commonwealth Club San Francisco, Am. Psychol. Assn., Calif. Juvenile Officers Assn. Presbyterian. Office: Ctr Marriage Family Therapy 1652 W Texas St #105 Fairfield CA 94533

SMOLUCHA, FRANCINE CAROL, psychology educator; b. Chgo., May 29, 1953; d. Leon Isadore and Frances Barbara (Olszewski) Ziemba; m. Larry Walter Smolucha, May 6, 1979. AA, City Colls. Chgo., 1972; BA, St. Xavier Coll., Chgo., 1973; MA, U. Chgo., 1975, postgrad., 1975-90. Adult edn. instr. City Colls. Chgo., 1974-76, St. Xavier Coll., 1974-76; prof. psychology Moraine Valley Community Coll., Palos Hills, Ill., 1976—. Contbr. to profl. publs. Mem. AAUW (recording sec. Oak Brook area unit 1989-91), Am. Psychol. Assn., Nat. Soc. Study of Edn., Interrnat. Assn. Empiracal Aesthetics, Am. Ednl. Rsch. Assn., Midwest Psychol. Assn. Office: MoraineValleyCommunity Coll 10900 S 88th Ave Palos Hills IL 60465

SMOOT, SAMANTHA SUE, corporate communications specialist, secretary; b. Excelsior, Mo., Mar. 13, 1966; d. William Kenneth Smoot and Shirley Jean (Miller) Rubino. Student, Cen. Mo. State U., 1984-85, Maple Woods Community Coll., 1987—. Office mgr. Crown Communications, Inc., Kansas City, Mo., 1987—. Mem. Mo. Notary Assn. Republican. Home: 28 NW 72d St Apt B Kansas City MO 64118 Office: Crown Communications Inc 4444 N Belleview Ste 106 Kansas City MO 64116

SMOOT, SHARENE LOWERY, social services administrator, educator; b. Niles, Mich., Oct. 2, 1940; d. Robert Francis and Eleanor Fay (Stock) Lowery; m. James Clinton Smoot III, Feb. 24, 1962; children: James IV, Gretchen Frances. BS, Mich. State U., 1961; MA, East Car. U., 1963; EdS, Ga. State U., 1982, PhD, 1989. Spl. Edn. Adminstr. Instr. E. Car. U., Greenville, N.C., 1963-65; instr. San Diego State U., 1968-70; tchr. Palm Beach County Schs., Boca Raton, Fla., 1971-77, Fulton County Schs., Conyers, Ga., 1979-81; spl. edn. tchr. Ga. Reg. Hosp. at Atlanta, Decatur, Ga., 1981-84; vocat. svcs. coord. Ga. Reg. Hosp. at Atlanta, Decatur, 1984—; waster safety instr. Am. Red Cross, Mich., Calif., Fla., Ga., 1961-87; dir. Palm Beach County Spl. Olympics, W. Palm Beach, Fla. 1973-76. Author: articles in profl. jours. 1961—, works listed in E.R.I.C., 1978. Leader Girl Scouts of Am., Fla. and Ga., 1975-85. Named Excellence in Progs. for Mentally Ill, Govs. Coun. of Mental Illness, 1987, Woman of the Week, Dekalb News Sun, Decatur, Ga., 1982. Mem. Nat. Rehabilitation Assn., Am. Assn. of ;U. Women, League of Women Voters, Nat. Orgn. for

Women., NAACP, Am. Civil Liberties Union. Office: Ga Reg Hosp of Atlanta 3073 Panthersville Rd Decatur GA 30037

SMULL, CYNTHIA ANN, administrative assistant; b. Borger, Tex., Jan. 8, 1944; d. Earl Arthur and Della Eddith (Brown) Wilmoth; m. Larry Lynn Smull, Aug. 25, 1963; children: Michael, Melissa, Paul. Cert. secretarial skills, Brown-Mackie Sch. Bus., Salina, Kans., 1963. Cert. vocat. tchr. in office edn., Kans. Sec., agt. Knapp Ins. Agy., Salina, ž, 1963-64; underwriting clk. Alliance Ins. Co., McPherson, Kans., 1964-65; bookkeeper, sec. Kans. Wesleyan U., Salina, 1965-66; income tax practitioner Clyde Beck, CPA, Salina, 1976-78; prin. Personalized Tax Svc., Salina, 1978-89; sec. Salina Pub. Libr., 1987-89, adminstrv. asst. to dir., 1989—; instr. income tax Salina Area Vocat.-Tech. Sch., 1981-88. Mem. NAFE. Nazarene. Home: 1301 E Ellsworth St Salina KS 67401 Office: Salina Pub Libr 301 W Elm St Salina KS 67401

SMUTS, MARY ELIZABETH, environmental scientist; b. Waterbury, Conn., Mar. 15, 1948; d. Thomas P. and Irene (Nest) Smith; m. R. Malcolm Smuts, June 10, 1972; children: Robert M., Felicia A. BA, Albertus Magnus Coll., New Haven, Conn., 1970; PhD, Temple U., 1974; MS, Harvard U., Boston, 1984. Postdoctoral fellow NIDR, NIH, Bethesda, Md., 1974-76; asst. prof. Cath. U. Am., Washington, 1976-78, Wheaton Coll., Norton, Mass., 1978-83; sr. indsl. hygienist R.I. Dept. Pub. Health, Providence, 1985-87; mgr. RTK prog. Mass. Dept. Pub. Health, Boston, 1987-89; environ. toxicologist U.S. EPA, Boston, 1990—. Exec. producer video: Understanding Material Safety Data Sheets; contbr. articles to profl. jours. Mem. Am. Pub. Health Assn., Am. Soc. Zoologists, Am. Conf. Govts. Indsl. Hygienists. Home: 45 S Washington St Norton MA 02766 Office: US EPA ATR 2311 JFK Federal Bldg Boston MA 02766

SMYTH, PAMELA ANN, nurse; b. Hiedelberg, Germany, Aug. 22, 1961; d. Joseph Francis and Loretta Kathryn (Yoder) Bender; m. James Douglas Smyth, Dec. 23, 1988. BSN, Ea. Memonite Coll., 1983. RN, Ariz. Staff nurse Sierra Vista (Ariz.) Community Hosp., 1983-84; staff nurse neonatal ICU Maricopa Med. Ctr., Phoenix, 1984-86, staff nurse, 1986-90; staff nurse ICU, 1986-89; asst. head nurse surg. ICU Maricopa Med. Ctr., Phoenix, 1988-90. Mem. Am. Assn. Critical Care Nurses, NAFE. Methodist. Home: 3090 W 4th Ave Apache Junction AZ 85220 Office: Maricopa Med Ctr 2601 E Roosevelt Phoenix AZ 85008

SMYTHE, MARSHA SUSAN HALLER, nurse practitioner, consultant; b. Joliet, Ill., Nov. 6, 1949; d. Eugene Keith and Margaret Evelyn (Hrebenyak) Haller; m. Bryan Edward Smythe, Nov. 15, 1969; children—Christopher, Jason. A.Arts and Scis. in Nursing, Joliet Jr. Coll., 1973; B.S. in Nursing with honors, Purdue U., 1983; postgrad., Med. U. of S.C., 1986—. R.N., cert. family nurse practitioner, Ill., S.C. Operating room nurse Silver Cross Hosp., Joliet, 1973-79; ob-gyn nurse practitioner Michael Reese Health Plan, Chgo., 1983, Joliet Med. Group, 1984-85; gynecol./pediatric nurse practitioner Kankakeeland Community Action Agy. (Ill.), 1983-84; nursing cons., Joliet, 1982-85, Charleston, 1985—; labor and delivery staff Trident Regional Med. Ctr., Charleston, S.C., 1985-88; family nurse practitioner Navcare, Charleston, S.C., 1988—. Mem. Am. Nurses Assn., Nurses Assn. of Am. Coll. Obstetricians and Gynecologists, Council Primary Care Nurse Practitioners, S.C. Nurses Assn., Trident Nurses Assn. Republican. Roman Catholic. Home: 2000-2E Waverly Place Ln Charleston SC 29418

SMYTHE, SHEILA MARY, government health policy advisor; b. N.Y.C., Nov. 1, 1932; d. Patrick John and Mary Catherine (Gonley) S. Student, Creighton U., 1952; BA, Manhattanville Coll., 1952; MS, Columbia U., N.Y.C., 1956; LHD (hon.), Manhattanville Coll., 1974. From rsch. assoc. to asst. dir. of rsch. and planning Blue Cross Assn., Chgo., 1957-63; exec. assoc. to pres. Empire Blue Cross & Blue Shield, N.Y.C., 1963-72, v.p., 1972-74, sr. v.p., 1974-78, exec. v.p., 1978-82, pres., chief oper. officer, 1982-85; health fin. and mgmt. cons. N.Y.C. and Washington, 1986-87; chief health policy advisor GAO, Washington, 1987—. Trustee Manhattanville Coll., Purchase, N.Y., 1981—; bd. dirs. Cath. Charities-U.S.A., 1989—, Nat. March of Dimes, 1989—; dir. Greater N.Y. March of Dimes, 1985-89. Recipient Elizabeth Cutter Morrow award YWCA, N.Y., 1977, Disting. Alumni award Manhattanville Coll., 1981, Excellence in Leadership award Greater N.Y. March of Dimes, 1989. Mem. Nat. Arts Club N.Y.C. Roman Catholic. Office: GAO 441 G St NW Rm 6856 Washington DC 20548

SNAPP, ELIZABETH, librarian, educator; b. Lubbock, Tex., Mar. 31, 1937; d. William James and Louise (Lanham) Mitchell; BA magna cum laude, North Tex. State U., Denton, 1968, MLS, 1969, MA, 1977; m. Harry Franklin Snapp, June 1, 1956. Asst. to archivist Archive of New Orleans Jazz, Tulane U., 1960-63; catalog librarian Tex. Woman's U., Denton, 1969-71, head acquisitions dept., 1971-74, coordinator readers services, 1974-77, asst. to dean Grad. Sch., 1977-79, instr. library sci., 1977-88, acting Univ. libr., 1979-82, dir. librs., 1982—; chair-elect Tex. Coun. State U. Librs., 1988-90, chmn., 1990—; mem. adv. com. on library formula Coordinating Bd. Tex. Coll. and Univ. System, 1981—; del. OCLC Nat. Users Council, 1985-87, mem. by-laws com., 1985-86, com. on less-than-full-services networks, 1986-87; project dir. Nat. Endowment for Humanities consultancy grant on devel. core curriculum for women's studies, 1981-82; chmn. Blue Ribbon com. 1986 Gov.'s Commn. for Women to select 150 outstanding women in Tex. history; project dir. math./sci. anthology project Tex. Found. Women's Resources. Co-sponsor Irish Lecture Series, Denton, 1968, 70, 73, 78. Sec. Denton County Democratic Caucus, 1970. Recipient Ann. Pioneer award Tex. Women's U., 1986. Mem. ALA (standards com. 1983-85), Southwestern, Tex. (program com. 1978, Dist. VII chmn. 1985-86, archives and oral history com. 1990—) library assns., Tex. Hist. Commn. (judge for Farenbach History prize 1990—), Women's Collecting Group (chmn. ad hoc com. 1984—), AAUW (legis. br. chmn. 1973-74, br. v.p. 1975-76, br. pres. 1979-80, state historian 1986-88), AAUW Ednl. Found. (rsch. and awards panel 1990—), So. Conf. Brit. Studies, AAUP, Tex. Assn. Coll. Tchrs. (pres. Tex. Woman's U. chpt. 1976-77), Woman's Shakespeare Club (pres. 1967-69), Beta Phi Mu (pres. chpt. 1976-78; sec. nat. adv. assembly 1978-79, pres. 1979-80, nat. dir. 1981-83), Alpha Chi, Alpha Lambda Sigma (pres. 1970-71), Pi Delta Phi. Methodist. Club: Soroptimist Internat. (Denton) (pres. 1986-88). Asst. editor Tex. Academe, 1973-76; contbg. author: Women in Special Collections, 1984, Special Collections, 1986; book reviewer Library Resources and Tech. Services, 1973—. Contbr. articles to profl. jours. Home: 1904 N Lake Trail Denton TX 76201 Office: TWU Sta PO Box 24093 Denton TX 76204

SNEARLY, SANDRA JO, accountant; b. East Chicago, Ind., May 13, 1954; d. Eugene John and Josephine Ann (Thomas) Smith; m. Dennis Dale Snearly, Oct. 2, 1976. BS, Ball State U., 1976. CPA, Ind., Ill. Cost reviewer Prudential Ins., Merrillville, Ind., 1976-78; acct. St. Pierre and Krafft, Merrillville, 1978-80; sr. acct. Krafft and Co., Merrillville, 1980-85, ptnr., 1985—. Chmn. panel Lake Area United Way, Griffith, Ind. 1984-86; bd. dirs. Lakes of the Four Seasons Property Owners Assn., 1988—, treas., 1988-89, pres., 1989—. Mem. AICPA, Ind. CPA Soc., Ind. St. Bd. Pub. Accountancy, Duneland Bus. and Profl. Women (founder, pres. 1986—, Woman of Yr. 1989-90), Lakeshore Bus. and Profl. Women (v.p. 1983-85, treas. 1981-83), Merrillville C. of C. (treas. 1988-89, Athena award 1986, 3d v.p. 1988-89, 1st v.p. 1989—). Republican. Roman Catholic. Home: 3381 W Lake Shore Dr LOFS Crown Point IN 46307 Office: Krafft and Co 398 W 80th Place Merrillville IN 46410

SNEDAKER, CATHERINE RAUPAGH (KIT SNEDAKER), editor; b. Fargo, N.D., Apr. 2; d. Paul and Charity (Primmer) Raupagh; B.A., Duke U., 1943; m. William Brooks, 1943; children—Eleanor, Peter William; m. 2d, Weldon Snedaker, Sept. 17, 1950. Pub. relations exec. United Seamen's Service, 1950-57; promotion mgr. sta. WINR-TV and WNBF-TV, Binghamton, N.Y., 1957-60; TV editor, feature writer Binghamton Sun, 1960-68; mem. staff Los Angeles Herald Examiner, 1968—, food editor, 1978—, restaurant critic, 1978-80, food and travel editor, 1980-86; editor The Food Package; columnist Copley News Service; instr. food/travel writing UCLA Extension. Author: The Great Convertibles; contbr. numerous articles on food and travel to nat. mags. and newspapers; guest editor Mademoiselle mag., 1942. Recipient 3 awards Los Angeles Press Club, VISTA award, 1979. Mem. Soc. Am. Travel Writers, Internat. PEN U.S.A. Ctr. West. Democrat. Home: 140 San Vicente Blvd Apt C Santa Monica CA 90402

SNEDAKER, DIANNE, advertising agency executive. Former sr. v.p. Ketchum Advt./San Francisco, pres., 1988—. Office: Ketchum Advt 55 Union St San Francisco CA 94111*

SNEED, EMOGENE MILDRED, nurse; b. Kingsport, Tenn., Nov. 11, 1929; d. O.H. and Ida Theresa (King) Cox; m. John H. Sneed, Jan. 11, 1956 (dec. Sept. 1988); children: Jerry Lee, Rex Ronald, Scott Donald. R.N., Knoxville Gen. Hosp., 1953; student U. Tenn., 1952, East Tenn. State U., 1955, postgrad. Margaret Hague Maternity Hosp., 1953. Staff nurse Holston Vally Hosp. Med. Ctr., Kingsport, Tenn., 1953—. Den mother Kingsport council Cub Scouts Am., 1965-66. Mem. ARC, Tenn. Nursing Assn., Am. Heart Assn., Tenn. Mental Health Assn., Am. Operating Nurses Assn. Baptist. Home: 2041 Sherwood Rd Kingsport TN 37664

SNEED, PAULA ANN, food products executive; b. Everett, Mass., Nov. 10, 1947; d. Thomas Edwin and F. Mary (Turner) S.; m. Lawrence Paul Bass, Sept. 2, 1978; children: Courtney Jameson. BA, Simmons Coll., 1969; MBA, Harvard U., 1977. Dir. plans, program devel. and evaluations Ecumenical Ctr. in Roxbury, Mass., 1971-72; program coord. Boston Sickle Cell Ctr., 1972-75; asst. product mgr. Gen. Food Corp., White Plains, N.Y., 1977-79, assoc. product mgr., 1979-80; product mgr. Gen. Foods Corp., White Plains, N.Y., 1980-82, sr. product mgr., 1982-83, product group mgr., 1983-86, category mgr., 1986-87; v.p. consumer affairs Gen. Foods Corp., White Plains, 1987-90, pres. food svc. div., 1990—. Bd. dirs. Crispus Attucks Scholarship Fund, Ridgewood, N.J., 1982—. Recipient Benevolent Heart award Graham-Windham, 1987, Black Achiever award Harlem YWCA, 1982; named MBA of Yr. Harvard Bus. Sch. Black Alumni Orgn., 1987. Mem. AAUW, Nat. Assn. Negro Bus. and Profl. Women, Coalition of 100 Black Women, Soc. Consumer Affairs Profls. Home: 158 Phelps Rd Ridgewood NJ 07450 Office: Gen Foods USA 250 North St White Plains NY 10625

SNELL, MARIE LETTY, artist; b. Detroit, May 15, 1924; d. Samuel Harris and Sylvia Doris (Cohen) Glucksman; m. John Richard Snell, Apr. 1, 1948 (dec. Oct. 1989); children: Jane Hannah Snell Fonfara, Florence Ann Snell Davis. Student, Wayne State U., 1941-43, 56, 75; B of Design, U. Mich., 1947; postgrad., Soc. Arts and Crafts, 1947-53. art therapist Pontiac Gen. Hosp., 1986; lectr. in field; juror various exhibits, 1985-86. One woman shows include Oak Park (Mich.) Pub. Library, 1980, Clerestory Gallery Pontiac Art Ctr., 1982, Southfield Civic Ctr., 1983, 86, COMERICA Hdqrs., 1983, State Capitol Bldg., 1986, Mich. Tech. U., 1987, Art of Crafts Gallery, Royal Oak, 1988, Unitarian Ch. Birmingham, 1989; group shows include Pontiac Art Ctr., 1981, 82, 89, Marygrove Coll., 1981, Mill Gallery, 1982, Oakland County Galleria, 1983, 87, 89, 90, Paint Creek Ctr. for the Arts, 1983, 87, 88, 89, Port con Toronto, 1982-83, Oak Park Pub. Library, 1983-87, La Galerie du Vitrail, Chartres, France, 1985, Artsource Gallery, 1986, Detroit Artists Market, 1987, 90, Corning (N.Y.) Mus. of Glass, 1987, Watertower Art Assn., Louisville, 1987, Birmingham Bloomfield Art Assn., 1989, Huntington Woods Libr. Gallery, 1989; work exhibited in permanent collections La Galerie du Vitrail, Chartres; designed stained glass windows for Temple Bapt. Ch., Windsor, Ontario, Can., 1988; contbr. articles to art mags. Mem. Oak Park Arts and Cultural Commn., 1982—; bd. dirs. Com. for Mich. Glass Month, 1981-85, Mich. Glass Guild, 1990, 2d Internat. Conf. Environ. Glass, Oklahoma City, 1990; panelist 1st Internat. Conf. Environ. Glass, Oklahoma City, 1989, 90. With USMC, 1944-46. Grantee Ohio Arts Council, Arts Council of Greater Toledo, 1985, Mich. Council for the Arts, 1981-82, 86. Mem. Stained Glass Assn. Am. (assoc., sec. 1980-84, exhibitor various group shows, Best of Show award 1981-83, 1st prize 1983, best use of opalescent glass award 1986), Mich. Glass Guild, Centre Internat. Vittrail, Women's Caucus for Art, Huntington Woods Studio Artists. Democrat. Home: 14201 Hart Oak Park MI 48237

SNELLING, LEE ANN, administrative assistant; b. Frankfort, Ky., July 11, 1963; d. Chester Lee and Elizabeth Ann (Williams) S. Student, Ky. State U. File clerk Ky. Div. of Fuel and Roadway Tax, Frankfort, Ky., 1982—; file room supervisor Ky. Div. of Fuel and Roadway Tax, Frankfort, 1982-83; sec. Ky. Div. of Vehicle Licensing, Frankfort, 1983; asst. mgr. McDonalds, Frankfort; dispatcher Kentucky State Police, Frankfort, 1983-85; pvt. Tan-Fastic Tanning Salon, 1985-86; word processor Ky. Disaster and Emergency Services, Frankfort, 1985-87, sec., 1987-88, adminstr. specialist, 1988-89; adminstrv. asst. Toyota Tsusho, Inc., Georgetown, Ky., 1989—. Exec. bd. Teresa Hatton Found., Frankfort, 1984—. Democrat. Home: 2046 Silver Lake Blvd Frankfort KY 40601 Office: Toyota Tsusho Inc 1001 Cherry Blossom Way Georgetown KY 40324

SNIDER, JUDY K., legal assistant; b. McMinnville, Oreg., June 9, 1945; d. Russell W. and Harriet E. (Deyoe) Jones; m. Gordon R. Domes (div. 1977); children: Robert G., Brian R.; m. Morris C. Snider. Student, Oreg. State U., 1963-64. Cert. profl. legal sec. Legal sec. Martin J. Hoffman, Philomath, Oreg., 1964-67, McCormick & Reynolds, Portland, Oreg., 1968-71, Robert L Abel, Salem, Oreg., 1971-72, Dan Ritter, Salem, 1972-74, McKinney, Churchill et al, Salem, 1974-77, Weatherford, Thompson et al, Albany, Oreg., 1977; legal sec./legal asst. Harland, Ritter et al, Salem, 1977—. Adult ldr. Amity 4-H Club, 1973-77; scout ldr. Boy Scouts Am., 1972; dir., officer Booster Club of Mill City, Oreg., 1982-88. Named Legal Sec. of the Yr., Marion Polk Legal Sec. Assn., 1976, 85, Oreg. Assn. Legal Secs., 1985. Mem. Marion-Polk Legal Secs. Assn. (pres. 1976-77, gov. 1977-78, treas. 1983-84), Oreg. Assn. Legal Secs. (pres. 1987-89, Nat. Assn. Legal Secs. (mem. continuing edn. council 1985-87). Democrat. Home: 204 3d Ct Sublimity OR 97385 Office: Harland Ritter et al 693 Chemeketa St NE Salem OR 97301

SNIDER, LOIS A. PHILLIPS, educator; b. Keokuk, Iowa, July 9, 1949; d. Forrest W. and Dorothy J. (Sisson) Phillips; m. Duane E. Snider, Apr. 3, 1970; children: David Duane, Leigh Anne. AA, Hannibal-LaGrange Coll., 1969; BA, Okla. Baptist U., Shawnee, 1971; MA, Northeast Mo. State U., Kirksville, 1985. Bus. tchr. Ind. (Mo.) Pub. Schs., 1971-77; bus. instr. Ind. (Mo.) Adult Edn., 1973-82; instr. Hannibal-LaGrange (Mo.) Coll., 1982-85, asst. prof. of bus., 1985—; mem., past chairperson Bus. Edn. Adv. Com. of the Hannibal Area Vocat. Tech. Sch., 1982-88. Mem. Solid Rock Bapt. Ch., Hannibal, 1987—. Mem. DAR, Mo. Assn. Acctg. Educators, Nat. Bus. Ednl. Assn. Republican. Home: 4935 College Ave Hannibal MO 63401 Office: Hannibal-LaGrange Coll 2800 Palmyra Rd Hannibal MO 63401

SNIDER, MARIE ANNA, communication executive; b. Croghan, N.Y., Aug. 9, 1927; d. Nicholas and Dorothy (Moser) Gingerich; m. Howard Mervin, Nov. 27, 1954; children: Vada Marie, Conrad Howard. BS, Goshen Coll., 1949; M in Religious Edn., Mennonite Bibl. Sem., 1957; MS, Kans. State U., 1980. High sch. tchr. Rockway Collegiate, Kitchener, Ont., Can., 1949-53; free-lance writer, 1953-54; pub. rels. Goshen Coll., Ind., 1955-57; free-lance writer, homemaker, 1957-67; info. editor Prairie View, Inc., Newton, Kans., 1967-76; dir., pub. info. & edn. Prairie View, Inc., Newton, 1976-85, dir. communications, 1985—; bd. dirs. Health Systems Agy. of S.E. Kans., 1981-86, v.p., 1986-87; workshop presenter Nat. Coun. of Community Mental Health Ctrs., Atlanta, 1980, N.Y., 1982, 89, Miami, 1987. Editor: Media and Terrorism--The Psychological Impact, 1976. pres. City Council, N Newton, 1977-79, pres. 1980. Recipient 1st Pl. MacEachern award Assn. of Hosp. Pub. Rels., 1981, 1st Pl. Media award Nat. Coun. Community Mental Health Ctrs., 1977, 84, runner-up Pub. Rels. award Nat. Assn. Pvt. Psychiat. Hosps., 1980. Mem. Pub. Rels. Soc. Am. Democrat. Home: Box 332 North Newton KS 67117 Office: Prairie View Inc 1901 E 1st St Box 467 Newton KS 67114

SNIPE, VALERIE BROOKS, social worker; b. Earle, Ark., Sept. 20, 1958; d. Clarence Vernice and Leona (Brown) Brooks; m. Maurice Ronea Snipe, Apr. 30, 1983; children: Brittany, Jennifer. BA, Ark. State U., 1982. Lic. social worker, S.C. Substitute tchr. Earle Elem. Sch., 1982-83; social worker Clark Sickle Cell Found., Columbia, S.C., 1987-90; edn. specialist and pub. info. officer East Tex. Coun. Alcoholism and Drug Abuse, Longview, 1990—; cons. Peer Helper Program, Columbia, 1990—; v.p. Interagy. Resource Com., 1989-90. Editor: Sickle Cell News, (newsletter) The Update. Sec. Challedon Precinct, Columbia, 1989-90; mem. support group S.C. Dept. Health and Environ. Control, 1989; bd. dirs. Friendship Ctr., Columbia, 1989-90. Mem. NAFE, NAACP, S.C. Assn. Vol. Adminstrn. (bd. dirs. 1990), S.C. Pub. Health Assn. (issues and answers com.). Democrat. Methodist. Home: 2600 Northbrook Dr Longview TX 75605 Office: East Tex Coun Alcoholism and Drug Abuse 1101 E Birdsong St Longview TX 75602

SNODGRASS, MARY ELLEN, freelance writer and editor; b. Wilmington, N.C., Feb. 29, 1944; d. William Russell and Lucy Ella (Hester) Robinson; m. Hugh Edwin Snodgrass, Nov. 16, 1984; 1 foster child, Deborah Eckard. AB, U. N.C., Greensboro, 1966; MA, Appalachian State U., 1968; gifted cert., Lenoir-Rhyne Coll., 1980. Tchr. Hickory (N.C.) High Sch., 1966-85; freelance writer and editor Hickory, 1985—. Writer/editor Cliffs Teaching Portfolios, 1985—, Great American English Handbook, 1987; writer Greek and Roman classics, Contests for Students, 1990. Named Star Tchr., Hickory C. of C., 1968, 69; AFL-CIO merit scholar, 1962, Leonard Hurley scholar, 1965. Mem. ACLU, Nat. Coun. Tchrs. English, Internat. Reading Assn., Phi Beta Kappa. Presbyterian. Home: 90 Ashley Ct Gold Creek Hickory NC 28601

SNODGRASS, SHERI L., corporate planning coordinator; b. Marshalltown, Iowa, Aug. 8, 1956; d. Marvin Lee and Betty Lou (Coffin) Katzer; m. William Kraig Snodgrass, Nov. 23, 1978. BS, BA, Drake U., 1985. Cert. systems profl.; assoc. in automation mgmt., in rsch. and planning, in mgmt. Bus. analyst, data entry supr. Am. InterInsur Exchange, Des Moines, 1980-84; bus. analyst Grinnell (Iowa) Mut. Reins. Co., 1986-87, work measurement specialist, 1987-89, planning coord., 1989—. Adult leader Boy Scouts Am., 1978—, advancement chmn., 1979-80. Mem. NAFE, Productivity Assn. (steering com. 1987—), Nat. Assn. Ins. Women, Mid-Iowa Ins. Women (pres. 1989-1990, long-range planning chmn. 1990—), Conf. Casualty Ins. Cos. (speaker methods/procedures div.), Am. Mgmt. Assn., Assn. Quality and Productivity, Iowa Geneological Soc. Mem. Worldwide Ch. of God. Office: Grinnell Mut Reins Co Interstate 80 at Hwy 146 Grinnell IA 50112

SNOW, CINDY (CYNTHIA DAWN SNOW), manufacturing executive; b. Carlsbad, N.M, Apr. 24, 1957; d. Amos Austen Snow; m. Steven W. Hallock, Jan. 19, 1984. Student, Pitzer Coll., Claremont, Calif., 1975, U. Calif., Berkeley, 1977, U. Calif., Santa Cruz, 1980. Export affairs advisor Taifung Flexible Tubing, Taipei, Rep. of China, 1980-82; v.p. Airmax Inc., Gilmer, Tex., 1983-87, pres., 1989—; owner, mgr. Applecart Enterprises, Inc., Mineola, 1989—. Organizer YWCA Big Sisters of Am., Monrovia, Calif., 1977; counselor YMCA, Los Angeles, 1977. Mem. Nat. Assn. Female Execs, Air conditioning and Refrigeration Inst., Air conditioning and Refrigeration Wholesalers Assn. Home: PO Box 495 Gilmer TX 75644 Office: Airmax Inc PO Box 159 400 Dean St Gilmer TX 75644

SNOW, EDWINA FEIGENSPAN (MRS. MACVICKER SNOW), editor, publisher; b. N.Y.C., July 14, 1927; d. Edwin Christian and Flora Marie (Russ) Feigenspan; student Barnard Coll., 1945-46, Columbia U., 1946, Juilliard Sch. Music, 1943; m. David Dodge Osborn, June 1946 (div. 1951); children: Dana Osborn de Tessan, Christopher Fairfield Osborn; m. MacVicker Snow, Dec. 19, 1964; children: Marina, Michael Snow. Model, John Robert Powers, N.Y.C., 1947-48, pub. relations dir. Powers cosmetics, 1948-50; model Ford Agy., N.Y.C., 1950-53, Jacques Heim, Paris, France, 1957; bilingual sec. Cofinindus, Brufina, Electrobel Belgian holding cos., 1960; co-editor, pub. Locust Valley (N.Y.) Leader, 1961-67; editor, pub. Oyster Bay-Syosset and Glen Cove-Sea Cliff Guardians, L.I., N.Y., 1967—; partner Locust Valley Pub. Co., Inc., 1965—; pres. Oyster Bay Pub. Co., Inc. Bd. dirs. Nassau chpt. ARC; benefit dir. Boys Town Italy, 1952-54. Recipient citation U.S. Dept. Def., 1952. Mem. ASCAP, Am. Horse Protection Assn. Kiwanian (hon.). Home: 103 Morris St PO Box 368 Oxford MD 21654 Office: 102 Audrey Ave Oyster Bay NY 11771

SNOW, ELIZABETH JEAN, university secretary; b. Northampton, Mass., Mar. 1, 1943; d. Dwight Clary and Jean Kennedy (Johnston) S. Student, Northampton Comml. Coll., 1958, 61-62, U. Mass., Tufts Sch. Mus. Fine Arts. Typist, sec., editor, proofreader, cons. various agys. including Kelly Svcs. Inc., Olsten Svcs. Inc., others, Boston, 1965-88; proctor Harvard U., Cambridge, Mass., 1986—. Author: (poetry) Emphasis on Best Care for a Patient, To Be or Are, 1990. Winner fourth place Boston Typing Contest at 84 words per minute, 1985. Home: PO Box No 21 Watertown MA 02272-0021 Office: Harvard Univ Massachusetts Ave Cambridge MA 02169

SNOW, JUDITH ROHLETTER, jewelry store executive, gemologist, jeweler; b. Miami, Fla., May 6, 1948; d. Guy Eugene and Mary Evelyn (York) Rohletter; student Miami-Dade Community Coll., 1966-67; cert. in diamond evaluation Gemological Inst. Am., 1979, cert. in colored stones and gem indentification, 1980; grad. Berlitz Sch. Langs., Coral Gables, Fla., 1987; m. Edward Hugh Snow, May 11, 1974; children: Judith Diane, Kelly Michelle, Mary Alice. Office mgr. Ross Printing Corp., Miami, 1965-74; corp. exec., gemologist Snow's Jewelers, Inc., Coral Gables, 1974—, also dir. Active Scott Kelly for Gov. of Fla. Campaign, 1965. Mem. Retail Jewelers Am., Jewelers Security Alliance, Coral Gables C. of C., Miracle Mile Mchts. Assn., Exec. Women Internat., Coral Bay Property Owner's Assn., Ferrari Club Am., Ferrari Owners Club, Zonta, Mus. Patrons. Democrat. Clubs: Ocean Reef, Coral Bay Yacht, Coral Reef Yacht, Fla. Philharm. Prelude, Noteworthy, Progress, Bimini (Bahamas) Big Game, Beach Colony. Office: 219 Miracle Mile Coral Gables FL 33134

SNOW, SARAH TURNBULL, telecommunications company executive; b. Winter Haven, Fla., June 2, 1952; d. James Phineas and Margaret Ann (Lawhon) Turnbull; m. T. Andrew Hunter, June 15, 1974 (div. Aug. 1980); children: Thomas, Catharine; m. Claude Henry Snow, Sept. 26, 1981. BA, Wesleyan Coll., Macon, Ga., 1974; cert. in teaching, U. N.C., Charlotte, 1975; cert. in info. systems, MIT, 1983. Communication cons. So. Bell Tel. Co., Atlanta, 1976-79; communications satellite relay systems designer So. Bell Tel. Co., Charlotte, 1979-83; staff mgr. policy adminstrn. AT&T Info. Systems, Atlanta, 1983, sr. tech. cons., 1983-85; div. mgr. tech. support MCI Telecommunications, Atlanta, 1985-89, exec. nat. accounts mktg., div. mgr., 1989—; chmn. program com. Women Info. Processing, Atlanta, 1983-85. Mem. pres.'s coun. SciTreck Mus., Atlanta. Mem. Women's C. of C., Atlanta, Henrietta Egleston Aux. (chmn. advanced sales com. 1984—), NAFE. Democrat. Episcopalian. Club: U. N.C. Chancellor's (Chapel Hill). Home: PO Box 88351 Atlanta GA 30356 Office: MCI Telecommunications 400 Perimeter Ctr Terr Atlanta GA 30346

SNOWDEN, BERNICE RIVES, former construction company executive; b. Houston, Mar. 21, 1923; d. Charles Samuel and Annie Pearl (Rorex) Rives; grad. Smalley Comml. Coll., 1941; student U. Houston, 1965; m. Walter G. Snowden; 1 dau., Bernice Ann Ogden. With Houston Pipe Line Co., 1944-45; clk.-typist Charles G. Heyne & Co., Inc., Houston, 1951-53, payroll asst., 1953-56, sec. to pres., also office mgr., 1956-62, sec. to pres., also controller, 1962-70, sec.-treas., 1970-77, chief fin. officer, also dir. Mem. Women in Constrn., Nat. Assn. Women in Constrn. (past pres.), San Leon C. of C. Methodist. Club: Lord and Ladies Dance. Home: 6611 Kury Ln Houston TX 77008

SNOWDEN, RUTH O'DELL GILLESPIE, artist; b. Gary, W.Va., Apr. 16, 1926; d. Haynes Thornton and Blanche Beaula (Boling) Gillespie; m. Eugene Louis Snowden, Dec. 21, 1946; children: Wanda Snowden Ballard, Eugene III, Ronald, Marian Snowden Warren, Jeffry. RN, Natharith Coll., 1946; postgrad., Transylvania U., 1983-84, U. Ky., 1985-89. Painter, publicity chmn. Artists's Attic Inc., Lexington, Ky., 1988-89. Exhibited in group shows at U. Ky. Art Mus., Lexington, 1988, 5th Internat. Juried Exhibition Pastels, Nyack, N.Y., 1988, Small Paintings Nat., Ky. Highlands Mus., Ashland, 1988, The Appalachian Cen., U. Ky., 1988, Ft. Wayne (Ind.) Mus. Art, 1986, John Howard Sanden Nat. Artists Seminar, Washington, Nat. Artists' Seminar, Chgo., Huntington (W.Va.) Galleries, Nat. Nursing Art Exhibit, Meth. Med. Cen., Peoria, Ill.; represented in the Director of American Portrait Artists, Am. Portrait Soc., Huntington Harbour, Calif. Recipient various watercolor and oil painting awards. Mem. Oil Pastel Assn., Nyack, N.Y., Winchester Art Guild, Lexington Art League, Ky. Watercolor Assn. (Bluegrass regional dir. 1988, 89). Home: 2800 Old Boonesboro Rd Winchester KY 40391 Office: Artists Attic Inc Victorian Square 401 West Main St Lexington KY 40507

SNOWE, OLYMPIA J., congresswoman; b. Augusta, Maine, Feb. 21, 1947; d. George John and Georgia G. Bouchles; m. John McKeenan. BA, U.

Maine, 1969; LLD (hon.), U. Maine, Machias, 1982, Husson Coll., 1981, Bowdoin Coll., 1985. Businesswoman; mem. Maine Ho. of Reps., 1973-76, Maine Senate, 1976-78; mem. 96th-102nd Congresses from 2d Maine Dist., 1979—, mem. fgn. affairs com., joint econ. com., select com. on aging; co-chair Congl. Caucus for Women's Issues; dep. Republican whip; corporator Mechanics Savs. Bank. Republican. Greek Orthodox. Club: Philoptochos Soc. Office: US Ho of Reps 2464 Rayburn House Office Bldg Washington DC 20515*

SNOW-WEBB, MARY ALICEN, hospital director; b. Jacksonville, Fla., July 7, 1953; d. A.D. and Ruth (Swiney) Snow; m. Michael Lynn Webb, Jan. 3, 1981; 1 child, Caitlin Snow. BS in Therapeutic Recreation, U. Ga., 1975, postgrad.; postgrad., Ga. Coll., 4 years. Dir. activity therapy College St. Hosp., Macon, Ga., 1975-78, Heritage Park Hosp., Macon, 1979-81, Coliseum Psychiat. Hosp., Macon, 1981—; activity therapy cons. Town and County Nursing Home, Macon, 1982-85, Bloomfield Nursing Home, Macon, 1988-89; instr. therapeutic recreation Ga. Coll., Milledgeville, 1986-87; gubernatorially apptd. master therapeutic recreation specialist rep. Ga. Bd. Recreation Examiners, Atlanta, 1987—. Mem. Nat. Assn. Activity Profls. (cert. activity dir.), Nat. Recreation Pks. Assn., Ga. Recreation Pks. Assn. Republican. Episcopalian. Home: 5071 Bowman Rd Macon GA 31210 Office: Coliseum Psychiat Hosp 340 Hospital Dr Macon GA 31208

SNYDER, ALLEGRA FULLER, dance educator; b. Chgo., Aug. 28, 1927; d. R. Buckminster and Anne (Hewlett) Fuller; m. Robert Snyder, June 30, 1951 (div. Apr. 1975, remarried Sept. 1980); children: Alexandra, Jaime. BA in Dance, Bennington Coll., 1951; MA in Dance, UCLA, 1967. Asst. to curator, dance archives Mus. Modern Art, N.Y.C., 1945-47; dancer Ballet Soc. of N.Y.C. Ballet Co., 1945-47; mem. office and prodn. staff Internat. Film Found., N.Y.C., 1950-52; editor, dance films Film News mag., N.Y.C., 1966-72; lectr. dance and film adv., dept. dance UCLA, 1967-73, chmn. dept. dance, 1974-80, 90—, acting chair, spring 1985, chair of faculty Sch. of the Arts, 1989—, prof. dance and dance ethnology, 1973—; vis. lectr. Calif. Inst. of Arts, Valencia, 1972; co-dir. dance and TV workshop Am. Dance Fest., Conn. Coll., New London, 1973; dir. NEH summer seminar for coll. tchrs. Asian Performing Arts, 1978, 81; coord. Ethnic Arts Intercoll. Interdisciplinary program, 1974-83, acting chmn., 1986; vis. prof. performance studies NYU, 1982-83; hon. vis. prof. U. Surrey, Guildford, Eng., 1983-84, chair faculty Sch. of Arts, 1989—; bd. dirs. Buckminster Fuller Inst.; cons. Thyodia Found., Salt Lake City, 1973-74; mem. dance adv. panel Nat. Endowment Arts, 1968-72, Calif. Arts Commn., 1974; mem. adv. screening com. Council Internat. Exchange of Scholars, 1979-82; mem. various panels NEH, 1979-85; mem. adv. bd. Los Angeles Dance Alliance, 1978-84; cons. dance film series Am. Film Inst, 1974-75. Dir. film Baroque Dance 1625-1725, in 1977; co-dir. film Gods of Bali, 1952; dir. and wrote film Bayanihan, 1962 (named Best Folkloric Documentary at Bilboa Film Festival, winner Golden Eagle award); asst. dir. and asst. editor film The Bennington Story, 1952; created films Gestures of Sand, 1968, Reflections on Choreography, 1973, When the Fire Dances Between Two Poles, 1982; created film, video loop and text Celebration: A World of Art and Ritual, 1982-83; supr. post-prodn. film Erick Hawkins, 1964, in 1973. Also contbr. articles to profl. jours. and mags. Adv. com. Pacific Asia Mus., 1980-84, Festival of the Mask, Craft and Folk Art Mus., 1979-84; adv. panel Los Angeles Dance Currents II, Mus. Ctr. Dance Assn., 1974-75; bd. dirs. Council Grove Sch. III, Compton, Calif., 1976-81; apptd. mem. Adv. Dance Com., Pasadena (Calif.) Art Mus., 1970-71, Los Angeles Festival of Performing Arts com., Studio Watts, 1970; mem. Technology and Cultural Transformation com., UNESCO, 1977. Fulbright research fellow, 1983-84; grantee Nat. Endowment Arts, 1981, Nat. Endowment Humanities, 1977, 79, 81, UCLA, 1968, 77, 80, 82, 85. Mem. Am. Dance Therapy Assn., Congress on Research in Dance (bd. dirs. 1970-76, chairperson 1975-77, nat. conf. chair 1972), Council Dance Administrs., Am. Dance Guild (chairperson com. awards, 1972), Soc. for Ethnomusicology, Am. Anthrop. Assn., Am. Folklore Soc., Soc. Anthropology of Visual Communication, Soc. Anthropol. Study of Play, Soc. Humanistic Anthropology, Calif. Dance Educators Assn. (conf. chair 1972), Los Angeles Area Dance Alliance (adv. bd. 1978-84, selection com. Dance Kaleidoscope project 1979-81), Fulbright Alumni Assn. Home: 15313 Whitfield Ave Pacific Palisades CA 90272 Office: UCLA Dept Dance 124 Dance Bldg Los Angeles CA 90024

SNYDER, ANN MCNELIS, educator; b. Hazleton, Pa., Sept. 21, 1940; d. Paul Dominic and Mildred Ann (DeCosmo) McNelis; m. Alvin Daniel Snyder III, Aug. 7, 1965; children: Anthony O'Malia, Rory McNelis. BA, Manhattanville Coll., 1962; MS, Marywood Coll., 1967. Cert. tchr., Pa. Tchr. reading Hazleton Area Sch. Dist., 1962-66; elem. tchr. Belmont Sch., Phila., 1970-88, Patterson Sch., Phila., 1988-89, McCall Sch., Phila., 1989—; realtor Century 21 Cochran Real Estate, Springfield, Pa., 1981—; guest lectr. various cruise lines, 1977—. Publicity chair Students for Kennedy and Johnson, Manhattanville Coll., Purchase, N.Y., 1959; alternate del. Dem. Nat. Conv., Miami, Fla., 1972; mem. Lansdowne (Pa.) Dem. Com., 1976—; campaign worker and coordinator Delaware County, Pa., 1976—; v.p. Hazleton chpt. Internat. Fedn. Catholic Alumnae, 1964-65, pres., 1965-66. Named fellow James Finnegan Com., 1960; recipient favorite Tchr. award Sta. WAZL Radio, 1964, Frances Perkins award U.S. Dept. Labor, 1980. Mem. U.S. Assn. Realtors, Pa. State Realtors, Del. County Assn. Realtors, Phila. Fedn. Tchrs. (labor relations rep. 1972-82). Roman Catholic. Club: Villager Jesuit Guild. Home: 277 Wayne Ave Lansdowne PA 19050 Office: McCall Sch 6th Delancey St Philadelphia PA 19106

SNYDER, ARLENE, water and wastewater materials distributor; b. Phila., Dec. 10, 1944; d. Henry and Phyllis (LaRocca) Bishop. Student, Peirce Bus. Coll., Phila. Sales rep. Pa. Water Works Supply, Horsham, pres.; pres., owner Pipeline Specialties, Inc., Horsham; pres. N.J. Water Works Supply, Mays Landing. Mem. NAFE, Am. Water Works Assn., Water and Sewer Distbn. Am., Nat. Utility Contractors Assn., Water Works Operators of Pa. Address: 730 Jarrett Rd Horsham PA 19044

SNYDER, BARBARA IRENE, freelance art director, retail executive; b. Pittsburg, Kans., Dec. 22, 1937; d. Ian and Vera Tomasene (Jones) Pierce; m. Herman Dale Snyder, July 5, 1959 (dec. May 1967). B.F.A., Kansas City Art Inst., 1959. Visual merchandising mgr. Coach House Stores, Kansas City, Mo., 1957-59; designer Hallmark Cards, Kansas City, Mo., 1959-61; advt. mgr. Kaufman's, Colorado Springs, Colo., 1961-65, 66-67, Bain's, Colorado Springs, 1965-66; advt. mgr. Regenstein's, Atlanta, 1967-69, visual merchandising dir., 1974-76; art dir. Davison's, Atlanta, 1970-72; instr. Atlanta Sch. Fashion and Design, 1972; art dir. Case/Hout, Atlanta, 1973-74, Richway Inc., Atlanta, 1976-78, Hahne's, 1978-79, direct mail advt. mgr., Newark, 1979-83; free-lance retail catalogue art dir., South Orange, N.J., 1983-89; pres., prin. Barbara Snyder Advt., 1989—. Designer Bicentennial Exhbn. at Southeastern State Fair, Atlanta, 1979. Democrat. Avocations: fine art; painting. Home and Office: 367 Vose Ave South Orange NJ 07079

SNYDER, CHRISTINE GLORIA, management consultant, information resource specialist; b. Balt., Oct. 10, 1955; d. Rowland Kenneth and Juliana (Trasarti) Hill; m. Larry D. Snyder, Apr. 16, 1988. BA in Fgn. Langs., Coll. of Notre Dame, 1977; MBA in Acctg., Loyola Coll., Balt., 1982. Sect. chief internal audit AT&T Tech. Inc., Balt., 1977-83; sr. mgr. electronic data processing auditing Black & Decker Corp., Balt., 1983-87; sr. mgr. mgmt. cons. services, info. resource Price Waterhouse, Balt., 1987—; speaker conf. Computer Audit, Control and Security, Chgo., 1985, North Jersey Inst. Internal Auditors, Newark, 1986. Mem. Electronic Data Processing Auditors Assn., Inst. Internal Auditors, Mid-Atlantic Top Secret User Group, Info. Systems Security Assn., Profl. Certs. Cert. Info. Systems Auditor, Cert. Systems Profl. Democrat. Roman Catholic. Office: Price Waterhouse 7 St Paul St Suite 1700 Baltimore MD 21202

SNYDER, GEORGIE ANN, elementary educator; b. Lewistown, Pa., Mar. 18, 1945; d. George Henry and Alice Roberta (Rowles) Stewart; m. Robert L. Snyder, Apr. 24, 1966 (div. 1989); children: Robert Jr., Timothy, Steven, Amber, Holly, Heather. BS in Edn., Calif. (Pa.) State U., 1966; postgrad., Pa. State U. Cert. elem. sch. tchr., spl. edn. tchr., Pa. Tchr. Pemberton Twp. Schs., Browns Mills, N.J., 1966-67, Mifflin County Schs., Lewistown, 1967—; stylist Beeline Clothes, Lewistown, 1968-69. Author: Tim's Trip, 1989. Cub scout den mother Boy Scouts Am., Vira, Pa., 1976-79; Brownie leader Girl Scouts Am., Maitland, Pa., 1990—. Mem. NAFE, NEA, Pa. Tchrs. Assn., Assn. Mifflin County Educators, Pa. Wildlife Assn., Am. Automobile Assn., Order Ea. Star. Democrat. Home: Box 120 RD 3 Lewistown PA 17044 Office: Strodes Mills Middle Sch RD 1 McVeytown PA 17051

SNYDER, GINGER LYNNE, communications specialist; b. North Vernon, Ind., Jan. 28, 1966; d. John Willis and Karen Colleen (Boling) Snyder. BA in Journalism, Ind. U., 1988. Feature editor North Vernon Plain Dealer & Sun, 1988-89; communications specialist Ind. Dept. Commerce, Indpls., 1989—. Mem. Nat. Assn. Female Execs. Democrat. Baptist. Home: 740-B Hardin Blvd Indianapolis IN 46241 Office: Ind Dept Commerce One North Capitol Indianapolis IN 46204

SNYDER, HELEN POHLABEL, retired educator, civic worker; b. Springfield, Ohio, Oct. 21, 1916; d. Carl Anthony and Josephine E. (Murray) Pohlabel; m. Henry R. Snyder, Apr. 9, 1950 (div. 1966); 1 child, Ann Elizabeth. BS in Edn., Wittenberg U., 1950. Elem. tchr. Springfield City Schs., 1934-75; ret., 1975. Author: (play) Never a Cubicle, 1982, (humor books) Criminy! It's the Preacher, 1977, Why Be Without A Gripe, 1978, A Shadow Slithering In, 1980, Shall We Take Down the Steeple, 1981, The Five Dollar Convention, 1982. Vol. Mercy Hosp., Springfield; former choir dir. Good Shepherd Luth. Ch.; mem. Oesterlen Repertory Theater Group; tchr. creative dramatics and theatrical make-up, dir. plays Springfield Jr. Civic Theatre; former mem. state bd. dirs. Luth. Ch. Women. Mem. Wittenberg Women's Guild (past sec., pres.).

SNYDER, JANE PETERS, public relations executive; b. Manassas, Va., July 23, 1925; d. James Walker and Alma Dorothy (Cross) Peters; student George Washington U., 1943-45, Columbia U. Sch. Public Health, 1962; div.; children—Susan Leland, James Peters. Reporter, Montgomery County (Md.) Sentinel, 1952-54, Chatham (N.J.) Courier, 1956-59, Morris County (N.J.) Daily Record, 1959-61; pub. relations asst. East Orange (N.J.) Gen. Hosp., 1962-64, United Hosp., Newark, 1964-65; dir. community relations Georgetown U. Hosp., Washington, 1966-68; dir. public relations Hosp. Council and Met. Regional Med. Program, Washington, 1968-70, Washington Hosp. Ctr., Washington, 1970-82; v.p. pub. relations The Pathfinder Corp., Washington, 1982-88 ; v.p. pub. relations and edn. Delaware Valley Hosp. Council, Phila., 1984—; appointed to adv. bd. Nat. Insts. of Health's Nat. Kidney and Urological Diseases, 1987—; lectr. George Washington U. Sch. Health Care Adminstrn., 1973, 78, 79, 80, 82. Recipient Excellence award Assn. Am. Med. Colls., 1981. Mem. Am. Soc. Hosp. Public Relations (dir. 1973-75), Acad. Hosp. Public Relations (treas. 1973, dir. 1973-78, MacEachern awards 1963, 72-81). Office: 5 Reaney Ct Philadelphia PA 19103

SNYDER, JANET RUTH, violinist, violist, music educator; b. Berkeley, Calif., Nov. 29, 1932; d. Harry Birge and Marion Virginia (Biggerstaff) O'Brien; m. John Valentine Snyder, Nov. 28, 1952; children—Carol Jeanne, Jeffrey William, Michael William. A.A. in Bus., Armstrong Coll., 1951. Exec. sec. Kaiser Steel Corp., Oakland, Calif., 1951-57; pvt. violin tchr., Idaho Falls, Idaho, 1955—; affiliate violin and viola instr. Idaho State U., Pocatello, Idaho, 1987—; tchr. strings Dist. 91, Idaho Falls, 1980-82; prin. violist Idaho Falls Symphony, 1980—; concert mistress Idaho State Civic Symphony, Pocatello, 1981—; concert mistress Idaho Falls Opera Assn., 1980—; violist Teton Music Festival Seminar, Jackson, Wyo., 1982. Mem. Idaho Music Educators Assn., Pocatello Music Club, Idaho Falls Music Club. Republican. Presbyterian. Home: 1675 Shasta St Idaho Falls ID 83402

SNYDER, JEAN MACLEAN, lawyer; b. Chgo., Jan. 26, 1942; d. Norman Fitzroy and Jessie (Burns) Maclean; m. Joel Martin Snyder, Sept. 4, 1964; children: Jacob Samuel, Noah Scot. BA, U. Chgo., 1963, JD, 1979. Bar: Ill. 1979, U.S. Dist. Ct. (no. dist.) Ill. 1979, U.S. Ct. Appeals (7th cir.) 1981. Ptnr. D'Ancona & Pflaum, Chgo., 1979—. Contbr. articles to profl. publs. Mem. ABA (mem. coun. litigation sect., editor-in-chief Litigation mag. 1987-88), Trial Bar Assn. of No. Dist. Ill. Office: D;Ancona & Pflaum 30 N LaSalle Ste 2900 Chicago IL 60602

SNYDER, JOAN, painter; b. Highland Park, N.J., Apr. 16, 1940; d. Leon D. and Edythe A. (Cohen) S.; 1 child, Molly Fink. A.B. in Sociology, Douglass Coll., 1962; M.F.A., Rutgers U., 1966. mem. faculty SUNY, Stony Brook, 1967-69, Yale U., 1974, U. Calif., Irvine, 1975, San Francisco Art Inst., 1976, Princeton U., 1975-77. One-women exhbns. include, Paley and Lowe, New Brunswick, N.J., 1971, 73, Michael Walls Gallery, San Francisco, 1971, Parker 470, Boston, 1972, Los Angeles Inst. Contempory Art, 1976, Portland (Oreg.) Center Visual Arts, 1976, Carl Solway Gallery, N.Y.C., 1976, Neuberger Mus., Purchase, N.Y., 1978, Hamilton Gallery Contemporary Art, 1978, 79, 82, 83, Nielson Gallery, Boston, 1983, 86, Hirshl & Adler Modern Art Mus., N.Y.C., 1985-87, 88, Jim Rose Gallery, Chgo., 1988; travelling one-woman show, San Francisco Art Inst., Grand Rapids Art Mus., Renaissance Soc., U. Chgo., Anderson Gallery, Va. Commonwealth U., Richmond, 1979-80, group exhbns. include, Whitney Ann., 1972, Whitney Bienniel, 1974, 80, Corcoran Bienniel, 1975, 87, Mus. Modern Art, N.Y.C. Grantee Nat. Endowment Art, 1974; Guggenheim fellow, 1981-82. Address: 105 Mulberry St New York NY 10013

SNYDER, JOYCE ELAINE, school principal; b. Wichita, Kans., Sept. 6, 1933; d. Milton James and Edna M.C. (Wiechman) Piotrowski; m. Fred A. Snyder, Jan. 13, 1951; children: Allen, Gwendolyn. BS, Ind. State U., 1969, MS, 1970, EdS, 1975, PhD, 1979. Cert, elem. tchr., adminstr., supr. Prin. Cruft Sch., Terre Haute, Ind., 1970-81, Warren Sch., Washington Center, Ind., 1981-87, Deming Sch., Terre Haute, 1987ú. Contbr. articles to profl. jours. Mem. Nat. Assn. Elem. Sch. Prins., Ind. Assn. Elem. and Middle Sch. Prins. (past treas.), Assn. for Supervision and Curriculum Devel., Ind. Assn. for Supervision and Curriculum Devel., Vigo County Adminstrs. Assn., Dist. 6 Prins. Assn., Wabash Valley Internat. Reading Assn., Ind. Sch. Women's Club, Delta Kappa Gamma Soc. Internat. Home: RR 21 Box 451 Terre Haute IN 47802

SNYDER, JULIA ANN, international trade and coffee company executive; b. Springfield, Mo., May 17, 1950; d. Arthur Jennings and Catheryn Laverna (Gallion) Swain; m. Orville Edward Kelley, Dec. 29, 1968 (div. 1972); 1 child, Adam Wayne; m. Ronald Warren Synder, May 29, 1982. Cert. Graff Vocat. Tech. Ctr., 1974. Sales sec. Paul Mueller Co., Springfield, 1971-73; surg. technician Cox Med. Ctr., Springfield, 1974-76; corp. sec., dir. OR&D, Inc., Springfield, 1979—; v.p., dir. Hey Mon Coffee Ltd., Everton, Mo., 1984—. Active Nat. Republican Com., 1980, Rep. Presdl. Task Force, 1981. Recipient Medal of Merit, Rep. Presdl. Task Force, 1982; named One of Outstanding Young Women of Am., 1984. Mem. Nat. Assn. Female Execs., Am. Notary Assn., Am. Film Inst. Mem. Assembly of God Ch. Avocations: latch hooking, stitchery, collecting depression era glassware, writing poetry, walking. Office: Hey Mon Coffee 294A Coffee Ln Everton MO 65646

SNYDER, MARIA LYNNE, software consultant; b. Orange, Calif., Mar. 21, 1962; d. Dante Anthony and Norma Jean (Pyle) Massarotti; m. David Louis Snyder, Sept. 15, 1984. Student, Augsburg Coll., Mpls., 1990. Lic. computer ops. and programming. Office svc. clk. Unisys, Eagan, Minn., 1982; records info. specialist, office svc. lead Unisys, Eagan, 1983, program terminal aide, 1984, programmer aide specialist, 1984-85, info. systems specialist, 1985-87, systems coord./programmer, 1987-89; software cons. Shared Resource Mgmt. of Minn., Inc., St. Louis Park, Minn., 1989—. Vol. United Way, Eagan, 1987-88, Adopt-A-Family Holiday Program, Eagan, 1987-88. Roman Catholic. Home: 6901 W 84th St #114 Bloomington MN 55438 Office: Shared Resource Mgmt Minn 5100 Gamble Dr Ste 125 Saint Louis Park MN 55416

SNYDER, ROBIN ESTHER, real estate broker; b. Balt., June 18, 1947; d. Robert Hutton and Kathryn Louise (Moesta) Siver; m. William A. Snyder Jr., june 29, 1968. BA cum laude, Western Md. Coll., 1969; MLA, Johns Hopkins U., 1981. Cert. residential specialist. Asst. br. mgr. Md. Nat. Bank, Balt., 1970-71; community vol. Balt. Symphony Orch., The United WAy, 1971-75; with pub. rels. Johns Hopkins U. and Loyola Coll., Balt., 1975-81; regional distbr. Bergwall Prodns., Garden City, N.Y., 1978-81; pres. Snyder Assocs., Balt., 1983-84; assoc. broker Chase Fitzgerald & Co., Balt., 1984—. Vice chmn. sustaining fund Balt. Symphony Orch., 1973-75; vice chmn. residential fund United Way of Central Md., Balt., 1978-79; conference coordinator Coll. Notre Dame, Balt, 1975-76. Recipient award AAUW, 1977, 83. Mem. Womens Coun. Realtors (program com. 1985-87), Nat. Assn. Realtors, Md. Assn. Realtors, Cert. Residential Specialists, Realtors Nat. Mktg. Inst., Greater Balt. Bd. Realtors (dir. 1987-89, strategic planning com. 1987-89). Democrat. Home: 1 Smeton Pl Apt 700 Towson MD 21204

SNYDER, SUSAN BROOKE, English literature educator; b. Yonkers, N.Y., July 12, 1934; d. John Warren and Virginia Grace (Hartung) S. B.A., Hunter Coll., CUNY, 1955; M.A., Columbia U., 1958, Ph.D., 1963. Lectr. Queens Coll., CUNY, N.Y.C., 1961-63; instr. Swarthmore Coll., Pa., 1963-66, asst. prof. English lit., 1966-70, assoc. prof., 1970-75, prof., 1975—, Eugene M. Lang research prof., 1982-86. Author: The Comic Matrix of Shakespeare's Tragedies, 1979; editor: Divine Weeks and Works of DuBartas, 1979, Othello: Critical Essays, 1988; editorial bd.: Shakespeare Quar., 1972—. Folger Library sr. fellow, 1972-73; Nat. Endowment for Humanities fellow, 1967-68; Guggenheim Found. fellow, 1980-81; Huntington Library summer grantee, 1966, 71; Folger Library grantee, 1969; Nat. Endowment for Humanities grantee, 1970; Nat. Endowment for Humanities summer grantee, 1976. Mem. Renaissance Soc. Am. (council 1979-81), Shakespeare Assn. Am. (trustee 1980-83), MLA, Spenser Soc. Office: Swarthmore Coll Dept English Swarthmore PA 19081

SNYDER, WANDA LORRAINE WEBBER, travel service executive; b. Detroit, Dec. 3, 1944; d. Wilbur Nathaniel and Marjorie Ellen (Schacht) Webber; m. Ervin David Snyder, June 7, 1965; children: Rani Elise, David Nathaniel, Sarah Joy. BA, Wheaton (Ill.) Coll., 1965. Cert. travel counselor. Tchr. U.S. Army dependent and GED schs., Gelnhausen, Budingen, Fed. Republic Germany, 1965-66; dir. tour ops. Wheaton Travel Inc., 1966-70, dir. ops., 1970-75; pres. World Travel Svc., Brunswick, Maine, 1975-89; bd. dirs. Coastal Bank, Portland, Maine, Regional Meml. Hosp., Brunswick. Bd. dirs. Brunswick C. of C., 1983-86; bd. dirs. Maine State Music Theatre, Brunswick, 1977—, pres., 1983-85; deacon, tchr. First Parish Ch., Brunswick, 1979—; vol. Tedford Homeless Shelter, Brunswick, 1989—. Mem. Town & Coll. Club. Home: 1 Colonial Dr Brunswick ME 04011

SNYDERMAN, BARBARA BLOCH, psychologist, educational consultant; b. Pitts., July 29, 1932; d. Louis J. and Selma (Stern) Bloch; m. Ruben Snyderman, Oct. 6, 1957; 1 child, Lynn Synderman Irwin. Student, Brown U., 1950-52; BS, U. Pitts., 1954, MS, 1956, PhD, 1965. Lic. psychologist, Pa. Clin. psychologist Children's Hosp. of Pitts., 1965-66, Pitts. Child Guidance Ctr., 1966-79; clin. asst. prof. child psychiat. U. Pitts., 1970-90; cons. in field. Co-author: The Motivation of Work, 1960; contbr. articles to numerous profl. jours. Trustee Winchester Thurston Sch., Pitts., 1971-77; mem. Gov.'s adv. com. mental health/mental retardation State of Pa., 1975-81; bd. dirs. Craig House, Pitts., 1990—. Mem. Am. Psychol. Assn., Ind. Ednl. Cons. Assn., Pa. Psychol. Assn., Greater Pitts. Psychol. Assn. Democrat. Jewish. Home: 5615 Aylesboro Ave Pittsburgh PA 15217 Office: 401 Shady Ave Ste C107 Pittsburgh PA 15206

SNYDERMAN, SELMA ELEANOR, pediatrician, educator; b. Phila., July 22, 1916; d. Harry Samuel and Rose (Koss) S.; m. Joseph Schein, Aug. 4, 1939; children: Roland M. H., Oliver Douglas. AB, U. Pa., 1937, MD, 1940. Diplomate Am. Bd. Pediatrics, Am. Bd. Clin. Nutrition. Instr. pediatrics Sch. Medicine NYU, N.Y.C., 1946-50, asst. prof. Sch. Medicine, 1950-57, assoc. prof. Sch. Medicine, 1957-67, prof. Sch. Medicine, 1967—; assoc. prof. Med. Br. U. Tex., Galveston, Tex., 1952-53; attending physician Bellevue Hosp., N.Y.C., 1947—, Tisch Hosp., N.Y.C., 1947—; mem. nutrition study sect. NIH, Bethesda, Md., 1973-77; dir. Pediatric Metabolic Disease Ctr., Bellevue Med. Ctr., N.Y.C., 1965—. Contbr. numerous med. articles to profl. jours. Named career scientist Health Rsch. Coun., 1961-75. Fellow Am. Acad. Pediatrics (Borden award 1975); mem. Am. Pediatric Soc., Soc. for Pediatric Rsch., Am. Soc. Clin. Nutrition, Soc. Study Inborn Errors Metabolism, Soc. Inherited Metabolic Disorders (pres., v.p.), Soc. Parenteral and Enteral Nutrition, Phi Beta Kappa. Jewish. Office: NYU Med Ctr 500 1st Ave New York NY 10016

SNYDER-SPEAK, CATHERINE GAIL, healthcare administrator; b. Chgo., June 16, 1960; d. L. Michael and Barbara Jane (Swartz) Snyder. BA in Biology, Brown U., 1982; MBA, U. Pa., 1986. Securities analyst State St. Rsch. & Mgmt., Boston, 1982-84; market rsch. analyst Merck, Sharp & Dohme, West Point, Pa., 1986-87; dir. new bus. devel. United Hosp., Inc., Cheltenham, Pa., 1987-88; health care cons. Fulton, Longshore & Assocs., Plymouth Meeting, Pa., 1988-90; dir. spl. projects AdvaCare, Inc., Horsham, Pa., 1990—. Mem. Wharton Health Care Alumni Bd., 1988—. Mem. Am. Coll. Health Care Exec. Home: 118 Clearfield Ave Trooper PA 19403

SOBEL, BERNESE PANZER, investment financial planner; b. Newark, June 4, 1920; d. Murray Alfred and Tess (Levy) Panzer; (div. May, 1976); children: Charles S., Jeffrey G., Maxine L. y. V.p. Assn. for the Help of Retarded Children, Bklyn., 1954-70; fin. planner Gold Team Fin. Plan, Melville, N.Y., 1976; fin. planner, mem. pres. adv. coun. IDS Fin. Svcs., Inc., Melville, 1986—. Mem. Nat. Assn. Life Underwriters, Women Life Underwriters Coun., Diamond Ring Club, Million Dollar Round Table Club. Office: IDS Fin Svcs Inc 225 Broad Hollow Rd Ste 116W Melville NY 11747

SOBER, DEBRA E., environmental services administrator; b. Oklahoma City, May 20, 1953; d. Donald E. and Zona E. (Taylor) Tillman; m. Gary L. Sober, May 24, 1980; children: Kara, Jeffrey, Kimberly. BS, Columbia Pacific U. Lic. water and wastewater operator; registered X-ray lab. technician; notary pub. Co-owner UMAS, Inc., Austin, Tex.; chmn. bd. PACE Corp., Austin; gen. mgr. Envir-O-Spec, Inc., Austin; pres., ind. practice Environ. Tng., Inc., Austin. Author numerous textbooks on water and wastewater treatment and operation. Founder ann. Just Fishin Show, Austin, 1989. Mem. Nat. Environ. Tng. Assn., Tex. Water Utilities Assn. (chmn. pub. rels. 1981-85, safety chmn. 1987-88), Okla. Water and Pollution Control Assn., Am. Water Works Assn., Water Pollution Control Fedn., Am. Bus. Women's Assn., N.W. Adult Athletic Assn. (founder and dir. 1986), N.W. Austin Women's Basketball Assn. (founder and pres. 1986), N.W. Austin Women's Soccer Assn. (founder and pres. 1986), Beta Sigma Phi. Baptist. Home: 11807 Highland Oaks Trail Austin TX 78759 Office: 11940 Jollyville Rd Synergy Pla South Ste 210 Austin TX 78759

SOBERON, PRESENTACION ZABLAN, legal association administrator; b. Cabambangan, Bacolor, Pampanga, Philippines, Feb. 23, 1935; came to U.S., 1977, naturalized, 1984; d. Pioquinto Yalung and Lourdes (David) Zablan; m. Damaso Reyes Soberon, Apr. 2, 1961; children—Shirley, Sherman, Sidney, Sedwin. Office mgmt., stenography, typing cert. East Central Colls., Philippines, 1953; profl. sec. diploma, Internat. Corr. Schs., 1971; student Skyline Coll., 1979, LaSalle Extension U., 1980-82; Assoc. degree, cert. in Mgt. and Supervision, Diablo Valley Coll., 1983—. Various clerical and secretarial positions U.S. Naval Base, Subic Bay, Philippines, 1955-73, adminstrv. asst., 1973-77; secretarial positions Mt. Zion Hosp. and Med. Center, San Francisco, 1977, Oakland City Hall (Calif.), 1978; secretarial positions gen. counsel div. State Bar of Calif., San Francisco, 1978, state bar ct. div., 1978-79, adminstrv. asst. fin. and ops. div., 1979-81, office mgr. sects. and coms. dept., profl. and pub. services div., 1981-83, adminstr. non-disciplinary standing coms. and appointment process of state bar entities, office of bar relations, 1983-86; adminstr. state bar sections bus. law section, estate planning, trust and probate law section, labor and employment law section, office of bar relations, 1986—, adminstr. antitrust and trade regulation law sect., labor and employment law sect., workers' compensation law sect., office of edn., 1989—; disc jockey/announcer Philippine radio stas. DZYZ, DZOR and DWHL, 1966-77. Organizer Neighborhood Alert Program, South Catamaran Circle, Pittsburg, Calif., 1979-80. Recipient thirteen certs. and awards U.S. Fed. Service, 1964-77, 20 Yr. pin and cert., 1975; Nat. 1st prize for community projects Inner Wheel Clubs Philippines, 1975; several plaques and award certs. for community and sch. activities, Olongapo City, Philippines. Mem. Nat. Assn. Female Execs., N.Y.C. Subic Bay-Olongapo City Assn. No. Calif. (Pittsburg rep. 1982-87, bus. mgr. 1988—), Castillejos Assn. of No. Calif. Roman Catholic. Home: 205 S Catamaran Circle Pittsburg CA 94565 Office: State Bar of Calif 555 Franklin St San Francisco CA 94102

SOBRALSKE, BARBARA NILA, educator; b. Wild Rose, Wis., May 10, 1949; d. Kenneth John and Beverly Janice (Rasmussen) Graydon; m. Michael John Sobralske Jr., Oct. 17, 1970; 1 child, Mark Michael. Cert.,

Waushara County (Wis.) Tchrs. Coll., 1969; BS, U. Wis., Oshkosh, 1974. Cert. elem. tchr., Wis. Tchr. elem. schs. Waupun (Wis.) Sch. Dist., 1969-72; title I aide Wild Rose Sch. Dist., 1975, tchr. elem. schs., 1975—. Mem. NEA, Wis. Edn. Assn., Wis. Assn. Environ. Edn., Wis. Soc. Sci. Tchrs., Wis. Elem. Sci. Tchrs., Internat. Reading Assn., Wis. State Reading Assn. Home: Rte 1 Box 88 Wild Rose WI 54984 Office: Wild Rose Sch Dist PO Box 276 Wild Rose WI 54984

SOCHEN, JUNE, historian; b. Chgo., Nov. 26, 1937; d. Sam and Ruth (Finkelstein) S. B.A., U. Chgo., 1958; M.A., Northwestern U., 1960, Ph.D., 1967. Project editor Chgo. Superior and Talented Student Project, 1959-60; high sch. tchr. English and history North Shore Country Day Sch., Winnetka, Ill., 1961-64; instr. history Northeastern Ill. U., 1964-67, asst. prof., 1967-69, assoc. prof., 1969-72, prof., 1972—. Author: books including The New Woman, 1971, Movers and Shakers, 1973, Herstory: A Womans View of American History, 1975, 2d edit., 1981, Consecrate Every Day: The Public Lives of Jewish American Women, 1981, Enduring Values: Women in Popular Culture, 1987, Cafeteria America: New Identities in Contemporary Life, 1988; contbr. articles to profl. jours. Nat. Endowment for Humanities grantee, 1971-72. Mem. Am. Studies Assn. Office: Northeastern Ill U 5500 N Saint Louis St Chicago IL 60625

SOCHET, MARY ALLEN, community organizer, psychotherapist, writer; b. Plattsburgh, N.Y., Feb. 10, 1938; d. Edwin Elisha and Mary Elizabeth (Thomson) Allen; m. Marvin J. Sochet, 1963; children: Melorra, David. BS in Childhood Edn., SUNY, Plattsburgh, 1958; MA in Human Rels., NYU, 1961, PhD in Human Devel., 1963. Tchr. kindergarten L.I. Pub. Schs., 1958-62; tchr. N.Y.C. Pub. Schs., 1962-64; prof. early childhood edn., child devel. and psychology Bklyn. Coll., 1964-71; program dir., acting exec. dir. Newark Pre-Sch. Coun., 1965-66; psychotherapist N.Y.C. Community Guidance Svc., 1966-78; staff cons. Human Resources Inst., 1966—; pvt. practice psychotherapy N.Y.C., 1966-87; writer, lectr., ednl. cons. and editorial cons. in field. Author: (with Robert Allen) Toward a Caring Community, 1980; contbr. articles on edn., community orgns., peace and mental health to various jours. Founding mem. Community Loft, 1971-74, Neighbor's Network, 1979—; organizing mem. Children's Free Sch., 1969-81; co-chmn. Kids Meeting Kids Can Make a Difference, 1982—. NCCJ fellow, 1961-61; recipient Founder's Day award NYU, 1963. Mem. Am. Psychol. Assn., Soc. Psychol. Study Social Issues, Psychologists for Social Responsibility. Home and Office: 380 Riverside Dr New York NY 10025

SOCOLOFSKY, IRIS KAY, lawyer; b. Davenport, Iowa, May 3, 1952; d. Forest Wesley and Josephine Jeanette (Barnett) Shaffer; 1 son, Eric Scott. BS, Mich. State U., 1976; JD, U. Mich., 1980. Bar: Mich. 1980, U.S. Dist. Ct. (we. and ea. dists.) Mich. 1980. Ptnr. Fraser, Trebilcock, Davis & Foster, P.C., Lansing., Mich., 1980—. Co-author: Michigan Usury Manual, 1982. Bd. dirs. Capitol Area council Girl Scouts U.S., 1986-88, Capital Area Polit. Action Com., 1990—, Capitol Enterprise Forum, 1989—; mem. planning bd. Ingham County Office for Young Children, 1986-87. Recipient Book award U. Mich. Law Sch., 1980. Mem. Ingham County Bar Assn., State Bar Assn. Mich., ABA, Lansing Regional C. of C. (bus. women's council 1984-87, bd. dirs. 1987—), Lansing Assn. Career Women (bd. dirs. 1983-85), Nat. Assn. Career Women (bd. dirs. 1985-87), Athena Found (bd. dirs. 1986-87). Home: 623 Bainbridge East Lansing MI 48823 Office: Fraser Trebilcock Davis & Foster 1000 Michigan Nat Tower Lansing MI 48933

SODEN, ARLENE JULIE, business manager; b. Superior, Wis., Aug. 6, 1957; d. Arthur Julius and Edna Mae (Roe) Anderson; m. Timothy James Soden, Nov. 28, 1981. BS in Social Work, U. Wis., Superior, Wis., 1983; postgrad., Coll. St. Scholastica, 1987-89, Western Ill. U., 1990. Writing skills tutor U. Wis.-Superior, 1982-83; adult svcs. coord. Crawford County Human Svcs., Prairie du Chien, Wis., 1983-84; program dir. The Salvation Army, Lacrosse, Wis., 1984-85; social svcs. dir. St. Francis Home, Inc., Superior, 1986-89; cen. zone mgr. Community Care Systems, Inc., Springfield, Ill., 1989—; workshop presenter Wis. Alzheimer's Info. & Tng. Ctr., Milw., 1988, 89. program com. Com. on Planning & Goals for Wis. & Upper Mich./The Salvation Army, Milw., 1986-88. Recipient Lavine Gerontology Scholarship Coll. St. Scholastica, 1988, Wis. Nursing Home Social Worker's Scholarship Wis. Assn. Social Workers, 1988, St. Vincent DePaul Scholarship, 1982, U. Wis.-Superior Alumni Scholarship, 1982. Mem. NAFE, Ill. Right to Life. Home: 1501 N Bruns Ln #16 Springfield IL 62702

SODERQUIST, KRISTINA SUE, controller; b. Peoria, Ill., June 6, 1960; d. Barbara Sue (Roseberry) Wallstrom. AA in Acctg., Kaskaskia Jr. Coll., Centralia, Ill., 1980; BSBA, So. Ill. U., 1982. Asst. mgr. Septembers Restaurant, Crystal Lake, Ill., 1983-84; staff acct. Pathfinder Computer Ctrs., Woodland Hills, Calif., 1984-86; sr. cost acct. NBC-TV, Burbank, Calif., 1986-89; dir. participations Hemdale Film Corp., L.A., 1989; controller LARGO Entertainment, L.A., 1989—; bookkeeping cons., L.A., 1990—. Vol. The Am. Child, Heal the Bay, The Tree People; active Adult Child of Alcoholics. Fellow Am. Film. Inst., NFL; mem. Sierra Club. Mem. Calvanist Ch. Home: 5005 Pacific Ave Apt #1 Marina Del Rey CA 90292 Office: LARGO Entertainment 10201 W Pico Blvd Los Angeles CA 90035

SOECHTIG, JACQUELINE ELIZABETH, telecommunications executive; b. Manhasset, N.Y., Aug. 12, 1949; d. Alvin Hermann and Regina Mary (Murphy) Venzke; m. James Decatur Miller, June 28, 1976 (div. Oct. 1982); M. Clifford Jon Soechtig, Oct. 19, 1983. B.A. cum laude, Coll. of New Rochelle (N.Y.), 1974; M.A. summa cum laude, U. So. Calif., 1978. Computer operator IBM, White Plains, N.Y., 1970-72, ops. job scheduler, 1972-74, various spl. assignments, 1974-75, mktg. rep., Bethesda, Md., 1975-76, Charleston, W. Va., 1979-81, adv. regional mktg. rep. Dallas, 1981-82; dist. mgr. Am. Speedy Printing Co., Dallas, 1982-83, nat. sales devel. mgr., Detroit, 1984; regional mgr. major and nat. accounts MCI Telecommunications, Southfield, Mich., 1984-85, dir. nat. accounts, 1985-86, v.p. nat. accounts, 1987-88, v.p. mktg. and customer svc., 1988-89, v.p. consumer segment, 1989—; interviewer, Sergio Segre, Bolonga, Italy, 1977, Radio Free Europe, Brussels, 1978, World Health Program, Rome, 1978, ITT, Brussels, 1977, Franz Josef Strauss, 1978. Recipient Golden Circle Achievement award IBM, 1980, Quar. Recognition award, 1980, 81; named New Bus. Pacesetter, 1980, 81. Republican. Club: German Am. Women's (v.p. Stuttgart, W.Ger. 1977-78). Office: MCI Telecommunications Corp 400 Perimeter Ctr Terrace Atlanta GA 30346

SOENKSEN, PATRICIA ANN, health administrator; b. Beaver Dam, Wis., Feb. 6, 1952; d. Robert Homer and Eileen Marie (Ewald) Brower; m. Gordon Douglas Soenksen, June 9, 1973. Student, Wartburg Coll., 1970-73; BS, Iowa State U., 1974; MA, U. North Iowa, 1975; MBA, Duke U., 1987. Speech pathologist N. Trails Area Edn. Agy., Mason City, Iowa, 1975-80; speech pathologist Holy Cross Hosp., Chgo., 1980, dept. mgr., 1981-83, adminstr. rehab. svcs., 1984; exec. dir. Triangle Hospice, Inc., Durham, N.C., 1985-87, Home Care Cen. Carolina, Inc., Greensboro, N.C., 1988—; pres. Superior Staffing Svcs., Inc., Greensboro, 1989—; guest lectr. Erikson Inst. Child Devel., Ill., 1981-83; chair Triangle Healthcare Exec. Forum, Raleigh-Durham, N.C., 1988-89, N.C. Hospice Dirs. Care Coun., 1987. Mem. Am. Cancer Soc., Durham, 1987. Mem. Triad Healthcare Exec. Forum, Ill. Assn. for Rehab. Facilities (exec. com. 1984), Durham C. of C. (community health svcs. com. 1987). Lutheran. Home: 1108 Hobbs Rd Greensboro NC 27410 Office: Home Care Cen Carolina PO Box 4205 Greensboro NC 27404

SOENNICHSEN, JEAN ELIZABETH, advocate; b. Denver, Nov. 3, 1926; d. George and Lillian May (Bitler) Nicodemus; m. John Melchior Soennichsen, Aug. 10, 1948; children: Richard Henry, Jeanne Eileen Serrano. BA, U. Nebr., Lincoln, 1949; MA, San Jose State Coll., 1968. Cert. Reading Specialist Tchr. Tchr. Moreland Sch. Dist., San Jose, Calif., 1963-83; cons. Moreland Sch. Dist., San Jose, 1983-88; sr. senator Calif. Sr. Legislature, Sacramento, 1988—; pres. Moreland Tchrs. Assn., Jan Sose, 1973-74, Moreland Retired Tchrs. Assn., San Jose, 1985-87; bd. dir. Calif. Ret. Tchrs. Assn., San Jose, 1987; sr. senator Calif. Sr. Legislature, 1988. Editor: CRTA Monitor, 1987; author: Moreland Spelling Program, 1986. Named Tchr. of the Year San Jose Jaycees, 1973. Mem. Calif. Tchrs. Assn., Coun. on Aging Adv. Coun., Legis. Task Force, Sr. Adult Forum, Nat. Coun., of Silver Haired Legislators, Moreland Ret. Tchrs. Assn., Calif. Ret. Tchrs. Assn., Nat. Ret. Tchrs. Assn., Sequoia Yacht Club. Republican. Presbyterian. Home: 4952 Northlawn Ct San Jose CA 95130

SOFFER, MIRIAM STEINHARDT, program director; b. Albany, N.Y., May 5, 1926; d. J. Milton and Evelyn (Stern) Steinhardt; m. Sanford Soffer, May 24, 1953; children: Jonathan Milton, Melinda Ann. AB, Bryn Mawr Coll., 1947; MS, Yale U., 1951. With advt. staff Flower Grower Mag., Albany, 1947-48; health educator N.Y. State Dept. Health, Albany, 1949-50, dir. publs., 1951-54; dir. pub. rels. Gov.'s Office Consumer Affairs, Albany, 1954-56, cons., 1957; ghostwriter for physicians various med. jours., Albany, 1958-60; mng. editor N.Y. State Mus., Albany, 1974-85; exec. dir. N.Y. State Mus. Assocs., Albany, 1985-86; dir. publs. N.Y. State Mus., Albany, 1986—; mem. commr.'s task force for community schs. N.Y. State Dept. Edn., 1988—; mem. N.Y.C.'s Cultural Instns./Schs. Collaborative, 1989—. Mng. editor: (mag.) NAHO, 1974-85, (newsletter) Affinities, 1990; contbr. editor: (mag.) New York Alive, 1985—, Upstate New York, 1990; author: How New York State Legislation Affects the Consumer, 1955. Active Bryn Mawr Scholarship Com., 1960; bd. dirs. ARC, Albany, 1957-59. Office: NY State Edn Dept 60 Commerce Ave Albany NY 12206

SOFLIN, DONNA LEE KRAJNIK, hospital pharmacist; b. Ord, Nebr., Feb. 15, 1952; d. George and Clarale (Blakeslee) Krajnik; m. John A. Soflin, Aug. 16, 1975. BS in Pharmacy, U. Nebr., 1975. Lic. pharmacist, Nebr. Resident in hosp. pharmacy U. Nebr. Med. Ctr., Omaha, 1976; dir. pharmacy and inservice edn. Tri-County Area Hosp., Lexington, Nebr., 1976—; vol. faculty rural hosp. clerkship U. Nebr. Med. Ctr., 1977—; instr. lic. practical nursing program Cen. Community Coll., Kearney, Nebr., 1983-85; instr. Long-term Care Nursing Asst. program, Lexington, Nebr., 1988. Contbr. articles to profl. jours. Mem., com. chmn., Dawson County Heart Assn., 1983-84; chmn. budget com., Lexington United Way, 1985-89; commr., Lexington Civil Svc. Commn., 1987—. Recipient leadership and practice awards, various pharm. orgns., 1985, 88. Mem. Am. Soc. Hosp. Pharmacists (bd. dirs. 1988-91), Nebr. Soc. Hosp. Pharmacists (pres. 1984-85; named Hosp. Pharmacist of Yr. 1981), Nebr. Pharmacists Assn., Bus. and Profl. Women's Club Lexington (pres. 1982-83; named Outstanding Young Careerist 1977). Republican. Methodist. Home: 1510 Liberty Dr Lexington NE 68850 Office: Tri County Area Hosp 13th at Erie St Lexington NE 68850

SOHMERS, BARBARA PEARL, actress; b. N.Y.C., July 7, 1930; d. Phillip Harry and Ethel (Grossman) S.; m. Claude Nicot, June 30, 1961 (div. 1977). Student, Antioch Coll., 1948-49. Actress Three Penny Opera, N.Y.C., 1955-56, Le Plus Grand Theatre Du Monde, Paris, 1962, Boeing-Boeing, Paris, 1959-60, Madame Princesse, Paris, 1966-67, Ne Reveillez Pas Madame, Paris, 1971-72, Long Wharf Tour, Pvt. Lives, Lion in Winter, U.S.A., 1980-81, Ned and Jack, N.Y.C., 1981, Legends, U.S.A., 1985-86, Tamara, Santa Barbara, L.A., 1989—. Author: The Fox and the Puma, 1988. Mem. SAG, AFTRA, Actors Equity Assn. Democrat. Buddhist.

SOHNEN-MOE, CHERIE MARILYN, management consultant; b. Tucson, Jan. 2, 1956; d. D. Ralph and Angelina Helen (Spiro) Sohnen; m. James Madison Moe, Jr., May 23, 1981. BA, UCLA, 1977. Rsch. asst. UCLA, 1975-77; ind. cons. L.A., 1978-83; cons. Sohnen-Moe Assocs., Tucson, 1984—. Author: Business Mastery, 1988; contbr. Compendium mag., 1987—, (jour.) Am. Massage Therapy Assn., 1989—. Vol. Am. Cancer Soc., Tucson, 1984—; charter mem. Civitan-El Conquistador, Tucson, 1986-87; mem. Ariz. Sonora Desert Mus., Tucson; pres. Women in Tucson. Recipient Outstanding Achievement award ASTD, 1987, Disting. Svc. award, 1988. Mem. NOW, NAFE, Resources for Women, Women in Tucson, Am. Soc. for Tng. and Devel. (dir. mem. svcs. 1988, Disting. Svc. award 1988), Pubs. Mktg. Assn., New Age Pub. and Retailing Alliance, Sierra Club. Office: Sohnen-Moe Assocs 3906 W Ina Rd #200-264 Tucson AZ 85741

SOKALSKI, DEBRA ANN, computer systems developer, programming consultant; b. Paterson, N.J., June 27, 1959; d. John Michael and Cecelia Ann (O'Brien) S. Computer program cert., Electronic Computer Prog.Inst., Paterson, 1978; student, Montclair State Coll., 1988. Programmer trainee Numerax, Inc., Paramus, N.J., 1978-79, programmer, 1979-82, programming supr., 1982-83, mgr. programming, 1983-84, mgr. data processing, 1984-88; dir. system devel. Numerax/McGraw-Hill, Inc., 1989-90; sr. programmer, analyst ADP, Roseland, N.J., 1990—; programming cons. Leslie Co., Parsippany, N.J., 1979-80. Mem. NAFE. Democrat. Roman Catholic. Home: 684 Main St Little Falls NJ 07424 Office: ADP One ADP Blvd Roseland NJ 07068-1728

SOKOL, ELENA, Russian educator; b. Chgo., July 17, 1943; d. Louis F. and Julia (Hajek) S.; m. Andras Furesz; 1 child, Sonja. BA, U. Colo., 1965; MA, U. Calif., Berkeley, 1967, PhD, 1974. Teaching asst. U. Calif., Berkeley, 1967-71; assoc. in Russian, U. Calif., Santa Cruz, 1972-73; vis. asst. prof. Reed Coll., Portland, Oreg., 1973-74; asst. prof. U. Wash., Seattle, 1974-82; vis. assoc. prof. Oberlin (Ohio) Coll., 1984-87; assoc. prof. Russian, Coll. of Wooster, Ohio, 1987—; lectr. Calif. State U., Hayward, fall 1970; resident dir. CIEE Russian Lang. Program, Leningrad, USSAR, 1982-83, ACM-GLCA Semester in USSR, Krasnodar, fall 1990; grad. student exchange Internat. Rsch. and Exchs., Moscow, 1971-72, sr. scholar exch., spring 1988. Author: Russian Poetry for Children, 1984; guest editor Soviet Studies in Lit., 1988; contbr. articles, revs. and transls. to profl. jours. Tchr. sewing Appalachian Vols., Compton, Y., 1967. Woodrow Wilson fellow, 1965-66, Nat. Def. Fgn. Lang. fellow, 1966-67. Mem. MLA, Am. Assn. for Advancement Slavic Studies, Am. Assn. Tchrs. Slavic and East European Langs., Phi Beta Kappa. Home: 1019 Forest Dr Wooster OH 44691 Office: Coll of Wooster Dept Russian Studies Wooster OH 44691

SOKOL, HILDA WEYL, physiology educator; b. St. Louis, Dec. 19, 1928; d. Walter H. and Kaethe (Schwettscher) Weyl; m. Robert Sokol, June 16, 1951; children: Kirstin Rosa, Niels Weyl, Heidi Rebecca. AB, Hunter Coll., 1950; AM, Radcliffe Coll., 1951; PhD, Harvard U., 1957. Teaching fellow in biology Harvard U., Cambridge, Mass., 1950-53; instr. in sci. Boston U., 1954-55; instr. zoology Wellesley (Mass.) Coll., 1955-58, Tufts U., Medford, Mass., 1958-59; rsch. assoc. in physiology Harvard Med. Sch., Boston, 1960-61; rsch. assoc. in physiology Dartmouth Med. Sch., Hanover, N.H., 1961-63, instr. physiology, 1963-67, asst. prof., 1967-75, assoc. prof. physiology, 1975—. Editor: The Brattleboro Rat, 1982; contbr. rsch. papers to sci. jours. Grad. fellow AAUW, 1953-54; Fogarty Sr. Internat. fellow NIH, Heidelberg (Fed. Republic Germany) U., 1975-76; sr. vis. fellow Anatomical Soc. Gt. Britain and Ireland, Oxford U., 1984. Fellow AAAS; mem. Endocrine Soc., Am. Soc. Zoologists, Assn. for Women in Sci., Phi Beta Kappa, Sigma Xi. Democrat. Home: 6 Storrs Rd Hanover NH 03755 Office: Dartmouth Med Sch Hanover NH 03756

SOLA, JANET ELAINE, government program official; b. New Britain, Conn., Oct. 23, 1935; d. Walter Andrew and Helen (Mandl) Sinkiewicz; m. Raymond Albert Sola,. BS, Cen. Conn. State U., 1957; MS, So. Conn. State U., New Haven, 1962; postgrad., U. Conn, 1969. Bus. tchr. Amity Reg. High Sch., Woodridge, Conn., 1957-60; bus. instr. Stone Coll., New Haven, Conn., 1962; instr. Manpower Devel. & Training Act, New Britain, Conn., 1970-74, So. Cen. Community Coll., New Haven, 1977; mgmt. lectr. II Quinnipiac Coll., Hamden, 1981-87; lectr. So. Cen. Community Coll., New Haven, 1987; mayor's aide Town of Hamden, 1987-89, recycling coord., 1989—; assessor, Credit for Life Quinn Coll. Hamden, Conn., 1986-89;. Author:(poetry) Contemporary, 1957, The Hamden Chronicle, 1978, The Hamden Chronicle, 1982. Campaigner Sola for Town Clk. Com., Hamden, 1981; community liaison Carusone for Mayor Com., Hamden, 1981-87; v.p., Am. Legion Aux. Unit 88, Hamden, 1985—. Mem. AAUW, Cen. Conn. State U. Alumni Assn. Bd., Conn. Bus. Educators. Home: 50 Vernon St Hamden CT 06518 Office: Town of Hamden 1125 Shepard Ave Hamden CT 06518

SOLAN, DEBORAH, public relations writer; b. Bklyn., Nov. 26, 1958; d. Stanley Markowitz and Maxine Herman; m. George M. Solan, Jr., Sept. 27, 1980. BS, W.Va. U., 1979. Reporter, office mgr. Aurora Advocate/Hudson Hub-Times/Record Pub. Co., Stow, Ohio, 1979-81; assoc. editor Hudson Hub-Times/Record Pub. Co., Stow, 1981-85; editor Aurora Advocate/Record Pub. Co., Stow, 1985-86; regional editor Record Pub. Co., Stow, 1986-87, exec. editor, 1987-88; pub. rels. writer coll. medicine Northeastern Ohio Univs., Rootstown, 1988—. Contbr. articles to Gospel Herald & Sunday Sch. Times, 1985—; newsletter editor Word of His Grace Fellowship, Cuyahoga Falls, Ohio, 1990. Youth group leader Victory Christian Fellowship, Hudson, Ohio, 1987-90, prison ministry, 1988-90; mem. communications com. Portage County United Way. Mem. Women in Communications Inc. Hebrew Christian. Office: Northeastern Ohio Univs Coll of Medicine 4209 St Rte 44 Rootstown OH 44272

SOLARZ, ANDREA LYNN, psychologist; b. Rockford, Ill., Oct. 9, 1955; d. Andrew Kasmer and Marilyn Dorothy (Safely) S. BA in Psychology, U. Va., 1973; MA in Psychology, Mich. State U., 1983, PhD in Psychology, 1986. Rsch. assoc. Ctr. for Innovation Rsch., Mich. State U., East Lansing, 1979-81; site rsch. dir. Univ. Assocs., Lansing, Mich., 1982-84; evaluation specialist, policy cons. Mich. Dept. Mental Health, Lansing, 1984-86, homelessness liaison, 1986-87; Am. Psychol. Assn. Congl. sci. fellow U.S. Senate Labor and Human Resources Subcom. on Handicapped, Washington, 1987-88; health policy analyst office tech. assessment U.S. Congress Carnegie Corp. N.Y., Washington, 1988—; cons. Detroit Cen. Cities Community Mental Health Ctr., 1987-89, Nat. Health Policy Coun., 1988-89. Contbr. articles to profl. jours. Health constituencies coord. Campaign '88, Dem. Nat. Com., 1988. Named one of Outstanding Young Women of Am., 1983; student rsch. grantee Mich. Dept. Mental Health, Lansing, 1985; recipient traineeship NIMH, 1978-80. Mem. Am. Psychol. Assn. (task force on health and behavior 1990—, div. 27 community psychology northeast regional coord. 1989-91, task force on homeless children and families 1989—), Soc. for the Psychol. Study Social Issues, Am. Pub. Health Assn., Am. Evaluation Assn. Democrat. Home: 3329 S Wakefield St B1 Arlington VA 22206 Office: Am Psychol Assn 1200 Seventeenth St NW Washington DC 20036

SOLBERG, ELIZABETH TRANSOU, public relations executive; b. Dallas, Aug. 10, 1939; d. Ross W. and Josephine V. (Perkins) Transou; m. Frederick M. Solberg, Mar. 8, 1969; 1 son, Frederick W. B.J., U. Mo., 1961. Reporter, Kansas City (Mo.) Star, 1963-70, asst. city editor, 1970-73; reporter spl. events, documentaries Sta. WDAF-TV, Kansas City, Mo., 1973-74; prof. dept. journalism Park Coll., Kansas City, Mo., 1975-76, advisor, 1976-79; mng. ptnr. Fleishman-Hillard, Inc., Kansas City, Mo., from 1979, now exec. v.p., sr. ptnr., gen. mgr. Kansas City br. Mem. Kansas City Commn. Planned Indsl. Expansion Authority, 1974—; mem. long-range planning com. Heart of Am. council Boy Scouts Am., 1980-82, bd. dirs., 1986—; mem. Clay County (Mo.) Devel. Commn., 1979-88; bd. govs. Citizens Assn., 1975—; mem. exec. com. bd. Kansas City Devel. Cpoun.; trustee Pembroke Hill Sch. Recipient award for contbn. to mental health Mo. Psychiat. Assn., 1973. Mem. Pub. Relations Soc. Am. (nat. honors and awards com., co-chmn. Silver Anvil Com. 1983; Silver Anvil award 1979-82), Mo. C. of C. Pub. Relations Council, Kansas City C. of C., Pi Beta Phi. Clubs: Jr. League, Kansas City, Carriage, Central Exchange. Office: Fleishman Hillard Inc 2405 Grand Ave Kansas City MO 64108*

SOLBERG, NELLIE FLORENCE COAD, artist; b. Sault Ste. Marie, Mich.; d. Sanford and Mary (McDonald) Coad; m. Ingvald Solberg, Aug. 24, 1930; children: Jeanne Elaine Solberg Unruh, Walter Eugene, Kay Louise Solberg Link. BA, Minot State Tchrs. Coll., 1930; MA, N.D. State U., 1963; postgrad. Wash. State U., 1960, U. Wyo., 1964, St. Cloud Coll., 1971. Tchr. Bismarck Elem. Schs., N.D., 1954-63, art dir. high sch., 1963-72; instr. art Bismarck Jr. Coll., 1964-67; cons. Bismarck Art Assn. Galleries, 1973-79, State Capitol Galleries, 1973-78; dir. arts festivals including Statewide Religious Arts Festival, Bismarck, 1969-85, State Treas.'s Gallery, 1977, N.D. State Capitol, Bismarck, 1973-78; co-dir. Indian Art Show, Nat. Congress Am. Indians, Bismarck, 1963. Artist: (print) Prairie Rose for N.D. centennial, 1989; one-woman shows include Minot State Coll., 1963, Dickinson State Coll., 1964, Jamestown Coll., 1964, U. N.D., Valley City State Coll., Bismarck Jr. Coll., 1963, 65, 68, 69, N.D. State U., 1970, 74, Linha Gallery, Minot N.D., 1972, 74-77, Bank of N.D., 1972-74, 76-77, Elan Gallery, 1982; exhibited in group shows at Gov. John Davis Mansion, 1960, Concordia Coll., Moorhead, Minn., 1965, N.D. Capitol, 1968, 69, Gov. William Guy Mansion, 1971, Internat. Peace Gardens, 1969. Mem. Indian Culture Found., 1964—, Civic Music Assn., 1942—; works included in numerous pvt. collections U.S., Can., Europe; religious arts com. Conf. Chs., 1973; bd. dirs. Citizens for Arts, 1978-81; mem. The Statue of Liberty/Ellis Island Found., 1984-89. Recipient numerous awards including Gov.'s award for arts, 1977, Gov. Allen Olson award, 1982, Gov.'s award Bismarck Art Show, 1982, Dakota Northwestern Bank award, 1983, Dr. Shari Orser Purchase award Religious Arts Festival, 1984, William Murray award Religious Arts Festival, 1984, Mandan Art Assn. award, 1986, 18th ann. 3d prize weaving Festivcal of Arts, 1987, Dr. Cy Rinkel watercolor purchase award, 1987, Heritage Centennial Art award Heritage Arts, Inc., 1988; named N.D. Woman Artist of Yr., 1974, Heritage Centennial award, 1989. Mem. Bismarck Arts and Galleries Assn. (membership com.), Bismarck Art Assn. (charter, Honor award 1960, pres. 1963-64, 71-72), Jamestown Art Assn., Linha Gallery (Minot), Nat. League Am. Pen Women (pres. N.D. 1964-66, pres. Medora br. 1972-74, treas. 1975-86), Mpls. Soc. Fine Arts, P.E.O. (pres. chpts. 1967-69), Bismarck Vets, Meml. Library (life), Soc. Preservation Gov.'s Mansion (charter, bd. dirs.), Women in the Arts Nat. Mus. (charter), Sigma Sigma Sigma. Republican. Lodges: Zonta, Order of Eastern Star. Home: 925 N 6th St Bismarck ND 58501 Office: 1021 N 6th St Bismarck ND 58501

SOLDO, BETH JEAN, demography educator, researcher; b. Binghamton, N.Y., Sept. 30, 1948; d. Frank E. and Ruth E. (Dayton) S.; m. T. Peter Bridge, Sept. 20, 1975. BA, Fordham U., 1970; MA, Duke U., 1973, PhD, 1977. Asst. dir. Ctr. Demographic Studies Duke U., Durham, N.C., 1974-77; sr. rsch. scholar Ctr. Population Rsch. Georgetown U., Washington, 1977-86, sr. rsch. fellow Kennedy Inst. Ethics, 1978—, assoc. prof. demography, 1985—, dept. chair, 1986—; cons. White House Conf. on Aging, Washington, 1980-81, U.S. House - Joint Econ. Com., 1987-88, U.S. Senate - Com. on Aging, Washington, 1984-86. Co-author: (with R.J. Struyk) Improving the Elderly's Housing: A Key to Preserving the Nation's Housing Stock and Neighborhoods, 1980; contbr. articles to profl. jours. and chpts. to books. Grantee Atlantic Richfield Found., 1984, Commonwealth Fund, 1984-85, Retirement Rsch. Found., 1986-88, competive grantee Nat. Inst. on Aging, 1986—. Fellow Gerontol. Soc. Am.; mem. Am. Pub. Health Assn. (sect. coun. 1986-88), Population Assn. Am. (bd. dirs. 1990—). Office: Georgetown U Dept Demography 233 Poulton Washington DC 20057

SOLENSKI, AGNES HELENE, advertising executive; b. Hazleton, Pa., Sept. 17, 1926; d. Joseph Thomas and Agnes Catherine (Stepien) S. Diploma, Western Union Telegraph Sch., Washington, N.J., 1945-46; student, Morse Coll., 1953, Hillyer Coll. U. Hartford, 1953-55; grad., Hanover Sch. Modeling, 1962. Advt. exec. F.W. Prelle Co. Advt. Agy., Hartford, Conn., 1954-69, WM Schaller Co., W. Hartford, Conn., 1969-73, Albee Trieber Co., W. Hartford, Conn., 1974-77; advt. agy. mgr. Robert T. Reynolds Assoc., Inc., W. Hartford, Conn., 1977-91. Mem. Women's Republican Assn., W. Hartford Conn. 1977--. Mem. Nat. Sec. Assn. (corr. sec. Hartford chpt. 1961-62), West Hartford Art League, New Britain Ski Club (sec., editor), Hartford Ski Club (corr. sec.). Office: Robert T Reynolds Assoc Inc 1010 Farmington Ave West Hartford CT 06107

SOLER, DONA KATHERINE, civic worker; b. Grand Rapids, Mich., Mar. 7, 1921; d. Melbourne and Katherine Anne (Herbst) Welch; 1 child, Suzette Maria. Student pvt. and pub. schs., Grand Rapids, Mich. Artist-instr., metaphys. councilor, researcher, editor, pub. Psychic Exchange, 1979—. Author: What God Hath Put Together, 1979, Our Heritage From the Angels, 1981, Expose the Dirty Devil, 1984, Contemporary Poets of America (anthology), 1984, For Love of Henry, 1985, Greyball, 1986, House of Evil Secrets, 1986. Founder, 1st pres. South Coast Art Assn., San Clemente, Calif., 1963-65, Orange Coast Cath. Christian Singles, 1970-73, Psychic Exchange, Orange County, 1979; founder, chief Lake Riverside Estates Communicators, Riverside, 1974-79. Mem. Rep. Nat. Com., Nat. Tax Limitation and Balanced Budget Com., Calif. Tax Reduction Movement, Halt Legal Reform, Internat. Platform Assn., Animal Assistance League of Orange County, Animal Protection Inst. Am., Greenpeace, People for the Ethical Treatment of Animals, Internat. Fund for Animal Welfare, World Wildlife Fund-U.S., Humane Soc. U.S., Am. Soc. Prevention Cruelty Toward Animals, In Def. of Animals, others.

SOLER, TERRELL DIANE, dramatic soprano, real estate and marketing executive; b. South Bend, Ind., Apr. 26; d. Harold J. Metzler and Margaret Terrell (Whiteman) Metzler-Fogarty. BA, Ithaca Coll., 1960; diploma, Brown's Bus. Coll., Decatur, Ill., 1960; postgrad. in real estate sales, NYU, 1984. Lic. securities dealer, real estate salesperson. Exec. legal asst. Carb Luria Glassner Cook & Kufeld, N.Y.C., 1962-64; Exec. legal asst. Graubard Moskovitz McGoldrick Dannett & Horowitz, N.Y.C., 1964-79; opera and concert singer N.Y.C., 1964—; real estate salesperson Rosemary Edwards Realty, N.Y.C., 1985, Kenneth D. Laub & Co., Inc., N.Y.C., 1987-89, GSW Realty, Inc., N.Y.C., 1990—; pres. Terrell Internat., Whiteman and Stewart Prodns., TS Assocs., TS Enterprises, DharMacduff Publs.; corr. sec., bd. dirs. Community Opera, Inc., N.Y.C., 1984—. Mem. internat. affairs com. and other coms. Women's Nat. Rep. Club, N.Y.C., 1968—; active Rep. County Vols., N.Y.C., 1976—; mem. nominating com. Ivy Rep. Club, N.Y.C., 1983-87; bd. dirs. Am. Landmark Festivals, 1986—. Named Female Singer of Yr., Internat. Beaux Arts, Inc., 1978-79, Princess Nightingale, Allied Indian Tribes N.Am. Continent-Cherokee Nation, 1985. Mem. Nat. Arts Club (music com. 1983-87), Wagner Internat. Instn. (dir. pub. rels. 1982-84), N.Y. Opera Club, Navy League U.S. (life, mem. N.Y. council), World Ship Soc., Assn. Former Intelligence Officers (assoc.), Friends of Spanish Opera (bd. dirs. 1982—), Finlandia Found., Inc. (life), World Ship Soc., Ziegfield Club. Home: 2 Tudor City Pl Apt 4-J s New York NY 10017

SOLES, ADA LEIGH, state legislator; b. Jacksonville, Fla., May 19, 1937; d. Albert Thomas and Dorothy (Winter) Wall; B.A., Fla. State U., 1959; m. James Ralph Soles, 1959; children—Nancy Beth, Catherine. Mem. New Castle County Library Adv. Bd., 1975-80, chmn., 1975-77; chmn. Del. State Library Adv. Bd., 1975-78; mem. Del. State Ho. Reps., 1980—. Adminstrv. asst. U. Del. Commn. on Status of Women, 1976-77; acad. advisor U. Del. Coll. Arts and Scis., 1977—. Mem. LWV (state pres. 1978-80), Phi Beta Kappa, Phi Kappa Phi, Mortar Bd., Alpha Chi Omega. Episcopalian. Office: Del Ho Reps Dover DE 19901

SOLLAMI, ROSEANN, teacher, politicial worker; b. Trenton, N.J., Dec. 30, 1935; d. Joseph Thomas and Anne Esther (Lipani) Bruno; m. Paul J. Sollami, May 4, 1963; children—Paula, Maryann. B.A., Douglass Coll., 1957; student Trenton State Coll., 1964, Rutgers U. Grad. Sch. Edn., 1959-61. Tchr. history, econs. Ewing Township, Trenton, 1957-59; asst. dir. admissions Rutgers U., New Brunswick, N.J., 1959-63; ascertainment coordinator Sta. NJP-TV Channel 52, N.J., 1975-81; tchr. English Ewing Twp. High Sch., 1985—; examiner acad. credential N.J. State Dept. of Edn. Committeewoman Dem. Party, Trenton, 1969—; polit. fundraiser Merlino for Gov., 1982; chairwoman fundraising dinner Mercer County Dems., 1978; active steering com. Women for Florio for Gov. of N.J., 1989. Mem. Douglass Coll. Alumni Assn., Ravine Club, Trenton Coll. Club, N.J. Fedn. Dem. Women. Avocations: drama, swimming, politics, photography. Home and Office: 11 Seven Oaks Ln Trenton NJ 08628

SOLLANO, ROSEMARIE, educator; b. Bklyn., Mar. 14, 1962; d. Gasper Anthony and Carmela (De Meo) S. BA, Fordham U., 1984; MA, U. Va., 1986. Cert. tchr., N.Y. Tchr. Spanish, St. Philip Neri Sch., East Northport, N.Y., 1987-88, St. Hugh of Lincoln Sch., Huntington, N.Y., 1987-88; tchr. Spanish and Italian, Herricks Sch. Dist., New Hyde Park, N.Y., 1988—. Mem. Am. Assn. Tchrs. Spanish and Portuguese, N.Y. State Assn. Fgn. Lang. Tchrs., L.I. Lang. Tchrs. Home: 4 Dorothy Ln Kings Park NY 11754 Office: Herricks Sch Dist Shelter Rock Rd New Hyde Park NY 11040

SOLLEY, MARY-SUE PASTORELLO, home entertainment products distributing executive; b. Chgo., Aug. 4, 1955; d. Daniel and Angela (Gatsos) Pastorello; m. Richard James Solley, Oct. 8, 1977; children—Daniel, Stephanie, Jennifer. Student Eastern Ill. U., 1973-76, Roosevelt U., 1980-82. Acct., office mgr. Burton's Shoes, Inc., Northbrook, Ill., 1976-80; asst. controller Sound Video Unltd., Inc., Niles, Ill., 1980-82, controller, 1982-86, chief fin. officer, 1986-87, also dir.; v.p., gen. mgr. Speedy Messenger Service, Inc., Arlington Heights, Ill., 1987—; treas., dir. JLT Films, Inc., Niles, 1983-87. Mem. exec. council St. John's Parish, Des Plaines. Mem. Nat. Assn. Accts., Bus. Planning Bd., Nat. Assn. for Female Execs., Controllers Council. Republican. Greek Orthodox. Club: St. John's Philoptochos (Des Plaines, Ill.). Avocations: piano, theatre, horseback riding, boating, swimming. Home: 811 E Appletree Ln Arlington Heights IL 60004 Office: Speedy Messenger Service 8 S Dunton Arlington Heights IL 60005

SOLLID, FAYE, volunteer; b. Milw., Aug. 31, 1913; d. George Walter and Jessie Belle (Davey) Eising; m. Erik Sollid, Aug. 1, 1936 (dec. Mar. 1977); 1 child, Jon Erik. BA, U. Wis., 1936; postgrad., U. Denver, 1947. Asst. in basic communications U. Denver, 1947. Editor Am. Hindi cookbook for Am. Women's Club New Delhi, 1956; mem. Clearwater (Fla.) Libr. Bd., 1981-89, liaison between libr. bd. and Friends of Libr. Bd., 1984-89; mem. Clearwater Beautification Com., 1989-90. Recipient Citation of Sincere Appreciation for pub. svc. as mem. libr. bd. 1981-89 Mayor City of Clearwater, 1989. Mem. Internat. Grapho-Analysis Soc. &Graphoanalyst, AAUW, PACT, Nat. Mus. Women inthe Arts, Fla. Pub. Interest Research Group, Upper Pinellas African Violet Soc. (v.p. 1973-74, pres. 1974-75), Sovereign Colonial Soc. Ams. Royal Descent, Plantagenet Soc., Soc. Descendants of Most Noble Order of the Garter, Order of Crown of Charlemagne in U.S.A., Suncoast Magna Charta Dames (recording sec. 1980-83), Colonial Dames XVII Century (v.p. 1983-85, 89). Democrat. Baptist.

SOLLINS, SUSAN, curator art museums; m. Earle Brown. BA, Sarah Lawrence Coll.; postgrad., Columbia U. Dir. studio art program Barnard Coll., U. Columbia, N.Y.C., 1964-66; editor Harry N. Abrams, Inc., N.Y.C., 1967; curator of Edn. Nat. Mus. Am. Art, Smithsonian Inst., Washington, 1968-71; producer arts interviews Nat. Pub. Radio, 1972-74; exec. dir., co-founder, curator Independent Curators Inc., N.Y.C., 1974—; dir. Inner City Art Program, Collegiate Sch., N.Y.C., 1965; instr. in Art History, NYU, 1965-66; guest curator Balt. Mus. of Art, 1972-73; cons. Balt. Pub. Schs., 1972, San Francisco Mus. of Art, 1975, Am. Assn. of Mus., 1975, London (Ontario) Art Gallery, 1976, The Neuberger Mus., SUNY, 1976, The Denver Art Mus. 1976, Portland (Oreg.) Art Mus., 1977, Georgetown U., 1988 and numerous other museums, ednl insts. and art galleries; curator contemporary art Art in Landscape, 1975, New Work, N.Y., 1977, Supershow!, 1979, New Sculpture: Icon and Environment, 1983, Points of View: Four Painters, 1985, Eternal Metaphors: New Art from Italy, 1988, Team Spirit, 1990. Author (tchr. instructional materials on art and art history) Great Ideas, 1976, The City-Project Ideas, 1977, The Decordova Lessons, 1979; (films) You're It, 1971, Learning to Look, 1977; contbr. articles to profl. jours., mags. and newspapers. Nat. Jury Awards in the Visual Arts, Southeastern Ctr. for Contemporary Art, 1988. Mem. Mass. Arts Coun., N.Y. State Arts Coun., Art Table Inc. (bd. dirs. 1984-87). Office: Independent Curators Inc 799 Broadway New York NY 10003

SOLLITT, BETTYE HERB, civic worker; b. Alton, Ill., June 4, 1911; d. Harrison Blaine Herb and Elizabeth (Green) Reticker; m. Harry Gale Nye, Jr., Dec. 4, 1935 (div. 1949); children—Julia Gale, Nancy Pogue, Sally Barbara; m. Sumner Shannon Sollitt, Nov. 30, 1949 (dec. 1964); 1 child, Bettye Martin. Student Northwestern U., 1929-31, U. Chgo., 1969-70. Acct. and circulation mgr. Barks Publs., Chgo., 1970-75; profl. fund raiser U. Mich. Coll. Engring. and Occidental Coll. L.A., 1975-78. Mem. women's bd. dirs., officer Arthritis Found., Chgo., 1951—, U. Chgo. Cancer Research Found., 1958—, Henrotin Hosp., Chgo., 1964-86; officer of bd. trustees Latin Sch. of Chgo., 1964-68; mem. Guild of Chgo. Hist. Soc., 1961—; past mem., officer Chgo. council Girl Scouts U.S., 1952-68, Parents Council Latin Sch., 1959-61, 64-68; bd. dirs. English Speaking Union, Chgo., 1981—. Republican. Episcopalian. Clubs: University, Chgo. Yacht (Chgo.). Avocation: sailing.

SOLOMON, A. MALAMA, state legislator; b. Honolulu, Mar. 3, 1961; d. Randolph Folau Solomon and Flora Beamer. B.Ed., U. Hawaii-Manoa, 1972, M.A., 1973; B.A., U. Hawaii-Hilo, 1974; Ph.D., Oreg. State U., 1980. Market and sales mgr. beef cattle Kohala Farms, from 1972; lectr. U. Hawaii-Hilo, 1973-75; program coordinator Aloha Week Festivals Inc., 1977-87. Trustee, Office Hawaiian Affairs, 1980-82; mem. Hawaii Senate, Dist. 3, 1983—. Native Am. Ford fellow, 1976-80; recipient Outstanding Community Service award Hilo Coll., 1973-75; Outstanding Leadership award Council Hawaiian Civic Clubs, 1982; named Outstanding Woman of Yr., Hawaii Nat. Women's Week, 1982. Mem. Kohala Community Assn., Dist. Council Hawaiian Civic Clubs. Congregationalist. Office: State Senate State Capitol Honolulu HI 96813 Home: PO Box 219 Kapaau HI 96755*

SOLOMON, BARBARA MILLER, retired history educator; b. Boston, Feb. 12, 1919; d. Benjamin Allen and Bessie (Pinsky) Miller Skirball; m. Peter Herman Solomon, May 13, 1940 (dec. 1987); children: Peter Herman Jr., Maida Elizabeth. AB, Radcliffe Coll., 1940; PhD, Harvard U., 1953; LittD (hon.), Regis Coll., 1986. Asst. prof. history Wheelock Coll., Mass., 1957-59; instr. Radcliffe Coll., Cambridge, Mass., 1960-61, assoc. dean, 1963-70, vis. scholar, 1989-90; lectr. history and lit. Harvard U., Cambridge, 1965-74, rsch. fellow, 1968-69, asst. dean, 1970-74, sr. lectr., 1974-85, lectr. Extension Sch., 1985-86; mem. adv. com. Arthur and Elizabeth Schlesinger Libr. for History Women Am., 1965—, chmn., 1975-76, hon. vis. scholar, 1989-91. Author: In the Company of Educated Women, 1984 (Frederick W. Ness award 1986), Ancestors and Immigrants, 1956, reprinted, 1965, 72, 89; editor: Educated Women, 12 vols., 1987. Guggenheim fellow, 1976-77; Radcliffe Mellon scholar, 1979-80. Mem. Cosmopolitan Club. Jewish.

SOLOMON, CATHY REBECCA, marketing communications executive; b. Toledo, Ohio, Feb. 8, 1957; d. Donald L. Solomon and Jan Sydney (Kadetsky) Cohn. Student, Mt. Holyoke Coll., 1974-75; BA, Carnegie Mellon U., 1979. Asst. buyer Kaufmann's Dept. Store, Pitts., Pa., 1979-80; prin. CR Solomon Assoc. Mfg. Rep., Pitts., 1980-81; pres. Porgy and Bass Specialty Seafoods, Pitts., 1981-83; mgr. Sweaterville USA, Colorado Springs, 1983-85; mktg. mgr. Nat. Assn. Realtors, Washington, 1985-87; political svcs. dir. Nat. Assn. of Realtors, Washington, 1987-89; assoc. dir. promotions and market rsch. Assn. Trial Lawyers Am., Washington, 1989—. Pres. Westmoreland Coop. Assn., Washington, 1989; trustee the Dublin Sch., 1987—; Dem. com. rep. Ward 1, Precinct 13, D.C. Mem. Am. Soc. Assn. Execs., Nat. Press Club, Am. Assn. Polit. Cons., AdClub of Met. Washington. Jewish. Home: 2122 California St NW Washington DC 20008 Office: Assn Trial Lawyers Am 1050 31st St NW Washington DC 20007

SOLOMON, DEBORAH ANTOINNETTE, volunteer; b. N.Y.C., Oct. 25, 1938; d. Robert Benjamin and Helene Catherine (Skaluba) Gross; m. Arthur Paul Solomon, Dec. 20, 1958; children: Melanie Elizabeth, Denise Carol, Russell David, Lauren Jodi. BA, Queens Coll., 1958, MEd, 1960. Profl. TV dancer June Taylor Dancers, Jackie Gleason Show, N.Y.C., 1955-59; high sch. tchr. William H. Maxwell Vocat. High Sch., Bklyn., 1959-61. Vol. Woman's Am. Orgn. for Rehab. Through Training, 1970—, dir. ORT Strolling Players, 1977—, co-convener Women's Pleas for Soviet Jewry through ORT, L.I., N.Y., 1986-87, chmn. exec. com. ORT, pres. North Shore Nassau Region, 1988—; choreographer fund-raising shows Temple Israel Great Neck, 1978-82. Named Woman of Yr. ORT, 1987. Democrat. Jewish. Home: 10 Somerset Dr S Great Neck NY 11020 Office: Women's Am ORT 275 Warner Ave Roslyn Heights NY 11517

SOLOMON, ELLEN JOAN, management consultant; b. Orange, N.J., Aug. 26, 1943; d. Abram Shrier and Mildred Elizabeth (Berger) S. BA in Psychology, U. N.C., Chapel Hill, 1965; MS in human resource devel. Am. U., 1985. Contract writer Conn. Gen. Life Ins. Co., Bloomfield, 1965-66; mgmt. trainee, asst. buyer G. Fox & Co., Hartford, Conn., 1966-68; account exec. WLAE-FM, Hartford, 1968; sr. analyst Travelers Ins. Co., Hartford, 1968-70; job analyst Conn. Blue Cross, New Haven, 1970-71; sr. ops. auditor Govt. Employees Ins. Co., Washington, 1972-75; employee devel. specialist Employment Standards Adminstrn., U.S. Dept. Labor, Washington, 1975-81, mgmt. analyst, 1981-82, supervisory mgmt. analyst, 1982-87; mgmt. cons. State Maine, 1986-87; program designer, cons. Eastman Kodak Co., Rochester, N.Y., 1987-89, mgr., 1989, sr. orgnl. cons., 1990—; conf. speaker; workshop leader; cons. Recipient spl. achievement award U.S. Dept. Labor, 1977, 78, 83, 85. Mem. NOW, Am. Soc. Tng. and Devel., OD Network, Gestalt Inst. Cleve., Rochester Women's Network (bd. dirs. 1990—), U. N.C. Alumni, Alpha Gamma Delta. Democrat. Jewish. Home: 67 Cornhill Pl Rochester NY 14608 Office: Eastman Kodak Co 343 State St Rochester NY 14650

SOLOMON, HILDA PEARL, wholesale executive; b. Conway, S.C., Dec. 15, 1948; d. Ezel and Dorothy (Gottlieb) S. BFA, U. S.C., 1968. Buyer Solomon Bros. Dept. Store, Conway, 1969-73; coutour saleswoman Julius Lewis, Memphis, 1973-75; buyer Helen of Memphis, 1975-78, George M. Muse Clothing Co., Atlanta, 1978-83; sales rep. Whiting & Davis Co. Inc., Plainville, Mass., 1983-84, exec. sales mgr. southeast dist., 1984—; sec. bd. dirs. Bur. Wholesale Accessory Reps., Atlanta, 1983-87, Accessories On 6 Atlanta Apparel Mart, 1986-87. Prin. works include Posh Petals, Atlanta, 1986—. Mem. Atlanta Hist. Soc., Young Careers High Mus. Art. Jewish. Home: 1430 Cambridge Common Decatur GA 30033

SOLOMON, JUDITH ANNE, music educator, pianist; b. Nutley, N.J., Apr. 25, 1943; d. Ernest and Rachael (Schecter) S. BA, Rutgers U., 1965; MMus, Yale U., 1968. Assoc. prof. music Tex. Christian U., Ft. Worth, 1968—. Contbr. articles to profl. jours. Instructional devel. grantee, Tex. Christian U., 1975, 87. Mem. Soc. Music Theory, Coll. Music Soc., AAUP, Ft. Worth Music Tchrs. Assn., Pi Kappa Lambda. Office: Texas Christian Univ Fort Worth TX 76129

SOLOMON, PHYLLIS, personnel firm executive; b. N.Y.C., May 9, 1935; d. Herman Aaron and Sylvia (Haymes) Kanarick; m. Harvey Charles Solomon, Feb. 5, 1955 (div. Oct. 1976); children: Deborah, William, David. Sec. Scovill Mfg., Montclair, N.J., 1955-56; co-owner, officer mgr. Bloomfield Glass Co., N.J., 1962-75; office mgr. Am. Service, Inc., Bronx, N.Y., 1975-76, PDI, Englewood Cliffs, N.J., 1976-77; pres., owner V.I.P. Exec. Personnel, Englewood Cliffs, 1977—; founder, chief exec. officer Park Ave. Faces, Inc., 1981—, Phyllis Temps, Inc., Englewood Cliffs, N.J., 1983—; pres., owner V.I.P. Temps IV, Ramsey, N.J., 1987—; pres. V.I.P. Temps V, Clifton, N.Y., 1988—. Pres. Women's Am. Orgn. Rehab. Tng., Verona, N.J., 1960-61; chair No. Valley dist. Boy Scouts Am., SME com. Fellow Healthcare Businesswomen's Assn.; mem. N.J. Assn. Personnel Counsellors (bd. dirs., 3d v.p.), Pharm. Advt. Coun., Englewood Cliffs C. of C., Fort Lee (N.J.) C. of C., Rotary (sec., v.p. Englewood Cliffs chpt.). Jewish. Avocations: golf, tennis, music, reading. Office: VIP Exec Personnel 140 Sylvan Ave Englewood Cliffs NJ 07632

SOLOMON, PHYLLIS LINDA, mental health sciences educator, researcher; b. Hartford, Conn., Dec. 6, 1945; d. Louis Calvin and Annabell Lee (Nitzberg) S. BA in Sociology, Russell Sage Coll., 1968; MA in Sociology, Case Western Res. U., 1970, PhD in Social Welfare, 1978. Lic. social worker, Ohio, Pa. Rsch. assoc. Inst. Urban Studies Cleve. State U., 1970-71; program evaluator Cleve. State Hosp., 1971-74; project dir. Ohio Mental Health and Mental Retardation Rsch. Ctr., Cleve., 1974-75; rsch. assoc. Psychiat. Rsch. Found. of Cleve., 1975; project dir. Ohio Mental Health and Mental Retardation Rsch. Ctr., 1977-78; rsch. assoc. dirs. rsch. and mental health planner Fedn. for Community Planning, 1978-88; prof. dept. mental health scis., dir. sect. mental health svcs. and systems research Hahnemann U., Phila., 1988—; grant reviewer numerous orgns.; cons. in field. Author: (with others) Community Services to Discharged Psychiatric Patients, 1984; co-editor: New Developments in Psychiatric Rehabiliation, 1990; mem. editorial adv. bd. Community Mental Health Jour., 1988—; contbr. articles to profl. jours. Trustee Cleve. Rape Crisis Ctr., 1981-84, CIT Mental Health Svcs., Cleve., 1985-88; mem. citizen's adv. bd. Sagamore Hills (Ohio) Children's Psychiat. Hosp., 1984-88. Named Evaluator of the Yr., Ohio Program Evaluators Group, 1987; recipient Ann. award Cuyahoga County Community Mental Health Bd., 1988. Mem. Internat. Assn. Psycho-social Rehab. Svcs. Jewish. Home: 220 E Mermaid Ln #186 Philadelphia PA 19118 Office: Hahnemann U Dept Mental Health Sci Broad and Vine Sts Philadelphia PA 19102

SOLOMON, RISA GREENBERG, video industry executive; b. N.Y.C., June 22, 1948; d. Nathan and Frances (Guttman) Greenberg; m. Philip Howard Solomon, June 21, 1970; children: Elycia Beth, Cynthia Gayle. BA, NYU, 1969, MA, 1970. Asst. editor Redbook Mag., N.Y.C., 1969-70; assoc. editor Greenwood Press, Westport, Conn., 1970-71; mng. editor Dushkin Pub., Guilford, Conn., 1971-72; free lance editor Yale U. Press, New Haven, 1972-75; v.p. ops. Videoland, Inc., Dallas, 1980-82; v.p. Video Software Dealers Assn., Cherry Hill, N.J. and Dallas, 1981-83; pres. Videodome Enterprises, Dallas, 1983—; cons. Home Recording Rights Coalition, Washington, 1983-84. Contbr. articles to video mags. Bd. dirs. Congregation Anshai Emet, Dallas, 1985-86. Mem. Video Software Dealers Assn. (founder, dir. 1981-82). Democrat. Jewish. Office: Videodome Enterprises 11420 St Michaels Dr Dallas TX 75230

SOLOMON, RUTH, state legislator, teacher; b. Phila., Apr. 16, 1941; d. David and Bella (Azeff) Epstein; m. Arthur Solomon; 1 child, Barry. BA, U. Ariz., 1971. Tchr. Tucson (Ariz.) Unified Sch. Dist., 1971—; mem. Ariz. Legislature; pres. Tucson Edn. Assn., 1983-85; dir. Ariz. Edn. Assn., Phoenix, 1986—. Bd. dirs. Pima County Community Action Agy., Tucson, 1986—, Mayor's Coun. Youth Initiatives, Tucson, 1987—. Mem. Bus. and Profl. Women's Coun., Alpha Delta Kappa, Phi Kappa Phi. Home: 7026 E Kenyon Dr Tucson AZ 85710 Office: Ariz Ho of Reps 1700 W Washington Phoenix AZ 85007

SOLOMON, SUSAN, scientist; b. Chgo., Jan. 19, 1956; d. Leonard Marvin and Alice (Rutman) Solomon; m. Barry Lane Sidwell, Sept. 20, 1988. BS in Chemistry, Ill. Inst. Tech., 1977; MS in Chemistry, U. Calif., Berkeley, 1979, PhD in Chemistry, 1981. Rsch. chemist aeronomy lab. Nat. Oceanic and Atmospheric Administrn, Boulder, Colo., 1981-88, program leader middle atmosphere group aeronomy lab., 1988—; head project sci. Nat. Ozone Expedition, McMurdo Sta., Antarctica, 1986, 1987; adj. faculty U. Colo., 1982—. Co-author: Aeronomy of the Middle Atmosphere, 1984; contbr. articles to sci. jours. Recipient: Gold Medal U.S. Dept. Commerce, 1989. Fellow Royal Meteorological Soc., Am. Geophysical Union (J. B. McElwane award, 1985).

SOLOMON, SUSAN LEE, marketing executive; b. Cin., May 6, 1946; d. Milton Bernard and Ida Pauline (Garber) Spiegel; m. Marshall David Solomon, Sept. 21, 1986; children: Tanya, Mira. BS in Edn., U. Cin., 1968; MED, Boston U., 1973. Pres. Access Telemarket Inc., Andover, Mass. Mem. New Eng. Bus. Owners, Greater Lawrence C. of C., State Office of Women and Minority Businesses. Office: PO Box 363 Andover MA 01810

SOLOMON-RICE, PATTI LYNN, speech pathology director; b. Milw., Sept. 27, 1955; d. Armin Irving and Sylvia (Nashban) S.; m. Gerald William Rice, Apr. 27, 1986; 1 child, Andrew Thomas. BEd in Speech Pathology with honors, U. Wis., 1977; M in Communication Scis. and Disorders, U. Mont., 1980. Lic. speech pathologist, Calif. Staff speech pathologist San Jose (Calif.) Speech and Lang. Clinic, 1981, sr. speech pathologist, 1981-83, supr. clinic, 1984; dir. dept. speech pathology Kentfield (Calif.) Med. Hosp., 1984-86; dir., pvt. practice Belmont, Calif., 1986—; Mem. Task Force on Disabilities, San Mateo County, chmn. recreation com. Mem. Am. Speech Lang. Hearing Assn. (com. mem. 1984—, Continuing Edn. award 1984, 87), Calif. Speech Lang. Hearing Assn. (adv. bd. 1984-86, program chmn. 1986), San Mateo County Speech Lang. Hearing Assn., Santa Clara County Speech Lang. Hearing Assn., Bay Area Group for Adult Communicative Disorders (pres. 1985, chmn. program com. 1986), Profl. Group for Adult Communicative Disorders (sec. 1982), Calif. Speech Pathologists and Audiologists in Pvt. Practice (publicity chair 1989—). Libertarian. Jewish.

SOLORZANO, ROSALIA, sociologist; b. El Paso, Tex., Mar. 18, 1953; d. Isidro and Isaura (Torres) S. BA in Psychology, U. Tex., El Paso, 1977; MA in Sociology, U. Tex., 1979; postgrad., Colegio de Mex., Mexico City, 1983; PhD in Sociology, Mich. State U., 1990. Rsch. assoc. Ctr. for U.S. Mex. Studies, La Jolla, Calif., 1981-83; assoc. dir. Ctr. for Inter-Am. and Border Studies, U. Tex., El Paso, 1983-85; vis. lectr. U. Colo., Boulder, 1985-87; instr. sociology, counselor El Paso Community Coll., 1988—; cons. in field. Author poems and contbg. author chpts. to books. Mem. bd. Chicano Humanities and Arts Coun., Denver, 1986-87. Nat. Minority Doctoral Competitive fellow, 1979-83, Tinker fellow, 1981-83, U. Mich. fellow, 1987, Stanford U. fellow, 1987, S.W. Inst. Rsch. for Women, U. Ariz., 1989. Mem. Assn. for Borderlands Scholars Conf., Western Social Svc. Assn. (site com.), Nat. Assn. Chicano Studies, Mujeres Activas en Letras (steering com. 1989-90, nat. com. coord. 1989-90), Phi Kappa Phi, Sigma Delta Pi (pres. 1975-76). Democrat. Roman Catholic. Office: El Paso Community Coll Women's Ctr El Paso TX 79998

SOLOVEI, MARION, clinical psychologist; b. Marburg, Germany, Dec. 20, 1936; came to U.S., 1964; d. Erwin Isaac and Henni (Walldorf) Hoechster; m. Norman Solovei, Jan. 11, 1959; children: Howard, Robyn. BA, Witwatersrand U., Johannesburg, Republic South Africa, 1958, Calif. State U., Long Beach, 1973; MA, Chapman Coll., 1975; PhD, U.S. Internat. U., 1987. Lic. psychologist, marriage, family and child counselor, Calif. Rsch. officer Franklin Rsch., Johannesburg, 1957-61; contract counselor Family Svc. Long Beach, 1975-80, supr., 1980-82, clin. dir., 1982—; mem. adv. bd. Child Care Ctr., Long Beach City Coll., 1986—. Chmn. Long Beach Community Mental Health Com., 1988—. Mem. Am. Psychol. Assn., Calif. Assn. Marriage and Family Therapists, Long Beach Child Trauma Coun. (pres. 1983-84), Phi Kappa Phi. Jewish. Office: Family Svc Long Beach 5500 Atherton Ste 416 Long Beach CA 90815

SOLTIS, ELIZABETH JEAN, banker; b. Chgo., June 18, 1961; d. Edward and Stanislawa (Chmura) Rogala; m. Philip E. Soltis, June 11, 1983. BS, DePaul U., 1983, MBA, 1988. With Continental Bank, Chgo., 1983—, sr. tng. cons., 1985-87, tng. mgr., 1987—. Mem. Am. Mktg. Assn., Am. Mgmt. Assn., Nat. Assn. Female Execs. Office: Continental Bank 231 S LaSalle Chicago IL 60697

SOLTYS, LOUISE R., fraternal benefit society executive; b. Woonsocket, R.I., Sept. 14, 1954; d. Laurier George and Jeannine Antoinette (Vincelette) Champigny; m. Martin John Soltys, Sept. 4, 1976. Ed., Community Coll. of R.I., Lincoln. Exec. sec., sec. to pres. Union St. Jean Baptiste, Woonsocket, R.I., corp. sec.; bd. dirs., corp. sec. 985 Corp., Woonsocket, R.I., 1988—, Exec. realty Co., 1983—; mem., sec. USJB Bd. Ednl. Assistance, Woonsocket, 1982—, SJB Ednl. Found., 1982—; mem. asst. sec. Associated Intermediaries Ins. Agys., Quincy, Mass., 1988—. Pres. New England Fraternal Congress, 1987-88, NFCA pub. rels. com. Nat. Fraternal Congress Am., Chgo., 1985-86; sec. Franco-Am. Hist. Soc., 1984-87; participant Nat. Alliance Bus. Career Exploration Program, Providence, 1980; mem. Mardi Gras com. Woonsocket Centennial Celebration, 1987-88; bd. dirs. NFCA Sec's. Sect., Chgo., 1986-87. Mem. Franco Am. Women's Fedn. (bd. dirs.), Club Richelieu, Ladies Woonsocket Richelieu Club (pres. 1989-90, Richelieu of Yr. 1986-87), Phi Theta Kappa.

SOLVANG, PAMELA JEAN, broadcast marketing executive, marketing consultant; b. Bellingham, Wash., Nov. 14, 1956; d. Merlin Nils and Phyllis Ann (Wynne) S. Student Clark Coll., Vancouver, Wash., 1975-77, Seattle U., 1977; B.A. in Communications, U. Portland, 1979. Copywriter Sugden-Freeman Advt., Portland, Oreg., 1979; writer, producer Ryan Advt., Portland, 1979-83; mktg. dir. KGON-KSGO Radio, Portland, 1983-85; corp. broadcast mktg. dir. Ackerley Communications, 1985-89; dir. mktg. London Broadcast Co., 1989-90; dir. mgtg. Ackerley Commuications, 1990—; video writer/producer Nat. Salon Edn. Tapes, KMS Shampoos and Research Labs., Bella Vista, Calif., 1985; writer, producer TV spl. Rose City Rock Awards, 1984, 85. Recipient Nat. Telly award Nat. Assn. TV Commls., 1982, 83, 86, 87, 88, 89. Mem. Broadcast Promotion/Mktg. Execs. (outdoor advt. gold medallion awards 1985, 86, 87, 88, 89; Audience Promotion gold medallion award 1987, 88; Print Advt. Gold medallion award 1988, Sales Promotion Gold medallion award 1990), Portland Advt. Fedn. Excellence award, Sales brochure, 1986, Nat. Assn. Broadcasters (recipient Best of the Best award in Sales Promotion, 1989). Avocations: traveling; snow skiing; scuba diving, golf. Home: care PO Box 255 Ferndale WA 98248

SOMA, ROSE SMERALDI, broadcaster, writer, women's rights activist, television and radio producer; b. Bronx, N.Y., Feb. 17, 1940; d. Albert and Jeanette (DiCostanzo) Smeraldi; attended NYC public schs. until 1955; m. Fraser Soma, Sept. 13, 1967; children: Michael, Carl, Paul, Steven, Nancy, Errol. Producer, interviewer, reporter WALK radio, L.I., N.Y., 1976—, producer weekly feminist radio program, 1976—; lectr., condr. workshops on women's rights; media public relations cons. feminist issues for radio and TV, 1978. Author: (survey questionnaire) Women Speak Out, 1990. Chmn. reprodn./abortion rights task force Suffolk (N.Y.) chpt. NOW, 1975—, chmn. media task force, 1975—; producer/host Women Speak Out and People Speak Out, Brookhaven Cable TV, Port Jefferson Sta., N.Y., 1979—, Women Speak Out, Sta. WYFA, Medford, N.Y., 1979—, Suffolk Cablevision, 1979—, Sta. WBLI-FM, 1980—; media coordinator, personal mgr. entertainment acts, 1981—; bd. dirs. Planned Parenthood of East Suffolk, 1977—; coordinator L.I. chpt. Nat. Coalition to Defend the Bill of Rights, 1978—; coordinator public relations and media for L.I. chpt. Internat. Women's Yr. Meeting for N.Y. State, 1977; exec. dir., co-founder Americans United to Save Legal Abortion, 1977—; founder Women Speak Out Internat., 1978; adv. bd. Women's Health Alliance L.I., 1978; chmn. abortion rights task force N.Y. State orgn. NOW, 1978; coordinator L.I. Coalition for Reproductive Rights; asso. Women's Inst. for Freedom of Press, 1976—. Mem. Am. Women in Radio and TV, Nat. Fedn. Press Women. Author: Women Speak Out About Abortion, 1978; contbr. numerous articles to profl. jours.; author monthly column for NOW newsletter, 1974—; editorial asst. and AdViews mag.; editorial asst. AdViews mag.; video editor, features editor Good Times mag. Home: PO Box AW Miller Place NY 11764 Office: UACC Brookhaven Cable TV Industrial Rd Port Jefferson Station NY 11776 also: Sta WBLI 106 FM Long Island NY 11763 also: AdViews Mag PO Box 268 Greenville NY 11548

SOMERS, ANNE RAMSAY, educator; b. Memphis, Sept. 9, 1913; d. Henry Ashton and Amanda Vick (Woolfolk) Ramsey; m. Herman Miles Somers, Aug. 31, 1947; children: Sara Ramsay, Margaret Ramsay. BA, Vassar Coll., 1935; postgrad., U. N.C., 1939-40; DSc (hon.), Med. Coll. Wis., 1975. Ednl. dir. Internat. Ladies Garment Workers Union, 1937-42; labor economist U.S. Dept. Labor, 1943-46; rsch. assoc. Haverford Coll., 1957-63; rsch. assoc. indsl. rels. sect. Princeton U., 1964-84; prof. U. Medicine and Dentistry of N.J.-R. Wood Johnson Med. Sch. (formerly Rutgers Med. Sch.), 1971-84, adj. prof., 1984—; adj. prof. geriatric medicine U. Pa. Sch. Medicine, 1990—; vice chmn., mem. adv. coun. Edn. for Health, 1978—; mem. Nat. Bd. Examiners, 1983-86; cons. in health econs., health edn., geriatrics, gerontology, related areas. Author: Hospital Regulation: The Dilemma of Public Policy, 1969, Health Care in Transition: Directions for the Future, 1971, (with H.M. Somers) Workmen's Compensation: The Prevention, Rehabilitation and Financing of Occupational Disability, 1954, Medicare and the Hospitals, 1967, Doctors, Patients and Health Insurance, 1961, Health and Health Care: Policies in Perspective, 1977; editor: (with D.R. Fabian) The Geriatric Imperative: An Introduction to Gerontology and Clinical Geriatrics, 1981. Mem. bd. visitors. Duke U. Med. Ctr., 1972-77, U. Tex. Health Scis. Ctr., Houston, 1980-86. Recipient Elizur Wright award Am. Risk and Ins. Assn. 1962. Fellow Am. Coll. Hosp. Adminstrs. (hon.), Coll. Physicians Phila. (hon.); mem. Inst. Medicine of Nat. Acad. Scis., Am. Pub. Health Assn., N.J. Hosp. Assn., Soc. Tchrs. Family Medicine (hon.). Home: 3300 Darby Rd Apt #3112 Haverford PA 19041-1095

SOMERS, MARION, gerontologist, retirement specialist; b. N.Y.C.; d. John Joseph and Lottie (Kramer) Strahl; m. John Cameron Somers; children: Lynne Caryl, Randy Mass, Craig Caryl; stepchildren: Carolyn Somers, Gail Sun, Matthew Somers. BA, CUNY, 1976; MS, Lehman Coll., 1980; PhD, The Fielding Inst., 1988. Activities dir. Wartburg Luth. Nursing Home, N.Y.C., 1980-82; prof. Lehman Coll., N.Y.C., 1982-84; pres. Marion Somers, Assoc., N.Y.C., 1985—; chief recreation therapist Kingsbrook Jewish Med. Ctr. and Rutland Nursing Home, 1989—; grant reader HHS, Washington, 1980—; observer White House Conf. on Aging, 1982; bd. dirs. Sr. Action in Gray Environ., 1980-84. Author: Viewers Guide for ABC-TV prodn. of The Shell Seekers, The Home. Advisor Sen. A. D'Amato, N.Y., 1981-82. Recipient Profl. award Met. Recreation & Pk. Soc., N.Y.C., 1985. Mem. Gerontol. Soc. Am., Nat. Coun. on Aging, Nat. Recreation and Pk. Assn. (Presdl. award 1984), N.Y. State Therapeutic Recreation Soc. (chair 1983-84, pres. 1984-85), Am. Therapeutic Recreation Soc., Nat. Assn. Retirement Profls., Internat. Soc. Retirement Planning.

SOMERVILLE, ROSEMARY ELAINE, nurse; b. Indpls., Jan. 20, 1955; d. Earnest H. and Leta Bernice (Biggs) Ellett; m. Scotty Nathan Bruer, Feb. 14, 1974 (div. 1976); m. James Michael Somerville, July 30, 1982. BS, Ind. Sch. Nursing, 1980. RN, Ind. Staff nurse CCU Wishard Meml. Hosp., Indpls., 1980-81; staff relief ICU, nurse CCU RN Registry of Pvt. Duty Nurses, Indpls., 1981-88; staff relief ICU, nurseCCU Norrell Health Care, Indpls., 1988—. Mem. Sigma Pi Alpha, Sigma Theta Tau. Home: 8433 S Sherman Dr Indianapolis IN 46237

SOMMER, VILMA EVELYN, electro-mechanical designer; b. N.Y.C., Sept. 1, 1933; d. Hermann August and Alwine (Becker) Schwarz; m. Gerald Arthur Sommer, Sept. 2, 1961; children: Robert, Caroline, Eric Arthur. BA, Hunter Coll., 1954; AAS, Suffolk County Community Coll., 1981. Art educator Lindenhurst (N.Y.) Pub. Schs., 1954-62; jr. drafter Coherent Communications Corp., Hauppauge, N.Y., 1982-85; designer, checker Chyron Corp., Melville, N.Y., 1985—. Mem. AAUW, Women in Electronics. Home: 6 Autumn Ct East Patchogue NY 11772

SOMMERS, ESTELLE JOAN, retail executive; b. Balt.; d. David Isaac and Mary Agnes (Curland) Goldstein; grad. high sch.; m. Ben Sommers, Dec. 2, 1962 (dec. Apr. 30, 1985); children: Gayle Joan, Cathy Harriet, Debbie Jane. Stylist, owner Loshins, Cin., 1948-62; mgr., owner Capezio Fashion Shop., N.Y.C., 1964-79; stylist, owner Estar Ltd., N.Y.C., 1969-79; head adminstr., joint owner Capezio Dance-Theatre Shops, N.Y.C., Boston, Chgo., Hollywood, 1970—. U.S. chmn. Dance Library of Israel, 1979—; bd. dirs. Dance Notation Bd., 1980—; bd. dirs. Am.-Israel Cultural Found., 1979-82, The Ctr. for Dance Medicine, 1983—; co-chmn. nat. adv. com. Internat Ballet Competition U.S.A., 1979—; acting pres. Internat. Dance Alliance, 1985—; bd. dirs. New Dance Group, 1985-86, New Dance Studios, 1985—, The Yard, 1986—; mem. Jacob's Pillow Bd. Overseers, 1988—, mem. artistic adv. com. Internat. Conf. Jews and Judaism in Dance, 1986; mem. nat. adv. bd. Career Transitions for Dancers, 1988—, adv. bd. Harkness Ctr. for Dance Injuries, 1989—. Recipient Peridance Annual award Peridance Dance Co., 1987.

SOMMERS, SHARI CATHERINE, management executive; b. Danville, Ill., July 31, 1950; d. Warren Albert and Shari Bernard (Hill) S.; m. Robert Wightman, Apr. 21, 1990; 1 child, Shane Anthony. BA in Polit. Sci. with distinction, U. Ill at Chgo., 1980; cert. legal asst., Roosevelt U., Chgo., 1980. Mgr., legal support AMOCO Corp., Chgo., 1981-86; legal asst. supr. Skadden, Arps, Slate, Meagher & Flom, Chgo., 1986-88; v.p., gen. mgr. Templeton & Assocs., Chgo., 1989—; mem. adv. bd. dirs. Roosevelt U. Lawyer's Asst. Program, 1985-88. Participant Conclave of Legal Assns., Baton Rouge, 1988. Mem. ABA, Ill. Paralegal Assn. Legal Asst. Mgmt. Assn. (v.p. Cen. region 1986, sec. 1987, adminstrv. v.p. 1988, bd. dirs. 1986-88). Republican. Roman Catholic. Office: Templeton & Assocs 333 W Wacker Dr Ste 700 Chicago IL 60606

SOMMERVILLE-O'BRIEN, EDITH LYNN, aerospace electrical engineer; b. Beverly Hills, Calif., Apr. 18, 1958; d. Harry Eugene and Mary Edith (Landman) Sommerville; m. William R. O'Brien Jr., June 23, 1984. BSEE, Pacific Coll., 1981. Jr. elec. specialist Grumman Aerospace, Point Mugu Nas, Calif., 1979-80, sr. elec. specialist, 1980-81; tech. writer, editor quality assurance Stanwick Corp., Ventura, Calif., 1980; test ops. engr. Martin Marietta Corp., Vanderberg AFB, Calif., 1981-83, integrated flight safety engr., 1984-85; group leader software safety engrs. Rockwell Internat., Vanderberg AFB, 1983; flight test engr. Gen. Dynamics/Convair, San Diego, 1983-84; night supr. field and project engring. All Systems, Inc. div. Eaton Corp., Edwards AFB, Calif., 1985—. Served with USAF, 1977-79. Fellow AAAS; mem. Nat. Assn. for Female Execs., Air Force Sgts. Assn. (life). Republican. Methodist. Home: 1608 W Lemon Pl Lompoc CA 93436

SOMMER-YEAGER, LINDA DIANNE, health science facility executive; b. Bklyn., Aug. 24, 1951; d. David and Blossom (Furman) Eskenazi; m. Marc Dennis Sommer, June 3, 1973 (div. 1974); m. Joseph Cornelius Yeager, Sept. 1, 1983; children: Joseph Benjamin, Rachel Leigh, Jeremiah David. BA in Edn. magna cum laude, Queens Coll., 1972; MS in Edn., Bklyn. Coll., 1976. Cert. neuro-linguistic programmer trainer. Tchr. N.Y.C Pub. Schs., Bklyn., 1973-82; pres. Eastern NLP Inst., Newtown, Pa., 1982—, also bd. dirs.; pres. CommTech Group, Inc.; bd. dirs. Reflections Unltd., N.Y.C., S.Am. Inst. of NLP, Buenos Aires; motivational and keynote speaker Fortune 500 cos. Author: (with others) Power of Persuasion, Teen Power, 1987. Trainer teenage scholarship program, Princeton, N.J., 1985—; vol. neurolinguistic programming trainer PTA, Bucks County, Pa., 1985—, Big Sisters Am., Bucks County, 1986. Fellow Soc. Neurolinguistic Programming (bd. dirs.); mem. Am. Soc. Tng. and Devel., Nat. Assn. Women Execs. Office: Eastern NLP Inst PO Box 697 Newtown PA 18940

SONCHIK, SUSAN MARIE, analytical chemist; b. Maple Heights, Ohio, Mar. 10, 1954; d. Stephen Robert and Gloria Ann (Hach) S. BS in Chemistry magna cum laude, John Carroll U., 1975; MS in Analytical Chemistry, Case Western Res. U., 1978, PhD in Phys. Chemistry, 1980. Asst. chemist Horizons Research Inc., Beachwood, Ohio, 1974-75; chemist specialist Standard Oil of Ohio, Warrensville Heights, Ohio, 1975-79; organic chemistry br. mgr. Versar, Inc., Springfield, Va., 1980-83; mgr. gas chromatography program IBM Instruments Inc., Danbury, Conn., 1983-87, radiation safety officer, 1985-87; expert witness, cons. Martin, Craig, Chester & Sonnenschein, Chgo., 1981-83; adv. engr. in advanced lithography IBM Corp., Essex Junction, Vt., 1987—; speaker in field. Author: African Walking Safari, 1985; editorial adv. bd. Jour. Chromatographic Sci., 1977—, guest editor, 1987. Mem. Danbury Conservation Commn., 1986-87, tchr. and tutor chemistry, 1987-89; troop leader Lake Erie coun. Girl Scouts U.S., 1972-80, Southeastern Conn. coun., 1983-87; leader Explorer Post, Greater Cleve. coun. Boy Scouts Am., 1977-78; managerial adviser Jr. Achievement, Warrensville Heights, Ohio, 1977-78; state sci. fair judge, 1977, 80, 81, 89, 90; asst. leader Internat. Folk Dancers, Newtown, Conn., 1985-87.town, Conn., 1985-87; religion tchr., 1981-84, 87-90. Recipient Overall Best Paper award Eastern Analytical Symposium, 1984, First Gas Chromatograph award IBM Instruments Inc., 1985, contbn. award (tech. paper) 10th Internat. Congress of Essential Oils, Flavors, Fragrances, Washington, 1986. Mem. ASTM (exec. com. E-19 1985—, subcom. chmn. 1989—), Am. Chem. Soc. (chmn. membership com. Green Mountain sect. 1988-90, chair elect Green Mountain sect. 1989-90, chmn. 1990—), Wilderness Soc., Nature Conservancy, No. Vt. Canoe Cruisers (treas. 1990—), Amnesty Internat., Green Mountain Club, Iota Sigma Pi (pres. N.E. Ohio chpt. 1978-79). Roman Catholic. Home: 14 Forest Rd Essex Junction VT 05452-3818 Office: IBM Corp Gen Tech Div Dept G40 Bldg 967-1 Essex Junction VT 05452

SONDERBY, SUSAN PIERSON, federal judge; b. Chgo., May 15, 1947; d. George W. and Shirley L. (Eckstrom) Pierson; m. James A. De Witt, June 14, 1975 (dec. 1978); m. Peter R. Sonderby, Apr. 7, 1990. AA, Joliet (Ill.) Jr. Coll., 1967; BA, U. Ill., 1969; JD, John Marshall Law Sch., 1973. Bar: Ill. 1973, U.S. Dist. Ct. (cen. and so. dists.) Ill. 1978, U.S. Dist. Ct. (no. dist.) Ill. 1984, U.S. Ct. Appeals (7th Cir.) 1984. Assoc. O'Brien, Garrison, Berard, Kusta and De Witt, Joliet, 1973-75, ptnr., 1975-77; asst. atty. gen. consumer protection div., litigation sect. Office of the Atty. Gen., Chgo., 1977-78; asst. atty. gen., chief consumer protection div. Office of the Atty. Gen., Springfield, Ill., 1978-83; U.S. trustee for no. dist. Ill. Chgo., 1983-86; judge U.S. Bankruptcy Ct. (no. dist.) Ill., Chgo., 1986—; adj. faculty De Paul U. Coll. Law, Chgo., 1986; spl. asst. atty. gen. 1972-78; mem. U.S. Trustee adv. com., consumer adv. council Fed. Reserve Bd., Sec. of State Fraudulent I.D. com., Dept. of Ins. Task Force on Improper Claims Practices. Mem. Fourth Presbyn. Ch., Westminster Presbyn. Ch., Art Inst. Chgo., Chgo. Coun. of Fgn. Rels.; bd. dirs. Land of Lincoln coun. Girl Scouts U.S.; mem. individual guarantors com. Goodman Theatre, Chgo.; chmn. clubs and orgns. Sangamon County United Way Capital Campaign; bd. dirs., chmn. house rules com. and legal subcom. Lake Point Towers; mem. Family Svc. Ctr., Aid to Retarded Citizens, Henson Robinson Zoo. Mem. Law Club of Chgo., Legal Club of Chgo. (hon.), Nat. Conf. of Bankruptcy Judges (legis. outreach com.), Am. Bankruptcy Inst., Comml. Law League Am. (exec. coun. bankruptcy and insolvency sect., bankruptcy com., vice chmn. U.S. Trustee Rev. com., edn. com.), John Marshall Law Sch. Alumni Assn. (bd. dirs., 2nd v.p., 1st v.p., chmn. Luncheon Series, chmn. Disting. Svc. Awards com., exec. com. Long-range Planning com., others), Zonta Club of the Chgo. Waterfront (charter), Union League Club (judicial privileges). Republican. Office: US Bankruptcy Ct 219 S Dearborn St #1650 Chicago IL 60604

SONDOCK, RUBY KLESS, former judge; b. Houston, Apr. 26, 1926; d. Herman Lewis and Celia (Juran) Kless; m. Melvin Adolph Sondock, Apr. 22, 1944; children: Marcia Cohen, Sandra Marcus. AA, Cottey Coll., Nevada, Mo., 1944; BS, U. Houston, 1959, LLB, 1961. Bar: Tex. 1961, U.S. Supreme Ct. 1977. Pvt. practice, Houston, 1961-73; judge Harris County Ct. Domestic Rels. (312th Dist.), 1973-77, 234th Jud. Dist. Ct., Houston, 1977-82, 83-89; justice Tex. Supreme Ct., Austin, 1982; of counsel Weil Gotshal and Manges, 1989—. Mem. ABA, Tex. Bar Assn., Houston Bar Assn., Houston Assn. Women Lawyers, Order of Barons, Phi Theta Phi, Kappa Beta Pi, Phi Kappa Phi, Alpha Epsilon Pi. Jewish. Office: Weil Gotshal & Manges 700 Louisiana Ste 1600 Houston TX 77002

SONGER, FRANCES VIRGINIA, marketing executive, consultant, public speaker; b. Atlanta, Feb. 13, 1957; d. Francis Harold and Lois Irene (Stringer) S. B.A. in Exptl. Psychology magna cum laude with honors, Ga. State U., 1982. Mgr., stores asst. Pepperidge Farm, Atlanta, 1976-82; mgr. S&A Corp., Atlanta, 1982-83; food and beverage asst. mgr., dir. meetings and banquets, sales dir., dir. mktg. Guest Quarters, Atlanta/Charlotte, 1983-87; hypnotherapist Hypnosis Motivation Inst., Atlanta, 1984-86; handwriting analyst, Atlanta, 1985-86; mktg. and image cons., public speaker Total Mind Cons., Charlotte, N.C., 1987-89; v.p. P.K.G.'s-Charlotte, N.C., 1988—. Mem. NAFE, Blue Key, Psi Chi, Phi Kappa Phi. Republican. Avocations: photography, racquetball, gardening. Home: 6120 Old Providence Ln Charlotte NC 28226 Office: 1534 East Blvd Charlotte NC 28203

SONG ONG, ROXANNE KAY, lawyer, judge; b. Phoenix, Apr. 24, 1953; d. Joe Henry and Sue (Tang) Song; m. Richard H. Ong, Nov. 25, 1978; children: Jocelyn, Bradley. BA, Ariz. State U., 1975; JD, U. Ariz., 1978. Bar: Ariz. 1979, U.S. Dist. Ct. Ariz. 1979, U.S. Ct. Appeals (9th cir.) 1986. Pvt. practice Phoenix, 1979, 85—; asst. city prosecutor Phoenix City Prosecutor's Office, 1979-82; asst. city prosecutor, asst. city atty. Scottsdale (Ariz.) City Atty.'s Office, 1982-85; pro tempore judge Scottsdale City Ct., 1986-89, assoc. judge, 1989—. Mem. community adv. bd. Sta. KAET-TV, Phoenix; mem. First Chinese Bapt. Ch.; mem. exec. bd. Ariz. So. Baptist Conv.; co-leader Arizona Cactus Pine Girl Scout/Brownie Troop; mem. parent adv. bd. YMCA, Paradise Valley/Scottsdale, Ariz. Named one of Outstanding Young Women of Am., 1988-89. Mem. ABA, Am. Judges Assn., Nat. Assn. Women Judges, Ariz. Magistrates Assn., Ariz. Cts. Assn., Maricopa County Bar Assn., Christian Legal Soc., Ariz. Women Lawyer's Assn., Outstanding Young Women Am., U. Ariz. Law Coll. Assn., Phi Delta Phi, Phi Kappa Phi, Alpha Lambda Delta, Kappa Delta Phi, Pi Lambda Theta. Republican. Office: Scottsdale City Ct 3739 N Civic Center Blvd Scottsdale AZ 85251 also: Scottsdale City Ct 3739 N Civic Ctr Blvd Scottsdale AZ 85251

SONGSIRIDEJ, VANEE, physician; b. Bangkok, Thailand, Feb. 21, 1949; Came to US 1977; d. Songsakdi and Mayuree (Wasantachat) S. MD, Siriraj Med. Sch Mahidol U., Bangkok, 1974. Residency in internal medicine St. Joseph Hosp. Affil. with Northwestern U., Chgo., Ill., 1977-80; fellow in allergy and clinical immunology U. Wis., Madison, 1980-82; allergist internist Gundersen Clinic, La Crosse, Wis., 1982—. Fellow Am. Coll. Chest Physicians; mem. Am. Lung Assn. Wis. (bd. dirs. 1989—), AMA, ACP, Am. Acad. Allergy and Clin. Immunology, Wis. Med. Soc., Wis. Allergy Soc., La Crosse County Med. Soc. Office: Gundersen Clinic 1836 S Ave La Crosse WI 54601

SONI, KUSUM KAPILA, mathematician, mathematics educator; b. Punjab, India, Nov. 14, 1930; came to U.S., 1959; d. Piare Lal and Sushila Devi (Bajaj) Kapila; m. Raj Pal Soni, Apr. 5, 1958; children: Poonam, Sushma. BA with honors, Punjab U., 1949, MA in Math., 1951; PhD, Oreg. State U., 1964. Lectr. Govt. Colls., Punjab, 1952-59; tchr. asst. Oreg. State U., Corvallis, 1959-64; asst. prof. math. U. Tenn., Knoxville, 1967-70, assoc. prof. math., 1970-83, prof. math., 1983—; vis. asst. prof. Oreg. State U., 1966-67; vis. prof. dept. applied math. Ctr. for Math. and Computer Sci., Amsterdam, 1987, Indian Inst. Sci., Bangalore, India, 1987; vis. mem. U. Dundee (Scotland), 1982; summer mem. Inst. for Advanced Study, Princeton, N.J., 1979; speaker Internat. Symposium, Winnipeg, Can., 1989. Contbr. approximately 40 rsch. articles to profl. jours. Recipient Women of Achievement Rsch. award, U. Tenn., 1983, rsch. and travel grants, 1969, 70, 80, 89. Mem. Am. Math. Soc., Math. Assn. of Am., Sigma Xi. Office: Dept Math/Univ Tenn Knoxville TN 37996-1300

SONKIN, MICHELLE ANNE EISEMANN, publisher; b. N.Y.C., Aug. 12, 1952; d. Ralph and Beatrice (Sichel) Eisemann; m. Richard Sonkin, May 30, 1976; 1 child, Lauren Sydney. BA in Psychology, Journalism, Syracuse U., 1974. Corp. dir. recruitment advt. Crain Communications, N.Y.C., 1974-75; pres. Eisemann & Assocs., N.Y.C., 1975-76; advt. dir. Fairchild Publs., N.Y.C., 1976-85; v.p., pub. Ave. Mag. Inc., N.Y.C., 1985—. Office: Avenue Mag Inc 145 E 57 St New York NY 10022

SONNENBERG, RONNIE, psychiatric social worker; b. N.Y.C., May 11, 1956; d. Leonard Jay and Eleanor (Green) S.; m. Paul Bernard Edelman, Oct. 5, 1985; 1 child, Jason Leigh. BA in Psychology, U. Mich., 1976; MSW, Ohio State U., 1979. Cert. social worker, N.Y. Child welfare worker Franklin County Children Svcs., Columbus, Ohio, 1979-82; pub. liaison, therapist Hauppauge (N.Y.) Consultation Ctr., 1982-85; therapist Smithtown (N.Y.) Psychol. Assocs., 1985-89; pvt. practice therapist Commack, N.Y., 1989—. Mem. Nat. Assn. Social Workers, B'nai B'rith. Democrat. Jewish. Office: 368 Veterans Memorial Hwy Commack NY 11725

SONNENFELD, JANET MARLOFF, lawyer; b. Long Branch, N.J., Feb. 9, 1948; d. Raymond James and Muriel (Goodkin) Marloff; B.A., George Washington U., 1970; J.D. cum laude, Howard U., 1973; m. Marc J. Sonnenfeld, Apr. 27, 1975. Bar: Pa. 1973, U.S. Dist. Ct. (ea. dist.) Pa. 1974, U.S. Ct. Appeals (3d cir.), 1975, U.S. Bankruptcy Ct. (ea. dist.) Pa. 1979, U.S. Supreme Ct., 1981. Assoc. firm Drinker Biddle & Reath, Phila., 1973-76; assoc. counsel consumer banking Fidelity Bank, Phila., 1976-77; sole practice, Phila., 1977-87; ptnr. Blackburn, Sonnenfield, Michelman & Tydall, Phila., 1988; pvt. practice law, 1988—; instr. Inst. Paralegal Tng., Phila., nat. seminars, 1983—; panelist Pa. Bar Inst., mem., panelist Ea. Dist. Pa. Bankruptcy Conf., 1988—. Author publs. in field. Committeewoman, Democratic Com., 1974-76, 78-82, mem. policy com., 1978—. Mem. Pa. Bar Assn. (com. on alcohol and drug abuse 1979—). Home: Wanamaker House 2020 Walnut St Philadelphia PA 19103 Office: Two Mellon Bank Ctr Ste 2000 Philadelphia PA 19102

SONNINO, ROBERTA ELENA, pediatric surgeon; b. N.Y.C., Aug. 14, 1952; d. Giorgio Guido and Sandra (Oreffice) S. BS, U. Mich., 1973; MD, U. Padova, Verona, Italy, 1979. Diplomate Am. Bd. Surgery. Surg. resident U. Minn., Mpls., 1980-82, Henry Ford Hosp., Detroit, 1982-86; rsch. assoc. Columbus (Ohio) Children's Hosp., 1986-87; fellow pediatric surgery Montreal (Que.) Children's Hosp., 1987-89; asst. prof. pediatric surgery Case Western Res. U., Cleve., 1989—; attending pediatric surgeon Rainbow Babies and Children's Hosp., Cleve., 1989—; prin. investigator Case Western Res. U., Cleve., 1989—. Contbr. articles to profl. jours. Rsch. grantee Henry Ford Hosp., Detroit, 1983, Case Western Res. U., Cleve., 1989-90. Fellow Am. Acad. Pediatrics (surg. com. Ohio chpt. 1990); mem. AMA, Assn. Acad. Surgery, Acad. Surg. Rsch., No. Ohio Pediatric Soc., Cleve. Acad. Medicine. Democrat. Jewish. Home: 22626 Rye Rd Shaker Heights OH 44122 Office: Rainbow Babies & Children 2101 Adelbert Rd Cleveland OH 44106

SONS, LINDA RUTH, mathematics educator; b. Chicago Heights, Ill., Oct. 31, 1939; d. Robert and Ruth (Diekelman) S. AB in Math., Ind. U., 1961; MS in Math., Cornell U., 1963, PhD in Math., 1966. Teaching asst. Cornell U., Ithaca, N.Y., 1961-63, instr. in maths., summer 1963, rsch. asst., 1963-65; asst. prof. maths. No. Ill. U., De Kalb, 1965-70, assoc. prof. maths., 1970-78, prof. maths., 1978—; vis. assoc. prof. U. London, 1970-71; dir. undergrad. studies math. dept. No. Ill. U., 1971-77, exec. sec. univ. coun., 1978-79; chair faculty fund No. Ill. U. Found., De Kalb, 1982—. Author: (with others) A Study Guide for Introduction to Mathematics, 1976, Mathematical Thinking in a Quantitative World, 1990; contbr. articles to profl. jours. Mem. campus ministry com. No. Ill. Dist. Luth. Ch./Mo. Synod, Hillside, 1977—; mem. ch. coun. Immanuel Luth. Ch., De Kalb, 1978-85, 87-89; pres. Luth. Women's Missionary League, 1974-87; bd. dirs., treas. De Kalb County Migrant Ministry, 1967-78. NSF Rsch. grantee, 1970-72, 74-75. Mem. Am. Math. Soc., Assn. for Women in Maths., Math. Assn. Am. (nat. bd. govs. 1989—), Ill. Math. Assn. (v.p. sect., pres. elect, pres., past pres. 1982-87, bd. dirs. 1989—), London Math. Soc., Phi Beta Kappa (pres. No. Ill. club 1981-85), Sigma Xi (chpt. pres. elect, pres., past pres. 1973-76). Office: No Ill U Math Scis Dept De Kalb IL 60115

SONTAG, SUSAN, author, film director. Author: (novels) The Benefactor, 1963, Death Kit, 1967, (stories) I, etcetera, 1978, (essays) Against Interpretation, 1966, Styles of Radical Will, 1969, On Photography, 1977, Illness as Metaphor, 1978, Under the Sign of Saturn, 1980, AIDS and Its Metaphors, 1989, (anthology) A Susan Sontag Reader, 1982, (film scripts) Duet for Cannibals, 1970, Brother Carl, 1974; editor, author introduction Antonin Artaud: Selected Writings, 1976, A Barthes Reader, 1982; dir.: (films) Duet for Cannibals, 1969, Brother Carl, 1971, Promised Lands, 1974, Unguided Tour, 1983. Guggenheim fellow, 1966, 75; Rockefeller Found. fellow, 1965, 74; recipient Ingram Merrill Found. award in lit. in field of Am. Letters, 1976; Creative Arts award Brandeis U., 1976; prize Nat. Book Critics Circle, 1978; named Officier de l'Ordre des Arts et des Lettres, France, 1984. Mem. Am. Acad. Inst. Arts and Letters (recipient Arts and Letters award 1976), PEN (pres. Am. Ctr. 1987-89). Office: Am Ctr PEN 568 Broadway New York NY 10012

SOOHOO, KAREN, pediatrician; b. L.A., Apr. 13, 1960; d. Don and Irene Soohoo; m. Stephen Monwei Chang, May 2, 1987. BA, Harvard U., 1981; MD, Baylor Coll. Medicine, 1987. Intern Children's Hosp. Nat. Med. Ctr., Washington, 1987-88; resident in pediatrics Cedars-Sinai Med. Ctr., L.A., 1988-90; pediatrician Sharp-Rees-Stealy Med. Group, San Diego, 1990—. Mem. AMA, Am. Acad. Pediatrics. Democrat. Home: 9838 Via Caceres San Diego CA 92129

SORDYL, LENORE MAUREEN, sales executive; b. Stutgart, Fed. Republic of Germany, Apr. 12, 1958; came to U.S., 1958; d. Ralph Aloysius and Jane Frances (Redel) S. BS, Ill. State U., 1979; MA, Roosevelt U., Chgo., 1983; tech. cert., Internat. Travel Tng. Sch., 1986. Registered music therapist. Keyboard instr. House of Music, Springfield, Ill., 1971-79; intern Ill. State Psychiat. Inst., Chgo., 1979-80; registered music therapist Northwest Community Hosp., Arlington Heights, Ill., 1980-81; pvt. practice Chgo., 1981-86; with reservations dept. Hilton Hotel Corp., Carrollton, Tex., 1990—; with sales and mktg. dept. Zig Ziglar Corp., Dallas, 1986—; profl. musician Springfield Symphony, 1973-75, Decatur (Ill.) Symphony, 1974-79, Galesburg (Ill.) Symphony, 1978-79. Music scholar Springfield Symphony, 1975. Mem. Internat. Assn. Music Therapists (editor quarterly newsletter 1984-86). Roman Catholic. Office: Zig Ziglar Corp 3330 Earhart Carrollton TX 75006

SOREL, CLAUDETTE MARGUERITE, pianist; b. Paris; d. Michel M. and Elizabeth S. Grad. with top honors, Juilliard Sch. Music, 1947, postgrad., 1948; student of, Sigismund Stojowski, Sari Biro, Olga Samaroff Stokowski, Mieczyslaw Horszowski, Rudolf Serkin; ensemble with, Felix Salmond; musicology with, Dr. Robert Tangeman; music history with, Marian Bauer; grad., Curtis Inst. Music, 1953; B.S. cum laude in Math., Columbia U., 1954. music faculty, vis. prof. Kans. U., 1961-62; assoc. prof. music Ohio State U., 1962-64; prof. music, head piano dept. SUNY Fredonia, 1964—, Disting. Univ. prof., 1969—, univ. artist, 1969—, faculty exchange scholar, 1976—; mem. internat. jury Van Cliburn Internat. Piano Competition, Tex., 1966, Que. and Ont. Music Festivals, 1967, 75; chmn. music panel Presdl. Scholars in Arts Program, 1979—; juror numerous nat. and internat. music competition; cons. Ednl. Testing Service, Princeton. Author: Compendium of Piano Technique, 1970, 2d edit., 1987, Japanese edit., 1987, Mind Your Musical Manners - Off and On Stage, 1972, 2d edit., 1975, The 24 Magic Keys, 3 vols, 1974, The Three Nocturnes of Rachmaninoff, 1974, 2d edit., 1975, 3d edit. with cassette in compact disc, 1988, Fifteen Smorgasbord Studies for the Piano, 1975, Arensky Piano Etudes, 1976; spl. editor: Music Insider; painter of oil portraits; contbr. articles to profl. mags.; Compiler: The Modern Music of Today, 1947, Serge Prokofieff - His Life and Works, 1947, The Ornamentations in Mozart's Music, 1948; Debut at, Town Hall, N.Y.C., 1943; since appeared in, leading cities of U.S., performed with, N.Y. Philharmonic, London Philharmonic, Zurich, Boston, San Antonio, Milw., NBC, Phila., New Orleans and Cin. symphony orchs., Youth Orch. of Am., 200 others; appeared at, Aspen, Berkshire, Chautauqua, other festivals, European concert tours, 1956, 57, 58, to, Eng., Sweden, Holland, Germany, Switzerland, France; appeared on various radio,

TV programs; made recordings for, R.C.A. Victor Rec. Co., Monitor Records, Musical Heritage.; 2000 solo appearances, U.S. and Europe. Bd. dirs. Olga Samaroff Found.; Jr. com. aux. bd. N.Y. Philharmonic Symphony Orch., N.Y. State Nat. Fedn. Music Clubs; mem. adv. bd. Univ. Library Soc. Winner Phila. Orch. Youth Auditions, 1950, to appear with orch. under direction of Eugene Ormandyn; mem. U.S. Senatorial Bus. Adv. Com. Fulbright scholar, 1951; Ford Found. Concert grantee, 1962; recipient Harry Rosenberg Meml., Frank Damrosch prizes, 1947; Nat. Fedn. Music Clubs Young Artist award, 1951; citation for service to Am. music Nat. Fedn. Music Clubs, 1966; citation Nat. Assn. Composers and Condrs., 1967; citation Mu Phi Epsilon, 1968; Fulbright fellow, 1951; nominated Kyoto Japan Humanitarian award, 1989. Mem. Nat. Music Council (dir. 1973—, chmn. performance com.), Music Critics Assn., Pi Kappa Lambda, Mu Phi Epsilon (dir. Meml. Found., nat. chmn. Sterling Staff Concert Series, citation 1968). Home: 333 West End Ave New York NY 10023

SORELL, CAROLE SUZANNE, public relations executive; b. N.Y.C., Oct. 6, 1940; d. Joseph and Lillian (Zeitlin) Spector; children: Melissa Bushell, Craig Bushell; m. Joel Thome, Oct. 16, 1988. BA with honors, Hunter Coll., 1961; MS, Cen. Conn. State Coll., 1966. Dir. pub. rels. Children's Mus. and Planetarium, Hartford, Conn., 1972-73; dir. media United Jewish Appeal, N.Y.C., 1973-75; sr. v.p. Ruder & Finn Fine Arts, N.Y.C., 1975-79; v.p. Adams & Rinehart, N.Y.C., 1979-80; pres. Carole Sorell Inc., N.Y.C., 1980—; author, moderator book revs. Hartford Times, 1970; writer, producer Sta. WNEW-TV, 1974; media coord. openings world hdqrs, insts. Chem. Bank, Philip Morris Cos. Inc., Nat. Bldg. Mus., Portland Mus. Art, Nat. Mus. Women in the Arts, Palazzo Grassi, Venice, Italy, others; publicistfor exhbns. Degas, Life the Sixties, A New World: Masterpieces of Am. Painting (The Gov.'s Arts award, Mayor's award for honor and culture, others). Fund raiser, publicity dir. Conn. Valley Regional Ballet, Hartford, 1971-72; mem. Mayor's All Am. Festival, Hartford, 1972; publicist South Bronx Community Action Theatre and Bronx Mus. Arts, 1978-79. Mem. Pub. Rels. Soc. Am., Am. Assn. Mus., ArtTable. Office: 30 Waterside Pla New York NY 10010

SORELL, KITTY JULIA, public relations executive; b. Vienna, Austria, Apr. 20, 1937; came to U.S. 1938; d. Bruno Alexander and Ilse (Fischl) Singerman. BA, Syracuse U., 1959. Spl. events coord. Gimbel's, N.Y.C., 1966-69; pub. rels./account exec. Hamra Assocs., N.Y.C., 1969-71; spl. events/pub. rels. dir. Stern Bros., Paramus, N.J., 1972; pub. rels. account exec. Zachary & Front, N.Y.C., 1972-76; dir. pub. rels. RSM&K Advt., N.Y.C., 1976-77; owner Kitty Sorell Pub. Rels., N.Y.C., 1977—; reporter Wisdom's Child, 1981-84, The Villager, 1986-88; lectr. in field. Contbg. editor Mktg. Maker mag., 1976. Fundraiser WNET-TV, N.Y.C., 1974-75; vol. pub. relations Sheridan Sq. Triangle Assn., N.Y.C., 1984—. Mem. Am. Soc. Profl. and Exec. Women, Publicity Club. Democrat. Jewish. Office: Kitty Sorell Pub Rels 250 W 57th St New York NY 10107

SORENSEN, CAMEY, writer; b. Boston, May 31, 1933; d. John Alabiso and Rose DiFrancesco; m. Charles F.; 1 child, Richard. Sec. Alford Mfg. Co., Woburn, Mass., 1984—; author, songwriter Camey's Freelance Svc., Woburn, 1986—; adminstrv. asst. Teleplex, Inc., Woburn; singer, actress WLHE Players. Author: It Could Happen to You, 1981; songwriter: Brown Eyes, How Could I Know, Your Guardian Angel, My Heart Went Bing-Bong and numerous other songs; hostess Job Search (Sta. WLHE), Woburn, Mass.; contbr. articles to many newspapers and mags. Office: Camey's Freelance Svc care Frank Paul Enterprises PO Box 113 Woburn MA 01801

SORENSEN, CANDACE LYNN, lawyer; b. Grand Rapids, Mich., May 6, 1960; d. Richard Allen and Connie Mae (Botma) Bos; m. Paul Thomas Sorensen, Oct. 4, 1985; 1 child, Jeffrey Paul. BA with honors, Calvin Coll., 1982; JD cum laude, Harvard U., 1985. Bar: Mich. 1985. Assoc. Dykema Gossett, Grand Rapids, 1985—; sec., bd. dirs. Sr. Neighbors, Inc., Grand Rapids, 1987—. Mentor Homeless Youth Svcs., Grand Rapids, 1988—. Mem. ABA, Mich. Bar Assn., Grand Rapids Bar Assn., Mich. Def. Trial Counsel. Republican. Office: Dykema Gossett 248 Louis Campau Promenade Grand Rapids MI 49503

SORENSEN, DEBRA LYNNETTE, computer training executive; b. Austin, Tex., Jan. 16, 1954; d. T.D. and Dolores E. (Walton) Williams; m. Audun I. Sorensen, June 10, 1972; children: Shawn M., Emily L., Jennifer L. Student, Kelsey-Baird Bus. Sch., Spokane, Wash., 1972-73, Spokane Community Coll., 1974, Lane Community Coll., Eugene, Oreg., 1976, 79, 86-87, U. Oreg., 1986-89, Linfield Coll., 1989—. Secretarial and word processing positions various, 1972-77; word processing mgr. Lane Council of Govts., Eugene, 1977-80; sales and tng. various word processing/computer vendors, Eugene, 1980-84; owner, mgr. Automation Plus, Eugene, 1984—; user svcs. mgr., computing and info. svcs. dept. Eugene Sch. Dist., 1987—; served on numerous panels related to word processing/computers for bus. and edn., including establishment of courses at Lane Community Coll., Eugene, 1979. Chmn. Lane County Affirmative Action Com., Eugene, 1980-82, Lane Community Coll. Women's Adv. Com., Eugene, 1980-82; mem. Bethel Sch. Dist. #52 Budget Com., Eugene, 1980-84, bd. dirs., 1984—, vice chmn., 1989-90, chmn., 1990—; bd. dirs. Lane Coun. of Govts., 1984—, vice chmn., 1986-88, chmn., 1989—; mem. Young Bd. Mems. Caucus Nat. Sch. Bd., 1986; pres. Willamette High Sch. Band Parents' Orgn., 1987-88; mem. Talented and Gifted Students Adv. Com., 1987-89; mem. Adult Transfer Task Force, 1989. Recipient scholarship Spokane Ednl. Secs. Assn., 1972. Mem. Eugene Word Processing Assn. (salary survey com. 1978, area dir. Willamette Valley chpt. 1977), Adminstrv. Mgmt. Soc. Republican. Mem. Ch. of Christ. Office: Automation Plus 3800 Barger Dr Eugene OR 97402

SORENSEN, ELIZABETH JULIA, cultural administrator; b. Kenora, Ont., Can., Nov. 24, 1934; d. John Frederick and Irene Margaret (Dowd) MacKellar; m. O. Leo P. Sorensen, July 7, 1956 (div. 1963); children: Lianne Kim Sorensen Kruger. BA, Lakehead U., 1970; MA, Brigham Young U., 1972; Assoc. Royal Conservatory, U. Toronto, 1978; Assoc., Mt. Royal Coll., Calgary, AB, 1978. Sec. Canadian Med. Assn. Manitoba div., Winnipeg, 1956-59; legal sec. Filmore, Riley & Co., Winnipeg, 1961-63; tchr. Fort Frances (Ont.) High Sch., 1963-70; instr. drama, speech, English Lethbridge (Alta.) Community Coll., 1972-77; tchr. bus. edn. Henderson Coll. Bus., Lethbridge, 1978-80; coordinator community services cultural programs City Medicine Hat, Alta., 1980—. Mem. Alta. Recreation and Parks Assn. (programming seminar com. 1987-88, chmn. 1989), Alta. Mcpl. Assn. for Culture (sec. 1982-87, treas. 1982—), Can. Conf. Arts. Mormon. Office: City of Medicine Hat, 580 1 St SE, Medicine Hat, AB Canada T1A 8E6

SORENSEN, JACKI FAYE, aerobic dance company executive, choreographer; b. Oakland, Calif., Dec. 10, 1942; d. Roy C. and Juanita F. (Bullon) Mills; m. Neil A. Sorensen, Jan. 3, 1965. B.A., U. Calif., 1964. Cert. tchr., Calif. Ptnr., Big Spring Sch. Dance, 1965; tchr. Pasadena Ave. Sch., Sacramento, 1968; founder, chmn. bd. dirs., choreographer Jacki's Inc., Northridge, Calif., 1969—; cons., lectr. on phys. fitness. Author: Aerobic Dancing, 1979, Jacki Sorensen's Aerobic Lifestyle Book, 1983; choreographer numerous dance exercises for records and videocassettes. Trustee Women's Sports Found. Recipient Diamond Pin award Am. Heart Assn., 1979; Individual Contbn. award Am. Assn. Fitness Dirs. in Bus. and Industry, 1981; Spl. Olympics Contbn. award, 1982; Contbn. to Women's Fitness award Pres.'s Council Phys. Fitness and Sports, 1982; Healthy Am. Fitness Leader award U.S. Jaycees, 1984; Lifetime Achievement award Internat. Dance Exercise Assn., 1985; New Horizons award Caldwell (N.J.) Coll., 1985; Legend of Aerobics award City Sports mag., 1985; Pres. Council award Calif. Womens' Leadership Conf., 1986; Hall of Fame award Club Industry mag., 1986. Mem. Am. Coll. Sports Medicine, AAHPER, Nat. Intramural and Recreation Assn., AFTRA. Office: Jacki's Inc PO Box 289 De Land FL 32721-0289

SORENSEN, MEREDITH JEAN, educator; b. Penn Yan, N.Y., May 23, 1940; d. Kenneth Edwin and Mary (Raiman) S. BA, Ottawa (Kans.) U., 1962; MA, No. Mich. U., 1976; postgrad., New Zealand Whole Lang. Mentorship Program, Hamilton, summer 1989. Cert. elem. tchr., elem. sch. prin. Tchr. Rochester (N.Y.) City Schs., 1962-63, Penfield (N.Y.) Cen. Sch., 1963-67, Marion (N.Y.) Cen. Sch., 1967—. Vol. (correctional facility) Industry (N.Y.) Sch., 1970-83, vis. dir., 1982—; bd. dirs. Ottawa U., 1970-74; mem. N.Y. State Legis. Adv. Com., Albany, 1977—; bd. dirs. Fairport Apts. for sr. citizens, 1981-83; founder Swinging Singles Western Sq. Dance Club, Rochester, 1967. Named one of Outstanding Young Women Am., 1971. Mem. Am. Federated Tchrs., N.Y. State United Tchrs., Marion Tchrs. Assn. (treas., chair legis. com. social and sunshine com., chair negotiations com.), Internat. Reading Assn., N.Y. State Reading Assn., Genesee Valley Devel. Learning Group, Phi Delta Kappa. Baptist. Club: Danish Sisterhood (Penn Yan). Office: Marion Cen Sch 3863 N Main St Marion NY 14505

SORENSEN, SHEILA, state legislator; b. Chgo., Sept. 20, 1947; d. Martin Thomas Moloney and Elizabeth (Koehr) Paulus; m. Wayne B. Slaughter, May, 1969 (div. 1976); 1 child, Wayne Benjamin III; m. Dean E. Sorensen, Feb. 14, 1977; (stepchildren) Michael, Debbie, Kevin, Dean C. BS, Loretto Heights Coll., Denver, 1965; postgrad. pediatric nurse practicioner, U. Colo., Denver, 1969-70. Pediatric nurse practicioner Pub. Health Dept., Denver, 1970-71, Boise, Idaho, 1971-72; pediatric nurse practicioner Boise (Idaho) Pediatric Group, 1972-74, Pediatric Assocs., Boise, 1974-77; rep. State of Idaho, Boise, 1987—. pct. committeman Ada County Rep. Party, Boise, 1982-86, dist. vice-chairperson, 1985—; polit. chmn. Idaho Med. Assoc. Aux., 1984-87, Ada County Med. Assocs., 1986-87. Mem. Nat. Conf. State Legislators, Nat. Orgn. Women Legislators, Am. Legis. Exch. Coun. Roman Catholic.

SORENSON, CAROL JOHNSON, minister, elder, pastoral counselor; b. Yakima, Wash., Dec. 28, 1953; d. Norman Burke and Eileen Winifred (Ricker) Johnson; m. Andrew Donald Sorenson Jr.; children: Andrew David, John Daniel. BA, Western Wash. State Coll., Bellingham, 1976; postgrad., Scarritt Coll., Nashville, 1976-77; MA in Christian Edn., Garrett Evang. Theol. Sem., 1979, MDiv, 1980. Ordained elder United Meth Ch. Pastor United Methodist, Sadorus, Ill., 1979-80, Urbana, Ill., 1980-81, Henning, Ill., 1981-84, Danville, Ill., Morton, Ill., 1985-88; chaplain resident Meth. Med. Ctr., Peoria, Ill., 1984-85; chair Clin. Pastoral Edn. Advanced Standing com., 1986—; Morton (Ill.) Ministerial Assn., 1987-88; mem. Dist. Com. on Ministry, Peoria, 1988—; liturgical dancer and workshop leader, 1970—. Author: Christian Ednl. material, 1979-80. Bd. mem., group therapy counselor, Shelter for Battered Wives and Children, Danville, Ill, 1982-84. Mem. AAUW, American Assn. Pastoral Counselors. Home: Box 52 Tremont IL 61568

SORENSON, SANDRA LOUISE, computer systems educator; b. Santa Monica, Calif., Nov. 30, 1948; d. Edward John and Gordon Dudley (Pollock) S. BA in Telecommunications, BS in Mktg., U. So. Calif., 1970. Merchandiser Montgomery Ward Inc., Los Angeles, 1970-82; sr. fin. planner Plums Co., Los Angeles, 1982-84; mgr. merchandising systems devel. and tng. Millers Outpost, Ontario, Calif., 1984-89; merchandising systems specialist Oshmans Sporting Goods, Santa Ana, Calif., 1989-90; mgr. merchandising systems devel. Clothestime, Anaheim, Calif., 1990—. Active Shakespeare Festival Guild, Garden Grove, Calif., 1985—; chairperson membership com. Gem Theatre Guild, Garden Grove, 1986—. Recipient Achievement award Bicentennial Com. Norwalk, Calif., 1976. Mem. Am. Soc. Tng. and Devel. (v.p.), Commerce Assocs., Assn. Retail Mgmt. Info. Systems, Mensa, Chi Omega, Phi Chi Theta, Alpha Epsilon Rho. Republican. Mem. Reformed Ch. Am. Club: Players of Orange. Home: 76 Carriage Way Phillips Ranch CA 91766 Office: Oshmans Sporting Goods 3300 Fairview St Santa Ana CA 92704

SORRENTINO, LAURA ANN, drilling engineer; b. N.Y.C., Oct. 24, 1959; d. Thomas Legenza and Carol Diane (Helbourg) S. BS, Colo. Sch. Mines, 1981. Roustabout, pumper Arco Oil & Gas Co., Gillette, Wyo., 1979; drilling engr. Arco Alaska, Anchorage, 1980, Gulf Oil Corp., New Orleans, 1982-85, Chevron U.S.A., New Orleans, 1985-86; prodn. technologist Amoco Prodn. Co., Liberal, Kans., 1981; teaching asst. Colo. Sch. Mines, Golden, 1981; sr. drilling engr. Mobil Exploration & Prodn. Svcs., Inc., New Orleans, 1987—. Campaign worker Henson Moore for Senate, New Orleans, 1986. Mem. Soc. Petroleum Engrs. (arrangements com. 1985), Alpha Gamma Delta. Republican. Roman Catholic. Home: 2236 Westmere St Harvey LA 70058 Office: Mobil Exploration & Prodn 1250 Poydras St New Orleans LA 70113

SORRENTINO, RENATE MARIA, illustrator; b. Mallnitz, Carinthia, Austria, June 21, 1942; came to the U.S., 1962; d. Johann and Theresia (Kritzer) Weinberger; m. Philip Rosenberg, Nov. 22, 1968 (dec. 1982); m. Francis J. Sorrentino, Sept. 4, 1988. Grad. tech. coll., Ferlach, Austria, 1961. Drafts woman Elecon Inc., N.Y., 1962-65; jr. designer Automatics Metal Prod. Corp., N.Y., 1965-70; designer, art dir. Autosplice, Inc., Woodside, N.Y., 1970--. Patentee, Quick Diconnect From continuous Wire, 1977. Office: Autosplice Inc 5912 37th Ave Woodside NY 11377

SORSTOKKE, ELLEN KATHLEEN, marketing executive, teacher; b. Seattle, Mar. 31, 1954; d. Harold William and Carrol Jean (Russ) S. MusB with distinction, U. Ariz., 1976; postgrad., UCLA Extension, 1979-83, L.A. Valley Coll., 1984-85, Julliard Extension, fall 1987. Cert. music specialist tchr., Ariz. Pvt. practice part-time music tchr. Music Land, Tucson, 1975-77; music tchr. Eloy (Ariz.) Elem. Schs., 1976-77, Whiteriver (Ariz.) Pub. Schs., 1977-78; from svc. writer to asst. svc. mgr. to acting svc. mgr. Alfa of Santa Monica, Calif., 1978-79; purchasing agt. Advance Machine Corp., L.A., 1979-80; asst. mgr. Atlantic Nuclear Svcs., Gardena, Calif., 1980-81; mgr. Blue Lady's World Music Ctr., L.A., 1981-83; instrument specialist Baxter-Northup Music Co., Sherman Oaks, Calif., 1983-85; dir. mktg. Mandolin Bros., Ltd., S.I., N.Y., 1985-89; product mgr. Gibson Guitar Corp., Nashville, 1989; sales mgr. Saga Musical Instruments, South San Francisco, 1990—; freelance mktg. cons. S.I., 1986-89; freelance music tchr., Tucson, L.A., N.Y.C., 1975-89; music cons. 20th Century Fox, L.A., 1984; freelance music copyist and orchestrator, Tucson, L.A., N.Y.C., 1972-89. Campaign worker Richard Jones for supr., Tucson, 1972; mem., program book designer Marina Del Rey-Westchester Symphony Orch., L.A., 1981-83. Scholar U. Ariz., 1973-76, ASCAP scholar, 1980-81. Mem. Am. Fedn. Musicians, NAFE, Soc. for the Preservation Film Music, Tucson Flute Club (publicity chmn. 1974-75, v.p. 1975-76). Republican. Office: Saga Musical Instruments 429 Littlefield Ave PO Box 2841 South San Francisco CA 94080

SORSTOKKE, SUSAN EILEEN, systems engineer; b. Seattle, May 2, 1955; d. Harold William and Carrol Jean (Russ) S. BS in Systems Engring., U. Ariz., 1976; MBA, U. Wash., Richland, 1983. Warehouse team mgr. Procter and Gamble Paper Products, Modesto, Calif., 1976-78; quality assurance engr. Westinghouse Hanford Co., Richland, Wash., 1978-80; supr. engring. document ctr. Westinghouse Hanford Co., Richland, 1980-81; mgr. data control and adminstrn. Westinghouse Electric Corp., Madison, Pa., 1981-82; mgr. data control and rcds mgmt. Westinghouse Electric Corp., Madison, 1982-84; prin. engr. Westinghouse Elevator Co., Morristown, N.J., 1984-87; region adminstrn. mgr. Westinghouse Elevator Co., Arleta, Calif., 1987-90; ops. rsch. analyst Am. Honda Co. Inc., Torrance, Calif., 1990—. Advisor Jr. Achievement, 1982-83; literacy tutor Westmoreland Literacy Coun., 1983-84, host parent EF Found., Saugus, Calif., 1987-88. Mem. Soc. Women Engrs., Am. Inst. of Indsl. Engrs. Republican. Methodist. Home: 21647 Spice Ct Saugus CA 91350 Office: Am Honda Motor Co Inc Parts Rsch and Planning Dept 1919 Torrance Blvd Torrance CA 90501-2746

SORTLAND, TRUDITH ANN, educator, speech and language therapist; b. Butte, Mont., Dec. 3, 1940; d. Kenneth Hjalmer Sortland and Sigrid V. (Kotka) Strand. BS, Minot (N.D.) State U., 1965. Tchr. Westby (Mont.) Sch., 1960-61, Glasgow (Mont.) Southside Sch., 1962-65; tchr., speech and lang. pathologist Mineral County Sch. Dist., Hawthorne, Nev., 1965-68, 78—; kindergarten tchr. Mineral County Sch. Dist., Mina, Nev., 1968-72; elem. tchr. Mineral County Sch. Dist., Mina, 1978-80; speech, language pathologist Mineral County Sch. Dist., Mina, Republic of Korea, 1980—; tchr. Dept. Def., Pusan, Republic of Kores, 1972-73, Illesheim, Fed. Republic Germany, 1973-78; tchr. Mohall (N.D.) Pub. Sch., 1964-65; cons. Mary Kay Cosmetics, tchr. Glasgow Air Force Base, 1965-68. Supt. Sunday sch. Bethany Luth. Ch., Hawthorne, 1987—, sec. Ladies Aid, 1987—. Mem. NEA, Nev. Edn. Assn., AAUW (past sec., pres.), Pair O Dice Square Dance Club (sec. 1989—), Delta Kappa Gamma. Home: PO Box 816 Hawthorne NV 89415 Office: Mineral County Sch Dist A St Hawthorne NV 89415

SOSNOWSKI, MARGARET ELIZABETH, nurse; b. Bklyn., July 19, 1959; d. Edward and Margaret (Ruggiero) S. BS in Nursing, L.I. U., 1981; MS in Nursing Edn., Wagner Coll., 1988. R.N., N.Y. Staff nurse Maimonides Med. Ctr., Bklyn., 1981-87; nursing instr. dept. staff devel. and continuing edn. Maimonides Med. Ctr., 1987—; instr. CPR, ARC, N.Y.C., 1987—, Am. Heart Assn., N.Y.C., 1989. Mem. NCAP, Am. Nurses Assn., N.Y. State Nurses Assn.. Home: 4206 Ave R Brooklyn NY 11234 Office: Maimonides Med Ctr 4802 10th Ave Brooklyn NY 11219

SOSVILLE, JERRI LYNN, English educator; b. Seattle, June 7, 1944; d. Richard William and Joan Elsie (Rose) Knowlton; m. Dennis John. BS in Econs., Rollins Coll., 1975; MA in English, Tex. A&M U., 1985, postgrad., 1989—. Tchr. Balt. City Schss., 1966-68; graphic artist, reporter Assabet Valley Pub. Co., Acton, Mass., 1968-70; sec. The Little Paper Newspaper, Melbourne, Fla., 1975-78; office mgr. Ron Stephens Corp., The Woodlands, Tex., 1979-82; tchr. Dept. English Tex. A&M U, College Station, Tex., 1983—; freelance pub. rels. for various orgns., Fla., 1968-88. Contbr. articles to profl. jours. Mem. Nat. Coun. Tchrs. English, Conf. Coll. Tchrs. English. Republican. Jewish. Home: 17A Raven's Nest Bryan TX 77802 Office: Tex A&M U College Station TX 77843

SOTO, ARLENE MARIE, owner; b. Oreg. City, Oreg., June 14, 1956; d. Harold Nelson and Mary Margaret (Edgell) Bigham; m. David Soto, Feb. 14, 1983. BA, Portland State U., 1985; MS, Marylhurst Coll., Marylhurst, 1988. Computer operations John Fought & Co. CPA'S, Portland, 1976-79; controller E.G. Stassens Realty, Portland, 1979-81, NW Power Planning Council, Portland, 1981-86; fin. analyst Oreg. Mutual Ins., McMinnville, Oreg.; owner Oasis Group, Inc., Portland, 1988--. Bd. dirs. fin. com. Found. for Women Owned Bus.'s, 1989—. Mem. Inst. Managerial & Profl. Women, Women Entrepreneurs (treas. 1988—, pres. 1989-90), Nat. Assn. Accts., Portland C. of C. Democrat. Home: 13311 S Glenn Dr Mulino OR 97042 Office: Oasis Group Inc 5100 SW Macadam Ste 250 Portland OR 97201

SOUHAMI, GLORIA, video producer, business writer; b. Wetzlar, Fed. Republic Germany, June 24, 1947; m. Sam Souhami, Mar. 26, 1966; 1 child, Annick Catherine. BJ, U. Tex., 1984. Editor Austin (Tex.) Community Coll., 1982-85; editor Ontra Cos., Austin, 1986—; TV talk show host, producer Austin Community TV, 1984—; video producer Premeditated Media, Austin, 1987—; cable commr. City of Austin, 1990—; freelance reporter United Press Internat.; bd. dirs. Austin Community TV, 1985-88. Producer (video documentary) Remembering the Darkness: Story of a Holocaust Survivor, 1990. Mem. Women in Communications, Austin Writers League, Soc. Profl. Journalists. Home: 2101 Newfield Ln Austin TX 78703

SOUKUP, JANE KLINKNER, services coordinator, consultant; b. New Ulm, Minn., June 6, 1958; d. Martin Paul and Clothildia Anne (Liebl) Klinkner; m. Michael Paul Soukup, Sept. 4, 1987. BA in Health, S.W. State U., 1980. Recreation asst. Willows Convalescent Ctr., Mpls., 1980-83; dir. recreation and vol. svcs. Beverly Enterprises, Mpls., 1983-86, St. Louis Pk., Minn., 1986-87; adult day svcs. coord. Health One-Sioux Valley Hosp., New Ulm, 1988—; mem. peer rev. team quality assurance dept. Beverly Enterprises, Mpls., 1986; bd. dirs. Community and Srs. Together, New Ulm, pres., 1990; group facilitator Caregiver Support Group, New Ulm, 1988—; recreation cons. Lafayette (Minn.) Good Samaritan Ctr., 1988-89. Vol. hostess Heritage Fest, New Ulm, 1988; mem. adv. bd. Sr. Peer Counseling-Sioux Trails, New Ulm, 1988-89; mem. Home Health Care Adv. Bd., New Ulm, 1988—; campaign co-chmn. Dem.-Farmer-Labor candidate for Minn. Ho. of Reps., 1988; mem. St. Mary's Parish Coun., Sleepy Eye, Minn., 1989—, mem. bd. edn., 1989—. Named Hon. Citizen, Marshall (Minn.) City Coun., 1978. Mem. Am. Assn. Ret. Persons, State Wide Activity Profls., Minn. Adult Day Care Assn. (bd. dirs. 1989—), SW State U. Alumni Assn. (bd. dirs. 1987—, scholar 1976-80), Minn. Valley Testing Softball. Home: Rte 1 Sleepy Eye MN 56085

SOULE, BEVERLY JEAN, data processing professional; b. Tacoma, June 9, 1949; d. Milton H. and Anna (Kubeck) S.; children: Angelique, Shannon. BS in Bus. Mgmt. cum laude, Linfield Coll., 1985. Credit and collection coord. Avon Fashions, Newport News, Va., 1973-77; sales and acctg. asst. Weyerhaeuser Co., Tacoma, 1980—, bus. support rep. Mem. NAFE. Office: Weyerhaeuser Co WSC-8 Tacoma WA 98477

SOULE, SALLIE THOMPSON, retired state official; b. Detroit, May 13, 1928; d. Hayward Stone and Elizabeth Robinson Thompson; A.B., Smith Coll., 1950; M.A., U. Vt., Burlington, 1952; m. Gardner Northup Soule, July 26, 1958; stepchildren: Gardner Northup, Nancy Soule Brown; children: Sarah Goodwin, Trumbull Dickson. Sec. trade sales dept. Macmillan Pub. Co., N.Y.C., 1952-57; tech. writer sales svc. div. Eastman Kodak Co., Rochester, N.Y., 1957-58; feature writer Brighton-Pittsford Post, Pittsford, N.Y., 1958-68; v.p., gen. mgr. F. H. Horsford Nursery, Inc., Charlotte, Vt., 1968-76; ptnr., v.p. Bygone Books, Inc., Burlington, Vt., 1978—; mem. Vt. Ho. of Reps., 1976-80, mem. ways and means com., 1976-80; mem. Vt. Senate, 1980-84, mem. appropriation com., energy and natural resources com. 1980-84; commr. Vt. Dept. Employment and Tng., Montpelier, 1985-88; chmn. Vt. Employment Security Bd., 1985-88; chmn. bd. Vt. Community Found., Inc.; trustee U. Vt., Wake Robin Continuing Care Retirement Community.

SOULES, BARBARA ANN, personnel professional; b. Gilmer County, Ga., June 19, 1947; d. Reuben and Doris V. (Thurman) Allen; m. Bud Soules, Oct. 19, 1980; children: Paula, Lewis. Student, Ga. Tech. U., 1987. Mgr. dist., br. and ter. DTI, Inc., Norcross, Ga., 1985-89; ops. mgr. Atlanta Pers. Svcs., Inc., 1989-90, Acctg. Alternatives, Atlanta, 1990—. Mem. ASPA, Nat. Assn. Temp. Svcs., Ga. Assn. Temp. Svcs., Atlanta C. of C., Cobb C. of C. Home: 113 Village Ct Woodstock GA 30188

SOULIOTIS, BARBARA ANNE, government official; b. Haverhill, Mass., July 8, 1942; d. Arthur Theodore and Rose Helen (Duma) S. Student, Katharine Gibbs Sch., Boston, 1961-62. Notary pub., Mass. Asst. to asst. dist. atty. Suffolk County, Boston, 1961-62; asst. for scheduling to Senator Edward M. Kennedy, U.S. Senate, Boston, 1962; appointments sec. U.S. Senate, Washington, 1962-69; chief scheduling U.S. Senate, Boston, 1970-86, state dir., adminstrv. asst., 1987—; bd. corporators Family Bank, Haverhill; bd. dirs. JKF Scholarship Fund, Friends of Pres. Kennedy Libr. Mem. Haverhill Dem. City Com.; scheduler Robert Kennedy for Pres., Ind., Oreg., Calif., 1968, Ted Kennedy for Pres., 1980., Ted Kennedy for Senate, 1962, 64, 70, 76, 82, 88; aide, mem. credentials com. Nat. Dem. Conv., 1980, 84, 88. Named Alumni of Yr. Haverhill High Sch., 1983. Mem. NAFE, U.S. Senate Staff Club, Crystal Springs Golf Club, M.I. Hummel Club. Roman Catholic. Home: 16 Edgewood Ave Haverhill MA 01832 Office: Office Senator Kennedy 2400 John F Kennedy Bldg Govt Ctr Boston MA 02203

SOUROUJON, BEATRICE, bank executive; b. Mexico City, Jan. 10, 1963; d. Ruben and Nelly (Muller) S. BS, Tex. A&M U., 1984; postgrad., Inst. Tech. Autonomo, Mexico City, 1987, NYU. Assoc. Chase Manhattan Bank NA, Mexico City; 2d v.p. Chase Manhattan Bank NA, N.Y.C. Mem. Phi Kappa Phi. Office: Chase Manhattan Bank NA 1 Chase Manhattan Plaza New York NY 10081

SOURWINE, KATHLEEN MARIE, payroll executive; b. Chgo., Apr. 7, 1951; d. Robert John and Barbara Ellen (Anderson) Crorkin; m. Richard Earl Burnham, Sept. 22, 1966 (div. 1972); m. 2d. Kerry Michael Sourwine, Sept. 20, 1975; 1 dau., Karen Michelle; 1 stepdau., Evelyn Marie. Student Northeastern U. Cashier, S.S. Kresge, Chgo., 1966. Cert. payroll prof., Ill. Switchboard receptionist Churchill Cabinet, Chgo., 1967-69, bookkeeper, 1972; mgr. payroll TSC Industries, Chgo., 1972-80; mgr. payroll Wilson Jones Co., Chgo., 1981-83, mgr. distribution services, 1983-86; mgr. Human Resources Hanley-Dawson, Chgo., 1986-87; payroll mgr. Cotter & Co. Merchandisers, Warehouse Distbrs. & Mfrs., Hardware, Variety & Related Lines, 1987—. Mem. NAFE (network dir. 1982—), Am. Payroll Assn. Democrat. Roman Catholic.

SOUSA, CONSUELO MARIA, pediatrician; b. New Bedford, Mass., Aug. 5, 1931; d. Edward Rogers and Candida Helena (Rogers) S.; m. Timothy Leonard Stephens, July 7, 1959; children: Timothy Leonard III, Susan Ellen, Amy Louise. BS, Howard U., Washington, 1953, MD, 1958; MPH, Harvard U., 1962; MBA, Case Western Res. U., Cleve., 1983. Diplomate Am. Bd. Pediatrics. Intern St. Luke's Hosp., New Bedford, 1958; resident pediatrics Freedmen's Hosp., Washington, 1959-61; fellow dept. maternal and child health Harvard Sch. Pub. Health, Boston, 1961-62; instr. preventive medicine Boston U. Sch. Medicine, 1962-63; asst. physician home med. svc. Mass. Meml. Svc. Hosp., 1962-63; pvt. practice, assoc. attending staff St. Luke's Hosp., New Bedford, 1963-66; pediatrician Well Child Conf., Fairhaven, Mass., 1965-66; clin. instr. pediatrics Case Western Res. U., Cleve., 1967—; mem. pediatric staff Rainbow Babes and Children's Hosp., Cleve., 1967—; chief pediatrics Hough Norwood Family Health Care Ctr., Cleve., 1967-76; vis. asst. pediatrics Cleve. Met. Gen. Hosp., 1967—; dir. health svcs. Buckeye Health Plan, Inc., Cleve., 1976-79, acting exec. dir., 1979, med. health svcs. dir., 1979-80; v.p., med. adminstr. Assocs. in Orthopaedics, Inc., Cleve., 1982—, cons., 1980-82; chmn. med. staff Health Hill Hosp., Cleve., 1982-84; mem. Headstart Health Adv. Com., Cleve., 1971-78, chmn., 1977-78. Contbr. articles to profl. jours. Mem. Citizens Adv. Bd. of Juvenile Ct. Cuyahoga County, 1975—, chmn. bd., 1985-89; appointed commr. Cuyahoga Met. Housing Authority, 1990; mem. bd., founding trustee Harambee Svcs. to Black Families, Cleve., 1979-85; mem. adv bd. Youth Svcs. Cuyahoga County, 1980—, chmn., 1980-85. Named Outstanding American, Cape Verdean Am. Vets., New Bedford, 1972. Fellow Am. Acad. Pediatrics; mem. AMA, Nat. Med. Assn., No. Ohio Pediatric Soc. Home: 13475 N Park Blvd Cleveland Heights OH 44118 Office: Assocs in Orthopaedics Inc 11201 Shaker Blvd Ste 328 Cleveland OH 44104

SOUTH, GRACE DEVITA, photo-graphic display designer; b. Boston, Jan. 9, 1957; d. Robert Allen and Sylvia Marcia (Roazen) Berman; m. James Alan Devita, Aug. 23, 1978 (div. Apr. 1980); 1 child, Jacob Elijah; m. Richard William South, June 30, 1985. Student, U. Md., 1974-75. Mgr. plant Color King, Hollywood, Fla., 1983; cons. Color Corp. Am., Tampa, Fla., 1984; sales rep. Berkey K&L, N.Y.C., 1984-85; owner Graphics Resource, Inc., Woodstock, Ga., 1985—. Mem. Photo Mktg. Assn., Soc. Photofinishing Engrs., Art Dirs. Atlanta. Home and Office: 1760 Old Country Pl Woodstock GA 30188

SOUTH, MARY ANN, pediatrics educator; b. Portales, N.Mex., May 23, 1933; d. John Anderson and Carrie (Schumpert) S.; m. Allard W. Loutherback, Dec. 29, 1983 (dec. June 1985); children: George Louie, Linda Lee Loutherback Putnam. Student, Baylor U., Waco, Tex., 1951-53; BA, Ea. N.Mex. U., 1955; MD, Baylor U., Houston, 1959. Diplomate Am. Bd. Pediatrics. Intern Presbyn.-St. Luke's Hosp., Chgo., 1959-60, resident in pediatrics, 1960-62; fellow in infectious diseasess Coll. of Medicine Baylor U., 1962-64; fellow in immunology, instr. in pediatrics U. Minn., Mpls., 1964-66; instr. pediatrics U. Minn., 1964-66; asst. prof., assoc. prof. Baylor U. Coll. Medicine, 1966-73; prof., chmn. dept. pediatrics Tex. Tech U. Health Scis. Ctr., Phila., 1973-77; prof., chmn. dept. pediatrics Tex. Tech U. Health Scis. Ctr., Lubbock, 1977-79, rsch. prof., 1979-83; med. officer Nat. Inst. Neurol.-Communicative Disorders and Stroke, NIH, Bethesda, Md., 1982-85; vis. scientist Gallaudet Coll., Washington, 1984-85; prof. pediatrics Meharry Med. Coll., Nashville, 1986-89, W.K. Kellogg disting. prof., program dir. clin. rsch., 1986—; program dir. Clin. Rsch. Ctr. Contbr. over 140 articles to med. jours., chpts. to books. Recipient Disting. Alumnus award Ea. N.Mex. U., 1969, rsch. career devel. award NIH, 1968-73. Fellow Infectious Diseases Soc. Am.; mem. Am. Pediatric Soc., Am. Assn. Immunology, Assn. for Gnotobiology, Am. Med. Women's Assn., Pediatric Infectious Diseases Soc., Alpha Omega Alpha. Home: 6666 Brookmont Terr Nashville TN 37205 Office: Meharry Med Coll 1005 DB Todd Blvd Nashville TN 37208

SOUTHARD, HELEN ELIZABETH FAIRBAIRN, psychologist; b. Buffalo, July 4, 1906; d. Robert Weatherston and Lorena May (Klock) Fairbairn; m. Paul John Southard, Feb. 24, 1934 (dec. 1961); children: John Brelsford, Robert Fairbairn. BA cum laude, U. Buffalo, 1927, MA, 1929; student, Columbia U., 1932-34, NYU, N.Y.C., 1987-89. Lic. psychologist, N.Y. Author: Sex Education Series, 1955, Sex Before Twenty, 1970, (manual) Handbook for Administrative Violaters, 1981; author poetry. Nat. Panhellmic grantee, 1932-33. Mem. Am. Psychol. Assn., Am. Orthopsychiatric Assn., N.Y. Psychol. Assn., Am. fEdn. Radio and TV Arts, AAUW, Woman's Club (chair literature and creative writin 1988-90). Home and Office: 100 E Palisade Ave Apt D55 Englewood NJ 07631

SOUTHERN, EILEEN (MRS. JOSEPH SOUTHERN), music educator; b. Mpls., Feb. 19, 1920; d. Walter Wade and Lilla (Gibson) Jackson; m. Joseph Southern, Aug. 22, 1942; children: April, Edward. A.B., U. Chgo., 1940, M.A., 1941; Ph.D., NYU, 1961; M.A. (hon.), Harvard U., 1976; D.A. (hon.), Columbia Coll., Chgo., 1985. Instr. Prairie View U., Hempstead, Tex., 1941-42; asst. prof. So. U., Baton Rouge, 1943-45, 49-51; tchr. N.Y.C. Bd. Edn., 1954-60; instr. Bklyn. Coll., CUNY, 1960-64, asst. prof., 1964-69; assoc. prof. York Coll., CUNY, 1969-71, prof., 1972-75; prof. music Harvard U., Cambridge, Mass., 1976-87, chmn. dept. Afro-Am. studies, 1976-79, prof. emeritus, 1987—. Concert pianist, 1940-55; author: The Buxheim Organ Book, 1963, The Music of Black Americans: A History, 1971, 2d edit., 1983, Readings in Black American Music, 1971, 2d edit., 1983, Anonymous Chansons in MS El Escorial Biblioteca del Monasterio, IV a 24, 1981, Biographical Dictionary of Afro-American and African Musicians, 1982, (with Josephine Wright) African-American Traditions in Song, Sermon, Tale, and Dance, 1630-1920: An Annotated Bibliography, 1990; editor, pub.: The Black Perspective in Music, 1973—; contbr. articles to profl. jours., encys. Active Girl Scouts U.S.A., 1954-63; chmn. mgmt. com. Queens Area YWCA, 1970-73. Recipient Alumni Achievement award U. Chgo., 1970; Deems Taylor award ASCAP, 1973; NEH grantee, 1979-83. Mem. NACCP, Internat. Musicol. Soc., Am. Musicol. Soc. (dir. 1974-76), Sonneck Am. Music Soc. (bd. dirs. 1986-88), Renaissance Soc., Phi Beta Kappa (hon. Radcliffe Coll.), Alpha Kappa Alpha. Home: 115-05 179th St Saint Albans NY 11434 Office: Harvard U Cambridge MA 02138

SOUTHWARD, L. LEILANI, consulting services company executive, coach; b. Hilo, Hawaii, Jan. 12, 1941; d. James Akoni and Margaret (Bray) Calles; m. Walter W. Southward, Mar. 30, 1963. Student, U. Hawaii, Hilo, 1965-68. Softball coach Waiakea High Sch., Hilo, 1978-80; sports dir. Sta. KIPA, Hilo, 1978-83; softball coach U. Hawaii, Hilo, 1988; owner Leilani's Svcs., Hilo, 1988—; gen. mgr. Hilo Comets Softball Assn., 1968-89. Named Sports Woman of Yr., Hukilau Assn., 1986; recipient Outstanding Vol. award State of Hawaii, 1982. Mem. Am. Numis. Assn., U. Hawaii Hilo Athletic Booster Club, Hist. Hawaii Found., Lyman House Museum Assn. Home: 94 Pakalana St Hilo HI 96720 Office: Leilani's Svcs PO Box 251 Hilo HI 96721

SOUTHWARD, PATRICIA FRANCIS, volunteer; b. Alexandria, La., Mar. 9, 1942; d. George Emerson and Mary Alice (Boland) Cilley; m. Arnold Lester Greenfield, May 18, 1963 (div. June 1968); m. Ernest Merritt Southward, Mar. 1970. BA, U. Fla., Gainesville, 1963; MS, Fla. State U., Tallahassee, 1966. Office mgr. Southward Gardens, Lake Mary, Fla., 1977-84, Southward Investment and Realty, Lake Mary, Fla., 1970-; city commr. Lake Mary, 1977-79, 82. Com. mem. Fla. Govs. Coun. on Housing Goals, 1980; sponsor, vol. and social worker Refugee Resettlement Office, Catholic, 1980—; bd. dirs., sec. Cen. Fla. Migrant and Community Health Clinic, Sanford, 1981-89; bd. dirs. LWV Seminole County, 1982-83; voters' svc. chair, bd. dirs. LWV Fla., 1989-90, 1st v.p., 1990—. Democrat. Home: One Stonegate N Longwood FL 32779 Office: PO Box 950730 Lake Mary FL 32795

SOUZA, MAURENE GLORIA, toy company executive; b. Providence, July 31, 1949; d. Joseph Antonio and Georgina Irene (Matta) S. BA in English, U. R.I., 1973. Copywriter, Outlet Dept. Stores, Providence, 1971-73; copywriter Hasbro Industries, Pawtucket, R.I., 1973-78, product mgr., 1978-81, mktg. dir., 1981-84, assoc. v.p. mktg., 1984-86, v.p. mktg. girls toys, 1986-89; v.p. mktg. Tyco Toys, 1989—. Bd. dirs. Children's Mus. of R.I. Named One of Top 50 Corp. Women to Watch, 1987, Top 100 Women in Corp. Am., 1989. Office: Tyco Toys 6000 Midlantic Ave Mount Laurel NJ 08054

SOUZA, VIRGINIA A., banker; b. New Bedford, Mass., Oct. 29, 1946; d. Frank and Palmira (Barros) Reis; m. Kenneth Paul Souza, Aug. 24, 1968; children: Kyle Paul, Aaron Joseph. Assoc. Bus., Fisher Jr. Coll., North Dart, Mass., 1986. Adminstrv. asst. First Nat. Bank, New Bedford, 1978-79; trust ops. officer First Nat. Bank/Shawmut Bank, New Bedford, 1980-89; asst. trust officer Shawmut Bank, New Bedford, 1989—. Chairperson devel. Am. Heart Assn., 1989 (appreciation award 1990). Mem. Am. Bus. Woman's Assn., Mass. Bankers (trust opera 1980—), Ideal Club, Inc. (sec. fin. 1990—). Roman Catholic. Office: Shawmut Bank NA 545 Pleasant St New Bedford MA 02740

SOVIE, MARGARET DOE, nursing administrator, college dean; b. Ogdensburg, N.Y., July 7, 1934; d. William Gordon and Mary Rose (Bruyere) Doe; m. Alfred L. Sovie, May 8, 1954; 1 child, Scot Marc. Student, U. Rochester, 1950-51; diploma in nursing, St. Lawrence State Hosp. Sch. Nursing, Ogdensburg, 1954; postgrad., St. Lawrence U., 1956-60; BS in Nursing summa cum laude, Syracuse U., 1964, MS in Edn., 1968, PhD in Edn., 1972; DSc (hon.), Health Sci. Ctr. SUNY, Syracuse, 1989. Staff nurse, clin. instr. St. Lawrence State Hosp., Odgensburg, 1954-55; instr. nursing St. Lawrence State Hosp., Ogdensburg, 1955-62; staff nurse Good Shepherd Hosp., Syracuse, 1962; nursing supr. SUNY Upstate Med. Ctr., Syracuse, 1963-65, insvc. instr., 1965-66, edn. dir. and coordinator nursing service, 1966-71, asst. dean Coll. Health Related Professions, 1972-84, assoc. prof. nursing, 1973-76, dir. continuing edn. in nursing, 1974-76, assoc. dean and dir. div. continuing edn. Coll. Health Related Professions, 1974-76; spl. assignment in pres.'s office SUNY Upstate Med. Ctr. and Syracuse U., 1972-73; assoc. dean for nursing U. Rochester, N.Y., 1976-88, assoc. prof. nursing, 1976-85, prof., 1985-88; assoc. dir. for nursing Strong Meml. Hosp., U. Rochester Med. Ctr., 1976-88; dir. nursing, assoc. exec. dir. Hosp. U. Pa., Phila., 1988—, assoc. dean for nursing practice, Jane Delano prof. nursing adminstrn. Sch. Nursing, 1988—; nursing coord. and project dir. Cen. N.Y. Regional Med. Program, Syracuse, 1968-71; mem. edn. dept. State Bd. Nursing, Albany, N.Y., 1974-84, chmn., 1981-83, chmn. practice com., 1975-80, mem. joint practice com., 1975-80, vice chmn., 1980-81; mem. adv. com. to clin. nurse scholars program Robert Wood Johnson Found., Princeton, N.J., 1982-88; adj. assoc. prof. Syracuse U. Sch. Nursing, 1973-76; mem. Gov.'s Health Adv. Panel N.Y. State Health Planning Commn., 1976-82, task force on health manpower policy, 1978, informal support networks sect. steering com., 1980; mem. health manpower tng. and utilization task force State N.Y. Commn. on Health Edn. and Illness Prevention, 1979; mem. task force on nursing personnel N.Y. State Health Adv. Council, 1980; mem. adv. panel on nursing services U.S. Pharm. Conv. Inc., Washington, 1985-90; cons. Nat. Ctr. for Services Research and Health Care Tech. Assessment, Rockville, Md., 1987—; mem. nursing standards task force Joint Commn. Accreditation Health Care Orgns., 1988-90; mem. various other adv. coms.; lectr. in field. Mem. editorial bd. Health Care Supr., 1982-87, Nursing Econs., 1983—; manuscript rev. panel Nursing Outlook, 1987—; contbr. articles to profl. jours., chpts. to books. Mem. bd. visitors Sch. Nursing U. Md., Balt., 1984-89; mem. bd. mgrs. Strong Meml. Hosp., Rochester, 1983-88; bd. dirs. Monroe County Assn. for Hearing, Rochester, 1979-82, Vis. Nurse Svc. Rochester and Monroe County, 1978. Ann. Margaret D. Sovie lectureship inaugurated Strong Meml. Hosp. U. Rochester, 1989; spl. nurse research fellow NIH, 1971-72; grantee various orgns.;. Fellow Am. Acad. Nursing (program com. 1980-81, task force on hosp. nursing 1981-83); mem. Inst. Medicine (com. design quality rev. and assurance in medicine 1988-90), Am. Nurses Assn. (nat. rev. com. for expanded role programs 1975-78, site visitor to programs requesting accreditation 1976-78, cabinet on nursing svcs. 1986-90, cert. bd. nursing adminstrn. 1983-86), Am. Orgn. Nurse Execs. (standards task force 1987), N.Y. State Nurses Assn. (med. surg. nursing group, chmn. edn. com. dist. 4 1974-76, chmn. community planning group for nursing dist. 4 1974-76, coun. on regional planning in nursing 1974-76, del. to conv. 1978, Nursing Svc. Adminstrn. award 1985), Sigma Theta Tau, Pi Lambda Theta. Republican. Roman Catholic. Office: Hosp U Pa 3400 Spruce St Philadelphia PA 19104-4283

SOVNER-RIBBLER, JUDITH W., information industry executive; b. N.Y.C., Feb. 1, 1947; d. Max and Esther Ribbler; children: Merrill, Nicholas. BA, Syracuse U., 1968, MLS, 1969. Librarian Stone & Webster Mgmt. Cons., N.Y.C., 1969-70; asst. prof. Westchester Community Coll., Valhalla, N.Y., 1970-72; dept. head ref. Boston Coll. Bapst Library, Chestnut Hill, Mass., 1972-75; library cons. Boston, 1975-78; dir. tech. search Warner-Eddison Assocs., Cambridge, Mass., 1978-81; pres. Searchline Assocs., Inc., Brookline, Mass., 1981—; database tng. cons. Info. Access Co., Forest City, Calif., 1983—; cons. Research Investment Advisors, Boston, 1985—; lectr. in field. Contbr. articles to profl. jours. Bd. dirs. Driscoll Extended Daycare Program, Brookline, 1982-84; v.p. bd. dirs. Clinton Path Presch., Brookline, 1977-81; mem. ann. fund com. The Computer Mus., Boston. Mem. Spl. Libraries Assn., New Eng. Online Users Group, Boston Computer Soc., Phi Beta Mu. Office: Searchline Assocs 8 Griggs Terrace Brookline MA 02146

SOWA, DOROTHY ROHRER, nursing administrator; b. Glasgow, Mont., June 15, 1938; d. Paul Revere and Sarah (Whitbread) Rohrer; divorced; children: Joan Pauline, Beverly Jeanne, Christine Marian. BS, Mont. State U., 1960, M Nursing, 1962. RN, Mont. Instr. nursing Mont. State U., Gt. Falls, 1960-61, 63-65, asst. prof., assoc. prof., 1967-81; staff nurse Deaconess Hosp., Bozeman, Mont., 1962-63, Gt. Falls, 1965-67; dir. nursing Mont. Deaconess Skilled Nursing Ctr., Gt. Falls, 1981—; mem. Coalition for Nursing Home Nurse Aide Cert., 1989—; mem. project on quality nursing care for grad. nursing Western Inst. Nursing. Mem. coun. Faith Luth. Ch., Gt. Falls, 1988—, chmn. edn. com., 1989—; bd. dirs. Cascade Mental Health Assn., Gt. Falls, 1986—, YWCA, Gt. Falls, 1989—. Mont. State U. grantee, 1979. Mem. Mont. Nurses Assn. (Dist 6 Nurse of Yr. award 1972), Long Term Dirs. Assn., Sigma Theta Tau. Office: Deaconess Skilled Nursing 1101 26th St S Great Falls MT 59405

SOWALD, DEBRA KAY, psychologist; b. Columbus, Ohio, Sept. 28, 1951; d. Martin Michael and Beatrice Fay (Kronick) S.; 1 child, Chad. BS, Case Western Res. U., 1973; MA, Ohio State U., 1975; D Psychology, Wright State U., 1982. Lic. psychologist, counselor, Ohio; cert. tchr., Ohio. Tchr. Groveport (Ohio)-Madison Schs., 1973-76; sch. counselor Centerville (Ohio) City Schs., 1976-79; tchr. Sinclair Community Coll., Dayton, Ohio, 1982-86; pvt. practice Dayton, 1984—; guest on TV programs including The Today Show. Mem. adv. bd. Make Today Count, Dayton, 1982—. Mem. Internat. Transactional Analysis Assn., Ohio Psychol. Assn., Am. Psychol. Assn., Ohio Women in Psychology (v.p. 1983-86, mem.-at-large 1986—), Am. Assn. Counseling and Devel., Ohio Assn. Counseling and Devel., Miami Valley Assn. Counseling and Devel., Dayton Assn. Female Execs., Dayton Women's Coalition, Dayton Area Psychol. Assn. (treas. 1988-89), Single Mothers by Choice, La Leche League Internat. Office: 28 E Rahn Rd Ste 105 Kettering OH 45429

SOWARDS, PATRICIA LUTIE (TRISH SOWARDS), psychologist; b. Buffalo, Wyo., Aug. 24, 1952; d. Charles Loyd and Lila Mae (Warrey) S. BA, Western State Coll., Gunnison, Colo., 1974; MS, Western Wash. U., 1978; PhD, U. Oreg., 1986. Lic. psychologist. Staff psychologist West River Mental Health Ctr., Spearfish and Rapid City, S.D., 1976-80; mental health profl. Peninsula Counseling Ctr., Port Angeles, Wash., 1980-83; intern in psychology Fed. Correctional Inst., Petersburg, Va., 1984-85; substance abuse coord. Island Mental Health Ctr., Coupeville, Wash., 1986; Powell (Wyo.) office supr. Park County Counseling, 1986—; acting dir. Park County Counseling, Powell and Cody, Wyo., 1990—; assoc. rep. Mental Health Assn., Lawrence County, S.D., 1977-78. Student counselor Help Phone Crisis Line, Brookings, S.D., 1970; vol. social svcs. worker Milton Olive III Meml. Clinic, Lexington, Miss., summer 1972; vol. Safe Home Rape Relief Network, Port Angeles, 1982-83; bd. dirs. Attention Ctr.-Run-a-Way Group Home, Spearfish, 1977-78, Adjustment Ctr.-Sheltered Workshop, Spearfish, 1977-78, Day Treatment Ctr., Port Angeles, 1982-83. Mem. Am. Psychol. Assn. Democrat. Home: 349 E 7th St Powell WY 82435 Office: Park County Counseling 639 Ave H Powell WY 82435

SOWDER, ELIZABETH ANNE, orthopedic center administrator; b. Roanoke, Va., Aug. 11, 1956; d. James Louis and Elizabeth Jeanne (Haley) S.; m. Mark H. Bower, Oct. 11, 1980. BBA, Coll. William and Mary, 1978. With McDonald and Co. Internat., Inc., Chgo. and Roanoke, 1980-83; dir. The Physicians Alliance of Roanoke, 1983-84; dir. mktg. Greater Roanoke Transit Co., 1985-87; mng. dir. Roanoke Orthopaedic and Athletic Rehab., 1987-88; adminstr. Roanoke Orthopaedic Ctr., 1988—. Bd. dirs. Am. Cancer Soc., Roanoke, 1987—. Mem. Med. Group Mgmt. Assn., Torch Club. Office: Roanoke Orthopaedic Ctr Inc 4064 Postal Dr SW Roanoke VA 24018

SOWERS, WILMA FRANCES, insurance agent; b. Templeton, Iowa, Nov. 21, 1933; d. Joseph E. and Mary Halbur Stevens; m. Gerald L. Sowers, Nov. 12, 1955 (div. Apr. 1983); 1 child, Cynthia Lee Winder. Student, U. Nebr., Omaha. Asst. to mgr. Breckenridge (Colo.) Inn, 1968-71; underwriter Great Am. Ins. Co., Omaha, 1971-73; agent Marcotte Ins. Agy. Inc., Omaha, 1973—. Vol. income tax assistant IRS program to assist elderly and poor, Omaha, 1988-89, Parent Assistance Line, Omaha, 1989. Mem. CPCU, Nat. Assn. Ins. Women (pres. local chpt. 1976), Independent Ins. Agents Am. Republican. Roman Catholic. Office: Marcotte Ins Agy Inc 3568 Dodge St Omaha NE 68131

SPACCIA, PIER'ANGELA, accounting professional; b. N.Y.C., Sept. 19, 1958; d. Francesco and Mary Yolanda (Soper) S.; 1 child, Sean. AA, Ventura Coll., 1983; BS in Bus. Mgmt., U. LaVerne, 1990. Acct. Alaska Constructors, Inc., Ventura, Calif.; office mgr. Bekins Moving and Storage, Ventura; acctg. mgr. City of Ventura, L.A. County Transp. Commn. Bd. dirs. Ventura County Fed. Credit Union. Mem. NAFE, Govt. Fin. Officers Assn., Mcpl. Fin. Officers Assn. Home: 2411 Harriman Ln #C Redondo Beach CA 90278 Office: LACTC 818 W Seventh St Ste 1100 Los Angeles CA 90017

SPACEK, SISSY (MARY ELIZABETH SPACEK), actress; b. Quitman, Tex., Dec. 25, 1949; d. Edwin S. and Virginia S.; m. Jack Fisk, 1974; children: Schuyler Elizabeth, Virginia Madison. Student, Lee Strasberg Theatrical Inst. Motion picture appearances include Prime Cut, 1972, Ginger in the Morning, 1972, Badlands, 1974, Carrie, 1976 (Acad. award nomination for best actress 1976), Three Women, 1977, Welcome to L.A., 1977, Heartbeat, 1980, Coal Miner's Daughter, 1980 (Acad. award for best actress 1980), Raggedy Man, 1981, Missing, 1982, The River, 1984, Marie, 1985, 'Night Mother, 1986, Crimes of the Heart, 1986, Violets Are Blue, 1986, The Long Walk Home, The Plastic Nightmare; TV movie appearances include The Girls of Huntington House, 1973, The Migrants, 1973, Katherine, 1975, Verna: USO Girl, 1978; guest host TV show Saturday Night Live, 1977; appeared in episode TV show The Waltons. Named Best Actress for Carrie, Nat. Soc. Film Critics, 1976, Best Supporting Actress, N.Y. Film Critics, 1977. Office: care Creative Artists 9830 Wilshire Blvd Beverly Hills CA 90212*

SPAGNA, GILDA, hospital administrator; b. Phila.; d. Francis Villone and Mafalda (Cortese) Spagna. BBA cum laude, U. Pa., 1981. Licensing agt. Ins. Co. N. Am., Phila., 1960-62; office mgr. Meth. Hosp., Phila., 1963-64; clin. dept. adminstr. dept. anesthesia U. Pa. Sch. Medicine, Phila., 1964—; mgmt. cons. Anesthesia Billing Office, U. Pa., 1985-87. Mem. Med. Group Mgmt. Assn., Del. Valley Med. Grp. Assn., Assn. Bus. Adminstrs. of U. Pa., Women's Faculty Club of U. Pa., Nat. Assn. Female Execs. Home: 1747 W Moyamensing Ave Philadelphia PA 19145

SPAID, ROBIN LOY, community college official, educator; b. Tucson, Feb. 10, 1947; d. Harlan Dean and Mary Natalie (Bartelt) Kosta; m. Glenn William Spaid, Mar. 5, 1966; 1 child, Natasha Kosta. AA, Hagerstown Jr. (Md.) Coll., 1974; BA, Hood Coll., 1975, MA in Human Sci., 1981; EdD, Va. Poly Inst. and State U., 1989. Part-time instr. in social studies; instr. social sci. Hagerstown Jr. Coll., 1975—, dir. adult reentry program, 1979—; field rep., manpower specialist Md. Gov.'s Com. To Promote Employment of Handicapped, Hagerstown, 1975-77. Contbr. articles to profl. publs. Bd. dirs. Pvt. Industry Coun., Hagerstown, 1985—; co-chmn. child care study Washington County Bd. Commrs., Hagerstown, 1988; trustee Washington County Free Libr., 1988—. Recipient Alumni Community Svc. award Hagerstown Jr. Coll. Alumni Assn., 1989; Carnegie-Mellon U. fellow, 1986. Mem. Am. Coun. on Edn. (rep. identification program for women adminstrs. 1987—), Hagerstown C. of C., AAUW (scholarship chmn. Hagerstown br. 1984-86, corp. rep. 1986—, Woman as Agt. of Change award 1985). Democrat. Office: Hagerstown Jr Coll 751 Robinwood Dr Hagerstown MD 21740

SPAINHOUR, ELIZABETH ANNE STROUPE, hospice official; b. Lenoir, N.C., July 13, 1944; d. Gustavus Lawson and Sara Arenna (Sharp) Stroupe; m. Jack Bryan Spainhour, Jr., June 20, 1965; children: Stephanie Leigh, Rebecca Anne, Jack Bryan III. Student, Lees-McRae Coll., Banner Elk, N.C., 1963; Accredited Record Technician Degree, Charlotte (N.C.) Meml. Hosp., 1964. Med. sec. Durwood Med. Clinic, Charlotte, 1964-65, Bowman Gray Sch. Medicine, Wake Forest U., Winston-Salem, N.C., 1965-69; rsch. sec. Med. Coll. Ga.-VA Hosp., Augusta, 1969-73; sec. Dr. Charles Freed, Danville, Va., 1973-74; adminstrv. asst. Hospice of Danville-Pittsylvania, 1986—. Sec., bd. dirs. Danville Mus. Fine Arts, 1987—; mem. Danville City Sch. Bd., 1988—; pres. Meml. Hosp. Aux., 1984-86, Aux. to Danville-Pittsylvania Acad. Medicine, 1988-89, Children's Theatre Danville, 1987-88. Republican. Methodist. Home: 260 Hawthorne Dr Danville VA 24541 Office: Hospice of Danville 115 S Main St Danville VA 24541

SPAK, DEBORAH GENDERNALIK, public relations specialist; b. Detroit, Aug. 24, 1963; d. Frank Edward and Gloria Jean (Gaucher) Gendernalik; m. David Gary Spak, June 15, 1986. BA in Communication, U. Mich., 1985. Legis. asst. Office of V.P. for Govt. Rels. U. Mich., Ann Arbor, 1983-85; intern Rosner & Liss Pub. Rels., Chgo., 1985; media rels. assoc. Weiser Group, Chgo., 1985-86, account exec., 1986-88, account supr., 1988—. Bd. dirs. City PAC, Chgo., 1990—; mem. communications com. March of Dimes of Chgo. Mem. Nat. Investor Rels. Inst., Pub. Rels. Soc. Am. Office: Weiser Minkus Walek 160 N Wacker Dr Chicago IL 60606

SPALDING, ALMUT MARIANNE, minister; b. Heidelberg, Fed. Republic Germany, July 19, 1957; came to U.S., 1979;p; d. Heinz-Peter Georg Alexander and Helga Kathe Ruth (Könnecke) Grutzner; m. Paul Stuart Spalding, May 27, 1978; children: Peter, James, Eckhart Arthur, Alex John. BA, U. Heidelberg, 1979; MDiv, McCormick Theol. Sem., 1984; MA, U. Iowa, 1985. Ordained to ministry, Presbyn. Ch., 1984. Student chaplain U. Iowa Hosps., Iowa City, 1980-81; co-pastor Elba (N.Y.) Presbyn. Ch., 1984-88; with pulpit supply Perry (Ill.) Presbyn. Ch., 1989—; chaplain Ill. Coll., Jacksonville, 1990; instr. Ill. Coll., Jacksonville, 1988, 90. Translator ABC Club, Damstadt, Fed. Republic Germany, 1987—. Mem. AAUW (sec. 1989—), Planned Parenthood Fedn. Am., Nat. Assn. Presbyn. Clergywomen. Home: 926 W Douglas Ave Jacksonville IL 62650

SPALDING, AMY JANETTE, accountant; b. Ann Arbor, Mich., Nov. 9, 1963; d. Martin John and Ruth Elaine (Wolter) S. BBA, Western Mich. U., 1985; postgrad., Walsh Coll., 1988—. Asst. br. mgr. Nat. Bank Detroit, 1985-86; mktg. cons. Promark Innovations, Southfield, Mich., 1986; staff acct. Molly Maid, Inc., Ann Arbor, 1986—. Vol. Friends of Mich. Parade Assn., Detroit, 1986, U. Mich. Hosp., Ann Arbor, 1987; founding mem. Detroit Inst. Arts, 1987. Mem. Am. Mktg. Assn., Western Mich. U. Alumni Assn. Lutheran. Home: 1669 Bloomfield Pl Bloomfield Hills MI 48013

SPALDING, DIANA J(ESUROGA), computer systems company executive; b. Miami, Fla., July 22, 1960; d. Richard Steven and Cleah June (Finley) S.; m. Richard Thomas Jesuroga, Feb. 16, 1982 (div. Feb. 1986). BA, U. Colo., 1983. Cert. paraprofl. counselor. Computer coder Dun & Bradstreet, N.Y.C., 1978, Parsippany, N.J., 1978-79; computer scientist NOAA/Program Regional Observing and Forecasting Services, Boulder, Colo., 1981-84; engr. NBI, Inc., Boulder, 1984-87; engr. Bell Labs, 1988—. Vol., counselor and pub. speaker Boulder County Safehouse, 1985—; peace activist, contbr. Women's Internat. League for Peace and Freedom, Boulder, 1985—, action chair, 1987; affiliate Friendship City Project, 1985—; suporting mem. N.Am. Congress on Latin Am., 1986—, ACLU, 1986—, Greenpeace, 1986—, Amnesty Internat., 1984—, Found. Nat. Progress, 1985—, Rocky Mountain Peace Ctr., 1985—; co-organizer Nat. Nonviolence Conf., 1988—; founding mem. Boulder Green Alliance Racial Justice Com., 1989—. Mem. Oxfam Am., The Nature Conservancy, Nat. Pub. Radio (KGNU), The Nation Assocs., Am. Peace Test, Nat. Hon. Soc. Clubs: Colo. Mountain. Avocations: hiking, bicycling, cross-country skiing. Office: Bell Labs PO Box 17054 Boulder CO 80308

SPALDING, ELAINE R., sales executive; b. Elmhurst, N.Y., June 26, 1940; d. John Arpod and Thelma (Smith) Rado; student Coll. Wooster, 1958-60; m. Larry Spalding, Dec. 24, 1966; children—Timothy A., Linda L., Med. sec. Duke U. Med. Center, Durham, N.C., 1967-70; adminstrv. sec. Tampa

Heights Hosp., Tampa, Fla., 1973-74; nat. distbr. Seyforth Labs., Inc., Dallas, 1975-79; nat. distbr. Futuron Industries, Inc., Dallas, 1979-83, dir. Futuron Distbr. Orgn., 1979-81, nat. distbr. Slendernow Internat., 1984—. Aide to Pinellas County Commr. Barbara Sheen Todd, 1980-89; v.p. Peninsula Republican Club, 1982-89. Recipient Distbr. of Year award, 1980, Spirit of Futuron award, 1981. Mem. Women in Mgmt. Address: 1211 Brookside Dr Clearwater FL 34624

SPALLA, ANNE BUCK, interior designer; b. Chgo., June 16; d. W. Gerald and Rita Bernadine (Maher) Buck; 1 child, Frank Gerald. BEd with honors, Chgo. State U., 1959, postgrad, 1965; postgrad, Roosevelt U., 1960-61; cert. in interior design with honors, Seminole Coll., 1986. Cert. tchr., Ill. Tchr. Chgo. Pub. Schs., 1959-61, 63-71, Huntsville (Ala.) Pub. Schs., 1961-62, Dallas Pub. Schs., 1971-72; artist Woodstock (Ill.) Gallery, 1975-77; interior designer Joan Carron Interiors, Lake Forest, Ill., 1977-79; pres. Anne Spalla Interiors, Inc., Longwood, Fla., 1980—; lectr. interior design Seminole Coll., Sanford, Fla., 1986; interior designer Orlando (Fla.) Opera Showhouse, 1985-86, March of Dimes Gourmet Gala, 1987-88; soloist Orlando Opera Edn. Program, 1979-82; mem. Orlando Opera Co., 1979—. Contbr. articles to various publs. Vol. Birth Edn. Tng. Acceptance, Orlando, 1979-82. Mundelein Coll. scholar, 1955-56; recipient Tchr. Certification Exam award, Chgo., 1959, Outstanding Future Tchr. award, 1959, Presdl. citation Am. Soc. Interior Design, 1987. Mem. Am. Soc. Interior Design (assoc., chmn. fund-raising com. Orlando chpt., Presdl. citation 1987), NAFE, Nat. Trust for Hist. Preservation, Horizon Club (Orlando, founder), Sweetwater Country Club (Longwood, founder). Republican. Roman Catholic. Clubs: Horizon (Orlando) (founder); Sweetwater Country (Longwood) (founder). Office: 820 W Gore St Orlando FL 32805 also: 186 S Pintail Chagrin Falls OH 44022

SPANDORFER, MERLE SUE, artist, educator; b. Balt., Sept. 4, 1934; d. Simon Louis and Bernice P. (Jacobson) S.; m. Lester M. Spandorfer, June 17, 1956; children: Cathy, John. Student, Syracuse U., 1952-54; BS, U. Md., 1956. Mem. faculty Cheltenham (Pa.) Sch. Fine Arts, 1969-90, dir. edn., 1970-90; instr. printmaking Tyler Sch. Art Temple U., Phila., 1980-84; faculty Pratt Graphics Ctr., N.Y.C., 1985-86; edn. dir., instr. Cheltenham (Pa.) Ctr. Arts, 1975—. One woman shows Richard Feigen Gallery, N.Y.C., 1970, U. Pa., 1974, Phila. Coll. Textiles and Sci., 1977, Ericson Gallery, N.Y.C., 1978, 79, R.I. Sch. Design, 1980, Syracuse U., 1981, Marian Locks Gallery, Phila., 1973, 78, 82, Temple U., 1984, Tyler Sch. Art, 1985, University City Sci. Ctr., 1987, Gov.'s Residence, 1988, Wenniger Graphics Gallery, Provincetown, Mass., 1989; group shows Bklyn. Mus. Art, 1973, San Francisco Mus. Art, 1973, Balt. Mus. Art, 1970, 71, 74, Phila. Mus. Art, 1972, 77, Fundacio Joan Miro, Barcelona, Spain, 1977, Del. Mus. Art, Wilmington, 1978, Carlsberg Glyptotek Mus., Copenhagen, 1980, Moore Coll. Art, Phila., 1982, Tyler Sch. Art, 1983, William Penn Meml. Mus., Harrisburg, Pa., 1984 Ariz. State U., 1985, Tiajin Fine Arts Coll., China, 1986, Beaver Coll., Phila., 1988, The Port of History Mus., Phila., 1987, Sichuan Fine Arts Inst., Chongging, People's Republic China, 1988, Glynn Vivian Mus., Swansea, Wales, 1989, Phila. Mus. Art, 1990; represented in permanent collections Met. Mus. Art, N.Y.C., Whitney Mus. Am. Art, N.Y.C., Mus. Modern Art, N.Y.C., The Israel Mus., Balt. Mus. (gov's prize and purchase award 1970), Phila. Mus. Art (purchase award 1977), Toyoh Bijutsu Gakko, Tokyo, Library of Congress, Temple U. Recipient Md. Inst. Art Balt. Mus., 1971; recipient Graphics Joan Mondale, Wallingford (Pa.) Art Ctr., 1978. Mem. Artist Equity, Am. Color Print Soc. (graphics 1980), Pa. Art Edn. Assn. (Outstanding Art Educator 1981-82), Coll. Art Assn. Jewish. Office: 307 E Gowen Ave Philadelphia PA 19119

SPANG, SARA CROSBY, publisher; b. Boston, Dec. 21, 1947; d. Carl Francis and Ruth Mary (Patterson) S.; m. Uzi Y. Bar-Gadda, Sept. 19, 1981; children: Rachel Ruth, David Carl. BA, U. Pa., Phila., 1969; PhD, Temple U., 1983. Rsch. assoc. Inst. for the Future, Menlo Park, Calif., 1979-81; mktg. mgr. Tymshare, Cupertino, Calif., 1981-83; founder Target Techs., Menlo Park, 1983-85, Spang Robinson, Menlo Park, 1985-88; founder, prin. Spang Robinson Wiley (merge with John Wiley & Sons), Menlo Park, 1988—. Contbr. articles to profl. jours. Grantee Ford Found., 1974-76, Nat. Sci. Found., 1974-76, Am. Inst. Pakistan Studies, 1974-76. Mem. Am. Assn. Artificial Intelligence, Palo Alto Jr. League. Republican. Office: Spang Robinson Wiley 830 Menlo Ave Ste 100 Menlo Park CA 94025

SPANGLE, TAMI RENEE, sales representative; b. Ft. Wayne, Ind., Dec. 7, 1965; d. Jimmy Franklin and Sharron Rose (Poyser) S. BS in Mktg., Ind. U., 1988, postgrad., 1988—. Pharm. sales rep. Marion Merrell Dow, Kansas City, Mo., 1988—. Dist. coord. United Way, Indpls., 1989—. Mem. Two Thousand Notable Am. Women, NAFE, Beta Gamma Sigma. Home: 1004 Lismore Dr S Apt E Indianapolis IN 46227

SPANGLER, DAISY KIRCHOFF, educator, educational consultant; b. Lancaster, Pa., Jan. 27, 1913; d. Frank Augustus and Lida Flaharty (Forewood) Kirchoff; BS, Millersville State Coll., 1963; MEd, Pa. State U., 1966, EdD, 1972; PhD, Stanton U., 1974; m. Francis R. Cosgrove Spangler, June 3, 1939 (dec.); children: Stephen Russell, Michael Denis. Tchr. rural sch., Providence, Pa., 1933-35, Rapho Twp., Pa., 1935-42, Mastersonville, Pa., 1942-51; elem. sch. prin. Manheim Cen., Pa., 1952-66; tchr., Manheim, Pa., 1967-68; assoc. prof. elem. edn. Millersville U., Pa., 1968-78, prof. emeritus, 1978—, advisor Kappa Delta Phi, 1968-88; tchr. Buckview Parachiol Sch., 1989-90; ednl. cons., 1978—; tchr. Amish Elem. Sch., Buckview, 1989—. Dist. chmn. ARC, 1965-66; mem. Hempfield PTA, 1966-67. Mem. Pa. Edn. Assn., Pa. Elem. Prins. Assn., Assn. Pa. State Coll. and Univ. Profs., Nat. Prin. Assn., Lancaster Prin. Assn. (pres. 1963-64), Pa. Assn. Ret. State Employees, Pa. Assn. State Retirees, Lancaster Area Ret. Pub. Sch. Employees Assn., Am. Ednl. Rsch. Assn., Manheim Tchrs. Assn. (pres. 1964-65), Hempfield Profl. Women, Am. Assn. Ret. Persons (chpt. pres. 1983-85, 89-90), Pi Lambda Theta (nat. com. 1980—, advisor Millersville U. 1968—, named outstanding advisor 1988, 89), Delta Kappa Gamma (pres. 1976-78), Order Eastern Star. Lutheran (pres. Luth. Women 1966-67, 79-81). Home and Office: Rte 7 Box 510 Manheim PA 17545

SPANGLER, MARGARET JOHNSON, nursing agency executive; b. Oceanside, N.Y., July 23, 1951; d. George Francis and Margaret Eileen (Sproat) Johnson; 1 child, Paul Scott. RN, St. Vincent Sch. Nursing, Birmingham, Ala., 1979; BS in Bus., Adelphi U., 1987, Litigation Legal Asst., 1987. Staff/charge registered nurse U. Ala. Hosp., Birmingham, 1979-82, Long Beach (N.Y.) Meml. Hosp., 1982-84; med. malpractice legal asst. Nathaniel Swergold, Esquire, Cedarhurst, N.Y., 1985-87; regional rep. Systel, Charlotte, N.C., 1988; sales rep. Health Care Svcs., Huntington, W.Va., 1989; br. mgr., dir. nursing Portamedic Healthcare, Charlotte, 1989—. Recipient Cert. of Appreciation, Gaston County, N.C., 1989. Mem. NAFE (assoc.). Office: Portamedic Healthcare 5701 Westpark Dr Suite 200 Charlotte NC 28217

SPANIEL, ROSALIE LOUISE SWANSON, public relations executive; b. Duquesne, Pa.; d. George S. and Louise B. (Stoehr) Swanson; m. William L. Spaniel, May 17, 1958; children: William George, Paul Maurice. BA, Frostburg State, 1975. Dir. alumni affairs Frostburg (Md.) State U., 1976-79; pub. info. officer City of Rock Hill, S.C., 1980-84; communications coord. Belk Stores Svcs., Inc., Charlotte, N.C., 1984-88; pub. info. specialist City of Charlotte, 1988—. Exec. bd. Greater Carolinas chpt. ARC, Charlotte, 1990-91. Recipient Achievement award Frostburg Alumni Assn., 1980. Mem. Pub. Rels. Soc. Am. (pres. Charlotte chpt. 1988, bd. dirs. Southeast dist. 1988), Pub. Rels. Soc. Roman Catholic. Office: City of Charlotte 600 E Fourth St Charlotte NC 28202

SPANN, REBECCA JANE, credit company manager; b. Corpus Christi, Tex., July 25, 1960; d. Bob J. and Billie Jane (Farr) S. Student, Del Mark Coll., Corpus Christi, 1979-80, U. Tex., Austin, 19j80-84. With sales and security Guarantee Sportswear, Corpus Christi, 1976-77; with sales and mgmt. J.C. Penney, Corpus Christi, 1978-80; sales clk. 3 Beau's Bros. 3, Corpus Christi, 1977-81; property mgr. Davis & Assocs., Austin, 1982-83; area mktg. dir., regional trainer Johnstown Am. Cos., Houston, 1983-85, with mgmt., mktg. maintenance specialist, 1985-86; dist. mgr. Balcor/Am. Express, Austin, 1986—. Mem. econ. devel. and bus. seminar coms. N.W. C. of C., Austin, 1986-88. Named Outstanding Young Woman Am., Outstanding Young Ams., 1988, recipient award Tex. Assn. Area Competitive Events Program Apparel and Accessories Series, Distributive Edn. Clubs Am., 1978, Exceptional Achievers award Johnstown Am. Cos. Tex., 1984. Mem. NAFE, Austin C. of C. (ambassador's coun., greeters com. 1985-88). Methodist. Home: 11215 Research Blvd Ste 2048 Austin TX 78759 Office: Balcor/Am Express 11215 Research Blvd Ste 1004 Austin TX 78759

SPARATORE, MARIA ANNA, pharmacist; b. Hartford, Conn., Dec. 18, 1964; d. Antonino Angelo and Maria Assunta (Malta) S. BS, U. Conn., 1987. Lic. pharmacist, Conn. Pharmacist Fay's Drugs, Bloomfield, Conn., 1988; pharmacist The Kay Drug Co., East Hartford, Conn., 1988-89, cons. pharmacist allcare medication svcs., 1989—. Mem. Am. Pharm. Assn., Conn. Pharm. Assn., Nat. Assn. Retail Druggists. Democrat. Roman Catholic. Home: 127 Main St East Hartford CT 06118 Office: The Kay Drug Co 112 Main St East Hartford CT 06118

SPARKS, DONNA THERESA, social worker; b. Freehold, N.J., July 16, 1946; d. Allen and Julia Louise (Lewis) S.; 1 child, Richard H. Davis III. BA in Psychology, Rutgers U., 1978, MSW, 1981. Pvt. practice therapy Newark, 1981; social worker N.J. Dept. Human Svcs., Newark, 1981. Investigative supr., coord. supr. staff Newark Alcoholism Awareness Day, North Jersey chpt. Nat. Coun. on Alcohol, 1980; mem. exec. com. and fundraising com. Boys and Girls Clubs of Newark, 1985—. Grad. scholar Rutgers U., 1979-81. Home: 583 Mount Prospect Ave Newark NJ 07104

SPARKS, ROBIN DALE, holding company executive; b. Hollywood, Calif., Feb. 15, 1940; d. Robert Lane and Elizabeth Jane (Wiehe) Snyder; m. John DeWitt Sparks Jr., July 26, 1958; children: Linda Kathleen, Jon Lane. Student, Woodbury Coll., L.A., 1957-58, Phoenix Coll., 1985-86. Typist Jerseymaid Milk Corp., L.A., 1959-62; with Harco Corp., Huntington Beach, Calif., 1963-70; bookkeeper Vika Corp., Costa Mesa, Calif., 1971-77; sales mgr. Vika Corp., Phoenix, 1977-80; adminstrv. asst. Vika Corp., 1980—; asst. asec. Lincoln Inst. Land Policy, Cambridge, Mass., 1987—, Lincoln Laser Co., Phoenix, 1985—; asst. sec.-treas. Jensen Patio Brick Co., Tempe, 1988—. Mem. Order DeMolay (dir. Sweethearts 1987—), Order Eastern Star. Republican. Home: 3680 W Aster Dr Phoenix AZ 85029 Office: Vika Corporation 55 E Thomas Rd Phoenix AZ 85012

SPARLING, MARY LEE, biology educator; b. Ft. Wayne, Ind., May 20, 1934; d. George Hewson and Velmah Evelyn (McClain) S.; m. Albert Alcide Barber, Sept. 1, 1956 (div. Jan. 1975); children: Bonnie Lee Barber, Bradley Paul Barber. BS, U. Miami, Coral Gables, Fla., 1955; MA, Duke U., 1958; PhD, UCLA, 1962. Lectr. UCLA, 1962-63; asst. prof. Calif. State U., Northridge, 1966-72, assoc. prof., 1972-76, prof., 1976—; mem. faculty senate, Calif. State U., Northridge, sec., 1978-79. Contbr. articles to profl. jours. NSF grantee Calif. State U., Northridge, 1971-72, 81-83, 89, NIH grantee Calif. State U., Northridge, 1987-89. Mem. Am. Soc. Cell Biology, Soc. for Devel. Biology, Am. Soc. Zoologists, AAUP (pres. 1981-82), Sigma Xi (bd. dirs. Research Triangle, N.C. 1974—). Home: 8518 White Oak Ave Northridge CA 91325 Office: Calif State U Biology Dept Northridge CA 91330

SPARR, BETSY CAROLYN, county official; b. Elizabethton, Tenn., June 24, 1960; d. Clyde D. and Agnes (Anderson) Atwood; m. Jeffrey L. Sparr, Oct. 10, 1987. BA, Coll. of Wooster, 1982. Program coord. Wayne County, Wooster, Ohio, 1984-85, asst. planner, 1985-88, dir. planning, 1988—; grantsperson Wayne County Airport Authority, 1985—; alt. NE Four County Regional Planning and Devel. Orgn., Akron, Ohio, 1985-89, mem., 1990—. Key person census statis. area Wayne County, 1985—. Mem. Ohio Planning Dir.'s Assn., Wayne County Women's Network. Office: Wayne County Planning Dept 428 W Liberty St Wooster OH 44691

SPARROW, BARBARA JANE, Canadian legislator; b. Toronto, Ont., Can., July 11, 1935; d. Thomas Henry and Alice (Musgrove) O'Connor; m. Robert Eugene Sparrow, Oct. 19, 1956 (dec.); children: Thomas, Jane, James, John. Student, Wellesley Hosp. Sch. Nursing. RN. Mem. from Calgary Southwest Ho. of Commons, Can., 1984—. Mem. Calgary C. of C., Glencoe Club, Calgary Golf and Country Club. Mem. Progressive Conservative Party. Anglican. Address: 68 Baycrest Pl SW, No 9, Calgary, AB Canada T2V 0K6*

SPARROW, LISSA CADLE, community relations official; b. Marietta, Ga., Jan. 14, 1964; d. William Reese and Sandra Lou (Wyatt) Cadle; m. Paul Maxwell Sparrow, Nov. 26, 1988. BA in Psychology, U. Ga., 1987. Asst. dir. undergrad. admissions Mercer U., Macon, Ga., 1987-88, market rsch. asst., 1988; dir. mktg. Barnes Drug Stores, Valdosta, Ga., 1989; regional referral coord. Sea Pines Rehab. Hosp., Jacksonville, Fla., 1989-90; community rels. rep. Charter Hosp. Jacksonville, 1990—. Chmn. pub. edn., mem. exec. com., bd. dirs. Am. Cancer Soc., Valdosta, 1989, pub. edn. vol., Jacksonville, 1989—. Republican. Episcopalian. Home: 4382 Carriage Crossing Dr Apt 401 Jacksonville FL 32257 Office: Charter Hosp Jacksonville 3947 Salisbury Rd Jacksonville FL 32216

SPARTI, CHERYL DIANE, principal; b. L.A., Feb. 3, 1930; d. Harold Emory and Lillian Nordica (Cosley) Counts; m. Norman Thomas Zahn Jr., Sept. 4, 1953 (div. Feb. 1958); children: Darrell H. and Farrell K. (twins); m. Carlo Sebastian Sparti, Aug. 12, 1961. AA, UCLA, 1951, BA with honors, 1953; MS, U. So. Calif., 1966. Tchr. L.A. Unified Sch. Dist., 1953-54, 56-58, tng. tchr., demonstration tchr., 1958-67, asst. prin., 1967-72, prin., 1972—; tchr. Pepperdine U., L.A., 1969-73; cons. mktg. rsch. in edn., L.A., 1956-87; panel mem. NBC-TV, L.A., 1973; ptnr. multi-million bus. bldg., Valencia, Calif., 1987—; adminstr. Sch.-Community Adv. Coun., L.A., 1966—, Local Sch. Leadership Coun., L.A., 1989—. Contbr. articles to profl. jours.; coord., spokesperson video Drug Abuse Edn., 1988. Vol. sch. activities, planting trees at schs., L.A., 1953-90; vol. XXIII Olympiad, L.A., 1984, TV Sportsathon PTA, L.A. Unified Sch. Dist., 1978; adminstr. Adopt-A-Sch. Program with Gen. Tel., L.A., 1981-90; hon. life mem. Calif. PTA, L.A., 1982. Recipient gold medallion L.A. Olympic Com., 1984, personal commendation L.A. City Coun., 1990, recognition for sch. L.A. City Coun., 1987. Mem. NAFE, Associated Adminstrs. L.A. (sec., com. mem. 1967-90, Plaque 1990), Am. Soc. Profl. and Exec. Women, Delta Kappa Gamma (pres. 1972-74, Plaque 1974), Kappa Delta Pi (pres. 1970-72, Plaque 1973), Alpha Gamma Delta.

SPARTIN, FLAVIA CLEO, government executive; b. N.Y.C., Sept. 15, 1935; d. Flaviano and Mary (Casuli) Coletta; m. William A. Spartin, Oct. 6, 1929; children: David William, Peter William, Steven William, Wilma Anne Rowe. BS, Queens Coll., N.Y.C., 1955; postgrad., Antioch Law Sch., 1979-81, George Wash. U., 1985. Research chemist E.I. DuPont de Nemours, Wilmington, Del., 1955-56, Dow Chem., Pitts., 1956-57; tchr. various schs., 1957-68; dir. research R.S. Landauer, Matteson, Ill., 1965-68; asst. dir EEO U.S. Dept of the Interior, Washington, 1972-81; dir. gov. wide women's program U.S. Office of Personnel Mgmt., Washington, 1981-84; assoc. dir., human resources U.S. Envir. Prot. Agy., Washington, 1984-88; dir. human resources U.S. Gov. Printing Office, Washington, 1988—; bd. dirs. Federally Employed Women, 1981-84, bd. mem. Fed. Women's Interagency Bd., 1981—, mem. White House Commn. on Women's Issues, 1981-84, Exec. Women in Govt., 1988—. Pres. PTA, sunday sch. tchr., Presbyterian Ch., Bethesda, Md., 1970—, dance com. Wolf Trap Farm Park Assn., Reston, Va., 1974-76, Project Hope, Washington, D.C., 1975—. Mem. AAUW, Bus. and Profl. Women, Republican Women's Club. Home: 10801 Stanmore Potomac MD 20854 Office: U S Govt Printing Office 732 N Capital St NW Washington DC 20401

SPATA, KATHLEEN MARIE, special events coordinator; b. Oak Park, Ill., Apr. 11, 1964; d. Charles P. and Rose Marie (Baldo) S. BA in Telecommunications, U. Miami, Coral Gables, Fla., 1986, MA in Communication, 1988. Spl. project coord. Miami-Dade Community Coll., 1988-89; program coord. Muscular Dystrophy Assn., Hollywood, Fla., 1988-90; coord. student affairs L.I.F.E. program Barry U., Miami Shores, Fla., 1990—. Mem. Women in Communications, Inc., Vizcayans, Phi Kappa Phi. Office: Barry U 11300 NE 2d Ave Miami Shores FL 33161

SPATARO, JANIE DEMPSEY WATTS, writer; b. Chattanooga, May 17, 1951; d. Ray Dean and Anne America (Dempsey) Watts; m. Stephen Anthony Spataro, June 18, 1977; children—Anthony Dempsey, Stephen Jackson. B.S. in Journalism, U. Calif.-Berkeley, 1974; M.A. in Broadcast Journalism, U. So. Calif., 1982. Writer, editor McGiffin Newspapers, South Gate, Calif., 1976; news bur. mgr. Loyola Marymount U., Westchester, Calif., 1976; asst. dir. pub. relations Hawthorne (Calif.) Community Hosp. 1977-78; writer, with pub. relations dept. Moneywise, Los Angeles, 1980-81; pub. relations cons. Security Pacific Bank, Los Angeles, 1978-82; writer Cable Card, Inc., Marina del Rey, Calif., 1983; writer Reality Prodns., Huntington Beach, Calif., 1983-86. Writer, producer, editor TV documentary: Who's Minding the Children?, 1983; contbr. articles to mags. and newspapers. Speaker on child care on TV, 1983-84. Beatrice E. Rice scholar U. Calif., 1973-74; Calif. State fellow, 1981-83. Mem. Women in Film, Women in Communications, DAR. Home and Office: 2629 Arizona Ave Santa Monica CA 90404

SPATTA, CAROLYN DAVIS, vice president university; b. Gauhati, Assam, India, Jan. 1, 1935; d. Alfred Charles and Lola Mildred (Anderson) Davis; m. John Robert Spatta, June 2, 1957 (div. Feb. 1964); children: Robert Alan, Jennifer Lynn Spatta-Harris; m. S. Peter Karlow, July 25, 1981. AB, U. Calif., Berkeley, 1964; MA, U. Mich., 1968, PhD, 1974. Rsch. asst. U. Calif., Berkeley, 1963-65; instr. Schoolcraft Coll., Livonia, Mich., 1968-74; corp. sec. Oberlin (Ohio) Coll., 1974-78; pres. Damavand Coll., Tehran, India, 1978-79; cons. pvt. practice, Washington, 1979-80; v.p., adminstr. E. Mich. U., Ypsilanti, Mich., 1980-81; Dir. Inst. grants programs, and adv. svc. Assn. Am. Colls., Washington, 1982-84; v.p., adminstrn. and bus. affairs Calif. State U., Hayward, 1984—; vis. lectr. E. Mich. U., Ypsilanti, 1969, 1970; mem. accreditation team Western Assn. Schs. Colls. Contbr. articles to profl. jours. bd. dirs. Wellness, Inc., mem. Trinity Parish, Menlo Pk., Calif. (pers., bldg. coms.), U. Mich. Alumni Assn., St. John's Episc. Ch. (pastoral care commn.), Chevy Chase, Md., Oberlin Open Space Com., Tenaya Guild, John Muir Hosp., Walnut Creek, Calif. (pres.), steering com. Ann Arbor Citizens for Good Schs. Recipient fellowship Nat. Defense Foreign Lang., 1966-68. Mem. Am. Assn. Higher Edn., Asian Studies on Pacific Coast, Assn. Asian Studies, Assn. Am. Geographers, Assn. Pacific Coast Geographers, Soc. Coll. and U. Planning. Office: Calif State U Hayward CA 94542

SPATZ, LOIS SETTLER, classics educator; b. Balt., Mar. 28, 1940; d. M. Martin and Esther Sonya (Levinson) Settler; m. Jonas Spatz, June 10, 1962; children: Stephen Dedalus, David Alexander. BA, Goucher Coll., 1960; MA in Teaching, Johns Hopkins U., 1961; MA, Ind. U., 1964; PhD, Ind. U , 1968. Lectr. in classics Bklyn. Coll., 1965-66; sr. tchr. Latin Sunset Hill Sch., Kansas City, Mo., 1967-68; prof. Western heritage Park Coll., Parkville, Mo., 1968-72; asst. prof. English U. Mo., Kansas City, 1973-80, assoc. prof. English, 1980-85, prof. English, co-dir. classical and ancient studies, 1985—; cons. magnet program Kansas City Sch. Dist., 1988—; bd. dirs. Interdisciplinary Courses in Humanities Program, 1985-89. Author: Aristophanes, 1978, Aeschylus, 1982; contbr. articles to profl. jours. Recipient Shelby Storck Teaching award U. Mo., Kansas City, 1988, Burlington No. Faculty Achievement award U. Mo., 1989. Mem. Am. Philological Assn., Soc. for Bibl. Lit., Assn. Integrative Studies, Archaeol. Inst. Am., Mo. Classical Assn. (pres. 1982-85), Classical Assn. Middle West and South, Phi Beta Kappa. Democrat. Jewish. Office: U Mo English Dept Cockefair Hall Kansas City MO 64110

SPAUDE, DORIS ANITA SCHROEDER, educator, freelance artist, interior decorator; b. Reedsburg, Wis., Sept. 7, 1942; d. Gilbert Edward and Anita (Mueller) Schroeder; children: Michelle Renee, Chantelle Kareen. BS in Elem. Edn., Wis. State U., Oshkosh, 1965; BS in Computer Graphics, Marycrest Coll., Davenport, Iowa, 1986; postgrad., Marycrest Coll., 1988—. Lic. tchr., Iowa. Tchr. various schs., various locations, 1964-74, Pleasant Valley (Iowa) Community Schs., 1974—; freelance artist Wis., Oreg., Ill., Iowa, and France, 1960—; freelance interior decorator and stenciler, Moline, Ill., 1979—. Copyright 7 computer graphic images. Mem. Computer Image Assn. Marycrest Coll., Davenport, Iowa, 1983-86, bldg. com. Prince of Peace Luth. Ch., Davenport, 1976-77, edn. chmn. ch. council; alt. sponsor Am.-Soviet Youth Exchange Initiative for Understanding, 1988-90; del. leader People to People, Am.-Soviet Friendship Caravan, 1990. Mem. NAFE, NEA, Iowa State Edn. Assn., Pleasant Valley Edn. Assn. (pres. 1990—), Nat. Mus. Women in Arts (charter). Home: 1923 13th St Moline IL 61265

SPAULDING, SUSAN KAY, advertising agency executive; b. St. Joseph, Mo., Aug. 24, 1955; d. Jack D. Baker and Polly (Weedin) Swafford; m. George T. Spaulding, June 24, 1978. BA in Journalism, U. Kans., 1977; MA in Mktg. & Mgmt., Webster U., 1988. Promotion dir. Metcalf South, Overland Park, Kans., 1977-78; account exec. SCG, Overland Park, 1978-79; assoc. dir. rsch. D'Arcy MacManus & Masius, Bloomington, Minn., 1979-81; v.p. rsch. and dir. mktg. Valentine-Radford, Kansas City, 1981—; guest tchr. Johnson Community Coll., Overland Park, 1987, U. Kans., Lawrence, 1987, Longview Coll., Kansas City, 1985, Pioneer Community Coll., Kansas City, U. Mo., Webster U. Contbr. articles to profl. jours. Cons. Parents Anonymous, Kansas City, 1982, Rehab. Inst. of Kansas City, 1983, Nat. Alcoholic Council, Kansas City, 1982. Mem. Am. Mktg. Assn., Direct Mktg. Assn., Market Research Assn., Ad Club, Austin Healey Club, EEA 200. Home: 17743 W 67th St Shawnee KS 66217 Office: Valentine-Radford 911 Main St Ste 1100 Kansas City MO 64105

SPAULDING, VANITA MARIE, forensic business valuation; b. Van Nuys, Calif., June 20, 1954; d. Vance Dalton Meyer and Patricia Ann (Stephan) Hadley; m. John Robert Spaulding; children: Brannon Robert, Erin Marie. BA in Fin., Calif. State U., Northridge, 1984, MBA in Fin. magna cum laude, 1987. Real estate sales broker Fred Sands, Woodland Hills, Calif., 1980-84; fin. analyst Hughes Aircraft, Canoga Park, Calif., 1982-83; bus. appraiser Desmond & Marcello, 1983; real estate appraiser Am. Real Estate Appraisal Co., Marina Del Rey, Calif., 1983-87; bus. valuation mgr. Touch Ross & Co., L.A., 1987-89; pres. forensic bus. valuation V.M. Spaulding & Assocs., Woodland Hills, Calif., 1990—. Coach Am. Youth Soccer Orgn. Mem. Am. Soc. Appraisers (sr. mem., chairperson bus. valuation com. L.A chpt.). Home and Office: V M Spaulding & Assocs 23040 Mariano St Woodland Hills CA 91367

SPAZIANI, JOANN, national sales manager; b. Monogehela, Pa., Dec. 26, 1952; d. Oscar Antonio and Ellen Rose (Franks) S. Assoc., Pa. State U., 1972. Buyer Gimbels Bros., Pitts., Pa., 1974-78, Emporium Capwell, Oakland, Calif., 1978-81; co-op sales dir. Sta. KNEW/KSAN, Oakland, Calif., 1981-83; acct. exec. Sta. KITS-FM, San Francisco, 1983-86, Sta. KYUU-FM, San Francisco, 1986-87; nat. sales mgr. Sta. KOIT AM/FM, Calif., 1987—. Volunteer, Cystic Fibrosis Found, San Francisco, 1987-89, Am. Heart Assn., 1987-89, Gerry Lewis Telethon Multiple Sclerosis, 1987--, March of Dimes Bid for Bachelors, 1988. Fellow: Northern Calif. Broadcasters Assn., Soc. of TV and Radio. Home: 105 Eucalyptus Knoll Mill Valley CA 94941 Office: Sta KOIT AM/FM 77 Maiden Ln San Francisco CA 94108

SPEAR, JEAN EVELYN HINSON, nurse; b. Quincy, Fla., Oct. 7, 1944; d. Wash Sr. and Emma Ree (Harris) Hinson; m. Thomas Robert Smith, Oct. 26, 1962 (div. 1983); children: Theophilus Rodney, Roderick O'Brien; m. Joshua Spear, July 26, 1986. BS, Fla. A&M U., 1976, postgrad., 1979; postgrad., Fla. State U., 1978, 79, 83, U. Fla., 1983. RN Fla. RN supr. Goodwood Manor, Tallahassee, Fla., 1978-79; crisis intervention counselor Apalachee Community Mental Health, Inc., Quincy, Fla., 1978-79; RN III, team leader Apalachee Community Mental Health, Inc., Quincy, 1977-79; sr. RN supr. State of Fla., Fla. State Hosp., Chattahoochee, Fla., 1979—; instr. Gadsden County Vocat. Sch., Quincy, Fla., 1987—; chmn. forensic nursing com., Chattahoochee, 1986-87; mem. Nursing Policy and Procedure Commn., Chattahoochee, 1981-82; substitute tchr. Gadsden County Bd. Edn., Quincy, 1978—; pres., chair, small bus. devel. Hinson Devel. Ltd., Inc., 1989—. Mem. Nat. Trust for Hist. Preservation, 1989—. Recipient Gov.'s Cert. Merit State of Fla., 1983. Mem. Am. Nurses Assn., Fla. Nurses Assn., Nat. Assn. Female Execs., Am. Bus. Women's Assn. Silver Dome chpt. Democrat. Missionary Baptist. Office: Fla State Hosp PO Box 1000 Chattahoochee FL 32324

SPEAR, MARY PATRICIA, sales and marketing executive; b. Sheridan, Wyo., May 4, 1954; d. Bradford Johnson and Patricia Ann (Brooder) S.; m. Kenneth Ray Gleason, June 3, 1972 (div. June 1982); children: Seth Kendy, Susan Michele. Grad. high sch., Dayton, Wyo. Bookkeeper Padlock Ranch,

Ranchester, Wyo., 1972; ranch ptnr. Eagle Point Ranch, Busby, Mont., 1972-82; purchasing agt. Top Office Products, Inc., Sheridan, 1982-86, sales rep., 1985-87; nat. sales and mktg. dir. GeoLearning Corp., Sheridan, 1988-89, gen. mgr., 1990—; ski sch. instr. Antelope Butte Corp., Sheridan, 1990—; property tax cons., 1989—. Bd. dirs. Sch. Dist. 17K Big Horn County, Kirby, Mont., 1980-82. Recipient Outstanding Skiing award Sheridan C. of C., 1970; named 1st Runner-up Mother of Yr. Big Horn County, 1980. Fellow NAFE; mem. Profl. Ski Instrs. of Am., Kiwanis (v.p. local club 1989—, pres. 1990-91), Future Farmers Am. Alumni Assn. (sec. 1988—), P.E.O. (treas. chpt. T), Young Farmers and Ranchers Edn. Assn. Republican. Episcopalian. Home: 355 Smith St Sheridan WY 82801 Office: Geolearning Corp 555 Absaraka Sheridan WY 82801

SPEARMAN, MAXIE ANN, financial analyst, accountant; b. Piedmont, S.C., Sept. 14, 1942; d. J. Mac and Margaret Cecille (Johnson) S. BS, U. S.C., 1965; student, Ga. State U., U. Ga. Internal auditor Sears, Roebuck & Co., Atlanta; acct. Econ. Opportunity Atlanta, Shell Oil Co., Atlanta; fin. analyst City of Atlanta. Mem. Rep. Presdl. task force, U.S. Senatorial Club. Office: 55 Trinity Ave Atlanta GA 30335

SPEARS, JAE, state legislator; b. Latonia, Ky.; d. James and Sylvia (Fox) Marshall; m. Lawrence E. Spears; children: Katherine Spears Cooper, Marsha Spears-Duncan, Lawrence M., James W. Student, U. Ky. Reporter Cin. Post, Cin. Enquirer newspapers; research Stas. WLW-WSAI, Cin.; tchr. Jiya Gakuen Sch., Japan; lectr. U.S. Mil. installations East Anglia, Eng.; del. State of W.Va., Charleston, 1974-80, state senator, 1980—; mem. adv. bd. W.Va. Women's Commn., Charleston, 1976—; mem. state visitors com. W.Va. Extension and Continuing Edn., Morgantown, 1977—. Mem. coun. W.Va. Autism Task Force, Huntington, 1981—; mem. W.Va. exec. bd. Lit. Vols. Am., 1985—; bd. dirs. Found. Ind. Colls. W.Va., 1986—; regional adv. com. Gov.'s Task Force for Children, Youth and Family, 1989; mem. USS W.Va. Commn., 1989; mem. exec. com. W.Va. Employer Support Group of Guard and Res., 1989; pres. litigation vols., W.V., 1990—. Recipient Susan B. Anthony award NOW, 1982, nat. award Mil. Order Purple Heart, 1984, Edn. award Profl. Educators Assn. W.Va., 1986, Ann. award W.Va. Assn. Ret. Sch. Employees, 1985, Meritorious Service award W.Va. State Vets. Commn., 1984, Vets. Employment and Tng. Service award U.S. Dept. Labor, 1984, award W.Va. Vets. Council, 1984; named Admiral in N.C. Navy, Gov. of N.C., 1982, Hon. Brigadier W.Va. N.G., 1984. Mem. Bus. and Profl. Women (Woman of Yr. award 1978), Nat. League Am. Pen Women (Pen Woman of Yr. 1984), Nat. Order Women Legislators, DAR, VFW (aux.), Am. Legion (aux.), Delta Kappa Gamma, Alpha Xi Delta. Democrat. Home and Office: PO Box 2088 Elkins WV 26241

SPEARS, JOYCE ANN, financial executive; b. St. Louis, Mar. 2, 1939; d. Roy Edward and Theda Irene (Stanley) Nunn; m. James Arnold Spears, May 13, 1972; children: Juliana Palmer, J.J. AA, Westark Community Coll., 1988; BS cum laude, U. Ozarks, 1988. Bookkeeper/sec. Graham Paper Co., Oklahoma City, 1959-66; legal asst. trainee/mgr. Wiliam M. Stocks, Atty., Ft. Smith, Ark., 1967-70; supr. lab. office Sparks Regional Med. Ctr., Ft. Smith, 1970-71, adminstrv. asst. dietary dept., 1971-74, payroll clerk, 1974-75, mgr. acct. dept., 1975-80, asst. controller fin., 1980—; fina. aid adminstr. Sparks Sch. Med. Tech., Ft. Smith, 1980—, Sparks Sch. Radiol. Tech., Ft. Smith, 1980—; Sparks Sch. Respiratory Service, Ft. Smith, 1980—, Ark. Assn. FAA, 1980—. Treas., vol., St. Jude Children's Research Hosp., Memphis, 1977-86; mem., tutor, The Ft. Smith Literacy Council, 1984—, bd. dirs., 1990—; mem., vol., The Ft. Smith Pub. Library, 1984—. Mem. LWV, Ark. Fedn. Bus. and Profl. Women (dist. dir. 1985-86, pres.-elect 1988, state pres. 1989-90, Best Conf. award 1985), Ft. Smith Bus. and Profl. Women (1st v.p. 1980-81, pres. 1982-83, Outstanding Bus. Woman 1982, Woman of Yr. 1983, best speaker competition), Bonneville House Assn. (pres. 1990—), Westark Community Coll. Profl. Women's Adv. Bd., Altrusa Club (pres., bd. dirs., award, community svc. and project chmn. for Taste of Ft. Smith, 1990), Leadership Ft. Smith (class of 25 1990—). Republican. Baptist. Home: 3034 S 58 St Fort Smith AR 72903 Office: Sparks Regional Med Ctr 1311 S I St Fort Smith AR 72901

SPECHALSKE, PHYLLIS VALAND, media specialist, educator; b. Stonega, Va., Mar. 18, 1931; m. Frank H. Spechalske, June 18, 1954; children: Richard, Janine, Jon, Robert. BA, Baldwin Wallace Coll., 1953; postgrad., Ea. Mont. U., 1969-71; MEd, U. South Ala., 1979. Cert. tchr., Ohio, Pa., Ala. Media specialist Billings (Mont.) Pub. Schs., 1972-77; tchr. Mobile (Ala.) County Pub. Schs., 1979-81, media specialist, 1982—. Mem. South Ala. Botanical Soc., Mobile, 1985-88. Recipient 4-H Club Leaders award, Ala. Coop. Extention Svc., 1985. Mem. Ala. Instructional Media Assn. (pres. 1985, 87), Ala. Libr. Assn., Bay Area Libr. Assn., Jubilee Story league, Mystic Maskers (Mobile, treas. 1986, recording sec. 1988), Nat. Assn. for Preservation and Perpetuation of Storytelling. Republican. Lutheran. Home: 3771 Swansea Dr Mobile AL 36608 Office: Theodore Middle Sch 5760 Theodore Dawes Rd Theodore AL 36582

SPECHT, DIANE ELIZABETH, publishing executive; b. Sunbury, Pa., July 14, 1944; d. David McKee Specht and Dorothy Ann (Rorick) Wagner. BA in Journalism, Pa. State U., State College, 1966; BS in Mktg., Fashion Inst. Tech., N.Y.C., 1989. Reporter Fashion Week, L.A., 1967-69; mng. editor Earnshaw Publs./Small World, N.Y.C., 1970-72, Earnshaw/Earnshaw's Rev., N.Y.C., 1973-76; editorial dir. Earnshaw Publs., Inc., N.Y.C., 1977-80, assoc. pub., 1980-87, pub. Plus Sizes, 1987—, exec. v.p., 1987—. Democrat. Episcopalian. Home: 720 Greenwich St Apt 4-C New York NY 10014 Office: Earnshaw Pubs Inc 225 W 34th St Ste 1212 New York NY 10014

SPECIAN, ROSEMARIE THERESE, entreprenuer; b. Somerville, N.J., Nov. 4, 1944; d. William Michael and Maryann (Dudek) S.; m. Edward J. Sinusas, Jr. Dec. 28, 1985. BS in Home Econs. (Ella Mae Shellshy Holmes award), Albright Coll., Reading, Pa., 1966; MS in Human Behavior and Devel., Drexel U., Phila., 1971; MBA, Loyola-Marymount U., L.A., 1980; cert. Comml. Flower Arranging, N.Y. Bot. Gardens, Bronx, 1987. Sales rep. Atlas Crown Brokerage, L.A., 1973-75; regional rep. Reynolds Metals Co., L.A., 1975-77; mktg. mgr. nat. accounts Glass Containers Corp., Anaheim, Calif., 1977-79; sr. package developer Lederle Labs., Pearl River, N.Y., 1980-89; pres. All Things Bright and Beautiful, Nanuet, N.Y., 1988—. Recipient various sales awards. Mem. AAUW, Am. Mktg. Assn., Packaging Inst., N.J. Mktg. Assn., N.J. Packaging Assn. Home: 60 Jonathan Dr Mahopac NY 10541 Office: 119 Rockland Ctr Nanuet NY 10954

SPECK, HILDA, social worker; b. Stalybridge, Cheshire, England, Mar. 2, 1916; came to U.S., 1923; d. John Robert and Rose Ethel (Tymns) Smith; m. Willmot Hilton Speck, Sept. 4, 1937 (dec. Jan 1968); foster children: Barbara Ann Beranek Renfrow, Winifred June Beranek Aguilar. Grad. high sch., Flint, Mich. Lic. social worker, Mich. Founder of Social Svc. Dept. and dir. social svcs. The Salvation Army, Flint, 1945-86; mem. establishing com. 4C Child Care Agy.; life mem. Salvation Army Adv. Bd., Flint, Mich. Assisted in establishing Safe House for Victims of Domestic Violence, Flint, 1976-80; mem. Churchwomen United Convalescent Home Com.; appt. clothing distbn. adminstr. Flint Civil Def.; mem. Red Feather Million Dollar Disaster Fund Salvation Army Rehab. Program, 1953; mem. Day Care com. Genesee County; mem. original planning com. Planned Parent Orgn.; mem. McLaren Gen. Hosp. Aux., 1988—. Recipient Hands of Mercy award The Salvation Army, 1967, Centennial Youth award The Salvation Army, 1965, 20 Year Service award Big Brothers of Genesee County; named Woman of Week local radio sta., 1957. Mem. Coun. Social Agys., Genesee County Commn. on Aging (v.p. 1971—), GLS Counties Health Planning Coun. Bd., Genesee County Emergency Task Force, Zonta. Home: 2015 Stoney Brook Ct Flint MI 48507

SPECTOR, BARBARA HOLMES, retired communications administrator; b. Manchester, N.H., June 15, 1927; d. Kenneth Morris and Frances A. (Hall) Holmes; m. Saul James Spector, Oct. 27, 1953 (dec. Apr. 1986); children: Pamela Jill, Mark James. Student, Hesser Bus. Sch., Manchester, 1945-46. Operator New England Telephone, Manchester, 1946-51, repair clk., 1951-54, repair observer, 1959-71; cen. office foreman New England Telephone, Nashua, N.H., 1972-73; staff instr., svc. ctr. foreman New England Telephone, Boston, Concord, N.H., 1973-75; asst. staff mgr. New England Telephone, Manchester, 1975-83, ret., 1983. Mem. N.H. Rep. Women's Club, 1987—. Mem. Telephone Pioneers. Episcopalian. Home: 662 Amherst St Manchester NH 03104

SPECTOR, ELEANOR RUTH, government executive; b. N.Y.C., Dec. 2, 1943; d. Sidney and Helen (Kirschenbaum) Lebost; m. Mel Alan Spector, Dec. 10, 1966; children: Nancy, Kenneth. BA, Barnard Coll., 1964; postgrad. sch. pub. adminstrn., George Washington U., 1965-67; postgrad sch. edn., Nazareth Coll., 1974. Indsl. investigator N.Y. State Dept. Labor, White Plains, 1964-65; mgmt. intern Navy Dept., Washington, 1965, contract negotiator, 1965-68, contract specialist, 1975-78, contracting officer/br. head, 1978-82, dir. div. cost estimating, 1982-84; dep. asst. sec. def. for procurement Dept. Def., Washington, 1984—; advisor Nat. Contract Mgmt. Assn., 1984—. Office: US Dept of Def Office of Procurement The Pentagon Room 3E144 Washington DC 20301-8000

SPECTOR, GAIL GREER, sales professional; b. Winston Salem, N.C., Sept. 25, 1950; d. John Baxter Greer and Edith (Walsh) Taylor; m. Samuel H. Spector (div. 1987); 1 child, Benjamin Randall. BA in Psychology, U. N.C., Chapel Hill, 1972. Sales cons., sales mgr. Royal Homes, Ft. Myers, Fla., 1978-80; sales cons. U.S. Home Corp., Ft. Myers, 1980—; mem. adv. coun. U.S. Home Corp. Nat. Sales, 1988. Mem. U. N.C. Alumni Assn., Phi Beta Kappa.

SPECTOR, JOHANNA LICHTENBERG, ethnomusicologist, emeritus educator; b. Libau, Latvia; came to U.S., 1947, naturalized, 1954; d. Jacob C. and Anna (Meyer) Lichtenberg; m. Robert Spector, Nov. 20, 1939 (dec. Dec. 1941). DHS, Hebrew Union Coll., 1950; MA, Columbia U., 1960. Rsch. fellow Hebrew U., Jerusalem, 1951-53; faculty Jewish Theol. Sem. Am., N.Y.C., 1954—, dir., founder dept. ethnomusicology, 1962-85, assoc. prof. musicology, 1966-70, Sem. prof., 1970-85, prof. emeritus, 1985—. Author: Ghetto-und Kzlieder, 1947, Samaritan Chant, 1965, Musical Tradition and Innovation in Central Asia, 1966, Bridal Songs from Sana Yemen, 1960; documentary film The Samaritans, 1971, Middle Eastern Music, 1973, About the Jews of India: Cochin, 1976 (Cine Golden Eagle 1979), The Shanwar Telis or Bene Israel of India, 1978 (Cine Golden Eagle 1979), About the Jews of Yemen, A Vanishing Culture, 1986 (Cine Golden Eagle 1986, Blue Ribbon, Am. Film Festival 1986); religious and folk recs. number over 10, 000; contbr. articles to encys., various jours.; editorial bd. Asian Music. Bd. dirs. Sino-Judaic Inst. Fellow Am. Anthrop. Assn.; mem. Am. Ethnol. Soc., Am. Musicol. Soc., Internat. Folk Music Council, World Assn. Jewish Studies, Yivo, Asian Mus. Soc. (v.p. 1964—, pres. 1974-78), African Mus. Soc., Soc. Ethnomusicology (sec.-treas N.Y.C. chapt. 1960-64), Soc. Preservation of Samaritan Culture (founder). Home: 400 W 119th St New York NY 10027

SPECTOR, KAREN, executive producer; b. Hackensack, N.J., June 20, 1951; d. Hyman and Shirley (Liss) Spector; m. James Steven Piotti, June 27, 1982. BFA magna cum laude, Syracuse U., 1972. Prodn. mgr. Bob Stewart Prodns., N.Y.C., 1972-75; tv producer Scali McCabe Sloves, N.Y.C., 1975-81; sr.v.p. exec. producer D'Arcy Masius Benton & Bowles, N.Y.C., 1981--. Recepient, silver medal, gold medal, Film and TV Festival, 1985-86, Mobius awards U.S. TV and Radio Festival, 1986-87. Office: D'Arcy Masius Benton & Bowles 1675 Broadway New York NY 10019*

SPEECH, ESTELLE GRACE, city manager; b. New Orleans, Feb. 6, 1951; d. Arthur and Mable Gladys (Lewis) Johnson; m. Charles Andrew Speech, June 25, 1983; children: Christopher A., Charles Arthur. BBA, Delgado Community Coll., 1983. Clk. safety and permits dept. City of New Orleans, 1973-75, account clk. police dept., 1975, clk. fin. dept., 1975-80, tax adminstr. fin. dept., 1980-86, instnl. bus. mgr. welfare dept., 1986—. Mem. Nat. Assn. Female Execs., La. Juvenile Detention Assn., City New Orleans Women Support Group. Democrat. Office: Youth Study Ctr Dept Welfare 1100 Milton St New Orleans LA 70122

SPEED, SHIRLEY ADAMS, data processing executive, consultant; b. Spokane, Wash., June 9, 1937; d. Claude M. and Berneice D. (Weiseger) Adams; m. Marvin E. Speed, July 9, 1958; children: Marva Jeanne Speed-Copeland, Marvin Ernest II. BA in Math., U. Wash., 1958; MBA, Calif. Coast U., 1985; postgrad., The Hartford Grad. Ctr. Tchr. math. U.S. Govt. HEW Schs., P.R., 1961-64, Upper Heyford, Eng., 1974-75; programmer, sr. analyst Aetna Life & Casualty, Hartford, Conn., 1976-79; data processing HE coord. Aetna Life & Casualty, Hartford, 1979-81, data processing HE cons., 1981-82, data processing HE adminstr., 1982-83, data processing HR adminstr., 1983-85; pvt. practice software cons. Del. and Conn., 1985-86; sr. software project specialist Digital Equipment Corp., Meriden, Conn., 1986-87; sr. software specialist with tech. sales support Digital Equipment Corp., Rocky Hill, Conn., 1987-88; prin. specialist, project mgr. Digital Equipment Corp., Rocky Hill, 1988—; keynote speaker UN Internat. Womens' Day in Eng., 1975; speaker at various univs. and colls., 1980-85, Impact, Hartford, 1984; mem., curriculum advisor Windsor (Conn.) Bd. Edn., 1984-85. Producer, co-editor, camera operator: (TV show) Graduation Days, 1986. Initiator, pres. Concerned Parents for Better Edn., Plattsburgh, N.Y., 1972; v.p. Plattsburgh Officers Wives Club, 1973, pres., 1974-75; organizer Windsor Edn. Perserve Arts, 1980-82; village rep. USAF Strategic Air Command, Plattsburgh and San Antonio, 1975. Mem. Am. Mgmt. Assn., Assn. Systems Mgrs., Data Processing Mgmt. Assn., Black Data Processing Assn., Am. Women in Computing (exec. bd. 1985-86, conv. speaker 1985). Home: 55 Windbrook Dr Windsor CT 06095 Office: Digital Equipment Corp 500 Enterprise Dr Rocky Hill CT 06067

SPEED, TANYA JO LENNARD, speech language pathologist; b. Dallas, Jan. 12, 1960; d. Robert Louis and Vera Mae (Kids) Lennard; m. David Lee Speed, Mar. 12, 1983. BS, S. Meth. U., Dallas, 1982; MS, N. Tex. State U., Denton, 1984. Speech pathologist Garland I.S.D., Garland, Tex., 1984--; speech pathologist Pvt. Practice Dallas, 1987,89. Recipient Outstanding Service D.A.S.P.A Dallas, 1988. Mem. Young Rep. Dallas, Phi Delta Kappa, Am. Speech Language, Hearing Assn., Tex. Speech Lang., Hearing Assn., Dallas Assn. Speech Pathology & Audiology (treas. 1987—), AAUW. Republic. Baptist. Home: 11236 Quail Run Rd Dallas TX 75238

SPEEDIE, MARILYN KAY, microbial biochemist; b. Salem, Oreg., Nov. 13, 1947; d. Arthur Alexander and Eleanor Ruth (Todd) Wilson; m. Stuart Mitchell Speedie, July 18, 1968; children: Andrea Elizabeth, Christopher Todd. BS Pharm., Purdue U., 1970, PhD, 1973. Asst. prof. Oreg. State U., Corvallis, Oreg., 1973-75; from asst. prof. to assoc. prof. dept. chmn. U. Md., Balt., 1975—. Contbr. articles to profl. jours. Mem. Am. Soc. Microbiology, Soc. Indusl. Microbiology, Am. Soc. Pharmacognosy (exec. com. 1987-89), Am. Assn. Colls. Pharmacy (bd. dirs.), Am. Chem. Soc., Sigma Xi, Rho Chi. Office: U Md Sch Pharmacy 20 N Pine St Baltimore MD 21201

SPEER, IREE SMITH, retired educator; b. Sycamore, Ga., Jan. 4, 1913; d. Ozzie W. and Pearl Smith; m. William Arthur Speer, Sept. 14, 1940; children: William A. Jr., Robert Allen. BS in Edn., Ga. State Coll. for Women, 1934; postgrad., U. Ga., 1936-38, Furman U., 1961. Elem. tchr. several cities Ga., 1934-40, elem. tchr., Clemson, S.C., 1956-62, Auburn, Ala., 1962-75; leader 5th grade unit teachers, Auburn, 1972-75. Sec.-treas. Frances McGehee Sunday Sch. Class, 1984-87. Named Outstanding Elem. Tchr. Am., 1974. Mem. Auburn Edn. Assn. (sec. 1964-66), Am. Childhood Edn. (treas. 1964-66), AAUW (sec. Clemson chpt. 1954-56), Delta Kappa Gamma (Clemson chpt., sec. 1958-60, treas. 1960-62). Democrat. Methodist. Home: 625 S Dean Rd Auburn AL 36830

SPEER, JESSICA CHRISTINE, marketing professional; b. Covington, Ky., Dec. 28, 1960; d. Russell E. and Mable F. (Martin) Wall; m. Casey L. Speer, Oct. 6, 1979; children: Aurora, Abigail, Augusta. BS, Ball State U., 1983, MA, 1985; MBA, Ind. Wesleyan U., 1990. Dir. audiological svcs. Johnson County Meml. Hosp., Franklin, Ind., 1986-87; mktg. mgr. St. John's Med. Ctr., Anderson, Ind., 1988-89; owner J.C. Secretarial Svcs., Bluffon, Ind., 1989—. Sch. bd. rep. local PTO, 1986-88, treas., 1990—; bd. dirs. Alternative, Inc., 1984-86; counselor alternative to abortions Ft. Wayne (Ind.) Clinic, 1989—; minister of music interim Franklin Rd. Bapt. Ch., Indpls., 1984-86; dir. youth Bethel Ch., 1989—. Mem. Am. Speech and Hearing Assn. (cert. in audiology), Ind. Speech and Hearing Assn., greater Indpls. Speech and Hearing Assn. Home and Office: 3088 E 500 S Bluffton IN 46714

SPEICHER, BETSY MARY ELIZABETH, psychologist; b. Reading, Pa., June 8, 1948; d. John Stanton Speicher and Elizabeth Ann (Barr) Moyer; 1 child, Elizabeth Brynne Dubin. BA, Bucknell U., 1970; MS, Purdue U., 1973; EdD, Harvard U., 1982. Cert. sch. psychologist, Mass.; lic. psychologist, Mass. Rsch. asst. Harvard U., Cambridge, Mass., 1972-78, teaching asst., 1973-75; psychol. cons. Brookline (Mass.) Pub. Schs., 1979-80; rsch. assoc. Radcliffe Coll., Cambridge, 1983-85; postdoctoral psychology intern Arlington (Mass.) Youth Consultation Ctr., 1985-86, Emerson Hosp., Concord, Mass., 1985-86; asst. prof. psychology U. R.I., Kingston, 1982-83, sch. psychology field supr., 1986-87; psychologist affiliated with Leonard Morse Hosp., Natick, Mass., 1987—; asst. prof. devel. studies and counseling Boston Univ., 1990—. Author: Measurement of Moral Judgement Vol. II, 1987. Chairperson mid. sch. guidance adv. com. Lexington (Mass.) Pub. Schs., 1987-90; bd. dirs. League Women Voters, Lexington, 1990—. Fellow Clin. Devel. Inst., 1990—. Mem. Am. Psychol. Assn., Mass. Psychol. Assn. Home: 11 Trotting Horse Dr Lexington MA 02173 Office: Leonard Morse Hosp Med Office Bldg Ste 404 67 Union St Natick MA 01760 also: Boston Univ Sch Edn 605 Commonwealth Ave Boston MA 02215

SPEIER, KAREN RINARDO, psychologist; b. New Orleans, Aug. 19, 1947; d. William Joseph Rinardo and Shirley Eva (Spreen) Christensen; m. Joe Max Sobotka, Nov. 27, 1970 (div. 1972); m. Anthony Herman Speier, May 29, 1982; children: Anthony Herman III, Austin Clay. Student, Vanderbilt U., 1965-67; BA, La. State U., New Orleans, 1969; MS, U. New Orleans, 1974; PhD, La. State U., 1985. Lic. psychologist, La. Tchr. spl. edn. Huntsville (Ala.) Achievement Sch., 1970-72; instr. neurology La. State U. Med. Ctr., New Orleans, 1972-78; clin. assoc. Dawson Psychol. Assocs., Baton Rouge, 1979-81; tchr. asst. dept. psychology La. State U., Baton Rouge, 1979-81; psychol. examiner La. Sch. for Deaf, Baton Rouge, 1979-80; psychology intern VA Med. Ctr., Martinez, Calif., 1981-82; psychology extern East La. State Hosp., Jackson, 1982-83; clin. assoc. Baton Rouge Psychol. Assocs., 1983-86, pvt. practice clin. psychology, 1986—; sec. bd. dirs. Baton Rouge Employment Devel. Svcs., 1987-89; mem. psychology cons. com. Meadow Wood Hosp., Baton Rouge, 1987-89; mem. psychology adv. com. Parkland Hosp., Baton Rouge, 1989—. Contbr. articles to profl. publs. Mem. steering com. Baton Rouge Stepfamily Support Group, 1983—; tchr. St. James Episcopal Sunday Sch., Baton Rouge, 1984-86. Mem. Orton Dyslexia Soc. (bd. dirs., chmn. nominating com. La. chpt.), Nat. Head Injury Found., Agenda for Children, Baton Rouge Area Soc. Psychologists, La. Psychol. Assn., Am. Psychology Assn., Internat. Soc. Child Abuse and Neglect, Mental Health Assn. La. Clubs: Baton Rouge, YWCA Connections. Office: Ctr Psychol Resources 2424 Bunker Hill Dr Ste 700 Baton Rouge LA 70808

SPEIR, BETTY SMITH, foundation administrator; b. Bethel, N.C., Mar. 3, 1928; d. William Jasper and Carolyn (Pollock) Smith; A.B., Duke U., 1949; M.A., East Carolina U., 1963; m. David Ordway Speir, June 10, 1950; children—Carolyn G. Speir Brown, Christine St. Clair Speir Price. Tchr. English, Farmville (N.C.) High Sch., 1949-50, Bain High Sch., Charlotte, N.C., 1950-51, Bethel High Sch., 1961-70; cotton buyer Bethel Mfg. Co. (N.C.), 1958-60; guidance counselor North Pitt High Sch., Bethel, 1970-86; exec. dir. Pitt Edn. Found, 1986—. Sec. N.C. Commn. on Edn. and Employment of Women, 1970-74; mem. N.C. State Bd. Edn., 1982—, N.C. Gov.'s Crime Commn., 1977-82, N.C. Commn. on Length of Sentencing, 1981-82; mem. Blue Ribbon Commn. to Study Needs of Tng. Schs.; mem. N.C. Commn. Edn. for Econ. Growth; vice chmn. N.C. Democratic Com., 1978-80, 81-84, chmn., 1980; mem. Dem. Nat. Com., 1978—; del. Dem. Nat. Conv., 1980, 84, 88, mem. site selection com., 1984, mem. credentials com., 1988; chmn. B.N. Duise Scholarship Adv. Com.; bd. trustees N.C. Ctr. for Advancement of Teaching, 1989—; mem. N.C. State Bd. Edn., 1982-87, N.C. Women's Forum. Named one of Winning Dem. Women of Decade, Nat. Fedn. Dem. Women, 1980. Mem. NEA, N.C. Assn. Educators, Delta Kappa Gamma. Methodist. Home: PO Box 340 Bethel NC 27812 Office: 1717 W 5th St Greenville NC 27834

SPEIR, MARCIA ANN, accountant; b. Tulsa, Oct. 20, 1935; d. Charles Henry and Pearl Jewell (Palmer) Hall; m. Jack Wesley Speir, June 17, 1955; 1 child, Andrea Renee. Student, Northeastern State Coll., Tahlequah, Okla., 1953-56, Am. River Coll., Sacramento, Calif., 1974-76. Acct. Commonwealth Life Ins. Co., Tulsa, 1953-56, Okla. Natural Gas Co., Tulsa, 1957-62; acct., systems analyst Shell Oil Co., Tulsa, 1962-69; staff acct. Trane Heating and Air Conditioning, Sacramento, 1975-79; owner Arapahoe County Steamway Carpet & Upholstery Cleaning Co., Denver, 1969-74; acct., office mgr. Sureway Corp., Sacramento, 1980—; career counselor Am. River Coll., 1974-76. Mem. NAFE, Sacramento Employer Adv. Group. Republican. Mem. Christian Ch. Home: 5424 Lequel Way Carmichael CA 95608 Office: Sureway Corp 2121 Arden Way Sacramento CA 95825

SPELL, LEE FAIRBANKS, artist; b. Janesville, Wis.; d. H.B. and Elizabeth (Abb) Fairbanks; children: Lawrence, Elizabeth. BA, Coll. William and Mary, 1970. Ind. practice property mgmt. and devel. Fair Banks, Inc., Swansboro, N.C.; artist Lee Side Designs, Swansboro. Mem. NAFE.

SPELLMIRE, SANDRA MARIE, systems analyst, programmer; b. San Francisco, Feb. 20, 1950; d. Robert Joseph and Catherine Louise (Sockett) S. BS, Calif. State U., L.A., 1977. Project controls analyst Ralph M. Parsons Co., Pasadena, Calif., 1978-81, C.F. Braun & Co., Alhambra, Calif., 1981-84; configuration mgr. software systems Burroughs Corp., Santa Ana, Calif., 1984-85; sr. scientific analyst, programmer Electronic Data Systems, L.A., 1985, Denver, 1985-87, Mpls., 1987-89; software cons. Shared Resource Mgmt., St. Louis Park, Minn., 1989—. Mem. AAAS, Nat. Assn. Female Execs., Assn. for Computing Machinery (assoc.).

SPELMAN, NANCY LATTING, psychologist, consultant; b. Oklahoma City, Sept. 13, 1945; d. Trimble Baggett and Patience Francelia (Sewell) Latting; m. Douglas Gordon Spelman, June 21, 1970; children: Brooke Patience, Erin Latting. BA in Polit. Sci., Boston U., 1967; MA in Psychology, Bucknell U., 1972; PhD in Psychology, U. Hong Kong, 1987. Lic. cognitive psychologist. Tour guide UN, N.Y.C., summer 1966; tchr. emotionally disturbed and retarded pre-sch. children Mass. Dept. Mental Health, Boston, 1968-70; coord. vols. campaign for mayor Patience Latting, Oklahoma City, 1971; lectr. psychology Petaling Jaya Community Coll., Kuala Lumpur, Malaysia, 1987-88, George Mason U., Fairfax, Va., 1989; interactive skills observer, facilitator mgmt. programs Xerox Corp. Edn. and Tng., Leesburg, Va., 1989—. Bd. dirs. Internat. Sch. Kuala Lumpur, 1986-87, sec., 1987-88; com. mem. Hong Kong Soc. for Disabled, 1976-77. Mem. Am. Psychol. Assn. Democrat. Home: 2023 Sarazen Pl Reston VA 22091

SPENCE, ANNA IOZZO, computer graphics specialist; b. Rome, N.Y., Oct. 16, 1964; d. Frank and Liberata (Sestito) I.; married. BS, Clarkson U., 1986. Sales rep. Newark Electronics, Waltham, Mass., 1986-87; with mktg. communications dept. Rise Tech., Cambridge, Mass., 1987; sr. application specialist Hell Graphics Systems, Woburn, Mass., 1988—. Republican. Roman Catholic. Home: 48 Dean Spring Dr Webster NY 14580 Office: Hell Graphics Systems 600 W Cummings Pk #2500 Woburn MA 01801

SPENCE, EVELYN BATTEN, insurance company executive; b. Huntington, W.Va., May 19, 1934; d. Lacy A. and Mary Frances (Wilhoit) B.; m. Charles I. Spence, May 28, 1954; 1 child, Larry S. Grad. high school, Huntington, 1952. CLU. V.p. Orange State LIfe Ins. Co., Largo, Fla., 1975-81; state regional mgr. Ministries Life Ins. Co., Lake Worth, Fla., 1981-83; asst. v.p. Am. Pioneer Life, Orlando, Fla., 1983-85; v.p., chief adminstrv. officer Fin. Benefit Life Ins. Co., Boca Raton, Fla., 1985-87, also bd. dirs.; v.p., chief underwriter Kanawha Ins. Co., Lancaster, S.C., 1987—. Editor company newsletter, 1980; free-lance photographer. Campaigner United Way, Orlando, 1984. Mem. Am. Coll. CLU's, Assoc. Photographers Internat. Club: Toastmasters. Office: Kanawha Ins Co 210 S White St Lancaster SC 29720

SPENCE, JANET BLAKE CONLEY (MRS. ALEXANDER PYOTT SPENCE), civic worker; b. Upper Montclair, N.J., Aug. 17, 1915; d. Walter Abbott and Ethel Maud (Blake) Conley; m. Alexander Pyott Spence, June

10, 1939; children: Janet Blake Spence Kerr, Robert Moray, Richard Taylor. Student, Vassar Coll., 1933-35; cert., Katharine Gibbs Sch., 1936. formerly active Jr. League, Neighborhood House, ARC, Girl Scouts U.S.A.; active various community drives; chmn. Darien (Conn.) Assembly, 1955-56; sec., chmn. Wilton Jr. Assembly, 1961-63; subscription chmn. Candlelight Concerts Wilton, Conn., 1963-65; rec. sec. Pub. Health Nursing Assn. Wilton Bd., 1964-67; corr., rec. sec. Royle Sch. Bd., Darien, 1952-55; fund raiser Vassar Class of 1937; mem. Washington Valley Community Assn.; mem. N.J. Symphony Orch. League, treas. Morris County br. 1978-83, corr. sec. 1982-83, pres. 1985-89, acting pres. 1989—, state coun. mem. 1985-89, acting pres. Morris br. 1989-90. Mem. Vassar Alumni Assn., Dobbs Alumni Assn., Jersey Hills Vassar Club, Wilton Garden Club, Washington Valley Home Econs. Club (life, corr. sec. 1977-82, pres. 1982-84, v.p. 1984-85, co-pres. 1985-86, treas. 1988—, chmn. membership com. 1987-89, mem. archives com. 1988—). Congregationalist. Home: Hilltop Washington Valley Rd Morristown NJ 07960 also: 8 Evergreen Ave Kennebunk ME 04043

SPENCE, MARY LEE, historian; b. Kyle, Tex., Aug. 4, 1927; d. Jeremiah Milton and Mary Louise (Hutchison) Nance; m. Clark Christian Spence, Sept. 12, 1953; children: Thomas Christian, Ann Leslie. BA, U. Tex., 1947, MA, 1948; PhD, U. Minn., 1957. Instr., asst. prof. S.W. Tex. State U., San Marcos, 1948-53; lectr. Pa. State U., State College, 1955-58; mem. faculty U. Ill., Urbana-Champaign, 1973—, asst. prof., assoc. prof., 1973-81, 81-89, prof. history, 1989—. Editor: (with Donald Jackson) The Expeditions of John Charles Fremont, 3 vols., 1970-84; contbr. articles to profl. jours. Mem. Children's Theater Bd., Urbana-Champaign, 1965-73. Grantee Nat. Hist. Pub. and Records Commn., Washington, 1977-78, 87-90; recipient Excellent Advisor award Liberal Arts and Sci. Coll., U. Ill., 1986. Mem. Western History Assn. (pres. 1981-82), Orgn. Am. Historians, Phi Beta Kappa (exec. sect. Gamma chpt. 1985-89), Phi Alpha Theta. Episcopalian. Home: 1107 S Foley Champaign IL 61820 Office: U Ill Dept History 810 S Wright St Urbana IL 61801

SPENCE, SHARON LLOYD, film, video director; b. Washington, Sept. 14, 1953; d. Franklin Lloyd and Mary Teresa (Riello) S. BSS, Northwestern U., 1975. Dir./producer NBC-TV, Cleve., 1975-79; writer J. Walter Thompson Advt., Chgo., 1979-80, Burson-Marsteller Pub. Relations, Chgo., 1980-82, Jack Lieb Prodns., Chgo., 1982-84; dir./producer Christian Sci. Monitor TV and freelance corp. films, Chgo., Boston, 1984-86, Ency. Britannica, Chgo., 1986-88; freelance producer, dir., travel writer Chgo., 1989—. Author: The Wall Street Journal Guide to Business Travel; contbr. articles to Asia Pacific Travel and Just 60 mags. Mem. Nat. Ghost Ranch Found., Abiquiu, N.Mex., 1987—, Chgo. Art Inst., 1986—. Recipient Cine Golden Eagle, Film Festival, 1989, U.S. Indsl. Film Festival, 1989; Ill. Arts Council screenwriting grantee, 1985, others. Mem. Women in Film Chgo. (founding mem., prog. dir.), Internat. TV and Video Artists. Home and Office: 5555 N Sheridan Rd Apt 306 Chicago IL 60640

SPENCE, SHIRLEY HARVEY, psychologist; b. Hopkins County, Ky., Jan. 20, 1939; d. G. Paul and Eula (Pool) Riley; m. Bobby Edward Harvey, Jan. 7, 1957 (div. 1964); 1 child, Bob; m. Richard C. Spence, July 2, 1969; children: Sean C., A. Marisa. BS, Western Ky. U., 1965; MEd, U. Mo., 1967; PhD, U. Wyo., 1969. Lic. psychologist. Elem. tchr. Hopkins County Schs., Madisonville, Ky., 1962-65, Maplewood/Richmond Heights Schs., St. Louis, 1965-66; sch. psychologist Laramie (Wyo.) Pub. Schs., 1967-69; vis. prof. U. Wyo., Laramie, summer 1968, Central Mich. U., Mt. Pleasant, summer 1969, 70; chief psychologist Penny Royal Mental Health Ctr., Madisonville, 1969-70; child devel. specialist Owensboro (Ky.) City Schs., 1971-77, Trover Clinic, Madisonville, 1978—. Pres. PTA, Madisonville, 1984; Sunday sch. tchr., Madisonville, 1985-86. Mem. Am. Psychol. Assn., Ky. Psychol. Assn.

SPENCER, ANITA LOUISE, psychologist, author, lecturer; b. Indpls., May 28, 1945; d. Paul Emory and Martha Jeanette (Terry) S.; m. Linden James Crawforth, Sept. 9, 1983; children: Steven, Scott, Christopher Quackenbush; stepchildren: Melissa Crawforth, Linden Crawford, Laurie Cooper. BA in Sociology, U. Calif., Santa Cruz, 1979; MA in Marriage, Family, Child Counseling, U. Santa Clara (Calif.), 1981; PhD in Clin. Psychology, Western Grad. Sch., Palo Alto, 1986. Lic. clin. psychologist, Calif., marriage, family and child counselor, Calif. Rehab. counselor Santa Clara County Sheriff's Dept., San Jose, Calif., 1979-81; dir. women and family svcs. YWCA, San Jose, 1981-86; clin. psychologist Affiliated Psychologists, San Jose, 1986-88; pvt. practice San Jose, 1988—; counselor Women's Community Clinic, San Jose, 1981-86; cons., crisis expert to TV and radio, San Francisco Bay area, 1989—; lectr. in field. Author: Seasons: A Woman's Search for Self through Life's Stages, 1982, Mothers Are People Too, 1984, Crisis and Growth: Making the Most of Hard Times, 1989. Mem. steering com. Women in Bus., San Jose, 1981—; sec. Quota Internat., San Francisco, 1984—. Mem. Am. Psychol. Assn., Calif. Psychol. Assn., Santa Clara County Psychol. Assn., Calif. Assn. Marriage & Family Counselors. Roman Catholic. Office: 4020 Moorpark Ave Ste 100 San Jose CA 95117

SPENCER, BARBARA JOYCE, antique store owner; b. Broken Bow, Nebr., Feb. 19, 1935; d. Gerald A. and Elizabeth (Field) Thurman; m. Berl W. Spencer, Aug. 28, 1955; children: Shannon Goertz, Stuart G., Stacia Elizabeth. BA in Edn., Nebr. State, 1956. Tchr. Omaha Pub. Schs., 1956-60, Nursery Sch., Ogallala, Nebr., 1964-70, St. Paul's Luth Sch., Ogallala, 1982-84; owner Party Bay Antique Store, Ogallala, 1982—. Mem. Keith County Hospice Bd. Mem. AAUW (pres.), Ogallala C. of C. (bd. dirs.), P.E.O. (pres.). Republican. Episcopalian. Office: Party Bay Originals 101 N Spruce St Ogallala NE 69153

SPENCER, BILLIE JANE, lawyer; b. Caro, Mich., Sept. 16, 1949; d. William Norman and Jane Isabel (Putnam) S. AB in Econs., U. Miami, Coral Gables, Fla., 1971, LLM in Tax, 1980; JD, U. Fla., Gainesville, 1973; course cert. St. Catherine's Coll., Oxford U., 1973; grad. with highest distinction, Naval War Coll., Washington, 1988. Bar: Fla., Calif. Assoc. Frates Floyd, et. al., Miami, Fla., 1973-74; commd. lt. (j.g.) USNR, 1974, advanced through grades to comdr., 1988; judge advocate USNR, Subic Bay, Pensacola, 1975-78; sole practice San Francisco, and Stuart, Fla., 1978-85; asst. staff judge advocate USNR, Lemoore, Calif., 1982-83; DOD liaison USNR, Washington, 1985-88; civilian atty. USN, Mechanicsburg, Pa., 1988-90; counsel Navy Pub. Works Ctr. USN, Norfolk, Va., 1990—; instr. econs. Fla. Inst. Tech., Jensen Beach, 1984-85; litigation cons. Castle & Cooke, Inc., San Francisco, 1979-83; clk. Ehrlichmann Watergate Trial team, Washington, 1974; del. state conf. on small bus., 1982; adj. analyst 6th quadrennial rev. of military compensation, 1987-88. Mem. U.S. Naval Inst., The Navy League. Republican. Unitarian.

SPENCER, DEBORAH JOYCE, school psychologist, consultant; b. Little Rock, Dec. 19, 1950; d. Virgil Roach and Frances Merle (Schafer) Moncrief; m. William Robert Price, Jr., June 14, 1970 (div. Dec. 1979), 1 child, Robert Geoffrey; m. James Leigh Spencer, Nov. 18, 1981; children: Alicia Joyce, Leslie Leigh. Student, Wesleyan Coll., Macon, Ga., 1068-69; BA in Psychology, Ga. State U., 1972, MEd in Sch. Psychology, 1973; EdD, Nova U., 1989. Lic. psychol. examiner, Ark.; nationally cert. sch. psychologist. Tchr. phys. edn. Immaculate Heart of Mary Sch., Atlanta, 1972-73; cons. sch. psychology West Ga. Coop. Ednl. Svcs. Agy., Newnan, Ga., 1973-76; dir., specialist in sch. psychology Hallandder Learning Ctrs., Vero Beach, Ft. Pierce, Fla., 1976-80; psychol. examiner Psychol. Testing Svc., Pine Bluff, Ark., 1981-84; sch. psychologist North Little Rock (Ark.) Sch. Dist., 1984—; Ark. field coord. Psychol. Corp., 1986-88; lectr. ann. conv. Ark. Assn. for Counseling Guidance and Devel., 1986-89. Vol. cons. devel. program alternative learning strategies for learning disabled students Christ the King Cath. Sch., Little Rock, 1988—. Grantee Rockfeller Found., 1988-89. Mem. Assn. for Measurement and Evaluation in Guidance (chmn. standards com. 1985-86), Nat. Assn. Sch. Psychologists, Ark. Assn. Sch. Psychologists (pres.-elect 1986-87, pres. 1987-88, exec. bd.), Learning Disabilities Assn. Kans., Mortar Bd., Phi Kappa Phi, Psi Chi. Republican. Roman Catholic. Home: 23701 Kanis Rd Little Rock AR 72211 Office: North Little Rock Sch Dist 2700 Poplar North Little Rock AR 72215

SPENCER, DOMINA EBERLE, mathematics educator; b. New Castle, Pa., Sept. 26, 1920; d. Andrew Berger and Ina May (Eberle) S.; m. Parry Moon, Aug. 17, 1961; 1 child, Euclid Eberle Moon. SB, MIT, 1939, SM, 1940, PhD, 1942. Asst. prof. physics Am. U., Washington, 1942-43, Tufts Coll., Medford, Mass., 1943-47, Brown U., Providence, 1947-50; assoc. prof. math. U. Conn., Storrs, 1950-60, prof. math., 1960—; cons. Sylvania, Salem, 1953-70, Ainsworth Lighting, L.I., 1943-53, Marlux Corp., Sommerville, Mass., 1948-61, Photo Rsch. Corp., Hollywood, Calif., 1945-58. Author: (with P. Moon) Lighting Design, 1947, Field Theory for Engineers, 1960, Field Theory Handbook, 1960, Foundations of Electrodynamics, 1960, Vectors, 1965, Partial Differential Equations, 1969, The Photic Field, 1981, Theory of Holors, 1986; co-inventor Aperture Lamp. Chmn. music com. St. Paul's Ch., Brookline, 1988—, pres. Back Bay Manor Tenants Assn., Boston, 1985—. Fellow Illuminating Engring. Soc. (gold medal 1974), Optical Soc. Am.; mem. Am. Math. Soc., Math Assn. Am., Am. Phys. Soc., MIT Nautical Assn. Democrat. Presbyterian. Home: 75 St Alphonsus St Boston MA 02120 Office: U Conn U-9 Storrs CT 06268

SPENCER, ELAINE THERESA, magazine editor; b. Kansas City, Kans., Feb. 21, 1949; d. Charles Clifford and Alice Patricia (Aaron) Blanton; m. Bradford Neal Spencer, Sept. 5, 1970 (div. Sept. 1982); children: Neal Patrick, Janelle Diane. BS in Journalism, Baker U., Baldwin City, Kans., 1971. Accredited advisor ins. With prodn. dept. Kans. State High Sch. Activities Assn., Topeka, 1972-77, MC Industries, Topeka, 1983; editor, staff reporter Resourceful Woman, Every Woman's Resource Ctr., Topeka, 1983-87; editor Kans. Ins. Mag., Ind. Ins. Agts. Kans., Topeka, 1985-87, Florists' Rev. Mag., Topeka, 1987—; cons. newsletter Girl Scouts U.S.A., Topeka, 1988. Bd. mem. Every Woman's Resource Ctr., Topeka, 1987. Republican. Home: 620 Vesper St Topeka KS 66606 Office: Florists Rev Enterprises Box 4368 Topeka KS 66604

SPENCER, ELIZABETH, author; b. Carrollton, Miss., 1921; d. James Luther and Mary James (McCain) S.; m. John Arthur Blackwood Rusher, Sept. 29, 1956. BA, Belhaven Coll., 1942; MA, Vanderbilt U., 1943; LittD (hon.), Southwestern U. at Memphis, 1968; LLD (hon.), Concordia U. at Montreal, 1988. Instr. N.W. Miss. Jr. Coll., 1943-44; reporter The Nashville Tennessean, 1945-46; instr. U. Miss., Oxford, 1948-51, 52-53; vis. prof. Concordia U., Montreal, Que., Can., 1976—, adj. prof., 1981-86; vis. prof. U. N.C., Chapel Hill, 1986—. Author: Fire in the Morning, 1948, This Crooked Way, 1952, The Voice at the Back Door, 1956, The Light in the Piazza, 1960, Knights and Dragons, 1965, No Place for an Angel, 1967, Ship Island and Other Stories, 1968, The Snare, 1972, The Stories of Elizabeth Spencer, 1981, Marilee, 1981, The Salt Line, 1984, Jack of Diamonds and Other Stories, 1988, (play) For Lease or Sale, 1989; contbr. short stories to mags. and anthologies. Recipient Women's Democratic Com. award, 1949, recognition award Nat. Inst. Arts and letters, 1952; Guggenheim Found. fellow, 1953; Richard and Hinda Rosenthal Found. award Am. Acad. Arts and Letters, 1957; Award of Merit medal for the short story Am. Acad. Arts and Letters, 1983; Kenyon Rev. fellow in fiction, 1957; 1st McGraw-Hill Fiction award, 1960; Bryn Mawr Col. Donnelly fellow, 1962; Henry Bellamann award for creative writing, 1968; Nat. Endowment for Arts grantee in lit., 1983, Sr. Arts Award grantee Nat. Endowment for Arts, 1988. Mem. Am. Inst. Arts and Letters. Home: 402 Longleaf Dr Chapel Hill NC 27514 Office: U NC Dept English Chapel Hill NC 27514

SPENCER, ELIZABETH J., air force officer; b. Tuscaloosa, Ala., Aug. 27, 1954; d. George and Alma (Richardson) Tukes. BA in Psychology, UCLA, 1977; MSHCM, Calif. State U., L.A. Commd. 2d lt. USAF, advanced through grades to maj.; exec. officer USAF, Wallace Air Sta., Rep. of Philippines; comdr. hdqrs. squadron USAF, Nellis AFB, Las Vegas, Nev.; adminstrv. systems officer Boeing Aerospace Co. USAF, Seattle; chief pub. div. USAF, Honolulu. Mem. NAFE, Orgn. Women Leaders. Home: Konigsberger St 13E, Leimen Germany 6906 Office: Hdqrs Fourth Allied Tactical Air Force Campbell Barracks APO New York NY 09403

SPENCER, GALE ALEXANDRA, real estate investment officer; b. N.Y.C., Aug. 13, 1951; d. Sylvester Joseph and Charlotte (Woitkiewicz) S. BA, Baruch U., 1973. Rsch. asst. MLA, N.Y.C., 1972; asst. mgr. New York Life Ins. Co., N.Y.C., 1973-81; asst. sec., appraiser Manufacturer Hanover Trust Co., N.Y.C., 1982-84; real estate investment officer New York State Pension Fund, N.Y.C., 1984—; mem. Real Estate Inst. Adv. Bd. Democrat. Roman Catholic. Office: New York State Pension Fund 270 Broadway New York NY 10007

SPENCER, JUDY SHIFFLETT, small business owner; b. Charlottsville, Va., Nov. 10, 1947; d. Russell Lowell and Mildred Louise Shifflett; ml. Clinton E. Jr., Aug. 30, 1969: children: Maari Ann, Ryan Scott. BS, Bridgewater Coll., 1970. Certi. Teaching. Tchr., originator home econs. dept. Home Econs. Dept. Internat. Sch. Bangsue, Bangkok, Thailand, 1970-73; tchr. Wm. Montoe High Sch., Stanardsville, Va., 1978-87; owner The Marypeg Dress Shop, Charlottesville, Va., 1987—; sponsor Future Homemakers Am., Stanardsville, Va., 1978-87, Home Econs. Related Orgn., Stanardsville, 1985-87. Organizer Greene County Fair, Stanardsville; mem. Greene County Fair Bd., Stanardsville, 1979-87. mem. Downtown Charlottesville Inv. Republican. Home: 101 Greene Lea Dr Stanardsville VA 22968

SPENCER, MARY EILEEN, biochemist, educator; b. Regina, Sask., Can., Oct. 4, 1923; d. John J. and Etta Christina (Hamren) Stapleton; m. Henry Anderson Spencer, July 3, 1946; 1 dau., Susan Mary. A.A., Regina Coll., 1942; B.A. with high honors in Chemistry, U. Sask., 1945; M.A. in Chemistry, Bryn Mawr Coll., 1946; Ph.D. in Agrl. Chemistry, U. Calif.-Berkeley, 1951. Chemist, Ayerst, McKenna and Harrison Ltd., Montreal, Que., Can., summer 1945; full time, 1946-47, Nat. Canners Assn., San Francisco, 1948; teaching fellow U. Calif.-Berkeley, 1949-51, faculty food chemistry, 1951-53; faculty U. Alta., Edmonton, Can., 1953-61, instr., asst. prof., assoc. prof., acting head biochem. dept., 1960-61, plant sci. dept., 1962, prof. plant sci., 1964-83, McCalla rsch. prof., 1983-84, univ. prof., 1984—; pres. Rootrainers Corp.; mem. NRC Can., 1970-73, 73-76, Task Force on Post-Secondary Edn., Alta. Govt. Com. on Ednl. Planning, 1970-72; chmn. nat. adv. com. on biology NRC, adv. bd. Prairie Regional Lab.; adv. bd. Atlantic Regional Lab.; chmn. ad hoc vis. com. in forestry rsch. NRC, 1975-76; bd. govs. U. Alta. 1976-79; mem. Agr. Can. Cons. Com. IBT Pesticides, 1981-82; bd. dirs. Natural Scis. and Engring. Rsch. Coun. Can., 1986-89, min. adv. com. Networks Ctrs. Excellence, 1989—; mem. Premier's Coun. on Sci. and Tech., 1990—. Recipient Queen Elizabeth II Silver Jubilee medal. Fellow Chem. Inst. Can., Royal Soc. Can.; mem. Can. Soc. Plant Physiologists (pres. 1971-72), Scandinavian Soc. Plant Physiology, Plant Growth Regulator Soc. Am., Am. Soc. Plant Physiologists, Can. Assn. Univ. Tchrs., Internat. Plant Growth Regulator Soc. Office: U Alta Dept Plant Sci, Faculty Agr & Forestry, Edmonton, AB Canada T6G 2E3

SPENCER, MARY MILLER, civic worker; b. Comanche, Tex., May 25, 1924; d. Aaron Gaynor and Alma (Grissom) Miller; 1 child, Mara Lynn. BS, North Tex. State U., 1943. Cafeteria dir. Mercedes (Tex.) Pub. Schs., 1943-46; home economist coordinator All-Orange Dessert Contest, Fla. Citrus Commn., Lakeland, 1959-62, 64; tchr. purchasing sch. lunch dept. Fla. Dept. Edn., 1960. Clothing judge Polk County (Fla.) Youth Fair, 1951-68, Polk County Federated Women's Clubs, 1964-66; pres. Dixieland Elem. Sch. PTA, 1955-57, Polk County Council PTA's, 1958-60; chmn. public edn. com. Polk County unit Am. Cancer Soc., 1959-60, bd. dirs., 1962-70; charter mem., bd. dirs. Lakeland YMCA, 1962-72; sec. Greater Lakeland Community Nursing Council, 1965-72; trustee, vice chmn. Polk County Eye Clinic, Inc., 1962-64, pres., 1964-82; bd. dirs. Polk County Scholarship and Loan Fund, 1962-70; mem. exec. com. West Polk County (Fla.) Community Welfare Council, 1960-62, 65-68; mem. budget and audit com. Greater Lakeland United Fund, 1960-62, bd. dirs., 1967-70, residential chmn. fund drive, 1968; mem. adv. bd. Polk County Juvenile and Domestic Relations Ct., 1960-69; worker children's services div. family services Dept. Health and Rehab. Services, State of Fla., 1969-70, social worker, 1970-72, 74-82, social worker OFR unit, 1977-81, pub. assistance specialist IV, 1984-89. Mem. exec. com. Suncoast Health Council, 1968-71; mem. Polk County Home Econs. Adv. Com., 1965-71; sec. bd. dirs. Fla. West Coast Ednl. TV, 1960-81; bd. dirs. Lake Region United Way, Winter Haven, 1976-81; mem. Polk County Community Services Council, 1978-88. Mem. Nat. Welfare Fraud Assn., Fla. Congress Parents and Tchrs. (hon. life; pres. dist. 7 1961-63, chmn. pub. relations 1962-66), AAUW (pres. Lakeland br. 1960-61), Polk County Mental Health Assn., Fla. Health and Welfare Council, Fla. Health and Social Service Council, North Tex. State U. Alumni Assn. Democrat. Methodist. Lodge: Order of Eastern Star. Mailing Address: PO Box 2161 Lakeland FL 33806

SPENCER, TRICIA JANE, wholesale manufacturing executive; b. Springfield, Ill., Dec. 8, 1952; d. Frank Edward and LaWanda (Edwards) Bell; m. Mark Edward Spencer, Aug. 21, 1982. Student pub. schs. Instr., Falcons Drum & Bugle Corps, Springfield, 1969-72; concert, stage, TV, film performer, 1970-82, part-time 1982—; guest dir. Sing out Salem, Ohio, 1973; contbg. writer Saddle Tramps Wild West Revue, 1977—; legal sec. to pvt. atty., Tustin, Calif., 1980-82; owner Am. Dream Balloons & Svcs., Orange, Calif., 1982-89; founder, corp. pres. Am. Dream Limousine Svc., Inc., Orange, 1983-90; founder, pres., designer Am. Dream Creations Co., Inc., Irvine, Calif., 1988—. Songwriter; designer greeting cards, T-shirts and wedding related gifts; one-of-a-kind automobile; producer, dir. mus. stage shows, 1974-82; author: TIPS - The Server's Guide to Bringing Home the Bacon, 1987. Performer, Up With People, 1972-73; organizer Bicentennial Com. Springfield, 1976; mediator Limousine and Chauffeur Council, Orange County, 1984—; vol. Orange County Performing Arts Soc., 1985—. Recipient Appreciation, Achievement awards Muscular Dystrophy Assn., 1977-79, Transp. Partnership award, 1988. Mem. Am. Entrepreneurs Assn., Internat. Platform Assn., Nat. Limousine Assn., So. Calif. Limousine Owners Assn., Nat. Assn. Female Execs., Orange County C. of C. Republican. Avocations: guitar, piano, writing. Office: Am Dream Creations Co Inc 15 Hammond #303 Irvine CA 92718

SPENCER-WILKINS, MARY LINDSEY, technical specialist; b. Big Spring, Tex., Oct. 8, 1964; d. Neil Douglas and Geraldine Ruth (Lindsey) S. BBA in Mktg., U. Tex., 1987. With Spencer Farm, Luther, Tex., 1980; salesperson Cinema Theatre, Big Spring, 1981-82; with telemktg. dept. TRAC, Austin, Tex., 1984; salesperson Helen's, Big Spring, summer 1984, 85; leasing agt. Greystone Mgmt., Austin, 1986-87; sales rep. II Gen. Mills, Inc., New Orleans, 1987-89; mktg. rep. Edward D. Jones & Co., St. Louis, 1990—. Vol. Spl. Olympics, Austin, 1985, 86. Mem. Nat. Bus. Women's Assn., Tex. Ex Students Assn., Phi Chi Theta. Home: 800 Woodpoint Dr Chesterfield MO 63017

SPENDER, VICTORIA THERESA, computer information specialist; b. Astoria, N.Y., Oct. 8, 1957; d. Herman Joseph and Ellen (Athanasas) Wullert; m. Stephen Allen Spender, Aug. 14, 1982. BA, Barnard Coll., 1979; MA, Rutgers U., 1982, Montclair State U., 1988. Copyright adminstr. European Am. Music, Totowa, N.J., 1982-84; trainer Allmilmo Corp., Fairfield, N.J., 1984-86; pc trainer Abbott Inst., Parsippany, N.J., 1986-87; pc training specialist Automatic Data Processing, Clifton, N.J., 1987--, Computer Applications Learning Ctr., Morristown, N.J., 1989; cons. Allmilmo Corp., Fairfield, 1986--, Kreg's Kitchens, Verona, N.J.,. Mem. Nat. Assn. Female Exec., Am. Soc. Training and Devel. Democrat. Office: Computer Appl Learning Ctr 100 Hanover Ave Morristown NJ 07962

SPERA, PATRICE, nurse; b. Cleve., May 22, 1953; d. Wilbur Timothy and Geraldine (Nachtigal) Helwig; married, Oct. 1, 1977. Student, St. Petersburg Coll., 1978, St. Leo's Coll., 1981-83, 87-88, U. South Fla., 1989. Registered nurse; cert. nurse operating room. Realtor assoc. ERA Seaview Realty, Belleair Bluffs, Fla., 1979; head nurse orthopedic surgery Largo (Fla.) Med. Ctr., 1981—; cons. Richards Med. Ctr., Clearwater, Fla.; interior decorator Spera Enterprises, Seminole, Fla., 1984—; travel agt. Largo Mall Travel '90. Chmn. Good Govt. Group Largo Med. Ctr., 1988—; mem. Fla. Realtor's Polit. Action Com., 1981—; vol. Dennis Jones campaign, Seminole, 1988, Don Sullivans campaign, 1990; co-chmn. Largo Olde Tyme Polit. Rally, 1990. Mem. Assn. of Oper. Rm. Nurses (pres. 1988, pres. elect 1990, v.p. 1988-89, nat. legis. com. 1990-91, chmn. nominating com. 1986), Nat. Assn. Orthopedic Nurses, Am. Nurses Assn., Fla. Nurses Assn. (legis. dist. coord.), Fla. Coun. Nurses (meeting chair 1988-89), Product Fair Assn. of Oper. Rm. Nurses (chmn.), NAFE, Meeting Planners, Fla. Coun. Operating Rm. Nurses (chmn.). Republican. Roman Catholic. Home: 9411 125th St N Seminole FL 34642

SPERBER, NANCY B., lawyer; b. L.A., Apr. 4, 1953. BA, UCLA, 1975; JD, Southwestern U., L.A., 1977. Bar: Calif. Staff atty. L.A. County Superior Ct., 1977-79; dept. dist. atty. County of L.A., 1979; pvt. practice L.A., 1979—; cons., lectr. Western Conf. on Criminal Justice, L.A., 1989—. Mem. Coaliton for Police Support, Inglewood, Calif., 1988—. Named Vol. of Yr., County of L.A., 1986, 88. Mem. South Bay Bar Assn., Inglewood Bar Assn., Calif. Homicide Investigators Assn., Internat. Assn. Bloodstain Pattern Analysts. Office: 1875 Century Park East 2605 Los Angeles CA 90067

SPHAR, GAIL LUFKIN, insurance company executive; b. LaPorte, Ind., Mar. 4, 1946; d. Edward R. and Dorothy Mae (Wallace) Trigg; 1 child. BS, U. S.C., 1966, MS, 1972; MBA, U. Ala.-Birmingham, 1984. Instr. U. S.C., Columbia, 1971-73; mgr. tng. and devel. Blue Cross and Blue Shield, Columbia, 1973-76, dir. tng. and devel., Birmingham, 1976-79, mgr. dept. human resources, 1979-82, v.p. human resources 1983-87, v.p. adminstrn. and human resources, St. Louis, 1987, sr. v.p. adminstrn., 1988, sr. v.p. corp. and med. adminstrn. 1989—. Chmn. funding and fin. Childcare Task Force, United Way, Birmingham, 1983-84, bd. dirs., chmn. personnel com. Childcare Resources of Jefferson, Shelby and Walker counties, 1984-86, pres., 1987—; v.p. membership, pres. FORUM, Birmingham, 1984—; mem. adv. bd. Masters in Pub. and Pvt. Mgmt. program Birmingham So. Coll., 1953-83; vice-chmn. pers. com. Confluence St. Louis, 1988-89, chmn., 1990-91, mem. Valuing Our Diversity Com., 1989—; mem. Vol. Svcs. St. Louis chpt. ARC, 1988—, mem. employee of the month selection com., 1989—; bd. dirs. The Caring Found. Mo., 1988—. Mem. Am. Assn. Indsl. Mgmt. (bd. dirs. 1989—, St. Louis chpt), Am. Soc. Pers. Adminstrs. (v.p. program 1984, pres.-elect 1985, pres. 1986), Am. Compensation Assn., Am. Soc. Tng. and Devel. (human resources exec. council Greater Birmingham chpt.), Birmingham C. of C. (chmn. pub. affairs com. 1985-86, chmn. edn. com. 1985-87, bd. dirs. 1987), Beta Gamma Sigma, Omicron Delta Epsilon. Clubs: Civitan (founding pres. local chpt. 1984-85, dist. tng. officer 1985-86), Young Men's Bus. (Birmingham chpt. bd. dirs. 1986). Avocations: reading, music, astronomy and astrophysics, volleyball. Office: Blue Cross-Blue Shield Mo 4444 Forest Park Saint Louis MO 63108

SPICAK, DORIS ELIZABETH, health services company executive; b. Balt., Sept. 6, 1943; d. Elwood Lee and Georgianna E. (Thomas) Fletcher; m. Marvin Ray Spicak, May 18, 1968; children: Charles Frank, Lisa Marie. Student, Towson State Coll., 1961-62, Balt. Jr. Coll., 1962-64; diploma in nursing, Sinai Sch. Nursing, Balt., 1965; AS, Bee County Coll., Beeville, Tex., 1976. RN, Md., Tex. Insvc. dir. Meml. Hosp., Beeville, 1975-76, dir. nurses, 1980-81; dir. nurses Hillside Nursing Ctr., Beeville, 1978-80; dir. br. agy. Coastal Bend Home Health, Victoria, Tex., 1981-85; adminstr. Crossroads Home Health, Victoria, 1985—, bd. dirs.; pres. bd. dirs. Crossroads Nursing Svc., Victoria, 1986—. Active John F. Kennedy Presdl. Campaign, Balt., 1960. 1st lt. U.S. Army, 1965-68, Vietnam. Mem. Tex. Assn. Home Health Agys. (medicare com. 1986—), Nat. Assn. for Home Care, Victoria C. of C., Coastal Plains Continuity of Care Club (Victoria, trea. 1983-84). Democrat. Roman Catholic. Home: 205 Kelly Crick Victoria TX 77904 Office: Crossroads Home Health 1501 E Mockingbird #403A Victoria TX 77904

SPICER, AUDREY ANN, manufacturing company executive; b. Dallas, Mar. 19, 1962; d. Frederick Thomas and Emma Jean (Poynor) Giesen; div. Student, Eastfield Community Coll., 1984, AA in Administrv. Asst., 1989. Credit clk. Gordon's Jewelers, Dallas, 1979-80; file clk., office mgr., mfr. rep. Jim Tuite Co., Dallas, 1980-87; customer service mgr. Triangle Plastic Wire & Cable Inc., DeSoto, Tex., 1987—. Office: Triangle PWC Inc 2050 Kestrel Ave DeSoto TX 75115

SPICER, CAROL INGLIS, freelance writer; b. Detroit, June 8, 1907; d. William Inglis and Carolyn (Clay) Rittenhouse; m. Robert Walker Spicer, 1936;1 child, Susan. AB, U. Mich., 1930. Free lancer Ann Arbor, Mich. Contbr. articles to House Beautiful, McCall's, Parents, Yankee, Better Homes and Gardens, Vogue, L.A. Times, Newsday, Boston Globe, Toronto Star, Cleve. Plain Dealer, Washington Post, Saturday Evening Post, others. Mem. Midwest Travel Writers Assn. (Best Mag. Article award 1979, Best Newspaper Article award 1981), Detroit Women Writers. Home: 740 Greenhills Dr Ann Arbor MI 48105

SPICER, CAROLYN MARIE, banker; b. Durand, Mich., July 31, 1947; d. Clarence Edward and Joyce Magdeline (McCarthy) Ackerman; m. Neal J. Spicer, Oct. 8, 1966 (div. Feb. 1978); children: Anthony J., Bethany L. Grad. with honors, Bank Adminstrn. Inst., 1988. Bookkeeper Genesee Mchts. Bank, Vernon, Mich., 1966-67; teller Citizens Comml. and Savs. Bank, Durand, 1967-69, Flint, Mich., 1976; teller State Savs. Bank, Fenton, Mich., 1976-78, asst. br. mgr., 1979, main br. mgr., 1980, administrv. asst. ops., 1981-82, ops. officer, 1983-86, v.p. ops., 1986—. Contbr. articles to profl. jours. Treas. Cliffview Assn., Fenton, 1980, pres., 1981. Named Profl. Banker of Yr., 1987. Mem. Am. Inst. Banking, NAFE, Sheshunoff Sr. Operators Officers Affiliation. Republican. Roman Catholic. Address: 247 Meadow Pointe Dr Fenton MI 48430

SPIECHA, ANNETTE JOAN, freelance artist; b. Pitts., July 9, 1939; d. Steven Albert and Mary Madeleine (Medvec) Kopelic; m. John Joseph Spiecha, Sept. 8, 1962; children: John Mark, Beth Ann, Michael David. Cert., Bus. Tng. Coll., 1959; BA in Sociology, Washington Jefferson Coll., 1980; cert. bus. mgmt., U. Utah, 1984; cert. legal asst. tng., Westminster Coll., 1986. Sales rep. Bell Telephone Co. of Pa., Pitts., 1957-59; data processing verifier Aluminum Co. of Am., Pitts., 1959-63; paralegal intern Van Cott, Bagley, Cornwall & McCarthy, Salt Lake City, 1986; paralegal Holme Roberts & Owen, Salt Lake City, 1986, Callister, Duncan & Nebeker, Salt Lake City, 1986-87; freelance artist Littleton, Colo., 1988—. Historian Sam Houston Elem. PTA, Maryville, Tenn., 1973-74, publicity chmn., 1973-74, mem. nominating com., 1973-74. Mem. Denver Art Mus., Newcomers (corr. sec. Maryville chpt. 1973). Republican. Roman Catholic. Home: 5374 E Otero Dr Littleton CO 80122

SPIEGEL, EVELYN SCLUFER, biology educator, researcher; b. Phila., Mar. 20, 1924; d. George and Helen (Laurantos) Sclufer; m. Melvin Spiegel, Apr. 16, 1955; children: Judith Ellen, Rebecca Ann. BA, Temple U., 1947; MA, Bryn Mawr Coll., 1951; PhD, U. Pa., 1954. Asst. program dir. for regulatory biology NSF, Washington, 1954-55; instr. in biology Colby Coll., Waterville, Maine, 1955-59; rsch. assoc. Dartmouth Coll., Hanover, N.H., 1961-74, rsch. assoc. prof. biology, 1974-78, rsch. prof. biology, 1978—; vis. scholar Calif. Inst. Tech., Pasadena, 1964-65, U. Calif.-San Diego, La Jolla, 1970, Nat. Inst. for Med. Rsch., Mill Hill, Eng., 1971, NIH, Washington, 1975-76, U. Basel (Switzerland) Biocenter, 1979, 80, 81, 82, 85. Contbr. numerous articles to profl. jours., chpts. to books and book reviews. Mem. Soc. for Devel. Biology, Marine Biol. Lab. Corp. (bd. trustees 1981-85, 88—). Office: Dartmouth Coll Dept Biol Scis Hanover NH 03755

SPIEGEL, KATHLEEN MARIE, hospital administrator, registered nurse; b. Erie, Pa., May 15, 1948; d. Julius B. and Helen K. (Schiller) S.; m. John Stuart Coffey, Nov. 14, 1970 (div. 1975). BS in Nursing, Villa Maria Coll., 1970; postgrad., Edinboro U., 1980; postgrad, Carnegie-Mellon U., 1989—. Diplomate Am. Bd. Quality Assurance and Utilization Rev. Staff nurse U. Hosps. of Cleve., 1970-71, Citizens Gen. Hosp., New Kensington, Pa., 1971-72; referral coordinator, staff nurse Kiski Valley Vis. Nurse Assn., Apollo, Pa., 1972-74; patient coordinator Medicenter Of Erie, 1974-75; coordinator, instr. St. Vincent Health Ctr. Sch. Nursing, Erie, 1975-82; asst. dir. Vis. Nurse Assn. of Erie County, Erie, 1982-85; mgr. discharge planning and ops. Equicor The Equitable HCA Corp., Pitts., 1986-87; dir. quality assessment and utilization rev. U. Health Services, Inc., Pitts., 1987-89; risk mgr. Magee Women's Hosp., Pitts., 1989—; bd. dirs. Pa. Hospice Network, 1983-87. Maj. USAR, 1978—. Mem. Am. Bd. Quality Assurance UR, Nat. Assn. Female Execs., Am. Mgmt. Assn., Assn. Quality Assurance Profls. Western Pa., The Carnegie, Assn. of Risk Mgrs., Sigma Theta Tau. Democrat. Roman Catholic. Club: The Carnegie. Home: 6 Oakville Dr Pittsburgh PA 15220 Office: Magee Womens Hops Forbes & Halket Sts Pittsburgh PA 15213

SPIEGEL, MARILYN HARRIET, real estate executive; b. Bklyn., Apr. 3, 1935; d. Harry and Sadie (Oscher) Unger; m. Murray Spiegel, June 12, 1954; children: Eric Lawrence, Dana Cheryl, Jay Barry. Grad. high sch., Bklyn. Exec. sec. S & W Paper Co., N.Y.C., 1953-54, Japan Paper Co., N.Y.C., 1954-58; salesperson Red Carpet Realtors, Los Alamitos, Calif., 1974-75, Coll. Park Realtors, Garden Grove, Calif., 1975-79; owner, broker S & S Properties, Garden Grove, 1979—. Named Realtor of Yr. Mem. Calif. Assn. Realtors (bd. dirs. 1984—), West Orange County Bd. Realtors (bd. dirs. 1984—, 1st v.p. 1987, pres. 1988), Million Dollar Sales Club, Long Beach C. of C., Seal Beach C. of C., Orange County C. of C., Summit Orgn., Toastmasters (pres. founders group Garden Grove, Calif. 1990). Home: 4765 Candleberry St Seal Beach CA 90740 Office: S & S Properties 5250 Lampson St Garden Grove CA 92645

SPIEGEL, ROSEMARY FORDHAM, project manager; b. Washington, July 30, 1953; d. Frank James and Layton (Wilks) Fordham; m. Richard Michael McMaster, May 12, 1989; 1 child, Brian Douglas; stepchildren: Richard Michael II, Christina Yong. BS, Georgetown U., 1975; AA in Acctg., No. Va. Community Coll., 1979. Staff asst. White House, Washington, 1974-75, Am. Revenue Bicentennial Adminstrn., Washington, 1975-77; internal auditor IRS, Washington, 1977-85, systems analyst, 1985-88, project mgr., 1988-90; project specialist OAO, Greenbelt, Md., 1990—; cons. Amera, Inc., Kennewick, Wash., 1990—. Treas., v.p. Nat. Coun. Career Women, Washington, 1980-84. Mem. NAFE, Cen. Springfield Little League. Home: 6842 Ben Franklin Rd Springfield VA 22150

SPIELMANN, LINDA GAIL, banker; b. Birmingham, Ala., Dec. 11, 1955; d. Amos Carson and Helen Patra (Holloway) Thompson; m. Peter Claus Spielmann, Sept. 3, 1988. BSBA, Jacksonville State U., 1979. Claims adjuster Liberty Mut. Ins. Co., Brentwood, Tenn., 1979-80; stockbroker Merrill Lynch, Huntsville, Ala., 1980-82; acct. rep. AT&T Communications, Atlanta, 1984-86; outside sales rep. Monroe Bus. Products, Chamblee, Ga., 1986, Electro Graphic Products, Norcross, Ga., 1986-87, Cone Bus. Forms, Decatur, Ga., 1987; sr. loan adjuster Citizens & So. Nat. Bank, Atlanta, 1987-88, FCC Nat. Bank, Elgin, Ill., 1988-89. Vol., Coun. for Battered Women, 1986, Young Democrats, 1980. Democrat. Presbyterian.

SPIER, LUISE EMMA, film editor, director; b. Laramie, Wyo., Aug. 22, 1928; d. Louis Constantine Cames and Vina Jane Cochran; m. John Spier, Sept., 1957 (div. 1962). Student, U. Wyo., 1947, U. Calif., Berkeley, 1948-53. Head news film editor Sta. KRON-TV, San Francisco, 1960-70, film editor, 1980—; freelance film editor, director San Francisco, 1970-80, 83—. Edited and directed numerous news specials and documentaries, including The Lonely Basque, Whaler, The American Way of Eating. Recipient numerous awards for film editing and directing, including Cine Golden Eagle, Best Med. Res. Film award John Muir Med. Found., Chris Statuette, Bronze and Silver Cindy awards Info. Film Producers Am. Democrat. Episcopalian.

SPIERING, NANCY JEAN, accounting executive; b. Park Ridge, Ill., Apr. 15, 1958; d. Richard Arthur and Helen Mary (Henry) S. BS, De Paul U., 1982; postgrad., U. Minn., 1989-90. CPA, Ill. Staff acct. Ruzicka & Assocs., Inc., Chgo., 1980-84; supr. acctg. Cargill, Inc., Carpentersville, Ill., 1984-87, regional asst. acctg. mgr., 1988-89; sr. internat. tax acct. Cargill, Inc., Minnetonka, Minn., 1989-90; acctg. mgr. Barnant Co. Div. Cole Parmer, 1990—; mgr. Twin Pines Janitorial Service, Elgin, Ill., 1980-89; pvt. practice tax service, Elgin, 1984-89. Official Michael Bakalis campaign, Chgo., 1980; vol. Disabled Am. Vets., Cin., 1987. Mem. Am. Soc. CPA's, Ill. Soc. CPA's, Chgo. Soc. Women CPA's. Roman Catholic. Club: Dundee Dart (Ill). Home: 875 Mohawk Dr Elgin IL 60120 Office: Barnant Co Commercial Ave Barrington IL

SPIERS, NEDRA BROWN, health care facility administrator; b. Kansas City, Mo., Nov. 3, 1929; d. Milton Bird and Blanche Sadie (McHenry) Brown; m. James Allyn Spiers, Mar. 17, 1950; children: James Allyn Jr., Susan, Lynn, Richard, Nancy, Jennifer, JoAnn. Student, Hendrix Coll., 1944-45, U. Ark., 1945-46; BA, Austin Seay State U., Clarksville, Tenn., 1972, MA, 1974. Dir. testing and counseling Ky. Better Living Ctr., Hopkinsville, Ky., 1974-79; clinic dir. Wayne County Community Mental Health Clinic, Jessup, Ga., 1979—; mem. adv. coun. Charter-By the Sea Hosp., St. Simmons, Ga., 1985—. Mem. Bus. and Profl. Women's Club, Jessup, 1980-89. Mem. Am. Psychol. Assn. (assoc.), Order of Eastern Star. Methodist. Home: 235 S Bamboo Jessup GA 31545

SPIES, CHERI LYNN, home economics consultant; b. Gloversville, N.Y., Aug. 26, 1957; d. Charles Pasquale and Marie Elizabeth (Sommella) Caputo; m. Ronald Dean Spies, May 4, 1985. BS, Marymount Coll., 1979. Coord. nutrition Nutrition Edn. and Tng. Program, Johnstown, N.Y., 1979-80; home economist Continental Baking Co., Rye, N.Y., 1980-84; mgr. consumer affairs Continental Baking Co., St. Louis, 1985-88; food technologist Best Foods CPC Internat., Union, N.J., 1984-85; pvt. practice cons. home econs. St. Louis, 1988—. Prototype developer Hostess Choco Bliss Cake, 1983. Mem. Women in Bus., Am. Home Economists Assn., Home Economists in Bus., Soc. Consumer Affairs Profls. (sec. 1986-87, v.p. 1987-88). Republican. Roman Catholic. Home and Office: 432 Graeser Rd Creve Coeur MO 63141

SPIGAI, FRANCES GAGE, electronic publishing consultant; b. Salina, Kans., Sept. 29, 1938; d. Frances Dana and Mina Lola (Jackson) Gage; m. Edwin B. Parker, Dec. 28, 1976. B.S., CCNY, 1960. Asst. prof. library and computer ctr. Oreg. State U., Corvallis, 1967-70; staff engr. Intrex, Cambridge, Mass., 1970-71; editor Becker & Hayes, Los Angeles, 1971-73; asst. to dir. Osshe Library Coun. Ashland, Oreg., 1974-76; mktg. dir. Dialog, Palo Alto, Calif., 1976-79; pres. Database Svcs. Internat., Los Altos, Calif. and Gleneden Beach., Oreg., 1979—; editor, pub. Microcomputer Index, 1984-88; instr. computer appreciation Linn-Benton Community Coll., Albany, Oreg., 1973; adj. assoc. prof. mktg. info. svcs. U. Hawaii, summer 1986; mem. adv. panel Office of Technology Assessment Fed. Info. Dissemination, 1987-88; keynote speaker Online '86, Chgo., Info. Online '87, Sydney, Australia; chair/co-chair nat. and internat. confs. and seminars., 1976—. Author: (with P. Sommer) Guide to Electronic Publishing, 1982; editor series Database Search Aids, 1980-82; contbr. articles to profl. jours. Recipient disting. svc. cert. Nat. Micrographics Assn., 1976; cert. of appreciation Am. Soc. Info. Sci., 1976. Mem. Info. Industry Assn. (bd. dirs. 1986-88). Address: Database Services Internat PO Box 366 The Marketplace at Salishan Gleneden Beach OR 97388

SPIKER, THECLA MARIE WAGNER, educator; b. Pitts., Aug. 28, 1948; d. Conrad A. and Thecla R. (Christof) Wagner; 1 child, David M. BEd, Duquesne U., 1970, MEd, 1973, postgrad., 1987; postgrad., U. Pitts., 1988—. Cert. reading specialist, tchr. bus. edn. Reading specialist Shaler Area Sch. Dist., Glenshaw, Pa., 1970—; instr. Community Coll. of Allegheny County, Pitts., 1972-73; tutor Duquesne U. Reading Clinic, Pitts., 1987—; bus. computer cons. Duquesne U., Pitts., 1988—, workshop presentor Tri-State Conf. on Vision and Reading, 1989, 90. Foster parent Profl. Family Care Svcs., Johnstown, Pa., 1984-86; co-chair Burchfield Parent Adv. Coun., Allison Park, Pa., 1988—. Recipient doctoral level award Annual Grad. Rsch. Colloquium U. Pitts., 1990. Mem. Three Rivers Reading Coun., Keystone State Reading Assn. (presenter workshop 1989, 90), Internat. Reading Assn. (presenter workshop 1990), Tri-State Bus. Edn. Assn., Pi Omega Pi (sec. 1968-70). Office: Shaler Area Sch Dist 1500 Burchfield Rd Allison Park PA 15101

SPIKES, DOLORES R., academic administrator. Vice chancellor acad. affairs So. U. and Agrl. and Mech. Coll., Baton Rouge, until 1987; chancellor So. U., New Orleans, from 1987; pres. So. U. and Agrl. and Mech. Coll. System, Baton Rouge, 1988—. Office: So U and Agrl and Med Coll Pres's Office Baton Rouge LA 70813*

SPILLANE, MARY CATHERINE, television producer; b. S.I., N.Y., Nov. 30, 1956; d. Joseph Bernard and Mary Catherine (Minoque) Spillane. BA, U. Hartford, 1978. Exec. sec. CBS Evening News, N.Y.C., 1978-80, asst. to producer, 1980; weekend producer/E.N.G. coordinator KTVI-TV, St. Louis, 1981-82, spl. projects producer, 1982-83, asst. news dir., 1983-86; assoc. producer CBS News, Detroit, 1986 , N.Y.C. 1986-87, sr. producer, 1987-89, Washington, 1989—. Avocations: reading, travel. Office: CBS News 2020 M St NW Washington DC 20036

SPILLER, MIRIAM BRITTON, fine arts appraiser; b. Reading, Pa., Sept. 4, 1926; d. William Wainwright and Katie Irene (Miller) Britton; student ceramics and sculpture Fleisher Art Meml., Phila., 1958, interior design Phila. Coll. Art, 1961; m. Raymond M. Spiller, Nov. 17, 1956. Practice interior design, 1958—; officer R.M. Spiller & Assos., appraisal, conservation and restoration fine arts, Phila., 1960—; mem. Strawberry Mansion, hist. preservation; slide lectr. in field. Cert. fine arts appraiser, Pa. Mem. Appraisers of Fine Arts Soc. (dir., sec., treas. 1975—), Phila. Mus. Art. Republican. Address: 1025 Westview St Philadelphia PA 19119

SPILLMAN, MARJORIE ROSE, dancer; b. Norfork, Va., Jan. 5; d. William Bert and Rose Marjorie (Naperski) S.; m. David E. Marks, Apr. 4, 1985; children: F. Oscar Marks, Miranda Rose. AS, Mt. Ida Jr. Coll., 1974; CT, Northeastern U., 1975; BS in Nursing, U. Mass., 1977. RN, Mass. Charge nurse VA Med. Ctr., Northampton, Mass., 1977-82; dancer N.E. Am. Ballet, Northampton, 1982, Ballet Theater Sch., Springfield, Mass., 1982-84; sales rep. Winthrop Pharm., N.Y.C., 1982—; dancer Smith Coll., Northampton, 1984—; prin. dancer Project Opera, Northampton, 1984-86; dancer Polobulus East St. Dance, Hadley, Mass., 1985. Dancer, creator part of Carmen in Carmen, 1985; dancer, choreographer A Victorian Evening, 1986; dancer Nutcracker Ballet Pioneer Valley Ballet, 1988; author, actor play Mary P. Wells Smith Narrates, 1987. Democrat. Lutheran.

SPIN, LILLIAN, psychologist; b. N.Y.C., Sept. 24, 1916; d. Charles and Rachel (Gimble) Shapiro;m. Milton Spin, Jan. 31, 1937; children: Ellen Spin-Weinstein, Frederick P. BA, CUNY, 1937, MS, CCNY, 1947; doctoral equivalent, NYU, 1961. Chief psychologist Children's Clinic, Brookdale Hosp., Bklyn., 1949-52; sch. psychologist Bur. Child Guidance, N.Y.C. Bd. Edn., 1949-55; condr. research, Vassar Coll., Poughkeepsie, N.Y., 1952, 54; chief psychologist, co-dir. Guidance Center of Flatbush, Bklyn., 1953—; psychol. cons. Vassar Coll., 1952-54, Early Childhood Ctr., Queens Coll., 1967-70; asst. examiner Bd. of Examiners N.Y.C. Bd. Edn. Lic., cert. psychologist, N.Y. State. Mem. Am. Psychol. Assn., N.Y. State Psychol. Assn., N.Y. Soc. Clin. Psychologists, Soc. of Personality Assessment. Home: 20 Lincoln Rd Putnam Valley NY 10579 Office: Guidance Ctr Flatbush 3619 Ave H Brooklyn NY 11210

SPINDLER, EUNICE MARIE, speech pathologist; b. Belvidere, Ill., Mar. 19, 1932; d. Robert Nathan and Lois Martha (Morehead) Sheley; m. Harry Keeler Spindler, June 1, 1929; children: Laura Boynton, Brian Spindler, Stanley Spindler. BA, Lindenwood Coll., 1954; MA, Coll. of St. Rose, 1975. Cert. clin. competence Am. Speech/Hearing Assn., speech pathology, N.Y. Speech pathologist North Colonie Sch. Dist., Latham, N.Y., 1975-76, 78-79, Parsons Child and Family Ctr., Albany, N.Y., 1976-78, Kenwood Individual Devel. Svcs., Albany, 1979-82; pvt. practice Delmar, N.Y., 1978—. Deacon, elder Presbyn. Ch. Mem. Cap ARea Speech/Hearing Assn., Am. Speech/Hearing Assn., Delmar Progress Club, Fed. Women's Clubs (v.p. 1984-86, pres. 1986-88, chmn. Albany County 3d dist. 1990—). Home and Office: 30 Longwood Dr Delmar NY 12054

SPINELLA, JUDY LYNN, nurse administrator; b. Ft. Worth, Apr. 8, 1948; d. Gettis Breon and Velrea Inez (Webb) Prothro; children: Scott Slater, Jennifer. BS, U. Tex., 1971; MS, Tex. Woman's U., 1973. RN, Tex. Asst. prof. U. Tex., Arlington, 1976-81; dir. emergency svcs. San Francisco Gen. Hosp., 1981-84, assoc. adminstr. for clin. svcs., 1984-88; exec. dir. for nursing svcs. Vanderbilt U. Med. Ctr., Nashville, 1988—. Wharton fellow Johnson & Johnson, 1987. Mem. Am. Orgn. Nurse Execs., Emergency Nurses Assn. (bd. dirs., treas. 1979-86), Tenn. Orgn. Nurse Execs. (bd. dirs. 1989—), Sigma Theta Tau. Home: 784 Harpeth Trace Dr Nashville TN 37221

SPINELLI, FRANCES MARKUNAS, academic official; b. Harrisburg, Pa., Mar. 6, 1950; d. Francis B. and Maud (Lyter) Markunas; m. Robert E. Spinelli, Nov. 15, 1975. BA, George Washington U., 1972, MA, 1974; cert. in lifelong edn., Harvard U., 1987. Asst. dir. Adult Edn. Resource Ctr., Montclair State Coll., Upper Montclair, N.J., 1974-76, dir. Nat. Adult Edn. Clearinghouse, 1976-80, assoc. dir. Ctr. for Continuing Edn., 1980—; cons. McGraw-Hill Book Co., N.Y.C., Coll. Bd., N.Y.C., Bound Brook (N.J.) Jointure for Community Adult Edn.; bd. dirs. N.J. Assn. Lifelong Edn. Editor Adult Edn. Clearinghouse Newsletter, 1976-88; mem. editorial bd. Educator, 1986—. Bd. dirs. Sr. Svc., Orange, N.J., 1984—, Autumn Stages: Sr. Adult Lifestory Theatre, Montclair, N.J., 1986—, Essex Literacy Consortium, N.J., 1989—; chmn. Essex County Ret. Sr. Vol. Program, Orange, 1984-87. Recipient Exemplary Program award Assn. for Adult Edn. N.J., 1978. Mem. Coalition Adult Edn. Orgns. (sec.-treas. 1979-81, pres.-elect 1981-82, pres. 1982-83), Am. Assn. for Adult Continuing Edn., Assn. for Continuing Higher Edn., N.J. Assn. for Lifelong Edn. Office: Montclair State Coll Ctr for Continuing Edn Upper Montclair NJ 07043

SPINGOLA, LAURA MARGARET, corporate executive; b. Chgo., Jan. 7, 1951; d. Joseph James and Anna Terese (Halper) S. BS in Bus., Ind. U., 1972; MBA, Loyola U., Chgo., 1988. Lic. real estate broker, cert. real estate appraiser. Coord. consumer rsch. dept. consumer services City of Chgo., 1973-77, asst. to commr. dept. consumer services, 1977-80, program coord. dept. econ. devel., 1980-81, asst. commr. dept. econ. devel., 1981-83; pres. Trade Resources Ltd., Chgo., 1984—; adj. prof. bus. Nat. Coll. Edn., Mundelein Coll., Chgo., 1989—; futures trader MidAmerica Commodity Exch., Chgo., 1978—; del. Ill. Conf. Small Bus. Exports, 1988; internat. bus. adv. bd. City Colls. Chgo. Author, contbg. author: International Business Council MidAmerica, 1982-86, International Business: Designing Effective Programs, 1988; contbr. articles to profl. jours. Vol. emergency room Northwestern U. Meml. Hosp., Chgo., 1984-86; telethon com. United Cerebral Palsy, Chgo., 1983-85; adv. com. Truman Coll., Chgo., 1982-83; women's aux. St. Joseph Carondelet Child Ctr., Chgo., 1974-78; active Mayor's Com. for Energy Conservation, Chgo., 1973-74. Recipient Partnership for Excellence award City Colls. Chgo., 1988. Mem. Chgo. Coun. Fgn. Relations, Chgo. Assn. Commerce and Industry, Acad. Internat. Bus., Japan Am. Soc., Ind. U. Alumni Assn. (life), World Future Soc. Roman Catholic. Office: Trade Resources Ltd 141 W Jackson Blvd Chicago IL 60604

SPINKS, RUTHANN, protective services official; b. Terre Haute, Ind., Sept. 4, 1959; d. Earl and Leota Ethel (Jantz) S. BS, Wichita (Kans.) State U., 1984; postgrad., U. Kans., 1986—. Cert. law enforcement officer, Kans. Paramedic Leavenworth (Kans.) Emergency Med. Svc., 1980-81; dep. sheriff Leavenworth Sheriff's Dept., 1981-86; dir. Saline (Kans.) County Community Corrections, 1986-87; officer U. Kans. Police Dept., Lawrence, 1987—. Author: Suicide Intervention for Law Enforcement Officers: A Law Enforcement Response to Domestic Violence, 1983. Com. mem. Kans. Women's Task Force on Crime and Delinquency, Topeka, 1986-89; bd. dirs. Hdqrs. Crisis Ctr., 1989—; v.p. classified senate U. Kans., 1988—. Mem. NAFE, Kans. Community Corrections Assn. (bd. dirs. 1986-89), Kans. Correctional Assn., Kans. Women in Criminal Justice, Domestic Violence Assn. of Kans. (bd. dirs. 1987-88), LWV, Am. Canoe Assn. (chpt. pres. 1984—). Office: U Kans Police Dept 302 Carruth-O'Leary Hall Lawrence KS 66045

SPIRE, NANCY WOODSON (MRS. LYMAN SPIRE), civic worker; b. Wausau, Wis., May 6, 1917; d. Aytchmonde Perrin and Leigh (Yawkey) Woodson; B.S., Radcliffe Coll., 1939; postgrad. Syracuse U., 1957—; m. Lyman J. Spire, June 29, 1940; children—Stephen Crittenden Woodson, Abigail Lyman. Vice pres. Woodson Fiduciary Corp., Wilmington, Del. Trustee Aytchmonde Woodson Found., pres., 1963—; trustee Corinthian Found., 1958-63, 68—, Syracuse Child and Family Service, 1957-62; trustee, sec. Crouse-Irving Meml. Hosp., Syracuse; trustee Syracuse Symphony Orch.; mem. exec. com. Syracuse U. Library Assos., 1958-63, trustee, 1958-—. Bd. visitors N.Y. State Tng. Sch. for Girls; v.p. bd. dirs. Leigh Yawkey Woodson Art Mus. Mem. Syracuse Symphony Guild (treas. 1958-59), U.S. Trotting Assn. Republican. Universalist (trustee). Club: Virgin Islands Game Fishing. Office: Yawkey Lumber Co Box 65 Wausau WI 54402-8065 also: 707 Kimry Moor Fayetteville NY 13066 also: 24 Windward Way Cowpet Bay W Saint Thomas VI 00802

SPIRER, JUNE DALE, marketing executive, psychologist; b. N.Y.C., May 14, 1943; d. Leon and Gloria (Wagner) Spirer; BA, Adelphi U., 1965; MS, Yeshiva U., 1980, PhD in Psychology, 1984, postgrad. NYU, 1988. TV/radio buyer BBD&O, 1965-66, SSC&B, 1966-68; sr. media planner Norman, Craig & Kummel, N.Y.C., 1968-71; assoc. media dir. Ted Bates Co., 1971-72; v.p., account supt. C.T. Clyne Co., N.Y.C., 1972-74; dir. advt. Am. Express, 1974-75; corp. dir. advt. Del Labs., Farmingdale, N.Y., 1975-79; pres. J. Spirer & Assocs., Inc., N.Y.C., 1978—; pres., chief exec. officer Media Placement Svcs., Inc., 1985—, Tactics, Inc., 1988—. Mem. Am. Psychol. Assn., N.Y. State Psychol. Assn., Soc. Personality Assessment (assoc.). Home: #1 S Ferry Rd North Haven NY 11963 Office: # 2 Horatio St New York NY 10014

SPIRITO, KATHRYN CECELIA, education educator; b. Elizabeth, N.J., Mar. 5, 1911; d. Patrick Joseph and Mary Frances (Mulvey) Gallagher; m. Michael William Spirito, June 21, 1941; children: Michael, Anthony, Maryellen, Catherine. BS, Mary Washington Coll., 1931; postgrad., Columbia U., 1932, Montclair State Tchrs. Coll., 1933, William and Mary Coll., 1934, Seton Hall U., 1959. Tchr. Union Twp. (N.J.) Sch. System, 1981-41; owner, operator Antique Kaye's Shop, Neptune, N.J., 1977-79; mgr. The Elegant Cabbage and Art Gallery, Wall Twp., N.J., 1979-81. Chaplain Fedn. Rep. Women, Monmouth County, N.J., bd. dirs., 1983—; charter mem. pres.' coun. Mary Washington Coll., Fredericksburg, Va., 1982-90. Recipient Silver Plate award Mary Washington Coll. Alumni Assn. Fellow AAUW (chmn. Elizabeth chpt. 1973-76, fund raiser Jersey Shore br. 1980), Monmouth County Ret. Educators Assn.; mem. Alexian Bros. Hosp. Aux. (charter and hon.), Ocean Grove Club (chaplain 1984—), Elderhostel. Republican. Roman Catholic. Home: 712 S Riverside Dr Shark River Hill NJ 07753

SPIRN, MICHELE SOBEL, communications professional, writer; b. Newark, Jan. 26, 1943; d. Jack and Sylvia (Cohen) Sobel; m. Steven Frederick Spirn, Jan. 27, 1968; 1 child, Joshua. BA, Syracuse U., 1965. Creative dir. Planned Communications Svcs., N.Y.C., 1966-72, EDL Prodns., N.Y.C., 1972-73; free-lance writer Bklyn., 1973-83; dir. pub. rels. Nat. Coun. Jewish Women, N.Y.C., 1983-90, dir. communications, 1990—; adj. lectr. CUNY, Bklyn., 1977-81. Author: The Fast Shoes, 1985, The Boy Who Liked Green, 1985; co-author: A Man Can Be..., 1981; editor, columnist Children's Entertainment Rev. mag., N.Y.C., 1982; columnist The Phoenix newspaper, Bklyn., 1983. Pres. Tenth St. Block Assn., Bklyn., 1989—; vol. Model Media Program, Bklyn., 1985—. Recipient Silver medal for pub. svc. film N.Y. Internat. Film and TV Festival, 1972. Mem. Jewish Pub. Rels. Soc. Am., Am. Mktg. Assn. Office: Nat Coun Jewish Women 53 W 23d St New York NY 10010

SPIRO, MARY JANE, biochemist, medical researcher; b. Syracuse, N.Y., Nov. 15, 1930; d. John A. and Julianne (Ellingsen) Paisley; m. Robert G. Spiro, June 21, 1952; children: David J., Mark D. AB, Syracuse U., 1952, PhD, 1955. Rsch. assoc. SUNY Med. Ctr., Syracuse, 1955-56; rsch. fellow Harvard Med. Sch., Boston, 1956-60, rsch. assoc., 1960-73, prin. assoc., 1974-84, assoc. prof. medicine (biochemistry), 1984—; sr. investigator Joslin Rsch. Lab., Boston, 1974—. Editor Biochem. Biophys. Acta, 1989—; contbr. articles to profl. jours. Grantee NIH, 1960—, Am. Diabetes Assn., 1989, Juvenile Diabetes Found., 1982, NSF, 1977, Nat. Found. for Infantile Paralysis, 1956-58, Med. Found., 1960-63. Mem. Am. Soc. Biol. Chemistry and Molecular Biology, Am. Diabetes Assn. Home: 19 Greylock Rd Newtonville MA 02160 Office: Joslin Diabetes Ctr Harvard Med Sch 1 Joslin Pl Boston MA 02215

SPISAK-GAMBLE, ANTONINA STANISLAWA, recording company executive; b. Krakow, Poland, Feb. 22, 1946; came to U.S., 1974; d. Mieczyslaw Roman and Zofia Helena (Tworzydlo) Spisak; divorced; 1 child, Dominik M. M in Math., Yagellonian U., Krakow, 1968, PhD in Math., 1974. Asst. prof. math. Yagellonian U., 1968-74; lectr. Grinnell (Iowa) Coll., 1975-80, Tufts U., Medford, Mass., 1980-86; pres. Cathedral Prodns. Inc., Toronto, Can., 1987—; bd. dirs. Dorian Digital Recordings, Toronto, Can.; pres. Assn. of Friends of Papal Organ, Vienna, Austria, 1983—. Author, editor, translator numerous articles in profl. jours. Republican. Roman Catholic. Office: Cathedral Prodns Inc, 9 Humewood Dr Ste 26, Toronto, ON Canada M6C 1C9

SPITSBERGEN, DOROTHY MAY, children's healthcare specialist; b. Eaton Rapids, Mich., May 13, 1932; d. Herbert Madison and Eva (Bunker) Van Aken; m. Merlin D. Spitsbergen, Dec. 27, 1952; children: Karen Richardson, Jan, Raymond, John, Claire Cooper. Student, Mich. State U.,

1960-63; BS in Sociology, Oakland U., 1973, MA in Teaching Early Childhood Edn., 1980. Cert. child life specialist. Child life specialist Crittenton Hosp., Rochester, Mich., 1980—; lectr. Oakland U., 1981—, Wayne State U., Macomb Community Coll., 1982—; creator Pediatric Edn. Program, 1981—, Child Body Safety Program, 1985—; state presentor in field. Bev Erikson Meml. grantee, 1987. Mem. Assn. for Care Children's Health (sec. state chpt. 1984-86, nat. presenter 1984, 87, state presentor 1983, 86), Child Life Coun., Rochester Tuesday Musicale Club (past pres., v.p., sec.), Delta Psi Kappa. Democrat. Home: 3959 Ellamae Rochester MI 48064 Office: Crittenton Hosp 1101 W University Dr Rochester MI 48063

SPITTLER, JAYNE ZENATY, advertising executive; b. Chgo., July 24, 1948; d. Ernest Frederick and Mary Winifred (McEvilly) Zenaty; m. Joseph R. Spittler, Aug. 22, 1987; 1 child, Brian Joseph. BA, Clarke Coll., 1971; PhD, Mich. State U., 1980. Asst. dir. pub. rels. Clarke Coll., Dubuque, Iowa, 1974-76; asst. prof. dept. telecommunications Ind. U., Bloomington, 1979-81; supr. media rsch. Leo Burnett Co., Inc., Chgo., 1981-82, mgr. media rsch., 1982-84, v.p., dir. media rsch., 1984—; guest lectr. Northwestern U., Evanston, Il., 1981—. Vol. ARC, McHenry County, Ill.; zoo parent Brookfield (Ill.) Zoo, 1975—. Named to Media Rsch. All Star Team, Media Decisions, N.Y., 1987; recipient Excellence in Teaching award, Mich. State U., 1979, grant broadcast ownership, FCC, 1979, grant VCR Usage, Corp. for Pub. Broadcasting, 1980. Mem. Advt. Rsch. Found. (video electronic media coun. 1985—, media communications coun. 1986—, radio rsch. coun. 1988—, people meter com. 1989—), Chgo. Advt. Club (bd. dirs. 1986—), Am. Assn. Advt. Agencies (media rsch. com. 1984—), Nat. Ski Patrol. Roman Catholic. Office: Leo Burnett Co Inc 35 W Wacker Dr Chicago IL 60601

SPITZER, KAREN DAWN, dentist; b. Mandan, N.D., Feb. 1, 1957; d. Myron J. and Dolores (Weinberger) S. AS, N.D. State Sch. Sci., 1977; student, U. Wis., LaCrosse, 1980-82; DDS, Marquette U., 1986. Dental hygienist for pvt. practice dentist Rothchild, Wis., 1977-78; dental hygienist for pvt. practice dentist LaCrosse, 1978-82, pvt. practice dentistry, 1986—; dental cons. St. Joe's Nursing Home, Bethany St. Joe Nursing Home, Bethany Riverside Nursing Home, LaCrosse, 1986—; mem. courtesy staff St. Francis Hosp. Mem. Am. Dental Soc., Acad. Gen. Dentistry, Delta Sigma Delta, Omicron Kappa Upsilon, Alpha Sigma Nu. Roman Catholic. Office: 3143 State Rd Ste 201 LaCrosse WI 54601

SPITZNAGEL, ANNE MOULTON SIRCH, psychologist; b. N.Y.C., Mar. 14, 1923; d. Thor Rheudy and Helen Trowbridge (Dutton) Sirch; m. John Keith Spitznagel, Feb. 2, 1947; children: John Jr., Jean, Margaret, Elizabeth, Paul. BA, Barnard Coll., 1944; BS in Nursing, Columbia U., 1947; MA, George Washington U., 1949; PhD, Duke U., 1981. lic. psychologist, Ga., 1982, marriage and family therapist, 1984. Rehab. counselor Tuberculosis Assn., Washington, 1948; RN in personnel dept. George Washington U. Hosp., Washington, 1947-48; RN Johns Hopkins Hosp., Balt., 1947, Barnes Hosp., St. Louis, 1950; research assoc. U. N.C. Child Study Project, Chapel Hill, 1962-65; psychometrist, chief research asst. Edn. Improvement Program Duke U., Durham, N.C., 1965-67; staff psychologist, devel. disabilities, rsch. asst., instr. dept. psychiatry U. N.C., Chapel Hill, 1969-76; grad. asst. Duke U., 1977-79; sch. psychologist Durham (N.C.) County Schs., 1977-79; psychologist Atlanta Pediatric Psychol. Assocs., Tucker, Ga., 1982-83; pvt. practice child psychology and family therapy Decatur and Lilburn, Ga., 1982—; child psychologist, marriage and family therapist Cath. Social Svcs., Atlanta, 1984-89; cons. Village of St. Joseph Residential Sch., Atlanta, 1985-89; mem. com. exceptional child Coun. for Children, Atlanta, 1983-85; therapist The Hub Counseling & Ednl. Ctr., Tucker, Ga., 1989-90. Author: I'll see You in the Morning, 1974. Past leader, den mother Girl Scout U.S., Boy Scouts Am., Chapel Hill; facilitator Parents Anonymous, Ga. Coun. Child Abuse, 1988-89, Adult Abuse Survivors Group, 1990, Ga. Coun. Child Abuse; mem. LWV. Mem. Am. Psychol. Assn., Am. Assn. Marriage & Family Therapy (clin. mem. 1987), Ga. Psychol. Assn., Assn. Children Learning Disabilities (past local pres., N.C. bd. dirs.). Democrat. Episcopalian. Office: 912 Killian Hill Rd Ste 104 Lilburn GA 30247

SPIVACK, ELLEN SUE, writer, food company executive; b. Trenton, N.J., Dec. 2, 1937; d. Chaim David and Beatrice (Safir) Knopf; m. Roger Elliot Spivack, May 15, 1960; children—Ira, Eileen, Basha. B.S. in Edn. and Sociol. Douglass Coll., New Brunswick, N. J., 1959. Tchr., N.Y., N.J., Pa., 1959-73; tchr. nat. foods cooking, Lewisburg, Pa., 1977—; writer articles and books, 1974—; ptnr. Deep Roots Trading and Foodworks Co., growers, Lewisburg, 1978-88, Williamsport, Pa., 1988—, Sprouted Foods, Inc.; owner Foodworks. Pres., bd. dirs. Johnny Alfalfa Sprout, Inc, assoc. dir. People to People. Author: Beginner's Guide to Meatless Casseroles, 1983; Whole Foods Experience, 1985; The Johnny Alfalfa Sprout Handbook, 1986; also others; editor newsletters in field. Vol. The Hunger Project, San Francisco Democrat. Jewish. Home: care Pinchak 3 Kings Gate Rd Suffern NY 10901 Office: 127 S Broadway Nyack NY 10960

SPIVAK, HELAYNE, advertising agency executive. Past sec. Della Femina, Travisano & Ptnrs., N.Y.C.; copywriter, then sr. v.p. and assoc. creative dir. Ally & Gorgano; v.p., assoc. creative dir., then sr. v.p. Ammirati & Puris, Inc., N.Y.C., 1986-88; sr. v.p., exec. creative dir. Hal Riney & Ptnrs., Inc., N.Y.C., 1988-90; exec. creative dir. Young & Rubicam N.Y., N.Y.C., 1990—. Recipient Clio awards. Office: Young & Rubicam NY 285 Madison Ave New York NY 10017*

SPIVAK, JACQUE R., bank executive; b. San Francisco, Nov. 5, 1929; d. Robert Morris and Sadonia Clardine Breitstein; m. Herbert Spivak, Aug. 26, 1960; children—Susan, Donald, Joel, Sheri. B.S., U. So. Calif., 1949, M.S., 1950, M.B.A., 1959. Mgr. Internat. Escrow, Inc., Los Angeles, 1960-65, Greater Los Angeles Investment Co., 1965-75; mgr. escrow Transam. Title Ins. Co., Los Angeles, 1975-78; mgr. escrow, asst. v.p. Wells Fargo Bank, Beverly Hills, Calif., 1979-80; adminstr. escrow, v.p. 1st Pacific Bank, Beverly Hills, 1980-85; escrow adminstr. Century City Savs. & Loan Assn., Los Angeles, 1986-87; pres. Producers Escrow Corp., Beverly Hills., 1987—. Recipient awards PTA, Girl Scouts U.S.A., Jewish Fedn. Los Angeles, Hadassah. Mem. Calif. Escrow Assn., Nat. Assn. Bank Women, Inst. Trustees Sales officers. Republican. Jewish. Office: Producers Escrow Corp 9328 Civic Ctr Dr Beverly Hills CA 90210

SPIVAK, JOAN CAROL, public relations executive; b. Phila., May 12, 1950; d. Jack and Evelyn Lee (Copelman) S.; m. John D. Goldman, May 17, 1980; children: Jesse, Marcus. AB, Barnard Coll., 1972; M of Health Scis., Johns Hopkins U., 1980. Freelance writer N.Y.C., 1980-84; project dir. Impact Med. Communication, N.Y.C., 1984-87; sr. v.p. Daniel J. Edelman Inc., N.Y.C., 1987—. Co-author: (pamphlet) Lead: New Perspectives on an Old Problem, 1978; contbr. The Book of Health, 1981. Bd. dirs. May O'Donnell Dance Co., N.Y.C., 1983-85, Chamber Ballet U.S.A., N.Y.C., 1985-87. Mem. N.Y. Acad. Sci. Democrat. Jewish. Office: Daniel J Edelman Inc 1500 Broadway New York NY 10036

SPLITT, CODY, lawyer; b. Wausau, Wis., Aug. 13, 1919; d. Anne Monahan Wendt; m. Harley B. Splitt, Apr. 17, 1948; 1 child, Leigh Rogers. BA, U. Wis.-Madison, 1947, LLB, 1949. Bar: Wis. 1949, U.S. Dist. Ct. (we. dist.) Wis. 1949. Sole practice, Appleton, Wis., 1949—; asst. dir. U.S. Agr. Census, 1955; dist. dir. U.S. Census, 1960; lectr., moderator Law for Laymen, Appleton, 1975-80; dir. Legal Service Northeastern Wis., Inc., 1984-85. Mem. Equal Rights Council, Wis., 1966-73, Equal Opportunities, Appleton, 1973-81, Wis. Coun. Mental Health, 1989—; vice chmn. Outagamie County Republican Club, 1965; pres. Outagamie County Rep. Women's Club, 1951, 88-89; co-pres. Appleton PTA, 1971; v.p. Appleton Big Sisters, 1974. Coun. Served with WAVES, 1942-45. Named Woman of Yr. Outagamie County, NOW, 1974. Mem. State Bar Wis. (sect. sec. 1974), Outagamie County Bar Assn. (exec. com. 1978-85, sec. 1985-86, pres. 1986-87), Fed. Bus. and Profl. Women (v.p. 1978), Fedn. Rep. Women. Home: 1611 W Glendale Ave Appleton WI 54914 Office: 103 W College Ave #1204 Appleton WI 54911-5706

SPOEGLER, CHRISTINA MARIE, foundation society executive; b. N.Y.C., June 2, 1950; d. Harvey F. Jr. and Lucille (D'Amiano) Goldsmith; m. Anton J. Spoegler, Nov. 16, 1971. BA, Hofstra U., 1979, MA, 1982. Rsch. asst. Hofstra U., Hempstead, N.Y., 1978-82, rsch. assoc., 1982-84; owner, mgr. Spoegler Stationery & News, Inc., Franklin Square, N.Y., 1984-85; reporter L.I. Bus. Newsweekly, Ronkonkoma, N.Y., 1986; adminstrv. asst. Merrill Lynch, Garden City, N.Y., 1987-88, fin. cons., 1988-89; asst. mgr. foundation affairs N.Y. Zool. Soc., Bronx, 1989—. Contbr. articles to profl. publs. Mem. regional adv. bd. Am. Kidney Fund, L.I., N.Y., 1989—. Mem. AAAS. Office: NY Zool Soc 185th St & So Blvd Bronx NY 11530

SPOEHEL, JERRI HOSKINS, volunteer agency executive; b. Oak Park, Ill., Mar. 13, 1932; d. George Alex and Myrtle Jean (McBean) Hoskins; BA in English cum laude, Coll. Wooster, 1953; m. Edwin H. Spoehel, Apr. 16, 1955; children: Ronald Ross, Jacqueline Jean. Instr., Success-Plus, 1974; columnist Daily News, San Fernando Valley, Van Nuys, Calif., 1970-85; community rels. dir. Sta. KCSN-FM, Nat. Pub. Radio, Northridge, Calif., 1975-85; exec. dir. Vol. Ctr. of San Fernando Valley, 1985-89; sec. Vol. Ctrs. of So. Calif.; mem. Pres. Assocs. Calif. State U., Northridge; panelist/seminar instr. Nat. Devel. Conf., Corp. Pub. Broadcasting. Recipient Nat. Abe Lincoln Merit award So. Bapt. Radio and TV Commn.; named Disting. Citizen of Northridge; other awards. Mem. AAUW (pres.), Pub. Rels. Roundtable, Dirs. Vols. in Agys., Soroptimists (pres.), Northridge Cultural Arts Club. Mem. Unity Ch.

SPOELMAN-KNOX, DEBORAH LEE, marketing executive; b. Bellair, Mich., Feb. 13, 1958; d. Nelson Lee and Karen Louise (Campau) Spoelman; m. Kerry Kyle Knox, Oct. 2, 1987. Student, Northwestern Mich. Coll., 1976-78; BA in Fine Arts, U. Maine, Presque Isle, 1980. Advt. mgr. Alaska Indsl. Hardware, Anchorage, 1981-83; creative dir. Mktg. Concepts, Anchorage, 1983-385; owner, mgr. Always Graphics, Anchorage, 1985-86, Indian (Alaska) Valley Mine & Gifts, 1988—; promotions coord. Carr Gottstein Properties, Anchorage, 1986-90, dir. mktg., 1990—. Bd. dirs. Big Bros.-Big Sisters, Anchorage, 1986-88, Am. Cancer Soc., Anchorage, 1989; com. chmn. Alaska Polit. Women's Caucus, 1989. Mem. Am. Mktg. Assn. (program chmn. 1989), Internat. Coun. Shopping Ctrs. Democrat. Office: Carr Gottstein Properties 6401 A St Anchorage AK 99518

SPOERR, WENDY SUE, educator; b. Sandusky, Ohio, Aug. 15, 1950; d. Everett J. and Shirley J. (Benton) S. BS in Early Childhood, Kent State U., 1975, MEd, 1979, specialist degree in curriculum and instruction, 1985. Tchr. Badger Local Schs., Kinsman, Ohio, 1975—; cons. Trumbull County Schs., Warren, Ohio, 1984-88; co-chmn. Hartford (Ohio) Library Constrn., 1987-88; presenter arts grant Trumbull County Inservice, Champion, Ohio, 1985, presenter NASA grant, 1987. Fundraiser Badger Levy Team, Kinsman, 1987-88. Psychomotor Skills grantee Trumbull County Schs., 1980, Sci./Health/Social Studies grantee Martha Holden Jennings, 1987; recipient Action award N.E. Ohio Tchrs. Assn., 1981-82; candidate tchr. in space NASA, 1986. Mem. Badger Edn. Assn. (pres. 1988-89), Phi Delta Kappa, Delta Kappa Gamma. Democrat. Home: 1128 Niles Cortland Rd NE Warren OH 44484

SPOHN, BEATRICE EVELYN, educator; b. Backus, Minn., Sept. 4, 1907; d. George Lawrence and Carolyn Jean (Hart) S. BS, U. Nebr., 1973, MEd, 1980. Profl. life Cert. in Teaching. Tchr. Plattsmouth, Nebr., 1927-28, Cook, Nebr., 1929-32, Weeping Water, Nebr., 1932-50, Sutton, Nebr., 1950-68; tchr. Campo Coll., 1968-72. Trustee Cedars Home for Children, Lincoln, Nebr., 1978. Recipient Outstanding Tchrs. award, 1972, Campo Coll. Mem. nat., state and local edn. orgns., AAUW, Pi Lambda Theta, Phi Delta Gamma (historian 1978-88). Republican. Mem. United Ch. Christ. Home: 1744 L St #2B Lincoln NE 68508

SPOLAR, GAIL TERESA, public relations specialist; b. Seattle, June 1, 1960; d. Paul Frederick and V. Teresa (Baysinger) Malinowski; m. Eric Thomas Spolar, July 9, 1983; 1 child, Grant Thomas. BA in Communications, Ea. Wash. U., 1982. News reporter, anchor Sta. KFBB-TV, Great Falls, Mont., 1982-83; pub. affairs specialist Sta. KREM-TV, Spokane, Wash., 1983-84; communications specialist ISC Systems Corp., Spokane, 1984-85; pub. rels. specialist ADP Dealer Svcs., Portland, Oreg., 1985—; advisor women in communcations com. Maryhurst Coll., Lake Oswego, Oreg., 1989-90. Mem. Women in Communications, Inc. (nat. v.p. 1982-83, v.p. 1987-88, nat. com. 1989-90). Roman Catholic. Office: ADP Dealer Svcs 2525 SW First Ave Portland OR 97201

SPOLTOREE, JANET DEE, psychologist; b. Bridgeton, N.J., Sept. 27, 1955; d. Duncan R. and Mildred (Joyce) S.; m. Len G. Guitar, May 13, 1989. BA, U. Del., 1978; MA, Fairleigh Dickinson U., 1980; PhD, U. So. Miss., 1983. Lic. psychologist, Mass., Conn. Clin. psychology intern Boston VA Med. Ctr., 1982-83; staff psychologist Tufts New Eng. Med. Ctr., Boston, 1984-87; instr. Tufts Med. Sch., Boston, 1984-87; dir. behavioral programming, community support program Brockton (Mass.) VA Med. Ctr., 1987—, asst. dir. psychology tng., 1989, dir. psychology tng., 1989—; pvt. practice psychotherapy Brookline, Mass., 1985—; clin. instr. Med. Sch. Harvard U., Boston, 1987—. Health Scis. Rsch. and Devel. grantee, 1989. Mem. Mass. Psychol. Assn. (profl. practice com.), Assn. Advancement of Behavior Therapy, New Eng. Soc. Behavior Analysis and Therapy, Am. Psychol. Assn., Nat. Registry Health Svc. Providers in Psychology. Roman Catholic. Office: Brockton VA Med Ctr 940 Belmont St Brockton MA 02401

SPOONER, LINDA GREER, lawyer; b. Huntington, Va., Mar. 31, 1950; d. Frank T. and Mary Lee (Hasty) G.; m. Lavoy Spooner Jr.; 1 child, Mary Michelle. BA in History, Cornell U., 1972, JD, 1975. Bar: Washington 1976, Md. 1982. Atty. U.S. Dept. HUD, Washington, 1975-79; assoc. Stroock & Stroock & Lavan, Washington, 1979-86, ptnr., 1986-88; ptnr. Blumenthal, Wayson, Downs & Offut, P.A., 1988—; bd. dirs. Prince George's Nat. Bank, Montgomery Bancorp. Appt. to Secs. panel on Tenant Participation of HUD by Sec. Patricia Harris, 1978; appt. to D.C. Tenant Housing Task Force by Mayor Marion Barry, 1984; appt. Prince George's County (Md.) Dep. People's Zoning Counsel by County Exec. Parris Glendening; mem. inmate grievance commn. State Md., 1989—; bd. dirs. Chrysalis House, Annapolis, Md., Prince George's County Hosp. Ctr. Found. Inc.; mem. adv. bd. Minority Bus. Resource Inst. Inc. Mem. D.C. Bar (real estate sect. 1988—), Nat. Urban League (housing task force), Nat. Assn. Black Women Attys. (Disting. Svc. award 1983), Nat. Assn. Bond Lawyers. Democrat. Episcopalian. Office: Blumenthal Wayson Downs & Offut PA 1801 McCormick Dr Ste 155 Landover MD 20785

SPOONER, VICTORIA ANNE, industrial engineer, statistician; b. Athens, Ga., Jan. 26, 1963; d. Joe Langley and June Dale (Taylor) S.; m. Michael Alan Bowman, Sept. 7, 1985 (div. 1990). BS in stats., U. Ky., 1983; MS in Indsl. Engring., Auburn U., 1986; MBA, Ohio State U., 1989. Computer programmer Diversified Products, Opelika, Ala., 1983; statistician Ampex Corp., Opelika, 1983-85; quality engr. GE, Worthington, Ohio, 1985-87, quality assurance mgr., 1987-89; staff assoc. Luftig & Assocs., Inc., Detroit, 1989—. Mem. 1st Bapt. Ch., Auburn, Ga. Mem. AAUW, Am. Soc. Quality Control (local chmn. 1987), Am. Statis. Assn., Mensa Chi Omega. Republican.

SPORE, STEPHANIE MCMANUS, chemical engineer, sales specialist; b. Darby, Pa., Mar. 24, 1962; d. Donald Gordon and Patricia Elizabeth (Hurley) McManus; m. James Sutherland Spore III, Feb. 14, 1990; children: James Sutherland IV, Jonathan Eric. BSChemE, Va. Poly. Inst. and State U., 1985; student, Exeter (Eng.) U., 1984; postgrad., Cen. Mich. U., 1985-87, Old Dominion U., 1990—. Registered engr.-in-tng., Va. Engring. technician Naval Sea Systems Command, Washington, 1980-85; govt. sales rep., with latex tech. svc. Dow Chem. USA, Midland, Mich., 1985; heat transfer specialist Dow Chem. USA, Moorestown, N.J., 1986, tech. sales rep., 1986-87; tech. sales rep. I Dow Chem. USA, Saddlebrook, N.J., 1987-88; tech. sales specialist Dow Chem. USA, Moorestown, 1988-89; tech. sales rep. Ethyl Corp., Mt. Olive, N.J., 1989—; pres. Crystal Bay Town Homes, 1987-88; group leader Dale Carnegie, Cherry Hill, N.J., 1987. Vol. Big Bros.-Big Sisters, N.J., 1986—; leader 4-H Club, Va., 1980—; corp. chmn. United Way, Burlington, N.J., 1989; coun. mem. County of Fairfax, Va., 1978-80. Scholar Allied Chem. Co., 1984. Mem. NAFE, N.J. Chem. Club, Phi Eta Sigma. Home: 500 Lord Dunmore Dr Virginia Beach VA 23464 Office: Ethyl Corp 500 Lord Dunmore Dr Virginia Beach VA 23464

SPORNICK, LYNNA BABS, physicist, lecturer; b. N.Y.C., Oct. 6, 1947; d. Louis and Jean (Schwartz) Kanney; m. Virgil Alexander Spornick, June 6, 1979. BS in Physics and Econs., Carnegie-Mellon U., 1969; PhD in Physics, Rutgers U., 1975; MS in Computer Sci., Johns Hopkins U., 1981. Teaching asst. dept. physics Rutgers U., 1970-73, rsch. intern, 1973-75; postdoctoral fellow Colo. State U., Ft. Collins, 1975-77; sr. staff physicist applied physics lab. Johns Hopkins U., 1977—, lectr., 1985—. NSF fellow, 1969-70. Mem. Am. Phys. Soc., Am. Assn. Physics Tchrs., Soc. for Computer Simulation. Office: Johns Hopkins U Applied Physics Lab Johns Hopkins Rd Laurel MD 20723

SPORT, BONNIE MONTROSE, elementary school teacher; b. Kansas City, Mo., Mar. 28, 1937; d. William Gus and Clara (Moore) McGinnis; m. Milton Sport, Dec. 25, 1960 (div. May 1964); 1 child, Lisa Jewell. Student, Cen. State Coll., Wilberforce, Ohio, 1957; BS in Edn., Kans. State U., 1960; postgrad., Pepperdine U., 1975, L.A. City Coll., 1974. Cert. elem. edn. tchr., Calif., Ohio, Mo.; cert. fashion designer. Tchr. Cleve. Pub. Schs., 1960, Edwards (Calif.) AFB, 1960-61, Pasadena (Calif.) City Schs., 1963-64, Kansas City Mo. Schs., 1965-71, L.A. City Schs., 1972-84, Compton (Calif.) Schs., 1985, Lynwood (Calif.) Schs., 1986, Lawndale (Calif.) Schs., 1987, Hawthrone (Calif.) Schs., 1987; tchr. Delta Sigma Theta Headstart, L.A., 1971, 85, Frederick Douglas Headstart, Calif., 1971-72, Child Care and Devel. Headstart, L.A., 1971, Fedn. of Sellemonta Headstart, Hawthrone, 1972. Fashion designer cocktail dress, wedding dress, sportswear, 1960-84; house designer, Acluff and Roada, Kansas City, 1988; designer mag. cover CBS studios, L.A., 1985. Parent asst. Greater Community Action Agy., L.A., 1974. Recipient scholarship Delta Sigma Theta, 1955. Mem. NAFE, Assn. of Childhood Educators, Calif. Tchrs. Assn., Kappa Alpha Psi, Beta Pi Zeta, Delta Sigma Theta. Republican. Baptist. Home: 2520 Park Ave Kansas City MO 64127 Office: Delta Sigma Theta Sorority 3740 Stockes St Los Angeles CA 90008

SPOTTSVILLE, DEBORAH DENISE, contract analyst; b. L.A., Apr. 26, 1955; d. Mitchell and Marilyn (Strickland) S. BBA, U. Redlands, 1981. Contract adminstr. Northrop Corp., Hawthorne, Calif., 1981-84, 87—; actress, movie extra, L.A., 1976-78, 84-87; co-host cable TV program, Compton, Calif., 1986. Mem. Youth Motivation Task Force, Industry High Sch. Instrs. Program. Mem. Black Women's Forum, Compton Alumni Assn. Democrat. Home: 5830 Green Valley Circle #316 Culver City CA 90230 Office: Northrop Corp Aircraft Div 1 Northrop Ave Hawthorne CA 90250

SPRABERY, PEGGY PEDEN, small business owner and administrator; b. Starkville, Miss., Oct. 21, 1950; d. William Aaron and Genevieve (McGuff) Peden; m. Donald L. Sprabery, Dec. 7, 1985; 1 child, Genevieve Anne. BS, Miss. U. for Women, 1972; MS in Edn. & Psychology, Miss Coll., 1974. Elementary educator Jackson (Miss.) Pub. Schs., 1972-76; English educator Long Beach (Miss.) Pub. Schs., 1976-79; food and beverage adminstr. Frenchman's Reef, St. Thomas, V.I., 1979-82; bus. owner Profl. Dressers, Gulfport, Miss., 1982—, Monograms, Etc., Gulfport, Miss., 1988—. Mem. Auxiliary (impaired phy. chmn. port Miss.), Civic League, Symphony bd. dirs. Home: Oaklawn Plantation Menge Pass Christian MS 39571 Office: Professional Dressers 1900 Pass Rd Gulfport MS 39501

SPRAGUE, AMARIS JEANNE, real estate broker; b. Jackson, Mich., Feb. 18, 1935; d. Leslie Markham and Blanche Lorraine (Basnaw) Reed; student Mich. State U., 1952-53; B.S., Colo. State U., 1965; m. John M. Vetterling, Oct. 1985; children by previous marraige—Anthony John, James Stuart. Real estate sales Seibel and Benedict Realty, Ft. Collins, Colo., 1968-69; salesman Realty Brokers Exchange, Ft. Collins, 1969-72; broker, pres. Sprague and Assos., Inc., Realtors, Ft. Collins, 1972-80; broker assoc. Van Schaack & Co., Ft. Collins, 1980-86; broker ptnr. The Group, Inc., 1986—; dir. Univ. Nat. Bank. Mem. bus. adv. council Colo. State U., 1976-84, chmn. 1979-80, mem. adv. council Coll. of Engring., 1981. Cert. real estate broker. Mem. Nat. Assn. Realtors, Colo. Assn. Realtors, Ft. Collins Bd. Realtors, Ft. Collins C. of C. (dir. 1975-78, 80-83, pres. 1982-83). Republican. Episcopalian. Home: PO Box 475 Fort Collins CO 80522 Office: 401 W Mulberry St Fort Collins CO 80521

SPRANG, PAMELA SUE, nurse educator; b. Columbus, Ohio, Sept. 6, 1953; d. Richard Gayle and Marie Elizabeth (Hafey) S. ADN, Columbus Tech. Inst., 1975; BSN in Nursing, U. S.C., Spartanburg, S.C., 1979; MS in Pub. Health Nursing, U. N.C., Chapel Hill, 1983. Cert. community health nurse. Supr., head nurse Luth. Sr. City, Columbus, Ohio, 1975-76; staff nurse SRMC Hosp., Spartanburg, S.C., 1976-77, Rutherford (N.C.) County Health Dept., 1986-87; staff nurse Spartanburg (S.C.) County Health Dept., 1979-81, supr. long term care, 1981, nurse coord. migrant program, 1987-89; nursing instr. Gardner-Webb Coll., Boiling Springs, N.C., 1983-87; asst. prof. comunity healthy nursing U. S.C., Spartanburg, 1987—. Tchr. first aid classes for Girl Scout leaders ARC, 1987—. Mem. Am. Nurses Assn., Am. Pub. Health Assn., S.C. Pub. Health Assn., Assn. Community Health Nurse Educators, S.C. Nurses Assn. (bd. dirs. Piedmont dist., editor newsletter 1988—). Lutheran. Home: The Bluffs Apt G2 100 Vanderbilt Ln Spartanburg SC 29301 Office: Mary Black Sch of Nursing 800 University Way Spartanburg SC 29303

SPRANKEL, CHARLENE MILDRED, mathematics educator; b. Waterloo, Ill., June 12, 1925; d. Charles Fredrick and Hulda Elizabeth (Fauss) S. BS in Edn., So. Ill. U., 1947; MS in Math., U. Ill., 1949; PhD in Edn., So. Ill. U., 1976. Grad. teaching asst. dept. math. U. Ill., Urbana, 1947-49; rsch. asst. in statistics agrl. econs. dept. U. Ill., 1949-52; tchr. 5th grade Rantoul (Ill.) City Schs., 1952-56; computer programmer Coordinated Sci. Lab., U. Ill., 1956-59; tchr. math. Niles Twp. High Sch., Skokie, Ill., 1959-61; instr. dept. math. Chgo. State U., 1961-67; instr. math. So. Ill. U., Carbondale, 1967-75; prof. math. Richland Community Coll., Decatur, Ill., 1975-89; ret. NSF scholar, 1962, 63; recipient Charles Neely award, AAUP, 1946, others. Mem. Am. Bus. Women's Assn. (treas. 1989-90), Ill. Mathematics Assn. for Community Colls. (sec. 1989-90), AAUW, AAUW Investment Club (sec. 1990). Republican. Methodist. Home: 120 Fenway Dr Decatur IL 62521

SPRANO, ESTHER JOHANNA, insurance executive; b. Waterbury, Conn., Oct. 17, 1958; d. Richard H. and Marie (Zello) S. BA in Communications cum laude, DePaul U., 1981. Editor Environ. Rsch. and Tech., Inc., Concord, Mass., 1981-82, State St. Bank, Boston, 1982; editor Arkwright Mut. Ins. Co., Waltham, Mass., 1982-83, publicity mgr., 1983-85, communications mgr., 1985-87, asst. v.p. mktg., dir. corp. communications, 1987—. Tutor Community Learning Ctr., Cambridge, Mass., 1981-83. Recipient Excellence award Paper Sources Internat., 1988, Cert. of merit Printing Industries of Am., 1988, Cert. of Excellence, Bus. Profl. Advt. Assn., 1989. Mem. NAFE, Advt. Club, Footlight Club, Toastmasters Internat. Office: Arkwright Mut Ins Inc 225 Wyman St Waltham MA 02254

SPRATT, ROBIN LOUISE, chemical engineer; b. Somerville, N.J., July 3, 1963; d. Robert and Frances Spratt. BS, Rutgers U., Piscataway, N.J., 1985. Process engr. Bell Labs., Murray Hill, N.J., 1986-87, Kalama Chem. Co., Garfield, N.J., 1987; applications engr. Kason Corp., Linden, N.J., 1988; instrument engr. chems. div. BASF Corp., Parsippany, N.J., 1988—. Fellow Am. Inst. Chem. Engrs. Office: BASF Corp Chems Div ML1-1 100 Cherry Hill Rd Parsippany NJ 07054

SPRECHMAN, EVELYN TERRY, nurse, consultant; b. N.Y.C., Feb. 25, 1930; d. Robert and Emma (Tewes) Redfield; m. Harry Sprechman, Dec. 3, 1950; children: Susan, David. Assoc. Degree in Nursing, State U. at Farmingdale, 1972. Asst. head nurse North Shore U. Hosp, Manhasset, N.Y., 1972-75; dir. in-service edn. Woodbury (N.Y.) Health Related Facility, 1975-81; supr. operating rm., endoscopy unit and laser surgery Dr's Howard J Eddy & Jian Chu Yu, Garden City, N.Y., 1986-89; cons. in field, 1986—. Mem. Soc. Gastrointestinal Assts. Hebrew. Office: Drs Howard J Eddy & Jian Chu Yu 520 Franklin Ave Garden City NY 11530

SPREITZER, CYNTHIA ANN, computer programming professional; b. Chgo., July 16, 1953; d. John Herbert and Patricia Virginia (Tieman) S. BS in Math., Loyola U., Chgo., 1975. Cert. data processor, 1986. Sr. Arthur Andersen and Co., Chgo., 1975-80; lead analyst Larimer County, Ft. Collins, Colo., 1980—. Mem. Assn. Inst. Cert. Computer Profls., Computer Security Inst., Data Processing Mgmt. Assn. Roman Catholic. Home: 610 Grove Ct

Loveland CO 80537 Office: Larimer County PO Box 1190 Fort Collins CO 80522

SPRIGGS, ANN JOHNSON, physicians assistant; b. Iowa City, Apr. 19, 1938; d. J. Garth and Zaida (Hutchins) Johnson; m. Richard Tuttle Spriggs, Aug. 27, 1960 (div. Mar. 1988); children: Jared Lewis, Matthew Crowell. BA, U. Rochester, 1959; MA, Cornell U., 1961; MS, U. Colo., 1979. Cert. physicians asst. Rsch. asst. Child Rsch. Coun., Denver, 1961-62; rsch. assoc. JFK Child Devel. Ctr., Denver, 1962-63; child health assoc. Mayer & Walters Pediatrics, Evergreen, Colo., 1979-81, Dept. Pediatrics, Fitzsimmons, Aurora, Colo., 1981-90; with emergency dept. The Children's Hosp., Denver, 1990—; clin. asst. Dept. Pediatrics, U. Colo. Health Scis. Ctr., Denver, 1981—; co-chairperson Com. for Licensing Day Care for Sick Children, State of Colo., 1989; reviewer Nat. Health Safety Standards for Day Care, 1990. Co-author: Test of Concept Utilization, 1972. Recipient Exceptional Performance award Fitzsimmons Army Med. Ctr., 1984-90. Democrat. Unitarian. Office: The Childrens Hosp Emergency Dept 19th and Downing Sts Denver CO 80218

SPRINGBORN, ROSEMARY KELLY, technical writer and editor; b. South Bend, Ind., June 2, 1932; d. Edward Joseph and Hazel Jeannette (Thompson) Kelly; m. Bruce Alan Springborn, Dec. 19, 1964. BS, Purdue U., 1953; postgrad., Northwestern U., 1954-55, U. Mich., 1960-61, No. Ill. U., 1974-75. Mng. editor Brewers' Digest jour., Bakers' Digest jour., Chgo., 1955-59; sr. tech. writer Systems div. Bendix Corp., Ann Arbor, Mich., 1960-63, Cadillac Gage div. Ex-Cell-O Corp., Warren, Mich., 1963-65; editor-in-chief books Soc. Mfg. Engrs., Dearborn, Mich., 1965-69; mng. editor Harper & Row, Pubs., Evanston, Ill., 1969-71; dir. contracts Harper & Row, Pubs., 1971-73; mng. editor Indsl. Rsch./Devel. jour., Barrington, Ill., 1973-75; editor-in-chief TPC Tng. Systems, Barrington, 1975-78; pres. Kelly/Springborn Assocs., Inc., Lakeland, Fla., 1978—; gen. adv. bd. Traviss Vocat. Tech. Ctr., Lakeland, 1982—, machine shop adv. bd., 1982—. Author: Basic Machine Shop, 1980, Measuring & Gaging, 1981, Concrete & Masonry Construction, 1985; editor: Non-Traditional Machining Processes, 1967; editorial adv. bd. Training mag., 1978-80; creator numerous tech. and indsl. skills tng. programs. Recipient Bruce Tyndall award Polk County Vocat. Assn., Fla., 1986. Mem. Soc. Mfg. Engrs. (sr.), Soc. Women Engrs. (sr.), Am. Inst. Plant Engrs., Am. Soc. for Tng. & Devel. (tech. & skills div. 1980-82), Am. Tech. Edn. Assn. Office: Kelly/Springborn Assocs Inc 2834 Elizabeth Pl Lakeland FL 33813

SPRINGER, DEBORAH R., business executive; b. Duluth, Minn.; m. E. Dean Springer; children: Stephanie, Susan, Brian. Student, Rose State Coll. Sr. counselor The Intercept Program, Riverside, Calif.; account rep. Southwestern Bell Mobile Systems, Oklahoma City; v.p. Am. Ednl. Svcs. Inc., Oklahoma City. Recipient Outstanding Young Bus. Woman award, 1974. Mem. NAFE, Oklahoma City C. of C. Address: PO Box 720364 Oklahoma City OK 73147

SPRINGER, PENNY ANN, broadcasting executive; b. Queens, N.Y., Apr. 9, 1952; d. Benjamin Herman and Florence (Goldman) Seltzman; m. Herbert J. Springer, Nov. 24, 1973 (dec. May 1985). BA, SUNY, Cortland, 1974. Resident mgr. Chelsea Townhouses, Cortland, 1974-75; pub. rels. asst. Am. Land Title Assn., Washington, 1976-78; promotions coord. Sta. WMAL-AM, Washington, 1978-81; dir. sta. rels. Washington Broadcast News, 1982-84; pres., treas. RGR Broadcasting Co., Gouverneur, N.Y., 1984-87, also bd. dirs., 1984-87; pres. AIRWAVES Ltd., San Francisco, 1988; bus. mgr. Mktg. Works, Marblehead, Mass., 1988-90; dir. ops. The Radio Mktg. Dept., Morristown, N.J., 1990—. Democrat. Jewish.

SPRINGER, SUSAN MAE, business consultant, educator; b. Grinnell, Iowa, Jan. 2, 1953. BA, U. Iowa, 1975; MA, U. No. Iowa, 1978. Grad. asst. dept. spl. edn. U. No. Iowa, 1978-79; tchr. Gerhard Kohn, Huntington Beach, Calif., 1978-79; resource specialist ABC Unified Sch. Dist., Cerritos, Calif., 1979—; dir. Total Achievement Cons., Sea Beach, Calif., 1986—; studio tchr. Affordable Svcs., Inc., Hollywood, Calif., 1987—; presenter Grinnell (Iowa) Coll., 1978. Contbr. articles to profl. jours. Mem. pub. rels. com. K. Latham for Congress, Newport Beach, Calif., 1988. Faculty scholar U. Iowa, 1977, 78; faculty grantee Chapman Coll., 1987-88. Mem. AAUW, Performing Arts Ctr., Newport Area Preferred Profls., Balboa Ski Club. Republican. Office: Total Achievement Cons PO Box 2022 Seal Beach CA 90740

SPRINGER, WILMA MARIE, educator; b. Goshen, Ind., Jan. 13, 1933; d. Noah A. and Laura D. (Miller) Kaufman; m. Walter Frederick Springer, May 25, 1957; children: Anita Daniel, Timothy, Mark. BA, Goshen Coll., 1956; MS, Bradley U., 1960. Tchr. Topeka (Ind.) Elem. Sch., 1956-57, Metamora (Ill.) Grade Sch., 1957-59, Bellflower (Calif.) Unified Sch. Dist., 1960-61, 68-89, Jefferson Elem. Sch., Bellflower, 1989—; chmn. gifted and talented edn. Lindstrom Elem. Sch., Lakewood, Calif., 1986-89; stage mgr. Hour of Power TV, Crystal Cathedral, 1983—; mem. program quality rev. team State of Calif., 1989—; mem. tchr. adv. bd. Nat. Tchrs. Weekly Reader, 1989—; mem. adv. bd. Weekly Reader, 1989—. Contbr. articles in field. Campaigner Sch. Bd. Mem., 1984, Bellflower City Council, 1988, State Senator and Assemblymen, 1986-87; petition circulator, State Initiatives, 1987-88; mem. Women's Ministries of Crystal Cathedral, Garden Grove, Calif. (bd. dirs. 1978-88, recipient Cathedral Star 1985); chairperson gifted and talented edn. Jefferson Elem. Sch., Bellflower, Calif., 1989—. Classroom Tchrs. Instructional Improvement Program grantee, State of Calif., 1986-87; recipient Recognition award Regional Ednl. TV Adv. Council, 1986. Mem. Bellflower Edn. Assn. (elem. dir. 1986-88, treas. 1988-89, v.p. 1989—), Calif. Tchrs. Assn. (del. 1986-87), Nat. Edn. Assn. (del. nat. conv. 1986, 87, 90), AAUW. Republican. Mem. Reformed Churches of Am. Home: 3180 Marna Ave Long Beach CA 90808 Office: Jefferson Elem Sch 10027 E Rose St Bellflower CA 90706

SPRINGFIELD, MARY SUSAN (MARY SUSAN PANCOAST), school services executive; b. Okmulgee, Okla., Feb. 25, 1944; d. Ardo Lee and Lula Mary (Matheney) Pancoast; m. Ronald Dean Springfield, Aug. 6, 1966; 1 child, Julie Lynn. BFA, U. Okla., 1966; MA, Central Okla. State U., Edmond, 1974. Cert. tchr., Okla. Secondary tchr. Mid-Del Pub. Schs., Midwest City, Okla., 1966-78; gen. mgr. Redland Constrn. & Supply, Norman, Okla., 1978-80; pres. Williams-Springfield Sch. Svcs., Inc., Moore, Okla., 1980—. Mem. Statue of Liberty-Ellis Island Centennial Commn., N.Y., 1984. Mem. Nat. Wildlife Fedn., U. Okla. Alumni Assn. (life), DAR, U. Okla. Found., Okla. Wildlife Fedn., Gamma Phi Beta (Psi chpt.). Methodist. Avocations: flying (pvt. pilot). Home: 3636 Rolling Ln Circle Midwest City OK 73110 Office: Williams-Springfield Sch Svcs Inc 2522 N Moore Ave PO Box 7008 Moore OK 73153

SPRINKEL, ANTOINETTE MILLER, insurance company representative; b. Dayton, Oct. 2, 1945; d. Paul Oldham and Helene Florence (Irion) Miller; m. Lee William Kessen, Nov. 23, 1963, (div. 1984); m. Robert E. Sprinkel, July 9, 1988; stepchildren: Kathy, Michael. BS magna cum laude, U. Dayton, 1978, MBA with scholastic honors, 1980. With distbn. dept. Frigidaire div. GM, Dayton, Ohio, 1965-78; advt. mgr. Frigidaire Parts Svc. Co., Dayton, Ohio, 1978-81; advt. acct. mgr. NCR Corp., Dayton, 1981-84; mktg. communications mgr. Reynolds and Reynolds, Dayton; mktg. mgr. L.M. Berry & Co., Dayton, 1985-87; agt., registered rep. Prudential Ins. Co. of Am., Dayton, 1987—. Mem. charitable giving com. Nat. Multiple Sclerosis Soc., Western Ohio. Mem. Nat. Assn. Life Underwriters, Ohio Assn. Life Underwriters, Dayton Assn. Life Underwriters, Prudential Leader's Roundtable. Republican. Lutheran. Home: 10108 Park Edge Dr Spring Valley OH 45370 Office: Prudential Ins Co 2621 Dryden Rd Ste 304 Dayton OH 45439

SPROCK, JUNE, psychologist; b. Paterson, N.J., Sept. 25, 1955; d. Joseph F. and Dorothy (Borden) S. BS in Psychology cum laude, U. Miami, 1976; MS in Clin. Psychology, San Diego State U., 1980; PhD in Clin. Psychology, U. Fla., 1986. Lic. psychologist, Ind. Asst. rsch. analyst vol. Passaic (N.J.) Clifton Community Mental Health Ctr., 1975; asst. recreational therapist vol. San Diego (Calif.) Community Mental Health Ctr., 1977-78; grad. rsch. asst. San Diego State U., 1978-79, teaching asst., 1979; rsch. asst. U. Calif., San Diego, 1979-81; grad. rsch. asst. U. Fla., Gainesville, 1981-85; psychology intern VA Med. Ctr., Gainesville, 1985-86; asst. prof. psychology Ind. State U., Terre Haute, 1986-90, assoc. prof. psychology, 1990—; clin. psychologist, Terre Haute, 1987—; exam item writer, SUNY - Regent's Coll. Examinations, Albany, 1989. Contbr. articles to profl. jours. Recipient rsch. grant Ind. State U., 1988-89. Mem. Am. Psychol. Assn., Phi Kappa Phi, Psi Chi. Office: Indiana State Univ Psychology Dept Root Hall Terre Haute IN 47809

SPRUCE, MICHELLE M., securities dealer; b. Tulsa, July 23, 1945; d. Robert Frances and Mary Nell (Lee) Finney; children from previous marriages: Richard Lobley, Ronald Lobley, Charles Spruce. BS, U. Tex., Dallas, 1960. Commodity broker Siegel Trading, Dallas; stockbroker Paine Webber Co., Dallas, Am. Gen Securities, Dallas; gen. securities prin. H.D. Vest Investments, Dallas; registered securities prin. Capitol Securities, Dallas. Mem. NAFE, Nat. Mus. Women in the Arts, U. Tex. Alumni Assn. Episcopalian. Home: 2706 S Surrey Dr Carrollton TX 75006 Office: Capitol Mcpl Securities Inc 609 Castle Ridge Ste 416 Austin TX 78746

SPRUILL, LOUISE ELAM, retired secondary educator; b. Mecklenburg County, Va., Aug. 17, 1918; d. William Llewellyn and Lillie Clayton (Puryear) Elam; m. Jacob Sipe Fleming, Aug. 12, 1941 (dec. Nov. 1957); 1 child, James Sipe; m. Edward Muse Spruill, Nov. 6, 1968; (stepdaughter) Florence Spruill Mackie. BA, East Carolina U., 1939, MA, 1961. cert. secondary tchr. Tchr. Washington County Bd. Edn., Plymouth, N.C., 1957-69; chmn. math. dept. Plymouth High Sch., 1965-69. Councilwoman Plymouth City Coun., 1980-87; trustee Pettigrew Regional Libr., 1983-88; chmn. Washington County Libr. Bd., 1985-88; bd. of adjustments, Plymouth, 1989—; mem. vestry, sec. Grace Ch., 1981-84. Named Outstanding Woman in Washington County, Washington County Coun. on Status of Women, 1988. Mem. N.C. Ret. Sch. Personnel, Washington County Hist. Soc. (bd. dirs. 1987-), Delta Kappa Gamma (v.p. Pi chpt. 1968-70, corresponding sec. Beta Upsilon chpt. 1986-88), Fortnightly Literary Club (Chase City, Va. pres. 1978-79). Democrat. Episcopalian.

SPRUILL, NANCY LYON, defense analyst; b. Takoma Park, Md., Mar. 24, 1949; d. John Nolon and Katherine Frances (Killeen) Lyon; m. Steven Gregory Spruill, Aug. 24, 1969. BS in Math., U. Md., 1971; MA in Math. Statistics, George Washington U., 1975, PhD in Math. Statistics, 1980. Assoc. prof., lectr. George Washington U., Washington, 1978-79; study dir., analyst Ctr. for Naval Analyses, Alexandria, Va., 1971-83; dir. support, liaison force mgmt. pers. Office Asst. Sec. of Def., Washington, 1983-89; ops. rsch. analyst program analysis and evaluation Office Asst. Sec. Def., Washington, 1989—. Contbr. articles to newspapers. Ctr. for Naval Analyses fellow, 1975. Mem. Am. Statis. Assn. (chair program sub-com. 1988-90), Sr. Profl. Women's Assn. (1st v.p. programs 1987, pres. 1988-90). Home: 123 N Park Dr Arlington VA 22203 Office: Office Sec Def OASD (PA&E) Pentagon Washington DC 20301-1800

SPRULES, MARCIA LYNN, librarian; b. Kearny, N.J., July 13, 1948; d. Francis James and Alice E. (Billman) S. AB, Cornell U., 1970; MS in Libr. Sci., Case Western Res., 1971; MA, Fairleigh Dickinson U., 1979. Asst. Slavic cataloger Ohio State U., Columbus, 1971-72; jr. libr. Newark (N.J.) Pub. Libr., 1972-74; med. libr. Peace Corps, Rabat, Morocco, 1974-75; asst. reference libr. Fairleigh Dickinson U., Teaneck, N.J., 1976-80; computer search coordinator U. S.D., Vermillion, 1980-86, libr. dir., 1986-88; computer svc. libr. Council Fgn. Rels., N.Y.C., 1988—; book reviewer Libr. Jour., N.Y.C., 1981—; cons. bookselling to librs., Middletown, N.Y., 1987—. Contbr. articles to profl. jours. Vol. Earthwatch, Watertown, Mass., 1986—. Mem. ALA (com. chmn. 1983-84), Special Librs. Assn., AAUW, Phi Alpha Theta, Beta Phi Mu, The Planetary Soc. Democrat. Episcopalian. Office: Council Fgn Rels 58 E 68th St New York NY 10021

SPRUNGL, JANICE MARIE, nurse; b. Brooklyn, Ohio, Mar. 9, 1960; d. Donald Edward and Delores Jane (Slys) S. BS in Nursing, U. Akron, 1982. RN, Ohio. Commd. 2d lt. U.S. Air Force, 1982, advanced through grades to capt., 1986; clin. nurse Med. Ctr. Keesler U.S. Air Force, Biloxi, Miss., 1982-86; charge nurse Med. Ctr. Keesler U.S. Air Force, 1986-88; charge nurse U.S. Air Force Acad. Hosp. U.S. Air Force, Colorado Springs, Colo., 1988—. Vol., Spl. Olympics, Keesler AFB, 1983-87; fundraiser, Biloxi unit Am. Cancer Soc., 1984. Mem. Ohio Nursing Assn., Soc. Peripheral Vascular Nursing, Air Force Assn.

SPURGEON, ROBERTA KAYE, lawyer; b. Genoa, Ohio, Sept. 2, 1938; d. Donald Howard and Audrey June (Schimmel). BS, U. Cin., 1963; MS, Yale U., 1965; JD, U. Calif., Berkeley, 1976. Bar: Ohio 1977, U.S. Dist. Ct. (no. dist.) Ohio 1977, U.S. Ct. Appeals (6th cir.) 1982. Staff nurse Vis. Nurse Svc., Toledo, 1960-61, VA Hosp., Cin., 1963; instr. Boston U. Sch. Nursing, 1965-67; asst. prof. Boston U. Sch. Nursing, Chestnut Hills, Mass., 1967-71; chmn., asst. prof. Yale U. Sch. Nursing, New Haven, Conn., 1971-73; pvt. practice Cleve., 1976—. Contbr. articles to profl. jours. Del. 8th dist. Jud. Conf., 1988, 89; mem. Holden Arboretum, Cleve., 1981—, Cleve. Mus. Art, 1980—. Mem. ABA, Def. Rsch. Inst., Ohio State Bar Assn., Cleve. Bar Assn., Cleve. Assn. Civil Trial Attys. Unitarian. Home: 2660 Edgehill Rd Cleveland Heights OH 44106 Office: 55 Public Sq Ste 1490 Cleveland OH 44113

SPURGIN, KAREN JOYCE, educator; b. Snyder, Tex., May 13, 1943; d. Owen Nail and Tennye Margot (Woody) S. Assoc., Mountaiview Coll., Dallas, 1976; BS, North Tex. State U., 1977; MEd, Tex. Woman's U., 1981. Cert. tchr., Tex. Tchr. Irving (Tex.) Ind. Sch. Dist., 1978-84, Waxahachie (Tex.) Ind. Sch. Dist., 1984—. Author: The Effects of Pracs & Positive Reinforcements on Behavior and Academic Achievement in an Elementary Classroom, 1981. Mem. Tex. Assn. Profl. Educators, Am. Cancer Soc., DAR, Aggie Mom's Club (v.p.). Republican. Mem. Ch. of Christ. Home: 1203 N Creek Cir Waxahachie TX 75165

SPURLOCK, DEBORAH QUIRK, nurse midwife; b. Hartford, Conn., Oct. 6, 1944; d. George Goble and Priscilla Aldrich (Greene) Quirk; m. Paul Edward Spurlock, Apr. 29, 1966 (div. Apr. 1981); children: Alexandra T., K-Shanti G. BS, U. Mass., 1965; MEd, U. Vt., 1974; Cert. nurse midwife, SUNY, Bklyn., 1976. RN. Charge nurse Maine Med. Ctr., Portland, 1966; indsl. nurse S.D. Warren Co., Westbrook, Maine, 1967; instr. Sch. Nursing U. Maine, Portland, 1967-70; asst. prof. dept. tech. nursing U. Vt., Burlington, 1970-75; instr., clin. nurse midwife Sch. Nursing Yale U., New Haven, Conn., 1976-77; coord. nurse midwifery program Univ. Assocs. in Ob-Gyn, Burlington, 1977-86; prenatal program dir., office mgr. Northwestern Med. Ctr., St. Albans, Vt., 1986-88; nurse practitioner Planned Parenthood of North New Eng., St. Albans, Burlington, 1988-89; coord. prenatal care ctr., nurse midwife dir. Cen. Vt. Hosp., Barre, 1989—; clin. instr. Coll. Medicine U. Vt., 1979-86, Sch. Nursing Yale U., 1981-88. Speaker State of Vt. Dept. Health, Schs. in Greater Burlington, various univs., continuing edn. programs. Lt. (j.g.) Navy Nurse Corps, 1965-66. Mem. Am. Coll. Nurse Midwives. Home: D7 Meadowbrook Joy Dr South Burlington VT 05403 Office: Prenatal Care Ctr Cen Vt Hosp PO Box 547 Barre VT 05641

SPURLOCK-DAHLKE, RHONDA, special events coordinator, retail administrator; b. San Antonio, May 9, 1959; d. Rosie Rosas; m. Edward A. Dahlke, Oct. 21, 1989. AA, Tex. Southmost Coll., 1979; BA in Journalism, U. Tex., 1981. Feature writer/prodn. Brownsville (Tex.) Times, 1977-79; sales assoc. Dillard's Dept. Stores., Brownsville and Austin, Tex., 1977-81; teen bd. coord. Dillard's Dept. Stores., Austin, 1979-83, spl. events coord., 1981-84; spl. events coord. 39 stores Dillard's Dept. Stores., San Antonio, 1984—; speaker Nat. Hispanic Inst., 1986; speaker on leadership, image and careers. Bd. dirs. Network Power/Tex., San Antonio, 1986—; mem. pastoral council St. Mark's Cath. Ch., San Antonio. Mem. Women in Communications Inc. (v.p. projects 1986-88), Exec. Women's Internat., San Antonio Women's C. of C. (founding bd. dirs., mktg. and communicating co-chmn.). Home: 1411 Loma Alto Apt 3 Apt 13 San Antonio TX 78232 Office: Dillard's Dept Stores Inc 9315 Broadway San Antonio TX 78217-5900

SQUARCY, CHARLOTTE VAN HORNE, lawyer; b. Chgo., June 8, 1947; d. Charles Marion and Ruth (Van Horne) S. BA, Smith Coll., 1969; JD, Ind. U., 1977. Bar: Ind. 1977, U.S. Tax Ct. 1977, Mich. 1978, U.S. Supreme Ct. 1980, D.C. 1980, Conn. 1983, Calif. 1986. Law clk. to presiding judge Ind. State Ct., Hammond, 1976-77; dep. atty. gen. State of Ind., 1977-78; mem. legal staff Gen. Motors Corp., Detroit, 1978-81; assoc. counsel Olin Corp., Norwalk, Conn., 1981-85; sr. assoc. Bishop, Barry, Howe & Reid, San Francisco, 1985-87, Carroll, Burdick & McDonough, San Francisco, 1987—. Exec. bd. dirs. U.S.O., No. Calif. Mem. ABA (vice chmn. products liability com., tort and ins. practice), Westchester-Fairfield County Corp. Counsel Assn. Republican. Methodist. Home: 51 Sulgrave Ln Peacock Gap San Rafael CA 94901 Office: Carroll Burdick & McDonough 44 Montgomery St #400 San Francisco CA 94104

SQUAZZO, MILDRED KATHERINE (MILDRED KATHERINE OETTIG), corporate executive; b. Bklyn., Dec. 22; d. William John and Marie M. (Fromm) Oetting; student L.I. U. Sec.-treas., Stanley Engrng., Inc. and v.p. Stanley Chems., Inc., 1960-68; founder, pres. Chem-Dynamics Corp., Scotch Plains, N.J., 1964-68; gen. adminstr., purchasing dir., Richardson Chem. Co., Metuchen, N.J., 1968-69; owner Berkeley Employment Agy. and Berkeley Temp. Help Service, Berkeley Heights, N.J., 1969—, Berkeley Employment Agy., Morristown, N.J., 1982, Bridgewater, N.J., 1987—; pres. M.K.S. Bus. Group, Inc., Berkeley Heights, 1980—; mgmt. cons.; personnel fin.; lectr. Served with Nurse Corps, U.S. Army, 1946-47. Mem. Nat. Bus. and Profl. Women's Club. Home and Office: 16 Heather Ln Warren Township NJ 07059-5258

SQUIBB, CHRISTINE PETERSON, non-profit agency executive; b. Omaha, Nov. 4, 1942; d. Stanley Schoolcraft and Marjorie (Rump) Peterson; m. John Wallace Squibb, Aug. 13, 1964; children: Wallace, Elizabeth, Lee. BS, Southwest Mo. State U., 1964; MBA, Drury Coll., 1968. Clk. Menorah Med. Ctr., Kansas City, Mo., 1962, Bapt. Hosp., Springfield, Mo., 1963-64; tchr. Springfield Pub. Schs., 1970-77; dir. Community Coordinating Coun., Springfield, 1977-83; exec. dir. Ozarks Nat. Coun. on Alcoholism, Springfield, 1983—; mem. Mo. State Adv. Coun. on Alcohol/Drug Abuse, 1988—; mem. Regional Adv. Coun. Psychiatric Svcs., Southwest Mo., 1989. Mem. Ash Grove (Mo.) R-4 Sch. Bd., 1984—. Mem. Young Woman of Yr., Springfield Jaycees, 1978, Mo. Jaycees, 1978. Mem. Jr. League. Democrat. Presbyterian. Home: Rte 1 Box 630 Bois D'Arc MO 65612 Office: Ozarks Nat Coun Alcoholism 407 Holland Bldg Springfield MO 65806

SQUILLANTE, JUDITH ANN, human resources executive; b. Providence, Jan. 29, 1942; d. David Joseph and Hilda Theresa (Jamiel) Ferris; m. John Emilio Squillante, Sept. 4, 1961 (div.); children: Mark David, Jason Richard. BS, Bryant Coll., 1960; mgmt. cert. program, U. R.I., 1965-67. Asst. to town treas. Town of Bristol, R.I., 1960-64; ops. coord. Speidel div. Textron, Providence, 1964-71; asst. v.p. CE Maguire, Inc., Providence, 1971-78; mgr. customer affairs Deltona Corp., Miami, Fla., 1978-79; v.p., dir. human resources, sr. assoc. Post, Buckley, Schuh & Jernigan, Miami, 1979—, mem. bd. exec. staff, trustee profit sharing plan, 1989—; bd. dirs. Tradcom Internat., Miami; cons. Modern Bus. Applications, Miami, 1986-88; founding mem. of Human Resource Mgmt. Inst. Adv. Bd. of the U. Miami, 1989—. Chmn. pack 22 Cub Scouts Am., Miami, 1985; mem. com. Miller-Sunset Homeowners Assn., Miami, 1986, liaison Beacon Coun., 1986; mem. personnel task group Tropical Fla. coun. Girl Scouts U.S.A., 1989; task force vice chmn. Drug Free Workplace Com., 1989. Named one of Outstanding Women in Bus. and Industry YWCA, Miami, 1983. Mem. Soc. for Human Resource Mgmt., Personnel Assn. Greater Miami (Outstanding Co. Achievement in Human Resources award 1987), Women's C. of C., NAFE, YWCA Women's Network, Greater Miami C. of C. (mem. personnel and labor mgmt. com. of econ. devel. group 1987—, co-editor bi-monthly bull.), Fla. C. of C. (drug issues com., human resources com.). Democrat. Roman Catholic. Home: 9725 SW 64th St Miami FL 33173 Office: Post Buckley Schuh & Jernigan Inc 8600 NW 36th St Miami FL 33166

SQUIRE, LAURIE RUBIN, media consultant; b. N.Y.C., Jan. 30, 1953; d. Daniel and Ruth Thelma (Deutsch) Rubin; m. Herbert E. Squire, Jr., Aug. 6, 1975; children: Amy Ruth and Julie Wynn (twins). BA cum laude (scholar), Finch Coll., 1974; MA, NYU, 1976; postgrad., Columbia U., 1977—. Actress TV commls., 1960-65; arts editor Finch/Metro newspaper, N.Y.C., 1970-74; co-editor Finch Alumnae mag., 1971-72; intern producer Sta. WBAI-FM, N.Y.C., 1973; music prodn. coord. Ballet Theatre spl. Sta. WNET-TV, 1973; coll. bd. writer Mademoiselle mag., 1973; intern asst. pub. affairs dir. N.Y. Cultural Ctr., 1974; mdse. coord. Sta. WOR-AM, N.Y.C., 1974-76, contbg. writer Bob and Ray's Mary Backstage serial, contbr. nostalgia features Joe Franklin Show, producer Jean Shepherd Show and sydicated markets, 1975-77, producer Bernard Meltzer What's Your Problem, 1977-80; broadcast stage mgr. Texaco Met. Opera, 1976—; dance critic Show Bus., theatre newspaper; bd. dir. publicity and advt. L.I. Playhouse, 1982—; press rep. Great Neck Pla.; writer Chanry Communications. Publicity cons. Nassau County Mus. Fine Art; v.p. pub. rels. United Community Fund. Recipient commendations for Leukemia Radiothons Peabody Broadcasting citation, 1983. Mem. Internat. Radio and TV Soc., Great Neck Hist. Soc. Home and Office: 892 Middle Neck Rd Great Neck NY 11024

SQUIRE, LISA SHARON, clinical psychologist; b. Glendale, Calif., Feb. 19, 1953; d. William Dean and Shirley Elizabeth (Mercer) S. BS in Psychology, San Diego State U., 1976, MS in Psychology, 1978; PhD in Clin. Psychology, U. N.D., 1983. Lic. cons. psychologist, Minn. Clin. psychologist West Cen. Human Svcs., Bismarck, N.D., 1983-85; clin. psychologist Mental Health Clinic Mpls. VA Med. Ctr., 1985—; vol. supr. Walk-In Counseling Ctr., Mpls., 1986-88. Contbr. articles to profl. jours. Mem. Am. Psychol. Assn., Minn. Psychol. Assn., Mid-Metro Bus. and Profl. Women's Assn. (v.p. 1988-89). Office: Mental Health Clinic 116A1 VA Med Ctr 1 Veterans Dr Minneapolis MN 55422 also: Midwest Ctr for Personal and Family Devel 2550 University Ave W Saint Paul MN 55114

SQUIRE, MOLLY ANN, management consultant; b. Highland Park, Mich., Aug. 18, 1953; d. George Edward and Dorothy Laura (Molteni) Squirrell; m. Arthur Bruce hanson, June 23, 1990. AA, NYU, 1978; BS, U. LaVerne, 1980; MA, Claremont (Calif.) Grad. Sch., 1982. Tchr. 2 colls.; health svcs. adminstr. health care delivery orgns., 1978-82; nat. dir. Huntington's Disease Rsch. Project, Calif., 1981-82; chief exec. officer Claremont Mgmt. Cons., Malibu, Calif., 1982—; instr. L.A. City Coll., L.A. Trade-Tech. Coll. Founding editor LASER; past editor Benezet Gazette, (yearbook) So. Calif. Com. to Combat Huntington's Disease; contbr. articles to jours. in field; patentee bus. and health care products. Past officer and sci. liaison So. Calif. Huntington's Disease Com.; benefit performer magic Crippled Children's Soc. Recipient Cert. Appreciation City of Ukiah, Calif., 1984, Western Square Dance Assn., 1986, Am. Heart Assn., 1990; grad. study fellow Claremont Grad. Sch., 1980-82. Mem. Am. Fedn. Tchrs., Coll. Guild, Am. Psychol. Assn., Soc. Indsl. and Orgnl. Psychologists, Soc. Profl. Mgmt. Cons. (cert.), Mensa, Soc. Am. Magicians (2 Certs. of Appreciation), Internat. Brotherhood Magicians (past pres. and sec., Best Mentalist trophy 1987, Zinger award, Cert. of Appreciation), Pacific Coast Assn. Magicians. Republican. Presbyterian. Office: PO Box 2312 Malibu CA 90265

SQUIRES, BONNIE STEIN, association administrator; b. Phila., May 12, 1940; d. Joseph and Lillian (Ponnock) Stein; children: Deborah Rose, David Abram. BE, U. Pa., MA. Various positions Temple U., 1983-89; asst. exec. dir. Pa. State Edn. Assn., Harrisburg, 1989—. Author: (poetry) New Eden, 1977; editor: (poetry) This Land of Fire, 1988, (student essays, poems and photos) A New Nation, 1976. Mem. Fedn. Jewish Agys., Citizens' Crime Commn., Ctr. UN Reform Edn.; bd. dirs. Phila. com. Am. Jewish Congress, Phila. Mus. Art, Am. Friends Hebrew U., Harrisburg Jewish Community Rels. Coun.; del. Israel's Prime Minister's Solidarity Conf., 1989, Pres. Bush's regional Edn. Summit, 1989. Recipient Torch award and Lillian Alpers award Am. Friends Hebrew U., Louise Waterman award Am. Jewish Congress. Mem. AAUW, LWV. Home: 11 Arthur's Round Table Wynnewood PA 19096 Office: Pa State Edn Assn 400 N 3d St Harrisburg PA 17105

SQUIRES, EDWINA RACHELS, microbiologist, researcher; b. N.Y.C., Sept. 12, 1942; d. James H. and Lorraine (Davis) Rachels; m. Lindley Sturges Squires, June 16, 1973. BA, Caldwell Coll., 1964. Asst. scientist I to mgr. microbiological svcs. Hoffmann-LaRoche Inc., Nutley, N.J., 1964—. Author numerous booklets. Mem. Am. Soc. Microbiology, N.Y. Acad. Sci., Theobald Smith Soc. Republican. Home: 62 Yantacaw Brook Rd Upper Montclair NJ 07043 Office: Hoffmann-LaRoche 340 Kingsland St Nutley NJ 07110

SQUIRES, PATRICIA EILEEN COLEMAN, free-lance journalist, writer; b. Beaver Falls, Pa., Jan. 28, 1927; d. John Wiley and Helen Marie (Barstow) Purtell; B.A. in Journalism, Ind. U., 1949; m. Mark B. Squires, Sr., June 30, 1951; children: Sally Regan, Mark B., Susan Barstow. Staff reporter LaPorte (Ind.) Herald-Argus, 1949-51, daily columnist, 1950-51, sect. editor, 1949-51; women's news and feature writer Muskegon (Mich.) bur. Grand Rapids Herald, 1956-57; editor suburban sect. North Shore Line, Chicagoland Mag., Chgo., 1967-69; staff writer Fairpress, Westport, Conn., 1972-73; regular contbr. New Canaan (Conn.) Advertiser, 1975-78, Bridgeport (Conn.) Sunday Post, 1976-78, Soundings, Essex, Conn., 1977-78, N.Y. Times, N.Y.C., 1976—; tchr. English, journalism, social studies jr. and sr. pub. high schs., Jackson, Mich., 1966-67, Niles Twp., Skokie, Ill., 1967-68; vol. tutor Social Cultural Ednl. Enrichment Program, Protestant Community Ctr., 1979-86. Public rels., promotion dir. Ella Sharp Mus., Jackson, 1964-66; publicity chmn. New Canaan Soc. for Arts, 1977-78; bd. dirs. Centennial Celebration Com., Winnetka, Ill., 1968-69; Community Coun. New Canaan, 1972-75; New Canaan Bicentennial Com., 1975-76; publicity chmn. parent-tchr. coun. Frost Jr. High Sch., Jackson, 1963-64; active Girl Scouts Am. Mem. Women in Communications, N.J. Press Women, Nat. Fedn. Press Women, Soc. Profl. Journalists, AAUW, Ind. U. Alumni Assn. Presbyterian. Clubs: Cedar Point Yacht (Westport, Conn.); Lake Mohawk Golf (Sparta, N.J.). Home and Office: 688 W Shore Trail Sparta NJ 07871 also: 6265 Sun Blvd 109 G Casa del Mar Saint Petersburg FL 33701

SQUIRES, REBECCA, public relations executive; b. Salt Lake City, Sept. 15, 1945. BA in English and Journalism, U. S.C. Press asst. U.S. Ho. of Reps., 1967-71; pub. info. officer Coun. on Wage and Price Stability, 1973-78, dep. dir. for Congl. rels., 1978-81; with Carl Byoir and Assocs., 1982-85, Needham Porter Novelli (now Porter/Novelli), from 1985; now sr. v.p. Porter/Novelli, Washington. Office: Porter Novelli 1001 30th St Nw Washington DC 20007*

SREENAN-AUGER, MELANEY KAY, social worker; b. Rockford, Ill., Dec. 19, 1955; d. Patrick and Barbara (Thomas) S.; m. Sherman Auger, Apr. 4, 1987. BSW, U. So. Fla., Tampa, 1979; MSW, Fla. State U., 1980; PHD, Grad. Sch., Cin., 1989. Adj. prof. Fla. So. Coll., Lakeland, 1981-86, Hillsborough Community Coll., Plant City, Fla., 1981-86; ptnr. Sreenan Human Resource Assocs., Lakeland, Fla., 1980—; preferred provider EAP Program, IMC Fertilizer, Lakeland, 1986—; psychotherapist Bartow Phys. Therapy, Lakeland Phys. Therapy, Winter Haven Phys. Therapy, XYZ Liquor, Inc.; cert. cons. Lakeland YMCA, Fla. So. Coll. Athletic Dept.; affiliate EAP program Cigna Co., Westvaco, Lakeland, Mulberry. Mem. Am. Assn. Marriage and Family Therapy, Am. Psychol. Assn., Am. Assn. Suicidiology, Nat. Assn. Social Workers (sec. Heartland unit 1983-87), Fla. Alcohol and Drug Abuse Assn., Fla. Soc. Clin. Hypnosis, Fla. Soc. Personality Assessment, Inc., Polk County Mental Health Assn. Office: Sreenan Human Resource 217 Hillcrest St Lakeland FL 33801

SRERE, LINDA JEAN, advertising executive; b. N.Y.C., Aug. 14, 1955; d. Rudolph Joseph and Muriel Evelyn (Weigand) Forquignon; m. David Benson Srere, Sept. 10, 1983. BA, SUNY, Oswego, 1975. Asst. account exec. to acct. exec. BBDO, Inc., N.Y.C., 1975-79; v.p., account supr. Ogilvy and Mather, Inc., N.Y.C., 1979-82, McCaffrey and McCall, Inc., N.Y.C., 1982; with Rosenfeld, Sirowitz, Humphrey, & Strauss, Inc., N.Y.C., 1983—, exec. v.p., 1986-90, pres., 1990—, also bd. dirs. Mem. Am. Mgmt. Assn., Advt. Women of N.Y. (mem. fashion group). Home: 235 E 22nd St Apt 8I New York NY 10010 Office: Rosenfeld Sirowitz Humphrey & Strauss Inc 111 Fifth Ave New York NY 10003

STAATS, MARY HORTENSE, nurse; b. Coshocton, Ohio, Mar. 22, 1908; d. Loyd Nichols and Ethel Jane (Fawcett) Staats. Diploma, RN, Mass. Gen. Hosp., 1937; student, Columbia U., 1953, Boston U., 1959. Chief deputy clk. Probate Juvenile Ct., Costochton, Ohio, 1930-33; vol. Community Vis. Nurse, Boston, 1937-39; nurse outpatient clinic Mass. Gen. Hosp., Boston, 1939-41; staff vis. nurse Assoc. & Sch. Nurse, Montclair, N.J., 1941-42; staff pub. health nurse Community Health Assn., N.Y.C., 1942-43; commd. ensign USN, 1943, advanced through grades to lt.; reg. staff nurse Nurse Corps. USN, Portsmouth, Va., 1943-64; nurse Mobile Hosp. 10, Solomon Islands, 3d Fleet Command, South Pacific, Korea, Vietnam; ret. USN, 1964; breeder Santa Gertrudis Beef & Shows, State, Coshocton, 1967-89. Author, pub: Samuel Cox Family of Virginia and Ohio, 1975, Eli Nichols Family of Virginia and Ohio, 1989, Joseph Staats (American Revolution Soldier) Family of Virginia and Ohio, 1989. Mem. ANA, Ohio Nursing Assn. (dist. 28), DAR (regent NS chpt. 1975-76), Nat. Children of Am. Revolution Soc., AAUW, DAV, Mass. Gen. Hosp. Alumnae Nursing Assn., Columbia U. Nursing Sch., Coshocton Town and Country Garden Club, Coshocton Bus. and Profl. Women's Club, Order of Ea. Star. Methodist. Home: 30515 Rabbit Ridge Rd Howard OH 43028

STABENOW, DEBORAH ANN, state legislator; b. Gladwin, Mich., Apr. 29, 1950; d. Robert Lee and Anna Merle (Hallmark) Greer; children: Todd Dennis, Michelle Deborah. BS magna cum laude, Mich. State U., 1972, MSW magna cum laude, 1975. With spl. svcs. Lansing (Mich.) Sch. Dist., 1972-73; county commr. Ingham County, Mason, Mich., 1975-78; state rep. State of Mich., Lansing, 1979—. Founder Ingham County Women's Commn.; co-founder Council Against Domestic Assault; mem. Dem. Bus. and Profl. Club, Mich. Dem. Women's Polit. Caucus, Grance United Meth. Ch. (past lay leader, chair Social Concerns Task Force, Sunday Sch. music tchr., Lansing Boys' Club, profl. adv. com. Lansing Parents Without Ptnrs., adv. com. Ctr. Handicapped Affairs, Mich. Council Family and Divorce Mediation Adv. Bd., Nat. Council Children's Rights, Big Bros./Big Sisters Greater Lansing Adv. Bd., Mich. Child Study Assn. Bd. Advisors, Mich. Women's Campaign Fund. Recipient Service to Children award Council for Prevention of Child Abuse and Neglect, 1983, Disting. Service to Mich. Families award Mich. Council Family Relations, 1983, Outstanding Leadership award Nat. Council Community Mental Health Ctrs., 1983, Snyder-Kok award Mental Health Assn. Mich., Awareness Leader of Yr. award Awareness Communications Team Developmentally Disabled, 1984, Communicator of Yr. award Woman in Communications, 1984, Lawmaker of Yr. award Nat. Child Support Enforcement Assn., 1985, Disting. Service award Lansing Jaycees, 1985, Disting. Service in Govt. award Retarded Citizens of Mich., 1986; named One of Ten Outstanding Young Ams. Jaycees, 1986. Mem. NAACP, Lansing Regional C. of C., Delta Kappa Gamma. Home: 2709 S Deerfield Lansing MI 48911 Office: Ho Reps PO Box 30014 Lansing MI 48909

STABILE, ROSE TOWNE (MRS. FRED STABILE), building and management executive, public relations consultant; b. Sunderland, Eng.; d. Stephen and Amelia Bergman; student English schs., Tchrs. Coll., Columbia; m. Wilfred Kermode (dec. Feb. 1934); m. 2d, Arthur Whittlesey Towne, May 29, 1936 (dec. 1954); m. 3d, Norbert Le Veillie, June 10, 1961 (div. Feb. 1969); m. 4th, Fred Stabile, May 30, 1970. Formerly auditor Brit. Govt., Whitehall, London; activities and membership dir. N.Y. League of Girls Clubs, N.Y.C.; real estate exec., now semi-ret. bldg. mgr. State Tower Bldg., Syracuse, N.Y.; cons. public relations, office designer and decorator; lectr. real estate dept. Syracuse U. An initiator Syracuse Peace Council; mem. area sponsoring com. Assn. for Crippled Children and Adults. Mem. English Speaking Union (membership com.), Nat. N.Y. assns. real estate bds., Nat. Assn. Bldg. Owners and Mgrs., Syracuse C. of C., League Women Voters, Assn. UN, Women of Rotary, Bus. and Profl. Women's Clubs, Everson Mus. Art Friends of Reading, Mus. Modern Art (N.Y.C.), Internat. Center of Syracuse. Unitarian (chmn. service com. 1956-57.). Club: Corinthian. Home: 304 Malverne Dr Syracuse NY 13208 Office: State Tower Bldg Syracuse NY 13202

STABLER, SARI BETH, lawyer; b. L.A., Aug. 23, 1960; d. Joseph and Ronna Lee (Cohen) S. AB, U. Calif., Berkeley, 1982; JD, U. So. Calif., 1985. Bar: Calif. 1986. Assoc. Memel, Jacobs and Ellsworth, L.A., 1985-86; legal recruiter Lee Jackson and Bowe, L.A., 1986-87, Kass, Abell and Assocs., L.A., 1987—; treas. Moca Contemporaries, L.A., 1986—, v.p., 1989-90. Mem. steering com. Big Bros./Big Sisters Am., 1989—. Mem. Calif. Bar Assn., L.A. County Bar Assn. Democrat. Jewish. Office: Kass Abell & Assocs 10780 Santa Monica Blvd Los Angeles CA 90025

STACEY, KATHLEEN MARY, writer, artist; b. Boston, Jan. 7, 1951; d. John Robert and Catherine Mary (Gray) Young; m. Gary Ronald Stacey, Feb. 10, 1984. BA, Northeastern U., Boston, 1974. Asst. producer WGBH-TV, Boston, 1971-73; asst. editor Arlington (Mass.) Advocate Century Publs., 1973-75; mng. editor New England Pubs., Bradford, Vt., 1975-78; free-lance writer Boston, 1978-80; mktg. communications dir. Dickinson Advt., Quincy, Mass., 1980-81; copywriter Berenson & Isham, Boston, 1981-82; chief writer The Interface Group, Needham, Mass., 1983-84; prin. Young-Stacey Assocs., Scituate, Mass., 1984—; cons. Laughlin-Winkler Galleries, Boston, 1985—, Candace Whittemore Lovely Editions, 1986-89, Lonborg-Feeney Fine Art, Scituate, 1988-89. Mem. The Copley Soc. Boston, South Side Arts Assn., Duxbury Arts Assn., North River Arts Soc. (bd. dirs. 1989—), Scituate C. of C., Talking Info. Ctr. Democrat. Roman Catholic. Home: 62 Maple St Scituate MA 02066 Office: Young-Stacey Assocs PO Box 221 Scituate MA 02066

STACEY, PAMELA, editor, writer; b. Salt Lake City; Mar. 29, 1945; d. Jack Nordvall Freeze and Peggy (Whelan) Sherman; m. Richard C. Murphy, Feb. 22, 1981; stepchildren—Greg, Jeanne. B.A. in English, UCLA, 1968, teaching credential, 1970; M.A. in English, Calif. State U.-Long Beach, 1985. Researcher, Drew Pearson-Journalist, Washington, 1964, 66; adminstr. UNESCO, Paris, 1968-69; Rand Corp., Santa Monica, Calif., 1972-76; editor, writer Cousteau Soc., Los Angeles, 1976—. Editor, creator (mag. for children) Dolphin Log for Cousteau Soc., 1981. Avocations: scuba diving; sailing; skiing. Office: Cousteau Soc 8440 Santa Monica Blvd Los Angeles CA 90069

STACIK, CAROLYN KAISER, nursing educator; b. Cleve., July 1, 1944; d. Russell Wakelee and Dorothy Alice (Faud) Mills; m. Richard Dean Kaiser, Aug. 2, 1969 (dec. Jan. 1984); m. Harold S. Stacik, May 26, 1990. BSN, Ind. U., Indpls., 1966; MA Guidance-Counseling, Western Mich. U., 1977. RN, Colo., Ohio, Mich., Ind. Sr. splty. nurse Ft. Logan Mental Health Ctr., Denver, 1966-68; asst. head nurse Luth. Hosp., Cleve., 1968-69; charge nurse Pipp Community Hosp., Plainwell, Mich., 1970-71; instr. nursing Southwestern Mich. Coll., Dowagiac, 1971-72, 74-76; staff nurse Lee Meml. Hosp., Dowagiac, 1973-74; asst. prof. pediatric and mental health nursing Lake Michigan Coll., Benton Harbor, Mich., 1977—; psychiat. cons. Mercy-Meml. Med. Ctr., St. Joseph, Mich., 1980-81, staff mental health nurse, 1984—; instr. St. Mary's Coll., South Bend, 1989; presenter burnout workshops, 1980—; community nurse Home Health Care, Benton Harbor, 1987; instr. RN completion program Ferris State U., Big Rapids, Mich., 1988; manuscript reviewer Addison-Wesley Pub. Co., 1980—, Saunders Pub. Co., 1986—. Youth group leader St. Paul's Episcopal Ch., St. Joseph, 1987-89. Mem. Nat. League for Nursing, Mich. League for Nursing, Berrien County Infant Mental Health Assn., Sigma Theta Tau (chpt. standing rules com. 1984), Eta Zeta. Office: Lake Michigan Coll 2755 E Napier Ave Benton Harbor MI 49022

STACK, JOAN MURPHY, producer; b. Stamford, Conn., Dec. 5, 1928; divorced; children: Patrick, Timothy, Nina. Postgrad., Low Heywood Sch., Stamford, 1946, Coll. New Rochelle, 1948. Tchr. French cooking Central Bucks YMCA, Doylestown, Pa., 1973-74; food program host WBUX AM Radio, Doylestown, Pa., 1974-75, daily talk show host, 1975—; univ. lectr. on media use. Contbr. articles to profl. jours. Pres., Chmn. Planned Parenthood 25th Anniversary, Bucks County, 1988-89. Mem. Art Matters (founding pres.), Am. Women in Radio and TV (pres.). Home: 2 Rivers Edge Lambertville NJ 08530 Office: Sta WBUX Box 2187 Doylestown PA 18901

STACK, MARY JUDITH, community college official; b. Balt., July 28, 1947; d. William and Gwendolyn (Reed) Owens; m. Stephen Smith Stack, Jr., Jan. 17, 1970; children: Michael Alan, Kenneth Andrew. AA, Anne Arundel Community Coll., Arnold, Md., 1967; BS, Towson State Coll., 1970. Communications analyst Md. Blue Cross-Blue Shield, Towson, 1970-72; owner, mgr. Stephen's Florist, Milford, Del., 1977-87; dir. Small Bus. Devel. Ctr., Cecil Community Coll., Elkton, Md., 1988—; agt. Western Union, Milford, 1977-87, Trailways, Milford, 1977-87. Mem. Delmarva Econ. Devel. Assn., Md. Econ. Devel. Assn., N.E. Indsl. Devel. Assn., NAFE. Democrat. Roman Catholic. Home: 49 Valley Forge Dr Milford DE 19963 Office: Cecil Community Coll 107 Rail Road Ave Elkton MD 21921

STACKELL, ESTHER ILANA, lawyer; b. Lvov, USSR, May 31, 1954; came to U.S. 1965, naturalized 1974; d. Joseph and Rose (Zilber) Goldstein; m. Isaac Barry Stackell, Jan. 8, 1977; 1 child, Zachary Alexander. BA, Lehigh U., 1974; JD, Hofstra U., 1979. Bar: N.Y. 1980. In-house counsel Jewish Hosp and Med. Ctr., Bklyn., 1979-81; assoc. gen. counsel Fedn. Jewish Philanthropies, N.Y.C., 1981; assoc. Bergner, Bergner, Blum & Ruditz, N.Y.C., 1981-84; sole practice, Bklyn., 1984-86; ptnr. Stackell and Wilner, N.Y.C., 1989—; asst. corp. counsel spl. services for children div. Family Ct. City of N.Y.; cons. in field. Chair 9425-9437 Shore Rd. Tenants Assn.; mem. Union Women's Ctr., Bklyn., 1985. Mem. N.Y. County Lawyers (medicine and mental health com.), N.Y. State Bar Assn., Suffolk County Women's Bar Assn., Greater N.Y. Hosp. Assn., Med. Malpractice Com., Nat. Assn. Female Execs. Republican. Club: Lehigh Alumni Greater N.Y. Lodge: B'nai B'rith Women. Avocation: stained glass design.

STACKPOLE, MARY PATRICIA, teacher; b. N.Y., Mar. 20, 1934; d. John and Mary T. (Durkin) Snee; children: John, Eugene, Christine. BA, Ladycliff Coll., Highland Falls, N.Y., 1955; MS, Hunter Coll., N.Y., 1961. Cert. techr. Actuarial clk. Equitable Life Assurance Soc., N.Y., 1955-58; tchr. Levittown (N.Y.) Sch. Dist., 1958-60; substitute tchr. Sachem Sch. Dist., Holbrook, N.Y., 1966-75, elem. tchr. Mem. Nokomis PTA, 1966-73, Waverly Ave. PTA, 1975—. Mem. Sachem Cen. Tchrs. Assn. Republican. Roman Catholic. Home: 82 Swezey Ln Middle Island NY 11953

STACY, PAULINE FRENCH, writer, artist; b. Pratt, Kans., Feb. 22, 1915; d. Leo Walter and Bessie Rosanna (Branson) French; m. Larcel Romain Stacy, July 21, 1934; children: Grace Romaine, Rosanna Pauline. BA, Ariz. State U., 1960; MS, Ft. Hays Kans. State U., 1971. With rentals & air conditioning Phoenix, 1949-62; tchr. Isaac Sch. Dist.High Sch., St. Mary of the Plains Liberty Jr. High Sch., Phoenix, Minneola, Dodge and Pratt, Kans., 1960-71; freelance artist Meade, Kans., 1971—; free lance writer poetry Long Beach, Calif., Phoenix and Meade, 1949—. Author: You Shall Not Want, 1975, As Long As We Both Shall Love, 1975, Ventriloquists: Here's How!, 1976; contbr. articles to profl jours. Vol. in field. Mem. AAUW, Mensa, The Rosicrucian Order. Home and Office: HCR 2 RR Box 10 Meade KS 67864

STADELMAIER, SHARON M., marketing professional; b. Elmira, N.Y., Aug. 24, 1946; d. Richard I. and Winifred N. (Genung) Narosky; m. John W. Stadelmaier, Nov. 21, 1970; children: Frank E., Amy M. Students, Corning Community Coll., 1967-70. Sec. LeValley McLeod Inc., Elmira, N.Y., 1964-66; exec. sec. Westinghouse, Electronic Tube Div., Elmira, 1964-72, Eastman Kodak CO., Rochester, N.Y., 1972-74, North Atlantic Industries, Inc., Hauppauge, N.Y., 1980-86; office mgr. North Atlantic Industries, Inc., Hauppauge, 1986-88, mgr., mktg. adminstr., 1988—. advt., publicity chmn. Boy Scouts Am., Troop 11, Nesconset, N.Y., 1984-86. Roman Catholic. Home: 8 Mildred Ct Nesconset NY 11767 Office: N Atlantic Industries Inc 60 Plant Ave Hauppauge NY 11788

STADLEN, DIANE ELIZABETH, marketing professional; b. Chgo., Nov. 10, 1953; d. Harvey O. and Regina E. (Kozlowski) Nottke; m. Richard W. Stadlen, Feb. 17, 1974; children: Jennifer Beth, Rachael Michelle. Student, Southwest Coll., Chgo., 1971-72. Traffic mgr. Sta WDAI-FM, Chgo., 1973-81; assoc. Creswell, Munsell, Fultz & Zirbel, Inc., Cedar Rapids, Iowa, 1981-88; sr. v.p., dir. Creswell, Munsell, Fultz & Zirbel, Inc., Cedar Rapids, 1988—. Mem. communications com. United Way East Cen. Iowa, 1986-88. Mem. Nat. Agr.-Mktg. Assn. (vice chair issues forum 1990), Nat. Assn. Farm Broadcasters (adv. bd. 1983—). Office: Creswell Munsell Fultz & Zirbel Inc 4211 Signal Ridge Rd NE Cedar Rapids IA 52406

STADLER, BETTY, registered nurse, educator; b. Terre Haute, Ind., Sept. 11, 1938; d. George Louis Sr. and Nellie E. (Bray) Merchant; children: Michelle Lynn, Ty Marc (dec.), Monique Renee. Diploma in Nursing, St. Anthony Hosp., Terre Haute, 1959; BS, U. Evansville, 1973; MS, U. Ky., 1982; cert. primary care nurse practitioner, U. Ill./Peoria Sch. Medicine, 1979. RN, Ind., Ill., Ky. Mgr. satellite clinic, student health svcs. So. Ill. U., Carbondale, Ill., 1972-73; sub. tchr. Herrin (Ill.) High Sch., 1973-74; asst. dir. nursing/insvc. dir. Hampton Nursing Home, Herrin, 1974-76; hypertension nurse specialist Comprehensive Health Svcs., Carbondale, 1976-78; nurse practitioner preceptorship Murphysboro, Ill., 1979; family nurse practitioner Jackson County Health Dept., Murphysboro, 1980-81; family nurse practitioner preceptorship Lexington and Evarts, Ky., 1981-82; asst. prof. nursing Murray (Ky.) State U., 1983-85; dept. mgr., nurse practitioner Carle Clinic Assn., Urbana, Ill., 1985-87; assoc. chief, nursing service for edn. VA Med. Ctr., Marion, Ill., 1987-88; med. svcs. dir. T.J. Maxx Distribution Ctr., Evansville, Ind., 1988-90; pvt. practice family nurse Nashville, 1990—; cons. Jackson County Health Dept., Murphysboro, 1980-81, Ky. Bluegrass ARNP Coun., Task Force, 1981, Murray State U. Grad. Rural Nurse Clinician Program, 1985-86. Contbr. articles to profl. jours. Adv. coun. So. Ill. Patient Edn., 1977-81; bd. dirs. Dist. 14 Nurses Assn., 1978-81; tech. adv. coun. So. Ill. Collegiate Common Market Assoc. Degree Nursing Program, 1976-78; health care advisor, summer day camp, Shagbark Girl Scouts USA Coun., 1973-75, bd. dirs., 1975-78, chairperson, 1977-78. Mem. Am. Assn. Occupational Health Nurses, Am. Nurses Assn., Ill. Nurses Assn., Ky. Nurses Assn., Ky. Advanced Regis. Nurse Practitioner Coun., Ky. Dist. Nurses Assn., Nat. Orgn. Nurse Practitioner Faculties, AAUW, So. Ill. Soc. of Healthcare Edn. and Tng., Phi Theta Kappa, Alpha Sigma Lambda, Sigma Theta Tau. Home: 7029 Reed Ct Brentwood TN 37027 Office: 393 Wallace Rd Ste 301 Nashvillee TN 37211

STADTMAN, THRESSA CAMPBELL, biochemist; b. Sterling, N.Y., Feb. 12, 1920; d. Earl and Bessie (Waldron) Campbell; m. Earl Reece Stadtman, Oct. 19, 1943. BS, Cornell U., 1940, MS, 1942; PhD, U. Calif.-Berkeley, 1949. Rsch. assoc. U. Calif., Berkeley, 1942-47; Rsch. assoc. med. sch. Harvard U., Boston, 1949-50; biochemist Nat. Heart, Lung and Blood Inst. NIH, USPHS, HHS, Bethesda, Md., 1950—. Editor Jour. Biol. Chemistry, Archives Biochemistry and Biophysics, Molecular and Cellular Biochemistry; editor-in-chief Bio Factors; contbr. articles on amino acid metabolism, methane biosynthesis, vitamin B12 biochemistry, selenium biochemistry to profl. jours. Helen Haye Whitney fellow Oxford U., Eng., 1954-55; Rockefeller Found. grantee U. Munich, 1959-60; recipient Rose award, 1987, Klaus Schwarz medal, 1988. Mem. Am. Soc. Microbiology, Biochem. Soc., Soc. Am. Biochemists, Am. Chem. Soc., Nat. Acad. Scis., Am. Acad. Arts and Scis., Sigma Delta Epsilon (hon.). Home: 16907 Redland Rd Derwood MD 20855 Office: Nat Heart Lung & Blood Inst HHS Bethesda MD 20892

STAFFORD, CARLENE ROUSSEL, small business owner; b. Baton Rouge, July 20, 1952; d. Adrien Arbour and Audrey (LeBlanc) Roussel; m. Steve A. Stafford, June 13, 1980; children: Christopher, Melissa. Office mgr., ins. clk. Automotive Wholesalers-La., Baton Rouge, 1975-82; owner, mgr. Checkcare Systems, Inc., Columbia, S.C., 1986—. Mem. Better Bus. Bur., Columbia, 1986—. Mem. NAFE, NRA, Am. Collectors Assn., State C. of C. (bank fraud com.), S.C. Convenience Stores Assn. Democrat. Roman Catholic. Office: Checkcare Systems Inc PO Box 11871 Columbia SC 29211-1871

STAFFORD, HELEN ELIZABETH THOMSON, management consultant; b. Port Chester, N.Y., Mar. 1, 1926; d. James Ramage and Helen Cunningham (McGill) Thomson; B.S. in Psychology, Coll. William and Mary, 1948; m. Paul Tutt Stafford, Dec. 14, 1951; children—Paul Tutt, Timothy Alden, Mark Thornton, Todd Lawton. Exec. asst. commn. on worship Nat. Council Chs., N.Y.C., 1950-51; co-founder, dir., treas., sr. v.p. Paul Stafford Assos., Ltd., Mgmt. Cons., N.Y.C., 1959-82. Bd. dirs. Princeton Area YWCA, 1985-87; active Commn. on the Tercentenary Observances of The Coll. of William and Mary. Mem. Assn. Exec. Recruiting Cons. (dir. 1968-70), Soc. Alumni Coll. William and Mary (dir. 1984—), Mortar Board, Phi Beta Kappa, Kappa Kappa Gamma. Republican. Presbyterian. Clubs: Bedens Brook, Nassau (Princeton, N.J.); Hillsboro (bd. dirs. 1986—, vice chmn. 1988—), (Pompano Beach, Fla.).

STAFFORD, REBECCA, college president, sociologist; b. Topeka, July 9, 1936; d. Frank C. and Anne Elizabeth (Larrick) S. A.B. magna cum laude, Radcliffe Coll., 1958, M.A., 1961; Ph.D., Harvard U., 1964. Lectr. dept. sociology Sch. Edn., Harvard U., Cambridge, Mass., 1964-70, mem. vis. com. bd. overseers, 1973-79; assoc. prof. sociology U. Nev., Reno, 1970-73, prof., 1973-80, chmn. dept. sociology, 1974-77, dean Coll. Arts and Scis., 1977-80; pres. Bemidji (Minn.) State U., 1980-82; exec. v.p. Colo. State U., Ft. Collins, 1982-83; pres. Chatham Coll., Pitts., 1983—; bd. dirs. Union Nat. Bank. Contbr. articles to profl. jours. Bd. dirs. Univ. Presbyn. Hosp., Pitts. Symphony, Winchester-Thurston Sch.; chmn. Harvard U. Grad. Soc. Council, 1987-89. Recipient McCurdy-Rinkle prize for rsch. Eastern Psychiat. Assn., 1970; named Man of Yr. in Edn., City of Pitts., 1986, Woman of Yr. in Edn., YWCA Tribute to Women, 1989; grantee Am. Coun. Edn. Inst. Acad. Deans, 1979, Inst. Ednl. Mgmt., Harvard U., 1984. Mem. Harvard U. Alumni Assn. (bd. dirs. 1985-87), Phi Beta Kappa, Phi Kappa Phi.

STAGEN, MARY-PATRICIA HEALY, investments executive; b. Ridgewood, N.J., Apr. 4, 1955; d. Bernard Patrick and Mary Patricia (O'Connor) Healy; m. Daniel A. Stagen, Oct. 31, 1987. BA, lic. in secondary edn.-libr. sci., Elms Coll., Chicopee, Mass., 1977. Adminstrv. asst. to meeting dir. Am. Inst. Chem. Engrs., N.Y.C., 1980-81, meetings coord., 1981-84, mgr. spl. projects to exec. dir., 1984-89; v.p. Wall St. Rsch. Svcs., Inc., Clifton, N.J., 1990—, VRH Constrn., Englewood, N.J., 1990—; meeting planner Am. Assn. Engring. Socs., Washington, 1984-85. Mem. NAFE. Republican. Roman Catholic. Home: 86 Blvd Passaic NJ 07055 Office: Wall St Rsch Svcs Inc PO Box 1343 Clifton NJ 07015-1343 also: 86 Boulevard Passaic NJ 07055 also: VRH Constrn 320 Grand Ave Englewood NJ 07631

STAGG, EVELYN WHEELER, educator, state legislator; b. Waterbury, Vt., Sept. 30, 1916; d. Aiton Grover and Edythe (Boyce) Wheeler; m. David Stagg, May 15, 1942; children: Christie Stagg Austin, Bonnie, Carol Stagg Kevan. BA, Middlebury Coll., 1939; MA, U. Vt., 1971. Assoc. prof. Castleton State Coll., Vt., 1966-82, mem. nursing adv. bd., 1987—; mem. Vt. Ho. of Reps., 1982—, chmn. house edn. com., 1982-88, vice chmn. health and welfare com., 1985-86, mem. ways and means com., 1989—; commr. Edn. Commn. of the States, 1987-88; mem. Gov.'s Commn., 1990—; cons. communications projects, Bomoseen, Vt., 1982—. Contbr. articles to profl. jours. Chmn. Women's Legis. Caucus, 1984-88; pres., bd. dirs. Rutland Area Vis. Nurse Assn., 1969-75, 89—; bd. dirs. Rutland Mental Health Assn., 1986-88; adv. bd. nursing Castleton State Coll.; trustee pub. funds, bd. civil authority, 1984—; justice of peace Town of Castleton, 1984—. Mem. Women's Caucus, Vt. Women's Polit. Caucus, Nat. Women's Polit. Caucus, AAUW, Inst. for Gen. Semantics, Internat. Soc. for Gen. Semantics, Am. Philatelic Soc., Castleton Hist. Soc. Democrat. Clubs: Women's, Rutland County Stamp. Avocations: stamp and coin collecting, sailing, skiing, traveling. Home: Mason's Point Bomoseen VT 05732 also: Naples FL 33940 Office: State House Montpelier VT 05602

STAGMEIER, TERRY DANIELS, information systems executive; b. Anniston, Ala., Sept. 9, 1948; d. Curtis J. and Dessie H. (Heathcock) Daniels; m. John H. Stagmeier, Jan. 5, 1980; 1 child, James H. BA in Acctg., Kennesaw (Ga.) Coll., 1986, MBA in Mktg., 1988. Asst. v.p., contr. info. systems and support Equifax Svcs., Inc., Atlanta, 1988—. Office: Equifax Svcs 1600 Peachtree St Atlanta GA 30309

STAGNOLIA, KATHI BLANTON, educational adminstrator; b. Knoxville, Tenn., Feb. 10, 1964; d. Dale Alexander and Sharon Ann (Brock) Blanton; m. Reecie Dean Stagnolia III, May 24, 1986. Assoc. Applied Sci., Southeast Community Coll., 1983; BS, Eastern Ky. U., 1985; postgrad., U. Ky., 1987—. Adminstrv. sr. specialist Ky. Dept. Edn., Frankfort, 1987—. Democrat. Baptist. Home: 489 Marblerock Way Lexington KY 40503 Office: Ky Dept Edn 1818 Capital Plaza Tower Frankfort KY 40601

STAHANCYK, JODY LEE, lawyer; b. Prineville, Oreg., July 26, 1948; d. Joseph and Bertie Lee (Farnham) S.; m. John G. Crawford, Jr., May 25, 1974; children: Seth, Kathryn. BA, Linfield Coll., 1970; student, Inst. for Am. U., Aix-en Provence, France, 1968-69; JD, U. Oreg., 1973. Bar: Oreg. 1973. Dep. dist. atty. Multnomah County, Portland, Oreg., 1973-79; hearing referee, pro tem judge Multnomah County Juvenile Ct., Portland, 1979-83; asst. atty. gen. Oreg. Atty. Gen., Portland, 1983; ptnr. Barnes & Stahancyk,

Portland, 1984-85, Stahancyk & Cohen, Portland, 1985—, Stahancyk & Assoc., Portland, 1988—. Bd. dirs. Parry Ctr., Portland, 1986—, Luth. Family Svc., 1981-85, Children's Charity Ball, 1987, Crime Commn., 1989, City/County Blue Ribbon Com. on Pub. Safety, 1986-87. Mem. Multnomah County Bar Assn. (membership com. 1987—). Episcopalian. Home: 2866 NW Shenandoah Terr Portland OR 97209 Office: Stahancyk & Assocs 720 SW Wasington St #215 Portland OR 97205

STAHELI, LANA RIBBLE, psychology counselor, management consultant; b. Battle Creek, Mich., June 21, 1947; d. Vercil LeRoy and Mildred Irene (Sponseller) Ribble; m. Lynn Taylor Staheli, June 11, 1977; children—Linda, Diane, Todd. B.A. cum laude, U. Wash., 1974, M.Ed., 1976; Ph.D., Union Grad. Sch.-San Francisco, 1978. Co-founder, bd. dirs. Human Alternatives, N.W., Seattle, 1973-74; adminstr. orthopedic med. office, Seattle, 1975-76; pres. Profl. Practice Cons., Seattle, 1974-79; pvt. practice psychol. counseling, Seattle, 1978—; pres. Staheli, Inc., 1979—; cons. orthopedic dept. Children's Orthopedic Hosp., 1974-76; exec. cons. Sundance Cruises, 1984-85, v.p. adminstrn., 1985-86; adj. faculty Antioch Coll., 1974. Bd. dirs. Univ. Tutoring Service, 1979-80, J. Silver, Glad Rags and Gt. Things. Founder, pres. Rainier Found. Fellow Orthopsychiat. Assn.; co-founder pediatric orthopedic fellowship for developing countries. Mem. Am. Psychol. Assn., Wash. Psychol. Assn., Orthopsychiat. Assn. (pres. Psychology Forum 1981-82). Club: U. Wash. President's. Office: 2301 Fairview E #402 Seattle WA 98102

STAHL, LESLEY R., journalist; b. Lynn, Mass., Dec. 16, 1941; d. Louis and Dorothy J. (Tishler) S.; m. Aaron Latham; 1 dau. B.A. cum laude, Wheaton Coll., Norton, Mass., 1963. Asst. to speechwriter Mayor Lindsay's Office, N.Y.C., 1966-67; researcher N.Y. Election unit London-Huntley Brinkley Report, NBC News, 1967-69; producer, reporter WHDH-TV, Boston, 1970-72; news corr. CBS News, Washington, from 1972; moderator Face the Nation, 1983—. Trustee Wheaton Coll. Recipient Tex. Headliners award, 1973. Office: CBS News 51 W 52nd St New York NY 10019

STAHL, RUTHANNE, legal administrator; b. Albuquerque, Dec. 3, 1939; d. Benjamin Byron and Newel Harriett (Webb) Crego; m. David Dale Stahl, Nov. 7, 1980; children: Ginger Le'Ann Davidson Wells, Lindsey Trey Davidson. Student, Colo. Woman's Coll., Denver, 1957-58, U. Denver, 1976-77, Ga. State U., 1979-80. Several mgmt. positions Pub. Service Co. N.Mex., 1965-74; mgr. regional credit and collection tng., field support JCPenney Co., Denver, 1975-80; dir. personnel and regional credit ops. JCPenney Co., Atlanta; project mgr. tng. and devel. corp. staff JCPenney Co., Dallas; corp. tng. dir. Peoples Gas System Inc., Tampa, Fla., 1980-81; dir. adminstrn. Schwall Ruff and Goodman Atty., Atlanta, 1982—; guest NBC TV Not For Women Only, 1979. Author: (tng. manual) Effective Collection, 1978. Mem. Assn. Legal Adminstrs., Legal Assts. Mgmt. Assn., Assn. Personnel Adminstrn., Atlanta Consumer Credit Assn., Nat. Assn. Female Execs., Pilot Club (dir. fin. 1972-74). Republican. Presbyterian. Lodge: Daus. of Nile. Office: Schwall Ruff and Goodman Atty 1615 Peachtree St NE Atlanta GA 30367

STAHL, THERESA, real estate agent; b. Defiance, Ohio, July 9, 1936; d. Nicholas J. and Gertrude J. (Hoeffel) Simonis; m. Roy P. Stahl, Apr. 4, 1989; stepchildren: Ron, Kathy, Sandy. BS in Med. Tech., Marian Coll., Fond du Lac, Wis., 1959; postgrad., Marquette U., 1963, U. Kans., 1967, 69, U. Colo., 1969; diploma, Hogan Sch. Real Estate, Tucson, 1989; grad., Realtors Inst. Asst. tech. dir. Chemistries Assocs. in Lab. Medicine, Tucson, 1982-84; med. technologist, supr., adminstr. Gamma Labs., ACC, Tucson, 1984-89; assoc. Realty Execs. of Tucson, 1989—. mem. profl. adv. panel Med. Lab. Observer. Mem. NAFE, DAV (aux.), Am. Soc. Med. Technologists (emeritus), Nat. Women's Coun. Realtors, Ariz. Women's Coun. Realtors, Tucson Women's Coun. Realtors, Tucson Bd. Realtors (mem. mktg. com.), Tucson Met. C. of C. Home: PO Box 31543 Tucson AZ 85751 Office: Realty Execs of Tucson 1610 N Kolb Rd Tucson AZ 85715

STAIGER, BONNIE LARSON, association executive; b. Bismarck, N.D., Sept. 23, 1947; d. Harvey C. and Jean (Burman) Larson; m. Raymond J. Staiger, June 7, 1980; 1 child, Stacy. BSc., Valley City State U., 1970. Owner Secs. Unltd., Bismarck, N.D., 1980-83; dir. pub. rels. Hart Agy., Bismarck, 1983-85; pres., owner Comml. Printing Co., Bismarck, 1985-89; exec. dir. N.D. Psychol. Assn., Bismarck, 1989—. Charter Mem. Symphony League Bismarck, N.D., 1976; Coun. Pres. Ch. the Cross Bismarck N.D., 1987. Recipient Outstanding Young Careerist award Bus. & Profl. Women 1976, Women Leaders award Greeter Mag., 1987; Named Woman of the Yr. Bus. & Profl. Women 1987. Mem. Bus. and Profl. Women, Am. Soc. Assoc. Execs., Bismarck Area C. of C. (bd. dirs. 1987-89), Rotary Club Internat., Am. Psychol. Assn. Republican. Lutheran. Home and Office: 1249 S Highland Acres Rd Bismarck ND 58501

STAINES, LAURA CATHERINE, architect; b. Bklyn., Nov. 25, 1953; d. Mariano and Giovanna (Yelovcich) Terdoslavich; m. Michael Laurence Staines, May 11, 1974; children: Leslie Myrra, Claire Alexandra. BArch in Design, U. Pa., 1975; postgrad., Drexel U., 1976-80. Registered architect, N.J., Pa., Va., Md., Del., N.Y., Conn., Vt., N.H., Colo., Ill., Maine, Mass., R.I.; Registered Planner, N.J. Designer The Architects Workshop, Phila., 1976-77, Schnadelbach/Braun, Phila., 1977-78, Hugh Zimmers & Assoc., Phila., 1978; with Martin Orgn., Phila., 1978-79, 80—; designer Wallace, Roberts & Todd (W.R.T.), 1979-80; sr. v.p. Martin Orgn., Phila., 1986-88, prin., 1988—; speaker in field. Mem. exec. com. ARC Starlight Ball, Phila., 1987, 88, U.S. Olympic rowing team, 1976. Mem. Comml. Real Estate Women, Art Alliance, Nat. Assn. Home Builders (design com.), Industry Residential Mktg., NAIOP, Riverton (N.J.) Yacht Club, Coll. Boat Club. Republican. Episcopalian. Office: The Martin Orgn 242 N 22d St Philadelphia PA 19103

STALDER, FLORENCE LUCILLE, educator; b. Fairmont, W.Va., Jan. 3, 1920; d. Brooks Fleming and Sally May (Odewalt) Clayton; m. Bernard Nicholas Stalder, Sept. 14, 1946; children: Kathryn Lynn Stalder Mirto, Susan May Stalder Woodard. BA in Edn. with honors, Fairmont State Coll., 1966; MA, W.Va. U., 1973; postgrad., Kent State U., 1973, U. Va., Charlottesville, 1981. Cert. elem. tchr., W.Va. Sec. to mgr. Hall Agy., Inc., Fairmont, W.Va., 1941-43; sec. to supt. Westinghouse Electric Corp., Fairmont, 1943-47; sec. to purchasing agt. Fairmont Supply Co., 1947-48; sec. to dist. mgtr. Ea. Gas & Fuel Assoc., Gen. Stores Div., Grant Town, W.Va., 1948-50; sec. to pres., v.p. Hutchinson Coal Co., Fairmont, 1950-52; sec. to personnel mgr. Consolidation Coal Co., Fairmont, 1957-61; sec. and asst. to adminstr. Fairmont Clinic (Monongahela Valley Assoc. Health Ctrs.), 1965-70; instr. Fairmont Jr. High, Miller Jr. High Schs., 1968-85; instr., dir. W.Va. Univ. Younger Youth Sci. Camps, Fairmont, 1966-72; workshop instr. W.Va. State Bd. Edn. Energy Workshops, Fairmont, 1973-74; adult edn. instr., Fairmont, 1985—. Pres. PTA, 1958-61; troop leader Girl Scouts USA, 1961-64; sec., mem. League of Women Voters, Fairmont, 1968—. Mem. AAUW (pres. 1972-74), Marion County Edn. Assn., W.Va. Edn. Assn., NEA, W.Va. Adult Edn. Assn., Daus. of Founders and Patriots of Am. (pres. 1979-85), DAR (1st v.p. regent 1986—), Daus. of Am. Colonists (vice regent 1988—), Alpha Delta Kappa (pres. 1979-81). Republican. Methodist. Home: 1208 Bell Run Rd Fairmont WV 26554

STALEY, ELAINE MARY, administrative assistant and grants manager; b. Wisconsin Rapids, Wis., Sept. 26, 1943; d. Maurice Philip and Mary Ann (Menke) S. B.S. in Communication Arts, U. Wis.-Madison, 1965. Registered profl. parliamentarian. Program specialist U. Wis. Extension, Madison, 1966-69; specialist, exec. sec. U. Wis. System-Faculty Coun. and Assembly, Madison, 1969-73; adminstrv. asst., exec. sec. Exec. Office, Wis. Coun. on Criminal Justice, Madison, 1973-75; asst. to chmn. dept. communication arts U. Wis.-Madison, 1975-80, adminstrv. asst., grants mgr. Sch. Social Work, 1980—; parliamentary cons. Nat. Assn. Parliamentarians, Kansas City, Mo., 1976—. Contbr. articles to profl. jours. Mem. Women's Polit. Caucus, Madison, 1973-77; mem. steering com. Dane County's Citizen Orgn., Madison, 1980-81; staff asst. Gov's Commn. on Edn., Wis., 1970-71; mem. Big Bros./Sisters Dane County, 1979—, bd. dirs., 1985—; chmn. Dane County Bowl for Kids Sake, 1987-88; bd. dirs. Madison Theatre Guild, 1974-76, treas., 1974-76; chmn. Dane County Bowl for Kids Sake, 1987-88; treas., bd. dirs. Madison Packer Backers, Inc., 1984-88; mem. Gov.'s Inaugural Ball Arrangements Com., Madison, 1979; mem. Madison Civic Opera Guild, 1977—, Madison Civic Ctr. Friends, 1983-86, Friends of WHA-TV, 1977-85, Friends of the Waisman Ctr., Madison, 1980—, pres., 1984-85. Recipient Merit awards Madison Theatre Guild, 1971-73, Exceptional Performance awards U. Wis.-State Wis., 1983, 84, 87, cert. of Appreciation United Way of Dane County, 1988. Mem. Commn. on Am. Parliamentary Practice of Speech Communication Assn. (chmn. 1978-80), Am. Inst. Parliamentarians, Nat. Assn. Parliamentarians (profl. registered parliamentarian 1976—, state bd. dirs. 1977—, chmn. newsletter 1989-91, state pres. 1981-93, co-chmn. publicity and newsletter coms. 1983-85, unit treas. 1985-87), Assn. Univ. Faculty Women and Univ. Extension League, 1968-74. Democrat. Roman Catholic. Avocations: downhill and cross-country skiing, golf, swimming, crafts, reading, sailing. Home: 933 Magnolia Ln Madison WI 53713 Office: U Wis-Madison Sch Social Work 425 Henry Mall Madison WI 53706

STALKER, JACQUELINE D'AOUST, academic administrator, educator; b. Penetang, Ont., Can., Oct. 16, 1933; d. Phillip and Rose (Eaton) D'Aoust; m. Robert Stalker; children: Patricia, Lynn, Roberta. Teaching cert., U. Ottawa, 1952; tchr. music, Royal Toronto Conservatory Music, 1952; teaching cert., Lakeshore Tchrs. Coll., 1958; BEd with honors, U. Manitoba, 1977, MEd, 1979; EdD, Nova U., 1985. Cert. tchr. Ont., Man., Can. Adminstr., tchr., prin. various schs., Ont. and Que., 1952-65; area commr. Girl Guides of Can., throughout Europe, 1965-69; administr., tchr. Algonquin community Coll., Ottawa, Ont., 1970-74; tchr., program devel. Frontenac County Bd. Edn., Kingston, Ont., 1974-75; lctr., faculty advisor Dept. Curriculum, Edn. U. Man., Can., 1977-79, U. Winnipeg, Man., Can., 1977-79; cons. Colls. Div. Man. Dept. Edn., Can., 1980-81; sr. cons. Programming Br. Man. Dept. Edn., 1981-84, Post-Secondary, Adult and Continuing Edn. Div. Man. Dept. Edn., 1985-88; dir. post secondary career devel. br. and adult and continuing edn. br. Man. Dept. Edn., 1989; asst. prof. higher edn. U. Man., 1989—; cons. lectures, seminars, workshops throughout Can. Mng. editor The Can. Jour. of Higher Edn., 1990—; contbr. articles to profl. jours. Mem. U. Man. Senate, 1976-81, 86-89, bd. govs., 1979-82; Can. rep. Internat. Youth Conf., Garmisch, Fed. Rep. Germany 1968; vol. Cancer Soc.; mem. Man. Assn. RN Accreditation Council, 1980-85, Leaf Women's Legal Edn. and Action Fund; chair Child Care Accreditation Com., Man., 1983-90; chair Task Force Post-Secondary Accessibility, Man., 1983; vol. United Way Planning and Allocations. Mem. Can. Congress Learning Opportunities Women (provincial dir.), Can. Soc. Study Higher Edn., Manitoba Tchrs. Soc., Alumni Assn. U. Manitoba, Alumni Assn. Nova U., Can. Club. Roman Catholic. Home: 261 Baltimore Rd, Winnipeg, MB Canada R3L 1H7 Office: U Man, Faculty Edn, Winnipeg, MB Canada R3T 2N2

STALKER, SUZY WOOSTER, human resources executive; b. Atlanta, Oct. 12, 1948; d. George Edward Wooster and Mary Evelyn (Dayton) Schmidt; m. James Marion Stalker, Nov. 11, 1966; children: Marian Paige, Jason Alexander. Student, Ga. State U., 1981—. Tng. rep. Rich's, Atlanta, 1980-81, tng. supr., 1981-82, regional tng. coord., 1982-84, employee communications specialist, 1983-84; dir. human resources Home Fed. Savs. & Loan, Atlanta, 1984-85, v.p. human resources, 1985-88; v.p. pers. Gulf States Mortgage Co., Inc., Atlanta, 1988—. Editor Richbits, 1983-84. Leader Girl Scouts U.S., Austell, Ga., 1975-76; pres. Clarkdale Elem. PTA, Austell, 1975-76. Mem. Nat. Assn. for Female Execs., Inc., Ga. Exec. Women's Network. Avocations: sailing, cross-stitching, watercolors. Home: 4820 Glore Rd Mableton GA 30059

STALLINGS-DORSETT, MARY ELLEN, academic administrator; b. Mount Dora, Fla., Sept. 5, 1941; d. James W. and Florence (Bailey) Moore; m. Herbert Franklin Dorsett, June 3, 1987. BA, Fla. Atlantic U., 1976; MS, Nova U., 1977, postgrad. Exec. dir. U. South Fla., Ft. Myers; pres. Dorsett and Dorsett Assn., Ft. Myers, Med. Dimensions, Ft. Lauderdale, Fla.; cons. sch. system West Palm Beach County, Fla., Broward County, Ft. Lauderdale, Fla. Mem. Govt. Coun. on Unemployment and Handicapped, S.W. Fla. Small Bus. Coun. Mem. Am. Mgmt. Assn. (pres. S.W. Fla. chpt.), Am. Soc. Tng. and Devel., Acad. Mgmt., Phi Theta Kappa. Home: 1319 Donna Dr Fort Myers FL 33919

STALLONE, SUSAN BETH, bank financial officer; b. Reading, Pa., Apr. 17, 1961; d. Albert Allen and Orpha Celeste (Dodge) S. BA in Econs., Wesleyan U., 1983; MBA in Acctg., NYU, 1989. Sr. acct. Arthur Andersen & Co., N.Y.C., 1983-86; chief fin. officer Banque Paribas, N.Y.C., 1986—. Mem. Wesleyan N.Y. Alumni Coun. (mgmt. com. 19896). Democrat. Methodist. Office: Banque Paribas 787 7th Ave New York NY 10019

STALLWORTH, ALMA GRACE, state legislator. Grad., Highland Park Community Coll., 1956; student, Wayne State U., 1956. Mem. Mich. Ho. of Reps., Lansing, 1970-74, 81—; dep. dir. Hist. Dept. City of Detroit, 1975-78, job developer, 1978-79; mem. exec. com. Nat. Conf. State Legislatures, 1986-89. Commr. Wayne County Charter, Detroit, 1978-79, Martin Luther King Commn., Detroit, 1987; chairperson bd. dirs. task force on infant mortality Mich. Legislature, 1987; pres. Nat. Black Child Devel. Inst., Detroit; vol. United Negro Coll. Fund, 1987—; founder, adminstr. Black Caucus Found. of Mich., 1987—. Recipient cert. of appreciation Mich. Dept. Edn., 1986, Advs. award Mich. Health Mothers, Health Babies Coalition, 1987; named Woman Leader in Pub. Health, Mi ch. Assn. Local Pub. Health, 1987, Woman of Yr., Minority Women's Network, 1988. Mem. NAACP, Nat. Conf. State Legislators (exec. commr. 1986), Nat. Black Caucus State Legislators, (sec. women's caucus), Mich. Legis. Black Causus (chair 1987), Alpha Kappa Alpha. Democrat. Clubs: Cameo, Top Ladies of Distinction. Home: 19793 Sorrento Detroit MI 48235 Office: Capitol Bldg Rm 12 Lansing MI 48909

STALLWORTH, DORIS A. CARTER, librarian, educator; b. Ala., June 12, 1932; d. Henry Lee Carter and Hattie Belle Stallworth; m. George Stallworth, 1950; children: Annette LaVerne, Vanzette Yvonne. BS, Ala. State U., 1955; MLS, CUNY, 1968; postgrad., Columbia U., St. John's U., N.Y.C. Cert. supr. and tchr. sch. libr. media, N.Y. Libr. media specialist N.Y.C. Bd. Edn.; head libr. Calhoun County High Sch., Hobson City, Ala.; cons. Libr. Unit, N.Y.C. Bd. Edn.; cons. evaluator So. Assn. Secondary Schs., Ala.; supr., adminstr., liason rep. Community Sch. Dist. #24 N.Y.C. Sch. System; previewer libr. media Preview Mag., 1971-73; mem. ednl. svcs. adv. coun. Sta. WNET, 1987-89; mem. coun. N.Y.C. Schs. Libr. System, 1987-90; turn-key tchr. trainer N.Y. State Dept. Edn., 1988; spl. guest speaker and lectr. Queens Coll., City U., Community Sch. Dist. #24, PTA, N.Y. City Sch. System, Libr. unit, 1980-90; curriculum writer libr. unit N.Y.C. Bd. Edn., 1985-86. Contbr. articles to ednl. publs. Mem. NAFE, ALA, Am. Assn. Sch. Librs. (spl. guest speaker and lectr. for conv. 1987), Am. Sch. Libr.'s Assn., Nat. Assn. Black Pub. Adminstrs., N.Y. State Libr. Assn., N.Y.C. Sch. Librs. Assn., Nat. Forum for Black Pub. Adminstrs., N.Y. Coalition 100 Black Women, Lambda Kappa Mu.

STALNAKER, JUDITH ANN, education educator; b. San Diego, Sept. 3, 1942; d. Harold Willard and Dorothy Ione (Maxwell) Growcock; m. Archie LaVern Stalnaker, Aug. 31, 1963; children: Dena Lyn Garcia, Keri Leigh Hale. BA, teaching credential, Calif. State U., San Diego, 1973; MA, reading specialist credential, San Diego State U., 1985. Cert. tchr., reading specialist. Tchr. El Centro (Calif.) Sch. Dist., 1976—; prof. San Diego State U., Calexico, Calif., 1987—; presenter critical thinking skills, Imperial County, Calif., 1986, El Centro, 1986, English/lang. arts framework, El Centro, 1989. Mem. Young Democrats, San Diego, 1962-63; mem. McKinley Sch. PTA, 1969-75, pres., 1971-72. Mem. AAUW, Imperial County Reading Coun. (v.p. 1988-89), Internat. Reading Assn., Lang. Arts Leadership Team, Jr. Women's 10,000 Club (pres. 1971-72), Calif. Fedn. Women's Clubs (jr. mem. De Anza dist., v.p. 1972-73, Calif. Jr. Citizen of Yr. 1972). Lutheran.

STALSBERG, GERALDINE MCEWEN, accountant; b. Springfield, Mo., May 10, 1936; d. Gerald Earl McEwen and Marie LaVerne (Pennington) Plautz; m. Bill Eugene Bottolfson, Mar. 10, 1956 (div. 1978); children: Bill Earl, Robert Edward, Brian Everett, Michelle Marie; m. Arvid Ray Stalsberg, Sept. 21, 1979; stepchildren: Angelite Renae, Neil Ray, Terry Jay. Diploma Hastings Beauty Acad., 1955; cert. in interior design, Cen. Tech. Community Coll., 1975; student Doane Coll., 1982; cert. computer programmer Lincoln Sch. Commerce, Nebr., 1984. Cosmetologist, Marinello Beauty Shop, Hastings, 1955-57; owner Nursery Sch. for Toddlers, 1958-67; acct. grain dept. Morrison-Quirk Elevator, Hastings, Nebr., 1968-69; acct., exec. sec., interior decorator Uerling's Home Furnishings, Hastings, 1970-79; acct., computer programmer, Lincoln Transp., Nebr., 1980-86, systems analyst, 1984-86; tax cons. H&R Block, Lincoln, 1983-86; programmer, tax cons., controller EBKO Industries, Hastings, 1987-90; pvt. practice acctg. and tax cons., 1987—. Emergency radio dispatcher Adams County Civil Def., Hastings, 1973-78; active YWCA, Girl Scouts USA, PTA, 4-H Clubs Am. Recipient Civic Achievement award City of Hastings, 1974. Mem. Nat. Assn. Govt. Employees, Bus. Profl. Women, Library Assn., Nat. Am. Mfrs. Assn., NAFE, Nat. Assn. Mfrs., Soroptimists Internat., Beta Sigma Phi (Woman of Yr. 1978, Order of Rose). Republican. Lutheran. Avocations: reading, bowling, fishing, swimming, jogging. Home and Office: 1620 W 12th St Hastings NE 68901

STAMATAKIS, CAROL MARIE, state legislator, lawyer; b. Canton, Ohio, Apr. 27, 1960; d. Emmanuel Nicholas and Catherine Lucille (Zam) S.; m. Michael Charles Shklar, Mar. 23, 1985. BA in Criminology and Criminal Justice, Ohio State U., 1982; JD, Case Western Res., 1985. Bar: N.H. 1985, U.S. Dist. Ct. N.H. 1985. Atty. Law Office Laurence F. Gardner, Hanover, N.H., 1985-87, Law Office William Howard Dunn, Claremont, N.H., 1987-90, Elliott Jasper, Newport, N.H., 1990—; state rep. N.H. State Legislature, 1988—; instr. Am. Inst. Banking, Claremont, 1987-88. Asst. editor: (jours.) Health Matrix: The Jour. of Health Services Mangement, 1983-85. Treas., mem. Town of Lempster N.H. Conservation Commn., 1987—; v.p. Sullivan County Transit Systems, Inc., Claremont, 1988—; bd. dirs. Orion House, Inc., Newport, N.H., 1987—; vice chair, solid waste chair Sierra Club (upper valley group), Hanover, N.H., 1980—; town chair N.H. Dem. Party, 1987—; mem. Town of Lempster Recycling Com., 1988—, Community Task Force on Drug and Alcohol Abuse, 1988. Mem. ABA, N.H. Bar Assn. Home: PO Box 807 Newport NH 03773

STAMBOULIAN, MARCIA ANN, medical office manager, cytotechnologist; b. Passaic, N.J., Feb. 28, 1951; d. Louis George and Martha S. (Tylicki) Mayer; m. Reinaldo Edwin Rivera, May 31, 1975 (div. Dec. 1980); m. Richard Edward Stamboulian, Apr. 4, 1987. BS, St. Peter's Coll., Jersey City, 1973; Cert. cytotechnology, Muhlenberg Hosp. Sch. of Cytot, Plainfield, N.J., 1974. Cytotechnologist Jersey City Med. Ctr., 1974-78; adminstrv. asst. to pres. Todd Logistics, Bayonne, N.J., 1979-81; asst. mgr. nat. distbn. Imperial Air Freight, Newark, N.J., 1981-83, internat. air freight shipping, 1981-83; office mgr. in sports medicine St. Joseph's Hosp., Clifton Family Practice, Paterson and Clifton, N.J., 1983—. Assoc. bd. mem., voting mem. Lionshead Lake Property Assn., Wayne, N.J., 1988; Eucharistic min. St. Andrew's Ch., Clifton, 1980—. Recipient scholarship Am. Cancer Soc., Passaic County, 1973. Mem. Garden State Games Com. (sec. 1984-87, bd. mem. 1983-87, advisory bd. 1987—). Roman Catholic.

STANALAND, SANDRA LEE, accounting firm administrator; b. Tucker, Ga., Apr. 10, 1946; d. Milton Willis and Doris Ella (Cain) Swann; m. Nathaniel B. Cosby, Sept. 10, 1966 (div. 1971); m. William W. Stanaland Jr., Dec. 1, 1971. AA, Inst. Religious Sci., L.A., 1976. Tech. and statis. clk. Fed. Res. Bank Atlanta, 1964-70; receptionist Claytons' Realty, Winter Park, Fla., 1971; sec., acctg. clk., now adminstr. Stanaland & Co., CPA's, Melbourne, Fla., 1973—. Lic. offshore capt. U.S. Coast Guard. Mem. NAFE. Home: Apt C20 441 N Harbor City Melbourne FL 32935 Office: Stanaland & Co CPAs 1600 Sarno Rd Ste 113 Melbourne FL 32935

STANDARD, ELIZABETH NEWTON, foundation executive; b. Boston, Nov. 1, 1963; d. Alan Lindsay and Teresa (Wesolowski) N. BA, William Smith Coll., 1985. Asst. office mgr. Project HOPE, Chevy Chase, Md., 1986-87; asst. dir. devel. and spl. events Cancer Rsch. Coun., Bethesda, Md., 1987-88; asst. project adminstr. Cafritz Co., Washington, 1988-89; devel. asst. People for the Ethical Treatment of Animals, Rockville, Md., 1989—. Democrat. Episcopalian.

STANDARD, MARY RUSSELL, computer software company executive, consultant; b. Orange, Tex., Mar. 8, 1926; d. Junius Brownrigg and Lily Amanda (McIlroy) Russell; m. Richard Clinton Armstrong, Jan., 1952 (div.); m. Jack Standard, Nov. 1955 (dec.). B.A., Baylor U., Waco, Tex., 1947; postgrad. U. So. Calif., 1948-49, NYU, 1964-66. Sr. computer systems analyst Continental Group, Stamford, Conn., 1959-82; pvt. practice consulting, N.Y.C., 1982—; v.p. software engrng. Signature Software & Services, Princeton, N.J., 1984-87. Mem. Data Processing Mgmt. Assn. Democrat. Office: 232 W 16th St New York NY 10011

STANDEFER, BETTY JEAN ALBURY, commercial bank branch manager; b. Chattanooga, May 17, 1951; d. Charles Franklin and Ida Louise (Roberts (Albury); m. Ronald L. Standefer, Oct. 5, 1947; children: Thomas Eugene, Candyce Lynn. Cert. achievement, Inst. Fin. Edn., Chgo., 1981. Credit collector Hamilton Nat. Bank, Chattanooga, 1969-75; asst. branch mgr. Cherokee Valley Bank, Hixson, Tenn., 1976-84; branch mgr. Volunteer Bank and Trust Co., Hixson, 1984—; tchr. law and banking application Chattanooga State Coll., 1988. Mem. Gideon Internat., Hixson, 1988—. Named Credit Profl. of Yr., 1982, 86, State Credit Profl. of Yr., 1982 CWI:Credit Profls., Chattanooga. Mem. CWI:Credit Profl. Chattanooga (pres. 1982-83), CWI:Credit Profl. Tenn. (pres. 1987-88), Internat. Credit Assn. of Chattanooga (pres. 1989-90), Hixson C. of C. (bd. dirs. 1986—, v.p. 1990), Optimist Club (bd. dirs. Hixson chpt. bd. dirs. 1987—, v.p. & bd. dirs. 1989-90). Republican. Baptist. Home: 1504 Caramel Circle Hixson TN 37343 Office: Volunteer Bank and Trust Co 5109 Hixson Pike Hixson TN 37343

STANDERFORD, MARILYN SUE, computer and business educator; b. Council Bluffs, Iowa, Dec. 7, 1957; d. Everett Gorm and Lois Audrey (Hansen) Nielsen. BA in Bus. Edn., Graceland Coll., 1980; postgrad. U. Iowa, Drake U., Iowa State U. Cert. bus. and multioccupational edn. tchr., Iowa. Tchr. bus. Council Bluffs Pub. Schs., 1980-88; instr. computer bus. applications Iowa Western Community Coll., Council Bluffs, 1988—, in-svc. facilitator, 1988-89; supr. typesetting Wright Spl. Finishing Co., Omaha, 1985—. Guest musician Ch. of Nazarene, Omaha, Mt. View Presbyn. Ch., Omaha, Reorganized Ch. of Jesus Christ of Latter Day Saints; mem. Met. Actors Guild, 1981-85, newsletter editor, 1982-84, bd. dirs., 1984-85, Nebr. Repertory Co., Omaha, 1986-88; mem. adv. coun. Norton Theatre; singer, actress, stage mgr. various community theatres, 1981—; mem. Heartland Consort, 1987—. Mem. Am. Vocat. Assn., Assn. for Supervision and Curriculum Devel., Nat. Bus. Edn. Assn., Iowa Bus. Edn. Assn., North Cen. Bus. Edn. Assn., Mountain Plains Bus. Edn. Assn., Nebr. Choral Arts Soc. Republican. Home: 6031 Hickory Omaha NE 68106 Office: Iowa Western Community Coll 815 N 18th St Council Bluffs IA 51502

STANDFAST, SUSAN J(ANE), health department administrator; b. Callicoon, N.Y., July 2, 1935; m. Theodore P. Wright Jr., 1967; children: Henry S., Margaret S., Catherine B. AB in Biology and Chemistry, Wells Coll., 1957; MD, Columbia U., 1961; MPH In Epidemiology, U. Calif., Berkeley, 1965. Cert. Am. Bd. Preventive Medicine. Intern King County Hosp., Swedish Hosp, Seattle, 1961-62; pediatric resident U. Wash., Seattle, 1963; sr. resident in epidemiology N.Y. State Health Dept., 1965-67; instr. dept. community health Albany (N.Y.) Med. Coll., 1965-67, asst. prof. dept. preventive and community medicine, 1968-72, cons. in epidemiology, 1968-72, adj. asst. prof. preventive and community medicine, 1975-80, adj. assoc. prof., 1980—, cons. preventive medicine dept. family practice, 1983—; research physician bur. cancer control, div. epidemiology N.Y. State Dept. Health, Albany, 1975-83, dir. cancer surveillance unit cancer control sect. bur. chronic disease prevention, 1983-85, asst. to dir. div. epidemiology, 1985-86, dir. injury control program div. epidemiology, 1986—; physician pub. health Albany, 1983—; vis. lectr. G.S. Med. Coll., Bombay, 1969-70, London Sch. Hygiene, 1974-75; cons. in epidemiology Bombay Cancer Registry Tata Meml. Hosp., Albany, 1968-72, cons. infectious disease sect. VA Med. Ctr., Albany, 1979; mem. ad hoc task force on data resource devel. for dir. epidemiology and biometry research program Nat. Inst. Child Health and Human Devel., Bethesda, Md., 1979-80; assoc. prof. epidemiology Sch. Pub. Health SUNY, 1987—; lectr. in field. Contbr. numerous articles to profl. jours. Mem. med. adv. bd. Hudson-Mohawk chpt. Nat. Founs. SIDS, 1976-84; mem. med. adv. bd. council on human sexuality Planned Parenthood, Albany, 1971-88; mem. Physicians for Social Responsibility, 1984—, Doctors Ought to Care, 1984—, also numerous pub. health task forces and coms. Fellow Am. Coll. Preventive Medicine, Am. Coll. Epidemiology; mem. Soc. Epideiologic Rsch., Am. Pub. Health Assn. Home: 27 Vandenburg Ln Latham NY 12110

STANDISH, LINDA SUE, lawyer; b. Indpls., Oct. 1, 1952; d. S. Miles and Gertrude Elizabeth (Eberle) S. BS, Ind. U., 1974; JD, Ind. U., Indpls., 1982. Bar: Ind. 1982. Staff med. tech. St. Vincent's Hosp., Indpls., 1974-79; assoc. White & Raub, Indpls., 1982-85; staff atty. Golden Rule Ins. Co., Indpls., 1985-87; corp. sec. and couns. Central Reserve Life Corp., Berea, Ohio, 1987—. Mem. Am. Soc. Corp. Sec., ABA, Ind. Bar Assn., Indpls. Bar Assn., Cleve. Bar Assn. Office: Central Reserve Life Corp 343 W Bagley Rd Berea OH 44017

STANFORD, KIMBERLEY ALICE, health science facility administrator; b. Concordia, Kans., Nov. 17, 1954; d. Cheslie Carl and Enola Evelyn (Steier) Boylan; m. Charles Stephen Stanford, Dec. 27, 1986. BS, U. Tex., 1976; MS, U. Houston, 1980. Occupational therapist Angels, Inc., Dallas, 1976-77, U. Tex. Med. Br., Galveston, 1977-79, Galveston Ind. Sch. Dist., 1980; supr. occupational therapy Bexar County Hosp. Dist., San Antonio, 1980-82; dir. occupational therapy Bexar County Hosp. Dist., 1982-83, adminstrv. dir. physical medicine and rehab., 1983—. Mem. Inst. Profl. Health Service Adminstrs., Am. Occupational Therapy Assn., Tex. Occupational Therapy Assn., Tex. Hosp. Assn., Nat. Assn. Female Execs. Baptist. Home: 6807 Forest Crest N San Antonio TX 78240

STANFORD, ROSE MARY, criminology educator, researcher; b. Portsmouth, Va., May 12, 1942; d. Robert Marion and Ruth (Watson) S.; children: Dion C. Greenwell, Cheryl L. Greenwell. BA magna cum laude, U. So. Fla., 1976, MA in Criminal Justice, 1979; PhD, Fla. State U., 1984. Interviewer U. South Fla., Tampa, 1975, researcher, interviewer, 1976; adj. instr. dept. criminal justice U. South Fla., St. Petersburg, 1977; parole and probation officer Fla. Dept. Corrections, Tampa, 1977-79; researcher Arthur Young and Co., Tallahassee, 1979-80; researcher, coder Office of State Cts. Adminstrs., Fla. Supreme Ct., Tallahassee, 1980; tutor dept. athletics Fla. State U., Tallahassee, 1981, teaching asst. Sch. Criminology, 1981; planner and evaluator planning and devel. Fla. Dept. Health and Rehab. Services, Tallahassee, 1980-81; asst. prof., intern coordinator dept. criminal justice Pan Am. U., Edinburg, Tex., 1982-85; asst. prof. dept. criminology U. South Fla., Ft. Myers, 1985—; cons. in field; chair 20th Jud. Cir. Task Force on Spouse Abuse, 1988-90; presenter Gender Bias Study Commn., 1988. Contbr. articles to profl. jours., chpts. to books. Book reviewer Criminal Justice, Rev., 1985. Mem. community rev. bd. Rio Grande State Ctr., Harlingen, Tex., 1985, Community Adv. Council, McAllen Halfway House and Parole, Tex., 1984-85, Inter-Agy. Council for Youth Services, Hidalgo County, Tex., 1983-85; mem. oral bd. for sgt. promotion, Mission Police Dept., Tex., 1982; mem. Tex. Council on Crime and Delinquency, 1982-85; active in media on child and spouse abuse. Grantee in field. Mem. Am. Soc. Criminology, Acad. Criminal Justice Scis. (program com. 1985-86, chmn. student affairs com. 1987-88, awards com. 1988—), Fla. Council on Crime and Delinquency (pres. chpt. 1, 1978-79, sec. chpt. 19, 1985-86, state bd. dirs. 1978-79, Criminal Justice plaque, award for contribution to criminal justice field, 1988), Alpha Phi Sigma, Phi Kappa Phi (pres. local chpt. 1989—), Phi Theta Phi. Democrat. Roman Catholic. Avocations: dancing; movies; reading. Office: U South Fla 8111 College Pkwy SW Fort Myers FL 33919

STANG, JUDY ANN, dietitian; b. Sidney, Ohio, Sept. 4, 1963; d. David Leo and Louise Alice (Siebeneck) S. BS in Dietetics, Bowling Green (Ohio) State U., 1985; MS in Nutrition, Case Western Res. U., 1987. Registered dietitian. Dir. nutrition svc. ARA Svcs./Van Wert City (Ohio) Hosp., 1987-89; asst. dir. patient svcs., nutrition dept. ARA Svcs./Grandview Hosp., Dayton, Ohio, 1989—. Bd. dirs. Am. Heart Assn., Van Wert, 1987-89; chmn. walk-a-thon March of Dimes, Van Wert, 1989. Named Assoc. of Yr., Am. Bus. Women, 1989. Mem. Am. Dietetic Assn., Ohio Dietetic Assn., Dayton Dietetic Assn., Diabetic Educators. Roman Catholic. Home: 636A Residenz Pkwy Kettering OH 45429

STANGA, BUCKLI MARLU, state bank examiner; b. Baton Rouge, Feb. 10, 1967; d. Lemuel Arnold and Helen Beatrice (Chaney) S. BS in Acctg. magna cum laude, Southeastern La. U., 1986. CPA, La. Securities examiner Office Fin. Insts., Baton Rouge, 1987, bank examiner, 1987—. Fellow NAFE. Democrat. Home: 8763 Airline Hwy Baton Rouge LA 70815

STANKEY, SUZANNE M., editor; b. Grand Rapids, Mich., Apr. 4, 1951; d. Robert Michael and Elizabeth (Rogers) Stankey. B.A., Ohio U., Athens, 1973; B.J., U. Mo., Columbia, 1977. Editor Living Today, The Blade, Toledo, 1980-82; editor Toledo Magazine, The Blade, Toledo, 1982—. Mem. Toledo Press Club. Home: 2510 Kenwood Blvd Toledo OH 43606 Office: The Blade 541 Superior St Toledo OH 43660

STANLEY, DEBORAH ALEXANDER, nurse; b. Columbus, Ohio, Mar. 19, 1952; d. James Howard and Ethelyn Marie (Aldrich) Alexander; m. David Charles Stanley, Aug. 15, 1970; children: Andrew, Matthew, Ryan. BSN, Ohio State U., Columbus, 1974; MSN, Ind. U., 1982. RN, Ohio, Calif. Nurse Warren (Pa.) Gen. Hosp., 1974-78; clin. instr. St. Mary's Sch. Nursing, Huntington, W.Va., 1978-79; clin. instr. Meth. Hosp., Indpls., 1980-81, nursing mgr., 1981-82; adminstrn. dir. St. Agnes Hosp., Fresno, Calif., 1982-83; instr. Calif. State U., Fresno, 1983-86; nursing mgr. Community Hosp. of Cen. Calif., Fresno, 1986-90, dir. nursing, 1990—; cons. for spl. projects Community Hosp. Cen. Calif., Fresno, 1986. Mem. Calif. Soc. for Nursing Svc. Adminstrs., Fresno Bus. Women's Network, Orgn. Healthcare Execs., Sigma Theta Tau. Republican. Office: Clovis Community Hosp 2755 Herndon Ave Clovis CA 93612

STANLEY, JEAN AGATHA FULLER, chemistry educator; b. White Hall, St. Thomas, Jamaica, Sept. 17, 1951; came to U.S., 1978; d. Clifford Alexander and Lovina Rebecca (Wilson) Fuller; m. Ernie Stanley, Oct. 4, 1976; children—Sofia, Nadia. B.Sc. with honors, U. London, 1976; M.S. in Chemistry, U. Nebr., 1980, Ph.D. in Organic Chemistry, 1984. Teaching asst. U. Nebr., Lincoln, 1978-84; asst. prof. chemistry Wellesley Coll., Mass., 1984—. Contbr. articles in organic chemistry to profl. jours. Mem. Am. Chem. Soc., Royal Soc. Chemistry, Am. Inst. Chemistry, Phi Lambda Upsilon, Sigma Xi. Avocations: sports; music; dancing; reading; sewing. Office: Wellesley Coll Sci Ctr Wellesley MA 02181

STANLEY, JEAN COOPER, accountant, food products executive; b. Atlanta, Sept. 7, 1953; d. Fleet R. and Evelyn (Parris) Cooper; m. Methen A. Stanley, June 22, 1984. BS in Acctg., Berry Coll., 1975, MBA, 1984. CPA, Ga. Acct. Coosa Baking Co., Rome, Ga., 1975-77, asst. officer mgr., 1977-78, mgr. office, 1978-79; sec.-treas. Skipco, Inc., Rome, 1979-85; controller Mondo Baking Co. (formerly S.E.M. Baking Co.), Rome, 1985-87, v.p. fin., 1987—; acct., 411 Mfg. Co., Rome, 1978—; cons. various small bus., Rome, 1982—; tax preparer, bus. and individuals, 1982—; owner, sec. M&J Mfg. With allocations and solications United Way, Rome, 1986-87. Mem. Am. Mgmt. Assn., Am. Assn. Accts., Am. Inst. CPA's, Ga. Soc. CPA's, Rome C. of C. (chmn. Women in Mgmt. 1985). Baptist.

STANLEY, KENDRA EUNICE, political consultant; b. Lynn, Mass., Apr. 12, 1936; d. Kendal Case and Eunice Aborn (Thompson) Ham; div. 1971; 1 child, Kelley Elizabeth. Student, No. Essex Coll., 1985—. Mem. Haverhill Republican City Com., Haverhill, Mass., 1978—, Haverhill Arts Commn. Adv. Bd., 1982-84; notary pub. Commonwealth of Mass., 1988—; mem. 3rd Essex Dist., Mass. Republican State Com., 1988—; mem., chmn.- Haverhill Arts Lottery Commn., 1989—; publicity coord. Haverhill Republican City Com., Women's Republican Club Essex County; mem. office/pub. relations Pepsicola Co., N. Conway, N.H., Lynn, Mass. Mem. citizens' panel Lawrence Eage Tribune; newsletter editor/publicity coord. N. Shore Square & Round Dance Assn.; past contbr. articles NECCO Observer. Publicity coord. Haverhill High Sch. Band, Haverhill Festival '83 Com.; publicity/spl. events chmn. 18th and 19th New Eng. Square & Round Dance Conv., Danvers, Mass.; coord. Ronald Reagan for Pres. campaign, Haverhill, 1980, 84, George Bush for Pres., Haverhill, 1988; pres., treas. Haverhill Women's Republican Club, pres., v.p. Haverhill Middle Sch. Band Parents, founder, pres. Single Eights Square Dance Club, Haverhill; pres. Happy Times Square Dance Club, Beverly, Mass. Mem. Breed Soc., (exec. bd.), Haverhill Armory Arts Assn. (bd. dirs.), Essex Club, Order of Eastern Star. Home and office: 231 Rosemont St Haverhill MA 01832

STANLEY, KIM, actress; b. Tularosa, N.Mex., Feb. 11, 1925; d. J.T. and Ann (Miller) Reid; m. Curt Conway (div.); children: Lisa, Jamison; m. Alfred Ryder (div.); m. Joseph S. Siegel, 1964. Actress with winter stock co. Louisville, 1946; with summer stock co. Pompton Lakes, N.J., 1947. First appeared on Broadway in play Montserrat, 1949; other Broadway plays include House of Bernarda Alba, The Chase, Picnic (N.Y. Drama Critics award 1953), Traveling Lady, 1954, Bus Stop, 1955, Clearing in the Woods, 1957, Cheri, 1959, A Far Country, 1961; TV appearances include The Bridge, You Are There, The Brownstone, A Young Lady of Property, Omnibus, Big Story, The Goddess, 1958, A Touch of the Poet, 1958; appeared in films The Goddess, 1958, Seance on a Wet Afternoon, 1964, Three Sisters, 1967, Frances, 1982, The Right Stuff, 1983. Recipient Donaldson award, 1953, (with Albert Salmi) Ann. Page One award N.Y. Newspaper Guild, 1955, Emmy award for A Cardinal Act of Mercy, 1963, for Cat on a Hot Tin Roof, 1985. Office: care Robert Lantz Agy 9255 Sunset Blvd Los Angeles CA 90069*

STANLEY, LANETT LORRAINE, state legislator; b. Atlanta, Nov. 5, 1962; d. Archie and Ethel Francis (Dixon) S. BS, U. Tenn., 1985. Children's reporter Sta. WXIA-TV, Atlanta, 1979-80; model, sales clk. Rich's Dept. Store, Atlanta, 1979-83; copy clk. Knoxville (Tenn.) Jour., 1984-85; reporter Atlanta Daily World, 1986; intern Sta. WTBS-TV, Atlanta, 1986; adminstrv. aide Bd. Commrs. Fulton County, Atlanta, 1986-87; mem. Ga. Ho. of Reps., Atlanta, 1987—; mem. Nat. and Ga. Legis. Black Caucus, 1987. Bd. dirs. Atlanta Southside Community Council, 1987. Democrat. Baptist. Office: Ga Gen Assembly Ga State Capitol Atlanta GA 30318*

STANLEY, LISA ANN, television reporter; b. Concord, N.H., Jan. 23, 1965; d. Richard Arnold and Marion Laura (Barrett) S. BA, Pembroke (N.C.) State U., 1986, M in English Edn., 1990. Asst. mgr. Nautilus Conditioning Ctr., Lumberton, N.C., 1983-86; bur. chief Sta. WECT-TV, Lumberton, 1986—; bd. dirs. Sta. WECT-TV Internship Program, Lumberton; pub. speaker, 1987—. Bd. dirs. ARC, Lumberton, 1988—; lector St. Francis DeSales Ch., Lumberton, 1986—. Recipient Golden Poet award World of Poetry, 1985, Silver Poet award, 1986. Mem. Zeta Tau Alpha (pres. 1987). Democrat. Roman Catholic. Home: 4900 Independence Blvd #14 Lumberton NC 28358

STANLEY, LISA MARIE, electrical engineer; b. Carlsbad, N.M., May 5, 1960; d. Willian Nall and Evelyn Marie (Perini) S.; m. Gary Walter Haass, May 28, 1983 (div. 1988). BSEE, Texas A and M U., 1982. Engr. LTV Missiles and Electronics, Grand Prairie, Tex., 1982-88; sr. support engr. Aptec Computer Systems Inc., Beaverton, Oregon, 1988--. Mem. Inst. of Electrical and Electronics Engrs., Dallas Navy Flying Club, Aircraft Owners and Pilot Assn. Republican. Office: Aptec Computer Systems 9605 SW Nimbus Ave Beaverton OR 97005

STANLEY, MARGARET KING, performing arts administrator; b. San Antonio, Tex., Dec. 11, 1929; d. Creston Alexander and Margaret (Haymore) King; children: Torrey Margaret, Jean Cullen. Student, Mary Baldwin Coll., 1948-50; BA, U. Tex., Austin, 1952; MA, Incarnate Word Coll., 1959. Tchg. cert. 1953. Elem. tchr. San Antonio Ind. Sch. Dist., 1953-54, 55-56, Arlington County Schs., Va., 1954-55, Ft. Sam Houston Schs., San Antonio, 1955-57; art, art history tchr. St. Pius X Sch., San Antonio, 1959-60; designer-mfr., owner CrisStan Clothes, Inc., San Antonio, 1967-73; founder, exec. dir. San Antonio Performing Arts Assn., 1976—, founder Arts Council of San Antonio, 1962; founding chmn. Joffrey Workshop, San Antonio, 1979; originator, first chairwoman Student Music Fair, San Antonio, 1963; radio program host On Stage, San Antonio, 1983—. Originator of the idea for a new ballet created for the City of San Antonio, "Jamboree," commd. from the Joffrey Ballet, world premiere in San Antonio, 1984. Pres. San Antonio Symphony League, 1971-74; v.p. Arts Council of San Antonio, 1975; bd. govs. Artists Alliance of San Antonio, 1982; v.p. San Antonio Opera Guild, 1974-76. Recipient Outstanding Tchr. award Arlington County Sch. Dist., 1954, Today's Woman award San Antonio Light Newspaper, 1980, Woman of Yr. in Arts award San Antonio Express News, 1983, Emily Smith award for outstanding alumni Mary Baldwin Coll., 1973, Headliner award Women in Communications Inc., 1982; named to Women's Hall of Fame, San Antonio, 1984; teaching fellow Trinity U., San Antonio, 1964-66. Mem. Internat. Soc. Performing Arts Adminstrs. (regional rep. 1982-85), Met. Opera Nat. Council, Women in Communications, Inc., Texas Arts Alliance (bd. govs. 1983-85), Assn. Performing Arts Presenters, Women in Communications (San Antonio chpt.), Jr. League of San Antonio, Battle of Flowers Assn., S.W. Performing Arts Presenters (chmn. 1988—). Avocations: traveling, reading. Office: San Antonio Performing Arts Assn 110 Broadway Suite 230 San Antonio TX 78205

STANLEY, PAMELA MARY, cell biologist; b. Melbourne, Australia, Mar. 25, 1947; came to U.S., 1977; d. John Patrick and Edith Della (Hart) Featherstonhaugh; m. Evan Richard Stanley, Feb. 6, 1970; children: Damian Alexander, Robert Fenton. BSc with honors, U. Melbourne, 1968, PhD, 1972. Rsch. assoc. U. Toronot, Ontario, Can., 1972-77; asst. prof. Albert Einstein Coll. Medicine, Bronx, 1977-82, assoc. prof., 1982-86, prof. of cell biology, 1986—; mem. study sect. NIH, Bethesda, 1989—. Editorial bd. Molecular and Cellular Biology, 1980—, Glycobiology, 1990—; contbr. articles to profl. jours. Bd. dirs. Kids Meeting Kids Can Make A Difference, N.Y., 1986—, Alaria Chamber Ensemble, N.Y., 1985—; mem. Educators for Social Responsibility, N.Y., 1985—; mem. review group Am. Cancer Soc., N.Y.C., 1981-85. NSF grantee, 1977, Am. Cancer Soc. grantee 1978, 80, NIH grantee, 1980, 83, 85, 86. Mem. Am. Assn. Biol. Chemists. Office: Albert Einstein Coll Medicine Dept Cell Biology Bronx NY 10461

STANLEY, PATRICIA MARY, microbiologist; b. Oneonta, N.Y., Mar. 28, 1948. BS, Cornell U., 1970; PhD, U. Wash., 1975. Mem. rsch. faculty U. Minn., Mpls., 1976-79; prin. microbiologist Ecolab, Inc., St. Paul, 1979-86, scientist, 1986—. Contbr. articles to sci. publs. Mem. Am. Soc. Microbiology, Soc. Indsl. Microbiology, Am. Soc. Testing and Materials, Assn. for Women in Sci., Grad. Women in Sci. Home: 3701 Pillsbury Ave S Minneapolis MN 55409 Office: Ecolab Inc 840 Sibley Hwy Saint Paul MN 55118

STANNARD, CAROLE CHRISTINE, cable administrator; b. Evanston, Ill., July 12, 1956; d. John Russell Stannard and Marjorie Jane (Garner) Suckow. Mgr. Stuarts, Niles, Ill., 1974-76; saleswoman Joannies Gift Boutique, Skokie, Ill., 1976-78; instr. Fred Astaire Dance Studios, Wilmette, Ill., 1979-81; asst. mgr. Fashionation, Skokie, 1981-83; with cash processing dept. Zayre's, Chgo., 1983-84; office mgr. TCI Ill., Skokie, 1984-87; exec. dir. N.W. Mcpl. Cable Coun., Arlington Heights, Ill., 1987—. Mem. Des Plaines (Ill.) Youth Commn., 1988-91. Mem. Nat. Assn. Telecommunications Officers and Advisors (assoc., co-chmn. pub. rels. com. Ill. chpt. 1990). Republican. Office: NW Mcpl Cable Coun 112 N Belmont Ave Arlington Heights IL 60004

STANTON, ELIZABETH MCCOOL, lawyer; b. Lansdale, Pa., Apr. 12, 1947; d. Leo J. and Helen M. (Gillooly) McCool; m. Robert J. Stanton, June 13, 1970; children: Jonathan R., James Alfred. BBA, Drexel U., 1969; JD magna cum laude, U. Houston, 1979. Bar: Tex. 1979, U.S. Dist. Ct. (so. dist.) Tex. 1980, Ohio 1982, U.S. Dist. Ct. (so. dist.) Ohio 1983, U.S. Ct. Appeals (6th cir.) 1986, U.S. Supreme Ct. 1990. Assoc. Friedman & Chaffin, Houston, 1979-80, Law Offices of Elaine Brady, Houston, 1980-81, Moots, Cope & Weinberger Co., L.P.A., Columbus, Ohio, 1981-86; prin. Moots, Cope and Kizer Co. L.P.A., Columbus, 1986-89, Moots, Cope, Stanton and Kizer. P.A., Columbus, 1989—. Mem. legal com. Met. Womens Ctr., Columbus, 1983-84. Drexel Bd. Trustees scholar, 1965-67, Internat. Ladies Garment Workers Union scholar, 1965-69. Mem. ABA, Ohio Bar Assn., Columbus Bar Assn., Nat. Assn. Women Lawyers, Plantiff Employment Lawyers Assn., Women's Lawyers Franklin County (treas. 1989-90, bd. dirs. 1990—), St. Thomas Moore Soc., Phi Kappa Phi, Beta Gamma Sigma. Democrat. Roman Catholic. Office: Moots Cope Stanton & Kizer Co 3600 Olentangy River Rd Columbus OH 43214-3913

STANTON, JANE GRAHAM, advertising executive, trade association executive; b. Rice, Tex., Mar. 4, 1922; d. William Edward and Kathryn Ruth (McKay) Tidwell; student Tex. State Coll. Women, 1938-39, Abilene Christian Coll., 1939-40, N. Tex. State Coll., 1941; m. Joseph Wesley Graham, Jan. 5, 1946 (div. Aug. 1974); 1 dau., Kathryn Ann; m. 2d, Hinds Victor Thomas, Dec. 18, 1975 (div. 1977); m. 3d, Hank Stanton, June 10, 1980. Profl. singer on radio, 1941-49; producer, writer radio-TV drama, N.Y.C., 1948-56; v.p. United Nat. Films, Dallas, 1957-59; with Tracy-Locke Advt., Dallas, 1964-66; owner Jane Graham Advt., 1967—; exec. dir. S.W. Apparel Mfrs. Assn., Dallas. Active United Fund. Recipient numerous awards Dallas Advt. League. Mem. Fashion Group. Editor Dallas Fashion Update, 1988—, Am. Fashion mag., 1974—; contbr. articles to profl. jours.; columnist Dallas Times Herald. Home: 4727 N Central Expy Dallas TX 75205

STANTON, JEANNE FRANCES, retired lawyer; b. Vicksburg, Miss., Jan. 22, 1920; d. John Francis and Hazel (Mitchell) S.; student George Washington U., 1938-39; BA, U. Cin., 1940; JD, Salmon P. Chase Coll. Law, 1954. Admitted to Ohio bar, 1954; chief clk. Selective Svc. Bd., Cin., 1940-43; instr. USAAF Tech. Schs., Biloxi, Miss., 1943-44; with Procter & Gamble, Cin., 1945-84, legal asst., 1952-54, head advt. svcs. sect. legal div., trade practices dept., 1954-73, mgr. advt. svcs., legal div., 1973-84, ret., 1984. Team capt. Community Chest Cin., 1953; mem. ann. meeting com. Archaeol. Inst. Am., 1983. Mem. AAAS, ABA (chmn. subcom. D of com. 307 copyright sect. 1987-88, 89, 90), Ohio Bar Assn. (chmn. uniform state laws com. 1968-70), Cin. Bar Assn. (sec. law day com. 1965-66, chmn. com. on preservation hist. documents 1968-71), Vicksburg and Warren County, Cin. hist. socs., Internat. Oceanographic Found., Otago Early Settlers Assn. (assoc.), Intercontinental Biog. Assn., Cin. Lawyers (pres. 1983, exec. com. 1978—), Cin. Women Lawyers (treas. 1958-59, nominating com. 1976), Terrace Park Country Club. Home: 2302 Easthill Ave Cincinnati OH 45208-2608

STANTON, JOANNE, securities trader; b. Lockport, N.Y., Apr. 30, 1944; d. Pauline Penwright; m. Edwin C. Stanton, Sept. 10, 1971; children: Kevin, Brian. AA, Niagara County Community Coll., Sanborn, N.Y., 1980; student, Niagara U., N.Y. Inst. Fin. Mgr. Peterson Drug Co., Middleport, 1971-79; tchr. Niagara County Community Coll.; broker Advest Inc., Lockport, 1980; leader personal growth and devel. seminars. Mem. common coun. City of Lockport, 1985-89. Recipient Outstanding Community Svc. Cert. of Merit, Senator John B. Daly. Mem. N.Y. State Bus. and Profl. Women's Club Inc. (Lockport chpt., named one of Outstanding Women in Field of Bus.), Toastmasters. Republican. Home: 214 Summit St Lockport NY 14094 Office: PO Box 372 Lockport NY 14095

STANTON, MARGARET ELIZABETH, musician; b. Chgo., Sept. 29, 1948; d. Henry Edmund and Evelyn Frances (Hayes) S.; m. William G. Christie, May 1, 1983. AB, Oberlin Coll., 1970; MusM, Juilliard Sch., NY, 1980. Pianist Anchorage Symphony, 1975-77, Anchorage Opera, 1976-77, 82, 86; music coordinator Alaska Pacific U., Anchorage, 1983-84; instr. No. Va. Community Coll., Woodbridge, Va., 1988; self-employed pianist, tchr. Arlington, Va., 1988--; performance tours State of Alaska, 1974-76, 79-82, 86-87, pianist Alaska Festival Music, 1974-75. vice chair Transp. Study Com., 1982-84, mem. Traffic Commn., Anchorage 1984-85. Mem. No. Va. Music Tchrs. Assn. Home: 1001 S Dinwiddie St Arlington VA 22204

STANTON-KELLEHER, CAROL, computer manufacturing sales executive; b. Ravenna, Ohio, Dec. 4, 1961; d. Robert Wendell and Helen Provan (Hamilton) Stanton; m. Joseph William Kelleher, Nov. 1, 1986; 1 child, Daniel Stanton. BS, Santa Clara U., 1983. Sales rep. McDonnell-Douglas Co., Cuperto, Calif., 1984-86; sr. sales rep. Atari, Sunnyvale, 1986-87; major account exec. Apple Computer Co., Independence, Ohio, 1987—. Community sponsor Orange (Ohio) High Sch., 1989. Mem. Cleve. Women's City Club. Presbyterian. Office: Apple Computer Co 6450 Rockside Woods Blvd Independence OH 44131

STANWICK, KATHY ANN, political and policy analyst; b. Utica, N.Y., Nov. 13, 1950; d. Anthony T. and Stella (Szarek) S. BA cum laude, SUNY, Buffalo, 1972; MA, Rutgers U., 1976. Rsch. asst. Ctr. for Am. Woman and Politics, Eagleton Inst., Rutgers U., New Brunswick, N.J., 1974-77, rsch. assoc., 1977-80, asst. dir., 1980-86; pres. Stanwick Assocs., Metuchen, N.J., 1986-90; dir. external affairs N.J. Dept. Transp., Trenton, 1990—; mem. Vocat. Equity Adv. Coun., Trenton, N.J., 1989—. Author: (report series) Bringing More Women into Public Office, 1984; editor: Women in Public Office, 1977. Del. Dem. Nat. Conv., 1984; asst. campaign mgr. Shapiro for Gov. N.J., 1985; exec. dir. Alliance for Affordable Housing, Metuchen, 1986-90; trustee Housing Coalition Middlesex County, New Brunswick, 1987—, Nat. Abortion Rights Action League, Montclair, N.J., 1990—. Grad. Leadership N.J., New Brunswick, 1989. Mem. LWV, AAUW, Women's Polit. Action Com. N.J. (trustee). Democrat. Office: NJ Dept Transp 1035 Parkway CN600 Trenton NJ 08625

STAPF, KRISTIN MARIE, management analyst; b. Albany, N.Y., Nov. 7, 1966; d. Joseph John Stapf and Mary Joy (Lloyd) Deyoe. BA, Siena Coll., Loudonville, N.Y., 1988. Editorial asst. Sec.'s Base Closure Commn., Dept. Def., Washington, 1988-89; mgmt. analyst Mitchell Systems Corp., Arlington, Va., 1989—. Mem. NAFE, Conservative Network. Republican. Roman Catholic. Home: 24 Hawk Run Ct Gaithersburg MD 20879 Office: Mitchell Systems Corp 4001 N Fairfax Dr Arlington VA 22203

STAPLES, JUDITH LINWOOD, healthcare administrator; b. Bklyn., Sept. 13, 1947; d. Sheldon Linwood and Gladys (Anthon) S.; m. Alan L. Smith, (div. Feb. 1979). AA in Fine Arts, Coll. of San Mateo, 1967; BFA, San Jose (Calif.) State U., 1970. Cert. employee assistance profl. Prodn. artist Beeline Specialty Printers, South San Francisco, 1972-73; advt. artist Transcontinental Music Corp., Burlingame, Calif., 1974; prodn. artist Schwabacher Frey, Inc., San Francisco, 1975-77; account exec. Schwabacher Frey, Inc., Emeryville, Calif., 1977-82; indsl. liaison Comprehensive Care Corp., Hayward, Calif., 1982-83; drug and alcohol services coordinator Comprehensive Care Corp., San Francisco, 1983-84, 1983-84; program mgr. St. Catherine's Care Unit for Women, San Francisco, 1984-86; program dir. Parkside Recovery Ctrs., Inc., San Jose, 1986-88; community rels. mgr. Parkside-San Jose Med. Ctr., San Jose, 1988—; also So. Bay Parkside Recovery Ctrs., El Camino Hosp., Good Samaritan Hosp. Producer numerous seminars on drug abuse. Fundraising chair Chem. Awareness and Treatment Services, San Francisco, 1984-87; chairperson exec. bd. Problems of Alcoholism in Labor and Mgmt., San Jose, 1986-89. Recipient Fine Art award Bank of Am., 1965. Democrat. Office: Parkside-San Jose Med Ctr 1101 S Winchester Blvd Bldg F 168 San Jose CA 95128

STAPLETON, CLAUDIA ANN, small business owner; b. Memphis, July 14, 1947; d. Ben Proctor and Mollie Jo (Johnson) Sivley; m. Cecil Dean Langham, Nov. 25, 1964 (div. Nov. 1984); m. Mark Phillip Stapleton, Sept. 18, 1985; children: Warren Scott Langham, Jeffrey Dean Langham, Lori Suzette Langham Calhoun. Student, Tex. Tech. U., 1976-77, Amarillo Coll., 1989—. Legal sec. Wm. A. Dyess Law Office, Stratford, Tex., 1973-75; code enforcement officer City of Lubbock, Tex., 1975-85; owner, operator Claudia Stapleton Consulting, Amarillo, Tex., 1985—; unit sec. Tex. Dept. Human Svcs., Amarillo, 1988-90; code enforcement officer City of Amarillo, 1990—; cons. in field. Mem. Nat. Elec. Sign Assn., Tex. Assn. Legal Secs., Tex. Heritage, Am. Bus. Women's Assn., Beta Sigma Phi Sorority. Republican. Methodist. Home: 3321 Lenwood Amarillo TX 79109 Office: City of Amarillo 509 E 7th St Amarillo TX 79186

STAPLETON, JEAN (JEANNE MURRAY), actress; b. N.Y.C.; d. Joseph E. and Marie (Stapleton) Murray; m. William H. Putch (dec.); 2 children. Student, Hunter Coll., N.Y.C., Am. Apprentice Theatre, Am. Actors Co., Am. Theatre Wing; student with, Harold Clurman; LHD (hon.), Emerson Coll.; hon. degree, Hood Coll., Monmouth Coll. Opera debut in Candide with Balt. Opera Co.; appeared in The Italian Lesson with Balt. Opera; first N.Y. stage role in The Corn is Green, Equity Library Theatre; starred as mother in Am. Gothic, Circle-in-the-Sq.; Broadway debut with Judith Anderson In The Summer House; also appeared on Broadway in Damn Yankees, Bells Are Ringing, Juno, Rhinoceros and Funny Girl; first major break in comic ingenue role as Myrtle Mae with Frank Fay in Harvey on-tour; played with nat. tour of Come Back, Little Sheba starring Shirley Booth; starred in tour of Morning's at Seven, The Show-Off, Daisy Mayme; appeared in motion pictures including Damn Yankees, 1958, Bells Are Ringin, 1960, Up the Down Staircase, 1967, Cold Turkey, 1971, The Buddy System, 1984, Klute; appeared in numerous TV shows including Golden Age, Studio One, Naked City, Armstrong Circle Theater, The Defenders, Jackie Gleason Show, PBS-TV appearances Grown-ups, Trying Times, The Boss, cable TV appearances Let Me Hear You Whisper, Mother Goose Rock and Rhyme; starred in the title role of Aunt Mary on Hallmark Hall of

Fame, 1979; most famous TV role as Edith Bunker on All In The Family, 1971-79; TV films include Dead Man's Folly, Tail Gunner Joe, 1977, Isabel's Choice, 1981, Angel Dusted, 1981, Eleanor: First Lady of the World, 1982, A Matter of Sex; appeared the Totem Pole Playhouse, Fayetteville, Pa., starred at Kennedy Ctr. in Daisy Mayme, 1978, The Late Christopher Bean, 1982, Bon Appetit; appeared on Broadway in Arsenic and Old Lace, 1986, (also nat. tour), nat. tour. Drood, 1986, The Birthday Party, 1989, Mountain Language, 1989; in CBS-TV series Bagdad Cafe, 1990—, La Opera's Oklahoma, 1990. U.S. commr. to Internat. Woman's Yr. Commn. and Nat. Conf. Women, Houston, 1977; bd. dirs. Women's Rsch. and Edn. Inst., Eleanor Roosevelt's Val-Kill; trustee Actors' Fund Am. Recipient Emmy award for best performance in comedy series 1970-71, 71-72, 78, Golden Globe awards Hollywood Fgn. Press Assn. 1972, 73, Obie award, 1990. Mem. Actors Equity Assn. (council 1958-63), Screen Actors Guild, AFTRA. Office: care Bauman & Hiller 5750 Wilshire Blvd Los Angeles CA 90036

STAPLETON, JOAN, publishing executive. Pub. New Republic mag., 1988—. Office: New Republic 1220 19th St NW Washington DC 20036*

STAPLETON, KATHARINE HALL (KATIE STAPLETON), food broadcaster, author; b. Kansas City, Mo., Oct. 29, 1919; d. William Mabin and Katharine (Hall) Foster; B.A., Vassar Coll., 1941; m. Benjamin Franklin Stapleton, June 20, 1942; children: Benjamin Franklin, III, Craig Roberts, Katharine Hall. Cookbook reviewer Denver Post, 1974-84; producer, writer, host On the Front Burner, daily radio program Sta. KOA-CBS, Denver, 1976-79, Sta. WGN, Portland, Maine, 1979-81, Cooking with Katie, live one-hour weekly, Sta. KOA, 1979-88; guest broadcaster Geneva Radio, 1974, London Broadcasting Corp., 1981, 82; tour leader culinaries to Britain, France and Switzerland, 1978-85. Eng., 1978. Chmm. women's div. United Fund, 1955-56; founder, chmn. Denver Debutante Ball, 1956, 57; hon. chmn. Nat. Travelers Aid Assn., 1952-56; commr. Denver Centennial Authority, 1958-60; trustee Washington Cathedral, regional v.p., 1967-73; mem. world service council YWCA, 1961-87; trustee, Colo. Women's Coll., 1975-80; pres. Harmes C. Fishback Found. Decorated Chevalier de L'Etoile Noire (France); recipient People-to-People citation, 1960, 66, Beautiful Activist award Altrusa Club, 1972, Gran Skillet award Colo./Wyo. Restaurant Assn., 1981; named Chevalier du Tastevin, 1989. Democrat. Episcopalian. Clubs: Denver Country, Denver. Author: Denver Delicious: 150 Past and Present Recipes from the Queen City, 1980, 3d. edit., 1983; High Notes: Favorite Recipes of KOA, 1984. Home: 8 Village Rd Englewood CO 80110

STAPLETON, MAUREEN, actress; b. Troy, N.Y., June 21, 1925; d. John P. and Irene (Walsh) S.; m. Max Allentuck, July 1949 (div. Feb. 1959); children: Daniel, Katharine; m. David Rayfiel, July, 1963 (div.). Student, Siena Coll, 1943. Debut in Playboy of the Western World, 1946; toured with Barretts of Wimpole Street, 1947; other plays include Anthony and Cleopatra, 1947, Detective Story, The Bird Cage, Rose Tattoo, 1950-51, The Sea Gull, Orpheus Descending, The Cold Wind and the Warm, 1959, Toys in the Attic, 1960-61, Plaza Suite, 1969, The Gingerbread Lady, 1970 (Tony award 1970), Country Girl, 1972, Secret Affairs of Mildred Wild, 1972, The Gin Game, 1977-78, The Little Foxes, 1981; motion pictures include Lonely Hearts, 1959, The Fugitive Kind, 1960, A View from the Bridge, 1962, Bye Bye Birdie, 1963, Trilogy, 1969, Airport, 1970, Plaza Suite, 1971, Interiors, 1978, The Runner Stumbles, 1979, Reds, 1981 (Oscar award as best supporting actress), The Fan, 1981, On the Right Track, 1981, The Electric Grandmother, 1982, Mother's Day, 1984, Johnny Dangerously, 1984, Cocoon, 1985, The Money Pit, 1986, Nuts, 1987, Made in Heaven, Cocoon: The Return; TV films include Tell Me Where It Hurts, 1974, Cat On a Hot Tin Roof, 1976, All the King's Men, 1958, For Whom the Bell Tolls, 1959, Save Me a Place at Forest Lawn, 1966, Mirror, Mirror, Off the Wall, 1969, Queen of the Stardust Ballroom, 1975, The Gathering, 1977, Part II, 1979, Letters From Frank, 1979, Little Gloria ... Happy at Last, 1982, Sentimental Journey, 1984, Private Sessions, 1985, Liberace: Behind the Scenes. Recipient Nat. Inst. Arts and Letters award, 1969. Office: care Silvia Gold Internat Creative Mgmt 8899 Beverly B Los Angeles CA 90048*

STAPLETON, SHARON MARIE, accountant; b. Chgo., June 17, 1957; d. Stephen W. and Patricia A. (Reidy) S. BSc in Accountancy, DePaul U., 1979, MBA in Fin., 1986. Mem. audit staff, supr. Coopers & Lybrand, Chgo., 1979-83; audit and spl. project mgr. Office Spl. Dep., Ill. Dept. Ins., Chgo., 1983-88; mgr. corp. acctg. CNA Ins., Chgo., 1988—; mentor DePaul U., Chgo., 1988—. asst. editor nat. sorority mag. The Compass, 1988—. Vol., vol. editor Northwestern Meml. Hosp. newsletter The Voice, Chgo., 1985-88; mem. alumni bd., com. chmn. DePaul U. Coll. Commerce, 1985-89; treas. Ledger and Quill DePaul U. Acctg. Alumni Group, 1990—. Fellow Life Office Mgmt. Inst.; mem. Health Ins. Assn. Am., Nat. Assn. Ins. Women (edn. com. Chgo. 1986-88), Theta Phi Alpha (dir. extension 1980-82, nat. treas. 1982-84, trustee 1984-88, conv. parliamentarian 1978, 82, conf. dir. 1990—, recipient Outstanding Chpt. Gov. award, 1990). Home: 21 W Goethe St Apt 5B Chicago IL 60610

STAPP, MIRIAM DOW, bank auditor; b. Jackson, Tenn., July 30, 1953; d. John Down and Miriam Faye (Boyett) Bryant; m. Al Stapp (div. June 1989); children: Wesley, Kellie. BS in Acctg., U. Tenn., Martin, 1975; MBA, Jacksonville U., 1989. Chartered bank auditor. Staff auditor First Tenn. Nat. Bank, Memphis, 1975-80, audit mgr., 1980-85; v.p., head audit dept. First Union Nat. Bank Fla., Jacksonville, 1985-89, v.p., head EDP audit dept., 1989—. Contbr. articles to profl. jours. Mem. Inst. Internal Auditors (bd. govs. 1988—), EDP Auditors Assn., Phi Kappa Phi. Methodist. Office: First Union Nat Bank Fla Mail Code 0140 PO Box 2080 Jacksonville FL 32231-0010

STAR, ANNE MARIE, educator; b. Phila., July 23, 1947; d. James H. J. and Anna M. Tate; m. Ernst Edward Star, Apr. 7, 1983; 1 child, Katharine Tate. BA, Chestnut Hill Coll., Phila., 1969; MS in Edn., U. Pa., 1972, postgrad., 1974-76. Cert. tchr., N.Y. Tchr. social studies Boston Pub. Schs., 1969-71, Vanguard High Sch., Phila., 1972-73, West Cath. High Sch. for Girls, Phila., 1973-74, Meml. Jr. High Sch., Valley Stream (N.Y.) Cen. Sch. Dist., 1988-89; edn. cons. Heuristics, Inc., Wellesley, Mass., 1977-78; ind. edn. cons., Newton, Mass., 1978; hearing officer Family Ct. Phila., 1978-83; tchr. Am. history South High Sch., Valley Stream Cen. Dist. Schs., 1989—. Mem. AAUW (coord. community action, 1988-89, legis. info. 1989-90, seminar week with Fgn. Policy Inst. 1988, 89), Nat. Coun. for Social Studies, L.I. Coun. for Social Studies, Phi Delta Kappa, Pi Lambda Theta. Office: Valley Stream Cen Sch Dist One Kent Rd Valley Stream NY 11582

STARFIELD, BARBARA HELEN, physician, educator; b. Bklyn., Dec. 18, 1932; d. Martin and Eva (Illions) S.; m. Neil A. Holtzman, June 12, 1955; children—Robert, Jon, Steven, Deborah. A.B., Swarthmore Coll., 1954; M.D., SUNY, 1959; M.P.H., Johns Hopkins U., 1963. Teaching asst. in anatomy Downstate Med. Center, N.Y.C., 1955-57; intern in pediatrics Johns Hopkins U., 1959-60, resident, 1960-62, dir. pediatric med. care clinic, 1963-66, dir. community staff comprehensive child care project, 1966-67, dir. pediatric clin. scholars program, 1971-76, prof. health policy, head health policy div., joint appointment in pediatrics, 1975—; cons. DHHS. Contbr. articles to profl. jours.; Mem. editorial bd.: Med. Care, 1977-79, Pediatrics, 1977-82, Internat. Jour. Health Services, 1978—, Med. Care Rev, 1980-84, Pediatrician, 1985—. Recipient Dave Luckman Meml. award, 1958; HEW Career Devel. award, 1970-75. Mem. Nat. Acad. Sci. Inst. Medicine (governing council 1981-83), Am. Pediatric Soc., Soc. Pediatric Research, Internat. Epidemiologic Assn., Ambulatory Pediatric Assn. (pres. 1980), Am. Public Health Assn., Sigma Xi, Alpha Omega Alpha. Office: Johns Hopkins Sch Hygiene 624 N Broadway Baltimore MD 21205

STARK, AGNES LOUISE, accountant; b. Omaha, Dec. 21, 1929; d. Arnold John Wichita and Mary Frances (Riha) Wichita Riedmann; m. Darrell Joseph Stark, Apr. 18, 1953; children: John, Mary, Anne, Christopher, Sally, Paul, Thomas. BS, Creighton U., 1952. Acct. Creighton U., Omaha, 1975—.

STARK, AMY LOUISE, clinical psychologist; b. St. Paul, May 13, 1954; d. Douglas Arvid and Irene Eleanor (Frokjer) S. BA, Gustavus Adolphus Coll., 1976; MA, Calif. Sch. Profl. Psychology, 1979, PhD, 1981. Lic. psychologist, Calif. Psychology intern Juarez-Lincoln Sch., Chula Vista, Calif., 1978-79, Cath. Family Services, San Diego, 1979-80, Southwood Mental Health Ctr., San Diego, 1980-81; clin. psychologist Orange County Children and Youth Services, 1982-84; clin. coordinator Western Youth Services, Tustin, Calif., 1986-88; indsl. psychologist Frederick Capaldi & Assocs., Tustin, 1982—; psychologist Tustin Psychology Ctr., 1985—; cons., presenter in field. Contbr. articles to profl. jours. Mem. Am. Psychol. Assn., Orange County Psychol. Assn., Newport Beach C. of C. Office: 131 N Tustin #210 Tustin CA 92680

STARK, BETTY R(UTH), interior designer; b. Bklyn., Jan. 29, 1935; d. Frank Philip and Leona (Cohen) Silverman; m. Richard M. Stark, Nov. 10, 1957; children: Thomas, John. BA, Cornell U., 1956. With artwork promotion dept. The New Yorker mag., N.Y.C., 1956-57; with advt. promotion House and Gerstin Advt., Washington, 1958-59; free lance interior designer N.Y.C., 1960-65; design coordinator Wendell Fabrics Corp., N.Y.C., 1965-70; prin., comml. interior designer Betty Stark Interiors, Roslyn, N.Y., 1970—; designer showcase area, Glen Cove, N.Y., 1977. Contbr. photographs and articles to mags. vol. interior designer Port Jewish Ctr., Port Washington, N.Y., 1985-87. Mem. Am. Soc. Interior Designers (assoc.), Designers Workshop. Office: 153 Main St Roslyn NY 11576

STARK, JOAN SCISM, education educator; b. Hudson, N.Y., Jan. 6, 1937; d. Ormonde F. and Myrtle Margaret (Kirkey) S.; m. William L. Stark, June 28, 1958 (dec.); children: Eugene William, Susan Elizabeth, Linda Anne, Ellen Scism; m. Malcolm A. Lowther, Jan. 31, 1981. B.S., Syracuse U., 1957; M.A. (Hoadly fellow), Columbia U., 1960; Ed.D., SUNY, Albany, 1971. Tchr. Ossining (N.Y.) High Sch., 1957-59; free-lance editor Holt, Rinehart & Winston, Harcourt, Brace & World, 1960-70; lectr. Ulster County Community Coll., Stone Ridge, N.Y., 1968-70; asst. dean Goucher Coll., Balt., 1970-73; asso. dean Goucher Coll., 1973-74; assoc. prof., chmn. dept. higher postsecondary edn. Syracuse (N.Y.) U., 1974-78; dean Sch. Edn., U. Mich., Ann Arbor, 1978-83, prof., 1983—; dir. Nat. Ctr. for Improving Postsecondary Teaching and Learning, 1986—. Contbr. numerous articles to various publs. Leader Girl Scouts U.S.A., Cub Scouts Am.; coach girls Little League; dist. officer PTA, intermittently, 1968-80; mem. adv. com. Gerald R. Ford Library, U. Mich., 1980-83; trustee Kalamazoo Coll., 1979-85; mem. exec. com. Inst. Social Research, U. Mich., 1979-81; bd. dirs. Mich. Assn. Colls. Tchr. Edn., 1979-81. Mem. Assn. Study Higher Edn. (dir. 1977-79, v.p. 1983, pres. 1984), Assn. Innovation Higher Edn. (nat. chmn. 1974-75), Am. Assn. for Higher Edn., Am. Edni. Research Assn., Assn. Instl. Rsch. (disting. mem.), Assn. Colls. and Schs. Edn. State Univs. and L and Grant Colls. (dir. 1981-83), Phi Beta Kappa, Phi Kappa Phi, Sigma Pi Sigma, Eta Pi Upsilon, Lambda Sigma Sigma, Phi Delta Kappa, Pi Lambda Theta. Office: U Mich 2002 Sch of Edn Ann Arbor MI 48109

STARK, KELLY SHIRA, lawyer; b. Ft. Warren, Wyo., Nov. 23, 1942; d. Malcolm D. and June (Buxton) Gish. BA, Tex. Tech U., 1965, MA, 1966; JD, Memphis State U., 1982. Bar: Tenn. 1982, U.S. Dist. Ct. Tenn. 1982, U.S. Supreme Ct. 1989. Prof. U. Oreg., Memphis State U. and others, Memphis and Eugene, Oreg., 1966-76; mem. Towery Press, Inc., Memphis, 1976-79; sole practice Memphis, 1982-83; ptnr. Dice, Burson & Stark, Memphis, 1983-86, Bernstein, McLean, Stark & Hinson, Memphis, 1986—; prof. law Memphis State U., 1982-90, mgmt. skills evaluator, 1986. Mem. Vollintine-Evergreen Community Assn., Memphis, 1985-87, Annesdale-Snowden Neighborhood Assn. Mem. Memphis Bar Assn. (pres. div. and family law sect. 1989—), Assn. Women Attys. (treas. 1984-86), LWV, ACLU, NOW. Office: McLean & Stark 44 N Second St Memphis TN 38104

STARK, MARY BARBARA, retired educator; b. Boston, Jan. 1, 1920; d. Charles Rathbone and Dorothea Brenton (Burge) S. BA, Whitworth Coll., 1965, MEd, 1968; EdS, U. of the Pacific, 1975; PhD, Southeastern U., New Orleans, 1981. Cert. elem. tchr., jr. high tchr., spl. edn. tchr. Play dir. Spokane (Wash.) Park Dept., 1937-41; tchr. Lanham Act Nursery Sch., Spokane, 1941-45; owner, mgr. Children's Play Room, Spokane, 1945-63; supr. Guild's Sch for Mentally Retarded, Spokane, 1962-66; tchr. primary educable mentally retarded Sacramento City Unified Sch. Dist., 1966-68, tchr. educable kindergarten mentally retarded, 1968-70; kindergarten educator Sacramento (Calif.) City Unified S.D., 1970-87. Mem. Sacramento Bus. and Profl. Women's Club (pres. 1973-74), Assn. Childhood Edn. Internat. (pres. 1983-85, state treas. 1984-86), Delta Kappa Gamma (pres. 1984-86), Phi Delta Kappa. Mem. United Ch. of Christ. Home: 5989 Lake Crest Way #1 Sacramento CA 95822

STARK, NELLIE MAY, forest ecology educator; b. Norwich, Conn., Nov. 20, 1933; d. Theodore Banjamin and Dorothy Josephine (Pendleton) Beetham; m. Oscar Elder Stark, Oct. 1962 (dec.). BA, Conn. Coll., 1956; AM, Duke U., 1958, PhD, 1962. Botanist Exptl. Sta., U.S. Forest Svc., Old Strawberry, Calif., 1958-66; botanist, ecologist Desert Rsch. Inst., Reno, Nev., 1966-72; prof. forest ecology Sch. Forestry, U. Mont., Missoula, 1972—; pres. Camas Analytical Lab., Inc., Missoula, 1987—. Contbr. articles to profl. jours. Named Distinguished Daughter Norwich C. of C., 1985; recipient Conn. award Conn. Coll., 1986, 40 grants. Mem. Ecol. Soc. Am. (chair ethics com. 1974, 76), Bot. Soc. Am., Soc. Am. Foresters (taskforce 1987-88), Internat. Soc. Tropical Foresters. Office: U Mont Sch Forestry Missoula MT 59812

STARK, PATRICIA ANN, psychologist; b. Ames, Iowa; d. Keith C. and Mary L. (Johnston) Moore. B.S., So. Ill. U., Edwardsville, 1970, M.S., 1972; Ph.D., St. Louis U., 1976. Counselor to alcoholics Bapt. Rescue Mission, East St. Louis, 1969; researcher alcoholics Gateway Rehab. Center, East St. Louis, 1972; psychologist intern Henry-Stark Counties Spl. Edn. Dist. and Galesburg State Research Hosp., Ill., 1972-73; instr. Lewis and Clark Community Coll., Godfrey, Ill., 1973-76, asst. prof., 1976-84, assoc. prof., 1984, coordinator child care services, 1974-84; mem. staff dept. psychiatry Meml. Hosp., St. Elizabeth's Hosp., 1979—; supr. various workshops in field, 1974—; dir. child and family services Collinsville Counseling Center, 1978-82; clin. dir., owner Empas-Complete Family Psychol. and Hypnosis Services, Collinsville, 1982—; cons. community agys., 1974—; mem. adv. bd. Madison County Council on Alcoholism and Drug Dependency, 1977-80. Mem. Am. Psychol. Assn., Ill. Psychol. Assn., Midwestern Psychol. Assn., Nat. Assn. Sch. Psychologists, Am. Soc. Clin. Hypnosis, Internat. Soc. Hypnosis. Office: 2802 Maryville Rd Collinsville IL 62234

STARK, ROBIN CARYL, psychotherapist, consultant; b. Yonkers, N.Y., Apr. 16, 1953; d. Louis and Bernice (Cooper) S. BA cum laude Psychology, Hunter Coll., 1979; MSW, NYU, 1982; CSW, N.Y.S., 1982. Cert. in psychoanalytic psychotherapy, Psychoanalytic Inst. of N.Y. Counseling and Guidance Svc., 1985. Pvt. practice psychotherapy N.Y.C., 1983—; social work supr./coordinator services for handicapped Plaza Head Start, N.Y.C., 1983-85; client coordinator Young Adult Inst., N.Y.C., 1985-88; mem. adj. field faculty Grad. Sch. Social Service, Fordham U., N.Y.C., 1986-87, Sch. Social Work, Hunter Coll., N.Y.C., 1987-88; coord. patient care svcs. Achievement and Guidance Ctrs. Am. Inc., N.Y.C., 1988-89. Recipient Service award Young Adult Inst., 1987; N.Y.C. Youth Bur. grantee, 1983-85. Mem. Acad. Cert. Social Workers, Nat. Assn. Social Workers, N.Y. State Soc. Clin. Social Work Psychotherapists (fellow), Am. Orthopsychiatric Assn., NAFE. Office: 110 East End Ave Suite 19 New York NY 10028

STARKE, MARY CELNIK, psychology professor; b. May 6, 1947; d. David and Eva (Rauf) Celnik; m. Charles L. Starke, Aug. 25, 1968; children: Katherine, Robert. BA summa cum laude, U. Pa., 1968; PhD, SUNY, Stonebrook, 1972. Cert. in clin. psychology. Prof. Ramapo Coll., Mahwah, N.J., 1972—; cons. Point of Woods Sch.-NIMH, Stonybrook, 1972-74, Inst. for Devel. of Human Resources, N.Y.C., 1973-74, Inst. for Behavior Therapy, N.Y.C., 1974-76, Harvey Resnick Psychiat. Assocs., Greenbelt, Md., 1976-78. Author: College Survival, 1987, Survival Skills for College, 1990; contbr. articles to profl. jours. Recipient Woodrow Wilson fellowship Woodrow Wilson Found., 1968, NDEA fellowship U.S. Govt., 1968-71. Mem. Am. Psychol. Assn., Eastern Psychol. Assn., Westchester Psychol. Assn., N.J. Psychol. Assn., Assn. for Advancement Behavior Therapy, Phi Beta Kappa. Office: Ramapo Coll SSHS Mahwah NJ 07430

STARKE, SANDRA, municipal government executive; b. Binghamton, N.Y., June 6, 1959; d. Thomas and Barbara Starke. BA in Pub. Justice, SUNY, 1981; MA in Pub. Fin., SUNY, Albany, 1983. Policy scholar N.Y. State Sears Grant Inst., Albany, 1983-87; budget analyst City of Albany, 1984-86, asst. budget dir., 1986, dep. budget dir., 1987—; treas. steering com. Capital Leadership, Albany, 1988—. Vice pres., treas. The Vol. Ctr., Albany, 1986—; vice pres. Community Svc. Sentencing Program, Albany, 1986—; panel mem. Auto Cap, Albany, 1988—; mem. League Women Voters, Albany, 1982-84. Mem. Am. Soc. Pub. Adminstrs. Office: City of Albany Eagle St Albany NY 12207

STARKMAN, BETTY PROVIZER, genealogist, writer, educator; b. Detroit, July 18, 1929; d. Jack and Rose (Bodenstein) Provizer; m. Morris Starkman, Dec. 25, 1952; children: Susan Lynn Starkman Rott, Robert David Starkman. AB, Wayne State U., 1951; postgrad., U.Wis., 1949; MA, Wayne U., 1954. Cert. social worker. Social worker Wayne County Social Aid, Detroit, 1951-54, B'Nai B'Rith Youth Orgn., Detroit, 1951-54; genealogist, historian Birmingham, Mich., 1979—; tchr. Midrasha Coll., Southfield, Mich., 1986-88, Coll. Jewish Studies, Birmingham, 1986-88; lectr. Jewish Community Ctr., West Bloomfield, Mich., 1986-89. Editor jour. Generations, 1986; contbr. articles to Jwish News, Generations, Search, others. Bd. dirs. Anti Defamation League, Detroit, 1980—, Jewish Community Council, Southfield, 1980—, Tribute Fund, Detroit, 1979-85; v.p. Maimonides, Detroit, 1966-67. Recipient 8 Gold Keys for debate and oratory, Wayne U., 1947-51; Humanitarian award State of Israel Bonds, 1980, Helping Hand award Israel Red Cross, 1980. Mem. Jewish Genealogy Soc. Mich. (founder, pres. 1984-86), Jewish Genealogy Soc. Ill., Jewish Genealogy Soc. Inc., Jewish Hist. Soc. (Mich. bd. dirs. 1986-88), Jewish genealogy socs. L.A., Phila., Washington, Toronto. Home and office: 1260 Stuyvessant Birmingham MI 48010

STARK WALSH, LISA CATHERINE, public relations executive; b. Amityville, N.Y., Mar. 10, 1955; d. Warren Alfred and Jean Anne (Baldwin) Stark; m. Francis Eugene Walsh, Dec. 20, 1981; 1 child, Benjamin Francis Walsh. BA, Alfred (N.Y.) U., 1977; MA in Pub. Relations, Ball State U., Muncie, Ind., 1981. Writer George B. Buck Cons., N.Y.C., 1977-79; communications asst. Tex. Med. Assn., Austin, 1982-86; asst. dir. pub. relations Tex. Med. Assn., 1986-88, dir. pub. relations, 1988—; pres. bd. dirs. Austin Wilderness Counseling Svcs., 1986-87. Mem. pub. info. com. Am. Cancer Soc., Austin, 1987—; vol. Loguna Gloria Art Mus., Austin, 1986. Recipient Best of Austin award IHBC, 1989. Mem. Pub. Rels. Soc. Am. (pres. 1985-86, chmn. southwest dist. 1988-89, Austin Star award 1989). Office: 1801 N Lamar Austin TX 78701

STARR, ILA MAE, teacher; b. La Grande, Oreg., Dec. 27, 1917; d. Samuel Fulmer Andrew and Ida Luella Perry; m. James Marion Starr, Mar. 2, 1940; children: Jacqueline Ann Starr Brandon, James Steven Starr. BA, U. Wash., 1939; BS, Eastern Oreg. Coll., LaGrande, Oreg., 1960, Tchr. Cert. Oreg., 1940. Cert. Wash. 1962, Calif. 1974. Mus. tchr. La Grande (Oreg.) Pub. Schs., 1939-40; girl scout exec. Girl Scouts of Am., Grand Coulee, Wash., 1940-41; Elem. Sch. Tchr. Centralia (Wash.) Pub. Schs., 1954; elem. sch. tchr. Wenatchee (Wash.) Pub. Schs., 1956-64, Lancaster (Calif.) Pub. Schs., 1964-68, Marysville (Calif.) Pub. Schs., 1968-79; pvt. mus. tchr., Seattle, Grand Coulee and Wenatchee, Wash., 1940—. Bd. dirs. Community Concert Assn., Yuba City, Calif., 1986-88; inspiration chmn. Republican Women, Yuba City, 1986-88. Recipient Hon. Pub. Sch. Award, Masonic Lodge 437, Lancaster, 1966; Nominee for Tchr. of Yr., Marysville Pub. Schs., 1978. Mem. Am. Assn. U. Women (program v.p. 1976; Grant Honoree 1977), PTA (hon. life mem. 1965), The Seminar Club (program chmn.), Innerwheel Club (pres. 1985-86). Mem. LDS Ch.

STARR, KIMBERLY GAIL, legislative research analyst; b. Ames, Iowa, Nov. 24, 1960; d. Paul Richard Jr. and Gail Marie (Walker) Josephson; m. Kenneth Irving Starr, Oct. 30, 1960. BA in Internat. Affairs, U. Colo., 1982, MBA, 1986. Sales assoc. May D&F Dept. Store, Ft. Collins, Colo., 1982-84; asst. dept. mgr. May D&F Dept. Store, Boulder, Colo., 1984-85; program and budget analyst Ariz. State U., Tempe, 1986-89; legis. rsch. analyst senate appropriations com. Ariz. State Senate, Phoenix, 1990—. Mem. Corvette Club of Ariz. (sec. Mesa chpt. 1988—). Republican. Methodist. Home: 2237 E Flossmoor Mesa AZ 85204 Office: Ariz State Senate Rsch Staff 1700 W Washington Phoenix AZ 85007

STARR, MIRIAM CAROLYN, telecommunications company executive; b. Pitts., Apr. 13, 1951; d. Donald Curtis and Virginia Ruth (Weise) S. BS in Math., Bucknell U., 1973; MBA in Fin., Drexel U., 1984. Mgmt. trainee Bell Pa., Allentown, 1973-75; equipment engr. Bell Pa., Phila., 1975-76, short range planner, 1976-77; chief switchman Bell Pa., Langhorne, 1977-78; long range planner Bell Pa., Phila., 1978-80, cost analyst, 1980-81, forecaster, 1981-83; inventory analyst AT&T, Parsippany, N.J., 1983-85, budget analyst, 1985-87, expense analyst, 1987-88, asst. controller gen. bus. systems, 1988-90, regional fin. mgr., 1990—. Treas. Stone Run II Neighborhood Assn., 1987-90, trustee, 1989-90. Mem. NAFE, Am. Soc. Profl. and Exec. Women, Delta Zeta. Home: 22 Springacre Irvine CA 92714 Office: AT&T 3355 Michelson Dr Ste 400 Irvine CA 92715

STARR, NANCY HAMBURGER, dentist; b. Lynn, Mass., Jan. 4, 1958; d. Joseph Murray and Sally Rose (Barry) Hamburger; m. Steven Frederick Starr, Oct. 6, 1985; 1 child, Zachary Aaron. BA, Brandeis U., 1980; DMD, Tufts U., 1983. Resident gen. dentistry Bellevue Hosp., N.Y.C., 1984; emergency med. technician Commonwealth Mass., Boston, 1977-81; dental hygienist Natick, Mass., 1982-83; preceptor in temporomandibular joint pain and dysfunction L.I. Jewish Hosp., Manhasset, N.Y., 1984-85; pvt. practice gen. dentistry N.Y., 1984—; gen. dentist Einstein Coll. Medicine, Bronx, N.Y., 1989—; attending dentist, faculty practice Montefiore Med. Ctr., Bronx, 1989—, clin. instr. in dentistry, 1989—. Mem. Am. Dental Assn., Acad. Gen. Dentists, Am. Assn. Women Dentists, Am. Assn. Dental Schs., Dental Soc. State of N.Y., Alpha Omega Gamma (pres. 1982-83). Jewish. Home: 11-29 Jackson Ave Scarsdale NY 10583 Office: 411 Bronx River Rd Yonkers NY 10704

STARR, NINA KENNEDY, university official, educator; b. Greensboro, N.C., Feb. 2, 1942; d. Vernon Wilson and Nell (Wagoner) Kennedy; m. William B. Starr, Aug. 22, 1964 (div. Aug. 1985); 1 child, Renée Lynn. BA in Sociology, U. N.C., Greensboro, 1964, MEd in Counsling, 1966, EdS in Counseling, 1980, EdD in Edni. Adminstrn., 1987. Nat. cert. counselor. Rsch. assoc. Sch. Edn., U. N.C., 1980-83, assoc. dir. Ctr. for Ednl. Studies, 1983-87, acting dir., 1987-89, dir., 1989—, lectr. dept. ednl. adminstrn., 1989—; observing del. White House Conf. on Aging, Washington, 1981; mem. rsch. adv. com. Human Svcs. Inst., 1984-85; mem. planning com. N.C. Legislature-State Conf. on Ednl. Equity, 1988-89; adminstrv. coord. Collegium for Advancement and Schs., Greensboro, 1989—. Contbr. articles to profl. jours. Bd. dirs. N.C. Arts Coun., Raleigh, 1981-84, Family Life Coun., Greensboro, 1982-87, Adolescent Post Detention Program, Greensboro, 1986-87; trustee Guilford Tech. Community Coll., Jamestown, N.C., 1983-91. Grantee N.C. Gen. Assembly, 1989-91. Fellow Am. Orthopsychiat. Assn.; mem. Nat. Assn. Women Deans, Adminstrs. and Counselors, Am. Assn. for Higher Edn., Alliance for Internat. Edn., N.C. Assn. Women Deans, Adminstrs. and Counselors, Chi Sigma Iota, Phi Delta Kappa. Office: U NC Ferguson Bldg Greensboro NC 27412

STARR, PAMELA THOMAE, public relations executive; b. Englewood, N.J., Nov. 18, 1966; d. Charles William and Vicki (Kohler) Thomae; m. Robert Alan Starr, May 24, 1987. BS in Advt., Fla. State U., 1987. Communication specialist Heidrick and Struggles, Chgo., 1988-90, mktg. materials specialist, 1990—. Mem. NAFE, Mensa. Office: Heidrick and Struggles 125 S Wacker Dr 2800 Chicago IL 60606

STARRATT, PATRICIA ELIZABETH, writer, actress, composer; b. Boston, Nov. 7, 1943; d. Alfred Byron and Anna (Mazur) S.; AB, Smith Coll., 1965; grad. prep. dept. Peabody Conservatory Music, 1961. Teaching asst. Harvard U. Grad. Sch. Bus. Aminstrn., 1965-67; mng. dir. INS Assocs., Washington, 1967-68; adminstrv. asst. George Washington U. Hosp., 1970-71; legal asst. Morgan, Lewis & Bockius, Washington, 1971-72; profl. staff energy analyst Nat. Fuels and Energy Policy Study, U.S. Senate Interior Com., 1972-74; cons., exec. asst. energy resource devel. Fed. Energy Adminstrn., Washington, 1974-75; sr. cons. energy policy Atlantic Richfield Co., 1975-76; energy cons., Alaska, 1977-78; govt. affairs assoc. Sohio Alaska Petroleum Co., Anchorage, 1978-85; legal asst. Hughes, Thorsness, Gantz, Powell and Brudin, Anchorage, 1989—; pres. Starratt Monarch Prodns., 1986—; Econ. Devel. Commn., Municipality of Anchorage, 1981; actress/ asst. dir. Brattle St. Players, Boston, 1966-67, Washington Theater Club 1967-68, Gene Frankel, Broadway 1968-69; actress Aspen Resident Theater,

Colo. 1985-86; writer and assoc. producer Then One Night I Hit Her, 1983; appeared Off-Broadway in To Be Young, Gifted and Black; performed as Mary in Tennessee, Blanche in A Streetcar Named Desire, Stephanie Dickinson in Cactus Flower, Angela in Papa's Wine, Elizabeth Procter in The Crucible, Candida in Candida, Zeuss in J.B., Martha in Who's Afraid of Virginia Woolf, Amy in Dinny and The Witches, as Columbina in Servant of Two Masters, as Singer in Death of Morris Biederman, as Joan in Joan of Lorraine, as Mado in Amadee, as Mrs. Rowlands in Before Breakfast, as the girl in Hello Out There, as Angela in Bedtime Story, as Hannah in Night of the Iguana, as Lavinia in Androcles and the Lion, as Catherine in Great Catherine, as Julie in Lilliom, as First Nurse in Death of Bessie Smith, as Laura in Tea and Sympathy, as Amelia Earheart in Chamber Music; appeared at Detroit Summer Theatre in Oklahoma, Guys and Dolls, Carousel, Brigadoon, Kiss Me Kate, Finnian's Rainbow; asst. to dir. Broadway plays A Cry Of Players, A Way Of Life, Off-Broadway play To Be Young, Gifted, and Black; screenwriter Challenge in Alaska, 1986, Martin Poll Films; asst. dir. Dustin Hoffman, 1974; contbr. articles on natural gas and Alaskan econ. policy to profl. jours. Bd. dirs. Anchorage Community Theatre; industry rep. Alaska Eskimo Whaling Commn.; mem. Alaska New Music Forum. Mem. Actors' Equity. Episcopalian. Avocations: skiing, horseback riding, biking, hiking. Home: 1054 W 20th Ave #2 Anchorage AK 99503

STARRETT, CAM, personnel executive; b. Apr. 5, 1949; d. William Henry and Jeanne (Koop) Bocklage; m. Peter M. Starrett, June 14, 1986. BA in Polit. Sci., U. Cin., 1971. Sales specialist bookstore W.Va. U., Morgantown, 1971-74; dept. mgr. Filene's, Boston, 1974, asst. store mgr., 1975, buyer, 1976-77, store mgr., 1978-79, v.p. pers., 1980-85; sr. v.p. pers. Avon Products, Inc., N.Y.C., 1985-88; v.p. pers. and adminstrn. Maxwell Macmillan, N.Y.C., 1989—; bd. advisors Catalyst, N.Y.C., 1986-89. Contbr. articles to profl. jours. Bd. dirs. Tufts U. Women's Ctr., Boston, 1981-85, N.Y.C. Alcohol Coun., 1985-88. Mem. Conf. Bd. (advisor 1987-89), Human Resource Planning Soc. (bd. dirs. 1989). Office: Macmillan Inc 866 3rd Ave New York NY 10022*

STARRS, ELIZABETH ANNE, lawyer; b. Detroit, Jan. 1, 1954; d. John Richard and Mabel Angeline (Gilchrist) S. BA, U. Mich., 1975; JD, Suffolk U., 1980. Bar: Mass. 1980, U.S. Dist. Ct. Mass. 1980, U.S. Ct. Appeals (1st. cir.) 1980, Colo. 1983, U.S. Dist. Ct. Colo. 1983, U.S. Ct. Appeals (10th cir.) 1983. Assoc. Denner & Benjoya P.C., Boston, 1980-83; assoc. Cooper & Kelley P.C., Denver, 1983-86, ptnr., 1986—; instr. bus. law Bay State Community Coll., Boston, 1981-82. Leader Girl Scouts U.S., Denver, 1984-85; mem. Denver Young Dems., 1983; sec., adv. council Colo. Taxpayers for Choice, Denver, 1985-88. Mem. Mass. Bar Assn., Colo. Bar Assn., Denver Bar Assn., Mass. Assn. Women Lawyers, Colo. Women's Bar Assn. (bd. dirs. 1984-85, v.p. 1988-89), Colo. Def. Lawyers Assn. Roman Catholic. Home: 115 S Clarkson Denver CO 80209 Office: Cooper & Kelley PC 1660 Wynkoop #900 Denver CO 80202-1197

STARTZMAN, SHIRLEY KAYLEEN, education specialist; b. Elwood, Ind., May 5, 1946; d. Hubert A. and Wilma Jean (Hutcheson) S.; divorced; children: Jill Carmen Carlyle, Tracie Kayleen Carlyle. AS in Bus., Vincennes U., 1982; BS in Journalism, Ball State U., Muncie, Ind., 1985, MA in Adult Edn., 1990. Reporter Lawrence (Ind.) & Suburban Jour., 1965-67; asst. editor Soldier Support Jour., Ft. Ben Harrison, Ind., 1980-84, editor in chief, 1984-87; edn. specialist Ctr. for Army Lessons Learned, 1987-88, Staff and Faculty Devel. div., Soldier Support Ctr., Ft. Harrison, Ind., 1988—; referee Ins. High Sch. Athletic Assn., Indpls., 1973—; varsity softball coach Mt. Vernon High Sch., Fortville, Ind., 1989—. Contbr. articles to profl. jours. Active Triple H. Softball, Hancock County, Ind., 1986-90. With U.S. Army, 1970—. Mem. Ind. High Sch. Athletic Assn., Assn. of U.S. Army. Lutheran. Home: 10808 Hoosier Rd Fishers IN 46038 Office: Soldier Support Ctr ATSG-DTS Fort Harrison IN 46216-5590

STASCO, DAPHNE JO, financial executive; b. Bronx, N.Y., Oct. 1, 1942; d. Paul Joseph and Joan Marie (Grimaldi) Ott; 1 child, Vanessa. Assoc. Applied Sci., SUNY, Farmingdale, 1962; BBA, Hofstra U., 1964. CPA, N.Y. Sr. acct. Peat, Marwick, Mitchell and Co., N.Y.C., 1962-68; controller Grolier, Inc., N.Y.C., 1968-73; pvt. practice acctg. Manhasset, N.Y., 1973-78; controller Off-Track Betting Corp., 1978-82; v.p. real estate and facilities N.Y.C. Offtrack Betting Corp., 1982-84; chief fin. officer, asst. sec. Sunnydale Farms, Inc., Bklyn., 1984—. Mem. NOW (bd. dirs. Nassau chpt.), Am. Soc. Women Accts. (bd. dirs.). Office: 400 Stanley Ave Brooklyn NY 11207

STASER, BETTY JO, model; b. Santa Ynez, Calif., Dec. 6, 1921; d. Rudolph Frederick and Josephine (Estelle) Thies; m. Bruce Ingle Staser, June 6, 1944; children: Merry Anna, Jeffrey Bruce, John Rud. BE, U. Alaska, 1943, postgrad., 1975-76; postgrad., U. So. Calif., L.A., 1942, U. So. Calif., Berkeley, 1954. High sch. tchr. Vass (N.C.) Sch. Dist., 1945; projectionist U.S. Army, Lathrop, Calif., 1945-46; tchr. jr. high sch. Elsinore (Calif.) Sch. Dist., 1955, Ft. Bragg (N.C.) Sch. Dist., 1956-57; pvt. practice interior design Honolulu, 1972-79; model Hensley Agy., Anchorage, 1982-89; sr. model Carlson's Co. Models & Talent, Anchorage, 1989—; v.p. Star Cruise, Anchorage, 1988—; model Nordstroms A.C. Bang, Anchorage, 1982—; hostess Miss Am. Pageant, Anchorage, 1986-87; judge Miss Co-ed Am. Pageant, Anchorage, 1987. Mem. Anchorage Women's Club, Symphony League. Mem. Anchorage Women's Commn, Am. Legion Aux., Pioneers of Alaska. Home: 1351 Hillcrest Dr #306 Anchorage AK 99503 Office: Carlson's Co Models & Talent 4011 Arctic Blvd Ste 206 Anchorage AK 99503

STASI, LINDA, writer, producer, screenwriter, editor; b. N.Y.C., Apr. 14, 1947; d. Anthony John and Florence (Barbera) Stasi; m. John Rovello, Nov. 22, 1970 (div.); 1 child, Jessica Stasi Rovello. BFA, N.Y. Inst. Tech., 1970; postgrad., Hofstra U., 1971. Editor edn. Seventeen mag., N.Y.C., 1970-74; freelance writer, N.Y.C., 1974—; producer, creator, host Good Looks Line, 1979-81; pres. Linda Stasi & Assocs., Inc., 1978-84; editor beauty and health New Woman mag., 1984-86; editor-in-chief Beauty Digest mag., 1986-88; editor health and beauty Elle mag., 1987-88; beauty editor Cosmopolitan mag., 1988—; columnist Inside N.Y., N.Y. Newsday, 1989—; contract screenwriter, 1989—. Author: Simply Beautiful, 1983, Looking Good is the Best Revenge, 1984, A Fieldguide to Impossible Men, 1987; syndicated newspaper writer N.Y. Daily News and Tribune Syndicate, 1984—, Times of London Syndicate; feature writer Redbook, Mademoiselle, Cosmopolitan, Elle, Harper's Bazaar, Newsday, Washington Post; on-camera host, producer 5-part health series Disney Channel, 1983. Home: 20 Waterside Pla New York NY 10010 Office: Newsday 235 Pinelawn Rd Melville NY 11747

STAUB, ANITA (ANITA KILPATRICK), management analyst, educator; b. Oakland, Calif., Dec. 24, 1947; d. Homer Lenel and Martha Bernice Kilpatrick; m. Jay Palmer Eickenhorst, Dec. 9, 1983. BA with honors, U. Calif., Berkeley, 1971, teaching cert., 1974; postgrad., Calif. State U., Hayward, 1972, U. Calif., Berkeley, 1973-74, Calif. Pacific U., 1986—. Cert. secondary tchr., Calif. Substitute tchr. Marin County Schs., San Francisco, 1974—; civil engring. tech. U.S. Army C. E., Sausalito, Calif., 1974-76; substitute tchr. Hendersonville (N.C.) City Schs., 1976-78, Henderson County (N.C.) Schs., 1976-79; park technician Nat. Park Service, Flat Rock, N.C., 1978-81; park technician Nat. Park Service, San Francisco, 1981-83, voucher examiner, 1983-85; mgmt. analyst intern Headquarters 6th U.S. Army, San Francisco, 1985-86; mgmt. analyst Hdqrs. 6th U.S. Army, San Francisco, 1986-89, U.S. Dept. Treasury, San Francisco, 1989—; cons. for interpretive prospectus Golden Gate Nat. Recreation Area, Nat. Park Service, San Francisco, 1981, recording sec. EEO com., 1984-85. Co-designer: Alcatraz Island interpretive display, 1981. Mem. NAFE, Am. Mgmt. Assn., Am. Soc. Mil. Comptrollers, , Calif. Nature Conservancy, Nat. Audubon Soc., Mus. Soc., San Francisco Opera Guild, Stinson Beach Allied Arts Guild, San Francisco Regional Fin. Ctr. Employees Assn. (bd. dirs.), Marin Conservation League. Home: PO Box 913 Stinson Beach CA 94970 Office: US Treasury Dept Fin Mgmt Svc San Francisco Regional Fin Ctr San Francisco CA 94119-3858

STAUBER, LEAH JOYCE, controller; b. Bklyn., Jan. 29, 1957; d. Wolf and Fay S. AAS in Acctg., N.Y. City Coll., 1986; BBA in Acctg., Pace U., 1990. Controller Comml. Movers Inc., N.Y.C., 1987-; dir. The Network Line, Bklyn., 1987—. Mem. NAFE, Exec. Networks, Network for Entrepreneurs Women (cons.). Office: Comml Movers 549 W 25th St New York NY 10001

STAUBER, PATRICIA MARRON, wholesale hardware company executive; b. Rock Island, Ill., Nov. 8, 1923; d. Leo Lyons and Carolyn W. (Ladehoff) Marron; m. Edward G. Stauber, June 29, 1952 (dec. 1981); children: Constance, Edward. Grad. in nursing, Moline Pub. Hosp., 1945. Pres., chief exec. officer E. Stauber Wholesale Hardware, Waukegan, Ill., also bd. dirs. Office: Edward Stauber Wholesale Hardware 2115 Northwestern Ave Waukegan IL 60087

STAUBLIN, JUDITH ANN, financial executive; b. Anderson, Ind., Jan. 17, 1936; d. Leslie Fred and Esta Virginia (Ringo) Wiley; student Ball State U., 1954-55, 69-70, Savs. and Loan Inst., 1962-67, U. Ga., 1974, Wright State U., 1975; children—Juli Jackson, Scott Jackson. Teller, Anderson Fed. Savs. and Loan Assn., Anderson, 1962-64, data processing mgr., 1965-70, loan officer, 1970-72, v.p. systems, 1972-74, fin. systems mktg., 1974-76; fin. dist. mgr. data centers div. NCR Corp., Atlanta, 1977-81, nat. sales mgr. EFT services Data Center Div., Dayton, Ohio, 1982-83; fin. dist. mgr. EFT and data services So. Thrift, Atlanta, 1983—. Active United Way. Mem. Am. Savs. and Loan Inst., Fin. Mgrs. Soc., Ga. Exec. Women's Network, Am. Soc. Profl. and Exec. Women, Anderson C. of C. Home: 6115 Woodmont Blvd Norcross GA 30092 Office: 130 Technology Pk Norcross GA 30092

STAUDENMAIER, MARY LOUISE, banker, lawyer; b. Marinette, Wis., Mar. 13, 1938; d. Louis W. and Hildegarde C. (Schmit) S. BA, Mt. Mary Coll., Milw., 1960; JD, Marquette U., 1971; postgrad. in banking, U. Wis., 1980; postgrad. in bus., Harvard U., 1980. Bar: Wis., 1971. Tchr. math. Milw. High Sch., 1960-66; security analyst 1st Wis. Trust, Milw., 1966-68, trust adminstr., 1968-70; v.p. Am. City Bank & Trust, Milw., 1970-75; trust officer Marine Nat. Exchange Bank, Milw., 1975; v.p., trust officer Heritage Trust Co., Milw., 1975-77; pres., chief exec. officer, trust officer Stephenson Nat. Bank and Trust, Marinette, 1977—, also bd. dirs., chmn.; speaker on estate planning; bd. dirs. Campbell Bruce Oil Co., Marinette, TYME Corp.; chmn. Wis. Banking Rev. Bd. Bd. dirs. Marinette Area Econ. Devel. Corp.; trustee Marinette County Hist. Soc.; bd. govs. Mt. Mary Coll.; mem. fin. coun. and investment com. Cath. Diocese Green Way (Wis.); mem. Marinette Downtown Revitalization Com.; past chmn. Marinette Downtown Adv. Com.; past pres. Marinette Voyageurs Com.; mem. fin. com. Our Lady of Lourdes Ch.; past bd. dirs. Marinette Area Indsl. Devel. Corp., United Way Marinette and others. Recipient Touhey award Marinette Cath. Cen. High Sch., 1988, Mary Neville Bielefeld award Marquette U., 1989. Mem. Wis. Bar Assn. (bd. dirs. corp., banking and bus. law com.), Wis. Bankers Assn. (br. banking task force), Marinette County Bar Assn. (past pres.), Wis. Trustees Assn. (past mem. legis. com.), Ind. Bankers Assn., Marinette Area C. of C. (bd. dirs.), Marquette U. Law Alumni Assn. (past mem. bd. dirs.), Assn. Marquette U. Women (past bd. dirs.). Home: 24ll Riverside Ave Marinette WI 54143 Office: Stephenson Nat Bank & Trust 1820 Hall Ave Marinette WI 54143

STAUFFER, JOANNE ROGAN, steel company official; b. Coatesville, Pa., Oct. 15, 1956; d. Joseph Chester and Anne Mary (Kauffman) Rogan; m. Robert Lee Marvin Stauffer, Oct. 15, 1988. AS in Bus. Adminstrn., Harrisburg Area Community Coll, 1979, postgrad., 1986—. Store acct. Giant Foods, Harrisburg, Pa., 1977-79; payroll clk. Bethlehem Steel, Steelton, Pa., 1980-83, material and cost acct., 1983-86, cost analyst, 1986—. Mem. NAFE, Am. Bus. Women's Assn., Bethlehem Mgmt. Club, Steelton Plant Engrs. Club (sec. 1982-85, v.p. 1985-86, Pres. 1986-87). Republican. Roman Catholic. Home: 401 Sheetz Rd Halifax PA 17032

STAUFFER, LOUISE LEE, retired educator; b. Altoona, Pa., Mar. 31, 1915; d. William Thomas and Mary Hall (Schroyer) Lee; m. John Nissley Stauffer, Aug. 20, 1938 (dec. Sept. 1983); children: Thomas Michael, Nancy Kay, John Lee, Donald David. BA, Juniata Coll., 1936; postgrad., Columbia U., U. Pa., Pa. State U. Tchr. Latin, Middletown (Pa.) High Sch., 1936-41; tchr. English and Latin, Roosevelt Jr. High Sch., Springfield, Ohio, 1949-57; tchr. French, North High Sch., Springfield, 1957-63; ret., 1963. Mem. Moorings Property Owners Assn., Naples, Fla., 1983—; v.p. King's Port Club, Inc., Naples, 1983—; sec. Emmanuel Luth. Ch., Naples, 1987-90; bd. dirs., editor newsletter, membership chmn. rec. sec. Naples Community Hosp., Aux., 1985—. Mem. AAUW, Am. Assn. Ret. Persons, Women's League (Juniata Coll.), Founders Club (Juniata Coll.), Moorings Country Club.

STAUFFER, PEGGY, small business owner; b. Rochester, N.Y., Apr. 25, 1944; d. William Joseph and Jeanette (Sullivan) Kelly; divorced; 1 child, Vivian Jeanette. Grad. high sch., Rochester, N.Y.; student in art courses, Rochester Inst. Tech.; student, Rochester Bus. Inst. Staff James Le Chase, Gen. Contractor, Rochester, N.Y., 1980-84, C.P. Ward Gen. Contractor, Rochester, 1984-86; pres. Stauffer Constrn. Co., Inc., Rochester, 1986—. Recipient Aetha award, Rochester C. of C., 1989. Mem. NAFE, Nat. Assn. Women Bus. Owners, Nat. Assn. Women in Constrn., Minority Coun. City of Rochester, Women's Coun. City of Rochester, Eagles Club. Roman Catholic. Home: 3264 Edgemere Dr Rochester NY 14612

STAUTBERG, SUSAN SCHIFFER, communications executive; b. Bryn Mawr, Pa., Nov. 9, 1945; d. Herbert F. and Margaret (Berwind) Schiffer; m. T. Aubrey Stautberg, Jr., Dec. 10, 1979. BA, Wheaton Coll., 1967; MA, George Washington U., 1970. Nat. TV corr., Washington, 1970-74; White House fellow, 1974-75; dir. communications U.S. Consumer Products Safety Commn., Washington, 1976-78, McNeil Consumer Products Co., 1978-80; v.p. Fraser/Assos., Washington, 1980; exec. asst. to pres. Morgan Stanley & Co., N.Y.C., 1980-82; dir. communications Deloitte & Touche, N.Y.C., 1982—. pres. MasterMedia Ltd., 1986—; bd. dirs. States, Inc.; Author: Making It in Less Than an Hour, 1976, Pregnancy Nine to Five: The Career Woman's Guide to Pregnancy and Motherhood, 1985, The Pregnancy and Motherhood Diary: Planning the First Year of your Second Career, 1988, Managing it All, 1989. Mem., nat. chmn. adv. coun. Ctr. for Study of the Presidency, 1976—; mem. Phila. Regional Panel for Selection White House Fellows; bd. dirs. Schiffer Pub., The Berwind Found.; mem. Reagan-Bush Presdl. Transition Team; mem. Commn. Presdl. Scholars; State Dept. speaker various countries. Selected as one of Wheaton's 10 Most Outstanding Grads., Alumnae Assn., Wheaton Coll., 1982. Mem. Pub. Rels. Soc. Am. (bd. dirs.), Pub. Affairs Profls., Nat. Soc. Colonial Dames, Acorn Club, City Tavern Club, Cosmopolitan Club, Colony Club, Radnor Hunt Club. Home: 17 E 89th St New York NY 10128 Office: Deloitte and Touche 1633 Broadway 7th Fl New York NY 10019

STAVENHAGEN, SANDI, insurance company official; b. N.Y.C., Feb. 6, 1958; d. Monroe S. and Geraldine (Diamond) S. BBA, U. Ga., 1979. Risk mgmt. analyst Wallace Murray Corp., N.Y.C., 1979-80; asst. risk mgr. Bradford Nat. Corp., N.Y.C., 1980-82; dir. risk mgmt. Penn Cen. Corp., Cin., 1982—. Mem. leadership div. United Jewish Appeal, N.Y.C., 1981-85, now mem. directions comm., campaign com., exec coun., Cin. Mem. Risk and Ins. Mgmt. Soc. (chmn. new risk mgrs. 1981-83, mem. editorial adv. bd. 1981-85). Home: 992 Paradrome St Cincinnati OH 45202 Office: Penn Cen Corp One E 4th St Cincinnati OH 45202

STAY, BARBARA, zoologist, educator; b. Cleve., Aug. 31, 1926; d. Theron David and Florence (Finley) S. A.B., Vassar Coll., 1947; M.A., Radcliffe Coll., 1949, Ph.D., 1953. Entomologist Army Research Center, Natick, Mass., 1954-60; vis. asst. prof. Pomona Coll., 1960; asst. prof. biology U. Pa., 1961-67; asso. prof. zoology U. Iowa, Iowa City, 1967-77; prof. U. Iowa, 1977—. Fulbright fellow to Australia, 1953; Lalor fellow Harvard U., 1960. Mem. Am. Soc. Zoologists, Am. Inst. Biol. Scis., Am. Soc. Cell Biology, Entomol. Soc. Am., Iowa Acad. Scis., Sigma Xi. Office: U Iowa Dept Biology Iowa City IA 52242

STEADMAN, LYDIA DUFF, elementary school educator, symphony violinist; b. Hollywood, Calif., Dec. 31, 1934; d. Lewis Marshall and Margaret Seville (Williams) Duff; m. John Gilford Steadman, Apr. 14, 1961. Student, Pepperdine U., 1952-55; BA in Music Edn., U. So. Calif., 1957. Cert. spl. secondary music, edn. tchr., Calif. Instrumental music tchr. Lancaster (Calif.) Sch. Dist., 1957-62; instrumental music tchr. Simi Sch. Dist., Simi Valley, Calif., 1962-70, elem. tchr., 1970—; tchr. Polynesian culture, dances, games, 1970—; hist. play wright for elem. grades, organizer elem. sch. dance festivals; dir. All Dist. Orch., Lancaster, Simi Valley Schs., 1957-70; compile Japanese Culture Study Unit for elem. grades Ventura County. 1st violinist San Fernando Valley Symphony, Sherman Oaks, Calif., 1962-75, Conejo Valley Symphony, Thousand Oaks, 1975-81, tour concert mistress, 1980; 2d violinist Ventura County Symphony, 1981—. Pres. San Fernando Community Concerts, Van Nuys, Calif., 1982—. Mem. AAUW, NAFE, Bus. and Profl. Women (pres. golden triangle 1988-90, issues and mgmt. chair 1990, ways and means chair Coast dist. 1990, editor golden triangle news letter 1988-90). Republican. Mem. Ch. of Chirst. Home: 32016 Allenby Ct Westlake Village CA 91361

STEARLEY, MILDRED SUTCLIFFE VOLANDT, foundation executive; b. Ft. Myer, Va., Aug. 3, 1905; d. William Frederick and Mabel Emma (Sutcliffe) Volandt; student George Washington U., 1923-24, 25-28; m. Ralph F. Stearley, Sept. 19, 1931. Elementary tchr. Brent Sch., Baguio, Philippines, 1929-30; staff aide vol. services ARC, also acting chmn., Charlotte, N.C., 1943, staff asst., Washington, 1943-47, Gray Lady vol., Okinawa, 1950-53, Brazil, Ind., 1954; trustee Air Force Village Found., San Antonio, 1975-78, sec. bd., 1975-77; sustaining mem. Tex. Gov.'s Com.; mem. 300 com. Bexar County Republican Com.; mem. decoration com. St. Andrew's Episc. Ch., San Antonio. Recipient commendation ARC, Washington, 1943. Mem. Army Daus., Am. Legion Aux., Army-Navy Club Aux., P.E.O. (life), Am. Security Council (nat. adv. bd.), San Antonio Mus. Assn., Smithsonian Inst., Pi Beta Phi. Episcopalian. Clubs: Ladies Reading (hon. mem.) (Brazil, Ind.); Lackland Officers Wives, Bright Shawl (San Antonio). Home: 4917 Ravenswood Dr Apt 311 San Antonio TX 78227

STEARNS, BETTY JANE, public relations executive; b. St. Paul. Ph.B., U. Chgo., 1945, M.A., 1948; cert. advt. studies, U. London, 1949. Editor Chgo. Stagebill, 1948-49; sec. U. Chgo. Cancer Research Found., 1949; writer Chas. A. Stevens & Co., 1949-50; account exec. The Pub. Relations Bd., Chgo., 1950-53, v.p., 1953-63, sr. v.p., 1963-78, mng. ptnr., 1978-85; exec. v.p. Porter Novelli (formerly Pub. Rels. Bd./Needham), Chgo., 1985-88, sr. counselor, 1989—; chmn. bd. dirs. Sta. WBEZ, Chgo., 1980-84, now dir.; dir. Chgo. Apparel Industry Bd. Author, editor: Careers in Music, 1976, Winning The Money Game, 1979; editor-writer, producer: book, radio series Instrumental Odyssey, 1970. Bd. dirs. Bus. Vols. for Arts. Recipient Golden Trumpet award Publicity Club of Chgo., 1959, 64, 68-70, 72-73, 76-79, 84, 85. Mem. Pub. Relations Soc. Am. (Silver Anvil award 1972, 76, 82), Home Fashions League, The Fashion Group of Chgo. (pres. 1967-68), Com. of 200, Chgo. Network (dir. 1982-85, 1989—), Arts Chgo. Club. Office: Porter Novelli 303 E Wacker Dr Chicago IL 60601

STEARNS, E(LIZABETH) CAROLYN, medical adminstrative officer, consultant; b. Mooresville, Ind., Aug. 16, 1928; d. Gale Able and Ercie Louise (Smith) Rose; grad. Mooresville public schs.; m. William Joseph Sawyers, Sept. 6, 1946, (div. May 1951); children: William Joseph, Sherry Lou; m. John Pershing Stearns, Oct. 4, 1954 (div. Mar. 1980); 1 son, Dennis Gale. Sec., Lab. Equipment Corp., Mooresville, 1946-49; sec. to chief surg. svc. VA Hosp., Indpls., 1950-57, sec. radiology svc., 1963-64, sec. to chief med. svc., 1964-66, adminstrv. asst. to chief med. svc., 1966-70, adminstrv. officer med. svc., 1970-72; staff asst. med. svc. VA Hosp., Tampa, Fla., 1972-80, adminstrv. officer. med. svc., 1981-88, adminstrv. cons., 1988—; adminstrv. officer dept. internal medicine U. So. Fla. Coll. Medicine, Tampa, 1972—. Mem. bus. edn. adv. com. J. Everett Light Career Ctr., Indpls., 1969-72. Mem. NAFE, Adminstrs. of Internal Medicine Assn., Med. Group Mgmt. Assn., Nat. Notary Assn., Am. Soc. Profl. and Exec. Women, Hillsborough County Med. Assts. Assn., Fla. Med. Group Mgmt. Assn., Acad. Practice Assembly. Office: Dept Internal Medicine 12901 Bruce B Downs Blvd Box 19 Tampa FL 33612

STEBBINS, MARILYN MASON, elementary educator; b. Trenton, N.J.; d. Alvin Pitman and Ida Rose (Brogley) Mason; m. Richard L. Stebbins, June 29, 1957; children: Shelley, Scott Mason. BS in Elem. Edn., Trenton State U., 1973, MS in Edn., 1977, cert. prin., 1981, cert. reading specialist, 1981. Sec. Trenton Bd. Edn., 1952-57, Princeton (N.J.) Borough Bd. Edn., 1957-61; tchr. DiPolvere Pvt. Nursery Sch., Hamilton Twp., N.J., 1967-72; tchr. Monroe Twp. (N.J.) Bd. Edn., 1973-89, curriculum cons., 1989—; curriculum intern, 1987-88; peer reviewer Internat. Reading Assn., 1986—, pres.; com. chmn. Mercer County Juvenile/Domestic Conf., Princeton Junction, 1977—. Pres. West Windsor Fire Co. Aux., Princeton Junction; mem. Alumni Coun. Trenton State Coll., 1989—; elder Presbyn. Ch., New Brunswick, N.J.; soprano Trenton Chorale Soc., 1986-87. Named to Churchwomen of Yr., Christian Edn. Orgn., 1982. Mem. Nat. Storytellers Assn., Garden State Storytellers Assn., N.J. Reading Assn. (v.p.-elect 1990—, membership dir. 1985-88, state coord. 1988—), Monroe Twp. Edn. Assn. (v.p. 1988—), Kappa Delta Pi.

STEBBINS, SHERYL BETH, retail company executive; b. Erie, Pa., May 23, 1953; d. Roger Harold and Helen Virginia (Shirley) S. BS in Communications Edn., Calif. U. of Pa., 1975. Store mgr. Waldenbooks, Erie, 1977-80; field trainer Waldenbooks, Stamford, Conn., 1980-81, asst. buyer, 1981-82, buyer books, 1982-85, mdse. mgr., 1985-87, dir. mdse. buying, 1987—. Republican. Methodist. Home: 208 Flax Hill Rd Apt 42 Norwalk CT 06854 Office: Waldenbooks 201 High Ridge Rd Stamford CT 06904

STECEWYCZ, KATHLEEN ANN, nursing educator; b. Youngstown, Ohio, July 7, 1958; d. Peter and Dorothy (Kuzio) S. Diploma, St. Elizabeth's Hosp., Youngstown, 1979; BSN, Youngstown State U., 1982; MS in Nursing, Kent State U., 1989. RN, Ohio,. Staff byrse St. Elizabeth Hosp. Med. Ctr., 1979-89, instr. nursing, 1989—. Mem. AACCN (cert., pres. Northeastern Ohio chpt. 1987-88, bd. dirs. 1988-89, pres.-elect 1989—), Sigma Theta Tau, Phi Kappa Phi.

STECHER, CHERYL CHADURGIAN, management consultant; b. Sweetwater, Tex., Oct. 16, 1950; d. Jack M. and Francis F. (McCreary) Chadurgian; m. Brian Mark Stecher, Dec. 30, 1983; children: Chad Daniel, Leah Alexandra. BA in Math., Fla. State U., 1972; PhD in Psychology, U. Calif., San Diego, 1978. Asst. prof. Calif. State U., San Bernardino, 1978-79; dir. rsch. Evaluation and Tng. Inst., L.A., 1979-83; devel. specialist L.A. Community Coll. Dist., 1983-84; mgr. Arthur Young & Co., L.A., 1985-89; ptnr. Applied Mgmt. and Planning Group, L.A., 1989—. Contbr. articles to various publs. Sec., bd. dirs. Family Planning Ctrs. Greater L.A., 1986-89. Mem. Phi Beta Kappa. Office: Applied Mgmt/Planning Group 12401 Wilshire Blvd Ste 304 Los Angeles CA 90025

STECHER, EMMA DIETZ, chemistry educator, researcher; b. N.Y.C., Sept. 23, 1905; d. Nicholas and Emma (Weidt) Dietz; m. Paul George Stecher, Feb. 18, 1944 (div. 1965). BA, Barnard Coll., 1925; MA, Columbia U., 1926; PhD in Organic Chemistry, Bryn Mawr Coll., 1929. Postdoctoral researcher Harvard U., Cambridge, Mass., 1929-34; rsch. chemist Hercules Powder Co., Wilmington, Del., 1935-37; adj. instr. Moravian Coll. Women, Bethlehem, PA., 1938-41; asst. prof. Conn. Coll., New London, 1941-43; rsch. chemist Gen. Aniline Co., Easton, Pa., 1943-45; instr. Barnard Coll., N.Y.C., 1945-47, from asst. to assoc. prof., 1947-59, prof., 1959-71, ret.; adj. prof. Pace U., N.Y.C., 1971-83, ret. Contbr. articles to profl. jours. AAUW fellow, Munich, 1934-35. Mem. Am. Chem. Soc. (edn. guidance com. 10 yrs., alt. councilor 1968-72), Sigma Xi, Iota Sigma Pi (former pres. Columbia chpt.). Home: 423 W 120th St Apt 74 New York NY 10027

STECK, AMY, advertising executive; b. Muncie, Ind., July 22, 1963; d. Thomas Hershchel and Patricia (Jenkins) S. BA, Ind. U., 1985. Copywriter WERK Radio, Muncie, 1985; acct. exec. WZZY Radio, Winchester, Ind., 1986, Majestic Group, Inc., Indpls., 1986—. Office: Majestic Group 501 Majestic Bldg 47 S Pennsylvania Indianapolis IN 46204

STECKEL, BARBARA JEAN, city financial officer; b. L.A., Mar. 9, 1939; d. John Herschel and Bernice Evelyn (Selstad) Webb Banta; m. Jimmie Raeburn Lugenbeel, Feb. 16, 1957 (div. 1962); Leanna Virgina, Debra Lynn; m. Dale Robert Steckel, Mar. 16, 1962; 1 child, Richard Alan. AA in Bus., Anchorage Community Coll., 1975; BBA, U. Alaska, Anchorage, 1980. City clk., treas. City of Kotzebue, Alaska, 1973-74, city mgr., treas., 1974-76; grants adminstr. Municipality of Anchorage, Alaska, 1976-79, contr., 1979-82, mcpl. mgr., 1982-84, chief fiscal officer, 1984-87; fin. dir., treas. City of Riverside, Calif., 1988—; bd. dirs. ICMA Retirement Corp., Riverside

Community Ventures Corp. Mem. adv. coun. sch. bus. and pub. adminstrn. U. Alaska, Anchorage, 1982-85; bd. dirs. Anchorage Parking Authority, 1984-87, Police and Fire Retirement System Mcpl. of Anchorage, 1982-87, chmn. 1986; devel. com. mem. Am. Heart Assn., Anchorage, 1987. Mem. Govt. Fin. Officers U.S. and Can. (bd. dirs. 1984-87), Mcpl. Fin. Officers of Alaska (pres. 1981-82), Nat. Assn. Accts. (bd. dirs. 1986-87), Am. Soc. Women Accts., Calif. Soc. Mcpl. Fin. Officers (chmn. cash mgmt. com. 1989—), Mcpl. Treas. Assn., Calif. Mcpl. Treas. Assn., Internat. City Mgrs. Assn., U. Alaska Alumni Assn., Rotary, Soroptomist, Elks, Moose. Home: 6947 Gladys Rd Riverside CA 92506 Office: City of Riverside 3900 Main Riverside CA 92522

STECKER, BONNIE YANKY, public relations executive; b. Balt., Dec. 1, 1958; d. Arthur Emil and Bette Emma (Muhl) Yanky; m. Richard George Stecker, Sept. 29, 1984; 1 child, Julie Marie. B.A., Salisbury State Coll., 1979. Pub. relations specialist Md. Nat. Bank, Balt., 1980-83; employee communications specialist Martin Marietta Aerospace, Balt., 1983-87, pub. relations officer Family and Children's Services of Cen. Md., 1987—. Mem. Internat. Assn. Bus. Communicators (treas. Balt. 1984), Phi Kappa Phi. Office: Family and Children Services of Cen Md 204 W Lanvale St Baltimore MD 21217

STECKER, DEBRA ANN, communications executive; b. Mt. Carmel, Pa., May 8, 1958; d. Raymond Paul Stecker and Alice (Katinsky) Welliver. Diploma, Mt. Carmel Area High Sch., 1976; BA in communications, East Stroudsburg U., 1980; postgrad., Glassboro State Coll., 1988. Accounts exec. BenePlus, Phila., 1981-83; prodn. specialist Towers, Perrin, Forster and Crosby, Phila., 1983-87; adv., sales promotion supr. West Chem./Penetone Corp., Cherry Hill, N.J., 1987-89; advisor, pub. rels. mgr. Metrologic Instruments, Blackwood, N.J., 1989—. Author: Book of American Collegiate Poets, 1979, (hon. award). Mem. Am. Soc. Advt. and Promotion, Am. Mgmt. Assn. Roman Catholic.

STECKLEIN, JONETTE MARIE, aerospace engineer; b. New Orleans, May 1, 1962; d. Carroll Lee and Barbara Jean (Ritter) S. BS in Aerospace Engring., U. Tex., 1985. Engring. technician Fed. Emergency Mgmt. Agy., Thomasville, Ga., 1981-82; intern Lockheed Missiles & Space Co., Austin, Tex., 1982-84; engr. advanced programs office Johnson Space Ctr. NASA, Houston, 1985—. Mem. AIAA (sci. fair judging chair 1987, 88, student affairs com. 1986—, treas. Houston chpt. 1988-89), Bay Area Rd. Rally Orgn. (bd. dirs., designer 1985—), Sigma Gamma Tau (pres. Austin chpt. 1984-85), Tau Beta Pi. Home: 9237 Midvale Dr Shreveport LA 71118 Office: NASA-Johnson Space Ctr Mail Code ED23 Houston TX 77058

STECKLER, PHYLLIS BETTY, publishing company executive; b. N.Y.C.; d. Irwin H. and Bertha (Fellner) Schwartzbard; m. Stuart J. Steckler, June 3, 1956; children: Randall, Sharon Steckler Slotky. BA, Hunter Coll., 1954; MA, NYU, 1957. Editorial dir. R.R. Bowker Co., N.Y.C., 1954-69, Crowell Collier Macmillan Info. Pub. Co., N.Y.C., 1969-71, Holt Rinehart & Winston Info. Systems, N.Y.C., 1971-73; pres., chief exec. officer Oryx Press, Scottsdale, Ariz., 1973-76, Phoenix, 1976—. Chair adv. coun. Ariz. Ctr. for the Book; pres. Friends of Librs. U.S.A.; mem. exec. com. ednl. resources info. Ctr. U.S. Dept. Edn. Elected to Hunter Coll. Hall of Fame, 1985. Mem. ALA, Spl. Libr. Assn., Ariz. State Libr. Assn., Am. Soc. Info. Sci. (bd. dirs.), Info. Industry Assn. (co-chmn. west coast com., bd. dirs.), Phoenix Pub. Libr. Friends (bd. dirs.), Univ. Club. Home: 5024 N 45th Pl Phoenix AZ 85018 Office: Oryx Press 4041 N Central at Indian School Rd Phoenix AZ 85012

STECKLING, ADRIENNE See ADRI

STEEBY, PATTY JEANNE, travel management company manager; b. Allentown, Pa., Jan. 14, 1955; d. William Kepner and H. Jeanne (Wentz) King; m. William Michael Steeby, Sept. 13, 1980. A. Bus. Adminstrn., Schoolcraft Coll., 1975. Sales asst. Am. Way Svc.Corp., Southfield, Mich., 1975-77; exec. asst. Ramco-Gershenson, Inc., Farmington Hills, Mich., 1977-79, Harley Ellington Pierce Yee Assoc., Southfield, 1979-81; office mgr. Byron W. Trerice Co., Birmingham, Mich., 1981-84; corp. travel mgr. 3PM-McKesson Corp., Livonia, Mich., 1984-87; client rels. mgr. IVI Travel Mgmt. Co., Troy, Mich., 1987-89, nat. accounts mgr., 1989—; speaker and cons. in field. Mem. Assn. Corp. Travel Execs. (chartered, com. chair 1989, 90), Nat. Bus. Travel Assn. (cons., exec. edn. com. 1985-88). Presbyterian. Office: IVI Travel Mgmt Co 2690 Crooks Rd Ste 200 Troy MI 48084

STEEDMAN, DORIA LYNNE SILBERBERG, advertising agency executive; b. L.A., July 14, 1936; d. Mendel B. and Dorothy H. (Howell) Silberberg; m. Richard Cantey Steedman, Feb. 19, 1966; 1 child, Alexandra Loren. BA magna cum laude, U. Calif., L.A., 1958. Sec., receptionist MPO Prodns., L.A., 1959-60; asst. producer EUE/Screen Gems, N.Y.C., 1961-62, producer, 1963-66; producer Jack Tinker & Ptnrs., N.Y.C., 1966-68, Telpac Mgmt., N.Y.C., 1968-72; v.p. broadcast prodn. and account mgmt. Geer DuBois Advt., N.Y.C., from 1972, exec. v.p., 1985—. Recipient Andy award Art Dirs. Club, 1968, 71. Office: Geer DuBois Inc 114 Fifth Ave New York NY 10011*

STEEG, ROSE MARY, interior designer; b. Ft. Worth, Sept. 30, 1958; d. Galen Ernest and Rose Marie (Sautter) S. BFA, So. Meth. U., 1981; BS, U. Tex., 1985. Intern InterDesign Corp., Austin, Tex., 1984; owner, designer RMS Interior Design, Arlington, Tex., 1985-87, 89—; interior designer Gabberts Bus. Interiors, Ft. Worth, 1987-88; outside sales agt. Russell and Assocs., Dallas, 1988-89. Mem. com. laser program So. Meth. U., Arlington, 1987-89. Recipient Outstanding Work award Hist. Preservation Soc. Tarrant County, 1986. Mem. Am. Soc. Interior Designers (assoc.), Inst. Bus. Designers (affiliate), Illuminating Engr. Soc. N.Am., U.S. Fencing Assn., NAFE, U. Tex. Alumni Assn. (chmn. membership 1987—), So. Meth. U. Young Alumni Assn. (mem. com.). Office: RMS Interior Designer PO Box 120094 Arlington TX 76012

STEEGE, DEBORAH ANDERSON, biochemistry educator; b. Boston, Oct. 2, 1946; d. Wayne Franklin and Jane (Carpenter) Anderson; m. Robert Lee Hill, Apr. 10, 1982. BA, Stanford U., 1968; PhD, Yale U., 1974. Postdoctoral fellow dept molecular biophysics & biochemistry Yale U., New Haven, 1974-76, postdoctoral fellow dept. biology, 1976-77; asst. prof. dept. biochemistry Duke U. Med. Ctr., Durham, N.C., 1977-83, assoc. prof. dept. biochemistry, 1983—. Predoctoral fellow NSF, 1968-72, postdoctoral fellow Am. Cancer Soc., 1974-76. Mem. AAAS, Am. Soc. for Biochemistry and Molecular Biology, Am. Soc. for Microbiology. Office: Duke U Med Ctr Dept Biochemistry Box 3711 Durham NC 27710

STEEL, CLAUDIA WILLIAMSON, artist; b. Van Nuys, Calif., Mar. 19, 1918; d. James Gordon and Ella (Livingston) Williamson; m. Lowell F. Steel, Aug. 15, 1941; children: Claudia Steel Rosen, Douglas Lowell, roger Conant. BA in Art, U. Calif., Berkeley, 1939, secondary credential, 1940; MFA, Mills Coll., 1967. Tchr. art Greenville Jr./Sr. High Sch., Calif., 1940-42; faculty Calif. State U., Chico, 1967-69; pvt. tchr. art, Chico; one-woman shows include Laboudt Gallery, San Francisco, 1958, Witherspoon Bldg., Phila., 1959, traveling show with Old Bergen Guild to nat. galleries, 1971-84, Redding (Calif.) Mus., 1973, Central Wyo. Mus. Art, Casper, 1976, U. Portland 1976, U. Wis., LaCrosse, 1978, Purdue U., West Lafayette, Ind., 1979, Pratt Inst., Manhatten Gallery, N.Y.C., 1980, Creative Arts Ctr., Chico, Calif., 1980, 84; exhibited in group shows Santa Barbara Art Mus., 1951, San Francisco Arts Festival (award), 1953, Oakland Art Mus., 1954, San Francisco Women Artists juried shows, 1958, 68 (award), 72, 73, 75, 76, Crocker Mus., Sacramento, 1958, 59, 60, 65, 67 (award), 73, Richmond Mus. (Calif.), 1960, DeYoung Mus. Art, San Francisco, 1960, San Francisco Mus. Art, 1959, 61 (award), Legion of Honor Mus., San Francisco, 1960, Mills Coll. Gallery, 1962, 67, 78, Berkeley Art Ctr. Gallery, 1969, San Francisco Art Commn. Gallery, 1972, Brandeis U., Mass., 1973, Ohio State U., Columbus, 1973, Brandt Gallery, Glendale, Calif., 1978, 1987, Chico State U., 1979, 1987, Fisher Gallery, Chico, Walnut Creek Art Gallery and Sonoma State U., 1979, Pratt Inst., Manhattan Gallery, N.Y.C., 1980, 1980, Calif. Soc. Printmakers traveling show, 1981, juried show, Singapore and Switzerland, 1984, Purdue U., 1982, U. Wis.-Eau Claire, 1982, Nat. Gallery, Bangkok, Malmo, Sweden, 1984-86, gallery show, Tokyo, 1985, Pacific Art League Gallery, Palo Alto, Calif., 1986, Tokyo Met. Mus., 1986, U.S.-U.K. Print Connection Barbican Ctr., London, 1989, others. Bd. dirs. Creative Art Ctr., Chico, 1977-81, Omni Arts, Chico, 1979-82. Recipient San Francisco Mus. of Art Serigraphy award, 1961; trustees' scholar Mills Coll., 1935, others. Mem. Calif. Soc. Printmakers (v.p., dir. 1973-77), Los Angeles Printmakers Soc., others. Republican.

STEEL, DANIELLE FERNANDE, author; b. N.Y.C., Aug. 14, 1947; d. John and Norma (Stone) Schuelein-Steel. Student, Parsons Sch. Design, 1963, NYU, 1963-67. Vice pres. pub. relations and new bus. Supergirls Ltd., N.Y.C., 1968-71; copywriter Grey Advt., San Francisco, 1973-74. Author novels Going Home, 1973, Passion's Promise, 1977, Now and Forever, 1978, The Promise, 1978, Season of Passion, 1979, Summers End, 1979, To Love Again, 1980, The Ring, 1981, Loving, 1980, Love, 1981, Remembrance, 1981, Palomino, 1981, Once in a Lifetime, 1982, Crossings, 1982, A Perfect Stranger, 1982, Thurston House, 1983, Changes, 1983, Full Circle, 1984, Family Album, 1985, Secrets, 1985, Wanderlust, 1986, Fine Things, 1987, Kaleidoscope, 1987, Zoya, 1988; (non-fiction) Having a Baby, 1984, Star, 1988, Daddy, 1989, (children's) Martha's Best Friend, Martha's New School, Martha's New Daddy, Max's New Daddy, Max and The Babysitter, Max's Daddy Does To The Hospital, Message From Nam, 1990; contbr. poetry to mags., including Cosmopolitan, McCall's, Ladies Home Jour., Good Housekeeping. Office: 598 Madison Ave New York NY 10017

STEEL, DAWN, motion picture studio executive; b. N.Y.C., Aug. 19, 1946; m. Charles Roven; 1 child, Rebecca. Student in mktg., Boston U., 1964-65; student in mktg., NYU, 1966-67. Sportswriter Major League Baseball Digest and NFL, N.Y.C., 1968-69; editor Penthouse Mag., N.Y.C., 1969-74; pres. O'Dawn!, Inc., N.Y.C., 1975-78; merchandising cons. Playboy mag., N.Y.C., 1978-79; v.p. merchandising Paramount Pictures, N.Y.C., 1979-80; sr. v.p. prodn. Paramount Pictures, L.A., 1980-85, pres. prodn., 1985-87; pres. Columbia Pictures, 1987-90; trustee Am. Film Inst. Served as prodn. co. pres. for numerous feature films incluwing Flashdance, Footloose, Top Gun, Star Trek IV, Beverly Hills Cop II, The Untouchables, The Accused, Fatal Attraction, 1985-87. Bd. mem. Inst. for Study Women and Men, U. So. Calif. Mem. Acad. Motion Picture Arts and Scis. Office: Columbia Pictures Office of Pres Columbia Pla Burbank CA 91505

STEELE, ANA MERCEDES, government official; b. Niagara Falls, N.Y., Jan. 18, 1939; d. Sydney and Mercedes (Hernandez) S.; m. John Hunter Clark, June 2, 1979. AB magna cum laude, Marywood Coll., 1958. Actress, 1959-64; sec. Nat. Endowment for Arts, Washington, 1965-67, dir. budget and research, 1968-75, dir. planning, 1976-78, dir. program coordination, sr. exec. service, 1979-81, assoc. dep. chmn. for programs, dir. program coordination, sr. exec. service, 1982—; guest lectr. George Washington U., 1987; trustee Marywood Coll., 1989—. Author, editor report: History of the National Council on the Arts and National Endowment for the Arts During the Johnson Administration, 1968; editor: Museums USA (Fed. Design Council award of Excellence 1975), 1974; National Endowment Arts 1965-1985; A Brief Chronology of Federal Involvement in the Arts, 1985. Former reader Rec. for the Blind, N.Y.C.; former tutor Future for Jimmy, Washington. Named Disting. Grad. in Field of Arts, Marywood Coll., 1976; recipient Sustained Superior Performance award Nat. Endowment for Arts, Washington, 1980, Disting. Service award, 1983, 84, 85, 89. Mem. Actors' Equity Assn., Screen Actors Guild, Delta Epsilon Sigma, Kappa Gamma Pi. Office: Nat Endowment for Arts Nancy Hanks Ctr 1100 Pennsylvania Ave NW Washington DC 20506

STEELE, BEVERLY LOUISE, educator; b. Alexandria, La., Jan. 1, 1944; d. Herman Theadore and Beverly Noel (Porter) Rauh; m. John Roy Steele; children: Josh Oliver, Matt Edward, Anne Elizabeth. BA, San Jose State U., 1965. Tchr. Cupertino (Calif.) Unified Sch. Dist., 1965-69; cons. math. Houghton Mifflin Publ. Co., Palo Alto, Calif., 1969-71; author math. program Ednl. Devel. Co., Palo Alto, 1971; tchr. math. resource Los Gatos (Calif.) Unified Sch. Dist., 1972; reading specialist Aurora (Ohio) Unified Sch. Dist., 1972-73; leader teaching team Hudson (Ohio) Unified Sch. Dist., 1973-74; office mgr. Century 21 Steele Realtors, Jackson, Calif., 1981-88; tchr. math. and sci. Amador County Unified Sch. Dist., Jackson, 1988-89; tchr. Amador County Unified Sch. Dist., Sutter Creek, Calif., 1989—; sec., treas. Sierra Mercantile Inc., 1981—; ptnr. Computer World, Jackson, 1983-85. Chmn. Sch. Site Improvement Program Jackson Elem. Sch., 1984-87; bd. dirs. Polar Bear Swim Team, Jackson, 1988-89. Mem. Nat. Tchrs. Math., Calif. Tchrs. Assn., Sacramento Coun. Sci. Tchrs., Amador C. of C., Odyssey of Mind (state bd. mem. 1987-89, regional dir. 1987-89, coord., 1987-89, coach state finals 1990), AAUW (Amador br. 1st v.p. 1983-84, pres. 1984-86). Home: 14355 E Hwy 88 PO Box 455 Jackson CA 95642 Office: Amador County Unified Sch Dist 217 Rex Ave Jackson CA 95642

STEELE, CAROLYN ANN, educator; b. Libertyville, Ill., Feb. 1, 1946; d. Charles Allen and Marion Elsing (Decker) Hudson; m. James Howard Steele, June 27, 1970. BS, Bradley U., Peoria, Ill., 1968; MA, Bradley U., 1975; postgrad., Ill. State U., So. Ill. U. Tchr. Bolin Elementary Sch., East Peoria, Ill., 1969-70, Neil Armstrong-Oakview Sch., East Peoria, 1971-85, Lincoln Elementary Sch., East Peoria, 1986-88, Cen. Jr. High Sch., East Peoria, 1989—. Lobbyist, Peoria Coalition; coach Intramural Basketball, East Peoria. Bradley U. grad. assistantship, 1969. Mem. AAUW, NEA, Ill. Edn. Assn., Cen. Ill. Bradley Alumni Assn., E. Peoria Elementary Edn. Assn., Delta Kappa Gamma, Beta Sigma Phi (Woman of the Yr.). Methodist. Home: 1701 Highview Rd East Peoria IL 61611 Office: 601 East Washington East Peoria IL 61611

STEELE, ELLEN LIVELY, business development executive, publishing executive; b. Fayette County, W.Va., Jan. 22, 1936; d. Alfred French and Sarah Ellen (Pritchard) L.; student N.Mex. State U., 1962-74; m. Henry Gilmer Steele, July 20, 1981; children: Gregory Benjamin Pake, Seana Ellen Pake. Civilian adminstrv. officer Dept. Army, White Sands Missile Range, N.Mex., 1962-67; mgr. Kelly Services Inc., Las Cruces, N.Mex., 1967-85; pres. Lively Enterprises, Inc., Las Cruces, 1967-76; sec., treas. Adam II, Ltd., Las Cruces, 1973-77; pres. Symposium Internat. Inc., Las Cruces, 1977-78, Asset & Resource Mgmt. Corp., Organ, N.Mex., 1978-83; lit. agt., prin. Ellen Lively Steele & Assocs., 1979—; mng. partner AVVA III, Las Cruces, 1981-82, Internat. Alliance Sports Ofcls., Las Cruces, 1982—; mng. ptnr. Steele Lehnert, 1986-88; pres., chief exec. officer Steele Svcs., Inc., Las Cruces, 1988—; ptnr., exec. producer Triple L Prodns., 1986—; chief exec. officer Mithra Corp., 1989—; dir. mktg. Las Cruces Conv. and Visitors Bur., 1984-85; dir. Santa Rosa Resources Corp., Denver; exec. GASCO Internat. Inc., Las Cruces, 1981-82; mem. N.Mex. State Senate, 1985-89, co-chmn. higher edn. reform com., 1985, 86, mem. interim coms., jud. com., edn. com., criminal justice com., Human Needs & Aids com., vice chmn. Children and Family Needs and Human Svcs., 1988; mem. nat. conf. state legislatures; N.Mex. Federated Rep. Women, Am. Legis. Exchange Commn.; mem. task force El Paso Electric Co. Rate Moderation; mem. firearms preemtion statute rev.; pres. N.Mex. Film Found., Inc., 1987-88. Served with USAF, 1954-57. Mem. Internat. Assn. Fin. Planners, Sales and Mktg. Execs. Internat., Am. Mgmt. Assn., DAR, La Croisee des Chemins Bruxelles, Belguim, Order Eastern Star, Picacho Hills Country (co-chmn. bd. dirs. 1980-84) (Las Cruces). Episcopalian. Home: PO Drawer 447 Organ NM 88052

STEELE, EVELYN JANE, public relations and advertising executive; b. Berkeley, Calif., Feb. 14, 1911; d. Carlos Louis and Jane Catherine (Jensen) de Clairmont; grad. Munson Bus. Coll., San Francisco, 1929-30; m. Donald Dickinson Steele, May 8, 1932; 1 son, Donald de Clairmont. Pvt. sec., 1930-32; engaged in public relations, publicity and advt., 1940—; v.p., dir. Steele Group, San Francisco, 1977—; sec.-treas. Internat. Pub. Relations Co., Ltd., San Francisco; sec.-treas. Internat. Bus. Interface, Inc., Don Steele Advt. Pres. Ladies Aid Retarded Children, San Francisco, 1977-78, bd. dirs., 1978-88. Mem. Fashion Group (regional dir. 1965-67). Republican. Unitarian. Clubs: Metropolitan (dir. 1961-68), Order Rainbow Girls. Office: 703 Market St San Francisco CA 94103

STEELE, HILDA HODGSON, retired home economist, consultant; b. Wilmington, Ohio, Mar. 24, 1911; d. George and Mary Jane (Rolston) Hodgson; AA, Wilmington Coll., 1931, BS, 1935; MA in Home Econs. Edn., Ohio State U., 1941; postgrad. Ohio U., 1954, Miami U., 1959; m. John C. Steele (dec. Jan. 1973). Tchr., Brookville (Ohio) Elementary Sch., 1932-37; tchr. home econs. Lincoln Jr. High Sch., Dayton (Ohio) Pub. Schs., 1937-40, coordinator home econs. dept., traveling exptl. home econs. tchr., 1940-45, supr. home econs., 1945-81, cons., 1981—; program dir. Family Life Adult Disadvantaged Program, 1969-81. Mem. Ohio Farm Electrification Com., 1964-66. Mem. town and country br. career com. Miami Valley br. YMCA, 1948-59. Adv. bd. Dayton Sch. Practical Nursing, 1951—; adv. com. Dayton Miami Valley Hosp. Sch. Nursing, 1951-63; jr. adv. com. Montgomery County chpt. ARC, 1940-80; mem. com. United Appeal, 1970—; bd. dirs. (Ohio) FHA-HERO, 1979-81. Recipient Outstanding Service recognition Dayton Met. Girl Scouts U.S., 1987, Outstanding Contributions to Edn. and Practical Nursing award Dayton Sch. Practical Nursing, 1989, Appreciation award, 1989; named Woman Owner in Agr. Bus. Ohio Dept. Devel., 1990. Mem. Dayton area Nutrition Council, Am. Home Econs. Assn. (del. 1961), Ohio Home Econs. Assn. (chmn. elem. and secondary edn. com. 1947-51, co-chmn. ann. conv. 1961-77, mem. housing and equipment coms. 1965-68, chmn. found. com. 1979-81), Dayton Met. Home Econs. Assn. (pres. 1949-50, 60-61); Nat., Ohio edn. assns., Ohio Council Local Adminstrs., Dayton Sch. Adminstrs. Assn., Elec. Women's Round Table, Dayton City Sch. Mgmt. Assn. (charter), Ohio Vocat. Assn. (Disting. Service award 1981), Am. Vocat. Edn. Assn., Ohio Vocat. Edn. Assn., Phi Upsilon Omicron (hon.). Mem. Ch. of Christ. Mem. Order Eastern Star. Club: Zonta (pres. Dayton 1950-52). Research in pub. sch. food habits, 1957. Home: 1443 State Rte 380 Xenia OH 45385

STEELE, KATHLEEN FRANCES, state legislator; b. Kansas City, Mo., Oct. 28, 1960. Admissions counselor N.E. Mo. State U., Kirksville, 1980-83, assoc. dir. admissions, 1983-86, programming coord. dept. pub. svcs., 1986-87; Iowa, N.H. dir. Gephardt for Pres., St. Louis, 1987-88; mem. Mo. Ho. of Reps., Jefferson City, 1988—; chairwoman Freshman Dem. Caucus, 1989—. Sec. Project 2000, Kirksville, 1986-88; bd. dirs. Adair County chpt. ARC, 1987—. Recipient Young Careerist award Kirksville Bus. and Profl. Women, 1988. Mem. Nat. Conf. State Legislators, Nat. Order Women Legislators, Am. Legis. Coun., Coun. State Govts., Lions, Shriners, Beta Sigma Phi. Roman Catholic. Home: 18 Grim Dr Kirksville MO 63501 Office: Mo Ho of Reps 115-J State Capitol Jefferson City MO 65101

STEELE, KATHRYN ANN, charitable organization administrator; b. Oelwein, Iowa, Mar. 9, 1949; d. John William and Lucy Clara (Langreck) McNamara; m. Richard George Steele; children: Scott, Jennifer, Timothy. AA, North Iowa Area Community Coll, 1969; student, U. Minn., 1970. Sec. Oelwein Daily Register, 1976, Oelwein Area United Way and C. of C., 1978-86; sec. Oelwein Area United Way, 1986—, exec. dir., 1987—. Bd. dirs., Oelwein Concert Series, 1976-78; mem. citizens adv. com., Oelwein Sch. Dist., 1977; coach, Girls' Little League Softball, Oelwein, 1980, 81; bd. dirs. Conestoga coun. Girl Scouts U.S., 1978-84, sec., 1981-84; pres. Mercy Hosp. Aux., Oelwein, 1981. Recipient Our Lady of Good Coun. award Roman Catholic Archdiocese of Dubuque, Iowa, 1977. Mem. Oelwein Area C. of C., Bus. and Profl. Women (sec. 1987-89), Cath. Daus. Am., Sacred Heart Rosary Soc. (treas. 1975). Home: 503 1st Ave NE Oelwein IA 50662 Office: Oelwein Area United Way 9 1st St SW Oelwein IA 50662

STEELE, MARY M., interior designer; b. DeMotte, Ind., Mar. 22, 1936; d. Leonard and Mary Catherine (White) Swart; children: Clarke Evan Hockney, Caryn Lynn Whitehead; m. Ray Allen Steele, Mar. 10, 1984. Student, Purdue U., 1965, Ind. U., 1965-74, N.Y. Sch. Interior Design, 1974, Ethan Allen Coll., Danbury, Conn., 1987. Interior designer, dir. floor display Georgetown Manor Ethan Allen, Merrillville, Ind., 1974—. Trustee First United Meth. Ch., Valparaiso, Ind., 1988—; chmn., fundraiser South Lake County Bus. Contbrs. to Meth. Hosp.; den mother local Boy Scouts Am., 1962-64; Brownie troop leader Girl Scouts U.S., 1966-68. Recipient Daughters of Am. Revolutionary award for Citizenship, 1954, Circle of Excellence award, 1987, 89. Mem. Interior Design Soc. (v.p N.W. Ind. chpt. 1978-80, pres. 1980-81), Kappa Kappa Kappa. Republican. Home: 1265 Vanderburgh Valparaiso IN 46383 Office: Georgetown Manor/Ethan Allen 8000 Broadway Merrillville IN 46410

STEELE, MILDRED ROMEDAHL, educator; b. Boone, Iowa, Jan. 13, 1924; d. Joe and Gladys Madeline (Bonebright/Cree) Romedahl; m. Otto Scott Steele Jr., Sept. 4, 1947; children: Martha Steele Knepper, John Joseph, Timothy Scott. BA, Simpson Coll., 1946; MA, Drake U., 1968; Edn. Specialist, U. Iowa, 1973, PhD, 1982. Instr. Des Moines Area Community Coll., Ankeny, 1972-73, Drake U., Des Moines, 1973, 1977; coord. communication Cen. Coll., Pella, Iowa, 1977-90, emirita, 1990. Co-author: 101 Voices and Guide, 1973; author numerous poems and contbr. numerous articles to profl. jours. Chmn. Higher Edn. and Campus Ministry, Iowa, 1984-88, Adminstrv. Coun., Pella United Meth. Ch., Pella, 1988—, chair, bd. trustees, 1990—; bd. dirs. Bd. Fellows Sch. Religion U. Iowa, 1986-88. Mem. Nat. Assn. Devel. Edn. (nat. sec. 1988-90, chmn. 1987-88), AAUW, Pi Lambda Theta, Sigma Tau Delta, Delta Delta Delta. Democrat. Home: 906 E Third St Pella IA 50219

STEELE, PAMELA BUSHER, real estate leasing representative; b. Hartford, Conn., Nov. 8, 1962; d. Roger King and Marilyn Grace (Macdonald) S. AA in Mktg. Mgmt., Harper Coll., 1983. Adminstrv. asst. property mgmt. 470 Atlantic Ave Mgmt Corp, Boston, 1984-85; residential leasing rep. Toll & Isenberg, Boston, 1986; retail leasing rep. MCM Assocs., Boston, 1986-89, Natural Wonders, Santa Clara, Calif., 1990—.

STEELE, PATRICIA KAY, recreational facilities chain executive; b. Staunton, Va., June 16, 1958; d. Emil Vincent and Betty J. (O'Brien) S.; 1 child, Emily Margaret Jarvis. BBA summa cum laude, James Madison U., 1980. Instr., asst. mgr. Skatetown USA, Harrisonburg, Va., 1977-80; mgr. Skatetown USA, Charlottesville, Va., 1980-82; gen. mgr. for Va., Tenn., Mass., Conn., Fla. Skatetown USA, Verona, Va., 1982—; mgr. rental property, 1985-88. Coordinator fundraising Va. Assn. Retarded Citizens, 1979-84, Muscular Dystrophy Assn., Whitman, Mass., 1985, Am. Cancer Soc., Harrisonburg, 1986; active Charlottesville Community Devel. Block Grant Task Force, 1981. Named Top Fundraiser Va. Assn. Retarded Citizens, 1980. Mem. U.S. C. of C., Staunton-Augusta C. of C., Roller Skating Rink Operators Assn. Am. (5 yr. award 1985), U.S. Amateur Confedn., Skating Club (v.p. 1985—). Republican. Lutheran. Office: Skatetown USA Roller Skating Ctrs PO Box 307 Verona VA 24482

STEELE, ROSE MARIE, government agency administrator; b. Nettleton, Miss., Aug. 27, 1949; d. Clyde and Maggie (Pierce) Griffin; m. Danny Ray Steele, Feb. 1973 (div. 1979). BS, Miss. Valley State U., 1971. Remedial reading tchr. Holmes County Pub. Sch., Lexington, Miss., 1971-73; claims rep. Social Security Adminstrn., Detroit, 1973-76, field rep., 1976-78; social ins. supr. Social Security Adminstrn., Wyandotte, Mich., 1979-80; supr. Social Security Adminstrn., Atlanta, 1981-84, social ins. specialist, 1988, operations and security analyst, 1984-86; br. mgr. Social Security Adminstrn., Winder, Ga., 1986-88; adminstr., dist. mgr. Social Security Adminstrn., Rome, Ga., 1988—. mem. Women of Harvest, Decatur, Ga. 1988. Mem. NAACP, Atlanta Region Mgmt. Assn., Chapel Hill Bus. and Prof. Women's Club, Alpha Kappa Mu. Democrat. Home: 17 Downing St SE Rome GA 30161 Office: Social Security Adminstrn 600 E First St Rome GA 30161

STEELE, YVONNE POTTS, university administrator; b. Indiana, Pa., Oct. 8, 1957; d. Clyde Leslie and Mildred Lucille (Kepner) Potts; m. Bruce Robert Steele, Aug. 27, 1978. BA, Point Park Coll., 1979; MA, U. Pitts., 1989. Dir. media rels. Chatham Coll., Pitts., 1979-82; program editor Pitts. Symphony Orchestra, Pitts., 1982-84; dir. mktg. and pub. rels. Three Rivers Shakespere Festival U. Pitts., 1984-88; dir. publs. Carnegie Mellon U., Pitts., 1988-89, dir. mtkg. communications, pub. rep. rep. Coll. Fine Arts, 1989—; pres. Pitts. Savoyards, 1989—, bd. dirs., mktg. cons., performer, 1983—. Author, actress one woman-shows include Mrs. Shakespeare, 1989, A Quiet Place to Live, 1986. Theatre Arts fellowship U. Pitts., 1984-86, Presdl. Merit scholarship Point Park Coll., 1977-78, Scripps Howard Found. scholarship, 1975-76. Mem. Women in Communications, Inc., Sherwood Forest Theatre. Democrat. Methodist. Office: Carnegie Mellon U 5017 Forbes Ave Pittsburgh PA 15213

STEELE-HERMAN, LISA MICHELLE, real estate broker; b. N.Y.C., Aug. 3, 1964; d. Alan Norton and Roslind Joan (Roush) Steele; m. Douglas Glen Herman, Nov. 17, 1989. BA in Communications, Am. U., 1986. Real estate sales agt. Time Equities, Inc., N.Y.C., 1986-88, broker, 1988—.

Republican. Jewish. Home: 454-338 Prospect Ave West Orange NJ 07052 Office: Time Equities Inc 55 Fifth Ave New York NY 10003

STEELE-WILLIAMS, RHEA L., marketing professional; b. Chgo., June 20, 1958; d. Johnny and Deloise Steele; m. James H. Williams III, Mar. 21, 1987. BS, U. Ill., 1981. Systems engr. IBM, Oak Brook, Ill., industry specialist, MR; adv. market support rep. IBM, Chgo., mktg. mgr. Active Literacy Coun. Chgo.

STEENBURGEN, MARY, actress; b. Newport, Ariz., 1953; m. Malcolm McDowell, 1980; children: Lilly, Charlie. Student, Neighborhood Playhouse. Films: Goin' South, 1978, Ragtime, 1981, A Midsummer Night's Sex Comedy, 1982, Time After Time, 1979, Romantic Comedy, 1983, Cross Creek, 1983, Melvin and Howard (Oscar for best supporting actress), 1980, One Magic Christmas, 1985, Dead of Winter, 1987, End of the Line, 1987, Parenthood, 1989, Miss Firecracker, 1989; exec. producer, The Whales of August, 1987; appeared in Showtime TV's Faerie Tale Theatre prodn. of Little Red Riding Hood and (miniseries) Tender Is the Night, 1985; TV films: The Attic: The Hiding of Anne Frank, 1988; theater appearance Holiday, Old Vic, London, 1987. Office: care Internat Creative Mgmt 8899 Beverly Blvd Los Angeles CA 90048*

STEENECK, REGINA A., information systems specialist; d. Albert M. and Hilda M. (Fields) Aultice; m. Lee R. Steeneck; children: Bradley, Darren. BA, Va. Poly. Inst., 1970. Programmer AT&T Long Lines, White Plains, N.Y., 1970-71, So. New Engl. Telephone Co., New Haven, 1971-72; systems specialist Aetna Life and Casualty, Hartford, Conn., 1972-76; systems analyst and programmer Miles Labs., West Haven, Conn., 1976-77; cons. Blue Cross/Blue Shield Conn., North Haven, 1978-79; account mgr. AGS Computers, Inc., Mountainside, N.J., 1977-79; systems cons. Communications Design Corp., Stamford, Conn., 1986-89; sr. CICS programmer Westinghouse Communications Software, Stamford, Conn., 1989—; systems cons. RAS Assocs., Trumbull, Conn., 1979—; co-owner Sunshine Flowers, 1980-81. Bd. dirs., fin. sec., chmn. computer com., vacation Bible Sch. supt., memls. com. chmn, mem. women' soc. Holy Cross Luth Ch., 1979—. Mem. NAFE, Assn. for Computing Machinery, Trumbull Woman's Club (bd. dirs. 1980-88, newspaper editor, miscellaneous coms.), Conn. Jr. Women's Club (bd. dirs., newsletter editor, Dist. VIII rep.), Conn. Assn. for Children with Learning Disabilities, Trumbull Parents Children with Spl. Needs. Lutheran. Home: 211 Putting Green Rd Trumbull CT 06611

STEESE, RUTH JUNIA, retired educator; b. Wapello, Iowa, Mar. 29, 1907; d. Christian Becker and Anna (Bechler) Zimmerman; m. Paul Alexander Steese, Apr. 3, 1931; children: Peter B., Paul R. BFA, U. Nebr., 1928; MMus, U. Rochester, 1933; postgrad., Northwestern U., summer 1930. Tchr. music Fairmont (Nebr.) pub. schs., 1927-29, Houghton (N.Y.) Coll., 1929-31, Washington Irving Elementary Sch., Gates, N.Y., 1941-48, Indian Landing Elementary Sch., Penfield, N.Y., 1948-54; dir. music Penfield Cen. Schs., 1954-67; ret.; guest lectr./tchr. Nazareth Coll., Rochester, N.Y., summers 1954-55; lectr. various univs. Author: Choral Music in American Colleges, 1933; contbr. articles to profl. jours. Mem. N.Y. State Congress of Parents and Tchrs. (hon. life). Republican. Presbyterian. Home: 1148 W Market St #412 Akron OH 44313

STEFAN, JILLIAN MARIE, communications professional; b. Evergreen Park, Ill., Nov. 29, 1965; d. James Thomas and JoAnn Marie (Galminas) Dencek; m. Robert John Stefan, Sept. 23, 1989. BS, Ill. State U., 1987. Account exec. Ave. M., Chgo., 1987, Southtown Economist Newspaper, Orland Park, Ill., 1987-88; communications mgr. Fed. Signal Corp., University Park, Ill., 1988—. Com. coord. Fed. Signal United Way.. Office: Fed Signal Corp 2645 Federal Signal Dr Park Forest IL 60466

STEFANICK, PATTI ANN, surgeon; b. Linden, N.J., Sept. 25, 1957; d. John Joseph and Johanna (Breza) S. BA in Biol. Scis., Rutgers U., 1979; DO, U. New England, 1983. Intern Kennedy Meml. Hosps., Stratford, N.J., 1983-84; resident in gen. surgery, chief resident Met. Hosp., Phila., 1984-88; breast cancer fellow Meml. Sloan-Kettering Cancer Ctr., N.Y.C., 1988-89; pvt. practice breast diagnostic surgery Johnstown, Pa., 1989—. Mem. AMA, Am. Osteopathic Assn., N.J. Assn. Osteopathic Physicians and Surgeons (alumni com. 1988, 89), Pa. Osteopathic Med. Assn., Rutgers Alumni Assn., Rutger's Scarlet R Club. Democrat. Roman Catholic. Office: 1111 Franklin St Ste 030 Johnstown PA 15905

STEFANKO, LEONA EVANS, minister; b. Chgo., Jan. 25, 1945; d. Hyman and Sophie Shapiro; m. George Stefanko; 1 child, Tony. BA in Religion, Ottawa U., 1985; MA in Religion, Park Coll., 1988. Ordained to ministry, Unity Ch., 1986. Instr. Unity Sch. Christianity, Unity Village, Mo., 1985-86, dept. chmn., 1986-89; min. Unity Ch. Christianity, Pensacola, Fla., 1989—. Active theatre, U.S., Can., South Am., Asia, 1963-76.

STEFFAN, FREDA REININGA, retired educator; b. Cañon City, Colo., May 22, 1911; d. George Charles and Lottie Avesta (Laws) Vahldick; m. Manfred Reininga (dec. 1979); m. Carl Frederick Steffan (dec.); children: Myron Eugene, Larry Joseph. BA, Western State Coll., Gunnison, Colo., 1934; postgrad., 5 univs., Colo., 1953-79. Tchr. Otero County Rural Sch., La Junta, Colo., 1931-32, Aurora (Colo.) Pub. Schs., 1953-55, Westminster Dist. 50, Denver Pub. Schs., 1941-48; interviewer various rsch. cos., Denver, 1946-53; tchr. remedial reading Westminster (Colo.) Sch. Dist. 50, 1955-70; libr. Canon City Pub. Libr., 1970-74; ret., 1975; mgr. craft store, Cripple Creek, summers, 1970-75. Co-author: A Walking Tour of Historical Canon City, 1981, About the Avenues, 1987. Bd. dirs. Canon City Mus., 1980—, Canon City Mcpl. Mus.; hist. libr. Canon City Pub. Libr., 1985-87. Mem. AAUW, NEA, Assn. for Childhood Edn. Internat., Internat. Reading Assn., Fremont-Custer Hist. Soc. (bd. dirs. 1974—, past sec., W.T. Little award 1986), Southeastern Colo. Hist. Soc. (bd. dirs.), Colo. Territorial Daus., Colo. Edn. Assn. (pres. Acads County chpt. 1967), Canon City Geology Club (bd. dirs.), Federated Woman's Club, Zeta Tau Alpha. Republican. Methodist. Home: 404 Sherman Ave Canon City CO 81212

STEFFEL, SHEILA GORMAN, lobbyist; b. Syracuse, N.Y., July 5, 1959; d. Francis Leo Jr. and JoAnne Delaney (Hopkins) Gorman; m. James John Steffel, Aug. 1, 1987. BS, Cornell U., 1981. Intern, lobbyist Dist. 1199 Nat. Union Hosp. and Health Care Employees, N.Y.C., 1980; adminstrv. resident Bedford-Stuyvesant/Crown Heights Demonstration Project, N.Y.C., 1980; programs specialist N.Y. State Assn. Counties, Albany, 1981-82; program assoc., lobbyist Bus. Coun. of N.Y. State, Albany, 1982-85; asst. exec. dir. N.Y. State Assn. of Counties, Albany, 1985-87; govt. rels. cons., lobbyist Karoub Assocs., Lansing, Mich., 1987—; vice chmn. Empire State Orgn. of Youth Employment, Albany, 1983-85. Mem. Cornell U. Coun., Ithaca, N.Y., 1986-89, Mich. Women's Hist. Ctr., Lansing, 1988—; reader for the blind Albany Pub. Library, 1982-86; bd. dirs. Cornell U. Coll. Human Ecology, Ithaca, 1985-89, N.Y. State Future Bus. Leaders of Am., Albany, 1984-85. Democrat. Roman Catholic. Office: Karoub Assocs 200 N Capitol Ste 500 Lansing MI 48993

STEFFEN, TINA MARIE, journalist, home economist; b. Amarillo, Tex., Apr. 10, 1958; d. Lynn Troy and Mary Lou (Odell) Bavousett; m. Gary Edgar Steffen, June 6, 1981; 1 child, Christopher Michael. Student, Sam Houston State U., 1976-78; BS in Home Econs., Tex. Tech U., 1981. Cert. home economist. Lifestyle writer Big Spring (Tex.) Herald, 1981-82, lifestyle editor, 1982-85, dir. creative svcs., 1985-86; reporter edn. beat Daily Ardmoreite, Ardmore, Okla., 1987; freelance writer home econs. reference books and curriculum guides Tex. Edn. Agy. and Tex. Tech U. Home Econs. Curriculum Ctr., Lubbock, Tex., 1987-89; feature writer, fashion editor Lubbock Avalanche-Jour., 1989—. Author: Hospitality Services, 1990; contbr. numerous articles to newspapers and mags. Mem. Tex. Press Women (treas. Dist. 14 1990, 1st pl. award for hist. articles 1990), Nat. Fedn. Press Women (1st pl. award hist. articles 1990), Women in Communication, Inc. (chair freedom of info. com. 1990—), Am. Home Econs. Assn., Home Economist in Bus. Mem. Christian Ch. Home: 5310 38th St Apt A Lubbock TX 79414 Office: Lubbock Avalanche-Jour 710 Ave J Lubbock TX 79401

STEFFEY, LELA, state legislator, banker; b. Idaho Falls, Idaho, Aug. 8, 1928; d. Orawell and Mary Ethel (Owen) Gardner; m. Carl A. Hendershott, Jr., Apr. 16, 1949 (div. 1961); children: Barry G., Bradley Carl, Barton P.; m. 2d Warren D. Steffey, July 13, 1973; children: Dean, Wayne, Luann, Scott, Susan. Grad. Am. Inst. Banking, 1972. With Pacific Tel. & Tel., San Diego, 1948-49, Bank of Am., San Diego, 1949-52, Gen. Dynamics/Astro, San Diego, 1960-61; escrow officer, mgr. consumer loans Bank of Am., San Diego, 1961-73; real estate agt. Steffey Realty, Mesa, Ariz., 1978—; mem. Ariz. Ho. of Reps, Phoenix, 1982-86, vice chmn. banking and ins. com., 1982-86, mem. house appropriations, judiciary, counties and municipalities coms., 1982—, chmn. counties and municpalities com., 1987—. Founder, Citizens Com. Against Domestic Abuse; precinct com. Legis. Dist. 29, 1978—, dep. registrar, 1978—; pres. Mesa Rep. Women, 1980; chmn. Mesa Mus. Adv. bd., 1981-83; del. to Rep. Nat. Conv., Dallas, 1984. Bd. dirs. Mesa Community Coun., 1985—, Ariz. Hist. Soc., Ariz. Life Found., Aide to Women Ctr. Mem. Nat. Order Women Legislators (v.p. 1987-88, pres. 1989-90), Am. Mothers Assn., Nat. Fedn. Rep. Women, Ariz. Fedn. Rep. Women (dir.), Ariz. Assn. of Women (dir.), Am. Legis. Exchange Coun., Pi Beta Phi. Mem. Ch. of Jesus Christ of Latter-Day Saints. Home: 1439 E Ivyglen St Mesa AZ 85203 Office: Ariz Ho Reps 1700 W Washington Phoenix AZ 85007

STEGALL, WENDY LEE, process engineer; b. Milw., Aug. 29, 1961; d. Roger McKee Hansen and Barbara June (Kovach) Hart; m. Bryan Hanson Stegall, Jan. 21, 1984. BSChemE, Auburn U., 1983. Jr. process engr. Engelhard Corp., Attapulgus, Ga., 1983-86; process engr. Engelhard Corp., Seneca, S.C., 1986-88; sr. process engr. Engelhard Corp., Edison, N.J., 1988—. Mem. Am. Inst. Chem. Engrs., Am. Soc. Quality Control. Office: Engelhard Corp Menlo Pk CN 28 Edison NJ 08818

STEGER-GRATZ, CHRISTINE, association publications editor; b. Detroit, Apr. 14, 1942; d. Chester and Josephine (Guy) Lonski; m. Douglas M. Steger, June 19, 1965 (div. 1983); children: Jennifer, Michael; m. James D. Gratz, Sept. 10, 1984. Student, Adrian (Mich.) Coll., 1960-62; BA, Ea. Mich. U., 1964; MA, Mich. State U., 1985; postgrad., Ea. Mich. U., 1967-68, 81-83. Cert. tchr., Mich. Tchr. English Tecumseh (Mich.) High Sch., 1964-68; tchr. adult edn. program Jackson (Mich.) Pub. Schs., 1975-79; tchr. English Lumen Christi High Sch., Jackson, 1979-83; mem. faculty Sch. Journalism. Mich. State U., East Lansing, 1983-87, publs. cons., adj. faculty Sch. Journalism, 1987—; mng. editor Mich. Dental Assn., Lansing, 1987-90, dir. communications, 1990—; corr. Jackson Citizen Patriot, 1985-86; freelance writer. Troop leader, conv. del. Jackson area Girl Scouts, 1977; mem. Queens Sch. Bd. Edn., Jackson, 1977-79. Mem. LWV (bd. dirs. Jackson County unit 1989-91), Women in Communications, Soc. Profl. Journalists (edn. com. 1989—, v.p. programs 1988-90). Home: 2223 Saines Manor Dr Jackson MI 49201 Office: Mich Dental Assn 230 N Washington St Ste 208 Lansing MI 48933

STEGGELL, SANDRA SUE, nurse; b. Wilmington, Del., Aug. 16, 1944; d. John R. and Mabel (Griffith) Fulton; m. Roger T. Underwood, June 12, 1967 (div. 1975); 1 child, Susan E.; m. Jack Steggell, Feb. 28, 1982; 1 child, Geoffrey. Diploma, Nursing Sch. Wilmington, 1969; BS, Wilmington Coll., 1982. RN, Del., Calif. Asst. head nurse Wilmington Med. Ctr., 1975-81; staff nurse Henry Mayo Newhall Hosp., Valencia, Calif., 1982—; coord., founder Infant and Pregnancy Loss Support Group, Valencia, 1988—; peer counselor Down Syndrome Support Group, L.A., 1990; organizer Down Syndrome Support Group, Santa Clarita Valley, Calif., 1990. Methodist. Home and Office: 27647 Open Crest Dr Saugus CA 91350

STEGMAR, PAMELA ANDERSON, communications executive; b. Sioux Falls, S.D., Dec. 16, 1959; d. Kenneth Wayne and Pearl Daisey (Sumption) A. B in Secondary Edn. & Bus. Adminstrn., Augustana Coll., 1982. Secondary tchr. West Allis (Wis.) Sch. Dist., 1982-83; network adminstr. Republic Telcom, Inc., Bloomington, Minn., 1983-85; telecommunications analyst Honeywell, Inc., Mpls., 1985-86, telecommunications specialist, 1986-87, supr. voice services, 1988—. Vol. Spl. Olympics, Mpls., 1985-87, Minn. Freeze Campaign, St. Paul, 1987; mentor Mpls. Bus. Mentor Program, 1986-87. Mem. Minn. Telecommunications Assn., Honeywell Women's Council, Kappa Delta Phi. Avocations: travel, reading, sailing, golfing, biking. Office: Honeywell Inc Honeywell Pla 5700 Smetara Dr MN02-1300 Minneapolis MN 55343

STEGNER, PHYLLIS YAWS, manager; b. Alton, Ill., Mar. 1, 1958; d. Phillip Andrew and Mary Jane (Huber) Yaws; m. Leslie Scott Stegner, . BBA in Mgmt., Texas A & M, Coll. Station, Tex., 1980. Compliance specialist Rotan Mosle, Houston, 1980-81; unit leader M Bank Dallas, 1981-84, mgr. funds, 1985, mgr. securities processing, 1985-86, mgr. asset service, 1986-87; mgr. asset acctg. M Trust Corp. N.A., Dallas, 1987--. Mem. Nat. Assn. Female Exec. Office: M Trust Corp NA PO Box 2320 Dallas TX 75221

STEIGER, BETTIE ALEXANDER, information industry specialist; b. Spirit Lake, Idaho, Jan. 27, 1934; d. Walter and Velma Esteline (Williamson) Alexander; m. Donald Wayne Steiger, Nov. 10, 1956; children: Craig Alexander Scott, Ann Alexander Carla. BS in Polit. Sci., Wash. State U., 1956, postgrad., 1957; AMP, Harvard U., 1987. V.p. Gartner Info. & Group, Inc., Stamford, Conn., Reference Tech. Inc.; exec. dir. Assn. for Image Mgmt., Silver Spring, Md.; dir. to prin. Rochester div. Worldwide Mktg. Xerox Corp., McLean, Va.; founder online system The Source. Founder Army Family Symposium, 1979; class sec. Harvard Bus. Sch., 1987—. Recipient Outstanding Alumni award Wash. State U., 1988. Mem. Nat. Womens' Econ. Alliance, Internat. Womans Forum (pres. 1985—), Army Officers Wives (pres. Greater Washington Area 1976), Info. Industry Assn., Videotex Industry Assn. (bd. dirs.), Am. Women's Club (pres. 1971), Pi Beta Phi (pres. alumnae prov. 1965). Republican. Presbyterian. Home: 6615 Malta Ln McLean VA 22101

STEIGER, JANET DEMPSEY, government official; b. Oshkosh, Wis., June 10, 1939; 1 son, William Raymond. B.A., Lawrence Coll., 1961; postgrad. U. Reading (Eng.), 1961-62, U. Wis., 1962-63. Legis. aide Office of Gov. Wis., 1965; v.p. The Work Place, Inc., 1975-80; commr. Postal Rate Commn., Washington, 1980-89, acting chmn., 1981-82, chmn., 1982-89; commr. and chmn. FTC, Washington, 1989—. Chmn. Commn. on Vets. Edn. Policy, 1987-90. Author: Law Enforcement and Juvenile Justice in Wisconsin, 1965; co-author: To Light One Candle, a Handbook on Organizing, Funding and Maintaining Public Service Projects, 1978, 2d edit., 1980. Woodrow Wilson scholar; Fulbright scholar, 1961. Mem. Phi Beta Kappa. Office: Fed Trade Commn Office of Chmn 6th and Pennsylvania Ave NW Washington DC 20580

STEIGERWALDT, DONNA WOLF, clothing manufacturing company executive; b. Chgo., Apr. 2, 1929; d. Harry Hay and Donna (Currey) Wolf; m. William Steigerwaldt, Dec. 31, 1969; children: Debra, Linda. BA, U. Colo., Colo. Springs, 1950, LHD (hon.), 1987. Ins. broker Conn. Mut. Life Ins. Co., Chgo., 1950-53; vice chmn. Jockey Internat., Inc., Kenosha, Wis., 1978-80, chmn., chief exec. officer, 1980—. Pres. Donna Wolf Steigerwaldt Found., Inc.; mem. Infant Welfare Soc., Evanston Hosp.-Glenbrook Hosp. Corp., N.W. Community Hosp. Aux., Aid to Animals No. Ill., Inc., Concerned Citizens Drug & Alcohol Coalition, Racine, Wis.; governing mem. Art. Inst. Chgo.; vice chmn. Carthage Coll., 1982—; bd. dirs. Sarasota Opera Assn.; mem. adv. bd. S.E. Wis. Coun. Boy Scouts Am. Paul Harris fellow, Rotary, 1984. Mem. Am. Apparel Mfrs. Assn., Navy League U.S., Glenview Hist. Soc., Exec. Women Internat. (hon.), Rotary (Paul Harris fellow 1984). Republican. Epsicopalian. Clubs: North Shore Country, Plaza, Valley Lo Sports; Meadows Country (Sarasota, Fla.). Office: Jockey Internat Inc 2300 60th St Kenosha WI 53140

STEIN, ADLYN ROBINSON (MRS. HERBERT ALFRED STEIN), jewelry company executive; b. Pitts., May 8, 1908; d. Robert Stewart and Pearl (Geiger) Robinson; Mus.B., Pitts. Mus. Inst., U. Pitts., 1928; m. F. J. Hollearn, Nov. 14, 1929 (dec.); children—Adlyn (Mrs. Brandon J. Hickey), Frances (Mrs. Ralph A. Gleim); m. Allen Burnett Williams, Dec. 5, 1955 (dec.); m. Herbert Alfred Stein, Nov. 28, 1963 (dec. Oct. 1980); 1 dau., Rachel Lynn (Mrs. Anthony Korzan). Treas., R. S. Robinson, Inc., Pitts., 1947—. Mem. Tuesday Musical Club, Pitts.; former mem. women's com. Cleve. Orch. Mem. DAR. Republican. Anglican. Clubs: Lakewood Country, Clifton (Cleve.). Home: 22200 Lake Rd Rocky River OH 44116

STEIN, BARBARA LAMBERT, marriage and family therapist; b. Detroit, Feb. 10, 1945; d. Joseph J. and Sylvia (Siegel) Lambert; m. David Joel Stein, Jan. 1, 1967; children: Craig Andrew, Todd Alexander. Student psychology Mich. State U., 1962-64; BA in Sociology, Wayne State U., 1966, postgrad. in psychiat. social work, 1972-74; MS in Counseling Psychology, Nova U., 1980; student, Art Inst. Ft. Lauderdale, 1985. Vol. abuse and neglect dept. Wayne County Juvenile Ct., Detroit, 1964-65; vol. D.J. Healy Shelter for Children, 1965-67; med. social worker Hutzel Hosp., Detroit, 1967-68; developer neighborhood teen drug program City of West Bloomfield (Mich.), 1970-71; med. social worker Extended Care Facilities, Inc., Birmingham, Mich., 1972-73; vol. group and occupational therapist Henderson Psychiat. Clinic Day Treatment Ctr., Ft. Lauderdale, Fla., 1977-78; pvt. practice family and marital therapy, Deerfield Beach, Coral Springs, and Boca Raton, Fla., 1980-85; mem. adv. bd. The Starting Place North, Pompano Beach, Fla., 1990—. Exhibited works (photography) at Iris Gallery, Boca Raton, Fla., 1989. Mem. Planned Parenthood, Simon Wiesenthal Ctr., Calif. Mem. Boca Raton Museum of Art (exec. chmn. antique show, sale and gala dinner fundraiser, 1988, co-chair mktg. mem. com.), The Friends of Photography, San Francisco, Mothers Against Drunk Driving, Sch. Edn. Bd. Temple Beth El of Boca Raton, until 1985; founding mem. Levis Jewish Community Ctr., Boca Raton; mem. adv. bd. The Starting Place North, Pompano Beach, Fla., 1990. Recipient cert. of Meritorious Achievement, Henderson Psychiat. Clinic Day Treatment Ctr. Mem. Am. Psychol. Assn. (assoc.), Wayne State U. Alumni Assn., Nova U. Alumni Assn., Photogroup Miami, Miami Design Preservation League, World Wildlif Fund, Friends of Photography of San Francisco, Nat. Trust Historic Preservation, Opera Soc. Ft. Lauderdale, Zool. Soc. Fla., Orton Dyslexia Soc., Assn. Children and Adults with Learning Disabilities, South County Jewish Fedn. (bd. dirs. until 1986, chmn. community relations council 1984-85, chmn. speakers bur. 1985-86).

STEIN, BETH ELLEN, elementary educator; b. Lafayette, Ind., Dec. 13, 1952; d. Kenneth Bartle and Merdith Annabel (Fowler) Cochran; m. Gary David Stein, Dec. 27, 1975; 1 child, Kent Adam. BA, Purdue U., 1975, MS, 1979. Cert. elem. tchr., Ind.; cert. tchr. gifted and talented, Ind. Elem. tchr. Twin Lakes Sch. Corp., Monticello, Ind., 1975-87; tchr. 5th grade North White Sch. Corp., Monon, Ind., 1987—; paper and yearbook sponsor Meadowlawn Elem., Monticello; active Meadowlawn and Reynolds Elem. NASA Young Astronauts, Rocket Club. Ind. state semi-finalist NASA Tchr. in Space program. Mem. NEA, Educator's Aerospace Edn. Assn., North White Classroom Tchrs., Ind. Sch. Tchrs. Assn., Psi Iota Xi (pres.), Alpha Nu (pres). Phi Kappa Phi, Kappa Delta Pi, Delta Pi. Republican. Methodist. Home: 1008 Hilltop Dr Monticello IN 47960 Office: Reynolds Elem Sch Gen Delivery Reynolds IN 47980

STEIN, CHERYL DENISE, lawyer; b. N.Y.C., Nov. 3, 1953; d. Arthur Earl and Joyce (Weitzman) S. BA magna cum laude, Yale U., 1974; postgrad., U. Chgo., 1974-75; JD, Yale U., 1977. Bar: D.C. 1978, U.S. Dist. Ct. 1983, U.S. Ct. Appeals (D.C. cir.) 1988. Atty. advisor CAB, Washington, 1978-79; assoc. Cohn & Marks, Washington, 1979-82; pvt. practice Washington, 1982—. Vol. reader radio reading svc. for the blind Washington Ear, Silver Spring, Md., 1982—. Mem. ABA, Bar Assn. D.C., Nat. Assn. Criminal Def. Lawyers. Democrat. Jewish. Office: 111 Massachusetts Ave NW Ste 200 Washington DC 20001

STEIN, ELEANOR BANKOFF, judge; b. N.Y.C., Jan. 24, 1923; d. Jacob and Sarah (Rashkin) Bankoff; m. Frank S. Stein, May 27, 1947; children: Robert B., Joan Jenkins, William M. Student, Barnard Coll., 1940-42; BS in Econs., Columbia U., 1944; LLB, NYU, 1949; grad. Ind. Jud. Coll., 1986. Bar: N.Y. 1950, Ind. 1976, U.S. Supreme Ct. 1980. Atty. Hillis & Button, Kokomo, Ind., 1975-76, Paul Hillis, Kokomo, 1976-78, Bayliff, Harrigan, Kokomo, 1978-80; judge Howard County Ct., Kokomo, 1980-89; ret., 1989; co-juvenile referee Howard County Juvenile Ct., 1976-78. Mem. Republican Women's Assn. Kokomo, 1980—; bd. dirs. Howard County Legal Aid Soc., 1976-80; dir. Howard County Ct. Alcohol and Drug Svcs. Program, 1982-89; bd. advisors St. Joseph Hosp., Kokomo, 1979—; bd. dirs. Kokomo Human Rels. Commn., 1967-70. Mem. law rev. bd. NYU Law Rev., 1947-48. Mem. Am. Judicature Soc., Ind. Jud. Assn., Nat. Assn. Women Judges, ABA (apptd. Ind. del. jud. adminstrn. div. 1987), Ind. Bar Assn., Howard County Bar Assn. Jewish. Clubs: Kokomo Country, Altrusa. Home: 3204 Tallyho Dr Kokomo IN 49602

STEIN, GERTRUDE EMILIE, educator, pianist, soprano; b. Ironton, Ohio; d. Samuel A. and Emilie M. (Pollach) S.; Mus.B., Capitol Coll. Oratory and Music, 1927; B.A., Wittenberg Coll., 1929, M.A., 1931, B.S. in Edn., 1945; Ph.D., U. Mich., 1948; piano and voice student Cin. Coll. Conservatory Music; cert. in piano Cin. Coll. Music, 1939. Music supr. Centralized County Schs. Ohio, Williamsburg, 1932-37; dir. jr. high sch. music, 1937-68, elem. music, 1968-71; mem. faculty Adult Evening Sch. Springfield (Ohio) Public Schs., 1951-68; head dept. music, asso. prof. piano and music edn. Tex. Lutheran Coll., Seguin, 1948-49. Donor, founder Rev. Dr. and Mrs. Samuel A. Stein Meml. Funds, 1955—. Mem. Am. Assn. Univ. Women, Am. Symphony Orch. League, NEA, Ohio Edn. Assn., Ohio Assn. Supervision and Curriculum Devel., Council for Exceptional Children, Assn. Tchr. Educators, Ohio Assn. Adult Educators, Associated Council Arts, Met. Opera Guild, Soc. Educators and Scholars, Am. Film Inst., Ohio Music Tchrs. Assn., Nat. Story League, Clark County Hist. Soc., Music Tchrs. Nat. Assn., Music Educators Nat. Conf., Nat. Assn. Schs. Music, Nat. Fedn. Music Clubs (spl. mem. Ohio), Fortnightly Musical Club, Amateur Chamber Music Players, Women's Assn. Springfield Symphony Orch., Springfield Authors Guild, Zonta Internat., Nat. Fedn. Bus. and Profl. Women, Phi Kappa Phi (hon.), Pi Lambda Theta (hon.). Lutheran. Contbr. articles to profl. jours.; research in field. Home: 133 N Lowry Ave Springfield OH 45504

STEIN, JANET ELLEN, civic worker; b. N.Y.C., June 9, 1955; d. Edward and Shirley Lucille (Freitag) S. BS, U. Hartford, 1976; MS, Hofstra U., 1979. Cert. spl. edn., nursery, kindergarten, elem. tchr., N.Y. Spl. edn. tchr. Valdosta (Ga.) Pub. Schs., 1976-78; ednl. evaluator N.Y.C. Bd. edn., South Ozone Park, 1978-79; spl. edn. tchr. N.Y.C. Bd. edn., Broad Channel, 1979-83; tchr. N.Y.C. Bd. edn., Bronx, 1983-84; religious sch. tchr. Temple Israel Valdosta, 1976-78, Temple Israel Jamaica, Holliswood, N.Y., 1978-84. Vol. Mental Health Assn., Ft. Lauderdale, Fla., 1987—; chmn. Plantation (Fla.) Adv. Com. for Handicapped, 1988—; chmn. Broward County Adv. Bd. for Disabled, 1988—; handicapped parking enforcement specialist Plantation Police Dept., 1988—. Recipient cert. of appreciation Am. Heart Assn., Orlando, Fla., 1987, Mental Health Assn., Ft. Lauderadale, 1988. Mem. Plantation C. of C., North Ridge Stroke Club. Home: 1380 SW 82d Terr Apt 711 Plantation FL 33324

STEIN, JODI LYNN, human resources consultant; b. Chgo., Dec. 5, 1959; d. Albert Morton And Phyllis Eileen (Orzte) S. BS, Ind. U., 1985; MBA, Keller Grad. Sch., 1986. Mgr. customer svc., purchasing, warehouse M.R. Enterprises, Chgo., 1984-86; sr. cons. Tom McCall & Assocs., Chgo., 1986—. Vice pres. Make-A-Wish Found., Chgo., 1986-87. Democrat. Jewish. Office: Tom McCall & Assocs 4145 Szuk Trail Richton Park IL 60471

STEIN, LINDA JOAN, commercial lending executive; b. Ridgewood, N.J., June 1, 1958; d. Herbert William and Dolores Ann (Suenderhauf) S. BS in Bus. Adminstrn., Bucknell U., 1980; MBA in Fin., Pace U., 1983; postgrad., Johns Hopkins U., 1988. Lic. ins., investments, securities broker. Internat. ops. mgr. Chem. Bank, N.Y.C., 1980-83, departmental contr., 1983-84; divisional contr. First Nat. Bank of Md., Balt., 1984-86; comml. lender, asst. v.p. First Nat. Bank of Md., Rockville, 1986—; fin. planner Lebowitz & Assocs., Ltd., Balt., 1985-87. Mem. Internat. Assn. for Fin. Planners, Balt. Chpt. for Fin. Planners, Montgomery County C. of C. Clubs: Columbia Athletic Assn. (Md.); Women's Internat. Bowling (Balt.) (team capt. 1986-87). Office: First Nat Bank of Md 15850 Crabbs Br Way Rockville MD 20855

STEIN, MARY See STEINMETZ, MARY DARLENE

STEIN, MARY KATHERINE, writer, editor, communications executive; b. Denver, Sept. 7, 1944; d. Robert Addison and Minta Mary (MacDonald) Dunlap; m. Lawrence Bronstein, June 29, 1970 (div. 1974); m. Donald L. Stein, Aug. 16, 1982. BS in Journalism, U. Kans., 1966. Sr. editor Am Family Physician mag., Kansas City, Mo., 1967-78; editor-in-chief Current Prescribing mag., Oradell, N.J., 1978-79; sr. editor Diagnosis mag., Oradell,

1979-83; mng. editor Advances in Reproductive Medicine, Bolton, Conn., 1983-85; pres. MD Communications, Laguna Niguel, Calif., 1983—. Author: Child Abuse, 1987, Caring for the AIDS Patient, 1987, Lifetime Weight Control, 1988, Substance Abuse, 1988, An Overview of HIV Infections and AIDS, 1989, Cardiovascular Disease: Evaluation and Prevention, 1989; mng. editor newsletter Eating Disorders Rev., 1990; contbr. numerous articles to mags. Mem. Women in Communications (pres. Greater Kansas City chpt. 1977-78, pres.-elect Orange County chpt. 1990-91), Am. Med. Writers Assn. Democrat. Lutheran. Home: 23791 Medinah Ln Laguna Niguel CA 92677 Office: MD Communications 23791 Medinah Ln Laguna Niguel CA 92677

STEIN, MINA BENEDICTE, librarian; b. Trosa, Sweden, July 19, 1933; came to U.S., 1958; d. Henry E. and Margit (Laeknaes) Anckarman; m. Benson I. Stein, Nov. 30, 1962; children: Erik Andrew, Thomas Frederik. Presch. degree, U. Upsala, Sweden, 1956; BS, Case Western Res. U., 1966; MS, U. So. Calif., 1981. Cert. tchr., N.J. Tchr. kindergarten Stockholm Bd. Welfare, 1956-58, Tenacre County Day Sch., Wellesley, Mass., 1958-59; instr. phys. edn. Pine Manor Jr. Coll., Wellesley, 1958-59; tchr. nursery sch. Cleve. Assn. for Nursery Sch. Edn., 1960-62; asst. children's libr. Cleveland Heights (Ohio) Pub. Libr., 1962-66; children's libr. Internat. Sch. Brussels, 1966-69; vol. ESL St. John's Internat. Sch. Brussels, 1972-83; children's libr. Mahwah (N.J.) Pub. Libr., 1984—; bd. dirs. St. John's Internat. Sch. Brussels, 1982-83; com. mem. youth div. Bergen-Passaic Libr. Coop., 1983—. Contbr. articles to Rendez-Vous jour. Bd. dirs. Am. Women's Club Madrid, 1969-71, founder librs. for mems., 1970; bd. dirs. Am. Women's Club Brussels, 1972-80, v.p., 1980-82, founder librs. for mems. 1969; den leader, coach Boy Scouts Am., Brussels, 1978-81. Mem. ALA, N.J. Libr. Assn., AAUW, USTA. Home: 22 Biscayne Dr Ramsey NJ 07446 Office: Mahwah Pub Libr 201 Franklin Turnpike Mahwah NJ 07430

STEIN, PAULA BARTON, international real estate executive; b. Chgo., July 29, 1929; d. Paul Everett and Helen (Taylor) Barton; m. Marshall Lowen Stein, May 29, 1954; children: George L., Guy Grant. BA, Lake Forest (Ill.) U., 1951; postgrad., Roosevelt U., Chgo., 1955-77, UCLA, 1978-79. Lic. internat. hotel and mgmt. broker, Ill. Adminstrv. asst. publicity Kefauver for Pres., Chgo., 1951-52; adminstrv. asst., writer Employers Assn. Am., Chgo., 1952; writer Woodworking Jobbers Assn., Chgo., 1953; cons. L.A., 1978-80; ptnr., pres. Steinvest, Inc., Chgo., 1980—; cons. Spindrift, Inc., hotels Nat. Diversified Svcs., Inc., Chgo., 1980—, Chatmar, Inc. Mem. Chgo. Coun. Fgn. Rels.; bd. dirs. Everybody's Village Art Ctr., Palm Springs, Calif., 1970; organizer New Trier West Fine Arts Assn., Northfield, Ill., 1976-77. Mem. NOW, Asia Soc., Cousteau Soc., Sierra Club, Alliance Francaise (chmn. various affairs 1947-89). Home and Office: Steinvest Inc 680 N Lakeshore Dr #1219 S Chicago IL 60611

STEIN, PHYLLIS ROSENSTEIN, educational program director; b. Hartford, Conn., Apr. 21, 1941; d. Nathan M. and Rachel (Schultz) Rosenstein; m. Maurice Robert Stein, Aug. 29, 1964; children: Paul Radin, Nina Rebecca Rosa. BA, Radcliffe Coll., 1963; MEd, Harvard U., 1970. Founder, coordinator Boston Area Reevaluation Counseling Community, Cambridge, Mass., 1971-76; dir. Radcliffe Career Svcs., Radcliffe Coll., Cambridge, 1976—. Home: 59 Parker St Cambridge MA 02138 Office: Radcliffe College 10 Garden St Cambridge MA 02138

STEIN, SANDRA LOU, educational psychologist, educator; b. Freeport, Ill., Oct. 6, 1942; d. William Kenneth and Marien Elizabeth (Dahlgren) S. BS, U. Wis., Madison, 1964; MS in Edn., No. Ill. U., 1967, EdD, 1969. Tchr. English Rockford (Ill.) Sch. Dist., 1964-65; tchr. Russian Jefferson County Sch. Dist., Lakewood, Colo., 1965-66; asst. prof. edn. U. S.C., Columbia, 1969-71, No. Ill. U., DeKalb, 1971-72; asst. prof. edn. Rider Coll., Lawrenceville, N.J., 1972-75, assoc. prof. edn., 1975-81, prof. edn., 1981—, dept. chair, 1983—; cons. on measurement and evaluation, women's edn., 1973—. Contbr. articles to ednl. publs. Treas. Lawrenceville Men's Breakfast Club, 1983-85; deacon Presbyn. Ch. Lawrenceville, 1984-87; contest judge N.J. Fedn. Bus. and Profl. Women, 1989; vol. Habitat for Humanity, Trenton, N.J., 1989. Recipient Disting. Teaching award Rider Coll. and Lindback Found., 1981. Mem. AAUP (Outstanding Achievement award Rider Coll. chpt. 1988), Am. Ednl. Rsch. Assn., Am. Psychol. Assn., Am. Assn. Colls. Tchr. Edn., Phi Delta Kappa (chpt. pres. 1986-87). Office: Rider Coll 2083 Lawrenceville Rd Lawrenceville NJ 08648

STEINBACH, ALICE, journalist; b. Balt.. Student, U. London. Feature writer Balt. Sun, 1981—; formerly dir. pub. info. Balt. Mus. Art. Recip. Pulitzer Prize for feature writing, 1985. Office: Balt Sun Calvert at Centre St Baltimore MD 21278*

STEINBACH, ELAINE THIELKE, product director; b. N. Tonawanda, NY, June 29, 1946; d. Norman Roland and Lucille (Knoell) T.; m. Robert Hugh Steinbach, June 19, 1965; children: Rebecca, Katherine. BS, Cen. Mo. State U., 1970. Tchr. Brklyn. Sch. Dist., 1970-73; mktg. mgr. Woodline Products, Villa Park, Ill., 1976-78; from asst. prodn. mgr. to asst. buyer Leewards Craft Stores, Elgin, Ill., 1978-81; buyer Ben Franklin Stores, Inc., Des Plaines, Ill., 1983-86; mktg. mgr. Ben Franklin Stores, Inc., Ill., 1986-87; dir. new prodn. devel. C.M. Offray & Son, Chester, N.J., 1987-88; import dir. Joseph Markovits, N.Y.C., 1988; product dir. Royal Cathay, South San Francisco, 1988—; mktg. com. Assn. of Creative Craft Industries, Zanesville Ohio, 1987-88. Mem. Hobby Industry of Am., Soc. of Craft Designers. Democrat. Lutheran. Home: 123 Coral Dr Orinda CA 94563 Office: Royal Cathay 570 Eccles Ave South San Francisco CA 94080

STEINBACH, LYNNE SUSAN, radiologist, educator; b. San Francisco, Dec. 28, 1953; d. Howard Lynne and Ilse (Rosengarten) S.; m. Eric Franklin Tepper, Aug. 14, 1977; 1 child, Mark Evan. Student, Vassar Coll.; BA, Stanford U., 1975; MD, Med. Coll. Pa., 1979. Intern Coll. Medicine and Dentistry N.J., Newark, 1979-80; resident radiology N.Y. Hosp.-Cornell Med. Ctr., N.Y.C., 1980-83; fellow musculoskeletal radiology Hosp. Spl. Surgery Cornell Med. Ctr., N.Y.C., 1983-84; asst. prof. radiology U. Calif., San Francisco, 1984—. Contbr. articles on radiology, chpts. on musculoskeletal radiology to profl. pubs. Mem. Radiologic Soc. N.Am., Am. Assn. Women Radiologists (mem.-at-large 1987-88, pres. San Francisco chpt. 1987-88, sec. 1989—), Am. Roentgen Ray Soc., Soc. Magnetic Resonance Imaging, Assn. Univ. Radiologists, Soc. Magnetic Resonance Imaging in Medicine, Am. Coll. Radiology. Democrat. Jewish. Home: 6 Burrell Ct Tiburon CA 94920

STEINBACH, SANDRA JOY, government executive; b. Waterloo, Iowa, July 24, 1950; d. Christopher G. and Joy J. (Johnson) S.; 1 child, Martin Jones. BS, Iowa State U., 1974; MA, U. Iowa, 1975. Dir. Seward (Nebr.) Pub. Library, 1976-78; first deputy auditor Johnson Co. Auditors Office, Iowa City, 1981-85; dir. of elections Sec. of State's Office, Des Moines, 1985—. Office: Sec of State's Office Capitol Des Moines IA 50319

STEINBERG, JANET ECKSTEIN, journalist; b. Cin.; d. Charles and Adele (Ehrenfeld) Eckstein; m. Irvin S. Silverstein, Oct. 22, 1988; children—Susan Carole Steinberg Somerstein, Jody Lynn Steinberg Lazarow. B.S., U. Cin., 1964. Free-lance writer; guest appearances Braun and Co., Sta.-WLW-TV. Contbr. numerous articles to newspapers, mags. and books, U.S., Can., Singapore, Australia, N.Z.; travel columnist Cin. Post, 1978-86, Ky. Post, 1978-86, Cin. Enquirer, 1986—; travel editor S. Fla. Single Living, 1988—; contbr. Singles Scene and Cin. Mag., 1980—; contbg. editor Travel Agt., 1986-88, Birnbaum Travel Guides, 1988—, The Writer, 1988—, Entree, 1986—; travel columnist Northeast mag., 1986-88, South Fla. Single Living, 1984—. Recipient Lowell Thomas travel journalism award, 1985, 86, Henry E. Bradshaw Travel Journalism award, 1st place, best of show, 1988. Mem. Am. Soc. Journalists and Authors, Soc. Am. Travel Writers (1st place award for best newspaper story 1981, 3d place award for best mag. story 1981, 1st place award for best newspaper article award 1984, best mag. article 1985, 2d place award best pathos article, 1984, 88, 2d place award specific category, 1989), Midwest Travel Writers Assn. (Best Mag. Story award 1981, Best Series award 1981, 84 Cipriani award 1981, 1st place award best article 1989, 2d place award for best article 1982, 83, 84, 89), Pacific Area Travel Assn., Internat. Food, Wine, and Travel Writers Assn. Club: Losantiville Country. Home: 2676 Fair Oaks Ln Cincinnati OH 45237

STEINBERG, JILL ENID, computer sales executive; b. Jersey City, Oct. 27, 1955; d. Edwin Jay and Renee Ruth (Kaufman) S. B.A., U. Miami (Fla.), 1979. Salesperson luggage Burdine's, Miami, Fla., 1979-80, asst. mgr. area, 1980-81, commn. sales advanced consumer electronics, 1981-83, asst. mgr. computer sales, 1983-87, mgr. Computerbanc booth, 1987—; participant Apple seminar, 1983. Named outstanding salesperson So. Region, Hartmann Luggage, 1980; mem. Burdine's B Club. Mem. AAUW (com.), Nat. Assn. Female Execs., Alpha Kappa Delta, Delta Phi Epsilon. Lodge: Hadassah (life). Home: 15725 SW 88th Ct Miami FL 33157 Office: Computerbanc at Burdine's 7303 N Kendall Dr Miami FL 33156

STEINBERG, MARCIA IRENE, national science foundation director; b. Bklyn., Mar. 7, 1944; d. Solomon and Sylvia (Feldman) S.; m. Nichael Flashner, Aug. 28, 1966 (div. 1978); 1 child, Eric Gordon. BS, Bklyn. Coll., 1964, MA, 1966; PhD, U. Mich., 1973. Rsch. scientist Meth. Hosp. Bklyn. Dept. Pathology, Bklyn., 1966-67, U. Mich. Dept. Surg. Rsch., Ann Arbor, Mich., 1967-68; post doctoral fellow Syracuse U. Dept. Biology, Syracuse, N.Y., 1973-76; from post doctoral fellow to assoc. prof. SUNY, Syracuse, N.Y., 1976-90; biochemistry program dir. NSF, Washington, 1990—; reviewer NATO fellowship NSF, San Francisco, 1988, Ad Hoc NSF, Syracuse, N.Y., manuscripts in field; vis. scientist Weizmann Inst. Renal Rsch. Fund, Weizmann Inst., Israel, 1987, 1988. Contbr. articles to profl. jours. Recipient Wellcome Rsch. Travel Grant, Wellcome Found. Cambridge U., U.K., 1985, Regents scholarship SUNY Bd. Regents, Bklyn., 1960-64. Mem. AAAS, Am. Soc. Biochemistry Molecular Biology, Am. Heart Assn. (Basic Rsch.Coun.), Assn. Women Sci., Sigma Xi. Office: Nat Sci Found Rm 325 1800 G St NW Washington DC 20550

STEINEGER, MARGARET LEISY, non-profit organization officer; b. Newton, Kans., Feb. 8, 1926; d. Ernest Erwin and Elva Agnes (Krehbiel) L.; m. John Francis Steineger, Dec. 2, 1949; children: John Steineger III, Cindy Blair, Melissa, Chris. B., So. Meth. U., 1947; M. in Social Work, U. Kans., 1949. County vice-chair United Way, Kansas City, Kans., 1960-61; bd., sec., treas. Wyandotte County Bar Aux., Kans., 1960-63; bd. Jr. League of Kansas City, 1962-66, County Coun. PTA, Wyandotte County, 1963-66, KCK Friends of the Arts, Kansas City, 1974-77; pres. Grinter Place Mus. Friends, Kans., 1977-78; bd. Kaw Valley Arts Coun., Kansas City, 1982-86; commr. Landmarks Commn., Kansas City, 1985-87; bd. Arts with the Handicapped, Wyandotte County, 1986—; bd. dirs. Kans. Arts Adv. Bd., Grinter Place Friends, Kans., Tri-County Tourism Coun., Kans. Vice-pres. Kans. Legis. Wives, Topeka, 1975-76; bd. dirs. KCK Friends of the Library, Kansas City, 1984—; founder Wyandotte County Libr., 1963-64, Creative Experiences, Kansas City, 1967; commr. Kans Arts Commn., 1965-85; pres., bd. dirs Kans. Arts Adv. Bd., 1983-85. Recipient Humanities award Kans. Com. for the Humanities, 1989; named Citizen of Yr. Kansas City, Kans., 1978. Democrat. Methodist. Home: 6400 Valley View Rd Kansas City KS 66111 Office: Security Bank Bldg Ste 600 Kansas City KS 66101

STEINEM, GLORIA, writer, editor, lecturer; b. Toledo, Mar. 25, 1934; d. Leo and Ruth (Nuneviller) S. BA, Smith Coll., 1956; postgrad. (Chester Bowles Asian fellow), India, 1957-58; D. Human Justice, Simmons Coll., 1973. Co-dir., dir. ednl. found. Ind. Rsch. Svc., Cambridge, Mass. and N.Y.C., 1959-60; editorial asst., editorial cons., contbg. editor, free-lance writer various publs. N.Y.C. and nat., 1960—; co-founder, contbg. editor New York Mag., 1968—; feminist lectr., 1969—; co-founder, editor Ms. Mag., 1971-87, columnist, 1980—, cons. editor, 1988—; Active various civil rights and peace campaigns including United Farmworkers, Vietnam War Tax Protest, Com. for the Legal Def. of Angela Davis (treas., 1971-72); active polit. campaigns of Adlai Stevenson, Robert Kennedy, Eugene McCarthy, Shirley Chisholm, George McGovern; Co-founder, bd. dirs. Women's Action Alliance, 1970—; convenor, mem. nat. adv. com. Nat. Women's Polit. Caucus, 1971—; co-founder, pres. bd. dirs. Ms. Found. for Women, 1972—; founding mem. Coalition of Labor Union Women, 1974; mem. Internat. Women's Year Commn., 1977. Author: The Thousand Indias, 1957, The Beach Book, 1963, Outrageous Acts and Everyday Rebellions, 1983, Marilyn: Norma Jeane, 1986; contbg. corr. NBC Today Show, 1987-88; contbr. to various anthologies. Bd. dirs. Voters for Choice, 1979—. Recipient Penney-Missouri Journalism award, 1970; Ohio Gov.'s award for Journalism, 1972; Bill of Rights award A.C.L.U. of So. Calif., 1975; named Woman of the Year McCall's mag., 1972; Woodrow Wilson Internat. Center for Scholars fellow, 1977. Mem. Nat. Orgn. for Women, AFTRA, Nat. Press Club, Soc. Mag. Writers, Authors' Guild, P.E.N., Phi Beta Kappa. Office: Ms Mag 1 Times Sq New York NY 10036

STEINER, GLORIA LITWIN, psychologist; b. Newark, Oct. 21, 1922; d. David Milton and Minna (Krasner) Litwin; m. Charles Steiner, Aug. 29, 1942; children: Charles Jr., Susan Steiner Sher, Jeanne. BA, U. Pa., 1944; MS, CCNY, 1956; EdD, Columbia U., 1965. Psychologist St. Michael's Hosp. and Mt. Carmel, Newark, 1956-62; chief psychologist Children's Hosp., Newark, 1965-78; prof. psychology, dir. psychol. svc. Child Study Ctr., Kean Coll., Union, N.J., 1971-78; vis. assoc. prof. grad. sch. applied and profl. psychology Rutgers U., Piscataway, N.J., 1976—; clin. assoc. prof., dir. psychology tng. U. Medicine and Dentistry N.J.-N.J. Med. Sch., Newark, 1978—. Co-author: Traumatic Abuse/Children, 1980; contbr. articles to profl. jours.; editorial bd. Jour. Psychotherapy, 1981—. Mem. N.J. State Task Force on AIDS, 1986-89, N.J. State Bd. Psychol. Exam., 1978-84, Regional Health Planning Coun., N.J., 1984-85, child adv. com. Mental Health Assn., N.J., 1974-80; trustee, founder N.J. Acad. Psychology, N.J., 1978-83. Grantee trg. health care workers Regional AIDS Edn. and Tng. Ctr. U. Medicine and Dentistry N.J., Newark, 1990. Fellow Am. Orthopsychiat. Assn.; mem. N.Y. Acad. Scis., N.J. Assn. for the Advancement Family Therapy (vice-chmn. 1979-81), Am. Psychol. Assn. Home: 35 Sequoia Dr Watchung NJ 07060 Office: U Medicine and Dentistry NJ Newark NJ 07103-2770

STEINER, JACQUE, state legislator; b. Pasadena, Calif., Sept. 4, 1929; d. John C. and Claire C. (Howard) Yelland; m. Frederick Karl III, Katherine Claire, Ann Carole. BA, Stanford U., 1951, MA, 1952. High sch. tchr. English, 1952-55; mem. Ariz. Ho. of Reps., 1976-80; state senator Ariz. Senate, 1981—. Named Citizen of Yr., Phoenix Bd. Realtors, 1976. Lutheran. Republican. Home: 2915 E Sherran Ln Phoenix AZ 85016 Office: Office of State Senate State Capitol Phoenix AZ 85007*

STEINFELS, MARGARET O'BRIEN, editor; m. Peter Steinfels, Aug. 31, 1963; 2 children: Gabrielle, John Melville. Founding editor, Church mag.; social sci. editor Basic Books; bus. mgr., later exec. editor Christianity and Crisis; dir. publications Nat. Pastoral Life Ctr.; editor Commonweal mag., 1987—. Office: Commonweal 15 Dutch St New York NY 10038*

STEINHART, CAROL (CAROL ELDER), writer, editor; b. Cleve., Mar. 27, 1935; d. Clayton Thomas and Carolyn Elise (Kalkbrenner) Elder; m. John Shannon Steinhart, Dec. 20, 1958 (div. 1988); children: Gail Shannon, Martha Reid, Geoffrey Blair. AB, Albion (Mich.) Coll., 1956; PhD, U. Wis., 1960. Biologist Gen. and Comparative Biochemistry Lab. NIMH, Bethesda, Md., 1961-66; biologist Office Rsch. Analysis and Evaluation Div. Rsch. Grants, NIH, Bethesda, 1966-70; freelance writer and editor Madison, Wis., 1970-77; project assoc. Water Resources Ctr. U. Wis., Madison, 1979-81; rsch. analyst, writer U. Wis. Extension/Wis. Dept. Agr. Trade and Consumer Protection, Madison, 1981-83; writer, editor VA Hosp., Madison, 1983—; editor newsletter Med. Com. for Human Rights, Washington, 1964-68; contract editor Am. Soc. Agronomy, Madison, 1984—. Author: (with others) Blowout: A Case Study of the Santa Barbara Oil Spill, 1972, Energy: Sources, Use and Role in Human Affairs, 1974, The Fires of Culture: Energy Yesterday and Tomorrow, 1975; contbr. articles to profl. jours, chpts. to books. Mem. Med. Com. for Human Rights, Washington, 1964-70; vol. Wis. Environ. Decade, Madison, 1980-85, Internat. Crane Found., Baraboo, Wis., 1988—. Mem. Phi Beta Kappa, Sigma Xi. Democrat.

STEINHART, KATHY SUE, secondary educator; b. Indpls., Dec. 1, 1952; d. John Glen Jr. and Ann Veronica (Mitsch) Steinhart. BS in Math. Edn., Ind. State U., 1975, MS, 1980. Lic. tchr. Tchr. Met. Sch. Dist. of Perry Twp., Indpls., 1981-84, Indpls. Pub. Schs., 1975-81, 84—; coordinator FAME, Shortridge Jr. High Sch., Indpls., 1988-89. Mem. Indpls. Edn. Assn. (exec. bd. 1989—), Ind. State Tchrs. Assn. (vice chmn. conf. on instrn. com. 1988-89, sec. 1987-88, issues and concerns com. 1985-89). Lutheran. Home: 8540 Conarroe Rd Indianapolis IN 46278 Office: Shortridge Jr High Sch 3401 N Meridian St Indianapolis IN 46208

STEINHAUER, GILLIAN, lawyer; b. Aylesbury, Bucks, Eng., Oct. 6, 1938; d. Eric Frederick and Maisie Kathleen (Yeates) Pearson; m. Bruce William Steinhauer, Jan. 2, 1960; children: Alison (Humphrey) Eric, John, Elspeth. AB cum laude, Bryn Mawr (Pa.) Coll., 1959; JD cum laude, U. Mich., 1976. Bar: Mich. 1976, U.S. Dist. Ct. (ea. dist.) Mich. 1976, U.S. Ct. Appeals (6th cir.), 1982. Assoc. Miller, Canfield, Paddock & Stone, Detroit, 1976-82, ptnr., then sr. ptnr., 1983—. Fellow Mich. State Bar Found.; mem. ABA, State Bar of Mich., Fed. Bar Assn., Fed. Jud. Conf. 6th Cir. (del. 1986-90), Assn. Def. Trial Counsel, Women Lawyers Assn. Episcopalian. Clubs: Detroit, Bryn Mawr (pres. 1970—). Home: 368 Notre Dame Ave Grosse Pointe MI 48230 Office: Miller Canfield Paddock & Stone 150 W Jefferson Ste 2500 Detroit MI 48226

STEINHAUSER, JANICE MAUREEN, arts administrator; b. Oklahoma City, Okla., Apr. 3, 1935; d. Max Charles and Charlotte (Gold) Glass; m. Stuart Z. Hirschman, Dec. 30, 1954 (div. 1965); children: Shayle, David, Susan; m. Sheldon Steinhauser, May 2, 1965; children: Karen, Lisa Steinhauser Hackel. BFA, U. Colo., Denver, 1972; student, U. Mich., 1953-55. Community affairs adminstr. United Bank Denver, 1973-76; dir. visual arts program Western States Arts Found., Denver, 1976-79; exec. dir. Artreach, Inc., Denver, 1980-82; v.p. mktg. Mammoth Gardens, Denver, 1982-83; dir. pub. rels. Denver Ctr. for Performing Arts, 1983-86; founder, pres. Resource Co., Denver, 1986-88. Bd. dirs. Met. Denver Arts Alliance, 1982-85, Denver Internat. Film Festival, 1983-86. Mem. Women's Forum Colo., Pub. Rels. Soc. Am., Colo. New Music Assn. (bd. dirs. 1987—), Asian Performing Arts Colo. (bd. dirs. 1989—), Art Students League Denver, Phi Beta Kappa, Kappa Delta Phi. Democrat. Jewish.

STEINHERZ, LAUREL JUDITH, pediatric cardiologist; b. N.Y.C., Jan. 5, 1947; d. Bernard and Adeline Weinberger; m. Peter Gustav Steinherz, July 4, 1967; children: Jennifer, Jonathan Daniel David. Student, Hebrew U., Jersualem, 1966; BA with distinction, U. Rochester, 1967; MD, Albert Einstein Coll. Medicine, 1970. Diplomate Am. Bd. Pediatrics, sub-bd. pediatric cardiology. Intern in pediatrics N.Y. Hosp.-Cornell Med. Ctr., N.Y.C., 1970-71, pediatric cardiology fellow, 1973-75, assoc. attending pediatrician, 1985—; resident in pediatrics St. Louis Children's Hosp., 1971-72; attending pediatrician State U. Hosp. and King County Med. Ctr., Bklyn., 1975-77; asst. prof. pediatrics med. coll. Cornell U., N.Y.C., 1977-85, assoc. prof. pediatrics, 1985—; asst. attending pediatrician, dir. pediatric cardiology dept. Meml. Sloan Kettering Cancer Ctr., N.Y.C., 1977—. Contbg. author: Adolescent Medicine !!, 1976; contbr. articles to profl. jours. Hutzler Found. grantee, 1987. Fellow Am. Acad. Pediatrics, Am. Coll. of Cardiology; mem. N.Y. Acad. Scis. Office: Meml Sloan Kettering Cancer Ctr 1275 York Ave New York NY 10021

STEINMAN, LISA MALINOWSKI, English literature educator, writer; b. Willimantic, Conn., Apr. 8, 1950; d. Zenon Stanislaus and Shirley Belle (Nathanson) Malinowski; m. James A. Steinman, Apr. 1968 (div. 1980); m. James L. Shugrue, July 23, 1984. BA, Cornell U., 1971, MFA, 1973, PhD, 1976. Asst. prof. English Reed Coll., Portland, Oreg., 1976-82, assoc. prof., 1982-90, prof., 1990—; cons. NEH, Washington, 1984-85; bd. dirs. Portland Poetry Festival. Author: Lost Poems, 1976, Made in America, 1987, All That Comes To Light, 1989; editor Hubbub Mag., 1983—; contbr. articles to profl. jours. Fellow Nat. Endowment for Arts, 1984, Oreg. Arts Commn., 1983-84, NEH, 1983, Danforth Found., 1971-75; recipient Pablo Neruda award, 1987; Rockefeller Found. scholar, 1987-88. Mem. MLA, Poets and Writers, PEN. Home: 5344 SE 38th Ave Portland OR 97202 Office: Reed Coll Dept English 3203 SE Woodstock Ave Portland OR 97202

STEINMETZ, MARY DARLENE (MARY STEIN), design company executive; b. Alexandria, Va., Feb. 16, 1959; d. Jerry Eugene and Jacqueline Mary (Bourne) Mackey; m. Wayne Michael Steinmetz, Mar. 1, 1953; children: John David, Jacqueline Mary. Student, No. Mich. U., 1979-83; student cosmetology, Citrus Heights Beauty Sch., Sacramento, 1985, Pacific Beauty Coll., Guam, 1986. Make-up artist Sacramento, 1984-85, Guam, 1985-87; pres. Stein Design, Inc., Ft. Worth, 1988—; pres. Beauty Visions Videos, Ft. Worth, 1989, Shootouts, Ft. Worth, 1989. Vol. Tarrant County Republican Party, Ft. Worth, 1988-89; pres. programs Officer Wives Club, Ill., Calif., Guam, 1984-89. Recipient 1st place medals make-up artist competition, Calif., 1988-89. Mem. Am. Woman Entrepreneurs, Nat. Assn. for Female Execs., Dallas Assn. Make-up Artist & Stylist, Nat. Pachyderms. Roman Catholic. Office: Stein Design Inc 6700 Duncan Fort Worth TX 76114

STEINRAUF, JEAN HAMILTON, biochemistry professor; b. Airdrie, Scotland, Feb. 5, 1938; came to U.S., 1962; d. Alexander Risk and Margaret Shaw Jarvie (Swann) Hamilton; m. Larry King Steinrauf, Nov. 28, 1968; children: Joseph Hamilton, Alexis Willa. BS, Glasgow (Scotland) U., 1959, PhD, 1962. Postdoctoral fellow U. Ill., Urbana, 1962-64; from resident assoc. to prof. sch. medicine Ind. U., Indpls., 1964—. Contbr. articles to profl. jours. Recipient Career Devel. awd. NIH, 1966-70, rsch. grants, NIH, 1966—. Office: Ind U Sch Medicine Dept Biochemistry 635 Barnhill Dr 450 Med Sci Bldg Indianapolis IN 46202-5122

STEITZ, JOAN ARGETSINGER, biochemistry educator; b. Mpls., Jan. 26, 1941; d. Glenn D. and Elaine (Magnusson) Argetsinger; m. Thomas A. Steitz, Aug. 20, 1966; 1 child, Jonathan Glenn. B.S., Antioch Coll., 1963; Ph.D., Harvard U., 1967; D.Sc. (hon.), Lawrence U., Appleton, Wis., 1982, Rochester U. Sch. Medicine, 1984, Mt. Sinai Sch. Medicine, 1989. Postdoctoral fellow MRC Lab. Molecular Biology, Cambridge, Eng., 1967-70; asst. prof. molecular biophysics and biochemistry Yale U., New Haven, 1970-74; assoc. prof. Yale U., 1974-78, prof. molecular biophysics and biochemistry, 1978—. Recipient Young Scientist award Passano Found., 1975, Eli Lilly award in biol. chemistry, 1976, U.S. Steel Found. award in molecular biology, 1982, Lee Hawley, Sr. award for arthritis research, 1984, Nat. Medal of Sci., 1986, Dickson Prize for Sci. Carnegie-Melloin U., 1988, Warren Triennial prize Mass. Gen. Hosp., 1989. Fellow AAAS; mem. Am. Acad. Arts and Sci., Nat. Acad. Arts and Sci. Home: 45 Prospect Hill Rd Stony Creek Branford CT 06405 Office: Yale U Sch Medicine 333 Cedar St PO Box 3333 New Haven CT 06510

STELK, MARIANNE BOYD, vocational rehabilitation specialist; b. Sharon, Pa., June 30, 1930; d. Harry S. and Carolyn Martha (Akers) Boyd; div.; 1 child, Carolyn Stelk Applegate. BS in Vocat. Home Econs., Colo. State U., 1953; MA in Guidance and Counseling, Chadron State Coll., 1988. Cert. tchr., Colo. Tchr. Logan County High Sch., Fleming, Colo., 1953-55, Minatare (Nebr.) High Sch., 1955-57, Bayard (Nebr.) Jr. and Sr. High Schs., 1960-66; extension home economist U. Nebr. Coop. Extension Svc., 1970-74; ind. living specialist Nebr. Vocat. Rehab. Svc., Scottsbluff, 1974—. Vol. Dem. party, 1958—. Mem. AAUW (past officer), PEO Sisterhood, North Platte Valley Home Economists, Rehab. Assn. Nebr., Nebr. Assn. Pub. Employees. Methodist. Office: Vocat Rehab Svc 4502 Ave I Scottsbluff NE 69361

STELLMAN, L. MANDY, lawyer; b. Toronto, Ont., Can., Aug. 22, 1922; came to U.S., 1946, naturalized, 1948; d. Abraham and Rose (Rubinoff) Mandlsohn; m. Samuel David Stellman, July 11, 1943; children—Steven D., Leslie Robert. B.Sc. summa cum laude, Ohio State U., Columbus, 1966; J.D., Marquette U., 1970. Bar: Wis. 1971. Tchr., Toronto Pub. Schs., 1943-46; recreation specialist, Toronto, 1942-46; educator, social worker Columbus (Ohio) Jewish Ctr., 1951-64; instr. U. Wis. Extension, Milw., 1970-76; sole practice, Milw., 1971—. Bd. dirs. Women's Crisis Line, Women's Coalition, Milw. Jewish Home for Aged. Recipient Disting. Alumni award Ohio State U., 1976; Hannah G. Solomon award Nat. Council Jewish Women, 1984. Mem. Assn. Trial Lawyers Am., Lawyers Assn. for Women, ABA, Milw. Bar Assn., Wis. Assn. Trial Lawyers, Nat. Council Jewish Women (life), Women's Polit. Caucus, Common Cause, NOW (Milw. Woman of Yr. 1977). Jewish. Home: 1545 W Fairfield Ct Glendale WI 53209 Office: 606 W Wisconsin Ave Ste 308 Milwaukee WI 53203

STELMACK, JOAN, optometrist, educator; b. Hartford, Conn., Oct. 13, 1948; d. Alfonso James and Geldra Rae (Burr) Antoinetti; m. Thomas R.

Stelmack, Dec. 24, 1977; children: Jenifer, Garret. Student, Case Western Res. U., 1966-68; BA, Conn. Coll., 1970; OD, Ill. Coll. Optometry, 1977. Lic. optometrist, Ill. Pvt. practice, Bartlett, Ill., 1978-84; chief optometry sect. Hines (Ill.) VA Hosp., 1984—; vision cons. Wesley Jessen, Inc., Chgo., 1977-78, S&C Electric, Chgo., 1983-84; cons. Innovate Employee Svcs. System, Plainfield, N.J., 1988—; clin. instr. Ill. Coll. Optometry, Chgo., 1977-84, adj. asst. prof., 19985-89, adj. assoc. prof., 1990—; dir. Dialogue Svcs. for Blind, Oak Park, Ill., 1988—, vice chmn., 1989-90. Contbr. articles to profl. jours. Grantee VA, 1985-87, 89, Ill. Soc. for Prevention Blindness, 1989-91. Fellow Am. Acad. Optometry (bd. dirs. Ill. br. 1989-90); mem. Am. Optometric Assn. (coun. low vision sect. 1989-91), Armed Svcs. Optometric Soc., Nat. Assn. VA Optometrists, Am. Pub. Health Assn. (coun. vision care sect. 1986-88, cert. of appreciation 1988). Office: Hines VA Hosp Bldg 13 Hines IL 60141

STELSEL, LINDA HOPE, librarian; b. Beaver Dam, Wis., Aug. 15, 1948; d. Robert Jones and Patricia (Eckstein) S. BS, U. Wis., La Crosse, 1970; MALS, U. Wis., Oshkosh, 1976. Asst. libr. Wauwatosa (Wis.) East High Sch., 1970-75, libr., 1975. Mem. Wis. Edn. Assn. Coun. Republican. Presbyterian. Office: Wauwatosa East High Sch 7500 W Milwaukee Ave Milwaukee WI 53213

STELTZLEN, JANELLE HICKS, lawyer; b. Atlanta, Sept. 18, 1937; d. William Duard and Mary Evelyn (Embrey) Hicks; divorced; children: Gerald William III, Christa Diane. BS, Okla. State U., 1958; MS, Kans. State U., 1961; JD, U. Tulsa, 1981. Bar: Okla. 1981, U.S. Dist. Ct. (no., ea. and we. dists.) Okla. 1981, U.S. Tax Ct. 1982, U.S. Ct. Claims 1982, U.S. Ct. Appeals (10th cir.) 1983, U.S. Ct. Appeals (Fed. cir.) 1984, U.S. Supreme Ct. 1986; lic. real estate broker. Sole practice Tulsa, 1981—; lectr. Coll. of DuPage, Glen Ellyn, Ill., 1976, Tulsa Jr. Coll., 1981—; dietitian, Tulsa. Christian counselor 1st United Meth. Ch., Tulsa, 1986—, lay pastor, 1987—; mem. Tulsa County Bd. Equalization and Excise Tax Bd. Mem. Okla. Bar Assn., Tulsa County Bar Assn., Vol. Lawyers Assn. (bd. dirs.), Am. Dietetic Assn., Delta Zeta. Republican. Methodist. Home: 6636 S Jamestown Place Tulsa OK 74136 Office: 1150 E 61st St Tulsa OK 74136

STEMEN, NOEL L. E., nursing educator; b. Port Huron, Mich., Aug. 29, 1946; d. Theron Noel and Agnes L. E. (Ford) Stuart; m. George William Stemen, Nov. 4, 1972; children: Gary, Jeremy. Diploma, Hurley Hosp. Sch. Nursing, 1967; BA, U. Detroit, 1975, MA, 1977; MSN, Wayne State U., Detroit, 1984. Staff nurse operating rm. McLaren Gen. Hosp., Flint, Mich., 1967-69, team leader surg. unit, 1969-73; pub. health nurse City of Flint Pub. Health Dept., 1973-75; educator Baker Bus. Coll., Flint, 1975-77, Mott Community Coll., Flint, 1977—. Mem. NEA, Am. Pub. Health Assn., Am. Nurses Assn., Coun. Community Health Nurses, Flint Dist. Nurses Assn. (pres. 1986-88), Mich. Nurses Assn. (bd. dirs. 1986-88). Baptist. Home: 5511 Lennon Rd Swartz Creek MI 48473 Office: Mott Community Coll 1401 E Court St Flint MI 48502

STEMPEL, RINA, educator; b. N.Y., July 31, 1936; d. Nathan and Irene (Gordon) Cheshes; m. Edward Stempel, Dec. 20, 1959; 1 child, Andrea. BS, Bklyn. Coll., 1958, MS, 1960. Cert. tchr., N.Y. Tchr. S.J. Tilden High Sch., Bklyn., 1958-68, dept. chmn., 1969-73; adjunct instr. Bklyn. Coll., Bklyn., 1971-74; asst. prin. S.J. Tilden High Sch., Bklyn.; deputy supt. Bklyn. High Schs., 1978-84; prin. S. Shore High Sch., 1984--; head counselor CAMP Roosevelt, Monticello, 1960-66. Mem. PTA, Canarsie Mental Health Assn., Nat. Assn. of Sec. Sch. Prins., Assn. for Supervision and Curriculum Devel., High Sch. Prins. Assn., Council of Suprs. and Adminstras. Office: South Shore High Sch 6565 Flatlands Ave Brooklyn NY 11236

STEMPER, MARY ELAINE, microbiologist, medical technologist; b. Spring Grove, Minn., June 30, 1964; d. Eugene and Saverna Mae (Scheckel) S. BS, U. Wis., La Crosse, 1987. Microbiologist Marshfield (Wis.) Clinic, 1987—, mem. med. tech. faculty, 1988—. Vol. Ronald McDonald House, Marshfield, 1989—. Scholar St. Joseph's Hosp. Aux., 1987. Mem. Am. Soc. for Med. Tech., Am. Soc. for Microbiology (registered), Am. Soc. Clin. Pathologists (cert. med. technologists). Democrat. Roman Catholic. Office: Marshfield Clinic JVL 1000 Oak St Marshfield WI 54449

STENANDER, SYLVIA LARSON, college administrator; b. Jamestown, N.Y., Oct. 3, 1947; d. Reece Williams and Winifred Ruthann (Johnson) Larson; m. Larry Roy Stenander, Aug. 16, 1969; children: Matthew Larry, Cherie Diane. BS Edn. summa cum laude, SUNY, Geneseo, 1969; postgrad., SUNY, Fredonia, 1972-75. Cert. tchr., N.Y. Tchr. Mesa (Ariz.) Pub. Schs., 1969-71, S.W. Central Sch., Jamestown, N.Y., 1971-76; needs analyst and cons. Cummins Engine Co., Lakewood, N.Y., 1985-86; tng. coord. Jamestown (N.Y.) Community Coll., 1986-87, acting dir. Bus. and Industry Ctr., 1987-88, dir. tng. svcs., 1988—; alt. governing bd. Regional Edn. Ctr., Depew, N.Y., 1988; mem. bus. and industryctr. bd. Jamestown Community Coll., 1987-88. Mem. So. Tier West Regional Planning Bd. Human Resource Devel. Com., Salamance, N.Y., 1987—. Named Outstanding Young Profl. Rochester Tchrs. Assn., 1969. Mem. Am. Soc. Tng. and Devel., Continuing Edn. Assn. N.Y., Parent-Student-Tchr. Orgn., Kappa Delta Pi. Republican. Lutheran. Office: Jamestown Community Coll 525 Falconer St Jamestown NY 14701

STENGER, LESLIE ANN, exercise physiologist, business owner, consultant; b. Pitts., Jan. 11, 1961; d. William Stenger and Ann Mcneely (Herndon) Green. BPE, Slippery Rock U., 1982, M in exercise physiology/cardic rehab., 1984. Cert. CPR instr. Fitness instr. Exec. Fitness Ctr., Pompano Beach, Fla., 1982-83; cardiac rehab. dir. Bioenergetiks, Health Maintenance, Beaver, Pa., 1983-86, Ohio Heart Inst., Youngstown, Ohio, 1986-90; co-owner Fitness Essentials, Inc., Pitts., 1990—; fitness cons. Alcoholic Clinic, Youngstown, 1986—. Co-author: Healthy Moves for Older Adults, 1984. Sponsor Big Sisters, Youngstown, 1988-89; vol. soccer and softball coach Community Recreation Program, 1988-89; vol. Spl. Olympics, Youngstown, 1988-89. Mem. NOW, Am. Coll. Sports Medicine, Am. Assn. Cardiopulmonary Rehab., Am. Heart Assn. (speakers bur.), Pa. Phys. Edn., Recreation, Health and Dance Assn. (presenter at state conv. 1985). Home: 1656 Citation Dr Pittsburgh PA 15129

STENMARK, JEAN KERR, education educator; b. Davis, Calif., Aug. 25, 1922; d. Norman and Rachel Minerva (Bledsoe) Kerr; m. Roy M., Aug. 24, 1952, (div. July 1975); children: Ruthann, John, Jane. BA, U. Calif., Berkeley, 1942; MS, Calif. State U., Hayward, 1978. Cert. elem. tchr., Calif. With civil svc. U.S. Navy-Aviation Supply, Oakland, Calif., 1942-45; acct. various acctg. firms, San Francisco, 1945-56; tchr. Oakland Unified Sch. Dist., 1969-80; maths. specialist EQUALS and Family Math. Programs U. Calif., Berkeley, 1980—; cons. Calif. Assessment Program, Sacramento, 1975—; mem. adv. bd. Coop. Maths. Project, Danville, Calif., 1987—, adv. com. Calif. Curriculum Info. for Parents, Sacramento, 1988-89. Author: Assessment Alternatives in Mathematics, 1989; co-author: Family Math, 1986, Math for Girls and Other Problem Solvers, 1981; editor: Sharing Resources. Named Alameda Contra Costa County Mathematics Educator of Yr., Oakland, 1978. Mem. Nat. Coun. Tchrs. Maths., Calif. Maths. Coun., Math/Sci. Network, Internat. Orgn. Women in Maths. and Sci., PTA (hon. life mem.). Democrat. Protestant. Home: 795-C Taft Ave Albany CA 94706 Office: U Calif EQUALS Lawrence Hall of Sci Berkeley CA 94720

STENQUIST, CONNIE UNDERWOOD, university administrative manager; b. Goldsboro, N.C., Dec. 20, 1949; d. Luther Rodney and Gouldia (Summerlin) Underwood; m. James Delvin Benton, Jan. 6, 1969 (div.); children: Jason, Jacob; m. 2d Ronald E. Stenquist, July 31, 1976; 1 dau., Brandy. AAS in Bus., Wayne Community Coll., 1974; postgrad. East Carolina U., 1979-80. Sec. Wayne Community Coll., Goldsboro, 1974-75; exhibit coordinator N.C. Assn. Educators, Raleigh, 1975-76; personnel sec. East Carolina U., Greenville, N.C., 1976-78, adminstr. dept. surgery, 1979-87; adminstrn. asst dept orolaryngology Vanderbilt U., Nashville, 1987— ; bus. mgr. Stonebranch Prodns., Lebanon, Tenn., 1983—. Mem. Phi Theta Kappa. Office: Dept Otolaryngology S-2100 MCN Vanderbilt Univ Nashville TN 37232

STENZEL, KAREN LOUISE, purchasing supervisor; b. Oct. 24, 1951; d. Frank Stenzel; children: Kim, Chris. Cert. purchasing mgr. Buyer, expeditor Borg-Warner Automotive, Dixon, Ill., supr. Mem. Nat. Assn. Purchasing Mgrs., Am. Legion (treas. aux. 1973). Office: Borg-Warner Automotive Inc 1350 Franklin Grove Rd Dixon IL 61021

STEORTS, NANCY HARVEY, management consultant; b. Syracuse, N.Y., Nov. 28, 1936; d. Frederick William and Josephine Elizabeth (Jones) Harvey; 1 dau., Deborah Joan. B.S., Syracuse U., 1959. Asst. buyer, public relations coordinator Woodward & Lothrop, Washington, 1958-61; home economist Washington Gas Light Co., 1961-64; sales assoc. real estate Summit, N.J., 1967-68; survey specialist Dept. Agr., Washington, 1968-69; chmn. Consumer Product Safety Commn., Washington, D.C., 1981-85; pres. Nancy Harvey Steorts & Assocs., Dallas, 1985-88, Washington and Dallas, 1988—; cons. Exec. Reorgn. Govt., Washington, 1971; nat. dir. women's speakers' bur. Com. Re-elect Pres., Washington, 1971-72; dir. candlelight dinners Presdl. Inaugural Commn., 1972-73, 81; expns. dir. Dept. Commerce, Washington, 1973; spl. asst. for consumer affairs to sec. agr., 1973-77; pres. Nancy Harvey Steorts & Assocs., 1977-81; disting. lectr., Strom Thurmond Inst. Govt. and Pub. Affairs, Clemson U.; mem. advisory council to bd. dirs., Adolph Coors Co.; mem. U.S. Dept. of Commerce Export Council for Texas, Nat. Adv. Com.; dir. People to People Trade Mission to Spain, 1987; mem. nat. consumer adv. coun. Fed. Res. Bd.; official U.S. rep. to 4th Pub. Health, Med. Equipment and Drugs Expn. Moscow USSR. Producer, host syndicated TV show spl. Trustee Food Safety Council Conf. Consumer Orgn.; bd. dirs. Women's Inst. Am. U.; bd. advisers Coll. Human Devel. Syracuse U.; commr. Montgomery County Commn. Women; pres. Welcome Wagon Clubs from 1986, Dallas Citizens Council, 1986—; bd. dirs. Council of Better Bus. Burs.; bd. adv. Am. U. Women's Inst.; bd. dirs. Med. Coll. Pa., Tex. Women's Alliance; bd. dirs., vice-chmn. regional devel. Nat. Assn. Women Bus. Owners; mem. internat. com. Com. 2000; bd. dirs. Jr. Achievement, United Way, Dallas, Goals of Dallas, Internat. Mayor's Ball; internat. del. 1st Women's Internat. Trade Mission to Europe for Women Entrepeneurs; chairwoman Trade Mission of Women Leaders to Taiwan, 1988; del. to USSR Internat. Women's Forum Mission; mem. advisory council to So. Meth. U. Dept. Economics; co-chmn. fundraising, Dallas Symphony; coord. bicentennial presdl. inaugural dinners, 1989; pres. Dallas Citizens' Coun., 1986-88. Recipient George P. Arents Pioneer medal Syracuse U., 1979, spl. award for consumer concern Nat. Diet Workshop, named one of five outstanding pub. servants Gallagher Report, 1984. Mem. Nat. Bd. Dirs., Am. Home Econs. Assn., AAUW, Nat. Consumers League, Am. Women in Radio and TV, Exec. Women in Govt. (chmn.), Nat. Conf. Consumer Orgns. Office: Nancy Harvey Steorts & Assocs 8101 Connecticut Ave Ste C-607 Chevy Chase MD 20815

STEPHENS, ALICE ELIZABETH (ALICE WANKE STEPHENS), artist; b. Portland, Oreg., Feb. 2, 1926; d. A.E. and Elfrieda I. (Strauch) Wanke; m. Farrold Franklin Stephens, Feb. 2, 1950; children: Scott, Lynn, Todd. Student, Oreg. State U., 1944-46; BA, Stanford U., Palo Alto, Calif., 1948. bd. dirs., cons. Wanke Cascade, Portland. Exhibited in numerous one-woman shows including City Auditors Office City Hall, Portland, 1990, World Forestry Ctr., Portland, 1989, Clackamas Community Coll., Oregon City, 1988, Beaverton (Oreg.) Arts Commn., 1988, George Fox Coll., Newberg, Oreg., 1987, Gazebo Gallery, Lake Oswego, Oreg., 1984, 82, 80, Unitarian Ch., Portland, 1976; represented at Rental Sales Gallery, Oreg. Art Inst., Gazebo Gallery. Sec. Portland Womens Union, 1990. Mem. Oreg. Soc. Artists, Pi Beta Phi. Democrat. Mem. Disciples of Christ. Home: 2323 SW Park Pl #805 Portland OR 97205

STEPHENS, ALISON AMY, cosmetics executive; b. Brainerd, Minn., May 29, 1949; d. Clark Merton and Amanda Elizabeth (Tufteland) Amy; m. Robert Gregory Stephens, Aug. 12, 1972 (div. Jul. 1983); m. B. Michael Stuppy, May 29, 1988. AA, Brainerd Coll., 1969; BS, U. Minn., 1971, postgrad. Cert. Lowthian Fashion Coll. Instr. Lowthian Fashion Coll., Mpls., 1969-79; tchr. English Hopkins (Minn.) Sch. Systems, 1971-79; profl. beauty cons. Mary Kay Cosmetics, Edina, Minn., 1977—, exec. sr. dir., 1985—. Mem. Nat. Assn. Female Exec., Nat. Assn. Women Bus. Owners, Edina C. of C., Mpls. C. of C. Republican. Clubs: U. Minn. Alumni Assn., Am. Legion. Office: Mary Kay Cosmetics 7101 Lanham Ln Edina MN 55435

STEPHENS, DEBORAH HAINES, chemical company official; b. Ann Arbor, Mich., Sept. 9, 1960; d. Richard F. and Marion (Thomas) Haines; m. Raymond H. Stephens, Mar. 28, 1987. BS in Indsl. and Ops. Engring., U. Mich., 1982. Sales rep. Dow Chem. USA, Chgo., 1982-86; account specialist Dow Chem. USA, Detroit, 1986-89, mgr. market devel., 1989-90; comml. supr. olefin feedstocks Dow Chem. USA, Houston, 1990—. Vol. various community orgns. and activities. Mem. Soc. Automotive Engrs., Am. Soc. Materials Internat., Alpha Delta Pi. Office: Dow Chem USA PO Box 3387 Houston TX 77253-3387

STEPHENS, GAY, not-for-profit foundation executive; b. Aurora, Ill., Sept. 29, 1951; d. Benjamin Mark Jr. and Joyce Audrey (Sinclair) S.; m. John Stephen Hauk, Mar. 24, 1973. BA magna cum laude, George Williams Coll., 1973, MS summa cum laude, 1975. Clin. dir. Village of Downers Grove (Ill.) Dept. Health and Human Svcs., 1975-78; exec. dir. Villages of Bloomingdale (Ill.) Police Program, 1978-81, Family Support Ctr., Aurora, 1981-83; devel. dir. Family Svc. & Mental Health Ctr. of Oak Park, Ill., 1983-88; mgmt. cons. United Way of Chgo., 1988-89; exec. Ill. Dept. Mental Health and Devel. Disabilities, Chgo., 1989—; prin. NPO Innovators, Chgo., 1988—. Mem. Unitarian Ch. of Naperville, 1973—; vol. Girl Scouts U.S. of DuPage County, Naperville, 1973-77. Mem. Nat. Soc. Fundraising Execs., Women in Mgmt., NAFE, CARA, Kappa Delta Phi. Democrat. Office: Ill Dept Mental Health 100 W Randolph St Ste 6-400 Chicago IL 60601

STEPHENS, LAURA LYNNE, psychology educator, researcher; b. Ft. Worth, Oct. 24, 1958; d. William Henry and Shirley Lynne (Anderson) S.; m. David Searle Noble, May 26, 1984 (div. Jan. 1990). BA, Purdue U., 1980; PhD, U. Mich., 1987. Asst. prof. dept. psychology N.Mex. State U., Las Cruces, 1987-89, Baylor U., Waco, Tex., 1989—. Contbr. articles to profl. jours. Mem. charging party EEOC, Albuquerque, 1988—. Fellow NSF, 1979, NIMH, 1980, 82, 87. Mem. Am. Psychol. Assn. (presenter convs. 1982, 86, 88), AAUP, People for Am. Way, Phi Beta Kappa. Office: Baylor U Box 7334 Waco TX 76798-7334

STEPHENS, LISA ANN, commodity broker; b. Brady, Tex., Aug. 21, 1959; d. Harold L. and Peggy (Shuffield) S. BS in Agrl. Econs., Tex. A&M U., 1982. Mgr., bookkeeper The Stephens Co., Stephens Wool & Mohair & Grain Elevators, Eden, Tex., 1982-83, Stephens Real Estate, San Angelo, Tex., 1983-86; residential appraiser Robert A. Elliott Real Estate, San Angelo, Tex., 1986-87; ptnr. H&L Ranch Co., Eden, 1986—; property mgr. City of San Angelo, 1987, div. asst. supt., 1985-87; right of way appraiser Dallas County, Tex., 1987-88. Mem. Nat. Assn. Realtors, Tex. Bd. Realtors, Southwestern Cattle Raiser's Assn., Tex. Cattle Raiser's Assn., Tex. Sheep and Goat Raisers Assn., San Angelo Stock Show and Rodeo Assn. (div. asst. supt. 1985-87). Methodist. Home and Office: PO Box 1693 Boune TX 76806

STEPHENS, MARY ELIZABETH, retirement communities chain executive; b. Lancaster, Pa., Feb. 20, 1949; d. Robert Eugene Detwiler and Sarah Louella (Hostetter) Weigand; m. George Frederick Stephens, Oct. 19, 1974. Grad. in nursing, St. Joseph's Hosp., Lancaster, 1970; BS with Nursing Emphasis, Castleton (Vt.) State Coll., 1977, MA in Edn. with Adminstrn. Emphasis, 1982. RN, Pa., Vt.; lic. nursing home adminstr., Pa. Asst. dir. nurses Masonic Homes, Elizabethtown, Pa., 1970-74; shift supr. Springfield (Vt.) Convalescent Ctr., 1975-78; dir. nurses Hanson Court Convalescent Home, Springfield, 1978-79; instr. Community Coll. Vt., Springfield, 1979; exec. dir. Springfield Area Hospice, 1979-80; adminstr. Leader Nursing and Rehab. Ctrs., Manor Care Inc., Valley Forge, Pa., and Silver Spring, Md., 1981-84; mgmt. cons. Health Care Resources, Inc., Valley Forge, 1985; health care coord. Armstrong World Industries, Inc., Lancaster, Pa., 1985-87; corp. dir. personal care svcs. and staff devel. George M. Leader Family Corp., Hershey, Pa., 1988—; lectr. Pa. Health Care Assocs., Harrisburg, 1985, 89. Home: 249 N Mt Joy St Elizabethtown PA 17022 Office: George M Leader Family Corp 830 Cherry Dr Hershey PA 17033

STEPHENS, NORMA J., hospital administrator; b. Beagle, Kans., Sept. 23, 1928; d. August F. and Flossie Mae (Matney) Loch; m. Charles C. Stephens, Oct. 16, 1948. BA in Health Care Adminstrn., Ottawa U., 1978; MPA, U. Kans., 1981. Cert. Mental Health Adminstr.; accredited med. record technician. Sec. to supt. Osawatomie (Kans.) State Hosp., 1946-50, med. records supr., 1950-55, registrar, 1955-82, dep. exec. officer, 1982-86, supt., 1986—; interim supt. Topeka State Hosp., 1988-89; bd. dirs. Am. State Bank, Osawatomie. Co-chairperson Osawatomie PRIDE com., 1982-86; chairperson fin. com. 1st United Meth. Ch., Osawatomie, 1971-77, 80-83. Named Woman of Yr., Bus. and Profl. Women, Osawatomie, 1986, Outstanding Pub. Adminstr. of Yr., Kans. chpt. Am. Soc. Pub. Adminstrn., Topeka, 1989. Mem. Am. Med. Record Assn., Assn. Mental Health Adminstrs. (mem. ethics com. 1984-86), Kans. Med. Record Assn., Ord. Ea. Star (officer 1960-64, worthy matron 1964-65, grand marshall 1967-68), Pi Sigma Alpha. Republican. Home: Box 500 Osawatomie KS 66064 Office: Osawatomie State Hosp Box 500 Osawatomie KS 66064

STEPHENS, PAMELA MITCHELL, airline pilot; b. Otis AFB, Mass., May 6, 1955; d. Gene Thomas and Rose Margaret (Jones) Mitchell; m. Robert Carroll Stephens, May 26, 1984. BFA, Colo. State U., 1975; postgrad., Webster Coll., 1981. Lic. pilot, Ill., comml. instr., airline transport pilot, jet rating, Boeing 747 and 727. Flight attendent United Airlines, Chgo., 1976-80; charter pilot Air Aurora, Sugar Grove, Ill., 1978-80; owner, operator Deliverance, Unltd. Ferry Co., Aurora, Ill., 1978-81; flight test pilot Cessna Aircraft Co., Wichita, Kans., 1981-82, nat. spokeswoman, 1982-83; airline pilot Rep. Airlines, Mpls., 1983-84, Northwest Airlines, Mpls., 1985—; pres., ptnr., half owner, artist Aerographics, Jacksonville, Fla., 1986—. Mem. Safety Coun. Airline Pilots Assn., 99's Internat. Women Pilots, Experimental Aircraft Assn., Aircraft Owners and Pilots Assn., Mooney Aircraft Pilots Assn., Internat. Women Airline Pilots Soc., Nat. Aviation Club, Northwest Airline Ski Team, Kappa Kappa Gamma. Republican. Presbyterian. Home: 4488 Fishing Creek Ln Jacksonville FL 32210 Office: Northwest Airlines Minn/St Paul Internat Airport Saint Paul MN 55111

STEPHENS, SHERYL LYNNE, family practice physician; b. Huntington, W.Va., Dec. 11, 1949; d. William Clayton Stephens and Virginia Eleanor (Hatten) Stephens Terry; 1 child, William Earl Hicks III (dec.); m. Lannie Dale Rowe, Jan. 17, 1981; 1 child, Seton Christopher. BA, U. Ky., 1972; MA, Marshall U., 1982, MD, 1988. Tchr. Wayne County Bd. Edn., Ceredo, W.Va., 1973-83; real estate developer Huntington, 1981-88; resident in family practice Grant Med. Ctr., Columbus, Ohio, 1988—; researcher, 1976-81. Counselor, instr. Contact of Huntington, 1975-88; polit. activist pro choice movement and ratification of equal rights amemdment, 1976-81. Recipient Leadership award Marshall U., 1985. Mem. Am. Assn. Family Practitioners (pres. 1984-85, Leadership 1985), Am. Med. Women's Assn. (sec. 1985-86), NOW (pres. 1976-78, 79-81, v.p. Huntington 1978-79, sec. 1981-82), Nat. Abortion Rights Action League. Democrat. Home: 703 French Dr Columbus OH 43228 Office: Grant MEd Ctr 111 s Grant Ave Columbus OH 43215

STEPHENS, SUSAN KAY, veterinarian; b. Elgin, Ill., Nov. 23, 1954; d. John Lewis and Marjorie Kay (Leonard) S. BS in Zoology, Iowa State U., 1976; postgrad., U. Ill., 1981. Owner, ptnr. Mt. Tabor Animal Hosp., Winston-Salem, N.C., 1981--. Bd. dirs. Forsyth Humane Soc., Winston-Salem, 1988--. Mem. Phi Zeta, Am. Vet. Med. Assn., Am. Animal Hosp. Assn., N.C. Vet. Med. Assn. Republican. Home: 2705 Windy Crossing Dr Winston-Salem NC 27127 Office: Mt Tabor Animal Hosp 4138 Robinhood Rd Winston-Salem NC 27106

STEPHENS, VICTORIA LYNN, marketing professional, consultant; b. Atlanta, Jan. 22, 1960; d. James Harry Jr. and Pauline June (Leighton) S. BSBA, U. So. Miss., 1981. Fin. analyst Conoco, Inc., Lafayette, La., 1981-85, B. Friedman Mktg.and Mgmt. Cons., Dallas, 1985-86; corp. sales mgr. Trammell Crow Co., Atlanta, 1986-88; divisional v.p., ops. physician mktg. svcs. Jackson And Coker, Atlanta, 1988—; pvt. practice real estate cons., Atlanta, 1986-87. Host ann. drive Am. Cancer Soc., Atlanta, 1988—. Mem. Am. Mktg. Assn., Am. Hosp. Assn. (healthcare mktg. and planning), U. So. Miss. Alumni Assn. (pres. 1983-84), Healthcare Women Execs., NAFE. Presbyterian. Office: Jackson and Coker 115 Perimeter Ctr Pl #380 Atlanta GA 30346

STEPHENSON, AMY MARIE, marketing executive; b. San Francisco, Sept. 5, 1960; d. Jay Floyd and Shirley Ann (Sims) S. AA, Coll. San Mateo, 1981. Personnel asst. Seton Med. Ctr., Daly City, Calif., 1980-81; office mgr., exec. sec. Container Transp., San Francisco, 1981-82; mktg. adminstrv. asst. Genentech, Inc., San Francisco, 1982-85, sales adminstrn. coord., 1985-88, nat. program mgr., 1988—. Mem. Am. Pediatric Soc. Exhibitors Adv. Coun., NAFE, Internat. Soc. Meeting Planners, Profl. Conv. Mgmt. Assn., Health Care Exhibitors Assn., Meeting Planners Internat., Internat. Exhibitors Assn. Office: Genentech Inc 460 Pt San Bruno Blvd San Francisco CA 94080 also: 746 Bounty Dr #4608 Foster City CA 94404

STEPHENSON, BETTE M., physician, former Canadian legislator; b. Aurora, Ont., Can., July 31, 1924; d. Carl Melvin and Clara Mildred (Draper) S.; grad. Earl Haig Coll. Inst.; M.D., U. Toronto, 1946; m. Gordon Allan Pengelly, 1948; children—J. Stephen A., Elizabeth Anne A., C. Christopher A., J. Michael A., P. Timothy A., Mary Katharine A. Mem. med. staff Women's Coll. Hosp., 1950—, chief dept. gen. practice, dir. outpatient dept., 1956-64; mem. med. staff N.Y. Gen. Hosp., from 1967; elected Ont. Legislature for York Mills, 1975, 77, 81, 85; minister labor, 1975-78; minister edn., minister colls. and univs., 1978-85, treas. and dep. premier, 1985-86; bd. dirs. Can. Inst. Advanced Rsch. Fellow Coll. Family Physicians Can. (chmn. nat. coordinating com. on edn. 1961-64, chmn. confs. on edn. for gen. practice 1961, 63), Acad. Med. Toronto; mem. Ont. Med. Assn. (dir. 1964-72, pres. 1970-71), Can. Med. Assn. (dir. 1968-75, pres. 1974-75), Art Gallery Ont., Royal Ont. Mus., Ont. Police Commn.

STEPHENSON, DEBORAH MAE, lawyer; b. Salem, Mass., Sept. 10, 1946; d. George Eustis Stephenson and Edythe Mae Geissinger Storrow; m. Philip C. Wysor, Aug. 23, 1969; children: Adam D., Nathaniel P., Jessica F. BA, Colby Coll., 1968; MBA, Boston U., 1982; JD, Suffolk U., 1982. Bar: Mass. 1982. Assoc. Hamel, Deshaies & Gagliardi, Amesbury, Mass., 1983-89, Goldman & Goldman, Swampscott, Mass., 1989—. Mem. Mass. Bar Assn., North Shore Women Lawyers Assn., Phi Beta Kappa. Office: Goldman & Goldman 990 Paradise Rd Swampscott MA 01907

STEPHENSON, IRENE HAMLEN, biorhythm analyst, consultant, editor, educator; b. Chgo., Oct. 7, 1923; d. Charles Martin and Carolyn Hilda (Hilgers) Hamlin; m. Edgar B. Stephenson, Sr., Aug. 16, 1941 (div. 1946); 1 child, Edgar B. Author biorhythm compatibilities column Nat. Singles Register, Norwalk, Calif., 1979-81; instr. biorhythm Learning Tree Open U., Canoga Park, Calif., 1982-83; instr. biorhythm character analysis 1980—; instr. biorhythm compatibility, 1982—; owner, pres. matchmaking service Pen Pals Using Biorhythm, Chatsworth, Calif., 1979—; editor newsletter The Truth, 1979-85, Mini Examiner, Chatsworth, 1985—; researcher biorhythm character and compatibility, 1974—, selecting a mate, 1985—, biorhythm columnist True Psychic Inquirer, 1989—, True Astrology Forecast, 1989—, Psychic Astrology Predictions, 1990—; author: Learn Biorhythm Character Analysis, 1980; Do-It-Yourself Biorhythm Compatibilities, 1982; contbr. numerous articles to mags; frequent guests clubs, radio, TV. Office: Irene Hamlen Stephenson PO Box 3893 WW Chatsworth CA 91313

STEPHENSON, JAN LYNN, professional golfer; b. Sydney, Australia, Dec. 22, 1951; d. Francis John and Barbara (Green) S.; m. Eddie Vossler, 1982. Student, Australian schs. Profl. golfer, 1972—; mem. Australian Ladies Profl. Golf Assn. tour, 1972-73, U.S. Ladies Profl. Golf Assn. tour, 1974—. Winner New South Wales (Australia) Jr. Championship, 1963-69; winner Australian Jr. Championship, 1968-71, Australian Title, 1973, Sarah Coventry Championship, 1976, Birmingham Championship Ala., 1976, Women's Internat., 1978, Sun City Classic, 1980, Peter Jackson Classic, 1981, Mary Kay Classic, 1981, United Va. Bank Classic, 1981, Ladies Profl. Golf Assn. Championship, 1982, Women's Tucson Open, 1983, Women's U.S. Open, 1983, Lady Keystone Open, GNA Tournament, 1985, French Open, 1985, Santa Barbara Open, 1987, Safeco Seattle Classsic, 1987, Konica San Jose Classic, 1987, 1st LPGA Skins Game, Frisco, Tex., 1990; named Rookie of Yr., U.S. Profl. Golfers Assn., 1974; Sportsman of Yr., Sportswriters Assn., Australia, 1976. Office: 6300 Ridglea Pl Ste 1118 Fort Worth TX 76116*

STEPHENSON, LINDA JEAN, magazine executive; b. Sacramento, Sept. 26, 1952; d. Homer Nixon and Jean (Hanson) S. BA in Communications, Brigham Young U., 1978. News anchorwoman Sta. KBYU-TV-FM, Provo, Utah, 1977-78; sales rep. Daily Universe, Provo, 1977-78; advt. sales rep. Sawyer Ferguson Walker, N.Y.C., 1978-80; account exec. Gannett Newspaper Advt. Sales, N.Y.C., 1980-84, Ms. mag., N.Y.C., 1985-86; New Eng. mgr. Met. Home, N.Y.C., 1984-85, spl. events mgr., 1986—. Democrat. Mormon. Office: Met Home 750 3d Ave New York NY 10017

STEPHENSON, LINDA SUE, cosmetic company executive; b. Monroeville, Ind., June 30, 1939; d. LeRoy Lloyd and Edith Lillian (Marquardt) Koehlinger; m. Jack Lynn Stephenson, Dec. 31, 1961. Student modeling Ft. Wayne Finishing Sch., 1959, instr. cert., 1961. Bus. mgr. Ft. Wayne Finishing Sch., Ind., 1960-64; dir., tchr. Cameo Finishing Sch., Ft. Wayne, 1964-65; assoc. dir. Fashion Two Twenty, Decatur, Ind., 1969-71; dir. Marjo Cosmetics, Ft. Wayne, 1971-81; founder, dir. Cozme Cosmetics, Ft. Wayne, 1981—; founder, tchr. Image Projection Workshops, Ft. Wayne, 1981—; dir. Your Total Look, Ft. Wayne. Author: New Dimensions, 1982; Eyes on Ft. Wayne, 1983, also articles. 4-H leader 4-H Horse and Pony Club, Monroeville, Ind., 1962-75; foster parent Adams County Welfare, Decatur, Ind., 1969-73, Indian Program, Ft. Wayne, 1970-72; choral dir. Community Youth Choir, Monroeville, 1967-80, Methodist Men's Chorus, 1980-87. Named Equity Queen, Nat. Farmers Equity, 1960. Mem. Ft. Wayne Better Bus. Bur., Ft. Wayne Women's Bur., Women Bus. Owner's Assn., Nat. Hairdressers and Cosmetologists Assn., Ft. Wayne C. of C., Am. Women Entrepreneurs. Avocations: physical fitness, music, bird watching, flower gardening. Home: RR 2 Monroeville IN 46773 Office: Cozme Cosmetics 5821 Decatur Rd Fort Wayne IN 46816

STEPHENSON, LISA G., social worker; b. Tacoma, June 29, 1955; d. Harold B. and Yvonne L. (Watkins) S.; 1 child, Natalie A. AAS, Wenatchee (Wash.) Valley Coll., 1986; BA, E. Wash. U., 1988. Bookkeeper Wenatchee (Wash.) Golf Country Club, 1978-79; from clk. typist to support enforcement officer Dept. Soc. and Health Svcs., Seattle, Wenatchee, 1979-90; regional rep. Wash. State Centennial Celebration Com., Wemathee, 1986-89; trainer/planner, Human Resource assts., Dept. Social and Health Svcs., Spokane, Wash., 1986-89. Vol. Gov. Dixy Lee Ray re-election campaign, Seattle, 1980; supporter Chelane County Demo. Com.; troop leader, Girl Scouts U.S., Wenatchee, Wash., 1984-87; mem. Chelan County Centennial Youth Com., Wenatchee, Wash., 1987-88; mem. exec. bd. Women's Resource Ctr., Wenatchee, 1990-91. Mem. AAUW (treas. 1989), Bus. Profl. Women (pres. 1988-90, asst. dist. dir., 1990-91, Evergreens), Internat. Order Job's Daus.(sec. 1990-91). Home: P O Box 2214 Wenatchee WA 98807

STEPHENSON, MARY RITA, association executive; b. Toronto, Ont., Can., Mar. 27, 1917; d. John Alexander and Marie Josephine (Kennedy) Pickett; m. Harald Jon Stephenson, June 19, 1945 (div. 1969); children—Helga Maria, Fridrik Jon, Helen Veronica, Donald Joseph. Student, U. Toronto, 1933-36. Advt., sales promotion mgr. Assos. Textiles, Montreal, Que., Can., 1941-45; head pub. relations dept. Cardon Rose Ltd., Montreal, 1968-73; exec. dir., founder Fashion Designers Assn. of Can. Ltd., Montreal, 1974—; pres. Mary Stephenson & Assocs. Inc., Toronto, 1979—; v.p. Fashion/Canada; bd. dirs. Can. Colour Service. Named Canadian Style's Hall of Fame, 1990. Mem. Fashion Group Internat. Roman Catholic. Home: 675 Roselawn Ave, Toronto, ON Canada M5N 1L2 Office: 675 Roselawn Ave #209, Toronto, ON Canada M5N 1L2

STEPHENSON, TONI EDWARDS, publisher, investment management executive; b. Bastrop, La., July 23, 1945; d. Sidney Crawford and Grace Erleene (Shipman) Little; BS, La. State U., 1967; grad. owner/pres. mgmt. program Harvard Bus. Sch.; m. Arthur Emmet Stephenson, Jr., June 17, 1967; 1 dau., Tessa Lyn. ; pres., dir. Gen. Communications, Inc., Denver; sr. v.p., founder Stephenson & Co., Denver, 1971—, Stephenson Mcht. Banking, 1980—; gen. ptnr. Viking Fund; ptnr. Stephenson Properties, Stephenson Ventures, Stephenson Mgmt. Co.; pres., dir. Starpak Internat., Inc., Lloyd's of London; founder Charter Bank & Trust. Pub., Law Enforcement Product News, Inside Product News; sec., HBS/OPM16, former dir. The Children's Hosp., St. Joseph's Hosp. Past pres. Children's Hosp. Assn. Vols. Mem. Harvard Bus. Sch. Clubs of Colo., So. Calif. and Orange County, Colo. Press Assn., DAR, Delta Gamma. Clubs: Rancho Mirage (Calif.), Annabel's (London), Thunderbird Country, Denver Petroleum. Office: Gen Communications Inc 100 Garfield St Denver CO 80206

STEPNER, LARAINE E. ADLER, public relations executive; b. Boston, Sept. 25, 1943; d. Neil and Sadie Adelman (Adler). BA in English, Wellesley Coll., 1978; MA in Econs., Internat. Studies, Johns Hopkins U., 1980; Cert., Washington Sch. Protocol, 1979. Airline rep. Can. Pacific Airlines, San Francisco, 1968-70; tour escort AAA, others, 1970-76; travel rep. Trans Nat. Travel, Boston, 1973-76; chief exec. officer Internat. Photography Soc., Washington, 1981-83; also bd. dirs. Internat. Photography Soc.; prin. Laraine Stepner & Assocs., Boston, 1983-85; pres. Stepner & Sayre PR Ltd., Natick, Mass., 1985—; Owner mag. The Social Calendar, 1986—. Cable TV Host Women on the Move, 1987—; contbr. articles to profl. jours. Fundraiser Presdl. campaign, Washington, 1980-81, Boston Ballet, 1984, Vietnam VA, Boston, 1985, Fulbright Alumni Assn., 1988—; com. mem. Fair Housing Panel, Natick, 1987, Affordable Housing Com.; chosen to C. of C. Leadership Acad., 1987. Mem. Bus. and Profl. Women, Women's Mus. Art, Mass. Women's Polit. Caucus. Office: Stepner & Sayre Ltd 5 Summer St PO Box 882 Natick MA 01760

STERLING, A. MARY FACKLER, federal official, lawyer; b. Pioneer, Ohio, Sept. 4, 1955. AB cum laude, Harvard U., 1976; MA, Ohio State U., 1977; JD, NYU, 1980. Bar: Mo. 1980, U.S. Dist. Ct. (we. dist.) Mo. 1980, U.S. Ct. Appeals (8th cir.) 1983, U.S. Ct. Appeals (10th cir.) 1985. Assoc. Watson, Ess, Marshall & Enggas, Kansas City, Mo., 1980-82; asst. U.S. atty. we. dist. Mo. U.S. Dept. Justice, Kansas City, 1982-85, fed. prosecutor organized crime and racketeering strike force, 1985-86; White House fellow, spl. asst. to U.S. Atty. Gen. U.S. Dept. Justice, Washington, 1987-88; atty. McDowell, Rice & Smith, Kansas City, 1989; asst. sec. labor-mgmt. standards U.S. Dept. Labor, Washington, 1989—; instr. U.S. Atty. Gen.'s Advocacy Inst., Washington, 1986, 88, FBI Acad., Quantico, Va., 1988; guest lectr. NYU Sch. Law, 1986, 88; bd. dirs. Dept. Labor Acad., 1989-90. Bd. dirs. Root-Tilden Scholarship program, NYU, 1982-89; bd. dirs. Urban Crime Prevention Authority, Kansas City, 1980-81, Friends of Art, Kansas City, 1982-89, Friends of the Symphony, Kansas City, 1982-89;exec. dir. Bush/Quayle '88 Campaign State of Mo., 1988. Recipient Thompson award Ohio State U. Alumni, 1988; named One of Top Ten Coll. Women in U.S., 1975, one of Ten Outstanding Young Working Women in Am., 1987; named Kansas City Career Woman of Yr., 1988; Ohio State U. fellow, 1976-77; Root-Tilden legal scholar NYU, 1977-80. Mem. ABA (assembly del. 1986-89, ho. of dels. 1986-89, assembly resolutions com. 1986-89, com. on govt. litigation counsel litigation sect., com. complex crimes litigation), Mo. Bar Assn. (bd. govs. 1986-89, chmn. pro bono task force 1984-86, young lawyers council 1983-86, Outstanding Service award 1984, Pro Bono Publico award 1986), Exec. Women in Govt., Harvard U. Alumni Assn. (bd. dirs. 1989—), Hasting Pudding Club, Harvard Club.

STERLING, DOROTHY ANNE, leasing company professional; b. Scranton, Pa., May 14, 1963; d. Albert Webster and Dorothy (Kanyuck) S. Student, Marywood Coll., 1981-82, Kutztown (Pa.) U., 1982-83, Lackawanna Jr. Coll., Keystone Jr. Coll., La Plume, Pa., 1989—. Sales clk. The Globe Store, Scranton, 1987; with Northeastern Bank of Pa., Scranton, 1984—, lease processing clk., 1988-89, vehicle leasing group leader, 1989—. Mem. NAFE, Greater Scranton C. of C. (membership com. 1990—). Lutheran. Home: 1902 Green Ridge St Dunmore PA 18512 Office: Northeastern Bank of Pa 201 Wyoming Ave Scranton PA 18503

STERN, ARLENE HELEN, human resources administrator; b. Bklyn., Nov. 7, 1950; d. Irving and Shirley Judith (Koretz) Stern. BS in Labor Relations, U. Bridgeport, 1971; postgrad. Pace U., 1972-75. Personnel asst. Pathmark, Woodbridge, N.J., 1971-72, regional personnel mgr., 1972-75, dir. human resource planning, 1975-77, dir. personnel and labor relations, Phila., 1977-81; v.p. human resources Howland-Steinbach-Hochschild's, White Plains, N.Y., 1981-85; sr. v.p. human resources and distbn. P.A. Bergner & Co., Milw., 1985-89, exec. v.p. human resources and distbn., 1989—; mem. Frederick Atkins Personnel Adv. Bd., N.Y.C., 1981-86, chmn., 1984. Bd. dirs. Clavis Theatre, 1986—, women's div. Milw. Jewish Fedn., 1987—, Milw. Jewish Council, 1987—, Wis. State of Israel Bonds, 1988—. Mem. Am. Soc. Personnel Adminstrs., Am. Soc. Tng. and Devel. Home: 4800 N Lake Dr Whitefish Bay WI 53217

STERN, GRACE MARY, state representative; b. Holyoke, Mass., July 10, 1925; d. Frank McLellan and Marguerite M. (Nason) Dain; m. Charles H. Suber, June 21, 1947 (div. 1959); children: Ann, Peter, Thomas, John; m. Herbert L. Stern, May 13, 1962; stepchildren: Gwen, Herbert III, Robert. Student, Wellesley Coll., 1942-45; LLD (hon.), Shimer Coll., 1984. Asst. supr. Deerfield Twp., Lake County, Ill., 1967-70; county clk. Lake County, Ill., 1970-82; mem. Ill. Ho. of Reps., Springfield, 1984—; candidate for lt. gov. Ill., 1982. Author: With a Stern Eye, 1967, Still Stern, 1969. Democrat. Presbyterian. Home: 291 Marshman St Highland Park IL 60035 Office: 559 Roger Williams Ave Highland Park IL 60035

STERN, MARIANNE, advertising agency executive; b. Elizabeth, N.J., July 17, 1950; d. Arthur Leo and Anne (De Paola) Monaghan; m. Manfred Joseph Stern, July 11, 1970 (div.); children: Kathryn Anne, Manfred Joseph III. Student, Montclair (N.J.) State Coll., 1970; BA in English summa cum laude, Kean Coll. of N.J., 1978. Copywriter Patrick J. Gallagher Advt., Westfield, N.J., 1978-79; media dir. Rapp Advt., Springfield, N.J., 1979-85; account exec. Spectrum advt., Springfield, 1985; pres., account exec. Whitney A. Morgan Advt., Montclair, 1985—; cons. Monadel, Inc., Rahway, N.J., 1985—; bd. dirs. Delatush Systems, Inc., Montclair. Mem. publicity com. 200 Club of Union County, N.J., 1978; pub. chmn. Boy Scouts Am. Union County chpt., 1987. Mem. NAFE, Phi Kappa Phi, Lambda Alpha Sigma, Alpha Sigma Lambda. Office: Whitney A Morgan Advt 37 N Fullerton Ave Montclair NJ 07042

STERN, MICHELE SUCHARD, biology educator; b. Chgo., Mar. 17, 1943; d. Henry Raymond and Thelma (Halkin) Suchard; m. Daniel Henry Stern, June 9, 1963 (div. Apr. 1982); 1 child, Alexander Daniel. BS, U. Ill., 1964; MS, Tenn. Tech. U., Cookeville, 1966; PhD, Tulane U., 1969. Asst. prof. biology U. Mo., Kansas City, 1969-75, assoc. prof., 1975—; cons. U.S. Fish and Wildlife Svc., U.S. EPA, U.S. Dept. Agr., Midwest Rsch. Inst. Contbr. articles to profl. publs. Served to maj. U.S. Army, 1982-85, maj. Res. Grantee Office Water Resources Rsch., U.S. Dept. Interior, 1969-80, C.E., U.S. Army, 1972-76, 1989, U.S. Fish and Wildlife Svc., 1978. Mem. AAAS, Am. Chem. Soc., Am. Soc. Limnology and Oceanography, Ecol. Soc. Am., Soc. Environ. Toxicology and Chemistry, N.Am. Benthological Soc., Health Physics Soc., Assn. Women in Sci., Kansas City Women's C. of C., Res. Officers Assn. Democrat. Jewish. Office: U Mo Dept Biology 5100 Rockhill Rd Kansas City MO 64110

STERN, NANCY ANN, lawyer; b. N.Y., Dec. 24, 1944; d. Harold H. and Evelyn (Fields) Stern; m. Samuel R. Karetsky, Dec. 1, 1974. BA, Goucher Coll., 1967; JD, NYU, 1970. Assoc. Cohn Glickstein Lurie & Ostrin, N.Y.C., 1970-71, Stern & Burns, N.Y.C., 1971-72; assoc. Barovick Konecky Schwartz Kay & Schiff and predecessor firms, N.Y.C., 1972-76, ptnr., 1977-82; ptnr. Kay Collyer & Boose, N.Y.C., 1983-87, of counsel, 1987—. Mem. N.Y. Women in Film, 1977-. Mem. Assn. of the Bar of the City of N.Y. Democrat. Office: Kay Collyer & Boose 1 Dag Hammarskjold Pla New York NY 10017

STERN, NANCY FORTGANG, professor; b. N.Y.C., July 15, 1944; d. Murray and Selma (Karp) Fortgang; m. Robert A Stern, Sept. 3, 1964; children: Lori Anne, Melanie. AB, Barnard Coll., 1965; MS, NYU, 1968; MA, SUNY, 1974, PhD, 1978. Programmer analyst ATT, N.Y.C., 1965-67; asst. prof. Nassau Community Coll., Garden City, N.Y., 1965-68; adj. prof. Dowling Coll. SUNY, 1968-77; prof. Hofstra U., Hempstead, N.Y.; rsch. cons. Am. Inst. Physics, N.Y.C., 1976-77; adv. editor John Wiley & Sons, 1977—. Contbr. articles to profl. jours. Mem. Annuals of the History Computing (asst. editor in chief, 1977-87), Charles Babbage Inst, Nat. Computing Com.

STERN, ROSLYNE PAIGE, magazine publisher; b. Chgo., May 26, 1926; d. Benjamin Gross and Clara (Sniderman) Roer; m. William E. Weber, May 3, 1944 (div. Mar. 1956); m. Richard S. Paige, June 28, 1958 (div. Apr. 1978); children: Sandra Weber Porr, Barbara Paige Kaplan, Elizabeth Paige; m. Robert D. Stern, June 5, 1978. Cert., U. Chgo., 1945. Profl. model, singer, 1947-53; account exec. Interstate United, Chgo., 1953-58; sales mgr. Getting To Know You Internat., Great Neck, N.Y., 1963-71, exec. v.p., 1971-78; pub. After Dark Mag., N.Y.C., 1978-82; assoc. pub. Dance Mag., N.Y.C., 1978-85, pub., 1985—; bd. dirs. Rudor Consol. Industries, Inc., N.Y.C. Founding pres. Dance Mag. Found., N.Y.C., 1984—; life mem. nat. women's com. Brandeis U., Waltham, Mass., 1958—. Mem. Pub. Relations Soc. Am., LWV, Am. Theatre Wing. Democrat. Jewish. Home: 2 Imperial Landing Westport CT 06880 Office: Dance Mag Inc 33 W 60th St New York NY 10023

STERN, RUTH, business executive; b. Bronx, N.Y., Oct. 14, 1929; d. Albert and Margaret (Karl) Nussbacher; student Hunter Coll., N.Y.C., 1947, cert. writing UCLA, 1988; m. Martin Szold, Apr. 10, 1949 (div. Sept. 1978); children—Lauren, Terry; m. James C. Stern, Aug. 22, 1982. Exec. legal sec. to sr. partner firm Paul, Weiss, Rifkind, Wharton & Garrison, N.Y.C., 1958-62; asst. to pres. M.E. Green & Co., brokerage co., N.Y.C., 1962-65; demonstrator and cons. for various cosmetic cos., 1965—; founder, pres. Ruth Szold Promotional Models, N.Y.C., 1968-84, Cosmetic Art, Inc., cosmetic and theatrical workshops, N.Y.C., 1979-85; founder, pres., designer, promoter cosmetic line Cosmetic Art, 1979-85; columnist Fire Island News, Ocean Beach, N.Y., 1985-89; asst. to pres., chief exec. officer Gladden Entertainment, L.A., 1989-90; exec. adminstr. C&O of Cogent Light and Techs., 1990—; demonstrator-lectr. for TV, also video tapes; condr. cosmetic workshops for N.Y. Salute to Fashion Industries, 1981; cons. in field. Mem. council Girl Scouts U.S.A., 1964-69; bd. dirs. Bleecker Tower Tenants Corp., N.Y.C., 1979-80, chmn. architecture and design com., 1979-80, chmn. maintenance, 1980—, pres., 1981-82; mem. Hunger Project, Financial Family; lectr., mem. panel Am. Women's Econ. Devel. Corp., 1981. Recipient Gold medal Deborah Fund Raising Dinner, 1955. Mem. Foragers of Am., Nat. Retail Mchts. Assn., Fragrance Found., Cosmetic Exec. Women. Clubs: Brandeis U., Hadassah. Home: 8787 Shoreham Dr 1202 Los Angeles CA 90069

STERNAD, SUSAN MARIE, social work administrator, educator; b. Cleve., July 20, 1957; d. Joseph Anthony and Mary Ann (Grabinski) S. BA, Lake Erie Coll., Painesville, Ohio, 1979; MS in Social Adminstrn., Case Western Res. U., 1981; postgrad., Alfred Adler Inst., Chgo., 1984-87. Lic. ind. social worker, Ohio; cert. chem. dependency counselor, Ohio. Asst. mgr. Greater Cleve. Vocat. Info. Svc., Inc., 1980, asst. adminstr., 1981-83; rsch. asst. Case Western Res. U., Cleve., 1981-83, mem. adj. faculty Mandel Sch. Applied Social Scis., 1983—; supr. spl. svcs. Ctr. for Human Svcs., Cleveland Heights, Ohio, 1982-89; adminstr. family programs USCG, Cleve., 1989—; cons. Inst. for Creative Living, Cleveland Heights, 1988—, Cleve. Pub. Schs., 1983—, Citizens Mental Health Assembly, Cleve., 1984-88, local civic and ch. orgns., Cleve., 1983—. Contbr. articles to profl. jours. Chmn. Teen Stress and Suicide Prevention Com., Cleve., 1986—; bd. dirs. Citizens Mental Health Assembly, 1988—; mem. Women Speak Out for Peace and Justice, Cleve., 1985—. Recipient outstanding svc. award Ctr. for Human Svcs., 1984. Mem. Orgn. Profls. for Adolescent Recovery (exec. bd. 1983—, sec. 1985-88), N.Am. Soc. Adlerian Psychology, Ams. Inst. Adlerian Psychology. Office: USCG 1240 E 9th St Cleveland OH 44199

STERNAL, SANDRA GAUNT, dietitian; b. Chgo., Oct. 1, 1946; d. George A. and Beatrice Gaunt; m. Joseph F. Sternal; children: Chandra, Karn, John, Joseph. BS in Dietetics and Instl. Mgmt., U. Wis., 1969. Adminstrv. dietitian Luth Hosp., LaCrosse, Wis., 1970-73; cons. State of Wis., Madison, 1973-76, specialist procurement, 1976-81; dir. dietetic svcs. SunHealth, Charlotte, N.C., 1981-85; dist. mgr. ARA, Hunt Valley, Md., 1985-87, Morrison's Custom Mgmt. Svcs., Mobile, Ala., 1987—. Mem. Am. Dietetic Assn., Fla. Dietetic Assn., Dietitians in Bus. and Industry (sec. 1986-87). Republican. Methodist. Office: Morrison's Custom Mgmt 3014 U S Highway 301 N Ste 500 Tampa FL 33619

STERN BELLOWE, JACQUELINE, physician; b. Syracuse, N.Y., May 2, 1958; d. Arthur Paul and Edith Marguerite (Samuel) Stern; m. Howard Lee Bellowe, Sept. 4, 1988; 1 child, Ilana Michelle. BS, UCLA, 1979; MD, U. Calif., San Diego, 1983. Diplomate Am. Bd. Family Practice. Intern, resident in family practice Mercy Med. Ctr., Denver, 1983-86; family physician Colo. Permanente Med. Group, Denver, 1986-89, Ponderosa Med. Group, Aurora, Calif., 1990—; mem. med. staff St. Joseph Hosp., Denver, 1986-89; mem. staff Aurora Humana Hosp., 1990—. Mem. Physicians for Social Responsibility, Am. Med. Womens Assn., Am. Acad. Family Physicians, St. Joseph Hosp. Med. Staff Peer Rev. and Quality Assurance, Colo. Acad. Family Physicians (bd. dirs. 1989—), Aurora Med. Soc., Colorado Med. Soc. Democrat. Jewish. Office: Ponderosa Family Physicians PC 14991 E Hampden Ave Ste 210 Aurora CO 80014

STERNBERG, DONNA UDIN, lawyer; b. Phila., May 3, 1951; d. Jack and Frances (Osner) Udin; m. Harvey J. Sternberg; children: Zachary Samuel, Zoe Sara. Student Tel Aviv U., 1971; BA, Northwestern U., 1973; JD, Loyola U., Chgo., 1976. Bar: Ill. 1976, Pa. 1979. Profl. actress, dancer, model, 1961-76; dancer Boishoi Ballet Co., 1965, 66, 67, Leningrad Kirov Ballet Co., 1966; actress Broadway prodn., 1966; appeared stage plays, TV and film roles, 1961-77; model nat. fashion mags. and publs., 1961-77; assoc. firm Ronald H. Balson & Assocs., Chgo., 1976-79, Mesirov, Gelman, Jaffe, Cramer & Jamieson, Phila., 1979-81; mem. firm Blank, Rome, Comisky & McCauley, Phila., 1981—. Active young leadership council Fedn. Allied Jewish Appeal, 1982-84; mem. Israel Bonds New Leadership Cabinet, 1982-87. Mem. ABA, Pa. Bar Assn., Phila. Bar Assn. Jewish. Club: Locust (Phila.). Office: Blank Rome Comisky & McCauley 4 Penn Ctr Plaza Philadelphia PA 19103

STERNE, BOBBIE LYNN, city council member; b. Ohio, Nov. 27, 1919; m. Eugene Sterne (dec.); children: Lynn, Cindy. Student, Akron U., 1941-42; student, U. Cin., 1946-47. City coun. mem. City of Cin., 1971—, mayor, 1976, 79; chair human resources com., 1987-89, mem. fin. and labor com., law and pub. safety com., pub. works and traffic safety com., chair intergovtl. affairs and environ. com. 1990—, urban devel. com. City Coun., Cin.; past chair fin. and labor com., human resources com., City Coun., Cin.; past mem. vice chair pub. wks. and traffic safety com. City Coun. Cin., also housing com.; trustee City of Cin. Retirement System, 1989-90; mem. Planning Commn., City of Cin., 1989-90, others. Mem. Adult Basic Edn. Bd.; mem. adv. com. Sch. Social Work U. Cin., Parents Anonymous, YWCA Alice Paul House, Bethesda Women's Network, Big Bros. and Big Sisters; mem. Arthritis Found., Cancer Control Coun., Caracole Bd., Charles P. Taft Meml. Fund Com., Community Chest, Drug and Poison Info. Ctr., Friends of Cin. Parks, Friends of the William Howard Taft Birthplace, gerantology community adv. bd. Deaconess Hosp., Greater Cin. Coalition People with Disabilities; chair Emergency Svcs. Coalition. Recipient Coun. Jewish Women Hannah G. Solomon award 1972, Citizens Com. on Youth's Most Valuable Citizen award, Achievement award Greater Cin. Beautiful Com., 1982, Anniversary award for work with Housing for Older Ams., Inc. Better Housing League, 1982, Orchid award Tri-State Air Com., 1982, Citizen's award Ohio Assn. for the Edn. Young Children, Advocate award Women in Communications, 1983, Betty Blake Award for Tourism, 1985, Others award Salvation Army, 1986. Home: 4033 Rose Hill Ave Cincinnati OH 45229

STERNER, JUDY MURTZ, legal administrator; b. Hollywood, Fla., Dec. 28, 1953; d. Richard John and Donna Jean (Freshley) Murtz; m. Michael Andrew Sterner, July 20, 1960. AS, DeKalb Community Coll., Clarkston, Ga., 1974; student, Ga. State U., 1983. Legal sec. McCurdy & Candler, Decatur, Ga., 1974-76, Gambrell & Mobley, Atlanta, 1976-77; office mgr. Bost & Ivy,/Scoggins Ivy, Goodman & Weiss, Atlanta, 1977-83; legal sec. BellSouth Corp., Atlanta, 1983-85, budget coord., 1986-87; asst. staff mgr. tax dept. So. Bell, Atlanta, 1985-86; legal adminstr. Bell South Corp., 1987—. Mem. Tel. Pioneers of Am. Lutheran. Office: BellSouth Corp 1155 Peachtree St NE #1800 Atlanta GA 30367-6000

STERRY, BARBARA REED, academic administrator; b. Cleve., Oct. 12, 1943; d. Marvin George and Ruth (Schneider) Reed; m. Leland Gerard Sterry, Nov. 15, 1963; 1 child, Anne Coleman. BA, Barry U., 1969; MBA, Nova U., 1990. Tchr. Broward County Pub. Schs., Ft. Lauderdale, Fla., 1970-75; with Fla. Dept. Health & Rehab. Svcs., Ft. Lauderdale, 1975-81, 82-86, detention supt., 1983-84, program mgr. children, youth and families, 1984-86; communications specialist Enfields/3M Co., Ft. Lauderdale and Miami, Fla., 1981-82; asst. dir. Inst. for Social Svcs. Nova U., Ft. Lauderdale, 1987-88, asst. dean, dir. continuing edn., 1988-89, program adminstr. rsch. svcs., 1990—; cons. Nova U., 1986-87. State of Fla. scholar, 1985; named Woman of the Yr., Women in Communicaton, 1986. Mem. LWV. Republican. Office: Nova U 3301 College Ave Fort Lauderdale FL 33314

STETS, DEBRA KAY, distribution company executive; b. Painesville, Ohio, Jan. 7, 1958; d. David L. and Phyllis J. (Lockard) Rosenbaum; m. Mark A. Stets, June 25, 1983; children: Courtney M., Joshua D. A in Bus., Lakeland Community Coll., Mentor, Ohio, 1986. Sec. to dir. sales Bowman Distbn../Barnes Group Inc., Cleve., 1977-79, sec. to dir. mktg., 1979-81, sec. to gen. mgr., 1981, asst. sales adminstr., 1981-87, sales adminstr., 1987-89, supr. customer svc., 1989—. Mem. Nat. Assn. for Female Execs., Inst. Cert. Profl. Mgrs. Roman Catholic. Office: Bowman Distbn Inc 850 E 72nd St Cleveland OH 44103

STETSON, NANCY E., college official, educator; b. Kitty Hawk, N.C., Sept. 24, 1936; d. Harold Clifton Stetson and Nannie Temperance (White) Mattern; children: Laurel Kroon Hair, Nancy Lee Kroon. AA, Wenatchee Valley Coll., Wenatchee, Wash., 1973; BA, Evergreen State Coll., Olympia, Wash., 1976; MS, Cen. Wash. U., 1980; EdD, Nova U., 1985. Info. specialist, pub. info. officer, dir. info. and devel. Wenatchee Valley Coll., 1972-80; interim dean North Campus Wenatchee Valley Coll., Omak, Wash., 1981; asst. to pres. Wenatchee, 1980-82, instr., 1972-79; dir. pub. affairs and devel. Marin Community Coll. Dist., Kentfield, Calif., 1982-86, interim adminstr. student svcs., 1984, dean devel. and info. svcs., 1986-87, acting v.p. for student and spl. svcs., 1987-88, v.p. for planning and devel., 1988—; instr. Coll. of Marin, Kentfield, 1982—; external cons., evaluator Cen. Ariz. Coll., Feather River Coll., Solano Community Coll., Foothill Coll., Olympia Tech. Contbr. numerous articles to profl. jours., also verse, short stories and poetry. Pres. Allied Arts Coun. No. Cen. Wash., Wenatchee, 1977-78; bd. dirs. Wenatchee Bd. Parks and Recreation, 1979-82; spl. gifts solicitor United Way Bay Area, Marin County, 1987—; instr. Coll. Commr. Sci., Boy Scouts Am., Vallejo, Calif., 1989. Recipient appreciation award Wenatchee Valley Coll. Students, 1974, Outstanding Svc. and Dedication to Students award Alpha Gamma Sigma, Coll. of Marin, 1987, 88. Mem. Am. Assn. Higher Edn., Am. Assn. Women in Community and Jr. Colls., Nat. Coun. for Resource Devel. (bd. dirs. 1977-84, v.p. 1983), Assn. Calif. Community Coll. Adminstrs., No. Calif. Community Coll. Rsch. Group (bd. dirs. 1989—, v.p.). Home: 222 Butterfield Rd San Anselmo CA 94960 Office: Marin Community Coll Dist College Ave Kentfield CA 94904

STETTLER, CARLA RICE, marketing executive; b. Louisville, Nov. 21, 1947; d. Rudolph Carl and Mildred N. (Sharp) Rice; m. John Austin Stettler, Sept. 19, 1967; children: Susan Romaine, Melissa Ann, Jennifer Jon. BA in Communications, Spalding U., Louisville, 1988. Freelance reporter Fern Creek Neighbor Newspaper, Louisville, 1978-79, Courier-Jour., Louisville, 1978-79; sec.-treas. Fern Creek United Meth. Ch., 1979-84; circulation mgr. Fern Creek Neighbor Newspaper, 1984-85; exec. sec. Spalding U., 1985-89; mktg. coordinator Genequip, Inc., Louisville, 1989—. Troop leader Girl Scouts Am., Louisville, 1974-80; bd. dirs. Fern Creek United Meth. Ch., 1979-84. Mem. Women in Communications, Nat. Assn. Female Execs., Louisville Bus. and Profl. Women. Office: Genequip Inc 1120 Ulrich Ave Louisville KY 40219

STEUART, SYBIL JEAN, elementary school educator; b. New Orleans, Aug. 6, 1954; d. John Thompson and Sybil Rose (Cousans) S. BS in Elem. Edn., Loyola U. of the South, New Orleans, 1976; postgrad., U. So. Miss., William Carey Coll. Cert. elem. sch. tchr., Miss. Tchr. 6th grade St. Rita Elem. Sch., New Orleans; tchr. kindergarten Sacred Heart Elem. Sch.,

D'Iberville, Miss.; presenter ednl. workshops. Lay mem. Mercy Assocs., St. Louis, 1985—; vol. aide Vets. Hosp., Biloxi, Miss., 1989; commentator, lector Sacred Heart Ch., Ocean Springs, Miss., Sacred Heart Ch., D'Iberville, Miss., 1988—; kindergarten tchr. Christian doctrine St. Elizabeth Seton Ch., Ocean Springs, 1982—, mem. confrat. of Christian doctrine, commentator, lector; v.p. Friends of Ocean Springs Libr., 1983—; vol. various civic and ch. orgns. Recipient Cert. of Appreciation, New Orleans Pub. Schs., 1974, Bishop's Svc. Cross award Diocese of Biloxi, 1985; named Outstanding Young Educator of Biloxi, Jaycees, 1986; named to Order of St. Louis, Archdiocese of New Orleans, 1980. Mem. ASCD, Nat. Cath. Educator's Assn., Mississippians for Ednl. Broadcasting, St. Elizabeth Seton Altar Soc. (chmn. spiritual com. 1988—), Coast Community Concert Assn., St. Mary's Dominican High Sch. Alumni Assn. (developer ednl. advancement programs), Loyola U. Alumni Assn. (developer ednl. advancement programs), Sacred Heart Auto League. Roman Catholic. Office: Sacred Heart Elem Sch 10482 LeMoyne Blvd D'Iberville MS 39532

STEUDTNER, MICHELLE ROTHER, management consultant; b. Houston, Nov. 5, 1965; d. Melvin Roy and Dorothy Gail (Warthan) Rother; m. Richard Todd Steudtner, Sept. 17, 1988. BBA, Tex. A&M U., 1988. System analyst Barrios Tech., Inc., Houston, 1984-87; conf. coord. Tex. A&M U., College Station, 1987; staff cons. Andersen Cons., Dallas, 1988—. Named one of Outstanding Young Women Am., 1986, 87; recipient Chapman Fund award Optimist Scholarship Found., 1987, 88. Mem. NAFE, Data Processing Mgmt. Assn., Phi Kappa Phi, Delta Zeta. Methodist. Home: 18081 Midway Rd #2821 Dallas TX 75287 Office: Andersen Cons 901 Main St Dallas TX 75202

STEUER, JOANNE, psychologist; b. Jersey City; d. George I. and Rose Levine. MS, U. So. Calif., L.A., 1974, PhD, 1977. Asst. rsch. psychologist UCLA, 1977-85; asst. rsch. prof. U. So. Calif., 1984-90, clin. assoc., 1990; chief psychol. svcs. White Meml. Med. Ctr., L.A., 1984—; dir. med. psychology group L.A., 1990. Contbr. articles to profl. jours. and chpts. in books. Mem. Am. Psychol. Assn., L.A. Soc. Clin. Psychologists (chair bd. hosp. practice 1986-90), L.A. County Psychol. Assn. (co-chair hosp. practice com. 1986-90, bd. dirs. 1990—). Office: 1555 N Ogden Dr Los Angeles CA 90046

STEVENS, ANN ROBINSON, dietitian; b. N.J., Feb. 10, 1951; d. Dexter and Virginia (Barney) S. BSHE, Hood Coll., 1973; MS, Ohio State U., 1975; MBA, Thomas Coll., 1989. Dietician Valley Hosp., Berlin, N.H., 1976-80; instr. U. N.H., Durham, 1979; cons. dietician Coos County Nursing Home, Berlin, 1978-80; dietician Meml. Hosp., Rochester, N.H., 1980-82; mgr., dietician Franklin Meml. Hosp., Farmington, ME, 1982-84; chief clin. dietician Mid Maine Med. Ctr., Waterville, ME, 1984-86, Masonic Home, Utica, N.Y., 1986-88; cons. dietician Eden Park Nursing Home, 1987-88; dist. dietitian Seiler Corp., Waltham, Mass., 1988—. Mem. Am. Dietetic Assn., N.Y. Dietetic Assn.

STEVENS, ANNE HAWLEY, executive search firm principal, consultant; b. Altoona, Pa., May 30, 1956; d. John King McLanahan and Carol (Bradford) S. BA, Boston U., 1978, MEd, 1981. Workshop/residential coordinator Task Oriented Communities, Waltham, Mass., 1978-80; clin. intern Counseling Services, Inc., Boston, 1980-81; dir. human resources, assoc. dir. Fee Mail Couriers, Boston, 1981-84; prin. A. H. Stevens Assocs., Boston, 1984—; housing renovator. Mem. Mass. Assn. Personnel Cons. (regional bd. dirs. 1984-87), Assn. Women in Psychology, New England Women in Real Estate, Associated Builders and Contractors, Thespian Soc., Nat Mus. of Women in Arts (charter), Nat. Assn. Female Execs. Democrat. Episcopalian. Avocations: water skiing, cooking. Home and Office: PO Box 279 North Scituate MA 02060

STEVENS, APRIL, legal administrator; b. Portsmouth, Ohio, Apr. 30, 1957; d. Gerald Rudolph Gilmore and Karen Nancy (Bowser) Wyant; divorced; 1 child, Patricia Jeannette Urban. Student, U. South Fla., 1972-75, 82-83; cert. as legal sec., Charron Williams Bus. Coll., Tampa, Fla., 1977. Office mgr. Cen. Account Systems, Inc., Tampa, 1977-78; legal asst., sec. G. Stewart McHenry, Esquire, Tampa, 1978-81; legal sec. G. Gregory Jones, Esquire, Tampa, 1981-82; legal asst., sec. R. Ray Brooks & Richard Blunt, Esquire, Tampa, 1982-83; pres. adminstrn. Profl. Office Assistance, Tampa, 1983-84; ops. mgr. Today's Temp., Tampa, 1984-86; office mgr. Sessums & Mason, P.A., Tampa, 1986—. Mem. Assn. Legal Adminstr. (Suncoast chpt., chmn. human resources sect. 1987-89, bd. dirs., chair membership 1990-91), Nat. Assn. Legal Adminstrs. Democrat. Office: Sessums & Mason PA PO Box 2409 307 S Magnolia Tampa FL 33601

STEVENS, BETTY NEVELS, real estate broker, accountant; b. Erwinville, La., Feb. 14, 1941; d. Marlin Martin and Ruth (Edwards) Nevels; 1 child, Glenn K. Grad. high sch., Baton Rouge; cert. acct., U. So. Miss., 1972. Cert. real estate broker, master appraiser. Bookkeeper, acct. Lyons Specialty Co., Baton Rouge, 1961-66; bookkeeper, sec. Builders Supply, Gloster, Miss., 1966-69, Southwest Miss. Devel. Co., Gloster, 1970-72, B&S Auto Sales, Gloster, 1972-76; owner, mgr. Fast Food Bus., Gloster, 1980-83; radio dispatcher Miss. Hwy. Patrol, Brookhaven, 1983-85; real estate broker Betty Stevens Real Estate, Gloster, 1985—; pub. acct. Gloster Tax Svc., 1969—; broker, owner Betty Stevens Real Estate, Gloster, 1985—. Mem. World Trade Ctr., New Orleans, 1988, Miss. Hist. Soc., Jackson, 1984, John James Audubon Found., Gloster, 1984. Mem. Southwest Bd. Realtors (sec.-treas. 1988—, Realtor of the Yr. 1989), Gloster C. of C. (pres. 1989—), Nat. Soc. Pub. Accts., Nat. Assn. Master Appraisers, Miss. Assn. Realtors, Nat. Assn. Realtors, Resdl. Sales Coun. Democrat. Pentecostal. Home: PO Drawer I Hwy 24 Gloster MS 39638 Offfice: Betty Stevens Real Estate Hwy 24 PO Drawer I Gloster MS 39638

STEVENS, CHRIS ANNE, food products company executive; b. Detroit, June 6, 1939; d. Frank and Angeline Malinowski; m. Walter S. Stevens (div. 1980); children: Linda Sue Stevens Fry, Laurie Ann, Lois Marie. Diploma in Nursing, Mercy Coll., Detroit, 1960; BA in Health Scis., Stephens Coll., 1975; postgrad., U. No. Colo., 1978-79. Coordinator Allied Health Program El Paso (Tex.) Community Coll., 1974-76; corp. mgr. health services Stanley Structures, Inc., Denver, 1976-80; pres. Chris Stevens Cons. Service, Sacramento, 1980-81; internat. cons. to mgmt. cons. Upjohn Health Care, Kalamazoo, Mich., 1981-87; pres. Crissy's Cheesecake Co., Ontario, Calif., 1986—. Contbr. articles to women's pubs. Mem. Bus. Women's Network, Nat. Assn. Female Execs., Am. Entrepreneurs Assn., Stephens Alumni Assn., Am. Soc. Profl. Cons. Roman Catholic. Office: PO Box 1340 Alta Loma CA 91701

STEVENS, CORNELIA ROCKWELL, public sailing club director; b. Lawrence, Mass., Apr. 22, 1953. BA in Art History, Franklin & Marshall, 1975. Asst. mgr. Community Boating, Boston, 1987-88; dir. Community Boating, 1988—. Mem. U.S. Yacht Racing Union, Mass. Bay Yacht Clubs Assn. (del. 1988-89). Office: Community Boating Inc 21 Embankment Rd Boston MA 02114

STEVENS, ELISABETH GOSS (MRS. ROBERT SCHLEUSSNER, JR.), writer, journalist; b. Rome, N.Y., Aug. 11, 1929; d. George May and Elisabeth (Stryker) Stevens; m. Robert Schleussner, Jr., Mar. 12, 1966 (dec. 1977); 1 child, Laura Stevens. B.A., Wellesley Coll., 1951; M.A. with high honors, Columbia U., 1956. Editorial assoc. Art News Mag., 1964-65; art critic and reporter Washington Post, Washington, 1965-66; free-lance art critic and reporter Balt., 1966—; contbg. art critic Wall Street Jour., N.Y.C., 1969-72; art critic Trenton Times, N.J., 1974-77; art and architecture critic The Balt. Sun, 1978-86;, 1989—; tchr. Am. lit. and writing The Writer's Ctr., Washington, 1990, Roland Park Country Sch., Balt., 1989-90. Author: Elisabeth Stevens' Guide to Baltimore's Inner Harbor, 1981, Fire and Water: Six Short Stories, 1982, Children of Dust: Portraits and Preludes, 1985, Horse and Cart: Stories from the Country, 1990; contbr. articles, poetry and short stories to jours., nat. newspapers and popular mags. Recipient A.D. Emmart award for journalism, 1980, citation for critical writing Balt.-Washington Newspaper Guild, 1980; art critics' fellow Nat. Endowment Arts, 1973-74, fellow MacDowell Colony, 1981, Va. Ctr. for Creative Arts, 1982, 83, 84, 85, 88, 89, 90, Ragdale Found., 1984, 89; Work in Progress grantee for poetry Md. State Arts Coun., 1986, Creative Devel. grantee for short fiction collection Mayor's Com. on Art and Culture, Balt., 1986. Mem. Coll. Art Assn., MLA, Balt. Writers Alliance, Balt. Bibliophiles, Popular Culture Assn., Authors Guild, Am. Studies Assn., Soc. Archtl. Historians. Home: 6604 Walnutwood Circle Baltimore MD 21212

STEVENS, FRANCES A., education administrator; b. Poteau, Okla., May 20, 1930; d. Clyde T. and Florence (Burns) Bennett; m. william C. Stevens, May 26, 1956 (dec. Feb. 1986); children: William Clyde, Sarah Stevens Gay. BS, U. N.Mex., 1951; MA, N.Mex. State U., 1966, EdD, 1971. Tchr. Albuquerque Pub. Schs., 1951-52; rsch. asst. N.Mex. State U., Las Cruces, 1967-70; tchr. Las Cruces Pub. Sch.s, 1957-63, counselor, 1965-67, program evaluator, 1970-85, coord. fed. programs, 1971-84; instr. N.Mex. State U., Las Cruces, 1975; dir. fed. programs Las Cruces Pub. Schs., 1984-85, assoc. supt. instrn., 1985—. Mem. adv. bd. Mesilla Valley Hosp., Las Cruces, 1988—, N.Mex. State U. Liaison Com.; v.p. Dona Ana County Drug and Crime Commn., 1987-88, mem. adv. bd. 1988—. Mem. AAUW, The Assn. (sec. 1987, v.p., pres. 1989), Assn. For Curriculum Devel., N.Mex. Adminstrs. Assn., Altrusa (v.p. 1987-89, treas. 1982-83), Phi Delta Kappa (sec., treas. 1982). Episcopalian. Home: 25 Las Casitas Las Cruces NM 88005

STEVENS, GEORGIANNA ANN, health resources executive; b. Indpls., Mar. 1, 1943; d. George Finley and Alice Patricia (Colson) Burk; m. John A Stevens. AD, Ind. U., 1963. Cert. radiologic technologist. Radiologist, technologist Meth. Hosp., Indpls., 1963-64; staff technologist Henry County Meml. Hosp., New Castle, Ind., 1964-65; chief technologist The Clinic, W. Lafayette, Ind., 1965-74; staff technologist Purdue U. Hosp., W Lafayette, Ind., 1974-77; med. asst. to nurse practitioner Purdue U. Hosp., W. Lafayette, Ind., 1977-82; asst. to radiation physician St. Elizabeth Hosp. Med. Ctr., Lafayette, Ind., 1982-87, dir. health resource ctr., 1987—; v.p. Ind. Soc. Radiologic Technologist, Lafayette, 1976-77. Bd. dirs. Am. Cancer Soc., Lafayette, 1986—, v.p. 1986-88, pres. Recipient Pres. award Am. Heart Assn., 1973, Merit award Am. Cancer Soc., 1986. Mem. Ind. Soc. Healthcare Edn. and Tng., Am. Registry Radiology. Republican. Roman Catholic. Office: St Elizabeth Hosp Med Ctr 1501 Hartford Lafayette IN 47904

STEVENS, HELEN JEAN, teacher, musician; b. Nevada, Iowa, July 11, 1934; d. Paul Ellison and Helen Margaret (Ives) S. MusB, U. So. Calif., L.A., 1956. Cert. secondary music tchr., Calif. Tchr. San Francisco Sch. Dist., 1956-58; prin. oboist Marin Symphony Orch., San Rafael, Calif., 1956—, Santa Rosa (Calif.) Symphony, 1956-86; tchr. Santa Venetia Mid. Sch., San Rafael, 1950-83; asst. prof. music Sonoma State Coll., Rohnert Park, Calif., 1963-76; tchr. Davidson Mid. Sch., San Rafael, 1984—; oboist Debut TV Show, L.A., 1954-55, Carmel (Calif.) Bach Festival, 1955-82; prin. oboist Light Opera Curren Theatre, San Francisco, 1966-67, Marin Opera Co., San Rafael, 1980-84. Active Sonoma County 4-H Guide Dog Project; leader Guide Dogs for Blind, Inc., 1974-87. Recipient Svc. award PTA, 1974, Golden Bell award Marin County Office of Edn., 1984; named Outstanding Tchr., Marin Edn. Found., 1986, Continuing Svc. award Calif. Congress Parents, Tchrs. and Students, Inc, 1989. Mem. German Shephard Dog Club Am. Democrat. Presbyterian. Home: 1450 Spring Hill Rd Petaluma CA 94952

STEVENS, JANE SEXTON, psychologist; b. Topeka, Apr. 3, 1947; d. Earl Luther and H. Eileen (Miller) Sexton; m. Robert David Stevens, Dec. 27, 1969; 1 child, James Robert. BA magna cum laude, Duke U., 1969, MEd, 1972, PhD, 1975. Lic. psychologist, N.C. Staff psychologist Children's Psychiat. Inst., Butner,, N.C., 1971-76, psychology program mgr., 1976-82, rsch. coord., 1982-88; pvt. practice Durham, N.C., 1982—; staff psychologist Butner,, 1989—; mem. adv. bd. Bragtown Project, Durham, N.C., 1976-82. Mem. Am. Psychol. Assn., N.C. Psychol. Assn. Home: 3439 Rugby Rd Durham NC 27707 Office: 20 W Colony Pl Ste 270 Durham NC 27705

STEVENS, JILL WINIFRED, control systems technologist; b. Southampton, Eng.; came to U.S., 1964; d. William Horace Routledge and Winifred Mabel (Richards) S. Asst. to producer BBC, London, 1961-64; governess pvt. home, Hillsboro, Calif., 1964-65; adminstrv. asst. Cambridge U. (Eng.), 1965-66; expediter, buyer, technician Bechtel Petroleum Inc., San Francisco, 1966-77, control systems technologist, Houston, 1978-83; control systems technologist Bechtel Power Corp., Houston, 1983-84; material planner Union Carbide/Bechtel Assn., Houston, 1988—. Recipient awards in English lang. and English lit. with honors, Royal Soc. Arts and Scis., London Day Coll., 1956. Mem. Instrument Soc. Am., Soc. Women Engrs. (assoc.). Roman Catholic. Home: 2121 Fountainview Condo E81 Houston TX 77057 Office: Bechtel Inc 3000 Post Oak Blvd Houston TX 77056

STEVENS, JOAN EVANS, computer programmer; b. Pitts., Feb. 17, 1950; d. J. Barry and Ruth Delouis (Ridgway) Evans; m. Robert L. Stevens; children: Robert B., Daniel L., Kyle A. BS in Math., Drexel U., 1973. Computer programmer U.S. AEC, N.Y.C., 1969-70, Abbotts Dairies, 1971, Del. Trust Co., 1971, NL Industries, 1972-73, Burroughs Corp., 1973-76, Ga. Iron Works, 1976-77, Augusta/Richmond County DPC, 1977, TRW, 1978; contract computer programmer Towanda, Pa., 1982—. Sch. dir. Towanda Area Schs., 1989—; chmn. com. Boy Scouts Am., 1987—, also den leader; pres. Barclay Friends Sch., 1985-87, bus. adminstr., 1987-88, treas., 1987-89. Mem. AAUW (2d v.p. Towanda 1988—). Home and Office: RR 5 Box 5202 Towanda PA 18848

STEVENS, LEOTA MAE, former educator; b. Waverly, Kans., Mar. 27, 1921; d. Clinton Ralph and Velma Mae (Kukuk) Chapman; m. James Oliver Stevens, Nov. 7, 1944; children: James Harold, Mary Ann Hooker. BA, McPherson Coll., 1954; MS, Emporia U., 1964, postgrad., 1969-77; postgrad., Wichita U., 1977. Educator Pleasant Mound Sch., Waverly, 1940-41; prin. educator Halls Summit Sch., Waverly, 1941-42; educator Waverly Grade Sch., 1942-43, Ellinwood (Kans.) Jr. High, 1943-45, Hutchinson (Kans.) Grade Sch., 1945-48, Lincoln Sch., Darlow, Kans., 1948-49; educator prin. Mitchell-Yaggy Consol. Sch., Hutchinson, 1949-57; educator elem. Hutchinson Sch. Dist. 308, 1957-85, ret., 1985; v.p. Reno County Tchrs. Assn. Hutchinson, 1956-57, pres. Assn. Childhood Edn. Internat., 1978-79. Author of numerous poems; compiler The Alexander-Kukuk Descendants: 1754 to 1985, 1985. Mem. Worker ARC Blood Mobile, 1986—, Hutchinson Community Concerts 1970—; ch. sch. tchr. Trinity United Meth. Ch., 1959-71; historian Woman's Civic Ctr., 1988—; den mother Cub Scouts 1963-66, leader Girl Scouts Ellinwood, 1944-45. Mem. AAUW (news reporter 1984-87), Ret. Nation State & Local Edn. Assn., Reno County Tchrs. Assn. (v.p. 1956-57), Assn. Childhood Edn. Internat. (pres. 1978-79), Rainbow Extension Club (pres. 1986—), Am. Legion Aux., Delta Kappa Gamma (sec. v.p. 1972-80, grant chmn. 1980-88). Republican. Home: 805 W 23d Ave Hutchinson KS 67502

STEVENS, LYDIA HASTINGS, state legislator; b. Highland Park, Ill., Aug. 2, 1918; d. Rolland T.R. and Ruth Shotwell (Beebe) Hastings; m. George Cooke Stevens, Nov. 2, 1940; children: Lydia Stevens Gustin, Priscilla Stevens Goldfarb, Frederick S., Elizabeth Stevens MacLeod, George H., Ruth Stevens Stellard. BA, Vassar Coll., 1939. State rep. 151st Dist. of Conn., Greenwich, 1988—. Pres. Greenwich YMCA, Conn., 1971-74; v.p. planning Greenwich United Way, 1973-76; pres. Greenwich Housing Coalition, 1982-86; warden Greenwich Christ Episcopal Ch., 1981-86; chmn. Diosecian Rev. Commn. Episcopal Diocese Conn., 1985-87; bd. dirs. Greenwich Libr., 1985—, Greenwich Hosp. Nursing Home Corp., 1987—; chmn. Greenwich Commn. Aging, 1987-89; pres., bd. dirs. Greenwich Broadcasting Corp., 1977-79; cons. Nat. Exec. Svc. Corps, N.Y.C., 1985. Protestant. Episcopal.

STEVENS, LYNN, financial consultant; b. Athens, Ga., Jan. 13, 1953; d. Joe A. Jr. and Eleanor W. (Mitchell) S.; m. Timothy L. Thomlinson, Apr. 5, 1974. BBA, Ga. So. Coll., 1974. Prin. examiner U.S. Govt. Nat. Credit Union Adminstrn., Atlanta; pres., chief exec. officer PWR Fed. Credit Union, Warner Robins, Ga.; v.p., comptr. Fla. State U. Credit Union, Tallahassee; chief exec. officer Stevens Cons., Macon, Ga.; mem. Gov.'s Commn. on Status of Women. Creator StevenSoft Acctg. and Fin. Analysis Software. Active Literacy Action. Recipient Ga. Courtesy Found. award. Mem. Credit Union Execs. Soc., Women in Credit. Office: 1060 Clairmont Pl Macon GA 31204

STEVENS, MARILYN RUTH, editor; b. Wooster, Ohio, May 30, 1943; d. Glenn Willard and Gretchen Elizabeth (Ihrig) Amstutz; BA, Coll. Wooster (Ohio), 1965; MAT, Harvard U., 1966; JD, Suffolk U., 1975; m. Bryan J. Stevens, Oct. 11, 1969; children: Jennifer Marie, Gretchen Anna. Bar: Mass. 1975. Tchr., Lexington (Mass.) Public Schs., 1966-69; in various editorial positions Houghton Mifflin Co., Boston, 1969—, editorial dir. sch. depts., 1978-81, editorial dir. math. and scis. Sch. Div., 1981-84, mng. editor, 1984—. Mem. ABA, Mass. Bar Assn.

STEVENS, PATRICIA ANN, executive director high education center; b. Rochester, N.Y., Dec. 16, 1946; d. Allee George and Alice Mae (Gray) Elliott; m. Dwight Morrow Stevens, Oct. 22, 1966; children: Kimberly Ori-Marie, Kenneth Todd. BS, SUNY, Brockport, 1970, MSED in Counseling, 1972; MSED in Higher Edn., SUNY, Rochester, 1979. Counselor Monroe Community Coll., Rochester, N.Y., 1970-76; asst. dir. Monroe Community Coll., Rochester, 1976-81, dir., 1981-89; exec. dir. Ednl. Opportunity Ctr. SUNY Brockport, Brockport, 1989—; continuing edn. counselor Monroe Community College, Rochester, 1975—; presentor at various conferences and workshops; cons. Onondaga Community Coll., Syracuse, N.Y., Community Coll. of the Finger Lakes, Canandaigua, N.Y. V.p. United Neighborhood Ctrs. of Greater Rochester; bd. mem. Genesee Settlement House, Inc.; chairperson Greater Rochester Area Spl. Programs; sec. Ralph Bunche scholarship bd.; bd. mem., sec. Ctr. for Ednl. Devel., others. Recipient Arthur O. Eve Dist. Community Svc. award, 1989. Mem. Nat. Assn. for Devel. Edn., N.Y. State Learning Skills Assn., Am. Fedn. Tchrs., N.Y. State Assn. Jr. Colls., N.Y. State United Tchrs., NAFE. Office: Ednl Opportunity Ctr 305 Andrews St Rochester NY 14604

STEVENS, PHYLISS ELIZABETH, fine art dealer; b. Balt., Dec. 30, 1953; d. Willie Reed and Rachel Mary (Brown) S. BS, Va. Commonwealth U., 1977. Gallery dir. KenWest Gallery, L.A., 1979-84; fine art cons. La Mirage Gallery, L.A., 1984-86; gallery dir. West 43rd St. Gallery, L.A., 1986-89; pres. Vibrant Fine Art, L.A., 1990—; dir., organizer Art in Pub. Places, L.A., 1984-86; creative dir. The Black Child/Art, L.A., 1986-88; art cons. NBC-TV Segment Series "Hill St. Blues", Hollywood, Calif., 1982. Editor Art Forum, 1984, American Black Artists Newsletter, 1988. Recipient Top Cons. Design Workshop award West Coast Art Stars, 1978, Community Involvement In the Arts award Founder's Women Club, 1980. Mem. NAFE, Am. Artist Club (pres. 1986-88). Democrat. Home: 2361 Pine St Long Beach CA 90806 Office: Vibrant Fine Art Los Angeles CA 90016

STEVENS, ROBERTA L., library administrator; b. Providence, Mar. 23, 1948; d. William F. and Emilia (Roselli) Leonelli; m. Henry J. Stevens; children: Michael H., John A.W. BA, Rosemont Coll., 1971; MLS, U. R.I., 1980. Asst. dir. Portsmouth (R.I.) Free Pub. Libr., 1979-87, assoc. dir., 1987—; mem. children's adv. coun. R.I. Dept. of State Libr. Svcs. Chairperson grad. libr. sci. sch. ann. gathering U. R.I., 1984. Recipient citation R.I. State Senate, 1988. Mem. R.I. Libr. Assn., R.I. Edn. Media Assn., N.E. Libr. Assn., Am. Assn. of Univ. Women (v.p. 1982-84 Newport chpt., women's issue chair 1985—), Portsmouth Garden Club (v.p.). Home: 381 Cory's Ln Portsmouth RI 02871 Office: Portsmouth Free Pub Libr E Main Rd Portsmouth RI 02871

STEVENS, ROSEMARY ANNE, public health educator; b. Bourne, Eng.; came to U.S., 1961, naturalized, 1968; d. William Edward and Mary Agnes (Tricks) Wallace; m. Robert B. Stevens, Jan. 28, 1961 (div. 1983); children: Carey, Richard. BA, Oxford (Eng.) U., 1957; Diploma in Social Adminstrn., Manchester (Eng.) U., 1959; MPH, Yale U., 1963, PhD, 1968. Various hosp. adminstrv. positions Eng., 1959-61; research assoc. Med. Sch. Yale U., 1962-68, asst. prof. Med. Sch., 1968-71, assoc. prof. Med. Sch., 1971-74, prof. pub. health Med. Sch., 1974-76; master Jonathan Edwards Coll., 1974-75; prof. dept. health systems mgmt. and polit. sci. Tulane U., New Orleans, 1976-78; chmn. dept. health systems mgmt. Tulane U., 1977-78; prof. history and sociology of sci. U. Pa., 1979—, chmn. dept., 1980-83, 86—, UPS Found. prof., 1990—; vis. lectr. Johns Hopkins U., 1967-68; guest scholar Brookings Instn., Washington, 1967-68; acad. visitor London Sch. Econs., 1962-64, 1973-74. Author: Medical Practice in Modern England: The Impact of Specialization and State Medicine, 1966, American Medicine and the Public Interest, 1971, In Sickness and in Wealth: American Hospitals in the Twentieth Century, 1989, (with others) Foreign Trained Physicians and American Medicine, 1972, Welfare Medicine in America, 1974, Alien-Doctors: Foreign Medical Graduates in American Hospitals, 1978. Bd. mgrs. Presbyn./Univ. Pa. Med. Ctr., bd. dirs. ednl. commn. for fgn. med. graduates. Mem. Inst. Medicine of Nat. Acad. Sci. (mem. coun.), History of Sci. Soc., Am. Assn. for History of Medicine, Am. Bd. Pediatrics (pub.), Cosmopolitan Club. Home: 319 S Hicks St Philadelphia PA 19102 Office: U Pa 215 S 34th St Philadelphia PA 19104-6310

STEVENS, SALLY ANN, interior and costume dsigner; b. Enid, Okla., Sept. 15, 1944; d. Ralph Leopold and Martha Loretta (Meyer) Richter; m. Donald Thompson Stevens, Jr., June 2, 1966; children: Zhawn, Angela, Amanda, Andrea. BEd, Phillips U., 1966, MEd, 1968; diploma interior design, LaSalle U., Chgo., 1972. Freelance designer SASI's (Sally Ann Stevens Interiors), Enid, 1970—; fashion designer under name Bare-None. Pres. Aquatic Club Enid; bd. dirs. Enid Joint Recreation and Trust; sustaining mem. Jr. Welfare League. Mem. NAFE, S.W. Home Furnishings Assn., P.E.O., Pi Beta Phi. Republican. Office: SASI's lll E Maine Enid OK 73703

STEVENS, SUSAN VIRGINIA, higher education administrator; b. Morlautern, Pfalz, West Germany, Jan. 25, 1955; d. James Montford and Eleanore (Edinger) S. BS in Biochemistry, Va. Poly. Inst. State U, Blacksburg, 1977; postgrad., Med. Coll. Va., Richmond, 1977-83; MS in Higher Edn. Adminstrn., Radford U., Va., 1985. Resident dir. Radford U., Va., 1983-85, Bloomsburg U., Pa., 1985-87; area coord. Memphis State U., 1987-90; asst. dir. residence life Mercer U., Macon, Ga., 1990—. Bd. Dirs. Va. Tech. Alumni Assn., Richmond, 1980-83. Named Grad. Teaching Asst. Yr. Va. Commonwealth U., Richmond, 1980. Mem. Am. Assn. Counseling & Devel., Am. Coll. Pers. Assn., Nat. Assn. Student Pers. Adminstrs., Tenn. Coll. & U. Housing Officers, Nat. Assn. Women Deans, Adminstrs. & Counselors, So. Assn. for Coll. Student Affairs, Assn. Coll. and U. Housing Officers Internat., Omicron Delta Kappa, Phi Kappa Phi. Republican. Home: 1347-C Adams St Macon GA 31201 Office: Mercer U Residence Life Office Macon GA 31217

STEVENS, VIOLET BERNICE, nursing administrator; b. Loris, S.C., May 17, 1940; d. Leroy and Carleen (Mincey) Sarvis; m. Jamed D. Stevens, May 7, 1961. Grad. in nursing, The McLeod Infirmary, Florence, S.C., 1961; BSN, Alaska Meth. U., 1975; MSN, U. Ariz., 1984. RN, S.C.; cert. nursing adminstr.; cert. quality assurance profl. Staff nurse St. Joseph's Hosp., Tucson, Sells (Ariz.) Indian Hosp.; nursing quality assurance coord. VA Med. Ctr., Tucson, supr. relief nursing, head nurse renal transplant unit. Mem. ANA, Am. Nephrology Nurses Assn., Ariz. Nurses Assn., Nat. Assn. Quality Assurance Profls.), Ariz. Assn. Quality Assurance Profls., Sigma Theta Tau. Home: 7550 S Placita de Cervecas Tucson AZ 85747 Office: VA Med Ctr S 6th Ave Tucson AZ 85723

STEVENSON, DENISE L., business executive, banking consultant; b. Washington, Sept. 18, 1946; d. Pierre and Alice (Mardrus) D'Auga; m. Walter Henry Stevenson, Oct. 17, 1970. AA, Montgomery Coll., 1967; BA in Econs./Bus. Mgmt., N.C. State U., 1983; cert. legal asst., Meredith Coll., 1989; cert. mgmt. Fin. Women Internat., 1990. Lic. ins. agt. Savs. counselor Perpetual Bldg. Assn. (now Perpetual Savs. Bank), Washington, 1968-70; regional asst. v.p. 1st Fed. Savs., Raleigh, N.C., 1971-83; pres., owner Diversified Learning Services, Raleigh, 1983—; instr. Inst. Fin. Edn., Raleigh, 1983—, Am. Inst. Banking, 1986; cert. leader Fin. Women Internat., 1987. Mem. NAFE, Inst. Fin. Edn. (2d v.p. 1982-83), Am. Bus. Women's Assn. (woman of yr. award 1982), Profl. Legal Assts., Nat. Assn. Bank Women (cert. leader 1987), Assn. Bank Trainers and Cons., Am. Soc. Tng. and Devel., Laurel Hills Women's Club (pres. 1974-75, Raleigh), Omicron Delta Epsilon. Avocation: fishing. Office: Diversified Learning Svcs PO Box 33231 Raleigh NC 27636

STEVENSON, FRANCES GRACE, small business owner; b. Colorado Springs, Colo., Aug. 4, 1921; d. Albert Earl and Grace Margaret (Cahill) Storey; m. Robert Louis Stevenson, Oct. 23, 1943; children: Donald Maurice, Nancy Jean, Richard Dean, James Kirk. Grad. high sch., Las Vegas, Nev.

Owner, mgr. Francie's Fancies, Napa, Calif., 1973-78, Cheyenne, Wyo., 1979—. Organizer Citizens Com. for Sylvan Dist. Schs., Citrus Heights, Calif., 1954; mem. Napa (Calif.) County Dem. Cen. Com., 1966-78, chmn., 1975-78; hdqrs. chmn. McGovern for Pres., Napa, 1972; mem. Calif. State Dem. Cen. Com., 1975-78; chmn. Klee for U.S. Congress, Napa County, 1976, Brown for Gov., Napa County, 1976; candidate 2d Congl. Dist. Calif. Assembly, 1976; elector Carter for U.S. Pres., Napa County, 1976. Mem. Am. Cut Glass Assn., Am. Carnival Glass Assn., Am. Bell Assn., Cheyenne C. of C. Episcopalian. Home and Office: 1715 Van Lennen Cheyenne WY 82001

STEVENSON, FRANCES KELLOGG, museum program director; b. Boston; d. Charles Summers and Alice deGueldry (Stevens) S. BA, Wells Coll., Aurora, N.Y., 1967; MA, Oxford U., 1972; postgrad., U. Pa., 1990—. News editor Sierra Club, San Francisco, 1970-71; copy editor Oxford (United Kingdom) U. Press, 1972-73; from editor to publs. officer Smithsonian Instn., Washington, 1974—. Co-editor: Abroad in America: Visitors to the New Nation, 1976; compiler: (book) National Portrait Gallery Permanent Collection Illustrated Checklist, 1982. James E. Webb fellow Smithsonian Instn., 1988-89. Mem. Sulgrave Club. Home: 2724 Ordway St NW Apt 4 Washington DC 20008 Office: Smithsonian Instn Portrait Gallery 8th and F Sts NW Washington DC 20560

STEVENSON, GRACE HOPE, retired social worker; b. Bradford, Yorkshire, England, Jan. 4, 1904; came to U.S., 1935; d. Archibald Campbell and Mary Helena (Robson) Hope; m. Kenneth Campbell MacDonald Stevenson, Dec. 21, 1939 (dec. 1940); 1 child, Kenneth Campbell MacDonald II. BA, U. B.C., Vancouver, Can., 1927, diploma in social work, 1930; MSW, U. Pa., 1964. Lic. social worker, N.J. Case worker, dist. sec. Family Welfare Assn., Montreal, Que., Can., 1930-35; asst. dist. sec. Bklyn. Bur. Charities, 1935-38; supr. family svc. Episc. City Mission, N.Y.C., 1938-40; case cons. Youth Conservation Svc., Trenton, N.J., 1945-47; supr. adoptions Children's Home Soc. N.J., Trenton, 1947-58; dir. rehab. svcs. Donnelly Hosp., Trenton, 1958-63; dir. rsch. congestive heart disease St. Peter's Hosp., New Brunswick, N.J., 1964-66; cons. N.J. Div. Mental Health and Hosps., Trenton, 1966-72; now ret.; mem.-at-large Social Svc. Coun., Princeton, N.J., 1964-67; del. NIH Conf., Calif., 1966, Internat. Conf. Social Welfare, Helsinki, Finland, 1968; bd. dirs. Nat. Assn. Social Workers, Cen. N.J., 1966-72. Watercolor artist, solo exhbns. include: Lambertville House, N.J., 1983, Lahaska, New Hope, Princeton, 1984, 85; exhibitor group shows in N.J., Pa.; contbr. articles to various publs., editorials to local newspapers. Del. Bucks County (Pa.) Housing Group, 1986—, Advocates for Human Needs, Bucks County, 1987—; mem. Village Improvement Assn., 1986—. Fellow Acad. Cert. Social Workers; mem. AAUW, LWV (bd. dirs. Bucks County chpt. 1987—), New Hope Art League, Sierra Club Southeastern Pa., Union Concerned Scientists, Bucks Alliance Nuclear Disarmament. Democrat. Episcopalian. Home: Holicong Rd Mechanicsville PA 18901

STEVENSON, HELEN ELIZABETH, pediatrician; b. Sumter, S.C., Jan. 14, 1955; d. William Hartin and Helen Elizabeth (Branche) S.; m. John Marcus Ellis; children: Lee Christopher, Anthony Kulvin, Renee Elizabeth. BS in Biohcemistry, Mich. State U., 1977; MD, Med. U. S.C., Charleston, 1981. Intern, resident Tulane Med. Ctr., New Orleans, 1981-84; staff pediatrician USAF, Maxwell AFB, Ala., 1985-89; pediatrician pvt. practice, Montgomery, Ala., 1989—; chief, dept. pediatrics Maxwell AFB Regional Hosp., Ala. 1988—. With USAF, 1985-89. Mem. Am. Acad. Pediatrics, Montgomery County Med. Soc. Home: 212 Deer Wood Dr Pratville AL 36067 Office: Pediatrics Clin Maxwell AFB AL 36112 also: 7020 Taylor Rd Ste 2200 Montgomery AL 36117

STEVENSON, JO ANN C., federal judge; b. 1942. AB, Rutgers U.; JD, Detroit Coll. Law. Admitted to bar, 1979. Bankruptcy judge U.S. Dist. Ct. (we. dist.) Mich. Office: US Dist Ct 240 Ford Fed Bldg Grand Rapids MI 49503*

STEVENSON, MARILYN ESTHER, consulting company executive; b. Chgo., June 9, 1933; d. John Michael and Mary Ann (Dusanic) Marchok; m. James Harold Stevenson, Aug. 13, 1955; children: J. Mark, Mary Linda, J. Scott, David H. Student, DePaul U., 1951-52; AB, U. Ill., 1955. Cert. tchr. Libr. asst. Purdue U., Lafayette, Ind., 1955-56; tchr. Tippecanoe County, Battleground, Ind., 1956-57; v.p., sec.-treas. James H. Stevenson, Inc., Palos Verdes, Calif., 1978—. Editorial bd. (book) Trustee Tool Kit for Libr. Trustees, 1988. Apptd. by Gov. to Vol. Calif. Libr. Svcs. Bd., Sacramento, 1979—, v.p. legis. chair; past bd. dirs.; mem., pres. bd. dirs. Palos Verdes Libr. Dist., Rolling Hills Estates, Calif., 1979-84. Named Woman of Yr. YWCA, Torrance, Calif., 1985. Mem. Am. Assn. Individual Investors, Calif. Assn. Libr. Trustees and Commrs. (pres. 1985, ALTA/ALA Trustee award 1989), LWV (pres. Palos Verdes chpt. 1977-79). Republican. Roman Catholic. Home: 2640 Via Carrillo Palos Verdes Estates CA 90274 also: La Paloma 234, Rosarito Baja California, Mexico Office: Calif Libr Svcs Bd PO Box 942837 Sacramento CA 94237-0001

STEVENSON, MAYBELLE IDA, nurse; b. Clinton, Mass., July 31, 1933; d. John Franklin and Doris Ardella (Hinsman) Sleeper; m. Alexander Stevenson, Aug. 27, 1960; 1 child, Scott. RN, Newton-Wellesley Hosp., 1951-54; BS in Profl. Arts, St. Joseph's Coll., 1980; MA in Health Care Adminstrn., Framingham State Coll., 1984. Asst. clin. instr., head nurse med. surg. Newton (Mass.) Wellesley Hosp., 1954-56; head nurse ICU Newton (Mass.)-Wellesley Hosp., 1959-62; office nurse Dr. William Taggart, Wellesley, Mass., 1963-65; staff nurse nursing home Needham, Mass., 1965-66; staff nurse float Newton-Wellesley Hosp., 1966-68, supr. nursing, 1968-80, staff edn. instr., 1980-84; assoc. dir. edn. ARC, Dedham, Mass., 1984-90, insvc. coord. long-term care, 1990—. Asst. dir. ARC Blood of edn. Svcs. Fellow Am. Nurses Assn., Am. Assn. Blood Banks, Mass. Nurses Assn. Republican. Home: 7-D Hawthorne Village Franklin MA 02038

STEVENSON, RUTH CARTER, art patron; b. Ft. Worth, Oct. 19, 1923; d. Amon Giles and Nenetta (Wiess) Carter; m. J. Lee Johnson III, June 8, 1946 (div. Feb. 1978); children: Sheila Broderick Johnson, J. Lee, Karen Carter Johnson Hixon, Catherine Johnson Tekstar, Mark Lehane; m. John R. Stevenson, May 21, 1983. BA, Sarah Lawrence Coll., 1945. Pres. Ft. Worth Jr. League, 1954-55; chmn. bd. Amon Carter Mus. Western Art, Ft. Worth, 1961—; pres. Amon G. Carter Found., 1982—, Arts Council Greater Ft. Worth, 1963-64; bd. regents U. Tex. at Austin, 1963-69; v.p. internat. council Mus. Modern Art, 1965-72; bd. dirs. Nat. Trust Historic Preservation, 1968-74, 89—, Nat. Coll. Fine Arts, Smithsonian Instn., Washington, 1966-70, U. Dallas, 1971-74; trustee Tex. Christian U., 1974-86, Nat. Gallery Art, Washington, 1979—; pres. Ft. Worth City Art Commn., 1960-80; nat. chmn. collector's com. Nat. Gallery Art, Washington, 1975—; mem. vis. com. Fogg Mus., Cambridge, Mass., 1978-83. Trustee Madeira Sch., Greenway, Va., 1989—. Roman Catholic. Home: 1200 Broad Ave Fort Worth TX 76107

STEVENSON, SANDRA JEAN, training specialist; b. Butler, Pa., Oct. 5, 1949; d. William Ross and Shirley Elizabeth (Pfaff) S. BA, Carlow Coll., 1975. Gen. mgr. Pa. Liquor Control Bd. Store, Harrisburg, Pa., 1980-82, 87-89; trainer Pa. Liquor Control Bd., Harrisburg, Pa., 1982-87; tng. specialist Tng. Sch., Pitts., 1989—. Author dramatizations and prototype for conf. on stigma and mental illness 1980. Office coord., bd. dirs. Lifeline of Southwestern Pa. (Crisis Pregnancy Ctr.), Butler, Pa., 1985-90; sec. Mental Health Assn. Pa., Harrisburg, 1981-83, regional v.p. 1979-81; mem. NAACP. Mem. NAFE, Mensa. Democrat. Roman Catholic. Club: Condor Aero. Office: Tng Sch #0200 1601 Liberty Ave 2nd Fl Pittsburgh PA 15222

STEVENS-SILVER, EMILY FABELLA, producer, director; b. Mexio, Mexico, Aug. 8, 1928; came to U.S., 1935; d. Raph and Leonor (Hernandez) Silver-Fabella. Student, L.A. City Coll.; student Scenic Designing, Goodman Theatre, Chgo. Founder Villeta Players, Woodstock, N.Y., The Loft Players, N.Y.C.; co-founder, co-producer, actress, prodn. mgr., stage mgr. Circle in the Square, N.Y.C.; various film and TV acting positions N.Y.C., Hollywood, Calif.; prin. various acting workshops; lectr. in theater Madrid, Hollywood, N.Y.C. Performed in and co-produced 35 theatrical productions including Summer & Smoke, Girl on the Via Flamina. Recipient OBIE award, 1977.

STEVER, MARGO TAFT, poet; b. Cin., Mar. 4, 1950; d. David Gibson and Katharine Longworth (Whittaker) Taft; m. Donald Winfred Stever Jr., July 31, 1976; children: David Whittaker, James Taft. A.B., Radcliffe Coll., 1972; Ed.M., Harvard U., 1974; MFA, Sarah Lawrence Coll., 1988. Asst. dir. N.H. Civil Liberties Union, Concord, 1976-77, dir. women's rights project, 1976-77; classroom tchr. learning disabled children The Kerbs Sch., Lexington, Mass., 1975-76; staff asst. Senator Ted Stevens, U.S. Senate, Washington, 1974-75; dir. Sleepy Hollow Poetry Series, Warner Library, Tarrytown, N.Y., 1983-89, Hudson Valley Writers' Ctr., 1988-89. Contbr. poetry to pub. mags., anthologies. Bd. dirs., sec. N.H. Pro Bono Referral System, N.H. Bar Assn., Concord, 1977-78; bd. dirs. Tarrytown Coop. Nursery Sch., N.Y., 1983-86, Sleepy Hollow Nursery Sch., Scarborough, N.Y., 1984-85, 1987-89. Mem. Poets and Writers, Acad. Am. Poets, Poetry Soc. Am. Democrat. Episcopalian. Clubs: Adirondack League; Abenakee (Biddeford Pool, Maine). Avocations: riding, tennis. Home: 157 Millard Ave North Tarrytown NY 10591

STEVICH-LARSON, ALISON JOY, office management executive; b. Chgo., Feb. 12, 1952; d. Crisalogo Mendoza and Ruby Marie (Johnson) Aguirre; m. David Charles Wiegel, Feb. 14, 1969 (div. 1972); 1 child, Yuri Christian; m. Wayne Herbert Larson, Apr. 21, 1989. AA, Kendall Coll., 1971. Shipping processor Gen. Products Corp., Chgo., 1972-73; med. biller Mason-Barron Labs. Inc., Chgo., 1973-74, Rheumatology Assocs., Chgo., 1974-76; sec. Tala Engel, Atty. at Law, Chgo., 1976-78; office mgr. Imrich A. Weiss, M.D., Chgo., 1978-84; med. biller Strauss Surg. Group, Chgo., 1984-85; office mgr. Lakeview Imaging & X-Ray Ltd., Chgo., 1985-86, Ibbotson Assocs. Inc., Chgo., 1986-87; office mgr. comml. loan dept. Columbia Nat. Bank Chgo., 1987-88; adminstrv. asst. Olympic Natural Foods, Oak Brook, Ill., 1988-89; sales assoc. Coldwell Banker Real Estate, Elmhurst, Ill., 1988—; cons. A&M Services, Chgo., 1985-87. Prodn. mgr.: Stocks, Bonds, Bills and Inflation, 1987. Mem. NAFE, Ill. Assn. Realtors, DuPage Bd. Realtors, Nat. Assn. Realtors. Club: Ice Skating Inst. Am. (Wilmette, Ill.). Home: 648 S York Rd Unit 115 Bensenville IL 60106 Office: Coldwell Banker Real Estate 695 W St Charles Rd Elmhurst IL 60126

STEWARD, BETTE ANN, computerized tomography technologist; b. New London, Conn., Mar. 13, 1949; d. Walter Andrew and Edith Margaret (Strickland) S.; m. Ivan Paul Klimko, May 3, 1969 (div. July 1976); m. Arthur Joseph Croteau III, July 15, 1989. Student radiologic tech., Lawrence and Meml. Hosp., New London, 1969. Staff technologist Lawrence and Meml. Hosp., 1969-71, spl. procedures technologist, 1971-78, computerized tomography technologist, 1978-87, supr. computerized tomography, 1987-89. Flutist Waterford (Conn.) Community Band, 1980-89, treas., 1982-89. Mem. New Eng. Conf. Radiologic Technologists (registration chmn. 1980-81, 88—), Conn. Soc. Radiologic Technologists (registration chmn. 1977-79), Thames Yacht Club. Democrat. Congregationalist.

STEWARD, PATRICIA ANN RUPERT, real estate executive, management consultant; b. Panama City, Panama, Apr. 20, 1945 (parents Am. citizens); d. Paul S. and Ernestina M. (Ward) Rupert; grad. Sch. of Mortgage Banking, Grad. Sch. of Mgmt., Northwestern U., 1979; m. Robert M. Levine, Oct. 28, 1978; children by previous marriage: Donald F. Steward, Christine Marie Steward. V.p. Assoc. Mortgage & Investment Co., Phoenix, 1969-71; v.p., br. mgr. Sun Country Funding Corp., Phoenix, 1971-72, Freese Mortgage Co., Phoenix, 1972-74, Utah Mortgage Loan Corp., Phoenix, 1974-81; pres. Elles Corp., 1982—, Elles Mgmt. Corp., 1987—, Elles Approvals Corp., 1987—; founder, The Elles Group, 1987; condr. numerous seminars on mortgage fin. Author: A Realtors Guide to Mortgage Lending, 1972. State chmn. Ariz. Leukemia Dr., 1977-78, mem. exec. com., 1979-80; troop leader Cactus Pine coun. Girl Scouts U.S., 1979-80; bd. dirs. Nat. Mental Health Assn., 1986-87, Ariz. Mental Health Assn., pres., 1986-87, bd. dirs., treas. Maricopa Mental Health Assn., 1984-85, v.p., 1985-86, pres., 1986-87; apptd. by state supreme ct. to Ariz. Foster Care Rev. Bd., 1984—, chairperson Bd. 8, 1986-87. Recipient cert. of appreciation Multiple Listing Svc., Phoenix Bd. Realtors, 1975, Multiple Listing Svc., Glendale Bd. Realtors, 1977. Lic. mortgage broker, Ariz. Mem. Ariz. Mortgage Bankers Assn. (bd. dir. 1981-82, chmn. edn. com. 1981-82, founder continuing edn. seminar series 1981), Young Mortgage Bankers Assn. (chmn. exec. com. 1980-81), Cen. Ariz. Homebuilders Assn. Republican. Office: Elles Corp 410 N 44th St Ste 175 Phoenix AZ 85008

STEWART, ALICE JEAN, pharmacist; b. Sigourney, Iowa, Dec. 12, 1958; d. Albert Friedrich and Gwendolyn Jean (Latimer) Goeldner; m. Jay Evan Stewart, May 25, 1985; 1 child, Lauren Elizabeth. BS in Pharmacy, U. Iowa, 1982. Lic. pharmacist, Iowa. Staff pharmacist Manly Drug Store, Inc., Grundy Center, Iowa, 1982—. Mem. pastor-parish relations com. Meth. Ch., Grundy Center, 1985-86. Mem. Am. Pharm. Soc., Iowa Pharm. Soc., Acad. of Long Term Care, Waterloo (Iowa) Met. Chorale, Grundy Ctr. C. of C., Order Eastern Star, Rho Chi. Republican. Home: 809 I Ave Grundy Center IA 50638 Office: Manly Drug Store Inc 621 G Ave Grundy Center IA 50638

STEWART, ANN HARLEMAN, English language educator. BA in English, Douglass Coll., 1967; PhD in Linguistics, Princeton U., 1972; MFA in Creative Writing, Brown U., 1988. Asst. prof. dept. English Rutgers U., New Brunswick, N.J., 1973-74; asst. prof. dept. English U. Wash., Seattle, 1974-79, assoc. prof. dept. English, 1979-84; vis. assoc. prof., research affiliate Writing Program MIT, Cambridge, 1984-86; vis. scholar Program in Am. Civilization Brown U., Providence, 1986—. Author: Graphic Representation of Models in Linguistic Theory, 1976, (with Bruce A. Rosenberg) Ian Fleming: A Critical Biography, 1989; contbr. 20 scholarly articles, poems and short stories to lit. mags. Guggenheim fellow, 1976-77, Huntington Libr. fellow, 1979-80, MacDowell Colony fellow, 1988, Fulbright-Hays lectr., 1980-81, R.I. State Coun. Arts, 1989-; ACLS/IREX sr. scholar, 1976-77; recipient grant Rockefeller Found., 1989, Raymond Carver prize, 1986, Nelson Algren runner-up award Chgo. Tribune, 1987, 3d prize Judith Siegal Pearson award, 1988, Chris O'Malley Fiction Prize Madison Rev., 1990. Mem. Modern Lang. Assn. (chair exec. com. Gen Linguistics), Linguistic Soc. Am.,Poets and Writers, Inc., Am Lit. Translators Assn. Home: 55 Summit Ave Providence RI 02906 Office: Brown U Program in Am Civilization Providence RI 02912

STEWART, ARLENE JEAN GOLDEN, designer, stylist; b. Chgo., Nov. 26, 1943; d. Alexander Emerald and Nettie (Rosen) Golden; m. Randall Edward Stewart, Nov. 6, 1970; 1 child, Alexis Anne. BFA, Sch. of Art Inst. Chgo., 1966; postgrad., Ox Bow Summer Sch. Painting, Saugatuck, Mich., 1966. Designer, stylist Formica Corp., Cin., 1966-68; with Armstrong World Industries, Inc., Lancaster, Pa., 1968—, interior furnishings analyst, 1974-76, internat. staff project stylist, 1976-78, sr. stylist Corlon flooring, 1979-80, sr. exptl. project stylist, 1980-89, sr. project stylist residential DIY flooring floor div., 1989—. Exhibited textiles Art Inst. Chgo., 1966, Ox-Bow Gallery, Saugatuck, Mich., 1966. Home: 114 E Vine St Lancaster PA 17602 Office: Armstrong Innovation Ctr 2500 Columbia Ave Lancaster PA 17604

STEWART, BARBARA ELIZABETH, free-lance magazine editor, artist; b. Ft. Dodge, Iowa, June 26, 1923; d. Warren Wheeler and Christine (Hubbard) Pickett; m. Charles Crombie Stewart, Sept. 2, 1943; 1 child, Charles Crombie IV. Student, Mt. Holyoke Coll., 1940-41, Wayne State U., 1941-42, So. Conn. State U., 1944-45; AA, Mercer County Community Coll., 1970; BA, Trenton State Coll., 1972. Cert. K-12 art tchr. Copywriter Fed. Dept. Stores, Goodwin's, Detroit, 1942-43; dept. coord. Sears, Roebuck & Co., Trenton, N.J., 1944; sec., writer Yale U., New Haven, Conn., 1945, 46; contbg. editor Mercer Bus. Mag., Trenton, 1980—. Oil and acrylic artist. Chmn. Stokes Sch. PTA, Trenton, 1952-58; pres. Rutgers Coop. Extension Mercer County, Trenton, 1970-82; charter mem. Hillcrest Civic Assn., Trenton, 1956-83; bd. dirs. Trenton YWCA, 1975-77; chmn. women's fellowship Covenant Presbyn. Ch., Trentton, 1978-88. Mem. Nat. Art Edn. Assn., N.J. Art Edn. Assn., AAUW (local chmn. 1965, 67), Torch Club (ofcl. del. 1985-88). Democrat. Home: 31 Clement Ave Trenton NJ 08638

STEWART, CAROL JOHNSON, library director; b. Mpls., June 30, 1949; d. William Steele and Constance Harriet (Mattson) Johnson; m. Robert Earl Stewart Jr., May 20, 1983. BA, Fla. Atlantic U., 1971; MS, Fla. State U., 1972. Br. librarian Memphis/Shelby County Pub. Library, Memphis, 1973-77, DeKalb Library System, Decatur, Ga., 1977-80; library coord. Clayton County Libraries, Jonesboro, Ga., 1980-81; dir. library svcs. Clayton County Library System, Jonesboro, 1981—. Mem. ALA, Southeastern Library Assn., Ga. Library Assn., Avondale Swim and Tennis. Office: Clayton County Libr 865 Battlecreek Rd Jonesboro GA 30236

STEWART, CATHERINE ANNE, sales professional; b. Orange, Calif., July 4, 1959; d. Alan W. and Margaret A. (Hoxsie) S. AA, Foothill Coll., Los Altos Hills, Calif., 1979; diploma, FIDM, San Francisco, 1978. Fashion coord. Atherton Industries, Menlo Park, Calif., 1980; account exec. Ernst Strauss, L.A., 1983; nat. sales mgr. Sir James, Inc., L.A., 1985; sales exec. Jakob Schlaepfer, Inc., L.A., 1988.

STEWART, CHARMAINE MARCIA, real estate broker; b. Kingston, Jamaica, West Indies, Nov. 20, 1954; came to U.S., 1981; d. Lancelot Watson and Barbara Jean (Jackman) Codrington; m. Stewart, Apr. 23, 1977; children: Nadira, Tarik. BS in Acctg., CUNY, 1985; postgrad., Touro Law Sch., Huntington, N.Y., 1989—. Lic. real estate broker. Corp. commercial paper adminstr. Chase Manhattan Bank, N.Y.C., 1981-84, acct., 1984-85; real estate sales person Spotlight Homes Realty, Queens Village, N.Y., 1985-89; broker, pres. Our Neighborhood Properties, Inc., Jamaica, N.Y., 1989—. Mem. Minority Bar Assn. (v.p. 1989-90). Office: Our Neighborhood Property 92-38 Guy Brewer Blvd Jamaica NY 11432

STEWART, CHERIE ANITA, painter/neo-impressionist; b. Gadsden, Ala., Sept. 20, 1945; d. Earl Donald Williams and Frances Morgan Bellenger; m. Walter Hurd Stewart, Apr. 2, 1966 (div. Sept. 1988); children: Don Paul, Virgina Elizabeth. BS, U. Ala., Tuscaloosa, 1968; BA, U. Ala.-Birmingham, 1983. One-man shows include Barker Gallery, Palm Beach, Fla., 1984, St. Vincent's Gallery, Birmingham, Ala., 1987, Tutwiler Gallery, Birmingham, 1988; exhibited in group shows at Birmingham Frame and Art Gallery, 1984-86, Maralyn Wilson Gallery, Birmingham, 1985—; Abstein Gallery, Atlanta, 1985—, Gateway Ctr., Newark, 1987, Ariel Gallery, N.Y.C., 1988, Windsors Gallery, Boca Raton, Fl., 1989; contbr. advt. layouts The Stewart Orgn., Birmingham, 1983-84; painter Shippee Gallery, N.Y.C., 1985—, Art South, Inc., Washington, 1987—, Archtl. Arts Co., Dallas. Recipient numerous awards. Mem. Birmingham Mus. Art, Birmingham Art Assn., Nat. Mus. Women in the Arts, Knickerbocker Artists N.Y. (assoc.), Allied Artists Am. (assoc.).

STEWART, CHRISTINE SUSAN, Canadian legislator; b. Jan. 1, 1941; d. Morris Alexander Leishman and Laura Anne Doherty; m. David Ian Stewart, Aug. 24, 1963; children: Douglas Alexander, John David, Catherine Ann. Ed., Neuchatel Jr. Coll., Switzerland, U. Toronto, Ont., Can. Nurse; mem. Ho. of Commons, 1988—. Founding exec. dir. Horizons of Friendship. Liberal. Roman Catholic. Office: House of Commons, Parliament Bldgs, Ottawa, ON Canada K1A 0A6*

STEWART, CLARA WOODARD, advertising executive; b. Mineola, N.Y., May 1, 1952; d. Samuel Woodard and Irene (Colm) S.; BA in Broadcasting and Psychology, Mich. State U., 1974; MA in Journalism and Communications, U. Fla., 1975. Sales rep. Sta. WSBR, Boca Raton, 1976-77; media dir. Fred Wagenvoord Assoc., Inc., Boca Raton, Fla., 1977-81; v.p., sr. account exec., media dir. Birkenes & Foreman Advt., Boca Raton, 1981-89, exec. v.p. Birkenes, Stewart & Rhine, 1989—. Bd. dirs. Boca Raton Community Theater, 1977-78, publicity chmn., 1977-78; bd. dirs. United Way Greater Boca Raton, 1979—; pres. Friends of Boca Raton Public Library, 1981-83; mem. adv. bd. Boca Raton Symphony Orch., 1983-85; mem. Young Pres.'s Council Norton Gallery; treas. Friends of Caldwell Playhouse, 1984—. Mem. B/PAA (treas. Southeast Fla. chpt. 1984-87, bd. dirs. 1988—), Women in Communications, Advt. Fedn. Greater Ft. Lauderdale (bd. dirs. 1986—, sec. 1987-88, treas. 1988—), Am. Mktg. Assn. (sr. v.p. spl. programs, Gold Coast chpt., 1987-88) Mensa (SE regional public relations asst. 1978-80, treas. Palm Beach County 1981-83), Palm Beach County Hist. Soc. (newsletter editor 1980-82), Palm Beach County Geneal. Soc., Greenpeace, Colonial Williamsburg, Nature Conservancy, Wilderness Soc., Clan Stewart Soc. Am., Dames of the Magna Carta, Am. Film Inst., Nat. Trust Historic Preservation, BMW Car Club of Am., DAR, Phi Kappa Phi. Home: 6443 Parkview Dr Boca Raton FL 33433 Office: 2900 N Military Tr Ste 200 Boca Raton FL 33431

STEWART, DEBORAH RUTH, public relations professional, broadcast executive, television producer and personality; b. Tokyo, May 4, 1954; came to U.S., 1959; d. Eugene M. and Ruth (Somerville) Owens; m. Lorenzo M. Stewart, Apr. 11, 1981 (div. June 1987); 1 child, Lynn M. Student, Hampton Inst., 1972-74; BS in Mass Media, Grand Valley State Colls., 1976. Project dir. Vols. in Probation, Hampton, Va., 1977-78; acting dir. Vols. in Probation City of Hampton, 1978-79; reporter, anchor Stas. WNOR-AM, WNOR-FM99, Norfolk, Va., 1979-80; anchor, dir. pub. svc. Sta. WCMS-AM-FM, Virginia Beach, Va., 1980-81; reporter, anchor Stas. WJNO-WRMF, West Palm Beach, Fla., 1982-84; asst. info. officer sch. bd. County of Palm Beach, West Palm Beach, 1984-87, pub. rels. planner sch. bd., 1987—; TV host, producer Sta. WPTV, West Palm Beach, 1985—; pres. Owens Broadcasting, Inc., West Palm Beach, 1989—; cons. pub. rels. Hall, Hewko & Leibovitz, P.A., West Palm Beach, 1989—. Sr. editor, contbr. Visions mag., West Palm Beach, 1989—; contbr. to monthly newsletter Insights. Bd. dirs. St. John's Home, Grand Rapids, 1975-76, Am. Cancer Soc., West Palm Beach, 1983-86, Northwood Inst., West Palm Beach, 1986—, Minority Cultural Consortium, West Palm Beach, 1988—; outreach worker Baxter Community Ctr., Grand Rapids, 1974-76; chmn. campaign com. United Way, West Palm Beach, 1987—; vol. Domestic Assault Shelter, 1989—. Recipient Disting. Svc. award St. John's Home, 1976, Urban League PBC, 1986, 87, Outstanding Coverage award in health category for radio news story, UPI, 1981, Appreciation award Alpha Kappa Alpha, 1989; named Community Leader Charmettes, West Palm Beach, 1989. Mem. Women in Communications (pres.), Nat. Sch. Pub. Rels. Assn. Democrat. Baptist. Home: 306 3d Way West Palm Beach FL 33407 Office: Palm Beach County Sch Bd 3930 RCA Blvd #3004 Palm Beach FL 33410

STEWART, DIANE BASNETT, mechanical engineer; b. Dallas, Aug. 18, 1955; d. William Marshall and Dorothea Louise (Tyler) Basnett; m. Thomas Wayne Stewart, Nov. 26, 1976; 1 child, Megan. BS in Biology, Stephen F. Austin State U., 1977; BSME, U. Fla., 1986. Registered engr.-in-tng., Tex. Engring. aid U.S. Army C.E., Lake Seminole, Fla., 1976, biol. technician, 1977; assoc. engr. Comanche Peak Nuclear Plant, TU-Electric, Glen Rose, Tex., 1986-88, engr., 1988—. Recipient First Use award Electric Power Rsch. Inst., 1990. Mem. ASME, Nat. Assn. Corrosion Engrs., Chec/Checmate Users Group (adv. com. 1990—), Breeders Internat. Office: TU-Electric CPSES PO Box 1002 Glen Rose TX 76043

STEWART, DOLORES ANN, court reporter; b. Ft. Worth, July 8, 1947; d. Charles David and Lupe (Brame) Mathis; m. Joseph W. Field III, Aug. 28, 1989; 1 child, Hollye. Diploma, Chapman Ct. Reporting Coll., 1976. Cert. ct. reporter, Tex. Ct. reporter Allied Stenotype Reporters, Ft. Worth, 1976-80, Kee, Meyer, Sturgess & Assocs., Ft. Worth, 1980-83, Hon. William Brigham, Ft. Worth, 1983-85, Adcock, Stewart & Assocs., Ft. Worth, 1985-86, Dolores Stewart & Assocs., Ft. Worth, 1986—. Mem. Tex. Shorthand Reporters Assn. (bd. dirs. 1986-89, v.p. 1989-90, pres. elect 1990—). Methodist. Office: Dolores Stewart & Assocs 222 W Exchange Fort Worth TX 76106

STEWART, DONNA RUTH, veterinarian; b. Kansas City, Mo., Feb. 24, 1947; d. Charles Edwin and Mattie Ruth (Galloway) Clark; m. Dale Lloyd Stewart, Oct. 18, 1968 (div. 1976); 1 child, Jason Clark. DVM, U. Mo., Columbia, 1972. Lic. veterinarian. Ptnr. Town and Country Animal Clinic, Richmond, Mo., 1972-76; assoc. Blue Pkwy. Animal Hosp., Kansas City, Mo., 1976-78; owner Blue Pkwy Animal Hosp., Kansas City, Mo., 1978-85, Bannister West Animal Clinic, Kansas City, Mo.; mem. bd. dirs. Animal Emergency Clinic, Independence, Mo., 1978; cons. Kansas City Animal Control, 1976-81; com. mem. small animal disease com., com. mem. peer assistance com. MUMA. Com. mem. Boy Scout of Am., Raymore, Mo., 1983—. Mem. Kansas City Vet. Med. Assn., Mo. Vet. Med. Assn., Am. Vet. Med. Assn., Lee's Summit Academic Support League, Lee's Summit Booster Club, Music Parents. Office: Bannister West Animal Clinic 4501 Bannuiter Rd Kansas City MO 64137

STEWART, DOROTHY ANNE, meteorologist; b. Beech Grove, Ind., June 2, 1937; d. Thomas Edward and Dorothy Anne (Browne) S.; BS, U. Tampa, 1958; MS, Fla. State U., 1961, PhD, 1966. Tchr. math, sci., high sch., Live Oak, Fla., 1958-59; rsch. physicist U.S. Army Missile Command, Redstone Arsenal, Ala., 1966-89, meteorologist, 1989—. Mem. Am. Meteorol. Soc., Am. Geophys. Union, AAAS, Ala. Acad. Scis., Sigma Xi. Contbr. articles to profl. jours. Home: PO Box 12067 Huntsville AL 35815-1067 Office: US Army Missile Command Attn AMSMI-RD-RE-AP Redstone Arsenal AL 35898-5248

STEWART, DORIS MAE, biology professor; b. Sandsprings, Mont., Dec. 12, 1927; d. Virgil E. and Violet M. (Weaver) S.; m. Felix Loren Powell, Oct. 8, 1956; children: Leslie, Loren. BS, Coll. Puget Sound, 1948, MS, 1949; PhD, U. Wash., 1953. Instr. U. Mont., Missoula, 1954-56, asst. prof., 1956-57; asst. prof. U. Puget Sound, Tacoma, 1957-58; head sci. dept. Am. Kiz Lisesi, Istanbul, Turkey, 1958-62; rsch. asst. prof. U. Wash., Seattle, 1963-67, rsch. assoc. prof., 1967-68; assoc. prof. Cen. Mich. U., Mt. Pleasant, 1970-72; assoc. prof. U. Balt., 1973-81, prof., 1981—. Contbr. numerous articles to profl. jours. Mem. Am. Physiol. Soc., Sigma Xi. Home: 1103 Frederick Rd Baltimore MD 21228

STEWART, EILEEN ROSE, real estate broker; b. Indpls., Oct. 20, 1942; d. Burgess Charles and Flora Clara (Schott) S.; m. Richard Michael Grindle, Feb. 12, 1966 (div. 1977). BS, Ind. U., 1965, MS, 1972. Lic. real estate broker, Ind., Fla. Tchr. pub. schs. various locations, Ind., Fla., 1965-72; sales rep. UARCO Bus. Forms, Ft. Lauderdale, Fla., 1972-74; staff trainer Palm Beach County Comprehensive Employment Tng. Act program, West Palm Beach, Fla., 1975-77; pres., cons. Untapped Resources, Inc., West Palm Beach, 1978-80; mgmt. cons. Profl. Mgmt. Assocs., Silver Spring, Md., 1980-82; sales rep. The St. George's Club, Washington, 1983-84; real estate broker Mascari Realty, Indpls., 1985—; innkeeper, pres. Stewart Manor, Inc., Indpls., 1987—; cons., Planned Parenthood, West Palm Beach, 1976-78, Jim Stewart Tire Co., Indpls., 1985—; chair adv. bd., Palm Beach County Displaced Homemakers Ctr., Lake Worth, 1977-78. Mem. Women's Bus. Initiative, Indpls. Bus. Network, Ind. Bed and Breakfast Assn. (cen. region coord. 1989), NOW (past officer South Palm Beach County chpt., asst. state coord. Fla. sect., 1978, nat. bd. dirs., 1978-79, newsletter editor 1976-77). Democrat. Home: 410 Ocean Dr PO Box 190558 Miami Beach FL 33139 Office: Era Real Estae Enterprises Inc 501 Alton Rd Miami Beach FL 33139

STEWART, ELAINE THELMA, artist; b. Ocean County, N.J., June 16, 1952; d. Clarence A. Stewart and Eleanor M. (Andrews); m. Richard V. Barth, May 16, 1970, (div. June 13, 1986); children: Richard Vincent, Tammy Lynn. Grad. high sch., Mommouth, N.J.; grad., Chubb Inst. Computer Tech., 1990. Picture framer, supr. Dupont Graphic Arts, Pinebrook, 1982-88; v.p. Art Magic, Inc., Rockaway, 1988--; arts dir., Hopatcong Recreation Program, 1983-84. Mem. Am. Radio Reley League, Profl. Picture Framers. Home: 14 Hillside Avenue 3A Rockaway NJ 07866 Office: Art Magic Incorporated 13 Union Street Rockaway NJ 07866

STEWART, ELIZABETH, textile industry executive; b. Chgo., Dec. 5, 1943; d. Louis P. and Lauretta (Kastelik) Buetow; m. William Stewart, July 9, 1977. Student, Amundsen Jr. Coll., Chgo., 1963. Talent dir. Monza Modeling Agy., Kansas City, Mo.; estimator Midwest Supply Co., Kansas City; adminstrv. asst. Chgo. Mus. Instrument, Lincolnwood, Ill.; pres., adminstr. contracts Stewart Draperies, Inc., Kansas City. Named Subcontractor of Yr., Mokan Contractors Assn., recipient Cert. of Appreciation. Mem. NAFE, NABOW, Kansas City Minority Contractors Assn.(Award of Appreciation), Builders Assn. Greater Kansas City. Home: 1720 Paseo PO Box 41325 Kansas City MO 64141

STEWART, ELLEN SMITH, psythotherapist; b. Greensboro, N.C., July 2, 1945; d. Arthur Raymond and Bertha (Edwards) Smith; m. Andrew Howard Stewart, Sept. 27, 1969; children: Elizabeth, Catherine. BA, Vanderbilt U., 1967; MS, Columbia U., 1971; postgrad., U. Minn., 1983—. Computer programmer IBM Corp., N.Y.C., 1967-70; head libr. Davis, Polk & Wardwell, N.Y.C., 1971-76; freelance book reviewer Louisville Courier Jour., 1980-81; asst. dir. Vocat. Psychology Rsch., Mpls., 1984-85; asst. to the chair psychology dept. U. Minn., Mpls., 1985-87, intern walk-in counseling ctr., 1987-89, team counselor walk-in counseling ctr., 1989—. Vol. Ky. Opera Assn., Louisville, 1976-81, Planned Parenthood, Louisville, 1979-80, polit. campaigns, Wayzata, Minn., 1982, ednl. activities, Wayzata, 1981-83. Mem. AACD, ACLU, NOW, Am. Psychol. Assn. (assoc.), Minn. Psychol. Assn., Minn. Women Psychologists, Assn. for Women in Psychology, Amnesty Internat., Minn. Civil Liberties Union, Nat. Abortion Rights Action League. Home and Office: 133 Chevy Chase Dr Wayzata MN 55391

STEWART, JANELLE HARAUGHTY, steel manufacturing company executive, accountant; b. Alva, Okla., Mar. 30, 1953; d. Charles Thomas and Edith Mildred (Tatro) Haraughty; m. Paul Lewis Stewart, Sept. 2, 1972 (div. Feb. 1987); 1 child, Jennifer Allyn. BBA, U. Okla., 1976; MBA, U. Tulsa, 1986. CPA, Okla., Cert. Mgmt. Acct. Audit supr. Coopers & Lybrand, Tulsa, 1976-80; v.p. fin. Century Geophys. Corp., Tulsa, 1980-84; contr. Sheffield Steel Corp., Sand Springs, Okla., 1985—. Mem. allocation com. Tulsa United Way, 1989—. Mem. AICPA, Okla. Soc. CPA's (legis. liaison person 1988, 89), Sand Springs C. of C. (race dir. 1989), Tulsa Running Club, Tulsa Ski Club, Tulsa Bicycle Club. Democrat. Presbyterian. Office: Sheffield Steel Corp PO Box 218 Sand Springs OK 74063

STEWART, JEAN CATHERINE, critical care nurse, educator; b. Pitts., July 12, 1948; d. Frank E. and Bertha G. (Drawdy) Henry. BSN, Ariz. State U., 1971; MSN, U. Tex., Houston, 1988. Cert. neurosci. RN; cert. emergency nurse; cert. trauma nurse; cert. instr. ACLS; cert. instr. BLS. Neurosurg. nursing cons. The Meth. Hosp., Houston, 1981-84; staff devel. instr. M.D. Anderson Hosp. and Tumor Inst., Houston, 1984-85; staff nurse Ben Taub Gen. Hosp., Houston, 1985-87, continuing edn. instr., 1987—; presenter meetings and confs. various profl. orgns.; announcer Dial A Shuttle program Nat. Space Insts. Mem. manuscript rev. bd. Jour. Neuroscis. Nurses.; editorial rev. bd. Dimensions in Oncology Nursing. Recipient Millie Fields Rsch. Assistance award U. Tex., 1987. Mem. NAFE, AACCN (rsch. award 1987), Emergency Nurses Assn., Am. Assn. Neurosci. Nurses (founding mem., past treas. S.C. chpt., pres. and program dir. Houston chpt.), World Fedn. Neurosci. Nurses, Am. Trauma Soc., Nat. Space Inst., Sigma Theta Tau. Home: 2829 Timmonshane #195 Houston TX 77027

STEWART, JOANNE, travel executive; b. Vancouver, Wash., Mar. 10, 1944; d. Edward Charles and Claudine Marie (Meilleur) Spencer; m. William Lemley Stewart, Sept. 2, 1966 (dec. June 1983); children: Amy Diane, Nicholas William. BS, Wash. State U., 1966, MA, 1973. Cert. tchr., Mont., Idaho, Wash., Calif. Tchr. foods Seaside High Sch., Monterey, Calif., 1966-67; tchr. home econs. Marysville (Wash.) High Sch., 1967-68, Palouse (Wash.) High Sch., 1968-73, Ennis (Mont.) High Sch., 1973-76, Genesee (Idaho) High Sch., 1976-77; instr. young family Missoula (Mont.) County High Sch., 1983-84; tchr. home econs. Woodman Sch., Lolo, Mont., 1985-86; travel cons. Travel Masters, Missoula, 1984-87; ticketing mgr. Blue Caboose Travel, Missoula, 1987—. Co-pres. Lolo PTO, 1980-81; v.p. Lolo Community Ctr., 1981; treas. Lolo Mosquito Control Bd., 1988—. Marysville Edn. Assn. scholar, 1962. Future Homemakers Am. scholar, 1962. Mem. AAUW (sec. 1986, program chmn. 1987), Forestry Triangle (pres. 1981-85, editor cookbook 1982), Future Homemakers Am. (hon.), Missoula Bus. Women's Network. Republican. Methodist. Home: 1200 Lakeside Dr Lolo MT 59847 Office: Blue Caboose Travel 410 E Pine St Missoula MT 59847

STEWART, JUDITH UNDERWOOD, securities analyst; b. Auburn, N.Y., Aug. 5, 1955; d. Martha (Davenport) Heard; m. Gordon Bennett Stewart III, June 13, 1981; children: Gordon Bennett IV, Charlotte Davenport. BA, Wellesley Coll., 1977; student, MIT, 1975-77; MBA, Wharton Grad. Sch. Bus., 1979. Corp. fin. assoc. Shearson Loeb Rhoades Inc., N.Y.C., 1979-80; asst. treas. Chase Manhattan Bank, N.Y.C., 1980-83; mgr. Citicorp, N.Y.C., 1983-85; rating officer Standard & Poor's Corp., N.Y.C., 1985—. Contbr. writer: Standard & Poor's Structured Finance Criteria, 1988. Mem. Wharton Grad. Bus. Sch. Club N.Y., Jr. League City of N.Y. (chmn. provisional com. winter ball 1984, vice-chmn. and treas. career awareness com. 1985-87), Am. Cancer Soc. N.Y. Div. (jr. com. 1982), French Library (jr. com. 1978), Soc. Mayflower Descendants, Nat. Soc. Colonial Dames, DAR Mary Washington Coll. chpt., New Eng. Soc. City of N.Y., Princeton Club N.Y., Wellesley Coll. Club N.Y., U. Pa. Club N.Y.C.

STEWART, JUNE, marketing manager; b. Melrose Park, Ill., Mar. 15, 1931; d. Harry John and Stephanie Gary; m. James Thomas Stewart, Sept. 13, 1953; children: Sue Anna Scribner, Linda, James, John. BA in Journalism, Northeastern U., 1973. Reporter Bugle Publ., Niles, Ill., 1970; editor Reminder Publ., Wheeling, Ill., 1970-73; reporter copy desk Topics Newspapers, Palatine, Ill., 1975—; area rep. Picwick Publs., Park Ridge, Ill., 1976; ad merchandiser Walgreens, Deerfield, Ill., 1976—; publisher, editor GS Publs., Mt. Prospect, Ill., 1983-84; correspondent Lerner Life Newspapers, Skokie, Ill., 1978-85; acting pres. Gary Stewart HVAC, Mt. Prospect, 1985; editorial dir., mktg. mgr. heating and air conditioning Gary Stewart Advt., 1984—; reporter Paddock Publs., Arlington Heights, Ill., 1966-69; founder Stewart Cosmetics Co., Wheeling, 1973-76. Editor Nomda Mag.; author, editor: Historical Grandma's Recipes, 1984. Chmn. Cub Scouts com., den mother Cub Scouts, Boy Scouts Am., Wheeling; chmn. mental health Bell Ringer March; vol. community producer Community Columnist Series, 1989, 90. With USAF, 1952-54. Mem. Chgo. Computer Soc., Nat. Writer's Union. Home: PO Box 497 Mount Prospect IL 60056

STEWART, KIM KRISTINE, protective services official; b. Lynwood, Calif., Nov. 11, 1952; d. Harry David and Marilyn Mathilda (Olson) S. BA in History, U. Calif., Irvine, 1974. Cert. peace officer, Calif. Exec. dir. Girls' Club of Laguna, Inc., Laguna Beach, Calif., 1973-75, Girls' Club of Santa Ana (Calif.), Inc., 1975-77; exec. v.p. Nat. Programmed Learning Inst., Newport Beach, Calif., 1978; loan adjustor Security Pacific Nat. Bank, Santa Ana, 1979-81; police officer Cypress (Calif.) Police Dept., 1981-83; sheriff's dep. Santa Barbara (Calif.) County Sheriff's Dept., 1983-89; dist. atty. investigator County of Ventura, 1989—. Active Santa Barbara Youth Charity Relay, 1986. Democrat. Office: County of Ventura Dist Atty 800 S Victoria Ventura CA 93003

STEWART, KIMBERLY KAY, data processing executive; b. Torrance, Calif., Feb. 1, 1964; d. Donald Gene and Barbara Ann (Tyykila) Jones; m. John Henry Thomas Stewart, Aug. 21, 1981 (div. Dec. 1985); 1 child, John Jacob; m. Jesse C. Stewart, Sept. 5, 1987. AAS, Lamar U., Port Arthur, Tex., 1985. Newspaper carrier Port Arthur News, 1978-80; waitress, cashier, cook Dairy Queen, Port Arthur, 1980-82; waitress, cashier Wyatt's Cafeteria, Port Arthur, 1982; computer lab. asst. Lamar U., Port Arthur, 1982-83; data engry clk. St. Mary's Hosp., Port Arthur, 1983; computer operator Mid-Jefferson Hosp., Nederland, Tex., 1983; systems operator support tech. St. Mary's Hosp., Port Arthur, 1983-85; software technician Calif. Connection, Inc., Austin, 1985-87; pres., systems analyst Profl. Systems and Svc., Round Rock, Tex., 1987—; pres. KST, Inc., Round Rock, 1987—. Democrat. Home and Office: 500 Greenlawn Round Rock TX 78664

STEWART, MARGARET JENSEN, chemist; b. Miami, Fla., Nov. 15, 1950; d. Arden Edward Jensen Sr. and Elizabeth Emma (Stevenson) Galliher; m. Lawrence Simpson Stewart, June 2, 1969 (div.); 1 child, Lawrence Simpson Jr. BS in Chemistry, Auburn U., 1972; postgrad., U. So. Miss., 1986—. Chemist Am. So. Dyeing and Finishing Corp., Opa Locka, Fla., 1972-74; sr. chemist Morton Internat., Inc., Moss Point, Miss., 1976—; treas. Dog River Fed. Credit Union, Moss Point, 1981-83. Mem. city and county taxation com. Miss. Econ. Council, Jackson, 1985-86; mem. vestry St. Johns Episcopal Ch., 1989—. Mem. AAUW (br. v.p. 1980-82, br. pres. 1984-87, Miss. state edni. found. chmn. 1984-86, Miss. state equity action vote chmn. 1986-87, crisis in higher edn. forum chmn. 1986). Clubs: Gulf Coast Orchid Soc.; Ocean Springs Yacht. Home: 43 Pittman Rd Ocean Springs MS 39564 Office: Morton Internat Corp PO Box 666 Moss Point MS 39563

STEWART, MARY AGNES, music critic, journalist; b. Battle Creek, Mich., Feb. 25, 1899; d. William Ray and Mary Ann (Hays) Simpson; student Pacific Union Coll., U. Wash., U. Md., Am. U., Southeastern U., Washington, San Diego State U.; m. William Robert Stewart, May 4, 1918, (dec. 1990); children: William Robert Jr., Ray Simpson, Stanley Hays. Assoc. editor Calif. Hawaii Hotel-Life and Ocean Travel, 1925-36; impresario L. E. Behymer, Honolulu, 1926-29, La Jolla, Calif., 1941-44; San Diego rep. Pacific Coast Musician, 1945-54; La Jolla corr. L.A. Times, 1952-60; interior decorator Mary Stewart Interiors, La Jolla, 1942-88; researcher: (books) The Spanish West, 1976, San Diego County Pioneer Families, 1976; free-lance writer, La Jolla, 1982-89; contbr. Opera News, San Diego Union, San Francisco Chronicle. Historian San Diego Opera Guild; chmn. San Diego Woman's Philharm. Com., La Jolla, L.A. Philharm. Orch., 1975-78; life mem. Scripps Meml. Hosp. Aux. Recipient Letter of Commendation, USN Hosp., San Diego, 1972; Agnes Ave. (North Hollywood) named in her honor. Mem. Nat. League Am. Pen Women (br. pres. 1960-62), DAR (chpt. registrar 1966-67), Women in Communications, Nat. Geneal. Soc., Nat. Soc. Colonial Dames Am., First Families Va., San Diego Geneal. Soc. (hon.), Social Svc. League La Jolla (life), Libr. Assn. La Jolla (life), Scottish Record Soc., Friends of Glasgow Cathedral (life), Magna Charta Dames, Owsley Family Hist. Sigma Alpha Iota, Woman's Club (La Jolla), Clan Hay (life). Home: 7118 Olivetas Ave La Jolla CA 92037

STEWART, MARY CATHERINE, psychologist; b. Sault Ste. Marie, Mich.; d. Alexander Pringle and Marguerite Louise (Mc Carron) S.; A.B., U. Miami, 1941, M.S., 1960; m. Charles William Marker, Nov. 14, 1942 (div.); 1 son, Kevin Charles Stewart Marker. Human engring. analyst Boeing Co., Seattle, 1960-69; cons., Seattle, 1969-71, MITRE Corp., McLean, Va., 1971-74; research contract mgr. U.S. Dept. Transp., Washington, 1974-76; supervisory auditor psychologist GAO, Washington, 1976-78; established human factors group Idaho Nat. Engring. Lab. EG&G Idaho, Inc., Idaho Falls, 1978, mgr., 1978-81; profl. staff TRW Ballistic Missiles Div., Norton AFB, Calif., 1982—. Mem. Human Factors Soc. (founder, 1st pres. Idaho chpt.). Office: TRW Ballistic Missiles Div Norton AFB CA 92402

STEWART, MARY LEEUW, writer; b. Holland, Mich., June 30, 1929; d. Edward and Elizabeth Alice (Nibbelink) L.; m. Richard Donald Stewart, June 14, 1952; children: Richard Scot, Gregory David, Mary Elizabeth. BA in English, Mount Mary Coll., 1979; MA in English and Writing, U. Wis., 1984. Lic. real estate broker. Auditor Sears, Roebuck & Co., Bay City, Mich., 1947-48; with payroll dept. The Dow Chem. Co., Midland, Mich., 1948-49, with advt. dept., 1949-52; broker N. Christensen Real Estate, Racine, Wis., 1986-87, Mrs. F.M. Hilpert Real Estate, Racine, 1987-88; ind. writer Racine, 1979—; real estate broker ind. referrals, Racine, 1988—. Contbr. articles to profl. jours. Befriender, Befriender Ministry program, Racine, 1987-89; program chmn. XYZ Elderly Group, Racine, 1989; docent Charles A. Wustum Mus. Fine Arts, Racine, 1990—. Mem. Inner Wheel of Racine West Corr., AAUW, Racine Bd. Realtors, Aux. Med. Soc., Book Club (chmn. 1986-87). Republican. Methodist. Home and Office: 5337 Wind Point Rd Racine WI 53402

STEWART, MARY LOU, business owner; b. Columbus, Ohio, Feb. 16, 1927; d. Raymond and Wilma Louise (Flowers) Stookey; m. Charles William Stewart, Aug. 30, 1952 (dec. June 1985); 1 child, Daniel William. Student, Cerritos Coll., 1960, Harbor Coll., 1961. Biller, typist Milani Foods, L.A., 1949-52; office mgr., biller Betty Brooks Sports Mfr., Maywood, Calif., 1952-57; sec., bookkeeper Harmony Homes, Temple City, Calif., 1958-60; office mgr., pvt. sec. Wesco Mdse. Co., L.A., 1972-75; owner Stewart World Trade, Hollywood, Calif., 1975-80, Stewart Trucking Co., Lake Arrowhead, Calif., 1980—. Reporter Chimes Newspaper, 1940-43. Mem. Star Route Mail Contractors Assn., NAFE, Am. Assn. Ret. Persons, Girls Athletic Assn., Ephebian Soc., Mensa. Democrat. Home and Office: 28771 Potomac PO Box 1153 Lake Arrowhead CA 92352

STEWART, MILDRED SIMPSON, social services administrator; b. Bath, Maine, Apr. 5, 1940; d. Herbert Peter and Lucy Gertrude (Ward) Simpson; m. Allan George Stewart, Feb. 4, 1967; children: Derek Allan, Ellen Simpson. BA in Journalism, U. Maine, 1962. Women's editor Daily Kennebec Jour., Augusta, Maine, 1962-66; reporter Bath (Maine) Daily Times, 1966-67, Bath-Brunswick Times Record, Brunswick, Maine, 1967-70, Portland Press Herald, Brunswick, Maine, 1970-72; staff writer/columnist Maine Sunday Telegram, Portland, Maine, 1972-86; dir. of vol. Reg. Mem. Hosp. and Bath Meml. Hosp., Brunswick, 1982—. Co-chmn.: cookbook, Merrymeeting Merry Eating, 1988; editor: hist. tour book, Falls to the Bay, 1980. Pub. chmn. Bath-Brunswick AAUW, Brunswick, 1968-88; chmn. 250th anniversary com., town of Brunswick, 1987-89; restorer Growstown Sch., Town of Brunswick, 1982-84; dir. Stevens Home, Brunswick, 1980—. Named Block "M", Gen. Alumni Assn. U. of Maine, Orono, Maine, 1976, Woman of Yr. Maine Press, Radio TV Women, Portland, 1972, Woman of Yr. Brunswick Bus. and Profl. Women, Brunswick, 1988. Mem. Maine Media Women, Main Soc. Hosp. Vol. Dir., N.E. Assn. Hosp. Vol. Dir., Bath-Brunswick AAUW, Village Improvement Assn., Pejepscot Hist. Soc. Republican. Congregational. Office: Reg Mem Hosp 58 Baribeau Dr Brunswick ME 04011

STEWART, ORA MARIE, library administrator; b. Monango, N.D., Sept. 14, 1927; d. Don C. and Edith Bernice (Hafey) Sprouse; m. Charles H. Stewart, June 1, 1946; children: Charles D., Terry, Aprill, Rock, Amy Jo, Reed. BS in Edn. and Natural Sci., Ellendale State Tchrs. Coll., 1947; MS in Libr. Sci, U. N.D., 1970. Dir. Carnegie Regional Libr. Grafton, N.D., 1965—. Dir. Grafton (N.D.) Community Theatre, 1975—. Mem. N.D. Com. for the Humanities, 1984-87, Mayor's Com. for Employment of Disabled, 1990; bd. dirs. Walsh County Hist. Soc., 1989—; sec. Foster Grandparent Program, 1987-89; adv. bd. for Grand Forks Pub. Radio, 1984; Dem. del. N.D. Dist. 16, 1982. Mem. N.D. Libr. Assn. (pres. 1980), N.D. Adv. Coun. for Librs., Northeastern Interlibr. Coop. Coun. of N.D., (pres. 1988—), Heritage Doll Collectors (pres. 1990). Democrat. Presbyterian. Home: 131 Prospect Ave Grafton ND 58237 Office: Carnegie Regional Libr 7th & Griggs Grafton ND 58237

STEWART, ORO ROZELLA, retail executive; b. Pendleton, Oreg., July 8, 1917; d. Joseph Allen and Oro Rozella (Overholtzer) Holiday; m. Ivan Stewart, Apr. 4, 1943 (dec.). BE, Oreg. State Coll., 1940; postgrad., Wash. State Coll., 1940-42. Owner, mgr. Stewart's Photo Shop, Anchorage, 1943—; owner Stewart's Jewel Jade Mine, 1970—; instr. TV Sch. Photograhpy; lectr. on Alaskan movies. Writer Alaskan directory on rockhound and internat. locations. Mem. Anchorage Centennial Com., 1967, organizer time capsule to be buried in Juneau; mem. Anchorage Downtown Assn., Fairview Homowners Assn. Recipient various awards at gem and mineral shows. Mem. Alaska Geol. Soc., Alaska Miners Assn., Chugach Gem and Mineral Soc. (chair field trips 1965-78, 81-84, pres. 1967, internat. chair 1967—), Am. Fedn. Lapidary Socs. (internat. relations com. 1977-80), N.W. Fedn. Mineral Socs., Nat. Businessmens Assn., Anchorage C. of C., Rifleman's Assn., Master Photo Dealers Assn., Profl. Photographers Alaska, Pioneers of Alaska. Democrat. Mem. Soc. of Friends. Clubs: Scottish, Tropical Fish. Lodge: Zonta (v.p. 1971). Home: 840 W 10th Anchorage AK 99501 Office: 531 4th Ave Anchorage AK 99501

STEWART, PAMELA TABOR, direct marketing professional; b. Plattsburgh, N.Y., July 18, 1958; d. David Kurtz and Sarah Anna (Kittinger) Tabor; m. Warren Allen Stewart, July 29, 1946. BA in History, Rollins Coll., 1980. Ferry boat pilot Walt Disney World, Orlando, Fla., 1976-80; legis. corr., campaign coord. U.S. Congress, Washington, 1980-83; confidential asst., sec. U.S. Dept. Agr., Washington, 1983-84; adminstrv. asst. Elliot L. Richardson for Senator campaign, Boston, 1984-85; asst. dep. polit. dir. Nat. Rep. Senatorial Com., Washington, 1985-86; sr. regional sales rep. Rexnord Data Systems, Milw., 1986-88; v.p. mktg. LMC, A Walter Karl Co., Richmond, Va., 1988-89; sales mgr. N.Am. Mktg., Richmond, 1989—. Campaign coord. McCollum for Congress, Orlando, 1980, 82; v.p. Boston Republican Women Club, 1988; mem. Va. Jefferson Assn., Richmond, 1988. Mem. Women's Direct Response Group, Direct Mktg. Assn. Washington, New Eng. Direct Mktg. Assn., Phila. Direct Mktg. Assn., Md. Direct Mktg. Assn., DAR, Omicron Delta Kappa (v.p. 1980). Lutheran. Home: 306 N Mulberry St 1 Richmond VA 23220 Office: NAm Mktg 3703 Carolina Ave Richmond VA 23222

STEWART, PATRICE LAFFERTY, securities trader; b. Sarasota, Fla., May 26, 1933; d. Chester James and Mable Marie (Stephens) Lafferty; m. John Wesley Stewart (div.); children: James Wesley, John David; m. William B. Chase II, Sept. 20, 1986. BBA, Fla. State U., 1958. Registered with N.Y. Stock Exch., Nat. Assn. Securities Dealers; registered option prin., br. office mgr., uniform state and interest rate options. With Merrill Lynch, 1963-85; ops. mgr. Merrill Lynch, Sarasota, 1965-79, asst. v.p., 1979-83; adminstrv. mgr. Merrill Lynch, Southfield, Mich., 1979-83; br. mgr. Merrill Lynch, Englewood, Fla., 1983-85; div. compliance adminstr. Paine Webber, Washington, 1985-86, S.E. div. tng. officer, 1986-88, S.E. div. adminstrv. mgr., 1988-90, v.p., 1985-90; pvt. practice as cons. Traverse City, Mich., 1990—. Fin. officer Luth. Ch., Ft. Myers, Fla., 1978. Mem. MADD, N.Y. Stock Exch., Nat. Assn. Securities Dealers, Phi Beta Psi (state pres. Fla. chpt. 1972). Home and Office: 2821 Forest Lodge Traverse City MI 49684

STEWART, PATRICIA ANN, bank executive; b. Phoenix, Nov. 3, 1953; d. Travis Delano and Ann Helen (Lopez) Hill; B.S., Ariz. State U., 1975. Programmer, analyst Victor Comptometer Corp., Phoenix, 1975-77, Lewis & Roca, Attys., Phoenix, 1977-79; data processing mgr. Central Mgmt. Corp., Phoenix, 1979-80; corp. systems cons. S.W. Forest Industries, Phoenix, 1981-87; human resources system mgr. Western Savs. and Loan, Phoenix, 1987—; ptnr. Abacus Group, 1981-83. Mem. Data Processing Mgmt. Assn. (pres. Phoenix chpt. 1982), Ariz. HP Users Group (mem. dir. 1987). Home: 15849 N 20th Pl Phoenix AZ 85022 Office: Western Savs 3200 E Camelback Suite 349 Phoenix AZ 85011

STEWART, PATRICIA CARRY, foundation administrator; b. Bklyn., May 19, 1928; d. William J. and Eleanor (Murphy) Carry; m. Charles Thorp Stewart, May 30, 1976. Student U. Paris, 1948-49; BA, Cornell U., 1950. Fgn. corr. Irving Trust Co., N.Y.C., 1950-51; with Janeway Rsch. Co., N.Y.C., 1951-60, sec., treas., 1955-60; with Buckner & Co. and successor firms, N.Y.C., 1961-73, ptnr., 1962-70, v.p.-treas., 1970-71, pres.-treas., 1971-73; pres., treas. Knight, Carry, Bliss & Co., Inc., N.Y.C., 1971-73; pres., treas. G. Tsai & Co., Inc., 1973; v.p. Edna McConnell Clark Found. Inc., 1974—; bd. dirs. Melville Corp., Borden Inc., Continental Corp., Bankers Trust Co., Bankers Trust N.Y. Corp.; allied mem. N.Y. Stock Exch., 1962-73; past mem. nominating com. Am. Stock Exch., N.Y. Stock Exch., dir., past chmn. Investor Responsibility Rsch. Ctr. Trustee, vice-chair Cornell U., bd. overseers Cornell Med. Coll.; vis. com. Grad. Sch. Bus., Harvard U., 1974-80; bd. dirs. NOW, Legal Def. and Edn. Fund, Women in Founds./Corp. Philanthropy 1980-86; v.p. fin. com. Women's Forum; vice chmn. CUNY, 1976-80; bd. dirs. United Way of Tri-State, 1977-81, Inst. for Edn. and Rsch. on Women and Work; voting mem. Blue Cross and Blue Shield Greater N.Y., 1975-82; trustee N.Y. State 4-H Found., 1970-76, Internat. Inst. Rural Reconstruction, 1974-79; mem. N.Y.C. panel White House Fellows, 1976-78; mem. bus. adv. coun. The Hosp. Chaplaincy. Recipient Elizabeth Cutter Morrow award YWCA, 1977, Catalyst award Women Dirs. in Corps., 1978, Trustee medal CUNY, 1983, Accomplishment award Wings Club N.Y., 1984, Women's Funding Coalition Innovators for Women$hare award, 1986, Banking Industry Acievement award Nat. Assn. Bank Women, 1987, Cert. Disting. Accomplishments Barnard Coll., 1989; named to YWCA Acad. Women Achievers. Mem. Fin. Women's Assn. N.Y., NOW (bd. dirs., treas.), Coun. Fgn. Rels., Pi Beta Phi. Clubs: University (N.Y.C.); Gullane Golf (Scotland). Home: 135 E 71st St New York NY 10021 Office: 250 Park Ave New York NY 10017

STEWART, PATRICIA LESLIE, international marketing executive; b. Kearny, N.J., May 17, 1956; d. Robert Hanna and Vivian (Buckley) S. Cert., 1st Sch. Paralegal, Paramus, Md., 1980; BA cum laude, William Paterson Coll., 1978; MBA in Mktg., Fairleigh Dickinson Coll., 1987. Theater critic Suburban Trends Newspaper, Butler, N.J., 1976-78; editorial asst. PDI Mktg. Svcs., Parsippany, N.J., 1978-79; legal asst. AT&T Bell Labs., Whippany, N.J., 1979-81; tech. writer, mgr. Western Electric, Whippany, 1981-82; tech. documentation mgr. Bell Communications Rsch., Morristown, N.J., 1983-84; mktg. mgr. AT&T Network Systems, Morristown, 1984-88; internat. mgr. AT&T Gen. Bus. Systems, Parsippany, 1988—. Pub. relations com. Morris County Young Reps., 1988. Mem. AT&T Profl. Women Assn. (Tri-State Sounding Bd. 1982—), Am. Mgmt. Assn., Am. Soc. Advt. Profls., Sierra Club, Audubon Soc., Pro Bono (Outstanding Community Pub. Rels. award 1986). Roman Catholic. Office: AT&T Gen Bus Systems 99 Jefferson Rd 1C12 Parsippany NJ 07054

STEWART, PATRICIA MARIA, air force personnel specialist; b. N.Y.C., Nov. 8, 1952; d. Edward Joseph and Marie Frances (Woytisek) S. BA, Our Lady of the Lake Coll., San Antonio, 1973; MBA, U. Tex., San Antonio,

1976. Personnel mgmt. specialist San Antonio Air Logistics Ctr., 1973-75, position classification specialist, 1975-76; labor rels. specialist Oklahoma City Air Logistics Ctr., 1976-80; civilian personnel officer 831 Combat Support Group, George AFB, Victorville, Calif., 1980-81; labor rels. specialist Hdqrs. USAF, Washington, 1981-86, personnel mgmt. specialist, 1986-88; civilian personnel officer Hdqrs. Alaskan Air Command, Anchorage, 1988—; vis. instr. Air U. Maxwell AFB, Ala., 1981-86, Profl. Personal Mgmt. Sch., Gunter AFB, Ala., 1981-88. Publicity chmn. Fairlington Players, Arlington, Va., 1984-86; mem. Alaska Women of the Wilderness, Eagle River, 1989. Office: Hdqrs Alaskan Air Command DPC Elmendorf AFB AK 99506

STEWART, PAULA WARD, health center administrator; b. Trenton, N.J., Apr. 11, 1949; d. Theodore and Vivian Emma (Huffington) Ward; m. Roosevelt Stewart Sr., Apr. 25, 1975 (div. July 1983); children: April C., Malaika M., Roosevelt Jr. BA, Webster Coll./Univ., 1978. Social work assoc. Yeatman/Union Sarah Health Ctr., St. Louis, 1972; genetic counselor Yeatman/Union Sarah Health Ctr., 1972-79; counselor, project dir. Metro Community Health Ctr., St. Louis, 1979-80; project dir. hi blood Metro Community Health Ctr., 1980-82, acting adminstr., 1982-85; dir. health promotion Plan de Salud Health Ctr., Ft. Lupton, Mo., 1983-85; adminstrv. resident Denver Health Hosps., 1985-86; exec. dir. Community Health Mgmt. Corp., Cordelia Martin Health Ctr., Toledo, 1986, Cordelia Martin Health Ctr., Toledo, 1986—; mem. community support svcs. com. Lucas County Mental Health Bd., 1988—; citizen adv. bd. Toledo Mental Health Ctr., 1987—. Contbr. articles to profl. jours. Chmn. polit. action com. NAACP, Toledo, 1987—, chmn. health com. Ohio conf., Columbus, 1988—. Recipient Community Svc. award Toledo Prince Hall Masons, 1988. Mem. Ohio Primary Care Assn. (sec. 1987-89), Ag. Exec. Dir. Assn. (sec. 1987-89), Ohio Pub. Health Assn., Am. Pub. Health Assn., Jack & Jill Club, Zonta Club I (co-chair svc. com. 1988—). Democrat. Methodist. Office: Cordelia Martin Health Ctr 905 Nebraska Ave Toledo OH 43607

STEWART, ROSALIND LANDIS, financial services executive; b. York, Pa., Nov. 27, 1941; d. Russell William and Viola Eletta (Leidig) Landis; m. Charles Edward Stewart June 24, 1983; 1 child, Charles Edward Jr. BS, U. Calif., Berkeley, 1973. Pres. Spectrum Unltd., Calif.; dist. rep. Aid Assn. for Lutherans, Appleton, Wis. Mem. Life Underwriters Luth. Charities, Fraternal Ins. Counselors (cert.). Peninsula Life Underwriters Assn. Home: PO Box 5544 South San Francisco CA 94083

STEWART, SANDRA GOWERS, marketing professional; b. Nephi, UT, Mar. 26, 1962; d. Fred Lewis and JoAnn (Price) G.; m. Scott Jay, Aug. 12, 1988. BS in Bus. Mgmt., U. Utah, Salt Lake City, 1984. Buyer, mdse. clerk Musician's Supply, Inc., El Cajon, Calif., 1979-81; bond clerk Northwestern Nat. Ins., Salt Lake City, 1983-84; purchasing clerk Teledyne Micronetics, San Diego, 1984-85, material control analyst, prodn. coord., 1985-86; buyer Teledyne Ryan Electronics, 1986-88; sr. buyer Teledyne Ryan Electronics, San Diego, 1988—. Counselor Young Women's Orgn. in Ch. Jesus Christ of LDS San Diego 1988—. Mem. Am. Prodn. and Inventory Control Soc. (sec. 1986-88, Cert. of Recognition), Teledyne Ryan Electronics Chap. of the Nat. Mgmt. Assn. (sec. 1988—), Beta Gamma Sigma. Republican. Mormon. Office: Teledyne Ryan Electronics 8650 Balboa Ave San Diego CA 92123

STEWART, SHEILA MARIE, medical services administrator; b. L.A., May 7, 1960; d. George Wallace and Philomena (Spillane) S. BA in Theatre, Radford (Va.) U., 1983. Adminstr. 70001 Tng. & Employment Inst., Washington, 1985-86; with ops. dept. Bloomingdales, McLean, Va., 1986-87; project adminstr. M. Rosenblatt & Son, Arlington, Va., 1987, Med. Svc. Corp. Internat., Arlington, 1988—. Mem. NAFE, Alpha Psi Omega (pres. 1980-81). Roman Catholic. Office: Med Svc Corp Internat 1716 Wilson Blvd Arlington VA 22209

STEWART, STEPHANIE, secretary; b. Bakersfield, Calif., Sept. 13, 1961; d. Troy L. and Carolyn Ann (Thurston) Childers; m. Brian C. Stewart, Aug. 18, 1984. BA in Pub. Adminstrn., Calif. State U., Bakersfield; cert., Kern County Bd. Suprs. Acad., Bakersfield. OMR clk., CTI investigator Contel, Bakersfield; legal sec. Hugie & Hugie Law Offices, Bakersfield, Hulsy & Hulsy Law Offices, Bakersfield; sec., asst. to dir. Emergency Med. Svcs. dept. Kern County, Bakersfield; motivational speaker various orgns. Active Kern County Child Abuse Prevention Coun., Kern County Women's Network. Mem. NAFE, Am. Assn. Pub. Adminstrs. Home: 3904 La Tonia Ct Bakersfield CA 93313

STEWART, SUE STERN, lawyer; b. Casper, Wyo., Oct. 9, 1942; d. Fraizer McVale and Carolyn Eliabeth (Hunt) Stewart; B.A., Wellesley Coll., 1964; postgrad. Harvard U. Law Sch., 1964-65; J.D., Georgetown U., 1967; m. Arthur L. Stern, III, July 31, 1965 (div.); children—Anne Stewart, Mark Alan; m. John A. Ciampa, Sept. 1, 1985. Admitted to N.Y. bar, 1968; clk. to Judges Juvenile Ct., Washington, 1967-68; mem. firm Nixon, Hargrave, Devans & Doyle, Rochester, N.Y., 1968-74, ptnr., 1975—; lectr. in field; trustee Found. of Monroe County (N.Y.) Bar, 1976-78. Sec., dir. United Community Chest of Greater Rochester, 1973-87; trustee, sec. Internat. Museum Photography at George Eastman House, Rochester, 1974—; Genesee Country Mus., Mumford, N.Y., 1976—; bd. dirs. Ctr. for Govtal. Research. Mem. Am. (chmn. task force on charitable giving, exempt orgns. com. tax sect. 1981—), N.Y. State (exec. com. tax sect., 1974-76, chmn. com. exempt orgns. 1975-76), Monroe County Bar Assn. (trustee 1974-78), BNA Portfolio, Pvt. Found. Distbns. Author: Charitable Giving and Solicitation. Office: Nixon Hargrave Devans & Doyle Lincoln First Tower Rochester NY 14603

STEWART, SUSAN COCHRAN, librarian; b. Houston, Feb. 8, 1954; d. John Wesley and Barbara Ann (McFall) Cochran; m. Leland E. Stewart, June 10, 1978 (div. Jan. 1988); 1 child, Erin Mariah. BA, Tex. Tech. U., 1975; MLS, U. Tex., 1978. Asst. libr. Bernard Johnson, Inc., Houston, 1978-79; supr. tech. records Chevron U.S.A., Houston, 1979-88; libr. Chevron Chems. Co., Houston, 1988—. Roman Catholic. Home: 7603 Mellowgrove Ct Spring TX 77379 Office: Chevron Chem Co PO Box 2100 Houston TX 77252-9987

STEWART, SUZANNE FLORENCE, hypnotherapist; b. Shreveport, La., Mar. 10, 1930; d. Fred Whitaker and Florence (Satterley) Michaud; children: Susan, David, Jim. BA in Psychology, U. Calif., L.A., 1964; grad., Profl. Hypnotism Inst., L.A., 1980. Cert. hypnotherapist Am. Coun. Hypnotist Examiners, hypno-anaesthesia therapist Nat. Bd. Hypnotic Anaesthesiology. Profl. hypnotist Thousand Oaks, Calif., 1980-84, pvt. practice hypnotherapist, 1985—; pvt. practice hypnotherapist/hypno-anaesthesia specialist, 1986—; owner, founder Med. and Dental Hypnotherapy Ctr., Thousand Oaks, Calif., 1986—. Recipient award for hypnosis for natural childbirth, Therapeutic Hypnosis Group, 1986. Fellow Nat. Bd. Hypnotic Anaesthesiology; mem. Hypnotist Examiners Coun. of Calif. (examiner 1989), U. Calif. Alumni Assn., Conejo Valley C. of C., Westlake Village C. of C. Office: Med/Dental Hypnotherapy Ctr 550 St Charles Dr Ste 204-A Thousand Oaks CA 91360

STEWART, SUZANNE LEIGH, computer software marketing consultant; b. Savannah, Ga., Sept. 20, 1963; d. Benjamin Leonard and Martha (Durham) Pike. BBA in Mktg., Ga. State U., 1986. Internat. sales and mktg. mgr. Information Tech., Atlanta, 1986-89; computer mktg. and sales consultant Atlanta, 1989—; mktg. comunications mgr. SofNet, Inc., 1989—.

STEWART, WHITNEY, children's book writer; b. Boston, Feb. 3, 1959; d. Richard Ramsdell Stewart and Carlin (Whitney) Scherer; m. Hans Christoph Andersson, Sept. 17, 1988. BA in Children's Lit. and Linguistics, Brown U., 1983. Puppeteer Le Theatre D'Avignon, France, 1977-78; children's libr. researcher Providence Athenaeum, Providence, 1981-82; travel agt., writer Parrish Travel Ctr., New Orleans, 1983-86; free lance writer, 1987—; editor Ctr. for Applied Linguistics, Washington, 1988—; lectr. elem. and high schs.; dir. Tibetan sponsorship program, Washington, 1988—. Author: To the Lion Throne, 1989, Clockwise Round the Stupa, 1989; former editor Tibet Today Newsletter, ERIC/CLL News. Former sec. Capital Area Friends of Tibet, Washington, 1988-89. Mem. Soc. Children's Book Writers, Writer's Ctr., Asia Soc. Mongolia Soc. Office: Ctr for Applied Linguistics 1118 22d St NW Washington DC 20037

STEWART-FRANK, JEAN HOOD, medical services sales executive; b. Lennoxtown, Scotland, Feb. 15, 1956; came to U.S., 1978; d. James and Janet (Hood) Stewart; m. David Frank, Dec. 20, 1985. Diploma, Vancouver (Can.) Sch. Nursing, 1977; B Health Sci., Chapman Coll., 1984; MBA, Loyola Marymount U., L.A., 1989. R.N., Calif. Staff nurse Vancouver Gen. Hosp., 1977-78, St. John's Hosp. and Health Ctr., Santa Monica, Calif., 1978-80, St. Paul's Hosp., Vancouver, 1980-81; charge nurse ICU St. John's Hosp., Santa Monica, 1982-86; liaison Lifeline Homecare, Downey, Calif., 1986-88; terr. mgr. Lifeline Homecare, Downey, 1988-90, area sales mgr., 1990—. Mem. NAFE, Nat. Nurses in Bus., Hosp. Discharge Planners Assn. Episcopalian. Home: 7533 McConnell Ave Los Angeles CA 90045 Office: Lifeline Homecare 12130 Paramount Blvd Downey CA 90242

STEWART-NEWMAN, CHERE LYNN, advertising company executive; b. Ashland, Ky., Aug. 27, 1955; d. James Henry and Fannie Mae (Ison) Stewart; m. James Edger Newman, July 14, 1972; children: James Edger II, Shannon Michael, Angela Kathryn. AA, U. Ky., 1980; BA, Marshall U., 1983, MA in Speech, Comm. and Broadcasting, 1990; postgrad. in bus. adminst, Morehead State U., 1985-88. Counselor, tutor Huntington (W.Va.) Learning Ctr., 1983; domestic violence counselor Pathways, Inc., Ashland, 1983-84; domestic violence pub. educator for Northwest Ky., procedure, 1984; owner, mgr. Advt. Promotional Svcs., Ashland, 1984—; advt., promotional cons., media writer-producer, TV comml. dir. Steele Plastics Co., Ashland, 1984-85; polit. advt. copywriter for local candidates, 1986; teaching asst. speech, communication Marshall U., Huntington, 1988—; speech instr., 1988—, bus. communication interviewer, 1989-90, spl. projects coordinaor Broadcast News; news writer WMUL, 1989, radio bus. mgr. and news anchor, 1989, newsletter writer/pur., 1989; video coordinator, ofcl. photographer Boyd County Football Assn., 1989—. Contbr. articles to profl. jours. Sec. Ironville Sch. PTA, 1986-88; coord. computer Lab. Ironville Sch., 1986-88; project chairperson Summit Jr. High Boosters Club, 1988-89. Recipient Students Choice award for teaching asst. of the yr., Marshall U. Speech/Communications Dept., 1988-89. Mem. Nat. Writers Club, Gamma Beta Phi, Psi Chi. Democrat. Home: 2815 Nolte St Ashland KY 41102

STEWART-PINKHAM, SANDRA MORRAL, pediatrician; b. Altoona, Pa., Jan. 14, 1942; d. F. Rolf and Lillie (Westberg) Morral; m. Alan D. Stewart, June 11, 1966 (div. 1983); 1 child, David Alan; m. Galen T. Pinkham, Oct. 1, 1979; children: Julia and Richard (twins). AB, Carleton Coll., 1962; MD, U. Rochester, 1968; MS, Ohio State U., 1973. Diplomate Am. Bd. Pediatrics. Intern Strong Meml. Hosp., Rochester, N.Y., 1968-69; resident in pediatrics Albany (N.Y.) Med. Ctr., 1969-70; fellow in pediatrics Children's Hosp., Columbus, Ohio, 1971-73; asst. prof. pediatrics Ohio State U., Columbus, 1974-78; pvt. practice Columbus, 1978—. Author pub. rsch. on heavy metal effects in children. Mem. Am. Acad. Pediatrics, Soc. Environ. Toxicology and Chemistry, Orton Dyslexia Soc., Learning Disabilities Assn. Office: 1890 Northwest Blvd Columbus OH 43212

STICKNEY, JESSICA, state legislator; b. Duluth, Minn., May 16, 1929; d. Ralph Emerson and Claudia Alice (Cox) Page; m. Edwin Levi Stickney, June 17, 1951; children: Claudia, Laura, Jeffrey. BA, Macalester Coll., St. Paul, Minn., 1951; PhD (hon), Rocky Mtn. Coll., Billings, Mont., 1986. Rep. State of Mont., 1989—; mem. Gov.'s Commn. on Post-Sec. Edn., Mont., 1973-75. Mem. Sch. Bd. Trustees, Miles City, Mont., 1968-74; mem., chmn. zoning bd., Miles City, 1975-89; mem. Govt. Study Commn., Miles City, 1974-76, United Ch. Christ Bd. Homeland Ministries, 1975-81; chmn., conf. moderator United Ch. Christ Bd. Mont.-Northern Wyo. Conf., 1980-82; chmn. Town Meeting on the Arts, Mont., 1980; mem., chmn. Miles Community Coll. Bd., 1975-89, chmn. 1978-80. Mem. Mont. Arts Coun. (chmn. 1982-85), Western States Arts Found. (vice chmn. 1984), Nat. Assembly State Arts Agys. (bd. dirs. 1982-88), AAUW (pres. 1964-66). Democrat.

STIELOW-LEACH, FAY ANN, interior designer; b. Oostburg, Wis., Apr. 20, 1939; d. Arnold Lloyd and May Annette (Steenweg) Wykhuis; m. Curtis G. Stielow, June 16, 1961 (div. 1978); m. Harrison Langford Leach, July 11, 1987. Student, Carroll Coll., 1957-58; BS, U. Wis., 1961; postgrad., U. Calif., Long Beach, 1962-63. Tchr. Long Beach Jordan High Sch., 1961-64, Shoales Jr. High Sch., Milw., 1964-66, McPherson Jr. High Sch., Orange, Calif., 1966-69; realtor Myers and Hill, Vienna, Va., 1971-74; sales rep. Ryland Homes, Manassas, Va., 1974-76, Fairfield Homes, Woodbridge, Va., 1976-79; v.p. Fairfield Design Studio, Woodbridge, 1980-86, pres., 1986—. Mem. No. Va. Builders Assn., Prince William County of C. of C. (com. chairperson 1984-87). Presbyterian. Office: Faifield Design Studio 15015A Farm Creek Dr Woodbridge VA 22191

STIENMIER, SAUNDRA KAY YOUNG, aviation educator; b. Abilene, Kans., Apr. 27, 1938; d. Bruce Waring and Helen E. (Rutz) Young; m. Richard H. Steinmier, Dec. 20, 1958; children: Richard, Susan, Julia, Laura. AA, Colo. Women's Coll., 1957; student, Temple Buell Coll., U. Colo.; ed., Embre Riddle Aviation U., Ramstein, Germany. Cert. FAA pilot. Dir. Beaumont Gallery, El Paso, Tex.; mem. grad. studies faculty Embre Riddle Aviation U.; mgr. Ramstein Aero Club, USAF, Peterson Aero Club, USAF, Peterson AFB, Colo. Named Outstanding S.W. Artist. Mem. AOPA, OES, Nat. Pilots Assn., Colo. Pilots Assn., Soc. Arts and Letters, 99's Club. Home: PO Box 14123 Peterson AFB CO 80914

STILES, HELEN, artist; b. N.Y.C., June 15; d. Max and Sophie (Gross) Brandwein; m. Joseph Richard Stiles, Sept. 2, 1943 (dec. Sept. 1975); 1 child, Richard Paul. BS, Bklyn. Coll., 1934; MS in Edn., Coll. of City of N.Y., 1936. Cert. art tchr., N.Y. Dir. Fresh Meadows Jr. Art Sch., N.Y.C., 1946-50; art tchr. Lewis Carrol Elem. Sch., N.Y.C., 1968-74; instr. of in svc. tchrs N.Y.C. Bd. Edn., 1971-72; appeared on radio and TV shows, N.Y.C., 1987. One-woman shows include European Am. Bank, Fresh Meadows N.Y., 1971, 81; exhibited in group shows at Artists Equity N.Y. Union Carbide Exhbn., 1975, Nat. Assn. Women Artists, 1975-82, 84-89 (Lillian Cotton Meml. prize 1976, Gayner award for printmaking 1985), Manhattan Graphics Artists at Associated Am. Artists Gallery, 1977, Provincetown Art Assn. and Mus., 1978-90, Allied Artists Am., 1978, Nat. Soc. Painters in Casein and Acrylics (Doris Kreindler Meml. award 1978), Nat. Acad. Gallery, N.Y.C., 1979, 80, Nat. Arts Club, N.Y., Pratt Graphics Ctr. Ann. Competition, 1980, Bergen Mus. of Art and Sci., 1983, Jacob K. Javits Fed. Bldg., N.Y.C., 1983-89, Outermost Gallery, Provincetown, 1984-90, Manhattan Graphic Artist at Sylvan Cole Gallery, 1988, Caton Rose Art Inst. (1st in Oil prize 1962), Marbella Gallery, N.Y.C., 1989, Wenniger Graphics, Provincetown, Mass., 1990, Audobon Arts Assn., N.Y.C., 1979, 80. Mem. Artists Equity N.Y., Provincetown Art Assn. and Mus., Nat. Assn. Women Artists (chmn. membership com. 1980-89, meml. com. 1989—). Home and Studio: 189-04 64th Ave Fresh Meadows NY 11365

STILES, MARY ANN, lawyer; b. Tampa, Fla., Nov. 16, 1944; d. Ralph A. and Bonnie (Smith) S. AA, Hills Community Coll., 1973; BS, Fla. State U., 1975; JD, Antioch Sch. Law, 1978. Bar: Fla. 1978. Legis. analyst Fla. Ho. of Reps., Tallahassee, 1973-74, 74-75; intern U.S. Senate, Washington, 1977; v.p., gen. counsel Associated Industries Fla., Tallahassee, 1978-81, gen. counsel, 1981-84, spl. counsel, 1986—; assoc. Deschler, Reed & Crichfield, Boca Raton, Fla., 1980-81; founding ptnr. Stiles, Allen & Taylor, P.A., Tampa and Tallahassee, Fla., 1982—; bd. dirs. Univ. Community Physicians Assn., Tampa, Six Stars Devel. Corp., Tampa, Uniphy Corp., Tampa. Author: Workers' Compensation Law Handbook, 1980-90 edit. Bd. dirs., sec. Hillsborough Community Coll. Found., Tampa, 1985-87; bd. dirs. Hillsborough Area Regional Transit Authority, Tampa, 1986-89; bd. dirs. Boys and Girls Club of Tampa, 1986—; mem. Gov.'s Oversite Bd. on Worker's Compensation, 1989-90, Judicial Nominating Commn. for Worker's Compensation Cts., 1990—. Mem. ABA, Fla. Bar Assn., Hillsborough County Bar Assn., Hillsborough Assn. Women Lawyers, Fla. Assn. Women Lawyers, Fla. Women's Alliance, Athena Soc., Hillsborough County Seminole Boosters (past pres.). Democrat. Baptist. Club: Tiger Bay (Tampa) (pres.). Office: 315 Plant Ave Tampa FL 33606 also: 216 S Monroe Tallahssee FL 30302

STILES, REBECCA ANN, organizational development consultant; b. Oelwein, Iowa, Apr. 30, 1951; d. Howard James and Elizabeth (Steimel) S. BA in Social Work, U. Minn., MSW, 1975; MPH, U. N.C., 1982; cert. human rels., Mid-Atlantic Assn. Tng. & Cons, Washington, 1988. Child treatment coord. Wis. Dept. Social Svcs., Fond du Lac, 1976-77;

juvenile ct. supr. Wis. Dept. Social Svcs., Madison, 1977-78; dir. Oakton-Arbor Treatment Ctr., Fairfax, Va., 1978-79; project assoc. Ctr. Devel. and Population Activities, Washington, 1982-83; health program coord. So. Sudanese Refugee Assistance Program, Juba, Sudan, 1983-85; cons. Overseas Devel. Office Episcopal Ch., N.Y.C., 1986; regional coord. Africa Salvation Army World Svc., Washington, 1987-88; indl. orgnl. devel. cons. Providence, 1989—; trainer, Mid-Atlantic Assn. Tng. and Consulting, Washington, 1989—; bd. dirs., Vols. in Action, Providence, Providence Haitian Project. Coord., Wis. Pub. Interest Rsch. Group, Madison, 1972-74; bd. dirs., Hotline Youth Agy., Fond du Lac, 1976-77; vol., Peace Corps, Sierra Leone, West Africa, 1979-81. Mem. Internat. Soc. Intercultural Edn., Tng. and Rsch., Assn. Creative Change, Soc. Internat. Devel., Organizational Devel. Network.

STILGENBAUER, NANCY KIEFFER, healthcare executive; b. National City, Calif., Feb. 16, 1934; d. Clinton Edward and Virginia (Grider) Kieffer; m. Marvin R. Stilgenbauer, Feb. 18, 1956; children: Debra Stilgenbauer-Miller, Holly S. Miller, Carey A. BA, Mo. Western U., 1953. Adminstrv. sec. Meml. Hosp., Inc., McPherson, Kans., 1976-80, purchasing dir., 1980-87, dir. materials mgmt., 1987—; advisor Kans. Hosp. Assn. Svc. Corp., Topeka, 1988. Contbr. articles to profl. publs. Deaconess, 1st Christian Ch., McPherson; mem. McPherson City Choir, 1980; active Campfire Girls, Inc., McPherson, 1968-75; vol. Hays and Wichita Spl. Olympics, 1989. Johnson & Johnson scholar, 1989. Fellow Am. Soc. Hosp. Materials Mgmt.; mem. Kans. Assn. Hosp. Purchasing and Materials Mgmt. (bd. dirs. 1984—, pres. 1988), Sweet Adelines (pres. local chpt. 1963), 20th Century Club (pres. 1974), Beta Omicron. Office: Meml Hosp Inc 1000 Hospital Dr McPherson KS 67460

STILLINGS, IRENE CORDINER, organization executive; b. Boston, Aug. 17, 1918; d. Matthew Wilson and Susan F. (Mason) Cordiner; m. Gordon A. Stillings, May 13, 1945; children: Daivd Gordon, Susan Irene. Student, Radcliffe Coll., 1936-39; diploma, Burdett Coll., 1941. Sec., bookkeeper Boston Refrigerator Co., 1941-42; sec., tchr. Burdett Coll., 1942-44; sec., bookkeeper Gertrude Rittenburg, Boston, 1944-46. Town chmn. Heart Fund, Woodland, Maine, 1953-61; Brownie leader Girl Scouts U.S., 1954-58; pres. Woodland Woman's Club 1961-63; sec. PTA, 1961-62; chmn. Baileyville Superintending Sch. Com., 1962-64; chmn. women's activities Nat. Found., East Washington County, 1959-61; pres. Hosp. Aid, 1961-63; chmn. Newcomers Coll. group YWCA, 1965-66, chmn. theatre group, 1968-70, pres. Suburbanites, 1970-71; Stamford chmn. Expt. in Internat. Living, 1965-68; bd. dirs. YWCA of Stamford, chmn. devotion, 1970-90, ann. Antique Show benefit, 1970-77. Mem. Mass. Hort. Soc., St. Luke's Guild (treas. 1954-63), Radcliffe Club, Stamford Woman's Club (treas. 1975-79, program com., co-chmn. Am. home dept. 1974, 75, pres. 1981-83, bd. dirs. 1985-87, 2d v.p. fin. 1983-85, 87-89, chmn. bldg. investment 1979-81, bd. dir. 1989-91), Theta Alpha Chi, Stamford Women's Club. Episcopalian. Home: 277 West Hill Rd Stamford CT 06902

STILLMAN, ANNE WALKER, fashion designer; b. Amsterdam, The Netherlands, Apr. 15, 1951; came to U.S., 1953; d. Edmund and Mary (Gwathmey) S. Student Barnard Coll., 1968-72. Pres., designer Sofia & Anne, Ltd., Bethel, Conn., Stratford, Conn. and N.Y.C., 1978—; designer Sofia & Anne Sportknit, 1983—, Sofia & Anne Children's Wear, 1985—, Go Cashmere for L'Zinger by Sofia & Anne, 1986. Mem. N.Y. Fashion Coun. Office: Sofia & Anne 37 W 39th St New York NY 10018

STILLMAN, ELINOR HADLEY, lawyer; b. Kansas City, Mo., Oct. 12, 1938; d. Hugh Gordon and Freda (Brooks) Hadley; m. Richard C. Stillman June 25, 1965 (div. Apr. 1975). BA, U. Kans., 1960; MA, Yale U., 1961; JD, George Washington U., 1972. Bar: D.C. 1973, U.S. Ct. Appeals (10th cir.) 1975, U.S. Ct. Appeals (9th cir.) 1976, U.S. Ct. Appeals (2d cir.) 1976, U.S. Supreme Ct. 1976, U.S. Ct. Appeals (5th cir.) 1983, U.S. Ct. Appeals (4th cir.) 1985. Lectr. in English CUNY, N.Y., 1963-65; asst. editor Stanford (Calif.) U. Press, 1967-69; law clk. to judge U.S. Dist. Ct. D.C., Washington, 1972-73; appellate atty. Nat. Labor Relations Bd., Washington, 1973-78; asst. to solicitor gen. U.S. Dept. Justice, Washington, 1978-82; supr. appellate atty. NLRB, Washington, 1982-86, chief counsel to mem. bd., 1986-88, chief counsel to chmn. bd., 1988—. Mem. ABA, D.C. Bar Assn. (steering com., adminstrv. law and agy. practice 1984-88), Order of the Coif, Phi Beta Kappa. Democrat. Office: Nat Labor Rels Bd 1717 Pennsylvania Ave NW Washington DC 20570

STILLMAN, MARTHA, interior designer; b. Chgo., Nov. 8, 1924; d. Frederick Arthur and Eva Mable (Ihle) Niestadt; m. Charles Harvey Stillman, Sept. 6, 1947; 1 child, Ann Elizabeth. Student, Beloit (Wis.) Coll., 1943-45; BS in Interior Design/Architecture, Northwestern U., 1947. Interior designer Interiors - Martha Stillman, New Canaan, Conn., 1961—; cons. in field. Pres. Wilmette Jrs. Infant Welfare Soc., 1953-60; mem. women's bd. Chgo. Infant Welfare Soc., 1957-60, Women's Rep.; advisor Girl Scouts U.S.A. Mem. Assn. Interior Designers (sec., bd. govs. 1964-75), Am. Soc. Interior Designers, Phi Beta Phi. Republican. Mem. United Ch. of Christ. Clubs: Woodway Country (Darien, Conn.); Skytop (Pa.). Home and Office: 301 W Hills Rd New Canaan CT 06840

STILLMAN, MARY ELIZABETH, librarian, administrator, educator; b. Phila., Oct. 31, 1929; d. Ernest E. and Rosalie (Burhans) Stillman; B.A., Wilson Coll., Chambersburg, Pa., 1950; M.S., Drexel U., Phila., 1952; Ph.D. (fellow), U. Ill., 1966. Librarian, USAF, 1953-63, Export-Import Bank U.S., 1965-68; asst. prof. Drexel U., 1968-72; mem. faculty Albright Coll., Reading, Pa., 1972-87, prof., librarian, 1975-87, spl. asst. to pres., 1987—; editor Drexel Library Quar., 1969-72; cons. research info. system Social and Rehab. Service, 1972-74; del. Pa. Gov.'s Conf. on Libraries, 1977; chmn. Pa. Library Week, 1978, 79; shareholder Reading Library Co., 1980—; mem. long-range planning com. Reading Pub. Library, 1982—, trustee, 1985—; pres. Reading Library, 1985—. Bd. dirs. Reading YWCA, 1981-83. Mem. ALA (reviewer Subscription Books Bull. 1969—), Pa. Library Assn. (dir. pub. relations task force 1974-79, editor bull. 1973-79, treas. colloquium on info. retrieval 1978-79), AAUP. Contbr. articles to profl. jours. Home: 1375 Pershing Blvd Apt 102 Reading PA 19607 Office: Albright Coll Reading PA 19604

STILLMAN, STEPHANIE MATUSZ, computer contract company executive; b. Middlesex County, N.J., July 16, 1946; d. William Stephan Matusz and Mary Jane (Van Horn) Falger; m. Dennis Edison DeMercer, Aug. 22, 1970 (div. 1977); m. Richard Alan Stillman, May 10, 1980; 1 child, Taylor Edison. B.A., Moravian Coll., 1968. Tchr., Hawaii Edn. Dept., Kohala, 1968-71; acct. exec. with various ins. agys., N.J., 1975-79; div. mgr. E.T. Lyons & Assoc., New Brunswick, N.J., 1979-80; sr. personnel adminstr. Systemp, Inc., New Brunswick, 1980-84; br. mgr. Officeforce, Inc., Cedar Knolls, N.J., 1984; pres., chief exec. officer The Resource Group, Inc., Cambridge, Mass., 1985—. Bd. dirs., pres. Rutgers-Livingston Day Care Ctr., Piscataway, N.J., 1978-80. Mem. Cambridge C. of C., Smaller Bus. Assn. New Eng., Data Processing Mgmt. Assn., Assn. Women in Computing. Republican. Avocations: skiing, travel, gourmet cooking. Office: The Resource Group Inc 122 Mt Auburn St Cambridge MA 02238

STILLS, GRACIE WIGGINS, teacher; b. Union Springs, Ala.; m. Lavaughn Clyde Still; 1 child, Kelvin Vaugh. BS, Ala. State U., 1966; MS, Ft. Valley State Coll., 1977; postgrad., Columbus Coll., 1988; postgrad. ednl. specialist program, Troy State U. V.p. Urban League Guild, Columbus, Ga., 1978; sec. Urban League Edn. Dept., Columbus, Ga., 1979-84; treas., chmn. Jr. Urban League, Columbus, Ga., 1982—; rep. HUB Auburn U., 1972-75, chmn. Knowledge Explosion Muscogee Sch. System, Columbus 1985-88. Com. mem. Boy Scouts of Am., Columbus 1979-82, bd. mem. YMCA, 1982-, Tenth St. Community Ctr.; hon mem. PTA. Recipient appreciation Continental Socs., 1976, recognition award Nat. Urban League, 1979; named Woman Achievement Concharty Coun. Girl Scouts U.S.A., 1989. Mem. AAUW (treas. Columbus br. 1990—), Ga. Edn. Assn., March of Dime (chmn. 1976-77), Nat. Assn. Negro Bus. and Profl. Women's Clubs (Community Svc. award 1982), Ala. State U. Alumni, Ft. Valley State Alumni, Ebonite Civic and Social Club, (pres. 1982—), Willie E Hatch Leadership Study Club (pres. 1964-66), Zeta Phi Beta (Women of Yr. award 1978), Phi Delta Kappa, Delta Sigma Theta. Home: 5335 Cleve St Columbus GA 31907

STILSON, CHRISTIE CAROL, publications executive, business owner; b. Portland, Oreg., Oct. 1, 1952; d. George Robert and Grace Carol (Zeller) Kammerer; m. Gregory H. Stilson, June 7, 1975; children: Maren Christine, Jeffrey Scott. BS, Portland State U., 1974, MS, 1978. Cert. tchr., Oreg. Adminstrv. asst. Office of the Chancellor, Portland, 1970-74; instr. Portland Pub. Schs., 1974-82; office mgr. Garden Home Chiropractic Ctr., Portland, 1981-83; pres. Paradise Pubs., Portland, 1983—. Author: Maui, A Guide for Everyone, 1985, Maui, A Paradise Guide, 2d edit., 1986, 3d, 1988; contbr. articles to profl. jours. Mem. Willamette Writers, N.W. Assn. Book Pubs., PEN Women, Internat. Food, Wine and Travel Writers Assn., Pubs. Mktg. Assn., Nat. Honor Soc., Alpha Chi Omega (pres. Portland chpt. 1972). Home and Office: 8110 SW Wareham Portland OR 97223

STIMPSON, CATHARINE ROSLYN, English language educator, writer; b. Bellingham, Wash., June 4, 1936; d. Edward Keown and Catharine (Watts) S. A.B., Bryn Mawr Coll., 1958; B.A., Cambridge U., Eng., 1960, M.A., 1960; Ph.D., Columbia U., 1967. Mem. faculty Barnard Coll., N.Y.C., 1963-80; prof. English, dean of grad. sch., vice provost grad. edn. Rutgers U., New Brunswick, N.J., 1980—; chmn. bd. scholars Ms. Mag., N.Y.C., 1981—. Author: Class Notes, 1979, Where The Meanings Are, 1988; founding editor: Signs: Jour. Women in Culture and Society, 1974-81; book series Women in Culture and Society, 1981. Chmn. N.Y. Council Humanities, 1984-87, Nat. Council Research on Women, 1984-89 ; bd. dirs. Stephens Coll., Columbia, Mo., 1982-85. Hon. fellow Woodrow Wilson Found., 1958; Fulbright fellow, 1958-60; Nat. Humanities Inst. fellow New Haven, 1975-76; Rockefeller Humanities fellow, 1983-84. Mem. MLA (exec. coun., chmn. acad. freedom com., 1st v.p., pres. 1990), P.E.N., AAUP, NOW. Democrat. Home: 62 Westervelt Ave Staten Island NY 10301 Office: Rutgers U Office of Grad Dean New Brunswick NJ 08903

STINE, ANNA MAE, publishing company executive; b. Monongahela, Pa., Sept. 6, 1938; d. Carlton Lee and Martha Regina (Graham) S.; B.S. in Edn., Calif. State Coll. (Pa.), 1959; elem. prin. cert. Duquesne U., 1962, masters in elem. edn., 1962; cert. reading specialist U. Pitts., 1963, postgrad., 1963-65. Tchr., student tchr. supr. Upper St. Clair Sch. Dist., Pitts., 1959-65; nat. lang. arts cons. Macmillan Pub. Co., N.Y.C., 1965-75, regional mgr., Riverside, N.J., 1975-78; v.p., nat. sales mgr. East of Macmillan Pub. Co., 1978-89, v.p., nat. sales mgr. McGraw Hill Sch. div. East of Macmillan Pub., 1989—. Recipient Robert Hann award Macmillan Pub. Co., 1965, Donald McGrew award 1967, NJRA award, 1985. Mem. Internat. Reading Assn., NEA, Regional Edn. Service Agy., Keystone Reading Assn., Upper St. Clair Tchrs. Orgn. (pres.). Republican. Roman Catholic. Home: 215 Haddon Commons Haddonfield NJ 08033

STINE, DEBORAH DIANE, environmental engineer; b. San Bernardino, Calif., Apr. 30, 1960; d. Harry Allen and Phyllis Marie (Konzem) S. BS in Mech. and Environ. Engring., U. Calif., Irvine, 1982; MBA, Corpus Christi State U., 1988; doctoral student, Am. U., 1988—. Registered profl. engr., Tex.; cert. asbestos coord., hazardous material supr., EPA. Mathematician Sch. Aerospace Medicine, Brooks AFB San Antonio, 1983; air pollution engr. Tex. Air Control Bd., Corpus Christi, Tex., 1983-88; air issues mgr. Chem. Mfrs. Assn., Washington, 1988-89; staff officer NAS, Washington, 1989—. Author: Exploring Careers in Engineering, 1985; contbr. articles to Women Engr., Minority Engr., 1985. Pres. LWV, Corpus Christi, 1987, bd. dirs., Tex., 1988. Named to Leadership Corpus Christi, Corpus Christi C. of C., 1986, Outstanding Young Woman Am., 1988. Mem. Am. Polit. Sci. Assn., Am. Soc. Mech. Engrs., Am. Soc. Pub. Adminstrn., Air & Waste Mgmt. Assn. Office: NAS 2101 Constitution Ave NW Washington DC 20418

STINE, LINDA FRANCE, archaeologist, educator; b. East Stroudsburg, Pa., Sept. 19, 1956; d. Donald Delbert and Barbara Marie (Shaffer) France; m. Roy Stanley. BA in Anthropology, U. N.C., 1978; MA in Anthropology, William and Mary Coll., 1984; PhD, U. N.C., 1989. Archaeological tech. N.C. Archaeology Br., Raleigh, 1979; archaeologist Soil Systems, Inc., Marietta, Ga., 1979-80, U. N.C., Occaneechi, N.C., 1985; instr., archaeologist Appalachian State U., Boone, N.C., 1986; archaeologist Brockington and Assocs., Atlanta, 1987, Garrow and Assocs., Atlanta, 1987; instr., rsch. fellow U. S.C., Columbia, 1988—. Contbr. articles to profl. jours. Chief Anthropological Student Soc., U. N.C., 1986; mem. Grad. Student. Mem. Soc. Hist. Archaeology, Soc. Am. Archaeology, Southeastern Archaeol. Conf., Leeward Island Sci. Assocs. Home: Rte 2 Box 385-G Bahama NC 27503 Office: U SC Dept Anthropology Columbia SC 29208

STINECIPHER, MARY MARGARET, research chemist, educator; b. Chattanooga, Feb. 26, 1940; d. Jesse Franklin and Florence Gladys (Marshall) S.; m. John David Fowler Jr. (div. Mar. 1979); children: John Christopher, Jesse David. AB, Earlham Coll., 1962; PhD, U. N.C., 1967. Postdoctoral researcher Research Triangle Inst., Research Triangle Park, N.C., 1966-68, 74-76; mem. staff Los Alamos (N.Mex.) Nat. Lab., 1976—; adj. prof. organic chemistry U. N.Mex. Grad. Ctr., Los Alamos, 1989—; instr. chemistry lab., 1989—; vis. scientist AFOSR (AFATL), Eglin AFB, Fla., 1980-81. Contbr. articles to profl. jours.; inventor ammonium nitrate explosive systems. Mem. AAUW (sec. 1972-74), Am. Chem. Soc., N.Mex. Network Women in Sci. and Engring. (v.p. 1985-86, pres. 1986-87), Los Alamos Women in Sci. (pres. 1986-87), Toastmasters Internat. (pres. 1988), 696 Club. Democrat. Unitarian. Office: Los Alamos Nat Lab MS C920 M-1 MS C920 Los Alamos NM 87545

STINGLE, SANDRA FROMER, psychologist, educator; b. N.Y.C., Feb. 10, 1946; d. Stephen and Irene Fromer; m. Walter H. Stingle, Aug. 3, 1967; children: Benjamin Adam, Jennifer Daisy. BA, Columbia U., N.Y.C., 1966; PhD, Columbia U., 1973; cert., Postgrad. Ctr. Mental Health, 1987. Lic. psychologist, N.Y. Pvt. practice N.Y.C., 1973—; mem. staff adult therapy clinic Postgrad. Ctr. for Mental Health, N.Y.C., 1973-77; asst. prof. psychology Columbia U., N.Y.C., 1973-80, adj. asst. prof. psychology, coord. psychology interns, 1980—; psychol. dir. Roosevelt Hosp. Biofeedback Tinnitus Program, N.Y.C., 1977-79; asst. dir. Early Care Ctr., N.Y.C., 1982-84; dean Barard Coll., 1982-85; bd. dirs., treas. YMCA Coop. Nursery, N.Y.C., 1987-89; mem. staff Cognitive Therapy Ctr., N.Y.C., 1989—. Hunter Coll. scholar, 1962, Grace Dodge scholar Columbia U., 1969-70. Mem. Am. Psychol. Assn., N.Y. State Psychol., Postgrad. Psychoanalytic Soc. Home and Office: 20 W 64th St Apt 39P New York NY 10023

STINSON, KATHARINE, aeronautical engineer; b. Raleigh, N.C., Sept. 18, 1917; d. William Elmond and Mary Katharine (Byrd) S. BSME, N.C. State U., 1941. Aero. engr. mfg. div. FAA, Washington, 1941-73; pvt. practice aviation cons. Glendale, Calif., 1973—; mem. engrs. council Washington. Conrbr. numerous articles to profl. jours. Recipient Disting. Women in Aerospace award Fedn. orgns. Profl. Women, 1984, Aerospace Pioneer award AIAA, 1987. Fellow Soc. Women Engrs. (pres. 1953-55); mem. Phi Kappa Phi, The Ninety Nines. Presbyterian. Lodge: Soroptimists. Home and Office: 1830 N Verdugo Rd Glendale CA 91208

STIVER, INEZETTA OREL ELIASON, accountant; b. Centerville, Ind., Mar. 26, 1916; d. Wood Esta and Pearl Mae (Davis) Eliason; m. Roy Carl Stiver, Nov. 24, 1940. Diploma, Ind. Bus. Coll., 1948. Pvt. practice acctg. Centerville, 1955-87; instr. acctg. Richmond (Ind.) Bus. Coll., 1945-48. Author: Wilderness Opportunity, 1964; columnist Centerville Crusader Silhouettes. Clk. Centerville Christian Ch., 1955-84; bd. dirs. Hist. Centerville Inc., 1969-84, 86—; mem. Centerville Planning Comn., 1975-77, Wayne County (Ind.) Resource Inventory Commn., 1985-88. Recipient civic award Centerville Jaycees, 1971, This Is Your Life award, 1978, Scouters Wife Heart of Gold award, 1979, Outstanding Citizen award Centerville Lions Club, 1986. Mem. Nat. Soc. Pub. Accts., Ind. Soc. Pub. Accts., Soc. Ind. Pioneers, Am. Legion Aux., Centerville Women's Cemetary Assn. (treas. 1980—), Alliance Wayne County Mus. (bd. dirs.), DAR, Colonial Dames 17th Century, Daus. Am. Colonists, Studebaker Family Assn., Ind. Genealogy Soc., Ill. Genealogy Soc., Iowa Genealogy Soc., Ohio Genealogy Soc., Md. Genealogy Soc., Del. Genealogy Soc., Pa. Genealogy Soc., Joshua Eliason Family Descendants (historian). Republican. Address: 116 E Plum St Centerville IN 47330

STOBB, MARGARET ANNE, teacher's aide; b. Astoria, N.Y., May 2, 1937; d. Anton Rudolph and Elizabeth Helene (Dudda) S. BA, Coll. St. Elizabeth, 1982; AA, Somerset County Coll., 1980. File clk. Stobb, Inc., Racine, Wis., 1956-62, Annandale, N.J., 1962-66; tchr.'s aide Keystone, Scranton, Pa., 1966, Head Start, Baptistown, N.J., 1966-67; file clk. Stobb, Inc., Annandale, 1967, Yale Transport, N.Y.C., 1967; tchr.'s aide Am. Inst. Mental Studies, Vineland, N.J., 1977-79. Mem. Hunterdon County Right to Life, Lebanon, N.J., Am. Assn. Retired Persons. Fellow AAUW (del. to conv. 1983, sunshine rep. Hunterdon br., women edn. chairperson Hunterdon br. 1983-85). Seventh-Day Adventist. Home: 110 Perryville Rd Pittstown NJ 08867

STOCK, MARGOT THERESE, nurse; b. Toronto, Ontario, Canada, Aug. 10, 1936; Arrived in US 1967.; d. Karl Dwight and Marguerite Anne (Lafitte) K.; m. Philip Anthony, Jan. 11, 1946; children: Dwight, Scott, Kayler, Travis & Anthony (twins) Sean. AAS, SuffolkŠ County Com. Coll., Selden, N.Y.C., 1981; BS in Nursing, U. S. Fla., Selden, N.Y., 1983; MS in Nursing, U. Tex., 1984; DPhil in Social Anthropology, U. Oxford, England, 1989. Nurse Sarasota Meml. Hosp., Fla., 1981-82, LW Blake Meml. Hosp., Bradenton, Fla., 1982-83, Med. Center Del Oro, Houston, 1983-85, Pitt County Meml. Hosp., Greenville, N.C.; asst. prof. E. Carolina U., Greenville, N.C., 1985-89; Cons. Gerontol. Nursing Network Greensboro N.C. Designer Game and Software (computer), Nursing Math Made Easy, Understanding Mgmt., Teaching Nursing Theory 1984; Author (with others) Book Clinical Pharmacology & Nursing 1987, Poetry Evolution Lycidas Jaso 1980-87. Mem. AAUW, Sigma Theta Tau, Sigma Kappa Found. (Houston Sigma Kappa award), Phi Theta Kappa (pres. 1981). Roman Catholic. Home: 1701 River Dr #1 Greenville NC 27858

STOCK, NAOMI FERGUSON, educational administrator; b. Middletown, Ohio, June 16, 1932; d. Oscar Daniel and Lydia Ellen (Carter) Ferguson; m. James D. Stock, May 11, 1951; 1 child, Jonathan Kent. BS in Edn. cum laude, Miami U., Oxford, Ohio, 1958, MEd, 1963. Tchr. Lakota City Sch. Dist., West Chester, Ohio, 1958-66; intern dir. Green County Joint Vocat. Sch. Dist., Xenia, Ohio, 1966-67; coord. home econs. dept. Princeton City Sch. Dist., Cin., 1967-69; curriculum and facilities planner Hamilton County Joint Vocat. Sch. Dist., Cin., 1970-71; supr. Gt. Oaks Joint Vocat. Sch. Dist., Cin., 1971—; mem. adv. com. curriculum redesign Miami U., 1979, dept. home econs. and consumer scis., 1980-86. Precinct leader West Chester (Ohio) Rep. Com., 1988—; mem. Butler County Rep. Cen. Com., 1988—; mem. bd. West Chester Ch. of Nazarene. Mem. Am. Home Econs. Assn. (cert.), Ohio Home Econs. Assn. (sec. 1968, pres. 1974), Am. Vocat. Assn., Ohio Vocat. Assn., Ohio Restaurant Assn., Internat. Food Svc. Execs. Assn., Home Econs. Edn. Assn., Nat. Assn. Local Suprs. Home Econs., Nat. Assn. for Edn. Young Children, Ohio Coun. on Hotel, Restaurant and Instnl. Edn., Ohio Trade and Indsl. Edn. Suprs. Assn., Nat. Restaurant Assn., AAUW, Phi Beta Kappa, Kappa Delta Pi, Phi Upsilon Omicron. Home: 8242 Shadybrook Dr West Chester OH 45069 Office: Gt Oaks JVSD 3254 E Kemper Rd Cincinnati OH 45241

STOCK, PEGGY A(NN), college president, educator; b. Jan. 30, 1936; married; 5 children. BS in Psychology, St. Lawrence U., 1957; MA in Counseling, U. Ky., 1963, EdD, 1969. Lic. psychologist, Ohio. Instr., research asst. dept. psychology and spl. edn. U. Ky., Lexington, 1958-59, 63-67, staff psychologist Med. Ctr., 1964-66; dir. edn. United Cerebral Palsy of the Bluegrass, Lexington, 1959-61; exec. dir. Community Council for Physically Handicapped and Mentally Retarded, Lexington, 1962-64; dir. clin. program No. Ky. Regional Community Mental Health Ctr., Covington, 1969-71; pres. Midwest Inst. Tng. and Edn., Cin., 1971-76; assoc. prof., counseling psychologist Coll. of Edn. Mont. State U., Bozeman, 1975-77, asst. dean Office of Student Affairs and Service, 1977-79; assoc. prof. Coll. of Edn. U. Hartford, Conn.; 1980-85, spl. asst. to pres., 1979-80, v.p. adminstrn., 1981-86; prof., pres. Colby-Sawyer Coll., New London, N.H., 1986—; vis. prof. dept. sociology and edn. Thomas Moore Coll., Fort Mitchell, Ky., 1970-71; panelist Nat. Inst. Edn., 1985; cons. and lectr. in field. Contbr. chpts. to books, articles to profl. jours. Mem. coun. N.H. Coll. and Univ.; nat. bd. dirs. Med. Coll. Pa.; mem. New London Bus. Adv. Bd.; active numerous other civic orgns. Recipient Disting. Alumna award St. Lawrence U., 1989; grantee in field, most recent George I. Alden Trust, Helen Fuld Health Trust, Surdna, Cogswell, U.S. Dept. Edn., 1981-89, numerous others; fellow U. Ky., 1966-68, Am. Council Edn., 1979-80, United Jewish Com., 1981. Mem. Am. Coun. on Edn., Am. Assn. for Higher Edn., Advancement Women in Higher Edn. Office: Colby-Sawyer Coll Office of Pres New London NH 03257

STOCKDALE, GAYLE SUE, wholesale florist, ornamental horticulturalist; b. Crawfordsville, Ind., July 3, 1955; d. Robert Lavern and Faye Louise (Ball) S. Student St. Joseph's Coll., 1973-74, Purdue U., 1974; BS in Tech. Horticulture, Eastern Ky. U., 1977. Reclamation foreman South East Coal Co., Irvine, Ky., 1977-79; asst. mgr., landscape designer Evergreen Garden Ctr., Lexington, Ky., 1979-80; asst. mgr., landscape designer, head grower South Trail Garden Ctr., Ft. Myers, Fla., 1980-82; floral designer Flowers by Jean, Cape Coral, Fla., 1982-83; floral designer, landscape designer Bev's Greenhouse, Owenton, Ky., 1983-84; co-owner Royalty Wholesale, Lexington, 1984-87, Imperial Fowers and Gifts, Lexington, 1988—. Contbr. poetry to anthologies. Sponsor, Save the Children, Korea, 1986. Moose lodge scholar, 1973. Mem. Nat. Assn. Female Execs. Democrat. Roman Catholic. Avocations: reading, movies, exercise. Office: Imperial Flowers & Gifts 393 Waller Ave Lexington KY 40504

STOCKHAUSEN, SHARRON RENEE, government official, educator, writer; b. Rochester, Minn., Aug. 19, 1948; d. Henry James and Bernice Gertrude (Foltz) LeCocq; m. Harry Stockhausen, May 4, 1968; children: Stacy Ann, Eric David. Student, U. Minn., 1966, Cameron U., 1979, Anoka-Ramsey Coll., 1980-87; BA in Bus., Metro State U., 1989. Cert. contract mgr. Purchasing agt. U.S. Army, Ft. Sill, Okla., 1976-80; procurement asst. Def. Logistics Agy., Mpls., 1980-84, contract adminstr., mgr. equal employment, 1984—, counselor equal employment, 1989—; tchr. Anoka (Minn.)-Hennepin Sch. Dist., 1980—. Editor: Comanche County Cookbook, 1978; newspaper columnist, 1979, 90—. Founder, pres. Homemaker's Plus Extension Group, Lawton, Okla., 1978; asst. coach men's softball Champlin/Dayton Athletic Assn., Anoka, 1988-89; pres. Presbyn. Women's Assn., 1990—. Mem. NAFE, Nat. Contract Mgmt. Assn. (hospitality chmn. 1986-88, publicity chmn. 1989—). Republican. Presbyterian. Home: 14314 Thrush Dr NW Andover MN 55304 Office: Def Logistics Agy Honeywell Plaza MN12-6254 2701 4th Ave S Minneapolis MN 55408

STOCKLIN, ALMA KATHERINE, academic administrator; b. New London, Conn., May 9, 1926; d. Stephen Sullivan and Theresa Catherine (Flynn) Sheehan; m. Philip L. Stocklin, Jan. 28, 1950 (div. 1984); children: Brian, Christopher, Virginia Katherine, Walter, Stephen. Student, U. Conn., 1945-46, Conn. Coll., 1946; cert., Sch. Modern Photography, N.Y.C., 1948; AA, Charter Oak Coll., 1979; BA, Eastern Conn. State U., 1981. Advt. photographer Gen. Electric Co., Bridgeport, Conn., 1948-49; pub. rels. cons. Norwich and Groton, Conn., 1983-86; asst. to dean Ea. Conn. State U., Willimantic, 1986—; coordinator videotape courses for submarines, New London, 1984—. Mem. Norwich Harbor Day Com., 1982-83, Catchment Area coun. 11 S.E. Conn. Mental Health Bd., 1989-90, Norwich Regional Mental Health Adv. Bd., 1987—, Norwich State Hosp. Adv. Bd., 1987—; vice chair Eastern Conn. Regional Mental Health Bd., 1988-89; founder, chmn. Norwich Nuclear Freeze Com., 1982; bd. dirs. Eastern Conn. Symphony Orch., New London, 1984-87, Friend of the Symphony, 1987—, Laurel Glen, Groton, 1984—; co-founder, bd. dirs. Newport Ch. Community Housing Corp., 1969-72. Mem. Assn. Continuing Higher Edn., Conn. Assn. Continuing Edn. Democrat. Roman Catholic. Home: 74-3 Buddington Rd Groton CT 06340

STOCKMAN, PAMELA YBARGUEN, performing company executive, choreographer; b. Plainview, Tex., Apr. 10, 1945; d. Frank Rufus and Orene (Biffle) Ybarguen; m. Jack Perry Stockman, Sept. 10, 1965; children: Nicholas Alexander Ybarguen-Stockman. Student, U. Houston, 1965. Exec. sec. St. Luke's Meth. Ch., Houston, 1965-66, Chevron Geophys., Houston, 1966-68; dancer Houston Ballet Found., 1966-68, asst. to mng. dir., 1969-71; dancer Discovery Dance Group, Houston, 1968-87, assoc. artistic dir., 1976-87, exec. dir., artistic dir., 1987—, also bd. dirs.; choreographer numerous ballets, modern and jazz dances, 1976—; lectr., artist drama dept. U. Houston, 1973-76; coord. dance program Jewish Community Ctr., Houston, 1974-82; bd. dirs. Houston Dance Coalition, 1989—. Mem. Cultural Arts Coun. Houston, 1982—; active Bus. Vols. for Arts, Houston, 1984—. Roman Catholic. Office: Discovery Dance Group 6427 Atwell Houston TX 77081

STOCKTON, BRENDA EVELYN, data processing executive; b. Houston, Feb. 26, 1949; d. Linzell Wilson and Evelyn Roberta (Barkuloo) Creel; m. James Harold Stockton, June 8, 1968; children: Matthew James, Martha Erin, Megan Lyn, Molly Kay. Student, U. Tex., 1967-72. Computer programmer Tex. Hwy. Dept., Austin, 1969-71, programmer, analyst, 1971-72; programmer, analyst State of Wyoming, Cheyenne, 1974-75; systems analyst, dir. fin. systems TRW Controls, Houston, 1975-76; data processing mgr. Marathon Gold Corp., Craig, Colo., 1981-83; systems designer Pegasus Data Systems, Craig, 1982-84, cons., tchr., 1983-84; systems analyst Tex. Dept. Mental Health/Mental Retardation, Austin, 1984-85; dir. data processing Williamson County (All County Agys.), Georgetown, Tex., 1985—; tech. cons. Craig Med. Clinic, 1982-85, Georgetown Weekly, 1985—; tech. advisor Tex. Dept. Pub. Safety, Georgetown, 1986—. Author: (weekly column) Austin Am./Statesman Newspaper; contbr. articles to profl. and popular publs.; author: (screenplays) Emily's Way, 1989, No Returns, 1989, The Storm, 1989, We Need Each Other, 1989, The Mystery of the Old Piano, 1989. Instr. ARC, Austin, 1984-86; advisor Girl Scouts U.S.A., Georgetown, 1985. Mem. Am. Bus. Women Assn., Data Processing Mgmt. Assn., Nat. Assn. Female Execs., Tex. Assn. Govtl. Data Processing Mgrs. (bd. dirs. 1986—). Republican. Episcopalian. Club: 12 O'Clock (Georgetown) (welfare com). Home: 3202 Sierra Dr Georgetown TX 78628 Office: Williamson County Courthouse 8th & Main St Georgetown TX 78626

STOCKTON, ROBERTA SUSAN, publishing professional; b. N.Y.C., Nov. 14, 1954; d. Milton I. and Rose (Robbins) S. BA in Polit. Sci., Vassar Coll., 1974. Prin. Roberta Stockton/Internat. Media, N.Y.C., 1985—. Mem. Arab-Am. Anti-Discrimination Com., N.Y.C., 1988. Office: Roberta Stockton/Internat Media 360 E 72d St New York NY 10021

STOCKTON, SANDRA LEE KEARSE, nurse; b. York, Pa., June 14, 1949; d. William and Dorothy Mae (Jackson) Smallwood; m. Joseph Kearse, Aug. 12, 1967 (dec. June 1968); children: Kimmy Jo, Kevin Scott, Karentrina Schevelle, Keenan Wynn; m. Aaron E. Stockton, Feb. 24, 1973. AA, Prince Georges Community Coll., 1978; BSN, George Mason U., Fairfax, Va., 1982; postgrad., Webster U., St. Louis, 1985. Med. tech. U.S.A.F. Reserve, Wash., 1979-82; charge nurse Mid Atlantic Nephology Ctr., Wash., 1983-85; from staff, charge nurse to asst. head nurse Vet. Adminstrn. Hosp., St. Louis, 1983-87; regional nurse, sub contractor Vet. Adminstrn. Hosp., Washington, 1985—; instr., sub. contractor, Prince Georges Doctors Hosp., Md., 1985--. Performed at Apollo Theatre, 1988. Capt. US Army, 1989—. Mem. George Mason Alumni Assn., Webster U. Alumni Assn. Democrat. Roman Catholic. Home: 5018 Brimfield Dr Upper Marlboro MD 20772

STOCKTON, VIRGINIA, marketing professional; b. L.A., Mar. 24, 1964; d. Fernando and Gaudalupe (Fernancez) Rueda; m. Patrick Duane Stockton, July 2. BS, Pepperdine U., 1986. Cert. sports medicine specialist. Sales, mktg. mgr. Jet Mgmt. Corp., L.A., 1987—. Republican. Mem. Church of Christ. Home: 4244 Via Marina 126 Marina del Rey CA 90292

STOCKWELL, AMY CAROL, food product executive; b. Toledo, Jan. 22, 1953; d. Bernard Reid and Rachel Francis (Nincehelser) S. BA magna cum laude, Ohio Wesleyan U., 1974; MBA, Wharton Sch., U. Pa., 1981. Mgr. bus. analysis Brown-Forman Corp., Louisville, 1981-86; treas. Mt. Eagle Corp, Louisville, 1986-88; v.p., gen. mgr. Nutrition Products Co., Louisville, 1988-90; mktg. dir. food starch A.E. Staley Mfg. Co., Decatur, Ill., 1990—. Treas. YWCA, Louisville, 1988; active Jr. Achievement, Louisville, 1988. Nat. Merit scholar, 1971. Mem. Am. Assn. Cereal Chemists, Inst. Food Technologists, Phi Beta Kappa. Methodist.

STODDARD, LINDA GANDRUD, veterinarian; b. Owatonna, Minn., Apr. 28, 1944; d. Ebenhard S. and Edith M. (Christensen) G.; m. Hannis L. Stoddard, Jr., July 10, 1973; children: Ebenhard C., Ryan M., Dahlen Ross. B.S. in Edn., U. Minn., 1966, B.S. in Vet. Medicine, 1968, D.V.M., 1970. Veterinarian, Dueland Animal Clinic, S.I., N.Y., 1970-72; dir. advt. Gandy Co., Owatonna, 1972-74, corp. dir., 1962—; owner Branford Vet. Clinic, Inc., Fla., 1974-83, Shamrock Vet. Clinic and Fisheries, fish diseases and aquaculture mgmt., Cross City, Fla., 1984—; guest lectr. U. Fla. Coll. Vet. Medicine, 1978-82; tchr. physics Branford High Sch., 1984; vice chmn. Fla. Dept. Edn. State Instructional Materials Coun.-Sci Grades K-8, 1987-88; mem. adv. com. Anderson Elem. Sch., 1986-88, 89-90, Dixie County High Sch., 1989-90; participant Fla.'s Gov.'s Summit on Edn., 1989. Grant writer Branford Sch. Adv. Coun., 1982-84. State of Fla. grantee, 1983. 84. Mem. AVMA, Suwannee Valley Vet. Med. Assn. (pres. 1980—), Am. Animal Hosp. Assn., Fla. Vet. Med. Assn. (4-H adv. com.), Am. Heartworm Soc., Alpha Delta Kappa. Avocations: reading, music, architecture.

STODDARD, SANDOL, writer; b. Birmingham, Ala., Dec. 16, 1927; d. Carlos French and Caroline (Harris) S.; m. Felix M. Warburg (div. 1966); children: Anthony, Peter, Gerald, Jason; m. Peter R. Goethals, May 1, 1984. BA magna cum laude, Bryn Mawr Coll., 1959. Author more than 20 books, including: Growing Time, 1971, The Hospice Movement, 1978, The Doubleday Children's Bible, 1983 (Lewis Citation 1983). Bd. dirs., co-founder Hospice of Kona, Kailua-Kona, Hawaii, 1985. Recipient Humanitarian Svc. award Forbes Health System, 1979, Notable Book award Am. Libr. Assn., 1964. Mem. Cosmopolitan Club. Democrat. Episcopalian. Home and Office: 78-6646 Mamalahoa Hwy Holualoa HI 97625

STODDARD, SUSAN, research firm executive, consultant; b. Modesto, Calif., May 11, 1942; d. Howard Augustus and Doris Ruth (Anderson) S.; m. Otto Pflueger Jr., June 12, 1970(div. 1977); children: Jeffrey, Justin. AB, U. Calif., Berkeley, 1964, M of City Planning, 1968, PhD, 1982. Evaluator Ctr. for Ind. Living, Berkeley, 1973-74; teaching asst. U. Calif., Berkeley, 1971-75; assoc. Sedway Cooke, Planners, San Francisco, 1971; v.p. sales Berkeley Planning Assoc., 1976-85; chmn., co-founder Inst. for the Study of Family, Work and Community, Berkeley and Larkspur, Calif., 1985—; pres. Info Use, Corte Madera, 1984—; adj. faculty U. San Francisco, 1985—; affiliated faculty inst. health and aging U. Calif., San Francisco, 1989, adj. faculty Calif. Sch. Profl. Psychology, 1988—. Author: Independent Living: Emerging Issues, 1978, Software Tools of Rehabilitation Managers, 1987. Bd. dirs. Larkspur Isle Condominium Assn., 1983—, pres., 1986—. Grantee Mott Found., 1986, 3 yr. expert systems Nat. Inst. Disability and Rehab. Research, 1988. Mem. Nat. Women's Polit. Caucus, Am. Planning Assn. (charter, chmn. human svcs. and planning div. 1983-85), Am. Inst. Cert. Planners (charter, profl. devel. trainer 1985—), Am. Mgmt. Assn. (on-site trainer 1985—). Democrat. Office: Info Use 100 Tamal Pla Corte Madera CA 94925

STOEBERMANN, MARINA NICOLE, banker; b. Akron, Ohio, June 27, 1963; d. John and Hilda (Kremer) S. BBA in Fin., Kent (Ohio) State U., 1985. Ops. analyst Ameritrust Co., Cleve., 1985-86; compensation analyst I Ameritrust Co., 1986-87, compensation analyst II, 1987, sr. compensation analyst, 1987-88, compensation officer, 1988-89, comml. lending officer, 1989—. Mem. Am. Compensation Assn. Republican. Roman Catholic. Home: 3941 Greentree Rd Stow OH 44224 Office: Ameritrust Company 900 Euclid Ave Cleveland OH 44115

STOECKL, SHELLEY JOAN, marketing professional; b. Buffalo, Feb. 24, 1951; d. Joseph T. and Joan (Carriere) S. AAS in Bus. Adminstrn., Bryant & Stratton, 1978; cert. in gen. banking, Am. Inst. Banking, 1982; cert. in pers. & human resource mgmt., Canisius Coll., 1983. Cert. profl. sec. Sr. sec. Mfrs. Hanover Trust Co., Buffalo, 1974-79, exec. sec., 1979-82, pers. asst., 1982-84, pers. mgr., 1984-87; account coord. Computer Task Group Direct Mktg. Svcs., Buffalo, 1987-89; project mgr. ANCOR Info. Mgmt., Inc., Buffalo, 1989—; adv. bd. office techs. dept. Niagara County Community Coll., Sanborn, N.Y. Co-author: (presentation) Go For The Gold: CPS, 1983—. Co. coord. United Way, Buffalo, 1980-87; vol. Jack Kemp for Congress, Buffalo, 1970. Recipient scholastic award Buffalo Clearing House Assn., 1982. Fellow Cert. Profl. Secs. Acad.; mem. NAFE, Profl. Secs. Internat. (bd. dirs. 1980-82, v.p. 1982-83, corr. sec. 1983-85, pres. 1986-87), Cert. Profl. Secs. Soc. N.Y. State (pres. 1987-88); Inst. for Certifying Secs. (rep. N.E. dist. 1988—), Toastmasters. Conservative. Roman Catholic.

Home: 239 Wimbledon Court West Seneca NY 14224 Office: ANCOR Info Mgmt Inc 5500 Main St Ste 300 Williamsville NY 14221-5723

STOELTJE, BEVERLY JUNE, university professor; b. Rotan, Tex., Apr. 1, 1940; d. Roger Caswell and Laura Inez (Kennedy) Smith; children: Gretchen, Rachael; m. Richard Bauman, Nov. 26, 1977; children: Mark D., Andrew. BA, U. Tex., 1961, MA, 1975, PhD, 1979. Asst. prof. of english U. Tex., Austin, 1983-86; assoc. prof. of folklore Ind. U., Bloomington, Ind., 1986—; cons. SW Ednl. Devel. Lab., Austin, 1976, Tex. Women's History Project, San Antonio, 1981; dir. Folk Arts Survey of Tex., Austin, 1977, 78. Author: Children's Handclaps, 1979; editor (essay collection) Feminist Revision in Folklore Studies, 1988; contbr. articles to profl. jours. Sec. CIBOLA Anthropological Assn., Southeast U.S., N.Mex., 1978-81. Recipient Media grant Tex. Commn. for the Humanitiesx, 1980, Fulbright fellowship U.S. Dept. Edn., Ghana, West Africa, 1989-90, S.W. Humanities Fulbright Rsch. fellow. Mem. African Studies Assn., Am. Folklore Soc. (mem. exec. bd. 1981-84), Am. Anthropological Assn., Modern Languages Assn., Nat. Womens Studies Assn., Am. Studies Assn. Office: Folklore Inst Ind Univ 504 N Fess Bloomington IN 47405

STOELZLE-MIDDEN, KAREN LYNN, educator; b. Carbondale, Ill., May 19, 1952; d. Robert Wilton and Mary Theda (William) S. AS, John Logan Jr. Coll., 1975; B PLSS, Southern Ill. U., 1977, M in Plant and Soil Sci., 1980; M in Landscape Architecture, U. Ga., 1983. Landscape designer Edward D. Stone Jr. & Assocs., Ft. Lauderdale, Fla., 1984-85, Cons., 1974—; instr. Southern Ill. U., Carbondale, 1985-87, asst. prof., 1987—; scientific illustrator, Consulting, 1978-; gaming/simulator, Consulting, 1983—; chrmn. Art/Garden Exhibit-SIU, Carbondale, 1987. Designer: gaming/simulation, Environmental Awareness, 1983, Recycling Awareness, 1988. Environ. designer, Clean & Green/Keep Am. Beautiful, Carbondale, 1988—, Recycling Com., Carbondale, 1989—. Mem. Ill. Acad. Sci., Inst. Ecology, Sigma Lambda Alpha, Phi Alpha Xi, Phi Theta Kappa.

STOGNER, JENNIFER DAWN, legal administrator; b. Glasgow, Ky., Sept. 5, 1961; d. Sidney E. Pruitt and Nancy E. (Smith) Rogers; m. Mark Kerley (div.); m. William L. Stogner, July 11, 1985; 1 stepchild, Dana D. Student, We. Ky. U., 1982-84. Legal adminstr. Kinsey Vincent Pyle, P.A., Daytona Beach, Fla., 1984—. Mem. NAFE, Assn. Legal Adminstrs., Nat. Soc. Pub. Accts. Home: 9 Fox Run Trail Ormond Beach FL 32174

STOICA, SUSANA, computer engineer, scientist; b. Tirgu Muresh, Romania, Apr. 26, 1946; came to U.S., 1985; d. Andrei and Clara (Heisikovitsch) Gerson; m. Vladimir Stoica, Sept. 5, 1970; 1 child, Andrei. MS, Polytech. Inst., Bucharest, Romania, 1969, postgrad., 1972-74. Reg. profl. engr., Ont., Can. Jr. rsch. engr. Inst. Computer Rsch., Bucharest, 1969-72, sr. rsch. engr., 1972-77; engr. Ramzorei Siemens Industry Ltd., Tel Aviv, 1977-78; sr. elec. engr. Control Data Can. Ltd., Toronto, Ont., 1979-85; sr. elec. engr. Control Data Corp., Mpls., 1985-86, cons., 1986-87, mgr. support, 1987-88; cons. very large scale integration/electronic computer aided design tech., 1988-90; chief scientist Delphax Systems, Toronto, 1990—. Contbr. articles to profl. jours.and confs.; inventor. Mem. IEEE, Assn. Prof. Engrs. Ont., Am. Assn. Artificial Intelligence, SIGNET.

STOKELY, EDITH MARGARET DAWLEY, medical technologist; b. Manhattan, Kans., Jan. 23, 1922; d. Earle Reed and Marion Erenay (Price) Dawley; m. Raymond Elmer Stokely, Dec. 6, 1942; children: Janet Mary Stokely Roe, Donna Rae Stokely Steward. BS, Kansas State U., 1943. Rsch. technologist Kansas State U., Manhattan, 1942-44; med. technologist Kecoughton (Va.) Sta. Hosp., 1944-45, Cleve. Clinic Blood Bank, 1945-47, Dr. H.G. Miskjian, Cleve., 1947-49, No. Ill. Blood Bank, Rockford, 1969-72, Dr. H.E. Zenisek, Dr. T.R. Glatter, Rockford, 1972-78, Pierce Chem. Co., Rockford, 1978-79, U. Ill. Coll. Medicine, Rockford, 1979-88; ret., 1988. Mem. Rockford Amateur Astronomers Club (sec. 1974-76, 86-88, bd. dirs. 1989—), Phi Kappa Phi, Omicron Nu, Dynamis, Alpha Xi Delta Alumnae (pres. 1964-66). Methodist. Home: 5427 Brookview Rd Rockford IL 61107-1659

STOKES, ELIZABETH HENDON, retired psychology educator; b. Richland, Tex., June 5, 1922; d. Walter Lee and Gertrude Arvette (McCord) Hendon; m. William Glenn Stokes. BS, Sam Houston State Coll., 1942, MA, 1947; Ed.S., George Peabody Coll., 1956; EdD, North Tex. State U., 1960. Lic. psychologist, Tenn.; nat. cert. sch. psychologist; cert. sch. psychologist, Tenn. Field worker Tex. State Dept. Pub. Welfare, Huntsville, Jacksonville, 1942-44; tchr. Richland Pub. Schs., 1945-46, 51-53; appraiser VA Guidance Ctr., Navarro Jr. Coll., Corsicana, Tex., 1949-50; sch. psychologist Clarksville (Tenn.) City Schs., 1955-57; asst. prof. psychology Northwest State Coll., Natchitoches, La., 1957-58; instr. psychology North Tex. State U., Denton, 1959-60; assoc. prof. psychology Austin Peay State U., Clarksville, 1960-87; pvt. practice psychologist Austin Peay State U., 1960-87; pres. Tenn. Assn. of Counselor Educators, 1966-67. Contbr. articles to profl. jours. Organizer, sponsor Saturday Recreation Program for Retarded, Clarkville, 1962-87; chmn. Human Rels. Coun., Clarksville, 1969-71; bd. dirs. Day Care Ctr., Clarksville, 1983-86; mem., officer Montgomery County Coun. for Retarded Citizens, Clarksville, 1960-87; vol. Austin (Tex.) Police Crisis Ctr., 1988-89; vol. instrn. parenting classes for low-income parents, Austin, 1988-89. Named Educator of Yr. Tenn. Assn. Retarded Citizens, 1975-76, Outstanding Retiring Educator, Phi Delta Kappa, Austin Peay Ch., 1986-87; recipient Award for Disting. Community Svc., Clarksville C. of C., 1986. Mem. Am. Psychol. Assn., Nat. Assn. Sch. Psychologists, Tenn. Assn. Sch. Psychologists (newsletter editor and v.p. 1975-85, bd. dirs., pres. 1978-79, Beth Stokes Award for Outstanding Sch. Psychology 1987, 88, 89, 90). Home: 10800 Culberson Dr Austin TX 78748

STOKES, LINDA P., telecommunications executive; b. Birmingham, Ala., Oct. 31, 1947; d. Marvin Louis and Juanita Myrle (Lee) Parker; m. Phillip W. Stokes, Apr. 1; children: Joseph, Michael. BS in Math., U. Ala., Birmingham, 1973. Br. mgr. Starnet Corp., Atlanta; founder, pres. Tele Designs, Inc., Atlanta, 1983—; co-founder, v.p. Speakeasy Systems, Inc. Columnist Ga. Bus. Forum. Republican. Roman Catholic. Home: 5110 Cameron Forest Pkwy Alpharetta GA 30201 Office: 4243 Dunwoody Club Dr Ste 103 Dunwoody GA 30350

STOKES, SARA MARGARET, computer analyst; b. Fort Worth, Mar. 5, 1945; d. John Roland and Cora Ellen (Canada) Reiser; m. William Thomas Stokes, June 23, 1963 (div. 1980); children: Jonathan Thomas, Corrie Elizabeth. BS in Math./Physics, U. Tex, Arlington, 1966; MA in Math., 1971. Math. tutor U. Tex., Arlington, 1963-66;, assoc. engr. Lockheed Electronics Co., White Sands Missile Range, N. Mex., 1966-67; computer programmer Systems Tech. Corp., Dallas, 1969-70; v.p. S & A Systems Inc., Mesquite, Tex., 1970—; bd. sec., 1988—. Deacon Royal Ln. Bapt. Ch., Dallas 1980-87; officer PTA, Stonewall Jackson Elem. Sch., Dallas, 1980-88, J. L. Long Mid. Sch., Dallas, 1984-90, Woodrow Wilson High Sch., Dallas (pres. 1990—). Mem. PTA (life). Republican. Home: 5519 McCommas St Dallas TX 75206

STOKES, THERESA EMMA (TERI STOKES), computer company executive; b. Boston, Apr. 9, 1943; d. Saverio L. and Mary Grace (Van Stratum) Santoro; m. Ivan L. Stokes, June 12, 1965 (div. 1977); children: Theresa-Ann, Eric M.; m. Peter R. Yensen, Apr. 30, 1982. BA in Biology, Boston U., 1965; cert. in chemistry and math, Wellesley (Mass.) Coll., 1970; MS in Applied Mgmt., Lesley Coll., 1987. Lic. med. technologist, (ASCP), Mass. Med. technologist Univ. and Hosp. Labs., 1966-72; sales mgr. Shaklee Products, Concord, Mass., 1972-76; lab. supr. Somerville Hosp. Bioran Med. Labs, Cambridge, Mass., 1976-77, dir. processing and communications, 1977-79; mgr. mktg. communications Digital Equipment Corp., Marlboro, Mass., 1979-81, specialist indsl. research and devel. bus. ops., 1981-83, mgr. internat. pharm. market, 1983-86, bus. mgr. life sci. and research Kodak corp. account team, 1986-90; cons. pharm. and chem. computer-integrated R&D Digital Equipment Corp., Basel, Switzerland, 1990—. Contbr. articles to profl. jours.; speaker in field. Advisor Jr. Achievement, Marlboro, 1983-85. Doctoral fellow Walden U., 1989—. Mem. AAAS, DAR, Drug Info. Assn., N.Y. Acad. Scis., Tridelta.

STOKES-ELIAS, JANICE ELAINE, nursing supervisor; b. Anamosa, Iowa, Apr. 10, 1952; d. John Morris and Eugenia Ann (Beaumont) Stokes; m. David Louis Elias, June 17, 1978. BSN, U. Iowa, 1974; postgrad., Des Moines Area Community Coll, 1988-89. RN, Iowa, Nev. Staff nurse Washoe Med. Ctr., Reno, Nev., 1974; staff nurse III U. Iowa Hosps. and Clinics, Iowa City, Iowa, 1975-84; clin. nurse II Mercy Hosp. Med. Ctr., Des Moines, 1985-86; nurse cons. Blue Cross/Blue Shield of Iowa, 1986-89; supr. medicare B IASD Health Svcs. Corp., Des Moines, 1989—. Precinct coord. state senate campaign, Des Moines, 1989; vol. Des Moines Bot. Ctr. Mem. Assn. Operating Rm. Nurses, NAFE, Health Ins. Assn. Am., Iowa Regional Health Care (program chairperson anti-fraud div. Des Moines chpt. 1989—), U. Iowa Alumni Coun. Home: 10486 Sunset Ter Clive IA 50325 Office: IASD/Health Svcs Corp 636 Grand Ave Sta #7 Des Moines IA 50309

STOLBERG, SHERYL GAY, journalist; b. N.Y.C., Nov. 18, 1961; d. Irving and Marcia Dawn (Papier) S. BA, U. Va., 1983. Reporter Providence Jour. Bulletin, 1983-87, L.A. Times, 1987—. Recipient Unity award Lincoln U., 1987. Office: LA Times Times Mirror Sq Los Angeles CA 90053

STOLEN, JOANNE SIU, immunologist, editor; b. Chgo., June 22, 1943; d. Paul and Helen (Ong) Siu; 1 child, Kit Stolen. BS, U. Mich., 1965; MS, Seton Hall U., 1968; PhD, Rutgers U., 1972. Prin. investigator Sandy Hook Lab., Highlands, N.J., 1973-85; tchr. sci. Ranney Sch., Tinton Falls, N.J., 1986-87; publisher, editor SOS Publs., Fair Haven, N.J., 1988—; adj. prof. Drew U., Madison, N.J., 1982-86, Brookdale Community Coll., Lincroft, N.J., 1989—; vis. prof. Rutgers U., Piscataway, N.J., 1986. Editor Fish Immunology, 1986; editor, pub. Techniques in Fish Immunology, 1990; pub.: So Blow Ye Winds, 1990. Office: SOS Publs 43 De Normandie Ave Fair Haven NJ 07704

STOLL, BARBARA J., pediatrics educator, neonatologist; d. Bernard and Miriam (Rubinstein) S.; m. Roger I. Glass, Mar. 12, 1975; children: Nina E., Michael G., Andrew. AB, Barnard Coll., 1971; MD cum laude, Yale U., 1975. Diplomate Am. Bd. Pediatrics, Am. Bd. Neonatal-Perinatal Medicine. Pediatric intern, jr. resident in pediatrics Babies Hosp.-Columbia Presbyn. Med. Ctr., N.Y.C., 1975-77; assoc. scientist Internat. Ctr. for Diarrhoeal Disease Rsch., Bangladesh, 1979-83; rsch. asst. prof. depts. medicine and pediatrics Uniformed Svcs. U. Health Scis., Bethesda, Md., 1984-85; fellow in neonatology Emory U. Sch. Medicine, Atlanta, 1977-79, asst. prof. pediatrics, 1986—; vis. scientist dept. med. microbiology U. Goteborg, Sweden, 1983; clin. cons. Walter Reed Army Med. Ctr., Washington, 1984-86, Naval Hosp., Bethesda, 1984-86. Contbr. numerous articles and abstracts to med. jours., chpts. to books. Fellow Am. Acad. Pediatrics; mem. Soc. Pediatric Rsch., Phi Beta Kappa. Democrat. Jewish. Office: Emory U Sch Medicine 80 Butler St Atlanta GA 30335

STOLL, KATHLEEN H., health management consultant; b. Boston, July 29, 1936; d. Vincent Lawrence and Mary Louise (Young) Hennessy; m. Myron Saunders Stoll, Aug. 26, 1961; children: Vincent Saunders, Sarah Louise, Heather Anne Wiard-Stoll. BA, Smith Coll., 1958; MS, Case Western Res. U., 1960, MBA, 1984. Lic. ind. social worker, Ohio. Social worker Cleve. State Hosp., 1960-62, 64-65, rsch. assoc., 1966-69; aftercare cons., then assoc. dir. Cuyahoga County Mental Health Bd., Cleve., 1970-78; interim dir. mental health Murtis H. Taylor Mental Health Ctr., Cleve., 1978; planning assoc. Univ. Hosps. Cleve., 1978-89; cons. health and mental health mgmt. Stoll & Assocs., Cleve., 1989—; sec. Mental Illness and Chem. Dependency task force, Cleve., 1984—. Chmn. mental health commn., Fedn. Community Planning, 1988—; bd. dirs., Aftercare Resource Ctr., Cleve., 1989—. Mem. Nat. Assn. Social Work (Social Worker of Yr. 1987), Smith Club (pres. Cleve. sect. 1989—), Smith Alumnae Assn. (medal com.). Democrat. Office: Stoll & Assocs 2943 S Park St Shaker Heights OH 44120

STOLLER, ALYCE, human resource administrator; b. Far Rockaway, N.Y., Mar. 31, 1955; d. Sam and Shirley (Sherman) Zimmerman; m. Gerald Stoller, June 14, 1984. BA magna cum laude, Coll. S.I., N.Y., 1977; MS magna cum laude, Herbert H. Lehman Coll., Bronx, N.Y., 1982; MBA, Adelphi U., 1989. Mgmt. trainee U.S. Postal Svc., Queens, N.Y., 1982-84; sr. tng., devel. specialist U.S. Postal Svc., Jamaica, N.Y., 1984-88, supr. employment, svcs., 1988-89, tng. officer airport mail facility JFK, 1989—; ad hoc instr. Empire State Coll. SUNY, 1990—; mem. exec. bd. Intergovernmental Tng. Council of N.Y.-N.J., 1985—; owner, mgr. Applied Action Career Cons., Long Beach, N.Y., 1985—. Vol. cons. Bezalel Health Related Facility, Far Rockaway, 1981-85. Mem. Am. Soc. for Tng. and Devel. (newsletter editor L.I. chpt. 1989—), Nat. Assn. Postal Suprs., Nassau County Police Wives Assn., Adelphi U. Grad. Bus. Students Assn. Office: US Postal Svc Airport Mail Facility JFK JFK Jamaica NY 11430-9408

STOLOVE, LORRAINE P. (LORRAINE P. AUGENFELD), gerontologist; b. Bronx, N.Y., Aug. 9, 1942; d. Erwin and Frances (Preminger) Augenfeld; m. Burt Stolove, Aug. 2, 1964; children: Evan Scott, Marc David. BSc, CCNY, 1964; cert. in gerontology, Rutgers U., 1980. Cert. Tchr., N.J., N.Y. Tchr. N.Y.C. Bd. Edn., Bklyn., 1964-67, Old Bridge (N.J.) Bd. Edn., N.J., 1967-68, Prince of Peace Nursery Sch., Howell, N.J., 1972-73, Interstudy Inc., Holmdel, N.J., 1979-80; supr., info. referral Monmouth County Office on Aging, Freehold, N.J., 1981-84; asst. exec. dir. Monmouth County Office, N.J., 1984—. Originator facilitator support group relatives of aging persons, 1984—; producer host cable TV, 1986—; coord. Sr. Health Ins. Program, 1986—. Chairperson Mayor's Adv. Com. on Sr. Citizens, Freehold Twp., N.J., 1979-81; trustee Ctr. for Aging, Freehold Area Hosp., 1989—, Health Care Affiliates, 1989—; adv. bd. Green Thumb of N.J., 1986—; profl. adv. com. Mental Health Bd. Monmouth County, 1986—; mem. Monmouth County Task Force on Women and Alcohol and Other Substance Abuse, 1987—; profl. adv. com., chair, county liaison Alcohol Outreach Sr. Project, 1988—; adv. bd. Svc. Learning Program Brookdale Community Coll., Lincroft, N.J., 1988—. Mem. AAUW (v.p. 1981-83), Gerontological Soc. N.J. (bd. trustees 1987-89). Home: Two Woods Rd Freehold NJ 07728

STOLPER, CAROLYN LOUISE, not-for-profit executive; b. Madison, Wis., Jan. 28, 1953; d. Warren H. and Jane (Hoeveler) Stolper; m. David L. Bither, June 3, 1978 (div. 1989). BA in Art History, U. Wis., 1975, MA in Arts Adminstrn., 1978. Cert. fundraising exec. Researcher Lincoln Ctr. for Performing Arts, N.Y.C., 1978; assoc. dir. Nat. Corp. Fund for Dance, N.Y.C., 1978-82; dir. devel. Nat. Theatre of the Deaf, Chester, Conn., 1982-83, Playwrights Horizons, N.Y.C., 1983-85, AFS Intercultural Progs., N.Y.C., 1985-88; v.p. devel. & pub. affairs AFS Intercultural Progs., 1988-89; chief devel. officer Mus. of Contemporary Arts, Chgo., 1989—; bd. advisor Ctr. for Arts Adminstrn. Grad. Sch. of Bus. U. Wis., 1989—. Author: Successful Fundraising for Arts and Cultural Organizations, 1989. U. Wis. grad. fellow, 1976-78. Mem. Nat. Soc. Fund-Raising Execs., Am. Ctr. for Internat. Leadership. Office: 237 E Ontario St Chicago IL 60611

STOLZENBERG, PEARL, fashion designer; b. N.Y.C., Oct. 9, 1946; d. Irving and Anna (Shenkman) S. Student, Fashion Inst. Tech., 1964-66. Textile stylist, designer Forum Fabrics Ltd., N.Y.C., 1966-68; dir. styling Beauknit Corp., N.Y.C., 1969-74; stylist, designer Mi-Bru-San Co., Inc., N.Y.C., 1983-84; gen. mgr. Laissez-Faire Inc., N.Y.C., 1984-85; merchandiser prodn. The Clothing Acad. Inc., N.Y.C., 1986-87; v.p. String of Pearls Knitwear, Inc., N.Y.C., 1988—; cons. Tam O'Shanter Textile Ltd., Montreal, 1974-79, Mitsui, Osaka, Japan, 1976-79, Sergio Valente English Town Sportswear, N.Y.C., 1980-84; cons. merchandiser The Fashion Acad., Hollywood Crossing, Inc., N.Y.C. Democrat. Jewish. Home: 8340 Austin St Apt. 5Y Kew Gardens NY 11415 Office: String of Pearls Knitwear Inc Jelo Fabrics 1350 Broadway New York NY 10018

STONE, (LARUE) BETH, golf professional; b. Harlingen, Tex., May 15, 1940; d. John Lewis and LaRue Beth (Packer) S. Student, Okla. U., 1958-61. Touring golf profl. Ladies PGA, Daytona Beach, Fla., 1961-82; pres., owner Golf Stop, Inc., Tucson, Ariz., 1982—. Golf tchr. Tucson Rd. Runners Assn. for Jr. Girl Golfers, 1987-90. Mem. Ladies PGA (Class A, past officer, bd. dirs. 1978-79), U.S. Golf Assn. (Bob Jones award com. 1978), Fellowship Christian Athletes (bd. dirs. 1979-80), Gamma Phi Beta. Republican. Baptist. Home: 5326 Paseo de la Terraza Tucson AZ 85715 Office: Golf Stop Inc 2440 S 34th Pl Tucson AZ 85713

STONE, BONNIE CAROL, railroad executive; b. Bklyn., Aug. 9, 1945; d. Michael and Sylvia (Silberling) S.; m. Peter Jeffrey Kaplan, Oct. 30, 1976 (div. 1987); m. John P. Deacy, Sept. 1989. BA, U. Wis., 1966; MA, Columbia U., N.Y.C., 1968; M in Urban Planning, NYU, 1974. Various positions N.Y.C., 1968-72; with N.Y.C. Health Dept., 1972-78, 86, dep. asst. commr., 1977-78, dep. commr., 1986; 1st asst. dep. commr. N.Y.C. Human Resources Adminstrn., 1978-85, dep. commr., 1985-86; v.p. L.I. R.R., Jamaica, N.Y., 1986—. NDEA fellow U. Wis., 1966. Mem. Women's Transp. Seminar. Democrat. Jewish. Home: 395 Broadway New York NY 10013 Office: LI Railroad Jamaica Station Jamaica NY 11435

STONE, BRENDA HEMPHILL, nurse practitioner; b. Hagerstown, Md., June 27, 1944; d. Harold Bruce and Lillian May (Gelsinger) Hemphill; m. Daniel Stewart Stone, June 11, 1966; children: Laura Stewart, Michael Watson. BS in Nursing, Duke U., 1966; MS in Nursing, U. Md., 1973. Cert. adult nurse practitioner. Clin. nurse Johns Hopkins Hosp., Balt., 1975-76, instr., 1976-78, clin. specialist, 1979-84, nurse practitioner, 1986—. Pres. Parents Assn. Waldorf Sch. Balt., 1985; bd. trustees Waldorf Sch. Balt., 1988-90; vol. Pets on Wheels, Dept. on Aging, Balt., 1985-88. Lt. nurse corp USNR, ret. Mem. Am. Nurses Assn., Md. Nurses Assn. Home: 602 Edgevale Rd Baltimore MD 21210 Office: Johns Hopkins Hosp 600 N Wolfe St Baltimore MD 21205

STONE, CAROLINE FLEMING, artist; b. N.Y.C., Mar. 26, 1936; d. Ralph Emerson and Elizabeth (Fleming) S.; m. Oakleigh B. Thorne, June 1956 (div. 1969); children: Oakleigh, Henry. Student, Art Students' League, 1954-57, 1973-74, Pratt Graphics, 1973-74. One-woman shows include Saginaw (Mich.) Art Mus., 1978, Jesse Besser Mus., Mich, 1979, Washington Art Assn., Conn., Ella Sharp Mus., Mich., 1980, San Diego Pub. Library, Diablo Valley Coll., Calif., 1981, Trustman Gallery Simmons Coll., Boston, 1985, Mary Ryan Gallery, N.Y.C., 1989; two-man shows include Miriam Perlman, Chgo., 1980, U. Mich., 1981, Mary Ryan Gallery, 1985, Katonah Gallery, N.Y., 1986, Davidson Gallery, Seattle, 1990; juried shows include Silvermine Nat. Printmaking, Conn., 1978, Print Club, Phila., 1981, Trenton State (nat. print exhibn. purchase award), 1982, Minot State Coll., N.D., 1985, Boston Printmakers (jurors commendation award), 1986; group shows include Mus. N.Mex., 1984, Wilhelm Gallery, Houston, 1985, De Cordova and Dana Mus., Nat. Acad. Art, N.Y.C., Boston Pub. Library, Mus. Contemporary Hispanic Art, N.Y.C., 1987, World Print Exhbn., San Francisco, Smith Coll. Gallery, Northampton, Mass., Mary Ryan Gallery, 1988, Virginia Lynch Gallery, R.I., 1989; invitational shows include Abington Ctr., Pa., Printmaking Workshop, N.Y., 1982; represented in permanent collections Art Inst. Chgo., Mid-West Mus. Am. Art, Ind., Mus. N.Mex., Nat. Mus. Am. Art, Saginaw Mus., Boston Pub. Library, U. Chgo., U. Mich., Exxon Corp. Chase Manhattan Bank, IBM, Mellon Bank; executed murals Revlon Inc. Mem. N.Y. Arts Group, The Kitchen (bd. dirs.). Episcopalian. Home and Office: C Stone Press 80 Wooster St New York NY 10012

STONE, CATHERINE LOUISE, perinatal consultant; b. Oakland, Calif., Jan. 7, 1956; d. Herbert Dean and Elizabeth Fisher (Burns) S.; m. Scott Clinton Burn, Aug. 6, 1978 (div. Sept. 1986); children: Sarah Adrielle Burn, Kaitlin Meredith Burn. BS, U. Calif., Davis, 1978; MA in Psychology, Calif. State U. Sonoma, Rohnert Park, Calif., 1990. Cert. childbirth educator, profl. birth asst. Environ. educator Orinda (Calif.) Union Schs., 1974-77, U. Calif.-Davis, 1976-78; childbirth educator Sacramento, 1979-81; health edn. coord. Lafayette (Calif.) Med. Group, 1982-86; mktg. dir. Westerbeke Ranch Conf. Ctr., Sonoma, 1986-88; cert. childbirth educator No. Calif, 1979—, midwife, 1980—; dir. BirthCare, El Verano, Calif., 1984—; trainer, educator Informed Birth & Parenting, U.S. and Can., 1985—; dir. tng. Informed Birth & Parenting, Ann Arbor, Mich., 1987—; coord. Challenge Sonoma Adventure Ropes Course, Eldridge, Calif., 1990—; lectr. Calif. State U-Sonoma, Rohnert Park, 1989; dir. Soc. for Humanized Birth, Sacramento, 1979-81. Vol. leader La Leche League, Sacramento, Moraga, Sonoma, Calif., 1980—, area conf. supr., 1981-83, area conf. adminstr., Calif., Oreg., Wash., Nev., Utah, Montana, Wyo., 1983-85; publicity chair Orinda Moraga Dem. Club, 1975. Recipient Dept. Citation, U. Calif.-Davis, 1978; March of Dimes grantee, 1982. Mem. Assn. Profl. Birth Assts. (dir. 1990—), Midwives Alliance N.Am., Assn. Humanistic Psychology, Assn. Transpersonal Psychology, Calif. Assn. Midwives (dir. 1984-86), Informed Birth and Parenting, Informed Homebirth, Internat. Childbirth Educators Assn., Psi Chi. Home: 18738 Railroad Ave Sonoma CA 95476 Office: Birthcare PO Box 426 El Verano CA 95433

STONE, CYNTHIA HUTCHINSON, real estate broker; b. Chgo., July 18, 1940; d. Charles White and Jeannette Naomi (White) Hutchinson; m. Thomas Richardson Stone, July 20, 1963; children: Sarah Bryden, Thomas Hutchinson. BA, Lawrence U., 1962. Tchr. Spanish Waukesha (Wis.) Pub. Schs., 1962-63; substitute tchr. various sch. dists., 1963-64, 73-77; adminstrv. asst. Graninger Realty, Inc., Stafford, Va., 1977-79; real estate sec. Realty World, Spike Hensel, Inc., Camp Hill, Pa., 1979-81, real estate salesperson, 1981-83; with Coldwell Banker MGM Realty, Inc., 1983-86; real estate assoc. broker, br. mgr. Coldwell Banker MGM Realty, Inc., Carlisle, Pa., 1987-88, Elizabethtown, Pa., 1988—. Mem. Nat. Assn. Realtors, Pa. Assn. Realtors, Lancaster County Assn. Realtors, Greater Harrisburg (Pa.) Assn. Realtors (non-resident), Officers Wives Club (various offices), P.E.O. (corr. sec. Carlisle chpt. 1985-87), Delta Gamma. Republican. Home: 6319 Stephen's Crossing Mechanicsburg PA 17055 Office: Coldwell Banker MGM Realty 1255 S Market St Elizabethtown PA 17022

STONE, DEBORAH LEE, actuary; b. Concord, N.H., Nov. 27, 1956; d. Philip M. and Barbara E. (Johnson) S. BS in Math. Edn., U. N.H., 1977; MBA, U. Pa., 1981. Outside plant engr. New Eng. Telephone Co., Somersworth, N.H., 1978-79; sr. analyst Exxon Corp., Florham Park, N.J., 1981-84; sr. actuarial asst. N.H. Ins. Group, Manchester, 1985-87; sr. actuarial analyst Nationale-Nederlanden N.A. Property and Casualty Group, Keene, N.H., 1987—. Mem. Jaycees. Republican. Jewish. Home: 317 Court St Keene NH 03431 Office: Nat Nederlanden NA P&C Grp 62 Maple Ave Keene NH 03431

STONE, DIANNE S., publishing company executive; b. Jamaica, W.I., Mar. 12, 1964; came to U.S., 1980; d. Troy and Sonia (Roberts) S.; 1 child, Jared Stone Rigg. BS, NYU, 1985. Asst. ops. mgr. Clark Boardman Co., Ltd., N.Y.C.; ops. mgr. Inspeco, N.Y.C., 1990—. Home: 336 E 9th St Brooklyn NY 11218 Office: Inspeco 99 Hudson St New York NY 10013

STONE, ELIZABETH CAECILIA, anthropology educator; b. Oxford, Eng., Feb. 4, 1949; d. Lawrence and Jeanne Cecilia (Fawtier) S.; m. Paul Edmund Zimansky, Nov. 5, 1976. BA, U. Pa., 1971; MA, Harvard U., 1973; PhD, U. Chgo., 1979. Lectr. anthropology SUNY, Stony Brook, 1977-78, asst. prof., 1978-85, assoc. prof., 1985—; participated archaeol. in Eng., Iran, Iraq, Afghanistan; dir. archaeol. projects Ain Dara, Syria, and Tek Abu Duwaii, Iraq. Author: Nippur Neighborhoods, 1987; co-author: (monograph) Old Babylonian Contracts from Nippur 1, 1976; contbr. articles to profl. jours. Assoc. trustee Am. Schs. of Oriental Rsch., 1983—. Fulbright fellow, 1986-87; rsch. grantee Ford Found., 1974, Nat. Geog. Soc., 1983, 84, 88, Am. Schs. of Oriental Rsch., 1987, 88, NSF, 1988, NEH, 1975-88. Office: SUNY Dept Anthropology Stony Brook NY 11794

STONE, ELIZABETH WENGER, emeritus dean; b. Dayton, Ohio, June 21, 1918; d. Ezra and Anna Bess (Markey) Wenger; m. Thomas A. Stone, Sept. 14, 1939 (dec. Feb. 1987); children: John Howard, Anne Elizabeth, James Alexander. A.B., Stanford U., 1937, M.A., 1938; M.L.S., Catholic U. Am., 1961; Ph.D., Am. U., 1968. Tchr. pub. schs. Fontana, Calif., 1938-39; asst. state statistician State of Conn., 1939-40; libr. New Haven Pub. Librs., 1940-42; dir. pub. relations, asst. to pres. U. Dubuque, Iowa, 1942-46; substitute libr. Pasadena (Calif. Pub. Libr. System), 1953-60; instr. Cath. U. Am., 1962-63, asst. prof., asst. to chmn. dept. libr. sci., 1963-67, assoc. prof., asst. to chmn., 1967-71, prof., asst. to chmn., 1971-72, prof., chmn. dept., 1972-80, dean Sch. Libr. and Info. Scis., 1981-83, prof. and dean emeritus, 1983—, lectr., 1990; libr. cons. U.S. Inst. of Peace, 1988-90; founder, exec. dir. Continuing Libr. Edn. Network and Exchange, 1975-79; founder Nat. Rehab. Info. Ctr., 1977, project mgr., 1977-83; co-chmn. 1st World Conf. on Continuing Edn. for the Libr. and Info. Sci. Professions, 1984-85. Author: Factors Related to the Professional Development of Librarians, 1969, (with James J. Kortendick) Job Dimensions and Educational Needs in Librarianship, 1971, (with R. Patrick and B. Conroy) Continuing Library and Information Science Education, 1974, Continuing Library Education as Viewed in Relation to Other Continuing Professional Movements, 1975, (with F. Peterson and M. Chobot) Motivation: A Vital Force in the Organization, 1977, American Library Development 1600-1899, 1977, (with others) Model Continuing Education Recognition System in Library and Information Science, 1979, (with M.J. Young) A Program for Quality in Continuing Education for Information, Library and Media Personnel, 1980, (with others) Continuing Education for the Library Information Professions, 1985; editor: D.C. Libraries, 1964-66; contbr. articles to profl. jours. Mem. Pres.'s Com. on Employment of Handicapped, 1972-88, Establishment of Elizabeth W. Stone Lectureship Cath. U. Am., 1990; pres. D.C. chpt. Am. Mothers, Inc., 1984-86, nat. v.p., pres.-elect, 1989—. Recipient DCLA Ainsworth Rand Spofford Pres's. award, 1990, Alumni Achievement award in libr. and info. sci. Cath. U. Am., 1990. Mem. ALA (coun. 1976-83, v.p. 1980-81, pres. 1981-82, chmn. Nat. Libr. Week 1983-85, Lippincott award 1986, hon. life), D.C. Libr. Assn. (pres. 1966-67), Spl. Librs. Assn. (pres. D.C. chpt. 1973-74), Assn. Am. Libr. Schs. (pres. 1974), Am. Soc. Info. Sci., Cath. Libr. Assn. (hon., life), Am. Soc. Assn. Execs., Am. Assn. Adult and Continuing Edn., Internat. Fedn. Libr. Assns. and Instns. (chmn. Continuing Profl. Edn. Round Table 1986—), Continuing Profl. Edn. Libr. and Info. Sci. Pers., fWashington Club, Cosmos Club, Phi Sigma Alpha, Beta Phi Mu, Phi Lambda Theta. Presbyterian. Home: 4000 Cathedral Ave NW 15B Washington DC 20016 Office: Catholic U Am Washington DC 20064

STONE, ELSA LOUISE, pediatrician; b. N.Y.C., June 18, 1943; d. Murry Hedley and Winifred Elizabeth (Carlsen) Stone; m. Richard Horace Granger, Jan. 1, 1983. BS, U. Chgo., 1964; MD, Albert Einstein Coll. Medicine, N.Y.C., 1970. Diplomate Am. Bd. Pediatrics. Intern/resident dept. pediatrics Yale/New Haven Hosp., 1970-73; fellow Yale U. Child Study Ctr., 1973-75; pediatrician Wallingford Pediatric Group, Conn., 1975-77; pvt. practice pediatrics North Haven, Conn., 1978—; mem. med. bd., adminstrv. com. Yale-New Haven Hosp. Fellow Am. Acad. Pediatrics (v.p. Conn. chpt. 1988—); mem. New Haven Individual Practice Assn. (pres. 1988—), New Haven Pediatric Soc. (v.p. 1987-89), New Haven County Med. Assn., Conn. Med. Soc. Democrat. Home: 25 Beechwood Ln New Haven CT 06511 Office: 25 Washington Ave North Haven CT 06473

STONE, GAIL HETZEL, sales and marketing executive; b. Middletown, Conn., Aug. 28, 1950; d. Raymond Francis and June Lavinia (Carlson) Hetzel; m. Stephen Thomas Nyerick (div. Jan. 1977); m. Christopher Odlin Stone, May 14, 1988. BE, U. Conn., 1972. Advt., sales promotion asst. Ames Dept. Stores, Inc., Hartford, Conn., 1973-74; customer svc. rep. Eli Lilly & Co. Elizabeth Arden Div., Enfield, Conn., 1975-79; announcer Sta. WMLB-FM, West Hartford, Conn., 1978; coordinating producer PM Mag., Hartford, 1979-80, program producer, 1981-83; dir. sales mktg. Monitor Prodns., Inc., Hartford, 1984-87; program marketing mgr. Conn. PBS, Hartford, 1988—; pres. GMH Enterprises, Portland, Conn., 1983-88; pub. rels. com. The Holiday Project, Hartford, 1982-83, Gov.'s Coun. on Vol. Action, 1990, Manchester Musical Players, 1989-90; asst. at Youth at Risk/The Breakthrough Found., Bridgeport, Conn., 1986. Friend of Goodspeed Opera House, Hartford Stage Company. Mem. Am. Mktg. Assn., Wadsworth Atheneum, Greater Hartford Ad. Club, Manchester Musical Players Club, Little Theatre Manchester Club. Roman Catholic. Office: Conn PBS 240 New Britain Ave Hartford CT 06106

STONE, JANE BUFFINGTON, artist; b. Madison, Wis., Dec. 1, 1942; adopted d. Marshall Buffington and Alvaretta (Smith) Atkinson; 1 child, Anthony Thomas. Grad. high sch., Eau Claire, Wis. Apprentice Karl Haagedorn, St. Paul, 1960-65; art instr. Head Start Program, St. Paul, 1965-67, Walker Art Inst., Mpls., 1967-69; founding mem., instr. Southside Free Sch., Mpls., 1968-69; free-lance artist Minn. and Oreg., 1965-73; art instr. Fairview Tng. Ctr., Salem, Oreg., 1974-77; founder, dir. 3 C's Sch. of Basic Carpentry, Salem, 1978-79; founder, pres. J. Stone Cards, Inc., Silverton, Oreg., 1980—. Author: Curriculum For Basic Carpentry Instruction, 1976. Newsletter editor NAACP, St. Paul, 1965-67, crisis counselor Mpls. Free Clinic, 1968-70, produce coord. Westbank Food Co-op, Mpls., 1968-70, counselor Womanspace, Salem, Oreg., 1978-80. Recipient Louie award Greeting Card Assn., N.Y.C., 1989. Mem. Am. Watercolor Assn., Oreg. Watercolor Assn. Unitarian. Office: J Stone Cards Inc One J Stone Pla Silverton OR 97381

STONE, KATHLEEN PATRICIA, nutritionist; b. Washington, Aug. 5, 1955; d. David Louis and Grace (Grubb) S.; 1 child, Meredith McCall. BS, W.Va. U., 1976, MS, 1979; MBA, U. Miami, 1985. Dietitian Uniontown (Pa.) Hosp., 1979-80; asst. dir. diet Mercy Hosp., Balt., 1980-82; patient feeding coord. Jackson Meml. Hosp., Miami, Fla., 1982-85; dir. clin. nutrition Boca Raton (Fla.) Community Hosp., 1985-86; pres. Strictly Nutrition, Boca Raton, 1986—. Author: Snack Attack: 30 Days to Conquer Craving, 1990. Bd. dirs. Am. Cancer Soc., Boca Raton, 1990. Recipient scholarship, ARA, 1983. Mem. Am. Dietetic Assn. (media spokesperson 1985-90, chmn. div. cons. and pvt. practice 1990—, pres.-elect Consulting Nutritionists, 1988-89), Broward Dietetic Assn. (pres. 1987-88), Boca Raton C. of C. Home: 4332 Brandywine Dr Boca Raon FL 33487 Office: Strictly Nutrition 1401 NW 9th Ave Boca Raton FL 33486

STONE, KATHRYN DOLORES, credit union executive; b. Pontiac, Mich., June 12, 1929; d. Durward South and Betty Marie (LaVelle) Young; student pub. schs.; m. James Macklin Stone, Oct. 19, 1946; children: James Durward, David Allan. Lic. realtor. With T&C Fed. Credit Union, Pontiac, 1955—, asst. gen. mgr., teller mgr., acctg. mgr., 1972-77, chief fin. officer, 1977—, treas. bd. dirs., exec. gen. mgr., 1977-83, pres., chief exec. officer, 1977-88; ret., 1988; pres., chief exec. officer, cons. Parda Fed. Credit Union; exec. com. Credit Union Data Acctg., 1972-74, 77—; mem. exec. com. Oakland County (Mich.), chpt. Credit Unions, 1980—; exec. bd. Credit Union Met. Area Advt. Coun., Detroit, chmn., 1983—; v.p. Joint Advt. Bd., Flint, Mich., 1983, dir., 1984-87. Chmn. community div. Pontiac United Way, 1972; fin. treas. 125th anniversary celebration City of Pontiac, also chmn. fundraising and promotion; golf instr. Alexander Sch. of Golf; bd. dirs. Waterford Township Planning Com. Recipient various svc. awards, certs. appreciation. Mem. Credit Union Execs. Soc., Jayno Heights Women's Assn., Pink Panthers (pres.), Golf League, Epsilon Sigma Alpha (chpt. pres. 1966, 76-77, pres. Mich. coun. 1968-69). Author manuals, policy books in field. Episcopalian. Office: 2525 N Telegraph Rd Suite 200 Bloomfield Hills MI 48013

STONE, LINDA LEE, retail specialist; b. Maywood, Calif., Sept. 14, 1942; d. Joseph Page and Ruth Irene (Brockett) Otero; m. Charles Rhodes Hamson, Dec. 28, 1960 (div. 1977); children: Gregory Page, Michael Rhodes. Student, U. Calif., L.A., 1960-68, Calif. Polytech., 1977. With sales dept. Ken Walker Realty, San Clemente, Calif., 1970-72; owner, mgr. Rumpelstiltskin Restaurant, San Clemente, 1972-74, A&B Woodworking, El Monte, Calif., 1975-82; cons. Ellington Wood Products, Commerce, Calif., 1982-84; with outside sales dept. United Wholesale Lumber, Montebello, Calif., 1984-86; door store mgr. Delaney Sash & Door, Los Alamitos, Calif., 1986—. Mem. Belmont Heights Assn., Long Beach, Calif., 1989—. Mem. NAFE. Republican. Office: Delaney Sash & Door Inc 10850 Portal Dr Los Alamitos CA 90720

STONE, LISA JANE, data processing executive; b. N.Y.C., June 30, 1944; d. Charles Haskel and Edith (Karlitz) Wald; m. Stephen Paul Stone, Mar. 1, 1969; children: Jason Harris, Erica Lauren, Charles David. BA in Spanish, Beaver Coll., Glenside, Pa., 1965; MBA, Sangamon State U., 1979. Systems analyst Ill. Dept. Pub. Health, Springfield, 1976—. Bd. dirs., sec., v.p., pres. Jr. League, Springfield, 1984-88, Springfield Sch. Found., 1981—; bd. dirs., sec. Habitat for Humanity-Sangamon County, Springfield, 1989—; mem. Young Women's Leadership Cabinet, United Jewish Appeal, 1981-84; bd. dirs., v.p. Springfield Jewish Fedn., 1984-87, 88—, campaign chmn., 1989-90; bd. dirs., v.p. Temple B'rith Sholom Sisterhood, pres., 1990, trustee, exec. com., 1990—, choir, soloist, 1985—; human svcs. com. United Way, 1988—. Named Vol. of Yr. Sch. Dist. 186, Springfield, 1985, YMCA, 1985, Commercial Svc. award Ill. Dept. Pub. Health, 1987. Mem. Orgn. for Rehab. and Tng., Hadassah, Go For Broke Investment Club. Home: 3013 Mill Bank Ln Springfield IL 62704 Office: Ill Dept Pub Health 535 W Jefferson Springfield IL 62761

STONE, MARTHA JANETTE STAFF, marketing communication executive; b. Pensacola, Fla., Dec. 25, 1953; d. Robert James and Harriet Gilda Staff; m. David Warren, May 21. 1977; children: Charmian Elizabeth, Timothy. MA, U. Michigan, 1977; BA magna cum laude, Kalamazoo Coll., 1976. Dir. of devel. rsch. Kalamazoo Coll., 1979-80; rsch. dir. Berrien County Pvt. Ind. Coun., Benton Harbor, Mich., 1980-82; writer and account exec. Mktg. Ptnrs./SMBR, Inc., St. Joseph, Mich., 1982-84; mgr. corp. mktg. communications Whirlpool Fin. Corp., Benton Harbor, 1984—. Contbr. articles to profl. jours. Parent coord. Girl Scouts U.S., 1987-88; mem. Stevensville United Meth. Ch. Recipient Advt. award Whirlpool Dealer Mgt. Group, Benton Harbor, Mich., 1985, Achievement award Dale Carnegie Inst., 1987, Book award, 1987, Human Rels. award, 1987. Mem. NAFE, Am. Mktg. Assn., Communicator's Forum, Phi Beta Kappa, Alpha Lambda Delta, Econ. Club of S.W. Mich., Whirlpool Mgmt. Club. Republican. Methodist. Home: 1668 Rhonda Saint Joseph MI 49085 Office: 553 Benson Rd Benton Harbor MI 49022

STONE, MAURINE RAINER, architect; b. Union Springs, Ala., Jan. 23, 1940; d. Joel Herron and Sara Eleanor (Floyd) Rainer; m. William Naylor Stone Jr., June 18, 1960; children: Elisa Marbury, William Naylor III, Sara Floyd. BS in Biology/Chemistry, U. Ala., Tuscaloosa, 1960; postgrad., Drew U., Madison, N.J., 1974-75, Princeton U., 1975-76; BArch, La. State U., 1979. Registered architect, N.J., N.Y.; registered profl. planner, N.J. Med. biologist radiol. health HEW, Montgomery, Ala., 1961; project mgr. James G. Howell, Architect, Baton Rouge, 1979-80; instr. Sch. Architecture, La. State U., Baton Rouge, 1980-81; contractor, craftsman Short Hills, N.J., 1981-82; project mgr. Becker, Bendixen, Murphy & Herbst, Newark, 1983-85; sr. assoc. James Goldstein & Ptnrs., Millburn, N.J., 1985-88; prin. Maurine Rainer Stone, AIA Architect/Planner, 1988—. Mem. Millburn Planning Bd., 1987—, vice chmn., 1990. Mem. AIA (regional liason to women in architecture com. 1989—), N.J. Soc. Architects (chmn. women in architecture 1989-90), Nat. Trust for Hwy. Preservation, Phi Beta Kappa, Phi Kappa Phi. Office: 24 Beechwood Rd Ste 27 Summit NJ 07901

STONE, MILDRED MARY-ANNE, writer; b. Sturgeon Bay, Wis.; d. Peter John and Catherine (Merget) Simon; m. Grant Clifford Stone, Feb. 7, 1933 (div.); children: Kathleen, K.K. Anderson, Bonnie Melody, Linda, Rebecca. BA in Journalism, U. Wis., 1931, MD, 1938. Pvt. practice medicine and allergy Berlin (Wis.) Hosp., 1939-51; staff physician ARC Blood Bank, Madison, 1951-52; health physician, head allergy clinic VA Hosp., Madison, 1952-60; health officer City of Berlin, 1941-51; chief staff Cuba City (Wis.) Hosp., 1967-80; staff writer Wis. State Jour., Madison, 1932-33. Author: HenMedic, 50 Years in Medicine, 1989; author poetry. Mem. Metro. Opera, Smithsonian Instn., Women in Communications, Theta Sigma Phi, AMA, Wis. Med. Soc. Democrat. Roman Catholic.

STONE, PAULA S., marketing and public relations professional; b. San Diego; m. William S. Johnson III. BS, Miss. State U., 1979, MA, 1981. Bur. chief InfoWorld, Dallas; v.p., dir. Ogilvy & Mather, Dallas; now prin. Soft Touch Technology, Plano, Tex.; presenter media tng. for execs.; speaker in field. Author 9 books, over 200 pub. articles. Mem. NAFE, Pub. Rels. Soc. Am. Office: 3305 Canyon Valley Plano TX 75023

STONE, TAMMY ANN, human resources professional; b. Springfield, Ill., June 11, 1963; d. Leroy John and Anna Marie (Seaborn) Schaddel; m. Richard L. Stone, Nov. 23, 1985. BS, Ill. State U., 1985. Manpower planner with div. econ. opportunity dept commerce and community affairs State of Ill., Springfield, 1986-90; human svc. grants coordinator dept commerce and community affairs State of Ill., 1990—. Contbr. to tech. and rsch. publs. Mem. NAFE, Jr. League Springfield (asst. chmn. wholesale cookbook 1989, chmn. Next-To-New fundraiser 1990), United Way (liaison to the Girl Scouts), Phi Gamma Nu. Home: 408 S MacArthur St Springfield IL 62704

STONE, TEENA MARIE, land corporation executive; b. Victoria, Tex., June 30, 1948; d. Allison Joseph and Vivian Marie (Tull) Hyak; m. Daniel Stone, July 3, 1982 (dec. 1985). Diploma in cosmetology, Papacs Beauty Sch., 1966; student, West Covina Coll., 1973. Mgr. Robert Houlihan, M.D., Pasadena, Calif., 1978-81; tchr. Western Coll. of Medicine, Van. Nuys, Calif., 1979-80; order desk operator Transo Envelope Co., Glendale, Calif., 1981-83; exec. adminstr. Edmund and Connie Chein, M.D., Beverly Hills, 1984-87; cons. acct. Charleen Chase, Beverly Hills, 1987; cons. sales Franklin B. Kirkbride, Inc., N.Y.C., 1987; pres. TNT Oley a Land Corp., Glendora, Calif., 1988—; ptnr., operator Sher's Mad About Cheesecake, 1989—. Mem. NAFE. Republican. Home and Office: 136 N Grand Ave #206 West Covina CA 91791

STONEKING, CAROLE LYNNE, former association executive, therapist, educator, consultant; b. Detroit, Mar. 28, 1937; d. Robert Frank and Esther Freda (Meier) S. BS, Wayne State U., 1963, MA, 1972. Program dir. Oakland br. YWCA, Clawson, Mich., 1961-63; program dir. no. br. YWCA, Highland Park, Mich., 1964-67; ctr. dir. Macomb br. YWCA, Warren, Mich., 1968-74; exec. dir. YWCA, East Detroit, 1974-79, Jacksonville, Fla., 1979-85; exec. dir. YWCA of the Midlands, Columbia, S.C., 1985-88; pres. Designs to Accommodate Madame Execs. (DAME), Columbia, S.C., 1988—, Stress Mgmt. Inst. Massage Therapy, Columbia, 1988—. Chmn. legis. com., mem. steering com. United Way of Midlands, 1986-87; pres. Coalition to Take Back the Night, Columbia, 1987-88, v.p., 1989; com. mem. Respite Care Council on Aging, Columbia, 1987—. Recipient Cert. Appreciation Am. Patriotic Commn., Jacksonville, Fla., 1982. Mem. Nat. Assn. YWCA Execs., Mich. Recreation and Park Assn. (registered profl.), Network of Female Execs., Fla. Council for Profl. Fundraisers (bd. dirs. 1983-85), Greater Columbia C. of C. (bd. dirs. 1987—, chair wellness com. 1987, sec. 1988—), Greater Columbia chpt. NOW (v.p. 1987, pres. 1988—), Independent Bus. Women (Columbia chpt. treas. 1988), Columbia Network for Female Execs. (com. mem. 1986—, sec. 1988), Cities in Schs. (Columbia) (bd. trustees, 1988). Office: Stress Mgmt Inst Massage Therapy 1005 Jackson Ave Columbia SC 29203

STONEKING, LILLIAN STANFORD, physician assistant; b. Corpus Christi, Tex., Aug. 25, 1951; d. Kermit Frate and Dorothy (Hausenfluck) Stanford; m. C. Nevin Anderson Jr., Jan. 19, 1974 (div. June 1987); m. Kim Stoneking, July 13, 1990; children: Daniel, Jennifer, Angela. Student, U. Tex., 1969-71; BS, U. Tex., Galveston, 1973. Cert. physician asst. Lab. aid Brackenridge Hosp., Austin, Tex., 1970; mem. med. staff Dr. George Bolmfalk, Weslaco, Tex., 1971; med. asst. Valley Bapt. Diagnostic Assocs., Harlingen, Tex., 1971; hosp. tech. asst. John Sealy Hosp., Galveton, Tex., 1972; co-therapist adolescent gorup therapy Gulf Bend Clinic, Victoria, Tex., 1974-76; physician asst. various clinics, Victoria, 1973-84; DRG coord. Victoria Regional Med. Ctr., 1984-85; DRG mgr. Tex., Fla., La. Universal Health Svcs. Inc., Victoria, 1985-86; dir. profl. devel./program devel. Victoria Regional Med. Ctr., 1986-87; exec. dir. Hospice Victoria, Inc., 1987-90; physician asst. II U. Tex. Health Sci. Ctr., Dept. Internal Medicine, Gen. Med., San Antonio, Tex., 1989-90; exec. dir., devel. Affectionate Arms Adult Day Health Care Ctr., Victoria, Tex., 1990—; found., dir. Women's Crisis Ctr., Inc., Victoria, 1982-86. Bd. dirs. Hospice Victoria, Inc. Mem. Nat. Hospice Orgn., Tex. Hospice Orgn., Am. Acad. Physician Assts., Tex. Acad. Physician Assts., Tex. Council Family Violence, Tex. Assn. Against Sexual Assaults, Nat. Coun. Cath. Women (chmn. community affairs 1988), Cath. Daus. Am. (cert. merit 1988), Stop Aids (Bekar County task force on women, children and aids 1989). Republican. Roman Catholic.

STONER, ELAINE BLATT, chemical patent literature analyst; b. Bklyn., Dec. 31, 1939; d. Joseph and Ann (Wertentheil) Blatt; m. Clinton Dale Stoner, Apr. 18, 1965; children—Robert, Michael. B.S., Bklyn. Coll., 1961; Ph.D., U. Calif.-Berkeley, 1965. NIH postdoctoral fellow U. Wis., 1964-65; with Chem. Abstracts Service, Columbus, Ohio, 1965—, sr. editor, 1976—. Mem. Am. Chem. Soc., Sigma Xi. Home: 1014 Kenway Ct Columbus OH 43220 Office: Chem Abstracts Svc PO Box 3012 Columbus OH 43210

STONER, FRANCES WYNETTE, city official, city secretary; b. Lake City, Fla., Oct. 2, 1943; d. Monroe Mattox Neveils and Freda Bryan (Mobley) Neveils Hollingsworth; m. Jerry Kay Stoner, Dec. 16, 1962; 1 child, Wynette Renae. Diploma Massey Bus. Coll., Jacksonville, Fla., 1962; student Alvin Community Coll., Tex., 1980-81. Legal sec. Crofton Holland & Starling, Titusville, Fla., 1962-63, Davis & Katz, Lebanon, Pa., 1963; dep. city clk. City of Titusville, 1964-68, sec., 1968-72; city clk. City of Alvin, Tex., 1974—. Recipient Cert. of Excellence award U.S. Dept. Labor, Washington, 1980. Mem. Assn. City Clks. and Secs., of Tex. (Salt Grass chpt. sec., treas., 1975, pres. 1978), Internat. Inst. Mcpl. Clks., Nat. Purchasing Inst., Alvin C. of C. Club: Soroptimist Internat. of Alvin (sec. 1984-85, v.p. 1985-86). Home: 113 S Jane St Alvin TX 77511 Office: City of Alvin 216 W Sealy St Alvin TX 77511

STONER, SUE, travel consultant; b. Seminole, Okla., June 8, 1942; d. E.D. and Atha Miriah (Brown) Burkhart; m. George M. Stoner, Jr., Sept. 5, 1964; children—Shelby Lynn, Steven Laird. B.A., Howard Payne Coll., 1964. Pres., Travel World, Inc., Gig Harbor, Wash., 1965—; sec.-treas. Travel Stamps, Inc., Gig Harbor, 1978—. Mem. distributive edn. com. Peninsula Sch. Dist., Gig Harbor. Mem. AAUW, Am. Soc. Travel Agts. (com. chmn.), Inst. Cert. Travel Agts. (cert. travel cons., nat. rep.), Assn. Retail Travel Agts. (com. chmn.), Gig Harbor C. of C. Republican. Baptist. Clubs: Toastmasters (pres. Gig Harbor chpt. 1987) Altrusa. Avocations: reading, travel, painting. Home: 15018 Sherman Dr NW Gig Harbor WA 98335 Office: PO Box 427 3116 Judson St Gig Harbor WA 98335

STOODT, BARBARA DERN, education educator; b. Columbus, Ohio, June 12, 1934; d. Millard Fissel and Helen Lucille (Taes) Dern; divorced; children: Linda Stoodt Neu, Susan Stoodt Price. BS in Edn., Ohio U., 1956; MA in Edn., Ohio State U., 1965; PhD, 1970; postgrad., U. Chgo., 1967. Tchr. North Charleston (S.C.) Schs., 1956-57, Cleveland Heights (Ohio) U., 1957-58, Mansfield (Ohio) Bd. Edn., 1958-59, 65-68; dir. reading, 1968; teaching assoc. Ohio State U., 1968-70; prof. edn. U. Akron, Ohio, 1970-77, Univ. N.C., Greensboro, 1977—. Author: Reading Instruction, 1981, 2nd edit., 1989, Teaching Language Arts, 1988; co-author: Secondary School Reading Instruction, 1987, 4th edit., 1991, Riverside Reading Program. U.S. Office Edn. research grantee, 1970. Mem. Nat. Conf. on Research in English, Internat. Reading Assn. (Outstanding Dissertation award), Am. Ednl. Research Assn., Nat. Council Tchrs. English (outstanding research award 1971), Assn. for Supervision and Curriculum Devel., Assn. for Childhood Edn. Internat. Methodist. Home: 1100 Forest Hill Dr Greensboro NC 27410 Office: U NC Curry Bldg Sch Edn Greensboro NC 27412

STOOP, NORMA MCLAIN, editor, author, photographer; b. Panama, C.Z., July 20, 1910; b. Harry Edward and Gladys (Brandon) McLain; student Penn Hall Jr. Coll., Carnegie Inst. Tech., New Sch., N.Y. U.; m. William J. Stoop, Jr., Sept. 20, 1932. Contbg. editor Dance Mag., N.Y.C., 1969-71, assoc. editor, 1971-79, sr. editor, 1979—; sr. editor After Dark, 1978-82, also feature writer; also photographer, theater, ballet and film critic; entertainment editor sr. edit. Sta. WNYC-AM, 1980-83; chief film critic Manhattan Arts, 1983-89, mem. editors panel Antioch U. summer writers workshop, 1988, 89, spl guest for dialogue sessions, 1990. Mem. Poetry Soc. Am., Acad. Am. Poets, Dance Masters Am., Dance Critics Assn., TV Acad. Arts and Scis., Overseas Press Club, Deadline Club, Sigma Delta Chi. Contbr. poems to Tex. Quar., Chgo. Rev., Plains Poetry Jour., Arts in Society, Quest, Atlantic Monthly, Puerto Del Sol, The Quarterly, Md. Poetry Rev., others, short stories to Portland Monthly, others, 1958—, essays to Book Week in N.Y. Herald Tribune; represented in Best Poems of 1973, Exhibit of Dance Photography, Harvard U., Tufts Coll., 1975, featured in 1990 Poet's Market; MacNeil Lehrer News, 1988. Recipient award Dance Tchrs. Club Boston, 1977.

STOPKEY, LINDA JOHANNA, electronics company official; b. Chgo., Mar. 3, 1960; d. Waldemar Dmitro and Lorraine (Bielenberg) S. B.S. in Mgmt. summa cum laude, Tulane U., 1981; M.B.A., U. Tex., 1984. Cost engr. IBM, Austin, 1981-84, cost engring. mgr., 1984-86, pricer, 1986-87, fin. planner, 1987—. Mem. Am. Soc. Women Accts., Am. Mgmt. Assn., Nat. Assn. Female Execs., Jaycees, Beta Alpha Psi, Phi Chi Theta.

STORB, URSULA BEATE, molecular genetics and cell biology educator; b. Stuttgart, Germany, July 6, 1936; came to U.S., 1966; d. Walter M. Stemmer and Marianne M. (Kämmerer) Nowara. MD, U. Freiburg, Fed. Republic Germany, 1960. Asst. prof. dept. microbiology U. Wash., Seattle, 1971-75, assoc. prof., 1975-81, prof., 1981-86, head. div. immunology, 1980-86; prof. dept. molecular genetics and cell biology U. Chgo., 1986—. Contbr. articles to profl. publs. NIH, NSF grantee, 1973—. Mem. Am. Women in Science, Am. Assn. Immunology, Am. Soc. Cell Biology. Office: U Chgo 920 E 58th St Chicago IL 60637

STORER, ROSEMARIE, sales executive; b. Salem, N.J., May 5, 1956; d. James William and Eileen Mary Spence; m. Patrick W. Storer, Mar. 19, 1983. BA in Communications, U. Wash., 1982; MBA, Seattle U., 1989. Mktg. rep. Parker Smith & Feek Inc., Seattle, 1983-86; mktg. coordinator Addington Baldwin & McDaniel Inc., Seattle, 1986-87; unit coordinator Sedgwick James of Wash. Inc., Seattle, 1988—. Mem. Nat. Assn. Female Execs., Nat. Inst. Bus. Mgmt., Nat. Assn. Sec. Office: Sedgwick James of Wash 2101 4th Ave Suite 1700 Seattle WA 98121-2344

STOREY, CHOMPUNUT, management consultant; came to U.S., 1972.; d. Amnuay Sumanaseni and Yuwahongsa Kongkeo; m. Robert F. Storey. BA in Polit. Sci., Chulalongkorn U., Bangkok, 1968; MA in Econs., Kent State U., 1970; postgrad., Temple U. Mem. faculty Chulalongkorn U.; internat. bus. negotiator, sr. cons., mktg. mgr. AT&T, Basking Ridge, N.J., 1978-87; economist, mgr. Wharton Sch., U. Pa., Phila., 1984-87, 89—; pres. Datatech Consulting, Media, Pa., 1987—. Author econometrics and math. models for telecommunications industry. Home: 1205 Hunt Club Ln Media PA 19063

STOREY, ISABEL NAGY, writer, television producer; b. Parry Sound, Ont., Can., July 2, 1955; came to U.S., 1961; d. Louis and Denise (Ktorza) N. Diploma in French lang. and lit., Inst. Etrangers, Aix-en-Provence, France, 1976; BA, Calif. State U., Northridge, 1979. Editor Burbank (Calif.) Scene, 1979; reporter Burbank Daily Rev., 1979; mng. editor San Fernando Valley Mag., Studio City, Calif., 1980; writer, producer Sta. KTLA News, L.A., 1980-82, Sta. KCBS News, L.A., 1982-87, Lifetime Med. TV, L.A., 1987-89; writer, producer Channel One Whittle Communications, 1989; segment producer syndicated mag. program Preview TV Program Enterprises, L.A., 1990—. Writer: Stuck in Traffic, Sta. KCET, 1990, The Nat. Driving Test, CBS, 1989, Rescue 911, CBS, 1989-90, The Nat. Emergency Test, ABC, 1990, The 2d Ann. Nat. Driving Test, CBS, 1990. Recipient Best Local TV Feature award Odyssey Inst., cert. appreciation Ctr. Improvement Child Caring, 1982. Mem. Writers Guild Am. (outstanding script award 1987), Acad. TV Arts Scis. (Emmy 1982), Internat. Documentary Assn. Office: Preview TPE 1438 N Gower St Box 56 Bldg 35 Hollywood CA 90028

STOREY, TAMMY JO, small business owner; b. Watertown, N.Y., Mar. 23, 1961; d. Paul John Vandermill and Kaye Francis (Ervay) McCabe; m. Douglas E. Bates, May 17, 1979 (div. 1980); m. Kenneth Alan Storey, Feb. 26, 1982; children: Richard Allen, David Joseph, Tiffany Irene. With quality control dept. Motorola Inc., Ft. Lauderdale, Fla., 1982-84; asst. foreman Times Pub. Co., St. Petersburg, Fla., 1984-86; mgr. Shady Acres, Flint, Mich., 1986-87; owner, operator Heather Hill Estates, Flint, 1987—. Democrat. Presbyterian.

STORSETH, JEANNIE PEARCE, insurance administrator; b. Casa Grande, Ariz., Sept. 24, 1948; d. Johnnie E. and Barbara (Dismukes) Pearce; m. Bryce Hallice Storseth, Aug. 15, 1981; 1 child, Michael Scott. B.S., U. Ariz., 1979. Mktg. rep. Group Health Coop., Seattle, 1981-83; dist. mgr. Health Plus/Blue Cross, Seattle, 1983-84; mktg. dir. Personal Health, Seattle, 1984-85; sales dir. Cigna Health Plan, Seattle, 1985-88; real estate agent John L. Scott Real Estate, Seattle, 1988—. Mem. Wash. Assn. Health Underwriters (v.p.), Am. Coll. Healthcare Mktg., Nat. Assn. Female Execs. Republican. Mem. Christian Ch. Avocations: oil painting; writing. Office: John L Scott Real Estate 15500 First Ave S Ste 100 Seattle WA 98148

STORSTEEN, LINDA LEE, librarian; b. Pasadena, Jan. 26, 1948; d. Oliver Matthew and Susan (Smock) Storsteen. AB cum laude in History, UCLA, 1970, MA in Ancient History, 1972, MLS, 1973. Librarian, L.A. Pub. Library, 1974-79; city librarian Palmdale City Library (Calif.), 1979—. Adv. bd. So. Calif. Inter-Library Loan Network, L.A., 1979-80; commr. So. Calif. Film Circuit, L.A., 1980—; council South State Coop. Library System, 1981—, chmn., 1982-83, 85-86, 87-88, chmn., 1989-90; pres. So. Calif. Film

Circuit, 1985-86; rec. sec. So. Antelope Valley Coordinating Council, Palmdale, 1983-84. Mem. ALA, Calif. Library Assn., Pub. Libraries Exec. Assn. So. Calif., Am. Saddle Horse Assn., Pacific Saddlebred Assn., So. Calif. Saddle Bred Horse Assn. (bd. dirs.), Chinese Shar-Pei Club of Am. Home: PO Box 129 Palmdale CA 93550 Office: Palmdale City Libr 700 E Palmdale Blve Palmdale CA 93550

STORTZ, LISA ANN, communications executive; b. Spencer, Iowa, May 12, 1958; d. Charles R. and Norma G. Stortz. BS in Journalism/Mass Communication, Iowa State U., 1980, BA in Polit. Sci. and Speech, 1980; postgrad., St. Thomas Coll., St. Paul, 1989—. With loan adminstrn. Midwest Fed. Savs. & Loan, Mpls., 1980-81; loan adminstr. Gill Savs. & Loan, Mpls., 1981-82; mktg. technician residential funding Norwest, Mpls., 1982-83, communications coord. residential funding, 1983-85, project mgr. residential funding, 1985-86; rsch. mgr. residential funding Salomon Bros., Mpls., 1987-88; program and communications mgr. residential funding Anchor Savs. Bank, Mpls., 1988-90, program and communications officer residential funding, 1990; asst. v.p. program and communications Gen. Motors Acceptance Corp. Residential Funding, Mpls., 1990—; cons. Design Svcs. and Interiors, Inc., Mpls., 1989-90, Litin Paper, Mpls., 1989-90. Instr. Minn. Literacy Coun., Mpls., 1990. Mem. NAFE, Internat. Assn. Bus. Communicators, Women in Communications, Nat. Assn. Desktop Pub. Office: GMAC Residential Funding Corp 8400 Normandale Lakes Blvd Ste 600 Minneapolis MN 55437

STORTZ, NANETTE ESTHER, communications company professional; b. Newark, July 27, 1944; d. Joseph C. and Kathleen E. (Baker) Shepard; m. Henry T. Stortz, June 27, 1975; children: Karen, Sandra, Kathleen, Cristin, Thomas. AA, Centenary Coll. for Women, 1964; cert., Babson Coll., 1988. Mgr. office systems Am. Bell, Inc., Morristown, N.J., 1983; dist. mgr. AT&T Info. Systems, Morristown, N.J., 1984; dist. mgr.Contract Svcs. Org AT&T Tech. Systems, Bridgewater, N.J., 1987; dist. mgr. AT&T, Bedminster, N.J., 1990. Mem. New Providence Fire Dept. Ladies Aux., 1975-85, AT & T Pioneers, 1987—. Mem. NAFE, Assn. Info. System Profls., Bldg. Ops. Mgmt. Assn. Home: 297 Livingston Ave Murray Hill NJ 07974 Office: AT & T Rte 202/206 N Rm 1A103 Bedminster NJ 07921

STORVICK, CLARA AMANDA, nutrition educator emerita; b. Emmons, Minn., Oct. 31, 1906; d. Ole A. and Elise A. (Opdahl) S. AB, St. Olaf Coll., 1929; MS, Iowa State U., 1933; PhD, Cornell U., 1941. Instr. chemistry Augustana Acad., Canton, S.D., 1930-32; rsch. asst. Iowa State U., Ames, 1932-34; nutritionist Fed. Emergency Relief Adminstrn., Brainerd, Minn., 1934-36; asst. prof. nutrition Okla. State U., Stillwater, 1936-38; rsch. asst. Cornell U., Ithaca, N.Y., 1938-41; asst. prof. nutrition U. Wash., Seattle, 1941-45; assoc. prof. nutrition to prof. Oreg. State U., Corvallis, 1945-72, prof. nutrition and head home econ. rsch., 1955-72, dir. nutrition rsch. inst., 1965-72; ret., 1972. Contbr. over 70 articles to profl. jours. Recipient Borden award Am. Home Econs. Assn., 1952, Disting. Alumni award St. Olaf Coll., 1955, Alumni Achievement award Iowa State U., Ames, 1955. Fellow AAAS, Am. Pub. Health Assn.; mem. Am. Inst. Nutrition, N.Y. Acad. of Scis., Am. Chem. Soc., Phi Kappa Phi, Sigma Xi, Iota Sigma Pi (nat. pres.), Omicron Nu. Republican. Lutheran. Home: 124 NW 29th St Corvallis OR 97330

STORY, ANNE WINTHROP, psychologist, engineer; b. Havenhill, Mass., Jan. 12, 1914; d. John Wintrop and Anna Louise (Fennelly) S. Diplôme supérieure, Sorbonne, Paris, 1933; AB, Smith Coll., Northampton, Mass., 1934; PhD, U. Calif., Berkeley, 1957. Registered profl. engr., Mass.; lic. psychologist, Mass. Rsch. psychologist USAF Flight Safety, San Bernardino, Calif., 1950; isntr. Pa. State U., 1947-50; assoc. prof. U. Mass., Boston, 1972-74; engring. psychologist USAF, Bedford, Mass., 1958-66, NASA, Cambridge, Mass., 1966-70, U.S. Dept. Transp., Cambridge, 1970-77; pvt. practice cons. Inventor, patentee flight safety devices.

STORY, MONA DEE, artist; b. Woodward, Okla., Dec. 9, 1945; d. Garnett Leroy and Georgia Thurlene (Trego) Frye; m. Keith Leon Story; children: Tray Lee, Stacy Leigh. Grad. high sch.; student, Southwestern Okla. State U., Weatherford, 1964-66, 70-71. Free-lance artist, instr. in field Sharon, Okla., 1974—; owner Country Woodworks, Sharon, 1980—; mgr., buyer Trego's Westwear & Gifts, Woodward, Okla., 1987—; ladies clothing designer Trego's Westwear, Inc. Mfg., 1987—. One woman exhibits in mus., galleries and banks, 1977-86. Mem. Plains Indians and Pioneers Hist. Found., Woodward, 1977—, bd. dirs. 1978-82; co-chmn. Paul Laune Meml. High Sch. Western Art Competition, Woodward, 1979—; co-chmn. Woodward Spring Arts Festival, 1986. Numerous awards art competitions, 1974-86. Mem. Woodward Artisans League (sec., reporter 1976, v.p. 1977, pres. 1978-80), Enid Art Assn. Democrat. Mem. Christian Ch. (Disciples of Christ). Home and Studio: Rt 1 Box 290 Sharon OK 73857

STOTLAR, CYNTHIA B., human resources professional; b. Atlanta, Aug. 23, 1953; d. Jesse Lee and Elizabeth Evelyn (Daniell) Byrd; m. David Stotlar, Feb. 5, 1983; children: Eric David, Jason William. BS, Middle Tenn. State U., 1975; MEd, Cen. Mich. U., 1982; student, St. Thomas Sch. Med.Technology, 1975. Asst. dir. pathology St. Thomas Hosp., Nashville; asst. dir. orgnl. devel. St. Paul Med. Ctr., Dallas; assoc. dir. human resources Michael Reese Health Plan, Chgo. Chair social ministries Meth. Ch., Riverwoods, Ill. Mem. Am. Mgmt. Assn., Am. Soc. Tng. and Devel., Orgn. Devel. Network. Home: 1175 Studio Ln Riverwoods IL 60015

STOTLER, ALICEMARIE H., federal judge; b. Alhambra, Calif., May 29, 1942; d. James R. and Loretta M. Huber; m. James A. Stotler, Sept. 11, 1971. BA, U. So. Calif., 1964, JD, 1967. Bar: Calif. 1967, U.S. Dist. Ct. (no. dist.) Calif. 1967, U.S. Dist. Ct. (cen. dist.) Calif. 1973, U.S. Supreme Ct. 1976. Dep. Orange County Dist. Atty.'s Office, 1967-73; mem. Stotler & Stotler, Santa Ana, Calif., 1973-76, 83-84; judge Orange County Mcpl. Ct., 1976-78, Orange County Superior Ct., 1978-83, U.S. Dist. Ct. (cen. dist.) Calif., L.A., 1984—. Active numerous civic orgns.; mem. exec. com. 9th Cir. Jud. Conf., 1989-90. Mem. ABA (jud. adminstrn. div., litigation sect.), Am. Law Inst., Fed. Judges Assn. (bd. dirs. 1988—), 9th Cir. Judges Assn. (9th cir. jud. conf. exec. com. 1989-90), Nat. Assn. Women Judges, Orange County Bar Assn. (mem. numerous coms., Franklin G. West award, 1984, Judge of Yr., 1978), Calif. Judges Assn. (mem. numerous coms.), Orange County Trial Lawyers Assn. (bd. dirs. 1975). Office: US Dist Ct 751 W Santa Ana Blvd PO Box 12339 Santa Ana CA 92701

STOTLER, PATRICIA S., interior designer; b. Mt. Pleasant Mills, Pa., Sept. 28, 1941; d. Lester Melvin and Sarah Louise (Schaffer) Sierer. BS, West Chester (Pa.) Coll., 1963; MS, Syracuse U., 1968. Ptnr. Stotler, Smithem, Loebe Design Group, Inc., West Palm Beach, Fla.; pres. Pat Stotler Interiors, Inc., Palm Beach Gardens, Fla. Trustee Fla. Repertory Theatre; bd. dirs. Nelle Smith Residence for Girls. Home: 105 Waterview Dr Palm Beach Gardens FL 33418

STOTT, BARBARA PAXTON, volunteer; b. Greenville, Miss., July 30, 1925; d. Lawrence Lipscomb Paxton and Elizabeth Lloyd; widowed; children: Sheila Stott Gourlay, Pamela Stott Kendall, Barbara Stott McCoy. Student, Gulf Park Coll., 1943. Appeared in TV Spl. "A Day in the Life of America." Mem. Am. Women's Club, London, 1977-78, Am. Women's Assn., Singapore, 1983-85, Am. Women's Club Bermuda, 1982-83. Mem. DAR, Colonial Dames, Magna Charta Dames, Delta Debutante Club (bd. dirs.). Republican. Episcopalian. Home: Osceola Plantation Rte 1 Box 351 Leland MS 38756

STOTTER, RUTH, college program director; b. Madison, Wis., July 26, 1936; d. Louis Marvin and Jeanne (Michael) Rapoport; m. Lawrence Henry Stotter, June 30, 1957; children: Daniel, Jennifer, Steven. BA, Ohio State U., 1958; MA, Stanford U., 1959; teaching cert., U. Calif., Berkeley, 1961; MA, Sonoma State U., 1984. Lifetime instr. credential (anthropology) Calif. Community Coll., lifetime teaching credentials (K-14) Calif. Bd. Edn. Free-lance storyteller and workshop leader, 1974—; storyteller Bookseller's Cafe, Kentfield, Calif., 1979-83; resident storyteller Renaissance Pleasure Faire, Novato, Calif., 1979-83, 85; instr. Sonoma State U., Rohnert Park, Calif., 1980, 89-90; producer, host radio program KUSF-FM, San Francisco, 1982-88; instr. Dominican Coll. Acad. for Profl. Devel., San Rafael, Calif., 1984-86, dir., tchr. cert.-in-storytelling program, 1986—; apptd. cons. Puppeteers of Am., 1989; rev. com. Nat. Assn. for the Preservation and Perpetuation of Storytelling; performing artist Youth-in-Arts, San Rafael, 1989-90; featured performer Mariposa (Calif.) Festival, 1990. Author: (book) Little Acorns, 1976, (calendar) The Storyteller's Calendar, 1988, 89, 91; contbr. to books Family Storytelling Handbook, 1987, Joining In, 1988; producer, narrator (audio cassettes) Tales From California History, 1989. Recipient Performance grant Alaska Arts Coun., Anchorage, 1980). Mem. Am. Folklore Soc. (panelist annual meetings, 1985, 87), Calif. Folklore Soc. (panelist annual meetings, 1980, 86, 90). Home: 2244 Vistazo East Tiburon CA 94920

STOTZ, NATALIE HAMER, underwriter; b. Gt. Falls, Mont., Oct. 22, 1921; d. Arthur C. Hamer and Gertrude H. (Kaufmann) Wallace; m. Theodore Philip Stotz, June 9, 1956. Student Great Falls Comml. Coll., 1939. C.L.U. Br. office cashier Occidental Life Ins. Co., Great Falls, 1939-44; sec. to underwriter, San Francisco, 1944-47; head claims dept. Friedman & Co., San Francisco, 1947-62; adminstrv. asst. to underwriter, San Jose, Calif., 1962—. Mem. Am. Soc. C.L.U.s. Sec.-treas. West Bay Opera Guild, Palo Alto, Calif., 1965-67. Republican. Christian Scientist. Avocation: ballet. Home: 988 N California Ave Palo Alto CA 94303 Office: 25 Metro Dr Ste 228 San Jose CA 95110

STOUDT, MARILYN ANN, educator; b. Allentown, Pa., Oct. 21, 1934; d. Ramsey Elmer and Edith Lovie (Prechtel) S. BS, East Stroudsburg State U., 1956, MPE, 1970. Tchr. Wellsboro (Pa.)-Charleston Sch. Dist., 1956-60, Allentown (Pa.) Sch. Dist., 1960—; coach cheerleading squad, Allentown Sch. Dist., 1956-76, coach girls basketball, 1960-76. Mem. NEA, Pa. State Edn. Assn., Allentown Edn. Assn., Women's Internat. Bowling Assn. Home: 13th and Fairmont Sts D-5 Whitehall PA 18052 Office: Harrison Morton Middle Sch 2nd and Turner Sts Allentown PA 18102

STOUFFER, NANCY KATHLEEN, publishing company executive; b. Hershey, Pa., Feb. 14, 1951; d. William Lawrence Sweeny O'Brian and Edna Luttrell; m. David Joel Stouffer, July 19, 1980; children: Jennifer Belle, Vance David. Pres. Andé Pub. Co., Inc., Camp Hill, Pa., 1985-88; pres., chmn. B.C.I., Camp Hill, Pa., 1988-90; v.p. R&D E.S.P. Inc., N.Y.C., 1989—; co-owner of Hons, Inc., Camp Hill, Pa. Contbr. articles on dyslexia and learning disabilities to popular mags.; author children's books. Exec. researcher com. on advanced studies in learning disabilities Med. and Ednl. Profl., SPECTRA, devel. of the EZ read program. Republican. Office: 3400 Trindle Rd Camp Hill PA 17011 Also: ESP Inc & SYN-Comm Group Penthouse 160 E 56th New York NY 10022

STOUT, GAIL BIELBY, publishing company executive; b. Hale, Mich., Dec. 29, 1946; d. Stanley Roy and Virginia (Bell) Bielby; m. David M. Stout, June 21, 1969; children: Courtney Ellen, Marianne Sevilla. BA, Coll. of Wooster, 1969; postgrad., U. Rochester, 1971. Tchr. English East Irondequist Sch., Rochester, N.Y., 1969-71; bus. mgr., editor, assoc. pub. Lake Pub. Corp., Libertyville, Ill., 1989—. Mem. Internat. Soc. for Hybrid Mircoelectronic (program chair 1988-89, edn. chair 1989-90). Democrat. Home: 25780 N St Marys Rd Libertyville IL 60048 Office: Lake Pub Corp 17730 W Peterson Libertyville IL 60048

STOUT, JUANITA KIDD, judge; b. Wewoka, Okla., Mar. 7, 1919; d. Henry Maynard and Mary Alice (Chandler) Kidd; m. Charles Otis Stout, June 23, 1942. BA, U. Iowa, 1939; JD, Ind. U., 1948, LLM, 1954; LLD (hon.), Ursinus Coll., 1965, Ind. U., 1966, Lebanon Valley Coll., 1969, Drexel U., 1972, Rockford (Ill.) Coll., 1974, U. Md., 1980, Roger Williams Coll., 1984, Morgan State U., 1985, Russell Sage Coll., 1966. Bar: D.C. 1950, Pa. 1954. Tchr. pub. schs. Seminole and Sand Springs, Okla., 1939-42; tchr. Fla. A&M U., Tallahassee, 1949, Tex. So. U., Houston, 1949; adminstrv. asst. to judge U.S. Ct. Appeals (3d cir.), Phila., 1950-54; pvt. practice law Turner & Stout, Phila., 1954-55; chief of appeals Dist. Atty.'s Office City of Phila., 1955-59, judge mcpl. ct., 1959-69; judge Ct. Common Pleas, Phila., 1969-88, sr. judge, 1989—; justice Supreme Ct. Pa., Phila., 1988-89. Recipient Jane Addams medal Rockford Coll., 1966, Disting. Svc. award U. Iowa, 1974; named to Hall of Fame of Okla., Okla. Heritage Soc., 1981. Mem. ABA, Pa. Bar Assn., Phila. Bar Assn., Nat. Assn. Women Judges, Nat. Assn. Women Lawyers. Democrat. Episcopalian. Home: 1919 Chestnut St Apt 2805 Philadelphia PA 19103

STOUT, KAREN LEE, supermarket executive; b. Charlotte, N.C., Mar. 30, 1959; d. Bill Edward and Catherine (Freeman) S. BA in Biology and Bus., U. N.C., Charlotte, 1982; postgrad., U. N.C., 1985; MBA, Queens Coll., 1987. Office asst. Harris Teeter Supermarkets, Charlotte, 1978-82, mgmt. trainee, 1982, store mgr., 1982-83, mgr. floral ops., 1984-87, mgr. produce, floral, 1988, dir. produce/floral, 1989, dir of perishables, 1989—. Fundraiser Pub. Sta. WTVI-TV, 1987. Named one of Outstanding Young Women Am., 1981. Mem. NAFE, Am. Mgmt. Assn., Produce Mktg. Assn. (dir. floral div. 1985-87, dir. 1987-90). Republican. Baptist. Home: 10223 Calloway Dr Charlotte NC 28277 Office: Harris Teeter Supermarkets 741 Crestdale Dr Matthews NC 28105

STOUT, LINDA ELAINE, marketing executive; b. Flint, Mich., Nov. 8, 1951; d. Ernest Junior and Donna Louise (Day) S. BA in Business with honors, Mich. State U., 1973; MBA, Ga. State U., 1978. Rsch. asst. Bank South, Atlanta, 1973-75; customer account auditor Norfolk So. Ry., Atlanta, 1975-77, sr. customer account auditor, 1977-81; mgr. Equifax Credit Bur. Inc., Atlanta, 1981-82, mktg. analyst, 1982-85, account exec., 1985-88, product devel. mgr., 1988-90; bus. cons. Atlanta, 1990—. Loaned exec. United Way, Atlanta, 1982. Mem. Am. Mktg. Assn. (Atlanta chpt. arrangements asst. v.p. 1985-86, treas. 1986-87, asst. v.p. mem. devel. 1988-89, sec. 1989-90, v.p. fin. 1990-91), Direct Mktg. Assn., Alpha Xi Delta. Home: 5512 Kingsport Dr Atlanta GA 30342 Office: Equifax Market Decision Sys Two Ravinia Dr Ste 500 Atlanta GA 30346

STOUT, MARGUERITE ANNETTE, physiology educator; b. Marion, N.C.; d. John Robert and Dorothy (Parsons) S. BS in Psychology, U. Wis., Madison, 1964; PhD in Physiology, Biophysics, U. Iowa, 1974; MBA in Mktg. Mgmt., Pace U., 1986. Rsch. scientist Galesburg (Ill.) State Rsch. Hosp., 1965-70; postdoctoral fellow U. Iowa, Iowa City, 1974-75; asst. prof. Univ. Medicine-Dentistry N.J. Med. Sch., Newark, 1975-82, assoc. prof. physiology, 1982—; vis. scientist Katholieke U. Leuven, Belgium, 1990-91; sci. cons. to pharm. industr. Contbr. rsch. papers to sci. publs., chpts. to books. NIH fellow, 1970-74, 74-75, Fogarty Sr. Internat. fellow, 1990-91. Office: Dept Physiology UMD-NJ Med Sch 185 S Orange Ave Newark NJ 07103-2714

STOUT, PATRICIA JOAN, educational specialist, counselor; b. Neptune, N.J., May 26, 1932; d. John Francis O'Keefe and Lillian Veronica (Olsen) Murray; m. Robert Paul Stout; children: Michael, Robin (dec.), Wendy Matson. BA in Edn., Kean Coll., 1974, MA in Guidance, 1978; EdS, Rutgers U., 1987. Tchr. English Holy Cross Sch., Rumson, N.J., 1962-64, St. James Sch., Red Bank, N.J., 1965-73; tchr. English Fair Haven (N.J.) Pub. Schs., 1974-84, guidance counselor, 1985—. Author poetry. Mem. Statewide Community Orgn. Project, Fair Haven, 1984, After-Sch. Program for Children, Fair Haven, 1985. Mem. Nat. Bd. Cert. Counselors, Nat. Mental Health Assn., NEA, Monmouth County Edn. Assn., Monmouth Ocean Guidance Counselors Assn., NAFE, Monmouth County Elem. Sch. Guidance Consortium. Democrat. Roman Catholic. Home: 162 Pinckney Rd Little Silver NJ 07739 Office: Fair Haven Bd Edn Hance Rd Fair Haven NJ 07704

STOUT, VIRGINIA FALK, chemist; b. Buffalo, Jan. 5, 1932; d. Stanley Geismer and Hannah (Brock) Falk; m. George Hubert Stout, June ll, 1955 (div. Dec. 1973); 1 child, Peter David; m. P. William Sieverling, Apr. 2, 1977; stepchildren: Eric David and Lisa Marie. BA, Cornell U., 1953; MA, Radcliffe Coll., 1955; PhD, U. Wash., Seattle, 1961; postgrad., Antioch U., 1987-90. Rsch. chemist US Dept. Interior, Bur. Comml. Fisheries, Seattle, 1961-70, US Dept. Commerce, Nat. Marine Fisheries Svc., Seattle, 1970—; assoc. prof., affiliate faculty U. Wash., Coll. Fisheries, Seattle, 1972-84; adv. com. Seattle Cen. Community Coll., 1975-86. Contbr. articles to profl. jours., chpts. in books in field; patentee in field. Vol. U. Adult Day Ctr. (pres. 1979-81), Seattle. Mem. Am. Chemical Soc., Puget Sound sect. (alt. 1979-82, nominating com. 1970, 1978, chmn. elect 1983, chmn. 1984, past chmn. 1985), Assn. Women in Sci.(Seattle chpt. mem. co-chmn. 1986-87), Pacific Fisheries Techs., Puget Sound Water Quality Authority. Democrat. Jewish. Home: 2822 10th E Seattle WA 98102

STOUT-PIERCE, SUSAN, radiologic technologist; b. Denver, June 6, 1954; d. Joseph Edward and Esther Mae (Miller) Hull; m. Jerry Lee Stout, Nov. 3, 1979 (div. Aug. 1984); m. Gary Myron Pierce, Nov. 21, 1987. AS, Denver Community Coll., 1975; BS, Met. State Coll., 1986. Cert. Radiologic Technologist, Calif., Am. Registry Radiologic Technologists. Radiologic technologist The Swedish Med. Ctr., Englewood, Colo., 1975-79, The Minor Emergency Clinic, Lakewood, Colo., 1979-80, The Children's Hosp., Denver, 1980-86, Merit Peralta Med. Ctr., Oakland, Calif., 1986-87, Am. Shared Hosp. Svcs., Oakland, 1987, HCA South Austin (Tex.) Med. Ctr., 1987-88, U. Calif., San Francisco, 1988-89; applications specialist OEC-Diasonics, Salt Lake City, 1989—. Active NOW. Mem. NAFE, Am. Soc. Radiologic Technologists. Home: 4220 D S Mobile Circle Aurora CO 80013

STOVALL, SHERYL ANN, computer technologist, consultant; b. Indpls., May 10, 1951; d. Clyde Albert and Mary Jane (Overman) Tindal; m. Roscoe Edward Stovall, Jan. 15, 1983; 1 child, Kristen Blair. BS in Bus. Edn., U. Indpls., 1974, MBA in Bus. Mgmt., 1986; MS in Counseling, Butler U., 1976. Dir. fin. aid, admissions counselor U. Indpls., 1974-77; mktg. specialist 1st Nat. Bank Brooksville, Fla., 1978-79; dir. scholarships and grants State of Ind., Indpls., 1980-83, sr. systems analyst info. svcs. div., 1983-84, systems analyst supr. info. svcs. div., 1984-86, sr. mgr. dept. adminstrn., 1986-89; dir. info. svcs. Employment and Tng. Svcs. State of Ind., Indpls., 1989—; instr. Pasco-Hernando Community Coll., Fla., 1978-79; guidance counselor Brooksville Jr. High Sch., 1978-79. Sec., bd. dirs. Southside Art League; bd. dirs. Indpls. Symphony Jr. Group, chmn. childrens concerts. Mem. Lawyers Aux. (past sec., bd. dirs.). Home: 886 Sleepy Hollow Pl Greenwood IN 46142

STOVER, ELLEN SIMON, health scientist, psychologist; b. Bklyn., Nov. 21, 1950; d. Ralph and Charlotte (Tulchin) Simon; m. Alan B. Stover, June 3, 1973; children: Elena Randall Simon, Randall Alan Simon, Samantha Anne Simon. BA with honors, U. Wis., 1972; PhD, Catholic U., 1978. Cons. NIMH, Rockville, Md., 1972-74, spl. asst. to assoc. dir. extramural programs, 1976-77, chief, small grants program, 1977-79, asst., acting & chief rsch. resources br., 1980-85, dep. dir., div. basic scis., 1985-88, dir., office of AIDS programs, 1988—; exec. sec., drug abuse rsch. rev. com. Nat. Inst. on Drug Abuse, Rockville, 1974-76; ex-officio mem. AIDS Adv. Com., Atlanta, 1989—. Recipient Superior Svc. award Pub. Health Svc., 1987. Mem. Am. Psychol. Assn. Office: NIMH 5600 Fishers Ln 17C-06 Rockville MD 20857

STOVER-POCK, ROBIN JO, lawyer; b. Hillsdale, Mich., Oct. 30, 1955; d. George F. Stover and Cornelia R. (Schmiege) Moore; m. William A. Pock, Oct. 30, 1984. BA, DePauw U., 1978; JD, Ind. U., Indpls., 1984. Bar: Ind. 1984, U.S. Dist. Ct. (no. and so. dists.) Ind. 1984. Pvt. practice Zionsville, Ind., 1984-88, 89—; assoc. McGinn, Webb & Warner, Attys., Peachtree City, Ga., 1988-89. Artist in oil painting, print-making. Mem. MADD, NOW, Greenpeace, Orgn. For Handgun Control, Ind. Bar Assn., ABA. Home and Office: 670 S St Rd 421 Zionsville IN 46077

STOWE, SUZANNE MARIE, company executive; b. Seattle, Wash., Aug. 16, 1952; d. Herbert Walter and Yvonne Marie (Henninger) S. BA, Calif. State U., Fullerton, 1985. Nurse aide Park Lido Superior Hosp., Newport Beach, Calif., 1971-73; service sec. Am. Optical, Newport Beach, Calif., 1975-78; sec. Gen. Crude O, Mobile Oil, Newport Beach, Calif., 1978-79; from program sec. to mgr. resources Am. Assn. Critical-Care Nurses, Newport Beach, Calif., mgr. mem. and chpts., 1989. Hot line counselor Ctr. for Creative Alternatives, Costa Mesa, 1972-74. Mem. Am. Soc. Assn. Execs., Women in Mgmt., Humane Soc. of U.S., Doris Day Animal League. Republican. Presbyterian. Office: Am Assn Critical-Care Nurses 1 Civic Pla Newport Beach CA 92660

STOWELL, DEANNA MARION, manufacturing company executive; b. Morrisville, Vt., Jan. 26, 1938; d. Urban Christopher and Marion (Anderson) Wakefield; m. Norman Leonard Stowell, Nov. 26, 1956; children: Jeffrey, Kimberly, Brian, Scott, Cynthia, Gregory, Patricia. Student, Lyndon Inst., 1955, U. Vt., 1955-56, Keene State Coll., 1976. Sales rep. Sta. WTSV-WECM, Claremont, N.H., 1977-78, sales mgr., 1978-79, sta. mgr., 1979-81; bookkeeper Homestead Cabinet Co. Inc., Newport, N.H., 1981-82; v.p., comptroller, co-owner Crown Point Mfg. Corp., Claremont, 1982—. Bd. dirs. United Way, Claremont, 1987. Republican. Methodist. Home: 64 Charlestown Rd Claremont NH 03743 Office: Crown Point Mfg Corp 153 Charleston Rd Box 1560 Claremont NH 03743

STOWES, PATRICIA ANNE, minister; b. Alexander City, Ala., Aug. 21, 1948; d. Ned and Thelma Odell (Glenn) S. Student, Tenn. State U., 1965-66, Ky. State U., 1966-67, Sarah Thomas Sch. Beauty, Louisville, 1968-69. Lic. cosmetologist, Ala., Ky. Cosmetologist Exclusive Beauty Salon, Louisville, 1968-82, Deeper Life Beauty Salon, Alexander City, 1984-88; minister Calvary Cathedral Ch., Louisville, 1988—. Mem. NAFE. Home: 2435 W Broadway #1 Louisville KY 40211

STOYKOVICH, CHRISTINE ANNE, psychologist; b. North Conway, N.H., Sept. 25, 1949; d. Voyin Petar and Aimee Hess (Rehr) S.; m. David B. VanDongen, Apr. 22, 1989; div. BA, Smith Coll., Northampton, Mass., 1972; MS, U. Wis., Milw., 1975; PhD, Vanderbilt U., Nashville, 1985. Rsch. asst. Peabody Coll., Vanderbilt U., Nashville, 1982-83; lectr. Vanderbilt U., Nashville, 1983-84; project coord. Brockton (Mass.) VA Med. Ctr., 1984-86, alcoholism rehab. technician, 1986-87; lectr. U. R.I. Coll. Continuing Edn., Providence, 1986; aswt. prof. R.I. Coll., Providence, 1986-87; sr. sensory assoc. Warner-Lambert, Morris Plains, N.J., 1987—. Mem. Am Psychol. Assn., ASTM, Inst. Food Technologist, Eastern Psychol. Assn., Sigma Xi.

STRABEL, HEIDI ANN, human resources executive, director; b. Detroit, July 14, 1963; d. John Harbison and Julie Ann (Van Loon) S. BA, Mich. State U., 1986. Dir. human resources Continental Mktg. Corp., Dearborn, Mich., 1986-88; corp. dir. human resources ATEC Assocs., Inc., Indpls., 1988-89; human resources mgr. Geo Engrs., Inc., Bellevue, Wash., 1989—. Mem. Am. Soc. Personnel Adminstrs. Home: 4323 Lake Washington Blvd NE #5203 Kirkland WA 98033

STRACHER, DOROTHY ALTMAN, education educator, consultant; b. N.Y.C., May 11, 1934; d. Joseph and Gussie (Newman) Altman; m. Alfred Stracher, July 4, 1954; children: Cameron Altman, Adam Reed, Erica Terri. BA, Bklyn. Coll., 1955; MA, Columbia U., 1957; postgrad., U. Copenhagen, 1958-59; acad. vis., Oxford (Eng.) U., 1973-74; PhD, Hofstra U., 1979. Cert. English and social sci. tchr., N.Y. Coordinator secondary reading Cen. Moriches (N.Y.) Sch. Dist., 1974-78; coordinator reading Ea. Williston (N.Y.) Sch. Dist., 1978-79; specialist reading and writing SUNY, Old Westbury, 1979-81; adj. prof. dept. reading Hofstra U., Hempstead, N.Y., 1979-82; asst. prof. edn. L.I. U., Bklyn., 1982-83, Coll. New Rochelle, N.Y., 1983-85; sr. learning diagnostic specialist child devel. div. L.I. Jewish Hosp., Bklyn., 1985-86; assoc. prof., dir. program for learning disabled coll. students Dowling Coll., Oakdale, N.Y., 1986—; cons. Johnson & Johnson, Inc., Princeton, N.J., 1982—, Sanford (Fla.) Sch. Dist., 1983, Lawrence (N.Y.) Sch. Dist., 1984, Sch. Dist. 7, N.Y.C., 1984—. Author: (with others) First the Fundamentals, 1980, What Do You Call a Well-Behaved Martian? A Manual For Thinkers' Parents, 1981, Integrating Assessment, 1982; editor: Differentiated Curricula, 1986, A Literature Based Integrated Curriculum: Grades Pre-K—, 1989; contbr. articles to profl. jours. Bd. dirs. Roslyn (N.Y.) Sch. Dist., 1975-84, v.p., 1980-82, pres., 1982-84; mem. adv. bd. Children's Sch. Sci., Woods Hole, Mass., 1976-82. Mem. Reading Forum Found., Orton Soc., Internat. Reading Assn., Nat. Assn. for Gifted Edn., League Women Voters (bd. dirs. 1961-70), NOW, Kappa Delta Pi. Home: 47 The Oaks Roslyn NY 11576

STRADA, CHRISTINA BRYSON, English language educator, library director; b. Dunoon, Argyll, Scotland, July 6, 1925; came to U.S., 1927; d. Alexander Paul and Margaret (Spencer) Bryson; m. Joseph Anthony Strada, Nov. 13, 1943; children: Michael, David, Elaine, Mary Margaret. AB, SUNY, Fredonia, 1968, MS, 1970; MLS, U. Buffalo, 1973. Library media specialist. Tchr. English Dunkirk (N.Y.) High Sch., 1969-70, Cardinal Mindzenty High Sch., Dunkirk, 1970-71; tchr. English Lake Shore Cen.

High Sch., Angola, N.Y., 1971-72, librarian, tchr., 1973-77; library dir. Darwin R. Barker Library and Mus., Fredonia, 1977-86, now vol. coordinator, cons.; instr. English composition, English lit., libr. rsch. Empire State Coll. N.Y., State Univ. Coll., Fredonia; cons. Friends of Barker Library and Mus., 1986—. Author short stories. Organizer Fredonia Hist. Preservation Soc., 1986—. Mem. N.Y. state Library Assn., N.Y. State Tchr. Assn., AAUW (chmn. telephone and reservations com. 1969—), LWV, Fredonia Shakespeare Club (v.p. 1988-89), Zonta Internat. (corr. sec., membership chmn. 1981-82). Democrat. Roman Catholic. Home: 15 Carol Ave Fredonia NY 14063

STRADER, ANN WALLACE, lawyer; b. Huntington, W.Va., Mar. 25, 1940; d. Robert Edwin and Hazel Virginia (Paul) Wallace; m. James David Strader, Feb. 8, 1964; children: James Jacob, Robert Benjamin. BS, W.Va. U., 1962; JD, U. Pitts., 1983. Bar: Pa. 1983, U.S. Dist. Ct. (we. dist.) Pa. 1983. Asst. v.p. 84 Lumber Co., Pa., 1983-84; pvt. practice Pitts., 1984—. Trustee Pressley Ridge Schs., Pitts., 1979—; committeewoman Allegheny County Dem. Com., 1988—; chmn. Mount Lebanon Community Rels. Bd., 1985-89, chmn., 1987-89; bd. dirs. Wesley Inst., 1989—; mem. Pa. Dem. Com., 1990—. Mem. ABA, Pa. Bar Assn., Allegheny County Bar Assn., Women's Bar Assn. of W.Pa. (charter mem. 1989—), Jr. League Pitts. Home and Office: 586 Audubon Ave Pittsburgh PA 15228

STRADER, JACQUELINE W., small business owner; b. Cin., Mar. 15, 1946; d. John Jacob and Joan (Ganne) S.; m. Don Michael Darragh, Sept. 17, 1965 (div. June 1979); children: Sean Marshall, John Cassilly. Lic. real estate agt. Owner, operator Premier Products dba The Brick House, Warm Springs, Ga., 1985—. Mem. Warm Springs Mchts. Assn. (v.p.), Meriwether County C. of C., Pilot Club Internat. Home: 30 Buck Smith Rd Hogansville GA 30230 Office: Premier Products Main St Warm Springs GA 30230 also: 3063 Hwy 34 Newnan GA 30265

STRAHAN, JULIA CELESTINE, electronics company executive; b. Indpls., Feb. 10, 1938; d. Edgar Paul Pauley and Pauline Barbara (Myers) Shawver; m. Norman Strahan, Oct. 2, 1962 (div. 1982); children: Daniel Keven, Natalie Kay. Grad. high sch., Indpls. With EG&G/Energy Measurements, Inc., Las Vegas, Nev., 1967—; sect. head EG&G Co., 1979-83, mgr. electronics dept., 1984—. Recipient award Am. Legion, 1952, Excellence award, 1986. Mem. NAFE, Am. Nuclear Soc., Internat. Platform Assn. Home: 5222 Stacey Ave Las Vegas NV 89108 Office: EG&G PO Box 1912 Las Vegas NV 89125

STRAHINE, PAMELA KAY, mathematics educator; b. Cleve., Aug. 12, 1957; d. Gaines Eugene and Mary Larue (Gooch) Norman. BS, Ohio State U., 1979, MA, 1981; postgrad., Mich. State U., 1989—. Cert. secondary tchr., Ohio. Tchr. Upper Arlington City Schs., Columbus, Ohio, 1981-83; instr. Franklin U., Columbus, 1987; asst. prof. mathematics Columbus State Community Coll., 1983—; cons. in field. Bd. dirs. Kid's N Kamp, Columbus, 1986-88. Mem. Nat. Coun. Tchrs. Mathematics. Home: 1351 Alstott Howell MI 48843 Office: Columbus State Comm College Columbus OH 43216

STRAHL-BOLSTORFF, DONNA MYRTLE, child care services educator; b. LeCenter, Minn., Apr. 22, 1940; d. Arthur John and Myrtle Gertrude (Overlee) Strahl; m. Aaron David Bolstorff, Sept. 9, 1961; children: Peter Aaron, Gretchan Elise, Anthony David. BS, U. Minn., 1963; MS, Mankato State U., 1986, specialist, 1989. Cert. tchr. Minn., Iowa. Owner, operator A Child's World, Forest City, 1975-81; chair edn. dept. Waldorf Coll., Forest City, Iowa, 1981-86; intern Waseca (Minn.) Community Edn., 1987-88; mem. home and family faculty U. Minn., Waseca, 1988—; project asst. Mktg./Resource Ctr., Rosemount-Apple Valley Community Edn., 1988; after-sch. tchr. Bloomington (Minn.) Community Edn., 1988; adv. bd. South Cen. Plus Child Care Resource Referrral, Mankato, 1988—; co-dir. Early Childhood Coun., Waseca, 1988—; seminar faculty Albert Lea (Minn.) Tech. Coll., 1989—; cons. Cummins Engine Co., Fleetguard Family Ctr., Lake Mills, Iowa, 1985-86. Cons. Waseca Parent Communication Network, 1987—; aqua instr. Waseca Community Edn., 1986; mem. Nat Rainbow Coalition, 1989; advisor African-Am. Club, Waldorf Coll., 1984. Grantee Evang. Luth. Ch., 1983, Minn. Dept. Human Svcs., 1989, U.S. Dept. Edn., 1989. Mem. Nat. Community Edn. Assn., Minn. Community Edn. Assn., NAFE, Nat. Assn. Edn. of Young Children, Assn. Childhood Edn. Internat., Women in Higher Edn. Home: 305 East Park Forest City IA 50436 also: 415 Western Ave #51 Faribault MN Office: U Minn 1000 University Dr SW Waseca MN 56093

STRAHLE, JULIA ANN, finance company executive; b. Kansas City, Mo., Nov. 8, 1946; d. Richard Henry and Ellen Catherine (Spinner) S.; m. Anthony R. DeFranco, Mar. 21, 1980 (div. Dec. 1986); m. Glin Tatum, Oct. 2, 1987. Student, Southwest Mo. State U., 1963-66, St. John's U., 1985. Lic. real estate agt., N.Y. V.p., registered prin. Equitec Fin. Group, San Francisco, 1974-75; sect. head Weeden & Co., N.Y.C., 1969 74, 76-78; pvt. practice cons. N.Y.C., 1978-84; pres. Securities Ops. Specialists, Staten Island, N.Y., 1984—; co-owner Glin-Glass & Mirror, Inc., Staten Island, N.Y., 1987—. Southwest Mo. State U. scholar, 1963. Mem. Am. Women Entrepreneurs, Nat. Assn. Female Execs.

STRAIN, GLADYS WITT, nutritionist, professor of medicine; b. Plymouth, Mich., Apr. 19, 1934; d. Elmer Milton and Iris Erleen (Palmer) Witt; m. James Joseph Strain, Sept. 3, 1956; children: Jay James, Jeffrey Witt, James Palmer. BS, Mich. State U., 1955; MS, Case Western Res. U., 1960, PhD, 1964. Diplomate Am. Bd. Nutrition. Dietetic intern Bronx VA, 1955-56; staff dietitian Harvard U., Cambridge, Mass., 1956-57; nutritionist Cleve. Welfare Fedn., 1958; pub. health trainee Case Western Res. U., Cleve., 1959-60; lectr. nutrition program Tchr.'s Coll. Columbia U., N.Y.C., 1974-75; nutrition cons. dept. medicine St. Luke's/Roosevelt Hosp. Ctr., 1975-85, rsch. assoc., 1985—; rsch. nutritionist clin. rsch. ctr. Montefiore Hosp. and Med. Ctr., 1977-81, rsch. assoc. oncology, 1980-81, rsch. nutritionist dept. medicine Beth Israel Med. Ctr., N.Y.C., 1981—; rsch. assoc. prof. medicine Mt. Sinai Sch. of Medicine, 1986. Mary Swartz Rose fellow; recipient Intern award Mich. Dietetic Assn., Hinman Donor award, Cleve. Found. award. Mem. Am. Dietetic Assn., Soc. for Nutrition Edn., Assn. for Women in Sci., AAAS, N.Y. Acad. Sci., A. Psychosomatic Soc., Am. Soc. for Clin. Nutrition, Am. Inst. Nutrition, Am. Pub. Health Assn., N.Am. Assn. for the Study of Obesity, Internat. Assn. for the Study of Obesity, Phi Kappa Phi, Omicron Nu. Office: Beth Israel Med Ctr 10 Nathan D Perlman Pl New York NY 10003

STRAIT, MARGARET JEAN, accounting executive; b. St. Albans, Vt., Apr. 1, 1945; d. Charles and Charlotte (Dewart) S.; m. Reginald F. Snow Jr., Dec. 3, 1988; children from previous marriage: Justin Bedell, Christopher Bedell. BA magna cum laude, U. Vt., 1967, MA, 1971; BS, Cin. U., 1985. CPA, Vt. Tchr. music Cin. and Burlington, Vt., 1967-83; office mgr. Stowe, Vt., 1980-83; staff acct. Urbach, Kahn & Werlin, P.C., Burlington, 1983-86; internal auditor Med. Ctr. Hosp. of Vt., Burlington, 1986-90; dir. acctg. Fanny Allen Hosp., Colchester, Vt., 1990—; soloist various choirs, Cin., 1971-75, Burlington, 1975-83. Contbr. articles to profl. jours. Mem. Assn. Healthcare Internal Auditors (regional coord. 1987-89), Green Mountain Inst. Internal Auditors (pres. 1989-90). Home: 50-1 Kim Ln Milton VT 05468 Office: Fanny Allen Hosp 101 College Pkwy Colchester VT 05446

STRAKOSCH, KATHERINE WENTON, executive recruiter; b. N.Y.C., Oct. 4, 1933; d. William J. and Elsie G. (Sullivan) Wenton; m. Raymond D. Strakosch, Nov. 10, 1956 (div. May 1977); children: Joanne, Mark, Gregory, Karen. B.A. cum laude, Coll. Mt. St. Vincent, 1955. Cert. personnel cons. Vice pres. Dunhill of Greater Stamford, Inc., Wilton, Conn., 1976-80, pres., 1980—; mem. Town of Wilton Personnel Policies Com., 1983—. Pres. bd. dirs. Wilton Playshop, 1971-73, vice chmn. bd. trustees, 1982-86, chmn. 1986-87; mem. Democratic Town Com., Wilton, 1976-79. Mem. Conn. Assn. Personnel Consultants (sec. 1979, mem. ethics com. 1981—, newsletter editor 1980), Nat. Assn. Pers. Cons., Women in Sales (v.p. membership Fairfield County chpt. 1989—). Roman Catholic. Avocations: tennis, travel, reading. Home: 28 Glen Ridge Wilton CT 06897 Office: Dunhill of Greater Stamford Inc 213 Danbury Rd Wilton CT 06897

STRALEY, JOANETTA SUE, interior design company executive; b. Williamson, W.Va., Mar. 12, 1950; d. John Edward and Marie (Marcum) Herald; m. David E. Straley, Apr. 20, 1968; 1 child, John David. Grad. high sch., Kenova, W.Va. Sec. Flair Furniture, Inc., Kenova, 1967-68; sec., bookkeeper, buyer Nap & Spence Furniture Co., Dover, Del., 1968-71; sec., bookkeeper R.W. Ashworth Constrn. Co., Huntington, W.Va., 1972-79; ptnr., bus. mgr. Design Connexion, Huntington, 1980—; mem. customer adv. bd. 1st Bank Ceredo W.Va., 1989—. Com. chmn. Boy Scouts Am., Huntington, 1980—, mem. bd. rev., chmn. merit badge, instr. drafting, Kenova, 1980—; active Big Bros.-Big Sisters, Huntington, 1983—. Named Outstanding Young Woman, Ashland (Ky.) Area Jaycettes, 1983. Mem. Am. Soc. Interior Designers, Nat. Fedn. Ind. Bus., Nat. Assn. Home Builders (silver pin, Spike Club award 1989), Tri-State Home Builders Assn. (bd. dirs., state and local sec., mem. state awards com., editor local newsletter 1987—, Assoc. of Yr. award 1987, Spl. President's award 1988), Women's Network Group (bd. dirs. 1983—), Huntington C. of C., Order Ky. Cols., Kenova Woman's Club (pres. 1983-86). Office: Design Connexion 615 20th St Huntington WV 25703

STRANBERG, WYNNE LEE, elementary educator; b. Carrington, N.D., Sept. 11, 1948; d. William Richard and Anne (O'Neill) Monk; m. John Theodore Stranberg, Aug. 2, 1975; children: Catherine, Erik. BS, N.D. State U., 1970; MS, U. Wis., 1976; cert. elem. educator, Silver Lake Coll., 1986. Lic. elem. educator, Wis. Psychology tchr. Sheboygan (Wis.) North High Sch., 1970-82; social studies tchr. Farnsworth Mid. Sch., Sheboygan, 1982-85; tchr. Grant Elem. Sch., Sheboygan, 1986—. Active couples program Big Bros./Big Sisters, 1976-79; group facilitator Alcohol and Other Drug Abuse, 1983-90; mem. bd. Christian edn. St. Paul's United Christian Ch., 1986-89. Mem. AAUW, NEA, Wis. Edn. Assn., Sheboygan Edn. Assn. Home: 3303 Hickory Circle Sheboygan WI 53081 Office: Grant Elem Sch 1528 N 5th Sheboygan WI 53081

STRAND, MARION DELORES, social service administrator; b. Kansas City, Mo., Dec. 19, 1927; d. Henry Franklin and Julia Twyman (Noland) Pugh; m. Robert Carmen Scipioni, Aug. 2, 1947 (dec. 1984); children: Mark, Brian, Roberta, Laura, Steven, Mary,Angela, Julie, Victor, Robert, Lawrence; m. Donald John Strand, Sept. 1, 1985. BA, U. Kans., 1948; MS, SUNY, Brockport, 1975. Counselor N.Y. Dept. Labor, Rochester, 1971-75, 77-79; regulatory adminstr. N.Y. Dept. Social Svcs., Rochester, 1976-77, 79-81; pres. Greater Rochester Svcs., Inc. (doing bus. as Scribes & Scripts), 1982—. Columnist, local newspaper. Active polit. campaigns for women candidates, 1981—; UN envoy, Unitarian Ch., Rochester, 1988—; fin. chair William Warfield Scholarship Com., Rochester, 1988—; mem. steering com., Citizens for a Quality Philharmonic, Rochester, 1988—; chair bd. govt. affairs, Genessee Valley Arthritis Found., Rochester, 1988—. Mem. Greater Rochester C. of C. (legis. com., small bus. coun. 1987—, bd. dirs. women's coun. 1986—, pres. 1989—), NOW (pres. child care com. Greater Rochester sect. 1987-88), Phi Beta Kappa, Psi Chi. Home and Office: Greater Rochester Svcs Inc 105 Elmwood Terr Rochester NY 14620

STRAND, NANCY MARIE, nurse; b. Phila., Dec. 27, 1926; d. Edward Joseph and Ella Frances (Waldron) McNelis; m. Bart Strand, Jan. 15, 1955; children: Deirdre, Maureen, Sheila. Student in Nursing, Coll. St. Rose, 1944-47; B.S., N.Y.U., 1951, M.A. in Counseling, 1954. Staff nurse, relief supr. VA Hosp., Bronx, N.Y., 1947-59; staff nurse Children's Hosp., Buffalo, 1959-61, VA Hosp., Buffalo, 1961-62; with U. Ark. Hosp., 1962-77, assoc. dir. nursing, 1966-73, dir. nursing, 1973-77; clin. coord. nursing VA Hosp., Little Rock, 1977-89; mem. nursing curriculum project So. Regional Edn. Bd.; mem. faculty research workshop U. N.C. R.N. Mem. Am. Nurses Assn. (cert. nursing adminstr.), Ark. State Nurses Assn., Nat. League Nursing, Ark. League Nursing (Ann. award of Merit 1971), Am. Coll. of Healthcare Exec. Student Assn., Sigma Iota Epsilon. Roman Catholic. Home: 464 Midland Ave Little Rock AR 72205

STRANG, SANDRA LEE, airline official; b. Greensboro, N.C., Apr. 22, 1936; d. Charles Edward and Lobelia Mae (Squires) S.; BA in English, U. N.C., 1960; MBA, U. Dallas, 1970. With American Airlines, Inc., 1960—, mgr. career devel. for women, N.Y.C., 1972-73, dir. selection and tng., 1974-75, sr. dir. selection, tng. and affirmative action, 1975-79, sr. dir. compensation and benefits, Dallas/Ft. Worth, Tex., 1979-84, dir. passenger sales tng. and devel., 1984—; regional sales mgr. Rocky Mountain Region, Denver, 1985—; pres. The SLS Group, Inc., (DBAs) Sales Leadership Seminars, Inc., Sr. Leadership Svcs., Inc., Svc. Leadership Seminars, Inc., Speakers, Lectrs., and Seminars, Inc, 1988—. Mem. Am. Mgmt. Assn., Assn. Advancement of Women into Mgmt., Am. Soc. Tng. and Devel., Am. Compensation Assn., Internat. Platform Assn., Am. Assn. Retired Persons. Home: 3493 E Euclid Ave Littleton CO 80121

STRASSER, JUDITH LOUISE, writer, radio producer; b. N.Y.C., Sept. 30, 1944; d. Alexander and Maxine H. (Hochberg) S.; m. Stephen W. Ela, Sept. 19, 1972 (div. 1990); children: Jedediah Smith Ela, Nathan Pell Ela. BA, Reed Coll., Portland, Oreg., 1966; MS, Stanford U., 1970, postgrad., 1970-72. Tech. writer Pacific Telephone and Telegraph Co., San Francisco, 1966-68; grants adminstr Wis. Ednl. Communications Bd., Madison, 1982-85; writer, producer Wis. Pub. Radio, Madison, 1984—; prin. Kaleidoscope Media Svcs., Madison, 1978—; bd. dirs. The Writers' Pl., Madison; guest editor Mademoiselle mag., N.Y.C., 1966. Writer, producer audio cassette series, audio documentary; contbr. articles to C.S. Monitor, Mademoiselle mag., other publs. Chair bd. dirs. Madison Children's Mus., 1982-85; bd. dirs. Wis. Pub. Radio Assn., 1980-81. Mem. Women in Communications, Phi Beta Kappa. Office: Kaleidoscope Media Svcs PO Box 1123 Madison WI 53701

STRASSER, NANCY SOWERS, nurse, healthcare executive; b. Englewood, N.J., Nov. 10, 1947; d. Forrest Wayne and Eva Marie (Bosstick) Sowers; m. Dermot Macaraugh Ross-Brown, June 3, 1978 (div. Dec. 1980); David Frederick Strasser, Sept. 17, 1982. Diploma, St. Luke's Hosp. Sch. Nursing, St. Louis, 1969; student, U. Colo., 1970-71, Am. Coll., Bryn Mawr, Pa., 1989—. Cert. critical care nurse practitioner. Staff nurse oper. rm. Barnes Hosp., St. Louis, 1969-70; staff nurse ICU, oper. rm. St. Anthony Hosp. Systems, Denver, 1971-75; clin. critical care crisis nurse Comprehensive Nursing Services, Denver, 1977-79; clin. specialist Pepin Distbg. Inc., Denver, 1979-80; asst. adminstr. NE Meml. Hosp., Houston, 1981; dir. nursing Med. Personnel Pool, Ft. Myers, Fla., 1982; head nursing operating room Lee Meml. Hosp., Ft. Myers, Fla., 1982; team leader S. Fla. Artificial Kidney Ctr., Ft. Myers, Fla., 1983; gen. mgr. Nat. Med. Homecare, Inc., Cape Coral, Fla., 1983-86; sales rep. Met. Life Ins. Co., 1987-90; case mgr. liaison Home Intensive Care, Inc., North Miami Beach, 1990—. Mem. Nat. Assn. Life Underwriters, Nat. Assn. Security Dealers, NAFE, DAR. Home: 9453 Palm Circle N Pembroke Pines FL 33025 Office: Home Intensive Care Inc 150 NW 168th St North Miami Beach FL 33169

STRATFORD, CAROL ANN DEERING, occupational therapist; b. Columbus, Ohio, Dec. 17, 1946; d. Earl Brent and Gladys May (Wade) Deering; A.A., Brevard Jr. Coll., 1966; B.S., U. Fla., 1968; m. Francis A. Stratford, Jr., Aug. 4, 1973. Staff occupational therapist Hosp. Albert Einstein Coll. Medicine, Bronx, N.Y., 1968-74; sr. research therapist Inst. Rehab. Medicine N.Y. U. Med. Center, N.Y.C., 1975-81, mem. developmental team voice recognition, wheel chair and environ. control system; supr. dept. occupational therapy Danbury (Conn.) Hosp., 1982-84; tech. aids cons., 1984—. Registered occupational therapist. Mem. Am. Occupational Therapy Assn. (resource person in rehab. engring.), Rehab. Engring. Soc. N. Am. Co-author, editor: (monograph) Environmental Control Systems and Vocational Aids for Persons with High Level Quadriplegia, 1979; contbr. articles to profl. jours. Methodist. Home: 16 N State St Dover DE 19901

STRATHY, JANETTE HANSEN, obstetrician, gynecologist; b. Duluth, Minn., Apr. 25, 1956; m. Gregg M. Strathy, Oct. 6, 1979; 1 child, Bryan. BS in Chemistry, Hamline U., 1977; MD, Mayo Med. Sch., 1981. Resident in ob-gyn. Mayo Med. Sch., Rochester, Minn., 1985; ob-gyn. Park Nicollet Med. Ctr., St. Louis Pk., Minn., 1985—; asst. clinical prof. U. Minn., 1988—. Mem. Am. Coll. Ob-Gyn. (Minn. sect. vice chrmn. 1989—). Lutheran.

STRATTON, LOIS JEAN, state legislator; b. Springdale, Wash., Jan. 5, 1927; d. Charles B. and Ann B. (Hill) Brunton; m. Allen F. Stratton, 1946; children—Alan Edward, Kathleen Prater, Mark Charles, Scott D., Karen Jeanne. Student Kinman Bus. U., 1944-45. Democratic precinct committeewoman, Spokane County, Wash., from 1958; mem. Spokane County Dem. Exec. Bd.; alt. del. Dem. Nat. Conv., 1976; co-chmn. Gov. Dixy Lee Ray Com., 1976; committeewoman Wash. State Dem. Com., from 1977; now mem. Wash. Senate, Dist. 3; exec. sec. pub. affairs Kaiser Aluminum & Chem. Corp., Spokane, from 1963; adminstrv. asst., exec. sec. to pres. Expo 74 World's Fair, Spokane. Recipient World's Fair Expo 74 Vol. Service citations Gov. of Wash. and Wash. State Commn., 1974. Mem. Spokane County Dem. Club (sec.), Jane Jefferson Dem. Club (1st v.p.). Roman Catholic. Office: State Senate Olympia WA 98504 Home: 1724 W Mansfield Spokane WA 99205*

STRATTON, NORMA JEAN, x-ray technician, swine farm owner; b. Bowling Green, Ohio, Jan. 13, 1936; d. Henry and Rozella (Loge) Tober; m. Lyndon T. Stratton, Apr. 26, 1963 (div. May 18, 1988); children: Benjamin, Richard, Debra. X-ray technican St. Rita's Hosp., Lima, Ohio, 1962-64, Blanchard Valley Hosp., Findlay, Ohio, 1964-65, Wood County Hosp., Bowling Green, Ohio, 1966-74; mgr. x-ray Thorn Hosp., Hudson, Mich., 1980—. With USN, 1954-62. Lutheran. Office: Thorn Health Ctr 458 Cross St Hudson MI 49247

STRAUB, DENISE MARGARET, utilities executive; b. Washington, June 19, 1959; d. Walter Albert and Margaret Elaine (Howell) S. AA in Bus. Adminstrn., Prince Georges Community Coll., 1981; BS in Acctg., U. Md., 1981; MBA in Fin., Marymount U., 1989. CPA, Md., Va. Acct. Washington Gas Light Co., 1981-84; auditor Washington Gas Light Co., Springfield, Va., 1984-86; tax acct. Washington Gas Light Co., Washington, 1986-88; assoc. rate analyst Washington Gas Light Co., Springfield, 1988—; tax cons. Beneficial Tax Service, Springfield, 1984-86; pvt. practice, Alexandria, Va., 1987—. Treas. Alexandria Christmas in April, Inc., 1988—. Mem. DC Inst. CPAs, Washington Gas Ski Club, Washington Gas Speakers Club, Delta Epsilon Sigma. Roman Catholic. Office: Washington Gas Light Co 6801 Industrial Rd Springfield VA 22151

STRAUGHAN, CAROL ANNETTE, human resource director; b. Oklahoma City, Apr. 29, 1935; d. Tom Henderson and Lou Abbot (Hannah) Sanders; m. Benjamin Earle Straughan; children: Lara, Caris, B. Kent. G-rad. high sch., Vaughn, N.Mex. Telephone operator Mountain Bell, Vaughn, N.Mex., 1952-53; asst. mgr. Vaughn Mercantile Co., 1963-65; correspondent Santa Rosa (N.Mex.) News., 1967-72; instr. Dale Carnegie Courses, El Paso, Tex., 1974-89; tng. dir. Ben E. Straughan & Assocs., El Paso, 1976-86; tng. dir. Whataburger of El Paso, 1987, human resource dir., 1987—; adv. bd. Whataburger of El Paso, 1987—. Author: True Value Through Effective Training, 1988. Seminar leader YMCA, El Paso, 1988; mem. bus. adv. com. torch of Hope, Inc., El Paso. Mem. NAFE, Am. Soc. Tng. Devel. (pres.-elect El Paso chpt., speaker 1987), Pod of the Pass, Chili Appreciation Soc. Internat. (area referee 1986-87), Order Eastern Star, Beta Sigma Phi, Order of Rainbow for Girls. Republican. Methodist. Home: 3608 Buxton El Paso TX 79927 Office: Whataburger of El Paso 9400 Montana El Paso TX 79925

STRAUGHN, CLAIRE VALENCIA LEE, airline sales executive; b. N.Y.C., June 18, 1953; d. William and Marjorie Media (Hoyt) S. BA in Polit. Sci., Bklyn. Coll., 1976, MA in Sociology, 1982. Asst. dir. Prison Reform in Devel. Edn., N.Y.C., 1973-75; researcher N.Y. Pub. Interest Research Group, N.Y.C., 1976; claims developer Social Security Adminstrn., N.Y.C., 1978-83; sales rep. Delta Airlines, Inc., N.Y.C., 1983—. Mem. Sheepshead Bay Citizen Action Com., Bklyn. Democrat. Baptist. Home: 3573 Nostrand Ave Apt 2-D Brooklyn NY 11229

STRAUS, ELLEN SULZBERGER, broadcast executive; b. N.Y.C., Mar. 11, 1925; d. David Hays and Louise (Blumenthal) S.; m. R. Peter Straus, Feb. 6, 1950; children—Diane Straus Tucker, Katherine Straus Caple, Jeanne Straus Tofel, Eric. B.A., Smith Coll., 1945; D.Comml. Sci. (hon.), St. John's U., 1985; L.H.D. (hon.), Franklin Pierce Coll., 1985. Program sec. N.Y.C. LWV, 1945-48; asst. dir. public info. U.S. AEC, 1948-49; campaign mgr. Herbert Lehman for Senate, 1949; fgn. corr. No. N.Y. newspapers, 1950-55; editor McCall's mag., N.Y.C., 1973-76; v.p. Sta. WMCA, 1976, pres., 1985—. Author: A Smith College Mosaic, 1974, A Survival Kit for New Yorkers, 1973, The Volunteer Professional: What You Need to Know, 1972, Women's Almanac, 1976, Women Behind Bars (broadcast series on prison reform 1983-84); monthly column McCall's mag, 1972-74. Pres., chairperson Nat. Call for Action, Inc., 1969-75; founder Vol. Profl., Inc., N.Y.C., 1970; aux. policeperson Mounted, Central Park precinct, 1974-77; chmn. exec. com. N.Y.C. Partnership, chmn. pub. safety com., 1981, acting pres., 1987-88; chmn. communications com. Pres.' Task Force on Pvt. Sector Initiatives, 1982; mem. adv. panel innovation tech. and regional econ. devel. Office of Tech., U.S. Congress, 1983; moderator Corp. in Contemporary Soc. Aspen Inst., 1983; mem. selection com. Dively Bus. award Harvard U., 1985; mem. The Bishop Desmond Tutu So. Africa Refugee Scholarship Program, 1985; mem. State-City Commn. on Integrity in Govt., 1986; pres. Exec. Service Strategies, 1988; mem. site selection com. Democratic Nat. Com., 1986; auxilary police person, 1986; acting pres. N.Y.C. Ptnrship., 1987-88; pres. Exec. Service Strategies, 1988. Recipient Woman of Conscience award, 1970, Hannah G. Solomon award, 1972, Nat. Council Jewish Women; recipient Louise Waterman Wise award Am. Jewish Congress, 1971,Medal of Honor Smith Coll., 1971, Am. Inst. Public Service award, 1974, B'nai B'rith Women Dist. One award, 1976; Consumer Crusader award Caveat Emptor Mag., 1978, Abram L. Sachar award Brandeis U., 1980, Amita Golden Lady achievement award, 1981, award for excellence Soc. for Advancement of Travel for the Handicapped, 1982, Olive award Council of Chs. of City of N.Y., 1983, Radio award Am. Women in Radio and TV, 1984, Caring New Yorker award Community Coucil Greater N.Y., 1986, Buddy award Legal Def. Fund NOW, 1987; named Woman of Yr. Ladies Home Jour., 1973, Woman of Outstanding Achievement Women's Equity Action League, 1984. Democrat. Jewish. Office: 1414 Avenue of the Americas New York NY 10019

STRAUS, HELEN LORNA PUTTKAMMER, educator; b. Chgo., Feb. 15, 1933; d. Ernst Wilfred and Helen Louise (Monroe) Puttkammer; m. Francis Howe Straus II, June 11, 1955; children: Francis Howe III, Helen E., Christopher M., Michael J. AB magna cum laude, Radcliffe Coll., 1955; MS in Anatomy, U. Chgo., 1960, PhD in Anatomy, 1962. With U. Chgo., 1964—, dean of students, 1971-82, dean of admissions, 1975-80, prof. anatomy and biol. scis., 1987—; trustee Radcliffe Coll., Cambridge, Mass., 1973-83. Recipient Excellence in Teaching award U. Chgo., 1970, Silver medal CASE Outstanding Tchr. Program, 1987. Mem. Nat. Sci. Tchrs. Assn., AAAS, Am. Assn. Anatomists, Nat. Collegiate Athletic Assn. (acad. requirements com. 1986—, chmn. 1990—), Harvard U. Alumni Assn. (bd. dirs.), Phi Beta Kapa (sec., treas. U. Chgo. chpt. 1984—). Home: 5642 Kimbark Ave Chicago IL 60637 Office: U Chgo 5845 Ellis Ave Chicago IL 60637

STRAUS, KATHLEEN NAGLER, education administrator, consultant; b. N.Y.C., Dec. 3, 1923; d. Maurice and Mildred (Kohn) Nagler; m. Everet M. Straus, May 29, 1948 (dec. Nov. 1967); children: Peter R., Barbara L. BA in Econs., Hunter Coll., 1944; postgrad., Columbia U., 1944-45, Am. U., 1946-47, Wayne State U., 1976-78. Various positions, 1944-50, 66; dep. dir. Model Neighborhood Agy., City of Detroit, 1968-70; dir. social svcs. Southeastern Mich. Coun. Govts., Detroit, 1970-74; staff coord. Edn. Task Force, Detroit, 1974-75; exec. dir. People and Responsible Orgns. for Detroit, 1975-76; staff dir. edn. com. Mich. Senate, Lansing, 1976-79; assoc. exec. dir. Mich. Assn. Sch. Bds., Lansing, 1979-86; dir. community rels. and devel. Ctr. for Creative Studies, Detroit, 1986-87, acting pres., 1987-88, pres., 1989—; mem. Edn. Commn. of States, Denver, 1979—; mem. Mich. Bd. for Pub. Jr. and Community Colls., Lansing, 1980—, v.p., 1989; com. mem. Met. Columbus (Ohio) Schs. Com., 1975-76; mem. steering com. Mich. Edn. Seminars, 1979-86; mem. adv. com. on Higher Edn. Needs in S.W. Mich., 1971-72, Ad Hoc Com. on Equal Access to Higher Edn., 1970-71, Citizens Action Com. on Sch. Fin. Contbr. articles to profl. jours. Active numerous civic orgns.; vice chmn. downtown br. Met. Detroit YWCA, 1970-74; bd. dirs. Citizens for Better Care, Inc., 1973-78; mem. edn. com. New Detroit, Inc., 1972—; trustee Detroit Sci. Ctr., Inc., 1975—; founder, pres. Mich. Tax Info. Coun., 1982—; v.p. bd. dirs. Univ. Cultural Ctr. Assn., 1986—; trustee Comprehensive Health Planning Coun. Southeastern Mich., 1977-78; mem. Wayne County Art and History Commn., 1988; co-chmn. Nat. Arts Program, 1987-88. Recipient Amity citation Congress, Detroit, 1966, Disting. Community Svc. award Am. Jewish Com., 1988, Disting. Community Svc. award Common Coun., Detroit, 1976, resolution Mich. Ho. of Reps., 1986, Mich. Senate, 1988. Mem. Nat. Soc. Fund Raising Execs., Am. Econ. Assn., Acad. Polit. and Social Sci., Econ. Club Detroit, Detroit Press Club, LWV (pres. Detroit 1961-63), Alpha Chi Alpha. Democrat. Home: 8801 Kingswood Detroit MI 48221 Office: Ctr for Creative Studies 201 E Kirby Detroit MI 48202

STRAUSBAUGH, TERESA ELAINE, economic forecaster, revenues analyst; b. Findlay, Ohio, Aug. 24, 1964; d. James Eugene and Madeline Lee (Shilling) Strausbaugh. BA summa cum laude, Ohio State U., 1986. Mgmt. intern/analyst United Telephone of Ohio, Mansfield, 1987-88, staff adminstr./revenues, 1988—; mem. forecasting com. United Telecom, Inc., Kansas City, Mo., 1988—. Vol. Am. Cancer Soc., Mansfield, 1990. Mem. Nat. Assn. Female Execs., Nat. Assn. Bus. Economists, Phi Beta Kappa, Mortar Bd. Office: United Telephone of Ohio 665 Lexington Ave PO Box 3555 Mansfield OH 44907

STRAUSE, GLYNIS HOLM, educator; b. McAllen, Tex., Sept. 11, 1952; d. Bertil Quinton and Vera Lea (Walters) Holm; m. Thomas Lynn Strause Jr., July 22, 1978; 1 child, Seth Rae; 1 stepchild, Renee Lynn. BS, Howard Payne U., 1975; MA in Teaching, U. Tenn., 1977. Cert. speech, theatre and English tchr., Tex. Vis. instr. Tex. A&I U., Kingsville, 1977-78; speech instr., forensics coach Bee County Coll., Beeville, Tex., 1978—. Author: A Rhetoric of Interpersonal Communication, 1984, Games: Games, Activities and Measures, Exercises in Speech, 1989. Adult leader 4-H Club, 1988-89; chmn. Dem. Precinct, George West, Tex., 1988. Mem. Tex. Intercollegiate Forensics Assn. (pres. 1986-87), Tex. Speech Jr. Coll. Speech Theatre Assn. (parlimentarian 1982-86), Tex. Speech Communications Assn. (dist. chmn. 1987-90), Tex. Fedn. Bus. and Profl. Women's Clubs, Inc. (state pres. 1989-90). Methodist. Home: PO Box 681 George West TX 78022 Office: Bee County Coll 3800 Charco Rd #159 Beeville TX 78102

STRAUSS, ANNETTE, mayor, public relations consultant; b. Houston, Jan. 26, 1924; d. Jacob B. and Edith (Weinberger) Greenfield; m. Theodore H. Strauss, Sept. 8, 1946; children: Nancy Strauss Halbreich, Janie Strauss McGarr. Student, Rice U., 1940-41; BA in Sociology, U. Tex., 1944; MA in Sociology and Psychology, Columbia U., 1945. Mayor City of Dallas, 1987—. Trustee John F. Kennedy Ctr. Performing Arts; chmn. nat. council Friends of Kennedy Ctr.; devel. bd. U. Tex, Dallas Inst. Humanities & Culture; chmn. bd. TACA; bd. dirs. nat. com. Arts with Handicapped, Dallas Symphony Orch., St. Paul Hosp. Found., Nat. Jewish Hosp., Children's Med. Ctr., Nat. Council Am. Jewish Com., Dallas Vol. Ctr., Dallas UN Assn., Creative Learning Ctr. Dallas, Jewish Fedn. Dallas, Timberlawn Found., Dallas Black Dance Theater, Community Chest Fund, Operation Lift, Women's Ctr. Dallas County; fundraiser for such programs as Downtown Dallas Family Shelter, U. Tex. Health Sci. Ctr., Dallas Assn. Retarded Citizens, Majestic Theatre, Dallas County Heart Found. Fund; former bd. mem. Dallas com. ARC, Planned Parenthood Dallas, Dallas Theater Ctr., Dallas Mcpl. Library Bd., others. Recipient John F. Kennedy Commitment to Excellence award, Headliner's award Press Club, Pro Bene Meritis award U. Tex., James K. Wilson award Dallas Performing Arts, Humanitarian award Nat. Jewish Hosp., Linz award, Brotherhood award Conf. Christians and Jews, Human Relations awards Am. Jewish Com., Zonta award, Arete award; named Woman of Yr., Nat. Jewish Hosp.; named to Honor Roll of Vol. Women, Town and Country mag., Citizen of Yr. Les Femmes du Monde, Dallas, YWCA Family of Yr. Women's Ctr., Dallas, Women Helping Women award, Person of Valor award Jewish Nat. Fund. Mem. Dallas C. of C. (steering com. Leadership Dallas), Dallas Arboretum Soc., Dallas Hist. Soc. Office: Office of Mayor City Hall 1500 Marilla 5EN Dallas TX 75201*

STRAUSS, CAROL KAHN, editor, consultant; b. N.Y.C., Sept. 21, 1944; d. Alfred and Lotte (Landau) K.; m. Peter Mathes, Dec. 1977 (div. 1980); m. Peter Strauss, June 1989. BS, Columbia U., 1970; MS, Hunter Coll., 1973. Asst. book editor Council on Fgn. Relations, N.Y.C., 1972-79; sr. editor, dir. pub. affairs Hudson Inst., Indpls., 1984-89; sr. editor, cons. 20th Century Fund, N.Y.C., 1990—; cons., writer, editor Ford Found., 20th Century Fund, Mayorial Task Forces, Kidder Peabody & Co., N.Y. Holocaust Commn. Editor: (books) The Coming Boom, 1982, Thinking About the Unthinkable in the 1980's, 1984; editor, co-author articles for profl. publs. Pres. Congregation Habonim, N.Y.C., 1984—; trustee Self-Help, Inc., N.Y.C., 1986—; mem. Leo Baeck Inst., N.Y.C., 1985—; v.p. Fedn. of Jews from Cen. Europe, 1990. Jewish. Club: Atrium (N.Y.C.). Home: 870 Fifth Ave New York NY 10021 Office: 20th Century Fund 41 E 70th St New York NY 10021

STRAUSS, DOROTHY BRANDFON, marital and family therapist; b. Bklyn.; d. Marcus and Beatrice (Wilson) Brandfon; widowed; 1 child, Josette Strauss Elliott. BA, Bklyn. Coll., 1932; MA, NYU, 1937, PhD, 1963. Diplomate Am. Bd. Sexology. Instr. Hunter Coll. CUNY, 1960-63; prof. Kean Coll., Union, N.J., 1963-77; pvt. practice and clin. supervision Bklyn. and, N.J., 1970—; clin. assoc. prof. psychiatry Downstate Med. Ctr., SUNY, Bklyn., 1974—; assoc. dir. Ctr. for Human Sexuality, 1974-82. Contbr. articles on gerontology and sexual dysfunctions to profl. jours. Mem. Am. Assn. for Marital and Family Therapy (clin. mem. 1971—, supr. 1981), Am. Assn. Sex Therapists, Counselors and Educators (chairperson task force on supervision 1984-86, chairperson supr. cert. com. 1986—), Am. Psychol. Assn., Kappa Delta Pi, Lambda Delta Theta, Sigma Phi Omega. Home and Office: 1401 Ocean Ave Brooklyn NY 11230

STRAUSS, HARLEE SUE, environmental consultant; b. New Brunswick, N.J., June 19, 1950; d. Robert Lemuel and Helene (Marcus) S. BA, Smith Coll., 1972; PhD, U. Wis., 1979. Postdoctoral fellow dept. biology MIT, Cambridge, 1979-81; congrl. sci. fellow U.S. House of Reps., Washington, 1981-83; spl. asst. Am. Chem. Soc., Washington, 1983-84; spl. cons. Environ. Corp., Washington, 1984-85; rsch. assoc. Ctr. for Tech., Policy and Indsl. Devel. MIT, Cambridge, 1985-86, rsch. affiliate, 1986—; sr. assoc. Gradient Corp., Cambridge, 1986-88; pres. H. Strauss Assocs., Inc., Natick, Mass., 1988—; adj. assoc. prof. Sch. of Pub. Health, Boston U., 1990; lectr. Tufts U. Sch. of Medicine, Boston, 1988—; steering com. Boston Risk Assessment Group, 1986—. Co-editor, author: Risk Assessment in Genetic Engineering, 1990; author: Biotechnology Regulations, 1986; author book chpts. in field. Active Instl. Biosafety Com., Army Rsch. Lab., Natick, 1989—. Predoctoral fellow, NIH, 1975-79; postdoctoral fellow, NIH, 1979-81. Mem. AAAS, Am. Chem. Soc., Am. Soc. Microbiology, Assn. for Women in Sci. (chmn. mem. com. New Eng. chpt. 1986-88, co-chmn. legis. com. 1985—), Biophys. Soc. (chmn. com. 1983-84, Congrl. Sci. fellow 181-83), Soc. for Risk Analysis. Jewish. Home: 21 Bay State Rd Natick MA 01760 Office: H Strauss Assocs Inc 21 Bay State Rd Natick MA 01760

STRAUSS, JEAN ANNE SACCONAGHI, writer; b. Martinez, Calif., Apr. 12, 1955; d. Louie Baldesare and Betty Lou (Wenger) Sacconaghi; m. Douglas W. Perez, Sept. 17, 1977 (div. 1982); m. Jon Calvert Strauss, June 14, 1985; children: Kristoffer Calvert, Jonathon Samuel Louis. BA in History, U. Calif., 1978; MA in Writing, U. So. Calif., 1988. Asst. adminstr. Olympic Planning U. of So. Calif., L.A., 1983-84, cons. personal computing, 1984-85; spl. assoc. Worcester Poly. Inst., Worcester, Mass., 1985—. Author: The Great Adoptee Search Book, 1990; columnist Reunions mag.; contbr. articles to profl. jours. Bd. dirs. Children's Friend Soc., 1986—; trustee Bancroft Sch., Worcester, 1986-89, New Eng. Sci. Ctr., Worcester, 1987—; chair Women's Olympic Rowing Com., 1984-88. Named: 100 most interesting women, Boston Woman's Mag., Boston, Mass., 1988. Ind. Office: Worcester Poly 100 Institute Rd Worcester MA 01609

STRAUSS, JUDITH FEIGIN, physician; b. N.Y., Mar. 7, 1942; d. Milton M. and Blanche (Tobias) Feigin; m. Harry William Strauss, June 14, 1964; children: Cheryl, Marcy. BS, Cornell U., Ithaca, 1963; MD, SUNY, 1967. Pediatrics. Pediatric resident SUNY, N.Y.C., 1976-68, Sinai Hosp., Balt., 1968-69; fellow pediatrics and psychiatry Johns Hopkins Hosp., Balt., 1969-70; pvt. practice in pediatrics Sacramento; cons. in pediatrics Bur. of Disability Ins. Social Security, Balt., 1973-74; pediatrician East Balt. Med. Plan, 1974-76; dir. USPHS Hosp., Boston, 1976-80; pvt. practice in pediatrics Boston, 1980-87; dir. med. svcs. Mediqual Systems, 1988—. Fellow Am. Acad. of Pediatrics; mem. Mass. Med. Soc., Am. Med. Women's Orgn., Alpha Lamda Delta. Office: Mediqual Systems 1900 W Park Dr Westborough MA 01581

STRAUSS, PHYLLIS R., professor of biology; b. Worcester, Mass., Mar. 19, 1943. BA, Brown U., 1964; PhD, The Rockefeller U., 1971. Rsch. fellow med. sch. Harvard U., Boston, 1971-73; asst. prof. biology Northeastern U., Boston, 1973-78, assoc. prof. biology, 1978-84, prof. biology, 1984-86; disting. prof. biology Northeastern U., Boston, Md., 1987—; vis. scholar Harvard U., Cambridge, Mass., 1988; reviewer NSF, NIH, Nat. Rsch. Coun., Alberta Heritage Found., U.S. Dept. Agrl. and numerous jours. and books. Author, editor: The Euraryotic Nucleus, 1990; contbr. articles to profl. jours. Grantee Am. Cancer Soc., 1973, NIH, 1977, Office of Naval Rsch., 1981, WHO, 1989, and others. Mem. AAAS, Am. Soc. for Cell Biology (coun. 1989-91), Am. Soc. Protozoologists, Am. Soc. Biol. Chemists, Am. Women in Sci. Office: Northeastern U 360 Huntington Ave Boston MA 02115

STRAUSS, SUSAN LOUISE, nurse, educator; b. Mpls., Nov. 17, 1946; d. Kenneth LeRoy and Jean Louise (Nelson) Strauss; children: Amy, Jill; m. Edward Hjermstad. RN, Abbott Hosp., 1967; BA, Metropolitan State U., 1967; MS, Mankato State U., 1981. RN, Minn. Nurse various hosps., Minn., 1967-74; nurse educator Waseca (Minn.) County Coop., 1974-78; cons. Strauss Cons., Chaska, Minn., 1978--; nurse educator Craver Scott Coop. Ctr., Chaska, 1978-89; dir. edn. and quality mgmt. Golden Valley (Minn.) Health Ctr.; cons. Minn. Dept. Edn., St. Paul, 1985—. Contbr. articles to profl. jours. Mem. Red Cross, St. Paul, 1976--, Minn., 1984--, NOW, Mo.,1983--, LWV,. Mem. Soc. Pub. Health Edn. Program, Am. Soc. Tng. and Devel., Nurse Healers Assn. Democrat. Methodist. Home: 891 Howard Ln Chaska MN 55318

STRAW, MICHELLE MARIE, critical care nurse; b. Laconia, N.H., May 19, 1958; d. John Casey and Nancy Althea (Brown) S. BS in Nursing, U. N.H., 1980; M in Nursing, U. Wash., 1986. RN, Wash., Ariz., N.H., Calif.; lic. critical care RN. Staff nurse Dartmouth-Hitchcock Med. Ctr., Hanover, N.H., 1980-82, U. Med. Ctr., Tucson, 1982-84, Va. Mason Med. Ctr., Seattle, 1984-87; critical care clin. nurse specialist MultiCare Med. Ctr., Tacoma, 1987—; clin. faculty U. Wash. Sch. Nursing, Seattle, 1987. Instr. basic and advanced cardiac life support Am. Heart Assn., Wash., 1988—. Research grantee Nursing Devel. Fund, 1986. Mem. Soc. of Critical Care Medicine, Am. Assn. of Critical Care Nurses (Puget Sound chpt., research grantee 1986), Sigma Theta Tau. Baptist. Home: 5702 N 33rd St #7A Tacoma WA 98407

STRAWDERMAN, VIRGINIA, education educator; b. Jacksonville, Fla., Sept. 6, 1949; d. William Richard and Gladys Virginia (Fritts) Wright. BS, U. Tenn., Chattanooga, 1972; MACT, Murray State U., 1975; PhD, Ga. State U., Atlanta, 1985. Tchr. Belen (N.Mex.) High Sch., 1972-73; teaching asst. Murray State U., 1973-75; instr. Chesterfield Marlboro Tech. Edn. Ctr., Cheraw, S.C., 1975-77; tchr. No. Fulton High Sch., Atlanta; instr. maths. dept. Ga. State U., Atlanta, 1980-83; instr. Div. of Devel. Studies Ga. State U., 1983-85; asst. prof. Ga. State U., Atlanta, 1986-88; math. instr. The Math Set, Atlanta, 1988—; co-chmn. Ga. Coun. of Tchrs. of Math., 1987-88. Author: Mathematics for Every Young Child, 1989, A Description of Mathematics Anxiety Using an Integrative Model, 1985. Mem. Nat. Coun. of Tchrs. of Math., Ga. Coun. of Tchrs. of Math. Christian Fellowships. Office: The Math Set 375 Pharr Rd Ste 222 Atlanta GA 30305

STRAWN, FRANCES FREELAND, real estate executive; b. Waynesville, N.C., Nov. 18, 1946; d. Thomas M. and Jimmie (Smith) Freeland; m. David Updegraff Strawn, Aug. 30, 1974; children: Laurel, Kirk, Trisha. AA, Brevard Community Coll., Cocoa, Fla., 1976; postgrad. U. Cen. Fla., 1976-77. acting sr. buyer Brevard County Purchasing Bd. of County Commns., Titusville, Fla., 1971-75; rsch. analyst Brevard Community Coll., Cocoa, 1977-78; realtor assoc., Orlando, Fla., 1979-82; realtor, broker, pres. Advance Am., Inc., Orlando, 1982-89; assoc. Ann Cross, Inc., Winter Park, Fla., 1988—; bd. dirs. Vol. Ctr. of Cen. Fla. (rec. sec. 1989), Cen. Fla. Zool. Pk., 1989—; program chmn. Young Rep. Women, Orlando, 1983; coord. Congressman Bill Nelson's Washington Internship Program; co-ticket chmn. Art and Architecture Orlando Regional Hosp.; mem. steering com. Fla. Heritage Homecoming, Orlando, 1987; sec. Mayor's Wife's Campaign Activities, Orlando, 1986-87; vice chmn. Horizon Exec. Bd., 1987-89, chmn., 1989; recording sec. Women's Bus. Edn. Council, 1988, mem. adv. bd. , 1987, bd. dirs. 1988—; active calendar com. Women's Resource Ctr., bd. dirs. 1989-90; lectr. Jr. Achievement., 1988—. Mem. Orange County Bar Aux. (bd. dirs. 1986-88, corr. sec. 1987), Creative Bus. Ownership for Women (adv. bd. 1986-88, grievance vice chmn. 1989), Nat. Assn. Realtors, Orlando Bd. Realtors (grievance com. 1985—), Orlando Area Bd. Realtors (membership com. 1980-84, profl. standards com. 1983-84, lectr. Success Series 1988—), Women's Coun. of Realtors, Women's Exec. Coun., Citrus Club (Orlando, social com. 1987-88, bd. dirs). Episcopalian. Avocations: travel, needlepoint, counted cross stitch, canoe trips, backpacking. Home: 105 NW Ivanhoe Blvd Orlando FL 32804 Office: Ann Cross Inc 213 W Comstock Ave Winter Park FL 32789

STRAWN, JUDY C., public relations professional; b. Walla Walla, Wash., Oct. 8, 1950; d. Warren Clarence and Nora Melissa (Riley) S. BA in Pub. Communications, Columbia Union Coll., 1975; postgrad., UCLA, 1985—. Sec., editor Mitsubishi Bank of Calif., L.A., 1977-78; adminstrv. asst., bookkeeper Young & Rubicam West, L.A., 1978-80; advertising media coord. Thriftimart Inc (now SFI), L.A., 1980-82; dir. pub. rels. Phipps Racing Corp., Beverly Hills, Calif., 1985-86; coord. spl. projects Nat. Hot Rod Assn., Glendora, Calif., 1988-89; pvt. practice pub. rels. L.A., 1982—; legal sec. Morrison and Forester, L.A., 1989—. Co-producer (play) Truth Be Told, 1989-90; contbr. articles to profl. jours.; author press releases. Vol. Red Cross. Mem. Am. Auto Racing Writers and Broadcasters Assn., Motor Press Guild, Smithsonian Assocs., L.A. County Mus. Art, Women in Theatre, Make a Wish Found., Windstar Found., Mothers Against Drunk Driving, Assn. Handcrafted Automobiles, Sports Car Club Am., Sierra Club. Democrat. Home: 634 S Pasadena #10 Glendora CA 91740 Office: 333 S Grand Ave 38th Fl Los Angeles CA 90071

STRAZDON, MAUREEN ELAINE, business information manager; b. Elizabeth, N.J., Aug. 6, 1948; d. Bruno H. and Leona E.(Sheehan) S.; m. Victor A. Bary, May 17, 1985. BA, Douglass Coll., New Brunswick, N.J., 1970; MLS, Rutgers U., New Brunswick, 1971; MBA, Drexel U., Phila., 1978; CLU, Am. Coll., Bryn Mawr, Pa., 1982. Bus., reference librarian Drexel U., Phila., 1971-78; head librarian Am. Coll., Bryn Mawr, Pa., 1978-82, Pa. State U., Abington, 1982-85; asst. dir. rsch. and devel. Am. Internat. Group, N.Y.C., 1985—. Editor Index, Database Ins. Periodicals Index, 1983—; author contbr. articles in profl. jours. 1979—. Named Outstanding Young Women Am. mem. Info. Services Adv. Council, Beta Gamma Sigma, Special Libraries Assn. Office: Am Internat Group 70 Pine St New York NY 10270

STREBEIGH, BARBARA, organization administrator, editor; b. Rye, N.Y., July 29, 1902; d. Harold Strebeigh and Blanche (Pierce) Bonaparte. Student Sargent Sch. Phys. Edn. (now Boston U.), 1923; sculpture student of Alexander Archipenko, 1940-41; student U. Calif.-San Diego Extension, 1924-25. Mem. phys. therapy staff U.S. Marine Hosp., San Francisco, 1923-24; head dept. field hockey Sargent Coll. Camp, N.H., 20 yrs.; dir. Firefly Diabetic Camp for Children, Pa., 1949; from sec. to v.p. to pres. Airedale Terrier Club Am., 1948-85, hon. pres., dir. 1985—; dog show judge, 1950—; bd. dirs. Animal Rescue League, Phila., 1975—. Author: Pet Airedale Terrier, 1960; Your Airedale. Editor newsletters for Airedale Terrier Club Am., 1948-85; contbr. to field hockey guides; columnist for various dog mags. Exhibitor terracotta sculpture in galleries. Mem. All-Am. Hockey Team, 1928-40. Mem. U.S. Field Hockey Assn. (sec. 1937-40, originator former editor Eagle, named to field hockey Hall of Fame, 1988). Republican. Episcopalian. Home: Beaver Hill Rd Birchrunville PA 19421

STREBER, BARBARA KOVACS, nutritionist; b. Allentown, Pa., Feb. 15, 1939; d. Louis and Julia (Elek) Kovacs; m. John Streber, Apr. 9, 1979; children: H. John, Gregory, Mark, Stephanie Dietrich. AA in Basic Studies, Broward Community Coll., 1981; BS in Dietetics and NTR with high honors, Fla. Internat. U., 1983; MS in Health Edn., Nova U., 1987. Cert. diabetes educator, vocat. tchr., Fla.; lic. dietitian nutritionist; registered dietitian, basic fitness instr. Nutrition educator Holy Cross Hosp., Ft. Lauderdale, 1986-89; behaviorist Holy Cross Weight Mgmt. Ctr., Ft. Lauderdale, 1987-90; instr. Broward Community Coll., Ft. Lauderdale, 1989—; pvt. practice Ft. Lauderdale, 1988—. Author: Weight Control for Ambulatory Patients with Diabetes Mellitus, The Lite 'N Up Program for Weight Control. Chairperson dietetic tech. adv. com. Broward Community Coll., 1984-85, 89-90; mem. nutrition com. Broward County Sch. Bd. Mem. NAFE, Am. Dietetic Assn., Fla. Dietetic Assn. (chairperson opening night com. 1987), Broward County Dietetic Assn. (pres.-elect 1988-89, pres. 1989-90, chairperson nominating com. 1990—), Am. Diabetes Assn. (profl. sect.), Am. Running and Fitness Assn., Am. Heart Assn. Address: 4520 NE 18th Ave #102 Fort Lauderdale FL 33334

STREBIG, MARY CATHERINE, small business owner, public relations consultant; b. Sunnyside, Wash., Dec. 13, 1948; d. Melvin E. and Catherine Virginia (Hathaway) Waller; m. James John Strebig II, Oct. 30, 1971; children: Rosina, Karina. BA, Linfield Coll., 1971. Secondary tchr. Cen. Point Sch. Dist., 1971-74; asst. worker Oreg. Pub. Welfare Div., Newport, 1975-76; interagency coord. Oreg. Dept. Human Resources, Newport, 1976-81; pub. rels. dir. Lincoln County Sch. Dist., Newport, Gresham Sch. Dists., 1986-89; owner, operator M.K. Hathaway Green Grocer, Portland, Oreg., 1989—; cons. Oreg. Sch. Bd. Assn. Bd. dirs. YMCA, 1986-89. Mem. Gresham Area C. of C. (v.p. 1988-89), Lincoln County Adoptive Parents, Oreg. Sch. Pub. Rels. Assn. (pres. 1988-89), Pub. Rels. Soc. Am. (accredited), Oreg. Confederation Sch. Adminstrs., Soroptimist Internat., Altrusa Internat. Democrat. Home: 4404 NE 24th Portland OR 97211

STRECKFUSS, MICHELLE ADRIENNE, benefits compensation specialist; b. Cin., Sept. 2, 1964; d. Ralph W. and Arleen A. (Arleth) S. BA in Communication Arts, U. Cin., 1986. Sr. plan adminstr. Assocs. Benefit Corp., Cin., 1987-88; account specialist United Benefits Agy., Cin., 1988-90; 401K account exec. Union Cen. Life Ins. Co., Cin., 1990—. Contbr. to World's Best Loved Poems, 1986 (Silver Poet award). Vol. League Animal Welfare, 1983—; cert. emergency med. technician Great Oaks Tng., Cin., 1989.

STREDDE, SHARON, community foundation executive; b. Aurora, Ill., May 24, 1946; m. Edward H. Stredde, Jan. 24, 1969; 1 child, Robert E. BA, U. Ill., 1968. Asst. to State Rep. Sue Deuchler, Aurora, 1980-82; devel. coordinator YWCA, Aurora, 1982-83; corp. sec. Aurora Found., 1986-87, exec. dir., 1987—. Mem. Coop. Planning and Budgeting, Aurora, Aurora Area Fundraisers; bd. dirs. YWCA, Aurora, 1983-86; mem. bd. edn. West Aurora, Ill., 1985—. Mem. Aurora C. of C. Republican. Congregational. Club: AAUW (Aurora) (asst. treas. 1985-86). Lodge: Rotary. Office: Aurora Found 111 W Downer Pl #312 Aurora IL 60506

STREEP, MERYL (MARY LOUISE STREEP), actress; b. Madison, N.J., June 22, 1949; d. Harry Jr. and Mary W. Streep; m. Donald J. Gummer, 1978; children: Henry, Mary Willa, Grace Jane. BA, Vassar Coll., 1971; MFA, Yale U., 1975, DFA (hon.), 1983; DFA (hon.), Dartmouth Coll., 1981. Ind. actress stage, screen, 1975—. Appeared with Green Mountain Guild, Woodstock, Vt.; Broadway debut in Trelawny of the Wells, Lincoln Center Beaumont Theater, 1975; N.Y.C. theatrical appearances include 27 Wagons Full of Cotton (Theatre World award), A Memory of Two Mondays, Henry V, Secret Service, The Taming of the Shrew, Measure for Measure, The Cherry Orchard, Happy End, Wonderland, Taken in Marriage, Alice in Concert (Obie award 1981); movie appearances include Julia, 1977, The Deer Hunter, 1978 (Best Supporting Actress award Nat. Soc. Film Critics), Manhattan, 1979, The Seduction of Joe Tynan, 1979, Kramer vs. Kramer, 1980 (N.Y. Film Critics' award, Los Angeles Film Critics' award, both for best actress, Golden Globe award, Acad. award for best supporting actress), The French Lieutenant's Woman, 1981 (Los Angeles Film Critics award for best actress, Brit. Acad. award, Golden Globe award 1981), Sophie's Choice, 1982 (Acad. award for best actress, Los Angeles Film Critics award for best actress, Golden Globe award 1982), Still of the Night, 1982, Silkwood, 1983, Falling in Love, 1984, Plenty, 1985, Out of Africa, 1985 (Los Angeles Film Critics award for best actress 1985), Heartburn, 1986, Ironweed, 1987, A Cry in the Dark, 1988 (named Best Actress N.Y. Film Critics' Circle, 1988, Best Actress Cannes Film Festival, 1989), She-Devil, 1989, Postcards From the Edge, 1990; TV film The Deadliest Season, 1977; TV mini-series Holocaust, 1978 (Emmy award); TV dramatic spls. Secret Service, 1977, Uncommon Women and Others, 1978; TV (narrator) A Vanishing Wilderness, 1990. Recipient Mademoiselle award, 1976, Woman of Yr. award B'nai Brith, 1979, Woman of Yr. award Hasty Pudding Soc., Harvard U., 1980, Best Supporting Actress award Nat. Bd. of Rev., 1979, Best Actress award Nat. Bd. of Rev., 1982, Star of Yr. award Nat. Assn. Theater Owners, 1983, People's Choice award, 1983, 85, 86, 87. Office: care Internat Creative Mgmt 40 W 57th St New York NY 10019*

STREET, KATHRYN CAROL, mortgage company executive; b. Rochester, N.Y., Dec. 22, 1960; d. John Phillips and Ann Featherstone (Hunt) S. BA, Smith Coll., 1983. Mortgage account exec. Sibley Mortgage Corp., Rochester, N.Y., 1983-85; branch mgr. Sibley Mortgage Corp., 1985—, asst. v.p., 1986—. Mem. Mortgage Bankers Assn., Women's Coun. Realtors, Sigma Xi. Democrat. Home: 592 Broadway Apt 2N Menands NY 12204

STREET, LINDA KAYE, management consultant; b. Memphis, Feb. 14, 1958; d. Elvin Lee and Pearlie B. Street. Student, Memphis State U., Tenn., 1981. Dept. mgr. Dillards Dept. Store, Memphis, 1982-83; mgr. Federal Express, Memphis, 1983-88; sr. mgr. Federal Express, Indpls., 1988—. Office: Federal Express Corp 3502 South High Sch Rd Indianapolis IN 46251

STREET, PATRICIA LYNN, educator; b. Lillington, N.C., May 3, 1940; d. William Banks and Vandalia (McLean) S.; m. Col. Robert Gest, June 2, 1962 (div. 1985); children: Robert, Roblyn Renee. BS, Livingstone Coll., 1962; MEd, Salisbury State U., 1974; postgrad., various, 1968-88. Tchr. Govt. of Guam Marianas Island, Agana, Guam, 1962-64; sec., typist USAF, Glasgow AFB, Mont., 1964-65, Syracuse (N.Y.) U. AeroSpace Engring., 1966-67; tchr. Syracuse (N.Y.) City Sch. System, 1967-69; lectr. U. of Md., Eastern Shore, Princess Anne, Md., 1970-72; tchr. Prince George's County Pub. Schs., Upper Marlboro, Md., 1973—; lectr. in bus. adminstrn. Bowie State U., Md., 1990—; instr. U. Guam, Anderson AFB, 1963, U.S. Armed Forces Inst., Anderson AFB, 1963, Yorktowne Bus. Inst., Landover, Md., 1987—, Cheseapeake Bus. Inst., Clinton, Md., 1983—; asst. advisor student tchrs. U. Md. Ea. Shore, Princess Anne, 1972; conv. speaker. Mem. Md. Bus. Edn. Assn. (pres.-elect 1987-88, pres. 1988-89), Md. Vocat. Assn. (regional rep. 1986-89, audit chmn. 1987-89, Vocat.-Tech. Educator of Yr. award 1989), Ea. Bus. Edn. Assn. (co-editor newsletter 1990—), D.C. Bus. Edn. Assn., Nat. Bus. Edn. Assn., Data Processing Mgmt. Assn., Assn. Supervision and Curriculum Devel., Internat. Soc. for Bus. Edn., Md. Bus. Edn. Com., Am. Vocat. Assn. Democrat. Baptist. Home: 8922 Goldfield Pl Clinton MD 20735 Office: Prince George's Pub Sch Upper Marlboro MD 20772

STREET, SHELBY BENNETT, educational administrator; b. Bakersville, N.C., Mar. 5, 1940; d. Jesse Simeon and Hattie (Campbell) Bennett; m. Buddy Eugene Street, June 10, 1961; children: Elizabeth Eujana, Johnathan David. BS, East Tenn. State U., 1961, MA in Elem. Edn., 1970; postgrad., Ea. Carolina U. Cert. adminstrv. and curriculum specialist, N.C. Tchr. Merrywood Elem. Sch., Greenwood, S.C., 1961-62, Fairmont Elem. Sch., Johnson City, Tenn., 1962-74, Louisburg (N.C.) High Sch., 1976-78, Louisburg Elem. Sch., 1978-80; prin. King Springs Sch., Johnson City, 1974-76; gen. supr. Franklin County Schs., Louisburg, 1980—. Mem. Am. Soc. for Curriculum and Devel., AAUW, NEA, N.C. Assn. Educators, Franklin County Assn. Educators, Delta Kappa Gamma (pres. Louisburg 1986-89). Methodist. Home: 304 Cottrell St Louisburg NC 27549 Office: Franklin County Schs 105 Bickett Blvd Louisburg NC 27549

STREETER, ANNE PAUL, state senator; b. Phila., July 21, 1926; s. Henry Neill and Marianne (Harris) Paul; m. Ronald Mather Streeter; children—Jean, Deborah, Stephen, Richard, Jonathan. B.A., Smith Coll., 1948. Tchr. Springside Sch., Phila., 1948-1949, Oxford Sch., West Hartford, Conn., 1949-1950; mem. Conn. Senate, Hartford, 1982-87, dep. majority leader, 1985-87. Mem. West Hartford Town Council, 1973-81, mayor, 1975-81. Named Woman of Year, Jr. C. of C., West Hartford, 1979, Hartford, 1981. Mem. LWV (pres. 1966-67, 1969-72). Republican. Congregationalist. Home: 31 Brookmoor Rd West Hartford CT 06107

STREETMAN, NANCY KATHERINE, cellist; b. Houston, Feb. 15, 1933; d. Sam and Christine (Norman) S. BS, U. Houston, 1953; Diploma, Juilliard Sch. Music, 1960; MA, Sarah Lawrence Coll., 1961. Instr. cello Manhattan Sch. Music, N.Y.C., 1967—, Manatee Community Coll., Bradenton, Fla., 1989—, Fla. W. Coast Symphony Youth Program, Sarasota, Fla., 1989—; instr. cello UN Internat. Sch., N.Y.C., 1967-84; free lance chamber musician various groups, N.Y.C. and on tour. Mem. Prospect Heights Neighborhood Assn. (pres. 1975-78), Bklyn. Mem. Sarasota/ Manatee Amiga Computer Group (v.p. 1988—). Democrat. Home: 1617 Bayhouse Ct 117 Sarasota FL 34231

STREISAND, BARBRA JOAN, singer, actress; b. Bklyn., Apr. 24, 1942; d. Emanuel and Diana (Rosen) S.; m. Elliott Gould, Mar. 1963 (div.); 1 son, Jason Emanuel. Grad. high sch., Bklyn.; student, Yeshiva of Bklyn. N.Y. theatre debut Another Evening with Harry Stoones, 1961; appeared in Broadway musical I Can Get It for You Wholesale, 1962, Funny Girl, 1964-65; rec. artist Columbia Records; motion pictures include Funny Girl, 1968, Hello Dolly, 1969, On a Clear Day You Can See Forever, 1970, The Owl and the Pussy Cat, 1970, What's Up Doc?, 1972, Up the Sandbox, 1972, The Way We Were, 1973, For Pete's Sake, 1974, Funny Lady, 1975, The Main Event, 1979, All Night Long, 1981, Nuts, 1987; star, producer film A Star is Born, 1976; producer, dir., star Yentl, 1983, The Prince of Tides, 1990; TV spls. include My Name is Barbra, 1965 (5 Emmy awards), Color Me Barbra, 1966; Gold record albums include People, 1965, My Name is Barbra, 1965, Color Me Barbra, 1966, Barbra Streisand: A Happening in Central Park, 1968, Barbra Streisand: One Voice, Stoney End, 1971, Barbra Joan Streisand, 1972, The Way We Were, 1974, A Star is Born, 1976, Superman, 1977, The Stars Salute Israel at 30, 1978, Wet, 1979, (with Barry Gibb) Guilty, 1980, Emotion, 1984, The Broadway Album, 1986, Til I Loved You, 1989; other albums include: A Collection: Greatest Hits, 1989. Recipient Emmy award, CBS-TV spl. (My Name Is Barbra), 1964, Acad. award as best actress (Funny Girl), 1968, Golden Globe award (Funny Girl), 1969, co-recipient Acad. award for best song (Evergreen), 1976, Georgie award AGVA 1977, Grammy awards for best female pop vocalist, 1963, 64, 65, 77, 86, for best song writer (with Paul Williams), 1977, Tony award (spl. award), 1970. Office: Creative Artists Agy care Fred Spector 1888 Century Pk E Ste 1400 Los Angeles CA 90067*

STRENGTH, JANIS GRACE, educator; b. Ozark, Ala., Jan. 31, 1934; d. James Marion and Mary Belle (Riley) Grace; m. Robert Samuel Strength, Sept. 12, 1954; children: Stewart A., James Houston (dec.), Robert David (dec.), James Steven (dec.). BS in Home Econs. and Edn., Auburn U., 1956; MA in Edn., Washington U., St. Louis, 1978, MA in Adminstrn., 1980. Home economist Gulf Power Co., Pensacola, Fla., 1956-59; tchr. sci. Northside Jr. High Sch., Greenwood, S.C., 1961-68; tchrs. home econs. Greenwood High Sch., 1968-70; chairperson dept. sci. Parkway West Jr. High Sch., Chesterfield, Mo., 1975-82; tchr. sci. Parkway West High Sch., Chesterfield, 1982-88; v.p.-sec. Product Safety Mgmt. Inc., Gulf Breeze, Fla., 1989—; chairperson dist. Phys. Scis. Curriculum Com., 1978-85, Sci. Fair Placement Com., 1978-82, Gifted Edn., 1983-84; leader Phys. Sci. Summer Workshops, Safety Sci. Lab. Workshop; sponsor Nat. Jr. Honor Soc., Parkway West Jr. Class. Supt. youth dept. Sunday sch. Greentrails Meth. Ch., sponsor summer camp; vol. fundraiser March of Dimes, Cerebral Palsy, Multiple Schlorosis, Cancer funds; judge Parkway/Monsanto/St. Louis Post Dispatch Sci. Fairs, 1978—; mem. citizens action com. Parkway Sch. Bd., 1980-84. Mem. NEA, Nat. Sci. Tchrs. Assn., Santa Rosa Women's Club, Greenwood Country Club, Cherry Hills Country Club (Glencoe, Mo.), Raintree Country Club (Hillsboro, Mo.). Republican. Methodist. Office: Product Safety Mgmt Inc Gulf Breeze FL 32561

STRETCH, SHIRLEY MARIE, marketing educator; b. Wauneta, Nebr., May 6, 1949; d. Lloyd Ray and Roberta Marie (Schroeder) S.; BS, U. Nebr., 1971; MS, Kans. State U., 1972; MBA, Ohio State U., 1977, PhD, 1982. Instr. clothing and textiles Bowling Green (Ohio) State U., 1972-75; grad. adminstrv. asso. Univ. Coll., Ohio State U., 1976-78, 80; asso. mgr. direct mktg. div. Ashland Petroleum Co. (Ky.), 1979-80; asst. prof. clothing and textiles Tex. Tech U., Lubbock, 1980-85; assoc. prof. mktg. Valdosta State Coll., Ga., 1985-87, Calif. State U., L.A., 1987—. Pres., mem. bd. adminstrn. Sunport Condominium. Ednl. Profl. Devel. fellow, 1971-73. Mem. Am. Mktg. Assn., So. Calif. Assn. MBA Execs., Nat. Assn. Female Execs., Am. Home Econs. Assn., So. Mktg. Assn., Southwestern Mktg. Assn., Western Mktg. Assn., Am. Collegiate Retailing Assn., Omicron Nu, Phi Upsilon Omicron. Republican. Methodist. Club: Toastmasters. Office: Calif State U Dept Mktg Los Angeles CA 90032

STRICK, SADIE ELAINE, psychologist; b. Masontown, Pa., May 5, 1929; d. Michael and Mary (Oziemblowski) Wierzbicki; m. John Macovjak, Aug. 10, 1947 (dec. Mar. 1972); children: Deborah, Susan; m. Ellis Strick, Aug. 11, 1974. BSW, U. Pitts., 1975, MEd, 1977, PhD, 1981. Lic. psychologist; clin. assoc. med. psychotherapist. Psychologist I Mayview State Hosp., Bridgeville, Pa., 1984-87; owner Counseling & Behavior Specialists, Pitts., 1981—; guest speaker Compassionate Friends, Pitts., 1986—, Womens Career Conv., Pitts., 1982. Bd. dirs. OAR/Allegheny, Pitts., 1981-82. Mem. Am. Psychol. Assn., Am. Mental Health Counselors Assn., Am. Assn. Counseling and Devel., Pa. Psychol. Assn., Press Club, Nat. Assn. Women Bus. Owners, Pitts. Assn. for Theory and Practice of Psychoanalysis, Am. Bd. Med. Psychotherapists (clin. assoc.). Home: 2160 Greentree Rd W 605 Pittsburgh PA 15220 Office: Counseling and Behavior Specialists 429 Forbes Ave Ste 1614 Pittsburgh PA 15219

STRICKHOLM, KAREN, corporate entertainment marketing specialist; b. Glen Cove, N.Y., July 19, 1958; d. Harry and Jean (Cason) S. BA, U. Mass., 1984; postgrad., UCLA, 1984-86. Account exec. Braun and Co., L.A., 1986-88; v.p. Rogers and Cowan, Inc., L.A., 1989—. Cons. Children Now, L.A., 1989—; activist Calif. State Transp. Com., Sacramento, 1989—. Mem. Women in Communications, Inc. (bd. dirs. L.A. chpt. 1989-90, exec. v.p. 1990-91), Women in Film. Democrat.

STRICKLAND, CHERYL ANN, small business owner; b. Elkhart, Ind., May 13, 1951; d. Charles Austin and Lois Jean (Kilmer) Wernicke; children: Tara, Shannon. Grad. high sch., Plantation, Fla. Pres. Drapery Arts Interiors, Swannanoa, N.C., 1979-89, Strickland Enterprises, Swannanoa, 1988—, Profl. Drapery Seminars, Swannanoa, 1988—; leader seminars in field. Author: Professional Drapery Seminars Handbook, 1988, rev. edit., 1990; feature writer for Draperies and Window Coverings. Mem. Bus. and Profl. Women's Assn., Black Mountain Swannanoa C. of C. (pres.). Home and Office: 230 Westwood Ave Swannanoa NC 28778

STRICKLAND, FRANCES MELVINA, personnel executive; b. Abbeville, S.C., June 2, 1957; d. Robert Monroe and Frances Beatrice (Coleman) S. BA, Duke U., Durham, N.C., 1978. From prodn. supr. to employee rels. rep. Union Carbide Corp., Greenwood, S.C., 1980-83, dept. supr., 1983-84; from employment specialist to sr. indsl. relations specialis Robert Bosch Corp., Charleston Heights, S.C., 1984-87, unit mgr., 1987—; Gospel singer North & South, Book II, ABC miniseries, 1986. Poet Let 'Em Go, 1988. Advisor Jr. Achievement of Greater Charleston, 1986-87, vice chmn. Charleston County Pvt. Ind. Coun., 1988—; vol. leadership com. YWCA, 1986-88, mem. leadership devel. com., 1989; mem. Gov.'s Bd., Cities in Schs. at Risk Youth Prog., 1988; mem. homeless steering com. for adminstrn. of McKinney Act Funds, Charleston Pvt. Ind. Coun., 1989-90, chmn. planning com., 1988-89. Mem. NAFE, Tri County Pers. Assn., North Charleston Alumni chpt. Delta Sigma Theta (sec. 1988—). Office: Associated Fuel Pump Systems Corp 2005 E Greenville St Ste 10 & 11 Anderson SC 29621

STRICKLAND, JULIA ALLISON, executive assistant; b. Laredo AFB, Tex., Jan. 6, 1963; d. Bryan Dalton and Charlotte Elizabeth (Stallings) S. BA cum laude, U. Ala., 1983. Intern HUD, Washington, 1983; jr. sec. Dominion Fed. Savs. & Loan, McLean, Va., 1984, exec. sec., 1984-86, secondary mktg. dir., 1985-86, exec. asst., 1986—. Participant Inst. on Comparative Polit. and Econ. Systems, Washington, 1983. Mem. Alumnae Assn., Alpha Delta Pi. Office: Trustbank Savings FSB 7799 Leesburg Pike Falls Church VA 22043

STRICKLAND, ROSE MARY NAMEE, marketing executive; b. Shreveport, La., Sept. 25, 1935; d. Ellis and Adele (George) Namee; children: David Boyd Jr., Donald Wayne, Darlene Adele. Owner Rose Mary & Assocs., Inc., Shreveport; demonstration supr. Foremost Foods, Coca-Cola. Mem. NAFE, Nat. Assn. Demonstration Cos., Shreveport C. of C. Democrat. Baptist. Home: 9155 Simmons Blvd Shreveport LA 71118 Office: 3034 Bert Kouns Industrial Loop Shreveport LA 71118

STRICKLIN, ALICE CAROLYN, publishing executive; b. Knoxville, Tenn., Nov. 11, 1959; d. William Joseph and Alice Carolyn (West) S.; m. Joseph Paul Chiarello, May 17, 1980 (div. May 29, 1988); 1 child, Mary Conner. BS, Rutgers U., 1987; MBA, St. Joseph's U., 1989. Fin. analyst Macmillan Pub. Co., Inc., Riverside, N.J., 1985-86; acctg. mgr. Macmillan Pub. Co., Inc., Riverside, 1986-88; bus. mgr. W.B. Saunders Co., Harcourt Brace Jovanovich, Inc., Phila., 1988-89, dir. bus. mgmt. & fin. adminstrn., 1989—. Contbr. articles to profl. jours. Com. chair Young Rep. Assn. South Jersey, Mt. Holly, 1989—; sponsor Phila. Mus., 1988—, Met. Opera Guild, N.Y.C., 1988—. Named Vis. Scholar/Russian Studies Internat. Studies Program Rutgers U., 1987. Mem. Young Rep. Assn. South Jersey (chmn. 1989—), New Eng. Women, DAR, Colonial Daughters of the Seventeenth Century, Inc., Delta Zeta Alumni Assn. South Jersey. Republican. Presbyterian. Office: W B Saunders Co Independence Sq W Philadelphia PA 19106-3399

STRIEFSKY, LINDA ANN, lawyer; b. Carbondale, Pa., Apr. 27, 1952; d. Leo James and Antoinette Marie (Carachilo) S.; m. James Richard Carlson, Nov. 3, 1984; children: David Carlson, Paul Carlson. BA summa cum laude, Marywood Coll., 1974; JD, Georgetown U., 1977. Bar: Ohio 1977. Assoc., Thompson, Hine and Flory, Cleve., 1977-85, ptnr., 1985—. Loaned exec. United Way of Northeast Ohio, Cleve., 1974. Mem. Am. Bar Found., ABA (mem. real estate fin. com. 1980—), Ohio State Bar Assn. (bd. govs. real property sect. 1985—), Greater Cleve. Bar Assn. (chmn. bar applicants com. 1983-84, exec. council young lawyers sect. 1982-85, chmn. 1984-85, mem. exec. council real property sect. 1980-84; Merit Svc. award 1983, 85), Pi Gamma Mu. Democrat. Roman Catholic. Home: 2222 Delamere Rd Cleveland Heights OH 44106 Office: Thompson Hine and Flory 1100 Nat City Bank Bldg Cleveland OH 44114-3070

STRIEGEL, PEGGY SIMSARIAN, advertising executive; b. Phila., July 12, 1941; d. Robert Ernest Samuel and Margaret (Miller) Thompson; m. James P. Simsarian, Sept. 4, 1965 (div. Sept. 1976); children: Catherine Ann, Sheila Thompson; m. Louis E. Striegel, Sept. 14, 1976 (div. June 1984). BA, Sarah Lawrence Coll., 1963. Asst. editor Oxford U. Press, N.Y.C., 1963-64; picture editor Western Pub. Co., N.Y.C., 1964-66; art editor Houghton-Mifflin, Inc., Boston, 1966-68; pres. Peggy's Graphics, McLean, Va., 1968-78, Striegel Advt. and Graphics, Inc., Broken Arrow, Okla., 1978—. Lower Merion (Pa.) area coordinator Shapp for Congress, Phila., 1970; area coordinator and graphic designer Phillips for U.S. Congress, McLean, 1972; mktg. cons. Striegel for U.S. Congress, Broken Arrow, 1982; bd. dirs. Gatesway Found., Broker Arrow, 1987—, Planned Parenthood N.E. Okla and Ea. Arks., 1988—; chmn. Community Playhouse Broken Arrow, 1979-81. Recipient numerous advt. awards including several Addies and citations Tulsa Advt. Club, 1980-88, Gold Quill, 1983, Cert. Merit Printing Industries Am., 1983, Award of Excellence Am. Inst. Graphic Arts, 1983. Mem. Advt. Fedn. Tulsa, Bus. and Profl. Advt. Assn. (Gold Ring award 1986, 87), Women in Communications (treas. Tulsa 1987, program chmn. 1988), Exec. Womens' Forum, Builders Assn. Met. Tulsa, Direct Mktg. Assn., Internat. Assn. Bus. Communicators, Met. Tulsa C. of C., Broken Arrow C. of C. Democrat. Presbyterian. Club: Art Directors. Home: 6110 S 221st E Ave Broken Arrow OK 74014 Office: 716 S Main St Broken Arrow OK 74012

STRIFE, MARY LOUISE, librarian; b. Lowville, N.Y., June 9, 1959; d. Kenneth Francis and Frances Katherine (Linck) S. BA in Biology, SUNY Coll., Potsdam, N.Y., 1981; MLS, SUNY, Buffalo, 1982. Reference libr. Cornell Univ., Ithaca, N.Y., 1982-85; libr. United Technologies Corp., East Hartford, Conn., 1985-86; reference libr. Syracuse (N.Y.) Univ., 1986-86, Univ. Rochester, Rochester, N.Y., 1986-89; coord. of pub. svcs. SUNY Inst. Tech., Utica, N.Y., 1989—. Mem. Upstate N.Y. Spl. Librs. Assn. (treas. 1990-91), N.Y. Libr. Assn. (Academic & Spl. Librs. sect. sec., treas. 1988-90), ALA, Spl. Librs. Assn., Gamma Sigma Sigma. Democrat. Roman Catholic. Office: SUNY Inst Tech Marcy Campus PO Box 3051 Utica NY 13504

STRIKER, SANDRA DARLENE, customer sales and service professional; b. Lorain, Ohio. Grad., Lorain Bus. Coll., 1958; BA, Lorain County Community Coll., 1985. Exec. sec. Elyria (Ohio) YMCA, 1974-77; communications cons. Elyria Telephone Co., 1977-81, bus. office mgr., 1981-88, mgr. customer sales and svc., 1988—; pub. rels. speaker Elyria Telephone Co., 1984—. Mem. allocations com. United Way; coord. March of Dimes, 1988; bd. trustees Ret. Sr. Citizens Com., 1990—; bd. dirs. bd. trustee YMCA, Elyria, 1981-85, treas., 1982-84. Mem. Women's Network. Home: 705 Cornell Ave Elyria OH 44035 Office: Elyria Telephone Co PO Box 4033 Elyria OH 44036

STRIN-GOLD, LAURIE MICHELLE, municipal government professional; b. Los Angeles, May 31, 1961; d. Marvin Arthur and Marilyn Barbara (Cohen) Strin; m. Harold Benjamin Gold, Mar. 20, 1983. BS in Polit. Sci., So. Meth. U., 1982, M of Pub. Adminstrn., 1985. Adminstrv. intern City of University Park, Tex., 1983-84; mgmt. asst. city mgr.'s office City of Dallas, 1985-86, adminstrv. asst. fin. dept., 1986-87, asst. mgr. tax collections Dept. Revenue and Taxation, 1987-90, spl. collections mgr. Dept. Revenue and Taxation, 1990—. Mem. women's com. Dallas Theatre Ctr.; del. Tex. Dem. Conv., 1982. Mem. Internat. City Mgmt. Assn., Am. Soc. Pub. Adminstrn., Urban Mgmt. Assts. North Tex. (program, profl. devel. coms.), ACLU, NOW, Greenpeace. Jewish. Office: City of Dallas Revenue and Tax Dept 1500 Marilla 2DN Dallas TX 75201

STRO, MARY ANNE, educational administrator; b. Chgo., Jan. 19, 1943; d. James Vicent and Edna Marcia (O'Connell) Routson; m. Jack Hugh Stro, June 21, 1969 (div. 1979). B.A., Northeastern Ill. State U., 1968; postgrad. U. Calif.-San Diego, 1969-74; M.S., San Diego State U., 1976; Ed.D., U.S. Internat., 1982. Counselor, Montgomery Jr. High Sch., San Diego, 1971-75, asst. prin., 1975-77, prin., 1982-84; asst. prin. Southwest High, San Diego, 1977-82; dir. curriculum and instrn. Sweetwater Union High Sch., Chula Vista, Calif., 1985—, dir. pub. info. and govt. relations, 1987—; mem. Western Assn. Schs. and Colls. Accredation Team, San Diego, 1982, 83, 84, 86; assessor, dir., trainer San Diego County Leadership Assessment Ctr., 1984—; mem. San Diego Council Adminstrv. Women Edn., 1984—. Active City Chula Vista Human Relation Commn., 1974; treas. South Bay Community Services, Inc., 1985—, pres. exec. bd., 1987—. Recipient Susan B. Anthony award NOW, 1983; twin honoree YWCA, 1986; named Woman of Achievement, Pres.'s Council 1983-84; Exec. Educator 100, 1985. Mem. Am. Bus. Women's Assn. (exec. bd. 1984—, NOW, Assn. Supervision and Curriculum Devel., Assn. Calif. Sch. Adminstrs., Southwest Adminstrn. Assn. (v.p. 1983-84), Mgmt. Assn. Sweetwater Dist. (pres.-elect 1985), Nat. Council Adminstrv. Women Edn. Office: Sweetwater Union High Sch Dist 1130 5th Ave Chula Vista CA 92011

STROBEL, SHIRLEY HOLCOMB, magazine editor, educator, non-profit organization writer; b. Hastings, Nebr., May 8, 1929; d. Dent Z. and Helen (Spriegel) Holcomb; m. Howard Austin Strobel, Aug. 26, 1953; children: Paul Austin, Gary Dent, Linda Susan Strobel Helgeson. BS, Northwestern U., 1951; MA, Duke U., 1953. Cert. counselor, N.C.; tchr., N.C. English tchr. Salem Acad., Winston-Salem, N.C., 1952-53; tchr. Durham city schs., N.C., 1954-55, Durham County schs., 1967-90; editor Ch. Tchrs. mag. Nat. Tchrs. Edn. Project, Durham, 1986-89; editor Ch. Tchrs. Harper-Collins, San Francisco, 1990—; team tchr. Duke U., Durham, 1986—; chmn. dept. English Jordan High Sch., Durham, 1967-75; reader Nat. Coun. Tchrs. of English, 1969-71; rsch. asst. CUNY, 1973-74; mem. accreditation team Duke U. Edn. Program, 1985. Co-author: Advanced Placement English, 1983. Founder, pres. Threshold Clubhouse for Mentally Ill, Durham, 1985, chmn. capital campaign, 1988—; active Area Bd. Mental Health, Durham, 1990—. Democrat. Baptist. Home and Office: 1119 Woodburn Rd Durham NC 27705

STROBLE, COLETTE MARY HOULE, plastering and stucco company executive; b. Manchester, N.H., Aug. 10, 1947; d. George Albert and Mary Agnes (Sala) H.; m. Randolph E. Stroble Jr. (div.); children: B.J., Danielle, Alden. Student, CAP Regional Staff Coll. Tex., 1985, 86. Lic. real estate agt., stucco/plasterer. Switchboard operator Leavitt's Dept. Store, Manchester, N.H., 1965-66, with credit office, 1966-67, merchandizer, advertiser, 1966-69; advt. marketer Ariz. wide K-Mart, Mesa; owner, mgr. Colette's Boutique, Mesa, 1980-82; co-founder, chief exec. officer, sec.-treas. Stroble Devel., Gilbert, Ariz., 1977—; cons. area wide constrn. firms, Phoenix, 1979-90; tchr. plastering and stucco, Phoenix, 1987-90; realtor personal real estate property, Phoenix, 1988-90. Author, editor Wing Tips, 1985-86; co-inventor, electronic locator transmitter. Maj., squadron leader, fin. officer, personnel officer CAP, Mesa, 1990; active Dept. Disabled/Disadvantaged, Phoenix. Recipient Humanitarian award Dept. Econ. Security, Mesa, 1989, Letters of Appreciation, Leper Colony, Mexico, 1989. Mem. Nat. Assn. Search and Rescue (life), World Wing Kung Fu Assn., Rosicrucian Fraternal Orgn. (dep. master, master). Office: Stroble Plastering & Stucco 721 N Monterey Ste 103 Gilbert AZ 85234

STROCCHIA-RIVERA, LENORE, psychologist; b. Queens, N.Y., Oct. 7, 1959; d. Ralph Joseph and Anne Carmela (Bellacicco) Strocchia; m. Carlos Strocchia-Rivera, Oct. 20, 1984. BS, Fordham U., 1981; MA, U. Tex., 1983, PhD, 1988. Cert. sch. psychologist; lic. psychologist, N.Y. Psychologist Carmel (N.Y.) Psychol. Assocs., 1990—, Rhinebeck (N.Y.) Psychol. Assocs., 1990—. Vol., Beyond War, Palo Alto, Calif., 1985—. Dwight D. Book award, U. Tex., 1981, Henderson Hewlitt scholar, 1982-84. Mem. Am. Psychol. Assn., N.Y. Assn. Sch. Psychologists. Home: 26 Bell Dr Highland NY 12528

STROCK, ANITA See SCHERER, ANITA

STRODEL, ADRIENNE MACATEE, education educator; b. Dallas, Oct. 9, 1962; d. George P. Macatee and Shirley Elizabeth (McBride) Macatee; m. Daniel. Student, St. Clare's Hall, Oxford, Eng., 1980-81, So. Meth. U., Dallas, 1983-84; BA with Spl. Honors, U. Tex., 1984; postgrad., U. North Tex., Denton, 1988—. Sec. tchr. Richardson Ind. Sch. Dist., Tex., 1985-. Tchr., leader Highland Park Presbyn. Ch., Dallas, 1982-87; Vol. I Have a Dream. Mem. Am. Assn. Tchrs. German, Nat. Coun. of Social Studies, Jr. League Dallas, Kappa Alpha Theta. Republican. Presbyterian. Home: 6604 Chevy Chase Dallas TX 75225

STROM, ELIZABETH (LIBBY) ANN, social worker; b. Edgefield, S.C., May 31, 1965; d. Wilson Lee and Doris (Hudson) Strom. BA in Sociology, U. S.C., Aiken, 1987; MSW, U. S.C., 1990. Lic. master social worker. Legis. intern S.C. Ho. of Reps., Columbia, 1988; social worker Univ. Hosp., Augusta, Ga., 1988-89, Eisenhower Army Med. Ctr., Augusta, 1988-90; program counselor Kid's HELP Family Counseling Svc., Inc., Aiken, S.C., 1990—; asst. mgr. Edgefield Billiard Parlor, 1983—; program counselor Kids' HELP Family Counseling Svc., Aiken, S.C., 1990—. Coach Spl. Olympics, Aiken, 1986. Mem. Nat. Assn. Social Workers. Baptist. Home: 427 Addison St Edgefield SC 29824

STROM, JULIE KAY, advertising executive; b. Oak Park, Ill., July 1, 1947; d. Harry Frank and Janette Henrietta (Nomden) Strom; m. Donald Robert Strandell, May 15, 1982; children: Strom Robert, Soni Karin. BS in Radio and TV, U. Ill., 1969. Copy writer, Post Keyes Gardner, Chgo., 1969-70; assoc. creative dir. Needham, Harper & Steers, Chgo., 1970-75; sr. v.p., creative dir. Benton & Bowles, Chgo., 1975-85; sr. v.p., exec. creative dir Darcy Masius Benton & Bowles, Chgo., 1985-89; pres. Strom Strandell, Inc., Chgo., 1989—. Office: Strom Strandell Inc 557 Arlington Pl Chicago IL 60614

STROM, SHIRLEY LONGETEIG, civic worker; b. Craigmont, Idaho, Jan. 28, 1931; d. Iver J. and Frances Willard (Mason) Longeteig; m. Robert C. Strom, June 15, 1952; children: Kristin, Trina, Camber. BA with honors, U. Idaho, 1952. Mem. Idaho Rep. Com., 1954-58, mem. exec. com., 1976-84; rep. Nat. Rep. Conv., 1968, 72; mem. Craigmont Plannign and Zoning Commn., 1965-70, justice of peace, 1967-70; trustee Lewis County Libr. Dist., 1980—, past chmn.; mem. letters and sci. adv. coun. U. Idaho, Moscow, 1986—, chmn. centennial fund U. Idaho Libr., 1988-90; chmn. Idaho Women's Polit. Caucus, 1975, Idaho Higher Edn. Polit. Action CCom., 1986-89; mem. Idaho Humanities Coun., 1988—; mem. community adv. coun. Lewiston (Idaho) Morning Tribune, 1988-89. Recipient cert. of appreciation Lewis County Rep. Com., 1984. Mem. NOW, Nat. Women's Polit. Caucus, U. Idaho Alumni Assn. (bd. dirs. 1977-84, pres. 1982-83, Alumni Svc. award 1988), Libr. Assocs. U. Idaho, Lewis County Hist. Soc., Order Eastern Star (grand Esther 1970), Pi Gamma Mu.

STROMAN, PATRICIA ANN HARRIS, systems analyst; b. Charleston, W.Va., Dec. 2, 1953; d. Paul Frederick and Faye Virginia (Shafer) Harris; m. Harry Jackson Stroman Oct. 23, 1980; children—James Harris, Virginia Louise. A.S., W.Va. Inst. Tech., 1973. Programmer, Carlton Industries, Richmond, Va., 1974-76; cons. SIS Inc., Richmond, 1976-77; team leader State of Va., Richmond, 1977-80, Airline Tariff Co., Dulles Airport, Washington, 1980-82; WITCO Chem. co., Woodeliffe Lake, N.J., 1982-84; cons. in field 1986; lead analyst Nat. Liberty Corp., 1987—; systems cons. Nat. Liberty Corp., 1988-89. Mem. Nat. Assn. Female Execs. Republican. Presbyterian. Home: 1022 Winfield Ct Lansdale PA 19446

STROMBERG, ANNE B., management consultant, executive recruiter; b. Sidney, Ohio; d. Joseph M. and Mary Louise (Marrs) Bell; children: Steve Stromberg, Anastasia Pflug. Student, Ohio No. U., 1949-50, Ind. U., 1950-51, Miami U., Oxford, Ohio, 1951-52, U. Dayton, 1953-54, Citrus Coll., 1955, U. Nev., 1960-61, Calif. State U., L.A., 1964-65. Tchr. various elem. schs., 1955-65; coord. corp. travel and relocations Mattel, Inc., Hawthorne, Calif., 1966-71; mng. dir. Morgan, Bentley, Bristol, Pasadena, Calif., 1974—; founder L.A. Travel and Transp. Coun., 1969; founder, speaker Careers in Transition Seminars. pub., editor Morgan Plus Four, 1964-65. Dir., mem. adv. bd. Cross Roads/New Life, Hemet, Calif., 1979—; participant Save the Books, L.A., 1986, L.A. Hist. Theater Found., 1989, 90. Named an Outstanding Woman in Bus., Orange County Register, 1976. Mem. DAR, Colonial Dames, Nat. Assn. Exec. Recruiters. Republican. Office: Morgan Bentley Bristol 115 W California Ste 293 Pasadena CA 91115

STROMBERG, PATRICIA ROBERTS, library media specialist; b. Cin., Apr. 23, 1932; d. Richard Bickmore and Ruth Hessler Roberts; children: Mark Alan, Ruth Ann Stromberg Bennet. BS in Edn., U. Cin., 1954; postgrad., Our Lady of the Lake Coll., San Antonio, 1973-75; MA in Edn., U. Colo., 1979. Tchr. Cin. Pub. Schs., 1954-56, Mt. Healthy (Ohio) Pub. Schs., 1972-73; library media specialist Jefferson County Pub. Schs., Golden, Colo., 1976—; mem. basic list com., 1976-77, 89-90; computer cons. JEFFCO Schs., 1983-88; co-chair gifted and talented com. Pleasant View Sch., Golden, Colo., 1987—; project dir. title IV C Child Drama Grant, 1980-84. Ruling elder on session, 1982-84, 88—, chair of worship and Christian edn. commns. of Green Mt. Presbyn. Ch., 1988, 89, Social Justice and Peacemaking Commn. Presbytery of Denver, 1989—. Mem. AAUW, Jefferson County Edn. Assn., Jefferson County Internat. Reading Assn. (sec. 1978-79), Colo. Coun. Internat. Reading Assn. (workshop presenter), Internat. Reading Assn., Phi Delta Kappa. Republican. Home: 12834 W Iliff Ave Lakewood CO 80228 Office: Peiffer Elem Sch 4997 S Miller Way Littleton CO 80401

STROM-PAIKIN, JOYCE ELIZABETH, nursing administrator; b. Syracuse, N.Y., Oct. 25, 1946; d. Paul H. and Elizabeth (Bartlett) Strom Black; m. Frank J. Iaconis, May 31, 1963 (div. Mar. 1974); children: Paul, Michael; m. Lester Paikin, June 26, 1982. AAS in Nursing, Cayoga Community Coll., Auburn, N.Y., 1976; BS, Nova U., Ft. Lauderdale, Fla., 1978, MS, 1980; PhD candidate, Saybrook Inst., San Francisco, 1988—. Diplomate Am. Bd. Med. Psychotherapy; cert. psychiat. nurse clinician. Surg. nurse Auburn Meml. Hosp., 1967-70; office nurse Auburn, 1971-74; charge nurse Mercy Rehab. Ctr., Auburn, 1974-75; nurse St. Joseph's Hosp., Syracuse, 1975-76, charge psychiat. nurse, 1976-77; staff psychotherapist, nursing adminstr. Psycho-Awareness Inc., Tamarac, Fla., 1980—; adj. prof. Nova U., 1976-79, Broward Community Coll., Ft. Lauderdale, 1980—; cons. Impaired Profls., Tallahassee, 1983—. Author: Medical Treason, 1989; contbr. articles to profl. jours. Mem. Am. Psychol. Assn., Am. Assn. Counseling and Devel., Am. Nurses Acad., Nat. Psychiat. Assn., Broward County Mental health Assn. Democrat. Episcopalian. Lodge: Soroptimists. Office: Psycho-Awareness Inc 5455 N State Rd 7 Fort Lauderdale FL 33319

STRONG, ALDA (MRS. LAVERNE STRONG), community service volunteer, realtor; b. Menan, Idaho, Sept. 22, 1911; d. William D. and Margaret (Hunting) Watson; grad. high school; nat. grad. Realestate Inst., 1977; m. LaVern Strong, June 14, 1930; children—Nalda (Mrs. Richard C. Powell), Harvey, Deanna (Mrs. Douglas Vollmer). Active Internat. Toastmistress Clubs, 1951—, organizer 4 local clubs, pres. council number 9, No. region, 1959-60, parliamentarian No. region, 1960-61; legislative chmn. Idaho Bus. and Profl. Women's Clubs, 1958-59, chmn. pub. relations, 1959-61, pres.; safety chmn. Idaho Gen. Fedn. Women's Clubs, 1960-61, Idaho chmn., 1964, state safety chmn.; sec. dist. South Central Bus. and Profl. Clubs, 1967; pres. 20th Century, Twin Falls, Idaho, 1962-63; bd. dirs. Twin Falls Salvation Army, chmn., 1975-78, life mem. Salvation Army; state rep. to President's Safety Conf. Mich. State U. Organizer 5 safety clubs Nat. Safety Council; safety chmn. So. Idaho Citizens Safety Council; regional dir. Idaho Women's Hwy. Safety Leaders, 1971-74; bd. dirs. Twin Falls Civic Auditorium, 1959-61; chmn. Twin Falls County chpt. Nat. Found.; sec. Idaho Hosp. Auxiliaries, 1959-60; pres. Twin Falls YWCA; mem. Salvation Army (life); sponsor Sigma chpt. Beta Sigma Phi; sec.-treas. Twin Falls County Civil Def.; past pres. Gem. State Writers Guild, editor Gem State News Letter, 1970-71; mem. Nat. Assn. Parliamentarians (Idaho pres. 1977-80). Candidate Idaho Ho. of Reps., 1960. Recipient Certificate of Merit award Nat. Safety Council, 1959; named Woman of Year, Bus. and Profl. Women's Clubs, 1966, Magic Toastmistress Club, Number 1002, No. region, 1959; Disting. Service award Jr. C. of C., 1960, merit award Idaho Safety Council; registered parliamentarian. Mem. Idaho Bd. Realtors (parliamentarian 1976—). Clubs: Greater Fedn. Women (past local pres.); 20th Century Federated (fine arts chmn. 2d v.p.). Lodges: Altrusa (internat. chmn.), Ladies of Elks (past pres.). Home: PO Box 31 Twin Falls ID 83301

STRONG, BARBARA IRENE, municipal official; b. Stoughton, Mass., Apr. 11, 1935; d. Alfred Strong and Irene Dorothy (Bellay) Woodward. Grad. high sch., Attleboro, Mass. Stenographer Phoenix-London Ins. Co., Providence, 1953-55; legal sec. Lyne, Woodworth & Evarts, Boston, 1955-57; sec. Transp. Displays, Inc., Boston, 1957-59, Hartford Fire Ins. Co., Boston, 1959-62; office mgr. Bicknell, Inc., Framingham, Mass., 1962-70, Paul J. Woods Co., Inc., Needham, Mass., 1970-73; adminstrv. asst. Devel. and Indsl. Commn., Attleboro, Mass., 1973-75; office mgr. Attleboro Redevel. Authority, 1975-85, exec. dir., 1985—. Home: 40 Bank St Attleboro MA 02703 Office: Attleboro Redevel Authority 7 Park St Rm 210 Attleboro MA 02703

STRONG, BETHANY JUNE, novelist, publisher, editor; b. Oklahoma City, June 13, 1906; d. Nicholas Henry and Anna Augusta (Spuhler) McLaughlin; m. John Donovan Strong, Sept. 2, 1928; children: Patricia, Virginia. BS in History of Ideas, Johns Hopkins U., 1966. Novelist, freelance writer, pub., editor Parable Press, Amherst, Mass., 1978—; cons. in field. Author: The King's Generalissima, 1976, First Love, 1978, Murder in the Mirror, 1985; also articles. Mem. Nat. Writers Club, Nat. League Am. Pen Women (pres. Conn. Valley br.). Roman Catholic. Avocation: photography.

STRONG, CAROLYN JEAN, educational administrator; b. Portland, Oreg., Feb. 3, 1947; d. Harold Joseph and Rose DeLima (Sevigny) Roetker; m. Gary Eugene Strong, Mar. 14, 1970; children: Christopher Eric, Jennifer Rebecca. BA, Marylhurst (Oreg.) Coll., 1969; MA, Calif. State U., Sacramento, 1986. Cert. life tchr., adminstr., Wash., Calif. Tchr. Portland Pub. Schs., 1970-73, St. Michael's Elem. Sch., Olympia, Wash., 1977-78; substitute tchr. Everett (Wash.) Parochial Schs., 1973-77, North Thurston Sch. Dist., Lacey, Wash., 1979-80; tchr. Sierra Sch., Sacramento, 1980-81, dir. pvt. sch., 1981-82; tchr. Folsom-Cordova Sch. Dist., Rancho Cordova, Calif., 1982-88, program mgr. attendance and due process, 1988—. Editor Snohomish County Foster Parents Newsletter, 1975-76, State of Wash. Legis. Newsletter, 1978-79. Religious edn. coord. Immaculate Conception Parish, Everett, 1974-75; v.p. Everett Opera Guild, 1975; bd. dirs. Mountain View Sch. PTA, Lacey, 1976-77, Statewide Polit. Campaign, Olympia, Wash., 1978; founder Calif. State Libr. Found., Sacramento, 1985—; tchr. religious edn. St John the Evangelist Ch., Carmichael, Calf., 1986-88; mem. parish coun., 1988—; pres. Del Campo Little League, Carmichael, 1986-87; leader Girl Scouts U.S., 1978-84; den mother Cub Scouts, 1978-84. Marylhurst Coll. grantee, 1965. Mem. Calif. Assn. Sch. Child Welfare and Attendance (sec. Delta-Sierra sect.), Calif. Consortium for Ind. Study (regional rep. 1987-89), Assn. Calif. Sch. Adminstrs. (chpt. legis. chair), AAUW (life, Wash. State legis. chmn. 1979-80, pres. Olympia 1980). Democrat. Home: 6247 Heathcliff Dr Carmichael CA 95608 Office: Folsom-Cordova Sch Dist 10850 Gadsten Way Rancho Cordova CA 95742

STRONG, CAROLYN RAY, electronics company official; b. Pasadena, Calif., Jan. 9, 1951; d. Albert Charles and Juliana (Ray) S. B.A. in Math., Whitworth Coll., 1973; postgrad., DeVry Inst. Tech., 1975-77, U. Oreg., 1986—. Math. and aerospace demonstrator Pacific Sci. Ctr., Seattle, 1970, 71; component info. specialist Tektronix, Inc., Beaverton, Oreg., 1973-75, tech. writer, 1975-76, tech. publs. group mgr., 1976-79, tech. communications mgr., 1979-85; tech. publs. and computer tng. mgr., 1985-86, mgr. lab. instruments documentation, 1986-89, mgr. lab. instruments mktg. support, 1989—; cons. Portland Community Coll., Chemeketa Community Coll. Bd. dirs. First Tech. Fed. Credit Union, 1984—, sec., 1985-86, vice chmn., 1986-87, chmn. 1987—. Mem. Soc. Tech. Communications (sr. mem., sec. Willamette Valley chpt. 1978, treas. 1979, pres. 1979-80). Home: 1325 NW 92nd Ave Portland OR 97229 Office: PO Box 500 Beaverton OR 97077

STRONG, GAY, industrial relations and human resources executive; b. Santa Monica, Calif., Jan. 13, 1930; d. Claude Roderick and Katherine Anna (Brown) Riley; m. Duane Gordon Strong, Aug. 20, 1949; children: Philip, Katherine, Patricia, Barbara. Student UCLA, 1947-49; AA, Pierce Coll., 1969; BA in English, Calif. State U., Northridge, 1973. With credit office, store ops., then asst. personnel mgr. Builders Emporium, Van Nuys, Calif., 1969-74, personnel mgr., 1974-78; dir. indsl. relations GC Internat., Hawthorne, Calif., 1978-81; personnel mgr. Lok Products Co., Fullerton, Calif., 1981-82; chief exec. officer Asset Recovery, Santa Monica, Calif., 1982-83; dir. Human Resource Targeted Coverage, Inc., Glendora, Calif., 1983-89, editor house organ, 1983-89; dir. human resources GC Internat., 1989—. Republican. Editor Builders Emporium house organ, 1972-78, Targeted Coverage house organ, 1983-88. Office: 907 S Magnolia Ave Monrovia CA 91016

STRONG, JOAN, designer; b. Wheeling, W. Va., Dec. 7, 1951; d. Harry and Madeline Margaret Mary (Cerrito) S. AAS in Communication tech, Community Coll. Air Force, 1980; BA in Bus. and Mgmt., U. Md., 1981; MS in Communication Design, Pratt Inst., Bklyn., 1985. Command, control engr. USAF, Pacific & European Theatre, 1979-81; freelance designer, art dir. NYC, 1982-84; art dir. Juhl Advt. Agy., Elkhart, Ind., 1984-87; section designer US News and World Report, Wash.; pub. affairs officer USAF Reserve, Md., N.J., Ind., 1983—. 1st Lt. USAF, 1976-82; capt. USAFR, 1990—. Mem. Reserve Officers Assn., Soc. of Newspaper Design, Cousteau Soc., Smithsonian Inst., Computer Graphics for Design Assn. Republican. Roman Catholic. Office: US News & World Report 2400 N St NW Washington DC 20037

STRONG, LAURA MARIE, cosmetics and retail business owner; b. Cortland, N.Y., May 13, 1963; d. Jack and Beatrice (Dyer) S. Grad. high sch., Groton, N.Y. Owner apparel shop and cosmetics line Peachy Keen, Groton, 1985—. Home: 129 Main St Groton NY 13073

STRONG, LOUISE CONNALLY, geneticist; b. San Antonio, Apr. 23, 1944; d. Ben Clarkson and Sarah Nell (Allen) Connally; m. Beeman Ewell Strong III, Jan. 10, 1970; children: Beeman Connally, Larkin Louise. BA, U. Tex., 1966; MD, U. Tex. Med. Br., Galveston, 1970. Diplomate Tex. State Bd. Med. Examiners. Faculty Grad. Sch. Biomed. Scis. U. Tex. Health Sci. Ctr., Houston, 1972—, rsch. assoc. Med. Genetics Ctr., 1972-73; asst. prof. pediatrics and biology, asst. geneticist U. Tex. M.D. Anderson Cancer Ctr., 1976-79, assoc. prof. exptl. pediatrics, assoc. geneticist, 1979—, Sue and Radcliffe Killam prof., 1981—; part-time asst. prof. U. Tex. Health Sci. Ctr., 1973-78; vis. prof. pediatrics, U. Tex. Med. Sch., U. Tex. Health Sci. Ctr., 1988—; nat. adv. bd. Dept. Health and Human Svcs., Nat. Cancer Inst., NIH, Bethesda, Md., 1984—, bd. scientific counselors Div. Cancer Etiology, Nat. Cancer Inst., 1981-84, mem. search com. for dep. dir. Div. Extramural Activities, Nat. Cancer Inst., speaker in field, others. Contbr. articles to profl. jours., books and abstracts. Named Warren E. Wheeler Vis. Prof., Children's Hosp., Columbus, Ohio, 1989; recipient Marjorie W. Margolin Award for Outstanding Achievement in Retina Rsch., Retina Rsch. Found., Houston, 1987, Outstanding Achievement in Field of Oncology, State Pres.'s BPW award Tex. Fedn. Bus. and Profl. Women's Clubs, 1984, several scholarships; grantee NIH, 1984-92, John S. Dunn Rsch. Found., 1989-91, Retina Rsch. Found., 1982-90, Joe and Jessie Crump Fund Med. Rsch., 1982-83, Kelsey-Leary Found., others. Mem. AAAS, Am. Assn. Cancer Rsch. AMA, Am. Med. Women's Assn., Am. Men and Women in Sci., Am. Soc. Human Genetics, Am. Soc. Preventive Oncology, Environ. Health Inst., Tex. Genetics Soc., Phil. Soc. Tex. Office: 1515 Holcombe Blvd HMB Box #209 Houston TX 77030

STRONG, MARCELLA LEE, music specialist, educator; b. East Liverpool, Ohio, Oct. 16, 1954; d. Carl and Ruth I. (White) Hinkle; m. David Lee Strong, Feb 19, 1977. BA magna cum laude, U. Toledo, 1976; MA in Early Childhood Edn., Kent State U., 1982. Cert. music, elem. tchr., Ohio. Music instr. Cardinal Local Schs., Parkman and Huntsburg, Ohio, 1977—. Choir dir. G.V. Nazarene Ch., Orwell, Ohio 1981-83; organist, mem. bd. deacons Huntsburg Congl. Ch., 1985—; mem., officer Orwell Farm Bur. Mem. Cardinal Edn Assn. (negotiator 1982, 84, 87, 90, sec. 1983-84, treas. 1984-85, pres. 1985-86, 89-90), Ohio Music Educators Assn., Kappa Delta Pi, Mu Phi Epsilon. Democrat. Home: 96 Penniman Rd Box 370 Orwell OH 44076

STRONG, SUSAN CLANCEY, communication consultant; b. Cin., Nov. 10, 1939; d. William Power and Elizabeth (Browne) Clancey; m. Oliver Swigert, 1957 (div. 1972); children: Silvia, David Mack; m. Richard Devon Strong, 1977. BA, Northwestern U., 1965; MA, U. Calif., Berkeley, 1972, PhD, 1979. Tchr. Helen Bush Parkside Sch., Seattle, 1965-66, Taipei (Taiwan) Lang. Inst., 1967-68; acting instr. U. Calif., Berkeley, 1972-78, teaching fellow, 1979, lectr., 1979-84; lectr. St. Mary's Coll., Moraga, Calif., 1982-85; pvt. practice Orinda, Calif., 1985-90; sr. rsch. assoc. Ctr. for Econ. Conversion, 1990—; mem. Contra Costa County Conflict Resolution Panels, Calif., 1987—; affiliate Support Ctr./CTD, San Francisco, 1987—. Author poetry, columnist, book reviewer, 1986—. Mem. Bay Area Global Tomorrow Com., 1988; mem. exec. com. Sane/Freeze, Washington, 1989; conf. co-chmn. Nat. San/Freeze Congress, 1989-90; rep. nat. bd. advisors Sane/Freeze, Washington, 1989—; mem. bd. advisors Peace and Environ. Project, San Francisco, 1986-88; chairperson No. Calif. Sane/Freeze, San Francisco, 1985-89. Mem. Bay Area OD Network, ASTD, Phi Beta Kappa. Democrat. Episcopalian.

STRONG-CUEVAS, ELIZABETH, sculptor; b. St. Germain en Laye, France, Jan. 22, 1929 (Am. citizen); d. George and Margaret (Strong) de Cuevas; 1 child, Deborah Carmichael. Student, Vassar Coll., 1946-48; AB, Sarah Lawrence Coll., 1952; postgrad., Art Students League, N.Y.C., 1963-68. One-woman shows include Lee Ault Gallery, N.Y.C., 1977-78, Tower Gallery, Southampton, N.Y., 1980, Iolas-Jackson Gallery, N.Y.C., 1983, 85, Guild Hall Mus., East Hampton, N.Y., 1985, Kerr Gallery, N.Y.C., 1988—, Ruth Vered Gallery, East Hampton, 1988; exhibited in group shows at Guild Hall, East Hampton, 1980, Art Students League of N.Y., 1982, Bruce Mus., Greenwich, Conn., 1984, 85, Tower Gallery, N.Y.C., 1984, Andre Zarre Gallery, N.Y.C., 1985, Kouros Gallery, N.Y.C. and Ridgefield, Conn., 1985, Susan Blanchard Gallery, N.Y.C., 1985-86, Ruth Vered Gallery, East Hampton, 1986-87, Benton Gallery, Southampton, 1987—, Kerr Gallery, N.Y.C., 1988—, Elaine Benson Gallery, Bridgehampton, N.Y., 1989, Portico, Inc., Cologne Art Fair, 1989, Feingarten Galleries, N.Y. Art Show, 1990; represented in pvt. collections. Club: Vassar of N.Y.

STRONG-TIDMAN, VIRGINIA ADELE, marketing and advertising executive; b. Englewood, N.J., July 26, 1947; d. Alan Ballentine and Virginia Leona (Harris) Strong; m. John Fletcher Tidman, Sept. 23, 1978. BS, Albright Coll., Reading, Pa., 1969; postgrad. U. Pitts., 1970-73, U. Louisville, 1975-76. Exec. trainee Pomeroy's div. Allied Stores, Reading, 1969-70; mktg. rsch. analyst Heinz U.S.A., Pitts., 1970-74; new products mktg. mgr. Ky. Fried Chicken, Louisville, 1974-76; dir. Pitts. office M/A/R/C, 1976-79; assoc. rsch. dir. Henderson Advt., Inc., Greenville, S.C., 1979-81; sr. v.p., dir. rsch. Bozell, Jacobs, Kenyon & Eckhardt, Inc., Dallas, 1981-86, sr. v.p., dir. rsch. and strategic planning Atlanta, 1986-88; sr. v.p., dir. mktg. svcs. Bozell, Inc., Atlanta, 1988—; cons. mktg. rsch. Greenville Zool. Soc., 1981; adj. prof. So. Meth. U., 1984-85. Mem. Am. Mktg. Assn. (Effie award N.Y. chpt. 1982). Republican. Episcopalian. Home: 1835 Johnson Ferry Rd Atlanta GA 30319 Office: Bozell Inc 3490 Piedmont Rd Ste 1400 Atlanta GA 30305

STRONZ, MICHELLE MARIE, real estate development executive; b. Canton, Ohio, Mar. 19, 1957; d. Michael Patrick and Helen Irene (Strebeck) S. BS in Journalism, Ohio U., 1979; MPA, U. Wash., 1984. Reporter Jamestown (N.Y.) Post Jour., 1976-78; editorial asst. Good Housekeeping Mag., N.Y.C., 1978; asst. mgr. pub. affairs Internat. Paper Co., N.Y.C., 1979-81; speechwriter, chancellor's office U. Mo., Columbia, 1981-82; asst. to pres. Wash. Coun. Internat. Trade, Seattle, 1982-84; econ. cons. U.S. Econ. Devel. Adminstrn., Meriden, Conn., 1984; asst. exec. dir. Meriden Econ. Devel. Corp., 1985; exec. dir. Middlesex Indsl. Devel. Corp., Middletown, Conn., 1985—. Chmn. community assessment component of strategic plan Middlesex United Way, 1988-89; team mem. Conn.-China Goodwill Mission, 1989. Mem. Pvt. Industry Coun. (vice chmn. 1985-89, chmn. 1989—), Conn. Assn. Mcpl. Devel. Commns. (v.p. 1986-89), Northeastern Indsl. Devel. Coun., Nat. Assn. Bus. Economists, Am. Econ. Devel. Coun. Democrat. Roman Catholic. Office: Middlesex Indsl Devel Corp 393 Main St Middletown CT 06457

STROOMER, KATHRYN PAULETTE, management analyst, real estate executive; b. Bridgeport, Conn., Feb. 28, 1949; d. Cornelius Jacob and Kathryn Harriet (Novak) S. BA in English, U. Conn., 1972; MBA, U. New Haven, 1987. Editorial asst. Golf Digest/Tennis, Norwalk, Conn., 1974; proposal coordinator Sikorsky Aircraft div. United Techs. Corp., Stratford, Conn., 1974-78, procedures analyst, 1979-82, supr. mfg. engrs., systems and procedures, 1982-87, supplier rating analyst, 1987; pres. Equity Enterprises, Ansonia, Conn., 1986—; specialist policy devel. Textron Lycoming, Stratford, 1988—; pres. The Prose Shop, Ansonia, 1986—; cons. in fin. Editor (textbook) Flexible Mfg. Systems, 1985. Contbr. community action com., Seymour, Conn., 1986. Mem. Am. Mgmt. Assn., Soc. Mfg. Engrs. (sec. 1984-87), Am. Congress on Real Estate, NAFE, Sikorsky Suprs. (mem. health/welfare com. 1986), Toastmasters (adminstrv. v.p. 1986-87, pres. 1988, area 11 gov. 1989-90), CEO Club. Republican. Home: PO Box 222 Ansonia CT 06401 Office: Textron Lycoming 550 Main St Stratford CT 06497 also: Equity Enterprises PO Box 286 Ansonia CT 06401

STROTHER, PAT WALLACE, author; b. Birmingham, Ala., Mar. 11, 1929; d. Claude Hunter and Gladys Eleanor (English) Wallace; m. Lee Levitt, 1951 (div. 1957); m. 2d, David G. Latner, 1958 (div. 1968); m. 3d, Robert A. Strother, 1980. Student, U. Tenn., 1947-51. Dir. women's programs WGNS Radio, Murfreesboro, Tenn., 1951-52; continuity dir. WMAK Radio, Nashville, 1952-54; asst. editor Civil Svc. Leader, N.Y.C., 1955-57; adminstrv. sec. Local 237 Teamsters, N.Y.C., 1957-76; works include: House of Scorpio, 1975, This Willing Passion, 1978, The Wand and the Star, 1978, Traitor in My Arms, 1979, The Voyagers, 1980, Once More the Sun, Silver Fire, 1982, My Loving Enemy, Summer Kingdom, 1983, Sweetheart Contract, Shining Hour, Objections Overruled, 1984, Love Scene, Star Rise, Unyielding Fire, 1985, Under the Sign of Scorpio, The Constant Star, A Wife for Ransom, 1986, Grand Design, 1988, Silvermore, 1989, Golden Windows, 1990. Mem. Authors Guild. Democrat.

STROTHMAN, ELEANOR SHAWFIELD JACOBS, communications executive; b. Harrisburg, Pa., July 22, 1940; d. William Wood and Emma Millie (Shawfield) Jacobs; m. James Edward Strothman, Sept. 9, 1961; children: Joseph E., Jill Emma Strothman Furuya, Stuart W. BA, Pa. State U., 1961; JD, NYU, 1976. Bar: N.Y. 1977. County govt. reporter Patent Trader newspaper, Mt. Kisco, N.Y., 1977-79; staff writer Con Edison, N.Y.C., 1979-81, sr. staff writer, 1981-87, dir. communications svcs., 1987—. Lay reader, newsletter editor Episcopal Ch. St. Mary the Virgin, Chappaqua, N.Y., 1989—. Home: 25 Bischoff Ave Chappaqua NY 10514 Office: Con Edison Rm 1640 4 Irving Pl New York NY 10003

STROTHMAN, WENDY JO, book publisher; b. Pitts., July 29, 1950; d. Walter Richard and Mary Ann (Hodtum) S.; m. Mark Kavanaugh Metzger, Nov. 25, 1978; children: Andrew Richard, Margaret Ann. Student, U. Chgo., 1979-80; AB, Brown U., 1972. Copywriter, mktg. U. Chgo. Press, 1973-76, editor, 1977-80, gen. editor, 1980-83, asst. dir., 1983; dir. Beacon Press, Boston, 1983—; trustee Brown U., 1990—. Bd. editors Brown Alumni Monthly, 1983-89, chmn., 1986-89. Bd. dirs. Editorial Project for Edn., trustee, 1987—, treas., 1988—. Mem. Renaissance Soc. (bd. dirs. 1980-83), Pubs. Lunch Club (N.Y.C.). Office: Beacon Press 25 Beacon St Boston MA 02108

STROUD, CASSANDRA INDIA, lawyer; b. Lynchburg, Va., May 22, 1960; d. James Wesley and Jeanette Lou (Garner) S. BA, U. Va., 1982; JD, N.C. Cen. U., 1985. Bar: Va. 1986, N.J. 1986, U.S. Dist. Ct. (ea. dist.) Va. 1987, U.S. Ct. Appeals (4th cir.) 1987, U.S. Bankruptcy Ct. (ea. dist.) Va. 1987. Law clk. Office Atty. Gen. State of Va., Richmond, summer 1984; law intern Office Dist. Atty. State of N.C., Durham, 1985; staff atty. Tidewater Legal Aid Soc., Chesapeake, Va., 1987-89; asst. atty. Commonwealth of Va., Petersburg, 1989-90; assoc. atty. Bland and Stroud, Petersburg, 1990; asst. pub. defender City of Petersburg, 1990—. Sec. Chesapeake Task Force Coun. on Youth Svcs., 1987-89; ch. directress and organist. Mem. Va. Bar Assn., Norfolk-Portsmouth Bar Assn., Old Dominion Bar Assn., Twin City Bar Assn., Virginia Beach Jaycees (community service dir. 1988), Chesapeake Bar Assn., NAACP, Phi Alpha Delta, Alpha Kappa Alpha. Democrat. Baptist. Club: Buddies (Lynchburg). Home: 189 Crater Woods Ct Petersburg VA 23805 Office: Office of Pub Defender Community Bank Bldg 212 N Sycamore St Petersburg VA 23803

STROUD, MEG DANIELSON, nurse; b. Salt Lake City, June 8, 1955; d. Paul Danielson and Bonnie Sue (Anderson) Paul. Assoc. degree, Brigham Young U., 1978; postgrad., Westminster Coll., 1990—. RN; cert. Post Anesthesia Nurse. Staff post-anesthesia recovery nurse St. Mark's Hosp., Salt Lake City, 1978-85, asst. coordinator post-anesthesia recovery and ministay, 1985-86, dir., 1986-89; product mgr. Utah Med. Products, Salt Lake City, 1989—. Assoc. editor Jour. Post Anesthesia Nursing, 1988-90; contbr. certification rev. texts, articles to profl. jours. Res. dep. sheriff Salt Lake County Sheriff's office, 1980-82. Mem. Am. Soc. Post Anesthesia Nurses (charter, bd. dirs. 1982-83, treas. 1983-85, v.p. 1985-86, pres. 1986-87), Utah Soc. Post Anesthesia Nurses (founding pres. 1982-83), NAFE, Am. Nurses Assn., Utah Nurses Assn., Am. Assn. Critical Care Nurses. Home: 5362 Old Trenton Way Murray UT 84123 Office: Utah Med Products 7043 S 300 West 1200 E 1300 S Midvale UT 84047

STROUP, ELIZABETH FAYE, librarian; b. Tulsa, Mar. 25, 1939; d. Milton Earl and Lois (Buhl) S. BA in Philosophy, U. Wash., 1962, MLS, 1964. Intern Libr. of Congress, Washington, 1964-65; asst. dir. North Cen. Regional Libr., Wenatchee, Wash., 1966-69; reference specialist Congl. Reference div. Libr. of Congress, Washington, 1970-71, head nat. collections Div. for the Blind and Physically Handicapped, 1971-73, chief Congl. Reference div., 1973-78, dir. gen. reference, 1978-88; city libr., chief exec. officer Seattle Pub. Libr., 1988—; cons. U.S. Info. Svc., Indonesia, Feb. 1987. Mem. adv. bd. KCTS 9 Pub. TV, Seattle, 1988—; bd. visitors Sch. Librarianship, U. Wash., 1988—; bd. dirs. Wash. Literacy, 1988—. Mem. ALA (pres. reference and adult svcs. div. 1986-87, div. bd. 1985-88), Wash. Libr. Assn., D.C. Libr. Assn. (bd. dirs. 1975-76), City Club, Ranier Club. Office: Seattle Pub Libr 1000 4th Ave Seattle WA 98104

STROUP, KALA MAYS, university president. BA in Speech and Drama, U. Kans., 1959, MS in Psychology, 1964, PhD in Speech Communication and Human Rels., 1974. V.p. acad. affairs Emporia (Kans.) State U., 1978-83; pres. Murray State U., Ky., 1983-90, S.E. Mo. State U., Cape Girardeau, 1990—. Mem. nat. exec. bd. Boy Scouts Am., chair profl. devel. com.; mem. nat. adv. bd. SBA Devel. Ctrs.; chair ACE Leadership Commn. Fellow Am. Assn. State Colls. and Univs. (sr.), Phi Beta Kappa. Office: SE Mo State U One University Pla Cape Girardeau MO 63701

STROUP, MARGARET ANN, manager; b. Louisville, Jan. 30, 1939; d. John William and Margaret Alberta (Neff) Menges; m. O. Keith Stroup Jr., June 10, 1960; children: O. Keith III, Andrew John. BA, Ctr. Coll. Ky., 1960; MA, Ind. U., 1961; postgrad., U. Calif., 1988. Chmn., history dept. Florissant Valley Community Coll., St. Louis, 1968-74; dir., dept. of human resources St. Louis County Govt., Clayton, 1974-79; from dir., social responsibility to dir., strategic issues a Monsanto, St. Louis, 1979-86; dir. planning Monsanto Chem. Co., St. Louis, 1986—. Author (chpt.) Strategic Issues Mgmt., 1988. Contbr. articls to profl. jours. Mem. Women's Forum, 1980—, St. Louis, trustee First Congregational Ch., Webster Goves, Mo., 1986—, treas. Productive Living Bd., St. Louis, 1987—; trustee Centre Coll. of Ky., 1989. Mem. The Nat. Planning Forum (dir. 1988—), Coms. on Fng. Rels.. Republican. Office: Monsanto Chem Co 800 N Lindbergh G4NR Saint Louis MO 63167

STROUSE, CAROL LOUISE KIRCHMAN, vocational educator; b. Bloomsburg, Pa., Sept. 14, 1947; d. George and Jessie Helen (Kitchen) Kirchman; m. William Earle Strouse, June 21, 1965; children: Matthew Alexander, Nathaniel Kirchman Stroue. B.S. in Health and Phys. Edn., Lock Haven U., Pa., 1970; M.S. in Phys. Edn., Ind. State U.-Terre Haute, 1976. Cert. tchr. health, phys. edn. and spl. edn., Md. Tchr. phys. edn., Charles County Bd. Edn., LaPlata, Md., 1970-78, tchr. phy. edn., 1978-85, vocat. tchr., 1978-85, work domain coordinator, 1983-86, team leader, 1981-84, cons. elementary career edn., 1986-90, learning coord., 1990—; spl. edn. reading teacher Milton Somers Middle Sch., 1986—; bd. dirs. Leonard Hall Jr. Naval Acad., 1989—; gymnastics instr., coach Charles County Dept. Parks and Recreation, La Plata, 1973-79. Area coordinator Charles County Spl. Olympics, 1976-78, 82-83; coach soccer St. Mary's County Recreation and Parks, Mechanicsville, Md., 1982-84; mem. Charles County Bd. Elections, 1986; del. MSTA, 1987, 88, 89, del. NEA, 1989. Recipient Outstanding Coach award Saint Gymnastics Club, Waldorf, Md., 1982; Recognition for Vocat. Guidance Project, Charles County Bd. Edn., 1982. Mem. Nat. Edn. Assn. (state del. MSTA 1987-89, nat. del. 1989, faculty rep. 1983-89), Nat. Assn. Female Execs. Democrat. Methodist. Avocations: reading; swimming; cycling; arts and crafts. Home: Route 2 Box 174 Charlotte Hall MD 20622 Office: Charles County Bd Edn La Plata MD 20646

STRUBEL, ELLA DOYLE, advertising executive; b. Chgo., Mar. 14, 1940; d. George Floyd and Myrtle (McKnight) D.; m. Richard Craig G'sell, Apr. 26, 1969 (div. 1973); m. Richard Perry Strubel, Oct. 23, 1976; stepchildren: Douglas Arthur, Craig Tollerton. BA magna cum laude, Memphis State U., 1962; MA, U. Ill., 1963. Staff asst. Corinthian Broadcasting Co., N.Y.C., 1963-65; dir. advt.& pub. rels. WANE-TV, Ft. Wayne, Ind., 1965-66; asst. dir. advt. WBBM-TV, Chgo., 1966-67, mgr. sales promotion, 1967-69, dir. advt. sales promotion & info. svcs., 1969-70; pres. Ctr. Pub. Rels., Chgo., 1970-73; dir. pub. rels. Walthaw Watch Co., Chgo., 1973-74; mgr. advt. promotion & pub. rels. WMAQ-TV, Chgo., 1974-76; v.p. corp. rels. Kraft, Inc., Glenview, Ill., 1985-87; sr. v.p. corp. affairs Leo Burnett Co., Inc., Chgo., 1987—. Bd. dirs. Rehab. Inst. Chgo., Found. Excellence Teaching, Chgo. Found. Edn., Mus. Broadcast Communications, Chgo. Pub. Libr. Found.; pres. Women's Bd. Rehab Inst., 1982-84; mem. women's bd. Art Inst., Goodman Theatre. Mem. Chgo. Network (women's bd., Northwestern U., U. Chgo.), Casino Club (Chgo.), Racquet Club (Chgo.). Democrat. Presbyterian. Home: 55 W Goethe Chicago IL 60610 Office: Leo Burnett Co Inc 35 W Wacker Chicago IL 60601 also: 35 W Wacker Chicago IL 60601*

STRUBLE, SUE ANN RUDOLPH, teacher, beauty consultant, real estate associate; b. Ft. Wayne, Ind.; d. Francis Robert and Mabel Helen (Hinds) Rudolph; (div. Mar. 1983); children: Kristine Sue, Kathleen Ann. BS, Purdue U., 1964; postgrad., Coll. of Mt. St. Joseph, 1984—, Xavier U., 1984—, Purdue U., 1984—. Cert. tchr., Ill., Ind. Tchr. Peoria (Ill.) City Schs., Canton (Ill.) Community Schs., 1978; tchr., adminstr., co-owner presch. St. Vincent's Sch., Logansport, Ind., 1979; prin. and pre-sch. adminstr. Walton, Ind., co-owner presch., 1979; real estate assoc., br. mgr. Terra Realty, Logansport, Ind.; tchr. Milan (Ind.) Elem. Sch., 1987-88, Cen. Elem. Sch., Lawrenceburg, Ind., 1988—; cons. curriculum rsch. com. Canton Bd. Edn. Sec. Women's Dem. Club, Lawrenceburg, 1989—, Am. Legion Aux., Logansport, 1983. Mem. Cen. Elem. Parent Tchr. Orgn., Canton Parent Tchr. Assn. (sec. 1968), Profl. Women's Club (pres., v.p.), AAUW (past v.p.), Alpha Delta Kappa (past pres.), Delta Kappa Gamma (hon. tchs.). Roman Catholic. Home: 70 Glenn Dr Lawrenceburg IN 47025

STRUNK, ROSEMARY, banker; b. Casper, Wyo., Dec. 29, 1959; d. Alvin Daniel and Eunice Edith (Wilson) S. BA, Grinell Coll., 1981; JD, Hamline Law Sch., 1985. Monetary specialist Security Rare Coin and Bullion Corp., Mpls., 1985-86; account exec. Dean Witter Reynolds Inc., Bloomington, Minn., 1986-88; personal banker 1st Bank Nat. Assn., Mpls., 1988-89, trust officer, 1989—; mem. fin. com. Chrysalis, Mpls., 1987—. Mem. adv. council Sr. Options/Sr. Fedn. of Minn., St. Paul, 1986—. Mem. ABA, Hennepin County Bd. Assn., Minn. Woman Lawyers (bd. dirs. 1987-88), NAFE (exec. dir. Monday's Network 1987-88). Office: 1st Trust 1st Nat Bank Assn PO Box 64704 Saint Paul MN 55164-0704

STRUPP, JACQUELINE VIRGINIA, executive assistant; b. Montevideo, Uruguay, July 24, 1963; d. Gunther and Silvia (Klemens) Strupp; m. Gonzalo Campruip-Soms, June 25, 1986; children: Matias, Mercedes. BA with hons. cum laude, NYU, 1986. Customer svc. mgr. Games Mag./Mail Order, N.Y.C., 1986-88; treas.; asst. to chief exec. officer Hudson Properties, Lyndhurst, N.J., 1986-90.

STRUTHERS, BARBARA JOAN, health/medical products executive; b. Bend, Oreg., May 4, 1940; d. Homer Hans and Elizabeth Ruth (Wilson) Oft; m. Allen B. Struthers, Aug. 29, 1959 (div. May, 1970); children: Debra S., Leslie J., Brent A. BS, Washington State U., 1962; MS, Oreg. State U., 1969, PhD, 1973. Diplomate Am. Bd. Toxicology. Project leader Ralston Purina Co., St. Louis, 1973-75, sr. project leader, 1975-78, assoc. scientist, 1979-81, mgr. of toxicology, 1981-82; assoc. dir. Office of Sci. Affairs G.D. Searle & Co., Skokie, Ill., 1982-87; dir. gynecol. products G.D. Searle & Co., Skokie, 1987-88, dir. GI and anti-infective products, 1988—; speaker on sexually transmitted diseases to local high schs., Cook and Lake Counties, Ill., 1984-90. Contbr. articles to profl. jours. Judge Ill. Sci. Fairs, Deerfield/Wheeling, Ill., 1983-90; reader Reading for the Blind, Chgo., 1989-90. Recipient undergrad. rsch. fellowship NSF, Oreg. State U., 1970-73. Mem. Soc. Toxicology (ethics com., Washington 1987-89), Soc. for Advancement Contraception (chmn. annual meeting Chgo. 1986, bd. dirs. 1985—), Am. Inst. Nutrition, Am. Oil Chemists Soc., Midwestern Regional Chpt. Soc. Toxicology (councilor 1986-88). Home: 1706 Garand Dr Deerfield IL 60015 Office: GD Searle & Co 4901 Searle Pkwy Skokie IL 60077

STRUTHERS, DEBORAH MARY, medical corporation executive; b. Sydney, N.S.W., Australia, Feb. 4, 1952; came to U.S., 1973; d. Anthony Eric and Mary Patricia (O'Mullane) Gray; m. Theodore Ralph Culbertson, July 31, 1971 (div. 1979); m. Scott Cameron Struthers, Jan. 31, 1981 (div. 1988). Student St. Petersburg Jr. Coll., 1978-85, Eckerd Coll., 1985—. Fin. counselor Wuesthoff Meml. Hosp., Rockledge, Fla., 1973-75; adminstrv. dir. Dresden & Ticktin, M.D.s P.A., St. Petersburg, Fla., 1976-80; exec. dir., v.p. Am. Med. Mgmt., Inc., Clearwater, Fla., 1980—; pres., dir. All Women's Health Ctr., Inc., St. Petersburg, 1980—, All Women's Health Ctr. North Tampa, Fla., 1980—, All Women's Health Ctr. Tampa Inc., 1980—, Women's Ob-Gyn Ctr. Countryside, Inc., 1984—, All Women's Health Ctr. Sarasota, Fla., 1980—, All Women's Health Ctr. Ocala, Fla., 1980—, All Women's Health Ctr. Gainesville, Fla., 1981—, Lakeland Women's Health Ctr., Fla., 1980—, Ft. Myers Womens Health Ctr., Fla., 1980—, All Women's Health Ctr. Jacksonville, Fla., 1980—, Nat. Women's Health Services, Inc., Clearwater, Fla., 1983—, D.M.S. of Ft. Myers, Inc., 1985—, Alternative Human Service, 1979; treas., v.p., dir. Birthing Mgmt. Inc., 1985—.

STRYCHALSKI, IRENE DOROTHEA, orthodontist; b. Linz, Austria, Sept. 21, 1948; d. Joachim Victor and Mathilde Theodora (Goerner) VonVarendorff; m. James Theodore Strychalski, June 28, 1969; children: Erika, Elizabeth, Wanda, Laura. BS, U. Rochester, 1972; DDS, SUNY, 1975, MS, 1977. Cert. orthodontist, N.Y. Pvt. practice Dunkirk, N.Y., 1977—; clin. asst. prof. Buffalo Sch. Dental Medicine SUNY, 1977—; clin. asst. prof. Buffalo sch. dental medicine SUNY, 1977—. Contbr. articles to profl. jours. Officer, Am. Cancer Soc., 1984. Recipient of various fraternal awards. Mem. ADA, Am. Assn. Orthodontists, AAUW, Lamda Lamda. Lutheran. Home: 5170 W Shorewood Dr Dunkirk NY 14048 Office: 415 Main St Dunkirk NY 14048

STUART, ALICE MELISSA, lawyer; b. N.Y.C., Apr. 7, 1957; d. John Marberger and Marjorie Louise (Browne) S. BA, Ohio State U., 1977; JD, U. Chgo., 1980; LLM, NYU, 1982. Bar: N.Y. 1981, Ohio 1982, N.Y. 1982, U.S. Dist. Ct. (so. dist.) Ohio 1983, U.S. Dist. Ct. (so. and ea. dists.) N.Y. 1985. Assoc. Schwartz, Shapiro, Kelm & Warren, Columbus, Ohio, 1982-84, Paul, Weiss, Rifkind, Wharton & Garrison, N.Y.C., 1984-85, Kassel, Neuwirth & Geiger, N.Y.C., 1985-86, Phillips, Nizer, Benjamin, Krim & Ballon, N.Y.C., 1987—. Surrogate Speakers' Bur. Mondale-Bush Campaign, N.Y.C., 1984; mem. Lawyers for Bush-Quayle Campaign, N.Y.C., 1988. Mem. ABA, N.Y. State Bar Assn., Winston Churchill Meml. Library Soc., Jr. League, Phi Beta Kappa, Phi Kappa Phi, Alpha Lambda Delta. Republican. Presbyterian. Club: Women's Nat. Rep. (N.Y.C.). Office: Phillips Nizer Benjamin Krim & Ballon 40 W 57th St New York NY 10019

STUART, ANNE ELIZABETH, journalist, freelance writer, educator; b. Lansing, Mich., Nov. 5, 1956; m. Kenneth E. Parker, Aug. 13, 1983. BA in English and Journalism with honors, Mich. State U., 1979; MS in Journalism, Columbia U., N.Y.C., 1986. Mng. editor Mich. Nurse, East Lansing, Mich., 1979-80; reporter, editor Star-Gazette/Sunday Telegram, Elmira, N.Y., 1980-83; reporter Knickerbocker News, Albany, N.Y., 1983-85; intern Newsday, Long Island, N.Y., 1985; freelance writer N.Y.C. and Boston, 1985-87; beat reporter The Patriot Ledger, Quincy, Mass., 1987—; instr. adult edn. programs Emerson Coll., Boston, Brookline (Mass.) Coll., Cambridge U, Boston U., 1987—, Northeastern U., spring 1990. Contbr. chpts. to books; contbr. articles to Boston Mag., Boston Woman Mag., Women's Day, Mass. Health Care and other profl. jours.; mng. editor Mich. State U. newspaper The State News, 1978-79; other state news reporting and editing, 1975-78. Knight Found. for Specialized Journalism fellow, 1988; Brookdale Inst. scholar, Scripps-Howard Found. Jacqueline Radin Newsday scholar, 1985-86, The State News scholar, 1976-79; recipient nat. 1st pl. in-depth reporting Sigma Delta Chi Mark of Excellence Competition, 1986, 1st pl. in-depth reporting and feature writing, 1986, statewide 3d pl. N.Y. State Assn. Press Competition. Am. Acad. Family Physicians, 1983, Nat. Well-Done award Gannett Co., 1982, statewide 2d pl. in news Detroit Press 1979, La Nacion Press award, 1990. Mem. Nat. Writers Union. Home: PO Box 364 Quincy MA 02269 Office: The Patriot Ledger PO Box 498 Quincy MA 02269-0498

STUART, BEVERLY ANN, professional society administrator, director; b. Providence, Oct. 20, 1937; d. Alfred George and Phoebe (Spinks) Davies; (div. 1982); children: Catherine A. Upchurch, Elizabeth E. O'Hern. Student, St. Augustine (Fla.) Tech. Ctr., 1984. Membership dir. Am. Culinary Fedn., St. Augustine, 1984—. Vol. Hist. St. Augustine Preservation, 1981-83, Lightner Mus., St. Augustine, 1981-85, Lighthousekeeper House, St. Augustine, 1989—. Recipient Cert. of Recognition, State of Fla., 1983. Mem. Am. Bus. Women Assn. Presbyterian. Home: 213 Queen Rd Saint Augustine FL 32086 Office: Am Culinary Fedn 10 San Bartola Rd Saint Augustine FL 32085

STUART, DOROTHY MAE, artist; b. Fresno, Calif., Jan. 8, 1933; d. Robert Wesley Williams and Maria Theresa (Gad) Tressler; m. Reginald Ross Stuart, Mar. 18, 1952; children: Doris Lynne Stuart Willis, Darlene Mae Stuart Cavalletto, Sue Anne Stuart Peters. Student, Calif. State U. Fresno, 1952-53, Fresno City Coll., 1962-64. Artist, art judge, presenter demonstrations at schs., fairs and art orgns. Calif., 1962—; editor and art dir. Centennial of Fresno High Sch.: 1889-1989; art advisor A Portrait of Fresno: 1885-1985. Editor, art dir.: (book) Centennial of Fresno High School: 1889-1989; art advisor: A Portrait of Fresno: 1885-1985; contbg. artist Heritage Fresno; graphics, oils and watercolor group shows include: M.H. De Young Mus., San Francisco, 1971, Charles & Emma Frye Mus., Seattle, 1971, Calif. State U.-Fresno tour Peoples Republic China, 1974. Mem. adv. com. Calif. State Senator Ken Maddy's Cen. Calif. Conf. on Women, 1989. Winner 53 art awards, 1966—. Mem. Soc. Western Artists (bd. dirs. 1968-74, v.p. 1968-70), Fresno Womens Trade Club (bd. dirs. 1986-88, pres. 1988-90), Fresno Art Mus., Fresno Met. Mus., Native Daus.

Golden West Fresno. Republican. Home and Office: 326 S Linda Ln Fresno CA 93727

STUART, JOAN MARTHA, fund raising executive; b. Huntington, N.Y., June 2, 1945; d. Ervin Wencil and Flora Janet (Applebaum) S. Student, Boston U., 1963-67. Cert. fund raiser. Prodn. asst. Random House, N.Y.C., 1968-69; book designer Simon & Schuster, N.Y.C., 1969-71; feature writer Palm Beach Post, West Palm Beach, Fla., 1971-72; co-founder, communications dir. Stuart, Gleimer & Assocs., West Palm Beach, 1973-84, pres., 1982—; fin. devel. dir. YWCA Greater Atlanta, 1984-86, Ctr. for the Visually Impaired, Atlanta, 1986—; regional dir. City of Hope, 1990—; adj. prof. Kennesaw Coll. Contbr. articles to profl. jours. Mem. crusade com. Am. Cancer Soc. Bd., 1981—; bd. dirs. Theatre Arts Co., 1980-81; community svcs. chmn., bd. dirs. B'nai B'rith Women, 1980-82; chmn. publicity Leukemia Soc. Atlanta Polo Benefit, 1983; com. chmn. Atlanta Zool. Beastly Feast Benefit, 1984; mem. Atlanta Symphony Assocs.; chmn. Salute to Women of Achievement, 1987-90. Recipient Nat. award B'nai B'rith Women, 1978, Regional award, 1979, cert. of merit Big Bros./Big Sisters, 1976. Mem. Nat. Soc. Fund Raising Execs., Ga. Exec. Women's Network, Diabetes Assn. (bd. dirs. 1990—), B'nai B'rith Women. Republican. Jewish. Office: Ctr for the Visually Impaired 763 Peachtree St NW Atlanta GA 30308

STUART, MARJORIE LOUISE, designer; b. St. Louis, Jan. 7, 1926; d. Herbert Judson and Vesta Jeannette (Winters) Browne; A.B., Fla. State U., 1947; m. John M. Stuart, Dec. 11, 1954; children: Jane Adkins, Alice Stuart, Richard Stuart. Designer of illusions, off Broadway magic show Make Me Disappear, 1969; designer of space stations, 1977—; lectr. on space architecture, 1977—. Mem. Nat. Space Soc., Internat. Brotherhood Magicians, Soc. Am. Magicians (life), Soc. Mayflower Descendants. Republican. Presbyterian. Author: (J. Marberger Stuart) You Don't Have to Slay A Dragon, 1975. Illustrator: Harbin on Magic, 1986. Home: 31 Westgate Blvd Plandome NY 11030

STUART, PAMELA ELIZABETH, cultural organization administrator; b. Louisville, Oct. 20, 1956; d. Herbert Joseph and Mary Elizabeth (Howell) Parsons; m. Edwin Brian Stuart, Feb. 25, 1989; children by previous marriage: Amy Elizabeth Marcum, Benjamin Allen Marcum. Student, U. Louisville, 1981. Office mgr. Transp. Engring. Svcs., Louisville, 1975-81; dir. fin. Ky. Opera Assn., Louisville, 1982—. Democrat. Baptist. Home: 824 Vannah Dr Louisville KY 40223 Office: Ky Opera Assn 631 S 5th St Louisville KY 40201

STUART, SANDRA JOYCE, computer information scientist; b. Wheatland, Mo., Aug. 15, 1950; d. Asa Maxville and Inez Irene (Wilson) Friedley; m. John Kendall Stuart, Apr. 17, 1971; 1 child, Whitney Renee. Student, Cen. Mo. State U., 1968-69; AA (hon.), Johnson County Community Coll., 1980; postgrad., Avila Coll., 1980—. Statis. asst. Fed. Crop Ins. Corp., Kansas City, Mo., 1978-83; mgr. Fed. Women's Program, Kansas City, Mo., 1979-80; mgmt. asst. Marine Corps Fin. Ctr., Kansas City, 1983-85, analyst computer systems, 1985-88; computer programmer analyst Corps of Engrs., Kansas City, 1988—. Author: The Samuel Walker History, 1983. Asst. supt. Sunday sch. Overland Park (Kans.) Christian Ch., 1979-80, supt., 1980-82. Mem. Wheatland High Sch. Alumni Assn. (pres.).

STUBBART, WANDA ESTELLE, communications company executive; b. Middletown, Ohio, Aug. 13, 1930; d. Oscar Roosevelt and Cora Ethel (Oliver) Thomas; m. Kenneth James Stubbart, Oct. 4, 1952; children: Bunni Lynn, Dale Alan, Robin Sue, Laura Dawn Irwin. BS in Edn., Denison U., Granville, Ohio, 1952; postgrad., Ohio State U., 1967. Med. asst. Gen. Practitioner's Practice, Pittsburg, Kans., 1952-53; pvt. piano tchr. Columbus, Ohio, 1957-86; elem. music tchr. Columbus Pub. Schs., 1968-71; typist AT&T, Dublin, Ohio, 1976-79, profl. editor, 1979-83, tech. writer, 1983-89, course developer, trainer, 1989—. Editor, composer: To Bethlehem: Family Activities for Christmas, 1978; composer: Heroes of the Book of Mormon, 1986. Entertainer rest homes, convalescent ctrs., retirement villages, Columbus, 1968—; pianist, organist Reorganized LDS Ch., Westerville, Ohio, Columbus, 1956—, elder, 1988—. Mem. Saturday Music Club, Phi Beta Kappa. Republican. Office: AT&T 5151 Blazer Meml Pkwy Dublin OH 43017

STUBBS, JAN DIDRA, travel industry executive; b. Waseca, Minn., June 19, 1937; d. Gordon Everett and Bertha Margaret (Bertsch) Didra; m. James Stewart Stubbs, Nov. 24, 1962; children: Jeffrey Stewart, Jacqueline Didra. BA in Speech/English, U. Minn., 1961. Sales agt. United Airlines, Mpls., 1961-64; interior decorator Lloyd and Assocs., St. Paul, 1964-66; v.p. Stubbs and Assocs., Textiles, St. Paul, 1966-83; account exec. Twin Cities Mag., Mpls., 1983-85; from group sales coord. to sales rep. Internat. Travel Arrangers, St. Paul, 1985-86, asst. dir. sales, 1986-88; mgr. Dayton's Group Holidays, Mpls., 1988—. V.p. Jr. Women's Assn. of Minn. Symphony Orch.; chairperson 60th anniversary Jr. League of St. Paul, sec., 1967—; deacon Ho. of Hope Presbyn. Ch., St. Paul, 1990. Mem. AAUW, Inst. Cert. Travel Agts. (mem. bylaws com. 1988-89), Am. Soc. Travel Agts., Minn. Exec. Women in Tourism, Minn. Exec. Women in Travel (by-laws chmn., sec. 1988-89, 90. fedn dir.), St. Paul Pool and Yacht Club, St. Paul Athletic Club, Alpha Omicron Pi (pres. 1958-59, alumni pres. 1962), Whitefish Chain Yacht Club (sec.). Republican. Home: 784 Lower Colonial Dr Saint Paul MN 55118 Office: Dayton's Group Holidays 12 S 6th St 320 Plymouth Bldg Minneapolis MN 55402

STUBITS, EVA SYLVIA, psychologist; b. Sopron, Hungary, Sept. 26, 1953; d. John and Emmy (Fozo) S.; m. Clifton Robert Gallagher, Apr. 22, 1988. BS with distinction, U. Mich., 1975; MS, U. Miami, Coral Gables, Fla., 1977, PhD, 1979. Psycho-diagnostican Highland Park Gen. Hosp., Miami, Fla., 1978; psychology intern Baylor Coll. Medicine, Houston, 1978-79; asst. prof. U. Houston-Clear Lake City, 1979-81; psychotherapist Neill Carson PhD, Houston, 1981; psychol. cons. Harris County Dept. Edn., Houston, 1979-82, Tex. Neurol. Clinic, Houston, 1982-83, Houston Headache Clinic, 1980-83; pvt. practice psychologist Houston, 1980-85; dir. Houston Psychol. Assocs., 1985—; clin. asst. prof. dept. psychiatry U. Tex. Med. Sch., Houston, 1985-90, dept. psychiatry Baylor Coll. Medicine, Houston, 1981-90. Co-author: Hypnosis for Stress Management, 1988, Stress Management with Headaches, 1988; contbr. articles to profl. jours. Vol. speaker Mental Health Assn., Houston, 1980—; patron mem. Mus. of Fine Arts, Houston. Fellow Mailman Ctr. for Child Devel., Miami, Fla., 1976-78. Mem. Am. Psychol. Assn., Assn. for Advancement Behavioral Therapy, Houston Behavior Therapy Assn. (treas., pres. 1984-86), Houston Psychol. Assn., Tex. Psychol. Assn., Am. Assn. for Study of Headache, Behavioral Medicine.

STUCHINS, CAROL MAYBERRY, nursing executive; b. Melrose, Mass., May 19, 1946; d. Robert Morton and Marion Evelyn (Fairchild) Mayberry; m. Robert Frederick Stuchins, Nov. 9, 1986. BS in Nursing, Boston U., 1969, MS, 1975. RN, Fla., Mass. Staff nurse Univ. Hosp., Boston, 1969-70, head nurse, 1970-74, 76-79, nursing supr., 1974-75, nurse mgr., 1979-81; clin. coord. Mt. Auburn Hosp., Cambridge, Mass., 1975-76; dir. nursing Meml. Hosp. Santa Barbara, Calif., 1981-84; v.p. nursing Bon Secours Hosp., North Miami, Fla., 1981—; mem. Commn. for Future Nursing in Fla., 1987—. Author: Coping with Neurologic Problems Proficiently, 1979. Mem. Assn. Nurse Execs., Assn. Rehab. Nurses, Am. Rehab. Nurses, Rehab. Nurses (pres. 1988-90), Sigma Theta Tau. Office: Bon Secours Hosp 1050 NE 125th St North Miami FL 33161

STUCK, NELDA MARIAN, journalist, piano teacher; b. Deep River, Iowa, Feb. 25, 1937; d. G. Malcolm and Agnes Mary (Crain) Trout; m. Monte Launfal Stuck, May 26, 1960; children: Brook Launfal, Holly Anne. BA magna cum laude, Mich. State U., 1959, MA, 1969. Stewardess United Air Lines, Denver, 1959; sec. Aerojet Gen., Rancho Cordova, Calif., 1960; piano tchr., Mass., Va., Calif., 1962-79; reporter Towne Courier, East Lansing, Mich., 1968, Redlands (Calif.) Daily Facts, 1979—; ch. organist USAF, George AFB, Calif., 1977-79. Bd. dirs. Redlands Panhellenic Assn., 1982-90, Redlands Music Boosters Inc., 1982-85; pres. The Spinet, federated music club, Redlands, 1986-88. Recipient Disting. Alumna award Mich. State U., 1972; named A Woman of Yr., U. Redlands Town and Gown, 1983. Mem. Redlands Symphony Guild (hon.), Assocs. Redlands Bowl (hon.), AAUW (v.p. Redlands 1989—, named gift honoree 1988), P.E.O., Mortar Bd., Theta Sigma Phi. Republican. Congregationalist. Home: 650 Center Crest Dr

Redlands CA 92373 Office: Redlands Daily Facts PO Box 2240 Redlands CA 92373

STUCKEY, HELEN S., advertising executive, marketing professional; b. Toronto, Ont., Can., Mar. 3, 1959. BS in Bus. and Econs., So. Conn. State U., 1982. Account exec. T-Views Publs., Danbury, Conn., 1982-84; mktg. and sales rep. Homes Mag., New Milford, Conn., 1984-86; dir. comml. mktg., regional mgr. Bus. Digest Mag., Danbury, 1986—; mktg. cons. Comml. Investment Div. of Realtors, Danbury. Mem. Danbury Bus. Execs., Greater Danbury C. of C., Ridgefield C. of C., Network One Bus. Assn. (mem. chmn. 1986-88). Office: Bus Digest Mag 275 Greenwood Ave Bethel CT 06801

STUCKEY, LINDALEE IRENE, librarian; b. Manitowoc, Wis., Nov. 9, 1952; d. Keith William and Lucy Grace (Ruffing) S.; m. Michael Walczak, Oct. 25, 1972; (div. 1978); m. Larry M. Cole, Feb. 22, 1984; 1 child, Lorelei Stuckey Cole. BS in Edn., U. Wis., Oshkosh, 1974, MLS, 1985; MLS, Rosary Coll., River Forest, 1988. Dist. librarian Southern Door Sch., Brussels, 1974-77; librarian Two Rivers Sch., Two Rivers, Wis., 1978-83, Greely & Hansen Engrs., Chgo., 1984-86, Oak Park (Ill.) Pub. Library, Cicero (Ill.) Sch., 1987-88, Queen Bee Sch., Ill., 1988—. Author: Fine Policy in 100 Wis. Sch., 1985. Vol. counselor, Domestic Violence Ctr., Manitowoc, Wis. 1978-83. Mem., Am. Library Assn.; Mem., DuPage SF&F, Dupage County, Ill. Office: Queen Bee Sch Glen Hill 2N 220 Bloomingdale Glendale Heights IL 60139

STUCKEY, SHEILA COSTNER, interior designer; b. Columbia, S.C., Sept. 8, 1954; d. Dennis Dale and Anita Louise (Whitener) Costner; 1 child, Robert Adam. B.S., Western Carolina U., Cullowhee, N.C., 1976. Asst. resident mgr. pub. relations/mktg. Club Regency/Governors Club, Myrtle Beach, S.C., 1976-78; designer, sales rep. S.S. Interiors, Myrtle Beach, 1978-83; comml. designer John Gore & Assocs., Myrtle Beach 1983-84; designer, owner Design Dimension, Myrtle Beach, 1984-85; dir. contract sales div., buyer, display coordinator Stuckey Furniture, Charlotte, 1985—. Mem. Am. Soc. Interior Designers, Inst. Bus. Designers, Nat. Assn. Female Execs. Avocations: art; golf; flying. Office: Stuckey Furniture 6600 N Tryon St Charlotte NC 28213

STUCYNSKI, SUSAN MOEN, information systems designer and implementer; b. Mpls., Sept. 25, 1950; d. Lorna M. (Bisek) Moen; m. Steven Louis Stucynski, June 7, 1974. BA in Liberal Arts with highest distinction, U. Minn., 1974; MBA in Acctg. and Pub. Mgmt., U. Pa., 1979. With accounts payable div. Valspar Corp., Mpls., 1974-75; supr. bus. office neurology dept. U. Pa. Hosp., Phila., 1975-77; sr. mgr. mgmt. info. cons. div. Andersen Cons., Phila., 1979—. Mem. steering com. Garden Court Plaza Tenants Assn., Phila., 1977-80; spl. cons. marathon fundraiser Phila. Orch., 1979-84; bd. dirs. Big Bros.-Big Sisters, Montgomery County, Pa., 1986-88. Recipient award Phila. YWCA, 1982. Mem. Nat. Assn. Female Execs., Phi Beta Kappa. Home: 515 W King Rd Malvern PA 19355 Office: Anderson Cons 5 Penn Center Plaza Suite 2600 Philadelphia PA 19103

STUDEBAKER, SANDRA SUE, nurse, director nursing program; b. Vinton, Iowa, Oct. 20, 1952; d. Howard Lee and Evelyn Mae (Peterson) Anderson; m. Keith Allen Studebaker, Aug. 20, 1971; children: Rebecca Sue, Bradley Dean. RN, St. Luke's Sch. Nursing, 1973; student, Kirkwood Community Coll., Cedar Rapids, 1984-86. Head nurse ICF Va. Gay Hosp., Vinton, 1973-74; surg. staff nurse St. Luke's Hosp., Cedar Rapids, 1974, dir. nursing acute and ICF, 1989—, nursing supr. acute care, 1987-89, med. staff nurse, 1986-87; sch. nurse Vinton Community Schs., 1976-77; office nurse Vinton Clinic, 1979-86. Office: Va Gay Hosp 502 N 9th Ave Vinton IA 52349

STUDINSKI, WENDY LEE, production executive; b. Pueblo, Colo., Feb. 16, 1955; d. Rush Ball and Nancy Lee (Speed) S.; m. Kevin Maurice Jennings, Oct. 14, 1977 (div. Mar. 1989); 1 child, Jorma Andrew. BFA, Colo. State U., 1977; Word Processing Cert., Barnes Bus. Coll., Denver, 1985. Potter Studinski Pottery, Denver, 1977-84; art tchr. gifted and talented Gilpin Extended Day Sch., Denver, 1983-84; sec. EPA, Denver, 1984-85; prodn. mgr. TIA/Tech. Info. Assocs., Denver, 1985—. Mem. K.E.E.P.S. User Group (exec. coun. 1987-89). Home: 4818 E 8th Ave Denver CO 80220 Office: Tech Info Assocs 600 S Cherry St #1100 Denver CO 80222

STUDLEY, HELEN ORMSON, artist, poet, writer, designer; b. Elroy, Wis., Sept. 8, 1937; d. Clarence Ormson and Hilda (Johnson) O.; m. William Frank Studley, Aug. 1965 (div.); 1 son, William Harrison. Owner RJK Original Art, Sherman Oaks, Calif., 1979—; designer Aspen Series custom greeting cards and stationery notes, lithographs Love is All Colors, 1982; represented in numerous pub. and pvt. collections throughout U.S., Can., Norway, Sweden, Austria, Germany, Eng., France; author poetry Love is Care, Changes, 1988. Active Luth. Brotherhood, Emmanuel Luth. Ch. Honors include display of lithograph Snow Dreams, Snow Queens at 1980 Winter Olympics, Lake Placid, N.Y., lithograph Summer Dreams, Summer Queens at 1984 Summer Olympics, Los Angeles; named finalist in competition for John Simon Guggenheim fellowship. Mem. Soc. Illustrators, Am. Watercolor Soc., Internat. Soc. Artists, Internat. Platform Assn., Calif. Woman's Art Guild. Club: Sons of Norway. Office: RJK Original Art 5020 Hazeltine Ave Sherman Oaks CA 91423

STUDSTILL, FELECIA GAYLE, bank officer; b. West Palm Beach, Fla., July 20, 1964; d. John H. and Nannie Jewell (Graham) S.; 1 child, Dawny-a. Cert. in darkroom tech., William Ford Vocat. Tech. Ctr., Westland, Mich., 1982; BS in Acctg., Fla. A&M U., 1986. Corr. credit analyst Bank of Boston, 1984; internal auditor RCA, Princeton, N.J., 1985; credit analyst Mfrs. Nat. Bank Detroit, 1985, account officer, 1987—; acctg. clk. Fla. A&M U. Tallahassee, 1985-86. Corp. adviser Jr. Achievement So. Mich., 1987—; Bd. dirs. Family and Neighborhood Svcs., 1990, vice chair fin. com. Mem. NAFE, Urban Bankers Forum (ways and means com. 1989—), Fla. A&M U. Alumni Assn. (chair social com. 1990). Home: 3122 John Daly Rd Inkster MI 48141 Office: Mfrs Nat Bank 100 Tower Renaissance Ctr Detroit MI 48243

STUDY, MARY MARGARET (MARY MARGARET TELLER), small business owner; b. Oklahoma City, Dec. 3, 1945; d. Ernest Leonard and Mary Ann Teller; m. Larry Lee Study, Jan. 3, 1970; 1 son, Darren Boyd. BA, U. No. Colo., 1967; MA in Pub. Rels., MA in Journalism, Ball State U., 1970. Report specialist, adminstrv. assistant, Avionics Rsch., Ohio U., Athens, 1971-73, exec. dean Coll. Engring. and Tech., 1973-74; instr., lectr. pub. rels. Sch. Mass Communications, Mara Inst. Tech., Shah Alam, Malaysia, 1974-76; owner, mgr. Alpha Graphics Ltd., Print Media Svc. Ctr., Muncie, 1976—; cons. advt. spltys., 1980—. Ad*mark Cons. Svcs., 1989; freelance pub. rels. writer, cons., Athens, 1970-74; freelance writer, pub. periodicals on small bus., graphics, advt. Editor, pub. Muncie Marketeer, 1978. Chmn. Oktoberfest, 1979; Muncie Am's. Hometown Taskforce Licensee, 1987-88; vol. Sta. WIPB-TV, 1986—, publicity release writer Mcht.'s Group, Muncie Mall, 1987—; mem. Downtown Bus. Coun. Retail Promotions and Spl. Events Com., 1987-88, chmn., 1979-81; mem. Try Muncie First Com.; mem. Pub. Rels. Task Force, 1972. Mem. Women in Communications (advisor Ball State U. chpt. 1969), C. of C. Muncie-Delaware County (small bus. coun. 1979), Muncie Advt. Club, Ad*libs Club (editor, pub. 1989), Muncie Marketeer (editor, pub. 1978), Alpha Gamma Delta. Office: 111 E Adams Muncie IN 47305

STUECK, LOIS ELAINE, retired association administrator; b. N.Y.C., Nov. 9, 1936; d. Charles Paul, Sr. and Catherine (Wehner) Hillicke; m. Clifford J. Stueck, July 14, 1956; children: Eileen Leech, Kathleen Kane, John, Paul, Florence. BA in French and Spanish Edn., Queens Coll., 1958; MS in Elem. Edn., U. Bridgeport, 1972. Tchr. Bridgeport (Conn.) Sch. System, 1969-81; first selectman Town of Easton, Conn., 1981-85; exec. v.p. Fairfield (Conn.) C. of C., 1985-89; adv. com. Inst. Pub. Service U. Conn., 1984. Elected official Bd. of Fin., Easton, 1979-81; mem. Greater Bridgeport Met. Planning Orgn., 1982-85, Gov.'s Task Force on Pvt. Sector Initiatives, 1985; dir. Conn. Conf. Municipalities, 1982-85; sec. bd. dirs. Coun. of Small Towns, 1982-85; hon. bd. dirs. Bridgeport Hosp., 1982-85; vol. Easton Ems, Easton Redding Safe Rides, Meals on Wheels; 1st vice chmn. adv. coun. Ctr. for Policy Issues Sacred Heart U., Fairfield, Conn.,

1988—; bd. dirs. Ridgefield High Sch. PTSA, 1990—, A Better Chance in Ridgefield, 1990—. Mem. LWV, Ridgefield High Sch. Rebound Club, Conn. Classic Soccer Club (sec., bd. dirs. 1989—), Soccer Booster Club (treas.), Rotary Internat. Roman Catholic. Home: 18 Shields Ln Ridgefield CT 06877

STULL, SYLVIA JOYCE, counselor; b. Lorain, Ohio, Sept. 29, 1939; d. Nicholas and Estelle (Petro) Tobicash; m. Harman A. Stull, June 28, 1963 (div. 1988); children: Nicholas, Kimberly, Christopher. BA, Heidelberg Coll., 1961; MA, Western Mich. U., 1976, postgrad., 1980. Tchr. English Centro Colombo-Americano, Barranquilla, Colombia, 1961-62; tchr. health and phys. edn. Bellefontaine (Ohio) High Sch., 1962-63; tchr. English and phys. edn. Mannheim (Fed. Republic of Germany) Am. High Sch., 1963-66; recreational dir. Ohio Reformatory for Women, Marysville, Ohio, 1967-68; tchr. drop-out prevention program Lewis Cass Ind. Sch. Dist., Cassopolis, Mich., 1975-76, vocat. counselor, 1977—; mem. career guidance program Mich. Ad Hoc Task Force, 1988-89; mem. adv. com. Vocat. Ednl. Counseling and Placement, 1984-88; mem. task force to rewrite Mich. Dept. Edn. Placement Guide, 1989—. Guidance rep. Mich. Coun. on Vocat. Edn., Lansing, 1989—. Mem. Mich. assn. Vocat. and Occupational Guidance (pres. 1984-88, Disting Svc. award 1988), Mich. Occupational Edn. Assn. (Secondary Vocat. Profl. of Yr. 1988), Berrien-Cass-Van Buren Counties Counselors (pres.), Mich. Assn. Counseling and Devel., Mich. Assn. Career Devel., Dowagiac Jr. Arts Club, Delta Kappa Gamma. Home: 210 Spruce St Dowagiac MI 49047 Office: Lewis Cass Ind Sch Dist 61682 Dailey Rd Cassopolis MI 49031

STUMBO, ANITA YVONNE, investment industry publishing executive, stockbroker; b. Dallas, Dec. 9, 1948; d. Earnest Eugene and Edna Maureen (Dill) Randall; m. Allen Stumbo, May 20, 1972; children: John Allen, Kelli Cathleen, James Michael. Student North Tex. State U., 1967-69. Mut. fund clk. Republic Nat. Bank, Dallas, 1969-72; asst. sec.-treas. Fund Mgmt. Co., Dallas, 1972-75; v.p., broker Schneider Bernet & Hickman, Dallas, 1975-83; br. mgr. mcpl. bond dept. Bateman Eichler Hill Richards, Dallas, 1983-84; pres. RR Publ. & Prodn. Co., Inc., Dallas, 1984—; stockbroker W.S. Griffith & Co. Inc., Dallas, 1986—; trustee Walnut Hill UMC Found., Dallas, 1984—; registered rep. N.Y. Stock Exchange, Am. Stock Exchange, Chgo. Bd. Options Exchange; assoc. Commodity Futures Trading Commn. Author, pub. book and study course: Winning Big with UIT Commissions, 1984; author, editor, pub.: The UIT Directory, 1984—; author, pub.: Wall Street Minder, 1985-86, The Wall Street Week with Louis Rukeyser (fin. calendar), 1987; contbr. articles to local newspapers, mags. Creator Parent to Parent, Dallas, 1980-84; active Edna Gladney Aux., Dallas; bd. dirs. Assn. Retarded Citizens Dallas, Walnut Hill UMC Creative Sch., Dallas, 1985—. Named Miss Denton, Denton Jr. C. of C., Tex., 1968. Mem. Nat. Assn. Security Dealers (registered rep. 1972—, registered prin. 1979—), Exec. Women Dallas, Dallas Women's C. of C. (bd. dirs. 1982-83). Methodist. Avocations: organ, piano. Office: RR Publ & Prodn Co Inc PO Box 294581 Lewisville TX 75029

STUMBO, HELEN LUCE, retail executive; b. Macon, Ga., Aug. 7, 1947; d. George Edgar and Willouise (Butts) Luce; m. Edward Paul Coppedge (div. Mar. 1980); 1 child, George Laurence; m. John Ellis Stumbo. BA, Fla. State U., 1969. With Rich's Design Studio, Atlanta, 1970-72; pres. Peachland Consortium, Inc., Ft. Valley, Ga., 1986—, Camellia & Main, Inc., 1987—; personal investor, 1972—; bd. dirs. Blue Bird Body Co., Ft. Valley, Cardinal Investment Co., Ft. Valley; chmn. bd. Bristol Books, Wilmore, Ky., 1988—. Dir. South Ga. United Meth. Home Aging, 1986—, Peach County Hosp. Authority, Ft. Valley, 1986—, also dir. capital campaign com., 1985-88; bd. dirs. United Meth. Gen. Bd. Global Ministries, 1984-88, Forum for Scriptural Christianity, Wilmore, Ky., 1972—; participant Leadership Ga. program, Bus. Coun. Ga., 1989. Recipient Athena award Peach County C. of C., Ft. Valley, 1986, Resolution of Commendation Ga. Ho. of Reps., Atlanta, 1987. Methodist. Home and Office: 305 Knoxville St Fort Valley GA 31030

STUP, JANET ANITA, county commissioner; b. Washington, Mar. 8, 1945; d. Louis Fillmore Jr. and Janet Leeman (Plummer) Watkins; m. William R. Stup, June 21, 1972; children: Scott Alan, Mark Louis. Student, Montgomery Jr. Coll., Takoma Park, Md., 1963-65; AA (hon.), Frederick Community Coll., 1988. Stewardess United Air Lines, Washington, 1965-66; faculty sec. Columbus Sch. Law, Cath. U. Am., Washington, 1966-68; sec. Univ. Legal Svcs., Washington, 1968; legal sec. Tomes and Spragins, Silver Spring, Md., 1968-70, Jackson Brodsky, Rockville, Md., 1970-74; legal sec. Wagaman, Klaven & Mannes, Rockville, 1972-74; office administr. Meyers, Wagaman, Corderman & Young, Hagerstown, Md., 1974-75; mem. Bd. County Commrs. for Frederick County, Frederick, Md., 1982—, pres., 1986—. Past mem. various coms. Frederick County Bd. Edn.; past chmn. govt. div. United Way; past mem. adv. bd. Community Commons; past bd. dirs. Arthritis Found.; past pres. Frederick Mid. Sch. PTA; hon. chmn. Big Bros.-Big Sisters; mem. Religious Coalition Frederick County; bd. dirs. Heartly House; mem. steering com. Way Sta., Elephant Club. Mem. Md. Assn. Elected Women, Bus. and Profl. Women, LWV, Frederick County Hist. Soc., DAR, Disabled Citizens Frederick County (life), Phi Theta Kappa. Republican. Lutheran. Home: 587 Pumphouse Rd Frederick MD 21701 Office: Bd County Commrs 12 E Church St Frederick MD 21701

STUPIN, SUSAN LEE, investment banker; b. Los Angeles, Sept. 14, 1954; d. Paul Alex and Elizabeth Lee (Williams) S.; m. Theodore Robert Gamble Jr., Mar. 3, 1984. AB cum laude, Princeton U., 1975; MBA, Harvard U., 1979. Rep. corp. bond sales Paine, Webber, Jackson & Curtis, N.Y.C., 1975-77; assoc. instl. fin. Eastdil Realty Inc., N.Y.C., 1979-83; assoc. real estate dept. Goldman, Sachs & Co., N.Y.C., 1983-85, v.p. real estate dept., 1985-88; prin. The Prescott Group Inc., N.Y.C., 1988—. Fellow Morgan Library; Bryant fellow Met. Mus. Art; exec. com., fund raiser Princeton Class of 1975. Mem. Urban Land Inst. (exec. group Comml. and Retail Devel. Council), Real Estate Bd. N.Y., Internat. Council Shopping Ctrs., Young Mortgage Bankers Assn., Doubles, N.Y. Jr. League, River Club, Harvard Club (N.Y.C., Boston). Republican. Episcopalian. Home: 860 United Nations Plaza New York NY 10017 Office: The Prescott Group Inc 767 Fifth Ave New York NY 10153

STURDIVANT, KELLY KEMP, consultant; b. Canonsburg, Pa., Apr. 28, 1957; d. Leonard and Mildred Marie (Brown) Kemp; m. Michael L. Sturdivant, Oct. 15, 1988. BS, Carnegie-Mellon U., 1979; MBA, U. Va., 1985. Engring. intern Gen. Foods, Dover, Del., 1977; systems intern IBM, Pitts., 1978; indsl. engr. Babcock & Wilcox, Beaver Falls, Pa., 1979-83; cons. Mgmt. Analysis, Inc., Vienna, Va., 1985-88, Westinghouse Productivity & Quality Ctr., Pitts., 1988—. Office: Westinghouse Productivity & Quality Ctr PO Box 160 Pittsburgh PA 15230-0160

STURDIVANT, SUSAN, psychotherapist; b. Amarillo, Tex., Dec. 12, 1944; d. Winton Charles and Betty Jane (Shoupe) S. BA, So. Meth. U., 1966; PhD in Clin. Psychology, Fielding Inst., 1977. Vocat. examiner Region X Ednl. Service Ctr., Richardson, Tex., 1971-72; psychologist Terrell State Hosp. Adolescent Ctr. (Tex.), 1972-79; pvt. practice psychotherapy, Dallas, 1979—; cons. Unit II, East Town Hosp., Dallas; pres. Human Svcs. Publs., Inc., 1984—. Mem. Dallas Mus. Fine Arts; bd. dirs. Tejas Council Girl Scouts U.S. Mem. Am. Acad. Psychotherapists, Am. Assn. Counseling and Devel., Exec. Women Dallas (bd. dirs.), Am. Psychol. Assn., Assn. Med. Psychotherapists, Internat. Transactional Analysis Assn., Greater Dallas C. of C. Author: Therapy with Women: A Feminist Philosophy of Treatment, 1980. Office: Human Svc Publs Inc 4514 Travis Ste 305 Dallas TX 75205

STURGEON, ANNA LOUISE, marketing and advertising executive; b. San Antonio, Mar. 11, 1951; d. Alfred and Anna (Pepe) Anzalua; m. William W. Cutter, Feb. 21, 1970 (div. 1976); children: Christopher John, Daniel Matthew, Celeste Angeline; m. Benjamin R. Sturgeon, Oct. 2, 1981. Student Ill. Cen. Coll., 1977-78; BS, Bradley U., Peoria, Ill., 1981. Intern Peoria County Bd., Ill., 1980-81; writing specialist/news analysis/film editing Cen. Ill. Light Co., Peoria, 1981-83; asst. advt. mgr. John P. Pearl & Assocs. Ltd., Peoria, 1984—, advt. mgr., 1984-90; mng. dir. Creating Images, Peoria, 1988—; mktg. mgr. Meth. Med. Ctr., Peoria, 1989—. Publicity chmn. Peoria Art Guild. Recipient mktg. methods award Profl. Ins. Mass Mktg. Assn., 1988. Mem. Internat. Assn. Bus. Communicators, Pub. Rels. Soc. Am. (v.p. 1988, pres. 1989—), Mem. of Yr. award 1989), Am. Women in

Radio and TV, Peoria Advt. and Selling Club, Phi Alpha Phi. Democrat. Roman Catholic. Home: 600 W Detweiller Peoria IL 61615 Office: Meth Med Ctr Ill 221 NE Glen Oak Ave Peoria IL 61636

STURGES, DARCY JEAN, investment analyst; b. Vancouver, British Co, Canada, Aug. 30, 1956; d. Everett Gerald and Olive (Harris) Wood. BS, Calif. State U., 1984; MBA, UCLA, 1986. CPA, Ill. Supr. Blue Cross Pet Hosp., North Hollywood, Calif., 1978-81; asst. mgr. Pay Fone Systems, L.A., 1981; administr. United Fin. Svcs., Torrance, Calif., 1981-82; asst. v.p. CSA Fin. Svcs., Torrance, Calif.; sr cons. Price Waterhouse, Boston, Mass., 1986-88; investment analyst Golder, Thoma & Cressey, Chgo., 1989—. Mem. MIT Enterprise Forum. Office: Golder Thoma & Cressey 875 N Dearborn St #7H Chicago IL 60610

STURGIS, LAURA MARIE, clinical psychologist; b. Appleton, Wis., Mar. 7, 1955; d. Harrison Jr. and Bette Jane (Schafhauser) S. BA in Psychology and Spanish, Edgewood Coll., 1977; MA in Gen. Exptl. Psychology, Calif. State U., Fresno, 1980; PhD in Profl. Sci. Psychology, Utah State U., 1986. Lic. psychologist, Hawaii; cert. hypnotherapist Am. Bd. Hypnotherapy, cert. neuro-linguistic programming practitioner Soc. Neuro-Linguistic Programming. Clin. psychology intern VA, Honolulu, 1982-83; cons. psychologist Sultan Easter Seals Sch., Honolulu, 1984—; clin. psychologist Waimano Tng. Sch. and Hosp., Pearl City, Hawaii, 1984-86, Children's Day Treatment Ctr., Honolulu, 1986-87, State of Hawaii Diamond Head Children's Team, Honolulu, 1987-88; pvt. practice psychologist Honolulu, 1988—; cons. psychologist Diamond Head Children's Mental Health Svcs. Branch, Honolulu, 1988—, Kauai Children's Mental Health Svcs. Team, Lihue, Hawaii, 1988—; presenter in field. Bd. dirs. New Musical Purposes Found., Honolulu, 1984-88. Mem. Am. Psychol. Assn. (Psi Chi Cert. of Excellence in Rsch. 1980), Hawaii Psychol. Assn. (legis. com. 1989), Hawaii Acad. of Hypnosis. Home: 3526 Sierra Dr Honolulu HI 96816 Office: 1110 University Ave Ste 510 Honolulu HI 96826

STURGULEWSKI, ARLISS, state senator; b. Blaine, Wash., Sept. 27, 1927; B.A., U. Wash. Mem. Assembly Municipality of Anchorage; vice chmn. New Capital Site Planning Commn., mem. Capital Site Selection Com.; chmn. Greater Anchorage Area Planning and Zoning Commn.; mem. Alaska State Senate, 1978—. Rep. nominee Office Gov. Alaska, 1986. Office: Alaska State Senate State Capitol Juneau AK 99811 Home: 2957 Sheldon Jackson Anchorage AK 99508

STURHAHN, BETTY J., corporate secretary; b. Coffeyville, Kans., Mar. 14, 1933; d. Charles Stephin and Edith Elizabeth (Sanders) Anderson; m. Edgar R. Sturhahn, July 10, 1967 (dec.); 1 child, Jama Nahlene Garvin. Student, Liberty U. Secretarial cons. Pub. Acctg. Office, Coffeyville; bus. mgr. Grace Episcopal Ch., Muncie, Ind.; corp. sec., bus. mgr. Lee's Supply of Muncie, Inc.

STURM, ANGELICA, commercial real estate broker; b. Chgo., July 31, 1955; d. Peter Nicholas and Phyllis (Booras) Maggos; m. William Douglas Sturm, Feb. 19, 1954. BBA, St. Mary's Coll. of Notre Dame, South Bend, Ind., 1977. Mgr. cash processing ctr. Allstate Ins., Northbrook, Ill., 1977-79; indsl. real estate broker Rubloff, Inc., Chgo., 1979-80; sr. v.p. Otis Realty Group, Deerfield, Ill., 1980-87, Lincoln Property Co., Chgo. and Deerfield, 1987-90; pres. Lincoln Corp. Real Estate Svcs., Chgo., 1990—. Mem Mayor's Energy Task Force, Chgo., 1989. Mem. Chgo. Ofcl. Leasing Brokers Assn. (treas. 1989—, sec. 1990), Internat. Alliance (del. 1989—), Women in Real Estate (v.p. 1989—), Chgo. Real Estate Exec. Women (treas. 1989-90, program chair 1990), Chgo. Ofcl. Leasing Brokers Assn. (bd. dirs. 1986—). Office: Lincoln Property Co 311 S Wacker Dr Ste 5450 Chicago IL 60606

STURM, EDITH S., telecommunications company finance executive; b. Hartford, Conn., Sept. 17, 1947; d. John J. and Jean R. Salling; m. John W. Sturm, Aug. 21, 1976. BS, Tufts U., 1969; MBA, Boston U., 1986. Former dist. mgr. acctg. New Eng. Telephone, Boston, asst. treas., 1986—; bd. dirs. Maine Self Ins. Guarantee Assn. Mem. Am. Mgmt. Assn., Fin. Mgmt. Assn., Nat. Bus. Adminstrn. Hon. Soc., Beta Gamma Sigma. Office: New Eng Telephone Co 125 High St Rm 309 Boston MA 02110

STURM, LORA ROSE, company executive; b. Lanesboro, Minn., June 22, 1956; d. Arthur Harley and Edith Marie (Guenther) Thompson; m. Georg Michael Sturm, Mar. 1, 1979 (div. May 1984); 1 child, Linda Marie; m. Richard Paul Thorn; 1 child, Matthew Arthur. Student, Schiller Coll., Heidelberg, Fed. Republic Germany, 1976-77; BA, Augsburg Coll., 1978. Asst. mgr. sports store Armed Forces Recreation Ctr., Berchtesgaden, Fed. Republic Germany, 1978-83; with prodn. and inventory control dept. Winona (Minn.) Van Norman, 1983-89; prodn. mgr. Wincraft, Winona, 1989—. Mus. vol. Minn. Hist. Soc., St. Paul, 1976. Mem. Am. Prodn. and Inventory Control Soc. (cert., sec. Winona 1986-88, v.p. 1988-89). Republican. Lutheran. Home: RR 3 Box 225B Winona MN 55987 Office: Wincraft 1205 E Sanborn Winona MN 55987

STURM, MAXINE SHIRLEE, fund raiser; b. Sioux City, Iowa, Aug. 21, 1934; d. Harry and Mary (Kiser) Rabiner; divorced; children: Robert, Melanie. BS in Edn., U. Nebr., 1956. Cert. elem. tchr., Nebr. Tchr. Jefferson County Schs., Denver, 1956-58; subsitute tchr. Denver public Schs., 1965-70. Bd. dirs. Opera Omaha, 1987—, Nat. Aging Blumkin Home, 1988—, Arthritis Found., 1988—; corp. fund raiser Ea. Nebr. Office Aging, 1988; apptd. by Gov. Kay Orr com. mem. Nebr. Capitol Environs Commn., 1989—; chair person George Shearing concert Nebr. Found. Visually Handicapped, 1989; chair person community benefit evening Firehouse Dinner Theatre, 1989; chair person arts awards dinner Bemis Found., 1989, mayoral com. Del. to Japan representing Sister City, 1989; state chmn. Nebr. State Holocaust Meml. Dinner, 1986; chmn. Women's div. Fedn. of Omaha, 1977-79 (1st place Nat. award, 1979); sponsor Danzig 39 exhibit Joslyn Art Mus., 1985. Mem. AAUW, Coun. Jewish Women, Children's Mus., Hadassah, Joslyn Mus., Nat. Conf. Christians and Jews, Temple Israel (sisterhood art com.), Omaha Jewish Fedn. Home: 8405 Indian Hills Dr Omaha NE 68114

STURM, RUTH FOSTER, lawyer; b. Bklyn., Jan. 3, 1911; d. Ernest and L. Elsie (Foster) S.; BA, Vassar Coll., 1932; LLB, Columbia, 1935; summer study U. Lausanne (Switzerland), 1929, U. Berlin, 1931. Admitted to N.Y. bar, 1936, pvt. practice N.Y.C., 1936-42, assoc. with Walter F. O'Malley, Esq.; law asst. Ct. of Appeals State N.Y., 1942-44; U.S. Customs Ct., 1944-76. Mem. Gov.'s Com. Edn. and Employment Women, 1964-65, adv. com. Hudson River Valley Commn., 1965-66. Mem. N.Y. County Lawyer's Assn., Fed. Bar Assn., Bus. and Profl. Women's Club Tarrytowns (pres. 1948-50, N.Y. State safety chmn. 1950-52, by-laws chmn. 1953-58, 2d v.p. 1958-60, 1st v.p. 1960-62, pres. 1962-64, parliamentarian 1972-76), Nat. Council Women, Phi Beta Kappa, Kappa Beta Pi. Republican. Presbyn. Author: A Manual of Customs Law, 1974, supplement, 1976; Customs Law and Administration, 1980, 3d edit. 1982, new edits., 1983, 84, 85, 86, 87, 88, 89. Home: Hudson House Ardsley-on-Hudson NY 10503

STURNICK, JUDITH ANN, college president, consultant; b. Mankato, Minn., Apr. 9, 1939. B.A. in English and History, U. N.D., 1961; M.A. in English, Miami U., Oxford, Ohio, 1963; Ph.D. in English, Ohio State U., 1967. Vis. asst. prof. U.S.C., Columbia, 1967-68; asst. prof. Ohio State U.-Newark, 1968-69; chmn. dept. English, dir. honors program Capital U., Columbus, Ohio, 1969-78; v.p. acad. affairs S.W. State U., Marshall, Minn., 1978-83; pres. U. Maine-Farmington, 1983-87, Keene (N.H.) State Coll., 1987—. Co-author: Women's Studies Guide, 1979; editor/contbr. A Suitable Job for a Woman: Leadership of Women Presidents/Chancellors in the Public Sector; contbr. articles to profl. jours. Mem. nat. adv. bd. Rural Am. Women, Washington, 1979-85; mem. nat. bd. AASCU, 1986-89, exec. com., 1987-88, chmn. coun. women, pres., chmn., 1986-88; bd. dirs. United Way, Farmington, 1983—; chmn. fundraising com. Maine Humanities Coun., 1984—; chair Nat. Commn. on Women in Higher Edn., 1986-87; trustee Cheshire County Hosp. Bd., 1988—. Recipient Praestantia award for Outstanding Teaching, Capital U., 1972; Woodrow Wilson fellow, 1961-62, Nat. Def. fellow, 1961-64. Mem. AAUW, Maine Bus. and Profl. Women, Am. Assn. State Colls. and Univs. (nat. bd. dirs. 1986-89, exec. com. 1987-88, chair coun. of pres.'s 1986-88), Maine Consortium for Health Professions

Edn. (trustee, pres. elect), Nat. Women's Studies Assn. (co-chmn. nat. coordinating coun. 1977-79), Nat. Coun. Edn., New Eng. Assn. Schs. and Colls. (chmn. accrediting teams 1985—, sch. and coll. related com. 1987—), Rotary. Lutheran. Office: Keene State Coll Office of Pres 229 Main Keene NH 03431-4183

STURZENACKER, LINDA M., management consultant; b. Weymouth, Mass., May 17, 1947; d. Reginald André and Betty May (Hill) Bouley; 1 child, Karen Renee. Student, Albright Coll., Reading, Pa., Northeastern U. Ptnr., instr. Computer Edn. Svcs. of Boston; pres., ptnr. P&L Cons., Ltd., also P&L Fin. Ltd., Braintree, Mass. Mem. adv. bd. Internat. Order of Rainbow for Girls, 1982, 83. Mem. NAFE, Am. Mgmt. Assn. Address: 71 Vinedale Rd East Braintree MA 02184

STUSNICK, MADELINE SEIDELLE, clinical psychologist; b. Bklyn., Oct. 27, 1943; d. Benjamin and Irma (Mendlowitz) Seidelle; m. Eric Stusnick, Aug. 20, 1967; 1 child, Harold Spencer. BA, Hofstra U., 1965; PhD, SUNY, Buffalo, 1970. Sch. psychologist Niagara-Wheatfield (N.Y.) High Sch., 1970-73; pvt. practice Niagara Falls, N.Y., 1973-77; dir. clin. svcs. Deveaux, Niagara Falls, 1973-74; lectr. George Mason U., Fairfax, Va., 1979-81; clin. psychologist Burke (Va.) Psychotherapy Assn., 1979—; dir. Burke Learning Lab., 1986—; coach, organizer Bowling League for Learning Disabled Children, Burke, 1980—. Mem. Am. Psychol. Assn., No. Va. Soc. Clin. Psychologists (pres. 1980-81), No. Va. Assn. for Children with Learning Disabilities (v.p. 1983-84), No. Va. Youth Coalition (bd. dirs. 1989—). Jewish. Office: 8992 Fern Pk Dr Burke VA 22015

STUSSY, PEGGY J., medical administrator; b. Salem, N.J., Aug. 21, 1957; d. Edward and Elizabeth (Thomas) Klessel. RN, Our Lady of Lourdes, Camden, N.J., 1979; BS in Nursing, Widener U., 1989. RN. Emergency room head nurse Salem Hosp.; med. adminstr., nuclear Pub. Svc. Electric and Gas, Newark, adminstr. project planning, compliance & safety programs, EEO & employee rels. and benefits, 1988—. Mem. NAFE, Emergency Nurses Assn.. Address: PO Box 20 Sayreville NJ 08872

STUTHEIT, LYNN SHERYL, public information officer; b. Englewood, Colo., Nov. 5, 1958; d. Wilbur Wallace and Geraldine Grace (Garrison) S. Student, U. N.Mex., 1976-78; BS, Colo. Women's Coll., 1981. Instr. in tennis South Suburban Pks. & Recreation, Littleton, Colo., 1975-80; reporter, photography, intern Denver Housing Authority, 1980-81; reporter, corr. The Denver Post, 1982; reporter Wyo. Eagle, Cheyenne, 1982-83, Aurora (Colo.) Sentinel, 1983-84; communications asst. Inst. Cert. Fin. Planners, Denver, 1985-86; pub. info. officer Durango (Colo.) Sch. Dist., 1985-90, 1990—. Author: (play) The Gov.'s Annual Senior Christmas Party, 1983 (guest columnist Durango Herald); World Book of Poetry, Gifted and Talented Mag., 1989. Vol. tchr. Four Corners Health Care Ctr., Durango, 1987-90; mem. Com. for Handicapped Citizens, Durango, 1989-90. Mem. nat. Sch. Pub. Rels. Assn., Colo. Sch. Pub. Rels. Assn., NOW (treas., v.p. Durango chpt. 1988-90), AAUW, Women in Communications (sec. Durango chpt. 1989-90), Optimists. Office: Durango Sch Dist 9R 201 E 12th St Durango CO 81302

STUTMAN, NANCY, calligrapher, graphic designer, educator; b. Detroit, Feb. 26, 1938; d. Albert E. and Pearl P. (Liebovich) Cook; m. William N. Stutman, Oct. 20, 1963; children—Michael, David. Student U. Ill., 1956-58; cert., grad. with honors Tobe Coburn Sch. for Fashion Careers, N.Y.C., 1959. Asst. buyer millinery R.H. Macy Co. Herald Sq., N.Y.C., 1959-60; exec. asst. Doris Weston, N.Y.C., 1960-64; account exec. Promotion Council Am., N.Y.C., 1965; v.p., co-owner Stutman Assocs., Inc., Fashion Publicity Agy., N.Y.C., 1965-83; prin. Nancy Stutman Calligraphics, Chappaqua, N.Y., 1982-87, Carlsbad, Calif., 1987—; workshop instr. for calligraphic socs. The Bus. of Calligraphy, 1984—, instr. Internat. Calligraphy Conf., 1987-89; vol. workshop instr. San Diego SBA, 1988-89, Communicating Arts Group, 1988-89; chairperson promotional gifts/lit N.Y. Soc. Scribes Internat. Calligraphy Conf., 1986. Juried show Master Eagle Gallery, N.Y.C., 1982, 85. chairperson fundraising tag sale Blythedale Children's Hosp., Valhalla, N.Y., 1983; vol. mem. Cancer Soc., White Plains, 1985-86, New Westchester Orch., 1985; vol. calligrapher Temple Beth El of No. Westchester, Chappaqua, 1978-88. Recipient Sisterhood Service award Temple Beth El of No. Westchester, 1982, 85. Mem. San Diego Fellow Calligraphers (workshop chmn. 1989-90), Advt. Club Westchester (hon. mem. 1984, bd. dirs. 1985-87, Gold design award 1984, 85, 86, 87, Hall of Fame award 1985, Chester award 1987), N.Y. Soc. Scribes, Westchester Assn. Women Bus. Owners (bd. dirs. 1981-87, Pres.'s award 1983), Women in Communications, Westchester County C. of C. (vol. Small Bus. Week, chairperson support network 1985), SanDi (Design in Excellence award 1988), Ad Club of San Diego (vol. Homburg awards 1988). Democrat. Home and Office: 3008 Rana Ct Carlsbad CA 92009

STUTZ, SANDRA LEE, real estate developer; b. Bklyn., Feb. 13, 1948; d. Albert and Miriam Stutz. BA, SUNY, Cortland, 1969. Pres., broker Trio Realty Inc., Bklyn., 1974-86; pres. Prominent Properties Inc., Bklyn., 1984—; sponsor 24 Remsen St. Housing Corp., Bklyn., 1982-88, 421-4th St. Housing Corp., Bklyn., 1984-86. Renovator landmark brownstone bldgs., 1982-88. Mem. Cert. Real Estate Appraisers, Bklyn. Bd. Realtors, Bklyn. Heights Assn. Home: 24 Remsen St Brooklyn Heights NY 11201

STUTZMAN, REBECCA LYNN, company executive; b. Iowa City, Apr. 11, 1953; d. Thomas Gene Bell and Lois Jean (Spurgeon) Mahanna; m. Thomas, Oct. Student, Drake U., Marguette U. Nurse's at. Iowa City Care Ctr., 1972-74; unit sec. St. Lukes Hosp., Cedar Rapids, Iowa, 1978; physical therapy asst. Rehabilitation Ctr., Cedar Rapids, 1974-77; v.p. 12th St. Repair, Marion, Iowa, 1979-. Mem. C. of C. Office: 12th St Repair 220 12th St Marion IA 52302

STUTZMAN, SANDRA LOUISE, nurse; b. Ashland, Pa., Nov. 10, 1953; d. Kenneth Robert and Mary (Tersavige) S. Diploma, Sacred Heart Hosp. Sch., Norristown, Pa., 1979; LPN, Pottstown Meml. Med. Ctr.; diploma, St. Joseph Sch. Nursing, Reading, Pa., 1983; student, Pa. State U., Reading. Staff nurse Med-Surg CCU and ICU Pottstown Meml. Med. Ctr., head nurse, telemetry.

STYERS, CAROLYN JEANETTE, business manager; b. Oxford, Miss., Oct. 28, 1939; m. Joe B Styers, June 22, 1958; children: Carole Jean, Bradley Joe. AA, N.W. Jr. Coll., Senatobia, Miss., 1982; BBA, U. Miss., 1988. Bookkeeper Hume's Dept. Store, Oxford; asst. bus. office mgr. Oxford Lafayette Med. Ctr., 1975-79, bus. office mgr., 1979-89; bus. office mgr. Bapt. Meml. Hosp., Oxford, 1989-90, Bolivar County Hosp., Cleveland, Miss., 1990—. Recipient Follmer award Healthcare Fin. Mgmt. Assn., 1986, Reeves award, 1989, O.K. Pearce award, 1989. Mem. Healthcare Fin. Mgmt. Assn. (treas. 1990—), Bus. and Profl. Women, Pilot Club (pres. 1989—). Home: Rte 3 Box 48 Oxford MS 38655 Office: Bolivar County Hosp Cleveland MS 38732

STYLES, BEVERLY, entertainer; b. Richmond, Va., June 6, 1923; d. John Harry Kenealy and Juanita Russell (Robins) Carpenter; m. Wilbur Cox, Mar. 14, 1942 (div.); m. Robert Marascia, Oct. 5, 1951 (div. Apr. 1964). Studies with Ike Carpenter, Hollywood, Calif., 1965—; student, Am. Nat. Theatre Acad., 1968-69; studies with Paula Raymond, Hollywood, 1969-70. Freelance performer, musician, 1947-81; owner Beverly Styles Music, Joshua Tree, Calif., 1971—. Composer (sheet music) Joshua Tree, 1975, I'm Thankful, 1978, Colour Chords (And Moods), 1990; records include The Perpetual Styles of Beverly, 1978, Wow, Wow, Wow, 1986; performer (album) The Primitive Styles of Beverly, 1977. Mem. ASCAP (Gold Pin award), Am. Fedn. Musicians. Republican. Office: PO Box 615 Joshua Tree CA 92252-0615

STYLES, ELLEN SANDERS, systems engineer; b. Rockville Centre, N.Y., Dec. 31, 1955; d. Shafton Dale and Ellen (Dragan) Dugal; m. Harold Roberts Sanders, Feb. 14, 1976 (div. 1986); children: Rosetta Yvonne, Paula Chérie, Valerie Elena; m. Robert Charles Styles, June 1, 1990. BSEE, U. Ala., Huntsville, 1985. Dancer, instr. Arthur Murray Studio, Huntsville, 1973-81; enumerator U.S. Census, Gurley, Ala., 1980; with coop. dept. Teledyne Brown Engring., Huntsville, 1982-85, engr. II, 1985-86; sr. systems engr. Intergraph, Huntsville, 1986—. Appeared in Guys and Dolls, A

Chorus Line, My Fair Lady, Music Man, Showboat, Annie Get Your Gun. Mem. Community Ballet Assn. (scholarship 1983-85), Omicron Delta Kappa, Tau Beta Pi, Eta Kappa Nu. Greek Catholic. Home: 2703 Peel St Huntsville AL 35805 Office: Intergraph One Madison Indsl Pk IW 1507 Huntsville AL 35807-4201

STYLES, MARGRETTA MADDEN, nursing educator; b. Mount Union, Pa., Mar. 19, 1930; d. Russell B. and Agnes (Wilson) Madden; m. Douglas F. Styles, Sept. 4, 1954; children: Patrick, Michael, Megan. B.S., Juniata Coll., 1950; M. in Nursing, Yale U., 1954; Ed.D., U. Fla., 1968; hon. doctorate, Valparaiso U., 1986. Staff nurse VA Hosp., West Haven, Conn., 1954-55; instr. Bklyn. Hosp. Sch. Nursing, 1955-58; supr. North Dist. Hosp., Pompano Beach, Fla., 1961-63; dir. nursing edn. Broward Community Coll., Ft. Lauderdale, Fla., 1963-67; asso. prof. Sch. Nursing, Duke U., Durham, N.C., 1967-69; dir. undergrad. studies Sch. Nursing, Duke U., 1967-69; prof., dean Sch. Nursing, U. Tex., San Antonio, 1969-73; dean, prof. Coll. Nursing Wayne State U., Detroit; prof. nursing U. Calif., San Francisco, 1977—, dean Sch. Nursing, 1977-87; chairperson Com. for Study of Credentializing in Nursing, 1976-79; mem. adv. group div. nursing HEW, 1977; asst. dir. nursing svcs. U. Calif. Hosps. and Clinics, 1978-87; mem. Nat. Commn. Nursing, 1980—; mem. Calif. Bd. Registered Nursing, 1985—; mem. Sec.'s Commn. on Nursing HHS, 1988—. Author: On Nursing: Toward a New Endowment (Am. Jour. Nursing Book of Yr. award 1982). Recipient Disting. Alumna award Yale U. Sch. Nursing, 1979; Am. Nurses' Found. 1st disting. scholar, 1983. Fellow Am. Acad. Nursing; mem. Nat. Acad. Scis., Am. Nurses Assn. (pres. 1986-88), Internat. Coun. Nurses (bd. dirs. 1989—), Sigma Theta Tau. Office: U Calif Sch Nursing N531C-D Box 0608 San Francisco CA 94143

STYLES, TERESA JO, producer, educator; b. Atlanta, Oct. 19, 1950; d. Julian English and Jennie Marine (Sims) S. BA, Spelman Coll., 1972; MA, Northwestern U., 1973. Researcher CBS News, N.Y.C., 1975-80, producer, 1980-85; instr. mass communications, English Savannah (Ga.) State Coll., 1985-89; asst. prof. English Savannah (Ga.) State Coll., 1990—; asst. prof. mass communications Bennett Coll., Greensboro, N.C., 1990—. Researcher documentary CBS Reports: Teddy, 1979 (Emmy cert.); assoc. producer documentaries for CBS Reports: Blacks: America, 1979 (Columbia Dupont cert. 1979), What Shall We Do About Mother?, 1980 (Emmy cert.), The Defense of the U.S., 1980 (Columbia Dupont cert.). Mem. Writers Guild Am., Internat. Platform Assn. Home: 311A College Rd Greensboro NC 27410

STYNES, BARBARA BILELLO, association administrator; b. N.Y.C., Apr. 24, 1951; d. Sylvester Francis and Jacqueline Marie (Giardelli) Bilello; m. Frank Joseph Stynes, Aug. 24, 1969; children: Christopher Francis, Jeremy Scott. BA, Rutgers U., 1976. Mktg. rep. McNeil Consumer Products Co., Fort Washington, Pa., 1979-82, Met Path Inc., Des Plaines, Ill., 1982-85; mktg. coordinator Life program Meml. Hosp. and YMCA, Chattanooga, 1986—; mem. Chattanooga Area Wellness Council, 1986—, Chattanooga Area Healthcare Coalition, 1986—; dir. mktg. and communications, met. YMCA, Chattanooga, 1986—, dir. internat. program, 1989—; fiber sculptor, 1975-77; weaver, 1976-79. Vol. communications com. Am. Heart Assn., 1972—, Spl. Olympics, Chgo., 1982-84; speaker Tenn. Safety Belt coalition, 1986—; clinic leader Am. Lung Assn., Chattanooga, 1986-88; chairperson fundraising, trustee Pine Grove Coop. Sch., New Brunswick, N.J., 1977-78; bd. dirs. Signal Mountain Newcomers Assn., Tenn., 1985-86. Mem. NAFE, Am. Bus. Womans Network Chattanooga (chair membership), Fiber Arts Guild, Assn. Profl. Dirs., Kiwanis (chair internat. rels. com. Chattanooga chpt.). Roman Catholic. Avocations: ballet, piano, aerobics. Home: 914 Dunsinane Rd Signal Mountain TN 37377

SU, HELEN CHIEN-FAN, research chemist; b. Nanping, Fujian, China, Dec. 26, 1922; came to U.S. 1949; d. Ru-chen and Sieu-Hsien (Wong) Su. BA, Hwa Nan Coll., China, 1944; MS, U. Nebr., Lincoln, 1951; PhD, U. Nebr., 1953. Cert. profl. chemist. Asst. instr. in chemistry Hwa Nan Coll., Fuzhou, Fujian, China, 1944-49; prof. chemistry Lambuth Coll., Jackson, Tenn., 1953-55; rsch. asst. Auburn Rsch. Found., Auburn, Ala., 1955-57; sr. chemist, project ldr. Borden Chem. Co., Phila., 1957-63; scientist Lockheed-Ga. Rsch. Lab., Marietta, Ga., 1963-67; rsch. chemist Agrl. Rsch. Svc., USDA, Savannah, Ga., 1968—. Contbr. articles to profl. jours., chpts. to books; patentee in field. Recipient IR-100 award, Indsl. Research Mag., 1966. Fellow Am. Inst. Chemists, Ga. Inst. Chemists; mem. ACS, AAAS, N.Y. Acad. Sci., Entomol. Soc. Am., Ga. Entomol. Soc., Sigma Xi, Sigma Delta Epsilon. Methodist. Home: 610 Highland Dr Savannah GA 31406 Office: USDA-ARS 3401 Edwin St Box 22909 Savannah GA 31403

SU, JUDY YA HWA LIN, pharmacologist; b. Hsinchu, Taiwan, Nov. 20, 1938; d. Ferng Nian and Chiu-Chin (Cheng) Lin; m. Michael W. Su; 1 child, Marvin. BS, Nat. Taiwan U., 1961; MS, U. Kans., 1964; PhD, U. Wash., 1968. Asst. prof. Dept. Biology U. Ala., Huntsville, 1972-73; rsch. assoc. dept. anesthesiology U. Wash., Seattle, 1976-77; acting asst. prof. Dept. Anesthesia U. Wash., Seattle, 1977-78, rsch. asst. prof., 1978-81, rsch. assoc. prof., 1981-89, rsch. prof., 1989—; mem. surg. anesthesiology & trauma study sect. NIH, 1987—; vis. scientist Max-Planck Inst. Med. Rsch., Heidelberg, West Germany, 1982-83; vis. prof. dept. anesthesiology Mayo Clinic, Rochester, Minn., Med. Coll. Wis., 1988; editorial bd. cons. Jour. Molecular & Cellular Cardiology, London, 1987—, European Jour. Physiology, Berlin, Germany, Muscle & Nerve, Kyoto, Japan, 1989—, Anesthesiology, Phila., 1987—, Molecular Pharmacology, 1988—, Jour. Biol. Chemistry, 1989—, Am. Jour. Physiology, 1990—. Contbr. articles to profl. jours. Grantee Wash. Heart Assn., 1976-77, 1985-87, Pharm. Mfrs. Assn. Found., Inc., 1977, Lilly Rsch. Labs, 1986-88, Anaquest, 1987—, NIH, 1978—; recipient Rsch. Career Devel. award NIH, 1982-87; rsch. fellowship San Diego Heart Assn., 1970-72, Max-Planck Inst., 1982-83. Mem. AAAS, Biophys. Soc., Am. Soc. for Pharmacology and Exptl. Therapeutics, Am. Physiol. Soc., Am. Soc. Anesthesiologists. Home: 13110 NE 33rd St Bellevue WA 98005 Office: University Washington Dept Anesthesiology RN-10 1959 NE Pacific St Seattle WA 98195

SUAREZ, SALLY ANN TEVIS, health care administrator, nurse, consultant; b. Jersey City, Jan. 23, 1944; d. Paul John and Gertrude Marie (Clancey) Tevis; divorced; 1 child, Maria E. Diploma, St. Mary Hosp. Sch. Nursing, 1965; BA in Health Edn. and Nursing, Jersey City State Coll., 1966, MA in Health Sci., 1977. Staff nurse St. Mary Hosp., Hoboken, N.J., 1965, Bayonne (N.J.) Hosp., 1966, Jersey City Med. Ctr., 1965-66; adminstr. Hoboken Med. Arts Family Health Ctr., 1969-75; adj. faculty Jersey City State Coll., 1976-77; adminstrv. supr. St. Mary Hosp., Hoboken, 1977-80; dir. North Hudson Commn. Action Corp. Clinic, West New York, N.J., 1979-88; nursing clin. dir. St. Mary Hosp., Hoboken, 1988-89; corp. dir. nursing Francisan Health System N.J., 1989—; instr. nursing St. Mary Hosp. Sch. Nursing; cons. Creative Concepts in Counseling, Rutherford, N.J., 1979-82, Com. for Cytogenetics, Newark, 1986—. Active March of Dimes, Hudson County, 1982—, Hudson County, 1984—, United Way, 1984—; Hudson County Perinatal Consortium Bd., 1987—. Mem. Am. Cancer Soc., Am. Nurses Assn., N.J. Nurses Assn., N.Y. Acad. Scis., Am. Pub. Health Assn., N.J. Pub. Health Assn., Am. Nursing Found., Nat. League Nursing, Nat. Assn. Dirs. Women's Health Programs, N.J. Family Planning Forum (exec. com. 1980-86), Family Planning Assn. N.J. (exec. com. 1986-88). Democrat. Roman Catholic. Home: 113 Wilson Ave Rutherford NJ 07070 Office: Franciscan Health System NJ 308 Willow Ave Hoboken NJ 07030

SUBAK-SHARPE, GENELL JACKSON, editor, writer; b. Great Falls, Mont.; m. Gerald Subak-Sharpe; children: David, Sarah and Hope (twins). B.A., Butler U., 1959; M.S. in Journalism with honors, Columbia U., 1961. Reporter Indpls. Star, 1958-61; copy editor N.Y. Times, 1962-70; exec. editor Family Health mag. (now Health), 1970-74; editor Med. Opinion mag., 1974-77; v.p., editor Biomed. Info. Corp., 1977-84; pres. G.S. Sharpe Communications Inc., N.Y.C., 1981—. Co-editor: The Physicians' Drug Manual, 1981; editor: The Compendium of Drug Therapy, 1982, The Compendium of Patient Information, 1982, The Physicians' Manual for Patients, 1984, (with Victor Herbert) Mount Sinai School of Medicine Guide to Complete Nutrition, 1990; author: (with Kathryn Schrotenboer) Freedom From Menstrual Cramps, 1981, Living with Diabetes, 1985, Overcomming Breast Cancer, 1987, Breathing Easy, 1988, (with James V. Warren) Frontiers in Medicine series: Surviving Your Heart Attack, 1984, Controlling Hypertension, 1984-87, Living with Diabetes, 1985, (with Joan Ness) The Calcium-Requirement Cookbook, 1985, (with Lois Jovanovic) Hormones: The Woman's Answerbook, 1987, (with Robert Weiss) Columbia University School of Public Health Complete Guide to Health and Well-Being After 50, (with Edward Frohlich) Take Heart, 1990; editoral dir.: Columbia University College of Physicians and Surgeons Complete Home Medical Guide, 1985, Columbia University College of Physicians and Surgeons Complete Guide to Pregnancy, 1988, Columbia University College of Physicians and Surgeons Complete Guide to Early Child Care, 1990; founding editor: Being Well Magazine, 1983; Off Hours, 1983; Health and Nutrition Newsletter, 1984, Physicians Lifestyle Magazine, 1989; mng. editor Home Health Handbook, 1988—. Pulitzer Traveling fellow Columbia U., 1961-62; recipient Russell L. Cecil Writing award Arthritis Found., 1972, Mag. Writing award Am. Dental Soc., 1977, Blakeslee award Am. Heart Assn., 1985. Mem. Authors Guild, Women's Press Club, Nat. Assn. Sci. Writers, Newswomens Club N.Y. Avocations: restoration historic houses, antique collecting. Home and Office: 606 W 116th St New York NY 10027

SUBERRI, KEREN CHANSKY, psychologist, consultant, educator; b. Oswego, N.Y., Sept. 3, 1957; d. Norman Morton and Elissa Ruth (Ellsas) Chansky; m. Moshe Suberri, Apr. 15, 1978; children: Gilad, Kinneret. Student, Tel Aviv U., 1975-78; BA, Temple U., 1979, MEd in Ednl. Psychology, 1981, PhD in Sch. Psychology, 1987. Nat. cert. sch. psychologist; cert. sch. psychologist, N.J. Sch. psychologist West Deptford (N.J.) Pub. Schs., 1986-88; cons. Phila. Early Childhood Evaluation ctr., 1988-89, St. John of God Community Svcs., Westville Grove, N.J., 1990—; adj. prof. Glassboro (N.J.) State Coll., 1989—; adj. faculty Camden County Coll., Blackwood, N.J., 1989—. Author: (with others) Children's Needs: Psychological Perspectives, 1987. Chairperson Early Childhood Parents' Com., Cherry Hill, N.J., 1986-87; bd. mgrs. Jewish Community Ctr. of South N.J., Cherry Hill, 1986-88; vol. tutor Jewish Family Svc. of South N.J., Cherry Hill, 1988-89. Mem. Am. Psychol. Assn., Nat. Assn. Sch. Psychologists, Am. Friends of Peace Now. Jewish.

SUBKOWSKY, ELIZABETH, insurance company executive; b. New London, Conn., Feb. 17, 1949; d. Thomas and Matilda (Mastroianni) Logan; m. Robert A. Subkowsky, June 9, 1972. BA with honors and dist., U. Conn., 1971; MBA, DePaul U., Chgo., 1977. Systems mgr. CNA Ins., Chgo., 1973—. Fellow Life Office Mgmt. Assn. (award 1977); mem. Woman's Club Evanston (aux. officer 1985-87, bylaws com. 1979—). Office: CNA Ins 1 CNA Pla Chicago IL 60685

SUCH, MARY JANE, nurse, service executive; b. Chgo., Dec. 15, 1942; d. Dr. Leon Raymond Wasielewski and Jane Genevieve (Guzik) Wallace; children from previous marriage: Jennifer, Kenneth, Christopher. BSN, Loyola U., Chgo., 1965. Clinical Instr. Dept. of Mental Health, Chgo., 1964-69, asst. chief of svc., 1969-72; charge nurse Luth. Gen. Hosp. Alcohol Treatment Ctr., Park Ridge, Ill., 1973-77; program coord. Malayali Cultural Assn., Chgo., 1977-79; psychiat. nurse con. Blue Cross Ill., Chgo., 1979-85; corp. adminstr. Forest Health Systems, Des Plaines, Ill., 1985—. Officer Parent-Tchrs. Coun., Sch. Dist. 64, Park Ridge, Ill., 1972-84; mem. Girl/Boy Scouts, Park Ridge, 1972-79. Mem. NAFE, Am. Hosp. Assn., Am. Coll. Utilization Rev. Physicians (cons. 1979-85), Am. Mgmt. Assn., Am. Coll. Healthcare Execs. Office: Forest Health Systems 555 Wilson Ln Des Plaines IL 60016

SUCHER, CYNTHIA CLAYTON CRUMB, hospital marketing executive; b. Washington, Dec. 19, 1943; d. Francis Paul and Jewell Evangeline (Sheets) Crumb; m. Theodore Richard Sucher III, Sept. 7, 1961 (div. Dec. 1980); children: Theodore Richard IV, Evangeline Leigh Sucher Gabrielson; m. Carlton Wayne Vaught, Dec. 20, 1982; 1 child Clayton Wayne. Student, Stetson U., 1959-61; BA in Communications summa cum laude, U. Cen. Fla., 1975. Reporter, anchorwoman Sta. WFTV-TV, Orlando, Fla., 1974-76, exec. producer, 1977-78; news anchorman Sta. KWTX-TV, Waco, Tex., 1976-77; editor, pub. Dining Out mag., Orlando, 1978-80; pub. info. officer Fla. Dept. Health and Rehabilitative Svcs., Orlando, 1980-82; dir. media communication Orlando Regional Med. Ctr., 1982-85; asst. adminstr. Winter Park (Fla.) Meml. Hosp., 1985-86; v.p. mktg. Winter Park (Fla.) Meml. Hsop., 1986—; mentor Crummer Sch. Bus., Rollins Coll., Winter Park, 1987—. Producer/reporter radio documentary Ted Bundy series, 1980 (UPI award). Media coordinator Bill Frederick Campaign, Orlando, 1980; bd. dirs. Vol. Ctr. Cen. Fla., 1983-87; commr. Winter Park Sidewalk Art Festival, 1984—; mem. Orlando Mayor's Nominating Bd., 1987—; mem. pres.'s council advisors U. Cen. Fla., Orlando, 1987—; chmn. ann. rev. com., City of Orlando, 1989. Recipient Healthcare Mktg. Report Merit award, 1986, 89. Mem. Am. Mktg. Assn. (bd. dirs. Cen. Fla. chpt. 1987-88), Acad. Health Svcs. Mktg. (bd. dirs. 1988—, chmn. nat. symposium, 1991, Internat. Mktg. award 1989), Soc. Profl. Journalists (pres. Cen. Fla. chpt. 1983), Fla. Exec. Women (pres. Orlando 1985-86), Town and Gown (council), Orlando C. of C. (chmn. community awards 1987), Winter Park C. of C. (bd. dirs. 1989—, v.p. internal affairs 1990). Democrat. Methodist. Home: 8617 Amber Oak Ct Orlando FL 32817 Office: Winter Park Meml Hosp 200 N Lakemont Ave Winter Park FL 32789

SUCHY, SUSANNE N., nurse; b. Windsor, Ont., Can., Sept. 20, 1945; d. Hartley Joseph and Helen Viola (Derrick) King; m. Richard Andrew Suchy, June 24, 1967; children: Helen, Hartley, Michael. Diploma, St. Joseph Sch. Nursing, Flint, Mich., 1966; BS in Nursing, Wayne State U., 1969, MS in Nursing, 1971. Staff nurse, head nurse, supr. St. John Hosp., Detroit, 1966-70; instr. Henry Ford Community Coll., Dearborn, Mich., 1972—; on leave 1988-90; case mgr. Harper Hosp., Detroit, 1988—; mem. Detroit DemonstrationSide Team for defining and differentioting ADN/BSN competencies, 1983-87. Contbr. articles to profl. jours. Past bd. dirs., pres. St. Pius Sch. Mem. Am. Nurses Assn. (apptd. legis. com. Detroit dist., elected nominating com.), N.Am. Nursing Diagnosis Assn., Mich. Nursing Diagnosis Assn. (pres.), Nat. League for Nursing, Daus. of Isabella (past regent, sec., trustee, now treas.), Ladies of Assembly (past 1st lady, 2d lady, scribe), Sigma Theta Tau. Roman Catholic. Home: 12666 Irene Southgate MI 48195 Office: Henry Ford Community Coll 5101 Evergreen Rd Dearborn MI 48128

SUDAKOFF, MARLENE MITCHELL MOOERS, lawyer; b. Mpls., Feb. 22, 1935; d. Henry Joseph and Frances O'Byrne Mitchell; m. Edwin Stanton Mooers II, July 31, 1965 (dec. 1970); 1 child, Edwin Stanton III; m. 2d, Michael Richard Sudakoff, Jan. 22, 1977. JD, U. Minn., 1958; postgrad., U. London, 1977, U. Pitts., 1977. Bar: Minn. 1959, Fla. 1980. Former ptnr. firm Mitchell & Pierce; ptnr. Golden Apple Dinner Theatre, Mpls., from 1971; now ptnr. firm Ahlquist & Sudakoff P.A., Sarasota, Fla.; bd. dirs. Three Arts Prodns. Inc., Coastal Prodns. Inc.; v.p. legal div. Ga. Am. Recovery, Inc., 1989—; participant Barbados Conf. Matrimonial Lawyers and Trial Lawyers. Asst. treas. Miller for Congress campaign, 1974; active Women Minn. Symphony Orch.; bd. dirs., historian Sarasota Opera Soc.; bd. dirs. Fla. Ballet Inc., Women's Ctr., Family Counseling Ctr.; treas. San Remo (Fla.) Assn., 1980-81; 1st woman chmn. bd. trustees Doctors Hosp., Sarasota, 1987-88, bd. trustees, 1988-89; v.p., dir. Project Rainbow, Inc., 1988—; mem. New Coll. Found. (life), Friends of Selby Libr. Mem. ABA, Minn. Bar Assn., Fla. Bar Assn., Sarasota County Bar Assn., Am. Judicature Soc., Assn. Trial Lawyers Am., Criminal Cts. Bar Assn., St. Andrew's Soc., English-Speaking Union, Century Club, World Trade Club (Atlanta), Kappa Beta Pi. Club: Sarasota City. Home: 3647 San Remo Terr Sarasota FL 33579 Office: 2088 Hawthorne St Sarasota FL 34239

SUDANOWICZ, ELAINE MARIE, government executive; b. Dorchester, Mass., Aug. 3, 1956; d. John Anthony and Helen Mary (Budzinski) S. Student, Fontbonne Acad., Milton, Mass., 1974; BA, Boston State Coll., 1978; MPA, Suffolk U., Boston, 1986. Pub. relations office mgr. MacDonald & Evans Inc. Litho., Dorchester, Mass., 1974-78; research asst. Nat. Commn. Neighborhoods, Wash., 1978; pol. cons. Various Nat. State & Local, Pol. Campaigns, 1974-86; telephonist supr., cons. ARC, Boston, 1980-81; adminstrv. asst. Suffolk County Courthouse Commn., Boston, 1981-82; exec. asst. sheriff Suffolk County Sheriff's Office, 1982-86; presl. mgmt. intern ESD/PK Air Force Systems Command, Hanscom AFB, Mass., 1986-89; advanced copper CAP Air Force Systems Command, Andrews AFB, Md., 1989-90; contract negotiatior Hdqrs., Electronic Systems div., Joint STARS Program, Hanscom AFB, Mass., 1990—. Author: Constitutional Vignette, Separation of Powers and Contracting in the Bureaucrat, 1987; contbr. PMInformer, 1989—; also articles; agt., cons Theatre Arts-Play 1988—. Vol., cons. City & State Pub. Agys.-Pub. Sector, Boston; literacy vol., 1988-89. Recipient Spl. Achievement award U.S. Dept. Transp., 1989, Outstanding Alumnus award Suffolk U., 1990. Mem. Nat. Contract Mgmt. Assn. (photographer No. Va. chpt. 1989-90), Am. Soc. Pub. Adminstrn. (rep. region 1 nat. young profls. forum 1988—), Profl. Mgrs. Assn., Presdl. Mgmt. Alumni Group (nat. bd. dirs. 1989-90, N.E. field bd. dirs. 1990—, Outstanding Alumnus award 1990), Pi Alpha Alpha. Democrat. Roman Catholic. Home: 108 Alban St Dorchester MA 02124-3711 Office: Air Force Systems Command Hdqrs Electronic Systems Div O'Neil Bldg Hanscom AFB MA 01731-5000

SUDARKASA, NIARA, academic administrator, anthropologist; b. Ft. Lauderdale, Fla., Aug. 14, 1938; d. Alex Charlton and Rowena (Evans) Marshall; m. John L. Clark; 1 child, Michael Sudarkasa. Student, Fisk U., 1953-56; AB, Oberlin Coll., 1957; MA, Columbia U., 1959, PhD, 1964; hon. degrees, Fisk U., Oberlin Coll., 1988, Sojourner-Douglass Coll., 1989, Franklin and Marshall Coll., 1990, Susquehanna U., 1990. Asst. prof. anthropology NYU, 1964-67; asst. prof. U. Mich., Ann Arbor, 1967-70, assoc. prof., 1970-76, prof., 1976-87, dir. Ctr. AfroAm./African Studies, 1981-84, assoc. v.p. acad. affairs, 1984-87; pres. Lincoln (Pa.) U., 1987—. Author: Where Women Work, 1973; co-editor: Women and National Development, 1977;contbr. numerous articles on African women, trade and migration to profl. jours.; articles on higher edn. in Chronicle of Higher Edn., Bull. Am. Assn. Higher Edn., Academe, other jours. Chair spl. adv. com. on minority enrollment State of Mich. Dept. Edn., 1985-86; bd. dirs. Ford Found. Project on New Emmigrants and Established Residents, 1987—, Pa. Econ. Devel. Partnership, 1987—, The Barnes Found., 1989—. Fulbright sr. research scholar, Republic of Benin, 1982-83; Ford Found. grantee, 1983-84; NEH grantee, 1983-84; Ford Found. Middle East & Africa research fellow, 1973-74; Social Sci. Research Council African Studies fellow, 1973-74; Ford Found. fgn. area tng. fellow, 1960-63; recipient numerous awards including Outstanding Achievement tributes and awards from Alpha Kappa Alpha, 1976, Zeta Phi Beta, U. Mich., 1971, 84, Zeta Phi Beta, Phila., 1987, Mich. State Senate, 1986, Mich. State Ho. of Reps., 1986, Pa. State Senate, 1987, Pa. State House of Reps., 1987 1986; Dr. Niara Sudarkasa Day, Ft. Lauderdale, 1976, Borough of Mahattan, 1987, Atlantic City, Atlanta, Detroit, 1987; E. Luther Cunningham award, 1988, Frederick D. Patterson award, 1988; named one of Top 100 Bus. & Profl. Women Dollars & Sense mag., 1988; included in I Dream A World: Portraits of Black Women Who Changed America, 1989. Mem. Am. Anthropol. Assn. (exec. bd. 1972-75), Am. Ethnol. Soc., African Studies Assn., Am. Assn. Higher Edn., Coun. on Fgn. Rels. Office: Lincoln U Office of Pres Lincoln University PA 19352

SUDBRINK, JANE MARIE, sales and marketing executive; b. Sandusky, Ohio, Jan. 14, 1942; niece of Arthur and Lydia Sudbrink. BS, Bowling Green State U., 1964; postgrad. in cytogenetics Kinderspital-Zurich, Switzerland, 1965. Field rep. Random House and Alfred A. Knopf Inc., Mpls., 1969-72, Ann Arbor, Mich., 1973, regional mgr., Midwest and Can., 1974-79, Can. rep., mgr., 1980-81; psychology and ednl. psychology adminstrv. editor Charles E. Merrill Pub. Co. div. Bell & Howell Corp., Columbus, Ohio, 1982-84; sales and mktg. mgr. trade products Wilson Learning Corp., Eden Prairie, Minn., 1984-85; fin. cons. Merrill Lynch Pierce Fenner & Smith, Edina, 1986-88; sr. editor Gorsuch Scarisbrick Pubs., Scottsdale, Ariz., 1988-89; regional mgr. Worth Publs., Inc., N.Y.C., 1989—. Mem. NAFE, Am. Ednl. Rsch. Assn. Lutheran. Home and Office: 3801 N Mission Hill Rd Northbrook IL 60062

SUDDOCK, FRANCES SUTER THORSON, gerontology educator; b. Estelline, S.D., Oct. 23, 1914; d. William Henry and Anna Mary (Oakland) Suter; m. Carl Edwin Thorson, July 6, 1941 (dec. Apr. 1976); children: Sarah Thorson Little, Mary Frances; m. Edwin Matthew Suddock, Aug. 7, 1982 (dec. Sept. 1986). BA, U. No. Iowa, 1936; postgrad., Syracuse U., 1940-41, U. Iowa, 1946; MA, Antioch U., San Francisco, 1981. Cert. tchr. Tchr. various high schs., Correctionville and Eagle Grove, Iowa, 1936-38, 38-40, 41-43, 45-47; chief clk. War Price and Rationing Bd., Eagle Grove, 1943-45; instr. (part time) Eagle Grove Jr. Coll., 1953-61; adminstr. Eagle Grove Pub. Library, 1961-77; tchr. Will Schutz Assocs., Muir Beach, Calif., 1987-88; facilitator indep. grief workshops, Anchorage, 1989—. Keynote speaker Nat. Widowed Persons Conf. of Am. Assn. Retired Persons, 1988. Vol. trainer Widowed Persons Svc., Am. Assn. Retired Persons, 1989—, retired sr. vol. program, Anchorage, 1988—; bd. dirs. North Iowa Mental Health Ctr., Mason City, 1959-76, Eagle Grove Community Chest, 1960, Help Line, Inc., Ft. Dodge, Iowa, 1976-77; chmn. Community Mental Health Fund, Eagle Grove, 1966-73; charter pres. Eagle Grove Concerned, Inc., 1973-77; active various civic drives. Mem. AAUW (charter pres. Eagle Grove br. 1973-75), Am. Soc. on Aging, Alaska Assn. Gerontology, P.E.O., Wright County Federated Women's Clubs (chmn. 1957-59), Kappa Delta Pi. Home: 333 M St Apt 404 Anchorage AK 99501

SUDLER, BARBARA WELCH, retired historical society administrator; b. Honolulu, Apr. 20, 1925; d. Leo F. and Barbara Lloyd (Petrikin) Welch; m. James Stewart Sudler, Dec. 30, 1950 (dec. 1982); children—Eleanor, James S.; m. William H. Hornby, Oct. 22, 1983. B.A., U. Colo., 1944. Exec. adminstr. Historic Denver, 1974-79; exec. dir. Colo. Hist. Soc., Denver, 1979-81, pres., 1981-89, ret.; historic preservation officer State of Colo., Denver, 1983—; dir. Women's Bank, Denver. Editor: Nothing Is Long Ago, 1975. Recipient Soroptimist award, 1980, Contbn. to Arts award Big Sisters, 1981, Contbns. to Community award AIA, 1982, Community Service award U. Colo., 1986, James Grafton Rogers award, 1987. Mem. Am. Antiquarian Soc., Nat. Conf. State Historic Preservation Officers. Republican. Episcopalian. Clubs: Denver County, University. Lodge: Rotary. Home: 180 High St Denver CO 80218 Office: State Hist Soc Colo 1300 Broadway St Denver CO 80203

SUELTENFUSS, ELIZABETH ANNE, university president; b. San Antonio, Apr. 14, 1921; d. Edward L. and Elizabeth (Amrein) S. B.A. in Botany and Zoology, Our Lady of Lake Coll., San Antonio, 1944; M.S. in Biology, U. Notre Dame, 1961, Ph.D., 1963. Joined Sisters of Divine Providence, Roman Catholic Ch., 1939; tchr. high schs. Okla. and La., 1942-49; mem. summer faculty Our Lady of Lake Coll., 1941-49, mem. full-time faculty, 1949-59, chmn. biology dept., 1963-73, pres., 1978—; mem. adminstrv. staff to superior gen. Congregation Divine Providence, 1973-77. Author articles in field. Bd. dirs. Am. Cancer Soc., San Antonio, Avance, Mind Sci. Found., YWCA, Sta. KLRN Pub. TV, S.W. Rsch. Found., I Have a Dream Found., Inst. Ednl. Leadership, Trim and Swim; chmn. edn. com. Pvt. Sector United San Antonio; mem. bd. visitors Air Force Inst. Tech. Recipient Achievement and Leadership award U. Notre Dame, 1979, Headliner award Women in Communications, 1980, Good Neighbor award NCCJ, 1982, Today's Woman award San Antonio Light, 1982, Outstanding Woman award San Antonio Express-News, 1983; named to San Antonio Women's Hall of Fame, 1985. Mem. AAAS, AAUP, AAUW, Am. Soc. Microbiology, Nat. Assn. Women Religious, Tex. Acad. Sci., San Antonio 100 and Tex. Women's Forum, Hispanic Assn. Colls. and Univs. (exec. com.), Greater San Antonio C. of C. (bd. dirs.), San Antonio Coun. Pres.'s (pres.), Zonta Internat. Home and Office: Our Lady of the Lake U 411 SW 24th St San Antonio TX 78207-4666

SUFFREDINI, KATHLEEN DEERY, physical therapist; b. N.Y.C., Apr. 25, 1951; d. James Gerard and Kathleen (Swift) Deery; m. Anthony Francis Suffredini, June 29, 1974; children: Dante Alexander, Giancarlo. BS magna cum laude, Boston U., 1973; MA in Motor Learning, Columbia U., 1979. Phys. therapist Greenwich (Conn.) Hosp., 1973-74, Clinica Moscati, Rome, 1974-76, St. Joseph's Hosp., Stamford, Conn., 1976-77, Hartford (Conn.) Hosp., 1977-79; supr. Med. Coll. Va., Richmond, 1979-82; clin. instr. U. Pitts., 1982-84; pvt. practice Rockville (Md.) Phys. Therapy, 1985—. Bd. dirs. College Gardens Elem. Sch. PTA, Rockville, 1989-90. Mem. Am. Phys. Therapy Assn. (coord. continuing edn. so. dist. Va. chpt. 1980-82), Physicians Health Plan Md. (quality assurance rev. com. 1986—). Home: 6 Rice Ct Rockville MD 20850 Office: Rockville Phys Therapy 966 Hungerford Dr Ste 30 A Rockville MD 20850

SUFFREDINI SASSETTI, ANN MARIA, insurance agency executive; b. Chgo., Apr. 1, 1932; d. Michael and Elia (Boggi) Suffredini; m. Frank R. Sassetti, June 10, 1972. Accredited ins. adviser, Chgo. Ins. Sch., 1986. Sec. Donchin-Hecht & Co., Chgo., 1950-54; asst. Arthur I. Bloom & Co., Chgo., 1954-62; ptnr. Erickson-Suffredini & Co. Inc., Chgo., 1962—; pres. MGA

Insurers Inc., Chgo., 1980—. Mem. Profl. Ins. Agts. Assn. (cert.), Italian-Am. C. of C. (pres. 1985-87). Roman Catholic. Office: Erickson-Suffredini & Co 7026 W North Ave Chicago IL 60635

SUGAR, SANDRA LEE, career counselor; b. Balt., May 18, 1942; d. Harry S. and Edith Sarah (Levin) Pomerantz; m. Fred N. Sugar, Oct. 11, 1963 (div. 1983); children: Gary Lee, Terry Lynn. BS in Edn. and English, Towson State U., 1965; MS in Edn. and Applied Behavioral Scis., Johns Hopkins U., 1986. Chairperson arts exhibit Balt. Arts Festival, 1979; med. interviewer Johns Hopkins Sch. of Hygiene, Balt., 1980-82; copy writer Concepts & Communications, Balt., 1984; instr. art history and world cultures Catonsville Community Coll., Balt., 1981-85; instr. English Community Coll. of Balt., 1981-85; instr. English and math. Info. Processing Tng. Ctr., Balt., 1985; info. specialist Info. of Md. New Directions for Women, Balt., 1986; trainer, job developer Working Solutions, Balt., 1987-88; art gallery dir. Renaissance Fine Art Gallery, Bethesda, Md., 1988—; judge nat. high sch. sci. fiction contests. Author poetry collection, juried exhibition, 1979, 80; editor mus. guides' newsletter Guidelines, 1978; painter juried exhibitions, 1979, 80. Docent Balt. Mus. of Art, 1973-86; festival coordinator Internat. Brass Quintet Festival, Balt., 1986; chairperson spl. events Balt. PTA, 1978-82; bd. dirs. Citizens Planning and Housing Assn., Balt., 1980-82; mem. women's com., ctr. stage hand Balt. Ballet, 1979-84, Balt. Symphony, 1979-80. Recipient F.J. Bamberger scholarship, Johns Hopkins U., 1985, Mayoral Vol. of Yr. award Balt. Mus. Art, 1979.

SUGGS, PATRICIA KAYLOR, health educator; b. Portsmouth, Ohio, Mar. 17, 1952; d. Charles Edward and Desdie Lenora (Woodbury) Kaylor; m. Douglas Lee Suggs, Mar. 5, 1977; 1 child, Christopher Jared. BS, Ill. State U., 1974; MDiv, Duke U., 1977; MS in Edn., U. N.C., 1981, PhD, 1985. Pastor Shiloh/Sparta (N.C.) United Meth. Chs., 1977-80; rsch. asst. U. N.C., Greensboro, 1982-85, assoc. project dir., 1986-87; dir. aging initiatives N.W. Area Health Edn. Ctr., Winston-Salem, N.C., 1987—; assoc. dir. Appalachian Geriatric Edn. Ctr., 1989—; asst. prof. Bowman Gray Sch. Medicine, Winston-Salem, 1988—. Contbr. numerous articles to profl. jours. Bd. dirs. Bethlehem Community Ctr., Winston-Salem, 1989; active N.C. Coalition Health Promotion for Older Adults. Mem. NAFE, Gertonol. Soc. Am., Soc. Gerontol. Soc., Am. Soc. Aging, N.C. Assn. Aging. Office: Appalachian Geriartric Edn Ctr 300 S Hawthorne Rd Winston-Salem NC 27103

SUGHRUE, KAREN MARIE, television news producer; b. Washington, Oct. 9, 1951; d. Richard Charles and Ruth Marie (Schultz) S. AA in Creative Writing, Bradford Coll., 1970; BA in Polit. Sci., Tufts U., 1972; MA in Communication, Am. U., 1975. Legis. aide to Sen. Adlai Stevenson III Washington, 1973-74; asst. news dir. Sta. WAMU-FM (Nat. PUb. Radio), Washington, 1976-79; news writer, producer Sta. WRC-TV, Washington, 1979; producer 6 and 11 p.m. news Sta. WCHS-TV, Atlanta and Charleston, W.Va., 1979-80; exec. producer Cable News Network, Washington and N.Y.C., 1980-82; assoc. producer Nightwatch CBS News, Washington, 1982-83; assoc. producer Face the Nation, CBS News, Washington, 1983-84, producer, 1984-85, exec. producer, 1985-90; bur. chief Berlin CBS News, 1990—; legis. caseworker Rep. John Erlenborn, Washington, 1972-73; speechwriter congl. campaign David Connor, Wausau, Wis., 1972. Trustee Bradford (Mass.) Coll., 1986—. Woodrow Wilson Found. fellow, Princeton, N.J., 1989. Mem. Radio and TV Corrs. Assn., White Ho. Corrs. Assn. Roman Catholic. Office: CBS News, Berlin Federal Republic of Germany

SUGHRUE, KATHRYN EILEEN, state legislator; b. Oketo, Kans., May 2, 1913; d. John and Charlotte Peterman; B.S. in Home Econs., Kans. State U., 1937; M.S. in Adminstrn., Colo. State U., 1962; m. Herbert Sughrue, May 3, 1941; children—Kathleen, Margaret, Patricia, John, Tim. Extension home economist, Ford County, Kans., 1937-41, Dodge City, Kans., 1949-61; dist. supt., asso. state leader Kans. State U., 1962-69; adv. Home Econs. Coll., Andra Pradesh U., Hyderabad, India, 1969; state leader N.D. State U., Fargo, 1969-73; freelance profl. speaker, 1973-76; mem. Kans. Ho. of Reps., 1976—. Vice pres., sec. Ford County Democratic Party. Recipient Top award Kans. 4-H Club Program, Finney County, 1958; Disting. Service award Kans. State U., 1981. Mem. Home Econs. Extension (pres. state chpt. 1957-58), Nat. Home Econs. Assn. (pres. state chpt. 1956-57), Kans. Home Econs. Assn. (pres. 1976-77), Home Econs. Club, Arts Council Speakers Guild, AAUW, Delta Kappa Gamma, Epsilon Sigma Phi (pres. state chpt. 1959-60). Roman Catholic. Clubs: Bus. and Profl. Women's, Women's Democratic. Philomat, PEO. Contbr. articles to mags.

SUGIYAMA, TOKU MARY, school administrator; b. Sacramento, Sept. 6, 1921; d. Sakae and Kuniko (Kosaka) Koda; m. Yone J. Sugiyama, Apr. 5, 1952; m. George Y. Morishita, Mar. 23, 1942; (dec. Mar. 1949); children—Maeona, Carolyn, George. Jr. cert. U. Calif.-Berkeley, 1941; B.A., Towson State U., 1980, M.A., 1984. Tchr., Poston Relocation Ctr., Ariz., 1941-44; purchasing agt. U.S. Dept. Def., Tokyo Ordnance Depot, 1952-56; instr. Ikebana Sogetsu Sch., Tokyo, 1956-67, exec. dir. Sogetsu USA, sch. Japanese flower arrangement, 1967—. Recipient Mohan Sho, Sogetsu Sch., 1960, Sofu Sho, 1967, Flower Arranger of yr. award Nat. Council State Garden Clubs, 1979. Mem. Md. Fedn. Garden Clubs, Ikebana Internat. (charter), Balt.-Kawasaki Sitster City Cultural Com. Home: 959 Ellendale Dr Towson MD 21204

SUHANDRON, INGRID, property management executive; b. Berlin, Germany, Oct. 24, 1938; came to U.S., 1956; d. George and Martha (Trostmann) Schmid; m. Joseph J. Suhandron, Sept. 16, 1956; 1 child, Kenneth. BA, Queens Coll., 1962. Photo model Powers Model Agy., N.Y.C.; lang. tchr. U.S. Army, Berlin; interrogator U.S. Army Intelligence Unit, Berlin; pres. Property Mgmt., Ft. Lauderdale, Fla. Mem. Am. Bus. Women Am. Republican. Home: 3912 S Ocean Blvd Highland Beach FL 33487 Office: 600 Prospect Pla NW 44th St Fort Lauderdale FL 33309

SUITS, VALERIE FAYE, medical transcription service owner; b. Syracuse, N.Y., Apr. 22, 1957; d. Allen P. and Margaret Faye (Umphlette) S. LPN, St. Joseph's Sch. Nursing, Nashua, N.H., 1977; AS, Hesser Coll., Manchester, N.H., 1986. Cert. med. asst. Lic. practical nurse Home Nursing Svc., Nashua, 1978; nurse Alexander-Eastman Hosp., Derry, N.H., 1978-80; lic. practical nurse Weeks Meml. Hosp., Lancaster, N.H., 1980; owner Scribe-Right Med. Transcription Svc., Manchester, 1987—. Episcopalian. Home and Office: 154 Longwood Ave Manchester NH 03103

SUKET, JUDITH ANN, nurse anesthetist, consultant; b. Milton, Mass., Oct. 28, 1942; d. Ralph Eugene and Mary Jane (Hall) S. B.S., St. Joseph Coll., Standish, Maine, 1975; M.S., Lesley Coll., 1986; R.N., Lynn Hosp. Sch. Nursing, 1964. Cert. nurse anesthetist. Staff anesthetist Quincy City Hosp., Mass., 1967-69, clin. instr. sch. nurse anesthesia, 1969-74, asst. dir., 1975-76; staff anesthetist New Eng. Bapt. Hosp., Boston, 1976-82, Met. Anesthesia Assn., Braintree, Mass., 1982—, Mass. Eye and Ear Infirmary, 1987—; cons. Cosgrove & Eisenberg, Quincy, 1974—. Mem. Am. Assn. Nurse Anesthetists, Am. Soc. Law and Medicine, New Eng. Assembly Nurse Anesthetists (bd. dirs. 1979-85, chmn. 1985—), Mass. Anesthesia Council Edn. (sec. 1978-80), Mass. Assn. Nurse Anesthetists (bd. dirs. 1984—, continuing edn. coordinator 1984—). Clubs: Altrusa Internat. (treas. 1982-83) (Quincy); Yankee Golden Retriever (sec. 1985—) (Andover, Mass.). Avocations: camping; gardening; cross country skiing; golden retrievers. Home: 38 Alroy Rd South Weymouth MA 02190 Office: Mass Eye and Ear Infirmary 243 Charles St Boston MA 02114

SUKHATME, SHASHIKALA BALKRISHNA, mathematics educator; b. Karad, India, Dec. 5, 1932; d. R.N. and Indira (Nagarkar) Chivate; m. Balkrishna Sukhatme, Apr. 12, 1956 (dec. Apr. 1978); 1 child, Vidya. BS with honors, U. Poona, India, 1954, MS, 1955; PhD, Mich. State U., 1960. Lectr. U. Dehli (India), 1963-67; assoc. prof. Iowa State U., Ames, 1967—. Co-author: Sampling Theory of Surveys with Applications, 1984; contbr. articles to Jour. Indian Soc. of Stats. Mem. Inst. Math. Stats., Am. Statis. Assn., Indian Statis. Soc., Assn. for Women in Math., Sigma Xi. Office: Dept of Statis Ames IA 50011

SULFARO, JOYCE A., school administrator; b. Bklyn., Oct. 23, 1948; d. John Joseph and Mildred Ann (Credidio) Carvelli; m. Guy Sulfaro, Aug. 1, 1971; children—Jacqueline Amber, Kristin Lynn. BA, Molloy Coll., 1970; postgrad. Fla. Atlantic U., 1979-80; MS in Adminstrn. and Supervision, Nova U., 1982. Tutor reading Our Lady of Loretto, Rockville Centre, N.Y., 1969-70; tchr. lang. arts and math. Resurrection Sch., Bklyn., 1970-73; tchr. Annunciation Sch., Hollywood, Fla., 1976-80, prin., 1980-84; tchr. St. Thomas More Sch., 1984-88; writer English curriculum for Jr. High for Archdiocese of Miami, 1979. Travel coordinator/sec. Rego Park (N.Y.) Met. Youth Orgn., 1969-70. Author: (with M. Sue Timmins) The Basket, 1980. Mem. Nat. Council Tchrs. Math., Fla. League Mid. Schs., Cath. Educators Guild Archdiocese of Miami, Nat. Cath. Ednl. Assn., Am. Mus. Natural History, Rocky Mt. Mental Health Assn. (bd. dirs. 1988-90), IBS Adv. Coun. Home: 1104 Waterloo Ct Rocky Mount NC 27804

SULLER, DEBRA JANE, accountant; b. Syracuse, N.Y., May 12, 1948; d. George Alan and Irma Mae (Winchell) Hammond; m. Robert George Suller, Dec. 31, 1973. BBA, Pace U., Pleasantville, N.Y., 1973; MBA, Pace U., 1982. CPA, N.Y. Staff acct. Jas. R. Frederick, CPA, Peekskill, N.Y., 1973-76; supr. Simmonds Precision Prod. Inc., Tarrytown, N.Y., 1976-82; mgr. Pepsi Co. Inc., Purchase, N.Y., 1982-88; prin. Debra J. Suller, MBA, CPA, Ossining, N.Y., 1985—. Troop advisor Girl Scouts U.S., Ossining, 1983—, treas. Westchester/Putnam chpt., Pleasantville, 1988—. Recipient appreciation pin Westchester/Putnam chpt. Girl Scouts U.S., 1988. Mem. AICPA, Nat. Conf. CPAs (sec. 1988, bd. dirs. 1989—), N.Y. State Soc. CPAs, Greater Ossining C. of C. (bd. dirs. 1985—, chmn. tax and budget 1985-89, Outstanding Vol. award, 1989), Ossining Bus. and Profl. Women (chmn. civic com. 1988—), Westchester Assn. Women Bus. Owners. Presbyterian. Office: 58 S Highland Ave Ossining NY 10562

SULLINS, JILL PACKALES, entrepreneur; b. N.Y.C., Aug. 16, 1945; d. Sidney A. and Shirley June (Burrows) Packales; m. Benjamin J. Hight, July 24, 1971 (div. Dec. 1981); children: David Matthew, Daniel Jeremy; m. H. Garland Sullins, Feb. 8, 1987. Student, Cornell U.; cert. profl. designation in advt., UCLA. Owner Hillside Graphics, Los Angeles, 1973-78, Dallas, 1978—; founding pres. Assn. Women Entrepreneurs Tex., Assn. Women Entrepreneurs Dallas, Inc.; exec. v.p. Nat. Assn. Women Govt. Contractors, Dallas; bd. dirs. Tech. Enterprises Devel. Ctr. U. Tex. Arlington Sch. Engring. Mem. adv. council U.S. Small Bus. Adminstrn., Dallas, steering com. Pres.'s Nat. Initiative Conf. on Women's Bus. Ownership, 1984, Gov.'s Conf. for Minority and Women-Owned Bus. Tex. Named Advocate of Yr. U.S. Small Bus. Administrn., 1985. Mem. Women in Communications, Ad League of Dallas, Bus. and Profl. Advt. Assn., LWV, Dallas Regional Minority Purchasing Council, Nat. Assn. Women Bus. Owners. Office: Hillside Graphics 6720 Robin Willow Ct Dallas TX 75248

SULLIVAN, ALMA JEAN, nurse; b. Vicksburg, Miss., Dec. 25, 1945; d. James B. Williams and Leila Mae (Stevens) Williams Deyamport; m. Louis Israel Sullivan, Sr., Mar. 10, 1966; children: Louis I. Jr., Michael Anthony, Reginald Jerome, Kenisha Erhonda. BSN, William Carey Coll., 1982. Various nursing positions Kuhn Meml. Hosp., Vicksburg, 1965-66, Vicksburg Hosp., 1968-69, Vicksburg Convalescent Home, 1969-72, Medgar Evers Comprehensive Ctr., Port Gibson, Miss., 1972-73, Care Inn Nursing Home, Clinton, Miss., 1973-74, Mercy Regional Med. Ctr., Vicksburg, 1974-79; head nurse med./surgical unit, relief asst. dir. nursing Vicksburg Med. Ctr., 1979—, sponsor teen hosp., 1987—. Sec. Miss. Action for Progress Adv. Bd., 1987—; mem. Title I Adv. Bd., Vicksburg, 1987-88, King Solomon's Choir, dir. Jr. Choir. Mem. Am. Nurses Assn., Dist. 12 Nurses Assn., Eliza Pillars R.N. Assn., Am. Heart Assn. (life support instr., Profl. Devel. in Gerontology award 1989), NAACP, Am. Legion Aux. (sec. unit 213), Bus. Profl. Women's Assn., Poinsetta Homemaker's. Baptist. Home: 2000 Rainey Dr Vicksburg MS 39180 Office: Vicksburg Med Ctr 3311 I-20 Frontage Rd Vicksburg MS 39180

SULLIVAN, BETTY JULIA, biochemist, consultant; b. Mpls., May 31, 1902; d. Thomas John and Blanche Lucille (Guilbert) Sullivan. BS, U. Minn., 1922, PhD, 1936; postgrad., U. Paris, 1924-25. Chief chemist Russell Miller Milling Co., Mpls., 1927-47; dir. rsch. Peavey Co., Mpls., 1947-58, v.p., dir. rsch., 1958-67; v.p. Experience, Inc., Mpls., 1967-69, pres., 1969-73, chmn. bd., 1973-75, bd. dirs., 1975—; bd. dirs. J.B. Short Milling Co., Chgo. Contbr. articles to profl. jours. Recipient Outstanding Achievement award U. Minn., 1956. Mem. AAAS, Am. Chem. Soc. (pres. Minn. sect.; Garvan medal 1954), Am. Assn. Cereal Chemists (Osborne Medal award 1948), Sigma Xi, Iota Sigma Pi. Roman Catholic.

SULLIVAN, CLAIRE FERGUSON, marketing educator; b. Pittsburg, Tex., Sept. 28, 1937; d. Almon Lafayette and Mabel Clara (Williams) Potter; m. Richard Wayne Ferguson, Jan. 31, 1959 (div. Jan. 1980); 1 child, Mark Jeffrey Ferguson; m. David Edward Sullivan, Nov. 2, 1984. BBA, U. Tex., 1958, MBA, 1961; PhD, U. North Tex., 1973. Instr. So. Meth. U., Dallas, 1965-70; asst. prof. U. Utah, Salt Lake City, 1972-74; assoc. prof. U. Ark., Little Rock, 1974-77, U. Tex., Arlington, 1977-80, Ill. State U., Normal, 1980-84; prof., chmn. mktg. Bentley Coll., Waltham, Mass., 1984-89; dean sch. bus. Met. State Coll., Denver, 1989—; cons. Gen. Tel. Co., Irving, Tex., 1983, Denver Partnership, 1989-90, McKnight Pub. Co., Bloomington, Ill., 1983, dental practitioner, Bloomington, 1982-83, Olympic Fed., Berwyn, Ill., 1982, Denver Partnership, 1990. Contbr. mktg. articles to profl. jours. Direct Mktg. Inst. fellow, 1981; Ill. State U. rsch. grantee, 1981-83. Mem. Am. Mktg. Assn. (faculty fellow 1984-85), So. Mktg. Assn., Southwestern Mktg. Assn., Denver World Trade Ctr., Rotary, Beta Gamma Sigma. Republican. Methodist. Home: 8101 E Dartmouth Ave #83 Denver CO 80231 Office: Met State Coll Sch Bus 1006 11th St Denver CO 80204

SULLIVAN, CONNIE CASTLEBERRY, artist, photographer; b. Cin., Jan. 8, 1934; d. John Porter and Constance (Alf) Castleberry; m. John J. Sullivan, June 6, 1959; children: Deirdre Kelly, Margaret Graham. BA, Manhattanville Coll., 1957. spl. lectr. Cin. Contemporary Art Ctr., 1984. One-woman shows include Contemporary Art Ctr. Cleve., 1982, Cin. Contemporary Arts Ctr., 1983, Fogg Art Mus., Cambridge, Mass., 1983, 90, Camden Arts Ctr., London, 1987, Jean-Pierre Lambert Galerie, Paris, 1988, David Winton Bell Gallery, Brown U., Providence, 1989, Toni Burckhead Gallery, Cin., 1989, The Fogg Art Mus., 1990; exhibited in numerous group shows including Dayton (Ohio) Art Inst., 1987, J.B. Speed Art Mus., Louisville, 1988, Ohio U., Athens, 1989, Centre Nat. Photographie, Paris, 1989; represented in permanent collections numerous mus., also pvt. collections; author: Petroglyphs of the Heart, Photographs by Connie Sullivan, 1983; work represented in numerous publs. Trustee Images Ctr. for Fine Photography, Cin., 1986—. Arts Midwest fellow NEA, 1989-90; recipient award Toledo Friends Photography Juried Show, 1986, Best of Show award, 1988; Best of Show award Images Gallery, Cin., 1986; Aid to Individual Artists grantee Summerfair, 1987. Mem. McDowell Soc. Home and Studio: 9 Garden Pl Cincinnati OH 45208

SULLIVAN, ELEANOR REGIS, editor; b. Cambridge, Mass., Oct. 19, 1928; d. Timothy Joseph and Katherine Irene (Dowd) S. B.S., Salem State Coll., 1950. Tchr. Clinton Grammar Sch., Conn., 1950-53, Russell Sch., Cambridge, Mass., 1953-57, George Washington Sch., White Plains, N.Y., 1957-60; editorial asst. Pocket Books, Inc., N.Y.C., 1961-62; editor Charles Scribner's Sons, N.Y.C., 1962-69, Davis Publs., Inc., N.Y.C., 1970—; tchr. writing workshops. Author: Whodunit: A Biblio-Bio-Anecdotal Memoir of Frederic Dannay, 1984; editor Ellery Queen anthologies, 10 Alfred Hitchcock anthologies; contbr. stories and articles to mags., newspapers, books. Vol. ARC, St. Albans Naval Hosp., Queens, N.Y., 1968-73; vol. tutor I Have A Dream Program, N.Y.C., 1986-87. Mem. Mystery Writers Am. (bd. dirs. 1974-77, 82-85, Ellery Queen award 1987), Dramatists Guild, Am. Film Inst. Democrat. Home: 236 E 49th St New York NY 10017 Office: Ellery Queen's Mystery Mag 380 Lexington Ave New York NY 10017

SULLIVAN, JANET SPRING, teacher; b. Plainfield, N.J., Mar. 19, 1944; d. Arthur Francis and Alice Mae (Marcasciano) Spring; m. Maurice Conrad Sullivan, Apr. 27, 1968; Sharon Louise Sullivan, Kimberly Alice Sullivan. AB in Eng., Coll. of St. Elizabeth, Convent Station, N.J., 1966. Jr. Systems Analyst Nat. State Bank, Linden, N.J., 1966-68; systems analyst Engelhard Minerals & Chemicals, Newark, N.J., 1968-69; English as a 2d lang. Instr. Mt. Diablo Sch. Dist., Concord, N.J., 1979—. Mem. Calif. Assn. Tchrs. of Eng. to Speakers of Other Languages, Calif. Coun. of Adult Edn., Am. Assn. of U. Women (pres. 1979-80; Grant Hon. 1980). Republican. Roman Catholic. Home: 28 Carpenter Ct Pleasant Hill CA 94523 Office: Mt Diablo Adult Sch 1266 San Carlos Ave Concord CA 94518

SULLIVAN, KATHRYN ANN, librarian; b. Elmhurst, Ill., Jan. 22, 1954; d. Joseph Terrence and Rose Marie (Wright) S. Student, Triton Jr. Coll., 1972-73; BA, No. Ill. U., 1975, MLS, 1977; postgrad., Nova U. Chief periodicals clk. No. Ill. U., Dekalb, 1976-77; periodicals librarian West Chgo. (Ill.) Pub. Library, 1977-78, Winona (Minn.) State U., 1978—. Contbr. articles to profl. jours. Grantee Winona State U., 1986, 88. Mem. ALA, Minn. Libr. Assn., Libr. and Info. Tech. Assn., N.Am. Serials Interest Group. Home: 651 Main Winona MN 55987 Office: Winona State U Maxwell Libr Winona MN 55987

SULLIVAN, KATHRYN D., geologist, astronaut; b. Paterson, N.J., Oct. 3, 1951; d. Donald P. and Barbara K. Sullivan. BS in Earth Scis., U. Calif., Santa Cruz, 1973; PhD in Geology, Dalhousie U., Halifax, N.S., Can., 1978, Dr. (hon.), 1985. With NASA, 1978—, astronaut, 1979—, mission specialist flight STS-41G, 1984, mission specialist flight STS-31, 1990; adj. prof. Rice U., Houston, 1985; mem. Nat. Commn. on Space, 1985—; mem. exec. panel Chief of Naval Ops., 1988—; first woman to perform extra-vehicular activity. Lt. comdr. USNR. Recipient Nat. Air and Space Mus. trophy Smithsonian Inst., 1985. Mem. AIAA, Geol. Soc. Am., Am. Geophys. Union, Soc. Women Geographers, Explorers Club, Sierra Club. Address: NASA Johnson Space Ctr Astronaut Office Houston TX 77058*

SULLIVAN, KATHRYN MEARA, computer company executive; b. Schenectady, N.Y., Sept. 20, 1942; d. Vincent Thomas and Agnes (Pendergast) Meara; m. Paul William Sullivan, Feb. 8, 1964; children: Mary Margaret, Paul Hammond, Patricia Eileen. BS in Physics, Bucknell U., 1964; MBA, Fairleigh Dickinson U., 1981. Software developer Gen. Electric Corp., Phila., 1964-65; account exec. Honeywell Corp., Phila., 1975-77; regional sales mgr. Nicolet Instrument Corp., Northvale, N.J., 1977-81; mktg. mgr. AT&T, Basking Ridge, N.J., 1981-83; bus. devel. mgr. AT&T, Berkeley Heights, N.J., 1983-86; pres. AT&T-Pixel Machines, Somerset, N.J., 1986-90; dir. sales ops. and support AT&T Computer Systems, Morristown, N.J., 1990—. Chairperson career options for women com. YWCA, Plainfield, N.J., 1989—. Recipient Anthony Gervino award Fairleigh Dickinson U., 1989. Mem. Nat. Computer Graphics Assn. (bd. dirs., chairperson internat. com. Fairfax, Va. 1989—), Rothman Inst. for Entrepreneurial Studies Fairleigh Dickinson U. (charter, adv. bd. 1989—).

SULLIVAN, LAURA PATRICIA, lawyer, insurance company executive; b. Des Moines, Oct. 16, 1947; d. William and Patricia (Kautz) S. B.A., Cornell Coll., Iowa, 1971; J.D., Drake U., 1972. Bar: Iowa 1972. Various positions Ins. Dept. Iowa, Des Moines, 1972-75; various legal positions State Farm Mut. Auto Ins. Co., Bloomington, Ill., 1975-81, sec. and counsel, 1981-88, v.p., counsel and sec., 1988—; v.p., sec., dir. State Farm Cos. Found., 1985—; v.p., counsel and sec. State Farm Fire and Casualty Co., 1988—, State Farm Gen. Ins. Co., 1988—; sec. State Farm Lloyd's, Inc., 1987—. Trustee John M. Scott Indsl. Sch. Trust, Bloomington, 1983-86; bd. dirs. Scott Ctr., 1983-86, Bloomington-Normal Symphony, 1980-85; chmn. Ins. Inst. for Hwy. Safety, 1987-88. Mem. ABA, Iowa State Bar Assn., Am. Corp. Counsel Assn. Office: State Farm Mut Automobile Ins Co 1 State Farm Pla Bloomington IL 61710

SULLIVAN, MARGARET WOLAN, research psychologist, educator; b. Elizabeth, N.J., Sept. 24, 1952; d. Julian and Bertha (Szpiech) Wolan; m. Dennis J. Sullivan, June 20, 1976; children: Heather Jean, Meredith Clare. BA magna cum laude, Kean Coll., 1974; MS, Rutgers U., 1976, PhD, 1979. Mem. rsch. staff Ednl. Testing Svc., Princeton, N.J., 1978-82; asst. prof. pediatrics and child devel. U. Medicine and Dentistry N.J. Robert Wood Johnson Med. Sch., Piscataway, N.J., 1982-90, assoc. prof., 1990—; dir. infant learning and emotion project Inst. for Study Inst. for Study of Child Devel., Piscataway, N.J., 1983—; coord. contingency intervention program for handicapped U. Medicine and Dentistry N.J. Robert Wood Johnson Med. Sch., Piscataway, N.J., 1986-89; presenter in field. Contbr. articles to profl. jours. Mem. N.J. Com. on Rehab. Tech. Nat. Inst. Child Health and Devel. grantee, 1983-85, 87-90, Robert Wood Johnson Found. grantee, 1986—. Mem. Soc. for Rsch. in Child Devel., Ea. Psychol. Assn., AAUW (pub. policy chmn. Somerville, N.J. br. 1984—), Polish Am. Univ. Club N.J. Roman Catholic. Office: UMDNJ-RWJ Med Sch 97 Paterson St New Brunswick NJ 08903-0019

SULLIVAN, SISTER MARIE CELESTE, hospital administrator; b. Boston, Mar. 18, 1929; d. Daniel John and Katherine Agnes (Cunniff) S. BBA, St. Bonaventure U., 1965. Joined Order Franciscan Sisters Roman Cath. Ch., 1952; bus. mgr. St. Joseph's Hosp., Providence, 1954-62; asst. adminstr. St. Joseph's Hosp., Tampa, Fla., 1965-70, adminstr., 1970-83, chief exec. officer, 1983—; mem. Adv. Council Hillsborough County, Emergency Med. Planning Council Hillsborough County; coord. health affairs Diocese of St. Petersburg, 1980—; mem. Fla. Cancer Control and Research Adv. Bd., 1980-90; bd. dirs. First Fla. Bank, N.A.; gen. councillor Franciscan Sisters of Allegany, 1984—. Contbr. articles to profl. jours. Trustee St. Francis Med. & Health Ctr., Miami Beach, Fla., 1986—; bd. dirs. local chpt. Am. Cancer Soc. Recipient Humanitarian award Judeo-Christian Health Clinic, Tampa, 1977, Athena award Fla. West Coast chpt. Women in Communications, 1978, Exec. Woman of Yr. award Tampa Bay chpt. Network Exec. Women, 1987. Fellow Am. Coll. Health Care Execs.; mem. Fla. Hosp. Assn. (trustee 1983-87), Am. Mgmt. Assn., Greater Tampa C. of C. (bd. govs. 1982-87). Democrat. Club: Centro (Tampa) (founding bd. govs.). Home: 2924 W Curtis St Tampa FL 33614 Office: St Joseph's Hosp PO Box 4227 Tampa FL 33677

SULLIVAN, MARJORIE ANN, nursing administrator; b. Worcester, Mass., Feb. 18, 1931; d. Mark W. and Cecelia R. (Ennis) Rice; m. Robert M. Sullivan, May 31, 1952; 1 child, Cathleen A. Student, St. Vincent Hosp., Worcester, Mass., 1951; BS, Anna Maria Coll., 1980, MS in Nursing, 1985. Staff nurse St. Vincent Hosp., Worcester, Mass., 1951-58, head nurse, 1959-65, from staff to head nurse, 1967-85, mgr. nursing, 1985—. Mem. Mass. Coun. Nurse Mgrs., Mass. Cath. Nurses, Coun. Nurse Mgrs., Nat. League of Nursing, St. Vincent Hosp. Alumni Assn. Democrat. Roman Catholic. Home: 5 Cabot St Worcester MA 01603

SULLIVAN, MARY JANE LEAHY, university program administrator; b. Bklyn., Mar. 11, 1939; d. George W. and Dorothy (Kane) Leahy; m. William Sullivan, Dec. 26, 1959 (dec. 1982); children: Deirdre, George, Mary-Laura; m. Albert B. Dickas, July 30, 1988. BA, Hunter Coll., 1960, MA, Ball State U., 1976, EdD, 1980. Freelance writer N.Y. Daily News, N.Y.C., 1959-69; tchr. English Westfield (N.J.) Pub. Schs., 1973-75; coordinator continuing edn. So. Ill. U., Carbondale, 1978-85; dir. Ctr. for Continuing Edn. and Univ. Relations U. Wis., Superior, 1985—. Mem. editorial panel Continuing Higher Edn. Rev.; contbr. articles to profl. jours. Bd. dirs. Dutton Found., Superior Meml. Hosp.; trustee Dutton Found. Grantee NSF. Mem. AAUW, LWV, Rotary. Office: U Wis Ctr for Continuing Edn 1800 Grand Ave Superior WI 54880

SULLIVAN, MARY LOU, communications executive; b. Evanston, Ill., Jan. 12, 1945; d. Charles Francis and Ann Louise (Hauck) Revelle; m. C.J. Sullivan, Aug. 13, 1966; 1 child, Mark Quinn. BS, U. Mich., 1966; postgrad., Harper Coll., 1986-88. Lic. speech and lang. pathologist; cert. tchr., Ill. Speech and lang. therapist Glenbrook North High Sch., Northbrook, Ill., 1968-70, Sch. Dist. #72, Skokie, Ill., 1972-75; speech and lang. cons. Stevenson High Sch., Prairie View, Ill., 1978-86; speech and lang. therapist Sch. Dist. #103, Lincolnshire, Ill., 1980-89; pres. Candere, Northfield, Ill., 1989—; sales cons. Spauldings Clothing, Wilmette, Ill., 1988-89. Bd. dirs. Lincolnshire Community Nursery Sch., 1978-80. Mem. North Suburban Speech and Lang. Assn., Image Industry Coun. Internat. (bd. dirs. Midwest chpt. 1989-91). Republican. Roman Catholic. Office: Candere One Northfield Plz Ste 300 Northfield IL 60093

SULLIVAN, MARY MAUREEN, naval officer; b. Hato Rey, P.R., Nov. 17, 1950; d. Maurice McKeen and Maria del Socorro (Viera) Stickney; m. Dennis Michael Sullivan, June 24, 1978; children: Heather Colleen, Michael Kelley. BA, Cath. U. Am., 1973; MEd, U. West Fla., 1984. Asst. to psychologist Head Start Program, Puerta de Tierra, P.R., 1973-74; commd.

ensign USN, 1977, advanced through grades to lt. comdr., 1986; dir. nonappropriated fund div. Naval Ordnance Sta., Indian Head, Md., 1977-79; manpower mgmt. officer Naval Air Res. Ctr., Patuxent River, Md., 1979-80; Naval ROTC at-sea tng. officer Office Chief Naval Edn. and Tng., Pensacola, Fla., 1980-84; Navy liaison officer, curriculum designer Def. Equal Opportunity Mgmt. Inst., Cocoa Beach, Fla., 1985-88; tng. officer U.S. Naval Acad., Annapolis, Md., 1988—; mem. Chief Naval Ops. Study Group for Equal Opportunity, Washington, 1989. Vol. Cath. Confraternity Doctrine tchr. Holy Name of Jesus Cath. Ch., Indiatlantic, Fla., 1984. Mem. NAFE, Am. Soc. Tng. and Devel., Women Officers Profl. Assn., Assn. Supervision and Curriculum Devel., Phi Kappa Phi, Psi Chi. Republican. Home: 1340 Blackwalnut Ct Annapolis MD 21403 Office: US Naval Acad Luce Hall Stop 7D Annapolis MD 21402

SULLIVAN, MAUREEN PATRICIA, academic administrator; b. Missoula, Mont., Nov. 13, 1946; d. James Edward Sullivan and Theresa Marie (Martin) Woolery; divorced; children: Cynthia Diane, Brenna Colleen, William Patrick. BA in English, Ea. Wash. U., 1983, postgrad.; postgrad., Mont. State U., 1985-86, U. Okla. Organizer Welfare Rights Orgn., Spokane, Wash., 1970-75; worker Spokane Falls Community Coll., 1973-75; tutor Ft. Wright Coll. Holy Names, Spokane, 1975-77; Title IV programmer Spokane Sch. Dist., 1979-81; substitute tchr. Loyola-Sacred Heart High Sch., Missoula, 1984-85; instr. reading Blackfeet Community Coll., Browning, Mont., 1985-86, grants writer, 1986, program dir., mem. devel. com., 1986; pres., founder, ednl./bus. cons. INK, Spokane, Wash., 1989—; supervising trainer Laubach Literacy Internat., Browning, 1985—, bd. dirs., 1985-86; tutor Blackfeet Literacy Program, Browning, 1985—, lead trainer, 1986—, pres., 1985-86; cons. Spokane Alliance for the Mentally Ill, Conf. for Ethnic Mental Health Svcs., Spokane Commn. Mental Health Ctr. Founder Sun Eagle, 1990—; mem. steering, task force Greater Spokane Abuse Coun., 1989—. Recipient writing grant award, 1989-90. Mem. Nat. Assn. Female Execs., Internat. Reading Assn. Democrat. Bahai. Home and Office: 2307 E 29th Ave L9 Spokane WA 99223 Office: Blackfeet Literacy Program Box 819 Browning MT 59417

SULLIVAN, NANCY JEAN, lawyer, insurance company executive; b. Americus, Ga., Oct. 9, 1957; d. James Howell and Margaret (Thomas) S. BA in Sociology and Polit. Sci., Queens Coll., Charlotte, N.C., 1978; JD, Mercer U., 1982. Bar: La., 1985. Law clk. Chattahoochee Jud. Cir. Ct., Columbus, Ga., 1982-85; dir. pub. rels. Am. Family Life Assurance Co., Columbus, 1986-90, 2d v.p., dir. conventions, meetings and spl. events, 1990—. Bd. dirs. Anne Elizabeth Shepherd Home, Columbus, 1982—, Girls Club Columbus, 1984—, Columbus Boy's Club, 1990; active contemporaries steering com. Columbus Mus., Hist. Columbus Found., Am. Cancer Soc.; mem. adminstrn. bd. St. Luke United Meth. Ch., 1988—. Named Outstanding Young Woman of Columbus, Columbus Jaycees and Columbus Civic League, 1989. Mem. ABA, La. Bar Assn., Youngers Lawyers Club, Jr. League Columbus, Columbus Symphony Women's Assn., Kiwanis, Network Execs. & Profls., Leadership Columbus. Home: 2625 Edgewood Rd Columbus GA 31906 Office: Am Family Life Assurance Co 1932 Wynnton Rd Columbus GA 31999

SULLIVAN, PATRICIA ANN, lawyer; b. Bklyn., Oct. 27, 1956; d. Francis E. and Catherine M. (Ryan) S.; m. Paul J. Kefer, Dec. 20, 1980; children: Ryan F. Kefer, John Sullivan Kefer. BA, Manhattanville Coll., 1977; JD, Fordham U., 1980. Bar: N.Y. 1981. Assoc. Barry, McTiernan & Moore, N.Y.C., 1980—. Mem. ABA, Assn. Trial Lawyers Am., N.Y. County Lawyers Assn. Democrat. Roman Catholic. Office: Barry McTiernan & Moore 22 Cortlandt St New York NY 10007

SULLIVAN, PATRICIA CLARE, hospital administrator; b. Cortland, Nebr., July 2, 1928. R.N. diploma, Mercy Hosp. Sch. Nursing, Denver, 1954; B.S.N., Coll. St. Mary, Omaha, 1955; M.H.A., St. Louis U., 1971, cert. for internal resources for renewal, 1971; cert. in gerontology, U. Nebr., Omaha, 1976. Instr. Mercy Hosp. Sch. Nursing, Des Moines, 1955-58; dir. Mercy Hosp. Sch. Nursing, 1960-64; nursing supr. pediatrics Mercy Hosp., Des Moines, 1955-58; adminstr. Mercy Hosp., 1977—; pres. Mercy Health Ctr. of Central Iowa, 1982—, Mercy Hosp. Med. Ctr., Mercy Found., Mercy Health & Human Services, Mercy Properties, ShareCare Ltd, Mercy Geriatric Services; coordinator rural hosp. nursing, nursing supr. ob-gyn Mercy Hosp., Durango, Colo., 1958-60, nursing supr., Williston, N.D., 1964-65; adminstr. St. Joseph's Mercy Hosp., Centerville, Iowa, 1965-69; resident Peter Bent Brigham Hosp., Boston, 1970-71; dir. Cen. Nat. Bancshares, First Interstate Bank Corp. Des Moines (formerly Bancshares), 1979—; in organizational renewal Province of Omaha, 1971-74; dir. community relations Archbishop Bergan Mercy Hosp., Omaha, 1974-77; mem. Province of Omaha Health Services Council, 1958—; provincial chpt. del. Province Omaha, 1970-74. Dir. film depicting tornado strike to Archbishop Bergan Mercy Hosp., 1975, numerous showings, including at Congl. hearing at Pentagon. Del. Mercy Gen. Chpt., 1981—; bd. dirs. Mercy Hosp., Devils Lake, N.D., 1972-81, Sub-Area IV, Iowa Health Systems Agy., 1977—, NCCJ, 1979-85, Health System of Mercy, 1979-83, Grand View Coll., Des Moines, 1982-87, Des Moines Better Bus. Bur., 1983-85; regional rep. Diocesan Pastoral Council, 1978-80; mem. Mercy Health Conf., 1979-83, Iowa Network Mercy Hosps. 1979—, IHA Coun. on Profl. Affairs, 1980—; bd. dirs. Convalescent Home for Children, 1980-84, Health System of Midlands, Omaha, 1984-86, Greater Des Moines Com., 1987—; chair Iowa Caucus Project, 1987-88; mem. pres.'s coun. Iowa State U., 1988—. Recipient Leadership award NCCJ, 1984, People of Vision award Iowa Soc. to Prevent Blindness, 1985; named Adminstr. of Yr. Des Moines Consortium of Family Practice Physicians, 1980-81; named to Iowa Women's Hall of Fame Iowa Commn. on Status of Women, 1988, Equestrian Order of Holy Sepulchre of Jerusalem, 1989. Mem. Nat. League for Nursing, Iowa League for Nursing (pres. 1966-69), Iowa Assn. Bus. Industry, Am. Acad. Med. Adminstrs. (pres. Iowa chpt. 1986-87, Adminstr. of Yr. 1984), Omaha League for Nursing (dir. 1976-77), Am. Hosp. Assn., Soc. Advancement Mgmt., Des Moines C. of C. (bd. dirs.), Cath. Health Assn. (bd. dirs. 1987—), Trendleaders of Ryan Club (advisor to chief exec. officers). Office: Mercy Hosp Med Ctr Office of the Pres 6th & University Ave Des Moines IA 50314

SULLIVAN, PATRICIA LANCE, writer, editor; b. Austin, Tex., Feb. 15, 1950; d. Frederick Lee and Betty Ellen (Leonard) Stead; m. John Edward Sullivan, Jan. 1, 1978. Student U. N.Mex., 1967-70; BA in English Lit., Calif. State U.-Northridge, 1978; M of Communication, Ga. State U., 1989. Clk., typist Adamson Co., Santa Monica, Calif., 1970-71; graphic artist Hughes Research Labs., Malibu, Calif., 1971-79; sales rep. In This Issue Mag., Costa Mesa, Calif., 1979-80; freelance writer, Atlanta, 1981—; writer, editor The Preferred Press, Atlanta, 1984-86; editor The Newsletter, Atlanta Occupational Medicine, 1985-86. Editor: Atlanta Professional Women's Directory, 1982-83; columnist Go mag., 1987-89; contbr. articles to profl. jours. Pub. relations staff Nat. MS Soc., Atlanta, 1982. Mem. Internat. TV Assn., AAUW, Nat. League Am. Pen Women (chmn. state letters com. Ga. 1986—, editor, pub. Pen-Graphs newsletter Atlanta br. 1987, 89-90, chmn. state conv. 1987, state historian 1988), Women in Communications Inc., Village Writers Group, Kappa Kappa Gamma, Sigma Delta Chi (scholar 1988). Republican. Presbyterian. Avocations: reading, computing, travel, writing. Home and Office: 3746 Wieuca Rd NE Atlanta GA 30342

SULLIVAN, PATRICIA SUE, aerospace executive, accountant; b. Phoenix, Apr. 1, 1956; d. Daniel John and Pauline (McCulloch) S.; m. Carl B. Martorana, Apr. 12, 1986; 1 child, Kelly Marie. BSBA in Acctg., Calif. State U., Long Beach, 1979. CPA, Calif. From staff auditor to sr. acct. Price Waterhouse, Newport Beach, Calif., 1979-84; corp. controller VERAC, Inc., San Diego, 1984-88; v.p. fin. and adminstrn. Ball Systems Engring. Div., San Diego, 1988—. Mem. AICPAs, Calif. Soc. CPAs. Republican. Roman Catholic. Office: Ball Systems Engring Div 9605 Scranton Rd Ste 500 San Diego CA 92121

SULLIVAN, PATRICIA W. (TERRY SULLIVAN), real estate manager; b. Hempstead, N.Y., July 25, 1936; d. Gilbert Hudson and Vera (Morgan) Wehmann; m. Richard J. Sullivan, June 8, 1957 (div. Apr. 1982); children: Katherine Sullivan-Irwin, Gillian Stewart, Adam W. BS, Skidmore Coll., 1958; MS, Syracuse U., 1965. Mgr. Purtell & Wigdale, Inc., Cedarburg, Wis., Merrill Lynch Real Estate, Cedarburg; office mgr. Coldwell Banker Real Estate, Cedarburg. Contbr. articles to profl. jours. Mem. Nat. Assn. Realtors (bd. dirs. 1989-90, Omega Tau Rho award 1983, Outstanding Educator of the Year award for medium states, 1989), Nat. Women's Coun. Realtors (pres. 1990), Women's Coun. Realtors (pres. Milw. chpt. 1982, bd. dirs. 1983-90, named WCR of Yr. 1983, LTG 1985), Ozaukee Bd. Realtors (pres. 1979, bd. dirs. 1977-79, Realtor of Yr. 1979), Realtors Nat. Mktg. Inst. (dir. RS coun. 1983-86, CRS 1978, CRB 1981), Wis. Realtors Assn. (v.p. 1982-83, bd. dirs. 1983-86, Instr. of Yr. 1988, GRI 1975), Wis. Cert. Residential Specialists (cert.; pres. 1982, Cert. Residential Specialist of Yr. 1983), Wis. Cert. Residential Brokers (cert.; pres. 1988). Address: Coldwell Banker 4309 Columbia Rd Cedarburg WI 53012

SULLIVAN, SANDRA JONES, designer, design company executive; b. Fredericksburg, Va., Jan. 26, 1948; d. Carle Hamilton and Lily Mae (Rose) Jones; m. Lehmer Kent Sullivan, July 11, 1970; children: Lehmer Cameron, Catherine Hollis. B.S. in Bus. Edn., Longwood, Coll., 1970. Tchr. James Monroe High Sch., Fredericksburg, 1970, Stafford High Sch., Va., 1971-72, 74-76; pres., designer Homespun Elegance Ltd., Fredericksburg, 1980—. Author, designer numerous needlework leaflets including Elegant Ducks, 1981, A Christmas Sampler, 1981, Wedding Folk Art, 1982, Candlewicking for Christmas, 1982, Tea Dyeing, 1982, Willow Tree Sampler, 1984, Antique Flowers, 1984, Cinnamon Stick Christmas, 1985, The Amish, 1985, created over 100 needlework publs.; established (product line): Prim and Proper Wares, 1989. Mem. jr. bd. Historic Fredericksburg, 1977—. Mem. Needlework Markets Inc., Nat. Needlework Assn., Am. Ind. Designers Assn., Embroiders Guild, Fredericksburg C. of C. Republican. Methodist. Avocations: antiques; gardening. Home: 104 Holly Cir Fredericksburg VA 22405 Office: Homespun Elegance Ltd 915A Sophia St Fredericksburg VA 22401

SULLIVAN, SARAH LOUISE, educator, researcher, consultant; b. Wilmington, Del., Sept. 24, 1954; d. Frederick William III and Ruth (Swavely) S. BS, Bowling Green U., 1975; MS, Ill. Inst. Tech., 1986, postgrad., 1986—. Programmer Computer Sci. Corp., Langley AFB, Va., 1975-77; sr. systems programmer JPLRCC, Perrysburg, Ohio, 1977-80; sr. systems engr. Kraft Inc., Glenview, Ill., 1980-83; project leader Siemens Gammasonics, Des Plaines, Ill., 1983-85; sect. mgr. Zenith Electronics, Glenview, Ill., 1985; mem. tech. staff AT&T Bell Labs., Naperville, Ill., 1986-87; asst. prof. North Cen. Coll., Naperville, Ill., 1988-89; cons., trainer Sarah L. Sullivan & Assocs., Morton Grove, Ill., 1988—; instr. Ill. Inst. Tech., Chgo., 1988; presenter in field. Mem. IEEE, Assn. for Computing Machinery, Oasis Ctr. for Human Potential. Home: 9417 Marion Ave Morton Grove IL 60053

SULLIVAN, SISTER SHARON, education educator; b. Austin, Tex., Sept. 22, 1947; d. Jack Davis and Jane Shelby (Strickland) S. AA with honors, Columbia (Mo.) Coll., 1967; BA in History, Maryville Coll., 1969; cert. elem. edn., spl. edn., Brescia Coll., 1975; MA in Edn., Western Ky. U., 1982; postgrad., U. No. Colo., 1987-88, Purdue U., 1990—. Cert. elem. tchr., spl. edn. tchr., Ky. Office mgr., bookkeeper Jerrico, Inc., Lexington, Ky., 1969-71; program and tng. dir. Pennyroyal coun. Girl Scouts U.S., Owensboro, Ky., 1971-73; village leader, program dir., asst. dir. Camp Kysoc, Ky. Easter Seal Soc., Louisville, 1974-77; tchr. learning disabilities resource rm. Daviess County Bd. Edn., Owensboro, 1975-82; pastoral care Mt. St. Joseph Ursulines, Maple Mount, Ky., 1983-84; dir. residential life, part-time faculty Brescia Coll., Owensboro, 1984-87, faculty, 1987—; diagnostician Brescia Coll. Ednl. Testing Ctr., Owensboro, 1985—; coord. summer tutoring, 1985-90, faculty 7th grad coll. experience, 1988-90; presenter State Literacy Coun., 1986-88. Participant Diocesan Choir, Owensboro, 1986-90; del. governing body Chpt. in Progress, Maple Mount, Ky., 1988-92; trainer, vol. Girl Scouts U.S., Owensboro, 1973—; instr. ARC, Owensboro, 1973-85; election official County Clk., Owensboro, 1973-81. Recipient Teaching Excellence award Alpha Chi, 1989; Presvc. Learning Strategies grantee Ky. Dept. Edn., 1988; Trustee's scholar Christian Coll., 1965. Mem. Coun. for Exceptional Children (pres. 1989-90), Coun. for Learning Disabilies, Ky. Assn. of Children with Learning Disabilities. Roman Catholic.

SULLIVAN, SHERRY E., educator; b. Cleve., Oct. 8, 1961. BSBA, Bowling Green State U., 1983; PhD, Ohio State U., 1988. Instr. Ohio State U., Columbus, 1983-88; prof. Memphis State U., 1988—; cons. Children's Hosp., Columbus, Ohio, 1982; reviewer Nat. Acad. Mgmt. Mtgs., 1988-89, S.W. Mgmt. Assn., 1988-89. Contbr. articles to profl. jours. Mem. Sta. WKNO Pub. TV, Memphis, 1989—, Provido, Memphis, 1988—. Grantee Fogelman Coll. Bus., Memphis, 1989, Ramsey Fowlers, 1989, Ohio State U., 1988; recipient McCoy Scholarship, 1987. Mem. Acad. Mgmt. Assn., Am. Psychol. Assn., So. Mgmt. Assn. (reviewer 1987-89). Office: Memphis State U Dept Mgmt Memphis TN 38152

SULLIVAN, SUSAN CAROL, assistant principal; b. St. Louis, Apr. 27, 1942; d. Charles Edward and Florence Mary (Corbett) Weniger; m. William Anthony Sullivan, Nov. 25, 1965; children: Kathleen, Tricia. Tchr. Parkway Sch. Dist., St. Louis, 1964-65, Cherry Hill (N.J.) Sch. Dist., 1970-78, Mt. Vernon (Ill.) Sch. Dist., 1978-80, Little Flower Sch., Springfield, Ill., 1980-82, Lincoln Land Community Coll., Springfield, 1982-83; tchr. Kirkwood (Mo.) Sch. Dist., 1982-90, lead tchr. gifted program, 1987-90; dir. Kirkwood Enrichment Program, 1986-88; asst. prin. Francis Howell Sch. Dist., St. Charles, Mo., 1990—; instr. Maryville Coll., St. Louis, 1990—; cons. in field of gifted edn. Chairwoman Neighborhood Watch Assn., Sunset Hills, Mo., 1983—. NSF grantee Glassboro (N.J.) State U., 1971. Mem. Nat. Assn. Gifted Children, St. Louis Assn. Gifted Children, Gifted Assn. of Mo., Assn. for Supervision and Curriculum Devel., Southside Imperial Dance Club. Office: Becky-David Elem Sch 1155 Jungs Station Rd Saint Charles MO 63033

SULLIVAN-HANLEY, CAROL, dean of faculty; b. Boston, June 21, 1956; d. June Edward and Marion L. (Cameron) S.; m. P.J. Hanley, Aug. 28, 1954. AA, Mt. Ida Coll., Newton, Minn., 1974-76; BS, Wheelock Coll., Boston, 1970-78; MEd., Lesley Coll., Cambridge, Mass., 1981-86. Tchr. Tufty Day Care, Medford, Mass., 1978-80, Children's Village, Cambridge, Mass., 1980-85, Mt. Ida Coll., Newton, Mass., 1985--. Mem. L.W.V., Situche Mass. 1988--, M.S.P.C.A., Boston 1988--. Mem. N.A.E.Y.C., Weelax Alumni Assn., Lesley Alumni Assn. Democrat. Roman Catholic.

SULLWOLD, CORLISS KAY, history educator; b. Kearney, Nebr., Feb. 9, 1946; d. Theodore Roslin and Floretta (Record) S.; 1 child, Christa Marie Britton. BA in Internat. Studies, Kearney State Coll., 1987, secondary teaching cert., 1989, postgrad., 1989—. Bank & loan officer Elm Creek (Nebr.) State Bank, 1968-72; statis. analyst Eaton Corp., Kearney, 1979-86; livestock producer Sullwold Farms, Inc., Elm Creek, 1985—; grad. teaching asst. history dept. Kearney (Nebr.) State Coll., 1990—; mem. pres.' planning coun. Kearney State Coll., 1989-90, grad. coun., 1989-90. Recipient Gene Hamacker scholarship Kearney State Coll., 1989, tuition waiver for grad. sch., 1989. Mem. AAUW (pres. 1989-90), N.Am. South Devon Assn., Nebr. Draft Horse Assn., Nat. Cattle Womens Assn., Kearney Country Club, Phi Alpha Theta (v.p. Pi Nu chpt. 1989-90, pres. 1990-91), Alpha Mu Gamma. Democrat. Home: 910 W 22nd St Kearney NE 68847 Office: Kearney State Coll Hist Dept Kearney NE 68848

SULTANA, NAJMA, psychiatrist; b. Nirmal, Andhra, India; July 22, 1948; came to U.S. 1973; d. Khaja Moinuddin and Mujib (Unnisa) Begum; m. Khaja Mohiuddin, July 8, 1971 (div. 1978); m. M. Rashid Chaudhry, Oct. 16, 1981. M.B.B.S. Gandhi Med. Coll., Hyderaba, India, 1973. Resident in psychiatry SUNY/Kings County Hosp. Ctr., Bklyn., 1976-78, fellow child psychiatry, 1978-80; asst. clin. physician S. Beach Psychiat. Ctr., S.I., N.Y., 1980-81; asst. clin. prof. SUNY Downstate Med. Ctr., N.Y.C., 1981—; attending psychiatrist King's County Hosp., Bklyn., 1981—. Mem. Am. Psychiat. Assn. Democrat. Muslim.

SULTON, ANNE THOMAS, lawyer, criminologist; b. Racine, Wis., Oct. 24, 1952; d. William Henry and Esther (Phillips) Thomas; m. James E. Sulton Jr., Aug. 1, 1981; children: James E. III, William Francis, Patrice Amandla. BA in Psychology, Wash. State U., 1973; MA in Criminal Justice, SUNY, 1975; PhD in Criminal Justice, U. Md., 1984; JD, U. Wis., 1985. Bar: Wis. 1985, U.S. Dist. Ct. (we. dist.) Wis. 1985. Instr. criminal justice and criminology Spelman Coll., Atlanta, 1976-78; rsch. assoc. Nat. Orgn. Black Law Enforcement Execs., Balt., 1978-80; lectr. criminal justice and criminology Howard U., Washington, 1980-84; asst. prof. criminal justice U. Wis., Oshkosh, 1984-85; project dir. Police Found., Washington, 1985-87; pvt. practice law Madison, Wis., 1985—; bd. dir. grad. criminal justice program U. Balt.; former instr. Atlanta U., Atlanta Fed. Penitentiary, Md. State Penitentiary, Balt. City Police Tng. Acad., Inst. Criminal Justice and Criminology, U. Md., Taycheeda Correctional Instn. for Women, Century 21 Sch. Real Estate; presenter, speaker, facilitator in field; numerous TV and radio appearances. Contbr. articles to various publs., poetry to books, mags. and newspapers. Bd. dirs. Washington Halfway Home for Women, 1983; pres. bd. dirs. Willard Thomas Scholarship Found., Inc., Racine, Wis., 1973—, South Madison Neighborhood Ctr., 1987-88; mem. allocations panel on un-and underemployment United Way Dane County, 1987-88; com. mem. Community Concerned Citizens; spokesperson Coalition African-Am. Orgns., Madison, 1987—; legal counsel NAACP Madison chpt. Recipient cert. Atlanta Commr. Pub. Safety, 1977, Outsdanding Citizen award Fulton County Commr.'s Office, 1977, cert. of appreciation Atlanta Crime Analysis Team, 1978; named to Washington Park High Sch. Hall of Fame, 1986; recipient Spl. Friend award Atlanta Fed. Penitentiray Bd., NAACP, 1978. Mem. ABA, Nat. African-Am. Braintrust on Criminal Justice and Criminology, Wis. Black Lawyers Assn. (sec. Madison chpt. 1987—), Nat. Inner-City Crime Prevention and Intervention Assn., Police Exec. Rsch. Forum, Madison Urban League. Office: PO Box 736 Middleton WI 53562

SUMERLIN, KATHERINE MARIE, retired librarian; b. Desdemona, Tex., Nov. 25, 1920; d. Julius Scott and Maude Ellen (Long) Strother; m. Claude Windell Summerlin, Sept. 2, 1947; 1 child, Neal Gordon. BS in Home Econs., Tex. Woman's U., 1942. Tchr. home econs. Mildred High Sch., Corsicana, Tex., 1942-43, Ozona (Tex.) High Sch., 1943; kindergarten tchr. East Hooks Elem. Sch., Hooks, Tex., 1944-46; lab. asst. Dow Chem. Co., Freeport, Tex., 1946-47; elem. tchr. Waco (Tex.) State Home, 1948-49; libr. asst. U. Mo., Columbia, 1962-63; periodicals librarian Ouachita Bapt. U., Arkadelphia, Ark., 1964-85. Vol. Community Store for Needy, Arkadelphia, 1987-88; librarian 1st Bapt. Ch. Media Ctr., Arkadelphia, 1960—. Mem. AAUW (sec. 1986-87), Arkadelphia Book Club. Democrat. Baptist.

SUMMER, DONNA (LA DONNA ADRIAN GAINES), singer, actress, songwriter; b. Boston, Dec. 31, 1948; d. Andrew and Mary Gaines; m. Helmut Sommer (div.); 1 child, Mimi; m. Bruce Sudano; children: Brooklyn, Amanda. has sold over 20 million records. Singer, 1967—; actress: (German stage prodn.) Hair, 1967-75, (Vienna Folk Opera prodns.) Porgy and Bess, (German prodns.) The Me Nobody Knows, (cable TV spl.) Donna Summer Special, 1980; recorded albums including The Wanderer, Star Collection, Love To Love You Baby, Love Trilogy, Four Seasons of Love, I Remember Yesterday, The Deep, Shut Out, Once Upon A Time, Bad Girls, On The Radio, Walk Away, She Works Hard For The Money, Cats Without Claws, All Systems Go, 1988, Another Place and Time, 1989; forerunner of disco style. Named Best Rhythm and Blues Female Vocalist, Nat. Acad. Rec. Arts and Scis., 1978, Best Female Rock Vocalist, 1979, Favorite Female Pop Vocalist, Am. Music Awards, 1979, Favorite Female Vocalist of Soul Music, 1979, Soul Artist of Yr., Rolling Stone mag., 1979; recipient Best Favorite Pop Single award, 1979, Best-selling Black Music Album for Female Artist award Nat. Assn. Record Merchandizers, 1979, Ampex Golden Reel award for album On the Radio, 1979, Best-selling Album for Female Artist, 1980, Ampex Golden Reel award for single On the Radio, 1980, Ampex Golden Reel award for album Bad Girls, Best of Las Vegas Jimmy award for best rock performance, 1980, Grammy award for best inspirational performance, 1984. Office: 1925 Century Pk E #920 Los Angeles CA 90067-2710*

SUMMER, LORAINE, psychologist; b. Easton, Pa., June 5, 1953; d. Harry and Ingrid (Weinberg) Son; m. Steven Jay Summer, Dec. 8, 1985. BA, Millersville (Pa.) State U., 1975; MA, Mich. State U., 1978, PhD, 1983. Lic. psychologist, Md. Psychologist Balt. Gas & Elec. Co., 1981—; adj. prof. U. Balt., 1989. Bd. dirs. Jewish Voc. Svc., Balt., 1989—, People Encouraging People, Balt., 1988-89. Mem. Am. Psychol. Assn., Soc. for Indsl./Orgnl. Psychology, Md. Psychol. Assn., Am. Compensation Assn., Personnel Testing Council of Met. Washington, Psi Chi. Office: Baltimore Gas & Electric Co 1 Center Plaza 4th Fl Baltimore MD 21203

SUMMERFIELD, JOANNE, business consultant; b. Brookline, Mass., June 30, 1940; d. Samuel J. and Edythe Bergel; m. Abraham Karlikow, 1988; children by previous marriage: Roberta, Sasha, Alexandra. Lyrics writer Buddah Records, N.Y.C., 1969-71; human resources dir. Fin. Acctg. Standards Bd., Stamford, Conn., 1973-76; v.p. mktg. U.S. Sports, Inc., Greenwich, Conn., 1976-79; communications cons. Today's World, N.Y.C., 1980—; pres. internat. costume jewelry mktg. Joanna K., Inc., Paris, France, 1990—; mktg. cons. Price Waterhouse Exec. Fin. Svcs., Can. govt.; presenter seminars on communications, selling, listening and ethics. Author: Legacy of Love, 1971; co-author: Corporate Lives, 1976, Listening-It Can Change Your Life, 1983, 2d edit. 1985 (also translated into Japanese, German), 101 Ways to Protect Your Job. Jewish. Home and Office: 315 W 57th St New York NY 10019 also: 62 Rue Spontini, Paris 75116, France

SUMMERFORD, SHERRY R., brokerage company executive; b. Hartselle, Ala., Jan. 21, 1948; d. James Benton and Lucy Ruby (Speakman) Roberts; m. Robert Copeland Summerford, Mar. 6, 1965 (dec. 1975); children: Cherie, Gina, Robin. Student, Calhoun Community Coll., Decatur, Ala., 1976-77. Collector Credit Bur. of Decatur (Ala.), 1976-78; collector, bookkeeper Wilson Equipment Co., Decatur, 1978; timekeeper Albert G. Smith Constrn. Co., Athens, Ala., 1978-79; bookkeeper, asst. mgr. Hogan's Ready Mix, Hartselle, Ala., 1979-82; rep. Dewline Trucking, Inc., Federalsburg, Md., 1982—; pres. Summerford & Summerford Enterprises Inc., Mgmt. Agy.-Environ., Decatur, 1987, SCL Warehouse Inc., Madison, Ala., 1988—. mgr. Sheriff Buford Burgess polit. campaign, Decatur, 1980. Mem. Credit Women of Ala. (pres. 1977-78), NAFE, Decatur C. of C., Nat. Fedn. Ind. Bus., Am. Legion Ladies Aux., North Ala. Traffic Club (v.p. 1988—), Tenn. Valley Traffic Club (pres. 1990—), Southeastern Transp. Forum (chairperson 1990—, vice chairperson 1989-90), Ala. Minority Supplier Devel. Coun., Inc., Jetplex Kiwanis. Republican. Methodist. Office: SCL Warehouse Inc 9310 Hwy 20 W Ste 9-19 Madison AL 35758

SUMMERLIN, KRISTIN LEE, editor, writer; b. Greenville, Mich., July 29, 1961; d. George Thomas Summerlin and Judy Ann (Dolamore) Stovall. BA in English Lit., U. of the South, Sewanee, Tenn., 1982. Reporter The Tullahoma (Tenn.) News, 1982-84; asst. editor World Wastes, Atlanta, 1984, Adhesives Age, Atlanta, 1984; assoc. editor Nat. Real Estate Investor, Atlanta, 1984-85; publs. coord., mng. editor Ga. ALERT Ga. Dept. Edn., Atlanta, 1985—. Contbr. articles to mags. Vol., editor Creative Options Inc., Atlanta, 1986—, Georgians for Children, 1990—. Nat. Merit scholarship U. of the South, 1979-82, named Order of Gownsmen; recipient Sch. Bell award Tenn. Edn. Assn., 1983. Mem. Ednl. Press Assn. Am., Ga. Sch. Pub. Rels. Assn. Democrat. Episcopalian. Home: 1055 Piedmont Ave C-3 Atlanta GA 30309 Office: Ga Dept Edn 2052 Twin Towers E Atlanta GA 30334-5010

SUMMERS, ANNE FAIRHURST, editor; b. Deniliquin, NSW, Australia, Mar. 12, 1945; came to U.S., 1986; d. Austin Henry Fairhurst and Eileen Frances (Hogan) Cooper; m. John Summers, Apr. 28, 1967. BA with honors, U. Adelaide, Australia, 1970; PhD, U. Sydney, Australia, 1979. Sr. writer Nat. Times, Sydney, 1975-78; fellow World Press Inst., St. Paul, 1978, now bd. dirs.; bur. chief Australian Fin. Review, Canberra, 1979-83; head Office of Status of Women Dept. of Prime Minister, Canberra, 1983-86; North Am. mgr. John Fairfax (U.S.) Ltd., N.Y.C., 1986-87; editor-in-chief Ms. Mag., N.Y.C., 1987-89, editor-at-large, 1990—; corr. Far Ea. Econ. Rev., Canberra, 1980-83, Le Monde, Canberra, 1983; bd. dirs. Matilda Publs., Inc., N.Y.C., 1988-89; mem. adv. bd. World Press Inst., 1989—. Author: Damned Whores and God's Police, 1975, Gamble for Power, 1983; co-author: Her Story: First Women in Print, 1979. Named to Order of Australia, Queen Elizabeth II, 1989; Young Writer's fellow Lit. Bd. Australia, 1974. Mem. Am. Soc. Mag. Editors. Home: 253 W 73d St New York NY 10023 Office: Ms Mag One Times Sq New York NY 10036

SUMMERS, BESSIE EVA, small business owner; b. Terry, Miss., May 21, 1937; d. Norwood and Maggie (Terrell) Thompson; children: Susie, Jonathan, Bruce, Mark. Student, Utica Jr. Coll., 1956, DePaul U., 1974-76. Claims clk. Social Security Adminstrn., Chgo., 1965-72; security supr. VA, Chgo., 1972-75; sr. officer Fed. Bur. Prisons, Chgo., 1975-77; owner Summers & Thompson Mail Svc., Chgo., 1977—. Mem. Urban League, Chgo. Named for Small Bus. of Yr., 2nd. Congl. Dist., Chgo., 1984. Mem. NAFE.

Office: Summers & Thompson Mailing Svc 2139 E 75th St Chicago IL 60649

SUMMERS, DENISE OTTINGER, university administrator; b. Crawfordsville, Ind., Sept. 4, 1951; d. Garold Richard and G. Josephine (Ocheltree) Ottinger; m. Neil Allen Wilson, June ll, 1971 (div. Dec. 1980); m. Ronald Lee Summers, Oct. 16, 1982; children: Jennifer L. and Holly M. (twins). BA, Purdue U., 1976, MS, 1980. Grad. asst. div. fin. aids Purdue U., West Lafayette, Ind., 1977, fin. aid asst., 1977-79, asst. dir. div. fin. aids, 1979-85, asst. to dean Sch. Vet. Medicine, 1985—; mem. supervisory com. Purdue Employees Fed. Credit Union, 1984-87, chmn. supervisory com., 1987-89; mem. Consumer Mail Panel, Chgo., 1980—. Mem. Nat. Acad. Adv. Assn., Ind. Assn. Coll. Admissions Counselors, Purdue Acad. Adv. Assn., Phi Kappa Phi. Office: Purdue U Sch Vet Medicine Lynn Hall West Lafayette IN 47907

SUMMERS, ELLEN SIDELLE, writer; b. N.Y.C., Oct. 21, 1932; d. Isidor Steckler and Anna Heuman; m. Zachary G. Summers, Dec. 21, 1958; children: Jayne, Valerie. BA, Bklyn. Coll., N.Y.C., 1954; MS, Hunter Coll., 1958. Tchr. Secondary English (permanent sec). Asst. prodn. mgr. Acad. Press, N.Y.C., 1954-55; tchr. Bd. Edn., N.Y.C., 1955-75, Great Neck Sch. Dist., Great Neck, N.Y., 1979-81; adj. instr. L.I. U., Brookville, N.Y.; rsch. assoc. Hunter Coll., N.Y., 1988-91. Contbr. short stories and poems to lit. jours. Bd. dir. Thomaston Civic Assoc., Great Neck, N.Y., 1974-75; campaign worker Dem. Party, Great Neck, 1976-82. Winner 24th Ann. Poetry Contest C.W. Post, L.I. U. Mem. NEA, Communication Workers, Kappa Delta Phi. Democrat. Office: LI U CW Post Campus Brookville NY 11548

SUMMERS, FRANCES PHAYE, vocational rehabilitation consultant; b. Klamath Falls, Oreg., Apr. 15, 1938; d. Phayo Grindol and Frances Ruth (Henry) Pfefferle; m. C. Oakley Summers Jr., Apr. 25, 1953 (div. Sept. 1969); children—Katherine , Anne, Donald O., Wayne P. Grad. in Social Work, Salvation Army Officers Tng. Coll., 1957; BS, U. Oreg., 1983, MS, 1985. Cert. rehab. counselor, Oreg. Exec. dir. Salvation Army, Oreg., Ariz. and Calif., 1957-69, exec. sec. Employment Div., Flagstaff, Ariz., 1970-75, placement specialist , Medford, Oreg., 1975-78; area supr. Workers Compensation Dept., Oreg., 1978-80; vocat. rehab. cons., Siskiyou, Cascade Rehab., Eugene, Oreg., 1980-85; regional mgr. Cooley/Assocs., Eugene, 1985-86; owner, exec. officer Oreg. Vocat. Solutions, Eugene, 1986—; conf. com. chmn. Oreg. Assn. Rehab. Profls., Eugene, 1982, edn. com. chmn. 1988. Bd. dirs. U. Oreg. Parents Assn., 1981-88, pres., 1986-88. Mem. Eugene C. of C., Nat. Rehab. Assn., Oreg. Assn. Rehab. Profls. in Pvt. Sector, Alpha Lambda Delta, Phi Eta Sigma. Contbr. articles to profl. jours. Avocations: swimming, hiking, antiques, boating, classical music.

SUMMERS, JANIE L., elementary school principal; b. Spartanburg County, S.C., July 22; d. Earl Dean and Bertha L. Willie (Miller) Irby; m. Johnnie W. Summers, Jr., July 3, 1958; childen: Amile Lemoin, Amy Renee. AB, Benedict Coll., 1954; MEd, S.C. State Coll., 1969; postgrad., U. Chgo., U. S.C., U. Nebr., Appalachian State U. Cert. elem. tchr., elem. guidance counselor, elem. prin. Adult edn. tchr., tchr. in migrant program, counselor Spartanburg Dist. One Schs., Campobello, S.C., prin. Mem. steering com. S.C. Sch. Improvement Council; bd. dirs. Spartanburg Educator's Fed. Credit Union; deaconess Mt. Pleasant Bapt. Ch. Named Tchr. of Yr., Optimist Club, 1989. Mem. NEA, S.C. Edn. Assn., S.C. PTA (life hon.), Internat. Reading Assn., S.C. Assn. Elem. and Middle Sch. Prins., Assn. for Supervision and Curriculum Devel., Nat. Assn. of Sec. Prin.'s (assessor), Kappa Delta Pi (chair incentive com.). Home: PO Box 513 100 Summers St Inman SC 29349 Office: O P Earle Elem Sch 100 Redland Rd Landrum SC 29356

SUMMERS, LORRAINE DEY SCHAEFFER, librarian, association official; b. Phila., Dec. 14, 1946; d. Joseph William and Hilda Lorraine (Ritchey) Dey; m. F. William Summers, Jan. 28, 1984. B.A., Fla. State U., 1968, M.S., 1969. Extension dir. Santa Fe Regional Library, Gainesville, 1969-71; pub. library cons. State Library of Fla., Tallahassee, 1971-78, asst. state librarian, 1978-84; dir. adminstrv. services Nat. Assn. for Campus Activities, Columbia, S.C., 1984-85; asst. state librarian State Library of Fla., Tallahassee, 1985—; cons. in field. Contbr. articles to profl. jours. Del. Pres.'s Com. on Mental Retardation Regional Forum, Atlanta. 1975; del. Fla. Gov.'s Conf. on Library and Info. Services, 1978, 90. Mem. ALA (orgn. com. 1979-83, council 1982-84, resolutions com. 1983-85), Assn. Specialized and Coop. Library Agys. (dir. 1976-82, chmn. planning and orgn. com. 1976-80, chmn. nominating com., 1980-81, chmn. by laws com. 1985-86, exec. bd. state library agy sect. 1983-86, pres. 1987-88), Southeastern Library Assn. (exec. bd. 1976-80), Fla. Library Assn. (sec. 1978-79, dir., 1976-80), Am. Soc. Pub. Adminstrn., Zonta. Democrat. Methodist. Office: State Library Fla RA Gray Bldg Tallahassee FL 32399

SUMMERSELL, FRANCES SHARPLEY, organization worker; b. Birmingham, Ala.; d. Arthur Croft and Thomas O. (Stone) Sharpley; student U. Montevallo, Peabody Coll., Nashville; m. Charles Grayson Summersell, Nov. 10, 1934. Ptnr., artist, writer Assoc. Educators, 1959—. Mem. D.A.R., Magna Charta Dames, U. Women's Club (pres. 1957-58), U.D.C. (state historian 1956-58, pres. Robert Emmet Rodes chpt. Tuscaloosa 1953-55), Daus. Am. Colonists (organizing regent Tuscaloosa 1956-63), English Speaking Union, Marquis Biog. Library Soc. (adv. mem.). Vice-chmn. Ft. Morgan Hist. Commn., 1959-63. Mem. Tuscaloosa County Preservation Soc. (trustee 1965-78, service award 1975), W. Ala. Art Assn., Nat. Trust Historic Preservation, Birmingham-Jefferson Hist. Soc. Clubs: Country, University (Tuscaloosa). Co-author: Alabama History Filmstrips, 1961; Viewing Alabama History Filmstrips, 1961; Florida History Filmstrips, 1963; Texas History Filmstrips, 1965-66; Ohio History Filmstrips, 1967 (Merit award Am. Assn. State and Local History 1968); California History Filmstrips, 1968; Illinois History Filmstrips, 1970. Home: 1411 Caplewood Tuscaloosa AL 35401

SUMMERVILLE, JESSICA DIANA, small business owner; b. June 19, 1950. BA, Clarion U., 1972; postgrad., U. London, 1972; MS, Clarion U., 1974; EdD, Columbia U., 1977. Asst. prof. U. Miss., Oxford, 1977-79; acct. exec. Data Communications Corp., Memphis, 1980-83; acct. mgr. Digital Equipment Corp., N.Y.C., 1983-90; small bus. owner N.Y.C., 1990—. Finance council Dem. Nat. Com., Washington, 1988. Mem. Emily's List, League Women Voters, ACT-PAC, Columbia Club.

SUN, LINDA CHRISTINE, commercial real estate broker; b. Shanghai, Peoples Republic of China, Mar. 9, 1943; came to U.S., 1961, naturalized, 1972; d. Richard T.L. and Sophie (Hsu) S.; m. Richard Jack Bishirjian, June 24, 1967 (div. 1984); children: Philip Edmund, Maria Stephanie. Student, Vienna (Austria) Acad. Music, 1961; BA in Biology, Coll. of St. Teresa, Winona, Minn., 1965; MBA in Mktg. Mgmt., Pace U., 1983; postgrad., D.C. Sch. Law, Washington, 1989—. Lic. real estate agent, Va., Md. Technician Microbiol. Assocs., Bethesda, Md., 1966-67; accompanist Westchester Conservatory of Music, White Plains, N.Y., 1974-75; research technician Sloan-Kettering Inst., Rye, N.Y., 1976-79; agt. Prudential Ins. Co., Fairfax, Va., 1984-85; ins. broker Prudential Ins. Co., Greenbelt, Md., 1986—; agt. The Equitable, Washington, 1986; mktg. mgr. Gen. Devel. Corp., Falls Church, Va., 1986—; agt. Am. Income Life, Arlington, Va., 1986—; real estate agt. Shannon and Luchs, Washington, 1987-89; negotiator Joint-venture between China and The ADCO Group, N.Y.C., 1989—; admitted to Vienna Acad. of Music, Vienna, 1961; panelist First Va. Asian Am. Bus. Conf., 1987. Fundraiser Orgn. of Chinese Americans, Washington, 1983-88; coord. Pace U. Alumni Reunion, Washington, 1987. Recipient scholarships Viterbo Coll., Coll. St. Teresa, Rosary Coll., fellowship George Washington U., Gold medal Nat. Assn. Piano Tchrs.; Solomon scholar D.C. Sch. Law, 1989-90. Mem. Bar Assn. D.C., Pace U. Alumni Assn. (reunion coordinator Washington chpt., 1987), Coll. St. Teresa Alumnae Assn. Republican. Roman Catholic. Home: 1301 Massachusetts Ave NW Apt 312 Washington DC 20005 Office: The ADCO Group 645 Fifth Ave New York NY 10022

SUNDERMAN, DEBORAH ANN, clothing designer and manufacturer; b. Detroit, Feb. 21, 1955; d. Eugene Wayne Sunderman and Nancy May (Reams) Sunderman-Elert. BS magna cum laude, No. Mich. U., 1978. Design instr. Newbury Coll., Boston, 1978-82; asst. to designers Clothware, Boston, 1978-82; designer, ptnr. Toute Nue Swimwear, Boston, 1982; designer Mast Industries, The Limited, Woburn, Mass., 1982-83; designer, founder Deborah Mann & Co., Boston, 1983-87, designer, owner, 1987—. Designer garment The Fiberarts Design Book, 1980. Organizer Neighborhood Crime Watch Group, Rossmore Rd., Boston, 1989—. Recipient 2d Pl. award Peter White Art Exhibit, Marquette, Mich., 1978, Fresh Start award Self Mag., Washington, 1985; named one of Boston's Most Interesting Women, Boston Woman Mag., 1990. Mem. Fort Pointe Arts Community, Boston Visual Artists Union, Nat. Assn. for the Self Employed. Office: Deborah Mann & Co 326 A St Ste 2C Boston MA 02210

SUNDERMAN, MARTHA-LEE, medical education administrator, editor; b. Norristown, Pa., July 5, 1934; d. William and Anna B. (Zeyn) Taggart; m. James Biscoe, Mar. 2, 1957 (div. 1971); children: Jennifer Lee Burke, Heather McLean; m. F. William Sunderman, May 3, 1980. AB, Beaver Coll., 1955; postgrad., Villanova U., 1967-71. Jr. engr. Philco Corp., Lansdale, Pa., 1955-57; med. research librarian Merck, Sharp, and Dohme, West Point, Pa., 1957-61; asst. to med. advisor Rohm and Haas Co., Phila., 1963; dir. alumnae affairs Beaver Coll., Glenside, Pa., 1964-67; dir. devel. Friends' Cen. Sch., Phila., 1967-71; asst. to dir. Inst. for Clin. Sci., Hahnemann U. Med. Sch., Phila., 1971-88; asst. dir. Inst. for Clin. Sci. Pa. Hosp., Phila., 1988—; asst. sec. bd. dirs. Inst. for Clinical Sci. Inc., Phila., 1985—. Editorial assoc. Annals of Clinical and Lab. Sci. jour., 1971—. Mem. instl. devel. bd. Beaver Coll., 1989—. Mem. Beaver Coll. Alumni Assn. (bd. dirs. 1986-90). Republican. Lutheran. Home: 1833 Delancey Pl Philadelphia PA 19103 Office: Inst for Clin Sci Duncan Bldg 3A 301 S Eighth St Philadelphia PA 19106

SUNERGREN, MARY ANNE, mental health nurse clinical specialist; b. Boston, Feb. 26, 1942; d. Ralph A. and Mildred Victoria Sunergren. BSN, Boston U., 1965, MSN, 1969. Child and family psychiatry Mass. Mental Health Ctr., Boston, 1965-67; with community mental health and pvt. consultation Corrigan Mental Health Ctr., Fall River, Mass., 1970-72; treatment team leader Human Resource Inst., Brookline, Mass., 1972-78; community mental health, pvt. cons., supr. acute admissions Glenside Hosp., Boston, 1978-83; pvt. practice William A. Rohde MD & Assocs., Dorchester, 1986—; clin. specialist Dorchester (Mass.) Mental Health Ctr., 1981—. Mem. Am. Nurses Assn. (cert. clin. specialist), Mass. Nurses Assn. Episcopalian. Home: Hingham MA 02043 Office: Dorchester Mental Health Ctr 591 Morton St Dorchester MA 02124

SUNIER, KATHERINE JOHNSON, nurse; b. Chgo., Mar. 16, 1952; d. Frank Richard and Mary Elizabeth (Pierce) J.; m. Richard Joseph Sunier, Oct. 15, 1983; children: Jessica Michelle, Leisa Amelia. B.S. in Nursing, Iowa Wesleyan Coll., 1975; postgrad. Rush U. Staff nurse Rush-Presbyn.-St. Luke's Hosp., Chgo., 1975-78, head nurse cardiovascular thoracic surgeries, 1979-82; staff nurse operating room Lake Forest Hosp., Ill., 1982—. Mem. Assn. Operating Room Nurses, Am. Endurance Ride Conf., Riding for the Handicapped Orgn., Upper Midwest Endurance and Competitive Riding Assn. Avocations: horseback riding, running, aerobics, handcrafts, computers. Home: 6618 88th Ave Kenosha WI 53140

SUNLIGHT, CAROLE, psychologist; b. DuBois, Pa., Aug. 19; d. Andy and Mary Ann Gaborick; Med. Tech., Carnegie Coll., 1959; BA in Psychology, Cleve. State U., 1971; MA in Psychology (Univ. scholar), Pepperdine U., 1973; PhD in Psychology, U.S. Internat. U., 1980. Med. technologist Doctors Piercy, Fertig, Schneider and Doran, Cleve., 1959-67; chief technologist med. dept. U.S. Steel Corp., Lorain, Ohio, 1967-69; office mgr. dept. philosophy and religious studies Cleve. State U., 1969-70; counselor Gardena Valley Counseling Svc., Gardena, Calif., 1971-72; clin. intern Pepperdine U. psychology clinic, 1972-73; testing technician Norco-Corona (Calif.) Sch. Dist., 1973; dir. treatment svcs. Unfinished Symphony Ranch, Inc., Agoura, Calif., 1973-77; pvt. practice, Westlake Village, Calif., 1977-78; staff Kaiser Permanente Mental Health Ctr., 1977-88; staff psychiatry dept. Kaiser Permanente, 1988—; pvt. practice, Torrance, Calif., 1980—; speaker in field. Bd. dirs. COMOSI Mental Health, Thousand Oaks, Calif., 1977-78. Registered med. technologist. Mem. Am. (sects on psychology of women, clin. neuropsychology, Calif. Psychol. Assn., Los Angeles County (newsletter editor 1982-84) Psychol. Assn., Am. Med. Technologists (Ohio State Soc. Publ. award 1972), Calif. Neuropsychol. Soc., Psychologists for Social Responsibility, Psi Chi. Office: 9449 Imperial Hwy Downey CA 90242 also: 19000 Hawthorne Blvd Ste 300 Torrance CA 90503

SUPINSKI, DAWN JACQUELINE, financial analyst, portfolio manager; b. N.Y.C., Jan. 9, 1961. BA summa cum laude, CUNY, 1982; MBA with distinction, NYU, 1984. Chartered fin. analyst. V.p., portfolio mgr., security analyst Bankers Trust Co., N.Y.C., 1984-89; pres. Supinski Assocs., N.Y.C., 1989—. Valedictorian CUNY, 1982. Mem. Fin. Analysts Fedn., Inst. Chartered Fin. Analysts, N.Y. Soc. Security Analysts (investment strategy/portfolio mgmt. com.), N.Y. Healthcare Analysts' Splinter Group, Nat. Investor Rels. Inst., Beta Gamma Sigma. Office: Supinski Assocs 444 E 82d St New York NY 10028

SUPPLE, DIANE MARIE, computer information scientist; b. Pasadena, Calif., Oct. 20, 1956; d. John Robert and Shirley Ann (Remy) S. AA, Pasadena City Coll., 1977; BS, Calif. Poly. State U. San Luis Obispo, 1980; MBA, Loyola Marymount, Westchester, Calif., 1984. Systems rep. Info. Internat., Inc., Culver City, Calif., 1980-83; jr. programmer analyst Xerox, El Segundo, Calif., 1983-86; sr. programmer analyst %, El Segundo, Calif., 1986-89; software computer tester Xerox, El Segundo, Calif., 1989—. Author: Online Computers Hyphenation and Justification, 1980. Republican. Roman Catholic. Home: 4902 W 97th St Inglewood CA 90301

SUPRIANO, SUSAN JEAN, radio producer; b. Evanston, Ill., July 31, 1938; d. Edwin H. Eichler and Carol Jean (McGraw) Root; m. Harold Supriano, Sept. 10, 1966 (div.); 1 child, Gregory. BA, U. Chgo., 1963; MSW, U. Calif., Berkeley, 1976; MPH, U. Hawaii, 1971. With CORE, Berkeley, 1963-64; civic worker, 1965-69; organizer in women's movement Honolulu, 1969-70; therapist, 1976-78; radio producer Pacifica Radio, Berkeley, 1980—, Radio for Peace Internat., San José, Costa Rica, 1987—; internat. adv. bd. Radio for Peace Internat., San José, Eugene, Oreg.; instr. communications World Peace U., Eugene; coord. San Francisco area antiwar groups; mem. staff Calif. Com. for New Politics; mem. Western Addition Com. Agianst the War in Vietnam, San Francisco. Producer documentaries. Mem. Rigpa Fellowship. Buddhist. Home: 2804 Piedmont Berkeley CA 94705 Office: Radio for Peace Internat PO Box 10869 Eugene OR 97440

SURFUS, SANDRA SUE, nurse; b. Knoxville, Tenn., Feb. 2, 1941; d. John Adolph and Ella Jane (McKittrick) Schaller; children: Kim Elizabeth, John Scott, Sara Lynn. BS in Nursing, U. Wis., 1963; MS in Nursing, Calif. State U., Los Angeles, 1980. RN, Calif., Wis. Staff nurse U. Hosps./Madison (Wis.) Gen. Hosp., 1963-74; staff nurse Huntington Meml. Hosp., Pasadena, Calif., 1974-80, cardiac rehab. nurse, 1976-80; mgr. cardiac rehab. and fitness ctr. St. Joseph Med. Ctr., Burbank, Calif., 1980—. Mem. Calif. Soc. Cardiac Rehab. (pres. 1984-86), Am. Assn. Cardiovascular Pulmonary Rehab. (founding fellow 1986). Office: St Joseph Med Ctr Cardiac Rehab Buena Vista and Alameda Sts Burbank CA 91505

SURGI, ELIZABETH BENSON, veterinarian; b. New Orleans, June 11, 1955; d. Andrew Ernest Jr. and Mary Elizabeth (Steinlage) Benson; m. Marion Rene Surgi, May 22, 1981; 1 child, Renee Elizabeth. BS in Med. TEch., U. New Orleans, 1977; DVM, La. State U., 1984. Assoc. veterinarian West Park Vet. Svcs., Houma, La., 1984, Animal Emergency Svc., Schaumburg, Ill., 1984-85; staff veterinarian Anti-Cruelty Soc., Chgo., 1985-86; assoc. veterinarian Terry Animal Hosp., Wilmette, Ill., 1986-89; owner, dir. Sauganash Animal Hosp., Chgo., 1989—. Bd. dirs., Cen. Evanston Child Care, Inc., 1988—, Edgebrook-Sauganash unit Am. Cancer Soc., 1990—. Mem. Am. Vet. Med. Assn., Am. Vet. Dental Soc., Ill. Acad. Vet. Medicine (v.p.), Assn. Avian Veterinarians, Ill. State Vet. Med. Assn., Chgo. Vet. Med. Assn. Republican. Episcopalian. Office: Sauganash Animal Hosp 4054 W Peterson Ave Chicago IL 60646

SURPRISE, JUANEE, chiropractor, nutrition consultant; b. Gary, Ind., Apr. 28, 1944; d. Glenn Mark and Willia Ross (Vasser) Surprise; m. Peter E. Coakley, Feb. 12, 1966 (div. Jan. 1976); children: Thaddeus, Mariah, Darius; m. Robert T.Howell, Feb. 24, 1984. RN, Phila. Gen. Hosp. Sch. Nursing, 1965; DrChiropractic summa cum laude, Life Chiropractic Coll. Marietta, Ga., 1981. Diplomate Nat. Bd. Chiropractic Examiners; cert. in acupuncture, Thompson technique, Nimmo receptor tonus technique. Staff nurse Children's Hosp., Balt., 1966-67; charge nurse Melrose (Mass.)-Wakefield Hosp., 1967-68; hosp. adminstr. Animal Hosp. of Wakefield, Mass., 1967-79; chiropractor Chiropractic Clinic of Greenville, N.C., 1982-84, Howell Chiropractic Clinic, Denton, Tex., 1984—; field coordinator Parker Coll. Chiropractic, Dallas, 1989—. Mem., chmn. Community Planning Commn., North Reading, Mass., 1976-79; chmn. bldg. com. Immaculate Conception Ch., Denton, 1987—, pres.-elect parish council, 1990—. Mem. Am. Chiropractic Assn., Bus. and Profl. Women's Assn., Tex. Chiropractic Assn., Pi Tau Delta. Republican. Roman Catholic. Office: Howell Chiropractic Clinic 1129 Ave C Denton TX 76201

SUSENS, MILLICENT MILANOVICH, writer, educator; b. Pitts.; d. Robert and Amelia (Merich) Milanovich; m. George Phelps Susens, Sept. 9, 1972; 1 stepchild, Karin. BS, Pa. State U., State College, 1965; MA in Creative Writing, San Francisco State U., 1985. Cert. elem. tchr., Mass. Asst. to the marshal Harvard U., Cambridge, Mass., 1966-67; conf. adminstr. Harvard Econ. Rsch. Project, Cambridge, 1967-68; tchr. English Attleboro (Mass.) High Sch., 1968-71; freelance writer San Francisco, 1986—; mem. publs. com. San Francisco Medicine, 1986—. Author: (three-act play) Poems for Last Acts, 1981 (Lawrence & Lee Playwriting award 1982); contbr. articles to profl. jours. Bd. dirs. San Francisco Med. Soc. Aux., 1982—, publ. com., 1986; bd. dirs. Enterprise for High Sch. Students, 1982-88, pres. bd. dirs. 1985-87; mem. Civil Grand Jury, San Francisco, 1988-89. Mem. Francisca Club. Eastern Orthodox. Home: 2134 Green St San Francisco CA 94123

SUSIE, SHARON KAY, sales representative; b. Sac City, Iowa, Apr. 4, 1951; d. Reed Elliott and Hattie Kathren (Cassens) S. Student, Wayne (Nebr.) State Coll., 1969-70. With Norkett Properties-John Maxson, Tulsa, 1981-82, John Maxson, Fairland, Okla., 1982, Gillean & Co., Tulsa, 1982, Don Lutz Constrn., Tulsa, 1982-83; lead person Bright Constrn., Tulsa, 1983-84; dist. mgr. Franklin Life Ins. Co., Tulsa, 1984-87; sales rep. United Ins. Co. of Am., Tulsa, 1987-88, Mut. of Omaha, Tucson, 1988—. Democrat. Office: Mut of Omaha 5151 E Broadway Ste 1250 Tucson AZ 85711

SUSMAN, KAREN LEE, lawyer; b. Austin, Tex., Oct. 26, 1942; d. Paul and Dorothy (Goudchaux) Hyman; m. Stephen D. Susman, Dec. 26, 1965; children: Stacy M., Harry P. BA, U. Tex., 1964; JD, U. Houston, 1981. Bar: Tex. 1981; bd. cert. in family law 1987. Tchr. high schs. Houston and Washington, 1964-68; realty broker Susman Realty, Houston, 1968-78; assoc. Saccomanno, Clegg, Martin & Kipple, Houston, 1981-83, Marian S. Rosen & Assocs., Houston, 1983-86; of counsel Webb & Zimmerman, Houston, 1986—. Editor Internat. Law Jour., 1980-81. Bd. dirs. Downtown YWCA, Houston, 1969-74, pres. 1974; bd dirs. Tex. Arts Alliance, Houston, 1975-78, Antidefamation League B'nai Brith, Houston, 1983-86, Lawyers and Accts. for Arts, Houston, 1985—; chmn. PBS TV Art Auction, Houston, 1975; mem. Tex. State Dem. Fin. Coun., 1983—, Harris County Dem. Chmn.'s Coun., 1984—, Candidate Selection Com., 1986—; bd. dirs. Houston Symphony, 1985—, Houston Grand Opera, 1988, Womens Advocacy Project, 1987—. Fellow Houston Bar Found.; mem. ABA (litigation sect. com. on individual and personal rights), Tex. Bar Assn., Houston Bar Assn., Gulf Coast Family Law Specialists, A.A. White Soc., U. Houston Alumni (bd. dirs., v.p., sec. 1983—), Houston Club, Phi Delta Phi. Home: 10 Shadder Way Houston TX 77019 Office: Post Oak Ctr 14th Fl 1990 S Post Oak Blvd Houston TX 77056-3814

SUSMAN, VIRGINIA LEHMANN, psychiatrist, educator; b. Bronxville, N.Y., Nov. 30, 1949; d. Arthur Edwin and Jeanne Anne (Uebelacker) Lehmann; m. William Mark Susman, June 24, 1973; children: Julianne Marie, Margaret Amanda. B.A., Fordham U., 1971; M.D., U. Rochester, 1975. Diplomate Am. Bd. Psychiatry and Neurology. Resident Bronx (N.Y.) Mcpl. Hosp. Ctr., 1975-78, asst. dir. psychiat. outpatient dept., 1978-79, assoc. dir. psychiat. outpatient dept., 1979-80, unit chief inpatient dept., 1980-81; unit chief Westchester div. N.Y. Hosp., White Plains, 1981—, acting. dir. med. student edn., 1984-87, dir. 1987; asst. prof. psychiatry Albert Einstein Coll. Medicine, Bronx, 1979-81, Cornell U. Med. Coll., White Plains, 1981-87, assoc. prof. 1987—; practice medicine specializing in psychiatry, White Plains, 1978—. Contbr. articles to profl. jours. Research grantee Cornell U. Med. Coll., 1982-85; Picker Found. grantee, 1986—. Mem. Am. Psychiat. Assn., Am. Med. Womens Assn., Physicians for Social Responsibility (acting chmn. Westchester County br. 1982), Assn. Women Psychiatrists. Office: NY Hosp Westchester Div 21 Bloomingdale Rd White Plains NY 10605

SUSOR, DOROTHY MARIE ALMA LEFFEL, volunteer; b. Wausau, Wis., Oct. 26, 1922; d. Richard and Nettie (Pophal) Leffel; m. Burt F. Susor, June 18, 1949; children: Patricia Ann, Barbara, Gary, Sandra. Grad. high sch., Wausau. Pvt. practice nurse's aide Wausau, 1936-42, 42-43, various positions, 1943-44; clk. Wausau Ins., 1944-53; co-owner B&D Sewing Ctr., Marshfield, Wis., 1981-89; ret., 1989. Vol. Faith Luth. Ch.. Mem. Smithsonian Inst. (exec.). Home: 802 W Blodgett St Marshfield WI 54449

SUSSAN, NANCY FREDERICK, writer, editor; b. Bklyn., Aug. 25, 1949; d. Selig Lester and Eleanor (Padgett) Frederick; m. David L. Sussan, Aug. 22, 1970 (div. 1980); 1 child, Alexandra Tracy. BA in English, Douglass Coll., 1971. Editor Astro Signs, Rye, N.Y., 1985—. Author: Love and Sex Under the Stars, 1989, Palmistry: All Lines Lead to Love, 1988, Tarot: Love is in the Cards, 1988, Love Games: Psychic Paths to Love, 1988, The Lover's Dream, 1988. Mem. Am. Fedn. Astrologers. Spiritualist.

SUSSER, CYNTHIA ROSE, town clerk, office manager; b. Boulder, Colo., Nov. 24, 1956; d. John Orville and Wilma Rose (Micklich) Mendenhall; m. David Susser, Apr. 5, 1976; children: Lisa Suzanne, David Adam, Clinton James. Comp. acct., pres. sec. Otterstein & Co., Inc., Pueblo, Colo., 1976-81; exec. v.p., sec. bd. dirs. main funding Otterstein & Co., Inc., Pueblo, 1986; town clk., office mgr. Town of Wellington, Wellington, Colo., 1987—. Bd. dirs., exec. sec. Pueblo (Colo.) Beautiful Assn., Inc., 1976-79; mem. Clean Community Commn., Pueblo, 1976-79, Colo. Resource and Recovery Commn., Pueblo, 1976. Mem. Colo. Mcpl. Clks. Assn., Internat. Mcpl. Clks. Assn. Office: Town of Wellington 3735 Cleveland Ave PO Box 127 Wellington CO 80549

SUSSMAN, DEBORAH EVELYN, design company executive; b. N.Y.C., May 26, 1931; d. Irving and Ruth (Golomb) S.; m. Paul Prejza, June 28, 1972. Student Bard Coll., 1948-50, Inst. Design, Chgo., 1950-53, Black Mountain Coll., 1950, Hochschule fur Gestaltung Ulm (Fulbright grantee), W.Ger., 1957-58. Art dir. Office of Charles and Ray Eames, Venice, Calif., 1953-57, 61-67; graphic designer Galeries Lafayette, Paris, 1959-60; prin. Deborah Sussman and Co., Santa Monica, Calif., 1968—; founder, pres. Sussman-Prejza and Co., Inc., Santa Monica, 1980-89, Culver City, Calif., 1990—; speaker, lectr. UCLA Sch. Architecture, Archtl. League N.Y.C., Smithsonian Inst., Stanford Conf. on Design, Am. Inst. Graphic Arts Nat. Conf. at MIT, Design Mgmt. Inst. Conf., Mass.; spl. guest Internat. Design Conf., Aspen, Colo., Fulbright lectr., India, 1976; speaker NEA Adv. Council, 1985, Internat. Council Shopping Ctrs., 1986, USIA Design in America seminar, Budapest, Hungary, 1988, participant exhbn., Moscow, 1989, Walker Art Ctr., Mpls., 1989. Mem. editorial adv. bd. Arts and Architecture Mag., 1981-85, Calif. Mag., Architecture Calif. Recipient numerous awards AIA Nat. Inst. Honors, 1985, 88, Am. Inst. Graphic Arts, Calif. Council AIA, Communications Arts Soc., Los Angeles County Bd. Suprs., Vesta award Women's Bldg. Los Angeles. Mem. AIA (hon.), Am. Inst. Graphic Arts (bd. dirs. 1982-85, founder Los Angeles chpt., chmn., 1983-84, numerous awards), Los Angeles Art Dirs. Club (bd. dirs., numerous awards), Alliance Graphique Internat., Architects, Designers and Planners Social Responsibility, SEGD. Democrat. Jewish. Avocation: photography. Office: Sussman/Prejza & Co Inc 3960 Ince Blvd Culver City CA 90232

SUSSMAN, GERTRUDE, buying service executive; b. N.Y.C., Dec. 8, 1933; d. Joseph Harry and Florence (Morowitz) Wechter; m. Paul Jerry Sussman. Student, Hunter Coll., 1955-59. Market rep. Independent Retail Syndicate, N.Y.C., 1963-67, Allied Stores Mktg. Corp., N.Y.C., 1967-78; porduct mgr. Associated Merchandising Corp., N.Y.C., 1978—.

SUSSMAN, RAQUEL ROTMAN, molecular biologist; b. Buenos Aires, Argentina, Oct. 22, 1921; came to U.S., 1948; d. Benjamin and Nina (Arensburg) Rotman; m. Maurice Sussman, Aug. 15, 1948; children: Paul, Michael, Daniel. BS, U. Chile, 1944; PhD, U. Ill., 1952. Rsch. assoc. Northwestern U., Evanston, Ill., 1950-58, Brandeis U., Waltham, Mass., 1958-73; sr. lectr. Hebrew U., Jerusalem, 1973-75; assoc. prof. U. Pitts., 1976-87; assoc. scientist Marine Biol. Lab., Woods Hole, Mass., 1987—. Mem. Am. Soc. for Microbiology, Soc. Sigma Xi. Office: Marine Biol Lab Water St Woods Hole MA 02543

SUTHERLAND, MARCIA ELIZABETH, psychology educator; b. Jamaica, W.I.; d. Norman Winston and Alice Victoria (Richards) S.; 1 child, Kalonji Garvey Sutherland. MS, Howard U., 1979, PhD, 1985. Grad. asst. Howard U., Washington, 1979-81, rsch. asst., 1983-85; asst. prof. psychology SUNY, Albany, 1985—. Contbr. articles to profl. jours. Coord. Nat. Conf. Commemorating 100th Birthday Marcus Garvey, Albany, 1987; speaker various black history orgns., 1987—. Recipient Marcus Garvey Outstanding Svc. award Orgn. Caribbean African Unity, 1987. Mem. Assn. Black Psychologists, Ea. Psychol. Assn., Assn. for Study Classical African Civilization. Office: SUNY Dept Psychology 1400 Washington Ave Albany NY 12203

SUTHERLAND, MONIKA LEA, educator, business owner; b. Hahn, West Germany, Apr. 13, 1955; d. Edsel Gavin and Katherin (Jones) S. BA in English, East Carolina U., 1976, MA in English, 1985, postgrad., 1985—. Writer, editor Productive Communications Agy., Greenville, N.C., 1978-80; instr. Enfield Acad., Whitakers, N.C., 1980-81; chairperson English dept. Edgecombe Community Coll., Tarboro, N.C., 1981—, dir. coll. transfer program, 1987—; cons., instr. continuing edn. Edgecombe Coll., 1982—. Author, co-editor: Awakenings-Eastern N.C. Women, 1978; contbr. articles to profl. jours. Speaker N.C. Humanities Coun., Kinston, 1989. Nat. Archives fellow, 1987. Mem. Nat. Coun. Tchrs. of English, N.C. Literary and Hist. Assn., So. Conf. English Tchrs., Orgn. of Am. Historians, N.C. Coll. English Instrs., AAUW (Woman of the Yr. 1988), Kiwanis, Gamma Beta Phi (Sci. award 1983). Baptist. Office: Edgecombe Community Coll 2009 Wilson St Tarboro NC 27886

SUTLIFF, DIANE LOUISE PEEK, associate director nursing; b. Ticonderoga, N.Y., Feb. 12, 1948; m. Walter N. Sutliff Jr.; children: Steven, Jason, Caleb. BS in Nursing, SUNY, 1969, MS in Edn., 1971. Coll. instr. nursing div. SUNY, Plattsburg, 1970-72; sch. nurse tchr. East Greenbush Cen. Sch. Dist., 1972-73; grad. instr. SUNY, summer 1972, 73; pub. health nurse Warren County Health Service, Lake George, N.Y., 1973-75; supervising nurse Warren County Health Service, Lake George, 1975-86; assoc. dir. Warren County Health Svc., Lake George, 1986—. Mem. Town of Kingsbury Planning Bd., Hudson Falls, N.Y., 1983-88; chariperson Town of Kingsbury Planning Bd., Hudson Falls, 1988--; adv. bd. Retired Sr. Vol. Program, Glens Falls, N.Y., 1988--; treas. Dirs. NENY Regional Home Health, Albany, N.Y., 1988--. Home: RD 1 Box 72B Hudson Falls NY 12839 Office: Warren County Health Svc Mcpl Ctr Lake George NY 12845

SUTLIN, VIVIAN, advertising executive; b. Chgo.; d. Samuel E. and Doris (Weinberg) S. BA, Roosevelt U. V.p. creative group head Grey North Advt., Inc., Chgo.; v.p. creative dir., founder Pilot Products, Inc., Chgo.; TV writer, producer Grey Advt., Inc., N.Y.; sr. writer Young and Rubicam, Inc., N.Y.; v.p. creative dir. Dodge and Delano, N.Y.; pres. Vivian Sutlin Advt., new products and consumer packaged goods specialist with full svc. TV and print, domestic and internat. ops.; creative supr. William Douglas McAdams, Inc., N.Y., Grey Med. Advt., Inc., N.Y.; pres. Vivian Sutlin Communications, N.Y.; advt. cons. consumer and med. pharm. Co-author: Industry Women Speak Out. Recipient Guacaipuro TV award Chgo. Fedn. of Advt. Clubs, Am. TV Commls. Festival award, TV award Art Dirs. Club of Chgo., Triangle award Med. Advt. Print, Internat. Broadcasting award.

SUTO, CARLA MARIE, biologist; b. Boston, Mar. 5, 1959; d. Carl Emil and Phylis Marie (Cronin) Swanson; m. Mark James Suto, July 15, 1988. BS, Simmons Coll., 1981; PhD, Brown U., 1986. Rsch. asst. Harvard U. Sch. Pub. Health, Boston, 1979-81, Brown U., Providence, R.I., 1981-85; teaching asst. Brown U., Providence, 1981-84; project investigator M.D. Anderson Hosp. Tumor Inst., Houston, 1985-87; scientist pharm. rsch. div. Parke-Davis, Ann Arbor, Mich., 1987-90, sr. sci., 1990—; reviewer Internat. Jour. Radiation, Oncology, Biology & Physics, 1987—. Contbr. many articles to profl. jours. Recipient Katherine Jones Witton Meml. Biology award Simmons Coll., 1981, NCI Predoctoral Tng. award Brown U., 1984-85; grantee M.D. Anderson Hosp. & Tumor Inst., 1986-87. Mem. Radiation Rsch. Soc., Am. Assn. Cancer Rsch., New Eng. Radiobiology Club. Office: Parke Davis Pharm Rsch Div 2800 Plymouth Rd Ann Arbor MI 48105

SUTTER, ELIZABETH HENBY (MRS. RICHARD A. SUTTER), civic leader, management company executive; b. St. Louis, May 15, 1912; d. William Hastings and Alvina (Steinbreder) Henby; A.B., Washington U., St. Louis, 1931; m. Richard A. Sutter, June 15, 1935; children: John Richard, Jane Elizabeth, Judith Ann (Mrs. William Hinrichs). Sec.-treas. Sutter Mgmt. Co., St. Louis, Sutter Clinic, St. Louis; v.p. Downtown Med. Bldg., Inc., St. Louis, until 1985. Chmn. com. on mental health AMA Aux., 1960-62, v.p., 1962-63, 63-64, pres. 1965-66, editor Direct Line newsletter, 1967-74; assoc. editor MD's Wife, 1973-80; mem. adv. bd. Deaconess Hosp. Sch. of Nursing, St. Louis; trustee John Burroughs Sch., 1958-61, v.p. 1959, devel. commn., 1960-61; mem. Hist. Bldgs. Commn. St. Louis County, 1957—, chmn., 1973—; bd. dirs. Gamma Phi Beta House Corp. Washington U., St. Louis; chmn. Com. for Preservation Children's Teeth; mem. planning bd. Health, Hosp. Health, Welfare Coun. Met. St. Louis, 1955-64; pres. Aux. Cen. States Soc. Indsl. Medicine and Surgery, 1960-61; pres. St. Louis County Med. Soc. Aux., 1948-49, Mo. Med. Soc. Aux., 1952-53; sec. St. Louis County Health and Hosp. Bd., 1956-61, chmn., 1961; bd. dirs. Am. Lung Assn. Eastern Mo., exec. com., 1956-85, v.p., 1960-61; pres. Tb and Health Soc. of St. Louis, 1962-65; adv. coun.vol. svcs. Nat. Assn. Mental Health, 1962-64; bd. dirs. Am. Cancer Soc., St. Louis, exec. com., 1954-64; bd. dirs. Mental Health Assn. St. Louis, 1960-61; mem. Practical Nursing Edn. Coun., chmn. exec. com., 1959-60; mem. AMA Coun. on Mental Health Planning for Nat. Conf. on Mental Health, 1961; mem. adv. com. on women in svcs. Dept. Def., 1969-72, vice chmn., 1971; participant 24th ann. global strategy discussion U.S. Naval War Coll., 1972; bd. govs. Washington U. Alumni, 1970-71, 75—, vice chmn. 1979-80, chmn., 1980-81; trustee Washington U., 1979-81; pres. Washington U. Arts and Scis. Century Club, 1970-71; bd. dirs. St. Louis Conv. and Tourist Bur., 1975-83, sec., 1980-82; bd. dirs. Health Svcs. Agy., 1975-82; mem. East West Gateway Coordinating Coun. Task Force on Hist. Preservation, 1975-81, U. City Hist. Preservation Commn., 1977; bd. dirs. Whitney Beach III Assn., Longboat Key, Fla., 1984-87; del. Mo. Rep. Conv., 1972, 76, 80, 84, del. Nat. Rep. Conv., 1984. Named 1 of 10 Women of Achievement in good citizen category St. Louis Globe-Democrat, 1961; Alumna of Yr., Gamma Phi Beta, St. Louis, 1966; recipient St. Louis County Med. Soc. award of merit, 1964; Disting. Alumni citation Washington U., 1968, Disting. Alumni Svc. citation, 1977; Life Style award Eastern Mo. chpt. Am. Lung Assn., 1982; Meritorious Svc. award Am. Park and Recreation Soc., 1985. Mem. Mo. Hist. Soc., St. Louis Symphony Soc., AMA Aux. (hon. life), Mo. Med. Aux. (hon. life), Met. St. Louis Med. Aux. (hon. life), Gamma Phi Beta (bd. found. St. Louis chpt. 1989, 90). Presbyterian. Endowed Richard A. and Betty H. Sutter Vis. Professorship in Occ. and Insdl. Medicine Washington U., St. Louis. Home: 7215 Greenway Dr Saint Louis MO 63130

SUTTER, EMILY MAY GEESEMAN, psychologist, educator; b. St. Louis, Nov. 18, 1939; d. George Robert and Cora Hamilton (Glasgow) Geeseman; m. Gordon Frederick Sutter, Aug. 13, 1960; children: John Blaine, Steven George. BS, U. Pitts., 1960, M of Retailing, 1961; MEd, Wayne State U., 1965; PhD, U. Tex., 1967. Lic. psychologist, Tex. Chief psychologist Richmond State Sch., Houston, 1967-71; dir. Fairhill Sch., Houston, 1971-72; assoc. dir. Battin Clinic, Houston, 1972-81; from asst. to assoc. prof. U. Houston, Clear Lake, 1981—, interim dean 1990—. Contbr. articles to profl. jours. Mem. Am. Psychol. Assn., Southwestern Psychol. Assn. (sec., treas. 1979-79), Tex. Psychol. Assn. (treas. 1978, liaison officer 1985-87, pres. 1990—), Houston Psychol. Assn. (pres. 1976-77). Avocation: gardening. Home: 15719 Heatherdale Dr Houston TX 77059 Office: U Houston 2700 Bay Area Blvd Houston TX 77058

SUTTER, MARGARET MOFFETT, public affairs executive; b. Schenectady, N.Y., Dec. 6, 1953; d. Edward Donald and Frances Mary (Behan) Moffett. Student, Schenectady Community Coll., 1971-72; BA in English Edn., SUNY, Albany, 1976, MA in English Edn., 1978; postgrad., Auburn U., 1981. Permanent teaching cert., N.Y. Reporter Schenectady Gazette, 1972-73; commd. lt. USAF, 1978; advanced through grades to maj. USAFR, 1989—; pub. affairs officer USAFR, Travis AFB, Calif., 1985-87, George AFB, Calif., 1985-87; pub. affairs officer Office of Sec. Air Force, Washington, 1987—; coll. programs coord./counselor Chapman Coll. Regional Campus, Travis AFB, Calif., 1987—. Contbg. writer The Dispatch newspaper, 1981-83; columnist, writer The Crosswinds mag., 1985-87; supr./editor several Air Force newspapers, 1985-87. Asst. leader Girl Scouts U.S., Falls Church, Va., 1989—; vol. Iliff Nursing Home, Falls Church, 1987-88, USAF Officer Wives Club, Calif., Va., 1985-89, Cath. Ch., Presbyn. Ch., Ala., Calif., 1981-83, 86-87. Capt. USAF, 1978-85, major USAFR, 1985—. Mem. Res. Officers Assn., Air Force Assn., Retired Officers Assn., Assn. Univ. Women, SUNY Alumni, Families Adopting Children Everywhere, Psi Gamma. Home: 2707 Westford Ct Falls Church VA 22043

SUTTIN, DORIS BETH, real estate broker and developer, mortgage broker; b. Chgo., July 5, 1940; d. Saul S. and Pearl (Goldberg) Siegal; m. Eugene N. Suttin, Feb. 1, 1961 (div. 1968); m. Myron J. Sponder, July 5, 1976 (div. 1977); 1 child, Adam L. B.S., U. Ill.-Urbana, 1961; Lic. real estate broker, Fla. Advt. mgr. Goldblatt Bros. Inc., Urbana, 1961-62; real estate salesperson Grand Bahama Devel. Co., Freeport, Grand Bahama, 1963-65; asst. sales mgr. Coral Beach Ltd., Freeport, 1968-70; owner-mgr. Saul S. Siegal Co., Miami, Fla., 1970-82; developer DLM Partnership, Miami, 1978—; owner, comml. real estate broker Doris B. Suttin Realty, Inc., Miami, 1981—; dist. official Miami Design Dist. Assocs.; real estate broker. V.p. membership Lowe Art Mus., Friends of Art, U. Miami; treas., bd. dirs. Hannah Kahn Poetry Found. Mem. Women in Communications, South Fla. Poetry Inst., Am. Acad. Poets, Vivian Laramore Rader Poetry Group (2d v.p.), Indsl. Assn. Dade County, Nat. Assn. Women Bus. Owners, Mensa, Assn. Comml. Real Estate Women. Home: 3900 Island Blvd Apt 203 Williams Island FL 33160 Office: Doris B Suttin Realty Inc 2875 NE 191st St Ste 401 North Miami Beach FL 33180

SUTTLES, VIRGINIA GRANT, advertising executive; b. Urbana, Ill., June 13, 1931; d. William Henry and Lenora (Fitzsimmons) Grant; m. John Henry Suttles, Sept. 24, 1977; step-children: Linda Suttles, Peg Suttles La Croix, Pamela Suttles Diaz, Randall. Grad. pub. schs., Mahomet, Ill. Media estimator and Procter & Gamble budget control Tatham-Laird, Inc., Chgo., 1955-60; media planner, supr. Tracy-Locke Co., Inc., Dallas and Denver, 1961-68; media dir., account exec. Lorie-Lotito, Inc., 1968-72; v.p., media dir. Sam Lusky Assos., Inc., Denver, 1972-86; ind. media buyer, 1984—; mktg. asst. mktg. dept. Del E. Webb Communities, Inc., Sun City West, Ariz., 1985-88, 89—, with telemarketing sales dept., 1989—; lectr. sr. journalism class U. Colo., Boulder, 1975-80; condr. class in media seminars Denver Advt. Fedn., 1974, 77; Colo. State U. panelist Broadcast Day, 1978, High Sch. Inst., 1979, 80, 81, 82, 83. Founder, Del E. Webb Meml. Hosp. Found.; patron founder Tree of Life Nat. Kidney Found. of Colo.- Rockies Snow Mountain YMCA Ranch, Winter Park, Colo. Mem. Denver Advt. Fedn. (bd. dir. 1973-75, program chmn. 1974-76, 80-82, exec. bd., v.p. ops. 1980-81, chmn. Alfie awards com. 1980-81, advt. profl. of Yr. 1981-82), Denver Advt. Golf Assn. (v.p. 1976-77, pres. 1977-78), Colo. Broadcasters Assn., Sun City West Bowling Assn. (bd. dirs. 1987-88), Sun City West Women's Social Club. Republican. Congregationalist. Club: Denver Broncos Quarterback. Home: 21022 Sunglow Dr Sun City West AZ 85375 Office: Del Webb Communities Inc 13323 Meeker Blvd Sun City West AZ 85375

SUTTON, BARBARA JEAN, financial planner; b. Fremont, Nebr., Apr. 12, 1949; d. James Lawrence and Beth Elaine (Dunn) Heywood; m. Byron Lee Sutton, Aug. 8, 1970 (div. Nov. 1980). BA in Edn., Wayne State Coll., Nebr., 1970; MEd, U. Nebr., 1976. Tchr. Genoa (Nebr.) Sch. Dist., 1970-74, Ashland-Greenwood (Nebr.) Unified Sch. Dist., 1974-77; fin. planner Profl. Planning Assocs. Ltd., Phoenix, 1978—; v.p. Profl. Planning Assocs., Ltd., Phoenix, 1980-89, sr. v.p., 1989—. Contbr. articles to profl. jours. Mem. adv. bd. Phoenix Econ. Growth Corp., 1988-89; bd. dirs. Valley Citizens League, 1987—; founding pres. Community Treatment Program, 1981-85; sec., pres. Phoenix Local Devel. Corp., 1986—; treas., 2d v.p. Phoenix City Club, 1986-88. Runner-up Phoenix C. of C., 1988; recipient Athena award, Small Bus. Woman of Yr. Mem. Am. Soc. CLUs and Chartered Fin. Cons's. (bd. dirs. Phoenix chpt. 1986-87), Nat. Assn. Health Underwriters, Greater Phoenix Assn. of Life Underwriters. Republican. Home: 3059 E Rose Ln Phoenix AZ 85016 Office: Profl Planning Assocs Ltd 1661 E Camelback Rd Ste 100 Phoenix AZ 85016

SUTTON, BEVERLEY ANN, hospital nursing services adminstrator; b. Albion, Ill., June 30, 1939; d. Henry Alvin and Mildred (Horton) Simpson; M. Thomas Wiley Sutton, Feb. 12, 1960; children: Debra, Elizabeth. Diploma, Alton Meml. Hosp., 1960. Unit leader recovery room Alton Meml. Hosp., Alton, Ill., 1968-79; patient care coord. Alton Meml. Hosp., 1979-84, asst. dir. nursing outpatient svcs., 1984-86, dir. nursing, 1986-88, v.p. for nursing svcs., 1988-89, v.p. for patient care svcs., 1989—; presenter on nursing retention 13th Annual Christian Health Systems Edn. Conf., San Antonio. Co-chair Upper Madison County, Am. Heart Assn., 1987. Recipient recognition Hist. Soc. for Women Healthcare Profls. Month, 1989, cert. of achievement DMT-II Advanced Mnagerial Strategies, cert. U. Pa. Wharton Sch. Fin. and Acctg. for the Non-Fin. Exec. Mem. Soc. for Ambulatory Care Profls., Ill. Assn. Nurse Execs., Am. Orgn. Nurse Execs., Alton Band and Orch. Builders (pres. 1984-85). Methodist. Office: Alton Meml Hosp 1 Memorial Dr Alton IL 62002

SUTTON, FRANCES HAMMER, computer science educator; b. Hillsboro, Md., Sept. 28, 1941; d. Arthur Walter and Mary Catherine (Coulby) Hammer; m. Thomas Townsend Sutton, July 14, 1962 (dec. June 1987); children: Thomas Arthur, Steven John, Michael David. AAS in Data Processing, Coll. of Albermarle, 1984; BS in Computer Sci., Elizabeth City State U., 1987. Sec./procurement asst. CIA, Washington, 1959-62; sec. Aeros. div. Mpls. Honeywell, St. Petersburg, Fla., 1962-63; cons. data base mgmt. system Watermark Assn. Artisans, Elizabeth City, N.C., 1986-87; instr. computer sci. Coll. of Albemarle, Elizabeth City, 1987—. Vol. campaign worker Winnie Wood for state senate, 1982. Cummings scholar, 1983, Chancellor's achievement scholar, 1984. Mem. Phi Theta Kappa, Alpha Kappa Mu. Roman Catholic. Home: 2206 Meads St Elizabeth City NC 27909 Office: Coll of Albemarle PO Box 2327 Elizabeth City NC 27906-2327

SUTTON, JOYCE ELAINE, medical records director; b. Chillicothe, Mo., Aug. 28, 1946; d. William Stanley and Helen Louise (Ashlock) Henderson; m. Ferold Rodrick Vermilyea, Jr., Feb. 7, 1964 (div. Aug. 1973); m. Ronald Eldon Sutton, Jan. 15, 1978; children: Sherra Wood, Janae Nezerka, Michael Sutton, Brian Sutton, Marcia Sutton. Accredited record technician. Ward clk. Heartland West Hosp. (formerly Meth. Med. Ctr.), St. Joseph, Mo., 1970-73; ward clk. Hedrick Med. Ctr., Chillicothe, 1973-74; med. records clk. Hedrick Med. Ctr., 1974-75, A.R.T. trainee, 1975-77, med. transcriber, 1977-82, asst. supr., 1982-85, med. records supr., 1985-89, med. records dir., 1989—, quality assurance cons., 1990—, also med. staff sec., treas., coord.; cons. Brookfield (Mo.) Nursing Ctr., 1987—, Excelsior Springs (Mo.) City Hosp., 1988—; dir. outpatient program, Hedrick Med. Ctr., Chillicothe, 1987—, dir. quality assurance/risk mgmt., 1988—. Mem. local civic orgns., Chillicothe, 1987—. Mem. Hedrick Med. Ctr. Aux. (life), Am. Med. Records Assn., Mo. Med. Records Assn., Kansas City Area Med. Records Assn. Republican. Baptist. Home: Box 114 Meadville MO 64659 Office: Hedrick Med Ctr 100 Central Chillicothe MO 64601

SUTTON, JUDITH KAY, library administrator; b. Salisbury, N.C., Sept. 13, 1947; d. Alex and Julia Mae (Webb) S. BS in History, U. N.C., 1969; MLS, U. N.C., Chapel Hill, 1970. Librarian Div. of State Library, Raleigh, N.C., 1970-72, librarian gen. and local history, 1972-73, cons. adult svcs., 1973-77; dep. dir. of libraries Pub. Library of Charlotte (N.C.) and Mecklenburg County, 1977—; mem. Mem. ALA, N.C. Library Assn. (pub. library sect. chmn. 1983-85), Southeastern Library Assn., Metrolina Library Assn., Women Execs. Democrat. Lutheran. Home: 3111 Stone Orchard Pl Charlotte NC 28209 Office: Pub Library Charlotte 310 N Tryon St Charlotte NC 28202

SUTTON, MARCELLA FRENCH, interior designer; b. Prague, Czechoslovakia, Sept. 4, 1946; came to U.S., 1952, naturalized, 1956; d. Eugen E. and Frances V. (Pruchovia) French; BS in Profl. Arts, Woodbury U., 1971; m. Michael D. Sutton, Feb. 11, 1978; 1 child, Kevin Christopher. Mgr. design dept. W. & J. Sloane, Beverly Hills, Calif., 1972-76; project dir. Milton I. Swimmer, Beverly Hills, 1977-78; owner, interior designer Marcella French Designs, Woodland Hills and La Crescenta, Calif., 1969—; v.p. Shepherd of the Valley Sch.; property mgmt. coordinator, interior designer Home Savs. and Loan., State of Calif., Los Angeles, 1979-82; regional premises officer, asst. v.p. regional hdqrs. Bank of Am., Los Angeles, 1981-86; v.p. M.D. Sutton Ins. Agy.; prin. designer Marcella French Designs, Woodland Hills; cons. pvt. residences. Mem. fund raising com. City of Canoga Park, 1987-88; enrichment chmn., fund raiser Shephard of the Valley Sch., 1990—; active Young Reps; treas. West Hills Baseball Aux., 1989—. Recipient various scholarships.

SUTTON, RENEE COLETTE, hospital administrator, pharmacist; b. Gettysburg, S.D., June 13, 1958; d. Anton and Betty Lou (Strong) Kost; m. William John Sutton, June 17, 1983; children: Dee Colette, Billie Harmon, Rehme Renee. BS in Pharmacy, U. Wyo., 1981. Pharmacist, mgr. Thompson Drug, Eagle Butte, S.D., 1981-83; relief pharmacist several drug stores, South and Cen., S.D., 1983-87; cons. pharmacist Bapt. Hosp., Winner, S.D., 1984—; cons. pharmacist Community Meml. Hosp., Burke, S.D., 1987—, adminstr., 1987—. Mem. Community Meml. Hosp. Aux., Burke, 1987—, Burke Community Club, 1987—, Burke Devel. Corp., 1987—; hon. mem. Dist. 4 S.D. Hosp. Assn., South Cen., 1985—. Mem. Rosebud Dist. S.D. Pharm. Assn. (pres. 1986), Rosebud Rancherette Cattlewomen (pres. Gregory County, S.D., 1987—). Democrat. Home: PO Box 98 Burke SD 57523 Office: Community Meml Hosp Inc 8th and Jackson Box 319 Burke SD 57523

SUTTON-SALLEY, VIRGINIA B., business executive; b. Miami, Fla.; d. Durward Belmont and Sarabelle (Burns) Sutton; m. George H. Salley, Aug. 28, 1961. Student, Sullins Coll., Rollins Coll. Assoc., jr. ptnr. D.B. Sutton Jewelry Co., Miami, 1948-50; singer (Gloria Manning, profl. name) with Vincent Lopez Orch., Ben Ribble Orch., 1951-60; owner, operator Wiscasset Antiques, 1960-62; owner, mgr., pres. Sutton Manning Corp., 1962—; guest artist WOR-TV, N.Y.C.; currently appearing on club singing engagements, Miami Beach. Co-author: Royal Bayreuth China; contbr. articles to Miami Beach Post and profl. jours. Mem Met. Dade County Zoning Apls. Bd., 1966-70, vice-chmn. 1970-71; mem. pres.'s adv. council Barry Coll., 1978-79; community advisor Beaux Arts, 1989—, U. Miami, Lowe Art Mus., 1975-78; bd. dirs. Big Bros., 1971-72, Gilded Lilies Dade County Soc. Crippled Children, 1982-83; founder, pres. Theatre Arts League, 1959, Jr. Theatre Guild of Miami, 1961. Mem. Nat. League Am. Pen Women, Am. Guild Variety Artists, Screen Actors Guild, DAR, Soc. Arts and Letters N.Y.C. , U.S. Croquet Assn., Palm Beach Croquet Club, Miami Yacht Club, Bath Club, Surf Club, Indian Creek Club, Boothbay Harbour Yacht Club. Mem. Christian Ch. Office: Sutton Manning Corp 100 N Biscayne Blvd Suite 700 Miami FL 33132

SUVA, SUZANNE, personnel relations executive, consultant, educator; b. Cleve., Feb. 15, 1947; d. James Patrick and Marie (Kohut) Monnolly; m. Robert J. Suva; children: Heather Marie, Sara Beth. BA in Psychology and Bus., Baldwin Wallace Coll., 1984; postgrad., Cleve. Marshall Law Sch., 1987—. Pers. asst. J.M. Smucker Co., Medina, Ohio, 1973-76; asst. mgr pers. Eaton Corp., Aurora, Ohio, 1976-85; mgr. personnel, supr. employee rels. Lubrizol Corp., Wickliffe, Ohio, 1985—; prof. reviewer Personnel Adminstr., Alexandria, Va., 1983—; mem. adv. bd. women starting over for success Cleve. State U., 1985—. Dep. registrar Summit County Bd. Elections, Akron, 1984—; clinic leader freedom from smoking Am. Lung Assn., Cleve., 1984—. Mem. Am. Soc. Personnel Adminstrs., Am. Humane Soc., Alpha Lambda Sigma. Roman Catholic. Home: 170 W Aurora Rd Sagamore Hills OH 44067 Office: Lubrizol Corp 29400 Lakeland Blvd Wickliffe OH 44092

SUWINSKY, PAM POKORNEY, book publisher; b. Pittston, Pa., Aug. 28, 1954; d. Walter Francis and Sophia Marie (Matthews) Pokorney; m. Henry Frank Suwinsky, Jr., Apr. 7, 1990. BA in Classics, English, Pa. State U., 1976; MA in English, U. Chgo., 1977; postgrad., U. Ill., Chgo., 1983-85. Permissions asst. U. Chgo. Press., 1977-79, design and prodn. asst., 1979-81, prodn. coord., 1981-83, sr. prodn. coord., 1983-85; prodn. mgr. Beacon Press, Boston, 1985-88, design and prodn. mgr., 1988—. Prin. author: Chicago Guide to Electronic MSS, 1987. Mem. Bookbuilders of Boston (bd. dirs. 1989-91), Chgo. Book Clinic, Am. Inst. Graphic Art. Roman Catholic.

SVADLENAK, JEAN HAYDEN, museum administrator; b. Wilmington, Del., Mar. 4, 1955; d. Marion M. and Ida Jean (Calcagni) Hayden; m. Steven R. Svadlenak, May 26, 1979. BS in Textiles and Clothing, U. Del., 1977; MA in History Mus. Studies, SUNY, Oneonta, 1982; postgrad., U. Calif., Berkeley, 1982. Curatorial asst. The Hagley Mus., Wilmington, 1976-77; curator of costumes and textiles The Kansas City (Mo.) Mus., 1978-82, chief curator, 1982-84, assoc. exec. collections, 1984-87, dir. for collection and exhibits mgmt., 1984-86, interim pres., 1986-87, pres., 1987-89; researcher, guest curator N.Y. State Hist. Assn., Cooperstown, 1980; grant reviewer Inst. for Mus. Svcs., 1985-89, accreditation vis. com., 1990—. Mem. Am. Assn. Mus. (mus. assessment program surveyor 1986—), Am. Assn. State and Local History, Costume Soc. Am., Heritage League of Kansas City (bd. dirs. 1987-89), Mo. Mus. Assocs. (bd. dirs. 1988—). Home: 624 Romany Rd Kansas City MO 64113

SVEC, CYNTHIA LILLIAN, business services administrator, building manager; b. Chgo., Jan. 20, 1941; d. George Mitchell Smith and Lillian (Mottl) Smith Trousil; m. 1964 (div. 1975); children—Victoria Lynn, Jacqueline Paige, Alison E. Student public schs., Cicero, Ill. Office mgr. Belmont Industries, Inc., Cicero, Ill., 1958-67; pres., exec., owner August Bus. Service, Inc., LaGrange, Ill., 1975—; v.p. Stewart's Indsl. Service Inc., LaGrange, 1979-83; owner, mgr. LaGrange Profl. Bldg., LaGrange, 1981—. Recipient Beautification award West Suburban C. of C., LaGrange, 1981. Mem. West Suburban C. of C., Midwest Assn. Commerce and Industry. Republican. Roman Catholic. Avocations: interior decorating and design; international travel; parapsychology, astrology; reading. Office: August Business Service Inc 110 N LaGrange Rd LaGrange IL 60525

SVEC, JANICE LYNN, military professional; b. Santa Anna, Calif., May 14, 1948; d. Leonard August Svec and Wanda Marcelle (Richards) McMillon; m. Lewis Eugene Humphrey, May 24, 1974 (div. 1977); 1 child, Jeromy Starbuck Svec. A.A. in Adminstrn. of Justice, Los Angeles Met. Community Coll., 1982; student criminal justice Thomas Edison State Coll., Trenton, 1985—. Adminstrv. supporter Naval Investigative Service, Subic Bay, Philippines, 1979-81; office supr. Naval Communication Ctr., Yokosuka, Japan, 1981-82; chief master at arms Naval Support Facility Security Dept., Diego Garcia, Brit. Indian Ocean Ter., 1982-83, U.S. Navy Drug Rehab. Ctr., San Diego, 1983-85; instr. U.S. Navy, Lakehurst, N.J., 1985-88, supr. Security Detachment Navy Support Office, La Magdalena, Italy, 1988—. Roman Catholic. Avocations: body building; horseback riding. Home: 120 Village Way Crockett TX 75835 Office: PO Box 578 Lakehurst NJ 08733

SVEC, SUSAN MARIE, social worker; b. Oak Park, Ill., Oct. 10, 1945; d. August Frank and Vera Agnes (Winfrey) S. AA, Morton Community Coll., 1965; BS, U. Ill., 1968; MSW, U. Ill., Chgo., 1988. Caseworker Misericordia Home, Chgo., 1968-74; field exec. West Cook Girl Scouts U.S., La Grange, Ill., 1974-79; exec. dir. Cloverleaf Girl Scouts U.S., Cicero, Ill., 1979-86; social worker West Town Hospice, Berwyn, Ill., 1985-88; dir. devel., social svc. coord. West Towns VNS & Hospice, Berwyn, 1988—. 1st aid inst. Mid-Am. chpt., ARC, Westchester, 1977-88; chmn. bd. trustees Morton Community Coll., Cicero, 1980-85; pres. Friends of Hospice, Berwyn, 1983-85; bd. dirs. Children's Ctr. of Cicero-Berwyn, 1986-88, Whispering Oaks Girl Scouts, 1988—; program chmn. Whisper Oaks Girl Scout Coun., 1989—, mem. long range planning com., 1988—, nominating com., 1989-91; mem. svc. com. Oak Park AIDS Network; mem. Berwyn Devel. Corp. Recipient Recognition Cert. ARC, Westchester, 1985, Recognition Plaque, Morton Community Coll., 1985, Thanks Badge, Cloverleaf Girl Scouts U.S., 1986, Honor Pin Whispering Oak Girl Scout Coun., 1990. Mem. Nat. Assn. Social Workers, Ill. Assn. Social Workers, Assn. Vol. Adminstrs., Berwyn Hist. Soc. (Appreciation cert. 1989), Nat. Soc. Fund Raising Execs.

SVEINSSON, LINDA RODGERS, computer scientist; b. Tuscaloosa, Ala., July 1, 1938; d. Eric and Sarah Ella (Haughton) Rodgers; B.A. in Math., Birmingham-So. Coll., 1960; M.S. in Indsl. Engring. (NSF trainee 1970-72), U. Ala., 1972; m. Hjalmar Sveinsson, May 29, 1971; children—Martha M. Reed, Stephen R.M. Moreno, III. Systems analyst U. Ala. Med. Center, Birmingham, 1967-69; systems mgr. Internat. Data Systems, New Orleans, 1969-70; computer scientist Computer Scis. Corp., Silver Spring, Md., 1973-76; computer systems specialist System Devel. Corp., McLean, Va., 1976-78; mem. tech. staff Bell Labs., Columbus, Ohio, 1978-85, tech. supr., 1979-85; mgr. bus. devel. No. Telecom, Inc., Research Triangle Park, N.C., 1985-88; dept. mgr. network ops. and mgmt. systems Contel Tech. Ctr., 1988— . Mem. Assn. Computing Machinery, Phi Beta Kappa, Alpha Pi Mu. Republican. Methodist. Home: 8911 Old Courthouse Rd Vienna VA 22182 Office: 1500 Conference Ctr Dr PO Box 10814 Chantilly VA 22021-3808

SVENDSEN, ELINE MARGUERITE, mathematics educator; b. Decatur, Ill., Feb. 7, 1924; d. Niels Jacob Svendsen and Johanne Moller. BA, James Millikin U., 1945; MA, Columbia U., 1948; MS, Purdue U., 1959. Math tchr. Decatur High Sch., 1945, 58-67, chmn. dept. math., 1958-67; math. tchr. Woodrow Wilson Jr. High Sch., Decatur, 1945-47, Roosevelt Jr. High, Decatur, 1948-58; instr. math. Lake Land Coll., Mattoon, Ill., 1968—; pres. IMACC, 1978-79, bd. dirs. 1975-78, 81-83, sec. 1983-89. Active PTA; WELC treas. Trinity Luth. Ch., Mattoon, 1988-90. GE Fellow Purdue U., 1957, 58, 59; NSF Fellow U. Ill., Ill. State U., U. Wis., U. Iowa, Rutgers U. Life mem. AAUW (v.p. membership Charleston-Mattoon br., pres. 1973-77, treas., legis. chmn., cen. conf. chmn. Lake Land Coll. br. 1989), NEA, Nat. Coun. Tchrs. Math.; mem. Math. Assn. Am. (bd. dirs. Ill. sect. 1989—), Delta Kappa Gamma (scholarship chmn., v.p. Gamma chpt. 1986-88, pres. 1988-90). Lutheran.

SVENDSEN, JOYCE ROSE, real estate company executive; b. Bayonne, N.J., Nov. 26, 1948; d. Peder and Rita Agnes (Bogert) S.; m. Stephen G. Takach, June 22, 1968; 1 child, Mark Stephen. Regional investigator Channel Co., Whippany, N.J., 1977-79; pres. Svendsen Studio, Clifton, N.J., 1979-82, Treasures, Sugar Loaf, N.Y., 1982-85; sales dir. M.L. Levine Real Estate, Clifton, 1985—. Mem. N.J. Assn. Realtors (million dollar sales club 1986, 87, 88, 89), Passaic County Bd. Realtors (assoc.), U.S. Coast Guard Aux. Republican. Unitarian. Office: M L Levine Real Estate 822 Clifton Ave Clifton NJ 07013

SVENSEN-SMITH, CAROL ALYCE, human resources manager; b. Erie, Pa., Dec. 8, 1947; d. Oscar and Lucille Irene (Hershelman) Svensen; m. Donald E. Furman Jr., Aug. 16, 1969 (div. 1980); m. Matthew L. Smith, Aug. 29, 1982; children: Sheridan Adam, Alexander Matthew. BA, Thiel Coll., 1969. Office mgr. Gen. Learning, Morristown, N.J., 1970-73; freelance photographer Jamestown, N.Y., 1973; personnel mgr. Falconer (N.Y.) Glass Industries, 1973-74; personnel technician City of Jamestown, 1974; labor rels. specialist Chautauqua County Govt., Mayville, N.Y., 1979-87; dir. of personnel Faculty Student Assn., Fredonia, N.Y., 1987-89; co-dir. Theatre of Young Artists, Jamestown, 1980—; organist, choir dir. St. John's Ch., Jamestown, 1983—; human resources mgr. The Resource Ctr., Jamestown, 1989—; Bd. dirs., sec. The Dance Experience, Fredonia, 1988—. Composer: Mass for St. Cecilia, 1988, various sacred songs, 1988-90; co-author various musicals, 1981-90. Pres. Jamestown Area Arts Coun., 1974-76; bd. dirs. Chautauqua Opportunities, Inc., Mayville, 1978. Mem. Little Theatre of Jamestown (bd. pres. 1983-85), Stagecraft Guild/Little Theatre, Jamestown Area Personnel Assn., Order Eastern Star. Lutheran. Home: 104 Sampson St Jamestown NY 14701 Office: The Resource Ctr 880 E Second St Jamestown NY 14701

SVETLOVA, MARINA, ballerina, choreographer, educator; b. Paris, May 3, 1922; came to U.S. from Australia, 1940; d. Max and Tamara (Andreieff) Hartman. Studies with Vera Trefilova, Paris, 1930-36, studies with L. Egorova and M. Kschessinska, 1936-39; studies with A. Vilzak, N.Y.C., 1940-57; D honoris causa, Fedn. Francaise de Danse, 1988. Ballet dir. So. Vt. Art Ctr., 1959-64; dir. Svetlova Dance Ctr., Dorset, Vt., 1965—; prof. ballet dept. Ind. U., Bloomington, 1969—; choreographer Dallas Civic Opera, 1964-67, Ft. Worth Opera, 1967-83, San Antonio Opera, 1983, Seattle Opera, Houston Opera, Kansas City Performing Arts Found. Ballerina original Ballet Russe de Monte Carlo, 1939-41; guest ballerina Ballet Theatre, 1942, London's Festival Ballet, Teatro dell Opera, Rome, Nat. Opera, Stockholm, Sweden, Suomi Opera, Helsinki, Finland, Het Nederland Ballet, Holland, Cork Irish Ballet, Paris Opera Comique, London Palladium, Teatro Colon, Buenos Aires, others; prima ballerina Met. Opera, 1943-50, N.Y.C. Opera, 1950-52; choreographer: (ballet sequences) The Fairy Queen, 1966, L'Histoire du Soldat, 1968; tours in Far East, Middle East, Europe, S.Am., U.S.; performer various classical ballets Graduation Ball; contbr. articles to Debut, Paris Opera. Mem. Am. Guild Mus. Artists (bd. dirs.), Conf. on Ballet in Higher Edn., Nat. Soc. Arts and Letters (nat. dance chmn.). Home: Dorset VT 05251 Office: 2100 Maxwell Ln Bloomington IN 47401 also: 25 W 54th St New York NY 10019

SVEZIA, VERA TISHEFF, concert pianist, educator; b. Alliance, Ohio, Sept. 5, 1937; d. Thomas and Anna (Tarpov) Tisheff; m. Rudolph Svezia, Mar. 14, 1970; children—Alexander, Alexandria. Study with Rosina Lhevinne Julliard Sch. Music, B Mich. State U., M Eastman Sch. Music, PhD Yale U. Founder, dir. Vera Tisheff Sch. of Music, N.Y.C. and Englewood, N.J., 1971— . Concert performances with leading orchs. in U.S. and Europe; solo concerts, U.S. and European cities. McDowell Music Colony scholar, 1964; recipient Martha Baird Rockefeller award, 1966, Internat. Platform Assn. award, U.S. Congl. Adv. Bd. citation. Mem. AAUW, Phi Omega, Delta Omnicron. Home: 130 E Hamilton Ave Englewood NJ 07631

SVIRSKY, ALLA, gymnastics coach, educational administrator; b. Moscow, July 13, 1939; came to U.S., 1974; d. Michael and Tatiana Schuldiner; m. Valentin Svirsky, 1960; children: Oleg, Tanya. M in Anatomy, Physiology and Phys. Edn., Odessa Pedagogical Inst., USSR, 1961; M Sports, USSR, 1959. Head coach Poly. U., Odessa, 1961-65; mem. USSR Gymnastics Nat. Team, 1959-64; head coach Lokomotif Nat. Club, Odessa, 1964-73, Odessa Lokomotif Club, 1971-74; head gymnastics coach U. So. Calif., L.A., 1975-81; U.S.A. nat. gymnastics coach, 1977-90, U.S.A. Olympic coach, 1984; exec. dir. L.A. Sch. Gymnastics, Culver, Calif., 1983—. Mem. U.S. Gymnastics Fedn. (internat. com. 1983—). Home: 2410 Hercules Dr Los Angeles CA 90046 Office: LA Sch Gymnastics 8675 Hayden Pl Culver CA 90232

SVOBODA, ELIZABETH JANE, state legislator, sales professional; b. Toledo, Iowa, Nov. 3, 1944; d. Ambrose and Bernadine D. (Doran) Kearney; m. Stanley J. Svoboda, Mar. 31, 1964; children: Brian, Kelly Marie, Jason, Nicholas. Advanced bus. degree, Bus. Inst. Tech., 1986. Sec. to supt. State Juvenile Home, Toledo, 1963-71; with sales dept. Home Interiors & Gifts, Dallas, 1979—; mem. Iowa Ho. of Reps., Des Moines, 1987—. Vol. lobbyist Iowa Citizens for Community Improvement, 1977-85. Named a Tama County Belle Ringer, 1980; named one of Outstanding Young Women Am., Tama County Pork Producers, 1982. Democrat. Roman Catholic. Office: Iowa Legislature State Capitol Bldg Des Moines IA 50319*

SWADOS, ELIZABETH A., composer, director, writer; b. Buffalo, Feb. 5, 1951; d. Robert O. and Sylvia (Maisel) S. B.A., Bennington Coll., 1972. Composer, mus. dir. Peter Brook, Paris, Africa, U.S., 1972-73; composer-in-residence La Mama Exptl. Theater Club, N.Y.C., 1977—; mem. faculty Carnegie-Mellon U., 1974, Bard Coll., 1976-77, Sarah Lawrence Coll., 1976-77. Author: The Girl With the Incredible Feeling, 1976 (screenplay adaptation 1977), Runaways, 1979, Lullaby, 1980, Sky Dance, 1980, The Beautiful Lady (musical), 1984, Listening Out Loud: Becoming a Composer, 1988; composer theatrical scores: Medea, 1972, Elektra, 1970, Fragments of Trilogy, 1974, Trojan Women, 1974, The Good Women of Setzuan, 1975, The Cherry Orchard, 1977, As You Like It, 1979, Haggadah, 1980, (with Garry Trudeau) Doonesbury, 1983; composer, dir., adapter, mem. cast: Nightclub Cantata, 1977; composer, adapter (with Andrei Serban) Agamemnon (on Broadway), 1977, The Incredible Feeling Show, 1979; composer, dir., adapter: Wonderland in Concert, N.Y. Shakespeare Festival, 1978; adapter, dir.: Dispatches, 1979, Lullaby and Goodnight (opera), 1980; adapter: Works of Yehuda Amichi, Book of Jeremiah; composer music for films: Step by Step, 1978, Sky Dance, 1979; composer music for PBS short stories, 1979, CBS-TV and NBC-TV spls., A Year in the Life (miniseries), 1987; composer: Rap Master Ronnie, 1986; composer, dir. Swing, Bklyn. Acad. Music, 1987; performer: Mark Taper Forum, Los Angeles, 1985, Jerusalem Oratorio, Rome, 1985. Recipient Obie award Village Voice, 1972, 77; Outer Critics Circle award, 1977; nominee for Tony awards, 1978; Creative Artists Service Program grantee, 1976; N.Y. State Arts Council playwriting grantee, 1977—; Guggenheim fellow. Mem. Broadcast Music Inc., Actors Equity. Jewish. Home: 112 Waverly Pl New York NY 10011 Office: care Sam Cohn Internat Creative Mgmt Co 40 W 57th St New York NY 10019*

SWAIN, DOROTHY JOY, microbiologist; b. Ashton, Iowa, Apr. 28, 1933; d. Joseph Johnathon and Josephine Anna (Miller) Wubbena; m. Daniel Wilbert Swain, Dec. 27, 1958; children: Elizabeth Ann, Amy Carolyn, William Joseph. BA, U. S.D., 1958, MA, 1959. Cert. infection control practitioner. Rsch. asst. U. Ky., Lexington, 1960-62; med. lab tech. St. Joseph Hosp., Sioux City, Iowa, 1954-58, St. Michaels Hosp., Sauk Centre, Minn., 1964-68; asst. dir. Fairfax County Health Lab., Alexandria, Va., 1969-70; microbiologist Children's Hosp., Washington, 1968-69; infection control practitioner Sioux Valley Hosp., Cherokee, Iowa, 1978—; microbiologist Sioux Valley Hosp., 1972—; continuing edn. presenter Western Iowa Tech., 1988-89. Ch. sch. tchr. Episcopal Ch., Storm Lake, Iowa, 1980—. Mem. AAUW (treas. 1988-90). Democrat. Episcopalian. Home: 471 Euclid Cherokee IA 51012

SWAIN, NANCY JANE COX (MRS. JAMES OBED SWAIN), retired educator; b. Elwood, Ind., Dec. 19, 1901; d. Alfred Thomas and Emma (Allen) Cox; A.B. with high distinction, Ind. U., 1923, postgrad., 1928; M.A., U. Tenn., 1951, postgrad., 1953; m. James Obed Swain, June 24, 1923; children—J. Maurice, J. Robert. Teaching missionary M.E. Ch., Costa Rica, 1923-28; instr. U. Tenn., Knoxville, 1943, 45, non-resident instr. corr. Extension Div., 1959-71; tchr. Oak Ridge High Sch., 1943-67, Hollins Coll., 1967. Mem. Am. Assn. Tchrs. Spanish and Portuguese, E. Tenn. Edn. Assn., S. Atlantic Modern Lang. Assn., Phi Beta Kappa, Phi Kappa Phi, Sigma Delta Pi, Pi Delta Phi, Pi Lambda Theta. Republican. Methodist. Mem. P.E.O. Home: 414 Forest Park Blvd Apt 622 Knoxville TN 37919

SWAIN, NOLA V., real estate appraiser; b. Tacoma, Wash., Mar. 10, 1942; d. Arthur and Viola Mafalda (Sirianni) De Caro; m. Lloyd E. Montgomery, Dec. 8, 1961 (div. 1971); children: Gina N. Montgomery, Melissa R. Montgomery; m. Walter B. Swain, Mar. 11, 1977. Student, U. Puget Sound, 1959-62. First woman cert. real estate appraiser, Wash. Appraiser/assesor Pierce County Assessors Office, Tacoma, 1971-77; chief appraiser Otero Savs. & Loan, Colorado Springs, 1977-78; pvt. fee appraiser, co-owner N.W.S. & Assocs., Colorado Springs, 1978—; pres., designer N.V.S. Enterprises, Colorado Springs, 1980—. Designer numerous gift items. Recipient Women at Work award Council on Working Women, 1985, Pub. Service award Colorado Springs Assn. Life Underwriters, 1985, Salesman With A Purpose Club Booster of Yr. award, 1986. Mem. NAFE, NOW, Urban League, Soc. Real Estate Appraisers (candidate, treas. 1978, bd. dirs. 1982-84), Chi Omega Alumnae. Democrat. Roman Catholic. Avocations: skiing, traveling, crafts.

SWAIN, SUSAN ELAINE, educator; b. Covington, Ky., July 4, 1950; d. Merrill and Martha Elaine (Taylor) S. BS, Pa. State U., 1972; MEd, U. Cin., 1977; postgrad., Xavier U., Cin., 1985-87. Sec. U. Cin., 1972-74; child care coordinator U. Hosp., Cin., 1974-75; grad. nursing sec. U. Cin., 1975-77; learning disability tchr. Twenhofel Jr. High Sch., Independence, Ky., 1977-80, Kenton Elem. Sch., Independence, 1980-85; tchr. Kenton Elem. Sch., 1985—; trainee TESA Prog., State Dept. Edn., Kenton County, Ky., 1988-89. Mem. Code of Conduct com. Kenton County Bd. Edn., Independenc , 1980-82; mem. recording sec. Kenton Elem. guidance com., 1980-84, guidance and steering com., 1989—. Mem. NEA, Ky. Edn. Assn., Pa. State Alumnae Assn., Phi Upsilon Omicron, Phi Delta Kappa. Republican. Episcopalian. Home: 5714 Bluegrass Dr Independence KY 41051 Office: Kenton Elem Sch 5577 Madison Pike Independence KY 41051

SWAN, JANET ELIZABETH, aviation company worker; b. Rutland, Vt., Aug. 22, 1944; d. Donald Pillsbury and Mary Elizabeth (White) S.; m. Robert James Malinowski, Dept. 21, 1972 (div. Mar. 1983). Student, Rutland Vo-Tech. Sch., 1989. Vet. asst. Rutland Vet. Clinic, 1962-70; rating and endorsement clk. Nat. Grange Mutual Ins. Co., Rutland, 1970-72; bus. mgr. Rutland Vet. Clinic, 1972-74; machine operator Metromail, Rutland, 1980, Mack Molding Co., Cavendish, Vt., 1980-85; machine operator Aircraft Engine div. GE, Rutland, 1985-87, ultrasonic tester, 1987—; skincare and beauty cons. Fashion Two Twenty Cosmetics, 1974-80.

SWAN, JOYCE ANN, comptroller; b. San Antonio, June 11, 1964; d. Richard Bronaugh II and Carolyn Ann (Gerhardt) Harn; m. Jesse G. Swan, June 3, 1983. BBA in Acctg., U. Tex., San Antonio, 1986. Bookkeeper Gerhardts Paint and Wallpaper Co., San Antonio, 1976-84, Ike Neumann & Assocs., San Antonio, 1983-86, Patrician Properties, San Antonio, 1984-86; gen. mgr. San Antonio Hermann Sons Home Assn., 1982-86; comptroller Courtesy Chevrolet Co., Phoenix, 1986—. Auditor bd. evaluators Valley of Sun United Way, Phoenix, 1988—. Mem. Nat. Assn. Accts. (bd. dirs. Scottsdale chpt. 1988-89, v.p. edn. 1989—), Am. Soc. Women Accts. (mem. com. Mesa East Valley chpt.), Internat. Credit Assn. Greater Phoenix, Retail Fin. Exec. Ariz., Valley Forward Assn., Ariz. Cash Mgmt. Assn., Am. Inst. Individual Investors, Exec. Bus. and Profl. Women's Club (auditor 1986-87, 88-89, sec. Phoenix chpt. 1986-88), Pershing Lodge. Office: Courtesy Chevrolet 1233 E Camelback Rd Phoenix AZ 85014

SWAN, MARTHA LOUISE, retired educator; b. Chadron, Nebr., May 6, 1912; d. Neal Watterson and Sarrah Abbie (Brower) Cook; m. Earle Jameson Swan; (dec. 1970); children: Judith Louise, Linda Camille, Calvin Lawrence, Noreen Adell. BA, Conn. Coll. for Women, New London, 1937; MEd, Lewis & Clark Coll., Portland, Oreg., 1964. Tchr. Norwich (Conn.) Free Acad., 1937-38; music-art tchr. Milwaukie (Oreg.) Sch. Dist., 1947-48; music tchr. Skyline Elem. Sch., Washington County, Oreg., 1951-52, Vancouver (Wash.) Sch. Dist., 1952-53, 57-58; tchr. Portland (Oreg.) Sch. Dist., 1958-64, French and Spanish tchr., 1965-72; ret., 1972; pvt. tchr. piano and voice, 1938—. Author: (book) American Cut and Engraved Glass of the Brilliant Period in Historical Perspective, 1986; contbr. articles and poems to numerous publs. Active in local church choirs and various social orgns. Winthrop scholar Conn. Coll. for Women, 1936. Mem. AAUW (antiques chpt. Portland 1980s, sec.-treas.), R.I. Honor Soc. (hon.), Willamette Writers, Am. Cut Glass Assn., Order Eastern Star (program chair 1938-40), Phi Beta Kappa.

SWAN, SANDRA SANDERSON, fund raising and marketing executive; b. Burbank, Calif., Aug. 18, 1942; d. J. Merlin and Wilma H. (Carpenter) Sanderson; m. Bruce Thomas Swan, Feb. 28, 1982; stepchildren: Bruce Thomas Jr., Lisa C., Rodney E. BA, U. Nebr., Kearney, 1963; MA, Baylor U., 1965; MBA, NYU, 1973. Various positions to mgr. publs. Am. Airlines, N.Y.C., 1965-79; devel. dir. Police Athletic League, N.Y.C., 1979-81; pres. Peer Publs., N.Y.C., 1982-83, Wonder Woman Found., N.Y.C., 1984-85, Nat. Corp. Theatre Fund, N.Y.C., 1985—; freelance writer, copy editor, 1988—. Editor, pub.: Footnotes, 1983; contbr. articles to profl. publs. Vice pres. N.Y.C. Opera Guild, 1984-86, 89—; pres. Jr. League N.Y.C., 1986-88. Recipient Vol. of Yr. award Jr. League N.Y.C., 1986; named One of 100 Women Who Run N.Y., Sara Lee Corp., 1987, 88. Mem. Nat. Assn. Fund Raising Execs., Women in Communications, Women in Found.-Corp. Philanthropy, Authors Guild. Republican. Episcopalian. Home: 347 W 22d St New York NY 10011 Office: Nat Corp Theatre Fund 22 Cortlandt St New York NY 10007

SWANBERG, CAROL JEAN, director of admissions; b. N.Y.C., Oct. 28, 1961; d. Raymond J. and Florence J. (Pietrowski) S. BS, U. Pitts., 1983, postgrad. Adminstrv. specialist office admissions and student aid U. Pitts., 1984-85, system adminstr. Grad. Sch. of Bus., 1985-89, asst. dir. admissions Grad. Sch. of Bus., 1989—. Contbr. articles to profl. jours. Mem. NAFE, Am. Mgmt. Assn., Internat. Platform Assn. Roman Catholic. Office: U Pitts Grad Sch Bus 276 Mervis Hall Pittsburgh PA 15260

SWANEY, CYNTHIA ANN, medical computer sales executive, business consultant; b. Garfield Heights, Ohio, Feb. 25, 1959; d. Peter John and Juanita Catherine (Crowle) Christ; m. C. Keith Swaney, Aug. 4, 1984; 1 child, Jason Scott. Grad. high sch., Pepper Pike, Ohio. With Park View Fed. S&L, Cleve., 1975-81; customer svc., teller, trainer Park View Fed. S&L, 1977-81; exec. sec., ops. mgr. Majestic Steel Svc., Solon, Ohio, 1981-84; v.p. adminstrn. Datashare Corp., Mayfield Heights, Ohio, 1984—; cons. Stenciler's Emporium, Hudson, Ohio, 1988—, Deep Springs Trout Club, Chardon, Ohio, 1988—, Hiram House Camp, Moreland Hills, Ohio, 1990—; numerous med. offices, 1986—. Office: Datashare Corp 6801 Mayfield Rd #540 Mayfield Heights OH 44124

SWANGER, CHRISTINA LETITIA, environmental engineer; b. Reading, Pa., July 6, 1963; d. Spencer Glenn and Susan May (Zehner) S. BSChemE, U. Colo., 1986; postgrad., St. Mary's Coll., Moraga, Calif., 1987-88. Design engr. Chevron Corp. Engring., San Ramon, Calif., 1986-88; design engr. Chevron Richmond (Calif.) Refinery, 1988-89, environ. engr., 1989—. tutor Tutor Richmond Youth, 1988-89; active vol. Habitat Restoration Project Gold Gate, Nat. Parks Svc., 1990—. Named Outstanding Sr. Am. Inst. Chem. Engrs., 1986. Mem. Am. Inst. Chem. Engrs., Western States Petroleum Alliance, Bay Area League Indsl. Assns., Sierra Club. Home: 227 Posada Del Sol Novato CA 94949

SWANN, MADELINE BRUCE, chemist, consultant; b. Washington, July 24, 1951; d. Edwin Everette and Ruth Madeline (Rice) S. BA, Fisk U., 1973; PhD, Howard U., 1980. Teaching asst. dept. chemistry Howard U., Washington, 1973-74, teaching fellow dept. chemistry, 1974-80; rsch. chemist U.S. Army Belvoir R & D Engring. Ctr., Ft. Belvoir, Va., 1981-89, chemist, phys. scientist, 1989-90; chemist U.S. Army Materiel Command, Adelphi, Md., 1990—; cons. Tech. Applications Inc., Arlington, Va., 1981. Mem. Am. Chem. Soc., N.Y. Acad. Sci., Orgn. of Black Scientists, Beta Kappa Chi, Sigma Xi. Office: US Army Materiel Command Attn AMCLD-PB 2800 Powder Mill Rd Adelphi MD 20783-1145

SWANN, PATRICIA LAMBERT, editor, periodical; b. Manhattan, Kans., Apr. 4, 1951; d. Jack Leeper and Beatrice (Holub) Lambert; m. Michael M. Swann, Dec. 30, 1978. BA, Kans. State U., 1973, MA, 1977; PhD, Syracuse U., 1989. Teaching asst. Kans. State U., Manhattan, 1973-75, English instr., 1975-76; teaching and rsch. asst. Syracuse (N.Y.) U., 1976-79; rsch. fellow Ctr. for Great Plains Studies U. Nebr., Lincoln, 1979-80, lectr., 1981-83; writer, editor Weather and Environ. Office U.S. Army, Fort Leavenworth, Kans., 1984-85, writer, editor Threats Directorate, 1985-86, editor Command and Gen. Staff Coll., 1986—; profl. indexer, Leavenworth, Kans., 1988—. Mem. Nat. Trust for Hist. Preservation, Washington, Hist. Kans. City (Mo.) Found., Kansas City (Mo.) Archtl. Found., Carnegie Ctr. for the Arts, Leavenworth. Recipient Robert Buzzard Graduate Award in Geography, Gamma Theta Upsilon, Kans. State U., 1974; rsch. grantee, Kans. State U., 1975, Syracuse U., 1978, U. Nebr., 1979-80. Home: 2706 Maple Ave Leavenworth KS 66048 Office: Command/General Staff Coll Bell Hall Fort Leavenworth KS 66027

SWANN, ROBERTA, program director; b. Bklyn., June 17, 1948; d. Louis and Eva (Shurnoff) Cheroff; m. Paul Metz (div. 1975); children: Derek, Nicole; m. Brian Swann, Feb. 14, 1980. Grad. high sch., Bklyn.; diploma, Brooklyn Coll., 1969. Fashion model, 1965-80; adminstr. Downstate Med. Ctr., 1969-75; tchr. Cooper Union, The New Sch., Ind. U., CUNY, 1979—; dir. The Great Hall, 1982—; co-founder Am. Jazz Orch., 1985—; treas., sec. Am. Jazz Orch., N.Y.C., 1985—. Author: Private Parts, 1978, Women the Children the Men, 1979, The Model Life, 1988, Everything Happens Suddenly, 1989. Bd. dirs. Zen Community of N.Y., Yonkers, 1987—. Recipient various awards Poetry Soc. Am., 1980—; McDowell Colony fellow, 1983. Mem. Poets and Writers, Poetry Soc. Am. Home: 19 Stuyvesant Oval New York NY 10003 Office: The Cooper Union 41 Cooper Sq New York NY 10003

SWANSIGER, ROSALIND ELAINE WINDSOR, analytical chemist; b. Anderson, Ind., Sept. 14, 1945; d. Clarence Vernon and Bernice Crystal (Wimmer) Windsor; m. William Andrew Swansiger, June 19, 1965; children: Susan Jeanne, James Andrew. BS in Chemistry, Antioch Coll., 1968. Intern in chemistry Aerospace Rsch. Lab., USAF, Dayton, Ohio, 1964-68; mem. tech. staff Monsanto Rsch. Corp., Dayton, 1968-69; mem. staff, chemist Lawrence Livermore (Calif.) Nat. Lab., 1974—. Mem. Am. Chem. Soc. Office: Lawrence Livermore Nat Lab PO Box 808 L-310 Livermore CA 94550

SWANSON, BEVERLY JANE, records and information management executive; b. Willmar, Minn., Jan. 27, 1949; d. Vernon Leroy and Betty Arlene (Schockley) Fullerton; m. Roger William Swanson, Mar. 21, 1970; children: Tammy Marie, Randolph William. BS in Speech, Mankato (Minn.) State U., 1971. Mgmt. analyst, records mgr. Minn. Dept. Hwys., St. Paul, 1974-76; chief records mgr. Minn. Dept. Adminstrn., St. Paul, 1977-79; records mgr. City of Mpls., 1980—. v.p. Ramsey Youth Athletic Assn.; advisory bd. Minn. Hist. Soc., 1981-83. Named Outstanding Records Mgr. of Yr. IRM mag., 1979. Mem. Assn. Records Mgrs. and Adminstrs. (cert., v.p. region IV 1982-86, membership chmn., sec., treas., v.p., pres. Twin City chpt. 1973-79, mgr. mcpl. county govt. industry action com. 1987—, chair long range planning com. 1987—, parliamentarian Twin City chpt. 1987—, Chpt. Mem. of Yr. award 1980), Inst. Cert. Records Mgrs. and Adminstrs. Lutheran. Home: 7003 164th Ave NW Anoka MN 55303 Office: City of Mpls 300 City Hall Minneapolis MN 55415

SWANSON, DARLENE MARIE CARLSON, speech therapist, educator; b. Boone, Iowa, Aug. 8, 1925; d. Arvid Wilhelm and Edith Marie (Peterson) Carlson; m. Reuben Theodore Swanson, Aug. 8, 1948; children: Conrad T., Joyce Marie Swanson Jobson. BA, Augustana Coll., 1947; postgrad., U. Chgo., 1949, Creighton U., 1972; student, Joslyn Art Mus., Omaha, 1975. Cert. tchr., Ill., Nebr. Speech therapist Rock Island and Rockford (Ill.) Pub. Sch. System, 1946-51, Omaha (Nebr.) Pub. Sch. System, 1963-64; ch. organist Calvary Luth. Ch., Moline, Ill., 1944-46; asst. organist Augustana Luth. Ch., Omaha, 1956-63; mortuary organist Swanson-Golden Mortuary, Omaha, 1956-63; freelance lectr., 1960—; freelance lectr. 1960—; chalk artist lectr. and pub. speaker, retreat leader; observer Luth. World Fedn. Assembly, Budapest, Hungary, 1984. Sunday sch. tchr. Kountze Meml. Luth. Ch., Omaha, 1964-74; Sunday sch. supr. St. Andrew's Luth. Ch., West Hempstead, N.Y., 1951-54; sec. Omaha PTA, 1968-70; mem. adv. coun. Cen. High Sch., Omaha, 1971-74, Omaha Pub. Schs., 1971-74; bd. dirs. Luth. Summer Music Program, 1990—; active Met. Opera Guild, 1986-90, Opera Omaha Guild, 1990—, Omaha Symphony Guild, 1990. Named Vol. of Yr. Omaha Head Start Program, 1965. Home: 11818 Oakair Pla Box 37448 Omaha NE 68137

SWANSON, FERN ROSE, retired educator; b. Kalmar Twp., Minn.; d. Henry E. and Susie (Hastings) Rose; student Winona (Minn.) Normal Coll., 1918-20; BS, St. Cloud (Minn.) State Coll., 1955, MS, 1958; m. Walter E. Swanson, June 24, 1928. Tchr. high sch. English, Latin, Eyota, Minn., 1920-21; tchr. jr. high sch. English, Appleton, Minn., 1921-22; tchr. elem. schs., Harmony, Minn., 1922-23; tchr. high sch. English, Latin, Augusta, Wis., 1923-24, South Haven, Minn., 1924-26; tchr. elem. and high sch. dramatics, Waterville, 1926-27; tchr. elem. schs., South Haven, 1927-41, 43-51, Silver Creek, Minn., 1941-43; tchr. elem. schs., Annandale, Minn., 1951-53, prin., 1953-67; tchr. elem. reading, Belgrade, Minn., 1967-71. Organizer, South Haven coun. Girl Scouts U.S., 1927, leader, 1927-30. Mem. Minn. Elem. Sch. Prins. Assn. (charter mem. 25 Year Club), Ret. Educators Assn. Minn., Minn. Edn. Assn., Nat. Coun. Tchrs. English, Cen. Minn. Reading Coun. (past dir.), Internat., Minn. reading assns., DAR, Ladies of Grand Army Rep. (registrar Lookout Circle, dept. pres. Minn. 1974-77, Betsy Ross Club (nat. pres. 1978, nat. historian 1980-89), nat. patriotic instr. 1981-84, nat. jr. v.p. 1984-85, nat. coun. adminstrn. 1985-88), Minn. Hist. Soc., Rebekah, Nat. Historian Pioneer Club, Delta Kappa Gamma (past chpt. pres., Minn. Woman of Achievement award 1982). Episcopalian. Home: 541 Fairhaven Av South Haven MN 55382

SWANSON, KARIN, hospital administrator, consultant; b. New Britain, Conn., Dec. 8, 1942; d. Oake F. and Ingrid Lauren Swanson; m. B. William Dorsey, June 26, 1965 (div. 1974); children: Matthew W., Julie I., Alison K.; m. Sanford H. Low, Oct. 14, 1989. BA in Biology, Middlebury Coll., 1964;

MPH, Yale U., 1981. Biology tchr. Kents Hill (Maine) Sch., 1964-66; laboratory instr. Bates Coll., Lewiston, Maine, 1974-78; asst. to gen. dir. Mass. Eye and Ear Infirmary, Boston, 1979-80; v.p. profl. services Portsmouth (N.H.) Hosp., 1981-83; v.p. Health Strategy Assn. Ltd., Chestnut Hill, Mass., 1983-85; v.p. med. affairs Cen. Maine Med. Ctr., Lewiston, 1986-89; health care mgmt. cons. Cambridge, Mass. Mem. Phi Beta Kappa. Home and Office: 73 Norfolk St Cambridge MA 02139

SWANSON, MARILYN ANN, food and nutrition specialist; b. Paterson, N.J., Apr. 20, 1945; d. John Lawrence and Florence Mildred (Danielson) Ribbe; m. Barry Grant Swanson, Apr. 4, 1970 (div. Feb. 1988); children: Alyssa Michelle, Krista Jo, Sara Beth; m. Craig George MacFarland, Mar. 19, 1988. BS in Foods and Nutrition, U. Del., 1967; MS in Food Sci., U. Wis., 1969; PhD in Nutrition, Wash. State U., 1987. Nutritionist Waisman Ctr., U. Wis., Madison, 1969-72; cons. dietitian Benewah Community Hosp., St. Maries, Idaho, 1973-79; pub. health nutritionist North Idaho Indian Health Svc., Lapwai, 1977-79; extension nutrition specialist U. Idaho, Moscow, 1979—; food preservation cons. Postharvest Inst. for Perishables, Moscow, 1983—; TV and radio speaker Biessen Communications, N.Y.C., 1987-88. Author: Everything About Exchange Values for Foods, 1973, 4th edit., 1986, Foods of the Pacific Northwest, 1988. Leader Idaho 4-H, Moscow, 1987-89; chmn. health subcom. Idaho-Ecuador Ptnrs. of Ams., Moscow, 1989-91. Recipient Leader award Idaho Home Econs. Assn., 1988, Nat. Leader award Am. Home Econs. Assn., 1989; fellow Nat. Ptnrs. of Ams., 1990. Mem. Am. Dietetic Assn., Inst. Food Technologists (sec. Lewis and Clark sect. 1984-85, regional communicator 1986—; exec. bd. nutrition div. 1989-91), Idaho Dietetic Assn. Lutheran. Home: 836 Mabelle St Moscow ID 83843 Office: U Idaho 108 Home Econs Moscow ID 83843

SWANSON, MARSHA KRISTIN, financial services registered representative; b. Kansas City, Mo., Sept. 3, 1953; d. Harold Albin and Betty Jo (Lusby) S.; m. D. Jefferey Cornett (div. Mar. 1988); children: Caylan Christine, Carla Chantal. BBA in Fin., U. Mo., Kansas City, 1989. Bus. mgr. Belmont Schs., Inc., Kansas City, 1985-89; registered rep. Equitable Fin. Svcs., Overland Park, 1989—. Vol. Children's Mercy Hosp., Kansas City, 1986. Home: 10901 W 102d St Overland Park KS 66214 Office: Equitable Fin Svcs 8500 W 110th St Overland Park KS 66210

SWANSON, MARTHA MADDEN, university student activities director; b. Utica, N.Y., Aug. 23, 1944; d. Eugene and Nancy Jane (Strohecker) Madden; m. David H. Swanson, July 8, 1967; children: Michael, Sarah. AB, Sweet Briar Coll., 1966; AM, Colgate U., 1967. Student activities comptroller Georgetown U., Washington, 1984-85, asst. dir. student activities, 1985-89, dir. student orgns., 1989—. Mem. AAUW, D.C. Coll. Personnel Assn., Am. Coll. Personnel Assn. Office: Georgetown U 37th and O Sts NW Box 2239 Washington DC 20057

SWANSON, PATRICIA K., librarian; b. St. Louis, May 8, 1940; d. Emil Louis and Patricia (McNair) Klick; 1 child, Ivan Clatanoff; m. Don R. Swanson, Aug 22, 1976. B.S. in Edn., U. Mo. 1962; postgrad., Cornell U., 1963; M.L.S., Simmons Coll., 1967. Reference librarian Simmons Coll., Boston, 1967-68; reference librarian U. Chgo., 1970-79, sr. lectr. Grad. Library Sch., 1974-83, 86-88, head reference service, 1979-83, asst. dir. for sci. libraries, 1983—, acting asst. dir. for tech. svcs., 1987-88; project dir. Office Mgmt. Svcs., Assn. Rsch. Librs., 1982-83; speaker in field; cons. on libr. mgmt., planning and space. Author: Great is the Gift that Bringeth Knowledge: Highlights from the History of the John Crerar Library, 1989; contbr. articles to profl. jours. Mem. ALA, Chgo. Library Club, Soc. for Scholarly Pub. Home: 5825 Dorchester Chicago IL 60637 Office: U Chgo John Crerar Libr 5730 S Ellis Ave Chicago IL 60637-1434

SWANSON, PATRICIA LOUISE, reinsurance company executive; b. Manilla, Iowa, June 20, 1948; d. Herbert and Irene (Stolz) S.; m. Jon J. Ebner, June 26, 1965 (div. Jan. 1979); 1 child, Antonette Maria Ebner. Student, U. Nebr., 1976-77. With claims and accounts dept. Mut. Protective Ins. Co., Omaha, 1965-68; claims mgr. Grace-Mayer Ins. Agy., Omaha, 1969-71; reins. claims supr. Nat. Indemnity Co., Omaha, 1972-84; asst. v.p., claims mgr. Cen. Nat. Ins., Omaha, 1984-89, G.L. Hodson & Son, Atlanta, 1989—. Editor: (textbook) Principles of Reinsurance, 1989. Pres. Intercultural Families Adoption Group, Omaha, 1978-79. Roman Catholic. Home: 360 Oak Terr Alpharetta GA 30201

SWANSON, RHONDA WOJAHN, hospital secretary; b. Windom, Minn., May 31, 1955; d. Melvin Ewald and Romelle Gail (Schneider) W.; m. Gregory Roy Swanson, June 3, 1978; 1 child, Erik Jon. AA, Cottey Coll., 1975; BA cum laude, Gustavus Adolphus Coll., 1977; MusM, Ind. U., 1980. Organist, choirmaster St. Timothy's Episcopal Ch., Indpls., 1978-81, Am. Ch. of Copenhagen, 1981-83; prin. sec. Ind. U., Bloomington, 1980-81, prin. records clk. Sch. of Music, 1983-84, dir. music svcs., 1984; dir. music 1st United Meth. Ch., Sparta, Tenn., 1985-86; tech. sec. Tenn. Technol. U., Cookeville, 1984-86; exec. sec. Bapt. Hosp., Nashville, 1986—. George C. Marshall grantee Am.-Scandinavian Found., Copenhagen, 1982. Mem. Am. Guild Organists (Nashville chpt., placement chmn. 1987—), PEO. Lutheran.

SWARDSON, MARY ANNE, mathematics educator; b. Atlanta, Sept. 10, 1928; d. Frank Wesley and Pearle (Spires) Thompson; m. Harold Roland Swardson, Sept. 10, 1949; children: Anne, Catherine, Christine. BA, Tulane U., 1949; MS, Ohio U., 1969, PhD, 1981. Instr. Am. Coll. Switzerland, Leysin, 1969-70; instr. Ohio U., Athens, 1970-80, asst. prof., 1980-89, assoc. prof., 1989—. Contbr. articles to profl. jours. Pres. League of Women Voters, Athens, 1960-62. Mem. Am. Math. Soc., Math. Assn. of Am., Am. Women in Math., Ohio Acad. Sci. (exemplar 1989), Phi Kappa Phi. Episcopalian. Office: Dept Math/Ohio Univ Athens OH 45701

SWARTOUT, JEAN ANN, travel agency executive; b. Catskill, N.Y., Feb. 28, 1945; d. Charles Richard and Vera Mildred (Bower) S. Cert. travel cons. Inst. Cert. Travel Agts. Clk., W.T. Grant Co., Albany, N.Y., 1962-63; mail clk. Mchts. Mut. Ins. Co., Albany, 1963-65; bookkeeper Mountain View Coachline, West Coxsackie, N.Y., 1965-73; mgr. Argus Travel, Inc., West Coxsackie, 1973-84; owner, mgr. Country Side Travel, West Coxsackie, 1984-86, ptnr. West Coxsackie, N.Y., 1986-89. Mem. Women In Travel Services, Town and Country Bus. and Profl. Women's Club (2d v.p. Coxsackie 1985-87, 1st v.p. 1987-89, pres. 1989-90). Roman Catholic. Avocations: music, reading, theatre, travel. Home: 3004 Parkway Blvd #108 Kissimmee FL 34746 Office: Country Side Travel Rt 9-W West Coxsackie NY 12192

SWARTZ, ANN LAMONTAGNE, insurance agent; b. Sanford, Maine, Aug. 6, 1966; d. Lionel J. and Jacqueline Lamontagne; m. Lawrence H. Swartz, June 4, 1988. BA, Clark U., 1988. Cert. LUTC. Ins. planner Mutual of Omaha, Cranston, R.I. Home: 81 Harbour Ave West Warwick RI 02893 Office: 105 Sockanoset Crossroads Ste 314-316 Cranston RI 02920

SWARTZ, MARIA CHRISTINA, financial recruiter; b. Harrisburg, Pa., Feb. 20, 1960; d. Kenneth Dale and Lena Annette (Detoma) S. BSBA, Shippensburg State, 1982; MBA, Loyola Coll., Balt., 1989. Tax staff Arthur Andersen & Co., Balt., 1982-84; acct. Enterprise Found., Columbia, Md., 1984-86; exec. recruiter Don Richard Assocs., Balt., 1986—; bd. dirs. Pet-Coke, Inc., Houston; part-time instr. U. Md. Baltimore County, 1989—. Bd. dirs. Santa Claus Anonymous, Balt., 1986-87. Mem. Nat. Assn. Accts. (bd. dirs. 1986-88), Balt. Jr. Assn. Commerce (bd. dirs. 1988-89, v.p. 1987-88, treas. 1986-87, Key Mem. award 1988, President's citation, 1986, 89, Outstanding New Mem. award 1986). Republican. Roman Catholic. Office: Don Richard Assocs 7 St Paul St Ste 1060 Baltimore MD 21202-1682

SWARTZ, RENEE BECKER, civic volunteer; b. Newark, N.J., Feb. 25, 1935; d. Sidney David and Adeline (Kleinberg) Becker; m. Harry Mason Swartz, Mar. 8, 1931; children: Stephen, Addi-Lyn, Sidney. Student, Rutgers U., 1950-52, Bryn Mawr Coll., 1952-53; BA, Barnard Coll.-Columbia U., 1955. Mem. planning com. N.J. White Ho. Conf. on Librs. and Info. Sci., 1975-79, mem. del. selection com., mem. programs com., 1978-79; chairperson of delegation White Ho. Conf., 1979; permanent N.J. rep. Nat. Commn. Follow-up Activities White Ho. Conf., chairperson nat. awards com., 1984-86, chairperson fund-raising com., 1989-90. Pres. Friends of the Monmouth County Library Assn., 1964-68; founding mem. N.J. Ci-

tizens for Better Libraries, 1982; chairperson bldg. com. Dorothy L. Spiwak Meml. Library, Rumson, N.J., 1971-73, trustee, 1971—; active N.J. Library Devel. Com., 1973-84; chairperson, bd. trustees Grad. Sch. of Communication, Info. and Library Studies, Rutgers U., 1980—, chairperson, 1983—; gov. appointee N.J. State Library Adv. Coun., 1975—, chairperson, 1986—; Monmouth County Library Commn., 1965—, chair, 1976—. Recipient Hannah G. Solomon award Greater Red Bank sect. Nat. Coun. Jewish Women, 1979, Pres. medal Barnard Coll.-Columbia U., 1984, Columbia U. medal, 1985. Mem. Nat. Citizens Com. for Pub. Libraries (steering com. 1980-84), Am. Library Trustee Assn. (pres. com. 1983, nat. intellectual freedom com. 1984—), N.J. Library Assn. (centennial com. 1986-89, chairperson N.J. Ednl. Inst. com. 1987-88, N.J. Trustee of the Yr. 1980), N.J. Library Trustee Assn. (exec. com. 1976-81, regional rep. 1983-86), Assn. N.J. Library Commrs. (pres. 1973-75), Lotus Club N.Y., Ocean Club of N.J. Home: 136 Rumson Rd Rumson NJ 07760

SWARTZ-BUCKLEY, RITA BRYNA, marketing and communications professional, writer; b. Brookline, Mass., June 10, 1955; d. Maxwell Goverman and Vera Edith (Rudman) Swartz; m. Richard Warren Buckley, Sept. 6, 1986. BS summa cum laude, Boston U., 1976; MBA, Northeastern U., Boston, 1978. Writer various publs., Boston, N.Y.C. and Newton, Mass., 1979-82; prof. Salem (Mass.) State Coll., 1982-88; pres. Buckley/Swartz, Inc., Swampscott, Mass., 1982—; contbr. fiction Bread Loaf Writer's Conf., Middlebury, Vt., 1988, 89, 90; pub. rels. dir. North Shore Creative Group, Salem, 1988—. Contbr. articles to Boston Sunday Globe and poetry to Am. Poetry Assn., 1988. Fund raiser Jewish Fedn. North Shore, Marblehead, Mass., 1986—, Am. Heart Assn., Needham, Mass., 1987—. Recipient Merit award North Am. Mentor mag., 1979. Mem. Greenpeace, Amnesty Internat. Democrat. Office: Buckley/Swartz Inc 25 Cedar Hill Terr Swampscott MA 01907

SWARTZELL, ANN GARLING, librarian; b. Elkhart, Ind., Jan. 23, 1955; d. Allen Henry and Barbara (Garling) S. AB, Ind. U., 1977, MLS, 1978. Preservation project librarian Harvard U. Library, Cambridge, Mass., 1978-84; Mellon intern in preservation adminstrn. Yale U. Library, New Haven, 1984; assoc. conservation librarian N.Y. State Libr., Albany, 1985-89; head preservation replacement and photographic svcs. U. Library, U. Calif., Berkeley, 1989—; mem. adv. com. N.E. Document Conservation Ctr., Andover, Mass., 1985-89. Contbr.: book Preservation Microfilm: A Guide for Libraries, 1986 (Leland award 1987). Mem. ALA (vice chair, chair reprodn. library materials sect. 1987-89).

SWATZELL, MARILYN, nurse; b. Johnson City, Tenn., July 31, 1942; d. Dallas Fred and Minnie Thelma (Clark) S. BS cum laude, East Tenn. State U., 1966, MS, 1967; BSN, U. Tenn., 1974. Chmn. pediatric nursing Meth. Hosp. Sch. Nursing, Memphis; head nurse LeBonefir Children's Med. Ctr., Memphis; dir. maternal child nursing Jackson (Tenn.) Madison County Gen. Hosp.; staff nurse Vanderbilt U. Hosp., Nashville; now supr. Meth. Hosp. Lexington, Tenn. Contbr. articles on care plans to profl. jours. Mem. ANA, Tenn. Nurses Assn., Tenn. Orgn. Nurse Execs. Address: 231 Law Loop Lexington TN 38351

SWAYZE, FRANCES GOEHRING, legislator, educator; b. Council Bluffs, Iowa, Feb. 11, 1901; d. William Alfred and Lilian (Huff) Goehring; m. THomas A. Swayze Sr., July 8, 1924 (dec. Oct. 1961); children: Shirley, Gretchen, Thomas A. Jr., Suzanne, George. Ba, U. Puget Sound, 1922. Dean of women U. Puget Sound, Tacoma, 1955-56, asst. to pres., 1957-65; state rep. State of Wash. Legislature, Olympia, 1952-65, trng. officer, 1965-71, ret., 1971. Freeholder City of Tacoma, 1948, 52; del. Meth. Ch. Gen. Conf., 1950-54; chmn. Commn. on Status of Women of the Meth. Ch., 1951-52. Named Mother of the Yr., State of Wash., 1955. Mem. P.E.O., AAUW, Bus. and Profl. Women's Assn., Avon Study Club, Pi Beta Phi. Republican. Home: 7400 Stinson #208 Gig Harbor WA 98335

SWAZEY, JUDITH POUND, institute president, sociomedical sciences educator; b. Bronxville, N.Y., Apr. 21, 1939; d. Robert Earl and Louise Titus (Hanson) Pound; m. Peter Woodman Swazey, Nov. 28, 1964; children: Elizabeth, Peter. AB, Wellesley Coll., 1961; PhD, Harvard U., 1966. Rsch. assoc. Harvard U., 1966-71, lectr., 1969-71, rsch. fellow, 1971-72; cons. com. brain scis. NRC, 1971-73; staff scientist neurosci. rsch. program MIT, Cambridge, Mass., 1973-74; assoc. prof. dept. sociomed. scis. and community medicine Boston U., 1974-77, prof., 1977-80, adj. prof. Schs. Medicine and Pub. Health, 1980—; exec. dir. Medicine in the Public Interest, Inc., Boston and Washington, 1979-82, 89—; pres. Coll. of the Atlantic, Bar Harbor, Maine, 1982-84, Acadia Inst., Bar Harbor, 1984—; mem. Army Sci. Bd. Author: Reflexes and Motor Integration, the Development of Sherrington's Integrative Action Concept, 1969, (with others) Human Aspects of Biomedical Innovation, 1971, (with R.C. Fox) The Courage to Fail, a Social View of Organ Transplants and Hemodialysis, 1975, rev. edit., 1978 (hon. mention Am. Med. Writers Assn., C. Wright Mills award Am. Sociol. Assn.), Chlorpromazine in Psychiatry, a Study of Therapeutic Innovation, 1974, (with K. Reeds) Today's Medicine, Tomorrow's Science, Essays on Paths of Discovery in the Biomedical Sciences, 1978; editor: (with C. Wong) Dilemmas of Dying, Policies and Procedures for Decisions Not to Treat, 1981, (with F. Worden and G. Adelman) The Neurosciences: Paths of Discovery, 1975; assoc. editor IRB: A Jour. of Human Subjects Rsch., 1979—; contbr. articles to profl. jours. Wellesley Coll. scholar, 1961; Wellesley Coll. Alumnae fellow Harvard U., 1966, NIH predoctoral fellow, 1966, Radcliffe Coll. Coll. grad. fellow, 1966. Mem. AAAS (sci. freedom and responsibility com. 1986-89), Inst. Medicine NAS (mem. health scis. policy bd. 1986-89, grad. record exam bd.), Sherrington Soc., Phi Beta Kappa, Sigma Xi. Office: Acadia Inst Bar Harbor ME 04609

SWEARINGEN, MARJORIE EILEEN, educator; b. Colorado Springs, Colo., Apr. 27, 1939; d. Carl Nelson and I. Velma (Young) Jackson; divorced Mar. 1979; children: R. Scott, Kent A., Lisa C. BA, U. No. Colo., 1960; MA, Colo. Coll., 1982. Elem. tchr. El Paso County, Colorado Springs Sch. Dist. #11, Colorado Springs, 1960—. Author unit on Am. History Freedom Found., 1965. Pub. rels. program dir. Am. Edn. Week, 1980-88; pres. Eve Circle St. Paul's United Meth. Ch., 1974-78. Recipient Tchrs. medal Freedoms Found., Valley Forge, 1966, Disting. Tchr. award Colo. Tchr. Award Found., 1983, George Washington Honor medal, 1967. Mem. NEA (life), Colo. Sci. Tchrs., Colo. Edn. Assn. (polit. action com. 1979—, Lion award 1983, Golden Apple award 1988, chair communications commn. 1982-88), Colorado Springs Edn. assn. (officer 1980-88), Colorado Springs High Sch. Palmer Alumni Assn. (publicity dir. 1984), Fun Finders Square Dance Assn., Phi Delta Kappa, Delta Kappa Gamma (profl. affairs com. 1982-86, scholar 1978). Democrat. Home: 1615 Querida Dr Colorado Springs CO 80909 Office: Sch Dist # 11 2400 E Van Buren Colorado Springs CO 80909

SWEASY, JOYCE ELIZABETH, government official, military reserve officer; b. Key West, Fla., Apr. 25, 1948; d. James Alfred and Josephine Mary (Fassel) Messick. BFA, Phila. Coll. Art, 1971; A in Bus. Adminstrn., Howard County Community Coll., 1985; grad., Army Command and Gen. Staff Co., 1988. Commd. 1st lt. U.S. Army, 1978, advanced through grades to maj., 1990; contract specialist U.S. Army, Adelphi, 1978-84, analyst procurement Lab. Command,, 1984-85, chief competition mgmt. office, spl. competition adv./ombuds, 1985—; owner, operator Hand Made 'N Ellicott City, Md., 1983—; ptnr., gen. mgr. Computelt. Contbr. numerous articles to profl. jours. Mem. Font Hill Citizens Orgn., Ellicott City, 1987—. Mem. U.S. Army Res. Officers Assn., Nat. Contract Mgrs. Assn., Am. Def. Preparedness Assn. Republican. Roman Catholic. Home: 4008 Arjay Circle Ellicott City MD 21043 Office: US Army Lab Command 2800 Powder Mill Rd Adelphi MD 20783

SWEC, DIANE MARIE, mechanical engineer, researcher; b. Cleve., Dec. 17, 1959; d. Joseph and Valeria Anne (Potoczak) S. BSChemE, Cleve. State U., 1983; MME, U. Toledo, 1988. Sr. engr. electo physics br. NASA Lewis Rsch. Ctr., Cleve., 1983-89, rsch engr. Stirling Tech. br., 1989—. Contbr. articles to profl. jours. Explorer post advisor Boy Scouts Am., 1984—. Mem. NAFE, Material Rsch. Soc., Internat. Soc. for Optical Engring., Am. Vacuum Soc., Soc. of Women Engrs., Bus. and Profl. Women's Orgn., Theta Phi Alpha (Greater Cleve. Alumni Assn. nat. fundraising chmn. 1988-90). Democrat. Roman Catholic. Home: 4783 Columbia Rd Apt 206

Olmsted OH 44070 Office: NASA Lewis Rsch Ctr 21000 Brookpark Rd. MS 301-2 Cleveland OH 44135

SWEEN, TERRI LYNN, computer analyst, consultant; b. Evanston, Ill., Mar. 29, 1963; d. James Bernard and Joyce Ann (Ellmer) S. BA, DePaul U., 1986, MS, 1988, postgrad., 1988—. Database adminstr. Lake Shore Country Club, Glenco, Ill., 1986-88; pres., founder The PC Pros, Chgo., 1988—; computer analyst DePaul U., Chgo., 1988—. Vol. Big Bros./Big Sister, Lawrence, Kans., 1988-89, Chgo. 49th Ward, 1989—, Miseracordia, Chgo., 1989—; editor DePaul U. Alumni Admissions Coun., Chgo., 1988—. Mem. ABA, Ill. Bar Assn., DePaul Student Bar Assn., Ill. Assn. for Inst. Rsch., NAFE. Home: 1330 W Birchwood Chicago IL 60626 Office: DePaul U 25 E Jackson Chicago IL 60604

SWEENEY, DOROTHY ANNE, real estate broker; b. Detroit, Mar. 25, 1927; d. Charles Louis and Mary Elizabeth (Kane) Jones; m. Donald Hogan, June 3, 1948 (dec. Mar. 1986); children: Sheila, Charles, Gerald, Marjorie; m. Louis Wright Sweeney. Apr. 25, 1987; stepchildren: Joann, Lois, Judy, Kathy, Mark. MusB, Marygrove Coll. Detroit, 1948; MusM, Ball State U., Muncie, 1968. Tchr. Warsaw Community Schs., Warsaw, Ind., 1957-78; realtor Lucas Realtors Better Homes and Gardens, Warsaw, 1980—; clinician St. Frances Coll., Ft. Wayne, 1969. Organist Sacred Heart Ch., Warsaw, 1950—; Bd. dir. Kosciusko Bd. of Realtors, Warsaw, 1981-84, Warsaw Community Devel. Corp., Warsaw, 1983—; Pres. Am. Assn. of U. Women, Warsaw, 1982-84. Named Woman of the Year Sacred Heart Ch., Warsaw, 1985. Mem. Kosciusko Bd. of Realtors (sec.), Kosciusko Bd. of Realtors (dir.), Am. Guild of Organists, Nat. Assn. of Realtors, Ind. Bd. of Realtor, Cert. Residential Specialists (Designee), C. of C. (past pres.), Warsaw Reading Club (pres. 1990). Republican. Roman Catholic. Home: 742 E Oak St Warsaw IN 46580 Office: Lucas Realtors Bh&G 525 E Center St Warsaw IN 46580

SWEENEY, ELIZABETH ANN, medical center executive; b. Birmingham, Ala., Nov. 9, 1946; d. Huretta and Elizabeth (Whisenant) Chappell; children from previous marriage: Wesley, Hugh L. Mitchell. BSN, U. Ala., 1973, MSN, 1975. Staff nurse VA Med. Ctr., Birmingham, 1972-74; asst. prof. nursing Sch. Nursing U. Ala., Birmingham, 1975-79; coordinator nursing services Cen. City Mental Health Ctr., Los Angeles, 1979-80; nurse educator VA Med. Ctr., Los Angeles, 1980—; asst. clin. prof. nursing Sch. Nursing U. Calif., Los Angeles, 1984—; dir. med. ctr. edn. and tng. Kaiser Permanente Med. Ctr., Woodland Hills, Calif., 1989—; asst. dir. Kaiser Permanente Med. Ctr., Bellflower, Calif., 1988; Guest faculty mem. Stanford U., Palo Alto, Calif., 1984; mem. conf. faculty United Nurses Assn. Calif., 1982, 83, 87, Calif. Park and Recreation Soc. Conf., Sacramento, 1985, 86; Equal Employment Opportunity investigator VA, Washington, 1985—. Contbr. articles to profl. jours. Recipient Commendation for Superior Performance Fed. Exec. Bd., Los Angeles, 1984. Mem. Ala. Nurses Assn. (exec. bd. dirs. 1976-79), Am. Nurses Assn., Calif. Nurses Assn., NAFE, Black Women's Network, Coun. Black Nurses. Office: Kaiser Permanente Med Ctr 5601 De Soto Ave Woodland Hills CA 91365

SWEENEY, JULIA, public relations executive; b. Ladonia, Tex., Feb. 2, 1927; d. Albert Earle and Julia (Nunn) S. Grad. Am. Acad., N.Y.C., 1946; student So. Meth. U., 1958-59. Asst. mgr. Ambrosia House, Milw., 1951-56; sec. Neiman-Marcus, Dallas, 1956-70, publicity dir. 1970-74; columnist, feature writer Dallas Times Herald, 1974-81; pres. Callas, Foster & Sweeney, Dallas, 1982—; bd. dirs. Fidelity Nat. Bank of Dallas. Bd. dirs. Boys' Clubs Dallas, Inc., No. Tex. chpt. Arthritis Found., N.E. Tex. chpt. Cystic Fibrosis Found.; trustee Protection of Animal World Soc.; mem. March of Dimes Women's Aux., Dallas Theater Ctr. Women's Com., Dallas Ballet Women's Com. Mem. Pub. Rels. Soc. of Am., Women in Communications, The Women's Found., Dallas C. of C., Dallas Symphony Orch. League, Dallas Mus. Art League, Dallas County Heritage Soc., Dallas Hist. Soc., Les Femmes Du Monde, Internat. Women's Forum, Fashion Industry Coun., Fashion Collectors, Charter 100. Episcopalian. Office: Callas Foster & Sweeney 2515 McKinney Ave Dallas TX 75201

SWEENEY, KAREN A., county official; b. Phila., Feb. 1, 1959; d. Gerald Patrick Sweeney and Kathryn Marie (Bulman) Detky. BS, East Stroudsburg (Pa.) U., 1981, postgrad., 1989—. Gameroom mgr. East Stroudsburg U., 1981-82; social dir. Polmont Lodge and Resort, Bushkill, Pa., 1982; asst. recreation dir. Rank-Ahnert Enterprise, Bushkill, 1982-83, recreation dir., 1984-85; recreation dir. Tree Tops Timesharing-Ahnert Enterprises, Bushkill, 1983-84; exec. dir. Monroe County Recreation and Park Commn., Stroudsburg, Pa., 1985—; mem. adv. coun. recreation dept. East Stroudsburg U., 1987—, practicum and intern supr., 1983—, com. chmn. alumni reunion recreation dept., 1988. Vol. crisis intervention counselor Woman's Resources, Monroe and Pike Counties, Pa., 1988—; cons. recreation Area Agy. on Aging, Monroe, County, 1985—. Mem. Nat. Recreation and Park Assn. ((cert. leisure profl.), Pa. Recreation and Park Soc. (cxonf. speaker 1986), Nat. Youth Sports Coaching Assn. (cert. clinician, chpt. bd. dirs. 1987—), Nat. Archery Assn., AAHPER and Dance, Smithsonian Assocs. Democrat. Roman Catholic. Home: 64 Lenox Ave East Stroudsburg PA 18301

SWEENEY, LISA ANNE, accountant; b. Plainfield, N.J., June 13, 1962; d. Walter James and Denise Jean (Macklin) Bennett; m. Terry Michael Sweeney, Oct. 17, 1987. BBA in Acctg. and Info. Systems, U. Wis., 1984; postgrad., Marquette U., 1989—. CPA, Wis. Asst. acct. Peat Marwick Main & Co., Milw., 1984-85, staff acct., 1985-86, sr. acct., 1986-87, supervisory sr. acct., 1987-88; sr. cost acct. EZ Paintr div. Newell, Milw., 1988-89, sr. cost analyst, 1989-90, supr. cost acctg., 1990, cost acctg. mgr., 1990—; income tax preparer, Waukesha, Wis., 1984—; micro computer cons., Waukesha, 1989—. Acct. St. John Vianney Cath. Ch., Brookfield, Wis., 1984-88; chmn., participant longest day of golf Am. Cancer Soc., Waukesha, 1982-88. Mem. AICPA, Wis. Inst. CPA's (chmn. membership task force 1989—), state membership com. 1989—), Nat. Assn. Accts., Inst. Cert. Mgmt. Accts., U. Wis. Alumni Assn., Mensa. Republican. Home: N24 W22700 Meadowood Pewaukee WI 53072 Office: EZ Paintr Corp 4051 S Iowa Ave Waukesha WI 53186

SWEENEY, SISTER MARGARET MARY, hospital administrator, nun; b. N.Y.C., Oct. 24, 1921; d. Jeremiah and Mary Jane (Dougherty) S. M.B.A., St. John's U., 1966; M.S. in Hosp. Adminstrn., Columbia U., 1970; DSc. (hon.), Iona Coll. 1987. Lic. nursing home adminstr., N.Y. joined Sisters of Charity, Roman Catholic Ch., 1946. Adminstrv. asst. St. Vincent's Hosp., N.Y.C., 1966-68, sr. v.p., 1970-80, pres., 1980—; adminstrv. resident Luth. Med. Ctr., Bklyn., 1969-70; trustee St. Joseph's Hosp., Yonkers, N.Y., 1977—, St. Vincent's Hosp., Harrison, N.Y., 1975—; assoc. prof. N.Y.C. Community Coll., 1973-77; preceptor hosp. adminstrn. Baruch U., George Washington U., N.Y.C., 1974-80; mem. bd. govs. trustee Greater N.Y. Hosp. Assn., 1983—, chmn.-elect, 1989—. Contbr. articles to profl. jours.; contbr. lecture series. Chmn. St. Joseph's Ch. Parish Council, Greenwich Village, N.Y., 1973; trusteeMedic Alert, vice chmn. bd. trustees, 1990—; trustee Coll. Mt. St. Vincent, Sisters of Charity Health Care System, Alliance for Cath. Health Care. Fellow Am. Coll. Hosp. Adminstrs.; mem. Hosp. Fin. Mgmt. Assn., N.Y.C Pub. Health Assn., N.Y. State Hosp. Assn., Delta Mu Delta. Office: St Vincent's Hosp Office of the Pres 153 W 11th St New York NY 10011

SWEENEY, MARY FRANCIS, human resources professional; b. Muncie, Feb. 19, 1938; d. Cecil L. and Irene V. (Gayheart) French; m. Charles H. Sweeney, May 16, 1959; children: Scott, Todd. BA, Ball State U., 1959. Various teaching positions elem. and secondary schs., colleges and adult edn. programs, 1959-75; v.p. human resources Brenton Banks, Des Moines, 1977—; instr. Am. Inst. Banking, Des Moines, 1987—. Bd. dirs. Des Moines Office Edn. Adv. Com., 1978—; chairperson Des Moines employers com., mem. state steering com. Job Svc. of Iowa, 1989—. Mem. Am. Adminstrv. Mgmt. Assn., Am. Compensation Assn., Soc. Human Resource Mgrs., Fin. Women Internat. (pres. Am. chpt. 1985—), Des Moines Fin. Industry Breakfast Group, Greater Des Moines C. of C. (chairperson employers com. 1989-90, fedn. bd. 1990—), Chamber Alliance.

SWEENEY, MARY MARGARET, dance educator, movement analyst; b. Dubuque, Iowa, Feb. 1, 1957; d. Merlin James and Marjorie Helen (Meltzer) S. BA, U. Iowa, 1979; MA, Ohio State U., 1984. Cert. labanotation tchr..

Rsch. assoc. Ohio State U., Columbus, 1982-84, instr., summer 1984, instr. creative arts program, 1985; artistic dir. Dublin (Ohio) Dance Centre, 1985-87; instr. Otterbein (Ohio) Coll., 1986-88; asst. prof. Calif. State U., Chico, 1988—; guest artist, Chico Unified Sch. Dist., 1989—, Greater Columbus (Ohio) Schs., 1985-87, Iowa Ctr. for the Arts, 1982. Mem. wellness planning com. Calif. State U., 1989-90; mem. tng. the young dancer Ohio Dance, 1986-87; editor ADMA newsletter, 1985-86. U. Iowa scholar, 1975-78, State of Iowa scholar, 1975, Lang. Dance Ctr. scholar, 1979. Mem. Nat. Dance Assn., Am. Dance Guild, Calif. Dance Educator's Assn., Laban/Bartenieff Inst., Congress on Rsch. in Dance.

SWEENEY, MAUREEN ROSE, real estate appraiser; b. N.Y., Aug. 21, 1963; d. Charles Hugh and Rose Patricia (Flynn) S. BA, SUNY, Geneseo, 1985. Sr. appraiser Henry Boeckmann Jr. & Assoc. Inc., Babylon, N.Y., 1985-88, N.Y.C., 1989—. Mem. Assn. of Real Estate Women (bd. dirs. 1988-90). Roman Catholic. Office: 306 5th Ave 7th Fl New York NY 10001

SWEET, DEE (MRS. HERBERT A. SWEET), business executive; b. Muskogee, Okla., June 3, 1913; d. Walter Oliver and Lola R. (Morris) McDaniel; student Butler U., 1931, 33, summer sch. Oxford U.; m. Herbert A. Sweet, Aug. 28, 1935; children: Judee Lo, Jill B. Sweet Bowles. Asst. to interior decorator L.S. Ayres & Co., Indpls., 1930-33; co-dir. Acorn Farm Camp, Carmel, Ind., 1933-77; owner Acorn Farm Antiques, Carmel, 1960—, Acorn Farm Workshops, 1972—; dir. TV programs WFBM, Indpls., 1949-54, WISH, Indpls., 1955-60; lectr. adult edn. Ind. U., Purdue U., 1959-69. Co-author Try It books for children. Mem. Appraisers Assn. Am. (sr.), Appraisers Soc. Am. (sr.), Associated Antique Dealers Am., Am. Camping Assn., Am. Women in Radio and TV, Ind. Hist. Soc., C. of C., Asso. Antique Dealers Am., Nat. Audubon Soc. Author newspaper column Ind. Soc. Auctioneers. Home: 15466 Oak Rd Carmel IN 46032

SWEET, MARGE JEAN, controller; b. London, Ky., Mar. 22, 1947; d. Clyde and Ruth (Lewis) Grimes; m. Michael D. Sweet, June 24, 1978; 1 child (by previous marriage) Jennifer Lyn. Student, Ind. U., Richmond, 1987-88. Time keeping coord. Huffman Mfg., Richmond, Ind., 1970-75; payroll mgr. City of Richmond, Ind., 1976-77, deputy controller, 1977-86, city controller; mem. Leadership Wayne Co., Richmond, 1987-. Mem. Gov. Fin. Assn., Controllers Assn. Baptist. Office: City of Richmond 50 N Fifth St Richmond IN 47374

SWEET, SUSAN COOKE, teacher, coach; b. Charleston, S.C., Oct. 9, 1944; d. Walter James Spurgeon and Helen Marie (Cook) Huff; m. James Andrew Sweet; 1 child, Jennifer Suzanne. BS, Ohio State U., 1966. Tchr. Frankfort (Ind.) Sr. High Sch., 1966-68, Frankfort Jr. High Sch., 1969-70; tchr., coach Toledo (Ohio) Schs., 1971-77, Maumee (Ohio) City Schs., 1977-80, L.A. Unified Sch. Dist., 1985—; head varsity basketball coach Toledo City Schs., 1972-76, varsity track coach, 1973-75; varsity/jr. varsity basketball coach Maumee City Schs., 1977-80, U.S. Grant High Sch., 1985—, softball coach, 1986—; coach Ohio State AAA Girls Basketball Championship, 1976. Vol. ARC, Frankfort, 1966, 70, Toledo, 1971-84. Named Coach of Yr. Ohio State AAA Girls Basketball Championship, 1976. Fellow NEA, United Tchrs. L.A., Calif. Tchrs. Assn., Doberman Pinscher Club of Maumee Valley, Alpha Xi Delta (v.p. 1965-66), Coaches of L.A. for Women's Sports, North Ranch Country Club. Republican. Presbyterian. Home: 16847 Bosque Dr Encino CA 91436 Office: US Grant High Sch 13000 Oxnard St Van Nuys CA 91401

SWEETING, LINDA MARIE, chemist; b. Toronto, Ont., Can., Dec. 11, 1941; came to U.S., 1965, naturalized, 1979; d. Stanley H. and Mary (Robertson) S.; BSc, U. Toronto, 1964, MA, 1965; PhD, UCLA, 1969. Asst. prof. chemistry Occidental Coll., Los Angeles, 1969-70; asst. prof. chemistry Towson (Md.) State U., 1970-75, assoc. prof., 1975-85, prof., 1985—; guest worker NIH, 1976-77; program dir. chem. instrumentation NSF, 1981-82; vis. scholar Harvard U., 1984-85. Bd. dirs. Chamber Music Soc. Balt. Mem. Md. Acad. Scis. (mem. sci. council 1975-83, 89—), Assn. for Women in Sci. (treas. 1977-78), Am. Chem. Soc. (mem. women chemists Conn. 1983-89), AAAS, Wilderness Soc. (exec. com. Exptl. NMR Conf. 1985-87), Nature Conservancy, Aircraft Owners and Pilots Assn., Sierra Club, Sigma Xi (sec. TSU Club 1979-81, pres. 1987-88, mid-Atlantic nominating com. 1987—, regional dir. 1988-89). Office: Towson State U Dept Chemistry Baltimore MD 21204*

SWEGER, GLENDA LEE, educator; b. Harrisburg, Pa., July 26, 1946; d. George Glenn and Bertha Alverta (Kitner) S. BS, Ind. U. of Pa., Indiana, Pa., 1968; MA, Calif. State U., Fullerton, 1981. Cert. tchr. Calif. Tchr. Greensburg-Salem (Pa.) Unified Sch. Dist., 1968-69, Covina-Valley (Calif.) Unified Sch. Dist., 1969—; bd. dirs. SCSPA, San Diego, 1972-82; publs. advisor Northview High Sch., Covina, 1970—, accreditation chmn. 1987—; lectr. Great Am. Lecture Series, Covina, 1988—; mentor tchr. 1989—; mem. Curriculum Devel. Adv. Bd., Staff Devel. Com.; chair Sch. Environment Com. Author: Male & Female Reporters: Differences in Readers' Perceptions, 1981. Active PTA, Covina, 1969—, SPRING, Seal Beach, Calif., 1987—, Orange County AIDS Found., Calif., 1987—, Ellis Island Found., N.Y.C., 1986—, Statue of Liberty Found., N.Y.C., 1984—. Recipient SCV Educators' grant, Covina-Valley Unifed Sch. Dist., 1986. Mem. Nat. Edn. Assn., Calif. Tchrs. Assn., Covina Unifed Edn. Assn., Nat. Coun. Tchrs of English, Calif. Assn. for Tchrs of English, Calif. Scholastic Press Assn., Columbia Scholastic Press Advisors Assn., Journalism Edn. Assn., So. Calif. Journalism Edn. Assn., So. Calif. Scholastic Press Assn. (sec. 1976-82, bd. dirs.), So. Calif. Scholastic Publs. Assn., Southland Assn. for Tchrs. of English, IUP Alumni Assn., Fullerton Alumni Assn. Democrat. Evagelical Lutheran. Home: 3372 Rowena Dr Rossmoor CA 90720 Office: Northview High Sch 1016 W Cypress Ave Covina CA 91722

SWEITZER, KAROL M., telephone company executive; b. Anna, Ill., May 26, 1959; d. Karl M. and Agnes M. (White) S.; m. Gary S. Gill, June 22, 1985. BS in Acctg., BSBA, MacMurray Coll., Jacksonville, Ill., 1981; BS in Bus. Adminstrn., Mac Murray Coll., Jacksonville, Ill., 1981. CPA. Mgr. Caterpillar Tractor Co., Peoria, Ill., 1982, Rockwell Internat., Iowa, 1983-85, Southwestern Bell Telephone Co., St. Louis, 1985—. Mem. Profl. Bus. Women Southwestern Bell. Home: 4891 Southridge Park Dr Saint Louis MO 63129

SWENN, GAYLENE LOUISE, pharmacist; b. Pampa, Tex., Aug. 11, 1953; d. Alexander and Leota Joye (Barnes) S. Student, Tex. Tech U., 1971-72; BS in Pharmacy, Southwestern Okla. State U., 1976. Intern Buffalo (Okla.) Clinic Pharmacy, 1976; staff pharmacist Cen. Plains Regional Hosp., Plainview, Tex., 1976-78; pharmacist, mgr. Revco Drug, Plainview, 1978-79, K-Mart Pharmacy, Plainview, 1979—; pharmacy cons. Buffalo Nursing Home, 1976; cons. Cen. Plains MHMR Crisis Unit. Mem. Hale County Foster Parent Assn., 1987. Recipient Outstanding Foster Parent award, 1987-88, Friend of MHMR award, 1988. Mem. Am. Pharm. Assn., Kappa Epsilon. Republican. Pentecostal. Home: 2709 Holliday Dr Plainview TX 79072 Office: K-Mart Corp 2801 Dimmitt Rd Plainview TX 79072

SWENSON, BARBARA A., business executive; b. Tacoma, Wash., Mar. 22, 1947; d. Robert Alan and Vivian Marie (Russell) Bartlett; children: Timothy, Julie, Aimee. BA, Pacific Luth. U., 1973; MEd, U. Puget Sound, 1974, MBA, 1983. Cert. tchr., ednl. adminstr. Market analyst Quinton Instrument Co., Seattle; v.p. sales and mktg. Corazonix Corp., Oklahoma City; dir. sales and mktg. Digital Medicine, Cambridge, Mass.; v.p. mktg. and sales Luxtex Corp., Sturbridge, Mass.; mng. ptnr., founder The Bartlett Co., Natick, Mass. Active United Way, C. of C., Dept. Employment Tng.. Mem. AMA, NOW, NAFE, New England Women Bus. Owners. Democrat. Address: 3 Hilldale Pl Ashland MA 01721 Office: 251 W Central St Ste 132 Natick MA 01760

SWENSON, KATHLEEN SUSAN, music and art teacher; b. Reno, Nev., Oct. 23, 1938; d. Harold Ruthaford McNeil and Hollyce Margaret (Scruggs) McNeil Biggs; m. James Michael Phalan, 1956 (div. 1974); children: David Michael, Jeanine Louise Phalan Lawrence, Gregory Shaun; m. Gerald Allen Swensen, Nov. 1976 (div. 1987); stepchildren: Craig Allen, Sarah Ann, Eric Sander. Student, U. Nev., Reno, 1956-58, Foothill Coll., 1966-68; AA, West Valley Coll.; BA, U. Calif., Santa Cruz, 1983. Concert pianist Nev.,Calif,

1950-64; pvt. piano instr. various locations, 1963—, pvt. art instr., 1970—, pvt. astrology instr., 1973—; founder, pres. AAM Triple Arts, Aptos, Calif., 1974—. Producer, instr. art instrn. videos. Mem. Soc Western Artists, Calif. Piano Tchrs. Assn., Los Gatos Art Assn. (pres. 1985-86), Saratoga Contemporary Artists (v.p. 1984-85), Nat. League Am. Pen Women (honorarian 1985). Republican. Episcopalian. Home and Office: AAM Triple Arts 3000 Wisteria Way Aptos CA 95003

SWENSON, VICTORIA SUE, optical company sales official; b. Denver, Apr. 6, 1956; d. Robert Edward and Sonja Anne (Ingersoll) Osborne; m. Fredrick E. Swenson, Sept. 20, 1975 (div. 1983). BA with distinction, U. Colo., 1978. Mktg. asst. Univ. Nat. Bank, Denver, 1978-79; mktg. cons. John A Pratt & Assocs., Inc., Lakewood, Colo., 1979-83; v.p., dir. mktg. Citizens Bank Aurora, Colo., 1983-84; ter. mgr. Allergan Pharms., Denver, 1984-87; product mgr. Allergan Optical, Irvine, Calif., 1987-89, mgr. sales tng., 1989—. Scholar U. Colo. Bd. Regents, 1977. Mem. U. Colo. Alumni Assn., Phi Beta Kappa. Democrat. Office: 2 Flagstone Apt 425 Irvine CA 92714 Office: Allergan Optical 2525 DuPont Dr Irvine CA 92715

SWERDLOW, AMY, historian, educator; b. N.Y.C., Jan. 20, 1923; d. Joseph and Esther (Rodner) Galstuck; m. Stanley H. Swerdlow, Nov. 27, 1949; children: Joan Swerdlow-Brandt, Ezra, Lisa Thomas. BA, NYU, 1963; MA, Sarah Lawrence Coll., 1973; PhD, Rutgers U., 1984. Prof. Sarah Lawrence Coll., Bronxville, N.Y., 1981—, dir. grad. studies in women's history, 1983—, dir. women's studies program, 1983—. Editor, co-author: Families in Flux, 1980, reprint, 1989; editor: Feminist Perspectives on Homework and Childcare, 1978; co-editor: Class, Race and Sex: The Dynamics of Control, 1983; contbr. articles to profl. jours. Rutgers U. fellow, 1977-81, Woodrow Wilson Dissertation fellow, 1980. Mem. Am. Hist. Assn. Home: 2 Hedges Banks Dr East Hampton NY 11937 Office: Sarah Lawrence Coll Bronxville NY 10708

SWERGOLD, MARCELLE MIRIAM, sculptor; b. Antwerp, Belgium, Sept. 6, 1927; came to U.S., 1939, naturalized, 1947; d. Gillel and Sarah (Matuzewitz) Elfenbein; student NYU, Art Students League, Sculptors Workshop; m. Maurice Swergold, June 12, 1949; children—Diane Botnick, Henry, Gary Swergold, Paul Kogan, George Kogan. Sculptor, 1965—; one-woman exhbns. include: Studio 12, N.Y.C., 1980, 82, 86, Nat. Fedn. Temple Sisterhoods, 1984; group exhbns. include Farleigh Dickinson U., Teaneck, N.J., 1972, Audubon Artist Ann., N.Y.C., 1978-86, Internat. Treasury Fine Arts, Plainview, N.Y., 1979, New Britain (Conn.) Mus., 1980, also Cork Gallery, Lincoln Center, N.Y.C., Allied Artists Nat. Acad. Galleries, N.Y.C., U.S. Custom House, N.Y.C., others; represented in permanent collection New Britain Mus. Am. Art Yad Vashem Sculpture Garden, Holocaust Mus., Jerusalem; represented in pvt. collection of Master Moshe Castel, Israel. Recipient Best in Show award for Tetons, Women's Art Gallery, N.Y.C., 1977, 1st prize for sculpture Stanley Richter Assn. Arts, 1985, Vincent Glinski Meml. award Audubon Artists, 1986. Mem. N.Y. Soc. Women Artists (pres. 1979-81, exec. v.p. 1981—), Artists Equity, Contemporary Artists Guild. Home: 43 Paul St Danbury CT 06810 Studio: 246 W 80th St New York NY 10024

SWETCHARNIK, SARA MORRIS, artist; b. Shelby, N.C., May 21, 1955; d. William Monroe and Nydia (Earley) Morris; m. William Norton Swetcharnik. Grad., Schuler Sch. Fine Arts, Balt., 1978, postgrad., 1978-79; student, Art Students League, N.Y.C., 1979-81. Monitor for Robert Beverly Hale Art Students League, N.Y.C., 1979-81. One-person exhbns. include Catepetl Gallery, Frederick, Md., 1977; exhibited in group shows at Christ Ch., Tarrytown, N.Y., 1982, Mt. St. Mary's Coll., Emmitsburg, Md., 1981, Weinberg Ctr. for the Arts, Frederick, 1980, Landon Sch., Bethesda, Md., Eikon Fine Arts, Frederick, 1979, Genesis Arts, Frederick, 1978, Foxhall Gallery, Washington, 1982-85, Harbor Gallery, Cold Spring Harbor, N.Y., Jaffae Gallery, Balt., 1979-81, Catepetl Gallery, 1975-79; competitive shows include Pastel Soc. of Am., N.Y.C., Miniature Painters, Sculptors and Gravers Soc., Washington; represented in pub. collections Haussner's Restaurant, Balt. Recipient Fulbright grant, 1987-88, 88-89, Art Students League, N.Y.C., 1987-89; scholarship, Schuler Sch. Fine Arts, Balt., 1978-79; 1st Pl. sculpture award, Miniature Soc. of Sculptors, Painters, and Gravers, Washington, 1976, Allegheny Internat. Miniature Art Exhibit, 1989. Home Studio: 7044 Woodville Rd Mount Airy MD 21771

SWETMON, SHARON THOMPSON, radiologic technologist; b. Rockwood, Tenn., June 10, 1957; d. Otis Garland Thompson and Willie Charlene (Brady) Smith; m. Kem English Morgan, Dec. 27, 1983 (div. July 1986); m. Carter Swetmon, June 13, 1988. AS in Radiologic Tech., Chattanooga State Tech., 1979; student, U. Tenn., Chattanooga, 1979, 83, 87. Staff technologist T.C. Thompson Children's Hosp., Chattanooga, 1976-84; staff technician South Pittsburg (Tenn.) Hosp., 1984-85; magnetic resonance technologist Diagnostic Imaging, Chattanooga, 1985-88; magnetic resonance tech. coord. Chattanooga Outpatient Ctr., 1985-88; magnetic resonance imaging tech. dir. Erlanger Plaza MRI, 1988—, instr., cons., 1989—; asst. dir. nurse asst. program Edmondson Jr. Coll., Chattanooga, 1983-84. Mem. U.S. Senatorial Bus. Adv. Bd., 1988—, Omni Adv. Bd., 1987-89. Mem. Soc. Magnetic Resonance Imaging, Am. Soc. Radiologic Technologists, Tenn. Soc. Radiologic Technologists, Possum Pack Ski Club, Scuba Club. Home: 3600 Gold Point Circle Hixson TN 37343 Office: Erlanger Plaza MRI 979 E 3d St Chattanooga TN 37403

SWIFT, EVANGELINE WILSON, lawyer; b. San Antonio, May 2, 1939; d. Raymond E. and Josephine (Woods) Wilson; 1 child, Justin Lee. Student So. Meth. U., 1956-59; LL.B., St. Mary's U., San Antonio, 1963. Bar: Tex. 1963, U.S. Ct. Appeals (5th cir.) 1972, D.C. 1976, U.S. Dist. Ct. D.C. 1976, U.S. Supreme Ct. 1980, U.S. Ct. Appeals (11th cir.) 1981, U.S. Ct. Appeals (10th cir.) 1982, U.S. Ct. Appeals (D.C. cir.) 1983, U.S. Ct. Appeals (fed. cir.) 1983. Atty.-adv. ICC, Washington, 1964-65; staff atty. Headstart Program, OEO, Washington, 1965; exec. legal asst. to chmn. spl. asst. to vice chmn. EEOC, Washington, 1965-71, chief decisions div., 1971-75, asst. gen. counsel, 1975-76; cons. to sec. Employment Standards Adminstrn., Dept. Labor, Washington, 1977-79; ptnr. Swift & Swift, P.C., Washington, 1977-79; gen. counsel Merit Systems Protection Bd., Washington, 1979-86, mng. dir., 1986—; dir. policy and evaluation, 1987—; bd. govs. U.S. Ct. Appeals (fed. cir.) Bar Assn., 1984—, treas., 1987-89, sec., 1989—; guest lectr. Drake U., U. Pa., MIT; mem. U.S. del. 23d Sessions UN Commn. on Status of Women, Geneva, 1970. Recipient Meritorious Service award Fed. Govt., 1967, Fed. Women's award, 1975, Performance award Merit Systems Protection Bd., 1981-86, 88-89, Gold award 1986, Presdl. CFC award, 1984, 86, EEO award Merit Systems Protection Bd., 1985, Theodore Roosevelt awrd, 1988. Methodist. Office: Merit System Protection Bd Office of Policy and Evaluation 1120 Vermont Ave NW Washington DC 20419

SWIGER, ELINOR PORTER, lawyer; b. Cleve., Aug. 1, 1927; d. Louie Charles and Mary Isabelle (Shank) Porter; m. Quentin Gilbert Swiger, Feb. 5, 1955; children: Andrew Porter, Clavin Gilbert, Charles Robinson. BA, Ohio State U., 1949, JD, 1951. Bar: Ohio 1951, Ill. 1979. Sr. assoc. Robbins, Schwartz, Nicholas, Lifton & Taylor, Ltd., Chgo., 1979—. Author: Mexico for Kids, 1971, Europe for Young Travelers, 1972, The Law and You, 1973 (Literary Guild award), Careers in the Legal Professions, 1978, Women Lawyers at Work, 1978, Law in Everday Life, 1977. Mem. Northfield Twp. (Ill.) Bd. Edn., 1976-83; mem. Glenview (Ill.) Fire and Police Commn., 1976-86; chmn. Glenview Zoning Bd. Appeals, 1987—. Mem. ABA (chmn. pub. edn. com. urban, state and local govt. sect. 1982-85), Ill. Bar Assn. (chmn. local govt. sect. 1986-87, vice chmn. legal edn. sect. 1990-91), Chgo. Bar Assn. (chmn. legis.-exec. com. 1990—), Women Bar Assn. Ill., Midland Authors. Republican. Home: 1933 Burr Oak Dr Glenview IL 60025 Office: Robbins Schwartz Nicholas Lifton & Taylor 29 S LaSalle St Ste 860 Chicago IL 60603

SWIGER, ELIZABETH DAVIS, chemistry educator; b. Morgantown, W.Va., June 27, 1926; d. Hannibal Albert and Tyreeca Elizabeth (Stemple) Davis; m. William Eugene Swiger, June 2, 1948; children: Susan Elizabeth Swiger Knotts, Wayne William. BS in Chemistry, W.Va. U., 1948, MS in Chemistry, 1952, PhD in Chemistry, 1964. Instr. math. Fairmont (W.Va.) State Coll., 1948-49, instr. math. and phys. sci., 1956-57, instr. chemistry 1957-60, asst. prof. chemistry, 1960-63, assoc. prof. chemistry, 1964-66, prof. chemistry, 1966—; NSF fellow rsch. W.Va. U., Morgantown, 1963-64; advisor Am. Chem. Soc. student affiliates, 1965-88. Author: Morton Family

History, 1984-90, Davis-Winters Family History, 1990; contbr. articles to profl. jours. Bd. mem. Prickett's Fort Meml. Found., Fairmont, 1988—; rep. Adv. Coun. to Bd. Regnets Fairmont State Coll., Charleston, 1977-79, rep. instl. bd. advisors, Fairmont, 1990—. NSF grantee, 1963; named Outstanding Prof. W.Va. Legislature, Charleston, 1990. Mem. Am. Chem. Soc. (sect. chmn. North W.Va. 1975, 83), W.Va. Acad. Sci. (exec. com., edn. chmn. 1990), The Nature Conservancy (bd. mem. W.Va. chpt. 1980-82). Republican. Methodist. Home: 1599 Hillcrest Rd Fairmont WV 26554 Office: Fairmont State Coll Locust Ave Fairmont WV 26554

SWIHART, PATRICIA PEARL, financial official; b. Mansfield, Ohio, Feb. 14, 1932; d. Charles Curtis and Catherine Lucille (Reiter) Lysinger; m. Murray Glen Swihart, June 16, 1951; children: Mark J., Marianne K. Swihart Witt. BS, Westminster Coll., Salt Lake City, 1989. Owner, mgr. acctg. co., Ohio, 1951-68; acct. Goodwill Industries, Sandusky, Ohio, 1976-78; bus. mgr. various automobile dealerships, Ohio, 1968-80; office mgr. Dave Jolley Chevrolet, Vernal, Utah, 1981-82, Myke & Gary's, Vernal, 1982-84; fiscal mgr. Utah Ind. Living Ctr., Inc., Salt Lake City, 1985—; owner, mgr. P.A.T.S. (Profl. Acctg. & Tax Svc.), NorthSalt Lake, Utah, 1990—. Designer costumes and sets for community theater, 1966-78. Pres. Shoestring Players, Milan, Ohio, 1978; treas. Community Action Program, Salt Lake City, 1987—; bd. dirs. Utah Issues, Salt Lake City. Ross Beason scholar Westminster Coll., 1988-89. Mem. NAFE. Democrat. Office: Utah Ind Living Ctr Inc 764 South 200 West Salt Lake City UT 84101-2700

SWINDALL, SARAH EARLENE, archivist; b. Stringtown, Okla., July 31, 1941; d. Earl Henry and Iona Belle (Welch) Magby; m. Donald Wayne Swindall, June 13, 1960; children: William Dennis Garrison, Earl Albert Garrison. BA, Cen. State U., Edmond, Okla., 1966; MS, U. North Tex, 1990. Cert. records mgr. Supr. records mgmt. Lone Star Gas Enserch Corp., Dallas, 1970-77; microforms analyst Bell Helicopter Textron, Ft. Worth, 1977-81; adminstrv. supr. Continental Telephone of Tex., Dallas, 1982-84; adminstrn. records mgmt. Dallas/Ft. Worth Internat. Airport Bd., Dallas, 1984-90; archivist records mgmt. Superconducting Super Collider Lab., Dallas, 1990—; speaker in field. Mem. adminstrv. bd., trustee St. Paul United Meth. Ch. Recipient Merit award Tex. State Libr. 1988, Olsten Disting. Achievement award Olsten Corp., 1989. Mem. Assn. Records Mgrs. and Adminstrs. (pres. Dallas chpt., Chpt. Mem. of the Yr. 1975, 87), Assn. Info. and Image Mgmt. (pres. Dallas-Ft. Worth chpt.), Spl. Librs. Assn., Soc. Am. Archivists, Soc. S.W. Archivists. Republican. Mailing: PO Box 1252 Hurst TX 76053 Office: Superconducting Super Collider Lab 2550 Beckleymeade Ave Dallas TX 75237

SWINDELLS, SUSAN PETERS, teacher; b. Newport News, Va., Sept. 17, 1952; d. Roger William and Sarah (Johnston) P.; m. Redd Stanley, May 25, 1985. BA, Lynchburg Clg., Va., 1974; MusM, Eastman Sch., Rochester, 1976. N.Y. State Teaching Certification. Elem. music teacher Fulton Consolidated Sch., N.Y.C., 1974-83, Oswego City Schools, N.Y., 1983; cons., singer, bd. mem. Oswego Opera Theatre Inc.; clinician N.Y. State Sch. Music Assn. Author: Teachers Guide to HMS Pinafore, Hansel and Gretel, Magic Flute, La Boheme, Barber of Seville, Tales of Hoffman, Noye's Fludde, La Cenerentola, Amahl and the Night Visitors. Performer Summer Lyric Theatre; mem. Heritage Found., Oswego Festival Chorus. Mem. Music Educator Nat. Conf., Oswego County Music Assn. Home: 134 E Seneca St Oswego NY 13126

SWIRE, EDITH WYPLER, music educator, musician; b. Boston, Feb. 16, 1943; d. Alfred Robert Jr. and Frances Glenn (Emery) Wypler; m. James Bennett Swire, June 11, 1965; 1 child, Elizabeth Emery. BA, Wellesley (Mass.) Coll., 1965; MFA, Sarah Lawrence Coll., Bronxville, N.Y., 1983; postgrad., Coll. of New Rochelle, 1984-85. Tchr. instrumental music The Windsor Sch., Boston, 1965-66; tchr., dir. The Lenox Sch., N.Y.C., 1967-76; music curriculum devel. The Nightingale-Bamford Sch., N.Y.C., 1968-69; head of fine arts dept. The Lenox Sch., N.Y.C., 1976-78, head of instrumental music, 1978-80; founder, dir., tchr. of string sch. Serpentine String Sch., Larchmont, N.Y., 1981—; mem. Founding Schs. com. of the Ind. Sch. Orch., N.Y.C., 1972; trustee Ind. Schs. Orchs., N.Y.C., 1976-87; designated panelist Nat. Assn. of Ind. Schs. Conf., N.Y.C., 1977. Mem. music and worship com., Larchmont Ave. Ch., 1978-82, 88. Mem. Westchester Musicians Guild, N.Y. State Music Tchrs. Assn., Music Tchrs. Nat. Assn., Music Tchrs. Coun. Westchester (program com.), Violin Soc. Am., Wellesley in Westchester. Republican. Home and Office: 11 Serpentine Trail Larchmont NY 10538

SWIRSKY, JUDITH PERLMAN, arts administrator, consultant; b. Bklyn., Oct. 31, 1928; d. Samuel and Rose (Klein) Perlman; m. Leo Jerome Swirsky, June 26, 1949; 1 child, Marjorie Ann Swirsky Zelner. BA, NYU, 1947; postgrad., Columbia U., 1947-48. Rsch. asst. The Bklyn. Mus., 1947-49, vol. coord., 1983-89; exec. dir. Grand Cen. Art Galleries Edn. Assn., N.Y.C., 1988-90; freelance curator Genest Gallery, Lamberville, N.J., 1990—; Dir. art sales and rental Gallery The Bklyn. Mus., 1974-77; del. Vol. Com. of Art Mus., Balt., 1973, panelist, 1979; mem., co-founder Vol. Program Administrs. N.Y.C. Cultural Inst., 1984—. Pres. Community Com. for the Bklyn. Mus., 1969-70; bd. dirs. Greater N.Y. Girl Scouts U.S., 1965-71; founder Children's Sch. Time Program and Women's League, Bklyn. Acad. Music, 1961-64; chmn. Bklyn. Guild for Opera, 1966-77; bd. dirs. Arthritis Found. Greater N.Y., 1969-79; trustee Bklyn. Home for Children, 1961-70, Julia Bernstein League of the Free Nurses Inst., 1952-60. Mem. Am. Assn. Mus., Assn. Vol. Adminstrn. (cert., editor region II newsletter), Am. Assn. Mus. Vols., Civitas. Home and Office: 57 Montague St Brooklyn NY 11201-3374

SWISTAK, IRENA, international management executive; b. Meriden, Conn., Oct. 18, 1964; d. Ben and Julia Swistak. BS in Internat. Mgmt., Cen. Conn. State U., 1987. With GE Capital Corp., Rocky Hill, Ct. Patentee sales limit indicator. Chair alumni adv. bd. Cen. Conn. State U. Recipient Spl. Merit award Meriden Record Jour.; named Alumna of Yr., Cen. Conn. State U. Sch. Bus., 1989-90. Mem. NAFE, Am. Mgmt. Assn. Home: 51 Carl St Meriden CT 06450

SWIT, LORETTA, actress; b. Passaic, N.J., Nov. 4, 1937. Student, Am. Acad. Dramatic Arts, Gene Frankel Repertoire Theatre, N.Y.C. Stage appearances include Same Time Next Year, Any Wednesday, The Mystery of Edwin Drood, toured in Maine, Shirley Valentine, Chgo., 1990; films include Stand Up and Be Counted, 1972, Freebie and the Bean, 1974, Race with the Devil, 1975, S.O.B, 1980, Beer, 1985; co-star: TV series M*A*S*H, 1972-83 (Emmy awards for Outstanding Supporting Actress in a Comedy series 1979-81); TV movies Mirror, Mirror, Valentine, Friendships, Secrets and Lies, Shirts and Skins, Coffeeville, Cagney and Lacey, Games Mother Never Taught You, First Affair, The Execution, Dreams of Gold, 14 Going on 30, My Dad Can't be Crazy, Can He?; star on maj. dramatic shows and musical variety shows, including Bob Hope Christmas Special. Mem. AFTRA, Screen Actors Guild, Actors Equity. Address: care Agy for Performing Arts 9000 Sunset Blvd Los Angeles CA 90069*

SWITALSKI, JOYCE DOOLEY, corporate communicatons specialist; b. Manville, N.J., Apr. 28, 1947; d. James Joseph and Mae (Melnyk) Dooley; m. Thomas Adam Switalski, June 13, 1970; children: Thomas J. Adam, Maureen. Student, Montgomery County Community, Blue Bell, Pa., 1988; grad. magna cum laude, Temple U., 1990. Flight attendant Delta Airlines, Boston, 1967-70; part-time pub. rels. cons. Kremp's Teh Am. Flower Market, Gwynedd, Pa., 1981-85; part-time pub. rels. liaison Simon Group, Spring Horse, Pa., 1985-86; market rsch. intern Earle, Palmer, Brown & Spiro, Phila., 1990—. Contbr. articles to profl. jours. pres. Jr. Colony Club of Ambler, 1978-80, St. Anthony's Sch. PTO, Ambler, 1982-84; mem. Lower Gwynedd Pk. & Recreation Bd., Spring Home, 1985-89; chmn. lobbist L.G. Residents Protection Zoning Laws, 1985-90. Mem. Am. Cancer Soc. (Ambler, Pa. info. chmn. hospice, driver 1978-87), Women in communications, Inc., AAUW, Student Govt. Assn., Kappa Tau Alpha, Phi Alpha Theta, Golden Key Nat. Honor Soc., Phi Theta Kappa. Home: Box 224 Spring House PA 19477

SWITTEN, MARGARET LOUISE, French language educator; b. Chgo., m. Henry N. Switten (dec.). B.Mus., Westminster Choir Coll., 1947; B.A., Barnard Coll., 1948; M.A., Bryn Mawr Coll., 1949, Ph.D., 1952. Asst. prof. music and French, assoc. prof., then prof. French Hampton Univ., 1952-63; mem. faculty Mt. Holyoke Coll., South Hadley, Mass., 1963—, Alumnae

MPH, Yale U., 1981. Biology tchr. Kents Hill (Maine) Sch., 1964-66; laboratory instr. Bates Coll., Lewiston, Maine, 1974-78; asst. to gen. dir. Mass. Eye and Ear Infirmary, Boston, 1979-80; v.p. profl. services Portsmouth (N.H.) Hosp., 1981-83; v.p. Health Strategy Assn. Ltd., Chestnut Hill, Mass., 1983-85; v.p. med. affairs Cen. Maine Med. Ctr., Lewiston, 1986-89; health care mgmt. cons. Cambridge, Mass. Mem. Phi Beta Kappa. Home and Office: 73 Norfolk St Cambridge MA 02139

SWANSON, MARILYN ANN, food and nutrition specialist; b. Paterson, N.J., Apr. 20, 1945; d. John Lawrence and Florence Mildred (Danielson) Ribbe; m. Barry Grant Swanson, Apr. 4, 1970 (div. Feb. 1988); children: Alyssa Michelle, Krista Jo, Sara Beth; m. Craig George MacFarland, Mar. 19, 1988. BS in Foods and Nutrition, U. Del., 1967; MS in Food Sci., U. Wis., 1969; PhD in Nutrition, Wash. State U., 1987. Nutritionist Waisman Ctr., U. Wis., Madison, 1969-72; cons. dietitian Benewah Community Hosp., St. Maries, Idaho, 1973-79; pub. health nutritionist North Idaho Indian Health Svc., Lapwai, 1977-79; extension nutrition specialist U. Idaho, Moscow, 1979—; food preservation cons. Postharvest Inst. for Perishables, Moscow, 1983—; TV and radio speaker Biessen Communications, N.Y.C., 1987-88. Author: Everything About Exchange Values for Foods, 1973, 4th edit., 1986, Foods of the Pacific Northwest, 1988. Leader Idaho 4-H, Moscow, 1987-89; chmn. health subcom. Idaho-Ecuador Ptnrs. of Ams., Moscow, 1989-91. Recipient Leader award Idaho Home Econs. Assn., 1988, Nat. Leader award Am. Home Econs. Assn., 1989; fellow Nat. Ptnrs. of Ams., 1990. Mem. Am. Dietetic Assn., Inst. Food Technologists (sec. Lewis and Clark sect. 1984-85, regional communicator 1986—; exec. bd. nutrition div. 1989-91), Idaho Dietetic Assn. Lutheran. Home: 836 Mabelle St Moscow ID 83843 Office: U Idaho 108 Home Econs Moscow ID 83843

SWANSON, MARSHA KRISTIN, financial services registered representative; b. Kansas City, Mo., Sept. 3, 1953; d. Harold Albin and Betty Jo (Lusby) S.; m. D. Jefferey Cornett (div. Mar. 1988); children: Caylan Christine, Carla Chantal. BBA in Fin., U. Mo., Kansas City, 1989. Bus. mgr. Justin Case Music, Inc., Overland Park, Kans., 1977-85; dir. spl. projects Belmont Schs., Inc., Kansas City, 1985-89; registered rep. Equitable Fin. Svcs., Overland Park, 1989—. Vol. Children's Mercy Hosp., Kansas City, 1986. Home: 10901 W 102d St Overland Park KS 66214 Office: Equitable Fin Svcs 8500 W 110th St Overland Park KS 66210

SWANSON, MARTHA MADDEN, university student activities director; b. Utica, N.Y., Aug. 23, 1944; d. Eugene and Nancy Jane (Strohecker) Madden; m. David H. Swanson, July 8, 1967; children: Michael, Sarah. AB, Sweet Briar Coll., 1966; AM, Colgate U., 1967. Student activities comptroller Georgetown U., Washington, 1984-85, asst. dir. student activities, 1985-89, dir. student orgns., 1989—. Mem. AAUW, D.C. Coll. Personnel Assn., Am. Coll. Personnel Assn. Office: Georgetown U 37th and O Sts NW Box 2239 Washington DC 20057

SWANSON, PATRICIA K., librarian; b. St. Louis, May 8, 1940; d. Emil Louis and Patricia (McNair) Klick; 1 child, Ivan Clatanoff; m. Don R. Swanson, Aug 22, 1976. B.S. in Edn., U. Mo., 1962; postgrad., Cornell U., 1963; M.L.S., Simmons Coll., 1967. Reference librarian Simmons Coll., Boston, 1967-68; reference librarian U. Chgo., 1970-79, sr. lectr. Grad. Library Sch., 1974-83, 86-88, head reference service, 1979-83, asst. dir. for sci. libraries, 1983—, acting asst. dir. for tech. svcs., 1987-88; project dir. Office Mgmt. Svcs., Assn. Rsch. Librs., 1982-83; speaker in field; cons. on libr. mgmt., planning and space. Author: Great is the Gift that Bringeth Knowledge: Highlights from the History of the John Crerar Library, 1989; contbr. articles to profl. jours. Mem. ALA, Chgo. Library Club, Soc. for Scholarly Pub. Home: 5825 Dorchester Chicago IL 60637 Office: U Chgo John Crerar Libr 5730 S Ellis Ave Chicago IL 60637-1434

SWANSON, PATRICIA LOUISE, reinsurance company executive; b. Manilla, Iowa, June 20, 1948; d. Herbert and Irene (Stolz) S.; m. Jon J. Ebner, June 26, 1965 (div. Jan. 1979); 1 child, Antonette Maria Ebner. Student, U. Nebr., 1976-77. With claims and accounts dept. Mut. Protective Ins. Co., Omaha, 1965-68; claims mgr. Grace-Mayer Ins. Agy., Omaha, 1969-71; reins. claims supr. Nat. Indemnity Co., Omaha, 1972-84; asst. v.p., claims mgr. Cen. Nat. Ins., Omaha, 1984-89, G.L. Hodson & Son, Atlanta, 1989—. Editor: (textbook) Principles of Reinsurance, 1989. Pres. Intercultural Families Adoption Group, Omaha, 1978-79. Roman Catholic. Home: 360 Oak Terr Alpharetta GA 30201

SWANSON, RHONDA WOJAHN, hospital secretary; b. Windom, Minn., May 31, 1955; d. Melvin Ewald and Romelle Gail (Schneider) W.; m. Gregory Roy Swanson, June 3, 1978; 1 child, Erik Jon. AA, Cottey Coll., 1975; BA cum laude, Gustavus Adolphus Coll., 1977; MusM, Ind. U., 1980. Organist, choirmaster St. Timothy's Episcopal Ch., Indpls., 1978-81, Am. Ch. of Copenhagen, 1981-83; prin. sec. Ind. U., Bloomington, 1980-81, prin. records clk. Sch. of Music, 1983-84, dir. music svcs., 1984; dir. music 1st United Meth. Ch., Sparta, Tenn., 1985-86; tech. sec. Tenn. Technol. U., Cookeville, 1984-86; exec. sec. Bapt. Hosp., Nashville, 1986—. George C. Marshall grantee Am.-Scandinavian Found., Copenhagen, 1982. Mem. Am. Guild Organists (Nashville chpt., placement chmn. 1987—), PEO. Lutheran.

SWARDSON, MARY ANNE, mathematics educator; b. Atlanta, Sept. 10, 1928; d. Frank Wesley and Pearle (Spires) Thompson; m. Harold Roland Swardson, Sept. 10, 1949; children: Anne, Catherine, Christine. BA, Tulane U., 1949; MS, Ohio U., 1969, PhD, 1981. Instr. Am. Coll. Switzerland, Leysin, 1969-70; instr. Ohio U., Athens, 1970-80, asst. prof., 1980-89, assoc. prof., 1989—. Contbr. articles to profl. jours. Pres. League of Women Voters, Athens, 1960-62. Mem. Am. Math. Soc., Math. Assn. of Am., Am. Women in Math., Ohio Acad. Sci. (exemplar 1989), Phi Kappa Phi. Episcopalian. Office: Dept Math/Ohio Univ Athens OH 45701

SWARTOUT, JEAN ANN, travel agency executive; b. Catskill, N.Y., Feb. 28, 1945; d. Charles Richard and Vera Mildred (Bower) S. Cert. travel cons. Inst. Cert. Travel Agts. Clk., W.T. Grant Co., Albany, N.Y., 1962-63; mail clk. Mchts. Mut. Ins. Co., Albany, 1963-65; bookkeeper Mountain View Coachline, West Coxsackie, N.Y., 1965-73; mgr. Argus Travel, Inc., West Coxsackie, 1973-84; owner, mgr. Country Side Travel, West Coxsackie, 1984-86, ptnr. West Coxsackie, N.Y., 1986-89. Mem. Women In Travel Services, Town and Country Bus. and Profl. Women's Club (2d v.p. Coxsackie 1985-87, 1st v.p. 1987-89, pres. 1989-90). Roman Catholic. Avocations: music, reading, theatre, travel. Home: 3004 Parkway Blvd #108 Kissimmee FL 34746 Office: Country Side Travel Rt 9-W West Coxsackie NY 12192

SWARTZ, ANN LAMONTAGNE, insurance agent; b. Sanford, Maine, Aug. 6, 1966; d. Lionel J. and Jacqueline Lamontagne; m. Lawrence H. Swartz, June 4, 1988. BA, Clark U., 1988. Cert. LUTC. Ins. planner Mutual of Omaha, Cranston, R.I. Home: 81 Harbour Ave West Warwick RI 02893 Office: 105 Sockanoset Crossroads Ste 314-316 Cranston RI 02920

SWARTZ, MARIA CHRISTINA, financial recruiter; b. Harrisburg, Pa., Feb. 20, 1960; d. Kenneth Dale and Lena Annette (Detoma) S. BSBA, Shippensburg State, 1982; MBA, Loyola Coll., Balt., 1989. Tax staff Arthur Andersen & Co., Balt., 1982-84; acct. Enterprise Found., Columbia, Md., 1984-86; exec. recruiter Don Richard Assocs., Balt., 1986—; bd. dirs. Pet-Coke, Inc., Houston; part-time instr. U. Md. Baltimore County, 1989—. Bd. dirs. Santa Claus Anonymous, Balt., 1986-87. Mem. Nat. Assn. Accts. (bd. dirs. 1986-88), Balt. Jr. Assn. Commerce (bd. dirs. 1988-89, v.p. 1987-88, treas. 1986-87, Key Mem. award 1988, President's citation, 1986, 89, Outstanding New Mem. award 1986). Republican. Roman Catholic. Office: Don Richard Assocs 7 St Paul St Ste 1060 Baltimore MD 21202-1682

SWARTZ, RENEE BECKER, civic volunteer; b. Newark, N.J., Feb. 25, 1935; d. Sidney David and Adeline (Kleinberg) Becker; m. Harry Mason Swartz, Mar. 8, 1931; children: Stephen, Addi-Lyn, Sidney. Student, Rutgers U., 1950-52, Bryn Mawr Coll., 1952-53; BA, Barnard Coll.-Columbia U., 1955. Mem. planning com. N.J. White Ho. Conf. on Librs. and Info. Sci., 1975-79, mem. del. selection com., mem. programs com., 1978-79; chairperson of delegation White Ho. Conf., 1979; permanent N.J. rep. Nat. Commn. Follow-up Activities White Ho. Conf., chairperson nat. awards com., 1984-86, chairperson fund-raising com., 1989-90. Pres. Friends of the Monmouth County Library Assn., 1964-68; founding mem. N.J. Ci-

tizens for Better Libraries, 1982; chairperson bldg. com. Dorothy L. Spiwak Meml. Library, Munson, N.J., 1971-73, trustee, 1971—; active N.J. Library Devel. Com., 1973-84; chairperson, bd. trustees Grad. Sch. of Communication, Info. and Library Studies, Rutgers U., 1980—, chairperson, 1983—; gov. appointee N.J. State Library Adv. Coun., 1975—, chairperson, 1986—; Monmouth County Library Commn., 1965—, chair, 1976—. Recipient Hannah G. Solomon award Greater Red Bank sect. Nat. Coun. Jewish Women, 1979, Pres. medal Barnard Coll.-Columbia U., 1984, Columbia U. medal, 1985. Mem. Nat. Citizens Com. for Pub. Libraries (steering com. 1980-84), Am. Library Trustee Assn. (pres. com. 1983, nat. intellectual freedom com. 1984—), N.J. Library Assn. (centennial com. 1986-89, chairperson N.J. Ednl. Inst. com. 1987-88, N.J. Trustee of the Yr. 1980), N.J. Library Trustee Assn. (exec. com. 1976-81, regional rep. 1983-86), Assn. N.J. Library Commrs. (pres. 1973-75), Lotus Club N.Y., Ocean Club of N.J. Home: 136 Rumson Rd Rumson NJ 07760

SWARTZ-BUCKLEY, RITA BRYNA, marketing and communications professional, writer; b. Brookline, Mass., June 10, 1955; d. Maxwell Goverman and Vera Edith (Rudman) Swartz; m. Richard Warren Buckley, Sept. 6, 1986. BS summa cum laude, Boston U., 1976; MBA, Northeastern U., Boston, 1978. Writer various publs., Boston, N.Y.C. and Newton, Mass., 1979-82; prof. Salem (Mass.) State Coll., 1982-88; pres. Buckley/Swartz, Inc., Swampscott, Mass., 1982—; contbr. fiction Bread Loaf Writer's Conf., Middlebury, Vt., 1988, 89, 90; pub. rels. dir. North Shore Creative Group, Salem, 1988—. Contbr. articles to Boston Sunday Globe and poetry to Am. Poetry Assn., 1988. Fund raiser Jewish Fedn. North Shore, Marblehead, Mass., 1986—, Am. Heart Assn., Needham, Mass., 1987—. Recipient Merit award North Am. Mentor mag., 1979. Mem. Greenpeace, Amnesty Internat. Democrat. Office: Buckley/Swartz Inc 25 Cedar Hill Terr Swampscott MA 01907

SWARTZELL, ANN GARLING, librarian; b. Elkhart, Ind., Jan. 23, 1955; d. Allen Henry and Barbara (Garling) S. AB, Ind. U., 1977, MLS, 1978. Preservation project librarian Harvard U. Library, Cambridge, Mass., 1978-84; Mellon intern in preservation adminstrn. Yale U. Library, New Haven, 1984; assoc. conservation librarian N.Y. State Libr., Albany, 1985-89; head preservation replacement and photographic svcs. U. Library, U. Calif., Berkeley, 1989—; mem. adv. com. N.E. Document Conservation Ctr., Andover, Mass., 1985-89. Contbr.: book Preservation Microfilm: A Guide for Libraries, 1986 (Leland award 1987). Mem. ALA (vice chair, chair reprodn. library materials sect. 1987-89).

SWATZELL, MARILYN, nurse; b. Johnson City, Tenn., July 31, 1942; d. Dallas Fred and Minnie Thelma (Clark) S. BS cum laude, East Tenn. State U., 1966, MS, 1967; BSN, U. Tenn., 1974. Chmn. pediatric nursing Meth. Hosp. Sch. Nursing, Memphis; head nurse LeBonheur Children's Med. Ctr., Memphis; dir. maternal child nursing Jackson (Tenn.) Madison County Gen. Hosp.; staff nurse Vanderbilt U. Hosp., Nashville; now supr. Meth. Hosp. Lexington, Tenn. Contbr. articles on care plans to profl. jours. Mem. ANA, Tenn. Nurses Assn., Tenn. Orgn. Nurse Execs. Address: 231 Law Loop Lexington TN 38351

SWAYZE, FRANCES GOEHRING, legislator, educator; b. Council Bluffs, Iowa, Feb. 11, 1901; d. William Alfred and Lilian (Huff) Goehring; m. THomas A. Swayze Sr., July 8, 1924 (dec. Oct. 1961); children: Shirley, Gretchen, Thomas A. Jr., Suzanne, George. BA, U. Puget Sound, 1922. Dean of women U. Puget Sound, Tacoma, 1955-56, asst. to pres., 1957-65; state rep. State of Wash. Legislature, Olympia, 1952-65, long time officer, 1965-71, ret., 1971. Freeholder City of Tacoma, 1948, 52; del. Meth. Ch. Gen. Conf., 1950-54; chmn. Commn. on Status of Women of the Meth. Ch., 1951-52. Named Mother of the Yr., State of Wash., 1955. Mem. P.E.O., AAUW, Bus. and Profl. Women's Assn., Avon Study Club, Pi Beta Phi. Republican. Home: 7400 Stinson #208 Gig Harbor WA 98335

SWAZEY, JUDITH POUND, institute president, sociomedical sciences educator; b. Bronxville, N.Y., Apr. 21, 1939; d. Robert Earl and Louise Titus (Hanson) Pound; m. Peter Woodman Swazey, Nov. 28, 1964; children: Elizabeth, Peter. AB, Wellesley Coll., 1961; PhD, Harvard U., 1966. Rsch. assoc. Harvard U., 1966-71, lectr., 1969-71, rsch. fellow, 1971-72; cons. com. brain scis. NRC, 1971-73; staff scientist neuroscis. rsch. program MIT, Cambridge, Mass., 1973-74; assoc. prof. dept. socio-med. scis. and community medicine Boston U., 1974-77, prof., 1977-80, adj. prof. in Schs. Medicine and Pub. Health, 1980—; exec. dir. Medicine in the Public Interest, Inc., Boston and Washington, 1979-82, 89—; pres. Coll. of the Atlantic, Bar Harbor, Maine, 1982-84, Acadia Inst., Bar Harbor, 1984—; mem. Army Sci. Bd. Author: Reflexes and Motor Integration, the Development of Sherrington's Integrative Action Concept, 1969, (with others) Human Aspects of Biomedical Innovation, 1971, (with R.C. Fox) The Courage to Fail, a Social View of Organ Transplants and Hemodialysis, 1975, rev. edit., 1978 (hon. mention Am. Med. Writers Assn., C. Wright Mills award Am. Sociol. Assn.), Chlorpromazine in Psychiatry, a Study of Therapeutic Innovation, 1974, (with K. Reeds) Today's Medicine, Tomorrow's Science, Essays on Paths of Discovery in the Biomedical Sciences, 1978; editor: (with C. Wong) Dilemmas of Dying, Policies and Procedures for Decisions Not to Treat, 1981, (with F. Worden and G. Adelman) The Neurosciences: Paths of Discovery, 1975; assoc. editor IRB: A Jour. of Human Subjects Rsch., 1979—; contbr. articles to profl. jours. Wellesley Coll. scholar, 1961; Wellesley Coll. Alumnae fellow Harvard U., 1966, NIH predoctoral fellow, 1966, Radcliffe Coll. Coll. grad. fellow, 1966. Mem. AAAS (sci. freedom and responsibility com. 1986-89), Inst. Medicine NAS (mem. health scis. policy bd. 1986-89, grad. record exam bd.), Sherrington Soc., Phi Beta Kappa, Sigma Xi. Office: Acadia Inst Bar Harbor ME 04609

SWEARINGEN, MARJORIE EILEEN, educator; b. Colorado Springs, Colo., Apr. 27, 1939; d. Carl Nelson and I. Velma (Young) Jackson; divorced Mar. 1979; children: R. Scott, Kent A., Lisa C. BA, U. No. Colo., 1960; MA, Colo. Coll. 1982. Elem. tchr. El Paso County, Colorado Springs Sch. Dist. #11, Colorado Springs, 1960—. Author unit on Am. History Freedom Found., 1965. Pub. rels. program dir. Am. Edn. Week, 1980-88; pres. Eve Circle St. Paul's United Meth. Ch., 1974-78. Recipient Tchrs. medal Freedoms Found., Valley Forge, 1966, Disting. Tchr. award Colo. Tchr. Award Found., 1983, George Washington Honor medal, 1967. Mem. NEA (life), Colo. Sci. Tchrs., Colo. Edn. Assn. (polit. action com. 1979—, Lion award 1983, Golden Apple award 1988, chair communications commn. 1982-88), Colorado Springs Edn. assn. (officer 1980-88), Colorado Springs High Sch. Palmer Alumni Assn. (publicity dir. 1984), Fun Finders Square Dance Assn., Phi Delta Kappa, Delta Kappa Gamma (profl. affairs com. 1982-86, scholar 1978). Democrat. Home: 1615 Querida Dr Colorado Springs CO 80909 Office: Sch Dist # 11 2400 E Van Buren Colorado Springs CO 80909

SWEASY, JOYCE ELIZABETH, government official, military reserve officer; b. Key West, Fla., Apr. 25, 1948; d. James Alfred and Josephine Mary (Fassel) Messick. BFA, Phila. Coll. Art, 1971; A in Bus. Adminstrn., Howard County Community Coll., 1985; grad., Army Command and Gen. Staff Co. 1988. Commd. 1st lt. U.S. Army, 1978, advanced through grades to maj., 1990; contract specialist U.S. Army, Adelphi, 1978-84, analyst procurement Lab. Command,, 1984-85, chief competition mgmt. office, spl. competition adv./ombuds, 1985—; owner Hand Made 'N Ellicott City, Md., 1983—; ptnr., gen. mgr. Computelt. Contbr. numerous articles to profl. jours. Mem. Font Hill Citizens Orgn., Ellicott City, 1987—. Mem. U.S. Army Res. Officers Assn, Nat. Contract Mgrs. Assn., Am. Def. Preparedness Assn. Republican. Roman Catholic. Home: 4008 Arjay Circle Ellicott City MD 21043 Office: US Army Lab Command 2800 Powder Mill Rd Adelphi MD 20783

SWEC, DIANE MARIE, mechanical engineer, researcher; b. Cleve., Dec. 17, 1959; d. Joseph and Valeria Anne (Potoczak) S. BSChemE, Cleve. State U., 1983; MME, U. Toledo, 1988. Research engr. electo physics br. NASA Lewis Rsch. Ctr., Cleve., 1983-89, rsch engr. Stirling Tech. br., 1989—. Contbr. articles to profl. jours. Explorer post advisor Boy Scouts Am., 1984—. Mem. NAFE, Material Rsch. Soc., Internat. Soc. for Optical Engring., Am. Vacuum Soc., Soc. of Women Engrs., Bus. and Profl. Women's Orgn., Theta Phi Alpha (Greater Cleve. Alumni Assn. nat. fundraising chmn. 1988-90). Democrat. Roman Catholic. Home: 4783 Columbia Rd Apt 206

Olmsted OH 44070 Office: NASA Lewis Rsch Ctr 21000 Brookpark Rd. MS 301-2 Cleveland OH 44135

SWEEN, TERRI LYNN, computer analyst, consultant; b. Evanston, Ill., Mar. 29, 1963; d. James Bernard and Joyce Ann (Ellmer) S. BA, DePaul U., 1986, MS, 1988, postgrad., 1988—. Database adminstr. Lake Shore Country Club, Glenco, Ill., 1986-88; pres., founder The PC Pros, Chgo., 1988—; computer analyst DePaul U., Chgo., 1988—. Vol. Big Bros./Big Sister, Lawrence, Kans., 1984-86, Chgo., 1988-, Ward 89, Misericordia, Chgo., 1989—; editor DePaul U. Alumni Admissions Coun., Chgo., 1988—. Mem. ABA, Ill. Bar Assn., DePaul Student Bar Assn., Ill. Assn. for Inst. Rsch., NAFE. Home: 1330 W Birchwood Chicago IL 60626 Office: DePaul U 25 E Jackson Chicago IL 60604

SWEENEY, DOROTHY ANNE, real estate broker; b. Detroit, Mar. 25, 1927; d. Charles Louis and Mary Elizabeth (Kane) Jones; m. Donald Hogan, June 3, 1948 (dec. Mar. 1986); children: Sheila, Charles, Gerald, Marjorie; m. Louis Wright Sweeney. Apr. 25, 1987; stepchildren: Joann, Lois, Judy, Kathy, Mark. MusB, Maygrove Coll. Detroit, 1948; MusM, Ball State U., Muncie, 1968. Tchr. Warsaw Community Schs., Warsaw, Ind., 1957-78; realtor Lucas Realtors Better Homes and Gardens, Warsaw, 1980-; clinician St. Frances Coll., Ft. Wayne, 1969. Organist Sacred Heart Ch., Warsaw, 1950—; Bd. dir. Kosciusko Bd. of Realtors, Warsaw, 1981-84, Warsaw Community Devel. Corp., Warsaw, 1983-; Pres. Am. Assn. of U. Women, Warsaw, 1982-84. Named Woman of the Year Sacred Heart Ch., Warsaw, 1985. Mem. Kosciusko Bd. of Realtors (sec.), Kosciusko Bd. of Realtors (dir.), Am. Guild of Organists, Nat. Assn. of Realtors, Ind. Bd. of Realtor, Cert. Residential Specialists (Designee), C. of C. (past pres.), Warsaw Reading Club (pres. 1990). Republican. Roman Catholic. Home: 742 E Oak St Warsaw IN 46580 Office: Lucas Realtors Bh&G 525 E Center St Warsaw IN 46580

SWEENEY, ELIZABETH ANN, medical center executive; b. Birmingham, Ala., Nov. 9, 1946; d. Huretta and Elizabeth (Whisenant) Chappell; children from previous marriage: Wesley, Hugh L. Mitchell. BSN, U. Ala., 1973, MSN, 1975. Staff nurse VA Med. Ctr., Birmingham, 1972-74; asst. prof. nursing Sch. Nursing U. Ala. Birmingham, 1975-79; coordinator nursing services Cen. City Mental Health Ctr., Los Angeles, 1979-80; nurse educator VA Med. Ctr., Los Angeles, 1980—; asst. clin. prof. nursing Sch. Nursing U. Calif., Los Angeles, 1984—; dir. med. ctr. edn. and tng. Kaiser Permanente Med. Ctr., Woodland Hills, Calif., 1989—; asst. dir. Kaiser Permanente Med. Ctr., Bellflower, Calif., 1988; Guest faculty mem. Stanford U., Palo Alto, Calif., 1984; mem. conf. faculty United Nurses Assn. Calif., 1982, 83, 87, Calif. Park and Recreation Soc. Conf., Sacramento, 1985, 86; Equal Employment Opportunity investigator VA, Washington, 1985—. Contbr. articles to profl. jours. Recipient Commendation for Superior Performance Fed. Exec. Bd., Los Angeles, 1984. Mem. Ala. Nurses Assn. (exec. bd. dirs. 1976-79), Am. Nurses Assn., Calif. Nurses Assn., NAFE, Black Women's Network, Coun. Black Nurses. Office: Kaiser Permanente Med Ctr 5601 De Soto Ave Woodland Hills CA 91365

SWEENEY, JULIA, public relations executive; b. Ladonia, Tex., Feb. 2, 1927; d. Albert Earle and Julia (Nunn) S. Grad. Am. Acad., N.Y.C., 1946; student So. Meth. U., 1958-59. Asst. mgr. Ambrosia House, Milw., 1951-56; sec. Neiman-Marcus, Dallas, 1956-70, publicity dir. 1970-74; columnist, feature writer Dallas Times Herald, 1974-81; pres. Callas, Foster & Sweeney, Dallas, 1982—; bd. dirs. Fidelity Nat. Bank of Dallas. Bd. dirs. Boys' Clubs Dallas, Inc., No. Tex. chpt. Arthritis Found., N.E. Tex. chpt. Cystic Fibrosis Found.; trustee Protection of Animal World Soc.; mem. March of Dimes Women's Aux., Dallas Theater Ctr. Women's Com., Dallas Ballet Women's Com. Mem. Pub. Rels. Soc. of Am., Women in Communications, The Women's Found., Dallas C. of C., Dallas Symphony Orch. League, Dallas Mus. Art League, Dallas County Heritage Soc., Dallas Hist. Soc., Les Femmes Du Monde, Internat. Women's Forum, Fashion Industry Coun., Fashion Collectors, Charter 100. Episcopalian. Office: Callas Foster & Sweeney 2515 McKinney Ave Dallas TX 75201

SWEENEY, KAREN A., county official; b. Phila., Feb. 1, 1959; d. Gerald Patrick Sweeney and Kathryn Marie (Bulman) Detky. BS, East Stroudsburg (Pa.) U., 1981, postgrad., 1989—. Gameroom mgr. East Stroudsburg U., 1981-82; social dir. Polmont Lodge and Resort, Bushkill, Pa., 1982; asst. recreation dir. Rank-Ahnert Enterprise, Bushkill, 1982-83, recreation dir., 1984-85; recreation dir. Tree Tops Timesharing-Ahnert Enterprises, Bushkill, 1983-84; exec. dir. Monroe County Recreation and Park Commn., Stroudsburg, Pa., 1985—; mem. adv. coun. recreation dept. East Stroudsburg U., 1987—; practicum and intern supr., 1983—, com. chmn. alumni reunion recreation dept., 1988. Vol. crisis intervention counselor Woman's Resources, Monroe and Pike Counties, Pa., 1986—; cons. recreation Area Agy. on Aging, Monroe, County, 1985—. Mem. Nat. Recreation and Park Assn. ((cert. leisure profl.), Pa. Recreation and Park Soc. (cxonf. speaker 1986), Nat. Youth Sports Coaching Assn. (cert. clinician, chpt. bd. dirs. 1987—), Nat. Archery Assn., AAHPER and Dance, Smithsonian Assocs. Democrat. Roman Catholic. Home: 64 Lenox Ave East Stroudsburg PA 18301

SWEENEY, LISA ANNE, accountant; b. Plainfield, N.J., June 13, 1962; d. Walter James and Denise Jean (Macklin) Bennett; m. Terry Michael Sweeney, Oct. 17, 1987. BBA in Acctg. and Info. Systems, U. Wis., 1984; postgrad., Marquette U., 1989—. CPA, Wis. Asst. acct. Peat Marwick Main & Co., Milw., 1984-85, staff acct., 1985-86, sr. acct., 1986-87, supervisory sr. acct., 1987-88; sr. cost acct. EZ Paintr div. Newell, Milw., 1988-89, sr. analyst, 1989-90, supr. cost acctg., 1990, cost acctg. mgr., 1990—; income tax preparer, Waukesha, Wis., 1984—; micro computer cons., Waukesha, 1989—. Acct. St. John Vianney Cath. Ch., Brookfield, Wis., 1984-88; chmn., participant longest day of golf Am. Cancer Soc., Waukesha, 1982-88. Mem. AICPA, Wis. Inst. CPA's (chmn. membership task force 1989—), state membership com. 1989—), Nat. Assn. Accts., Inst. Cert. Mgmt. Accts., U. Wis. Alumni Assn., Mensa. Republican. Home: N24 W22700 Meadowood Pewaukee WI 53072 Office: EZ Paintr Corp 4051 S Iowa Ave Waukesha WI 53186

SWEENEY, SISTER MARGARET MARY, hospital administrator, nun; b. N.Y.C., Oct. 24, 1921; d. Jeremiah and Mary Jane (Dougherty) S. M.B.A., St. John's U., 1966; M.S. in Hosp. Adminstrn., Columbia U., 1970; DSc. (hon.), Iona Coll. 1987. Lic. nursing home adminstr., N.Y. joined Sisters of Charity, Mount St. Vincent's Hosp., 1946. Adminstrv. asst. St. Vincent's Hosp., N.Y.C., 1966-68, sr. v.p., 1970-80, pres., 1980—; adminstrv. resident Luth. Med. Ctr., Bklyn., 1969-70; trustee St. Joseph's Hosp., Yonkers, N.Y., 1977—, St. Vincent's Hosp., Harrison, N.Y., 1975—; assoc. prof. N.Y.C. Community Coll., 1973-77; preceptor hosp. adminstrn. Baruch U., George Washington U., N.Y.C., 1974-80; mem. bd. govs., trustee Greater N.Y. Hosp. Assn., 1983—, chmn.-elect, 1989—. Contbr. articles to profl. jours.; contbr. lecture series. Chmn. St. Joseph's Ch. Parish Council, Greenwich Village, N.Y., 1973; trusteeMedic Alert, vice chmn. bd. trustees, 1990—; trustee Coll. Mt. St. Vincent, Sisters of Charity Health Care System, Alliance for Cath. Health Care. Fellow Am. Coll. Hosp. Adminstrs.; mem. Hosp. Fin. Mgmt. Assn., N.Y.C. Pub. Health Assn., N.Y. State Hosp. Assn., Delta Mu Delta. Office: St Vincent's Hosp Office of the Pres 153 W 11th St New York NY 10011

SWEENEY, MARY FRANCIS, human resources professional; b. Muncie, Feb. 19, 1938; d. Cecil L. and Irene V. (Gayheart) French; m. Charles H. Sweeney, May 16, 1959; children: Scott, Todd. BA, Ball State U., 1959. Various teaching positions elem. and secondary schs., colleges and adult edn. programs, 1959-75; v.p. human resources Brenton Banks, Des Moines, 1977—; instr. Am. Inst. Banking, Des Moines, 1987—. Bd. dirs. Des Moines Office Edn. Adv. Com., 1978—; chairperson Des Moines employers com., mem. state steering com. Job Svc. of Iowa, 1989—. Mem. Am. Adminstrv. Mgmt. Assn., Am. Compensation Assn., Soc. Human Resource Mgrs., Fin. Women Internat. (pres. 1983-84, edn. com. 1985—), Des Moines Fin. Industry Breakfast Group, Greater Des Moines C. of C. (chairperson employers com. 1989-90, fedn. bd. 1990—), Chamber Alliance.

SWEENEY, MARY MARGARET, dance educator, movement analyst; b. Dubuque, Iowa, Feb. 1, 1957; d. Merlin James and Majorie Helen (Meltzer) S. BA, U. Iowa, 1979; MA, Ohio State U., 1984. Cert. labanotation tchr..

Rsch. assoc. Ohio State U., Columbus, 1982-84, instr., summer 1984, instr. creative arts program, 1985; artistic dir. Dublin (Ohio) Dance Centre, 1985-87; instr. Otterbein (Ohio) Coll., 1986-88; asst. prof. Calif. State U., Chico, 1988—; guest artist, Chico Unified Sch. Dist., 1989—, Greater Columbus (Ohio) Schs., 1985-87, Iowa Ctr. for the Arts, 1982. Mem. wellness planning com. Calif. State U., 1989-90; mem. tng. the young dancer Ohio Dance, 1986-87; editor ADMA newsletter, 1985-86. U. Iowa scholar, 1975-78, State of Iowa scholar, 1975, Lang. Dance Ctr. scholar, 1979. Mem. Nat. Dance Assn., Am. Dance Guild, Calif. Dance Educator's Assn., Laban/Bartenieff Inst., Congress on Rsch. in Dance.

SWEENEY, MAUREEN ROSE, real estate appraiser; b. N.Y., Aug. 21, 1963; d. Charles Hugh and Rose Patricia (Flynn) S. BA, SUNY, Geneseo, 1985. Sr. appraiser Henry Boeckmann Jr. & Assoc. Inc., Babylon, N.Y., 1985-88, N.Y.C., 1989—. Mem. Assn. of Real Estate Women (bd. dirs. 1988-90). Roman Catholic. Office: 306 5th Ave 7th Fl New York NY 10001

SWEET, DEE (MRS. HERBERT A. SWEET), business executive; b. Muskogee, Okla., June 3, 1913; d. Walter Oliver and Lola R. (Morris) McDaniel; student Butler U., 1931, 33, summer sch. Oxford U.; m. Herbert A. Sweet, Aug. 28, 1935; children: Judee Lo, Jill B. Sweet Bowles. Asst. to interior decorator L.S. Ayres & Co., Indpls., 1930-33; co-dir. Acorn Farm Camp, Carmel, Ind., 1933-77; owner Acorn Farm Antiques, Carmel, 1960—, Acorn Farm Workshops, 1972—; dir. TV programs WFBM, Indpls., 1949-54, WISH, Indpls., 1955-60; lectr. adult edn. Ind. U., Purdue U., 1959-69. Co-author Try It books for children. Mem. Appraisers Assn. Am. (sr.), Appraisers Soc. Am. (sr.), Associated Antique Dealers Am., Am. Camping Assn., Am. Women in Radio and TV, Ind. Hist. Soc., C. of C., Asso. Antique Dealers Am., Nat. Audubon Soc. Author newspaper column Ind. Soc. Auctioneers. Home: 15466 Oak Rd Carmel IN 46032

SWEET, MARGE JEAN, controller; b. London, Ky., Mar. 22, 1947; d. Clyde and Ruth (Lewis) Grimes; m. Michael D. Sweet, June 24, 1978; 1 child (by previous marriage) Jennifer Lyn. Student, Ind. U., Richmond, 1987-88. Time keeping coord. Huffman Mfg., Richmond, Ind., 1970-75; payroll mgr. City of Richmond, Ind., 1976-77, deputy controller, 1977-86, city controller; mem. Leadership Wayne Co., Richmond, 1987—. Mem. Gov. Fin. Assn., Controllers Assn. Baptist. Office: City of Richmond 50 N Fifth St Richmond IN 47374

SWEET, SUSAN COOKE, teacher, coach; b. Charleston, S.C., Oct. 9, 1944; d. Walter James Spurgeon and Helen Marie (Cook) Huff; m. James Andrew Sweet; 1 child, Jennifer Suzanne. BS, Ohio State U., 1966. Tchr. Frankfort (Ind.) Sr. High Sch., 1966-68, Frankfort Jr. High Sch., 1969-70; tchr., coach Toledo (Ohio) Schs., 1971-77, Maumee (Ohio) City Schs., 1977-80, L.A. Unified Sch. Dist., 1985—; head varsity basketball coach Toledo City Schs., 1972-76, varsity track coach, 1973-75; varsity/jr. varsity basketball coach Maumee City Schs., 1977-80, U.S. Grant High Sch., 1985—, softball coach, 1986—; coach Ohio State AAA Girls Basketball Championship, 1976. Vol. ARC, Frankfort, 1966, 70, Toledo, 1971-84. Named Coach of Yr. Ohio State AAA Girls Basketball Championship, 1976. Fellow NEA, United Tchrs. L.A., Calif. Tchrs. Assn., Doberman Pinscher Club of Maumee Valley, Alpha Xi Delta (v.p. 1985-86), Coaches of L.A. for Women's Sports, North Ranch Country Club. Republican. Presbyterian. Home: 16847 Bosque Dr Encino CA 91436 Office: US Grant High Sch 13000 Oxnard St Van Nuys CA 91401

SWEETING, LINDA MARIE, chemist; b. Toronto, Ont., Can., Dec. 11, 1941; came to U.S., 1965, naturalized, 1979; d. Stanley H. and Mary (Robertson) S.; BSc, U. Toronto, 1964, MA, 1965; PhD, UCLA, 1969. Asst. prof. chemistry Occidental Coll., Los Angeles, 1969-70; asst. prof. chemistry Towson (Md.) State U., 1970-75, assoc. prof., 1975-85, prof., 1985—; guest worker NIH, 1976-77; program dir. chem. instrumentation NSF, 1981-82; vis. scholar Harvard U., 1984-85. Bd. dirs. Chamber Music Soc. Balt. Mem. Md. Acad. Scis. (mem. sci. council 1975-83, 89—), Assn. for Women in Sci. (treas. 1977-78), Am. Chem. Soc. (mem. women chemists Com. 1983-89), AAAS, Wilderness Soc. (exec. com. Exptl. NMR Conf. 1985-87), Nature Conservancy, Aircraft Owners and Pilots Assn., Sierra Club, Sigma Xi (sec. TSU Club 1979-81, pres. 1987-88, mid-Atlantic nominating com. 1987—, regional dir. 1988-89). Office: Towson State U Dept Chemistry Baltimore MD 21204*

SWEGER, GLENDA LEE, educator; b. Harrisburg, Pa., July 26, 1946; d. George Glenn and Bertha Alverta (Kitner) S. BS, Ind. U. of Pa., Indiana, Pa., 1968; MA, Calif. State U., Fullerton, 1981. Cert. tchr. Calif. Tchr. Greensburg-Salem (Pa.) Unifed Sch. Dist., 1968-69, Covina-Valley (Calif.) Unified Sch. Dist., 1969—; bd. dirs. SCSPA, San Diego, 1972-82; publs. advisor Northview High Sch., Covina, 1970—, accreditation chmn. 1987—; lectr. Great Am. Lecture Series, Covina, 1988—; mentor tchr. 1989—; mem. Curriculum Devel. Adv. Bd., Staff Devel. Com.; chair Sch. Environment Com. Author: Male & Female Reporters: Differences in Readers' Perceptions, 1981. Active PTA, Covina, 1969—, SPRING, Seal Beach, Calif., 1987—, Orange County AIDS Found., Calif., 1987—, Ellis Island Found., N.Y.C., 1986—, Statue of Liberty Found. N.Y.C., 1984—. Recipient SCV Educators' grant, Covina-Valley Unified Sch. Dist., 1986. Mem. Nat. Edn. Assn., Calif. Tchrs. Assn., Covina Unified Edn. Assn., Nat. Coun. Tchrs of English, Calif. Assn. for Tchrs of English, Calif. Scholastic Press Assn., Columbia Scholastic Press Advisors Assn., Journalism Edn. Assn., So. Calif. Journalism Edn. Assn., So. Calif. Scholastic Press Assn. (sec. 1976-82, bd. dirs.), So. Calif. Scholastic Publs. Assn., Southland Assn. for Tchrs. of English, IUP Alumni Assn. Democrat. Evangelical Lutheran. Home: 3372 Rowena Dr Rossmoor CA 90720 Office: Northview High Sch 1016 W Cypress Ave Covina CA 91722

SWEITZER, KAROL M., telephone company executive; b. Anna, Ill., May 26, 1959; d. Karl M. and Agnes M. (White) S.; m. Gary S. Gill, June 22, 1985. BS in Acctg., BSBA, MacMurray Coll., Jacksonville, Ill., 1981; BS in Bus. Adminstrn., Mac Murray Coll., Jacksonville, Ill., 1981. CPA. Mgr. Caterpillar Tractor Co., Peoria, Ill., 1982, Rockwell Internat., Iowa, 1983-85, Southwestern Bell Telephone Co., St. Louis, 1985—. Mem. Profl. Bus. Women Southwestern Bell. Home: 4891 Southridge Park Dr Saint Louis MO 63129

SWENN, GAYLENE LOUISE, pharmacist; b. Pampa, Tex., Aug. 11, 1953; d. Alexander and Leota Joye (Barnes) S. Student, Tex. Tech U., 1971-72; BS in Pharmacy, Southwestern Okla. State U., 1976. Intern Buffalo (Okla.) Clinic Pharmacy, 1976; staff pharmacist Cen. Plains Regional Hosp., Plainview, Tex., 1976-78; pharmacist, mgr. Revco Drug, Plainview, 1978-79, K-Mart Pharmacy, Plainview, 1979—; pharmacy cons. Buffalo Nursing Home, 1976; cons. Cen. Plains MHMR Crisis Unit. Mem. Hale County Foster Parent Assn., 1987. Recipient Outstanding Foster Parent award, 1987-88, Friend of MHMR award, 1988. Mem. Am. Pharm. Assn., Kappa Epsilon. Republican. Pentecostal. Home: 2709 Holliday Dr Plainview TX 79072 Office: K-Mart Corp 2801 Dimmitt Rd Plainview TX 79072

SWENSON, BARBARA A., business executive; b. Tacoma, Wash., Mar. 22, 1947; d. Robert Alan and Vivian Marie (Russell) Bartlett; children: Timothy, Julie, Aimee. BA, Pacific Luth. U., 1973; MEd, U. Puget Sound, 1974, MBA, 1983. Cert. tchr., ednl. adminstr. Market analyst Quinton Instrument Co., Seattle; v.p. sales and mktg. Corazonix Corp., Oklahoma City; dir. sales and mktg. Digital Medicine, Cambridge, Mass.; v.p. mktg. and sales Luxtex Corp., Sturbridge, Mass.; mng. ptnr., founder The Bartlett Co. Natick, Mass. Active United Way, C. of C., Dept. Employment Tng.. Mem. AMA, NOW, NAFE, New England Women Bus. Owners. Democrat. Address: 3 Hilldale Pl Ashland MA 01721 Office: 251 W Central St Ste 132 Natick MA 01760

SWENSON, KATHLEEN SUSAN, music and art teacher; b. Reno, Nev., Oct. 23, 1938; d. Harold Ruthaford McNeil and Hollyce Margaret (Scruggs) McNeil Biggs; m. James Michael Phalan, 1956 (div. 1974); children: David Michael, Jeanine Louise Phalan Lawrence, Gregory Shaun; m. Gerald Allen Swensen, Nov. 1976 (div. 1987); stepchildren: Craig Allen, Sarah Ann, Eric Sander. Student, U. Nev., Reno, 1956-58, Foothill Coll., 1966-68; AA, West Valley Coll.; BA, U. Calif., Santa Cruz, 1983. Concert pianist Nev.,Calif.

1950-64; pvt. piano instr. various locations, 1963—, pvt. art instr., 1970—, pvt. astrology instr., 1973—; founder, pres. AAM Triple Arts, Aptos, Calif., 1974—. Producer, instr. art instrn. videos. Mem. Soc Western Artists, Calif. Piano Tchrs. Assn., Los Gatos Art Assn. (pres. 1985-86), Saratoga Contemporary Artists (v.p. 1984-85), Nat. League Am. Pen Women (honorarian 1985). Republican. Episcopalian. Home and Office: AAM Triple Arts 3000 Wisteria Way Aptos CA 95003

SWENSON, VICTORIA SUE, optical company sales official; b. Denver, Apr. 6, 1956; d. Robert Edward and Sonja Anne (Ingersoll) Osborne; m. Fredrick E. Swenson, Sept. 20, 1975 (div. 1983). BA with distinction, U. Colo., 1978. Mktg. asst. Univ. Nat. Bank, Denver, 1978-79; mktg. cons. John A Pratt & Assocs., Inc., Lakewood, Colo., 1979-83; v.p., dir. mktg. Citizens Bank Aurora, Colo., 1983-84; ter. mgr. Allergan Pharms., Denver, 1984-87; product mgr. Allergan Optical, Irvine, Calif., 1987-89; mgr. sales tng., 1989—. Scholar U. Colo. Bd. Regents, 1977. Mem. U. Colo. Alumni Assn., Phi Beta Kappa. Democrat. Home: 2 Flagstone Apt 425 Irvine CA 92714 Office: Allergan Optical 2525 DuPont Dr Irvine CA 92715

SWERDLOW, AMY, historian, educator; b. N.Y.C., Jan. 20, 1923; d. Joseph and Esther (Rodner) Galstuck; m. Stanley H. Swerdlow, Nov. 27, 1949; children: Joan Swerdlow-Brandt, Ezra, Lisa Thomas. BA, NYU, 1963; MA, Sarah Lawrence Coll., 1973; PhD, Rutgers U., 1984. Prof. Sarah Lawrence Coll., Bronxville, N.Y., 1981—, dir. grad. studies in women's history, 1983—, dir. women's studies program, 1983—. Editor, co-author: Families in Flux, 1980, reprint, 1989; editor: Feminist Perspectives on Homework and Childcare, 1978; co-editor: Class, Race and Sex: The Dynamics of Control, 1983; contbr. articles to profl. jours. Rutgers U. fellow, 1977-81, Woodrow Wilson Dissertation fellow, 1980. Mem. Am. Hist. Assn. Home: 2 Hedges Banks Dr East Hampton NY 11937 Office: Sarah Lawrence Coll Bronxville NY 10708

SWERGOLD, MARCELLE MIRIAM, sculptor; b. Antwerp, Belgium, Sept. 6, 1927; came to U.S., 1939, naturalized, 1947; d. Gillel and Sarah (Matuzewitz) Elfenbein; student NYU, Art Students League, Sculptors Workshop; m. Maurice Swergold, June 12, 1949; children—Diane Botnick, Henry, Gary Swergold, Paul Kogan, George Kogan. Sculptor, 1965—; one-woman exhbns. include: Studio 12, N.Y.C., 1980, 82, 86, Nat. Fedn. Temple Sisterhoods, 1984; group exhbns. include Farleigh Dickinson U., Teaneck, N.J., 1972, Audubon Artist Ann., N.Y.C., 1978-86, Internat. Treasury Fine Arts, Plainview, N.Y., 1979, New Britain (Conn.) Mus., 1980, also Cork Gallery, Lincoln Center, N.Y.C., Allied Artists Nat. Acad. Galleries, N.Y.C., U.S.Custom House, N.Y.C., others; represented in permanent collection New Britain Mus. Am. Art Yad Vashem Sculpture Garden, Holocaust Mus., Jerusalem; represented in pvt. collection of Master Moshe Castel, Israel. Recipient Best in Show award for Tetons, Women's Art Gallery, N.Y.C., 1977, 1st prize for sculpture Stanley Richter Assn. Arts, 1985, Vincent Glinski Meml. award Audubon Artists, 1986. Mem. N.Y. Soc. Women Artists (pres. 1979-81, exec. v.p. 1981—), Artists Equity, Contemporary Artists Guild. Home: 43 Paul St Danbury CT 06810 Studio: 246 W 80th St New York NY 10024

SWETCHARNIK, SARA MORRIS, artist; b. Shelby, N.C., May 21, 1955; d. William Monroe and Nydia (Earley) Morris; m. William Norton Swetcharnik. Grad., Schuler Sch. Fine Arts, Balt., 1978, postgrad., 1978-79; student, Art Students League, N.Y.C., 1979-81. Monitor for Robert Beverly Hale Art Students League, N.Y.C., 1979-81. One-person exhbns. include Catepetl Gallery, Frederick, Md., 1977; exhibited in group shows at Christ Ch., Tarrytown, N.Y., 1982, Mt. St. Mary's Coll., Emmitsburg, Md., 1981, Weinberg Ctr. for the Arts, Frederick, 1980, Landon Sch., Bethesda, Md., Eikon Fine Arts, Frederick, 1979, Genesis Arts, Frederick, 1978, Foxhall Gallery, Washington, 1982-85, Harbor Gallery, Long Island, N.Y., Jaffae Gallery, Balt., 1979-81, Catepetl Gallery, 1975-79; competitive shows include Pastel Soc. of Am., N.Y.C., Miniature Painters, Sculptors and Gravers Soc., Washington; represented in pub. collections Haussner's Restaurant, Balt. Recipient Fulbright grant, 1987-88, 88-89, Art Students League, N.Y.C., 1987-89; scholarship, Schuler Sch. Fine Arts, Balt., 1978-79, 1st Pl. sculpture award, Miniature Soc. of Sculptors, Painters, and Gravers, Washington, 1976, Allegheny Internat. Miniature Arts Exhibit, 1989. Home Studio: 7404 Woodville Rd Mount Airy MD 21771

SWETMON, SHARON THOMPSON, radiologic technologist; b. Rockwood, Tenn., June 10, 1957; d. Otis Garland Thompson and Willie Charlene (Brady) Smith; m. Kem English Morgan, Dec. 27, 1983 (div. July 1986); m. Carter Swetmon, June 13, 1988. AS in Radiologic Tech., Chattanooga State Tech., 1979; student, U. Tenn., Chattanooga, 1979, 83, 87. Staff technologist T.C. Thompson Children's Hosp., Chattanooga, 1976-84; staff technician South Pittsburg (Tenn.) Hosp., 1984-85; magnetic resonance technologist Diagnostic Imaging, Chattanooga, 1985-88; magnetic resonance tech. coord. Chattanooga Outpatient Ctr., 1985-88; magnetic resonance imaging tech. dir. Erlanger Plaza MRI, 1988—, instr, cons., 1989—; asst. dir. nurse asst. program Edmondson Jr. Coll., Chattanooga, 1983-84. Mem. U.S. Senatorial Bus. Adv. Bd., 1988—, Omni Adv. Bd., 1987-89. Mem. Soc. Magnetic Resonance Imaging, Am. Soc. Radiologic Technologists, Tenn. Soc. Radiologic Technologists, Possum Pack Ski Club, Scuba Club. Home: 3600 Gold Point Circle Hixson TN 37343 Office: Erlanger Plaza MRI 979 E 3d St Chattanooga TN 37403

SWIFT, EVANGELINE WILSON, lawyer; b. San Antonio, May 2, 1939; d. Raymond E. and Josephine (Woods) Wilson; 1 child, Justin Lee. Student So. Meth. U., 1956-59; LL.B., St. Mary's U., San Antonio, 1963. Bar: Tex. 1963, U.S. Ct. Appeals (5th cir.) 1972, D.C. 1976, U.S. Dist. Ct. D.C. 1976, U.S. Supreme Ct. 1980, U.S. Ct. Appeals (11th cir.) 1981, U.S. Ct. Appeals (fed. (10th cir.) 1982, U.S. Ct. Appeals (D.C. cir.) 1982, U.S. Ct. Appeals (fed. cir.) 1983. Atty.-adv. ICC, Washington, 1964-65; staff atty. Headstart Program, OEO, Washington, 1965; exec. legal asst. to chmn., asst. asst. to vice chmn. EEOC, Washington, 1965-71, chief decisions div., 1971-75, asst. gen. counsel, 1975-76; cons. to sec. Employment Standards Adminstrn., Dept. Labor, Washington, 1977-79; gen. counsel Merit Systems Protection Bd., Washington, 1979-86, mng. dir., 1986—, dir. policy and evaluation, 1987—; bd. govs. U.S. Ct. Appeals (fed. cir.) Bar Assn., 1984—, treas., 1987-89, sec., 1989—; guest lectr. Drake U., Pa., MIT; mem. U.S. del. 23d Sessions UN Commn. on Status of Women, Geneva, 1970. Recipient Meritorious Service award Fed. Govt., 1967, Fed. Women's award, 1975, Performance award Merit Systems Protection Bd., 1981-86, 88-89, Gold award 1986, Presdl. CFC award, 1984, 86, EEO award Merit Systems Protection Bd., 1985, Theodore Roosevelt awrd, 1988. Methodist. Office: Merit System Protection Bd Office of Policy and Evaluation 1120 Vermont Ave NW Washington DC 20419

SWIGER, ELINOR PORTER, lawyer; b. Cleve., Aug. 1, 1927; d. Louie Charles and Mary Isabelle (Shank) Porter; m. Quentin Gilbert Swiger, Feb. 5, 1955; children: Andrew Porter, Clavin Gilbert, Charles Robinson. BA, Ohio State U., 1949, JD, 1951. Bar: Ohio 1951, Ill. 1979. Sr. assoc. Robbins, Schwartz, Nicholas, Lifton & Taylor, Ltd., Chgo., 1979—. Author: Mexico for Kids, 1971, Europe for Young Travelers, 1972, The Law and You, 1973 (Literary Guild award), Careers in the Legal Professions, 1978, Women Lawyers at Work, 1978, Law in Everday Life, 1977. Mem. Northfield Twp. (Ill.) Bd. Edn., 1976-83; mem. Glenview (Ill.) Fire and Police Commn., 1976-86; chmn. Glenview Zoning Bd. Appeals, 1987—. Mem. ABA (chmn. pub. edn. com. urban, state and local govt. sect. 1982-85), Ill. Bar Assn. (chmn. local govt. sect. 1986-87, vice chmn. legal edn. sect. 1990-91), Chgo. Bar Assn. (chmn. legis.-exec. com. 1990—), Women Bar Assn. Ill., Midland Authors. Republican. Home: 1933 Burr Oak Dr Glenview IL 60025 Office: Robbins Schwartz Nicholas Lifton & Taylor 29 S LaSalle St Ste 860 Chicago IL 60603

SWIGER, ELIZABETH DAVIS, chemistry educator; b. Morgantown, W.Va., June 27, 1926; d. Hannibal Albert and Tyreeca Elizabeth (Stemple) Davis; m. William Eugene Swiger, June 2, 1948; children: Susan Elizabeth Swiger Knotts, Wayne William. BS in Chemistry, W.Va. U., 1948, MS in Chemistry, 1952, PhD in Chemistry, 1964. Instr. math. Fairmont (W.Va.) State Coll., 1948-49, instr. math. and phys. sci., 1956-57, instr. chemistry, 1957-60, asst. prof. chemistry, 1960-63, assoc. prof. chemistry, 1964-66, prof. chemistry, 1966—; NSF fellow rsch. W.Va. U., Morgantown, 1963-64; advisor Am. Chem. Soc. student affiliates, 1965-88. Author: Morton Family

History, 1984-90, Davis-Winters Family History, 1990; contbr. articles to profl. jours. Bd. mem. Prickett's Fort Meml. Found., Fairmont, 1988—; rep. Adv. Coun. to Bd. Regents Fairmont State Coll., Charleston, 1977-79, rep. instl. bd. advisors, Fairmont, 1990—. NSF grantee, 1963; named Outstanding Prof. W.Va. Legislature, Charleston, 1990. Mem. Am. Chem. Soc. (sect. chmn. North W.Va. 1975, 83), W.Va. Acad. Sci. (exec. com., edn. chmn. 1990), The Nature Conservancy (bd. mem. W.Va. chpt. 1980-82). Republican. Methodist. Home: 1599 Hillcrest Rd Fairmont WV 26554 Office: Fairmont State Coll Locust Ave Fairmont WV 26554

SWIHART, PATRICIA PEARL, financial official; b. Mansfield, Ohio, Feb. 14, 1932; d. Charles Curtis and Catherine Lucille (Reiter) Lysinger; m. Murray Glen Swihart, June 16, 1951; children: Mark J., Marianne K. Swihart Witt. BS, Utah State U., 1989. Owner, mgr. acctg. co., Ohio, 1951-68; acct. Goodwill Industries, Sandusky, Ohio, 1976-78; bus. mgr. various automobile dealerships, Ohio, 1968-80; office mgr. Dave Jolley Chevrolet, Vernal, Utah, 1981-82, Myke & Gary's, Vernal, 1982-84; fiscal mgr. Utah Ind. Living Ctr., Inc., Salt Lake City, 1989—; owner, mgr. P.A.T.S. (Profl. Acctg. & Tax Svc.), NorthSalt Lake, Utah, 1990—, mgr. Shoestring players Milan, Ohio, 1977-78; treas. Community Action Program, Salt Lake City, 1987—; bd. dirs. Utah Issues, Salt Lake City. Ross Beason scholar Westminster Coll., 1988-89. Mem. NAFE. Democrat. Office: Utah Ind Living Ctr Inc 764 South 200 West Salt Lake City UT 84101-2700

SWINDALL, SARAH EARLENE, archivist; b. Stringtown, Okla., July 31, 1941; d. Earl Henry and Iona Belle (Welch) Magby; m. Donald Wayne Swindall, June 13, 1980; children: William Dennis Garrison, Earl Albert Garrison. BA, Cen. State U., Edmond, Okla., 1966; MS, U. North Tex, 1990. Cert. records mgr. Supr. records mgmt. Lone Star Gas Enserch Corp., Dallas, 1970-77; microforms analyst Bell Helicopter Textron, Ft. Worth, 1977-81; adminstrv. supr. Continental Telephone of Tex., Dallas, 1982-84; adminstr. records mgmt. Dallas/Ft. Worth Internat. Airport Bd., Dallas, 1984-90; archivist records mgmt. Superconducting Super Collider Lab., Dallas, 1990—; speaker in field. Mem. adminstrv. bd., trustee St. Paul United Meth. Ch. Recipient Merit award Tex. State Libr. 1988, Olsten Disting. Achievement award Olsten Corp., 1989. Mem. Assn. Records Mgrs. and Adminstrs. (pres. Dallas chpt., Chpt. Mem. of the Yr. 1975, 87), Assn. Info. and Image Mgmt. (pres. Dallas-Ft. Worth chpt.), Spl. Librs. Assn., Soc. Am. Archivists, Soc. S.W. Archivists. Republican. Mailing: PO Box 1252 Hurst TX 76053 Office: Superconducting Super Collider Lab 2550 Beckleymeade Ave Dallas TX 75237

SWINDELLS, SUSAN PETERS, teacher; b. Newport News, Va., Sept. 17, 1952; d. Roger William and Sarah (Johnston) P.; m. Redd Stanley, May 25, 1985. BA, Lynchburg Clg., Va., 1974; MusM, Eastman Sch., Rochester, 1976. N.Y. State Teaching Certification. Elem. music teacher Fulton Consolidated Sch., N.Y.C., 1974-83, Oswego City Schools, N.Y., 1983; cons., singer, bd. mem. Oswego Opera Theatre Inc.; clinician N.Y. State Sch. Music Assn. Author: Teachers Guide to HMS Pinafore, Hansel and Gretel, Magic Flute, La Boheme, Barber of Seville, Tales of Hoffman, Noye's Fludde, La Cenerentola, Amahl and the Night Visitors. Performer Summer Lyric Theatre; mem. Heritage Found., Oswego Festival Chorus. Mem. Music Educator Nat. Conf., Oswego County Music Assn. Home: 134 E Seneca St Oswego NY 13126

SWIRE, EDITH WYPLER, music educator, musician; b. Boston, Feb. 16, 1943; d. Alfred Robert Jr. and Frances Glenn (Emery) Wypler; m. James Bennett Swire, June 11, 1965; 1 child, Elizabeth Emery. BA, Wellesley (Mass.) Coll., 1965; MFA, Sarah Lawrence Coll., Bronxville, N.Y., 1983; postgrad., Coll. of New Rochelle, 1984-85. Tchr. instrumental music The Windsor Sch., Boston, 1965-66; tchr., dir. The Lenox Sch., N.Y.C., 1967-76; music curriculum devel. The Nightingale-Bamford Sch., N.Y.C., 1968-69; head of fine arts dept. The Lenox Sch., N.Y.C., 1976-78, head of instrumental music, 1978-80; founder, dir., tchr. of string sch. Serpentine String Sch., Larchmont, N.Y., 1981—; mem. Founding Schs. com. of the Ind. Sch. Orch., N.Y.C., 1972; trustee Ind. Schs. Orchs., N.Y.C., 1976-87; designated panelist Nat. Assn. of Ind. Schs. Conf., N.Y.C., 1977. Mem. music and worship com., Larchmont Ave. Ch. 1978-82, 88. Mem. Westchester Musicians Guild, N.Y. State Music Tchrs. Assn., Music Tchrs. Nat. Assn., Music Tchrs. Coun. Westchester (program com.), Violin Soc. Am., Wellesley in Westchester. Republican. Home and Office: 11 Serpentine Trail Larchmont NY 10538

SWIRSKY, JUDITH PERLMAN, arts administrator, consultant; b. Bklyn., Oct. 31, 1928; d. Samuel and Rose (Klein) Perlman; m. Leo Jerome Swirsky, June 26, 1949; 1 child, Marjorie Ann Swirsky Zelner. BA, NYU, 1947; postgrad., Columbia U. 1947-48. Rsch asst. The Bklyn. Mus., 1947-49, vol. coord., 1983-89; exec. dir. Grand Cen. Art Galleries Edn. Assn., N.Y.C., 1988-90; freelance curator Genest Gallery, Lamberville, N.J., 1990—; Dir. art sales and rental Gallery The Bklyn. Mus., 1974-77; del. Vol. Com. of Art Mus., Balt., 1973, panelist, 1979; mem., co-founder Vol. Program Administrs. N.Y.C. Cultural Inst., 1984—. Pres. Community Com. for the Bklyn. Mus., 1969-70; bd. dirs. Greater N.Y. Girl Scouts U.S., 1965-71; founder Children's Sch. Time Program and Women's League, Bklyn. Acad. Music, 1961-64; chmn. Bklyn. Guild for Opera, 1966-77; bd. dirs. Arthritis Found. Greater N.Y., 1969-79; trustee Bklyn. Home for Children, 1961-70, Julia Bernstein League of the Free Nurses Inst., 1952-60. Mem. Am. Assn. Mus., Assn. Vol. Adminstrn. (cert., editor region II newsletter), Am. Assn. Mus. Vols., Civitas. Home and Office: 57 Montague St Brooklyn NY 11201-3374

SWISTAK, IRENA, international management executive; b. Meriden, Conn., Oct. 18, 1964; d. Ben and Julia Swistak. BS in Internat. Mgmt., Cen. Conn. State U., 1987. With GE Capital Corp., Rocky Hill, Ct. Patentee sales limit indicator. Chair alumni adv. bd. Cen. Conn. State U. Recipient Spl. Merit award Meriden Record Jour.; named Alumna of Yr., Cen. Conn. State U. Sch. Bus., 1989-90. Mem. NAFE, Am. Mgmt. Assn. Home: 51 Carl St Meriden CT 06450

SWIT, LORETTA, actress; b. Passaic, N.J., Nov. 4, 1937. Student, Am. Acad. Dramatic Arts, Gene Frankel Repertoire Theatre, N.Y.C. Stage appearances include Same Time Next Year, Any Wednesday, The Mystery of Edwin Drood, toured in Maine, Shirley Valentine, Chgo., 1990; films include Stand Up and Be Counted, 1972, Freebie and the Bean, 1974, Race with the Devil, 1975, S.O.B, 1980, Beer, 1985; co-star: TV series M*A*S*H, 1972-83 (Emmy awards for Outstanding Supporting Actress in a Comedy series 1979-81; TV movies Mirror, Mirror, Valentine, Friendships, Secrets and Lies, Shirts and Skins, Coffeeville, Cagney and Lacey, Games Mother Never Taught You, First Affair, The Execution, Dreams of Gold, 14 Going on 30, My Dad Can't be Crazy, Can He?; star on maj. dramatic shows and musical variety shows, including Bob Hope Christmas Special. Mem. AFTRA, Screen Actors Guild, Actors Equity. Address: care Agy for Performing Arts 9000 Sunset Blvd Los Angeles CA 90069*

SWITALSKI, JOYCE DOOLEY, corporate communicatons specialist; b. Manville, N.J., Apr. 28, 1947; d. James Joseph and Mae (Melnyk) Dooley; m. Thomas Adam Switalski, June 13, 1970; children: Kristen, T. Adam, Maureen. Student, Montgomery County Community, Blue Bell, Pa., 1988; grad. magna cum laude, Temple U., 1990. Flight attendant Delta Airlines, Boston, 1967-70; part-time pub. rels. cons. Kremp's Teh Am. Flower Market, Gwynedd, Pa., 1981-85; part-time pub. rels. liaison Simon Group, Spring Horse, Pa., 1985-86; market rsch. intern Earle, Palmer, Brown & Spiro, Phila., 1990—. Contbr. articles to profl. jours. mem. Jr. Colony Club of Ambler, 1978-80, St. Anthony's Sch. PTO, Ambler, 1982-84; mem. Lower Gwynedd Pk. & Recreation Bd., Spring Home, 1985-89; chmn., lobbist L.G. Residents Protection Zoning Laws, 1985-90. Mem. Am. Cancer Soc. (Ambler, Pa. info. chmn. hospice. driver 1978-87), Women in communications, Inc., AAUW, Student Govt. Assn., Kappa Tau Alpha, Phi Alpha Theta, Golden Key Nat. Honor Soc., Phi Theta Kappa. Home: Box 224 Spring House PA 19477

SWITTEN, MARGARET LOUISE, French language educator; b. Chgo.; m. Henry N. Switten (dec.). B.Mus., Westminster Choir Coll. 1947; B.A. Barnard Coll., 1948; M.A., Bryn Mawr Coll., 1949, Ph.D., 1952. Asst. prof. music and French, assoc. prof., then prof. French Hampton Inst., Va., 1952-63; mem. faculty Mt. Holyoke Coll., South Hadley, Mass., 1963—. Alumnae

Found. prof. French, 1975-83, Lucia, Ruth and Elizabeth MacGregor prof. French, 1983-86, Class of 1926 prof. medieval and 18th Century French lang., lit. 1986—, chmn. dept., 1969-76, 82-83. Author: The Cansos of Raimon de Miraval, Medievel Academy, 1985; editor: The Medieval Lyric: Anthologies and Cassettes for Teaching, 1988; contbr. articles to profl. jours. Mary Andersen fellow, 1951-52, Fulbright fellow, 1956-57, Am. Council Learned Socs. fellow, 1969-70. Mem. MLA, Am. Assn. Tchrs. French, Medieval Acad., Modern Humanities Research Assn. Office: Mount Holyoke Coll South Hadley MA 01075

SWITZ, MARY ANN, funeral home executive; b. Massillon, Ohio, July 1, 1944; d. Harold Homer and Margaret Ann (Abel) Hartel; m. David Lee Switz, Oct. 13, 1962 (div. 1970); children: Bethany Lynne, Philip David. Student Cleve. Inst. Music, 1974-75, Cuyahoga Community Coll., Cleve., 1976—. Sec., Calvin Woodward, Atty., Warren, Ohio, 1969-73, Univ. Circle Rsch. Ctr., Cleve., 1973-74; program coord. Univ. Circle Center Community Programs, Cleve., 1974-77; bus. office mgr. Johnson-Romito Funeral Homes, Bedford, Ohio, 1977-90; dir. music Luth. Ch. of Covenant, Maple Heights, Ohio, 1982-86. Mem. bd., accompanist, keyboard prin., soloist Chagrin Valley Choral Union, and Orch., Cleve., 1981-89; accompanist, concertmistress Solon Players Community Theatre and Orch. (Ohio), 1981-83; organist Forest Hill Presbyn. Ch., Cleveland Heights, Ohio, 1987-88. Mem. Chagrin Valley Choral Union, Am. Guild Organists. Lutheran. Home: 400 Vineyard Dr #402 Broadview Heights OH 44147

SWOGER, MARCIA KAY, training and development specialist; b. Elkins, W.Va., July 26, 1951; d. James H. and Carrie M. (Arnold) Chandler; m. Timothy Mark Swoger, Nov. 19, 1983; children: Carrie, Joshua. AS in Bus., W.Va. Career Coll., 1972; student, W.Va. U., 1980. Fin. aid officer W.Va. U., Morgantown, 1972-73; adminstrv. asst. W.Va. Mountain Lair, Morgantown, 1973-75; res. mgr., 1977-80, facilities mgr., 1980-82, asst. dir., 1982-85; div. mgr. ETCON, Inc., Gainesville, Ga., 1985-87; mgr. human resources and devel. ETCON, Inc., Duluth, Ga., 1987-89; tng. and devel. specialist US Achievement, Duluth, Ga., 1989—. Mem. Am. Bus. Women's Assn., Nat. Assn. Female Execs., Am. Cons. League, Am. Soc. Tng. and Devel. Bus. Council Ga. Democrat. Methodist. Office: 3473 Satellite Blvd Ste 200 1879 Buford Hwy Duluth GA 30136

SWOPE, ELAINE HELEN, education educator; b. Lancaster, Pa., Oct. 2, 1947; d. Donald Groff and Helen Beatrice (Gerlitzki) Swope; m. Richard Warren Bakove. BA (with distinction), U. Colo., 1969; MA, U. N. Mex., 1977. Cert. benefit specialist;. Evaluator City & County of Denver, 1970-76; researcher Nat. Inst. Drug Alcohol Abuse, Denver, 1977-81; ins. agt. State Mutual Am., Denver, 1981-83; benefits dir. Univ. Denver, 1984-90; dir. personnel U. Denver, 1990—; lect. Univ. Denver, 1988--. Ptnr. Big Sister Program, Denver, 1977-81; vol. March of Dimes, Denver,. Fellow Internat. Soc. CEBS; mem. Colo. Safety Assn., Colo. Soc. Personnel Adminstrs., Coll. and Univ. Personnel Assn., Nat. Assn. Coll. Univ. Bus. Officers, Am. Soc. Personnel Adminstrs., Phi Beta Kappa, Colo. CEBS (chpt. pres. 1989). Home: 1560 Cook St Denver CO 80206 Office: U Denver 2020 E Evans Denver CO 80208

SWYSTUN-RIVES, BOHDANA ALEXANDRA, dentist; b. Kopychynci, Ukraine, USSR, Jan. 31, 1925; came to U.S., 1951; d. Peter and Maria (Ottawa) Swystun; m. John Rives, June 20, 1952 (div. 1960); 1 child, Peter A. DMD, Ludwig Maximillians Universitat, Munich, 1951; DDS, NYU, 1960. Dentist Dr. Joseph Matriss, East Rutherford, N.J., 1960-61; gen. practice dentistry Clifton, N.J., 1961—. Vol. dentist Felician Sisters Orphanage, Lodi, N.J., 1982—; mem. Presdl. Task Force, Washington. Mem. ADA (award for commitment to professionalism and health), Ukrainian Med. Assn., Ukrainian Nat. Assn., Ukrainian Inst. Am., Clifton-Pasaic (N.J.) C. of C. Republican. Ukrainian Catholic. Office: 1 Portland Ave Clifton NJ 07011

SYDNEY, DORIS S., sports touring company executive, interior designer; b. N.Y.C., Feb. 18, 1934; d. Morris and Frances (Terrace) Steinman; m. Herbert P. Sydney, Oct. 20, 1957; children: Madeleine Jane, Peter Samuel. Student, Vassar Coll., 1950-52; BS, Columbia U., 1952-55; postgrad., NYU, 1956-57, N.Y. Sch. Interior Design, 1974. Cert. documentor Equitable Life Ins. Co., N.Y.C., 1955-57; researcher Fairchild Publs., N.Y.C., 1957-58; furniture sales Steinman's Inc., N.Y.C., 1958-60; interior designer, prin. Doris S. Sydney Interiors, Armonk, N.Y., 1975; exec. asst. Tennis Europe Inc., Conn., 1984--. Pres. Coman Hill Sch. PTA., 1971-72, Byram Hills High Sch. PTA, 1977-79, Byram Hills Scholarship Fund, 1980-82, Non-Partisan Nominating Com, 1982-84; council delegate Vassar Coll. Alumnae Assn., Poughkeepsie, N.Y., 1973-77; chmn. Fred Caruolo Meml. Fund, 1979-81; pres. bd. trustees North Castle Pub. Library, 1981--; treas., pres. Armonk Hadassah, 1980—. Republican. Jewish. Home: 65 Windmill Rd Armonk NY 10504

SYDNOR, EDYTHE LOIS, volunteer executive Bungoma Projects; b. Newark, Dec. 24, 1920; d. Samuel LeRoy and Sarah Lillian (Gaffney) S. Grad. high sch., Newark; cert. in engine repair, Casey Jones Sch. Aeronautics, 1942; student, NYU, 1956-57. Clk. typist U.S. Q.M. Depot, Jersey City, 1940-42; airplane engine mechanic U.S Army Air Depot, Rome, N.Y., 1942-45; exec. sec. Neighborhood Ctr., Montclair, N.J., 1945-53; office mgr. pub. rels. div. Salvation Army, Newark, 1953-56; sec. to dir. fgn. ops. Morey Machinery Co., N.Y.C., 1956-58; adminstrv. supr. Essex County Div. Youth Svcs., Belleville, N.J., 1959-83, ret., 1983; founder, pres. Bungoma Projects, Inc., Montclair, 1983—. Contbr. articles to profl. jours. Participant, leader civil rights activities including March on Washington; mgr. hdqrs. for local and nat. polit. candidates, 1950-70; organizer of voter registration drives in Montclair, Essex County and N.J., 1950-70; 1st woman candidate for Town Commn. Election, Montclair, 1963. Named in proclamation N.J. State Senate, 1983; Edythe Sydnor Day in Essex County proclaimed by Essex County Executive, May 12, 1983; 1 of 15 finalists Salute Black Women Who Make It Happen Nat. Coun. Negro Women and Frito-Lay, 1987. Mem. Essex County League of Vol. Workers, Inc. (pres. 12 yrs. between 1958-82), NAACP. Democrat. Baptist. Office: Bungoma Projects Inc PO Box 1326 Montclair NJ 07042

SYKORA, SANDRA LYNN, graphic artist; b. Slayton, Minn., Jan. 28, 1954; d. Donald D. and Beverly Jo (Dawson) Sykora; m. Steven D. Ross, Oct. 8, 1983. BA, U. Tex., 1976; JD, U. Houston, 1980; Dipl. Comml. Art, Art Inst. Houston, 1982. Legal asst. immigration law Law Offices of Harry Gee, Jr., Houston, 1979-82; graphic artist Radian Corp., Austin, 1984—. Assoc. editor Houston Internat. Law Jour., 1978-79. Coordinator Amnesty Internat., Austin, 1987. Mem. Austin Graphic Arts Soc., Internat. Law Soc. (pres. 1978-79), Delta Theta Phi, Alpha Lambda Delta. Democrat. Roman Catholic. Home: 6308 Lakewood Hollow Austin TX 78750

SYMANK, OLETA MARLENE, educator; b. Elkins, W.Va., Aug. 24, 1957; d. Odis Milton and Oleta Frances (Owen) McNeill; m. Clarence Theodore Symank, May 3, 1986. BS in Edn., Baylor U., 1980. Cert. tchr., Tex. Tchr. kindergarten St. Mary's Cath. Sch., Waco, Tex., 1980-85; tchr. H.O. Whitehurst Elem. Sch., Groesbeck, Tex., 1985—. Mem. Assn. Tex. Profl. Tchrs. Republican. Baptist. Home: Rt 1 Box 1037-L Waco TX 76712

SYMONDS, JOHNNIE PIRKLE, retired pscyhologist; b. Wynnewood, Okla., Apr. 5, 1900; d. John Thomas and Lillie Belle (Driver) Pirkle; m. Percival Mallon Symonds, Dec. 25, 1922. BA, U. Tex., 1920, MA, 1921; postgrad. Columbia U., 1921-22, 26-27, 28-29, 30-31, NYU, 1975. Asst. dept. psychology U. Tex., Austin, 1919-21; rsch. assoc. Inst. Ednl. Rsch. Tchrs. Coll. Columbia U., N.Y.C., 1921-22; psychologist Family Svc. Soc., Yonkers, N.Y., 1937-46; ret., 1946. Editor: Jour. Cons. Psychology, 1937-46; contbr. articles to profl. jours. Mem: Columbia Com. for Community Svc., 1972—; active English in action program, English speaking union Riverside Ch., N.Y.C., 1974-75, honored 50th anniversary mem., 1979. Named disting. grad. Tchrs. Coll. Columbia U. Trustees, 1990. Mem. Am. Psychol. Assn., N.Y. Acad. of Scis., N.Y. State Psychol. Assn., Am. Assn. Applied Psychology, AAAS, AAUW, Ednl. Press Assn., World Fedn. Mental Health, Pi Lambda Theta, Kappa Delta Pi, Appalachian Mountain Club (Honor award 50th anniversary mem. 1981). Home: 106 Morningside Dr Apt 71 New York NY 10027

SYTSMA, KAREN L., public relations and publishing executive; b. West Allis, Wis., May 7, 1964; d. Charles Frank and Carol Jean (Kotowski) Meyer; m. James Kenneth Sytsma, June 21, 1986. BA in Mass Communication, U. Wis., Milw., 1985. Staff asst. publications Women's Internat. Bowling Congress, Greendale, Wis., 1986-88, editor Woman Bowler mag., asst. mgr. pub. rels., 1988—. Mem. Pub. Rels. Soc. Am., Bowling Writers Assn. Am., Nat. Women Bowling Writers.

SZABLAK, LAURA ROSEMARY, controller; b. Bridgeport, Conn., Nov. 12, 1957; d. Leo Anthony and Augustina (Angelo) S. BS in Acctg., Fairfield U., 1979. Acct. Citytrust Bancorp, Bridgeport, 1979-85, fin. analyst, 1985-87, acctg. mgr., 1987-90; asst. contr. First Nat. Bank Litchfield, Conn., 1990—. Instr., advisor color guard Cheshire (Conn.) High Sch. Mem. NAFE. Roman Catholic. Home: 48-2 Harper Ave Waterbury CT 06705 Office: First Nat Bank Litchfield PO Box 578 Litchfield CT 06759

SZABO, DENISE ZAROTNEY, insurance company executive; b. New Britain, Conn., Aug. 3, 1953; d. Henry and Jacquelyn (Frank) Zarotney; m. John Frederick Szabo, June 6, 1981. Student, Tunxis Community Coll., 1972-73. Office adminstr. Lenko Finishing Inc., Plainville, Conn., 1971-75; customer service rep. Aetna Life & Casualty Co., Hartford, Conn., 1975-76, sr. pension analyst, 1976—. Roman Catholic. Club: Tuesday Bowling (Plainville, Conn.) (v.p. 1985-86). Home: 421 Burritt St New Britain CT 06051 Office: Aetna Life & Casualty Co 151 Farmington Ave Hartford CT 06156

SZALAY, CAROLYN RUTH O'CONNOR, catering company executive; b. Carmel, Ind., Apr. 8, 1943; d. Charles Milburn and Ruth Isabelle (West-Covert) O'Connor; m. Robert Eugene Szalay, Sept. 7, 1963; children: Robert Scott Albert Charles Richard David Lawrence, Theresa Ruth Pearl Isabelle Mary Margaret Anne Szalay-Vester. Student, Internat. Corrs. Schs., 1989. Asst. mgr. Pickett's, Indpls., 1965-70; mgr. Feminine Accents, Indpls., 1970-75; co-mgr. Sizes Unltd., Indpls., 1975-81; owner, mgr. Carol's Catering, Indpls., 1983—; co-owner, mgr. Treasured Moments Tea Room, Indpls., 1989—. Vol. Community Hosp., Indpls, 1969—. Mem. Wesleyan Ch. Home and Office: 2320 N Courtney Rd Indianapolis IN 46219-1202

SZALKOWSKI, MARY B., chemist; b. Cleve., Nov. 24, 1951; d. Michael and Mary (Hornik) S. BS in Chemistry magna cum laude, Cleve. (Ohio) State U., 1972, MS in Chemistry, 1976. Cert. med. writer. Rsch. chemist Diamond Shamrock, Plainesville, Ohio, 1976-79; sr. rsch. chemist Diamond Shamrock, Plainesville, 1979, rsch. supr., 1979-81; clin. rsch. assoc. Amaric Corp., Mentor, Ohio, 1981-82; project mgr. Amaric Corp., Mentor, 1982-83, asst. dir. clin. planning, 1983-84; dir. corp. planning Amaric Corp., Austin, Tex., 1984-86; v.p. corp. planning Amaric Corp., Austin, 1986-87; pres. Amaric Corp., Seven Hills, Ohio, 1987—; Mem. Edison Biotechnology Ctr. Author to numerous sci. papers, 1975-89. Mem. Womenspace, Cleve., 1990. Recipient YWCA Career Woman of Achievement award, Cleve. Mem. NAFE, Am. Chem. Soc., Am. Med. Writer's Assn., Drug Info. Assn., N.E. Ohio Biotechnology Assn. (chair-elect 1990), Iota Sigma Pi (past pres. and v.p.). Office: Amaric Corp 5700 Lombardo Ctr Dr Ste #235 Seven Hills OH 44131

SZARO, JUDITH SALOMEA, advertising executive, artist, political worker; b. Elizabeth, N.J., Aug. 2, 1952; d. Albert Stanley and Mary Stella (Turon) S. BA, Douglass Coll., 1974; MBA, Rutgers U., 1989; cert. in art, Albert Pels Sch. Art, 1980. Mktg. researcher Phila. Mftr. Mut. Ins. Co., N.Y.C., 1976-78; advt. bd. artist Spiros Assocs., N.Y.C., 1980-82; freelance comml. artist, polit. fundraiser N.J., 1982-85; advt. exec. Grey Advt., Inc., N.Y.C., 1985—. Corr. sec. Greater Elizabeth Dem. Club, Union County, N.J. 1982-85; local fundraiser, campaign promoter Raymond J. Lesniak for N.J. State Senator, 1982-85, fin. sec., 1982-85. Democrat. Roman Catholic. Office: Grey Advt Inc 777 3d Ave New York NY 10017

SZCZESNIAK, ALINA SURMACKA, food scientist, researcher; b. Warsaw, Poland, July 8, 1925; came to U.S., 1946; d. Wladyslaw Tadeusz and Zofia (Szukiewicz) Surmacki; m. Walter Szczesniak, June 18, 1949 (dec. June 1984); 1 child, Andrew. AB in Chemistry, Bryn Mawr (Pa.) Coll., 1948; DSc in Food Tech., MIT, 1952. With Gen. Foods Corp., Tarrytown, N.Y., 1952—; rsch. scientist, 1974-81, sr. scientist, 1981-86, ret., 1986; mem. adv. bd. food sci. dept. Rutgers U., New Brunswick, 1989—. Mem. editorial adv. bd. Food & Nutrition Press, 1977—, AVI Pub. Co., 1981-85; author book chpts.; editor-in-chief Jour. Texture Studies, 1969-80; inventor in field. Bd. dirs., sec. Polish Inst. Arts & Scis. of Am., N.Y.C., 1986—. Fellow Inst. Food Technologists (Disting. Scientist of the Yr. 1982, Nicolas Appert medal 1985); mem. N.Y. Acad. Scis., Soc. Rheology, Sigma Xi, Phi Tau Sigma. Republican. Roman Catholic. Home: 22 Wilson Block Mount Vernon NY 10552

SZCZESNY, FRANCES EVELYN, human resources executive; b. Bklyn., Aug. 23, 1951; d. Charles and Anne Betty (Lerner) Feurman; m. Thomas A. Szczesry, July 15, 1972; 1 child, Spencer Evan. BA in English, SUNY, Buffalo, 1972; MS in Mgmt., Poly. Inst. N.Y., 1977. Editor John Wiley & Sons, Inc., N.Y.C., 1974-76; asst. dir. personnel Vis. Nurse Service N.Y., N.Y.C., 1977-81; dir. employee relations, 1984-87; pres. HRM Services, Marlboro, N.J., 1987—; human resources cons. Vis Nurses Assn., S.I., 1981-84, Women Aware, Inc., New Brunswick, N.J., 1986-87, Metaplex Mgmt. Svcs. Inc., Red Bank, N.J., 1987—, Inst. Bus. Careers, Highland Park, N.J., 1987, Elite Diversified HealthCare Inc., New Brunswick, 1988, Howell (N.J.) Coll. System, 1988, N.J. Shore Savs. and Loan Assn., 1989; adj. lectr. Brookdale Coll., Lincroft, N.J., 1987—, Ocean County Coll., Toms River, N.J., 1988—. V.p. Whitter Oaks Civic Assn., Morganville, N.J., 1980-81. Mem. Am. Soc. for Hosp. Personnel Adminstrn., Am. Soc. Personnel Adminstrn. (speaker), Internat. Assn. Personnel Women (speaker, bd. dirs., program chmn. 1987-89, pres.-elect 1989—), N.J. Home Health Assembly (speaker, chmn.), Western Monmouth County C. of C., AAUW, NAFE, Hadssah, Soroptimists. Club: Hadassah (Marlboro, N.J.) Lodge: Soroptimists. Home: 45 Georgian Bay Dr Morganville NJ 07751

SZEBENYI, DOLETHA MARIAN EVANS, crystallographer; b. Arlington, Mass., Nov. 27, 1947; d. Gordon Goodwin and Doletha Soorn (Watt) Evans; m. Thomas Akos Szebenyi, Sept. 3, 1972; 1 child, Gordon K. AB, Bryn Mawr Coll., 1968; PhD, U. Conn., 1972. Computer programmer DCA Inc., Linden, N.J., 1972-75; rsch. assoc. Cornell U., Ithaca, N.Y., 1975—. Contbr. articles to profl. jours. Mem. AAAS, Am. Crystallographic Assn. Home: 176 Jackson Hollow Rd Newfield NY 14867 Office: Cornell U 209 Biotechnology Bldg Ithaca NY 14853

SZEGO, CLARA MARIAN, cell biologist, educator; b. Budapest, Hungary, Mar. 23, 1916; came to U.S., 1921, naturalized, 1927; d. Paul S. and Helen (Elek) S.; m. Sidney Roberts, Sept. 14, 1941. A.B., Hunter Coll., 1937; M.S. (Garvan fellow), U. Minn., 1939, Ph.D, 1942. Instr. physiology U. Minn., 1942-43; Minn. Cancer Research Inst. fellow, 1943-44; research asso. OSRD, Nat. Bur. Standards, 1944-45, Worcester Found. Exptl. Biology, 1945-47; research instr. physiol. chemistry Yale U. Sch. Medicine, 1947-48; mem. faculty UCLA, 1948—, prof. biology, 1960—. Researcher, author numerous publs. on steroid protein interactions, mechanisms of hormone action and lysosome participation in normal cell function. Named Woman of Year in Sci. Los Angeles Times, 1957-58; Guggenheim fellow, 1956; named to Hunter Coll. Hall of Fame, 1987. Fellow AAAS; mem. Am. Physiol. Soc., Am. Soc. Cell Biology, Endocrine Soc. (CIBA award 1953), Soc. for Endocrinology (Gt. Britain), Biochem. Soc. (Gt. Britain), Internat. Soc. Rsch. Reprodn., Phi Beta Kappa (pres. UCLA chpt. 1973-74), Sigma Xi (pres. UCLA chpt. 1976-77). Home: 1371 Marinette Rd Pacific Palisades CA 90272 Office: U Calif Dept Biology Los Angeles CA 90024

SZEREMETA-BROWAR, TAISA LYDIA, endodontist; b. Geneva, N.Y., Mar. 21, 1957; d. Swiatoslaw Bohdan and Stefania (Melnyk) Szeremeta; m. Andrew Wlodymyr Browar, Sept. 19, 1981. BS in Dentistry, Case Western Res. U., 1978, DDS, 1980; cert. specialty endodontics magna cum laude, U. Ill., Chgo., 1982. Pvt. practice Hinsdale (Ill.) Periodontics and Endodontics, 1982—; asst. clin. prof. Northwestern U. Dental Sch., Chgo., 1986—. Counselor, mem. Plast-Ukrainian Scouting, Cleve., 1976-77; presenting team Worldwide Marriage Encounter, Chgo., 1985—; parish coun. Sts. Volodymyr and Olha, Chgo., 1985—. E. Wach rsch. grantee U. Ill., Chgo., 1980. Mem.

ADA, Am. Assn. Endodontists, Am. Coll. Stomatologic Surgeons, Ukrainian Med. Assn. (membership chair 1983-88), Ill. Assn. Endodontists (pres. 1990-91), Ill. State Dental Soc., Chgo. Dental Soc. (sec. table clinic 1990, vice chair 1991), Hinsdale C. of C. Ukrainian Catholic. Office: Hinsdale Periodontics and Endodontics 40 S Clay St Ste 111W Hinsdale IL 60521

SZESKO, DEBORAH PULDA, microbiologist; b. New Brunswick, N.J., Mar. 5, 1958; d. William Francis and Patricia Ann (Van Orden) Pulda; m. Michael Joseph Szesko, June 11, 1983. BA in Microbiology, Rutgers U., 1980, MS in Indsl. Microbiology, 1990. Fermentation microbiologist New Brunswick Sci. Co., Inc., Edison, N.J., 1980-82; in process control scientist Cell Products Inc., New Brunswick, 1982-83, quality assurance microbiologist, 1983-85; assoc. scientist I, Schering Corp., Union, N.J., 1985-86, assoc. scientist II, 1986-88; coord. process devel. and prodn. Agri-Diagnostics Assocs., Cinnaminson, N.J., 1988—; book reviewer for edn. materials AAAS, Washington, 1989—. Tchr. St. Robert Bellarmine Ch., Freehold, N.J., 1989-90. Mem. Soc. for Indsl. Microbiology, Am. Soc. for Microbiology, Am. Chem. Soc., Theobald Smith Soc. (banquet com.). Roman Catholic. Home: 325 Georgia Rd Freehold NJ 07728 Office: Agri-Diagnostics Assocs 2611 Branch Pike Cinnaminson NJ 08077

SZLYK, PATRICIA CAROL, research physiologist, consultant; b. Worcester, Mass., Dec. 24, 1952; d. Stanley John and Felicia Geraldine (Kislak) S. BA summa cum laude, Elmira Coll., 1974; postgrad., Clark U., 1974-75; PhD with distinction, SUNY, Buffalo, 1980. Rsch. asst. Worcester Found. for Exptl. Biology, Shrewsbury, Mass., 1974-75; lectr. dept. physiology SUNY, Buffalo, 1977-78, Queen's U., Kingston, Ont., Can., 1980-83; rsch. physiologist heat rsch. div. U.S. Army Rsch. Inst. Environ. Medicine, Natick, Mass., 1983—; biochemist 373d Army Gen. Hosp., Boston, 1985—; cons. Dept. Army, Natick, 1983—, Inst. Chem. Def., Aberdeen, Md., 1984-87; reviewer Jour. Aviation Space Environ. Medicine, 1985—. Contbr. numerous articles on fluid intake, heat injuries, dehydration and breathing-circulation control to profl. jours. Vol. Boston Marathon, 1984-88; judge Worcester Regional Sci. Fair, 1987-89, Internat. Sci. and Engring. Fair, 1988, 89, 90, Mass. Sci. Fair, 1989—. Can. Heart. Found. fellow, 1981-83. Mem. Am. Physiol. Soc., Can. Physiol. Soc., N.Y. Acad. Scis., Boston Bicycle Road Club, Phi Beta Kappa, Sigma Xi (admissions com., pres. Natick chpt.), Beta Beta Beta. Roman Catholic. Home: 45 Curtis Sq Marlborough MA 01752-2677 Office: USA Rsch Inst Environ Med Heat Rsch Div Natick MA 01760

SZMYT, DAVENA D., retail executive; b. Brockton, Mass., Nov. 18, 1939; d. David Elroy Dart and Lorena (Young) Love; m. Henry Joseph Szmyt, Aug. 3, 1969; children: Paul Scott, Steven Todd, Christopher Henry. Diploma, Peter Bent Brigham Hosp. Sch. Nursing, 1960. Charge nurse Boston Lying-In Hosp., 1960-62; supr. operating room Beverly Hills (Calif.) Doctors Hosp., 1962-64; nurse Peter Bent Brigham Hosp., Boston, 1964-65; organizer, head nurse Boston City Hosp. and Harvard Surg. ICU, Boston, 1967-68; instr. nursing Lawrence (Mass.) Gen. Hosp. Sch. Nursing, 1968-70; asst. dir. nursing, dir. inservice edn. Hunt Meml. Hosp., Danvers, Mass., 1970-77; organizer 1st regional health ctr. Urgent Care Unit, Wilmington, Mass., 1977-80; co-owner, bus. mgr. Freedman Fur Assocs., Inc., Lawrence, Mass., 1980-84, owner, pres., 1984—; owner, pres. Freedman Furs of N.H. Inc., Plaistow, N.H., 1984—; bd. dirs. Rockingham County Trust Bank. Founder, sec. Timberlane Civic Assn., Plaistow, 1972; founder, past pres., trustee Plaistow Area Commerce Exch. Inc., 1985-87, bd. dirs. 1989-90, treas. 1990—; sec. Plaistow Safety Complex Com., 1984-86, bldg. com. 1985-87; mem. Plaistow Budget Com., 1985, bd. of selectmen, 1985—; sec. property com. First Bapt. Ch., Plaistow, 1986-88; dir. Plaistow Civil Def., 1980-87; select liaison Budget Com., 1987—. Recipient Outstanding Vol. award Gov. N.H., 1986; named one of Outstanding Women Achievement Mem. Plaistow Bus. and Profl. Women Fedn. (pres. 1985-86), Plaistow Area C. of C., Master Furrier Guild, Exptl. Merchant Assn. Republican. Home: 22 Forrest St Plaistow NH 03865 Office: Freedman Furs of NH Inc 12 Plaistow Rd #4 Plaistow NH 03865

SZUCH, STEPHANIE, administrative assistant; b. Czechoslovakia, Mar. 8, 1936; d. Abraham and Charlotte (Deutsch) Berkowitz; m. Rudy S. Szuch, Mar. 13, 1955 (div. 1975); children: Randy Scott, Jamie Dee Corallo, Mike Lee. BA in English, Rutgers U., 1974. Communications specialist Airco Indsl. Gases, Murray Hill, N.J., 1974-79; adminstrv. asst. Wakefern Food Corp., Elizabeth, N.J., 1979—. Editor, reporter for local newspaper, 1976-80; editor Boy Scouts Am./Cub Scouts, 1987-88. Mem. com. Fanwood (N.J.) Reps., 1976-80; co. rep. communications United Way, N.J., 1976-79; sec., chmn. Fanwood Recreation Commn., 1977-80; active Boy Scouts and Cub Scouts Am., Scotch Plains, N.J., 1987-89; co-chmn. Meml. Day Parade Commn., Scotch Plains, 1984-87; fund raiser Am. Cancer Soc., scotch Plains, 1985-89; vol Ronald Reagan Campaign, Thomas Kean Campaign, N.J.; del. state Rep. caucuses. Jewish. Home: 325 Forest Rd Scotch Plains NJ 07076

SZUETS, JUDIE ELIZABETH, information processing executive; b. Tatatovaros, Hungary, Aug. 19, 1956; came to U.S., 1956; d. Ervin Antal and Maria Cecilia (Valyi) S. AS, Sacred Heart U., Bridgeport, Conn., 1981. Project sec. Crawford and Russell, Inc., Stamford, Conn., 1977-80; adminstrv. asst., risk mgmt. Xerox Corp., Stamford, 1980-82; mgr. svc. bur./tng. edn. All Bus. Assistance, Norwalk, Conn., 1982-87; owner computer svc. bur. Advanced Bus. Support, Norwalk, 1987—. Mem. NAFE. Office: 266 Main Ave Ste 6 Norwalk CT 06851

SZUMYLO, HELEN BARBARA, national cemetery administrator; b. Pfaffenhofen, Germany, Nov. 10, 1946; d. Wojciech and Stanislawa (Witkowska) Szumylo. Student, Calif. Coast U., Kalamazoo Community Coll., Nazareth Coll., Parson's Bus. Sch. Dir. Marion (Ind.) Nat. Cemetery; asst. dir. L.I. Nat. Cemetery, Farmingdale, N.Y.; dir. L.A. Nat. Cemetery. Mem. NAFE, ALTRUSA. Address: 2901 S Sepulveda Apt 368 West Los Angeles CA 90064

SZYMANSKI, KAREN ANN, marketing executive; b. Chgo., Aug. 22, 1951; d. Casimir and Frances (Wojtecki) S. BA, Mundelein Coll., 1971; MA, Syracuse U., 1975, PhD, 1980. Admissions counselor Mundelein Coll., Chgo., 1971-73; instr., postdoctoral teaching fellow Syracuse (N.Y.) U., 1973-81; mgr. communications Magnavox CATV, 1982-85; mgr. mktg. communications GE Aerospace, 1985-90; mktg. cons. Highland Park, Ill., 1990—; communications cons., Syracuse, 1980-82; presenter in field. Contbr. to Guide to American Women Writers. Mem. Internat. Assn. Bus. Communicators (bd. dirs. Syracuse chpt. 1983—, pres. 1985), Soc. for Tech. Communications.

SZYMONIAK, ELAINE EISFELDER, state senator; b. Boscobel, Wis., May 24, 1920; d. Hugo Adolph and Pauline (Vig) Eisfelder; Casimir Donald Szymoniak, Dec. 7, 1943; children: Kathryn, Peter, John, Mary, Thomas. BS, U. Wis., 1941; MS, Iowa State U., 1977. Speech clinician Waukesha (Wis.) Pub. Sch., 1941-43, Rochester (N.Y.) Pub. Sch., 1943-44; rehab. aide U.S. Army, Chickasha, Okla., 1944-46; audiologist U. Wis., Madison, 1946-48; speech clinician Buffalo Pub. Sch., 1948-49, Sch. for Handicapped, Salina, Kans., 1951-52; speech pathologist, audiologist, counselor, resource mgr. Vocat. Rehab. State Iowa, Des Moines, 1956-66; mem. Iowa Senate, Des Moines, 1989—. Coun. mem. Des Moines City Coun., 1978-88; bd. dirs. Nat. League Cities, Washington, 1982-84; chair Greater Des Moines United Way, 1987-88. Named Woman of Achievement Young Women's Christian Assn., 1982. Mem. Am. Speech Lang. and Hearing Assn., Iowa Speech Lang. (and Hearing Assn. (pres. 1977-78), Nat. Coun. State Legislators, Women's Polit. Caucus, Nexus (pres. 1981-82). Home: 2116 44th Des Moines IA 50310 Office: State Senate State Capitol Des Moines IA 50319

SZYSZKEIWICZ, REGINA F., marketing director; b. Chgo., July 6, 1962; d. Joseph Stanley and Mary Bernadette (Flondro) S. BA, U. Ill., 1985, MA, 1987. Project mgr. market rsch. SRI Gallup, Chgo., 1985-88; asst. dir. mtkg. Charter Hosp. of Long Beach, Calif., 1980-89; dir. mktg. Charter Hosp. of Torrance, Calif., 1989—. Mem. Am. Mtkg. Assoc. Office: Charter Hosp Torrance 4025 N 226th St Torrance CA 90505

TABACHUK, EMELIA, banker; b. Passaic, N.J., Aug. 3, 1926; d. Michael and Fannie (Stefanyk) T.; student Drake Bus. Coll., 1956, N.Y. Inst. Credit, 1978-80. With Marine Midland Bank. N.Y.C., 1946—; adminstrv. asst. 1975-76, ops. asst., 1976-78, comml. banking officer, 1978—, asst. v.p., 1982-85; retired 1985. Mem. Nat. Assn. Bank Women, Nat. Assn. Female Execs., Am. Soc. Profl. and Exec. Women. Home: 78 Stadtmauer Dr Clifton NJ 07013 Office: 140 Broadway New York City NY 10015

TABAKIN, LORAINE SMITH, lawyer; b. Cambridge, Mass., July 2, 1940; d. Albert Frances Smith and Eileen (Mullett) Boynton; m. Frank Tabakin, Sept. 1, 1963; children: Jennifer, Steven. BS, Simmons Coll., 1962; MSW, Columbia U., 1964; JD, U. Pitts., 1976. Bar: Pa. 1976, U.S. Supreme Ct. 1980, U.S. Ct. Appeals (3d cir.), 1984. Psychiat. social worker Altro Health Rehab. Service, N.Y.C., 1964-65, Pitts. Child Guidance Ctr., 1965-67; asst. county solicitor Allegheny County Law Dept., Pitts., 1976-80; assoc. atty. Strassburger, McKenna, Pitts., 1980-83; ptnr. Tabakin, Carroll & Curtin, Pitts., 1984—. Mem. exec. bd. 14th Ward Dem. Club, Pitts., 1972-73, 80-86; bd. dirs. ACLU, Pitts., 1978-82. Mem. ABA, Pa. Bar Assn., Allegheny County Bar Assn. (council family law sect.), Pa. Trial Lawyers Assn. Office: Tabakin Carroll & Curtin 1430 Grant Bldg Pittsburgh PA 15219

TABATCHNICK, MERYL S., American history educator; b. Bklyn., Nov. 10, 1950; d. Lester and Marcelle (Applebaum) Schwartz; m. Bruce J. Tabatchnick, Feb. 7, 1971; 1 child, Ian Joshua. BS in Edn., CUNY, 1971; postgrad., Hunter Coll., 1972-73; MEd, Fla. Atlantic U., 1979. Cert. social studies instr., elem. instr., early childhood edn., Fla., N.Y. Early childhood educator The Dalton Sch., N.Y.C., 1971-73; history instr. Ramblewood Middle Sch., Coral Springs, Fla., 1981-88; Am. history educator Forest Glen Middle Sch., Coral Springs, 1988—; acad. competitions coord. Ramblewood Middle Sch., 1985-88, team leader, 1987-88; acad. competitions coord. Forest Glen Middle Sch., 1988-89, team leader, 1988-89, prime grant steering com., 1988—; educator Jr. Achievement Project Bus., Coral Springs, 1983—. Educator Coalition of Essential Schs., Broward County, Fla., 1989—; vol. March of Dimes, Ft. Lauderdale, 1974-76, Lubb Dubb Club U. Miami, Fla., Sch. of Medicine, Jackson Meml. Hosp., Miami, 1979—, Pine Crest Sch. Ann. Fund, Ft. Lauderdale, 1988—; mem. English Channel Swim Fundraising Com., 1988—. Mem. Broward Coun. for the Social Studies (Tchr. of Yr. 1987-88), Fla. Coun. for the Social Studies, Fla. Coun. for the Social Studies Conv. (steering com., registration chairperson), Phi Kappa Phi. Jewish. Office: Forest Glen Middle Sch 6501 Turtle Run Blvd Coral Springs FL 33067

TABBERT, RONDI JO, accountant; b. Dallas, Mar. 14, 1953; d. Jack H. and June F. (Williams) Russell; m. William Henry Tabbert, Nov. 16, 1979. A.A., Tarrant County Jr. Coll., 1975; B.S. in Bus., U. Tex.-Dallas, 1980; M.B.A., U. Dallas, 1984. C.P.A., Tex. Bookkeeper, Kelly-Moore Paint, Dallas, 1976-78; corp. acct. Gen Portland, Dallas, 1978-80; chief acct. W.R. Grace & Co., Dallas, 1980-83; controller Little & Assocs., Dallas, 1983-85; prin. Rondi J. Tabbert, CPA, Desoto, Tex., 1985—; accting. instr., Cedar Valley Community Coll., 1987—. Weekly fin. columnist De Soto Tribune, 1986-87. Bd. dirs., treas. Unity Ch. Duncanville, 1989—; mem. adv. bd.DeSoto Cultutal Ctr., 1989—. Mem. AICPA, NAFE, Tex. Soc. CPAs (vice chmn. tax edn. com. 1988-89, chmn. 1989—, communication coun. steering com. 1989—, bd. dirs. 1988-89), Dallas chpt. 1989—. Nat. Soc. Tax Profls., Dallas Soc. CPAs (tax edn. com. 1985-86, vice chmn. 1986-87, chmn. 1987-88), Am. Women's Soc. CPAs, Am. Bus. Women's Assn. (program com. 1986-87, program chmn. 1987—), DeSoto C. of C. Mem. Libertarian party. Home: 1055 Turner Ave Dallas TX 75208 Office: 911 N Hampton #104 DeSoto TX 75115

TABER, CAROL A., magazine publisher. AA, Green Mountain Coll., 1965. Network mgr. Media Networks, Inc., 1970-74; N.Y. advt. mgr. Ladies' Home Jour., 1974-79; assoc. publisher, advt. dir. Working Woman, N.Y.C., 1979-83, publisher, 1984—. Office: Working Woman Mag 342 Madison Ave New York NY 10173*

TABER, ELSIE, medical educator; b. Columbia, S.C., May 3, 1915; d. Stephen and Bessie (Ray) T. BS, U. S.C., 1935; MS, Stanford U., 1936; PhD, U. Chgo., 1947. Biology tchr. Greenwood, S.C., 1936-38; instr. Lander Coll., Greenwood, 1938-41; instr. U. Chgo., 1944-48, asst. dean student affairs, 1947-48; asst. prof. to prof. anatomy Med. U. S.C., Charleston, 1948-80, prof. emerita, 1980—, asst. dean, 1980—; bd. dirs U.S.C. Edul. Found., Columbia; councilor Soc. Anatomy, 1968-70, 76-78. Contbr. chpts. to scientific books. Bd. dirs. Episcopal Retirement Community, Charleston, 1984—. Mem. U.S.C. Acad. Sci. (pres. 1954-55), Colonial Dames of Am., Phi Beta Kappa, Delta Delta Delta, Sigma Xi, Alpha Omega Alpha. Republican. Home: 216 Molasses Ln Mount Pleasant SC 29464 Office: Deans Office Coll Med U SC 171 Ashley Ave Charleston SC 29425

TABER, LINDA PERRIN, public relations executive; b. Marshalltown, Iowa, Dec. 30, 1941; d. Burr H. Perrin and Luella (Memler); m. Roy Howard Pollack, Oct. 1, 1983; m. Allan D. Taber, Apr. 26, 1969 (div. 1976). B.A., U. Iowa, 1964; M.A., Syracuse U., 1969. Account supr. Ketchum, Macleod & Grove, N.Y.C., 1969-73; v.p. Carol Moberg, Inc., N.Y.C., 1973-78; dir. Ketchum Pub. Relations, N.Y.C., 1979-83; sr. v.p. Ketchum Pub. Relations, 1983—. Mem. Pub. Relations Soc. Am., The Fashion Group, Women Execs. in Pub. Relations, Women in Communications. Office: Ketchum Pub Rels 1133 Ave of Americas New York NY 10036*

TABNER, MARY FRANCES, educator; b. Rochester, N.Y., Dec. 11, 1918; d. William Herman and Mary Frances (Willenbacher) Arndt; m. James Gordon Tabner, June 27, 1942; 1 child, Barbara Jean. BA, SUNY, Albany, 1940, MA, 1959; postgrad., U. Rochester, N.Y., 1944, 45, Northwestern U. (John Hay fellow), 1963-64, U. Manchester (Eng.), 1971-72. Tchr. history pub. schs. Mattituck, N.Y., 1940-43, Gorham, N.Y., 1943-46; tchr. pub. schs. Waterford, N.Y., 1949-55; tchr. social studies Shaker High Sch., Latham, N.Y., 1959-83, now also dir. Russian studies seminar, 1959-83, ret., 1983; tchr. ch. history Our Lady of Assumption Ch., Latham. Author bibliographies on Russian history, Am. studies. Mem. Citizens Exch. Coun. N.Y. State Regents independent study grantee, 1966. Mem. Nat. Coun. Social Studies, N.Y. State United Tchrs., Assn. Advancement Slavic Studies, SUNY, Albany Alumni Assn., Albany Inst. History and Art, Capital Dist. couns. for social studies, Shaker Heritage Soc. (trustee, guide, tchr.), Nat. Trust for Hist. Preservation, English Speaking Union, Am. Assn. Ret. Persons. Republican. Roman Catholic. Home: 557 Columbia St Cohoes NY 12047

TABORSKY, CAROL JEANNE, chemist, research scientist; b. Balt., Feb. 19, 1947; d. Emil D. and Louise (Zeman) T.; m. James H. Reamer, Dec. 23, 1969 (div. 1980); children: David, Brian, Angela Kristina. BS in Chemistry, Am. U., 1970. Chemist trainee drug rsch. div. FDA, Washington, 1968-70; rsch. chemist U.S Pharmacopeia, Washington, 1972-78; mgr. chemistry Copanos Drug Co., Balt., 1978-79; supr. quality control chemistry Noxell Corp., Balt., 1981-85; sr. chemist Noxell Corp., 1985-88, analytical chemist, 1988-89; formulation scientist, mgr. clin. supplies Nova Pharm. Corp., Balt., 1989—; cons. in thermal analysis, Balt. Contbr. rsch. articles to pharm. publs. Mem. Thermal Analysis Network (treas. 1987, 88, sec. 1989—), Soc. Cosmetic Chemists (chair Mid Atlantic chpt. 1988-89), Nat. Soc. Cosmetic Chemists. Methodist. Home: 6333 Summercrest Dr Columbia MD 21045 Office: Nova Pharm Corp 6200 Freeport Ctr Baltimore MD 21224

TACHA, DEANELL REECE, federal judge; b. Jan. 26, 1946. BA, U. Kans., 1968; JD, U. Mich., 1971. Spl. asst. to U.S. Sec. of Labor, Washington, 1971-72; assoc. Hogan & Hartson, Washington, 1973; assoc. prof. law U. Kans., Lawrence, 1974-77, prof., 1977-85, assoc. dean, 1977-79, as. soc. vice chancellor, 1979-81, vice chancellor, 1981-85; assoc. Thomas J. Pitner, Concordia, Kans., 1973-74; dir. Douglas County Legal Aid Soc. Concordia, Kans., 1974-77; judge U.S. Ct. Appeals (10th cir.), Denver, 1985—. Office: US Ct Appeals 4830 W 15th St Ste 100 Lawrence KS 66049-3846

TACKI, BERNADETTE SUSAN, principal; b. Kenosha, Wis., Oct. 21, 1913; d. Peter Frank and Anna (Rathke) T. BS in Edn., Dominican Coll., 1952; MA in Edn., Northwestern U., 1958. Tchr. Whitley Sch., Brighton

Twp., Wis., 1932-33, Highland Sch., Pleasant Prairie, Wis., 1933-41, Victory Sch., Pleasant Prairie, 1941-47, Paris (Wis.) Consol. Sch., 1947-53, Southport Sch., Kenosha, 1953-61; prin. Harvey Sch., Kenosha, 1961-80; tchr. St. Casimir, Kenosha, 1980-83, vol. tchr. part-time, 1983—. Pres. Kenosha County Hist. Soc., 1985-89, St. James Parish Coun., Kenosha, 1975-89. Recipient Disting. Svc. award Wis. State Dept., 1980. Mem. Ret. Tchrs. Assn., AAUW, PTA, Kenosha County Tchrs. Assn. (past pres.), Kenosha Edn. Assn. (past pres.), Schubert Club, Delta Kappa Gamma. Roman Catholic. Republican. Roman Catholic. Home: 7527-37th Ave Kenosha WI 53142

TACKOVICH, JO ANN, retired tire company executive, fashion and image consultant; b. Hampton, Tenn., May 4, 1938; d. John Paul and Lena Jane (Cooke) Greer; m. Sidney Clayton Jones, Dec. 22, 1956 (div. Apr. 1959); 1 child, Randall; m. Martin David Tackovich, June 18, 1966. Student U. Arkon, 1974-75. Cert. profl. sec. Tech.-chem. sec Goodyear Tire & Rubber Co., Akron, 1959-69, corp. law sec., 1969-75, corp. law paralegal, 1975-81, consumer relations profl., 1981-87; owner, pres. Exclusively Jo Ann, fashion image and wardrobing cons., Akron, 1986—. Mem. Akron Women's Network (founder 1978, mem. bd. 1978-81, sec.-treas. 1978-80). Republican. Avocations: fashion, running, aerobics, weight lifting, reading. Home: 1052 N Portage Path Akron OH 44313 Office: Exclusively Jo Ann 1835 W Market St Akron OH 44313

TAESCHLER, DEBRA ANN, advertising executive; b. Jersey City, Jan. 7, 1953; d. Edward George and Marion Madeline (Naas) Miller; m. John Paul Taeschler, June 24, 1978. BA summa cum laude, Rutgers U., 1975. With mech. arts dept. Vornado, Inc., Garfield, N.J., 1975-76; asst. account exec. Clifton (N.J.) Graphix Assn., 1976-77; advt. mgr. Davis Printing Corp., Carlstadt, N.J., 1977-80; v.p. account mgr. Landmark Assocs., Whippany, N.J., 1980-85; account mgr. R.Z.A. Advt., Inc., Park Ridge, N.J., 1985-86; pres. Grafica, Inc., Chester, N.J., 1986—. Mem. Phi Beta Kappa. Roman Catholic. Office: Grafica Inc 50 Main St Chester NJ 07930

TAFFER, DEBORAH BATTS, hospital laboratory director; b. Cairo, Ill., Mar. 24, 1954; d. Clyde Turner and Martha Rachel (Viets) Batts; m. Edward Bruce Taffer, June 12, 1957. BS, Western Ky. U., 1976; cert. in med. tech., Lourdes Hosp., 1976. Registered med. technican Ann. Soc. Clin. Pathologists. EKG tech. Lourdes Hosp., Paducah, 1972, 74, 75; phlebotomist Lourdes Hosp., 1976, staff tech., 1976-78; staff tech. Marshall County Hosp., Benton, Ky., 1978, Mo. Delta Community Hosp., Sikeston, Mo., 1979; staff technologist Western Bapt Hosp., Paducah, 1979-80; blood bank supr. Western Bapt Hosp., 1980-86, lab. dir., 1986—. Mem. blood svcs. com. Tennessee Valley region ARC, Paducah, Ky., 1986—. Mem. Am. Soc. Med. Technologists (registered med. technologist), Ky. Soc. Med. Technologists (western area dir. 1984-85, bd. dirs. 1985-88, New Mem. of Yr. award 1984), Paducah Area Med. Technologists Soc. (v.p. 1983-84). Democrat. Home: Rte 2 Box 69 Kevil KY 42053

TAFFET, ELIZABETH ROSE, national fund raising consultant; b. Bklyn., July 10, 1934; d. Morris and Sylvia (Samovitz) Gropper; m. Arthur S. Taffet, June 11, 1953 (div. Dec. 1982); children—George, Allen, Mimi. Cert. in Fin. Planning Adelphi U., 1979-84, Clark U., Worcester, Mass., 1952-53, Philanthropy Tax Inst., N.Y.C., 1981, 84. Research dir. Douglas Lawson, Inc., N.Y.C., 1979-80; dir. planned giving Jewish Nat. Fund, N.Y.C., 1980-81, nat. dir. major gifts and bequests, 1981-85, Deferred Planning Concepts, 1985—, Planned Giving Concepts, 1986—; asst. coordinator Found. Caucus White House Conf. Library and Info. Services, 1979; account exec. Juvenile Diabetes Research, Miami, 1979; preparer planned giving instruments Care, Inc., N.Y.C., 1979. Research editor Foundation 500, 1979. Vice pres. Hadassah, Oceanside, N.Y., 1975, also editor newspaper; community rep. Middle States Evaluation Com., Oceanside, 1976; pres. Oceanside council PTA, 1977, also editor newsletter; mem. Adult Edn. Adv. Com., Oceanside, 1978; dir. Women's Orgn. Yeshiva U., 1987-89; dir. devel. Zionist Orgn. of Am., 1989. Mem. Nat. Soc. Fund-Raising Execs., N.Y. League of Bus. and Profl. Women, Nat. Speakers Assn., Internat. Assn. Fin. Planning, Women in Fin. Devel., Am. Women's Econ. Devel. Assn., Women's Econ. Devel. Assn. Corp., N.Y. Planned Giving Assn., Nat. Assn. Female Execs. Democrat. Home: 135 Irma Dr Oceanside NY 11572

TAGGART, SONDRA, financial planner, investment advisor; b. N.Y.C., July 22, 1934; d. Louis and Rose (Birnbaum) Hamov; children: Eric, Karen. BA, Hunter Coll., 1955. Cert. fin. planner, registered investment advisor; registered prin. Nat. Assn. Securities Dealers. Popular dir. Copyright Service Bur., Ltd., N.Y.C., 1957-69; dir. officer Maclen Music, Inc., N.Y.C., 1964-69; pres. Westshore, Inc., pub. internat. bus. materials, Mill Valley, Calif., 1965-80; pres. securities broker dealer The Taggart Co. Ltd., 1981—; The Beatles, Ltd., 1964-69. Mem. Internat. Assn. Fin. Planners, Registry Fin. Planning Practitioners. Republican. Clubs: Bankers. Editor: The Red Tapes: Commentaries on Doing Business With The Russians and East Europeans, 1978. Office: 1875 Century Pk E #1400 Los Angeles CA 90067-2501

TAI, JULIA CHOW, chemistry educator; b. Shanghai, China, Dec. 15, 1935; came to U.S., 1957; d. Fei-chen and Jean-tson (Liao) Chow; m. Hung-Chao Tai, Aug. 14, 1960; children: Eve, Helen, Michael. BS in Chemistry, Nat. Taiwan U., 1957; MS in Chemistry, U. Okla., 1959; PhD in Chemistry, U. Ill., 1963. Rsch. assoc. Wayne State U., Detroit, 1963-66, 67-68; vis. assoc. prof. Nat. Taiwan U., Taipei, Republic of China, 1968-69; asst. prof. U. Mich., Dearborn, 1969-73, assoc. prof., 1973-79, prof. chemistry, 1979—. Contbr. articles to sci. jours. Mem. Am. Chem. Soc., Quantum Chemistry Program Exch., Mich. Coll. Chemistry Tchrs. Assn. Office: Univ Mich Dearborn 4901 Evergreen St Dearborn MI 48128-1491

TAIRA, FRANCES SNOW, nurse educator; b. Glasgow, Scotland, Feb. 27, 1935; came to U.S., 1959, naturalized, 1964; d. Thomas and Isabel (McDonald) Snow; m. Albert Taira, June 20, 1962; children—Albert, Deborah, Paul. B.S.N., U. Ill., 1974, M.S.N., 1976; Ed.D., No. Ill. U., 1980. Staff nurse various hosps., 1959-73; instr. nursing Triton Coll., 1976-81; asst. prof. nursing Loyola U., Chgo., 1981—. Mem. Am. Nurses Assn., Ill. Nurses Assn., U. Ill. Nursing Alumni Assn., Sigma Theta Tau, Phi Delta Kappa. Roman Catholic. Author: Aging: A Guide for the Family, 1983, Home Nursing: Basic Rehabilitation Care of Adults, 1986, Independence: Building Upon the Strengths pf Aging People, 1988; contbr. articles to profl. jours.; contbg. author Saunders Rev. for NCLEX-RN, 1990. Home: 404 Atwater Ave Elmhurst IL 60126 Office: Loyola U Lake Shore Campus 6525 N Sheridan Rd Chicago IL 60626

TAJON, ENCARNACION FONTECHA (CONNIE TAJON), retired educator, association executive; b. San Narciso, Zambales, Philippines, Mar. 25, 1920; came to U.S., 1948; d. Espiridion Maggay and Gregoria (Labrador) Fontecha; m. Felix B. Tajon, Nov. 17, 1948; children: Ruth F., Edward F. Teacher's cert., Philippine Normal Coll., 1941; BEd, Far Eastern U., Manila, 1947; MEd, Seattle Pacific U., 1976. Cert. tchr., Philippines. Tchr. pub. schs. San Narciso and Manila, 1941-47; coll. educator Union Coll. Manila, 1947-48; tchr. Auburn (Wash.) Sch. Dist., 1956-58, Renton (Wash.) Sch. Dist., 1958-78; owner, operator Manila-Zambales Internat. Grill, Seattle, 1980-81, Connie's Lumpia House Internat. Restaurant, Seattle, 1981-84; founder, pres. Tajon-Fontecha, Inc., Renton, 1980—, United Friends of Filipinos in Am. Found., Renton, 1985—; founder Labrador Fontecha and Balfovi-Tajon Permanent Scholarship Fund of The Philippine Normal Coll., 1990, U. Wash. Alumni Assn. Endowed Scholarship Fund, World Div. of the Gen. Bd. of Global Ministries of the United Meth. Ch., 1982-84. Bd. dirs. women's ch. Gen. Bd. Global Ministries United Meth. Ch., 1982-84; bd. dirs. Renton Area Youth Svcs., 1980-85, Girls' Club of Puget Sound, Ethnic Heritage Coun. of Pacific N.W.; mem. Mcpl. Arts Commn. Renton, 1980—; chair fundraising steering com. Washington State Women's Polit. Caucus, 1985-89; governing mem. nat. steering com. Nat. Women's Polit. Caucus Wash. State Coun., 1990—, mem. vol. action; amb. 1990 Goodwill Games, Seattle. Recipient spl. cert. of award Project Hope, 1976, U.S. Bicentennial Commn., 1976, UNICEF, 1977; named Parent of Yr. Filipino Community of Seattle, Inc., 1984. Mem. NEA, U. Wash. Alumni Assn. (life), U. Wash. Filipino Alumni Assn. (pres. Wash. State chpt. 1985-87), Renton Retired Tchrs. Assn., Wash. State Edn. Assn. (bd. dirs. 1990—), Am. Assn. Ret. Persons, Nat. Ret. Tchrs. Assn., Renton Hist. Mus. (life), Internat. Platform Assn., United Meth. Women, Pres.'s Forum, Am. Biog.

Inst. Rsch. Assn. (dep. gov.), Alpha Sigma, Delta Kappa Gamma. Democrat. Home and Office: 2033 Harrington Pl NE Renton WA 98056

TAKACH, MARY JO ANN, public relations consultant, freelance writer; b. Buffalo, Sept. 1, 1945; d. Steve Richard and Mary Ann (Wurtz) Takach. BA in Biology and Journalism, U. Maine, 1967; MA in Journalism and Medicine, U. Wis., 1970. Advt. asst. Boyd Corp., Cambridge, Mass., 1967-68; tchr. sci. St. Joseph's High Sch., Somerville, Mass., 1968-69; sci. writer U. Wis., Madison, 1969-70; med. editor Enterprise Sci. News, N.Y.C., 1971-72; pub. info. officer U. R.I., Kingston, 1973-79; pub. info. specialist Bradley Hosp., East Providence, R.I., 1980-84; pub. relations account supr. FitzGerld & Co., Inc., Cranston, R.I., 1986-89; pub. relations cons. Takach Pub. Relations & Publs., Wakefield, R.I., 1989—; cons. R.I. div. Girl Scouts U.S., R.I. Office Higher Edn., Johnson & Wales U. Author: The Right Way to Walk for Health, 1972. Bd. dirs. Am. Cancer Soc./R.I., 1988—. Recipient 1st place/community svc. Nat. Assn. Press Women, 1987, 3d place/ann. reports, 1983; 1st place/community relations New Eng. Hosp. Pub. Relations Assn., 1984. Mem. Pub. Relations Soc.Am. (editor 1984-86, bd. dirs. 1985-89). Office: Takach Pub Relations & Publ 25 Prospect Ave Wakefield RI 02879

TAKAHASHI, TOMOKO, education educator; b. Ageo, Saitama, Japan, Jan. 25, 1955; came to U.S., 1975; d. Kiyoshi and Sachiko (Takahashi) T.; m. Jitsuro Jason Yamamoto, Oct. 12, 1984. BA magna cum laude, Albertus Magnus Coll., New Haven, Conn., 1977; MA, Columbia U., 1980, MEd, 1981, EdD, 1984. Researcher tchrs.' coll. Columbia U., N.Y.C., 1984-89; instr. of edn. grad. edn. Coll. New Rochelle, N.Y., 1985-89, asst. prof. edn., 1989—. Author: Conversational Strategies, 1990, Oral Communication, 1989, A Study on Leico-Semantic Transfer, 1984; contbr. numerous articles to profl. jours. Mem. Tchrs. of English to Speakers Other Langs., Am. Assn. for Applied Linguistics, MLA. Home: 517 Windsor Dr Palisades Park NJ 07650

TAKANE, EVELYN SACHIE, dentist; b. Honolulu, June 24, 1954; d. Robert Fujio and Jane Fumie (Nakahara) T. BA in Japanese Lang., BS in Fashion Merchandising, U. Hawaii, Honolulu, 1977; DDS, Loma Linda (Calif.) U., 1986. Pvt. practice Orange County, Calif., 1987—. Vol. dentist SOS Dental Clinic, Costa Mesa, Calif., 1988, Laguna Beach (Calif.) Community Clinic, 1990—; vol. in-take interviewer Legal Aid Soc., Santa Ana, Calif., 1990; vol. dentist cons. Poverty Law Ctr., Santa Ana, 1990. Mem. ADA, Calif. Dental Assn., Orange County Dental Soc.

TAKKUNEN, CANDYCE SUE, leadership development consultant; b. Moose Lake, Minn., June 10, 1947; d. Fred E. and Lillian Virginia (Lennartson) Kovanen; m. Leonard Allen Takkunen, Aug. 5, 1967; children: Brooke Nicole, Blake Dillon. BS in Edn. and Math., U. Minn., 1968. Elem. tchr. Burnsville (Minn.) Pub. Schs., 1968-76; student coun. advisor Chaska (Minn.) Pub. Schs., 1987-89, youth svc. cons., 1989; leadership development cons., 1987—. Co-author: Rasing Minnesota Leaders, 1988. Mem. Chanhassen (Minn.) Pub. Safety Commn., 1981-89; mem. Chaska Youth Devel. Com., 1988-89; bd. dirs. Waconia (Minn.) Ridgeview Hosp. Found., 1989—, West Suburban Teen Clinic, Excelsior, Minn., 1989—. Mem. LWV (pres. Carver County, Minn. 1983-85, v.p., bd. dirs. Minn. 1985-89). Lutheran.

TALAG, TRINIDAD SANTOS, education educator; b. Manila, Philippines, June 12, 1932; came to the U.S., 1954; d. Telesforo Dunca and Felisa Abriol (Santos) T. BS in Edn., U. Philippines, Quezon City, 1953; BS in Physical Edn., U. Oreg., 1955, MS in Physical Edn., 1956; PhD, U. Md., 1972. Instr. Centro Escolar U., Manila, Philippines, 1957-60; asst. prof. Northeastern U., Boston, 1962-66, Slippery Rock (Pa.) State Coll., 1966-73; assoc. prof. Elizabeth City (N.C.) U., 1980-90, prof., 1990—. NIH fellow, 1976. Mem. Bus. Profl. Women's Club, Am. Coll. Sports Medicine, Am. Alliance for Health, Phys. Edn., Recreation and Dance. Home: 861 Westway Elizabeth City NC 27909 Office: Elizabeth City State U Parkview Dr Elizabeth City NC 27909

TALBOT, CAROL LYNN, educator; b. Akron, Ohio, Jan. 3, 1952; d. Frederick Rollin and Margaret (Rens) T. BS, La. State U., 1974; MEd, U. New Orleans, 1979; PhD, U. Tex., 1988. Tchr. New Orleans Pub. Schs., 1974-89, after care tchr., 1983-88; tchr. Loudoun County Pub. Schs., Leesburg, Va., 1989—; cooperating tchr. U. New Orleans, 1979-88, Tulane U., New Orleans, 1979-81; teaching asst. U. Tex., Austin, 1985-86; curriculum cons. Child Inc. Head Start, Austin, 1985-86; workshop condr. Nat. Sci. Tchrs. Conv., New Orleans, 1985. Vol. reader Sta. WRBN Radio for Blind, New Orleans, 1983-84. Mem. Assn. for Childhood Edn., Nat. Assn. Educators for Young Children, Internat. Assn. for Child's Right To Play, Kappa Delta Pi (joint convocation workshop 1988). Home: 666 Gateway Dr Apt 509 Leesburg VA 22075

TALBOT, PAMELA, public relations executive; b. Chgo., Aug. 10, 1946. BA in English, Vassar Coll., 1968. Reporter Worcester, Mass. Telegram and Gazette, 1970-72; account exec. Daniel J. Edelman, Inc., Chgo., 1972-74, account supr., 1974-76, v.p., 1976-78, sr. v.p., 1978-83, exec. v.p., 1983—, exec. sr. gen. mgr., 1984—. Office: Edelman Pub Rels 211 E Ontario St Chicago IL 60611

TALBOTT, SUSAN ELLEN, social worker; b. Augsburg, Germany, Apr. 4, 1962; d. Peter Bruce and Barbara Anne (Howell) T. BS, So. Conn. State U., 1984. Social worker Wedgewood Health Care, St. Petersburg, Fla., 1985; social worker, discharge planner St. Anthony's Hosp., St. Petersburg, 1985-88; dir. social svc. Shore Acres Nursing Home, St. Petersburg, 1988; social svc. cons. Lindsey Cons. Svcs., St. Petersburg, 1989; dir. social svc. The Oaks of Clearwater, Fla., 1989—. Mem. Fla. Assn. Health and Social Svcs., Fla. Healthcare Social Workers Assn. Presbyterian. Home: 4410 9th Ave N Saint Petersburg FL 33713 Office: The Oaks of Clearwater 420 Bay Ave Clearwater FL 34615

TALBOTT, YVONNE CHATELAIN, management consultant; b. Syracuse, N.Y., Aug. 19, 1942; d. Charles Walrath and Yvonne (Merriman) T.; children: Peter, Geoff, Michelle, Leigh Ann. BS, Syracuse U., 1967; MS, Marshall U., 1977; Ed.S., U. N.C., Greensboro, 1988. Tchr. Richmond, Va. and Rochester, N.Y., 1968-78; instr. U. Wyo., Laramie, 1979-80, Guilford Community Coll., Greensboro, 1980-84; dir. Edul. Concepts, Inc., Greensboro, 1983-85; sr. cons. Human Dynamics, Inc., Greensboro, 1985—. Leader Triad coun. Girl Scouts Am., Greensboro, 1984-86; mem. Greensboro PTA; mem. stewardship com. Jamestown Presbyn. Ch., 1988—; mem. Ragsdale Booster Club, Greensboro. Mem. Am. Soc. Tng. and Devel., Tchrs. Math., Internat. Reading Assn., Phi Delta Kappa. Republican. Episcopalian. Home: 5134 Autumncrest Ct Greensboro NC 27407 Office: Human Dynamics Inc 5815 High Point Rd PO Box 7241 Greensboro NC 27417

TALESE, NAN AHEARN, publishing company executive; b. N.Y.C., Dec. 19, 1933; d. Thomas James and Suzanne Sherman (Russell) Ahearn; m. Gay Talese, June 10, 1959; children: Pamela Frances, Catherine Gay. B.A. Manhattanville Coll. of Sacred Heart, 1955. Fgn. exchange student 1st Nat. City Bank, London and Paris, 1956; editorial asst. Am. Eugenics Soc., N.Y.C., 1957-58, Vogue mag., N.Y.C., 1958-59; copy editor Random House Pub., N.Y.C., 1959-64; assoc. editor Random House Pub., 1964-67, sr. editor, 1967-73; sr. editor Simon & Schuster Pubs., N.Y.C., 1974-81; v.p. Simon & Schuster Pubs., 1979-81; exec. editor, v.p. Houghton Mifflin Co., N.Y.C., 1981-83, v.p., editor-in-chief, 1984-86, v.p., pub., editor-in-chief, 1986-88; sr. v.p. Doubleday & Co., N.Y.C., 1988-90; pres., editorial dir. Nan A. Talese Books, 1990—. Home: 109 E 61st St New York NY 10021

TALEVI, MELISSA ANN MARIE, designer/fabricator of stained glasses; b. Middletown, Conn., Oct. 15, 1959; d. Nicholas Edward and Rose Phyllis (Pitruzzello) Salafia; m. Christopher Tracy Talevi, Oct. 11, 1958; 1 child, Christopher Kyle. Kitchen aide Middlesex Convalescent Ctr., Middletown, Conn., 1976-77; file clk., coding dept. Middlesex Mutual Assurance Co., Middletown, 1977-78; full charge bookkeeper Talco Insulation Inc., Berlin, Conn., 1978-88, office mgr.; bookkeeper Middlesex Opera House Restaurant, Middletown, 1988; owner/designer/fabricator MT Glass Studio, Higganum, Conn., 1981—; bookkeeper Plumb & Level Constrn. Corp., Higganum,

Conn., 1988—. Designer custom stained glass pieces Deer, Freedom, 1986, Floral Scene New Awakening, 1987. Recipient: Dog Sled Races, NBSDC Rhode Island, 1986, Dog Show, CVSHC, Middletown, 1987. Ind. Catholic. Home and Office: 144 Nedobity Rd Higganum CT 06441

TALLCHIEF, MARIA, ballerina; b. Fairfax, Okla., Jan. 24, 1925; d. Alexander Joseph and Ruth Mary (Porter) T.; m. Henry Paschen, Jr., June 3, 1957; 1 child, Elise. DFA (hon.), Lake Forest (Ill.) Coll., Colby Coll., Waterville, Maine, 1968, Ripon Coll., 1973, Boston Coll., Smith Coll., 1981, Northwestern U., Evanston, Ill., 1982, Yale U., 1984, St. Mary-of-the-Woods (Ind.) Coll., 1984, Dartmouth Coll., 1985, St. Xaviar Coll., 1989. Ballerina Ballet Russe de Monte Carlo, 1942-47; with N.Y.C. Ballet Co., 1947-65, prima ballerina, 1947-60; former artistic dir. Lyric Opera Ballet Chgo.; founder Chgo. City Ballet, 1979—; now artistic dir. Lyric Opera Ballet; prima ballerina Am. Ballet Theatre, 1960; founder Sch. Chgo. Ballet. Guest star, Paris Opera, 1947, Royal Danish Ballet, 1961. Named Hon. Princess Osage Indian Tribe, 1953; recipient Disting. Service award U. Okla., 1972, award Dance mag., 1960, Jane Addams Humanitarian award Rockford Coll., 1973, Bravo award Rosary Coll., 1983, award Dance Educators Am., 1956, Achievement award Women's Nat. Press Club, 1953, Capezio award, 1965, Leadership for Freedom award Roosevelt U. Scholarship Assn., 1986. Mem. Nat. Soc. Arts and Letters.

TALLETT, ELIZABETH EDITH, biopharmaceutical company executive; b. London, Apr. 2, 1949; d. Edward and Edith May (Vickers) Symons; m. Martin Richard Tallett, Oct. 3, 1970; children: James Edward, Alexander Martin. BS with honors, U. Nottingham (Eng.), 1970. Ops. rsch. analyst So. Gas Bd., 1970-73; mgmt. svcs. mgr. Warner-Lamber (UK), Eastleigh, Eng., 1973-77, strategic planning mgr., 1977-81; internat. dir. strategic planning Warner-Lambert, Morris Plains, N.J., 1981-82, corp. dir. strategic planning, 1982-84; dir. mktg. ops. Parke-Davis, Morris Plains, 1984-87; exec. v.p. therapeutic products Centocor, Malvern, Pa., 1987-89, exec. v.p. pharms., 1989, pres. pharms. div., 1989—; bd. dirs. Med. Edn. System. Contbr. articles to profl. jours. Mem. Ch. of Eng.

TALLEY, CAROL LEE, newspaper editor; b. Bklyn., Sept. 10, 1937; d. George Joseph and Viola (Kovash) T.; children—Sherry, Jill, Scott. Student, U. Ky., 1955-57, Ohio U., 1957-58. Reporter Easton (Pa.) Daily Express, 1958-60; reporter N.J. Herald, 1962-64, edn. editor, 1964-66; reporter Daily Advance, Dover, N.J., 1966-68, polit. editor, investigative reporter, from 1969, mng. editor, 1974-81; editor Evening Sentinel, Carlisle, Pa., 1982—; Mem. A.P. Task Force N.J., 1970, Pa. Associated Press Mng. Editor's Bd. Dirs. Bd. dirs. Helen Stevens Community Mental Health Ctr., Carlisle, Stevens Mental Health Ctr., Carlisle. Recipient pub. service awards Nat. Headliners, 1971, Sigma Delta Chi, 1971, George Polk Meml. award for local reporting, 1974, Dew Meml. award Pa. Newspaper Pub.'s Assn., 1985. Mem. Pa. Newspaper Editors Soc., Kiwanis Club. Office: 457 E North St Carlisle PA 17013

TALLEY, JODY ELIZABETH, educator; b. Columbus, Ga., Mar. 14, 1958; d. Bill Ray and Jaqueline (Hay) T. BS in Edn., West Ga. Coll., 1979, MEd, 1982; EdD, Auburn U., 1988. Cert. tchr., Ga. Tchr. Cen. Primary Sch., Carrollton, 1979-88; tchr. gifted student program Cen. Middle Sch., Carrollton, 1988—. Mem. Carroll County Community Chorus. Mem. Internat. Reading Assn., Phi Delta Kappa, Phi Kappa Phi, Alpha Gamma Delta. Presbyterian. Office: Cen Middle Sch 633 Stripling Chapel Rd Carrollton GA 30117

TALLEY, RONDA CAROL, educational administrator; b. Glasgow, Ky., Nov. 21, 1951; d. Jack Howard and Ronda Mae (McCoy) T. BS, Western Ky. U., 1973; MEd, U. Louisville, 1974, EdS, 1976; PhD, Ind. U., 1979. Spl. edn. tchr. Jefferson County Public Schs., Louisville, 1973-76; research assoc. U. Calif., Riverside, 1977, Ind. U., Bloomington, 1977; adminstrv. intern Bur. Edn. Handicapped, HEW, Washington, 1978-81; adj. prof. dept. spl. edn. U. Louisville, 1981-83; adj. prof. Spalding U., 1984-86; coordinator assessment/placement services exceptional child edn. Jefferson County Public Schs., Louisville, 1981-86, coord. instrnl. support svcs. and placement, 1986-88; coord. innovative projects, rsch. and program evaluation, 1988-90; dir. policy and advocacy in schs. APA, Washington, 1990—; founder, pres. Tri-T Assocs., 1982—. Sta. WHAS Crusade for Children grantee, 1974-76; Bur. Edn. for Handicapped student research grantee, 1978; cert. sch. psychologist, lic. psychologist. Mem. Am. Psychol. Assn. (chmn. adminstrs. sch. psychol. services), Am. Ednl. Research Assn., Nat. Assn. Sch. Psychologists, Women in Sch. Adminstrn., Ky. Assn. Sch. Adminstrs., Ky. Psychol. Assn., Ky. Assn. Psychology in the Schs. (past pres.), Council Exceptional Children, Phi Delta Kappa, Kappa Delta. Republican. Methodist. Editor: Special Education in Transition: Administrator's Handbook on Integrating America's Mildly Handicapped Students, 1982. Home: 9104 Hurstwood Ct Louisville KY 40222 Office: APA 1200 17th St NW Washington DC 20036

TALLMAN, FRANCINE R., financial manager; b. Palmer, Mass., May 1, 1966; d. Gerald E. and Carol R. Trombly. BS, U. Mass., 1989. Mortgage technician County Bank for Savs., Ware, Mass.; fin. mgmt. trainee Monarch Capital Corp., Springfield, Mass. Mem. Golden Key Nat. Honor Soc. Address: 76 Palmer Rd Three Rivers MA 01080

TALLMAN, KAREN RAMSEY, government agency administrator; b. Maryville, Tenn., July 16, 1951; d. O.L. and Iva (Pickell) Ramsey; m. Herman J. Tallman, Oct. 31, 1976. ABS, Knoxville Bus. Coll., 1970. Sec. Levi Strauss Co., Knoxville, Tenn., 1971; editorial clk. TVA, Knoxville, 1971-78, community info. specialist, 1978-84, mgr. pub. participation, 1984-88, sr. specialist community and visitor rels., 1988-90, specialist, spl. events planning, 1990—; sec. TVA Coop. Conf., Knoxville, 1977, co-leader, 1978. Mem. LWV, Soc. Consumer Affairs Profls., Nat. Mgmt. Assn., Federally Employed Women. Republican. Methodist. Home: 7502 Rivertrace Blvd Knoxville TN 37920 Office: TVA 400 W Summit Hill Dr Knoxville TN 37902

TALLY, LURA SELF, state legislator; b. Statesville, N.C., Dec. 9, 1921; d. Robert Ottis and Sara (Cowles) Self; A.B., Duke U., 1942; M.A., N.C. State U., Raleigh, 1970; m. J.O. Tally, Jr., Jan. 30, 1943 (div. 1970); children—Robert Taylor, John Cowles. Tchr., former guidance counselor Fayetteville (N.C.) city schs.; mem. N.C. Ho. of Reps. from 20th Dist., 1971-83, chmn. com. higher edn., from 1975, also 1980-83, vice chmn. com. appropriations for edn., 1973-86; state senator from 12th Dist. N.C., 1983-90; chmn. N.C. Senate Com. on Natural Resources, Community Devel. and Wildlife, 1987, Environment and Natural Resources, 1989-90. Past pres. Cumberland County Mental Health Assn., N.C. Historic Preservation Soc.; trustee Fayetteville Tech. Inst., 1981-90; mem. Legis. Research com. Mem. Am. Personnel and Guidance Assn., Fayetteville Bus. and Profl. Women's Club, Kappa Delta, Delta Kappa Gamma. Methodist. Club: Fayetteville Woman's (past pres.). Office: NC Legis Bldg W Jones St Raleigh NC 27611

TALMA, LOUISE J., composer, educator; b. Arcachon, France, Oct. 31, 1906. Student, Inst. Mus. Art, N.Y.C., 1922-30; pupil, Isidore Philipp and Nadia Boulanger, Fontainebleau Sch. Music, 1926-39; B.Mus., NYU, 1931; M.A. in Music, Columbia U., 1933; L.H.D. (hon.), Hunter Coll, CUNY, 1983; D.Arts (hon.), Bard Coll., 1984. Tchr. Manhattan Sch. Music, 1926-28, Fontainebleau Sch. Music, summers 1936-39, 78, 81-83, 87; mem. faculty Hunter Coll., 1928-79, prof. music, 1952-76, prof. emeritus, 1976—; Clark fellow Scripps Coll., 1975; Sanford fellow Yale, 1976; mem. Pres.'s Circle, Hunter Coll., 1977; Bd. dirs. League-ISCM. Compositions include: (with Thornton Wilder as librettist) opera The Alcestiad, premiered Frankfurt, West Germany (Marjorie Peabody Waite award Nat. Inst. Arts and Letters 1960); 2 piano sonatas, 6 études for piano, 1 string quartet, 1 sonata for violin and piano, Toccata for orch., Dialogues for piano and orch., Clarinet Quintet; chamber opera Have you heard? Do you know?, Diadem; Flute Quartet; Full Circle for Chamber Orch. Recipient Koussevitzky Music Found. commn., 1959, Nat. Fedn. Music Clubs award, 1963, Nat. Assn. Am. Composers and Condrs. award, 1963, Sibelius medal, 1963, numerous others; Guggenheim fellow, 1946, 47; sr. Fulbright research grantee, 1955-56; Nat. Endowment of the Arts grantee, 1966, 75. Fellow Am. Guild Organists; mem. League of Composers (dir. 1950—), Fontainebleau Fine Arts and Music Assn. (trustee 1950, v.p. 1982-86), Edward MacDowell Assn. (corporate mem.), ASCAP, Am. Inst. Arts and Letters, Phi Beta Kappa, Sigma Alpha Iota (hon.). Office: 30 W 26th St 250 W 54th St New York NY 10010

TALMADGE, MARY CHRISTINE, educator; b. Monticello, Ga., Nov. 6, 1940; d. Herbert Pope and Margaret (Allen) T.; m. Larry Benson, Aug. 10, 1962 (div. 1975). Diploma, Crawford W. Long Hosp. Sch. of Nursing, Atlanta, 1961; BSN, U. Dayton, 1966; MPH, U. Hawaii, 1971, PhD, 1989. RN. Staff charge nurse Crawford W. Long Hosp., Atlanta, 1961-62; instr. LPN program Dayton (Ohio) Bd. Edn., 1963-66; instr. Miami Valley Hosp. Sch. of Nursing, Dayton, 1967-69; clin. nurse specialist Hawaii State Hosp., Kaneohe, 1970-77, dir. nursing, 1978-80; adminstrv. asst. to dir. health Hawaii State Dept. of Health, Honolulu, 1977-78; clin. nurse specialist Windward Community Counseling Ctr., Kaneohe, 1980-83; asst. prof. U. Hawaii, 1983-85; assoc. prof., assoc. program dir. Hawaii Loa Coll., Kaneohe, 1987-89; assoc. prof. Ga. So. U., Statesboro, 1990—; cons. Tokyo Women's Med. Coll. Sch. of Nursing, 1988—; local and internat. healthcare orgns. Sec., mem. Gov.'s Commn. on Mental Health and Criminal Justice, Honolulu, 1978-80; mem., chmn. Windward Oahu Svc. Area Bd. on Mental Health and Substance Abuse, Honolulu, 1985-86; candidate Neighborhood Bd. Kaneohe, 1988. Mem. Nat. League for Nursing, Am. Sociol. Soc., Sigma Theta Tau. Democrat. Methodist. Home: 201 Buckston Ct Statesboro GA 30458

TALMADGE, SHARON SUE, municipal government official; b. Ft. Belvoir, Va., Jan. 5, 1950; d. Walter Harvey and Genevieve (Harrison) Hall; (div.); 1 child, Stacy Lynn. Cert. latent print examiner. Fingerprint tech. FBI, Washington, 1970-71; supr., latent print examiner Balt. Police Dept, 1971—; lectr. in field various orgns. Recipient Law Enforcement medal Md. Soc. SAR, 1981, Bronze Star, Balt. Police Dept., 1981. Mem. Internat. Assn. for Identification (pres. Chesapeake Bay div. 1984-85). Republican. Office: Balt Police Dept 601 E Fayette St Baltimore MD 21202

TALTY, LORRAINE CAGUIOA, accountant; b. Makati, Manila, Philippines, July 3, 1957; came to U.S., 1973, naturalized, 1983; d. Leon Perez and Asuncion (Rodriguez) Caguioa; m. Kevin Michael Talty, Jan. 23, 1982; 1 child, Leah Marie. BBA in Acctg. magna cum laude, Chaminade U., Honolulu, 1979. Office mgr., comptr. Caro of Honolulu, 1976-82; acct. David Schenkein, CPA, Latham, N.Y., 1984-86; sales rep. Caromat Corp., Torrance, Calif., 1985-86; owner Kevlor Internat., mfrs. rep. agy., Fairport, N.Y., 1985—; acct. Cortland L. Brovitz & Co., CPA's, Rochester, N.Y., 1986-87; pvt. practice acctg., Fairport, 1986—. Newsletter editor Country Knolls West Civic Assn., Clifton Park, 1984-85, civic com. rep., 1985-86. Home: 8 Silver Fox Dr Fairport NY 14450

TAMASHIRO, LYNN YOSHIKO, technical writer, pharmacy technician; b. Chgo., July 25, 1967; d. Stanley Yoshio and Caroline Yoshea (Arakaki) Tamashiro. Student, DePaul U., Chgo., 1990. Clk., pharmacist asst. Medicare Pharmacy, Chgo., 1983-85; pharmacy technician, apprentice N.H. Ballin Pharmacy Inc., Chgo., 1986—; office asst., receptionist Small Assemblies Inc., Chgo., 1987-88; typist, adminstrv. stay-in-schooler asst. Social Security Adminstrn., Chgo., 1989-90; tech. writer, project specialist Cole Parmer Instrument Corp., Niles, Ill., 1990—. Mem. Women in Communications. Home: 4322 N Oakley Chicago IL 60618

TAMBURO, CONSTANCE DOLORES, sales representative; b. Englewood, N.J., Oct. 6, 1940; d. Anthony M. and Carmella (Masci) Merlino; m. Vincent A. Tamburo, Aug. 4, 1962; children: Robert M., Theodore V. A.B., Chatham Coll., 1962. Cert. tchr. Tchr., Fox Chapel and Penn Hills, Pa., 1962-64, 73-76; real estate agt. Koenig & Strey, Lake Forest, Ill., 1977-79; sales rep. Commerce Clearing House, Chgo., 1980—. Docent, Midwest Mus. Am. Art, Elkhart, Ind., 1980-84; pres. Pitts. Opera Guild, 1972-76; mem. Pitts. Opera Aux., 1986—. Andrew Smalley scholar, 1960-62. Mem. Art Inst. Chgo., South Bend Art Ctr., 1988—, Friends of the Shite Mus., 1989—. Mem. NAFE, AAUW (v.p. Lake Forest 1976-79), Pitts. Peace Inst., Christ Child Soc., Chatham Coll. Alumnae Assn. (exec. bd. 1986-87), Mortar Board. Roman Catholic. Avocation: tennis. Home: 1124 Aline Ct South Bend IN 46614

TAMEN, HARRIET, lawyer; b. Yonkers, N.Y., May 17, 1947; d. Saul and Lily (Balglau) T. A.B., Bryn Mawr Coll., 1969; J.D., George Washington U., Washington, 1973. Bar: N.Y. 1974, U.S. Dist. Ct. (so. dist.) N.Y. 1975. Atty., W.T. Grant, N.Y.C., 1974-76; atty. City of N.Y. Office Econ. Devel., Div. Real Property, N.Y.C., 1977-81; atty. Credit Lyonnais Bank, N.Y.C., 1981-86, Chase Manhattan Bank, 1986-89; v.p., counsel internat. corp. fin. Citibank, 1989—. Bd. dirs. Dromenon Theatre, N.Y., 1980-86, Nat. Dance Inst., N.Y., 1982, chmn. bd. dirs., 1984-87; chmn. bd. dirs. Theatre & Dance Alliance, 1989—; del. exch. program Women in Law, South Am., 1987—; mem. campaign staff Ed Koch for Mayor, N.Y.C., 1977. Mem. ABA, Bar of Assn. of City of N.Y.

TAMM, GERALDINE KURCZ, communications professional; b. Lakewood, Ohio, Apr. 11, 1932; d. Raymond Bennett and Helen (Haynik) Whittock; m. Robert A. Kurcz, Aug. 21, 1954 (div. Aug. 1971); children: Timothy J., Stephen M., Laura B., Joseph A.; m. Jerome T. Tamm, Aug. 8, 1973. BA magna cum laude, Wayne State U., 1954, MA magna cum laude, 1971, PhD magna cum laude, 1976. Speech therapist Detroit Orthopaedic Clin., 1954-56; grad. asst. Wayne State U., Detroit, 1971-74; instr. Henry Ford Community Coll., Dearborn, Mich., 1976-82, Detroit Coll. Bus., Dearborn, 1977-82; dir. communications J.T. Tamm Assocs., Dearborn, 1983—. Contbr. poetry to mags. and anthologies; co-editor: Mingled Threads, 1982. Parliamentarian, co-author by-laws River Oaks Estates Community Assn., Dearborn Heights, Mich., 1959-61. Recipient grad. fellowship Wayne State U., 1975. Mem. Detroit Women Writers (treas. 1988—), Soc. Children's Book Writers, Poetry Soc. Mich., AAUW. Lutheran.

TAMONDONG-HELIN, SUSAN DAET, international social worker; b. Quezon City, Philippines, Jan. 31, 1957; came to U.S.A., 1986; d. Marcelino R. and Concepcion (Daet) T.; m. William Henry Helin, Apr. 11, 1985. BS cum laude, U. Philippines, 1979; MA in Internat. Communication and Internat. Devel. with honors, Am. U., 1990. Asst. mgr., social worker BPF Found., Palawan Island, Philippines, 1979-80; supervising orgnl. devel. specialist Ministry of Human Settlements, Manila, 1980; resettlement counselor, field officer United Nations High Commr.for Refugees, Manila, 1980-82; field resettlement officer United Nations High Commr. Regional Office, Bangkok, Thailand, 1987; project mgmt. cons. Asiatrust Bank, Quezon City, 1983-84; info., pub. relations officer PNVSCA Office of the Pres., 1983-84; social svcs. counselor United Nations High Commr. for Refugees, Mogadishu, Somalia, 1984-86; health, family svcs. coordinator El Centro De La Raza, Seattle, 1986-87; area rep. AFS Internat. Intercultural Programs, Seattle, 1986-87; field dir. Girl Scouts, USA, Seattle, 1987; researcher Export-Import Bank of the USA, dir. Social and Cultural Affairs Grad. Student Council, grad. fellow asst. to Dr. Mitch Hammer, SIS, TAU, Internat. Communications Dept., Washington, D.C., 1988-89; founder Tanglaw publ., Seattle, 1986. Author: poem, Someday, 1978; editor and project adminstr.: The World Bank, Washington and Latin America. Advocate Cen. Am. Peace Campaign, mem. Women's Internat. for Peace and Justice, Filipino Assn. for Community Edn., Amnesty Internat., 1986-87, Alliance for Philippine Concerns, Seattle, 1986-89. Fellow Sch. of Internat. Svc.; mem. Soc. for Internat. Devel., Soc. for Intercultural Edn., Tng. and Research, AFS Returnees, Kappa Alpha Phi. Roman Catholic. Home: 4607 Connecticut Ave NW Apt 316 Washington DC 20008

TANAKA, LEILA CHIYAKO, lawyer; b. Honolulu, Mar. 11, 1954; d. Masami and Bernice Kiyoko (Nakamura) T. B Arts and Scis. with distinction in Japanese Lang. and Am. Studies, U. Hawaii, Manoa, 1977; JD, U. Santa Clara, 1980. Bar: Hawaii 1980, U.S. Dist. Ct. Hawaii 1980. Pvt. practice Hawaii, 1980-81; law clk. to judge U.S. Ct. Appeals (2d cir.) Hawaii, Wailuku, 1981-82; spl. dep. atty. gen. Dept. of Atty. Gen., Hawaii, 1983, dep. atty. gen., 1983-88; housing unit supr., 1987-88; eviction hearings trial examiner Hawaii Housing Authority, 1986-88; mgr. departmental liability Dept. Transp., Hawaii, 1988—. Mem. Pacific Rim Found., People to People Internat. Mem. Smithsonian Instn., Bishop Mus. Assn., Soroptimist, Phi Kappa Phi. Democrat. Buddhist. Office: Hawaii Dept Transp 869 Punchbowl St Honolulu HI 96813

TANCRETI, CHERYL ANN, marketing specialist; b. New Haven, Conn., May 15, 1960; d. Leo Joseph and Helen Joyce (Scillia) T. Student, Siena Coll., 1978-80; BS in Bus., Quinnipiac Coll., 1982. Dir. mktg. East Coast Environ. Svcs. Inc., New Haven, Conn., 1983—; exec. mgr. Tancreti Stables, North Haven, Conn., 1988—. Editor Jour Conn. Environ. Regulations, 1988, The East Coast Informer; exec. editor Conn. Recycling Manual. Treas. State rep. campaign. Mem. Conn. Forum of Regulated Environ. Profls. (seminar mgr., 1987, bd. dirs. 1988—), NAFE, New England Morgan Horse Assn. (conf. planner 1989—), New Haven Harbor Petroleum Coop (nat. conf. mgr. 1984—), Environmentally Regulated Conn. Industries (founding mem.), New Haven Ski Club. Office: East Coast Environ Svcs Inc 454 Quinnipiac Ave New Haven CT 06513

TANCS, LINDA ANN, paralegal technician; b. Elizabeth, N.J., Sept. 27, 1963; d. Tibor Louis and Rose (Cecere) T. Student U. Warwick, Coventry, Eng., 1984; BA, Rutgers Coll., 1985. Sales asst. McCrory Corp., Union, N.J., 1980-83; sales assoc. People Express Airlines, Newark, 1984-85; substitute tchr. Roselle Park (N.J.) Schs., 1984-85; editorial asst. Enslow Pubs., Hillside, N.J., 1985; paralegl technician Fox and Fox, Counsellors at Law, Newark, 1985-88; paralegal technician, asst. legal services coordinator Vol. Lawyers for Arts, N.Y.C., 1988; corp. paralegal Wilentz, Goldman & Spitzer, Woodbridge, N.J., 1988-90. Editor German newsletter Der Trichter, 1984-85. Mem. NAFE, N.J. Assn. for Female Execs., Phi Beta Kappa, Phi Sigma Iota, Delta Phi Alpha. Republican. Home: 411 Roosevelt St Roselle Park NJ 07204

TANCZAK-DYCIO, MARY, anesthesiologist; b. Rybnyky, Ukraine, July 10, 1922; came to U.S., 1950, naturalized, 1955; d. Basil and Helen (Cisyk) Tanczak; student U. Lviv, 1940-41, Med. Sch., 1942-44, U. Erlangen (Germany), 1945-49; m. George Dycio, Nov. 11, 1949; children—George Myron, Mark Roman. Resident, Contagious Disease Hosp., Belleville, N.J., 1951-52; intern Mercy Hosp., Canton, Ohio, 1952-53, resident anesthesia, 1952-55; practice medicine specializing in anesthesiology, 1955-58; mem. staff Irvington (N.J.) Gen. Hosp., 1955-58; staff St. Mary's Gen. Hosp., Lewiston, Maine, 1958—, chief anesthesia dept., 1960—, also dir. Sch. Nurse Anesthetists. Fellow Am. Coll. Anesthesiologist; mem. AMA, Am.-Ukrainian, Maine. Androscoggin County med. socs. Office: 300 Pine St Lewiston ME 04240 also: 3 Bayberry Ln Lewiston ME 04240

TANDOURJIAN, REBECCA ELLEN DONZANTI, sales consultant; b. Abington, Pa., Jan. 21, 1957; d. Adam Paul and Phyllis R. (D'Amicodatri) Donzanti; m. Aaron Tandourjian, Sept. 6, 1987. AA, Bucks County Community Coll., Newtown, Pa., 1977; B of Nursing, Widener U., 1979. RN, Pa. Staff nurse St. Mary Hosp., Phila., 1979-82, Thomas Jefferson U. Hosp., Phila., 1982-85; nurse cons. Support Systems Internat., Charleston, S.C., 1985-87, med. sales cons., 1987—, field trainer for nurse cons., 1986-87; mem. presdl. adv. com. Support Systems Internat., 1986, mem. nurse cons. task force, 1987-88. Co-author: (copyrighted info. packet) Diabetic Keto-Acidosis: A Self Learning Guide for Nurses, 1981. Participant task force, vol. Project Ninos, World Servants, Dominican Republic, 1990. Mem. NAFE, Christian Career Women (Newtown). Office: Support Systems Internat 4349 Corporate Rd Charleston SC 29405

TANDY, JESSICA, actress; b. London, Eng., June 7, 1909; d. Harry and Jessie Helen (Horspool) T.; m. Jack Hawkins, 1932 (div. 1940); 1 dau., Susan (Mrs. John Tettemer); m. Hume Cronyn, 1942; children: Christopher Hume, Tandy. Student, Dame Alice Owens Girls Sch., 1919-24, Ben Greet Acad. Acting, 1924-27; LL.D., U. Western Ont., 1974; LHD (hon.), Fordham U., 1985. Dramatic adviser Goddard Neighborhood Center, N.Y.C., 1948. First profl. acting role in: Manderson Girls; later appeared in: London debut in The Rumor, 1929; Comedy of Good and Evil, 1929, Alice Sit-By-The-Fire, 1929, Yellow Sands, 1929; other theatre appearances in Twelfth Night, 1930, Man Who Pays the Piper, Autumn Crocus, Port Said, 1931; various engagements, Old Vic, London, including Midsummer Night's Dream, Hamlet, King Lear, 1933-40; first stage appearance U.S., 1930; on Broadway in Time and Conways, 1938, White Steed, 1939, Yesterday's Magic, 1942, Streetcar Named Desire, 1947, Four Poster, 1951-53, Madame Will You Walk, 1953, The Honeys, 1955, A Day by the Sea, 1955, The Man in the Dog Suit, 1958, Five Finger Exercise, 1959, The Physicists, 1964, Noel Coward in Two Keys, 1974; played in Mpls. Hamlet, Three Sisters, Death of a Salesman, 1963, Rose, 1981; Foxfire; in The Glass Menagerie; summer theatre prodns. The Caucasian Chalk Circle, 1950-55; appeared: Triple Play, 1958-59, Big Fish, Little Fish, London, 1962; (with husband) reading tour U.S. Face to Face, 1954; A Delicate Balance, 1966-67, The Miser, 1968, Heartbreak House, Shaw Festival, 1968, Tchin-Tchin, Chgo., 1969, Camino Real, Lincoln Center, N.Y.C., 1970, Home, Morosco, N.Y., 1971, All Over, N.Y.C., 1971; (with husband) in Samuel Beckett festival, Lincoln Center, N.Y.C., 1972, tour Promenade All, 1972-73, Not I, 1973; limited concert recital tour Many Faces of Love, 1974, 75, 76, also Seattle Repertory theatre; tour (with husband) Noel Coward in Two Keys, 1975; appeared in Eve, Stratford (Ont.) Festival, 1976; played Mary Tyrone in Long Day's Journey into Night, Theater London, Ont., Can., 1977; star of The Gin Game, at Long Wharf Theatre, New Haven, 1977, Golden Theatre, N.Y.C., 1978; on tour in U.S., Toronto, London, USSR, 1978-79, Rose, Cort Theater, N.Y.C., 1981; appeared (with husband) in Foxfire, Stratford Festival, Ont., 1980, The Guthrie Theatre, Mpls., 1981, Ahmanson Theatre, Los Angeles, 1985-86, Ethel Barrymore Theatre, N.Y.C., 1982-83; in The Glass Menagerie, Eugene O'Neill Theatre, N.Y.C., 1983-84; off-Broadway in Salonika, 1985; (with husband) in The Petition, Golden Theatre, N.Y.C., 1986; motion pictures include A Light in the Forest, 1958, Valley of Decision, Green Years, Desert Fox, The Birds, 1962, Butley, 1973, Honky Tonk Freeway, 1980, Garp, 1981, Still of the Night, 1981, Best Friends, 1982, The Bostonians, 1983, Cocoon, 1984, Batteries Not Included, 1986, The House on Carroll Street, 1988, Cocoon: The Return, 1988, Driving Miss Daisy, 1989; TV prodns. Portrait of a Madonna, 1948, Christmas 'Till Closing, 1955, Marriage; series, 1954, The Fallen Idol, 1959, The Moon and Sixpence, 1959, Tennessee Williams' South, Many Faces of Love, 1977, The Gin Game, 1979, Foxfire, 1987. Recipient Antoinette Perry award, Twelfth Night Club award for performance in Streetcar Named Desire, 1948, for Five Finger Exercise, 1960, bronze medallion (with husband) for performance in The Four Poster Comedia Matinee Club, 1952, Obie award for Not I, 1973, Drama Desk award for Happy Days and Not I, Creative Arts award Brandeis U., 1978, Antoinette Perry (Tony) award for The Gin Game, 1978, Drama Desk award, 1978, Los Angeles Critics award, 1979, Sarah Siddons award, 1979; named to Theatre Hall of Fame, 1979; recipient Antoinette Perry award for Foxfire, 1982, Common Wealth award, 1983, Alley Theatre award, 1987, Acad. Sci. Fiction, Fantasy and Horror Films award for Batteries Not Included, 1987, Franklin Haven Sargeant award Am. Acad. Dramatic Arts, 1988, Emmy award for Foxfire, 1988; nominated for Tony award as best actress in The Petition, 1986; Acad. award for Driving Miss Daisy, 1990; honoree Kennedy Ctr. Honors, 1986. Office: 63-23 Carlton St Rego Park NY 11374

TANENBAUM, SUSAN G., lawyer, human resources specialist. BA, Queen's Coll., 1961; MA, Syracuse U., 1967; JD, U. Santa Clara, 1974. Bar: Calif. 1974. Assoc. McCutchen, Doyle, Brown & Enerson, 1974-76; labor counsel Bank of Am., 1976-81; with Advanced Micro Devices, Inc., Sunnyvale, Calif., 1981—, now v.p. human resources ops. Office: Advanced Micro Devices Inc PO Box 3453 Sunnyvale CA 94088*

TANG, ESTHER DON, development consultant, retired social worker; b. Tucson, Mar. 5, 1917; d. Don Wah and Yut (Gnan) Fok; m. David W. Tang, June 14, 1942; children: Patricia Karen Tang Crowley, Diane Cherly Tang Simones, David Jr., Elizabeth Carol. Student, Draughn's Bus. Sch., San Antonio, 1936, U. Ariz., 1938-41. Owner, operator supermarket, Tucson, 1940-66; exec. dir. Pio Decinio Ctr. Cath. Diocese, Tucson, 1966-85; cons., ptnr., vice chmn. bd. Netwest Devel. Corp., Tucson, 1985—. Mem. Tucson Airport Authority, 1975—; vice chmn. Tucson-Taichung Sister Cities, 1979-88; chmn. Tucson Sister Cities Steering Com., 1984—, Ariz. Pers. Bd.; chmn. bd. dirs. Pima Community Coll., 1975-85; pres. bd. dirs. Pima Coun. on Aging, 1986-90; coord. U.S. Bicentennial, Tucson; mem. adv. bd. Ariz. Dept. Econ. Security. Named Woman of Yr., City of Tucson, 1955, Woman of Yr. in Adminstrn., 1968; recipient Univ. Alumni award U. Ariz., 1976, Jefferson award Ariz. Daily Star, 1987, svc. award Pima Coun. on Aging, 1987-89, Disting. Svc. award U. Pima Community Coll. Found., 1988, Rosie award So. Ariz. Ctr. Against Sexual Assault, 1990. Mem. Soroptimist (hon.).

Roman Catholic. Home: 701 Camino de Los Padres Tucson AZ 85718 Office: Netwest Devel Corp 2221 E Broadway Ste 211 Tucson AZ 85719

TANGNEY, JUNE PRICE, psychology educator, researcher; b. Buffalo, Aug. 11, 1958; d. James Robert and Roberta June (Woods) Price; m. John Francis Tangney, July 20, 1985. BA, SUNY, Buffalo, 1979; MA, UCLA, 1981, PhD, 1985. Lic. psychologist, Md.; lic. clin. psychologist, Va. Rsch. and clin. psychologist Regional Ctr. for Infants and Young Children, Rockville, Md., 1985-86; lectr. human devel. Bryn Mawr (Pa.) Coll., 1986-88; asst. prof. psychology George Mason U., Fairfax, Va., 1988—; testifier Congl. Subcom. on Sci. Misconduct, 1988. Author: Measures of Self-Conscious Affective Styles; contbr. articles to profl. jours. NIMH fellow, 1979, 80; NIH-Nat. Inst. Child Health and Human Devel. grantee, 1988-90, 90—. Mem. Am. Psychol. Assn., Am. Psychol. Soc., Soc. for Rsch. in Child Devel., AAAS, Soc. for Personality Assessment. Office: George Mason U Dept Psychology Fairfax VA 22030

TANGUAY, ANITA WALBURGA, real estate broker; b. Oberndorf, Fed. Republic of Germany, July 31, 1936; came to U.S., 1958, naturalized, 1968; d. Karl W. and Luise (Roescheisen) Ederle; m. Donald M. Tanguay, Jan. 21, 1958; children: Elizabeth Ivy, Aimee Marie. Student various schs., Oberndorf and Heidelberg, Fed. Republic of Germany; grad. in real estate, Middlesex (N.J.) Coll., 1981. Sales assoc. Lois Schneider Co., Summit, N.J., 1978-82; pres. Tanguay Assocs. Inc., Millburn, N.J., 1982—. Co-founder Hospice Overlook Hosp., Summit, 1978—, bd. dirs., 1980-84; mem. adv. bd. Summit Child Care Ctr. Recipient Women of Achievement award Greater Millburn (N.J.)/Short Hills (N.J.) Bus. and Profl. Women Inc., 1988. Mem. Bd. Realtors Maplewood Oranges (trustee), N.J. Assn. Realtors, Nat. Assn. Realtors, Indsl. Comml. Real Estate Women (exec. bd., treas. 1983—, past pres., indsl./comml. real estate women, N.J. del. nat. network), Nat. Comml. Real Estate Women (N.J. del.). Republican. Roman Catholic. Avocations: gardening, classical music. Home: 11 Ferndale Rd Short Hills NJ 07078 Office: 89 Millburn Ave Ste 101 Millburn NJ 07041

TANIGUCHI, ELSIE LEILANI (ELSIE LEILANI YOTSUUYE), travel consultant; b. Tacoma, Oct. 3, 1936; d. Tom Toju and Kazue (Uchida) Yotsuuye; m. Harry H. Taniguchi, July 14, 1957; children: Harry H. Jr., Elaine Taniguchi Ingram. BA in Edn., U. Wash., 1958. Cert. bus. and elem. tchr., Wash. Owner, tchr., costume designer Leilani Taniguchi's Polynesian Dance Studio, Seattle, 1970-80; travel cons., agt. T.A.C. Holidays-Burien, Seattle, 1980-84, Southcenter br. Univ. Travel, Seattle, 1984—. First v.p., program chmn. Des Moines Elem. Sch. PTA, 1967-69, Marvista Elem. Sch. PTA, 1971-72; 1st v.p., chmn. ways and means Olympic Jr. High Sch. PTA, 1974-75; 1st v.p., program chmn. Mt. Rainier High Sch. PTSA, 1975-76; former presch. dept. leader, tchr. Southminster Presbyn. Ch.; organizer Southminster Christian Coop. Presch., 1963; chaperone Seattle Seafair. Recipient Golden Acorn award Des Moines Elem. Sch. PTA, 1969, award Marvista Elem. Sch. PTA, 1971; outstanding svc. award Olympic Jr. High Sch. PTA, 1976, Mt. Rainier High Sch. PTSA, 1979. Mem. Am. Soc. Travel Agts., Pacific Area Travel Assn., Caribbean Tourism Assn., Internat. Fedn. Women in Travel, Seattle Women in Travel, AAUW (travel chmn. Highline br.), NAFEA,Bus. and Profl. Women's Club, U. Wash. Alumni Assn., Hawaii Hula Tchr.'s Assn., Japanese Am. Citizens League (corr. sec. Puyallup Valley), Tacoma Nikkeijin Kai, Lions, Mortar Bd., Totem Club, W-Key. Home: 225 SW 197th Pl Normandy Park Seattle WA 98166 Office: Univ Travel Southcenter Br 16400 Southcenter Pkwy 104 Seattle WA 98188

TANKERSLEY, MICHELE ANN, teacher; b. Trenton, Mich., Sept. 2, 1966; d. Garry Fay Tankersley and Carol Ann (Wanhapiha) Matthews. B of Social Work, Ferris State U., 1989, AAS in Child Devel., 1989. Day care worker Mrs. Cheryl DePew, Big Rapids, Mich., 1988-89; social work intern Mecosta-Osceola Alternative Sch., Big Rapids, 1989; presch. dir. Downriver Parent Coop. Presch., Inc., Southgate, Mich., 1989; tchr., child devel. specialist II Westwood Child Devel. Ctr. Wayne County Imtermediate Sch. Dist., Inkster, Mich., 1989—. Mem. NAFE, Nat. Assn. for the Edn. of Young Children, FRAEYC, Assn. for Childhood Edn. Internat., Assn. for Supervision and Curriculum Devel., Blueline Hockey Club, Phi Sigma Sigma. Democrat. Lutheran. Home: 20490 Coachwood Rd Riverview MI 48192 Office: Wayne County ISD Westwood Child Devel Ctr Inkster MI 48141

TANKOOS, SANDRA MAXINE, court reporting services executive; b. Bklyn., Nov. 12, 1936; d. Samuel J. and Ethel (Seltzer) Rich; m. Kenneth Robert Tankoos, Mar. 17, 1957; children: Robert Ian, Gary Russell, Jenine Sheryl. AA, Stenotype Inst., 1957; BA, Queens Coll., 1969; MA, C.W. Post Coll., 1973. Cert. stenotype reporter, 1959. Ct. reporter free lance, N.Y.C., 1957-70; tchr. Spanish, various high schs., L.I., 1970-76; pres. Tankoos Reporting, N.Y.C., 1976—, Ar-Ti Recording, Mineola, N.Y., 1977—. Contbr. articles to profl. jours. exec. v.p., bd. dirs. Temple Sinai, Roslyn Hts., N.Y., 1989—, Am. Jewish Acad., West Hempstead, 1984—, LWV, Roslyn, 1969-75, NOW, Nassau County, 1975-77. Mem. Nat. Assn. Shorthand Reporters, Principal's Assn., Numismatic Club (pres. 1973-78). Avocations: writing, piano. Home: 77 Shepherd Ln Roslyn Heights NY 11577 Office: Ar-Ti Recording Inc 223 Jericho Turnpike Mineola NY 11501 also: Tankoos Reporting Co 11 John St New York NY 10038

TANNENWALD, LESLIE KEITER, educator; b. Boston, May 5, 1949; d. Irving Jules and Barbara June (Caplan) Keiter; m. Robert Tannenwald. BA, Brandeis U., 1971, MA, 1976; MAT in Social Studies, Simmons Coll., Boston, 1972. Cert. Social Worker, Tchr., Mass. Sr. assoc. Combined Jewish Philanthropies of Greater Boston, 1977-84; interim dir., asst. dir. Cambridge (Mass.) Community Svcs., 1984-85; ednl. cons. Bur. Jewish Edn., Boston, 1985-87; ednl. dir. Congregation Shalom Emeth, Burlington, Mass., 1987—; cons. Selected Ednl. Orgns. Boston 1972. Author: Curriculum, Male and Female, 1979 (Honors award 1971), Understanding the Holocaust, 1990. Officer, bd. dirs. Combined Jewish Philantropies of Greater Boston 1972—; mem. Am. Jewish Congress, Boston 1976—. Recipient Leadership award Inst. Leadership Devel. and Fund Raising. Mem. Nat. Alliance Profl. & Exec. Women, Alumni Assn. Benjamin S. Hornstein Program of Jewish Communal Svc., Assn. Jewish Community Personnel. Democrat. Home: 6 Clifton Rd Newton Center MA 02159 Office: Congregation Shalom Emeth 16 Lexington St Burlington MA 01803

TANNER, ALEXANDRA, marketing professional; b. San Francisco, June 21, 1951; d. Frederick Chauncey Tanner and Alexandra (Todd) Holmyard; m. Nigel Broughton Russell, Jan. 5, 1986. AA, Pine Manor Coll., Chestnut Hill, Mass., 1971; BS in Mktg., NYU, 1980, MBA in Mktg., Fin., 1981. Vice pres. Letitia Baldridge Pub. Rels., N.Y.C., 1975-79; cons. Dunham & Marcus Mktg. Cons., N.Y.C., 1982-86; sr. planner Bob Dorland Advt., London, 1986-87, assoc. planning dir., 1987-88, planning dir., 1988-89, planning dir. mktg. consulting unit, 1986-89; mgmt. supr., dir. account planning Perkins/Butler Direct Mktg., N.Y.C., 1989—. Mem. Direct Mktg. Assn., Direct Mktg. Women's Group, Account Planning Group (London), Beta Gamma Sigma. Office: Perkins Butler 79 Fifth Ave New York NY 10003

TANNER, COURTENAY TYLER, law office administrator; b. Ft. Lewis, Wash., Aug. 20, 1948; d. Henry Samuel and Dorothy Elizabeth (Connor) Tyler; m. Richard Brevard Tanner, May 25, 1974; children: Timothy Tyler, Richard Brevard Jr. BA in Teaching, Sam Houston State U., 1970. Tchr. Livingston (Tex.) Ind. Sch. Dist., 1970-71, San Antonio Acad., 1972-74; substitute instr. McKinney (Tex.) Job Corps, 1975-77, 80-82; demonstrator, salesperson Krups-McBride & Allen, Dallas, 1983-85; salesman, agt. Fenwick & Assocs. Realtors, Dallas, 1985-87; coord. corp. mktg. Remax Preston Rd. North Realtors, Dallas, 1987-89; law office adminstr. Richard B. Tanner, atty., 1989—. Touring docent Dallas County Heritage Soc., 1975-83, docent candelight tours Christmas Festival, 1977—, salesman on-site tickets 1981-83, 88—, chmn.-elect, 1984, chmn., 1985, chmn. decorations 1986-87, mem. Grand Heritage Ball Com., 1989—; v.p. 101 Club Dallas County Hist. Soc., 1983-84; chmn. women's com. Wayback House, Inc., Dallas, 1985-86, v.p., 1986-87, mem. adv. bd., 1987—; sec. Women's Wayback House Bd., Dallas, 1983-84, v.p., 1984-85, pres., 1985-86; artists chmn. Irish Fair com. Women's Com. of Dallas Ballet, 1985-86; mediator Neighborhood Youth Services, Richardson, Tex., 1986-88; vol. Office of Internat. Affairs, Dallas, 1988—; sustainer Jr. League of Richardson, 1984-88; leader, pack com. Cub Scouts Boy Scouts Am., 1981-83, 86-89; communication chairwoman Richardson Symphony Guild, 1989—, pres., 1999-91; bd. dirs. Richardson Arts Assn., 1988—, pres., 1990-91; bd. dirs. Victims Outreach, 1990-91, Children's Internat. Summer Villages, 1990-91; mem. adv. bd. Victims Svc. Sect., Tex. Dept. of Criminal Justice, 1989-91. Recipient Gold Pin award Dallas County Heritage Soc., 1986. Roman Catholic. Clubs: P.E.O. (Dallas) (chaplain 1983-84), Young Lawyer's Wives Inc. (Dallas) (Women's Wayback chmn. 1982-83, luncheon chmn. 1983-84, v.p. ways and means 1984-85).

TANNER, HELEN HORNBECK, historian; b. Northfield, Minn., July 5, 1916; d. John Wesley and Frances Cornelia (Wolfe) Hornbeck; m. Wilson P. Tanner, Jr., Nov. 22, 1940 (dec. 1977); children—Frances, Margaret Tanner Tewson, Wilson P., Robert (dec. 1983). A.B. with honors, Swarthmore Coll., 1937; M.A., U. Fla., 1949; Ph.D., U. Mich., 1961. Asst. to dir. pub. rels. Kalamazoo Pub. Schs., 1937-39; with sales dept. Am. Airlines Inc., N.Y.C., 1940-43; teaching fellow, then teaching asst. U. Mich., Ann Arbor, 1949-53, 57-60, lectr. extension svc., 1961-74, asst. dir. Ctr. Continuing Edn. for Women, 1964-68; project dir. Newberry Libr., Chgo., 1976-81, rsch. assoc., 1981—; dir. D'Arcy McNickle Ctr. for Indian History, 1984-85; cons., expert witness Indian treaties; mem. Mich. Commn. Indian Affairs, 1966-70. Author: Zespedes in East Florida 1784-1790, 1963, 89, General Green Visits St. Augustine, 1964, The Greeneville Treaty, 1974, The Territory of the Caddo Tribe of Oklahoma, 1974; editor: Atlas of Great Lakes Indian History, 1987. NEH grantee, 1976, fellow 1989. Mem. Am. Soc. Ethnohistory (pres. 1982-83), Am. Hist. Assn., Conf. Latin Am. History, Soc. History Discoveries, Orgn. Am. Historians, Chgo. Map Soc., Fla. Hist. Soc., Hist. Soc. Mich. Home: 5178 Crystal Dr Beulah MI 49617 Office: The Newberry Libr 60 W Walton St Chicago IL 60610

TANOOS, ANN, travel consultant; b. Marks, Miss., July 7, 1940; d. Earl Wayne and Martha Ann (Locke) Varner; m. George F. Tanoos, July 8, 1988; children: Donna Tipton Ridgeway, David Tipton. Student, Banking Sch., 1960, U. Tex., Arlington, 1962. Cert. travel agt. Office mgr., sec., treas. Tipton Cons. Engrs., Garland, Tex.; sec. Texaco Oil Corp., Dallas, First Nat. Bank, Dallas; travel cons. Lakeside Travel Agy., Rockwall, Tex. HALT mem. Am. for Legal Reform; active Rep. Women of Rockwall County, Prestonwood Bapt. Ch., Dallas. Recipient Travel Career Devel. award. Mem. NAFE, Am. Soc. Profl. and Exec. Women, Rockwall Newcomers Club, Rockwall Investment Club. Address: 213 Tanya Dr Rockwall TX 75087

TANOUS, HELENE MARY, physician; b. Zanesville, Ohio, Oct. 22, 1939; d. Joseph Carrington and Rose Marie (Mokarzel) T.; m. John Camp, 1986. BA, Marymount Coll., 1961; MD, U. Tex., 1967. Diplomate Am. Bd. Radiology. Intern County Hosp., L.A., 1967-68; resident in radiology U. So. Calif. Hosp., L.A., 1969-71; pvt. practice medicine specializing in radiology, L.A., 1972-73; instr. radiology U. So. Calif. Med. Sch., L.A., 1971-72; asst. prof. diagnostic radiology Baylor Med. Sch., Houston, 1973-75; dir. med. student elective in diagnostic radiology Ben Taub Hosp., Houston, 1973-75; pvt. practice diagnostic radiology, Largo, Fla., 1975—; asst. prof. diagnostic radiology U. South Fla. Med. Sch., 1980—; asst. prof., dir. of med. student edn. in diagnostic radiology U. Tex., Galveston, 1988—. Pres., founder Children's Advs., Inc.; bd. dirs. Fla. Endowment for Humanities, 1979-83. Decorated Chevalier des Palmes Academiques Govt. of France, 1988. Mem. AMA, So. Med. Assn., Internat. Platform Assn., L'Alliance Francaise of Tampa (bd. dirs. 1984—, pres. 1985-87), Fedn. Alliances Francaises U.S.A. (bd. dirs. 1987—). Office: U Tex Med Sch Dept Radiology G-09 Galveston TX 77550

TANUR, JUDITH MARK, sociologist, educator; b. Jersey City, Aug. 12, 1935; d. Edward Mark and Libbie (Berman) Mark; m. Michael Isaac Tanur, June 2, 1957; children: Rachel Dorothy, Marcia Valerie. BS, Columbia U., 1957, MA, 1963; PhD, SUNY, Stony Brook, 1972. Analyst Biometrics Rsch., N.Y.C., 1955-67; lectr. SUNY, Stony Brook, 1967-71; asst. prof. SUNY, 1971-77, assoc. prof., 1977-85, prof. sociology, 1985—; cons. NBC, N.Y.C., 1976-89, Lang. of Data Project, Los Altos, Calif., 1980—; mem. Com. on Nat. Statistics of the Nat. Acad. of Scis., 1980-87; trustee, NORC, U. Chgo., 1987—. Editor, Internat. Encyc. of Social Scis., N.Y.C., 1963-67, Statistics: A Guide to the Unknown, 1972, Internat. Encyc. of Statistics, 1978, Cognitive Aspects of Survey Methodology, 1984; contbr. articles to sci., statis. and social sci. jours. Bd. dirs. Vis. Nurse Svc., Great Neck, N.Y., 1970—; bd. govs. Gen. Soc. Survey, Chgo., 1989—. Sr. rsch. fellow, Am. Statis. Assn./NSF/Bur. Labor Statistics, 1988-89. Fellow, AAAS, Am. Statis. Assn.; mem. Internat. Statis. Inst., Phi Beta Kappa. Home: 17 Longview Pl Great Neck NY 11021 Office: Dept Sociology SUNY Stony Brook NY 11794-4356

TAN-WONG, LILY, textile executive; b. Medan, Sumatra, Indonesia, Aug. 10, 1947; came to U.S., 1968; d. Eng Chuan and Sor Choo (Peh) T.; m. Wilson Wong, Feb. 16, 1990. BA, I.K.I.P., Medan, 1967, Gustavus Adolphus Coll., St. Peter, Minn., 1972; MM, U. So. Calif., L.A., 1974. Adminstrn. officer Lloyds Bank, Los Angeles, 1974-80; v.p. Comml. Flooring Assn., Marina Del Rey, Calif., 1981-83; contract mgr. Harbinger Co., L.A., 1983-86; v.p. regional sales Princeton Techs., Ltd., L.A., 1986-87; v.p. export Bentley Mills, Inc., City of Industry, Calif., 1987—. Mem. Network Exec. Women in Hospitality, Indonesian Bus. Soc. Office: Bentley Mills Inc 14641 E Don Julian Rd City of Industry CA 91746

TANZOSH, ERMA CAROLYN, reinsurance brokerage executive; b. Caribou, Maine, Nov. 29, 1936; d. Martin and Mildred Otilia (Aronson) Akerson; m. Charles Francis Tanzosh, Feb. 16, 1939. Student, Coll. Ins., N.Y.C., 1985. Lic. real estate agt., N.Y. With Loring AFB, Limestone, Maine, 1954-57, 60-65; sec. AEC, Limestone, 1957-60; mgmt. asst., reporting stenographer USPHS Hosp., S.I., N.Y., 1965-81; broker's asst. Paul Napolitan, Inc., N.Y.C., 1983—. Vol. Snug Harbor Cultural Ctr., S.I., 1982-83. Recipient Achievement award Am. Internat. Group, 1986. Mem. Assn. Profl. Ins. Women, Nat. Assn. Ins. Women, Am. Spl. Risk Assn. Republican.

TAPLETT, LYNN CRAVEN, health facility administrator. Diploma in nursing, Alexandria (Va.) Hosp. Sch. Nursing. RN; cert. nursing administrator. Chief exec. officer TM Assocs., Del Mar, Calif.; dir. critical care svcs. Grossmont Hosp., LaMesa, Calif.; ind. nurse cons. Tyler, Tex.; dir. critical care nursing svcs. Mother Frances Hosp., Tyler. Author: Quick Reference to Critical Care Nursing. Lt. USN, 1975-76. Recipient Mary Gremish Outstanding Leadership award. Mem. AACN (charter pres. San Diego chpt.). Address: 402 Woodland Hills Dr Tyler TX 75701

TAPP, JUNE LOUIN, psychology educator; b. N.Y.C.; d. R.B. Louin and Ann Revier-Wacholder. B.A. magna cum laude in Sociology, U. So. Calif., 1951; M.S. in Ednl. Psychology, 1952; Ph.D. in Psychology, Syracuse U., 1963. Registered psychologist, Ill. Instr. ednl. psychology and psychology St. Lawrence U., Canton, N.Y., 1952-55; adminstrv. asst. to dean Moran Crime Inst., 1954-60; asst. instr. in citizenship Maxwell Grad. Sch., Syracuse U., N.Y., 1955-56; tutor in psychology and sociology Albert Schweitzer Coll., Churwalden, Switzerland, 1957-58; asst. prof. psychology Harvey Mudd Coll., Claremont, Calif., 1961-64; organizer behavioral scis. program, 1961-64; lectr., cons. Indian Coll. Youth Project, U. Poona, India, 1963-64; asst. prof., research assoc. com. on human devel. U. Chgo., 1964-67; assoc. prof., research assoc. com. on human devel., 1964-67, assoc. prof. in social scis., 1968-72; co-investigator, project adminstr. Children's Socialization into Compliance Systems, 1965-70; sr. research social scientist Am. Bar Found., Chgo., 1967-72; affiliated scholar, 1972-74; fellow in law and psychology Harvard U. Law Sch., Cambridge, Mass., 1971-72; prof. psychology U. Calif.-San Diego, La Jolla, 1976-78; provost Revelle Coll., 1976-78; chmn. humanities program, 1976-77, chmn. law and society program, 1977-78; prof. child psychology and criminal justice studies, adj. prof. law, adj. prof. family studies U. Minn., Mpls., 1972—; participant U. Calif.-Irvine Mgmt. Inst., 1977; cons. in field; lectr. profl. confs. and symposia. Author: (with F. Krinsky) Ambivalent America: A Psycho-political Dialogue, 1971; (with F.J. Levine) Law, Justice and Individual in Society, 1977. Mem. numerous editorial bds. of profl. jours. Manuscript reviewer for numerous profl. jours. Contbr. articles to profl. jours., chpts. to books. Mem. numerous civic, govtl. and profl. orgns. Recipient numerous civic and profl. awards; grantee in psychology and law from numerous profl. and govtl. agys. and orgns. Fellow Am. Psychol. Assn. (council 1981-84); mem. Am. Psychology-Law Soc. (pres. 1972-73), Soc. Psychol. Study Social Issues (pres. 1978-79), Soc. Research Child Devel., Internat. Assn. Polit. Psychology (council 1979-82), Assn. Advancement Psychology (trustee 1980-84), Interam. Soc. Psychology (v.p. 1985—), Internat. Assn. Cross-Cultural Psychology, Internat. Assn. Philosophy (exec. com. 1974-75), Law and Soc. Assn. (sec. 1973-74, trustee 1980-82), Soc. Exptl. Social Psychology (mem. forum White House Conf. on Children 1970). Address: Inst Child Devel 51 E River Rd U Minn Minneapolis MN 55455

TAPP, MARA ANNE, journalist; b. Canton, N.Y., July 22, 1956; d. Robert Berg and June (Louin) Tapp; m. Michael Silverstein, May 18, 1986; children: Ariella Beryl Silverstein-Tapp, Gabrielle Eve Silverstein-Tapp. Student, Macalester Coll., St. Paul, 1972-74; BA, U. Wis., 1976; MA, U. Chgo., 1977; MSJ, Northwestern U., Evanston, Ill., 1980. Poetry co-editor Chgo. Rev., 1977-79; legal adminstr. Isham, Lincoln & Beale, Chgo., 1977-79; coord. Chg. Rev. Speaker Series, 1978-80; producer/reporter Minn. Pub. Radio, St. Paul, 1981-82; staff writer U. Chgo. News Office, 1982-84, Chgo. Daily Law Bull., 1984-85; pub. info. officer City of Chgo. Law Dept., 1985-86; sr. writer, feature editor Chgo. Daily Law Bull./Sullivan's Rev., 1986-89; mng. editor Merrill's Ill. Legal Times, Chgo., 1989-90; free-lance writer, 1990—; mem. standing com. on media Ill. State Bar Assn., Chgo., 1989—. Recipient AP Sweepstakes Trophy, 1987, first prize, Ill. AP Editors Assn., 1987, Ill. Press Assn. Newspaper contest, 1988, Meritorious Achievement award, 1989. Home: 420 W Grand Ave Chicago IL 60610

TAPP, SHELLEY RAYE, marketing educator; b. Paducah, Ky., June 5, 1953; d. David Donald and Beatrice (Guill) T. BA, Agnes Scott Coll., 1975; MS, Ga. Inst. Tech., 1977; PhD, Ind. U., 1986. Lectr. Murray (Ky.) State U., 1978-79; assoc. instr. Ind. U., Bloomington, 1979-84; asst. prof. U. Nebr., Lincoln, 1984-89, St. Louis U., 1990—. Contbr. articles in consumer research field, 1982—. Cons. Goodwill Industries, Lincoln; pres. Lincoln Civic Chorus, 1986-89. George Holmes fellow U. Nebr., 1986, Ind. U. fellow, 1979-82, 83. Mem. Assn. Consumer Rsch., Am. Acad. Advt., Am. Mktg. Assn. (v.p. 1985-87), Jr. Women's League (cons.), Lincoln Needleworkers Guild (pres. 1987-89). Democrat. Home: 139 N 11th St #305 Lincoln NE 68508 Office: St Louis Univ Sch Bus 3674 Lindell Blvd Saint Louis MO 63108

TARAN, CAROLE, vocalist, actress; b. London, Sept. 7; d. Michael G. Kent and Mickey (Cummings) Novack; m. Robert S. Taran; 1 child, Adam Scott. Vocalist various night clubs and cabarets, 1978—; v.p. Adam Prodns., Inc., Miami Beach, Fla., 1979—; record producer Atlantic Records, 1987; rec. artist Fabulous New Jimmy Dorsey Orch., 1987; spl. events cons. numerous cos., 1979—. Actress: (films) Super Fuzz, 1981, Making Mr. Right, 1986; various TV appearances and commls.; producer (album) Dorsey Then and Now, 1987; lead vocalist Dorsey, Then and Now orch., 1988—; vocalist/producer: The South Beach Band "Limba Limba Lambada, Wizard Records, 1990. Recipient Carbonell award South Fla. Entertainment Writers. Mem. Screen Actors Guild, AGVA, Am. Fedn. Musicians. Club: Props Women of Show Bus. (past pres. Miami, Fla. chpt.). Office: Adam Prodns PO Box 414314 Miami Beach FL 33141

TARASCON-AURIOL, REGINE GINETTE, research chemist; b. Oran, Algeria, Mar. 6, 1957; came to U.S., 1981; m. Jean-Marie Tarascon, Sept. 5, 1981. BS in Phys. Chemistry, U. Abidjan, Ivory Coast, 1977; MSChemE, U. Bordeaux, 1981. Vis. scientist Cornell U., Ithaca, N.Y., 1981; mem. tech. staff AT&T Bell Labs., Murray Hill, N.J., 1982—. Contbr. articles on microlithography to profl. jours. Mem. Am. Chem. Soc., Internat. Soc. for Optical Engring., Materials Research Soc. Office: AT&T Bell Labs 600 Mountain Ave Murray Hill NJ 07974

TARBOX, KATHARINE RIGGS, investor relations executive; b. N.Y.C., Feb. 8, 1948; d. Henry Fisk and Mary (Powell) T.; m. Jeremy M.F. Warner, Sept. 25, 1975 (div. Nov. 1982); m. Donald O. McLeod, May 25, 1983. BA in Econs., Wellesley Coll., 1970. Cash mgr., specialist Citibank, N.A., N.Y.C., 1970-75, sr. account officer, 1975-77; cash mgr. Chesebrough-Ponds, Inc., Greenwich, Conn., 1977-79, mgr. investor relations, 1979-82; dir. investor relations Chesebrough Ponds, Inc., Westport, Conn., 1982-86; v.p. investor relations Colgate-Palmolive Co., N.Y.C., 1987—. Alumnae gov. Westover Sch., Middlebury, Conn., 1987—. Mem. Nat. Investor Relations Inst. (dir. N.Y.C. chpt. 1981-82). Office: Colgate-Palmolive Co 300 Park Ave New York NY 10022

TARDIF, MONIQUE BERNATCHEZ, Canadian legislator; b. Que., Can., Jan. 8, 1936; d. Henri and Aline (LaRue) B.; m. Louis Tardif (dec.); children: François, Michel, Dominique, Danielle (dec.). Student, Laval U. Dir. for consumer protection Que. Auto Club, 1976-80; mem. Can. Ho. of Commons, 1984—; re-elected as mem., 1988—, parliamentary sec. to minister of supply and svcs., 1989—. Mem., bd. dirs. Les Grands Ballets Canadiens, Montreal, 1969-70. Mem. Progressive Conservative Party. Roman Catholic. Office: House of Commons, Room 325 Confederation Bldg, Ottawa, ON Canada K1A 0A6

TARGAN, LYNNDA LEWIS, business owner, consultant; b. Reading, Pa., July 22, 1948; d. Sidney Irving and Bernice Lewis; m. Larry Edward Targan, Dec. 1, 1968; children: Eric, Beth. BS, Temple U., 1971. Corr. Meyers Pub. Co., Chgo., 1975-78; nat. dir. pub. rels. Friends of AKIM, U.S.A., 1982-83; assoc. cons. Toplin & Assocs., Phila., 1985-86; prin. LT Communications, Ambler, Pa., 1981—; instr. in pub. rels. continuing edn. dept. Temple U., 1990—; co-chair community resource com. Abington (Pa.) Hosp. Contbr. articles to profl. jours. Bd. dirs. pub. rels. Linda Creed Found., Phila., 1987—. Mem. Pub. Rels. Soc. Am., Phila. Pub. Rels. Assn., Nat. Soc. Fundraising Execs., Women in Communications, Inc., Am. Mktg. Assn. Democrat. Jewish. Home and Office: 1429 Treetop Ln Ambler PA 19002

TARNOSKI, LORI M., clothing company executive; b. 1940. With V F Corp., Wyomissing, Pa., 1961—, adminstrv. asst. to v.p., 1970-73, asst. sec., 1973-74, sec., 1974—, v.p., 1979—. Office: VF Corp 1047 N Park Rd Wyomissing PA 19610

TARNOVE, ELIZABETH JOY, journalism educator; b. Pasadena, Calif., Oct. 29, 1955; d. Norman and Jean (Miller) T.; m. Calvin Barry Pomeroy, June 24, 1984; 1 child, Sarah Rebecca. BA, Calif. State U., Long Beach, 1977; MS, Northwestern U., Evanston, Ill., 1978; postgrad., Claremont U., 1984—. Cert. community coll. journalism tchr., Calif. Editorial editor Macon (Ga.) Telegraph, 1978; feature editor Palos Verdes Peninsula News, Rolling Hills Estates, Calif., 1978-79; reporter San Gabriel Valley Tribune, Covina, Calif., 1979-81; instr. L.A. Harbor Coll., Wilmington, Calif., 1981, East L.A. Coll., Monterey Park, Calif., 1981-85; lectr. Calif. State Polytechnic U., Pomona, 1983-86, asst. prof., 1986-89; lect. Calif. State U., Northridge, 1989—. Editor: The Drawings of Van Dyck, 1976, More Drawings of Rubens, 1976. Recipient 1st place News Feature, Greater L.A. Press Club, 1979, 1st place Feature Writing, Calif. Press Women, 1979. Mem. Soc. Profl. Journalists (Outstanding Grad. 1977), Women in Communications (advisor 1985-87, Outstanding Grad. 1977), Assn. for Edn. in Journalism and Mass Communications. Democrat. Jewish. Office: Calif State Univ 18111 Nordhoff St Northridge CA 91330

TARPLEY, BRENDA MAE See LEE, BRENDA

TARSELL, THOMASINE MISSOURI, insurance brokerage executive, financial advisor; b. Shamokin, Pa., Sept. 27, 1941; d. Walter Thomas and Missouri Elizabeth (Haas) T.; m. David Charles Cohen, Aug. 13, 1969 (div. Jan. 1982). Grad. Phoenixville Area High Sch., Pa. Cert. ins. counselor. Mfrs. rep. Ardlee Assocs., Phila., 1963-66; v.p. mktg., nat. sales mgr. Marlee Creations, Phila., 1965-66; owner Schneider, Hill & Spangler, 1966-68; account exec., ins. broker Schaprio-Shadline & Balser, Inc., Balt., 1968-71; gen. mgr., ins. broker Bruce Ins. Corp., Balt., 1971-77; founder, chief exec. officer Tomco Ins. Corp. and Tomco Money Mgmt. Corp., Towson, Md., 1977—; exec. v.p. 7 Services Inc., Balt., 1984—; dir. Care First Health Maintenance Orgn., Balt., now advisor; founder, exec. First Comprehensive Directory of Women Owned Businesses in State Md., 1983—, First Women in Exporting Trade Mission, 1985—; chairperson Bus. Ptnrs. Inc., 1987—. Founder, treas. Pooling of Women Entrepreneurial Resources Polit. Action Com., 1984—; mem. Md. Indsl. Devel. Fin. Authority, 1987—; mem. small bus. adv. coun. trade policy matters, U.S. Dept. Commerce, 1987—. Named

Woman of Yr., Nat. Assn. Women Bus. Owners, 1981. Mem. Ind. Ins. Agts. Assn., Cert. Fin. Planners Assn., Nat. Assn. Women Bus. Owners, Minority Bus. Council Md. (bd. advisors), U.S. SBA (counselor, lectr., mem. adv. coun. region III 1989—, Woman Bus. Adv. of Yr. 1984). Republican. Lutheran. Avocations: golf, racquetball, reading, sailing, boating. Office: Tomco Ins Corp 22 West Rd Ste 202 Towson MD 21204-2366

TARSITANO, BETTY JEANNE, nursing educator; b. Spalding, Nebr., Aug. 11, 1930; d. Edward William and Dorothy Sophie (Hinze) Patterson; m. Robert Leo Tarsitano, Dec. 27, 1969. BS, Creighton U., 1958; MS in Nursing, Catholic U. Am., 1960; PhD, U. Nebr., 1971. RN, Ill. Staff nurse Creighton Meml. St. Joseph Hosp., Omaha, Nebr., 1952-53, 57-60, U. Mich. Hosp., Ann Arbor, 1953-55; asst. prof. Creighton U., Omaha, 1960-69, U. Ill. Med. Ctr., Chgo., 1970-74, Loyola U. Sch. Nursing, Chgo., 1977-83; assoc. prof. nursing Rush Coll., Chgo., 1974-77, Northwestern U., Chgo., 1983-88, Elmhurst (Ill.) Coll., 1989—; bd. dirs. Elmhurst Meml. Home Health Care, Villa Park, Ill.; cons. in field. Contbg. editor to book chpts. USPHS grantee 1958, 64, 76. Mem. Ill. Nurses Assn. (pres. 1976-78, bd. dirs. dist. 19, 1974-76, 78-80, 87-89), Chgo. Heart Assn., Nat. Coun. Family Rels., Lombard Hist. Soc., Sigma Theta Tau (counselor chair com. 1977). Republican. Roman Catholic. Home: 305 Elm Lombard IL 60148 Office: Elmhurst Coll 190 Prospect Elmhurst IL

TARTTER, VIVIEN CAROL, psychology educator; b. Flushing, N.Y., June 13, 1952; d. John and Gertrude Phyllis (Ullmann) Rothman; m. Paul Ian Tartter, Oct. 13, 1972; children: Eric Walter, Alexander Charles. AB, Brown U., 1973, MA, 1975, PhD, 1977. Postdoctoral fellow Bell Labs., Murray Hill, N.J., 1977-79, cons., 1979-84; asst. prof. Rutgers U., Camden, N.J., 1979-84, assoc. prof., 1984-88, chmn. psychology, 1985; assoc. prof. psychology CUNY, 1988—; cons. Salk Inst., La Jolla, Calif., 1980, Air Force Aerospace Med. Research Lab. Contract U. Dayton, 1984-86, Cochlear Implant Project Manhattan Eye and Ear Hosp., 1986—; vis. research assoc. dept. otolaryngology U. Melbourne, 1987. Author: Language Processes, 1986; contbr. articles to profl. jours. Recipient Charles Johanna Busch Meml. Fund award Rutgers U., 1985-87; James Gordon Bennett Meml. scholar, 1969; Deafness Research Found. grantee, 1988; NIH predoctoral fellow, 1975-77, NIH-Fogarty Sr. Internat. fellow, 1987; recipient Career Advancement award for women NSF, 1989. Mem. Acoustical Soc. Am., AAAS, Am. Psychol. Assn., Psychonomic Soc., N.Y. Acad. Scic., Phi Beta Kappa, Sigma Xi. Democrat. Jewish. Avocations: cooking, sailing, scuba diving, hiking. Office: City College Psychology Dept 138th St & Convent Ave New York NY 10031

TARULLI, BEVERLY ANN, telecommunications company manager; b. Union, N.J., Nov. 23, 1954; d. Joseph John and Catherine Joan (Zieleniewska) T. BA, Franklin & Marshall Coll., 1976; MA, U. Akron, 1983, PhD, 1987. Lic. psychologist, Ga. Cons. Organizational Cons. Group, Akron, Ohio, 1976, The Standard Oil Co., Cleve., 1979-80; instr. Kent State U., 1985, U. Akron; mgr. BellSouth Corp., Atlanta, 1989—. Mem. Atlanta chpt. Franklin and Marshall Coll. Alumni Bd. Mem. Am. Psychol. Assn., Am. Soc. Tng. and Devel., Soc. Indsl. Organizational Psychology, Atlanta Human Resource Planning Group, Franklin and Marshall Coll. Psychology Club (pres. 1975-76). Office: BellSouth Corp 13E04 1155 Peachtree St Atlanta GA 30367

TASHJIAN, JOY MARIE, entertainment consultant; b. San Francisco, Aug. 2, 1958; d. Simon John and Shirley Ann T. BSBA in Broadcasting summa cum laude, San Francisco U., 1980. Advt. asst. J.L. Marsh, Burlingame, Calif., 1973-76; advt. buyer STAR-TV, San Bruno, Calif., 1981-83; v.p. DIC Entertainment, Burbank, Calif., 1983-88; pres. Entertainment Trademark Consultants, N.Y.C., 1988-90; pres., chief exec. officer Entertainment Merchandising Enterprises, San Francisco. Contbr. articles to various publs. Com. mem. Spl. Olympics, San Francisco, 1981-83. Mem. Licensing Industry Assn. (com. mem. 1984-86, bd. dirs. 1986-90). Office: Entertainment/Enterprises 1 Market Pla Steuart Tower Ste 1780 San Francisco CA 91405

TASHJIAN, JULIA ZAKARIAN, state official; b. Providence, June 8, 1938; d. Harry and Eliza (Kaffeian) Zakarian; m. James Samuel Tashjian, Nov. 29, 1959; children: Sherri Lynn, James Edward, Lisa Helene, Charles Harry. Dep. registrar of voters Town of Windsor, Conn., 1968-82, chmn. jury com., 1969-75; adminstrv. asst. State and Urban Devel. Com., 1965-75, Govt. Adminstrn. and Policy Com., 1975-76, Human Svcs. Com., 1977-78; spl. asst. fin. com. Conn. Legislature, 1979-81, interim intern coord., 1979-81; sec. of state State of Conn., Hartford, 1982—; adminstrv. asst. House Asst. Majority Leaders, 1981. Mem. Dem. State Cen. Com., 1978-82; del. Dem. Nat. Conv., 1980, 84, Dem. Nat. Party Conf., 1981. Mem. Nat. Assn. Secs. of State (exec. com., chmn. bylaws com., sec. 1986, v.p. 1987, pres. 1989-90). Office: Sec of State Office State Capitol Hartford CT 06106

TASSANI, SALLY MARIE, communications executive, marketing consultant; b. Teaneck, N.J., Dec. 30, 1948; d. Peter R. and Marie Irene (Sorbello) T. BA, Am. U., 1970. Elem. sch. tchr., Washington, 1970-73; asst. prodn. and promotion mgr. First Nat. Bank of Chgo., 1973-74; exec. dir. Jack O'Grady Graphics, Inc., Chgo., 1974-76; creative dir. Dimensional Mktg., Inc., Chgo., 1976-78; pres., founder Tassani Communications (formerly Nexus, Inc.), Chgo., 1978—. Elected to Com. of 200; nat. trustee Boys and Girls Clubs Am. Named one of Ad Age's Best and Brightest Women in Advt., Top Women Entrepreneur Crain's Chgo. Bus., Entrepreneur of Yr. women's category INC, 1990. Mem. Alliance Roundtable for the Art Inst. Chgo., Northwestern Univ's. Com. on Fgn. and Domestic Affairs, Chgo. Coun. on Fgn. Rels., Old Town Triangle Assn., Terra Mus. Mem. Internat. Assn. of Bus. Communicators (Spectra award 1987, guest speaker 1988), Women's Advt. Club of Chgo., Am. Mktg. Assn. (guest speaker 1988), Pub. Rels. Soc. of Am. (guest speaker), Young Pres's. Orgn., Econ. Club, Chgo. Advt. Club, The Executives Club Chgo., Women's Athletic Club, East Bank Club. Avocations: race walking, sailing, photography, Am. crafts, graphic design. Home: 1735 N Orleans St Chicago IL 60614 Office: Tassani Communications Inc 625 N Michigan Ave Ste 1600 Chicago IL 60611

TASSO, MARIA GERALYN, pediatrician; b. Bklyn., Apr. 25, 1958; d. John P. and Marion D. (Paccione) T. BS, SUNY, Binghamton, 1980; MD, SUNY Health Sci. Ctr., Syracuse, 1984. Diplomate Am. Bd. Pediatrics. Internship and residency in pediatrics SUNY Health Sci. Ctr., Syracuse, 1984-87; pvt. practice Pediatric Assocs. of Conn., Waterbury, 1987—; assoc. attending physician Waterbury Hosp., 1987—, St. Mary's Hosp., Waterbury, 1987—. Fellow Am. Acad. Pediatrics. Roman Catholic. Office: Pediatric Assoc of Conn PC 1078 W Main St Waterbury CT 06704

TASSONE, GELSOMINA (GESSIE TASSONE), steel fabricating executive; b. N.Y.C., July 8, 1944; d. Enrico and A. Cira (Petriccione) Gargiulo; children: Ann Marie, Margaret, Theresa, Christine; m. Armando Tassone, Mar. 20, 1978. Student, Orange County Community Coll., 1975-79. Head bookkeeper Gargiulo Bros. Builders, N.Y.C., 1968-72; pres., owner A&T Iron Works, Inc., New Rochelle, N.Y., 1973—, Gessie Realty, New Rochelle, N.Y., 1980-86, Majestico Iron Works, Inc., N.Y.C., 1980-89, A&G Distbg. of West, New Rochelle, 1987—, Orsogril USA, Inc., N.Y.C., 1988—. Recipient Profl. Image award Contractors Coun. Greater N.Y.C., 1986; named Businesswoman of Yr., Contractors Coun. Greater N.Y.C., 1985, N.Y. State Small Bus. Person of Yr., 1988, Entrepreneur of Yr. Inc. mag., 1990; company named a Successful Small Bus. Co. Westchester County C. of C./BSBA, 1986-88. Mem. Nat. Ornamental and Miscellaneous Metal Assn., Builders Inst. Westchester and Putnam County, Westchester Assn. Women Bus. Owners, Profl. Women in Constrn., Westchester C. of C. Office: A&T Iron Works Inc 25 Cliff St New Rochelle NY 10801

TASSOTTI, TERESA, college administrator; b. New Kensington, Pa., Feb. 10, 1957; d. Oliver and Julia (Cecchini) T. BA, Gannon U., 1979, MS, 1983. Nat. cert. counselor. Assoc. dir., operation pathway program Gannon Univ., Erie, Pa., 1979-80, counselor, upward bound program, 1980-82, dir., upward bound program, 1982—, instr. self devel., 1984—. Vol. United Way of Erie County, 1984-89; bd. mem. Shiloh Day Care Ctr., Erie, 1983-87; class reporter Gannon Univ. Alumni Assn., Erie, 1987—. Mem. Pa. Assn. Ednl. Opportunity Program Pers. (treas. 1987-90, pres. 1990—, Conf. presenter 1987—), Mid-Eastern Assn. Ednl. Opportunity Program Pers., Am. Assn. for Counseling and Devel., NAFE, Am. Coll. Pers. Assn., Assn. for Multicultural Counseling and Devel. Democrat. Roman Catholic. Office: Gannon Univ University Square Erie PA 16502

TATE, CHARLOTTE ANNE, biochemist; b. Mt. Clemens, Mich., Sept. 15, 1944; d. Howard Belverd and Beth (Wilkerson) T. BS, Tex. Woman's U., Denton, 1969; MA, S.W. Tex. State U., San Marcos, 1972; PhD, U. Tex., 1976. NIH postdoctoral fellow Inst. Environ. Stress, U. Calif., Santa Barbara, 1976-77; postdoctoral fellow sect. cardiovascular scis. Baylor Coll. Medicine, Houston, 1977-79, instr., 1979-80, asst. prof., 1980-86, assoc. prof., 1986-90; prof. dept. pharmacology U. Houston, 1990—. Assoc. editor Medicine and Sci. in Sports and Exercise, 1986—; contbr. articles to profl. jours., chpts. to books. Named Disting. Alumnus, S.W. Tex. State U., San Marcos, 1983; NIH grantee, 1986—. Fellow Am. Coll. Sports Medicine (bd. trustees 1987-89, pres. Tex. chpt. 1980); mem. AAAS, ACLU, Am. Physiol. Soc., Biophys. Soc. Democrat. Home: 5702 Arboles Houston TX 77035 Office: Dept Pharmacology U Houston Houston TX 77204-5515

TATE, ELLIENNE TODD, dean of school of nursing; b. Lake Charles, La., Sept. 30, 1940; d. Donald Wilbur and Marie (Young) Todd; m. W.O. Tate Jr., Nov. 19, 1966; 1 child, Walton Todd. BS, Northwestern State U., Natchitoches, La., 1962; MS, U. Md., 1964; EdD, La. State u., 1978. Staff nurse Lake Charles Meml. Hosp., Lake Charles, La., 1962-63; mem. faculty Northwestern State U., Baton Rouge, La., 1964-67; mem. faculty Southeastern La. U., Hammond, La., 1967-70, dean, school of nursing, 1970—; chmn. bd. of commrs. Seventh Ward Gen. Hosp., Hammond, 1989—. Mem. Am. Nurses' Assn., Coun. Adminstrn. of Nursing Edn., So. Coun. on Collegiate Edn. for Nursing, Sigma Theta Tau. Republican. Presbyterian. Home: 1628 E Pleasant Ridge Hammond LA 70403 Office: Southeastern La U Coll Nursing U Sta Box 781 Hammond LA 70402

TATE, EVELYN RUTH, real estate broker; b. Ottumwa, Iowa, Sept. 21; d. Frank Edward and Ella Belle (Smith) Ross; student public schs., Huntington Park, Calif.; m. William Tate (dec.); 1 son, William. Owner, mgr. Evelyn R. Tate Realty Co., Sherman Oaks, Calif., 1943-53, Beverly Hills, Calif., 1942—; owner, mgr. Evelyn Tate Fine Arts, San Francisco, 1976—; mgr. Beverly Hills Galleries, Hyatt Regency Hotel, San Francisco, 1979—; mgr. art gallery Fairmont Hotel; owner, mgr. Tate Gallery, St. Frances Hotel, San Francisco, Hyatt Regency Hotel San Francisco, Fairmont Hotel, Dallas. Mem. Nat. Assn. Female Execs., The Exec. Female. Home: 999 Green St Apt 1003 San Francisco CA 94133

TATE, FRAN M., small business owner; b. Auburn, Wash., Oct. 5, 1929; dau. Frank Joseph and Theresa Mary (Bingesar) Pfulg; m. Rory Tate, Sept. 30, 1970 (div.); children—Michael C., Joseph M.; m. 2d, Juan Ramon Ramirez, Sept. 6, 1981 (div. May 1986). Student U. Wash. Gen. mgr., Sorensen Heating Co., Auburn, 1952-70; cons. Success Motivation Inst., Bellevue, Wash., 1970-72; field engr., draftsman, J. Dalton and Assocs., Point Barrow, Alaska, 1973-75; pres., owner Inupiat Water Delivery Co., Barrow, Alaska, 1977—; pres., owner Elephant Pot Sewage Haulers, Barrow, 1977—; pres., owner, operator Pepe's North of the Border Restaurant, Barrow, 1978—, pres., owner Tate Enterprises, Inc.; Burger Barn, Barrow, 1984—; disc jockey, Sta. KBRW, Barrow. Mem. Barrow Zoning commn.; mem. citizens adv. bd. Barrow Mus. and Cultural Ctr., 1989-90; regional coord. Gov.'s Conf. for Small Bus., 1989-90. Recipient Boss of Yr. award Credit Women Internat., 1969; Outstanding Service award Barrow PTA; Alaska's Outstanding Women State Comm. for Status of Women, 1984. Mem. Barrow C. of C. (pres. 1989—, bd. dirs.), Blues Alley Music Soc., Nat. Geog. Soc., Smithsonian Instn., Jazz Heritage Found., Arctic Slope Scholarship Found., Nat. Assn. Female Execs. Roman Catholic. Club: Las Vegas Jazz.

TATE, GERALDINE WILLIAMS, financial planner; b. Montgomery, Ala., Feb. 10, 1954; d. Willie Paul Williams and Mary Maude (Moore) Stansbury; m. James Edward Tate, June 16, 1973; children: James, Gennifer, Jessica. BS, Wayne State U., 1979; MS, Cen. Mich. U., 1983. EKG technician Henry Ford Hosp., Detroit, 1977-78, monitor scanner, 1978-79, EKG supr., 1979-86, billing coor., 1985-89; spl. agent, registered rep. Prudential Life Ins., Southfield, Mich., 1989—. Leader Girl Scouts Am., Detroit, 1986—; vol. State Rep., Detroit, 1988; treas. Rosedale Pk. Assn., Detroit, 1985. Recipient Achievement award Girl Scout Am., 1987. Mem. Nat. Assn. Exec. Women, Nat. Assn. Life Underwriters, Greater Detroit Assn. Life Underwriter, Greater Detroit Optimist Club, Am. Heart Assn., Nat. Assn. Technicians, Mich. Assn. Ins. Billers. Democrat. Baptist. Home: 14923 Grandville Detroit MI 48223

TATE, JO OSBORNE, electronics engineer; b. Princeton, Ind.; d. Riley Frederick Jr. and Connie Ruby (Phillips) Osborne; m. Timothy Alan Tate, June 1, 1980; children: Jeffrey, Justine. BSEE, Purdue U., 1980; postgrad., U. Ariz., Air Force Inst. Tech., Wright-Patterson AFB. Cert. in EIT. Electronics engr. Emerson Electric, St. Louis, USAF Systems Command, Wright-Patterson AFB, U.S. Army Info. Systems Engring., Ft. Huachuca, Ariz.; computer specialist Office of Dir. Info. Systems for Command, Control, Communications and Computers Hdqrs. Dept. of the Army, 1989—. Author: Local Area Network Specification for Army Minicomputer; editor Army OSI Implementation and Transition Plan, Army Minicomputer Menu Specification. Recipient Sustained Superior Performance award, 1985, Exceptional Performance award, 1987, Quality Step Increase award, 1987, Spl. Act award, 1988. Mem. IEEE, Assn. Computing Machinery, Armed Forces Communications and Electronics Assn., Soc. Women Engrs. Republican. Baptist. Home: 3 Forester Ct Sterling VA 22170 Office: HQDA ODISC4 SAIS-ADM The Pentagon Rm 1C670 Washington DC 20310-0107

TATE, MERZE, educator; b. Blanchard, Mich., Feb. 6, 1905; d. Charles H. and Myrtle Katora (Lett) T.; BA Western Mich. U. 1927; MA Columbia U. 1930, BLitt Oxford U. 1935, PhD Harvard U. 1941; LLD (hon.) Morgan State U., Bowie State Coll. 1977, Lincoln U. 1978; DHL, Havard U., 1986. Tchr., Crispus Attucks High Sch., Indpls. 1927-32, Barber Scotia Coll. Concord, N.C. 1935-36, Bennett Coll. 1936-41, Morgan State U. 1941-42; faculty Howard U. 1942-74, now prof. emeritus; Fulbright prof. India 1950-51. Fellow and grantee in field; recipient Nat. Urban League Disting. Achievement award 1948; Western Mich. U. Disting. Alumna award 1970; Mayor of Detroit award 1978; Am. Black Artist's Pioneer award 1978; award The Prometheans, Inc., 1980; Am. Assn. State Colls. and Univs. award, 1982. Mem. Am. Hist. Assn., Assn. Study Afro-Am. History, AAUW (Disting. Mem. award D.C. chpt. 1983), Phi Beta Kappa, Alpha Kappa Alpha (3d fgn. fellow), Pi Gamma Mu, Radcliffe Club of Washington, Harvard Club of Washington, Writers Club, Howard U. Women's Club, Howard U. Retirees Club, Bridge Builders Club, Bridge Eights Club. Roman Catholic. Author: The Disarmament Illusion—The Movement for a Limitation of Armaments to 1907, 1942, The United States and Armaments, 1948, The United State and the Hawaiian Kingdom, 1965, Hawaii: Reciprocity or Annexation 1968, Diplomacy in the Pacific, 1973; contbr. numerous articles to profl. jours.

TATE, OCTAVA LOUISE, social worker; b. Hardin, Mont., July 30, 1940; d. Elmo and Lucy Louise (English) T.; m. Antonio Sanchez-Vargas, Sept. 1975 (div. 1976); children: Jamie Jewel Anna, James Montie. BS, Ea. Mont. Coll., 1985. Floral asst. Waterman Floral, Hardin, 1954-64; community catalyst Billings (Mont.) Community Action, 1966-67; ward clk. St. Vincent Hosp., Billings, 1967-71, discharge clk., 1971-74; parking enforcement attendant City of Billings, 1974-78, pers. asst., 1978-80; secretarial asst. Student Union Ea. Mont. Coll., Billings, 1980-86; community social worker Dept. of Family Svcs. State of Mont., Billings, 1986—. Mem. Community Focus, Billings Housing Com., bd. dirs., 1988-89. Recipient Community Svc. award City of Billings, 1967. Mem. AAUW, South Park Task Force (chairperson 1986-88), People Against Poverty, Inc. (chairperson, organizer). Democrat. Mormon. Home: 124 S 38th St Billings MT 59101

TATE, SHEILA BURKE, public relations executive; b. Washington, Mar. 3, 1942; d. Eugene L. and Mary J. (Doherty) Burke; m. William J. Tate, May 2, 1981; children: Hager Burke Patton, Courtney Paige Patton. BA in Journalism, Duquesne U., 1964; postgrad. in mass communications, U. Denver, 1975-76. Rsch. asst. Westinghouse Air Brake Co.; asst. account exec. Falhgren and Assocs.; copywriter Ketchum, MacLeod and Grove, 1964-66; account exec. Burson-Marsteller Assocs., Pitts., 1967; sr. v.p. Burson-Marsteller Assocs., Washington, 1985-87; public rels. mgr. Colo. Nat. Bank, Denver, 1967-71; account exec. Hill and Knowlton, Inc., Houston, 1977-78; v.p. Hill and Knowlton, Inc., Washington, 1978-81; dep. to the chmn. Hill and Knowlton Inc., Washington, 1987-88; press sec. to First Lady White House, Washington, 1981-85; press sec. George Bush for Pres. Campaign, 1988; press sec. to Pres.-elect George Bush, 1988-89; vice chmn. Cassidy and Assocs. Pub. Affairs, Washington, 1989—; bd. dirs. Corp. for Pub. Broadcasting. Mem. Nat. Press Club, Nat. Press Found. (bd. dirs.). Republican. Clubs: Duquesne U. Century, F Street, Washington Golf and Country. Office: 655 15th StNW Washington DC 20005

TATEM, NANCY GAUER, nursing services administrator; b. Newark, N.J., Aug. 16, 1942; d. Harry and Jean (Hill) Gauer; m. H. Randolph Tatem, 3d, Sept. 14, 1963 (div. 1979); children: Jeffrey Randolph, Kyra Elizabeth. RN, Hahnemann U., 1963; BS in Nursing, Gwynedd-Mercy Coll., Gwynedd, Pa., 1984. Cert. gerontol. nurse Am. Nurses Assn., 1985. Med.-surg. nurse Hahnemann U., Phila., 1963-65; health info. coordinator Nat. Found. March of Dimes, Bucks County, Pa., 1977-78; nurse/instr. Upjohn, Doylestown, Pa., 1978-80; head nurse Doylestown Manor (Pa.), 1980-82; surg. asst. AJL Simoes Assocs., Lansdale, Pa., 1982-84; dir. nursing Doylestown Manor, 1984-85; co-founder, dir. nursing services, pres. exec. bd. Geriatric Svcs. T.H.E. Respite, alternative adult day program, Mechanicsville, Pa., 1986—; cons. ElderFair Inc.; vol. nurse ARC, Bucks County, 1977-80. Com. mem. Bucks County Hist. Soc., 1972-78; founding mem. PAK Teen Drug and Alcohol Program, 1976-78; bd. dirs. Bucks County chpt. March of Dimes, 1979-80. Mem. Bucks County RN's Assn. (sec. 1980-84), Pa. Nurses Assn., Forum for Advancement Nursing Excellence, 1984-88, Am. Nurses Found, AAUW, Pa. Adult Day Care Assn., Nat. Gerontol. Nursing Assn., Cen. Bucks C. of C., Sigma Theta Tau (Iota Kappa chpt.). Republican. Presbyterian. Club: PEO. Home: 54 Spring Dr Doylestown PA 18901 Office: T H E Respite Route 413 PO Box 294 Mechanicsville PA 18934

TATHAM, JULIE CAMPBELL, writer; b. N.Y.C., June 1, 1908; d. Archibald and Julia deFres (Sample) Campbell; student pvt. schs., N.Y.C.; m. Charles Tatham, Mar. 30, 1933; children—Charles III, Campbell. Author more than 30 juvenile books including: The Mongrel of Merryway Farm, 1952; The World Book of Dogs, 1953; To Nick from Jan, 1957; author Trixie Belden series, 1946—, Ginny Gordon series, 1946—; co-author Cherry Ames and Vicki Barr series, 1947—; author: The Old Testament Made Easy, 1985; many series books transl. into fgn. langs.; contbr. numerous mag. stories and articles to popular publs., 1935—; free-lance writer, 1935—; contbr. numerous articles to Christian Sci. publs., including Christian Sci. Monitor, 1960—. Address: 1202 S Washington St Apt 814 Alexandria VA 22314

TATLOCK, ANNE M., trust company executive; b. White Plains, N.Y., July 1, 1939; d. John and Kathleen (McGrath) McNiff; m. William Tatlock, Apr. 29, 1967; children: Julina, Kerry, Christopher. BA, Vassar Coll., 1961; MA in Econs., NYU, 1968. 1st v.p. Smith Barney Harris Upham, N.Y.C., 1962-84; sr. v.p. Fiduciary Trust Internat., N.Y.C., 1984—, also bd. dirs. Treas., bd. dirs. West Side Day Nursery, N.Y.C.; bd. dirs. Stanley Isaacs Neighborhood Ctr., N.Y.C., 1988—; trustee Cultural Instns. Retirement System, N.Y.C., 1989—. Elected to Acad. Women Achievers, YWCA, N.Y.C., 1983.

TATUM, DEBORAH ELAINE, industrial sales executive; b. Maxwell AFB, Ala., May 24, 1952; d. Cecil Richard Tatum and Ethel Cleo (Covan) Matuska. Student, U. Philippines, 1970-71; BS, Troy State U., 1974; MS in Edn., Auburn U., 1980. State history and contemporary world affairs tchr. T.R. Miller High Sch., Brewton, Ala., 1974-78; grad. resident, advisor Auburn (Ala.) U., 1978-80; lighting sales engr. Gen. Electric Co., El Monte, Calif., 1980-83, sales engr., 1983-84; region sales adminstr. GE, Brea, Calif., 1984-88; mgr. indsl. sales GE, El Monte, Calif., 1990—. Mem. NAFE. Republican. Methodist. Home: 24 Hollyhock Ln Laguna Hills CA 92656 Office: GE 9350 E Flair Dr Ste 200 El Monte CA 91731

TAUB, MARCIA JEAN, marketing and display design executive; b. N.Y.C., Oct. 9, 1957; d. Ronald Herbert and Ethel Betty (Flecker) T. Student, Northwestern U., winter 1975, summer 1978; BA, U. Denver, 1979; M of Mgmt. and Human Resource Devel., Nat. Coll. Edn., Evanston, Ill., 1983. Account exec. creative displays div. Saatchi and Saatchi, London, 1980-85, now v.p. ops., 1989—; display mgr. Max Factor & Co., Stamford, Conn., 1985-87; cons. Creative Displays, Inc./Mktg. Services Group, Chgo., 1987—. Vol. Haddasah, Jewish United Fund, Starlight Found. Mem. Am. Mktg. Assn., Cosmetic Exec. Women, Point-of-Purchase Advt. Inst., Chgo. Bus. Women of Pi Beta Phi (pres. Chgo. chpt. 1983-85), Phi Alpha Theta. Clubs: Carlton (Chgo.); Merchandising Exec.

TAUB, PATRICIA GAIL, nurse; b. Detroit, Jan. 28, 1954; d. Ross Freeman and Gertrude C. (Eldred) Shader; m. Martin Taub, Oct. 22, 1983. AS, Columbia Greene Community Coll., Greene, N.Y., 1972; diploma in nursing, Columbia Meml. Hosp. Coll., Hudson, N.Y., 1972; diploma in nurse anesthesia, Norfolk (Va.) Gen. Hosp., 1979; BS in Environ. Health., Old Dominion U., 1981. RN, Md., Calif., Va. Staff anesthetist Louise Obici Hosp., Suffolk, Va., 1979-80, Kaiser Permanente Med. Ctr., Anaheim, Calif., 1983-84, Calvert Anesthesia Assocs., Prince Fredrick, Md., 1986-87; staff anesthetist, clin. instr. Norfolk Gen. Hosp., 1980-82; staff anesthetist R. Adams Cowley Shock and Trauma Ctr., Balt., 1987-88, assoc. dir. nurse anesthesiology, 1988—; guest lectr. dist. 1 Ala. Assn. Nurse Anesthetists, Dothan, 1988, Nurse Anesthesiology Faculty Assocs., Williamsburg, Va., 1989; cons. aviation div. Md. State Police,. Mem. Am. Assn. Nurse Anesthetists (cert. nurse anesthetist), Anesthesia Care Team Soc. (steering com.), Internat. Trauma Anesthesia and Critical Care Soc. (lectr. 1989, co-dir. presymposium session 1990), Med. Assn. Nurse Anesthetists (lectr. ann. conv. 1990), Pan Am. Trauma Soc., Anesthesia Care Team Soc. (steering com.). Home: 12800 Stonecrest Dr Silver Spring MD 20904 Office: R Adams Cowley Shock and Trauma Ctr 22 S Greene St Baltimore MD 21201

TAUBER, KATHLEEN GRISANTI, business owner, consultant; b. Chgo., Mar. 15, 1949; d. Joseph Leonard and Anne (Masi) Grisanti; m. David Wendel Tauber, May 22, 1971 (div. June 1980); children: Amy Suzanne, Lory Lyn. BA, Tex. Christian U., 1971; postgrad., Houston Bapt. U., 1988—. Mgr. Ruggles Corp., Houston, 1980-82, gen. mgr., 1982-85; pres., owner Great Gatherings, Inc., Houston, 1985—. Named Outstanding Vol., Juvenile Diabets Found., 1987, 88. Mem. Meeting Planners Internat. (v.p. 1987-88, Nominee Planner of Yr. 1986, 87), Internat. Spl. Event Soc. (bd. of govs. L.A. chpt. 1989—).

TAUBITZ, FREDRICKA, financial executive; b. Los Angeles, Feb. 25, 1944; d. Ferdinand C. and Marie L. (Stewart) T. AA, Pasadena City Coll., 1963; BSBA, U. Calif., Berkeley, 1965; MSBA, UCLA, 1967; grad. advanced mgmt. program, Harvard U., 1980-81. CPA, Calif. Acct. Coopers & Lybrand, Los Angeles, 1965-75, ptnr., 1976-85; exec. v.p., chief fin. officer Zenith Nat. Ins. Corp., Woodland Hills, Calif., 1985—; founding dir. First Women's Bank Calif., Los Angeles, 1974-76. Bd. dirs. Soroptimist Found. Los Angeles, 1978-79; bd. dirs. Girls' Club, Pasadena, Calif., 1973-84, pres., 1981-83; mem. Calif. Mus. Found. Adv. Bd., 1978-81. Recipient Outstanding Young Bus. Leader award Los Angeles Jr. C. of C., 1978, Internat. Achievement award Soroptimist Internat., 1977. Mem. AICPA (ins. coms. com. 1990—), Calif. Soc. CPAs, L.A. C. of C. (bd. dirs. women's coun. 1978-81), Fin. Execs. Inst., Phi Beta Kappa. Office: Zenith Nat Ins Corp 21255 Califa St Woodland Hills CA 91367

TAUBMAN, JANE ANDELMAN, Russian literature educator; b. Boston, Oct. 23, 1942; d. Hyman M. and Esther (Rosenthal) Andelman; m. William Chase Taubman; children: Alexander, Phoebe. BA, Radcliffe Coll., 1964; MA, Yale U., 1968, PhD, 1972. Instr. Russian Smith Coll., Northampton, Mass., 1968-72; asst. prof. Russian Amherst (Mass.) Coll., 1973-83, assoc. prof. Russian, 1983-89, prof. Russian, 1989—. Author: A Life Through Poetry: Marina Tsvetaeva's Lyric Diary, 1989; co-author: Moscow Spring, 1989; contbr. articles to profl. jours. Woodrow Wilson Found. fellow, 1964—, Am. Coun. Learned Socs.-SSRC, 1974; trustee-faculty fellow Amherst Coll., 1978, IREX grantee USSR, 1988. Mem. AAUP, Modern Langs. Assn., Am. Assn. Tchrs. Slavic and East European Langs., Am. Assn. Slavic Studies. Office: Amherst Coll Dept Russian Amherst MA 01002

TAUNTON, KATHRYN JAYNE, accountant; b. Thomaston, Ga., Nov. 3, 1953; d. Mack Doudal and Martha Jayne (Goolsby) T. AA, Cypress Coll., 1973; BA in Accounting, Calif. State U., 1977. Circulation clk. Buena Park Library Dist., Buena Park, Calif., 1973-76; account supr. Orange County State Employees Credit Union, Santa Ana, Calif., 1977-78, Santa Ana City Credit Union, 1978-79; self employed Reliable Credit Union Service, Buena Park, 1979—.

TAUNTON-RIGBY, ALISON, healthcare company executive; b. Barnsley, Yorkshire, Eng., Apr. 23, 1944; d. Charles Francis and Joan (Willis) Forster; m. Roger Taunton-Rigby, June 2, 1966 (div. 1985); children: Jonathan, Rolf, Jason, Liv. BS, Bristol U., Eng., 1965, PhD, 1968; postgrad., Harvard Bus. Sch., 1985. V.p. rsch. and devel. Collaborative Rsch., Boston, 1969-83; v.p. bus. devel. Biogen., Boston, 1983-84; v.p., gen. mgr. Vivotech (Damon Biotech), Boston, 1984-86; health mgr. Arthur D. Little, Boston, 1986-87; sr. v.p. therapeutics Genzyme Corp., Cambridge, Mass., 1987—; bd. dirs. Mass. Biotech Coun., Boston, New Eng. British Bus., Boston. Contbr. articles to profl. jours., books; patentee in field. Mem. Gov. Dukakis' innovation com., Boston, 1986-88, Blueprint 2000 com., Boston, 1989. Mem. AAAS, N.Y. Acad. Sci., Boston Club, New Eng. British Bus. Assocs. Home: Farrar Rd Lincoln MA 01773 Office: Genzyme Corp 1 Kendal Sq Cambridge MA 02139

TAVARES, JOAN CHRISTINE, management consultant; b. Owatonna, Minn., June 12, 1941; d. John and Lillian Valborg (Ordal) Boyum; m. Pedro Julio Tavares, May 21, 1965. BA, Gustavus Adolphus, St. Peter, 1962; MA, U. Minn, Mpls., 1969; PhD, U. Minn., 1978. Tchr. St. Louis Park High Sch., 1962-66; instr. U. Minn., Mpls., 1968-75; adminstr. U. Minn., 1972-75; mgr. Prudential NCHO, Mpls., 1980-85; mgmt. exec. devel. cons. Ctr. for Creative Leadership, Greensboro, N.C., 1985-. Fellow, Fulbright Com., Paris, 1963-64, U.S. Govt., Minn., 1966-69, NYU, 1979; named Outstanding Young Woman of Am., 1968, 72. Mem. Am. Soc. for Training Devel. Office: Ctr for Creative Leadership PO Box P 1 Greensboro NC 27410

TAVEL, DIANA M., real estate broker; b. Havana, Cuba, Mar. 20, 1941; came to U.S., 1962; d. Eleusipo A. and Graciela (Corrons) Hernandez; m. Alberto F. Tavel, Oct. 7, 1961; children: Diana J. Tavel Williams, Lizette Tavel Martin-Hidalgo, Alberto Jr. BArch, U. Havana, 1962; cert. residential appraisal, Miami Dade Jr. Coll.; cert. in real estate broker, Bert Rodgers Sch., 1985. Lic. real estate broker, mortgage broker, Fla. Chief engr. Suntrol Products, Miami, Fla., 1966-75, Sun Railings, Miami, 1975-78; architect designer Burger King Corp., Miami, 1978-87; real estate broker, salesman Open Realty, Miami, 1984-87; real estate broker Jaen Realty, Miami, 1987-88; broker, pres. Save Money Realty, Miami, 1988—. Mem. Nat. Assn. Realtors (cert. residential specialist), Fla. Assn. Realtors (honor soc. 1990), Miami Bd. Realtors (grievance com. 1988-89, communication com. 1988-90, honor soc. 1989). Republican. Roman Catholic. Home: 2680 SW 92d Ave Miami FL 33165 Office: Save Money Realty 8890 Coral Way Ste 213 Miami FL 33165

TAYLOR, ALISON JEAN, mortgage officer, financial planner; b. Ann Arbor, Mich., Aug. 30, 1952; d. William Ralph and Janice Gwynne (Lowe) T. BS in Human Nutrition, U. Md., 1977. With Nat. Heart Assn., Bethesda Md., 1977-78; food technicianMeat Sci. Rsch. Lab. USDA, Beltsville, Md., 1978-79; statis. asst. Food Consumption Rsch. Group USDA, Hyattsville, Md., 1979-80; fin. planner Investors Diversified Svcs., Bethesda, Md., 1981-82, FSC Securities Corp., Silver Spring, Md., 1982-86, Internat. Money Mgmt. Group, Greenbelt, Md., 1986—; v.p. Wallace Mortgage Co., Inc., Silver Spring, 1983-86; real estate agt. Classic Properties, Inc., Landover, Md., 1983-87; mortgage officer United Security Mortgage Corp., Kensington, Md., 1986-88, Mortgage Funding Corp., 1988-89. Mem. Internat. Assn. Fin. Planners, Nat. Assn Realtors, Am. Dietetic Assn., D.C. Dietetic Assn. Republican. Mem. non-demonimational ch. Home: 13101 Dauphine St Silver Spring MD 20906

TAYLOR, ANN LOUISE, marketing executive; b. Fairmont, Minn., Aug. 8, 1937; d. Eugene and Celia Ethel (Fulton) Lundahl; m. James Harold Taylor, May 23, 1959; children: Kimberly Taylor Locey, Jayme K. BA in Edn., U. Minn., 1959; postgrad., Am. Inst. Banking, 1985—. Tchr. Nokomis Jr. High Sch., Mpls., 1959-61, Helen Keller Mid. Sch., Easton, Conn., 1973-75; photojournalist Suburban & Wayne Times, Berwyn, Pa., 1975-80; cons. pub. relations Fla. Internat. Bank, Miami, Fla., 1981-84; v.p. Fla. Internat. Bank, Miami, 1984—. Contbr. articles to profl. jours. Adv. bd., community participation Dade County Pub. Schs., 1987—. Mem. Am. Inst. Banking (v.p. mktg. 1986-87), Am. Soc. Tng. and Devel., Am. Pen Women/Miami, Women in Communications (pres. 1987-88, so. region v.p. 1989—), Greater South Dade C. of C. (bd. dirs. 1987—, pres. elect 1989—), Founders of South Dade (pres. 1987-88). Republican. Presbyterian. Office: Fla Internat Bank 17945 Franjo Rd Miami FL 33157

TAYLOR, ANNA DIGGS, federal judge; b. Washington, Dec. 9, 1932; d. Virginius Douglass and Hazel (Bramlette) Johnston; m. S. Martin Taylor, May 22, 1976; children: Douglass Johnston Diggs, Carla Cecile Diggs. BA, Barnard Coll., 1954; LLB, Yale U., 1957. Bar: D.C. 1957, Mich. 1961. Atty. Office Solicitor, Dept. Labor, W, 1957-60; asst. prosecutor Wayne County, Mich., 1961-62; asst. U.S. atty. Eastern Dist. of Mich., 1966; ptnr. Zwerdling, Maurer, Diggs & Papp, Detroit, 1970-75; asst. corp. counsel City of Detroit, 1975-79; U.S. dist. judge Eastern Dist. Mich. Detroit, 1979—; adj. prof. labor law Wayne State U. Law Sch., Detroit, 1976. Trustee Receiving Hosp. Detroit, Detroit Symphony, United Found., Community Found., Southeastern Mich., Orch. Hall, Detroit, Greater Detroit Health Coun. Mem. Fed. Bar Assn., State Bar Mich., Wolverine Bar Assn., Yale Law Assn. (exec. com. 1989—). Episcopalian. Office: US Dist Ct 231 W Lafayette Blvd 740 US Courthouse Detroit MI 48226

TAYLOR, BARBARA ALDEN, public relations executive; b. Dallas, Aug. 21, 1943; d. Harold Earl and Sally Alden (Howard) T.; BA, Smith Coll., 1965; MA, Antioch Coll., 1971. Vol., Peace Corps, India, 1966-68; tchr. Upper Merion Sch. Dist., King of Prussia, Pa., 1969-70; tchr. Cheltenham Sch. Dist., Elkins Park, Pa., 1970-74; pub. relations dir. Princess Hotels Internat., N.Y.C., 1974-75; chmn. Taylor & Hammond Ltd., N.Y.C., 1975-84; pres. Doremus/Marketshare, 1984-86; exec. v.p. Porter/Novelli, N.Y.C., 1986-90; sr. v.p. Hill and Knowlton, Inc., N.Y.C., 1990—. Bd. dirs. Madison Square Boys' and Girls' Club N.Y., 1978—, also mem. women's bd. Boys' Club N.Y. Named to Acad. of Women Achievers YWCA, 1985; bd. dirs. Up With People, Tucson, 1990—. Mem. Women in Communications, Pub. Relations Soc. Am. (counselors acad.), Soc. Am. Travel Writers, Advt. Women N.Y., Doubles Internat. Club, Smith Coll. Club N.Y., Lyford Cay Club, Jr. League City N.Y. Avocations: tennis, walking. Office: Hill and Knowlton Inc 420 Lexington Ave New York NY 10017

TAYLOR, BARBARA ANN, psychologist, consultant; b. St. Croix Falls, Wis., Aug. 29, 1944; d. George Fallon and Helen Romelle (Ols) T.; (div.); children: Joseph Taylor Cerutti, Lara Jan Taylor Cerutti; m. Robert George Blaikiock, June 22, 1980. Student, U. Minn., 1962-64; BA, SUNY, Albany, 1966; MA, Montclair (N.J.) State Coll., 1977; PhD, Fordham U., 1985. Lic. psychologist, N.J., N.Y.; nationally cert. sch. psychologist. Cons. psychologist Straight & Narrow, Inc., Paterson, N.J., 1978-80; sch. psychologist Pascack Valley Bd. Edn., Hillsdale, N.J., 1979-83; rsch. cons. N.Y.C. Bd. Edn., 1985-87; cons. psychologist Lord Stirling Sch., Basking Ridge, N.J., 1984—; pvt. practice psychologist Cedar Grove, N.J., 1988—. Mem. Am. Psychol. Assn., N.J. Psychol. Assn., N.J. Assn. Sch. Psychology, Internat. Assn. Applied Psychology, Assn. Advancement Behavioral Therapy. Office: 466 Pompton Ave Cedar Grove NJ 07009

TAYLOR, BARBARA JO ANNE HARRIS, government official, librarian, educator, civic and political worker; b. Providence, Sept. 9, 1936; d. Ross Cameron and Anita (Coia) Harris; m. Richard Powell Taylor, Dec. 19, 1959; 1 child, Douglas Howard. Student, Tex. Christian U., 1952, Salve Regina Coll., 1952-53; Student, Our Lady of the Lake Coll. and Convent, 1953-54, St. Mary's U., 1954, Incarnate Word Coll., 1954-55, Georgetown U., 1956-59, 62-63; BS cum laude, Georgetown U., 1963. Adminstrv. asst. profl. devel. and welfare NEA, Washington, 1956-59; asst. to dir. Georgetown U., Washington, 1956-59; exec. asst. All Am. Conf. to Combat Communism, Washington, 1960; spl. legis. asst. mil. affairs to chmn. mil. R & D subcom. U.S. Senate Armed Svcs. Com., 1971-72; U.S. nat. commr. UNESCO, 1982—, mem. exec. com. U.S. nat. commn., 1983—, sr. advisor 22d gen. conf., 1983. Del. numerous internat. confs.; U.S. Commr. Nat. Commn. Librs. and Info. Sci., 1985-89, mem. various coms.; gen. chmn. George Bush for Pres. Md. State Steering Com., 1987-88; co-chmn. Md. del. 1988 Rep. Nat. Convention; dep. chmn. Md. Victory '88, Bush-Quayle Campaign; mem. Nat. Fin. Com. Reagan for Pres., 1980, Reagan-Bush, 1984; state fin. chmn. Md. Rep. Party, 1980; mem. Nat. Rep. Club; mem. exec. bd. Salvation Army Aux., Washington, 1967-75, chmn. membership com., 1969-70, chmn. fund-raising com. 1968-69, mem. exec. com. of exec. bd., 1970-75, treas., mem. fin. com., 1970-71, v.p., 1971-72, historian, 1972-73, editor newsletter, 1968-69, chmn. nominating com., 1974-75, spl. awards for exceptional vol. svc., 1969, 72; mem. exec. bd. Welcome to Washington Internat., 1969-74, bd. advisers, 1969-74, dir. workshop, 1969-74; exec. bd. Am. Opera Sch. Soc., Washington, 1970—, v.p., 1974—; mem. Episcopal Ch. Home for Aged Women's Aux., 1970-75, Episc. Ctr. for Emotionally Disturbed Children Women's Aux., 1970-75; exec. bd. St. David's Episcopal Ch. Aux., 1970-72, 73-74; bd. dirs., treas. Spanish-Portuguese Study Group, 1970-72; mem. exec. bd. League Rep. Women D.C., 1964-67, 75-77, treas., 1964-67; mem. nat. coun. Women's Nat. Rep. Club, N.Y.C., 1969—, chmn. Washington-Md.-Va. legis. com., 1970-75; mem. Nat. Fedn. Rep. Women, 1964—; mem. nat. fin. com. Reagan for Pres., 1979-80; mem. governing bd. Capital Speakers Club, 1973-75, chmn. by-laws com., 1973-74; mem. exec. bd. Nat. Vols. in Action, 1975-77; mem. adv. com. Rock Creek Found. Mental Health, 1982-87; mem. 50th anniversary com. Save the Children; mem. fund-raising com. Washington Choral Arts Soc., 1982-84; state fin. chmn. Reagan-Bush campaign Md. Rep. Com., 1980; Md. coord.Nat. Inaugural Com., 1981, 85; trustee Crossnore Sch., Inc., N.C., 1983—, vice-chmn. bd.; trustee Kate Duncan Smith DAR Sch., Grant, Ala., 1983-86, Tamassee (S.C.) DAR Sch., 1983-86; adviser Bacone Am. Indian Coll., Inc., Muscogee, Okla., 1983-88. Mem. ALA, Spl. Librs. Assn., Coun. on Libr. Resources (commn. on preservation and access), Am. Libr. Trustees Assn., Libr. Adminstrn. and Mgmt. Assn., Assn. Coll. and Rsch. Librs., Am. Antiquarian Soc., Internat. Platform Assn., Spanish-Portuguese Study Group, Nat. Lawyers' Wives, Nat. Capital Law League, DAR (chmn. nat. resolutions com. 1980-83, chmn. nat. DAR sch. com. 1983-86; state historian 1978-80, mem. state bd. mgmt., 1973—, libr. gen., mem. exec. com. 1978-80, 86-89, numerous other offices), Nat. Soc. Children Am. Revolution (sr. nat. asst. registrar 1978-80, mem. sr. nat. bd. mgmt. 1978-80, sr. nat. exec. com. 1978-80), Nat. Assn. Parliamentarians, World Affairs Council, League of Rep. Women, Md. Fedn. Rep. Women, WNRC, Nat. Fed. Rep. Women, Commn. on Preservation and Access, Lit. Vols. Am. (D.C. affiliate), Exec. Women in Govt., Am. News Women's Club, Internat. Club, Capitol Hill Club, Washington Club, Congl. Country Club (Potomac, Md.).

TAYLOR, BEVERLY W., psychology educator; b. New Hampton, Iowa, Mar. 27, 1941; d. Walter A. and Hazel Weidler; m. LaRue E. Taylor, Aug. 29, 1970. BA, Wartburg Coll., 1963; MA, U. No. Iowa, 1967, EdS, 1968; PhD, U. Iowa, 1975. Elem. tchr. St. Paul Luth. Sch., Michigan City, Ind., 1963-66; prof. U. No. Iowa, Cedar Falls, 1968-85, Grand Canyon Coll., Phoenix, 1985-86, Cen. Ariz. Coll., Coolidge, 1986—; coord. profl. sequence U. No. Iowa, Cedar Falls, 1975-77, coord. of deans grant, 1982, dir. comprehensive study of tchr. edn., 1981-82; honors dir. Cen. Ariz. Coll., Coolidge, 1989-90; presenter in field. Author: Case Studies in Child Development, 1982; contbr. articles to profl. jours. Named Sponsor of Yr., Student Iowa State Edn. Assn., 1971. Mem. Am. Psychol. Assn., Phi Theta Kappa. Republican. Lutheran. Home: Rte 1 Florence Gardens 289 Florence AZ 84232 Office: Cen Ariz Coll 8470 N Overfield Rd Coolidge AZ 85228

TAYLOR, CARMELA MAE, post closing specialist; b. St. Paul, Feb. 12, 1962; d. William Dale and Mary Ann (Feldhous) Lamminen; m. Richard Leon Taylor, Mar. 22, 1989; children: April, Caleb, Sommer. BBA (finance), UW-Eau Claire, Eau Claire, 1985; BBA (mgmt.), UW Eau Claire, Eau Claire, 1985. Post closing specialist Investors Mortgage, Minnetonka, Minn., 1988-89; govt. insuring examiner Norwest Mortgage Inc., Mpls., Minn., 1989—; post closing specialist Investors Mortgage, Minnetonka, Minn., 1989—. Dem. Methodist. Home: 22874 Poppy St Saint Francis MN 55070 Office: Norwest Mortgage Inc 800 Marquette Ave S Minneapolis MN 55402

TAYLOR, CAROL ROSE, nurse; b. Salem, Mo., Sept. 3, 1950; d. Lloyd Wendell and Jo Ann (Adams) Ellerman; children: Lisa, Gina. A, Lincoln U., 1983. Operator Salem Meml. Hosp., 1975-77, ins. clk., 1977-78, adminstr. sec., 1978-81, charge nurse, 1981-85, asst. dir. nurses, 1985-86, dir. nurses, 1986—. Bd. dirs. Extended Studies S.W. Bapt. U., Salem, 1988—. Mem. Mo. Assn. Healthcare Educators (bd. dirs. 1987—), Mo. Orgn. Nursing Execs. Republican. Office: Salem Meml Hosp PO Box 774 Salem MO 65560

TAYLOR, CAROLYN SUE, insurance agency owner; b. Shattuck, Okla., Jan. 26, 1936; d. Mack Russell Heiserman and Helen Fay (Sills) Landon; m. George Raymond Taylor, Sept. 11, 1955; children: Pamela Sue, Mark Edward (dec.). Student, Okla. State U., Stillwater, 1954-55, So. Meth. U., 1987, 88. Asst. sales mgr. Red Comet, Inc., Littleton, Colo., 1955-57; sec. Continental Oil Co., Ponca City, Okla., 1967-70; exec. sec. Citizens' Utilities Co., Stamford, Conn., 1970-73; corp. sec. Guaranty Trust Co., Ponca City, Okla., 1973-75; co-owner The Place, Columbus, Tex., 1978-81; owner Pat Walker's Figure Salon, Columbus, 1982-83; office mgr. H.F. Halcom, Atty. at Law, Columbus, 1982-86; exec. v.p. Columbus Area C. of C., 1986-89; agt. Nat. Farm Life Ins. Co., 1989—. Bd. dirs. Colo. Count Mental Health/Retardation, Columbus, 1981-85; sec. Colo. County Cancer Soc., Columbus, 1983-86, pres., 1989-90, 90-91; mem. Inst. for Orgn. Mgmt. So. Meth. U. Mem. Nat. Assn. Female Execs., Rotary Internat., Pilot of Columbus (pres.-elect 1985-86, pres. 1986-87). Republican. Methodist. Club: Pilot of Columbus (pres.-elect 1985-86, pres. 1986-87).

TAYLOR, CLAUDIA ANN, psychotherapist, registered nurse; b. Knoxville, Tenn., May 22, 1946; d. Darlene M. Moore; m. Kendryl S. Taylor (div. 1974). RN, Grady Nursing Sch., 1966; BSN, Ga. State U., 1979, MEd, 1982. Acting head nurse Grady Meml. Hosp., Atlanta, 1966, psychiatric clin. coordinator, 1969—; instr. in counseling Barbara King Sch. of Ministry, Atlanta, 1982-83; workshop, seminar coordinator and facilitator Atlanta, 1977—; pvt. practice psychotherapist, cons. C. Ann Taylor & Assocs., Atlanta, 1983—; assoc. trainer, counselor The Inst. for Effective Living, Trinidad, 1983—; producer Relationships on Cable Atlanta, 1984—; cons. Ga. Inst. Tech., Atlanta, 1985-87, Psychiatric Inst. Atlanta, 1986-87, AT&T, Atlanta, 1988, IRS, Atlanta, 1988. Bd. dirs. Community Friendship, Inc., Atlanta; group leader Dept. Offender Rehab., Atlanta, 1980. Maj. USAFR. Mem. Assn. Black Psychologists (chmn. 1986-88), Mental Health Assn., Ga. Nurses Assn., Res. Officers Assn., Internat. Transactional Analysis Assn., Nat. Coun. Negro Women (chmn. Atlanta 1983—, award of appreciation 1985, 87), Delta Sigma Theta (award of appreciation 1986). Democrat. Home: 410 Mary Erna Dr Fairburn GA 30213 Office: Carter Newkirk & Assocs 600 W Peachtree St Suite 1570 Atlanta GA 30308

TAYLOR, CORA HODGE, social worker; b. Fayetteville, N.C., Nov. 25, 1942; d. John Marlin and Cora Louise (Mitchell) Hodge; B.S., N.C. Coll., Durham, 1963; M.S.W., U. N.C., Chapel Hill, 1965; m. Charles L. Taylor, June 26, 1965; children—Charles L., John M. Clin. social worker VA Hosp., Bedford, Mass., 1965-68, 73-79; chief social worker Regional Health Center, Wilmington, Mass., 1978-79; clin. social worker VA Hosp., Bedford, Mass., 1979—; field instr. Boston U. Sch. Social Work, 1979-87, Smith Coll. Sch. of Social Work, 1986— ; instr., cons. primary care residents Tufts U. Med. Sch., Regional Health Center, Wilmington, Mass., 1978-79. Mem. Town Meeting, Billerica, Mass., 1981—; precinct clk., 1981, 82, 89, precinct chmn., 1984, 85, 86; deacon First Congl. Ch., 1986—. Recipient Superior Performance award VA Hosp., Bedford, 1966, 84-88. Mem. LWV (dir. 1970-73), Acad. Cert. Social Workers, Nat. Assn. Social Workers. Home: 35 Wildwood Rd Pinehurst MA 01866 Office: 200 Springs Rd Bedford MA 01730

TAYLOR, CYNTHIA ROBERTS, human resources professional; b. Washington, Sept. 26, 1958; d. Howard Richard and Marylyn Anne (Morrissey) Roberts; m. Douglas Robert Taylor, Sept. 26, 1987. B, Va. Tech., Blacksburg, 1981; M, George Mason U., 1987. Student intern U.S. Customs Svc., Washington, 1978-81, pers. staffing specialist, 1981-85, employee rels. specialist, 1984-87; sr. pers. analyst City of Richmond (Va.), 1987-88, employment svcs. and employee rels. mgr., 1988—. Mem. Am. Soc. Pub. Adminstrn., Internat. Pers. Mgmt. Assn., Am. Bus. Women's Assn., Va. Tech. Alumni Assn. (bd. dirs., pres.). Office: City of Richmond 900 E Broad St Rm 900 Richmond VA 23219

TAYLOR, DEBORAH LYNN, nurse; b. Street, Md., Apr. 24, 1953; d. Robert Bradley and Marie Estell (Krilko) Beamer; m. Richard Bray Taylor, Jr., Aug. 19, 1972 (div.). BSN, Temple U., 1989. RN., Pa. Histotechnician Milford (Del.) Meml. Hosp., 1977-82, Nat. Cancer Inst., Frederick, Md., 1983-85, McNeil Pharmaceutical, Springhouse, Pa., 1986; staff nurse Albert Einstein Med. Ctr., Phila., 1989—. Mem. Sigma Theta Tau. Republican. Methodist. Home: 9578-B State Rd Philadelphia PA 19114

TAYLOR, DELLA MAE, nurse; b. Johnson City, Tenn., Apr. 15, 1932; d. Lee Roy and Honolulu Cornelius (Holly) Brewer; Diploma, Meml. Hosp., Johnson City, 1953; student E. Tenn. State U.; diploma newspaper writing Newspaper Inst. Am., 1968; BS, Steed Coll., 1978; postgrad. Emmanuel Sch. Religion, 1987-89; m. John R. Taylor, Jr., Feb. 12, 1955 (dec. Oct., 1986); children: Aliesa Benea, Celeste Taylor. RN, Tenn. Pediatric polio head nurse Meml. Hosp., Johnson City, 1953-54; staff nurse VA, Mountain Home, Tenn., 1954-55, 1961-64, part-time pvt. duty. 1964-78; staff nurse Meml. Hosp., Clarksville, Tenn., 1955-56; pediatric nurse U.S. Army Hosp., Augsburg, Germany, 1957-61; nurse for life ins. exams, Jonesboro, Tenn., 1978—; instr. nursing, 1986—; instr. Draughrons Fr. Coll., Johnson City, Tenn., 1986-87; owner Mama Bear's Fudge; owner, innkeeper Country Side Bed/Breakfast, 1989—; owner Taylor Paramedical, Jonesboro, Tenn. Contbr. article to newspaper. Pres., Pageants III, Jonesboro, 1980-82; coord. Pageants III Nationwide Youth Scholarship Pageant Corp., 1980-82. Chmn. precinct, 15th Dist. Dem. Com., 1977-78; mothers' chmn. Washington County March of Dimes; youth coord. Washington County Heart Assn.; chmn. Dr. Charles Underwood Scholarship Fund, 1984. Recipient 2d prize for party time sausage pie Litton. Mem. Nurses Christian Fellowship, E. Tenn. State U Alumni Assn., Steed Coll. Alumni Assn., Nat. Assn. Female Execs., Unicoi C. of C., U.S. Pageants Assns., Bus. and Profl. Women's Club. Washington County Farm Bur. Democrat. Baptist. Home: RR #8 Taylor Rd Jonesboro TN 37659

TAYLOR, DIANA LYNN, sales representative; b. Greensburg, Pa., May 25, 1957; d. Alfred Lawrence Jr. and Garnet Elizabeth (Rahl) T. BSBA, W.Va. Wesleyan Coll., 1979. Sales asst. Liberty Mut. Ins. Co., Dallas, 1979-83, Knoll Internat., Dallas, 1983-84; sales rep. Pentel of Am., San Antonio, 1984-87, Max Factor & Co., Dallas, 1987—. Mem. AAUW, Nat. Assn. Female Execs. Club: Cimarron (Dallas). Home and Office: 2228 Cedarbrush Dr Carrollton TX 75006

TAYLOR, DONNA BLOYD, vocational rehabilitation consultant; b. Louisville, Ky., July 15, 1958; d. Donald Ray Bloyd and Georgia Carmen (Bryant) Whitehead; 1 child, Stephanie Micah Taylor. BS, U. Louisville, 1981, MEd, 1982. Program coord. Hazelwood ICF-MR, Louisville, 1981-83; lead vocat. therapist Rehab. Ctr. Southeastern Ind., Clarksville, 1983-85; regional supr., vocat. cons. Rehab. Coords., Inc., Louisville, 1985; asst. mgr., rehab. cons. Nat. Rehab. Cons., Cin., 1985-88; dist. mgr., vocat. cons. Recovery Unlimited, Inc., Cin., 1988—; vocat. expert Social Security Adminstrn.; cert. rehab. counselor U.S. Dept. Labor, 1987—. Mem. Nat. Assn. Rehab. Profls. in Pvt. Sector, Ohio Assn. Rehab. Profls., Nat. Assn. Ins. Women, Nat. Forensic Ctr., Nat. Disting. Svc. Registry, Sierra, NOW, U. Louisville Alumni Assn., Phi Kappa Phi Honor Soc. Democrat. Presbyterian. Office: Recovery Unlimited Holiday Park Tower 644 Linn St Ste 1034 Cincinnati OH 45203

TAYLOR, DONNA MARIE, educator; b. Bonne Terre, Mo., May 18, 1960; d. Thomas Jerome and Jane Lorraine (Watts) T. BGS, S.E. Mo. State U., 1983, BS in Elem. Edn., 1986. Cert. elem. tchr., Mo. Nurse aide St. Genevieve (Mo.) County Hosp., 1980-81, Riverview Manor Nursing Home, St. Genevieve, 1982; kindergarten aide St. Genevieve Region II Sch. Dist., 1983-84, substitute tchr., 1986-87, parent educator, 1987-89; library clk. Migrant Edn. Ctr., Cape Girardeau, Mo., 1984-85; day care ctr. worker Wee Care Child Ctr., Cape Girardeau, 1985-86; tutor S.E. Mo. State U., Cape Girardeau, 1985-86; desk clk. Chateau Deville Motel, Bonne Terre, 1987; ednl. cons. Intelligy, Pleasanton, Calif., 1990—; in-svc. workshops Parents As Tchr. Nat. Ctr., Flat River, Mo., 1987-88, Cape Girardeau, 1987—. Home and Office: 515 S Knott Ave Apt 207 Anaheim CA 92804

TAYLOR, DORIS DENICE, physician; b. Indpls., Sept. 19, 1955; d. Eugene and Mary Catherine (Ryder) T. BA, U. Minn., 1976, cert. behavior analyst, 1977, MD, 1983; BS, Purdue U., 1979. Diplomate Nat. Bd. Med. Examiners. Pvt. practice Indpls., 1988—. Lange scholar, U. Minn., 1980, Joseph Collins Found. scholar, 1980-81, Nat. Med. Fellowship scholar, 1980-81. Mem. AMA, Am. Soc. for Therapeutic Radiology and Oncology, Am. Soc. Clin. Oncologists.

TAYLOR, DOROTHY HARRIS, real estate broker; b. Richmond, Va., Nov. 3, 1931; d. Edgar Alan and Sadie (Wheeler) Harris; m. Gethsemane Jess Taylor (dec. Nov. 1964); children: Marlene J., Eric M., Andre E. Student, L.I. U., 1959, John J. Criminal Coll., 1974, Queen's Coll., 1983, 90—; diploma in Mgmt. of Residential Properties, Queen's Coll., 1987; student, St. John's U., 1984, 86. Lic. real estate broker. Toll collector Port of N.Y. and N.J. Authority George Washington Bridge (formerly Port of N.Y. Authority), N.Y.C., 1967-80, tolls dispatcher, 1967; transp. driver George Washington Bridge/Port Authority of N.Y. & N.J., Ft. Lee, N.J., 1972-75, acting supervising toll collector, 1974-75; transp. driver Port of N.Y. and N.J. Authority George Washington Bridge (formerly Port of N.Y. Authority), Ft. Lee, N.J., 1972-75; acting supervising toll collector Port of N.Y. and N.J. Authority George Washington Bridge (formerly Port of N.Y. Authority), Ft. Lee, 1974-75; sales exec. Flushing Tribune, 1979; real estate salesperson Parkfield Realty, Queens Village, N.Y., 1982-83, Arro of Queens, 1983-84; real estate broker Arro of Queens, Queens Village, 1984-85; residential appraiser Arro of Queens, N.Y.C., 1986—. Active Nat. Arbor Day Found., North Shore Animal Shelter League; mem. com. for disabled children Queens Coll.; charter mem. Nat. Mus. Women in Arts; mem. Nat. Trust for Hist. Preservation, The Smithsonian Assocs., Am. Mus. Natural History, N.Y.C., ace program Queens Coll., Flushing, N.Y. Named Hon. Citizen, City of Williamsburg, Va.; John F. Kennedy Libr. hon. fellow, Boston. Mem. NAFE (network dir. 1983-84), Am. Assn. Ret. Persons, Nat. Assn. of Unknown Players for Film, TV, and Print Modeling Arts, Inc. (charter), Queen's Coun. on Arts, Nat. Geog. Soc., Am. Entrepreneurs' Assn., United Christian Evangelistic Assn., Dorcas Soc. (Bklyn., pres. 1957-58), Queens Coll. Women's Club, Order Ea. Star, Heroines of Jericho, Lady of Knights. Democrat.

TAYLOR, DOROTHY JANE, biologist, consultant; b. Waco, Tex.; d. Mat E. and Sulee (Damon) Taylor. BA, Rice U., 1943; MS, Iowa State U., 1947; PhD, George Washington U., 1957. Chem. technician Humble Oil Co. (now Exxon), Bay Town and Ingleside, Tex., 1943-45; instr. zoology and physiology Iowa State U., Ames, 1945-47; parasitologist Lab. Tropical Diseases, NIH, Bethesda, Md., 1947-58; biologist Nat. Cancer Inst., Bethesda, 1958-61, head endocrine related tumor systems sect., 1961-73, asst. br. chief breast cancer program coordinating br., 1973-75; chief breast cancer coordinating br., exec. sec. task force Nat. Cancer Inst., 1975-82; sci. adminstr. Stehlin Found. for Cancer Rsch., Houston, 1982-88; cons. cancer adminstrn. and mammography Houston, 1989—; pres. NIH Fed. Credit Union, 1963-64; bd. dirs. Nat. Alliance Breast Cancer Orgns., N.Y.C., 1983—; mem. adv. bd. Cancer Fighters Houston, Inc., 1989—; mem. adv. bd. Rose Mammography Ctrs., Houston, 1990—. Editor: Tumors of Endocrine Glands, 1966; coeditor: Commentaries on Research in Breast Cancer, vol. 1, 1979, vol. 2, 1981, vol. 3, 1983; contbr. articles to profl. jours. Named Woman of Yr., Breast Dis. Assn. Am., 1979; recipient numerous awards. Fellow AAAS; mem. Am. Assn. for Cancer Rsch., Sigma Xi, Sigma Delta Epsilon. Home: 5001 Woodway Dr Apt 605 Houston TX 77056

TAYLOR, E.J., employment counselor; b. Flint, Mich., May 16, 1934; d. Leonard Lee and Wynona Ruth (Davis) Harvey; children: Wynona Jane MacDonald, Cynthia Lee Zellmer. BS, No. Ariz. U., 1963; MEd, U. Ariz., 1967. Tchr. high sch. Sunnyside Sch. Dist., Tucson, 1963-68; employment program counselor employment devel. dept. State of Calif., Canoga Park,

1968—. Mem. adv. coun. Van Nuys Community Adult Sch., Calif., 1983-90, elected to steering com., 1989-90; mem. adv. coun. Pierce Community Coll., Woodland Hills, Calif., 1979-81; first aid instr., recreational leader ARC. Mem. NAFE, Internat. Assn. of Pers. in Employment Security, Delta Psi Kappa. Office: State of Calif Employment Devel Dept 21010 Vanowen St Canoga Park CA 91303

TAYLOR, ELISABETH COLER, teacher; b. N.Y.C., Jan. 24, 1942; d. Gerhard Helmut and Judith (Horowitz) C.; m. Billie Wesley Taylor II, Jan. 27, 1960; children: Letitia Rose, Billie Albert. Postgrad. Wilmington Coll., 1959-60; BS, Wayne State U., Detroit, 1969; MS, The Ohio State U., 1980; MEd, Wright State U., Dayton, Ohio, 1989-. Tchr. Dayton (Ohio) City Schs., 1972—. Bd. mem. Camp Fire Girls, 1970-71, vol. Detroit Mus. of Art, 1970-71, group leader Camp Fire Girls, Boy Scouts, Detroit, 1968-74. Mem. AAUW, NEA, Home Econs. Assn. (cert. home economist), Ohio Edn. Assn., Dayton Edn. Assn., Mensa. Home: 2461 S Patterson Blvd Kettering OH 45409

TAYLOR, ELIZABETH, actress; b. London, Feb. 27, 1932; d. Francis and Sara (Sothern) T. Student, Byron House, Hawthorne Sch., Metro-Goldwyn-Mayer Sch. Motion pictures include Lassie Come Home, 1942, There's One Born Every Minute, 1942, The White Cliffs of Dover, 1943, Jane Eyre, 1943, National Velvet, 1944, Life With Father, 1946, Courage of Lassie, 1946, Cynthia, 1947, A Date With Judy, 1948, Julia Misbehaves, 1948, Little Women, 1948, Conspirator, 1949, The Big Hangover, 1949, Father of the Bride, 1950, Father's Little Dividend, 1950, A Place in the Sun, 1950, Love is Better Than Ever, 1951, Ivanhoe, 1951, Elephant Walk, 1954, Rhapsody, 1954, Beau Brummel, 1954, The Last Time I Saw Paris, 1955, Giant, 1956, Raintree County, 1957, Cat on a Hot Tin Roof, 1958, Suddenly Last Summer, 1959, Holiday in Spain, 1960, Butterfield 8, 1960 (Acad. award best actress), Cleopatra, 1962, The V.I.P.'s, 1963, The Sandpiper, 1965, Who's Afraid of Virginia Woolf (Acad. award 1966), Taming of the Shrew, 1967, The Comedians, 1967, Reflections in a Golden Eye, 1967, Dr. Faustus, 1968, Boom!, 1968, Secret Ceremony, 1968, The Only Game in Town, 1969, X, Y and Zee, 1972, Under Milk Wood, 1971, Hammersmith is Out, 1972, Night Watch, 1973, Ash Wednesday, 1974, The Driver's Seat, 1975, The Blue Bird, 1976, A Little Night Music, 1977, Victory at Entebbe, 1977, The Mirror Crack'd, 1980, Return Engagement (TV), 1979, Between Friends, 1983, Malice in Wonderland (TV film), 1985, North and South (TV miniseries), 1985, The Young Toscanini, 1988; Broadway debut in The Little Foxes, 1981; narrator film documentary Genocide, 1981; appeared in play Private Lives, 1983; Hotel (TV series); TV films include: There Must Be a Pony, Poker Alice, Sweet Bird of Youth, 1989; author: (with Richard Burton) World Enough and Time; poetry reading, 1964, Elizabeth Taylor, 1965, Elizabeth Taylor Takes Off-On Weight Gain, Weight Loss, Self Esteem and Self Image, 1988. Active philanthropic, relief, charitable causes internationally; initiated Ben Gurion U.-Elizabeth Taylor Fund for Children of the Negev, 1982; nat. chmn. Am. Found. AIDS Research, 1985—, internat. fund, 1985—. Named Comdr. Arts and Letters (France), 1985; awarded Legion of Honor (France), 1987; recipient Aristotle S. Onassis Found. award, 1988. Office: Chen Sam & Assocs Inc 315 E 72d St New York NY 10021

TAYLOR, ELIZABETH JANE, investment consultant, real estate company executive; b. Tiffin, Ohio, Oct. 27, 1941; d. Albert Joseph Lucas and Mary Jane Siebenaller-Swander; m. Gaylen Lloyd Taylor, July 11, 1977. Student, Heidelberg Coll., 1961, Austin Community Coll., Tex., 1983-84; grad. Real Estate Edn. Ctr., 1984, Inst. Real Estate, 1988, Real Estate Inst., 1989, Tex. Realtors Inst., 1989. Cons., Hypnosis Conn., Ohio and Tex., 1967—; dir. regional mktg. Sibrow, Inc., Ottawa, Can., 1981-83; realtor assoc. Alliance Sales, Austin, 1985-88; assoc. Broadway Comml. Investments, 1988—; prin., Taylor & Assocs., Internat. Mktg. & Bus. Devel., Hong Kong, U.S., 1980—; tchr. mktg. and bus. develop., 1980—. Author: profl. column Austin Women Mag., 1984-86; (poetry) Letters from Home, 1986, Best New Poets of 1986, American Poetry Anthology, vol. VI., #3, 1986. V.p. Am. Congress on Real Estate, 1982-83; arbitrator Better Bus. Bur., 1984-89, sr. arbitrator, 1989—; mem. speakers bur. Austin Woman's Ctr., 1985-88; v.p. Austin World Affairs Council, 1984—; mem. adv. panel Austin Woman Mag., 1984-86. Nominated to Tex. Womens Hall of Fame, 1984. Mem. NAFE (network dir. 1980-88), Am. Biog. Inst. Rsch. (hon., bd. advisers 1988). Avocations: writing, behavior research. Home: 1414 Cardinal Hill Dr Austin TX 78758

TAYLOR, ELLEN BORDEN BROADHURST, civic worker; b. Goldsboro, N.C., Jan. 18, 1913; d. Jack Johnson and Mabel Moran (Borden) Broadhurst; student Converse Coll., 1930-32; m. Marvin Edward Taylor, June 13, 1936; children: Marvin Edward, Jack Borden, William Lambert. Bd. govs. Elizabethan Garden, Manteo, N.C., 1964-74; mem. Gov. Robert Scott's Adv. Com. on Beautification, N.C., 1971-73; mem. ACE nat. action com. for environ. Nat. Coun. State Garden Clubs, 1973-75; bd. dirs. Keep N.C. Beautiful, 1973-85; mem. steering com., charter mem. bd. dirs. Keep Johnston County (N.C.) Beautiful, 1977—; life judge roses Am. Rose Soc.; chmn. local com. that published jointly with N.C. Dept. Cultural Resources: An Inventory of Historic Architecture, Smithfield, N.C., 1977; co-chmn. local com. to survey and publish jointly with N.C. Div. Archives and History: Historical Resources of Johnston County, 1980—. Mem. Nat. Coun. State Garden Clubs (life; master judge flower shows), Johnston County Hist. Soc. (charter), Johnston County Arts Coun. (Spl. award for 1987 projects of Pub. Libr. Johnston County & Smithfield 1965-87), N.C. Geneal. Soc. (charter), Johnston County Geneal. Soc. (charter), Hist. Preservation Soc. N.C. (life), N.C. Art Soc. (life). Democrat. Episcopalian. Clubs: Smithfield (N.C.) Garden (charter; pres. 1969-71), Smithfield Woman's (v.p. 1976), DAR (organizing vice-regent chpt. 1976), Gen. Soc. Mayflower Descs. (life), Descs. of Richard Warren, Nat. Soc. New Eng. Women (charter mem. Carolina Capital chpt.), Colonial Dames Am. (life), Magna Charta Dames, Nat. Soc. Daus. of Founders and Patriots Am. Home: 616 Hancock St Smithfield NC 27577

TAYLOR, EVA MARIETTA, interior designer; arrived in Can., 1956; came to U.S., 1967; d. Istvan Domolky and Lea Maria (Koszegi) Coan; m. Craig Allan Taylor, Apr. 28, 1972 (div. Feb. 1978); 1 child, Renee Christine. BS, So. Ill. U., 1972. Dir. mktg. Lococo Design, St. Louis, 1982-83; project mgr., nat. dir. mktg. hosp. div. Hotel Restaurant Planners div. Profl. Interiors, St. Louis, 1983-87; with Interior Solutions Inc., Willowbrook, Ill., 1987—; mem. adv. com. interior Meramec Community Coll., St. Louis 1985-. Mem. AIA (assoc.), Nat. Assn. Women Bus. Owners, Am. Soc. Interior Design (chairperson 1984-86), Nat. Assn. Indsl. Office Pks. Roman Catholic. Office: 6109 Knollwood Rd Ste 101 Willowbrook IL 60514

TAYLOR, FRANCES MARIE, office manager; b. Rapid City, SD, Mar. 10, 1942; d. Frank Eldon and Roberta (Jacobi) Cottle; m. Duane R., June 7, 1964, (div. Oct. 1984); children: Ashleigh L., Meagan B. BA, U. Denver, Denver, 1964. Sec. Montana Power Co., Butte, 1964-65; dept. sec. U. of Denver, Denver, 1965-66; bus. owner Housing Distbrs., Inc., Ashland, 1972-85; office mgr. Christopher Briscoe Studio, Ashland. Mem. Jr. Svc. League, Tudor Guild/Ore Shakespeare, Shakespeare Festival Assn., AAUW, YMCA, Delta Gamma Alumni Assn. Methodist.

TAYLOR, FRANCINE MARIE CONAT, TV producer, writer; b. Long Beach, Calif., Mar. 25, 1937; d. Francis William and Maria (Mary) Magdalena (Riestras Bustos) Conat; m. Charles Lastufka, June 29, 1957 (div. May 1980); children: Marta Ann, Carlos; m. Richard Clinton Taylor, Aug. 4, 1987; children: Anna Zoachney Taylor, Andrew. BA in Interdisciplinary Studies, U. Alaska, 1977. TV columnist Anchorage Daily News, 1975-77; TV producer, dir. U. Alaska, Anchorage, 1977-86; pres. Lastufka & Assocs., Anchorage, 1986-89, Taylor Prodns., Anchorage, 1989—; mem. media panel Alaska State Coun. on the Arts, 1984—; cons. Prime Cable Community Access Channel, Anchorage, 1989—; statewide coord. Alaskans Hot on the Arts, 1989—. Founding dir. Anchorage Arts Coun., 1970; co-founder Alaskans Hot on the Arts, 1989; founding dir. Visual Arts Ctr. of Alaska, Anchorage, 1972; bd. dirs. Alaska Festival of Native Arts, Anchorage, 1966. Mem. Women in Communicaton, Inc., Alaska Press Women. Democrat. Home and Office: 3740 Winterset Dr Anchorage AK 99508

TAYLOR, GRACE ELIZABETH WOODALL (BETTY TAYLOR), law educator, law library administrator; b. Butler, N.J., June 14, 1926; d. Frank E. and Grace (Carlyon) Woodall; m. Edwin S. Taylor, Feb. 4, 1951 (dec.); children: Carol Lynn Taylor Crespo, Nancy Ann. AB, Fla. State U., 1949, MA, 1950; JD, U. Fla., 1962. Instr. asst. librarian Univ. Libraries, U. Fla., 1950-56, asst. law librarian, 1956-62; dir. Legal Info. Ctr., 1962—, prof. law, 1976—; cons. law libraries; chmn. LAWNET network legal info. Fla. Legislature Lewis scholar, 1946-50. Contbr. numerous articles on automation and law to library publs. Nat. Endowment for Humanities grantee, 1981-82; Council Library Resources grantee 1984-86. Mem. Am. Assn. Law Libraries (exec bd.), Am. Assn. Law Schs., ABA, Am. Soc. Info. Scis., Fla. Library Assn, Online Computer Library Council (past pres. users council), West Law Adv. Bd. Democrat. Methodist. Office: U Fla Legal Info Ctr Gainesville FL 32611

TAYLOR, HILLARY, personnel placement service executive; b. N.Y.C., Feb. 20, 1950; d. Adam T. and Sylvia Eve (Park) T. Counselor Mahoney Pers., N.Y.C.; sr. v.p. Stanton Pers., N.Y.C.; owner Treasure Trove Antiques, N.Y.C.; owner, pres. Hillary Taylor Pers. Cons., N.Y.C., Hillary Taylor Word Porcessing Annex, N.Y.C., 1990—. Named Rookie of Yr. 1975, Counselor of Yr., 1977-85. Address: 139 Fulton St #301 New York NY 10038

TAYLOR, JACQUELINE DIANE, college official; b. Fife Lake, Mich., July 8, 1934; d. John Orville Richardson and Margaret Loretta (Bishop) Brewer; divorced; children: Kevin Zachary, Kip Nathan. AS, Lansing Community Coll., 1977; BS, Aquinas Coll., Grand Rapids, Mich., 1980; MA, Mich. State U., 1982, PhD, 1986. Office mgr. physician's office, Lansing, Mich., 1966-69; dir. fin., contr. Grand Ledge (Mich.) Pub. Schs., 1969-79; adminstrv. sec. to pres. Lansing Community Coll., 1979-82, adminstrv. sec. to bd. trustees, 1982—, adminstrv. asst. to pres., 1982-84, v.p. coll. and community rels., 1984—; cons., instr. Nat. Taipei (Republic of China) Inst. Tech., 1981—, Nat. Taitung (Republic of China) Tchrs. Coll., 1988—. Co-author: Japan Adventure, 1987; editor EPIC East West Conf., 1987. Bd. dirs. United Way, Lansing, 1986-90, chmn. planning and admissions, 1987-89, mem. agy. rels. and vol. com., 1989—; bd. dirs. Mich. Festival, Inc., East Lansing, Mich., 1987—; sec., mem. bd. mgrs. Sparrow Hosp., Lansing, 1989—; bd. dirs. Boy Scouts Am., Lansing, 1988—; mem. St. Davids Vestry Commn., 1988—. Named Woman of Yr., Am. Bus. Women's Assn., 1978, Leader of 80's, League for Innovation and AACJC, 1984; recipient resolution for outstanding svc. Grand Ledge Bd. Edn., 1979, Tri County Unsung Heroine award Mich. Sesquicentennial, 1987. Mem. Mich. State U. Coll. Edn. Alumni Assn. (bd. dirs. 1985—), Zonta Club. Episcopalian. Office: Lansing Community Coll PO Box 40010 Lansing MI 48901

TAYLOR, JAN HUDSON, insurance company official; b. Port Arthur, Tex., May 17, 1949; d. Henry and Vivian Corine (Duncan) Hudson. BBA, Stephen F. Austin U., 197l. Claim rep. Travelers Ins. Co., Houston, 197l-73, asst. supr., 1973-78, sr. rep., 1978-87, regional gen. adjuster, 1987—. Author software program Business Interruption, 1988. Mem. Women for Reagan, Houston, 1983. Recipient cert. of achievement Am. Ednl. Inst., 1974, G.A.B. Bus. Interruption, 1988. Mem. NAFE, Ford's of 50's (treas. 198l-82). Republican. Baptist. Office: Travelers Ins Co l0800 Richmond Houston TX 77042

TAYLOR, JERRY LYNN, microbiologist, educator; b. Warrenton, Mo., Jan. 12, 1947; d. Albert Marcus and Naomi Azalee (Greer) Hafner; m. William Carl Taylor, June 12, 1971. BA in Microbiology, U. Mo., Columbia, 1969, MA in Botany, 1971; PhD in Microbiology, So. Ill. U., 1976. Asst. prof. microbiology Calif. State U., Long Beach, 1976-77; postdoctoral fellow Med. Coll. Wis., Milw., 1977-79, instr., 1979-80, asst. prof. microbiology, 1980-81, asst. prof. microbiology, ophthalmology, 1981-84, assoc. prof. microbiology and ophthalmology, 1984-90, prof., 1990—, vice-chmn. microbiology, 1988—, prof. microbiology and ophthalmology, 1990—. Contbr. sci. papers to jours. Mem. AAAS, Am. Soc. Microbiology, Am. Soc. Virology, Internat. Assn. Antiviral Rsch., Internat. Assn. Interferon Rsch., Assn. Rsch. in Vision and Ophthalmology, Phi Beta Kappa, Sigma Xi. Office: Dept Microbiology Med Coll Wis 8701 Watertown Plank Rd Milwaukee WI 53226

TAYLOR, JOAN K(OSLOSKY), psychologist; b. Mpls., Nov. 7, 1929; d. Dawson J. Dinsmore and Ione E. Koslosky; m. Richard Wirt Taylor, July 6, 1957; children: Laura (dec.), Martha. BA in Psychology and Sociology, Coll. St. Catherine, St. Paul, 1951; MA in Clin. Psychology, Catholic U. Am., 1954; PhD, Columbia U., 1958. Diplomate Am. Bd. Family Psychology; lic. psychologist, N.J. Clin. asst. prof. dept. psychiatry, mental health sci. Coll. Medicine and Dentistry N.J., 1979-81; chief supervising psychologist Family Svc., Child Guidance Ctr. Orange, Maplewood, Millburn, Orange, N.J., 1962-76; pvt. practice Chatham, N.J., 1965—; supr. grad. students Sch. Applied and Profl. Psychology Rutgers U., 1976-82; cons. Orange Head Start Program, 1972-76, Barrett House Foster Home for Girls, Summit, N.J., 1974-76, Arlington Ave. Pre-Sch., East Orange, 1975-76, Gen. Med. Hosp. VA, East Orange, 1977-79, Family Therapy Tng. Program: Child and Adolescent Unit, St. Clare's Hosp., Denville, 1980-81, N.J. Acad. Psychology, 1979-81; founder N.J. Ctr. Family Studies, 1976—. Contbr. articles to profl. jours.; lectr. various profl. groups. Apptd. by Gov. B. Byrne to State Bd. Psychol. Examiners, 1975-78; mem. Summit Drug Adv. Com., 1972-73. Mem. Am Psychol. Assn. (assoc. chair membership com. div. 43 1987, chair state network com. div. 35 1987-90), Am. Assn. Marriage and Family Therapists (approved supr. 1985—), Am. Family Therapy Assn., Nat. Register Health Care Providers in Psychology, N.J. Psychol. Assn. (bd. dirs. 1981-83, 85-88, ethics com. 1990), Psychology Found. Trust N.J. Psychol. Assn. (charter), Assn. Advancement Family Therapy N.J. (co-founder, pres. 1981), Consortium Family Therapy Edn. N.J. (co-founder, chair 1985—). Office: 291 Main St Chatham NJ 07928

TAYLOR, JOANNA WANDA, philatelist, show promoter; b. Jersey City, May 17, 1942; d. Jan and Victoria Pelagia (Malecki) Sliski; m. Phillip Gray Vincent, Dec. 22, 1961 (div. May 1969), 1 child, Laurie Yvonne; m. Scott Harry Taylor, Jan. 5, 1970, 1 child, Joanna Victoria. BS in Microbiology, U. Md., 1966. Sanitarian Prince Georges County Dept. Health, Cheverly, Md., 1968-72; co-founder Scojo Stamps, Ridgely, Md., 1972—; co-founder, promoter S & S Enterprises, Balt., 1974—; auction agt. Scott H. Taylor, Ridgely, 1979—; boothholder World Expo '89. Vice-chmn. Rep. Cen. Com.; sec. Caroline County Rep. Women, Caroline County Gypsy Moth Control Bd. Recipient Merchandising Excellence award at Nat., '81 Show, Ameripex '86 (Internat. Stamp Show). Mem. Am. Stamp Dealers Assn. (sec.), Am. Philatelic Soc. (life, expert com.), Scandinavian Collectors Club, Tidewater Stamp Club (sec. 1985) (Easton, Md.). Office: Scojo Stamps PO Box 423 Ridgely MD 21660

TAYLOR, J(OCELYN) MARY, museum administrator, zoologist, educator; b. Portland, Oreg., May 30, 1931; d. Arnold Llewellyn and Kathleen Mary (Yorke) T.; m. Joseph William Kamp, Mar. 18, 1972. B.A., Smith Coll., 1952; M.A., U. Calif., Berkeley, 1953, Ph.D., 1959. Instr. zoology Wellesley Coll., 1959-61, asst. prof. zoology, 1961-65; assoc. prof. zoology U. B.C., 1965-74; dir. Cowan Vertebrate Mus., 1965-82, prof. dept. zoology, 1974-82; collaborative scientist Oreg. Regional Primate Research Ctr., 1983-87; prof. (courtesy) dept. fisheries and wildlife Oreg. State U., 1984—; dir. Cleve. Mus. Nat. History, 1987—; adj. prof. dept. biology Case Western Res. U., 1987—. Assoc. editor Jour. Mammalogy, 1981-82. Contbr. numerous articles to sci. jours. Trustee Benjamin Rose Inst., 1988—, Western Res. Acad., 1989—; bd. dirs. Holden Arboretum, 1988—. Fulbright scholar, 1954-55; Lalor Found. grantee, 1962-63; NSF grantee, 1963-71; NRC Can. grantee, 1966-84; Killam Sr. Research fellow, 1978-79. Mem. Soc. Woman Geographers, Am. Soc. Mammalogists (1st v.p. 1978-82, pres. 1982-84), Australian Mammal Soc., Cooper Ornithol., Northwest Sci. Assn. (trustee 1980-83), Assn. Sci. Mus. Dirs. (v.p. 1990—), Sigma Xi (rodent specialist group of species survival commn., chmn. 1989—). Episcopalian. Office: Cleve Mus Natural History U Circle Wade Oval Cleveland OH 44106

TAYLOR, JULIA W., bank executive. Student, N.C. Cen. U., Stonier Graduate Sch. of Banking. With Mechanics and Farmers Bank, Raleigh, 1955-60, asst. cashier, 1966-77, v.p., mgr., 1967-78, sr. v.p., city exec. officer, 1978-83, pres., chief exec. officer, 1983-87, chmn., pres. and chief exec. officer, 1987—; With Bank of Am., L.A., 1960, Broadway Fed. Savs. and Loan Assn., L.A., 1961-63; bd. dirs., exec. com. Mechanics and Farmers Bank, Durham; bd. dirs. Am. Inst. of Banking, Triangle Better Bus. Bur., Downtown Raleigh Devel. Corp., Wheeler Flying Svc., Inc.; mem. N.C. Assembly on Women and Economy; bd. trustees U. N.C., Wilmington. Trustee Bd. St. Joseph's African Meth. Episcopal Ch., Durham; vice chmn. N.C. State Ednl. Assistance Authority; bd. dirs. Jr. Achievement of Raleigh and Wake Co., N.C. Bus. Adv. Bd. Fuqua Sch. of Bus. Duke U., N.C. 4-H Devel. Fund, Inc.; mem. Raleigh Civic Ctr. Authority; bd. assocs. N.C. Child Advocacy Inst. Named Women of Achievement award Silver Medallion in Bus. and Industry YWCA, 1985, The Tarhell of the Week News and Observer, 1986, Atlanta Regional Minority Bus. Advocate of Yr. award U.S. Dept. of Commerce Minority Bus. Devel. Agy., 1987, Nat. Minority Bus. Advocate of Yr. award U.S. Dept. Commerce, 1987; recipient Citizen award Ind. Weekly 1988, 1989. Mem. N.C. Cen. U. Sch. Law (bd. vis.), N.C. Citizens for Bus. & Industry, Conf. State Bank Suprs. (regional rep.), Forest at Duke (bd. dirs.), Africa News (bd. dirs.), N.C. Bankers Assn. (bd. dirs.). Office: Mechanics & Farmers Bank 116 W. Parrish Durham NC 27701

TAYLOR, KATHLEEN MARY, nuclear pharmacist; b. New Haven, Nov. 29, 1964; d. Edward Allen and Kathleen Ann (Reilly) T. BS in Pharmacy, Mass. Coll. of Pharmacy, 1987. Cert. Nuclear Pharmacy. Nuclear pharmacy residency Mass. Gen. Hosp., 1987; critical care pharmacist South Shore Hosp., South Weymouth, Mass., 1987-88; retail pharmacist Wellesley (Mass.) Pharmacy, 1987—; staff pharmacist Brockton (Mass.) Hosp., part time 1989; nuclear pharmacist joint program in nuclear medicine Harvard Med. Sch., Boston, 1988—; tchr. cardiac rehab. class South Shore Hosp., South Weymouth, 1987-88; lectr. Mass. Assn. Pharmacy Technicians, Mass., 1989—. Contbr. U.S. Disabled Olympic Team, 1988—; moderator polit. forum Mass. Coll. of Pharmacy, Boston, 1984; contbr. to appeal Archdiocese of Boston, 1989—. Mass. Coll. Pharmacy scholar, 1982-87. Mem. Am. Diabetes Assn., Soc. Nuclear Medicine, Am. Soc. Hosp. Pharmacists, Rho Pi Phi (vice chancellor Boston chpt. 1985-86). Republican. Roman Catholic. Home: 18 Cherry Ln PO Box 237 Minot MA 02055 Office: Radiopharmacy Brigham & Womens Hosp 75 Francis St Boston MA 02115

TAYLOR, KATHRYN EVANS, communications executive; b. Douglas, Ariz., May 8, 1929; d. Joseph Wesley and Maurine (Forehand) Evans; m. Otwell C. Taylor, Aug. B Gen. Studies, Coll. S.W., N.Mex., 1979. Billing clk. Lea County Electric, Lovington, N.Mex., 1956-57, bookkeeper, 1957-68, computer operator, 1969-73; bookkeeper Leaco Rural Telephone, Lovington, 1974-77, acct., 1978-79; office mgr. Five Area Tel. Cooperative Inc., Muleshoe, Tex., 1980—; advisor Rural Tel. and Electric Credit Union, 1987-90. Pres. Jennyslippers-Women's div. C. of C. and Agr., 1984; bd. dirs. C. of C., 1984-86, treas., 1985; mem. Tex. Statewide Coop. Inc., chmn. region x accts. 1982-83, program com. 1988-90. Mem. Tex. Telephone Assn. (program com. 1990, Beta Sigma Phi (pres. Lovington). Democrat. Home: 706 West Ave K Muleshoe TX 79347 Office: Five Area Tel PO Box 448 Muleshoe TX 79347

TAYLOR, KENDALL FRANCES, arts administrator, educator; b. N.Y.C., May 9; d. Alexander and Sophie (Tannenbaum) Finne; m. David R. Garner, Nov. 23, 1979; BA, Fairleigh Dickinson U., Rutherford, N.J., 1962; MA, Vanderbilt U., 1963, MAT, 1964; MA, Syracuse U., 1977, PhD, 1979. Lectr., U. Md., 1964-71; writer, producer Stas. KNBC-TV, KTTV-TV, KPIX-TV, 1971-73; dir. Brainerd Art Gallery SUNY, Potsdam, 1979-80, chmn. Council of SUNY Gallery and Exhibit Dirs., 1979-80; asst. prof. Grad. Sch. George Washington U., 1980—; dir. traveling exhbn. program Library of Congress, 1980-84; dir. Arts Mgmt. Assocs. and subs. ARTBANK, Washington, 1984—; acad. dir. Washington Seminar Program in Art and Architecture, The Am. U., 1988—; nat. speaker represented by Ross Assocs. Speakers Bur., N.Y.C. Author: (with Lila Weingarten) Arts and Crafts in Los Angeles, 1974, Never Separate from the Heart: The Life and Work of Philip Evergood, 1987; contbr. articles to profl. jours. Field rep. N.Y. State Council on the Arts, N.Y.C., 1980—; mem. steering com. Women Adminstrs. in Higher Edn. Adminstrn., Washington, 1983-84. Ford Found. fellow, 1963-64, Syracuse U. Florence fellow (Italy), 1974-75; Smithsonian fellow, 1977-78. Mem. Am. Assn. Mus. (mem. accreditation com. 1983—, chmn. Women Mus. Dirs. Caucus 1983-84, reviewer Mus. Assessment program 1984), Coll. Art Assn., Nat. Assn. Women Deans & Adminstrs. (presider conf. 1984, 85), Writers Guild Am. Democrat. Jewish. Home: 2707 Adams Mill Rd NW Apt 401 Washington DC 20009

TAYLOR, KRISTIN CLARK, media specialist, federal official; b. Detroit, Mar. 26, 1959; d. James W. and Mary Elizabeth (Moore) Clark; m. Lonnie Paul Taylor; children: Paul II, Mary Elizabeth. BA in Classical Lit., Mich. State U., 1982. Editor, writer USA Today, Washington, 1982-86; corp. writer Gannett Co., Inc., Washington, 1986; bus. corr. Gannett News Svc., Washington, 1987; asst. press sec. to Vice Pres. White House, Washington, 1987-88, spl. asst. to Vice Pres. for press rels., 1988-89, dir. media rels., 1989—. Republican.

TAYLOR, LESLI ANN, pediatric surgeon; b. N.Y.C., Mar. 2, 1953; d. Charles Vincent Taylor and Valene Patricia (Blake) Garfield. BFA, Boston U., 1975; MD, Johns Hopkins U., 1981. Surg. resident Beth Israel Hosp., Boston, 1981-88; rsch. fellow Pediatric Rsch. Lab. Mass. Gen. Hosp., Boston, 1984-86; fellow pediatric surgery Children's Hosp. of Phila., Phila., 1988-90; asst. prof. pediatric surgery U. N.C., Chapel Hill, 1990—. Author: (booklet) Think Twice: The Medical Effects of Physical Punishment, 1985. Recipient Nat. Rsch. Svc. award NIH, 1984-86. Mem. AMA.

TAYLOR, LINDA LEE, behaviorist anthropologist; b. Ft. Dodge, Iowa, Dec. 9, 1948; d. Fredric and Peggy Elaine (Newberg) T. Student, Ariz. State U., 1977; BA in Anthropology, San Diego State U., 1978; MA in Anthropology, Washington U., 1980, PhD in Anthropology, 1986. Adminstrv. asst. art conservation lab. ctr. for archaeometry Washington U., St. Louis, 1979-81; instr. anthropology dept. social scis. Jefferson Coll., Hillsboro, Mo., 1980; primate technician primate ctr. Duke U., Durham, N.C., 1982, vis. scholar in anthropology primate ctr., 1982-85; sr. rsch. asst. behavioral medicine lab. Dept. Physiology an Medicine, SW Found. for Biomed. Rsch., San Antonio, 1985-86, postdoctoral scientist behavioral medicine lab., 1986-88; sessional instr. dept. anthropology U. Calgary (Can.), 1988-89; rsch. asst. prof. dept. anthropology U. Miami, Coral Gables, Fla., 1989—; behavioral primatologist Specific Pathogen Free Rhesus Monkey Breeding Ctr., U. Miami, Coral Gables, 1989—; rsch. asst., logistics coord. Dr. K. Glander's Earthwatch Expedition to Hacienda La Pacifica, Costa Rica, 1983; adj. asst. prof. dept. anthropology U. Calgary, 1989—; cons. specific pathogen free rhesus monkey breeding ctr. U. Miami, Coral Gables, 1988; presenter in field. Editor, tech. writer A.D.E.P.T. Consulting Svc., Inc., Honolulu, 1984-87; editor, tech. writer: Technical Report on the IDMS/R Systems, 1986; editor: (with J.C. Wooten) IDMS/R Systems Desk Reference, 1987; contbr. articles and abstracts to profl. jours. NSF dissertation grantee, 1983-85, U.S. Dept. Energy grantee, 1985-87, NIH grantee div. rsch. resources U. Miami, 1988—; Univ. Grad. fellow Washington U., 1982-85. Mem. Am. Assn. Lab. Animal Sci., Am. Assn. Phys. Anthropologists, Animal Behavior Soc., Am. Soc. Primatologists, Am. Assn. Zool. Parks and Aquariums, Internat. Primatological Soc., Sigma Xi (grantee 1982-83), Phi Beta Kappa, Phi Kappa Phi. Home: 9950 SW 161 St Miami FL 33157 Office: U Miami 12500 SW 152 St Bldg C Miami FL 33177

TAYLOR, LINDA RATHBUN, investment banker; b. Rochester, N.Y., May 25, 1946; d. Lewis Standish and Elizabeth Florence (Hunt) Rathbun; m. Donald Gordon Taylor, Mar. 1, 1975; children: Alexander Standish, Abigail Elizabeth, Elizabeth Downing. BA, Vassar Coll., 1968; MBA, Harvard U., 1973. Chartered fin. analyst, D.C. Assoc.; corp. fin. Donaldson, Lufkin & Jenrette, N.Y.C., 1973-75; cons. World Bank, Washington, 1975; fin. analyst U.S. Treas. Dept., Washington, 1976-78; chief investment officer United Mine Workers Fund, 1978-85; investment mgr. Cen. Pension Fund of Internat. Union Oper. Engrs., Washington, 1985-86; investment banker The Saranow Co., 1986-89; pvt. investor, 1990—. Bd. dirs. Fluid Mgmt., Ltd.; trustee Montgomery County Md. Employees' Retirement System, 1987—. Contbr. articles to profl. jours. Mem. Jr. League Washington, 1975-80. Mem. Washington Soc. Investment Analysts (bd. dirs. 1984-85), Fin. Analyst Fedn. Republican. Presbyterian.

TAYLOR, LISA MARLENE, museum director; b. N.Y.C., Jan. 8, 1933; d. Theo and Martina (Weincerl) von Bergen-Maier; m. Bertrand L. Taylor III; children: Lauren, Lindsay. Student, Corcoran Sch. Art, 1958-65, Georgetown U., 1958-62, Johns Hopkins U., 1956-58; D.F.A. (hon.), Parsons

Sch. Design, 1977, Cooper Union, 1984. Adminstrv. asst. President's Fine Arts Com., 1958-62; membership dir. Corcoran Gallery Art, 1962-66; program dir. Smithsonian Instn., 1966-69; dir. Cooper-Hewitt Mus. Decorative Arts and Design, Smithsonian Instn., 1969-87, dir. emeritus, 1987—; mem. adv. bd. Design Mus. (London), N.Y. Hist. Soc., Katonah Gallery, Ctr. for Childhood, 1989. Co-dir. (film) A Living Museum, 1968; editor: Urban Open Spaces, 1979, Cities, 1981, The Phenomenon of Change, 1984, Housing: Symbol, Structure, Site, 1990. Recipient Thomas Jefferson award, 1976; Bronze plaque Johns Hopkins YMCA, 1958; medal of honor Am. Legion, 1951; Bronze Apple award Am. Soc. Indsl. Designers, 1977; named Trailblazer of Yr. Nat. Home Fashion League, 1981, Mcpl. Art Soc. award 1987, Joseph Henry medal, 1987, Dame of Honour Order of St. John of Jerusalem. Mem. Smithsonian Instn. (hon. life, Exceptional Service award 1969, Gold medal 1972, Women's Council award 1979), Am. Soc. Interior Designers (hon.), AIA (hon.). Home: Seven Gates Farm Vineyard Haven MA 02568 Office: Cooper-Hewitt Mus 2 E 91st St New York NY 10128-9990

TAYLOR, LUCILLE MARIE, insurance company administrator; b. Youngstown, Ohio, Oct. 16, 1939; d. Victor Emanuel Scarpine and Elizabeth (Louise) Partezana; m. Norman Eugene Taylor, May 15, 1961 (div.); children: Mark Eugene, Stephen Emanuel. RN, St. Elizabeth Med. Ctr., Youngstown, 1960. RN, Ohio. Surg. nurse St. Elizabeth Med. Ctr., Youngstown, 1960-62, Ohio State U. Hosp., Columbus, 1962-65; surg. supr. Salem (Ohio) City Hosp., 1965-66; mgr. divisional claims Equitable Life Assurance, Youngstown, 1967-84; 2d v.p. Dun & Bradstreet Plan Services, Youngstown, 1984-86, v.p., 1986—, asst. v.p., 1990. Democrat. Roman Catholic. Office: Plan Svcs Inc 7655 Market St Suite 3800 Youngstown OH 44512

TAYLOR, LYNN BOGGESS, college dean; b. South Bend, Ind., Aug. 13, 1945; d. W.A. and Jean B. (Petree) Slaughter. B.A., Western Mich. U., 1967; M.Ed., Kent State U., 1977, Ph.D., 1984. Tchr. Delton (Mich.)-Kellogg Schs., 1967-68; supr. Grad. Sch. of Edn. Kent (Ohio) State U., 1973-78; counselor Cuyahoga Valley CMHC, Cuyahoga Falls, Ohio, 1979-83; dir. of counseling, assoc. dean of students Hiram (Ohio) Coll., 1983—, acting dean of student, 1986-87; cons. Womemchelter, Kent, 1977. Presenter numerous presentations at profl. conferences. Vol. Akron City Hosp. Emergency Room, Ohio, 1983. Mem. Nat. Assn. Women Deans, Adminstrs., and Counselors (exec. bd. 1978-79, nominations com. 1982-84, steering com. counseling and individual devel. div. 1988-90), Ohio Assn. Women Deans, Adminstrs., and Counselors, Am. Coll. Personnel Assn., Am. Assn. Counseling and Devel., Nat. Assn. Student Personnel Adminstrs., Am. Psychol. Assn., Ohio Assn. Student Personnel Adminstrs. (conf. planning com. 1987-89). Club: Ohio Pinto (past pres.), Ohio High Sch. Rodeo Assn. Avocation: exhibiting horses. Home: 3652 Porter Rd Rootstown OH 44272 Office: Hiram Coll Bates Hall Hiram OH 44234

TAYLOR, MARGARET LEE, English educator; b. Albany, Ga., July 15, 1949; d. Thomas Will and Mathie Lee (Harris) T. BA, Albany State Coll., 1970; MEd, Ga. Southwestern Coll., 1977. Dir. speech, drama Dougherty High Sch., Albany, 1987-90; instr. English Dougherty County Bd. Edn., 1970—; cons. Ga. Writing Project, 1981; moderator Nat. Issues Forum, Albany, 1988. Author: (poems) Selected Writings of 1987. Dir. Bapt. Student Union, Albany, 1987-90; founder, dir. Taylor's Players, Albany, 1976—; bd. dirs. Albany Mus. Art, Albany, 1984-90; cert. dean Cristian edn. Friendship Bapt. Ch., Albany. Mem. Dougherty County Edn. Assn., Ga. Coun. Tchrs. English, NEA, Ga. Assn. Educators, Internat. Reading Assn., Zeta Phi Beta (chmn. scholarship, sec. 1988—). Democrat. Baptist. Home: 1205 S Davis St Albany GA 31701 Office: Dougherty High Sch 1800 Pearce Ave Albany GA 31701

TAYLOR, MARGARET TURNER, clothing designer, economist, writer, planner; b. Wilmington, N.C., May 7, 1944. A.B. in Econs., Smith Coll., 1966; M.A. in Econ. History, U. Pa., 1970, now Ph.D. candidate in City and Regionel Planning. Tchr. Jefferson Jr. High Sch., New Orleans, 1966-69; instr. econs. U. Tex.-El Paso, 1974-75; adj. prof. econs., Salisbury State Coll., (Md.), 1976-78; prin. mgr., designer Margaret Norriss, women's clothing, Salisbury, Md., 1980—; planner at Wharton Ctr. Applied Research, Phila., 1985-86; planning cons., freelance writer.

TAYLOR, MARGARET UHRICH, academic official, consultant; b. Lebanon, Pa., Nov. 27, 1952; d. William Murray and Anne (Shultz) Uhrich; m. Timothy Norman Taylor, Sept. 29, 1979; 1 child, Walter Marshall. B.A., Shippensburg U., 1974. Adminstrv. asst. Patriot-News Co., Harrisburg, Pa., 1974; reporter Pub. Opinion sect., Chambersburg, Pa., 1975-78; assoc. editor, Miami bur. chief OAG, Inc., N.Y.C., 1978-79; dir. mktg., pub. affairs Wilson Coll., Chambersburg, 1980—, co-founder women in transition program, 1985; pres. Margaret Taylor's Mktg. Communications, 1989; adj. faculty Shippensburg U., Pa., 1981—. Founding mem. Commonwealth Assn. Students, 1972; charter mem. Friends of Fulton County Library, McConnellsburg, 1975; founder Unforgettable Charity Ball, Chambersburg, 1983-86; active Gotemba Sister-City Com., Borough of Chambersburg, 1981-90; pub. relations counsel Greater Chambersburg Area United Way, 1985-90; cons. dir. Straight Love Franklin County, Chambersburg, 1982-83; founder Women's Network Franklin County, 1982—; bd. dirs. Fulton County Med. Ctr. Corp., 1987—, sec., 1989-90. Mem. Soc. Profl. Journalists (treas. Central Pa. chpt. 1981-82, v.p. 1982-83, pres. 1983-84, chmn. freedom of info. com. 1980-81, chpt. del. nat. conv. 1977), Women in Communications, Pa. Pub. Relations Soc., Chambersburg Area C. of C. (active Leadership Com. 1985-88). Home: PO Box 552 Hustontown PA 17229 Office: Wilson Coll Pub Affairs Office 1015 Philadelphia Ave Chambersburg PA 17201

TAYLOR, MARGARET W., educator; b. Terre Haute, Ind., Aug. 5, 1920; d. Carl and Grace (Riehle) Wischmeyer; m. John Edward, Sept. 5, 1942; children: Deborah Ann, Tobin Edward, Mary Leesa. BA magna cum laude, Duke U., Durham, 1941; MA, John Carroll U., Cleve., 1973. Feature writer Dayton Daily News, Dayton, 1945-53; freelance writer Cleve., 1953—; asst. to Dr. Joseph B. Rhine Duke U. Parapsychology Lab., Durham, 1941; asst. prof. English, journalism Cuyahoga Community Coll. Ea. Campus, Cleve., 1973—; writing cons., editor various cos. and pubs., Cleve., 1973—; bd. dir. Writers Conf. Cuyahoga Community Coll., Cleve; adviser to campus newspaper Cuyahoga Community Coll., Cleve., 1973-84, founder and operator. Active Grammar Hot Line, 1987—. Recipient Best Ednl. Story, Best Overall Story award Am. Heart Assn., 1970. Mem. Mensa, Phi Beta Kappa. Presbyterian. Home: 27900 Fairmount Blvd Pepper Pike OH 44124 Office: Cuyahoga Community Coll Ea Campus 4250 Richmond Rd Cleveland OH 44122

TAYLOR, MARY A., public relations executive; b. Detroit, June 20, 1948; d. Robert George and Elizabeth A. (Murphy) Klein; m. Alexander Lindsay Taylor III, Apr. 21, 1983; children: Alexander, Madeleine. BS in Mktg., Wayne State U., 1972; BA in English, Fordham U., N.Y.C., 1983. Officer tng. prog. City Nat. Bank, Detroit, 1971-72; mgr. pub. rels. City Nat. Bank, 1972-73, dir. pub. rels., 1973-75, asst. v.p. pub. affairs, 1975-78; dir. invester rels. The Pittston Co., Greenwich, Conn., 1978-83; mgr. communications Philip Morris Cos., Inc., N.Y.C., 1983-86; dir. communications Philip Morris Cos., Inc., 1986-89, dir. spl. projects, 1989—. Contbr. articles to profl. jours. Mem. Civitas. Office: Philip Morris Co Inc 120 Park Ave New York NY 10017

TAYLOR, MARY CUTIS SMITH, musician; b. Shepherdsville, Ky., Jan. 9, 1937; d. Curtis Waldo and Hazel Dell (Trunnell) Smith; m. John G. Taylor, Aug. 16, 1958; children: John Gordon Jr., Tiffany May, Whitney Adams. Student, U. Louisville, 1954-55, postgrad., 1966; B Music Edn., Murray State U., 1958, MA in Edn., 1960, Cert. in Sch. Libr. Media, Sch. Adminstrn. and Supervision, 1981; postgrad., U. So. Calif., 1976; MLS, Vanderbilt U., 1985. Pvt. tchr. music, 1954-80; switchboard operator Murray (Ky.) State U., 1956-58, asst. prof., supr., student tchr., 1974-76; tchr. music and phys. edn. Benton City Schs., Ky., 1958-60; tchr. music Jefferson County Sch. Dist., Louisville, 1960-64; with Nashville Symphony Orch., Nashville, 1969—; libr. technician Ky. Dept. for Librs. and Archives Field Svcs., 1981-89; dir. Calloway County Pub. Library, Murray, Ky., 1989—; music tchr. upward bound project Alice Lloyd Coll., Pippa Passes, Ky., 1967; music instr. string class Bethel Coll., McKenzie, Tenn., 1980; coord. KENCILIP/Inter-Libr. Loan, Murray, 1980. Touring Broadway musicals: Sound fo Music, Hello, Dolly!, A Funny THing Happened on the Way to the Forum, West Side Story, Carnival, Nutcracker Suite (concertmaster), Fiddler on the Roof. First violinist Nashville Symphony Orch., 1963—; concertmaster Jackson Symphony Orch., 1974-88; first violin sect. Paducah (Ky.) Symphony Orch., 1981—, The Des Moines Metro Summer Festival of Opera, Indianola, Iowa, 1978, Murfreesboro Symphony Orch. Middle Tenn. State U., 1973-76, 89, Nashville Baroque Orch., 1974-76, Jackson Symphony Orch., 1969—, Louisville Symphony Orch., 1969-76, Owensboro (Ky.) Symphony; concertmaster Louisville Youth Orch., 1955, Louisville Civic Orch., 1954-55. Mem. ALA, So. Libr. Assn., Ky. Libr. Assn., AAUW, Am. Fedn. Musicians, Colonial Dames 17th Century, Sigma Alpha Iota. Home: Rte 7 Box 21 Murray KY 42071 Office: Calloway County Pub Library 710 Main Street Murray KY 42071

TAYLOR, MARY D., counselor; b. Manitow, Okla., July 24, 1936; d. Hoye S. and Grace (Herrell) Rayburn; children: James, Joel, Paul, Steven, Denise. AA in Mental Health, Arts and Scis. Social Welfare, Pierce Coll., 1978; BA, Pacific Luth. U., 1979. Registered counselor; cert. tchr., property mgr., child and family welfare. Instr., trainer Tahoma Industries, Tacoma; supr. City of Tacoma; counselor Episcopal Svc. for Youth, Tacoma, Rainier State Sch., Buckley, Wash.; owner, mgr. Taylor Apts., Tacoma. Advocate for mental illness; past bd. dirs. group health Larchmont Sr. Ctr. Recipient award Ret. Sr. Vol. Program. Mem. DAV Women's Aux., ARC, Am. Fedn. Tchrs. Address: 7629 Pacific Ave Tacoma WA 98408

TAYLOR, MARY ELIZABETH, dietitian; b. Medina, N.Y., Dec. 10, 1933; d. Glenn Aaron and Viola Hazel (Lansill) Grimes; m. Wilbur Alvin Fredlund, Apr. 12, 1952 (div. Jan. 1980); 1 child, Wilbur Jr.; m. Frederick Herbert Taylor, Mar. 15, 1981; children: Martha Dayton, Jean Grout, Beth Stern, Cindy Hey, Carol McLellan, Cheryl, Robert. BS in Food and Nutrition, SUCB, Buffalo, 1973; MEd in Health Sci. Edn. and Evaluation, SUNY, 1978. Registered dietitian, 1977. Diet cook Niagara Sanitorium, Lockport, N.Y., 1953-56; cook Mount View Hosp., Lockport, N.Y., 1956-60, asst. dietitian, 1960-73, dietitian, food svc. dir., 1973-79, cons. dietitian, 1979-81; instr. Erie Community Coll., Williamsville, N.Y., 1979-81; sch. lunch coord. Nye County Sch. Dist., Tonopah, Nev., 1982—; cons. dietitian Nye Gen. Hosp., Tonopah, 1983-88; adj. instr. Erie Community Coll., Williamsville, 1978-79; nutrition instr. for coop. extension Clark County Community Coll., 1990—; cons. Group Purchasing Western N.Y. Hosp. Adminstrs., Buffalo, 1975-79, vice-chmn. adv. com., 1976-78; cons. BOCES, Lockport, 1979-81. Nutrition counselor Migrant Workers Clinic, Lockports, 1974-80; mem. Western N.Y. Soc. for Hosp. Food Svc. Adminstrn., 1974-81; nutritionist Niagara County Nutrition Adv. Com., 1977-81. Recipient Outstanding Woman of the Yr. for Contributions in the field of Health award YWCA-UAW Lockport, 1981, Disting. Health Care Food Adminstrn. Recognition award Am. Soc. for Hosp. Food Svc. Adminstrs., Chgo., 1979, USDA award for Outstanding Lunch Program in Nev. and Western Region, 1986. Mem. Am. Dietetic Assn., Nev. State Dietetic Assn., Nutrition Today Soc., Am. Sch. Food Svc. Assn. (bd. dirs. 1987, cert. dir. II 1987, mem. 5 yr. planning com. 1990, mem. annual conf., 1988-90), Nev. State Food Svc. Assn. (mem. annual meeting 1990), AARP. Republican. Baptist. Home: 481 N Murphy PO Box 656 Pahrump NV 89041 Office: Nye County Sch Dist Mil Circle PO Box 113 Tonopah NV 89049

TAYLOR, MARY JOAN, lawyer; b. Kenton, Ohio, Dec. 24, 1926; d. Maurice A. and Martina (Dolan) McMahon; student St. Mary Springs Coll., 1944-45; Asso. Degree in Bus. Adminstrn. Franklin U., 1946-49; J.D. with high distinction, Ohio No. U., 1951; postgrad., U. Wyo., 1954-56; m. Edward McKinley Taylor, Jr., Apr. 23, 1952; 1 dau., Mary Margaret. Admitted to Ohio bar, 1951; gen. practice law, Kenton, 1951-52, Wichita Falls, Tex., 1953—; ptnr. law firm Taylor and Taylor, Dayton, Ohio, 1957—; law librarian Franklin U., 1948-49. Trustee, Harrison Twp., 1980—. Mem. Ohio Bar Assn., Montgomery County Law Library Assn., Ohio No. U. Alumni Assn. (sec. Miami Valley 1958-60), Iota Tau Lambda, Kappa Beta Pi. Club: Soroptimist. Address: 7417 N Main St Dayton OH 45415

TAYLOR, MERRILY ELLEN, university librarian; b. Winchester, Mass., May 24, 1945; d. Philip Forbes and Ruth Ellen (Piper) T. A.A., St. Petersburg Jr. Coll., 1965; B.A., U. South Fla., 1967, M.A., 1973; M.S. in L.S., Fla. State U., 1968. Reference librarian U. South Fla. Library, Tampa, 1968-69, head circulation dept., 1969-74, head collection devel., 1974-77; asst. to univ. librarian Yale U. Library, New Haven, 1977-78; dir. services group Columbia U. Libraries, N.Y.C., 1978-82; univ. librarian Brown U., Providence, 1982—; pres. Consortium R.I. Acad. and Research Libraries, 1985-87. Author: The Yale University Library 1901-1978, 1978; author, editor: Remembering P.D. Ouspensky (exhbn. catalog), 1978. Mem. R.I. State Commn. on the Pricing Libr. Svcs., 1987-88; mem. adv. com. R.I. Libr. Study, 1987-88; mem. R.I. Coun. on the Preservation Rsch. Resources, 1989—. Acad. Library Mgmt. intern Council on Library Resources Washington, 1976. Mem. ALA, R.I. Library Assn. (chmn. pub. rels. com. 1985), Rsch. Libraries Group (bd. govs. 1982—, chmn. bd. govs. system comm. 1989—, chmn. pub. services com. 1984-86), Assn. Rsch. Libraries (com. on library edn., chmn. com. on gov. policies 1989—, adv. com. pub. services self study program 1982-84, com. on gov. policy 1986—, bd. mem. 1986-89), Nat. Trust for Hist. Preservation, Providence Preservation Soc. Democrat. Methodist. Home: 55 Charlesfield Providence RI 02906 Office: Brown U Libr Box A Rockefeller Libr Providence RI 02912

TAYLOR, MILDRED JUANITA, controller; b. Delray Beach, Fla., Nov. 21, 1947; d. Le Roy and Lula Bell (Comb) Weiss; m. Ronald I. Taylor, Oct. 8, 1965 (div. July 1967); 1 child, Cheryl. BS in Acctg., Kingsenton Coll., 1969. Mgr. bldg. dept. City of Boca Raton, 1970-78; adminstr. constrn. dept. Arvida Corp., Boca Raton, Fla., 1978-80; cont. Seiko Time Corp., U.S.A., Boca Raton, 1978-88, Lytal & Reiter, West Palm Beach, Fla., 1988—; pres. Troublefree Acctg., Inc., Boynton Beach, Fla., 1987—. Mem. Orgn. Women Execs. Democrat. Baptist. Home: 96 Mayfair Ln Boynton Beach FL 33462 Office: Troublefree Acctg Inc PO Box 3438 Boynton Beach FL 33424

TAYLOR, MINNA, lawyer; b. Washington, Jan. 25, 1947; d. Morris P. and Anne (Williams) Glushien; m. Charles Ellett Taylor, June 22, 1969; 1 child, Amy Caroline. BA, SUNY, Stony Brook, 1969; MA, SUNY, 1973; JD, U. So. Calif., 1977. Bar: Calif. 1977, U.S. Dist. Ct. (cen. dist.) Calif. 1978. Field atty. NLRB, L.A., 1977-82; dir. employee rels., legal svcs. Paramount Pictures Corp., L.A., 1982-85, v.p. employee rels. legal svcs., 1985-89; dir. bus. and legal affairs Wilshire Ct. Prodns., L.A., 1989—. Editor notes and articles: U. So. Calif. Law Rev., 1976-77. Mentor MOSTE, L.A., 1986-87, 88-89; pres. Beverly Hills chpt. ACLU, L.A., 1985. Fellow Women in Film, ABA, L.A. County Bar Assn.; mem. Order of Coif. Office: Wilshire Ct Prodns 5750 Wilshire Blvd Ste 222 Los Angeles CA 90036

TAYLOR, NANCY ELIZABETH, dentist, educator; b. Elkins, W.Va., Sept. 12, 1953; d. Odbert Haymond and Dorothy Elizabeth (Cox) T.; m. Stephen Lee Swadley, Aug. 14, 1976 (div. Sept. 1983); m. George D. Milam, June 17, 1990. Student, Davis and Elkins Coll., 1970-71; BA, W.Va. U., 1973, DDS, 1978. Cert. dentist, N.E. regional bd. Pub. health dentist Monongalia County Health Dept., Morgantown, W.Va., 1978—; asst. prof. community dentistry Sch. Dentistry W.Va. U., Morgantown, 1979—; participating dentist in behavioral medicine rsch. Sch. Medicine W.Va. U., 1981-83; mem. doctoral dissertation com. dept. psychology W.Va. U., 1982-83. Mem. Adult Community Band, Morgantown, 1982-83. Recipient Bd. Regents Acad. scholarship W.Va. U., 1971-73. Mem. Dental Sect. W.Va. Pub. Health Assn. (chmn. 1981-83, vice chmn. 1988-89, chmn. dental sect. 1990—). Democrat. Home: 27 Orchard Acres Morgantown WV 26505 Office: Monongalia County Health Dept 453 Van Voorhis Rd Morgantown WV 26505

TAYLOR, NANCY STIRLING, securities analyst; b. Balt., July 29, 1960; d. Clarence Jr. and Janet (Stevenson) T. BS in Fin., Towson State U., 1982; MBA, Loyola U., Balt., 1989. Cert. fin. analyst. Staff acct. Legg Mason, Inc., Balt., 1982-85, securities analyst, 1985—. Mem. Inst. Chartered Fin. Analysts, Balt. Soc. Chartered Fin. Analysts, Jr. Assn. of Commerce. Republican. Methodist. Office: Legg Mason Inc 111 S Calvert St Baltimore MD 21203-1476

TAYLOR, NATHALEE BRITTON, nutritionist; b. Lubbock, Tex., June 8, 1941; d. Nathaniel E. and Dessie Pauline (Moss) Britton; children by previous marriage: Clay H., Bret N. Courtney. BS in Home Econs., Tex. Tech U., 1963. Home economist Pioneer Gas, Lubbock, Tex., 1963-65; dietician Tex. Tech U., Lubbock, 1966-71; home economist South Plains Electric Co-op., Lubbock, 1986; mgr. quality control Rip Griffins Enterprises, Lubbock, Tex., 1987; sales rep. Time Chem., Lubbock, 1987—; with Sentry, Lubbock. Co-author: (cookbook) From Our House to Yours, 1975; columnist: Lubbock Lights mag.; presenter TV show Southwestern Cooking Sta. KTXT. Bd. dirs. Am. Heart Assn., Lubbock, 1985-87; mem. Home Economist in Bus. (pres. Lubbock chpt., 1985); culinary co-chmn. Lubbock C. of C. Arts Festival, 1982, 83, 84. Named Lincoln County Fair Queen. Mem. Tech. Home Ec Alumns (sec./treas.), Am. Home Econs. Assn. (v.p., sec./treas.), Soroptomist (v.p. Lubbock club). Democrat.

TAYLOR, PATRICIA MAY, retired coordinator deaf and blind services, consultant; b. Orange, N.J., May 31, 1919; d. Prescott and Edith Mirian (Stevenson) May; m. Richard Porter Taylor (dec. May 1971); children: Richard Bingham, Jeremy Stevenson, Ann Taylor Jackson. BA, Middlebury Coll., 1940; edn. for blind degree, Harvard U., Perkins Sch. Blind, 1941; MS, So. Conn. State U., 1971. Cert. elem. tchr., Mass., tchr. of blind., Conn. Pvt. sec. to dir. Seeing Eye, Inc., Morristown, N.J., 1941; elem. tchr. Perkins Sch. for Blind, Watertown, Mass., 1942-44, Shore Country Day Sch., Beverly, Mass., 1958-62; edn. cons. N.J. Commn. for Blind, Newark, 1941-42; edn. cons. Bd. Edn. and Svcs. for Blind, Wethersfield, Conn., 1964—, coord. for deaf and blind svcs., 1978-89; ret., 1989; transitional planner N.E. Regional Ctr. for the Deaf Blind, Perkins and Watertown, Mass., summers, 1980—. Recipient award N.E. chpt. Assn. Educators and Rehab. Counselors, 1986, award for svc. to deaf-blind children and adults Deaf-Blind Assn. Conn., 1989. Mem. Internat. Assn. Educators of Deaf Blind (Ann Sullivan award 1987), Assn. Educators of Blind and Visually Handicapped (bd. dirs. 1975-82), Assn. Educators and Rehab. of Blind and Visually Handicapped, Conn. Braille Assn. (1st v.p., bd. dirs. 1964—, pres. 1990—, svc. award 1979), Kappa Kappa Gamma, Wilton Riding Club. Democrat. Home: 306 Chestnut Hill Rd Wilton CT 06897

TAYLOR, PEARLIE BEATRICE, real estate executive, investment executive; b. Monroe, La.; d. Lee Andrew Taylor and Josephine (Curington) Dotray. BA in Sociology, So. Ill. U., 1965; MA in Bus., Cen. Mich. U., 1977. Lic. real estate salesperson, Mo. Social caseworker Mo. Div. Welfare, St. Louis, 1965-71; social planner Domino Planning & Devel. Corp., Kansas City, Mo., 1971-72; sch. social worker Kansas City Sch. Dist., 1972-73; mgmt. asst. Midwest Asset Mgmt. Group, Kansas City, 1973-75, adminstrv. asst., 1975-79, exec. v.p., 1979—; bd. dirs., sec. Cen. States Housing, Kansas City, 1982—. Vol. nursing homes; vol. Svc. Project for Battered Women, Kansas City, 1990—, Sponsorship of a Child, South Africa, 1990—. Mem. NAFE, Alpha Kappa Alpha. Presbyterian. Office: Midwest Asset Mgmt Group 1903 Woodland Ave Kansas City MO 64108

TAYLOR, PEGGY LOUISE, educator; b. Oak Park, Ill., Nov. 18, 1946. BS, Ea. Ill. U., 1969; MEd, Nat. Coll. Edn., Evanston, Ill., 1987. Tchr. Dist. 41, Glen Ellyn, Ill., 1969—; mem. faculty Ill. Benedictine Coll., Lisle; math. cons. sch. dists. Westchester and Geneva, Ill., 1990; presenter Ednl. Svc. Ctr. 4, DuPage County, Ill., 1989, Ill. Kindergarten Conf., Oakbrook, 1990. Named Outstanding Young Educator, Glen Ellyn Jaycees, 1976. Mem. NEA, Nat. Coun. Tchrs. Math., Nat. Assn. Educators Young Children, Ill. Assn. Supervision and Curriculum Devel., Wheaton-Glen Ellyn Tchrs. Applying Whole Lang., AAUW, Phi Delta Kappa. Office: Dist 41 380 Greenfield Ave Glen Ellyn IL 60137

TAYLOR, PRISCILLA W., college director; b. Alameda, Calif., July 8, 1941; d. Ruben A. and Harriet L. (Porter); children: Mark Barrett, Michelle Renee. Student, San Francisco State Coll., Bethany Bible Coll. Cert. real estate and life ins. agt., securities analyst. Sales rep. Sitcler Assocs. Realty, Roseville, Calif., Bus. Men's Assurance, Roseville; dir. food svc. Bethel Ch., San Jose, Calif.; dir. conferencing and food svc. Bethany Coll., Scotts Valley, Calif. Pres. Ladies' Aux. Bethany Coll.; active numerous local ch. orgns. Address: 800 Bethany Dr Scotts Valley CA 95066 Office: 800 Bethany Dr Scotts Valley CA 95066

TAYLOR, RAMONA GARRETT, financial services company executive; b. Dallas, 1930. Student So. Meth. U. Sec. to pres. Universal Fin. Co., Dallas, 1957-61; corp. sec., exec. asst. to chmn. bd. dirs., chief exec. officer Lomas Fin. Corp., 1965—. Office: Lomas Fin Corp PO Box 655644 Dallas TX 75265-5644

TAYLOR, ROBBIE R., manager; b. Atlanta, Ga., Feb. 19, 1947; d. James Robert and Frankie (Barker) McDonnold; m. Carlton Wesley Taylor, May 18, 1974; 1 child, Sheila Kaye. ABA, Georgia State U., 1970; posrgrad., Kennesaw Coll., 1988. Acct. John Portman & Assoc., Atlanta, 1970-74; adminstrv. asst. Attorney's Title Guaranty Fund, Inc., Marietta, Ga., 1978-85; v.p. Attorney's Title Guaranty Fund, Inc., Cartersville, Ga., 1986-. Pres. Christian League for Battered Women, Cartersville. Mem. NAFE, Nat. Assn. Bar-Related Title Insurers, Ga. Title Insurers Assn. (sec.), C. of C. Bartow-Cartersville (bd. dirs., v.p. community affairs), Bus. and Profl. Womens Club (3d v.p.), Pilot Club. Democrat. Home: 126 Duncan Dr SW Cartersville GA 30120 Office: Attys' Title Guaranty 121 N Erwin St Cartersville GA 30120

TAYLOR, ROSANNE CAPPIELLO, small business owner; b. Darby, Pa., June 14, 1945; d. Frank S. and Louise Ann (Moreschi) Cappiello; m. A. Jeffrey Taylor, Apr. 27, 1984; stepdau., Jackie. AB, Immaculate Coll., 1967; Cert. Bus., Villanova U., 1977; postgrad. in Bus. Adminstrn., Wilmington Grad. Sch., 1980-81. Clk. typist AMP Products Corp., Valley Forge, Pa., 1975-76, sales corr., 1976-77, tng. coordinator, 1977-78, supr. and trainer, 1978-80, sales rep., 1980-83, asst. product mgr., 1983-85; dir. mktg. Spitz Space Systems, Chadds Ford, Pa., 1985-86; pres., owner R.C. Taylor & Assocs. Tng. Cons., West Chester, Pa., 1986—. Chmn. Friends for Maggie Found., West Chester, 1984-85; bd. dirs. YWCA, West Chester. Mem. Main Line Women's Network, Women's Referral Network (co-founder), Step-up Support Group for Step-parents, Bus. and Profl. Women, Nat. Assn. Female Execs. (area dir. 1982—), Women in Electronics, Del. C. of C., Delaware County C. of C., Westchester C. of C. Republican. Roman Catholic. Avocations: racquetball; bicycling; reading; cooking. Home: 20 Cannon Hill Rd West Chester PA 19382 Office: R C Taylor & Assocs 20 Cannon Hill Rd West Chester PA 19382

TAYLOR, ROSEMARY, artist; b. Joseph, Oreg.; d. Theodore and Sarah A. (Lambright) Resch; student Cleve. Inst. Art, 1937-40, NYU, 1947; m. Robert Hull Taylor; children—Barbara Taylor Ryalls, Robert H. Tchr. pottery Rahway (N.J.) Art Center, 1950-55; one-woman shows: Paterson (N.J.) Coll., 1964, Westchester (Pa.) Coll., 1970, Gallery 100, Princeton, N.J., 1967, George Jensen's, N.Y.C., 1972, Artisan Gallery, Princeton, 1974, Am. Crafts (Ohio), 1979-89, Guild Gallery, 1986-90, Little Art Gallery, N.C., 1985-90, Olde Queens Gallery (N.J.), 1987, N.J. Designer Craftsmen, 1990 (bd. dirs. 1986-87); group shows include: Mus. Natural History, N.Y.C., Newark Mus., Trenton (N.J.) Mus., Montclair (N.J.) Mus., Phila. Art Alliance, Pa. Horticulture Soc., 1988, Nat. Design Center, N.Y.C.; represented in permanent collection Westchester Coll.; pottery cons. McCalls Mag., 1962-72. Bd. dirs. Solebury Community Sch.; mem. Fulbright award com., 1982, 83. Mem. LWV (pres. Plainfield, N.J. chpt.). Mem. Am. Craft Council, N.J. Designer-Craftsmen, Phila. Craft Group, Bucks County (Pa.) C. of C., Visual Artists and Galleries Assn., Nat. Assn. Am. Penwoman, Women in the Arts (charter). Democrat. Unitarian. Home: PO Box 46 River Rd Lumberville PA 18933 Office: PO Box 282 Stockton NJ 08559

TAYLOR, SALLY JANE, guidance counselor, educator; b. Marion, Ky., Jan. 1, 1948; d. William Donald and Bette (Kinneman) T.; m. Daniel Buie, May 13, 1989. BS, Murray (Ky.) State U., 1970, MA, 1976, postgrad., 1980. Careers tchr. Barkley Boys Camp Sch., Benton, Ky., 1971-72; tchr. phys. edn. Bayonet Park Jr. High Sch., New Port Richey, Fla., 1973-74; elem. tchr., counselor Hopkins County Sch. System, 1974-78; tchr. English and health White Plains (Ky.) Elem. Sch., 1978-85; tchr. health and phys. edn., sch. guidance counselor South Hopkins High Sch., Nortonville, Ky., 1987—. Amb. to Fed. Republic Germany, Friendship Force, 1981; del. Nat. Dem. Conv., 1984; pub. rels. chmn. Champions Against Drugs, 1987—; chmn. curriculum com. Teenage Pregnancy Coalition, 1987—; pres. Homemakers, 1986—. Mem. NEA, Ky. Edn. Assn. (assembly del., Best

Newsletter award 1983), Hopkins County Edn. Assn. (pres. 1983), Ky. Assn. for Counseling and Devel., Ky. Sch. Pub. Rels. Assn., Madisonville Bus. and Profl. Women (past pres., historian, treas., sec.), Greater Madisonville C. of C., NOW, LWV, Beta Sigma (First Lady of Yr. award 1981), Alpha Delta Kappa (past pres., sec.). Presbyterian. Home: 585 Evergreen Circle Madisonville KY 42431

TAYLOR, SANDRA LYNN, marketing executive; b. Wadesboro, N.C., Oct. 19, 1962; d. William Steve and Brenda Joy (Eddins) T. BSBA, U. N.C., Chapel Hill, 1984. POS rep. Jefferson Standard Life Ins., Greensboro, N.C., 1984-85; advt. markets rep. Sun Life Ins. Co., Atlanta, 1985-88, mktg. rep., 1988; mktg. support mgr. Life of Ga., Atlanta, 1988—. Fellow Cert. Life Underwriters Assn.; mem. Life Office Mgmt. Assn. Republican. Methodist. Office: Life of Ga 5780 Powers Ferry Rd NW Atlanta GA 30327

TAYLOR, SARAH LOUISA, import company official; b. Porthcawl, Wales, Feb. 27, 1942; came to U.S., 1964; d. Alfred Norman and Joan (Harrington) Butler; m. Philip Liddon Taylor, July 16, 1966; children: Camilla Bronwen, Imogen Ruth. BS in Biology, Univ. Coll., London, 1964. Mem. rsch. staff Case Western Res. U., Cleve., 1964-70; exec. sec. Young People's Petition, Cleve., 1982-88; pres. Ariel Co., Cleve., 1976—. Founder Cleve. Pub. Radio, 1975. Democrat. Home: 2894 Meadowbrook Blvd Cleveland Heights OH 44118-2872

TAYLOR, SARAH WIGHTMAN, broadcasting executive; b. Westport, Conn., Mar. 8, 1956; d. Sherrill Wightman and Phylis June (Whitmeyer) T.; m. Roger William Lockhart, Sept. 26, 1987; 1 child, Roger William. BA in Anthropology, Rollins Coll., 1978. With Sta. WTOP, Washington, 1978—, gen. sales mgr., 1985-87; gen. sales mgr. Sta. WTOP-WASH, Washington, 1987—. Mem. com. New Yr.'s Eve Ball, ARC, Washington, 1987-88; mem. com. Make-A-Wish Found., Washington, 1989—; external v.p. Downtown Jaycees, Washington, 1985-86, mem., 1987-88. Mem. Wash. Bd. Trade, Wash. Ad Club, Am. Women in Radio and TV, Wash. Area Broadcasters Assn., Bravo. Republican. Episcopalian. Home: 6009 Ramsgate Rd Bethesda MD 20816 Office: Sta WTOP-WASH 3400 Idaho Ave NW Washington DC 20016

TAYLOR, SHIRLEY ANN, educator; b. Oakland, Calif., Oct. 5, 1948; d. Elmore and Clara Taylor; 1 child, Demar Richardson. AA, Merritt, Oakland, 1969; BA, San Francisco State, 1973, MA, 1975. Cert. elem. tchr. (life), Calif. Educator Oakland Pub. Schs., 1974—. Big Sister Big Bros./Big Sisters, Oakland, 1988-89; den mother Cub Scouts Am., Oakland, 1982-83. Tchr. grant San Francisco State, 1986-88; new notions grant Marcus Foster Inst., 1982. Mem. NEA, Claif. Tchrs. Assn., Calif. Assn. Student Counselors, Phi Delta Kappa.

TAYLOR, SUSANNE GREGORY, security company executive; b. New Haven, July 19, 1946; d. Frederick Miles and Meriel (Marston) G.; m. Louis Rome, July 21, 1971 (div.); m. Mark Francis Taylor, Sept. 11, 1982. BA, George Washington U., 1969; postgrad., Fairfield U. Licensed pvt. detective, Conn. Personnel dir. NESS Corp., Milford, Conn., 1974-78, v.p., 1978-85, pres., 1985—. Editor NESS newsletter. Mem. Am. Soc. for Indsl. Security, Am. Soc. for Human Resource Mgmt., Am. Mmgt. Assn. (pres. assn.), Conn. Bus. and Industry Assn., Young Pres.'s Orgn., Am. Assn. Marriage and Family Therapists. Office: NESS Corp 7 Lafayette St Milford CT 06460

TAYLOR, TESSA JANE, wholesale corporation assistant; b. Stout, Ohio, Aug. 27, 1964; d. Raymond and Mattie Melissa (Evans) Taylor; m. Phillip Lee Swayne, June 2, 1990. Student, Shawnee State U., 1983-87; cert. computer studies, Scioto County Joint Vocat. Sch, Portsmouth, Ohio, 1989. Receptionist Wil-Car Enterprises, Inc., Wheelersburg, Ohio, 1983-86, purchase processor, 1983-88, mktg. sec., 1987-88, adminstrv. asst., 1988—; recreation chmn. Wil-Car Enterprises, Inc., 1988—, safety com. mem., 1989. Editor (newsletter) Wil-Car Pride, 1989-90. In-house chmn. United Way Campaign, Portsmouth, 1989; advisor 4-H Club, Adams County, 1988—. Office: Wil-Car Enterprises Inc 10451 Old Gallia Pike Wheelersburg OH 45694

TAYLOR, TOBY TERET, sales representative, accountant; b. Bklyn., Apr. 16, 1945; d. Herbert and Judith (Shapiro) Friedman; m. Lester Norris Friedman, Nov. 1, 1962 (div. Nov. 1964); m. Steven Roy Teret, Sept. 15, 1968 (div. May 1974); children: George Friedman, Carrie Teret; m. Jeffrey Elliot Taylor, Oct. 1, 1988. BS in Acctg. magna cum laude, Bklyn. Coll., 1984. Adminstrv. supr. VA Hosp., N.Y.C., 1976-79; account exec. Crafton Graphic Co., N.Y.C., 1980-85, account mgr., 1985-86; sales rep. Penn Colour Graphics, N.Y.C., 1986-88; asst. sec., dir. sales adminstrn. Milocraft, Inc. (merger Crafton Graphics and Milo Press 1989), N.Y.C., 1988-90; ind. distbr. Nuskin, Internat., 1990—; mem. edn. com. Women In Prodn., 1982—; profl. singer. Mem. Am. Inst. Graphic Arts. Jewish. Home: 3395 Nostrand Ave Brooklyn NY 11229 Office: Grid Typographic Svcs Inc 124 W 24th St New York NY 10011

TAYLOR CLARK, ANDREA, educational consultant; b. Warrenton, Va., Nov. 5, 1952; d. Andrew Earl and Catherine (Dennis) Taylor. BS, Norfolk State U., 1974, MA, 1983; postgrad., Old Dominion U., 1975-76, 89. Profl. collegiate cert. in learning disabilities, mentally handicapped and emotionally handicapped. Classrm. tchr. Facquier County Sch. System, Warrenton, 1974-75; child devel. specialist, team leader Norfolk Pub. Schs., Norfolk, Va., 1976-82; ednl. diagnostician Norfolk Pub. Schs., 1982-87; ednl. cons. Va. State Dept. Edn., Norfolk, 1987—; v.p. DECAA Enterprises, Norfolk, 1983—. Mem. Lindenwood Civic League, Norfolk, 1st Bapt. Ch., Norfolk; troop leader Girl Scouts U.S.A., Norfolk, 1977-79. Named Dubutante, Norfolk Med. Soc. Aux., 1969. Mem. NAFE, NEA, Va. Edn. Assn., Norfolk Edn. Assn., Coun. Exceptional Children, Delta Sigma Theta. Democrat. Office: Tidewater Child Devel Clinic 401 A Colley Ave Norfolk VA 23507

TAYLOR-HUNT, MARY BERNIS BUCHANAN, educator, artist; b. Marion, Ind., Aug. 16, 1904; d. Walter Scott and Nora Elizabeth (Kinslear) B.; m. Robert Rush Taylor, Jan. 26, 1929 (dec. Mar. 1975); m. Ralph Van Nice Hunt, May 20, 1978; stepchildren: Penelope Clark, Diane Stockmar. AB in English, UCLA, 1926; MA in Drama, U. So. Calif., 1931. Tchr. speech and dramatics Los Angeles City Schs., 1929-44; vol. instr. Ikebana (Japanese Flower Arranging) Huntington Library, San Marino, Calif., 1957—,; produced Japanese Festival at Huntington Library, for Olympic Fine Arts Festival in L.A., 1984. represented in permanent collection at Japanese House in Japanese Garden at Huntington Library, 1957—. Recipient Gold Crown award Pasadena Arts Coun. Mem. L.A. Soc. Ikenobo (bd. dirs. 1987-88, 89), San Marino League (fine arts projects), Valley Hunt Club, Calif. Club. Republican. Mem. Christian Ch. Club: San Marino League (founding pres. 1954-55). Home: 1300 Sierra Madre Blvd San Marino CA 91108

TAYLOR-LITTLE, CAROL J(OYCE), state legislator, real estate agent; b. Berkeley, Calif., Aug. 13, 1941; d. Harold Robert and Marjorie Evelyn (Strawn) Hochmuth; m. Nicholas G. Kappas, Aug. 29, 1959 (div. Sept. 1980); children: Anthony N., Katherine M.; m. Donald L. Little, June 19, 1982. Student in real estate Red Rocks Community Coll., 1978; cert. degree adminstrn. non-profit agys. Met. State Coll., Denver, 1981, postgrad. in urban studies and polit. sci., 1981—. Lic. in real estate, Colo. Recreation instr. North Jefferson Recreational Dist. (Colo.), 1970-82; real estate sales agt. Crown Realty/Better Homes & Gardens, Arvada, Colo., 1979-88, Realty Ptnrs. Referral Network, Lakewood, Colo., 1989—; mem. Colo. Ho. of Reps., 1982-84, 84-86, 86-88, 88-90, House majority whip, 1984-86; chmn. House Majority caucus, 1988-90. Chairperson Med. Malpractice Task Force; vice chmn. Victims' Assistance Adv. Council; mem. Met. Air Quality Council. Named Legislator of Yr. Colo. Univ. Alumni Assn., 1988; Spl. Recognition Colo. Spl. Olympics, 1988, Colo. Bankers Assn., 1988; recipient Cert. Appreciation United Veterans Com., 1988, 90. Mem. Nat. Fedn. Ind. Bus., Colo. Adv. Small Bus., Nat. Conf. State Legislators's, Nat. Fedn. Rep. Women, Colo. Hist. Soc., Arvada C. of C. (bd. dirs.), Arvada Ctr. for Arts and Humanities. Office: Ho Reps State Capitol Denver CO 80203

TAYLOR-SMITH, CHEMINNE, writer, editor; b. Key West, Fla., Oct. 29, 1963; d. Carl Todd and Anne (Shelor) T.; m. Matthew Channing Smith, Oct. 24, 1987; 1 child, Aana Cheminne. BA, Winthrop Coll., 1985. News dir. Sta. WHEO, Stuart, Va., 1985-86; reporter The Enterprise, Stuart, 1985-86; freelance copywriter Fox Enterprises, Charlotte, N.C., 1986; with mgmt. Ivey's, Charlotte, N.C., 1986-88; mng. editor Programmer's Update, Boston, 1988-90; freelance writer, editor High Point, N.C., 1990—. Contbr. articles to prof. jours. Mem. AIDS Action Com., Boston, 1989-90; publicity chmn. Am. Heart Assn., Patrick County, Va., 1985. Mem. Mass. Press Assn., Patrick County C. of C. (bd. dir. 1985-86.), Alpha Epsilon Rho. Democrat. Home: 519 Nova Ave High Point NC 27260

TAYLOR WILLIAMS, TERESA KATHERINE, executive, financial consultant; b. Queens, N.Y., Feb. 5, 1957; d. Robert Lee and Sophie Estelle (Craft) Taylor; m. Eric Steven Williams, Sept. 14, 1953; 1 child, Justin Alexander. BA, CUNY, 1978, MA, 1982; MEd, Columbia U., 1986, EdD, 1988. Tchr., adminstr. N.Y.C. Bd. Edn., 1978-85; pres., chief exec. officer TTW Assocs., Inc., N.Y.C., 1984—; exec. dir. N.Y. Voice, Inc., N.Y.C., 1988—; cons. TTW Associates, Inc., N.Y.C., 1989—. Contbr. articles to profl. jours. Mem. Nat. Assn. Minority Doctors, Bus. and Profl. Women's Club, NAACP, Phi Delta Kappa. Office: TTW Assocs Inc 15 W 43rd St 20 New York NY 10036

TCHERKASSKY, MARIANNA ALEXSAVENA, ballerina; b. Glen Cove, N.Y., Oct. 28, 1952; d. Alexis and Lillian (Oka) T.; m. Terrence S. Orr. Student, Washington Sch. Ballet (scholar), 1965-67, Sch. Am. Ballet and Profl. Children's Sch., 1967-70; pupil of Edward Caton. Appeared with Bolshoi Ballet in Ballet Sch., 1961, 62, N.Y.C. Ballet in A Midsummer Night's Dream, 1963; profl. debut with Andre Eglevsky Ballet Co., 1968; mem., Am. Ballet Theatre, 1970—, soloist, 1972-76, prin. dancer, 1976—, guest appearances throughout U.S. and in Europe, also on TV; created lead female roles in Configurations, Grand Pas Romantique (Fernando Bujones), 2d female role in Push Comes to Shove (Twyla Tharp). Winner Nat. Soc. Arts and Letters competition, 1967; Ford Found. scholar, 1967-70. Office: care Am Ballet Theatre 890 Broadway New York NY 10003*

TEAFORD, JANE BROWN, state legislator; b. Hunter, Kans., July 1, 1935; d. Fred Welch and Antoinette Prendergast (Lawson) Brown; m. William John Teaford, Feb. 8, 1959; children: Sarah Ellen, Phillip Allen. BS, Kans. State U., 1957. Agt. home econs. Wabaunsee County Extension Council, Alma, Kans., 1957-59; library clk. Downers Grove (Ill.) Pub. Library, 1959-61, U. Ill. Library, Champaign, 1961-62; mem. Iowa Gen. Assembly, Des Moines, 1985—. Bd. dirs., v.p. LWV Iowa, 1973-79, pres., Des Moines, 1979-81, dir. Iowa caucus info. project, 1983-84; mem. Black Hawk County Bd. Social Welfare, Iowa, 1983-84, Profl. and Occupational Regulation Commn., Des Moines, 1983-86; mem. Midwestern Legis. Conf. of the Coun. State Govts., 1987—. Mem. NAACP (life). Democrat. Methodist. Home: 3913 Carlton Dr Cedar Falls IA 50613 Office: Iowa Ho Reps Des Moines IA 50319

TEAGLE, MADELINE LOUISE, learning products company executive, minister, researcher; b. Altoona, Pa., May 8, 1924; d. Phillip Norbert and Georgiana (Shadle) Pottsgrove; m. William James Teagle, Nov. 10, 1947; children: William II, Carol Ann, Susan Elizabeth, Sheryl Lynn, Roy Elan. DD, Life Science Sch., Rolling Meadows, Ill., 1970. Pres., founder Omono Sun Systems & Rsch. (formerly OM-ON-O Rsch.), Cuyahoga Falls, Ohio, 1977—, OMONO Enterprises, Cuyahoga Falls, 1986—; bd. dirs. Kindrid Spirits. Mem. Akron Regional Devel. Bd. Mem. Med. and Sci. Network, Noetic Scis., Life Extension Found., Spiritual Emergence, Psychotronics Assn. Home and Office: 548 Steeles Corners Rd Cuyahoga Falls OH 44223 Office: OM-ON-O Rsch/OMONO Enterprises 1640 Akron-Penninsula Rd Akron OH 44313

TEAGUE, RICHALYN ELAINE, school system administrator; b. Cleburne, Tex., Nov. 21, 1941; d. Richard F. and Dorothy (Allen) Johnston; m. William E. Houser, May 27, 1962 (dec. Mar. 1982); children: Bryan Allen, Barbara; m. Marvin O. Teague, July 2, 1988. BA in Biology, Edn., Baylor U., 1962; MS in Edn., Adminstn., Tex. So. U., 1977; postgrad., U. Houston, 1981. Tchr. English Manhattan (Kans.) Pub. Schs., 1962-63; tchr. biology Houston Pub. Schs., 1972-75, coordinator instructional sci., 1975-76, tchr. gifted and talented, 1976-79, cons. tchrs., 1979-81, adminstr. program, 1981-82; coordinator instructional dept. Magnet Schs., Houston, 1982-85, asst. prin., 1985-88; dean of instruction, fiscal policy specialist Tex. Edn. Agy., Austin, 1988—; cons. magnet schs. Washington D.C. Pub. Schs., 1984-85; bd. dirs. Local Close=Up Found., Washington 1982-86. Mem. Tex. Assn. Secondary Prins., Houston Assn. Sch. Adminstrs., Tex. Council Women Sch. Exec. Democrat. Home: 1122 Colorado #1409 Austin TX 78701 Office: 1701 N Congress Austin TX 78701

TEASCHNER, PATRICIA ANN, small business owner; b. Portland, Oreg., Jan. 13, 1943; d. Albert Ernest Puckett and Mary Elizabeth (Messer) Briggs; m. Gerald Albert Droste, Aug. 20, 1959 (div. 1975); 1 child, Diane Marie; m. Timothy Keene Teaschner, Jan. 18, 1986. Student, U. Kans., 1971, Coll. Cosmetology, Dodge City, Kans., 1972, Amarillo Coll., 1987. Owner, sec., bookkeeper Mid-Way Constrn. Co., Dodge City, 1964-68; sec. St. Rose of Lima Sch., Great Bend, Kans., 1969-70; hairdresser House of Beauty, Dodge City, 1972-73; dist. mgr. Greencrest Meml. Gardens, Dodge City, 1974, Twin Oaks Meml. Gardens, Corvallis, Oreg., 1974-75; ins. agt. Met. Life Ins., Albany, Oreg., 1975-76; prin. Pat's Bookkeeping Service, Dodge City, Amarillo, 1977—; tax preparer Mayfield-Rogers and Pendleton, Amarillo, Tex., 1985—. Author: From the Heart, 1975. Vol. Rep. Cen. Com., Amarillo, 1984, Pro Life, Amarillo, 1986—, Hope, Inc., Great Bend, Kans., 1969-70. Mem. Howell Extension Unit (pub. relations com. 1972-73), Am. Hairdressers Assn. (pub. relations com. 1972-73), Am. Bus. Womens Assn. (pub. relations com. 1975-76, pres. 1978-79), Cameo Club (pres. 1971-72), Womens Ministries, Caring Program. Mem. Trinity Fellowship Ch. Home: 3311 Winton Dr Amarillo TX 79121

TEASLEY, ANNA DELORES, corporate executive, engineer; b. Detroit, July 20, 1949; d. Pete Turner and Ruth Roberta Teasley. AS, Wayne County Community Coll., 1974; postgrad., Oakland U., 1976. Lic. engr., Mich. Water plant operator City of Detroit, 1977-79; power plant operator State of Mich., Pontiac, 1979-80; stationary engr. U.S. Postal Svc., Detroit, 1984; mech. maintenance specialist Mich. Consol. Gas Co., Detroit, 1983-88; bldg. engr. Detroit Bd. of Edn., 1980-90; pres. Home Search Insps., Inc., Detroit, 1987—. Contbr. articles to profl. jours. Mem. Nat. Polit. Congress Black Women, Detroit, 1988. Mem. Nat. Assn. Home Insps., Am. Soc. Home Insps., Am. Inst. Home Insps., Nat. Assn. Women Bus. Owners, Inc. (chair membership com. 1990), Nat. Polit. Congress Black Women, Profl. Women in Sales, Mich. Assn. Housing Ofcls. Office: Home Search Insps Inc PO Box 27132 Detroit MI 48227

TEBBITT, BARBARA VOLK, hospital administrator, nurse. BS in Nursing, Alverno Coll., 1966; MS in Med.and Surg. Nursing, U. Minn., 1970. Nursing supr. Oakes (N.D.) Community Hosp., 1966-67; gen. staff nurse U. Minn. Hosps., Mpls., 1967-70; nursing dir. Met. Med. Ctr., Mpls., 1970-71, dir. ambulatory and rehab. svcs., 1971-72, dir. med. nursing svcs., 1972-73, dir. ambulatory care and community health svcs., 1973-74; assoc. dir. nursing svcs. Meth. Hosp., St. Louis Park, Minn.; coord. consultation/edn. and nursing svcs. U. Minn. Hosps. and Clinic, Mpls., 1976-79, sr. assoc. dir., dir. nursing svcs., 1979—; Chairperson nurse exec. coun. Univ. Hosp. Consortium, Chgo., 1987-88, 88-89; bd. dirs., vice chairperson, chair Am. Jour. Nursing Co., N.Y.C., 1985—. Contbr. articles to profl. jours. Capt. USAFR, 1970-73. Mem. Am. Nurses Assn., Nat. League for Nursing, Am. Orgn. Nurse Execs. (bd. dirs. 1985-86, 86-89, mem. prog. com. 1983, mem. nursing edn. com. 1987), Minn. Nurses Assn., Minn. League for Nursing, Minn. Orgn. Nurse Execs. (mem. bylaws com. 1985-87, Moline recognition award 1986), Midwest Alliance in Nursing (past bd. dirs., chmn., past treas.), Minn. Hosp. Assn. (co-chairperson nursing edn. 1988-89, bd. trustees 1989—), Sigma Theta Tau (Zeta chpt.). Office: Minn U Hosp 420 Delaware St NE Minneapolis MN 55455

TEBEDO, MARY ANNE, state legislator; m. Don Tebedo. Former mem. Colo. Ho. of Reps.; now mem. Colo. Senate; profl. parliamentarian. Republican. *

TECCE, SUSAN MARILYN, forensic scientist; b. Holyoke, Mass., Mar. 6, 1961; d. Robert H. and Marilyn E. (Long) Tibbetts; m. Albert M. Tecce. BS in Biology, L.I. U., 1983; MS in Forensic Chemistry, Northeastern U., 1985. Intern in forensic sci. Westchester County, Valhalla, N.Y., 1984; forensic chemist K-Chem. Labs., Boston, 1985; asst. forensic scientist Westchester County Dept. Labs. and Research, Valhalla, 1986-88, forensic scientist, 1988—; lectr. Crime Scene Sch. FBI, Valhalla, 1987. Mem. Am. Acad. Forensic Scis., Northeastern Assn. Forensic Scis., Northeastern U. Justice Alumni Assn. Office: Westchester County Dept Labs and Research Grasslands Reservation Valhalla NY 10595

TEDESCO, KRISTINE J., benefits consultant; b. Jamaica, N.Y., Jan. 21, 1961; d. Ralph A. and Jeanette M. (Santacruce) T. BA in Math., Manhattanville Coll., 1983. Life and health ins. underwriter Met. Life Ins. Co., N.Y.C., 1983-85; asst. v.p. benefits Frank Crystal & Co., Inc., N.Y.C., 1985-89; benefits cons. Corroon and Black Co. of N.Y., N.Y.C., 1989—. Roman Catholic. Home: 300 E 40th St Apt 4F New York NY 10016 Office: Corroon & Black Co of NY 7 Hanover Sq New York NY 10004

TEDESCO, SHELBY ANN, transportation planner; b. Bristol, Conn., May 3, 1965; d. Frederick C. and Carol (Gallant) T. BS, Cornell U., 1987, M Regional Planning, 1989. Staff technician Peat Marwick Main & Co., Boston, 1987-88; transp. planner Sverdrup Corp., Boston, 1989, TAMS Consultants, Inc., Boston, 1990—. Organizer Cornell Career Fair Com., Boston, 1989-90. Mem. Cornell Club Boston, Sigma Delta Tau. Office: TAMS Consultants Inc 320 W Second St #204 South Boston MA 02127

TEDESCO, SUSAN MARY, pharmacy technician; b. Chgo., Sept. 22, 1954; d. Edmund L. and Viola M. (Cote) T. BA, U. St. Thomas, Houston, 1976. Cert. pharmacy technician, Ill. Pharmacy technician, IV specialist Children's Meml. Hosp., Chgo., 1978—; pres., cons. Aseptech, Inc., Chgo., 1989—. Mem. Am. Soc. Hosp. Pharmacists, Ill. Coun. Hosp. Pharmacists (rep. bd. dirs. 1984-88, President's award 1987, voting technician mem., bd. dirs. 1990—). Home: 2245 N Magnolia Chicago IL 60614 Office: Children's Meml Hosp 2300 Children's Pla Chicago IL 60614

TEED, C. CASON, author; b. Dallas, Mar. 9, 1941; d. Jack Charles and Gladys (Swope) Cason; m. William Banta, Feb. 19, 1971 (div. 1977); children: Bayard Swope and Bret Cason (twins); m. John E. Teed, 1978 (dec. 1979). B.A., Newcomb Coll., 1962; M.A., Middlebury Coll., 1963; postgrad. Sorbonne, Paris, 1964, U. Dijon (France), 1967, So. Meth. U., 1987—. Lectr. in langs. U. Houston, 1965-66, 79-82; tour guide Mus. Fine Arts, Houston, 1975-81; now freelance lang. writer. Author: Guidebook for American Bar Association; Walking Tour of Museum of Fine Arts, Houston, 1981; Conversational Spanish for Medical and Allied Health Personnel, 1983. Vol. translator Ben Taub Hosp., Houston, 1968-70. Govt. of Spain travel stipend, 1962. Mem. AAUP, Soc. Profl. Journalists, Kappa Kappa Gamma. Episcopalian. Home and Office: 3203 Drexel Dr Dallas TX 75205

TEEGEN, EVELYN IRENE HOOPES, diplomat; b. Muscatine, Iowa, Nov. 17, 1931; d. John Wendell and Laura Nevola (Kennedy) Hoopes; m. Richard Frank Teegen, Aug. 9, 1952; children: Susan Elaine, Martha Ellen Teegen Adolph. Student, Cornell Coll., Mt. Vernon, Iowa, 1949-50; BS, Iowa State U., 1953. V.p. Teegen & Assocs., Mpls., 1986-89; U.S. amb. to Fiji, Tuvalu, Tonga, Republic of Kiribati, 1989—. State vice chair Minn. Ind. Reps., 1975-80; mem. Rep. Nat. Com., Minn., 1980-89; bd. dirs. Minn. Citizens Coun. on Crime and Justice, Mpls., 1982-89; mem. Nat. Hwy. Safety Com., 1982-85; mem. 55 mile per hour study NAS, Washington, 1984-85; exec. dir. Minn. Seat Belt Coalition, Mpls., 1985-89. Recipient Outstanding Achievement award City of Edina (Minn.), 1989, Outstanding Achievement award Minn. Exec. Women in Travel, Mpls., 1989, Recognition of Svc. award Ind. Reps. of Minn., 1989. Mem. Philanthropic and Ednl. Orgn., Woman's Club (Mpls.), Pi Beta Phi Alumnae Club (pres. Mpls. chpt. 1971-73). Presbyterian. Home and Office: Am Embassy, 31 Loftus St, PO Box 218, Suva Fiji

TEEL, SANDRA LOUISE, health science facility administrator; b. Culbertson, Nebr., Feb. 28, 1944; d. Paul Vincent Moore and Mary Louise (Copley) Case; m. Willis Dale Teel, Dec. 6, 1969 (div. Apr. 1980); 1 child, Jeffrey Lynn. Student, St. Catherine Jr. Coll., 1962-65; BS, Sienna Coll., Memphis, 1967; postgrad., St. Joseph Hosp., Memphis, 1967. Lab. supr. Rosary Hosp., Campbellsville, Ky., 1967-68; lab. mgr. Phelps County Meml. Hosp., Holdrege, Nebr., 1968-70; med. technologist Santa Rosa (Calif.) Meml. Hosp., 1970-76; lab. mgr. Med. Sci. Lab., Santa Rosa, 1976-80; sect. head Cen. Oreg. Dist. Hosp., Redmond, 1980-83; tech. field svc. rep. Skonie Mktg. Bio-Dynamics, Oreg., 1982-83; lab. mgr. Mountain View Hosp., Madras, Oreg., 1983-86, Physicians Med. Ctr., McMinnville, Oreg., 1986—. Fin. v.p. Peewee Baseball League, Rohnert Park, 1979, treas. Cub Scouts Boy Scouts Am. Redmond coun., 1981. Mem. AAUW, Am. Soc. for Med. Technology, Am. Soc. Clin. Pathologists, Toastmasters, McMinnville Athletic Club. Democrat. Roman Catholic. Home: 1698 Shelton St McMinnville OR 97128

TEETER, MARTHA MARY, biophysical chemistry researcher, educator; b. Boston, Oct. 15, 1944; d. Charles Edwin and Lura May (Shaffner) T.; m. Curtiss Joel DuRand, Dec. 31, 1988. BA, Wellesley Coll., 1966; PhD, Pa. State U., 1973. Rsch. scientist Oil Additives Div. Rohm & Haas, Spring House, Pa., 1973-74; postdoctoral assoc. dept. biology MIT, Cambridge, Mass., 1974-76; postdoctoral assoc. in molecular structure Naval Rsch. Lab., Washington, 1976-77; vis. asst. prof. dept. chemistry Boston U., 1977-78, instr., 1978-80, rsch. asst. prof., 1980-86; assoc. prof. Boston Coll., Chestnut Hill, 1986—; cons. Data Commn. Internat. Union Crystallography, 1986—. Contbr. numerous articles to profl. jours. Rsch. grantee NSF, 1980—, Shared Instrument grantee, 1987—, rsch. grantee: prediction NIH, 1982—, Shared Instrument grantee, 1984-85, rsch. grantee: cloning, 1988—. Mem. Am. Chem. Soc., Macromolecule Group of Am. Crystallographic Assn. (chair 1990-91), U.S. Nat. Com. Crystallography (interdisciplinary affairs 1986—), Biophysical Soc. (coun. 1987-90, exec. com. 1988-90). Office: Boston Coll Dept Chemistry Chestnut Hill MA 02167

TEETERS, NANCY HAYS, economist; b. Marion, Ind., July 29, 1930; d. S. Edgar and Mabel (Drake) Hays; m. Robert Duane Teeters, June 7, 1952; children: Ann, James, John. A.B. in Econs., Oberlin Coll., 1952, LL.D. (hon.), 1979; M.A. in Econs., U. Mich., 1954, postgrad., 1956-57, LL.D. (hon.), 1983; LL.D. (hon.), Bates Coll., 1981, Mt. Holyoke Coll., 1983. Teaching fellow U. Mich., 1954-55, instr., 1956-57; instr. U. Md. Overseas, Germany, 1955-56; staff economist govt. fin. sect. Bd. Govs. of FRS, Washington, 1957-66; mem. bd. Bd. Govs. of FRS, 1978-84; economist (on loan) Coun. Econ. Advs., 1962-63; economist Bur. Budget, 1966-70; sr. fellow Brookings Instn., 1970-73; sr. specialist Congl. Rsch. Svc., Library of Congress, Washington, 1973-74; asst. dir., chief economist Ho. of Reps. Com. on the Budget, 1974-78; v.p., chief economist IBM, Armonk, N.Y., 1984-90. Author: (with others) Setting National Priorities: The 1972 Budget, 1971, Setting National Priorities: The 1973 Budget, 1972, Setting National Priorities: The 1974 Budget, 1973; contbr. articles to profl. pubs. Recipient Comfort Starr award in econs. Oberlin Coll., 1952; Disting. Alumnus award U. Mich., 1980. Mem. Nat. Economists Club (v.p. 1973-74, pres. 1974-75, chmn. bd. 1975-76, gov. 1976-79), Am. Econ. Assn. (com. on status of women 1975-78), Am. Fin. Assn. (dir. 1969-71). Democrat. Home: 243 Willowbrook Ave Stamford CT 06902

TEICH, THERESA MARIE, educator; b. Duluth, Minn., May 14, 1948; d. Kenneth William Teich and Charlotte Marie (Kouba) Hughes. BS in Home Econs., U. Minn., Duluth, 1971, BS in English, 1975; MS in Reading, U. Wis., Superior, 1979. Tchr. home econs. and English Ordean Jr. High Sch., Duluth, 1972-75, tchr. English and media, 1976-78; tchr. home econs. and English West Jr. High Sch., Duluth, 1975-76, tchr. remedial reading, 1978-80; tchr. devel. reading and English Lincoln Jr. High Sch., Duluth, 1980-82; tchr. English and journalism Washington Jr. High Sch., Duluth, 1982—; mem. reading com.Ind. Sch. Dist. 709, Duluth, 1983-87; freelance demonstrator. Author: Lake Superior Mag., 1980-83. Com. chmn. for tng. and community rsch., vol. Jr. League of Duluth, 1980-89. Mem. Duluth Pub. Library Minn. (trustee, bd. mem., pres. 1980—), AAUW (publicity and arrangements chmn. Duluth chpt. 1976-79), Minn. Home Econs. Assn. (dist. pres. 1977), Internat. Reading Assn., Nat. Coun. Tchrs. English, Keel Club (editor). Unitarian. Home: 1318 N 19th Ave East Duluth MN 55812

TEICHMAN, EVELYN, antiques appraiser, educator; b. N.Y.C., Mar. 13, 1929; d. Bernard and Minnie (Goldenberg) Mensch; m. Milton Teichman, Jan. 16, 1949; children: David, Jeb, Sondra. Student, CUNY, 1946-49. Tchr. Bergen County Adult Schs., N.J., 1976—; freelance appraiser Paramus, N.J., 1978—. Home: 56 Bush Pl Paramus NJ 07652

TEIXEIRA, CATHY ANN, corporate executive; b. East Hartford, Conn., Sept. 12, 1956; d. Joseph R. and Shirley (Landry) T. BA in Psychology, East Conn. State U., 1978; MS in Mgmt., Rensselaer Poly. Inst., 1983. Personnel generalist Conn. Transit, Hartford, 1978-82; supr. receiving J.C. Penney Catalog, Manchester, Conn., 1982-83, supr. inventory control, 1983-84; mgr. telephone sales ctr. J.C. Penney Telemktg., Manchester, 1985; mgr. mdse. fulfillment Avon Direct Response, Hampton, Va., 1985-86; mgr. order processing Avon Direct Response div., Hampton, 1986-87, mgr. customer service, telephone sales ctr., 1987-88; mgr. customer relations Chadwick's of Boston, Stoughton, Mass., 1988; dir. office ops. Rapidforms, Inc., Thorofare, N.J., 1988-90; dir. ops. Bedford Fair, Inc., Wilmington, N.C., 1990—. Mem. NAFE, Am. Mgmt. Assn., Internat. Customer Svc. Assn.

TEIXEIRA, MARYANN C., counseling administrator; b. Bessemer, Ala., Jan. 18, 1948; d. Howard Samuel and Vonceil Louise (Latham) Crowder; m. Milton James Teixeira; 1 child, Samuel James. BA, Avila Coll., 1976. Cert. addictions profl., alcohol and drug abuse counselor. Dir. The Salvation Army Childcare Facility, Lafayette, La., 1980-81; br. dir. LaPetite Acad., Ft. Worth, 1981-82; dir. oncology preschl. Cook's Childrens Hosp., Ft. Worth, 1982; adminstrv. asst. All Saints Hosp., Ft. Worth, 1982-83; ednl. specialist Tarrant Coun. on Alcohol and Drug Abuse, Ft. Worth, 1983-84; community svc. rep. Brookwood Recovery Ctr., Dallas, 1984-86, LaHacienda Treatment Ctr., Hunt, Tex., 1986; program mgr. LaHacienda Outpatient Svcs., San Antonio, 1986-87; owner, dir. LaNube Gris Counseling, San Antonio, 1987—; program mgr. Pinellas County chpt. Nat. Safety Coun., Clearwater, Fla., 1988-89; addictions specialist PCAS, Clearwater, Fla., 1989—. Author: Branching Out, 1984; editor: Lifting the Cloud of DUI, 1987. Mem. Alamo Area Coun. Govts., San Antonio, 1986-87, substance abuse comm., 1988; treas. Rep. Bus. Women Bexar County, San Antonio, 1988. Mem. Bus. and Profl. Women Internat., NAFE, Nat. Assn. Drug and Alcohol Counselors, Beta Sigma Phi (past pres., v.p., sec., Women of the Yr. award 1983). Republican. Roman Catholic. Home: 2051 Imperial Way Clearwater FL 34624 Office: Nat Safety Coun Pinellas County Chpt 2358 Sunset Point Rd Clearwater FL 34625

TELBAN, SHARON GRACE, nursing educator; b. Pittston, Pa., May 10, 1944; d. Joseph F. Telban and Grace (Love) Jones. BS in Nursing Edn., Wilkes Coll., Wilkes-Barre, Pa., 1969, MS in Edn., 1979; MS in Nursing, Pa. State U., University Park, 1980, postgrad. Cert. gerontologic nurse. Staff nurse Moses Taylor Hosp., Scranton, Pa., 1964-66, asst. head nurse, 1966-68; instr. Bryn Mawr (Pa.) Hosp. Sch. Nursing, 1969-74; instr., asst. prof. Wilkes Coll., Wilkes-Barre, Pa., 1974-87, assoc. prof., 1987—; dir. grad. program in nursing Wilkes U., Wilkes-Barre, 1988—; lectr. continuing edn. Pa. State U., University Park, 1985—; mem. task force older adult ministries Presbytery of Lackawanna, Scranton, Pa., 1989—; USPHS trainee, 1976, 78-79. Elder Presbyn. Ch., Moosic, Pa., 1979-85, 86-89. Mem. Pa. Nurses Assn. (pres. dist. 3 1986-88, dir. 1989—), Sigma Theta Tau (faculty advisor Zeta Psi chpt. 1989—, exec. com. 1989—), Phi Delta Kappa, Pi Lambda Theta. Presbyterian. Home: 1500 N Main St Moosic PA 18641 Office: Wilkes U Wilkes-Barre PA 18766

TELESHA, MEREDITH CAROL, employment specialist and training coordinator; b. Hershey, Pa., Oct. 24, 1948; d. Carl Eugene and Ada Kann (Wagner) Cope; m. Edward A. Telesha, Feb. 14, 1987. Cert., York Thompson Bus. Coll., 1967; student, Pa. State U., 1972, Elizabethtown Coll., 1978. Sec. Milton S. Hershey Med. Ctr. of Pa. State U., Hershey, 1967-74, pers. asst., 1975-80, employment specialist, 1980-81, employment specialist, training coordinator, 1981-87, employmnet specialist procedures analyst, 1987—; speaker at high schs., bus. schs.; conductor of in-house tng. programs. Mem. Bus. Adv. Com., Hershey, 1978—; sec. Employee Safety Com., Hershey, 1981—; mem. Com. for the Disabled, Hershey, 1986; cons. Right-to-Know Task force, Hershey, 1987—; mem. presdl. task force, 1980-86, Nat. Rep. Com., Pa. Rep. Com. Served with USAR, 1973-76. Recipient Problems of Democracy study award Am. Legion, 1965, Cert. of Merit Gov. of Pa., 1965. Mem. Leadership Found., U.S. Senatorial Club, Am. Bus. Women's Assn. (recording sec. 1979-80, 82-83, v.p. 1980-81, pres. 1981-82, treas. fall frolics 1982), Nat. Secs. Assn., Am. Soc. Personnel Amdminstrn. Lutheran. Lodges: Women's Auxillary to Elks, Order Rainbow. Home: 2267 E Harrisburg Pike Middletown PA 17057 Office: The Milton S Hershey Med Ctr PO Box 850 Hershey PA 17033

TELLEM, SUSAN MARY, public relations executive; b. N.Y.C, May 23, 1945; d. John F. and Rita C. (Lietz) Cain; divorced; children: Tori, John, Daniel. BS, Mt. St. Mary's Coll., L.A., 1967. Cert. pub. health nurse; RN. Pres. Tellem Pub. Rels. Agy., Marina del Rey, Calif., 1977-80, Rowland Grody Tellem, L.A., 1980-89, Tellem, Inc., Beverly Hills, Calif., 1990—; chmn. The Rowland Co., L.A., 1989-90; instr. UCLA Extension, 1983—; speaker numerous seminars and confs. on pub. rels. Editor: Sports Medicine for the '80's, Sports Medicine Digest, 1982-84. Bd. dirs. Marymount High Sch., 1984-87, pres., 1984-86; bd. dirs. L.A. Police Dept. Booster Assn., 1984-87; mem. Cath. Press Coun. Mem. Am. Soc. Hosp. Mktg. and Pub. Rels., Healthcare Mktg. and Pub. Rels. Assn., Pub. Rels. Soc. Am., L.A. Counselors (vice counselor). Roman Catholic. Club: Sports (L.A.). Office: Tellem Inc 270 N Canon Dr Ste 2039 Beverly Hills CA 90210

TELLER, BARBARA GORELY, curator, writer, consultant; b. Wellesley, Mass., Mar. 14, 1920; d. Charles Percival and Jean Niven (Watt) Gorely; m. Graham Prescott Teller, Dec. 14, 1950; children—Grafton, Diana, Christopher. B.A., Wellesley Coll., 1943, M.A. in Am. Social and Cultural History, 1944, postgrad., 1946. Registrar Soc. for Preservation New Eng. Antiquities, Boston, 1969-74, asst. to curator, 1970-74; dir., curator Wellesley Hist. Soc. Mus., 1983—; researcher, writer, cons. hist. socs., mus. on decorative arts exhbns., house mus. interior restoration projects; lectr. mus. seminars and forums, hist. socs., clubs, groups. Co-author: (with others): Domestic Pottery of the Northeastern United States, 1625-1850, 1985; contbr. articles on ceramics, other aspects of decorative arts in colonial, fed. periods of New Eng. to hist., antique jours. Mem. Soc. Am. Hist. Archaeology, Wellesley Career Assns., Am. Ceramic Circle, Wedgwood Soc. Boston (dir.), Nat. Trust Hist. Preservation, Nat. Mus. Women in Arts (charter), Mus. Nat. Heritage, Am. Assn. Mus.

TELLER, DAVIDA YOUNG, psychology, physiology and biophysics educator; b. Yonkers, N.Y., July 25, 1938; d. David Aidan and Jean Marvin (Sturges) Young; m. David Chambers Teller, June 18, 1960 (div. May 1986); children: Stephen, Sara. BA, Swarthmore Coll., 1960; PhD, U. Calif., Berkeley, 1965. Lectr., research prof. U. Wash., Seattle, 1965-69, asst. prof. psychology, physiology and biophysics, 1969-71, assoc. prof., 1971-74, prof., 1973—; rsch. affiliate Regional Primate Rsch. Ctr., Child Devel. & Mental Retardation Ctr.; mem. com. on vision Nat. Acad. Scis.-Nat. Rsch. Coun., 1971—, vision rsch. program com. Nat. Eye Inst. and NIH, 1973-76, visual scis. B study sect. NIH, 1981-85, chmn. 1983-85; U. Wash. appointments include chmn. Univ. Com. on Vision, 1971; mem. Univ. Coun. Women, 1971-76, Faculty Senate Spl. Com. Faculty Women, 1972-75, ad hoc com. Evaluation Dir. Black Studies Program, 1976, faculty adv. bd. Women Studies, 1980-82, ad hoc com. to search for Chmn. Psychology, 1981, standing com. Women Studies, 1982-83, faculty senate coun. Grants & Contract Rsch., 1985—, Univ. Acad. Coun., 1986—; dept. psychology appoints include Exec. Com., 1973-75, 77-79; chmn. Budget and Facilities Com., 1979-81; mem. ad hoc com. Staff Employment, 1982-83; honors advisor and dir. Honors Program, 1982—; mem. planning com. 1984-87. Mem. editorial bd. Infant Behavior and Development, 1981-85, Behavioral Brain Research, 1984-87, Vision Research, 1985—, Clinical Vision Sciences, 1986-87; contbr. numerous articles to profl. jours.; patentee in field. Recipient Sabbatical award James McKeen Cattell Fund, 1981-82. Fellow AAAS, Optical Soc. Am. (program com. vision 1986-88, vice chmn. vision tech. group 1986-87, chmn. 1988-89, tech. coun. 1988-89, Tillyer award 1987, dir.-at-large 1989—); mem. Assn. Rsch. Vision & Ophthalmology, Assn. Women Sci., Am. Acad. Ophthalmology (Glenn Fry award 1982). Office: U Wash Dept Psychology NI-25 Seattle WA 98195

TELLER, JUDITH L., management consultant; b. Phila., June 25, 1949; d. Oscar and Estelle (Simon) T.; m. David N. Kaye, Aug. 30, 1973. BS in Econs., U. Pa., 1971. Mgmt. analyst GSA, N.Y.C. and Boston, 1971-74; ptnr. Andersen Cons., N.Y.C., 1971—. Pres. 10 W. 66th Street Corp., N.Y.C., 1983-84. Office: Andersen Cons 1345 Ave of Americas New York NY 10105

TELLER, MARY MARGARET See STUDY, MARY MARGARET

TELLESBO, MARSHA LOUISE, business consultant; b. Mt. Vernon, Wash., Feb. 16, 1948; d. Alfred M. and Georgia M. (Waltner) T. BA, Seattle U., 1970, MBA, 1977; MS in Fin. Svcs., Am. Coll., 1985. Mem. ops. staff duPont Glore Forgan, Seattle, 1971-72; ops. mgr. duPont Glore Forgan, Paris, 1972-73; office mgr. Western Mgmt. and Investment, Seattle, 1973-77; prin., cons. Tellesbo & Co., Seattle, 1977—; vol., seminar presenter, Seattle area Small Bus. Adminstrn. Mem. Employee Benefit Planning Assn., MBA Alumni Com. Seattle U., Seattle C. of C. (bd. dirs. bus. action coun. 1988—, chmn. editorial bd. 1988—), Women's Bus. and Entrepreneurial Network, Women Bus. Owners, Rainier Club, Seattle Club. Republican. Home: 3612 W Fulton Ave W Seattle WA 98199 Office: Tellesbo & Co 999 3rd Ave Ste 4100 Seattle WA 98104

TELLIER, DIANE ANGELA, state official; b. Providence, Jan. 30, 1953; d. Donato Costanzo and Lucia Maria (Di Cicco) Del Mastro; m. Leslie Clayton Tellier, Nov. 18, 1972. AS, Community Coll. R.I., Warwick, 1986. Clk. R.I. Hosp. Trust Nat. Bank, Providence, 1970-7l; salesclk. Outlet Dept. Store, Providence, 1970-7l; sr. clk.-stenographer R.I. Dept. Human Svcs., Cranston, 197l-75; owner, operator Grist Mill Village Plant Shop, Seekonk, Mass., 1975-76; prin. clk.-stenographer R.I. Dept. Human Svcs., Cranston, 1976-77; exec. sec. div. drug control R.I. Dept. Health, Providence, 1977—; v.p., treas. Dew Rite Jewelry Co., Inc., Providence, 1974—; sec.-treas. Import Svc. Specialists R.I., West Warwick, 1984-85. Contbr. articles to profl. jours. Mem. Chief of Police Secs. Assn., Am. Rabbit Breeders Assn., Phi Theta Kappa. Roman Catholic. Home: 639 Oak Hill Rd North Kingstown RI 02852 Office: RI Dept Health Three Capitol Hill Rm 304 Providence RI 02908

TELLO, DONNA, accounting company executive; b. Annapolis, Md., Mar. 23, 1955; m. Gregory Tello, July 5, 1975 (div. 1978); m. Dennis R. Thompson, Apr. 1, 1987; children: Jesse Elliott Timothy Tello, Kimbrelle Shey Thommasson. Owner, tax strategist Tax Savers, San Diego, 1981—. Libertarian party candidate for state assembly, 1984. Mem. Internat. Platform Soc., Inland Soc. Tax. Cons. (sec. San Diego chpt. 1989—), Nat. Taxpayers Union, Nat. Assn. Enrolled Agts., Calif. Assn. Enrolled Agts., Mensa (columnist on taxes in monthly newsletter, treas. San Diego chpt. 1985-87), Camelopard Club (co-founder, treas. 1988—), Toastmasters (v.p. edn. Liberty chpt. 1987). Office: 4114 Adams Ave San Diego CA 92116

TEMA-LYN, LAURIE, management consultant; b. Bklyn., Mar. 25, 1951; d. Morton and Jeanne (Lite) Carlin; m. Chris Holley, May 13, 1984 (div. 1990). BA, Bklyn. Coll., 1972. Mgmt. supr. Rapp & Collins, Inc., N.Y.C., 1972-78, v.p., 1978-80; assoc. Synectics, Cambridge, Mass., 1980-83; founder, gen. ptnr. IdeaScope Assocs., Cambridge, 1983—; presenter European Conf. on Innovation and Creativity, 1987. Contbr. articles to bus. publs. Bd. dirs. Arica Inst., N.Y.C., 1979-80. Mem. Creative Problem Solving Inst. (presenter, leader), Am. Mktg. Assn., Direct Mktg. Assn. (presenter at industry meetings), Sharing a New Song. Office: IdeaScope Assocs 25 Mount Auburn St Cambridge MA 02138

TEMELKOFF, VONDA LEE, counselor, therapist; b. Sharon, Pa., July 12, 1937; d. Edward Hopkins and Alberta (Mae) Bakondy; m. Thomas B. Temelkoff, Nov. 10, 1956; children: Linda Temelkoff Schuller, Thomas C., Timothy B., Todd A. BS in Edn., Youngstown State U., 1970, MS in Edn., 1986; postgrad., Kent State U., 1981, Akron State U., 1981, Mt. St. Joseph, Cin., 1987, Bowling Green State U., 1989, Ashland Coll., 1990, Drake U., 1990. Cert. sch. counselor, Ohio, tchr., Ohio. Tchr. elem. Woodside Elem. Sch., Austintown, Ohio, 1971-84; tchr. Am. history Austintown Middle Sch., 1984-85; tchr. math. and sci. Frank Ohl Middle Sch., Austintown, 1986-87; guidance counselor five elem. schs. Austintown, 1987—; children's therapist Regional Assocs. in Counseling, Canfield, Ohio, 1989—; presenter parent workshop Austintown Elem. Sch., winter 1989; speaker Rotary and Kiwanis, 1987, 90, Rescue Mission/Canfield Presbyn. Ch., Youngstown, Ohio, 1989; resource person Davis Sch., Austintown, 1988-90; intern NEOUCOM Cancer Rsch. Ctr., Rootstown, summer 1986. Writer, producer (video) It's Your Choice, 1986. Participant NEORCA-Community Intervention, Youngstown, 1987, ONTASC-Tng., East Liverpool, Ohio, 1989; mem. panel, participant NEORCA-At Risk Kids, Youngstown, 1988; com. mem. St. John's Soup Kitchen, 1985-86. Youngstown State U. scholar, 1985-86. Mem. AACN, AAUW (bd. dirs. 1987, program v.p. 1988), NEA, Ohio Edn. Assn., Austintown Edn. Assn. (bldg. rep. 1978), Am. Assn. for Curriculum Devel., Ohio Assn. for Counseling and Devel., Internat. Reading Assn. (bd. dirs. membership com. 1989), Friends of Am. Art, Chi Sigma Iota, Delta Kappa Gamma Soc. Republican. Episcopalian. Home: 4454 Canfield Rd Canfield OH 44406

TEMKIN, MAIRLYN LISA, cardiologist, educator; b. Bklyn., June 8, 1954; d. Max Temkin and Sarah (Braun) T.; m. Mitcehll Coleman Pollack; 1 child, Stephanie Leigh. B.A., Johns Hopkins U., 1975; M.D., med. Coll. Pa., 1979. Diplomate Am. Bd. Internal Medicine. Intern internal medicine Nassau County Med. Ctr., East Meadow, N.Y., 1979-80; resident internal medicine, 1980-82; cardiology fellow, 1982-84; rsch. asst. Johns Hopkins U., Balt., 1973-74; clin. supr. SUNY-Stony Brook Med. Sch., 1981-82, clin. instr., 1986—; asst. dir. cardiology Brookhaven Meml. Hosp. Med. Ctr. Patchogue, N.Y., 1984-89; med. dir. cardiac rehab., 1987—. Mem. ACP, AMA, Am. Coll. Cardiology. Office: PO Box 2037 Setauket NY 11733-0704

TEMKIN, PENELOPE CATHERINE, English educator; b. Buffalo, Nov. 7, 1947; d. Edward C. and Sophia (Dzeizic) Carney; m. Ascher M. Temkin, May 31, 1964 (dec. Nov. 1982); children: Nicole Alanna, Alexei Primrose. BA in English and French summa cum laude, SUNY, Brockport, 1974; MA in English, U. Rochester, 1989, postgrad., 1987—. Artist mgr. Ascher M. Temkin, 1975-82; program dir. for internat. programs N.Y. Festival, Inc., Rochester, 1977-82, bd. dirs., 1977—; cons. mktg. dir., editor Rochester Women mag., 1983-85; instr. writing and lit. U. Rochester and Nazareth Coll., 1989—. Mem. MLA. Home: 30 Glen Ellyn Way Rochester NY 14618

TEMPEL, JEAN C., bank executive. Former sr. v.p. Conn. Bank & Trust, Hartford; now exec. v.p. Boston Safe Deposit & Trust Co. Office: Boston Safe Deposit & Trust Co 1 Boston Pl Boston MA 02106*

TENBRINK-WYNGARDEN, HELEN DOROTHEA, retired public health nursing educator; b. Ottawa County, Mich., Oct. 29, 1921; d. Eugene James and Ida (Dykstra) TenB.; m. Herman J. Wyngarden, Nov. 24, 1984 (dec. Nov. 1988); children: stepchildren: Nan Vosburg, Mary Ellen Haan, James. Diploma, Butterworth Sch. Nursing, Grand Rapids, Mich., 1945; BS in Pub. Health Nursing, U. Mich., 1952; MPH, U. N.C., 1969. RN, Conn., Mich. Staff nurse psychiat. unit Inst. of Living, Hartford, Conn., 1945-46; pub. health nurse Kalamazoo City-County Health Dept., 1948-50, Poonamalee Child Guidance Unit, Madras, India, 1952-59, Allegan County Health Dept., Allegan, Mich., 1960-62; instr. pediatrics Hagerstown (Md.) Hosp. Sch. Nursing, 1962-63; pub. health nurse cons. Wis. Dept. Pub. Health, Fond du Lac, 1963-67, WHO, New Delhi, 1970-78; asst. prof. U. Ark. Sch. Nursing, Little Rock, 1969-70; assoc. prof. pub. health nursing W.Va. Wesleyan Coll., Buckhannon, 1978-84; ret., 1984. Bd. dirs. Area Agy. on Aging, Tampa, Fla., 1985-88; elem. sch. vol. on teen parenting, Sebring, Fla. Mem. AAUW (pres. 1985-87), Federated Women's Club. Democrat. Presbyterian. Home: 207 Lakeview NE Apt 402 Sebring FL 33870

TENCZA, PATRICIA ANN, university admissions executive; b. Melrose Park, Ill., Nov. 20, 1962; d. Chester A. and Loretta A. (Materna) T. BS, Bradley U., Peoria, 1984. Mktg. cons. Gen. Investment & Devel., Peoria, Ill., 1984-85; mktg. rep. Salem Services, Inc., Skokie, Ill., 1985-86; Chgo. area admissions rep. St. Louis Coll. Pharmacy, 1986-88; admissions rep. Bradley U., Peoria, 1988—; collegiate province officer Sigma Kappa Sorority Indianapolis 1988-89. Mem. Nat'l Assoc. Coll. Admission Counselors , Ill. Assoc. Coll. Admission Counselors. Republican Party. Roman Catholic. Home: 23682 N Echo Lake Rd Lake Zurich IL 60047 Office: Bradley U 1501 W Bradley Ave Peoria IL 61625

TENEWITZ, MARYROSE CLARK, vision specialist; b. Wilkes-Barre, Pa., Sept. 7, 1952; d. George Daniel and Mary (Buttson) Clark; m. F. Edward Tenewitz, June 1975. AA, Palm Beach (Fla.) Jr. Coll., 1972; BSc., Fla. State U., 1974; MSc., U. Fla., 1978; student, Fla. Atlantic U., 1987. Tchr. of learning disabled Thomas Co. Schs., Thomasville, Ga., 1975-76; tchr. of physically impaired Putman Co. Schs., Palatka, Fla., 1976-78; vision cons. Berkeley Co. Schs., Moncks Corner, S.C., 1978-83; dress designer Boca Raton, Fla., 1983--; vision specialist Palm Beach Co. Schs., Fla., 1984-88, Marietta (Ga.) City Schs., 1988--. Author: Curriculum, Resource Guide for Tchrs. VI Students, 1983, Computers and Spl. Edn. 1986. Named Outstanding New Small Bus. C. of C. Palm Beach Bus. Women 1985. Mem. Coun. of Exceptional Children. Roman Catholic. Office: Dept Spl Svcs 353 Lemon St Marietta GA 30060

TEN EYCK, MARY ELIZABETH, pharmacist; b. Columbus, Jan. 17, 1953; d. Laurence Earl and Helen Elizabeth (Cunningham) Bidwell; m. Richard Clarence Januszewski, Sept. 28, 1975 (div. Nov. 1981); 1 child Cynthia Mary; m. Charles Leonard, May 14, 1983; 1 child Robert Charles. BS, U. Minn., 1976. Registered pharmacist. Pharmacist Northwestern Hosp., Mpls., 1976-77, Snyder Drug, Shakopee, Minn., 1977-88, Dahm Drug, Jordan, Minn., 1988-89, Relief Pharmacist, Inc., 1989—. mem. Am. Pharmaceutical Assn., Minn. Pharmaceutical Assn. Democrat. Presbyterian. Home: 1026 Jackson St Shakopee MN 55379

TENNANT, GERALDINE B., judge; b. Clarendon, Tex., Aug. 31, 1922; d. James D. and Josephine (Chamberlain) Browder; m. James P. Tennant, Dec. 28, 1952 (dec. 1962); children: James B., Lucile B., Josephine A. BA, Tex. Christian U., 1943; postgrad., So. Methodist U., 1946; JD, U. Tex.-Austin, 1949. Bar: Tex. 1949, U.S. Dist. Ct. (so. dist.) Tex. 1970, U.S. Ct. Appeals (5th cir.) 1970. Pvt. practice Ft. Worth, Houston, 1949-67; probate asst. to county judge Harris County, Houston, 1967-73, referee for juvenile cts., 1973-80; pvt. practice Houston, 1980-83; dist. judge State of Tex., Houston, 1983--. Contbr. to book: Desk Book for Juvenile Courts, 1980. Bd. dirs. YWCA, Houston, 1970, Mental Health Assn. Tex., Austin, 1980, LWV, Houston, 1967. Mem. ABA, Assn. Women Attys., Nat. Assn. Judges, State Bar Tex., Houston Bar Assn., Tex. State Bar Coll., Rotary. Democrat. Roman Catholic. Home: PO Box 130289 Houston TX 77219 Office: State of Tex Dist Judge Harris County Ct House Rm 600 Houston TX 77002

TENNANT, MARY JO, educator; b. Tacoma, Jan. 6, 1938; d. Glenn Everett and Adelia Maurine (Converse) Sigler; m. Charles Edward Tennant, June 27, 1959; children: Stephen Victor, Catherine J. Mc Guire, Susan M., William G. AB, Cornell U., 1959; MT, U. Ariz., 1976. Tchr. Yuma (Ariz.) Dist. 1, 1975-77, Children's Way Sch., Fairfax, Va., 1977-78, St. Michael Sch., Annandale, Va., 1978-84; substitute tchr. Conejo Valley Unified Dist., Thousand Oaks, Calif., 1985; tchr. English Newbury Park High Sch., 1986-87, Redwood Intermediate Sch., Thousand Oaks, 1987—, chmn. dept. English, 1989—; mem. secondary schs. com. Cornell U., Cornell Club of Washington, 1979-84, Cornell Club So. Calif., 1984—; v.p. sch. bd. Am. Sch. Vientiane, Laos, 1973-74, sec. sch. bd., 1972-73. Neighborhood chmn. Ariz. Cactus-Pine council Girl Scouts U.S., 1974-77, bd. dirs., 1976-77. Recipient Service award Lao Mil. Wives, 1974. Mem. NEA, Calif. Tchrs. Assn., Alpha Phi (dist. alumnae chmn. 1985-89). Republican. Roman Catholic. Avocations: reading, sewing, walking. Home: 1317 Breckford Ct Westlake Village CA 91361 Office: Redwood Intermediate Sch 233 W Gainsborough Rd Thousand Oaks CA 91360

TENNESSEN, CAROL, academic administrator; b. Milw., Nov. 2, 1938; d. Norman Lester and Jane Marie (Geittman) Schmeichel; m. William Lewis Tennessen, Dec. 29, 1962; children: Margaret Beth, Charles Sherwood, Kathryn Jane. BA, Depauw U., 1956-60; MA, U. Wis., 1976; PhD, U. Wisc., 1985. Tchr. Glendale (Wis.) Schs., Wauwatosa (Wis.) Schs., 1960-64; program coord. U. Wis., Milw., 1977—, acting dir., sr. adminstrv. program mgr. Ctr. for 20th Century Studies, 1989; dir. Study in Paris program, U. Wis., 1985. Judge art show, Wis. State Prison, photo shows, King Community Ctr., 1978—, mem. adv. bd. Martin Luther King Library, 1983, cons. Ko-Thi Dance Co., Milw., 1989; vice-chair Wis. Humanities Com., 1989, sec.-treas. 1987-88. Mem. Wis. Humanities Com. Office: Univ of Wis PO Box 413 Milwaukee WI 53201

TENNEY, DELLA WOOTEN, court reporter, writer; b. Chattanooga, May 5, 1930; d. Charles Madison Wooten and Belle (Davis) Knight; m. Gene William Ailor, Aug. 2, 1948 (div. May 1959); children—Linda Hughie, Sandra Barnwell, Angela Ailor; m. Frank Leonard Stilin, Feb. 21, 1964 (div. Apr. 1971); 1 child, Andrew; m. Edward Jewett Tenney, II, Feb. 17, 1983; stepchildren—Cyndra Fontaine, Edward B. II, Jill. Grad. Gregory Bus. Coll., Knoxville, Tenn., 1950-52; student U. S.C., 1958-59, Stenotype Inst., Jacksonville Beach, Fla., 1972-74, Lippert Sch. Ct. Reporting, Plainview, Tex., 1974. Cert. court reporter, Ga., Fla., Tenn., Guam, N.H. Former personal sec. to lt. gov. of Ga., Atlanta; legal sec. Witt-Gaither-Abernathy, Chattanooga, 1971-72; pres. Accurate Reporting Service, Chattanooga, 1975-78; dean, chief exec. officer The Stenotype Ctr., Chattanooga, 1978-79; ofcl. ct. reporter Guam Superior Ct., 1979-80, N.H. Superior Ct., Concord, 1980—. Author, editor, pub. Basic Stenotype Manual, 1979. Sec., Am. Cancer Soc., Aiken, S.C., 1952-53; campaign mgr. election com. for supt. edn., Aiken, 1954. Mem. N.H. Shorthand Reporters Assn. (sec., v.p.), Nat. Shorthand Reporters Assn., Nat. Assn. Female Execs. Republican. Roman Catholic. Club: Kaypro Users Group. Avocations: traveling; reading; book collecting; motorcycling; photography. Home: PO Box 322 River Rd Claremont NH 03743 Office: NH Superior Ct 163 N Main St Concord NH 03743

TENNIS, JANE SUZANNE, pharmacist; b. St. Louis, Nov. 10, 1948; d. Jack S. Tennis and Betty J. (Lukens) Baltmeskis; m. Harold E. Rose, Feb. 14, 1975 (div. Mar. 1978). BS in Pharmacy, St. Louis Coll. of Pharmacy, 1972. Pharmacist Mo. Baptist Hosp., St. Louis, 1972-75, IV room lead pharmacist, 1978-81; pharmacy mgr. Med-X Drug, Tulsa, 1975-78; IV room supr. Barnes Hosp., St. Louis, 1981-82; pharmacist St. Louis County Hosp., 1982-85; pharmacy supr. St. John's Regional Health Ctr., Springfield, Mo., 1985-89; dir. pharmacy Owen Healthcare, Houston, Tex., 1989—. Author: poster presentation, Unique Approach to UD Dispensing, 1988. Mem. Am. Soc. Hosp. Pharmacists, Mo. Soc. Hosp. Pharmacist (sec. 1983-85), Mo. Soc. Hosp. Pharmacist Rsch. and Edn. Found., (exec. dir. 1986—), Ozark Soc. Hosp. Pharmacists, Ronald McDonald House of the Ozarks. Democrat. Presbyterian. Home: 1732 W Spruce Olathe KS 66061

TENOFSKY-EALY, DEANNA V., lawyer; b. Keene, N.H., Sept. 13, 1956; Jack M. and Sheila A. (Horne) Tenofsky; m. Robert Tenofsky-Ealy, May 29, 1982. AB, Franklin and Marshall Coll., Lancaster, PA, 1978; JD, W. New England Coll., Sch. of Law, Springfield, MA, 1982; LL.M. in Taxation, John Marshall Law Sch., Chgo, IL, 1985. Tax analyst G.D. Searle, Skokie, IL, 1984-87; tax lawyer Kraft, Inc., Glenview, Ill., 1987-88; internat. tax atty. Motorola, Inc., Schaumburg, Ill., 1988—. Recipient of Excellence in Piano award, Nat. Piano Student's Guild, 1968-74; named to All-State Orch. as first chair flute, New Hampshire, 1971; recipient of Trustee Scholarship, Franklin and Marshall Coll., Lancaster, PA, 1975. Mem. ABA, 1983—, Chgo. Bar Assn., 1984—, Ill. Bar Assn., 1984—, Women's Bar Assn., 1986—, ABA Sect. Taxation and Com. on Gen. Income Tax Problems, 1987—, ABA's Spl. Task Force Com. on Rates and Credits, 1987—, Chgo. Tax Club, 1987—. Democrat. Jewish. Office: Kraft Inc Kraft Ct Tax Dept 4W Glenview IL 60025

TENOPYR, MARY LOUISE WELSH (MRS. JOSEPH TENOPYR), psychologist; b. Youngstown, Ohio, Oct. 18, 1929; d. Roy Henry and Olive (Donegan) Welsh; AB, Ohio U., 1951, MA, 1951; PhD, U. So. Calif., 1966; m. Joseph Tenopyr, Oct. 30, 1955. Psychometrist, Ohio U., Athens, 1951-52, also housemother Sigma Kappa; personnel technician to research psychologist USAF, 1953-55, Dayton, Ohio, 1952-53, Hempstead, N.Y.; indsl. research analyst to mgr. employee evaluation N.Am. Rockwell Corp., El Segundo, Calif., 1956-70; asso. prof. Calif. State Coll.-Los Angeles, 1966-70; assoc. research educationist UCLA, 1970-71; program dir. U.S. CSC, 1971-

72; dir. selection and testing AT&T, N.Y.C., 1972—; lectr. U. So. Calif., Los Angeles, 1967-70; vice chmn. research com. Tech. Adv. Com. on Testing, Fair Employment Practice Commn. Calif., 1966-70; adviser on testing Office Fed. Contract Compliance, U.S. Dept. Labor, Washington, 1967-73. Pres., ASPA Found., 1985-87; mem. Army Sci. Bd. Fellow Am. Psychol. Assn. (bd. profl. affairs, edn. and training bd., mem. council reps., pres. div. indsl. organizational psychology); mem. Eastern Psychol. Assn., Am. Soc. Personnel Adminstrn. (bd. dirs. 1984-87), Nat. Acad. Sci. (coms. on ability testing, math. and sci. edn., panel on secondary edn.), Soc. Indsl. and Organizational Psychology (Recipient Profl. Practices award 1984), Nat. Council Measurement in Edn., Psychometric Soc., Met. N.Y. Assn. Applied Psychology, Am. Ednl. Research Assn., Sigma Xi, Sigma Kappa, Psi Chi, Alpha Lambda Delta, Kappa Phi. Editorial bd. Jour. Applied Psychology, 1972-87, Journal Voctional Behavior; assoc. editor Am. Psychologist; contbr. chpts. to books and articles to profl. jours. Home: 557 Lyme Rock Rd Bridgewater NJ 08807 Office: One Speedwell Ave Morristown NJ 07960

TENORE, MARILYNN JOYCE, sales executive; b. Highland Park, Mich., Mar. 12, 1948; d. Morley Austin and Joyce Margaret (Griffiths) Winegarden; m. James Griffin, Mar. 17, 1974 (div. Mar. 1978); m. Arthur Phillip Tenore, Nov. 22, 1979;1 1 child, Phillip. Grad. high sch., Taylor, Mich.; student, Huntington (Ind.) Coll., 1965-66. Sales adminstr. Andrew Jergens Sugar Beet Products, Saginaw, Mich., 1975-78; mkt. mgr. Knapp King Size Corp., Brockton, Mass., 1978-80; office mgr. Mich. Indsl. Shoe, Detroit, 1980-83; telemktg. mgr. Epson Am., Southgate, Mich., 1983-87; sales rep. Entire Supply, Farmington Hills, Mich., 1987-88, Procomp Computers, Troy, Mich., 1988—. Mem. Altrusa Internat., Saginaw, Mich., 1976-78; vol. Big Sisters Am., Brockton, Mass., 1978-79; worker Dem. candidates, Taylor, Mich., 1988-89; Cub scout den leader Boy Scouts Am., Taylor, 1988-89; mem. exec. com. H.A.N.D.S., Inc., Detroit. Named Vol. of Yr., Big Sisters Am., 1978. Episcopalian. Office: Procomp Computer 72 W Maple Troy MI 48084

TENUTA, JEAN LOUISE, sports reporter, medical technologist; b. Kenosha, Wis., Apr. 12, 1958; d. Fred and Lucy Ann (Taylor) Tenuta; m. Robert Lewis Bennett, Nov. 22, 1989. BS in Biology, U.Wis., 1979; BA in Journalism, Marquette U., 1983; MS in Print Journalism, Northwestern U., 1989. Sports reporter Kenosha News, 1978-84, Washington Post, 1984-86, Jour. Messenger, Manassas, Va., 1986, Jour. Times, Racine, Wis., 1988-89; med. technologist St. Therese Med. Ctr., Waukegan, Ill., 1980-83, 86-87, Suburban Hosp., Bethesda, Md., 1985-86, Group Health Assn., Washington, 1985-86, St. Francis Hosp., Milw., 1988-89; sports reporter Jour.-Gazette, Ft. Wayne, Ind., 1989—. Recipient 1st place in sports writing Capital Press Women, 1986, 87, Women's Press Club. of Ind., 1990. Mem. Assn. Women in Sports Media (midwest region coord. 1990-91), Nat. Fedn. Press Women (treas. 1985-87, 1st place in sports writing 1986), Soc. Profl. Journalists, Women in Communications (v.p., sec., Milw. chpt.), Nat. Writers Club. Democrat. Home: 5203 Coventry Pkwy Fort Wayne IN 46804 Office: Ft Wayne Jour-Gazette 600 W Main St PO Box 88 Fort Wayne IN 46801-0088

TEPOEL, DONNA LEE FULLER, former education educator; b. Lewiston, Maine, Aug. 6, 1942; d. Francis Robinson and Gertrude Louise (Keene) Fuller; m. William Gagne, June 25, 1966 (div. 1972); m. Louis Dean TePoel, July 4, 1974; children: Jamie Lee, Sarah Louise. BS in Edn., Farmington State Coll., 1964; MA, U. Colo., 1973; EdD, U. No. Colo., 1980. Tchr. Westbrook (Maine) Sch. Dist., 1964-72, right to read dir., 1973-74; reading specialist Manning Jr. High Sch., Jefferson County, Colo., 1974-78; instr. Casper (Wyo.) Coll., 1978-79; instr. for extension classes U. Wyo, Gillette, 1982-83; asst. prof. edn. U. Mary, Bismarck, N.D., 1985-88; mem. consortium, rep. from Westbrook, New Eng. Consortium for Right to Read, 1973-74; presenter, staff Devel. Workshops, Greeley, Colo. Mem. Internat. Reading Assn., Delta Kappa Gamma, Phi Delta Kappa (life, membership chmn. 1986-88). Mem. United Ch. of Christ. Home: 136 Ella Peery Addn Tazewell VA 24651

TEPPER, LISA DICKSON, management professional; b. Davis, Calif., Oct. 6, 1960; d. Herbert Bernard and Antoinette (Petrusa) T. BA, Syracuse U., 1983; postgrad., Monterey Inst. Internat. Studies, 1984-85. Licensed Pvt. Sch. Agent, N.Y. Admissions rep. The Stratford Sch., Syracuse, N.Y., 1985-88, dir. admissions, 1988—. Dance scholarship The Joffrey Sch. Dance, N.Y.C. 1977-78. Mem. NAFE. Democrat. Roman Catholic. Home: 204 Gilbert Ave Syracuse NY 13208 Office: The Stratford Sch 2301 James St Syracuse NY 13206

TEPPER, NANCY BOXLEY, lawyer; b. Richmond, Va., Mar. 7, 1933; d. Joseph Harry and Mathilda (Appell) Boxley; children: Amanda, Nicholas, Eliza. Student, U. Richmond, 1951; BA, Radcliffe Coll., 1953; LLB, Harvard U., 1958. Bar: N.Y. 1958, Calif., 1969. Assoc. Simpson, Thacher & Bartlett, N.Y.C., 1958-63, Robertson, Howser & Garland, Laguna Hills, Calif., 1969-70, Kindel & Anderson, Laguna Hills, 1970-77; freelance legal editor, writer Prentice-Hall, Inc., Englewood, N.J., 1963-69; pres. Nancy Boxley Tepper, Inc., Laguna Hills, 1977—; instr. U. Calif., Irvine, 1971-72. Contbr. articles to legal publs. Endowment counsel Orange County Ctr. for Performing Arts, Costa Mesa, Calif., 1985—; mem. fund raising com. Saddleback Hosp., Laguna Hills, 1989. Mem. ABA, Calif. Bar Assn., Orange County Bar Assn., Orange County Estate Planning Coun., Harvard Club (Santa Ana, Calif., bd. dirs. 1970-72), Phi Beta Kappa. Office: 24031 El Toro Rd Ste 130 Laguna Hills CA 92653

TERBORG-PENN, ROSALYN MARIAN, historian, educator; b. Bklyn., Oct. 22, 1941; d. Jacques Arnold Sr. and Jeanne (Van Horn) Terborg; 1 dau., Jeanna Penn. B.A. in History, Queens Coll., CUNY, 1963; M.A. in History, George Washington U., 1967; Ph.D. in Afro-Am. History, Howard U., 1978. Day care tchr. Friendship House Assn., Washington, 1964-66; program dir. Southwest House Assn., Washington, 1966-69; adj. prof. U. Md.-Balt. County, Catonsville, 1977-78, Howard Community Coll., Columbia, Md., 1970-74; prof. history Morgan State U., Balt., 1969—, project dir. oral history project, 1978-79, coord. grad. programs in history, 1986—; project dir. Assn. Black Women Hist. Research Conf., Washington, 1982-83. Author: (with Thomas Holt and Cassandra Smith-Parker) A Special Mission: the Story of Freedmen's Hospital, 1862-1962, 1975. Editor (with Sharon Harley) The Afro-American Woman: Struggles and Images, 1978, 81; (with Sharon Harley and Andrea Benton Rushing) Women in Africa and The African Diaspora, 1987. History editor Feminist Studies, 1984-89; mem. editorial bd. Md. Hist. Mag., 1988—. Founding mem. Howard County Commn. for Women. Ford Found. fellow, 1980-81, Smithsonian Instn. fellow, 1982; Howard U. grad. fellow in history, 1973-74, recipient Rayford W. Logan Grad. Essay award Howard U., 1973. Mem. Assn. Black Women Historians (co-founder, 1st nat. dir. 1980-82, nat. treas. 1982-84, cert. outstanding achievement 1981), Am. Hist. Assn. (mem. com. on women historians 1978-81), Orgn. Am. Historians (mem. black women's history project adv. com. 1980-81), Alpha Kappa Alpha. Office: Morgan State U Baltimore MD 21239

TERHAAR, ANN, food, hotel and tourism management educator; b. N.Y.C.; d. John Sullivan and Ada Conrad; children: Susan, Kevin, Mark, Laura. BS, Hunter Coll.; MS, Kans. State U.; MS in Edn., SUNY, Brockport. Mem. faculty NW Mo. State Coll., Maryville; assoc. prof. food, hotel and tourism mgmt. Monroe Community Coll., Rochester, N.Y. Mem. Am. Dietetics Assn., Am. Home Econs. Assn., Nat. Restaurant Assn. (registered food svc. mgr.). Home: 10 LacKine Dr Rochester NY 14618 Office: Monroe Community Coll 1000 E Henrietta Rd Rochester NY 14623

TERNBERG, JESSIE LAMOIN, pediatric surgeon; b. Corning, Calif., May 28, 1924; d. Eric G. and Alta M. (Jones) T. A.B., Grinnell Coll., 1946, Sc.D. (hon.), 1972; Ph.D., U. Tex., 1950; M.D., Washington U., St. Louis, 1953; Sc.D. (hon.), U. Mo., St. Louis, 1981. Diplomate: Am. Bd. Surgery. Intern Boston City Hosp., 1953-54; asst. resident in surgery Barnes Hosp., St. Louis, 1954-57; resident in surgery Barnes Hosp., 1958-59; research fellow Washington U. (Sch. Medicine), 1957-58; practice medicine specializing in pediatric surgery St. Louis, 1966—; instr., trainee in surgery Washington U., 1959-62, asst. prof. surgery, 1962-65, assoc. prof., 1965-71, prof. surgery in pediatrics, 1975—, prof. surgery, 1971—, chief div. pediatric surgery, 1972—; mem. staff Barnes Hosp., pediatric surgeon in chief, 1974—, mem. operating room com., 1971—, mem. med. adv. com., 1975—; mem. staff Children's Hosp., dir. pediatric surgery, 1972—. Contbr. numerous articles on pediatric surgery to profl. jours. Recipient Alumni award Grinnell Coll., 1966. Fellow A.C.S.; mem. Am. Pediatric Surg. Assn., Western Surg. Assn., St. Louis Med. Assn., Soc. Surgery of the Alimentary Tract, Am. Acad. Pediatrics, Soc. Pelvic Surgeons, AAAS, Brit. Assn. Paediatric Surgeons, Mo. State Surg. Soc., St. Louis Surg. Soc. (pres. 1980-81), St. Louis Pediatric Soc., Soc. Surgical Oncology, St. Louis Childrens Hosp. Soc. (v.p. 1977-78, pres. 1979-80), Barnes Hosp. Soc., Sigma Xi, Phi Beta Kappa, Iota Sigma Pi, Alpha Omega Alpha. Office: St Louis Childrens Hosp 400 S Kingshighway Ste 5W12 Saint Louis MO 63110

TERNULLO, KAREN MARIE, software engineer; b. Stoughton, Mass., June 26, 1965; d. Daniel and Janet Marie (Ramsdell) Sheehan; m. James Ternullo, June 16, 1990. BSEE, U. Lowell, 1987. Programmer Digital Equipment Corp., Marlboro, Mass., 1984; technician Prime Computer, Inc., Framingham, Mass., 1985-86; programmer Prime Computer Inc., Framingham, 1986-87; hardware engr. Digital Equipment Corp., Maynard, Mass., 1987-88; software engr. Digital Equipment Corp., Maynard, 1988—. Fellow Tau Beta Pi, Eta Kappa Nu. Roman Catholic.

TERPELUK, DIANE GUGLIELMINO, government official; b. Glendale, Calif., Dec. 22, 1957; d. Donald and Flora Augusta (Nau) Guglielmino; m. Peter Terpeluk Jr., Nov. 29, 1986; 1 stepchild, Meredith. BA in Polit. Sci., U. So. Calif., 1980. Staff asst. to Senator Robert Kasten, Washington, 1981-82; confidential asst. to adminstr. SBA, Washington, 1982-83; exec. asst. to conv. mgr. 1984 Rep. Nat. Conv., Washington and Dallas, 1983-84; exec. asst. to chmn. 1985 Presdl. Inaugural, Washington, 1984-85; spl. asst. to Vice-Pres. Bush Washington, 1985-89; dir. Office of Bus. Liaison Dept. Commerce, Washington, 1989—. Mem. Jr. League Washington. Republican. Roman Catholic. Home: 4374 Westover Pl NW Washington DC 20016 Office: US Dept Commerce Bus Liaison 14th & Constitution Ave NW Rm H-5898C Washington DC 20230

TERPENING, VIRGINIA ANN, artist; b. Lewistown, Mo., July 17, 1917; d. Floyd Raymond and Bertha Edda (Rodifer) Shoup; m. Charles W. Terpening, July 5, 1951; 1 child by previous marriage, V'Ann Baltzelle Dlatrick. Studies with William Woods, Fulton, Mo., 1936-37; student Washington U. Sch. Fine Arts, St. Louis, 1937-40. Exhibited in one-woman shows at Culver-Stockton Coll., Canton, Mo., 1956, Creative Gallery, N.Y.C., 1968, The Breakers, Palm Beach, Fla., 1976; others; exhibited in group shows Mo. Ann., City Art Mus., St. Louis, 1956, 65, Madison Gallery, N.Y.C., 1960; Ligoa Duncan Gallery, N.Y.C., 1964, 78, Two Flags Festival of Art, Douglas, Ariz., 1975, 78-79, Internat. Art Exhibit, El Centro, Calif., 1977, 78, Salon des Nations, Paris, 1985, UN World Conference of Women, Narobi, Kenya, 1985; represented in permanent collection Nat. Mus. Women in Art; lectr. on art; jurist for selection of art for exhibits Labelle (Mo.) Centennial, 1972; chmn. Centennial Art Show, Lewiston, 1971, Bicenntenial, 1976; dir. exhibit high sch. students for N.E. Mo. State U., 1974; supt. ann. art show Lewis County (Mo.) Fair; executed Mississippi RiverBoat, oil painting presented to Pres. Carter by Lewis County Dem. Com., Canton, 1979. Mem. Lewistown Bicentennial Hist. Soc.; charter mem. Canton Area Arts Coun. N.E. Mo. Recipient cert. of merit Latham Found., 1960-63, Mo. Women's Festival Art, 1974, Bertrand Russell Peace Found., 1973, Gold Medallion award Two Flags Festival Art, 1975, Safeco purchase award El Centro (Calif.) Internat. Art exhibit, 1977; 1st pl. award LaJunta (Colo.) Fine Arts League, 1981; diploma Universita Delle Arti, Parma, Italy, 1981; Purchase award Two Flags Art Festival, 1981; award Assn. Conservation and Mo. Dept. Conservation Art Exhbt., 1982; paintings selected for Competition '84 Guide by Nat. Art Appreciation Soc., 1984; 1st pl. award New Orlean Internat. Art Exhibit, 1984, with Am. Women Artists at United Nations Conf. on Women, Nairobi, Kenya, 1985, Two Flags Festival of Art, 1986; named artist laureate, Nepenthe Mondi Soc., 1984, cert. on Arts for the Parks Nat., 1987. Mem. Artist Equity Assn., Inc., Internat. Soc. Artists, Internat. Platform Assn., Nat. Mus. Women in Art (charter), Canton Area Art Coun., Animal Protection Inst. Mem. Disciples of Christ Ch.

TERRANA, JUDITH ANNE HAHN, air traffic manager; b. Braddock, Pa., Dec. 7, 1942; d. Gustava J. and Gesine Eva (Mower) Hahn; m. Charles Joseph Terrana, July 31, 1976. Student, Marietta Coll., Elizabethtown Coll. Air traffic control specialist ea. regional office FAA, Jamaica, N.Y., tng. specialist ea. regional office; area supr. FAA, Dubois, Pa.; air traffic mgr. FAA, Parkersburg, W.Va. Recipient Pres.'s award for excellence Profl. Women Controllers. Mem. Profl. Women Controllers (past pres., past bd. dirs.), Air Traffic Control Assn. (Tech. Writing award), NAFE. Home: 201 Woodlawn Ave Martinsburg PA 16662 Office: FAA Altoona FSS Blair County Airport Martinsburg PA 16662

TERRANOVA, TERESE-MARIE CHRISTINE, optician; b. Buffalo, May 13, 1958; d. Carmelo John and Marie Elizabeth (Sinaguglia) T. Student, Canisius Coll., 1976-79; A.A.S. with honors, Erie Community Coll., Buffalo, 1981. Registered spectacle lens dispenser, contact lens dispenser, Calif.; cert. optician Am. Bd. Opticianry; cert. ophthalmic dispenser N.Y. State Bd. Regents. Mgr. Michael's Optical, E. Aurora, N.Y., 1981-82; mgr. U.S. Vision, Buffalo, 1982-83; ophthalmic dispenser Site for Sore Eyes Opticians, Oakland, Calif., 1983-84; contact lens fitter Site for Sore Eyes Opticians, Daly City, Calif., 1984-87; asst. mgr. Site for Sore Eyes Opticians, 1987-89, mgr., 1989; ophthalmic dispenser/contact lens fitter Kaiser Permanente-San Francisco Optical Sales, 1989—. Fellow Nat. Acad. Opticianry; mem. Bay Area Career Women. Democrat.

TERRAS, AUDREY ANNE, mathematics educator; b. Washington, Sept. 10, 1942; d. Stephen Decatur and Maude Mae (Murphy) Bowdoin. B.S. with high honors in Math., U. Md., 1964; M.A., Yale U, 1966, Ph.D., 1970. Instr. U. Ill., Urbana, 1968-70; asst. prof. U. P.R., Mayaguez, 1970-71; asst. prof. Bklyn. Coll., CUNY, 1971-72; asst. prof. math. U. Calif.-San Diego, La Jolla, 1972-76, assoc. prof., 1976-83, prof., 1983—, vis. positions MIT, fall 1977, 83, U. Bonn (W.Ger.), spring 1977, Inst. Mittag-Leffler, Stockholm, winter, 1978. Inst. for Advanced Study, spring 1984; dir. West Coast Number Theory Conf., U. Calif.-San Diego, 1976, AMS joint summer research conf., 1984; lectr. in field. Author: Harmonic Analysis on Symmetric Spaces and Applications, Vol. I, 1985, Vol. II, 1988; assoc. editor Trans. Am. Math. Soc. Contbr. articles and chpts. to profl. publs. Woodrow Wilson fellow, 1964; NSF fellow, 1964-68; NSF grantee Summer Inst. in Number Theory, Ann Arbor, Mich., 1973; prin. investigator NSF, 1974-88. Fellow AAAS; mem. AAAS (nominating com. math. sect.), Am. Math. Soc. (com. employment and ednl. policy com. on coms., council, transactions editor), Math. Assn. Am. (program com. for nat. meeting 1989-90), Soc. Indsl. and Applied Math., Assn. for Women in Math., Assn. for Women in Sci. Research in harmonic analysis on symmetric spaces and number theory. Office: U Calif San Diego Dept Math C-012 La Jolla CA 92093

TERREBONNE, ANNIE MARIE, medical technologist, educator; b. Isola, Miss., Mar. 17, 1932; d. Tommy and Alpha (Whitfield) Patterson; m. Frank Paul Terrebonne, May 7, 1960. A.A., Co-Lin Jr. Coll., 1950; B.S., Miss. State U., 1952; grad. Knoxville Gen. Hosp. Sch. Med. Tech., 1953. Cert. Nat. Cert. Agy. Med. Lab. Personnel. Med., x-ray and EKG technician Layman-Saffold Clinic, Knoxville, Tenn., 1952-55; med. technologist in bacteriology St. Dominic's Hosp., Jackson, Miss., 1956-58; parasitologist Oschner's Clinic and Hosp., New Orleans, 1959-65; sr. med. technologist II spl. hematology dept. U. Tex. Med. Br., Galveston, 1969—, mem. research and devel. staff, 1974—, instr. med. tech. students, 1981-86, instr. med. students, residents, and hematology fellows, 1987—. Contbr. articles to profl. jours. Mem. Am. Assn. Med. Technologists, Galveston Dist. Soc. Med. Technologists, Tex. Soc. Med. Technologists, Am. Soc. Clin. Pathologists (cert.), Miss. State U. Alumni Assn. Democrat. Methodist. Clubs: Loyalty, Found. for Christian Living, Bayou Vista Recreation, Positive Thinkers'. Lodge: Order of Eastern Star, Grand 1984 Opera House. Home: 353 Ling Dr Hitchcock TX 77563 Office: U Tex Med Br Spl Hematology Dept 425 Clin Sci Bldg 300 University Blvd Galveston TX 77550

TERRELL, ANNTOINETTE YVONNE, pharmaceutical sales representative; b. San Leandro, Calif., Apr. 3, 1963; d. Cleo Visor Dunn; 1 child, Darnell Terrell-Fryer. BS, Calif. State U., 1985, postgrad, 1985—. Cert. loan rep. Teller Wells Fargo Bank N.A., Hayward, Calif., 1980-85; banking svcs. rep. II Wells Fargo Bank N.A., Union City, Calif., 1985-87; banking svcs. officer Wells Fargo Bank N.A., San Ramon, Calif., 1987-89; ter. sales rep., credit lender Summit Pharms., Walnut Creek, Calif., 1989—. Mem. NAFE. Democrat. Home and Office: Summit Pharms 3868 Oakes Dr Hayward CA 94542

TERRERI, MALINDA ANN, television producer; b. Columbus, Ohio, Aug. 28, 1964; d. David H. and Ann (Farley) Ferry; m. Michael John Terreri, Oct. 1, 1988. BSBA, Northeast Mo. State U., 1986. Fin. cons. Merrill Lynch Pierce Fenner & Smith, St. Louis, 1986-88; prin., producer Preview of Homes, Lancaster, Pa., 1988—. Contbr. articles to profl. jours. Active Citizens Against Crime, St. Louis, 1984-88, Mo. Taxpayers Watchdog Assn., 1988, Pa.'s Campaign for Choice, 1990; asst. dir. fundraising Shelter for Abused Women, Pa., 1989. Named Young Entrepreneur of 1985 Mentors of Mo., 1985; recipient Achievement award Citizens Against Crime, 1987, Golden Triangle award Women in Broadcasting, 1990. Mem. NOW, Female Exec. Mgmt. Assn., Lancaster C. of C. (co-chmn. membership 1990—), Am. Bus. Women's Assn. (treas. 1989), Sertoma. Office: Preview of Homes 1935 Fruitville Pike Ste 115 Lancaster PA 17601

TERRIS, LILLIAN DICK, psychologist, association executive; b. Bloomfield, N.J., May 5, 1914; d. Alexander Blaikie and Herminia (Doscher) Dick; BA, Barnard Coll., 1935; PhD, Columbia U., 1941; m. Louis Long, Apr. 22, 1935 (dec. Sept. 1968), 1 son, Alexander Blaikie Long; m. Milton Terris, Feb. 6, 1971. Instr. psychology Sara Lawrence Coll., Bronxville, N.Y., 1937-40; jr. pers. tech. SSA, Washington, 1941; sr. pers. clk. OWI, N.Y.C., 1941-43; dir. profl. examination svc. Am. Pub. Health Assn., N.Y.C., 1943-70, pres., 1970-79, pres. emeritus, 1979—. Assoc. editor Jour. Pub. Health Policy, 1979—. Bd. dirs. Profl. Exam. Svc., 1979—; chair bd. Vis. Nurse Assn. Chittenden County, Vt., 1989. Recipient Nat. Environ. Health Assn. award, 1976, Cert. of Svc. award Am. Bd. Preventive Medicine, 1979. Diplomate Am. Bd. Examiners in Profl. Psychology. Fellow Am. Psychol. Assn.; mem. Am. Pub. Health Assn., N.Y. State Psychol. Assn., Am. Coll. Hosp. Adminstrs. (hon. fellow), Phi Beta Kappa, Sigma Xi. Contbr. articles in field to profl. jours. Home: 208 Meadowood Dr South Burlington VT 05403 Office: 475 Riverside Dr New York NY 10027

TERRONE, MARIA, college administrator; b. N.Y.C., May 21, 1951; d. Dalio Dominick and Concetta (Malvagna) Rotondi; m. William Michael Terrone, June 26, 1971. BA in English, Fordham U., Bronx, N.Y., 1972. Editorial asst. to commr. N.Y.C. Dept. Mental Health, 1972-73; staff writer N.Y.C. Dept. Social Svcs., 1973-74; asst. to pres. Peabody Orgn. Devel., N.Y.C., 1974-76; sr. editor I-Am Mag., N.Y.C., 1976-78; publs. editor Clairol Inc., N.Y.C., 1979-82; exec. editor Attehzione Mag., N.Y.C., 1982-83; editor Grey Matter Grey Advt. Inc., N.Y.C., 1983-84; mgr. corp. pub. rels. Avon Products Inc., N.Y.C., 1984-89; dir. pub. info. and community rels. Hunter Coll. CUNY, 1990—; cons., freelance writer Avon Products Inc., N.Y.C. Researcher, editor: The Mental Breakdown of a Nation, 1974; author: Beauty, A Year Round Guide, Wives' Legal Rights. Mem. Jackson Heights Beautification Group, Queens, N.Y., 1990; pres. 105-20th St Jackson Heights Inc., Queens, 1986-88, sec., 1989—. Recipient peotry award Writers' Digest mag., 1977. Mem. Women in Communications, Phi Beta Kappa, Kappa Gamma Phi. Home: 35-56 77th St Jackson Heights NY 11372 Office: Hunter Coll 695 Park Ave Rm E1212 New York NY 10021

TERRY, KAY ADELL, temporary help and executive search services company executive; b. Portland, Oreg., July 11, 1939; d. Langdon Alcott and Emma Francis (Meyer) Howard; m. Frank F. Terry, Aug. 31, 1963 (div. Mar. 1988); 1 child, Kimberly Sue. CPC, CIPC. Office mgr. Merck Sharp & Dohme, Portland, 1959-63; asst. dir. admissions Seattle Pacific U., Seattle, 1963-66; owner United Personnel Svc., Seattle, 1966-86; pres., chief exec. officer Ram Force Cos., Seattle, 1986—; bd. dirs. Ram Force Cos., Seattle Acctg. Force, Inc., Seattle, Office Force, Inc., Seattle, Data Force, Inc., Seattle. Contbr. articles to profl. jours. Mem. Seattle C. of C., 1989; vol. Spl. Olympics, Seattle. Recipient fellow award Seattle Pacific U., 1989. Mem. Women Bus. Owners, Nat. Assn. Accts. (bd. dirs. 1985-87, Mem. Achievement award 1987, Disting. Svc. award 1987), Nat. Assn. Personnel Cons. (nat. bd. dirs., pres. Washington chpt.), Nat. Assn. Temp. Svcs., Pacific N.W. Personnel Mgmt. Assn., Wash. Athletic Club. Republican. Office: Ram Force Companies Plaza 600 Bldg Ste 800 Seattle WA 98101

TERRY, MARY SUE, state official, lawyer; b. Martinsville, Va., Sept. 28, 1947; d. Nathaniel Chatham and Nannie Ruth T. B.A., Westhampton Coll., 1969; M.A., U. Va., Charlottesville, 1970, J.D., 1973. Bar: Va., 1973. Asst. commonwealth's atty. Patrick County, Va., 1973-77, mem. house dels., 1977-85; ptnr. B.H. Cooper Farm, Inc., Stuart, Va., from 1978, Terry & Rogers, Stuart, Va., from 1978; atty. gen. State of Va., Richmond, Va., 1986—; dir. First Nat. Bank of Stuart. Mem. Piedmont Planning Dist. Crime Commn., 1974-77; bd. dirs. West Piedmont Health Planning Coun., 1975-77; bd. dirs. Patrick Henry Mental Health Ctr., 1975-77; mem. Pres. Bd. Advisors Ferrun Coll., Va., 1978-83; bd. dirs. Va. YMCA, 1980—; trustee U. Richmond, Va., 1980—; chmn. Gov.'s Task Force to Combat Drunk Driving, 1982. Recipient Svc. to Youth award Va. YMCA, 1981, Disting. Alumna award U. Richmond, 1984. Mem. Va. Trial Lawyers Assn., ABA, Omicron Delta Kappa. Democrat. Baptist. Office: Office of Atty Gen 101 N 8th St Richmond VA 23291*

TERRY, SEAN M., health science association administrator; b. Portsmouth, Ohio, July 25, 1959; d. Melvin M. and Peggie Sue (Carver) T. BSN, Capital U., Columbus, Ohio, 1982. Reg. Nurse. Staff nurse Mt. Carmel East Hosp., Columbus, Ohio, 1982-84; RN mgr. Vis. Hours, Inc., Columbus, Ohio, 1984-85; nursing specialist Portamedic Health Care, Columbus, Ohio; owner, nursing dir. Cen. Ohio Nursing Svc., Worthington, Ohio, 1986—; site coord., 1986, 1987, Northland, site coord., sponsor, Worthington, Ohio, 1987, HealthCheck, 1989, Columbus, Ohio., cons. Bay Area Home Health and Nursing Svcs., La Porte, Tex., 1987—. Chmn. HealthCheck Vol. Com., Columbus, Ohio, 1988-89; vol. coord. for community, 1991. Mem. Cen. Ohio Continuity of Care Coords., Zonta HealthCheck Com., Zonta. Methodist. Office: Cen Ohio Nursing Svc 870 High St Ste 201 Worthington OH 43085

TERRY, STEPHANIE ANN, editor; b. Sherman, Tex., June 15, 1947; d. Franklin Ireneus and Vivian (Laney) Easom; m. Brooks Dessain Terry, June 7, 1969; 1 child, Lauren Michal. BA in English, Okla. Christian Coll., 1969. Cert. sec. edn. tchr. Tchr., pvt. tutor Comstock (Tex.) ISD, 1970-72; pvt. tutor Laredo, Tex., 1972-74; proofreader Laredo Citizen, 1974-76; pvt. English tutor San Antonio, Tex., 1976-79; adminstrv. asst. Campaign For Christ, Arlington, Tex., 1980-85; editor Sweet Pub., Ft. Worth, Tex., 1985-89; freelance editor Editorial Cons., Canton, Tex., 1989—; sec., treas. Worldwide Campaign for Christ, Salt Lake City, 1988—; cons. Mission Printing, Inc., Arlington, 1985—. Contbg. editor Teach Newsletter, Ft. Worth, 1985—; editor: How to Win Your Mate to Christ, 1978, Speaking From the Heart, 1986, International Children's Bible Handbook, 1986, It Couldn't Just Happen, 1987. Recipient Gold Medallion award, Evangelical Christian Pub. Assn., Christian Booksellers Assn., 1987, 88. Republican. Ch. of Christ. Home: 1725 Ridge Rd Canton TX 75103 Office: Editorial Consultants 1725 Ridge Rd Canton TX 75103

TERZIAN, MARY, senior internal auditor, business owner; b. Cairo, Sept. 18, 1932; came to U.S., 1967; d. Dikran Kevork and Rebecca (Demirjian) T.; (div.); 1 child, Ani Nayri Tertzakian. Student, Columbia U., 1967-69; BSBA, Calif. State U., L.A., 1977, postgrad., 1978; postgrad., UCLA, 1982, 84. From adminstrv. asst. to personnel asst. UN, Alexandria,, Arab Republic Egypt, Kinshasa, People's Republic Congo, Lome, Togo, 1957-65; bilingual sec. Gedeon Bus. Forms, Beirut, Lebanon, 1965-67, Givaudan Corp., N.Y.C., 1967-69, L.A. County Dept. Health, 1970-74; internal auditor Transam. Occidental Life Ins., L.A., 1980-82, The Aerospace Corp., El Segundo, Calif., 1982—; owner, mgr. Nayri Internat. Gifts, L.A., 1988—. Mem. Inst. Internal Auditors (sec. Beach Cities, Calif. chpt. 1988—), Armenian-Am. M.E. Club (treas. L.A. chpt. 1979), Toastmasters (pres., edn. v.p., editor Aerospace #401 chpt.). Republican. Armenian Orthodox. Home: 7830 Paseo del Rey Playa del Rey CA 90293

TESAR, JENNY ELIZABETH, freelance writer and editor; b. Rockville Centre, N.Y., Mar. 24, 1937; d. Joseph Anthony and Mary Elizabeth (Schedlbower) T. BS, Cornell U., 1959; MS, Oreg. State U., 1964. Sci. tchr. Oceanside (N.Y.) Pub. Schs., 1959-60; sci. tchr., chmn. sci. dept. Monterey (Calif) Pub. Schs., 1960-65; editor Grolier Inc., N.Y.C., 1969-74; mng. editor The Stonehouse Press, N.Y.C., 1974; founding editor Columbia Today

Simmons-Boardman, N.Y.C., 1975-77; freelance writer and editor Tesar Communications, N.Y.C., 1977-80, Bethel, Conn., 1980—; cons. product devel. Program Design, Inc., Greenwich, Conn., 1979-83; cons. sci. Sci. Rsch. Assocs., 1977. Author: Introduction to Animals, 1980, Preparing for the SAT and Other Aptitude Tests, 1982, Parents as Teachers, 1987; author/designer ednl. software including Alphabet Arcade (Arcade Awards Cert. of Merit 1983), others; editor textbooks and reference works; contbr. numerous articles to nat. mags. and reference publs. Pres. Chestnut Hill Village Assn., Bethel, 1981-87. Mem. Nat. Assn. Sci. Writers, Cornell Assn. Class Officers (class of 1959 officer 1972—), Toastmasters (pres. West-Conn. chpt. 1988). Office: Tesar Communications 97A Chestnut Hill Village Bethel CT 06801

TESCH, JULIA, security officer; b. Winston-Salem, N.C., Oct. 16, 1956; d. Felix Lee and Eloise (Garwood) T.; m. William A. Caldwell III, Feb. 28, 1976 (div. 1989); children: Jennifer N., William A. IV, Dana K. Pulmonary technician N.C. Bapt. Hosp., Winston-Salem, 1977-80; receptionist, file clk. dept. ob.-gyn. Bowman Gray Med. Sch., Winston-Salem, 1984-86; pharmacy technician N.C. Bapt. Hosp., Winston-Salem, 1986-88; security officer Allied Security/N.C. Bapt. Hosp., Winston-Salem, 1988—; agt. Spl. Response Corp., Towson, Md., 1990—; instr. Karate Internat., Winston-Salem, 1988—. Office: Allied Security / NC Bapt Hosp 300 S Hawthorne Rd Winston-Salem NC 27104

TESCHNER, ANNE FARRAR, video artist; b. Worcester, Mass., Apr. 11, 1956; d. Charles William Teschner Jr. and Margaret Edna (Farrar) Richardson; m. Russell Steven Powell, May 22, 1976; 1 child, Rita Teschner. Cert., Dynamy Inc., Worcester, 1974; BA, U. Mass., 1984. Founding dir. family day care program YMCA, Southbridge, Mass., 1979; dir. Family Violence Program, Lebanon, N.H., 1980-82; assoc. dir. internship program U. Mass., Amherst, 1984-86, dir. spl. projects Ctr. for New Eng. Culture, 1986-87; community developer Mass. Office for Children, Westfield, Mass., 1987-88; dir. Primal Time TV Workshop, Amherst, 1988—. Writer, dir., actor TV programs Primal Time TV, 1988, Primal Time II, 1989, Primal Time and A Half, 1990. Mem. Tantasqua Regional Sch. Com., Sturbridge, Mass., 1977-80; vice chmn., bd. dirs. Crocker Care, Amherst, 1986-87; founding dir. Holyoke (Mass.) Teen Pregnancy Coalition, 1988—; speaker N.H. Commn. on Status of Women, 1981, Children's Def. Fund., Holyoke, 1989; founding coord. El Arco Iris-Teen Arts Ctr., Holyoke, 1989. Recipient 2d place Conn. Screening Room, 1988; grantee Amherst Arts Coun., 1988. Office: Primal Time TV Workshop 1260 West St Amherst MA 01002

TESKE, PATRICIA LOOS, retired educator; b. Murphysboro, Ill., Sept. 13, 1921; d. Alvin Carl and Esther (Ruehling) Loos; m. Glenn Duane Teske, Apr. 24, 1943; children: Paul G., Pamela E., David C. BA, Carthage Coll., 1943; MS, Tex. Tech U., 1967. Cert. tchr. Tchr. pub. sch. Lovington, N.Mex., 1963-80. Mem. AAUW (various offices Lovington br.), Am. Home Econs. Assn., Am. Fedn. Woman's Clubs, Order of Ea. Star, Omicron Nu, Beta Beta Beta, Delta Kappa Gamma (various offices Lambda chpt.). Home: 1011 West Ave H Lovington NM 88260

TESONE, JUDY, educator; b. Youngstown, Ohio, Jan. 28, 1943; d. Walter V. and Millie (Erkman) Dragelevich; m. F. Nicholas Tesone, Dec. 4, 1965; children: Mark, Denise. BS in Edn., Youngstown State U., 1966. Cert. reading specialist, Ohio, Pa. Tutor Youngstown Schs., 1981-83, reading specialist, 1983-88; reading specialist North Allegheny Schs., Pitts., 1988-89; reading tutor Huntington Learning Ctr., Pitts., 1988—. Mem. North Hills Welcome Wagon, Pitts., 1988—. Mem. Ohio Reading Tchrs. Assn., AAUW, Youngstown Symphony Guild, Pitts. Symphony Guild,. Republican.

TESORO, GIULIANA CAVAGLIERI, chemistry research educator, consultant; b. Venice, Italy, June 1, 1921; came to U.S., 1939; d. Gino and Margherita (Maroni) Cavaglieri; m. Victor Tesoro, Apr. 17, 1943; children: Claudia, Andrew. PhD, Yale U., 1943. Rsch. chemist Am. Cyanamid Co., Boundbrook, N.J., 1943-44; asst. dir. rsch. Onyx Chem. Co., Jersey City, 1944-58, J. P. Stevens & Co., Inc., Garfield, N.J., 1958-68; dir. chem. rsch. Burlington Industries, Greenboro, N.C., 1968-72; sr. scientist, adj. prof. MIT, Cambridge, 1973-82; rsch. prof. Poly. U., Bklyn., 1982—; Mem. nat. materials adv. bd. NRC, Washington, 1979-82. Contbr. numerous articles to profl. publs.; patentee in field. Recipient Am. Dyestuff Reporter award, 1959, Achievement award Soc. Women Engrs., 1978. Fellow Textile Inst. Gt. Britain; mem. AAAS (co-chmn. polymer combustion and fire retardance conf. 1977), Am. Assn. Textile Chemists and Colorists (Olney medal 1963), Am. Chem. Soc., Am. Inst. Chemists, Info. Coun. Fabric flammability, N.Y. Acad. Sci., Textile Rsch. Inst. (editorial bd.jours.), Fiber Soc. (pres. 1974-75). Democrat. Home: 278 Clinton Ave Dobbs Ferry NY 10522 Office: Poly U 333 Jay St Brooklyn NY 11201

TESSA, MARIAN LORRAINE, talk show host, writer and producer; b. N.Y.C., Sept. 23, 1950; d. Sylvester Joseph and Emma Carol (Chimento) T. BA in English, SUNY, Cortland, 1972; postgrad., N.Y. Sch. Broadcasting, 1972-73. Writer CBS, N.Y.C., 1972-75; show host, producer, writer Manhattan Cable, N.Y.C., 1975—, S.I. Cable, 1988—. Spokesperson Miss Universe/Miss U.S.A. Beauty Pageants, 1976, promotion benefits; guest appearances include David Susskind Show, 1978, ABC Wide World Spl., 1978, The Joe Franklin Show, 1980, The You Show, 1979, Natural Living Program, 1981; talk show host Kaleidoscope, 1983-85; voice over on cable TV,1975—; performer Broadway in the Streets, 1969; photographic model Penzo Spagnoli Gallery, Florence Italy, 1984, San Francisco, N.Y.C. and London, 1988. Com. mem. Am. Cancer Soc. Recipient Forensic award. Mem. TV Acad. Arts and Scis. Office: Tessa Prodns 10 Wagner St Staten Island NY 10305

TESSIER, KAREN PATRICIA, nursing service executive; b. Manchester, Conn., June 12, 1943; d. Chester Marion and Patricia Mae (Chartier) Jedrzewski; m. Stephen Joseph Tessier, Oct. 8, 1966; children: Nicole Karen, Stephanie Michele. BS with honors, U. Conn., 1965; MS, U. Hawaii, 1986. RN; cert. in nursing adminstrn. Staff nurse pediatrics UCLA Med. Ctr., 1965-69, asst. head nurse pediatrics, 1969-71, asst. nursing coord. II, 1971-73, sr. staff nurse pediatric ICU, 1973-74; staff nurse pediatrics St. John's Hosp., Oxnard, Calif., 1976-77; staff nurse neonatal and pediatric ICU Kapiolani Med Ctr. for Women and Children, Honolulu, 1977-80, from asst. supr. to supr. pediatric intensive care unit, 1980-89, dir. pediatric svcs., 1989—. Bd. dirs. Iroquois Point Preschool, Ewa Beach, Hawaii, 1978; adult vol. Youth Ambassadors Internat., Honolulu, 1989—; vol. Lifespring, Honolulu, 1989. Recipient Leadership award YWCA, 1989. Mem. Am. Orgn. Nurse Execs., Am. Assn. Critical Care Nurses (membership chmn. 1987-89, Achievement award 1989), U. Conn. Alumni Assn., 4-H Club Alumni Assn., Sigma Theta Tau. Roman Catholic. Home: 91-574 Pupu St Ewa Beach HI 96706 Office: Kapiolani Med Ctr 1319 Punahou St Honolulu HI 96826

TESSLER, JULIA ANN, sales executive; b. McPherson, Kans., May 22, 1959; d. George Washington and Roberta Jean (McGuire) Willard; m. George Fair Tessler, July 17, 1982, 1 child, Logan Trey. Grad. high sch. With Far-Mar-Co., Inc., Hutchinson, Kans., 1978-82; data entry clk. Contemporary Communications, Wichita, Kans., 1982, office mgr., 1982-84; inside salesperson Massco, Inc., Wichita, 1984-85, inside sales mgr., 1985, inside sales and telemarketing mgr./customer svc. mgr., 1985-86, customer svcs. mgr., ops. mgr., 1987-89; telemarketing-teleservices ops. mgr. Beal Office Supply, Wichita, 1989—. Recipient Century Sales award Butcher Polish Co., 1986. Mem. Nat. Assn. Female Execs., Bus. and Profl. Women's Club. Republican. Office: 1501 E First Wichita KS 67214

TESTA, SHARON ANNE, business consultant; b. Lawrence, Mass., Mar. 6, 1948; d. Joseph Robert and Carmela Mary (Palermo) T.; 1 child, Michael Antony. AA, Middlesex Community Coll., 1977; BS in Bus. Edn., Salem State coll., 1981; MBA, N.H. coll., 1985. Sec. Atty. Gen. of Mass., Boston, 1968-69; legal asst. to pvt. atty. Lawrence, 1969-81; owner, bus. cons. M.T. Assocs., Danville, N.H., 1981—; instr. Castle Jr. Coll., Windham, N.H., 1986—; acad. coord. No. Essex Community Coll., Haverhill, Mass., 1987—. Mem. NAFE, Nat. Assn. Bus. Educators, N.H. Coll. Alumni Assn., New Eng. Bus. Educators Assn., N.H. Bus. Educators Assn. Democrat. Roman Catholic. Office: MT Assocs PO Box 607 Danville NH 03819

TETERYCZ, BARBARA ANN, entrepreneur, advertising executive; b. Chgo., Jan. 23, 1952; d. Sylvester and Anne (Deutsch) T.; m. Robert Nathan Estes, Oct. 13, 1984. BA, U. Ill., 1974; postgrad. Parkland Coll., 1975-76, U. Ill., 1976-77; student Second City Tng. Ctr. Teller, First Fed. of Champaign, Ill., 1974-75; cashier Kroger Co., Champaign, 1975-77; merchandise rep. RustCraft Greeting Cards, Champaign, 1977-78; sales rep. Hockenberg-Rubin, Champaign, 1978, John Morrell & Co., Champaign, 1978-80; account exec. Sta. WICD TV, Champaign, 1981-86; owner Left-Handed Compliments, Champaign; creator 1987, 88 left-handed calendar. Contbg. editor mag. Champaign County Bus. Reports, 1986; inventor Left-Behind Sweat Pants and Shorts. Vol. Am. Cancer Soc., 1985, Ill. Radio Readers for the Visually Impaired, U. Ill. Alumni Assn., 1985-88, Mercy Hosp. Aux., coms. to Elect and Re-elect Beth Beauchamp to City Council, Champaign, 1984, 87. Ill. State scholar, 1970-74; grad. players workshop Second City, 1989. Mem. NAFE, Ad Club of Champaign (finalist several copywriting contests), Internat. Platform Assn., Entrepreneurs Roundtable (founding), Women's Bus. Coun., Urbana C. of C., Champaign C. of C. (pub. rels. com., pres.'s club), Alpha Omega. Roman Catholic. Avocations: reading, writing, bicycling, bodybuilding. Home: 1615 Harbor Point Dr PO Box 873 Champaign IL 61820

TEVLIN, LOIS PENKETH, hospital official; b. Bklyn., Jan. 16, 1935; d. Aloysius Joseph and Louise Marie (Rooney) Penketh; m. William Joseph Tevlin, Sept. 29, 1957; children: Nora, Kyle, Catherine, William Joseph III, David. Grad., Kings County Hosp. Sch., Bklyn., 1956; BA, Upsala Coll., 1977. RN, N.Y. Staff nurse Kings County Hosp Ctr., 1956-57; coord. utilization rev. Mountainside Hosp., Montclair, N.J., 1980-84, quality assurance analyst, 1984-88, supr. quality assurance, 1988—. Pres. Glen Ridge (N.J.) Music Parents Assn., 1976-78. Mem. Am. Soc. Hosp. Risk Mgrs., Soc. Healthcare Risk Mgmt., Assn. Quality Assurance Profls. N.J., Phi Alpha Theta. Home: 37 Devon Rd Essex Fells NJ 07021 Office: Mountainside Hosp Bay and Highland Aves Montclair NJ 07042

TEWS-YOCUM, EVE LYNN, insurance adjuster; b. Berea, Ohio, Aug. 11, 1956; d. Clee Cliffton Leatherman and Marlene J. (Shepard) Findlay; m. James Edward Tews, May 24, 1975 (div.); m. Bryan E. Yocum, Aug. 29, 1987; children: James Wesley Tews, Dianne Marie Yocum. Grad. high sch. Sec., Toensmeier Adjustment, Allentown, Pa., 1974-78, adjuster, 1978-81; resident adjuster Gemmill Adjustment, Reading, Pa., 1981-84; ins. adjuster/owner E.L. Tews Adjustment, Allentown, 1984—. Mem. NAFE, Nat. Assn. Self-Employed, Reading Claims Assn., Lehigh Valley Claims Assn. (sec., 1984-85, 1st v.p. 1985-86, pres. 1986-87). Republican. Avocations: aerobics; reading; crocheting.

THALL, LETTY DERMAN, social services administrator; b. New Orleans, Jan. 6, 1947; d. Herbert and Mary Virginia (Coughlin) Derman; m. Bruce Louis Thall, June 23, 1968; children: Gregory Coughlin, Mary Courtney. B.A., Skidmore Coll., 1968; M.S.S., Bryn Mawr Coll., 1974. Trainer, cons. Bell Telephone Co., Phila., 1968-71; policewoman Phila. Police Dept., 1971; planning cons. Health and Welfare Council, Phila., 1974-75; dir. WOAR, Phila., 1975-77; program coordinator Hall-Mercer Ctr., Phila., 1978-80; div. dir. and planner Community Services Planning Council, Phila., 1980-85; exec. dir. Delaware Valley Child Care Council, 1986—; pres. bd. CHOICE, 1977-80; alumni com. mem. Community Leadership Seminars, Phila., 1978-83. Coordinator Shirley Chisholm for Pres., Miami, Fla., 1972; fin. dir. Bill Gray for Congress Com., Phila., 1978; co-chairperson Marion Tasco for City Commr., Phila., 1983; mem. Phila. Mayor's Commn. for Women, 1980-85, vice-chair., 1983-85; bd. dirs. City Parks Assn., 1986-89, Ctr. Responsible Philanthropy, 1987—. Mem. Mid Atlantic Assn. for Tng. and Counseling (trainer, group facilitator 1979—), Women's Way (co-founder; bd. dirs. 1975-81), Delaware Valley Assn. for Edn. Young Children, Nat. Assn. Social Workers, Assn. for Creative Change. Democrat. Office: 401 N Broad St Ste 818 Philadelphia PA 19108

THALMANN, JOAN LOUISE, environmental health scientist; b. Salt Lake, Jan. 15, 1952; d. John Fredrick and Emma Shara (May) T. Student, Weber State Coll., 1970-71; BS, U. Utah, 1975; M of Urban & Regional Planning, Va. Poly. State U., 1979. Housing resource specialist Utah Migrant Coun., Salt Lake, 1975-76; land use planner, engrng. technician Wasatch Front Regional Coun., Salt Lake, 1976; program analyst State Planning Coord. Office, Salt Lake, 1979-80; tech. writer Templeton Linke & Assoc., Salt Lake City, 1980-84; environ. health sci. I Bur. Air Quality, Salt Lake City, 1984-86, environ. health sci. II, 1986-89, environ. health sci. III, 1989—; instr. Nat. Edn. Program on Asbestos, Salt Lake City, 1990—, Rocky Mountain Ctr. for Occupation & Environ. Health, Salt Lake City, 1990—. Author: Keep the Home Fires Burning, 1985 (Work Performed 1985), (bur. report) The Emission Inventory, 1984-90; editor: (newsletter) The Utah Air Monitor, 1985-88. Recipient 2000 Notable Women in Am. in 1990 award, 1990, Wood Burning Brochure award State of Utah, 1985. Mem. Utah Pub. Employees Assn., Local & Nat. Asbestos Assn., Nat. Assn. Bus. & Profl. Women, Nat. Wildlife Fedn., Wasatch Mountain Club. Republican. Mormon. Home: 3575 S 3200 W #9D West Valley City UT 84119

THARP, TWYLA, dancer, choreographer; b. Portland, Ind., July 1, 1941; 1 son, Jesse. Student, Pomona Coll.; grad., Barnard Coll.; D of Performing Arts (hon.), Calif. Inst. Arts, 1978, Brown U., 1981, Bard Coll., 1981; LHD, Ind. U., 1987; DFA, Pomona Coll., 1987; studies with, Richard Thomas, Merce Cunningham, Igor Schwezoff, Louis Mattox, Paul Taylor, Margaet Craske, Erick Hawkins. With Paul Taylor Dance Co., 1963-65; freelance choreographer with own modern dance troupe and various other cos. including Joffrey Ballet and Am. Ballet Theatre, 1965—; teaching residencies various colls. and univs. including U. Mass., Oberlin Coll., Walker Art Ctr., Boston U. Choreographer: Tank Dive, 1965, Re-Moves, 1966, Forevermore, 1967, Generation, 1968, Medley, 1969, Fugue, 1970, Eight Jelly Rolls, 1971, The Raggedy Dances, 1972, As Time Goes By, 1974, Sue's Leg, 1975, Push Comes to Shove, 1976, Once More Frank, 1976, Mud, 1977, Baker's Dozen, 1979, When We Were Very Young, 1980, Amadeus, 1984, White Nights, 1985, (film) Hair, 1979, (video spls.) Making Television Dance, 1977, CBS Cable Confessions of a Corner Maker, 1980, (Broadway shows) Sorrow Floats, 1985, Singin' In The Rain, 1985. Recipient Creative Arts award Brandeis U., 1972; Dance mag. award, 1981; Univ. Medal for Excellence, Columbia U., 1987. Office: Am Ballet Theatre 890 Broadway New York NY 10003*

THATCHER, BEVERLY ROSE, senior programmer analyst; b. S.I., N.Y., Dec. 8, 1965; d. George Edward and Rita Marie (Durbrow) T. BS in Computer Sci., St. John's U., N.Y.C., 1986; MBA in Fin., St. John's U., 1990. Clk. Advt. Coun., N.Y.C., 1979; data processor Am. Internat. Group, N.Y.C., 1983; mktg. rep. Compu-Media Supplies, S.I., 1984-85; computer operator, sec. Norrell Svcs., N.Y.C., 1985; analyst Family Radio Programming, N.Y.C., 1985-86; tech. support staff mem. Info Centre, N.Y.C., 1986-87; programmer analyst Tishman Realty & Contrn., N.Y.C., 1987-88, Gold Fields Mining Corp., N.Y.C., 1988—; cons. Pet Tracks, S.I., 1981-83, Thatcher & Assocs., S.I., 1985—; computer instr. Holland Am. Cruise Line, 1988; adj. computer tchrs. Barnard Baruch Coll., 1990. Editor sch. periodical Aries mag., 1981. Vol. Mt. Lorretto home for children, S.I., 1986, United Cerebral Palsy, S.I., 1982. Mem. NAFE (network dir. 1988-89), Am. Computing Machinery Assn., St. John's Alumni Assn., Bus. and Profl. Woman's Club (exec. bd. 1988-89, roster chmn. Young Careerist award 1988), Speedware Users Group, Cognos Users Group, NYPC, SigSmall PC Spl. Interest Group. Republican. Roman Catholic. Home: 266 Oakland Ave Staten Island NY 10310 Office: Gold Fields Mining Corp 230 Park Ave New York NY 10169

THATCHER, KRISTINE MARIE, actress, writer; b. Lansing, Mich., June 22, 1950; d. Joseph and Marjorie Suzanne (McKeone) Schneider; m. Timothy T. Thatcher, Apr. 24, 1971 (div. Nov. 1977); m. David Darlow, May 11, 1990. Grad. high sch., Lansing. Appeared numerous theatre prodns. including Hunting Cockroaches, The Taming of the Shrew, Angel Street, The Real Thing, The Life and Adventures of Nicholas Nickleby, The Browning Version, Twelve Pound Look, You Never Can Tell, A Tinker's Dam, Boy Meets Girl, Custer, A Doll's House, As You Like It, Merton of the Movies, The Nerd, Translations, Arms and the Man, Of Mice and Men, Cat on a Hot Tin Roof, Macbeth, The Threepenny Opera; TV appearances include Trial of the Moke, Hyde and Seeke, Another World, Search for Tomorrow, Modern Parenting; playwright: The Adventures of Captain Karma, 1976, Michigan Bio (The Rustic Village), 1983, Niedecker, 1985, (with Larry Shue) Waiting for Tina Meyer, 1989; honorary mem. Milw. Repertory Theater. Mem. Actors' Fund Am., N.Y.C., 1985—, Dem. Nat. Com., Washington, 1988—; vol. Greenpeace, Chgo. and Washington, 1987-88. Nominated for Plays in Process Theatre Communications Group, 1987, Joseph Kesselring award Nat. Arts Club, 1987, Joseph Jefferson award, 1985, Susan Smith Blackburn award, 1985; finalist Nat. One-Act Play Contest, 1990. Mem. AFTRA, Actors Equity Assn., Dramatists' Guild, Soc. Stage Dirs. and Choreographers, Inc. Roman Catholic. Home and Office: 6722 N Bosworth Ave Chicago IL 60626

THAU, ROSEMARIE BRIGITTE, population council director, scientist; b. Vienna, Austria, Mar. 15, 1936; came to U.S., 1963; d. Leopold Caspar and Wilfriede (Kern) Widl; m. Joseph Zischka, July 20, 1955 (div. 1959); m. Albert Thau, May 19, 1970. BS, U. Vienna, 1954, PhD, 1963. Rsch. assoc. exptl. surgery, med. ctr. Duke U., Durham, N.C., 1963-65; instr. pediatrics SUNY, 1965-67, asst. prof., 1967-72; scientist Population Coun., N.Y.C., 1972-87, assoc. div. dir., dir. contraceptive devel., 1987—; cons. WHO. Contbr. numerous articles to profl. jours., chpts. to books; subject of numerous radio and TV interviews, 1987—. Fellow N.Y. Zool. Soc.; mem. Soc. Immunology Reproduction, Soc. Endocrinology, Sigma Xi (pres. Rockefeller U. chpt. 1985-86). Office: Population Coun 1230 York Ave New York NY 10021

THAWLEY, MARY NANCY, photographer; b. Cambridge, Mass., Oct. 20, 1947; d. George Clifton and Mary Agnes (Glennon) T. BA, U. Mass., Boston, 1969; postgrad., Northeastern U., 1981, Harvard U., 1984, Harvard U., 1986. Tchr. Boston Sch. Com., 1969; rep. Nynex Info. Resources Co., Lynn, Mass., 1970-88; photographer, sports reporter South End News, Boston, 1983-85; photographer sports Lynn Sunday Post, 1986—; photographer Boston Celtics, 1985—. Contbr. articles to profl. jours. Active McGovern Dem. campaign for Pres. of U.S., Boston, 1972; founding mem. Rainbow Coalition, Boston, 1982; mem., photo contbr. New Eng. Sports Mus., 1985—; photographer Joe Kennedy campaign, Cambridge, 1986—; spokesperson Berkeley Residents Tenants Orgn., Boston, 1987, also chmn., 1988; photographer Make-a-Wish Found. of Boston, 1989—. Fellow John F. Kennedy Library Assn. (hon., founding mem.); mem. Nat. Press Photographers Assn., Associated Photographers Internat., Communications Workers Am., Nat. Marfan Found., Internat. Platform Assn., Greater Lynn Camera Club. Roman Catholic. Home: 40 Berkeley St Apt 207 Boston MA 02116

THAYER, EDNA LOUISE, service executive, nurse; b. Madelia, Minn., May 21, 1936; d. Walter William Arthur and Hilda Engel Emily Ann (Geistfeld) Wilke; m. David LeRoy Thayer, Aug. 30, 1958; children: Scott, Tamara, Brenda. Diploma in nursing, Bethesda Luth., 1956; BS in Nursing Edn., U. Minn., 1960; MSN, Washington U., St. Louis, 1966; MS, Mankato (Minn.) State U., 1972. Nurse Bethesda Luth. Hosp., St. Paul, 1956-58, U. Minn. Hosp., Mpls., 1958; from nurse to asst. head nurse supr., edn. dir. Fairmont (Minn.) Community Hosp., 1959-63; instr. Alton (Ill.) Meml. Hosp., 1963-66; mem. faculty, acting dean nursing dept. Mankato State U., 1966-77; asst. adminstr. Rice County Dist. One Hosp., Faribault, Minn., 1977-89; RN, adminstrv. supr. St. Peter (Minn.) Regional Treatment Ctr., 1990—; bd. dirs. Hospice, Faribault; nurse surveyor Minn. Dept. Tech. Edn., St. Paul, 1980—; mem. adv. co. LPN and MA programs Tech. Inst., Faribault, 1977—. Mem. Rice County Extension Bd., Faribault, 1986—; adult leader 4-H Club, Rice County and St. Paul, 1971—; advisor Med. Explorers, Faribault, 1977—, Rep. Rodosovich Health Com., Faribault, 1984—; coun. mem. Our Savior's Luth. Ch., Faribault, 1984-87. Recipient Alumni award Nat. 4-H Club, 1983. Mem. Minn. Orgn. Nurse Execs. (bd. dirs. 1987-89), Dist. F Nursing Svc. Adminstrs. (pres. 1980-82), Minn. Nurses Assn. (bd. dirs. 1985-87, Pres.'s award 1983), AAUW, Sigma Theta Tau, Hosp. Aux. Republican. Home: RR 1 Box 7B Elysian MN 56028 Office: St Peter Regional Treatment Ctr 100 Freeman Dr Saint Peter MN 56082

THAYER, JANE See WOOLLEY, CATHERINE

THAYER, JANE HILLIS, psychologist; b. N.Y.C., June 17, 1930; d. Harold Lee and Ruth Evelyn (Caldwell) Hillis; m. Roger Eugene Thayer, June 16, 1951; children: Peggy, David, Cynthia. BA in Psychology, Cornell U., 1952; MA in Clin. Psychology, George Washington U., 1956, PhD in Clin. Psychology, 1969. Lic. psychologist, D.C. Intern in psychology St. Elizabeth's Hosp., Washington, 1965-66, intern in rsch., 1966-68; staff psychologist Alexandria (Va.) Community Mental Health Ctr., 1968-71, acting chief psychologist, 1969-70; pvt. practice Washington, 1971—; cons. in field; pres. Gestalt Inst., Washington, 1973; book reviewer A.P.A. div. Family Psychology, Washington, 1990—. Mem. AAAS, D.C. Psychol. Assn., Am. Psychol. Assn., Sigma Xi, Psi Chi. Democrat. Office: 1231 Potomac St NW Washington DC 20007

THAYER, NINA NICHOLS, image processing scientist; b. Akron, Ohio, July 29, 1945; d. Stanbery J. and Maxine Lavonne (Snyder) Nichols; m. Gary R. Thayer, June 20, 1970; children: Timothy, Tamra Marie. BA in Physics, Earlham Coll., 1967; MS in Physics, U. Md., 1972. Rsch. asst. chemistry dept. U. Ill., Urbana, 1970-73; digital image analyst Jet Propulsion Lab. Mariner X, Pasadena, Calif., 1974; scientist EG&G Energy Measurements, Los Alamos, N.Mex., 1978—, lab. mgr., 1986-88, project leader, 1984—. Bd. dirs. N.Mex. Network for Women in Sci. and Engring., 1986-89, sec., 1987-89. Recipient Pub. Svc. Group Achievement award NASA, 1974, Excellence award Office Mil. Applications Dept. of Energy, 1984. Mem. AAUW (bd. dirs. 1980-90, pres. 1984-86, Eleanor Roosevelt grantee 1990).

THAYER, WANDA E., business owner; b. Tuscaloosa, Ala., July 27, 1943; d. Herman Springer and Anita (Rogers) Parker; m. Cameron Jones (div. 1976); children—Bryan Keith, Kimberly Ann. Student Foothills Jr. Coll., Palm Beach Jr. Coll. Co-owner Aluma Loc Awning, San Jose, Calif., 1964-67; sec.-treas. A&A Air Conditioning, Boca Raton, Fla., 1968-76; pres. Personalized Air Conditioning, Inc., Boca Raton, 1978—. Chmn. BACPAC, 1979-81; bd. dirs. SAFEPAC, 1983—, Boca Raton United Way, 1984—; mem. bd. of rules and appeals City of Boca Raton, 1986; appointed to Boca Raton Planning and Zoning Bd., 1986—; dep. mayor City of Boca Raton, 1987-88; bd. dirs. Cities in Schs., Inc., 1987—. Mem. Boca Raton C. of C. (dir., treas. 1986-87), Fla. Atlantic Builders Assn. (past 2d v.p., past sec.; Assoc. of Yr. 1983), Nat. Fedn. Ind. Bus., Fla. Air Conditioning Contractors Assn., Better Bus. Bur. Republican. Lutheran. Avocations: tennis; travel; reading. Home: 149 NW 70th St #205 Boca Raton FL 33487 Office: Personalized Air Conditioning 121 NW 11th St Boca Raton FL 33432

THEESFELD, CAROLE ANN, educator; b. Elmwood Park, Ill., Apr. 29, 1943; d. Howard Maurice and Ann (Romcoe) Kumlin; m. David Alan Theesfeld, Aug. 7, 1965; children: Michael Dean, Michelle Sue. BS in Edn., Ill. State U., 1965; MS in Math. Edn., U. Ill., 1968. Cert. tchr., Ill. Tchr. math. Fremd High Sch., Palatine, Ill., 1965-70, Harper Jr. Coll., Palatine, 1970—; tchrs. aide math. Arlington Heights (Ill.) Grade Schs. Dist. 25, 1976-82; tchr. math. Rolling Meadows (Ill.) High Sch., 1982-83, East Leyden High Sch., Franklin Park, Ill., 1983-84, Addison (Ill.) Trail High Sch., 1984—; dir. plays Addison Trail High Sch., 1984—; speaker in field. Author: Essentials of Algebra (TRB), 1987; co-author: Geometry, 1990. Recipient Excellence award for Exemplary Educators Ill. Math. Sci. Acad., 1989. Mem. Nat. Council Tchrs. Math., Ill. Council Tchrs. Math, Kappa Mu Epsilon. Lutheran. Club: Addison Trail Fishing (sponsor run 1985—). Home: 712 N Kennicott Arlington Heights IL 60004 Office: Addison Trail High Sch 213 N Lombard Addison IL 60101

THEISS, SALLY ANN, laboratory administrator; b. Massillon, Ohio, Jan. 26, 1950; d. Duane G. and Thelma A. (Ruwadi) Fetrow; m. Nicholas J. Theiss, July 25, 1987; children: Alison, Nichole, Leigh Ann. BS, Mt. Union Coll., 1972; MA in Counseling and Human Devel., Walsh Coll., North Canton, Ohio, 1986. Registered med. technician. Immunohematology supr., med. technician Aultman Hosp., Canton, Ohio, unit dir. immunohematology/hematology/venipuncture. Mem. adv. bd., quality circle facilitator Stark Tech. Coll. Mem. Am. Soc. Clin. Pathologists, Chi Sigma Iota. Address: 7283 Thatcher NW North Canton OH 44720

THELIAN, LORRAINE, public relations executive; b. N.Y.C., Jan. 13, 1948; d. Anthony G. and Inez (Gelfo) Bufano; m. Helmuth Thelian, Sept. 11, 1942. BA, Molloy Coll., 1969. Account coordinator Basford Pub. Rels., N.Y.C., 1969-71; from asst. account exec. through v.p. Paluszek & Leslie Assoc., N.Y.C., 1971-74; sr. v.p., assoc. dir. Ketchum Pub. Rels., Washington, 1985—; mem. Washington Bd. Trade, 1987—. Mem. Pub. Relations Soc. Am. (accredited, chmn. accreditation com. Washington chpt. 1987—), Washington Communications Assn. Roman Catholic. Office: Ketchum Pub Rels 1201 Connecticut Ave NW Washington DC 10036

THEOBALD, JEAN ANN, marketing and public relations executive; b. N.Y.C., Apr. 1, 1958; d. Edward Joseph and Alberta Lorraine (Terrell) T.; m. Leonard Joseph Williams, Feb. 17, 1989. Assoc. Media Arts, Dutchess Community Coll., 1984; BFA summa cum laude, N.Y. Inst. Tech., 1986. Retail sales clk. Mays Dept. Store, Fishkill, N.Y., 1974-76; bank teller Marine Midland Bank, Hopewell Junction, N.Y., 1976-78; order expediter Gen. Vending Co., Poughkeepsie, N.Y., 1978-79; receptionist Witco/Chemprene, Beacon, N.Y., 1979-81; v.p., founder Williams Auto Restoration, Fishkill Plains, N.Y., 1981—; promotions asst. WTZA-TV Channel 62, Kingston, N.Y., 1987; dir. mktg. and pub. rels. Bardavon 1869 Opera House, Poughkeepsie, 1987-89; regional account exec. DK & R Advt., Hopewell Junction, N.Y., 1989; asst. dir. student activities Dutchess Community Coll., Poughkeepsie, N.Y., 1989—; freelance rsch. asst. to Caroline Bird (published author), 1989—. Pub. rels. and media coord. Dutchess County Tricentennial Com., Poughkeepsie, 1988; prodn. com. Bicentennial of the Ratification of the Constitution, Poughkeepsie, 1988; mem. adv. com. Communications and Media Arts Program Dutchess Community Coll., 1988—. Mem. Hudson Valley Mktg. Assn. Democrat. Roman Catholic. Office: Bardavon Opera House 35 Market St Poughkeepsie NY 12601

THERIOT, ROSEMARY, health educator; b. New Orleans, Feb. 22, 1954; d. Wilbert and Mildred (Harris) Williams; m. Henry Theriot, Apr. 21, 1973 (div. 1978); 1 child, Natasha Danielle. BS, Western Ky. U., 1981, MS in Pub. Health, 1982; EdD, Ind. U., 1985. Operator S. Central Bell Telephone Co., New Orleans, 1973-74; grad. asst. Western Ky. U., Bowling Green, Ky., 1980-81; health educator Warren County Health Dept., Bowling Green, 1982; adminstrv. intern U. Louisville, 1984; adminstrv. asst. Ind. U., Bloomington, 1983-85; asst. dir. student affairs Ind. U., Indpls., 1986-87; teller Bloomington Nat. Bank, 1985-86; asst. prof. health Meharry Med. Coll., Nashville, 1987—; cons. in field; presenter confs. and workshops in field. Contbr. articles to profl. publs. Mem. faculty Consortium on Adolescent Pregnancy, Nashville, 1989. With U.S. Army, 1975-78. Recipient Pres.' Phys. Fitness award Vandebilt High Sch., 1972. Mem. Am. Coll. Healthcare Execs., AAUP, Bus. and Profl. Women. Democrat. Roman Catholic. Home: 1303 Tiffany Ln Hendersonville TN 37075 Office: Meharry Med Coll 1005 D B Todd Blvd Nashville TN 37208

THEROS, CHRISTINA MARIE, photographic company executive; b. Mpls., Nov. 12, 1962; d. George Frank and Zoi C. Theros. BFA, Coll. St. Catherines, St. Paul, 1987. Account exec., mgr. Photog. Specialties, Mpls., 1986-89; account exec. Slide Svcs., Inc., Mpls., 1989—. Mem. Minn. Commercial Indsl. Photographers Assn.

THEVENOT, MAUDE TRAVIS, retired home economist; b. Many, La., Dec. 31, 1914; d. Rennie L. and Fairy D. (Minter) Travis; m. Aubrey J. Thevenot, July 4, 1952 (dec. Sept. 1981); 1 stepchild, Peter A. BA, Northwestern State U., 1939; MS, La. State U., 1963. Tchr. home econs. Bienville Parish High Sch., Jamestown, La., 1940-41; parish home mgmt. supr. Farmers Home Adminstrn., USDA, Natchitoches, Oak Grove, Winnefield, La., 1942-47; state home mgmt. supr. Farmers Home Adminstrn., USDA, Alexandria, La., 1948-52; social worker La. Dept. Pub. Welfare, New Roads, Alexandria, Marksville, La., 1952-56; home economist La. State U.-La. Coop. Extension Svc., Makrsville, Alexandria, 1957-74; specialist expanded food & nutrition edn. program La. State U.-La. Coop. Extension Svc., Baton Rouge, 1975-79; co-advisor in home econs. Ptnrs. of Am. La./El Savador and La. Home Econs., 1975. Author: Central District Louisiana Home Economics Association, 1984 Louisiana Federation of Chapters of the National Association of Retired Federal Workers, 1989; co-author: A Taste of Yesterday, 1988. Mem. Kent Plantation House, Inc., Alexandria, 1970—, com. mem. for orgn., 1970, exec. bd., 1985-88, cookbook chmn., 1985-90; mem. Friendship House-Adult Day Care Ctr., Alexandria, 1982-90, exec. bd., 1982-88, organizer, pres. vol. orgn., 1978-90; advisor Anchors as Pilot Club of Alexandria Outreach Com., Anchor Club of Pineville (La.) High Sch., 1978-90; mem. La. Avoyelles & Rapides Parish Farm Bur., Marksville, Alexandria, 1967-90, Avoyelles & Rapides Cowbelles, Alexandria, Marksville, 1967-70. Recipient Plaque for Svc. Rapides Parish Coun. on Aging, Alexandria, 1971, Plaque for Outstanding Leadership & Svc., Rapides Parish Homemakers Coun., Alexandria, 1974, Plaque of Appreciation as Coord., Expanded Food and Nutrition Ednl. Program La. State U., Baton Rouge, 1978, 11 Certs. of Appreciation, Anchor Club of Pineville High Sch., 1980-90, Cert. of Recognition (3) Friendship House-Day Care for Adults, 1983, 84, 85, Plaque for Outstanding Svc., Rapides Coun. on Aging 20th Ann., 1967-87. Mem. Internat. Fedn. Home Econs., Am. Home Econs. Assn., La. Home Econs. Assn. (v.p. 1972-73), Cen. Dist. Home Econs., Nat. Assn. Extension Home Economist, La. Assn. Extension Home Economist, AAUW, La. Assn. Nat. Assn. Retired Fed. Employees, CENLA, Am. Assn. Retired Persons, La. State U. Alumni, La. State U. Home Econs. Retiree, Northwestern State U. Alumni, La. Retired Tchrs. Assn., Pilot Club Internat., Epsilon Sigma Phi, Gamma Sigma Delta. Democrat. Baptist. Home: 507 Tanglewood Dr Alexandria LA 71303

THEVENOW, ANNA VICTORIA, court system executive; b. Madison, Ind., June 29, 1954; d. Thomas Joseph and Anna Louise (Hoffman) T.; m. Richard Scott Harrison, Sept. 17, 1983; children: Jordan Thomas, Quincy Scott. BS in Forensic Studies, Ind. U., 1976, MS in Counseling, 1985. Cert. probation officer, Ind. Dep. probation officer Monroe Unified Ct. System, Bloomington, Ind., 1975-76, adult probation officer, 1977-80, dep. chief probation officer, 1981, chief probation officer, 1981-85, dir. ct. svcs., 1985—; mem. adv. bd. probation com. Ind. Jud. Ctr., Indpls., 1980—. Vice chmn., bd. dirs. Monroe County Community Corrections Adv. Bd., 1983—; pres., bd. dirs. Monroe County Youth Shelter, Bloomington, 1984-86; bd. dirs. YMCA Monroe County, 1985—; mem. Ind. Gov.'s Task Force To Reduce Drunk Driving, 1986-88. Recipient gov.'s exemplary project award State of Ind., 1984, 85, 87. Mem. Am. Correctional Assn. (merit award 1989), Nat. Assn. for Ct. Mgmt., Am. Probation and Parole Assn., Ind. Correctional Assn. (membership chmn. 1981, scholar 1980, 83, 85), Probation Officers Profl. Assn. Ind., Rotary (chmn. pub. rels. Bloomington 1989—). Office: Monroe Unified Ct System Justice Bldg 301 N College Bloomington IN 47401

THIBEAULT, DALE WILKINS, construction services executive, consultant; b. Manchester, Conn., Sept. 10, 1938; d. Edgar Thomas Richard Wilkins and Jessie Morgan Roberts; widowed; children: Craig, Fleur, Clayton, Danielle. Student, U. Hartford, 1960, Long Beach Community Coll., 1972, Flat River Community Coll., 1974, Santa Rosa Community Coll., 1978. Asst. adminstr. Enfield (Conn.) Extended Care Facility, 1967-68; asst. v.p. Lewten Industries, Inc., Hartford, Conn., 1968; office mgr. Buell-Lungren-Todd, Long Beach, Calif., 1969-73; dir. 8 country region East Mo. Community Action Agy., Flat River, 1974-75; sales mgr. Western region A-L Woodworks, Inc., Lynwood, Calif., 1975-77; corp. sec., controller X-L Homes, Inc., Santa Rosa, Calif., 1978-82, Northridge Corp., Santa Rosa, 1980—; pres. Thibeault & Assocs., Ltd., Santa Rosa, 1984—; gen. ptnr. Highland Ventures, Clearlake, Calif., 1984—; v.p., gen. ptnr. Highland Ventures, Inc., Santa Rosa, 1985—. Author or co-author various tng. manuals. Mem. Gov.'s Adv. Bd., Jefferson City, Mo., 1974-75, Southeastern Mo. Regional Rev. Bd., Cape Girardeau, 1973-75; pres., founder Vols. in Action, Cape Girardeau, 1974-75; sec. LWV, Manchester, Conn., 1963, NOW, Cerritos, Calif., 1971-73; den leader, coach Boy Scouts Am., Conn. and Calif., 1965-73. Recipient Achievement awards U. Mo., 1974, Lincoln U., 1974, Regional Area on Aging, Kansas City, Mo., 1974, Inst. Real Estate Mgmt., Sacramento, Calif., 1983. Mem. NAFE (charter mem. Sonoma County chpt.), Rural Builders Council, Sonoma County Apt. Assn., North Coast Builders Exchange, Windsor C. of C. Republican. Episcopalian. Lodges: Elks, Peacemakers. Office: Thibeault & Assocs Ltd 1055 W College Ave #289 Santa Rosa CA 95401

THIBODEAUX, LYNNE W., youth development specialist, consultant, speaker; b. Liberty, Tex., Nov. 1, 1946; d. Roger Warren and Melba Dee (Franklin) Lewis; m. Amar P. Thibodeaux, Nov. 26, 1977; 1 child, Jeffrey P. BS, Lamar U., 1968; MS, Tex. A&M U., 1973, PhD, 1983. Tchr. Poteet (Tex.) Ind. Sch. Dist., 1967-68, Pasadena (Tex.) Ind. Sch. Dist., 1968-69; community agt. Tex. Agrl. Extension Svc., Hempstead, 1969-72; family resource specialist Tex. Agrl. Extension Svc., Prairie View, 1972-79; nutrition specialist Tex. Agrl. Extension Svc., College Station, 1979-80, 4 H youth specialist, 1980—; pres., chmn. McCord & Co., Cypress, Tex., 1983—; edn. dir. BMW Farms, Brookshire, Tex., 1987-88. Author: Seymour Safety, 1983, 84, Food & Fiber, 1986, 87, It's Up to Me, 1988. Advisor to 4 H Vol. Leaders Assn., College Station, 1986—; com. mem. Tower Oakes Player Assn., Cypress, Tex., 1980—; peer educator Literacy Program, Houston, 1988. Recipient Meritorious Svc. award 4 H Vol. Leaders, 1988. Mem. Agrl. Specialists Assn. (historian, sec.), 4 H Agts. Assn., Epsilon Sigma Phi (state-regional mid career award 1988), World Future Soc., A&M Future Soc. Office: Tex Agrl Extension Svc 809 University East St D-E College Station TX 77843-2473

THIEL, SANDRA SCHOOFS, rehabilitation center administrator; b. Milw., Aug. 4, 1956; d. Lawrence Alfonse and Dorothy Ann (Schlaefer) Schoofs; m. Larry Melvin Thiel, Apr. 27, 1985; 1 child, Deidre Ann. BS in Spl. Edn., Univ. Wis., Eau Claire, 1978. Cert. Vocat. evaluator, 1984. 3rd grade tchr. Sheridan (Wyo.) County Sch. Dist. #2, 1978-81; resource counselor, program mgr. Rehab. Enterprises of North Eastern Wyo. (RENEW), Sheridan, 1982-82; vocat. evaluator RENEW, Sheridan, 1982-85, dir. of residential svcs., 1985-89; v.p. RENEW, 1989—; summer program group leader, No. Wyo. Mental Health Ctr., Sheridan, 1979; summer program supr., No. Wyo. Mental Health Ctr., Sheridan, 1980-81; cons. summer children's program, No. Wyo. Mental Health Ctr., Sheridan, 1982; trainer McCarron-Dial Work Evaluation System, Dallas, 1985—. Surrogate parent Sheridan (Wyo.) Sch. Dist. #2, 1988—; Baptism instr. Holy Name Ch., Sheridan, 1987—; active Civic Theatre, Sheridan, 1981-87, Community Choir, Sheridan, 1978-85; coed softball coach Sheridan Recreation Dist., 1978-85; coord., coach Spl. Olympics, 1982-84; Sunday sch. tchr. Holy Name Ch., Sheridan, 1979-80; group leader for handicapped scouts Boy Scouts of Am., 1976-77; and more. Mem. Nat. Rehab. Assn., Nat. Assn. for Ind. Living, Vocat. Evaluation and Work Adjustment Assn. (nat. chpt., Wyo. chpt. sec. 1987-89), NAFE. Democrat. Roman Catholic. Home: 1407 Highland Ave Sheridan WY 82801 Office: RENEW 245 Broadway Sheridan WY 82801

THIEL, SUSAN, veterinarian; b. Tulsa; d. John E. and Mary A. (Arnold) T. BSc in Biochemistry, Okla. State U., Stillwater, 1980, DVM, 1983. Vet. Greenville Animal Hosp., Tex., 1984—. Mem. Am. Vet. Med. Assn., N.E. Tex. Vet. Med. Assn. (v.p., sec. treas. 1988), Okla. Vet. Med. Assn., Am. Assn. Bovine Practitioners. Home: 3201 Kari Ln #1114 Greenville TX 75401

THIELE, GLORIA DAY, retired librarian, small business owner; b. Los Angeles, Sept. 4, 1931; d. Russell Day Plummer and Dorothy Ruby (Day) Th.; m. Donald Edward Cools, June 13, 1953 (div.); children: Michael, Ramona, Naomi, Lawrence, Nancy, Rebecca, Eugene, Maria, Charles. MusB, Mt. St. Mary's Coll., Los Angeles, 1953. Library asst. Anaheim (Calif.) Pub. Library, 1970-73, head Biblioteca de la Comunidad, 1973-74, children's library asst., 1974-76, children's br. specialist, 1976-78, children's librarian, 1978-81; head children's services Santa Maria (Calif.) Pub. Library, 1981-85; cons. Literature Continuum, Santa Maria Sch. Dist., 1981-85; cons. Organizational Ch.-Sch. Library, Los Angeles, 1980; guest lectr. children's lit. Allan Hancock Coll., Santa Maria, 1981-85; owner Discovery Garden, Grass Valley, Calif., 1989—. Library liaison Casa Amistad Community Service Group, Anaheim, 1973-74; mem. outreach com. Santiago Library System, Orange County, 1973-74, mem. children's services com., 1971-81; mem. Community Services Coordinating Council, Santa Maria, 1982-85; chairperson children's services com. Black Gold Library System, 1983-84; cons. children's library programs, 1986—; profl. storyteller, 1989—. Mem. ALA, Calif. Library Assn., Am. Booksellers Assn., Assn. Booksellers for Children, No. Calif. Booksellers Assn., Ednl. Dealers and Suppliers Assn., So. Calif. Council Lit. for Children and Young People, AAUW, Nevada County C. of C., Women's Network, Minerva Club, Delta Epsilon Sigma. Republican. Roman Catholic.

THIELE, IRMA E., educator; b. Buffalo, Sept. 26, 1918; d. Charles Adolph and Elizabeth Gertrude (Rauschnick) Gritzke; m. George Adolph Burgasser, Sept. 8, 1938 (dec. May 1973); children: Joanne Burgasser Gatz, Patricia Burgasser Doebler, Raymond, George Charles; m. Eugene W. C. Thiele, June 29, 1976 (dec. Apr. 1980); stepchildren: Claudia LoJacano, Janet Leslein, Marion Bay. BS in Edn., SUNY, Buffalo, 1964, MA in Supervision, 1968, postgrad., 1977, 82-83, 87. Cert. elem. tchr., supr., sch. prin., early childhood. Sec. to office mgr. AM&A's Dept. Store, Buffalo, 1935-39; tax preparer IRS, North Tonawanda, N.Y., 1958-59; tchr. Niagara Falls (N.Y.) Bd. Edn., 1964-88; tchr. exercise at Sr. Citizen Ctr. North Tonowonda Bd. Edn. Continuing Edn. program, 1988—; head tchr. math. and lang. arts summer sch. Niagara Falls Bd. Edn., 1977, head tchr. sci., 1985; dir. on youth bd., North Tonawanda, 1982-86. Numerous offices PTA, North Tonawanda, 1945-58; leader Girl Scouts U.S.A., North Tonawanda, 1947-52; local campaign chmn. Eisenhower for U.S. Pres., North Tonawanda, 1956; chmn. March of Dimes, North Tonawanda and Niagara Falls, 1956-57; mem. Luth. Women's Missionary League, Pres. Reagan's Task Force, Bush Task Force, DeGraff Hosp. Aux.; Sunday sch. tchr. Luth. Ch., supt. Vacation Bible Sch.; tchr. calanetics continuing edn., North Tonawanda, 1978—. Mem. Assn. Supervision and Curriculum Devel., Bus. and Profl. Women, Early Childhood Assn., NEA (Elem., Kindergarten, Nursery Edn. div.), SUNY-Buffalo Alumni Assn., Kappa Delta Phi. Republican. Home: 1276 Wurlitzer Ct North Tonawanda NY 14120 Office: 1201 16th St NW Washington DC 20036

THIEMAN, ALICE ANNE, psychology educator; b. Quincy, Ill., Jan. 2, 1941; d. Lloyd Herman and Emery Eloise (Clark) T.; m. James Edward Woods, Aug. 13, 1960 (div. Jan. 1981); children: Michael, Teresa, Cathy, Shari; m. Lloyd Lee Avant, May 26, 1989. BS in Psychology, Iowa State U., 1977, MS in Child Devel., 1980, PhD in Psychology, 1982. Asst. prof. Wartburg Coll., Waverly, Iowa, 1982-85, Briar Cliff Coll., Sioux City, Iowa, 1986-89; specialist human devel. Iowa State U., Ames, 1985-86, asst. prof., 1989—; cons. Pub. Svc. Co. Small Grant, State of Iowa, 1985-86; cons. evaluator Found. for Improvement in Postsecondary Edn. Grant to Briar Cliff Coll., Sioux City, 1988-89. Contbr. articles to profl. publs. Mem. Am. Psychol. Assn., Midwestern Psychol. Assn. Office: Iowa State U MacKay 125 Ames IA 50010

THIGPEN, NORMA JEAN, health education specialist; b. Youngstown, Ohio, Jan. 8, 1957; d. Joseph and Christine L. (Keys) T. BA in Biology, San Jose State U., 1982, MPH, 1988. Lab. supr. PharmChem Labs., Menlo Park, Calif., 1979-87; quality control chemist Becton Dickinson Co., Mountain View, Calif., 1988—; health edn. specialist Santa Clara County (Calif.) Health Dept.; exec. asst., Stanford (Calif.) U., 1986-87; health educator, Menlo Park Police Dept., 1986-87, St. John Missionary Bapt. Ch., Palo Alto, Calif., 1988—. Author diabetic tng. guide, 1988. Bd. dirs., Mothers for Equal Edn., Palo Alto, 1988. Mem. Calif. Assn. Lic. Med. Technologists, Soc. Pub. Health Educators, Queen Esther Lodge. Democrat. Baptist. Home: 8164 Del Monte Ave Newark CA 94560

THOELE-RYAN, SYLVIA KATHLEEN, librarian, artist; b. Springfield, Ill., Dec. 15, 1949; d. Charles Edward and Dorothy May (Douglas) Thoele; m. William John Ryan. BA, U. Wis., 1971, MA, 1973. Med. librarian VA Med. Ctr., North Chicago, Ill., 1973—. Mem. Health Sci. Librarians Ill., Med. Library Assn. Midwest, Art League Lake County, Art Inst. Chgo., AAUW (bd. dirs. Waukegan, Ill. chpt.). Home: 35775 N Greenplace Waukegan IL 60087 Office: VA Med Ctr 3001 Buckley Rd North Chicago IL 60064

THOMAS, ALVA LEE, university administrator; b. Houston, July 23, 1929; d. Young and Luvenia (Dickinson) Lee; m. Aug. 12, 1948 (div. 1964); 1 child, Leiana Thomas Gary. BA in Sociology, Lincoln U., Jefferson City, Mo., 1949; MSE, Chgo. State U., Chgo., 1973. Cert. Tchr., Ill., Calif. . Case worker Cook County Dept. Pub. Welfare, Chgo., 1950-56; tchr. Chgo. Pub. Schs., 1956-75; asst. prof. mgmt. Chgo. State U. Coll. Bus. Adminstrn., 1975-80; mgr. job devel. W.L. Dawson Tech. City Coll. Chgo.; dept. chairperson, lectr. Coll. Edn. Kafanchan, Kaduna State, Nigeria, 1981-84; counselor Chgo. Pub. Schs., 1984-86; dir. career planning placement Chgo. State U., 1986—; coll. cons. Black Collegian Mag., New Orleans 1987--. Cook County Bd. Commrs. Chgo. 1988--. Author, Editor: Training Manuals, Internships, Promotional Lit., Features Newsletters 1979. Pres. Chgo. chpt. Lincoln U. Alumni Assn., 1970-78; bd. dirs. Chgo. State U., 1972-76; mem. Senator Paul E. Simons So. Africa Adv. Com., Chgo., 1985—; chairperson Career Svcs. Adv. Coun., Chgo., 1987—; publicity co-chair Chgo. Alumnae, 1988—; bd. mem. The Jane Addams Conf. Recipient 1st Black History Exhibit award Ahmada Bello U., Zaria Kadunu Nigeria 1983, Women's Devel. Services award Evangelical Ch. Nigeria, Kagaro, Kaduna Nigeria 1984, Recruitment Placement Services award USAF, Chgo. 1987--. Mem. Midwest Coll. Placement Assn., Am. Assn. Coll. U. Personnel, Coll. Placement Assn., Ill. Minority Women's Caucus, Women's Support Ctr., Women in Mgmt., Delta Sigma Theta Inc. Democratic. Office: Chgo State U 95th King Dr Chicago IL 60628

THOMAS, ANDRA CAROL, nurse, scientific studies administrator, health policy strategist; b. Decatur, Ill., Dec. 7, 1948; d. Elmer Jr. and Mary Katherine (Patteson) T. Diploma in Nursing, Barnes Hosp. Sch. Nursing, 1969; student, U. Md., 1971-72, Johns Hopkins U., 1976-79, Coll. Notre Dame, Md., 1980-81, SUNY, 1981—; grad. Minn. Mgmt. Inst., U. Minn., 1990. Staff nurse operating rooms Johns Hopkins Hosp., Balt., 1971-72, head nurse operating rooms, 1972-81; clin. rep. Intec Systems, Inc., Pitts., 1981-83, mgr. clin. research, 1983-85; mgr. clin. research implantable defibrillation devices Cardiac Pacemakers, Inc., St. Paul, 1985, mgr. clin. programs, 1985-88, mgr. sci. studies, 1988—. Mem. Pitts. Ballet Theater Guild, 1981-84; aux. vol. St. Margarets Meml. Hosp., Pitts., 1984-85. Mem. Am. Heart Assn. Clin. Couns., Assn. Operating Room Nurses, Am. Mgmt. Assn., NAFE, N.Am. Soc. Pacing and Electrophysiology, Nat. Health Lawyers Assn., Regulatory Affairs Profl. Soc. Office: Cardiac Pacemakers Inc 4100 Hamline Ave N Saint Paul MN 55112

THOMAS, ANN LOUISE, personnel services administrator; b. West Green, Ga., Sept. 5, 1930; d. Alpheus Albert and Martha Josephine (Williams) Hazard; div.; children—Rodney, Michael, Karen. Student Wayne State U., 1948-50, Harlem Sch. Nursing, N.Y.C., 1951, Wayne County Community Coll., 1969, Henry Ford Community Coll., 1970. Nat. recruiting dir. Internat. Personnel, Detroit, 1962-69; EEO recruiting specialist Blue Cross/Blue Shield Mich., Detroit, 1969-72; assoc. dir. Detroit Indsl. Mission, 1972-76; personnel adminstr. Parke-Davis div. Warner & Lambert Co., Detroit, 1976-79; adminstr. Comprehensive Health Services Detroit, 1979—. Organizer, planner Focus Hope, Detroit, 1970, bd. dirs., 1970—; advisor-cons. Mich. Inter-Collegiate Black Bus. Students Assn., Detroit, 1970-74; co-founder, mem. Detroit Metro EEO Forum, 1973—; chair bd. dirs. Eastwood Clinics, Detroit, 1986—; active in civil rights movement, 1970's—. Named one of 10 Outstanding Detroit Women, Detroit News, 1972. Democrat. Avocations: travel; gourmet cooking; reading; stamp collecting; classical and jazz music. Home: 17334 Santa Rosa Dr Detroit MI 48221

THOMAS, ANNE ELIZABETH, journalist; b. Taunton, Mass., June 28, 1920; d. George and Tamena Barbara (John) Thomas. BS in Journalism, Boston U., 1941, MA in Govt. and History, 1969. Reporter Taunton Daily Gazette, 1941-42, U.P., Boston, 1942-45, Congl. Quar. News Features, Washington, 1948-52; reporter, feature writer Boston Post, 1954-58; dir. news and promotion Newsome Pub. Relations Agy., 1946-47; speech writer Gov. John A. Volpe of Mass., 1960-63; info. officer Mass. Dept. Edn., 1964-66; polit. rsch. and writing, 1978-85; editor, program mgr. Ginn Pub. Co., Boston, 1969-78. Co-author: Leading the Way, 1984. Mem. AAUW. Roman Catholic. Home: The Pelham 1284 Beacon St Brookline MA 02146

THOMAS, BARBARA SINGER, trust company executive; b. N.Y.C., Dec. 28, 1946; d. Jules H. and Marcia (Bosniak) Singer; m. Allen Lloyd Thomas, Mar. 12, 1978; 1 child, Allen Lloyd Jr. B.A. cum laude, U. Pa., 1966; J.D. cum laude (John Norton Pomeroy scholar 1968-69, editor law rev. 1968-69, Jefferson Davis prize public law 1969), NYU, 1969. Bar: N.Y. 1969. Assoc. Paul, Weiss, Rifkind, Wharton & Garrison, N.Y.C., 1969-78; assoc. Kaye, Scholar, Fierman, Hayes & Handler, N.Y.C., 1973-77, ptnr., 1978-80; commr. SEC, Washington, 1980-83; pres. Samuel Montagu Holdings Inc., N.Y.C., 1984-86; regional dir. Asia Pacific Samuel Montagu Ltd., London, 1984-86; sr. v.p., group head The Internat. Pvt. Bank, Bankers Trust Co., N.Y.C., 1986—; mem. Council on Fgn. Relations; adv. council K.H.D. Deutz Am. Corp., KHD Deutz, N.Y.C.; trustee Inst. East-West Securities Studies, N.Y.C. Mem. adv. coun. Women's Econ. Roundtable; internat. adv. bd. Am. U.; mem. women's forum Women's Trusteeship L.A., N.Y.C.; bd. dirs. N.Y.C. Opera; gov. U. Pa. Joseph H. Lauder Inst. Mgmt. and Internat. Studies; mem. bd. overseers Sch. Arts and Scis.; trustee Youth for Understanding, U. Pa. Alumni Assn., Washington Opera, Fin. Women's Assn., N.Y. Law Rev. Alumni Assn.; adv. com. Nat. Mus. Women's Art; internat. com. N.Y.C. BAllet. Recipient award for outstanding service in govt. Fin. Mktg. Council Greater Washington, 1982, Woman of Achievement award WETA-FM, 1983; named one of Outstanding Young Women in Am., 1981, mem. of Men and Women Under 40 Changing Am., Esquire Mag., 1984, Baylor U. Woman of Yr., 1987. Mem. Young Pres.' Orgn., ABA, Washington Bar Assn. (sect. on corp., banking and bus. law), N.Y. State Bar Assn., Internat. Bar Assn., Assn. Bar of City of N.Y. (chmn. corp. law com. 1979-80), Global Econ. Action Inst., Order of Coif, Econ. Club N.Y., NAFE (bd. dirs., Cosmopolitan Club, River Club. Office: Bankers Trust Co 280 Park Ave 33W New York NY 10017

THOMAS, BETH EILEEN WOOD (MRS. RAYMOND O. THOMAS), editor; b. North Vernon, Ind., May 12, 1916; d. Fayette J. and Emma J. (Ream) Wood; m. Raymond O. Thomas, Feb. 28, 1941; 1 son, Stephen W. Comml. diploma, Bedford High Sch., 1934; student, Lockyear Bus. Coll., 1936. Sec. WPA, Vincennes, Ind., 1935-36, Evansville, Ind., 1937-38, Indpls., 1939-41; sec. to adj. AAF Storage Depot, Indpls., 1941-44; sec. Coll. Life Ins., Indpls., 1957-58, Indpls. Sch. Bd., 1958-59; classified office mgr. North Side Topics Newspaper, Indpls., 1960-67. Editor: Child Life mag., 1967-71, Brownie Reader, 1971-73, Children's Playmate mag., 1968—; editorial assoc.: Saturday Evening Post, 1971; exec. editorial dir.: Jack and Jill mag., 1971—, Young World mag., 1971-79, Child Life mag., 1971—, Design mag., 1977-80, Turtle mag. for Presch. Kids, 1979—, Humpty Dumpty's mag., 1980—, Children's Digest, 1980—; exec. editorial dir. juvenile mags., Children's Better Health Inst., 1980—. Mem. Women in Communications, Indpls. Press Club, Soc. Children's Book Writers. Club: Thetis. Home: 6172 Compton B Indianapolis IN 46220 Office: Children's Better Health Inst 1100 Waterway Blvd Box 567 Indianapolis IN 46206

THOMAS, BETTY, actress; b. St. Louis. BFA, Ohio U. Former sch. tchr.; co-star Hill St. Blues, from 1981; Joined Second City Workshop, Chgo.; appeared on Second City TV, 1984; appeared in after sch. spl. The Gift of Love, 1985, Prison of Children, 1986. Appeared in The Fun Factory game show, 1976; film: Troop Beverly Hills, 1989; in TV film Outside Chance, 1978, Nashville Grab, 1981, When Your Lover Leaves, 1983; star TV series Hill Street Blues, 1981-87 (Emmy nominations 1981, 82, 83). Emmy Best Supporting Actress, 1985. Office: care Internat Creative Mgmt 8899 Beverly Blvd Los Angeles CA 90048*

THOMAS, BEVERLY PHYLLIS, state management analyst; b. Ashland, Ky., June 11, 1938; d. Ernest Vincent Runyon and Samye Beaire (Maynard) Burns; m. Lawrence Smith, Apr. 10, 1955 (div. 1958); 1 child, Jeffery Lawrence Smith; m. Jack Lee Thomas, Sept. 20, 1959 (dec. 1982); 1 child, Samye Ann Thomas Davies. Student, Ohio U., Chillicothe, 1972-74. Bookkeeper John R. Burns Acctg. Office, Chillicothe, Ohio, 1964-71; bookkeeper Chillicothe-Ross County Health Dept., 1971-75; bookkeeper, asst. mgr. Holiday Inn, Chillicothe, 1975-76; computer programmer Chillicothe-Ross County Health Dept., 1976-78; mgmt. analyst State of Ohio Dept. Health, Columbus, 1978—; chairperson South East Ohio Pub. Health assn., Columbus, 1981-82. Editor (newsletters) Greenroom Gazette, 1987—, Dateline: Data Svcs., 1987—. Recipient Editors Choice award Nat. Libr. Poetry, 1988. Mem. Ohio Community Theatre Assn. (named for Excellence in Newsletters 1988, del. 1986-89), Ohio Pub. Health Assn. (chairperson 1979-80, chairperson Ohio profl. clerical unit 1983-86, mem. pub. policy com. 1980-85), Nat. Assn. for Female Execs., Gallery Players Assn. (pres. 1988-89). Republican. Home: 1077 Rumsey Rd Columbus OH 43207

THOMAS, BONNIE LOU, real estate sales; b. Berwick, Pa., Apr. 17, 1942; d. Ammon Phillip and Virginia Mae (Slusser) Bowersox; m. J.H. Hindman, June 1959 (div. 1965); m. Francis Lamar Thomas, July 17, 1965; 1 child Jamie Lou. Office clk. J.M. Fields, Winter Park, Fla., 1966-68, Bankamericard Barnett Bank, Winter Park, Fla., 1968-70; sec., bookkeeper Bio-clinical Lab., Maitland, Fla., 1970-77; payroll supr. Harcar Aluminum Products, Sanford, Fla., 1977-80; office mgr. Seminole Work Opportunity Program, Sanford, Fla., 1980; data processing mgr. Robalo/AMF, Fla., 1981-83; sales assoc. Bowles Realty, Longwood, Fla., 1984—. Treas. Christ Ch. Family Group, Longwood, Fla., 1972-75, Cent. Fla. Assoc. for the Deaf, Orlando, 1972-74. Mem. Oceanview Towers Condo Assn. (bd. dirs. 1986—), Wayside Woods Homeowners Assn (treas. 1988—). Republican. Episcopalian. Home: 201 Woods Trail Sanford FL 32771

THOMAS, BRENDA E., paralegal; b. Columbia, S.C., Apr. 2, 1957; d. William and Sarah Mae (Butler) Peterson; m. William L. Thomas, Jan. 1, 1987. AA, Kings Coll., Charlotte, N.C., 1976; BS, U. S.C., 1981; diploma for paralegal studies, Vt. Inst. for Paralegal Studies. Vol. paralegal, court advocate The Family Place Ctr. for Battered Women, Dallas, 1986; paralegal R. Kenneth Mundy Assocs., Washington, 1986, Fowler, Smith and Tieman, Dallas, 1987, Baron and Budd, Dallas, 1987—; owner Paralegal Assistance Assocs. Mem. NAFE, State Bar Tex. (legal assts. div.), Nat. Assn. Legal Assts., Dallas Assn. Legal Assts. (co-chair environ. sect.), Nat. Fedn. for Paralegal Assns. Baptist. Home: PO Box 141199 #226 Dallas TX 75214

THOMAS, CAROL TODD, executive director law firm, consultant; b. Rochester, Pa., May 24, 1952; d. Horace J. and Sarah Evelyn (Pack) T.; m. Robert E. Young, Aug. 16, 1975 (div. Dec. 1985); m. Geoffrey J. Suszkowski, Nov. 26, 1988. MPA, U. Denver, 1975, BA, 1974. Coord. manpower scvs. Onondaga County, Syracuse, N.Y., 1976-78; coord. community assistance Cen. N.Y. Regional Planning and Devel. Bd., Syracuse, 1978-79; from dir. adminstrn. to city mgr. Twp. of O'Hara, Pa., 1979-86; pres. OPUS, Inc., Coraopolis, Pa., 1986; city mgr. Municipality of Monroeville, Pa., 1986; exec. dir. Babst, Calland, Clements and Zomnir, P.C., Pitts., 1987—; ptnr., cons. Mcpl. Cons. Assoc., Upper St. Clair, Pa., 1986—. Participant Leadership Pitts., 1986; mem. exec. com., treas. Civic Light Opera Assocs., Pitts., 1989—; mem. Civic Light Opera Guild, 1986—; charter mem. Citizens League, Pitts., 1988. Mem. Assn. Legal Adminstrs., Govt. Fin. Officers Assn. (bd. dirs. 1982-86, state rep. 1984-86), Internat. City Mgmt. Assn., NAFE, Oakmont Country Club, Longvue Club, Rivers Club, Sigma Iota Epsilon, Gamma Phi Beta. Republican. Presbyterian. Home: 120 Millstone Ln Pittsburgh PA 15238 Office: Babst Calland Clements & Zomnir PC 2 Gateway Ctr 8th Fl Pittsburgh PA 15222

THOMAS, CAROLYN ELISE, educator; b. Mt. Clemens, Mich., Mar. 8, 1943; d. Jack W. and Agnes E. (Anderson) T.; B.A., Western Mich. U.; M.S., U. Wash.; Ph.D., Ohio State U. Instr., U.Idaho, 1966-70; asst. prof. phys. edn. Denison U., Brockport State U., 1972-73; asst. prof. SUNY, Buffalo, 1973-76, asso. prof., 1976—, chmn. dept. phys. edn., 1976-83, chmn. dept. phys. therapy and exercise sci., from 1983. Mem. Philosophic Soc. for Study Sport, Nat. Assn. Sport and Phys. Edn., Soc. Health and Human Values, Nat. Assn. Phys. Edn. in Higher Edn. Author: Sport in a Philosophic Context, 1983; editor: Aesthetics and Dance, 1980. Office: 405 Kimball Tower SUNY Buffalo NY 14214

THOMAS, CHRISTINA JOAN, publishing executive; d. J.C. and Bonnie Mae (Harden) King; 1 child, Julie Anna. Ed., Memphis State U. Cert. practitioner neuro-linguistic programming. Pres. Chela Publs., Memphis, 1986—; founder Inner Light Ctr. Author: Secrets: A Practical Guide to Undreamed of Possibilities. Mem. Am. Mensa. Mailing Address: PO Box 40299 Memphis TN 38174

THOMAS, CLARA MCCANDLESS, emeritus English language educator, biographer; b. Strathroy, Ont., Can., May 22, 1919; d. Basil and Mabel (Sullivan) McCandless; m. Morley Keith Thomas, May 23, 1942; children: Stephen, John. B.A., U. Western Ont., London, 1941, M.A., 1944; Ph.D., U. Toronto, 1962; DLitt (hon.), York U., 1986. Instr. English U. Western Ont., London, 1947-61, U. Toronto, 1958-61; asst. prof. English York U., Toronto, 1961-68; prof. York U., 1969-84, prof. emeritus, 1984—; acad. adv. panel Social Scis. and Humanities Research Council, 1981-84; mem. Killam Awards Selection Bd., 1978-81. Author biography of Anna Jameson, 1967, biography of Egerton Ryerson, 1969, biographies of Margaret Laurence, 1969, 75, biography of William Arthur Deacon, 1982; mem.: (editorial bd.) Literary History of Canada, 1980—. Recipient Internat. Coun. of Can. Studies prize No. Telecom, 1989; grantee Can. Coun., 1967, 73, Social Sci. and Humanities Rsch. Coun. Can., 1978-80. Fellow Royal Soc. Can.; mem. Assn. Can. Univs., Tchrs. English (pres. 1971-72), Assn. Can. and Que. Lit., Bus. and Profl. Women's Club, Assn. for Can. Studies. New Democratic. Office: York U 305 Scott Libr, 4700 Keele St, Downsview, ON Canada M3J 2R2

THOMAS, DEBI (DEBRA J. THOMAS), ice skater; b. Poughkeepsie, N.Y., Mar. 25, 1967; d. McKinley and Janice T.; m. Brian Vanden Hogen. Student, Stanford U. Competitive figure skater, 1976-88. Winner U.S. figure Skating Championship, 1986, 88, Women's World Figure Skating Championship, 1986, World Profl. Figure Skating Championship, 1988, 89. Recipient Am. Black Achievement Award, Ebony mag., named Women Athlete of Yr., 1986; winner Bronze medal Olympic Games, 1988. Address: care IMG 22 E 71st St New York NY 10021

THOMAS, DEBORAH ANNE, librarian, councilwoman; b. Phila., Aug. 14, 1957; d. Joseph Henry and Maryellen Rita (Berry) T. BS in Edn., Shippensburg (Pa.) U., 1979, MLS, 1981. Media specialist North Hagerstown (Md.) High Sch., 1980-81; reference libr. St. Joseph's U., Phila., 1982-84, head of reference libr., 1985-86, head pub. svcs., 1987—. Chairperson Colwyn (Pa.) Dem. Com., 1990—; founder, organizer Polit. Action in Neighborhoods, Colwyn, 1989—; sec. Southeastern Del. County Dems., Colwyn, 1990—; councilwoman Borough of Colwyn, 1990. Mem. ALA, Assn. Coll. Rsch. Librs., Phila. Inter-Libr. Loan Group (pres. 1987-89), Phila. Area Reference Librs. Info. Exch., NAFE, NOW, Greenpeace. Home: 401 Thatcher Ave Colwyn PA 19023-2721 Office: St Josephs U 5600 City Ave Philadelphia PA 19131-1399

THOMAS, DEBORAH BROOKS, artist, educator; b. Pitts., Sept. 25, 1951; d. Joseph Warren Jr. and Gladys Mae (Brooks) T. AB with honors, U. Mich., 1973; MA, U. Pa., 1974, postgrad., 1974-79; student, atelier Janine Falk-Vairant, Geneva, 1982-84, Art Students League, 1984-85. tchr. dept. Am. civilization U. Pa., Phila., 1975-78; tchr. dept. de langue et littérature anglaises U. de Genève, 1979-82; tchr. English seminar U. Bern Switzerland, 1980, 82-83; tchr. art dept. Vassar Coll., Poughkeepsie, N.Y., 1985-86, Bklyn. Friends Sch., 1989. Exhibited at Art Students League, 1984, 85, TAI Artists Group, 1987, 88, Multi Media Arts Gallery, 1988, 89. Intern to dir. Pa. Acad. Fine Arts Bicentennial Exhbn., 1975; curator Robert L. McNeil Jr. Americana Collection, 1977-79; researcher U. Pa. Archives, 1978; curator, founding mem. TAI Artists Group, 1987-88. Mem. N.Y. Artists' Equity, Coll. Art Assn. Episcopalian. Studio: 129 W 56th St New York NY 10019

THOMAS, ELIZABETH ANNE, advertising executive; b. Chgo., June 6, 1959; d. Kenneth Warren and Sharon Diane (VanMatre) T. BS in Journalism, U. Fla., Gainesville, 1980. Sales assoc. RKO Radio Sales, L.A., 1980-81; leasing cons. R & B Enterprises, Inc., L.A., 1981; owner, operator Thomas Mktg. Svcs., Ft. Lauderdale, Fla., 1981-82; editorial asst. First Mktg. Corp., Pompano Beach, Fla., 1981-82, account exec., 1982-83, sr. account exec., 1983-84, group supr. retail publ., 1984-87, v.p. nat. accounts mgr., 1988-90; regional advt. mgr. UDC Homes, Boynton Beach, 1990—. Editor: Fin. Newsletter, Money Matters 1987 (awarded Printing Industries of Fla. award of Excellence 1988). Mem. Broward County Young Reps., Ft. Lauderdale 1983-85. Named Advt. Student of Yr., Bus. & Profl. Advt. Assn., S.E. Region, 1980. Mem. Pompano Players Theater. Republican. Roman Catholic. Office: UDC Homes 4965 LeChalet Blvd Boynton Beach FL 33437

THOMAS, ELLEN DILLON, marketing executive; b. Nashville, Oct. 29, 1958; d. William Wesley and Ellen Wallace (White) Dillon; m. James Anderson Thomas, June 20, 1981; 1 child, Warner Grant. BS, Vanderbilt U., 1980; MBA, 1981. Mktg. dir. corr. banking div. U.S. Bank, Nashville, 1981-83; advt. dir. Jacques-Miller, Inc., Nashville, 1983-86; sec., treas. Silver Lining, Inc., 1982—, owner, Vol. Ventures Inc., 1987—. Mem. Am. Mktg. Assn. (pres. Nashville chpt.), Nashville Acad. Theatre Guild, Jr. League of Nashville, Pi Beta Phi. Mem. Christian Ch. Avocations: gardening, skiing, traveling. Home: 716 Cantrell Ave Nashville TN 37215 Office: PO Box 159009 Nashville TN 37215

THOMAS, ELLEN MCVEIGH, human resources executive; b. Manchester, N.H., Aug. 14, 1952; d. John Joseph and Margaret Mary (Devan) McVeigh; m. Stephen David Thomas, Nov. 6, 1983. BS, St. Anselm Coll., 1974; MBA, Rivier Coll., 1989. Asst. dir. admissions Cath. Med. Ctr., Manchester, 1975-76, dir. admissions, 1976-77, adminstrv. coordinator, 1978-80, asst. dir. personnel, 1981-83, personnel mgr., 1983-85, dir. personnel, 1985-86, v.p. of human resources, 1986-89; v.p. of human resources Cen. Maine Healthcare Corp., Lewiston, Maine, 1989—; mgmt. cons. Porter-McGee, Manchester, 1983-85, Creative Entertainment Corp., Manchester, 1981—. Bd. dirs. Anselmian Summer Theatre, Manchester, 1973-76; bd. dirs. Big Bros./Big Sisters of Greater Manchester, 1987-89, N.H. Performing Arts Ctr., 1988-89. Mem. Maine Soc. for Healthcare Human Resources, N.H. Soc. for Healthcare Personnel Adminstrn. (treas. 1983-84, v.p., 1984-85, pres. 1985-86), Manchester Soc. Personnel Adminstrs., N.H. Hosp. Assn. (council for mgmt. and recruitment task force 1984-88). Office: Cen Maine Med Ctr PO Box 4500 Lewiston ME 04240

THOMAS, ESTHER MERLENE, educator; b. San Diego, Oct. 16, 1945; d. Merton Alfred and Nellie Lida (Von Pilz) T. AA, Grossmont Coll., 1966; BA, San Diego State U., 1969; MA, U. Redlands, 1977. Cert. elem. and adult edn. tchr. Tchr. Cajon Valley Union Sch. Dist., El Cajon, 1969—; tchr. Hopi and Navajo Native Americans, Ariz, Calif., Utah, 1964-74, Goose and Gander Nursery School, Lakeside, Calif., 1964-66; dir. bible and Sunday schs. various chs., Lakeside, 1961-87. Contbr. articles to profl. jours. Mem. U.S. Senatorial Club, Washington, 1984—, Conservative Caucus, Inc., Washington, 1988—, Ronald Reagan Presdl. Found., Ronald Reagan Rep. Ctr., 1988, Rep. Presdl. Citizen's Adv. Commn., 1989—, 1988 Rep. Platform Planning Com., Calif., 1988, health articulation com. project AIDS, Cajon Valley Union Sch. Dist., 1988—, Concerned Women Am., Washington, Recruit Depot Hist. Mus., San Diego, 1989—, Citizen's Drug Free Am., Calif., 1989—, The Heritage Found., 1988—; charter mem. Marine Corps; mem. Lakeside (Calif.) Centennial Com., 1985-86; hon. mem. Rep. Presl. Task Force, Washington, 1986. Mem. Nat. Tchrs. Assn., Calif. Tchrs. Assn., Cajon Valley Educators Assn., Christian Bus. & Profl. Women, Lakeside Hist. Soc., Capitol Hill Women's Club. Republican. Home: 13594 Hwy 8 Apt 3 Lakeside CA 92040 Office: Flying Hills Elem Sch 1251 Finch St El Cajon CA 92020

THOMAS, ETHEL COLVIN NICHOLS (MRS. LEWIS VICTOR THOMAS), educator; b. Cranston, R.I., Mar. 31, 1913; d. Charles Russell and Mabel Maria (Colvin) Nichols; Ph.B., Pembroke Coll. in Brown U., 1934; M.A., Brown U., 1938; Ed.D., Rutgers U., 1979; m. Lewis Victor Thomas, July 26, 1945 (dec. Oct. 1965); 1 child, Glenn Nichols. Tchr. English, Cranston High Sch., 1934-39; social dir. and adviser to freshmen, Fox Hall, Boston U., 1939-40; instr. to asst. prof. English Am. Coll. for Girls, Istanbul, Turkey, 1940-44; dean freshman, dir. admission Women's Coll. of Middlebury, Vt., 1944-45; tchr. English, Robert Coll., Istanbul, 1945-46; instr. English, Rider Coll., Trenton, N.J., 1950-51; tchr. English, Princeton (N.J.) High Sch., 1951-61, counselor, 1960-62, 72-83, coll. counselor, 1962-72, sr. peer counselor, 1986—. Mem. NEA, AAUW, Nat. Assn. Women Deans Adminstrs. and Counselors, Am. Assn. Counseling and Devel., Bus. and Profl. Women's Club (named Woman of Yr., Princeton chpt. 1977), Met. Mus. Art, Phi Delta Kappa, Kappa Delta Pi. Presbyn. Clubs: Brown University (N.Y.C.); Nassau.

THOMAS, FLORENCE KATHLEEN, army officer; b. Torrington, Conn., June 20, 1945; d. James Dudley and Nova Lee (Campbell) T. B.A. in Mass Communications, U. Tex.-El Paso, 1970; M.A. in Adminstrn. of Justice, Wichita State U., 1984. Commd. 2d lt. U.S. Army, 1969, advanced through grades to lt. col., 1990; chief ops. tng. devels. U.S. Mil. Police Sch., Ft. McClellan, Ala., 1979-80; exec. officer criminal investigation div. Kaiserslautern, Germany, 1980-82; comdr. criminal investigation div. Nuernberg Field Office, Fed. Republic Germany, 1982-83; corrections officer Forces Command, Provost Marshal, Ft. McPherson, Ga., 1985; chief law enforcement mgmt. div., 1985-87, chief evaluations, exercise div., dir. ops., 1987-88; chief force deployment br. plans div. office of dir. for ops. HQ USAREUR & 7A, Heidelberg, Germany, 1988—; mil. cons. law enforcement activities, 1977—. Mem. Assn. U.S. Army, Nat. Assn. Female Execs., U.S. Golf Assn., Mid-Ga. Women's Golf Assn., Am. Correctional Assn. Avocation: running, golf, fishing. Home: PO Box 45 APO New York NY 09063 Office: HQ USAREUR DCSOPS APO New York NY 09043

THOMAS, GEORGIA MAE, service executive; b. Racine, Wis., Sept. 22, 1939; d. Arthur E. and Alma S. (Baker) Bengtson; m. Monroe Thomas, Aug. 1, 1968. Diploma, Swedish Hosp. Sch. Nursing, Mpls., 1960; BA, U. Wis., Kenosha, 1972. RN. Staff nurse The Swedish Hosp., Mpls., 1960-61; staff nurse, head nurse, supr. St. Luke's Hosp., Racine, Wis., 1961-70; instr. St. Luke's Sch. Nursing, Racine, 1970-74; v.p. Quality Services, Inc., Racine, 1974-80, Cardinal Profl. Bldg. Maintenance and Supplies, Cardinal Express div. M.G.T. Holdings, Inc., Racine and Milw., 1980—; del. White House Conf. Small Bus., 1986, exec. bd. Wis. Gov.'s Conf. Small Bus., 1987; bd. dirs. Nat. Small Bus. United, Washington, MGT Holdings Inc., Cardinal Express, Cardinal Profl. Bldg. Maintenance, Cardinal Janitorial Supplies. Vol. St. Luke's Hosp. Aux., Racine, 1985—; bd. dirs. Rep. Fedn., Racine County, 1986—; mem. Bus. Ptnrs. Inc., Washington, 1987, elected bd. Nat. Small Bus. United, Washington, 1988—. Mem. Wis. Women Entrepreneurs (legis. chair Milw. 1986-87, state pres. 1988-89), Ind. Bus. Assn. Wis. (bd. dirs. 1988—, v.p. fed. programs 1989—), Nat. Fedn. Ind. Bus., Nat. Assn. Women Bus. Owners. Lutheran. Home: 1564 Maria St Racine WI 53404 Office: MGT Holdings Inc 1515 16th St PO Box 1885 Racine WI 53401

THOMAS, GEORGIE A., state official. B.A., Cornell U., 1965; M.B.A., Columbia U., 1973. Asst. portfolio mgr. Money Mgmt. dept. R.W. Pressprich & Co. Inc., N.Y.C., 1968-71; portfolio analyst Bache & Co., N.Y.C., 1971-72; with Exxon Corp., N.Y.C., 1973-76, consolidation analyst Treas. dept., 1975-76; treas. Penntech Papers Inc., N.Y.C., 1976-79; budget dir. Yankee Publishing Inc., Dublin, N.H., 1982-85; treas. State of N.H., Concord, 1985—; mem. econ. growth and productivity and tech. coms. Bus. Research Adv. Council of Bur. Labor Statistics, 1978-79; mem. alumni counseling bd. Columbia U. Bus. Sch., 1973-79. Editor: Jour. World Bus., Columbia Bus. Sch. Mem. Fin. Women's Assn. N.Y. (mem. exec. bd. 1977-78), Womens Econ. Roundtable. Club: Cornell of Fairfield County (Conn.). Home: Ashley Rd Antrim NH 03440 Office: State NH State House Annex Rm 121 Concord NH 03301

THOMAS, GLADYS ROBERTS, foundation executive. BA, Bryn Mawr Coll. Pub. relations mgr. Am. Internat. Group, N.Y., 1978-80, dir. corp. communications, 1980-90; v.p. The Starr Found., N.Y.C., 1990—. Mem. Insurers Pub. Rels. Coun., India House. Republican. Office: Starr Found 70 Pine St New York NY 10270

THOMAS, HELEN A. (MRS. DOUGLAS B. CORNELL), journalist; b. Winchester, Ky., Aug. 4, 1920; d. George and Mary (Thomas) T.; m. Douglas B. Cornell. BA, Wayne U., 1942; LLD, Eastern Mich. State U., 1972, Ferris State Coll., 1978, Brown U., 1986; LHD, Wayne State U., 1974, U. Detroit, 1979; LLD, St. Bonaventure U., 1988, Franklin Marshall U., 1989, No. Michigan U., 1989. With UPI, 1943—; wire svc. reporter UPI, Washington, 1943-74; White House bur. chief UPI, 1974—. Author: Dateline White House. Recipient Woman of Yr. in Communications award Ladies Home Jour., 1975, 4th Estate award Nat. Press Club, 1984. Mem. Women's Nat. Press Club (pres. 1959-60, William Allen White Journalism award, U. Mo. Journalism award, Dean of Schs. of Journalism award), Am. Newspaper Women's Club (past v.p.), White House Corrs. Assn. (pres. 1976), Sigma Delta Chi (fellow, Hall of Fame), Delta Sigma Phi (hon.). Home: 2501 Calvert St NW Washington DC 20008 Office: UPI World Hdqrs 1400 I St Washington DC 20005

THOMAS, JACQUELYN MAY, librarian; b. Mechanicsburg, Pa., Jan. 26, 1932; d. William John and Gladys Elizabeth (Warren) Harvey; m. David Edward Thomas, Aug. 28, 1954; children: Lesley J., Courtenay J., Hilary A. B.A. summa cum laude, Gettysburg Coll., 1954; student U. N.C., 1969; M.Ed., U. N.H., 1971. Libr., Phillips Exeter Acad., Exeter, N.H., 1971-77, acad. libr., 1977—, chair governing bd. Child Care Ctr., 1987—; chair Com. to Enhance Status of Women, Exeter, 1981-84; dir. Loewenstein Com., Exeter, 1982—; pres. Cum Laude Soc., Exeter, 1984-86. Editor: The Design of the Libr.: A Guide to Sources of Information, 1981, Rarities of Our Time: The Special Collections of the Phillips Exeter Academy Libr. Trustee, treas. Exeter Day Sch., 1965-69; mem. bd. Exeter Hosp. Vols., 1954-59; mem. Exeter Hosp. Corp., 1978—; mem. bldg. com. Exeter Pub. Libr., 1986—; chair No. New Eng., Council for Women in Ind. Schs., 1985-87; chmn. Lamont Poetry Program, Exeter, 1984-86. N.H. Council for Humanities grantee, 1981-82; Nat. Endowment Humanities grantee, 1982; recipient Lillian Radford Trust award, 1989. Mem. ALA, New Eng. Libr. Assn., N.H. Ednl. Media Assn., New Eng. Assn. Ind. Sch. Librs., Am. Assn. Sch. Librs. (program com. for non-pub. sch. sect. 1985—), Phi Beta Kappa. Home: 16 Elm St Exeter NH 03833 Office: The Library Phillips Exeter Acad Exeter NH 03833

THOMAS, JEANETTE MAE, public accountant; b. Winona, Minn., Dec. 19, 1946; d. Herbert and Arline (Shank) Harmon; m. Gerald F. Thomas, Aug. 9, 1969; children: Bradley, Christopher. BS, Winona State U., 1968; postgrad., Colo. State U.; CFP, Coll. for Fin. Planning, Denver, 1985. Enrolled agt.; cert. fin. planner; registered investment advisor. Tchr. pub. schs. systems Colo., N.Mex., Mich., 1968-72; adminstrv. asst. Bus. Men's Svcs., Ft. Collins, Colo., 1974-75; tax cons. Tax Corp. Am., Ft. Collins, Colo., 1972-80; chief acct. Jayland Electric, La Porte, Colo., 1981—; owner Thomas Acctg. & Tax Svcs., Ft. Collins, 1980—. Contbr. articles to newspapers and profl. newsletters. Bd. dirs. local PTO, 1984-85; treas. Boy Scouts Am., 1985-88; master food preserver coop. extension Colo. State U., 1988—; speaker, mem. steering com. Women's Fin. Info. Program, 1988—. Mem. Internat. Assn. for Fin. Planning (various offices including pres. 1984—), Am. Soc. Women Accts. (bd. dirs. 1984-86), Pvt. Industry Coun. (fin. com. 1987—), Nat. Soc. Pub. Accts., Am. Notary Assn., Ft. Collins C. of C. (mem. red carpet com. 1989—). Home: Box 370 La Porte CO 80535

THOMAS, KAREN M., physical therapist; b. Fulton, N.Y., Oct. 21, 1949; d. Harold Edwin and Mary Fullerton (MacTurk) Blance; m. Bruce Jay Thomas, June 12, 1971; children: Krista Marie, Bryan Jay. BS, Ithaca Coll., 1971. Grad. Realtors Inst. Staff phys. therapist Anchorage Hosp. and Med. Ctr., 1981-82; team leader cons. Mary Kay Cosmetics, Inc., Dallas, 1984-86; salesperson Gallinger Real Estate, Inc., Baldwinsville, N.Y., 1986-90; staff phys. therapist SUNY Health Sci. Ctr., Syracuse, 1990—. Mem. Am. Bus. Women's Assn. (rec. sec. 1988-89, pres. 1989-90, Woman of Yr. 1989, v.p. 1990—), Am Phys. Therapy Assn. Democrat. Episcopalian. Home: RD 8 Box 70 Fulton NY 13069

THOMAS, KAY LEE, optician, secondary school educator; b. Cleve., Mar. 21, 1942; d. John Henry and Ethelmae (Petee) Aufdenhaus; children: Teri Panter-Thomas, Tracy. BA in Secondary Edn., Kent State U., 1964, postgrad., 1974-75. Lic. optician, Ohio. Tchr. high sch. Streetsboro (Ohio) Bd. Edn., 1964-65; substitute tchr., pvt. tutor Wickliffe (Ohio) City Schs., 1966-75, Euclid (Ohio) Pub. Schs., 1965-75; optician Case Optical Co., Warrensville Hts., Ohio, 1975-80, mgr., 1980—. Fellow Nat. Acad. Opticianry; mem. Sigma Delta Pi.

THOMAS, LAURA MARLENE, artist, social services; b. Chico, Calif., Apr. 29, 1936; d. Boyd Stanley Beck and Lois Velma (Behrke) Lyons; m. Charles Rex Thomas; children: Tracy Loraine, Jeffory Norris. AA in Fine Arts, Sacramento City Coll., 1978; BA in Fine Arts, Calif. State U., 1981. Tchrs. asst. Hanford Elem. Sch., Hanford, Calif., 1963-68; asst. dir. RSVP: Retired Sr. Vol. Program, Hanford, 1971-74; dir. of Art Bank Sacramento City Coll., Sacramento, 1976-78; pub. asst. Student Activities Calif. State Univ., Sacramento, 1978-81; antique dealer pvt. practice, Sacramento, 1981--, arts and crafts bus., 1976--; social worker Cath. Social Svcs., Sacramento, 1985--. Artist: weaving, Double Image, 1977, 2nd Place 1977; ceramic sculptor, Bird. Charter mem. YWCA, Sacramento, 1972, Folsum Hist. Soc., 1988. Cert. of appreciation, Carmellia City Ctr. Adv. Council, Sacramento, 1986. Mem. Statue of Liberty-Ellis Island Found., 1985, North Shore Animal League (Benefactors award 1985), Internat. Platform Assn., Calif. State U. Alumni Assn., Hanford Sportsman Club (v.p. 1963-68). Republican. Protestant. Home: 2721 I St #8 Sacramento CA 95816 Office: Cath Social Svcs 1121 9th St Sacramento CA 95814

THOMAS, LEONA MARLENE, medical records educator; b. Rock Springs, Wyo., Jan. 15, 1933; d. Leonard H. and Opal (Wright) Francis; m. Craig L. Thomas, Feb. 22, 1955; (div. Sept. 1978); children: Peter, Paul, Patrick, Alexis. BA, Govs. State U., 1982, MHS, 1986; cert. med. records adminstrn. U. Colo., 1954. Dir. med. records dept. Meml. Hosp. Sweetwater County, Rock Springs, 1954-57; staff assoc. Am. Med. Records Assn., Chgo., 1972-77, asst. editor, 1979-81; asst. prof. Chgo. State U., 1984—, faculty esnator, 1989-90, chairperson com. Coll. Allied Health Pers., 1986-88; statistician Westlake Hosp., Melrose Park, Ill., 1982-84. Co. pres. Ill. Dist. 60 PTA, Westmont, Ill., 1972. Mem. editorial rev. bd. Assembly On Edn. newsletter. Mem. Assembly on Edn., Am. Med. Records Assn., Ill. Med. Records Assn., Chgo. and Vicinity Med. Records Assn., Am. Pub. Health Assn., Ill. Assn. Allied Health Profls., Internat. Platform Assn., Chgo. and Vicinity Med. Records Assn. (publicity com. 1989—), Governors State Alumni Assn. Democrat. Methodist. Home: 6340 F Americana Dr Apt 1101 Clarendon Hills IL 60514 Office: Chgo State U Coll Allied Health 95th at King Dr Chicago IL 60608

THOMAS, LINDA B., accounting administrator; b. Hudson, N.Y., Dec. 16, 1946; d. Emil Jr. and Edith Gloria (Sauer) Bitterlich; m. Delbert C. Thomas, Dec. 3, 1967; children: Robert Allen, James Emil. Sec. IBM Corp., Poughkeepsie, N.Y., 1965-67, Raleigh, N.C., 1967-70; officer First Quality Electric, Inc., Monroe, N.C., 1988—. Home: 8116 Potter Rd S Waxhaw NC 28173 Office: 8608 Potter Rd S Waxhaw NC 28173

THOMAS, LORI RAE, lawyer; b. Ft. Morgan, Colo., Dec. 24, 1954; d. Arlo Acton Watchorn and Carlene Joyce Miller; m. Frank Nelson Thomas, Aug. 21, 1976; 1 child, Allison Leigh. BA, U. S.D., Vermillions, S.D., 1976; Student, Stenotype Inst., Sioux Falls, 1978-79, 81; JD, Tex. Tech. U., Lubbock, 1988. Freelance ct. reporter Fremont, Neb., 1982-83; ct. stenographer Dodge County Ct., Fremont, Nebr., 1983; placement coordinator Tex. Tech. U. Sch. Law, Lubbock, Tex., 1983-85; atty. Shannon, Gracey, Ratliff & Miller, Ft. Worth; contbg. author for lender liability seminar Tarrant County Civil Trial Lawyers, 1989. Editor: Tex. Tech. Law Review, 1986-88. Sec. Ballet Lubbock Bd. Dir. Lubbock, 1984-86, Ballet Lubbock Bd. Dir., Lubbock, 1984-88, V.P./Pres. Ballet Lubbock Guild, Lubbock, 1984-86. Recipient C.J.S. Award Tex. Tech. Sch. Law Faculty, Lubbock, 1986, Am. Jurisprudence Awards Tex. Tech. Sch. Law, 1986, 1988, Outstanding Young Women of Am. Mem. ABA, Tex. State Bar Assn., Tex. Young Lawyers' Assn., Tarrant County Bar Assn., Tarrant County Young Lawyers' Assn., Conf. Consumer Fin. Law, Order of Coif, Phi Kappa Phi, Phi Delta Phi. Am. Baptist. Home: 7612 Meadowlark Dr Fort Worth TX 76133 Office: Shannon Gracey Ratliff & Miller 201 Main #2200 Fort Worth TX 76102

THOMAS, LUCILLE COLE, librarian; b. Dunn, N.C., Oct. 1, 1921; d. Collie and Minnie (Lee) Cole; m. George Browne Thomas, May 24, 1943; children: Ronald C., Beverly G. Effatt. BA, Bennett Coll., 1941; MA, NYU, 1955; MS, Columbia U., 1957. Tchr., Bibb County Bd. Edn., Macon, Ga., 1947-55; libr. Bklyn. Pub. Libr., 1955-56; libr. N.Y.C. Bd. Edn., Bklyn., 1956-68, supr. librs., 1968-77, dir. elem. sch. librs., 1977-83; program dir. Weston Woods Inst., Weston, Conn., 1984-85; founder Sch. Libr. Media Day, N.Y. State, 1973; cons. Putnam Pub. Group, N.Y.C., 1983, bd. examiners N.Y. City Bd. Edn., 1983—; bd. dir. Am. Reading Coun., N.Y.C., 1976-89; mem. adv. bd. Regents' Adv. Council on Learning Tech., Albany, N.Y., 1982—; reviewer U.S. Office Ednl. Rsch. & Improvement, 1988—; adj. prof. CUNY, 1987—; coord. UNESCO/Internat. Assn. Sch. Librarianship Book Program for devel. countries, 1980—; trustee N.Y. Met. Ref. &

Rsch. Libr. Agy., N.Y.C., 1979-83; liaison Freedom to Read Foundation. Editor: Insight, 1974. Contbr. articles to profl. publs. Treas., Bklyn. Home for Aged Commn., 1967—, vestry mem. St. John's Episcopal Ch., Bklyn., 1988-90, chair stewardship com., 1987—; mem. Gould Found. Recipient Disting. Alumna award Bennett Coll., 1981, Edn. award Bus. and Profl. Women's Club, Bklyn., 1983, Merit award Bklyn. Coun. Suprs., 1983, Achievement award Columbia U. Sch. Libr. Svcs., 1987, Grolier Found. award, 1988, Disting. Pub. Svc. award SUNY, Albany, 1989. Mem. ALA (councilor 1980—, exec. bd. personnel com. 1988-89, chair Nominations and Spl. Assignments Com. 1987-88, chair Hqtrs. Libr. Rev. Accountability Com. 1987-88, disaster relief com. 1989-90, direction and rev. com. 1989-90, exec. bd. found. 1987-89, chair ALA/AASL disting. svc. award com. 1989-90), N.Y. Libr. Assn. (pres. 1977-78, Appreciation cert. 1983, pres. sch. libr. media sect. 1973-74, Outstanding Achievement award 1984, Achievement award 1988), Internat. Assn. Sch. Librarianship (pres. 1989—), Internat. Fedn. Libr. Assn. (sec. 1985-89, chair sch. librs. sect. 1989—), N.Y. Libr. Club (pres. 1977-78), N.Y.C. Sch. Librs. Assn. (pres. 1970-72, chair sch. librs. sect. 1989—), Bklyn. Hist. Soc. (named one of Outstanding Women of Bklyn. 1985), Schomburg Soc., Schomburg Commn., Alpha Kappa Alpha, Pi Phi Omega, Women's City of N.Y.C. Club (bd. dirs. 1986—, vice chmn. 1987-89, chair edn. com. 1989—). Democrat. Home: 1184 Union St Brooklyn NY 11225

THOMAS, LYN ELLEN, software engineer; b. Pitts., Dec. 17, 1958; d. Frederick Albert and Grace Bollens T. BS in Computer Sci., U. Pitts., 1983; AS in Computer Engring., Tampa Tech. Inst., 1986. Software engr. Honeywell, Tampa, Fla., 1983-85, Fotomat, Tampa, 1986-88, Precision Software Inc., Tampa, 1989—. Home: 3719 Alabama Ave Saint Petersburg FL 33703

THOMAS, MABLE, state legislator; b. Atlanta, Nov. 8, 1957; d. Bernard and Madie Thomas. BS in Pub. Adminstrn., Ga. State U., 1982, postgrad., 1983—. With acctg. dept. Trust Co. Bank, Atlanta, 1977; recreation supr. Sutton Community Sch., Atlanta, 1977-78; data transcriber Ga. Dept. Natural Resources, Atlanta, 1978-79; clk. U.S. Census Bur., Atlanta, 1980; laborer City of Atlanta Parks and Recreation, 1980-81; student asst. Ga. State U., Atlanta, 1981-82; state rep. Ga. House Reps., Atlanta, 1984—; mem. exec. com. Ga. Legis. Black Census, Atlanta, 1985—. Mem. adv. youth council Salvation Army Bellwood Club, 1975; founder Vine City Community Improvement Assn., Atlanta, 1985; mem. Neighborhood Planning Unit, Ga. State U. Adv. Bd. of Comprehensive Youth Services, 1988—, Nat. Black Woman's Health Project, Ga. Housing Coalition; actively involved in Say No to Drugs Program; bd. dirs. Am. Cancer Soc., 1988—. Recipient Bronze Jubilee award City of Atlanta Cultural Affairs, 1984, Disting. Service award Grady Hosp., 1985, Human Service award for community and political leadership for disadvantaged, 1986, Exceptional Service award Young Community Leaders, 1986, Citizenship award Salvation Army Club; named Outstanding Freshman Legislator, 1986, one of Outstanding Young People of Atlanta, 1987. Mem. Ga. Assn. Black Elected Officials (mem. housing and econ. devel. com.), Conf. Minority Pub. Adminstrn. (Outstanding Service award), Nat. Polit. Congress Black Women (bd. dirs.). Democrat. Methodist. Home: PO Box 573 Atlanta GA 30301

THOMAS, MARGARET ANN, psychologist; b. Cleve., June 2, 1945; d. Frank Robert and Marie (Prochazka) Wiesenberger; m. Charles Walter Geggie, Aug. 30, 1969 (div. 1978); 1 child, Anne Marie; m. James Blake Thomas, Sept. 14, 1978. BA, Albion Coll., 1967; MA, Mich. State U., 1969, PhD, 1981. Lic. psychologist, Mich. Head advisor Albion (Mich.) Coll., 1967-68; head advisor Mich. State U., East Lansing, 1970-72, assoc. dir. Holmes Hall, Lyman Briggs Coll., 1972-74, grad. asst. dept psychiatry, 1974-79, psychology intern, 1977-79; cons. Stress Mgmt. Inc., Okemos, Mich., 1979-80; staff psychologist James B. Thomas, M.D., P.C., Okemos, Mich., 1980-89; psychologist Psychol. Health Systems, P.C., Lansing, Mich., 1989-90; clin. instr. Dept. Psychiatry, Mich. State U., East Lansing, 1980-86. Pres. parent adv. com., Mich. State U. Day Care Ctr., 1975-77; mem. Friends of Bob Carr for U.S. Ho. Reps., East Lansing, 1982; parent adv. com. Mason (Mich.) Middle Sch., 1985-86. Mem. Am. Psychol. Assn., Mich. Psychol. Assn., Greater Lansing Area Women Therapists (founder, chairperson 1983-84), Nat. Assn. Career Women (sec. Lansing Founding chpt. 1985-87). Democrat. Episcopalian. Home: RFD Box 66 Penobscot ME 04476

THOMAS, MARGARET JEAN, clergywoman, religious research consultant; b. Detroit, Dec. 24, 1943; d. Robert Elcana and Purcella Margaret (Hartness) T. BS, Mich. State U., 1964; MDiv, Union Theol. Sem., Va., 1971; D Ministry, San Francisco Theol. Sem., 1991. Ordained to ministry United Presbyn. Ch., 1971. Dir. rsch. bd. Christian edn. Presbyn. Ch. U.S., Richmond, Va., 1965-71; dir. rsch. gen. coun. Presbyn. Ch. U.S., Atlanta, 1972-73; mng. dir. rsch. div. support agy. United Presbyn. Ch. U.S.A., N.Y.C., 1974-76; dep. exec. dir. gen. assembly mission coun. United Presbyn. Ch. U.S.A., 1977-83; dir. N.Y. coordination Presbyn. Ch. (U.S.A.), 1983-85; exec. dir. Minn. Coun. Chs., Mpls., 1985—; mem. permanent jud. commn. Presbyn. Ch., 1985—, moderator, 1989—; sec. com. on ministry Twin Cities Area Presbytery, Mpls., 1985—, dir. joint religious legis. coalition, 1985—; bd. dirs. Franklin Nat. Bank, Mpls. Contbr. articles to profl. jours. Mem. adv. panel crime and victim svcs. Hennepin County Atty.'s Office, Mpls., 1985-86, Police and Community Rels. Task Force, St. Paul, 1986, Hennepin County Crime Victim Coun., Mpsl., 1990—; bd. dirs. Minn. Foodshare, Mpls., 1985—; co-chair Minn. Interreligious Com., 1988—; bd. dirs. Minn. Coalition on Health, St. Paul, 1986—, Minn. Black-on-Black Crime Task Force, 1988, Twin Cities Coalition for Affordable Health Care, 1986-87; bd. dirs. Abbott Northwestern Counseling Pastoral Ctr., 1988—, vice chmn., 1989—, chmn., 1990—. Recipient Human Rels. award Jewish Community Rels. Coun./Anti-Defamation League, 1989. Mem. Nat. Assn. Ecumenical Staff, Religious Edn. Assn. (sec. 1974-76), People for the Am. Way, NOW (Outstanding Woman of Minn. 1986), Amnesty Internat. Democratic Farm Laborer. Office: Minn Coun of Chs 122 W Franklin Ave #100 Minneapolis MN 55404

THOMAS, MARJORIE BEKAERT, lawyer, television producer and syndicator; b. N.Y.C., Jan. 3, 1947; d. Charles J. and Marjorie (Dew) Bekaert; m. Bryan M. Thomas. BA with honors, Duke U., 1969; postgrad., Trinity Coll., 1975; JD, U. Fla., 1976. Bar: Fla. 1976. Assoc. van den Berg, Gay & Burke, Orlando, Fla., 1976-79; mng. ptnr. Thomas and Thomas, P.A., Orlando, 1979—; chief exec. officer Ivanhoe Communications Inc., Orlando, 1982—. Creator internat. TV program Today's Breakthroughs: Tomorrow's Cures. Fellow NEH, 1979. Mem. Fla. Bar Assn., Orange County Bar Assn. (chmn. estate planning com. 1982), Fla. Assn. for Women Lawyers (pres. 1982), Fla. Exec. Women (pres. 1981), Order of Coif. Democrat. Home: 242 Chase Ave Winter Park FL 32789 Office: Ivanhoe Communications 401 S Rosalind Ste 100 Orlando FL 32801

THOMAS, MARJORIE OLIVIENE, health care administrator; b. Spaldings, Jamaica, Sept. 5; came to U.S., 1971; d. Cedrick Milo and Avis Clair (Morgan) West; m. Carol Oswald Thomas, Sept. 10, 1977; children—Chandra, Brian. A.A., Kendall Coll., 1973; B.S., U. Ill.-Chgo., 1975; M.P.A., Roosevelt U., 1977. Asst. to dir. utilization rev. Bellevue Hosp., N.Y.C., 1977-81, risk mgr., 1981-83, assoc. dir./dir. quality assurance, 1983-85; dir. risk mgmt. svcs. Adminstrs. for the Professions, Inc., Manhasset, N.Y., 1985—. Mem. Am. Soc. for Healthcare Risk Mgmt., Assn. Hosp. Risk Mgmt. N.Y. Mem. Christ Temple. Avocations: reading, writing, traveling.

THOMAS, MARLO (MARGARET JULIA THOMAS), actress; b. Detroit, Nov. 21, 1943; d. Danny and Rose Marie (Cassanti) T.; m. Phil Donahue, May 22, 1980. Ed., U. So. Calif. Theatrical appearances in Broadway prodn. Thieves, 1974, London prodn. Barefoot in the Park, Broadway play Social Security, 1986; star: TV series That Girl, 1966-71; appeared in TV films: The Last Honor of Kathryn Beck, 1984, Consenting Adults, 1985, Nobody's Child, 1986; conceived book and record, starred in TV spl. Free to Be. . . You and Me, 1974 (Emmy for best children's show); films include Thieves, 1977, In the Spirit, 1990; author: Free to Be...A Family, 1987. Recipient George Foster Peabody award; Tom Paine award Nat. Emergency Civil Liberties Com. Office: care Michael Ovitz Creative Artists Agy Inc 1888 Century Pk E #1400 Los Angeles CA 90067*

THOMAS, MARSHA L., telecommunications and management consultant; b. Pittsfield, Mass., June 14, 1947; d. Joseph A. Guarda and Rita M (Harrison) Perrone; m. Allen P. Gobbo, Aug. 31, 1967; (div. 1982); m. Dr. B. Lewis Thomas, July 28, 1984; children: Scott, Kellie, Erin. Student, Loretto Heights Coll., Denver, 1983. Pub. telecommunications coord. Mesa County Commissioners, Grant Junction, Colo., 1979-87; project dir. Corp. for Pub. Broadcasting Grant, Washington, 1981, Colo. Pub. Radio Expansion Planning Project, Denver, 1982-83; founder, gen. mgr. Pub. Radio KPRN, Grand Junction, 1983-88; ptnr. Walker Consulting Services, Denver, 1989, Feedback Resources Unltd., Denver, 1989—; bd. dir. Nat. Fedn. Wash. 1988, Community Broadcasters, Nat. LP-TV Translator Ac. Salt Lake City 1979-83, Colo. Translator Assoc. Colo. 1979-83. Author: Colo. Pub. Radio Resource Book, 1983; Editor: Industry Publication New LPTV Reporter, 1983. Bd. Mem. Mesa County Found. Grand Junction 1983-85, Mem. United Way Allocations Bd. Grand Junction, Co-founder Rape Crisis Ctr. Grand Junction, Publicity Ch. Mesa County Med. Auxiliary Grand Junction, 1987. Mem. NFCB Bd., Soc. for Tng. and Devel. (pres. western Colo. chpt. 1990—). Dem. Catholic. Home: 1733 Crestview Dr Grand Junction CO 81506 Office: Mellon Fin Ctr 1775 Sherman St Ste 1900 Denver CO 80203

THOMAS, MARTHA JANICE, ground transportation company executive; b. Hyden, Ky., Aug. 30, 1949; d. John Maynard and Nell (Hensley) Baker; m. Robert Eugene Ripberger, May 23, 1970 (div. April 1982); children: Amy Elizabeth, Robert Eugene II; m. Jerry Allen Thomas, Jan. 21, 1984. Grad. high sch., Indpls., 1967. Sub-distbr., salesperson Jhirmack, Indpls., 1978-79; real estate salesperson Heritage Estates, Brownsburg, Ind., 1979-81; br. mgr. Home Mark, Inc., Indpls., 1981-82; trade broker The Trade Arranger, Indpls., 1982-84; owner AAA Delivery System, Inc., Indpls., 1984—; participant Women's Initiative Conf., 1985—. Mem. mktg. com. Indpls. Conv. and Visitors Bur., 1984—. Mem. Nat. Assn. Women Bus. Owners, Nat. Passenger Traffic Assn., NAFE, Nat. Def. Transp. Assn., Airport Mgr.'s Club (officer).

THOMAS, MARTHA WETTERHALL, advertising agency executive; b. Ann Arbor, Mich., Aug. 23, 1949; d. Roy Christner and Doreen (Armstrong) Wetterhall; m. James William Thomas, May 22, 1982. BA cum laude, U. Mich., 1971. Copywriter McCaffrey & McCall, N.Y.C., 1972-76, Cunningham & Walsh, N.Y.C., 1976-78; sr. copywriter Grey/2 Advt., N.Y.C., 1978-79, Symon, Thomas & Hilliard, N.Y.C., 1979-82; pres. Thomas & Thomas Advt., N.Y.C., 1983—. Writer, producer 1st paid TV advt. campaign for art mus., 1985. Recipient Encore award N.Y. Arts and Bus. Council, 1985, Effie award Am. Mktg. Assn., 1987, Telly award for local and regional TV commls., 1988. Mem. Advt. Women of N.Y., Am. Women's Econ. Devel. Corp., Ad Net (2d v.p.). Office: Thomas & Thomas Advt Inc 432 Park Ave S New York NY 10016

THOMAS, MICHELLE ROCHON, financial analyst; b. Dallas, Jan. 22, 1962; d. Bernard and Audrey Mae (Scott) T. BS, U. Okla., 1984; postgrad., Dallas Bapt. U., 1989—. Adminstrv. asst. 1st RepublicBank of Dallas, 1980-88; fin. analyst NCNB Tex. Nat. Bank, Dallas, 1988—. Mem. Dallas Black MBA Assn., Dallas Urban League, Alpha Kappa Alpha. Democrat. Methodist. Home: 5429 Cherry Glen Ln Dallas TX 75232

THOMAS, MIRIAM HIGGINS, chemist; b. Chgo., June 22, 1920; d. William Henry and Mame (Mason) H.; m. Lucius Howard Thomas, Jr., Sept. 6, 1947 (dec. Nov. 1963); 1 child, Brian Kevin. BS, Bennett Coll., 1940; MS, U. Chgo., 1942. Rsch. assoc. U. Chgo., 1942-45; rsch. chemist Q.M. Food and Container Inst. for Armed Forces, Chgo., 1945-62, U.S. Army Natick Rsch. and Devel. Ctr., Mass., 1962-85, ret., 1985; vis. lectr. MIT, 1975-82. Contbr. articles to profl. jours. and books. Dept. Army fellow, 1975-76. Mem. Inst. Food Technology, Sigma Xi. Avocation: travel.

THOMAS, MONICA G., savings bank administrator; b. Jamaica, W.I., Aug. 28, 1939; came to U.S., 1967.; d. Reuben and Kathleen (Daley) Blake; children: Patrick, David, Dalton, Denise, Karen. Ed., Am. Inst. Banking, Hofstra U. Cert. in consumer lending, comml. lending. V.p., area mgr. Crossland Savs. Bank, Bklyn. Active in ch. young peoples group. Mem. Lions. Office: Crossland Savs Bank 2145 Ralph Ave Brooklyn NY 11234

THOMAS, PATRICIA ANNE, law librarian; b. Cleve., Aug. 21, 1927; d. Richard Joseph and Marietta Bernadette (Teevans) T.; B.A., Case Western Res. U., 1949, J.D., 1951. Admitted to Ohio bar, 1951, U.S. Supreme Ct. bar, 1980; librarian Arter & Hadden, Cleve., 1951-62; asst. librarian, then librarian IRS, Washington, 1962-78; library dir. Adminstrv. Office, U.S. Cts., 1978—. Mem. Am. Assn. Law Libraries, Law Librarians Soc. D.C. (pres. 1967-69). Office: US Cts Adminstrv Office Legal Rsch & Library Svcs Washington DC 20544

THOMAS, PATRICIA GRAFTON, educator; b. Michigan City, Ind., Sept. 30, 1921; d. Robert Wadsworth and Elinda (Oppermann) Grafton; student Stephens Coll., 1936-39, Purdue U., summer 1938; BEd magna cum laude, U. Toledo, 1966; postgrad. (fellow) Bowling Green U., 1968; m. Lewis Edward Thomas, Dec. 21, 1939; children: Linda L. (Mrs. John R. Collins), Stephanie A. (Mrs. Andrew M. Pawuk), I. Kathryn (Mrs. James N. Ramsey), Deborah (Mrs. Edward Preissler). Tchr., Toledo Bd. Edn., 1959-81, tchr. lang. arts Byrnedale Sch., 1976-81. Dist. capt. Planned Parenthood, 1952-53, ARC, 1954-55; mem. lang. arts curriculum com. Toledo Bd. Edn., 1969, mem. grammar curriculum com., 1974; bd. dirs. Anthony Wayne Nursery Sch., 1983—; bd. dirs. Toledo Women's Symphony Orch. League, 1983—, sec., 1985—. Mem. AAUW, Toledo Soc. Profl. Engrs. Aux., Helen Kreps Guild, Toledo Artists' Club, Spectrum, Friends of Arts (bd. dirs. 1989), Phi Kappa Phi, Phi Delta Kappa, Kappa Delta Pi, Pi Lambda Theta (chpt. pres. 1978—), Delta Kappa Gamma (chpt. pres. 1976-78, area membership chmn. 1978-80, 1st place award for exhbn. 1985). Republican. Episcopalian. Home: 4148 Deepwood Ln Toledo OH 43614

THOMAS, PENELOPE JANE, human resources administrator; b. Cardiff, Wales, May 9, 1949; came to U.S., 1980; d. Tydwg Lewis and Emily Irene (Cook) T.; m. Eric Lindy Bostick, Aug. 30, 1972 (div. Feb. 1980). BS in Gen. Studies, Pace U., 1989, BS in Indsl. Relations, 1989. Head cartographer Aero Precisa, Beirut, 1969-72; office mgr. Aviation Devel. Cons. Airlines, Sharjah, United Arab Emirates, 1976-78; exec. asst. UN Relief and Works Agy., N.Y.C., 1980-81, Lee Nat. Corp., N.Y.C., 1981-84; office mgr. Operation Sail 1986 South St. Seaport Mus., N.Y.C., 1985-86, coord. vols., 1986-87; office mgr. Peterson & Blyth Assocs., N.Y.C., 1987-89; pub. program coord. Staten Island Inst. Arts & Scis., N.Y.C., 1989—; adminstrv. asst. Beth Israel Hosp., 1989—; fin. dir., hon. sec. East River Charter, Inc., N.Y.C., 1985-88; hon. sec. Ship Trust of N.Y., N.Y.C., 1986—; dir. Columbia Sailing Assn./N.Y. Harbor Sailing Ctr., N.Y.C., 1987—. Ship restoration vol. Wavertree Soc., South Street Seaport, N.Y., 1982—, hon. sec., fin. dir., 1986—; lay reader Christ Ch., Staten Island, N.Y., 1986—. Episcopalian. Home: 49 Clinton Ave Staten Island NY 10301 Office: Beth Israel Med Ctr 421 E 14th St New York NY 10009

THOMAS, SANDRA PAUL, nurse, educator; b. Moline, Ill., Mar. 9, 1940; d. Raymond Spencer and Oceana Lee (Agee) Paul; m. Eddie King Thomas, Dec. 17, 1960 (div. June 24, 1977); children: Kenneth, Tommy, Shana; m. Nurhan Elias Takvoryan, Mar. 20, 1988. BEd, U. Tenn., 1974, MEd, 1977, PhD in Edn., 1983, MS in Nursing, 1984. Staff nurse East Tenn. Bapt. Hosp., Knoxville, 1964-74; instr. psychiat. mental health nursing East Tenn. Bapt. Sch. Nursing, Knoxville, 1975-80; project dir. Kellogg grant U. Tenn., Knoxville, 1983-87, assoc. prof., 1989—, dir. Ctr. for Nursing Rsch., 1986—. Contbr. articles to profl. jours. and rsch. presentations to nat. and internat. confs. Mem. governing bd. East Tenn. Health Improvement Coun., Knoxville, 1976-82; mem. Knoxville Mental Health Assn.; bd. dirs. Greater Knoxville Epilepsy Found., 1980-83; bd. dirs. Internat. Coun. Women's Health Issues, 1986—. Recipient Jessie Harris award U. Tenn., 1983, Writing award Am. Jour. Nursing, 1989; fellow Nat. Inst. Edn., 1981-82. Mem. Am. Nurses Assn., Tenn. Nurses Assn. (dist. pres. 1978-80, vice chmn. nurse educators spl. interest group 1984-85, chmn. nurse educators coun. 1985-86, mem. coun. nurse researchers, Nursing Scholarship award dist. 2 1987, Hall of Fame award Dist. 2 1989), chmn. rsch. com. 1985—, bd. dirs. 1986-88, Nurse of Yr. award 1980), Am. Psychol. Assn., Soc. Behavioral Medicine, Internat. Coun. on Women's Health Issues, So. Nursing Rsch. Soc. (charter), So. Coun. Collegiate Edn. for Nursing, Inst. Advancement Health, Nat. League for Nursing, Internat. Platform Assn., Sigma Theta Tau (faculty adv. Gamma Chi chpt. 1987-89), Phi Kappa Phi. Avocations: travel, writing, music. Contbr. articles to profl. jours. Democrat. Presbyterian. Office: U Tenn Coll Nursing 1200 Volunteer Blvd Knoxville TN 37996

THOMAS, SARAH BETH, marketing director; b. Paola, Kans., July 21, 1957; d. Ernest L. and Verla Jean (Achey) T. BS in Journalism, U. Kans., 1979. Cert. mem. Am. Soc. for Hosp. Mktg. & Pub. Relations. Asst. dir. pub. relations Children's Mercy Hosp., Kansas City, Mo., 1979-84; dir. community relations Med. Ctr. Independence, Mo., 1984-86; dir. mktg., pub. relations HCA Med. Ctr., Plano, Tex., 1986—. Exec. com. North Tex. Legis. Conf., Dallas, 1988; bd. dirs. United Way of Plano, 1979—. Mem. Am. Soc. Hosp. Mktg. and Pub. Rels., Tex. Soc. Hosp. Mktg. and Pub. Rels. Republican. Presbyterian. Home: 6000 Ohio Dr #524 Plano TX 75093 Office: HCA Med Ctr of Plano 3901 W 15th St Plano TX 75075

THOMAS, SHERYL ELAINE, insurance company executive; b. Detroit, Aug. 26, 1950; d. John David and Dorothy Lucille (Cleveland) T. BS, Western Mich. U., 1972. From claim rep. to claim supr. Allstate Ins., Livonia, Mich., 1973-81; from unit claim mgr. to casualty claim mgr. Allstate Ins., Dearborn, Mich., 1981-87; mkt. claim mgr. Allstate Ins., Mt Clemens, Mich., 1987-88; sr. mkt. claim mgr. Allstate Ins., Lansing, Mich., 1988-89; home office field casualty claim mgr. Allstate Ins., Northbrook, Ill., 1989—; teaching cons. Jr. Achievement, Farm Hills, Mich., 1983-85. Participant March of Dimes com., United Way com., Green Peace, Lansing C. of C., 1988. Mem. Detroit Econ. Club, Alpha Kappa Alpha, Kappa Delta Pi, Mortar Bd. Democrat. Office: Allstate Ins Co Allstate Pla North Northbrook IL 60062

THOMAS, SHIRLEY, author, educator, business executive; b. Glendale, Calif.; d. Oscar Miller and Ruby (Thomas) Annis; m. W. White, Feb. 22, 1949 (div. June 1952); m. William C. Perkins, Oct. 24, 1969. Student pvt. schs. Actress, writer, producer, dir. numerous radio and TV stas., 1942-46; v.p. Commodore Prodns., Hollywood, Calif., 1946-52; pres. Annis & Thomas, Inc., Hollywood, 1952—; prof. technical writing U. So. Calif., L.A., 1975—; Hollywood corr. NBC, 1952-56; editor motion pictures CBS, Hollywood, 1956-58; corr. Voice of Am., 1958-59; now free lance writer; cons. biol. scis. communication project George Washington U., 1965-66; cons. Stanford Rsch. Inst., 1967-68, Jet Propulsion Lab., 1969-70. Author: Men of Space vols. 1-8, 1960-68, Spanish trans., 1961, Italian, 1962; Space Tracking Facilities, 1963, Computers: Their History, Present Applications and Future, 1965; The Book of Diets, 1974. Organizer, chmn. City of L.A. Space Adv. Com., 1964-73, Women's Space Symposia, 1962-73; founder, chmn. aerospace hist. com. Calif. Mus. Sci. and Industry. Mem. AIAA, AAAS, Internat. Soc. Aviation Writers, Air Force Assn. (Airpower Arts and Letters award 196l), Internat. Acad. Astronautics, Nat. Aero. Assn., Nat. Assn. Sci. Writers, Soc. for Tech. Communications, Brit. Interplanetary Soc., Am. Astronautical Soc., Nat. Geog. Soc., Am. Soc. Pub. Adminstrn. (sci. and tech. in govt. com. 1972—), Achievement Rewards for Coll. Soc. (nat. bd. dirs.) Muses of Calif., Theta Sigma Phi, Phi Beta. Home: 8027 Hollywood Blvd Hollywood CA 90046

THOMAS, TERESA ANN, microbiologist, educator, consultant; b. Wilkes-Barre, Pa., Oct. 17, 1939; d. Sam Charles and Edna Grace T. B.S. cum laude, Coll. Misericordia, 1961; M.S. in Biology, Am. U. Beirut, 1965; M.S. in Microbiology, U. So. Calif., 1973. Tchr., sci. supr., curriculum coord. Meyers High Sch., Wilkes-Barre, 1962-64, Wilkes-Barre Area Public Schs., 1961-66; research assoc. Proctor Found. for Research in Ophthalmology U. Calif. Med. Ctr., San Francisco, 1966-68; instr. Robert Coll. of Istanbul (Turkey), 1968-71, Am. Edn. in Luxembourg, 1971-72, Bosco Tech. Inst., Rosemead, Calif., 1973-74, San Diego Community Coll. Dist., 1974-80; prof. math.-sci. div. Southwestern Coll., Chula Vista, Calif., 1980—, pres. acad. senate, 1984-85, del., 1986-89; mem. steering com. project CREATE Southwestern Coll.-Shanghai Inst. Fgn. Trade; coord. Southwestern Coll. Great Teaching Seminar, 1987, 88, 89, coord. scholars program, 1988—; mem. exec. com. Acad. Senate for Calif. Community Colls., 1985-86, Chancellor of Calif. Community Colls. Adv. and Rev. Council Fund for Instrnl. Improvement, 1984-86; adj. asst. prof. Chapman Coll., San Diego, 1974-83; asst. prof. San Diego State U., 1977-79; chmn. Am. Colls. Istanbul Sci. Week, 1969-71; mem. adv. bd. Chapman Coll. Community Center, 1979-80; cons. sci. curriculum Calif. Dept. Edn., 1986—; pres. Internat. Relations Club 1959-61; mem. San Francisco World Affairs Council, 1966-68; chmn. land use, energy and wildlife com. Congressman Duncan Hunter's Environ. Adv. Council, 1982-84; v.p. Palomar Palace Estates Home Owners Assn., 1983-85, pres. 1987—. mem. editorial rev. bd. Jour. of Coll. Sci. Teaching, NSTA, 1988—. Mem. Internat. Friendship Commn. (vice chmn. 1989—), Chula Vista, Calif., 1987—. NSF fellow, 1965; USPHS fellow, 1972-73; recipient Nat. Teaching Excellence award Nat. Inst. Staff and Orgnl. Devel., 1989; recognized at Internat. Conf. Teaching Excellence, Austin, 1989, ; Pa. Heart Assn. research grantee, 1962; named Southwestern Coll. Woman of Distinction, 1987. Mem. Am. Soc. Microbiology, Nat. Sci. Tchrs. Assn. (life, internat. com., coord. internat. honors exchange lectr. competition sponsored with Assn. Sci Educators Great Britain, 1986), Nat. Assn. Biology Tchrs., Soc. Coll. Sci. Tchrs. (Calif. membership coordinator 1984—), S.D. Zool. Soc., Calif. Tchrs. Assn., NEA, Am. Assn. Community and Jr. Colls., MENSA, Arab Am. Med. Assn., Am.-Lebanese Assn. San Diego (chmn. scholarship com., pres. 1988—), Am. U. of Beirut Alumni and Friends of San Diego (1st v.p. 1984—) Kappa Gamma Pi (pres. Wilkes-Barre chpt. 1963-64, San Francisco chpt. 1967-68), Sigma Phi Sigma, Phi Theta Kappa, Alpha Pi Epsilon (advisor Southwestern Coll. chpt. 1989—). Club: Am. Lebanese Syrian Ladies (pres. 1982-83). Office: Southwestern Coll 900 Otay Lakes Rd Chula Vista CA 92010

THOMAS, VALERIE MICHELLE, lawyer, educator; b. Quitman, Ga., July 16, 1963; d. Frank Leroy and Deloris (Adams) T.; m. Darryl Louie Bryant, June 30, 1990. BA, U. Ga., 1985, JD, 1988. Bar: Ga. 1988. Law clk. Thurmond & Thurmond, Athens, Ga., 1987-88; assoc. Copeland Firm, Valdosta, Ga., 1988-89; ptnr. Copeland and Thomas, Valdosta, 1990—; adj. prof. Valdosta State Coll., 1988-89; seminar leader, Valdosta, 1988-90. Recipient Challenging Address award Quitman Elem. Sch., 1989, Outstanding Achievement award Delta Sigma Theta. Mem. ABA, Ga. Bar Assn., Nat. Bar Assn., NAFE, AAUW, Capital City Club, Alpha Kappa Alpha (Outstanding Achievement award 1988). Democrat. Mem. African-Methodist-Episcopalian Ch. Home: 1708 Chatham Pl Valdosta GA 31601 Office: 102 E Adair St Valdosta GA 31601

THOMAS, VERA MARLINE, career and personal development specialist; b. Columbia, S.C., Nov. 17, 1953; d. John C. Thomas and Myrtis (Davis) Cole; 1 child, Miles J. PR communications, Kent State U., Stark County Branch, 1974-76. Cert. Trainer - Personal and Career Devel. Pres. student govt. Kent State U., Stark County Branch, Ohio, 1976-77; asst. dir. Stark County Bd. Edn., Stark County, 1977-79; cons. personal devel. specialist VM Thomas & Assoc., Canton, Ohio, 1979-82; career personal devel. cons. State Calif. Nuri Webber & Assoc., L.A.; career personal devel. specialist Job Training Partnership, L.A. and Stark County, Ohio, 1987—; profl. speaker Visions & Treasures, Ohio, 1988—; trainer, youth coordinator Visions & Treasures, 1988---; radio, tv. promotions Visions & Treasures, Canton, 1988—; writer, poet Visions & Treasures, 1989—; pub. seminars YWCA, Community Based Orgns, 1989; profl. speaker Sch. Groups, Orgns., 1989--; motivational prog. Sch., Youth Oriented Prog.; instr. creative arts programs Project for Academic Excellence. Contbg. editor: News, Personal Development; Creator Posters designed by youth; producer: Public Service Awareness; guest: My Involvement with Projects. Pub. Rels. Habitat for Humanity Bd. Dir., Canton, 1988—, family nurturing com. chairperson, Stark County Bus. League Bd. Canton, 1988, ABCD, Inc. YWCA, Canton, 1989, nominating com.; Vol. Various Political Campaigns, L.A. and Stark County, 1988; Stark County organizer for Housing NOW! March on Washington; active Leadership Canton, 1990-91, Jr. League, 1990-91. Recipient Outstanding Poet Award N. Canton Playhouse, Ohio, 1988, Award of Appreciation Brunswick Kiwanis Club, Columbus, 1988, Award of Appreciation Youth Union Baptist Ch. Canton, 1988. Mem. Ohio Speakers Forum, Nat. Assn. of Female Exec., Nat. Bus. League, Stark County Bus. League. Home: 301 Chicago Pl NW Canton OH 44703 Office: Job Tng Partnership 300 Market Ave N Canton OH 44702

THOMAS, VICKIE MARTIN, sales and management training executive; b. Garrett, Ind., June 18, 1951; d. Edmund Norris and Dorothy Pearl (Leiter) Martin; m. Richard Z. Thomas, Nov. 25, 1987; 1 child, Jason Matthew. BA, Ind. U., 1980. Cert. in advanced sales, sales mgmt. skills. Asst. to mktg. mgr. Gen. Telephone Co., Ft. Wayne, Ind.; local indsl. devel. coord. Arabian Am. Oil Co., Dhahran, Saudi Arabia; gen. sales mgr. N.Am. Transp., Washington; pres., sales mgmt. cons. Thomas Martin and Assocs., Highlands Ranch, Colo. Contbr. articles to profl. jours. Recipient Presdl. Achievement award Pres. Ronald Reagan, 1985; award Nat. Assn. Women Bus. Owners. Mem. NAFE, Nat. Assn. Profl. Saleswomen, Highland C. of C. (chmn. mem. com.). Home and Office: 9918 Falcon Creek Dr Highlands CO 80126

THOMAS, VIOLETA DE LOS ANGELES, real estate broker; b. Buenos Aires, Dec. 21, 1949; came to U.S., 1968; d. Angel and Lola (Andino) de Rios; m. Jess Thomas, Dec. 23, 1974; 1 child, Victor Justin. BA, Pine Manor Coll., 1970; BBA, U. Bus. Adminstrn., Buenos Aires, 1971. Mgr. book div. Time-Life, N.Y.C., 1970-74; real estate broker First Marin Realty, Inc., Mill Valley, Calif., 1985—. Bd. dirs. City of Tiburon, Calif., 1987—, Art and Heritage Commn., Tiburon. Named Woman of Yr. City of Buenos Aires, 1977, Agt. of Yr. Marin County and San Francisco, 1987-89. Home: PO Box 662 Tiburon CA 94920

THOMAS, VIRGINIA LEE, microscopist, consultant; b. Traer, Iowa, Sept. 22, 1916; d. Paul and Zenaide (Kahler) T.; grad. Gates Coll., 1939, U. Mich., 1943. Spectrographer Rock Island (Ill.) Arsenal, 1943-45; electron microscopist U.S. Rubber Research Labs., Passaic, N.J., 1945-54; group leader Interchem. Research Labs., N.Y.C., 1954-62; research scientist Am. Standard Research Lab., Piscataway, N.J., 1962-68; lectr., supr. microscopy U. Medicine and Dentistry, Rutgers U. Med. Sch., Piscataway, 1968-84; cons. on electron and light microscopy, 1984—. Active New River Trading Coop., Graham House Preservation Soc., ACLU, Mercer County Peace Coalition. Fellow N.Y. Microscopical Soc. (pres. 1960-61, Ashby award 1962); mem. Electron Microscopical Soc. Am., N.Y. Soc. Electron Microscopists. Clubs: Sierra, Porsche Club Am., Nat. Wildlife Assn., Nature Conservancy. Contbr. chpts. to books in field, articles to profl. jours. Home and Office: 268 Main St Hinton WV 25951

THOMAS-BUCKLE, SUZANN REMINGTON, public policy and planning educator; b. Elizabeth City, N.C., Jan. 22, 1945; d. James Ernest Thomas and Marion (Blackwell) Dodson; m. Leonard Gould Buckle, June 4, 1966. B.A. in English Lit., Wellesley Coll., 1962-66; Ph.D. in Urban Studies and Planning, MIT, 1974. Instr. pub. policy and planning MIT, Cambridge, 1970-74, asst. prof., 1974-78, assoc. prof., 1978-85; community and environ. mediator, 1984—; assoc. prof., dir. law, policy and soc. programs Northeastern U., Boston, 1985—; research assoc. John F. Kennedy Sch. Govt., Harvard U., Cambridge, 1979-81; cons. U.S. Dept. Labor, Nat. League of Cities, 1971-76, Mus. Fine Arts, Boston, 1972-75; reporter ABA, Washington, 1973-77; research cons. U.S. Dept. Justice, Washington, 1975-76; chmn. trustees Am. Legal Studies Assn., 1987—; mem. Forum on Negotiation, Harvard Law Sch., also adv. bd. specialization in negotiation Program on Negotiation. Author: Bargaining for Justice, 1977; Standards Related to Planning for Juvenile Justice, 1980; mem. editorial bd. Law and Society Rev., 1985—; publisher: Legal Studies Forum and Transformations, 1987—; contbr. articles to profl. jours. Trustee Mass. Council for Pub. Justice, Boston, 1982—. Recipient Everett Moore Baker award MIT, 1972; Eli Lilly postdoctoral fellow, 1974; German Marshall fellow, 1979. Mem. Am. Sociol. Assn., Soc. Profls. in Dispute Resolution, Law and Soc. Assn., Soc. for Study of Social Problems. Office: Northeastern U Programs in Law Policy and Soc Boston MA 02115

THOMAS-COTE, NANCY DENECE, manufacturing company executive; b. Long Beach, Calif., Feb. 20, 1959; d. Alan and Barbara Jean (Rush) Tuthill; m. Gary Cote, Sept. 1, 1988; 1 child, Liana Barbara. V.p. BTE, Inc., Long Beach, 1978-88; gen. mgr. BTE, Inc., Huntington Beach, Calif., 1982-88, pres., 1988—; pres. Omni Label, Inc., Huntington Beach, 1985—; co-owner LeMac Leasing, La Canada, Calif., 1985—. V.p. Long Beach Spl. Charities, Inc., 1987; pres. Long Beach Spl. Charities, Inc., 1988. Mem. NAFE, Nat. Office Products Assn., Young Execs. Forum, Am. Med. Records Assn., Calif. Med. Records Assn., Office Products Mfg. Assn., Wholesale Stationers Assn. Office: BTE Inc 5672 Bolsa Ave Huntington Beach CA 92647

THOMASON, ANN WENNINGER, public relations and marketing executive; b. Bucyrus, Ohio, June 22, 1934; d. Clifford Earl and Helene (Hall) Wenninger; m. Lyon Burks Hutcherson Jr., June 9, 1956 (div. Mar. 1976); children: Steven Burks, Leighan Hutcherson Hunt, Michael Hall; m. William Olin Thomason, Nov. 24, 1977. Student, U. Ky., 1952-56; profl. cert., N.Y. Sch. Interior Design, 1963. Prin. Ann Hutcherson Interiors, Glasgow, Ky., 1963-76; part-owner Bucky Farnor & Assocs. (flower, gift and design shop), Nashville, 1977-81; co-owner William Thomason & Assocs., Nashville, sec., treas., bd. dirs., 1981-85, v.p. pub. relations, 1986-87, exec. v.p., 1988—; presenter in field, 1963—. Active Nashville Symphony Guild, pres., 1982-83, mem. exec. com., bd. dirs., 1979-86, decorations chmn. Symphony Ball, 1986, pub. rels. chmn., 1987; active Nashville Symphony Assn., bd. dirs. 1982-89; projects chairperson Tenn. Homecoming '86', Nashville/Davidson Co., Nashville, 1985-86; co-chairperson Heart Gala, Mid Tenn. Heart Assn., Nashville, 1985; mem. adminstrv. bd. West End United Meth. Ch.; founder, bd. dirs. Nashville Tree Found., Inc., 1989—, Cumberland Valley Girl Scouts, 1989—; bd. dirs. ARC, 1989—, Heart Gala Benefit Inc., 1990—; benefit chmn. Sr. Citizens, Inc., 1990. Recipient Ky. Col. award Gov. Ky., 1968, Outstanding Vol. award Nashville Symphony Guild, 1979, cert. recognition Nashville Symphony Assn., 1983; named to Outstanding Young Women Am., U.S. Jaycees. Mem. Nashville C. of C., Nat. Assn. for Female Execs., Royal Chase Com., Peak Investment Club. Republican. Methodist. Office: Annotations 510 Armistead Pl Nashville TN 37215

THOMASON, JANICE MARTECHIA, accountant; b. Welch, W.Va., July 6, 1945; d. Michael and Georgia (Corner) Rock; m. David F. Thomason Sr., Feb. 22, 1964 (div. Jan. 1988); children: David Jr., Michael, Markus. AAS, Davidson County Community Coll., Lexington, N.C., 1984. Ins. clk. Southern Ins. Co., Lexington, 1964; payroll and shipping clk. Burlington Industries, Lexington, 1964-65; ins. clk., switchboard operator Lexington Meml. Hosp., 1967-68; receptionist Thomasville (N.C.) Med. Assocs., 1968-69; tax cons. H&R Block, Lexington, 1970-80; gen. acct. Lexington Telephone Co., 1975—. Mem. Davidson County Photography Club, Lexington, 1984-87; treas. North Davidson Band Boosters, Lexington, 1983-85, New Friendship United Ch., Lexington, 1980-85. Link Taylor Furniture Industries scholar, 1963. Mem. Carolina Crescent Pioneer Club, Order of Eastern Star (worthy matron Lexington chpt. 1984-85). Home: Rt 13 Box 2378 Lexington NC 27292

THOMAS-RINGLEY, CATHY J., pharmaceutical sales manager; b. La Plata, MD, Sept. 2, 1958; d. Roger C. and Emily Ann (Bauer) T.; m. Giles P. Ringley. BS, U. Md., 1979. Hosp. sales rep. Glaxo, Inc., Balt.; assoc. product mgr. Glaxo, Inc., Research Triangle Park, N.C., product mgr., mgr. pharm. sales. Mem. Am. Heart Assn., Omicron Nu. Address: 104 W Kirkfield Cary NC 27511

THOMPKINS, GAYLE LYNETTE, marketing professional; b. Clinton, La., Feb. 20, 1960; d. Tommy Isaac and Gloria D. (Hayes) T. BA, U. New Orleans, 1982. Pub. relations liaison Mullican Communications, Matairie, La., 1983; pvt. practice Cleve., 1986-87; mktg. specialist Cuyahoga Met. Housing Authority, Cleve., 1987—; coun. mem. Sr. Companion Program Adv. Coun., Cleve., 1989—. Mem. NAFE. Democrat. Buddhist. Office: 1441 W 25th St Cleveland OH 44113

THOMPSEN, JOYCE ANN, sales executive; b. Owatonna, Minn., Mar. 21, 1946; d. Stanley Albert and Elda Margaret Elsie (Buehring) Moeckly; children: James Paul, Matthew John. BS Bus. Edn, Mankato (MN) State U., 1984; MBA, Coll. St. Thomas, St. Paul, MN, 1988. Exec. sec. Josten's Co., Owatonna, MN, 1964-71; univ. rels. supr. U. Minn., Waseca, 1971-72; v.p. employee and community rels., corp. sec. E.F. Johnson Co., Waseca, 1972—, corp. sec., 1977-81, v.p. adminstrn., corp. sec., 1981-86, v.p. employee and community relations, corp. sec., 1986-88, v.p. human resources, 1988-89, mgr. employee Devel. and adminstrn., 1989-90; acct. exec. Devel. Dimensions Internat., 1990—; chmn. Mgmt. Devel., Waseca, Minn., 1983—; mem. rsch. adv. bd., dir. Minn. Coop. Office, Greater Minn. Corp.; asst. prof., adj. lectr. St. Mary's Coll., St. Thomas Coll. Trustee E.F. Johnson Co. Found., Waseca, 1984-89; mem. Gov.'s Coll. Edn. Coun., 1984-88; chmn. adv. coun., Mankato (Minn.) State U., 1986—; mem. adv. coun. grad. mgmt. programs Coll. St. Thomas, 1987—. Mem. Am. Soc. Tng. and Devel., AAUW, Am. Electronics Assn. (exec. coun. Minn. chpt. 1983—), Minn. High Tech. Coun. Lutheran. Home: 830 4th Ave NE Waseca MN 56093 Office: DDI 820 Fourth Ave NE Waseca MN 56093

THOMPSON, ANNE ELISE, federal judge; b. Phila., July 8, 1934; d. Leroy Henry and Mary Elise (Jackson) Jenkins; m. William H. Thompson, June 19, 1965; children: William H., Sharon A. B.A., Howard U., 1955, LL.B., 1964; M.A., Temple U., Phila., 1957. Bar: D.C. bar 1964, N.J. bar 1966. Staff atty. Office of Solicitor, Dept. Labor, Chgo., 1964-65; asst. dep. public defender Trenton, N.J., 1967-70; mcpl. prosecutor Lawrence Twp., Lawrenceville, N.J., 1970-72; mcpl. ct. judge Trenton, 1972-75; prosecutor Mercer County, Trenton, 1975-79; U.S. dist. judge Dist. of N.J., Trenton, 1979—; vice chmn. Mercer County Criminal Justice Planning Com., 1972; mem. com. criminal practice N.J. Supreme Ct., 1975-79, mem. com. mcpl. cts., 1972-75; v.p. N.J. County Prosecutors Assn., 1978-79; chmn. juvenile justice com. Nat. Dist. Attys. Assn., 1978-79. Del. Democratic Nat. Conv., 1972. Recipient Assn. Black Women Lawyers award, 1976, Disting. Service award Nat. Dist. Attys. Assn., 1979, Gene Carte Meml. award Am. Criminal Justice Assn., 1980, Outstanding Leadership award N.J. County Prosecutors Assn., 1980, John Mercer Langston Outstanding Alumnus award Howard U. Law Sch., 1981; also various service awards; certs. of appreciation. Mem. Am. Bar Assn., Fed. Bar Assn., N.J. Bar Assn., Mercer County Bar Assn. Democrat. Office: 343 US Courthouse 402 E State St PO Box 401 Trenton NJ 08608*

THOMPSON, ANNE MARIE, newspaper publisher; b. Des Moines, Feb. 7, 1920; d. George Horace and Esther Mayer Sheely; m. J. Ross Thompson, July 31, 1949; children: Annette McCracken, James Ross. BA, U. Iowa, 1940; postgrad. U. Colo., 1971. Co-pub. Baca County Banner, Springfield, Colo., 1951-54, Rocky Ford (Colo.) Daily Gazette, 1954-82, pub., 1982—. Editor Colo. Bus. Prof. Women Mag. Colo. Bus. Women, Rocky Ford, 1981—, The Sage Quar. Publ. Toastmasters dist. 26, 1983—. Mem. Otero Jr. Coll. Counc., 1987—, Colo. Ho. of Reps., 1957-61; Colo. presdl. elector, 1972; chmn. Colo. adv. com. SBA, 1979-81. Recipient Community Service award Rocky Ford C. of C., 1975; named Colo. Woman of Achievement in Journalism, 1959, Colo. Bus. Person of Yr., Future Bus. Leaders of Am., 1981; elected to Colo. Community Journalism Hall of Fame, 1981. Mem. Nat. Fedn. Press Women (dir. 1971-81), Nat. Newspaper Assn. (Emma C. McKinney award 1984, Inland Daily award 1984), Colo. Press Assn. (dir. 1981-83), Colo. Press Women, PEO, Bus. and Profl. Women's Club. Republican. Methodist.

THOMPSON, BETTY LUCILLE, educator; b. Billings, Mont., May 18, 1943; d. Chester G. and Helen L. (Bullis) Scott; m. James J. Thompson, Mar. 21, 1964; children: Garth Scott, Ashli Elise. BS, Mont. State U., 1965; MEd, U. Mont., 1972. Cert. home economist, Mont. Social worker Flathead Welfare Office, Kalispell, Mont., 1965-66, Pettis County Welfare Office, Sedalia, Mo., 1966-68; edn. counselor USAF Edn. Office, Bitburg Air Base, Fed. Republic Germany, 1969-71; tchr. Kalispell Jr. High Sch. and Flathead High Sch., 1972—, head vocat. dept., 1987—. Mem. Assn. for Supervision and Curriculum Devel., Nat. Home Econs. Assn., Mont. Home Econs. Assn., Mont. Edn. Assn. (instrn. and profl. devel. com. 1985—), Kalispell Edn. Assn. (sec. newsletter 1986-89), AAUW, LWV. Methodist. Home: 160 River View Dr Kalispell MT 59901 Office: Kalispell Jr High Sch Northridge Heights Kalispell MT 59901

THOMPSON, BLANCHE LEE, employment and training officer; b. Washington, Dec. 30, 1958; d. Arthur Norman and Helen (Calos) Lee; m. Tom B. Thompson, May 21, 1977 (div. July 1985). BA magna cum laude, No. Ill. U., 1982. Behavior counselor Nutri/Systems, Aurora, Ill., 1983-84, ctr. mgr., 1984-87, area mgr., 1987-89; employment and tng. officer KDK Tng., Employment and Bus. Svc., Geneva, Ill., 1989—; seminar leader Coll. DuPage, Glen Ellyn, Ill., 1989—. Sponsor Compassion, Colorado Springs, 1989. Mem. NAFE (pub. rels. chmn.), Aurora Profl. Bus. Womans Assn. (pub. rels. chmn.). Home: 526 Grand Ave Aurora IL 60506

THOMPSON, BRENDA CLARE, public relations executive; b. Waterloo, Iowa, May 5, 1961; d. Thomas Henry and Diane Sargent Thompson. BJ, U. Tex., 1984. Features editor/reporter Hill Country News, Austin, Tex., 1985-86; asst. editor Austin Mag., 1986-88; dir. pubs. and pub. rels. St. Edward's U., Austin, 1988—. Mem. Women in Communications (v.p. programs Austin chpt.). Democrat. Roman Catholic. Office: St Edwards U 3001 S Congress Ave Austin TX 78704

THOMPSON, CARYN ELIZABETH, banker; b. Palo Alto, Calif., Mar. 22, 1954; d. Robert Louis and Harriet Elizabeth (Jeffs) Hildebrand; m. Terence William Thompson, Aug. 30, 1975; children: Cory Elizabeth, Christopher William. Student, U. Ariz., 1972-75; BS, Ariz. State U., 1979, MBA, 1984. Asst. treas. Great Western Bank, Phoenix, 1984-85; asst. v.p. Citibank (Ariz.), Phoenix, 1985-87; v.p. Nat. Processing Co., Phoenix, 1987—. Dem. precinct committee-person, dist. 26, Phoenix, 1983; registrar Ariz. State Govt., 1980. Mem. Nat. Assn. Female Execs., Nat. Assn. Banking Women (bd. dirs. 1985), Ariz. Bank Assn. (bank rep.), Delta Gamma. Democrat. Home: 202 W Lawrence Rd Phoenix AZ 85013 Office: Nat Processing Co 16402 N 28th Ave Phoenix AZ 85023

THOMPSON, CHRISTINE EPPS, educator; b. Ft. Worth, Nov. 1, 1940; d. John Robert Epps and Eva May (Taylor) Epps McKee; m. Robert Edgar Thompson Jr., Sept. 28, 1957; children: Thomas Len, Robert Kearn. BA, North Tex. State U., 1964, MA, 1966, MLS, 1970, PhD, Tex. Woman's U., 1989. Teaching asst. North Tex. State U., Denton, 1964-65, library clk., 1968-70; librarian Tarleton State U., Stephenville, 1970-83; teaching asst. Tex. Woman's U., Denton, 1983-84; head original cataloging dept. Tex. A&M U. Library, College Station, 1984-85, acting head processing div., 1985-86, head original cataloging/copy cataloging dept., 1986-88; asst. prof. U. Wis., Milw., 1989—. Author: The Works of Zbigniew K. Brzezinski; Mgmt. Information Systems Bibliography, Decision Support Systems: A Bibliography, 1980-84; spl. editor Reference Services Rev., 1986; contbr. numerous articles to profl. jours. Mem. ALA, Assn. Coll. Research Libraries (sec. LPSS 1987-89), Tex. Library Assn. (chmn. scholarship com. 1980-81, chmn. intellectual freedom com. 1983-84), Tex. Assn. Coll. Tchrs. (exec. bd. 1980-81, 87-88, nomination com. 1983-84), chmn., Com. for Acad. Freedom and Defense, 1987-88, Assn. for Libr. and Info. Sci. Educators, Wis. Libr. Assn. Democrat. Baptist.

THOMPSON, CHRISTINE KLENA, public relations executive; b. San Antonio, July 30, 1960; d. Martin Daniel and Margaret Patricia (Schilling) Klena; m. James Garfield Thompson, Feb. 4, 1989. BS, Fla. State U., Tallahassee, 1982. Telemarketer, sales rep. Lanier Bus. Products, Tallahassee, 1982-83; advt. coord. Fla. AGC Coun., Tallahassee, 1983-85; mgr. seminars and contracts Fla. C. of C., Tallahassee, 1985-87; pub. rels. adminstr. Cen. Telephone Co. of Fla., Tallahassee, 1987—. bd. dirs. exec. com. March of Dimes N.W. Fla. chpt., 1988—. Mem. Cen. Mgmt. Club (v.p. 1989-90, pres. 1990—), Tallahassee Soccer Assn., Women In Communications, Fla. Pub. Rels. Assn., Tallahassee Jaycees, Fla. C. of C., Tallahassee C. of C. Office: Centel Fla 1313 Blair Stone Rd Tallahassee FL 32316

THOMPSON, DEBORAH KEMP, association executive; b. Mobile, Ala., Mar. 3, 1947; d. Hattie Isabele (Robinson) Kemp; div.; children: Michelle R. Taylor, LuVeidya A., SaBella A. AA, Fla. Community Coll., 1967; student, Ky. State Coll., 1968; BA, U. Minn., 1970; postgrad., Cen. Mich. U., 1980. Adminstrv. asst. Small Bus. Devel. Ctr. Jacksonville (Fla.) Urban League, 1973-75, dir. housing counseling program, 1975-80; exec. dir. Jacksonville Neighborhood Resource Ctr., 1980-82; project dir. Old Stanton, Inc., Jacksonville, 1982-84; prin. Profl. Investors assn., Jacksonville, 1984-86; counselor U. North Fla., Jacksonville, 1986; dir. minority econ. devel. program Jacksonville Urban League, 1986-89; loan officer specialist 1st Coast Black Bus. Investment Corp., Jacksonville, 1989—; self-employed mortgage broker, Jacksonville, 1986-90; cons. Fla. Jr. Coll., Jacksonville, 1988. Mem. Bus. and Profl. Women's Club, Exec. Women Internat., NAFE, Nat. Assn. Parliamentarians, Nat. Assn. Notary Pubs. Democrat. Home: 3471 Docksider Dr S Jacksonville FL 32202 Office: 1st Coast Black Bus Invest 101 E Union St Ste 309 Jacksonville FL 32202

THOMPSON, DEBRA JEAN, paralegal; b. Manchester, N.H., Apr. 12, 1954; d. William Crawford and Jeanne Delene (Coffin) T. BA in Edn., Notre Dame Coll., 1976, MA in Reading, 1980, cert. paralegal, 1986; postgrad., Rivier Coll., 1980-81. Tutor learning disabilities Hudson (N.H.) Meml. Sch., 1976-77; tutor Londonderry (N.H.) Jr. High Sch., 1977-78, Bakersville Sch., Manchester, 1978-79; tchrs. aide Adult Learning Ctr., Manchester, 1979-80; librarian Hillsborough County Law Library, Manchester, 1985-89; paralegal Thornton & Thornton, P.A., Manchester, 1985-88; law librarian, paralegal Kfoury & Elliot, Manchester, 1986-88; paralegal Hillsborough County Atty.'s Office, Manchester, 1988-89, Kfoury & Elliott, P.A., Manchester, 1989—; asst. to paralegal studies program Notre Dame Coll., Manchester, 1985-86; guest speaker N.H. Paralegal Assn., 1988. Book reviewer: Legal Research: How to Find and Understand the Law, 1986, Personal Injury Paralegal, 1987. Mem. Notre Dame Coll. Paralegal Adv. Com., 1986—. Mem. Notre Dame Coll. Alumni Assn., N.H. Paralegal Assn. Roman Catholic. Home: 41 Wayland Ave Manchester NH 03103 Office: Kfoury & Elliott PA 106 Market St Manchester NH 03101

THOMPSON, DIANE JANELLE, financial planning professional; b. Boone, Iowa, Nov. 11, 1950; d. Jerome Mauritz and Dolores Marie (May) Pearson; m. Douglas Dwight Wells, Nov.17, 1990; children: Stacia, Kristin, Alex. BS, Iowa State U., 1971; MBA, Drake U., 1981. Fin. analyst Hydro-Transmission div. Sundstrand Corp., Ames, Iowa, 1971-81; supr. plant site acctg. Hydro-Transmission div. Sundstrand Corp., Freeport, Ill., 1981-82; sect. mgr. fin. planning Sundstrand Corp., Rockford, Ill., 1982-85, mgr. fin. planning advanced technology group, 1985-88; mgr. fin. Aerospace Mech. Systems div. Sundstrand Corp., Rockford, 1988—. Tutor Rockford Area Literacy Coun., 1987-90. Mem. Nat. Assn. Accts., Fin. Execs. Inst. (dir. academics 1990-91). Office: Sundstrand Corp 4747 Harrison Ave Rockford IL 61125-7002

THOMPSON, DIDI CASTLE (MARY BENNETT), writer, editor; b. Terre Haute, Ind., Feb. 7, 1918; d. Robert Langley Bennett and Marjorie Rose (Tyler) Castle; student U. Ill., Champaign, 1935-36, U. Ky., 1936-39; m. Jamie Campbell Thompson, Jr., June 24, 1939; children—Jamie III, Julia King Balko, Langley Stewart Ruede. News editor Glen-Echoes, Glencoe, Ill., 1930; columnist Ky. Kernel, U. Ky., Lexington, 1937-39; radio script writer Modern Am. Music, 1940-42; asst. pub. relations dir. Salem Coll., Winston-Salem, N.C., 1945; pub. relations chmn. Barrington (Ill.) Horse Show, 1959-67; staff writer, columnist Barrington Press Newspapers, 1958-84; editor ECHO, Defenders of the Fox River, Inc. newsletter, 1970-80; travel editor Barrington Press Newspapers, 1973-84; columnist The Daily Herald, Paddock Publs., 1984-86; columnist Rapid City (S.D.) Journal, 1990—; freelance writer, 1943—. Past bd. mem. Barrington chpt. Lyric Opera Guild Chgo., Barrington Sr. Center, Infant Welfare Soc. Chgo., Art Inst. Chgo., Barrington Assos.; elected trustee Village of Barrington Hills, 1969-73, health, pub. relations chmn., 1969-73; mem. Barrington Hills Plan Commn., 1986. Mem. Women in Communications (past dir.), Citizens for Conservation (past dir.), Barrington Countryside Assn. (past dir.), Barrington Hist. Soc., Spring Creek Basset Hounds Club, Barrington Hills Riding Club (past dir.), Pan Hellenic Council, DAR, Chgo. Press Club, Chi Omega. Episcopalian. Address: 11 Glendale Ln #D Rapid City SD 57702-4992

THOMPSON, DONNA MARIE, data processing company official; b. L.I., N.Y., July 27, 1956; d. Raymond Joseph and Sally Rose (Freda) Pontecorvo; m. Gary Richard Thompson, Mar. 15, 1981; children: Alexander J., Jessica Anne, Garrett A. BA, Drew U., 1978; MBA, Seton Hall U., 1986. Lic. tchr., N.J. Restaurant mgr. Strade, Inc., Elmwood Park, N.J., 1976-78; client field rep. Union Photo Co., Clifton, N.J., 1979-80; client service rep. Automatic Data Processing Corp., Clifton, 1980-82, software support specialist, 1982-84, supr. support, 1984-86, mgr. support, 1986-87, mgr. product, 1987—. Vol. Chitton Meml. Hosp., Pequannock, N.J., 1970-74. Mem. Am. Mgmt. Assn., Nat. Assn. Female Execs., Beta Gamma Sigma. Roman Catholic. Office: Automatic Data Processing Corp WDS 205 Main Ave Clifton NJ 07015

THOMPSON, DORIS LEONE ARDOLF, consultant radio; b. Sherburn, Minn., July 23, 1958; d. Leo Albert and Gladys (Popelka) Ardolf; m. Theodore Francis Stecker, Sept. 19, 1981. BA, Coll. St. Benedict, 1977; MA, West Georgia Coll., 1986; postgrad., U. Tex., San Antonio, 1986-87, Columbia Pacific U., 1988—. On-air personality Sta. KNIA, Knoxville, Iowa, 1980; on-air personality, engr. Sta. KIOZ, Laramie, WY, 1980; on-air personality, music dir., asst. program dir. Stas. KHYS/KPAC, Port Arthur, Tex., 1981-82; program dir. Stas. WSAI/WKXF, Cin., 1983-84; v.p. Stecker-Thompson Assocs., San Antonio, 1984-88; Dallas/Ft. Worth; pres., Arlington (Tex.) and Ft. Worth, 1988—. Vol. various animal protection groups, San Antonio, 1985—. Mem. NOW, Mensa. Democrat. Roman Catholic. Club: Intertel (San Antonio). Home and Office: Stecker-Thompson Assocs 5206 Independence Ave Arlington TX 76017

THOMPSON, DOROTHY BROWN, writer; b. Springfield, Ill., May 14, 1896; d. William Joseph and Harriet (Gardner) Brown; m. Dale Moore Thompson, July 2, 1921; 1 child, William B. (dec. 1978). AB., U. Kans., 1919. Began writing professionally, 1931; contributed verse to nat. mags. and newspapers including Saturday Rev., Saturday Evening Post, Va. Quar. Rev., Poetry, Commonweal, Good Housekeeping and others, author research articles for various hist. jours.; poems pub. in over 200 collections and textbooks; mags. and textbooks pub. in Eng., Australia, N.Z., Can., India, Sweden; 25 in Braille. Author: (poetry) Subject to Change, 1973. Leader poetry sect. Writers' Conf., U. Kans., 1953-55, McKendree Coll., 1961, 63, Creighton U., Omaha, 1966; lectr. writers' conf. U. Kans., 1965, Am. Poets Series, Kansas City, Mo., 1973; mem. staff Poets Workshop, Cen. Mo. State U., 1974; poet-in-schs. residency for Mo. State Council of Arts, 1974. Recipient Mo. Writers' Guild Award, 1941, Poetry Soc. Am., nat. and local awards. Mem. Diversifiers, Poetry Soc. Am., Nat. Soc. Colonial Dames, First Families of Va. (Burgess for Mo.). Mem. Christian Ch. Clubs: Woman's City, Filson (Louisville). Address: 221 W 48th St Apt 1402 Kansas City MO 64112

THOMPSON, E. JOYCE, English educator; b. Quanah, Tex., Nov. 9, 1943; d. Harvey Grant and Claudie Elizabeth (Crume) T. BA in Math., Tex. Tech. U., 1967, MA in English, 1969, PhD in English, 1972. Asst. to assoc. supt. for devel. Dallas Ind. Sch. Dist., 1973-74; prof. English Texas Woman's U., Denton, 1974—. Author: Marking a Trail, 1982; editor: Texas Women: The Myth, The Reality, 1986. Mem. South Cen. MLA, Nat. Coun. Tchrs. English, Popular Culture Assn. Democrat. Office: Tex Womans U Box 23972 Denton TX 76204

THOMPSON, EARLENE, civic volunteer; b. Pelzer, S.C., Nov. 12, 1942; d. Tobie and Sallie (Moss) Tate; m. Willie J. Thompson, Apr. 19, 1958; children: Quenton, Quentena, Quenleasa, Quendrida. Foster parent Ventura County DPSS, Simi Valley, Calif., 1969-73, L.A. County, 1983-87; exec. dir. Wilene's Re-Growth Ctr., Fontana, Calif., 1986—. Mem. Soroptimist (photographer 1988-89). Democrat. Office: Wilene's Re-Growth Ctr Inc 403 E Arrow Hwy #303 San Dimas CA 91773

THOMPSON, EDITH MAUREEN, education program administrator; b. Midland, Md., June 24, 1938; d. Thomas Earl and Mary Catherine (Hammersmith) Brinegar; m. Roger Leonard Thompson, Oct. 23, 1943; children: Jose, Roger, Catherine, Michael, Bradford, Nikki, Eric. RN, St. Agnes Hosp., Balt., 1959; BS in Health Sci., Columbus (Ga.) Coll., 1987; MS in Edn., Troy State U., Phenix City, Ala., 1988; MS in Counseling, Troy State U., 1990; postgrad., Ga. State U. RN, cert. med. asst. Clk. Murphy's 5 & 10, Frostburg, Md., 1952-56; staff nurse Sacred Heart Hosp., Cumberland, Md., 1960-61; nursing instr. St. Joseph. Hosp. Sch. Nursing, Balt., 1961-64, Balt. City Hosp. Sch. Nursing, 1964-66; supr. nurses ARC, Ft. Lewis, Wash., 1973-75; dir. Phys. Measurements, Inc., Columbus, Ga., 1975-78; instr. nursing Columbus (Ga.) Tech. Inst., 1978-84, program dir., med. asst., 1984—. Chmn. bd. Columbus Specialized Sch., 1989—; treas. Columbus Alliance for Battered Women, 1989—, State Health Occupations Assn., 1985—. Mem. Health Occupations Ednl. Assn. (treas. 1986—), Am. Voc. Assn., Am. Assn. Med. Asst., Am. Assn. Counseling & Devel., Ga. Voc.

Assn., Am. Mental Health Counselors Assn., Phi Kappa Phi, Kappa Delta Pi. Republican. Roman Catholic. Home: 3437 Sue Mack Dr Columbus GA 31906 Office: Columbus Tech Inst 928 45th St Columbus GA 31995

THOMPSON, ELEANOR DUMONT, nurse; b. Derry, N.H., May 26, 1935; d. Louis Arthur and Florence Berthae (Gendreau) D.; m. Carl Hugh Thompson, Aug. 22, 1959; children: Justine, Julie. Student, Dartmouth Hitchcock Nur. Sch., 1956; BA, New Eng. Coll., 1977; MS, Drake U., 1984. Registered art therapist. Pediatric instr. Hanover (N.H.) Sch. Practical Nursing, 1958-61; pub. W.B. Sanders Co., Phila., 1962—; pediatric instr. St. Joseph Hosp., Nashua, N.H., 1978-81; clin. nurse specialist Mercy Hosp. Med. Ctr., Des Moines, 1987-90; puppetteer St. Joseph's Hosp. Sch. Nursing, Nashua, 1981-82; created and conducted shows on hospitalization for children; nursing cons. Hospice Cen. Iowa, Des Moines, 1982-89. Author: Pediatric Nursing An Introductory Text, 1965, 5th edit., 1990, Introduction to Maternity and Pediatric Nursing, 1990. Vol. nurse Vietnam Vets. Ctr., Des Moines, 1985-87, Camp Apanda Childrens Cancer Camp Boone, Iowa, 1984-86; organist Holy Trinity Ch. Des Moines, 1982, St. Pius Ch., Des Moines, 1982. Mem. Am. Art Therapy Assn., Iowa Art Therapy Assn., Drake Alumnae Assn., Hospice Cen. Iowa, Iowa Nurses Assn., Am. Nurses Assn. Republican. Roman Catholic. Home: 24 Peninsula Dr Stratham NH 03885

THOMPSON, ELIZABETH ABRAMS, painter; b. N.Y.C., Mar. 26, 1954; d. Jerome and Linda (Kaplan) Abrams; m. Richard Martin Holden Thompson, Dec. 16, 1978. BA, Mount Holyoke Coll., 1975; MFA, Pratt Inst., 1977. With Pratt Inst. Art Gallery, Bklyn, 1977, Galerie Les Arts Plastiques Modernes, Paris, 1978, Plan Gallery Knokke le Zoute, Belgium, 1979, Andrew Crispo Gallery, N.Y.C., Albermarle Gallery, London, 1989, Lavigne Bastille, Paris, 1989. Jewish. Home: 116 E 64th St New York NY 10021 Office: 849 Lexington Ave New York NY 10021

THOMPSON, ELIZABETH JANE, sociology educator; b. Ithaca, N.Y., Jan. 11, 1927; d. Merle Godley and Nellie Gray (Trowbridge) T. AB, Syracuse U., 1948, MA, 1962, PhD, 1971. Writer, editor Cornell U., Ithaca, N.Y., 1950-53; dir. pub. rels. Taylor Ward Advt., Ithaca, 1953-54; account exec. Doug Johnson Assocs., Syracuse, N.Y., 1954-58; assoc. in community rels., Youth Devel. Ctr. Syracuse U., 1958-66, grad. asst., 1967-68; asst. prof., assoc. prof., now prof. sociology Shippensburg (Pa.) U., 1968—, dir. Fashion Archives, 1980—; lectr. on costume, fashion and sociology of dress to numerous civic and ednl. groups. Co-editor: Among the People: Studies of the Urban Poor, 1968; contbr. articles on sociology of dress to numerous publs. Mem. Costume Soc. Am. (bd. dirs. region II 1985—), Am. Sociol. Soc., Popular Culture Assn., Assn. for Edn. in Journalism and Mass Communications. Dutch Reform. Home: 19 S Prince St Shippensburg PA 17257 Office: Shippensburg U Sociology Dept Shippensburg PA 17257

THOMPSON, EVE LLOYD, public relations executive; b. Teaneck, N.J., Aug. 31, 1934; d. Francis Van Duyne and Evelyn (Roth) Lloyd; m. Joseph J. Scherschel, Dec. 6, 1959 (div. 1964); m. Richard Knight Thompson, Jr., Dec. 15, 1966. BA, Cornell U., 1956; postgrad., U. Md., 1975-77, NYU, 1957. Asst. buyer Saks Fifth Ave., N.Y.C., 1956-57; buyer Peck and Peck, N.Y.C., 1958-60, Garfinckel's, Washington, 1961-69, Hecht Co., Washington, 1970-71; pres. Fashion Abilities, Poolesville, Md., 1971-82; exec. dir. Washington Internat. Horse Show, 1983-88; spl. projects coord. Harwood Lloyd, Hackensack, N.J., 1989—; TV commentator horse sports, Home Team Sports, Washington, 1983—, Sports Channel Am., nationwide, 1989—, Madison Square Garden Network, N.Y.C., 1984—; dir. Internat. Hunter Futurity, Lexington, Ky., 1990—; treas., sec. Bernice Barbour Found., Inc., Hackensack, 1989—; treas. Fashion Group Internat. of Washington, 1968-70, 77-78, regional dir. 1970-74. Mem. Am. Horse Shows Assn. (chmn. planning com. 1989—, chmn. scholarship com. 1988—, hearing com. 1983—, steward 1983), Am. Horse Coun. (horse show adv. com. 1990—), Md. Horse Shows Assn. (pres. 1979-81, John A. Wagner award 1980). Republican. Presbyterian. Home: 14431 Sugarland Lane Poolesville MD 20837

THOMPSON, FRANCES ANN, English educator; b. Havre, Mont., Nov. 2, 1945; d. William Compton and Bess Irene (Harrison) T. B.A. in English, U. Tex.-Arlington, 1967; M.A. in English, East Tex. State U., 1973, Ed.D. in Elem. Edn., 1983. Cert. tchr. all levels and ESL, Tex. Kindergarten tchr. Mrs. Schaeffer's Sch., Arlington, 1967-68; tchr. English, Crystal City Ind. Sch. Dist., Tex., 1969-71; elem. and English tchr. Mirando City Ind. Sch. Dist., Tex., 1974-81; ESL tchr. Como-Pickton Ind. Sch. Dist., Como, Tex., 1981—. Contbr. articles to profl. jours., also poetry to Poor Richard's Poetry, 1968 (1st Pl. award). Mem. Tex. State Tchrs. Assn., Phi Kappa Theta. Republican. Baptist. Avocations: reading; crafts; needlework. Office: Como-Pickton Ind Sch Dist PO Box 18 Como TX 75431

THOMPSON, GENEVA FLORENCE, medical technologist, cytotechnologist; b. Zionsville, Ind., Apr. 5, 1915; d. Alfred Seymour and Grace Viola (Kutz) T. Cert. in cytotechnology, Ohio State U., 1964; BA, Ind. U./Purdue U., Indpls., 1972. Cert. Am. Soc. Clin. Pathologists. Med. technician Noblesville (Ind.) Hosp., 1948-52; med. technician Riverview Hosp., Noblesville, 1952-56, med. technologist, 1956-60; med. technologist Office of Robert Harris, M.D., Noblesville, 1960-64; cytotechnologist Office of Thornton, Haymond, Costin, Buehl & Bolinger, M.D., Indpls., 1965-78; ret., 1978. Active with local church; served with U.S. W.A.C., 1944-46. Mem. AAUW (chmn. literature study group), Ind. U. Women's Club of Indpls., Am. Soc. Clin. Pathologists, Noblesville Tourist Club (sec.), Sr. Citizens Orgn., Inc. Republican.

THOMPSON, HELEN VIRGINIA, nurse; b. Frederick, Md., May 14, 1941; d. William Linwood and Bertha Mae (Horman) T. BS, Frostburg (Md.) State U., 1963; diploma, Broofs AFB Sch. Aerospace Medicine, 1969, Frederick meml. Hosp. Sch. Nursing, 1968; MA, W.Va. Grad. Studies, 1985. Staff RN, asst. charge nurse Frederick Meml. Hosp., 1968-69; classroom instr. Charleston (W.Va.) Area Med. Ctr. Sch. Anesthesia, 1973-79, asst. dir., 1975-79; staff anesthetist Herbert J. Thomas Meml. Hosp., South Charleston, W.Va., 1979—; counselor Women's Counseling Ctr., Charleston, 1982-85; tchr. Woodburn jr. High Sch., Balt. Chair W.Va. Nurses Polit. Action Com., 1983-89. Named Politically Active Nurse of Yr. State of W.Va., 1985. Mem. Assn. Mil. Surgeons U.S., Am. Nurses Assn., W.Va. Nurses Assn. (Recognition award 1989), Am. Assn. Nurse Anesthesists, NRA, Nat. Guard Assn. Democrat. Mem. Disciples of Christ. Home: Rt 1 Box 166 Walton WV 25286 Office: Herbert J Thomas Meml Hosp MacCorkle Ave SW South Charleston WV 25309

THOMPSON, HENRIETTA SPOTTS, educator; b. Georgetown, Ky., Dec. 15, 1920; d. Henry Simpson and Margaret (Generals) Spotts; m. Clarence Thompson (dec.). BS, Ky. State Coll., 1942; MS, Cornell U., 1957; postgrad., U. Ky., 1953-57. Home econs. tchr. Augusta County Schs. of Va., Staunton, 1943-48, Lexington (Va.) Ind. Schs., fall 1952, Charlottesville (Va.) Ind. Schs., 1952-57, Lexington (Ky.) Schs., 1957-84. Contbr. letters to editor local newspapers, also articles on clothing to textbooks. Pioneer Bus. Integration, Waynesboro, Va., 1947; pub. speaker various orgns., 1950—; v.p. Tennant Svcs., Lexington, 1984—; pres. Blind Buddies, Lexington, Trinity Bapt. Ch., Ky., 1985-86; active Trinity; with job interview panel Mayor's Office, 1990—. Mem. Fayette Vocat. Tchrs. (chair 1976-82, scholarship 1984), LWV (vol.), New Homemakers Am. (co-organizer Richmond, Va. chpt. 1945), Fayette County Tchrs. (pres. Lexington chpt. 1963-64), Kappa Delta Pi. Democrat. Baptist. Home: 544 Haskins Dr Lexington KY 40508

THOMPSON, JANE JOHNSON, retail executive; b. Charleston, W.Va., July 13, 1951; d. Robert Paul and Phyllis Jane (Judson) Johnson; m. t. Stephen Thompson, Aug. 28, 1976; children: Robert Baker, Catherine Brooke. BBA, U. Cin., 1977; MBA, Harvard Coll., 1978. Brand mgr. Procter & Gamble, Cin., 1973-77; prin., ptnr. McKinsey & Co., Inc., Chgo., 1978-88; v.p. Sears Specialty Merchandising div. Sears Roebuck & Co., Chgo., 1988-89; v.p. corp. planning Sears Roebuck & Co., Chgo., 1989—. Bd. dirs. Lincoln Park Zool. Soc. Aux. 1988—. Baker scholar Harvard U., 1978. Office: Sears Roebuck & Co Sears Tower 902P 61st Fl Chicago IL 60684

THOMPSON, JANET KEITH, accountant; b. Denver, Aug. 27, 1929; d. Douglas Lee Keith and Florence Rita (McLaughlin) Rush; m. Duane E. Thompson, Aug. 26, 1951 (div. Apr. 1965). Student, Colo. State U., 1948, U. Colo., 1949. Staff acct. Harold C. Greager CPA, Ft. Collins, Colo., 1948-52; bookkeeper Bruce Anderson Independent Oil Co., Denver, 1957-64; office mgr., book keeper Jack Grynberg & Co., Denver, 1965-66, Willam Branch & Co., Denver, 1966-69; pvt. practice book keeper Denver, 1969—; ptnr. J.E. Thompson & Son, Ft. Collins, Colo., 1951-65, 32d Street Venture, Denver, 1982—, Badger Drilling Co., Colo. and N.Mex., 1984—; rehabber hist. Denver homes, 1977-84. Mem. League of Women Voters, Thornton County, Colo., 1962-64. Mem. Friday Morning Breakfast Club. Democrat. Episcopalian. Home and Office: 955 Eudora #402 Denver CO 80220

THOMPSON, JANICE, office manager; b. Dodge City, Kans., Feb. 11, 1955; d. John Gilbert and Gladys Nadine (Allen) Olson; 1 child, Tamara. Office mgr. Chouteau AutoMart, Kansas City, Mo. Address: 7201 N Forest Kansas City MO 64119

THOMPSON, JEAN DUNIVANT, medical alumni association director; b. Wright City, Mo., June 21, 1927; d. Claude Lawrence Dunivant and Lela Snow (Niblack) Dunivant-Shears; m. John Goral, Feb. 5, 1946 (div. Nov. 1978); 1 child, Daniel; m. Paul W. Thompson, June 23, 1984. Student, U. Md. Br. mgr., dist. sec. Singer Co., Balt., 1969-71; sec. to exec. v.p. Balt. Fed. Savs., 1971-74; exec. dir. med. alumni assn. U. Md., Inc., Balt., 1974—. Mem. Fed. Hill and Fells Point Preservation Soc., Preservation of Md. Antiquities. Mem. Am. Soc. Assn. Execs., Md. Soc. Assn. Execs., Assn. Am. Med. Colls., Nat. Preservation Soc. Republican. Office: U Md Med Alumni Assn 522 W Lombard St Box 2198 Baltimore MD 21203

THOMPSON, JILL ELLEN, school system administrator; b. Newton, N.J., Dec. 11, 1951; d. Charles Edward and Helen Marie (Funk) T. BA, Mary Washington Coll., 1970; diploma, Swedish Inst. Massage Therapy, 1977; MDiv, Union Theol. Sem., 1978. Lic. massage therapist, N.Y. Faculty instr., dept. chairperson Swedish Inst. Massage Therapy, N.Y.C., 1978—, asst. dir., 1984-86; cons. N.Y. State Bd. for Massage, Albany, 1980-85, N.Y. State Dept. Edn., Albany, 1985—. Editor: Intro. to Pathology for the Massage Practitioner, 1985. Clergy on staff Met. Community Ch., N.Y.C., 1980-85; mem. Sri Chinmoy Marathon Team, 1985-90. Mem. AAUW. Democrat. Home: 85-12 160th St Jamaica Hill NY 11432 Office: Swedish Inst Massage Therapy 226 W 26th St New York NY 10001 Also: New York State Bd for Massage Cultural Edn Ctr Albany NY 12230

THOMPSON, JOAN KATHRYN, university official; b. Portsmouth, Va., Jan. 24, 1956; d. Alfred Colbein and Ruby (Skeie) Lee; m. David Lee Thompson, May 24, 1975; children: Chad David, Allison Rae. BS in Bus. Edn., Drake U., 1977. Tchr. Des Moines Pub. Schs., 1978-80; commodity broker R.G. Dickinson, Des Moines, 1980-82; investmment officer 1st Interstate Bank, Des Moines, 1982-87, v.p., sales mgr., 1987-88; treas. Iowa State U., Ames, 1988—. Treas. Iowa 4-H Found., Ames, 1988—. Mem. Nat. Cash Mgmt. Assn., Iowa Cash Mgmt. Assn. Republican. Lutheran. Office: Iowa State U 122 Beardshear Hall Ames IA 50011

THOMPSON, JOYCE ELIZABETH, cultural association executive; b. Pasadena, Tex., Aug. 15, 1951; d. James Little and Ruth Lake (Skinner) Wilkison; divorced; children: Christine Joy, Cassidy Jane. BA in Psychology, David Lipscomb Coll., 1974; MA in Speech, Theater, Murray State U., 1976; postgrad., U. Tex., 1978; MA in Arts Adminstrn., Ind. U., 1981. Asst. prof. speech Vincennes (Ind.) U., 1976-79; asst. dir. mktg. Hartford (Conn.) Ballet, 1981-82; touring dir. Hartford Ballet/Conn. Opera, 1982-84; exec. dir. Wyo. Coun. on Arts, Cheyenne, 1984—; adj. instr., Manchester (Conn.) Community Coll., 1982-84, Chapman Coll., 1990—; mem. selection com. Coca-Cola Scholars Found., 1989, 90. Mem. adv. bd., Cheyenne Little Theatre Players, 1986, Cheyenne Civic Ctr., 1987-88. Mem. Assn. Performing Arts Producers, Speech Communication Assn., Western States Arts Fedn. (bd. dirs. 1984—, chair performing arts com. 1985-87). Democrat. Office: Wyo Coun on Arts 2320 Capitol Ave Cheyenne WY 82002

THOMPSON, JOYCE LURINE, information systems specialist; b. White Oak Twp., Mich., Mar. 5, 1931; d. Orla Jacob and Ethel Inita (Thayer) Sheathelm; m. Robert E. Thompson, Dec. 10, 1949 (div. 1972); children: Wendy, Robin, Kristen. Student, Mich. State U., 1972-78, Lansing (Mich.) Community Coll, 1976-77. Programmer, analyst Mich. State U., East Lansing, 1966-73; tech. programmer Mich. State Police, East Lansing, 1973-77; database coord. Mich. Dept. Treasury, Lansing, 1977-79; systems engr. 4-Phase Systems, Grand Rapids, Mich., 1979-81; mktg. rep. Motorola, Grand Rapids, 1981-84; data analyst Whirlpool Corp., Benton Harbor, Mich., 1984-88, data adminstr., 1988—. Activity chmn. Girl Scouts U.S.A., East Lansing; leader 4-H Clubs, East Lansing; vol. Stepping Stones, South Haven; vol. Lake Mich. Maritime Mus., South Haven. Mildred Erickson fellow Mich. State U., EAst Lansing, 1974-78. Mem. Assn. Systems Mgmt. (sec. 1984), Data Adminstrn. Mgmt. Assn. Office: Whirlpool Corp 2000 M63 Benton Harbor MI 49022

THOMPSON, JUDITH CURFMAN, association executive; b. Cin., Sept. 7, 1942; d. William Kenneth Rogers and Pauline Patricia (Paterson) Curfman; m. Robert Smith Thompson, June 17, 1967; 1 child, Pauline Alexandra. MusB, Westminster Choir Coll., Princeton, 1964. Dir. music and christian edn. Front Royal (Va.) Meth. Ch., 1964-67; music tchr. Wayne County (Mich.) Sch. Dist., 1967-68, Belleville (Mich.) Sch. Dist., 1968-70; cons. affiliated facilities U. S.C., Columbia, 1970-83; music tchr. Internat. Sch. Beijing, People's Republic of China, 1983-84; cons. Human Resources Mgmt. Div., 1985-86; exec. dir. S.C. Nurses' Assn., Columbia, 1985—. Author: Political Participation Handbook, 1978; mng. editor: Know Your State, S.C., 1982. Pres. LWV, (S.C., 1980-83, Columbia area, 1977-80), Planned Parenthood Cent. S.C., Columbia, 1979, ; bd. dirs. S.C. Christian Action Coun., Columbia, 1984-87; docent Hist. Columbia Found., 1970-74. Mem. Am. Nurses Assn. (exec. com. constituent forum, 1988-90). Democrat. Home: 2509 Monroe St Columbia SC 29205

THOMPSON, JULIA ANN, physicist, educator; b. Little Rock, Mar. 13, 1943; d. Erwin Arthur and Ruth Evelyn (Johnston) T.; m. Patrick A. Thompson, Mar. 22, 1964 (div. 1974); 1 child, Diane E.; m. David E. Kraus, Jr., June 22, 1976; children: Vincent Szewczyk, Larry Lynch. B.A., Cornell Coll., Mt. Vernon, Iowa, 1964; M.A., Yale U., 1966, Ph.D., 1969. Research assoc. Brookhaven Lab., Upton, N.Y., 1969-71; research assoc./assoc. instr. U. Utah, Salt Lake City, 1971-72; asst. prof. physics U. Pitts., 1972-78, assoc. prof., 1978-85, prof., 1986—; mem. users coms. Brookhaven Nat. Lab., 1983-86; condr. experiments at Ctr. Europeene Recherche Nucleaire, Switzerland, Brookhaven Natl. Lab., L.I., Fermi Natl. Accelerator Lab., Chgo. Contbr. articles to profl. jours. Bd. dirs. 1st Unitarian Ch., Pitts., 1980-83; zone councillor Soc. Physics Students, 1986-88. Woodrow Wilson fellow, 1964-65. Mem. Am. Phys. Soc. (com. on status of women in physics 1983-86). Democrat. Unitarian. Avocations: promoting effective science education, hiking, reading, music.

THOMPSON, KAREN ELAINE, manufacturing company executive; b. Palo Alto, Calif., Aug. 24, 1958; d. Herbert Walter and Mary Muriel (Thickett) Thompson. BSIE, San Jose State U., 1982, MBA, 1986. Indsl. engr. Atari, Inc., Sunnyvale, Calif., 1982-83, H & K Mfg. Co., Dublin, Calif., 1983-86; pres. H & K Mfg. Co., 1986—; dir. H & K Mfg. Co. Contbr. articles to profl. jours. Leader 4-H, Alameda County, 1985—. Soc. Women Engrs. scholar, 1976; San Jose State U. pres.'s scholar, 1981, 82. Mem. Am. Inst. Indsl. Engrs., Soc. Mfg. Engrs., Nat. Assn. Female Execs., NorCal Western Club. Repubican. Office: H&K Manufacturing Co 7112 Village Pkwy Dublin CA 94568

THOMPSON, LAVERNE ELIZABETH THOMAS, English language educator; b. Bklyn., July 17, 1945; d. Roscoe Lee and Mary Elizabeth (Blackwell) Thomas; m. Robert Louis Thompson, Sept. 28, 1968. BA in English, Bluffton Coll., 1967; MS in Ednl. Adminstrn./Supervision, U. Dayton, 1977; postgrad., U. Toledo. Cert. sch. prin., Ohio; cert. secondary sch. supr., Ohio; cert. realtor, Ohio; cert. notary public, Ohio. Instr. English, speech Piqua (Ohio) Cen. High Sch., 1967-68; instr. Lima (Ohio) Sr. High Sch., 1968-77, Shawnee High Sch., Lima, 1977-86; grad. asst., U. Toledo, 1986-90, interim adminstrv. asst., 1990, interim counsel adminstrn. student support svcs., 1989, adminstrv. asst. multicultural student devel., 1990; real estate agt. Alberta Lee Realty, Lima, Ohio, 1978-82, Slonaker Realty, Lima, 1982-84, Gooding Co., Lima, 1985-90. Editor Higher Edn. newsletter, 1987. Bd. dirs. Lima YWCA, 1971; co-chair Brotherhood Dinner Sr. High Sch., Lima, 1976; participant 17th annual Nat. Conf. on Citizenship, Washington, 1962. Mem. Va. Assn. New Homemakers Am. (pres. 1962), New Homemakers Am. (nat pres. 1963), Blackwell Family Assn., NAFE, M.I. Hummel Club, Lladro Collectors Soc., Internat. Platform Assn., Belleek Collectors Soc., Club Anri, Gartland USA Collectors League, Lalique Soc. Am., G. Armani Soc., Royal Doulton Internat. Collectors Club, Duncan Royale Collectors' Club, All God's Children Collectors' Club, Phi Delta Kappa (charter mem. west cen. Ohio chpt.). Home: 24501 W River Rd Perrysburg OH 43551

THOMPSON, LILLIAN HURLBURT, communications company executive; b. Bennington, Vt., Apr. 27, 1947; d. Paul Rhodes and Evelyn Arlene (Lockhart) Hurlburt; m. Wayne Wray Thompson, June 28, 1969. BS, Skidmore Coll., 1969; MS, U. So. Miss., 1975. Communication cons. Southwestern Bell Telephone, San Antonio, 1978-80; acct. exec. C&P Telephone, Washington, 1980-82, Am. Bell, Washington, 1983; staff mgr. AT&T Info. Systems, Rosslyn, Va., 1984; mgr. sales intermediary mktg. dept. Bell Atlantic Corp., Silver Spring, Md., 1984-89, mgr. product line mgmt. dept., 1989—. Home: 9203 St Marks Pl Fairfax VA 22031 Office: Bell Atlantic 13100 Columbia Pike Silver Spring MD 20904

THOMPSON, LINDA LEE, educational consultant; b. Ottumwa, Iowa, Sept. 21, 1940; d. Clarence Adelbert and Ollie Mae (Easley) Andrews; m. Richard Bruce Thompson, Aug. 13, 1961 (div. Nov. 1986); children: Bruce Edward, Curtis Lowell. BA, U. No. Iowa, 1961; postgrad., U. Wis., 1962-66, U. Ariz., 1967-68. Cert. tchr. Math. tchr. Franklin Jr. High Sch., 1961-63; tchr., head math. dept. LaFollette High Sch., Madison, Wis., 1963-67; cons., editor, writer Tucson, 1968—; cons. Ariz. State Dept. Edn., Phoenix, 1981. Author: General Mathematics, 1977; co-author: Consumer Mathematics, 2d edition, 1986, McGraw-Hill Mathematics, 1987, You, The Consumer, 1987, Business Mathematics, 1988; contbr. articles to Scholastic Math mag., Creative Classroom mag. Chairperson, bd. dirs. Tucson Jr. Strings, 1981-84; com. mem. Rincon/Univ. High Sch. Drug Impact Group, Tucson, 1986-90, co-chair 1989-90; mem. Univ. High Sch. Parents Bd., co-chair 1989-90. Mem. Math. Assn. Am., Nat. Coun. Tchrs. Math., Nat. Coun. Suprs. Math. Home and Office: 2370 Manion Dr Warrenton OR 97146

THOMPSON, LOIS JEAN ORE, psychologist; b. Chgo., Feb. 22, 1933; d. Harold William and Ethel Rose (Neumann) Heidke; m. Henry Thomas Ore, Aug. 28, 1954 (div. May 1972); children: Christopher, Douglas; m. Joseph Lippard Thompson, Aug. 3, 1972; children: Scott, Les, Melanie. BA, Cornell Coll., Mt. Vernon, Iowa, 1955; MA, Idaho State U., 1964, EdD, 1981. Lic. psychologist, N.Mex. Tchr. pub. schs. various locations, 1956-67; tchr., instr. Idaho State U., Pocatello, 1967-72; emp./org. dev. specialist Los Alamos (N.Mex.) Nat. Lab., 1981-84, tng. specialist, 1984-89, sect. leader, 1989—; pvt. practice Los Alamos, 1988—; sec. Cornell Coll. Alumni Office, 1954-81, also other orgns.; bd. dirs. Parent Edn. Ctr., Idaho State U., 1980; counselor, Los Alamos, 1981-88. Editor newsletter LWV, Laramie, Wyo., 1957; contbr. articles to profl. jours. Pres. Newcomers Club, Pocatello, 1967, Faculty Womens Club, Pocatello, 1968; chmn. edn. com. AAUW, Pocatello, 1969. Mem. Am. Psychol. Assn., N.Mex. Psychol. Assn. (div. II bd. dirs. 1990—, sec. 1988-90, chair 1990—), N.Am. Soc. Adlerian Psychology, N.Mex. Soc. Adlerian Psychology (pres. 1990—), Am. Assn. Counseling and Devel., Soc. Indsl. and Orgnl. Psychology, Nat. Career Counseling Assn. Mormon, Christian Scientist. Home: 340 Aragon Los Alamos NM 87544 Office: Los Alamos Nat Lab MS M589 HRD-3 Los Alamos NM 87545

THOMPSON, LOLA MAY, music educator, volunteer; b. Mpls., Mar. 10, 1931; d. Jens Christian and Lydia Mathilda (Ronsberg) Jensen; m. Wayne Leo Thompson, July 27, 1957; children: Mark Wayne, Scott Christopher. BS, U. Minn., 1953. Music supr. Little Falls (Minn.) Pub. Schs., 1954-57; music coord. Bloomington (Minn.) Pub. Schs., 1957-61; tchr., owner Thompson Piano Studio, St. Paul, 1961—; sr. choir dir. Holy Trinity Ch., Mpls., 1953-54, 1st English Luth. Ch., Little Falls, Minn., 1954-57, dir. Jr. Sunday Sch. Choir Cen. Luth. Ch., Mpls., 1970—; benefit co-chmn. Dale Warland Singers, 1989, benefit chmn., 1989—; bd. dirs. Friends of Dale Warland Singers. Composer numerous children's songs, choir piece Twenty-seventh Psalm, 1949 (received award). Pres. Friends of St. Paul Chamber Orch., 1974-77, pres. coun., 1977—, benefit chmn., 1978, 79, 80, 88; gen. chmn. Minn. Orch. and Women's Assn. for Young Artist Competition, 1982-84, repertoire chair, 1984—; advisor Women's Assn. Minn. Orch., 1986—; benefit chmn. U. Minn. Found., 1984-85; mem. Minn. Hist. Soc. Women's Orgn. Recipient Good Neighbor award WCCO Radio, 1985. Mem. AAUW, Music Tchrs. Nat. Assn., Minn. Music Tchrs. Assn. (state chair grants and funding), Minn. Opera Assn., Sigma Alpha Iota (nat. province v.p. 1979-82, pres. St. Paul-Mpls. chpt. 1699-72, 83-85, Sword of Honor 1969, Rose of Honor 1970). Republican. Lutheran.

THOMPSON, MARCIA LYNN, nurse; b. Zanesville, Ohio, Jan. 18, 1956; d. Harry Loyd and Catherine J. (Swendryck) Miller; m. Victor Herbert Thompson, Sept. 7, 1975; children: Justin Michale, Jordan Matthew. AAS, Ohio U., Zanesville, 1984, BS in Health, 1989. Lic. optician Dr. R.C. England, Zanesville, Ohio, 1975-82; lic. optician, mgr. Royal Optical, Zanesville, 1984-85; RN Midwest Allergy, Zanesville, 1985-86, Bethesda Hosp. Nurse Asst., Zanesville, 1982-86, Zanesville City Schs., 1986—; childbirth educator Bethesda Hosp., Zanesville, 1984-87. Advisor Girls Athletic Assn., Zanesville, 1986—; vol. Salvation Army, Zanesville, 1986; bd. dirs. Am. Heart Assn., Zanesville, 1989-90. Mem. Zanesville Edn. Assn., Ohio Edn. Assn., NEA, Ohio Sch. Nurses Assn. Methodist.

THOMPSON, MARGARET DOUGLAS, geology educator; b. Wilmington, Del., May 12, 1947; d. Collins Thompson and Margaret (Porch) Lips; m. E. Randy Shull, June 25, 1983; children: Jessica Marshall, Eleanor Nicholas. AB, Smith Coll., 1969; MA, Harvard U., 1974, PhD, 1976. Asst. prof. geology Wellesley (Mass.) Coll., 1976-83, assoc. prof. geology, 1983—. Office: Wellesley Coll Dept Geology Wellesley MA 02181

THOMPSON, MARGUERITE MYRTLE GRAMING (MRS. RALPH B. THOMPSON), librarian; b. Orangeburg, S.C., Apr. 23, 1912; d. Thomas Laurie and Rosa Lee (Stroman) Graming; m. Ralph B. Thompson, Sept. 17, 1949 (dec. Oct. 1960). BA in English cum laude, U. S.C., 1932, postgrad., 1937; BLS, Emory U., 1943. Tchr. English pub. high schs., S.C., 1932-43; libr. Rockingham (N.C.) High Sch., 1943-45, Randolph County (N.C.) Libr., Asheboro, 1945-48, Colleton County (S.C.) Libr., Walterboro, 1948-61; dir. Florence (S.C.) County Libr., 1961-78. Sec. com. community facilities, svcs. and instns. Florence County Resources Devel. Com., 1964-67; vice chmn. Florence County Coun. on Aging, 1968-70, exec. bd. 1968-82, bd. treas., 1973-75, bd. sec., 1976-77, bd. v.p., 1979; mem. Florence County Bicentennial Planning Com., 1975-76; mem. rels. and allocations com. United Way, 1979-80. Named Boss of Yr. Nat. Secs. Assn., 1971. Mem. ALA (coun. 1964-72), Southeastern Libr. Assn., S.C. Libr. Assn. (pres. 1960, chmn. assn. handbook revision com. 1967-69, 80, sect. co-chmn. com. standards for S.C. pub. librs. 1966-75, fed. rels. coord. 1972-73, planning com. 1976-78), Greater Florence C. of C. (women's div. chmn. 1969-70, bd. dirs. 1975-77), S.E. Regional Conf. Women in C. of C. (bd. dir. 1970-71), Florence Bus. and Profl. Women's Club (2d v.p. 1975-76, Career Woman of Yr. 1974, parliamentarian 1980-81, chmn. scholarship com. 1981-82), Delta Kappa Gamma (county chpt. charter pres. 1963-65, treas. 1966-70, chmn. com. on expansion 1977-80, 82-84, state chpt. chmn. state scholarship com. 1967-73, state 2d v.p. 1971-73, state 1st v.p. 1973-75, state pres. 1975-77, chmn. policy manual 1977-81, chmn. adv. coun. 1978-85, chmn. fin. com. 1981-83, parliamentarian 1987—, cons. bylaws com. and adv. coun. 1987—, chmn. nominations com. 1989—, dir. S.E. Region 1978-80, coord. S.E. Regional Golden Anniversary Conf. 1979, internat. scholarship com. 1970-74, internat. exec. bd. 1975-77, 78-80, internat. adminstrv. bd. 1978-80, internat. constn. com. 1980-82, internat. achievement award com., 1986-88), Florence Literary Club (sec. 1964-66, 79-82, pres. 1970-72). Methodist (chmn. ch. libr. com. 1965-71, chmn. com. ch. history, 1968-69, sec. adminstrv. bd. 1979-82). Home: 1000 Live Oaks Dr SW #8B Orangeburg SC 29115

THOMPSON, MARY E., automobile lubricants manufacturing executive; b. Richmond, Va.. BA in English, James Madison U., 1972. Dist. sales rep. Kayser-Roth Hosiery, Inc., Richmond, 1979-83; ter. sales mgr. Castrol, Inc., Richmond, 1983-87; nat. sales tng. mgr. Castrol, Inc., Wayne, N.J., 1987—. Mem. Am. Soc. Tng. and Devel., Am. Mgmt. Assn., NAFE, President's Club of Castrol, Inc. Office: Castrol Inc 1500 Valley Rd Wayne NJ 07470

THOMPSON, MARY EILEEN, chemistry educator; b. Mpls., Dec. 21, 1928; d. Albert C. and Blanche (McAvoy) T. B.A., Coll. St. Catherine, 1953; M.S., U. Minn., 1958; Ph.D., U. Calif.-Berkeley, 1964. Math. and sci. tchr. Derham Hall High Sch., St. Paul, 1953-59; faculty Coll. St. Catherine, St. Paul, 1964—, prof., chmn. dept. chemistry, 1969-90. Contbr. articles to profl. jours. Mem. Am. Chem. Soc., N.Y. Acad. Sci., Chem. Soc. London, AAAS, Sigma Xi, Phi Beta Kappa. Democrat. Roman Catholic. Avocations: tennis; biking; camping. Office: Coll St Catherine 2004 Randolph Ave Saint Paul MN 55105

THOMPSON, MARY KOLETA, sculptor, arts consultant; b. Portsmouth, Va., Dec. 27, 1938; m. James Burton Thompson, May 5, 1957; children: Burt, Suzan, Kate, Jon. BFA, U. Tex., 1982; postgrad., Boston U. Asst. dir. communications TXPTA; pres. Fine Art Traditions, Austin, Tex., 1986—; dir. Tex. Children's Mus. Fredericksburg, 1987-88, Internat. Hdqrs. Share Command Arts & Crafts Ctr., 1985-86; com. chair Symposium for Encouragement of Women in Math and Natural Sci., U. Tex., Austin, 1990; bd. dirs. Teenage Parent Coun. of Austin, Inc., 1990—; exhibit chair Tex. Soc. Sculptors, Austin, 1988—. Sculptor portrait busts; contbr. The Arts Edn. Rev. of Books, 1990. Asst. dir. communications Tex. PTA, Austin, 1990—. Named U.S. Vol. of Yr., Belgium, 1986; grantee NEA, 1988. Mem. AAUW (life, pub. info. com. 1989-90, pres. 1990-92), U. Tex. Ex-Student Assn. (life), Tex. Hist. Found. (life), Leadership Tex., Raleigh Tavern Soc. (founding mem.). Office: Fine Art Traditions PO Box 12885 Austin TX 78711

THOMPSON, MAUREEN FIELDER, emergency-trauma nurse; b. Edmonton, Alta., Can., Feb. 5, 1951; came to U.S., 1961; d. William H. and Natalia Irene (Plawiuk) Fielder; 1 child, Kelley Fielder. AS in Nursing magna cum laude, Gadsden (Ala.) State Coll., 1982. RN, Ala.; cert. in basic cardiac life support, basic cardiac life support instr., advanced cardiac life support, advanced cardiac life support instr., pediatric advanced life support, basic trauma life support, trauma nursing core course instr. Office nurse N.D. VanMarter, M.D., Anniston, Ala., 1975-77, S.P. Sanchetti, M.D., Gadsden, 1978-79; charge nurse emergency room Thomas Hosp., Fairhope, Ala., 1982—. Chairperson Ala. Leukemia Soc., 1978. Mem. Am. Nurses Assn. (cert. gen. practice nurse), Ala. Nurses Assn. (nurse day com.), Emergency Nurses Assn. (cert.), Phi Theta Kappa. Jewish. Home: 212 Perdido Ave Fairhope AL 36532 Office: Murphy Ave Fairhope AL 36532

THOMPSON, MAVIS SARAH, physician; b. Newark, June 22, 1927; d. Nathaniel Albert and Mavis Carolyn (Smart) T.; m. James Blaize, Apr. 17, 1955; children: Clayton, Marcia, Sidney, Ronald, Kevin. BA Hunter Coll., 1947; MD, Howard U., 1953. Intern, then resident in internal medicine Kings County Hosp., Bklyn., 1953-57; pvt. practice medicine specializing in internal medicine, Bklyn., 1957-76; med. dir. Lyndon B. Johnson Health Complex, Inc., Bklyn., 1970-71, 74-76; sch. med. insp. N.Y.C. Bd. Edn., Bklyn., 1962-85; family physician Kingsboro Med. Group, Bklyn., 1976—; tchr. dept. nursing Medgar Evers Coll., 1975-76; mem. adv. com. Gerontol. Svcs. Adminstrn. program New Sch. Social Rsch., N.Y.C.; cons. in field. Contbr. articles to med. jours. Bd. dirs. Camp Minisink, 1973-85; active local Boy Scouts Am.; lic. lay reader St. George's Eplsc. Ch., Bklyn., vestry mem., 1985-88. Recipient Community Svc. award St. Mark's Meth. Ch., N.Y.C., 1973; Alberta T. Kline Svc. award Camp Minisink, 1980. Mem. Am. Public Health Assn. (pres. Black caucus health workers 1976-77), Nat. Med. Assn., Am. Mgmt. Assn., Am. Geriatrics Soc., Am. Med. Women's Assn., Kings County Med. Soc., Delta Sigma Theta. Episcopalian. Office: 1000 Church Ave Brooklyn NY 11218

THOMPSON, MOLLIE SUE, manager; b. Hestand, Ky., Nov. 9, 1939; d. James M. and Grace (Baxter) Oliver; m. James V. Thompson, Dec. 28, 1963, (div. May 1977); children: Cynthia, Kevin. Nutrition degree, Vocat.-Tech. Sch., Bowling Green, Ky., 1982; Secretarial Sci., Morrison Bus. Sch., Glasgow, Ky., 1962. Dep. county ct. clk. Barren County, Glasgow, Ky., 1965-75; supr. Scottie Lanes Glasgow, 1975-78, Holiday Inn Glasgow, 1978-82; restaurant mgr. Bolton's Landing Restaurant, Glasgow, 1982-84; conv. coordinator Cave City (Ky.) Conv. Ctr., 1984-86; food svc. mgr. Warren Cen. High Sch., Bowling Green, 1986-88; master chef Citizens Nat. Bank, Bowling Green, 1988; gen. mgr. Bowling Green Country Club, 1989—; guest speaker Ark. Food Svc. Conf., State Food Svc. Conf. First organizer Glasgow Highland Games. Recipient Louise Sublett Award of Excellence, 1988. Mem. Kay Bledsoe Bus. and Profl. Women's Club (past pres., v.p., treas.), Ky. Restaurant Assn., Order of the Eastern Star (numerous chpt. offices, dist. officer), City-County Food Svc. Assn. (past v.p.), Ky. Restaurant Assn. (v.p. Cave Country chpt.). Home: 556 Shady Lane Alvaton KY 42122

THOMPSON, NANCY ETHELYN, association executive; b. Greene County, Ark., June 10, 1925; d. James Samuel and Nancy Theresa (Jackson) T. B in Philosophy, U. Chgo., 1949; postgrad. in journalism Northwestern U., 1950. Asst. to counsel to Pres. White House, Washington, 1964-65; sec., asst. treas. Internat. Econ. Policy Assn., 1967-84, v.p., sec., treas., 1984-88; sec. Internat. Econ. Studies Inst., Washington, 1974-88. Mem. Literacy Coun. of No. Va., 1976—, pres., 1983-84, bd. dirs., 1981-85; del. Action in Community Through Svc., Prince William County, Va., 1982-84, bd. dirs., 1986-89; chmn. Winter Harmony Fest., Prince William County, 1984-85; editor U.S. Internat. Trade Commn., 1988; advisor task force on Internat. Trade Coun. Great Lakes Govs. Econ. Devel. Com., 1988; program specialist Action, 1989—; trustee funds Protestant Episcopal Ch. in Diocese Va., 1988—. Mem. Nat. Assn. Execs., Nonprofit Fin. Mgrs. Roundtable, Women in Econs. Roundtable, Asia Soc. Republican. Episcopalian. Clubs: Montclair Country (Dumfries, Va.), Nat. Press. Home: Box 807 Dumfries VA 22026 Office: 304A LeVeque Tower Columbus OH 43215

THOMPSON, NANCY LYNN, chemist; b. Charlotte, N.C., Sept. 28, 1956; d. Fred Leonard and Lena Verne (Miller) T. BS in Physics, Math., Guilford Coll., 1977; MS in Physics, U. Mich., 1979, PhD in Physics, 1982. Postdoctoral rsch. assoc. chemistry dept. Stanford (Calif.) U., 1982-85; asst. prof. chemistry U. N.C., Chapel Hill, 1985-90, assoc. prof., 1990—; mem. biomed. rsch. tech. rev. com. NIH, Bethesda, Md., 1987—; lectr. Sesquicentennial Alumni Guilford Coll., 1988. Contbr. articles to sci. jours. Charles Dana fellow Guilford Coll., 1976-77, Damon Runyon-Walter Winchell Cancer Fund fellow, 1982-85; named Pres. Young Investigator NSF, 1986. Mem. AAAS, Biophys. Soc. (Margaret Oakley Dayhoff award 1989), Am. Phys. Soc., Am. Chem. Soc. Office: U NC Dept of Chemistry Campus Box #3290 Chapel Hill NC 27599-3290

THOMPSON, OLIVIA, publishing executive. Pub. Women's Wear Daily, N.Y.C. Office: Women's Wear Daily 7 E 12th St New York NY 10003*

THOMPSON, PAMELA ASHLEY, advertising executive; b. St. Louis, Oct. 17, 1954; d. Quentin Miles and Betty K. (Kaner) Knussmann; m. David Beck Thompson, Sept. 12, 1981; 1 child, Taylor Beck. BA in Bus., U. Tenn., 1976. Copywriter McCann-Erickson, Inc., Chgo., 1976-81; v.p., creative dir. Foote, Cone & Belding, Chgo., 1981—. Copywriter Volume Shoes 1986, 87 (Omni award 1986, Addy award 1987). Named Copywriter of Yr. Screen mag., Chgo., 1987, one of Best and Brightest Women of 1988 Advt. Age, N.Y.C., 1988. Democrat. Office: Foote Cone & Belding 101 E Erie St Chicago IL 60611

THOMPSON, PAMELA KAY, human resources director; b. Wilmington, Ohio, Feb. 18, 1951; d. Robert L. and Ruth Marie (Roberts) T. BS in Bus. Mgmt. summa cum laude, Webster U., 1984. Personnel asst. Buckeye Molding Co., New Vienna, Ohio, 1978-81; benefit counselor Benefit Communications, Inc., St. Louis, 1982-84; personnel dir. United Mo. Bank of St. Louis, 1984-87; dir. human resoures Becton Dickinson Accu-Glass, St. Louis, 1987—. Named one of Outstanding Young Women of Am., 1986. Mem. St. Louis Women's Commerce Assn., Internat. Assn. of Personnel Women, St. Louis Personnel Assn. (bd. dirs., project chairperson 1987-88), Human Resources Mgmt. Assn. of Greater St. Louis, Am. Inst. of Banking (bd. dirs., chairperson of benefit, compensation and selection coms., 1986-87), Am. Assn. Indsl. Mgmt. (chairperson banking benefit & compensation task force 1985-86), Mo. Women's Action Fund. Republican. Home: 798 W Oak Dr Saint Louis MO 63122 Office: 10765 Trenton Ave Saint Louis MO 63132

THOMPSON, PHEBE KIRSTEN, physician; b. Glace Bay, N.S., Can., Sept. 5, 1897; d. Peter and Catherine (McKeigan) Christianson; M.D., C.M. Dalhousie U., Halifax, N.S., 1923; m. Willard Owen Thompson, M.D., June 21, 1923 (dec. Mar. 1954); children—Willard Owen, Frederic, Nancy, Donald. Came to U.S., 1923, naturalized, 1937. Intern Children's Hosp., Halifax, N.S., 1922-23; asst. biochemistry, dept. applied physiology Harvard Sch. Pub. Health, 1924-26; asst. and research fellow in medicine, thyroid clinic, Mass. Gen. Hosp., Boston, 1926-29; asst. in metabolism dept. (endocrinology) Rush Med. Coll. of U. Chgo. and The Central Free Dispensary Chgo., 1930-46; assoc. with husband in practice medicine, Chgo., 1947-54; mng. editor Jour. Clin. Endocrinology and Metabolism, 1954-61, cons. editor, 1961-65; editor Jour. Am. Geriatrics Soc., 1954-82; cons. editor Endocrinology, 1961-65; free-lance editor and writer. Recipient Thewlis award Am. Geriatrics Soc., 1966; cert. of appreciation Am. Thyroid Assn., 1966. Fellow Am. Med. Writers' Assn. (adv. com. 1955-60, v.p. Chgo. 1962), Am. Geriatrics Soc., Gerontological Soc. Am.; mem. Endocrine Soc., AAAS, Am. Genetic Assn., Am. Pub. Health Assn., Ill. Pub. Health Assn., Ill. Acad. Scis., Art Inst. Chgo. (life), Chgo. Hist. Soc. (life). Clubs: Univ.; Harvard; Canadian (corr. sec. 1968-73; mem. bd. 1973-76). Address: care Nancy K Thompson 4319 N Dayton Chicago IL 60613

THOMPSON, RANDI EILEEN, public relations executive; b. Summit, N.J., June 25, 1952; d. Henry Gilbert and Betty Jane (Fritz) T.; m. Ronald W. Moreland, June 3, 1984; 1 child, LindseyAllison Thompson-Moreland; stepchildren: Michael C. Moreland, Susan J. Moreland. B.A. in Arts and Humanities, U. Md., 1973, M.A. in Communications, 1975. Radio intern Democratic Nat. Com., Washington, 1974; newsletter intern Marriott Corp., Washington, 1974; instr. interpersonal communication U. Md., College Park, 1974-75; assoc. Porter, Novelli & Assocs., Washington, 1975-78, sr. assoc., 1978-80, v.p., research dir., 1980-81, v.p., gen. mgr., Los Angeles, 1981-83, sr v.p., gen. mgr., 1983-86; exec. v.p., Western regional mgr. Porter Novelli, L.A., 1986-88, exec. v.p., corp. strategic planning and bus. devel., 1989—. Mem. Pub. Rels. Soc. Am., Am. Assn. Bus. Communicators, Am. Mktg. Assn., Am. Pub. Health Assn., L.A. Women. Democrat. Office: Porter Novelli 11755 Wilshire Blvd Los Angeles CA 90025

THOMPSON, ROLANDA G. (RO THOMPSON), art director, graphic artist, publications administrator; b. Henryetta, Okla., July 2, 1950; d. Rolland Glen and Jane Evelyn (McClendon) T. BFA, U. Tex., 1975; cert. in graphic arts, Tex. Edn. Agy. Owner, art dir. Ro Thompson Design & Illustration, Austin, 1968—; tech. dir. Paul Thorpe Women's Spa, Midland, Tex., 1970-71; asst. mgr. Johnson Tobacco Co., Austin, 1972; prodn. mgr., designer Craig & Co., Dallas, 1975-76; owner, chief exec. officer, cons. RGT Cons. Svcs., Austin, 1981—; mem. faculty Austin Community Coll., 1978-88, head dept. comml. art, 1981-88; dir. publs. State Property Tax Bd., Austin, 1989-90. Mem. coordinating bd. of post secondary graphic arts task force Tex. Edn. Agy., 1984-87; judge art competitions Austin Community Coll., 1976, VA, 1979, Austin C. of C., 1983; bd. dirs. Headliner's East Hist. 6th St. Grantee NEH, 1979-82, ACC, 1984, 85, 87, NEA, 1989. Mem. NAFE, Tex. Jr. Coll. Tchrs. Assn., Austin Graphic Art Soc. (charter; bd. dirs.), Austin Visual Arts Assn. (charter), Sierra Club, Zeta Tau Alpha. Home: 9001 Wagtail Dr Austin TX 78748

THOMPSON, SALLY, state official. Elected treas. of Kans., 1990. Democrat. Offices: Office of State Treasurer Landon State Office Bldg Topeka KS 66612*

THOMPSON, SHARON ANDREA, lawyer; b. New Bedford, Mass., May 31, 1948; d. Russell Edwin and Elma (Andreasen) T. BS, Mich. State U., 1970; JD, Antioch Sch. Law, 1976. Bar: N.C. 1976, U.S. Dist. Ct. (ea. and mid. dists.) N.C. 1976. Ptnr. Mailman & Thompson, Raleigh, N.C., 1976-79; prin. Thompson & McAllaster, P.A., Durham, N.C., 1979-89; ptnr. Thompson & Burgess, Durham, 1989—; adminstrv. hearing officer N.C. Dept. Human Resources, 1981-86. Mem. Durham Human Rels. Commn., 1979-82. Mem. N.C. Bar Assn., Durham County Bar Assn., N.C. Acad. Trial Lawyers, N.C. Assn. Women Attys. (bd. dirs. 1979-81, 83-85); elected to N.C. Ho. of Reps., 1987-89, re-elected, 1989-90. Home: 1809 Glendale Ave Durham NC 27701 Office: Thompson & Burgess PO Box 2164 Durham NC 27702

THOMPSON, STACY JO, food brokerage company executive; b. Mpls., Apr. 24, 1958; d. H.A. and Violet (Calhoun) T.; m. Clark David Champeau, Dec. 19, 1987. BA, Gustavus Adolphus Coll., 1980; MA in Psychology, Mankato (Minn.) State U., 1986. Behavioral analyst Christian Concern Inc., Mankato, 1977-79; regional sales mgr. No. Star Co., Mpls., 1979-83; nat. sales mgr. Med-Diet Labs., Mpls., 1982-84; indsl. sales mgr. Lampson and Tew Brokerage Co., Mpls., 1984-87; territorial sales mgr. Nabisco Brands, Mpls., 1987-88; dist. franchise mgr. parent corp. office Pepsi-Cola Bottling Co. div. Pepsico, Mpls., 1988-89; regional sales mgr. Redken Labs., Inc, Eden Prairie, Minn., 1989—; buying group mgr. The Pillsbury Co., Mpls., 1989-90; ind. contractor, cons. Sol-nuts Inc., St. Joseph, Wis., 1986—; cons. small cos. in food industry, 1986—; cons. small cos. in food industry, 1986—. Active Aid to Retarded Citizens. Mem. Nat. Assn. Female Execs., Am. Assn. Cereal Chemists, Indsl. Food Technologists, Minn. Indsl. Suppliers Assn. Republican. Lutheran. Home: 16320 Millford Dr Eden Prairie MN 55347

THOMPSON, SUSAN LYNNE, cosmetics executive; b. Flint, Mich., Apr. 30, 1950; d. John Seth and Doris Adelia (Almeling) T. BS in Edn., Cen. Mich. U., 1971; MFA, Eastern Mich. U., 1974; diploma in art, Universita Per Straneri, Perugia, Italy, 1972; postgrad., Princeton Theol. Sem., 1987-90. Art tchr. Lapeer (Mich.) Pub. Sch. System, 1974-75; beauty advisor Estée Lauder, Inc., Chgo., 1975-77; acct. coordinator Estée Lauder, Inc., Peoria, Ill., 1977-78; acct. exec. Estée Lauder, Inc., St. Louis, 1978-81; regional mktg. mgr. Estée Lauder, Inc., Oklahoma City, 1981-86; regional acct. mgr. Estée Lauder, Inc., St. Louis, 1986-87; instr. art therapy Oak Theraputic Sch., Chgo., 1975-76. Recipient 1st Place award Flint Inst. Art, 1972, 5th Place award Detroit Inst. Art, 1972; named one of Outstanding Young Women Am., 1983, one of 2000 Notable Am. Women, 1989. Republican. Presbyterian. Home: 300 Harrison St Apt 3 Charleston IL 61920

THOMPSON, TARA DENISE, illustrator, writer; b. Borger, Tex., June 7, 1962; d. Sammy Jo and Jeannean (Johansen) T. AA, Tex. State Tech. Inst., 1982. Art dir. Dalco Athletic Lettering, Garland, Tex., 1983-85; office mgr. Jean West Enterprises, Dallas, 1985-86; dept. adminstr. Dean Witter Reynolds, Inc., Dallas, 1986-87; info. specialist, pub. relations asst. Anderson Fischel Thompson Advt., Dallas, 1986-87, office mgr., 1987-89, traffic mgr., 1989-90; illustrator, writer Garland, Tex., 1990—. Mem. NAFE, Internat. Platform Assn. Office: 2618 Centennial Dr Garland TX 75042

THOMPSON, TINA DIANE, editor; b. L.A., Aug. 20, 1950; d. Gordon W. Thompson and F. Eileen (Knoles) Thompson-Baschky; m. Rainer Freytag, Aug. 17, 1985. BA in Journalism, Calif. State U., Long Beach, 1976. Editorial asst. Systems and Energy and Quest Mags. TRW, Redondo Beach, Calif., 1977-78; assoc. editor Systems and Energy Mag. TRW, Redondo Beach, 1978-81, assoc. editor Quest Mag., 1978-84, editor Editions, Tech. Briefs, 1983-84; promotional writer TRW Mktg. Communications, Redondo Beach, 1984-85; editor TRW Space Log, Redondo Beach, 1985—; v.p. pub. relations Sounds of Space Group, San Bernardino, Calif., 1985-88. Author: We've Proven It Can Fly, 1987; author, producer (records) Sounds of Saturn, 1982, Sounds of Space, 1985; contbr. articles to profl. jours. Recipient Pro award L.A. Publicity Club, 1981, Maggie award West Coast Mag. Pubs., Manhattan Beach, Calif., 1981. Mem. Internat. Assn. Bus. Communicators (Gold Quill award 1980, Helios award 1984), Aviation Space Writers Assn. (Co. Communications award 1979), Sigma Delta Chi. Office: TRW Space and Tech One Space Park Redondo Beach CA 90278

THOMPSON, TRACY KATHLEEN, public relations administrator; b. Charlotte, N.C., Mar. 9, 1961; d. Samuel Jackson and Alice Elizabeth (Joyner) T. AB in Polit. Sci., Davidson Coll., 1983; MS in Journalism, Boston U., 1989. Customer svc. rep. Graftech, Corp., Charlotte, 1983-84; asst. dir. communications and mktg. St. Andrew's Presbyn. Coll., Laurinburg, N.C., 1985-86; coord. printing and pub. info. Vance-Granville Community Coll., Henderson, N.C., 1986-89; coord. pub. info. N.C. Dept. Community Colls., Raleigh, 1989—. Mem. NAFE, N.C. Community Coll. Assn. for Mktg. and Pub. Rels., Women in Communications, Inc., N.C. Assn. of Govt. Info. Officers, Am. Assn. for Women in Community and Jr. Colls. Republican. Methodist. Office: NC Dept Community Colls 200 W Jones St Raleigh NC 27603

THOMPSON, VIRGINIA WILLIAMS, college vice-president; b. Moscow, Idaho, Oct. 26, 1938; d. James Kenneth and Marion (Edwards) Williams; m. David Jerome Thompson, Aug. 11, 1962; children: Keith David, Craig Marshall. BS, Baylor U., 1959; MS, U. Wis., 1961, PhD, 1963. Instr. in chemistry Coll. of Lake County, Grayslake, Ill., 1970-77, assoc. dean, 1977-88; v.p. instrn. Sauk Valley Community Coll., Dixon, Ill., 1988—. Mem. AAUW, Dixon C. of C. and Industry (bd. dirs. 1989—), Rotary Internat. Home: 826 Fair Way Libertyville IL 60048 Office: Sauk Valley Community Coll 173 Ill Rt 2 Dixon IL 61021

THOMPSON, VIVIAN OPAL, retired nurse; b. Lebanon, Va., Nov. 30, 1925; d. Luther Smith and Cora Belle (Baugh) Thompson. R.N., Knoxville (Tenn.) Gen. Hosp., 1947. Supr. obstetrical dept. Knoxville Gen. Hosp., 1947-48; gen. duty nurse Clinch Valley Clinic Hosp., Richlands, Va., 1948-52, supr., 1957-61, 68-88; ret., 1988; indsl. nurse Clinch Valley Clinic Hosp., Morocco, Va., Africa, 1952-56; charge nurse Bluefield Sanitarium, Morocco, W.Va., Africa, 1961-65, Rochingham Meml. Hosp., Harrisonburg, Va., Africa, 1965-68; part-time nurse, 1988—. Democrat. Presbyterian. Home: 205 Pennsylvania Ave Richlands VA 24641

THOMPSON, WYNELLE DOGGETT, chemistry educator; b. Birmingham, Ala., May 25, 1914; d. William Edward and Dollie Odessa (Ferguson) Doggett; m. Davis Hunt Thompson, Sept. 17, 1938; children: Carolyn Wynelle, Helen Hunt, Cynthia Carle, Davis Hunt, jr. BS summa cum laude, Birmingham Southern, 1934, MS, 1935; MS, U. Ala., 1956, PhD, 1960. From grad. lab. asst. to instr. chemistry Birmingham (Ala.) Southern Coll., 1934-36,39-44; tchr. Bd. Edn., Sheffield, Ala., 1936-37; jr. chemist Bur. Home Econs. USDA, Washington, 1937-38; instr. chemistry U. Ala. extension ctr., Birmingham, 1950-54; grad. asst. biochemistry U. Ala. Med. Coll., Birmingham, 1954-55; from asst. prof. chemistry to prof. emerita Birmingham (Ala.) Southern Coll., 1955-76; rsch. assoc. U. Ala. Dept. Biochemistry, Birmingham, 1965, 1968, 1969, Dept. Biophysics, 1976-78; adj. prof. chemistry New Coll. Tuscaloosa, Ala., 1980—. Contbr. articles to profl. jours. Bd. dirs. Cahaba Coun. Girl Scouts U.S. (vol. chmn. troop orgn., camping.). Recipient grants NSF, Appleton, Wis., Emory U. Atlanta. Fellow Am. Inst. Chemists; mem. AAUW (bd. dirs., treas.), Am. Chem. Soc. (sec. 1942-44, 1972-73, chmn. elect 1966-67, chmn. 1967-68), Ala. Acad. Sci. (chmn. chem. edn. sect. 1960-62), Soc. Sigma Xi (sec. 1970-72), Theta Chi Delta, Delta Phi Alpha, Theta Sigma Lambda, Kappa Delta Epsilon, Delta Kappa Gamma. Republican. Methodist. Home: 917 Valley Rd Pl Birmingham AL 35208-1020

THOMPSON, YVONNE ELIZABETH, business executive; b. Charleston, S.C., Jan. 10, 1948; d. Lurie Darwin and Constance (Morrison) Thompson. B.A. in Polit. Sci., Fisk U., 1969; M.B.A., U. Calif.-Berkeley, 1975. Gen. mgr. Ventures Mgmt. Co., San Francisco, 1974-75; pres. The Venture Group, Inc., San Francisco, 1975-80; pres. Puget Sound Pet Supply Co., Oakland, Calif., 1976-80; v.p. Fulcrum Venture Capital Co., Washington, 1980-81; v.p. mktg. Gen. R.R. Equipment & Services, Inc., East St. Louis, Ill., 1981—; participant Career Pathfinders, St. Louis pub. schs. 1986—. Mem. Gov.'s Club, Springfield, Ill., 1984—; bd. dirs. Arthritis Found., St. Louis, 1985—; mem. adv. council U.S. SBA, 1979-80; vice chmn. Minority and Female Bus. Enterprise Council, Chgo., 1984-86; mem. small bus. com. Minority Bus. Brain Trust, Ho. of Reps., Washington, 1979—. Mem. Nat. Assn. Female Execs., Profl. Women in Constrn., NAACP, Alpha Kappa Alpha. Club: Citizens for Thompson. Avocations: art collecting; travel; skiing; tennis. Home: 4501 Lindell Blvd Saint Louis MO 63108 Office: Gen RR Equipment & Services Inc PO Box 159 East Saint Louis IL 62202

THOMSEN, MARCIA ROZEN, marketing executive; b. St. Louis, Sept. 23, 1958; d. Saul and Ruth (Burstein) Rozen; m. Timothy Lars Thomsen, Sept. 23, 1984; 1 child, David Rozen Thomsen. B in Journalism, U. Mo., 1980. Media planner, buyer Leo Burnett Co., Chgo., 1980-82, asst. acct. exec., 1982-83; acct. exec. D'Arcy Masius, Benton & Bowles, St. Louis, 1983-85, acct. supr., 1985-86, v.p., 1986-89; dir. mktg. Pizza Hut, Inc. div. Pepsi Co., St. Louis, 1989—; chmn. com. DMB&B Account Mgmt., St. Louis, 1988—. Mem. Chgo. Advt. Club. Office: Pizza Hut of St Louis 760 Rue St Francois Florissant MO 63031

THOMSEN, MICHELLE FLUCKEY, physicist; b. Burlington, Colo., June 25, 1950; d. James Orville and Annette E. (LeVert) Fluckey; m. Robert John Thomsen, Aug. 18, 1973; children: Davis Robert, Kristine Marie. BA, Colo. Coll., 1971; postgrad., U. Minn., 1971-72; MS, U. Iowa, 1974, PhD, 1977. Rsch. investigator U. Iowa, Iowa City, 1977-78, asst. rsch. scientist, 1978-79, assoc. rsch. scientist, 1979-80; vis. scientist Max Planck Inst. for Aeronomy, Lindau, Fed. Republic of Germany, 1980-81; staff mem. Los Alamos (N.Mex.) Nat. Lab., 1981—; geosci., space sci., and astrophysics adv. group Los Alamos Nat. Lab., 1986-88, lab fellow screening com., 1989; mgmt. ops. working group NASA, 1989—. Editor: Geophysical Research Letters, 1989—; contbr. articles to profl. jours. Bd. dirs. Little Forest Playsch., Los Alamos, 1988-89; treas. Self Help, Inc., Los Alamos, 1987-89; program chmn. Barranca Mesa Elem. Sch. PTO, Los Alamos, 1988—; adult leader Girl Scouts Am., Los Alamos, 1989—. Recipient Editor's Citation for Excellence in Referencing Journal of Geophysical Research, 1983, Disting. Alumni award U. Iowa, 1985. Mem. Am. Geophys. Union. Office: Los Alamos Nat Lab MS D438 Los Alamos NM 87545

THOMSON, BARBARA JEANNE, purchasing executive; b. Cardiff, Calif., Feb. 10, 1929; d. Zack Rowden and Zula Mae (Tuckness) Taylor; m. Robert Allyn San Clemente, Feb. 8, 1946 (div. Aug. 1954); children—Robert Allyn Jr., Frances Irene, Michael George; m. Seeth Lyle Thomson, Aug. 7, 1954; 1 child, David Seeth. Grad. high sch., Encinitas, Calif. Various positions Gen. Dynamics Convair, San Diego, 1957-73; purchasing agt. Systems, Sci. & Software, San Diego, 1973-78; sr. buyer Gen. Dynamics Electronics, San Diego, 1978-80; sr. buyer LSI Products div. TRW, San Diego, 1980-84, purchasing mgr., 1984—. Named Employee of Yr., Gen. Dynamics Electronics, San Diego, 1978. Mem. Ry. Hist. Soc. (sec. San Diego 1957-60), Pacific Beach Model R.R. Club (sec. 1955-65), Nat. Assn. Female Execs., Nat. Mgmt. Assn., San Diego Hospice Assn. Democrat. Avocations: model railroading; photography; baseball; football. Home: 3204 McGraw St San Diego CA 92117 Office: TRW LSI Products Div 4243 Campus Point Ct San Diego CA 92121

THOMSON, GRACE MARIE, nurse, minister; b. Pecos, Tex., Mar. 30, 1932; d. William McKinley and Elzora (Wilson) Olliff; m. Radford Chaplin, Nov. 3, 1952; children: Deborah C., William Earnest. Assoc. Applied Sci., Odessa Coll., 1965; extension student U. Pa. Sch. Nursing, U. Calif., Irvine, Golden West Coll. RN, Calif., Okla., Ariz., Md., Tex. Dir. nursing Grays Nursing Home, Odessa, Tex., 1965; supr. nursing Med. Hill, Oakland, Calif.; charge nurse pediatrics Med. Ctr., Odessa; dir. nursing Elmwood Extended Care, Berkeley, Calif.; surg. nurse Childrens Hosp., Berkeley; med-surg. charge nurse Merritt Hosp., Oakland, Calif.; adminstr. Grace and Assocs.; advocate for emotionally abused children; active Watchtower and Bible Tract Soc.; evangelist for Jehovah's Witnesses, 1954—.

THOMSON, KATHLEEN RUTH, librarian; b. St. Joseph, Mo., Jan. 23, 1934; d. Oscar S. and Ruth W. (Lodholz) Meyer; m. James L. Thomson, Aug. 30, 1955; children: William, Robert, Ruth Ellen, David, Steven. BA, Park Coll., Parkville, Mo., 1955; MS, U. Ill., 1978. Libr. asst. Carnegie-Stout Pub. Libr., Dubuque, Iowa, 1955-56, 57-58; tchr. Thurston (Nebr.) High Sch., 1956-57; dir. Kinder Kare Day Care Ctr., Montevideo, Minn., 1969-70; libr. asst. Dawson (Minn.) Pub. Libr., 1974-75; tchr., dir. Little Dragons Nursery Sch., Madison, Minn., 1975-76; libr. tech. asst. Dept.

Natural Resources State of Ill., Springfield, 1978-79; coord. youth svcs. Manitowoc (Wis.) Pub. Libr., 1979-86; mgr. children's svcs. Kenosha (Wis.) Pub. Libr., 1986, mgr. west br. and bookmobile, 1986—. Mem. AAUW (pres. Manitowoc/Two Rivers chpt. 1984-86), Am. Libr. Assn., Wis. Libr. Assn. (chmn. sect. children's and young adult svcs.), Wis. Alliance for Arts Edn., Racine-Kenosha Reading Coun., Tri-County Liars, Elaborators, and Storytellers. Presbyterian. Office: West Br Libr 2419 63d St Kenosha WI 53140

THOMSON, MABEL AMELIA, retired elementary educator; b. Lancaster, Minn., Oct. 28, 1910; d. Ernest R. and Sophie Olinda (Rotert) Poore; m. Robert John Thomson, June 20, 1936; children: James Robert, William John. BS, U. Ill., 1933; MEd, Steven F. Austin Coll., Nacogdoches, Tex., 1959. Tchr. La Harpe (Ill.) Sch. Dist., 1930, Scotland (Ill.) Sch. Dist., 1934, Washburn (Ill.) Sch. Dist., 1935-36, Tyler (Tex.) Ind. Sch. Dist., 1959-76; ret., 1976; substitute tchr. Tyler (Tex.) Ind. Sch. Dist., 1976-86. Past pres. Woman's Soc. Christian Svc. of local Meth. Ch. Mem. AAUW (pres. Tyler chpt. 1947-48), Am. Childhood Edn. (pres. 1960-61), Alpha Delta Kappa (charter Tyler br.), Phi Mu (life). Republican. Methodist.

THOMSON, MARGARET FAITH, nurse; b. Williams, S.C., Dec. 25, 1941; d. Rex Nolan and Margaret (Fitzgerald) Coulter; m. Thomas Michael Thomson, Nov. 23, 1963 (div. July 1986); children: Thomas Michael Jr., Margaret Elizabeth. AA, Prince Georges Community Coll., Largo, Md., 1974. RN, Md.; lic. broker, Tex.; cert. residential specialist, Tex. Clin. nurse to head nurse Nutri System, Dayton, Ohio, 1977-79; saleswoman, broker, office mgr. Halmark Bradfield Real Estate, San Antonio, 1982-86; renal transplant nurse Med. U. S.C., Charleston, 1987-88, staff and charge dialysis nurse, 1988; radiology nurse St. Luke Luth. Hosp., San Antonio, 1989—. Mem. San Antonio Bd. Realtors. Roman Catholic. Home: 4411 Gardendale 7C San Antonio TX 78240 Office: Med U SC Hosp 171 Ashley Ave Charleston SC 29400

THOMSON, MARY OTTEN, marketing professional, director; b. Crawford, Tex., Sept. 7, 1940; d. Julio and Maria (Acosta) Quiroz; 1 child, Dawn Rochelle. BA, U. Mary Hardin-Baylor, 1963; postgrad., Govenors State U., 1987—. Tchr. Dist. 218 Blue Island, Ill., 1963-67, Dist 111 Kankakee, Ill., 1967-84; cons., assoc. BFD Assocs., Kankakee, Ill., 1984; counselor, tchr. Kankakee Community Coll., 1984—; mktg. dir., retirement couselor Riverside Med. Ctr., Kankakee, 1989—. Named: Toastmaster of The Year, Key City Toastmasters, Kankakee, Ill., 1986. Mem. Kankakee C. of C., Working Women's Council, Women in Bus. Seminar Comm., Ambassador Club. Republican. Methodist. Office: Westwood Oaks Info Ctr 1905 W Court St Kankakee IL 60901

THOMSON, SUSAN MARIE, business owner, director, counselor, therapist; b. Tucson, Dec. 10, 1951; d. Quentin Robert and Nihla (Hanks) T.; m. Darryl Jude Tschirn. BA, U. Ariz., 1973, MED, 1976; MA, Tulane U., 1983, PhD, 1985. Lic. counselor, La. Tchr. psychology Pima Coll., 1976; tchr. Tanque Verde Elem. Sch., Tucson, 1974-76, Parkland Jr. Coll., Champaign, Ill., 1976-78; therapist Thompson Med. Clinic, New Orleans, 1979-86; pres., owner Dr. Susan M. Thomson's Clinic, New Orleans, 1986—. Mem. Am. Psychol. Assn. Republican. Home: 5 Miller Ln Metairie LA 70006 Office: 4420 Conlin St #205 Metairie LA 70002

THOMSON, THYRA GODFREY, former state official; b. Florence, Colo., July 30, 1916; d. John and Rosalie (Altman) Godfrey; m. Keith Thomson, Aug. 6, 1939 (dec. Dec. 1960); children—William John, Bruce Godfrey, Keith Coffey. B.A. cum laude, U. Wyo., 1939. With dept. agronomy and agrl. econs. U. Wyo., 1938-39; writer weekly column Watching Washington pub. in 14 papers, Wyo., 1955-60; planning chmn. Nat. Fedn. Republican Women, Washington, 1961; sec. state Wyo. Cheyenne, 1962-86; mem. Marshall Scholarships Com. for Pacific region, 1964-68; del. 72d Wilton Park Conf., Eng., 1965; mem. youth commn. UNESCO, 1970-71, Allied Health Professions Council HEW, 1971-72; del. U.S.-Republic of China Trade Conf., Taipei, Taiwan, 1983; mem. lt. gov.'s trade and fact-finding mission to Saudi Arabia, Jordan, and Egypt, 1985. Bd. dirs. Buffalo Bill Mus., Cody, Wyo., 1987—; adv. bd. Coll. Arts & Scis., U. Wyo., 1989. Recipient Disting. Alumni award U. Wyo., 1969, Disting. U. Wyo. Arts and Scis. Alumna award, 1987; named Internat. Woman of Distinction, Alpha Delta Kappa; recipient citation Omicron Delta Epsilon, 1965, citation Beta Gamma Sigma, 1968, citation Delta Kappa Gamma, 1973, citation Wyo. Commn. Women, 1986. Mem. N.Am. Securities Adminstrs. (pres. 1973-74), Nat. Assn. Secs. of State, Council State Govts. (chmn. natural resources com. Western states 1966-68), Nat. Conf. Lt. Govs. (exec. com. 1976-79). Home: 3102 Sunrise Rd Cheyenne WY 82001

THOMSON, VIRGINIA WINBOURN, history educator, author; b. Oakland, Calif., Aug. 6, 1930; d. Harry Linn and Jennie Cook (Vineyard) T. A.A., San Mateo Coll., 1949; B.A., San Jose State Coll., 1951; M.A., U. Calif.-Berkeley, 1952. Cert. secondary tchr., Calif. Social sci. tchr. Capuchino High Sch., San Bruno, Calif., 1952-54, Watsonville High Sch., Calif., 1954-87; saleswoman and storyteller Home Interiors, San Mateo, 1963-64. Author: The Lion Desk, 1965; Short Talks Around The Lord's Table, 1985; numerous poems published in anthologies, 1988. Recipient Silver Pitcher award Home Interiors, 1964; poem selected as Editor's Choice The Nat. Library Poetry, 1988. Mem. Nat. Geog. Soc. (life), AAUW (life), Calif. Alumni Assn. (life), Phi Alpha Theta. Republican.

THONG-HORTON, JULIETTA KHANTEYA, systems documentation administrator; b. Battambang, Cambodia, Jan. 9, 1960; came to U.S., 1981, naturalized, 1986; d. Henry Sareth and Sarom (Som) Thong; m. Thomas Edward Horton, Dec. 1-3, 1988. AA, Long Beach City Coll., 1984; BS, Calif. State U., Long Beach, 1986. Cert. nurse's aide; office tech. cert. Vol. translator Swiss Caritas, Khao-I-Dang, Thailand, 1979, World Relief Corp., Philippines, 1980; nurse's aide Empress Convalescent Ctr., Long Beach, 1981-82; tchr.'s asst. Long Beach Unified Sch. Dist., 1982-84; asst. coach Transwestern Inst., Long Beach, 1984-86; adminstrv. intern Port of Long Beach, 1986-87; in systems documentation Met. Stevedore Co., Wilmington, Calif., 1987—. Author health booklet for refugees in Philippines camp, 1980. Mem. Long Beach Port Ambs.; pres. Cambodian Student Soc. of Calif. State U., Long Beach, 1984-85. Named Miss Port Princess of Port of Long Beach, Port Ambs., 1989-90. Mem. Nat. Assn. for Female Execs., Long Beach Area C. of C., Internat. Bus. ASsn. Home: 462 E 61st St Long Beach CA 90805

THOR, LINDA M., college president; b. Los Angeles, Feb. 21, 1950; d. Karl Gustav and Mildred Dorrine (Hofius) T.; m. Robert Paul Huntsinger, Nov. 22, 1974; children: Erik, Marie. BA, Pepperdine U., 1971, EdD, 1986; MPA, Calif. State U., Los Angeles, 1980. Dir. pub. info. Pepperdine U., Los Angeles, 1971-73; pub. info. officer Los Angeles Community Coll. Dist., 1974-75, dir. communications, 1975-81, dir. edn. services, 1981-82, dir. high tech., 1982-83, sr. dir. occupational and tech. edn., 1983-86; pres. West Los Angeles Coll., Culver City, Calif., 1986—; bd. dirs. Calif. Industry Edn. Council, West Los Angeles Coll. Found., Tech. Exchange Ctr. Editor: Curriculum Design and Development for Effective Learning, 1973; author: (with others) Effective Media Relations, 1982, Performance Contracting, 1987. Bd. trustees Woodbury U.; bd. dirs. United Way Western Region, Culver-Palms YMCA, Calif. Assn. Community Colls., Commn. on Pub. Rels. Tri-Valley Alliance Higher Edn. Recipient Delores award Pepperdine U., 1986, Alumni Medal of Honor, 1987, Outstanding Achievement award Women's Bus. Network, 1989; named Woman of the Yr., Culver City Bus. and Profl. Women, 1988. Mem. Calif. Community Colls. Chief Exec. Officers. Lodge: Optimists. Office: West Los Angeles Coll 4800 Freshman Dr Culver City CA 90230

THORLAKSON, ROSEMARY AHEARN, nursing administrator; b. Columbus, Ohio, July 12, 1947; d. Joseph Edmond and Elizabeth Sabrina (Morse) Ahearn; children: AmySue, Stephen. AAS in Nursing, Gemanna Community Coll., Locust Grove, Va., 1975; BS in Nursing, U. Va., 1977, MEd. RN; cert. critical care nurse, emergency care nurse, trauma nurse instr., others. Critical care contract nurse various states; supr. emergency svcs. Minidoka Meml. Hosp., Rupert, Idaho. Contbr. articles to profl. jours. Community educator in CPR and First Aid. Mem. Am. Nurses Assn., Emergency Nurses Assn., Am. Assn. Critical Care Nurses, Nat. Assn. Search and Rescue, Nat. Assn. Underwater Rescue and Recovery. Democrat. Roman Catholic. Office: 1224 8th St Rupert ID 83350

THORN, SUSAN HOWE, interior designer; b. Washington, Apr. 22, 1941; d. James Bennett Cowdin and Lois (Fiesinger) Howe; BA cum laude, Syracuse U., 1962; postgrad. N.Y. Sch. Interior Design, 1965, lighting design Parsons Sch. Design, 1975-77; m. William D. Thorn, June 22, 1963; children—Melissa Ann, William David. Owner, designer Susan Thorn Interiors, Inc., Cross River, N.Y., 1965—; designer total bldg. Cooper Labs, Bedford Hills, N.Y., 1973, total redesign Nycrest Corp., Cold Spring, N.Y., 1973-75, showrooms, model rooms stylist and coordinator France Voiles Co. Inc., N.Y.C., 1976, total design new corp. hdqrs. in Gen. Dynamics Bldg. (with Marjorie Borradaile Helsel), Robert E. Eastman Co., N.Y.C., 1967, Cummin & Friedland Capital Corp., 1982; designer offices, stores, employee areas comml., public, residential clients, including Waccabuc (N.Y.) Country Club, 1969, S. Salem (N.Y.) Library; instr. adult edn. dept. John Jay High Sch., Jr. League No. Westchester, Caramoor Mus.; speaker civic orgns. Mem. Am. Soc. Interior Designers (profl.), Internat. Assn. Lighting Designers (asso.). Episcopalian. Club: Waccabuc Country; Decorators (bd. dirs. N.Y.C. chpt.). Home: Rte 121 Cross River NY 10518

THORNBER, JUDY PAULENE, real estate developer, consultant, lawyer; b. Chgo., May 26, 1941; d. Paul and Irene (Swanson) Davis. BA, U. Chgo., 1963, MBA, 1969; JD, Harvard U., 1966. Bar: Ill. 1967. Vice pres. Rubloff Devel. Corp., Chgo., 1970-72; sr. v.p. Am. Invesco, Chgo., 1975-76; pres. Thorndev Corp., Chgo., 1978—; v.p. Fogelson Properties, Chgo., 1989—; adminstrv. v.p. Cen. Sta. Devel. Corp., Chgo., 1990—. Mem. Com. of 200, Chgo. Mem. Nat. Assn. Homebuilders, Chgo. Bar Assn., Chgo. Real Estate Bd., Chgo. Fin. Exchange (bd. dirs. 1984). Office: Thorndev Corp 7105 Higgins Rd Chicago IL 60656

THORNBERRY, SUSAN L., artist, educator; b. Long Beach, Calif., Aug. 7, 1944; d. Charles Gallemore Thornberry and Virginia (Irving) Beeks; ; children: Kathryn Ann, August Ann Mitchell. BFA in Painting, Calif. Coll. Arts, Oakland, 1977; MA in Art Edn., Ariz. State U., 1988; cert., Western Arts Mgmt. Inst., 1988; postgrad., Phoenix Coll., 1990, Glendale Community Coll., 1990. Part-time instr. art Phoenix Art Mus., 1984-85, Phoenix Coll., 1988, Glendale (Ariz.) Community Coll., 1989—; chmn. exhibition Women in Design, Phoenix, 1987-88. Exhibitions include Harry Wood Gallery, Ariz. State U., Shemer Art Ctr. and Mus., Phoenix, Tubac (Ariz.) Ctr. for the Arts, Renoir Art Gallery, Western Fedn. of Watercolor Socs., San Antonio, U. Ariz., 1st Interstate Bank, Phoenix, Prescott Fine Arts Gallery, Yavapai Coll. Art Gallery, Meml. Union Gallery, Mathes Cultural Ctr., Escondido, Calif., West First St. Restaurant and Gallery, Humana Hosp. Artists Program, Miracle Mile Deli, Phoenix Little Theatre, 1987-89, Don Ruffin Meml. Art Exhbn., Paradise Valley Community Coll., 1989, Western Fedn. Watercolor Socs., Tex. Tech. U. Mus., Ariz. State U. Hayden Libr., Women Image Now Exhbn., Glendale Community Coll. Gallery coord. Phoenix Little Theatre, 1987—; mem. Phoenix Art Mus/Contemporary Forum, Phoenix Artist's Coalition, Arizonans for Cultural Devel., Mars Artspace, Nat. Mus. for Women, Scottsdale Cultural Coun. Mem. AAUW, Ariz. Watercolor Assn. (Coatamundi award 1987), Women's Caucus for Art (v.p. 1986), Nat. Watercolor Soc., Nat. Art Edn. Assn., Nat. League of Am. Pen Women (rec. sec. Phoenix br. 1990—), Women in Design (sesec. 1988), Soc. of Layerists in Multi Media (assoc.), Women Image Now (Ariz. State U. chpt.). Democrat. Episcopalian.

THORNER, PRUDENCE MARIA, hospital administrator; b. Lancashire, Eng., July 4, 1944; Came to U.S., 1977; d. Bernard and Lily Ross; m. Michael Oliver Thorner; Jan. 14, 1945; children: Benjamin, Anna. Assoc., London U. Coll. Estate Mgmt., 1967; MA, U. Va., 1981. Chartered surveyor Allsop & Co., London, 1962-65, Knight Frank & Rutley, London, 1965-70, Britton Poole & Burns, London, 1974-77; mgmt. engr. U. Va. Hosp., Charlottesville, 1981-85, dir., hosp. supply, 1985--; asst. dir. gen. services div. U. Va. Hosp., 1988--; mem. adv. bd. Thomas Jefferson Adult Day Care Ctr., Charlottesville, 1987--; chair, task force on status of women U. Va., Charlottesville, 1986-88. Author: (Book) Simplicity of Breastfeeding, 1973. Recipient Woman of Achievement award, U. Va., 1988. Office: U Va Hosp Hosp Box 413 Charlottesville VA 22908

THORNHILL, LOIS, photographer; b. Boston, Apr. 7, 1945; d. Fred S. and Mary (Evans) T.; B.A., Middlebury Coll., 1966; postgrad. U. St. Thomas, Houston, 1967-69; M.A., N.Y. U., 1971; cert. in graphic design U. Calif.-Santa Cruz, 1983; m. Edward J. McCluskey, Feb. 14, 1981. Research technician dept. virology Baylor Sch. Medicine, Houston, 1966-68; with Kelly Girls, Palo Alto, 1971-72; slide curator dept. art Stanford (Calif.) U., 1972-80; founder, pres. Stanford Design Assocs., Palo Alto, 1981—; cons. copy and museum photography; designer, producer custom lecture slides. Mem. Smithsonian Assos., Coll. Art Assn. Am. Home: 895 Northampton Dr Palo Alto CA 94303 Office: PO Box 60451 Palo Alto CA 94306

THORNLOW, CAROLYN, law firm administrator, consultant; b. Kew Gardens, N.Y., May 25, 1954. B.B.A. magna cum laude, Bernard M. Baruch Coll., 1982. Gen. mgr. Richard A. Ramm Assocs., Levittown, N.Y., 1972-78; adminstr. Tunstead Schechter & Torre, N.Y.C., 1978-82, Cowan Liebowitz & Latman, P.C., N.Y.C., 1982-84, Rosenberg & Estis, P.C., N.Y.C., 1984-85; controller Finkelstein, Borah, Schwartz, Altschuler & Goldstein, P.C., N.Y.C., 1986—; pres. Concinnity Services, Hastings, N.Y., 1984—; instr. introduction to law office mgmt. seminars Assn. Legal Adminstrs., N.Y.C., 1984. Contbr. numerous articles to profl. jours. Mem. N.Y. Assn. Legal Adminstrs. (v.p. 1982-83), Internat. Assn. Legal Adminstrs. (asst. regional v.p. 1983-84, regional v.p. 1984-85), Adminstrv. Mgmt. Soc. (cert.), ABA, Mensa, Beta Gamma Sigma, Sigma Iota Epsilon.

THORNTON, ANN MURPHY, retired military officer; b. Fargo, N.D., Sept. 8, 1920; d. Matthew William and Ethel Geneva (Brink) Murphy; m. William Aloysius Curtin Jr., Nov. 20, 1948 (div. Apr. 1958); m. Clarke Wayne Thornton Jr., Aug. 21, 1961 (dec.). BS, N.D. State U., 1942. Reporter Fargo Forum, 1942-43; commd. 2d lt. U.S. Army, 1944, advanced through grades to maj., 1959; served as feature writer pub. rels. office 9th Svc. Command, Ft. Douglas, Utah; conf. officer, officer in charge overseas conf. rm. Office of Chief of Staff, U.S. Army, The Pentagon, 1944-49; asst. advt. dir. Army Navy Air Force Jour. U.S. Army, Washington, 1949-50, 56-57; liaison officer to Def. Dep., pictorial officer Office of Chief of Staff, U.S. Army, The Pentagon; security, shift officer, pub. info. officer, USAREUR, Frankfurt, Paris, Fed. Republic Germany; exec. officer, officer tng. co. 1st WAC Tng. Ctr., Ft. Mclellan, Ala., 1950-56; asst. sec. XIIth Conf. Mil. Advisors to SEATO, Washington (D.C.); asst. exec. officer, officer in charge women's recruiting Hdqrs. 6th U.S. Army, Presidio San Francisco, 1957-61; ret. U.S. Army, 1961. Wife of USIA officer, Pretoria, Capetown, Republic of South Africa, 1961-66; bd. dirs. Mil. Retiree's Benefit Found. Mem. Res. Officers Assn. U.S., Ret. Officers Assn. Episcopalian. Home: 32 15th Ave San Francisco CA 94118

THORNTON, ELIZABETH DEE KAPLAN, chemistry educator; b. Bklyn., June 4, 1940; d. Leo and Eva (Sable) Kaplan; m. Edward R. Thornton. AB, Mount Holyoke Coll., 1961; PhD, U. Pa., 1966. Post doctoral fellow Swiss Fed. Inst. Tech., Zurich, Switzerland, 1966-68, U. Pa., Phila., 1968; asst. prof. chemistry Widener Coll., Chester, Pa., 1968-75; assoc. prof. chemistry Widener U., Chester, 1975—; curriculum coordinator of sci. Widener Coll., Chester, 1987—. Co-author: Book Chpt. entitled Isotope Effects in Chemical Reactions, 1971, Transition States of Biochemical Processes, 1978. Mem. ACLU, Sierra Club, Environ. Defense Fund., NOW, Action on Smoking and Health. Recipient NSF Instructional Sci. Equipment Program Grant, 1970. Mem. Am. Chem. Soc., AAAS, AAUW, Am. Assn. Univ. Professors, Sigma Xi. Home: 7 Swarthmore Pl Swarthmore PA 19081 Office: Widener Univ Kirkbride Hall Chester PA 19013

THORNTON, ELIZABETH SHARON ECKART, librarian, library director; b. Southington, Conn., Mar. 30, 1960; d. Frederick and Jean Virginia (Bailey) Eckart; m. Michael Craig Thornton, Oct. 15, 1983. BS, Central Conn. State U., 1982; MLS, So. Conn. State U., 1985. Reference librarian Southington Pub. Library, 1977-83; legis. fellow Legis. Rsch. Library, Hartford, Conn., 1984-85; librarian Conn. Conf. United Ch. of Christ, Hartford, 1985-88; reference librarian Hartford Grad. Ctr., 1985-86; dir. Bentley Meml. Library, Bolton, Conn., 1988—; librarian, workshop leader Conn. Conf. United Ch. of Christ, Hartord, 1987. Mem. ALA, New Eng. Library Assn., Conn. Library Assn., Zeta Delta Epsilon. Home: 17 Hickory Dr Hebron CT 06248 Office: Bentley Meml Library 206 Bolton Ctr Rd Bolton CT 06043

THORNTON, KATHRYN C., physicist, astronaut; b. Montgomery, Ala., Aug. 17, 1952; d. William C. and Elsie Cordell; m. Stephen T. Thornton; children: Carol Elizabeth, Laura Lee; stepchildren: Kenneth, Michael. BS in Physics, Auburn U., 1974; MS in Physics, U. Va., 1977, PhD, 1979. NATO postdoctoral fellow Max Planck Inst. Nuclear Physics, Heidelberg, Fed. Republic Germany, 1979-80; physicist U.S. Army Fgn. Sci. & Tech. Ctr., Charlottesville, Va., 1980-84; with NASA, 1984—; astronaut Lyndon B. Johnson Space Ctr. NASA, Houston, 1985—, mission specialist Space Shuttle Discovery flight STS-33, 1989. Mem. AAAS, Am. Phys. Soc., Sigma Xi, Phi Kappa Phi. Address: NASA Johnson Space Ctr Astronaut Office Houston TX 77058*

THORNTON, KATHY ELIZABETH, secondary educator; b. Decatur, Ill., Jan. 14, 1955; d. Woodrow William and Mary Elizabeth (Hughes) T. AB in Latin Edn., U. Ill., 1977; MS in Guidance, Ea. Ill. U., 1981. Latin tchr. Highland (Ill.) High Sch., 1977-78, MacArthur High Sch., Decatur, Ill., 1979-87; counselor Brush Coll./Baum Sch., Decatur, 1988; Latin tchr. McArthur High Sch., Decatur, 1988-89; counselor Brush Coll. Sch., Decatur, 1988-89, Eisenhower High Sch., Decatur, 1989—; Latin tchr. MacArthur High Sch., Decatur, 1989—. Steering com. Hands Across Am., 1986; events chairperson Decatur Celebration, 1986—; supporter and com. mem. Nat. Tax Limitation Com., 1989—. Mem. AAUW (program v.p. Decatur br. 1989—, pub. policy chair 1986—), NEA, Classical League, Ill. Classical Conf., Ill. Edn. Assn. Republican.

THORNTON, LINDA WIERMAN, research institute executive; b. Charleston, S.C., Oct. 16, 1942; d. Robert Wendell and Frances (Bass) Wierman; m. Alan Farrar Thornton, Dec. 7, 1968 (div. May 1982); children: Robert Bass, Andrew Farrar. BA, U. Kans., 1966. Economist Midwest Rsch. Inst., Kansas City, Mo., 1964-69; sr. economist, cons. Hare & Hare, Inc., others, Kansas City, 1969-76; dir. rsch. and mgmt. svcs. dept. Midwest Rsch. Inst., Kansas City, 1976—. Contbr. articles to profl. jours. Mem. Nat. Assn. Bus. Econs., Kans. City Assn. Bus. Economists, Mo. Valley Econ. Assn., Am. Econ. Devel. Coun. Office: 425 Volher Blvd Kansas City MO 64110

THORNTON, MARY JANICE, artist; b. Andalusia, Ala.; m. Harry Thornton. Student, Judson Coll., Marion, Ala., Fla. State U., Met. Art Sch., N.Y.C., Arthur Schwieder Sch. Art, N.Y.C. mem. Pensacola (Fla.) Mus. Art, Met. Mus. Art, N.Y.C., Modern Mus. Art, N.Y.C. Exhibited in over 50 one-woman shows, Paris, Mexico City; represented in permanent collections at Sears Roebuck, Pensacola Mus. Art, Anderson House, Washington, Mus. Norte Americana y Mexico City, Mus. Fine Arts, Montgomery, Ala., Zarzuela Palace, Madrid, Spain, Tefair Mus., Savannah, Ga., Bernheim Gallery, Palette Bleu, Paris, various prvt. collections; commd. muralist Anderson House, Washington, Soc. of Cin.; developer Striatism, 1960s, 1970s. Life patron Internat. Biograph. Inst., Cambridge, Eng.. Recipient Soc. Cin. award, citation USN, award Mus. of Arts, Pansacola; named Woman of Yr., 1990. Mem. Pastel Soc. N. Fla. (hon.). Home and Studio: PO Box 30032 Pensacola FL 32503

THORPE, BETSY TUCKER, contracting company official; b. South Hill, Va., Jan. 14, 1956; d. Grattan Howard Jr. Tucker and Phyllis Freese (Draper) Haislip; m. Brady Bennett, Feb. 8, 1975 (div. Oct. 1980); 1 child, Jaime Elizabeth; m. Burton Walter Thorpe, Jr., Jan. 25, 1986; 1 child, Brittney Leigh. BTech., U. North Fla., 1982. Cert. gen. contractor, Fla.; lic. real estate agt., Fla. Project engr. Blosam Contractors, Inc., St. Petersburg, Fla., 1982-84, Condel Constrn. Co., Jacksonville, Fla., 1984-85; asst. project mgr. McDevitt & Street Co., Jacksonville, 1985-86; owner, mgr. Tucker-Thorpe Gen. Contractors, Jacksonville, 1984-88; qualifying agt. Dynamic Land Devel., Inc., Jacksonville, 1987—. N.E. Fla. Home Builders Assn. scholar, 1982. Republican. Episcopalian. Office: Dynamic Land Devel Inc 10520 Atlantic Blvd Jacksonville FL 32225

THORPE, MARTHA CAMPBELL, retired nuclear magnetic resonance spectroscopist; b. Tullahoma, Tenn., Apr. 28, 1922; d. Donald B. Campbell and Martha Blanche (Bingham) Dupont; m. Frederick Edward Thorpe, June 19, 1943; children: Susan Thorpe Dean, Florence Thorpe Eddins. BA in Chemistry, Vanderbilt U., 1944; MA in Math., Samford U., 1968. Chemist E.I. duPont, Old Hickory, Tenn., 1944-45; spectroscopist So. Rsch. Inst., Birmingham, Ala., 1961-84, ret., 1984; cons. in field, 1961-84. Contbr. articles to profl. jours. Vol. Civil Def. Radiological Def. instr., Jefferson County, Ala., Homewood, Ala., 1959-80. Recipient Founder's Medal Arts & Scis. Vanderbilt U., 1944. Mem. Am. Chem. Soc., Phi Beta Kappa. Episcopalian. Home: 2161 Kent Way Birmingham AL 35226

THORPE, SUSAN M., real estate company recruiting executive; b. Sept. 12, 1956; d. Yolande Macerollo; children: Patricia Anne, Norman. BA, Brock Univ.; postgrad. U. N.C., Greensboro. Real estate salesperson, trainer and mgr. Century 21 Carolinas; dir. recruiting Century 21 Real Estate Corp., Irvine, Calif. Mem. NAFE, Nat. Assn. Realtors, Nat. Speakers Assn., Toastmasters. Home: 251 Temple Ave Apt 3 Long Beach CA 90803

THORSEN, NANCY DAIN, real estate broker; b. Edwardsville, Ill., June 23, 1944; d. Clifford Earl and Suzanne Eleanor (Kribs) Dain; m. David Massie, 1968 (div. 1975); 1 child, Suzanne Dain Massie; m. James Hugh Thorsen, May 30, 1980. B.Sc. in Mktg., So. Ill. U., 1968, M.Sc. in Bus. Edn., 1975; grad. Realtor Inst., Idaho, 1983. Cert. resdl. and investment specialist. Personnel officer J.H. Little & Co. Ltd., London, 1969-72; instr. in bus. edn. Spl. Sch. Dist. St. Louis, 1974-77; mgr. mktg./ops. Isis Foods, Inc., St. Louis, 1978-80; asst. mgr. store Stix, Baer & Fuller, St. Louis, 1980; assoc. broker Century 21 Sayer Realty, Inc., Idaho Falls, Idaho, 1981-88, RE/MAX Homestead Realty, 1989—; mem. RE/MAX 100% Club; speaker RE/MAX Internat. Conv., 1990. Bd. dirs. Idaho Vol., Boise, 1981-84, Idaho Falls Symphony, 1982; pres. Friends of Idaho Falls Library, 1981-83; chmn. Idaho Falls Mayor's Com. for Vol. Coordination, 1981-84. Recipient Idaho Gov.'s award, 1982, cert. appreciation City of Idaho Falls/Mayor Campbell, 1982, 87, Century 21 Gold Assoc. award, 1987, 88; named to Two Million Dollar Club, Three Million Dollar Club, 1987, 88; named Top Investment Sales Person for Eastern Idaho, 1985, No. 1 Century 21 Agt. in Idaho, 1986, 87, 88. Mem. Idaho Falls Bd. Realtors (chmn. orientation 1982-83, chmn. edn. 1983, chmn. legis. com. 1989, chmn. program com. 1990), Idaho Assn. Realtors (pres. Million Dollar Club 1988-90), So. Ill. U. Alumni Assn., Idaho Fallls C. of C., Newcomers Club, Civitan (pres. Idaho Falls chpt. 1988-89, Civitan of Yr. 1986, 87, outstanding pres. award 1990), Re/Max Exec. Club. Office: RE/MAX Homestead Inc 1301 E 17th St Ste 1 Idaho Falls ID 83404

THORSON, BARBARA ANN, media specialist; b. Hamlet, N.C., July 24, 1949; d. Franklin Paul and Betty Louise (Collins) Thompson; m. Bradley Dean Thorson, May 3, 1969; children: Jennifer Lee, Jeanny Louise. MEd, U. N.C., Greensboro, 1986; cert. in supervision, U. N.C., Charlotte, 1987, cert. in adminstrn., 1988. Media coord. Carteret County Bd. Edn., Beaufort, N.C., 1979-83, Bertie County Bd. Edn., Windsor, N.C., 1983-84, Iredell County Bd. Edn., Statesville, N.C., 1984—. Co-chmn. communications Broad St. United Meth. Ch., Statesville, 1987—. Mem. N.C. Assn. Educators (policies com. 1988—), N.C. Sch. Libr. Assn. (awards and scholarship com. 1986—), AAUW (corr. sec. Statesville 1987—). Democrat. Home: 1512 Country Dr Statesville NC 28677 Office: East Iredell Elem Sch Rte 1 Box 8 Statesville NC 28677

THORSON, CONNIE CAPERS, librarian, professor; b. Dallas, July 25, 1940; d. Ewing Ashby and Constance (Romberg) Capers; m. James Llewellyn, June 6, 1970. BA, U. Ark., 1962, MA, 1964; PhD, U. N.Mex., 1970; MS in Library Sci., U. Ill., 1977. Instr. English S.E. Mo. State U., Cape Girardeau, 1963-67; with U. N.Mex., Albuquerque, 1970-71, 79—, acquistitions libr., 1980—, assoc. prof. libr., 1984-90; prof. U. N.Mex., 1990—. Editor: A Million Stars, 1981, Pocket Companion for Oxford, 1989. Mem. South Cen. Soc. for 18th Century Studies (pres. elect 1988-89, pres. 1989-90), Modern Lang. Assn. Am., Am. Soc. for 18th Century Studies, ALA. Office: U NMex Library Albuquerque NM 87131

THORSON, DIANE RAE, health administrator; b. Fergus Falls, Minn., Oct. 15, 1953; d. Carl Frank and Lena E. (Boeder) Rocholl; m. Douglas R. Thorson, July 28, 1973; 1 child, Matthew. BA in Nursing, St. Scholastica, 1975. Staff nurse Lake Region Hosp., Fergus Falls, 1975-78; dir. Otter Tail Pub. Health, Fergus Falls, 1978—; bd. dirs. Lakeland Hospice, Fergus Falls; chairperson Minn. League for Nursing Assembly of Home Health Nursing Agys., Mpls., 1986-87; chair-elect Minn. Assn. Community Health Adminstrs., 1989-90. Tche. Sunday sch., Henning, Minn., 1982—. Recipient Cert. of Recognition, Minn. Dept. Health, 1988. Mem. Nat. League Nursing, Minn. Nurses Assn., Sigma Theta Tau. Lutheran. Office: Otter Tail Pub Health Ct House Fergus Falls MN 56537

THORSON, GRETCHEN, educator; b. Janesville, Wis., Oct. 8, 1957; d. Floyd V. and Winnifred A. (Goldsmith) T. BS in Edn., U. Wis., 1979; MEd, U. So. Fla., Tampa, 1985. Cert. tchr., Fla. Tchr. Hillsborough County Schs., Tampa, 1980-88, Brewster SED Ctr., Tampa, 1982-88; learning resources tchr. Fla. Diagnostic & Learning Resource System, Sarasota, 1988-89; software reviewer Fla. Ctr. for Instructional Computing, Tampa, 1984—; curriculum resource tchr. Bett Tackett Sch., Sarasota, 1989—; speaker in field. Mem. Coun. for Children with Behavioral Disorders (pres. 1987-89), Coun. for Exceptional Children, ASCD, Fla. Assn. for Computers in Edn. Home: 3720 Delta St Sarasota FL 34232 Office: Betty Tackett Sch 4430 Beneva Sch Sarasota FL 34233

THORSON, MARCELYN MARIE, applied art educator; b. Houston, Dec. 18, 1927; d. Oliver Herbert and Helene Marie (Brown) Fritts; m. Edward L. Thorson, June 16, 1956. BS, Pratt Inst., N.Y.C., 1950. Cert. home economist, tech. tchr. Apparel designer Dallas Sportswear Co., 1954-64, Srader Sportswear Co., Dallas, 1964-65; instr., coordinator apparel design program and pattern design program El Centro Coll., Dallas, 1966-88; cons. computer research Camsco, Inc., Richardson, Tex., summer 1976-77; project devel. coordinator state grant Fashion Design Series, North Tex. State U., summer 1978-79, instr. Indsl. Tng. Lab., summer 1978. Instr. Adult Christian Edn. Found., Bethel Bible Series, Luth. Ch., 1965-80. Mem. Costume Soc. Am., AAUW, Am. Home Econs. Assn., The Fashion Group (edn. com. 1975—, scholarship chmn. 1975-85, dir. fashion mus. 1963-65, Silver Tray award 1965). Republican. Home: 11229 Lanewood Circle Dallas TX 75218

THRAILKILL, FRANCIS MARIE, college president; b. San Antonio, Sept. 21, 1937; d. Franklin E. and Myrtle M. (Huggins) T. B.A. cum laude, Coll. New Rochelle, N.Y., 1961; M.A., Marquette U., Milw., 1969; Ed.D., Nova U., Ft. Lauderdale, Fla., 1975. Joined Ursuline Order of Sisters, Roman Catholic Ch., 1955; tchr. Ursuline Acad., Dallas, 1961-64; prin. Ursuline Acad., 1970-77; vice prin. Ursuline Acad., New Orleans, 1965-70; pres. Springfield (Ill.) Coll., 1978-87, Coll. of Mt. St. Joseph, Ohio, 1987—. Trustee Community, Found. Ind. Colls., Little Miami Inc.; mem. Leadership Cin.; mem. edn. com. Cin. At Mus.; bd. dirs. Dan Beard Coun., Ursuline Acad., Cin. Assn. for Blind, Coun. Ind. Colls., Summit Country Day, Joy Outdoor Edn. Ctr., Community Mut. Blue Cross/Blue Shield. Mem. Assn. Cath. Colls. and Univs., Assn. Governing Bds. of Colls. and Univs., Assn. Ind. Colls. and Univs., Greater Cin. Corsortium Colls., Nat. Assn. Ind. Colls. and Univs., Ohio Bd. Regents, Council Ind. Colls. Office: Coll of Mt St Joseph Mount Saint Joseph OH 45051

THRASHER, BESSIE G., real estate company executive; b. St. Louis; d. George and Maude Mae (Haggin) Chouris; children: Bessie, Robert. BA, U. Mo., St. Louis, 1981. Cert., Dale Carnegie Inst.; grad. Realtors Inst. Br. mgr. Gundaker Realtors, St. Louis. Mem. NAFE, Warson Village Mchts. Assn. (past pres.) Women's Assn. (past pres.), St. Louis Coun. Realtors, St. Louis Bd. Realtors. Address: 2601 Sun Meadow Dr Chesterfield MO 63005

THRONE, MARILYN ELIZABETH, professor of English; b. Cleve., Oct. 24, 1939; d. Charles George and Clara Elizabeth (Kieffer) T. AB, Miami U. in Oxford, 1961, MA, 1962; PhD, Miami U. in Oxford, Ohio State, 1969. Instr. Miami U., Oxford, Ohio, 1964-69; asst. prof. Miami U., Oxford, 1969-79, assoc. prof., 1979-90, prof., 1990—. Author: Walter Havighurst: Novelist of the Heartland, 1979. Office: English Dept Miami U Oxford OH 45056

THRONE, ROBIN M., language professional; b. Bklyn., May 5, 1954; d. Lawrence Harold and Pearl Janet (Small) T. AB, U. Mich., 1976; MA, U. Ill., 1978. Spanish tchr. U. Richmond (Va.), 1978-81, Elisabeth Irwin High Sch., N.Y.C., 1981-82; account exec. Font and Vaamonde Inc., N.Y.C., 1982-83, Smith, Greenland Inc., N.Y.C.; spanish tchr. NY City Bd. Edn., Bklyn., 1985--, Herricks High Sch., NY, 1989; translator, interpreter NY City Bd. Edn., Bklyn. 1985--, freelance translator, Queens 1985--. Democrat.

THRYFT, ANN R., marketing communications writer, editor; b. San Francisco, Dec. 22, 1950; d. William Boyd and Margaret Evelyn (Wilson) T.; m. Alfred Stephens Nelson, May 15, 1971 (div. 1983); m. Mark J. Tussman, Mar. 2, 1985 (div. 1988). BA in Anthropology, Stanford U., 1976. Cert. bus. communicator U.S.A. Mktg. communications specialist Franklin Electric, Sunnyvale, Calif., 1981-82; advt. specialist Lear Siegler Inc., Menlo Park, Calif., 1982-83; mktg. communications mgr. Buscom Systems, Santa Clara, Calif., 1983-84; corp. communications mgr. Nat. Tech. Systems, Calabasas, Calif., 1985-86; mktg. communications mgr. Forth, Inc., Manhattan Beach, Calif., 1986-88; cons. in field, 1989—. Contbr. articles to profl. jours. Rep., sec. Los Trancos Woods Community (Calif.) Assn, 1978-79, pres., 1979-80. Mem. Bus.-Profl. Advt. Assn. (bd. dirs. L.A. chpt.), Stanford Alumni Assn., Publicity Club L.A., Phi Beta Kappa. Avocations: historical research, research history of religions, poetry, writing fiction.

THUERMER, KAREN ELAINE, editor; b. Dayton, Ohio, Sept. 23, 1955; d. Russell Lee and Elinore Elaine (Seelig) T. BA, Denison U., 1977; post-grad., Richmond Coll., London, 1975-76; MA, Pa. State U., 1979. Editor Air Force Sgts. Assn., Camp Springs, Md., 1979-82; editor, writer Electronic Industries Assn., Washington, 1982-85; editor Nat. Assn. Indsl. and Office Parks, Arlington, Va., 1985—. Editor Ladies Golf Mag., 1982, Am. Friends of Turkey, McLean, Va., 1986, 87; contbr. articles to mags. and newspapers. Vol. Reagan Presdl. Election Campaign, Arlington, 1979; v.p., singer Alexandria (Va.) Singers, 1980-88; asst. curator Orleans House Gallery, Twickenham, Eng., 1975-76. Recipient Scholastic Award of Achievement, Achievement Key-So. Ohio-No. Ky. Scholastic Art Awards, State of Ohio, 1977, Merit award (oil painting) Art League, Alexandria, 1990. Mem. Am. Soc. Assn. Execs., Nat. Assn. Real Estate Editors, The Writers Group, PEO, Performing Arts Coun. Alexandria (bd. dirs. 1983-84), Art League, Toastmasters, Sigma Delta Chi. Republican. Presbyterian. Home: 212 N Pitt St Alexandria VA 22314 Office: NAIOP 1215 Jefferson Davis Hwy Arlington VA 22202

THUESTAD, LORI LYNN, small business owner; b. Elgin, Ill., June 21, 1957; d. Harry Ashbaugh and Patricia Ann (Porter) Burnidge; m. Ronald Bernard Thuestad, Jan. 26, 1981; children: Rebecca Ann, Patricia Ann. G-rad. high sch., Elgin, 1975. lic. real estate, 1987, notary public, 1988. Pres., owner Ashbaugh Stable, Elgin, 1975—; sales rep. Pace Constrn. Co., Elgin, 1986-89, sales mgr., 1989—; co-mgr. horse shows Impressive Farm, Elgin, 1984—. Mem. Elgin Bd. Realtors. Republican. Roman Catholic. Home: 1414 Kaskaskia Elgin IL 60123 Office: Pace Constrn Co 450 Shepard Dr Elgin IL 60123

THURAISINGHAM, BHAVANI MARIENNE, computer scientist; b. Colombo, Sri Lanka, July 11, 1954; came to U.S. 1980; naturalized, 1985; d. Nitchingam and Gnanam (Thalayasingham) Armstrong; m. Thevendra S. Thuraisingham, Apr. 2, 1975; 1 child, Breman. BSc in Math., Physics, U. Sri Lanka, 1975; MSc in Math., U. Bristol, Eng., 1977; PhD in Math., U. Wales, Swansea, U.K., 1979; MS in Computer Sci., U. Minn., 1984. Mem. faculty computer sci. N.Mex. Inst. Mining and Tech., Socorro, 1980-81; mem. faculty in math. U. Minn., Mpls., 1981-82, adj. prof. computer sci., 1984-89; sr. analyst Control Data Corp., Arden Hills, Minn., 1984-86; prin. rsch. scientist Honeywell, Inc., Golden Valley, Minn., 1986-89; lead engr. The Mitre Corp., Bedford, Mass., 1989—. Contbr. over 40 rsch. papers to refereed jours. and confs. Mem. Assn. Computing Machinery, IEEE Computer Soc., Sigma Xi. Home: PO Box 822 West Acton MA 01720

THURMAN, JANET LOUISE, management executive; b. Denison, Tex., May 18, 1957; d. David Arthur and Joan Louise (Collins) H.; m. Ray Thurman, Aug. 18, 1990. BS, W. Tex. State U., 1979 and 1980; MBA, Tex. A&M U., 1987. Tchr. Arlington (Tex.) Ind. Sch. Dist., 1980-84; dir. adminstrn., sec. bd. dirs. Biophor Corp., College Station, Tex., 1987-89; adminstrv. asst. Pub. Policy Resources Lab., Tex. A&M U., College Station, 1989—. Mem. Brazos Valley Pers. Assn. Republican. Home: 5808 Knightsbridge Ln Bryan TX 77802 Office: Texas A&M U Pub Policy Resources Lab College Station TX 77843-4476

THURMAN, KAREN, state senator; b. Rapid City, S.D., Jan. 12, 1951; d. Lee Searle and Donna (Altfillisch) Loveland; m. John Patrick Thurman, 1973; children—McLin Searl and Liberty Lee. B.A., U. Fla., 1973. Mem. Dunnellon City Council (Fla.), 1974-82; mayor of Dunnellon, 1979-81; mem. Monroe Regional Med. Ctr. Governancy Com.; mem. Comprehensive Plan Tech. Adv. Com.; del. Fla. Democratic Conv.; Dem. Nat. Conv., 1980; mem. Regional Energy Action com.; mem. Fla. State Senate, 1982—. Recipient Service Above Self award Dunnellon C. of C., 1980; Regional Planning Council Appreciation for Service award. Mem. Dunnellon C. of C. (dir.), Fla. Horseman's Children's Soc. (charter). Episcopalian. Office: State Senate Tallahassee FL 32301*

THURMOND, SANDRA BARKER, health facilities administrator; b. Richmond, Va., Dec. 26, 1961; d. Oscar Bayne III and Betty Jean (Vaughn) Barker; m. Andrew Jackson Thurmond III, Nov. 26, 1983. BS in Biology, Birmingham-So. Coll., 1984; MS in Health Adminstrn., U. Ala., 1988. Anesthesia clk. U. Ala. Health Services Found., Birmingham, 1980-81; operating room aide Children's Hosp. Ala., Birmingham, 1981, adminstrv. resident, 1988, asst. in ops., 1988, asst. v.p. ops., 1989—; with Kelly Girl, Birmingham, 1984; office mgr. Mech. Service and Erection Corp., Birmingham, 1984-85; acctg. asst. SMI Steel, Inc., Birmingham, 1985-86. Mem. Healthcare Fin. Mgmt. Assn., Am. Hosp. Assn., Ala. Hosp. Assn., DAR (state teller's commn. 1988—, registrar Cahawba chpt. 1987—, chmn. pub. rels. 1985—), Birmingham So. Colll. Alumni Leadership Bd. (bd. dirs. 1987—), U. Ala. Alumni Assn. (Acad. Excellence award 1988), Kiwanis (bd. dirs.), Alpha Eta Soc., Phi Kappa Phi, Omicron Delta Kappa. Republican. Episcopalian. Office: Childrens Hosp Ala 1600 7th Ave S Birmingham AL 35233

THURRELL, MARIAN, technical sales representative; b. Wilmington, Del., Mar. 12, 1960; d. Lawrence Alden and Helen (Czerniakowski) T. BA in Chemistry and Biology, Bucknell U., 1982. Contract chemist duPont, Glasgow, Del., 1983-84; chemist Witco, 1984; tech. rep. EM Diagnostic Systems, Atlanta, 1984-85; chemist Himont USA Inc., Wilmington, 1985-87, tech. rep., 1987-89, tech. sales rep., 1989—. Sec. Linden Green Condo Coun., Wilmington, 1986, pres., 1987-89; mem. Wilmington Handbell Choir. Mem. Wilmington Ski Club. Republican. Home: 5418 Valley Green Rd B4 Wilmington DE 19808

THURSTON, ANNE ELIZABETH, college official; b. Greensboro, N.C., Jan. 31, 1957; d. Robert Lee and Margaret Daniel (Wilkerson) T. AA, Peace Coll., Raleigh, N.C., 1977; BA, U. N.C., 1979; MEd, N.C. State U., 1990. Customer svc. rep. Standard Savs. & Loan, Winston-Salem, N.C., 1979-81; residence dir. Greensboro Coll., 1981-82; dir. student activities Peace Coll., Raleigh, N.C., 1982-86, dir. alumnae affairs, 1987-90, assoc. dir. adminssions, 1990—; ops. mgr. Norrell Svcs., Inc., Raleigh, 1986-87. Mem. N.C. Assn. Women Deans, Adminstrs. and Counselors, Coun. for Advancement and Support Edn., AAUW, Peace Coll. Alumnae Assn. Presbyterian. Home: 3731 Browning Pl Raleigh NC 27609 Office: Peace Coll 15 E Peace St Raleigh NC 27604

THURSTON, DORIS, municipal administrator, nurse; b. Louisville, May 7, 1929; d. Lloyd Leith Robertson and Elsie May Sullivan; m. Donald Rice Thurston, July 3, 1952 (div. 1983); children: Christine Ann, Edwin Rice, John Donald; m. Norman Francis Parker, Dec. 6, 1987. AA, RN, L.A. County Med. Ctr., 1951; student, UCLA, 1952; BS, U. So. Calif., 1954; MA, U.S. Internat. U., San Diego, 1974. RN., Calif. Tchr. Compton (Calif.) Coll., 1954-55, ARC, San Diego, 1955-60; charge nurse Physicians Med. Office, Escondido, Calif., 1960-65; nursing supr. Palomar Meml. Hosp., Escondido, 1965-72; tchr. Regional Occupational Program, Poway, Calif., 1972-74; mem. San Diego Trauma Rsch., 1988, Home Nursing Care Advance Bd., Escondido, 1986-90. Contbr. articles to profl. jours. Mayor Escondido City, 1988-90; mem. city coun., 1982-90; mem. League of Calif. Safty Com., Sacramento, 1988-90; chmn. Community Devel. Com., Escondido, 1988-90, Mayors Resource Panel, Escondido, 1988-90; pres. Palomar-Pomerado Hosp. Dist. , Escondido, 1976-82; organizer and founder Child Abuse Prevention Coalition, Escondido, 1984-90. Recipient cert. of appreciation Calif. Legislature, 1987; named to Hon. Order Ky. Cols. Mem. League of Calif. Cities (Del.), PEO, (pres. 1977-79), Rotary. Republican. Presbyterian. Office: City of Escondido Mayor 201 N Broadway Escondido CA 92025

THURSTON, ELLA ISABELLE, health facility administrator; b. Concordia, Kans., Sept. 9, 1925; d. Gasper Viateur and Lottie Elizabeth (Green) Fraser; m. Bryant Edward. Diploma in Nursing, St. Joseph Hosp., 1946. Staff, private duty nurse St. Joseph Hosp., Concorda, Kans., 1946-56; staff nurse, supr. Mitchell Co. Hosp., Beloit, Kans., 1956-67; adminstr. Jamestown Nursing Home, Kans., 1967--. Mem. Kans. Nursing Home Assn., Kans. Profl. Nuring Home Adminstr. Assn.

TIBBELS, NANCY ANN, instructor; b. Omaha, Nov. 9, 1963; d. Terrence Edward and Mary Jean (Belitz) T. BA in Sociology and Communication Study, U. Calif., Santa Barbara, 1985. Pub. svc. announcement coord. KMGQ, Santa Barbara, 1984; seminar coord. Target Fitness, Santa Barbara, 1985; instr. Jazzercise, Santa Barbara, 1984—; area mgr. Jazzercise, Santa Barbara and Ventura, 1986-89; instr., trainer Jazzercise Know More Diet, Carlsbad, 1989—; mem. com. Coun. Christmas Cheer, Santa Barbara, 1984-88; mem. com. Dance for Heart-Am. Heart Assn., Santa Barbara, 1986. Mem. Internat. Dance Exercise Assn., U. Calif.-Santa Barbara Alumni Assn. Office: Jazzercise Inc 2808 Roosevelt St Carlsbad CA 92008

TIBBETTS, CATHY D., optometrist; b. Elizabeth City, N.C., Sept. 8, 1954; d. Lawrence Stewart and Carolyn Ruth (Evans) T. BS in Microbiology, U. Maine, Orono, 1976; BS in Optometry, Pa. Coll. Optometry, Phila., 1977, OD, 1980. Optometrist John Gundzik, M.D., P.A., Santa Fe, N.Mex., 1980-83, N.Mex. State Penitentiary, Santa Fe, 1982-84; pvt. practice Farmington, N.Mex., 1984—. Vol. United Way, Farmington, 1989. Mem. Am. Bus. Women's Assn. Home: 5542 Beech St Farmington NM 87401 Office: 4601 E Main St Farmington NM 87401

TIBERI-SMOLENSKI, SANDRA JOSEPHINE, copywriter, retail advertiser, fitness educator; b. Chgo., Mar. 4, 1964; d. Jerome Charles and Diane Marie (Malatia) T.; m. Michael Joseph Smolenski, June 23, 1990. BS in Advt., U. Ill., 1986. Instr., with sales and pub. rels. depts. Health & Tennis Orgn. Am., Chgo., 1987-89; copywriter, advt. exec., nat. catalog hdqrs. Sears, Roebuck & Co., Skokie, Ill., 1988—; fitness instr. Webster Fitness Club, Chgo. 1989-90, Jamnastics, Chgo., 1989—, Second Wind, Inc., Chgo., 1990—, U. Chgo., 1990. Basic life saver Am. Heart Assn., Chgo., 1988—. Mem. Internat. Dance-Exercise Assn. (cert.), Greenpeace, Amnesty Internat. Office: Sears Roebuck & Co Nat Catalog Hdqrs 7447 Skokie Blvd BSC 3-2 Skokie IL 60077

TIBURZI, ANITA M(ARIE), marketing and public relations firm executive, consultant; b. Englewood, N.J., Aug. 14, 1944; d. August Robert and Gunvor Inga Britt (Dahlberg) T.; m. Stephen F. Johnson, Aug. 3, 1973; 1 child, James Wood. B.A., U. Stockholm, 1966; postgrad. Centre Universitaire Mediterrannee, Nice, France, 1967. Dir. corp. communications Kenton Corp., N.Y.C., 1968-72; dir. bus. devel. L.M. Rosenthal, N.Y.C., 1972-73; cons. Monsanto Corp., Simplicity Corp., Helena Rubenstein, N.Y.C., 1973-78; v.p. Perrier Group, Greenwich, Conn., 1978-83; pres., owner Atwood Internat. Inc., N.Y.C., 1983-89, Atwood Design Group, 1989—; cons. mktg./pub. relations and creative spl. events, etc.; dir. Salt-Free Gourmet Corp., N.Y.C.; trustee Philharmonia Virtuosi, N.Y.C., 1985—. Patentee ednl. toy. Com. mem. Am. Cancer Soc., N.Y.C., 1975—, Millay Colony for Arts, N.Y.C., 1977—, Just One Break, Inc., N.Y.C., 1978—; mem. Inner Circle Republican Com., Washington, 1984—, The Seeing Eye Orgn., N.J., 1986—. Episcopalian. Avocations: art and antique collecting, historical preservation and conservation, riding, tennis, skiing. Office: Atwood Internat Inc 1202 Lexington Ave Ste 307 New York NY 10028

TICE, CAROL HOFF, teacher, consultant; b. Ashville, N.C., Oct. 6, 1931; d. Amos H. and Fern (Irvin) Hoff; m. (div.); children: Karin E., Jonathan H. BS, Manchester Coll., North Manchester, Ind., 1954; MEd, Cornell U., 1955. Cert. tchr., Mich., N.Y., N.J. Tchr. Princeton (N.J.) Schs., 1955-60; tchr. Ann Arbor (Mich.) Schs., 1964—; dir. of intergenerational programs, Inst. for the Study of Children and Falmilies Eastern Mich. U., Ypsilanti, 1985—; Founder & pres., Lifespan Resources, Inc., Ann Arbor, 1979—; commr. U. S. Nat. Commn. Internat. Yr. of the Child, Washington, 1979-81. Innovator; program, Tch. Learning Intergenerational Communities, 1971; author: Guide Books and articles, Community of Caring, 1980; co-producer, Film, What We Have, 1976 (award, Milan, Italy Film Festival 1982). Mem. Democratic Party, Ann Arbor; trustee Blue Lake Fine Arts Camp, Twin Lake, Mich., 1975—. Recipient Ford Found. Fellowship, Ithaca, N.Y., 1955, Program Innovation, Mich. Dept. Edn. ESEA-3C, Ann Arbor, 1974-80, C.S. Mott Found., Ann Arbor, 1982, Nat. Found. Improvement in Edn., Washington, 1986, Disting. Alumni, Manchester Coll., N. Manchester 1979. Mem. Am. Soc. of Curriculum Devel., Am. Assn. U. Women (Agt. 1979), Generations United (Pioneer Award 1989), Optimist Club. Democrat. Presbyterian. Office: Lifespan Resources Inc 1212 Roosevelt Ann Arbor MI 48104

TICE, CAROLYN KAY, magazine editor; b. Kans. City, Mo., June 20, 1945; d. Clyde Prather and Hazel Adelyn (Best) Coleman; m. Arthur Raymond Tice, June 1, 1968. AA, Kans. City Community Coll., 1965. Office mgr. Litho-Comp Art Assocs., Kans. City, 1965-67; layout editor Spencer Printing Co., Kans. City, 1967-68; prodn. mgr. InterTec Pub. Co., Lenexa, Kans., 1968-70; assoc. editor Farm and Power Equipment Mag., St. Louis, 1970-79; exec. sec. Custodis Constrn. Co., Salt Lake City, 1979; mng. editor Fin. Freedom Report Mag., Salt Lake City, 1980—. Active Nat. Humane Soc., Washington, 1988—, Humane Soc. Salt Lake City, 1988—. Mem. Nat. Assn. Real Estate Editors, Phi Theta Kappa. Republican. Lutheran. Home: 7268 Macintosh Ln Salt Lake City UT 84121 Office: Fin Freedom Report 1831 Fort Union Blvd Salt Lake City UT 84121

TICE, PATRICIA KAYE, counselor, entrepreneur, teacher; b. Grinnell, Iowa, May 22, 1953; d. Ronald Stephen and Shirley Ann (Arthur) Tice. BS, Iowa State U., 1975, MS, 1983. Tchr. St. Augustin Sch., Des Moines, 1975-77; tchr. S.E. Polk Schs., Runnells, Iowa, 1977-84, guidance counselor, 1984-86; prevention coordinator Nat. Council on Alcoholism, Des Moines, 1986-87; owner, pres. The Hug Lady, Des Moines, 1987—; Bd. dirs. Children's Oncology Svcs. Iowa, Inc., Des Moines, 1986—, pres., 1988—. Author: Alpha Delta Pi Pledge Manual, 1975; creator registered trademark The Hug Lady. Active Des Moines Ronald McDonald House, 1977—. Mem. Greater Des Moines C. of C. Fedn., Entrepreneurs Breakfast Group, Assn. Retarded Persons (human rights commn. 1988—), AAUW, Nat. Assn. Women Bus. Owners, Men's Garden Club, Alpha Delta Pi, Alpha Delta Pi Alumni Assn. Office: The Hug Lady PO Box 2242 Des Moines IA 50310

TICHIK, EVELYN KAY, office administrator, bookkeeper; b. Detroit, Jan. 7, 1942; d. Clarence Valentine and Beatrice Lavere (MCCarty) Rodocker; m. Mel Tickik, Dec. 19, 1963; children: Jacqueline Ellen, Erik Brian. Student, U. Detroit, 1959-61, Henry Ford Community Coll., 1961-63, Wayne State U., 1963, Oakland Community Coll., 1986—. Salesperson Woolworth Co., Detroit, 1959-60, J.L. Hudson Co., Detroit, 1960-61; accounts payable staff Ditzler div. PPG, Detroit, 1961-64; asst. to office mgr. Drake Inc., Detroit, 1964-64; service rep., comml. accounts Mich. Bell Telephone Co., Detroit, 1965-68; bookkeeper, office mgr., data processing mgr., sec. Bonded Guard Services Inc., Detroit, 1972-87; controller Small & Berris, Southfield, Mich., 1987-88; pres. Bookkeeping Alternatives Inc., Oak Park, Mich., 1988—; office administrator, bookkeeper Simon, Deitch, Friedman, Siefman & Green, Southfield, 1988-90; office/pers. adminstr. Simpson Moran, Birmingham, Mich., 1990—. Sec. Edn. Advancement Found., Oak Park Bd. Edn., 1985, vice chmn., 1986; pres. Tourette Syndrome Assn., 1981—; treas. Womens Am. Orgn. Rehab. Through Tng., Detroit, 1977-79. Mem. NAFE, Met. Small Systems Mgmt., Am. Entrepreneurs Assn., B'nai B'rith Jewish Profl. Network, Roundtable of Christians and Jews, DAR, B'nai'Brith Women (pres. Deborah chpt. Detroit 1970-75, sec., pres. Metro coun. 1975-77), Asns. Legal Adminstrs., Phi Theta Kappa. Republican. Home and Office: 14450 Elm Oak Park MI 48237

TICKETT, DEBORAH L., insurance company executive; b. Jacksonville, Fla., May 18, 1951; d. Charles T. Jr. and Isabelle Lee (Capers) Laney; m. Kenneth Tickett, Mar. 15, 1969; children—Kenneth II, Steven Lee. Student Pinellas Vocat. Tech. Inst., Tampa U.; lic. ins. agent. Sec. Laney & Assocs., Clearwater, Fla., 1974-75, bookkeeper, 1975-77, ins. agent, 1977—, asst. mgr., 1977-79, v.p., mgr., 1979-85, pres., owner, 1986—; sec./treas., majority ptnr. Debco Electric, Inc. Tchr. Episc. Ch. of Good Samaritan, 1972-79, counselor youth group, 1975-79. Mem. Ind. Ins. Agts. Am., Ins. Women St. Petersburg, Nat. Assn. Female Execs., Fla. Assn. Ins. Agts., Clearwater C. of C., Beta Sigma Phi (v.p.). Democrat. Episcopalian. Avocations: design, decorating. Office: Laney & Assocs 516 N Fort Harrison Ave PO Box 1508 Clearwater FL 34617

TIDBALL, M. ELIZABETH PETERS, physiology educator; b. Anderson, Ind., Oct. 15, 1929; d. John Winton and Beatrice (Ryan) Peters; m. Charles S. Tidball, Oct. 25, 1952. BA, Mt. Holyoke Coll., 1951, LHD, 1976; MS, U. Wis., 1955, PhD, 1959; ScD (hon.), Wilson Coll., 1973, Trinity Coll., 1974, Cedar Crest Coll., 1977, U. of South, 1978, Goucher Coll., 1979; HHD (hon.), St. Mary's Coll., 1977, Hood Coll., 1982; LittD (hon.), Regis Coll., 1980, Coll. St. Catherine, 1980; LLD (hon.), St. Joseph Coll., 1983; LHD (hon.), Skidmore Coll., 1984, Marymount Coll., 1985, Converse Coll., 1985, Mt. Vernon Coll., 1986; DSc (hon.), St. Mary-of-The-Woods Coll., 1986; LittD (hon.), Alverno Coll., 1989; MTS summa cum laude, Wesley Theol. Sem., 1990. Teaching asst. physiology dept. U. Wis., 1952-55, 58-59; research asst. anatomy dept. U. Chgo., 1955-56, research asst. physiology dept., 1956-58; USPHS postdoctoral fellow NIH, Bethesda, Md., 1959-61; staff pharmacologist Hazleton Labs., Falls Church, Va., 1961; cons. Hazleton Labs., 1962; asst. research prof. dept. pharmacology George Washington U. Med. Center, 1962-64, assoc. research prof. dept. physiology, 1964-70, research prof., 1970-71, prof., 1971—; Cons. FDA, 1966-67, assoc. sci. coordinator sci. assocs. tng. program, 1966-67; mem. com. on NIH tng. programs and fellowships Nat. Acad. Scis., 1972-75; faculty summer confs. Am. Youth Found., 1967-78; founder, dir. Summer Seminars for Women Am. Youth Found., 1987—; cons. for instl. research Wellesley Coll., 1974-75; exec. sec. com. on edn. and employment women in sci. and engring. Commn. on Human Resources, NRC/Nat. Acad. Scis., 1974-75, vice chmn., 1977-82; cons., staff officer NRC/Nat. Acad. Scis., 1974-75; cons. Woodrow Wilson Nat. Fellowship Found., 1975—, NSF, 1974—, Assn. Am. Colls., 1986—; Lucie Stern Disting. vis. prof. in natural scis. Mills Coll., 1980; scholar in residence Coll. Preachers, 1984, Salem Coll., 1985; disting. scholar in residence So. Meth. U., 1985; cons. Assn. Am. Colls. Project on Status and Edn. of Women, 1986-90; rep. to D.C. Commn. on Status of Women, 1972-75, nat. panelist Am. Council on Edn., 1983—; panel mem. Congl. Office of Tech. Assessment, 1986-87. Contbr. sci. articles and research on edn. of women to profl. jours.; mem. editorial bd. Jour. Higher Edn, 1979-83, cons. editor, 1984—; mem. editorial adv. bd. Religion and Intellectual Life, 1983—. Trustee Mt. Holyoke Coll., 1968-73, vice chmn., 1972-73, trustee fellow, 1988—; trustee Hood Coll., 1972-84, 86—, exec. com., 1974-84, 89—; overseer Sweet Briar Coll., 1978-85; trustee Cathedral Choral Soc., 1976—, pres. bd. trustees, 1982-84; trustee Skidmore Coll., Saratoga Springs, N.Y., 1988—; councillor Coll. of Preachers, 1979-85, chmn., 1983-85; trustee Washington Cathedral Found., 1983-85, mem. exec. com., 1983-85; bd. vis. Salem Coll., 1986—; ctr. assoc. Nat. Resource Ctr., Girls Clubs Am., 1983—. Shattuck fellow, 1955-56; Mary E. Woolley fellow Mt. Holyoke Coll., 1958-59; USPHS postdoctoral fellow, 1959-61; recipient Alumnae Medal of Honor Mt. Holyoke Coll., 1971, Chestnut Hill Medal for Outstanding Achievement Chestnut Hill Coll., Phila., 1987; named Outstanding Grad. The Penn Hall Sch., 1988. Mem. AAAS, Am. Physiol. Soc. (chmn. task force on women in physiology 1973-80, com. on coms. 1977-80), Am. Assn. Higher Edn., Mt. Holyoke Alumnae Assn. (dir. 1966-70, 76-77), Histamine Club, Sigma Delta Epsilon, Sigma Xi. Episcopalian. Home: 4100

Cathedral Ave NW Washington DC 20016 Office: George Washington U Med Ctr 2300 I St NW Washington DC 20037

TIDMORE, TERRI LACEY, utilities executive; b. Neodesha, Kans., July 12, 1955; d. Norman John Lacey and Mitzie Ann (Riddle) Northcutt; m. Bill D. Tidmore; children: J. Daniel, Ian B. Student, Tex. Tech. U., 1973-75, U. Calif., Riverside, 1975-76. With Continental Natural Gas, Tulsa, 1983-87; v.p. mktg. Golden Gas Energies, Inc., Tulsa, 1987—. Mem. Natural Gas Assn. Okla., Natural Gas Soc. North Tex., Natural Gas Assn. Houston, Nat. Transp. and Exch. Assn., NAFE, Indian Spring Country Club, Gamma Phi Beta. Office: Golden Gas Energies Inc 7060 S Yale Ste 900 Tulsa OK 74136

TIDWELL, TRUDY, mathematics educator; b. Oxford, Miss., May 4, 1948; d. Andrew Barnett and Lottie Trus (Billingsley) T. BA, U. Miss., 1970; MA, U. N.C., Chapel Hill, 1980; cert., N.C. Cen., 1989. Cert. tchr. Educator Granville County Schs., Oxford, 1970-72; educator Vance County Schs., Henderson, N.C., 1972-86, 89—, observer, evaluator, 1986-89; adj. instr. Vance Granville Community Coll., Henderson, 1983-84; reader Ednl. Testing Svc., Princeton, N.J., 1986-90; tchr. Nat. Sci. Found. Summer Program, Western Carolina U., 1974. Adminstrv. bd. sec. First United Meth. Ch., Henderson, 1985-87, treas. 1985-87; pres. Henderson Jr. Woman's Club, Henderson, 1975, ways and means chmn. 1976, dist. lit. chmn. 1977. Recipient Outstanding Club Woman of Yr. Henderson Jr. Woman's Club, 1978. Mem. Nat. Coun. of Tchrs. of Math., N.C. Coun. of Tchrs. of Math., Assn. for Supervision and Curriculum Devel., Phi Delta Kappa, Alpha Delta Kappa (pres. 1986-88, treas. 1978-80, chmn. 1988-90, Scholarship 1976-78). Democrat. Home: 859 Nelson St Henderson NC 27536 Office: Northern Vance High Sch Rt 6 Box 285 Henderson NC 27536

TIEDE, PATRICIA LEE, association administrator; b. Butte, Mont., Mar. 17, 1937; d. Harry Elwin and Martha Adele (Prentice) Chisholm; m. Tom R. Tiede, 1959 (div. 1982); children: Kristina Anne, Thomas Patrick. BA in Sociology, Wash. State U., Pullman, 1959. Exec. asst. Wandell Elem. Sch., Saddle River, N.J., 1970-74, Congl. Country Club, Bethesda, Md., 1974-75; with adminstrv. mktg. dept. Nat. Bus. Systems, Rockville, Md., 1975-78; exec. asst. Club Mgrs. Assn. of Am., Bethesda, 1978-89; mgr. adminstrv. svcs. Indsl. Rsch. Inst., Washington, 1989—. Pres. Manor Country Club Community Assn., Rockville, 1975; mem. house com. Promenade Housing Assn., Bethesda, 1989. Mem. Am. Soc. Assn. Execs., Greater Wash. Assn. of Assn. Execs., NAFE, Alpha Chi Omega Alumnae Group (pres. Bergen County chpt. 1969). Home: 5225 Pooks Hill Rd #1520N Bethesda MD 20814 Office: Indsl Rsch Inst 1550 M St NW Washington DC 20005

TIEDEKEN, KATHLEEN HELEN, health facilities administrator; b. Camden, N.J., Aug. 6, 1945; d. Joseph Henry and Katherine Rita (Byrne) T. RN, Our Lady of Lourdes Sch., Camden, 1966; BSN, U. Pa., 1974, MSN, 1979. RN, N.J. Staff nurse Our Lady of Lourdes Med. Ctr., Camden, 1966-68, head nurse, 1968-76, asst. dir. staffing, 1976-78; asst. dir. nursing Our Lady of Lourdes Med. Ctr., 1978-80, assoc. dir. nursing, 1980-83; assoc. exec. dir. nursing West Jersey Health System, Voorhees, N.J., 1983-87; assoc. adminstr. nursing Meml. Hosp. Burlington County, Mt. Holly, N.J., 1986—; clin. adj., faculty nursing Widener U.; speaker in field. Contbg. author: Emotion and Reproduction, 1979, New Directions for Nursing in the '80s, 1980. Mem. ANA (cert. nursing advanced adminstrn.), Orgn. Am. Nurses Execs. (bd. dirs., chmn. ednl. dialogue com.), N.J. State Nurses Assn. (legis. com., role of honor com. 1980-85), N.J. Bd. Nursing (ad hoc com. on unlicensed personnel role), Vol. Hosps. Am. (N.J. nursing coun.), Am. Coll. Obstetricians and Gynecologists (nurses assn.), Nat. Perinatal Assn., Sigma Theta Tau. Roman Catholic. Home: 1610 Beechwood Clementon NJ 08021 Office: Meml Hosp Burlington County 175 Madison Ave Mount Holly NJ 08060

TIEFENTHAL, MARGUERITE AURAND, school social worker; b. Battle Creek, Mich., July 23, 1919; d. Charles Henry and Elisabeth Dirk (Hoekstra) Aurand; m. Harlan E. Tiefenthal, Nov. 26, 1942; children: Susan Ann, Daniel E., Elisabeth Amber, Carol Aurand. BS, Western Mich. U., 1941; MSW, U. Mich., 1950; postgrad., Coll. of DuPage, Ill., 1988-90. Tchr. No. High Sch., Flint, Mich., 1941-44, Cen. High Sch., Kalamazoo, 1944-45; acct. Upjohn Co., Kalamazoo, 1945-48; social worker Family Svc. Agy., Lansing, Mich., 1948-50, Pitts., 1950-55; sch. social worker Gower Sch. Dist., Hinsdale, Ill., 1962-70; sch. social worker Hinsdale (Ill.) Dist. 181, 1970-89, cons., 1989—; sch. social worker Villa Park (Ill.) Sch. Dist. 45, 1989; addictions counselor Mercy Hosp., 1990—; field instr. social work interns U. Ill., 1979-88; impartial due process hearing officer; mem. adv. com. sch. social work Ill. State Bd. Edn. approved programs U. Ill. and George Williams Coll.; speaker Nat. Conf. Sch. Social Work, Denver, U. Tex. Joint Conf. Sch. Social Work in Ill.; founder Marguerite Tiefenthal Symposium for Ill. Sch. Social Work Interns. Co-editor The School Social Worker and the Handicapped Child: Making P.L. 94-142 Work; sect. editor: Sch. Social Work Quarterly, 1979. Sec. All Village Caucus Village of Western Springs, Ill., mem. village disaster com.; deacon Presbyn. Ch. Western Springs, Sunday sch. tchr., mem. choir; instr. Parent Effectiveness, Teacher Effectiveness, STEP; trainer Widowed Persons Service Tng. Program for Vol. Aides AARP. Recipient Ill. Sch. Social Worker of Yr., 1982. Mem. Nat. Assn. Social Workers (chmn. exec. council on social work in schs.), Ill. Assn. Sch. Social Workers (past pres., past conf. chmn., conf. program chmn.), Sch. Social Workers Supervisors Group (del. to Ill. Commn. on Children), Programs. for Licensure of Social Work Practice in Ill., LWV, DKG, PEO. Home: 4544 Grand Ave Western Springs IL 60558

TIEGEN, ELAINE MALIN, accounting company executive; b. Elizabeth, N.J., May 22, 1944; d. Bernard Edwin and Estelle (Radin) Malin; m. Robert A. Tiegen, Feb. 2, 1973 (div. Nov. 1975); 1 child, Heike-Ann M. BS in Acctg., Fairleigh Dickinson U., Madison, N.J., 1966. CPA, Fla. Staff auditor Peat, Marwick, Mitchell and Co., Miami, 1968-69; sr. staff auditor J.H. Cohn and Co., CPA's, Newark, N.J., 1969-71; with Clarence Rainess and Co., CPA's, N.Y.C., 1971-73; spl. asst. to sr. ptnr. Wiener, Stern and Hantman, CPA's, Miami, 1973-74; sr. specialist Laventhol & Horwath, Coral Gables, Fla., 1974-78, supr. dept. total acctg. svcs., 1978-79, mgr., 1979, head dept., 1980-83; prin. Elaine Malin Tiegen CPA, PA, Miami, 1983—; v.p. So. Fla. Interprofl. Coun., 1984-85, pres., 1985-86; mem. small bus. rep. of adv. coun. Fed. Res. Bank of Atlanta, 1986-89, chmn. 1988-89. Mem. Am. Women's Soc. CPA's, Am. Soc. Women Accts (chpt. pres. 1975-76; Fla. Acct. of Yr. award 1976), Am. Inst. CPA's (small bus. coun. 1984-87, small bus. taxation com. 1987—), Fla. Inst. CPA's (recipient Disting. Svc. award Dade County chpt. 1980, 81, 82, gov. 1983-85, pres. chpt. 1984-85), Am. Arbitration Assn., Mensa. Office: 2861 SW 73d Way #2001 Davie FL 33314

TIEGS, CHERYL, model, designer; d. Theodore and Phyllis T. Student, Calif. State U., Los Angeles. Profl. model, appearing in nat. mags., including, Time, Life, Bazaar, Sports Illustrated, Glamour; appeared weekly on ABC's Good Morning America; also appearing in TV commls., Cheryl Tiegs line of sportswear, Cheryl Tiegs nationally-distributed line of women's eyeglass frames. Author: The Way to Natural Beauty, 1980; Sports Illustrated video Aerobic Interval Training with Cheryl Tiegs. Address: care Eileen Ford 344 E 59th St New York NY 10022

TIEMAN, SUZANNAH BLISS, neurobiologist; b. Washington, Oct. 10, 1945; d. John Alden and Winifred Texas (Bell) Bliss; m. David George Tieman, Dec. 19, 1969. AB with honors, Cornell U., 1965; postgrad., MIT, 1965-66, Calif. Inst. Tech., 1971-72; PhD, Stanford U., 1974. Postdoctoral fellow dept. anatomy U. Calif., San Francisco, 1974-77; rsch. assoc. Neurobiology Rsch. Ctr. SUNY, Albany, 1977-90, rsch. assoc. prof. dept. biol. scis., 1984-90, rsch. prof., 1990—, sr. rsch. assoc., 1990—, assoc. prof. dept. biomed. scis., 1988; adj. asst. prof. dept. biol. scis., SUNY, Albany, 1977-84. Contbr. articles to profl. jours., chpts. to books in field. Recipient predoctoral fellowship NSF, NIH, Stanford U., 1970-73, 73-74, postdoctoral fellowship Nat. Eye Inst., U. Calif. San Francisco, 1974-77, rsch. grant, SUNY, Albany, 1979-83, NSF, SUNY, 1983-86, 1988-91. Mem. AAAS, Soc. for Neurosci., Hudson Berkshire Chpt. Sci. (steering com. 1980-81), Assn. Rsch. in Vision and Ophthalmology, Am. Assn. Anatomists, Assn. Women in Sci., Women in Neurosci., Nat. Audubon Soc., Nature Conservancy. Office: Neurobiology Rsch Ctr SUNY 1400 Washington Ave Albany NY 12222

TIENDA, MARTA, demographer, educator; b. Tex. Ph.D. in Sociology, U. Tex., 1976. From asst. prof. to prof. rural sociology U. Wis., Madison, 1976-87; vis. prof. Stanford U., 1987; prof. sociology U. Chgo., 1987—; assoc. dir. Population Research Ctr. Co-author: Hispanics in the U.S. Economy, 1985, Divided Opportunities, 1988; contbr. articles to profl. jours. Mem. Am. Sociol. Assn., Population Assn. Am., Internat. Union for the Sci. Study Population, Nat. Council on Employment Policy, Population Assn. Am. (adv. com.). Office: U Chgo Dept Sociology Chicago IL 60637*

TIERNAN, JULIE FLETCHER, financial executive; b. Cin., June 1, 1952; d. Joseph Harrison Sr. and Hazel Virginia (Kinnaird) Fletcher. Student, St. Petersburg Jr. Coll. Owner, restaurateur Seafood & Sunsets At Julie's, Clearwater, Fla.; fin. mgr. Johazel Corp., Clearwater Beach, Fla. Mem. Discover Fla.'s Suncoast div. Tourist Devel. Coun. Mem. NAFE. Address: 450 N Gulfview Blvd Clearwater Beach FL 34630

TIETJE, GERDA ALICE, grease lubricators manufacturing company executive; b. Bklyn., Mar. 24, 1929; d. Emil C. and Cecilie I. (Toenissen) Petersen; m. Helmut G. Tietje, Aug. 22, 1948 (dec. Jan. 1988); children: Arno Paul, Donna Alice Tietje Herndon, Alan Christopher. Grad. high sch., Leonia, N.J. Pres. TM Industries, Inc., Hampton, N.J., 1988—. Patentee in field in U.S., Japan and Europe. Mem. N.J. Bus. and Industry Assn. Republican. Lutheran. Office: TM Industries Inc Plaza 78 Rte 1 PO Box 386C Hampton NJ 08827

TIFFANY, MARSHA BELMONT, systems engineer; b. Ingolstadt, Bavaria, Fed. Republic Germany, Oct. 31, 1954; came to U.S., 1956; d. John Laing and Joyce (Ferris) T. BS in Engring., Physics and Math., Southeast Mo. State U., 1977. Physicist USAF, Wright Patterson AFB, Ohio, 1977-79, electronics engr., 1980-85, computer specialist, 1985-86, sr. engr., 1986-87; systems analyst Nat. Cash Register, Dayton, Ohio, 1979-80; systems engr. Armco Research, Middletown, Ohio, 1987—. Instr. Cardio-Pulmonary Resuscitation, Dayton, 1985-89; vol. United Way. Mem. IEEE, NAFE, Armco Rsch. PC Users Group (pres. 1987-89), Smithsonian Instn., Dayton Art Inst. Democrat. Unitarian. Office: Armco Rsch 703 Curtis St Middletown OH 45043

TIFFANY, MARY MARGARET, communications company executive; b. Carbondale, Pa., May 19, 1947; d. Curtis Hilton and Margaret Mary (Livsey) Abney; m. Richard Allen Tiffany, Aug. 13, 1976; children: Colleen Denise O'Day, Thomas Edward O'Day. Dir. pub. info. Parkland Healthcare Ctr., Orlando, Fla., 1980-82; mgr. pers. RCS, Inc., Orlando, 1982-84; mgr. adminstrv. svcs. AT&T, Orlando, 1983-84, mgr. tng. programs, 1984-86, mgr. mktg., 1986-88; owner, pres. Tng. Plus, Orlando, 1986—. Mem. Rep. Women Fla., Orlando, 1985-87, Goals 2000 Health and Human Services Task Force, Orlando City Planning Coun. Trans. Com., pub. svcs. com.; bd. dirs. Am. Diabetes Assn., Orlando, 1987, sec., Women's Exec. Coun.; chmn. Orlando Women's Achievement Week; trustee U. Cen. Fla. Alumni Trustee Found.; bd. dirs. So. Ballet. Recipient Appreciation award Vietnam Vets. Assn., 1983. Mem. NAFE, Adminstrv. Mgmt. Soc., Orlando C. of C. (chair bus.-after-hours com. 1986, orange juice forum com. 1986), Am. Soc. Tng. and Devel., Downtown Orlando Ptnrship., Orange County Conv. and Visitors' Bur., Am. Soc. Tng. Dirs. Republican. Roman Catholic. Home: 3488 Exeter Ct Orlando FL 32812 Office: TPI 605 E Robinson St Ste 610 Orlando FL 32801

TIFT, MARY LOUISE, artist; b. Seattle, Jan. 2, 1913; d. John Howard and Wilhelmina (Pressler) Dreher; m. William Raymond Tift, Dec. 4, 1948. BFA cum laude, U. Wash., 1933; postgrad., Art Ctr. Coll., L.A., 1945-48, U. Calif., San Francisco, 1962-63. Art dir. Vaughn Shedd Advt., L.A., 1948; asst. prof. design Calif. Coll. Arts & Crafts, Oakland, Calif., 1949-59; coord. design dept. San Francisco Art Inst., 1959-62. Subject of cover story, Am. Artist mag., 1980, studio article, 1987; one woman shows, Gumps Gallery, San Francisco, 1977, 1986, 90, Diane Gilson Gallery, Seattle, 1978, Oreg. State U., 1981, group shows include, Brit. Biennale, Yorkshire, Eng., 1970, Grenchen Triennale, Switzerland, 1970, Polish Biennale, Crakow, 1972, Nat. Gallery, Washington, 1973, U.S.-U.K. Impressions, Eng., 1988; represented in permanent collections, Phila. Mus. Art, Bklyn. Mus., Seattle Art Mus., Library Congress, Achenbach Print Collection, San Francisco Palace Legion of Honor. Served to lt. USNR, 1943-45. Mem. Print Club Phila., World Print Council, Calif. Soc. Printmakers, Phi Beta Kappa, Lambda Rho. Christian Scientist. Studio: 112 Industrial Ctr Bldg Sausalito CA 94965

TIGER, LYNNE FORRESTER, artist; b. Paterson, N.J., Aug. 26, 1938; d. Howard Bradford and Harriet (Forrester) Parker; m. James Patrick Tiger, Dec. 31, 1960; children: Blair Andrew, Jill. Student, Wood Secretarial Sch., N.Y.C., 1958. Owner Snoop Shop, Pompton Lakes, N.J., 1971—; sec. Pack-A-News Inc., Wayne, N.J., 1964-66, 72-74; editor Pack-A-News Inc., Wayne, N.Y., 1968-70, 76-78, 88—; pres. Pack-A-News Inc., Wayne, N.J., 1970-72, 78-80, 86-88. Contbr. articles to prof. jours. Pres. Fire Ladies Aux. No. 5, 1972-74; trustee Healing the Children Midlantic, Inc., 1986—, dir. med. trips, 1987—. Mem. Nat. Plastercraft Assn. (adv. com. 1978-83). Home: 154 Beechwood Dr Wayne NJ 07470 Office: Snoop Shop 715 Hamburg Turnpike Pompton Lakes NJ 07442

TIGHE, PEGGY JO, army officer; b. Lynchburg, Va., Sept. 2, 1949; d. JoAnn Stephenson. AA, El Paso Community Coll., 1987. Enlisted U.S. Army, 1967;; advanced through grades to sgt. maj. U.S. Army, 1989; stenographer, legal clk., adminstr. U.S. Army, various locations, 1968-82; drill sgt., 1st sgt. U.S. Army, Ft. McClellan, Ala., 1982-86; sr. adminstrv. sgt. U.S. Army, Ft. Monroe, Va., 1986-89; comdr. sgt. maj. U.S. Army, Ft. Dix, N.J., 1989—. Home: 34 Phyllis Ln Hampton VA 23666 Office: HHD 42d A6 Bn PO Box 233 Fort Dix NJ 08640

TIGHE, SONIA, publisher; b. Paris, Tenn., Jan. 15, 1957; d. James Lemuel and Barbara (Smith) Muzzall; m. Mark Thomas Tighe, Aug. 21, 1982; 1 child, Sean. BS in Journalism, U. Tenn., 1979; postgrad., Northwestern U., 1988. Asst. circulation mgr. Vance Pub. Corp., Shawnee Mission, Kans., 1979-83, circulation mgr., 1983-85, assoc. pub., 1985-87, pub., 1987-90, pub. dir., 1990—; mem. nat. sales tng. com. Vance Pub. Corp., Lincolnshire, Ill., 1988-89, chmn. database com. produce div., Shawnee Mission, 1988-90, steering com. computer acquisition, Lincolnshire, 1986-88. Mem. mag. adv. group, U. Kans., 1990—. Mem. Nat. Agri-Mktg. Assn. (treas. 1984-89, program com. 1989-90), Phi Kappa Phi. Methodist. Office: Vance Pub Corp 7950 College Blvd Overland Park KS 66210

TIJERINO LESHER, CARMENZA, creative writing educator, artist; b. Matagalpa, Nicaragua, Sept. 27, 1917; came to U.S., 1944; d. Trinidad Ramon and Zoraida (Rizo) Tijerino; m. George William Lesher, Feb. 21, 1947 (dec. 1965); children: Arthur Barry, Narda Lesher Gaskell; m. Louis Antonin Guette, Sept. 23, 1986. BA magna cum laude, Pepperdine Coll., 1959, MA, 1964; MA, UCLA, 1973. Instr. Spanish, Notre Dame Coll., Belmont, Calif., 1944-45, U. Calif., Santa Barbara, 1966-68; pres. Sch. Art and Decoration, Mexico City, 1950-53, AAA Lang. Svcs., L.A., 1975-83; tchr. Spanish, Inglewood (Calif.) High Sch., 1959-64, Santa Barbara High Sch., 1964-66; instr. art history Pepperdine U., 1974; instr. creative writing UCLA, 1986. Author: Prepositions: The Key to Idiomatic English, 1989; contbr. articles and essays to profl. publs.; one-woman show Gumps Gallery, San Francisco, 1945, Palace Fine Arts, Mexico City, 1946. UCLA grantee, 1969-70, Alpha Beta Phi grantee, 1970-71; UCLA Chancellor's doctoral fellow, 1971-72. Home: 823 Java St No 5 Inglewood CA 90301

TILGER, JUSTINE THARP, research director; b. New Point, Ind., Sept. 11, 1931; d. Joseph Riley and Marcella Lorene (King) Tharp; m. Clarence A. Tilger II, Aug. 22, 1959 (div. Nov. 1972); children: Evelyn Mary, Clarence Arthur III, Joseph Thomas. AB, U. Chgo., 1951; BA, St. Mary's Coll., Notre Dame, Ind., 1954; MA, Ind. U., 1962, PhD, 1971. Mem. Sisters of the Holy Cross, Notre Dame, 1954-58; teaching fellow Ind. U., Bloomington, 1959-61; asst. editor Ind. Mag. History, Bloomington, 1962-64; bookkeeper Touche Ross, Boston, 1974-77; mgr. account services Harvard U., Cambridge, Mass., 1977-81; dir. research and records Bentley Coll., Waltham, Mass., 1982-84; dir. support services Sta. WGBH-TV, Boston, 1985; dir. research Tufts U., Medford, Mass., 1986—; cons. Laduke Assocs., Framingham, Mass., 1972-74, New Eng. Ballet, Sudbury, Mass., 1981-82. v.p. Potter Rd. Sch. Assn., Framingham, 1968-69; chmn. vols. St. Anselm's, Sudbury, 1970-71. Mem. Am. Soc. for Info. Sci, Council for Advancement and Support Edn., New Eng. Online User's Group, Soc. for Competitor Intelligence Profls., Mass. Bus. and Profl. Women (sec. 1981-82), Mensa. Democrat. Roman Catholic. Club: Gem (Framingham) (sec. 1981-83). Home: 15 Auburn St #6 Framingham MA 01701 Office: Tufts U Packard Hall Medford MA 02155

TILGHMAN, MICHELLE LYNN, veterinarian; b. St. Petersburg, Fla., Feb. 5, 1957; d. Henry Woodville and Elizabeth Ann (Wiegand) T.; children: Naia, Rosemary Catherine. BS, Berry Coll., Mt. Berry, Ga., 1978; DVM, U. Ga., 1982. Veterinarian Murray County Vet Svc., Chatsworth, Ga., 1982-83, LBJ Animal Clinic, Balch Springs, Tex., 1983-86; owner, veterinarian Loving Touch Animal Ctr., Stone Mountain, Ga., 1986—; lectr. in field. Mem. Internat. Vet. Accupuncture Soc., Am. Holistic Vet. Soc. (bd. dirs.), Am. Vet. Assn., Stone Mountain Bus. Assn., Audubon Soc., Nat. Wildflower Soc., Dogwood Akita Club. Office: Loving Touch Animal Center 5398 E Mountain St Stone Mountain GA 30083

TILIPKO, LAURA, nursing administrator, educator, consultant; b. N.Y.C., Mar. 16, 1953; d. Peter and Alfreda (Jankowski) T. BA in Polit. Sci., Lebanon Valley Coll., 1975; MS, Pace U./N.Y. Med. Coll., 1979, cert. nurse practitioner, 1979; MPA, Baruch Coll., 1986. RN, N.Y. Staff nurse ICU New York Hosp., N.Y.C., 1979-80; family nurse practitioner Roosevelt Hosp., N.Y.C., 1980-81; adult nurse practitioner Bellevue Hosp., N.Y.C., 1981-82; nursing supr. St. Barnabas Hosp., N.Y.C., 1982-84; asst. dir., project dir. Met. Hosp., N.Y.C., 1984-85; asst. adminstr., dir. nurses No. Dutchess Hosp., Rhinebeck, N.Y., 1985—; advisor nursing curriculum Dutchess Community Coll., Poughkeepsie, N.Y., 1985; advisor Ulster Community Coll., Stone Ridge, N.Y., 1985; advisor econs. com. SUNY-New Paltz, 1986. Mem. com., faculty Am. Heart Assn., Poughkeepsie, 1985-86, chmn. nursing edn. com.; bd. dirs. Hospice of Dutchess Ct. Mem. Am. Nursing Assn. (cert. family nursing practice), Sigma Theta Tau, Pi Gamma Mu. Avocations: scuba diving, skiing, swimming. Home: 245A Patrick Dr La Grangeville NY 12540

TILLER, KATHLEEN BLANCHE (KAY TILLER), public relations consultant; b. Dallas, Nov. 11, 1925; d. Frank L. and Blanche Carrington (Hillyer) T. AA, Whitworth Coll., 1944; BJ, U. Tex., 1946. Reporter Laurel (Miss.) Leader Call, 1946; editor Winnsboro (Tex.) News, 1947-48, Seguin (Tex.) Gazette and others, 1955-56; account exec. Van Cronkhite & Maloy Pub. Rels., Dallas, 1970-73; dir. pub. rels. Crume & Assocs., Dallas, 1973-74; owner, pres. Kay Tiller Pub. Rels., Richardson, Tex., 1974—; v.p. Women in Communications, Inc., Dallas, 1973-74. Contbr. articles to newspapers, mags., and books. Mem. Dallas County Hist. Commn., Dallas, 1977-83. Recipient Matrix award Women in Communications, Dallas, 1975. Pub. Relations Soc. Am. (com. chair N. Tex. chpt. 1988-89, accredited, 1990), Am. Soc. Landscape Architects (pub. relations chmn. Tex. chpt. 1981-90), Garden Writers Am., Tex. Golf Writers Assn., Press Club Tex. (bd. dirs. 1983-85, 90—, pub. relations dir. 1983-89). Republican. Baptist. Home and Office: Kay Tiller Pub Rels 625 Kirby Ln Richardson TX 75080

TILLINGHAST, META IONE, civic worker; b. Newark, Nov. 14; d. Ralph Vincent and Florence Virginia (MacDonald) Muldoon; m. Frederick William Tillinghast; children: Anne (Mrs. Robert Riley), Patricia (Mrs. Charles McLaughlin). Student, Leland Powers Sch. of Spoken Word, Boston. Bd. dirs. Balt. chpt. ARC, 1955-58, chmn. Queen Anne's chpt. 1964-66, nat. bd. govs., 1966-69, Md. state fund chmn., 1969-71, Delmarva div. chmn. mems., funds, 1971-73, vols., 1971-74, coord. community relations Eastern area, 1975-76; chmn. vols. nat. field office (now Eastern field office) ARC, Alexandria, Va., 1976-83, regional chmn. Eastern ops., 1983-86, chmn. vols. Del. chpt., 1986-88, chmn. vols. Nat. Hist. Resources, 1986—, mem. nat. hist. resource com.; dir. ch. plays; chmn. United Fund Baltimore County (Md.) Women's div., 1950. Named vol. of year Md., ARC, 1965; recipient award Gen. Fedn. Women's Clubs, 1952. Mem. Md. No. Dist. Fedn. Women's Clubs (pres. 1953-55), Women's Glyndon Club (pres. 1949-51), Talbot County Women's Club (pres. 1962-64), Women's Ten Hills Club (pres. 1940-42). Home: Nesbit Rd Rt 3 Box 24 Queenstown MD 21658

TILLIS, ROSALYN BRANTLEY, educational consultant; b. Johnson County, Ga., June 6, 1932; d. Grady Harmon and Nevelyn Oree (Colston) Brantley; m. C. Richard Tillis; children: Marcia Jeralyn, Grady Brantley. BS in Elem. Edn., Ga. So. U., 1952; MS in Curriculum and Instrn., Fla. Atlantic U., 1966. Cert. tchr., Fla. Elem. tchr. Burke County Bd. Edn., Waynesboro, Ga., 1952-56, Chatham County Bd. Edn., Savannah, Ga., 1956-57, Palm Beach County Bd. Pub. Instrn., West Palm Beach, Fla., 1957-68; planner, tchr. summer program Pine Jog Environ. Ctr., West Palm Beach, 1967-69; environ. specialist Fla.-Caribbean dist. U.S. Nat. Park Svc., Tallahassee, 1972-74; project assoc. Fla. State U., Tallahassee, 1975-76; coord. energy edn. Fla. Gov.'s Energy Office, Tallahassee, 1976-82; cons., owner, mgr. RBT Enterprises, Tallahassee, 1974-75, 82—; cons. Dozier Sch. for Boys, Marianna, Fla., 1988-90. Author, co-author tchr. guides for energy education. Mem. environ. awards com. Bd. Leon County Commrs., Tallahassee, 1989-91; vol. Chiles-MacKay for Gov., Tallahassee, 1990. Recipient award of distinction Ga. So. U., 1972, Alumnus of Yr. award, 1973, Fla. Conservationist of Yr. award Sears, Roebuck and Co., 1979; named hon. citizen City of Daytona Beach, Fla., 1982. Mem. Fla. Wildlife Fedn. (regional rep. 1983-85, Fla. Conservationist of Yr. award 1979), Fla. Fedn. Garden Clubs (regional environ. and energy officer 1989-90). Democrat. Primitive Baptist. Home and Office: 2812 Roscommon Dr Tallahassee FL 32308

TILLMAN, KAY HEIDT, real estate executive; b. Tampa, Fla., Jan. 24, 1945; d. Clarence Eugene and Doris (Tyson) Heidt; m. Thomas E. Barnes, Mar. 18, 1967 (div. 1972); children: Britton H., William H.; m. Herbert A. Tillman, Oct. 7, 1988. BA with honors, Rollins Coll., 1975, MS with honors, 1979. Lic. real estate sales person, Fla. Tchr. art Orange County Sch. Bd., Orlando, Fla., 1976-79; pres., owner Internat. Handcraft Ctr., Winter Garden, Fla., 1980-83, Decors Internat., Inc., Winter Garden, Fla., 1980-83, Mohamad & Barnes Investment Co., Orlando, Fla., 1983—, Eagle Investment Properties, Orlando, 1985—, Eagle-One Internat., Winter Garden, 1986—; v.p., ptnr. Eagle Mktg. Group, Inc., Winter Garden, 1989—; cons. Nigerian Govt., Lagos, Nigeria, 1987-88, Mid-East Investment Group, Orlando, Fla., 1986-89. Pres. coun. Orlando C. of C., 1987-88. Miss. Fla., Am. Beauty Pageant, Long Beach, Calif., 1975. Mem. Am. Soc. Ind. Sec., Orlando Bd. Realtors, Alpha Chi Omega (v.p. 1966). Republican. Methodist. Home: 215 Valencia Shores Dr Winter Garden FL 34787 Office: Eagle One Internat PO Box 770397 Winter Garden FL 34777-0397

TILLMAN, MARY ANNE TUGGLE, pediatrician; b. Bristow, Okla., Sept. 4, 1935; d. Thomas Gus and Ruthie (English) Tuggle; B.S., Howard U., 1956, M.D., 1960; postgrad. Harvard Grad. Med. Sch., 1965; m. Daniel Tillman, Apr. 20, 1957; children—Dana, Daniel. Intern, Homer G. Phillips Hosp., St. Louis, 1960-61, resident pediatrics, 1961-63; practice medicine, specializing in pediatrics, St. Louis, 1963—; dir. nurseries Homer G. Phillips Hosp., St. Louis, 1964-79, St. Louis City Hosp., 1979-85; mem. staffs St. Louis Children's, Deaconess, Barnes, Jewish hosps.; asst. prof. Washington U. Sch. Medicine, St. Louis, 1963—, pediatric cons. Project Head Start, 1969—. Recipient Woman of Year award Zeta Phi Beta, 1970; Woman of Achievement, St. Louis Globe Democrat, 1982. Diplomate Am. Bd. Pediatrics. Fellow Am. Acad. Pediatrics (nat. com. adoptions 1969—); mem. Am., Nat. med. assns., Am. Med. Women's Assn. Presbyterian. Contbr. articles to profl. publs. Home: 26 Washington Terr Saint Louis MO 63112 Office: Northland Office Bldg 330 W Florissant at Lucas Hunt Saint Louis MO 63136

TILLMAN, MARY NORMAN, urban affairs consultant; b. Atlanta, Jan. 31, 1926; d. Mary Nellie Shehee; B.A., Morris Brown Coll., 1947; postgrad. U. Minn., 1964, Old Dominion U., 1975—; m. James A. Tillman, Jr., Apr. 11, 1952; children—James A., Gina G. Asst. bus. mgr. Morris Brown Coll., Atlanta, 1947-53; race relations and urban affairs cons. Tillman Assos. Cons. Social Engrs., Atlanta and Syracuse, N.Y., 1963—, sr. partner, treas., from 1965, now pres.; clin. prof. United Theol. Sem., New Brighton, Minn.; adj. prof. Gordon-Conwell Theol. Sem., South Hamilton, Mass. Mem. adv. council to urban ministries dept. So. Bapt. Conv.; bd. dirs. Christian Council Met. Atlanta, Tillman Inst. Human Relations. Mem. Tidewater Assn. Public

Adminstrs. (dir.), Am. Acad. Consultants, Nat. Black Writers Consortium (v.p.), Joint Ctr. for Polit. Studies. Author: What is Your Racism Quotient?, 1964; (with James A. Tillman, Jr.) Why America Needs Racism and Poverty, 1972; (with J.A. Tillman, Jr.) Black Intellectuals, White Liberals and Race Relations: An Analytic Overview, 1973;What Is Your Exclusivity Quotient, 1978; also articles. Office: 1765 Glenview Dr SW Atlanta GA 30331

TILLY, LOLA CREMEANS, retired home economics educator; b. Wayside, Ill., Jan. 16, 1898; d. John W. and Samantha Jean Cremeans; m. Gray S. Tilly, May 17, 1937 (dec. 1973); 1 foster child, Gray Wangelin. BA, U. Ill., 1920, MS, 1921; HHD (hon.), U. Alaska, 1963. Tchr. Benton (Ill.) High Sch., 1921-23; instr. home econs. Ill. Normal U., 1922, U. Minn., St. Paul, 1927-29; tchr., head home econs. dept. West Cen. Sch., Morris, Minn., 1923-27; prof. home econs., head dept. U. Alaska, Fairbanks, 1929-63, prof. emeritus, 1963—; weekly columnist Daily News Miner, Fairbanks, 1942—; announcer radio sta., Fairbanks, 1942—. Contbr. articles to profl. jours. Past camp dir. 4-H Club, Harding Lake, Alaska; past pres. Presbyn. Women's Group, Fairbanks, Farthest North coun. Girl Scouts U.S.A.; past elder Presbyn. Ch., Fairbanks. Lola Tilly Commons Bldg., U. Alaska, named in her honor, 1985; recipient Disting. Alumnus award U. Ill., 1987, Dir.'s award Sch. Human Resources and Family Studies, 1987; named Disting. Illumnus U. Ill., 1988. Mem. Nat. Ret. Tchrs. Assn. (chmn. bd. dirs. 1980-82, joint chmn. bd. dirs. with Am. Assn. Ret. Persons 1978-82),, VFW Ladies Aux. (past pres. Fairbanks), P.E.O. (past pres. chpt. B), Order Eastern Star, Phi Beta Kappa, Omicron Mu, Phi Delta Kappa, Iota Sigma Pi. Home: Pioneers' Home 2221 Eagan St Fairbanks AK 99701

TILLY, LOUISE AUDINO, history and sociology educator; b. Orange, N.J., Dec. 13, 1930; d. Hector and Piera (Roffino) Audino; m. Charles Tilly, Aug. 15, 1953; children: Christopher, Kathryn, Laura, Sarah. BA, Rutgers U., 1952; MA, Boston U., 1955; PhD, U. Toronto, 1974. From instr. to asst. prof. Mich. State U., East Lansing, 1972-75; from asst. prof. to prof. U. Mich., Ann Arbor, 1975-84; prof. history and sociology, chair com. hist. studies New Sch. for Social Rsch., N.Y.C., 1984—; assoc. dir. studies Ecole des Hautes Etudes en Sciences Sociales, Paris, 1979, 80, 88; fellow Shelby Cullom Davis Ctr., Princeton (N.J.) U., 1978; vis. mem. Inst. for Advanced Study, Princeton, 1987-88; bd. dirs. Social Scis. Rsch. Coun., N.Y.C., 1983-86. Co-author: The Rebellious Century, 1975; Women, Work and Family, 1978, rev. edit., 1987; co-editor: Class Conflict and Collective Action, 1981; co-author, co-editor Women, Politics and Change, 1990; also articles. Active com. on women's employment and related social issues Nat. Acad. Scis., 1981-86, chmn., co-editor report Panel on Tech. and Women's Employment, 1984-86. Grantee Rockefeller Found., 1974-76, Am. Philos. Soc., 1977-78, 85-86, Russell Sage Found., 1985-86; Guggenheim Found. fellow, 1991—. Mem. Am. Hist. Assn. (coun. 1985-87), Social Sci. History Assn. (pres. 1981-82), Coun. on European Studies (exec. com. 1980-83), Berkshire Conf. Women Historians. Democrat. Home: 61 Irving Place Apt 6C New York NY 10003 Office: Com on Hist Studies 64 University Pl New York NY 10003

TILSON, KATHERINE ANNE, medical practice manager; b. Cin., Mar. 21, 1951; d. Paul Joseph Walter and Anne Elizabeth (Kleemann) Centner; m. Dennis Bascombe Tilson, II, June 8, 1974. B.S. in Nursing, Med. Ctr. U. Kans.-Kansas City, 1973; M.B.A., Avila Coll., 1983. R.N., Kans., Mo. Staff nurse U. Kans. Med. Ctr., Kansas City, 1973-76, Menorah Med. Ctr., Kansas City, 1976-78; nursing coordinator Kelly Health Care, Inc., Kansas City, 1978, nursing supr., 1978-79, br. mgr., service dir., 1979-83; mgr. ServiceMaster Home Health Care Services, Kansas City, 1983, adminstr., 1983-84; cons. Am. Nursing Resources, Inc., Kansas City, 1984, adminstr. Am. Nursing Resources Home Health Agy., Inc., 1985-88, exec. dir. Am. Nursing Resources, Inc., Kansas City, Mo., 1984-88; med. practice mgr. Drs. Brothers and Centner, Kansas City, 1988—; jr. faculty liaison for home health nursing practice residency tng. program S.S.M. Family Practice, Kansas City, 1982-83; mem. in-home services com. Johnson County Area Agy. on Aging, 1982-83. Mem. Challinor Guild, St. Andrew's Episcopal Ch., 1981-89, choir, 1980—, Scola Cantorum, 1984-85, Metro Discharge Planners Group, 1985-88, Mayor's Corps of Progress for Greater Kansas City, 1980-83. Mem. Broadway Bus. Assn., Mid-Am. Regional Council (in-home services task force 1980-87, in-home services com. 1979-87), Kansas City Regional Home Health Assn. (bd. dirs. 1979-83, mem., chmn. coms.), Kansas City C. of C. Republican. Avocations: piano; singing; sailing; swimming; sports; sewing; gardening. Home: 4600 W 66th St Prairie Village KS 66208 Office: Drs Brothers and Centner 2727 Main Suite 201 Kansas City MO 64108

TILTON, BERNICE SHEPPARD (MRS. EARLE BARTON TILTON), civic worker; b. Chgo.; d. Samuel Charles and Elizabeth (Keith) Sheppard; Mus.B., Wis. Coll. Music, 1954; m. Earle Barton Tilton, Mar. 12, 1940. Performed as soloist and two-piano team for orgns., Ill., Wis., Fla., 1947—. Pres., Symphony Club, Clearwater, Fla., 1958-60; founder Mus. Arts Soc., Clearwater, 1960, pres., 1960-62, 81-83; chpt. pres. Delta Omicron, 1964-66, Fla. chmn. alumnae-at-large, 1965-67, internat. v.p. alumnae, internat. bd. dirs., 1967-71; pres. Fla. West Coast Panhellenic Assn., 1967-68, chpt. adv. bd., 1968—. Bd. dirs. Clearwater Community Concert Assn., 1963-74. Recipient Gold Star Delta Omicron, 1967, Recognition award, 1971. Mem. Nat. Soc. Arts and Letters (local sec., v.p. 1972-73), Henry Solomon Lehr Soc. (life), Delta Omicron (alumnae chpt. pres. 1973-74, 81-84, rec. sec. 1985-88). Home: 6 Belleview Blvd Apt 608 Belleair FL 34616

TILTON, TANYA TYLENE, naval officer; b. Anamosa, Iowa, Aug. 25, 1960; d. Terold Tilman and Wylma Rose (Doty) T.; m. Robert Benton Spengler, Nov. 26, 1988. BBA, Iowa State U., 1983; MBA, Golden Gate U., 1987. Commd. ensign USN, 1983, advanced through grades to lt., 1987; adminstrv. asst. to chief naval ops. USN, Washington, 1984-87; exec. officer for pers. and leadership USN, Memphis, 1987-89; staff readiness and automated processing officer USNR, San Diego, 1989—. Decorated Navy Commendation medal (2). Mem. NAFE, Naval Res. Assn. Methodist. Office: 960 N Habor Dr San Diego CA 92132-5108

TIMANUS, DEBRA DUNSTON, public relations professional; b. Dyersburg, Tenn., Jan. 31, 1953; d. Nally B. and Winnie (Turner) Dunston; m. Richard Anthony Timanus, Feb. 13, 1988. BS, U. Tenn., Martin, 1975; MBA, Memphis State U., 1977. Employability counselor State of Tenn., Dyersburg, 1976-84; dir. mktg. Meth. Hosp. Dyersburg, 1984-87; pub. rels. mgr. Charter Lakeside Hosp., Memphis, 1987—. Rep., Corp. Vol. Assn., Memphis, 1987—. Mem. Am. Soc. Hosp. Mktg. and Pub. Rels., Kappa Delta Alumni Orgn. Democrat. Mem. Ch. of Christ. Home: 346 Meadow Trail Cove Cordova TN 38018 Office: Charter Lakeside Hosp 2911 Brunswick Rd Memphis TN 38133

TIMM, MARIANNA, nurse; b. Passaic, N.J., Mar. 25, 1947; d. Wolfgang Richard and Ann Patricia (Kress) T. Nursing diploma, St. Mary's Hosp. Sch. Nursing, Passaic, 1967; BS in Nursing, Rutgers U., Newark, 1982; MS in Nursing, U. Pa., 1988. Staff nurse St. Mary's Hosp., 1967-69, 73-75, head nurse, 1969-73, 75-78, staff nurse, 1978-82; staff nurse Mountainside Hosp., Montclair, N.J., 1982-83, 84-87, patient care coordinator, 1987-88; inservice instr. St. Mary Hosp., Hoboken, N.J., 1983-84; clin. nurse specialist U. Medicine and Surgery N.J., Newark, 1989—. Bd. dirs. Am. Heart Assn., Clifton, N.J., 1987-89; chmn. speakers bur., 1988-89. Mem. Am. Nurses Assn. (cert. med.-surg. nurse), N.J. Nurses Assn. (bylaws com. 1988-90), Oncology Nursing Soc., Sigma Theta Tau. Roman Catholic. Home: 71 E 6th St Clifton NJ 07011 Office: U Medicine & Dentistry NJ 150 Bergen St Newark NJ 07103

TIMMERMANN, BARBARA NAWALANY, phytochemical educator; b. Bury St. Edmunds, England, May 30, 1947; came to U.S., 1970; d. Tadeusz and Helena (Komarowska) Nawalany; m. Ricardo G. Timmermann, Oct. 17, 1969 (div. 1980); Erik R., Dirk A. BA, U. Cordoba, Argentina, 1969; MA, U. Tex., Austin, 1977, PhD, 1980. Rsch. assoc. U. Ariz., Tucson, 1981-85, asst. rsch. scientist, 1985-87, asst. prof., 1987-90, assoc. prof. dept. pharm. sci., 1990—; chair Arid Lands Resource Scis. PhD com., Tucson, 1988-89. Editor: Phytochemical Adaptations to Stress, 1984, Arid Lands Today and Tomorrow, 1985; contbr. articles to profl. jours. Grantee NSF, 1983—, Tinker Found., N.Y.C., 1988. Mem. AAAS, Phytochem. Soc. N.Am., Phytochem. Soc. Europe, Internat. Soc. Chem. Ecology, Botan. Soc. Am. Office: Univ Ariz Dept Pharm Sci Tucson AZ 85721

TIMMONS, ALFREDA JOYCE, human resources administrator; b. Montgomery, Ala., July 4, 1956; d. Romie and Maurice (Green) Mays; m. James Timmons, July 17, 1977; children: Brian Cory, Jason Michael. BS with honors, Ala. State U., 1976. Sr. design assoc. AT&T Bell Labs., Naperville, Ill., 1977-79, employment rep., 1979-83, pub. rels. rep., 1983-86, supr. tng. and edn., 1986-87; employment specialist Argo-Tech Corp., Cleve., 1988; recruitment and security coord. Internat. Gear Corp., Cleve., 1989—; cons., Solon, Ohio, 1987—; sec. Career Edn. Adv. Coun., Naperville, 1983-87; chmn. Synergy in Action Seminar, Naperville, 1986. Contbr. articles to profl. jours. Chmn. United Way/Crusade of Mercy Campaign, Naperville, 1986. Mem. Success Net, Delta Sigma Theta. Home: 7381 Cheshire Pl Solon OH 44139 Office: Internat Gear Corp 23555 Euclid Ave Cleveland OH 44117

TIMMONS, ANITA ABBOTT, entrepreneur; b. Kokomo, Ind., Oct. 13, 1938; d. Charles Robert and Nedra Margaret (Seagrave) Abbott; m. James Donald Timmons, Aug. 26, 1961; children: Amy Louise (dec.), Daniel Barnes, Sean Abbott, James Donald Jr. AA, Christian Coll., Columbia, Mo., 1958; BA magna cum laude, Montclair State Coll., 1976. Advt. trainee Huntington (Ind.) Herald Press, 1952-56; claims adjuster Lincoln Nat. Life Ins. Co., Ft. Wayne, Ind., 1958, Washington, 1960; marine ins. supr. David R. Wallace Ins. Co., Washington; exec. asst. Reynolds & Co., N.Y.C., 1961-62; tchr. Montclair (N.J.) Kimberly Acad., 1975-78; ptnr. Taj Enterprises, St. Simons Island, Ga., 1985—; chmn. Taj FBO Corp., Brunswick, Ga., 1986—; pres. Taj Adventure Travel, St. Simons Island, 1988—. Trustee No. Essex Devel. & Action Com., 1981-84, N.J. Chamber Music Soc., 1984—, Phillips Exeter Acad., 1986—, Golden Isles Chamber Music Festival, St. Simons Island, 1989—; pres., trustee, Montclair Kimberly Acad. Parents Assn., 1981-83; v.p. women's com., Montclair Art Mus., 1982-84. Mem. Women's Bus. Orgn., Montclair Golf Club, Jr. League, Williams Club. Republican. Office: Taj Enterprises PO Box 1099 Saint Simons Island GA 31522

TIMMONS, EVELYN DEERING, pharmacist; b. Durango, Colo., Sept. 29, 1926; d. Claude Elliot and Evelyn Allen (Gooch) Deering; m. Richard Palmer Timmons, Oct. 4, 1952 (div. 1968); children: Roderick Deering, Steven Palmer. BS in Chemistry and Pharmacy cum laude, U. Colo., 1948. Chief pharmacist Meml. Hosp., Phoenix, 1950-54; med. lit. rsch. librarian Hoffman-LaRoche, Inc., Nutley, N.J., 1956-57; staff pharmacist St. Joseph's Hosp., Phoenix, 1958-60; relief mgr. various ind. apothecaries, Phoenix, 1960-68; asst. then mgr. Profl. Pharmacist, Inc., Phoenix, 1968-72; mgr. then owner Mt. View Pharmacy, Phoenix and Paradise Valley, Ariz., 1972—; pres. Ariz. Apothecaries, Ltd., Phoenix, 1976—; mem. profl. adv. bd., bereavement counselor Hospice of Valley, 1983—; mem. profl. adv. bd. Upjohn Health Care and Svcs., Phoenix, 1984-86; bd. dirs. Am. Council on Pharm. Edn., Chgo., 1986—, v.p. 1988, 89. Author poetry; contbr. articles to profl. jours. Mem. Scottsdale (Ariz.) Fedn. Rep. Women, 1963; various other offices Rep. Fedn.; mem. platform com. State of Ariz., Nat. Rep. Conv., 1964; asst. sec. Young Rep. Nat. Fedn., 1963-65; active county and state Rep. coms. Named Outstanding Young Rep. of Yr., Nat. Fedn. Young Reps., 1965, Preceptor of Yr., U. Ariz./Syntex, 1984; recipient Disting. Public Svc. award Maricopa County Med. Soc., 1962, Disting. Alumni award Wasatch Acad., 1982, Leadership and Achievement award Upjohn Labs., 1985-86, Outstanding Achievement in Profession award Merck, Sharp & Dohme, 1986, Disting. Coloradoan award U. Colo., 1989. Fellow Am. Coll. of Apothecaries (v.p. 1982-83, pres. 1984-85; chmn. bd. dirs. 1985-86, adv. council 1986—, Chmn. of Yr. 1980-81 Victor H. Morganroth award 1985); mem. Ariz. Soc. of Hosp. Pharmacists, Am. Pharmacy Assn. (Daniel B. Smith award 1990), Ariz. Pharmacy Assn. (Svc. to Pharmacy award 1976, Pharmacist of Yr. 1981, Bowl of Hygeia 1989), Maricopa County Pharmacy Assn. (pres. 1977, Svc. to Pharmacy award 1977), Am. Soc. of Hosp. Pharmacists, Aux. to County Med. Soc. (pres. 1967-68), Am. Aircraft Owners and Pilots Assn., Nat. Assn. of Registered Parliamentarians. Lodge: Civinettes (pres. Scottsdale chpt. 1960-61). Avocations: flying, skiing, swimming, backpacking, hiking. Office: Mt View Pharmacy 10565 N Tatum Blvd Suite B-118 Paradise Valley AZ 85253

TINDALL, JILL DENISE, music educator; b. Akron, Iowa, Aug. 25, 1958; d. Rollin Jay and Mary Alice (Clark) T. MusB, Morningside Coll., 1980; MusM, Fla. State U., Tallahassee, 1981; postgrad., Ind. U., 1982-83, U. Iowa, 1983-84. Cert. music tchr., Ariz. Freelance violinist Sioux City (Iowa) Symphony Orch., 1976-80, S.D. Symphony Orch., Sioux Falls, 1976-80; asst. condr. Fla. State U. Orch., Tallahassee, 1980-81; coach, asst. condr. Ind. U. Opera Theater, Bloomington, 1982-83; asst. condr. U. Iowa Orchs., Iowa City, 1983-84, Greater Miami (Fla.) Opera Assn., 1984-85; freelance musician Siouxland Region, 1985-87; instr. in music Ea. Ariz. Coll., Thatcher, 1987—; pres., artistic dir. Gila Valley Arts Coun., Safford, Ariz., 1989—. Friend Sta. KUAT, Tucson, 1989—. Mem. Am. Symphony Orch. League, Chamber Music of Am., Music Educators Nat. Conv., Ariz. Music Educators (sec. 1989—), Met. Opera Guild. Methodist. Home: 2807 12th Ave Apt 606 Safford AZ 85546 Office: Ea Ariz Coll 600 Church St Thatcher AZ 85552

TINDALL, MONICA ELAINE, marketing professional; b. Jacksonville, Fla., Feb. 12, 1953; d. Douglas Campbell and Lucy (Balestrini) T. BA, U. North Fla., 1976. Mktg. exec. Am. Hosp. Supply, Cin., 1977-79; mgr. nat. account programs Gen. Electric Med. Systems, Milw., 1979-85; mgr. mktg. svcs. Internat. Imaging, Chgo., 1985-88; mgr. strategic mktg. Toshiba Am. Med. Systems, Tustin, Calif., 1988—.

TINER, DONNA TOWNSEND, nurse; b. Memphis, Dec. 14, 1947; d. Jack Edwin and Anne Coolidge (Burleigh) Townsend; m. Clinton William Matson, Aug. 30, 1969 (div. 1976); m. Dow David Tiner, Apr. 15, 1978; children: Jeffrey David, Cynthia Leigh, Catherine Renee. Grad., Bapt. Meml. Hosp. Sch. Nursing, Memphis, 1969. RN, Ark. Nurse Bapt. Meml. Hosp., Memphis, 1969, New Bern (N.C.) Surgical Assocs., 1970-71, Bapt. Meml. Hosp, 1971-72, Meml. Hosp., North Little Rock, Ark., 1972-73, Bapt. Med. Ctr., North Little Rock, Ark., 1974-87; practice nursing specializing in post-anesthesia care Little Rock, 1987-89; post-anesthesia care specialist Freeway Surgery Ctr., Little Rock, 1989—. Instr., ARC, 1975—, Instr. Am. Red Cross, 1975-80; leader Park Hill Bapt. Ch., 1986—. 1st. lt. U.S. Army Med. Unit 1976-79. Mem. Am. Soc. Post Anesthesia Nurses (chartered), Ark. Post Anesthesia Care Nurses, Alumnae Assn. Bapt. Hosp. Sch. Nursing. Republican. Home: 12 Knights Bridge Sherwood AR 72116

TINGEY, CAROL, psychologist, educator; b. St. James, Mo., Sept. 24, 1933; d. Willis Alma and Lola (Madsen) T.; children: Richard, Blaine, James, Neil, Trish. BS magna cum laude, U. Utah, 1970, MEd, 1971, PhD, 1976. Tchr. public schs., Salt Lake City, 1970, spl. edn. tchr., 1971-72; clin. instr. spl. edn. U. Utah, Salt Lake City, 1972-74; dir. staff devel. Utah State Tng. Sch., American Fork, Utah, 1974-75; asst. prof. spl. edn. U. No. Iowa, Cedar Falls, 1975-77; asst. prof. spl. edn. Trinity Coll., Washington, 1977-78; asst. prof. spl. edn. of severely handicapped George Mason U., Fairfax, Va., 1978-79; assoc. prof. edn. and tng. physically and multi-handicapped Northwestern State U. of La., Natchitoches, 1979-81; assoc. prof. spl. edn. Ill. State U., Normal, also coordinator program for physically handicapped, 1981-83; assoc. prof. psychology Utah State U., Logan, 1983-88; psychologist Bear River Mental Health, Brigham City, Utah, 1988-90; psychologist Western Rehab. Inst., Salt Lake City, 1990—; bd. dirs. Nat. Down Syndrome Congress; researcher, cons. in field. Fellow Am. Assn. on Mental Retardation (sec. Utah chpt. 1975, ednl. chmn. region VIII 1976-77, treas. edn. div. 1979-80, editorial com., chair Down Syndrome Spl. Interest Group, mem. edit. adv. bd., 1989—) mem. Assn. for Severely Handicapped, Council for Exceptional Children (pres. Utah chpt. 1974-75), Assn. for Retarded Citizens, Phi Delta Kappa, Phi Kappa Phi. Author: Home and School Partnerships in Exceptional Education; Handicapped Infants and Children: Handbook for Parents and Professionals; New Perspectives on Down Syndrome; Down Syndrome: A Resource Handbook; Implementing Early Intervention; contbr. articles to profl. jours.; recorded albums: Self Help Skills, Adaptive Behavior; Socialization Skills; Adaptive Behavior; Daily Living Tasks, Housekeeping Skills, Vocational Awareness, Community Helpers; editorial adv. bd. Exceptional Parent mag., Infants and Young Children mag. Home: Essex Ct Midvale UT 84047 Office: 195 W 7200 S Midvale UT 84047

TINKER, CYNTHIA ALOMA, teacher; b. Miami, Fla., May 13, 1953; d. George Whitfield and Verne Elizabeth (Taylor) Tinker. AA, Miami Dade Community Coll., 1973; BS, Fla. Meml. Coll., 1976. Cert. tchr., Fla. Substitute tchr. Dade County Schs. Mem. Unrepresented People, Positive Action Coun., Opalocka, Fla., 1986-. With U.S. Army, 1979-82. Mem. AAUW, NAACP, Daus. of the King, Alpha Kappa Alpha, Gamma Zeta Omega. Democrat. Episcopalian. Home: 2501 NW 162 St Opalocka FL 33054

TINKER, DEBRA ANN, systems analyst; b. Cleve., June 27, 1951; d. Keith Donald and Rita Patricia (Rowinski) T.; m. Charles Earl Enos, Aug. 6, 1983; children: Christopher Tinker Enos, Matthew Tinker Enos. BS in Edn. cum laude, Ohio U., 1973; MA in Clin. and Community Psychology, Chapman Coll., 1988. Tchr. English, remedial reading Northmont Jr. High Sch., Clayton, Ohio, 1973-76; dance instr. Schehera's Studio, Dayton, Ohio, 1974-76; substitute tchr. Knox County Schs., Mt. Vernon, Ohio, 1976; tchr. English, remedial reading Ohio Youth Commn., Massillon, Ohio, 1977; coord. spl. needs program Knox County Joint Vocat. Sch., Mt. Vernon, 1977-82; life ins. sales Belding and Assocs., Mt. Vernon, 1980-82; student control officer Naval Air Tng. Unit, Sacramento, 1982-85; dir. Navy Counseling and Assistance Ctr., Charleston, S.C., 1985-88; chief counseling svcs. Navy Family Svc. Ctr., Charleston, 1988-89; program analyst Navy Drug and Alcohol Program Hdqrs., Washington, 1989—. Leader Girl Scouts U.S., Dayton, Ohio Counsel, 1975-76, mem., cons. North Charleston, S.C., 1987-88; exec. producer Mt. Vernon AWARE, 1977-81; mem. Charleston Area DUI Prevention Coun., 1987-88; mem. Navy Family Advocacy Support Team, Charleston, 1985-89, Navy Alcohol and Drug Adv. Coun., Charleston, 1985-88, chairwoman, 1988; bd. dirs. Exch. Club Ctr. for the Prevention of Child Abuse, Charleston, 1987-88, mem. adv. com. Promulgation Child Abuse and Neglect Definitions, 1989. Lt. USNR, 1982—. Mem. Am. Psychol. Assn. (assoc.), Women Officer's Profl. Assn., Soc. Mayflower Descendants, Mensa, Kappa Delta Pi. Lutheran. Home: 202 Brailsford Rd Summerville SC 29485 Office: Navy Drug and Alcohol Program COMMAUMICPERSCOM Code N-63C Washington DC 20370

TINKLE, F. LORAIN, lawyer; b. Sioux City, Iowa, Jan. 4, 1913; d. David Alexander and Flora Mary (McKay) Aitken; m. Lloyd LaVern Tinkle, Dec. 25, 1940. BA, Morningside Coll., 1934; JD, U. S.D., 1948; MLS, Vanderbilt U., 1967. Bar: S.D. 1948, Iowa 1957. Tchr. bus. edn. various pub. schs., 1936-40, 1965; instr. in law Joliet (Ill.) Jr. Coll., 1967-78, ret., 1978, part-time instr. in law, 1969—. Bd. dirs. Sioux City Mus. Hist. Soc., 1985. Mem. AAUW, S.D. Bar Assn., Iowa Bar Assn., Federated Woman's Club, Order of Eastern Star. Republican. Presbyterian. Home: 1903 Rebecca St Sioux City IA 51103

TINNELL, CAROL ANN, non-profit association administrator; b. Seattle, Apr. 20, 1959; d. Ernest Elmer and Thelma Aletha (Keebaugh) Wentz; m. Michael Warren Tinnell, July 11, 1981 (div. Apr. 1988). BA in Communications, U. Portland, 1981. Reporter, photographer Daily Jour. Commerce/Sports People N.W., Portland, Oreg., 1981; sr. assoc. United Way of the Columbia-Willamette, Portland, 1982—; cons. Chapman Howarth Dental Group, Portland, 1982. Contbr. articles to newspapers. Vol., Multnomah County Spl. Olympics, Portland, 1987—; mem. pub. relations com. Global Vision Found., Portland, 1989—; vol. editor Lions Eyebank Oreg., Portland, 1990. Mem. Women in Communications Inc. (nat. bd. dirs., regional v.p. 1989—, pres. Portland chpt. 1987-88, Outstanding Membership Contbn. 1989), Order of the Amaranth (sec. 1985-87), Eastern Star. Democrat. Nazarene. Home: 3729 NE 47th St Portland OR 97213

TINSLEY, SHELIA C., nurse; b. Roanoke, Va., Nov. 8, 1955; d. Irvin Daniel and Mary Davis (Flippen) Childress; m. Carl Terrie Tinsley, Sept. 4, 1976; children: Carl, De Anthony. Assoc Degree in Nursing, CHRV Coll. Health Sci., Roanoke, 1989. RN. Staff nurse Friendship Manor Nursing Home, Roanoke, Meml. Hosp., Roanoke, Lewis Gale Clinic, Salem, Va. Dir. youth choir Ebenezer A.M.E. Ch. Recipient Award for Nursing Excellence, 1989; Med. Found. scholar. Mem. ANA. Home: 3864 Red Fox Dr NW Roanoke VA 24017 Office: R M Hosp Belliview and Jefferson St SE Roanoke VA 24017

TINSMAN, MARGARET NEIR, state senator; b. Moline, Ill., July 14, 1936; d. Francis Earl and Elizabeth (Laurie) Neir; m. Robert Hovey Tinsman Jr., Feb. 23, 1958; children: Robert Hovey III, Heidi Elizabeth, Bruce McAllister. BA in Sociology, U. Colo., 1958; MSW, U. Iowa, 1974. Health care coord. Community Health Care, Inc., Davenport, Iowa, 1975-77; assoc. dir. Scott County Info., Referal, and Assistance Svc., Davenport, Iowa, 1977-79; county supr. Scott County Bd. Suprs., Davenport, Iowa, 1978-89; senate State of Iowa, Des Moines, 1989—; chair Iowa adv. commn. on inter-govt. rels, 1982-84; U.S. county rep. to the German-Am. Symposium German Marshall Plan, 1983; commr. Iowa Dept. Elder Affairs, Des Moines, 1983-89; senate coms. Appropriations, Edn., Human Resources, Local Govt., Appropriations Subcom., ranking mem. health and human rights, 1989—. Chairperson Planning Com. Quad City United Way, Davenport; bd. dirs. Bi-State Met. Planning Commn., Davenport, 1981-89, Quad City Devel. Group, Davenport, 1988—. Named Iowa Social Worker of Yr., 1978. Mem. Am. Lung Assn. (bd. dirs. 1989—), Davenport C. of C. (local/state govt. com. 1989—), Nat. Assn. Legislators, Nat. Assn. of Counties (bd. dirs. 1984-89, pres. Women Ofcl. 1984-89), Iowa State Assn. of Counties (bd. dirs. 1983-89, chair), Jr. League (sustaining mem. 1989), Vol. Action Ctr. (pres. 1989). Republican. Episcopalian. Home: 2865 Hickory Hill Ln Bettendorf IA 52722 Office: c/o Twin State 3541 E Kimberly Rd Davenport IA 52807*

TINUCCI, GEORGIA MAE, small business owner, designer; b. Chgo., May 12, 1930; d. Philip Arthur and Lillian Georgia (Lish) Sandblom; m. Raymond Peter Tinucci, Aug. 21, 1954; children: Crystal Marie, Peter Steven, Christopher Andrew. Student, Bradley U., 1948-51. Comml. artist Patton, Haggerty & Sullivan, Chgo., 1951-53; color cons. Crafton & Assocs., Chgo., 1953-55; tchr., mgr. publicity Tinucci Music Ctr., Elmwood Park, Ill., 1966-81; pres. Cove Wax Works, Melrose Park, Ill., 1981—. Republican. Home: 1117 8th Ave Addison IL 60101 Office: Cove Wax Works 2311 W Main St Melrose Park IL 60160

TIONGCO, DOLORES DONATO, child psychiatrist; b. Santa Rosa, The Philippines, Apr. 30, 1949; came to U.S., 1979; d. José Zavalla and Antonia (Donato) T. Degree in medicine, U. of East, Quezon City, The Philippines, 1973. Diplomate Am. Bd. Psychiatry, Am. Bd. Child Psychiatry. Intern No. div. Albert Einstein Med. Ctr., 1979-80; resident in psychiatry U. Mich., Ann Arbor, 1983, fellow in child psychiatry, 1984, fellow in adult psychiatry, 1986; dir. adolescent I unit Meadows Psychiat. Ctr., Centre Hall, Pa., 1986—; pres. med. staff Meadows Psychiat. Ctr., 1988—. Recipient fellowship in Child Psychiatry, U. Mich., 1984. Mem. Am. Psychiat. Assn., Am. Acad. Child Psychiatry. Home: 578 Westgate Dr State College PA 16803 Office: Meadows Psychiat Ctr Rd 1 Box 259 Centre Hall PA 16828

TIPPS, TINA J., training and development specialist; b. Clearfield, Utah, June 3, 1962; d. Gordon Eugene and Jeanie Irene Tipps. Ed., Orange Coast Coll. Tng. specialist, sr. tng. specialist Businessland; tng. specialist Computer Consoles, Inc.; sr. courseware devel. specialist, corp. trainer Ashton-Tate, Torrance, Calif.; mgr. tng. and devel. Curaflex Health Svcs. Mem. NAFE. Address: 14156 Sawston Circle Westminster CA 92683

TIPTON, JENNIFER, lighting designer; b. Columbus, Ohio, Sept. 11, 1937; d. Samuel Ridley and Isabel (Hanson) T.; m. William F. Beaton., Aug. 29, 1976. B.A., Cornell U., 1958. Lighting designer Paul Taylor Dance Co., Twyla Tharp and Dancers, 1965, Pa. Ballet Co., 1966, Macbeth, Am. Shakespeare Festival, Stratford, Conn., Harkness Ballet Co., 1967, Dan Wagoner Dancers, Richard II, Love's Labour's Lost, Am. Shakespeare Festival, HB Studios N.Y., 1968, Horseman Pass By, Fortune Theatre, Les Grands Ballet Canadiens, Yvonne Rainer Co., City Center Joffrey Ballet, Our Town Anta Theatre, 1969, Anta Theatre Dance Series, 1971, 72, Eliot Feld Ballet Co., Am. Ballet Theatre from 1971; numerous ballets include Airs, Amnon V'Tamar, Bach Partita, The Little Ballet, N.Y. Export: OP Jazz, Triad, Kazuko Hirabayashi Dance Co., A Ballet Behind the Bridge, Negro Ensemble Co., Delacorte Dance Festival, Houston Ballet Co., 1972, Nat. Ballet Co., Hartford Ballet Co., Celebration: The Art of Pas de Deux, Jerome Robbins, Jose Limon Dance Co., 1973; lighting designer The Tempest, Macbeth, Midsummer Night's Dream, N.Y. Shakespeare Festival-Newhouse Theatre, The Killdeer, Newman Theatre, Jerome Robbins' The Dybbuk, N.Y.C. Ballet, Dreyfus in Rehearsal, Barrymore Theatre, 1974, San

Francisco Ballet Co., Anthony Tudor's The Leaves Are Fading, Am. Ballet Theatre, Habeas Corpus, Martin Beck Theatre, Murder Among Friends, Biltmore Theatre, 1975, Rex, Lunt-Fontanne Theatre, For Colored Girls Who Consider Suicide When the Rainbow is Enuf (Drama Desk award), Booth Theatre, Cleve. Ballet Co., Mikhail Baryshnikov's The Nutcracker, Am. Ballet Theatre, 1976, The Landscape of the Body, Newman Theatre, The Cherry Orchard (Drama Desk award, Tony award 1977), Agamemnon, Beaumont Theatre, Happy End, Martin Beck Theatre, Agamemnon, Delacorte Theatre, 1977, Museum, Public Theatre, Runaways, Public Theatre and Plymouth Theatre, All's Well That Ends Well, Taming of the Shrew, Delacorte Theatre, After the Season, Academy Festival Theatre, A Month in the Country, Williamstown Theatre Festival, Mikhail Baryshnikov's Don Quixote, Am. Ballet Theatre, The Goodbye People, Westport Playhouse, Funny Face, Buffalo Studio Arena, Drinks Before Dinner, Public Theatre, Alice in Wonderland, The Pirates of Penzance, Public Theatre, 1978, Lunch Hour, 1980, Billy Bishop Goes to War, 1980, The Sea Gull, 1980, Sophisticated Ladies, 1981, The Wake of Jamie Foster, 1982, Uncle Vanya, 1983, Orgasmo Adulto Escapes from the Zoo, 1983, Baby with the Bathwater, 1984, Hurlyburly, 1984, Whoopie Goldberg, 1984, Endgame, 1984, The Ballad of Soapy Smith, 1984, Jerome Robbins' Broadway, (Antoinette Perry award, 1989); assoc. dir. Goodman Theatre, Chgo.; lighting instr. Yale U. Sch. Drama. Recipient Creative Arts award Brandeis U., 1981. Office: care Joffrey Ballet 130 W 56 St New York NY 10019*

TIPTON, MARILYN OGLESBY, advertising company executive, consultant; b. Chester, Pa., Nov. 22, 1944; d. Samuel and Martha (Marsden) Oglesby; m. James William Godwin, July 17, 1970 (div. Sept. 1984); m. Noah Ray Tipton, Jan. 3, 1986. BS, Fla. State U., 1966. Tchr. A.V. Clubbs/Gulf Breeze Mid. Sch., Pensacola, Fla., 1966-76; freelance designer Pensacola, 1976-78; exec. dir. Pensacola Escambia Clean Community Commn., 1978-86; cons., nat. rep. Keep Am. Beautiful, Inc., Pensacola, 1979—; pres. Talley Neon & Advt., Richmond, Va., 1988—. Pres. Pensacola Mus. Art, 1979-81; trustee Pensacola Jr. Coll. Found., 1987-89; bd. dirs. Pensacola Symphony Orch., 1987-90. Named Outstanding Young Woman of Am., 1981. Mem. Pensacola Heritage Found., Pensacola Area C. of C., Womens Com. of Richmond Symphony, Jr. League Pensacola. (profl. chmn. 1976), Keep Fla. Beautiful, Inc. (chmn. awards com. 1989—). Republican. Presbyterian. Home: 2010 Park Ave Richmond VA 23220 Office: Talley Neon & Advt Co 1908 Chamberlayne Ave Richmond VA 23222

TIPTON, MARY DAVISON, banker; b. Atlanta, Jan. 11, 1947; d. W. Kay and M. Estelle (Reynolds) T. MA in History, Emory U., 1969, postgrad. in fin., 1978, MBA, 1986. Asst. bank examiner Fed. Res., Atlanta, 1969-72; credit officer 1st Nat. Bank, Atlanta, 1975-77; asst. treas. Bankers Trust, N.Y.C., 1979-81, asst. v.p., 1982; asst. v.p. Amro Bank, N.Y.C., 1983-84; fin. mgr. Reynolds Properties, 1984-86; cons. to Office of Gov. Ga., 1986—; independent fin. cons., 1987—. Author essay: The Analysis of Foreign Banks (Robert Morris Assocs. Contest Southeastern winner 1977), 1977. Vol. tutor adult literacy Martin Luther King Assn., Atlanta, 1975-79; sec. bd. dirs. North Ga. chpt. March of Dimes Birth Defects Found., 1988-90. Mem. Ga. Hunter Jumper Assn., Emory Alumni Club, Phi Beta Kappa, Phi Kappa Phi.

TIRAKIS, JUDITH ANGELINA, financial company executive; b. Bristol, Conn., Oct. 11, 1938; d. Dante and Ines (Paravella) Follandri; m. George Tirakis, July 15, 1967. BA, St. Joseph Coll., West Hartford, Conn., 1956-60; postgrad., St. Joseph Coll., 1960-61. With Engelhard Minerals and Chem. Corp., Menlo Park, N.J., 1964-67; supr. Sci. Info. Ctr. Ciba Geigy Pharm. Co., Summit, N.J., 1967-78; records mgr. research info. Ortho Pharm. Corp. div. Johnsn & Johnson, Raritan, N.J., 1978-86; v.p., corp. records mgr. AMBAC Indemnity Corp., N.Y.C., 1985—. Mem. Assn. Records Mgrs. and Adminstrs., Am. Mgmt. Assn., Nat. Assn. Female Execs., Assn. Image and Info. Mgmt. Office: AMBAC Indemnity Corp 1 State St Plaza New York NY 10004

TIRRELL, JANE MARIE RUTTER, volunteer; b. Phillipsburg, N.J., Apr. 25, 1924; d. John Anthony and Marie M. (Kilpatrick) Rutter; m. James A. Tirrell, Jr., Sept. 17, 1949; 1 child, Gerard Patrick. BA, Conn. Coll., 1946. Chemist cen. rsch. lab. Gen. Aniline & Film Corp., Easton, Pa., 1946-49. Vol. ARC, Phillipsburg, N.J., 1959—, life mem.; trustee Warren County Community Coll., Washington, N.J., 1982— (Svc. award 1983-87), Easton Area YWCA, 1980—; former sec., pres., bd. dirs. jr. aux. Easton Children's Home; former pres. jr. aux. Easton Hosp., Jr. Svc. League Easton; former bd. dirs., v.p. Easton YWCA; former bd. dirs., vice chmn. Phillipsburg Red Cross; former chmn. Warren County Children's Com.; former coll. leader Girl Scouts U.S. Rotary Citizenship award Rotary Club, Phillipsburg, 1985, Svc. award Children's Home Easton, 1972, 7000 Hour award Warren Hosp., Phillipsburg, 1987. Mem. Northampton Country Club. Republican. Roman Catholic. Home: 3050 Belvidere Rd Phillipsburg NJ 08865

TIRRELL, JANET ANTHONY, public relations generalist; b. Piedmont, Calif., July 13, 1938. BA in Polit. Sci., U. Calif., Berkeley, 1961, MA in Edn., 1968; postgrad. in bus. adminstrn., Fordham U. Tchr. English Orinda Union Sch. Dist., Calif., 1962-68; coordinator ednl. research, edn. counselor Hill & Knowlton Inc., N.Y.C., 1968-70; cons., writer Ednl. Systems & Designs, Westport, Conn., 1974; writer, producer Producers Row Inc., N.Y.C., 1975. Mem. championship synchronized swimming team; appearances include Australian Olympics, Brussels World Fair, Ed Sullivan Show. Recipient Helms award, 1963 (All-American 1956-61).

TISHKIN, NANCY ANN, university administrator; b. San Francisco, Aug. 18, 1959; d. Constantine Alexis and Pamela Ann (Maddock) T. BS, Bowling Green (Ohio) State U., 1981; postgrad., Case Western Res. U., 1981—. Sec. Case Western Res. U., Cleve., 1981-85, dept. asst., 1985-86, asst. to sec. of corp., 1986-89, asst. sec. of corp., 1989, acting sec. of corp., 1989-90; sec. corp. Case Western Res. U., 1990—. Mem. AAUW (treas. 1986-90, corr. sec. 1990—, grantee 1988). Office: Case Western Res U 2040 Adelbert Rd Cleveland OH 44106

TISINGER, CATHERINE ANNE, university executive; b. Winchester, Va., Apr. 6, 1936; d. Richard Martin and Irma Regina (Ohl) T. BA, Coll. Wooster, 1958; MA, U. Pa., 1962, PhD, 1970; LLD (hon.), Coll. of Elms, 1985. Provost Callison Coll., U. of Pacific, Stockton, Calif., 1971-72; v.p. Met. State U., St. Paul, 1972-75; v.p. acad. affairs S.W. State U., Marshall, Minn., 1975-76, interim pres., 1976-77; dir. Ctr. for Econ. Edn., R.I. Coll., Providence, 1979-80; v.p. acad. affairs Cen. Mo. State U., Warrensburg, Mo., 1980-84; pres. North Adams State Coll., Mass., 1984—; cons. North Cen. Assn. Colls. and Schs., 1980-84, New Eng. Assn. Schs. and Colls., 1978-79, 85—, Minn. Acad. Family Physicians, 1973-77; mem. adv. bd. First Agrl. Bank, North Adams, 1985—; pres. No. Berkshire Cooperating Colls., 1986—; v.p. Coll. Consortium for Internat. Studies, 1989—. V.p. Med. Simulation Found., 1986-88; bd. dirs. Williamstown Concerts, 1988—. Mem. No. Berkshire C. of C. (bd. dirs. 1984-89, v.p. 1986-89). Avocations: fiber/textile arts, photography, choral and instrumental music. Office: North Adams State Coll Office of Pres Church St North Adams MA 01247

TISZA, VERONICA BENEDEK, psychiatrist; b. Szeged, Hungary, Aug. 7, 1912; came to U.S., 1941; d. Maurice and Lidia (Raisz) Benedek. MD, Med. Sch. Budapest, 1937. Diplomate Am. Bd. Pscyhiatry and Neurology; cert. Nat. Bd. Med. Examiners. Intern New Eng. Hosp., Boston, 1942-43; tng. pediatrics Boston Floating Hosp., Childrens Med. Ctr., Haynes Meml., Boston, 1943-46; clin. fellow Mass. Gen. Hosp., 1948-49, resident in psychiatry, 1949-51; resident in psychiatry Children's Med. Ctr., 1951-52; dir. psychiat. svc. for children New Eng. Med. Ctr., 1952-61; assoc. dir. psychiat. clinic Children's Hosp. of Pitts., 1961-68, sr. assoc., 1969—, dir. tng. pediatric residents in psychiatry, 1969—; asst. prof. psychiatry Harvard Med. Sch., Boston, 1969—. Contbr. articles to profl. jours. Home: 221 Mount Auburn St Cambridge MA 02138

TITCOMB, BONNIE L., state legislator; m. Fred Titcomb; 3 children. Mem. Maine State Senate. Democrat. Office: Maine State Senate State Capitol Augusta ME 04330*

TITTERTON, JUDITH LESLIE, customer support services professional; b. N.Y.C., Aug. 19, 1951; d. William DeWitt and Winifred (Bosch) T.; m. Patrick William McCormack, Oct. 8, 1983. BS in Indsl. Arts Edn., Millersville State U., 1978; postgrad., Marymount U. Recreation supr. Nassau County Dept. Parks and Recreation, East Meadow, N.Y., 1971-72; graphic artist Sci. Applications, Inc., Arlington, Va., 1978-80; sr. technical illustrator System Planning Corp., Arlington, 1980-83; grp mgr., customer support svcs. Analysis & Tech., Inc., Arlington, 1983—; designer, framer, Titterton Graphics, Alexandria, Va., 1978—. Vol., Fairfax County Adult Softball Coun., 1986—, Alexandria Vol. Bur., 1988. Mem. NAFE, Nat. Fedn. Bus. and Profl. Women's Clubs, Art Dirs. Club Met. Washington. Office: Analysis & Technology Inc 2121 Crystal Dr Arlington VA 22202

TITTLE, CAROLE JEAN, computer programmer; b. Temple, Tex., June 5, 1959; d. Lloyd Melvin Johnson and Shirley Faye (Bruss) Druley; m. Jerry Allen Tittle, Oct. 1, 1977; 1 child, James Adam. AA, NE Wis. Tech. Coll., 1988. Bookkeeper, sec. White House Music, Waukesha, Wis., 1976-77; acct. Lamplight Farms, Brookfield, Wis., 1979; prodn. clk. W.A. Krueger, Brookfield, Wis., 1979-80; data processing asst. Video Images, West Allis, Wis., 1980-85; adminstrn. asst. Jones Intercable, Brookfield, 1985; computer programmer Anamax Corp., Green Bay, Wis., 1988-89; quality assurance analyst Nielsen Mktg. Rsch., Green Bay, Wis., 1989; applications programmmer N.E. Wis. Tech. Coll., Green Bay, 1990. Democrat. Roman Catholic. Office: NWTC 2740 W Mason St Green Bay WI 54307

TITUS, ALICE CESTANDINA (DINA TITUS), political science educator, state legislator; b. Thomasville, Ga., May 23, 1950; m. Thomas Clayton Wright. AB, Coll. of William and Mary, 1970; MA, U. Ga., 1973; PhD, Fla. State U., 1976. Prof. polit. sci.; mem. Nev. State Senate. Author: Atomic Testing and American Politics, 1986. Chmn. Nev. Humanities Com., 1984-86. Mem. Western Polit. Sci. Assn. Democrat. Greek Orthodox. Home: 1637 Travois Crescent Las Vegas NV 89119*

TITUS, BARBARA, advertising agency executive. Former v.p. and rsch. dir. Scali, McCabe, Sloves, Inc., N.Y.C., now exec. v.p. and rsch. dir. Office: Scali McCabe Sloves Inc 800 3d Ave New York NY 10022*

TITUS, PAMELA LOUISE, real estate leasing representative; b. Ft. Wayne, Ind., Aug. 15, 1953; d. Gene W. Eby and Louise Miller. BS in Speech and Hearing, Purdue U., 1975, MS in Speech Pathology with highest distinction, 1976. Speech pathologist Speech Pathology Assocs., Houston, 1977-80; profl. recruiter Diversified Human Resources Group, Houston, 1980-81, Key Pers. Pty., Ltd., Sydney, Australia, 1981-82; computer sales rep. ComputerLand, Houston, 1982-84; broker Coldwell Banker Comml. Real Estate Svcs., 1985-89; real estate broker Homart Devel. Co., 1989—. Mem. Tex. Assn. Realtors, Internat. Coun. Shopping Ctrs. Presbyterian. Home: 11711 Memorial Dr #112 Houston TX 77024

TOAL, JEAN HOEFER, lawyer, state supreme court justice; b. Columbia, S.C., Aug. 11, 1943; d. Herbert W. and Lilla (Farrell) Hoefer; m. William Thomas Toal; children: Jean Hoefer, Lilla Patrick. BA in Philosophy, Agnes Scott Coll., 1965; JD, U. S.C., 1968. Bar: S.C. Assoc. Haynsworth, Penny, Bryant, Marion & Johnstone, 1968-70; ptnr. Belser, Baker, Barwick, Ravenel, Toal & Bender, Columbia, 1970-88; assoc. justice S.C. Supreme Ct., 1988—; mem. S.C. Human Affairs Commn.; mem. S.C. Ho. of Reps., 1975-88, chmn. house rules com., constitutional laws subcom. house judiciary com.; mem. parish council and lector St. Joseph's Cath. Ch. Mng. editor S.C. Law Rev. Bd. visitors Clemson U., 1978; trustee Columbia Mus. Art. Named Legislator of Yr., Greenville News, Woman of Yr., U. S.C. Mem. Columbia Bus. and Profl. Women (Career Woman of Yr. 1974), S.C. Mcpl. Assn., John Belton O'Neill Inn of Ct., Phi Alpha Delta. Office: Supreme Ct SC PO Box 12456 Columbia SC 29211

TOBACH, ETHEL, curator; b. Miaskovka, USSR, Nov. 7, 1921; came to U.S., 1923; d. Ralph Wiener and Fanny (Schechterman) Wiener Idels; m. Charles Tobach, 1947 (dec. 1969). BA, Hunter Coll., 1949; MA, NYU, 1952, PhD, 1957; DSc (hon.), Southampton Coll., 1975. Lic. psychologist, N.Y. Rsch. fellow Am. Mus. Natural History, N.Y.C., 1958-61, assoc. curator, 1964-69, curator, 1969—; rsch. fellow NYU, N.Y.C., 1961-64; adj. prof. psychology CUNY, N.Y.C., 1964—. Editor: Internat. Jour. of Comparative Psychology, 1987; (with others) (series) T.C. Schneirla Conference Series, 1981, Genes 2 Gender, 1975. Recipient Disting. Sci. Career, Assn. Women in Sci., 1974, Disting. Sci. Publ., Assn. for Women in Psychology, 1982. Fellow Am. Psychol. Assn. (pres. comparative psychol. div. 1985); Interant. Soc. Comparative Psychology (pres. 1984-86), N.Y. Acad. Scis. (v.p. behavioral scis. 1973-76), Eastern Psychol. Assn. (pres. 1987). Office: Am Mus Natural History Central Pkwy @ 79th St New York NY 10024-5192

TOBE, SUSAN BRING, lawyer; b. N.Y.C., 1949; d. Ira and Sylvia (Stevelman) Bring; m. Richard M. Tobe, 1980. B.A., State U. Coll., Buffalo, 1971; J.D., SUNY-Buffalo, 1974. Bar: N.Y. 1975, U.S. Dist. Ct. (we. dist.) N.Y. 1976. Asst. gen. counsel Carborundum Co., Niagara Falls, N.Y., 1974-75; asst. corp. counsel City of Buffalo, 1975-78; atty.-advisor U.S. Dept. HUD, Buffalo, 1978-81; asst. atty. gen. State of N.Y., Buffalo, 1981—; supervising atty. Pub. Interest Law Clinic, 1982; program lectr. St. Law Inst., N.Y., 1978; guest lectr. various high schs., colls., 1975—; dir. SUNY Sch. Law Alumni Assn., Buffalo, 1979-82. Vol. Leukemia Soc., Buffalo, 1981—, United Way Campaign, Buffalo, 1977, 88, 89, Friends Community Music. Sch., Buffalo, 1984—; com. person Dem. Party, Buffalo, 1976-78; com. mem. Instnl. Advancement State U. Coll. at Buffalo, 1987—; mem. strategic planning com. Buffalo State Coll. Found., 1989—. Mem. Erie County Bar Assn., N.Y. Civil Liberties Union, ABA, Women Lawyers of Western N.Y., N.Y. State Bar Assn. (profl. ethics com. 1984-87, profl. discipline com. 1986—, profl. ethnic com. 1984-87, profl. discipline com. 1986-89), State Univ. Coll. Buffalo Alumni Assn. (bd. dirs. 1984-86, v.p. 1986-88, pres. 1988—), Leadership Buffalo. Office: NY State Atty Gen's Office Dept of Law 125 Main St Buffalo NY 14203

TOBER, BARBARA D. (MRS. DONALD GIBBS TOBER), editor; b. Summit, N.J., Aug. 19, 1934; d. Rodney Fielding and Maude (Grebbin) Starkey; m. Donald Gibbs Tober, Apr. 5, 1973. Student, Traphagen Sch. Fashion, 1954-56, Fashion Inst. Tech., 1956-58, N.Y. Sch. Interior Design, 1964. Copy editor Vogue Pattern Book, 1958-60; beauty editor Vogue mag., 1961; dir. women's services Bartell Media Corp., 1961-66; editor-in-chief Bride's mag., N.Y.C., 1966—; dir. Gen. Brands Corp., sec.-treas.; adv. bd. Traphagen Sch.; coordinator SBA awards; Am. Craft Council Mus. Assoc., 1983—, benefit food com. chmn., 1984-87. Author: The ABC's of Beauty, 1963, China: A Cognizant Guide, 1980, The Wedding . . . The Marriage . . . And the Role of the Retailer, 1980, The Bride: A Celebration, 1984. Mem. Nat. Council on Family Relations, 1966; nat. council Lincoln Center Performing Arts, Met. Opera Guild; mem. NYU adv. bd. Women in Food Service, 1983; NYU Women's Health Symposium: Steering Com., 1983—. Recipient Alma award, 1968, Penney-Mo. award, 1972, Traphagen Alumni award, 1975, Diamond Jubilee award, 1983. Mem. Fashion Group, Nat. Home Fashions League (v.p., program chmn.), Am. Soc. Mag. Editors, Am. Soc. Interior Designers (press mem.), Intercorporate Group, Women in Communications (60 yrs. of success award N.Y. chpt. 1984), Nat. Assn. Underwater Instrs., Pan Pacific and S.E. Asia Women's Assn., Asia Soc., Japan Soc., China Inst., Internat. Side Saddle Orgn., Millbrook Hounds, Golden's Bridge Hounds, Wine and Food Soc., Chaines des Rotisseurs (chargée de press) (bd. dirs.), Dames d'Escoffier, Culinary Inst. Am. Home: 620 Park Ave New York NY 10021 Office: Bride's Magazine 350 Madison Ave New York NY 10017*

TOBIAS, JUDY, university development executive; b. Pitts.; d. Saul Albert Landau and Bess (Previn) Kurzman; m. Seth Tobias (dec. May 1983); children: Stephen Frederic, Andrew Previn; m. Lewis F. Davis, 1990. Student Silvermine Artists Guild, 1951-55. Art cons. Westchester Mental Health Assn., White Plains, N.Y., 1968-69; cons. sch. social work NYU, 1973-74, devel. exec. 1976—; conf. coord. Today's Family: Implications for the Future, N.Y.C., 1974-75; cons. Playschools, Inc., N.Y.C., 1975. Bd. dirs. St. John's Place Family Ctr. (bd. dirs. 1987—), Gov.'s Commn. on Continuing Edn., Albany, N.Y., 1968-70, Nat. Coun. on Children and Youth, Washington, 1974-75, Manhattan Inter-Hosp. Group on Child Abuse, 1975-76; chmn. N.Y. met. com. for UNICEF, 1976-77; mem. exec. com. Town Hall Found., N.Y.C., 1979—, vice chmn., 1986—; founder, bd. dirs. N.Y. chpt. WAIF, Inc., 1961—, nat. pres., 1978-82; bd. dirs., v.p. Citizen's Com. for Children, City of N.Y., 1975—, Am. br. Internat. Social Svc.; bd. dirs. Andrew Glover Youth Program, 1965-80, 86—, Goddard Riverside Community Svcs., 1985—, Dance Mag. Found., 1986—, Capitol Hall Preservation Corp., 1989—. Mem. Child Study Assn. Am. (bd. dirs. 1963-71, pres. 1969-71), Child Study Assn./Wel-Met, Inc. (bd. dirs. 1972-85). Democrat.

TOBIAS, SHEILA, writer, educator; b. N.Y., Apr. 26, 1935; d. Paul Jay and Rose (Steinberger) Tobias; m. Carlos Stern, Oct. 11, 1970 (div. 1982); m. Carl T. Tomizuka, Dec. 16, 1987. BA, Harvard Radcliffe U., 1957; MA, Columbia U., 1961, MPhil, 1974. Journalist W. Germany, U.S. and Fed. Republic Germany, 1957-65; lect. in history C.C.N.Y., N.Y.C., 1965-67; univ. adminstr. Cornell U., Wesleyan U., 1967-78; lect. in women's studies U. Calif., San Diego, 1985—; lect. in war, peace studies U. So. Calif., 1985—; lectr. in war, peace studies U. So. Calif., 1985-89. Author: Overcoming Mathematics Anxiety, 1978, Succeed with Math, 1987; co-author: The People's Guide to National Defense, 1982, Women, Militarism and War, 1989, They're Not Dumb, They're Different, 1990. Chmn. bd. dirs. The Clarion newspaper. Mem. Coll. Sci. Tchrs. Assn., Nat. Women's Studies Assn., Phi Beta Kappa. Office: Univ Ariz Polit Sci Dept Tucson AZ 85721

TOBIN, AVIS ANN, educational association executive; b. Helena, Mont., Mar. 24, 1920; d. Richard D. Tobin and Blanche H. Sites. Student, U. Mont., Missoula. Exec. v.p. Montana Hardware & Implement Assn., Helena, Mont., 1954-82; dir. Western Fed. Savings Bank, Missoula, 1970—; coun. mem. Mont. Vo-Tech. Coun., Helena, 1980—. Trade Jours., 1975. Protestant. Home: 1525 Beavershead Rd Helena MT 59601

TOBIN, ILONA LINES, psychologist, marriage and family counselor, educator, consultant; b. Trenton, Mich., Apr. 15, 1943; d. Frank John and Marjorie Cathalean (Lines) Kotyuk; m. Roger Lee Tobin, Aug. 20, 1966. BA, Ea. Mich. U., 1965; MA, 1968; MA, Mich. State U., 1975; EdD, Wayne State U., 1978. Diplomate Am. Bd. of Sexology; cert. marriage, family counselor; cert. sex educator and counselor; cert. sex therapist. Tchr., counselor Willow Run Pub. Schs., Ypsilanti, Mich., 1966-72; prof. Macomb County Community Coll., Mt. Clemens, Mich., 1974-79; psychotherapist Identity Ctr., Inc., Mt. Clemens, 1974-79; dir. treatment Alternative Lifestyles, Inc., Orchard Lake, Mich., 1979-80; psychologist Profl. Psychotherapy and Counseling Ctr., Farmington Hills, Mich., 1980-83; pvt. practice clin. psychology, Birmingham, Mich., 1983—; psychologist William Beaumont Hosp., 1989—; lectr. Wayne State U., Detroit, 1977—; recruitment dir. Upward Bound Ea. Mich. U., Ypsilanti, 1969-72. Creator Doc's Dolls. Cochmn. Birmingham Families in Action, 1982-83; bd. dirs. HAVEN-Oakland County's Phys. and Sexual Abuse Ctr. and Oakland Area Counselors Assn., 1984-85; mem. exec. bd., v.p. pres. Birmingham Community Women's Ctr., 1984-85, also bd. dirs.; mem. adv. bd. Woodside Med. Ctr. for Chemically Dependent Women, 1984-86. NIMH fellow, 1976-78; Wayne State U. scholar, 1976-78. Mem. Am. Psychol. Assn., Mich. Psychol. Assn., Am. Assn. Sex Educators, Counselors and Therapists, Am. Assn. for Counseling and Devel., Pi Lambda Theta, Phi Delta Kappa. Presbyterian.

TOBOLOWSKY, SARAH, retired librarian; b. Dallas; d. A.B. and Lena (Skibell) T. B.A., So. Meth. U., 1934, M.A., 1938; M.S. in Library Sci., Columbia U., 1952; postgrad. U. So. Calif., Northwestern U., U. Hawaii, Boston U. Sch. Tchr. Dallas Ind. Sch. Dist., 1935-80; sch. librarian Benjamin Franklin Jr. High Sch., Dallas, 1957-80, ret. 1980; libr. Lisbon Sch., 1935-57; instr. North Tex. State U., 1966-69. Honors Day speaker Tex. Woman's U., Denton, 1981. Mem. NEA (life), ALA (joint com. mem. with NEA), Am. Assn. Sch. Librarians (regional bd. dirs.), Dallas Classroom Tchrs. Assn. (pres. 1952-54), Tex. Classroom Tchrs. Assn. (legis. chmn. 1952-53, adv. bd. 1953-55), Tex. State Tchrs. Assn. (life), Tex. Library Assn., Dallas Sch. Librarians (pres. 1947-49), Delta Kappa Gamma (chpt. pres. 1956-58, state pres. 1963-65, State Achievement award 1963, Internat. Achievement award 1984; internat. pres. 1980-82), Kappa Kappa Iota. Home: 6838 Orchid Ln Dallas TX 75230

TOCKLIN, ADRIAN MARTHA, insurance company executive; b. Miami, Fla., Aug. 4, 1951; d. Kelso Hampton and Patricia Jane (Crook) Cook Atkins; m. Gary Michael Tocklin, Nov. 23, 1974. B.A., George Washington U., 1972. Regional claim examiner Interstate Nat. Corp., St. Petersburg, Fla., 1973-74; branch supr. Underwriter's Adjusting Co. subs. Continental Corp., Tampa, Fla., 1974-77, asst. dir. edn. tng. adminstrn., N.Y.C., 1977, asst. regional mgr. adminstrn. ops., Livingston, N.J., 1977-78, br. mgr., Paramus, N.J., 1978-80, sr. v.p. mktg., N.Y.C., Piscataway, N.J., 1980-84, regional v.p., mgr., Livingston, N.J., 1984-86, exec. v.p., 1986—, sr. v.p. Continental Corp., 1988—, also bd. dirs.; pres. U.S. Protection Indemnity Agy., Inc., N.Y.C., 1983-85, also dir.; bd. dirs. Underwriters Adjusting Co., Arbitration Forums, Inc., Tarrytown, N.Y., 1986—; v.p. Continental Risk Services, Inc., Hamilton, Bermuda, 1983-86; editor-in-chief Profl. Ins. Bulletin Update, N.Y.C., 1977-79. Mem. YWCA Acad. Women Achievers. Mem. Nat. Assn. Ins. Women (Outstanding Ins. Woman in N.Y.C.), NOW. Democrat. Lutheran. Office: Continental Corp 180 Maiden Ln New York NY 10038

TOD, MARTHA ANN, small business owner; b. Nogales, Ariz., Dec. 20, 1927; d. Robert Thomas and Beatrice Martha (Jones) F.; m. James William Tod, April 18, 1952; children: James, Bill, Bob, John, Gerry. BA, U. Ariz., 1952; postgrad., Ariz. State U., 1977. Cert. elem. and spl. edn. tchr. Spl. edn. tchr. Paradise Valley. Schs., Phoenix, 1976-77, Round Valley Schs., Springerville, 1977-88; resort owner Tod's Antler Ridge, Greer, Ariz., 1977—. Mem. Title XX Bd., Town Hall; treas. WMC Hosp. Bd. Springerville, 1980; pres. Cocopah PTA Paradise Valley, 1967. Named Tchr. of Yr. Springerville Rotary, 1985. Mem. Assn. for Children and Adults with Learning Disabilities, Greer Civic Club. Home: Box 72 Greer AZ 85927

TODARO, LAURA JEAN, lawyer; b. Neligh, Nebr., June 8, 1956; d. Andrew Robert and Mary Louise (Leenerts) T. BS, U. Ill., 1978; JD, Loyola U., New Orleans, 1981. Bar: La. 1981, U.S. Dist. Ct. (ea. and mid. dists.) La. 1981, U.S. Ct. Appeals (5th cir.) 1981, U.S. Supreme Ct. 1985. Assoc. Dutel & Dutel, New Orleans, 1981-85; ptnr. Todaro & Todaro, Kenner, La., 1985—; city atty. City of Kenner, 1985-87, prosecutor, 1987-88, exec. counsel to Mayor, 1987—. Bd. dirs., sec., met. bd. rep., chmn. maj. gifts campaign Kenner YMCA, 1988; mem. Jefferson Parish Alliance for Good Govt.; bd. dirs. Met. New Orleans Battered Womens' Program. Mem. ABA, Fed. Bar Assn., Jefferson Parish Bar Assn., Kenner Bus. Women's Assn., U. Ill. Alumni Assn. (local organizer), Kiwanis, Phi Delta Phi. Republican. Roman Catholic. Home: 720 Vanderbilt Ln Kenner LA 70065 Office: City Kenner Legal Dept 1801 Williams Blvd Kenner LA 70062

TODARO, RAPHAELE ANN, lawyer, physician; b. Wilmington, Del., Aug. 23, 1952; d. Andrew Charles and Raphaele Mary (Facciolo) T.; m. L.S. Rubin. BA, U. Del., 1975; JD, Widener U., 1979; MD, St. George's U., Grenada, W.I., 1988. Bar: Pa. 1980, N.J. 1981. Ptnr. Rubin & Todaro, Media, Pa., 1980—; resident Northeastern Hosp., 1990—. Mem. Widener U. Law Rev., 1978. Mem. Mortar Bd., Phi Beta Kappa, Phi Delta Phi. Home: 103 Baynard Blvd Wilmington DE 19803 Office: 337 W State St Carrcroft Woods Media PA 19063

TODD, BARBARA ANN, dentist; b. Conway, S.C., Sept. 8, 1954; d. Junior B. Todd and Myrna Loy (Roberts) Murphy. ASc., Florence Darlington Tec. Coll., S.C., 9179; BSc., Francis Marion Coll., Florence, S.C., 1983; DMD, Med. U. Sci., Charleston, S.C., 1987. Cert. DDM, S.C. Dental hygienist Dr. C.F. Fishburne, Rock Hill, S.C., 197981; dentist Medical Plaza, Murrells Inlet, S.C., 1987—. Named Outstanding Young Women in Am. Montgomery Ala. 1987. Mem. ADA, Acad. Gen. Dentistry, Am. Acad. Implant Dentistry, Horry-Georgetown Dental Soc., ABWA, S.C. Dental Assn., Grand Strand Dental Soc., Psi Omega. Office: Barbara A Todd DMD 103 Mount Gilead Ste 2 Murrells Inlet SC 29576

TODD, DEBORAH J., public health advisor; b. Seattle, July 27, 1951; d. Charles Hunt and Katherine Anne (Galbraith) T. BS in Nursing, U. Wash., 1983; MPH, Johns Hopkins U., Balt., 1986. Nurse practitioner II Harborview Med. Ctr., Seattle, 1983-85; pub health edn. cons. Chinese Acad. Preventive Medicine, Beijing, China, 1986-88; pub. health advisor State of Wash. Dept. Social and Health Svcs., Seattle, 1989—. Co-author, editor: English for Public Health, 1989. Mem. Am. Pub. Health Assn., Nat. Coun. Internat. Health, Am. Assn. World Health. Baha'i.

TODD, JACKIE STEELE, personnel administrator; b. Mt. Gilead, N.C., Nov. 30, 1950; d. Arthur B. Todd; children: Marlita LaShea Steele, Alissa Brianna. BS, SUNY, Brockport, 1977. Cert. elem. tchr., N.Y. Pers. coord. Xerox Credit Corp./Xerox Fin. Svcs., Stamford, Conn., 1985-87, pers. specialist, pers. coord., credit analyst, 1987; pers. ops. mgr. LMV Leasing/ Xerox Fin. Svcs., Niagara Falls, N.Y., 1988—. Sec. Niagara Falls, N.Y. chpt. NAACP, 1990—; mem. task force Citizens Against Substance Abuse, Niagara Falls, 1990—; mem. African-Am. Task Force, Niagara Falls, 1990—; caseworker for child protective svcs. Mem. NAFE, NEA, Am. Sociologists Assn.

TODD, JESSIE A., social worker; b. New London, Conn., Apr. 1, 1946. AS, Bryant Coll., Smithfield, R.I., 1966; BA, Cen. Conn. State U., 1971; MSW, U. Conn., 1974. Tchr., tutor, med. asst. Peace Corps, India, 1966-68; child-care worker Klingberg Children's Home, New Britain; teen counselor Mitchell House, Hartford, Conn., 1968-71; tchr. spl. edn. Ben Haven Resdl. Treatment Ctr., New Haven, 1972-73; interviewer/personal care prog. Hartford, 1975; social worker Meriden (Conn.) Reg. Ctr., 1975-77; substitute tchr. New Haven Schs., 1978; legal sec. New Haven, 1979-84; sales rep. Better Bus. Bur., Albuquerque, 1986; word processing profl. Digital Corp., Mass., 1986-87; account exec. recruitment advt. New Eng. Times, Norwood, Mass., 1987-88; secondary edn. prin. Cen. Conn. State U., 1990—. Republican. Address: 226 Ellsworth Ave New Haven CT 06511

TODD, JOYCE ANDERSON, social service agency director; b. Lumberton, N.C., June 2, 1940; d. Irvin L. and Esther (Huggins) Anderson; m. William H. Strickland, Dec. 9, 1960 (div. Oct. 1976); 1 child, William (dec.); m. John Wendell Todd, July 6, 1979; 1 stepchild, Stephanie Leigh. B.A., Coker Coll., 1960. Social worker Horry County Dept. Social Services, Conway, S.C., 1962-66, casework supr., 1966-73, county dir., 1973—. Mem. S.C. Assn. County Human Service Adminstrs., S.C. County Dirs. and Suprs. Assn., Am. Pub. Welfare Assn., Child Welfare League Am. Democrat. Baptist. Avocations: cooking; snow skiing; golf. Office: Horry County Dept Social Services PO Drawer 1465 Conway SC 29526

TODD, KRISTIN KORF, freelance writer, consultant; b. Waukesha, Wis., July 11, 1956; d. Gerald James and Carol Elizabeth (McKelsen) Korf; m. Robert Kim Todd, June 9, 1984; 1 child, Kelly Alison. BS, U. Wis., 1979. Editor, membership and spl. projects coord. Greater Madison (Wis.) C. of C., 1979-88; freelance writer Madison, 1988—. Pub. rels. advisor Very Spl. Arts, Madison, 1988-89. Mem. Women in Communications (scholarship chair Madison chpt. 1988—). Lutheran.

TODD, NORMA JEAN ROSS, retired government official; b. Butler, Pa., Oct. 3, 1920; d. William Bryson and Doris Mae (Ferguson) Ross; m. Alden Frank Miller, Jr., Apr. 16, 1940 (dec. Feb. 1975); 1 child, Alden Frank III; m. Jack R. Todd, Dec. 23, 1977. Student, Pa. State U., 1944-46, Yale U., 1954-57. Exec. mgr. Donora (Pa.) C. of C., 1950-57, Donora Community Chest, 1950-57; office mgr. Donora Golden Jubilee, 1951; staff writer Herald-Am., Donora, 1957, city editor, 1957-70; assoc. editor Daily Herald, Donora, 1970-73; svc. rep. Pitts. Teleservice Ctr., Social Security Adminstrn., HHS, 1977-83. Mem. Mayor's Adv. Council, Donora, 1965-69, Citizens' Adv. Council, Donora, 1965-69; mem. Donora Bd. Edn., 1954-60, pres., 1960; mem. Donora Borough Council, 1970-72; bd. dirs. Mon Valley chpt. ARC, 1964—, sec. bd., 1966—; bd. dirs. Washington County Tourism Agy., 1970—, sec., 1972—; bd. dirs. Washington County History and Landmarks Found. 1971-80, sec., 1975-80; bd. dirs. Mon Valley council Camp Fire Girls, 1965-79, Mon Valley Drug and Alcoholism Council, 1971-78; hon. life mem. Pa. Congress PTAs; bd. dirs. United Way Mon Valley, 1973-82, chmn. pub. rels., 1973-74. Recipient Fine Arts Festival of Pa. Poetry first prize award Fedn. of Women's Clubs, 1987, 1st and 2nd pl. awards for photography Washington County Fine Arts Festival, County Fedn. of Women's Club, 1990. Mem. Pa. Soc. Newspaper Editors, Pitts. Press Club, Donora C. of C. (pres. 1971-72), DAR (regent Monongahela Valley chpt. 1974-77), Washington County Poetry Soc. (pres. 1967-69), Family of Bruce Soc. (descendants of King Robert the Bruce of Scotland 1987—), Washington County Fedn. Women's Clubs (rec. sec. 1964-66). Clubs: Order Ea. Star (worthy matron 1966-67), White Shrine of Jerusalem (high priestess 1973-74), Order of Amaranth (royal matron 1966, dist. dep., grand rep. W.Va. 1979-80), Donora Forecast (pres. 1962-63), Donora Unidon (pres. 1965-66, 56-57). Avocation: genealogy. Home: Overlook Terr Donora PA 15033 also: 1310 McKean Ave Donora PA 15033

TODD, PATRICIA, sewing school operator; b. Cin., Oct. 27, 1946; d. Ralph and Agnes (Klenk) Pfalz; m. Paul Todd, June 24, 1972; children: Rita, Tricia, Scott, Alfred, Daniel, Matthew, Amelia, Nathan, Paula, Donald. Ed., Am. River Coll., Sacramento. Owner Sewing Sch., Fair Oaks, Calif. Author: Rainbows, Butterflies and Roses. Trainer, Pony Express dist. Boy Scouts Am.; vol. Girl Scouts. U.S. Mem. Nat. Writers Club. Mem. LDS Ch. Home: 4932 Papaya Dr Fair Oaks CA 95628

TODD, RENATE KLÖPPINGER, financial executive, consultant; b. Bensheim, Fed. Republic of Germany; came to U.S., 1976; d. Heinrich and Gertrud (Schubert) K.; 1 child, Christopher. BS, Goethe U., Frankfurt, Federal Republic of Germany, 1973, MS in Psychology, 1976; MBA in Finance, UCLA, 1981. Treasury analyst intern Carnation Internat., Los Angeles, 1980-81; corp. fin. assoc. Drexel Burnham Lambert, Inc., N.Y.C., 1981-83; v.p. Fulcrum Venture Capital Corp., Washington, 1983-88, Citibank Leveraged Capital, Frankfurt, Fed. Republic Germany, 1988—; Bd. dirs. Applied Intelligent Systems, Inc., Ann Arbor, Mich., PKS, Inc., Maecomp, Inc. Com. mem. Nat. Assn. of Investment Cos., Washington, 1984—; com. mem. D.C. Com. for Women, Washington, 1986—. Recipient Sister Cities Internat. award, 1981. Mem. OEF Internat. Women in Bus. (cons. 1986, advisor/small bus. San Jose, Costa Rica, 1986), Phi Beta Kappa (named Outstanding Member 1981).

TODD, SHIRLEY ANN, guidance director; b. Botetourt County, Va., May 23, 1935; d. William Leonard and Margaret Judy (Simmons) Brown; m. Thomas Byron Todd, July 7, 1962 (dec. July 1977). B.S. in Edn., Madison Coll., 1956; M.Ed., U. Va., 1971. Cert. tchr., Va. Elem. tchr. Fairfax County Sch. Bd., Fairfax, Va., 1956-66, 8th grade history tchr., 1966-71, guidance counselor James F. Cooper Intermediate Sch., McLean, Va., 1971-88, dir. guidance, 1988—; chmn. mktg. Lake Anne Joint Venture, Falls Church, Va., 1979-82, mng. ptnr., 1980-82. Del. Fairfax County Republican Conv., 1985. Fellow Fairfax Edn. Assn. (mem. profl. rights and responsibilities commn. 1970-72, bd. dirs. 1968-70), Va. Edn. Assn. (mem. state com. on local assns. and urban affairs 1969-70), NEA, No. Va. Counselors Assn. (hospitality and social chmn., exec. bd. 1982-83), Va. Counselors Assn. (exec. com. 1987), Va. Sch. Counselors Assn., Am. Assn. for Counseling and Devel., Chantilly Nat. Golf and Country Club (v.p. social 1981-82, Centreville, Va.). Baptist. Avocations: golf, tennis. Home: 6543 Bay Tree Ct Falls Church VA 22041 Office: James F Cooper Intermediate Sch 977 Balls Hills Rd McLean VA 22101

TODD COPLEY, JUDITH ANN, materials and metallurgical engineering educator; b. Wakefield, West Yorkshire, Eng., Dec. 13, 1950; came to U.S., 1978; d. Marley and Joan Mary (Birkinshaw) Booth; m. David Michael Todd, June 17, 1972 (div. June 1981); m. Stephen Michael Copley, Aug. 3, 1984. BA, Cambridge (Eng.) U., 1972, MA, PhD, 1977. Research asst. Imperial Coll. Sci. and Tech., London, 1976-78; research assoc. SUNY, Stonybrook, 1978; research engr. U. Calif., Berkeley, 1979-82; asst. prof. materials sci. and mech. engring. U. So. Calif., L.A., 1982-90; assoc. prof. metall. and materials engring. Ill. Inst. Tech., Chgo., 1990—; mem. task force Materials Property Coun., N.Y.C., 1979—. Contbr. articles to profl. jours. Recipient Faculty Research award Oak Ridge (Tenn.) Nat. Lab., 1986, Brit. Univs. Student Travel award 1972, Brit. Fedn. Univ. Women award 1972, Vanadium award British Inst. Metals 1990; Kathryn Kingswell Meml. scholar 1972. Mem. AIME (research award, 1983), ASTM, Soc. Women Engrs. (sr.), ASM Internat. (chmn. Los Angeles chpt. 1986-87, council mem. materials sci. div. 1984—), Electron Microscopy Soc. Am., Assn. Women in Sci., Hist. Metallurgy Soc., Nat. Soc. Corrosion Engrs. (Seed Grant award 1983), Microbeam Analysis Soc. Home: 307 Briargate Terr Hinsdale IL 60521 Office: Ill Inst Tech Dept Metall and Materials Engring Chicago IL 60616

TOEDTE, SHARON LYNN SIMON, communications executive; b. Coral Gables, Fla., Mar. 19, 1957; d. Gerald Tobias and Faye Marion (Fields) S.; m. Ross John Toedte, Sept. 6, 1987. BA in Econs., Coll. William & Mary, 1978; MBA in Mktg., U. Tenn., 1987. Asst. buyer Davison's, Atlanta, 1978-79, sales mgr., 1979-80; project dir. Leonard & Assocs., Atlanta, 1980-82; rsch. account exec. D'Arcy, MacManus, Masius, Atlanta, 1982-84; rsch. mgr. Whittle Communications, Knoxville, Tenn., 1984-87, rsch. dir., 1987—; speaker mktg. classes U. Tenn., Knoxville, 1986—; adj. faculty mem. Tenn. Wesleyan Coll., 1989—. Active Knoxville Arts Coun., 1985—, Knoxville Mus. Art, 1985—, Knoxville Symphony Orch., 1987—; contbr. Victor Ashe for Mayor, Konxville, 1987. Mem. Am. Mktg. Assn. (program chmn. Knoxville chpt. 1988—, v.p. programs 1988-89, v.p. community edn. 1989-90, outreach, 1990—, speaker 1989—). Republican. Jewish. Office: Whittle Communications LP 505 Market St Knoxville TN 37902

TOENSING, VICTORIA, lawyer; b. Colon, Panama, Oct. 16, 1941; d. Philip William and Victoria (Brady) Long; m. Trent David Toensing, Oct. 29, 1962 (div. 1976); children: Todd Robert, Brady Cronon, Amy Victoriana; m. Joseph E. diGenova, June 27, 1981. BS in Edn., Ind. U., 1962; JD cum laude, U. Detroit, 1975. Bar: Mich. 1976, D.C. 1978. Tchr. English Milw., 1965-66; law clk. to presiding justice U.S. Ct. Appeals, Detroit, 1975-76; asst. U.S. atty. U.S. Atty.'s Office, Detroit, 1976-81; chief counsel U.S. Senate Intelligence Com., Washington, 1981-84; dep. asst. atty. gen. criminal div. Dept. Justice, Washington, 1984-88; spl. counsel Hughes Hubbard & Reed, Washington, 1988-90; ptnr. Cooter and Gell, Washington, 1990—; with U.S. Sentencing Commn. Working Group on Corp. Sanctions, 1988-89; co-chair Coalition for Women's Appts. Justice Judiciary Task Force, 1988—. Author: Bringing Sanity to the Insanity Defense, 1983, Mens Rea: Insanity by Another Name, 1984; contbg. author: Fighting Back: Winning The War Against Terrorism; contbr. articles to profl. jours. Founder, chmn. Women's Orgn. To Meet Existing Needs, Mich., 1975-79; chmn. Republican Women's Task Force, 1979-81; bd. dirs. Project on Equal Edn. Rights, Mich., 1980-81, Nat. Hist. Intelligence Mus., 1987—. Recipient Spl. Commendation award Office U.S. Atty. Gen., 1980, Agy. Seal medallion CIA, 1986. Mem. ABA (standing com. on law and nat. security, council criminal justice sect., adv. bd. com. complex crimes and litigation, vice chmn. white collar crime com., chmn. subcom. on corp. criminal liability), U. Detroit Law Sch. Alumnae (bd. dirs.).

TOEPFER, SUSAN JILL, editor; b. Rochester, Minn., Mar. 9, 1948; d. John Bernard and Helen Esther (Chapple) T.; m. Lorenzo Gabriel Carcaterra, May 16, 1981; children: Katherine Marie, Nicholas Gabriel. B.A., Bennington Coll., 1970. Mng. editor Photoplay Mag., N.Y.C., 1971-72; freelance writer, N.Y.C., 1972-78; TV week editor N.Y. Daily News, N.Y.C., 1978-79, leisure editor, 1979-82, features editor, 1982-84, arts and entertainment editor, 1984-86, exec. mag. editor, 1986-87; sr. writer People Mag., 1987-89, sr. editor, 1989—. Democrat. Presbyterian. Office: People Mag Time-Life Bldg Rockefeller Ctr New York NY 10020

TOFANI, LORETTA A., journalist; b. N.Y.C., Feb. 5, 1953; d. Lucio M. and Olga R. (Danise) T. B.A., Fordham U., 1975; M.J., U. Calif., 1976. Reporter UPI, Los Angeles, 1977, Washington Post, D.C., 1978-87, Phila. Inquirer, 1987—. Author: newspaper series Rape in the County Jail, 1982 (Pulitzer Prize for local investigative reporting 1983, Soc. Profl. Journalists award for general reporting 1983, Investigative Reporters and Editors Bronze medal 1983, Henry Miller award for enterprise reporting 1983, Robert F. Kennedy citation for reporting on the disadvantaged 1983); feature story A Shared Habit: Addict Gives Birth, Addict is Born, 1989 (feature writing finalist Pulitzer Prize 1989). Fulbright scholar Japan-U.S. Ednl Commn., Tokyo, 1983; recipient Mark Twain award, 1981, 82, Front Page award Washington-Balt. Newspaper Guild, 1980, 81, 82, Keystone Press award Pa. Soc. Newspaper Editors, 1988, 1st place for excellence in writing Soc. Profl. Journalists Greater Phila. chpt., 1989. Roman Catholic. Home: 114 Conway Ave Narberth PA 19072 Office: Philadelphia Inquirer 400 N Broad St Philadelphia PA 19101

TOIA, MARGARET ELIZABETH, sales executive; b. Naha, Okinawa, Dec. 26, 1962; came to U.S., 1970; d. Frank Philip Toia and Amanda Lee (McConnell) Brush. BA, Hood Coll., Frederick, Md., 1985. Customer svc. rep. Whittaker Bioproducts, Walkersville, Md., 1985-86, equipment coord., 1986-87, telemarketing specialist, 1987-88; sales rep. Life Techs., Gaithersburg, Md., 1988—; mktg. and sales assoc. My Forge, Rohrersville, Md., 1988—; freelance tech. writer, Rohrersville, 1989—. Mem. NAFE, Smithsonian Instn. Republican. Episcopalian. Home: 4801 Woodstock Ln Rohrersville MD 21779

TOKAR, MAUREEN TANSEY, architect; b. Cin., Mar. 4, 1931; d. Bernard Joseph and Cecile Marie (Sunman) Tansey; B.S. in Architecture, U. Cin., 1955; m. Edward Tokar, June 29, 1974. Job capt. Hixson, Tarter & Merkel, Cin., 1964-68; dir. interior architecture Ferry & Henderson, Springfield, Ill., 1968-72; project coordinator Skidmore, Owings & Merrill, Chgo., 1972-76; rev. architect Ill. Capital Devel. Bd., Chgo., 1977-82; v.p. Planning and Design Cons., 1975—. Active, Art Inst. Chgo. Mem. AIA, Chgo. Women in Architecture, Alpha Omicron Pi. Club: Chgo. Altrusa.

TOKOLY, MARY ANDREE, microbiologist; b. Manila, Dec. 4, 1940; (parents Am. citizens) d. Robert Francis Tokoly and Ruby Waunita (Shriner) Kaderli. BS, Tex. Woman's U., 1962, MS, 1964, PhD, 1974. Instr Victoria (Tex.) Coll., 1964-66; asst. prof. Kans. State Coll., Pittsburg, 1966-68, Kans. Newman Coll., Wichita, 1974-75; grad. teaching asst. Tex. Woman's U., Denton, 1968-74; microbiologist Nix Hosp., San Antonio, 1975-77, Humana Hosp. Met., San Antonio, 1977—. Sec. Bexar County chpt. Czech Heritage Soc. Tex., San Antonio, 1988—. Robert A. Welch Found. grantee, 1971, 72. Mem. Am. Soc. Clin. Pathologists (registered microbiologist), Am. Soc. Microbiology, Tex. Soc. Microbiology, South Tex. Assn. Microbiology Profls., Am. Soc. Med. Tech., N.Y. Acad. Scis., AAUW, S.W. Assn. Clin. Microbiologists, Sigma Xi. Roman Catholic. Office: Human Hosp Met 1310 McCullough Ave San Antonio TX 78212

TOKUBO, CATHLEEN C., accountant; b. Fresno, Calif., Dec. 7, 1958; d. Akira and Betty Harumi (Obata) T. BS, Calif. State U., Fresno, 1981. Bookkeeper, asst. office mgr. Mack Lazarus Mobilhomes, Kerman, Calif.; staff acct. Ben Nakamura P.A., Fresno, Moore, Grider, Griggs, Cowan and Co., Fresno; gen. acctg. supr. Van Beurden Ins. Svcs., Inc., Kingsburg, Calif.; acct. Accountemps, Fresno. Calif. State scholar; Wishon Meml. scholar. Mem. NAFE, Cen. Calif. Asian Pacific Women (pres., treas.), Asian Pacific Women's Network (treas.). Republican. Buddhist. Home: 523 LaCrosse Fowler CA 93625

TOLAND, JOY E., marketing professional; b. Newark, Apr. 8, 1965; d. William D. Cartwright; m. Mark E. Toland, Sept. 10, 1988. BS, Montclair State Coll., 1987. Staff acct., acctg. clk., billing clk. Delta Dental Plan of N.J., Parsippany; product specialist, mktg. support specialist PyMah Corp., Somerville, N.J.; dir. mktg. Am. Multi-Svcs. Unltd., Inc., Manville, N.J. Mem. NAFE, Kiwanis (treas. Circle K 1983-84).

TOLBERT, AMY SUE SCHROEDER, training program consultant; b. Rochester, Pa., Feb. 10, 1964; d. James Samuel and Margaret Elizabeth (Schroeder) T.; m. Andres Alonzo Parra, June 30, 1990. BA in Radio and TV Prodn., SUNY, Geneseo, 1985; MEd in Career and Tech. Edn., Bowling Green (Ohio) State U., 1986; PhD in Edn., U. Minn., 1990. Coord. mgmt. devel. and in-house degree program Westinghouse Electric, Lima, Ohio, 1986-87; researcher, tng. manual coordinator Bus. Incentives, Mpls., 1987; independent cons. MST Assocs., Rochester, 1985—; field trainer intercultural programs Am. Field Svc., Mpls., Minn., 1989—; cons., trainer, ptnr. Effective Cross-Cultural Orgns., Mpls.-St. Paul, 1989—; producer, tng. specialist, ptnr. VenUS Directions, St. Paul, 1989—; presenter confs. in field. Fellow Bowling Green State U., 1985-86, U. Minn., 1987-88; Ruth Eckert scholar, 1988-89; named to 200 Notable Am. Women, 1990. Mem. Am. Soc. Tng. and Devel., NAFE, Internat. Soc. Intercultural Edn., Tng. and Rsch., Women in Communications, Inc. Home and Office: 24 Pine Dr Circle Pines MN 55014

TOLCHIN, SUSAN JANE, public administration educator, writer; b. N.Y.C., Jan. 14, 1941; d. Jacob Nathan and Dorothy Ann (Markowitz) Goldsmith; m. Martin Tolchin, Dec. 23, 1965; children: Charles Peter, Karen Rebecca. B.A., Bryn Mawr Coll., 1961; M.A., U. Chgo., 1962; Ph.D., N.Y.U., 1968. Lectr. in polit. sci. City Coll., N.Y.C., 1963-65, Bklyn. Coll., 1965-71; adj. asst. prof. polit. sci. Seton Hall U., South Orange, N.J., 1971-73; assoc. prof. polit. sci., dir. Inst. for Women and Politics, Mt. Vernon Coll., Washington, 1975-78; prof. pub. adminstrn. George Washington U., Washington, 1978—. Co-author (with Martin Tolchin): To The Victor: Political Patronage from the Clubhouse to the White House, 1971, Clout-Womanpower and Politics, 1974, Dismantling America-The Rush to Deregulate, 1983, Buying Into America-How Foreign Money Is Changing the Face of Our Nation, 1988. Bd. dirs. Cystic Fibrosis Foun., 1982—; pres. Wyngate Elem. Sch. PTA, Bethesda, Md., 1981-82; county committeewoman Democratic Party, Montclair, N.J., 1969-73. Dilthey fellow George Washington U., 1983, Aspen Inst. fellow, 1979; named Tchr. of Yr., Mt. Vernon Coll., 1978; recipient Founder's Day award NYU, 1968. Mem. Am. Polit. Sci. Assn. (pres. Women's Caucus for Polit. Sci. 1977-78), Am. Soc. Pub. Adminstrn. (chairperson sect. Natural Resources and Environ. Adminstrn. 1982-83). Democrat. Jewish. Office: George Washington U Dept Pub Adminstrn Washington DC 20052

TOLER, MELISSA ANN, health organization executive; b. Carrollton, Mo., Nov. 18, 1953; d. Billy Gene and Sarah Ann (Schnell) T. Diploma, Newman Hosp. Sch. Nursing, 1974; student, Christopher Newport Coll., 1979-80; BA in Bus. Mgmt. with honors, U. South Fla., 1983; MBA in Health Svcs. Mgmt., Fla. Inst. Tech., 1987. With USN Nurse Corps, Orlando, Fla., 1974-76, Portsmouth, Va., 1976-78; adminstr. Wooten, Honeywell, Kest & Martinez, Orlando, 1983-84; dir. physician recruitment CIGNA Health Plan of Fla., Inc., Orlando, 1984-86, dir. recruitment and provider rels., 1986-87; program mgr. Diabetes Treatment Ctr. at Orlando Regional Med. Ctr., 1987-88; mktg. coord., RN Mediplex Rehab-Bradenton, 1988-89; asst mgr. Prospective Payment Mgmt. for Comml. and Contract Care, 1989—. Lt. comdr. USNR, 1978—. Mem. Fla. Hosp. Assn., NAFE, Phi Kappa Phi, Beta Gamma Sigma, Sigma Iota Epsilon. Republican. Avocations: swimming, scuba diving. Office: Dept Prospective Payment Mgmt Orlando Regional Med Ctr 1414 S Kuhl Ave Orlando FL 32806

TOLETE-VELCEK, FRANCISCA AGATEP, pediatric surgeon, surgery educator; b. Santo Domingo, Ilocos Sur, The Philippines, Mar. 16, 1943; came to U.S., 1966; d. Celedonio Alvarez Tolete and Cristeta (Lopez) Agatep; m. Damir Velcek; children: John, Jennifer. BS, U. Philippines, 1961, MD, 1966. Diplomate Am. Bd. Surgery, Am. Bd. Pediatric Surgery. Intern U. Philippines, Manila, 1965-66; straigt surg. intern St. Clare's Hosp., N.Y.C., 1966-67, resident, 1967-71; surg. asst. St. Barnabas Hosp., N.Y.C., 1971-72; rsch. fellow in pediatric surgery Health Sci. Ctr., Bklyn., 1972-73, pediatric surg. chief res., 1973-75; asst. instr. surgery SUNY Downstate Med. Ctr., Bklyn., 1972-75, asst. prof., 1975-81, assoc. prof., 1981—; attending-in-charge pediatric surg. ICU, Kings County Hosp. Ctr., Bklyn.; attending staff L.I. Coll. Hosp., Bklyn., St. Vincent's Med. Ctr., S.I., N.Y., Meth. Hosp., Bklyn., Interfaith Med. Ctr., Bklyn., St. John's Episc.-South Shore, Far Rockaway, N.Y., State Univ. Hosp., Health Sci. Ctr., Kings County Hosp. Contbr. articles to med. jours. Named Most Outstanding Alumnus, U. Philippines, 1987. Fellow ACS, Am. Acad. Pediatrics; mem. Am. Pediatric Surg. Assn., Am. Assn. for Surgery of Trauma, Soc. Internat. De Chirurgie, John Madden Surg. Soc., N.Y. Surg. Soc., Sigma Xi, Phi Sigma, Phi Kappa Phi. Roman Catholic. Home: 471 Summit St Englewood Cliffs NJ 07632 Office: Health Sci Ctr at Bklyn 450 Clarkson Ave Brooklyn NY 11203

TOLL, ROBERTA DARLENE (MRS. SHELDON S. TOLL), clinical psychologist; b. Detroit, May 14, 1944; d. David and Blanche (Fischer) Pollack; married, Aug. 11, 1968; children: Candice, John, Kevin. B.A., U. Mich., 1966; M.S.W., U. Pa., 1971; postgrad., 1986. Dir. counselors Phila. Family Planning, Inc., 1971-72; psychologist Lafayette Clinic, Detroit, 1972-73; social worker Project Headline, Detroit, 1973-75; pvt. practice clin. psychology, Bloomfield Hills, Mich., 1975—; adj. prof. U. Detroit, Oakland Community Coll. Bd. dirs. Detroit chpt. Nat. Council on Alcoholism. Cert. social worker, Mich. Fellow Masters and Johnson Inst.; mem. Nat. Assn. Social Workers. Democrat. Club: Franklin Hills Country. Home and Office: 640 Lone Pine Hill Rd Bloomfield Hills MI 48013

TOLL-CROSSMAN, JACQUELINE JOY, accountant; b. Iola, Kans., Mar. 23, 1947; d. Clarence Leslie and Marie Irene (Pearman) Robinson; m. Benjamin Thomas Toll, Nov. 24, 1967 (div. Nov. 1987); children: Dacia Ianthe, Thaddeus Nathaniel, Allegra Alexandra; m. Duane Arlen Crossman, Feb. 13, 1988; children: Chad Anthony, Shannon Elaine. A.A., Kansas City Community Coll. Kans., 1973; B.S., Avila Coll., 1979, M.B.A., 1981. Cert. mgmt. acct. Assoc. adminstr. Clinicare, Kansas City, 1979-82; chief fin. officer Alexian Bros. Health Mgmt., St. Joseph Home, Kansas City, Kans., 1982-86; asst. controller Truman Med. Ctr., West Kansas City, Mo., 1986—; field acct. Hillhaven Corp. , Overland Park, Kans., 1987-88; reimbursement specialist Bapt. Med. Ctr., Kansas City, Mo. Mem. Nat. Assn. Accts., Health Care Fin. Mgmt. Assn., Dimensions Unlimited. Baptist. Avocations: cooking; sightseeing; computer operations.

TOLLETT, GLENNA BELLE, accountant, mobile home park operator; b. Graham, Ariz., Dec. 17, 1913; d. Charles Harry and Myrtle (Stapley) Spafford; m. John W. Tollett, Nov. 28, 1928; 1 child, Jackie J., 1 adopted child, Beverly Mae Malgren. Bus. cert., Lamson Coll. Office mgr, Hurley Meat Packing Co., Phoenix, 1938-42; co-owner, sec., treas. A.B.C. Enterprises, Inc., Seattle, 1942—; ptnr. Bella Investment Co., Seattle, 1962—, Four Square Investment Co., Seattle, 1969—, Warehouses Ltd., Seattle, 1970—, Tri State Partnership, Wash., Idaho, Tex., 1972—; pres. Halycon Mobile Home Park, Inc., Seattle, 1979—; co-owner, operator Martha Lake Mobile Home Park, Lynwood, Wash., 1962-73. Mem. com. Wash. Planning and Community Affairs Agy., Olympia, 1981-82, Wash. Mfg. Housing Assn. Relations Com., Olympia, 1980-84; appointed by Gov. Wash. to Mobile Home and RV Adv. Bd., 1973-79. Named to RV/Mobile Home Hall of Fame, 1980. Mem. Wash. Mobile Park Owners Assn. (legisl. chmn., lobbyist 1976-85, cons. 1984, pres. 1978-79, exec. dir. 1976-84, This is Your Life award 1979), Wash. Soc. of Assn. Execs. (Exec. Dir. Service award 1983), Mobile Home Old Timers Assn., Mobile Home Owners of Am. (sec. 1972-76, Appreciation award 1976), Nat Fire Protection Assn. (com. 1979-86), Aurora Pkwy. North C. of C.)sec. 1976-80), Fremont C. of C. Republican. Mormon. Home: 18261 Springdale Ct NW Seattle WA 98177 Office: ABC Enterprises Inc 3524 Stone Way N Seattle WA 98103

TOLLEY, CAROLYN JACKSON, audiologist, audiometric service executive; b. DeQueen, Ark., Aug. 27, 1953; d. Carlton Conway and Charlie Mae (Chaney) Jackson; m. Philip Austin Tolley, June 25, 1977. BSE, U. Ark., 1975; MS (grantee), So. Methodist U., 1979. Tchr. of deaf Mo. State Sch. for the Deaf, Fulton, 1975-76, Tex. Regional Day Sch. for the Deaf, Kenedy, 1976-77; clin. audiologist E.N.T. Surg. Assn., Richardson, Tex., 1979-81; indsl. audiologist, pres. Audiometric Services, Inc., Dallas, 1982—. Mem. Tex. Safety Assn. (bd. dir. 1983—, officer 1988-89), Nat. Hearing Conservation Assn. (bd. dirs. 1985—, pres. elect 1988, pres. 1989), Am. Speech Lang. Hearing Assn. (cert. clin. competence in audiology), Am. Soc. Safety Engrs., Am. Indsl. Hygiene Assn. Avocations: sailing, travel. Office: Audiometric Services Inc 2718 Hollandale Ste 200 Dallas TX 75234

TOLLIVER, DOROTHY OLIVIA, educational association administrator; b. Cleve.; d. Enoch and Olivia (Smith) Greenwood; m. Stanley E. Tolliver Sr., Aug. 21, 1951; children: Stephanie, Sherrie, Stanley E. Jr. BS in Edn., Kent State U.; MA in Supervision, Baldwin-Wallace Coll., 1980; postgrad., U. Akron, 1985, 87. Cert. family life educator. Elem. sch. tchr. Cleve. Bd. Edn., 1945-51, music educator, 1969-82, 85-87, social studies tchr., 1982-85; instr. Dyke Coll., Cleve., 1987; dir. Parent Info. Ctr., Cleve., 1962—. Mem. citizen's adv. bd. Cuyahoga County Juvenile Ct., 1973-86; mem. adv. bd. Upward Bound Program Case Western Res. U., Cleve., 1982—; state chmn. juvenile justice task force Ch. Women United, Columbus, Ohio, 1975-76; mem. Cleve. Orchestra Chorus, 1972-75, Cuyahoga County Youth Svcs. Bd., 1982-88, Joint Ctr. Polit. Studies. Mem. AAUW (v.p. Cleve. chpt. 1975-76), LWV, Nat. Assn. Social Workers, Nat. Coun. on Family Rels., Am. Assn. for Counseling and Devel., Gerontol. Soc. Am., Nat. Coun. for Social Studies, Ohio Counsel for Social Studies, Internat. Platform Assn., Acad. Family Mediators, Cleve. Bar Aux., Fortnightly Club, Women's City Club. Congregationalist. Office: Parent Info Ctr PO Box 1893 Cleveland OH 44106

TOLOSKO, KAREN LYNN, mathematics teacher; b. Chgo., Jan. 26, 1965; d. Paul A. and Betty Ann (Dumerer) T. Student, Northwestern U., 1983-85; BA, Ariz. State U., 1987. Math. tchr. Mesa (Ariz.) Pub. Schs., 1987—; tutor Learning Dynamics, Tempe, Ariz., 1986—. Tchr. Venture grantee PCS, Inc., 1988-89. Mem. Mesa Educators Assn., Ariz. Educators Assn., Kappa Delta. Roman Catholic. Home: 625 S Westwood Mesa AZ 85210

TOLSON, SHARON GRACE, director, educator; b. Elyria, Ohio, June 4, 1947; d. Robert D. and Belva M. (Hawke) Hoskin; m. William D. Tolson, Aug. 16, 1969 (div.). BA, Kent State U., 1969, MS, 1972; postgrad., Stetson U., 1980-82. Cert. ednl. adminstr.; speech pathology and audiology. Exptl. lang. tchr. Akron (Ohio) Bd. Edn., 1969-70; speech pathologist Cuyahoga Falls (Ohio) Bd. Edn., 1970-71; lang. coordinator Goodwill Rehab. Ctr., Canton, Ohio, 1971-74; ednl. coordinator Child Guidance Ctr., Akron, 1974-78; behavior disorders tchr. Green Bd. Edn., Greensburg, Ohio, 1978-79; lang. diagnostician Sch. Bd. Brevard County, Titusville, Fla., 1979-80; placement specialist Sch. Bd. Brevard County, Titusville, 1980-85; dir. Fla. Diagnostic & Learning Resource System, Merritt Island, Fla., 1985—; mem. State Com. on Comprehensive System Personnel Devel., Tallahassee, Fla., 1988-89, Multiagency Network, Brevard County, 1986—; tng. com. Parent Edn. Network, State of Fla., 1987—. Coordinator Very Spl. Arts, Kennedy Found., Brevard County, 1988—; adv. bd. Parent to Parent, Tampa,. Fla., 1985-89; mem. Gov.'s Constituency for Children, Daytona, Fla., 1987-89. Mem. Am. Speech & Hearing Assn., Bus. & Profl. Women, Indian River Yacht (dir. 1983-86, sec. 1979-81). Home: 840 Sandgate St Merritt Island FL 32953 Office: Fla Diagnostic System 1450 Martin Blvd Merritt Island FL 32952

TOM, ELIZA, college administrator, marketing executive; b. N.Y.C., Apr. 9, 1963; d. Henry G.F. and Gloria (Lui) T. BBA, Bernard M. Baruch Coll., 1984. Office asst. Bernard M. Baruch Coll., N.Y.C., 1984-85, asst. registrar, 1985—; v.p. Tridium, Inc., N.Y.C., 1986—. Active Asian Pacesetters, N.Y.C., 1986—. Mem. NAFE, Asian Fin. Soc.

TOMA, JEANNE BROEMMELSICK, editorial consultant; b. St. Louis, Nov. 21, 1950; d. Howard August and Doine Edith (Williams) Broemmelsick; m. Richard L. Toma, Dec. 30, 1972; children: Richard A. R., John S. H. BA, U. Mo., 1971. Assoc. editor C.V. Mosby Co., St. Louis, 1972-78; editor and dir. communications Retina R & D Found., St. Louis, 1978-89; devel. editor Manning Co., St. Louis, 1989—; freelance editorial cons. and writer. Mem. Women in Communications, Inc. (Ruth Philpott Collins award 1980). Republican. Home: 329 Planthurst Saint Louis MO 63119

TOMAO, DOREEN ELIZABETH, sales executive; b. Yonkers, N.Y., Dec. 23, 1949; d. Robert Fitzgibbon and Doris Theresa (Farrell) Rodenhizer; m. Richard Tomao, Oct. 25, 1980; 1 child, Lindsey Elizabeth. AS with honors, Housatonic Community Coll., Bridgeport, Conn., 1974; BS in Mgmt. summa cum laude, U. New Haven, 1981. With Raymark Friction Co., 1967—; mgr. strategic mktg. and bus. planning Raymark Friction Co., Trumbull, Conn., 1983-84; dir. sales and mktg. Raymark Friction Co., Manheim, Pa., 1984—. Conn. Bus. Educators Assn. scholar, 1974. Mem. Automotive Parts Rebuilder's Assn., Friction Materials Standards Inst., Automotive Market Rsch. Coun., Friction Materials Standards Inst., Pootatuck Yacht Club (sec., bd. of govs. Stratford chpt. 1979), Alpha Sigma Iota Alpha. Roman Catholic. Home: 106 Hammersmith Ln Lititz PA 17543 Office: Raymark Friction Co 123 E Stiegel St Manheim PA 17545

TOMASCH, MARIA CHRISTINE, marketing professional; b. Bayshore, N.Y., Dec. 13, 1964; d. Louis John and Cleopatra (Triglianos) Gianaro; m. Kenneth Henry Tomasch, Sept. 30, 1989. BS in Telecommunication, U. Fla., 1988. Prodn. asst. WINK-TV, Ft. Myers, Fla., 1983-85; mem. spl. pub. rels. com. Coll. Health and Human Performance, Gainesville, Fla., 1986-87; assoc. producer WINK-TV, Ft. Myers, Fla., 1988-89; reporter WUFT-FM radio sta., Gainesville, 1987; mktg. adminstr. Missimer & Assocs., Inc., Cape Coral, Fla., 1989—; preview editor U. Fla., Gainesville, videographer Coll. of Edn.; pub. svc. announcer, writer WUFT-TV. Author, editor newsletter The Missimer Report, 1990. Mem. Aerho Nat. Broadcasting Soc., NAFE, Fla. Pub. Rels. Assn. Home: 5233 Red Cedar Dr Apt 7 Fort Myers FL 33907

TOMASCHEWSKY, MICHAELA MARIA, history educator; b. Munich, Dec. 22, 1947; came to U.S., 1949; d. Mikhail Vikentivich and Ingeborg F. (Albrecht) T. BA, Roosevelt U., 1974; MA, Northeastern Ill. U., 1977, U. Ill., Chgo., 1980. Contract adminstrv. Head Start svcs. Worthington, Hurst & Assocs., Chgo., 1970-75; adminstrv. asst. Affirmative Action Office, Northeastern Ill. U., Chgo., 1976-77; mem. faculty dept. psychiatry Med. Sch., U. Ill., Chgo., 1977-79, teaching assts. depts. history and women's studies, 1978-86, rsch. asst. Inst. for Humanities, 1985; instr. depts. history and polit. sci. Roosevelt U., Chgo., 1982-83; instr. depts. history and women's studies Northwestern U., Chgo. and Evanston, Ill., 1987—; vis. asst. prof. dept. history and philosophy U. Ind. NW, Gary, 1988—. Contbr. articles to profl. jours. Sec.-treas. Women in Crisis Can Act, Chgo., 1975-80; victim adv. Chgo. Rape Victim Advs., Chgo., 1976-78; interpreter Nat. Assn. Housing and Redevel. Ofcls., Lake County, Ind., 1990; bd. dirs. West Andersenville Neighbors Together, Chgo. James scholar U. Ill., Urbana, 1964-65; Fulbright fellow, Frankfurt, Fed. Republic Germany, 1981-82; Univ. fellow U. Ill., Chgo., 1983-84. Mem. Nat. Women's Studies Assn., Am. Hist. Assn., Assn. Ind. Historians, Women Historians Midwest, Chgo. Area Women's Studies, Friends George Sand, Women in German. Office: U Ind NW Dept History 3400 Broadway Gary IN 46408

TOMASZEWICZ, ELIZABETH ELEONORA, corporate training executive; b. Trani, Bari, Italy, July 11, 1946; came to U.S., 1951; d. Stanislaw and Ludmila (Aleksandrowicz) Mroczkowski; m. George Roman Tomaszewicz, Aug. 1, 1970. BA in Russian and Math., U. Mass., 1968; postgrad., NYU, 1968-69, Worcester Poly. Inst., 1972-73. Programmer Conn. Gen., Bloomfield, Conn., 1970-72; systems programmer Worcester (Mass.) Poly. Inst., 1972-73; project mgr. Am. Optical, Southbridge, Mass., 1973-75; dist. mgr. Advanced Systems, Inc., L.A. and Boston, 1975-81; v.p. S.W. region Advanced Systems, Inc., Dallas, 1981-83; v.p. sales Advanced Systems, Inc., Arlington Heights, Ill., 1983-87; sr. v.p. sales Applied Learning Internat., Naperville, Ill., 1987-88; exec. v.p. Applied Learning Internat., Naperville, 1988-89; founder, sr. v.p. The Roach Orgn., Rolling Meadows, Ill., 1989—. Mem. Am. Soc. for Tng. and Devel. Republican. Roman CAtholic. Home: 10 Lakewood Dr Bannockburn IL 60015 Office: The Roach Orgn 3501 W Algonquin Rd #200 Rolling Meadows IL 60008

TOMCZAK, NANCY JEAN, educator; b. Erie, Pa., June 23, 1938; d. Edward Leo and Jean Sophia (Wojnakowski) T. Student, Mercy Coll., 1970; postgrad., St. John's Coll., 1971-73, St. Thomas U., 1988--. Cert. Tchr. Tchr. Cath. Sch. System, Detroit, 1958-70; founder, dir. Hope House Inc., Cleve., 1970-75; tchr. Cerebral Palsy Ctr., Liberty, N.Y., 1976-78; dir. home svcs. Cerebral Palsy Ctr., Liberty; coord. Lazar House Hospice, East Ridge, N.Y., 1981-83; program supr. Assn. for Retarded Adults, N.Y., 1983-84; pre-sch. tchr. First Bapt., Huntsville, Tex., 1984-86; dir. religious edn. St. Thomas the Apostle Cath. Ch., Huntsville, 1987-90, pastoral assoc., 1990—. Bd. dirs. Coalition for Black Students, Cleve., Organized Labor, Cleve., Assn. for Retarded Children, Monticello; fund raiser Hope House, Cleve., 1972-74; grant writer 1970-72. Mem. Mental Health Assn., Female Execs., Nat. Assn. Catechists. Republican. Home: 77 Bull Run Conroe TX 77302 Office: St Thomas Cath Ch 1323 16th St Huntsville TX 77340

TOMCZYK, REBECCA BLOOMFIELD, communications executive; b. Chgo., Jan. 27, 1942; d. Henry H. and Beatrice A. (Ronz) Bloomfield; m. 1961 (div. 1974); children: Joshua A. Hillman, Pamela J. Hillman; m. Casimir J. Tomczyk, Sept. 6, 1980. Writer, researcher Project Wingspread U. Chgo., 1966-68; writer Sta. WBBM-TV/Chgo. Bd. Rabbis, 1969-72; assoc. creative dir., v.p. Leo Burnett Advt., Chgo., 1972-89; pres. Bright Star Enterprises, Chgo., 1989—; advt. cons. Chgo. Symphony Marathon, 1979-82, Ill. Spl. Olympics, Carbondale, Ill., 1983-86, Little Bros., Chgo., 1987, Found. for Excellence in Tech., Chgo., 1988-89. Writer, producer, actor and designer play The Revolutionary Mrs. Adams, 1988. Bd. dirs. Arve Connection Dance Co., Chgo., 1978-80, Rejoice Repertory Theatre Co., Chgo., 1986-87, Voyagers Theatre Co., Chgo., 1988; pres. bd. dirs. Chgo. Chamber Brass, 1982-85. Recipient Emmy award, 1971, Starch award Publ. Readership Report, 1978, Effie award Am. Mktg. Assn., 1987, 88, Addy award Am. Assn. Advt. Agys., 1989, Gold Lion award Cannes Internat. Film Festival, 1989. Mem. Chgo. Ad Club, Women's Bus. Devel. Ctr. Jewish. Office: Bright Star Enterprises 9063 Niles Ctr Rd Skokie IL 60076

TOMICH, NANCY ELLEN, editor; b. Belleville, Ill., May 17, 1945; d. John and Ethel Frieda (Bender) T.; m. Charles W. Puffenbarger, June 15, 1968 (div. Nov. 1974); m. John S. Zapp, May 22, 1976; 1 child, Vanessa. BS, U. Ill., 1967. Reporter Champaign (Ill.)/Urbana Courier, 1965-67, News Jour., Wilmington, Del., 1967, U.S. Transport, Washington, 1968; writer George Washington U., Washigton, 1969; reporter U.S. Medicine, Washington, 1970-78, editor, 1978—. Washington Journalism Ctr. fellow, 1968. Mem. Nat. Press Club, Soc. Profl. Journalists, AAAS, N.Y. Acad. Scis. Office: US Medicine 2033 M St NW Ste 505 Washington DC 20036

TOMISKA, CORA LORENA, civic worker; b. Fontana, Calif., July 30, 1928; d. Riley Royston and Winifred Lillian (Humphry) Green; m. Joseph Frank Tomiska, June 19, 1950; children: Jo Ann, William Joseph, Robert Royston, Charity Lillianne, Angelina Kathleen. AA, Chaffey Jr. Coll., 1948; BA, Calif. State Coll., San Bernardino, 1976, postgrad., 1976—. Owner Tomiska Aviaries, Fontana, 1963—. Pres. Redwood PTA, 1976, Sequoia Jr. High PTA, 1969-70, Fontana Council PTA, 1972-74; mem. exec. bd. 5th Dist. PTA, 1972-83, historian, 1976-79, v.p., dir. health, 1979-81, v.p., dir. parent edn., 1981-83; mem. Redwood PTA; sec. consol. projects adv. com. Fontana Unified Sch. Dist., 1972-81, sec. family life edn. project, 1982-86; mem. Mayoral Candidacy Com., 1978: counselor jr. gardening Fontana Redwood Blue Jays, 1964-83; pres. Fontana Garden Club, 1974-77; vol. Fontana Youth Svc. Ctr., Am. Heart Fund, Am. Cancer Soc., Christian Youth Edn., Valley Bible Ch., Fontana United Way; scholarship chmn. San Bernardino Valley dist. Calif. Garden Clubs, 1974-83; sec.-treas. Fontana Family Svc. Agy., 1976-79, pres., 1980-82; mem. Arthritis Found., Westside Bapt. Ch.; mem., personal care provider, estate mgr. Fellowship of the Living Water, 1984-88. Recipient 1st place award Calif. Jr. Flower Shows, 1969-73. Mem. AAUW (edn. chmn. 1981-82), ARC, San Bernardino County Mus. Assn., Fontana Hist. Soc., Am. Fedn. Aviculture. Address: 8365 Redwood Ave Fontana CA 92335

TOMKIEL, JUDITH IRENE, small business owner; b. St. Louis, Nov. 4, 1949; d. Melvin Charles William and Mildred Neva (Kayhart) Linders; m. William George Tomkiel, Dec. 15, 1972; children: Soteara, William, Kimberli, Christopher. Order filler Baker & Taylor Co., Sommerville, N.J., 1972-74; owner, founder The Idea Shoppe, Garden Grove, 1983--; seamstress, crafts person Cloth World, Anaheim, Calif.; vol. Reading Is Fundamental Program, Garden Grove, 1988—; freedom writer Amnesty Internat., Garden Grove, 1988—. Author numerous poems; pub., editor (newsletter) Shoppe Talk, 1987. Fellow World Literary Acad.; mem. Nat. Writer's Club, NAFE, Soc. Scholarly Pub. Office: The Idea Shoppe PO Box 323 Garden Grove CA 92642

TOMLIN, LILY, actress; b. Detroit, 1939. Student, Wayne State U.; studied mime with Paul Curtis, studied acting with Peggy Feury. Appearances in concerts and colls. throughout U.S.; TV appearances include Lily Tomlin, CBS Spls., 1973, 81, 82; 2 ABC Spls., 1975; formerly cast mem. The Music Scene, Laugh In; motion picture debut in Nashville, 1975 (N.Y. Film Critics award); also appeared in The Late Show, 1977, Moment by Moment, 1978, The Incredible Shrinking Woman, 1981, Nine to Five, 1980, All of Me, 1984, Big Business, 1988; one-woman Broadway show Appearing Nitely, 1977 (Spl. Tony award), The Search for Signs of Intelligent Life in the Universe (Drama Desk award, Outer Critics Circle award, Tony award 1986), 1985; recs. include This is a Recording, And That's The Truth, Modern Scream, On Stage. Recipient Grammy award 1971, 5 Emmy awards for CBS Spl. 1973, 81, Emmy award for ABC Spl. 1975. Address: PO Box 27700 Los Angeles CA 90027*

TOMLINSON, JANICE MEYER, insurance company executive; b. Axtell, Kans., Apr. 29, 1950; d. Henry Herman and Clara Catherine (Haug) Meyer; m. Thomas Fred Tomlinson, Nov. 24, 1973; 1 child, Ryan Thomas. BA, Marymount Coll., 1972. Underwriter trainee St. Paul Cos., Springfield, Mass., 1972-73; casualty underwriter, then casualty mgr. Chubb Group of Ins. Cos., New Haven, 1973-78; comml. lines mgr. Chubb Group of Ins. Cos., White Plains, N.Y., 1978-81, New Haven, 1981-85; adminstrv. mgr. Chubb Group of Ins. Cos., N.Y.C., 1985-86; br. mgr. Chubb Group of Ins. Cos., White Plains, 1986-90; nat. mgr. human resources Chubb & Son Inc., Warren, N.J., 1990—; instr., Inroads Nat. Tng. Seminar, Lawrence, Kans., 1987. Advisor, FIRST, White Plains, 1986—. Mem. NAFE. Roman Catholic. Office: Chubb & Son Inc 15 Mountain View Rd Warren NJ 07059

TOMLINSON-KEASEY, CAROL ANN, psychology educator; b. Washington, Oct. 15, 1942; d. Robert Bruce and Geraldine (Howe) Tomlinson; m. Charles Blake Keasey, June 13, 1964; children: Kai Linson, Amber Lynn. BS, Pa. State U., 1964; MS, Iowa State U., 1966; PhD, U. Calif., Berkeley, 1970. Lic. psychologist, Calif. Asst. prof. psychology Trenton (N.J.) State Coll., 1969-70, Rutgers U., New Brunswick, N.J., 1970-72; prof. U. Nebr., Lincoln, 1972-77; prof. U. Calif., Riverside, 1977—, acting dean coll. humanities and social scis., 1986-88, chmn. dept. psychology, 1989—. Author: Child's Eye View, 1980, Child Development, 1985; also numerous chpts. to books; articles to profl. jours. Recipient Disting. Tchr. award U. Calif., 1986. Mem. Am. Psychol. Assn., Soc. Rsch. in Child Devel., Riverside Aquatics Assn. (pres. 1985). Office: U Calif Dept Psychology Riverside CA 92521

TOMMASO, ANNE KATHRYN, health care consultant; b. Bklyn., July 25, 1960; d. Nicholas and Vincenza Jean (DiGiovanna) T. BS in Mgmt., St. John's U., Jamaica, N.Y., 1982, MBA, 1988; MPA, Columbia U., 1986. Adminstr. Boulevard Hosp., Long Island City, N.Y. 1982-84; health care cons. Healthscope Mgmt. Services Corp., Mount Vernon, N.Y., 1985-87, Peat Marwick Main & Co., N.Y.C., 1987—. Treas. 33d AD Democratic Club, Queens, N.Y., 1979. Mem. N.Y. Soc. Health Planning, Nat. Assn. Female Execs. Roman Catholic. Avocations: skiing, flying, reading. Home: 6 Milton St Maplewood NJ 07040 Office: Peat Marwick Main & Co 345 Park Ave New York NY 10154

TOMMEY, BELINDA STOKES, hospital administrator; b. Columbia, S.C., July 23, 1957; d. Robert Joseph and Betty (Harrod) Stokes; m. Rodney Edmond Tommey, June 4, 1983; children: Lindsey Morgan, Joseph Oliver. BS in Nursing, Tex. Woman's U., 1979, MS, 1986. RN, Tex. RN Presbyn. Hosp., Dallas, 1983-85; adminstrv. fellow Baylor U. Med. Ctr., Dallas, 1985-86, mktg. mgr., 1986-87, adminstrv. dir. transplant svcs., 1987—. Mem. Am. Coll. of Healthcare Execs. Office: Baylor University Med Ctr 3500 Gaston Ave Dallas TX 75246

TOMPKINS, A. KATHLEEN KELLY, civic worker; b. St. Johns, Mich., Jan. 15, 1903; d. William Thomas and Harriet A. (Wright) Kelly; grad. U. Cin. Conservatory of Music, 1926; m. Neil Wright (dec.); children—Neil, Ross; m. 2d, Raymond McLaughlin, June 1961 (dec.); m. 3d, Lawrence E. Tompkins, June 5, 1976 (dec. Apr. 1985). Concert pianist, 1932-37; social dir. Lakeside Hotel, Eaglesmere, Pa., 1938-47; publicity dir. Pocono Manor, 1947-49; resident mgr. Gulf Winds Apts., St. Petersburg, Fla., 1949-50; social dir. Marshall House, York Harbor, Maine, 1951. Bd. dirs. Sarasota Music Club, 1964—, pres., 1966-68, parliamentarian, 1976-81; bd. dirs. Fla. Fedn. Music Clubs, 1968—; piano chmn., mem. artists selection com. Community Concerts Bd., 1971—; pres. Golden Gate Point Assn., 1962—, cons., 1977-81, also bd. dirs. Named Realtor of Yr., Sarasota Realtors Assn., 1960. Mem. Delta Omicron (nat. pres. 1931-37). Episcopalian. Home: 7979 S Tamiami Trail #214 Sarasota FL 34231-6869

TOMPKINS, DONNA ELLEN, communications specialist; b. Baton Rogue, Dec. 19, 1959; d. Edward Madison and Agnes (Sproha) T. BA in Journalism, U. N.C., 1981. Vol. Vol. Ministries Community, Harrisonburg, Va., 1981-82; coord. of youth ministry Youth Ministry Diocese of Raleigh, Smithfield, N.C., 1982-85; spl. projects ass. Capitol Broadcasting Co., Raleigh, 1985; adminstrv. asst. Sta. WRAL-FM, Raleigh, 1986; sr. communications specialist Carolina Power & Light Co., Raleigh, 1986—. Assoc. exec. dir. Hugh O'Brian Youth Found., 1989, dir. pub. rels., 1988. Mem. Women in Communications Inc. (bd. dirs., pres. 1987-89, publicity chair 1987, job info. chair 1989-90, newsletter chair 1990—). Office: Carolina Power & Light Co 411 Fayetteville St Mall Raleigh NC 27601

TOMPKINS, MARY MOULTON, pyschiatric nurse; b. Montpelier, Vt., July 10, 1951; d. Walter Redmond and Marie (Bisson) Moulton; m. William Andrew Tompkins, Nov. 28, 1981. Student, U. Colo., 1977-79; BS in Nursing, U. Ariz., 1981. RN, Ariz., Calif. Mem. nursing staff Kino Community Hosp., Tucson, 1981-84, Mercy Hosp., San Diego, 1984; charge nurse, supr. Alvarado Pkwy. Inst., La Mesa, Calif., 1985—, insvc. instr., 1986—; instr. Nursing Advancement Ctr., San Diego, 1985-86. Active in The Hunger Project, San Francisco, 1980—, Save the Children, San Diego, 1988, Prison Possibilities, Carlsbad, Calif., 1988—. Named psychiatric "Nurse of Yr.", Alvarado Parkway Inst., 1989.

TOMPKINS, PAMELA SUE, land manager; b. Duncan, Okla., May 3, 1955; d. Henry Oliver and Patsy Jean (Fulton) T. Student, U. Okla., Norman, 1977-79. Stenographer Gulf Oil Corp., Oklahoma City, 1977-78, accounts payable clk., 1978, sr. clk., 1978-80; in-training landman O-Tex Energy Inc., Oklahoma City, 1980-81; jr. landman, lease records supr. HG&G Inc., Oklahoma City, 1981-82; land analyst Wilshire Oil Co. Tex., Oklahoma City, 1982-84; land mgr. Berry Petroleum Corp., Oklahoma City, 1984-85; pvt. practice land and div. order cons., 1985—; owner Wonder Weaves Inc., Oklahoma City. Vice-chmn. Oklahoma City Planning Commn., 1988-89; Okla. planning commr., 1988-89; mem. Oklahoma City Plan Update Steering Com.; mem. N.E. 63d St. devel. com. City Oklahoma City, landscaping com.; chmn. front yard parking com. City Oklahoma City; pres. Gatewood Neighborhood Assn., 1987-88, dist. steering com. Mem. Am. Planning Assn., Oklahoma City Assn. Petroleum Landmen. Republican. Baptist. Home: 924 NW 17th St Oklahoma City OK 73106-4026

TOMS, KATHLEEN MOORE, nurse; b. San Francisco, Dec. 31, 1943; d. William Moore and Phyllis Josephine (Barry) Stewart. RN, AA, City Coll. San Francisco, 1963; BPS in Nursing Edn., Elizabethtown (Pa.) Coll., 1973; MS in Edn., Temple U., 1977; MS in Nursing, Gwynedd Mercy Coll. 1988; m. Benjamin Peskoff; children from previous marriage: Kathleen Marie Toms Myers, Kelly Terese Toms. Med.-surg. nurse St. Joseph Hosp., Fairbanks, Alaska, 1963-65; emergency room nurse St. Joseph Hosp., Lancaster, Pa., 1965-69, blood, plasm and components nurse, 1969-71; pres. F.E. Barry Co., Lancaster, 1971—; dir. inservice edn. Lancaster Osteo. Hosp., 1971-75; coord. practical nursing program Vocat. Tech. Sch., Coatesville, Pa., 1976-77; dir. nursing Pocopson Home, West Chester, Pa., 1978-80, Riverside Hosp., Wilmington, Del., 1980-83; assoc. Coatesville VA Hosp., 1983-89; chief Nurse, 1984-89; with VA Cen. Office; supr. psychiat. nursing Martinez (Calif.) VA Med. Ctr., 1989—; trainee assoc. chief Nursing Home Care Unit, Washington; mem. Pa. Gov.'s Council on Alcoholism and Drug Abuse, 1974-76; mem. Del. Health Council Med.-Surg. Task Force, 1981-83; dir. Lancaster Community Health Ctr., 1973-76; lectr. in field. Lt. col. Nurse Corps, USAR, 1973—. Decorated Army Commendation medal, Meritorious Svc. medal; recipient Community Service award Citizens United for Better Public Relations, 1974; award Sertoma, Lancaster, 1974; Outstanding Citizen award Sta. WGAL-TV, 1975; U.S. Army Achievement award, 1983. Mem. Elizabethtown, Temple U. Alumni Assns., Pa. Nurses' Assn. (dir.), Sigma Theta Tau, Beta Gamma. Inventor auto-infuser for blood or blood components, 1971. Home: 208 Sea Mist Dr Vallejo CA 94591 Office: Martinez VA Med Ctr John Muir Dr Martinez CA 94553

TOMSETT, JANET MOFFAT, legal administrator; b. Windsor, Ont., Can., June 3, 1943; d. Arthur William and Jean Elizabeth (Lee) Moffat; m. Robert W. Tomsett, June 20, 1964 (div. 1979); children: Robert W., Duncan M. Student, U. Windsor, 1961-62, Oakland Community Coll., Royal Oak, Mich., 1988—. Sec. All Saints Episcopal Ch., Detroit, 1975-78; reg. sec. IDS, Oak Park, Mich., 1978-81; reg. rep. IDS, 1981-82, 83; agt. John Hancock, Southfield, Mich., 1982-83; agy. mgmt. sec. Prin. Fin. Group, Birmingham, Mich., 1984; legal adminstr. Glotta, Adelman, Dinges & Riley, Detroit, 1984-85, Maddin, Weiner, Hauser, Wartell, Roth, Southfield, 1985, Harness, Dickey & Pierce, Birmingham, 1985-89, Mager, Monahan, Donaldson & Alber, Detroit, 1989—. Active various polit. campaigns. Mem. Assn. Legal Adminstrs. Episcopalian. Office: Mager Monahan Donaldson & A lber 2400 First National Detroit MI 48226

TONELLI, EDITH ANN, art gallery director, art historian; b. Westfield, Mass., May 20, 1949; d. Albert Robert and Pearl (Grubert) T. B.A., Vassar Coll., 1971; M.A., Hunter Coll., 1974; Ph.D., Boston U., 1981; grad., Mus. Mgmt. Inst. U. Calif.-Berkeley, 1981. Arts curriculum coordinator Project SEARCH, Millbrook, N.Y., 1972-74; curator DeCordova Mus., Lincoln, Mass., 1976-78; dir. art gallery, asst. prof. art U. Md., College Park, 1979-82, dir. mus. studies program, 1979-82; project dir. Summer Inst. Artists U. Md., 1981-82; dir. Frederick S. Wight Art Gallery, 1982—; adj. asst. prof. art UCLA, 1982—; reviewer pub. programs NEH, 1977—. Author exhbn. catalogs. Fellow Nat. Endowment Arts, 1981; predoctoral fellow Smithsonian Instn., 1979; doctoral and teaching fellow Boston U., 1974-76; mem. Helen Squire Townsend fellow Vassar College, 1971-72; recipient dissertation award Boston U. Vis. Com., 1979. Mem. Am. Assn. Museums, Coll. Art Assn., Women's Caucus for Art, Am. Fedn. Arts (advisor profl. tng.), Assn. Art Mus. Dirs. (trustee 1987—), Am. Studies Assn., Art Table Inc. Office: UCLA Wight Art Gallery 1100 Gallery Bldg 405 Hilgard Los Angeles CA 90024

TONELLI, GIOVANNA MARIE, professional development consultant, social worker; b. Phila., Nov. 13, 1951; d. Peter Paul and Mary Rita (Campagna) T. AAS, Community Coll. of Phila., 1972; B of Social Work, Temple U., 1974, MSW, 1981. Lic. social worker, Pa. Med. social worker Bio-Med. Applications, Phila., 1976-79; with foster care program Tabor Children's Svcs., Doylestown, Pa., 1981; with adoption program, cons. Tabor Children's Svcs., Doylestown, 1982; social worker City of Phila., 1982; program dir. Italian Home for Children, Boston, 1983-87; trainer, cons. Temple U., Phila., 1987; social worker Support Ctr. for Child Advocates, Phila., 1987-88; trainer/ cons. profl. devel. Becoming, Phila., 1987—; mem. exec. bd. Today's Child, Boston, 1985-87. Vol. Boston Dept. Social Svcs., 1986-87; adv. Nat. Abortion Rights Action League, Phila. and Boston, 1974-89. Recipient Achiever award Success Motivation Inst., Inc., Waco, Tex., 1988. Mem. Nat. Assn. Social Workers (mem. child welfare task force 1984-87), Nat. Assn. Female Execs., Phila. Women's Network. Home and Office: Becoming 905 Mountain St Philadelphia PA 19148

TONEY, EDNA, playwright, actress; b. N.Y.C., Mar. 22, 1914; d. Henry and Frieda (Berger) Greenfield; m. Anthony Toney, Apr. 8, 1947; children: Anita Karen, Adele Susan. Student New Theatre Sch., 1936; Columbia U., 1953-55, New Sch. Social Research, 1975. Actress WPA Theatre Project, N.Y.C., 1937; writer Kraft Music Hall, N.Y.C., 1946; writer, producer, actress schs., community ctrs., colls., libraries, etc., 1972-82; playwright Meet Miss Lucy Stone (video prodn. written by and starring Edna Toney 1988), Lincoln Ctr. Library's Museum of the Performing Arts, 1977, Baby Brother Prodn., Mid-Hudson Arts and Sci. Ctr., Poughkeepsie, N.Y., 1980; writer, dir., actress, producer Katonah Community Theatre, N.Y., 1984; columnist Queries and Theories. Author: Once Told Tales, 1967, How to Become a Famous Playwright, 1987; featured in The Rosenbergs: Collected Visions of Artists & Writers by Rob Okun, 1988, Book of Spoofs, edited by Norman Cousins, 1989. Benefit performance Meet Miss Lucy Stone, North Westchester-Putnam County Women's Resource Ctr., Mahopac, N.Y., 1986; featured performer Sane/Freeze of No. Westchester Hiroshima Day meeting, 1989; performer for Rosenberg Commemoration Program, NYU Law Sch., 1990. Recipient acting awards 10th Annual Arts Festival, 1976. Mem. NOW, Women's Internat. League Peace and Freedom, SANE, Katonah Gallery. Democrat. Avocation: swimming. Home: 16 Hampton Pl Katonah NY 10536

TONGE, MURIEL SMITH, educator; b. Biddeford, Maine, Apr. 28, 1926; d. Donald Oscar and Ruth (Means) Smith; m. Robert Morgan Tonge, June 15, 1948; children: Robert, James, Richard. BA, Vassar Coll., 1948. Geneticist Detroit Inst. Cancer Rsch., 1949-54; tchr. sci. Coburn Classical Inst., Waterville, Maine, 1963-69; substitute tchr. Waterville Sch. Dept., 1970—. Mem. Maine Libr. Commn., Augusta, 1975-80, Maine Arts Commn., Augusta, 1986-88; pres. Maine Libr. Trustees, Augusta, 1975-80; master judge Nat. Coun. of State Garden Clubs, Inc., 1980—. Mem. Cen. Maine Garden Club (pres. 1978-80). Republican. Baptist. Home: 5 Greylock Rd Waterville ME 04901

TONINI, CARRIE BEAL, real estate executive; b. Cleve., Jan. 3, 1950; d. Joe Leon and Catherine L. (Gallucci) Beal; m. Richard B. Tonini, Feb. 16, 1980 (div. 1986); children: Ammon B., Cydon J., Carly C. AA, Palomar Coll., San Marcos, Calif., 1978. Pres., prin. Video-Go, Leucadia, Calif., 1978-84; real estate agt. Jelley Co., Encinitas, Calif., 1984-86; real estate mgr. Jelley Co., La Jolla, Calif., 1986—; speaker, trainer Jelley Co., Del Mar, Calif., 1986—; speaker Bldg. Industry Assn., San Diego, 1990—. Pres. PTA, Encinitas, 1982, chmn. fundraising, 1980-82; video prodn. Leucadia Hist. Soc., 1981-82. Mem. Real Estate Brokers La Jolla, San Diego Assn. Realtors (speaker 1989—). Office: Jelley Co 7825 Fay Ave La Jolla CA 92037

TONUCCI, ELIZABETH FOX, human resources director; b. Hartford, Conn., Feb. 19, 1944; d. Wesley Vincent and Gertrude Clarissa (Sibley) Birge; m. Armand William Tonucci, July 8, 1967 (div. Jan. 1983); children: Karen, Katherine. BS in Elem. Edn., U. Conn., 1966; cert. profl. in human resources, Personnel Accreditation Inst. Tchr. Salem (Conn.) Elem. Sch., 1966-67, John Fitch Sch., Windsor, Conn., 1967-69; dir. vols. Manchester (Conn.) Meml. Hosp., 1979-86; mgr. personnel Shipman & Goodwin, Hartford, 1986-87; dir. human resources St. Joseph Coll., West Hartford, Conn., 1987—. Mem. Citizens Adv. Com. for Ednl. Goals, Manchester, 1980-81, Manchester Human Relations Commn., 1982-85; co-chmn. Manchester Interracial Council, 1981-84. Mem. Soc. for Human Resource Mgmt., So. New Eng. Coll. and Univ. Pers. Assn., Human Resource Assn. of Cen. Conn. (chmn. profl. devel./accreditation 1986-87, sec. 1988-90). Democrat. Congregationalist. Home: 21 Croft Dr Manchester CT 06040 Office: St Joseph Coll 1678 Asylum Ave West Hartford CT 06117

TOODLE, BRENDA ELAINE, computer software specialist; b. Detroit, Feb. 26, 1940; d. Harold Monroe and Raciene Maurice (Ison) Simmons; m. George Nathaniel Kimbrough, June 9, 1962 (div. 1981); children: Craig Harold, Traci Lynn; m. Charles Daniel Toodle, June 17, 1989. BS, Wayne State U., 1962; MA, U. Mich., 1967; cert. edn. specialist, Wayne State U., 1984. Cert. tchr. spl edn. K-12 mentally impaired, counseling and guidance K-12. Spl. edn. tchr. Detroit Bd. Edn., 1962-67, elem. tchr., 1967-78, counselor, 1978-1983, computer trainer, 1984-85, microcomputer software coordinator, 1985—; cons. Detroit Fedn Tchrs., 1979, Mich. Assn. Computer Users, 1985, Delta Kappa Gamma, 1986, WDTR Radio, 1985-86; mem. Metro Detroit Reading Coun., 1974—, mem. adv. bd., 1986-87. Editor: Detroit Pub. Schs. Software Catalog, 1985—. Mem. NAACP, 1975—, adv. bd. Metro Detroit Reading Coun., 1986-87; tutor TAIOPS, Detroit Pub. Libr., 1976-79. Mem. Detroit Assn. Computer Users (treas. 85—), Metro Detroit Alliance Black Adminstrs., Mich. Assn. Computer Users In Learning, Wayne State U. Coll. Edn. Alumni Assn. (bd. govs. 1987—), Beta Sigma Phi, Phi Delta Kappa, Delta Sigma Theta, Delta Kappa Gamma (treas. Zeta chpt. 1986-90). Office: Detroit Pub Schs 9345 Lawton Detroit MI 48206

TOOHILL, CAROL MARIE, dental group administrator; b. Chgo., May 23, 1961; d. Robert James and Kathryn Louise (Dennett) T. BA in Journalism, U. Wis., 1983. Systems mgr. Wauwatosa (Wis.) Dental Group, 1983-87, adminstr., 1987—. Mem. Internat. Assn. Bus. Communicators, Dental Group Mgmt. Assn., Wis. Dressage and Combined Tng. Assn. (publicity chmn. 1988—). Office: Wauwatosa Dental Group 2600 N Mayfair Rd Wauwatosa WI 53226

TOOHILL, VIVIAN ELAINE, manufacturing company executive; b. L.A., Jan. 29, 1943; d. George Grenade Toohill and Elaine Andrea (Lingwood) Fortney. Student, Hillsdale (Mich.) Coll., 1961-64; BA in Social Sci., Mich. State U., 1980, M of Labor and Indsl. Relations, 1984. Exec. asst. Roberts Corp., 1978-82; dir. personnel Quality Dairy Co., Lansing, Mich., 1984-86; pers. adminstr., team success coord. Simpson Industries, Inc., Litchfield, Mich., 1986-87; mgr. employee rels. NI Automotive Trim div. Masco Industries, Novi, Mich., 1987-89; human resource mgr. Libbey-Owens-Ford Co., Clinton, Mich., 1989—; cons. PMA, Mason, Mich., 1985—; faculty Lansing (Mich.) Community Coll., 1984—. Editor Newsgram Newsletter, 1981-82, Robert's Round-Up Newsletter, 1981-82. Mem. Am. Soc. Personnel Adminstrs., Indstl. Relations Research Assn. (Lansing chpt.), Personnel Assn. Mid-Mich., Alumni Bd. Mich. State U. Sch. Labor and Indusl. Relations. Lutheran. Office: Libbey-Owens-Ford 11700 Tecumseh-Clinton Rd Clinton MI 49236

TOOTE, GLORIA E. A., lawyer, developer, columnist; b. N.Y.C.; d. Frederick A. and Lillie M. (Tooks) Toote. Student, Howard U., 1949-51; J.D., NYU, 1954; LL.M., Columbia U., 1956. Bar: N.Y. 1955, U.S. Dist. Ct. (so. and ea. dists.) N.Y. 1956, U.S. Supreme Ct. 1956. With firm Greenbaum, Wolff & Ernst, 1957; mem. editorial staff Time mag., 1957-58; asst. gen. counsel N.Y. State Workmen's Compensation Bd., 1958-64; pres. Toote Town Pub. Co. and Town Sound Studios, Inc., 1966-70; asst. dir. Action Agy., 1971-73; asst. sec. Dept. HUD, 1973-75; vice chmn. Pres.'s Adv. Council on Pvt. Sector Initiatives, 1983-85; housing developer, 1976—; pres. Trea Estates and Enterprises, Inc.; newspaper columnist. Former bd. dirs. Citizens for the Republic, Nat. Black United Fund, Exec. Women in Govt., Am. Arbitration Assn., Consumer Alert; bd. overseers Hoover Inst.; vice chair Nat. Polit. Congress of Black Women; former mem. Council Econ. Affairs, Rep. Nat. Com.; pres. N.Y.C. Black Rep. Council; exec. trustee Polit. Action Com. for Equality. Recipient citations Nat. Bus. League, Alpha Kappa Alpha, U.S. C. of C.; YMCA World Service award. Mem. Nat. Assn. Black Women Attys., N.Y. Fedn. Civil Service Orgns., Nat. Assn. Real Estate Brokers, Nat. Citizens Participation Council, Nat. Bar Assn., Delta Sigma Theta, others. Address: 282 W 137th St New York NY 10030

TOPHAM, MARGARET ANN, prison counselor; b. Brown City, Mich., May 8, 1950; children: Diane, Dennis, Daniel. BS in Corrections, No. Mich. U., 1988, BS in Sociology, 1988. Mental health aide Mich. Dept. Mental Health, Lapeer, 1976-83; prison counselor Mich. Dept. Corrections, Marquette, 1983-86; corrections officer Mich. Dept. Corrections, Clarkston, 1988-89; prison counselor Plymouth, 1989—.

TOPINKA, JUDY BAAR, state legislator; b. Riverside, Ill., Jan. 16, 1944; d. William Daniel and Lillian Mary (Shuss) Baar; BS, Northwestern U., 1966; 1 son, Joseph Baar. Features editor, reporter, columnist Life Newspapers, Berwyn and LaGrange, Ill., 1966-77; with Forest Park (Ill.) Review and Westchester News, 1976-77; coordinator spl. events Dept. Fedn. Communications, AMA, 1978-80; research analyst Senator Leonard Becker, 1978-79; mem. Ill. Ho. of Reps., 1981-84; mem. Ill. Senate, 1985—, judiciary I com., senate transp. com., appropriations I com., co-chmn. Citizens Council on Econ. Devel., U.S. Commn. for Preservation of Am.'s Heritage Abroad, serves on legis. ref. bur. ; former mem. minority bus. resource ctr. adv. com. U.S. Dept. Transp.; mem. adv. bd. Nat. Inst. Justice. Founder, pres., bd. dirs. West Suburban Exec. Breakfast Club, from 1976; Republican candidate Ill. Senate, 1984; chmn. Ill. Ethnics for Reagan-Bush, 1984, Bush-Quayle 1988; spokesman Senate Health, Welfare, Corrections Com., Fin. Instns. Com., Nat. Coun. State Legislatures Health Com.; mem nat. adv. coun. health professions edn. HHS; mem., GOP chairwoman Legis. Audit Commn. of Cook County.

TOPJIAN, MENA ROSE, educator; b. Cambridge, Mass., Sept. 7, 1936; d. Daniel and Siran T. B.S. in Edn., Boston U., 1958, M.Ed. in Sch. Librarianship, 1966. Tchr., Deep River Elem. Sch., Conn., 1958, Prospect Sch., Beverly, Mass., 1959, Oak Grove Sch., North Miami Beach, Fla., 1960, Franklin Sch., Lexington, Mass., 1961-83, Bowman Sch., Lexington, 1983—. Author articles and reports in field of Native Am. studies. Mem. Nat. Council Social Studies Tchrs., Mass. Council Social Studies Tchrs., NEA, Mass. Tchrs. Assn., Lexington Tchrs. Assn., Pan Am. Soc., Cultural Survival Soc. Club: Victorian, World Affairs Council (Boston); Peabody Mus. (Cambridge, Mass.). Home: 36 F Jacqueline Rd Waltham MA 02154 Office: Bowman Sch Lexington MA 02154

TOPP, BARBARA HARRISON, library administrator; b. L.A., Oct. 2, 1937; d. Reuben Lionel and Rita (Ramella) Harrison; m. James Parker Topp (div. 1984); children: Gretchen, Krista, Margot. BA, San Jose State State U., 1960; MLS, SUNY, Geneseo, 1983. Dir. Arcade (N.Y.) Free Libr., 1980-82; asst. dir. Pub. Libr. Steubenville, Ohio, 1983—. Contbr. articles to profl. jours. Sec. Old Ft. Steuben Project, Inc., Steubenville, 1986—. Mem. ALA, Ohio Libr. Assn. (div. chmn. 1989-90), Southeastern Ohio Libr. Assn. (chmn. Steubenville 1989-90). Home: 483 Lovers Ln Apt 11 Steubenville OH 43952

TOPPAN, CLARA ANN RAAB (MRS. FREDERICK WILLCOX TOPPAN), accountant; b. Cheyenne, Wyo., Nov. 9, 1910; d. Cornelius Emil and Gizella (Marczelly) Raab; m. Frederick Willcox Toppan, July 23, 1949 (dec. Nov. 1966). BS, U. Wyo., 1931. CPA, Wyo., D.C. Sec. Yellowstone Nat. Park, 1934, Nat. Park Svc., Washington, 1934-37; chief clk. Grand Teton Nat. Park, Moose, Wyo., 1937-42; acct. Cordle Raab & Roush CPA, Casper, Wyo., 1942-45; owner Clara Raab Toppan CPA, Jackson, Wyo., 1945-53; ind. part-time acct., 1954—; instr. acctg. U. Wyo., 1967. Treas. Community Bldg. Fund, Jackson, 1952-54, Teton County Libr. Fund, Jackson, 1950-53. Clara Raab Toppan Day proclaimed by Gov. of Wyo., 1990. Mem. AICPA, AAUW, Am. Women's Soc. CPAs, Wyo. Soc. CPAs (hon. lifetime mem. 1990), Bus. and Profl. Women (organizer Jackson Hole club 1953), Jackson Hole C. of C. (an organizer), U. Wyo. Alumni Assn., Jackson Hole Trap Club, Jackson Hole Golf and Country Club, Brandenton Country Club, Phi Gamma Nu. Republican. Home: 3605 Sun Eagle Ln Bradenton FL 34210

TOPPING, NANCY GRACE, educator; b. Pitts., Nov. 5, 1934; d. Frank Williamson and Helen Luther Arnold (Wilson) T.; m. Maurice Jacques Bazin, Dec. 21, 1958 (div. June 1978); children: Michel Francois, Christine Nicole. BA, Ohio Wesleyan U., 1956; MA, Middlebury Grad. Sch. French, 1958; PhD, Stanford U., 1969; postdoctoral, Inst. Higher Edn. Adminstrn., 1977. Asst. English prof. Rutgers U., New Brunswick, N.J., 1970-71; dir. women's studies U. Pitts., 1977-78; assoc. prof. English and women's studies Old Dominion U., Norfolk, Va., 1978-84; dir. women's studies Old Dominion U., Norfolk, 1978-85, chair dept. English, 1985-89, prof. English & women's studies, 1984—; v.p. Women's Caucus Modern Lang., 1978-81; mng. editor Doris Lessing Newsletter, 1980-82; reader for various jours.; speaker in field. Author: Virginia Woolf and the Androgynous Vision, 1973; co-editor: Conversations with Nadine Gordimer, 1990; contbr. articles to profl. jours. Named for Faculty Devel. Trips to China, Japan, Ivory Coast, Tanzania. Mem. MLA, Nat. Women's Studies Assn., African Lit. Assn., nat. Coun. Tchrs. English, South-Atlantic MLA, Women's Caucus of Modern Lang. Democrat. Home: 4005 Gosnold Ave Norfolk VA 23508-2917

TOPPINS, SARAH ELIZABETH, real estate agent; b. Lake Village, Ark., Jan. 18, 1952; d. John Edwin and Anne (Davis) T. BS in Radio-TV-Film, U. Tex., 1973; MS in Polit. Sci., U. Ala., Tuscaloosa, 1977. Real estat lic., Md., Washington; Grad. Realtors Inst. Ops. mgr. WUOA Radio, Tuscaloosa, 1974; news dir. Sta. WQTY-WFMI Radio, Montgomery, Ala., 1974-76; reporter, anchor Ala. Radio News Network, Montgomery, 1976; capital bur. chief Fla. Info. Network, Tallahassee, 1976; instr. U. Ala., Tuscaloosa, 1976-77; producer, reporter, news dir. Ala. Pub. TV, Tuscaloosa, Montgomery, 1977-79; asst. prof. U. Ill., Urbana, 1979-86, Am. U., Washington, 1986-89; real estate agt. Long & Foster, Kensington, Md., 1987—; chair bd. Illini Media Co., Urbana, 1983-86; exec. sec. Ill. News Broadcasters Assn., Urbana, 1985-86; writing cons. NEA, Washington, 1988. Reporter, producer radio and TV stories. Actress, singer community theatre, Urbana, Tuscaloosa, 1972—. Recipient Ala. AP awards, 1975, Ala. Soc. Proj. Journalist award, 1979, Troy State Univ. Hector award, 1979, Coltrane Award for Media Excellence, Internat. Radio TV Soc., N.Y.C., 1989. Mem. Radio TV News Dirs. Assn. (bd. dirs. 1985-86), Soc. Profl. Journalists (local officer 1976), Montgomery County Bd. Realtors (Washington com. mem. 1988—), D.C. Assn. Realtors, Prince Georges County Assn. Realtors, Md. Assn. Realtors, Nat. Assn. Realtors (editorial bd. Realtor mag. 1988-89). Home: 12503 Valleywood Dr Silver Spring MD 20906

TORAN, YANCIE ANTOINETTE, hotel executive; b. Liberty, Tex., Nov. 9, 1962; d. James Emmitt and Arthola Marie (Tellis) T. BS, Sam Houston State U., 1988. With Four Seasons Hotel, Houston, 1983—, asst. mgr. Terrace Cafe, 1985-86, mgr. lobby lounge, 1986-87, asst. mgr. hotel, 1987-88, asst. exec. dir. housekeeping, 1988-89, reservtions mgr., 1989—. Mem. NAFE, Smithsonian assocs. Baptist. Home: 1300 Lamar St Houston TX 77010 Office: Four Seasons Hotel 1300 Lamar St Houston TX 77010

TORETTI, CHRISTINE JACK, gas company executive; b. Pitts., Feb. 24, 1957; d. Samuel Williams and Nell Jacqueline (Gibson) Jack; m. Michael Joseph Toretti, Aug. 15, 1981; children: Joseph Jack, Maxwell Jack. BS in Commerce, U. Va., 1981. Ptnr. C & N Co., Indiana, Pa., 1972—; pres. S. W. Jack Drilling Co., Indiana, 1984—; owner The Jack Co. and Plum Prodn., Inc., Indiana, 1989—; bd. dirs. The Savings and Trust Co. of Pa. Bd. mgrs. U. Va., 1984—; trustee Chi Omega Found., Cin., 1984—; pres. Found. Indiana U. of Pa., 1984—, YMCA of Indiana County, 1985—. Mem. Zonta Club (pres. 1986—). Republican. Presbyterian. Home: 2428 Oak Dr Indiana PA 15701 Office: SW Jack Drilling Co 43 S 9th St Indiana PA 15701-0697

TORKELSON, LUCILE EMMA, writer; b. Fond du Lac, Wis., Sept. 24, 1915; d. Joseph Michael Julka and Matilda (Elz) Pickart; m. Ivar John Torkelson, Sept. 24, 1945; children: Jean, David. PhB in Journalism, Marquette U., 1938; postgrad., U. Minn., 1950. Reporter Fond du Lac Reporter, 1938-41, Milw. Jour., 1941-45; movie critic South Bend (Ind.) Tribune, 1945; editor LWV Mag., Mpls., 1961-62; office mgr. Midwest Bearing Corp., Milw., 1963-89; book features writer Milw. Sentinel, 1963-75, book reviewer, 1990—; freelance writer Wauwatosa, Wis., 1990—. Contbr. articles to popular jours., mags. Active LWV, Mpls., 1957-62. Mem. Women in Communications (50 Years of Svc. cert. 1988), Great Books Assn., Theta Sigma Phi. Republican. Roman Catholic. Home: 6511 Washington Circle Wauwatosa WI 53213

TOROK, MARGARET LOUISE, insurance company executive; b. Detroit, June 22, 1922; d. Perl Edward Ensor and Mary (Seggie) Armstrong; m. Leslie A. Torok, Aug. 14, 1952; 1 child, Margaret Mary Ryan. Lic. Ins. Agy. Ins. agy. Grendel-Wittbold Ins., Southgate, Mich., 1961-68, corp. officer, 1968-72; pres. of corp. Grendel-Wittbold Ins., Southgate, 1972--; bd. dirs. Ind. Ins. Agts. of Mich., Lansing, 1984, Ind. Ins. Agts. of Wayne County, Dearborn, 1979—, pres. 1978. Bd. dirs. So. Wayne County C. of C., Taylor, 1974—, Downriver YMCA, Wyandotte, 1980, City of Southgate Econ. Devel., 1982—, City of Southgate Tax Increment, 1984—; lay chmn. Cath. Svc. Appeal for Archdiocese of Detroit, 1989. Recipient Capital award Ind. Ins. Agents of Mich., 1988; Advancing the Status of Women Wyandotte Southgate Taylor, 1988. Mem. Wyandotte Yacht Club, Soroptimist Club of Wyandotte, Southgate, Taylor. Roman Catholic. Office: Grendel Wittbold Agy Inc 12850 Eureka PO Box 1422 Southgate MI 48195

TORRANCE, CAROL LOUISE, computer scientist; b. Rahway, N.J., Dec. 9, 1936; d. John Vincent Gray Williams and Clara Catherine (Coons) Schade; m. Robert Edmund Torrance III, June 28, 1958; children: Robin Ellen, Robert Edmund IV, John Douglas. BS, Maryville (Tenn.) Coll., 1958; MEd, William Paterson Coll., Wayne, N.J., 1979. Cert. elem. tchr., media specialist, early childhood tchr. Tchr. Bd. Edn., Rutherford, N.J., 1958-60; tchr. Bd. Edn., Kearny, N.J., 1971-88, media specialist, computer coord., 1988—. Author: Listen, Laugh, Learn, 1979, Sound of the Week, 1984. Mem. county com. Rep. party Hudson County, N.J., 1984-89; treas. Lincoln Sch. PTA, Kearny, 1985-87, 88-90; elder First Presbyn. Ch., Arlington, N.J., 1975-78, 86-89; chmn. Midatlantic region Operation Friendship of Am., Palmer, Mass., 1983-88; chm. Woman's Club of Arlington, EMD, 1985-87. Recipient Jersey Jour. Woman of Achievement award, 1984. Mem. NEA, Ednl. Media Assn. N.J., N.J. Edn. Assn., Kearny Edn. Assn. (sch. rep. 1985-87, 89—), Hudson County Edn. Assn., Kindergarten Educators Assn. (Hudson County rep. 1985-88). Republican. Presbyterian. Home: 41 Alpine Pl Kearny NJ 07032 Office: Lincoln Sch 121 Beech St Kearny NJ 07032

TORRE, ELIZABETH LASSITER, social worker, educator; b. Winston-Salem, N.C., June 17, 1931; d. Vernon Clark and Mary (Pfohl) Lassiter; m. Mottram Peter Torre, Apr. 13, 1957 (dec.); m. Andrew Joseph Reck, June 17, 1987. student Wellesley (Mass.) Coll., 1948-49; BA, Duke U., 1952; MRE, Union Theol. Sem., 1957; MSW, Tulane U., 1966, PhD, 1972; cert. social worker, La. Field dir. undergrad. admissions Duke U., Durham, N.C., 1952-53; head tchr. primary dept. Riverside Ch., N.Y.C., 1957-60; instr. Sch. Social Work, Tulane U., New Orleans, 1966-72, assoc. prof., 1972—, coord. Indsl. Social Work Program, 1982-89; mem. faculty senate Tulane U., 1982—. Non-govtl. orgn. rep. UNICEF, World Fedn. Mental Health, 1957-61; cons. to v.p. community affairs WETA, Washington, 1979; cons. Office Spl. Symposia and Seminars, Smithsonian Instn., Washington, 1979-86. Treas., N.Y. Jr. League, 1961-62, v.p., 1962-63; bd. dirs. Community Vol. Svcs., New Orleans, 1965-68; mem. profl. adv. com. Project Pre-Kindergarten, Orleans Parish Sch. Bd., New Orleans, 1967-69; mem. adv. bd. DePaul Community Mental Health Ctr., New Orleans, 1971-72; mem. citizens adv. com. Orleans Parish Juvenile Ct., New Orleans, 1970-73; mem. Coun. on Social Work Edn. Task Force on Prevention, 1981-87 ; mem. New Orleans Women's Coalition Task Force on Employers and Working Parents, 1985—. NIMH grantee; Summer Inst. grantee Nat. Endowment Humanities, 1982; Newcomb Coll. fellow, 1989-90. Mem. Coun. Social Work Edn., Nat. Assn. Social Workers (bd. dirs. La. chpt. 1987-89), Am. Orthopsychiat. Assn., AAUP (treas. Tulane chpt. 1984-86, 88—), AAUP, World Future Soc., AAUW, Phi Beta Kappa. Office: Tulane U Sch Social Work New Orleans LA 70118

TORRENCE, MARGARET ANN, company executive; b. Memphis, Apr. 25, 1946; d. Simon Robert and Earline Juanita (Parker) Johnson; m. Tony Horace Robinson, Oct. 16, 1965 (div. 1968); 1 child, Veronica Antoinette; m. David Torrance, Oct. 16, 1968; 1 child, Erika Joyce. BS in BA, Pacific Western U., L.A., 1989; postgrad., Pacific Western U., 1989—. Adminstrv. sec. Lockheed Aircraft Svc. Co., Ontario, Calif., 1978—; paralegal Torrence Lawn Care, Rialto, 1985—; contract adminstr. Torrence Lawn Care, 1985—; asst. adminstr. Torrence Scholarship Svc., 1986—; counselor Torrence Group Home, San Bernardino, Calif., 1990—. With USAF, 1964-65. Mem. NAFE, Nat. Assn. Legal Secs., Nat. Mgmt. Assn., Inland Counties Assn. Paralegals. Office: Torrence Scholarship Svc 420 E Cerritos St Rialto CA 92376

TORRES, CHRISTINE MARIE, hospital administrator; b. Phila., Aug. 24, 1962; d. Luis Raul and Mildred Mary (DiLorenzo) T. BS in Biology, Villanova U., 1981. Cert. surg. technologist; cert. central svc. technician. Sr. surg. rsch. technician Hahnemann U. and Hosp., Phila., 1978-80, sr. operating rm. technician, 1980-84; operating rm./SPD coord. Pa. Hosp., Phila., 1984-86, asst. dir. SPD, 1986-87; SPD mgr. Bryn Mawr (Pa.) Hosp., 1987-89, asst. dir. materials mgmt., 1989—. Contbr. articles to surg. jours. Mem. Internat. Assn. Cen. Svc. Mgrs., Am. Hosp. Soc. Cen. Svc. Personnel, Assn. for Advancement Med. Instrumentations, Am. Asns. Cert. Surg. Technologists. Democrat. Roman Catholic. Office: Bryn Mawr Hosp 130 S Bryn Mawr Ave Bryn Mawr PA 19010

TORRES, CYNTHIA ANN, banker; b. Glendale, Calif., Sept. 24, 1958; d. Adolph and Ruth Ann (Smith) T.; m. Michael Victor Gisser, Mar. 11, 1989. AB, Harvard U., 1980, MBA, 1984. Research assoc. Bain & Co., Boston, 1980-82; assoc. Goldman, Sachs & Co., N.Y.C., 1984-88, v.p., 1988; v.p. First Interstate Bancorp, L.A., 1989—. Mem. judiciary rev. bd. Bus. Sch. Harvard U., Boston, 1983-84. Rockefeller Found. scholar, 1976; Harvard U. Ctr. for Internat. Affairs fellow, 1979-80; recipient Leadership award Johnson and Johnson, 1980; by Council for Opportunity in Grad. Mgmt. Edn. fellow, 1982-84. Mem. Acad. Polit. Sci., L.A. World Affairs Council, Harvard Club of So. Calif. (mem. schs. com. 1988—). Office: First Interstate Bancorp 707 Wilshire Blvd Los Angeles CA 90017

TORRES, HELEN ROSEMARIE, real estate company executive; b. N.Y.C.; d. Henry and Rosa (Stader) T. BS, NYU. Asst. buyer Saks Fifth Avenue, N.Y.C., 1946-48; buyer Wm. H. Block, Indpls., 1949-55, Filene's Dept. Store, Boston, 1956-60; owner, mgr. boutiques, Boston, 1961-72; brownstone rehabilitator Boston, 1973-78; assoc. Cooke Realty, St. Petersburg, Fla., 1984-87; owner, mgr., broker Homes By Helen, Inc., St. Petersburg, 1988—. Vol. Meals on Wheels, St. Petersburg, 1987. Mem. St. Petersburg Real Estate Bd., St. Petersburg Women's Coun. (sec. 1989, v.p. 1990), Nat. Assn. Realtors (sec. Women's Coun. of Realtors), Toastmasters (treas. St. Petersburg 1988). Roman Catholic. Home and Office: 656 15th Ave NE Saint Petersburg FL 33704-4709

TORRES, LOIS ANN, accountant; b. Mobile, Ala., Feb. 19, 1954; d. John and Eunice (Harris) T. B in Interior Design, La. State U., Baton Rouge, 1976, MS in Acctg., 1979. CPA, Tex., La.; CMA. Tax acct. Tenneco Oil Co., Houston, 1979-89, Sonat Inc., Houston, 1989-90, Mitchell Energy Corp., Houston, 1990—. Author: Dimensions in Elementary School Design, 1976. Pres., v.p., sec., treas. St. Michael's Single Adult Club, Houston, 1980-86; co. vol. United Fund, Houston, 1989; vol. Am. Heart Assn., Houston, 1988-89. Mem. La. State U. chpt. Am. Soc. Interior Design (charter), Tex. Soc. CPAs, Western Oil and Gas Assn. (tax com.). Home: 15519 Blakeway Houston TX 77032 Office: Mitchell Energy Corp 2204 Timbercock PO Box 4000 Woodlands TX 77387-4000

TORRES, YOLANDA, education educator; b. San Antonio, June 13, 1936; d. Roland and Bertha (Garza) Parga; children: Denise, Peter, Tina, Paul. BA in English, Incarnate Word Coll., San Antonio, 1957; MA in Psychology, St. Mary's U., San Antonio, 1975. Tchr. Edgewood Jr. and High Sch., San Antonio, 1957-61, Edgewood High Sch., San Antonio, 1964-65, Jeff Davis High Sch., Houston, 1961-62, Fox Tech. High Sch., San Antonio, Edison High Sch., San Antonio, 1980—; mem. State Bd. Edn. 20th Congl. Dist., San Antonio, 1975-77. Mem. Democratic Women Bexar County, San Antonio, 1970-80. Methodist. Home: 1811 Moreshead San Antonio TX 78231

TORRES-REAVES, CARMEN NELLIE, religious lay worker; b. Bklyn., Jan. 5, 1954; d. Ferdinand and Felicita (Castro) Torres; m. Robert McKinley Reaves Jr., Feb. 14, 1976; 1 child, Robert McKinley Reaves 3rd. AAS, Bronx Community Coll., 1982; cert. ministry, N.Y. Theol. Sem., 1987; BA in Religious Studies, Coll. New Rochelle, 1989; MDiv, Harvard U., 1989. Lay speaker United Meth. Ch., Bronx, N.Y., 1987-89; staff asst., bilingual tchr. Coll. New Rochelle (N.Y.), 1988-89; workshop leader Bonds of Difference Conf., Cambridge, Mass., 1990; pastoral counselor Windsor House, Cambridge; youth counselor Hispanic Coun. Inc., Cambridge. Scholar bd. higher ed. United Meth. Ch., 1989-90, N.Y. annual conf. United Meth. Ch., 1989-90; Hispanic fellow Fund for Theol. Edn., 1989-90, 90-91. Mem. Phi Theta Kappa. Democrat. Methodist. Office: Harvard Divinity Sch 45 Francis Ave Cambridge MA 02138

TORRES-ULLAURI, MARIÁ ISABEL, banker; b. Valencia, Spain; d. José Manuel and Vicenta (Soriano) Mazás; m. Modesto Ignacio Torres-Ullauri. Student, U. Madrid; cert., Cambridge (Eng.) U.; BA, NYU; MBA, Adelphi U., 1977. Mgr. corp. banking Royal Bank Can., N.Y.C., 1975-85; v.p., rep. N.Am. Banque de la Soc. Financiere Europeenne, N.Y.C., 1986—. Bd. dirs. Kennedy Child Study Ctr., N.Y.C., 1984-87; lectr. St. Patrick's Cathedral, N.Y.C., 1985—. Mem. Am. Mgmt. Assn., Univ. Club. Office: Banque Soc Fin Europeenne 375 Park Ave Ste 2707 New York NY 10152

TORRIE, R. ELAINE, public relations professional; b. Columbus, Ohio, Sept. 3, 1961; d. James Clarence and Dolores Evelyn (Brown) Torrie. BA in English, Ohio State U., 1982, MA in Journalism, 1989. Script- and copywriter ICOM, Inc., Columbus, 1985; pub. rels. cons. Columbus, Ohio, 1984-86; news bur. specialist Battelle Meml. Inst., Columbus, 1986-88; mgr. communication svcs. Mt. Carmel Health, Columbus, 1988-89; program communicator Borden, Inc., Columbus, 1990—. Mem. communcations com. St. Johns Episc. Ch., Worthington, Ohio, 1986—. Mem. NAFE, Pub. Rels. Soc. Am. (publicity chairperson Columbus chpt. 1987-88), Internat. Assn. Bus. Communicators, Women in Communications Inc., Kappa Tau Alpha, Phi Kappa Phi. Democrat. Office: Borden Inc 180 E Broad St Columbus OH 43215-3799

TORRIERI, JOAN MARIA, newspaper advertising executive; b. Mt. Vernon, N.Y., Apr. 23, 1950; d. Carmine and Angela (Masocchi) T. BS in Music and Journalism, Ind. U., 1972; MBA, SUNY, Binghamton, 1983. Profl. musician Indpls. Symphony, 1972-73, Jalapa (Veracruz, Mex.) Symphony, 1976-80, Veracruz Symphony, 1980-81; freelance musician, various locations, 1974-76; asst. mktg. dir. Greater Miami (Fla.) Opera, 1983-85; classified mktg. mgr. Miami Herald, 1985-87, classified, gen., El Nuevo Herald mktg. mgr., 1987-89, advt. promotion mgr., 1989—; bd. dirs. Builders Assn. South Fla., Miami, 1988-90. Vol. cons. Bus. Vols. for Arts, Miami, 1986—; mem. vol. bd. Insight Miami; mem. founding bd. dirs.

Fanfare, supporters New World Symphony, 1988-89. Office: Miami Herald 1 Herald Pla Miami FL 33132

TORRIERO, DOLORES FRANCES, human resources director; b. Bklyn., Mar. 5, 1957; d. Robert Nicholas and Naomi (Abrahms) T. BA, SUNY, Oswego, 1979; MPA, Kent State U., 1982. Rsch. assoc. Clemens, Nelson and Assocs., Columbus, Ohio, 1983; labor rels. asst. to mayor's office City of Cleve., 1983-84, labor rels. officer utilities dept., 1984-88; dir. human resources City of Canton, 1988—. Past pres., charter mem. S.W. Unitarian Universalist Ch. Mem. Ohio Pub. Employer Labor Rels. Assn. (sec.-treas.), Pub. Sector Labor Rels. Assn., Internat. Personnel Mgmt. Assn. Home: 931 Tollis Pkwy Broadview Heights OH 44147 Office: City of Canton 218 Cleveland Ave SW Canton OH 44702

TOSH, JUANITA PRILLAMAN, tire company executive; b. Axton, Va., Jan. 13, 1930; d. Stuart Owen and Ann Halvorsen (Jamison) Prillaman; attended public schs., Bassett, Va.; m. James Cleavon Tosh, June 5, 1961; children—Rebecca Ann Craze, Cheryl Sue Layton, Mark Cleavon. Owner, Russ Auto Service Co., Norfolk, Va., 1954-59; v.p. Russ & Prillaman Auto Service Inc., Collinsville, Va., 1959-68; co-owner John Allen Estates, Collinsville, 1975—; v.p. Town Gun Shop, Collinsville, 1983—; owner Tosh Tire Town, Collinsville, 1969—; sec.-treas. Cash Oil Sales Inc., Collinsville, Va., 1982-85. Mem. Retail Mchts. Assn., Va. Tire Dealers and Retreaders Assn., Nat. Tire Dealers and Retreaders Assn., Nat. Alliance Stocking Gun Dealers. Baptist. Home: 208 Ferndale Dr Collinsville VA 24078

TOSH, NANCY PECKHAM, magazine editor; b. Clinton, Iowa, May 5, 1932; d. George Taylor, III and Mildred Amelia (Smallfeldt) Peckham; m. David Warren Tosh, July 5, 1958 (div. Dec. 1978); children—Murray, Warren, Amy; m. Robert Louis Knop, Feb. 24, 1990. Student, Sullins Coll., Bristol, Va., 1950-52; B.A. in Journalism, State U. Iowa, 1954. Copywriter Sears, Roebuck & Co., Chgo., 1954-58; copywriter, staff writer Clapper Pub. Co., Inc., Park Ridge, Ill., 1973-76, copy editor Crafts 'N Things mag., 1976-77, asst. editor, 1977-79, editor, 1979—. Mem. P.E.O., Gamma Alpha Chi, Phi Theta Kappa. Republican. Home: 732 Park Plaine Park Ridge IL 60068 Office: Crafts 'N Things Mag 701 Lee St Ste 1000 Des Plaines IL 60016

TOSIC, SILVANA CECELIA, computer systems analyst; b. Buenos Aires, Argentina, June 9, 1961; came to U.S., 1963; d. Frank Anthony and Beatriz H. (Ruiz) Moffa; m. Andrej Budimir Tosic, May 19, 1985; 1 child, Kristina Andrea. BS in Computer Sci., Loyola U., Chgo., 1984, MS in Computer Sci., 1989. Methods analyst Commonwealth Edison, Chgo., 1984-89, systems analyst, 1989—. Roman Catholic.

TOSKOS, ELIZABETH ANN, ferret breeder; b. Newberry, S.C., Dec. 22, 1941; d. John Wallace and Margaret Elizabeth (Thomas) Bedenbaugh; m. Albert Charles Truitt, Apr. 6, 1970 (div. 1978); 1 child, Kimberly Anne; m. George Ernest Toskos, Nov. 24, 1978. Student, U. S.C., 1960-61, U. Md. Far East, Tokyo, 1967-69. Kennel operator Am. Kennel Club Show Dogs, Mt. Holly, N.J., 1961-66; pub. trainer harness horses U.S. Trotting Assn., various race tracks, N.Y., 1972-80; ferret breeder Internat. Ferret Assn., Roanoke, Va., 1980—, Ga. state dir., Gulfshore dir., sr. judge, 1985—, adminstrv. dir., 1989—. Contbr. to profl. publs. Mem. Internat. Ferret Assn. (life, Breeder of Yr. 1988). Republican. Episcopalian. Home and Office: 3604 Reese Circle Talmo GA 30575

TOSTI-VASEY, JOANNE LOUISE, research psychologist; b. N.Y.C., Aug. 8, 1953; d. Louis Peter and Martha Magdaline (Bowery) Tosti; m. Joseph John Vasey, Jr., July 13, 1975. BS with distinction, Va. Poly. Inst. and State U., 1974, MS, 1977; postgrad., Radford U., 1979-81; PhD, Pa. State U., 1987. Teaching asst. Va. Poly. Inst. and State U., Blacksburg, 1974-75; co-counselor Marriage & Family Consultation Ctr., Blacksburg, 1975-76; instr. Ohio State U. Coop. Extension Svc., Woodsfield, 1976-77; social worker Mental Health Svcs. of New River Valley, Blacksburg, 1978-81; teaching asst. Pa. State U., University Park, 1981-83, rsch. asst., 1981-87, instr., 1982-85; rsch. assoc. Hubbard & Revo-Cohen, Inc., Reston, Va., 1987-88; rsch. coord. Data Base, State College, Pa., 1988-90; pvt. practice J.L. Tosti-Vasey Applied Rsch. Analysts; dept. rep. Grad. Student Assn. Assembly Pa. State U., University Park, 1985-87; adminstrv. aide Ctr. Women Students Pa. State U., 1986-87; apptd. mem. Commn. Women Pa. State U., 1984-87; conf. dir. Sisterhood is Global Conf. Pa. State U., 1986. Author: (with others) Contemporary Approaches to Professional Updating, 1990; contbr. articles to profl. jours. Mem. NOW (pres. Montgomery City chpt. 1980-81, mem. Va. state policy coun.), Am. Psychol. Assn. (Psychology of Adult Devel & Aging div., Psychology of Women div.), Assn. Women in Psychology, Gerontol. Soc. Am., Bellefonte Hist. & Cultural Assn., Mortar Bd., Phi Kappa Phi, Omicron Nu, Phi Upsilon Omicron. Democrat. Home and Office: 231 W Linn St Bellefonte PA 16823

TOTELS, DARLENE, legal secretary; b. Beaumont, Tex., Sept. 6, 1958; d. Larry Earl and George Ann (Wilson) Tillotson; m. Richard Totels, July 17, 1984; 1 child, Laci Elizabeth. Student, Angelina Coll., Jasper, Tex., Lamar U., Port Arthur, Tex. Payroll clk. Setco Gen. Contractors, Beaumont; legal sec. Wright & Pitre, Neches, Tex., Seale, Stover, Coffield, Gatlin & Bisbey, Jasper, Tex., Mehaffy, Weber, Keith, Gonsoulin, Beaumont. Mem. exec. bd. Diocese of Beaumont; treas., jr. advisor St. Elizabeth CYO. Recipient 2nd pl. award in flashtype MDA, 1987, 88; recipient Golden Poet award, 1989. Mem. Beaumont Legal Sec. Assn. (pres., cert. of completion in legal edn.). Home: 2920 Oleander Groves TX 77619 Office: Mehaffy & Webber PO Box 16 Beaumont TX 77704

TOTER, KIMBERLY MROWIEC, nurse, medical company representative; b. Chgo., Apr. 22, 1956; d. A. Kenneth and Megan Dawson (Schiefer) Mrowiec; m. William Frank Toter, Dec. 16, 1978; children: William Kenneth, Kimberly Helen, Tod Frank, Matthew Jonathan, Haley Victoria. BS in Biology, Millikin U., 1978; grad. sch. nursing, Decatur (Ill.) Meml. Hosp., 1978. RN, Ill.; cert. operating room nurse. Operating room nurse Riddle Meml. Hosp., Media, Pa., 1979-89; pres., chief exec. officer Towic Med., Inc., Park Ridge, Ill., 1984—; instr. Delaware Community Coll., Media, 1986. Contbg. author: Decision Making in Perioperative Nursing, 1987; contbr. article to profl. jours.; patentee gastric drainage system. Mem. Assn. Operat. Rm. Nurses (v.p. Southeast Pa. chpt. 1983-85, pres.-elect 1985-86, pres. 1986-87, edn1. chmn. 1983-85, chmn. bylaw and policy com. 1987—, bd. dirs. 1983-89, chmn. 1987-89), Pa. Coun. Oper. Rm. Nurses, Am. Tech Mgmt. (bd. dirs. 1989—), Am. Reprographics Mgmt. (bd. dirs. 1989—), Pi Beta Phi. Roman Catholic.

TOTH, ANNE PATTEN, convalescent center administrator; b. Bridgeport, Conn., Dec. 14, 1947; d. Albert Allen and Harriet Ellen (Leib) Garofalo; m. Kevin Randall Meyer, July 29, 1967 (div. June 1972); 1 child, Nicole Marie; m. Michael Edward Toth, Oct. 6, 1978; children: Alexis Patten, Aaron Michael. Student Quinnipiac Coll., Wharton Sch., Harvard Bus. Sch. OPM Programmer, Save the Children, Westport, Conn., 1966-69; systems analyst Burndy Corp., Norwalk, Conn., 1969-70; pvt. practice systems analyst cons., Fairfield, Conn., 1970—; adminstrv. asst. Southport (Conn.) Manor, 1974-75, adminstr., chief exec. officer, 1975—, pres. 1987—. Chpt. pres. Am. Field Service, Greens Farms, Conn., 1984-86; chairwoman Daffodil Festival, Am. Cancer Soc., Fairfield, 1984; chairwoman Gourmet Gala March of Dimes, Stamford, Conn., 1985; mem. Nat. Child Safety Coun., 1986. Mem. Young Pres. Orgn., Fairfield C. of C. (treas. 1986), Am. Coll. Health Adminstrs. (cert.), Concerned Women's Colleagues, Am. Mgmt. Assn, Mountain Reach Home Owners Assn. (pres. 1987—). Democrat. Roman Catholic. Club: YWCA-100 Com. (bd. dirs. 1982—). Avocations: scuba diving, skiing, swimming, horseback riding, travel. Home: 160 Farmstead Hill Rd Fairfield CT 06430 Office: Southport Manor Convalescent Ctr 930 Mill Hill Terr Southport CT 06490

TOTH, ELIZABETH LEVAY, educational organization executive, lawyer; b. Woodbridge Twp., N.J.; d. Nicholas and Elizabeth (Nagy) Levay; m. Frederick Louis Toth; children: Frederick Albert, Thomas Franklin. BA, Rutgers U., 1970; JD, Seton Hall U., 1973; LLM, NYU, 1980. Bar: N.J. 1973. Mgr., dispatcher, prin. Tri-R-Bus Svc., Inc., Metuchen, N.J., 1959-71; arbitration atty. Robert J. Casulli, East Orange, N.J., 1973; mediator, hearing officer N.J. Pub. Employment Relations Commn., Trenton, 1974-75; assoc. dir. employee relations Woodbridge (N.J.) Twp. Pub. Schs., 1975-81; dir. govt. and community relations Ariz. Sch. Bd. Assn., Phoenix, 1981-85; exec. dir. Greater Phoenix Ednl. Mgmt. Coun., 1985—; completed Insts. for Orgnl. Mgmt., San Jose (Calif.) State U. and Stanford U., Calif., 1985-90. Mem. community adv. bd. Sta. KAET-TV, Ariz. State U., Tempe, 1985—; bd. dirs. North Community Behavioral Health Ctr. (merged into Terros Community Mental Health Orgn. 1988), Phoenix, 1984-88, Ariz. Partnership, 1988—, Ariz. Alliance Sci., Math. & Tech., 1989—; arbitrator Better Bus. Bur., Phoenix, 1987—; judge Acad. Decathlon, 1988—. Recipient plaque and pub. recognition North Community Behavioral Health Ctr., 1987. Mem. Am. Arbitration Assn. (arbitrator), Nat. Panel Mediators, Am. Soc. Assn. Execs., Ariz. Soc. Assn. Execs. (bd. dirs. 1987-88, Exec. of Yr. award 1987), Soc. Profls. in Dispute Resolution (sec. 1986-87), Pub. Affairs Profls. Ariz., Rutgers U. Alumni Club (bd. dirs.), Ariz. State U. West-Alumni Assn. (sec. 1990—), Phi Alpha Delta, Alpha Sigma Lambda. Home: 3142 W Marconi Ave Phoenix AZ 85023 Office: Greater Phoenix Ednl Mgmt Coun 415 E Grant St Ste 106 Phoenix AZ 85004

TOTH, GWENDOLYN JOYCE, musician; b. Cleve., July 28, 1955; d. Ernest J. and Ruth M. (Office) Toth; m. Philip M. Rosenberg, May 31, 1981 (div. 1988); m. Dongsok Shin, Sept. 10, 1989; 1 child, Samantha Emily. BA, Middlebury (Vt.) Coll., 1977; postgrad., So. Meth. U., 1977-78; MA, CUNY, 1979; D in Mus. Arts, Yale U., 1981; postgrad., Sweelinck Conservatory, 1981-82. Solo performer Am. and Europe, 1981—; artist-in-residence Ala. Shakespeare Festival, Anniston, 1982-85; music dir. Festivanni '85', Anniston, 1985; artistic dir. Art of the Early Keyboard, N.Y.C., 1986—; music dir. The Artek Ensemble, N.Y.C., 1987—, Monteverdi Music Festival, Milw., N.Y., 1988; acting dir. Maplewood Music Festival, Essex County, N.Y., 1988; music dir. St. Francis of Assisi Ch., N.Y.C., 1989—. Composer (choral work) Light, 1981, "Orion's Voice", 1984. Organist Union Temple, N.Y.C., 1985—. Named one of 10 Top Condrs., Opera News, 1989. Mem. Am. Guild Organists (bd. dirs. N.Y.C. chpt. 1987-90, 1st prize 1977, 79). Home: 170 W 73d St #3C New York NY 10023

TOTH, LAURA ANNE, psychotherapist; b. Evanston, Ill., Sept. 26, 1949; d. Walter Steven and Mary E. (Kendall) T.; m. Richard LaDue, Dec. 9, 1967 (div. 1971); 1 child, Mark K. Toth; m. Errol Dean Hackett, Oct. 19, 1984. B in Social Welfare, U. Wis., 1981, MSW, 1982. Bd. Cert. Diplomate in Clinical Social Work. Adj. clin. instr. U. Wis., Milw., 1983-86; social worker Rosalie Manor/Mother Care, Milw., 1983-86; psychotherapist Life Skills Ctr. and St. Agnes Counseling Ctr., Fond du Lac, Wis., 1986—; dir. outpatient eating disorders program St. Agnes Hosp. Counseling Ctr., Fond du Lac, Wis., 1987—; cons., speaker, employee asst. counselor, St. Agnes Hosp., 1987-90. Program dir. Parents without Ptnrs., Milw., 1978. Mem. Internat. Assn. Eating Disorder Profls., Nat. Assn. Social Workers, Women in Mgmt. (Fond du Lac chpt.), Am. Assn. Marriage and Family Therapists (clin.), Acad. Cert. Social Workers. Office: St Agnes Hosp Counseling Ct 430 E Division St Fond du Lac WI 54935

TOU, JEN-SIE HSU, biochemistry educator; b. Lai-yang, China, Sept. 17, 1936; came to U.S., 1962; d. Pei-min and Jing-yu (Chang) Hsu; m. Patrick P. Tou, May 29, 1965. BS in Agrl. Chemistry, Nat. Taiwan U., 1959; MS in Biochemistry, Baylor Coll. Medicine, 1964; PhD in Biochemistry, Tulane U., 1968. Rsch. asst. Harvard Med. Sch., Boston, 1964-65; rsch. fellow Tulane U. Med. Sch., New Orleans, 1968-71, instr. biochemistry, 1971-73, asst. prof., 1973-80, rsch. assoc. prof., 1980-88, assoc. prof. biochemistry, 1988—. NIH rsch. fellow, 1972-74, recipient rsch. career devel. award, 1975-80. Mem. Am. Soc. Biochemistry and Molecular Biology. Home: 4641 Ithaca St Metairie LA 70006 Office: Dept Biochemistry Tulane U Med Sch 1430 Tulane Ave New Orleans LA 70112

TOUCHSTONE, MARTHA JONES, public relations executive; b. Detroit, Nov. 3, 1948; d. Robert Everett and Bess Alice (Johnson) Jones; m. John N. Touchstone, Jan. 24, 1987. Student, Williams Coll., 1969; BA, Vassar Coll., 1970. With radio and TV news dept. Burson Marsteller, N.Y.C., 1974; account exec. Hill & Knowlton, N.Y.C., 1975-78; dir. public relations and environ. affairs Fla. Phosphate Council, Lakeland, 1978-81; pres. Jones & Assocs., Lakeland, 1981-87, Houston, 1987—. Apptd. commr. edn. Fla. Adv. Council on Sci. Edn., 1979, vice chmn., 1980-81, chmn., 1981-82; mem. Gov.'s Task Force on Phosphate-Related Radiation, 1979-80; trustee Learning Resource Ctr., Lakeland, 1979-82; bd. dirs. Campfire Inc., Lakeland, 1982-85; mem. Lakeland Young Life Council, 1985; del. Diocesan Conv., St. Stephen's Episcopal Ch., 1982-85, lay reader, 1983-86, mem. vestry, 1984-86; mem. adv. council Fla. Defenders of Environ., 1980, United Way, 1980, Hist. Lakeland, 1979-80, Fla. Assn. Sci. Tchrs., 1981; active Leadership Lakeland, 1985-86. Recipient nat. 1st place Addy award Am. Advt. Fedn., 1978. Mem. Fla. Pub. Relations Assn. (bd. dirs. Polk chpt. 1983-84, Golden Image awards 1979-80, 82, Grand All Fla. award 1982), Leadership Lakeland, Lakeland C. of C., Jr. League Houston, Meml. Dr. Country Club. Episcopalian. Home and Office: 2205 Fulham Ct Houston TX 77063

TOURETZ, LILLIAN CAROLE CONRAD, psychotherapist; b. N.Y.C., Oct. 17, 1923; d. Philip and Rose Helen Stetsky;m. Martin Conrad, June 3, 1944; children David, Donna; m. 2d, Arthur Touretz, May 28, 1977. BA, Hunter Coll., 1944; MSW, NYU, 1968. Diplomate Am. Bd. Examiners Social Work. Asst. mgr. N.Y.C. Housing Authority, 1946-49; pres. Profl. Workers AFL-CIO, 1947-49; lectr., cons. in field, 1952-78; psychotherapist Pelham (N.Y.) Family Svc., 1968-77; pvt. practice psychotherapy, Hartsdale, N.Y., 1977—; field instr. Adelphi U., 1972-77. Chmn. United Jewish Appeal; v.p. regional bd. B'nai B'rith, chpt. pres., 1981-84, pres. Coun. of Pres. Mem. Nat. Assn. Social Workers (diplomate), Soc. Clin. Social Work Psychotherapists, Ortho Psychiat., Hunter Coll. Alumni Assn., NYU Alumni Assn. Democrat. Address: 55 Edgewood RD Hartsdale NY 10530

TOURTET, CHRISTIANE ANDRÉE, writer; b. Grenoble, France, June 18, 1945; came to U.S., 1965; d. André Tourtet. Cert. completion humanistic psychology, Fla. Jr. Coll., Jacksonville, 1969, AA with high honors, 1972, AS with high honors, 1973; BA, Jacksonville U., 1975. Hostess interpreter-translator Credit Lyonnais, Grenoble, 1963-65; instr. French Albany (N.Y.) Acad. for Girls, 1965-66; instr. French, asst. lang. lab. Coll. of St. Rose, Albany, 1966-67; instr. French Bartram Sch., Jacksonville, 1970; instr. French and modeling Fla. Jr. Coll., Jacksonville, 1971-74; producer-dir. ednl. French program Sta. WFAM FM radio, Jacksonville, 1977-79; interpreter, translator French Lang. Bank, Jacksonville, 1980-83; tutor pvt. and small group classes in French; model for publicity ads, brochures in major mags., newspapers; lectr. in field. Author: Fruits of Life (Silver medal Arts, Scis, Letter, Paris, 1977) 1973, editor, writer newsletter, recordings Flamingo Studios, Tallahassee, Fla., 1986-87; paintings exhibited in France, Monte Carlo and U.S.; participant in over 28 TV commls. Pres. Le Cercle Francais, Albany, 1965. Recipient Medal of Olympic City of Grenoble, France, 1977, Medal of Dauphine County, 1977, Medal of Chevalier of Order of Merit, Paris, 1976, medal Chevalier o f French Courtesy, Paris, 1977, Medal of Nat. Merit, Paris, 1976. Mem. NAFE, Am. Acad. Environ. Medicine (assoc.), Environ. Illness Assn. Tallahassee (founder, pres. 1989), Nat. Ctr. for Environ. Strategies, SZhare, Care, Prayers, H.E.A.L., Am. Pub. Health Assn., India Assn. Tallahassee (publicity officer), Phi Theta Kappa.

TOUSLEY, MARTHA MERRITT, clinical mental health specialist; b. Dallas, Tex., Feb. 10, 1943; d. Harry Eugene and Evelyn Cecilia (Hebert) Merritt; m. Michael John Tousley, Aug. 7, 1965; children: Christopher, Benjamin. BS in Nursing, U. Mich., 1965; MS in Psychiat. Nursing, Rutgers U., 1980. Psychiat. nurse Traverse City (Mich.) State Hosp., 1965-67; instr. Northwestern Mich. Coll., Traverse City, 1968-72, Ferris State Coll., Traverse City, 1972-76; psychotherapist Psychol. Services Assoc. P.C., Traverse City; dir. edn. Fair Oaks Hosp., Summit, N.J., 1980-85; psychiat. nursing cons. mental health and hosp. div. N.J. Dept. Human Svcs., 1985-87; clin. specialist Princeton (N.J.) House, 1987-88; pvt. practice, Boston, 1988—. Mng. editor Internat. Jour. Psychiaty in Medicine, 1983-85; mem. editorial bd. Jour. Psychosocial Nursing, 1984—; contbr. articles to profl. jours., chpts. to books. Named Psychiat. Nurse of Yr., N.J. Nurses Assn., 1987. Mem. Am. Nurses Assn. (cert. clin. specialist in adult psychiat. mental health nursing), Cabinet Continuing Edn. N.J., U. Mich. Alumni Club, Rutgers U. Alumni Club, Sigma Theta Tau. Home and Office: 2001 Marina Dr 304-W Boston MA 02171

TOUSSAINT, JEANNE ISABELLA, electrical engineer; b. Havre de Grace, Md., Apr. 30, 1964; d. Melvin Edward and Karen Jean (Diley) T. BSEE, Johns Hopkins U., 1986; postgrad. bus. adminstrn., U. Md. Textbook asst. Barnes and Noble, Balt., 1982-86; asst. mgr. Chesapeake & Potomac Telephone Co. subs. Bell Atlantic Co., Silver Spring, Md., 1986-89; specialist in network svcs., sr. engr. Bell Atlantic Corp., Silver Spring, 1990—. Vol. Lifespring, Inc., Washington, 1990. Mem. IEEE, Toastmasters. Home: 15799 Haynes Rd Laurel MD 20707

TOUSSAINT, ROSE MARIE, renal transplant surgeon; b. Haiti, June 15, 1956; came to U.S., 1971; d. Alfred Paul Marie and Justine T. BS in Biology, Loyola U., New Orleans, 1978; MD, Howard U., 1983. Diplomate Am. Bd. Surgery. Gen. surgery resident Howard U. Hosp., Washington, 1983-88; liver, kidney transplant fellow U. Pitts., 1988—; research asst. Nat. Inst. Health, Bethesda, Md., 1980, 81. Named Best Gen. Surgery Resident D.C. Gen. Hosp., 1986. Mem. AMA, AMORC, Am. Coll. Surgeons, Nat. Med. Assn. (speaker conf. seminar 1986, presentation award 1986), All African Physicians N.Am., A.M.O.R.C., Delta Sigma Theta. Democrat. Home: 5 Bayard Rd #607 Pittsburgh PA 15213

TOVAR, DORA OLIVIA, land use analyst; b. L.A., June 7, 1963; d. Maria (Garcia) Huerta. BA, UCLA, 1986; postgrad., LBJ Sch. Pub. Affairs, Austin, Tex., 1987—. Legis. aid Tex. House of Reps., Austin, 1986-87; state policy analyst Mexican-Am. Legal Def. Fund, San Antonio, 1987-88; south Tex. field desk rep. Campaign 88/Dukakis-Bentsen, Austin, 1988; policy analyst, land mgmt. Tex. Gen. Land Office, Austin, 1989, policy analyst, redistricting, 1989—; conf. coord. Hispanic Women's Network of Tex., San Antonio, 1987-88; founder Gen. Land Office, Hispanic Women's Group, Austin, 1989—; chmn. Cinco de Mayo com., Austin, 1990—. Del. State Dem. Conv., Houston, 1988; mem. Tex. Women's Polit. Caucus, 1988—, Mexican-Am. Dems. of Tex., 1989—. Mem. Hispanic Women's Network of Tex. (Outstanding Svc. award 1988), Mexican-Am.Bus. and Profl. Women's Assn. Office: Texas General Land Office 1700 N Congress Austin TX 78701-1495

TOW, SUZANNE, personnel manager; b. Queens, N.Y., Apr. 7, 1950; d. Arthur Theodore and Lillian (Saltzman) T. BS cum laude, SUNY, 1972. Mgr. various places, N.Y., 1972-84; adminstrv. mgr. N.Y. State Sch. of Indsl. and Labor Rels., Cornell U., N.Y.C., 1984-88; personnel mgr. The Salvation Army Social Services for Children, N.Y., 1988—. Sch. vol. N.Y.C. Pub. Sch., 1985—. Mem. Am. Soc. for Human Resource Mgmt., Voluntary Agy. Pers. Assn., NAFE, Amateur Chamber Music Players, Inc., Queens Symphonic Band (bd. dirs. 1980-87). Jewish. Home: 38-15 Bowne St # 6H Flushing NY 11354

TOWE, NANCY ELLEN CARPENTER, electronics manufacturing company executive; b. Kildav, Ky., July 28, 1941; d. John Henry and Nora Jenny (Snyder) Carpenter; m. Marshall Towe, Sr., Dec. 1, 1958 (div. 1981); children: Marshall, Jr., Michael Lee; m. John Edward Lescher, July 26, 1986. AAS in Mktg. Mid-Mgmt., McHenry Community Coll., 1981; BA in Orgnl. Psychology, Nat. Coll. Edn., 1982. Switchboard operator Malibu Answering Service, Chgo., 1964-71; corr. Seaboard Life Ins. Co., Chgo., 1972-74; sales corr. Chgo. Miniature div. Gen Instrument Co., Chgo., 1975-77; product mgr. Oak Industries, Crystal Lake, Ill., 1978-82; pres., chief exec. officer Lamptronix Co., Ltd., Crystal Lake, 1982—; speaker in field. Den mother Chgo Area council Boy Scouts Am., 1970-75; active Pierce Sch. PTA, Chgo., 1973; mem. Lake in the Hills Property Owners Assn., 1978-82; founder Woodstock Ctr. for Women, Ill., 1982. Recipient Disting. Service scroll Ill. Congress PTA, 1973, Award of Achievement SBA, 1989. Mem. Women in Electronics, Nat. Network of Women in Sales, Aerospace Lighting Inst., Crystal Lake C. of C. (bd. dirs.). Congregationalist. Home: 2412 N Orchard Beach McHenry IL 60050 Office: Lamptronix Co Ltd 81 N Williams Crystal Lake IL 60014-4443

TOWER, JANET MAY, retired educator; b. Mount Pleasant, Mich., Sept. 19, 1925; d. Adrian L. and Nina (Mahoney) Fraidenburg; m. Richard B. Tower (dec.); children: Ronald B., Kenneth L. BS, U. Ariz., 1963, MEd, 1964. Tchr. Tucson pub. schs., 1963-87, asst. prin., 1984-87; ret.; ch. librarian St. Mark's Presbyn. Ch., Tucson, 1986—. Active various charitable orgns. Mem. U. Ariz. Alumni Assn., Pi Lambda Theta, Alpha Delta Kappa, Phi Delta Kappa. Repubican. Presbyterian. Home: 8085 Shadow Canyon Dr Tucson AZ 85715

TOWER, JOAN PEABODY, composer, educator; b. New Rochelle, N.Y., Sept. 6, 1938. B.A., Bennington Coll., 1961; M.A., Columbia U., 1964, D.M.A., 1978. Pianist, Da Capo Chamber Players, 1969-84; compositions include: Amazon II (premiered by Hudson Valley Philharmonic), Sequoia (premiered by Am. Composers Orch.), Silver Ladders, 1985 (premiered by St. Louis Symphony, Grawemeyer award, U. Louisville, 1990), Breakfast Rhythms, Black Topaz, Amazon (original scoring for quintet), Wings (solo clarinet), Fantasy (clarinet and piano), Cello Concerto, Piano Concerto, Clarinet Concerto; works recorded; commns.: Contemporary Music Soc., Jerome Found., Mass. State Arts Council, Schubert Club St. Paul, Richard Stoltzman, St. Louis Symphony, Elmar Oliveira, N.Y. Philharm., Chgo. Symphony, Fromm Found., Nat. Endowment Arts; assoc. prof. Bard Coll., N.Y.C., from 1972; composer-in-residence St. Louis Symphony, 1985-87. Recipient N.Y. State Council for Arts award, 1980; award in music Am. Acad. and Inst. Arts and Letters, 1983; Guggenheim fellow, 1976; Nat. Endowment Arts fellow, 1974, 75, 80, 84, Koussevitzky Found. grantee, 1982.*

TOWER, RONI BETH, psychologist; b. Akron, Ohio, Dec. 11, 1943; d. Arnold Edward Weinstein and Elva Hermoine (Gross) MacRae; m. Stuart James Lowenthal, June 2, 1983 (dec. 1984); m. M. Barry Schlosser, Jan. 1, 1989; children: Jennifer, Daniel. BA, Barnard Coll., N.Y.C., 1964; MS, Yale U., 1977, M in Philosphy, 1979, PhD, 1980. Lic. in clinical psychology, Conn. Psychologist Silver Hill Found., New Canaan, Conn., 1979-81; pvt. practice Westport, Conn., 1981—; co-founder, treas. Clarity Cons. Corp., Westport, 1990—; lectr. in psychology Yale U., New Haven, 1981—, Am. Bd. Profl. Psychology Seminar, Portland, Oreg., 1990; cons. in field. Cons. editor Jour. of Imagination Cognition and Personality, 1983—; contbr. numerous articles to profl. jours. Active Jr. League of Eastern County, Fairfield County, Conn. Recipient Traineeship award U.S. Pub. Health, 1979-80. Mem. Am. Assn. for Study of Mental Imagery (pres. 1988-89, conf. organizer New Haven 1988), Am. Psychol. Assn., Conn. Psychol. Assn., LWV (Fairfield chpt.). Office: Clarity Cons Corp 6 Signal Ln Westport CT 06880

TOWERS, JUNE CROZIER, home economist; b. Hedley, Tex., June 28, 1922; d. Paul Haskell and Ruby Leah (Shaw) Crozier; m. Quentin Edward Nelson, May 5, 1942; children: Paul Eric Nelson, Diane Louise Millington, Charlotte Kay Nixon. Student, U. Tex., 1942, U. Houston, 1953-55; BA in English, Eastern New Mex. U., 1956; M in Liberal Arts, Houston Bapt. U., 1989; postgrad., U. Houston, 1989—. Asst. Booz Allen & Hamilton, Chgo., 1943-44; office mgr. Golemon & Rolfe, Architects, Houston, 1949-50; v.p. Quentin Nelson & Co., Houston, 1952-67; home Econ. dir. Tracy Locke Advt., Houston, Brown Communications, Richardson, Tex., 1975-89; freelance Food Cons., Food Stylist. Author: 6 cookbooks, 1974-80. Mem. Houston Culinary Guild, AAUW (pres., v.p. 1975-89). Republican. Lutheran. Address: 2515 Fairway Dr Sugar Land TX 77478

TOWEY, MARIE ELIZABETH, nursing administrator, educator; b. Salem, Mass., Jan. 13, 1934; d. Daniel and Mary Catherine (Buckley) Linehan; m. Carroll Francis Towey, Aug. 24, 1957; children: Mary Ellen Towey Roth, Michael Carroll, Kevin James. Diploma Burdett Coll., 1952; R.N., Salem Hosp. Sch. Nursing, 1955; postgrad. Boston Coll. Sch. Nursing, 1956-61; B.S., Salem State Coll., 1975, M.Ed. in Health Counseling and Guidance, 1978. R.N., Mass., Va., D.C. Md., W.Va. Staff nurse Salem Hosp. and Mass. Gen. Hosp., 1955; nursing instr. Salem Hosp. (Mass.), 1955-59, med. nursing supr., 1960-61; staff nurse Twin Oaks Nursing Home, Danvers, Mass., 1961-71, Mt. Pleasant Hosp., Lynn, Mass., 1971; social worker, nurse NIMH Tng. Grant, Malden Ct. Clinic (Mass.), 1972-73; region IV coord. North Shore Coun. on Alcoholism, Danvers, 1973-74; community mental health nurse Danvers-Salem Community Mental Health Resources Unit, Salem, 1974-78; nurse instr. Med. Aid Tng. Sch., Washington, 1978-79, Fairfax County Div. Continuing Edn. med. div., Woodson High Sch. (Va.), 1979-80; dir. nursing and health svcs. ARC, Alexandria, 1980-81; dir. nursing svcs. Med. Pers. Pool, Alexandria, 1981-82, adminstr., 1982-84; adminstr. ambulatory care ctr. Medic 24-Ltd., Baileys Crossroads, Va., 1984—; adminstr. Am. Med. Svcs., Springfield, Va., 1984-85; dir. nursing svc. Camelot Hall Nursing Facility, Arlington, Va., 1985-86, Clinton Convalescent Ctr., Md., 1986; auditing supr., trainor Intracorp, Falls Church, Va., 1986—; lectr. in field. Co-author planning grant in mental health and mental retardation, 1978. Sec. Mass Soc. of D.C.,1987; area chmn. Burke Centre Conservancy (Va.), 1981-88; mem. town meeting Danvers Town Govt., 1971-78; pres. Mass. Region IV Mental Health and Mental Retardation Adv. Coun., 1977-78; sec., treas. Mass. Area Bd. Coalition, 1977-78; trustee Danvers State Hosp., 1977-82; community mental health resources devel. unit com. chmn. Danvers-Salem Area Mental Health Retardation Bd., 1973-78, pres., 1975-77; chmn. emergency med. svcs. com. North Shore Coun. on Alcoholism, 1972-76; mem. adv. com. for adult edn. North Shore Region, 1974-75; mem. Danvers Task Force on Deinstitutionalization, 1975-76; bd. dirs. Archdiocesan Coun. Cath. Nurses, 1969-72. Recipient Merit and Appreciation certs. various agys., socs. and hosps. Mem. Am. Nurses Assn. (membership com. 1983—), Va. Assn. Rehab. Nurses, Va. Nurses Assn. (hospitality com. 1983), Va. Assn. Home Health Agys. (chmn. region I legis., rep. 1984-86), D.C. Nurses Assn. (conf. com. 1982), Health Adminstrs. Assn. of Nat. Capitol Area, Salem Hosp. Alumnae Assn. (past treas. and chmn. program 1956-58, 60-64), Alexandria C. of C. Republican. Club: Danvers Garden (pres., chmn. civic beautification 1972-77). Home: 10639 Canterberry Rd Fairfax Station VA 22039 Office: Intracorp 5205 Leesburg Pike Falls Church VA 22041

TOWLE, NADINE VALERY, college administrator, educator; b. Weymouth, Mass., Feb. 14, 1947; d. Clayton Ellsworth Towle and Alise (Rostan) Dowling. BS with high honors, Northeastern U., 1978, MBA, 1983, postgrad., 1986—; postgrad., Harvard U., 1986. Asst. dir. personnel Northeastern U., Boston, 1972-84, mem. faculty coll. bus., 1980—; exec. dir. human resources/affirmative action Emerson Coll., Boston, 1984—; cons. Whale Communications, N.Y.C., 1978-80, Images, Hull, Mass., 1982-88; exec. v.p., cons. Mgmt. Concepts, Hull, Mass., 1989—. Founder New Eng. Retirement Planners Council, 1974; co-chair Gov's. Adv. Coun. for Affirmative Action, Boston, 1990—; mem. pers. bd. Town of Hull. Mem. Personnel Mgrs. Council (chair employment com. 1989—), Internat. Assn. Personnel Women (editor newsletter 1982-83, pub. rel. com. 1983-84, chair employment com. 1989—), Nat. Assn. Female Execs. (dir. network 1985-86), Am. Soc. Personnel Adminstrs., Mass. Assn. Affirmative Actions Profls., Coll. and Univ. Personnel Assn., Small Coll. Personnel Mgr.'s Assn. (founder), Fringe Benefits Adminstrs.' Council (founder), Greater Boston C. of C. (speaker Bus. Expo 1985). Democrat. Methodist. Home: 24 Halvorsen Ave Hull MA 02045 Office: Emerson Coll 100 Beacon St Boston MA 02115

TOWN, SUSAN BARBARA, social worker; b. Des Moines, May 25, 1947; d. Robert Walton and Donna Jean (Firman) Goode; m. David Robert Wilkins, Dec. 4, 1965 (div. 1967); 1 child, David Robert Jr.; m. Leslie Robert Town, Aug. 18, 1990. BA, Drake U., Des Moines, 1971. Social worker dept. human svcs. State of Iowa, Des Moines, 1972—; custody study preparation Hope, Inc., Des Moines, 1989—; lectr. in field. Mem. Alpha Kappa Delta. Democrat. Meth. Office: State of Iowa Dept Human Svcs Warren Co Box 729 Indianola IA 50125

TOWNE, RUTH WARNER, history educator; b. Kirksville, Mo., June 19, 1917; d. Frank Warner and Mary Elizabeth (McCoy) T. BS in Edn., NE Mo. State Tchrs. Coll., 1939; MA, U. Mo., 1940, PhD, 1953. Cert. tchr., Mo. Tchr. history Sr. High Sch., Kirksville, Mo., 1940-51; asst. prof. history NE Mo. State Tchrs. Coll., Kirksville, 1952-57, assoc. prof. history, 1957-65; prof. history NE Mo. State Tchrs. U., Kirksville, 1965—, dean grad. studies, 1983-88; thesis reader grad. office NE Mo. State U., Kirksville, 1988—. Author: A Winner Never Quits: The Life and Times of Walter Harrington Ryle, 1970, Senator William J. Stone and the Politics of Compromise, 1979, From These Beginnings: A History of First Methodis Church Kirksville, 1984; contbr. articles to profl. jours. Mem. history and archives commn. Mo. east annual conf. United Meth. Ch., 1981—. Mem. Orgn. Am. Historians, AAUW, Delta Zeta (coll. chpt. dir. 1953-87, Achoth award 1973). Democrat. Office: NE Mo State U Kirksville MO 63501

TOWNER, NAOMI WHITING, fiber artist, educator; b. Providence, May 8, 1940; d. Basil J. and Nellie (Woolhouse) Whiting; B.F.A. in Textile Design, R.I. Sch. Design, 1962; postgrad. (Textron fellow) Foreningen Handarbetets Vanner, Stockholm, 1962-63; M.F.A. in Textile Design, Rochester Inst. Tech., 1965. Internat. studies with faculty Ill. State U., People's Republic of China 1986; Teaching grad. asst. Sch. Am. Craftsmen, Rochester (N.Y.) Inst. Tech., 1963-65, instr. textile design, summer 1964; instr. Ill. State U., Normal, 1965-68, asst. prof., 1968-72, assoc. prof., 1972-76, prof. art, 1976—; lectr. various art guilds and schs., 1967—; pres., ptnr. Smiling Camel Choklits, Ltd., Bloomington; dir. workshops on weaving and textile design, 1964—. One person shows art fabrics include: Fox Valley Art League, St. Charles, Ill., 1968, Fine Arts Ctr. Clinton (Ill.), 1971, Old Town Gallery, St. Charles, Mo., 1973, Lincoln Coll., Lincoln, Ill., 1974, Craft Alliance Gallery, St. Louis, 1974, Unitarian Ch., Bloomington, Ill., 1975, The Art-In, Riverton, Wyo., 1975; numerous group shows including: Mus. Contemporary Crafts Fabrics Internat. travelling exhibit, 1961-62, Security Trust Co., Rochester, N.Y., 1965, Ill. State U., Normal, 1965-68, 71, 73-86, Old Town Art Ctr., Chgo., 1967, Brooks Meml. Art Gallery, Memphis, 1967, Lakeview Ctr. for Arts, Peoria, Ill., 1967-68, Ill. State Mus., 1968, Wis. State U., Oshkosh, 1969, Art Inst. Chgo., 1971, No. Ill. U., DeKalb, 1971, U. Mass. Art Gallery, Amherst, 1972, Evansville (Ind.) Mus. Arts and Scis., 1973, 88, Eureka Coll. (Ill.), 1973, Mills Coll., Oakland, Calif., 1974, Columbus (Ga.) Mus. Arts and Crafts, 1974, Wright Art Center, Beloit (Wis.) Coll., 1975, Lowe Art Mus., U. Miami (Fla.) Goldstein Gallery, 1976, U. Minn., St. Paul, 1977, Paul Sargent Gallery, Eastern Ill. U., Charlestown, 1977, Boise (Idaho) State U., 1978, Cin. Art Mus., 1978, Kearney (Nebr.) State Coll. Art Gallery, 1979, Coll. Art Gallery, 1979, Rahr-West Mus., Manitowoc, Wis., 1979, Ill. State Mus., Springfield, 1979, No. Calif. Handweavers, Inc., San Mateo, 1979, Ill. Arts Council Gallery, Chgo., 1979, Tex. Tech U., Lubbock, 1980, Caterpillar Internat., Peoria, Ill., 1980, No. Ill. U., Midwest Constructed Fibers, 1940-80, travelling exhibit, 1980-82, Loveland (Colo.) Mus., 1981, Ft. Collins (Colo.) Mus., 1981, Fiber Art Trends, 1982, Pyramid Arts Ctr., Rochester, 1983, U. Wis.-Green Bay travelling exhibit, 1984-85, Ariel Gallery, Naperville, Ill., 1984, Premonitions, Nashville, 1985, Ill. State Fair Profl. Art Exhbn., Springfield, 1986 (1st place award craft media, merit award 1987), 7th ann. Cen. Ill. Arts Consortium Visual Arts Touring Exhbn., 1984-86 (merit award), Juror's Exhbn.: New Dimensions in Fiber II, Coll. Du Page, Ill.; represented in permanent collections Ill. State Mus., Springfield, Washington U., St. Louis, Eureka (Ill.) Coll., corp. and pvt. collections; juror exhbns. Recipient numerous awards including Silver Shuttle award U. Rochester, 1964, Owens-Corning Fiberglas competition, 1964, award of excellence Ill. Craftsmen's Council Invitational, 1967, Merit award Springfield Art Assn., 1976, Hon. mention Tchr. of Yr. awards, 1986; grantee Handweavers Guild Am. and Ill. Arts Council, 1975-78. Mem. Am. Crafts Council, Midwest Weavers Conf., Am. Fedn. Tchrs., AFL-CIO, Handweavers Guild Am. (rep. 1973-77, bd. dirs. 1978-80), ACLU, Surface Design Assn. Contbr. articles on textile design and weaving to profl. publs.; editor Fiber News, 1975-85; mem. editorial bd. Ars Textrina, 1985—. Home: 610 E Taylor St Bloomington IL 61701 Office: Ill State U Art Dept Normal IL 61761

TOWNLEY, LINDA ROSE, financial analyst; b. Gainesville, Ga., Nov. 5, 1947; d. Herbert William and Bobbie (Talley) Goswick; m. Randall Wiley Townley, July 18, 1969; children: Seth and Shelly (twins), Audra. AS, Young Harris Coll., Ga., 1967; BS, North Ga. Coll., 1969. With Lockheed Aero. Systems Corp., Marietta, Ga., 1969—; sr. pricing and control analyst Lockheed Aero. Systems Corp., 1976—. Mayor, City of Dawsonville, Ga., 1988—; bd. dirs. Ga. Mountains Area Planning Devel. Commn., 1988—, Reg. Planning Commn. Mem. Nat. Mgmt. Assn., Nat. Estimating Soc. (cert.), Ga. Mcpl. Assn. (3rd v.p., bd. dirs. 1989), Women in Govt. Club. Baptist. Home: RR1 Box 1904 Dawsonville GA 30534 Office: City of Dawsonville PO Box 6 Dawsonville GA 30534

TOWNSEND, ALAIR ANE, city official; b. Rochester, N.Y., Feb. 15, 1942; d. Harold Eugene and Dorothy (Sharpe) T.; m. Robert Harris, Dec. 31, 1970. BS, Elmira Coll., 1962; MS, U. Wis., 1964; postgrad. Columbia U., 1970-71. Assoc. dir. budget priorities Com. on Budget, U.S. Ho. of Reps., Washington, 1975-79; dep. asst. sec. for budget HEW, Washington, 1979-80, asst. sec. for mgmt. and budget, 1980-81; dir. N.Y.C. Office Mgmt. and Budget, 1981-85; dep. mayor for fin. and econ. devel. City of N.Y., 1985-89; pub. Crain's N.Y. Bus., N.Y.C., 1989—; vice chmn., trustee Elmira Coll. Mem. Am. Soc. Pub. Adminstrn., Women's Forum, Nat. Acad. Pub. Adminstrn., Fin. Women's Assn. N.Y., Advt. Women N.Y., N.Y.C. Partnership, N.Y. State Bus. Coun. Office: Crain's NY Bus 220 E 42d St New York NY 10017

TOWNSEND, ANNA STOFFLET, civic worker, retired educator; b. Vicksburg, Mich., Sept. 12, 1899; d. John Howard and Ada (Rosenberry) S.; m. Ray Winthrop Townsend, Dec. 20, 1931. BA in English summa cum laude, U. Wis., 1920; postgrad., U. Calif., 1932-40; MA in English, U. S.C., 1940. Tchr. Cen. High Sch., Tulsa, 1920-25; tchr. Woodrow Wilson High Sch., Long Beach, Calif., 1927-61, head English dept., 1931-61; ret., 1961. Sustaining mem. Nat. Com. GOP Congl. Com., 1960—. Mem. AAUW (pres. L.B. br. 1937-38, Calif. div. com. 1939-44, v.p. 1945-47, pres. Calif. 1950-52, nat. v.p. So. Pacific region 1955-63, Anna S. Townsend Internat. Fellowships Endowment founded in her honor Calif. div. 1968—), Woodrow Wilson High Sch. City Tchrs. Club (pres. 1955-56), Nat. Support Pub. Schs., P.E.O. (pres. 1965-67), Ebell Club, Phi Beta Kappa, Phi Kappa Phi, Delta Kappa Gamma, Alpha Xi Delta. Republican. Presbyterian. Home: 4520 Pepperwood Ave Long Beach CA 90808

TOWNSEND, IRENE FOGLEMAN, accountant, tax analyst; b. Birmingham, Ala., May 29, 1932; d. James Woods and Virginia (Martin) Fogleman; m. Kenneth Ross Townsend, Mar. 18, 1951; children: Marietta Irene, Martha Shapard, Kenneth Ross Jr., Elizabeth Buchanan. BSBA, East Carolina U., 1980. Acct. Norwood P. Whitehurst & Assocs., Greenville, N.C., 1981-86; tax mgr. Psychiat. Inst. Am., Washington, 1986—. Fellow AICPA, N.C. Assn. CPA's, D.C. Inst. CPA's; mem. DAR, N.C. Soc. Daughters of the Colonial Wars, Colonial Dames 17th Century. Democrat. Episcopalian (lay reader, chalice bearer). Home: 2521 Paxton St Lake Ridge Woodbridge VA 22192 Office: Psychiat Inst Am 1010 Wisconsin Ave NW Ste 900 Washington DC 20007

TOWNSEND, JACQUELINE ARIZA, civil engineer; b. Summit, N.J., Apr. 29, 1961; d. Hector and Carmen (Gil) Ariza; m. Dale Edward Townsend, July 26, 1986. BS in Engring., U. N.C., 1984. Civil engr. I City of Charlotte (N.C.), 1985-87, civil engr. II, head systems and records sect., 1987—. Contbr. articles to profl. jours. Vol. Charlotte Arts & Scis., 1987—. Mem. Am. Water Works Assn. (meter and pipe sch. cross connection control programs com. 1988—, program com. 1988—), Am. Backflow Prevention Assn., Internat. Backflow Prevention Assn., Charlotte Profl. Mgmt. Club (bd. dirs. 1985—, chmn. membership 1987—), Zeta Tau Alpha (gen. advisor to collegiate chpt. 1987—, historian 1988—). Democrat. Roman Catholic. Office: Charlotte Mecklenburg Util Dept City of Charlotte 5100 Brookshire Blvd Charlotte NC 28216

TOWNSEND, JANE KALTENBACH, zoologist, educator; b. Chgo., Dec. 21, 1922; B.S., Beloit Coll., 1944; M.A., U. Wis., 1946; Ph.D., U. Iowa, 1950; m. 1966. Asst. in zoology U. Wis., 1944-47; asst., instr. U. Iowa, 1948-50; asst., project assoc. in pathology U. Wis., 1950-53; Am. Cancer Soc. research fellow Wenner-Grens Inst., Stockholm, 1953-56; asst. prof. zoology Northwestern U., 1956-58; asst. prof. to assoc. prof. zoology Mt. Holyoke Coll., South Hadley, Mass., 1958-70, prof., 1970—, chmn. biol. scis., 1980-86. Fellow AAAS (sec. sect. biol. sci. 1974-78); mem. Am. Assn. Anatomists, Am. Inst. Biol. Scis., Am. Soc. Zoologists, Corp. of Marine Biol. Lab., Sigma Xi, Phi Beta Kappa. Office: Mount Holyoke Coll Dept of Biology South Hadley MA 01075

TOWNSEND, JENNIFER ELIZABETH, advertising and promotion professional; b. Austin, Tex., June 23, 1967; d. Edward Allen and Patricia Lois (Nulty) T. BS in Journalism, Tex. A&M U., 1989. Mktg. coord. Profl. Impressions, Inc., Austin, 1989-90; editor, advt. and promotion assoc. KLRU-Pub. TV, Austin, 1990—. Mem. Women in Communications Inc. Office: KLRU-TV PO Box 7158 Austin TX 78713

TOWNSEND, JOSEPHINE CATHERINE, sergeant; b. Utica, N.Y., Feb. 11, 1960; d. Robert Israel and Frances (Kaminski) T. AA, Mohawk Valley Community Coll., 1981. Police officer Cazenovia (N.Y.) Police, 1981-83; trooper N.Y. State Police, Albany, 1983-86, sgt., 1986-88. Instr. Am. Red Cross, Albany, N.Y., 1978—. Sgt. U.S. Army, 1978-81. Mem. Nat. Orgn. for Women. Republican. Home: 456 Dix Rd Rome NY 13440 Office: NY State Police Rt 5 Box 300 Oneida NY 13471

TOWNSEND, LISA CAMILLE, computer programmer, systems analyst; b. Washington, Apr. 29, 1965; d. John Lionel and Mary Elizabeth (Check) T. BBA, Howard U., 1988. Adminstrv. asst. Sch. Bus., Howard U., Washington; programmer/analyst Gen. Mills, Inc., Mpls.; jr. programmer/analyst IBM, Bethesda, Md., assoc. programmer/analyst. Active Big. Sisters Am. Mem. NAFE, NAACP, Beta Gamma Sigma. Home: PO Box 30987 Washington DC 20030 Office: 1041 Fernwood Rd Bethesda MD 20817

TOWNSEND, MARJORIE RHODES, aerospace engineer, business executive; b. Washington, Mar. 12, 1930; d. Lewis Boling and Marjorie Olive (Trees) Rhodes; m. Charles Eby Townsend, June 7, 1948; children: Charles Eby Jr., Lewis Rhodes, John Cunningham, Richard Leo. BEE, George Washington U., 1951. Registered profl. engr., D.C. Electronic scientist Naval Research Lab., Washington, 1951-59; research engr. to sect. head Goddard Space Flight Ctr.-NASA, Greenbelt, Md., 1959-65, tech. asst. to chief systems div., 1965-66, project mgr. small astronomy satellites, 1966-75, project mgr. applications explorer missions, 1975-76, mgr. preliminary systems design group, 1976-80; aerospace and electronics cons. Washington, 1980-83; v.p. systems devel. Space Am., 1983-84; aerospace cons. Washington, 1984-90; dir. space systems engring. BDM Internat., Inc., Washington, 1990—. Patentee digital telemetry system. Decorated Knight Order Italian Republic, 1972; recipient Fed. Women's award., 1973, Eur. Culture Assn. award, Rome, 1974, Engr. Alumni Achievement award George Washington U., 1975, Gen. Alumni Achievement award, 1976, Exceptional Service medal NASA, 1971, Outstanding Leadership medal, 1980. Fellow IEEE (chmn. Washington sect. 1985), AIAA (assoc.), Washington Acad. Sci. (pres. 1980-81); mem. AAAS (coun. del. 1985-88), Internat. Acad. Astronautics, Am. Geophys. Union, Soc. Women Engrs., Sigma Kappa, DAR, Daus. Colonial Wars, Mensa. Republican. Episcopalian. Home: 3529 Tilden St NW Washington DC 20008-3194

TOWNSEND, PATRICIA LEE, manufacturing company executive; b. Mansfield, Ohio, July 9, 1955; d. Leo Thomas and Eleanor Anne (Wheatley) T. Grad., Madison Comprehensive High Sch, Mansfield, Ohio, 1973. Office clk. Alsco Anaconda, Mansfield, 1972-74; prodn. and inventory control mgr. Indsl. Tech. Sales & Svc., Mansfield, 1974-79; purchasing agt. Weiss Industries, Mansfield, 1979—. Mem. Nat. Assn. Purchasing Mgmt. of N. Cen. Ohio (named Mem. of Yr. 1989, dir. nat. affairs 1988-89, sr. dir. 1989-90). Democrat. Lutheran. Home: 359 N Illinois Ave Mansfield OH 44905 Office: Weiss Industries 2480 N Main St Mansfield OH 44903

TOWNSEND, RHONDA JOYCE, small business owner; b. Dayton, Ohio, Aug. 10, 1960; d. Newman Jr. and Bedelia Belle (Hymes) T. AAS, Sinclair Community Coll., 1984; BA, Capital U., 1989. Clk. Bowman Funeral Chapel, Dayton, Ohio, 1980, Math Dept. Otterbein Coll., Westerville, Ohio, 1980; asst. sec. Bethel Bapt. Ch., Dayton, 1982-84; apprentice typographer J&L Graphics, Dayton, 1984; typesetter Design Graphics, Dayton, 1984-86; print shop asst. Fletchers' Printing Service, Dayton, 1986; owner Grapes Graphics, Dayton, 1983—; mgr., graphic arts technician Curry Printing, Dayton, 1987-89; ptnr. A.S.A.P. Printing/Photo Ctr., Dayton, 1989; mgr. Cheryl's Creation, Dayton, 1990—; cons. career day Nettie Lee Roth Intermediate Magnet Sch., 1987, 89; artist, keyline type designer logo 1988 Night Run of Dayton. Editor: 90th Anniversary at Bethel, 1983; editor/pub. (newsletter) Dayton Urban League, 1987. Bd. dirs. Bethel Bapt. Fed. Credit Union, 1983—, asst. treas., 1987-90; treas. Bethel Bapt. Gospel Ensemble, 1987-90; asst. treas., 1990—. Mem. 600 Bowling Club. Democrat. Club: Women Inter. Bowling Conf. Home: 4144 Shenandoah Dr Dayton OH 45417

TOWNSEND, SUSAN ELAINE, social service institute administrator, hostage survival consultant; b. Phila., Sept. 5, 1946; d. William Harrison and Eleanor Irene (Fox) Rogers; m. John Holt Townsend, May 1, 1976. BS in Secondary Edn., West Chester State U., 1968; MBA, Nat. U., 1978; PhD in Human Behavior, La Jolla U., 1984. Biology tchr. Methacton Sch. Dist., Fairview Village, Pa., 1968-70; bus. mgr., analyst profl. La Jolla Research Corp., San Diego, 1977-79; pastoral asst. Christ Ctr. Bible Therapy, San Diego, 1980-82, also bd. dirs.; v.p., pub. relations World Outreach Ctr. of Faith, San Diego, 1981-82, also bd. dirs.; owner, pres., cons. Townsend Research Inst., San Diego, 1983—; teaching assoc. La Jolla U. Continuing Edn., 1985-86. Author: Hostage Survival-Resisting the Dynamics of Captivity, 1983; contbr. articles to profl. jours. Religious vol. Met. Correctional Ctr., San Diego, 1983—, San Diego County Jail Ministries, 1978—. Served to comdr. USN, 1970-76, USNR, 1976—. Mem. Naval Res. Assn. (life), Res. Officers Assn. (Outstanding Jr. Officer of Yr. Calif. chpt. 1982), Navy League U.S. (life), West Chester U. Alumni Assn., Nat. U. Alumni Assn. (life), La Jolla U. Alumni Assn., Gen. Fedn. Women's Clubs (pres. Peninsula club 1983-85, pres. Parliamentary law club 1984-86, Past Pres.' Assn.), Calif. Fedn. Women's Clubs (v.p.-at-large San Diego dist. 25 1982-84). Office: 1060 Alexandria Dr San Diego CA 92107

TOWNSEND, TERRY, publishing executive; b. Camden, N.J., Dec. 14, 1920; d. Anthony and Rose DeMarco; B.A., Duke U., 1942; m. Paul Brorstrom Townsend, Dec. 8, 1961; 1 son, Kim. Public relations dir. North Shore Univ. Hosp., Manhasset, N.Y., 1955-68; pres. Theatre Soc. L.I., 1968-70; pres. Townsend Communications Bur., Ronkonkoma, N.Y., 1970—, L.I. Communicating Service, Ronkonkoma, 1977—; columnist, writer L.I./Bus., Ronkonkoma, 1970-75, pub., 1978—; pub. L.I. Bus. News, 1978—; v.p. Parr Meadows Racetrack, Yaphank, N.Y., 1977. Assoc. trustee North Shore U. Hosp., 1968—; bd. govs. Adelphi U. Friends Fin. Edn., 1978-85; chmn. ann. archtl. awards competition N.Y. Inst. Tech., 1970-83; trustee Dowling Coll., 1984—, L.I. Fine Arts Mus., 1984-85; bd. dirs. Family Svc. Assn. Nassau County, 1982—; dinner chmn. L.I. 400 Ball, 1987. Recipient Media award 110 Center Bus. and Profl. Women, 1977, Enterprise award Friends of Fin. Edn., 1981, L.I. Loves Bus. Showcase Salute, 1982, Community Svc. award N.Y. Diabetes Assn., 1983, Disting. Long Islander in Communications award L.I. United Epilepsy Assn., 1984, Spl. award Dowling Coll. Spring Tribute, 1989, Disting. Svc. award Episcopal Health Svcs., 1989; named First Lady of L.I., L.I. Public Relations Assn., 1973, L.I. Woman of Yr. L.I. Assn. Action Com., 1989. Mem. Public Relations Soc. Am. (pres. L.I. chpt. 1979). Office: LI Bus News 2150 Smithtown Ave Ronkonkoma NY 11779

TOWNSEND, TERYL ARCHER, artist, educator; b. Coronado, Calif., May 9, 1938; d. Robert Lee and Elizabeth (Archer) T.; m. Arthur W. Viner; children: Shawn Elizabeth, Don Philip Jr. Studies with Chen Chi, Millard Sheets, Edgar Whitney, Carl Molno, Glen Bradshaw, Maubry Brown, Edward Betts, Robert E. Wood., 1971—. Free-lance tchr. Nantucket, Mass., Conn., 1974—. Designer book covers; exhibited at Veerhoff Gallery, Washington, James Hunt Barker Gallery, Palm Beach, Nantucket, Mass. Recipient Merit award Art League Houston, 1975, 77, 82, 3d place award Nat. Small Painting Show, 1976, Merit award So. Watercolor Soc., 1977. Mem. Am. Watercolor Soc., Nat. Watercolor Soc., Rocky Mountain Nat. Watermedia Soc. (Century award 1974, 77), Southwestern Watercolor Soc. (awards 1974-76, 78, 84), Nantucket Artists Assn. (bd. dirs., advisor, exec. com. 1986—, Merit award 1980, 82, 83, 86), Houston Watercolor Soc. (v.p., pres. 1974-75, advisor profl. standards 1976-82, various awards 1975-76, 82-83), Nantucket C. of C., Houston C. of C. (advisor cultural com. 1975-76). Episcopalian. Home and Office: 109 Rosebrook Rd New Canaan CT 06840

TOWNS-SPENCER, GINA ANITA, public relations professional; b. Gary, Ind., May 19, 1965; d. Edward Windsor and Dorothy (Waddell) Towns. BA, Hampton U., 1986. Pub. rels. intern Lake County Conv. and Visitor's Bur., Merrillville, Ind., 1984; news reporter The Daily Press, Inc., Newport News, Va., 1985; revenue supr. Hotel Nikko/Chgo., 1987-88; pub. affairs intern Sta. WVEC-TV (ABC), Norfolk, Va., 1985; pub. affairs rep. Patrick Media Group, Chgo., 1988—. Bd. dirs. Chgo. Internat. Film Festival, 1990; mem. Women for Commr. John Stroger, Chgo., 1990, Thornton Twp. Regular Dem. Orgn., Cook County, Ill., 1989, Women for Commr. Sam Vaughan, Chgo., 1989. Named Most Outstanding Youth of Northwest Ind., Info Newspaper, Gary, 1981. Mem. Chgo. Area Pub. Affairs Group, Women in Communications, Outdoor Advt. Assn. Am. (congl. lobby team 1990), Outdoor Advt. Assn. Ill., Women in Govt., LWV, Delta Sigma Theta (undergrad. historian 1985), Alpha Kappa Mu, Kappa Tau Alpha. Democrat. Baptist. Office: Patrick Media Group Inc 4000 S Morgan St Chicago IL 60609

TOY, KAREN W., army officer; b. Tokyo, Aug. 3, 1962; d. Edward S. and Toku (Koasa) Wall; m. Robert P. Toy, May 30, 1989. AA, N.Mex. Mil. Inst., 1982; postgrad., U. Hawaii, 1987; BS in Biology, Tex. Tech U., 1985. Commissioned USAR, 1982, advanced through grades to capt.; maintenance officer USAR, Harrisburg, Pa.; supply distbn. officer Hawaii Army NG, Honolulu. Recipient undergrad. physics rsch. scholarship. Mem. Nat. Student Nurse Assn., Assn. uartermaster Officers, Quartermaster. Home: 170 J Ave NCAD New Cumberland PA 17070

TOY, MADELINE SHEN, chemistry scientist; b. Shanghai, Republic of China, Nov. 6, 1926; came to U.S., 1947; d. Zee and She-Ven (Hwang) Shen; m. Stephen Moy Toy, Dec. 26, 1951; 1 child, Stephanie Moy. BS, Coll. St. Theresa, Winona, Minn., 1949; MS, U. Wis., 1951, Ohio State U., Columbus, 1957; PhD, U. Pa., 1959. Mgr. organic lab. Freelander Research Devel. Lab. div. Dayco Corp., Hawthorne, Calif., 1959-60; staff mem. ITT Fed. Lab., San Fernando, Calif., 1961-62; sec. chief, research scientist McDonnell Douglas Corp., Newport Beach and Huntington Beach, Calif., 1964-70; sr. chemist Stanford Research Inst., Menlo Park, Calif., 1971-75; head chem. lab. Sci. Applications Internat. Corp., Sunnyvale and Los Altos, Calif., 1975-88, Carter Analytical Lab. Inc., Campbell, Calif., 1988—; cons. NASA, Houston, 1972. Author books in field; contbr. numerous articles profl. jours.; patentee in field. Recipient Certs. of Recognition NASA, Houston, 1978,80, Pasadena, Calif., 1977, New Tech. award NASA, Pasadena, 1970. Fellow Royal Chem. Soc. London; mem. Am. Chem. Soc. (exec. com. div. fluorine chems. 1975-77), Am. Inst. Chemists (sec. treas. Golden Gate chpt. 1975). Club: Lydia Health.

TOY, THERESA MAUREEN, educator; b. Chester, Pa., Aug. 17, 1947; d. Harry Reese and Mary (Gordon) T. BA in Elem. Edn., Loyola Coll., Balt., 1975, MEd in Spl. Edn., 1980, MEd in Adminstrn./Supervision, 1983. Tchr. Personnel sec. Wilmington Planning Com., Wilmington, Del., 1965; tchr. Ourlady of Fatima Parish, New Castle, Del., 1968-69; spl. edn. tchr. The Benedictine Sch. of Exceptional Children, Ridgely, Md., 1969-77, Am. Inst. for Mental Studies, Vineland, N.J., 1977-78, Talbot Co. Bd. Edn., Easton, Md., 1978-82; dir. outreach ctr. for social programs The Benedictine Sisters, Md., 1982-84; spl. edn. tchr. Maurice River Twp. Elem. Sch., Port Elizabeth, N.J., 1985-86; asst. supr. edn. So. State Correctional Facility, Delmont, N.J., 1986-88; spl. edn. tchr. Woodbine Elem. Sch., Woodbine, N.J., 1989—; supr. of mgmt. N.J. Cert. Pub. Mgrs. Program, Trenton, N.J., 1987. Bd. dirs. Caroline Co. Dept. of Social Svcs., Denton, 1983, United Concerned Christians, Denton, 1983; Founder Tri-County Special Olympics, Ridgely, 1971; Mem. State Edn. Adv. Com. Edn. Consolidation & Improvement, Balt., 1981; instr. water safety ARC, Honesdale, Pa., 1972. Mem. NAFE, N.J. Edn. Assn., Woodbine Edn. Assn., Alpha Sigma Nu. Democrat. Roman Catholic. Home: PO Box 186 Station Rd Leesburg NJ 08327 Office: Woodbine Elem Sch Webster St Woodbine NJ 08270

TOYNE, MARGUERITE CASTLES, management consultant, business executive; b. Batesburg, S.C., Jan. 7, 1942; d. Hal Ross and Myrtle (McKeown) Castles; m. Gerald Bump; children from previous marriage: Susanne Marguerite, Ross Brian. BA, U. S. Fla., 1970; M Bus. Edn., Ga. State U., 1971, PhD, 1974. Bookkeeper Erlangen (Fed. Republic Germany) Rod and Gun Club, 1964, Inmark, Inc., Kensington, Md., 1968; evening instr. DeKalb Tech. Sch., Clarkston, Ga., 1971; grad. instr. Ga. State U., Atlanta, 1972; instr. DeKalb Community Coll., Clarkston, 1974; mgmt. cons. Mescon, Inc., Atlanta, 1974-75; chair dept. bus. and econs., founder adv. bd. for dept. Columbia (S.C.) Coll., 1975-79; dir. mgmt., edn. and tng. programs Office Textile and Apparel, Dept. Commerce, Washington, 1979-82; sales support, nat. account exec. AT&T Info. Systems, 1982-85; pres. Bus. Resource Network, Atlanta, 1985—; cons. orgn. design tng. programs, strategic planning for human resource devel.; planner, organizer, leader seminars, workshops for women in mgmt., 1975-78; cons. state and local govt., ednl. TV; leader presentations U.S.C., Columbia Coll., Ga. Vocat. Assn., Ga. Libr. Assn., others; speaker ann. mtg. Internat. Alliance, Emory U., ann. conf. Soc. for Info. Mgmt. Contbr. articles to profl. publs. V.p. liaison Am. Field Svc.; del. Internat. Community Conf., Cali, Colombia, 1978; mem. pub. ednl. workgroup task force S.C. Heart Assn., 1978—; mem. S.C. exec. com. Internat. Women's Yr., 1977; bd. dirs. Coun. on Battered Women, One Peachtree Battle Townhouses. Recipient awards S.C. Ednl. Resources Found., 1977, United Fund, others; named one of Outstanding Young Women Am., 1976; fellow NDEA, 1971-74, faculty forum fellow Exxon Corp., Houston, 1976; grantee AID, 1978. Mem. Columbia Sales and Mktg. Execs. (v.p. 1978-79, bd. dirs., fun raising com.), Ga. Exec. Women's Network (bd. dirs.), Am. Bus. Communication Assn. (nat. bus. practice and problems com. 1975), Am. Soc. Tng. and Devel., Data Processing Mgmt. Assn., Am. Mtg. Assn., Assn. Computing Machinery, Ptnrs. of the Ams., Bus. and Profl. Women's Assn., Coldstream Country Club (bd. govs.), Kappa Delta Pi, Delta Pi Epsilon. Home: One Peachtree Battle Ave Townhouse 14 Atlanta GA 30305

TOYSER, FRANCINE, home remodeling equipment company executive; b. Chgo., Feb. 13, 1946; d. Angelo Ralph and Gilda (Stellato) Trozzolo; m. Frank J. Amabile, Apr. 12, 1970 (div. Sept. 1977); 1 child, Laura Rose; m. Richard Walter Toyser, Aug. 26, 1978; step-children: Tammy J. Toyser Kopera, Wendy J. Toyser Woodbury. A.A., Coll. of St. Francis, Joliet, Ill., 1967. Tech. writer GTE, Northlake, Ill., 1976-78; dir. services Lion-Hearted Remodeling, Inc., Elmhurst, Ill., 1978-85, corp. sec., 1978—; pres., chief exec. officer Pride Kitchens & Baths, Inc., Villa Park and Streamwood, Ill., 1985—. Sec. South Barrington Plan Commn. and Zoning Bd. Appeals. Mem. Nat. Assn. Remodeling Industry, Nat. Kitchen and Bath Assn., U.S. C. of C. Republican. Roman Catholic. Avocation: sailing.

TRACTON, SYNDI ROBIN, actress, stuntwoman; b. Wyndmoor, Pa., Aug. 12, 1961; d. James Barry and Roslyn Frieda (Katz) T. AA, U. So. Fla., 1981; BS with honors, Fla. Internat. U., 1986; Student, Am. Acad. Dramatic Arts, 1987-88. Actress Murder Mystery's Inc., Miami, Fla., 1988—; stage mgr., actress Apple City-Miami Repertory Theater, Kendall, Fla., 1989; stunt double Chains of Gold, Miami, 1989; appeared on Miami Vice, 1986-89, Making Mr. Right, 1986; asst. dir. mus. Aranoff Prodns., N.Y.C., 1988; asst. stage mgr. Actor's Playhouse, Miami, 1989,Playhouse Equity. Chair com. Spl. Olympics and Talent Olympics, Miami, 1989; reader, recorder Taping for the Blind, N.Y.C., 1988. Mem. SAG, AFTRA, Women of Motion Picture Industry, Fla. Motion Picture and TV Assn., Am. Film Inst., Screen Extra's Guild. Democrat. Jewish. Home: 12700 N Bay Shore Dr North Miami FL 33181 Office: 4441 Tujunga Ave #2 North Hollywood CA 91602

TRACY, ALOISE See SHOENIGHT, PAULINE ALOISE SOUERS

TRACY, BARBARA MARIE, lawyer; b. Mpls., Oct. 13, 1945; d. Thomas A. and Ruth C. (Roby) T. BA, U. Minn., 1971; JD, U. Okla., 1980. Bar: Okla. 1980, U.S. Dist. Ct. (we. dist.) Okla. 1980, U.S. Supreme Ct., 1988. Assoc. Pierce, Couch, Hendrickson, Johnston & Baysinger, Oklahoma City, 1980-82; ptnr. Rizley & Tracy, Sayre, Okla., 1982-84; pvt. practice Oklahoma City, 1984—; bd. dirs. HOYA Inc., Oklahoma City. Mem. citizens adv. bd. O'Donoghue Rehab. Inst., Oklahoma City. Mem. ABA, Okla. Bar Assn. Democrat. Roman Cathlic. Office: 1501 Classen Blvd Ste 105 Oklahoma City OK 73106

TRACY, CARLEY DEAN, educator; b. Bluefield, W.Va., May 27, 1923; d. Cecil Stephen and Ola Mae (Hamblin) Henderson; m. Don Hubert Tracy, May 6, 1943 (div. 1954); children: Don Henderson, Norma Lee, Patricia Kaye. BS, U. Akron, 1966. 1st grade tchr. Woodford Sch., Barberton, Ohio, 1957-58; kindergarten tchr. Hazelwood Sch., Barberton, 1958-76; pre-sch. tchr. head start Lincoln Sch., Barberton, Ohio, 1966; pre-sch. tchr. head start Washington Sch., Barberton, 1967, 2nd grade tchr., 1976-80; 2nd grade tchr. Oakdale Sch., Barberton, 1980-84; owner, sr. exec. Teachers Aid. Author and pub.: Trace a Pattern, 1979, visual aid, Number Clowns, 1978; contbr. articles to profl. jours. State Dept. Edn. scholar, 1956. Mem. Toastmistress Club (pres. local club 1972, treas. com. 1 1974, workshop leader state conv. 1973), Parliamentary Law Study Club (treas. 1987), Kappa Kappa Iota (local pres. 1980-82, state pres. 1984-85). Democrat. Methodist. Home: PO Box 226 Tallmadge OH 44278 Office: PO Box 226 Tallmadge OH 44278

TRACY, DOROTHY SHEA, financial planner; b. Pitts., Oct. 4, 1920; d. Thomas Francis and Frances Marie (Gilhouse) Shea; widow; children: Patrick, Thomas, Nancy, Christine, Michael, Kathleen. BBA in Econs., Ga. State U., 1967. Tchr. Ga. Continuing Edn., Atlanta, 1978-85; fin. planner Atlanta, 1980—; lobbyist Coun. for Children, Atlanta, 1979-8l; rep. Legislex, Washington, 1980-8l; legis. aide to Rep. Eleanor Richardson, Ga. Gen. Assembly, Atlanta, 1983-90. Author: ABC's of School Finance in Georgia, 1983. Mem. Atlanta Civil Svc. Rev. Bd., 1985—; bd. dirs. Atlanta Regional Commn. Task Force on Elderly, 1988—. Recipient Outstanding Cath. Woman award Archdiocese of Ga. Coun., 1977, community svc. award Atlanta Women's C. of C., 1984, Gov.'s commendation State of Ga., 1988. Mem. LWV (task force for tax study Ga. 1987-88, task for marital property study 1988), AAUW (legis. chmn. Ga. and Atlanta 1983-87), Am. Arbitration Assn., Am. Assn. Ret. Persons. Democrat. Home and Office: 3037 Slaton Dr NW Atlanta GA 30305

TRACY, KAREN ANN, instructional designer; b. Oil City, Pa., Jan. 15, 1963; d. James Leroy and Mary Louise (Beichner) McClelland; m. Edward C. Tracy, Oct. 5, 1985. BS, Pa. State U., 1984; MA, Marymount U., 1990. Antepartum coord. Goldfarb Adult Devel., Baylor Coll. Medicine, Houston, 1984-85; project coord. family communication project Am. Assn. Counseling and Devel., Alexandria, Va., 1986-88; cons. ARC, Nat. Hdqrs., 1988-89; instructional designer grad. sch. of govt. Audit Tng. Inst., 1990—. Mem. ASTD, Nat. Soc. Performance and Instrn., Delta Epsilon Sigma. Home and Office: 5140 Maris Ave #100 Alexandria VA 22304

TRACY, MARY ELIZABETH, librarian; b. Joliet, Ill., Aug. 18, 1922; d. Charles Joseph and Catherine (Fay) Tracy; B.A. cum laude, Coll. St. Francis, 1944; M.A., Rosary Coll., 1958. Tchr., librarian Joliet pub. schs., 1944-52, 54-61, Am. schs., Bremerhaven and Frankfurt, Germany, 1952-54; librarian Cen. Campus Joliet Twp. High Sch., 1961-86; librarian Coll. St. Francis, 1987—; chmn. Joliet Local Archives Com., 1981-87. Sec., v.p., and mem. adv. bd. Alumnae of the Coll. of St. Francis. Mem. Am., Ill. Library Assns., Ill. Assn. for Media in Edn., Ill. Audio-Visual Assn., Will County Library/Media Assn. (pres. 1976), Joliet Jr. Cath. Woman's League (pres. 1950-51), Joliet Area Hist. Soc. (bd. advisors 1986—). Home: 1010 Glenwood Ave Joliet IL 60435

TRADER, MARY ELIZABETH, home health care professional; b. Aurora, Ill., Mar. 2, 1936; d. Herbert Anthony Ostergrant and Helen Opal (Combs) Stone; m. Donald Eugene Trader, May 9, 1954 (dec. 1967); children: Timothy E., Laura E., Tami E., Julia E., Thomas E., Todd E. AS in Humane Svcs., Sauk Valley Coll., Dixon, Ill., 1980, AS in Criminal Justice, 1983. Lic. cosmetologist, Ill. Credit bur. mgr. Ogle County Credit Bur., Oregon, Ill., 1975-78; fin. aid officer Sauk Valley Coll., 1978-80; social worker Rockford (Ill.) Child and Family Svcs., 1980-82; probation officer Lee County Probation Dept., Dixon, 1982-83; ind. home health care provider Smyrna, Ga., 1984—. Active Feed the Hungry programs, Help the Homeless programs various churches in Dixon, Smyrna and Marietta, Ga., 1988—; foster parent, Dixon, 1968-73. Home: 4985 Crowe Dr Smyrna GA 30082

TRADUP, JANETTA FREEMAN, nursing educator; b. Pawhuska, Okla., Jan. 12, 1951; d. Foy Eugene and Cora Ellen (Anderson) Freeman; m. Steven William Tradup, Aug. 10, 1969 (div. Oct. 1977); 1 child, Gregory Mark. AD in Nursing, U. Albuquerque, 1979; BS in Nursing, West Tex. State U., 1982; MS in Nursing, U. Tex. Health Sci. Ctr., 1984. Staff nurse Lubbock (Tex.) Gen. Hosp., 1979-80, charge nurse, 1980-82; staff nurse Meth. Hosp., Lubbock, 1982, instr. Sch. Nursing, 1985-89; head nurse Health Sci. Ctr. Tex. Tech. U., Lubbock, 1983, asst. prof. nursing, 1989—; sec. Meth. Hosp. Faculty, Lubbock, 1985-86. Com. mem. Boy Scouts Am., Lubbock, 1982; caseworker Family Outreach, Lubbock, 1986. Mem. Am. Nurses Assn. (cert. high risk perinatal nurse), Tex. Nurses Assn. (faculty cons. student's assn. 1986—), Council on Maternal Child Nursing, Tex. Nurses Assn. (treas. local dist. 1986, v.p. local dist. 1988-89), Nat. League Nursing, Tex. League Nursing, Tex. Nursing Assn. (state fin. com. 1988—), Sigma Theta Tau. Home: 4209 40th St Lubbock TX 79413 Office: TTUHSC Sch Nursing Lubbock TX 79430

TRAFAS, NAN, telemarketing professional; b. Quantico, Va., June 1, 1960; d. Richard A. and Mary M. (Minton) T. BA in Psychology, Miami U., Oxford, Ohio, 1982; postgrad., Fla. Internat. U., 1990—. Supr. reservations Jartran, Inc., Miami, Fla.; adminstrv. asst. Enterprise Leasing, Miami; fundraiser Sta. WPBT-TV, PBS, Miami; mgr. telemktg. Interval Internat., Miami. Mem. NAFE. Home: 14895 NE 18 Ave Bldg #1 Apt #2D North Miami FL 33181 Office: 6262 Sunset Dr Penthouse 1 South Miami FL 33143

TRAHAN, ELLEN VAUNEIL, non-profit association executive, public administrator; b. Rosie, Ark., June 30, 1941; d. Jess James Ross and Ellen Alabama (Spears) Massey; m. Terrance Dale Trahan, June 9, 1961; children: Ginny-Marie, Anthony Scott, Julie Jeanette. BA in Home Econs., Magic Valley Christian Coll., Albion, Idaho, 1962; BA in Psychology, Pepperdine U., 1966; postgrad., Willamette U., 1983-84; MBA, Chaminade U., Honolulu, 1985. Social worker Los Angeles Dept. Social Service, 1966-70; adminstr. Socialization Ctr. Marion County Mental Health Clinic, Salem, Oreg., 1973; social service worker Fairview Hosp. and Tng. Ctr., Salem, 1973-85; exec. dir. Autistic Vocat. Edn. Ctr., Honolulu, 1986-89; supr. adult clin. svcs. community mental health Cen. Oahu Community Mental Health, Mental Health Div. Hawaii, Pearl City, 1989—. Mem. bus. adv. com. Supported Employment Task Force, Goodwill Corp, 1986-87; orgn. cons. Fairview Parents Club, Salem, 1977-85; advisor Honolulu Dept. Health Community Service to Developmentally Disabled, 1986—. Mem. NAFE, ACLU, NOW, Nat. Soc. Autistic Citizens, Assn. Retarded Citizens, Nat. Alliance for the Mentally Ill. Home: 250 Ohua Ave 3E Honolulu HI 96815 Office: Dept Health Hawaii Cen Oahu Community Mental Health 860 4th St Pearl City HI 96782

TRAIGIS, MARY ELIZABETH, nurse; b. Mt. Holly, N.J., Feb. 15, 1963; d. William Peter and Mary(Frankovich) T. AA in Nursing summa cum laude, Walters State Community Coll., Morristown, Tenn., 1989; cert. emergency med. technician, State Tech. Inst., Knoxville, Tenn., 1983. RN, Tenn. Firefighter, emergency med. technician Rural Metro Fire Dept., Knoxville, 1981-87; emergency med. dispatcher Knox County Govt., Knoxville, 1983-86; nurse extern, monitor technician St. Mary's Hosp., Knoxville, 1987-89; staff nurse U. Tenn. Hosp., Knoxville, 1989-90; staff nurse coronary care unit Washington Hosp. Ctr., 1990—; mem. dive rescue team, leader dispatch team, Jr. squad adviser, sec., historian Knoxville Vol. Rescue Squad, 1983-85; basic life support instr. Am. Heart Assn., Knoxville, 1987—; nursing del. People to People, People's Republic China, 1990. Mem. NAFE, Am. Assn. Critical-Care Nurses, Tenn. Nurse's Assn. Roman Catholic. Home: 9314 Cherry Hill Rd Apt 214 College Park MD 20740

TRAINOR, LILLIAN (MIDGE TRAINOR), elections official; b. Norma, N.J., Oct. 30, 1936; d. Loenell Lesley and Lillie Ara (Kenyon) Barber; m. Arthur James Trainor, Mar. 9, 1959; children: Michael, Arthur, Lynn Marie. Student pub. schs., Pleasantville, N.J. Chair Burlington County Bd. Elections, Mount Holly, N.J., 1978-81, commr. of registration, 1981-83, chair, 1983-90; dir. N.J. Div. Elections, 1990—. Vice chair, mem. exec. bd. Burlington County Dem. Com., 1977-90; chair Southampton Twp. Dem. County Com., 1976-79, Bd. County Canvassers, Burlington County, 1978-90; v.p. Southeastern Dem. Coalition, 1977-87; mgr. Florio for Gov. Campaign, N.J., 1981, Carter for Pres. Campaign, Burlington County area, 1980; del. Dem. Nat. Conv., 1984, 88; coord. Women for Florio Gubanatorial campaign, 1989. Served with WAC, 1955-57. Mem. N.J. State Assn. Election Ofcls., VFW Aux. Club: Big Six (pres. 1973-79). Avocations: accordian, piano, birdwatching, reading. Home: PO Box 256 Vincentown NJ 08088 Office: NJ Div Elections 315 W State St Trenton NJ 08625 Mailing: PO Box 256 Vincentown NJ 08088

TRAMONTE, BARBARA PATURICK, bookstore owner; b. Bklyn., Nov. 26, 1946; d. Arthur and Sarah (Zander) Paturick; m. Robert Joseph Tramonte, Mar. 23, 1972; children: Rachel, David. BA, Fordham U., 1984. Asst. editor Worth Pubs., N.Y.C., 1978-80; pub. Blue Star Press, Bklyn., 1982—; poet-in-residence Packer Collegiate Inst., Bklyn., 1987-88, Poets-in-Pub. Svc., N.Y.C., 1989-90; owner bookstore Cousin Arthur's Bookshop, Bklyn., 1984—; lect. on children's books various schs. and colls., N.Y.C., 1985—. Arthor: (poetry book) Letter to a Friend, 1986. Office: Cousin Arthurs Bookshop 82 Montague St Brooklyn NY 11201

TRANER, DONNA MARIE, accountant; b. Tokoma Park, Md., Mar. 6, 1958; d. Albert Alexander and Florence Louise (Kluth) Angeline; m. James Frank Traner, May 20, 1989. AA, PG Community Coll., Largo, Md., 1984. Acctg. supr. Tower Fed. Credit Union, Annapolis Junction, Md., 1983-85; acctg. asst. Trammel Crow Co., Boca Raton, Fla., 1985-86; acctg. supr. Trammel Crow Co., Boca Raton, 1986-88, asst. controller, 1988-89; controller Trammel Crow Co., Atlanta, 1989—. Mem. NAFE. Democrat. Roman Catholic.

TRANSOU, LYNDA LEW, advertising art administrator; b. Atlanta, Dec. 11, 1949; d. Lewis Cole Transou and Ann Lynette (Taylor) Putnam. B.F.A. cum laude, U. Tex.-Austin, 1971. Art dir., The Pitluk Group, San Antonio, 1971, Campbell, McQuien & Lawson, Dallas, 1973-74, Bozell & Jacobs, Dallas, 1974-75; art dir., ptnr. The Assocs., Dallas, 1975-77; art dir. Belo Broadcasting, Dallas, 1977-80; creative dir., v.p. Allday & Assocs., Dallas, 1980-85; owner Lynda Transou Advt. & Design, 1986—. Recipient Merit award N.Y. Art Dirs. Show, 1980; Gold award Dallas Ad League, 1980, Silver award, 1980, Bronze award, 1981, 82, 2 Merit awards Houston Art Dirs. Club, 1978-86; Merit award Broadcast Designers Assn., 1980, 82; Merit awards Dallas Ad League, 1978, 87; Silver award Houston Art Dirs. Show; Gold award Tex. Pub. Relations Assn., 1982, 85; Gold award N.Y. One Show, 1982, Creativity award Art Direction mag., 1986, Print award Regional Design Annual, 1988, Telly Finalist, 1987. Mem. Am. Inst. Graphic Arts, Dallas Soc. Visual Communications (Bronze award 1980, Merit awards, 1978-86), Delta Gamma (historian 1969-70).

TRAPHAGAN, KATHLEEN E., electrical engineer; b. East Chgo., June 2, 1958; d. Kenneth E. and Martha L. Peters; children: Elizabeth, Sarah. BA, U. Mich., 1980; AAS, Purdue U., South Bend, Ind., 1987. Elec. engr. Mfg. Tech. Inc., Mishawaka, Ind.; engrng. technician Johson Controls, Goshen, Ind. Mem. NAFE, Soc. Mfg. Engrs.

TRAPHAGAN, TRACY LYNNE, product engineer; b. Wheatridge, Colo., Feb. 11, 1964; d. Robert Patrick and Phyllis Pauline (Kotschwar) T. BBA with high distinction, Colo. State U., 1986, C.I.S., 1986, Cert. Criminal Justice, 1986. Bookkeeper Valley Water Dist., Wheatridge, 1976-81; kitchen aide Columbine Manor Nursing Home, Lakewood, Colo., 1979; maintenance Colo. Athletic Club, Wheatridge, 1980-81; pers. receptionist U.S. Geol. Survey, Denver, 1981; receptionist, office clk. in physical edn. dept. Colo. State U., Ft. Collins, 1982-85; asst. mgr. Twilite Motel & Grocery Store, Eads, Colo., 1983, Fla. Park Condominium Assn., Lakewood, 1982, 84; programmer, analyst Nat. Ctr. for Animal Health Info. Systems USDA, Ft. Collins, 1985-86; sr. programmer, analyst Hewlett-Packard, Palo Alto, Calif., 1986-90; product support engr. Hewlett-Packard, MountainView, Calif., 1990—. Vol., fund-raiser Big Bros./Big Sisters, Santa Clara, Calif., 1989; vol. Spl. Olympics, Denver, 1983-86; team capt. Hewlett Packard Volleyball League, Palo Alto, 1986-89, fundraiser United Way, Santa Clara, Calif., 1990, Jr. Achievement, Santa Clara, 1990. Colo. State U. Women's Assn. scholar, 1985-86, President's scholar Colo. State U., 1982-86, Agnes Kragh Hearn scholar Agnes Kragh Hearn Found., 1982-85. Mem. Data Processing Mgmt. Assn., Beta Gamma Sigma (v.p. 1985-86), Phi Kappa Phi (honorable recognition 1986-89), Phi Eta Sigma (sec./treas. 1983-84), Alpha Lambda Delta. Democrat. Roman Catholic. Home: 1357 Floyd Ave Sunnyvale CA 94087 Office: Hewlett Packard 100 Mayfield Ave Mountain View CA 94043

TRAPP, KATHRYN ANNE, marketing professional; b. Indpls., Oct. 23, 1957; d. Wayne Charles and Mary Anne (Bills) T. BS, Bowling Green State U., 1980; MS, Ind. State U., 1982. Cert. Home Economist. Co-mgr. Kroger, Indpls., 1982-86; customer service mgr. Kroger, Ft. Wayne, Ind., 1986-87, deli and bakery merchandising rep., 1987-89; deli and bakery specialist Super Valu Stores, Inc., 1989—. Author: Effects of Selected Socioeconomic Factors On The Consumer Competencies of Coll. Coeds. Vol. SPCA, March of Dimes, Switchboard, Ft. Wayne, 1988. Mem. Home Economists in Bus., American Home Econs. Assn., Nat. Assn. of Female Execs. Home: 3927 Ravenscliff Pl Fort Wayne IN 46804

TRASK, BETTY M., journalist; b. Laconia, N.H., Jan. 28, 1928; d. James Edwin and Clemency (Anstey) Burbank; m. Allison Keith Trask, June 28, 1947; children: Frank Edwin, Michael Thomas, Rory Scott, Allison Keith, Jr. Women's editor Laconia Evening Citizen, 1966-70, county editor, 1970-89, life style editor, 1989—, travel columnist editor, 1981—; mem. adv. bd. N.H. Vocat.-Tech. Coll., Laconia, 1972-78; treas. N.H. Commn. on Status of Women, Concord, 1974-76; mem. state adv. bd. N.H. Vocat.-Tech. Coll. and Inst., Concord, 1981-84. Bd. dirs. Laconia Salvation Army, 1973-89, aux. 1984—, Belknap Easter Seals, 1980—; trustee Gilford Village Knolls, Inc., N.H., 1985—; mem. task force on alcohol and drug abuse N.H. Gov.'s Commn. on Criminal Adminstrn. and Juvenile Delinquency, 1969-71; mem. adv. bd. Lakes Region YMCA, Belknap County Unit Am. Cancer Soc., Lake Region Community Concert Assn., Child and Family Svcs., N.H. Orgn. for Drug Abuse Community Control. Recipient Recognition award Laconia Lions Club, 1977, Lakes Region Citizenship award N.H. Vocat. Tech. Coll., 1978. Mem. Internat. Platform Assn., Laconia Altrusa Club (past pres., dist. pub. rels. chmn.), Laconia Bus. and Profl. Women's Club (past pres., dist. dir.), Sigma Delta Chi. Republican. Avocations: travel, photography. Home: 120 Liberty Hill Rd Gilford NH 03246 Office: PO Box 40 171 Fair St Laconia NH 03246

TRAURIG, LEONA, researcher, orthomolecular therapist; b. Chgo., Aug. 14, 1934; d. Daniel and Sonia (Lemson) Leviton; m. Walter Bernard Traurig, Nov. 6, 1955; children: Marcia, William, Donald. R.N., Jackson Meml. Hosp., Miami, Fla., 1955. Asst. charge nurse labor and delivery Jackson Meml. Hosp., 1955-56; dir. employee health svcs. Larkin Gen. Hosp., Miami, 1972-73; med. examiner, Miami, 1973-82; pres. Miami Med. Assocs., 1982—; cons. Life Extension Found., Hollywood, Fla., 1982—; organizer-vol. Sch. Systems Clinics, Dade County, Fla., 1970-79; cons. Girl Scouts Am., 1968-74, Home for Aged, 1979— (both Miami). Contbr. articles to profl. jours. Vol. examiner Am. Cancer Soc., Miami, 1982—; vol. counselor health fairs Am. Heart Assn., Miami, 1980-83; vol. coord. summer camp clinics clinics Girl Scouts U.S.A., Miami, 1971-73. Recipient Best All Round Nurse award Alumnae Assn. Jackson Meml. Hosp., 1955; Appreciation award Dade County (Fla.) Sch. Bd., 1979. Mem. Am. Heart Assn., Am. Nurses Assn., Nat. Bus.-Profl. Assn., Ctr. Chinese Medicine, Life Extension Found. Address: 13149 SW 91 Ct Miami FL 33176

TRAVER, PHYLLIS ANNE, food products company executive; b. N.Y.C., Mar. 31, 1952; d. Harold August and Barbara Lucille (Seifert) T.; m. C. Carl Muscari, June 30, 1979 (div. Nov. 1982). BA, Northwestern U., 1974; MBA, Harvard U., 1978. Dir. rsch. Staub, Warmbold and Assocs., N.Y.C., 1974-75; dir. rsch., assoc. cons. Coopers and Lybrand, N.Y.C., 1975-76; asst. product mgr. Nestle Food Corp., White Plains, N.Y., 1978-79, product mgr., mktg. mgr., 1979-83; bus. dir. Nestle Food Corp., Purchase, N.Y., 1983-90; pres. PT Ventures, 1990—. Contbr. articles to mktg. jours. Named to Acad. Women Achievers YWCA. Republican. Episcopalian. Club: Harvard U. Bus. Sch. Home: 198 Ivy Hill Crescent Rye Brook NY 10573

TRAVERS, JUDITH LYNNETTE, human resource executive; b. Buffalo, Feb. 25, 1950; d. Harold Elwin and Dorothy (Helsel) Howes; m. David Jon Travers, Oct. 21, 1972; 1 child, Heather Lynne. BA in Psychology, Barrington Coll., 1972; cert. in paralegal course, St. Mary's Coll., Moraga, Calif., 1983; postgrad., Southland U., 1982-84. Exec. sec. Sherman C. Weeks, P.A., Derry, N.H., 1973-75; legal asst. Mason-McDuffie Co., Berkeley, Calif., 1975-82; paralegal asst. Blum, Kay, Merkle & Kauftheil, Oakland, Calif., 1982-83; exec. v.p. Dela Pers. Svcs. Inc., Concord, Calif., 1983—; pres. All Ages Sitters Agy., Concord, 1986—. Vocalist record album The Loved Ones, 1978. Vol. local Congl. campaign, 1980, Circle of Friends, Children's Hosp. No. Calif., Oakland, 1987—; mem. Alameda County Sheriff's Mounted Posse, 1989, Contra Costa Child Abuse Prevention Coun., 1989. Mem. NAFE, Am. Assn. Respiratory Therapy, Calif. Soc. Respiratory Care, Am. Mgmt. Assn., Gospel Music Assn., Palomino Horse Breeders Am., DAR, Barrington Oratorio Soc., Commonwealth Club Calif., Nat. Trust Hist. Preservation, Alpha Theta Sigma. Republican. Baptist. Home: 3900 Brown Rd Oakley CA 94561 Office: Western Med Pers Inc 1820 Galindo St Ste 225 Concord CA 94520

TRAVERS, LORRAINE A., tax director; b. Fall River, Mass., Oct. 21, 1943; d. Leo A. and Elaurienne (Gelinas) M.; m. Louis A. Travers, Sept. 26, 1964; children: Louis A., Terri Lyn. BS in Acct., SMU, N. Dartmouth, Mass., 1975; Masters in Taxation, Bryant Coll., N. Smithfield, 1989. CPA. With J.G. Hodgson & Co., Inc., New Bedford, Mass., 1977-80, audit mgr., 1980-85, audit partner, 1985-86, tax dir.; mem. audit com. Mass. Soc. CPAs, Boston, 1985—; asst. treas. S.E. Econ. Devel. Corp., Taunton, Mass., 1985-90. Named Outstanding Career Woman YWCA New Bedford Mass. 1984. Mem. Mass. Soc. CPAs, AICPAs. travel, sports, tennis, reading, hiking. Home: 97 Hollister Rd Swansea MA 02777

TRAVERS, ROSE ELAINE, nursing administrator; b. Aberdeen Proving Grounds, Md., July 30, 1056; d. Calvin Mace and Margaret Rose (Duncan) T. AS, Harford Community Coll., Belair, Md., 1976; B magna cum laude, Towson State U., 1985; postgrad., Cen. Mich. U. Nursing asst. Brevin Nursing Home, Havre de Grace, Md., Citizen's Nursing Home, Havre de Grace; staff nurse Harford Meml. Hosp., Havre de Grace; RN supr. Keswick Home for Incurables, Balt.

TRAVIS, ANITA HARTMAN, state official; b. Frankfort, Ky., Jan. 26, 1944; d. Howard Fredrick and Rosalie (Page) Hartman; m. Zane Grey Travis, July 22, 1961 (div. July 1981); children: Deborah Grey, Kevin Thomas, Gwendolyn Louise. Cert., Capitol Bus. Sch., Frankfort, 1959; student, Ky. State U., 1971-78, 87—. Pub. health rep. consumer health protection div. Ky. Dept. for Health Svcs., Frankfort, 1978-80, adminstrv. supr. sanitation programs info. system, 1980-82, unit supr. environ. health data unit, 1982-84, supr. data info sect., 1984-86, mgr. info. and support br. food and sanitation div., 1987—; mem. planning com. statewide regional health confs., 1986—; mem. Computer Network Steering Com., Frankfort, 1986—; mem. processing steering com. Cabinet for Human Resources Data, Frankfort, 1986-87; mem. local health dept. funding formula study group Ky. Dept. Health Svcs., 1988—. Co-editor Ky. Sanitarian's and Fieldmen Jour., 1978-80; contbr. articles to profl. jours. Mem. Ky. Pub. Health Assn. (nomination and election chmn. 1987, membership chmn. 1989), Ky. Assn. Milk, Food and Environ. Sanitarians (sec., treas., chmn., mem. various coms., Environ. Svc. award 1986), Assn. Food and Drug Ofcls. So. States, Ten-Ure Assn. Democrat. Baptist. Home: 191 Travis Rd Frankfort KY 40601 Office: Ky Dept for Health Svcs Info and Support Br 275 E Main St Frankfort KY 40621

TRAVIS, ERIN JANE, student; b. York, Pa., Aug. 20, 1969; d. Ralph Gordon and Jane Amelia (Bowser) T. Student in journalism, Temple U., 1988—. Libr. asst. Widener U. Libr., Chester, Pa., 1987-88; sec. Aberdeen (Md.) Proving Grounds, 1988; program coord. Shadowfax Corp., York, Pa., 1989; freelance The Free Press, Shrewsbury, Pa., 1989; with sales and mktg. St. WRTI-FM, Phila., 1988-90; with pub. rels. Earle Palmer Brown & Spiro, Phila., 1990; writer The Dome, The Free Press. Mem. Women in Communications, Pub. Rels. Student Soc. Am. (v.p.), Temple U. Singers and Diamond Marching Band. Democrat. Presbyterian. Home: PO Box 122 Fawn Grove PA 17321

TRAVIS, KAREN ANNE, computer administrator; b. Watertown, Aug. 9, 1965; d. Van Cleft and Clara Ann (Miller) T. BS, Cornell U., Ithaca, N.Y., 1987. Asst. dir. for adminstrn. NYU. Office: NYU Univ Computer Ctr 715 Broadway 9th Fl New York NY 10003

TRAVIS, NANCY, marketing executive, program administrator; b. Brownwood, Tex., Feb. 29, 1936; d. John Clyde and Annie (Bynum)

Goosby; m. Floyd J. Travis (div. 1983); children: J. Barrett, Timothy Allen. BS, U. Tex., 1962; MS, U. So. Calif., 1976. Adminstr. U.S. Army Dept. Continuing Edn., Fed. Republic Germany, 1975-79; dir. Clear Creek County (Colo.) Dept. Community Edn., 1980-83, Dept. Social Svcs., Central City, Colo., 1980-82; program dir. Am. Ednl. Complex, Killeen, Tex., 1983-85; dir. mktg. Herring Marathon Group, Killeen, 1985-87; program dir. Am. Ednl. Complex Pacific Far East Campus, 1987-89; regional dir. Am. Heart Assn., 1989—; lectr. and cons. in field. Author: English Text, 1985; editor: Training in Communication Skills, 1985. Bd. dirs. Bluebonnet coun. Girl Scouts Am., Cen. Tex., 1986-87, Am. Heart Assn., 1986-87, regional dir., 1989—; mem. Dem. Cen. Com., Colo., 1982-83; advisor Ethiopian Ministry Social Welfare, Addis Ababa, 1971-74. Recipient Comdrs.' award U.S. Army, 1987. Mem. Assn. Am. Bus. Women, Internat. Coun. Shopping Ctrs. (Merit award 1986), Mil. Educators and Counselors Assn., Delta Kappa Gamma.

TRAVIS, SUSAN KATHRYN, real estate broker; b. Charleston, W.Va., Aug. 31, 1940; d. James Edward and Iva Catherine (Mangus) Roberts; m. Ray Ransleur Collins, Apr. 15, 1960 (dec. May 10, 1965); children: Cary Calvin, Camala Kathryn; m. Burr James Travis, Oct. 8, 1966 (div. Oct. 1979); children: Tammi Jill and Terry James (twins). Student, Gulf Pk. Coll., Gulfport, Miss., 1957-58, Coll. Conservatory Music, Cin., 1958-59. Dir. rental svcs. Nat. Computerized Property Mgmt. Inc., Cin., 1970-75; real estate broker First Comml. Realty Inc., Florence, Ky., 1978—; prin. First Comml. Realty Inc., Florence, 1978—; cons. market analysis and concept E.W. Richmond Retirement Ctr. and Nursing Home, Owensboro, Ky., 1985-86. Founder Tri-State rehabilitation and counciling program Kids Helping Kids, 1980, sec. 1980-88, chmn. fund raising 1987—, trustee, 1987; appointee Gov.'s Drug Abuse Bd. Trustees for Commonwealth of Ky., Frankfort, 1983; mem. Internat. Econ. Devel., Louisville, 1987, ACT for Covington, Ky., 1988, Govt. Affairs Council, No. Ky., 1988; initiated House Bill No. 26 in Gen. Assembly in Commonwealth of Ky., 1982. Named Outstanding Woman Mo., Women's World News, No. Ky., 1981. Mem. No. Ky. C. of C., Small Bus. Council (steering com. 1982), Econ. Devel. Bus. and Industry (com. mem. 1988), Greater Cin. C. of C., Women Entrpreneurs, Inc. Democrat. Home: 1082 Cayton Rd Florence KY 41042 Office: First Comml Realty 8172 Mall Road Ctr Ste 239 Florence KY 41042

TRAWIN, NANCY LYNN, psychologist; b. Glen Ridge, N.J., Sept. 16, 1947; d. Donald MacLeay and Merilea Charlotte (Schultze) Trawin; m. John Weston Simes III, Dec. 4, 1982; 1 child, John Weston Simes IV. BA, Ohio Wesleyan U., Delaware, Ohio, 1969; MA, Montclair State Coll., N.J., 1971; EdD, Lehigh U., Bethlehem, Pa., 1982. Lic. psychologist, Pa. Sch. psychologist Newark Sch. Sys., 1971-73, 74-76; clin. intern N.J. Intership Prog., 1973-74; sch. psychologist Allentown (Pa.) Sch. Dist., 1976-78; grad. asst. Lehigh U. Counseling Svc., Bethlehem, Pa., 1978-80; psychologist Lehigh Valley Guidance Clinic, Allentown, 1980-85; psychologist in pvt. practice Wescosville, Pa., 1980—; clin. dir. Lehigh Valley Guidance Clinic, Allentown, 1985-86; cons. Sacred Heart Hosp. Family Practice Residency Prog., Allentown, 1987—; lectr. in field. Mem. Am. Psychol. Assn., Pa. Psychol. Assn., Lehigh Valley Psychol. Assn. (ethics com. 1989—). Home: RD1 Box 1650 New Tripoli PA 18066 Office: 758 N Brookside Rd Wescosville PA 18106

TRAXLER, RITA ARIANOUTSOS, telecommunications executive; b. Valparaiso, Ind., Dec. 22, 1957. BS, Purdue U., 1985. Svc. technician Taito Am., Elk Grove Village, Ill., 1980-81; customer svc. rep. Mylstar Electronics, Northlake, Ill., 1982-84; pres. Svc. Cen. Inc., Monee, Ill., 1984—. active anti-drug campaigns, 1986-87, employment of rehabilitated drug users. Mem. South Suburban C. of C. (bd. dirs.).

TRAYLOR, CHERIE LEE, psychiatric social worker; b. Oswego, N.Y., June 20, 1944; d. Donald Elton and Harriete (Lee) Gais; BA, SUNY, Buffalo, 1966, MSW, 1972; m. Jean LaRue Traylor, Jr., Nov. 11, 1965 (div. Dec. 1970). With psychiat. clinic, Buffalo, 1967-70; psychiat. social worker Hillcrest Childrens Ctr., Washington, 1972-74; asst. dir. outpatient svcs. Comprehensive Community Mental Health Ctr. #2, Seat Pleasant, Md., 1974-77; psychiat. social worker Arlington (Va.) Mental Health Ctr., 1977-78, So. Calif. Permanente Med. Group, San Diego, 1978—; pvt. practice psychotherapy La Jolla, Calif., 1983—; NIMH fellow, 1970-72. Mem. Nat. Assn. Social Workers (cert.), Nat. Assn. Black Social Workers. Democrat.

TRAYLOR, CLAIRE GUTHRIE, state senator; b. Kansas City, Mo., Jan. 18, 1931; d. Frank and Janet Guthrie; m. Frank A. Traylor, 1954; children: Nancy, Frank, Susan, David. BS, Northwestern U., 1952; MA, Washington U., St. Louis, 1955. Primary sch. tchr., 1955-57; mem. Colo. Ho. of Reps., 1978-82, majority caucus chmn., 1980-82; mem. Colo. State Senate, 1987—, chair bus. affairs and labor, 1985—, capital devel. com., 1988; mem. health, environ. and insts., audit coms., 1987—; mem. Colo. Commn. on Aging, Colo. Commn. on Children and Families, Colo. Housing Fin. Authority Bd., Colo. Guaranteed Student Loan Bd., Colo. Indsl. Commn. Adv. Com., Colo. Internat. Trade Adv. Commn., Colo. Capital Complex Commn., Wheat Ridge, Golden, Arvada, Lakewood, Jefferson County, Rep. Cen. Coms., del. rules com. Rep. Nat. Com., 1988; Jr. League, Clear Creek (Colo.) Valley Med. Aux., pres. bd. Highland West-Highland So. (Colo.). Presbyterian. Mem. Lakewood C. of C., Nat. Conf. State Legislators (dir. western region), Women's Network (chair Human Svcs. com. 1988-89), vice chair internat. trade com.). Office: Colo State Senate State Capitol Bldg Rm 259 Denver CO 80203

TRACY, SANDRA JOANNE PRATT, art educator, artist; b. New Haven, Aug. 5, 1934; d. Willis Hadley Jr. and Gladys May (Gell) P.; m. Gillette van Nuyse, Aug. 27, 1955; 1 child, Jonathan Todd. BFA, R.I. Sch. Design, 1956. Cert. elem. and secondary tchr., N.J. Tchr. art and music Pkwy. Christian Ch., Ft. Lauderdale, Fla., 1964-66; developer Pequannock Twp. Bd. of Edn., Pompton Plains, N.J., 1970-72, tchr. art, 1972-76; vol. art tchr. Person County Bd. of Edn., Roxboro, N.C., 1978-80, tchr. art, 1980-90; tchr. art So. Jr. High Sch., Roxboro, 1989-90, Woodland Elem. Sch., Roxboro, 1989—; instr. elem. art, mem. faculty Bethel Hill Sch., Roxboro, 1974-79; instr. basic art, vol. all elem. schs. of Person County, Roxboro, 1981; tchr. arts and crafts, summers, 1981-82. Artist, illustrator. Mem. Roxboro EMTs, 1979-81; bd. dirs. Person County Arts Coun., 1980-81, pres., 1981-82; piano and organ choir accompanist Concord United Meth. Ch., 1981-90. Mem. NEA, Nat. Mus. of Women in the Arts (continuing charter), Smithsonian Assocs., N.C. Assn. Arts Edn., N.C. Assn. Educators, N.C. Art Soc. Mus. of Art, Internat. Platform Assn., Womans Club (tchr. Pompton Plains chpt. 1974-79), Person County Saddle Club (rec. sec. 1981-84), Puddingston Pony Club (dist. sec. 1974-75), Roxboro Garden Club (continuing, commr. 1980-82, pres. 1982-84, 87—), Roxboro Woman's Club (arts dept.). Republican. Methodist. Home: Rt 1 Box 38 Leasburg NC 27291

TREADWAY, ANTOINETTE, arts administrator, author; b. Hartford, Conn.; d. David Fowle and Edith T. BS in Journalism, Boston U., 1972. Ptnr. Brodsky & Treadway, Somerville, Mass., 1976—; founder, pres. Internat. Ctr. for 8mm Film and Video, Inc., Somerville, 1983—. Contbg. editor: (jour.) AIVF's, (film and video monthly) The Independent, 1982—; co-producer: (film) John Lindquist Photographer of the Dance, 1980; co-author: (book) Super 8 in the Video Age, 1982, 3d ed., 1988. Mem. Nat. Alliance of Media Arts Ctrs. (bd. dirs. 1982-84), Boston Film-Video Found. (bd. dirs. 1980-83, pres. 1982), Women in Film and Video, Assn. Ind. Video and Filmmakers (Indy award 1988). Office: Internat Ctr 8mm Film/Video 10-R Oxford St Somerville MA 02143

TREADWAY, SUSAN MARIE, technical writer; b. West Palm Beach, Fla., June 14, 1951; d. Karl Paul and Margaret Elizabeth (Ross) Casseur; m. Oscar Gaines Owen, June 7, 1969 (div. 1979); 1 child, Angela (dec.); m. Ronald Jay Treadway, Nov. 22, 1980 (div. 1989); children: Cassandra Erin, Kimberly Dawn. Student, Craven Community Coll., Havelock, N.C., 1981, Mid. Ga. Tech. Inst., Warner Robins, 1987-89. NDI radiographer Space Sci. Services, Inc., Riviera Beach, Fla., 1968-69; with Hayes Internat. Corp., Napier Field, Ala., 1970-71; oper. rm. tech. Flowers Hosp., Dothan, Ala., 1971-75; inventory programmer Barr Co., Niles, Ill., 1985-86; tech. writer Jana, Inc., Warner Robins, Ga., 1987-89; prodn. assoc. McDonnell Douglas, 1989; tech. writer HEBCO, Inc., Macon, Ga., 1989—. Author: Reflections of Feelings, 1980. Family services asst. coord. USAF, 1987. Sgt. USMC, 1978-83. Mem. Internat. Platform Assn., NAFE. Presbyterian. Club: Mensa. Home: 101 Port Terr Warner Robins GA 31088 Office: HEBCO Inc 380 Allied Industrial Pk Macon GA 31206

TREADWELL, ANN, art director, artist, consultant; b. Cleve., Apr. 17, 1957; d. Verne Franklin and Mary Ann Treadwell; m. William Everett McKee, June 9, 1984. BFA, Cleve. Inst. Art, 1981; MFA, Cranbrook Acad. Art, 1984; postgrad., Local Arts Leadership Inst., 1987, Skowhegan Sch. Painting and Sculpture, 1980. Co-owner Treadwell-McKee Constrn., Pontiac, Mich., 1984—; exec. dir. Creative Arts Ctr., Pontiac, 1985—; cons. various cos., Mich.; grant panel rev. mem. Ky. Arts Coun., Frankfort, 1990, Mich. Coun. Arts, Detroit, 1988—. Exhibited in group shows at Detroit Artists Market, 1985, 87, 89, Art Works Gallery, Erie, Pa., 1986, Mary Inst., St. Louis, 1986, Paint Creek Ctr. Arts, Rochester, Mich., 1987, 89, U. Houston, 1988, Michigan Gallery, Detroit, 1988; contbr. articles to profl. jours. Mem. steering com. United Way, 1989. Mem. NAFE, Coll. Art Assn., Detroit Artists Market. Home: 29 W Howard Pontiac MI 48058 Office: Creative Arts Ctr 47 Williams Pontiac MI 48053

TREADWELL, DEBBIE J., neonatalogical nurse; b. Pell City, Calif., May 29, 1963; d. Douglas E. and Mildred F. (Singleton) T. Cert. in religious edn., Bible Missionary Inst., Rock Island, Ill., 1982; BS in Nursing, Azusa Pacific U., 1987. RN, Calif. Staff nurse neonatal ICU Pomona (Calif.) Valley Hosp. Med. Ctr. Pell grantee. Mem. Nat. Assn. Neonatalogical Nurses. Democrat. Home: 624 E Grand Ave Pomona CA 91766 Office: 1798 N Garey Ave Pomona CA 91768

TREBILCOT, JOYCE, feminist philosopher, educator; b. San Diego, Feb. 15, 1933; d. Earl and Angela (Dameral) T. B.A. in Philosophy, U. Calif.-Berkeley, 1957; M.A., U. Calif.-Santa Barbara, 1966, Ph.D., 1970. NEH teaching fellow Bryn Mawr Coll., 1967-69; vis. scholar/tchr. women studies U. N.Mex., Albuquerque, 1977-78; asst. prof. philosophy Washington U., St. Louis, 1970-77, assoc. prof., 1977—, coordinator women's studies, 1980—; vis. prof. feminist thought Wheaton Coll., Norton, Mass., 1979-80. Author: (pamphlet) Taking Responsibility for Sexuality, 1983, In Process: Adventures of a Radical Lesbian Philosopher, 1990; editor: Mothering: Essays in Feminist Theory, 1984, spl. issue Jour. Social Philosophy, 1984; mem. editorial bd. Hypatia: Jour. Feminist Philosophy, 1977—, Social Theory and Practice, 1979—, Jour. Social Philosophy, 1981—; contbr. essays to jours. NEH fellow, 1974-75; Washington U. grantee. Mem. Soc. for Women in Philosophy, Nat. Women's Studies Assn., Am. Philos. Assn., Am. Soc. Social Philosophy (dir. 1982). Office: Washington U Campus Box 1073 Saint Louis MO 63130

TRECO-JONES, SHERYL LYNN, public relations professional; b. Winchester, Mass., Nov. 19, 1948; d. Richard Mitchell and Helen (Pleskus) T. BA in English, Beaver Coll., 1970. Assoc. editor nat. hdqrs. United Ch. of Christ, Phila., 1971-74; assoc. Ken Smith Pub. Relations, Atlanta, 1976-78; sr. pub. relations specialist Dept. Archives and History State of Ga., Atlanta, 1978-80; dir. pub. relations Scottish Rite Childrens' Hosp., Atlanta, 1980-85; account supr. Ketchum Pub. Relations, Atlanta, 1985-89; pub. rels. cons. Atlanta, 1989—. Mem., 3rd v.p. of bd. dirs. N.W. Ga. Coun. Girl Scouts Am., Atlanta, 1986—, rep. nat. roundup, 1965. Recipient Bronze award Southeastern Art Dirs., 1986, Golden ADDY-TV award AD Club, 1986, Champagne Edit. Gold Flame award Internat. Assn. Bus. Communicators, 1987. Mem. Am. Hosp. Assn., Atlanta Women's Network, Pub. Rels. Soc. Am. (Silver Phoenix award 1988), Phi Sigma Tau. Democrat. Methodist. Home: 543 Stratford Green Avondale Estates GA 30002 Office: Box 8 Avondale Estates GA 30002

TREE, MARIETTA PEABODY, city planner; b. Lawrence, Mass.; d. Malcolm Endicott and Mary Elizabeth (Parkman) Peabody; m. Desmond FitzGerald, Sept. 2, 1939; 1 dau., Frances; m. Ronald Tree, July 28, 1947; 1 dau., Penelope. Student, La Petite Ecole Florentine, Florence, Italy, 1934-35, U. Pa., 1936-39; LL.D., U. Pa., 1964; L.H.D., Russell Sage Coll., 1962, Bard Coll., 1964, Hobart and William Coll., 1967; LL.D., Drexel Inst. Tech., 1965; LL.D. hon. degrees, Franklin Pierce Coll., Coll. New Rochelle, Skidmore Coll. With hospitality div. Office Coordinator Inter-Am. Affairs, 1942-43; researcher Life mag., 1943-45; mem. Fair Housing Practices Panel, N.Y.C., 1958; mem. bd. commrs. N.Y.C. Commn. on Human Rights, 1959-61; U.S. rep. to Human Rights Commn. of UN, 1961-64; mem. U.S. del. UN, 1961; U.S. rep. Trusteeship Council of UN with rank of ambassador, 1964-65; mem. staff U Thant, UN Secretariat, 1966-67; partner Llewelyn-Davies Assocs. (city planners), 1968-80; dir. Llewelyn-Davies, Sahni Inc., Pan Am. Airways, N.Y.C., CBS; sr. cons. Hill & Knowlton, Inc.; editor-at-large Archtl. Digest. Del. N.Y. State Constl. Conv., 1967; mem. N.Y. State Dem. Com., 1954-60; mem. civil rights com. Dem. Adv. Coun., 1959-60; founder Syndenham Hosp., N.Y.C., 1943; past bd. dirs. UN Assn., Citizens Housing and Planning Coun., Ctr. Internat. Studies-NYU; bd. dirs. Am. Coun. for Ditchley; vice chmn. Cooper-Hewitt Mus., Am. Friends of Australia Nat. Gallery; chmn. Citizens Com. for N.Y.C., Friends of Arthur Ross Gallery, U. Pa.; bd. dirs. Franklin D. Roosevelt Four Freedoms Found., Marconi Internat. Found., Coun. Am. Ambassadors, Fund for Free Expression. Mem. Pilgrim Soc. (vice chmn.), Coun. Fgn. Rels. Episcopalian. Home: 1 Sutton Pl S New York NY 10022

TREECE, ELEANOR MAE, nurse researcher; b. Mansfield, Ohio, Feb. 11, 1921; d. Clarence Samuel and Helen LaDonna (Marmet) Walters; m. James William Treece Jr., Apr. 11, 1954. Diploma, Mansfield Bus. Tng. Sch., 1939, Missionary Tng. Inst., Nyack, N.Y., 1944; grad., Mansfield Gen. Hosp. Sch. Nursing, 1948; BA, Ashland Coll., 1952; MEd, U. Minn., 1962, PhD, 1967. RN, Ohio. Dir., instr. Mpls. Vocat. Sch. Practical Nursing, 1958-61; adminstrv. head St. Paul (Minn.) unit S.D. State U., 1967-68; curriculum coord., instr. Arthur B. Ancker Meml. Sch. Nursing St. Paul-Ramsey Hosp. and Med. Ctr., St. Paul, 1968-71; chairperson dept. nursing Liberty U., Lynchburg, Va., 1978-86; adj. prof. Coll. St. Thomas, St. Paul, 1978, St. Paul Bible Coll., St. Bonifacius, Minn., 1965-67; cons. PAHO/WHO, Sch. Nursing, U. Panama, Minn. League Nursing, Va. League Nursing; profl. nurse traineeship USPHS, 1961-62. Contbr. articles to profl. publs. Mem. Multiple Sclerosis Assn., trustee, 1985—. Recipient cert. of recognition Minn. State Dept. Edn., Corp. of Lynchburg, cert. of appreciation Nat. Multiple Sclerosis Soc., citation of merit Nat. Multiple Sclerosis Soc., 1988; spl. nurse predoctoral fellow USPHS, 1963-65. Mem. AAUW, Am. Nurses Assn., Va. Nurses Assn., Am. Ednl. Rsch. Assn., Internat. Platform Assn., Nat. League Nursing, Va. League Nursing, Coun. Nurse Researchers, Va. Vocat. Assn. Am. Assn. Higher Edn., Am. Vocat. Assn., Phi Delta Kappa, Gamma Alpha Kappa, Sigma Theta Tau (Beta Kappa chpt.). Republican. Home: PO Box 234 Forest VA 24551-0234

TREECE, MALRA CLIFFT, educator, author; b. Oxford, Ark., Nov. 19, 1923; d. Joseph A. and Ruth (Thompson) Clifft; B.S., Ark. State U., 1947; M.A., Memphis State U., 1956; Ph.D., U. Miss., 1971; m. Guy Treece, Jan. 18, 1946; children: Diana, Mark David. Prof. bus. communication Memphis State U., 1957—. Recipient Nat., State, Mid-South Poetry awards. Mem. Am. Bus. Communication Assn., Tenn. Poetry Soc., Phi Kappa Phi, Delta Pi Epsilon. Methodist. Author: Communication for Business and the Professions, 1978; 2d edit., 1982, 3d edit., 1986, 4th edit., 1989; Successful Business Communication, 1980, 2d edit., 1984, 3d edit., 1987, 4th edit., 1990; Effective Reports, 1982, 2d edit., 1985, 3rd edit., 1990; contbr. articles to profl. jours. Home: 1064 Estate Memphis TN 38119 Office: Memphis State U 317 Bus Adminstrn Bldg Memphis TN 38152

TREES, CANDICE D., clerk of the circuit court; b. Springfield, Ill., July 18, 1953; d. Clarence L. and Peggie D. (Neal) Senor; m. John F. Trees, Sept. 28, 1974; children: Peggi F., Jessi M., Johanna F. BA, Sangamon State U., 1981. Teller Town & Country Bank, Springfield, 1976-77; exec. correspondent Office of Gov., State of Ill., Springfield, 1977-79; city clk. City of Springfield, 1979-86; clk. of cir. ct. Sangamon County, Ill., 1986—; various offices Mcpl. Clks. Ill., 1980-86. Precinct committeeman Sangamon County Republican, Springfield, 1977-80; various offices Jerome Irwin Republican Club, Springfield, Sangamon County Young Republicans, Springfield, Capitol City Republican Women's Club, Springfield. Mem. Internat. Inst. Mcpl. Clks., Ill. Assn. Ct. Clks., Salvation Army Bd., Mental Health of Cen. Ill. Bd., United Way Bd., Delta Sigma Theta. Republican. Methodist. Home: 1106 N 32nd Springfield IL 62702 Office: Clerk of the Circuit Ct 412 County Bldg Springfield IL 62701

TREHY, JOAN ELLEN, aerospace company executive; b. N.Y.C., Jan. 28, 1942; d. William Ignatius T. and Winifred Ann (Dodge) Campbell. BS, SUNY, Oneonta, 1963; postgrad., Chapman Coll., Orange, Calif., 1987—. Tchr. third grade Elwood Sch. Dist., Huntington, N.Y., 1963-64; asst. to exec. v.p. Conover-Mast Div., Cahners Publ., N.Y.C., 1964-71; prodn. coordinator The Dreyfus Corp., N.Y.C., 1971-75; sales supr. Gorsuch Ltd., Vail, Colo, 1976-77; asst. sec. Vail Nat. Bank, 1977; subcontract adminstr. Ford Aerospace Corp., Newport Beach, Calif., 1978-83, sr. subcontract adminstr., 1983—. Active Street People In Need Minstry to feed the homeless, Our Lady Queen of Angels Ch., Newport Beach, 1987—. Mem. Nat. Contract Mgmt. Assn., Nat. Assn. Purchasing Mgmt. Republican. Roman Catholic. Toastmasters (Newport Beach) (treas. 1985-86, sec. 86-87). Home: 102 Stanford Irvine CA 92715 Office: Ford Aerospace Corp Ford Rd Newport Beach CA 92658-8900

TREI, ALICE ROSALIE, retired occupational therapist; b. Estonia, Oct. 17, 1909; d. Prüdu and Müna (Kraun) Roost; came to U.S., 1929, naturalized, 1938; certificate occupational therapy, Columbia U., 1948; B.S., N.Y. U., 1954; m. Peter Trei, Sept. 20, 1928 (dec. Jan. 1962); children—Astra (Mrs. Felix Bottenhorn), Alan. Occupational therapist N.Y. State Psychiat. Inst., N.Y.C., 1948-53, head occupational therapist, 1953-79; clin. instr. occupational therapy Columbia U., 1966-79. Recipient Outstanding Employee award N.Y. State Dept. Mental Hygiene, 1975. Mem. Am., N.Y. State (treas. 1959-62, 69-73) occupational therapy assns., Met. N.Y. Dist., World Fedn. Occupational Therapists. Home: 15 Sickles St New York NY 10040

TREICHEL, JEANIE NIERI, computer company executive; b. South San Francisco, May 23, 1931; d. Robert Tancredi and Lena Marie (Borelli) Nieri; m. Georg Treichel, Mar. 14, 1955; 1 child, Carl Stanford. BA, San Jose State U., 1952, MA, 1955; MBA, Golden Gate U., 1983. Tchr. San Mateo (Calif.) City Sch. Dist., 1952-55; research assoc. The Conservation Found., Africa, 1956-58; from research sec. to systems doc., administrn. Xerox Palo Alto (Calif.) Research Cnt., 1974-82; asst. treas. Sutherland, Sproull & Assoc., Menlo Park, Calif., 1982—. Mem. Assn. Computing Machinery, Stanford PC Users' Group, Telecommunications Assn., Alpine Hills Tennis Club, Sequoia Yacht Club. Republican. Roman Catholic. Office: Sutherland Sproull and Assocs 1000 El Camino Real Ste 360 Menlo Park CA 94025

TREIMAN, JOYCE WAHL, artist; b. Evanston, Ill., May 29, 1922; d. Rene and Rose (Doppelt) Wahl; m. Kenneth Treiman, Apr. 25, 1945; 1 child, Donald. A.A., Stephens Coll., 1941; B.F.A. (grad. fellow 1943), State U. Iowa, 1943. Vis. prof. San Fernando Valley State Coll., 1968; lectr. UCLA, 1969-70; vis. prof. State U. Calif., Long Beach, 1977. One-man shows include Paul Theobald Gallery, Chgo., 1942, John Snowden Gallery, Chgo., 1945, Art Inst. Chgo., 1947, North Shore Country Day Sch., Winnetka, Ill., 1947, Fairweather-Garnett Gallery, Evanston, 1950, Edwin Hewitt Gallery, N.Y.C., 1950, Palmer House Galleries, Chgo., 1952, Glencoe (Ill.) Library, 1953, Elizabeth Nelson Gallery, Chgo., 1953, Charles Feingarten Gallery, Chgo., 1955, Cliff Dwellers Club, Chgo., 1955, Fairweather-Hardin Gallery, Chgo., 1955, 58, 73, 81, 86, Marian Willard Gallery, N.Y.C., 1960, Felix Landau Gallery, Los Angeles, 1961, 64, La Jolla (Calif.) Mus., 1962-72, Forum Gallery, N.Y., 1963, 66, 75, 81, Adele Bednarz Gallery, Los Angeles, 1969-71, 74, Palos Verdes (Calif.) Art Mus., 1976, Mcpl. Art Gallery L.A., 1978, monotypes UCLA, 1979, drawings Art Inst. Chgo., 1979, Tortue Gallery, Santa Monica, Calif., 1980, 83, 86, 88-90, Schmidt-Bingham Gallery, N.Y.C., 1986, 88, Portland (Oreg.) Art Mus., 1988, Rochester Meml. Art Gallery, 1988, U. So. Calif. L.A., 1988, U. So. Calif. Retrospective, 1987, L.A., Rochester Meml. Art Gallery, Rochester, N.Y., 1988, Portland (Oreg.) Art Mus., 1988; numerous exhbns. including Carnegie Internat., 1955, 57, Met. Mus., 1950, Whitney Mus., 1951, 52, 53, 58, Art Inst. Chgo., 1945-59, John Herron Art Inst., 1953, Library of Congress, 1954, Cocoran Gallery, 1957, Pa. Acad. Fine Arts, 1958, Mus. Modern Art, 1962, Am. Acad. Arts and Letters, N.Y.C., 1974, 75, 76, Retrospective Exhbn., Mcpl. Art Gallery, Los Angeles, 1978; represented in permanent collections Kemper Ins. Co., Chgo., Met Mus. Art, N.Y.C., Denver Mus. Art, State U. Iowa, Ill. State Mus., Long Beach (Calif.) Mus., Whitney Mus. Am. Art, N.Y.C., Tupperware Art Mus., Orlando, Fla., Art Inst. Chgo., Utah State U., Abbott Labs., Oberlin Allen Art Mus., Internat. Mineral Corp., Pasadena Art Mus., U. Calif. at Santa Cruz, Grunwald Found., UCLA, Santa Barbara Mus. Art, Calif., Oakland Mus., Calif., Security Pacific Nat. Bank, Los Angeles, Rochester (N.Y.) Art Mus., L.A. County Art Mus., Met. Mus., N.Y., Portland (Oreg.) Mus., Santa Barbara (Calif.) Mus.; pub. collections include Art Inst. Chgo., Whitney Mus., Met. Mus., Santa Barbara (Calif.) Mus., Portland (Oreg.) Mus. Recipient numerous awards including Logan purchase prize Art Inst. Chgo., 1951, Martin B. Cahn prize, 1959, 60, Pauline Palmer prize, 1953, Saratosa Am. Painting Exhbn. award, 1959, Ford Found. purchase prize, 1960, Purchase prize Ball State Coll., 1961, prize La Jolla Art Mus., 1961, Purchase prize Pasadena Art Mus., 1961; Tiffany fellow, 1947-48; Tupperware Art Fund fellow, 1955; Tamerind Lithography fellow, 1961; Nat. Endowment for the Arts Visual Artist Fellowship grantee, 1989—. Assoc. mem. Nat. Acad. Design. Address: 712 Amalfi Dr Pacific Palisades CA 90272

TREINAVICZ, KATHRYN MARY, software engineer; b. Brockton, Mass., Nov. 25, 1957; d. Ralph Clement and Frances Elizabeth (O'Leary) T. BS, Salem State Coll., Mass., 1980. Tchr., Brockton Pub. Schs., 1980-81; instr. Quincy CETA Inc., Mass., 1981-82; programmer Systems Architects Inc., Randolph, Mass., 1982, programmer analyst, Dayton, Ohio, 1982-84; sr. programmer analyst System Devel. Corp., Dayton, 1984-86; project mgr. Unysis Inc., Dayton, 1986-87; software engr. Systems and Applied Scis. Corp., 1987-89, project mgr. Atlantic Rsch. Corp., Fairborn, Ohio, 1989—. Mem. NAFE. Democrat. Roman Catholic. Avocations: Steven King novels, needlepoint, knitting, crocheting.

TREMPE, NANCE JOAN, communications executive; b. Duluth, Minn.; children: Christian, Louis. BS in Edn., U. Minn. Personnel cons. Staff One, Mpls., 1973-79; owner Nance Trempe & Assoc., Chgo., 1979-82; dir. sales and mktg. div. U.S. Sprint, Chgo., 1982-88; v.p. telecenter Ottenheimer & Co., Bannockburn, Ill., 1988—. Office: Ottenheimer & Co 2275 Half Day Rd Bannockburn IL 60515

TREMPER, KIMBERLY ANN, public relations executive; b. Pasadena, Calif., Sept. 24, 1963; d. Gary Lyle and Vera Jean (Williams) T. BA in Speech Communications, Calif. State U., Long Beach, 1985. Pub. rels. asst. Grand Prix Assn. of Long Beach, 1985-86; adjustment sec. Factory Mut. Engring., Orange, Calif., 1986-87; office coord. Persona Personnel Svc., Irvine, Calif., 1987-88; dir. bus. devel. Azeka De Almeida Planning, Costa Mesa, Calif., 1988—. Mem. Orange County Bldg. Industry Assn., Antelope Valley Bldg. Industry Assn. Office: Azeka De Almeida Planning 10 Corporate Pk Ste 210 Irvine CA 92714

TRENT, JOYCE MILLER, librarian; b. Dayton, Ohio, Dec. 7, 1946; d. Fielding Leo and Joyce (Henry) Miller; m. Robert Cody Trent, Mar. 17, 1973; children—Michael Frederick Cody, Paul Templeton, Mark Fielding. B.A., Stephen F. Austin State U., 1969; M.L.S., U. Tex., Austin, 1975. Pub. service librarian Deer Park Pub. Library, Tex., 1969-73; system interlibrary loan librarian San Antonio Pub. Library, 1975-76; dir. system, county librarian Atascosa County Library System, Jourdanton, Tex., 1976-81; library dir. Leon Valley (Tex.) Pub. Library, 1981—. Biweekly columnist N.W. Leader, 1981—. Pres. parish council St. Brigid's Ch., San Antonio, 1980-81; del. Met. Congl. Alliance, San Antonio, 1982—; mem. civic affairs com. Tex. Sesquicentennial Com., Leon Valley, 1984—. Mem. ALA, Tex. Library Assn. (treas. dist. 10, vice chair-elect, then chair), Leon Valley Bus. and Profl. Assn., San Antonio Geneal. Hist. Soc. (sec. 1977-78). Democrat. Roman Catholic. Home: 5903 Forest Rim San Antonio TX 78240 Office: Leon Valley Pub Library 6500 Evers Rd San Antonio TX 78238

TRENT, ROSE MARIE, accounting firm executive; b. Chgo., July 10, 1943; d. William and Katherine (Kristman) Schweitzer; divorced; children: Anna Marie, Tracy Neal, Jeffrey Earl, Stoney Alexander, Sunny Eric. Student, LaSalle Extension U., Chgo., 1966-69; BS, Cen. State U., Edmond, Okla., 1982. Pres. J & R Ranch, Inc., Yukon, Okla., 1972—, My-Co Acctg. Plus, Inc., Yukon, 1982—; v.p. Hillman's Taxidermy Studio, Inc., Yukon, 1976-82, Reliable Lawn Care, Inc., Yukon, 1982—; bd. dirs. South Tex. Electric, Houston, 1977-82, 33 Welding, Inc., Kingfisher, Okla., 1982—, B & B Air Express, Inc., Oklahoma City, 1984-88; owner, prin. RJ Transp. Co., Yukon,

1988—; pres. Tax Plus Inc., Missoula, Mont., 1990—; bd. dirs. Rowland Enterprises, Inc., Oklahoma City, Okla.; pres. Tax Plus, Inc., Missoula, Mont., 1990—. Mem. ABWA, Nat. Soc. Pub. Accts., Okla. Soc. Pub. Accts., Nat. Taxidermists Assn., NAFE, NRA, Mont. Soc. Pub. Acctg. Avocations: hunting, fishing, boating. Home: 819 Poplar Yukon OK 73099 Office: J&R Ranch Inc PO Box 850708 Yukon OK 73085

TRENTHAM, BARBARA NEWTON, biology educator; b. Hamilton, Ala., July 27, 1939; d. Lew Allen and Burladine (Rudisell) Newton; m. Jimmy N. Trentham, July 31, 1965; children: Allen N., Laura Lee. BS, U. Montevallo, 1961; MS, Vanderbilt U., 1965. Microbiologist Health Dept. State of Tenn., Nashville, 1962-65; tchr. Weakley County Schs., Martin, Tenn., 1965-69; instr. U. Tenn., Martin, 1971—. Active Weakley County Libr. Bd., Dresden, Tenn., 1975—, C.E. Weldon Libr. Bd., Martin, Tenn., 19756, chmn., 1975-85; treas. Reelfoot Libr. Bd., 1980—; sec. Martin Planning Commn., 1990—; mem. Weakley County Bd. Edn., Dresden, 1989—. Mem. AAUW (various offices 1970-90), Faculty Women's Club (pres. U. Tenn. Martin 1976-77). Methodist. Home: 429 Raven St Martin TN 38237

TREPANOWSKI, JUDITH MARY, trust company executive; b. Bklyn., June 12, 1948; d. Raymond Edward and Elizabeth (Zenty) T.; m. Giuliano Boni, July 21, 1979 (div. 1983). BBA, Baruch Coll., 1969. Asst. investment officer Marine Midland Bank, N.Y.C., 1969-79; v.p. U.S. Trust Co. of N.Y., N.Y.C., U.S. Trust Co. of Calif., 1979—. Mem. Nat. Assn. of Bank Women. Republican. Roman Catholic. Office: US Trust Co of New York 144 W 47th St New York NY 10036

TREPPLER, IRENE ESTHER, state senator; b. St. Louis County, Mo., Oct. 13, 1926; d. Martin H. and Julia C. (Bender) Hagemann; student Meramec Community Coll., 1972; m. Walter J. Treppler, Aug. 18, 1950; children: John M., Steven A., Diane V. Anderson, Walter W. Payroll chief USAF Aero. Chart Plant, 1943-51; enumerator U.S. Census Bur., St. Louis, 1960, crew leader, 1970; mem. Mo. Ho. of Reps., Jefferson City, 1972-84; mem. Mo. Senate, Jefferson City, 1985—. Mem. Oak-Le-Mehl Rep. Club, Concord Twp. Rep. Club; alt. del. Rep. Nat. Conv., 1976, 84; charter mem., bd. dirs. Windsor Community Ctr. Mem. Nat. Order Women Legislators (rec. sec. 1981-82, pres. 1985), Nat. Fedn. Rep. Women. Republican. Mem. Ch. of Christ. Office: Mo State Senate Rm 328 Jefferson City MO 65101

TRESMONTAN, OLYMPIA DAVIS, psychotherapist, marriage and family counselor; b. Boston, Nov. 27, 1925; d. Peter Konstantin and Mary (Hazimanolis) Davis; B.S., Simmons Coll., 1946; M.A., Wayne State U., 1960; Ph.D. (Schaefer Found. grantee), U. Calif., Berkeley, 1971; m. Dion Marc Tresmontan, Sept. 15, 1957 (dec. Mar. 1961); m. 2d, Robert Baker Stitt, Mar. 21, 1974. Child welfare worker San Francisco Dept. Social Service, 1964-66; sensitivity tng. NSF Sci. Curriculum Improvement Study, U. Calif., Berkeley, 1967-68; individual practice psychol. counseling, San Francisco, 1970—; dir. Studio Ten Services, San Francisco, Promise for Children, San Francisco, 1981-88; tchr. U. Calif. extension at San Francisco, 1971-72, Chapman Coll. Grad. Program in Counseling, Travis AFB, 1971-74; clin. cons. Childworth Learning Ctr., San Francisco, 1976-80; cons. project rape response Queen's Bench Found., San Francisco, 1977; adv. bd. Childrens' Multicultural Mus., San Francisco, 1988—. Active Friends San Francisco Pub. Library; bd. dirs. Childworth Learning Center, 1976-80. Mem. Am. Psychol. Assn., Am. Orthopsychiat. Assn., Am. Assn. Marriage and Family Therapists, Calif. Assn. Marriage, Family and Child Therapists. Club: Commonwealth. Author: (with J. Morris) The Evaluation of A Compensatory Education Program, 1967; (Karplus edit.) What is Curriculum Evaluation, Six Answers, 1968. Home: 2611 Lake St San Francisco CA 94121

TREYBIG, EDWINA HALL, sales representative; b. Ft. Worth, Dec. 12, 1949; d. George Edward and Lillian Wanita (Herring) Hall; m. Jerry Kenneth Treybig, Sept. 20, 1980; children: Allison Lindsey, Gifford Carl, Brick Edward. BS in Home Econs., Tex. Tech U., 1972. Office mgr. Am. Internat. Rent-A-Car, Dallas, 1973, gen. mgr., 1973-74; sales rep. Martinez Mud Co., Denver, 1977-80, Am. Mud Co., Denver, 1980-83, Robinson Construction Co., Denver, 1983-87, Dig-It, Inc., N.Y.C., 1987-88; sales rep., corp. sec. Treybig Enterprises, Littleton, Colo., 1984—. Organizer Mile High Golf Tournament, Denver, 1980-84; mem. subcom. Colo. Devel. Disabilities Planning coun., Denver, 1989-90; mem. Coalition to Insure the Uninsurable, Denver, 1989-90. Mem. Soc. Petroleum Engrs. (organizer golf tournament), Internat. Assn. Drilling Contractors, Ind. Producers Assn. Mountain States, Assn. Retarded Citizens, Denver Petroleum Club (organizer golf tournament), Alpha Chi Omega (social chmn. 1970-72). Republican. Mem. Ch. of Christ. Home and Office: 7397 S Fillmore Cir Littleton CO 80122

TRIBBLE, B. JODIE, broadcasting executive; b. Burnet, Tex., Sept. 10, 1932; d. Bill Essex and Annie Lee (Dizard) Essex-Pabst; m. Elton Ray Johnson (dec.); children: Elton Wayne, Steven Denis, Mark Alan Tribble, Tandra Sue Tribble-Findlay. Student, Draughon's Bus. Coll., San Antonio, 1951, So. Tex. Jr. Coll., 1960-62, U. Tex., 1974-75, U. Houston, 1974-75, Houston Community Coll., 1975-79. Bookkeeper Southland Corp., Houston, 1957-65; office mgr., acct. Bldg. & Rsch. Corp., Houston, 1965-67, Reliable Incubator Corp., Houston, 1967-70; acct. Gaylord Broadcasting Corp., Houston, 1970-77; bus. mgr., pers. dir. Crest Broadcasting, Houston, 1977-78, Metromedia Broadcasting Inc., Houston, 1978-80; comptr. Schindler Broadcasting, Houston, 1980-86; v.p., gen. mgr. Silver King Broadcasting of Houston, Inc., Alvin, Tex., 1986—, v.p., mgr. Sta. KHSH-TV, 1986—; with Broadcasting Cons., Houston, 1980-87. past sec./dir. Parents without Ptnrs., Houston; vol. Mayor Kathryn Whitmire campaign, Houston, 1981, 83. Mem. Nat. Assn. Broadcasters, Am. Women in Radio and TV, Tex. Assn. Broadcasters, Tex. Cable TV Assn., Alvin (Tex.) C. of C. (chairperson 1988, 89). Democrat. Mem. Ch. of Christ. Office: Silver King Broadcasting 2522 Highland Square Mall Alvin TX 77511

TRIBBLE, HARRIETT GEE, government official; b. Charleston, S.C., Sept. 19, 1944; d. John Thomas III and Alice G. (Easterling) Forehand; 1 child, Gary Warren Gee Jr. BA, U. Ala., 1977, MBA, 1983. With U.S. Army Materiel Command, Huntsville, Ala., 1967—; dir. Mgmt. Engring. Agy., 1984—. Pres. Huntsville Women's Ctr., 1977; treas., mem. exec. bd. Hope Pl., Huntsville, 1987-88. Mem. Am. Soc. Mil. Comptrollers (1st v.p. 1987, pres. 1988), Assn. U.S. Army, Am. Mgmt. Assn., Huntsville Mus. Art, Huntsville Lit. Assn. Republican. Baptist. Home: 702 Versailles Dr Huntsville AL 35803 Office: US Army Materiel Command Mgmt Engring Agy 4940-B Research Dr Huntsville AL 35805

TRICARICO, LINDA MARIE, fashion designer; b. Bklyn., June 8, 1961; d. John William and Phyllis Jean (D'Addario) T. Student, Bucks County Community Coll., 1978-79, Fashion Inst. Tech., 1979-80. Mgr. retail Canadians, 1980-83; coord. sales and design Sure Snap Corp., N.Y.C., 1983-84; asst. designer E.S. Sutton Inc., N.Y.C., 1984-86; designer Good 'N Plenty Inc., N.Y.C., 1986—; free-lance illustrator, designer. Contbr. fashion trend reports, Milan, Italy, 1984, Rome, 1985, Milan and Florence, Italy, 1986, London and Paris, 1987, Montreal, Can., 1988. Mem. Fashion Soc., NAFE. Democrat. Roman Catholic. Home: 84-25 118th # 6F Kew Gardens NY 11415

TRICE-DAUGHDRILL, ANN MORTON, emergency physician; b. Madisonville, Ky., Sept. 15, 1932; d. Joel Dabney and Hallie (Traylor) Trice; m. William Eugene Daughdrill, Nov. 18, 1961; children: Brian Evan, Cheryl Ann. BA, Newcomb Coll., 1954; MD, Tulane U., 1959. Resident in internal medicine Tulane Charity Hosp.-So. Bapt. Hosp., New Orleans, 1960-63; pvt. practice New Orleans, 1963-66, Metairie, La., 1966-69; emergency physician South Ga. Med. Ctr., Valdosta, 1973-89; infirmary physician Valdosta State Coll., 1989—; guest lectr. Valdosta State Coll., 1976, Lowndes High Sch., Valdosta, 1979, Sta. WALB-AM-TV, Albany, Ga., 1979; med. dir., bd. dirs. ABC Home Health Svc., Valdosta, 1985—. Vice chmn. Valdosta Dem. Com., 1979; del. Ga. Dem. Conv., 1980; condr. seminar on rape to local civic clubs; speaker on sexually transmitted diseases to chs. and local schs.; mem. Valdosta Choral Guild, 1988—, mem. governing bd., 1990—. Recipient cert. of merit South Ga. Med. Ctr., 1978. Mem. Am. Coll. Emergency Physicians, AMA, Am. Med. Women's Assn., Med. Assn. Ga., Lowndes County Med. Assn., AAUW (governing bd. Valdosta 1979-80, 86-89), DAR (governing bd. Gen. James Jackson Chpt. 1989—), Camelia Garden Club, Delta Zeta. Republican. Presbyterian. Home: 110 Brookview Terr Valdosta GA 31602

TRIFOLI, LAURA CATHERINE, psychologist, consultant; b. L.I., N.Y., June 8, 1958; d. Peter Nicholas and Susan Maria (Graziano) T. BA, Hofstra U., Uniondale, N.Y., 1980, MA, 1982, PhD, 1986. Founder, prin. Quality Cons., West Islip, N.Y., 1980-87; sr. tng. officer Norstar Bank, Garden City, N.Y., 1985-87; asst. v.p. mgmt. devel. First Boston Corp., N.Y.C., 1987—; cons. Am. Mgmt. Assn., N.Y.C., 1981-83, AT&T, Basking Ridge, N.J., 1982-83; instr. dept. psychology Hofstra U., 1983-85. Author: Vietnam Veterans: Post Traumatic Stress and its Effects, 1986; contbr. articles to profl. publs. Shift coord. Islip Hotline, 1976-78; eucharistic min. Hofstra U. Cath. Soc., 1980-85, Good Samaritan Hosp., West Islip, N.Y., 1988—. Scholar, Hofstra U., 1978-81, fellow, 1980, 81. Mem. Am. Psychol. Assn., Am. Soc. Tng. and Devel., Nat. Psychol. Honor Soc. Roman Catholic. Home: 11 Edmore Ln S West Islip NY 11795 Office: First Boston Corp 12 E 49th St New York NY 10017

TRIFONE, CAROL A., advertising agency executive; b. N.Y.C., Sept. 6, 1953; d. William Howard and Marie Teresa (Kurtz) Strubbe; m. Richard J. Trifone, April 6, 1974. BA, Lehman Coll., 1975. With Ogilvy & Mather, N.Y.C., 1972-77; advt. mgr. O'Henry's Film Works, N.Y.C., 1977-79; acct. exec. Castagne Communications, Bedford, N.Y., 1979-80, Conrad & Co., Hingham, Mass., 1980-81; acct. supr., 1981-82; sr. acct. exec. Quinn & Johnson, Boston, 1982-83; v.p. acct. supr., 1984-86; v.p. mgmt supr. Ingalls Quinn & Johnson, Boston, 1986—. Mgmt. supr T.J. Maxx TV & Radio; acct. supr. Friendly Ice Cream TV. Mem. Advt. Club of Boston, New England Broadcasting Assn. *

TRIFONIDIS, BEVERLY ANN, opera company manager, accountant; b. Dallas, Dec. 19, 1947; d. Philo McGill and Mary Elizabeth (Sikes) Burney; m. Paul Douglas Spikes, June, 1968 (div. 1976); m. Chris Trifonidis, August 1979 (div. 1986); 1 child, Alexandra. BBA, U. Tex., 1971, M in Profl. Acctg., 1976. CPA, Tex. Mgmt. trainee J.C. Penney Co., Austin, Tex., 1971-72; acctg. clk. SW Ednl. Devel. Lab., Austin, 1972-73; editorial asst. Jour. of Mktg., Austin, 1974-76; staff auditor Hurdman & Cranstoun, CPA's, San Francisco, 1976; instr. acctg. U. Tex., San Antonio, 1976-77; lectr. acctg. Simon Fraser U., Burnaby, B.C., Can., 1978-79, 81-84; gen. mgr. Vancouver (Can.) Opera, 1984—. Bd. dirs. United Way, 1988; mem. spl. coun. Com. on Arts, Vancouver, 1987; exec. bd. Vancouver Cultural Alliance, 1987. Mem. AICPA, Tex. Soc. CPAs. Presbyterian. Office: Vancouver Opera, 1132 Hamilton St, Vancouver, BC Canada V6B 2S2

TRIGERE, PAULINE, fashion designer; b. Paris, Nov. 4, 1912; came to U.S., 1937, naturalized, 1942; d. Alexandre and Cecile (Coriene) Trigère; children: Jean-Pierre, Philippe Radley. Student, Victor Hugo Coll., Paris. Began career at Martial et Armand, Place Vendôme, Paris, before 1937; became asst. designer at Hattie Carnegie, N.Y.C.; started own bus. House of Trigère with bro., N.Y.C., 1942. Recipient Coty Am. Fashion Critics award, 1949, Return award, 1951, Neiman-Marcus award, 1950, Cotton award Nat. Cotton Council, 1959, award Filene's, 1959, Coty Hall of Fame award, 1959, Silver medal City of Paris, 1972. Office: Trigere Inc 550 7th Ave New York NY 10018*

TRIGG, KAREN ANN, marketing company exeutive; b. Cleve., July 15, 1947. Sales mdse. mgr. Clorox Co., Oakland, Calif.; dir. mktg. Ampex Corp., Redwood City, Calif.; v.p. TMF Ptnrs., San Francisco; owner Mktg. Mgmt., Alameda, Calif. Mem. NAFE. Address: 153 Oak Park Dr Alameda CA 94501

TRIGGS, JONNA FRANCES, child psychologist; b. Sharon, Pa., Feb. 5, 1950; d. John Frank and Estelle Frances (Dankoff) Conticelli; m. Vincent Lovell Triggs, Feb. 14, 1980. BA, Pa. State U., 1973; MEd, U. Nev., Las Vegas, 1975, EdD, 1981. Tchr. spl. edn. Clark County Sch. Dist., Las Vegas, 1975-76, 77-78; child devel. specialist Las Vegas Mental Health, 1978-80; teaching parent Triggs Group Home for Disturbed Youth, Las Vegas, 1979-82; psychologist Clark County Juvenile Ct., Las Vegas, 1981-83, So. Nev. Child and Adolescent Mental Health, Las Vegas, 1984—; mem. faculty Clark County Community Coll., 1979, U. Nev., 1983-85. Mem. Clark County Dem. Cen. Com., 1988. Mem. Am. Psychol. Assn., Assn. for Child Support Enforcement (bd. dirs. 1989), Nev. Assn. for Handicapped (cons. 1982—). Roman Catholic. Home: 4132 Butterfield Way Las Vegas NV 89103 Office: So Nev Child-Adolescent MH 6171 W Charleston Blvd Las Vegas NV 89158

TRIGLIONE-WEINER, JANICE, management consultant; b. Medford, Mass., Jan. 13, 1956; d. Anthony James and Clementina Sylvia (D'Errico) Triglione; m. Richard Weiner, May 22, 1983; children: Jenna, Michael. BS in Nursing, Georgetown U., 1978; MBA, Babson Coll., 1984. Asst. head nurse surg. ICU New Eng. Med. Ctr., Boston; mktg. coord. Omni-Flow, Inc., Wilmington, Mass.; ops. mgr. Health Data Inst., Lexington, Mass.; ind. mgmt. cons. Address: 15 Thomas Dr Reading MA 01867

TRIHAS, MARIA, airline executive; b. Athens, Greece, Jan. 10, 1942; came to U.S., 1963; d. Stelios Garyfalidakis and Kaliopi Anagnostaki; m. Lefteris Trihas, Oct. 20, 1963; children: Anastasia, Christina. Student, NYU, 1963-66, cert. in travel, tourism, 1972. Sec. Dorothy Gray, N.Y.C., 1965-66; sec. Olympic Airways, N.Y.C., 1966, supr., 1967-70, supr. purchasing, 1971-77, mgr. purchasing, 1977—; cons. Philoptochos Soc. Archdiocesan Cathedral, N.Y.C., 1987—. Singer radio, Athens, 1962; actress Athens Tragas Theater, 1962; announcer station WEVD Athas Show, 1965.

TRIMBLE, CELIA DENISE, lawyer; b. Clovis, N.Mex., Mar. 3, 1953; d. George Harold and Barbara Ruth (Foster) T. BS, Ea. N.Mex. U., 1976, MA, 1977; JD, St. Mary's U., San Antonio, 1982. Bar: Tex. 1982, U.S. Dist. Ct. (no. dist.) Tex. 1983, U.S. Ct. Appeals (5th cir.) 1985, U.S. Supreme Ct. 1986. Instr. English, Eastern N.Mex. U., Portales, 1977-78; editor Curry County Times, Clovis, 1978-79; assoc. Schulz & Robertson, Abilene, Tex., 1982-85, Scarborough, Black, Tarpley & Scarborough, 1985-87; ptnr., Scarborough, Black, Tarpley & Trimble, Abilene, Tex., 1988—; instr. legal research and writing St. Mary's Sch. Law, 1981-82. Legal adv. to bd. dirs. Abilene Kennel Club, 1983-85; mem. landmarks commn. City of Abilene, 1989—. Recipient Outstanding Young Lawyer of Abilene, 1988. Mem. ABA, State Bar Tex. (mem. disciplinary rev. com. 1989—), Am. Trial Lawyers Assn., Tex. Trial Lawyers Assn., Tex. Criminal Def. Lawyers Assn., Tex. Acad. Family Law Specialists, Tex. Bd. Legal Specialization (cert. 1987), Abilene Bar Assn. (bd. dirs. 1985-86, 87-88, sec./treas. 1985-86), Abilene Young Lawyers Assn. (bd. dirs. 1985-86, 87-89, treas. 1985-86, pres.-elect 1987-88, pres. 1988-89), NOW, ACLU, Phi Alpha Delta. Democrat. Avocations: needlework, gardening. Office: Scarborough Black Tarpley & Scarborough PO Box 356 104 Pine St Ste 500 Abilene TX 79604

TRIMBLE, LORA NELLE GARRETSON (MRS. JAMES CURTIS TRIMBLE), writer; b. Wichita Falls, Tex., Aug. 12, 1935; d. Jesse Columbus and Alma Geneva (Higgenbottom) Garretson; m. James Curtis Trimble Sr., Sept. 4, 1954; children: James Curtis Jr., Mary Kristi. Student, Sul Ross State Tchrs. Coll., 1954, Midwestern U., 1956; BA, So. Meth. U., Dallas, 1961. Free-lance writer, 1961-67; dir. Royal Lane Lang. Ctr., Dallas, 1969-77; English lang. tchr. to fgn. adults, 1969-77. Mem. Theta Sigma Phi.

TRIMBLE, ROSE MARIE, substitute teacher; b. Macon, Miss., July 21, 1956; d. Jerry Perry and Laura Mae Trimble. Student, Rust Coll., 1977, Miss. U., 1977-78, East Miss. Jr. Coll., 1978-80. Substitute tchr. Profl. Nox County Schs., Macon, Miss., 1980-90; tchr. Prairie Oportunity Inc., Macon, 1980. Sec. Women's New Hope Ch., Macon, 1983-92, New Hope Ch. Choir, 1985-90. Democrat. Methodist. Home: 925 Ceadar Creek Rd Macon MS 39341 Office: Womens Soc New Hope 925 Ceadar Creek Rd Macon MS 39341

TRIMBY, MADELINE JEAN, management consultant; b. Ann Arbor, Mich., Aug. 15, 1943; d. Robert Hosea and Dorothy Eleanor (Shutt) T. BA in English, U. Mich., 1965; MLS, Rutgers U., 1967; PhD in Edn. Systems Devel, Mich. State U., 1982. Assoc. prof., coord. libr. tech. program Ferris State Coll., Big Rapids, Mich., 1967-79; cons. GM, Flint, Mich., 1979-80; various positions Mich. State U., East Lansing, 1977-81; pres. Dynamic Directions, East Lansing, 1981—; cons., facilitator Gen. Motors Corp., Troy, Mich., 1984—; part-time faculty Lansing Community Coll., Lansing, Mich., 1982—, Mich. State U., East Lansing, 1984—; cons. NCR Corp., Dayton, Ohio, 1986. Co-author: Instructional Development, 1984; contbr. articles to profl. jours. Bd. dirs. Wardcliff Assn., Okemos, Mich., 1987-88. Clifford Erickson scholar, 1980, Arthur & Pearl Butler scholar, 1979 Mich. State U.; Okoboji fellow Assn. Edn. Communications and Tech., 1979. Mem. Am. Soc. for Tng. & Devel. (local chpt. pres. 1984-85), GAPS (membership chair), Jug & Mug Club, U. Mich. Alumnae Club, Phi Delta Kappa, Beta Phi Mu. Republican. Home and Office: Dynamic Directions 2759 Brentwood East Lansing MI 48823

TRINKAUS-RANDALL, VICKERY, biochemistry educator; b. Albuquerque, Jan. 11, 1953; d. Robert and Dawn (Weathersby) Randall; m. Gregor Trinkaus-Randall, May 22, 1976; children: Jennifer, Christopher. BS, Kenyon Coll., Gambler, Ohio, 1974; PhD, U. Wis., 1981. Rsch. assoc. Harvard U., Boston, 1981-84; rsch. assoc. Boston U. Sch. Medicine, 1984-85, asst. prof. dept. biochemistry and ophthalmology, 1985—; cons. MIT, Boston, 1989—. Contbr. numerous articles to profl. jours.; patentee in field. Instr. Nashoba Ski Patrol, 1984—; organizer Com. Concerned Parents, 1990—. Whittaker fellow MIT. Mem. Assn. Rsch. in Vision and Ophthalmology, Soc. Cell Biology, Soc. Biochemistry and Molecular Biology. Office: Boston U Sch Medicine Dept Biochemistry and Ophthalmology 80 E C Boston MA 02118

TRIPATHI, BRENDA JENNIFER, ophthalmology researcher, educator; b. Rochford, Essex, Eng., July 5, 1946; came to U.S., 1977, naturalized, 1983; d. Charles Edward and Kathleen Lane; m. Ramesh Chandra Tripathi, May 20, 1969; children: Anita, Paul. BS with honors, U. London, 1967, PhD, 1971. Research asst. Univ. Coll. Hosp., London, 1967-69; lectr. pathology U. London, 1969-77; research assoc. (asst. prof.) U. Chgo., 1977-84, research assoc., assoc. prof. ophthalmology, 1984—, asst. prof. lectr., 1979-84, assoc. prof. lectr., 1984—, ocular microbiologist dept. ophthalmology, 1977—; apptd. co-prin. investigator Med. Research Council, 1973-76, Nat. Eye Inst., USPHS, 1981; apptd. prin. investigator Nat. Soc. to Prevent Blindness, 1978-80; cons. Krogh Found., NSF. Contbg. editor: Exptl. Eye Research, Cornea, Lens Research, Ophthalmic Research; contbr. over 170 articles and communications to profl. jours. and chpts. to books. Recipient Outstanding Citizen award Chgo. Citizenship Council, 1984. Recipient Honor award Alcon Research Inst., 1987. Mem. N.Y. Acad. Scis., AAAS, Am. Acad. Ophthalmology (assoc.; Service award 1987), Assn. for Research in Vision and Ophthalmology, Soc. for Exptl. Biology and Medicine, Midwest Soc. Electron Microscopists, Assn. Indians in Am. (life), Assn. Research Scientists, Sigma Xi. Office: U Chgo Visual Scis Ctr 939 E 57th St Chicago IL 60637

TRIPOLITIS, ANTONIA, religion, classics and comparative literature educator; b. Phila.. PhD, U. Pa., 1971. Rsch. assoc. Inst. for Antiquity and Christianity, Claremont, Calif., 1971—; asst. dean acad. affairs Rutgers U., New Brunswick, N.J., 1975-76, assoc. dean acad. affairs, 1976-79, chair, grad. dir. classical studies, 1979-87, assoc. prof. classics, comparative lit. and religion, 1987—. Author: Doctrine of Soul in Thought of Plotinus and Origen, 1978, Origen: A Critical Reading, 1985; contbr. numerous articles to profl. jours. Nat. Geographic Soc. grantee, 1968-69. Mem. AAUW (fellowship 1969-70), Am. Literacy Translaters Assn., Am. Soc. Ch. History, Internat. Soc. for Neoplatonic Studies, N.Am. Patristic Soc. Office: Rutgers U New Brunswick NJ 08903

TRIPP, DOROTHY, town official; b. N.Y.C., Feb. 21, 1922; d. Daniel A. and Marguerite (Vanni) Clarke; m. Edward J. Tripp, Oct. 9, 1943; children: Edward J. Jr., Robert, Thomas, Dorothy, Raymond, Lawrence, Richard. Student, Rochester Inst. Tech., 1975, N.Y. Inst. Tech., 1976, Hofstra U., 1986. Indsl. devel. cons. industry and commerce dept. Town of Hempstead, N.Y., 1973-88, dir. Office Tourism,, 1988—; dir. L.I. Tourism and Conv. Commn., Uniondale, N.Y., 1980-89, L.I. White House Small Bus. Coun., Commack, 1986—; dir. arboretum com. Hofstra U., Hempstead, N.Y., 1989—; dir., mem. steering com. N.Y. Gov.'s L.I. Regional Econ. Devel. Coun., Plainview, 1988—; indsl. devel. cons. Author: Joys and Pitfalls of Starting Your Own Business, 1975, ABC's of Starting Your Own Business, 1976, Financing Your Business, 1977, also guides on available activities and facilities, 1988—. Pres., bd. dirs. Franklin Square (L.I.) East Rep. Club, 1978—; advisor North Shore Bus. Forum, Port Washington, L.I., 1988—; mem. arts in edn. program Bd. Coop. Ednl. Svcs., Nassau and Suffolk Counties, L.I., 1989—; mem. small bus. coun. L.I. Assn., Commack, 1988—. Recipient cert. of appreciation Distributive Edn. Clubs Am., N.Y. State, 1982, 83, spl. award N.Y. State Econ. Devel. Coun., 1984, Originator-Coord. award L.I. Tourism and Conv. Commn., 1985, Achiever's award L.I. Ctr. for Bus. and Profl. Women, 1988. Mem. Women Econ. Developers L.I. (founder, pres., bd. dirs. 1985—), L.I. Innkeepers Assn., Advancement for Commerce and Industry (advisor 1988-89), 110 Action-Bus. Group (advisor 1989—), Confrat. Christian Mothers (pres. 1979-80), St. Catherine of Sienna Club (numerous offices). Republican. Roman Catholic. Home: 1008 Shelburne Dr Franklin Square NY 11010 Office: Town of Hempstead Office Tourism 1 Washington St Hempstead NY 11550

TRIPP, PATRICIA MARIE, business owner, consultant; b. Ft. Worth, Oct. 1, 1948; m. John H. Tripp Jr.; 1 child, Michael. Grad. high sch., Ft. Worth. Owner, telecommunications cons. Decisions! Decisions!, Carrollton, Tex., 1987—. Counselor Crisis Pregnancy Ctr., Dallas, 1988; mem. speakers bur. Dallas Epilepsy Assn., 1989; bd. dirs. region II, Odyssey of Mind. Mem. Toastmasters (sgt.-at-arms 1989—, club speaking award 1989). Republican. Baptist.

TRISCHETTA, ELAINE ANNE, insurance company executive; b. N.Y.C., June 29, 1951; d. Eugene S. and Anne Marie (Fanelli) T. BA in Econs., CUNY, 1972; postgrad., NYU, 1977-78. Underwriter Home Ins. Co., N.Y.C., 1972-78; excess casualty mgr. Home Ins. Co., 1978-80; corp. sec. Cameron & Colby Co., N.Y.C., 1980-85; asst. v.p. Am. Internat. Underwriters, N.Y.C., 1985-87; sr. v.p. Reliance Nat. Risk Specialists, N.Y.C., 1987—. Mem. Assn. Profl. Ins. Women, Met. Mus. Art. Republican. Roman Catholic. Office: Reliance Nat Risk Specialists 77 Water St New York NY 10005

TRISSEL, SANDRA LYNNE, university administrator; b. Albia, Iowa, June 28, 1941; d. Clyde Melvin and Frances Lucille (Sweet) Harris; m. William Albert Trissel, Aug. 10, 1968; 1 child, Daniel Allyn. Sr. underwriting clk. Farmers Elevator Mutual, Des Moines, 1961-66; jr. underwriting clk. Crum and Forester Group, Des Moines, 1966-69; sec. Giltner Ins. Agy., Fort Collins, Colo., 1973-75; loan clk. Home Fed. Savs. and Loan, Fort Collins, 1975-77; adminstrv. officer risk mgmt. Colo. State U., Fort Collins, 1977—. Bd. dirs. Larimer County Alcohol Svcs., Fort Collins, 1981-85. Fellow Nat. Prima; mem. Colo. Prima (past pres. 1989—). Mem. Ch. of Christ. Office: Colo State U 309 Administration Bldg Fort Collins CO 80523

TRITES, BEATRICE VIRGINIA, educator; b. Underwood, Minn., Sept. 3, 1917; d. Sylvanus Baughman and Gladys Mary (Shepley) T. BS, U. Minn., 1944; MEd, Mont. State U., 1963; postgrad., Utah State U., 1965. Cert. tchr. Mont., Minn. County club agt. Minn. Extension, Mahnomen, 1944-45, Dodge Center, 1946-47, Redwood Falls, 1947-48; tchr. home econs. Eyota (Minn.) High Sch., 1948-49, Clarissa (Minn.) High Sch., 1949-51, Glasgow (Mont.) High Sch., 1951-85. Mem. Minn. State County Club Agt. Assn. (pres. 1946-47), Mont. Home Econs. Vocat. Assn. (pres 1962-63), AAUW (treas. 1976, sec. 1989), N.E. Retired Tchrs. Assn. (pres 1988—), N.E. Home Econs. Group (v.p. 1989—), Mont. Edn. Assn., Mont. Edn. Assn., NEA. Home: 58 Heather Ln Glasgow MT 59230

TRIVISON, MARGARET ANN, librarian; b. Cleve., Aug. 9, 1942; d. Amilio S. and Louise (Zaccagnini) Trivison. BA, Notre Dame Coll. (Ohio), 1964; postgrad. Columbia U., 1965; MS in Libr. Sci., Case Western Res. U., 1969. Instr., Cath. Bd. Edn., Cleve., 1964-66; sch. libr. Cleve. Bd. Edn., 1966-69; reference libr. Cuyahoga County Libr., Cleve., 1969-71; libr. III, San Diego County Libr., 1971-88, libr. coord., 1971-83, govt. documents libr., 1982-83, outreach svcs., 1983-85, dir. adult literacy project, 1985-87, media coord., 1987-88; part-time law libr. Pepperdine U. Sch. Law, 1990; sch. libr. Pilgrim Sch., 1990. Mem. Calif. Libr. Svcs. Bd., Sacramento, 1978-82, L.A. County Mus. Art. Mem. ALA, Am. Assn. Law Librs., Spl. Librs.

Assn., Calif. Libr. Assn., UN Assn. Democrat. Home: 441 W Burchett St Apt 201 Glendale CA 91203

TRIVITT, ROXANNA S., technical writer; b. Columbus, Ga., Dec. 3, 1962; d. Dwight William and Brenda Lou (Avery) Bland; m. Gary Dean Trivitt, June 10, 1983; children: Chelsey Nicole, Hannah Marie. BS, Oakland City Coll., 1985. Assoc. documentation analyst Humana, Inc., Louisville, 1985-87, documentation analyst, 1987-89, sr. documentation analyst, 1989—. Tchr. Dover Chapel Gen. Baptist Ch., Louisville, 1987—. Mem. Soc. of Tech. Communication (publicity mgr. 1989-90), Women in Communication, Inc. Home: 4320 Dover Rd Louisville KY 40216

TROELLER, LINDA, photographer, educator; b. Springfield, N.J., June 26, 1949; d. Raymond Samuel and Marion (MacDonald) T.; m. James M. Hollmom, Dec. 20, 1981 (div. 1990). Student, W.Va. U., 1967-71; MS, Syracuse (N.Y.) U., 1972, MFA, 1975. Vis. lectr. Ind. U., Bloomington, 1975-76; instr. photography Stockton State Coll., Pomona, N.J., 1976-79; dir. Troeller Photography and Pub. Rels., Lawrenceville, N.J., 1986—; prof. photography workshops U. Calif., Santa Cruz, 1989—, New Sch., Parsons, Paris, 1989—. Exhibited in group shows at Ohio State U., Film in the Cities, John Jay Coll. Criminal Justice, N.Y.U., Trenton State Mus., Clarence Kennedy Gallery, Polaroid Corp., 1989. Stockton State Coll. grantee, 1977. Mem. Soc. for Photographic Edn. (sec. Mid Atlantic chpt. 1987—), Friends of Photography (Ferguson award 1989), Ctr. for Photography at Woodstock, Coll. Art Assn., Print Club. Home and Office: 718 Polk Ave Lawrenceville NJ 08648

TROFIMENKOFF, SUSAN MANN, university official, history educator; b. Ottawa, Ont., Can., Feb. 10, 1941; d. Walter and Marjorie Mann; m. Nicholas Trofimenkoff; 1 child, Britt. BA in Modern History, U. Toronto, 1963; MA in History, U. Western Ont., 1965; PhD, U. Laval, Que., Can., 1970; LLD (hon.), Concordia U., Montreal, Que, Can., 1989. Lectr. English Toyo Eiwa Jogakuin, Tokyo, 1963-64; lectr. in history U. Montreal, 1966-70; asst. prof. history U. Calgary, Alta., Can., 1970-72; from asst. to assoc. prof. U. Ottawa, Ont., Can., 1972-83, prof. history, 1983—, chmn. dept. history, 1977-80, vice rector acad., 1984-90; participant Nat. Forum on Post-Secondary Edn., Sask., 1987; mem. stamp adv. com. Can. Post Corp., Ottawa, 1988—; chmn. adv. bd. Nat. Archives Can., 1989—. Author: Action Française: French Canadian Nationalism in the 1920s, 1975, Stanley Knowles: The Man From Winnipeg North Centre, 1982, Dream of Nation: A Social and Intellectual History of Quebec, 1983 (Sec. of State Canadian Studies prize 1984), Visions nationales: Une historie du Québec, 1986; editor: The Twenties in Western Canada, 1972, Abbé Groulx: Variations on a Nationalist Theme, 1973, (with Alison Prentice) The Neglected Majority: Essays in Canadian Women's History, vol. I, 1977, vol II, 1985; acad. editor Social Scis. in Can., 1974-76; assoc. editor Social History, 1982-84; contbr. articles to profl. jours. Assessor of projects SSHRCC, 1972—; chmn., aid to scholarly publs. com. Social Sci. Fedn. Can., 1976-79; mem. appraisals com. Ont. Coun. Grad. Studies, 1983-84; pres. Canadian Hist. Assn., 1984-85; chair status of women com. Coun. Ont. Univs., 1985-88; mem. Summer Inst. Women in Higher Edn. Adminstrn. Bryn Mawr (Pa.) Coll., 1986; co-organizer Sr. Women Acad. Adminstrs. Can. Publ. grantee SSHRCC, 1975, Leave fellow, 1980-81, Doctoral fellow Can. Coun., 1968-70; U. Toronto scholar, 1959-61, U. Western Ont. scholar, 1964. Fellow Royal Soc. Can., Canadian Rsch. Inst. Advancement Women (hon., life, founder, bd. dirs. 1976-78). Home: 12 Bower St, Ottawa, ON Canada K1S 0K1 Office: U Ottawa, Dept of History, Ottawa, ON Canada K1N 6N5

TROIANO, THERESA MARIE, advertising professional; b. Winthrop, Mass., May 29, 1963; d. Robert Francis and Karen Joan (Andrews) T. BS, Springfield (Mass.) Coll., 1985. Layout prodn. artist Tello's, Cambridge, Mass., 1985-87; asst. to prodn. supr. May Co., L.A., 1987; freelance graphic designer L.A., 1987-88; media traffic coord. L.A. Gear, 1988—; graphic designer, pres. Le Physique, L.A., 1988—. Mem. Graphic Artist Guild. Home: 245 26th St Hermosa Beach CA 90254 Office: LA Gear 4221 Redwood Ave Los Angeles CA 90066

TROLAN, KAREN LYNN WEINMAN, real estate executive; b. Las Cruces, N.Mex., May 8, 1958; d. Herbert Lee and Beverly (Brewer) Weinman; m. Steven Terrill Trolan, Mar. 19, 1983; 1 child, Terrill James. BS in Dietetics, San Jose (Calif.) State U., 1981. Stable mgr. The Ranch, Los Gatos, Calif., 1972-76; head mgr. The Antique, Los Gatos, 1976-79; rep., mgr. CRS, Mountain View, Calif., 1979-83; sales mgr. Honolulu Club, 1983-85; v.p., mgr. Cornish & Carey Real Estate, Palo Alto & Mountain View, 1985—; chem. lab. technician Van Water & Rogers, San Jose, 1981-83. Mem. Beta Psi of Alpha Phi (corp. bd. pres. San Jose chpt. 1986-88, pub. rels. com. Palo Alto chpt. 1988—). Office: Cornish & Carey Real Estate 2754 Middlefield Rd Palo Alto CA 94306

TROLINGER, JANE CATHERINE, plant pathologist; b. Greensboro, N.C., Sept. 14, 1952; d. James Henry Trolinger and Thelma Jane (Wright) Hill. BA, Greensboro Coll., 1974; MS, W.Va. U., 1978; PhD, N.C. State U., 1983. Field pathologist Yoder Bros., Inc., Alva, Fla., 1984-86, plant certification mgr., 1986—; editor newsletter for fin. bus. group Yoder Bros., Inc., Alva, 1988—. Author: chpt. Botrytis Diseases, 1985. Mem. Am. Path. Soc., Mycol. Soc. Am., Sigma Xi. Republican. Methodist. Office: Yoder Bros Inc PO Box 68 Alva FL 33920

TROMBETTA, VICTORIA, office manager; b. Bklyn., Nov. 15, 1961; d. Michael and Rose (Occhini) T. AS, S.I. Coll., 1986, BS, 1988. Typist Fed. Res. Bank, N.Y.C., 1979-81; sec. Man Han T/C, N.Y.C., 1981-84; adminstrv. asst. Salomon Bros., N.Y.C., 1984-88; office mgr. South Shore Physicians, S.I., N.Y., 1988—. Treas. United Activities Unltd., S.I., 1989. Mem. NAFE. Office: South Shore Physicians 4108 Hylan Blvd Staten Island NY 10308

TROPF, CHERYL GRIFFITHS, accountant, mathematician; b. Newark, Oct. 15, 1946; d. Frank R. and Shirley J. (Magnusson) Griffiths; m. William Jacob Tropf, III, Aug. 31, 1968; 1 child, Andrew Zachary. BS, Coll. William and Mary, 1968; MS in Acctg., Georgetown U., 1983; MAM, U. Va., 1972, Ph.D., 1973. CPA, Md. Sr. physicist Johns Hopkins Applied Physics Lab., Laurel, Md., 1973-80; mem. profl. staff U.S. Senate Commerce Com., Washington, 1980-81; project mgr. U.S. Nuclear Regulatory Commn., Washington, 1981-82; asst. prof. U. Balt. Sch. Bus., 1983-85; pvt. practice acctg., Columbia, Md., 1984—. Vice chmn. Howard County Commn. for Women, 1983-84, chmn., 1984-85; vice chmn. United Way, 1985, Landlord/Tenant Rels. Task Force, 1986. Congl. Sci. fellow, 1980-81; named Outstanding Bus. Woman Howard County C. of C., 1986. Mem. AICPA, Md. Assn. CPAs, Soc. Indsl. and Applied Math., Phi Beta Kappa, Sigma Xi. Avocation: stocks. Home: 13060 St Patricks Ct Highland MD 20777

TROPIANO, MARIE JOYCE, educational administrator; b. Rochester, N.Y., Sept. 30, 1942; d. Frank Michael and Jennie (Cimino) T. BA, Mercyhurst Coll., 1964; MS in Edn., Nazareth Coll., 1977. Cert. tchr., N.Y., Ariz. Tchr. St. Thomas Sch., Rochester, 1964-68, St. Cecilia Sch., Rochester, 1968-78, Christ the King Sch., Mesa, Ariz., 1978-84; dir. religion edn. St. Timothy Cath. Community, Mesa, 1984—; presenter workshops, slide shows in field. Workshop presenter St. Timothy Parish, Mesa and Diocese of Phoenix, 1984—, mem. Parish Liturgical Commn., dir. Children's Liturgy Com. Mem. Coords. and Dirs. of Religious Edn. Roman Catholic. Home: 1921 N Bull Moose Dr Chandler AZ 85224 Office: St Timothy Cath Community 1730 W Guadalupe Mesa AZ 85202

TROPP, LOUISE CONSTANCE VELARDI, aircraft spare parts company executive; b. Phillipsburg, N.J., Apr. 30, 1942; d. John Francis and Julia Cecilia (Pisaniello) Velardi; BA, New Sch. Social Research, 1976; MA, NYU, 1988; m. Howard S. Tropp, June 6, 1964; children—Josephine, Philip. Elem. sch. tchr., Princeton, N.J., 1962-64; owner MPT Enterprises div. Aero. Procurement and Tech. Inc., N.Y.C., 1976-86; owner, Apple Aviation Corp., Washington, N.J., 1986—; dir. Jefferson Towers Inc., N.Y.C., 1976—, chmn., 1979-81, v.p., 1982-83, sec., 1983-84; asst. coord. for disabled students Hunter Coll., CUNY, 1987; dir. Tall Timbers, Sussex, N.J., 1980-83, chmn., 1981-83, cons ex-officio, 1983—. Fellow Deaf Rehabilitation N.Y.U., 1987-88. Mem. bd. Parents Assn. of Columbia Prep. Sch., 1981-83. Mem. Am. Women's Econ. Devel. Corp., Women Bus. Owners N.Y., N.Y. Chamber Commerce and Industry, La Leche League (chpt. treas. 1970-89). Address: 700 Columbus Ave Apt 7C New York NY 10025

TROSPER, MARY SUE, research laboratory administrator; b. Ontonogon, Mich., May 8, 1953; d. Joseph Thompson and Martha Grace (McCullough) Robison; m. Robert Thomas Trosper, Dec. 22, 1978. BS in Biology magna cum laude, U. Utah, 1978. Lab. technician hematology dept. Holy Cross Hosp., Salt Lake City, 1973-78; lab. supr. oncology Drs. Glassburg, Rosenbaum, San Francisco, 1979; supr. analytical lab. Norton Co. Diamond Tech. Ctr., Salt Lake City, 1980—; coord. quality assurance Eastman Christensen, Salt Lake City, 1980—. Contbr. articles to profl. jours. Coord. Neighborhood Watch, 1981, Sub for Santa Program, 1988; asst. coord. United Way, 1982. Mem. Electron Microscopy Soc. Am., Microbeam Analysis Soc., Phi Kappa Phi. Republican. Presbyterian. Office: Norton Co Diamond Tech Ctr 2532 S 3270 W Salt Lake City UT 84119

TROSSEN, MARGARET ANNE, marketing consultant; b. Chgo., Apr. 21, 1952; d. Raffaele and Ruth Agnes (Crowe) Suriano; m. Brian John Trossen, Dec. 28, 1974; children: Brendan James, Meghan Anne. BA, U. Md., 1972; MBA, Va. Poly. Inst. and State U., 1979. Sales mgr. L'Oreal, N.Y.C., 1974-76, Purdue Frederick, Norwalk, Conn., 1976-80; prof. bus. Mt. Vernon Coll., Washington, 1980-88, chmn. dept., 1984-87; owner, mgr., cons. Trossen Associates, Washington, 1984—; dir. mktg. Med Test Systems Inc., Bethesda, Md., 1986-88. Bd. dirs., membership sec. McLean (Va.) Citizens Assn., 1984—; bd. dirs. McLean Rep. Women's Club; mem. spl projects staff Coleman for Gov., McLean, 1989. Recipient Outstanding Prof. award Mt. Vernon Coll., 1987. Mem. McLean Bus. and Profl. Women. Republican. Roman Catholic. Home and Office: 7621 Huntmaster Ln McLean VA 22102

TROTTER, BETTY LOU, retired educator; b. Junction City, Kans., Mar. 20, 1925; d. Claude Frank and Mertie (Ware) Short; m. James Brown Trotter, June 4, 1946; children: James B., Jay M., Mark R., Lee R.F. AA, Stephens Coll., 1945; BA cum laude, U. N.Mex., 1948; MA, U. Mo., Kansas City, 1972. Cert. music and secondary English tchr., Mo. Substitute tchr. Denver Pub. Schs., 1960-63; tchr. English, Consol. Sch. Dist. 2, Raytown, Mo., 1966-84; ret., 1984; sales assoc. Jones Store Co., Kansas City, 1987—. Vice pres. Independence (Mo.) Neighborhood Coun., 1985-89. Recipient outstanding svc. award Nat. Coun. Tchrs. English, 1979. Mem. AAUW (pres. Raytown 1980-82), Mortar Bd., Phi Kappa Phi, Pi Lambda Theta, Sigma Alpha Iota (pres. Denver 1960-62). Democrat. Mem. Ch. of Christ. Home: 12900 E 50th Terr Independence MO 64055 Office: Jones Store Co 4700 Blue Ridge Blvd Kansas City MO 64141

TROTTER, DEBRA MILLS, educator; b. Tallahassee, Aug. 16, 1953; d. Hugh Roland and Alfreddia (Gainous) Mills; m. Gary Lionel Trotter, June 20, 1980; 1 child, India Ashlei. BA, Spelman Coll., 1975; MFA, Cranbrook Acad. Art, 1977. Cert. tchr., Fla. Art librarian Spelman Coll., Atlanta, 1973-74; asst. instr. children's art program Cranbrook Acad., Bloomfield Hills, Mich., 1975-76; coordinator ednl. program Loch Haven Art Ctr., Orlando, Fla., 1977-78; tchr. art Orange County Pub. Schs., Orlando, 1978-80; comml. artist Fla. Sun Review News, Orlando, 1978-80; tchr. art Crealde Art Ctr., Orlando, 1979; artist D. Mills-Trotter Inc., Ft. Lauderdale, Fla., 1986—; tchr. Broward County Schs., Ft. Lauderdale, 1980—; vendor D. Mills-Trotter Inc., Ft. Lauderdale, 1988—; instr. supr. Orange County Schs., Orlando, 1978-80. One-woman shows include Broward County Main Library, 1987, Von D. Mizell Ctr., 1982; designer costumes for Kids Stuff (musical), 1986, Costumes kids, 1986; vis. artist Sistrunk Hist. Festival, 1987, also judge, 1985; judge Promenade Arts Festival, 1986. Ann. Sistruck Festival. Mem. evaluating team accrediation high sch., Palm Beach, Fla. 1982; bd. dirs. Lauderhill Arts Council. Mem. Broward Tchrs. Union, Am. Fedn. Tchrs., Nat. Assn. Female Execs., Interested Members Performing Arts Ctr. Team. Democrat. Methodist. Home: 7139 NW 49th St Lauderhill FL 33319

TROUT, MARGIE MARIE MUELLER, civic worker; b. Wellston, Mo., Apr. 27, 1923; d. Albert Sylvester and Pearl Elizabeth (Jose) Mueller; student Webster Coll., 1944-45; cert. genealogist Bd. Cert. Genealogy; m. Maurice Elmore Trout, Aug. 24, 1943; children—Richard Willis, Babette Yvonne. Sec. offices Robertson Aircraft Corp., St. Louis, 1942; speed lathe and drill press operator Busch-Selzer Diesel Engine Co., St. Louis, 1942-43; Cub Scout den mother, Vienna, Austria, 1953-55, Mt. Pleasant, Mich., 1955, London, 1956-57; leader Nat. Capitol council Girl Scouts U.S.A., Bethesda, Md., 1963-65; co-chmn. Am. Booth YWCA and Red Cross Annual Bazaars, Bangkok, Thailand, 1970-72; worker ARC, Vientiane, Laos, 1959-60, Bangkok, 1970-72; activities co-chmn., exec. bd. mem. Women's Club Armed Forces Staff Coll., Norfolk, Va., 1975-77; mem. Am. Women's Clubs, Embassy Clubs, Internat. Women's Clubs Vienna, 1952-55, London, 1956-59, Vientiane, 1959-61, Munich, Germany, 1965-69, Bangkok, 1969-72, Norfolk, 1975-77. Crochet articles exhibited Exhibition of Works of Art by the Corps Diplomatique, London, Eng., 1958. Home: 6203 Hardy Dr McLean VA 22101

TROUTNER, JOANNE JOHNSON, computer resource educator, consultant; b. Muncie, Ind., Sept. 9, 1952; d. Donal Russel and Lois Vivian (Hicks) Johnson; m. Lary William Troutner, May 17, 1975. BA in Media and English, Purdue U., 1974, MS in Edn., 1976. Media specialist Lafayette (Ind.) Sch. Corp., 1974-77, 81-83, computer resource tchr., 1983-84; media specialist, Tippecanoe Sch. Corp., Lafayette, 1984-85, ednl. computer coordinator, 1985-87, coordinator instrl. support, 1988—; instrnl. specialist edn. IBM, 1987-88; tchr. English, Minot Pub. Schs. (N.D.), 1978-79, media specialist, 1979-81; vis. prof. continuing edn. U. S.C., Columbia, summer 1983; instr. Purdue U., West Lafayette; vis. prof. continuing edn. U. N.D. Author: The Media Specialist, The Microcomputer and the Curriculum, 1983; contbr. materials rev. column Sch. Library Media Quar.; computer literacy columnist Jour. Computers in Math. and Sci. Teaching; pub.: Computers and the Gifted Student; editor newsletter Indiana Computer Educators. Active Greater Lafayette Leadership Acad. Alumni Group, 1983—; bd. dirs. Lafayette Family Service Agy., 1987-89. Mem. ALA, Ind. Assn. Media Educators (chmn. computer div. 1982-84), Am. Assn. Sch. Librarians (sec. 1983-84, 2d v.p. 1985-86), Internat. Council for Computers in Edn. (interactive video spl. interest group newsletter editor 1986-87), Ind. Computer Educators (bd. dirs. 1986—, pres. 1990—), Phi Beta Kappa, Kappa Delta Gamma, Phi Delta Kappa (v.p. programs 1987-88, v.p. memberships 1988-89, pres. 1989-90). Home: 4001 Penny Packers Mill Rd Lafayette IN 47905-3557 Office: Tippecanoe Sch Corp 21 Elston Rd Lafayette IN 47905

TROUTWINE-BRAUN, CHARLOTTE TEMPERLEY, psychologist, educator, clergywoman; b. Newton, Mass., Nov. 27, 1906; d. Joseph and Libbie (Kempton) Temperley; m. Arklay S. Richards, Nov. 28, 1928 (div. 1942); children: Whitman Albin, Lincoln Kempton, Sylvia Caroline; m. Harry Troutwine, May 3, 1945 (div. 1954); m. Charles E. McCrum, 1961 (div. 1965); m. Lester Lewis Walsh, Feb. 16, 1968 (div. Feb. 1972); m. George Braun, Feb. 6, 1975 (dec. Oct. 1975). BS, Simmons Coll., 1927; postgrad. Boston U., 1947-49; MA, Northeastern U., 1966; BES, Internat. Ch. Ageless Wisdom, 1981. Pvt. sec. pres. Hygrade Sylvania Electric Corp. Salem, Mass., 1927-28; pvt. and dept. exec. sec. Dr. Stanley Cobb, Bullard prof. neuropathology Harvard U. Med. Sch., 1928-31; part-time caseworker Friends of Framingham Reformatory, 1928-31, others, 1931-51; exec. dir. Postgrad. Med. Inst., 1951-57; mgr. Postgrad. Information Services, Lederle Labs. div. Am. Cyanamid Co., Pearl River, N.Y., 1957-61; exec. sec. postgrad. med. edn., Hahnemann Med. Coll. and Hosp. also exec. dir. Mary Bailey Inst. Cardiovascular Research, 1961; counselor, tchr. psychology Holliston High Sch., 1965-66. Counselor Falmouth (Mass.) High Sch., 1966-74; psychotherapist Hallgarth Clinic, 1974-75. Speaker for Am. Epilepsy League. Mem. Mass. Tchrs. Assn. (life), Spiritual Frontiers Assn. (life), N.E.A. (life), Nat. Ret. Tchrs. Assn. (life), Nat. Assn. Sch. Counselors (charter, life), Assn. Research Enlightenment, Soc. Mayflower Descs. (life), Simmons Coll. Alumnae Assn., AAUW, Med. Soc. Execs. Assn. (emeritus), Am. Soc. Psychical Research, States Med. Postgrad. Assn. (past sec.), Mass. Psychol. Assn. (life), Spiritual Frontiers Fellowship (life), World Fedn. Healers (healer mem.), Mass. Healers Assn. Author articles in med., spiritual and psychol. fields. Mem. Soc. of Friends. Home: 83 Falmouth Ct Bedford MA 01730

TROVER, ELLEN LLOYD, lawyer; b. Richmond, Va., Nov. 23, 1947; d. Robert Van Buren and Hazel (Urban) Lloyd; m. Denis William Trover, June 12, 1971; 1 dau., Florence Emma. A.B., Vassar Coll., 1969; J.D., Coll. William and Mary, 1972. Asst. editor Bancroft-Whitney, San Francisco, 1973-74; owner Ellen Lloyd Trover Atty.-at-Law, Thousand Oaks, Calif., 1974-82; ptnr. Trover & Fisher, Thousand Oaks, 1982-89; pvt. practice law, Thousand Oaks, 1989—. Editor: Handbooks of State Chronologies, 1972. Trustee, Conejo Future Found., Thousand Oaks, 1978—, vice chmn., 1982-84, chmn., 1984-88; pres. Zonta Club Conejo Valley Area, 1978-79; trustee Hydro Help for the Handicapped, 1980-85. Mem. Conejo Simi Bar Assn. (pres. 1979-80, dir. 1983-85), Ventura County Bar Assn. (state del. 1984), State Bar Calif., Va. State Bar, Phi Alpha Delta. Democrat. Presbyterian. Home: 11355 Presilla Rd Camarillo CA 93010 Office: 1107E Thousand Oaks Blvd Thousand Oaks CA 91362

TROW, JO ANNE JOHNSON, university official; b. Youngstown, Ohio, Feb. 10, 1931; d. Raymond Leonard Johnson and Mary Belle Beede; m. Clifford W. Trow, Oct. 10, 1969. BA, Denison U., 1953; MA, Ind. U., 1956; PhD, Mich. State U., 1965. Case worker Office Pub. Assistance, Cleve., 1953-54; asst. dean women Denison U., Granville, Ohio, 1956-59, Wash. State U., Pullman, 1959-63; asst. dir. resident program Mich. State U., East Lansing, 1964; dean women Oreg. State U., Corvallis, 1965-69, assoc. dean students, 1969-83, v.p. student affairs, 1983—, program dir., 1972-83; presenter, speaker in field. Contbr. articles to profl. jours. Bd. dirs. Benton County Mental Health Assn., 1975-79, United Way Benton County, 1977—, United Way Oreg., 1977-80; mem. adv. bd. Old Mill Sch., 1979—, chmn., 1983; mem. Oreg. Community Corrections Adv. Bd., 1988—; moderator 1st Congl. Ch., 1977, trustee, 1979-83; mem. Oreg. Gov.'s Com. on Status Woman, 1972-78, vice chmn., 1976-77; mem. fund campaign Good Samaritan Hosp. Found. Cancer Care Ctr., 1982-83. Recipient Corvallis Woman of Achievement award, 1974, Boss of Yr. award Oreg. State U. Office Personnel Assn., 1979, White Rose award March of Dimes, 1987, Elizabeth A Greenleaf Disting. Alumna award Ind. U., 1987, Scott Goodnight award, 1989. Mem. Nat. Assn. Women Deans, Adminstrs. and Counselors (pres. 1981-82), Am. Coll. Personnel Assn. (sec. 1969-70), Nat. Assn. Student Personnel Adminstrs., Am. Coun. on Edn., N.W. Assn. Schs. and Colls., Am. Assn. for Higher Edn., N.W. Coll. Personnel Assn. (life, pres. 1969-70), Assn. Oreg. Faculties, AAUW (state and local bd. dirs.), LWV (bd. dirs., v.p. Corvallis 1966-69, 79-80), Corvallis Area C. of C. (bd. dirs. 1972-74, 78-80), Mortar Bd., Phi Delta Kappa, Phi Kappa Phi, Alpha Lambda Delta. Democrat. Office: Oreg State U AdS A632 Corvallis OR 97331-2128

TROWBRIDGE, VICKI JANE, education educator; b. Middletown, Ohio, June 27, 1950; d. Fredric Robert and Patricia (Van Camp) Harbach; m. Dale Martin. AA, Mt. Vernon Nazarene, Ohio, 1970; student, Trevecca Nazarene, Nashville, Tenn., 1970-71, Miami U., Middletown, 1972-74, Pensacola Christian, Fla., 1987. Substitute tchr. Franklin City Schs., Ohio, 1972-74; early childhood tchr. First Baptist Daycare, Middletown, 1976-78; headstart lead tchr. Butler County Headstart, Middletown, 1978-79; kindergarten dir., tchr. Little People's Day Nursery, Middletown, 1979-83, PJ's Preschool Junction, Middletown, 1983-87; owner, dir., tchr. Madison Nursery Sch., Middletown, 1988—; governing bd. Nat. Assn. for the Edn. Young Children, Butler County Ohio. Author: Poem pub. in Our World's Best Loved Poems, 1984 (Golden Poet award 1985). Presentation Judge FHA Hero (Regional Rally) Fairfield Ohio 1984; Adv. Recipient Citizenship award Daughters of the Am. Revolution, Franklin Ohio 1968, Valedictorian award Sr. Class of Franklin high sch. Ohio 1968, Honor Soc. award Mt. Vernon Nazarene Coll., Ohio 1968-70. Republican. Home: 1801 Panama Ave Middletown OH 45042 Office: Madison Nursery Sch 1052 Middletown Eaton Rd Middletown OH 45042

TROXELL, DEBORAH ANNE, realtor, developer, personnel consultant; b. Meridian, Miss., Jan. 2, 1950; d. Carl Hebron and Marianne (Dean) Graves; m. Brent Allen Garrison, June 16, 1973 (div. Sept. 1987); children: Blaine Graves, Ryan Richmond; m. Mark Fillmore Troxell Jr., Nov. 21, 1987. BA in Psychology, Mich. State U., 1972; postgrad., U. N.C., Greensboro, 1975. Lic. real estate salesperson, site agt. Rehab. counselor Dept. Corrections, Greensboro, 1973-75; realtor/builder James River Corp., Richmond, Va., 1983—, Twin Rivers Devel., Richmond, 1988—; substitute tchr. Henrico County Pub. Schs., Richmond, 1988—; cons. pers. evaluation Personal Devel., Inc., Richmond, 1990—; co-founder Entrepreneur's Resource Group, Richmond, 1989; cons. in field. Author: Survival Handbook for Real Estate Agents, 1984; writer, performer on local radio. Mem. archtl. rev. com. Glen Gary Civic Assn., Memphis, 1969-70; mem. com. St. Mary's Hosp., Richmond, 1982; mem. Byrd Mid Sch. PTA, Richmond, 1989—; banquetchmn. Booster Club, 1989—. Recipient Bronze award Sales/Mktg. Council, Bd. Realtors, Richmond, 1988. Mem. Network of Enterprising Women (project com. 1989—), Bd. Realtors, Raintree Swim and Racquet Club. Home: 11900 Glen Gary Ct Richmond VA 23233

TROXELL, JANE LEE, editor, author; b. Cumberland, MD, Nov. 25, 1963; d. Edward Wheatley and Bonnie Lou (McClellan) T. BA, U. Md., 1986. Buyer women's books Lambda Rising Bookstore, Washington, 1987; editor Lambda Book Report, Washington, 1988—; editor, mem. steering com. Pub. Triangle News, N.Y.C., 1989—; dir. Lambda Lit. Awards, Washington, 1988—. Contbr.: Gay and Lesbian Events, 1989, The Big Gay Book, 1990. Bd. dirs. Gay Women's Alternative, Washington, 1988-89. Democrat. Office: Lambda Book Report 1625 Connecticut Ave NW Washington DC 20009

TROXELL, REBECCA LYNNE, information systems professional; b. Winston-Salem, N.C., July 23, 1959; d. John Cline and Elevee Era (Ammons) T. BS, U. N.C., 1983. Cert. info. systems profl. Instr. Guilford Tech. Community Coll., Jamestown, N.C., 1982; info. system staff AT&T Tech., Greensboro, N.C., 1983—. Mem. N.C. Clogging Coun., Inc., treas. 1988—, Nat. Clogging Hoedown Coun. Mem. NAFE, Quill & Scroll, Am. Clogging Hall of Fame, Clog Leaders Orgn. Am., N.C. Clogging Council. Republican. Club: Deep River Cloggers (dir. 1987—).

TROY, DALE WINOKUR, legal recruiter; b. New Haven, Mar. 16, 1958; d. Richard Malcolm and Joan Carol (Heller) Winokur; m. Alexander Troy, July 27, 1986. BA summa cum laude, Yale U., 1980, JD, 1983. Bar: N.Y. 1984. Assoc. Weil, Gotshal & Manges, N.Y.C., 1983-84, Paul, Weiss, Rifkind, Wharton & Garrison, N.Y.C., 1984-86, Richards & O'Neil, N.Y.C., 1986-87; legal recruiter Elaine P. Dine, Inc., N.Y.C., 1987—. Mem. Vols.-in-Ct., New Haven, 1977-78, Big Bro./Sister program, New Haven, 1978-80. Mem. N.Y. State Bar Assn., Phi Beta Kappa. Office: Elaine P Dine Inc Ste 1210 115 E 57th St New York NY 10022

TRUAN, SUSAN CAROL, software analyst; b. Logansport, Ind., May 23, 1952; d. William Carl and Barbara Jean (Boyer) Kerber; m. Robert W. Truan, Mar. 15, 1974; 1 child, Nicholas. BS in Edn., Ind. U., 1974. Sr. programmer College Park Corp., Indpls., 1976-79; programmer, analyst Harcourt Brace & Jovanovich, Cleve., 1981-85; sr. software engr., R & D project mgr. DBMS, Inc., Naperville, Ill., 1985-87; project mgr. Pansophic Systems, Naperville, 1987; sr. systems analyst, project mgr. contingency planning Dow Chem. Co., Freeport, Tex., 1987—, supr. info. systems. Mem. AAUW. Home: 117 Strawberry Dr Lake Jackson TX 77566 Office: Dow Chem Co Rte 288 Freeport TX 77541

TRUAX, BONNIE M., university program administrator; b. Reed City, Mich., Dec. 2, 1945; d. Arthur Roy and Lois Ellen (Gould) T.; m. Kevin Charles Earle, Nov. 28, 1987. BA, Mich. State U., 1968; MA, Western Mich. U., 1973, EdD, 1985. Cert. counselor. Asst. dir. univ. placement svcs. Western Mich. U., Kalamazoo, 1982-87; ptnr., cons. Pers. Devel. Associates, Kalamazoo, 1980-87; dir. career planning and placement ctr. U. N.C., Greensboro, 1980-87, adj. grad. faculty edn., 1987—. Mem. task force sexual abuse Kalamazoo Child Abuse and Neglect Coun., 1978-83; mem. Mayor's Coun. for Handicapped, 1987-90. Mem. NAFE, Am. Assn. for Counseling and Devel., N.C. Placement Assn., Am. Assn. for Schs., Coll. and Univ. Staffing, S.E. Assn. for Schs., N.C. Career Devel. Assn. (treas. 1989—), Southeastern Assn. Sch., Coll. and Univ. Staffing (bd. dirs.), N.C. Assn. Women Deans, Adminstrs. and Counselors (rsch. com. 1990—), Am. Mgmt. Assn., Assn. for Psychol. Type, Am. Coll. Pers. Assn., Coll. Placement Coun., Am. Soc. for Tng. and Devel., Am. Mental Health Counselors Assn., Assn. for Counselor Edn. and Supervision, Greensboro Area C. of C. (task force on edn. and bus. 1989-90). Home: 2711 Bears Creek Rd Greensboro NC 27406 Office: U NC Career Planning and Placement Ctr 208 Foust Bldg Greensboro NC 27412

TRUDEL, MARY, public relations executive. Exec. v.p., gen. mgr. N.Y. ops. Rowland Co. Worldwide, N.Y.C. Office: Rowland Co Worldwide 1675 Broadway New York NY 10019*

TRUE, CLAUDIA, geologist; b. Kingsville, Tex., Sept. 15, 1948; d. Elmer Conrad and Gift Jeanette (Haralson) T.; m. Michael Frank Driggs, Mar. 31, 1983. B.A. in Geology, Trinity U., 1971; M.S. in Geology, Pa. State U., 1978. Research aide Tex. Bur. Econ. Geology, Austin, 1972-73; coal petrologist coal research sect. Pa. State U., University Park, 1974-77; cons. in coal petrology, University Park, 1975-77; coal geologist U.S. Geol. Survey, Denver, 1977-80; prodn., exploration geologist Mobil Alternative Energy, Inc., Denver, 1980-85; prodn. geologist Mobil Oil Corp., Denver, 1986—; art cons.; speaker in field. Contbr. articles to profl. publs. Mem. Am. Assn. Profl. Geologists, Am. Inst. Profl. Geologists, RMAG, Denver Coal Club (program chmn. 1984-85, bd. dirs. 1985-87), Women in Mining (scholarship awards chmn., tech. adviser 1986-87, sec. 1987-88, v.p. 1988-89, pres. 1989-90), Colo. Mining Assn. (bd. dirs. 1989-90), Western Mus. of Mining and Industry (bd. dirs. 1989-90). Republican. Methodist. Avocations: arts, music, travel, photography. Home: 5801 Lugene Ave Bakersfield CA 93313 Office: Mobil Oil Corp 5001 Commerce Center Ave Bakersfield CA 93309

TRUE, JEAN DURLAND, entrepreneur, oil company executive; b. Olney, Ill., Nov. 27, 1915; d. Clyde Earl and Harriet Louise (Brayton) Durland; m. Henry Alfonso True, Jr., Mar. 20, 1938; children: Tamma Jean (Mrs. Donald G. Hatten), Henry Alfonso III, Diemer Durland, David Lanmon. Student, Mont. State U., 1935-36. Ptnr. True Drilling Co., Casper, Wyo., 1951—, True Oil Co., Casper, 1951—, Eighty-Eight Oil Co., 1955—, True Geothermal Energy Co., 1980—, True Ranches, 1981—; officer, dir. Toolpushers Supply Co., Casper, White Stallion Ranch, Inc., Tucson; dir. Belle Fourche Pipeline Co., Casper, Black Hills Trucking, Smokey Oil Co., True Geothermal Drilling Co., True Wyo. Beef. Mem. steering com. YMCA, Casper, 1954-55, bd. dirs., 1956-58; mem. exec. bd. trustees Gottsche Rehab. Ctr., Thermopolis, Wyo., 1966—, v.p., 1973-90; mem. adv. bd. for adult edn. U. Wyo., 1966-68; mem. Ft. Casper Commn., Casper, 1973-79; bd. dirs. Mus. of Rockies, Bozeman, Mont., 1983-87, bd. dirs. Nicolaysen Art Mus., 1988—; mem. Nat. Fedn. Rep. Women's Clubs; del. Rep. nat. conv., 1972. Mem. Rocky Mountain Oil and Gas Assn., Casper Area C. of C., Alpha Gamma Delta, Casper Country Club, Petroleum Women's Club (Casper). Episcopalian. Office: Rivercross Rd PO Box 2360 Casper WY 82602

TRUESDELL, CAROLYN GILMOUR, lawyer; b. Oak Park, Ill., July 15, 1939; d. William Bonney and Gladys (Chapman) Gilmour; m. J. Richard Cheney, June 26, 1982; children by previous marriage—Kelly Elizabeth, Robin Suzanne. Student Stanford U., 1957-59; B.A., Case Western Res. U., 1961; J.D., U. Houston, 1975. Bar: Tex. 1975. Law clk. Chief Judge John R. Brown, U.S. Ct. Appeals, 5th Cir., Houston, 1975-76; assoc. Vinson & Elkins, Houston, 1976-83, ptnr., 1983—. Mem. ABA, Nat. Assn. Bond Attys. Office: Vinson & Elkins 3300 First City Tower 1001 Fannin Houston TX 77002

TRUFFELMAN, JOANNE, advertising company executive; b. N.Y.C., Sept. 22, 1943; d. Henry and Selma (Schwartz) T. Student, Queens Coll., 1960-63. Asst. prodn. clk. Maxwell Sackheim Co., N.Y.C., 1960-63; mgr. prodn. Sherman Sackheim Co., N.Y.C., 1963-67; v.p., mgr. prodn. Wells, Rich, Green Inc., N.Y.C., 1967-77; v.p., dir. creative svcs. McDonald & Little Inc., Atlanta, 1977-82; mgr. graphic svcs. and bottler advt. Coca-Cola USA, Atlanta, 1982-86; owner, pres. T.G. Madison Adv. Svcs., Atlanta, 1986—; instr. Atlanta Advt. Inst. Mem. Humane Soc., Friends Atlanta Zoo, 1987—. Mem. Ad Club (Atlanta chpt.), Atlanta Art Dirs. Club, Advt. Club, Print Prodn. Club. Office: TG Madison Inc 3210 Peachtree Rd NE Ste 11 Atlanta GA 30305

TRUITT, EVELYN MACK, corporate consultant; b. Los Angeles, July 2, 1931; d. Everett E. and Celeste (Pratt) Mack; m. Edwin A. Truitt, (div.). Student Los Angeles City Coll., UCLA, Sawyer Sch. Bus. Sec., United Calif. Bank, Los Angeles, 1951-57; group tour coord. Gray Line Tours, Los Angeles, 1957-60; corp. exec. sec. Signal Cos., Inc., La Jolla, Calif., 1960-78, v.p., 1978-85; chair Allied-Signal (West) Found., La Jolla, 1985-87; cons. The Henley Group, La Jolla, 1988—. Author: Who Was Who on Screen, 1974, 76, 83. Bd. dirs. Old Globe Theatre, San Diego, 1981, Girl Scouts U.S.A., San Diego, 1983, Nat. Corp. Theatre Fund, N.Y., 1985. Republican. Office: The Henley Group 11255 N Torrey Pines Rd La Jolla CA 92037

TRUITT, PHYLLIS LYNN, financial executive; b. Evansville, Ind., Aug. 25, 1945; d. Richard Lynn and Mary Louise (Christmas) McNabb; m. Curtis Michael Truitt, July 3, 1964; children: Erick Todd, Michael Sean. Assoc. Bus. Acctg., U. So. Ind., 1983. Bookkeeper Evansville Printing Corp., 1967-69; asst. controller, office mgr. Peerless Pottery, Evansville, 1969-79; credit, office mgr. Shelby Steel, Inc., Evansville, 1979-87; corp. credit, collections mgr. Atlas Van Lines, Inc., Evansville, 1987—. treas. Concordia Lutheran Ch., Evansville, 1984-85; active Ohio Valley Hospice, Evansville, 1985-87. Mem. Nat. Assn. Credit Mgrs. (bd. dirs. 1986—), Women's Credit Group NACM (membership chmn. 1986-87), Aid Assn. Luths. (treas. 1986-87), Women's Group Nat. Assn. Credit Mgrs., Nat. Orgn. Female Execs., Toastmaster (treas. Evansville chpt. 1989), Credit and Fin. Devel. (pres. Evansville chpt. 1988-89). Democrat. Home: 1819 Sweetser Ave Evansville IN 47715 Office: Atlas Van Lines Inc 1212 Saint George Rd PO Box 509 Evansville IN 47703

TRUITT, VICTORIA MIZE, management consultant; b. Danville, Va., Aug. 21, 1949; d. Douglas F. and Jeanne (Daniels) Mize; m. K. Ray Truitt, Aug. 23, 1975. BA, Stratford Coll., Danville, Va., 1971; MS, Va. Commonwealth U., 1973. Mgmt. engr. Med. Coll. Va Hosp., Richmond, 1973-75; health planner Mid-Am. HSA, Kansas City, Mo., 1975-76; mgmt. cons. Bethany Med. Ctr., Kansas City, Kans., 1976-78, Medicus Sys., Kansas City, Mo., 1979-81, The Kennedy Group, Redwood City, Calif., 1988—. Mem. Rep. Congl. Leadership Coun., Washington, 1980; chmn. Mayor's Beautification Com., Shawnee, Kans., 1989; master gardener Kans. State U., Johnson County, 1989—. Mem. Friends of Johnson County Library, Friends of Nelson Atkins Mus., Kans. Women's Golf Assn., Lake Quivira Garden Club (pres. 1989). Home: 5096 Mullen Rd Shawnee KS 66216

TRUMAN, MARGARET, author; b. Independence, Mo., Feb. 17, 1924; d. Harry S. (Pres. U.S.) and Bess (Wallace) T.; m. E. Clifton Daniel, Jr., Apr. 21, 1956; children: Clifton T., William, Harrison, Thomas. L.H.D., Wake Forest U., 1972; H.H.D., Rockhurst Coll., 1976. Concert singer, 1947-54, actress, broadcaster, author, 1954—; author: Souvenir, 1956, White House Pets, 1969, Harry S. Truman, 1973, Women of Courage, 1976, Murder in the White House, 1980, Murder on Capitol Hill, 1981, Letters from Father, 1981, Murder in the Supreme Court, 1982, Murder in the Smithsonian, 1983, Murder on Embassy Row, 1985, Murder at the FBI, 1985, Murder in Georgetown, 1986, Bess. W. Truman, 1986, Murder in the CIA, 1987, Murder at the Kennedy Center, 1989, Murder in the National Cathedral, 1990; editor: Where the Buck Stops: The Personal and Private Writings of Harry S. Truman, 1989. Trustee Harry S. Truman Inst.; sec. Harry S. Truman Scholarship Found.

TRUMP, BECKY ANN, hospital administrator; b. Lancaster, Pa., Oct. 28, 1955; d. John Raymond and Shirley Ann (Hess) Snyder; m. Peter Martin Trump, June 26, 1976 (div. Mar. 1984); children: Gretchen Marie, Savannah Lee. Diploma in nursing, St. Joseph Hosp., Lancaster, 1976; BS summa cum laude, Chapman Coll., Orange, Calif., 1981; MBA in Health Adminstrn., St. Joseph's U., Phila., 1989. RN. Mem. nursing staff Bass Meml. Bapt. Hosp., Enid, Okla., 1976-77, Columbus (Miss.) Hosp., Inc., 1982-83; supr. nursing Beverly Manor, Riverside, Calif., 1978-82; charge nurse Lancaster Gen. Hosp., 1984-85; from head nurse mental health to dir. clin. support svc. Ephrata (Pa.) Community Hosp., 1985-89, asst. v.p. for ancillary svcs., 1989—, aux. treas., 1990—. Recipient Great Am. Family award Children and Youth Svcs. County of Lancaster, 1987. Mem. NAFE, Am. Coll. Healthcare Execs. Republican. Lutheran. Home: 404 Hilton Dr Lancaster PA 17603 Office: Ephrata Community Hosp 169 Martin Ave PO Box 1002 Ephrata PA 17522-1002

TRUSLER, SUZANNE SMALL, construction company executive; b. Crow Agency, Mont., Nov. 12, 1949; d. Clinton and Victoria (Roundstone) Small; m. Thomas William Trusler, June 15, 1968; children: Tom Dale, Suzanne Adel, Mary Florence. BS in Bus., U. Mont., 1973; MS in Econs., Mont. State U., 1975. Adminstr. asst. Big Sky of Mont., 1973; econ. cons. Northern Cheyenne Tribe, Lame Deer, Mont., 1974-76; v.p. Morning Star Enterprises, Inc., Lame Deer, 1975—; v.p., dir. Northern Cheyenne Devel. Corp., Lame Deer, 1988—; fiscal agt. Morning Star Prodns., Lame Deer, 1988—. Pres. St. Labre Parish Coun., 1976-81; bd. dirs. Govs. Small Bus. Coun., 1985-86, Govs. Econ. Devel. Bd., 1986-87, Helena Mont., Cath. Social Svcs., Helena, 1984, Chairmans Coun., Helena, 1987—, No. Cheyenne Econ. Devel. Commn.; mem. Mont. State U. Pres. Coun., 1987—. Named Mont. Small Bus. Person of Year, 1982, Constr. Co. of Year, SBA, Region 7, 1983. 0em. Minority Contractor's Assn. (founder Mont. chpt.), Women in Construction, Assn. Builders & Contractors, No. Cheyenne C. of C. (founder). Democrat. Roman Catholic. Home: Box 155 Ashland MT 59003 Office: Morning Star Enterprises PO Box 328 Lame Deer MT 59043

TRUSSLER, PHYLLIS ANN, police officer; b. Vienna, Ill., Sept. 24, 1936; d. John Carlos Barrett and Virginia (Pippins) Recotta; m. Winsford Wheatley (div. 1963); children: Wendy M. Fishburn, Randi Corder, Jeffrey Wheatley; m. JOhn Edward Trussler (div.); 1 child, Joelle E. Trussler. Student, U. Calif., San Jose, 1975-76. Police officer San Jose Police Dept., 1962—; instr. West Valley Coll., Saratoga, Calif., 1981—; bd. dirs. Dept. Corrections Vocat. Bd., Sacramento, 1986—. Co-leader US-USSR Initiative, USSR, 1987, 89, 90; com. mem. US-USSR Peace Walk, Santa Cruz, Calif., 1988; bd. dirs. Women's Alliance, San Jose, 1985-86. Mem. Internat. Assn. Women Police (chair conf. 1989), San Jose Women Police Inc. (v.p. 1984-85), San Jose Police Officers Assn. (charter), San Jose Police Benevolent Assn. (bd. dirs. 1962—), Commonwealth Club (San Francisco), Keith Kelley Club (bd. dirs. 1985—). Office: San Jose Police Dept 201 W Mission St San Jose CA 95110

TRUSTY, ARLINE LOIS, government official; b. Amityville, N.Y., Jan. 21, 1950; d. Armand Edward Bernagozzi and Lois Vivian (Budd) Aversano; m. Dennis Byrne, 1969 (div. 1972); children: Blair, Drew; m. Danny C. Trusty, July 19, 1980. BBA, U. Albuquerque, 1986. Clk. IRS, Holtsville, N.Y., 1973-75; tax fraud investigative aide criminal investigation div. IRS, Bklyn., Smithtown, N.Y., 1975-77; spl. agt. IRS, Albuquerque, 1977-87; supervisory criminal investigator IRS, San Antonio, 1987-89; sr. regional analyst criminal investigation div. IRS, Dallas, 1989—. Mem. South Tex. Assn. Women in Law Enforcement (pres. 1988—), N.Mex. Assn. Women in Law Enforcement (pres. 1986-87), Internat. Assn. Women Police, Nat. Assn. Female Execs., Frat. Order Police, Delta Epsilon Sigma. Office: IRS Criminal Investigation SW Region 4050 Alpha Rd 12th Fl Dallas TX 75244-4203

TRUTA, MARIANNE PATRICIA, oral and maxillofacial surgeon; b. N.Y.C., Apr. 28, 1951; d. John J. and Helen Patricia (Donnelly) T.; m. William Christopher Donlon, May 28, 1983. BS, St. John's U., 1974; DMD, SUNY, Stonybrook, 1977. Intern The Mt. Sinai Med. Ctr., N.Y.C., 1977-78, resident, 1978-80, chief resident, 1980-81; asst. prof. U. of the Pacific, San Francisco, 1983-85, clin. asst. prof., 1985—; asst. dir. Facial Pain Rsch. Ctr., San Francisco, 1986—; pvt. practice oral and maxillofacial surgery Peninsula Maxillofacial Surgery, South San Francisco, Calif., 1985—, Burlingame, Calif., 1988—, Menlo Park & Redwood City, Calif., 1990—. Contbr. articles to profl. jours. Mem. Am. Assn. Oral Maxillofacial Surgeons, Am. Dental Soc. Anesthesiology, Am. Soc. Cosmetic Surgery, Am. Assn. Women Dentists, Western Soc. Oral Maxillofacial Surgeons. No. Calif. Soc. Oral Maxillofacial Surgeons. Office: Peninsula Maxillofacial Surgery 1860 El Camino Real Ste 300 Burlingame CA 94010

TRYON, GEORGIANA SHICK, psychologist; b. Glendale, Calif., Mar. 28, 1945; d. Norman Alton and Nancy Emily (Shaffer) Shick; m. Warren W. Tryon, July 31, 1970; 1 child, Elizabeth. B.A., Pa State U., 1966; M.A., Kent State U., 1969, Ph.D., 1971. Lic. psychologist, N.Y. Psychologist to outpatients N.Y. Hosp., N.Y.C., 1971-72; dir. Counseling Ctr., Fordham U., N.Y.C., 1972-75, Bronx, N.Y., 1975—; pvt. practice psychology, Briarcliff Manor, N.Y., 1973—. Author, editor: The Professional Practice of Psychology, 1986. Contbr. articles to psychology jours. Mem. Am. Psychol. Assn., Assn. for Advancement Behavior Therapy, Nat. Assn. Women Deans, Counselors and Adminstrs., Eastern Psychol. Assn., N.Y. State Psychol. Assn. Office: Fordham U 226 Dealy Hall Bronx NY 10458

TRZEPACZ, PAULA TERESE, physician, consultant, researcher; b. Pittsfield, Mass., Oct. 13, 1952; d. Edward John and Mary Purina (Monticone) T.; m. Robert Winfield Baker, M.D., Sept. 20, 1986. BA, Wellesley (Mass.) Coll., 1974; MD, Dartmouth Med. Sch., 1978. Cert. Psychiatry, Am. Bd. of Psychiatry and Neurology, 1983. Med. intern. Berkshire Med. Ctr., Pittsfield, Mass., 1978-79; psych. residency Dartmouth Med. Sch., Hanover, N.H., 1979-82; fellow, C/L psych. Dartmouth Med. Sch., Hanover, 1982-83; asst. prof. psych. U. Pitts. Sch. of Med., 1983-87, dir., C/L Svc. dept. psychiatry, 1983-87, assoc. prof. psychiatry, 1989—; assoc. prof. psychology Med. Coll. Pa., Pitts., 1988-89; clinical dir. Allegheny Neuropsychiat. Inst., Pitts., 1987-88; assoc. editor, Journ. of Neuropsychiatry and Clinical Neurosciences, Washington; examiner, oral exams, Am. Bd. of Psych. and Neurology, Chgo. Author: scientific articles for profl. jours., 1976-89, chpts. in science books,(with others) book, Mental Status Examination, Oxford U. Press. First Award grantee, NIMH, Bethesda, Md., 1988—; Sarah Perry Wood fellow Wellesley (Mass.) Coll., 1976-78; recipient Joseph Collins Found. award, N.Y., 1976-78. Mem. Soc. of Biol. Psychiatry, Am. Psych. Assn., Wellesley Coll Alumnae Assn., N.H. Br. (treas. 1980-82), Fox. Chapel Yacht Club. Republican. Roman Catholic. Office: Western Psychiat Inst and Clinic 3811 O'Hara St Pittsburgh PA 15213

TSCHINKEL, SHEILA LERNER, banker, economist; b. N.Y.C., Nov. 21, 1940; d. Abraham and Mira (Nevelova) Lerner. BA, Hunter Coll., 1961; MA, Yale U., 1963, postgrad., 1967-68; grad. advanced mgmt. program, Harvard Bus. Sch., 1988. Asst. prof. U. Alaska, Fairbanks, 1963-65, U. Conn., Storrs, 1967-68; instr. Yale U., New Haven, 1968-69; asst. v.p. Fed. Res. Bank, N.Y.C., 1970-79; v.p., dir. global asset mgmt. Chase Manhattan Bank, N.Y.C., 1979-81; exec. v.p. MPH Commodities Corp., N.Y.C., 1982-83; sr. v.p., dir. research Fed. Res. Bank, Atlanta, 1984—. Mem. Com. on Future of South. Fellow Yale U., 1961-63, Ossabaw Island Project, Ga., 1977. Mem. Am. Econ. Assn., So. Econ. Assn., Ga. Exec. Women's Network, Money Marketeers N.Y. (bd. govs. 1979-82), Rotary, Phi Beta Kappa. Office: Fed Reserve Bank 104 Marietta St NW Atlanta GA 30303-2713

TSCHINKEL, VICTORIA JEAN, environmental and technology consultant, former state official; b. Mt. Vernon, N.Y., Oct. 30, 1947; d. William Aaron and Edith (Meyerson) Nierenberg; m. Walter Rheinhardt Tschinkel, June 15, 1968; 1 child, Erika Lotte Elizabeth. AB in Zoology, U. Calif.-Berkeley, 1968. Biologist, libr. Tall Timbers Rsch. Sta., Tallahassee, 1970-74; field insp. Trustees for Internal Improvement Trust Fund, Tallahassee, 1974-76; environ. specialist Dept. Environ. Regulations, Tallahassee, 1976; asst. to sec. Dept. Environ. Regulations, 1976-77, asst. sec., 1977-81, sec., 1981-87; sr. cons. Landers and Parsons, 1987—; mem. energy rsch. adv. bd. Dept. Energy, 1979-86; mem. adminstrv. toxic substances adv. council EPA, 1982-84; dir. Environ. and Energy Inst., Washington, 1984—; mem. Gas Rsch. Adv. Council, Chgo., 1983—, NRC, Washington, Space Applications Bd., 1983-85; mem. adv. panel on energy in city bldgs. Office Tech. Assessement, 1980-81; chmn. adv. bd. Solar Energy Inst., 1985; mem. Electric Power Rsch. Inst. Adv. Council, NAS site selection com. for superconducting supercollider; bd. dirs. Environ. & Energy Study Inst., 1986, German Marshall Fund, 1989; mem. adv. com. Nuclear Facility Safety, 1988—; bd. dirs. Fla. Defenders of the Environment, 1987—, 1000 Friends of Fla., 1988—. Mem. Capital Womens Network, Tallahassee, 1983-84, Community Adv. Bd., Ctr. for Profl. Devel., 1983-84. Named North Fla. Pub. Aminstr. of Yr., Am. Soc. Pub. Adminstrs., 1984. Mem. Women Execs. in State Govt., Nat. Acad. Pub. Adminstrn. Office: Landers & Parsons PO Box 271 Tallahassee FL 32302

TSE, CHARLENE KIT-YU, director educational programming, consultant; b. Hong Kong, Mar. 2, 1958; came to U.S., 1965; d. William Cho-Yee and Maria Man-Jin (Lai) T. BS, U. Pa., 1982; MBA, MS, U. Wis., 1984; post-grad., Harvard U., 1988. Instr. Roxbury Community Coll., Boston, 1985-86; dir. health ins. project Robert Wood Johnson Found. Harvard U., Boston, 1987-89; dir. ednl. programming and satellite campuses Bunker Hill Community Coll., Boston, 1989—, dir. Bilingual Vocat. Tng. Ctr., 1986-87; mktg. cons. Minority Bus. Tng. and Resources Ctr., Boston, 1986; rsch. cons. Bell Assocs., Cambridge, Mass., 1989; planning cons. South Cove Manor Nursing Home, Boston, 1990—. Cons. Chinatown Neighborhood Coun., Boston, 1986-88; mem. South Cove Community Health Ctr., 1987—. Mem. Am. Pub. Health Assn. (speaker financing health care in inner city 1988), NAFE. Mem. Christian Ch. Home: 16 Winter St Unit 34A Waltham MA 02154 Office: Bunker Hill Community Coll New Rutherford Ave Boston MA 02129

TSENG, JOAN LIU, librarian; b. Chengtu, China, Jan. 5, 1939; came to U.S., 1963, naturalized, 1973; d. Yi-chiang and Chin-feen (Chou) Liu; m. Gan-tai Tseng, Sept. 5, 1965; children—Carol, Michelle. B.A., Nat. Taiwan U., Taipei, 1961; M.L.S., Tex. Woman's U., 1965. Children's librarian San Mateo County (Calif.) Library, 1965-66; periodical librarian Loyola Maymount U., Los Angeles, 1966-70, cataloging librarian, 1977-80; catalog librarian Palos Verdes (Calif.) Library Dist., 1980-84, asst. supr. tech. services, 1984-86, supr. cataloging services, 1986-87; librarian The Charles C. Lauritsen Library, The Aerospace Corp., Los Angeles, 1987—. Vol., Maurice Hawks Sch., Princeton Junction, N.J., 1975-77, Montemalaga Elem. Sch., Palos Verdes Estates, Calif., 1977. Scholar Nat. Taiwan U., 1957-61. Mem. ALA, Calif. Library Assn. (councilor 1983-85), Chinese-Am. Librarians Assn. Office: Charles Lauritsen Library Aerospace Corp Mail Sta M /199 PO Box 92957 Los Angeles CA 90009-2957

TUAN, DEBBIE FU-TAI, professor of chemistry; b. Kiangsu, China, Feb. 2, 1930; came to U.S., 1958; d. Shiau-gien and Chen (Lee) T.; m. John W. Reed, Aug. 15, 1987. BS in Chemistry, Nat. Taiwan U., Taipei, 1954, MS in Chemistry, 1958; MS in Chemistry, Yale U., 1960, PhD in Chemistry, 1961. Rsch. fellow Yale U., New Haven, 1961-64; rsch. assoc. U. Wis., Madison, 1964-65; asst. prof. Kent (Ohio) State U., 1965-70, assoc. prof., 1970-73, prof., 1973—; rsch. fellow Harvard U., Cambridge, 1969-70; vis. scientist SRI Internat., Menlo Park, Calif., 1981; rsch. assoc. Cornell U., Ithica, N.Y., 1983; vis. prof. Academia Sinica of China, Nat. Taiwan U. and Nat. Tsing-Hwa U., summer 1967. Contbr. articles to profl. jours. U. Grad. fellow Nat. Taiwan U., 1955-58, F.W. Heyl-Anon F fellow Yale U., 1960-61, U. Faculty Rsch. fellow Kent State U., 1966, 68, 71, 85, Pres. Chiang's scholar Chinese Women Assn., 1954, 58, grad. scholar in humanity and scis. China Found. Mem. Am. Chem. Soc., Am. Phys. Soc., Sigma Xi. Office: Chemistry Dept Kent State U Williams Hall Kent OH 44242

TUBBERT, MARGARET A., biology educator; b. Syracuse, N.Y.; d. Robert Frederick and Jane Agnes (Healy) T. BA in Biology, Syracuse U., 1962; MS in Biology, Northwestern U., 1966; MA in Cell Biology, SUNY, Buffalo, 1972, PhD in Cell Biology, 1973. Lab. asst. biology Utica (N.Y.) Coll. Syracuse U., 1962; instr. Onondaga Community Coll., Syracuse, 1964-66, asst. prof., 1966-68, assoc. prof., 1968-76, prof., 1976—, chmn. biology dept., 1981-84; researcher embryogenesis Utica (N.Y.) Coll. of Syracuse U., 1962; established, coordinator Pre-biotech. Option, Onondaga Community Coll., 1984—; cons. NASA Life Sci. Program in Space, 1975. Molecular Biology Tng. fellow SUNY, Buffalo, 1970-72; scholar Summer Inst. Biotech., U. Rochester, N.Y., 1986; recipient Chancellor's award SUNY, 1980, Onondaga Community Coll. Trustees' Recognition award, Syracuse, 1980. Mem. AAAS, N.Y. Acad. Scis., Beta, Beta, Beta. Republican. Roman Catholic. Home: 4250 Onondaga Blvd Syracuse NY 13219 Office: Onondaga Community Coll Onondaga Hill Campus Syracuse NY 13215

TUCCERI, CLIVE KNOWLES, library administrator, science educator, educational consultant; b. Bryn Mawr, Pa., Apr. 20, 1953; d. William Henry and Clive Ellis (Knowles) Hulick; m. Eugene Angelo Tucceri, Sept. 1, 1984; stepchildren: Heather Deann, Christopher Eugene; 1 child, Clive Edna. BA in Geology, Williams Coll., 1975; MS in Coastal Geology, Boston Coll., 1982. Head sci. dept. Stuart Hall Sch., Staunton, Va., 1975-77; sci. faculty William Penn Charter Sch., Phila., 1977-79; sci. faculty Tower Sch., Marblehead, Mass., 1982-86; sci. faculty Bentley Coll., Waltham, Mass., 1986-88; adminstrv. dir., co-founder Stout Aquatic Libr., Nat. Marine and Aquatic Edn. Resource Ctr., Wakefield, R.I., 1982-89; sci. faculty Mabelle B. Avery Sch., Somers, Conn., 1989-90; cons. Addison-Wesley Publ. Co., Menlo Park, Calif., 1986—. Bd. dirs. People against Rape, Staunton, 1976-77. Mem. AAUW (bd. dirs., br. pres.-elect 1975-77, v.p. 1985-86, sec. 1986-87), Nat. Marine Edn. Assn. (sec. 1986-87, chpt. rep. 1987—), Assn. for Supr. and Curriculum Devel., Mass. Marine Educators (pres. 1987-89, bd. dirs. 1983—), Cousteau Soc., Oceanic Soc., Woods Hole Oceanographic Inst., Internat. Oceanographic Found., Mass. Environ. Edn. Soc. (bd. dirs. 1985-88), Sigma Xi, Longmeadow Newcomers Club (bd. dirs. 1989—). Episcopalian. Avocations: renovating old homes, sailing, gardening, reading. Home and Office: 15 Berwick Terr Longmeadow MA 01106

TUCCI, CAROLYN, management consultant; b. Westchester, N.Y., Oct. 21; d. Edward Joseph and Catherine (Giordano) Menninger; m. Thomas David Tucci, Sept. 22, 1984. BS, U. Ill., 1982. Rsch. analyst Market Facts, Inc., Chgo., 1983-85; mktg. mgr. Bekins Van Lines, Hillside, Ill., 1985-88; owner, v.p. mktg. Impact Prodns., LaGrange, Ill., 1988-90; mgmt. cons. Elmhurst (Ill.) Mgmt. Svc., 1990—. Mem. NAFE, Chgo. Area Meeting Profls.

TUCK, APRIL ELIZABETH, speech pathologist; b. Washington, Mar. 17, 1956; d. William Arthur and Elaine Elizabeth (Macomber) T.; m. Ronald R. Carter, Apr. 24, 1987. BS, Ithaca (N.Y.) Coll., 1978; MS, U. Wis., 1980. Sr. speech pathologist New Eng. Med. Ctr., Boston, 1980-87; speech pathologist Doylestown (Pa.) Hosp., 1987-88; clin. coord. In-Speech/Nova Care, Charlotte, N.C., 1989—; lectr. Emerson Coll., Boston, 1980-87; pvt. practice cons., Boston, 1980—; vocat. specialist Doylestown Hosp., 1987-88. Mem. Am. Speech-Hearing Assn., Mass. Speech-Hearing Assn. (regional rep. 1984-85, v.p. 1985-86), Greenpeace, Cousteau Soc., World Wildlife Fund, WLPA. Home: 1115 Burnley Rd Charlotte NC 28210

TUCK, LYNNE, writer; b. Amarillo, Tex., Dec. 10, 1938; d. Alfred James and Maude Emma (Best) Weiser; m. Jay Nelson Tuck, Dec. 12, 1970 (dec. 1985). BA, U. Tex., 1961. Clerk typist U.S. Senate, Washington, 1961-62; writer, reporter Space Bus. Daily, Washington, 1962-65, The Blue Sheet, Washington, 1964-65, Med. Tribune, Washington, 1965-68, Med. World News, Washington, 1968-70; pvt. practice Andover Township, N.J., 1974—; cons. Ames Rubber Corp., Hamburg N.J. 1986—. Co-author: Report, Dept. Health, Edn. and Welfare 1972; author: Video. Pres. Vis. Nurse Assn., Frankford, N.J., 1981-86; mem. Zoning Bd. Democrat. Episcopalian. Home: Rd 3 Box 2242 Lafayette NJ 07848

TUCKER, ANNETTE LA VERNE, nurse, health care administrator; b. N.Y.C.; d. Roy L. and Gwendolyn (Cush) Tucker; 1 child, Aaron Nathaniel. Diploma in Nursing, Misericordia Sch. Nursing, 1976; BS in Health Care Adminstrn. with distinction, Iona Coll., 1984; MPS, New Sch. for Social Research, 1988. Cert. long term care mgmt., 1988, counselor. Charge nurse med. Jacobi Hosp., 1976-77; charge nurse pediatrics Bronx (N.Y.) Mcpl. Hosp., 1977-78, asst. head nurse neonatal ICU, 1978-83, coord. utilization rev., 1983-84; charge nurse hematology Van Etten Hosp., Bronx, 1984-85; asst. dir. Salem Home Care, N.Y.C., 1985-87, dir., 1987-90; adminstr.-in-tng. Morningside House Nursing Home, Bronx, 1990—. Fellow Hunter-Brookdale Coll. on Aging; mem. NAFE, Harlem Health Forum Coun., Home Care Field Practice Com., Home Care Coun. N.Y.C.

TUCKER, BARBARA HARTMAN, public affairs executive, consultant, lobbyist; b. Hartford, Conn., July 19, 1942; d. Howard Lowell and Mildred Janet (Deady) Hartman; m. William Quoos Tucker, Dec. 16, 1967; children: Garrett Todd, Lisa Kristen. AA, Briarcliff Coll., 1962; student, Radcliff Coll., 1962; BA in Edn. and Polit. Sci., Rollins Coll., 1964. Tchr. Hartford (Conn.) Pub. Sch. Systems., 1965-66; legis. liaison, asst. to dir. Conn. Conf. of Mayors, Hartford, 1967; chief lobbyist Glass Constructors, Inc., Newington, Conn., 1974-75; dir. Conn. Citizen's Lobby, Hartford, 1975-76; exec. asst. to sen. leadership State Sen., Hartford, 1976-82; chief-of-staff to Sen. Minority Leader, Hartford, 1980-82; mgr. Conn. State News Bur., Hartford, 1983-84; exec. dir. Conn. Safety Belt Coalition, Hartford, 1985; exec. asst to the pres. Traffic Safety Now, Inc., Detroit, 1985-89; pres. Concorde Enterprises, Inc., Hartford, Conn., 1989—; Press sec. Spl. Congrl. Election, 1981. Assoc. editor: Repub. Courier, 1978, editor: Conn. State News Bur., 1982-84.

Mem. statewide steering com. Reagan for Pres., 1980; campaign coordinator, Conn. 5th Sen. Dist., 1978, Conn. Gubernatorial Race, 1980; mem. Gubernatorial Draft com., 1974; co-chmn. goods and services com. for ann. auction, Conn. Pub. Broadcasting, 1978; mem. exec. bd. PTO Norfedlt Sch., Hartford, 1973; mem. West Hartford Rep. Women's Club, 1st v.p., program chmn., legis. liason, corresp. sec., exec. bd. mem. Mem. Conn. Bus. and Industry Assn., Conn. World Trade Assn., Internat. Vis. Execs. Network, Greater Hartford C. of C., Pi Beta Phi Alumni Assn. Episcopalian. Office: Concorde Enterprises Inc 56 Arbor St Hartford CT 06106

TUCKER, BEVERLY SOWERS, information specialist; b. Trenton, N.J., Dec. 1, 1936; d. Eldon Jones and Verbeda Eleanor (Roberts) Sowers; m. Harvey Richard Tucker, Dec. 27, 1958 (div. Nov. 1983); children: Randall Richard, Brian Alan. BS in Chemistry with distinction, Purdue U., 1958; MS in Geology, No. Ill. U., 1985; MA in Library and Info. Sci., Rosary Coll., 1989. Asst. rsch. librarian CPC Internat., Argo, Ill., 1958-62; chem. patent searcher Chgo., 1962-66; info. specialist C. Berger & Co., Wheaton, Ill., 1986, Amoco Corp., Naperville, Ill., 1987—; faculty Coll. Du Page, Glen Ellyn, Ill., 1989—. Mem. Spl. Libraries Assn., Ill. Fedn. Women's Club (treas. 5th dist. 1979-81, Outstanding Jr. Clubwoman award 1979-80), Garden Club Council Wheaton (pres. 1981-82), Wheaton Jr. Woman's Club (pres. 1977-78, Single Parent scholar 1984), Gardens Etc. Club (pres. 1978-79), Alpha Lambda Delta, Delta Rho Kappa, Theta Sigma Phi, Alpha Chi Omega (grantee 1985). Republican. Presbyterian. Home: 1507 Paula Wheaton IL 60187 Office: Amoco Corp PO Box 3083 Warrenville Rd and Mill St Naperville IL 60566

TUCKER, DEBORAH DIANE, lawyer; b. Oakland, July 6, 1952; d. Merle Guy and Mavis Irene (Reid) T. BA (with honors), U. Calif., Santa Cruz, 1973; JD, U. Puget Sound, Tacoma, 1983. Judge adv. 2nd Combat Support Group, Barksdale AFB, 1983-86, Oklahoma City Air Logistics Ctr., Tinker AFB, 1986-87; atty.-advisor Acquisition Law Div., Tinker AFB, 1987-88; atty. 12th Air Div., Ellsworth AFB, 1988-90, GE Aircraft Engines, Cin., 1990—. Recipient Meritorious Service Medal, Air Force Commendation Medal, AF Achievement Medals (3), USAF. Mem. Federal Bar Assn., Nebraska Bar Assn., Nat. Guard Assn. Republican. Office: GE Aircraft Engines 1 Neumann Way Cincinnati OH 45215

TUCKER, EDITH MCMILLAN, editor; b. Concord, Mass., Feb. 25, 1938; d. John Endicott and Caroline (Cutter) McMillan; m. Dan Stuart Tucker, Apr. 18, 1958; children: Susan, Sarah, Margaret, Andrew. Researcher Prof. J.K. Galbraith, Cambridge, Mass., 1980-87; editor United Retirement Bull., Boston, 1987—. Chmn. Wellesley (Mass.) Adv. Com., 1977; mem. Wellesley Sch. Com., 1978-87. Democrat. Home: 18 Arlington Rd Wellesley MA 02181

TUCKER, FRANCES LAUGHRIDGE, civic worker; b. Anderson, S.C., Dec. 4, 1916; d. John Franklin and Sallie V. (Cowart) Laughridge; m. Russell Hatch Tucker, Aug. 30, 1946 (dec. Aug. 1977); children—Russell Hatch, Pamela Tucker. Student U. Conn., 1970, Sacred Heart U., Fairfield, Conn., 1977, 79, Fairfield U., 1978, U. S.C., 1984. Sec. to atty., Asheville, N.C., 1935-37; sec. to gen. mgr. Ga. Talc Mining & Mfg., Asheville, 1937-42; sec. engring. dept. E.I. duPont de Nemours, Wilmington, Del., 1942-46. Chmn. radio com. D.C. chpt. ARC, 1947-48, bd. dirs., Beaufort County chpt., 1982-87, chmn. pub. rels., Hilton Head Island, S.C., 1980-87, 89—; mem. pub. relations com. United Fund, Westport-Weston, Conn., 1968-69; bd. dirs. communications media St. Luke's Episcopal Ch., Hilton Head Island, 1980—; media pub. relations Bloodmobile Hilton Head Hosp. Aux., 1984-88. Clubs: Sea Pines Golf; Princeton of N.Y.C. Home: 13 Willow Oak Rd Hilton Head Island SC 29928

TUCKER, JANEE MICHELLE, technical services consultant; b. New Orleans, Apr. 12, 1946; d. Walbert Francois and Pauline (Mathieu) Mercadel; m. Robert Do Qui, Apr. 25, 1969 (div. 1978); 1 child, Robert; m. Robert Houston Tucker, Jr., June 24, 1979; 1 child, Iam. Student, Los Angeles City Coll., 1965; studied with Lee Strasberg, Actors Studio West, Los Angeles, 1966. Image cons. various polit. candidates New Orleans, 1970-73; staff producer Essence of Life Kwanza Found., New Orleans, 1976, Vanderhorst Tng. Systems, New Orleans, 1983; program coordinator Popeye's Famous Fried Chicken, New Orleans, 1977-85; cons. Tucker & Assocs., New Orleans, 1980-84, pres., chief operating officer, 1985—. Bd. dirs. New Orleans City Ballet, Daishiki Theater of New Orleans; mem. Met. Area Com., Planned Parenthood Advocacy Com. New Orleans. Named Person to Watch New Orleans mag., 1985; recipient Outstanding Women-Owned Bus. Enterprise Award U.S. Dept. Transp., 1986. Mem. Nat. Coalition of 100 Black Women (3d v.p. Greater New Orleans), Women's Am. ORT, Nat. Bus. League, Nat. Assn. Female Execs. Democrat. Home: 3610 Carondelet St New Orleans LA 70115

TUCKER, JANET LYNN, marketing professional; b. Pitts., Feb. 20, 1956; d. William Phillip and Helen Marie (Platt) T. BS, Penn. State U., 1978; MBA, U. Pitts., 1984. Buyer Ametek, Thermox Instruments Div., Pitts., 1979-82; contracts adminstr. Westinghouse Electric Corp., Pitts., 1982-86; v.p., mktg. Raymond James Fin. Corp., St. Petersburg, Fla., 1986--. Co-author: The Advisor's Guide to Asset Management, 1988. Mem. Nat. Assn. Female Execs., Toastmasters Internat. Office: Raymond James Investment 880 Carillon Pkwy Saint Petersburg FL 33716

TUCKER, JOYCE ELAINE, lawyer, state human rights administrator; b. Chgo., Sept. 21, 1948; d. George M. and Vivian Louise T. B.S., U. Ill., 1970; J.D., John Marshall Law Sch., 1978. Bar: Ill. 1978. Substitute tchr. Chgo. Public Schs., 1970-71; mental health specialist Tinley Park (Ill.) Dept. Mental Health, 1970-74; coordinator Title VII Program, Ill. Dept. Mental Health, Chgo., 1974-76, chief mental health equal employment opportunity officer, 1976-79; acting dir. Ill. Dept. Equal Employment Opportunity, Chgo., 1979-80; dir. Ill. Dept. Human Rights, Chgo., 1980—. Mem. Nat. Bar Assn., Cook County Bar Assn. (Spl. Achievement award 1980), Am. Bar Assn., Chgo. Bar Assn. Mem. African Methodist Episcopal Ch. Office: 619 Stratton Office Bldg Springfield IL

TUCKER, LINDA WISE, real estate operations manager; b. Prospect, Tenn., Oct. 3, 1955; d. Johnnie Ester and Hattie Will (Gatlin) Wise; m. Marc Lory Tucker, June 9, 1979. BS, U. Ala., Florence, 1977. Fin. counselor U. Tenn. Hosp., Memphis, 1978-81; credit mgr. Wilson Electronics, Las Vegas, 1981-82; office mgr. Upjohn Healthcare Services, Abilene, Tex., 1982-83, Computer Optical Products, Chatsworth, Calif., 1983-84; ops. mgr. Merrill Lynch Realty, Calabasas, Calif., 1984—; v.p. Marlin Corp., Las Vegas, Nev., 1980—, Futura Services, Woodland Hills, 1988—. Mem. LWV. Mem. NAFE, Nat. Assn. Meeting Planners, Lead's Club. Home: 22291 Cass Ave Woodland Hills CA 91364-3009 Office: Merrill Lynch Realty 26541 Agoura Rd #180 Ste #180 Calabasas CA 91302

TUCKER, MARY LOUISE, social worker; b. Washington, June 16, 1945; d. Robert Moxley and Catherine E. (Sellner) Underwood; m. Randolph Leon Tucker, June 29, 1967; children: Mary Catherine, Jesse Berkley, Theresa Ann, Randolph Jr. AS, Stratford Coll., Danville, Va., 1967; postgrad., Tex. Womens U.; BS, Longwood Coll., Farmville, Va., 1969; postgrad., Averett Coll., Danville. Side asst. oral surgery Marlow Heights, Md., 1965-66; sci. tchr. Sanford (Fla.) Naval Acad., 1967; owner, operator Tucker Electronics, South Boston, Va., 1970-74; biology and sci. tchr. Halifax (Va.) Sch. Bd., 1970, 72; social worker Halifax Dept. Social Svcs., 1973—. Chmn. Family Life Action Com., Halifax, 1983-84, Health Fair Com., Halifax, 1984-85, Holiday Living Show Com., Halifax, 1985-86; active Head Start Adv. Bd., Halifax, 1985, 4-H Adv. Bd., Halifax, 1984-85, Mental Health Adv. Bd., Halifax, 1984; vol. 4-H, Halifax, 1984-86. Mem. NAFE. Roman Catholic. Office: Halifax Dept Social Svcs PO Box 666 Halifax VA 24558

TUCKER, MELODY SUE, health facility administrator; b. Louisville, Nov. 9, 1947; B.S., Ind. U., 1970: M.P.A., Ariz. State U., 1985. Trainer, U.S. Office Edn. Alcohol and Drug Abuse Prevention Program, Chgo., 1974-77; coordinator prevention activities for alcohol, drug abuse, and mental health prevention activities Ariz. Dept. Health Services, Phoenix, 1978-83, contracts coordinator, 1983-84, trainer, 1984-85; planning analyst Community Hosps. of Central Calif., 1985-87; dir. Women's Health Ctr., Tulare (Calif.) Dist. Hosp., 1987—; owner Phoenix Designs, 1988—; cons. various human service orgns., 1976—. Mem. staff Ariz. Gov.'s Task Force on Alcohol and Hwy. Safety, 1982; bd. overseers Calif. Sch. Profl. Psychology. Home: 1128 Jefferson Tulare Tulare CA 93274 Office: Tulare Dist Hosp 869 Cherry St Tulare CA 93274

TUCKER, PAMA LEE, administrative assistant; b. Big Spring, Tex., May 19, 1953; d. William Thomas and Patty Jo (Heffelfinger) Kiehl; children: Tammie N. Pennebaker, Melissa D. Student, Pima Community Coll., Tucson, 1982-88. Cert. pub. mgr., Ariz. Office mgr. for pvt. physician Phoenix, 1973-76, 78-80; quality reviewer, office mgr. Dept. Econ. Security Family Assistance Adminstrn., Mammoth, Ariz., 1981-84; head cashier, bookkeeper Safeway Food Stores, Tucson, Ariz., 1985-88; with Child Support Enforcement Adminstrn., Tucson, 1984—, br. office mgr., supr., 1988-90; adminstrv. asst. Child Support Enforcement Adminstrn., Phoenix, 1990—; speaker Dept. Econ. Security, Mammoth and Tucson, 1981-90; trainer Child Support Enforcement Adminstrn., Tucson, 1988-90; coord. people's law Ariz. Trial Lawyers Assn., Tucson, 1988. Recruiter state employee's campaign United Way, Tucson, 1988, 89. Mem. Family Support Coun. Ariz., 2000 Notable Am. Women, NAFE. Baptist. Home: 6821 N 45th Ave #15 Glendale AZ 85301 Office: Child Support Enforcement 2222 W Encanto PO Box 40458 Phoenix AZ 85067

TUCKER, PATRICIA S., juvenile corrections; b. Amarillo, Tex., Dec. 19, 1944; d. L. Alex and Dorothy Lou (Barrier) White; m. Jim Tucker, Apr. 3, 1965 (dec. Apr. 1981). BS, West Tex. State U., 1970, MA, 1979. Cert. Social Worker; 1989. Parole officer Tex. Youth Commn., Amarillo, 1970-77; randall county probation officer Amarillo, Tex., 1977-78; parole officer, office mgr. Tex. Youth Commn., Amarillo, 1978-82; adminstr. interstate compact Tex. Youth Commn., Austin, community specialist, resource vol. coordinator, 1983-86; statewide monitor contract program Tex. Youth Commn., 1986-87; asst. program mgr. training, staff devel. Tex. Youth Commn., Austin, 1987--; criminal justice adv. bd. City of Amarillo, 1974-75; vice chmn. parole Tex. Corrections Assn., Austin, 1981-82. Author: Kids Who Kill, 1979.

TUCKER, SUSAN CAROL, state legislator; b. Winfield, Kans., Nov. 7, 1944; d. Allen and Jeanne (Lawrence) Shaffer; m. Mike A. Tucker, Dec. 2, 1967; children: Mark, David. Student, U. Nigeria, 1965; BA magna cum laude, Mich. State U., 1966. English tchr. Lexington (Mass.) High Sch., 1966-69; legis. aide Mass. Legislature, Boston, 1980-82; mem. Ho. of Reps. Mass. Great and Gen. Ct., Boston, 1983—, vice chair edn. com., chair spl. commn. on child abuse, mem enery com., ethics com.; chair Mass. Caucus Women Legislators. V.p. Mass. LWV, Boston, 1977-80. Recipient Environ. Schievement award Environ. Lobby Mass., 1984. Mem. Nat. Women's Polit. Caucus. Democrat. Office: Mass State House R 473-C Boston MA 02133

TUCKER, THERESA PETERSON, health systems specialist; b. Vandalia, Ill., Dec. 24, 1946; d. David Carl and Loretta Joan (Lindner) Peterson; m. William Ed Dearing, Jan. 10, 1965 (div. June 1973); children: Jeff Edward, Laura Rachelle, Mark Allen; m. Lloyd Dale Tucker, Jan. 11, 1975; children: Rhonda Elaine, William Dale. BS, Columbia Pacific Coll., San Rafael, Calif., 1988. Asst. dir. quality assurance VA Hosp., Lexington, Ky., 1981-84; dir. quality assurance Alvin C. York VA Med. Ctr., Murfreesboro, Tenn., 1984—; with Quality Assurance Cons., Murfreesboro, 1989—. Mem. Nat. Assn. Quality Assurance Profls., Am. Med. Records Assn., Tenn. Quality Assurance Utilization Rev. Profls., Blue Grass Med. Record Assn. (v.p. 1979-80), Toastmasters (sec., treas., adminstrv. v.p. Heart of Tenn. club 1987-89). Democrat. Office: Alvin C York VA Med Ctr 3400 Lebanon Rd Murfreesboro TN 37130

TUCKER, WANDA HALL, writer, editor; b. Los Angeles, Feb. 6, 1921; d. Frank Walliston and Hazel Gladys (Smith) Hall; m. Frank R. Tucker, Apr. 16, 1943; children: Frank Robert, Nancy Irene. AA, Citrus Coll., 1939. Society editor Azusa (Calif.) Herald, 1939-42, editor, 1942-43; city editor San Marino (Calif.) Tribune, 1943-45; editor Canyon City (Calif.) News, 1953; reporter Pasadena (Calif.) Star-News, 1953-73, city editor, 1973-75, day mng. editor, 1975, mng. editor, 1975-81, sr. mng. editor, 1981-84, dir. internship program, 1976-79, mem. editorial bd., 1982-84; editor, assoc. pub. Foothill Inter-City Newspapers, 1984-86; communications cons., freelance writer, Palm Desert, Calif., 1986-90. Editor, editorial cons.: The Internat. Fine Art Collector Mag., 1990—. Mem. rent rev. commn. City of Palm Desert, Calif.; sec. Shadowcliff Colony Home Owners Assn.; former mem., bd. dirs. Silver Spur Ranch Assn. Recipient writing award Calif. Newspaper Pubs. Assn., 1965; named Woman of Year, Pasadena Women's Civic League, 1974, Pasadena chpt. NAACP, 1977, Emer Bates Meml. award, 1981. Mem. Nat. Soc. Newspaper Columnists, Soc. Profl. Journalists, Shadowcliff Homeowners Assn. (bd. dirs.), Desert Press Club, Greater Los Angeles Press Club (writing awards 1971-72).

TUCKER-DIGGS, FRANCINE MARIE, state official; b. Newark, Nov. 11, 1949; d. Frank and Dorothy Inez (Penn) Tucker; m. Ronald Clayton Diggs, Feb. 20, 1980. BA cum laude, Howard U., 1971; MBA, U. Pa., 1973. Pres., chief exec. officer Yogurt Whirl, Inc., Balt., 1979-82; instnl. bond salesperson Pryor, Govan & Counts, N.Y.C., 1982-84, Legg Mason, Inc., Balt., 1984-86, Kidder Peabody, Inc., Balt., 1986-89; dep. treas. State of Pa., Harrisburg, 1989—. Fellow Cen. Pa. Investment Mgrs. Assn.; mem. Nat. Assn. Security Dealers (registered rep.). Home: Water St RD8 Box 282B York PA 17403

TUCKER-GRIFFITH, GAIL SUSAN, biology educator, researcher; b. N.Y.C., Aug. 30, 1945; d. Albert Eugene and Frances Anna (Kennedy) Tucker; m. Robert Philip Griffith, Aug. 1, 1987. BA, Mercy Coll., 1967; PhD, U. Kans., 1973. Postdoctoral fellow Coll. of Physicians and Surgeons Columbia U., N.Y.C., 1973-76; vis. instr. in biology Mercy Coll., Dobbs Ferry, N.Y., 1974-75; head asst. oceanography field practicum Woods Hole (Mass.) U. Mich., Woods Hole, Mass., 1973; rsch. assoc. Sch. of Medicine U. Miami, Fla., 1976-80, asst. prof. biology, 1980-87; postdoctoral Biol. Lab. Harvard U., Boston, 1980; tchr. sci. New World Sch. of the Arts, Miami, 1987—; cons. gifted in sci. program Dade County Pub. Schs., Miami, 1977-86, cons. motivation in depth summer sci. program, 1978-86. Pres. Women in Eye Rsch., nationwide, 1982-84. NIH Rsch. grantee U. Miami, 1981-84, United Way grantee, 1971, 79. Mem. AAAS, Soc. for Neurosci., Zonta (sec., treas., pres., bd. dirs. 1980—). Home: 2121 N Bayshore Dr Apt 1410 Miami FL 33137 Office: New World Sch of the Arts 25 NE 2nd St Miami FL 33132

TUCKER-PARRISH, FLORENCE DENSLOW, writer, retired government official; b. Greenville, Miss.; d. Victor Amos and Martha Buchannan (Binkley) Denslow; m. Joseph Nathaniel Tucker Jr., Nov. 9, 1946 (dec.); children: Joseph Nathaniel III, Frederick Steven, James Denslow; m. Noel Francis Parrish, June 25, 1983 (dec. Apr. 1987). Diploma piano, Ward-Belmont Coll., Nashville, 1945; studied piano with Michael Field, N.Y.C., 1945-46; B of Music Edn., Delta State U., Cleveland, Miss., 1960; MS in Counseling, U. So. Miss., 1971; EdD, George Washington U., 1982. Tchr. music Gulfport (Miss.) pub. schs., 1959-63; recreation therapist VA Hosp., Gulfport, 1964-70; edn. counselor USAF, Miss. and Japan, 1971-74, edn. svcs. officer, Republic of Korea, 1974-75, asst. dir. sr. tng. CAP nat. hdqrs., 1975-77; EEO officer D.C. Dept. Labor, 1977-80; bur. chief complaints processing and adjudication Office EEO, U.S. Geol. Survey, Reston, Va., 1980-82, mgr. human resources, Dept. Interior, 1982-84; internat. forum coord. Pres.'s Com. on Employment of Handicapped, 1985; commr. Alexandria Commn. on Aging, Va., 1985-88, chmn. edn. and cultural affairs com., 1985-88, sec., 1987-88, 90—; lead scholar pilot project Nat. Coun. on Aging; vis. prof. Kunsan Tchrs. Coll., Kunsan Jr. Coll., 1974-75; apptd. mem. del. People-to-People Internat. Amb. Program, Beijing, Peoples Republic China and Hong Kong, 1988; mem. steering com. Va. Home Care Alliance, 1990—; workshop leader, cons. and lectr. in field; bd. dirs. Wake Assocs., Ltd., Washington, 1980-84. Columnist on aging issues, Alexandria (Va.) Gazette-Packet, feature writer, 1986—; contbr. articles to profl. jours. Organizer, pres. Gulfport chpt. Parents-Without-Ptnrs., 1962-64; charter mem. Westminster Presbyn. Ch., Gulfport, 1961; mem. Nat. Coun. on Aging; mem. Military Classics Seminar. Recipient Outstanding Vis. Prof. award Kunsan Tchrs. Coll., 1974, Kunsan Jr. Coll. award for promoting tchr. exchange program, also certs. of commendation, Brigadier Gen. Noel F. Parrish award Tuskegee Airmen, Inc. Mem. Women in Communication, Washington Opera Guild, USAF Assn., NATO Def. Coll. Anciens Assn., Am. Wine and Food Inst., Am. Inst. Wine and Food, Va. Assn. on Aging, Nat. Press Club, Miss. Soc. Washington, Ret. Officers Assn., Tex. Soc. Washington, Friends of Kennedy Ctr., Smithsonian Assocs., The Famous Tuskegee Pilots Nat. Orgn. Home: Stonehurst 9302 Arlington Blvd Fairfax County VA 22031

TUCKETT, RHONA BENNETT, bank administrator, consultant; b. Rochester, N.Y., Sept. 13, 1947; d. Lawrence F. and Irene (Fowler) Bennett; m. Michael Tuckett, Apr. 17, 1982. BS, Mansfield (Pa.) State Coll., 1969. Tchr. Randolph (Mass.) Pub. Schs., 1969-76, Hudson (N.H.) Pub. Schs., 1977-83; tng. officer Indian Head Banks Inc., Nashua, N.H., 1983-85; tng. specialist Fed. Res. Bank, Boston, 1985-89, training adminstr., 1990—; tax preparer, planner, Epping, N.H., 1978—. Mem. Am. Soc. Tng. and Devel., NAFE, Nat. Assn. Desktop Pubs., Boston Computer Soc. Home: 15 Blake Rd Epping NH 03042 Office: Fed Res Bank 600 Atlantic Ave Boston MA 02106

TUDOR, INA POLLACK, retail manager; b. Pitts., Oct. 7, 1955; d. Harold B. Pollack and Dorothy Natalie (Kabat) Kirby; m. Thomas William Tudor, Nov. 27, 1977 (div. 1979); m. Alan John Herlitzka, July 10, 1987. Student, Grinnell Coll., 1972-74, U. Iowa, 1975-77, Gemological Inst. Am., 1987. Mgr. downtown location Hand's Jewelers, Iowa City, Iowa, 1977-81, Gray's Jewelers, Inc., Tulsa, 1981-89; corp. ops. mgr. Samuel's Jewelers, Davenport, Iowa, 1989—; ops. mgr. Herlitzka Ina Lynn. Bd. dirs., Am. Theater Co., 1985-87, TUL Ctr., Inc., 1984—; charter mem. Arts & Humanities Coun. Tulsa; corp. sponsor, Tulsa Heart Assn.; Leadership Tulsa XII, 1986. Mem. Okla. Jewelers Assn. (v.p. 1981—), Gemol. Inst. Am. Alumni Assn., Gemol. Inst. Am., Am. Gem Soc., Downtown Tulsa Unlimited (exec. com. 1981—), Bohemian Soc. (bd. dirs. 1987—), Downtown Tulsa Retail Mchts. Assn., Tulsa Urban League. Democrat. Jewish. Home: 324 Main St #606 Davenport IA 52801 Office: Samuel's Jewelers PO Box 3744 Davenport IA 52808

TUFANO, MANUELA, typesetter; b. Wyk, Fohr, Germany, July 27, 1957; came to U.S., 1961; d. Erich Adolf and Ilse (Henkel) Eggert; m. John Robert Tufano; 1 child, Michael Robert. AAS, N.Y.C. Coll., 1978. Paste-up artist TMP, Inc., N.Y.C., 1978-80, asst. art dir., 1980-81; studio mgr. Milbin Printing, Farmingdale, N.Y., 1981-82; typesetter Precision Type & Form, Hauppauge, N.Y., 1982-84; typesetter, dept. head Keller Pub., Great Neck, N.Y., 1984-86; owner Maris Graphics, Ltd., Holliswood, N.Y., 1985-90. Mem. NAFe. Office: Maris Graphics Ltd 87-80 202d St Holliswood NY 11423

TUGGLE, JUDY GAIL, educator; b. Birmingham, Ala., Aug. 23, 1946; d. Newton and Lurla (Key) T. MusB, Samford U., 1968; MEd, U. Louisville, 1976; cert. in edn. specialist, Ga. State U., 1981, PhD, 1984. Supr., house parent Greenwich Home for Children, Phila., 1976-77; edn. dir. Phila. Assn. for Retarded Citizens, 1976-77; tchr. Clayton County Schs., Jonesboro, Ga., 1977-78, Dekalb County Schs., Decatur, Ga., 1978—; guest lectr. Ga State U., instr. part-time; intern Ga. State Dept.Dem., Atlanta; vocat. coord. Margaret Harris Ctr., 1978-83; coord. Project Svc., 1983-86, instructional coord., 1986—. Mem. Assn. for Supervision Devel., Coun. for Exceptional Children (career devel. div.), Am. Vocat. Assn., Kappa Delta Pi (pres. 1984-85). Democrat. Home: 3749 Gleneagles Ln Tucker LA 30084 Office: Dekalb County Sch System Rehoboth Instructional Ctr 2652 Lawrenceville Hwy Decatur GA 30033

TUGWELL, CYNTHIA KAY, materials management executive; b. Gladewater, Tex., Sept. 9, 1954; d. Floyd Calvin Jr. and Margery R. (Shelton) Tugwell. Student, Kilgore (Tex.) Jr. Coll., 1972-73, Ouachita Bapt. U., 1974-75. Typist, proofreader Kilgore News Herald, 1974; nurse aide Roy H. Laird Meml. Hosp., Kilgore, 1975-77, PBX operator, 1977-78, respiratory therapy technician, 1981-88, dir. materials mgmt., 1988—; receptionist Charles F. Campbell, M.D., Longview, Tex., 1978-80, Kilgore Ins. Agy., 1980-81. Recorded (album) Without Him, 1976. Pianist, organist Friendship Bapt. Ch., Kilgore, 1978-80; pianist 1st Bapt. Ch., Kilgore, 1989—, mem. sanctuary choir, 1981—. Home: 704 Parkview Kilgore TX 75662

TUHOLSKI, ELIZABETH MURRAY, nurse, educator; b. Portsmouth, Va., Oct. 20, 1956; d. William Michael and Nora (Bryan) Murray; m. Richard Allen Tuholski, July 3, 1983; 1 child, Eric William. BS in Nursing, Northeastern U., 1979. RN, Calif.; cert. diabetic educator, Calif., ACLS, CCRN. Staff nurse Centinela Hosp., Inglewood, Calif., 1979-80; charge nurse Little Co. Mary Hosp., Torrance, Calif., 1980-81; staff nurse ICU Centinela Hosp., Inglewood, Calif., 1981-86, clin. instr., coord. diabetic teaching, 1987—; instr. nusing ICU Calif. State U., L.A., 1987—, Am. Heart Assn., 1987—; mem. BSLC Provider, 1988—; tchr. prepatory classes for RN state bd. exams. Mem. AACCN (cert. critical care nurse), Am. Assn. Diabetes Educators (cert. diabetes educator). Democrat. Roman Catholic. Home: 5134 W 139th St Hawthorne CA 90250 Office: Centinela Hosp 555 E Hardey St Inglewood CA 90307

TUHY, MARIE RUTH, medical technologist; b. Neubrücke, Fed. Republic Germany, Aug. 15, 1961; came to U.S., 1965; (parents Am. citizens); d. Melvin Henry and Margaret Ann (Ehen) Droege; m. Edwin Eugene Tuhy, Jr., Apr. 1, 1989. BS in Med. Tech., No. Ill. U., 1983. Cert. med. technologist Am. Soc. Clin. Pathologists; cert. clin. lab. scientist Nat. Certification Agy. Clin. Lab. Pers. Med. technologist Hines (Ill.) VA Hosp., 1983-89, asst. supr., 1986-89; med. technologist Meml. Hosp. DuPage County, Elmhurst, Ill., 1983-85, White Earth (Minn.) Pub. Health Ctr., 1989—. Mem. Am. Found. for Vision Awareness, Detroit Lakes Jaycees, Detroit Lakes Women of Today (treas. 1990-91). Republican. Lutheran.

TUKUAFU, ROSE A., compensation and human resource development specialist; b. Mauston, Wis., Apr. 13, 1954; d. Ray Harrison and Mary Louise (Leshley) Palmer; m. Manu P. Tukuafu, Apr. 20, 1989; children: Jesse, Ryan. BS, Brigham Young U., Laie, Hawaii, 1988; student, USAF Tech. Tng. Sch., Biloxi, Miss., 1976. Cert. air traffic controller. Compensation specialist Polynesian Cultural Ctr., Laie. Mem. NAFE, Am. Mgmt. Assn., Soc. for Human Reousrce Devel. Address: BYUH Box 1864 Laie HI 96762

TULEY, SISTER MARGARET, hospital administrator; b. Boston. BS in Nursing, St. Joseph's Coll., Emmitsburg, Md., 1961; MS Nursing Svc. Adminstrn, Boston U., 1969; MA in Hosp. and Health Care Adminstrn., St. Louis U., 1976. Lic. to practice nursing, Mass., Va., Maine, N.Y., Mo., Tex., Washington. Staff nurse, head nurse DePaul Hosp., Norfolk, Va., 1961-62; med.-surgical nursing supr. DePaul Hosp., 1962-67; dir. nursing svcs., bd. dirs. Seton Hosp., Waterville, Maine, 1969-70; adminstrv. asst. St. Mary's Hosp., Rochester, N.Y., 1970-71; assoc. adminstr. sec. bd. trustees St. Mary's Hosp., Rochester, 1971-74; pres., chief exec. officer, chmn. bd. trustees Carney Hosp., Boston, 1976-85; pres., chief exec. officer, chmn. bd. dirs. Our Lady of Lourdes Meml. Hosp., Binghamton, N.Y., 1985-89, pres., chief exec. officer, vice chmn., bd. dirs., 1989—; adv. bd. SUNY-Ctr. for Leadership Studies, Binghamton, 1988—; bd. dirs. St. Mary's Hosp., Rochester, Good Samritan Hosp., Pottsville, Pa. Mem. United Way, Binghamton, 1987—, State U. Binghamton Found., 1986—. Recipient Leboure medal Laboure Coll., 1986. Fellow Am. Coll. Healthcare Execs. (nominating com. 1987—); mem. Am. Hosp. Assn. (search com. for pres. 1985—, regional adv. bd. II Chgo. 1985-87), N.Y. State Cahtolic Healthcare Coun. (exec. com. 1987—), Hosp. Assn. N.Y. State (strategic planning com. 1987—), Cen. N.Y. Hosp. Assn. (exec. com. 1986—), Broome County C. of C., Rotary. Office: Our Lady Lourdes Meml Hosp 169 Riverside Dr Binghamton NY 13905

TULL, RENEÉ MARTIN, communications executive; b. Monroe, La., Feb. 13, 1950; d. William Otis and Betty Mae (Roan) Martin; m. Haskell Eugene Tull Jr., Jan. 29, 1972; 1 child, Haskell Eugene Tull III. BA in Speech Edn., N.E. La. U., 1972, MA in Rhetoric/Pub. Address, 1974. High sch. tchr. Ouachita Parish Sch. System, Monroe, 1974-76; newspaper editor Ouachita Citizen, Monroe, 1976-80; farm market editor La. Dept. Agriculture, Baton Rouge, 1980-84, agriculture communications and promotions dir., 1984—; agriculture advt. cons., West Monroe, 1977-80; promotional cons. State Wide Farm Assns., La., 1978-85; cons. dir. La. State Fair, Shreveport, 1984—; pageant dir. Ark.-La.-Miss. Stampede Rodeo, Monroe, 1986—; lectr. Domestic Mktg. Inst., New Orleans, 1985-89, USMC, 1985-89. Author, editor Louisiana Foods, 1985-89;. Named Outstanding Young Women,

Jaycees, 1985; recipient Disting. Svc. La. Meat Industry Coun., 1987. Mem. Quota Internat. of Monroe (sec. 1982), Farm Bur. Fedn. (Nat. speaker award), Monroe C. of C. (bd. dirs. agriculture div. 1981-86), La. State U. Agriculture Commn. (bd. dirs. 1982-89). Democrat. Baptist. Home: 5257 New Natchitoches West Monroe LA 71292 Office: LA Dept Agriculture 122 St John Ste 231 Monroe LA 71201

TULL, THERESA ANNE, foreign service officer; b. Runnemede, N.J., Oct. 2, 1936; d. John James and Anna Cecelia (Paull) T. B.A., U. Md., 1972; M.A., U. Mich., 1973; postgrad., Nat. War Coll., Washington, 1980. Fgn. svc. officer Dept. State, Washington, Brussels and Saigon, 1963—; assigned to Brussels and Saigon, Vietnam, 1973-75; dep. prin. officer Am. Embassy, Danang, Vietnam; prin. officer Cebu, Philippines, 1977-79; dir. office human rights, 1980-83; charge d'affaires Am. Embassy, Vientiane, Laos, 1983-86; ambassador to Guyana, 1987—. Recipient Civilian Service award Dept. of State, 1970, Meritorious Honor award, 1977. Mem. Am. Fgn. Service Assn., Cathedral Choral Soc. (Washington). Home: care Waldis 416 N Washington Ave Moorestown NJ 08057 Other: Am Embassy, 31 Main St, Georgetown Guyana

TULLIS, LUCY MERYL, therapist; b. Osceola, Iowa, July 21, 1906; d. Perry Zebulon and Martha Lenora (Carter) Fogle; m. Edward Langdon Tullis (dec. May 1968); children: Highland Kent (dec.), Terry Edson, Alan Langdon. BA, U. Denver, 1927; postgrad., U. Chgo., 1932-33, Stanford (Calif.) U., 1964-65. Rsch. technician Sch. Medicine Child Rsch. Coun., Denver, 1927-30; instr. psychology S.D. Sch. of Mines and Tech., Rapid City, 1955-64; pvt. practice family therapist Rapid City, 1966-68, 81—; family therapist Luth. Social Svcs., Rapid City, 1969-73; family therapist addiction dept. Rapid City Regional Hosp., 1974-81; mem. staff Va. Satir's Avanta Process Community, 1981, 82; adj. prof. U. Okla., Norman, 1987—, U. N.D., Grand Forks, 1987-88; cons. Hazelden Treatment Ctr., Center City, Minn., 1977-78, Minn. Men's Maximum Security Prison, St. Cloud, 1977-79, Luth. Social Svcs., Columbus, Nebr., 1977-78, State Mental Health Dept., Mandan, N.D., 1978. Author: chpt. Satir, Banman Anthology, 1989. Recipient Svc. award Tiyospaye, 1984, Svc. award Indian-White Coun., 1986; inducted into S.D. Hall of Fame, 1985. Mem. Internat. Human Resources Network, Avanta Satir Network, AAUW. Home: 2911 Tomahawk Dr Rapid City SD 57702 Office: 2911 Tomahawk Dr Rapid City SD 57702

TULLY, CAROL THORPE, social work educator, administrator; b. Portsmouth, N.H., Sept. 16, 1946; d. Francis William and Laura Alice (Thorpe) T. BA, U. Ariz., 1968; MSW, Va. Commonwealth U., 1977, PhD, 1983. Licensed social worker. Indexer Nat. Geog. Soc., Washington, 1968-69; social worker Richmond (Va.) City Pub. Welfare, 1971-77; tng. specialist Va. Dept. Welfare, Richmond, 1977-79; asst. prof. W. Va. U. Sch. Social Work, Charleston, W.Va., 1983-86; exec. dir. Ga. Council on Aging, Atlanta, 1986-90; asst. prof. Sch. Social Work U. Ga., Athens, 1990—; cons. in field; adv. council Council on Elder Abuse/Neglect, Atlanta, 1986-87, Ctr. for the Hearing Impaired, Atlanta, 1989—. Contbr. several articles to profl. jours. Bd. dirs. Nat. Assn. Social Workers, Atlanta, 1988—, Atlanta Women's Network, Black Diamond Girl Scout Coun., Charleston, 1985-86; house of dels. Coun. on Social Work Edn., Washington, 1987-89. Recipient Presdl. Recognition award Kanawha Valley United Way, 1985. Mem. Am. Assn. for Higher Edn., AAUP, So. Gerontol. Soc. Home: 750 Yorkshire Rd NE Atlanta GA 30306 Office: U Ga Sch Social Work Tucker Hall 101 Athens GA 30602

TULP, GAYE G.K., oil and gas company executive, artist; b. Bismarck, N.D., Aug. 26, 1947; d. Virgil Ralph and Violet Flora (Burg) T.; grad. Famous Artist Sch., 1975; bus. mgmt. Houston Community Coll., Blinn Coll., also profl. seminars; 1 son, Travor Will Rogers. Sec., Thomas W. Moore, Atty., Houston, 1969-70; underwriter Gt. So. Life Ins. Co., Houston, 1970-71; temporary sec. Top Girls, Houston, 1972-73; sec. to v.p. Rex Supply Co., Houston, 1973; office mgr. John L. Skalla Agy., Houston, 1973-74; traffic coordinator Nat. Supply Co. div. Armco Inc., Houston, 1974-79; owner Gaye Tulp Studio; cons. Internat. Transp. Mgmt. Assn. Served with USN, 1965-68; Vietnam. Mem. Internat. Transp. Mgmt. Assn., Nat. Assn. Female Execs. (network dir.), Brenham Fine Arts League, Lone Star Fine Arts League, Houston Women's Bus. Club. Home and Office: Route 1 Box 45C Brenham TX 77833

TUMBLESON, TREVA ROSE, writer; b. Willits, Calif., June 23, 1927; d. Lloyd Arthur and Ruth (Selvage) Launer; m. John Raymond Tumbleson, Sept. 1949; children: Lisa Ruth, Paul Arthur, Raymond Dana. BS, So. Oreg. Coll., Ashland, 1968; MS, So. Oreg. Coll., 1970; PhD, U. Oreg., 1981. Actor Savoy Opera Co., San Francisco, 1944-45, The Drunkard Co., San Francisco, 1945; singer Ken Murray Show (TV), N.Y.C., 1950; actor Round-Up Revue, N.Y.C., 1950, Indsl. Show - Happy Acres, 1951; instr. S.O.C., Ashland, Oreg., summer 1971; tchr. Dist. #549 C, Medford, Oreg., 1970-73; teaching fellow U. Oreg., Eugene, 1973-74; freelance writer Ashland, 1981—. Author: Three Female Hamlets: Charlotte Cushman, Sarah Bernhardt and Eva Le Gallienne, 1981; contbr. articles to profl. jours. and newspapers. Mem. AAUW (pres. 1989, parliamentarian 1990, internat. rels. rep. 1988-89), Friends of the Ashland Pub. Libr. (v.p. 1990), Beta Sigma Phi (pres. 1989—). Democrat. Home: 655 Leonard St Ashland OR 97520

TUMELSON, BETSY MARTIN, consulting and training company executive; b. Paris, Tenn., July 29, 1943; d. Frank and Bassie Destine (Moore) Martin; m. Ronald Adrian Tumelson, Dec. 14, 1963; children: Arlene Dawn Dettler, Gretchen Loraine, Ronald Adrian, Karen Destine. BS in Human Relations Organ. Behavior, U. San Francisco, 1982; MS in Human Resource Mgmt. Devel., Chapman Coll., 1984. Cert. orgn. cons. Cons. to city mgr. Heidelberg Am. Community, Fed. Republic Germany, 1979-80; cons., trainer U.S. Army Organizational Effectiveness Ctr. and Sch., Ford Ord, Calif., 1980-84; instr. Hartnell Coll., Salinas, Calif., 1985-87; expert community leader Dept. of Def., Washington, 1983—; pres. Betsy Tumelson, Cons., Monterey, Calif., 1980-84, Systems Excellence, Monterey, 1984—; pres. tng. Mgmt. Inst. Monterey, 1986—, bd. dirs.; cons. Smith/Trahern Mansion, Clarksville, Tenn., 1986—. Author: Moving In and Moving Up, 1982, Managerial Competencies, 1982, Volunteer Motivational Index, 1981. Founder Leaderspirit, 1990. Named one of Outstanding Women in Leadership, County of Monterey (Calif.), 1990. Mem. NAFE, Profl. Women's Network (membership com.), Salinas C. of C. (coord., bd. dirs. 1987). Democrat. Methodist. Club: German/Am. (chmn. protocol, hospitality) (Heidelberg), Am. Woman's (Heidelberg). Home: 54 Castro Rd Ste A 3784 Monterey CA 93940 Office: Systems Excellence SYSTEX 177 Webster St Ste A3784 Monterey CA 93940

TUNG, ROSALIE LAM, b. Shanghai, China, Dec. 2, 1948; came to U.S., 1975; d. Andrew Yan-Fu and Pauline Wai-Kam (Cheung) Lam. BA (Univ. scholar), York U., 1972; MBA, U. B.C., 1974, PhD in Bus. Adminstrn. (Univ. fellow, Seagram Bus. fellow, H.R. MacMillan Family fellow), 1977; m. Byron Poon-Yan Tung, June 17, 1972; 1 child, Michele Christine. Lectr. diploma div. U. B.C., 1975, lectr. exec. devel. program, 1975; asst. prof. mgmt. grad. sch. mgmt. U. Oreg., Eugene, 1977-80; assoc. prof. U. Pa., Phila. 1981-86; prof., dir. internat. bus. ctr. U. Wis., Milw., 1986—; vis. scholar U. Manchester (Eng.) Inst. Sci. and Tech., 1980; vis. prof. UCLA, 1981, Harvard U., 1988; Wis. disting. prof. U. Wis. System, 1988—. Mem. Acad. Internat. Bus. (mem. exec. bd., treas. 1985-86), Acad. Mgmt. (bd. govs. 1987-89), Internat. Assn. Applied Psychology, Am. Arbitration Assn. (comml. panel arbitrators). Author: Management Paractices in China, 1980, U.S.-China Trade Negotiations, 1982, Chinese Industrial Society After Mao, 1982, Business Negotiations with the Japanese, 1984, Key to Japan's Economic Strength: Human Power, 1984, The New Expatriates: Managing Human Resources Abroad, 1988; editor: Strategic Management in the U.S. and Japan, 1987. Oppehheimer Bros. Found. fellow, 1973-74, U. B.C. fellow, 1974-75, H.R. MacMillan Found. fellow, 1975-77; named Wis. Disting. Prof., 1988. Roman Cathlic; recipient Leonore Rowe Williams award U. Pa., 1990. Avocation: creative writing. Home: PO Box 17441 Milwaukee WI 53217 Office: U Wis Sch Bus PO Box 742 Milwaukee WI 53217

TUNGPALAN, ELOISE YAMASHITA, state legislator; b. Maui, Hawaii, July 22, 1945; married; 3 children. BA, U. Hawaii. Former instr. U. Hawaii; legis. aide to coms., former mem. Hawaii Ho. of Reps.; now state senator Hawaii Senate; legis. aide and researcher for govt. coms. and depts. State of Hawaii. Mem. Phi Beta Kappa, Phi Kappa Phi. Democrat. Office: Hawaii State Senate State Capitol Honolulu HI 96813*

TUNGSVIK, MARY ELIZABETH, real estate associate; b. Kirkland, Wash., Nov. 16, 1932; d. Reginald and Elizabeth Hunt; m. Cecil Clement Tungsvik, Aug. 24, 1956; children: James Emory, Jane Elizabeth. Student, U. Wash., 1955-56. Various office positions, 1951-79; sec., tax preparer Taylor's Acctg., Inc., Auburn, Wash., 1979-84; adminstr. asst. property mgmt. div. W.E. Ruth Real Estate, Renton, Wash., 1984-90; ptnr. Team Corp. aka Around the Clock Property Mgmt., Kent, Wash., 1990—. Recipient Mayor's Spl. Recognition award City of Auburn, 1981, Disting. Citizen award Elks, 1980, 81, Svc. award Auburn C. of C., 1980. Republican. Presbyterian. Home: 1905 Dogwood Dr SE Auburn WA 98002 Office: Team Corp 25018-104th Ave SE Ste A Kent WA 98031

TUNKIEICZ, MARY URSULA, farm company executive, clown; b. Chgo., Sept. 28, 1937; d. Gunnar and Jennie Adella (Howe) Gram; student public schs., Mich. and Ill.; m. Charles Tunkieicz, Feb. 23, 1957; children—Charlene, John, Jennie, Robert. Vice pres. Charles Tunkieicz Farms, Inc., Kenosha, Wis., 1972—, sec., 1972-80, sec.-treas., 1980—, v.p., sec., 1982-86, chmn. bd., 1985-86; clown Kenosha Unified Sch. Dist., 1979—; dir. I Am Sorry God, Somers Clowns Circus film, Alpha Film Corp.; clown ambassador Cousin Otto's Alley #22, Franzen Bros. Traveling Circus, Delavan, Wis. Leader for cooking Somers 4-H Club, 1974-75, clown project leader, 1976-80; chairperson Kenosha Farm Bur., 1975-78, pres. women's group, 1982-84; pres. Homemakers Club, 1986. Mem. Somers Clowns Clubs (dir.), Soc. Am. Magicians, Wis. Magical Entertainers Club. Democrat. Roman Catholic. Lodges: Moose, Eagles. Contbr. poetry to various publs. Home: 8410 W 60th St Kenosha WI 53142 Office: 8418 38th St Kenosha WI 53142

TUNNELL, CLIDA DIANE, air transportation specialist; b. Durham, N.C., Nov. 20, 1946; d. Kermit Wilbur and Roberta (Brantley) T. BS cum laude, Atlantic Christian Coll., 1968; pvt. pilot rating, instr. rating, Air Care, Inc., 1971, 83. Cert. tchr. Tchr. Colegio Karl C. Parrish, Barranquilla, Colombia, S. Am., 1968-69, Nash County Schs., Nashville, N.C., 1969-86; ground sch. instr. Nash Tech. Schs., Nashville, 1984-85; specialist, technician Am. Airlines, Dallas-Ft. Worth Airport, Tex., 1987—, A300 lead developer, 1988-89, with flight ops. procedures, 1990—; ednl. cons., Euless, Tex., 1989—. State Tchrs. Scholar N.C., 1964-68, Bus. and Profl. Women Scholar, 1980-81. Mem. 99, Internat. Orgn. Women Pilots (various offices), AMR Mgmt. Club. Republican. Home: 1800 Fuller-Wiser #318 Euless TX 76039

TUNSTALL, SHARON SUE, advertising executive; b. Houston, Oct. 19, 1949; d. O. Ray and Etta Mae (Stodghill) T. BA, U. Houston, 1973, MA, 1977, PhD, 1981. Tchr. Dulles High Sch., Stafford, Tex., 1974-77; asst. prof. Oakland U., Rochester, Mich., 1980-85; v.p., dir. human resources D'Arcy Masius Benton & Bowles, Bloomfield Hills, Mich., 1985—, dir. corp. tng. N.Am. div., 1986-90; v.p., dir. human resources B.H. and Corp, Tng., 1990—; polit. cons. U. Houston; guest speaker Advt. Ednl. Found., N.Y.C., 1988—. Mem. Am. Soc. Tng. and Devel., Am. Mgmt. Assn. Democrat. Office: D'Arcy Masius Benton & Bowles Inc 1725 N Woodward Ave PO Box 811 Bloomfield Hills MI 48303

TUOHEY, SUSAN KRUMHOLZ, nursing administrator, consultant, expert witness; b. Fairmont, Minn., June 14, 1945; d. Francis William and Ruth Ardelle (Jacobson) Krumholz; m. Edward Luke Halloran, July 5, 1983; children: Stephanie, Susan. Diploma, St. Mary's Sch. Nursing, Mpls., 1966; MBA, U. Houston, 1987. Supr., asst. dir. ICU, assoc. dir. nursing St. Luke's Episcpoal and Tex. Med. Ctr., Houston; asst. adminstr., dir. nursing Tex. Children's Hosps., Houston; cons. health care mgmt., 1990—; expert witness for pediatrics, nursing, hosp. adminstrn.; mem. nursing team which cared for first heart transplant recipient in U.S., 1968. Mem. Am. Orgn. Nurse Execs. (bd. dirs.), Exec. MBA Assn. (bd. dirs.) Houston Orgn. Nurse Execs., Fedn. Houston Profl. Women, Tex. Nurses Assn., Forum Club of Houston. Address: 7918 Redding Houston TX 77036

TUPLER, HARRIETT GLORIA, television producer; b. Bronx, N.Y., Dec. 10, 1935; d. Louis and Rose (Cohen) Harris; m. Dec. 17, 1956 (div. 1976); children: Larry N., Anne T., Diana L. AA, U. Fla, 1955; B in Edn., U. Miami, 1959; postgrad., Fla. Atlantic U., 1978. Cert. tchr., early childhood and elem. edn., Fla.; cert. in journalism. Tchr. Dade County Sch. Bd., Miami, 1959-64, Alachua County Sch. Bd., Tallahassee, 1964-65, Broward County Sch. Bd., Ft. Lauderdale, 1970-72, 75-77, 89, Temple Beth Torah, Tamarac, Fla., 1983-88; co-owner, dir. Discovery Preschool, Ft. Lauderdale, 1968-69; coord. handicapped program Fla. Internat. U., Miami, 1977-78; staff writer Miami Herald, Tamarac, 1979—; producer Changing Directions, Inc., Ft. Lauderdale; pres., cons. Harriett Tupler Assocs., Ft. Lauderdale, 1990; co-producer TV show on handicapped concerns, Ft. Lauderdale, 1990. Author: Legal Rights of the Handicapped, 1978. Foster parent Seed Drug and Alcohol Abuse Ctr., Ft. Lauderdale, 1974-75; sec. Broward Ostomy Assn., Hollywood, Fla., 1974-75; mem. Gov.'s Com. on Employment of the Handicapped, Tallahassee, 1977-82. Named Outstanding Woman of Yr., Women in Communications, 1989; recipient Pres.'s award Plantation Kiwanis Clubs, 1989. Mem. Pompano Ostomy Assn., Against All Odds (chair 1989), Quota Club of Plantation (charter mem., program chair 1989), Kiwanis Club of Deaf. Democrat. Jewish. Home: 430 N Commodore Dr #314 Plantation FL 33325 Office: Changing Directions Inc PO Box 25082 Fort Lauderdale FL 33320

TURBEN, SUSAN HANRAHAN, child development consultant, parent educator; b. Buffalo, Nov. 6, 1936; d. James Edward and Sylvina (Tubbs) Hanrahan; m. Newton Shepard Kimberly, Feb. 9, 1957 (dec. 1976); children: Newton Shepard Jr., James Hanrahan, Mary Kimberly Rademacher; m. John Franklin Turben, Mar. 13, 1976. AA, Bradford (Mass.) Coll., 1956; BA in Child Devel., SUNY, Albany, 1972; MEd, Kent State U., 1978, PhD, 1987. Cert. tchr., Ohio. Head tchr., home trainer Head Start Albany County, Albany, N.Y., 1966-69; dir. family life project Albany Trinity Inst., 1969-72; staff devel. trainer N.Y. State Dept. Mental Hygiene, Albany, 1972-75; exec. dir. Multiple Sclerosis Soc., Cleve., 1975-76; instr. child devel. positive edn. program Lakeland Community Coll., Mentor, Ohio, 1976-79; dir. continuing edn. Lake Erie Coll., Painesville, Ohio, 1979-83; pres. Turben Devel. Svcs., Mentor, 1983—; cons. Cleve. Sight Ctr., 1979—, Lake County Early Intervention, 1987—; advisor, trainer Lake County Soc. Rehab., Mentor, 1987—; trainer Inst. Human Svcs., Columbus, Ohio, 1988—. Contbr. articles to profl. jours. Mem. exec. com., v.p. Cleve. Sight Ctr., 1979—; bd. dirs. Breckenridge Village, Ohio Presbyn. Retirement Svcs., 1986—, Sta. WCPN, PBS, Cleve., 1988—; mem. adv.. bd. Preveniton Child Abuse and Neglect, Lake County, 1987—. Recipient Recognition award Cleve. Sight Ctr., 1987, award Ohio Hosp. Assn., 1988; grantee Ohio Dept. Mental Retardation/Devel. Disabilities, 1979, Ohio Dept. Health, 1987, 88. Mem. Nat. Assn. for Edn. Young Children, Assn. for Persons with Severe Handicaps, Nat. Ctr. for Clin. Infant Programs, Soc. for Rsch. in Child Devel., Ohio Rehab. Assn. (President's award 1988), Ohio Coun. for Exceptional Children, Foster Parents Assn. Presbyterian. Home: 8966 Booth Rd Mentor OH 44060 Office: Interstate I Ste 200 4230 Chillicothe Rd Willoughby OH 44094

TURBEVILLE, BECKY LUANN, chemist; b. Cleve., July 22, 1964; d. Arthur E. and Margaret Radin; m. Wayne Turbeville, Apr. 2, 1988. BA in Chemistry, Ea. Ky. U., 1086. Quality control chemist Andrew Jergens Co., Cin., 1986-87; process engr. Showa Aluminum Corp. Am., Mt. Sterling, Ohio, 1987-89; analytical chemist Roxane Labs., Columbus, Ohio, 1989—. Mem. Am. Chem. Soc. Office: Roxane Labs Wilson Rd Columbus OH 43228

TURCO, JENIFER, microbiology researcher and educator; b. Morgantown, W.Va., July 24, 1950; d. Mario Samuel and Elizabeth Jane (Lamus) T. BS in Biology, Marywood Coll., Scranton, Pa., 1972; MS in Biology, W.Va. U., 1975, PhD in Med. Microbiology, 1978. Tchg. asst. W.Va. U., Morgantown, 1972-74; postdoctoral fellow U. South Ala., Mobile, 1978-82, instr., 1983-84, asst. prof. microbiology, 1984-90, assoc. prof. microbiology, 1990—. Co-editor: Interferon and Nonviral Pathogens, 1988; contbr. articles to profl. jours. Competitive Acad. scholar Marywood Coll., 1968-72; W.Va. U. Found. fellow, 1974-77, Benedum Found. fellow, 1977-78; NSF postdoctoral fellow, 1979-80; recipient Nat. Rsch. Svc. award nat. Inst. Allergy and Infectious Diseases, NIH, 1980-82. Mem. Am. Soc. Microbiology, Am. Assn. Immunologists, Internat. Soc. for Interferon Rsch., Am. Soc. for Rickettsiology and Rickettsial Diseases (councilor-at-large 1989—). Roman Catholic. Office: U South Ala Lab Molecular Biology Dept Microbiology and Immunology Mobile AL 36688

TURCONI, TERI LYNN, pharmaceutical company executive; b. Beaver Falls, Pa., Apr. 28, 1962; d. Joseph Louis and Patricia Jean (Masson) T. BS cum laude, U. Fla., 1984; MEd, U. Va., 1986. Asst. dir. Mesa (Ariz.) Luth. Hosp., 1986, Classics Gymnastic Ctr., Charlottesville, Va., 1984-85, 86-87; supr. quality assurance and clin. monitoring Pharm. Rsch. Assn., Charlottesville, 1987-89; pharm. sales rep. Parke-Davis div. Warner-Lambert, Chesapeake, Va., 1989—; Counselor Sports Psychology, Charlottesville, 1985. Witness asst. program City of Chesapeake, 1990. Recipient Brownie-Wrona Gymnastics award, 1980; various Gymnastics awards U.S. Gymnastic Fedn., 1967-80. Home and Office: 1716P Birch Trail Circle Chesapeake VA 23320

TURCOT, MARGUERITE HOGAN, innkeeper, medical researcher; b. White Plains, N.Y., May 19, 1934; d. Joseph William and Marguerite Alice (Barrett) Hogan; children: Michael J., Susan A. Turcot, William R. Student, Syracuse U., 1951-54; BS in Nursing, U. Bridgeport, 1968. RN, Conn., N.C. Staff nurse Park City Hosp., Bridgeport, Conn., 1968-69, Meml. Mission Hosp., Asheville, N.C., 1969-70; instr. St. Joseph's Hosp., Asheville, 1970-71; oper. rm. nurse St. Joseph's Hosp., 1973-77, charge nurse urology-cystoscopy, 1977-85; tchr. Asheville-Buncombe Tech. Coll., Asheville, 1971-72, Buncombe County Child Devel., Asheville, 1972-73; researcher VA Med. Ctr., Asheville, 1988—; owner Reed House Bed & Breakfast, Asheville, 1985; bd. dirs. RiverLink. Charter mem. French Broad River Planning Com., Asheville, 1987—; mem. Asheville Bicentennial Commn., 1990—. Faculty scholar Syracuse U., 1951-54, U. Bridgeport, 1967-68. Mem. Am. Urology Assn. (presenter VA urology workshop 1981, Ashville chpt., nat. meeting, allied), Am. Bd. Urologic Allied Health Profls., Nat. Trust for Hist. Preservation, Preservation Found. N.C., Blue ridge Pkwy. Assn., Preservation Soc. Asheville and Buncombe County (past pres.), Asheville Newcomers Club (founder, 1st pres.). Republican. Roman Catholic. Home: 119 Dodge St Asheville NC 28803 Office: VA Med Ctr Tunnel Rd Asheville NC 28805

TURCOTTE, MARGARET JANE, nurse; b. Stow, Ohio, May 17, 1927; d. Edward Carlton and Florence Margaret (Hanson) McCauley; R.N., St. Thomas Hosp., Akron, Ohio, 1949; m. Rene George Joseph, Nov. 24, 1961 (div. June 1967); 1 son, Michael Lawrence. Mem. nursing staff St. Thomas Hosp., 1949-50; pvt. duty nurse, 1950-57; polio nurse Akron's Children Hosp., 1953-54; mem. nursing staff Robinson Meml. Hosp., Ravenna, Ohio, 1958-67, head central service, 1963-67; supr. central service Brentwood Hosp., Warrensville Heights, Ohio, 1967, emergency med. technician. Mem. St. Thomas Hosp. Alumni Assn. Democrat. Roman Catholic. Home: 6037 Highview St Lot 14-F Ravenna OH 44266 Office: 4110 Warrensville Center Rd Warrensville Heights OH 44122

TURCZYN-TOLES, DOREEN MARIE, pharmaceutical executive; b. Chelsea, Mass., Aug. 5, 1958; d. Francis Henry and Rosalie (Lomba) Turczyn; m. Ronald Eugene Toles, Oct. 19, 1986. BA cum laude, Boston U., 1981; MA, U. Chgo., 1984. Programming subcontr. Abbott Labs., Abbott Park, Ill., 1983-84; programmer, analyst Nat. Opinion Research Ctr., Chgo., 1984-88; statis. computing analyst G.D. Searle & Co., Skokie, Ill., 1988-90; supr. Parke-Davis Pharms., Ann Arbor, Mich., 1990—. Mem. Nat. Assn. Female Execs., NOW. Democrat. Roman Catholic.

TURECK, ROSALYN, concert artist, author, editor, educator; b. Chgo., Dec. 14, 1914; d. Samuel Tureck and Mary (Lipson) Tureck-Wise; (w. 1964). Studies with Sophia Brilliant-Liven, 1925-29, with Jan Chiapusso, 1929-31, with Gavin Williamson, 1931-32; BA cum laude, The Juilliard Sch. Music, 1935; studies with Olga Samaroff; MusD (hon.), Colby Coll., 1964, Roosevelt U., 1968, Wilson Coll., 1968, Oxford U., Eng., 1977, Music and Arts Inst., San Francisco, 1987. Mem. faculty Phila. Conservatory Music, 1935-42, Mannes Sch., N.Y.C., 1940-44, Juilliard Sch. Music, N.Y.C., 1943-55, Columbia U., N.Y.C., 1953-55; prof. music, lectr. U. Calif., San Diego, 1966-72; vis. prof. Washington U., St. Louis, 1963-64, U. Md., 1981-85; vis. fellow St. Hilda's Coll., Oxford (Eng.) U., 1974, hon. life fellow, 1974—; vis. fellow Wolfson Coll., Oxford, 1975—; lectr. numerous ednl. instns., U.S. and Eng., Spain, Denmark, Holland, Can., Israel, Brazil, Argentina, Chile; hon. mem. adv. coun. Ams. for Music Libr., Hebrew U., Israel; bd. dirs., founder Internat. Bach Soc., Inst. for Bach Studies; founder Composers of Today, 1949-53, Tureck Bach Players, 1955, London, 1981, New York, Tureck Bach Inst., Inc., 1981, Symposia 1983, 84, 86—; was 1st woman invited to conduct N.Y. Philharm., 1958, San Antonio Symphony, Okla. Symphony, 1962, World Tour, U.S., Eng., Holland, Turkey, Israel, 1985-86; soloist at White House State Dinner for Can. Prime Minister, 1986. Debut 2 solo recitals, Chgo., 1924; soloist Chgo. Symphony Orch., 1926, 2 all-Bach recitals, Chgo., 1930; N.Y.C. debut Carnegie Hall with Phila. Orch., 1936; series 6 all-Bach recitals, Town Hall, N.Y.C., 1937, ann. U.S.-Can. tours, 1937—, ann. series 3 all-Bach recitals, N.Y.C., 1944-54, 59—; European debut Copenhagen, 1947; organizer, dir. soc. for performance internat. contemporary music: Composers of Today, Inc, 1951-55; extensive European tours, 1947—; condr., soloist, London Philharmonia, 1958, founder, dir., Tureck Bach Players, London, 1957, N.Y.C., 1981, Bach festivals cities, Eng., Ireland, Spain, 1959—; TV series Well-Tempered Clavier, Book I, Granada TV, Eng., 1961; BBC series Well-Tempered Clavier, Books 1 and 2, 1976; numerous TV appearances, U.S., 1961—, including Wm. F. Buckley's Firing Line, 1970, 85, 87, 89, Today Show, Camera Three, Bach recitals on piano, harpsichord, clavichord, antique and electronic instruments, 1963—; world tours in Far East, India, Australia, Europe, 1971, S.Am., 1986, 87, 88, 89, Europe, Israel, Turkey, Spain, 1986, Argentian, Chile, 1989; N.Y.C. series, Met. Mus. Art and Carnegie Hall, 1969—; appeared with leading orchs. U.S., Can., Europe, South Africa, S.Am., Israel; recs. for HMV, Odeon, Decca, Columbia Masterworks., Everest, Allegro, Classical Music, Inc; condr., soloist, Israel Philharmon., Tel Aviv, Haifa and Kol Israel orchs., 1963, Israel Festival, Internat. Bach Soc. Orchs., 1967, 69, 70, Washington Nat. Symphony, 1970, Madrid Chamber Orch., 1970, Tureck Bach Players, London, 1957—, N.Y. 1981, 84, 85; author: An Introduction to the Performance of Bach, 3 vols, 1960; contbr. articles to various mags.; editor: Bach-Sarabande, C minor, 1960, Tureck Bach Urtext Series: Italian Concerto, Schirmer Music, Inc., 1983, Lute Suite, E minor, 1984, C minor, 1985, Carl Fischer Paginini-Tureck—Moto Perpetuo, A. Scarlatti—Air and Gavotte; films: Fantasy and Fugue: Rosalyn Tureck Plays Bach, 1972, Rosalyn Tureck plays on Harpsichord and Organ, 1977, Joy of Bach, 1978, Camera 3: Bach on the Frontier of the Future, CBS film, Ephesus, Turkey, 1985; numerous recs. Decorated Officers Cross of the Order of Merit Fed. Republic Germany, 1979; recipient 1st prize Greater Chgo. Piano Playing Tournament, 1928; Winner Schubert Meml. Contest, 1935, Nat. Fedn. Music Clubs Competition, 1935; Phi Beta award, 1946, 1st Town Hall endowment award, 1937; NEH grantee; named Musician of Yr., Music Tchrs. Nat. Assn., 1987. Fellow Guildhall Sch. Music and Drama (hon.); mem. Royal Mus. Assndon, Am. Musicological Soc., Inc. Soc. Musicians (London), Royal Philharmonic Soc. London, Sebastian Bach de Belgique (hon.), Am. Bach Soc., Oxford Soc. Clubs: Cosmopolitan (N.Y.C.), Bohemians (N.Y.C.) (hon.). Office: care Columbia Artists Mgmt 165 W 57th St New York NY 10019*

TURETSKY, JUDITH, librarian, researcher; b. Bklyn., Jan. 19, 1944; d. Samuel and Ruth (Moskowitz) Turetsky. BS, Boston U., 1965; MS, Long Island U., 1969. Tchr. Trumbull (Conn.) Bd. Edn., 1965-66; libr. Darien (Conn.) Bd. Edn., 1968-69, Albert Einstein Coll., Bronx, 1969-74; researcher Koskoff, Koskoff & Bieder, Bridgeport, Conn., 1977-86. Author:(book and micro film), The History and Development of the D. Samuel Gottesman Library of Albert Einstein College of Medicine. Mem. Med. Library Assn., Conn. Assn. Health Sci. Libraries, N. Atlantic. Democrat. Home and Office: 496 W Mckinley Ave Bridgeport CT 06604

TURIACE, ELEANOR MARIE, manufacturing executive; b. Waynesburg, Oct. 23, 1939; d. John Richard Hlipala and Mary Isabelle Zimmerman; m. Samual Lazar Sander, June 10, 1961; (div. Nov. 1971); children: Eric Ben, Gregory Robert; m. Frank Anthony, July 14, 1973. BA, George Washington U. Owner King Mirror & Door Corp., L.A., 1978—. Fin. dir., Am. Med. Ctr., L.A., 1967. Republican. Jewish. Home: 125 Topsail Mall

Marina Del Rey CA 90292 Office: King Mirror & Door Corp 2040 Davie Ave Los Angeles CA 90040

TURK, CATHERINE H., educational administrator; b. Goldsboro, N.C., May 7; d. James H. and Elizabeth (Rhodes) Holmes; m. Willie C. Turk, June 8, 1969; 1 child, Marcus. Student, East Carolina U., Clark-Atlanta U.; BA, N.C. Cen. U., 1968; MEd, Ga. State U., 1975. Cert. tchr. English; cert. in adminstrn./supervision. Tchr. Goldsboro City Schs., Newton County Sch. System, Covington, Ga.; tchr., dept. chmn. DeKalb County Bd. Edn., Decatur, Ga., instructional coord. Co-chair fundraising United Negro Coll. Fund, 1980—; pres. Keller Lake PTA, 1977-79; bd. dirs. Glenwood Hills Athletic Assn., 1976-83. Recipient numerous awards. Mem. NAACP, Assn. for Supervision and Curriculum Devel., DeKalb Adminstrn. Assn., Am. Bus. Women's Assn., Ga. Coun. Tchrs. English, Alpha Kappa Alpha, Phi Delta Kappa. Baptist. Office: DeKalb County Sch System 3770 N Decatur Rd Decatur GA 30032

TURK, CYNTHIA COHEN, advertising executive; b. Medford, Mass., Mar. 16, 1953; d. Irving M. and Marie Santa (Liata) Cohen; m. Harry Nathan Turk, Apr. 8, 1989. BSBA, Boston U., 1977. Fin. mgr. Digital Equipment Corp., Maynard, Mass., 1977-80; cons. Touche Ross, Boston, 1980-83; v.p. fin. Leach & Garner/Interchain Corp., Hialeah, Fla., 1983-84; prin. Deloitte & Touche, N.Y.C., 1984—; bd. advisers Ben Gurion program Boston U., 1990—, commencement speaker, 1990; speaker in field. Mem. Women's Campaign Fund (leadership circle 1990), Fashion Group. Democrat. Office: Deloitte & Touche 666 Fifth Ave New York NY 10103 Also: Deloitte & Touche 4649 Ponce de Leon Blvd Coral Gables FL 33146

TURK, ELAINE ELIZABETH, school system administrator; b. Elizabeth, N.J., Nov. 8, 1946; d. Stephen Anthony and Mary Theresa (Sotak) T.; m. Paul Frank Tomaino, June 29, 1969 (div. June 1975). BA, Trenton State Coll., 1968, MEd, 1974; postgrad., Rutgers U., 1977-79; EdD, No. Ill. U., 1985. Bus. tchr. Carteret (N.J.) High Sch., 1968-75; asst. to dean Middlesex County Coll., Edison, N.J., 1975-77, asst. prof., 1977-82; grad. asst., instr. No. Ill. U., DeKalb, 1982-84; asst. prof. La. State U., Shreveport, 1984-85; bus. edn. program specialist N.J. Dept. Edn., Trenton, 1985—; evaluator Assoc. Ind. Colls. and Schs., Washington, 1986—; speaker McGraw-Hill Book Co., N.Y.C., 1986—. Contbr. articles to profl. jours. Vol. Hand-in-Hand, Edison, 1978-82. Mem. N.J. Bus. Edn. Assn. (exec. bd. 1987-88), Ea. Bus. Edn. Assn. (com. chmn.), Nat. Assn. Bus. Edn. State Suprs. (editor 1988-89), Delta Pi Epsilon, Beta Gamma Sigma. Roman Catholic. Home: 674 Danbury Ct Newtown PA 18940 Office: NJ Dept Edn 240 W State St CN 500 Trenton NJ 08625

TURLEY, JUNE WILLIAMS, chemical company official; b. Boston, Apr. 12, 1929; d. Fred Russell and Hazel Marion (Warnick) Williams; m. Sheldon Gamage Turley, Sept. 2, 1950; children: Sheldon Gamage, Jr., Cynthia Kingsbury, Linda Barrow. BS in Chemistry, Wilkes Coll., 1950; MS in Phys. Chemistry, Pa. State U., 1951, PhD in Agrl. and Biol. Chemistry, 1957. Rsch. chemist Dow Chem. Co., Midland, Mich., 1957-64, rsch. specialist, 1964-71, analytical mgr., 1971-74, sr. econ. planner, 1974-84, rsch. assoc., 1984—. Contbr. articles on x-ray crystallography and molecular structure to tech. jours. Organizer, bd. dirs., officer Career Women's Forum, Midland, 1972-83; mem. adv. coun. Midland Pub. Schs., 1980; bd. dirs. Unitarian Universalist Fellowship, Midland, 1983. Fellow AAAS; mem. Am. Chem. Soc., Natural Resources Def. Coun., Worldwatch Inst., AAUW (bd. dirs., officer Midland chpt. 1959-64), Midland Figure Skating Club (hon. life, bd. dirs., officer 1970-90), Sigma Xi, Sigma Delta Epsilon, Iota Sigma Pi. Home: 1208 Wakefield Dr Midland MI 48640 Office: Dow Chem Co 1603 Bldg Midland MI 48674

TURLEY, SARA JEAN, educator; b. Indiana, Pa., Jan. 31, 9135; d. Harry James and Edna Mabel (George) Lunn; m. Donald Richard Turley Sr., June 15, 1957; children: Donald Richard Jr., Debra Lynn. BS, Indiana U. Pa., 1956; MS, W.Va. U., 1962. Cert. home economist; cert. tchr., Pa. Tchr. Penns Manor Sch. Dist., R.D. Clymer, Pa., 1956-62; substitute tchr. Frankling Area Schs., Philo, Ohio, 1962-64; substitute tchr. Clearfield (Pa.) Area Schs., 1964-72, tchr., 1972—. Pres. Penns Manor Edn. Assn., Clymer, Pa., 1958-59, Clearfield Third Ward PTA, 1969-70, Presbyn. Women, Clearfield, 1988-89, treas., 1989-90. Mem. Am. Home Econs. Assn., Pa. Home Econs. Assn., NEA, Pa. State Edn. Assn. Nat. Coun. for Social Studies, Am. Psychol. Assn. (affiliate), AAUW (v.p. Clearfield chpt. 1973-74), Sigma Kappa (life). Republican. Home: 312 SW 3rd Ave Clearfield PA 16830 Office: Clearfield Area High Sch Box 910 Clearfield PA 16830

TURNBOLE, KATHLEEN MCCOMBE, minister; b. N.Y.C., Oct. 2, 1951; d. John Harold and Dorothy Mae (Skove) McCombe; m. David Paul Turnbole; children: Samantha, John, Katherine, Heath. BA, Baldwin-Wallace Coll., Berea, Ohio, 1974; MDiv, Princeton Theol. Sem., 1977. Minister Nicholville (N.Y.) Parish, 1977-79, First United Meth. Ch., Little Falls, N.Y., 1979-81, Four Steeples Parish, Belleville, N.Y., 1981-82, Summerfield United Meth. Ch., Staten Island, 1983-86, First United Meth. Ch., E. Hampton, N.Y., 1986-90; chaplain, bereavement coord. Hospice of Jefferson County, Inc., Watertown, N.Y., 1990—. Author poetry, Sojourner, 1982; lyricist, We Are One..., 1972. Pres. E. Hampton Town Clericus, 1988-89; bd. dirs. Bd. Ethics, Town of E. Hampton, 1988-89; soloist, chorister Choral Soc. of the Hamptons, 1987-89. Mem. AAUW, NAFE, Am. Guild Organists.

TURNBULL, CHERYL LANKARD, investment banker; b. Chicago Heights, Ill., Aug. 21, 1960; d. David Reid and Bettina Anne (Priamvera) L.; m. Michael Lambo Turnbull. BBA, Miami U., 1982; postgrad., Kellogg Grad. Sch. Mgmt., 1987. Mem. Kellogg Alumni Assn. Office: Prudential Bache Capital 199 Water St New York NY 10292

TURNBULL, DOREEN JOYCE, electronic data processing consultant; b. Evanston, Ill., Jan. 10, 1938; d. Dale M. and Juliet L. (Van Buskirk) T. B.S. in Bus. Mgmt., Calif. State Poly., Pomona, 1969; M.A. in Mgmt., Claremont Grad. Sch., 1984. Sr. systems analyst Sunkist Growers Inc., Sherman Oaks, Calif., 1969-74; EDP systems analyst Ralphs Grocery Co., Compton, Calif., 1974-77; propr. DJT Cons., 1977-80; project mgr., sr. systems analyst, Xerox Corp., Pasadena, Calif., 1980-84; project mgr. DHL Corp., San Bruno, Calif., 1984-86; propr. DJT Cons., 1986; MIS acct. rep., Westinghouse Marine div., Sunnyvale Calif., 1986—. Mem. Data Processing Mgmt. Assn. (chpt. dir., sec.), Am. Mgmt. Assn., Nat. Assn. Female Execs., Women in Mgmt., IS/DP Alumni Assn. (dir.). Club: Altrusa (past treas., past sec.) (Arcadia, Calif.). Home and Office: 760 Edgemar Ave Pacifica CA 94044

TURNBULL, FIONA MARY, librarian, information broker; b. Welwyn Garden City, Eng., Jan. 6, 1954; came to U.S., 1963; d. Douglas James and Mary Paula (Sperring) T.; m. George Avery Grimes, Dec. 29, 1984; 1 child, Christopher. BA in History, St. Bernard Coll., 1976; MLS, Rutgers U., 1981. Cert. profl. libr., Nebr., Washington. Dir. libr. svcs. Daniel Hale Williams U., Chgo., 1977-78; serials asst. Coll. of Physicians Phila., 1978-79; serials libr. Franklin Inst., Phila., 1979-80; head cataloger Mo. Bot. Garden Libr., St. Louis, 1982-84; circulation supr. Vancouver (Wash.) Pub. Libr., 1985-86; info. specialist Nat. Coun. Against Health Fraud, Kansas City, Mo., 1987-88; asst. libr. U.S. Ct. Appeals, St. Louis, 1981-82, Ralston Purina, St. Louis, 1984, Coll. St. Mary, Omaha, 1988-90; dir. libr. svcs. Bellevue (Nebr.) Coll., 1990—; cons. Kansas City Med. Soc., 1987, Infomore, Omaha, 1989—. Mem. Women's Devel. Ctr., Omaha, 1988—. Mem. Econ. History Assn., Nebr. Libr. Assn. (exec. sec. 1990), Nebr. On-Line Users Group, Omaha Health Scis. Consortium. Home: 1831 N 54th St Omaha NE 68104 Office: Bellevue Coll Galvin Rd at Harvell Dr Bellevue NE 68005

TURNBULL, VERNONA HARMSEN, retired residence counselor; b. Teeds Grove, Iowa, Dec. 6, 1916; d. Henry Ferdinand and Ida Amelia (Dohrmann) Harmsen; m. Alexander Turnbull, Oct. 12, 1961. BA, Cornell Coll., Mt. Vernon, Iowa, 1939; MEd, U. Colo., Boulder, 1947, profl. cert. edn., 1955. Cert. secondary and high sch. tchr. Tchr. English, Latin and phys. edn. Winslow (Ill.) High Sch., 1939-45; dir. women's activities, instr. Trinidad (Colo.) State Jr. Coll., 1947-53; counselor women, assoc. prof. edn. Western State Coll., Gunnison, Colo., 1953-54; instr., residence counselor Stephens Coll., Columbia, Mo., 1955-61. Active Salvation Army Aux. Mem. AAUW, Am. Assn. Ret. Persons (corr. sec. 1986-87), Kena Kampers Camping Club.

TURNER, ANN COFFEEN, educator; b. Evanston, Ill., Oct. 16, 1930; d. Carl Roy and Louise Glatz (Groser) Coffeen; m. Harvey Stewart Turner, Sept. 7, 1952; children: Catharine Whitford, Victoria Louise. BA, Cornell U., 1952; MAT, Seton Hall U., S. Orange, N.J., 1980; MA, Kean Coll., Union, N.J., 1984; cert. learning disabilities tchr., Montclair State Coll., 1985. Reading tchr. Pediatric Lang. Disorder Clinic/Columbia Med. Ctr., N.Y.C., 1955-57, Far Brook Sch., Short Hills, N.J., 1963-77, Gill St. Bernard's Sch., Bernardsville, N.J., 1978—. Singer, mem. chorus bd. Masterwork Chorus, Convent Station, N.J., 1982—. Cornell U. nat. scholar, 1948-52. Mem. Orton Dyslexia Soc., Kappa Delta Pi. Home: RD4 Mountainside Rd Mendham NJ 07945 Office: Gill St Bernards Sch PO Box 604 St Bernard's Rd Gladstone NJ 07934-0604

TURNER, ANNE HALLIGAN, chemist, spectroscopist; b. Columbus, Ohio, Feb. 3, 1941; d. William Thomas and Mary Louise (Clements) Halligan; m. Noel Hinton Turner, Aug. 13, 1966; children: Deborah Lynn, Laura Elizabeth. AB, Middlebury Coll., 1963; PhD, U. Rochester, 1969. Instr. Prince Georges Community Coll., Largo, Md., 1969-79; NMR lab. mgr. and instr. dept. chemistry Howard U., Washington, 1979—. Contbr. articles to profl. jours. Mem. Am. Chem. Soc., Chem. Soc. Washington, Iota Sigma Pi (treas. 1979-81, pres. 1981-82). Office: Howard U Dept Chemistry Washington DC 20059

TURNER, C. DENISE YARBROUGH, lawyer; b. Tulsa, May 23, 1956; d. John Floyd and Eileen Denise (Sheppard) Yarbrough; m. Robert W. Turner Jr., Oct. 9, 1982; children: Bonnie Lynne, Robert W. III. BA, Barnard Coll., 1978; JD, U. Mich., 1982. Bar: N.Y. 1983, N.J. 1984. Assoc. Shea and Gould, N.Y.C., 1982-84, Szold and Brandwen, P.C., N.Y.C., 1985-86; v.p., atty. corp. Young and Rubicam, Inc., N.Y.C., 1986—; bd. dirs., corp. sec. Damce Forum, Inc., N.Y., 1986-89. Vestry mem. Christ Ch., Glen Ridge, 1990—. Mem. Phi Beta Kappa. Democrat. Episcopalian. Home: 273 Baldwin St Glen Ridge NJ 07028 Office: Young & Rubicam Inc 285 Madison Ave New York NY 10017

TURNER, CHERI ANNE, financial executive; b. Spring City, Pa., Apr. 7, 1949; d. Harold William and Evelyn Virginia (Wagner) T. Student Syracuse U., 1967-69; Cert. Fin. Paraplanner, Coll. Fin. Planning, Denver, 1986. Pub. relations mediator Don Poindexter & Assocs., St. Petersburg, Fla., 1969-72; exec. sec. Honeywell Inc., Largo, Fla., 1972-75; sec., design coordinator SCM Design Ctr., Syracuse, N.Y., 1975-76; personnel dir. Jay Galbraith's Penthouse, St. Petersburg, 1977-79; cert. fin. paraplanner R. A. Siebern & Assocs., St. Petersburg, 1982-87, pres. C.A. Turner Services Inc., 1987— ; real estate sales rep. Corwin Realty Inc., St Petersburg 1988—; registered rep. gen. securities Mut. Benefit Fin. Service Co. Inc., Tampa, Fla., 1985—; music dir. Capt. Anderson Cruises, Clearwater, Fla., 1982-88; pres. CA Turner Services, Inc., Clearwater, Fla., 1987; pvt. practice music tchr., Largo, 1964—. Composer, illustrator children's music book: Ditties for Kiddies, 1980. Mem. Nat. Assn. Female Execs., Inst. Cert. Fin. Planners (soc. adminstr. 1988-89), Am. Soc. Notaries, Hospitality Industry Assn. Inc., Nat. Assn. Security Dealers, Internat. Assn. Reg. Fin. Planners, U.S. Figure Skating Assn. (preliminary test judge 1975—), Sun Coast Figure Skating Club. Avocations: figure skating, music, fishing, gemology, rock hounding. Office: CA Turner Svcs Inc 4161 103d Ave N Clearwater FL 34622

TURNER, CLAUDIA MARJORIE, corporate technical support executive; b. Summit, N.J., Oct. 28, 1939; d. Claude Swanson and Mary Marjorie (Whitfield) Finney; m. Samuel Hamilton Turner, Feb. 10, 1984; children: Gayle Lois Dotson, Gary William Dotson. BS, D.C. Tchrs. Coll., 1974; MEd, U. Md., College Park, 1981. Office mgr. Univ. Legal Services, Washington, 1969-1975; from asst. dir. continuing edn. to assoc. dean Strayer Coll., Washington, 1976-81; div. mgr. edn. Wang Labs., Inc., Bethesda, Md., 1982-86, div. support dir., 1986—; cons. World Bank, The Office, TRW Washington Group, South Western Pub. Co., Washington, 1978-84. Mem. continuing edn. adv. bd. U. D.C., 1985; advisor Washington area Upward Bound Program; v.p., sec. Plyers Mill Crossing Homeowners Assn., Silver Spring, Md.; mem. program com. March of Dimes. Named one of Outstanding Afro-Am. Bus. and Profl. Women Dollars and Sense Mag., 1990, one of 100 Best and Brightest Black Women in Corp. Am. Ebony Mag., 1990. Democrat. Baptist. Office: Wang Labs Inc 7500 Old Georgetown Rd Bethesda MD 20814

TURNER, DANA JOAN, insurance sales and marketing professional; b. N.Y.C., Dec. 8, 1956; d. Leonard and Ruth (Fine) Levin. BA in Psychology/Communication cum laude, Queens Coll., 1978. Account mgr. Speare and Co., Santa Monica, Calif.; mgr. employee benefits Grosslight, Inc., Los Angeles; account mgr., account exec. Martin J. Wolff and Co., Inc., Los Angeles; ins. specialist Fin. Design Group, Woodland Hills, Calif. Home: 10825 Blix St Toluca Lake CA 91602

TURNER, DENISE MICHELLE, educator; b. Yonkers, N.Y., Nov. 22, 1951; d. George Henry and Lillian Estelle (Crier) T. BA in Psychology, Manhattanville Coll., 1973; MA in Edn., NYU, 1974. Cert. elem. tchr., spl. edn. tchr., learning disabilities, N.Y. Tchr. Adult Edn. Program, Yonkers, 1973-74; tchr., tutor Graham Home for Children, Hastings, N.Y., 1974-77; counselor, tchr. Youth Employment Tng. Program, Yonkers, 1977-79; tchr., tutor Nepperhan Community Ctr., Yonkers, N.Y., 1980-81; tchr. Ednl. Opportunity Ctr., Yonkers, 1979-80; tchr. spl. edn. Yonkers Bd. Edn., 1974—; dir., supr., tchr. Community Meml. Ch. Tutorial Program, 1973-75; cons. Lifestyles Enterprise, Yonkers, 1987—; pres., counselor Deja Ltd. Inc., Yonkers, 1985—. Chmn. Westchester Women's Polit. Black Caucus, Yonkers, 1979; organizer voter registration drive, Westchester County, 1976-78; mem. Westchester Women's Polit. Caucus, 1989—. Recipient cert. of achievement City of Norwalk (Conn.), 1980, achievement award Womens Civic Club o Nepperhan Inc., Yonkers, 198l, Jenkins award Nat. PTA, 1989; NYU fellow, 1974. Mem. NEA, N.Y. State United Tchrs., Yonkers Fedn. Tchrs., Yonkers Assn. Minority Sch. Educators, Black Alumni Assn. Manhattanville Coll., Delta Sigma Theta. Clubs: Westside Polit., Christian Youth Fellowship (Yonkers) (bd. Christian edn. pres. 1973-75). Home: 380 N Broadway C-5 Yonkers NY 10701

TURNER, DORIS SEWELL, counselor; b. Memphis, Mar. 18, 1925; d. Oscar James and Lois Marie (Parke) Sewell; m. Max Wesley Turner, June 23, 1950 (dec. 1979). AB, U. Ill., 1946; MS, So. Ill. U., 1949. Counselor Stephen's Coll., Columbia, Mo., 1946-47; dean women So. Ill. U., Carbondale, Ill., 1947-49; staff, dean women U. Ill., Champaign, Ill., 1949-50; tchr., student tchr. supr. Pub. Schs., Champaign, Ill., 1950-55; from lectr., psychology dept. to acad. adv. So. Ill. U., Carbondale, Ill., 1956-83; mem. Nat. Acad. Advising Assn. (program com., 1979-83), So. Ill. U. Women's Studies Com. (chmn. Ccuuiculum Com., 1982-83), Carbondale (Ill.) Edn. Assn. (pres. 1954-55). Named A Regional Woman of So. Ill, Women's History Assn., Carbondale, Ill., 1983, grantee fellowship AAUW (Carbondale branch, 1975). Mem. AAUW, Ariz. LWV. Democrat. Presbyterian. Home: 3417 W St Moritz Phoenix AZ 85023

TURNER, DOROTHY BREMER, real estate company official; b. Danville, Ill.; d. J. Fred and Dorothy Eva (Hiskey) Bremer; m. Charles Preston, June 19, 1948 (div. 1964); children: Robert, Carol Preston Grassel, Lawrence; m. Dean H. Turner, Dec. 4, 1965. BS, U. Ill., 1946; postgrad., Nat. Coll., Evanston, Ill., 1967-68. Head Illini Ctr. U. Ill., Chgo., 1946-48; tchr. Middleton Sch., Skokie, Ill., 1948-50; real estate saleswoman Koenig & Strey, Wilmette, Ill., 1968-86; sales assoc. Prudential Preferred Property, Winnetka, Ill., 1986—. Pres. Wilmette Ctr. Infant Welfare Soc., Chgo.; bd. dirs. Interfaith, Sun City, Ariz. Mem. Million Dollar sales Club (life), Wilmette-Kenilworth Club (pres.). Republican. Methodist. Home: 3l15 Country Ln Wilmette IL 60091 Office: Prudential Preferred Property 586 Lincoln Ave Winnetka IL 60093

TURNER, E. VICTORIA, immunologist; b. Columbia, Mo., Jan. 23, 1946; d. M. Samuel and Dorothy M. (Holmes) Offutt; m. James Ethridge Turner, Aug. 27, 1966; children: Laura Elizabeth, Stephen James. BA with hons., U. Ark., 1967; PhD, U. Louisville, 1973. Faculty Spalding Coll., Louisville, 1972; rsch. asst. U. Louisville, 1973-74, postdoctoral rsch. assoc., 1974-78, adj. asst. prof., 1978-80; cons. Jewish Hosp., Louisville, 1977-80; dir. HLA lab. St. Jude Children's Rsch. Hosp., Memphis, 1983—. Mem. Am. Assn. Histocompatibility & Immunogenetics, S.E. Organ Procurement Found., Sigma Xi, Phi Beta Kappa, Phi Kappa Phi. Office: St Jude Childrens Hosp 332 N Lauderdale Memphis TN 38101

TURNER, ELIZABETH ADAMS NOBLE (BETTY TURNER), mayor, management consultant; b. Yonkers, N.Y., May 18, 1931; d. James Kendrick and Orrel (Baldwin) Noble; m. Jack Rice Turner, July 11, 1953; children: Jay Kendrick, Randall Ray. BA, Vassar Coll., 1953; MA, Tex. A&I U., 1964. Ednl. cons. Noble & Noble Pub. Co., N.Y.C., 1956-67; psychometrist Corpus Christi Guidance Ctr., 1967-70; psychologist Corpus Christi State Sch., 1970-72, dir. programs, 1972, dir. vol. svc., 1972-76, dir. rsch. and tng., 1977-79, psychologist Tex. Mental Health and Mental Retardation, 1970-79; program cons. Tex. Dept. Mental Health and Mental Retardation, dir. alumni Corpus Christi State U., 1976-77; coord. vols. Summer Head Start Program, Corpus Christi, 1967. Chmn. spl. gifts coml United Way, Corpus Christi, 1970; mem. Corpus Christi City Coun., 1979—; mayor pro tem Corpus Christi, 1981-85, mayor, 1987—; pres. Barnes and Noble, N.Y.C.; pres. Turner Co. Leadership, Corpus Christi, 1980—; founder Com. of 100 Goals for Corpus Christi; pres. USO; bd. dirs. Coastal Bends Coun. Govts., Corpus Christi Mus. Harbor Playhouse, Communities in Schs., Del Man Coll. Found., Food Bank; bd. govs. Southside Community Hosp., Admiral Tex. Navy; apptd. Gov.'s Commn. for Women, 1984-85, Leadership Tex. Class I; active Goals for Corpus Christi Bay Area Sports, Assn. Coastal Bend Mayor's Alliance, Mayor's Commn. on the Disabled, Mayor's Task Force on the Homeless. Recipient Love award YWCA, 1970, Y's Women and Men in Careers award, 1988, Commander's Award for Pub. Svc. U.S. Army, Scroll of Honor award Navy League, award Tex. Hwy. Dept., Road Hand award Tex. Hwy. Commn., 1989; named Newsmaker of Yr., 1987. Mem. Tex. Psychol. Assn. (pres., mem. exec. bd.), Psychol. Assos. (pres., founder), Tex. Mcpl. League (bd. dir.), Jr. League Corpus Christi, Tex. Bookman's Assn., Tex. Assn. Realtors, Kappa Kappa Gamma, Corpus Christi Country Club, Corpus Christi Yacht Club, Jr. Cotillion Club. Home: 4466 Ocean Dr Corpus Christi TX 78412

TURNER, GLORIA TOWNSEND BURKE, social services association executive; b. Lumberton, N.C., Nov. 16, 1938; d. John B. and Alice (Haite) Townsend; m. James Rae Burke, June 3, 1957 (dec. 1974); children: William H., Sonya Kyle; m. Robert R. Turner,June 23, 1977. Student, U. S.C., 1974; degree in nursing, York Tech. Coll./U. S.C., 1976. RN, S.C. Staff nurse, head nurse York Gen. Hosp., Rock Hill, S.C., 1976-78; head med. dept., indsl. nursing J.P. Stevens Plant, Rock Hill, 1976-78; hsop., nursing home auditor S.C. Med. Found., Columbia, 1978-79; exec. dir. Kershaw County Coun. on Aging, Camden, S.C., 1979—; bd. dirs. S.C. Fedn. Older Ams., 1988—; mem. state adv. com. on Alzheimers, Columbia, 1984—; trustee Kershaw County Meml. Hosp., Camden, 1989—. Mem. Camden C. of C. Methodist. Home: 1092 Pepper Ridge Lugoff SC 29078 Office: Kershaw County Coun Aging 906 Lyttleton St Camden SC 29020

TURNER, JANET SULLIVAN, painter; b. Gardiner, Maine, Nov. 15, 1935; d. Clayton Jefferson and Frances (Leighton) Sullivan; m. Terry Turner, Oct. 6, 1956; children: Lisa Turner Reid, Michael Ross, Jonathan Brett. BA cum laude, Mich. State U., 1956; Diploma in Painting, Haystack Mountain Sch. Arts and Crafts, Deer Isle, Maine, 1964. lectr. Student Cultural Exch. Program Pa. State U., Harrisburg, 1985; rep. Am. Women in Art, UN World Conf. on Women, Nairobi, Kenya, 1985; pres. Phila chpt. Artists Equity, 1987-88, Artists Equity newsletter, 1985-86, editor; newsletter editor 1985-87, pres. 1988-89. One-artist shows include San Diego Art Inst., 1971, Villanova (Pa.) U. Gallery, 1982, Pa. State U. Gallery, Middletown, 1985, Temple U. Gallery, 1986, Widener U. Art Mus., Chester, Pa., 1987, Suzanne Gross Gallery, Phila., 1986-89, Ariel Gallery Soho, N.Y.C., 1986-89; group shows include Del. Art Mus., Wilmington, 1978, Woodmere Art Mus., Phila., 1980, Port of History Museum, Phila., 1984, Allentown Art Mus., 1984, Trenton City Mus. Ellarslie Open VIII, Trenton, N.J., 1989, Gettysburg Coll., Ammo Gallery, Bklyn., 1989; represented in permanent collections Nat. Mus. Women in Arts, Washington, Mich. State U., East Lansing, ARA Services Inc., Phila., Blue Cross/Blue Shield, Phila, Am. Nat. Bank and Trust Co., Rockford, Ill., Burroughs Corp., Lisle, Ill.; contbg. writer and art critic Art Matters, Phila., 1987; artists of the 1990's series featured in Manhattan Arts mag., N.Y.C., 1990. Bd. dirs. Rittenhouse Sq. Fine Arts Ann., Phila., 1984-86. Recipient 2d pl. award San Diego Art Inst. 19th Ann. Exhbn., 1971. Mem. Artists' Equity (bd. dirs. 1985-86, 1st v.p. Phila. 1986-87, newsletter editor 1985-86, pres. 1987-88, honorable mention traveling exhbn. Stedman-Gallery 1985), Phila. Watercolor Club, Delta Phi Delta. Democrat. Roman Catholic. Home and Studio: 88 Cambridge Dr Glen Mills PA 19342

TURNER, JANICE MARIA, occupational therapist; b. Washington, Oct. 15, 1951; d. Alvin McShayne and Catherleen (Edwards) Harvey; m. Gary Harold Turner, Jan. 28, 1950; children: Gary Harold, Ashely Tiara. BS, U. LaVerne, 1973; MS, Western Mich. U., 1976. Staff therapist D.C. Gen. Hosp., Washington, 1976-78, chief therapist pre-vocat. evaluation, 1978-81; chief occupational therapy VA Med. Ctr., Washington, 1981-86; ind. contract therapist Washington, 1986—; contract therapist Vis. Nurses Assn., Washington, 1983—; cons. SunShine Multi-Service Inc., Washington, 1985-86; mem. admissions bd. occupational therapy Howard U., Washington, 1983-85. Mem. Capital View Bapt. Ch., Washington, 1961, PTA, Washington, 1986. Mem. Am. Occupational Therapy Assn., Arthritis Found. Allied Health (sec. 1977-80), D.C. Occupational Therapy Assn. (co-chairperson continuing edn. com. 1981-82). Democrat. Baptist. Home: 2927 W Street SE Washington DC 20020

TURNER, JENNY LEE, psychotherapist, consultant; b. Parkersburg, W.Va., Nov. 20, 1954; d. Raymond Lee and Rose Louise (Corra) T. BS in English Edn., U. Va., 1977; MEd in Clin. Counseling, The Citadel, 1986. Cert. English and sec. tchr., Va.; lic. profl. counselor, S.C.; lic. ind. social worker, S.C.; nat. cert. counselor. Tchr. English Pub. Schs., Virginia Beach, Va., 1977-78; social worker S.C. Dept. Social Svcs., Charleston, 1979-88; psychotherapist Anxiety and Stress Treatment Ctr., 1987-88; dir. Anxiety and Stress Counseling Ctr., Charleston, S.C., 1989—. Chair support svcs. Palmetto AIDS Life Support Svcs., Charleston, 1986-88. Named Vol. of Yr., Palmetto AIDS Life Support Svcs., 1988. Mem. Am. Assn. for Counseling and Devel., Chi Sigma Iota. Office: Anxiety/Stress Counseling PO Box 31133 Charleston SC 29407

TURNER, KAREN M., broadcast executive; b. Trenton, N.J., May 23, 1954; d. Arthur H. and Gloria (Scott) Turner. AB, Dartmouth Coll., 1976; JD, Northwestern U., 1979; MS, Columbia U., 1985. Staff dir. ABA, Chgo., 1980-84; intern Manhattan Community Bd. #7, N.Y.C., 1984-85, Newsweek mag., 1985, Greater Media, Inc., East Brunswick, N.J., 1985-86; news reporter, anchor Sta. WCTC, New Brunswick, N.J., 1986-87; news/pub. affairs dir. Sta. WIZF-FM, Cin., 1987-89; reporter, anchor, talk show host Sta. WPEN-AM, Phila., 1989—. Bd. dirs. Hyde Park-Kenwood Community Health Ctr., Chgo., 1983-84, NIA Comprehensive Ctr. for Devel. Disabilities, Chgo., 1982-84. RCA/NBC Broadcast fellow. Mem. Cook County Bar Assn., Dartmouth Alumni Council (exec. commn. Hanover, N.H. 1982-85), Dartmouth Black Alumni Assn. (sec. Hanover 1979-85, pres. 1989-92), Phila. Assn. Black Journalists, Greater Cin. Assn. Black Communicators (exec. com.), Nat. Black Assn. Journalists (founding), Greater Cin. Assn. Radio News Dirs. (founding), Phi Alpha Delta. Author: Reaching Out: Bringing Minority Lawyers Into the Fold; author, editor: Model Lawyers Guide to Legal Services, 1983; co-author: The Father of Black Aviation, Legal Self-Help is on the Way; editor: Lawyers See Yourselves as Others See You: Feasibility Study on Institutional Advertising, 1984, Everybody's mag.

TURNER, KATHLEEN, actress; b. Springfield, Mo., June 19, 1954; m. Jay Weiss, 1984; 1 child, Rachel Ann. Student, Cen. Sch. of Speech and Drama, London, Southwest Mo. State U.; M.F.A., U. Md. Various theater roles, Broadway debut: Gemini, 1978, Cat on a Hot Tin Roof, 1990; appeared in TV series The Doctors, 1977; films include Body Heat, 1981, The Man With Two Brains, 1983, Crimes of Passion, 1984, Romancing the Stone, 1984, Prizzi's Honor, 1985, The Jewel of the Nile, 1985, Peggy Sue Got Married, (D.W. Griffith award for best actress) 1986, Julia and Julia, 1988, Switching Channels, 1988, Accidental Tourist, 1988, The War of the Roses, 1989. Office: care Gersh Agy Inc 222 N Canon Dr Beverly Hills CA 90210*

TURNER, L. ALDORA, secondary educator; b. Richmond, Va., Mar. 11, 1939; d. Oakley Julius and Bessie Baker (Easley) Greene; m. Clinton V. Turner, Dec. 21, 1968; children: Clinton V., Michael. BS, St. Paul's Coll., Lawrenceville, Va., 1962; postgrad., U. Va., 1965, James Madison Coll., Harrisburg, Va., 1074, Va. Commonwealth U., others. Cert. coll. profl. Tchr., dept. head Halifax County Sch. Bd., Halifax, Va., prin., tchr.; tchr., guidance asst. Culpeper County Sch. Bd., Culpeper, Va.; coop. office edn. coord. Richmond Pub. Schs. Sponsor, Future Bus. Leaders Am. Recipient Jefferson award, 1985, numerous others. Mem. NEA, Richmond Edn. Assn., So. Bus. Edn. Assn., Am. Vocat. Assn., Va. Vocat. Assn., Assn. for Supervision and Curriculum Devel. Home: 3000 Kenmore Rd Richmond VA 23225 Office: John F Kennedy High Sch 2300 Cool Ln Richmond VA 23223

TURNER, LAURA SMITH, enrolled agent; b. Dallas, Tex., May 17, 1955; d. Charles Clinton and Louise (Gartman) Smith; m. Blake S. Turner, Sept. 7, 1984. Student history, fgn. langs, U. Tex., 1973-79; student, Edinburgh U., Edinburgh, Scotland, 1975-76; student acctg., Austin Community Coll., 1988—. Owner Bookkeeping & Tax Svc., Marble Falls, Tex., 1983—. Author: Articles, The Ledger 1988. Bd. dirs., treas. Family Crisis Ctr., 1990—. Mem. TAPA (past pres. Capital Area chpt., Austin dist. IRS/practitioner liaison com., mem. edn. com., chpt. pres. of yr. 1989, chair publs. com. 1990—, editor The Ledger 1990—), Nat. Soc. Pub. Accts., Nat. Assn. Tax Practitioners. Office: Commonsense 700 East Highway 1431 Marble Falls TX 78654

TURNER, LAWALTA DEAN, education educator; b. Clarksdale, Mo., July 31, 1941; d. Harry Delmar and Helen Norine (West) Heyde; m. Darrell E. Class, May 31, 1964 (div. 1981); 1 child, Heyde Faye; m. Kenneth Duane Turner, Aug. 28, 1982; stepchildren: Mauricia, Scott. BS in Edn., U. Kans., 1964. Educator Detroit Pub. Sch., 1964-66, Palatine (Ill.) Rolling Meadows Pub. Sch., 1966-71, Dodge City (Kans.) Pub. Sch., 1971-73, Enid (Okla.) Pub. Sch., 1974—. Author: Gifted and Talented Curriculum Guide Kindergarten to 3rd Grade, 1984, Outdoor Education, 1976. Mem. LWV. Grantee Soil Conservation Svc., 1975-78. Mem. Nat. Edn. Assn., Okla. Edn. Assn., Enid Edn. Assn., Delta Kappa Gamma, Beta Sigma Phi. Democrat.

TURNER, LILLIAN ERNA, nurse; b. Coalmont, Colo., Apr. 22, 1918; d. Harvey Oliver and Erna Lena (Wackwitz) T. BS, Colo. State U., 1940, Columbia U., 1945; cert. physician asst., U. Utah, 1978. Commd. 2d lt. Nurse Corps, U.S. Army, 1945; advanced through grades to lt. comdr. USPHS, 1964; dean of women U. Alaska, Fairbanks, 1948-50; head nurse Group Health Hosp., Seattle, 1950-53; adviser to chief nurse Hosp. Am. Samoa, Pago Pago, 1954-60; head nurse Meml. Hosp., Twin Falls, Idaho, 1960-61; shift supr. Hosp. Lago Oil and Transport, Siero Colorado, Aruba, 1961-63; chief nurse, advisor Truk Hosp., Moen, Ea. Caroline Islands, 1964; nurse advisor Children's Med. Relief Internat., South Vietnam, 1967-76; physician's asst. U. Utah, 1976-78, Wagon Circle Med. Clinic, Rawlins, Wyo., 1978-89, Energy Basin Clinic Carbon County Meml. Hosp., Hanna, Wyo., 1989—. Mem. Wyo. Acad. Physician Assts. (bd. dirs. 1982—), Am. Acad. Physician Assts., Nat. Assn. Physician Assts. Home: PO Box 337 Hanna WY 82327

TURNER, LISA PHILLIPS, marketing executive; b. Waltham, Mass., Apr. 10, 1951; d. James Sinclair and Virginia (Heathcote) T. BA in Edn. and Philosophy magna cum laude, Washington Coll., Chestertown, Md., 1974; AS in Electronics Tech., AA in Engring., Palm Beach Jr. Coll., 1982; MBA, Nova U., 1986, DSc, 1989; PhD, Kennedy Western U., 1990, Kennedy Western U., 1990. Cert. pers. adminstr., quality engr., human resource profl.; lic. USCG capt. Founder, pres. Turner's Bicycle Svc., Inc., Delray Beach, Fla., 1975-80; electronics engr., quality engr. Audio Engring. and Video Arts, Boca Raton, 1980-81; tech. writing instr. Palm Beach Jr. Coll., Lake Worth, Fla., 1981-82; adminstr. tng. and devel. Mitel Inc., Boca Raton, 1982-88; mgr. communications and employee rels. Modular Computer Systems, Inc., Ft. Lauderdale, Fla., 1988-89; corp. communications mgr. Modular Computer Systems, Inc., Ft. Lauderdale, 1989-90; U.S. mktg. project mgr. Mitel, Inc., Boca Raton, Fla., 1990—. With USCG Aux. Mem. Am. Soc. for Pers. Adminstrn., Am. Soc. Tng. and Devel., Internat. Assn. Quality Circles, Am. Soc. Quality Control, Fla. Employment Mgmt. Assn., Am. Acad. Mgmt., Employment Assn. Fla., Am. Capts. Assn. Home: 2027 SW 12th Ct Delray Beach FL 33445-6206 Office: Mitel Inc 5400 Broken Sound Blvd NW Boca Raton FL 33437

TURNER, LISA SUZANNE, dental society administrator; b. Ventura, Calif., Apr. 12, 1962; d. Robert Elam and Caroline (Jackson) Turner; 1 child, Jennifer Morgan. Student, Ventura Coll. Registered dental asst. Dental asst. Dr. Robert Turner, Oxnard, Calif., 1979-85; small claims cons. Ventura, 1981-86; adminstrv. asst. Santa Barbara, Uta County Dental Soc., Ventura, 1986—; mgr., ptnr. Cal-Coast Constrn. Co., Ventura, 1988—. Vol. Oxnard Police Dept. Olympics, 1989. Mem. Bus. and Profl. Women, Ventura County Contractor's Assn. Republican. Seventh Day Adventist. Home: 1185 Pittsfield Ln Ventura CA 93001 Office: Santa Barbara Dental Soc 1607 E Thompson Blvd Ventura CA 93001

TURNER, LOUISA ALINE, psychologist; b. Newport, R.I., Oct. 21, 1953; d. Clyde Templeton and Aline Louisa (Stouse) T. BA in psychology, SUNY, Geneseo, 1976; PhD in psychology, SUNY, Buffalo, 1987. Lic. clin. psychologist, Ohio. Asst. prof. psychology Case Western Res. U. Sch. of Medicine Dept. Psychiatry, Cleve., 1987—; co dir. CWRU Gender Identity Clinic, Cleve. Contbr. articles to numerous profl. jours. Woodburn fellow State of N.Y., 1978-81. Mem. Am. Psychol. Assn., Soc. for Sex Therapy and Rsch. (at-large mem. 1990—), Harry Benjamin Internat. Gender Dysphoria Assn. (sec. 1987-89). Office: Ctr for Human Sexuality 11400 Euclid Ave Cleveland OH 44106

TURNER, LYNNE, small business owner; b. Leavenworth, Kans., Sept. 27, 1943; d. Robert Correll and Hazel Elizabeth (Barnes) T. BA, Whitman Coll., Walla Walla, 1965; MFA, Mills Coll., Oakland, 1970. Tchr. Instr., program coord. Chabot Coll., Hayward, Calif., 1973-87; instr. Ohlone Coll., Fremont, Calif., 1975-80; owner, artist Quicksilver Pottery Studio, Berkeley, Calif., 1979—. Crafts Project grantee Nat. Endowment for Arts, Washington, 1980-81; Recipient First Place Purchase award Hayward Area Festival, 1979, W.E. Mushet Co. award Assn. of San Francisco Potters, 1979. Mem. West Berkeley Area Plan Com., 1985. Democrat. Home and Office: 225 Clifton St #108 Oakland CA 94618

TURNER, MARTA DAWN, youth program specialist; b. Morgantown, W.V., Oct. 7, 1954; d. Trubie Lemard and Dorothy Genevieve (Helmick) T.; m. David Michael Dunning, Mar. 1, 1980. Student, Royal Acad. Dramatic Art, London, 1975; BA with honors, Chatham Coll., 1976; grad. cert. in arts adminstrn., Adelphi U., 1982; MA Devel. Drama, Hunter Coll., 1988. Cert. video prodn. specialist. Asst. dir. Riverside Communications, N.Y.C., 1985-88; dir. drama, video youth environ. group Water Proof, Cornell Coop. Extension, 1989—. Exec. producer video projects including Hispanic City Sounds, Time for Peace, Home, Home In Inwood, 1985—; asst. dir./dir. video series Riverside at Worship, 1985-88. Bd. dirs. Trinity Presbyn. Ch., N.Y.C, 1980—; mem. Am. Diabetes Assn. Mem. Am. Assn. Theatre Edn., W.Va. Soc. N.Y.C. (bd. dirs. 1986-87). Home: 540 W 55th St #6V New York NY 10019 Office: Cornell Coop Extension 4-H Youth Devel 1360 Fulton St Rm 515 Brooklyn NY 11216

TURNER, MARY LOUISE, computer specialist; b. Glens Falls, N.Y., June 24, 1954; d. Gilmore Eldridge and Joan (Ringrose) T. AAS, Adriondack Community Coll., Glens Falls, 1974. Computer operator Glens Falls Nat. Bank & Trust Co., 1974-89; computer specialist Ace Rent A Car, Newport News, Va., 1989—; refreshment mgr. Lake George Opera Festival, Glens Falls, summer 1974. Author: (novel) Today Begins Tomorrow, 1986; (poetry) Why Me, 1983, Auf Wiedersehen, 1988, Jealousy (poetry), 1988, You've Got To Be Kidding (poetry), 1988, What If Time Stood Still (poetry), 1989. Republican. Home: 372A Circuit Ln Newport News VA 23602

TURNER, MELANIE ANN, horticulturist; b. Houston, May 13, 1957; d. Wayland Byron and Martha Ann (Brown) T. BS in Biology, Tex. A&M U., 1979, Master, 1980, PhD in Horticulture, 1984. Rsch. technician USDA, Coll. Sta., Tex., 1979-80; rsch. asst. Tex. Agrl. Extension Svc., Coll. Sta., 1980; teaching asst. Tex. A&M U., Coll. Sta., 1981-83; sales rep. W.R. Grace & Co., Dallas, 1984-86, br. mgr., 1986-89; ter. mgr. Grace-Sierra, Richardson, Tex., 1990—. Contbr. articles to profl. jours. Mem. Profl. Plant Growers Assn., Am. Soc. Horticultural Sci. Republican. Home: PO Box 1351 Lewisville TX 75067

TURNER, NANCY ELIZABETH, artist, designer; b. Cumberland Mountains, Ky., Sept. 7, 1955; d. Earl K. and Mary Lee (Jones) T.; m. Peter Alvet, Mar. 31, 1989. BA in Liberal Arts, U. Southwestern La.; Master Painter and Restorer, Yelland Acad. Fine Art, Calif.; cert. completion, Interior Decorators Inst. of L.A., 1990. Owner, chmn. The Turner Studio, Los Angeles; head artist/designer The Art Connection, Beverly Hills, Calif. Work includes fine paintings, artwork and decorative svcs. for residential and comml. interiors, trompe l'oeil murals, hand painted furniture and standing screens; creator bestselling collector's plates Michael's Miracle, 1982, Susan's World, 1983. Leader nat. multi-ch. religious freedom crusade, 1985-86. Winner Lithograph of Yr. award, 1982. Mem. Am. Inst. Fine Arts, Am. Soc. Interior Designers (accessorizing cons.). Address: 270 N Canon Dr #1433 Beverly Hills CA 90210

TURNER, PAMELA WALKER, retired educational administrator; b. Montgomery, Ala., July 28, 1943; d. Frederick J. and Yvonne L.B. (Chaplin) Walker; m. F. Cort Turner III, Oct. 19, 1968; children: Frederica Chaplin, F. Cort IV. BA in Econs., Wellesley Coll., 1965; S.M. in Mgmt., Sloan Sch., MIT, 1971. Cons. energy econs. Arthur D. Little, Inc., Cambridge, 1965-67; mem. corp. orgn.-info. staff, dept. mgr. mktg. div. Soc. Nationale de Siderurgie, Algiers, Algeria, 1970-72; dir. recruitment and placement, Sloan Sch. Mgmt., M.I.T., 1975-79, mgr. accelerated master's program, 1978-79, dir. external rels., 1979-82, lectr. in mgmt., 1978-82; cons. in field. Treas., Buckingham, Browne & Nichols Parents Assn., P.A., 1984-86; bd. dirs., treas., 1984-88; bd. dirs. Ten Ten Meml. Dr. Corp., 1984-89; bd. dirs., treas. Hospice of Cambridge, 1989—. Mem. Wellesley Coll. (Boston) Club, Longwood Cricket Club, Cambridge Skating Club (pres. 1983—), Badminton and Tennis Club. Address: 4 Fayerweather St Cambridge MA 02138

TURNER, PATRICIA BUSBY WHITNEY, city government and cultural organization administrator; b. Chgo., Sept. 25, 1923; d. Percy Shelley Busby and Vivian Richardson; m. Daniel Rockefeller Whitney, July 19, 1944 (dec. 1952); m. Admiral Stansfield Turner, Dec. 23, 1953 (div. 1984); children: Laurel Armbuster, Geoffrey Whitney Turner. Student, Northwestern U, 1941-44, U. Hawaii, 1959-60. Docent, tchr. Muses Prog. in Grade Sch., Sedona, Ariz., 1986-89; Indian story teller Muses, Primary Sch. Classes, Sedona, 1986-89; art instr. Art Reach (subs. Sedona Arts and Cultural Commn.), 1988—. City Councilman 1st city coun., Sedona, 1988; 1st city clk. newly inc. city established city govt. mechanisms, 1988; founding chmn. Sedona's Arts and Cultural commn.; founding bd. mem., sec. Red Rock Arts Coun., 1990. Mem. Muses (Support Group for Mus. N. Ariz. pres. 1987-88), Sedona Arts Ctr. Arts and Craftsmens Guild (sec. 1985-87). Democrat. Christian. Home: 90 Yavapai Tr Sedona AZ 86336 Office: Sedona Arts and Cultural Commn PO Box 30002 Sedona AZ 86336

TURNER, PHYLLIS IRENE, business executive; b. Walker, Minn., Aug. 10, 1935; d. Lewis Edward and Ethel Irene (Marx) Wilson; m. Ralph James Turner, Feb. 25, 1956; children: Sage Russell, Theresa Dawn, Rosalind, Ruth, Alys Renee. BA, U. Ariz., 1971. Newsletter editor Pima Assn. Govts., Tucson, 1972-73; tech. editor Kaiser Permanente Health Svcs. Rsch. Ctr., Portland, Oreg., 1973-78; news editor The Sun, Sheridan, Oreg., 1979-84; asst. to antiquarian bookdealer Phillip J. Pirages Fine Books, McMinnville, Oreg., 1985—. Vice pres. Sheridan Woman's Study Club, 1986-88, pres. 1988-90; sec. Rock Creek Road Community Club, Sheridan, 1987—. Oreg. Newspaper Pubs. Assn. Wendell Webb fellow U. Oreg. Sch. Journalism, 1984. Office: Phillip J Pirages Fine Book 965 W 11th St McMinnville OR 97128

TURNER, RUTH ELAINE, librarian, educator; b. Kaysville, Utah, July 28, 1922; d. Walter Scott and Mabel Ella (Holt) T. BS in English cum laude, Weber State Coll., 1965; MLS, Brigham Young U., 1969. Acquisitions libr. Weber State Coll., Ogden, Utah, 1965-69, social sci. and reference libr., 1969-70, head social sci. and gen. coll. libr., 1970-71, govt. documents libr., 1971-72, head govt. documents and periodical libr., 1972-75, head pub. svcs., 1975-79, head govt. documents dept., 1979-88, faculty emeritus, 1988—; ret., 1988; Nat. com. mem. Govt. Documents Round Table, ALA, 1972, 78, 80, 82, asst. coordinator, 1975-77, coordinator, 1977-78; active Govt. Docs Round Table, Utah Liberation Assn. Contbr. articles to profl. jours. Participant Utah Women: Artists Exhibition Com., Utah Div. AAUW, 1988-89, co-chmn., 1989-91; pres. Am. Cancer Soc., Kaysville, Fruit Heights, Utah, 1987. Recipient grants, Weber State Coll., 1980-85. Mem. AAUW (pres. Kaysville br. 1985-87, 89-91, program v.p. Utah div. 1987-89, Ogden br. 1972-74), Athena Club (pres. 1989-90, treas. 1985-86, 87-88), Lambda Iota Tau, Phi Beta Mu. Home: 261 South 300 West Kaysville UT 84037

TURNER, SALLY ANN, veterinarian; b. South Bend, Ind., Oct. 30, 1934; d. Charles and Mary Roma (Olmstead) Etter; (div. Feb. 1983); children: Steven, Mary. BS, Mich. State U., 1956, D in Vet. Med., 1958. Pvt. practice, Battle Creek, Mich., 1960—. Trustee Battle Creek Bd. Edn., 1982, pres., 1989-90. Mem. Calhoun County Vet. Assn. (pres. 1980-82), Mich. Vet. Med. Assn. (pres. 1952), Am. Vet. Assn. (pres. 1952--), Am. Animal Hosp. Assn. (1952--). Home: 3070 W Michigan Ave Battle Creek MI 49017 Office: Turner Vet Clinic 3070 W Michigan Ave Battle Creek MI 49017

TURNER, SANDRA STEPHENS, publisher, writer; b. Oneida, Tenn., Aug. 21, 1945; d. Ray and Gladys (Tinch) Stephens; m. Kenneth Leon Turner, June 28, 1975; 1 child, Erin Lee. BA in Liberal Arts, U. Tenn., 1965, MS in Communications, 1974. Reporter Herald-Citizen, Cookeville, Tenn., 1966, Tennessean, Nashville, 1966-67; tchr. York Inst., Jamestown, Tenn., 1967-69, Clarkrange (Tenn.) High Sch., 1971, 73; editor Campbell County Times, LaFollette, Tenn., 1972; writer, editor TVA, Chattanooga, 1974-78; publisher, editor Singles Scene, Crossville, Tenn., 1981—. Contbr. articles to various jours. Home and Office: PO Box 310 Crossville TN 38555

TURNER, SHEILA GAYE, federal agency official; b. Bklyn., Feb. 23, 1949; d. William and Betty Louise (Lindsey) T.; m. Alonzo Cartlidge, Mar. 27, 1988. BS, N.Y. Inst. Tech., 1970; MS, L.I. U., 1977. With IRS, N.Y., 1971—; group mgr. examination IRS, N.Y.C., 1982-84, chief examination br., 1984, staff asst. appeals, 1984-85; assoc. chief appeals IRS, Long Island, N.Y., 1985-88; asst. chief appeals IRS, N.Y.C., 1988—. Mem. NAFE, Federally Employed Women (fundraising chair, pres. 1982-85). Democrat. Roman Catholic. Office: IRS 90 Church St New York NY 10008

TURNER, TAMARA ADELE, medical librarian; b. Seattle, Mar. 27, 1940; d. Fredrick Patrick and Florence Elfreda (Puntenney) T. B.A., U. Wash., 1972, M.L.S., 1974. Staff librarian Rainier Sch., Wash. State Library, Buckley, 1974-77; dir. med. library Children's Hosp. and Med. Ctr., Seattle, 1977—. U.S. Dept. Edn. fellow, 1973-74. Mem. Wash. Med. Librarians Assn., Seattle Area Hosp. Library Consortium (pres. 1980), Med. Library Assn., Am. Soc. Info. Sci. (pres. Pacific northwest chpt. 1987-88). Home: 1931 E Calhoun Seattle WA 98112 Office: Childrens Hosp and Med Ctr PO Box 5371 Seattle WA 98105

TURNER, TINA (ANNA MAE BULLOCK), singer; b. Brownsville, Tenn., Nov. 26, 1939; m. Ike Turner, 1956 (div. 1978); children: Craig, Ike Jr., Michael, Ronald. Singer with Ike Turner Kings of Rhythm, and Ike and Tina Turner Revue; appeared in films: Gimme Shelter, 1970, Soul to Soul, 1971, Tommy, 1975, Mad Max Beyond Thunderdome, 1985; concert tours of Europe, 1966, Japan and Africa, 1971; albums with Ike Turner include Hunter, 1970, Ike and Tina Show II, Ike and Tina Show, 1966, Ike and Tina Turner, Bad Dreams, 1973, solo albums include Let Me Touch Your Mind, 1972, Tina Turns the Country On, 1974, Rough, 1978, Airwaves, 1979, Private Dancer, 1984, Break Every Rule, 1986, Foreign Affair, 1989; performed with USA for Africa on song We are The World, 1985. Recipient Grammy award, 1972, 85 (three), 86. Address: care Roger Davies Mgmt 3575 Cahuenga Blvd W Los Angeles CA 90068*

TURNIPSEED, PAMELA JEAN, insurance company executive; b. Lake Arrowhead, Calif., Mar. 28, 1947; d. Robert Earl and Dean Ann (Pitcher) T. BA, U. Calif., Santa Barbara, 1970. Claims adjuster Allstate Ins. Co., Los Angeles, 1970-74; claims mgr. Allstate Ins. Co., Honolulu, 1974-78, Tucson, 1978-79, Las Vegas, 1979-81, San Diego, 1981-83, Santa Ana, Calif., 1983-86; pres., chief exec. officer Creative Settlements, Honolulu, 1986—; mgmt. cons. Peak Performance Systems, HonoluLu, 1986—. Mem. NAFE, Nat. Assn. Life Underwriters, Am. Bus. Women's Assn. Office: Creative Settlements 212 Merchant St Ste 229 Honolulu HI 96813

TURNLUND, JUDITH RAE, nutrition scientist; b. St. Paul, Sept. 28, 1936; d. Victor Emanuel and Vida Mae (Priddy) Hanson; m. Richard W. Turnlund, Nov. 9, 1957; children: Michael Wayne, Mark Richard, Todd Hanson. BS in Chemistry and Psychology, Gustavus Adolphus Coll., 1958; PhD in Nutrition, U. Calif., Berkeley, 1978. Postdoctoral fellow U. Calif., Berkeley, 1978-80, vis. lectr., 1984-89; research nutritionist Western Regional Research Ctr., USDA, Albany, Calif., 1980-84, Western Human Nutrition Research Ctr., USDA, Albany, 1984—; vis. asst. prof. Am. U., Beirut, 1989, 90; adj. assoc. prof., U. Calif., Berkeley, 1989—. Editor: Stable Isotpes in Nutrition, 1984; contbr. articles to profl jours. Recipient Disting. Alumni citation Gustavus Adolphus Coll., 1988; grantee USDA, 1980, 82, 84, 85, Nat. Dairy Council, 1986. Mem. Am. Inst. Nutrition (chmn. adv. bd. Nutrition Notes, 1985-86), Am. Soc. Clin. Nutrition, Am. Chem Soc. (sec.-treas. nutrition sect. 1982-83), Am. Dietetics Assn. Home: 2276 Great Highway San Francisco CA 94116-1555 Office: USDA/ARS Western Human Nutrition Rsch Ctr PO Box 29997 Presidio of San Francisco San Francisco CA 94129

TUROCK, BETTY JANE, information scientist, educator; b. Scranton, Pa., June 12; d. David and Ruth Carolyn (Sweetser) Argust; B.A. magna cum laude (Charles Weston scholar), Syracuse U., 1955; postgrad. (scholar) U. Pa., 1956; M.L.S., Rutgers U., 1970, Ph.D., 1981; m. Frank M. Turock, June 16, 1956; children: David L., B. Drew. Library and materials coordinator Holmdel (N.J.) Public Schs., 1963-65; story-teller Wheaton (Ill.) Public Library, 1965-67; ednl. media specialist Alhambra Public Sch., Phoenix, 1967-70; br. librarian, area librarian, head extension service Forsyth County Public Library System, Winston-Salem, N.C., 1970-73; asst. dir. Montclair (N.J.) Public Library, 1973-75, dir., 1975-77; asst. dir. Monroe County Library System, Rochester, N.Y., 1978-81; asst. prof. Rutgers U. Grad. Sch. Communications, Info. and Library Studies, 1981-87, assoc. prof. 1987—, dept. chair, 1989—, dir. M.L.S. program, 1990—; dir. Grass Roots, Inc., Montclair, 1974—; vis. prof. Rutgers U. Grad. Sch. Library and Info. Studies, 1980-81. Trustee, Raritan Twp. (N.J.) Public Library, 1961-62; mem. Bd. Edn. Raritan Twp., 1962-66; mem. Title VII Adv. Bd., Montclair Public Schs., 1975-77; ALA mem. coordinating council Task Force on Women, 1978-84; treas. Social Responsibilities Round Table, 1978—. Named Woman of Yr., Raritan-Holmdel Woman's Club, 1975. Mem. ALA (councilor 1984—), Public Library Assn., NOW, Rutgers U. Grad. Sch. Library and Info. Studies Alumni Assn. (pres. 1977-78), Phi Theta Kappa, Psi Chi, Beta Phi Mu, Pi Beta Phi. Unitarian. Author: Serving Older Adults, 1983; editor: The Bottom Line, 1984—; contbr. articles to profl. jours. Home: 11 Undercliff Rd Montclair NJ 07042 Office: Rutgers U 4 Huntington St New Brunswick NJ 08903

TUROCK, JANE PARSICK, nutritionist; b. Peckville, Pa., Apr. 15, 1947; d. Paul Charles and Elizabeth Dorothy (Mistysyn) Parsick; m. Michael John, July 12, 1968; children: Eric Matthew, Nathan Andrew, J. Seth, Melanie Kay. BS, Marywood Coll., Scranton, 1969; MS, Marywood Coll., 1982. Registered Dietitian. Registered dietitian Jane P. Turock, Scranton, Pa., 1985--; founder and chief dietitian Gastric Bubble, Scranton, Pa., 1986--; prof. Penn State Coll., Scranton, Pa., 1987--; dir. & chief Dietitian Northeast Fitness Spa, Moosic, Pa.; dietitian & presenter WNEP TV Healthwatch, Avoca, Pa., 1988--; dir. & chief dietitian Vascular Inst. of Northeast Pa., Pa., 1989--; cons. Home Health Care Assn., Clarkes Summit, 1985--; dietitian Clarks Summit, 1985--. Treas. Lackawanna County Med. Soc. Auxiliary, 1974-76; Pres. Lackawanna County Med. Soc. Auxiliary, 1979-80; Bd. dir. Lackawanna County Med. Soc. Auxiliary, 1980-81. Mem. Am. Dietic Assn., Northeast Dist. Pa. Dietic Diet Therapy, Consultng Nutritionists in Pvt. Practice, Am. Diabetic Assn. Republican. Roman Catholic. Office: Jane P Turock MS RD 381 North Ninth St Scranton PA 18504

TUROFF, DEBORAH DRYDEN, printing company official, councilwoman; b. Springfield, Mass., July 22, 1944; d. James Murray and Gloria Rebecca (Johnson) Dryden; m. Stuart James Turoff, Nov. 19, 1966 (dec. Aug. 1983); children: Beth, Tammy, Jamey. BA in Psychology, Ohio State U., 1966. Caseworker Franklin County Welfare Dept., Columbus, Ohio, 1966-68; social worker Richland County Welfare Dept., Mansfield, Ohio, 1968-69; instr. cooking and sewing Sears & Roebeck Co., Mansfield, 1971-81; instr. sewing Stretch & Sew, Mansfield, 1980-82; psychiat. social worker Linn Ctr., Norwalk, Ohio, 1984-86; customer svc. rep. R.R. Donnelley & Sons, Willard, Ohio, 1986—. Mem. Willard City Coun., 1978—, pres., 1983—; sec. Huron County Econ. Coun., 1982-86; mem. City Devel. Commn., Willard, 1983—. Named Woman of Yr., Mansfield News Jour., 1980. Republican. Episcopalian. Home: 330 E Howard St Willard OH 44890 Office: Donnelley & Sons 1145 Conwell St Willard OH 44890

TUSA, KATHRYN SMITH, lawyer; b. Newton, N.J., Aug. 22, 1958; d. Robert Blakeslee and Dolly Mae (Mayberry); m. Robert Paul, May 26, 1984; 1 child, Samantha Marie. BA, Wilson Coll., Chambersburg, 1980; JD, U. Bridgeport, 1984. Lawyer. Claims adjuster Amerisure, Jericho, N.Y., 1985; atty. J. Milfred Hull, P.C., Smithtown, N.Y., 1986-89, Flower and Plotka Esqs., Bay Shore, N.Y., 1990—. Recipient Law Review U. Bridgeport, 1983. Mem. N.Y. Bar Assn., Suffolk County Bar Assn., Suffolk County Women's Bar Assn., Legal Services Club, Bus. Profls. & Bus. Women's Assn. Republican. Office: Flower and Plotka Esqs 24 E Main St PO Box P430 Bay Shore NY 11706

TUTAK, VICTORIA MARY, chiropractic doctor; b. Dearborn, Mich., Dec. 10, 1955; d. Walter J. and Victoria (Sawaya) Gorney; m. Dean. R. Tutak, Mar. 21, 1976 (div. 1980); 1 child, Dean Kalon Gorney-Tutak; m. Alvie J. Farley, June 3, 1989. BS, Wayne State U., 1979; D of Chiropractic, Los Angeles Sch. Chiropractic, 1987. Diplomate of Am. Bd. Orthopedics. Funeral dir. South Field (Mich.) Funeral Home, 1976-77; intern Clin. Internship, Whittier, Ga., 1986-87; doctor, owner South Lane Chiropractic, Cottage Grove, Oreg., 1988—. Contbr. articles to newspapers. Mem. Lane County Drug Abuse Council, Cottage Grove, 1989. Mem. Am. Chiropractic Assn., Oreg. Chiropractic Assn., Calif. Chiropractic Assn., Am. Pub. Health Assn., Lions Club (Cottage Grove). Home and Office: South Lane Chiropractic 145 Hwy 99 S Cottage Grove OR 97424

TUTELMAN, JACKI DEENA, textile company executive, consultant; b. Roslyn, N.Y., Nov. 14, 1954; d. Paul and Elaine (Kligman) T. BS in Mass Communications, Emerson Coll., Boston, 1976. Group buyer European and Am. designer collections for women Bloomingdale's, 1976-86; v.p. Jakob Schlaepfer, Inc., St. Gallen, Switzerland, N.Y.C., 1986—. Mem. Fashion Group, Emerson Coll. Alumni Assn.

TUTINO, ROSALIE JACQUELINE, college administrator; b. Bklyn., Dec. 28, 1937; d. Peter Rocco and Rose (Oliva) T. BA, St. Joseph's Coll., 1959; MA, NYU, 1964. Licensed ins. broker, N.Y. Publ., annuity mgr. Equitable Life Assurance, N.Y.C., 1959-62; instr., dept. chmn. Our Lady Perpetual Help High Sch., Bklyn., 1962-70; dir. coll. relations St. Joseph's Coll., Bklyn., 1970-75, devel. and coll. rels. dir., 1975-77, v.p. devel. and coll. rels., 1977—; pres. Rosalie Tutino Assn., Bklyn., 1980—. Bd. dirs. Suffolk coun. Boy Scouts Am., 1988—, Suffolk Coun., 1988—. Mem. L.I. Coalition for Fair Broadcasting (bd. dirs.), Nat. Soc. Fundraising Execs., Pub. Rels. Soc. Am., L.I. Assn., CASE. Republican. Roman Catholic. Home: 49 Romana Dr Hampton Bays NY 11946 Office: Saint Josephs Coll 155 Roe Blvd Patchogue NY 11772

TUTT, GLORIA J. RUTHERFORD, insurance company executive; b. Texarkana, Ark., Sept. 1, 1945; d. William Thomas and Lois Elizabeth (Vic) Rutherford; m. F. David Tutt, Nov. 27, 1964; children: David Wayne, Danny Ray, Darryl Wilson. Student, Texarkana Jr. Coll., 1962-63. Agy. adminstr. Nat. Found. Life Ins., Oklahoma City, 1973-77; office mgr. NFC Assocs., Little Rock, 1977-78; owner, corp. sec. So. Capitol Enterprises, Baton Rouge, 1980—; exec. sec. Ins. Mgmt. & Assocs., 1989—; exec. v.p., chief oper. officer Southern Capitol Enterprises, Inc., Baton Rouge, 1990—.

Scoutmaster Boy Scouts Am., Baton Rouge, 1977-78; officer PTA, Bethany, Okla., 1971-74; PTF v.p. Parkview Bapt. Sch., Baton Rouge, 1989-90. Democrat. Baptist. Office: So Capitol Enterprises 10915 Perkins Rd Baton Rouge LA 70810

TUTTLE, DONNA FRAME, public relations executive, consultant, former government official; b. Los Angeles, Apr. 21, 1947; d. Les Frame and Marilyn (Dunton) Simpson; m. Robert Holmes Tuttle, Mar. 25, 1972; children—Tiffany Noel, Alexandra Christina. B.A. in History, U. So. Calif., 1969; Edn. credential, UCLA, 1970. Tchr. Los Angeles City Schs., 1970-75; nat. chmn. Youth for Reagan-Bush Campaign, Los Angeles, 1980; under sec. for travel and tourism U.S. Dept. Commerce, Washington, 1983-88, dep. sec., 1988-89; chmn., chief exec. officer Ayer Tuttle Advt., Beverly Hills, Calif., 1989—, Ayer Tuttle, L.A., 1990—. Bd. dirs. Coro Found., Los Angeles, 1978—, John F. Kennedy Ctr., Washington, 1982. Recipient Travel Woman of Yr. award Travel Industry of Am., 1984; Travel Leader of Yr. award Nat. Tour Assn., 1984; Golden Wheel award Am. Bus. Assn., 1984; Travel South Leader of Yr. award Travel South USA, 1985. Republican. Office: Ayer Tuttle 888 S Figueroa 12th Fl Los Angeles CA 90017

TUTTLE, DOROTHY EDITH LORNE, writer, communications consultant; b. Seattle, Dec. 7, 1916; d. William Henry and Maude alice (Fuller) T. Student U. Wash., 1936-37, U. Richmond, 1946, Stanford U., 1945-46; Banking/Econs. grad. Am. Inst. Banking, 1941; BA, Am. U., Washington, 1955; postgrad. Mich. State U., 1960-61; grad. nat. security mgmt. Indls. Coll. Armed Forces, 1969. Pub. rels. dir. Mich. Coun. State Coll. Pres., Lansing, 1961; pub. rels. dir. woman's div., dir. weekly press and small dailies Rep. Nat. Com., Washington, 1962-64; pub. info. officer, div. dir., br. chief Dept. Navy, Washington, 1965-71; info. and editorial specialist Assn. Am. R.R.s, Washington, 1973-75; writer, communications cons. DELT Communications Svcs., Washington, Ithaca, Mich., 1976-84; internat. press corr. and editor USIA, 1948-59; freelance writer, 1989-90; communications cons., Ithaca, 1984—; nat. communication cons., 1989; Mid-Mich. Farm owner, producer, mgr., 1988, 89, 90; mem. Farm Bur., 1990. Editor USA Life, 1950, Navy Mgmt. Rev., 1965-69; contbr. articles to nat. to nat. periodicals and govt. publs. Mem. pres.'s circle Am. U.; mem. Republican Congl. Com.; mem. Emerson Twp. Women's Club, Mich. With USN-USCG, 1942-46. Am. Inst. Banking fellow, 1936-42; recipient Outstanding Performance award Navy Bur. Supplies and Accounts, 1966; Superior Accomplishment award and Cash award Dept. Navy, Washington, 1967, Fed. Civilian Svc. award, 1969, Civilian Meritorious Service award, 1971. Mem. AAUW, Nat. Press Club, Am. Newspaper Women's Club (1st v.p., bd. dir.), Am. Legion, Res. Officers Assn., Internat. Fedn. Univ. Women, Washington Press Club (officer, com. mem.), Am. U. Alumni Assn., Stanford U. Alumni Assn., Mich. State U. Alumni Assn., Women in Communications, Inc., Pub. Soc. of Am. Republican. Episcopalian. Home: 636 N Baldwin Rd Ithaca MI 48847

TUTTLE, LINDA SUZANNE, nurse; b. Middletown, Conn., Apr. 8, 1953; d. Wallace Monroe and Marjorie Jean (Goodrich) T. AS, Middlesex Community Coll., Middletown, 1983; AS in Nursing, Greater Hartford Community Coll., 1984. RN, Conn. Sec. Middlesex Community Coll., 1975-81; nurse's aide Queens Convalescent Home, Middletown, 1981; pvt. home health aide Middletown, 1981-82; staff nurse Conn. Valley Hosp., Middletown, 1984—. Recipient scholarship Rotary Club, 1974. Home: 150 Newfield St Middletown CT 06457

TUTTLE, LYNDA LEE, account systems engineer; b. Amityville, N.Y., May 11, 1947; d. Kenneth Lynwood (dec.) and Hazel Marie (Wanser) (dec.) T. AA, Suffolk County Community Coll., Selden, N.Y., 1968. Data processing supr. oil firm Oyster Bay, N.Y., 1968-70; computer operator oil firm Oyster Bay, 1970-71, application programmer oil firm, 1971-73; assoc. customer engr. IBM Corp., Garden City, N.Y., 1973-74, customer engr., 1974-77, acct. customer engr., 1977-81; program support rep. IBM Corp., Jericho, N.Y., 1981-87, acct. ops. specialist systems engr., 1987-89, acct. system engr., 1989—; commodities trader Stotler and Co., Los Angeles, 1987—; computer cons. various firms, N.Y., 1980—. Mem. Blue Point (N.Y.) Community Assn., Inc., 1978—. Mem. NAFE, Am. Assn. Individual Investors, IBM Metropolitan Credit Union (supr. com. 1973-75), Assn. Rsch. and Enlightenment, Blue Point Racquet Ball Club, IBM Sands Point Country Club, Omega Delta Psi. Methodist. Office: IBM Corp Two Jericho Plaza Jericho NY 11753

TUTTLE, M(ARGARET) DIANE, infosystems executive; b. Kansas City, Mo., Aug. 11, 1945; d. Allen T. and Vernia Margaret (Pugh) Ashbaugh; m. Robert Stephen Tuttle; 1 child, Robert Stephen II. BBA, Baker U. Supr. bus. officer South Cen. Bell Tel. Co., 1975-80, supr. network adminstrn., 1980-81, project mgr. billing adminstrn. and contracts, 1981-83, mgr. data telecommunications data systems, 1983-85; sr. mgr. telecommunications, mgmt. infosystems Fed. Express, Memphis, 1985—. Active Alcohol and Drug Coun., Memphis, 1987. Fellow Data Processing Mgmt. Assn.; mem. Christian Bus. Women's Club. Republican. Baptist. Home: 2093 Glenalden Germantown TN 38138 Office: Fed Express 2828 Business Park Dr Memphis TN 38138

TUTTLE, MARGARET GOSS, publishing executive; b. Cook County, Ill., May 24, 1958; d. Frederick Goss Tuttle and Jeanne Adele (Dondanville) Brown. BA, Princeton U., 1980. Mem. sales and mktg. staff Addison-Wesley Pub. Co., Reading, Mass., 1980-84; mktg. mgr. Bantam Books, N.Y.C., 1984-86; mktg. rep. McGraw-Hill, Inc., N.Y.C., 1986-89; editor Consumers Union, Mt. Vernon, N.Y., 1989-90; publs. mgr. Assn. for Computing Machinery, N.Y.C., 1990—; cons. Quinn & Tuttle Pub., N.Y.C., 1990—. Tutor Literacy Vols. Am., N.Y.C., 1988-89. Home: 319 Garfield Pl Brooklyn NY 11215 Office: ACM 11 W 42d St New York NY 10036

TUTTLE, PHYLLIS FAYE, small business owner; b. Parthenon, Ark., Nov. 5, 1947; d. Hugh Rondall and Susie Viola (Harris) Champlin; m. Stephen Laird Tuttle, May 22, 1965; children: Stephen Jr., Rondall Blake, Sarah Suzanne. AS, Northland Pioneer Coll., 1983; student in chemistry and math., No. Ariz. U., 1983-85. Electronic tester Western Electric Co., Northglenn, Colo., 1971-73; lab. dir. City of Winslow, Ariz., 1983-85; prin. Abel Gift and Christian Supply, Winslow, 1985-88, Abel Travel Agy., Winslow, 1985—. Leader Boy Scouts Am., Phoenix, 1974; officer PTO Bonnie Brennan Sch., Winslow, 1976-81; chmn. Georgia Metzger for Mayor, Winslow, 1982-86; rep. precinct person, 1983. Mem. Indsl. Devel. Endeavor Assn., Bapt. Women, Winslow Club. Office: Abel Travel Agy 114 E 2d St Winslow AZ 86047

TUTTLE, ROSE MARY GUERRA, editor; b. Syracuse, N.Y., July 22, 1920; d. Isaia and Angela Marie (DeIulio) Guerra; m. Franklin Halbert Tuttle. BS, Syracuse U., 1943, MS, 1961. Cert. Home Economics Edn., 1961. Lab. tech. Sealtest Corp., Syracuse, 1943-44; child welfare svcs. Onondaga County Social Svcs., Syracuse, N.Y., 1944-48; home economist Onondaga Supply Co., Syracuse, N.Y., 1948-49; range product rep. to regional home economist Crosley div. Avco Mfg., Chgo., 1949-50, Cin., 1950-51; assoc. editor The American Home Mag., N.Y.C., 1951-52; nat. home svc. dir. Easy Div., Murray Corp., N.Y., 1952-56; home equipment editor Farm Jour. Town Jour. Magazines, Phila., 1956-58; copywriter Cl & B Advt. Agy., Syracuse, N.Y., 1958-59; tchr. Syracuse (N.Y.) Pub. Schs., 1959-61, North Syracuse (N.Y.) Pub. Schs., 1961-85; self-employed cons., Syracuse, N.Y., 1985--. Mem. NEA, American Home Econs. Assn., Home Economists, in Bus., Electrical Women's Round Table, Nat. Council on Family Relations, N.Y. State Tchrs. Assn., Skaneateles Country Club. Republican. Roman Catholic. Home: Twisting Ln Skaneateles NY 13152

TUTTON, REBECCA SUE, hospice executive; b. Charleston, W. Va, Aug. 27, 1950; d. Dan David and Betty Jean Oliver (Conroe); m. James E. Tutton, III, July 28, 1968; 1 child, Regan Boone. AA, Sante Fe Jr. Coll., Gainesville, 1972-73; BS, U. Fla., Gainesville, 1976; Degree in Nursing, St. Petersburg Jr. Coll., Clearwater, 1981. RN. Sec. CMHU U. Fla., Gainesville, 1969-72; instr. Northeast High Sch., Gainesville, 1976-77, Safety Harbor Middle Sch., Safety Harbor, Fla., 1977-79; registered nurse Morton Plant Hosp., Clearwater, Fla., 1979-83; nurse clinician Fla. Ctr. for Knee Surgery, Clearwater, 1983-85; nurse coord. Commonwealth Rehab., 1985-86; program dir. Hospice Citrus County, Inverness, Fla., 1986-88; exec. v.p. Hospice Citrus County, Inverness, 1988-89, exec. dir., 1989—; asst. track coach Northeast High Sch., Gainesville, 1976-77; tennis coach Safety Harbor Middle Sch., Safety Harbor, 1978-79. Bd. dirs. CASA, Inverness, 1988; mem. Dist. Adv. Coun. State of Fla., 1988, Countinuity of Care Coun., Inverness. Mem. Rotary, Nat. Hospice Orgn., Tri-County C. of C., Fla. Nursing Assn., Altrussa, Women's Med. Auxillary (pres. 1989-90). Democrat. Home: 8694 E San Ramon Ct Inverness FL 32650 Office: Hospice Citrus County PO Box 368 Inverness FL 32651

TUTWILER, MARGARET DEBARDELEBEN, federal agency official; b. Birmingham, Ala., Dec. 28, 1950; d. Temple Wilson and Margaret (DeBardeleben) Tutwiler, II. Student, Finch Coll., 1969-71; B.A., U. Ala., 1973. Sec. Ala. Rep. Party, Birmingham, 1974; scheduler Pres. Ford Com., Birmingham, 1975-78; exec. dir. Pres. Ford Com. Ala., Birmingham, 1976; pub. rels. rep. Nat. Assn. Mfrs. for Ala. and Miss., Birmingham and Washington, 1977-78; dir. scheduling George Bush for Pres. Com., Houston and Washington, 1978-80; spl. asst. to Pres. Reagan and exec. to Chief of Staff The White House, Washington, 1981-85; asst. sec. Dept. Treasury, 1985-88; sr. advisor transition team U.S. Dept. State, Washington, 1988-89, asst. sec. pub. affairs, spokesman, 1989—; dep. chmn. Bush-Quayle '88, Washington, 1988. Recipient Woman of Yr. award Wake Forest U., 1986, Alexander Hamilton award, 1988. Republican. Episcopalian.

TUZZIO, MARGARET, loss prevention company executive; b. Jersey City, Apr. 3, 1962; d. Vito Michael and Grace (Castellitto) T. Securitydir. Saks Fifth Ave., N.Y.C.; dir. internal audit R&S Strauss, Union, N.J.; pres. Ultra Protection Systems, Inc., Hoboken, N.J. Mem. NAFE, Soc. Profl. Investigators, Associated Locksmiths Am., Nat. Locksmith Assn., Nat. Fire Prevention Assn., Am. Soc. for Indsl. Security, Internat. Assn. Credit Card Investigators, Nat. Burglar Alarm Assn., John Jay Coll. Criminal Justice, Nat. Assn. Chiefs Police, Nat. Law Enforcement Acad., Internat. Systems Security Assn., N.Y.-N.J. Detective Crime Clinic. Roman Catholic. Office: 601 Grand St Hoboken NJ 07030

TVEITARAAS, RANDI ANNE, state government official; b. Detroit, Sept. 9, 1959; d. John Tveitaraas and Kari Bye. Student, U. Madrid, 1980; BSBA, Colo. State U., 1981; M. in Internat. Mgmt., Am. Grad. Sch. Internat. Mgmt., 1986. Internat. account rep. Storage Tech. Corp., Louisville, Colo., 1981-85; mktg. and devel. coord. Internat. Classics, Ltd., Boulder, Colo., 1987; internat. devel. dir. Kans. Dept. Commerce, Topeka, 1988—. Literacy tutor Adult Learning Ctr., Topeka, 1988-89. Mem. AAUW, Kans. Indsl. Developers Assn., Phi Sigma Iota. Home: 2901 University Dr A Lawrence KS 66049

TWA, INEZ LOUISA ARBUTHNOT, author; b. Boulder County, Colo., Nov. 9, 1905; d. George John and Nancy Louisa (Brammeier) Arbuthnot; student Coll. Commerce, Stockton, Calif., 1929; m. Norman Osbert Twa, Nov. 7, 1929 (dec.); children: Lois, Gordon, Audrey. Office positions, U.S. and Can., 1929-57; with FAA, 1957-75, sec. CAA, Grand Junction, Colo., 1957-63; adminstrv. asst. to dist. chief FAA, Reno, 1963-65, mgmt. tech./specialist area office, Salt Lake City, 1965-68; mgmt. specialist, asst. motor fleet mgr. Dept. Transp., L.A., 1968-72, regional motor fleet mgr. Rocky Mountain Region, Denver, 1972-75, ret., 1975; author short stories pub. 1977—; editor Buckingham Gardens News and Revs. newsletter, 1984-86; contbr. stories to Colo. Old Times mag., Denver Post newspaper. Active Mental Health Assn., 1958-63. Recipient award C. of C., 1963; Svc. citation CSC, 1975. Mem. Profl. Secs. Internat., Arbuthnot Family Internat. Assn. Aurora Geneal. Soc., Nat. Mus. Women in the Arts (charter). Presbyterian. Home: 800 S Ironton St Apt #77 Aurora CO 80012

TWADDLE, JOAN BOTHAM, secondary school headmistress; b. Manchester, N.H., Aug. 9, 1927; d. Arthur Eastman and Ruth Carolyn (McQuesten) T. BA, Wellesley Coll., 1947, MA, 1949. Tchr. Columbia Sch., Rochester, N.Y., 1949-64, headmistress, 1964-72; assoc. dir. Allendale (Mass.) Columbia Sch., 1972-77; asst. headmistress MacDuffie Sch., Springfield, Mass., 1977-85; head upper sch. Barnard Sch., N.Y.C., headmistress, 1986-88; head upper sch. Cathedral Sch., 1988--. Mem. Head Mistress Assn. East (treas.), Nat. Assn. Prins. Sch. for Girls (treas.). Republican. Home: 67 Leonard Dr Tiverton RI 02878

TWEEDIE, CAROL E., owner real estate company; b. Elgin, Ill., July 29, 1942; d. William J. and Gladys (Speicher) Y.; m. John V. Healy (div.); m. Edward J. Tweedie, Aug. 7, 1978; children: Stephanie A. Student, So. Ill. U., 1961. Owner Best Real Estate, Dundee, Ill., 1967—. Mem. Valley Garden League Elgin. Home: One Chateau Dr W Dundee IL 60118 also: 1200 Windward Ct Punta Gorda Isles FL 33950

TWEEDY, ISABELLA G., healthcare administrator; b. Los Angeles, Feb. 22, 1915; d. Clifford E. and Aimee Estelle (Miller) McMartin. BA in Philosophy and Psychology cum laude, U. Wash., 1977, MA in Psychology, 1982, PhD, 1984. Outpatient counselor, aftercare and inpatient counselor Fairbanks (Alaska) Native Assn.; outpatient and program dir. Horizon Recovery Ctr., Fairbanks; outpatient and inpatient counselor, facility adminstr. Milam Recovery Ctrs., Fairbanks; pres. alcohol and drug abuse counseling ctr. Isabella Inc., Fairbanks. Mem. Am. Mental Health Counselors Assn., Nat. Assn. Alcohol and Drug Addictions Counselors. Home: PO Box 72709 Fairbanks AK 99707

TWEITO, ELEANOR MARIE, social services administrator; b. Westgate, Iowa, Dec. 25, 1909; d. Henry Christopher and Amanda Marie (Fink) Frese; m. Thomas E. Tweito, Aug. 26, 1936; children: David Henry, Thomas Elling. Student, Wartburg Coll., 1926-28; BA, Morningside Coll., 1940; MA, U. Mo., 1966. Tchr. Pub. Rural Sch., Waverly, Iowa, 1928-30; exec. sec. Century Life Ins. Co., Waverly, 1930-36, State U. Iowa, Iowa City, 1938-40; prof. Tri-State Bus. Coll., Sioux City, Iowa, 1940-42; tchr. Bronson Consolidated High Sch., Bronson, Iowa, 1942-59; founder, prof., chair bus. edn. dept. Mo. Valley Coll., Marshall, 1960-77; adminstr. Sr. Ctr. Dist. III Area Agy. on Aging, Marshall, 1987—; sec. of faculty Mo. Valley Coll., Marshall, 1965-70; lectr. workshop St. Paul's Coll., Concordia, Mo., 1979. Editor, contbr. The Evangel, 1976-86; co-author: Lest We Forget, 1988; contbr. articles to newspapers. Pres. Luth. Daughters of the Reformation, Sioux City, 1957-60; sec., fin. sec. Luth. Ch., Marshall, 1976-86; bd. dirs., sec.-treas. Dist. III Area Agy. on Aging, Marshall, 1980—. Fellow AAUW (bd. dirs. Marshall chpt. 1970—), AAUP, AARP (sec., treas. 1977—), Nat. Assn. Retired Tchrs., Sorosis Club, Faculty Women Club, Pi Gamma Mu, Zeta Sigma, Pi Lambda Theta. Home: 1108 Sunrise Dr Marshall MO 65340

TWINING, LYNNE DIANNE, psychotherapist; b. Midland, Mich., Aug. 14, 1951; d. James and Dorothy Twining; m. Alan Howard Mass. BA in Psychology, Oakland U., 1974; MSW, Wayne State U., 1977; Cert., Bkln. Inst. Psychotherapy, 1990. Social work supr. non-profit orgn., Detroit, 1977-83; co-founder, co-dir. Women Psychotherapists Bklyn., 1986—; pvt. practice Bklyn. and N.Y.C., 1987—. Author: (with other) Metro Detroit Guide, 1975; contbr. articles to profl. jours.; contbg. editor: Detroit Guide, 1983; asst. producer docudrama. Bd. dirs. Progressive Artists and Educators Coalition, Detroit, 1977-79. Mem. N.Y. Acad. Scis., Nat. Trust for Hist. Preservation, Tng. Inst. Mental Health Practitioners, Nat. Assn. Advancement Psychoanalysis (affiliate), Am. Orthopsychiatric Assn., Women Psychotherapists Bklyn. (founding mem.), ACLU (sec. exec. bd. Mich. chpt. 1982-83), Amnesty Internat. (freedom writer), NOW. Office: 55 Eastern Pkwy Ste 3A Brooklyn NY 11238

TWINING, MARILYN J., travel agency and college executive; b. Spooner, Wis., May 30, 1939; d. Lloyd L. and Mary C. (Talarico) T. BS, U. Wis., La Crosse, 196l; MA, U. No. Colo., 1967; edn. specialist, U. Wis., Stout, 1977. Tchr., coach Whitnall High Sch., Hales Corners, Wis., 1961-64, Cen. High Sch., Mpls., 1964-65, Joliet (Ill.) Cen. High Sch., 1966-67; chmn. phys. edn. dept. South St. Paul (Minn.) High Sch., 1965-66, West Chicago (Ill.) High Sch., 1967-69; coord. leisure careers Moraine Valley Community Coll., Palos Hills, Ill., 1969-89; owner, pres. Gold Star Travel Inc., Wheaton, Ill., 1988—; dir. Roberta Fisher Coll. Travel and Tourism, Elk Grove Village, Ill., 1988—; instr. North Cen. Coll., Naperville, Ill., 1970-85; rsch. asst. U. Wis., Stout, 1976-77; cons. on leisure careers to various colls., 19776—; curriculum cons. Madison (Wis.) Tech. Coll., 1978-79. Author: Leisure Service Careers Model for Post Secondary Schools, 1977. Tres. bd. dirs. Holy Covenant Ch., Hinsdale, Ill., 1979-89; campaign vol. Hinsdale Rep. Com., 1988. Recipient Outstanding Svc. award Ill. Assn. Health, Phys. Edn. and Recreation, 1974; Ill. Gt. Tchr. award Moraine Valley Community Coll., 1972, Student Contbn. award, 1979; Disting. Svc. award South Suburban Park and Recreation Assn., 1982. Mem. Nat. Parks and Recreation Assn., AAHPER and Dance, Chgo. Women in Travel, AAUW, Delta Kappa Gamma. Roman Catholic. Home: 4440 Fairview Downers Grove IL 60515

TWISS, WANDA MAY, interior designer; b. Marengo, Ind., Oct. 28, 1934; d. Gamford Ingle and Anjie Pearl (Beld) Tate; m. Eugene Clyo Twiss, Nov. 27, 1952; children: Sheryll Lynn, Carol Ann. Student pub. schs., Newcastle, Ind. Decorator Decorating Den, Leesburg, Fla., 1970-85, franchise owner, 1983—, regional coordinator, instr., 1984—, designer, 1985—. Mem. Leesburg Bus. and Profl. Women. Mem. Ch. of Nazarene. Home: 41640 County Rd 25 Weirsdale FL 32195 Office: Decorating Den 1031 W Main St Leesburg FL 34748

TWOMEY, ELIZABETH ANN, aerospace engineer; b. N.Y., Jan. 22, 1965; d. Thomas Jerome and Elizabeth Veronica (Costello) T. AS in Engring. Sci., Westchester Community Coll., Valhalla, 1985; BS in Aerospace Engr., Syracuse U., 1988. Tutor Westchester Community Coll., Valhalla, N.Y., 1984-85; researcher Syracuse U., 1986-87, aircraft engr., 1986-87; tech. writer Volvo Cars of N.Am., Rockleigh, N.J., 1987—. Co-author: The Pup: A Design for an Advanced Personal Aircraft, 1987-88; author: Subsonic Pressure Measurement using Digital Pressure Transducers, 1987. Mem. Am. Inst. of Aeronautics and Astronautics, Soc. of Women Engrs. Home: 317 N Main St Spring Valley NY 10977

TWOMEY, JANET LOUISE WILKOV, banker; b. Washington, Oct. 17, 1952; d. Harry and Minnie S. Wilkov; m. Thomas N. Twomey, June 6, 1981. Student, Inst. d'Etudes Politiques, Paris, 1972-73; AB, Mt. Holyoke Coll., 1974; MBA, Columbia U., 1980. Corp. lending officer Chem. Bank, N.Y.C., 1980-84; asst. v.p. SE Bank, N.A., Melbourne, Fla., 1984-85, v.p., dept. mgr. corp. bank, 1985-87; sr. v.p. Chem. N.J., 1987—. Mary Vance Young scholar Mt. Holyoke Coll., 1972, Falk Found scholar Mt. Holyoke Coll., 1974. Mem. Commerce and Industry Assn. N.J. Club: Mt. Holyoke Coll. (South Hadley, Mass., class treas. 1984-89, class agt. 1989—).

TWOMEY, MARY REGINA, women's rights activist, writer; b. Trenton, N.J., Oct. 11, 1941; d. Anthony James and Beatrice Mary (Burns) Moran; div.; children: Moira, William III, Kathleen. Student, Rider Coll., Trenton, 1959, Trenton Jr. Coll., 1960, U. N.H., 1984. Engrs.' asst. U.S. Govt., Burlington, Mass., 1961-62; ptnr. nursing home business various orgns., Mass., 1969—; tchr. Sacred Heart Sch., Amesbury, Mass., 1974-75; sports writer Rockingham County Newspapers, Hampton, N.H., 1986-88; exec. planning com. Women in Sports Coer., New Agenda/Northeast, 1987, 88, 89; runner NOW/NAGWS Run for Equality, Washington to Phila., 1986. Candidate for N.H. State Legislature, 1990; del. to Dem. nat. conv., 1984, 88; bd. dirs. Rockingham County Family Planning Program, 1988-90; mem., lobbyist Epilepsy Found. Am., Landover, Md., 1970—. JFK Libr. fellow, 1989, 90. Mem. NOW (past state and local v.p., N.H. pres., local publicity chmn., named 1 st Woman of Yr., 1990), Dem. Alliance for Women in N.H. (founding mem.), N.H. Women's Lobby, Seacoast Women's Svc. Orgn. (founding mem., bd. dirs.), Women's Sports Found. (lobbyist, N.H. chmn. Nat. Women's Sports Day in 1989, 90), Assn. for Women in Sports Media. Democrat. Roman Catholic. Home: 7 Hedman Ave Hampton NH 03842

TWYNER, ALEXIS CHERYLE, special education educator; b. Iowa City, Iowa, Sept. 19, 1946; d. Lafayette James and Rosemary Lucille (Roberts) T.; B.A. in Edn. and History, U. Iowa, 1964-68; M.A. in Reading and Learning Disabilities, Marycrest Coll., 1971; Ph.D. in Adminstrn., U. Iowa, 1978. Tchr. Pleasant Valley Community Sch. Dist., LeClaire, Iowa, 1968-73; reading specialist Lincoln Elem. Sch., 1973-75; specific learning disability tchr. North High Sch., Davenport, 1975—; adult edn. instr. Davenport Community Sch. Dist., 1980—; reading specialist McKinley Elem. Sch., 1990—. Mem. NEA, Iowa State Edn. Assn., Davenport Edn. Assn., Internat. Reading Assn., Assn. for Children with Learning Disabilities, Pi Lambda Theta. Republican. Office: 1716 Kenwood Ave Davenport IA 52803

TYAU, GAYLORE CHOY YEN, business educator, academic administrator; b. Honolulu, May 13, 1934; d. Moses M.F. and Bessie (Amana) T. BS, U. Calif., Berkeley, 1956, MBA, 1959. Cert. bus. tchr., Calif. Tchr. bus. Richmond (Calif.) Union High Sch., 1959-64, Westmoor High Sch., Daly City, Calif., 1964-90; instr. bus. City Coll. San Francisco, 1978-87, 88—; office mgr. P.F. Freytag Assocs., San Francisco, 1978-86. Coordinator Pacific Telephone Co.'s Adopt-a-Sch. Program, Colma, Calif, 1987. Mem. Nat. Bus. Edn. Assn., Calif. Bus. Assn. (chairperson program com. 1979, mem. program com. 1981-82, Pacific Bell contract edn. grantee 1989), Am. Vocat. Assn., Assn. for Supervision and Curriculum Devel., Western Bus. Edn. Assn., City Coll. Faculty Assn., Jefferson Union High Sch. Dist. Tchrs. Assn., Beta Phi Gamma. Republican. Episcopalian. Home: 4050 17th St #1 San Francisco CA 94114

TYLER, ANNE (MRS. TAGHI M. MODARRESSI), author; b. Mpls., Oct. 25, 1941; d. Lloyd Parry and Phyllis (Mahon) T.; m. Taghi M. Modarressi, May 3, 1963; children: Tezh, Mitra. B.A., Duke U., 1961; postgrad., Columbia U., 1962. Author: novels If Morning Ever Comes, 1964, The Tin Can Tree, 1965, A Slipping-Down Life, 1970, The Clock Winder, 1972, Celestial Navigation, 1974, Searching for Caleb, 1976, Earthly Possessions, 1977, Morgan's Passing, 1980, Dinner at the Homesick Restaurant, 1982, The Accidental Tourist, 1985, Breathing Lessons, 1988, (Recipient Pulitzer prize for fiction); contbr. short stories to nat. mags. Home: 222 Tunbridge Rd Baltimore MD 21212

TYLER, GAIL MADELEINE, nurse; b. Dhahran, Saudi Arabia, Nov. 21, 1953 (parents Am. citizens); d. Louis Rogers and Nona Jean (Henderson) T. AS, Front Range Community Coll., Westminster, Colo., 1979; BS in Nursing, U. Wyo., 1989. RN. Ward sec. Valley View Hosp., Thornton, Colo., 1975-79; nurse Scott and White Hosp., Temple, Tex., 1979-83, Meml. Hosp. Laramie County, Cheyenne, Wyo., 1983-89; dir. DePaul Home Health, 1989—. Avocations: collecting international dolls, sewing, reading, traveling.

TYLER, JEAN B., public information executive; b. Pitts., Dec. 17, 1929; d. Harvey Kellog and Margaret Irene (Hatfield) Breckenridge; m. Edward Alton Tyler, June 30, 1950 (div. Sept. 1973); children: William Breckenridge, Jeffrey Alan, James Edward. BA, Smith Coll., 1950; postgrad., U. Pitts., 1952; MA, U. Wis., 1974. Dir. Legis. Reference Bur., Milw., 1974-81, Goals for Greater Milw. 2000, Milw., 1981-83, UWM Partnership Program, Milw., 1983-84, Pub. Policy Forum, Milw., 1984—; adj. prof., lectr. numerous colls. and U.; Gov. appointments various coms. dealing with edn. bd. dirs. Greater Milw. Edn. Trust, Coun. Health and Human Svcs., Wis. Econ. Edn. Coun., Neighborhood Devel. Ctr. Recipient Frye Community awd. Milw. Found., 1983, Woman of Yr., B'nai B'rith Indpls., 1970; named leadership in Govt. Polit. YWCA, Milw., 1978, Achievement in Urban Design/ Devel., Profl. Dimensions, Milw., 1986. Mem. LWV (nat. bd. 1970-72, state bd. 1969-72, local pres. 1964), Am. Soc. Pub. Adminstrs. (nat. coun. 1983-85, editorial bd. 1988-90, Wis. pres. 1987), Govtl. Rsch. Assoc. (pres. elect 1989, six rsch. awds. 1987-89). Home: 2857 N Lake Dr Milwaukee WI 53211

TYLER, MARIE O., healthcare products professional; b. Washington, Ga., May 14, 1959; d. Webster Thaxton and Josephine Marie (Wilson) Orr; m. Stephen H. Tyler, Dec. 15, 1979. BS, Med. Coll. Ga., 1981; MBA, Merced U. Cert. in med. tech., Am. Soc. Clin. Pathologists. Asst. head chemistry sect. N.E. Ga. Med. Ctr., Gainesville; tech. svc. specialist, tech. system specialist Baxter Health Care, Inc., Atlanta, field. svc. region mgr. Sci. Products div. Mem. NAFE, Am. Mgmt. Assn., Kappa Lambda, Phi Mu. Baptist. Address: 3215 Pond Ridge Trail Snellville GA 30278

TYNAN, LAURIE FRANCINE, librarian; b. N. Tonawanda, N.Y., July 14, 1951; d. Bruce Homer and Marie Rosalie (De Ryck) T. AB, Bucknell U., 1973; MS, Columbia U., N.Y.C., 1975. Asst. dir. Meadville (Pa.) Pub. Library, 1975-80, Sussex County Library System, Newton, N.J., 1980-81; dir. Huntingdon (Pa.) County Library, 1982-87; dist. cons. Montgomery County-Norristown (Pa.) Pub. Library, 1987—; exec. dir. Montgomery County-Norristown Pub. Library, 1989—; chair Pa. Interlibrary Loan Adv. Coun.,

Harrisburg, Pa., 1987—. Treas. Women's Svcs., Inc., Meadville, 1979-80, Huntingdon House, Inc., 1985-87. Mem. Am. Library Assn., Pa. Library Assn. (legis. day coord. 1989, chair Juniata-Conemaugh, Pa. chpt. 1985-86), ACLU, NOW, AAUW (pres. Huntingdon chpt. 1984-86, treas. 1988—). Office: Montgomery County Library Swede & Elm Sts Norristown PA 19401

TYNER, LEE REICHELDERFER, lawyer; b. Annapolis, Md., Mar. 12, 1946; d. Thomas Elmer and Eleanor Frances (Leland) Reichelderfer; m. Carl Frederick Tyner, Aug. 31, 1968; children: Michael Frederick, Rachel Christine, Elizabeth Frances. BA, St. John's Coll., 1968; MS, U. Wash., 1970; JD, George Washington U., 1975. Bar: Wash., D.C., U.S. Dist. Ct. (D.C.), U.S. Ct. Appeals (4th cir., 1st cir., 9th cir., D.C. cir., 5th cir., 8th cir., 11th cir., 10th cir.), U.S. Ct. Claims, U.S. Supreme Ct. Profl. staff U.S. Senate Commerce Com., Washington, 1970-72; trial atty. Land and Natural Resources div. U.S. Dept. Justice, Washington, 1975-85; atty. Office of Gen. Counsel U.S. EPA, Washington, 1985—. Bd. dirs. Grace Episcopal Day Sch., Silver Spring, Md., 1987-89; den leader, cubmaster Boy Scouts Am., Silver Spring, 1987—. Recipient Bronze medal, U.S. EPA, 1988. Mem. Order of the Coif. Episcopalian. Home: 1416 Geranium St NW Washington DC 20012 Office: US EPA 401 M St SW Washington DC 20460

TYNG, ANNE GRISWOLD, architect; b. Kuling, Kiangsi, China, July 14, 1920; d. Walworth and Ethel Atkinson (Arens) T. (parents Am. citizens); 1 child, Alexandra Stevens. A.B., Radcliffe Coll., 1942; M.Arch., Harvard U., 1944; Ph.D., U. Pa., 1975. Assoc. Stonorov & Kahn, Architects, 1945-47; assoc. Louis I. Kahn Architect, 1947-73; pvt. practice architecture Phila., 1973—; adj. assoc. prof. architecture U. Pa. Grad. Sch. Fine Arts, 1968—; assoc. cons. architect Phila. Planning Commn. and Phila. Redevel. Authority, 1952-54, Mill Creek Redevel. Plan, 1954; vis. disting. prof. Pratt Inst., 1979-81, vis. critic architecture, 1969; vis. critic architecture Rensselaer Poly. Inst., 1969, 78, Carnegie Mellon U., 1970, Drexel U., 1972-73, Cooper Union, 1974-75, U. Tex., Austin, 1976; lectr. Archtl. Assn., London, Xian U., China, Bath U., Eng., Mexico City, Hong Kong U., 1989; panel speaker Nat. Conv. Am. Inst. Architects, N.Y.C., 1988, also numerous univs. throughout U.S. and Can.; asst. leader People to People Archtl. del. to China, 1983. Subject of films Anne G. Tyng at Parsons School of Design, 1972, Anne G. Tyng at University of Minnesota, 1974, Connecting, 1976, Forming the Future, 1977; work included in Smithsonian Travelling Exhbn., 1979-81, 82; contbr. articles to profl. publs.; prin. works include: Walworth Tyng Farmhouse (Hon. mention award Phila. chpt. AIA 1953); builder (with G. Yanchenko) Probability Pyramid, Nat. Math. Conf., Smithsonian Mus. Am. History, 1984; patentee Tyng Toy. Graham Found. for Advanced Study in Fine Arts fellow, 1965, 79-81. Fellow AIA (Brunner grantee N.Y. chpt. 1964, 83, dir., mem. exec. bd. Phila. chpt., 1976-78); mem. NAD (asso.), Nat. Assn. Archtl. Historians, C.G. Jung Center Phila. (planning com. 1979—), Form Forum (co-founder, mem. planning com. 1978—). Democrat. Episcopalian. Home: 2511 Waverly St Philadelphia PA 19146 Office: Univ Pa Dept Architecture Grad Sch Fine Arts Philadelphia PA 19107

TYRRELL, ELEANORE DAY, medical research administrator; b. Phila., Aug. 9, 1938; d. Peter Aloysius Tyrrell and Elsie Amelia Day. BA in Psychology, U. Richmond, 1960; MA in Psychology, Pepperdine U., 1980. Rsch. assoc. U. Pa. Med. Sch., Phila., 1961-62; with UCLA, 1962—, rsch. assoc. to lab. supr. to co-adminstr. Marijuana Rsch. Program, 1973-77; now project coord. program in psychiatry, law and human sexuality Neuropsychiatric Inst. program coord. Program in Psychiatry, Law & Human Sexuality, 1987—; exec. dir. Ctr. for Drug Edn. and Brain Rsch., L.A., 1987-88; cons., researcher Beverly Hills Headache and Pain Med. Group, L.A., Los Alamos (N.Mex.) Nat. Labs., SUNY, Stony Brook, Southern Calif. Neuropsychiat. Inst., La Jolla, Southern Calif. Ctr. for Sleep Disorders, Santa Monica, and others. Contbr. articles and rsch. papers to profl. jours. Pres. The Opera Assocs., L.A.; dir. publicity and pub. rels. L.A. and western regions Met. Opera Nat. Coun. Auditions. Mem. Psi Chi. Home: 1436 Butler Ave Los Angeles CA 90025

TYSON, CHARLOTTE ROSE, electrical engineer; b. San Mateo, Calif., Aug. 14, 1954; d. Herbert Parry and Rose (Goldner) T.; m. Edward Philip Sejud, Aug. 11, 1979; children: Laura Rose, Elizabeth Ann. A.A. in Physics, DeAnza Coll., 1974; B.S. in Elec. Engring., U. Calif.-Berkeley, 1976. Engr. IBM, Boulder, Colo., 1976-82, project engr. mgr., 1982-84, devel. engr. mgr., 1984—, staff to lab. dir., 1986-87,; 3820 program mgr., 1987-89, project office mgr. 3825, 1988-89, mgr. svc. process support, 1990—. Mem. Soc. Women Engrs. (life), IEEE (Debt of Gratitude award 1981, 82, 83, chmn. Denver sect. 1982-83), Electromagnetic Compatability Soc. (bd. dirs. 1985-90, awards and membership chmn. 1986-90). Avocations: gardening, reading, sewing, skiing. Home: 1213 Twin Peaks Circle Longmont CO 80503 Office: IBM PO Box 1900 Boulder CO 80302

TYSON, CICELY, actress; b. N.Y.C.; d. William and Theodosia Tyson; m. Miles Davis, 1981 (div.). Student, N.Y. U., Actors Studio; hon. doctorates, Atlanta U., Loyola U., Lincoln U. Former sec., model; co-founder Dance Theatre of Harlem; bd. dirs. Urban Gateways. Stage appearances include: The Blacks, 1961-63, off-Broadway, Moon on a Rainbow Shawl, 1962-63, Tiger, Tiger, Burning Bright, Broadway; star: film Sounder, 1972; other film appearances include Twelve Angry Men, 1957, Odds Against Tomorrow, 1959, The Last Angry Man, 1959, A Man Called Adam, 1966, The Comedians, 1967, The Heart is a Lonely Hunter, 1968, The Blue Bird, 1976, The River Niger, 1976, A Hero Ain't Nothin' but a Sandwich, 1978, The Concorde-Airport 79, 1979; TV appearances include: series East Side, West Side, 1963; spl. TV films The Autobiography of Miss Jane Pittman, 1973, 1974, A Woman Called Moses, 1978, The Marva Collins Story, 1981, Benny's Place, 1982; TV miniseries: Roots, 1977, King, 1978, The Women of Brewster Place, 1989; TV movie Just An Old Sweet Song, 1976; named best actress for Sounder, Atlanta Film Festival 1972, Nat. Soc. Film Critics 1972, nominee best actress for Sounder, Acad. awards 1972, Emmy award for best actress in a spl. 1973. Trustee Human Family Inst.; trustee Am. Film Inst. Recipient Vernon Price award, 1962; also awards NAACP Nat. Council Negro Women; Capitol Press award. Address: care Larry Thompson 345 N Maple Dr Ste 183 Beverly Hills CA 90210*

TYSON, CYNTHIA HALDENBY, college administrator; b. Scunthorpe, Lincolnshire, Eng., July 2, 1937; came to U.S., 1959; d. Frederick and Florence Edna (Stacey) Haldenby; children: Marcus James, Alexandra Elizabeth. BA, U. Leeds, Eng., 1958, MA, 1959, PhD, 1971. Lectr. Brit. Council, Leeds, 1959; faculty U. Tenn., Knoxville, 1959-60, Seton Hall U., South Orange, N.J., 1963-69; faculty, v.p. Queens Coll., Charlotte, N.C., 1969-85; pres. Mary Baldwin Coll., Staunton, Va., 1985—; bd. dirs. Am. Frontier Culture Edn., Staunton, Va. Lottery Bd., Am. Coun. on Edn.; commr. Am. Council on Edn./Commn. on Higher Edn. and Adult Learner, Washington, 1981—. Contbr. articles to profl. jours. Commr. Va. Internat. Trade Commn., Richmond, 1987—; trustee Woodrow Wilson Birthplace Found., Staunton, 1985—; bd. dirs. United Way, Staunton, 1986—. Fulbright scholar, 1959; Ford Found. grantee Harvard U., 1981; Shell Oil scholar Harvard U., 1982. Fellow Soc. for Values in Higher Edn.; mem. Am. Mgmt. Assn. (council ops. enterprise 1985—), So. Assn. Colls. for Women (pres. 1980-81). Republican. Presbyterian. Office: Mary Baldwin Coll Staunton VA 24401

TYSON, GRETA ENGLAND, entomology and biology educator; b. Medford, Mass., Nov. 12, 1933; d. Wightman Shearer and Thelma Mary (England) T.;m. Albert M. Rosenburg, Jan. 2, 1986. BS, State Coll., Bridgewter, Mass., 1955; MS, U. N.H., 1957; PhD, U. Calif., Berkeley, 1967. Instr. U. Wash., Seattle, 1970-72; asst. prof. U. Md., Balt., 1972-76; dir., assoc. prof. Miss. State U., Starkville, 1976-80, prof., dir. electron microscope ctr., 1980—. Contbr. articles to profl. jours. Recipient Fulbright Student award U. Queensland (Australia), 1957-58, NIH traineeship U. Wash., 1969-70; NIH predoctoral fellow U. Calif., Berkeley, 1964-67, NIH postdoctoral fellow U. Wash., 1969-70; Rsch. grantee USPHS, NIH, 1974-77. Mem. Ala. Electron Microscopy Soc., Am. Soc. Zoologists, Electron Microscopy Soc. Am., La. Soc. for Electron Microscopy, Southeastern Electron Microscopy Soc., The Crustacean Soc. Home: 2610 Persimmon Dr Starkville MS 39759 Office: Miss State U Drawer EM Electron Microscope Ctr Mississippi State MS 39762

TYSON, HELEN FLYNN, civic leader; b. Wilmington, N.C.; d. Walter Thomas and Fannie Elizabeth (Smith) Flynn; Student Guilford Coll., Am. U., Washington; m. James Franklin Tyson, Dec. 25, 1940 (dec.). U.S. Civil Svc. auditor, Disbursing Office, AUS, Ft. Bragg, N.C., 1935-46, chief clerical asst. Disbursing Office, Pope AFB, N.C., 1946-49, asst. budget and acctg. officer, 1949-55, supervisory budget officer hdqrs. Mil. Transport Command, USAF, 1955-57, budget analyst Hdqrs. USAF, Washington, 1957-74, ret. Active Arlington Com. 100, Ft. Belvoir, U.S. Army Engr. Ctr., Civilian-Mil. Adv. Coun., Salvation Army Women's Aux., Inter-Svc. Club Coun. of Arlington; pres. Operation Check-Mate Coun. of Arlington, 1981; friend of Arlington County Libr. Recipient awards U.S. Treasury, 1945, 46, U.S. State Dept., 1970; Good Neighbor award Ft. Belvoir Civilian-Mil. Adv. Coun., 1978; awards U.S. First Army, 1973, ARC, 1977; named Arlington Woman of Yr., 1975; recipient Cert. of Recognition, 1981, Vol. Activists award Greater Washington Met. Area, 1981. Mem. Nat. Fedn. Bus. and Profl. Women's Clubs, Am. Assn. Ret. Fed. Employees, Am. Soc. Mil. Comptrs. (Outstanding Mem. award Washington chpt. 1988), Friends of the Kennedy Ctr., Nat. Assn. Female Execs., Am. Inst. Parliamentarians, Guilford Coll. Alumni Assn., N.C. Soc. Washington, Altrusa Internat., Alexandria (Va.) City Hosp. Found., Arlington Hosp. Found. Home: 4900 N Old Dominion Dr Arlington VA 22207

TYSON, KAREN ELAINE, management consultant, director; b. Romulus, N.Y., Dec. 19, 1945; d. Alvia Theodore Hilliard and Shirley Reba (Henderson) Gurtler; m. Wayne McKenny Tyson, Dec. 23, 1965 (div. May 1986); 1 child, Janice Elaine. Student, James Madison U., 1963-66; AA, U. Md., 1977, BS, 1979, M, 1990. With Naval Air Test Ctr., Patuxent River, Md., 1975—, mgmt. analyst Force Warfare Aircraft, test directorate, 1983-86; dep. dir. Force Warfare Aircraft, test directorate Naval Air Test Ctr., Patuxent River, 1986—; chmn. master planning com. Naval Air Test Ctr., 1988-90; participant naval sr. exec. mgmt. devel. program, Patuxent River, 1987—. Translator, interpreter USN Family Svcs., Patuxent River, 1985-90; Brownie leader Girl Scouts U.S., Rota, Spain, 1972-73; ways and means chmn. Leonardtown (Md.) Sch. PTA, 1975-76; pres. Great Mills (Md.) High Sch. Band Boosters, 1983-84. Mem. Nat. Contracts Mgmt. Assn. (instr. 1986). Republican. Presbyterian. Office: Naval Air Test Ctr Force Warfare Aircraft Test Patuxent River MD 20670

TYSON, PATTI BIRGE, lawyer; b. Sherman, Tex.; d. John Sinclair and Evelyn (Wolverton) Birge; m. Bruce Spivey, Dec. 20, 1987. AB, U. Tex.; JD, George Washington U. Bar: Tex. 1979, D.C. 1979. Exec. asst. to rep. Joe Pool Washington, 1964-68; asst. to vice chmn. Equal Employment Opportunity Commn., Washington, 1968; exec. asst. to rep. Margaret M. Heckler Washington, 1968-72; asst. to dir. of peer rev. HEW, Washington, 1972-75; adminstrv. asst. to U.S. Rep. Gillis Long Washington, 1975-76; chief counsel, staff dir. sub-com. on legis. process House Com. on Rules, Washington, 1976-79, 1979-83; exec. asst. to sec. health and human services Washington, 1983-85; mem. U.S. Postal Rate Commn., Washington, 1985—, vice chmn., 1987-89; adv. coun. Fogarty Internat. Ctr. NIH, Bethesda, Md., 1985-88. Pres. Tex. State Soc., Washington, 1985-86, Tex. U. Ex-Students Assn., D.C. chpt., 1990-91; trustee St. John's Child Devel. Ctr., Washington, 1987-90; adv. coun. U. Tex., 1987—; adv. commn. Congrl. Asst. Program, Conf. Bd., Washington, 1986—. Mem. ABA, Tex. Bar Assn., D.C. Bar Assn., Nat. Assn. Regulatory Utility Commrs., Nat. Women's Econ. Alliance (exec. adv. com. 1985—), Exec. Women in Govt., Found. for Coll. of Liberal Arts (adv. coun. U. Tex./Austin chpt.), Charter 100 Club, Club Sulgrave. Democrat. Office: Postal Rate Commn Office of Chmn 1333 H St NW Ste 300 Washington DC 20268

TYSON, PHOEBE WHATLEY, painter, artist; b. Wichita Falls, Tex., May 5, 1926; d. Mertic Boyd and Susie Phoebe (Creath) Whatley; student Abilene Christian U., 1943-45; BA, North Tex. State U., 1946, MA, 1951; m. Josiah William Tyson, Jr., Dec. 20, 1946; children: Josiah William III, Phoebe Creath Tyson McDavid. Elem. art tchr. Ft. Worth Ind. Sch. Dist., 1946-47; pvt. tchr. art, Haskell, Tex., 1948-50; painter watercolors, acrylics, Seabrook, Tex., 1971-79. Represented in exhbns. (solo) Scurry County Mus., Snyder, Tex., (group) Biennial Exhbn., Nat. League Am. Pen Women, Kennedy Center, Washington (award of distinction), 1976, Rocky Mountain Nat. Watermedia Exhbn., Golden, Colo., 1977, 82, 85, McNay Art Mus., San Antonio, Tex. (purchase prize), Tex. Tech. Mus., Lubbock (excellence award), Trinity U., San Antonio, St. Edward's U., Austin (best of show), Madison (Wis.) Nat. Watercolor Exhbn., Watercolor Art Soc. Ann. Exhbn.; represented in permanent collections Univ. Ave Ch. of Christ, Austin, Tex. Water Quality Assn. Mem. McLean (Va.) Art Club (pres. 1970-71), Nat. League Am. Pen Women (nat. art bd. 1972-74, Tex. v.p. 1972-74, Meml. br. pres. 1976-78), Art League Houston, AAUW (v.p. Austin 1955-56), Nat. Watercolor Soc. (assoc.), Watercolor Art Soc. Houston, San Antonio Watercolor Group, Waterloo Watercolor Group, Austin. Mem. Church of Christ. Home: 8600 Appalachian Austin TX 78759

TYSON, SHIRLEY ANN, hospital administrator; b. Columbiana, Ohio, Nov. 24, 1934; d. Kenneth Goerge and Sarah Ann (Gray) T. Diploma Nursing, Youngstown Hosp. Assn. Sch. Nursing, 1956; BS in Nursing, Youngstown State U., 1970; MBA, Baldwin-Wallace Coll., 1986. RN, Ohio, Calif. From staff to head nurse Youngstown (Ohio) Hosp. Assn., 1956-61; staff nurse Cedars of Lebanon Hosp., Los Angeles, 1961-63; night supr. Kaiser Found. Hosp., Los Angeles, 1963-66; supr. inservice edn. Salem (Ohio) Community Hosp., 1966-72, dir. personnel, 1972-78, asst. adminstr., 1978—; instr. part time Kent State U., Salem, 1980-84. Mem. adv. bd. Kent State U., Salem, 1987—; adminstrv. advisor Med. Explorers Scout Troupe, Salem. Mem. Am. Orgn. Nursing Execs., Ohio League Nursing (state dir. 1981-82), Northeast Ohio Nursing Service Adminstrs. (sec. 1982-83), Columbiana Bus. and Profl. Women (pres. 1983-85). Lutheran. Office: Salem Community Hosp 1995 E State St Salem OH 44460

TYTLER, LINDA JEAN, marketing executive, state legislator; b. Rochester, N.Y., Aug. 31, 1947; d. Frederick Easton and Marian Elizabeth (Allen) T.; m. George Stephen Dragnich, May 2, 1970 (div. July 1976). AS, So. Sem., Buena Vista, Va., 1967; student U. Va., 1973; student in pub. adminstrn. U. N. Mex., 1981-82. Spl. asst. to Congressman John Buchanan, Washington, 1971-75; legis. analyst U.S. Senator Robert Griffin, Washington, 1975-77; ops. supr. Pres. Ford Com., Washington, 1976; office mgr. U.S. Senator Pete Domenici Re-election, Albuquerque, 1977; pub. info. officer S.W. Community Health Service, Albuquerque, 1978-83; cons. pub. relations and mktg., Albuquerque, 1983-84; account exec. Rick Johnson & Co., Inc., Albuquerque, 1983-84; dir. mktg. and communications St. Joseph Healthcare Corp., 1984-88; mktg. and bus. devel. cons., 1987—; mgr. communications and pub. affairs Def. Avionics Systems div., Honeywell Inc.; mem. N.Mex. Ho. of Reps., Santa Fe, 1983—, vice chmn. appropriations and fin. com., 1985-86, interim com. on children and youth, 1985-86, mem. edn. com., transp. com., interim com. environ., land use and solid waste, 1989—; chmn. Rep. Caucus, 1985-88; chmn. legis. campaign com. Rep. Com.; mem. hosp. cost containment task force Nat. Conf. State Legislatures; del. to Republic of China, Am. Council of Young Polit. Leaders, 1988. Bd. dirs. N. Mex. chpt. ARC, Albuquerque, 1984. Recipient award N.Mex. Advt. Fedn., Albuquerque, 1981, 82, 85, 86, 87. Mem. Am. Soc. Hosp. Pub. Relations (cert.), Nat. Advt. Fedn., Soc. Hosp. Planning and Mktg., Am. Mktg. Assn. Republican. Baptist.

TZAVARAS, ANASTASIA, research company executive, economist; b. Athens; d. Anastasios and Despina (Kotsafti) T. BA, Coll. of Wooster, 1983; MPP, Harvard U., 1985; postgrad., Am. U., 1981. Rsch. and devel. trainee UN Devel. Program, Islamabad, Pakistan; assoc. Abacus and Associs., N.Y.C.; devel. mgmt. specialist Developmental Alternatives Inc., Washington; exec. officer internat. Univ. Rsch. Corp., Bethesda, Md. Author numerous devel. publs. Harvard Inst. for Internat. Devel. fellow; Compton scholar; Helen Graham scholar; recipient Blanchard award for promotion of internat. understanding. Mem. Devel. Mgmt. Network, Omicron Delta Epsilon. Address: 1260 21st St NW Apt 309 Washington DC 20036

UAZZANO, JANICE DEMICCO, strategic information systems official; b. Montclair, N.J., Nov. 13, 1948; d. Emilio A. and Georgia (Ciccarelli) Demicco; m. John M. Armentrout, Oct. 25, 1973. Student, Allegheny Coll., Pitts., 1970, Carnegie Mellon U., Pitts., 1971. Dir., mgmt. info. Pine Tree Orgn. for Profl. Standards Review, Augusta, Maine, 1978-80; project dir. Va. Mason Med. Ctr., Seattle, Maine, 1980-81; dir., mgmt. info. Mercy Hosp., Portland, Maine, 1981-84; pres., owner CompuMed Corp., Portland, Maine; asst. dep. commissioner Office Info. Services, Augusta, Maine, 1987—; cons. Commonwealth Mass., Pa. Small Bus., US Dept. Health and Human Services. Chair Woolwich Dem. Com., 1984, Conservation Commn., 1985, mem. Audobon Soc., Falmouth, Nature Conservancy, Topsham, Maine, 1988. Mem. Data Processing Mgmt. Assn., Hosp. Mgmt. Systems Soc. Democrat. Office: Office Info Svcs Sta #61 Augusta ME 04333

UDEN, JANICE LYNN, chemical and metallurgical engineer; b. Columbus, Nebr., Aug. 11, 1958; d. Marvin Lavern and Carol Ann (Struss) U.; m. Lawrence W. Monroe, Aug. 19, 1978 (div. Feb. 1982); 1 child, Jennifer Ann. BSChemE., U. Nebr., 1980, MS in Metall. Engring., 1989. Registered profl. engr., Nebr. Engr. Omaha Pub. Power Dist., 1980-85, sr. engr., 1987—; lead nuclear engr. reactor performance, grad. tchr., researcher U. Nebr., Lincoln, 1985-86; with tech. staff Sandia Nat. Labs., Albuquerque, 1986-87. Instr. fitness YMCA, 1984—, soccer coach, 1988—; Stephen min. Mem. NSPE, Am. Nuclear Soc. (chmn. elect, sec. 1987-90, chmn. Nebr. chpt. 1990—), Am. Inst. Chem. Engrs., Am. Soc. for Metals (sec.), Cousteau Soc. Lutheran. Home: 2010 N 53d St Lincoln NE 68504 Office: Omaha Pub Power Dist 444 S 16th St Omaha NE 68102

UDOW, ROSALYN LONG, education and civil liberties specialist, lecturer, lobbyist, local government official; b. Malden, Mass., Jan. 17, 1926; d. Harry A. and Anna Florence (Jacobson) Long; m. Alfred Bernard Udow, Nov. 16, 1951; children—Marianne, Henry Adam. Student Bennington Coll., Vt., 1943-45; A.B., U. Mich, 1947. Exec. dir. N.Y. State Com. for Legal Abortion, 1971, N.Y. State Coalition for Family Planning, N.Y.C., 1971-76; dir. govt. policy affairs Planned Parenthood of N.Y.C., 1976-80; N.Y. regional dir. People for the Am. Way, N.Y.C., 1981-84; dir. edn. and pub. affairs Nat. Coalition Against Censorship, N.Y.C., 1985—; coordinator Hofstra U. Sch. Bd. Forum, Hempstead, N.Y., 1985-87; trustee, bd. chair Nassau Community Coll., Garden City, N.Y., 1984—. Editor: Great Neck Regional Plan, 1966; (with others) This is Great Neck, 1956. Contbr. articles to profl. publs. Founder, voters service chair LWV, Great Neck, N.Y., 1954-59; bd. dirs. N.Y. State LWV, 1962; chair Village of Great Neck Planning Bd., 1959-66; sec. Great Neck Regional Planning Bd., 1960-66; trustee, pres. Great Neck Bd. Edn., 1966-70; bd. dirs. Planned Parenthood, Nassau County, N.Y., 1980-83, Family Planning Advocates of N.Y. State, 1977-80, Nat. Coalition Against Censorship, N.Y.C., 1983—, Citizens for Family Planning, N.Y. State, 1982—; mem. nat. advance team Ferraro V.P. Campaign, 1984. Recipient Margaret Sanger award Family Planning Advocates of N.Y. State, 1980; Eleanor Roosevelt award Am. Jewish Congress, 1982. Mem. ACLU, Govt. Affairs Profls., Intellectual Freedom Found. Avocations: watercolor, monotype, gardening. Home: 3 Bly Ct Great Neck NY 11023 Office: Nat Coalition Against Censorship 2 W 64th St New York NY 10023

UDZIELA, LORETTA ANN, educator; b. Blue Island, Ill., July 30, 1933; d. John Joseph and Stephanie Matilda (Parzygnot) U. BA, De Paul U., 1963; MS, U. Wis., Milw., 1971, reading specialist lic., 1973. Elem. tchr. Archdiocese of Chgo., 1952-66; elem. tchr. Milw. Pub. Schs., 1966-76, reading clinician, 1976-82, pod coord. grade 4, 1982—; cooperating tchr. Alverno Coll., Milw., 1969-74, Marquette U., Milw., 1982-83, U. Wis., Milw., 1988—. Tchr. rep. Jeremiah Curtin Sch. PTA, Milw., 1972-74; mem. Intergroup Coun. for Women, Milw., 1978-80; coord. Stamp Club, 21st Street Sch., Milw., 1984—; vol. food distbr. Marquette U. High Sch., Milw., 1986—. Mem. Internat. Reading Assn. (membership com. 1972-78), Disabled Reading Assn., Delta Kappa Gamma (2d v.p. 1978-80), Phi Delta Kappa (scholarship com. 1986-87), Pi Lambda Theta. Democrat. Roman Catholic. Home: 5642 S 27th St Milwaukee WI 53221 Office: Milw Pub Schs 2121 W Hadley Milwaukee WI 53206

UEHLING, BARBARA STANER, educational administrator; b. Wichita, Kans., June 12, 1932; d. Roy W. and Mary Elizabeth (Hilt) Staner; m. Stanley Johnson; children: Jeffrey Steven, David Edward. B.A., U. Wichita, 1954; M.A., Northwestern U., 1956, Ph.D., 1958; hon. degree, Drury Coll., 1978; LL.D. (hon.), Ohio State U., 1979. Mem. psychology faculty Oglethorpe U., Atlanta, 1959-64, Emory U., Atlanta, 1966-69; adj. prof. U. R.I., Kingston, 1970-72; dean Roger Williams Coll., Bristol, R.I., 1972-74; dean arts scis. Ill. State U., Normal, 1974-76; provost U. Okla., Norman, 1976-78; chancellor U. Mo.-Columbia, 1978-86, U. Calif., Santa Barbara, 1987—; sr. vis. fellow Am. Council Edn., 1987; sr. vis. fellow Am. Coun. Edn., 1987; cons. higher edn. State of N.Y., 1973-74; cons. North Cen. Accreditation Assn., 1975-86; mem. nat. educator adv. com. to Comptroller Gen. U.S., 1978; mem. commn. on mil.-higher edn. rels. Am. Coun. on Edn., 1978-86; bd. dirs. Coun. on Postsecondary Edn., 1986-87, 90—; bd. dirs. Merc Bancorp, Inc., 1979-86, Meredith Corp., 1980—. Author: Women in Academe: Steps to Greater Equality, 1978; editorial bd. Jour. of Higher Edn. Mgmt., 1986—; contbr. articles to profl. jours. Bd. dirs., chmn. Nat. Ctr. Higher Edn. Mgmt. Systems; bd. dirs. Am. Council on Edn., 1979-83, treas., 1982-83; trustee Carnegie Found. for Advancement of Teaching, 1980-86, Santa Barbara Med. Found. Clinic, 1989—; bd. dirs. Resources for the Future; mem. NCAA Select Com. on Athletics, 1983-84, NCAA Presdl. Commn.; mem. Nat. Council on Ednl. Research, 1980-82; mem. Bus.-Higher Edn. Forum, Am. Council on Edn. Social Sci. Research Council fellow, 1954-55; NSF fellow, 1956-57; NIMH postdoctoral research fellow, 1964-67; named one of 100 Young Leaders of Acad. Change Mag. and ACE, 1978; recipient Alumni Achievement award Wichita State U., 1978, Alumnae award Northwestern U., 1985, Excellence in Edn. award Pi Lambda Theta, 1989. Mem. Am. Assn. Higher Edn. (dir. 1974-77, pres. 1977-78), Western Assn. Schs. and Colls. (pres.-elect 1988-89, pres. 1990—), Internat. Com. for Study of Ednl. Exchange (chair 1988—), Gold Key Nat. Honor Soc., Sigma Xi. Office: U Calif Cheadle Hall Santa Barbara CA 93106

UFFORD, ELIZABETH, pediatrician; b. Elmira, N.Y., Aug. 19, 1909; d. William Mandeville and Fanny O. (Henry) U.; 1 child, Joseph H. Carpenter. AB, Vassar Coll., 1931; MD, Columbia U., 1937. Diplomate Am. Bd. Pediatrics. Intern Bellevue Hosp., N.Y.C., 1937-38, Sydenham Hosp. Contagious Diseases, Balt., 1939; asst. resident The Babies Hosp., Columbia Presbyn. Med. Ctr., N.Y.C., 1939-40; pvt. practice Port Washington, N.Y., 1940-75; sch. physician Port Washington Manhasset, N.Y., 1941-46, 72-75, Waterbury, Conn., 1976-78; asst. dir. health Southbury, Conn., 1978-84; researcher Nat. Inst. Nervous Dieseases and Blindness, Coll. Phys. and Surgs., 1965-75; clinician HIP Orgn., Hempstead, N.Y., 1973, Pediatric Health Clinic, Freeport, N.Y., 1969-73; asst. prof. pediatrics Columbia U. Babies Hosp., 1940-75; mem. staff pediatrics North Shore Unive. Hosp., Manhasset, 1954-75, The Babies Hosp., Columbia Presbyn. Med. Ctr., N.Y., 1940-75; asst. dir. health Southbury, Conn., 1980-85. Bd. dirs. Pomperaug Woods Life Care Ctr., Southbury, 1979-90; chmn. libr. com.; chmn. health com. Pomperaug Woods. Mem. Am. Acad. Pediatrics, Hezekiah Beardsley Pediatric Soc. Home: 167 Pomperaug Woods Southbury CT 06488

UGISS-ALTIERI, CAROLYN, real estate consulting and development company executive, broker; b. Scott Field, Ill., Nov. 19, 1947; d. Philip Patrick and Marcia (Truxton) U.; m. Donald R. Altieri, Dec. 12, 1982. B.S., Cornell U., 1969. Lic. real estate broker, N.Y., Colo.; lic. real estate salesperson, Calif. Pub. relations dir. Smoke Watchers Internat., N.Y.C., 1969-73; mktg. dir. Environ. Research & Devel., N.Y.C., 1973-76; exec. v.p. CPC/Corp. Planners and Coordinators, Inc., N.Y.C., 1976—, dir. subs. cos.; dir. Beri, Inc., Salem, Oreg. Mem. Real Estate Bd. N.Y. Club: Cornell of Fairfield County (Conn.). Office: CPC Corp Planners and Coordinators 645 Fifth Ave 21st Floor New York NY 10022

UHL, DIANA LOIS, health services administrator; d. Alton L. and Bette B. (Winters) Brown; m. Kenneth Uhl, Nov. 21, 1975. BS magna cum laude, Saginaw Valley State U., 1977; MBA, So. Ill. U., 1982. Cert. quality engr. Mgr. tech. svc. and devel. CD Med., Inc., Miami Lakes, Fla., 1989—. Mem. Am. Soc. for Quality Control, Assn. for Advancement Med. Instrumentation, Beta Gamma Sigma. Address: 9601 NW 16th St Plantation FL 33322

UHLENBECK, KAREN KESKULLA, mathematician, educator; b. Cleve., Aug. 24, 1942; d. Arnold Edward and Carolyn Elizabeth (Windeler) Keskulla; m. Olke Cornelis, June 12, 1965 (div.). B.S. in Math., U. Mich., 1964; Ph.D. in Math., Brandeis U., 1968. Instr. math. MIT, Cambridge, 1968-69; lectr. U. Calif.-Berkeley, 1969-71; asst. prof., then assoc. prof. U. Ill.,

Urbana, 1971-76; assoc. prof., then prof. U. Ill., Chgo., 1977-83; prof. U. Chgo., 1983-88; Sid W. Richardson Found. Regents' Chair in Math. U. Tex., 1988—; speaker plenary address Internat. Congress Maths., 1990. Author: Instantons and Four Manifolds, 1984. Contbr. articles to profl. jours. NSF Grad. fellow, 1964-68, Sloan Found. fellow, 1974-76, MacArthur Found. fellow, 1983-88; recipient Alumni Achievement award Brandeis U., 1988. Mem. AAAS. Nat. Acad. Scis., Alumni Assn. U. Mich. (Alumnae of Yr. 1984), Am. Math. Soc., Assn. Women in Math., Phi Beta Kappa. Office: U Tex Dept Math Austin TX 78712

UHRMAN, CELIA, artist, poet; b. New London, Conn., May 14, 1927; d. David Aaron and Pauline (Schwartz) U. BA, Bklyn. Coll., 1948, MA, 1953; PhD, U. Danzig, 1977; postgrad. Tchrs. Coll., Columbia U., 1961, CUNY, 1966, Bklyn. Mus. Art Sch., 1956-57, PhD (hon.), LittD, 1973; cert. Koret Living Library U. of San Francisco, 1982. One-woman shows: Leffert Jr. High Sch., Bklyn., 1958, Flatbush C. of C., N.Y.C., 1963, Conn. C. of C., New London, 1962; exhibited in group shows: Smithsonian Instn., Washington, 1958, Springfield (Mass.) Mus. Fine Arts, 1959, Bklyn. Mus., 1959, Old Mystic (Conn.) Art Center, 1959, Carnegie Endowment Internat. Center, N.Y.C., 1959, Lyman Allyn Mus., New London, 1960, Palacio de La Virrelna, Barcelona, Spain, 1961, YMCA, Bklyn., 1962, UFT Art Exhibit, N.Y.C., 1963, Soc. of 4 Arts, Palm Beach, Fla., 1964, Perspective 68, Monte-Carlo, Monaco, 1968, George W. Wingate High sch., Bklyn., 1967, Premier Salon Internat., Charleroi, Belgium, 1968, Palme d'or Beaux Arts, Monte-Carlo, 1970, 72, Dibuix-Joan Miro Premi Internacional, Barcelona, 1970; N.Y. Art Festival, 1970, Internat. Platform Assn. Art Show, Washington, 1971, 73, Ovar Mus., Portugal, 1974, others; represented in permanent collections: Bklyn. Coll., Ch. of Evangel, Bklyn.; tchr. N.Y.C. Sch. System, 1948-82; ptnr. Uhrman Studio, 1973-83; hon. rep. U.S., Centro Studi E Scambi Internazionali, Rome, mem. Internat. Com., 1969. Hon. life mem. World Poetry Day Com., Inc. and Nat. Poetry Day Com., 1977. Recipient award Freedoms Found., George Washington medal of honor, 1964, Diplome d'Honneur Palme d'Or des Beaux Arts Exhbn., Monaco, 1969, 72, Diploma and Gold medal, Centro Studi E Scambi Internazionali, 1972; decorated Order of Gandhi Award of Honour, Knight Grand Cross, 1972; personal poetry certificate WEFG Stereo, 1970; Gold Laurel award Esposizione Internazionale D'Art Contemporain, Paris, 1974; named Poetry Translator Laureate World Acad. Lang. and Lit., 1972, Poet of Mankind Acad. Philosophy, 1972; cert. of appreciation Bd. Edn. of N.Y.C., 1982. Fellow World Lit. Academy Eng.; mem. Internat. Arts Guild (comdr. 1966—), World Poetry Soc. Intercontinental (rep. at large 1969—), Internat. Acad. Poets (founding fellow), N.Y. Artists Equity. Author: Poetic Ponderances, 1969, A Pause for Poetry, 1970, Poetic Love Fancies, 1970, A Pause for Poetry for Children, 1973, The Chimps Are Coming, 1975, Love Fancies, 1987. Home: 1655 Flatbush Ave Apt and Studio C106 Brooklyn NY 11210

UILKEMA, GAYLE BURNS, vice-mayor, councilwoman; b. Detroit, Sept. 2, 1938; d. Joseph A. and Pearl (Rasmussen) Burns; children: Lynn, Sharon. BS in Edn., U. Mich., 1959; MPA, Calif. State U., Hayward, 1987. Tchr. bus. edn. and vocat. subjets Heald Coll., Oakland, Calif., 1961-62; tchr. bus. edn. dept. Oakland High Sch., 1962-66; lectr. Grad. Sch. Mgmt. John F. Kennedy U., Orinda, Calif., 1988—; lectr. in field. Commr. Contra Costa Local Agy. Information Commn., 1986, 88, chmn., 1987, vice-chmn., 1990—; Lafayette rep. Cen Contra Costa Transit Authority, 1978-90, chmn., bd. dirs., 1980, bd. dirs., chmn. fin. com., 1981-85, bd. dirs., chmn. ops. and scheduling, 1986, dir. ops. and scheduling com., 1987, chmn. exec. and ops. scheduling coms., 1989, bd. dirs., 1990—; mem. Lafayette City Coun., 1978—, vice mayor, 1980, mayor 1981-82, 1983-84. Recipient MTC award, 1981. Mem. AAUW (bd. dirs. 1971-78, pres. 1972-73, state bd. dirs. 1974-76, nat. rep. 1977-78, Disting. Woman award 1978), Soroptimists Internat. Republican. Roman Catholic. Home: 670 Sky Hy Circle Lafayette CA 94549 Office: City of Lafayette 251 Lafayette Circle Lafayette CA 94549

UITERMARK, HELEN JOAN, computing services executive; b. Zandvoort, Netherlands, May 4, 1941; came to U.S., 1968, naturalized, 1977; d. Peter Theodore and Maria Francisca (Castien) U.; ed. London, Ont., Can. With Drug Trading Co., London, 1957-59, Richard-Wilcox, London, 1959-62, Friden Bus. Machines, Toronto, Ont., 1962-68, Permatex, West Palm Beach, Fla., 1968-70, Singer Bus. Machines, London, Ont., Can., 1970-72, Los Angeles, 1972-74; with Safariland Leather Co., Monrovia, Calif., 1974-81, v.p. adminstrn., 1975-81; ind. systems analyst, Los Angeles, 1981-83; owner Timor Computing Services, Azusa, Calif., 1983—; exec. dir. Forum Internat., 1983—. Mem. Forum Internat., Aircraft Owners and Pilots Assn.

ULANSEY, VIVIENNE K., psychologist, consultant; b. Phila., July 22, 1922; d. Allen and Rose (Daroff) Kaplan; m. Judson Thomas Ulansey, June 25, 1950; children: Raymond, Charles. AB in Psychology, Temple U., 1944; MA in Clin. Psychology, U. Pa., 1945, postgrad., 1946-50; student, Inst. Nervous & Mental Disease, 1948. Lic. psychologist, Pa. Psychologist pediatric and psychiat. clinic Med. Sch. Temple U., 1943-44; psychologist U.S. Army Induction Ctr., Phila., 1945; pvt. practice psychologist West End, N.C., 1945—; cons., psychologist Centenniel Sch. Dist., Warminster, Pa., 1976-83; cons. Pennswood Village, Newtown, Pa., 1980-87; lectr. in field. Utilization rev. chmn. Bucks County, Pa., 1974-75; majority insp. voting dist. Doylestown Twp., Bucks County, 1968-72, judge of elections, 1972-75; clk. of elections New Hope Borough, Bucks County, 1980-83, asst. com. person, 1981-86; developer old newsboy day drive Variety Club, 1990; bd. dirs. Children of Aging Parents, 1984-86; mem. adv. coun. Ret. Srs. Vol. Program, 1988—; spl. registration commr. Moore County, N.C., 1989. Recipient Membership award Four Chaplains Legion of Honor, 1975, Cert. of Appreciation, AFL-CIO, 1976. Mem. Am. Psychol. Assn., Pa. Psychol. Assn., Eastern Psychol. Assn., Soc. for Personality Assessment, Nat. Health Svc. Providers Register, Rorschach Internat., LWV (fin. chmn., v.p.). Home: Seven Lakes Box 1003 West End NC 27376

ULICHNY, BARBARA L., state legislator; b. Milw., June 10, 1947; d. Clarence and Karmen (Egge) Seybold. BA in Econ., Northwestern U., 1969. Tchr. Nicolet High Sch., Milw., 1969-74; adminstr. bicentennial City of Milw., 1975-76; program staff YWCA, Milw., 1976-78; mem. Wis. Assembly, Madison, 1978-84, Wis. Senate, Madison, 1984—; chmn. senate com. econ. devel., crime victim's council. Mem. Common Cause, Italian Community Ctr., Profl. Dimensions, Wis. Heritages, Watertower Landmark Trust, Milw. Task Force on Rape/Sexual Assault and Domestic Violence, Hist. Lower E. Side Neighborhood Assn.; adv. bd. ctr. study of entrepreneurship Marquette U.; bd. dirs. Milw. Ballet, Visiting Nurses Corp. Recipient Pub. Interest award Ctr. for Pub. Representation, 1977, Wis. Women's Polit. Caucus award, 1979, 81, Woman of Yr. award, NOW, 1980, Nat. Orgn. Victim Assistance award, 1981, Meritorious Service award Phi Kappa Phi, 1984. Mem. Nat. Conf. State Legislature (com. fed. taxation, trade and econ. devel.), Council State Govt. (bus. devel. task force), Wis. Women's Network, LWV. Democrat. Lutheran. Office: Wis State Senate PO Box 7882 Madison WI 53707-7882 Other: 3063 N Murray Ave Milwaukee WI 53211*

ULLERY, JUDITH ANN, nursing home management company executive, nurse; b. Memphis, May 15, 1945; d. Howard and Dorothy (Hyatt) Smith; m. Curtis Adrian Ullery, June 21 1965; children: Russ, Adrienne. Diploma, Meth. Hosp. Sch. Nursing, Memphis, 1966. RN, Tenn.; lic. nursing home adminstr., Tenn. Staff nurseemergency rm. Meth. Hosp., Memphis, 1966-69; staff nurse surgery Lebonheur Children's Hosp., Memphis, 1970-71; with Aetna Ins., Memphis, 1970-71; dir. nurses Mid-South Hosp., Memphis, 1971-74, Doctors Hosp., Memphis, 1974-75; nursing supr. Mid South Comprehensive Home Health, Memphis, 1975-76; cons. on med. mgmt. Batesville, Miss., 1976-79; adminstr. Layton Watson Nursing Home, Gallaway, Tenn., 1979-81, Care InnNursing Home, Memphis, 1981-87; sr. v.p. VHA, Long Term Care, Memphis, 1987—. Active various ch. related assns.; nurse ARC, Memphis. Mem. Am. Coll. Health Care Adminstrs., Tenn. Health Care Assn. (bd. dirs. 1982-89, pres. 1987). Home: 3535 Marietta Blvd Memphis TN 38134 Office: VHA Long Term Care 5050 Poplar St 18th Fl Memphis TN 38157

ULLMAN, MARIE, manufacturing company executive; b. Linlithgo, N.Y., Mar. 19, 1914; d. Max and Sarah (Jaffe) Michaelson; R.N., Bklyn. Hosp., 1935; m. Robert Ullman, Aug. 15, 1935. Pres., sec.-treas. Ullman Devices Corp., Ridgefield, Conn., 1938—; dir. State Nat. Bank Conn., Ridgefield. Mem. C. of C. Ridgefield, Bklyn. Hosp. Nurses Alumnae. Home: 43 Chestnut Hill Rd Wilton CT 06897 Office: PO Box 398 Ridgefield CT 06877

ULLMAN, NELLY SZABO, statistican, educator; b. Vienna, Austria, Aug. 11, 1925; came to U.S., 1939; d. Viktor and Elizabeth (Rosenberg) Szabo; m. Robert Ullman, Mar. 20, 1947; children: Buddy, William John, Martha Ann, Daniel Howard. BA, Hunter Coll., 1945; MA, Columbia U., 1948; PhD, U. Mich., 1969. Rsch. assoc. MIT Radiation Lab, Cambridge, Mass., 1945; instr. Polytechnic Inst. of Bklyn., 1945-63; asst. prof. to prof. Ea. Mich. U., Ypsilanti, 1963—. Author: Study Guide To Actuarial Exam, 1978; contbr. articles to profl. jours. Mem. Am. Math. Assn., Am. Stat. Assn., Biometric Soc., Am. Assn. Univ. Profs. Office: Ea Mich Univ/Dept Math Ypsilanti MI 48197

ULLMAN, TRACEY, actress, singer; b. Slough, Eng., Dec. 30, 1959; m. Allan McKeown, 1984; 1 child, Mabel Ellen. Student, Itaia Conti Stage Sch., London. Appeared in plays Gigi, Elvis, Grease, Four in a Million, 1981 (London Theatre Critics award), The Taming of the Shrew, 1990; films include The Rocky Horror Picture Show, Give My Regards to Broad Street, 1984, Plenty, 1985, Jumpin' Jack Flash, 1986, I Love You To Death, 1990; Brit. TV shows include Three of a Kind, A Kick Up the Eighties, Girls on Top; actress TV series: The Tracey Ullman Show, from 1987 (Emmy award 1990); album You Broke My Heart in Seventeen Places (Gold album). Recipient Brit. Acad. award, 1983. Office: Fox Broadcasting Co care Antonia Coffman 10201 W Pico Blvd Los Angeles CA 90035*

ULMER, EVONNE GAIL, health science administration admission executive; b. Bagley, Minn., Sept. 12, 1947; d. John Ferdinand and Elsie Mabel (McCollum) Lundmark; m. G. Bryan Ulmer, Jan. 11, 1969; 1 child, G. Bryan. Diploma, St. Luke's Hosp., Duluth, Minn., 1968; BS, St. JOseph's Coll., N. Windam, Maine, 1981; MHA, U. Minn., 1984. Staff nurse Baton Rouge Gen., 196970, St. Luke's Hosp., Duluth, Minn., 1968-69, 71-72; asst. adminstr. Hickory Heights Care Ctr., Metarie, La., 1972--73; asst. head nurse Eisenhower Hosp., Colorado Springs, Colo., 1973-74; dir. pt. care svcs. St. Vincent's Gen. Hosp., Leadville, Colo., 197478; inservice, quality assurance dir. Watsatch Hosp., Heber City, Utah, 1979; adminstr. Prospect Park Living Ctr., Estes Park, Colo., 1982-84; asst. adminstr. Estes Park Med. Ctr., Colo., 1979-84; chief exec. officer Weston Co. Hosp. and Manor, Newcastle, Wyo., 1984—. Mem. Am. Hosp. Assn. Chgo. (Tech. Adv. Com. 1989, com. on ethics, del. small and rural governing coun., del. region and policy bd.), Small or Rural Am. Republican. Lutheran. Home: 3306 Latigo Newcastle WY 82701 Office: Weston County Meml Hosp 1124 Washington Newcastle WY 82701

ULMER, HARRIET GLASS, health services adminstrator; b. St. Louis, June 7, 1940; d. Melvin Gabriel and Deenie Joy (Laskowitz) Shcolnik; m. Allen L. Glass, Sept. 4, 1956 (div.); children—Bonnie Nielson, Bernard J., Laura L.; m. 2d, Raymond A. Ulmer, Feb. 26, 1980 (div.). A.B. in English, UCLA, 1976; M.P.A. in Health Services Adminstrn., U. So. Calif., 1980. Regional project coordinator Kaiser Found. Health Plan, Los Angeles, 1977-80; dir. planning and mktg. Hosp. of Good Samaritan, Los Angeles, 1981, v.p. mktg. and bus. devel., 1981-86; cons. healthcare Laventhol & Horwath, Los Angeles, 1986-87; Western regional dir. provider services Provident Life and Accident Ins. Co., Los Angeles, 1987-88; exec. dir., chief exec. officer Med. Research Found., Ventura, Calif., 1988—; cons. Humana Corp., Los Angeles Health Planning and Devel. Agy. Mem. Coro Assocs.; mem. Los Angeles Area Planning Com. Mem. Am. Hosp. Assn., Am. Coll. Healthcare Execs., Women in Health Adminstrn., Healthcare Execs. of So. Calif., So. Calif. Soc. for Hosp. Planners, Am. Soc. Hosp. Planning, Am. Mktg. Assn. (founder, pres. health care div. So. Calif. chpt. 1984-85), Am. Heart Assn. (chmn. pub. policy edn. com. Greater Los Angeles affiliate 1982-84), Acad. Health Services Mktg. (nominating com. 1985, award coordinator and presentation com. 1987), U. So. Calif. Health Services Adminstrn. Alumni Assn. (treas. 1983-84, v.p. 1984-85).

UMBDENSTOCK, JUDY JEAN, educator, farmer, feed and pet store owner; b. Aurora, Ill., Feb. 12, 1952; d. Alfred Alloyuisious and Mary Emma (Orha) U. AA, Elgin (Ill.) Community Coll., 1972, AS, 1973; BA, Aurora U., 1977. Cert. elem., secondary and spl. edn. tchr., Ill. Phys. edn. tchr., head volleyball and track coach St. Laurence Sch., Elgin, 1970-75; asst. coach varsity basketball East Aurora High Sch., 1976-77; jr. varsity coach softball St. Charles (Ill.) High Sch., 1978-79, phys. edn. tchr., 1978-79; head coach volleyball and basketball, math. tchr. Canton Jr. High Sch., Elgin, Ill., 1979-82; varsity coach volleyball and softball Elgin High Sch., 1982-85, phys. edn. tchr., 1982-86; elem. phys. edn. tchr. Sch. Dist. U-46, Elgin, 1986—; substitute tchr. Elgin, St. Charles and Burlington (Ill.) High Sch., 1977-78; referee sports Elgin and St. Charles Area High Sch., 1970—; cons. Draft and Carriage Horse Assn., Kane County, 1981—; owner feed and seed store, 1988—. Leader, youth counselor 4-H (farming and animal husbandry), Northern Ill. area, 1970—; campaign supporter state and local Reps. for re-election, Kane county, 1974-86. Served with U.S. Army, 1976-77, with USNR, 1981-87. Named one of Outstanding Young Women Am., 1983; Elgin Panhellenic Soc.scholar, 1972. Mem. NEA, NAFE, Ill. Edn. Assn., Nat. Farmers Orgn. (pub. relations 1967-80), Airplane Owners and Pilots Assn., Am. Assn. Health, Phys. Edn. and Recreation, Elgin Tchrs. Assn., Ill. Coaches Orgn., Am. Draft Horse Assn., Kane County Tchrs. Credit Union. Clubs: Barrington (Ill.) Carriage, 99's Women's Pilot Assn. Home: 8N129 Umbdenstock Rd Elgin IL 60123 Office: Sch Dist U-46 E Chicago St Elgin IL 60120

UMLAUF, MARY GRACE, nurse; b. Houston, Mar. 26, 1949; m. Arthur W. Umlauf; children: Simon Matthew, Shane Michael. BA, U. Tex., Austin, 1970, BS in Nursing, 1979, PhD, 1988; MS, Tex. Women's U., 1983. Assoc. chief nursing svc. for edn. VA, Marlin, Tex., 1985-88; asst. prof., dir. rsch. devel., grant program coord. Sch. Nursing Tex. Tech U. Health Scis. Ctr., Lubbock, 1988—. Co-author: (with Sue Hamby) The Road to Personal Success: A Travelers Pocket Guide, 1990. VA scholar, 1982-83, VA grantee, 1984-85. Mem. AAUW (v.p. membership 1989—), Tex. Nurses Assn., Am. Nurses Assn., Am. Assn. Spinal Cord Injury Nurses (mem. program com. and rsch. com. 1985—), Sigma Theta Tau (v.p. Iota Mu chpt. 1988—). Office: Tex Tech U Health Svcs Ctr Sch Nursing Lubbock TX 79430

UMPHERS, LUCRETIA SNELLING, elementary school educator, retired; b. Frederick, Okla., Feb. 2, 1912; d. Orange C. and Delia (Redeker) Snelling; m. Audie T. Umphers, Nov. 24, 1949 (dec.). AB, Cen. State U., Edmond, Okla., 1938; student, U. Hawaii, 1949-50, Trinity U., 1954, U. Okla., 1964. Elem. tchr. Lawton, Okla., 1934-45, Paaulo, Hawaii, 1945-46, Pahala, Hawaii, 1946-48, Helemano, Hawaii, 1948-49; elem. tchr. Hickham Air Force Base, Hawaii, 1949-50, Fort Sam, Houston, 1951-53, Lawton, 1953-54, 61-76. Mem. P.E.O. (officer 1963-70), Assn. Childhood Edn. (past pres.), Eastern Star, United Meth. Women (dist. sec., treas. 1977-85). Democrat. Home: 1812 NW 23rd St Lawton OK 73505

UMPHRESS, AGNES ELLEN, clin. therapist; b. Ashland, Oreg., June 27, 1925; d. Charles Albert and Mabel (Rice) White; B.A., Willamette U., 1947; M.S.W., U. Wash., 1961; m. Rupert Hampton Umphress, Jan. 20, 1962. Supr., Harry & David, Medford, Oreg., 1947-56; med. social worker Oreg. Welfare Commn., 1956-59; clin. therapist U. Wash., 1961-68; chief therapist Children's Home Soc. Wash., Tacoma, 1968-78; co-owner, therapist Counseling Resource Ctr., Inc., Chehalis, Wash., 1979—; adv. bd. Child Abuse Program, 1974-78, Sexual Assault Program, 1977-78, Family Planning Assn., 1975-80. Cert. Acad. Cert. Social Workers. Mem. Nat. Assn. Social Workers, Nat. Assn. Clin. Social Workers, Am. Assn. Psychiat. Services for Children, Am. Orthopsychiat. Assn. Republican. Club: Sertoma. Contbr. articles to profl. jours. Rsch. on therapeutic programs in technologically advanced and Third World nations. Home: 625 Tauscher Rd Chehalis WA 98532

UNDERDOWN, JOY, educator; b. Boston, Feb. 21, 1935; d. Nathaniel Ridley and Eleanor Johnston (Abbe) U. AA, Stephens Coll., 1954, BA, 1972; MEd, U. Mo., 1974. Cert. tchr., Mo. Tchr. kindergarten Buckley Sch., Sherman Oaks, Calif., 1955-57; tchr. nursery and kindergarten John Thomas Dye Sch., L.A., 1959-63; tchr. kindergarten Palm Valley Sch., Palm Springs, Calif., 1963-66; tchr. Buckley Sch., Sherman Oaks, Calif., 1966-70, Fairview Elem. Sch., Columbia, Mo., 1974—. Mem. Nat. Sci. Tchrs. Assn. (com., presenter), Coun. for Elem. Sci. Internat. (treas. 1982-86, presenter), Columbia Community Tchrs. Assn. (chair com.), Mo. State Tchrs. Assn. (dist. com. chair 1982-83), AAUW, Phi Delta Kappa (treas. 1981-82), Delta Kappa Gamma, Pi Lambda Theta (pres. 1974-76). Home: 2610 Wee Wynd Columbia MO 65203 Office: Fairview Elem Sch 909 Fairview Rd Columbia MO 65203

UNDERHILL, ANNE BARBARA, astrophysicist; b. Vancouver, B.C., Can., June 12, 1920; d. Frederic Clare and Irene Anna (Creery) U. BA, U. B.C., 1942, MA, 1944; PhD, U. Chgo., 1948; DSc (hon.), York U., Toronto, Ont., 1969. Sci. officer Dominion Astrophys. Obs., Victoria, B.C., 1949-62; prof. astrophysics U. Utrecht, The Netherlands, 1962-70; lab chief Goddard Space Flight Ctr./NASA, Greenbelt, Md., 1970-77, sr. scientist, 1978-85; hon. prof. U. B.C., Vancouver, 1985—. Author: The Early-type Stars, 1966; author/editor: B Stars with and without Emission Lines, 1982, O, Of and Wolf-Rayet Stars, 1988; contbr. articles to profl. jours. Fellow NRC, 1948, Can. Fedn. Univ. Women, 1944, 47. Fellow Royal Soc. Can., Royal Astron. Soc.; mem. Internat. Astron. Union (pres. commn. #36 1963-66), Am. Astron. Soc., Can. Astron. Soc. Anglican. Office: U BC, Dept Geophysics & Astronomy, Vancouver, BC Canada V6T 1W5

UNDERHILL, MARTHA JEAN, educator; b. Greenville, Miss., Mar. 29, 1948; d. Thomas Eugene and Matilda Blanton (McDowell) U. BS in Edn., Delta State U., Cleveland, Miss., 1970, MEd, 1972, EdS, 1975. Cert. elem. tchr., Miss. Tchr. math. Coleman Jr. High Sch., Greenville, 1970-71; elem. tchr. Washington Sch., Greenville, 1971—, head tchr. 2d grade, 1980-90. Pianist Avon (Miss.) United Meth. Ch., 1970—; mem. Community Concert Assn., Greenville, Delta Ctr. Stage, Greenville. Mem. Miss. Pvt. Sch. Edn. Assn. (dist. chmn. 1976-77), DAR (2d vice regent), AAUW (sec. 1974-75, treas. 1988-90, named gift honoree to Ednl. Found. 1988), Phi Delta Kappa, Delta Kappa Gamma (sec. 1986-88). Democrat. Home: 567 Cypress Ln Apt F-2 Greenville MS 38701

UNDERHILL, PHYLLIS LOUISE JAYNES, automotive executive; b. Tucumān, Argentina, Sept. 23, 1928; d. Harold Andrus and Virginia (Bier) Jaynes; m. Charles Edward Underhill, Mar. 1, 1947 (dec.); children: C. Edward Jr., James J. Sec. Danbury Auto Haus, Danbury, Conn., 1965-80; pres., dealer Danbury Auto Haus, 1980—. Mem. Eastern Star. Republican. Congregationalist. Office: Danbury Auto Haus Inc 32 Federal Rd Danbury CT 06810

UNDERWOOD, ELLEN FRANKLIN, healthcare administrator, radiologic technologist; b. Summerville, Ga., Dec. 2, 1955; d. John Albert and Irene (Westbrook) Franklin; m. Rodney Dale Underwood, Aug. 24, 1974; children: Amanda Faith, Clinton Kyle. AS, Chattanooga State U., 1976. Radiologic technologist Hutcheson Med. Ctr., Ft. Oglethorpe, Ga., 1974-83; owner TAG Healthcare Staffing, Inc., Ft. Oglethorpe, 1986—. Mem. Dalton Steering Com., Ringgold, Ga., 1988-89. Mem. Nat. Assn. Temp. Svcs., Chattanooga Area Med. Mgrs., Radiologic Technologists Soc., Catoosa County Area C. of C. (dir. 1989). Democrat. Office: TAG Healthcare Staffing Inc 208 Lafayette Rd Fort Oglethorpe GA 30742

UNDERWOOD, KARON M., finance company executive; b. Orlando, Fla., Nov. 29, 1945; d. E. Raymond and Edna (Wehner) Mayfield; m. Robert E. Underwood, Feb. 19, 1987. Banker Sun Bank, Melbourne, Fla., 1965-76; realtor Century 21, Titusville, Orlando, Fla., 1981-86; stockbroker Dean Witter, Winter Park, Fla., 1986—. Mem. ABWA, Sanford (Fla.) C. of C. (com. chmn. 1988-89), Econs. Club (pres. 1987—). Office: Dean Witter Reynolds 200 E New England Ave Winter Park FL 32789

UNDERWOOD, SHIRLEY ANN, business administrator; b. Washington, Aug. 2, 1958; d. George Albert Jr. and Shirley Mae (Simms) U. AS, No. Va. Community Coll., 1983; diploma, Temple Bus. Sch., Alexandria, 1981, Cappa Chell Modeling Sch., 1983. Staff asst. U.S. Senator, adminstrv. asst., staff asst.; exec. asst., adminstrv. asst. BDM Corp.; support coord. Systems Mgmt. Am. Corp. Contbr. atricles to newsletters and mags. Sec.-treas. Alexandria Bowling Ctr., 1989; mem. budget and fin. com. Saxony Square Condominium, Alexandria, 1990, chairperson Ad Hoc com. on mgmt. rev., 1990, chairperson covenants com., 1987-88; pres. Seminary Fair Lanes, 1986-87; participant Super Cities Walk Multiple Sclerosis Soc., 1990. Mem. NAFE, Profl. Secs. Internat. (NOVA chpt.), Henson Creek Golf Club (Oxon Hill, Md.) (named Most Improved Female Golfer 1989, winner Women's Longest Drive 1989, Pres's. Cup 3d Low Gross 1989). Home: 487 N Armistead St Apt T-1 Alexandria VA 22312 Office: 1225 Jefferson Davis Hwy #1209 Arlington VA 22202

UNDERWOOD, VIRGIE DUNMAN, insurance executive; b. Roanoke, Va., Dec. 7, 1951; d. Latane Wilmer and Hennie Virginia (StClair) Dunman; m. Ronald G. Underwood, Mar. 19, 1971 (div. June 1986); 1 child, Stephen D. Degree cum laude, Va. Western Community Coll., 1972. Cert. ins. agt., CPR. With prodn. planning Eli Lilly & Co., Roanoke, Va., 1973-74, exec. sec., 1975-76; exec. sec. Curtis Mathes HEC, Roanoke, 1976-78, bookkeeper, 1978-80, rental mgr., 1980-83, regional rental mgr., 1984-85, store mgr., 1986-89, regional ops. mgr., 1989—; owner, pres. All Around Ins. Agy. Co., Roanoke, 1989—; trainer, cons. NE dist. Curtis Mathes, 1983—. Author guides and manuals, 1982; originator newspaper ads, 1983. Home: 8519 Muirfield Circle Roanoke VA 24019 Office: Curtis Mathes HEC 2138 Colonial Ave SW Roanoke VA 24015

UNGARSOHN, LORI SUE, small business owner; b. N.Y.C., Jan. 23, 1956; d. Harry and Eva (Beckerman) U. AA, Sullivan County Community Coll., 1976; BA, SUNY, Stony Brook, 1978. Pvt. practice photography South Fallsburg, N.Y., 1974-76; free-lance reporter N.Y.C., 1976-77; pres. Nation-Wide Reporting and Conv. Coverage, Inc. and affiliate, Simultaneous Wireless Interpretations, N.Y.C., 1985—. Contbr. articles to profl. jours., 1983—. Mem. Nat. Assn. for Female Execs., Smithsonian Inst., Phi Beta Kappa. Republican. Jewish. Home: 200 E 94th St Apt 404 New York NY 10028 Office: Simultaneous Wireless Interpretations 350 Broadway Suite 1108 New York NY 10013

UNGER, BARBARA FRANKEL, educator, poet; b. N.Y.C., Oct. 2, 1932; d. David and Florence (Schuchalter) Frankel; m. Bernard Unger, 1954 (div. 1976); m. Theodore Sakano, 1987. B.A., CCNY, 1955, M.A., 1957; advanced cert. NYU, 1970; children: Deborah, Suzanne. Grad. asst. Yeshiva U., 1962-63; edn. editor County Citizen, Rockland County, N.Y., 1960-63; tchr. English, N.Y.C. Pub. Schs., 1955-58, Nyack (N.Y.) High Sch., 1963-67; guidance counselor Ardsley (N.Y.) High Sch., 1967-69; prof. English, Rockland Community Coll., Suffern, N.Y., 1969—; poetry fellow Squaw Valley Community of Writers, 1980; writer-in-residence Rockland Ctr. for Arts, 1986. Author: (poetry) Basement, 1975, Learning to Fox Trot, 1989, The Man Who Burned Money, 1980, Inside the Wind, 1986; (fiction) Dying for Uncle Ray, 1990; contbr. poetry to over 40 lit. mags., including: Kans. Quar., Carolina Quar., Beloit Poetry Jour., Minn. Rev., Poet and Critic, The Nation, Poetry Now, Invisible City, Thirteenth Moon, So. Poetry Rev., Mass. Rev., Nebr. Rev., Wis. Rev., So. Humanities Rev.; contbr. to Anthology Mag. Verse, Yearbook Am. Poetry, 1984, 89; contbr. fiction to True to Life Adventure Stories, Midstream, Esprit, Am. Fiction '89 and numerous others; poetry reading in colls. and libraries throught N.Y. and elsewhere; critical reviewer Contact II. Ragdale Found. fellow, 1985, SUNY Creative Writing fellow, 1981-82, Edna St. Vincent Millay Colony fellow, 1984; NEH grantee, 1975. Recipient Goodman Poetry award, 1989, Anna Davidson Rosenberg award Judah Magnes Mus., 1989; finalist Am. Fiction Competition, 1989, W.Va. Writing Competition, 1982; honorable mention Chester Jones Nat. Poetry Contest. Mem. Poets and Writers, Poetry Soc. Am., Writers' Community. Office: Rockland Community Coll 145 College Rd Suffern NY 10901

UNGER, ELIZABETH BETTY, hospital chaplain; b. Manitoba, Can., Mar. 4, 1936; came to U.S. 1962; d. Johann Cornelius and Ottillie (Hirsch) U. BA, Andrews U., 1967, MA in Teaching, 1972. Office clk. Overland Express, St. Catherines, Ont., Can., 1954-55; bookkeeper G.A. Moggridge Printing Co., St. Catherines, Ont., Can., 1955-56; sec., receptionist, asst. to cost acct. Anthes-Imperial, St. Catherines, Ont., Can., 1956-60; ins. claims dir. North York Branson Hosp., Ontario, Toronto, Can., 1960-62; teaching, registrar Mt. Pisgah Acad., Chandler, N.C., 1967-79; spiritual counselor, chaplain Portland (Oreg.) Adventist Med. Ctr., 1971-83; chaplain Hinsdale (Ill.) Hosp., 1984—. Fellow Coll. of Chaplains. Seventh-day Adventist. Home: 304 Scotts Ct Bolingbrook IL 60439 Office: Hinsdale Hosp 120 N Oak St Hinsdale IL 60521

UNGER, MARIANNE LOUISE, computer graphics artist, consultant; b. Reading, Pa., June 8, 1957; d. Paul Richard and Virginia Ruth (Moyer) U. BS in Art Edn., Kutztown U., 1982. Art tchr. 7 local sch. dists., Reading, 1982-83; sec. Berks Cable, Reading, 1983-84, project asst. new bus. devel., 1984-85; art educator Reading Area Community Coll., 1983-87; pres. Unger Computer Graphics, Reading, 1985—; cons. in field, video and multi-image producer, dir., animator. Grantee NET Ben Franklin Advanced Tech. Ctr., 1986-87. Mem. Nat. Computer Graphics Assn., Berks Women's Network, Berks County C. of C. Office: 1313 Good St Reading PA 19602

UNGERICHT, RHONDA DIANE, insurance adjuster; b. Troy, Ohio, Nov. 1, 1949; d. Robert Dwight Ungericht and Irene (Pickett) Adams. Sec. State Farm Fire and Casualty Co., Greenville, S.C., 1968-76; claim svc. rep. State Farm Fire and Casualty Co., Jacksonville, Fla., 1976-79; claim specialist State Farm Fire and Casualty Co., Columbia, S.C., 1979—; supr. State Farm Spl. Disaster Svc. Mem. Internat. Assn. Arson Investigators (S.C.), Habitat for Humanity, Riverbanks Zool. Soc., Soc. Prevention Cruelty to Animals. Office: State Farm Fire/Casualty Co 454 Berry Hill Rd Columbia SC 29210

UNKEFER, BARBARA MORGAN BAXTER, plastics manufacturing company executive, educator; b. Cleve., Apr. 14, 1939; d. James Clifford and Mildred Elizabeth (Button) Baxter; m. David S. Unkefer, Dec. 28, 1956 (div. Jan. 1989); children: Rachel, Clifford David, Elizabeth, Monica, Todd James. BSBA in MIS, Bowling Green State U., 1977, MBA, 1979, postgrad. in psychology, 1984; postgrad. in psychology, Wright State U., 1984-85. Clk. J.C. Baxter Co., Minerva, Ohio, 1962-66; v.p., co-founder Sherwood Plastics, Inc., Fostoria, Ohio, 1966-75, pres., chief exec. officer, 1975-89; mem. adj. faculty Tiffin (Ohio) U., 1984—; MIS cons. to small bus., 1984—. V.p. Carroll County Young Reps., 1960-61; mem. Carroll County Rep. Cen. and Exec. Com., 1961-65, Wood County Rep. Com., 1967-70; troop leader, troop organizer, badge cons. Girl Scouts U.S., 1967-81; vestrywoman, sr. warden Trinity Episcopal Ch., Fostoria,, 1972-75; therapist Community Hospice Care Seneca County, Tiffin, 1987-89; del. U.S.-China Trade Talks People to People, Spokane, Wash., 1988; adv. bd. Tiffin U. Students in Free Enterprise, 1986-87; tchr. applied econs. Jr. Achievement, 1988-89. Mem. Nat. Fedn. Ind. Bus., Order Eastern Star, Ladies Oriental Shrine N.Am., Fostoria Shrine Club (pres. 1982-83), DAR, Alpha Lambda Delta. Home: 435 Park Ave Fostoria OH 44830

UNSOELD, JOLENE, congresswoman; b. Corvallis, Oreg., Dec. 3, 1931; m. William F. Unsoeld (dec.), 1951; children: Regon, Devi (dec.), Krag, Terres. Student, Oreg. State U., 1950-51. Dir. U.S. Info. Svc. English Lang. Inst., Kathmandu, Nepal, 1965-67; mem. Wash. Ho. of Reps., 1985-88, 101st, 102nd Congresses from 3d Dist. Wash., 1989—. Office: US Ho of Reps Office House Mems 1508 Longworth HOB Washington DC 20515

UNTERBERGER, BETTY MILLER, history educator, writer; b. Glasgow, Scotland, Dec. 27, 1923; d. Joseph C. and Leah Miller; m. Robert Ruppe, July 29, 1944; children: Glen, Gail, Gregg. B.A., Syracuse U., N.Y., 1943; M.A., Harvard U., 1946; Ph.D., Duke U., 1950. Asst. prof. E. Carolina U., Greenville, 1948-50; assoc. prof., dir. liberal arts ctr. Whittier Coll., Calif., 1954-61; assoc. prof. Calif. State U.-Fullerton, 1961-65, prof., chmn. grad. studies, 1965-68; prof. Tex. A&M U., College Station, 1968—; vis. prof. U. Hawaii, Honolulu, summer 1967, Peking U., Beijing, People's Republic of China, 1988; vis. disting. prof. U. Calif., Irvine, 1987—; mem. adv. com. fgn. relations U.S. Dept. State, 1977-81, chair, 1981; mem. U.S. Dept. Army Hist. Adv. Com., 1980-82; commr. Nat. Hist. Publs. and Records Commn., 1980—. Author: America's Siberian Expedition 1918-1920: A Study of National Policy, 1956, 69 (Pacific Coast award Am. Hist. Assn. 1956); editor: American Intervention in the Russian Civil War, 1969, Intervention Against Communism: Did the U.S. Try to Overthrow the Soviet Government, 1918-20, 1986, The United States, Revolutionary Russia and the Rise of Czechoslovakia, 1989; contbr.: Woodrow Wilson and Revolutionary World, 1982; editorial adv. bd.: The Papers of Woodrow Wilson, Princeton U., 1982; bd. editors: Diplomatic History, 1981-84, Red River Valley Hist. Rev., 1975-84. Trustee Am. Inst. Pakistan Studies, Villanova U., Pa., 1981—, sec., 1989—. Fellow Woodrow Wilson Found., 1979; named Disting. Teacher State of Calif. Legislature, 1966; recipient All-Univ. Disting. Teaching award Tex. A&M U., 1975. Mem. LWV, NOW, AAUW, Am. Hist. Assn. (chair 1982-83, nominating com. 1980-83), Orgn. Am. Historians (govt. relations com.), Soc. Historians of Am. Fgn. Relations (exec. council 1978-81, 86-89, govt. relations com. 1982-84, v.p. 1985, pres. 1986), Am. Soc. for Advancement Slavic Studies, Coordinating Com. on Women in Hist. Profession, Rocky Mountain Assn. Slavic Studies (program chair 1973, v.p. 1973-74), So. Hist. Assn., Asian Studies Assn., Assn. Third World Studies, Czechoslovak History Conf., Women's Fgn. Policy Coun., Beyond War, Sierra Club, Phi Beta Kappa, Phi Beta Delta. Office: Tex A&M U College Station TX 77843*

UNTERMEYER, SALLE PODOS, lawyer; b. Bklyn., Oct. 1, 1938; d. David Meyer and Rose (Ifshin) Garber; m. Steven Maurice Podos, June 20, 1959 (div. Dec. 1978); children: Richard Lance Podos, Lisa Beth Podos; m. Walter Untermeyer, Jr., May 2, 1982. BA, Vassar Coll., 1959; MA, Brandeis U., 1960; JD, Columbia U., 1977. Bar: N.Y. 1978. Assoc. Paul, Weiss, Rifkind, Wharton & Garrison, N.Y.C., 1977-79; gen. counsel, v.p., sec. MacAndrews & Forbes Group, Inc., N.Y.C., 1979-81; sr. assoc. Sage Gray Todd & Sims, N.Y.C., 1981-84, Proskauer Rose Goetz & Mendelsohn, N.Y.C., 1984-87; pres., gen. counsel Untermeyer Mace Ptnrs., 1987—. Class fund-raising chmn. Vassar Coll., 1977-80; bd. dirs. Vassar Club N.Y., 1978-80; chmn. women's div. U.S. Senate Campaign, 1970; regional chmn. U.S. Presdl. Campaign, 1972; chmn. State Rep.'s Campaign, 1973; del.-elect Interim Dem. Conv., 1974, Lawyers Com. for Gov. Carey, 1978; chmn. Mo. state legis. Nat. Coun. Jewish Women, 1969-75, mem. nat. affairs com., 1969-77, chmn. Mo. juvenile justice project, 1970-75, mem. legis. coordinating com. Midwestern region, 1971-75, mem. nat. task force on constl. rights, 1974-77; v.p., bd. dirs. St. Louis Jewish Community Rels. Coun., 1970-75, chmn. ch.-state and Black Jack Amicus Curiae coms.; v.p., bd. dirs. St. Louis chpt. Am. Jewish Com., 1969-75, chmn. urban affairs and placement for ex-offenders coms., mem. com. on status of women, 1974-77; mem. legis. liaison Coalition for Environment, St. Louis, 1970-74; bd. dirs. St. Louis Jewish Community Ctrs. Assn., 1970-74, chmn. urban affairs and legis. affairs coms.; bd. dirs. St. Louis Jewish Family and Children's Svc., 1972-74, chmn. welfare rights and health svcs. coms.; bd. dirs. Glaucoma Found., 1986—; vol. coord. Poor People's Campaign, 1968; founder, bd. dirs. Consumer's Assn., 1967-69; founder, chmn. Urban Corps program St. Louis Mayor's Com. on Youth, 1969-72; panelist White House Conf. on Children and Youth, 1970, 72, White House Conf. on Aging, 1974; founder, bd. dirs. Mo. chpt. PEARL (Pub. Edn. and Religious Liberty), 1972-75. Woodrow Wilson Found. fellow, 1959, NDEA fellow, 1959. Mem. ABA, Assn. of Bar of City of N.Y. (mem. continuing legal edn. com., com. on lecture), N.Y. State Bar Assn. Home: 950 Park Ave New York NY 10028

UNTERREINER, KAREN ANN, consulting actuary; b. Hartford, Conn., Feb. 17, 1959; d. Francis Leo Unterreiner and Beverly Jean Robichaud. BS in Maths., Rensselaer Poly. Inst., 1981. Actuarial assoc. Aetna Life and Casualty, Hartford, Conn., 1981-86; cons. actuary Milliman & Robertson, Inc., Albany, N.Y., 1986—. Fellow Soc. Actuaries; mem. Am. Acad. Actuaries, Adirondack Actuaries Club (treas. 1988—). Democrat. Home: 3 Flintlock Ln Clifton Park NY 12065

UNTI, SHARON MARSHA, pediatrician; b. Chgo., Dec. 30, 1957; d. Marshall Robert and Dolores Amelia (DiPiero) Hejza; m. James Alan Unti, June 12, 1982; 1 child, Kristen Marsha. BMS, Northwestern U., Evanston, Ill., 1980; MD, Northwestern U., Chgo., 1982. Resident pediatrics Children's Meml. Hosp., Chgo., 1985, intern, 1982; pediatrician Prucare HMO, Chgo., 1985-89; pediatrician, assoc. dir. pediatric edn. Children's Meml. Hosp., Chgo., 1989—; dir. pediatrics Northwestern U. Med. Sch., Chgo., 1985—. Fellow Am. Acad. Pediatrics; mem. AMA. Home: 1000 S Knight Ave Park Ridge IL 60068 Office: Childrens Meml Hosp 2300 N Children's Plaza Chicago IL 60614

UNZICKER, RAE ENGLES, mental health services professional; b. Monett, Mo., Aug. 20, 1948; d. Robert Jefferson and Mildred Evon (Willis) Engles; m. James L. Unzicker, Nov. 9, 1974. BA, U. Kans., 1969. Pres., chief exec. officer Midwest Films, Sioux Falls, S.D., 1973-79; creative group head Bozell and Jacobs Advt., Omaha, 1976-79; dir. S.D. Mental Health Advocacy Project, Sioux Falls, 1978-80; pvt. practice Sioux Falls, 1980—. Candidate S.D. Legislature, Minnehaha County, 1980; bd. dirs. Sioux Falls Community Playhouse, 1979-82; planning coun. Sioux Falls United Way, 1979. World Inst. on Disability fellow, 1990; named one of Outstanding Women in U.S. Woman's Day Mag., 1986; recipient Heart of Gold award Gannett Found., 1985, Humanitarian award YWCA Leader, 1983, Vail Advocacy award Nat. Mental Health Assn., 1989. Mem. Nat. Assn. Psychiat. Survivors (coord. 1985—, editor journal 1986—), Nat. Assn. for Rights Protection/Advocacy (bd. dirs. 1982—), Mental Health Assn. S.D. (pres. 1979-81, Watson award 1980), Nat. Abortion Rights Action League, Nat. Women's Polit. Caucus (Foremothers award 1981). Home: 804 S Phillips Sioux Falls SD 57104 Office: Nat Assn Psychiat Survivors PO Box 618 Sioux Falls SD 57104

UPBIN, SHARI DOLORES KIESLER, talent agent, instructor, theatrical producer; b. N.Y.C.; m. Hal J. Upbin, May 29, 1960; 3 children. Master tap instr. Talent mgr. Goldstar Talent Mgmt., Inc., N.Y.C., 1989—; guest tchr. Total Theatre Lab., N.Y.C. Asst. dir. 1st Black-Hispanic Shakespeare prodn. Julius Ceasar, Coriolanus at Pub. Theatre, N.Y., 1979; dir., choreographer Matter of Opinion, Players Theatre, N.Y., 1980, Side by Side, Sondheim Forum Theatre, N.J., 1981; producer, dir. Vincent, The Passions of Van Gogh, N.Y., 1981; producer Bojangles, The Life of Bill Robinson, Broadway, 1984, Captain America, nat. Am. tour; dir. Fiddler on the Roof, Cabaret, Life with Father, Roar of the Grease Paint, regional theatre, 1979-82; co-producer One Mo' Time, Village Gate, N.Y., nat. and internat. tour.; producer/dir. off-Broadway musical Flypaper, 1990—. Founded Queens Playhouse, N.Y., Children's Theatre, Flushing, N.Y.; mem. Willy Mays' Found. Drug Abused Children. Recipient Jaycees Service award Jr. Miss Pageants Franklin Twp., N.J., 1976. Mem. NAFE, League Profl. Theatre Women, Soc. Stage Dirs. Choreographers, Actors Equity Assn., Villagers Barn Theatre (1st woman pres.), Drama League N.Y. Home: 45 E 89th St New York NY 10128 Office: Total Theatre Lab 622 Broadway New York NY 10012

UPDEGROVE, KIMBERLY KAY, health educator; b. Camden, N.J., Nov. 15, 1963; d. John Roy Horton and Joanne Lee (Ament) Horton Mikulski; m. Daniel Allen Updegrove, May 29, 1988. BS in Nursing, William Paterson Coll., 1985; MPH, Robert Wood Johnson Med. Sch., Piscataway, N.J., 1989. RN, N.J. Office mgr., nurse Dr. C. Renna, Morristown, N.J., 1987; with Health Rsch. and Edn. Trust, Princeton, N.J., 1988—; program coordinator adult immunization edn. Health Rsch. and Edn. Trust, 1988—. Devel. com. Trenton Healthy Mothera/Healthy Babies, Trenton, 1988—. Mem. Am. Pub. Health Assn., N.J. Pub. Health Assn., Am. Soc. Healthcare Edn. and Tng., N.J. Soc. Healthcare Edn. and Tng., Soc. Profl. Health Educators, Aurthur Murray Dance Studio Club. Democrat. Lutheran. Home: 13 Viburnum Ct Lawrenceville NJ 08648

UPDIKE, HELEN HILL, economist, consultant, educator; b. N.Y.C., Mar. 27, 1941; d. Benjamin Harvey and Helen (Gray) Hill; m. Charles Bruce Updike, Sept. 7, 1963 (div. 1989); children: Edith Hill, Nancy Lamar. B.A., Hood Coll., 1962; Ph.D., SUNY-Stony Brook, 1978. Asst. prof. Suffolk U., Boston, 1965-67; lectr. SUNY-Stony Brook, 1969-75, vis. asst. prof., 1977-78; asst. prof. U. Mass., Boston, 1975-77; asst. prof. Hofstra U., Hempstead, N.Y., 1978-85, assoc. prof., 1985-90, chmn. dept. econs. and geography, 1981-84; assoc. dean Hofstra Coll. Hofstra U., 1984-87; pres. Interfid Capital Corp., 1987—; bd. dirs. McCrory Corp., E-II Holdings; cons. environ. econs., 1973-87. Author: The National Banks and American Economic Development, 1870-1900, 1985. Trustee, v.p. L.I. Forum for Tech., 1979-85; trustee Madeira Sch., Greenway, Va., 1984-88, N.Y. Outward Bound Ctr.; mem. nat. adv. bd. Outward Bound. H.B. Earhart fellow Georgetown U., 1962-63; Georgetown U. fellow, 1963-64. Mem. AAAS, Am. Econ. Assn. Office: Interfid Capital Corp 1 Dag Hammarskjold Pla 47th Fl New York NY 10017

UPHOLD, MARGE BROADWATER, public relations executive, marketing professional; b. Keyser, W.Va., Oct. 27, 1948; m. Rodger Lee Uphold, May 19, 1968; 1 child, Teresa. AA, Allegany Community Coll., Cumberland, Md., 1982; BS, Frostburg (Md.) State U., 1984, postgrad., 1989—. Sec. USDA, Hyattsville, Md., 1966-68; bank teller 1st Nat. Bank, Oakland, Md., 1968-69; freelance transcriber, editor Oakland, 1969-77; adminstrv. sec. Sacred Heart Hosp., Cumberland, 1977-80, sec., staff writer, 1984-85, staff asst., 1985-87; dir. mktg. and community relations Frostburg Community Hosp., 1987—; writer Allegany Hearing and Speech Assn., Cumberland, 1988-89, Whitewater Internat., McHenry, Md., 1989—. Author poetry. Mem. Am. Soc. Hosp. Mktg. and Pub. Rels., Bus. and Profl. Women's Assn., Beta Sigma Phi (v.p. Cumberland chpt. 1989-90). Republican. Methodist. Home: 18621 Woodlawn Dr Rawlings MD 21557 Office: Frostburg Community Hosp 48 Tarn Terr Frostburg MD 21532

UPJOHN, MARY KIRBY, communications educator; b. Kansas City, Mo., Sept. 30, 1948; d. William Bryant and Mary Analaura (Harrington) U.; B.A., Pomona Coll., 1970; M.S., Boston U., 1977. Dir. product devel. and promotion Urban Systems, Inc., Cambridge, Mass., 1970-73; pres., co-founder Funktions, Inc., Watertown, Mass., 1973-75; mng. editor Decade Mag., Boston, 1978-79; assoc. prof. Boston U. Coll. Communication, 1978—, mem. exec. com., 1986—; sr. analyst Urban Systems Research and Engring., Cambridge, 1988-89; cons. Urban Systems Research and Engring., 1975—, bd. dirs., 1982-89; cons. Economica, Inc., Goodmeasure, Inc., Speedwell, Inc., Info. Architects, Inc.; TV panelist, Media Watch, Brookline Cablevision, 1989—. Recipient Matrix award, 1987, awards of merit New Eng. Newspaper Execs., 1978, 79, 80, 81, 82, 83, 85, Women Grad. award Boston U., 1981. Mem. Women in Communications, Inc. (Nat. Outstanding Adviser award 1980, 81, 83 v.p. Boston chpt. 1981-82, pres. 1983, nat. v.p. 1986-88), Informational Film Producers Assn., Pomona Coll. Alumni Assn. (bd. mem. New Eng. chpt.). Author: Urban Homsteading: A Guide for Local Officials, 1978; (with Kathleen Heintz) Neighborhood Planning Primer, 1979; (with others) Television Literacy, 1981; prin. author Case Study of the Alaska National Communication Program. Home: 39 Marion Rd Watertown MA 02172 Office: Urban Systems Rsch & Engring 2067 Massachusetts Ave Cambridge MA 02140

UPPLEGER, RUTH SIMPSON, magazine and newspaper controller; b. Grand Ridge, Fla., Dec. 1, 1943; d. Chester Leon and Nellie Ada (Middleton) Jeter; m. James Bernard Simpson, Sept. 14, 1962 (div. 1984); children: Tonya Ruth, Michael James; m. Lawrence Franklin Uppleger, Jan. 25, 1986. Student Chipola Jr. Coll., 1961-62, Canal Zone Coll., 1971-73; BBA, Austin Peay State U., 1985. Bookkeeper, Leaf Chronicle, Clarksville, Tenn., 1976-78, office mgr., 1978-81, asst. controller, 1981-84; controller Music City News, Gallatin News Examiner, Nashville Record, Hendersonville Star News (subs. Multimedia Inc.), Nashville, 1984—. Mem. Nat. Assn. Accts., Nat. Assn. Female Execs. Democrat. Baptist. Club: Civitan (officer, bd. dirs.). Avocations: hiking, dancing, reading, horticulture. Home: 512 Lisa Ct Clarksville TN 37043

UPRIGHT, DIANE WARNER, auction house executive; b. Cleve.; d. Rodney Upright and Shirley (Warner) Lavine. Student, Wellesley Coll., 1965-67; BA, U. Pitts., 1969; MA, U. Mich., 1973, PhD, 1976. Asst. prof. U. Va., Charlottesville, 1976-78; assoc. prof. Harvard U., Cambridge, Mass., 1978-83; sr. curator Ft. Worth Art Mus., 1984-86; dir. Jan Krugier Gallery, N.Y.C., 1986—; sr. v.p., head contemporary art dept. Christie's, N.Y.C., 1990—. Author: Morris Louis: The Complete Paintings, 1979, Ellsworth Kelly: Works on Paper, 1987, various exhbn. catalogues; contbr. articles to art jours. Mem. Coll. Art Assn., Art Table, Inc. Office: Christies 502 Park Ave New York NY 10022

UPSHAW, LISA GAYE, business management systems analyst; b. Alamogordo, N.Mex., June 27, 1959; d. James Leroy Upshaw and Margaret (Shackelford) Carrell; m. Michael J. Zamora, Nov. 3, 1976 (div. July 1983); 1 child, Jeremy Brandon; m. Eddie Gonzalez, Mar. 19, 1984. BS in Bus. Computer Systems, U. N.Mex., 1983. Govt. and large account system analyst Office Systems, Alburquerque, 1982-84; sr. system analyst, nat. accounts mgr. Bell Atlantic/CompuShop, Houston, 1984-89; nat. account mgr. CompuCom Systems, Inc., Houston, 1988—, mem. president's coun., 1988-89; br. mgr. CompuCom Systems, Inc., Atlanta, 1990—; cons. Bell Atlantic President's Club, Dallas, 1986-87, 88, Bell atlantic Leaders Club, 1986-89. Chmn. publicity Ronald McDonald House, Alburquerque, 1982, chairwoman spl. events, 1983; chairwoman Rep. Vol. Community, Houston, 1986; sponsor Houston Ballet, Theatre of Arts, Fundraising Heart Assn. Mem. NAFE (network dir. 1987-88), Assn. Info. System Profls., Houston Area League Personal Computer Specialists, NOW, VFW, CompuCom Leaders Club. Home: 3551 Robinson Rd NE Marietta GA 30068 Office: CompuCom Systems 2580 Cumberland Pkwy #400 #400 Atlanta GA 30339

UPSHAW, MARGE LAVERNE HARPER, anesthesiologist; b. Atlanta; d. William Nichols and Marge Clark (Few) Harper; m. James Milton Upshaw, Jr., Nov. 14, 1970; children: Sujuan LaVerne, James Milton III. BA, Fisk U., 1966; MD, Meharry Med. Coll., 1970. Rotating intern Hubbard Hosp., Nashville, 1970-71; resident in anesthesiology Emory U. Affiliated Hosps., Atlanta, 1971-73; anesthesiologist John Andrew Community Hosp., Tuskegee, Ala., 1973-87; dir. anesthesia Community Hosp., Tallassee, Ala., 1987—. Life mem. Tuskegee Civic Assn. Fellow Am. Coll. Anesthesiologists; mem. AMA, Am. Soc. Anesthesiologists, Med. Assn. State Ala., Ala. State Med. Assn., Ala. Soc. Anesthesiologists, Nat. Med. Assn., Am. Heart Assn. (instr. BLS), Nat. Coun. Negro Women, Montgomery Mus. Fine Arts, Phi Beta Kappa, Alpha Kappa Alpha (anti basileus 1987—). Office: Community Hosp PO Box 707 Friendship Rd Tallassee AL 36078

UPSHAW-MCCLENNY, LOUISE ADAMS, marketing and sales professional; b. Chgo., Aug. 16, 1953; d. Aubrey Russell Jr. and Evelyn Adams (Torbert) U.; m. Bruce Barron McClenny, Oct. 2, 1976; 1 child, Russell Ferguson Upshaw. BA, Auburn U., 1975, M in French Studies, 1976. Fin. asst. Elf Aquitaine Oil & Gas, Houston, 1977-79; sales coordinator Hotel Meridien Houston, 1979-80, sales rep., 1980-81, sales mgr., 1981-82; sales mgr. Four Seasons Hotel, Houston Ctr., Houston, 1982-84, nat. sales mgr., 1984-85, dir. sales, 1985-86, dir. sales, mktg., 1986—. Co-author: Foreign Languages and International Trade: A Global Perspective. Mem. L'Alliance Francaise de Houston, 1977—. Mem. Hotel Sales and Mktg. Assn. (bd. dirs. 1982-83), Meeting Planners Internat. (sec. 1985-86, bd. dirs. 1986—), Sales and Mktg. Execs. Internat., Downtown Houston Assn., Tex. Exec. Women (v.p. 1985, sec. 1986). Unitarian. Office: Four Seasons Hotel Houston Ctr 1300 Lamar Houston TX 77010

UPSHUR, CAROLE CHRISTOFK, psychologist, educator; b. Des Moines, Oct. 18, 1948; d. Robert Richard and Margaret (Davis) Christofk; 1 child, Emily. A.B., U. So. Calif., 1969; Ed.M., Harvard U., 1970, Ed.D. (NIMH fellow), 1975. Lic. psychologist, Mass. Planner, Mass. Com. on Criminal Justice, Boston, 1970-73; licensing specialist, planner, policy specialist Mass. Office for Children, Boston, 1973-76; asst. prof. Coll. Public and Community Svc., U. Mass., Boston, 1976-81, assoc. prof., 1982—, chmn. Center for Community Planning, 1979-81, 84-86; cons. to govt. and community agys. on mental health and social svc. policy and mgmt., 1970—; cons. Harvard Family Rsch. Project, 1983-86; assoc. in pediatrics, sr. rsch. assoc. U. Mass. Med. Sch., 1983—; adj. prof. Heller Sch. Social Welfare, Brandeis U., 1985—. Commr. Brookline Human Rels.-Youth Resources Commn., 1988—. Mem. Am. Psychol. Assn., Am. Assn. on Mental Retardation (cons. editor Mental Retardation, Amer. Jour. on Mental Retardation 1981—). Office: U Mass Coll Pub and Community Service Boston MA 02125

UPTON, MARY DAVIS, director of admissions; b. N.Y.C., Jan. 12, 1942; d. John Davis and Kate Hurd (Rennell) U. Student, Conn. Coll., 1960-62. Registrar Harvard Law Sch., Cambridge, Mass., 1971-78; asst. dean Harvard Law Sch., 1978-80, dean students, 1980-87; dir. admissions Washington Coll. Law, Am. Univ., Washington, 1987—. Mem. Am. Assn. Collegiate Registrars & Admissions Officers, Nat. Assn. Women Deans, Counselors, Adminstrs. Democrat. Episcopalian. Office: Am Univ Washington Coll Law 4400 Massachusetts Ave NW Washington DC 20016

UPTON, SUSAN HOLLIS, nurse; b. Pitts., Apr. 16, 1950; d. Richard Joseph and Dorothy Naoma (Havener) Hollis; m. Joe Thomas Upton, Apr. 5, 1950; children: Mary-Ellen, James Richard. BA, Tenn. Tech. U., 1989. RN, Tenn. Staff nurse Baptist Meml. Hosp., Memphis, 1972-73; staff Tenn. Psychiatric Hosp. and Inst., Memphis, 1973-74; instr. Livingston (Tenn.) State Area Vocat.-Tech. Sch., 1974-75; nurse cons. for Medicare Fentress County Nursing Home, Jamestown, Tenn., 1976; gen. office nurse Overton County Med. Ctr., 1976-78; staff nurse Livingston Community Hosp., 1980; nurse cons. Medicare Overton County Nursing Home, Livingston, 1981, tng. coordinator, 1986-87; office receptionist Joe T. Upton, DDS, Livingston, 1982; staff nurse Livingston Community Hosp., 1982-83, 87—; instr. health occupations edn. Livingston Area Vocat.-Tech. Sch., 1983-85; childbirth educator Livingston Regional Hosp., 1978-81, 1987—. Pres. Tenn. Homemakers Council, Livingston, 1986—; county chmn. blood svcs. div. ARC, Overton County, 1987—; leader Girl Scouts U.S., 1986. Mem. Middle Tenn. 4th Dist. Dental Soc. Aux., German Club (sec. 1986), Livingston Home Demonstration (pres. 1987), Civic and Garden (dist. 4 v.p. 1984-86), Christian Women's Fellowship. Republican. Mem. Christian Ch. Home: 31 S Golf Lane Livingston TN 38570

URATO, BARBRA CASALE, entrepreneur; b. Newark, Oct. 10, 1941; d. Dominick Anthony and Concetta (Castrichini) Casale; m. John Joseph Urato, June 20, 1965; children: Concetta U. Graves, Gina E., Joseph D. Student, Seton Hall U., 1961-63. File clk. Martin Gelber Esquire, Newark, 1956-58; policy typist Aetna Casualty Ins., Newark, 1959-61; sec. to dean Seton Hall U., South Orange, N.J., 1961-63; paralegal sec. Judge Robert A. McKinley, Newark, 1963-66; office mgr. Valiant I.M.C., Hackensack, N.J., 1971-73; asst. mgr. Degussa Inc., Teterboro, N.J., 1975-77; night mgr. The Ferryboat Restaurant, River Egde, N.J., 1976-78; mgr. Fratello's and Ventilini's, Hilton Head, S.C., 1978-80; day mgr. Ramada Inn Restaurant, Paramus, N.J., 1980-82; mgr. Gottlieb's Bakery, Hilton Head, 1982-83; asst. mgr. closing dept. Hilton Head Mortgage Co., 1983-85; owner, mgr. All Cleaning Svc., Hilton Head, 1985—. Mem. Nat. Assn. Female Execs., Profl. Women of Hilton Head, Assn. for Rsch. and Enlightenment, Rosicrucian Order, Low Country Property Mgmt. Roman Catholic.

URBACH, PHYLLIS ANN ROSE, clothing executive; b. Mpls., June 29, 1936; d. Charles George and Mildred Eileen (Conover) Rose; m. Thomas Arnold Andersen, Sept. 14, 1953 (div. Apr. 1970); children: Debra, Ramona, David, Mark, Brad, Michael; m. Robert Dale Urbach, Feb. 12, 1978 (dec. Feb. 1979). Student, Normandale Coll., 1976-77. Owner, pres., artist Andersen Originals Inc., Burnsville, Minn., 1966-84; activities dir. Lake View Nursing Home, Mpls., 1977-78; owner, pres. designer Lady Huntress Fashions by Phyllis Rose, Edina, Minn., 1983—; co-founder Midwest Fashion and Design Consortium, 1989-90, bd. dirs., editor-in-chief publ. New Lines, 1990—; substitute tchr. Burnsville Sch. Dist., 1977-79. Editor: Jim Peterson Outdoor News, 1985-86; patentee canvas paint tote, 1985. Leader Cub Scouts Am., Girl Scouts USA, 4-H Club, Burnsville, 1965-68; spiritual instr. Burnsville Jr. High and Newbrighton Sr. High, 1975-81; developer, promoter Mpls. Aquatennial Bicentennial, Mpls., 1975-76; vol. cons. various women's entrepreneurial Orgns., Mpls. Recipient Merit award Mpls. Aquatennial, 1975. Mem. Women's Entrepreneur's Network, Bus. and Profl. Women's Assn., Ducks Unltd. (chmn. Minn. Valley Womnen's chpt.), VFW, Nat. Sporting Goods Assn. Home and Office: 110 1st Ave NE Apt 1002 Minneapolis MN 55413

URBACH, SUSAN KAY, small business development administrator; b. York, Nebr., June 30, 1956; d. James Floyd and Mary Jane (Schwab) U. B. Mus., Oklahoma City U., 1978, M in Mus., 1980. Comml. loan asst., sec. Citizens Nat. Bank, Oklahoma City, 1983-86; loan svc. asst. SBA, Oklahoma City, 1986-88; dir. Small Bus. Devel. Ctr., Edmond, Okla., 1988—; mem. adv. bd. Okla. Home Based Bus. Assn.; mem. steering com. Gov.'s Conf. on Small Bus. Editor: (songbook) Sigma Alpha Iota Songbook Supplement vols. I and II, 1981, 84. Mem., choir dir. Chapel-Tinker AFB, Midwest City, Okla., 1982-88, St. Francis Assisi Cath. Ch., Oklahoma City, 1988—; mem. Gatewood Neighborhood Bd., 1990. Mem. Edmond C. of C., Oklahoma City C. of C., Sigma Alpha Iota. Republican. Roman Catholic. Home: 2012 NW 19th St Oklahoma City OK 73106 Office: Cen State U Small Bus Ctr 100 N University Dr Edmond OK 73034

URBAN, ANNE HOLMES, marketing executive; b. Chgo., Aug. 1, 1954; d. Vernon Francis and Evelyn (Tait) Holmes; m. Lawrence Donald Urban, Aug. 25, 1979. BA, U. Ill., 1976. Pubs. editor Nat. Assn. Clin. Lab. Scis.,

Chgo., 1976-78; asst. editor Trailer Dealer Pub., Chgo., 1978-80; mng. editor Profl. Press Div. Fairchild Pubs., Chgo., 1980-82; copy dir. Delos Advt., Des Plaines, Ill., 1982-84; pub. rels. dir. Inland Real Estate, Oak Brook, Ill., 1984-87; mktg. communications mgr. Citicorp Savs., Chgo., 1987-88; mktg. specialist On-line Fin. Svcs., Oak Brook, 1988—. Contbr. articles to profl. ours. Active Salvation Army, Chgo., 1983—. Recipient (2) Cert. Merit Bus. and Profl. Advt. Assn., 1989. Office: On-Line Fin Svcs 900 Commerce Dr Oak Brook IL 60521

URBAN, JEANNE MARIE, federal agency administrator; b. Clearfield, Pa., Mar. 29, 1950; d. Donald Alvin and Martha (Mick) U. BS in Animal Sci., Pa. State U., 1972. Floral designer Undercoffer Florist, Clearfield, 1972-77; program asst. USDA, Clearfield, 1977-81, county exec. dir., 1981—. Activist Concerned Citizens Clearfield Mcpl. Authority. Mem. AAUW (pres. 1979-80), VFW Aux., Am. Legion Aux., Nat. Assn. County Office Employees (scholarship com. 1989-90), Pa. Assn. County Office Employees (alt. rep.), U.S. Trotting Assn. (charter, clk. course 1989-90). Democrat. Office: USDA-ASCS Jefferson County Svc Ctr RD#5 Brookville PA 15825

URBAN, MARY H(ELEN), educator; b. Newark, June 2, 1942; d. John and Helen (Smrha) U. BS in Edn., SUNY, Geneseo, 1965; MRE, Boston U., 1967, MSW, 1979. Dir. Christian edn. Holy Trinity Luth. Ch., Buffalo, 1970-73; coordinator telephone counseling services Crisis Services, Buffalo, 1973-77; coordinator tng. Sch. Social Work Boston U., 1979-81, asst. prof., coord. B Social Work program, 1986—; pvt. practice in psychotherapy Boston, 1979—. Mem. Nat. Assn. Social Workers (cert., chair ethics com.). Office: Boston U 808 Commonwealth Ave Boston MA 02215

URBAN, SHARON KAY, educator; b. Thornton, Iowa; d. Samuel John and Esther Mae (Sorensen) Will; m. Rudolf John Urban, Aug. 14, 1971 (dec. Apr. 1986); m. Rudolf John Urban. BS in Edn., Ill. State U., 1966, MS in Reading, 1969; postgrad., Bradley U., 1983, No. Ill. U., Western Ill. U., 1988. Tchr. Wilson Sch., Pekin, Ill., 1966—. Bd. dirs. Pekin Community Concerts Assn., 1973—, pres., 1987-89; pres. Tazewell County Med. Aux., Pekin, 1975-76; bd. dirs. YWCA, Pekin, 1987—. Mem. NEA, Ill. Edn. Assn., Edn. Assn. Pekin (pres. 1974-76, v.p. 1990—), AAUW (bd. dirs. Pekin 1973-88, 89—, pres. 1983-85, honoree Ednl. Found. 1983), Alpha Delta Kappa (bd. dirs. 1974-80, pres. Alpha Theta chpt. 1978-80). Republican. Lutheran. Home: 3 Prestwick Dr Pekin IL 61554 Office: Wilson Sch 900 Koch St Pekin IL 61554

URBANOWICZ, LYNNE JENNIFER, legal assistant; b. Jersey City, N.J., Feb. 20, 1965; d. Henry F. and Carolyn J. (Raczkowski) U. Student, U. London, 1986; BA, NYU, 1987; JD, Seton Hall Univ, 1990. Owner, mgr. Every 'Wear' A Bead, Watchung, N.J., 1983-88; legal asst. Hurley and Vasios, P.A., Short Hills, N.J., 1986, paralegal, 1987, law clk., 1988; summer assoc. Shanley and Fisher, P.C., Morristown, N.J., 1989, law clk., 1989-90; assoc. Shanley & Fisher, PC, Morristown, N.J., 1990—; legal intern Legal Svcs. Clinic, Newark, 1989-90. Mem. Law Sch. Young Reps., ABA, N.Y. State Bar Assn. (student div.), Phi Alpha Delta (v.p. 1988-89).

URBAUER, KRISTINE JOANNE, military officer; b. Chgo., June 3, 1964; d. Joseph Harold and Carmen Dorinda (Arroyo) U. BSCE, U.S. Mil. Acad., West Point, N.Y., 1986. Commd. 2d lt. U.S. Army, 1986, advanced through grades to capt., 1990; vertical constrn. platoon leader U.S. Army, Ft. Riley, Kans., 1986-88, horizontal constrn. platoon leader, 1988-89; dep. facility engr. U.S. Army, Uijonbu, Republic of Korea, 1990—; exec. officer Medium Girder Bridge Co., 1989-90; dep. dir. engring. U.S. Army, Uijongbu, Korea, 1990. Mem. Soc. Am. Military Engrs. Republican. Home: 10615 S Albany Chicago IL 60655

UREEL, PATRICIA LOIS, retired manufacturing company executive; b. Detroit, Nov. 29, 1923; d. Peter Walter and Ethel Estelle (Stewart) Murphy; grad. Detroit Bus. Inst., 1941; student Wayne State U., 1942, U. Detroit, 1943, U. Miami, 1945-46; m. Joseph Ralph Ureel, Jan. 4, 1947; children—Mary Patricia, Ronald Joseph. Exec. sec. to chmn. bd. and pres. Detroit Ball Bearing Co. of Mich., 1965-67; exec. sec. to partner charge Mich. dist. Ernst & Ernst, Detroit, 1967-71, Clubs of Inverrary, Lauderhill, Fla., 1971-72, partner charge of group Coopers & Lybrand, Miami, Fla., 1972-74; corp. sec., personnel mgr. Sanford Industries, Inc. and 4 subsidiaries, Pompano Beach, Fla., 1974-81; corp. sec., asso. Asphalt Assos., Ft. Lauderdale, 1982-86. Named Sec. of Yr. for City of Detroit, 1966; cert. profl. sec. Mem. Nat. Secs. Assn., Women's Econ. Club Detroit. Republican. Roman Catholic. Club: Moose. Home: 2504 Seagate Ln Saint Augustine FL 32084

URIOSTE, MARY LOUISE, insurance executive; b. Pueblo, Colo., Sept. 2, 1947; d. Jesus Felix and Victoria (Munoz) Martinez; m. Andrew Lee Urioste, Jan. 12, 1963 (dec. 1968); children: Daniel L., David A., John R., Victoria S. Student, So. Colo. State Coll., 1973-75. Comml. rater Comml. Union Ins., Denver, 1975-78; underwriter CNA Ins. Cos., Denver, 1978-86; supr. Md. Casualty Co., Denver, 1986-89; property mgr. Crum & Forster, Denver, 1989—. Foster mother City of Lakewood, Colo., 1984. Roman Catholic. Office: Crum & Forster 5445 DTC Pkwy Denver CO 80111

URMER, DIANE HEDDA, management firm executive, financial officer; b. Bklyn., Dec. 15, 1934; d. Leo and Helen Sarah (Perlman) Leverant; m. Albert Heinz Urmer, Sept. 2, 1952; children: Michelle, Cynthia, Carl. Student U. Tex., 1951-52, Washington U., St. Louis, 1962-63; BA in Psychology, Calif. State U.-Northridge, 1969. Asst. auditor Tex. State Bank, Austin, 1952-55; v.p., controller Enki Corp., Sepulveda, Calif., 1966-70, also dir., 1987—; v.p., fin. Cambia Way Hosp., Walnut Creek, Calif., 1973-78; v.p., controller Enki Health & Research Systems, Inc., Reseda, Calif., 1978—, also dir. Contbr. articles to profl. jours. Pres. Northridge PTA, 1971; chmn. Northridge Citizens Adv. Council, 1972-73. Mem. Women in Mgmt. Club: Tex. Execs. Avocations: bowling, sailing, handcrafts, golf. Office: Enki Health and Rsch Systems Inc 6660 Reseda Blvd #203 Reseda CA 91335

URNESS, CINDY LYNN, insurance manager; b. Kansas City, Mo., June 13, 1963; d. Orville Jack and Virginia Lee (Bradshaw) Washam; m. Terrence Brian Urness, Apr. 16, 1983. Grad. high sch., Raytown, Mo., 1981. Clk. Kansas City Life Ins. Co., 1981, clk. typist, 1981-82, jr. examiner, 1982-83, sr. examiner, 1983-87, supr., 1987-88, project coor., 1988-90; systems mgr., claims systems mgr. Forrest T. Jones/Fidelity Security Life, 1990—; real estate agt. Brady Investments, Independence, Mo., 1987-88. Active Greenpeace. Mem. NAFE.

USHER, JONELL ADAIR, college dean; b. Hartsville, S.C., Feb. 19, 1947; d. John Jarman and Nell Carolyn (Rolader) Adair; children: Christoher Todd, Ellen Leigh. BA, Ga. State U., 1981; MA, Emory U., 1986, PhD, 1989. Tchr. High Meadows Sch., Roswell, Ga., 1981-83; academic counselor Emory Coll., Atlanta, 1987-88, asst. dean, 1988—, faculty rep. Fulbright Fellowships, 1989-90; cons. Roswell High Sch., 1986-90. Mem. APA, Psychonomics Soc. Office: Emory Coll Office 218 White Hall Atlanta GA 30322

USHER-KERR, MARVA DIANNE, corporate records manager; b. Henderson, N.C., Feb. 24, 1955; d. Millie Lucille (Usher) Johnson; m. Eric Sylvester Kerr, June 20, 1981. BA, SUNY, Stony Brook, 1977; postgrad., N.Y. Inst. Tech., 1989—. With customer svc. dept. F.W. Woolworth's, N.Y.C., 1977-82; with Gen. Bd. Global Ministries, N.Y.C., 1983—, records supr., 1985-87, corp. records mgr., 1987—. Founder Nat. Network of Minority Info. Profls., N.Y., 1988—; youth organizer L.I. West Dist. United Meth. Ch., Jamaica, N.Y., 1988-89. Mem. Assn. Records Mgrs. and Adminstrs. (v.p. info. and resources N.Y.C. chpt. 1989—, program com. 1989—), Assn. Image and Info. Mgmt. Democrat. Home: 91-35 193rd St New York NY 11423 Office: Gen Bd Global Ministries 475 Riverside Dr New York NY 10115

USHIJIMA, CAROL M., utility executive; b. Santa Monica, Calif., Mar. 15, 1958; d. Tadami Ernie and Jean Miyoko (Miwa) U. BA in Econs. and History, UCLA, 1979. Research asst. Nat. Econ. Research Assocs., Los Angeles, 1979-80; jr. adminstrv. asst. Office of City Adminstrv. Officer City of Los Angeles, 1980-81, jr. adminstrv. asst. Dept. Water and Power, Water Exec. Office, 1981-82, cons. energy utilization Dept. Water and Power, Conservation Div., 1982-87, sr. utility conservation rep., supr. mktg. services, Systems Devel. Div., 1987—. Mem. allocations com. region V United Way, Los Angeles, 1986—; team leader LADWP Asian Community Affiliates, Los Angeles, 1984-85; bd. dirs. West Los Angeles Japanese Am. Citizens League, 1984—. Marina Mercy Hosp. scholar, 1975; recipient Outstanding Community Service award West Los Angeles Japanese Am. Citizens League, 1986. Mem. Asian Pacific Women's Network, Nat. Assn. Female Execs., Leadership Edn. for Asian Pacifics, Assn. Profl. Energy Mgrs., Profl. Women's Network (chairperson LADWP system devel. div. 1986-87), Calif. Scholarship Fedn. (life). Methodist. Office: Los Angeles Dept Water & Power PO Box 111 Room 1169 Los Angeles CA 90051

USHIJIMA, JEAN MIYOKO, city official; b. San Francisco, Feb. 14, 1933; d. Toyoharu George and Frances Fujiko (Misumi) Miwa; m. Tad E. Ushijima; 1 child, Carol M. BS, U. San Francisco, 1981. City clk. City of Beverly Hills, Calif., 1973—. Bd. dirs. West L.A. Japanese Am. Citizens League, 1979—, pres., 1988—, also chmn. bd.; bd. dirs. Leadership Edn. for Asian Pacifics, 1985—. Mem. Acad. Advanced Edn., City Clks. Assn. Calif. (pres. 1986, City Clerk of Yr. award 1989), Calif. Women in Govt. (program chmn. 1978-79), Leadership Edn. for Asian Pacific (chmn. bd. 1987), League Calif. Cities (adminstrv. svcs. com. 1982-86), Internat. Inst. Mcpl. Clks. (bd dirs. 1988). Avocations: reading, Japanese dancing. Office: City Ck 450 N Crescent Dr #102 Beverly Hills CA 90210

USHKOW, CHARMAINE MARIE, advertising company executive; b. Wyondotte, Mich., July 22, 1955; d. Carl Lyle and Sara Therese (Ruvolo) Cantrell; m. Bruce Scott Ushkow. AAS in Mktg., Corning Community Coll., 1975. Asst. mgr. Hedleys (Retail, Women's), Trenton, Mich., 1975-76; account exec. Yellow Pages dept. Meldrum & Fewsmith Advt., Cleve., 1976-78, Sta. WSYE-TV, Elmira, N.Y., 1978-79, Sta. WSYR-TV (now Sta. WSTM-TV), Syracuse, N.Y., 1979-82, Greater Dayton Cable (Interconnect), 1982-84; local sales mgr. Cable Sales Inc. (Interconnect), Syracuse, 1984-88; gen. sales mgr. Capital Dist. Cable Advt. Network (Interconnect), Albany, 1988--; guest speaker Dale Carnegie, Syracuse, 1988. Mem. Albany Advt. Club, Cleve. Advt. Club, Syracuse Advt. Club. Democrat. Office: Capital Dist Cable Advt Net 130 Washington Ave Albany NY 12203

USINGER, JANE ELIZABETH, management consultant, educator; b. E. Chicago, Ind., Sept. 20, 1951; d. Richard Lewis and Vera Wheeler (Nickell) U.; m. Dennis Joseph Goginsky, May 16, 1987; 1 child, Matthew. BA in Edn., Purdue U., 1973, MS in Edn. with honors, 1974; MBA, DePaul U., Chgo., 1983. Cert. tchr. Tchr. neurologically impaired Stewart Jr. High Sch., Tacoma, 1974-75; supr., adminstr. Seattle Crisis Clinic, Inc., 1975-78; program coord. State Dept. Pub. Instrn. ESD 121, Seattle, 1978-80; sales rep. N.W. Airlines, Chgo., 1980-81; tng. coord. Montgomery Ward, Inc., Chgo., 1981-83; tng. mgr. Calvary Hosp. and Palliative Care Inst., N.Y.C., 1983-85; prin. Omega Assocs., Columbia, S.C., 1985—; mem. continuing edn. faculty Kennesaw (Ga.) Coll., Trident Tech. Coll., Charleston, S.C., Midlands Coll., Columbia, S.C., U. S.C. Daniel Mgmt. Ctr., S.C.; bd. dirs. Ga. Image Cons., Atlanta. Author: One in Fifty, 1978; contbr. articles and poetry to various mags; inventor wheelchair laptray (Purdue Commendation award), 1973. Vol. Rape Relief Ctr, Chgo., 1981-83, AIDS Speakers Bur., 1987—; bd. dirs. Puget Sound chpt. Big Sisters, Seattle, 1975-77, Charleston Big Bros./Big Sisters, 1988-89. Mortar Bd. fellow, 1973-74. Mem. Am. Soc. Tng. and Devel. (membership com. 1982-83), Fedn. Bus. Profl. Women (chair 1979-80, young career woman program, Young Career Woman award Wash. chpt. 1979), Orgn. Devel. Network, Bus. Network, Atlanta C. of C., Am. Assn. U. Women, Nat. Orgn. Women, Nat. Speakers Assn., Kappa Delta Pi. Roman Catholic. Home: 112 Cricket Hill Rd Columbia SC 29223 Office: Omega Assocs Columbia SC 29223

USINGER, MARTHA PUTNAM, educator; b. Pitts., Dec. 10, 1912; d. Milo Boone and Christiana (Haberstroh) Putnam; m. Robert Leslie Usinger, June 24, 1938 (dec. Oct. 1968); children: Roberta Christine, Richard Putnam. AB cum laude, U. Calif., Berkeley, 1934; postgrad., Oreg. State U., 1936, U. Ghana, 1970, Coll. Nairobi, 1970. Tchr. Oakland (Calif.) Pub. Schs., 1936-38; tchr. Berkeley (Calif.) Pub. Schs., 1954-57, dean West Campus, counselor, 1957-78; lectr., photographer in field. Author: Ration Books and Christmas Crackers, 1989. Mem. adv. coun. Lifespan Alta Bates Hosp. Mem. DAR (lifespan), Berkeley Ret. Tchrs., U. Calif. Emeriti Assn., U. Calif. Alumnae Assn., Prytanean Alumnae Assn. (pres. 1952-54), Mortar Bd., Delta Kappa Gamma. Congregationalist.

USREY, EULETA GUSTAVA, writer, advertising consultant; b. Harrison, Ark., May 19, 1956; d. Carson E. and Bonnie Ree (Phillips) U. BS, U. Tulsa, 1979; postgrad., U. Ark., 1980-81. Con., writer Comedy Creations, Washington, 1986-87; attendee Screenwriting A to Z, Dallas, 1987, Ozark Creative Writers Conf., Eureka Springs, Ark., 1988, Story Structure So. Meth. U., Dallas, 1988. Author numerous fiction stories, articles for mags. including Woman's World, 1973—; author screenplay Nob Hill, 1988, Love Line, 1990. Vol. re-election com. Gov. Clinton, Carroll County, Ark., 1984. Mem. Ozark Writer's League, Stephaine Rogers Agy., Berryville (Ark.) C. of C., Phi Theta Kappa. Office: PO Box 122 Berryville AR 72616

USTICK, MARYANN INTERMONT, city official; b. East Orange, N.J., Oct. 30, 1947; d. Robert John and Anne Marie (Nork) Intermont; m. Perry W. Ustick, Jr., June 3, 1967; children: Perry Intermont, Tarah Intermont. BA in History, St. Mary's Coll. Md., St. Mary's City, 1971; MA in History, Old Dominion U., 1974, MPA, 1987. Instr. St. Leo Coll., Norfolk, Va., 1975-76; tchr. Christ the King Sch., Norfolk, 1976-77; enforcement agt. Va. Dept. Commerce, Virginia Beach, 1981-84; coord. consumer edn. City of Virginia Beach, 1977-79, coord. community devel. program, 1979-81, dir. dept. housing, 1984—; cons. on consumer edn. Tidewater Community Coll., Virginia Beach, 1978-79. Counselor vol. Navy Relief Soc., Corpus Christi, Tex., 1968-69; vol. tchr. Good Neighborhood Child Devel., Virginia Beach, 1971-74; discrimination counselor NOW, Virginia Beach, 1973-75; citizen coord. Virginia Beach Dept. Pub. Utilities, 1982-83; mem. fund distbn. com. United Way, Norfolk, 1990; mem. subcom. Va. Housing Study Commn., Richmond, 1987-90; bd. dirs. Va. Housing Coalition, 1987-90; legis. chmn. Hampton Roads (Va.) Housing Coalition, 1987-89. Named Mgr. of Yr., City of Virginia Beach, 1989; rsch. grantee Old Dominion U., 1973. Mem. ASAP, Va. Assn. Housing and Community Devel. Ofcls., Phi Alpha Theta, Phi Kappa Phi. Democrat. Roman Catholic. Home: 628 Ft Raleigh Dr Virginia Beach VA 23451 Office: Virginia Beach Dept Housing Municipal Ctr Virginia Beach VA 23456

UTESCH, DOROTHY MARIE (DOROTHY MARIE DALLMEYER), retired secretary and administrator; b. Brenham, Tex., Jan. 30, 1923; d. Charles Dietrich and Lydia Marie (Fuchs) Dallmeyer; m. Luther Paul Utesch, Nov. 23, 1946; children: Cassandra Ann Utesch Ehlert, Karen Marie Utesch Boardman. AA, Blinn Jr. Coll., Brenham, 1942; BBA, U. Tex., Austin, 1944. Editor safety mag. Exxon Corp. (formerly Humble Oil and Refinery Co.), Houston, 1944-46, McBee Systems organizer and sec., 1946-55; ret., 1955. Pres. Bluebonnet Garden Club, 1962-63; mem. Coastal Prairie Coun., Tex. Gardens Clubs, program chmn. 1986-88; treas. Brehnham U. Women, 1988-, St. Paul's Ch. Women, 1955—; pres. St. Paul's Ch. Women Cir.; mem. St. Paul's Sunday Sch., Intermediate Dept., prin. 1957-89; active local Girl Scouts, 1958-73; v.p. local PTA, 1960-62. Mem. Washington-on-the-Brazos State Park Assn. (bd. dirs. 1987-), Barrington Hist. Soc. (bd. dirs., sec., treas. 1975-80), Spouces of Nat. Am. Whole Groceries Assn. (bd. dirs. 1987-90), Tex. Fedn. Womens Clubs (bd. dirs. 1976-, past dist. pres., pres. San Jacinto dist. 1980-82, state bd. dirs. 1960-, named Outstanding Club Woman 1973), Washington County Hist. Soc. (life, v.p. 1965), Am. Legion Aux., Fortnightly Club (pres. 1960-62, 83-84), Sigma Iota Epsilon, Alpha Delta Pi.

UTGOFF, KATHLEEN PLATT, economist, pension fund executive; b. Trenton, N.J., Feb. 5, 1948; d. Francis J. and Helen Platt; m. Victor Utgoff; children: Anna, Margaret. Student, Rutgers U., 1966-68; BA in Econs., Calif. State U., Northridge, 1971; PhD in Econs., UCLA, 1978. Employment counselor Dept. Human Resources, Van Nuys, Calif., 1971-72; economist Ctr. for Naval Analysis, Alexandria, Va., 1974-83; sr. staff economist Council Econ. Advisors, White House, Washington, 1983-85; exec. dir. Pension Benefit Guaranty Corp., Washington, 1985—. Mem. Women in Govt. Relations, Am. Econ. Assn., Women in Employee Benefits. Republican. Office: Pension Benefit Guaranty Corp 2020 K St NW Washington DC 20006

UTLEY, DONNA LAVELLE, hospital administrator; b. Tulare, Calif., June 30, 1948; d. Donald Raymond and Vivian Lee (Baber) Rogers; B.S., Calif. State U., Fresno, 1970; M.P.A., U. So. Calif., 1985; m. July 23, 1970. Resources and devel. asst. Concentrated Employment Program, Fresno, Calif., 1970-72; personnel analyst Fresno County Personnel Dept., 1972-74; personnel mgr. Fresno County Health Dept., 1974-79; personnel dir. Merced (Calif.) Community Med. Ctr., 1979-81; dir. human resources Bay Area Hosp., Coos Bay, Oreg., 1981-85; asst. adminstr. human resources, St. Elizabeth Med. Ctr., Yakima, Wash., 1985—; bd. dirs. Enterprise for Progress in the Community, 1986—, sec., 1989-90, chair personnel com., 1987, 88, 89. Mem. Wash. Soc. Hosp. Human Resources Adminstrn., Am. Soc. Healthcare Human Resources Adminstrn., Cen./S.E. Wash. Healthcare Personnel Dirs. Assn. (pres. 1987, 88), Pacific N.W. Personnel Mgmt. Assn.. Republican. Methodist. Office: 110 S 9th Ave Yakima WA 98902

UTLEY, SUSAN G., pollution control specialist; b. Little Rock, Nov. 2, 1957; d. Bobby D. and Dorothy J. (Rutledge) U. BS, Ark. Tech. U., 1981. Engr. technologist Hoffman-Brixey and Assocs., Ft. Smith, Ark.; reclamation specialist Ark. Dept. Pollution Control, Russellville; pretreatment coord., ops. mgmt. intern Ark. Dept. Pollution Control, Fayetteville. Mem. NAFE, Water Pollution Control Fedn., Ark. Water Pollution Control Assn. Address: 1500 N Foxhunter Rd Fayetteville AR 72701

UTZ, DEBORAH E., real estate executive; b. Rochester, N.Y., June 8, 1961; d. Fredrick A. and Marlene (Culligan) U. BS, Ithaca Coll., 1982; MBA, St. John Fisher Coll. Lic. real estate broker; cert. neuro associative conditioning specialist, residential brokerage mgr. Producer WICB-TV, Ithaca, N.Y., 1980-82; news dir., disc jockey WICB-FM, Ithaca, 1979-82; tech. editor, job mgr. Xerox Corp., Webster, N.Y., 1982-84; v.p., gen. mgr. Coldwell Banker Utz Realty, Inc., Webster, 1984—. Vol. Compeer, 1990; mem. Webster C. of C., 1984—. Mem. NAFE, Nat. Assn. Realtors, N.Y. State Assn. Realtors, Greater Rochester Assn. Realtors (dir. 1991, staff instr.), Women's Coun. of Realtors (pres. Rochester chpt. 1990, pres. elect N.Y. state chpt. 1991), Cert. Residential Brokerage Mgrs., Realtors Nat. Mktg. Inst., Real Estate Brokerage Coun., Real Estate Buyers Agents Coun. Address: 162 S Estate Dr Webster NY 14580

UTZ, SARAH WINIFRED, nursing educator; b. San Diego; d. Frederick R. and Margaret M. (Gibbons) U.; B.S., U. Portland, 1943, Ed.M., 1958; M.S., UCLA, 1970; Ph.D., U. So. Calif., 1979. Clin. instr. Providence Sch. Nursing, Portland, Oreg., 1946-50, edn. dir., 1950-62; edn. dir. Sacred Heart Sch. Nursing, Eugene, Oreg., 1963-67; asst. prof. nursing Calif. State U., Los Angeles, 1969-74, assoc. prof., 1974-81, prof., 1981—, assoc. chmn. dept. nursing, 1982—; cons. in nursing curriculum, 1978—; past chmn. ednl. adminstrs., cons., tchrs. sect. Oreg. Nurses Assn., past pres. Oreg. State Bd. Nursing; mem. research program Western Interstate Commn. on Higher Edn. in Nursing; chmn. liaison com. nursing edn. Articulation Council Calif. Served with Nurse Corps, USN, 1944-46. HEW grantee, 1970-74, Kellogg Found. grantee, 1974-76, USDHHS grantee, 1987—; R.N., Calif., Oreg. Mem. Am. Nurses Assn., Calif. Nurses Assn. (edn. commr. region 6 1987—, chair edn. interest group region 6 , 1987—), Am. Ednl. Research Assn., AAUP, Phi Delta Kappa, Sigma Theta Tau. Formerly editor Oreg. Nurse; reviewer Western Jour. Nursing Research. Home: 1409 Midvale Ave Los Angeles CA 90024 Office: 5151 State University Dr Los Angeles CA 90032

UTZINGER, PAULINE ROSE, public relations librarian; b. Rochester, Minn., Apr. 9, 1925; d. Lyle Chester and Mabel Regina (Schanke) U. BA in Psychology, Carleton Coll., 1947; MS in Counseling, Winona State U., 1966; postgrad. in ednl. psychology, Bryn Mawr Coll., 1948-51. Cert. secondary educator, librarian (K-12). Testing svc. Carleton Coll., Northfield, Minn., 1947-48; warden Bryn Mawr (Pa.) Coll, 1948-51; dean of freshmen women U. Wis., Madison, 1951-52; asst. to dean women Carleton Coll., Northfield, 1953-55; dir. women's club Mayo Clinic, Rochester, Minn., 1956; librarian, tchr. Pine Island (Minn.) Sch. Dist., 1957-58; sr. high counselor Winona (Minn.) Pub. Schs., 1959-69; pub. relations Rochester Pub. Library, 1975—; community edn. tchr. Rochester, 1979—; class agt. Carleton Coll., Northfield, 1984—, alumni bd. dirs., 1978-80, alumni admissions rep., 1947—; alumni admissions rep., Bryn Mawr (Pa.) Coll., 1947—. Bd. dirs. Olmsted County Hist. Soc., Rochester, 1980—, pres. bd. trustees, 1987-89; pres. Winona YWCA, 1965-67; bd. dirs. Lakeview Homeowners Assn., Rochester, 1984—. Mem. Minn. Libr. Assn., Nat. Geneal. Assn., Minn. Geneal. Soc., Wis. Geneal. Soc., Iowa Geneal. Soc., Ind. Geneal Soc., N.C. Geneal Soc., German Geneal. Soc., Olmsted County Geneal Soc., AAUW (bd. dirs. 1970—, Woman as Agt. of Change Award Minn. 1987, named fellowship Rochester br. 1986), AFSCME (pres. local chpt. 1982-84), All the Good Old Girls. Methodist. Home: 1900 Lakeview Ct SW Rochester MN 55902-4203 Office: Rochester Pub Library 11 First St SE Rochester MN 55904-3743

UZENDA, JARA CARLOW, technical writer; b. Brookline, Mass., May 24, 1946; d. Roscoe William and Gloria Pauline (St. Jacques) Carlow; m. William ANthony Perry, June 1, 1963 (dec. Dec. 1971); children: Troy Anthony, William Lance; m. Richard Paul Matsumoto Sr., May 24, 1981; 1 child, Richard Paul Jr. Student, R.I. Jr. Coll., 1965-67, U. R.I., 1967-68; BS in Journalism, U. Colo., 1975, MS in Telecommunications, 1978. Mktg. mgr. Humidor Smoke Shoppes, Warwick, R.I., 1965-69; telecommunication cons. Arthur D. Little, Inc., Boston, 1976-78; dir. research Horizon House Internat., Boston, 1978-80; market analyst Internat. Telecommunications, Boulder, Colo., 1980-81; field service engr. Allied Info. Systems, Boulder, 1981-83; gen. ptnr. Kentucky Gold Ltd., San Jose, Calif., 1984; sr. tech. writer Paradyne Corp., Largo, Fla., 1984-86; sales and mktg. Piedmont Airlines Golf Resort Directory, Myrtle Beach, S.C., 1986-87; cons. Data Security, Little River, S.C., 1987—; v.p. mktg. So. Golfer, 1989—; vis. prof. Prescott Coll., Flagstaff, Ariz., 1972; film dir. Niel Minority News, Estes Park, Colo., 1973-74; featured artist Denver Post, 1973; spl. expert Latin Am. Telecommunications, Washington, 1980. Author: Electronic Fund Transfer, 1978; contbr. articles to Flatiron Mag., Telecommunications Mag., Security Management Mag. Grantee Nat. Endowment Arts, 1973. Mem. Council Internat. Relations & UN Affairs, Internat. Relations Club, Soc. Women Engrs., U. Colo. Alumni Assn., Mortar Bd. Lodge: Optimists. Home: PO Box 603 Little River SC 29566

VACHER-MORRIS, ELIZABETH MICHELE, lay worker; b. Morgantown, W.Va., July 2, 1963; d. John Michael Vacher and Carole Jean (Doughton) Vacher-Mayberry. BA in Communications, Carson-Newman Coll., 1986; postgrad., Div. Sch., Duke U., 1990—. Intern Sta. WBIR-TV, Knoxville, Tenn., 1986; camera operator Media Svcs. Ctr., Jefferson City, Tenn., 1986, 87; advt. account exec. Sta. WKJQ-WJFC-AM-FM, Jefferson City, 1986-87; reporter Sta. WKPT-TV, Kingsport, Tenn., 1986, 87; prodn. specialist Sta. WTVK-TV, Knoxville, 1987-88; electronic graphics producer Sta. WATE-TV, Knoxville, 1988-90. Vol. Blount Meml. Hosp., Maryville, Tenn., 1981, Contact Teleministries, Knoxville, 1982; mem. choir, pres. Sunday sch., adminstrv. bd. coun. on ministries, worship coord., pres. jr. class Cokesbury United Meth. Ch., Knoxville, 1987—, sponsor mission family, 1988—, dir. singles, 1990—. Mem. Alpha Xi Delta. Republican. Home: 2752 Middleton Ave #31E Durham NC 27705

VADNEY, LAURA LECLAIR, social worker; b. Memphis, Oct. 3, 1945; d. William James and Elsye LeClair (Schultz) Johnson; m. Paul H. Vadney, Jan. 21, 1967 (div. Jan. 1984); children: Timothy Vadney, Joshua Vadney. Student, U. Tenn., 1963-65; BS, Memphis State U., 1967; MS, Troy State U., 1981. Cert. assoc. counselor. Welfare worker Dept. Health & Rehab. Svcs., Jacksonville, Fla., 1967-69; vol. coord. Naval Air Station Clinic, Beeville, Tex., 1970-73; pub. rels. specialist Brunswick (Maine) Area Humane Soc., 1973-77; edn. worker Humane Soc., Pensacola, Fla., 1978; protective svcs. counselor Dept. of Health and Rehab. Svcs., Milton, Fla., 1978-82; founding dir. Key West (Fla.) Help Line, 1982-83; exec. dir. Armed Svcs. YMCA, Key West, 1983; dir. of vol. svcs. and pub. rels. B'nai B'rith Home, Memphis, 1984-89, dir. social svcs., 1989—. Author, facilitator seminar series, Coping With Deployment, 1983; author series of publs. Home Edition/BBH News, 1984-88. Docent Memphis (Tenn.) Zoo & Aquarium, 1988—, mem. adv. com., 1989—; telephone crisis counselor Crisis Ctr.,

Memphis, 1985-87; pres. Memphis Area Assn. Dir. of Vols., 1987-88. Mem. Tenn. Health Care Assn. Social Work Dirs. Office: Bnai Brith Home 131 N Tucker Memphis TN 38104

VAGNEUR, KATHRYN OTTO, accountant, rancher; b. Aurora, Ill., Feb. 23, 1946; d. Harold William and Afton (Bryner) Otto; m. Gerald Ronald Terwilliger, Oct. 19, 1968 (div. 1974); 1 dau., Jocelyn Marie; m. Clyde O. Vagneur, Aug. 24, 1979. BS in Math., U. Utah, 1968; MS in Agribus. Mgmt., Ariz. State U., 1979. CPA, Colo. Computer systems designer U. Utah Libraries, Salt Lake City, 1966-68; rsch. asst. in computer systems Carnegie-Mellon U., 1968-70; owner, mgr. Evening at Arthurs Restaurant, Aspen, Colo., 1973-76; self-employed tax cons. Phoenix, 1977-78; with Touche Ross & Co., Colorado Springs, Colo., 1978-82; ptnr., fin. mgr. V Bar Lazy V Ranch, Peyton, Colo., 1978—; ptnr. Vagneur & Firth, Colorado Springs, 1982—; pres. The Marlwood Corp., Colorado Springs; chmn. Excellence in Bus. Seminar Series, 1987-88; lectr. in field. Chmn. bd. dirs. Pikes Peak Ctr.; del. Rep. State Conv., 1982, White House Small Bus. Conf., 1986; bd. dirs. Springs Into Action Econ. Devel. Strategy, 1987-88, Colo. Springs Children's Mus.; chmn. Pvt. Industry Coun., 1989—; mem. Gov.'s Econ. Devel. Action Coun., 1988; trustee Colo. Springs Econ. Devel. Coun., 1988—; 4-H leader; advisor Colo. Small Bus. Devel. Ctrs., 1988—. Mem. AICPA, Nat. Soc. Accts. for Coops., Colo. Soc. CPAs, Nat. Assn. Accts., Jr. League, Am. Salers Assn., Nat. Cattlemen's Assn. (featured speaker 1986 Beef Profit Conf.), Nat. Fedn. Ind. Bus., Colorado Springs C. of C. (com. chmn.), Am. Quarter Horse Assn., Beta Alpha Psi, Alpha Zeta. Author: A Financial Analysis of Cooperative Livestock Marketing, 1978; contbr. articles to mags. Home: 14725 Jones Rd Peyton CO 80831 Office: Vagneur & Firth 830 N Tejon Ste 303 Colorado Springs CO 80903

VAIL, IRIS JENNINGS, civic worker; b. N.Y.C., July 2, 1928; d. Lawrence K. and Beatrice (Black) Jennings; grad. Miss Porters Sch., Farmington, Conn.; m. Thomas V.H. Vail, Sept. 15, 1951; children: Siri J., Thomas V.H. Jr., Lawrence J.W. Exec. com. Garden Club Cleve., 1962—; mem. women's coun. Western Res. Hist. Soc., 1960—, Cleve. Mus. Art, 1953—; chmn. Childrens Garden Fair, 1966-75, Public Square Dinner, 1975; bd. dirs. Garden Center Greater Cleve., 1963-77; trustee Cleve. Zool. Soc., 1971—; mem. Ohio Arts Coun., 1974-76, pub. sq. com. Greater Cleve. Growth Assn., pub. sq. preservation and maintenance com. Cleve. Found., 1989, chmn. pub. sq. planting com. Recipient Amy Angell Collier Montague medal Garden Club Am., 1976, Ohio Gov.'s award, 1977. Chagrin Valley Hunt Club, Cypress Point Club, Kirtland Country Club, Union Club, Colony Club, Women's City of Cleve. Club (Margaret A. Ireland award). Home: Hunting Valley Chagrin Falls OH 44022

VAILE, JEAN ELIZABETH, association executive; b. Cut Bank, Mont., July 18, 1938; d. Leo M. and Evelyn A. (Hensrude) Baker; m. Alvin L. Vaile (div.); children—Arthur Henry, Sheila Jean, Leo Michael. Student Kinman Bus. Sch., 1956-57, Fresno City Coll., 1975-76, U. San Francisco, 1980, State Center Community Coll., Fresno, Calif., 1981-82. Lic. life disability ins. agt., real estate agt., Calif.; notary pub., Calif. Mgr., Glacier Drug, Browning, Mont., 1958-60, Club Cafe, Browning, 1960-67; office mgr. J.C. Penny Co., Mont., 1967-69, Bob Ward & Sons, Inc., Missoula, Mont., 1970-73; acct. Sun Fruit, Ltd., Fresno, 1973-76; bus. adminstr. Assn. for Retarded Citizens, 1976-82; adminstrv. asst. to sr. v.p. Guarantee Savs., Fresno, 1985—; Amway distbr., 1975—; owner part-time income diversification and 2d income devel. bus. Chmn. supervisory com. Fresno Consumers Credit Union, 1979; voting mem. two social service health orgns., 1979—. Mem. Republican Presdl. Task Force. Lutheran. Club: Toastmasters. Home: 2007 E Austin Fresno CA 93726

VAJDA, DEBORAH LOUISE, editor; b. Tarentum, Pa., Oct. 30, 1956; d. Jaroslav J. and Louise Margaret (Mastaglio) Vajda. BA in English, U. Mo., Kans. City, 1979. Copy clerk Kans. City Star, 1977; music, dance reviewer Kans. City Star & Times, 1978; intern Family Cir. Mag., N.Y., 1978; editor Insight, Darcy Macmanus & Masius, St. Louis, 1979-80, Networth, St. Paul, Minn., 1982-83; sr. editor TWA Ambassador Mag. Webb Co., Minn., 1981-84; mgng. editor Twin Cities Mag. Dorn Comm., Mpls., 1985-88; editor, writer Self-Employed, St. Paul, Minn., 1989; editorial bd. Info. A Three Dimensional Design Journal, Mpls., 1988--. Contbr. articles to profl. jours. Democrat. Lutheran.

VAJDOS, VANESSA ELLEN, chiropractor, pharmacist; b. Karnes City, Tex., Aug. 28, 1951; d. Joseph Melick and Cecilia (Zezuela) Vajdos. BS in Pharmacy, U. Tex., 1973; Dr of Chiropractic, Tex. Chiropractic Coll., 1986. Owner Good Health Chiropractic Ctr., Seattle, 1990—. Winner Houston Marathon; 10th in the Arron Internat. World Championship. Mem. United Chiropractors of Wash., Wash. Chiropractic Assn., Queen Anne Runners for the Goodwill Games. Home: 1401 5th West Apt 105 Seattle WA 98119

VALANCE, MARSHA JEANNE, library director, story teller; b. Evanston, Ill., Aug. 2, 1946; d. Edward James Jr. and Jeanne Lois (Skinner) Leonard; m. William George Valance, Dec. 27, 1966 (div. 1976); 1 child, Marguerite Jeanne. Student Northwestern U., 1964-66; AB, UCLA, 1968; MLS, U. R.I., 1973. Children's libr. trainee N.Y. Pub. Libr., N.Y.C., 1968-69; reference libr. Action Meml. Pub. Libr. (Mass.), 1969-70; mgr. The Footnote, Cedar Rapids, Iowa, 1976-78; assoc. editor William C. Brown, Dubuque, Iowa, 1978-79; dir. Dubuque County Libr., Dubuque, 1979-81, G.B. Dedrick Pub. Libr., Geneseo, Ill., 1981-84, dir. Grand Rapids (Minn.) Pub. Libr., 1984-89; mgmt. libr., Wis. Regional Libr. for Blind and Physically Handicapped, 1989—; workshop coord., participant, sect. chmn. profl. confs. Author: (with others) Mystery, Value and Awareness, 1979; Pluralism, Similarities and Contrast, 1979; contbr. articles to publs. Troop leader Miss. Valley Coun. Girl Scouts U.S., Cedar Rapids, 1976-78; mem. liturgy com. St. Malachy's Roman Cath. Ch., Geneseo, 1983; com. judging clinic 4-H, Moline, Ill., 1984; trustee KAXE No. Community Radio, 1986-89, ICTV, 1988-90; sec. Grand Rapids Community Svcs. Coun., 1986; coach Itasca County 4-H Horse Bowl Team, 1987; dir. Grand Rapids Storyfest, 1987-89;sprogram chmn. Spotlight on Books Conf., 1989; bd. dirs., trustee Vols. in Svc. to the Handicapped, 1989—. Iowa Humanities Bd. grantee, 1981, Minn. Libr. Found. grantee, 1985, 86, 87, Blandin Found. grantee, 1986, Arrowhead Regional Arts Coun. grantee, 1987, 89, Ms. Soc. grantee, 1989. Mem. ALA, Minn. Libr. Assn., Iowa Librs. of Medium Size (sec. 1981), Northlands Storytelling Network (bd. dirs. 1988—, v.p. 1989, pres. 1990), Nat. Assn. Preservation and Perpetuation Storytelling, Nat. Clearinghouse for Info. on Storytelling, Alliance Info. and Referral Svcs., DAR (constn. chmn. 1983-84), Am. Morgan Horse Assn., Ill. Morgan Horse Assn., Geneseo Jr. Women's Club (internat. chmn. 1983-84), Alpha Gamma Delta. Home: 6639 Dodge Pl Milwaukee WI 53220 Office: Wis Regional Libr for Blind & Physically Handicapped 814 W Wisconsin Ave Milwaukee WI 53233

VALCIC, SUSAN JOAN, judge; b. N.Y.C., Mar. 23, 1956; d. Joseph and Eve (Manderville) Caciola; m. Alexander C. Valcic, July 28, 1979. BA magna cum laude, Columbia U., 1983; JD, Cardozo Sch. Law, 1986. Assoc. attorney Bailey, Marshall & Hoeniger, N.Y.C., 1986-87, Zalkin, Rodin & Goodman, N.Y.C., 1987-89; pvt. practice N.Y.C., 1989—. Apptd. adminstrv. law judge, N.Y., 1990. Mem. Assn. Bar City N.Y., N.Y. County Lawyers Assn., N.Y. State Bar. Assn., Fed. Bar. Assn., Columbia Club, Phi Beta Kappa.

VALDES-DAPENA, MARIE AGNES, pediatric pathologist, educator; b. Pottsville, Pa., July 14, 1921; d. Edgar Daniel and Marie Agnes (Rettig) Brown; m. Antonio M. Valdes-Dapena, Apr. 6, 1945 (div. Oct. 1980); children: Victoria Maria Valdes-Dapena Hiltebeitel, Deborah Anne Valdes-Dapena Malle, Maria Cristina Valdes-Dapena, Andres Antonio, Antonio Edgardo, Carlos Roberto, Marcos Antonio, Ricardo Daniel, Carmen Patricia Valdés-Dapena Fater, Catalina Inez, Pedro Pablo. BS, Immaculata Coll., 1941; MD, Temple U., 1944. Diplomate: Am. Bd. Pathology. Intern Phila. Gen. Hosp., 1944-45, resident in pathology, 1945-49; asst. pathologist Fitzgerald Mercy Hosp., Darby, Pa., 1949-51; dir. labs. Woman's Med. Coll. Pa., Phila., 1951-55; instr. pathology Woman's Med. Coll. Pa., 1947-51, asst. prof., 1951-55, assoc. prof., 1955-59; assoc. pathologist St. Christopher's Hosp. for Children, Phila., 1959-76; dir. sect. pediatric pathology U. Miami-Jackson Meml. Hosp., Miami, 1976-81, pediatric pathologist, dir. div. edn. in pathology, 1981—; cons., lectr. U.S. Naval Hosp., Phila., 1972-76; instr. pathology Sch. Medicine U. Pa., 1945-49; instr. Sch. Medicine U. Pa. (Sch. Dentistry), 1947, Sch. Medicine U. Pa. (Grad. Sch. Medicine), 1948-55, vis. lectr., 1960-62; asst. prof. Temple U. Med. Sch., 1959-63, assoc. prof., 1963-67, prof. pathology and pediatrics, 1967-76; prof. pathology and pediatrics U., Miami, 1976—; cons. pediatric pathology div. med. examiner Dept. Pub. Health Phila., 1967-70; mem. perinatal biology and infant mortality research and tng. com. Nat. Inst. Child Health and Human Devel., NIH, 1971-73; mem. sci. adv. bd. Armed Forces Inst. Pathology, 1976-82; assoc. med. examiner, Dade County, Fla., 1976—; chmn. med. bd. Nat. Sudden Infant Death Syndrome Found., 1961-81, 87—, pres., 1984-87, chmn. bd., 1985-88. Contbr. articles to profl. jours. NIH grantee. Mem. U.S. and Can. Acad. Pathology, Coll. Physicians Phila., Internat. Assn. Pediatric Pathology, Soc. for Pediatric Pathology (pres. 1980-81), Dade County Med. Soc., Alpha Omega Alpha. Roman Catholic. Home: 179 Morningside Dr Miami Springs FL 33166 Office: U Miami Sch of Med Dept Pathology PO Box 016960 Miami FL 33101

VALDÉS-VALLE, NANCY ZAIDA, foreign language educator; b. Havana, Cuba, Jan. 21, 1938; came to U.S., 1961; d. Abelardo Luis and Maria Zaida (Cabrera) Barba Inclán; m. Jorge L. Valdés-Valle, Feb. 4, 1967 (div. Jan. 1978); 1 child, Lissette. Assoc. degree, U. Havana, 1961; BA, St. Thomas U., 1975. Cert. elem. and Spanish tchr., Fla. Tchr. pvt. sch. Havana, Cuba, 1956-61; tchr. fgn. lang. Acad. La Castellana, Caracas, Venezuela, 1965-71, Centro Venezolano Americano, Caracas, 1965-71, George Washington Carver Elem. Sch., Miami, Fla., 1975-79, David Fairchild Elem. Sch., Miami, 1979-83, Kendale Lakes Elem. Sch., Miami, 1983—; curriculum writer for bilingual programs Dade County Pub. Schs., Miami, 1982-88; cons. Nat. Text Book Co., Miami, 1988-89, Santillana Pub., Miami; asst. supt. Dade County Youth Fair Spanish Dance, Miami, 1990. Named to Order Academica Don Miguel de Cervantes Saavedra Instituto de Cultura Hispanica, Miami, 1988-90. Mem. Am.-Hispanic Edn. Assn. of Dade County, Fgn. Lang. Assn. Dade County (v.p. 1988-89, 89-90). Roman Catholic.

VALENT, MICHELE D., production manager; b. Milw., Apr. 25, 1965; d. John M. and Barbara J. (Kowski) V. BS, U. Wis., Platteville, 1987; student, U. South Fla. Prodn. engr. Centercom, Inc., Milw., 1986-88; mgr. prodn. Centercom, Inc., Tampa, Fla., 1988—. Mem. Fla. Motion Picture and TV Assn., Internat. TV Assn., Soc. Broadcast Engrs., Alpha Epsilon Rho.

VALENTE, PATRICIA LUCILLE, counselor; b. Chgo., June 30, 1940; d. Joseph James and Mae L. (Durand) V.; m. Robert J. Maxwell, Jan. 19, 1963 (div. Feb. 1974); children: Kim Maxwell, Robert Maxwell; m. Robert W. Witzke, Aug. 4, 1977. BA, No. Ill. U., 1962, MS, 1967; MS, George Williams Coll., 1976. Cert. sex educator, sex therapist. Tchr. English Hinsdale (Ill.) High Sch., 1963-69; tchr. English Morton Coll., Cicero, Ill., 1969-71, counselor, sex therapist, 1971—; cons. West Chgo. (Ill.) Community High Sch., 1965-66; mem. north cen. visitation team Ill. State Dept. Edn., Springfield, 1968; presenter in field. Author: (with others) Community College Career Alternatives, 1981, The WOW Group: The New Frontier, 1984. Named Educator of Yr., Morton Coll., 1979. Mem. CWP (exec. bd. dirs. 1983—), ASSECT, IGPA, AGPA. Roman Catholic. Home: 17 W 507 Portsmouth Dr Westmont IL 60559 Office: Morton Coll 3801 S Central Ave Cicero IL 60650

VALENTE, SANDRA DEBRA, fund raising consultant; b. Bklyn., Aug. 6, 1940; d. Anthony and Theresa V.; m. Henry J Jansen, June 19, 1960 (div. Feb. 1976); children: Gregory Joseph, Scott Henry, Anthony William. BAin Psychology cum laude, Kean Coll., 1976, BA in History cum laude, 1976. Cert. Social Sutdies Tchr., 1976. Purchasing clk. Johnson & Johnson, New Brunswick, N.J., 1957-58; library clk. ER Squibb & Sons, New Brunswick, 1959-61; psychology tchr. Manalapan High Sch., Freehold, N.J., 1976-79; community rels. dir. Bonnie Brae Found., Millington, N.J., 1980-81; dir. devel. Sussex County Assn. for Retarded Citizens Found., Newton, N.J., 1982-86; exec. dir. Sussex County Assn. for Retarded Citizens Found., Newton, 1986; dir. devel. Yosemite Community Coll. Dist., Modesto, Calif., 1986-87; cons. Fund Devel. Assocs., Sacramento, Calif., 1988-89; exec. dir. Calif. Multi-Cultural Park, Sacramento, Calif., 1989—; cons., vol. Samaritan Inn, Newton, 1984-85; adv. bd. mem. County Coll. of Morris, Succasunna, N.J., 1983-85, com. mem. Outstanding Bus. in Community Sussex County C. of C., 1986. Pres. Jr. C. of C. Wives, Hightstown, N.J., 1965-66; sec. Boy Scouts Am., Freehold, 1968, Cub Scouts Am., Freehold, 1975; state chmn. Jaycee-ettes, Hightstown, N.J., 1966 (named Outstanding Pres. 1966). Mem. Nat. Soc. Fund Raising Exec. (com. chmn., 1985-86, bd. dirs.), Sacramento C. of C. (ambassador). Office: Calif Multi-Cultural Pk 3711 Branch Center Rd Sacramento CA 95827

VALENTEKOVICH, MARIJA NIKOLETIC, diagnostic chemist, executive; b. Dubrovnik, Yugoslavia, Feb. 5, 1932; came to U.S., 1965; d. Miroslav-Adam Nikoletic and Vinka (Brangjolica) Sepic; m. Duro A. Valentekovich, Feb. 3, 1962; children: Vladimir M., Robert J. MS in Chem. Engring., U. Zagreb, Yugoslavia, 1957, PhD in Chemistry, 1963. With U. Ill., Urbana, 1965-67; rsch. assoc. U. So. Calif., L.A., 1967-68; dir. quality assurance Cyclo Chem. Co., L.A., 1968-72; head radiochemistry Curtis Nuclear Co., L.A., 1972-74; dir. quality assurance Nichols Inst., San Pedro, Calif., 1974-79; prin. chemist Beckman Instruments Inc, Brea, Calif., 1979-83; v.p. tech. Innotron-Diagnostic Co., Irvine, Calif., 1983-87; tech. dir., ops. mgr. Merrel Inc., Gardena, Calif., 1987-88; assoc. dir. quality control Diagnostic Product Corp., L.A., 1989—. Contbr. articles to profl. jours. Mem. Am. Chemical Soc., Am. Assn. Clin. Chemistry. Home: 33 Silver Spring Dr Rolling Hills Estates CA 90274

VALENTIN, ANN MARGARET, foundation administrator; b. Waltham, Mass., July 4, 1936; d. William Bemish and Violet Mary (Ferguson) Clarke; m. William Valentin, May 2, 1964 (div.); children: Lisa, David. Cert., Newton Bus. Sch., 1955; cert. real estate broker, Lee Inst., Boston, 1960. Statistical clk. John Hancock Mut. Life Ins., Boston, 1954-59; real estate broker Mass., 1959-63; real estate advt. G.H. Powell Humphrey Realtor, San Francisco, 1960-61; broker's gal Friday Shoemaker, Pritchard & Wheeler, San Francisco, 1961-71; stocks and bonds supr. Crocker Bank, Western Bradford, San Francisco, 1971-77; property mgmt. Vallejo, Calif., 1977-79; restaurant mgmt. J.C. Penney, Inc., Richmond, Calif., 1979-83; cost acctg., personnel Grove Value, Emeryville, Calif., 1983-85; co-founder, exec. v.p., sec., treas. Share Found., S.E.E. Pub., Co., Santa Clara, Calif., 1985—; bd. dirs. SHARE Found., Santa Clara, 1986—, lectr., 1986—. Co-author: Cosmic Revelation, 1987, Descent of the Dove, 1988. Mem. NAFE, Greenpeace, Cousteau Soc., World Wildlife Fund, Nat. Audubon Soc. Office: 968 Admiral Callaghan Ln Ste 219 Vallejo CA 94591

VALENTIN, NILDA, psychologist; b. Manati, P.R., Oct. 2, 1950; d. Juan and Aurora (Colón) V.; m. Nigel A.L. Brooks, Oct. 23, 1988. BA, U. P.R., Rio Piedras, 1972; PhD, Caribbean, Santurce, P.R., 1981. Lic. psychologist, N.Y., P.R. Pvt. practice N.Y.C.; unit dir. Fordham-Tremont Community Mental Health Ctr., Bronx, N.Y., 1983-89; clin. supr. NYU Med. Sch., N.Y.C., 1987—. Apptd. by gov. Cuomo to adv. coun. Com. on Quality Care for Mentally Disabled, 1986—; mem. Legis. Adv. Com. Mental Health, 1987—. Mem. NAFE, Am. Assn. Sex Educators, Counselors and Therapists. Office: 168 5th Ave 2d Fl North Ste New York NY 10021

VALENTINE, CAROL ANN, director educational program, consultant; b. Mt. Clemens, Mich., Dec. 5, 1942; d. Joseph Eldon and Erna Fredericka (Brandt) V.; married; children: Christopher, David. BA, U. Mich., 1964, MA, 1965; PhD, Pa. State U., 1971. Tchr. Oak Park (Ill.)-River Forest High Sch., 1965-67; research assoc. U. Md., College Park, 1967; dir. grants Pa. State U., State College, 1967-78; asst. prof. Oreg. State U., Corvallis, 1970-74; vis. prof. U. Oreg., Eugene, 1974-75; assoc. prof. Ariz. State U., Tempe, 1975-85, assoc. dir. women's studies, 1975—; cons. Tempe, 1975—. Author: First Impressions, 1980, Women and Communicative Power, 1988. Bd. dirs. Tempe Pub. Library, 1984—. Named Outstanding Woman of Phoenix, 1987. Mem. Zeta Phi Eta. Democrat. Presbyterian. Home: 2607 S Forest Ave Tempe AZ 85282 Office: Ariz State U Stauffer Hall 412 Tempe AZ 85287

VALENTINE, MARYANN, health care consultant; b. Durango, Colo., Feb. 25, 1935; d. Otto and Concetta (di Ubaldo) Serroni; m. William Ellsworth Valentine, Sept. 21, 1962; children: Antony Alexander, Anna Maria. BS, U. Colo., 1956. Dir. med. records Presbyn. Med. Ctr., Denver, 1959-74; health care cons. Denver, 1974—, Health and Human Svcs., Denver, 1988—; ptnr. Paramount Pub., Denver, 1970-79. Editor, pub.: Elitch Theatre Program, 1974-79, Colo. Tourist Guide, 1974-79. Docent Colo. Hist. Soc., Denver, 1986-89; vol. Homeless Groups, Denver, 1985-89; mem. Denver Botanic Gardens, 1988-89; mem. Colo. Commn. on Status of Women, 1970. Recipient Employer Merit award, Pres. Commn. on Employment of Handicapped, Washington, 1973. Mem. Am. Med. Record Assn. (instr. med. record technician program 1969-74, del. 1970), Colo. Real Estate Commn., Colo. Med. Record Assn. (pres. 1970). Republican. Roman Catholic. Home: 5636 E 17th Ave Denver CO 80220

VALENTINE, MELINDA STAUFFER, speech pathologist; b. Wichita Falls, Tex., Aug. 20, 1954; d. Charles Dee and Loretta Jean (Webster) Stauffer; m. James T. Valentine, July 31, 1976. BS, Okla. State U., 1976; MS, So. Meth. U., Dallas, 1977. Cert. speech-lang. pathologist. Speech and lang. pathologist Dallas Ind. Sch. Dist., 1977-82, Dallas Easter Seal Soc., 1982-90; speech-lang. pathologist pvt. practice, Dallas, 1990—. Mem. Internat. Soc. Alternative and Augmentative Communication, Tex. Speech-Lang.-Hearing Assn. (task force chair), Am. Speech-Lang.-Hearing Assn. (liaison), Dallas Assn. Speech-Lang. Pathologists and Audiologists, Neurodevel. Treatment Assn. Home and Office: 12832 Noel Rd #1029 Dallas TX 75230

VALENTINI, SUSAN MARIE, sales official; b. Lynwood, Calif., Jan. 24, 1963; d. Peter Angelo and Sally Ann (Stafford) V.; m. Brian Kevin McFadden, Aug. 31, 1985 (div. Oct. 1986); 1 child, Joseph. BBA, U. S.D., 1985, MBA, 1988. Cashier, bookkeeper Wild West Store, Encinitas, Calif., 1979-81; asst. mgr. Parisian, Encinitas, 1981-85; sales assoc. Robinsons, La Jolla, Calif., 1990—. Scholar U. S.D., 1981. Mem. NAFE. Office: Robinson's PO Box 9317 4425 LaJolla Village Dr San Diego CA 92122

VALENTINO, RENE X., drummer, recording artist; b. Passaic, N.J., Dec. 18, 1961; d. Michael Anthony and Filomena (Campitiello) V. BA cum laude, Fairleigh Dickinson U., 1987. Ambassador Internat. Symphonic Wind Orch., Kinnelon, N.J., 1980, 82; computer, mktg. exec. ITT DCD, Nutley, N.J., 1981-89; pub. rels. exec., drummer, recording artist Hari Kari, N.Y.C., 1988—; mgr. for Eric Carr-Kiss; mgr. Eric Carr - Kis. Composer, arranger musical compositions. Music diplomate People to People Internat. Coun. for Understanding. Mem. Percussive Arts Soc. Office: Hari Kari PO Box 4744 Clifton NJ 07015-4744

VALERIO, HELEN JOSEPHINE, restaurant company executive; b. Chelsea, Mass., Nov. 23, 1938; d. William P. and Helen (Hoffman) Kazukonis; m. Michael A. Valerio, Oct. 6, 1957; children—Michael A., Laura L., Linda M. Acct., Piece O Pizza, of Am. Inc., Arlington, Mass., 1958-63; treas. Papa Gino's of Am., Inc., Needham Heights, Mass., 1963—, sr. v.p., 1980-81, exec. v.p., 1981—; chmn. bd. Helen Broadcasting. Bd. dirs. Cath. Charitable Bur. Boston, Family Counseling Service Boston; chmn. Nat. Adv. Council Women's Ednl. Programs; trustee Nichols Coll., Dudley, Mass. Mem. Nat., Mass. restaurant assns., Fin. Execs. Inst., Small Bus. Adminstrn. (nat. adv. council). Roman Catholic. Clubs: Weston Community League, St. Julia's Women's (pres. 1977-78). Lodge: Dames of Malta. Home: 1064 Grove St Framingham MA 01701 Office: 600 Providence Hwy Dedham MA 02026

VALERY, LENORE DOROTHY, health services executive; b. Liberty, N.Y., June 20, 1947; d. Isaac and Eva (Kanter) V. Diploma, Kree Electrolysis, N.Y.C., 1967, Traphagen Fashion Design Sch., N.Y.C., 1969, Hoffman Electrolysis, N.Y.C., 1970, Internat. Sch. Esthetics, N.Y.C., 1971. Bd. cert. electrologist. Pres. Lenore D. Valery, Ltd., N.Y.C., 1973—. Fellow Soc. for Clin. and Med. Electrologists (cert.); mem. Internat. Guild Profl. Electrologists, Skin Care Assn. Am. Home and Office: 119 W 57th St New York NY 10019

VALESKIE-HAMNER, GAIL YVONNE, infosystems specialist; b. San Francisco, May 16, 1953; d. John Benjamin and Vera Caroline (Granstrand) Valeskie; m. David Bryan Hamner, May 21, 1983. Student, Music Conservatory, Valencia, Spain, 1973, U. Valencia, 1973; BA magna cum laude, Lone Mountain Coll., 1973, MA, 1976. Fgn. exchange broker trainee Fgn. Exchange Ltd., San Francisco, 1978-79; fgn. exchange remittance supr. Security Pacific Nat. Bank, San Francisco, 1979-81; exec. sec. Bank of Am., San Francisco, 1981-83, fgn. exchange ops. supr., 1983-84; word processing specialist Wolborg-Michelson, San Francisco, 1984-86; office mgr. U.S. Leasing Corp., San Francisco, 1986-88; cons. Valeskie Data/Word Processing, San Francisco, 1987-89, pres., 1989—. Soc. chmn., mem. mission edn. com. Luth. Women's Missionary League, Vallejo, Calif., 1986—; vol. Luth. Braille Workers, Vallejo, 1987; organist Shepherd of Hills Luth. Ch., San Francisco, 1988—. Mem. NAFE, Profl. Assn. Secretarial Svcs., Embarcadero Ctr. Forum, Profl. Womens Network. Office: Valeskie Data Word Process 611 Front St San Francisco CA 94111

VALETTE, REBECCA MARIANNE, educator; b. N.Y.C., Dec. 21, 1938; d. Gerhard and Ruth Adelgunde (Bischoff) Loose; m. Jean-Paul Valette, Aug. 6, 1959; children: Jean-Michel, Nathalie, Pierre. BA, Mt. Holyoke Coll., 1959, LHD (hon.), 1974; PhD, U. Colo., 1963. Instr., examiner in French and German U. So. Fla., 1961-63; instr. NATO Def. Coll., Paris, 1963-64, Wellesley Coll., 1964-65; asst. prof. Romance Langs. Boston Coll., 1965-68, assoc., 1968-73, prof., 1973—; lectr., cons. fgn. lang. pedagogy; Fulbright sr. lectr., Germany, 1974; Am. Council on Edn. fellow in acad. adminstrn., 1976-77. Author: Modern Language Testing, 1967, 77, French for Mastery, 1975, 81, 88, Contacts, 1976, 81, 85, 89, C'est comme ca, 1978, 86, Spanish for Mastery, 1980, 84, 89; albums: Cuentos del mundo hispanico, 1984, French for Fluency, 1985, Situaciones, 1988; contbr. numerous articles to fgn. lang. pedagogy and lit. pubs. Mem. MLA (chmn. div. on teaching of lang. 1980-81), Am. Coun. on Teaching Fgn. Langs., Am. Assn. Tchrs. French (v.p. 1980-86), Am. Assn. Tchrs. German, Phi Beta Kappa, Alpha Sigma Nu. Home: 16 Mount Alvernia Rd Chestnut Hill MA 02167 Office: Boston Coll Lyons 311 Chestnut Hill MA 02167

VALK, SHIRLEY ROUNELLE, construction company executive; b. Trenton, Mich., Feb. 18, 1948; d. Granvel William and Blance Lophia (Pratt) Curtis; (div. 1983); children: Jennifer Dawn Beedy, Joshua Mark; m. Howard Leroy Valk, Aug. 11, 1984. Grad. high sch., Whittier, Calif. Telephone operator Gen. Telephone Co., Whittier, 1967-68; bookkeeper Major Motor Supply Co., Downey, Calif., 1971-73; owner, mgr. Shirley's Daycare, Riverside, Calif., 1971-80; office mgr. Dr. Mastakas, Kingman, Ariz., 1981-84; fin. officer, co-owner Affordable Constrn. Co., Riverside, Calif., 1988—; with Steel Roof Systems, Riverside; cons. Mary Kay Cosmetics, Riverside. Mem. Nat. Assn. Female Execs., MADD. Democrat. Lutheran. Office: Comml Svcs Realty Inc Amargosa Rd Victorville CA

VALLBONA, RIMA-GRETEL ROTHE, Spanish educator, writer; b. San José, Costa Rica, Mar. 15, 1931; d. Ferdinand Hermann and Emilia (Strassburger) Rothe; m. Carlos Vallbona, Dec. 26, 1956; children: Rima-Nuri, Carlos-Fernando, María-Teresa, María-Luisa. BA/BS, Colegio Superior de Señoritas, San José, 1948; diploma, U. Paris, 1953; diploma in Spanish Philology, U. Salamanca, Spain, 1954; MA, U. Costa Rica, 1962; D in Modern Langs., Middlebury Coll., 1981. Tchr. Liceo J.J. Vargas Calvo, Costa Rica, 1955-56; faculty U. St. Thomas, Houston, 1964—, prof. Spanish, 1978—, Cullen prof. of Spanish, 1989—, head dept. Spanish, 1966-71, chmn. dept. modern fgn. lang., 1978-80; Cullen Chair Spanish, 1989—; vis. prof. U. Houston, 1975-76, Rice U., 1980-81, U. St. Thomas, Argentina, 1972, vis. prof. U. St. Thomas Merida program, 1987—; vis. prof. Rice U. program in Spain, 1974. Author: Noche en Vela, 1968, Yoland Oreamuno, 1972, La Obra en Prosa de Eunice Odio, 1981, Baraja de Soledades, Las Sombras que Perseguimos, 1983; (short stories) Polvo de Camino, 1972, La Salamandra Rosada, 1979, Mujeres y Agonias, 1982, Cosecha de Pecadores, 1988, El arcángel del perdón, 1990; mem. editorial bd. Letras Femeninas, U.S.; co-dir. Foro Literario, Uruguay, Alba de América; contbr. numerous articles and short stories to lit. mags. Mem. scholarship com. Inst. Hispanic Culture, 1978-79, 88, chmn., 1979, bd. dirs., 1974-76, 88—, chmn. cultural activities, 1979, 80, 85, 88-89; bd. dirs. Houston Pub. Libr., 1984-86. Recipient Aquileo J. Echeverria Novel prize, 1968, Agripina Montes del Valle Novel prize, 1978, Jorge Luis Borges Short Story prize, Argentina, 1977, Lit. award S.W. Conf. Latin Am. Studies, 1982; Constantin Found. grantee for rsch. U. St. Thomas, 1981; Ancora Lit. award, Costa Rica, 1984, Civil Merit award King Juan Carlos I of Spain, 1989. Mem. MLA, Am. Assn. Tchrs. Spanish and Portuguese, Houston Area Tchrs. of Fgn. Langs., South Cen. MLA, S.W.

conf. Orgn. Latin Am. Studies, Latin Am. Studies Assn., Inst. Internat. de Lit. Iberoam., Latin Am. Writers Assn. of Costa Rica, Inst. Hispanic Culture of Houston, Casa Argentina de Houston, Inst. Lit. y Cultural Hispanico, Phi Sigma Iota, Sigma Delta Pi (hon.), Nat. Writers Club. Roman Catholic. Home: 3002 Ann Arbor St Houston TX 77063 Office: 3812 Montrose Blvd Houston TX 77006

VALLE, GEORGETTE WALD, state legislator; b. Blue Earth, Minn., Oct. 31, 1924; d. George Wilhelm Endre and Emily (Tenold) Vikingstad; m. Odd Valle, June 30, 1951; children: Peter Odd, Christine Georgette. AA, Waldorf Jr. Coll., 1945; BS, U. Minn., 1949. Occupational therapist Mpls. Curative Workshop, 1949-50; dir. occupational therapy Swedish Polio Rehab. Ctr., Mpls., 1950-51; mem. Wash. Ho. of Reps., Olympia, 1965-67, 72—, chair, exec. chair appropriations com., vice chair environ. affairs, local govt., sci. and tech. coms., ranking minority mem. edn., natural resources and environ. affairs appropriations, human services com., mem. ways and means, rules coms.; clk. Wash. Senate Senator Mike McCormack, Olympia, 1967; cons. occupational therapy Seattle Queen Anne Nursing Home, 1970; dir. occupational therapy Valley Gen. Hosp., Kent, Wash., 1971-72. Mem. state adv. bd. Fed. Water Pollution Act; mem. Coalition Against Oil Pollution, Air Quality Coalition, Wash. Lung Assn., Highline YMCA, Highline West Seattle Mental Health Ctr., Wash. State Environment Policy Act Commn., Fauntleroy Environ. Assn., Adult Literacy Bd., Mothers Against Drunk Drivers; mem. Gov.'s Task Force on High Level Nuclear Waste; bd. dirs. West Seattle Sr. Ctr., Highline Community Council, S.W. Youth Service Bur. Seattle, Wash. State Seismic Safety Bd.; mem. adult edn. bd. Plymouth Congl. Ch.; v.p. bd. dirs. Shoreline Community Hosp.; chair Green River Murder Reward Com. Recipient Friend of Edn. award Highline Ednl. Assn., 1980, Disting. Service award Wash. Lung Assn., Outstanding Achievement for Edn. award Wash. Edn. Assn., 2,000 award Am. Lung Assn., 1985, placque West Seattle Jaycees, Outstanding Alumni award Waldorf Jr. Coll., 1987; cited for Outstanding Dedication for Clean Air Fresh Air for Non-Smokers, Inc., 1987; named Woman of Yr. Evergreen Dem. Club, West Seattle Bus. and Profl. Women, 1985. Mem. NOW, LWV (chair natural resources com. King county South chpt.), Wash. Environ. Council (Outstanding Elected Official 1980), Sierra Club, World Affairs Council (Seattle chpt.), West Seattle C. of C., Highline Assn. Am. Univ. Women. Clubs: Hurstwood Community, West Seattle Garden. Home: 1434 SW 137th St Seattle WA 98166 Office: Wash State Ho Reps 401 Legislative Bldg Olympia WA 98504

VALLEAU, NORMA KATHRYN SASS, lawyer; b. Dearborn, Mich., Mar. 9, 1933; d. Norman Ralph and Dorothy Lorraine (Mullreed) Sass; m. Kenneth William Valleau, Sept. 2, 1953 (div. 1956); children—Bobbee Leota Kovar, Carla Renee Margolis; m. 2d John Henry Metz, July 15, 1983. A.S., Henry Ford Coll., 1974; B.S., Western State Coll., Fullerton, Calif. 1980, J.D., 1980. Bar: Ind. 1981. Actress, singer, dancer Kennedy Artists, N.Y.C., 1960-78; actress Eastside/Westside Repertory, N.Y.C., 1960-63, Herbert Berghof Studios, N.Y.C., 1963-64; legal intern Screen Actors Guild, Hollywood, Calif., 1978-80; ptnr. Metz & Valleau, Indpls., 1981-82; law clk. U.S. Bankruptcy Ct., Indpls., 1982-85; atty. legal div., bankruptcy specialist FDIC, 1985-87, sr. ptnr. Valleau, Coney & Metz, Indpls., 1987—; program dir. Lawyers in the Classroom project, N.Y. State Bar Assn., 1977; outstanding dir. Fullerton Children's Theatre, 1979. Mem. Friends of Benjamin Harrison House, Indpls., 1983—, Indpls. Hist. Soc., 1983—; instr. Free U., Indpls., 1983; v.p. Women's Caucus, Fullerton, Calif., 1978-81. Women's Caucus Book scholar, 1978-80. Mem. ABA, Ind. Bar Assn., Indpls. Bar Assn., Screen Actors Guild, Actors Equity Assn., Am. Guild Variety Artists, AFTRA, DAR (Caroline Scott Harrison chpt.). Lutheran. Home: 3663 N Pennsylvania Indianapolis IN 46205 Office: Valleau Coney & Metz 3663 N Pennsylvania -B Indianapolis IN 46205

VALLEE, MARTHA RUTH, music educator; b. Beaumont, Tex., Sept. 15, 1942; d. Oliver Bee and Katherine Venona (Ryals) Netterville; m. Simon Peter Vallee, Jr., Jan. 3, 1963; children: Peter Scott, Simon Sean. BS, Lamar U., 1967. Tchr. music, English, art Beaumont (Tex.) Ind. Sch. Dist., 1979-85; tchr. music Austin (Tex.) Ind. Sch. Dist., 1985-86, 1st grade tchr., 1986-87, tchr. music, 1987—; organist Anderson Mill Bapt. Ch., Austin, 1985-86; dir. children's choir St. Andrews Presbyn. Ch., Beaumont, 1983-84; pianist, choir dir. N. End Bapt. Ch., Beaumont, 1969-79. Author musical: Sesquincentennial Mayfete, 1986. Chaplain PTO, Beaumont, 1971-72; dep. dir. Cub Scouts, Beaumont, 1974-76; mem. Humane Soc. 1974-84; vol. United Appeals, 1980. Mem. Beaumont Music Tchrs. Assn. (treas. 1974-76), NEA, Tex. Tchrs. Assn., Austin Assn. Tchrs., Beaumont Classroom Tchrs. Assn., Woman's Club (pianist 1977-85), Tex. Fedn. Music Clubs. Republican. Baptist. Home: 1111 Terjo Ln Austin TX 78732 Office: Austin Independent Sch Dist 6100 Guadalupe St Austin TX 78752

VALLEJOS, ROBERTA F., social worker; b. Cheyenne, Wyo., Dec. 17, 1944; d. Stanley J. and Clementena J. (Palu) Sheldon; m. John B. Vallejos, Apr. 1, 1987 (div.); children: Juanita M., John B. BSEd, Chadron State Coll., 1966; BA in Social Work, Colo. State U., 1981, MSW, 1986. Cert. social worker, Colo. From caseworker to gen. social svc. supr. Huerfano County Dept. Social Svc., Walsenburg, Colo., 1966—; developer, cons. Domestic Violence Elimination Program, Walsenburg, 1985-89; chmn. Human Svc. Coun., Walsenburg, 1984—. Contbr. articles to profl. publs. Chmn. sr. svcs. adv. coun. AAA, 1989—. Mem. Nat. Assn. Social Workers (area rep. 1987—), Am. Pub. Welfare Assn., NAFE. Home: Box 172 Walsenburg CO 81089 Office: Huerfono Co Dept Social Svc 121 W 6th Walsenburg CO 81089

VALLERY, JANET ALANE, industrial hygienist; b. Lincoln, Nebr., Apr. 4, 1948; d. Gerald William and Lois Florence (Robertson) V.; BS, U. Nebr., Lincoln, 1970; diploma Bryan Meml. Sch. Med. Tech., Lincoln, 1971. Med. technologist Lincoln Gen. Hosp., 1971-72; congressional sec., 1973; lab. scientist Nebr. Dept. Health, 1973-79; sr. indsl. hygienist Nebr. Dept. Labor, 1979-85; indsl. hygienist U.S. Dept. Labor OSHA, 1985-89; indsl. hygienist supr. VA Med. Ctr., Omaha, Nebr., 1989—. Mem. Am. Conf. Govt. Indsl. Hygienists, Am. Soc. Clin. Pathologists (assoc.), Arabian Horse Assn. Nebr., Nebr. Dressage Assn., Am. Indsl. Hygiene Assn., Am. Legion Aux. Republican. Methodist. Home: 4900 S 30th St Lincoln NE 68516 Office: VA Med Ctr 4101 Woolworth Ave Omaha NE 68105

VALO, CAROLYN ROSE, healthcare consultant; b. Mpls., Dec. 29, 1952; d. Pierson John and Dancia (Bubalo) Kirk; m. David Allen Valo, Oct. 12, 1985. A.A.S., St. Mary's Jr. Coll., 1977; B.A., Metro State U., 1982. Cert. Am. Med. Record Assn. Sec. Nat. Assn. Ind. Businessmen, Mpls., 1969-70; clk., typist, data clk. Mpls. Health Dept., 1970-75, health info. mgr., 1977-84; faculty asst. St. Mary's Jr. Coll., Mpls., 1976-77, adj. faculty, 1978—; client svc. rep. Code 3 Health Info. Systems 3M, Mpls., 1984-85; asst. dir. med. records Fairview-Southdale Hosp., Mpls., 1985, dir. med. records, 1985-88; healthcare cons. MediQual Systems, Inc., 1988—, mem. Patient Care Task Force; adj. faculty Moorhead Area Vocat. Tech. Inst., 1986—; mem. faculty St. Catherine's Coll., St. Mary's Campus, 1987; pvt. practice cons. Ambulatory Care, Mpls., 1983; cons. severity systems, quality assurance MediQual Systems Inc., 1988; speaker profl. groups in field. Contbr. articles to profl. jours. Mem. Am. Med. Record Assn. (appeals panel), Minn. Med. Record Assn. (pres. 1984-85, award, bd. dir.), Twin Cities Women in Computing, Assn. Record Mgrs. and Adminstrs., NAFE. Home: 1897 Carroll Ave Saint Paul MN 55104 Office: MediQual Systems Inc 5200 W 73rd St Edina MN 55435

VALO, MARTHA ANN, hospital dietary executive, consultant; b. West Aliquippa, Pa., Apr. 6, 1938; d. George and Susan Helen (Pollak) V.; m. John Daniel Dempsey, Dec. 17, 1974. B.S., Carlow Coll., 1960; postgrad. U. Pa. Registered dietitian. Food service mgr. Stouffer's Mgmt. Co., Phila., 1960-76; restaurant mgr. Strawbridge & Clothier, Phila., 1976-78; food service dir. Saunders House, Phila., 1978-80; dir. dietary services Kennedy Meml. Hosp., U. Med. Ctr., Stratford, N.J., 1980—; cons. dietitian Pinecrest Nursing Home, Sewell, N.J., 1980—; chmn. N.J. Hosp. Assn. Dietary Group Purchasing, Princeton, 1980—; adj. faculty Camden County Coll., Blackwood, N.J., 1985—. Mem. Am. Dietetic Assn., N.J. Dietetic Assn., Phila. Dietetic Assn., So. N.J. Nutritional Council, Am. Soc. for Hosp. Food Service Adminstrs. Home: 135 Fenway Dr Atco NJ 08004 Office: Kennedy Meml Hosps Univ Med Ctr 18 E Laurel Rd Stratford NJ 08084

VALOIS, RENÉE MARIE, copywriter; b. Mpls., June 27, 1958; d. Robert Donald and Sharon Marie (Knutson) V.; m. David Wayne Housewright, Dec. 1, 1984; 1 child, Nicholas Valois. BA summa cum laude, U. Minn., 1980, MA, 1981. Freelance journalist Mpls., 1981-83; writer Ryter Advt., Mpls., 1983, Carmichael-Lynch, Mpls., 1983-86, Kauffman Stewart, Mpls., 1986-88; freelance writer Roseville, Minn., 1988—; judge, Fargo/Moorhead Advt. Show, Fargo, N.D., 1987. Recipient N.Y. Art Dirs. Club, One Show, Athena, Clio, and Andy awards, Effie silver and bronze awards, Telly awards, Adweek's newspapers advt. awards. Mem. Phi Beta Kappa, Phi Kappa Phi, Art Dirs. and Copywriters Club. Roman Catholic. Home and Office: 2014 N Cleveland Ave Roseville MN 55113

VALOON, PATRICIA LOUISE, nursing and hospital administrator; b. Nov. 11, 1936. Diploma, Western Pa. Hosp. Sch. Nursing, Pitts., 1957; BS, Duquesne U., 1965; MS, U. Colo., 1971. Staff nurse Western Pa. Hosp., 1957-58; staff nurse, relief head nurse Allegheny Gen. Hosp., Pitts., 1958-61, asst. dir. nursing, 1961-65, instr., 1965-66; sr. instr. U. Colo. Sch. Nursing, Denver, 1970-72; supr. pediatrics NYU Med. Ctr.-Univ. Hosp., N.Y.C., 1966-70, asst. dir. nursing for clin. practice, 1972-74, assoc. dir. nursing, 1974-79, acting dir. nursing, asst. adminstr., 1979-80, dir. nursing, assoc. adminstr., 1980—; adj. instr. nursing program Skidmore Coll., Sarasota Springs, N.Y., 1972-74; mem. adj. faculty NYU, 1990—; presenter in field. Contbr. articles to profl. jours., chpts. to books. Mem. Am. Nurses Assn., Nat. League for Nursing, Am. Orgn. Nurse Execs., Sigma Theta Tau. Home: 67 Chestnut St Dumont NJ 07628

VALVERDE-WARD, DEBORAH LOUISE, engineering psychologist; b. Phoenix, Nov. 6, 1957; d. Anselmo and Francis Elaine (McCrary) Valverde; m. Frank Alan Ward, Aug. 21, 1982 (separated); 1 child, Ryan David Ward. BA in Psychology, N.Mex. State U., 1981, MA in Exptl. Psychology, 1986. Edn. facilitator Ctr. for Learning Assistance, N.Mex. State U., Las Cruces, 1981-83; statistics teaching asst. Exptl. Statistics Dept., N.Mex. State U., Las Cruces, 1983-84; engring. psychologist U.S. Dept. Army, White Sands Missile Range, N.Mex., 1984—. Mem. Women in Sci. and Engring., AAUW, Rio Grande Human Factors Soc., Associated Women Students (pres. N.Mex. State U. chpt. 1980-81). Democrat. Presbyterian. Office: Dept of Army White Sands Missile Range STEWS TE RE White Sands MR NM 88002

VAN ALSTYNE, JUDITH STURGES, English educator; b. Columbus, Ohio, June 9, 1934; d. Rexford Leland and Wilma Irene (Styan) Van A.; m. Dan C. Duckham (div. 1964); children: Kenton Leland, Jeffrey Clarke. BA, Miami U., Oxford, Ohio, 1956; MEd, Fla. Atlantic U., 1967. Sr. prof. Broward Community Coll., Ft. Lauderdale, Fla., 1967—; spl. asst. for women's affairs Broward Community Coll., 1972—, dir. community svcs., 1973-74, dir. cultural affairs, 1974-75, dir. Broward Community Coll. Found., Inc., 1973-89; speaker, cons. Malaysian Coll., 1984. Author: Professional and Technical Writing Strategies, 1986, Write It Right, 1980; contbr. articles to profl. jours. Active Sister Cities/People to People, Ft. Lauderdale, 1988—; docent Ft. Lauderdale Mus. Art, 1988—. Recipient Award of Achievement Soc. for Tech. Communication, 1986, Award of Distinction Fla. Soc. for Tech. Communication, 1986. Mem. English-Speaking Union (bd. dirs. 1984-89). Democrat. Episcopalian. Home: 1688 S Ocean Ln #265 Fort Lauderdale FL 33316

VANAMAN, LINDA BELL, telecommunications company executive; b. Lexington, Ky., Aug. 13, 1941; d. William Herald and Velma (Hill) Bell; m. Thomas Clark Vanaman, Mar. 1962 (div. Dec. 1983); children: Thomas Randolph, John Tyler. BA magna cum laude, Duke U., 1982. Office mgr., then pers. asst. Foam Design, Inc., Research Triangle Park, N.C., 1982-84; staffing-recruiting specialist Sumitomo Electric RT, Inc., Research Triangle Park, 1985-87; coord. relocation and immigration No. Telecom, Inc., Research Triangle Park, 1987-88, mgr. staffing svcs., 1988—, sr. human resources rep., 1989—; chmn. Spouse Employment Assistance Program, Research Triangle area, 1990. Contbr. articles to profl. jours. Mem. exec. bd. Spouse Employment Assistance Program, Research Triangle Park, 1987—, chmn., 1990; bd. dirs. Durham Chamber Pvt. Industry Coun., 1985-87; v.p. adv. bd. Duke U. Art Mus. Mem. Am. Soc. Pers. Adminstrs., Durham-Triangle Pers. Assn. (v.p. 1987-88, pres.-elect, 1988-89, pres. 1989-90). Home: 3102 Eubanks Rd Durham NC 27707 Office: No Telecom Inc 4001 E Chapel Hill-Nelson Hwy PO Box 13010 Research Triangle Park NC 27709

VAN ANDEL, BETTY JEAN, household products company executive; b. Mich., Dec. 14, 1921; d. Anthony and Daisy (Van Dyk) Hoekstra; A.B., Calvin Coll., 1943; m. Jay Van Andel, Aug. 16, 1952; children—Nan Elizabeth, Stephen Alan, David Lee, Barbara Ann. Elementary sch. tchr., Grand Rapids, Mich., 1943-45; service rep. and supr. Mich. Bell Telephone Co., Grand Rapids, 1945-52; bd. dirs. Amway Corp., Grand Rapids, 1972—. Treas., LWV, 1957-60; chmn. Eagle Forum, Mich., 1975—; bd. dirs. Christian Sch. Edn. Found. Found., Pine Rest Christian Hosp., Grand Rapids Opera, 1982, exec. com. Mem. Nat. Trust Hist. Preservation, St. Cecelia Music Soc., Smithsonian Assos. Republican. Club: Women's City of Grand Rapids. Home: 7186 Windy Hill Rd SE Grand Rapids MI 49506 Office: PO Box 172 Ada MI 49301

VAN ANDEL-GABY, BARBARA A., marketing professional; b. Grand Rapids, Mich., May 9, 1962; d. Jay and Betty Jean (Hoekstra) Van Andel; m. Richard Douglas Gaby, June 29, 1985. BA, Hope Coll., 1983; MBA, Ind. U., 1985. Mktg. intern Marriott Corp., Bethesda, Md., 1984; mgmt. specialist Amway Corp., Grand Rapids, Mich., 1985-87; sales mgr. Amway Grand Plaza Hotel, Grand Rapids, 1987-88, resident mgr., 1988-89; v.p., chief exec. officer Amway Hotel Corp., Grand Rapids, 1989—. Bd. dirs. Better Bus. Bur. of Western Mich., Grand Rapids Conv. Bur., Downtown Mgmt. Bd., Inc., Ferguson Hosp. Found., United Way. Mem. NAFE, Assn. MBA Execs., Am. Mktg. Assn., Am. Soc. Travel, Nat. Restaurant Assn., Am. Hotel and Motel Assn., Mich. Loging Assn. Republican. Home: 7046 Riverwood Ln SE Grand Rapids MI 49546 Office: Amway Grand Plaza Hotel Pearl at Monroe Grand Rapids MI 49503

VAN ANDEN, ANNE LINDA, real estate broker, retail executive; b. N.Y.C., Dec. 5, 1945; d. Lester Manuel and Gertrude (Parnes) Kaeck; m. Norman Edward Van Anden, July 13, 1975; children: Jason Ian, Heather Andrea, Wesley Harold. AAS magna cum laude, Rockland Community Coll., Pomona, N.Y., 1975; BS magna cum laude, St. Thomas Aquinas Sch., Sparkill, N.Y., 1975. Lic. real estate broker, Va. Computer programmer rsch. ctr. Columbia U., Orangeburg, N.Y., 1962-65; broadcast news reporter Sta. WRKL, New City, N.Y., 1972-73; counsellor Rockland County Community Mental Health Ctr., Pomona, N.Y., 1975-76, MultiCounty Community Devel. Corp., New Paltz, N.Y., 1976; educator Peekskill (N.Y.) Spl. Schs., 1976-77; retail entrepreneur Yorktown Crafts Depot, Yorktown Heights, N.Y., 1977-83; realtor Long & Foster Realtors, Woodbridge, Va., 1983-88; assoc. broker Old Mill Properties, Inc., Woodbridge, 1988-90; chief exec. officer NEV Enterprises, 1985—; prin. broker Van Anden Assocs., Woodbridge, 1990; v.p. Va. South, Potomac Realty Inst., 1990—; pres. Van Anden Referrals, Woodbridge, 1990—. Chair, Americans for Hart, Prince William County, Va., 1983-84; exhibits chair Nat. Womens Polit. Caucus, Washington, 1983-84; fundraising chair Prince William County Dem. Com., 1983-85; treas. Occoquan Dem. Dist., Woodbridge, Va., 1983-85. Mem. Realtors nat. Mktg. Inst., Nat. Assn. Realtors, Va. Assn. REaltors, Prince William Bd. Realtors, NAFE, Nat. Orgn. for Women. Home: 11690 Bacon Race Rd Woodbridge VA 22192 Office: Van Anden Assocs 12866B Harbor Dr Woodbridge VA 22192

VAN ANTWERPEN, REGINA LANE, underwriter, insurance company executive; b. Milw., Aug. 16, 1939; d. Joseph F. Gagliano and Sophia B. (Johannik) Wolfe; widowed; children: Thomas II, Victoria. Student, U. Wis., Milw., 1954-57. Office mgr. Gardner Bender Inc., Milw., 1972-80; mfg. rep. Rosenbloom & Co., Chgo., 1980-81; spl. agt. Northwestern Mut. Life Equities Inc., Milw., 1981-88, registered rep., 1985-88; account rep. Fin. Instn. Mktg. Co., Milw., 1988—. Author: (poetry) One More Time Its Christmas, 1978, True Friendship, 1979. Mgr. Sch. Bd. Elections, Fox Point, 1969; v.p. Suburban Rep. Women's CLub, Milw., 1968-72; vol. tchr. St. Eugene Sch., Milw., 1968-72. Mem. Milw. Life Underwriters, Women's Life Underwriters (v.p. 1982-83), Legis. Orgn. Life Underwriters, Nat. Assn. Securities Dealers (lic.), Investment Club (sec. 1989-90). Republican. Roman Catholic. Office: Fin Instn Mktg Co 111 E Kilbourn Ave Ste 1850 Milwaukee WI 53202-6611

VAN ARK, JOAN, actress; d. Carroll and Dorothy Jean (Hemenway) Van A.; m. John Marshall, Feb. 1, 1966; 1 child, Vanessa Jeanne. Student, Yale Sch. Drama. Appeared at Tyrone Guthrie Theatre, Washington Arena Stage, in London, on Broadway; appeared in plays: Barefoot in the Park, School for Wives, Rules of the Game, Cyrano de Bergerac, Ring Round the Moon; appeared on TV series: Temperatures Rising, We've Got Each Other, Dallas, Knots Landing, 1979—; motion pictures for TV: The Judge and Jake Wyler, 1972, Big Rose, 1974, Shell Game, 1975; The Last Dinosaur, 1977, Red Flag, 1981, Shakedown on the Sunset Strip, 1988, My First Love, 1989, Murder at the PTA, 1990; TV miniseries: Testimony of Two Men, 1978. Recipient Theatre World award, 1970-71, L.A. Drama Critics Circle award, 1973, Outstanding Actress award Soap Opera Digest, 1986, 89. Mem. Actors Equity Assn., SAG, AFTRA. Club: San Fernando Valley Track. Office: care William Morris Agy Inc 151 El Camino Beverly Hills CA 90212

VAN ARNAM, BARBARA JUNE, artist; b. Plainfield, N.J., Aug. 4, 1946; d. Thomas and Dorothea Julia (Phillips) Van A.; m. Michael David Alch, July 9, 1973. BA, U. San Francisco, 1974; MA, Calif. State U., Fresno, 1984. Freelance artist, Fresno, 1981—; dir., founder Fresno 277, 1985; pres. Gallery 25, Fresno, 1987-88, exhbns. dir., 1987—, historian and publicity dir. 1988—. Executed mural Poverello House, Fresno, 1987, Holy Cross Ctr. for Women, Poverello House, 1988. Recipient 1st award Calif. State Fair, Sacramento, 1981, 3d award Yosemite Curry-County Nat. Park County 1988. Office: Van Arnam Studio 1782 N De Wolf Fresno CA 93727

VAN ARSDALE, NANCY P., publishing executive; b. Phila., June 8, 1957; d. Ellsworth A. and Elizabeth A. (Navitt) Van A.; m. Thomas M. Brody, Apr. 2, 1982; 1 child, Nicholas. BA, Bucknell U., 1979; MA, NYU, 1981, PhD, 1990. Instr. NYU, 1980-83; promotion writer, mgr. Time Mag., N.Y.C., 1983—. Mem. Advt. Women N.Y. (chmn. ADDY competition 1986-88, treas., bd. dirs. 1989—), Phi Beta Kappa. Home: 99 Haddon Pl Upper Montclair NJ 07043 Office: Time Mag 1271 Ave of the Americas New York NY 10020

VAN BALEN, CISSY, executive search firm executive; b. L.A., Dec. 11, 1941; d. William Parke and Agnes Rachel (Clement) Murdaugh. BA in Anthropology, U.N.C., 1963; MS in Counseling Psychology, Dominican Coll., 1987. Personnel cons. IBM Corp., Cape Canaveral, Fla., 1964-70, Yorktown Heights, N.Y., 1970-71; sr. mktg. rep. IBM Corp., San Francisco, 1971-80; mgmt. cons. Profls. for Computing, Inc., San Francisco, 1980-85; pres. King and Van Balen, Inc., San Francisco, 1985—. Mem. Commonwealth Club of Calif., Cary (N.C.) C. of C., Meadow Club, Wachasaw Plantation Club, DAR, Employment Mgmt. Assn., Phi Psi Soc. Republican. Episcopalian. Home: 17 Newhall Dr San Rafael CA 94901 Office: King and Van Balen Inc 222 Kearny St Ste 204 San Francisco CA 94108

VANBARRIGER, CAROL LYNNE, healthcare consultant; b. Connellsville, Pa., Apr. 26, 1941; d. Charles Lynn and Iola Grace (Sembower) Sliger.; m. George Van Barriger, May 27, 1966 (div. Feb. 1972). RN, Montefiore Hosp., 1962; BS, Coll. St. Francis, 1985; MA in Mgmt., Nat. Coll. Edn., 1988. Pub. health nurse Kendall County Health Dept., Yorkville, Ill., 1970-72; team leader Edward Hosp., Naperville, Ill., 1972-73; emergency nurse Cen. Dupage Hosp., Winfield, Ill., 1973-74; staff nurse and head nurse Palos Community Hosp., Palos Heights, Ill., 1974-77, surg. nurse, 1977-82; auditor Med-Charge Analysis, Chgo., 1982-83; mgr. Intracorp CIGNA, Glen Ellyn, Ill., 1983-86, Metlife Healthcare Network, Schaumburg, Ill., 1986; project mgr. Healthcare Intermedaries, Lombard, Ill., 1986-88; dir., provider services Multicare HMO, Chicago, IL, 1988—; ptnr. Greenberg Assocs., 1989—; Mem. group comparison studies healthcare delivery/costs USSR, 1981, China, 1982, England, 1985. V.p. Indian Oak Condominium Assn., Bolingbrook, Ill., 1972-76; treas. Hickory Heights Condominium Assn., Hickory Hills, Ill., 1978-83, bd. dirs. 1983-89. Mem. Nat. Assn. Quality Assurance Profls., Ill. Assn. Quality Assurance Profls., Midwest Assn. Billing Auditors (treas. 1986-87), Nat. Assn Female Execs., Women's Health Exec. Network, Chgo. Health Exec. Forum. Home: 9450 Greenbriar Dr Hickory Hills IL 60457

VAN BERGEN, MARILYN ANNE, lawyer, academic administrator. BA in Psychology, Ind. U., 1979, MPA in Pub. Adminstrn. and Mgmt., 1982, JD, 1985. Editor, validator Westat, Inc., Rockville, Md., 1977-78; residential supr. Coun. for the Retarded, South Bend, 1978-81; assoc. instr. Sch. Pub. and Environ. Affairs Ind. U., Bloomington, 1981-82, resident asst., 1983-85; adminstrv. coord. Employment and Devel. Systems, Inc., Goshen, Ind., 1986-88, contract mgr., 1988; project coord. U. Notre Dame (Ind.), 1989—. Mayoral appointee Disability Rights Commn. St. Joseph County, 1986; mem. endowment com. Literacy Network Elkhart County, Inc., 1987-88, Jr. League of South Bend, 1990—. Ind. U. fellow, 1982-84. Mem. Elkhart Area C. of C. (edn. com. 1988), Phi Alpha Theta, Psi Chi, Pi Alpha Alpha. Home: 205 N Hawthorne Dr South Bend IN 46617

VAN BOOVEN, JUDY LEE, data processing manager; b. Kansas City, Mo., Oct. 26, 1952; d. Gene Warren and Jane Lewis (Wallace) Pulley; m. Cecil Carlin Van Booven, Aug. 19, 1972; children: Walter Matthew, Leia Christine, Kelly Diane, Matthew Carlin. Student, Cen. Mo. State U., Warrensburg, 1970-72; AAS, Penn Valley Community Coll., Kansas City, Mo., 1981; BS, William Jewell Coll., 1988. Bookkeeper Century Mills, Wilmington, N.C., 1972-73; acctg. clk. Forest Siding, North Kansas City, Mo., 1974-75, computer operator, 1975-77, programmer/ops. mgr., 1977-80; programmer/analyst Western Water Mgmt., Inc., North Kansas City, Mo., 1980-88, data processing mgr., 1989—; freelance programmer Modern Window Co., North Kansas City, 1978-80, Forest Lumber, Oklahoma City, 1975-80, Kay-Dee Systems, North Kansas City, 1980-82; systems cons. Forest Siding, 1980-82. Author 1st place essay, North Kansas City Centennial, 1988. Founder/chmn. Children's Book Drive, Kansas City, 1983-90; mem. parent adv. com./Gracemor Sch., Kansas City, 1988-89, bd. dirs. Gracemor PTA, 1989-90, co-chmn. newsletter, 1989-90. Recipient scholarship Bus. and Profl. Women's Assn., 1970, Bd. Regents, Mo., 1970. Mem. ABWA (treas. 1983-84, sec. 1985-87, named Woman of the Yr. 1986), NAFE, Phi Theta Kappa. Baptist. Home: 5143 North Richmond Kansas City MO 64119 Office: Western Water Mgmt Inc 1345 Taney North Kansas City MO 64116

VAN BRUNT, MARCIA ADELE, social worker; b. Chgo., Oct. 21, 1937; d. Dean Frederick and Faye Lila (Greim) Slauson; student Moline (Ill.) Pub. Hosp. Sch. Nursing, 1955-57; B.A. with distinguished scholastic record, U. Wis., Madison, 1972, M.S.W. (Fed. tng. grantee), 1973; M.O.E. Bartholomew; children—Suzanne, Christine, David. Social worker div. community services Wis. Dept. Health Social Services, Rhinelander, 1973, regional adoption coordinator, 1973-79, chief adoption and permanent planning no. region, 1979-83, asst. chief direct services and regulation no. region, 1983-84, adminstr., clin. social worker No. Family Services, Inc., 1984—; counselor, public speaker, cons. in field of clin. social work. Home: 5264 Forest Ln Rte 1 Rhinelander WI 54501 Office: Box 237 Rhinelander WI 54501

VAN BULCK, MARGARET WEST, accountant, financial planner, educator; b. Chgo., Nov. 25, 1955; d. Lee Allen and Margaret Ellen (Sauls) West; m. Hendrikus E.J.M.L. van Bulck, Aug. 7, 1976; children: Marcel Allen, Sydney Josette. BS in Mktg., U. S.C., 1978; MA in Econs., Clemson U., 1981. CPA, S.C. Econs. instr. St. Andrews Presbyn. Coll., Laurinburg, N.C., 1980-82; staff acct. L. Allen West, CPA, Sumter, S.C., 1982-84; ptnr. West & van Bulck, CPA's, Sumter, 1984-88, Van Bulck & Co. CPA's, Sumter, 1989—; part time instr. U. S.C., Sumter, 1985-87, mem. full time faculty, 1989—. Contbr. articles to profl. jours. Treas. Make-A-Wish Found., Sumter, 1985-87, wish granting chmn. 1987-88; edn. found. chmn. Laurinburg/Scotland County chpt. AAUW, 1981-83; treas. Friends Sumter County Library, 1986-88, Sumter Gallery of Art, 1989—; mem. Jr. Welfare League, Sumter; Circle Bible leader, Sunday Sch. tchr. Recipient Sunrise Found. award, Clemson U., 1978, 79; grantee U.S. Dept. Labor, 1979-80. Mem. AICPA, S.C. Assn. CPAs, Fla. Inst. CPAs, Internat. Assn. Fin. Planning, Sumter Estate Planning Council (past treas.), Omicron Delta Epsilon. Presbyterian. Home: 234 Haynsworth St PO Box 1327 Sumter SC

29151-1327 Office: Van Bulck & Co CPAs PO Box 1327 Sumter SC 29151-1327

VAN BUREN, PHYLLIS EILEEN, foreign language educator; b. Montevideo, Minn., June 4, 1947; d. Helge Thorfin and Alice Lillian (Johnsrud) Goulson; m. Barry Redmond Van Buren, Apr. 4, 1970; children: Priscila Victoria Princesa, Barry Redmond Barán. Student, Escuela de Bellas Artes, Guadalajara, Mex., 1968; BS, St. Cloud (Minn.) State U., 1969, MS, 1976; postgrad., Goethe Inst., Mannheim, West Germany, 1984, U. Costa Rica, 1989, Union Grad. Sch., Cin., 1990—. Instr. in Spanish Red Wing (Minn.) Pub. Schs., 1969-70; instr. in Spanish and German St. Cloud Pub. Schs., 1970-80; prof. German and Spanish St. Cloud State U., 1975, 79—; advance placement reader Ednl. Testing Svc., Princeton, N.J., 1987—; translator in field. Coord. children's programs St. Cloud, 1970—; vol. ESL instr. St. Cloud Community Coll., 1973—, mem. task force com., 1979—; reviewer St. Cloud Pub. Schs., 1985-89. U.S. Dept. Def. fellow, 1969, Goethe Inst. fellow, 1983; N.W. Area Found. grantee, 1985-86, Bush Found. grantee, 1986. Mem. Am. Assn. Tchrs. Spanish and Portuguese, Am. Assn. Tchrs. of German, Am. Coun. Tchrs. of Fgn. Langs. (tester 1989—), Minn. Coun. Tchrs. of Fgn. Langs., MLA (cen. states adv. bd.), AAUW (exec. bd. 1988—), Modern Lang. Assn., Phi Kappa Phi, Sigma Delta Pi. Republican. Lutheran. Home: 3001 Co Rd 146 Clearwater MN 55320 Office: St Cloud State U 720 4th Ave S Saint Cloud MN 56301

VANBURKALOW, ANASTASIA, retired geography educator; b. Buchanan, N.Y., Mar. 16, 1911; d. James Turley and Mabel Ritchie (Ramsay) VanB. BA, Hunter Coll., 1931; MA, Columbia U., 1933, PhD, 1944. Rsch. asst. in geomorphology Columbia U., N.Y.C., 1934-37; rsch. and editorial asst. Am. Geog. Soc., N.Y.C., 1945-48; from tutor to prof. geography Hunter Coll. CUNY, 1938-45, 48-75, prof. Hunter Coll., 1961-75, prof. emeritus Hunter Coll., 1975—; cons. geologist E.I. DuPont deNemours & Co., Wilmington, Del., 1945-59. Editor: Megalopolis (Jean Gottman), 1961, Geol. Edn., 1954-56; contbg. editor Geog. Rev., 1949-72; contbr. articles to profl. jours.; composer hymns. Trustee John Street United Meth. Ch., N.Y.C., 1972-84; bd. dirs. Five Points Mission, 1975-89. Kemp fellow, 1937-38. Mem. Fellow Geol. Soc. Am., AAAS, N.Y. Acad. Scis. (sec. geology sect. 1955-57), Hymn Soc. Am. (rec. sec. 1974-80); mem. Assn. Am. Geographers, Am. Geophys. Union, Am. Guild Organists, Soc. Woman Geographers (exec. com. 1974-80, 83-87), United Meth. City Soc. (bd. dirs. 1974—), Bethany Deaconess Soc. (bd. dirs. 1980—), N.Y. Deaconess Assn. (bd. dirs. 1982—), Phi Beta Kappa, Sigma Xi. Home: 160 E 95th St New York NY 10128

VAN CASPEL, VENITA WALKER, financial planner; b. Sweetwater, Okla.; d. Leonard Rankin and Ella Belle (Jarnagin) Walker. Student, Duke, 1944-46; B.A., U. Colo., 1948, postgrad., 1949-51; postgrad., N.Y. Inst. Fin., 1962. Cert. fin. planner. Stockbroker Rauscher Pierce & Co., Houston, 1962-65, A.G. Edwards & Sons, Houston, 1965-68; founder, pres., owner Van Caspel & Co., Inc., Houston, 1968—, Van Caspel Wealth Mgmt.; owner, mgr. Van Caspel Planning Service, Van Caspel Advt. Agy.; sr. v.p. investments Raymond James and Assocs.; owner Diamond V Ranch; moderator PBS TV show The Money Makers and Profiles of Success, 1980; 1st women mem. Pacific Stock Exchange. Author: Money Dynamics, 1978, Money Dynamics for the 1980's, 1980, The Power of Money Dynamics, Money Dynamics for the New Economy, Money Dynamics for the 1990's, Money Dynamics for Your Retirement Years, 1990; editor: Money Dynamics Letter; columnist The Sat. Evening Post. Bd. dirs. Boy Scouts Am., Horatio Alger Assn., Robert Schuller Ministries. Recipient Matrix award Theta Sigma Phi, 1969, Horatio Alger award for Disting. Americans, 1982, Disting. Woman's medal Northwood Inst., 1986, George Norlin award U. Colo. Alumni Assn., 1987. Mem. Internat. Assn. Fin. Planners, Inst. Cert. Fin. Planners, Phi Gamma Mu, Phi Beta Kappa. Methodist. Office: Raymond James & Assocs Inc 2700 Post Oak Blvd #2325 Ste 2325 Houston TX 77056

VANCE, DOROTHY SAUNDERS, real estate consultant; b. Ogden, Utah, Jan. 16, 1944; d. Heber Clyde Saunders and Norma Leone (Phillips) Devorss; m. John T. Ferrier, Mar. 8, 1962 (div. 1970); 1 child, John T. Ferrier. m. Kimball Roland Vance, July 17, 1976; children: Amanda Keturah, Richard James. Student, Pacific State Hosp., Pomona, Calif., 1970, Weber State U., Ogden, Ut., 1974-75, Lumbleau Coll., Salt Lake City, 1978. Lic. Real estate. Dispatcher Pomona (Calif.) Police Dept., 1968; psychiatric tech. Pacific State Hosp., Pomona, Calif., 1970-71; real estate cons. Motel Hotel Sales and Mgmt., Salt Lake City, 1981—; v.p. Worldwide Inst. Mktg., Salt Lake City; owner, mgr. Macks Inn (Ida.) Resort, 1982; hotel cons. Motel Hotel Sales and Mgmt., Salt Lake City. Author: Vance Family Genealogy. Mem. Utah Alliance for Mentally Ill, Salt Lake City; worker Rep. Group, 1989—; vol. Utah State Prison, 1981-89, Head Start, 1989. Mem. Relief Soc., Bd. Realtors. Home: 8756 Snow Mountain Circle Sandy UT 84093 Office: Worldwide Inst Mktg 1800 SW Temple #406 Salt Lake City UT 84115

VANCE, ZINNA BARTH, artist, writer; b. Phila., Sept. 28, 1917; d. Carl Paul Rudolph Barth and Dorothy Ellice (Wilson) Hart; m. Nathan E. Curry (div. 1959); m. Samuel Therrel Vance, Dec. 2, 1960; children: Barry, Scott Hart. BS in Edn. summa cum laude, Southwestern U., Georgetown, Tex., 1965; MA in Communications, U. Tex., 1969. Cert. in teaching langs., Tex. Freelance writer various publs., 1946-56; assoc. editor, newspaper Canacao Clipper, Philippines, 1956-58; dir. Region One Tex. Fine Arts Assn., Austin, 1962-63; curricular cons. U. Tex. Curricular Conf., 1966; sec. Tex. Fgn. Langs. Assn., 1967; publicity dir. Burnet (Tex.) Creative Arts, 1983—; freelance portrait artist, Liberty Hill, Tex.; owner Gallery Zinna Portrait Studio, Liberty Hill, Tex., 1978—; artist registry Hill Country Arts Found., Ingram, Tex., 1984—; art columnist two newspapers Burnet, 1983—. Contbr. numerous articles to profl. jours.; exhibited in pvt. and corp. collections; illustrator children's books; numerous one-woman shows. Active Hill Country Arts Found., 1978—, Burnet Creative Arts, 1980—, Hill Country Council of Arts, 1986—. Named one of Tex. Emerging Artists, Hill Country Arts Found., 1985; featured as Cover Story Philippines Internat. mag., 1957, featured in (book) Artists of Texas, 1989. Mem. Nat. Mus. Women in Arts (charter mem.), Nat. Portrait Inst., Alpha Chi, Phi Kappa Phi. Republican. Episcopalian. Home: Rt 2 Box 135 Liberty Hill TX 78642

VANDAVEER, LINDA IRENE, psychologist; b. Peoria, Ill., Sept. 19, 1944; d. Kenneth Eugene and Gwendolyn Esther Vandaveer; m. Anton Peter Krasovec, Aug. 6, 1966 (div. 1983); children: Teresa Ann, Tamara Lynne, Michael Anton. BA, Calif. State U., Northridge, 1982; MA, Loyola Marymount U., L.A., 1983, 84; postgrad., U. So. Calif., L.A., 1987—. Psychologist Simi Valley (Calif.) Unified Sch. Dist., 1984—. Mem. Nat. Assn. Sch. Psychologists, Calif. Assn. Sch. Psychologists, Ventura County Assn. Sch. Psychologists (recording sec. 1987, 88), Am. Psychol. Assn., Assn. Calif. Sch. Adminstrs., Phi Delta Kappa. Republican. Home: 4136 Lincoln Ave Culver City CA 90232

VAN DE BOVENKAMP, SUE ERPF, charitable organization executive; b. N.Y.C.; d. George Norton and Bettina Lions (Hearst) Mortimore; student Gardner Sch., Art Students League, Cooper Union; m. Armand Grover Erpf, 1965; children: Cornelia Aurelia, Armand Bartholomew; m. Gerrit Pieter Van de Bovenkamp, Aug. 11, 1973. Pres. Armand G. Erpf Fund, N.Y.C., 1971—; founder, hon. chmn. Erpf Catskill Cultural Ctr., 1972—. Bd. advisors, founder N.Y. Zool. Soc., 1971—, William Beebe fellow, 1983—; fellow in perpetuity Met. Mus. Art, 1977; life fellow Pierpont Morgan Libr., 1974—; mem. coun.of friends Whitney Mus. Am. Art, 1971-77; mem. Whitney Circle, 1978—; bd. dirs. Catskill Ctr. for Conservation and Devel., 1983-86; mem. adv. coun., dept. art history and archaeology Columbia U., 1972—, established univ. seminar on uses of oceans, 1977, mem. adv. coun. Translation Ctr., 1986; life conservator N.Y. Pub. Libr., 1980; fellow Frick Collection; 1971—; mem. coun. Agribus. Coun., Inc., 1979-87; founder, life mem. World Wildlife Fund, 1973—, bd. dirs., 1984-89; mem. pres.'s coun. Columbia U., 1973-78; life mem. Mus. City N.Y., 1972—, mem. pres.'s coun., 1971—. Mem. N.Y. Acad. Scis., The Planetary Soc., Soc. of Tufts Fellows. Office: The Armand G Erpf Fund 640 Park Ave New York NY 10021

VAN DE CAR, DIANA LEE, lawyer; b. Honolulu, Apr. 28, 1952; d. Robert Albert and Dolores (Souza) Pelletier; m. Lloyd Xavier Van De Car, Nov. 11, 1978; children: Nicola E.K., Hannah P.S. BA, U. Hawaii, 1974, JD, 1977. Bar: Hawaii 1977, U.S. Dist. Ct. Hawaii 1977, U.S. Ct. Appeals (9th cir.) 1980. Assoc. Case, Kay, Clause & Lynch, Honolulu, 1977-79; of counsel Stanley H. Roehrig, Esq., 1979-80; sole practice Hilo, 1979-81; assoc. Case & Lynch, Hilo, Hawaii, 1981-85, ptnr., 1985—; mem. Bd. of Bar Examiners, 1987—. Mem. adv. coun. Am. Lung Assn., Hilo, 1983-87. Mem. Hawaii Bar Assn. (chmn. com. guardianships 1985-87), Hawaii Island Bar Assn. (treas. 1980-81), Hawaii Island C. of C. (bd. dirs. 1984-89), Rotary. Office: Case & Lynch 275 Ponahawai St Hilo HI 96720

VANDELL, DEBORAH LOWE, educational psychology educator; b. Bryan, Tex., June 5, 1949; d. Charles Ray and Janice (Durrett) Lowe; m. Kerry Dean Vandell, May 16, 1970; children: Colin Buckner, Ashley Elizabeth. AB, Rice U., 1971; EdM, Harvard U., 1972; PhD, Boston U., 1977. Tchr. Walpole (Mass.) Pub. Schs., 1972-73; researcher Ralph Nader Congress Project, Washington, 1972; asst. prof. U. Tex., Dallas, 1976-81; vis. scholar MacArthur Rsch. Network, Cambridge, Mass., 1985-86; assoc. prof. U. Tex., Dallas, 1981-89; vis. scholar U. Calif., Berkeley, 1988-89; prof. ednl. psychology U. Wis., Madison, 1989—; steering com. nat. study of young children's lives, Washington, 1989—. Editorial bd. Child Devel., 1980-90, Jour. Family Issues, 1983-89, Devel. Psychology, 1989—; co-author books; contbr. articles to profl. jours. Mem. bd. Huffman Sch., 1987-88, Tex. Infant Mental Health Assn., 1988-89, Community Coordinated Child Care, Madison, Wis., 1990—; den mother Cub Scouts, Plano, 1987-88; Sunday sch. tchr. Ch. of the Epiphany, Richardson, Tex., 1986-88. Named Outstanding Young Scholar, Found. for Child Devel., 1982; grantee infant child and family processes NIH, 1989. Mem. Am. Psychol. Assn. (exec. com. div. 7 1985-88), Southwestern Soc. Rsch. in Human Devel. (pres. 1988-90), Am. Psychol. Soc., Soc. for Rsch. in Child Devel., Phi Beta Kappa. Episcopalian. Office: U Wis Dept Ednl Psychology 1025 W Johnson St Madison WI 53706

VAN DEMARK, RUTH ELAINE, lawyer; b. Santa Fe, N. Mex., May 16, 1944; d. Robert Eugene and Bertha Marie (Thompson) Van D.; m. Leland Wilkinson, June 23, 1967; children: Anne Marie, Caroline Cook. AB, Vassar Coll., 1966; MTS, Harvard U., 1969; JD with honors, U. Conn., 1976. Bar: Conn. 1976, U.S. Dist. Ct. Conn. 1976, Ill. 1977, U.S. Dist. Ct. (no. dist.) Ill. 1977, U.S. Supreme Ct. 1983, U.S. Ct. Appeals (7th cir.) 1984. Instr. legal research and writing Loyola U. Sch. Law, Chgo., 1976-79; assoc. Wildman, Harrold, Allen & Dixon, Chgo., 1977-84, ptnr., 1985—. bd. dirs., sec. Systat, Inc., Evanston, Ill. Assoc. editor Conn. Law Rev., 1975-76. Mem. adv. bd. Horizon Hospice, Chgo., 1978—; del.-at-large White House Conf. on Families, Los Angeles, 1980; mem. adv. bd. YWCA Battered Women's Shelter, Evanston, Ill., 1982-86; mem. alumni coun. Harvard Divinity Sch., 1988—; vol. atty. Pro Bono Advocates, Chgo., 1982—; bd. dirs. Friends of Pro Bono Advocates Orgn., 1987-89, New Voice Prodns., 1984-86, Byrne Piven Theater Workshop, 1987—; founder, bd. dirs. Friends of Battered Women and their Children, 1986-87. Mem. ABA, Ill. Bar Assn., Conn. Bar Assn., Chgo. Bar Assn., Appellate Lawyers Assn. Ill. (bd. dirs. 1985-87, treas. 1989—), Women's Bar Assn. Ill., AAUW, Jr. League Evanston (chair State Pub. Affairs Com. 1987-88, Vol. of Yr. 1983-84). Clubs: Chgo. Vassar (pres. 1979-81), Cosmopolitan (N.Y.C.). Home: 1127 Asbury Ave Evanston IL 60202 Office: Wildman Harrold Allen & Dixon 225 W Wacker Dr Chicago IL 60606

VANDENBERG, SISTER PATRICIA CLASINA, health system executive; b. N.Y.C., Mar. 15, 1948; d. Paul John and Alice Margaret (Walters) V. BS in Nursing cum laude, Hunter Coll., 1970; MHA, Duke U., 1979. Nurse critical care staff Roosevelt Hosp., N.Y.C., 1967-69, St. Vincent's Hosp., N.Y.C., 1970; nurse specialist, instr. Meth. Hosp. Bklyn., 1970-71; cons., instr. St. John's Hosp., Anderson, Ind., 1972; nurse critical care, ambulatory svcs. Mt. Carmel Med. Ctr., Columbus, Ohio, 1974-77; v.p. clin. svcs., apostolic devel. Holy Cross Hosp., Silver Springs, Md., 1979-83; pres., chief exec. officer St. Alphonsus Regional Med. Ctr., Boise, Idaho, 1983—; trustee St. Alphonsus Regional Med. Ctr., Boise, 1983-88; sr. v.p. Holy Cross Health System Corp., South Bend, Ind., 1988-89; pres., chief exec. officer Holy Cross Health System Corp., South Bend, 1989—; trustee Holy Cross Hosp., Blue Cross Idaho, Boise, 1986—. Mem. task force United Way, Boise, 1985; bd. dirs. ARC, Boise, 1984-85. Mem. Idaho Hosp. Assn. (trustee), Greater Boise C. of C. (bd. dirs. 1987), Sigma Theta Tau. Roman Catholic. Office: Holy Cross Health System Corp 3606 E Jefferson Blvd South Bend IN 46615

VAN DEN BOOM, ESPERANZA (HOPE VAN DEN BOOM), speech and language pathologist, educator; b. Adrian, Mich., Aug. 31, 1953; d. Bennito Christino Hernandez and Enriqueta Mendez; m. Wayne Jerome Van Den Boom; children: Sean, Kristine. AA, Delta Coll., 1974; BS in Spl. Edn., Ea. Mich. U., 1977, M Spl.Edn. SLI, 1978, M Spl. Edn., 1986. Cert. speech and lang. pathologist, tchr. of learning impaired, art and early childhood tchr. Tchr's. aide Bay City (Mich.) Pub. Schs., 1972-74; receptionist Cen. Mich. U., Mt. Pleasant, Mich., 1974, Ea. Mich. U., Ypsilanti, Mich., 1975-76; dir. speech pathology Emma L. Bixby Hosp., Adrian, Mich., 1981-83; learning disabiltiy tchr. Utica (Mich.) Community Schs., 1986; speech lang. pathologist Grand Ledge (Mich.) Pub. Schs., 1978-81, Rochester (Mich.) Community Schs., 1986-; dir. speech dept. E. L. Bixby Hosp., Adrian, 1981-83; supr. tchr. tng. in learning disabilities Oakland U., Rochester, 1988--. Mem. Women's Bus. Assn., Grand Ledge, Mich., 1978-81, U. Mich. Hosp. Med. Rsch. Team,Ann Arbor, Mich., 1981-83. Mem. NEA, Mich. Edn. Assn., Mich. Speech Hearing and Lang., Oakland County Speech and Hearing Assn., Macomb St. Clair Speech and Hearing Assn., Mich. Assn. Learning Disabilities Educators, Mich. Assn. for Learning Disabled, Coun. for Exceptional Child (mental retardation div., communication disorder div., learning disabilities div., early childhood div.). Home: 46347 Franks Ln Utica MI 48087 Office: Rochester Community Schs 4th and Wilcox Rochester MI 48063

VANDENBURG, MARY LOU, psychologist; b. Passaic, N.J., Dec. 18, 1943; d. Nicholas and Louise (Rosiello) Yacono; m. James Joseph Vandenburg, Jr., July 2, 1966; 1 child, James Joseph III. BA, William Paterson, 1965; MA, Montclair Coll., 1982; MS, Pace U., 1986, D of Psychology, 1988. Cert. tchr., sch. guidance counselor, sch. psychologist, N.J., N.Y. Elem. tchr. various, 1966-67, 76-80; therapist Pequannock Valley Mental Health Ctr., 1985—; sch. psychologist Andover Schs., 1988—; lectr. ednl. enrichment programs, 1980—; psychotherapist various schs., clinics, hosps.; pvt. tutor, other. Author children's books; contbr. articles to profl. jours. Recipient honor cert. Freedom Found., Valley Forge, Pa., Merit Scholarship, Pace U. Mem. N.J. Assn. Sch. Psychologists, Nat. Assn. Sch. Psychologists, Am. Psychol. Assn., Sussex County Assn. of Sch. Psychologists. Home: Rt 1 PO Box 462-B Highland Lake NJ 07422 Office: 1395 Rt 23 Ste 4 Butler NJ 07405

VANDENBURG, ROBIN CORDARY, public relations executive; b. Oneida, N.Y., Dec. 2, 1964; d. Robert Paul and Mary Louise (Battle) Cordary; m. David H. Vandenburg, Oct. 27, 1988. Grad. high sch., St. Petersburg, Fla. Mktg. dir. Harriett Stein & Assocs., St. Petersburg, 1986-87; program asst. Suncoast C. of C., Clearwater, Fla., 1987-88; sales and mktg. rep. Mktg. Concepts, Largo, Fla., 1988; pub. rels. dir. Meridian Design Group, Inc., Clearwater, 1988—; com. mem. Pinellas Econ. Devel. Coun., Clearwater, 1989—. Mem. NAFE, CBA (affiliate dir. ambassador's com. 1990—, tng. and edn. com. 1990—), Gulfcoast Exec. Women's Club, Fla. Pub. Rels. Com. Republican. Roman Catholic. Home: 2636 27th Ave N Saint Petersburg FL 33713

VANDERBEEK, HELEN FREE, entrepreneur; b. Caliente, Nev., Nov. 28, 1944; d. Lory M. and Myrtle Joy (Wadsworth) Free; m. Ronald VanderBeek, May 29, 1968; children: Simone Ane, Margo Joy, David Lory. BA in Clothing, Textiles, Brigham Young U., Provo, Utah, 1968; BA in English, Brigham Young U., 1970. Grad. asst. Brigham Young U., Provo, 1969-70; tchr. Adult Edn. Provo pub. schs., 1971-72, Idaho Falls (Idaho) pub. schs., 1972-74; faculty Brigham Young U.-Ricks, Idaho Falls, 1978-86; tech. writer EG&G Svcs., Idaho Falls, 1984-85; distbr. Melaleuca, Inc., 1987—; writer Word Engring.; owner VanderBeek Ent., 1987—; lectr. in field; cons. in field. Contbr. articles to profl. jours. Com. mem. Bonneville County Centennial Com., Idaho Falls, 1989—; sec. Pub. Comm. Council, Idaho Falls, 1988—. Mem. Idaho Press Women (registrar 1989), Nat. Fedn. press Women, AAUW (bd. dirs.). Republican. Mem. Ch. of Jesus Christ of Latter Day Saints. Home: 1987 N 55th St W Idaho Falls ID 83402 Office: VanderBeek Enterprises PO Box 50476 Idaho Falls ID 83405

VANDERBILT, GLORIA MORGAN, artist, actress, fashion designer; b. N.Y.C., Feb. 20, 1924; d. Reginald Claypoole and Gloria (Morgan) V.; m. Pasquale di Cicco (div.); m. Leopold Stokowski, 1945 (div. 1955); children—Stanislaus, Christopher; m. Sidney Lumet, 1956 (div.); m. Wyatt Emory Cooper, 1963; children—Carter V. (dec.), Anderson H. Attended, Mary C. Wheeler, Miss Porter's schs.; studied acting with, dir. Sanford Meisner, beginning 1955. Exhibited in one-man shows at Rabun Studio, N.Y.C., 1948, Bertha Shaeffer Gallery, N.Y.C., 1954, Juster Gallery, N.Y.C., 1956, Hammer Gallery, N.Y.C., 1966, 68, Cord Gallery, N.Y.C., 1966, Washington Gallery Art, 1968, Neiman-Marcus, Dallas, 1968, Vestart Gallery, N.Y.C., 1969, Parish Museum, Southampton, N.Y., also in Nantucket, Mass., Houston, Reading, Pa., Monterey, Calif., Nashville; exhibited in group shows, Washington Gallery Art, 1967, Hoover Gallery, San Francisco, 1971, stage career; acted in summer stock prodn. The Swan; made Broadway debut in The Time of Your Life, 1955; other stage appearances include Picnic, 1955, The Spa, 1956, Peter Pan, 1958, The Green Hat; made TV debut in Tonight At 8:30; other TV appearances include Colgate Comedy Hour, 1955, Flint and Fire on U.S. Steel Hour, 1958, Family Happiness on U.S. Steel Hour, 1959, Very Important People; appeared in film Johnny Concho, 1955; dir. design film, Riegel Textile Corp., N.Y.C., from 1970; designer stationary and greeting cards, Hallmark Co., fabrics, Bloomcraft Co., bed linens, Martex Co., table linens, Peacock Co., Gloria Vanderbilt jeans; also china, glassware, scarves. Recipient Sylvania award 1959, Fashion award Neiman-Marcus 1969. Author: Love Poems, 1955, (with Alfred Allen Lewis) Gloria Vanderbilt Book of Collage, 1970, Woman to Woman, 1979, Once Upon a Time: A True Story, 1985, novel Never Say Good-Bye, 1989; author: (with Alfred Allen Lewis) play Three by Two, early 1960's, Black White, White Knight, 1987; poems and short stories. Mem. Actors Equity, Screen Actors Guild, AFTRA, Authors League Am., Am. Fedn. Arts. *

VANDERBURG, KATHLEEN, surgical nurse; b. Milw., Feb. 2, 1951; d. Raymond Lawrence and Louise Mary (Jelich) Ksobiech; m. Richard John, July 27, 1975. Diploma, Mt. Sinai Hosp. Sch. Nursing; BS, Chapman Coll., 1979; BS in Nursing, McKendree Coll., 1988; MS, Health Sci. Chapman Coll., 1981. RN, Ariz. Supr. oper. room svcs. USAF, Luke AFB, Ariz.; commd. USAF, advanced through grades to lt. col. Decorated Meritorious Svc. medal (3), Commendation medal (2). Mem. Air Force Assn., Assn. Operating Rm. Nurses. Home: 11133 Ashbrook Pl Phoenix AZ 85039 Office: USAF 832d Med Group Luke AFB AZ 85309

VANDERLINDE, SUSAN KAY, lawyer; b. Balt., Nov. 28, 1951; d. Raymond Edward and Ruth Louise (Hansen) V.; m. Gary Kelley Bove, Aug. 23, 1975 (dec. July 1977); m. Albert Matthew Miller, June 19, 1981; children: Molly, Brooke. BA, Coll. William and Mary, 1973; MA in Psychology, Vanderbilt U., 1975; JD, SUNY, Buffalo, 1979. Bar: Md. 1980, U.S. Dist. Ct. Md. 1980. Assoc. Miles & Stockbridge, Balt., 1979-80, Weinberg & Green, Balt., 1980-81; ptnr. Miller & Vanderlinde, Balt., 1982-83; sr. atty. U.S. Fidelity & Guaranty Co., Balt., 1983-84, counsel and officer, 1984-89, sr. counsel, 1989—. Counsellor, bd. dirs. Soc. of Mayflower Descendants in Md., 1981-87; bd. dirs. Balt. Coun. for Equal Bus. Opportunity, 1990—, Montessori Soc. Cen. Md., 1989—. Mem. ABA, Md. Bar Assn. (program chmn. 1984-85), Women's Bar Assn. Md. (program chmn. 1981-83, sec. 1983-84, v.p. 1984-85, treas. 1987-88). Democrat. Methodist. Home: 135 W Montgomery Baltimore MD 21230 Office: US Fidelity & Guaranty Co 100 Light St Baltimore MD 21202

VANDERLINDEN, CAMILLA DENICE DUNN, quality assurance development, management executive and human resources executive, educator; b. Dayton, July 21, 1950; d. Joseph Stanley and Virginia Danley (Martin) Dunn; m. David Henry VanderLinden; Oct. 10, 1980; 1 child, Michael Christopher. Student, U. de Valencia, Spain, 1969; BA in Spanish and Secondary Edn. cum laude, U. Utah, 1972, MS in Human Resource Econs., 1985. Asst. dir. Davis County Community Action Program, Farmington, Utah, 1973-76; dir. South County Community Action, Midvale, Utah, 1976-79; supr. customer service Ideal Nat. Life Ins. Co., Salt Lake City, 1979-80; mgr. customer service Utah Farm Bur. Mutual Ins., Salt Lake City, 1980-82; quality assurance analyst Am. Express Co., Salt Lake City, 1983-86, quality assurance and human resource specialist, 1986-88; mgr. quality assurance & engring. Am. Express Co., Denver, 1988—; adj. faculty Westminster Coll., Salt Lake City, 1987-88. Vol. translator Latin Am. community. Republican. Christian. Office: Am Express Info Svcs Co Integrated Payments Systems Div 181 Inverness Dr W Englewood CO 80112

VAN DER POL, DENISE MARIE, rehabilitation center executive; b. Santa Ana, Calif., Nov. 25, 1955; d. A.C. Murhyle and Mary Carolyn (Steiner) Sales. Student, Fullerton (Calif.) Community Coll., 1975-76, Saddleback Coll., Mission Viejo, Calif., 1979-81; BLA in Social Sci., U. Alaska S.E., 1990. Grant evaluator Calif. Dept. Edn., Sacramento, 1981; credential specialist Calif. Assn. Alcohol and Drug Counselors, Newport Beach, 1981-83; rehab. counselor Orange County Halfway House, Anaheim, Calif., 1981-83; alcohol edn. instr., group facilitator Safety Cons. Services, Westminster, Calif., 1981-83; dir. counseling Cascade Rehab. Ctr., Anchorage and Juneau, Alaska, 1984-86; owner, dir. counseling S.E. Rehab. Services, Juneau, 1986—; program coordinator Statewide Conf. Foster Parent Devel., Orange County, 1981. Commr. Capistrano Unified Sch. Dist. Rev. Bd., 1980; bd. dirs. Gastineau Human Services, Juneau, 1988. Named to Nat. Disting. Svc. Registry: Rehab., 1989. Mem. Nat. Rehab. Assn., Nat. Assn. Rehab. Profls. in the Pvt. Sector, Calif. Assn. Alcohol and Drug Educators, Saddleback Coll. Alumni Assn., Ducks Unltd., Nat. Fedn. of Independent Bus. Club: Rotary. Office: Southeast Rehab Svcs 130 Seward St Ste 212 Juneau AK 99801

VANDERSLOOT, VALDA ILZE, financial executive; b. July 14, 1947; m. Donald L. Vandersloot. BA, Wayne State U., 1968, MA, 1974, MBA, 1982. Cert. secondary tchr., counselor, Mich. English tchr. Livonia (Mich.) Pub. Schs., 1968-75, counselor, 1975-78, adminstr., 1978-82; fin. planner IDS Fin. Svcs., Inc., Farmington Hills, Mich., 1984-89, tng. mgr., 1985-87, dist. mgr., 1987—. Sec. Livonia Zoning Bd. of Appeals, 1988—; mem. Livonia League of Womens Voters, bd. dirs. 1985-87. Mem. Women's Econ. Club, Livonia C. of C. (leg. com. 1985—), Beta Gamma Sigma. Office: IDS Fin Svcs 30840 Northwestern Hwy Ste 300 Farmington Hills MI 48018

VANDERSYPEN, RITA DEBONA, English educator; b. Alexandria, La., Sept. 13, 1953; d. Sam S. and Myrtle (Genova) DeBona; m. Robert Louis Vandersypen, Aug. 17, 1974; children: Regina Marie, Ryan Matthew. BA summa cum laude, La. Coll., 1975; MEd, La. State U., 1980, postgrad., 1982; postgrad., Northwestern State U., Natchitoches, La., 1982. Eligibility worker Rapides Parish Office Family Svcs., Alexandria, 1975-78; welfare social worker Rapides Parish Foster Care Svcs., Alexandria, 1978-79; tchr. A. Wettermark High Sch., Boyce, La., 1979-84; tchr. English Alexandria Sr. High Sch., 1984—. Contbr. to handbook and curriculum guide. Sponsor Future Voters Am. Club, 1984-89, 4-H Club, 1988—. Mem. AAUW, Rapides Council English Tchrs., Rapides Fedn. Tchrs., Rapides Parish Livestock Club, Belgian-Am. Club, Am. Quarter Horse Assn., St. Rita Altar and Rosary Soc., Phi Kappa Phi. Roman Catholic. Office: Alexandria Sr High Sch 800 Ola Ln Alexandria LA 71301

VANDER TUIG, JANE MARIE, educator; b. Sioux City, Iowa, Nov. 16, 1951; d. Edwin Carl and Pearl Louise (Higgins) Fick; m. Stephen George Vander Tuig, Jan. 30, 1972; children: Adam Cory, Marci Nicole. BA in Elem. Edn., Augustana Coll., 1973; postgrad., Kearney State Coll., 1980-90. Cert. tchr., Nebr. Tchr. 1st grade Holy Ghost Sch., Dubuque, Iowa, 1974-75; tchr. pre-sch. Mary Moppets Day Care Ctr., Lakewood, Colo., 1975; salesperson Fortress Ch. Supply, Denver, 1975-77; tchr. 1st grade Glenvil (Nebr.) Elem. Sch., 1978-82, sch. libr., 1982-83, substitute tchr., homemaker, 1983-84; coord., head tchr. Aurora (Nebr.) Literacy and GED Programs, 1986—. Mem. Friends of the Library, Aurora, 1989—. Mem. AAUW. Democrat. Lutheran. Home: 907 2d Ave Aurora NE 68818

VANDERVELDE, ANN ELIZABETH, watercolorist; b. Milw., Aug. 21, 1946; d. Cuthbert Kellogg and Evalyn Cecelia (Roberts) V.; m. Brian W. Bergemann, Aug. 26, 1967 (div. 1976); children: Christopher, Jennifer; m. Peter Robert Cavanagh, Apr. 18, 1981; 1 child, Drew; 1 stepchild,

Sasha. BS in Art, U. Wis., 1968; Student, Pa. State U., 1989-90. Graphic illustrator Pa. State U., State College, 1974-81. Artist: (book) Physiology and Biomechanics of Cycling, 1978, The Running Shoe Book, 1980. Jurer Art Alliance Exhibit, Lemont, Pa., 1987; vol. Dem. Com., State College, 1988; co-chairwoman fundraising Friends of Sch., 1989. Recipient 2nd prize watercolor State College Arts Festival, 1987; Merit award watercolor Images 89. Mem. Nat. Orgn. Women in the Arts (chartered), Pa. Watercolor Soc., Nat. Watercolor Soc. (assoc.), Art Alliance Central Pa. (v.p. 1988—, Merit award 1986), Am. Coun. for the Arts, Nat. Abortion Rights Action League, NOW. Home and Office: 1352 Deerfield Dr State College PA 16803

VANDER WAAL, DEBORAH KAY, insurance broker; b. Ft. Meade, Md., Dec. 26, 1952; d. James Dewey and Frances Harding (Kidd) Vander Waal. BS in Gen. Bus., Va. Poly. Inst. and State U., 1974. CPCU; assoc. in underwriting; cert. profl. ins. woman. All lines rater Aetna Ins. Co., Camp Hill, Pa., 1974-77; underwriter trainee Md. Casulaty Ins. Co., Camp Hill, 1977-78; sr. personal lines underwriter Gt. Am. Ins. Co., Lancaster, Pa., 1978-82; malpractice underwriter Phico Ins. Co., Mechanicsburg, Pa., 1983-87; sr. comml. underwriter Va. Profl. Underwriters, Richmond, Va., 1987-88; asst. v.p. Corroon & Black, Nashville, 1988—. Recipient award for acad. excellence Conf. Spl. Risk Underwriters, 1987. Mem. Soc. CPCU (edn. com. 1989—), Nat. Assn. Ins. Women, NAFE, Am.Bus. Womens Assn. (chpt. pres., Chpt. Woman of Yr. 1981). Democrat. Methodist. Home: 609 Darlington Pl Nashville TN 37211 Office: Corroon & Black 1 Commerce Pl Ste 1500 Nashville TN 37239

VANDERWIEL-SCHLEENVOIGT, CAROLE JEAN, publishing company executive, research scientist; b. Cleve., May 6, 1950; d. Henry Charles and Dorothy Marie (Kloepfer) VanderWiel; m. Felix Richard Schleenvoigt III, Mar. 20, 1976; children: Kyle Andrew, Mindy Kathryn. BS, U. Tex., 1972; PhD, Baylor U., 1976. Cert. bone physiologist. Biochem. technician U. Tex. Health Sci. Ctr., Dallas, 1968-70; serology technician Harris Hosp., Ft. Worth, 1970-72; grad. asst. Baylor Coll.Dentistry, Dallas, 1973-76; doctoral fellow NIH, Chapel Hill, N.C., 1977-79; asst. prof. U. N.C. Sch. Medicine, Chapel Hill, 1979-82; dir. S.W. Metabolic Bone Inst., Plano, Tex., 1982-85; co-owner Castille Properties Real Estate, Ft. Worth, 1982—; pres. Charles Pub. Corp., Weatherford, Tex., 1986—; cons. VanderWiel & Assocs. Real Estate, Ft. Worth, 1982—. Contbr. chpts. to books, articles to profl. jours. Mem. campus improvement team Weatherford Ind. Schs., 1987-89. Recipient Rsch.Scientist award Parathyroid Conf., Japan, 1983; Investigator's award Pfizer Pharm., 1982; grantee NSF, 1983, NIH, 1980, Nat. Inst. Dental Rsch., 1976. Fellow Am. Acad. Orthopedic Rsch.; mem. Am. Soc. Bone and Mineral Rsch. (program coordinator 1984), AAAS. Republican. Presbyterian. Home: 141 Vista Dr Weatherford TX 76087 Office: Charles Pub Corp Box 577 Weatherford TX 76086

VAN DER WOUDE, MARY ELIZABETH, French hornist, writer, educator; b. Grand Rapids, Mich., Dec. 1, 1939; d. John William and Elizabeth (ten Hoor) Monsma. French horn studies with Philip Farkas, Chgo., 1957-64; French horn studies with Lorenzo Sansone, N.Y.C., 1964-67; BS, Chgo. City Coll., 1965; BA, St. Xavier Coll., Chgo., 1968; postgrad. in piano, Am. Conservatory of Music, Chgo., 1974-76, postgrad. in French horn, 1983-84. French hornist Grand Rapids Symphony Orch., 1955-57, Grand Rapids Chamber Orch., 1955-57, Chgo. Civic Orch., 1958-60, Chgo. Chamber Orch., 1959-64; composer French horn texts Summy-Birchard Co., Evanston, Ill., 1960-62; free-lance musician St. Louis, 1970-71; composer French horn Fema Publs. div. Interlochen Press, Naperville, Ill., 1974-75; French hornist Bach & Madrigal Soc., Phoenix, 1977-80, Ariz. Ballet, Phoenix, 1977-80, Phoenix Chamber Orch., 1977-80; freelance French hornist, writer Chgo., 1988—; mem. faculty U. Ill., Chgo., 1988—. Composer: Virtuoso Series, 12 vols., 1961-65; contbr. articles to profl. jours. Mem. Am. Fedn. Musicians, Chgo. Fedn. Musicians, Phoenix Fedn. Musicians. Home and Office: 1130 S Michigan Ave #3606 Chicago IL 60605

VAN DEVANTER, SUSAN EARLING, health care marketing executive; b. Washington, Dec. 12, 1960; d. Willis and Ann Pemberton (Cutler) Van D. BA, Skidmore Coll., 1983. Customer svc. rep. GTE-Sprint, Arlington, Va., 1984; mktg. rep. TDX Systems, Inc., Vienna, Va., 1984-85, sr. sales rep., 1985; account exec. TDX Systems, Inc., Norfolk, Va., 1986; mktg. cons. Mktg. Inst. Internat. Corp., Herndon, Va., 1986-88; mktg. coordinator Nat. Rehab. Hosp., Washington, 1988—. Editor bus. and econs. newspaper, 1983. Vol. Rep. Nat. Com., Washington, 1981; mem. Friends of the Kennedy Ctr., Washington, 1987—; mem. disability awareness com. Nat. Rehab. Hosp. Mem. Am. Mktg. Assn. (Washington chpt.), Acad. Health Svcs. Mktg., Washington Met. Soc. for Hosp. Mktg. and Pub. Rels. (bd. dirs.), Capital Area Soc. Healthcare Planning and Mktg. Episcopalian. Office: Nat Rehab Hosp 102 Irving St NW Washington DC 20010

VANDEVENDER, BARBARA JEWELL, reading specialist, farmer; b. Trenton, Mo., Dec. 4, 1929; d. Raleigh Leon and Rose Rea (Dryer) S.; m. Delbert Lyle Vandevender, Aug. 15, 1948; children: Lyle Gail, James R. BS, Northeast Missouri State U., Kirksville, 1971; MA, Northeast Mo. State U., 1973. Elem. tchr. Williams Sch., Spickard, Mo., 1948-49; reading specialist Spikard R-2 Sch., 1971-74, Princeton (Mo.) R-5 Sch., 1974-89; speaker Mo. State Coun. of IRA, Columbia, 1987-89, Plains area IRA, 1988. Dir., writer Children's Drama, 1964-72, Comedy, 1967-68. Pres. Spickard PTA, 1963-64, Women's Ext. Club, Galt, Mo.; foster mother Family Svcs., Trenton, Mo., 1972-79. Recipient Mo. State Conservation award Goodyear Tire Co., Akron, Ohio, 1972, Balanced Farming award Gulf Oil Co., N.Y.C., 1972, Mo. State Farming award Kansas City C. of C., 1974, FHA State Farming award, Jefferson City, Mo., 1974, Outstanding Leadership Mo. U., Columbia, 1976, Ednl. Leadership award MSTA, Columbia, 1984, Outstanding Contbn. to Internat. Reading Assn., Newark, Del., 1988. Pres. Internat. Reading Assn., 1985-86. Republican Baptist.

VAN DE VYVER, SISTER MARY FRANCILENE, academic administrator; b. Detroit, Sept. 6, 1941; d. Hector Joseph and Irene Cecilia (Zygailo) V. BA, Madonna Coll., 1965; MEd, Wayne State U., 1970, PhD, 1977. Joined Sisters of St. Felix of Cantalice, Roman Cath. Ch., 1967. Tchr. Ladywood High Sch., 1965-74; adminstrv. asst. to pres. Madonna Coll., Livonia, Mich., 1974-75, acad. dean, 1975-76, now pres. Office: Madonna Coll Office of Pres 36600 Schoolcraft Rd Livonia MI 48150-1173*

VAN DE WORKEEN, PRISCILLA TOWNSEND, small business executive; b. Denver, July 9, 1946; d. Reginald and Ruth (Poor) Townsend; m. Melvin Charles Van de Workeen, Oct. 27, 1973; 1 stepchild, Scott Minot. BA in Chinese History, Wheaton Coll., Norton, Mass., 1968; postgrad., Cornell U., 1965. Asst. dir. Nat. Info. Bur., N.Y.C., 1969-73; dep. dir. Harkness Fellowships, N.Y.C. and London, 1973-83; owner, mgr. Vernalwood Enterprises, splty. and custom crafts, Dudley, Mass., 1984—; co-owner, mgr. Vernalwood Bed & Breakfast, Dudley, 1989—, Folkstone/Cen. Mass. Bed & Breakfast Reservation Svc., Dudley, 1989—. Bd. dirs. Hubbard Regional Hosp. Guild, Webster, Mass., 1986—, Internat. Ctr., Worcester, Mass., 1989-90; coord. Nat. Coun. for Internat. Visitors, Washington, 1989-90; mem. Worcester County Conv. and Visitors Bur. Mem. Tri-Community Area C. of C., Webster-Dudley Garden Club. Democrat. Home and Office: Vernalwood RR 3 Box 375 Dudley MA 01570

VANDINE, MARYANN ELIZABETH, educator; b. Kansas City, Kans., Jan. 30, 1953; d. Edgar William and Ruth Ann (Gatchell) Eikermann; m. Wayne Russell VanDine, July 30, 1977; 1 child, Corey Marie. BS, Kans. State U., 1975; MS in Sports Sci., U.S. Sports Acad., Mobile, Ala., 1987. Cert. tchr., Mo., Kans. Tchr. St. John LaLande Sch., Blue Springs, Mo., 1979-81; tchr. phys. edn. Kansas City (Kans.) Pub. Schs., 1975-77, tchr. phys. edn. and dance K-5th grade, 1981—; dance instr., asst. artistic dir. Kansas City Pub. Sch. Dist. #500, Wyandotte High Sch. All City Dance Ensemble, 1986—. Mem. drug core team Welborn Elem. Mem. AAUW, P.E.O., Delta Kappa Gamma, Alpha Xi Delta. Office: Welborn Elem Sch 5200 Leavenworth Kansas City KS 66104

VAN DUYN, MONA JANE, poet; b. Waterloo, Iowa, May 9, 1921; d. Earl George and Lora G. (Kramer) Van D.; m. Jarvis A. Thurston, Aug. 31, 1943. B.A., U. No. Iowa, 1942; M.A., U. Iowa, 1943; D.Litt. (hon.), Washington U., St. Louis, 1971, Cornell Coll., Iowa, 1972. Instr. in English U. Iowa, Iowa City, 1943-46; instr. in English U. Louisville, 1946-50; lectr. English Univ. Coll., Washington U., 1950-67; poetry reader, 1970—; poetry editor, co-pub. Perspective, A Quar. of Lit., 1947-67; lectr. Salzburg (Austria) Seminar Am. Studies, 1973; adj. prof. poetry workshop Washington U., Spring 1983; vis. Hurst prof. Washington U., 1987; poet-in-residence Sewanee Writing Conference, 1990. Poet-in-residence, Breadloaf Writing Conf., Mass., 1974, 76; author: Valentines to the Wide World, 1959, A Time of Bees, 1964, To See, To Take, 1970, Bedtime Stories, 1972, Merciful Disguises, 1973, Letters from a Father and Other Poems, 1983, Near Changes, 1990. Recipient Eunice Tietjens award, 1956, Helen Bullis prize, 1964, 76, Harriet Monroe award, 1968, Hart Crane Meml. award, 1968, Borestone Mountains 1st prize, 1968, Bollingen prize, 1970, Nat. Book award, 1971, Loines prize Nat. Inst. Arts and Letters, 1976, Sandburg prize Cornell Coll., 1982, Shelley Meml. prize Poetry Soc. Am., 1987, $25,000 Lilly Prize for Poetry, 1989, Mo. Arts award, 1990; grantee Nat. Council Arts, 1967; grantee in poetry NEA, 1985; Guggenheim fellow, 1972; fellow Acad. Am. Poets, 1980. Mem. Nat. Inst. Arts and Letters, Acad. Am. Poets (chancellor 1985).

VAN DYCK, DAWN CORNELIA, journalist; b. Albany, N.Y., Feb. 16, 1962; d. H. David and Roxa Ann (Becker) Van D. BA, Principia Coll., 1984. Environ. researcher N.Y. State Pub. Svc. Commn., Albany, 1982; tech. writer Albany Energy Recovery System, 1985; news writer Sta. WAMC-FM, Albany, 1985; program coord. Conversations with the Christian Sci. Monitor, Boston, 1985-86, exec. producer, 1986-87; radio producer, editor World Svc. of Christian Sci. Monitor, Boston, 1987-89; editorial and audio production cons. Milton, Mass., 1989—. Mem. exec. bd. 1st Ch. of Christ, Scientist, Quincy, Mass., 1988-89, 2d reader, 1989—.

VAN DYKE, JEAN ANITA, clinical nurse specialist; b. Hazleton, Pa., July 11, 1953; d. William David and Anita Jean (Morgan) Van D. BS, Pa. State U., 1975; MS in Nursing, U. Pitts., 1983. Staff nurse Altoona (Pa.) Hosp., 1975-77; staff nurse adult inpatient unit We. Psychiatric Inst. and Clinic, Pitts., 1977-79; nurse clinician/diagnostic and evaluation ctr. We. Psychiatric Inst. and Clinic, 1979-83, clin. specialist/project interviewer, 1987-88, clin. specialist Cognitive Disorders Clinic, 1983—. Vol. Animal Friends, Pitts., 1982, Vita - Tax Prepared, Pitts., 1987. Mem. Sigma Theta Tau. Democrat. Office: 3811 O'Hara St Pittsburgh PA 15213

VANDYKE, JILL, geophysicist; b. Douglas, Mich., Apr. 11, 1954; d. Arthur John VanDyke and Suzanne (Leonard) Simmons. BA in Geophysics, Hope Coll., 1976; MS in Geophysics, U. Minn., 1979. Geophysicist Gulf Oil, Houston, 1979-81, exploration geophysicist, 1981, petroleum geophysicist, 1981-82, sr. geophysicist, 1982-84, project geophysicist, 1984-85; geophysicist Chevron U.S.A., San Ramon, Calif., 1985-90; petroleum geophysicist Chevron U.S.A., Bakersfield, Calif., 1990—. Recipient Bausch & Lombe Sci. award, 1972, Pres. scholarship, 1972-76; named one of Notable Women of Tex., 1984. Mem. Soc. Exploration Geophysicists, Am. Assn. Petroleum Geologists, Geophys. Soc. Houston, Bay Area Geophys. Soc., Geol. Soc. Am.

VAN DYKE, SUSAN CAROL, educator; b. St. Louis, Mar. 7, 1945; d. John Howard and Margaret Mary (Brubaker) Van D. BS, E. Stroudsburg (Pa.) U., 1967; MEd, Colo. State U., Ft. Collins, 1973; PhD, Temple U., 1983. Phys. edn. instr. Pennridge Pub. Schs., Perkasie, Pa., 1968-71, Glassboro (N.J.) State Coll., 1973-75; sports sci. instr. Colo. Women's Coll., Denver, 1975-76; sports sci. prof. Fla. Internat. U., Miami, 1982, U. Denver, 1980-81, 82-84; fitness cons. Porter Hosp., Denver, 1988; kinesiologist Rolf Inst., Boulder, Colo., 1986—, Chapman Coll. Ext., Denver, 1988—; phys. fitness cons.; editor Health Beat, 1987-88; kinesiologist Boulder Sch. of Massage, 1990—. Contbr. articles to profl. jours. Bd. dirs. Urban Drainage & Flood Control, Denver, 1988—; chmn., creator Englewood Downtown Task Force, 1987—; mayor City of Englewood, 1988—; com. chairperson Gov.'s Task Force on Solid Waste Mgmt., 1989, 90; chairperson Englewood Econ. Coalition, 1989. Office of Energy Conservation grantee, 1989—. Mem. Colo. Mcpl. League, South Metro Denver C. of C. (bd. dirs. econ. devel. 1988-89, mem. leadership group 1989), Greater Englewood C. of C., Denver Community Leadership Forum, Profls. Against Fitness Fraud (co-founder). Republican. Home: 570 E Amherst Englewood CO 80110 Office: City of Englewood 3400 S Elati St Englewood CO 80110

VAN DYKE-COOPER, ANNY MARION, financial company executive; b. Howard, Ont., Can., Sept. 30, 1928; d. Anthony and Anna (Koolen) Van D.; m. John Arnold Cooper, Apr. 9, 1983. BA, Concordia U., 1959. Chartered fin. analyst. Tchr. Lanoraie Sch. Bd., 1946-47; sec. Can. Nat. Rys., Montreal, Que., Can., 1947-51; sec. Sorel Industries Ltd., Sorel, Que., Can., 1952-53; with Bell Investment Mgmt. Corp. and BIMCOR, Inc. subs. Bell Canada, Montreal, 1953-83; portfolio mgr. U.S. Equities, 1971-83; chmn., dir. Cooper, Van Dyke Assocs. Inc., Birmingham, Mich., 1983—. Mem. Inst. Chartered Fin. Analysts (trustee 1979-80), Fin. Analysts Soc. Detroit, Montreal Soc. Fin. Analysts (program chmn., pres. 1974-75), Can. Coun. Fin. Analysts (vice-chmn. 1976-77), Fin. Analysts Fedn. (treas. 1977-78, vice chmn. 1978-79, chmn. 1979-80). Home: 1111 N Woodward Ave Apt C 236 Birmingham MI 48009 Office: 1100 N Woodward Ave Birmingham MI 48009

VAN DYNE, MICHELE MILEY, information engineer; b. Harrisburg, Pa., Sept. 8, 1959; d. Joseph Lawrence Miley and Tina Theresa (Dudash) Smollack; m. David Franklin Buck, Aug. 8, 1981 (div. July 1984); m. David George Van Dyne, Sept. 9, 1989. BA in Psychology, U. Mont., 1981, MS in Computer Sci., 1985. Div. sr. tech. programmer, analyst Allied-Signal Aerospace, Kansas City, Mo., 1985-89; knowledge engr. United Data Svcs., Inc., United Telecom, Overland Park, Kans., 1989-90; pres. IntelliDyne, Kansas City, Mo., 1990—; cons. Comprehensive Devel. Ctr., Missoula, Mont., 1984; speaker Sigart, Kansas City, 1988, Allied Corp., Teterboro, N.J., 1988; mem. Silicon Prairie Tech. Assn., Kansas City, 1989. Vol. Palnned Parenthood Greater Kansas City, 1986. United Bldg. Ctrs. scholar, 1976. Mem. IEEE Computer Soc., Am. Assn. Artificial Intelligence, Internat. Neural Network Soc., Alpha Lambda Delta. Democrat. Episcopalian. Home: 6040 Wornall Rd Kansas City MO 64113 Office: 6040 Wornall Rd Kansas City MO 64113

VANE, MARY KATHLEEN, chemical company executive; b. Washington, Apr. 27, 1951; d. Calvin Chaplin and Grace Rachel (Van Zant) V. BS with honors and distinction, Cornell U., 1973. Research chemist DuPont Co., Wilmington, Del., 1973-75, tech. service rep., 1976-77; mktg. rep. DuPont Co., N.Y.C., 1978-79, sales rep., 1979-80, mktg. supr., 1981-83; mktg. mgr. DuPont Co., Wilmington, 1983-86, N.Y.C., 1983-86; bus. mgr. DuPont Co., Wilmington, 1986-88, bus. planning mgr., 1988—; lectr. Cornell U., Ithaca, N.Y., 1974—, mem. adv. council, 1986—. Vol. Rep. campaign, 1982, 84, 86, 88; sponsor Christian Children's Fund, Richmond, Va., 1986—; commr. Del. Commn. for Women, 1990. Mem. Nat. Assn. Female Execs., Human Ecology Alumni Assn., Wilmington Women in Bus. Republican. Methodist. Office: DuPont de Nemours Textile Fibers Dept Chestnut Run Plaza Laurel Run 2E15 Po Box 80 705 Wilmington DE 19898-0705

VANE, SYLVIA BRAKKE, anthropologist, cultural resource management company executive; b. Fillmore County, Minn., Feb. 28, 1918; d. John T. and Hulda Christina (Marburger) Brakke; m. Arthur Bayard Vane, May 17, 1942; children: Ronald Arthur, Linda, Laura Vane Ames. AA, Rochester Jr. Coll., 1937; BS with distinction, U. Minn., 1939; postgrad., Radcliffe U., 1944; MA, Calif. State U., Hayward, 1975. Med. technologist Dr. Frost and Hodapp, Willmar, Minn., 1939-41; head labs. Corvallis Gen. Hosp., Oreg., 1941-42; dir. lab. Cambridge Gen. Hosp., Mass., 1942-43, Peninsula Clinic, Redwood City, Calif., 1947-49; v.p. Cultural Systems Rsch., Inc., Menlo Park, Calif., 1978—; pres. Ballena Press, Menlo Park, 1981—; cons. cultural resource mgmt. So. Calif. Edison Co., Rosemead, 1978-81, San Diego Gas and Elec. Co., 1980-83, Pacific Gas and Elec. Co., San Francisco, 1982-83, Wender, Murase & White, Washington, 1983-87, Yosemite Indians, Mariposa, Calif., 1982-84, San Luis Rey Band of Mission Indians, Escondido, Calif., 1986—, U.S. Ecology, Newport Beach, Calif., 1986—, Riverside County Flood Control and Water Conservation Dist., 1985—, Infotec, Inc., 1989—, Alexander & Karshmer, Berkeley, Calif., 1989—, Desert Water Agy., Palm Springs, Calif., 1989—. Author: (with L.J. Bean), California Indians, Primary Resources, 1977, rev. edit., 1990, The Cahuilla and the Santa Rosa Mountains, 1981; contbr. chpts. to several books. Bd. dirs. Sequoia Area coun. Girl Scouts U.S., 1954-61; bd. dirs., v.p., pres. LWV, S. San Mateo County, Calif., 1960-65, cons. San Francisco coun. Girl Scouts U.S., 1962-69. Fellow Soc. Applied Anthropology; mem. Southwestern Anthrop. Assn. (program chmn. 1976-77, newsletter editor 1976-79), Am. Anthropology Assn., Soc. for Am. Archaeology. Mem. United Ch. of Christ. Office: Ballena Press 823 Valparaiso Ave Menlo Park CA 94025

VANEK, BARBARA S., hospital administrator; b. Oskaloosa, Iowa, June 21, 1957; d. Ralph and Helen VerPloeg; m. Wayne E. Vanek, July 25, 1981. BSN, Olivet Nazarene U., Kankakee, Ill., 1979. Staff nurse Ingalls Meml. Hosp., Harvey, Ill., 1979-81; clin. supr. ATC Ingalls Meml. Hosp., 1981; head nurse St. Croix Valley Meml. Hosp., St. Croix Falls, Wis., 1981-83, Ctr. for Recovery, JFK Hosp., Atlantis, Fla., 1983-84, Transylvania Community Hosp., Brevard, N.C., 1984-86; intensive care nurse St. Croix Valley Meml. Hosp., 1986-87; prog. designer/cons. Sharing AB, Blentarp, Sweden, 1987; asst. adminstr. St. Croix Valley Meml. Hosp., 1987—; trainer Hazelden Found., Center City, Minn., 1988—. Bd. dirs. Local Emergency Planning Com. for Polk County, 1988—; clk. of session, elder Westminster Presbyn. Ch., Palm Beach Gardens, Fla., 1985. Mem. Am. Nurses Assn., Nat. Assn. Quality Assurance Profls., Wis. Assn. Risk Mgmt. Profls., Wis. and Minn. Assn. Quality Assurance Profls., Wis. Safety Assn., Hazardous Resource Assn., Dist. 20 of Wis. Nurses Assn. (sec. 1988—), NOW, Greenpeace, Nat. Wildlife Fedn. Democrat. Presbyterian. Office: 204 S Adams St Saint Croix Falls WI 54024

VAN ERT, BARBARA MARIE, retail executive; b. Superior, Wis., Jan. 16, 1943; d. Edward Theodore and Hazel Marie (Nelson) Van Ert. Student, Wis. Ind. Tech. Sch., Superior, 1961-63, U. Wis., Superior, U. Minn., Duluth, Carroll Coll. Acctg. clk. Cooperative Wholesale, Superior, 1961-82; tax preparer H & R Block, Superior, 1976—; owner Barbara Van Ert Bookkeeping Svc., Superior, 1983—, The Yarn Basket, Superior, 1984—; fin. planning cons. 1983—; occasional instr. H&R Block tax sch., seminars. Author brochure: I Don't Have Time, 1967. Elder New Hope & Itasca Chs., Superior, Wis., 1958-83. Mem. Am. Profl. Needlework Retailers. Presbyterian. Office: The Yarn Basket 1211 Tower Avenue Superior WI 54880

VANESS, MARGARET HELEN, artist, consultant; b. Seattle; d. Paul Edward and Alma Magdalena Lauch; B.F.A., U. Wash., Seattle, 1970, 71, M.F.A., 1973; cert. bus. Drexel U., Phila., 1975; m. Gerard Vaness; children—Bette, Bruce, Barbara, Helen-Cathleen. Teaching asst. Sch. Art, U. Wash., 1971-73; illustrator DuPont Co., Wilmington, Del., 1973-74, Boeing Vertol Co., Phila., 1974-75; illustrator, program mgr. Boeing Co., Seattle, 1978-84; judge art shows, 1969—; executed mural for Dr. L. Mellon-Boeing Vertol Med. Ctr., 1974; commd. by USIA, 1973. Mem. Coll. Art Assn., Soc. for Tech. Communication, Photog. Soc. Am. (area rep. 1985-88, dist. rep. 1988—), Seattle Photographic Soc. (editor official bulletin Cable Releases 1985-89, bd. dirs. 1986-88), U. Wash. Alumni Assn. (life), U. Wash. Arboretum Found. (unit pres. 1981-83), Nat. Mus. of Women in the Arts (charter mem.), Lambda Rho (past pres.). Address: 17128 2d Ave SW Seattle WA 98166-3521

VANET, JUDITH ANN, art dealer; b. Coffeyville, Kans., Feb. 19, 1951; d. Donald Joseph and Wanda (Couch) Strain; m. M. Randall Vanet, Dec. 11, 1974. AA, Stephens Coll., 1971, BA, 1973. Substitute tchr. Kansas City (Mo.) Pub. Schs., 1974-75; art dealer LaGaleria, Kansas City, 1976-83, Leawood, Kans., 1983—; free-lance writer Leawood, 1983—. Author: Missouri Poets, 1974, Best Loved Poems, 1980, Best Contemporary Poems, 1982. Mem. Jr. Women's Symphony Alliance, Kansas City, Mo.; co-chmn. 150th Anniversary Reunion Stephens Coll., 1983. Named Boss of Yr. Am. Bus. Womens, 1980; recipient Disting. Svc. award Stephen Coll. Mem. Rainbow Girls Grand Cross of Color. Democrat. Presbyterian. Home and Office: 12306 Overbrook Ct Leawood KS 66209

VAN EVERA, MARY PATRICIA, retired nurse, civic volunteer; b. Chgo., Apr. 30, 1920; d. Earle Delavan and Harriette Edith (Sessions) Andrews; m. Carl C. Van Evera, July 8, 1942; children: Richard Kepler, Patricia Lynn. Student, Coe Coll., 1938-40; diploma Sch. of Nursing, St. Luke's Hosp., Chgo., 1943. RN, 1943. Pub. health nurse Mo. State Health Dept., 1943-46; nurse doctor's office Ill., 1946-48, sch. nurse, 1952-65; health officer Village of Western Springs, Ill., 1952-65. Bd. dirs. Presbyn. Home of Md., Towson, Md.; elder Christ Our King Presbyn. Ch., Bel Air, Md.; bd. dirs. ARC, Hartford County chpt.; active Girl Scouts U.S., 1935—, leader, camp nurse, camp dir., svc. com., cons. Recipient Hall of Fame award, ARC Balt. regional chpt., 1973. Mem. AAUW Hartford County. Republican. Home: 507 Linwood Ave Bel Air MD 21014

VANGHEL, RUTH MARGARET, advertising agency administrator; b. Buffalo, Apr. 12, 1950; d. Russell Short and Emma Pleasant (Wear) Garrick; m. Jeffrey George Vanghel (dec. 1988). Grad. high sch., Williamsville, N.Y. Sec. McKesson & Robbins Drug Co., Cheektowaga, N.Y., 1972-78; sales rep. Nasco Inc., Springfield, Tenn., 1978-80; telemktg. sales rep. L.M. Berry & Co., Amherst, N.Y., 1980-81, mgr. telemktg. sales unit, 1981-83, mgr. telemktg. sales dept., 1984—; grad. asst. Dale Carnegie Inst., Buffalo, 1985. Mem. Nat. Assn. Female Execs. Home: 129 Beale Ave Cheektowaga NY 14225 Office: LM Berry Co Creekside Ctr 2825 Niagara Falls Blvd N Tonawanda NY 14120

VAN GILDER, BARBARA JANE DIXON, interior designer, consultant; b. South Bend, Ind., Dec. 6, 1933; d. Vincent Alan and Wanda Anita (Rapell) Dixon Van Gilder; student Mich. State U., 1951-55; postgrad. St. Mary's Coll., 1956-57, N.Y. Sch. Design, 1956-58; m. Erwin Dalton VanGilder, May 25, 1959; children: Eric Dalton, Marc David. Factory color cons. Smith-Alsop Paint Co., Terre Haute, Ind., 1955-56; archtl. design cons., Mishawaka, Ind., 1956-58; residential-comml. designer, South Bend, Chgo., 1958-63; designer industrialized housing industry, Ga., Fla., Ind., Mich., 1962—; design cons. Skyline Corp., Ind., Calif., Pa., 1962-66; v.p. design Treasure Chest Corp., Sturgis, Mich., 1969, also dir.; pres., dir. Sandpiper Art, Inc.; v.p. T.C.I. Ltd.; design cons. C.O. Smith Ind. Peachtree Housing, Moultrie, Ga., Nobility Homes, Ocala, Fla.; head merchandising and design Sandpiper Originals, clothing boutique, 1978-87; pres., owner mktg. design firm, 1987—; placement dir. specialized design mktg. STS Corp., South Bend, 1989—; currently pub. relations ofcl. Am. Mktg. Assn., adj. tchr. Lakeshore Sch. System. also coordinator trade show displays; nat. advt. rep. Studebaker-Packard Corp., Mercedes Benz, Clark Equipment, 1959-63; writer series on decorating for 2 Mich. newspapers, 1961-63; participant TV show Know Your Decorator, Calif. and Maine, 1962, 77. Officer, Shoreham Village (Mich.) Bd. Zoning, 1960-63. Named Woman of Year, Profl. Model's Club, 1952; recipient 1st pl. furniture design hardwoods Nat. Hardwoods Assn., 1956; 1st pl. Best in Show award, Louisville, Atlanta, 1964-65, 66, 69, 70-74, 76; others. Mem. Design Council Industrialized Housing (award 1974), Nat. Soc. Interior Designers, Mich. State U. Alumni Assn., Internat. Platform Assn., Internat. Biog. Assn. Contbg. editor Skyliner mag., 1962-66; permanent guest editor, contbr. Today's Home mag., 1974—. Home: 3630 S Lakeshore Dr Saint Joseph MI 49085 Office: PO Box 244 Stevensville MI 49127 also: PO Box 1100 Dunedin FL 33528

VAN GILDER, CARON HOWELL, art administrator; b. Manchester, N.H., Nov. 8, 1947; d. Winfred Dennis and Gloria (Caron) Howell; m. Lynn C. Van Gilder, Nov. 28, 1970 (div. 1989). BS, Ind. U., 1970, MA, 1975. Community art adv. Arts Extn. Service U. Mass., Amherst, Mass., 1974-77; exec. dir. Ashtabula (Ohio) Arts Ctr., 1976-84; instr. Lake Erie Coll., Painesville, Ohio, 1978-80; dir. Anderson Ctr. for the Arts, Binghamton, N.Y., 1984-86, Summer Music Festival, Binghamton, 1984-86; dir. Govs. Challenge for Excellence grant Montclair (N.J.) State Coll., 1986—; cons. Univ. Mass., Amherst, 1974-77, Ohio Arts Council, Columbus, 1978-82. Editor: (booklet) Arts Festivals Workkit, 1977. Bd. dirs. Friends of Sch. Fine and Performing Arts, Montclair, Opera Music Theatre Inst. Found., Arts Coun. of Greater Essex (N.J.) Area, TheatreFest. Recipient numerous orgn. grants. Mem. Met. Opera Guild, Met. Museum, Am. Council Fine Arts. Home: 828 Bloomfield Ave 7B Montclair NJ 07042

VAN GORDER, BARBARA ELLEN, editor; b. Washington, Aug. 18, 1958; d. James Lee and Ursula Virginia (Bruce) Beller. BA, U. Md., 1980, paralegal cert., 1982. Editor TV Digest, Inc., Washington, 1980-86; dir. communications Info. Industry Assn., Washington, 1986-89; exec. editor Am. Fin. Svcs., Washington, 1989—. Editor: (directory) Information Sources, 1988 (Best Ann. Assn. Directory 1988). Fund raiser Multiple

Sclerosis, Washington, 1987-89. Mem. Am. Soc. Assn. Execs. Office: Am Fin Svcs Assn 1101 14th St NW Washington DC 20005

VAN GROUW, MARGARET ELLEN, educator, counselor; b. Lansing, Mich., Mar. 15, 1935; d. Theodore Roosevelt and Margaret Annette (Shadduck) Foster; m. Steven Van Grouw, Aug. 5, 1961; children: Todd Allen, Richard Lee. BA, Mich. State U., 1957, MA, 1961. Tchr. elem. Holland (Mich.) Pub. Schs., 1957-60, 1974—, coord., tchr. gifted and talented, 1978-86; co-founder Citizen's Adv. Com. for Gifted and Talented, Holland, 1978—; mem. steering com. Strategic Planning Task Force, Holland, 1987-89. Contbr. articles to profl. jours. Chair Holland City Zoning Bd. Appeals; chair City Hist. Dist. Commn., Holland; pres. PTA, Holland, 1972-74. Mem. AAUW (pres., v.p., bd. dirs. Mich. div.), Mich. Edn. Assn., Mich. Assn. Educators Gifted, Talented and Creative, Mich. Assn. Academically Talented, Peninsula Writers, Holland Hist. Soc. (trustee 1985—), Pi Beta Phi, Phi Kappa Phi, Alpha Lambda Delta, Kappa Delta Pi. Office: Holland Pub Schs 633 Apple Ave Holland MI 49423

VAN HAGEY, CONNIE W., speech and language pathologist; b. Effingham, Ill., Sept. 2, 1946; d. Edward A. and Martha Winnogean (Cohea) Wittenberg; m. William Van Hagey, Sept. 3, 1966; children: Catherine E., Willia Colin. BS, U. Ill., Champaign, 1968, MA, 1970. Dir. speech and lang. pathology Good Shepherd Hosp., Barrington, Ill.; speech and lang. pathologist Condell Hosp., Libertyville, Ill., Lake Forest (Ill.) Hosp., Lake County Spl. Edn. Dist., Gurnee, Ill. Leader local club Cub Scout; mem. Barrington United Meth. Ch. Mem. Am. Speech/Language/Hearing Assn., Ill. Speech/Langauge/Hearing Assn., Dean's Club U. Ill., Phi Beta Kappa, Phi Beta Phi.

VAN HAMEL, MARTINE, dancer; b. Brussels, Nov. 16, 1945. Student, Nat. Ballet Sch. Can. Debut with Nat. Ballet Can., 1963; guest dancer Royal Swedish Ballet, Royal Winnipeg Ballet, Joffrey Ballet; with Am. Ballet Theatre, 1970—, soloist, 1971-73, prin. dancer, 1973—; created leading female roles in Estuary (Lynn Taylor-Corbett), Bach Partita (Twyla Tharp), Field, Chair, and Mountain (David Gordon), Push Comes to Shove (Twyla Tharp), Sphinx (Glen Tetley); choreographer Amnon V'Tamar, many others; founder New Amsterdam Ballet, N.Y.C. Winner Gold medal internat. competition, Varna, Bulgaria, 1966, Prix de Varna for best artistry all categories, 1966; recipient Cue mag. award, 1976, Dance mag. award, 1983. Office: care Am Ballet Theatre 890 Broadway New York NY 10003

VAN HECKE, MADELEINE LOUISE, psychology educator, consultant; b. Chgo., Nov. 19, 1943; d. George L. and Charlotte (Grondin) Van H.; m. Roy Martin Wulatin, Feb. 19, 1966 (div. June 1981); children: Kalyn Ann, David Jon; m. Gregory F. Risberg, Sept. 12, 1987. BA in Psychology, DePaul U., 1969, MA in Psychology, 1975, PhD in Psychology, 1978. Lic. psychologist, Ill. Assoc. prof. psychology North Cen. Coll., Naperville, Ill., 1979—; lectr. Elmhurst (Ill.) Coll., 1977-79; cons. in field. Contbr. articles to profl. jours. Coord. coat drive Mental Health Assn. Greater Chgo., 1988, 89. Mem. Am. Psychol. Assn., Midwest Psychol. Assn., Perry Network, AAUP, Ctr. for Partnership Studies. Home: 295 E Church St Elmhurst IL 60126 Office: North Cen Coll 30 N Brainard PO Box 3063 Naperville IL 60566-7063

VAN HEMERT, JUDY, manufacturing executive; b. Dallas, Feb. 8, 1947; d. Marion Everett and Thelma Rhea (Robinson) Van H.; children: Christopher Martin, Matthew Everett. BA, Vanderbilt U., Nashville, 1969; cert. lang. therapist Scottish Rite Hosp., Dallas, 1971. Cert. secondary tchr., Tex., lang. therapist. Lang. therapist Scottish Rite Hosp., Dallas, 1970-72, The Winston Sch., Dallas, 1975-82; mktg., purchasing S.V. Mfg., Richardson, Tex., 1982-84; pres. Bullet Electronics, Rockwall, Tex., 1984—; owner C-Power, Inc. Elder Presbyn. Ch. Named Miss Park Cities; finalist Arthur Young Entrepreneur of Yr., 1989. Mem. Assn. Women Entrepreneurs of Dallas, Nat. Assn. Women Bus. Owners, Small Bus. Owners, Tex. Bus. Coun., Rockwall C. of C. (exec. bd. dirs.), SBA (Sta. WNET mentor), Soroptimist Internat. Republican. Avocations: golf, tennis. Office: C-Power Products Inc 2007 Industrial Ln Rockwall TX 75087

VAN HERIK, JUDITH, psychology and religion educator; b. Rochester, Minn., Aug. 18, 1947; d. Martin and Jeanette (Wilchinski) Van H. AB, U. Chgo., 1968, MA in Teaching, 1971, MA in Divinity, 1973, PhD in Divinity, 1978. Instr. Pa. State U., University Park, 1977-78, asst. prof., 1978-84, assoc. prof., 1985—. Author: Freud on Femininity and Faith, 1982; contbr. articles to profl. jours. Mem. Am. Acad. Religion, Am. Psychol. Assn., Pa. Humanities Coun. (acad. mem. referee for jours., presses and founds. 1986—). Office: Pa State University 219 Sparks University Park PA 16802

VAN HORN, JOANNE MARIE, speech/language pathologist, consultant; b. Elizabeth, N.J., Aug. 13, 1953; d. Peter Salvatore and Anne Eve (Calavano) Caterinicchio; m. Leon Charles Van Horn Jr., Dec. 28, 1975; children: Leon Charles III, Allison Anne. BS, Purdue U., 1975; MS, Douglass Coll., 1979. Cert. speech/language pathologist. Speech therapist Woodbridge (N.J.) Twp. Bd. Edn., 1975-79, Speech Pathology Assocs., Neptune, N.J., 1979-80, Matawan (N.J.) Bd. Edn., 1983-85; pre-sch. head tchr. City of Cape May, N.J., 1986-88; speech therapist Sea Isle City (N.J.) Bd. Edn., 1987—; cons. head tchr. Pelican Place Child Devel. Ctr., Cape May, 1988-90; cons. Borough of Wildwood Crest (N.J.0 Recreation Dept., 1990. Co-author: (preschool packet) Chapter I Preschool The Good Apples and The Sunshine Kids, 1986. Bd. mem. Dennis Twp. Bd. Edn., Dennisville, N.J., 1989—; exec. bd. mem. Cape May (N.J.) County Sch. Bd. Assn., 1989-90. Recipient cert. of merit U.S. Dept. Edn., Washington, 1985. Mem. AAUW (corr. sec. 1988-89, pub. rels. chairperson 1989-90), N.J. Sch. Bds. Assn. Roman Catholic. Home: 10 Tressler Ln Cape May Court House NJ 08210

VAN HORN, LECIA JOSEPH, television newswriter; b. L.A., Jan. 19, 1963; d. McKinley Joe and Opal Geneva (Ivie) Joseph; m. Philip Dale Van Horn, Apr. 19, 1986; 1 child, Kari Christine. BA in Journalism, U. Southern Calif., 1984. News reporter KSCR Radio, L.A., 1983; consumer news researcher KCBS-TV, L.A., 1983, KABC-TV, L.A., 1983-84; newswriter Headline News, Atlanta, 1984-85; newswriter, field producer KNBC-TV, Burbank, Calif., 1985-86; newswriter, producer WYFF-TV, Greenville, S.C., 1986; free lance newswriter, assoc. producer WSB-TV, Atlanta, 1987-88; network newswriter Cable News Network, Atlanta, 1987—. Author: Thoughts and Inspirational Sayings, 1985; contbr. poetry and articles to newspapers. Mem. Nat. Assn. of Broadcast Employees and Technicians, Univ. So. Calif. Alumni, Zonta Club. Mem. Science of Mind. Office: Cable News Network 1 CNN Ctr Atlanta GA 30348

VAN HORN, REBECCA ANN, presentation specialist; b. Cleve., Feb. 10, 1957; d. Ross Edward and Virginia Mary (Connell) V. BA, Ohio State U., 1979. Dental hygienist Dr. Michael Zimmerman DDS, Columbus, Ohio, 1980-85, St. Mary of Nazareth Hosp. Dental Ctr., Chgo., 1985-87, Dr. Katherine Lauterbach DDS, Chgo., 1985-87; profl. programs area mgr. Oral-B Lab., Chgo.; pres., Ohio State U. Dental Hygiene Alumni Assn., Columbus, Ohio, 1982-83. Mem., Am., Dental Hygienists Assn., Ill. Chgo. Dental Hygienists Assn., NOW. Roman Catholic.

VAN HOUTEN, ELIZABETH ANN, corporate communications executive; b. Washington, Feb. 22, 1945; d. Raymond R. and Marian Edna (Hovemann) Van H. BA, Mary Washington Coll., 1966. Analyst U.S. Gov., Washington, 1966-68; dep. chief of publs. Found. for Coop. Housing, Washington, 1968-72; editor Nat. League of Savs. Inst., Washington, 1972-76; dir. pub. relations Fed. Nat. Mortgage Assn., Washington, 1976-83; v.p. communications & investor relations Student Loan Mktg. Assn., Washington, 1983—. Appointed by city coun. to Master Plan Task Force, Alexandria, 1987—; vice chmn. Dance Exch.; mem. campaign com. for Del Pepper, Alexandria, 1987; bd. dirs. Watergate of Alexandria (Va.), 1984-89, pres., 1988-89. Mem. Nat. Assn. Real Estate Editors (bd. dirs. 1970). Office: Student Loan Mktg Assn 1050 Thomas Jefferson St NW Washington DC 20007

VAN HOUTEN, OLIVIA LEE, legal mediator; b. Atlanta, June 6, 1955; d. Thomas Embry Jr. and Elizabeth Olive Van H. BA, Emory U., 1977, JD, 1989; MEd, Ga. State U., 1980. Adminstrv. asst. Scott Hudgens Cos., Atlanta, 1977-78; counselor, staff mem. Mt. Paran Counseling Ctr., Atlanta, 1979-80; tchr. English, soccer, swimming and tennis coach Westminster Schs., Atlanta, 1981-82; asst. dir., then assoc. dir. alumni rels. Emory U., Atlanta, 1982-85; account exec. Bus. Interiors div. House of Denmark, Atlanta, 1985-86; legal intern State Bar Ga., Atlanta, 1987, 88, law clk., 1988, 89; legal intern pvt. practice of Elizabeth M. Leonard, Atlanta, 1988, Legal Aid of Atlanta, Marietta, Ga., 1989; cert. mediator Justice Ctr. of Atlanta, 1989-90; assoc. Autrey & Parker, Marietta, Ga., 1990—. Home: 2230 Vistamont Rd NE Decatur GA 30033

VAN HOWE, ANNETTE EVELYN, real estate agent; b. Chgo., Feb. 16, 1921; d. Frank and Susan (Linstra) Van Howe; m. Edward L. Nezelek, Apr. 3, 1961. BA in History magna cum laude, Hofstra U., 1952; MA in Am. History, SUNY-Binghamton, 1966. Editorial asst. Salute Mag., N.Y.C., 1946-48; assoc. editor Med. Econs., Oradell, N.J., 1952-56; nat. mag. publicist Nat. Mental Health Assn., N.Y.C., 1956-60; exec. dir. Diabetes Assn. So. Calif., L.A., 1960-61; corp. sec., v.p., editor, pub. rels. dir. Edward L. Nezelek, Inc., Johnson City, N.Y., 1961-82; mgr. condominium, Fort Lauderdale, Fla., 1982-83; dir. Sky Harbour East Condo, 1983-88; substitute tchr. high schs., Binghamton, N.Y., 1961-63. Editor newsletters Mental Health Assn., 1965-68, Unitarian-Universalist Ch. Weekly Newsletter, 1967-71. Bd. dirs. Broome County Mental Health Assn., 1961-65, Fine Arts Soc., Roberson Ctr. for Arts and Scis., 1968-70, Found. Wilson Meml. Hosp., Johnson City, 1972-81, Found. SUNY, Binghamton, Ann White Theatre, 1988—; mem. Fla. Women's Alliance; v.p. Fla. Women's Polit. Caucus, 1989—; pres. Fla. Women's Consortium, 1989—; trustee Broome Community Coll., 1973-78; v.p. Broward County Commn. on Status of Women, 1982—; bd. dirs. Ft. Lauderdale Women's Coun. of Realtors, 1986-88, Broward Arts Guild, 1986; grad. Leadership Broward Class III, 1985, Leadership Am., 1988; trustee Unitarian-Universalist Ch. of Ft. Lauderdale, 1982-89. Mem. AAUW (legis. chair Fla. div. 1986-87), NAFE, Am. Med. Writers Assn., LWV (bd. dir. Broome County 1969-70), Alumni Assn. SUNY Binghamton (bd. dir. 1970-73), Am. Acad. Polit. and Social Sci., Fla. Women's Alliance, Am. Heritage Soc., Nature Conservancy, Nat. Hist. Soc., Ft. Lauderdale Women's Coun. Realtors (corr. sec.), Zonta (Internat. Women's Polit. Caucus), Alpha Theta Beta, Phi Alpha Theta, Phi Gamma Mu, Binghamton Garden Club, Binghamton Monday Afternoon Club, Acacia Garden Club (pres.), 110 Tower Club, Tower Forum Club (bd. dirs. 1989—), Downtown Coun. Club, Ft. Lauderdale Woman's Club. Home: 2100 S Ocean Dr Fort Lauderdale FL 33316 Office: 1554 Cordova Rd Fort Lauderdale FL 33316

VANIMAN, JEAN A., manufacturing executive; b. Huntsville, Ala., Dec. 3, 1960; d. Jerold L. and Janis (Taylor) V. BSChemE, U. Ala., Tuscaloosa, 1984; MBA, Utah State U., 1989. Program mgr. advanced launch vehicle ops. Morton Thiokol, Inc., Brigham City, Utah, mgr. trident program R & D; rsch. analyst dept. chem. engring. U. Ala.; program mgr. space shuttle program Thiokol Corp., Huntsville, 1989—; dir. Thiokol Recreation Coun., 1987-89. Vol. counselor Huntsville Crisis Line. Mem. NAFE, Am. Inst. Chem. Engrs., Capstone Engring. Soc. (bd. dirs.), Am. Mgmt. Assn., Soc. Women Engrs., Tau Beta Pi Alumni Assn., Chi Omega Alumni Assn. Home: 319 Spring Valley Ct Huntsville AL 35802 Office: Thiokol Corp Progress Ctr Bldg No 4 6767 Madison Pike NW Huntsville AL 35806

VAN KIRK, CHERYL ANN, legal assistant; b. Dearborn, Mich., July 7, 1964; d. Donald John and Wyva Arlis (Moore) Van K. BS, U. Mich., Dearborn, 1989; AA, Henry Ford Community Coll., 1985. Legal asst. Feikens, Foster, VanderMale and DeNardis, Detroit, 1985-88, Hayduk, Dawson, Andrews and Hypner, Detroit, 1988-89, Plunkett and Cooney, Detroit, 1988-89, Vandeveer, Garzia, Detroit, 1989-90; pres., owner Freelance Paralegals, Dearborn, 1990—; paralegal coord. , paralegal/legal asst. program Utica Adult Edn. Mem. NAFE, State Bar Mich. (affiliate), Nat. Assn. Legal Assts., Legal Assts. Assn. Mich. (newsbrief editor), Good Bears of World (life). Office: 23917 Rockford St Dearborn MI 48124

VANKIRK, MARSHA LAUTERBACH, legal professional; b. Worchester, Mass., Nov. 23, 1949; d. Robert Emil and Jane (Stonerod) Lauterbach; m. Thomas Lee VanKirk, Jan. 5, 1980 (div. 1983). BS in Sociology, U. Pitts., 1975. Stock trader Pitts. Nat. Bank, 1970-73; research assoc. U. Pitts., 1974; sr. legal asst. Buchanan Ingersoll, P.C., Pitts., 1975—. Contbr. to profl. jour. Mem. citizens review com. United Way Allegheny County, 1987—; adv. bd. Renaissance Too, 1986—; bd. dirs. United Mental Health, Inc., 1986—. Mem. Pitts. Paralegal Assn. (v.p. 1977-80). Democrat. Presbyterian. Office: Buchanan Ingersoll PC 600 Grant St 57th floor Pittsburgh PA 15219

VANLEEUWEN, LIZ SUSAN (ELIZABETH VANLEEUWEN), farmer, state legislator; b. Lakeview, Oreg., Nov. 5, 1925; d. Charles Arthur and Mary Delphia (Hartzog) Nelson; B.S., Oreg. State U., 1947; m. George VanLeeuwen, June 15, 1947; children—Charles, Mary, James, Timothy. Secondary sch. and adult tchr., 1947-70; news reporter, feature writer The Times, Brownsville, Oreg., 1949—; co-mgr. VanLeeuwen Farm, Halsey, Oreg.; mem. Oreg. Ho. of Reps., 1981—; weekly radio commentator, 1973-81. Mem. E.R. Jackman Found., PTA, sch. adv. com.; precinct committeewoman; founder Linn County Ct.-Apptd. Spl. Advs. Recipient Outstanding Service award Oreg. Farm Bur., 1975, Oreg. Farm Family of Yr. award, 1983; Chevron Agrl. Spokesman of Yr. award, 1975. Mem. Oreg. Women for Agr. (pres.), Oreg. Women for Timber, Linn-Benton Women for Agr. (pres.), Linn County Farm Bur., Am. League (aux.), Linn County Econ. Devel. Com., Grange, Am. Agri-Women. Republican. Office: Capitol Bldg H386 Salem OR 97310

VAN LEEUWEN, PATRICIA ANN SZCZEPANIK, toxicologist; b. Chgo., May 27, 1939; d. Marion Edward and Ruth Hazel (Brophy) Szczepanik; m. G. Dale Van Leeuwen, May 27, 1978. BS in Chemistry, U. Ill., Urbana, 1961; MPH, U. Ill., Chgo., 1987. Research asst., research assoc. BIM div. Argonne (Ill.) Nat. Lab., 1961-76, biochemist, 1976-82; biochemist RER div. Argonne Nat. Lab., 1980-82; research assoc. U. Ill. Coll. Pharmacy, Chgo., 1982-87; research specialist U. Ill. Sch. Pub. Health, Chgo., 1987—; research assoc., asst. prof. Dept. Medicine U. Chgo., 1976-80. Contbr. 48 articles to sci. jours. Co-recipient Distinguished Performance award U. Chgo., 1978. Mem. Am. Assn. Study Liver Disease, Am. Soc. Mass Spectometry, Nat. Environ. Health Assn., Air Pollution Control Assn., Am. Chem. Soc., Am. Pub. Health Assn., Phi Kappa Phi. Episcopalian. Office: US EPA Region V Superfund Mgmt Program Tech Support Unit 230 S Dearborn Chicago IL 60604

VAN LENGEN, KAREN, architect, educator; b. Syracuse, N.Y., Apr. 9, 1951; d. Robert Warner and Carol P. (Freiberger) Van L. BA cum laude, Vassar Coll., 1973; MArch, Columbia U., 1976. Registered architect, N.Y., Fla. Assoc. I.M. Pei & Ptnrs., N.Y.C., 1976-82; ptnr. Heisel/Van Lengen Architects, N.Y.C., 1986-88, Karen Van Lengen Architects, N.Y.C., 1988—; asst. adj. prof. Columbia U., N.Y.C. 1986—. Fulbright fellow, Rome, 1982-83, AAUW fellow, 1976; winner 1st prize Am. Meml. Libr. competition, Berlin, 1989. Mem. AIA, Nat. Council Archtl. Registration Bd. Democrat. Office: 424 Broome St New York NY 10013

VAN LEUVEN, HOLLY GOODHUE, social scientist, consultant, researcher; b. Salem, Mass., Dec. 2, 1935; d. Nathaniel William and Elizabeth VanClowes (Crowley) Goodhue; m. John Jamison Porter, II, Oct. 16, 1954 (div. 1974); children: Donald J. II, Nathaniel G., Alison A. Dionne, Erin E.; m. Robert Joseph VanLeuven, Dec. 31, 1976. BA with honors, Western Mich. U., 1971, MA with honors, 1975. Exec. dir. Community Confrontation and Communication Assocs., Grand Rapids, Mich., 1969-73; coordinator tng., research Nat. Ctr. for Dispute Settlement, Washington, 1973; tng. dir. Forest View Psychiat. Hosp., Grand Rapids, 1974; case coordinator Libner, Van Leuven, & Kortering, P.C., Muskegon, Mich., 1982-87; pres. Genesis Group, Muskegon, Mich., Phoenix, 1987—; v.p. devel. Motion Pictures Makers, Grand Rapids, Mich., 1990—; talk show host Sta. WTRU-TV, Muskegon, 1985; cons. U.S. Dept. Justice, Washington, 1969-73, No. Ireland Dept. Community Relations, Belfast, 1971; jury selection cons. various law firms in Midwest, 1975—. Contbr. articles to profl. jours. Bd. dirs. Planned Parenthood Western Mich., Grand Rapids, 1964-72, Jr. League Grand Rapids, 1955—, YFCA, Muskegon, 1981-83, Girl Scouts U.S., 1988—; chmn. Student Showcase, Inc., Muskegon, 1983—; candidate for Mich. State Rep. 97th Dist., Muskegon, 1978; pres. Planned Parenthood Assn., Muskegon, 1980. Mem. Am. Sociol. Assn., Am. Soc. Trial Cons. Clubs: Muskegon Country, Century; Women's City (Grand Rapids). Lodges: Zonta, Compass. Home: 966 Mona Brook Rd Muskegon MI 49441 Office: Motion Pictures Makers Inc 6660 Old 28th St Grand Rapids MI 49506

VAN LINGEN, GABRIELE, psychologist, educational administrator; b. Potsdam, Germany, June 1, 1944; came to U.S., 1954; d. Job van Lingen and Gisela Marie (Schwanz) Gurski; m. Norman G. Darling, Aug. 8, 1988. AB cum laude, Cornell U., 1966; MA, U. Calif., 1973, PhD, 1982. Cert. sch. adminstr., sch. psychologist, Va. Tchr., social worker, researcher, other positions Calif. Dept. Edn., Calif., 1962-74; edn. program specialist Calif. Regional Resource Ctr., L.A., 1974-78; project coord., clin. psychologist IDEA, GmbH, Berlin, 1978-81; mgr. cen. nervous section Dr. Thiemann GmbH, Luenen, Fed. Republic Germany, 1982-83; guidance counselor U.S. Dept. Def. Dependent's Schs., Stuttgart, Fed. Republic Germany, 1983-84; cons. Western Europe, 1984-86; sch. psychologist Round Valley Unified Sch. Dist., Covelo, Calif., 1986-87; therapist Grafton Sch., Berryville, Va., 1988; sch. psychologist Loudoun County Pub. Schs., Leesburg, Va., 1988-89; supr. rsch. Prince William County Pub. Schs., Manassas, Va., 1989—; workshop presenter, organizer, trainer U.S. Office Edn., 1966-67. Grantee Cornell U., 1962-66. Mem. Nat. Assn. Sch. Psychologists. Democrat. Lutheran. Office: Prince William County Schs PO Box 389 Manassas VA 22110

VAN LOAN, MARY KIRKWOOD, financial counseling officer, educator, author; b. Mitchell, S.D., Dec. 18, 1934; d. Robert Campbell and Virginia Viola (Bates) Kirkwood; m. Richard Rodman Van Loan, July 11, 1959 (div. 1977); children—Richard Rodman, Lynn Virginia Van Loan Brainerd, Robert Edward; m. John William Twiddy, Aug. 23, 1980 (div. 1989); stepchildren—John Peter, Susan Twiddy Slink. B.A. in English, Mt. Holyoke Coll., 1956; postgrad. in Secondary Edn., Boston U., 1957-58. Cert. fin. planner, tax preparer. English tchr. Castilleja Sch. for Girls, Palo Alto, Calif., 1956-57, Andrew Warde High Sch., Fairfield, Conn., 1958-60; substitute tchr. Town of Greenwich, Conn., 1974-79; co-owner, developer Assoc. Budget Cons., Greenwich, 1979-80; personal fin. counseling officer Union Trust Co., Greenwich, 1980-89; instr. fin. planning adult edn., Greenwich, 1983—. Author various articles. Officer, Young Republicans, Greenwich, 1961-62; mem. Greenwich council Boy Scouts Am., 1968—, exec. bd., 1985—, asst. treas. 1986—, Explorer post advisor banking and fin., 1986-87. Recipient awards Boy Scouts Am., 1974, Greenwich YWCA BRAVO award, 1989. Mem. Internat. Assn. Fin. Planning (chmn. So. Conn. Chpt. 1986-87, pres. 1985-86, sr. adv. bd. 1987—), Inst. Cert. Fin. Planners (bd. dirs. Westchester, Rockland, Fairfield socs. 1985—, sec. 1987-88, treas. 1988—, pres. elect 1989—), Nat. Assn. Bank Women, Lower Fairfield County Estate Planning Council, AAUW, Mt. Holyoke Fairfield Villages Alumnae Assn., Nat. Assn. Female Execs. Mormon. Avocations: handcrafts; sports; travel. Home: Old Forge Rd Greenwich CT 06830 Office: Union Trust Co Pvt Banking Group One Centre St Darien CT 06820

VAN METER, LINDA LIESELOTTE, psychologist, consultant; b. N.Y.C., Feb. 27, 1950; d. William Dirk and Gretel Lieselotte (Dietrich) Groon; m. William Isaac Van Meter, May 22, 1976; children: Matthew William, Alisa Lieselotte. BA in Psychology, East Stroudsburg State Cll., 1972; MA in Psychology, Marywood Coll., 1985. Intern Pocono Hosp., East Stroudsburg, Pa., 1971-72; caseworker, therapist Mental Health/Mental Retardation of Carbon, Monroe and Pike Counties, Stroudsburg, Pa., 1972-76; psychologist Pocono Neuropsychiat. Ctr., East Stroudsburg, Pa., 1976-87; psychologist, clin. suprs. Pocono Neuropsychiat. Ctr., East Stroudsburg, 1987-88; psychologist, cons. Coll. Hill Med. Ctr., East Stroudsburg, 1986—; cons. Winco Health Care and Cons., Inc., East Stroudsburg, 1986—. Mem. Biofeedback Soc. Am., Pa. Psychol. Assn., Pa. Soc. Behavioral Medicine and Biofeedback, Psi Chi. Lutheran. Club: Pocono Environ. (East Stroudsburg). Home: 80 Clermont Ave Stroudsburg PA 18360 Office: College Hill Med Ctr 329 E Brown St East Stroudsburg PA 18301

VANN, LORA JANE, educator; b. Chgo.; d. Amos Alva and Mary Prudie (Ellery) V. BA, Marian Coll., Indpls., 1958; MA, Ball State U., 1963, EdD, 1985. Cert. life tchr., reading specialist, supr., Ind. Elem. tchr., asst. prin. Indpls. Pub. Schs., 1959-71; instr. dept. edn. William Woods Coll., Fulton, Mo., 1972-73; tchr. reading, supr. Washington Twp. Schs., Indpls., 1973—; teaching fellow Ball State U., Muncie, Ind., 1980-81; cons. Advanced Tech., Inc., Indpls., 1987; vis. cons. North Cen. Assn., Bloomington, Ind., 1988. Author: Self-Concept and Parochial School Children, 1985, Sigma's Outstanding Women of the 20th Century, 3 vols., 1986, 88; editor newsletters Reading Timely Topics, 1974-80, AS News, 1985—. Pres. St. Rita Bd. Edn., Indpls., 1987-89; founder Afro-Am. Children's Theatre, 1987. Cath. Interracial Coun. scholar, 1954; NDEA grantee, 1964, 65, Fulbright grantee, Birmingham, Eng., 1967-68, Ball State U. grantee, 1980-81. Mem. Internat. Reading Assn., Nat. Coun. Negro Women (charter, sec. Cen. Ind. sect. 1981-84), Washington Twp. Edn. Assn. (chmn. polit. action com. 1987-88, co-chmn. 1988-89), AAUW, Fulbright Assn., Kappa Delta Pi, Phi Delta Kappa, Sigma Gamma Rho (treas. cen. region 1981-86, chpt. pres. 1986—). Roman Catholic. Home: 2615 Hillside Ave Indianapolis IN 46218 Office: Washington Twp Schs 3801 E 79th St Indianapolis IN 46240

VANN, ROBIN IRIS, makeup artist; b. N.Y.C., Aug. 9, 1952; d. Sydney and Seena (Wagman) Vann; m. Amos Nir, Apr. 3, 1976 (div. 1977). AA, George Washington U., 1979; postgrad. Prodn. makeup/hair artist Cinema Makeup Madness, Boca Raton, Fla., 1984—. Mem. Green Peace, 1989—, Doris Day Animal League, Washington, 1989—, ASPCA, Washington, 1990; mem. NABET Local 15, Miami, Fla, N.Y.C., 1985-88. Mem. Women of the Motion Picture Industry. Roman Catholic. Home and office: Cinema Makeup Madness 464 Lakeside Blvd Boca Raton FL 33434

VAN NAME, JUDITH ANN, consumer economist, educator; b. Cin., July 14, 1945; d. Glen Albert and Lena Anna (Woerner) Beyring; B.S., Miami U., Oxford, Ohio, 1967; M.S., Ohio State U., 1968. Instr. home econs. U. Del., Newark, 1968-71, asst. prof., 1971-77, assoc. prof. Coll. Human Resources, 1977—, chmn. textiles, design and consumer econs., 1978-83; dir. Computer Input Services, Inc. Pres., White Haven Poconos Homeowners Assn., 1975-76, dir., 1976-79. HEW grantee, 1974-76, Dept. Health, Human Services grantee, 86-88. Mem. Am. Home Econs. Assn., Am. Assn. Univ. Profs., Am. Council Consumer Interests, Assn. for Fin. Counseling and Planning Edn., Phi Upsilon Omicron. Author: (with James D. Culley and Barbara H. Settles) Understanding and Measuring the Cost of Foster Family Care, 1975; contbr. articles and revs. to profl. jours. Home: 125 Dallam Rd Newark DE 19711 Office: Textiles Design and Consumer Econs U Del Newark DE 19716

VAN NESS, PATRICIA CATHELINE, composer, violoinst; b. Seattle, June 25, 1951; d. C. Charles and Marjorie Mae (Dexter) Van N.; m. Wendell James Ketcham, Dec. 16, 1972 (div. 1977)); m. Adam Sherman, June 26, 1983. Student, Wheaton Coll., 1969-70; degree in conservatory of music, Gordon Coll., 1972. Founding mem. Pvt. Lightning, 1975-82. Composer: Ballet Score for Beth Soll, 1985, 87, Ballet Score for Monica Levy, 1988, Ballet Score for Boston Ballet, 1988, 90; various dance scores, 1985, 87, 88; recording violoinst A&M Records, Private Lightning, 1980, founding mem. 1975-82. Grant New England Biolabs Found., 1989, Mass. Arts Lottery Coun., 1988. Mem. Am. Women Composers.

VANNIER, THERESA MARIE, electronic buyer; b. Denver, Mar. 1, 1955; d. Joseph George and Margaret Alta (Jones) Matzura; m. Michael Thomas Vannier, Oct. 4, 1980; children: Clarissa Ruth, Thomas Joseph. BS in Law Enforcement, Jacksonville State U., 1977. With inventory control & mgmt. Paints, Crafts & Hobbies, Jacksonville, Ala., 1976-78; office mgr. New World Coll. Bus., Anniston, Ala., 1978; inventory coord. Harris/Lanier, Atlanta, 1987; planner purchasing Harris/Lanier, 1987—; buyer Panasonic, 1990, NCR, 1990. Chmn. Spl. Olympics, Myrtle Beach, S.C., 1986; lectr. Catholic Ch., Myrtle Beach, 1985-86. Capt. USAF, 1979-86, USAFR. Mem. Nat. Assn. Purchasing Mgrs., Res. Officers Assn., County Grade Officer's Coun. (recorder, sec. 1979-80, v.p. 1986), Toastmasters (edn. v.p. Blytheville, S.C. 1980). Republican. Roman Catholic. Home: 406 Burgess Point Peachtree City GA 30269

VAN NORMAN, PEGGY SHINN, social worker, healthcare administrator; b. Seattle, Dec. 31, 1951; d. Albert William and Betty Jane (Richardson) Shinn; m. Timothy S. Van Norman, Aug. 2, 1980; children: Megan Ann,

Michael Frederick. BS in Social Work, Calif State U., Sacramento, 1974. Crisis interventionist Suicide Prevention Svc., Sacramento, Calif., 1971-74; pre-parole counselor Calif. State Med. Facility, Vacaville, Calif., 1973-74; mental health specialist Warm Hands Co., Sacramento, 1974; site mgr. Sr. Now Generation, Tucson, 1974-78; pers. cons. Republic Personnel, Tucson, 1978-79; habilitation specialist Rehab. & Work Adjustment Ctr., Tucson, 1979-82; social worker Flower Square Healthcare, Tucson, 1984-90, asst. adminstr., 1990—. Active Friends of Vista. Recipient Job Tng. Partnership Act grant Pima County, Tucson, 1984. Mem. Nat. Assn. of Social Workers, Am. Soc. on Aging. Democrat. Office: Flower Square Healthcare 2502 N Dodge Blvd Tucson AZ 85716

VAN NORTWICK, BARBARA LOUISE, administrator, librarian; b. Johnson City, N.Y., Jan. 3, 1940; d. Joseph John and Mary Louise (Hamzik) Goodwin; B.A., Harpur Coll., 1961; M.L.S., State U. N.Y. at Albany, 1976; D.A. Info./Library Adminstrn. (U.S. Govt. Title II B fellow in library adminstrn.), Simmons Coll., Boston, 1986; m. David Harry Van Nortwick, Nov. 17, 1962; children: Kimberly Lynn, Craig Michael. Coordinator ednl. facilities Maine-Endwell High Sch., Endwell, N.Y., 1961-64; tchr. English, Guilderland High Sch. (N.Y.), 1965-66; audiovisual librarian So. Colonie (N.Y.) High Sch., 1974-76; head librarian Westfield (Mass.) High Sch., 1976-78, Columbia High Sch., East Greenbush, N.Y., 1978-79; library dir. N.Y. State Nurses Assn., 1979-84; dir. Com. Aging and Subcom. libraries N.Y. State Senate, 1983-84, dir. Select Com. Interstate Coop., 1985-89; assoc. prof. govt. documents and social scis. Skidmore Coll., Saratoga Springs, N.Y., 1989—; del. Mass. Gov.'s Conf. Libraries and Info. Services, 1978-79; cons. HEW grant on self-directed continuing edn. for nurses; prof. Sch. Library and Info. Sci., SUNY-Albany, 1983-84. Mem. ALA, N.Y. Library Assn., Med. Library Assn. Methodist. Home: Rural Delivery 1 Box 292 Nassau NY 12123 Office: Lucy Scribner Library Skidmore Coll Saratoga Springs NY 12866

VAN NOSTRAND, CATHARINE MARIE HERR, human resource development company executive; b. Dubuque, Iowa, June 17, 1937; d. King George and Julia Marie (Hansen) Herr; m. David Michael Van Nostrand, July 16, 1960; children: Laura Susan Caviani, Catharine Louise, Maren Thyra. Student, Grinnell (Iowa) Coll., 1955-57; BA in Music Edn., U. Iowa, 1959; MA in Human Devel., St. Mary's Coll. of Minn., Winona, 1989. Music specialist Bound Brook, N.J. and Brookline, Mass., 1959-62; coord. music and worship First United Meth. Ch., St. Cloud, Minn., 1970-75; radio interviewer Minn. Pub. Radio and WJON Radio, Collegeville, St. Cloud, Minn., 1976-77; founder, prin. cons. Catharine Van Nostrand & Assocs., St. Cloud, 1975—; guest lectr. area colls. and univs., regional, statewide, nat. acad. symposia, 1975—; tng. and devel. cons. numerous bus., health and ednl. orgns., 1975—; keynote speaker and workshop facilitator confs., convs., 1975—; designer custom-tailored workshops, 1975—; presenter, panelist, discussant profl. devel. confs., 1980—. Contbr. articles to profl. jours. capt. profl. div. fundraising for area family YMCA, St. Cloud, 1975; founding bd. mem. St. Cloud Civic Orch. Mem. AAUW, Forum Exec. Women, Nat. Speakers Assn., Minn. Speakers Assn., St. Cloud Area Tng. and Devel. Group, St. Cloud Area C. of C. Democrat. Methodist. Home: 36854 Winnebago Rd Saint Cloud MN 56303 Office: 14 N 7th Ave Ste 034 Saint Cloud MN 56303

VAN NOY, CHRISTINE ANN, executive assistant; b. Oakland, CA, Mar. 25, 1948; d. Julio Ceaser and Bernice Thelma (Rose) Lucchesi; m. David Craik Van Noy, July 10, 1971; children: James Allan, Joseph Julio. Student, U. Calif., Berkeley, 1971-73. Exec. sec. Kaiser Permanente Med. Care Program, Oakland, 1966-76; owner Secret Closet Boutique, Moraga, Calif., 1972-82; owner, operator The Wordshop, Moraga, 1976-86; owner, cons. Van Noy & Assocs., Moraga, 1979—; exec. sec. to sr. v.p., regional mgr. Kaiser Permanente Med. Care Program, 1986-88, asst. to vice chmn., 1988—; instr. U. Calif., Santa Cruz, 1983-84, Diablo Valley Coll., Concord, Calif., 1984; cons. Nat. Alliance Homebased Businesswomen, San Francisco, 1981-84. Author: Homebased Business Guide, 1982, (with others) Women Working Home, 1982. Mem. bd. Moraga Sch. Dist., 1983-84, Calif. Federated Jr. Women's Clubs, 1972-77; bd. dirs. Orinda/Moraga Recreational Swimming Assn., 1984-85, St. Mark's United Methodist Ch., Moraga, 1983-84; pres. bd. Protect Our Nation's Youth Baseball Assn., 1987-90. Mem. Women Health Care Execs. Democrat. Roman Catholic. Home: 181 Paseo Del Rio Moraga CA 94556 Office: Kaiser Permanente Med Program 1 Kaiser Pla Oakland CA 94612

VAN NOY, ELENE MEURY, math and computer supervisor; b. Buffalo, Apr. 30, 1943; d. Herman J. Meury and Marian (McLean) Lane; children: Richard, Jennifer, Gretchen. BA cum laude, Beaver Coll., 1965; MA, Trenton State Coll., 1973; postgrad., Rutgers U., 1975-82. Cert. secondary math., edn. supervision, N.J. Math tchr. Hamilton Twp. Schs., Trenton, N.J., 1965-66, Ewing Twp. Schs., Trenton, 1975-77; adj. prof. Trenton (N.J.) State Coll., 1977-79; math tchr. Hopewell Valley Regional Schs., Pennington, N.J., 1979-80; math and computer supr. Hopewell Valley Regional Schs., Pennington, 1980—; trustee, vice-chmn. Mercer County Community Coll., Trenton, 1980—. Mem. Assn. Math. Tchrs. N.J., Nat. Coun. Tchrs. Math., N.J. Prins. and Suprs. Assn., AAUW (Trenton br. fellowship). Republican. Presbyterian. Office: Hopewell Valley Regional Sch Dist Pennington NJ 08534

VAN NUFFEL, JEANNETTE THERESE W., educator; b. Abington, Pa., Sept. 27, 1932; d. Earl Harvey and Jeannette Justine (Heppe) Woodroffe; m. William J. Scott (div. Sept. 1979); children: Jeannette S. Ohmae, William, James Scott; m. Vincent Louis van Nuffel, 1979. BA with high honors, Trenton State Coll., 1966, MA with high honors, 1969. Cert. in elem. edn. and secondary social studies. Tchr. Council Rock Sch. Dist., Newtown, Pa., 1965—; NEH seminar participant U. Puget Sound, Tacoma, 1985. Mem. NEA, Pa. Edn. Assn., Council Rock Edn. Assn., Pa. Assn. Gifted Educators, AAUW (officer Doylestown, Pa. 1986—). Republican. Office: 116 Richboro Rd Newtown PA 18940

VAN OOSBREE, CHARLYNE SELMA NELSON, librarian; b. Alta, Iowa, Jan. 19, 1930; d. John Albin and Albertina (Rydstrom) Nelson; m. Anton Van Oosbree, Dec. 30, 1950 (dec. 1965); children: Tina Van Oosbree Taylor, Jon, David. BS in English, Iowa State U., 1970; MLS, U. Mo., 1973. Hosp. librarian Army Hosp., Ft. Leonard Wood, Mo., 1970-72; head sch. libr. Tng. Sch. for Boys, Boonville, Mo., 1973-76; head br. library Mid-Continent Pub. Libr., Independence, Mo., 1976-82; head base libr. Whiteman AFB, Mo., 1982-86; head base libr. Florennes AFB, Belgium, 1986-87; head base libr. Scott AFB. Ill., 1987—; mem. adv. coun. U. Mo. Sch. Libr. and Info. Sci., Columbia, 1978-80, sec., 1978-79; coord. Writers' Group, Platte Woods, Mo., 1980-82. Contbr. articles to libr. publ. and newspapers, poems in Poetry Anthologies. Bd. mem. Tri-County Mental Health Assn., Kansas City, Mo., 1980-82, Park Hill Sch. Adv. Coun., Kansas City, 1977-78, Synergy House, Parkville, Mo., 1976-77; mem. youth adv. coun. Whiteman AFB; counselor Widowed Persons Svc., Kansas City, 1977-78. Named SAC Libr. of Yr., 1984; Mo. State Libr. scholar, 1972. Mem. ALA, Fed. Librs. Round Table, Humane Soc. U.S., St. Louis Poetry Ctr., Beta Phi Mu. Home: 4416 S Park Dr Belleville IL 62223 Office: USAF Base Libr Scott AFB IL 62225

VAN ORMAN, JEANNE, planning consultant; b. N.Y.C., Apr. 9, 1939; d. Wayne and Jean (O'Gara) Van O.; m. Robert F. Brown, May 25, 1963 (div. 1975); children: Frank Van Orman Brown, Virginia Corbin Brown. BA, Smith Coll., 1961; M in City Planning, Harvard U., 1974. Land use planner Mass. Exec. Office of Communities and Devel., Boston, 1979-83, mgr. planning grants program, 1984-85, dir. strategic planning program, 1985-87; prin. Van Orman & Assocs., Easton, Mass., 1987—. Contbr. articles to profl. jours. Mem. Easton Charter Commn., 1971-72, mem. fin. com., 1982-83, libr. com., 1984-86, selectman, 1973-75; mem. Housing Partnership, 1988—; bd. overseers Moses Brown Sch., Providence, R.I. Mass. Housing Partnership grantee, 1987, NEA grantee, 1981; recipient Disting. Svc. award, Jaycees, 1973. Mem. Am. Planning Assn. (exec. bd. Mass. sect.), Westport (Mass.) Yacht Club. Mem. Soc. of Friends. Home: 479 Bay Rd South Easton MA 02375 Office: 50 Oliver St North Easton MA 02356

VAN PELT, FRANCES EVELYN, management consultant; b. Oregon, Ill., Aug. 25, 1937; d. Henry Benjamin and Bessie May (Himes) Ulferts; m. R. Richard Van Pelt, Oct. 28, 1953; children: R. Richard Jr., Robin F. Van Pelt Dobbs, Raymond Scott, Ronda Jean. Student, Waubonsee Coll., Sugar Grove, Ill., 1971-75. Adminstrv. asst. Sears, Roebuck & Co., Aurora, Ill., 1960-73; owner, mgr., pres. Outdoor World, Inc., Aurora, 1973-87; mgmt. cons. Spader Mgmt. Groups, Inc., Sioux Falls, S.D., 1988—; bd. dirs. RV Consumer Care Commn., Fairfax, Va., 1985-88. Contbr. articles to profl. jours. Bd. dirs. Breaking Free, Aurora, 1988—; cellist Fox Valley Symphony, Aurora, 1961-81. Mem. Aurora C. of C. Recrational Vehicle Dealers Assn. (bd. dirs. 1978-79, exec. bd. 1980-82, pres. 1983, chmn. bd. dirs. 1984), Ill. RV Dealers Assn. (pres., bd. dirs. 1978-79, exec. bd. 1980-82, pres. 1983, chmn. bd. dirs. 1984). Republican. Roman Catholic. Home: 1050 N Farnsworth #107 Aurora IL 60505 Office: PO Box M Sioux Falls SD 57101

VAN PELT, JANET RUTH, insurance executive; b. Baltimore, Md., Jan. 28, 1948; d. John Francis and Helen Janet V. BA, Fla. State U., 1969, MA, 1972. Instr. Wayne State U., Detroit, Mich., 1971-72; promotion asst. Actors Theatre of Louisville, Ky., 1972-73; lecturer Towson State U., Towson, Md., 1973-75; workers compensation Harry T. Campbell Sons' Co., Towson, 1973-74; claims representative Atlantic Mutual Companies, Hunt Vly., Md., 1974-78; claims supr. Atlantic Mutual Co., N.Y., 1978-79; home office claims examiner Atlantic Mutual Co., N.Y., 1979-88; supr. home office excess claims Am. Home Assurance Co., East Orange, N.J., 1988, sr. supr. home office excess claims, 1989-90; claims mgr. GRE Am., Princeton, N.J., 1990—. Mem. Assn. of Research and Enlightment, Holistic Health Assn. Democratic. Episcopalian. Office: GRE America 4390 US Rte 1 Princeton NJ 08540

VAN RAALTE, POLLY ANN, educator; b. N.Y.C., Sept. 22, 1951; d. Byron Emmanuel and Enid (Godnick) Van R.; student U. London, 1972; BA, Beaver Coll., 1973; MS in Edn., U. Pa., 1974, postgrad., 1975—, West Chester State Coll., 1975-77; student, Bank St. Coll.. Title I reading tchr. Oakview Sch., West Deptford Twp. Sch. Dist., Woodbury, N.J., 1974-75, Title I reading supr., summer 1975; lang. arts coord. Main Line Day Sch., Mitchell Sch., Haverford, Pa., 1975-76; reading supr. Salvation Army, Phila., summer 1976; reading Huntingdon Jr. High Sch., Abington (Pa.) Sch. Dist., 1976-78; reading specialist No. 2 Sch., Lawrence Pub. Sch., Inwood, N.Y., 1978-87, high sch. reading specialist, Cedarhurst, N.Y., 1988—, Lawrence (N.Y.) High Sch., 1988—; reading specialist Hewlett Elem. Sch., Hewlett-Woodmere Pub. Sch., Hewlett, N.Y., 1987-88; instr. reading and spl. edn. dept. Adelphi U., 1979—; cons. to sch. dists.; advisor Am. Biog. Inst., Inc.; speaker at reading convs. Coord., Five Towns Young Voter Registration, Hewlett, N.Y., summer, 1971; chmn. class fund Beaver Coll., also mem. internat. rels. com. U. Pa. scholar, 1977-78; mem. assoc. div. Jewish Guild for Blind. Mem. Internat. Reading Assn., Wis. Reading Assn., Nat. Council Tchrs. English, Nassau Reading Coun., N.Y. Reading Assn., Coun. Exceptional Children, Coun. for a Beautiful Israel, Nat. Assn. Gifted Children, Am. Assn. of the Gifted, Nat./State Leadership Tng. Inst. on the Gifted and Talented, Children's Lit. Assembly, N.Y. State English Coun., Assn. Curriculum Devel., Am. Israel Pub. Affairs Com., New Leadership com. of Jewish Nat. Fund, State of Israel Bonds New Leadership, Simon Wiesenthal New Leadership Soc., Nat. Polit. Action Com, Am. Friends of Hebrew U. (torch com.), Technion Soc., Am. Friends David Yellin Tchr's. Coll., Am. Friends Ben Gurion U., Am. Friends Israel Philharm., Am. Friends of Tel Aviv Univ., Friends of N.Y.C. Sports Commn., Cooper-Hewitt Mus., Mus. Modern Art, Met. Mus. Art, Whitney Mus., Phila. Mus. Art, Smithsonian Inst., Friends of Carnegie Hall, Friends of Am. Ballet Theatre, U. Pa. Alumni Assn. N.Y.C., Dorot Soc., Human Rels. Club (sec.), Pi Lambda Theta, Kappa Delta Pi (sec.). Home: 26 Meadow Ln Lawrence NY 11559 Office: Lawrence High Sch Reading Dept Reilly Rd Cedarhurst NY 11516

VAN RADEN, TOYA ANN, school system administrator; b. Salina, Kans., Jan. 8, 1936; d. Alvin John and Marianne (Black) Hegwer; m. Harry Lee Schnatterly, Dec. 24, 1954 (div. 1966); 1 child, Michael Dean; m. Roy C. Van Raden, Feb. 20, 1971 (div. 1972). BS, Ft. Hays Kans. U., 1959, MS, 1967. Cert. tchr., supr., prin., S.C. Tchr. Hays (Kans.) pub. schs., 1959-71; Tchr. Greenville (S.C.) County Schs., 1971-72, chpt. I coordinator, 1972-84, coord. Edn. Improvement Act, 1984—; cons. Dept. Youth Svcs., Columbia, S.C., 1977-81; change agt. S.C. State Dept. Edn., McCormick, 1983-84. Mem. adv. com. Greenville (S.C.) Tech. Coll., 1987—. Mem. Internat. Reading Assn. (chmn. literacy com. 1987—), Assn. for Supervision and Curriculum Devel., Mensa, Phi Delta Kappa, Delta Kappa Gamma (pres. 1990—). Republican. Episcopalian. Home: 808B Townes St Greenville SC 29609 Office: Greenville County Schs PO Box 2848 301 Camperdown Way Greenville SC 29602

VAN RHYN, CONSTANCE CAREY, interior designer; b. White Plains, N.Y., July 15, 1960; d. Neil James and Joan Marie (Gorman) C. BFA in Interior Design, Syracuse U., 1982. Jr. designer Sherburne/Hurst Inc., N.Y.C., 1980-81; draftsperson, furniture coord. The Space Design Group, Inc., N.Y.C., 1982-83; designer G.T.E. Corp., Stamford, Conn., 1983-86; sr. designer PepsiCo, Inc., Purchase, N.Y., 1986—. Mem. Internat. Facility Mgmt. Assn., Am. Soc. Interior Designers (bd. dirs. Conn. chpt. 1986—), Stamford Art Assn. (bd. dirs. 1985-88), PepsiCo Runners Club. Home: 5 Manor Rd Old Greenwich CT 06870

VANSANT, JOANNE FRANCES, school system administrator; b. Morehead, Ky., Dec. 29, 1924; d. Lewis L. and Dorothy (Greene) VanS. BA, Denison U., Granville, Ohio; MA, The Ohio State U.; postgrad., U. Colo. and The Ohio State U.; LLD (hon.), Albright Coll., 1975. Tchr., health and phys. edn. Mayfield, Kentucky High Sch., 1946-48; instr. Denison U., Granville, Ohio, 1948; instr. Women's Phys. Edn. Dept. Otterbein Coll., Westerville, Ohio, 1948-52, asst. prof., 1952-55, assoc. prof., 1955-62, departmental chmn., 1950-62, chmn. of the div. of profl. studies, 1961-65, dean of women, 1952-60, 62-64, dean of students, 1964—, v.p. student affairs, dean of students, 1968—. Co-pres. Directions for Youth, 1983-84, pres., 1984-85; bd. dirs. North Area Mental Health; trustee Westerville Civic Symphony at Otterbein Coll., 1983-88; active numerous other community orgns.; ordained elder Presbyn. Ch., 1967. Named to hon. Order of Ky. Cols., 1957; recipient Focus on Youth award Columbus Dispath, 1983, Vol. of the Yr. award North Area Mental Health Svcs., 1982. Mem. Ohio Personnel and Guidance Assn., Ohio Assn. Women Deans, Adminstrs., Counselors (treas., mem. exec. bd. 1972-73), Nat. Assn. Student Personnel Adminstrs., Zonta Internat. (pres. Columbus, Ohio chpt. 1978-80, gov. dist. V 1988-90), Cap and Dagger Club, Torch and Key Club, Order of Omega, Alpha Lambda Delta, Theta Alpha Phi, others. Home: 9100 Oakwood Point Westerville OH 43081 Office: Otterbein Coll Student Pers Office Westerville OH 43081

VAN SCHAICK, MARY JANE, supervisor medical records; b. Sidney, N.Y., Nov. 15, 1958; d. Karl L. and Ann (Bennett) Van S. AAS, Alfred State Coll., 1979; BS in Bus., Elmira Coll., 1990. Data analyst Tioga Gen. Hosp., Wavenly, Wyo., 1979-87; record technician, supr. med. records Arnot Odgen Meml. Hosp., Elmira, N.Y., 1987—. Mem. NAFE, Am. Med. Record Assn., Stray Haven Humane Soc. Democrat. Home: Rt 2 PO Box 303 Waverly NY 14892 Office: Arnot Odgen Meml Hosp 600 Roe Ave Elmira NY 14902

VAN SCHUYVER, CONNIE JO, geophysicist; b. Tulsa, Oct. 10, 1951; d. Lloyd Lee and Mary Ellen (Scott) Parks; m. Larry Gene Van Schuyver, May 15, 1972 (div. 1982). Student, Okla. State U., Stillwater, 1969-71; BS, Tex A&M U., 1977; postgrad., Houston Community Coll., 1990, Univ. Houston, 1990—. Geophysicist Seiscom Delta, Inc., Houston, 1978-81; sr. geophysicist Champlin Petroleum Corp., Houston, 1981-84, BKW Seismic Processing (later ESP Earth Scis.), Houston, 1984-85, Geophys. Devel. Corp., Houston, 1987—; paralegal analyst, Conoco, Inc., Houston, 1986. Mem. Soc. Exploration Geophysicists, Geophys. Soc. Houston, Sports Car Club of Am. Office: Geophys Devel Corp 8401 Westheimer Rd Ste 150 Houston TX 77063

VAN SETERS, VIRGINIA ANN, writer; b. Columbia, S.C., Apr. 11, 1947; d. Garret and Virginia Carolina (Motley) Van S. BA in Journalism, U. S.C., 1968. Research div. publs. editor Coll Bus. Adminstrn. U. S.C., Columbia, 1969—; editorial adv. bd. Studies in Econ. Analysis jour. U. S.C., Columbia, 1979—. Author: 22 Object Talks for Children's Worship, 1986, 3d edit., 1989, 26 Object Talks for Children's Worship, 1988, 26 More Object Talks for Children's Worship, 1990; contbr. articles to profl. jours. and consumer mags. Singer Beulah Bapt. Ch., 1959—, tchr. 1973—, pianist 1975—, substitute children's minister, 1980—; supr. children's counselors Billy Graham Evangelistic Assn., Columbia, 1987. Home: 245 Chateau de Ville Columbia SC 29204 Office: Univ SC Coll Bus Adminstrn Columbia SC 29208

VANSICKLE, BARBARA JEAN, computer services coordinator; b. Parkersburg, W.Va., Oct. 18, 1948; d. Robert Syrl and Evelyn June (Anderson) McGraw; m. John Vernon Morrison Jr., Oct. 7, 1968 (dec. June 1981); children: John Vernon III, Deborah Margarette; m. Danny Ray Vansickle, Oct. 1, 1983. AS, Shawnee State Community Coll., 1984; BA, Wilmington Coll., 1990, 1990. Keypunch operator Columbus (Ohio) Mut. Life Ins. Co., 1966-67, Steele Data Processing, Washington Court House, Ohio, 1971-74; data entry operator F&R Lazarus, Columbus, 1978-79; clk. III Parker Hannifin Corp., Waverly, Ohio, 1979-80; computer programmer Shawnee State U., Portsmouth, Ohio, 1981-88; coord. computer svcs. Wilmington (Ohio) Coll., 1988—; instr. part-time Southeastern Bus. Coll., Portsmouth, 1982-83. Mem. Valley High Sch. PTA, Lucasville, Ohio, 1982-85; pres. Valley High Sch. Band Boosters, 1986-87, v.p., 1985-86. Mem. Data Processing Mgmt. Spl. Interest Group for Edn., Data Processing Mgmt. Assn., Digital Equip. Corp. Users Soc. (assoc.). Republican. Home: PO Box 921 Wilmington OH 45177 Office: Wilmington Coll Pyle Ctr Box 1204 Wilmington OH 45177

VANSITTERT, CAROL ANN, computer programmer; b. Kansas City, Mo., Dec. 18, 1936; d. Clarence Alfred and Adelaide Harriet (Hurst) Hallberg; m. Joseph VanSittert, Jr., Mar. 18, 1956; children: Sarah Lynn VanSittert Goodman, Jeanne Marie VanSittert Glidewell. Student, Baker U., 1955-56; AA, Johnson County Community Coll., Overland Park, Kans., 1975. Lead programmer Pyramid Life Ins. Co., Mission, Kans., 1965-68, Wolf & Co., Kansas City, 1971-74; programmer Interstate Securities Corp., Kansas City, 1968-69; sr. programmer Hercules, Inc., De Soto, Kans., 1969-71; supr. datapoint ops., programmer Bayvet div. Cutter Labs., Shawnee, Kans., 1974-79; programmer, analyst III, North Supply Co. subs. United Telecommunications., Industrial Airport, Kans., 1979—. Mem. NAFE, USCG Aux. Republican. Mem. Unity Ch. Home: 5006 Garnett Shawnee KS 66203 Office: North Supply Co 600 Industrial Pkwy Industrial Airport KS 66031

VAN SLETT, KAREN ANN, researcher, nurse; b. Milw., Sept. 13, 1950; d. Theodore Ernst and Regina Viola (Orlikowski) Voss; m. Gene Francis Van Slett, Nov. 6, 1971. BS, U. Wis., Milw., 1972. RN, Wis., Calif. Nursing instr. County Hosp. Sch. Nursing, Milw., 1973-75; nursing supr. Project Involve, Milw., 1976-77; pub. health nurse Home Kare, Inc., San Jose, Calif., 1977-78; br. mgr. Quality Care, Inc., San Jose, 1978-79; ops. mgr. Cardiodyne Gen., Los Gatos, Calif., 1979-83; clin. research assoc. Barnes-Hind, Inc., Sunnyvale, Calif., 1983-86, Genentech, Inc., 1986—. Mem. Assocs. Clin. Pharmacology, Nat. Assn. Female Execs. Democrat. Mem. AAAS. Home: 44467 Arapaho Ave Fremont CA 94539

VANTERPOOL, ELEANOR LORETTA, educator; b. Bronx, N.Y., Dec. 31, 1955; d. William Ulrich and Gladys Constancia (Bronstorph) V. BA, Herbert Lehman Coll., 1979; MS, CCNY, 1981, advance cert. adminstrn., 1983, postgrad., 1986-87. Cert. adminstr., supr., speech and hearing scis., spl. edn., speech tchr., N.Y. Spl. edn. tchr. N.Y.C. Bd. Edn., Bronx, 1979—, speech therapist, 1983—; lectr., cons. on talent search Bronx Community Coll., 1986-87; bd. dirs. Home Tutoring Svcs., Bronx; parent counselor Chama Intervention Program, 1989—. Sch. coord. United Negro Coll. Fund, N.Y.C., 1980-82, Spl. Olympics, Bronx, 1985-87; organizer, sch. coord. Jump Rope for Heart, N.Y. Heart Assn., Bronx, 1982-85; fund raiser Bronx Dem. Club, 1984—; mem. Black Citizens for Fair Media, N.Y.C., 1983-86; mem. exec. bd. Upper Manhattan Health Ctr. Recipient certs. for vol. work, 1982, 89. Mem. Am. Speech and Hearing Assn., United Fedn. Tchrs., Afro Am. Guild Performing Arts. Roman Catholic. Home: 30-12G Richman Pla Bronx NY 10453 Office: 1260 Franklin Ave Rm 408 Bronx NY 10456

VANTREASE, ALICE TWIGGS, marketing executive; b. Augusta, Ga., Mar. 29, 1943; d. Samuel Warren and Harriett Alice (Wright) Twiggs; m. John Mulford Marks, July 8, 1964 (div. Oct. 1972); children: John Mulford, Sarah Elizabeth; m. James David Vantrease, May 9, 1980 (div. Mar. 1988). Student Winthrop Coll., 1961-62, Augusta Coll., 1962-64. Sales staff Chalker Publ. Co., Waynesboro, Ga., 1972-74; with Creative Displays, Inc., Tuscaloosa, Ala., 1974-78; sales mgr. GMC Bdcasting, Chattanooga, 1978-80; corporate sales, mktg. dir. Creative Displays Inc., Augusta, 1980-83; pres. Creative Mktg. Svcs., Augusta, 1983—. Bd. dirs. Better Bus. Bur., 1987-89; pres. Good Luck Found., 1988—. Editor: The Met. Spirit Newspaper, 1989—. Named to Co-op Advt. Hall of Fame, 1989. Mem. Outdoor Advt. Suppliers Assn. (v.p. 1984-87, pres. 1987-88, editor newspaper 1985-88), Nat. Speakers Assn., Am. Assn. Coop Advt. Profls., Outdoor Advt. Assn. Am. Instr. Episcopalian. Avocations: painting, writing. Home: 1203 Bay St Beaufort SC 29902 Office: Creative Mktg 825 Russell St Augusta GA 30914-2247

VAN TUYL, KATHRYN URSULA LEACH, retired high school teacher; b. New Bethlehem, Pa., Jan. 10, 1909; d. Alonzo and Catherine (Hoelzel) Leach; m. George Henry Van Tuyl Jr., Aug. 10, 1933; children: George Henry III, John Steelman. BA, Bucknell U., 1930; postgrad., Columbia U., 1932. Permanent teaching cert. Tchr. Summerville (Pa.) High Sch., 1930-33; part time teaching various high schs., Pa., N.Y., 1946-55; part time substitute tchr. various high schs., Garden City, N.Y., 1955-65; real estate sales person Garden City (N.Y.) Realty, 1965-72; high sch. drama coach, newspaper coach, Pa., N.Y.; founder English in Action Group Adelphi U.up, Garden City. Sunday sch. tchr. McKeesport, Pa., Garden City, 1940-80. Recipient scholarship Bucknell U., Lewisburg, Pa., 1926. Mem. AAUW (various positions), PEO. Republican. Methodist. Home: 20 Lincoln Ave N Lehigh Acres FL 33936

VAN TYNE, NATALIE CHRISTINE T., chemical engineer; b. Somerville, N.J., Oct. 31, 1952; d. Steve and Helen (Sudillo) Trehubets; m. Chester John Van Tyne, May 23, 1981; children: Mary Helen, Daria Natalie, Kathryne Christine, Fiona Marion. BA in Russian Lang., Rutgers U., 1976, BSChemE, 1976; MSChemE, Lehigh U., 1978, MBA, 1986. Rsch. engr. J.T. Baker Chem. Co., Phillipsburg, N.J., 1978-86, sr. rsch. engr., 1986-87; sr. supr. J.T. Baker, Inc., Phillipsburg, 1987-88; prin. process engr. Rockwell Internat., Golden, Colo., 1989-90, EG&G Rocky Flats, Inc., Golden, 1990—. Editor engring. mag. Rutgers U., 1974-76. Mem. Am. Chem. Soc., Am. Inst. Chem. Engrs. (pub. rels. chairperson Rocky Mountain chpt. 1988-89, bd. dirs. Lehigh Valley chpt. 1987-88, exec. staff Rocky Mountain sect. 1988—), Inst. Food Technologists, Soc. Women Engrs. Democrat. Roman Catholic. Home: Cimarron Pines 318 Parkview Ave Golden CO 80401 Office: EG&G Rocky Flats Inc PO Box 464 Golden CO 80401

VAN UMMERSEN, CLAIRE A(NN), university administrator, biologist, educator; b. Chelsea, Mass., July 28, 1935; d. George and Catherine (Courtovich); m. Frank Van Ummersen, June 7, 1958; children: Lynn, Scott. BS, Tufts U., 1957, MS, 1960, PhD, 1963; DSc (hon.), U. Mass., 1988. Rsch. asst. Tufts U., 1957-60, 60-67, grad. asst. in embryology, 1962, postdoctoral teaching asst., 1963-66, lectr. in biology, 1967-68; asst. prof. biology U. Mass., Boston, 1968-74; assoc. prof. U. Mass., 1974-86, assoc. dean acad. affairs, 1975-76, assoc. vice chancellor acad. affairs, 1976-78, chancellor, 1978-79, dir. Environ. Sci. Ctr., 1980-82; assoc. vice chancellor acad. affairs Mass. Bd. Regents for Higher Edn., 1982-85, vice chancellor for mgmt. systems and telecommunications, 1985-86; chancellor Univ. System N.H., Durham, 1986—; cons. Mass. Bd. Regents, 1981-82; asst. Lancaster Course in Ophthalmology, Mass. Eye and Ear Infirmary, 1962-69, lectr., 1970—; reviewer HEW; mem. rsch. team which established safety standards for exposure to microwave radiation, 1958-65. Recipient Disting. Svc. medal U. Mass., 1979, Am. Cancer Soc. grantee Tufts U., 1960. Mem. AAAS, Am. Coun. on Edn. (com. on self-regulation 1987—), State Higher Edn. Exec. Officers (fed. rels. com., cost accountability task force), Nat. Ctr. for Edn. Stats. (network adv. com. 1989—, chair accreditation teams 1988—, exec. com. 1990—), Nat. Assn. Systems Heads (exec. com. 1990—), New Eng. Assn. Schs. and Colls., New Eng. Bd. Higher Edhn., Am. Soc. Zoologists, Soc. Devel. Biology, Bus. and Ind. Assn. N.H. (bd. dirs. 1988—, chair Rhodes scholarship selection com. N.H. chpt. 1986—, N.H. ct. system rev. task force), Phi Beta Kappa, Sigma Xi. Office: NH U System Dunlap Ctr Durham NH 03824

VAN VALIN, SHARON F., educator; b. Twin Falls, Idaho, Dec. 16, 1939; d. Frank and Bessie (Broyles) Zlatnik; m. Victor van Valin, June 26, 1964 (div. 1984); children: Vanessa, Jonathan. MusB, Whitman Coll., 1962; degree, U. Wash., Seattle, 1963; MPA, Seattle U., 1985. Tchr. Cascade Jr. High Sch., Seattle, 1963-65; pvt. practice tchr. Seattle, 1965—; tchr. Canyon Pk. Jr. High Sch., Bothell, Wash., 1966-68; job line coord., counselor State Employment Security Dept., Bothell, 1968-69; workshop instr. Wash. State Music Tchrs. Assn., 1980—. Mem. LWV, Seattle, 1965-70. Mem. Wash. State Music Tchrs. Assn. (program chair Eastside chpt. 1982, v.p. 1983), Nat. Guild Piano Tchrs. (adjudicator 1988-90), Nat. Fedn. Music Clubs. Home: 18135 SE 42d Pl Issaquah WA 98027

VAN VEEN, KATHLEEN LOUISE, plant propagator; b. Portland, Oreg., Jan. 6, 1947; d. Theodore Vincent and Frances Kathryn (Ackerman) Van V. Student, U. Portland, 1965-67; BS in Geology, U. Wash., Seattle, 1970, BS in Oceanography, 1970, postgrad., 1970-73. Rhododendron propagator Van Veen Nursery, Portland, Oreg., 1973—. Mem. Internat. Plant Propagators Soc., MENSA. Roman Catholic. Office: Van Veen Nursery 4201 SE Franklin St Portland OR 97206

VAN VELZER, VERNA JEAN, research librarian; b. State College, Pa., Jan. 22, 1929; d. Harry Leland and Golda Lillian (Cline) Van V. BS in Library Sci., U. Ill., 1950; MLS, Syracuse U., 1957. Head librarian Orton Library, Ohio State U., Columbus, 1952-54; serials assoc. Syracuse (N.Y.) U. Library, 1954-57; head cataolger SRI Internat., Menlo Park, Calif., 1957-58; head librarian GE Microwave Lab., Palo Alto, Calif., 1958-64, Fairchild Rsch. and Devel. Lab., Palo Alto, 1964-65, Sylvania Intelligence Library, Mountain View, Calif., 1965-66; rsch. librarian ESL Inc. subs. TRW, Sunnyvale, Calif., 1966—; cons. in field. Vol. Lantos Re-election Campaign, San Mateo, Calif., 1972—, Wildlife Rescue, Palo Alto, 1980—; mem. Barron Park Assn., Palo Alto, 1975—; mem. Calif. Polit. Action Com. for Animals, San Francisco, 1986—. Recipient Commemorative medal of Honor, Am. Biographical Inst., 1946, Paul Revere Cup, Santa Clara Camellia Soc., 1968, Internat. Cultural Diploma of Honor, Am. Biographical Inst., 1988. Mem. Spl. Libraries Assn., IEEE, AIAA, Calif. Holistic Vet. Assn., Internat. Primate Protection League, People for Ethical Treatment of Animals, Assn. Old Crows. Home: 4048 Laguna Way Palo Alto CA 94306 Office: ESL Inc subs TRW 495 Java Dr PO Box 3510 Sunnyvale CA 94088-3510

VAN VLECK, PAMELA KAY, real estate broker, consultant; b. St. Cloud, Minn., Aug. 26, 1951; d. Kipp James Gillespie and Lorraine Marie (Johnson) Storck; m. Clinton Eugene Van Vleck, Jan. 29, 1985. Student, St. Cloud State U., 1970, Washburn U., 1971-72. Mgr., broker Coldwell Banker-Pioneer Realty, Jackson, Wyo., 1980-85; owner, broker Tri-Corp Realty, Ltd., Scottsdale, Ariz., 1985-87, Affiliated Properties Group, Inc., Phoenix, 1987—; mgr., broker Machan Hampshire Properties, Las Vegas, Nev., 1990—; bd. dirs., owner Affiliated Properties Group Inc., Phoenix, 1985—; bd. dirs., cons. Realty Software Svcs. of Ariz., Inc., Phoenix, 1986—, MHP Realty & Mgmt., Inc., Las Vegas, 1989—. Mem. NAFE, Women in Comml. Real Estate, Nev. Devel. Authority, Wome's Conv. Sales Assn., Internat. Coun. Shopping Ctrs. Republican. Office: Machan Hampshire Properties 4435 W Spring Mountain Rd Las Vegas NV 89102

VAN WAGNER, NANCY LEE, educator; b. Bklyn., Aug. 8, 1938; d. Antonio and Julia Kathryn (Frieri) Mercaldo; m. Arthur L. Van Wagner (div. 1979); 1 child, Anthony Burton. Student, Pine Crest Bible Inst., 1959-62; BA, Roberts Wesleyan Coll., 1964; MEd, Mich. State U., 1970; diploma in legal assistance, Oakland U., 1984. Elem. tchr. Holly (Mich.) Sch. Dist., 1966-69, Clarkston (Mich.) Sch. Dist., 1969—; legal asst. intern George Dovas, Southfield Mich., summer 1984; mem. first task force to establish requirements for spl. edn., Mich., 1970-71; sec. to bd. dirs. WE Restaurant Corp., 1989—. Precinct del., 1984—, mem. exec. com. Oakland County Democratic Com., 1986—; Sunday sch. leader Brightmoor Tabernacle. Mem. NEA, Mich. Edn. Assn., Clarkston Edn. Assn. (region 7 del. to Mich. Edn. Assn. 1981—, region 7 Mich. at large del. to Nat. Edn. Assn. Conv. 1990). Home: 8564 Elizabeth Lake Rd PO Box 402 Union Lake MI 48387 Office: Pine Knob Elem Sch 6020 Sashabaw Rd Clarkston MI 48085

VAN WART, GAY ANN, hospital contract administrator; b. Detroit, Jan. 19, 1937; d. Edwin Pelham and Gay Martin (Teasdale) Baugher; m. Calvin Thomas Van Wart, June 3, 1956 (div. Apr. 1971); children: Brenda Kay, Pamela Gay, Charles Wayne (dec.). Student, Draughon's Bus. Coll., 1955-56, Richland Coll., 1977-78. Adminstr. asst. L-M Div. Ford Motor Co., Dallas, 1967-73; asst. sec. TCC, Inc., Dallas, 1973-74; asst. gov., affairs dir. Flower Mound New Town, Lewisville, Tex., 1974-75; asst. dir. of fund raising Yale U., New Haven, Conn., 1976-78; mgr. customer service Blue Cross Blue Shield of Tex., Dallas, 1978-81; sr. assoc. Abrams, Warrick & Winstead, Dallas, 1981-82; account exec. CIGNA Health Plan, Dallas, 1982-84; sales mgr. Whittaker Health Services, Los Angeles, 1984-87; dir. contracting City of Hope Nat. Med. Ctr., Duarte, Calif., 1987—; sec. Forward Looking Strategies Coalition, Los Angeles, 1987-88. Bd. dirs., chmn., Mothers Against Drunk Drivers, Dallas, 1981-84; pres. Remove Intoxicated Drivers, Dallas, 1981-84; founder Dallas County Driving While Intoxicated Task Force, Dallas, 1983; fundraiser Dallas Met. Opera, 1982. Mem. Bus. and Profl. Women (sec. v.p. Los Angeles chpt. 1985-88, Dallas chpt. 1983-84), High Quality Child Care Coalition, Am. Mktg. Assn., Soc. for Healthcare Planning & Mktg. Republican. Episcopalian. Home: 3450 Fairpoint St Pasadena CA 91107

VAN WHY, REBECCA RIVERA, counseling administrator; b. Casa Blanca, N.Mex., Sept. 14, 1932; d. Charles and Doris (Thompson) Rivera; m. Raymond Richard Van Why, Aug. 27, 1955; children: Raymond R., Ronald R., Randall R. BS, U. N.Mex., 1959. Tchr. Bur. of Indian Affairs, Albuquerque, 1960-62, guidance counselor, 1969—, tchr., supr., 1973-74, acting dir. student life, 1987; head tchr. Laguna (N.Mex.) Headstart OEO, 1967-69, acting dir., 1969. Recipient Cert. of Recognition, Sec. of Interior, 1975, Cert. of Appreciation, State of N.Mex., 1986; named honoree Internat. Women's Day, U. N.Mex., 1987. Republican. Home: 6328 Cuesta Pl NW Albuquerque NM 87120 Office: Bur of Indian Affairs 9169 Coors Blvd NW Albuquerque NM 87184

VAN WINKLE, NICKIE JOAN, real estate manager; b. Taylorville, Ill., Feb. 13, 1938; d. Richard Carl and Violet Josephine (Franklin) V.; m. Philip Michael Santella, Nov. 28, 1957 (div. 1963); 1 child, Ernest Michael Santella. V.p. Maxwell Mgmt. Corp., N.Y.C., 1972--; v.p., sec. 20166 Tenants Corp, N.Y.C. 1987--. Mem. Nat. Ctr. for Housing Mgmt., Nat. Assn. Home Builders. Democrat. Home: 201 East 66th St New York NY 10021 Office: Maxwell Mgmt Corp 101 West 55th St New York NY 10019

VAN ZANDT, ELAINE MARIAN, computer programmer; b. Albany, N.Y., Jan. 21, 1945; d. Joseph John and Katherine Mary (Fisher) DeRusso; m. Walter F. Mucha, 1966 (div. 1978); 1 child, Walter David; m. Lloyd Van Zandt, Mar. 23, 1979; 1 stepson, Mark. Student, Albany Med. Ctr. Sch. Nursing, 1962-63, Hudson Valley Community Coll., 1965, Albany Bus. Coll., 1974-76. Lic. practical nurse, N.Y. Various positions Sterling Drug, Inc., Rensselaer, N.Y., 1964-78; data entry operator N.Y. State Higher Edn. Svcs. Corp., Albany, 1979; computer operator N.Y. State Dept. Mental Hygiene, Albany, 1979-81, computer program trainee, 1981-82; computer programmer N.Y. State Office of Mental Health, Albany, 1982-85, sr. computer programmer, analyst, 1985-89, assoc. computer programmer/analyst, 1989—. Dir. nursery, deaconess New Life Assembly of God, East Greenbush, N.Y., 1987—. Office: NY State Office of Mental Retardation and Devel Disabilities 800 N Pearl St Albany NY 12204

VAN ZANDT, GLORIA JEAN, real estate company executive; b. Ft. Worth; m. James Cribbs, Nov. 26, 1988; 2 children. Student, East Tex. State U., 1959-61, U. Tex., Arlington, 1970-72. Lic. realtor, Tex. With various airlines and stock brokerage cos.; pres., prin. broker, owner, chief exec. officer Van Zandt, Realtors, Arlington; mem. nat. adv. bd. Real Estate Leaders Am., 1985—, Relocation Resources, Inc., 1987—; instr. real estate continuing edn. dept. U. Tex., Arlington, 1983-84; bd. dirs. N.W. Nat. Bank. Active numerous civic orgns., including bd. dirs. YMCA, 1980-81; appointee Arlington Econ. Devel. Found., 1987—, Tarrant County Econ. Devel. Com., 1989, exec. com. Metroplex Relocation Forum, 1989, Tarrant 2000 Task Force Facilities and Distbn. of Svc. Com., 1987-89; 1st pres., charter mem. Friends of the Libr. Adv. Coun. Univ. Tex.-Arlington, 1987—; dir. Arlington Quality of Life Found., 1987-90; chmn. fundraising com. Arlington United Arts, 1987. Recipient numerous award including appreciation award Arlington Parks and Recreation Dept., 1987; named Broker of the Yr., Travelers Realty Network, 1985, 86, 87. Mem. Nat. Assn. Realtors (mem. realtor active in politics team 1988—, econ. and rsch. com. 1987—, life mem. realtors nat. polit. action com. 1985—), Realtors Nat. Mktg. Inst. (cert. real estate brokerage mgr., residential specialist), Tex. Assn. Realtors (bd. dirs. 1985—, chmn. realtor-lawyer com. 1988—, TREPAC life mem. 1985—, legis. com. 1979—), Arlington Bd. Realtors (bd. dirs. 1982, mem. Arlington Bd. Realtors 1974—, chmn. realtor-lawyer 1988-89, Realtor of Yr. award 1987), Nat. Assn. Homebuilders, Tex. Relocation Network, Arlington Jr. League (community adv. coun. 1988-91), Alpha Delta Pi. Republican. Mem. Christian Ch. (Disciples of Christ). Office: 1300 S Bowen Rd Arlington TX 76013

VAN ZANTEN, DOROTHY JUNE, controller; b. Calif., May 11, 1934; d. Harold and Goldie June (Harris) Branch; m. Ben E. Van Zanten, Feb. 9, 1980. AA, Armstrong Coll., 1956. Acct. Berkeley Plywood Co., Oakland, Calif, 1956-65; controller Hubbard Structures Inc., Redwood City, Calif., 1965—. Vol. Kainos Orgn. for Retarded Adults, Redwood City, 1985—; elder, deacon United Presbyn. Ch., San Mateo, Menlo Park, Calif., 1978-88. Mem. Constrn. Fin. Mgmt. Assn., Women's Coun. C. of C., Soroptimists. Republican. Presbyterian. Office: Hubbard Structures Inc PO Box 5765 Redwood City CA 94063

VAN ZILE-STABINS, CHRISTINE HELEN, travel consultant; b. Rochester, N.Y., May 9, 1958; d. Fayette Cameron and Martha (Holcomb) Van Zile; m. Richard Keith Stabins, July 3, 1983; children: Keith Edward, Benjamin Michael. AA, SUNY, Morrisville, 1978. Cert. travel counselor. Receptionist Van Zile Travel Service, Rochester, 1980-83; travel agt. Van Zile Travel Service, Fairport, N.Y., 1983—, office mgr., 1986—. Mem. Rochester Area Travel Agts. Assn. Republican. Office: Van Zile Travel Service 380 Cedarwood Office Pk Fairport NY 14450

VARELLAS, SANDRA MOTTE, lawyer, judge; b. Anderson, S.C., Oct. 17, 1946; d. James E. and Helen Lucille (Gilliam) Motte; m. James John Varellas, July 3, 1971; children: James John III, David Todd. BA, Winthrop Coll., 1968; MA, U. Ky., 1970, JD, 1975. Bar: Ky. 1975, Fla. 1976, U.S. Dist. Ct. (ea. dist.) Ky. 1975, U.S. Ct. Appeals (6th cir.) 1976, U.S. Supreme Ct. 1978. Instr. Midway Coll., Ky., 1970-72; adj. prof. U. Ky. Coll. Law, Lexington, 1976-78; instr. dept. bus. adminstrn. U. Ky., Lexington, 1976-78; atty. Varellas, Pratt & Cooley, Lexington, 1975—; Fayette County judge exec., Ky., 1980—; hearing officer Ky. Natural Resources and Environ. Protection Cabinet, Frankfort, 1984-88. Committeewoman Ky. Young Dems., Frankfort, 1977-80; pres. Fayette County Young Dems., Lexington, 1977; bd. dirs. Ky. Dem. Women's Club, Frankfort, 1980-84; grad. Leadership Lexington, 1981; chairwoman Profl. Women's Forum, Lexington, Ky., 1985-86. Named Outstanding Young Dem. Woman, Ky. Young Dems., Frankfort, 1977, Outstanding Former Young Dem., Ky. Young Dems., 1983. Mem. Ky. Bar Assn. (treas. young lawyers div. 1978-79, long range planning com., 1988-89), Fla. Bar, Fayette County Bar Assn. (treas. 1977-78, bd. govs. 1978-80), LWV (nominating com 1984-85). Club: Philharm. Women's Guild (Lexington, Ky., bd. dirs. 1979-81, 86—). Office: Varellas Pratt & Cooley 167 W Main St Lexington KY 40507

VARESCHI, SUSAN LUIGS, technical computer resource planning executive; b. Paducah, Ky., Aug. 9, 1951; d. Andrew Charles and Bertha Leland (Jones) Luigs; m. William John Vareschi, May 17, 1980. BS, Western Ky. U., 1972. With fin. mgmt. program GE Appliances, Louisville, 1973-74; fin. analyst GE Motors and Drives, Bridgeport, Conn., 1975-76; mem. corp. audit staff GE Corp., Schenectady, N.Y., 1976-79; mgr. fin. analysis GE Corp. Cons. Svcs., Schenectady, N.Y., 1979-82; mgr. fin. planning GE Info. Svcs., Rockville, Md., 1982-84; mgr. finance GE Silicones Europe, The Netherlands, 1984-87; mgr. mktg. analysis and forecasting GE Lighting, Cleve., Ohio, 1988-90; mgr. tech. computer resource planning GE Aircraft Engines, Cin., 1990—. Treasurer, YWCA, Schenectady, 1981-82. Democrat. Roman Catholic.

VARGA, FRANCES ANDREA IRMA, telecommunications specialist; b. Trenton, N.J., May 23, 1956; d. Frank G. and Marguerita A. (Drosdick) V. BBA, Marywood Coll., 1978; postgrad., Liberty U., 1987—. Intern Internat. Salt Co., Clark Summit, Pa., 1978; auditor Cen. Labor Coun., Altoona, Pa., 1978-90; fin. auditor So. Alleghenies Planning, Altoona, 1978-81; jr. acct. Edward Jesse, CPA, Silver Spring, Md., 1981; directory operator C&P, Silver Spring, 1982-84; libr. asst. AT&T, Bedminister, N.J., 1984-87; assoc. mgr. AT&T, Morristown, N.J., 1987-90; asst. staff mgr. AT&T, Somerset, N.J., 1990—; mem., instr. Accounts for the Pub. Interest, Plainfield, N.J., 1988-90; instr. adopt-a-sch. program AT&T, Somerset, 1990—. Mem. Future Telephone Pioneers Am. (pres. 1989—). Home: 7 Bennington Pkwy Franklin Park NJ 08823 Office: AT&T 290 Davidson Ave Somerset PA 08875

VARGA, L. ELIZABETH, community health nurse; b. Marysville, Calif., Mar. 3, 1922; d. Alva Henry and Bertha (Heinrich) Nunes; m. Steven Alexander Varga, Oct. 16, 1945; children: Darian, Stevan, Tracey, Lesley, Kendal. BS in Pub. Health Nursing, U. Calif., Berkeley, 1950, MPH, 1968. RN, Calif., Md. Program clin. specialist Montgomery County (Md.) Health Dept., 1971-76; community health nurse various pub. schs., 1968-76; nurse coord. interagy. project Devel. Evaluation Svcs. for Children, Montgomery County, 1976-81, sect. head div. sch. health svcs., 1981-89; ret. Devel. Evaluation Svcs. for Children, 1989; part-time staff asst. Senator DeCancini of Ariz., Washington, 1989—; freelance cons. Montgomery County Health Dept., 1989—. 1st lt. A.C., U.S. Army, 1944-46. Fellow Am. Sch. Health Assn.; mem. APHA, ANA, AAUW (sec., treas. 1987-90), Sigma Theta Tau. Republican. Home: 6714 Tildenwood Ln Rockville MD 20852

VARGAS, LENA BESSETTE, nursing administrator; b. Hardwick, Vt., Dec. 26, 1922; d. Leon Alphonse and Dorilla Leah (Boudreau) Bessette; m. Jose Emilio Vargas, Sept. 3, 1949; children: Jose Emilio, Maria del Carmen, J. Ramon, Vicente Andres, Yolanda Teresa. BS in Nursing Edn., U. Vt., 1949. Instr. basic nursing Mary Fletcher Hosp., Burlington, Vt., 1947-49; clin. instr. St. Francis Hosp., Evanston, Ill., 1949-50; nurse participant streptomycin therapy research H.M. Biggs Meml. Hosp., Ithaca, N.Y., 1950-51; supr. ancillary personnel Providence Hosp., Washington, 1953-55, asst. dir. nursing, 1965—. Mem. coun., del. coop. congress Greenbelt Coop., Savage, Md., 1983-86; bd. dirs. Providence Hosp. Fed. Credit Union, Washington, 1977-80, v.p. bd. dirs., 1983-85. Mem. AAUW (chmn. various coms.), Am. Nurses Assn. (cert. nursing adminstr.), Nat. League for Nursing, Christ Child Soc. Roman Catholic. Avocations: bridge, travel, real estate, horseback riding. Home: 10706 Keswick St Garrett Park MD 20896 Office: Providence Hosp 1150 Varnum St Washington DC 20017

VARHEGYI, PATRICIA ILONA, financial services company executive; b. N.Y.C., Oct. 19, 1960; d. Laszlo Carl and Evelyn Liane (Schauer) Varhegyi; m. Ahmed Sharif Al-Azzawe, Jan. 2, 1986. BS, Seton Hall U., 1982; MBA, Rutgers U., Newark, 1987. Statis. analyst UN, Vienna, Austria, 1983-85; cons., tutor, N.J., 1985-87; assoc. mgr. strategy and devel. AT&T, Basking Ridge, N.J., 1987-88; market mgr. microelectronics AT&T, Berkeley Heights, N.J., 1988-89; sr. product mgr. data systems group AT&T, Morristown, N.J., 1989; sr. fin. analyst Am. Express Travel Related Svcs. Co., N.Y.C., 1989—; internat. cons., N.J., 1985—; interpreter, translator, N.J., 1987—. Mem. NAFE, Am. Mgmt. Assn. Home: 14 King James Ct Scotch Plains NJ 07076 Office: Am Express Travel Related Svcs Co WFC 200 Vesey St Amex Tower New York NY 10285-2850

VARHOLAK, DOROTHY MALISEK, nurse, hospital administrator; b. Bridgeport, Conn., Nov. 3, 1939; d. Joseph M. and Frances I. (Lampart) Malisek; m. Edward Michael Varholak, Sept. 23, 1961; children: Kathryn, Carolyn, Laurie, Edward Jr., Suzanne, Peter, James. BS, U. Conn., 1961; MS, Hartford Grad. Ctr., 1980; EdD, Columbia U., 1989. RN, Mass., Conn. Instr. sch. nursing Baystate Med. Ctr., Springfield, Mass., 1976-78, supr., head nurse, 1978-82; v.p. nursing Wing Meml. Hosp., Palmer, Mass., 1982-83, v.p. pvt. care svcs., 1983-85; v.p. nursing Hebrew Home & Hosp., Hartford, Conn., 1985—; researcher in field. Mem. Am. Orgn. Nurse Execs. (Excellence in Nursing Adminstrn. award), Conn. Nurses Assn., Conn. League for Nursing, Am. Nurses Assn., Conn. Assn. Non-Profit Homes for Aged, Conn. Hosp. Assn., New Eng. Orgn. Nurses, Sigma Theta Tau, Kappa Delta Pi. Home: 1788 Hill St Suffield CT 06078

VARMA, ASHA, research administrator, chemist; b. Bareilly, India, Mar. 19, 1942; came to U.S., 1966; d. Gulzari Mall and Javitri Devi Varma; m. Vinod Shanker Agarwala, Feb. 14, 1967; children: Veena V., Vinay. BSc, Agra U., Bareilly, 1958, MSc, 1960; PhD, Banaras Hindu U., Varanasi, India, 1963; def. mgmt. diploma, Nat. Def. U., 1988; exec. mgmt. diploma, Office Pers. Mgmt., 1988. Rsch. fellow Banaras Hindu U., 1960-64, Nat. Rsch. Coun., Poona, India, 1964-66; asst. dir. Forensic Sci. Lab., Sagar, India, 1966-68; sci. officer Coun. Sci. and Indsl. Rsch., Kanpur, 1969-70; rsch. assoc. U. Conn., Storrs, 1973-76; rsch. scientist U. Pa., Phila., 1977-82; rsch. chemist Naval Air Devel. Ctr., Warminster, Pa., 1983-88, asst. dir. Office Sci. and Tech., 1988—; chmn. Fed. Women's Program, Warminster, 1987-88, Navy R & D Info. Exch. Conf., Washington, 1989—. Author: Handbook of Atomic Absorption Spectroscopy, 1984, Handbook of Furnace Atomic Absorption, 1990, Handbook of Inductively Coupled Plasma Spectroscopy, 1990; contbg. author CRC Press Inc. Former mem. Indo-U.S. Orgn., Phila. Recipient performance award Naval Air Devel. Ctr., 1983-89, award of appreciation Office Personnel Mgmt., 1988; scholar Govt. of India, 1954-66, fellow, 1963-75; fellow U.S. govt., 1963-75. Fellow Am. Inst. Chemists (cert. profl. chemist); mem. Am. Chem. Soc., Coblentz Soc., Am. Mus. Natural History, Nat. Wildlife Fedn., Internat. Wildlife Fedn. Home: 1006 Marian Rd Warminster PA 18974 Office: Naval Air Devel Ctr Warminster PA 18974

VARMECKY, BETTY JO, electronic instrumentation executive; b. Tulsa, Jan. 22, 1927; d. Walter Jonathon and LaVinia (Clear) Eyestone; m. Joseph Dean Varmecky, Jan. 11, 1947 (dec.); children: Joseph Dean Jr., Diane Louise, David Charles. Student U. Tulsa, 1945, Okla. State U., 1946. Sec. Tri-State Instrument Lab. Inc., Tulsa, 1959-75, pres., 1975—. Mem. Instrument Soc. Am. Democrat. Christian Scientist. Avocations: travel; exercise; reading. Office: Tri-State Instrument Lab Inc 6801 E 15th St Tulsa OK 74112

VARNER, CHARLEEN LAVERNE MCCLANAHAN (MRS. ROBERT B. VARNER), educator, administrator, nutritionist; b. Alba, Mo., Aug. 28, 1931; d. Roy Calvin and Lela Ruhama (Smith) McClanahan; student Joplin (Mo.) Jr. Coll., 1949-51; B.S. in Edn., Kans. State Coll. Pittsburg, 1953; M.S., U. Ark., 1958; Ph.D., Tex. Woman's U. 1966; postgrad. Mich. State U., summer, 1955, U. Mo., summer 1962; m. Robert Bernard Varner, July 4, 1953. Apprentice county home agt. U. Mo., summer 1952; tchr. Ferry Pass Sch., Escambia County, Fla., 1953-54; tchr. biology, home econs. Joplin Sr. High Sch., 1954-59; instr. home econs. Kans. State Coll., Pittsburg, 1959-63; lectr. foods, nutrition Coll. Household Arts and Scis., Tex. Woman's U., 1963-64, research asst. NASA grant, 1964-66; asso. prof. home econs. Central Mo. State U., Warrensburg, 1966-70, adviser to Colhecon, 1966-70, adviser to Alpha Sigma Alpha, 1967-70, 72, mem. bd. advisers Honors Group, 1967-70; prof., head dept. home econs. Kans. State Tchrs. Coll., Emporia, 1970-73; prof., chmn. dept. home econs. Benedictine Coll., Atchison, Kans., 1973-74; prof., chmn. dept. home econs. Baker U., Baldwin City, Kans., 1974-75; owner, operator Diet-Con Dietary Cons. Enterprises, cons. dietitian, 1973—. Mem. Joplin Little Theater, 1956-60. Mem. NEA, Mo., Kans. state tchrs. assns., AAUW, Am., Mo., Kans. dietetics assns., Am., Mo., Kans. home econs. assns., Mo. Acad. Scis., AAUP, U. Ark. Alumni Assn., Alumni Assn. Kans. State Coll. of Pittsburg, Am. Vocat. Assn., Assn. Edn. Young Children, Sigma Xi, Beta Sigma Phi, Beta Beta Beta, Alpha Sigma Alpha, Delta Kappa Gamma, Kappa Kappa Iota, Phi Upsilon Omicron. Methodist (organist). Home: Main PO Box 1009 Topeka KS 66601

VARNER, JOYCE EHRHARDT, librarian; b. Quincy, Ill., Sept. 13, 1938; d. Wilbur John and Florence Elizabeth (Mast) Ehrhardt; m. Donald Giles Varner, Sept. 12, 1959; children: Amy, Janice, Christian, Matthew, Nadine. BA, Northeastern Okla. State U., 1980; MLS, U. Okla., 1984. Lab. analyst Gardner Denver Co., Quincy, 1956-60; sales rep. Quincy, 1963-69, seamstress,, 1969-73; libr. clk. U. Ill., Urbana, 1973-75; libr. tech. asst. Northeastern Okla. State U., Tahlequah, 1976-86; asst. reference libr. Muskogee (Okla.) Pub. Libr., 1986—. Editor Indian Nations Audubon Nature Notes, 1977-81; contbr. articles to newspaper. Vol. Lake-Wood coun. Girl Scouts U.S.A., 1975—; sec.-treas. Cherokee County Rural Water Dist. 7, 1987—; edn. chmn. Indian Nations chpt. Nat. Audubon Soc., 1989—. Recipient Thanks Badge, Lake-Wood coun. Girl Scouts U.S.A., 1990. Mem. ALA, Okla. Libr. Assn. (nominating com. 1989), Okla. Acad. Sci., Okla. Ornithol. Soc. (chmn. libr. com. 1978-88), AAUW, Alpha Chi, Beta Beta Beta, Phi Delta Kappa. (Found. rep. 1984-86). Home: RR 1 Box 1 Welling OK 74471 Office: Muskogee Pub Libr 801 W Okmulgee Muskogee OK 74401

VARNER, NELLIE MAE, real estate investment broker; b. Lake Cormorant, Miss., 1935; d. Tommie and Essie (Davis) V.; m. Louis S. Williams (div. Feb. 1964). AA, Highland Park Community Coll., 1956; BS, Wayne State U., 1958, MA, 1959; PhD, U. Mich., 1968. Tchr. pub. schs. Detroit Bd. Edn., 1959-64; spl. asst. to dean Coll. Lit., Sci. and Arts U. Mich., Ann Arbor, 1968-70, faculty assoc. Ctr. Russian and Ea. European Studies, asst. prof. polit. sci., 1968-79, dir. affirmative action programs, 1972-75, assoc. dean Grad. Sch., 1976-79; research assoc. Russian Research Ctr., research fellow Ctr. Internat. Affairs Harvard U., Cambridge, Mass., 1970-71; assoc. sales Real Estate One, Farmington, Mich., 1971-75; v.p. Strather & Varner, Inc., Southfield, Mich., 1978—; pres. Primco Foods, Inc., Southfield, 1988—; chmn. Mich. Real Estate Adv. Bd., Lansing, 1979-80; bd. dirs. Community Investment Adv., Washington, Am. Inst. for Bus., Detroit, New Detroit, Inc.; del. White House Conf. on Small Bus., 1980. Bd. regents U. Mich., Ann Arbor, 1980—; bd. dirs. Highland Park YMCA, 1980-82. Wilton Park fellow, 1969, Social Sci. Research Council tng. fellow, 1970-71; U. Mich. grantee, 1970-71. Mem. Nat. Assn. Realtors, Mich. Assn. Realtors, NAACP, S. Oakland County Bd. Realtors, Nat. Assn. Women Bus. Owners, Phi Kappa Phi, Pi Sigma Alpha, Delta Sigma Theta (bd. dirs. Detroitchpt.). Democratic. Baptist. Office: Strather & Varner Inc 3000 Town Ctr #2460 Southfield MI 48075

VARNEY, SUZANNE GLAAB, hospital program administrator, civilian military employee; b. Ft. Meade, Md., Dec. 17, 1951; d. Lawrence Harrold and G. Sue (Strain) Glaab; m. Richard Alan Varney, Dec. 31, 1983; children: Alysen Suzanne, Judson Dietrick. Student, Ohio U., Lancaster, 1969. Transp. asst. U.S. Army, Seoul, Republic of Korea, 1979-81; pers. specialist U.S. Army Hosp., Ft. Knox, Ky., 1982-84, credentials specialist, 1984-86; adminstrv. asst. Brooke Army Med. Ctr., Ft. Sam Houston, Tex., 1987, adminstr. credentials program, 1988—; seminar leader office basic course AMEDD, Ft. Sam Houston, 1988-90. Rep. Brookwood Neighborhood Assn., San Antonio, 1987-90; mem. N.E. Ind. Sch. Dist. PTA, San Antonio, 1986-90; den leader Cub Scouts/Boy Scouts Am., San Antonio, 1986-90. Named one of 2,000 Notable Am. Women, 1990. Mem. NAFE, Nat. Assn. Med. Staff Coords., Tex. Hosp. Assn., Tex. Soc. Med. Staff Svcs. Home: 1093 Loran Court Grand Valley VA 22066 Office: Walter Reed Army Med Ctr Washington DC 20307

VAROGLU, MARY, wholesale distribution executive; b. Mt. Vernon, N.Y., Apr. 11, 1960; d. Jack Walter and Jean (Kish) Milder; m. Salih Varoglu, Oct. 9, 1982. Student, Pace U., 1979-81. Adminstrv. dir. Jingles Internat., N.Y.C., 1982-85; pres. Elite Salon Svcs., Ossining, N.Y., 1985—. Mem. Beauty and Barber Supply Inst. Roman Catholic. Home: 611 Briarcliff Dr S Ossining NY 10562

VARTANIAN, ELSIE VIRGINIA, real estate broker; b. Haverhill, Mass., July 19, 1930; d. Minott Laforrest and Nellie Phyllis (Berry) Brown; m. David Vartanian, Nov. 9, 1952; children: David (dec.), Corey Jay. Student, MacIntosh Bus. Sch., 1948. Pres. Elsie Vartanian Real Estate, Inc., Salem, N.H., 1977—; legislator N.H. Ho. of Reps., 1979—; chmn. State Insts. and Housing Com., 1983-86; chmn. Gov.'s Office on Voluntarism, 1983-87; asst. majority leader, 1987—. Committeewoman Rep. Nat. Com., 1988, vice chmn. N.E. Region, 1989, chmn. N.E. Regional Chmn.'s Assn., 1987, chmn. N.E. Leadership Conf., 1988; chmn. N.H. Rep. State Com., 1985-88; vice chmn. Bush-Quayle 88 Coalition Am. Nationalities; del. Rep. Nat. Convs., 1984, 88, mem. com. on call, 1988; town chmn. Reagan-Bush campaign; mem. Town & Country Rep. Coms., 1979—; steering com. Gov. John Sununu campaign, election coms., 1983-89; past pres. local PTA. Mem. Nat.

Rep. Legislators Assn. (pres. 1989-90, Bill Brock award), Nat. Conf. State Legislatures (vice chmn. state and fed. assembly 1989-90, mem. exec. com. 1990-91). Address: 44 Brady Ave Salem NH 03079

VARVIL, CANDACE JOAN, psychologist; b. Marquette, Mich., Dec. 11, 1950; d. Dana Vane and Fern Marie (O'Donnell) v. BS, No. Mich., Marquette, 1968-72; MA, U. N.D., Grand Forks, 1972-75; PhD, U. N. D., 1975-77. Psychologist Traverse City State Hosp., Mich., 1978-80, Escambia Co. Mental Health Ctr., Pensacola, Fla., 1980-82, Cen. Counties MHMR, Killeen, Tex., 1982-84, Mid Coast MHC, Belfast, Maine, 1984-86; dir. Children's Psychiatric Program., Carrollton, Tex., 1986-88; psychologist Alger Marquette Community Mental Health Ctr., Mich., 1988--; bd. dirs. Home Builders, Rockland Maine 1984-8; cons. Waldo County Hosp., Belfast Maine 1984-86, Trinity Med. Ctr., Carrollton Tex. 1986-88,. Recipient Chi Omega Scholarship award No. Mich. U., 1971. Mem. Am. Psychol. Assn., Chi Omega Marquette Mich. (sec. 1970). Republican. Roman Catholic. Home: 176 Timberlane Marquette MI 49855 Office: Alger County CMHC Ridge St Marquette MI 48955

VASA, ROBIN LEAH, architect; b. San Diego, Calif., Sept. 29, 1953; d. Ralph Leonard and Irene Ellen (Jarvis) V. BArch, U. Tenn., 1976. Licensed architect in the District of Columbia. Draftsperson, designer Morton, Sweetser and Assoc., Knoxville, Tenn., 1973-74; volunteer architect Vice Ministry Urban Planning, Managua, Nicaragua, 1974; project architect Chatelain, Samperton and Carcaterra, Wash., 1976-78; project mgr. The E/A Design Group, Wash.; assoc. prin. Kresscox Assocs. P.C., Wash., 1981—; instr. Mt. Vernon Coll., 1984-85. Contbr. articles to prof jours. Mayoral appointee adv. com. DC/BLDG Codes, 1986-90, subcom. chmn., 1988—. Mem. AIA (treas. 1990), Young Architects Forum (mem., chmn. steering com. 1990), Constrn. Specifications Inst. (cert.), Wash. Bldg. Congress (bd. dirs.), Greater Wash. Bd. of Trade, Housing for Humanity (bldg. com. 1990). Jewish. Office: Kresscox Assoc PC 2909 M St NW Washington DC 20007

VASCONCELLOS, MURIEL, linguist; b. N.Y.C., May 5, 1933; d. Wenzel and Eleanore (Brown) Habel; m. Sylvio de Vasconcellos, Oct. 22, 1970 (dec. Mar. 1979). BS in Langs., Georgetown U., 1958, MS in Linguistics, 1982, PhD in Linguistics, 1985. Editor Orgn. Am. States, Washington, 1963-69; editor Pan. Am. Health Orgn., Washington, 1969-77, chief machine translation program, 1977-89, chief translation svc., 1989—; lectr. Georgetown U., Washington, 1976-78, 80-87. Editor: Technology as Translation Strategy, 1988; mem. editorial bd. Machine Translation, 1985—, Jerome Quarterly, 1985—, Lang. Internat., 1989—; contbr. over 45 articles to profl. jours. Nat. Endowment for Humanities grantee, 1978-80, U.S. Agy. for Internat. Devel. grantee, 1983-85. Mem. Am. Assn. Lang. Specialists (treas., exec. sec.), Am. Translators Assn., Linguistic Soc. Am., Assn. for Computational Linguistics, Nat. Capital Area Translators Assn., Washington Linguistics Soc. Unitarian. Home: 17391/2 Corcoran St NW Washington DC 20009 Office: Pan Am Health Orgn 525 Twenty Third St NW Washington DC 20037

VASIL, VIMLA, research scientist; b. New Delhi, India, Dec. 11, 1932; came to U.S., 1967; d. Hayat Singh and Revati (Bisht) Negi; m. Indra K. Vasil, May 15, 1959; children: Kavita, Charu. BS with honors, U. Delhi, India, 1953; MS, U. Delhi, 1955, PhD, 1959. From asst. rsch. scientist to rsch. scientist U. Fla., Gainesville, 1967—. Contbr. over 75 sci. articles to profl. jours. Office: U Fla Dept Vegetable Crops Lab Plant Cell Molecular Biology Gainesville FL 32611

VASS, JOAN, fashion designer; b. N.Y.C., May 19, 1925; d. Max S. and Rose L.; children by previous marriage—Richard, Sara, Jason. Student Vassar Coll., 1941; B.A., U. Wis., 1946. Pres., Joan Vass Inc., N.Y.C., 1977—. Recipient Prix de Cachet, Prince Machiabelli, 1980; Coty award, 1979; Disting. Woman in Fashion award Smithsonian Instn., 1980. Office: Joan Vass Inc 117 E 29th St New York NY 10016

VASS, LISA TAYLOR, software executive; b. Balt., Dec. 17, 1953; d. George Henry and Cannie Marion (Chandler) Mueller; m. Garry James Vass, June 28, 1981; 1 child, Carmen Abigail. BFA, Towson State Coll., Balt., 1975; student, Columbia U., 1986. Pres. Emmet/Taylor Assocs., Balt., 1976-78; mgr. Mothercare, Gaithersburg, Md., 1979-80; asst. mgr. Stein's, Arlington, Va., 1980-81; pres. Telemachus Software Assocs., West New York, N.J., 1982—. Author play, Money, 1977; composer of songs. Bd. dirs. Columbia Community Theatre, Md., 1972-76; v.p. PTA, West N.Y., 1987, treas., membership chmn., 1990—, pres., 1990—; chmn. founder's day program Howard County PTA, 1990—; mem. Partnership for Homeless, N.Y.C. Mem. Am. Women Entrepreneurs Assn., Am. Entrepreneurs Assn., Metro Opera Guild, Assn. Research and Enlightenment. Democrat. Club: Wagner Soc.

VASSALLO, JO ANN, child care company executive and co-founder; b. Atlantic City, Feb. 6, 1960; d. Anthony Emil and Sera Fina (Damiano) V.; m. Karl D. Conrad, Mar. 14, 1987; 1 child, Ryan V. BS in Aerospace Engring., Ga. Inst. Tech., 1982; cert. in investment, mktg. and appraisal, Champions Sch. Real Estate, Houston. Vehicle performance analyst Acurex Corp., Mountain View, Calif., 1982-83; propulsion engr. Lockheed Missiles and Space Co., Sunnyvale, Calif., 1983-87; apprentice aircraft mechanic Vanguard Aviation, Palo Alto, Calif., 1985-86; pres. Progressive Child Care Inc., Houston, 1989—; owner, builder custom speculative home, Cupertino, Calif., 1987-88. Tutor Center City (N.J.) Elem. Sch., 1975-77; tutor, vol. Ga. Inst. Tech. Big Sister Program, 1980-82. Republican. Office: 1618 Willowbrook Mall Houston TX 77070

VASSAR, TINA MARRIE, nurse; b. Portsmouth, Va., Oct. 29, 1956; d. John Dixie and Hazell (Barr) V. BS in Nursing, Radford U., 1979; MS in Nursing, U. Va., 1983. Staff nurse U. Va. Hosp., Charlottesville, 1979-80, head nurse, 1980-83; cardiothoracic surgery clin. nurse specialist N.C. Meml. Hosp., Chapel Hill., 1983—; adj. instr. U. N.C. Sch. Nursing, Chapel Hill, 1986—. Bd. dirs. ARC, Chapel Hill. Mem. Am. Nurses Assn. (bd. dirs., research chmn. Dist. II 1984-88), Am. Assn. Critical Care Nurses (bd. dirs., workshop chmn. Triangle chpt. 1984-85, chpt. treas. 1986-87), Alpha Delta Pi. Republican. Baptist. Avocations: swimming, music. Office: NC Meml Hosp Manning Dr Chapel Hill NC 27514

VASSER, LYNN TRACY, retail marketing professional; b. Valley Stream, N.Y., Sept. 10, 1961; d. Charles S. and Elaine (Senk) Danzker; m. Jeffrey S. Vasser, Apr. 12, 1987. BS, Cornell U., 1983. Asst. buyer Abraham & Straus, Bklyn., 1983-84; dept. mgr. Abraham & Straus, Massapequa, N.Y., 1984-85; assoc. buyer Montgomery Ward Co., N.Y.C., 1985-86; asst. market rep. May Merchandising Corp., N.Y.C., 1986-90; merchandiser Seiko Corp. of Am., Maitwah, N.J., 1990—. Home: 12 Lessing Rd West Orange NJ 07052

VASUTA, LORINDA, dog groomer; b. Akron, Ohio, Feb. 4, 1955; d. George Thomas and Loretta M. (Tomaz) V. Grad. high sch., Akron. Sec. Firestone Tire & Rubber Co., Akron, 1972-78; owner, groomer Lorinda's Dogs of Distinction, Akron, 1978—. Mem. North Akron Bd. Trade (pres. 1984, 85), Medina Kennel Club, Ohio Valley Pomeranian Club. Home and Office: Lorinda Dogs of Distinction 63 E Cuyahoga Falls Ave Akron OH 44310

VATH, ELIZABETH MARIE, nurse; b. Buffalo, Jan. 12, 1951; d. Joseph George and Beatrice Elizabeth (Trapper) V. BSN, SUNY, 1985; AAS, Corning Community Coll., 1972; postgrad., State U. Buffalo, 1993. RN, N.Y. Staff nurse West Seneca (NY) Devel. Ctr., 1972-73; staff nurse operating room Children's Hosp. Buffalo, 1973—, team leader orthopedics operating room, 1988—; basic and advanced emergency med. technician, Buffalo, 1982—; pediatric advanced life support nurse certification Md. Inst. Emergency Med. Svcs. System, Balt., 1988. Eucharistic minister, lector, mem. music ministry, worship com. Mem. Nat. Assn. Orthopedic Nurses, Critical Care Nurses Assn., American Trauma Soc., Assn. Operating Room Nurses, Trauma Nurse Network. Republican. Home: 4615-E Chestnut Ridge Rd Amherst NY 14228 Office: Children's Hosp Buffalo 219 Bryant St Buffalo NY 14222

VAUGHAN, ELIZABETH ARDREY, television commerical producer; b. N.Y.C., Sept. 22, 1963; d. Rushton Leigh Jr. and Sally (David) Ardrey; m. Steven J. Vaughan. Grad. cum laude, Choate Rosemary Hall, Wallingford, Conn., 1981; student, Carnegie Mellon U., 1982-83; BA, Tulane U., 1985. Editorial asst. Rolling Stone Mag., N.Y.C., 1984; asst. assignment editor Sta. WDSU-TV, New Orleans, 1984; prodn. asst. Fairbanks Films, N.Y.C., 1985; asst. casting dir. McCaffrey and McCall Advt., N.Y.C., 1986, asst. producer, 1987; asst. producer, sales rep. The Ptnrs.'/USA, N.Y.C., 1988—. Contbr. Meml. Sloan Kettering, 1985—; exec. com. Madison Sq. Boys Club, 1986—, Youth Counseling League, 1985—, N.Y.C. Republican. Episcopalian. Home: 2315 Alcyona Dr Los Angeles CA 90068

VAUGHAN, FRANCES ELIZABETH, psychologist; b. N.Y.C., Jan. 1, 1935; d. Frederick V. and Caroline (Willis) V.; m. Reece R. Clark, July 12, 1957 (div. 1975); children: Reece Robert, Leslie Elizabeth; m. Roger N. Walsh, June 30, 1985. BA with great distinction, Stanford U., 1956; MA, Calif. State U., Sonoma, 1969; PhD, Calif. Sch. Profl. Psychology, Berkeley, 1973. Lic. psychologist, Calif. Pvt. practice Mill Valley, Calif., 1975—; prof. psychology, Inst. Transpersonal Psychology, Menlo Park, Calif., 1975-85; presenter workshops, 1975—; asst. clin. prof. U. Calif. Med. Sch., Irvine, 1987—; bd. dirs. Transpersonal Inst., Palo Alto. Consulting editor: ReVision, 1979—; Author: Awakening Intuition, 1979, The Inward Arc, 1986; co-editor: Beyond Ego, 1980, Accept This Gift, 1983, A Gift of Peace, 1986, A Gift of Healing, 1988. Mem. Am. Psychol. Assn., Calif. State Psychol. Assn., Assn. Transpersonal Psychology (pres. 1975-77), Assn. Humanistic Psychology (pres. 1987-88), Internat. Transpersonal Assn. (bd. dirs. 1982-84, 89—), Phi Beta Kappa. Democrat. Episcopalian. Office: 10 Millwood St Ste 3 Mill Valley CA 94941

VAUGHAN, MARGARET EVELYN, psychologist, consultant; b. Mpls., Nov. 9, 1948; d. Robert Bergh and Evelyn (Glockner) Cedergren; m. William Vaughan Jr., July 30, 1981. BA, St. Cloud (Minn.) State U., 1972; MA, Western Mich. U., 1977, PhD, 1980. Asst. prof. psychology Kalamazoo (Mich.) Coll., 1979-81; postdoctoral fellow Harvard U., Cambridge, Mass., 1981-82, rsch. assoc., 1982-83, rsch. assoc. Sch. of Bus., 1983-84; asst. prof. psychology Salem (Mass.) State Coll., 1984-88, assoc. prof. psychology, 1988—; cons. Shore Ednl. Collaborative, Medford, Mass., 1984—; bd. dirs. B.F. Skinner Found., Cambridge. Author: (with B.F. Skinner) Enjoy Old Age, 1983; mem. editorial bd. The Behavior Analyst Jour. Mem. Am. Psychol. Assn., Assn. for Behavior Analysis, Phi Kappa Phi, Psi Chi. Office: Salem State Coll Dept Psychology Salem MA 01970

VAUGHAN, MARTHA, biochemist; b. Dodgeville, Wis., Aug. 4, 1926; d. John Anthony and Luciel (Ellingen) V.; m. Jack Orloff, Aug. 4, 1951 (dec. Dec. 1988); children: Jonathan Michael, David Geoffrey, Gregory Joshua. Ph.B., U. Chgo., 1944; M.D., Yale U., 1949. Intern New Haven Hosp., Conn., 1950-51; research fellow U. Pa., Phila., 1951-52; research fellow Nat. Heart Inst., Bethesda, Md., 1952-54, mem. research staff, 1954-68; head metabolism sect. Nat. Heart and Lung Inst., Bethesda, 1968-74; acting chief molecular disease br. Nat. Heart, Lung and Blood Inst., Bethesda, 1974-76, chief cell metabolism lab., 1974—; mem. Metabolism Study Sect. NIH, 1965-68; mem. bd. sci. counselors Nat. Inst. Alcohol Abuse and Alcoholism. Mem. editorial bd. Jour. Biol. Chemistry, 1971-76, 80-83, 88-90; mem. editorial adv. bd. Molecular Pharmacology, 1972-80; editor Biochemistry and Biophysics Rsch., 1990—; cons. editor Acad. Medicine; contbr. articles to profl. jours., chpts. to books. Bd. dirs. Found. Advanced Edn. in Scis. Inc., Bethesda, 1979—, exec. com., 1980—, treas., 1984-86, v.p. 1986-88, pres. 1988-90; mem. Yale U. Council com. med. affairs, New Haven, 1974-80. Recipient Meritorious Service medal HEW, 1974, Disting. Service medal HEW, 1979, Commd. Officer award USPHS, 1982. Mem. Nat. Acad. Scis., Am. Soc. Biol. Chemists (chmn. pub. com. 1984-86), Assn. Am. Physicians, Am. Soc. Clin. Investigation. Home: 11608 W Hill Dr Rockville MD 20852 Office: Nat Heart Lung & Blood Inst Bldg 10 Rm 5N-307 NIH Bethesda MD 20892

VAUGHAN, MARY KATHLEEN, anatomy educator; b. Houston, Sept. 7, 1943; d. William Asa and Ana Maria (Lopez) Cotten; m. George Martin Vaughan, July 2, 1966; children: Thomas Emanuel, Charles Martin, Christopher Nicholas. BA in Biology, U. St. Thomas, Houston, 1965; PhD in Anatomy, U. Tex., Galveston, 1970. Lectr. U. Rochester, N.Y., 1970-71; asst. prof. U. Tex. Health Sci. Ctr., San Antonio, 1975-80, assoc. prof., 1980—. Contbr. numerous chapters to books and articles to profl. jours. Mary Gibbs Jones scholar, 1961-65, USPHS spl. rsch. fellow, 1974-75. Mem. Am. Assn. Anatomists, Endocrine Soc., Soc. for Experimental Biology and Medicine, Neurosci. Soc., Am. Physiol. Soc., Internat. Soc. Neuroendocrinology, Sigma Xi. Democrat. Roman Catholic. Office: U Tex Health Sci Ctr Dept Cellular Structural 7703 Floyd Curl San Antonio TX 78284-7762

VAUGHAN, MITTIE KATHLEEN, journalist; b. Waycross, Ga., Mar. 18, 1950; d. Charles N. and Kathleen (Howell) V.; m. Bill Crews, Apr. 21, 1975 (div. Oct. 1978); 1 child, R. Hannah. Student, Abraham Baldwin Coll., 1968-70. Women's editor Waycross (Ga.) Jour.-Herald, 1970-73; staff writer Daily Tifton (Ga.) Gazette, 1973-74; news editor Wiregrass Shopper, Alma, Ga., 1976-78; assoc. editor The Alma Times, 1978-79; pub. Pierce County Press, Blackshear, Ga., 1980—. 2d vice chmn. Pierce County Dem. Exec. Com., Blackshear, 1988-89; chmn. parent anonymous program Child Abuse Coun., 1988-89. Mem. Ga. Collegiate Press Assn. (dir. 1969-70, sec. 1970-71), Blackshear Exchange Club (sec.-treas. 1988-89, sec. 1989—), Blackshear Woman's Club (publicity chmn. 1986-88, outstanding new mem. 1987). Democrat. Baptist. Office: Pierce County Press 125 S Central Ave Blackshear GA 31516

VAUGHAN, PEGGY THORPE, personnel interviewer, home economist; b. Emporia, Va., May 12, 1942; d. Neuit Henry Thorpe Sr. and Ruth Ethel (Harris) Thorpe Harrell; m. Joseph Kelley Vaughan, Dec. 21, 1962; children: Jody, Thorpe, Andy. BS in Home Econs. Edn., Longwood Coll., 1964. Lic. tchr. Tchr. spl. edn. Emporia Elem. Sch., 1964-65; tchr. home econs. Southampton High Sch., Courtland, Va., 1965-66, Greensville High Sch., Emporia, 1968-69; elem. grade tchr. Roanoke Christian Sch., Roanoke Rapids, N.C., 1979-80; part-time instr. Halifax Community Coll., Weldon, N.C., 1969-80, Southside Va. Community Coll., Alberta, Va., 1984-85; interviewer U.S. Dept. Commerce, Charlotte, N.C., 1984—; consumer council rep. Farm Fresh Supermarkets, 1986-88, regional rep., 1988—; judge Future Homemakers Am./Home Econs. Related Occupations contest Deep Creek High Sch., Norfolk, Va., 1988. Vol. Am. Cancer Soc. Bazaar, 1987—; mem. Va. Bluegrass and Country Music Found., Richmond, 1988—; v.p. Emporia Jr. Women's Club, 1965-69, Greenville County Hist. Soc., 1988; com. chmn. Emporia Federated Garden Club, 1967-69; co-chmn. campaign Henry Howell for Gov., 1969-78. Named one of Outstanding Young Women of Am., 1978. Mem. Am. Home Econs. Assn., Va. Home Econs. Assn. (spl. edn. sect. 1964-65, Tidewater Home Economists (pres. 1986-88), Home Economists in Homemaking (yr. book chmn. 1979), United Daus. Confederacy (com. chmn. 1986—, recording sec. 1987—), Emporia Hist. Soc. (com. chmn. 1985—), Archeol. Soc., Early Am. Soc., Am. Rose Soc. Baptist. Lodges: Rotary (surrogate mother for Mexican Rotary exchange student 1987—), Order Ea. Star (officer 1988). Home: 204 Battery Ave Emporia VA 23847

VAUGHN, ALEASE JUET, nurse anesthetist; b. Akron, Ohio, June 30, 1945; d. William and Doris Madeline (Woods) Tolbert; m. DorLan Vaughn, Sept. 24, 1964 (div. Mar. 1976); children: Kimberly Annette, Candace Marie. Diploma in nursing, Akron Gen. Hosp. Sch. Nursing, 1967; diploma in nurse anesthesia, Aultman Sch. Nurse Anesthesia, 1977; BA in Allied Health, Malone Coll., 1986. Staff nurse Akron Children's Hosp., 1968-73, recovery rm. charge nurse, 1973-75; staff anesthetist, clin. instr. Aultman Anesthesia Inc. at Canton (Ohio) Aultman Hosp., 1977-78, 80-90; staff anesthetist Akron City Hosp. Profl. Anesthesia Svcs., 1990—; mem. curriculum com. Canton Aultman Sch. Nurse Anesthesia, 1984-85, mem. admission com., 1986, 87. Mem. AAUW, Am. Assn. Nurse Anesthetists, Zonta Internat. (bd. dirs.), Nat. Black Nurses Assn., Inc. Democrat. Home: 863 Castle Blvd Akron OH 44313

VAUGHN, CINDY GAIL, real estate executive; b. N. Myrtle Beach, S.C., Feb. 10, 1953; d. Harry Lee and Hellon Marie (Smith) Bellamy; m. Anthony Kirby Vaughn, Jan. 7, 1976; 1 child, Crisler Lee. BA in English, Limestone Coll., Gaffney, S.C., 1974; real estate broker, Harry Georgetown Tech., Myrtle Beach,S.C., 1984. Lic. real estate broker. Tchr. English Boiling Springs (S.C.) High Sch., 1974-75; office mgr. Elliott Realty, North Myrtle Beach, S.C., 1975-83; gen. mgr. Condos Unltd., Inc., North Myrtle Beach, 1983—. Cons. Chateau by the Sea Homeowners Assn., North Myrtle Beach, 1983—; sec. Waipani Homeowners Assn., North Myrtle Beach, 1983—. Mem. North Myrtle Beach Aerobics Club. Baptist. Office: Condos Unlimited 7th Ave S North Myrtle Beach SC 29582

VAUGHN, ELEANOR, state legislator; b. Troy, Idaho, Nov. 12, 1922; m. Benjamin Vaughn Sr.; 3 children. Grad., Kinman Bus. U. Mem. Mont. State Senate. Democrat. Home: 251 Mahoney Rd PO Box 45 Libby MT 59923

VAUGHN, ELIZABETH MARIE, county official; b. Ada, Minn., June 26, 1958; d. Glen Walter and Vivian Hazel (Johnson) Hanson; 1 child, David Gregory. BS in Acctg., Moorhead (Minn.) State U., 1982. Commns. clk. Maintenance Engring., Ltd., Fargo, N.D., 1980-83; account clk. hwy. dept. Norman County, Ada, 1983—. Candidate City Coun., Ada, 1989; participant Community Leadership Series, Ada, 1990; fin. sec. Grace Luth. Ch., Ada, 1985—. Mem. Moorhead State U. Alumni Assn., Am. Legion Aux., VFW Aux., NAFE, AFSCME (sec.-treas. local 3064 1990—). Democrat. Office: Norman County Hwy Dept Hwy 9 N Ada MN 56510

VAUGHN, JOYCE ELAINE, special education educator; b. Kewanee, Ill., May 16, 1946; d. Earl Walter and Borgia Catherine (Wetzel) Grant; m. Laurence Eugene Vaughn, Aug. 17, 1968; children: Noah Andrew, Mieke Maureen. BS in Edn., Ill. State U., Normal, 1968; MA, Bradley U., Peoria, Ill., 1986. Tchr. Farmington (Ill.) Sch. Dist., 1968-71; tchr. learning disabilities East Peoria (Ill.) Sch. Dist. 86, 1980-81; resource tchr. North Pekin (Ill.) Sch. Dist. 102, 1983-85; lang. impaired tchr. East Peoria Sch. Dist. 86, 1985—; video producer Regional Supts. Office, Tazewell County, 1989; mem. Tchr. Assistance Teams, East Peoria, 1989-90; coord. Arts Day Program, 1987, 88, 89. Pres. East Peoria Youth Coun., 1972-79. Peoria Area Arts and Sci. Coun. fine arts grantee, 1987-90. Mem. AAUW (Young Career award 1970), Coun. Exceptional Children, Ill. Edn. Assn. (del. 1970). Roman Catholic. Home: 615 Fondulac Dr East Peoria IL 61611 Office: E Armstrong Sch 1848 Highview Rd East Peoria IL 61611

VAUGHN, MARY, healthcare facilities executive; b. Trafford, Ala., Apr. 20, 1930; d. Grover Webster and Vivian Lenora (Dorman) V.; student Birmingham Bus. Coll., 1952, Howard Coll., 1959, U. Ala., 1960, 62, Balboa Intermediate Care Facility, San Diego, 1969-76; certificate in therapeutic activities tng. Grossmont Adult Sch., 1975; m. James T. Lovvorn, Mar. 1952 (div. 1959). Owner, pres., treas. Balboa Manor Inc. and Balboa Manor Health Facility, San Diego, 1969-79. Charter pres. Quota Club of Birmingham (Ala.), 1967-68; lt. gov. 8th dist. Quota Internat., 1968-69; supr. adv. com. to Jim Bates, 4th Dist. Supr. San Diego County, 1973—; mem. San Diego County Com. on the Handicapped, 1979—; mem. support com. Community Video Center, pub. access TV, 1979—. Pres., bd. dirs. Girls Club San Diego, 1987-88. Recipient Safety award Indsl. Indemnity, 1973, 75, cert. of appreciation Jim Bates, 1975, 11th Woman award Women's Internat. Ctr., 1988; named Citizen of Month Congl. Service award, 1987; recipient Wuzzer trophy Southland Club for Bus. and Profl. Women of San Diego, 1975, 83, 89; notary pub., cert. nursing home adminstr., Calif. Mem. Am. Health Care Assn., Am. Coll. Nursing Home Adminstrs., Am., Calif. nursing home assns., Com. of 100 of San Diego Klee Wyk Soc., San Diego Opera, Bus. and Profl. Women's Club (pres. Birmingham chpt. 1967-69), San Diego Mus. Natural History, San Diego Mus. of Man, Nat. Notary Assn. Republican. Methodist. Author: Exploring Mental Therapy. Home: 2804 C St San Diego CA 92102

VAUGHN, MARY ANN, real estate professional; b. Moulton, Ala., July 25, 1947; d. James and Ruby Lee (Welborn) Stewart; m. James Columbus Vaughn, Jan. 27, 1965; children: Pamela, Michael. Student, Calhoun Coll., 1977-78. Clk./stenographer State of Ala., Decatur, 1965-67; exec. sec. Mut. Savs. Life Ins. Co., Decatur, 1975-77; adminstrv. asst. Ala. Farmers Coop., Decatur, 1977-78; mgr. Aquadome Pool City of Decatur, 1979-80; mgr., owner The Golden Door Personal Improvement Studio, Decatur, 1980-84; adminstrv. asst. trust dept. Am. South Bank, Decatur, 1984-85; realtor Morgan County Bd. Realtors, Decatur, 1986—; mem. computer com. Morgan County Bd. Realtors, 1987-89, mem. awards com., 1988-89, chmn. computer com., 1989. Active Decatur Christian Women's Club, 1983-89; chmn. Morgan County Jr. Miss Assn., 1987-89; vol. ARC, 1974-89, Voluntary Action Ctr., 1985-89. Mem. NAFE, Nat. Assn. Realtors, Ala. Assn. Realtors, Cert. Residential Specialists (Ala. chpt.), Realtors Nat. Mktg. Inst., Residential Sales Coun., Morgan County Bd. Realtors, Women's C. of C., Decatur Area C. of C., Decatur Area PC Users Group. Democrat. Baptist. Home: 1212 Fremont St SW Decatur AL 35601 Office: Real Estate Plus Inc 809 6th Ave SE Decatur AL 35601

VAUGHN, VIRGINIA A., data processing executive; b. Wilmington, Del., Apr. 3, 1956; d. Joseph Edward and Catherine Irene (Wallace) V. AA, Del. Tech. Coll., Newark. Word processing technician; sec. Div. Vocat. Rehab., Wilmington, EDP technician III; pres. Rainbow Word Processing Svcs., New Castle, Del.; adminstrv. asst., word processing coord. Div. Vocat. Rehab., Wilmington. Editor 3 newsletters. Recipient Nat. Sec. Svc. award, Mid Atlantic Sec. Svc. award, others. Mem. NAFE, First State Assn. Rehab. Secs. (v.p. 1985, sec. 1986, pres. 1988-90), Del. Rehab. Adminstrs. Assn. (sec. 1986-90). Democrat. Home: 25 Revelle St New Castle DE 19720

VAUGHT, JANET MAUREEN BURGER, city official; b. Indpls., Jan. 23, 1952; d. Clifford Robert and Opal June (McKinnon) Burger; m. Charles H. Vaught, Jr., Sept. 15, 1977; children: Patricia Lynn, Jennifer Leigh. BS in Edn., So. Ill. U., 1974, MS in Edn., 1984. Registered mcpl. clk.; cert. mcpl. clk. Research asst. So. Ill. U., Carbondale, 1974, sec., 1974-75, researcher, 1976; sec. City of Carbondale, 1976-77, dep. city clk., 1977-79, city clk., 1979—. Vol. Girl Scouts Am.; bd. dirs. LWV, 1988). Ill. tchr. edn. scholar State of Ill., 1970. Mem. Internat. Inst. Mcpl. Clks. (bd. dirs. 1988), Nat. Bus. Edn. Assn. (award of merit 1974), Ill. Bus. Edn. Assn. (scholar 1973), So. Ill. Bus. Edn. Assn., Ill. Mcpl. Clks. Ill. (pres. 1987, Mem. of Yr. 1988), Carbondale Bus. Profl. Women (2d v.p. 1987), Delta Pi Epsilon, Pi Omega Pi, Pi Lambda Theta, Kappa Delta Pi. Methodist. Avocations: travel, reading, being with children. Home: 620 Glenview Dr Carbondale IL 62901 Office: City of Carbondale PO Box 2047 Carbondale IL 62902

VAUPEL, JANE KATHRYN, journalist; b. Pitts., June 23, 1963; d. John Rodney and Joanne Kathryn (Pettican) Vaupel. BS in Journalism, Ohio U., 1985. Sales coordinator Ocean Communications, Ocean City, N.J., 1986-87; fashion editor Sun newspaper, Absecon, N.J., 1987-89; mng. editor She newsmagazine, Ocean City, 1989—. Mem. Humane Soc., Ocean City, 1987-88. Mem. Women in Communications, Press Club Atlantic City, Ocean City C. of C. Home: 620 Atlantic Ave Ocean City NJ 08226

VAUTIER, ALICE FORSHA, nurse, administrator; d. George Oliver abd Elna Margareta (Nordberg) F.; m. Robert Arthur Vautier, Oct. 6, 1967; children: Robert Arthur, Charlene Elisabeth. Diploma in Nursing, Cooper Med. Ctr., 1961; BS in Nursing U. Pa., 1981; MS in Nursing Villanova U., 1983; postgrad. Columbia U.; mem. staff St. Christopher Hosp. for Children, Phila., 1963-65, coord. nursing edn., 1965-77, asst. v.p. nursing, 1977-81; nursing cons. O'Leary and Assocs., Wayne, Pa., 1983-85; v.p. patient svcs. Cabell Huntington Hosp., Huntington, W.Va., 1985—. Mem. Am. Orgn. Nurse Execs., W.Va. Orgn. Nurse Execs. (pres. 1987—), Nat. League Nursing, W.Va. League Nursing. Episcopalian. Home: RD 2 Box 99A Ona WV 25545 Office: Cabell Huntington Hosp 1340 Hal Greer Blvd Huntington WV 25701

VAUX, DORA LOUISE, sperm bank official, consultant; b. White Pine, Mont., Aug. 8, 1922; d. Martin Tinus and Edna Ruth (Pyatt) Palmlund; m. Robert Glenn Vaux, Oct. 25, 1941; children: Jacqueline, Cheryl, Richard, Jeanette. Grad. high sch., Bothell, Wash. Photographer Busco-Nestor Studios, San Diego, 1961-68; owner, mgr. Vaux Floors & Interiors, San Diego, 1968-82; cons., mgr. Repository for Germinal Choice, Escondido, Calif., 1983—. Mem. Escondido Country Club, Escondido Fish and Game

Club. Republican. Home: 1255 LaCienega San Marcos CA 92069 Office: Found for Advancement Man 450 S Escondido Blvd Escondido CA 92025

VAVRICK, ELLAN FINMAN, insurance company executive; b. Pensacola, Fla., Aug. 28, 1943; d. Maurice Max Finman and Rosalie (Buchman) Rotwein; m. Samuel Dunham Harris Jr., Dec. 30, 1971 (div. Feb. 1982); children Marcia Harris Francis, Julie Harris Prommasit; m. Richard Anthony Vavrick, Mar. 12, 1987. AA, Pensacola (Fla.) Jr. Coll., 1967; BA, U. W. Fla., 1970. Registered health underwriter; cert. fin. planner Nat. Assn. Securities Dealers. Exec. asst. Amy's Shop's, Inc., Pensacola, Fla., 1961-68; exec. asst. to pres. Pensacola Rug & Shade, Co., Pensacola, 1968-69; account exec. WBOP radio, Pensacola, 1971; owner, artist Grand Lagoon Gallery, Pensacola, 1971-77; sales rep. in tng. Travelers Ins. Co., Pensacola, 1977-78, agy supr., 1978-80, prodn. mgr., 1980-85; dir. disability income sales Pan-Am. Lif Ins. Co., New Orleans, 1985-89; disability income regional specialist N.Y. Life Ins. Co., 1989—; instr. mktg. Life Office Mgmt Assn., Pan Am., New Orleans, 1986-87; mem. Ins. Commrs. Cost Containment com., Baton Rouge, 1986-87; speaker Internat. Assn. Fin. Planners workshop, New Orleans, 1986, La. State Health Underwriters conv., Baton Rouge, 1986. Contbr. articles to profl. jours.; author: (monthly column) Panorama, 1985-87. bd. dirs. La. Multiple Sclerosis Soc., New Orleans, 1985-87, U.S. Councils of Navy League, Pensacola, 1980-84, v.p. 1985; mem. museum expansion com., U.S. Naval Aviation Museum Found., Pensacola, 1984; ops. officer Assn. Naval Aviation, New Orleans, 1987; bd. dirs. mentor program Covenant House New Orleans, 1987—. Mem. U.S. Marine Corps Assn. (life), Inst. Cert. Fin. Planners, Nat. Assn. Health Underwriters, New Orleans Registered Health Underwriters Assn. (bd. dirs. 1988—), Beta Sigma Phi. Republican. Roman Catholic. Clubs: Ikebana Internat. (Pensacola) (exhibition chair 1974-77, treas. 1975, sec. 1976); Krewe of Shangri-La (New Orleans). Home: 3025 Esplanade Ave New Orleans LA 70119 Office: Pan Am Life Ins Co 3025 Esplanade Ave 12 Floor New Orleans LA 70130

VAZ, KIM MARIE, research psychologist, writer; b. Springfield, Ill., Aug. 30, 1960; d. Winston and Lois Alice (White) V.; 1 child, Iya-Alice L. Vaz-Kale. BA in Psychology, Newcomb Coll., 1981; MEd, Tulane U., 1983; PhD in Ednl. Psychology, Ind. U., 1990. Rsch. assoc. La. State U., New Orleans, 1989-90; asst. prof. women's studies program U. South Fla., 1990—. Dir. Third World Women's Forum, Bloomington, Ind., 1984-85. Recipient Legis. scholarship State Senate, 1978-81; grantee Dept. Edn., Washington, 1985-86, 87-88; recipient Dist. Young Investigator award Soc. for Life Hist. Rsch., 1990. Mem. Am. Psychol. Assn. (assoc.), Soc. for Study of Social Psychol. Issues. Office: U South Fla Women's Studies Program Tampa FL 33613

VAZIRI, FAKHRI FAY, financial consultant, insurance broker; b. Teheran, Iran, July 4, 1929; came to U.S., 1947; d. Abass and Hamiyat (Monif) V.; divorced; 1 child, Kew. BA in Drama, Hofstra U., 1953; M in Dramatic Art, Columbia U., N.Y.C., 1954-56; postgrad., Life Underwriters Tng. Coun. Actress Bombay Film Co., 1942-47; film reporter Iranian Dept. Info. and Radio, U.S.; radio MC Voice of Am., N.Y.C., 1952-54; scriptwriter, announcer featured as "Star of the East" Voice of Am., Washington, 1954-61; agent Reserve Life Ins. Co., Dallas, 1962-81; fin. cons., ins. broker Vaziri Ins. Agy., Bethesda, Md., 1982—. Actress in numerous Persian films, including Shirin-Farhad, one of first Persian films made. Named Woman of the Yr. Reserve Life Ins. Co., 1966, named to All-Star Honor Roll issue of Insurance mag., 1967, ; one of few women to be named a charter member for Nat. Sales Achievement award, Nat. Assn. Life Underwriters, 1966; named Agent of Yr. Atlantic Terr. Pruduential Ins. Co. Am., 1980; recipient numerous other awards from ins. industry, also subject of articles for industry publs. Mem. NOW, Women Leaders Roundtable of Nat. Assn. Life Underwriters, D.C. Life Underwriters Assn., Bus. and Profl. Women's Assn. (pres. Washington chpt. 1987, woman of yr. award 1988), Muslim Women Assn. of Washington (co-founder, chairwoman postgrad. scholarship for Muslim girls, 1986—). Office: 5317 Sangamore Rd Bethesda MD 20816

VAZQUEZ, CARMEN INOA, clinical psychologist; b. Bonao, Dominican Republic, July 16, 1942; came to U.S., 1958; d. Laureano and Victoria (Vargas) Inoa; m. Hector Vazquez, Dec. 18, 1965; children: Jaime Alberto, Miguel Angel. BA, Queens Coll., 1976; PhD, CUNY, 1981. Lic. psychologist, N.Y. Bilingual neuropsychol. testing intern Morrisania Neighborhood Clinic, N.Y.C., 1979-80; psychology intern Nassau County Med. Ctr., East Meadow, N.Y., 1980-81; pvt. practice psychotherapy N.Y.C., 1984—; dir. psychology intern tng. program NYU-Bellevue Hosp. Ctr., N.Y.C., 1984—; dir., founder Bilingual Treatment Program, N.Y.C., 1988—; sr. psychologist Bellevue Psychiat. Hosp., N.Y.C., 1982—; clin. supr. South Bronx (N.Y.) Mental Health Coun. Alcoholism Clinic, 1981-82; mem. faculty NYU Sch. Medicine, 1983—, St. John's U., 1983-87, New Sch. Social Rsch., 1980—, Hostos Community Coll.-CUNY, 1977; presenter tng. programs, seminars in field. Contbr. to profl. publs. Grantee Am. Psychol. Assn., 1977-80, NIMH, 1985—.

VEAL, TRACEY YVONNE, marketing professional; b. Atlanta, Mar. 16, 1962; d. Jonas Harry and Lavada (Morton) V.; m. Allen David Booker, Aug. 12, 1989. BA, Agnes Scott Coll., Decatur, Ga., 1984; MBA, Atlanta U., 1989. Asst. student health svcs. Agnes Scott Coll., 1981-84; compensation analyst Sun Life Ins. Co., Inc., Atlanta, 1984-86, supr., 1986-87; intern Digital Equipment Corp., Marlboro, Mass., 1988; market rsch. analyst Allergan, Inc./Herbert Labs. Div., Irvine, Calif., 1989—; intern in family planning Emory U., Atlanta, 1982; gov.'s intern Ga. Dept. Med. Assistance, Atlanta, 1983, Contiuum Alliance for Healthcare, Atlanta, 1984. Vol. Planned Parenthood of Am., Atlanta, 1982, Grady Meml. Hosp., Atlanta, 1983-84; mem. Atlanta Bus. League, 1987-89. Mem. NAFE, Am. Mktg. Assn., Nat. Black MBA Assn., Med. Mktg. Assn., Pharm. Mktg. Rsch. Group, Atlanta U. Entrepreneurs Club (pres. 1988-89). Home: 1380 Village Hwy #E205 Costa Mesa CA 92626

VEALE, ANGELA M., banking executive; b. Oct. 2, 1948; d. Robert Andrew and Ollie (Ushry) V. B in Econ., Spelman Coll., 1970; MPA, Pepperdine, 1974; postgrad., U. Wash., 1980, UCLA, 1984. Tng. officer Security Pacific Bank, Encino, Calif., 1972-74, asst. mgr. loans, 1974-77, asst. v.p., 1977-79, v.p., 1979-81, div. credit adminstr., 1981-84, div. pers. adminstr., 1984-85, regional v.p., 1985-88, div. adminstr., 1989-90, sr. v.p., 1990—. Bd. dirs. San Fernando Valley Girl Scout Coun., United Negro Coll. Fund Adv. Bd. Named Outstanding Black Woman of Achievement NAACP Legal Defense Fund, 1986, Top 100 Best and Brightest Black Women Execs. in Corp. Am. Ebony Mag., 1990. Mem. Alpha Kappa Alpha. Methodist. Office: Security Pacific Nat Bank 333 S Hope St Los Angeles CA 90071

VEGA, BETH SUSAN, personnel director; b. Johnson, Vt., June 7, 1950; d. Kenneth Eugene and Lenor (Kaufman) Brimmer; children: Lilian Anna, Jose G. III. Student, U. Wyo., 1967-68; BS, Met. State Coll., 1971; MPA, U. Colo., 1979. Asst. affirmative action officer Met. State Coll., Denver, 1973-76; affirmative action adminstr. United Bank of Denver, 1977-78; personnel mgmt. specialist City of Aurora, Colo., 1979-80; personnel technician City of Pueblo, Colo., 1981-83, dir. personnel, 1984—; instr. part-time U. So. Colo., Pueblo, 1987-88. Pres.-elect bd. Girls Club of Pueblo, 1988—, bd. dirs., 1982-89, pres., 1989; bd. dirs. YWCA of Pueblo, 1989—, v.p., 1990; mem. choir St. Peters Episcopal Ch., 1988—. Mem. So. Colo. Assn. Human Resource Profls. (pres. 1985-86), Nat. Pub. Employer Labor Rels. Assn., Am. Soc. for Personnel Adminstrn. Office: City of Pueblo PO Box 1427 Pueblo CO 81002

VEGA, ROSA ELIA, financial service secretary; b. East Chgo., Ind., Oct. 16, 1952; d. Domingo and Maria Natividad (Mendoza) V. Student, Ind. U., Gary, 1985-88. Payroll sec. Gary (Ind.) Community Sch. Corp., 1978—; recording sec. SEIU, Local 208, Gary, 1983—; counselor Lake Area United Way Union Counselors, Griffith, Ind., 1985—. Active voter registration, Local 208, Gary, 1983—, various campaign activities, 1983—. Mem. Ind. Assn. Ednl. Secs., Lake Area Hist. Soc., Coalition of Labor Union Women, Friends of Gary Pub. Libr., Latin Am. Hist. Soc. Democrat. Roman Catholic. Office: SEIU Local 208 3750 Hayes St Gary IN 46312

VEHAR, NILA A., manager; b. Butler, Pa., Mar. 28, 1940; d. John Jacob and Helen Regina (Pocorus) V. BS in Economics, Robert Morris Coll., Pitts., 1975; grad. studies, Georgetown U., Wash.; grad., George Wash. U. Mgr. purchasing Koppers Co., Inc., Pitts., 1960-75; congl. fellow The Conf. Bd., Wash., 1975-76; mgr., govt. affairs Koppers Co., Inc., Pitts., 1977-80; dir., the congl. asst. program The Conf. Bd., Wash., 1980-89; exec. dir. A Presdl. Classroom for Young Americans, Alexandria, Va., 1989—; adv. mem. Elmer B. Staats Fund for Pub. Svc., Wash., 1986—; mem. evaluation com. Leader Found. Fellowship Program, Wash., 1987; bd. mem. Leadership Greater Wash., 1989. Author: Research Report, Bus. Role in Federal Adv. Com., 1987. Home: 4242 East West Hwy #805 Chevy Chase MD 20815

VEIHMEYER, CAROL ANNE, management consultant, nurse; b. Columbus, Ohio, June 23, 1957; d. Francis Xavier and June (Lamphear) V.; m. Douglas Donald Cecil, July 6, 1985. BSN, Fla. State U., 1979; MBA, U. N.C., 1987. RN, Ga., N.C. Staff nurse Henrietta Egleston Hosp. for Children, Atlanta, 1980; asst. head nurse adolescent psychiatry charter Chatee Peachford Psychiat. Hosp., Atlanta, 1980-81; charge nurse pediatric ICU Duke U. Med. Ctr., Durham, N.C., 1981-82; pediatric neonatal svc. supr. N.C. Meml. Hosp., Chapel Hill, 1982-85; mgmt. cons. ops. and productivity practice FLR Health Resources, Atlanta, 1987-89; sr. consult Ernst & Young, Atlanta, 1989—; bd. dirs. Second Start, Inc., Durham. Instr. ARC, 1977-88. Mem. Am. Coll. Healthcare Cons., Ga. Nurses Assn., Am. Nurses Assn. (coun. on nursing adminstrn. 1988—). Democrat. Roman Catholic. Office: Ernst & Young 2100 Gas Light Tower Atlanta GA 30303

VEIT, CHRISTINE MARIA, management consultant; b. Syracuse, N.Y., May 25, 1959; d. Leonard G. and Jadwiga (Dziekanski) Kot; m. Richard Joseph Veit, June 20, 1981. BS in Fin., U. Ill., 1981; MBA in Fin., U. Puget Sound, 1985. Bank balancer Busey 1st Nat. Bank, Champaign, Ill., 1979-81; fin. analyst SAFECO Corp., Seattle, 1981-84; with Thousand Trails, Bellevue, Wash., 1984-88; sr. fin. analyst, 1984-86; supr. acctg. analysis Thousand Trails, Bellevue, Wash., 1986-87, mgr. ops., 1987-88; owner, cons. Veit Cons. Assocs., Seattle, 1988—; mem. bd. trustees Neighborhood House, Inc., Seattle, 1985—, bd. devel. chair, 1986—. Meeting chairperson Sr. Transp. Coun., Seattle, 1987. Mem. Planning Forum, Women's Bus. Exch., Nat. Assn. for Women Execs. Home: 927 N 81st St Seattle WA 98103 Office: Veit Cons Assocs 1415 Western Ave Ste 600 Seattle WA 98101

VELASQUEZ, GERALDINE KHANER, artist, educator; b. N.Y.C., Dec. 24, 1943; d. Barney and Lillian (Yones) Khaner; m. Jose Manuel Velasquez, Aug. 31, 1963; children: Brenda, Mark. BFA, Hunter Coll., 1964; MA in Fine Art, Montclair State U., 1976; EdD, Rutgers U., 1987. Textile designer Batista Studio, N.Y.C., 1964-65; textile stylist Stien-tex Fabrics, N.Y.C., 1966-68; adj. prof. art Monmouth Coll., West Long Branch, N.J., 1969-80; assoc. prof. art Georgian Court Coll., Lakewood, N.J., 1980—; guest curator Bell Labs., Prudential Ins. Co., Johnson & Johnson, 1976—; mem. grants awards panel N.J. Coun. on Arts, 1983-85; curator art Long Beach Island (N.J.) Arts Found., 1986-89; presenter papers, speaker at profl. confs. Solo and group shows Monmouth (N.J.) Mus., Pen and Brush Club, N.Y.C.; author nat. study on attitudes of contemporary crafts people; contbr. to N.Y. Times, The Crafts Report. Pres. Great Lincroft (N.J.) Civic Assn., 1980-83. Invited Woman Artist of 1976, Ft. Monmouth, N.J. Mem. N.J. Designer Craftsmen (dir. orgn. devel. 1984-86), Am. Crafts Coun. (nat. panel on crafts conf. 1987), Jersey Shore Pub. Rels. and Advt. Assn., Northeastern Edn. Assn., AAUW (v.p. for programs 1980-81), Soroptomists. Home: PO Box 223 Lincroft NJ 07738 Office: Georgian Court Coll Lakewood NJ 08701

VELASQUEZ-WALSH, KELLIE ELAINE, retail company executive; b. Inglewood, Calif., Oct. 8, 1961; d. Theodore Adrian Velasquez and Ann Veronica (Abel) Walsh; m. Dennis L. Smith,Sept. 24, 1988. Student, Calif. State U., Fullerton, 1979-82, Nat. U., 1984-85. Loss prevention agt. Mervyn's, Huntington and Tustin, Calif., 1983-85; loss prevention mgr. J.W. Robinsons, Anaheim and Escondido, Calif., 1985-86; dist. loss prevention mgr. J.W. Robinsons, 1986-87; dir. loss prevention dept. Three D Depts., Inc., Costa Mesa, Calif., 1987—. Mem. Am. Soc. for Indsl. Security. Republican. Roman Catholic. Office: Three D Depts Inc 3200 Bristoe #800 Costa Mesa CA 92626

VELAZQUEZ, ANABEL, sales executive; b. Havana, Cuba, June 26, 1958; came to U.S, 1966; d. Joe and Elsa (Miranda) V. BS in Nursing, Fla. Internat. U., 1987; AS, So. Coll., Collegedale, Tenn., 1979. Cert. emergency room nurse, trauma nurse specialist. Staff nurse Hialeah (Fla.) Hosp., 1980-85; home care supr. Med. Pers. Pool, Miami, 1985-88; regional mgr. Peninsular Rehab. Assocs., Winter Park, Fla., 1988-89; med. sales specialist Bristol Myers-Squibb, Evansville, Ind., 1989—. Recipient award Am. Legion. Mem. Fla. Nurses Assn., Coun. on Future of Nurses. Address: 5415 NW 173d Dr Miami FL 33055

VELDMAN, VICKI LYNN, software engineer; b. Rock Rapids, Iowa, Oct. 5, 1963; d. Gerald Henry and Sherrie Lee (Nelson) V. BA, Dordt Coll., 1986. Intern U.S. State Dept. AID, Washington, 1985; software engr. Dynamics Research Corp., Arlington, Va., 1987—. Mem. Smithsonian Assoc., Friends of the Kennedy Ctr., Friends of Hist. Mt. Vernon. Republican. Home: 8046 St Annes Ct Alexandria VA 22309 Office: Dynamics Rsch Corp 1755 Jefferson Davis Hwy Arlington VA 22202

VELLENGA, KATHLEEN OSBORNE, state legislator; b. Alliance, N.C., Aug. 5, 1938; d. Howard Benson and Marjorie (Menke) Osborne; m. James Alan Vellenga, Aug. 9, 1959; children: Thomas, Charlotte Vellenga Landreau, Carolyn. BA, Macalester Coll., 1959. Tchr. St. Paul Pub. Schs., 1959-60, Children's Ctr. Montessori, St. Paul, 1973-74, Children's House Montessori, St. Paul, 1974-79; mem. Minn. Ho. of Reps., St. Paul, 1980—, mem. fin. div. edn./health and human services com., 1981-82, 87—, mem. judiciary com., 1981—, chmn. St. Paul del., 1985-89, chmn. criminal justice div., 1987—, chmn. crime and family law div., 1987—, mem. Dem. steering com., 1987—; mem. Gov.'s Council on Youth, St. Paul, 1983-86. V.p. LWV, St. Paul, 1979; mem. steering com. Alliance for Sci., St. Paul, 1982-84; 9; bd. dirs. Landmark Ctr., St. Paul, 1985-87; chmn. Healthstart, St. Paul, 1987—. Democrat. Presbyterian. Office: Minn Ho Reps 549 State Office Bldg Saint Paul MN 55155

VELLENOWETH, CAROLE LELAND, social services administrator; b. Washington, Dec. 1, 1941; d. Theodore Walter and Elizabeth Polk (Warfield) Leland; m. James Randolph Vellenoweth, July 28, 1962 (div. 1966); 1 child, Holly Augusta; m. Fred Douglass Green, Mar. 16, 1985. BA, Davis and Elkins Coll., 1967; MSW, Va. Commonwealth U., 1984. Lic. social worker, Va. Social worker Loudoun County Dept. Social Services, Leesburg, VA., 1968-73, Charlottesville (Va.) Dept. Social Services, 1977-82; tchr., counselor Glaydin Sch., Leesburg, 1973-77; social worker, trainer Refugee Unaccompanied Minors Program, Falls Church, Va., 1984-85; social work supr. Fairfax (Va.) Dept. Social Services, 1985-86, adminstrv. supr., 1986—; adminstrv. supr. Turnabout Counseling Ctr., Lewes, Del.; trainer, workshop presenter, cons., 1980—; guest lectr. Piedmont Community Coll., 1980, 82, U. Va., 1982, George Mason U., 1985. Author: Handbook for Parent Education for Low Income Families, 1981, The Parent Aide Primer and Trainer's Manual, 1985; producer, dir. videos Mon's Bag of Tricks, 1981, On the Edge, 1988. Founding mem. bd. dirs. Fauquier-Loudoun Day Care Ctr., 1969-73; active Loudoun County Housing Coun., 1971-73, Loudoun County Environ. Group, 1970-73, Goose Creek Friends Social Concerns Com., 1974-77; bd. dirs. Piedmont Coun. Arts, 1980-82; bd. dirs., v.p. Four County Players, 1978-82. Merit scholar Va. Commonwealth U., 1983, Am. Friends Service Com. nat. merit scholar, 1983. Mem. Nat. Assn. Social Workers. Democrat. Mem. Soc. of Friends. Home: Box 407 AFTB Lewes DE 19958 Office: Turnabout Counseling Ctr Lewes DE 19958

VELLER, MARGARET PAXTON, physician; b. Beaver Dam, Ky., Dec. 14, 1925; d. Darrell K. and Gladys (Myers) V.; B.A., Vanderbilt U., 1947, M.D., 1950. Intern, resident Vanderbilt U. Hosp., Nashville, 1950-54; practice medicine, 1954—. Mem. Am., Miss. (com. maternal and child care 1956-72), Homochitto Valley med. assns., Miss. Obstet. and Gynecol. Soc., Phi Beta Kappa, Alpha Omega Alpha. Baptist. Club: Pilgrimage Garden. Home: 28 S Circle Dr Natchez MS 39120 Office: Natchez Med Clinic 49 Sgt S Prentiss Dr Natchez MS 39120

VELTMAN, JAMIE DAWN, pilot; b. Clarksburg, W.Va., Nov. 20, 1958; d. Charles Leslie Akers and Mary Kelly (Gerrard) Williamson; m. Gregory David Veltman, June 9, 1979 (div. May 1987); 1 child, Christina Dawn. Cert., West. Fla. Helicopters, 1986; cert. flight tng., Bell Helicopter Textron, 1986. Cert. rotocraft-helicopter flight instr.; lic. real estate agt., Fla. Salesperson Largo, Fla., 1986—. Mem. Concerned Women for Am. Mem. The Whirly-Girls, Inc., Internat. Women Helicopter Pilots, Am. Helicopter Soc., Inc., Aircraft Owners and Pilots Assn. Republican. Home and Office: 821 Jacaranda Dr Largo FL 34640

VENABLE, PATRICIA LENGEL, educator; b. Elyria, Ohio, Aug. 6, 1930; d. Manhatten John and Marcelyn Marie (Ketchum) Lengel; m. Baxter Venable, June 12, 1965; children: Mark, Amy. BA, Coll. Wooster, 1952; MS, Ohio State U., 1954, PhD, 1963. Instr. Hanover (Ind.) Coll., 1954-55, Muskingum Coll., New Concord, Ohio, 1955-56, Coll. Wooster, Wooster, Ohio, 1956-60; teaching asst. Ohio State U., Columbus, 1960-63, Ohio State U.-Lakewood, Cleve., 1963; assoc. prof. SUNY, Buffalo, 1963-65; vis. prof. Rider Coll., Lawrenceville, N.J., 1966-70; tchr. Lawrenceville Sch., 1974-79; co-adjutant prof. Trenton State Coll., Trenton, N.J., 1979-80; edn. dir. Stonybrook-Millstone Watershed, Pennington, N.J., 1980-81; tchr. Princeton (N.J.) Day Sch., 1981—. Treas. fin. chmn. Lawrence Twp. LWV, Lawrenceville, 1971-74; mem. adv. com. coun. Landscape Com. Lawrence Twp., Lawrenceville, 1974-81. Mem. Am. Inst. Biol. Sci., Ohio Acad. Sci., N.J. Acad. Sci., Am. Orchid Soc., Cen. Jersey Orchid Soc. (sec. Lawrenceville chpt. 1987-89), Sigma Xi. Republican. Presbyterian. Home: 10 Monroe Ave Lawrenceville NJ 08648 Office: Princeton Day Sch The Great Rd PO Box 75 Princeton NJ 08542

VENCILL, GAY T., human resources executive; b. Moline, Ill., July 30, 1944; d. Jack Wiley and Evelyn (Baxter) Thompson; m. Robert W. Taylor, May 4, 1967 (dec. Feb. 1971); m. James A. Vencill Jr., June 11, 1976; 1 child, Michael. AA, Black Hawk Jr. Coll., Moline, 1964; BA, Marycrest Coll., 1967; postgrad., U. Tex., Dallas, 1990—. Adminstrv. intern IRS, Dallas, 1973-74; employee devel. specialist IRS, Austin, Tex., 1974-75; staffing specialist IRS, Austin and Dallas, 1975-78; employee rels. specialist IRS, Dallas, 1978-83, labor rels. specialist, 1983-84; employee rels. and tng. mgr. Intecom-Wang, Allen, Tex., 1984-86; mgr. human resources Integrated Tech-Tandem, Plano, Tex., 1986-88; dir. human resources Dallas Semiconductor, 1988—; instr. Zenger-Miller mgmt. tng., Allen, 1984-86, mgmt. tng. Allen Community Svc., 1986. chairperson awards Boy Scouts Am., Plano, 1988-89; Sunday sch. tchr. St. Mark's Ch., 1982—. Mem. Am. Mgmt. Assn., Human Resources Mgmt. Assn., Dallas Human Resources Mgmt. Assn., Plano C. of C. (indsl. rels. com. 1986-88), Farmers Br. C. of C. (edn. com. 1989—). Republican. Roman Catholic. Office: Dallas Semiconductor 4401 S Beltwood Pkwy Dallas TX 75244

VENDLER, HELEN HENNESSY, literature educator, poetry critic; b. Boston, Apr. 30, 1933; d. George and Helen (Conway) Hennessy; 1 son, David. A.B., Emmanuel Coll., 1954; Ph.D., Harvard U., 1960; Ph.D. (hon.), U. Oslo; D.Litt. (hon.), Smith Coll., Kenyon Coll., U. Hartford, Union Coll., Columbia U., Marlboro Coll. Instr. Cornell U., Ithaca, N.Y., 1960-63; lectr. Swarthmore (Pa.) Coll. and Haverford (Pa.) Coll., 1963-64; asst. prof. Smith Coll., Northampton, Mass., 1964-66; asso. prof. Boston U., 1966-68, prof., 1968-85; Fulbright lectr. U. Bordeaux, France, 1968-69; vis. prof. Harvard U., 1981-85, Kenan prof., 1985—, Porter U. prof., 1990—, assoc. acad. dean, 1987—, sr. fellow Harvard Soc. Fellows, 1981—; poetry critic New Yorker, 1978—. Author: Yeats's Vision and the Later Plays, 1963, On Extended Wings: Wallace Stevens' Longer Poems, 1969, The Poetry of George Herbert, 1975, Part of Nature, Part of Us, 1980, The Odes of John Keats, 1983, Wallace Stevens: Words Chosen Out of Desire, 1985, Harvard Book of Contemporary Am. Poetry, 1985; editor: Voices and Visions: The Poet in America, 1987, The Music of What Happens, 1988. Fulbright fellow, 1954; AAUW fellow, 1959; Guggenheim fellow, 1971-72; Am. Council Learned Socs. fellow, 1971-72; NEH fellow, 1980, 85; Overseas fellow Churchill Coll., Cambridge, 1980; recipient Lowell prize, 1969, Explicator prize, 1969, award Nat. Inst. Arts and Letters, 1975, Radcliffe Grad. Soc. medal, 1978, Nat. Book Critics Circle award, 1980. Mem. MLA (exec. council 1972-75, pres. 1980), English Inst. (trustee 1977-85), Am. Acad. Arts and Scis., Norwegian Acad. Letters and Sci., Nat. Humanities Ctr. (bd. dirs. 1989—), Phi Beta Kappa. Home: 54 Trowbridge St #2 Cambridge MA 02138 also: Harvard U Warren House Cambridge MA 02138

VENEZIA, JOYCE ANN, journalist; b. Englewood, N.J., Sept. 26, 1960; d. Rocco Peter and Maria L. (Matera) V.; m. Sherwin Alan Suss, Mar. 3, 1990. BA in Journalism and Am. Studies, Pa. State U., 1982. News. clk. Asbury Pk. (N.J.) Press, 1982; copy editor Montgomery County Record, Jenkintown, Pa., 1982-83; newswoman AP, Augusta, Maine and Hartford, Conn., 1983-85; corr. AP, Evansville, Ind., 1985-86, Atlantic City, 1986-89; reporter The Star-Ledger, Newark, 1989—. Roman Catholic. Office: The Star Ledger Press Rm Bergen County Courthouse Hackensack NJ 07601

VENEZIANO, PATRICIA JOAN MORSE, educator, librarian, poet; b. Waterbury, Conn., Apr. 4, 1931; d. Eugene Lester and Rosemary (Martone) Morse; m. Santo Sebastian Veneziano, Feb. 20, 1965 (dec. Nov. 1979). Student, Fordham U., 1952-54, So. Conn. State U., 1955-57, U. Conn., Waterbury, 1960-62. Cert. libr. III, Conn. Libr. asst. Silas Bronson Libr., Waterbury, 1954-60; libr. I S. Las Bronson Libr., Waterbury, 1961-69, libr. II, 1970-72, head of art, music and theatre dept., 1973-84; substitute tchr. Crosby High Sch., Waterbury, 1986—. Author numerous poems. Chmn. Nat. Young Adult Coun. YWCA, N.Y.C., 1961, 64, del. internat. conf., Kingston, Jamaica, 1961, U.S. Youth Coun., N.Y.C., 1965-68; site dir. latchkey prgram Cheshire YMCA, 1988—. Mem. AAUW (chmn. edn. found. program 1987-89, program v.p. 1989—, chmn. cultural interests 1990—), Conn. Poetry Soc. Home: 170 Hillside Ave Waterbury CT 06710 Office: Crosby High Sch 300 Pierpont Rd Waterbury CT 06705

VENINGA, KAREN ANN, human service facility administrator; b. Marshalltown, Iowa, Sept. 19, 1944; d. Pieter and Katherine (Borchardt) Smit; m. Robert Louis Veninga, Dec. 29, 1967; 1 child, Brent Karl. BS in Biology, Sioux Falls Coll., 1967; MPH in Pub. Health Nutrition, U. Minn., 1976. RN, Minn. Staff nurse intensive coronary care Midway Hosp., St. Paul, 1967-68; occupational health nurse, curriculum coordinator, instr. Mounds-Midway Sch. Nursing, St. Paul, 1968-74; lectr. dept. nursing Coll. St. Catherine, St. Paul, 1976-77; instr. dept. nursing St. Olaf Coll., Northfield, Minn., 1978-86; dir. human resources Bapt. Hosp. Fund, Inc., St. Paul, 1986-88; mgr. recruitment and retention HealthEast, St. Paul, 1988-89; employment mgr. North Meml. Med. Ctr., Robbinsdale, Minn., 1989—; cons. N.D. Health Care Assn., Bismarck, 1980. Author: article book Readings in Community Health Nursing, 1986; also contbr. nutritional health care articles to profl. jours. Pres. Brimhall Elem Sch. PTA, St. Paul, 1977-78; cons. Soc. for Nutrition Edn. to March of Dimes, Mpls., 1978; chairperson worship com. Centennial United Meth. Ch., St. Paul, 1985-87. Mem. Am. Nurses Assn., Minn. Nutrition Council (chairperson edn. com. 1979-80), Twin City Health Care Personnel Assn., Sigma Theta Tau. Methodist. Office: North Meml Med Ctr 3300 N Oakdale Robbinsdale MN 55422

VENINGA, LOUISE ANN, trade association executive; b. Dallas, Aug. 3, 1948; d. Frederick William and Dolores M. (Meehan) V.; m. Benjamin R. Zaricor, Dec. 23, 1971; children: Tanya, Carl, Karen. BA, Webster Coll., 1970; MA, Washington U., St. Louis, 1972. Bd. dirs., exec. v.p., founder Fmali Corp., Santa Cruz, Calif., 1973—. Author: The Ginseng Book, 1973, The Golden Seal Book, 1975. Mem. Monterey Bay Internat. Trade Assn., Herbal Trade Assn. (sec., treas. 1979). Office: Fmali Corp 831 Almar Ave Santa Cruz CA 95060

VENNESLAND, BIRGIT, biochemistry educator; b. Kristiansand, Norway, Nov. 17, 1913; came to U.S, 1917; d. Gunnuf Olav and Sigrid Kristine (Brandsborg) V. BS in Biochemistry, U. Chgo., 1934, PhD in Biochemistry, 1938; D.Sc. (hon.), Mt. Holyoke Coll., 1960. Asst. biochemistry U. Chgo., 1938-39; fellow biochemistry Harvard Med. Sch., Boston, 1939-41; instr. biochemistry U. Chgo., 1941-44, asst. prof. biochemistry, 1944-48, assoc. prof. biochemistry, 1948-57, prof. biochemistry, 1957-68; dir. Max-Planck Inst. for Cell Physiology, Berlin, 1968-70; leader Forschungsstelle Vennesland, Berlin, 1970-81; adj. prof. biochemistry and biophysics U. Hawaii, Honolulu, 1986—. Editor: Cyanide in Biology, 1981; contbr. rsch. papers and rev. articles to sci. jours. Study sec. mem. NSF, USPHS, Washington, 1954-63; mem. Wooldridge Com., Washington, 1964. kRecipient Hales award Am. Soc. Plant Physiology, 1950. Fellow AAAS, N.Y. Acad. Scis.;

mem. Am. Chem. Soc. (Garvan medal 1964), Am. Soc. Biol. Chemistry, Am. Soc. Plant Physiology. Home: 1206 Mokapu Blvd Kailua HI 96734

VENTIMIGLIA, KATHARINE JANE GARVER, education educator; b. Muncie, Ind., Sept. 1, 1949; d. Edwin Gilmore and Sybil Marie (Daughtry) Garver; m. Joseph John Ventimiglia, June 17, 1972; children: Joseph Marc, Robert Edwin, Jeffrey Peter, Matthew Patrick. BA in Edn., NE La. U., 1971; postgrad., Dowling Coll., 1988—. Cert. nursery and elem. tchr., Ill., N.Y. Tchr. Archdiocese of Chgo., 1971-72, Diocese of Bklyn., 1972-74; adj. instr. edn. Suffolk Community Coll., Selden, N.Y., 1986—; tutor learning disabled postsecondary students Dowling Coll., Oakdale, N.Y., 1989—. Treas. Sagamore Jr. High Sch. PTA, Holtsville, N.Y., 1987-88, bd. dirs. 1986—; treas. Gatelot Ave. PTA, Lake Ronkonkoma, N.Y., 1983—, mem. exec. bd. 1979—, project coord. Reading Is Fundamental, 1989—. Mem. AAUW, DAR, Internat. Reading Assn.

VENTRES, JUDITH MARTIN, lawyer; b. Ann Arbor, Mich., Feb. 10, 1943; d. D. Lawrence and Donna E. (Webb) Moran; children: Laura C. Martin, Paul M. Martin, A. Lindsay Martin; m. Daniel B. Ventres Jr., Dec. 27, 1984. BA, U. Mich., 1963; postgrad., Universite de Jean Moulin, Institut du Droit, Lyon, France, 1981; JD, U. Minn., 1982. Bar: Minn. 1982, U.S. Tax Ct. 1989, U.S. Dist. Ct. 1989, U.S. Ct. Appeals (8th cir.) 1989; CLU, Chartered fin. cons. Tax supr., dir. fin. planning, asst. nat. dir. Coopers & Lybrand, Mpls., 1981-84; dir. fin. planning Investors Diversified Services subs. Am. Express, Mpls. and N.Y.C., 1984-85; sr. tax mgr., dir. fin. planning KPMG Peat Marwick Main & Co., Mpls., 1985-89; prin. Martin & Assocs., P.A., Edina, Minn., 1989—. Author contg. edn. materials on taxation and income and estate planning. Mem. Mpls. C. of C. campaign, Downtown Council Coms., Mpls., 1982-84, Metro Tax Planning Group, 1984-86, Mpl. Estate Planning Council, 1985—; class chmn. fundraising campaign U. Minn. Law Sch., Mpls., 1985; usher Christ Presbyn. Ch., Edina, Minn., 1983—; mem. adv. council on planned giving ARC. Mem. ABA (task force on legal fin. planning), Minn. Bar Assn., Hennepin County Bar Assn., Minn. Soc. CPAs (instr. continuing legal edn. 1983-84, continuing profl. edn. 1986, individual trust and estate provisions 1986 tax reform act 1983-86) Am. Assn. Ind. Investors (speaker), Am. Soc. CLUs, Minn. Soc. CLUs, Minn. Women Lawyers, Lex Alumnae, U. Mich. Alumni Assn. (coun. govs. 1989—), U. Minn. Alumni Club (coun. govs. 1988—), Minn. World Trade Assn., Internat. Assn. Fin. Planners. Clubs: Interlachen, Athletic, Lafayette (Mpls.). Home: 1355 Vine Pl Orono MN 55364 Office: Martin & Assocs PA 3209 W 76th St Ste 200 Minneapolis MN 55435

VENTRESCA, DEBORAH ANNE, nurse; b. Boston, Oct. 12, 1948; d. H. Vincent and M. Helen (Butler) Strout; m. Anthony L. Ventresca Jr.; 1 child, Amy L. AS in Nursing, North Shore Community Coll., 1980; BS in Nursing cum laude, U. Mass, 1986, postgrad., 1988—. Staff nurse J.B. Thomas Hosp., Peabody, Mass., 1980-87; staff nurse home health J.B. Thomas Home Care/Vis. Nurses, Peabody, 1987; staff devel coorinator Lenox Hill Nursing and Rehabilitative Care Facility, Lynn, Mass., 1987-88; community health nurse J.B. Thomas Health Care, Peabody, 1988—. Vol. nurse Make Today Count, Beverly, Mass., 1982-84; nurse admission assessment Hospice North Shore, 1983, vol. coordinator, 1983-84, bd. dirs., 1984-86; bd. dirs. Am. Cancer Soc., Lynn, 1987—. Margaret Anderson Meml. scholar. Mem. Sigma Theta Tau. Republican. Club: Lothrop (Beverly). Home: 200 Vantage Terr Unit 308 Swampscott MA 01907 Office: JB Thomas Home Health Care 100 Lowell St Peabody MA 01960

VENTRONE, PENNY JAMES, financial executive; b. Concord, Calif., Feb. 3, 1960; d. Richard Austin and Helen Louise (Miller) James; m. Angelo Ventrone, Sept. 14, 1985; children: Abbey, Nicholas. BS, Ferris State U., Big Rapids, Mich., 1982. CPA. Controller ITI, Inc., Bridgeport, Mich.; staff acct. Stricoff & Okray, CPAs, Birmingham, Mich.; sr. fin. analyst Ameritech Pub., Troy, Mich.; v.p., treas. Telesupply Inc., Drayton Plains, Mich. Recipient various citizenship awards. Address: 5087 Williams Lake Rd Waterford MI 48329

VENTRY, CATHERINE VALERIE, lawyer; b. Bronxville, N.Y., Feb. 19, 1949; d. Victor and Catherine Regina (Dillon) V. AB in Logic and Philosophy, Vassar Coll., 1971; postgrad., Boston U., 1972; JD, N.Y. Law Sch., 1978. Bar: N.Y. 1979, U.S. Dist. Ct. (so. and ea. dists.) N.Y. 1979. Adj. asst. prof. John Jay Coll. of Criminal Justice, N.Y.C., 1978-80; adj. asst. prof. bus. law Coll. Mount St. Vincent Lehman Coll., N.Y.C., 1978-82; staff atty. City of N.Y. Dept. Housing Preservation and Devel. Litigation Bureau, N.Y.C., 1981-84; pvt. practice N.Y., 1984—; Tax editor Prentice-Hall Pub. Co., Englewood Cliffs, N.J., 1980-81. Mem. N.Y. State Bar, Rockland County Women's Bar, Rockland County Bar Assn., MENSA. Office: 876 Union Ave Newburgh NY 12550

VENTURA, JUDY, beauty salon professional; b. Providence, Feb. 10, 1951; d. Michael and Adeline (Verissimo) V.; m. Paul Alexander Turchetta, May 10, 1969 (div. 1984); 1 child, Gina M.; m. William A. Ross, Aug. 10, 1986 (div. 1989). Student, R.I. Jr. Coll., 1969-70, Joann's Sch. Beauty Culture, 1969, Costins R.I. Acad. Beauty, 1982, Guilford Tech. Community Coll., 1989. With Glemby Internat. of N.Y., London and Can., 1969-86; instr. Costin's R.I. Acad. Cosmetology, 1983, Leon's Beauty Sch., 1984; supr. beauty salons Esannele Co. N.Y., 1986-88; dir. beauty salon div., instr., recruiter, adminstrv. asst. Dudley Products, Inc., 1988—; prin. GMT Cons., Greensboro, N.C., 1988—. Author mgmt. and procedure materials. Vol. Wesley Long Community Hosp., Multiple Sclerosis Orgn. Mem. Nat. Cosmetology Assn. Greensboro (sec. 1989—). Republican. Baptist. Home: 381 E Montcastle Dr Ste F Greensboro NC 27406

VEON, DOROTHY HELENE, educator; b. Oxford, Nebr., May 31, 1914; d. John B. and Ella V. (Robertson) V.; B.Sc., U. Nebr., 1935; M.A., George Washington U., 1939; Ed.D., Columbia U., 1947; M. Med. Sci. (fellow), Tulane U., 1969. Asst. prof. edn. dept. George Washington U., Washington, 1941-50; prof. edn. Pa. State U., Phila., 1950-66; asst. dir. Sch. of Nursing, Thomas Jefferson U., Phila., 1966-68; vis. prof. Ariz. State U., 1959-60, Drexel U., Phila., 1973-74, Temple U., Phila., 1974-75; ednl. and bus. cons., Phila., 1972—; prof., dir. div. econs. and bus. adminstrn. Community Coll. Phila., 1976-88; vis. prof. U. Vt., summer 1966, Bradley U., summers 1956-58, U. Oreg., summer 1964. U.S. Del. to World Congress of Women, Moscow, 1987; organizer, speaker UN Decade for Women Conf., Nairobi, Kenya, 1985; mem. confs. Internat. Fedn. Univ. Women, Mexico City, 1966, Helsinki, Finland, 1989; conf. del. Trinity Coll., Dublin, Ireland, Oxford (Eng.) U.; bd. dirs. Va. Guildersleeve Internat. Found. for Univ. Women, 1982—, convener for pub. rels., v.p. Recipient Nat. Research award Delta Pi Epsilon, 1949; Internat. Disting. Service award for Status of Women, 1986; Radcliffe research scholar, 1986—. Mem. AAUW (nat. grantee 1968, 84, v.p. Pa. div. 1964-66, Disting. award 1985, pres. Phila. br. 1983-85), Am. Acad. Natural Scis., Am. Mgmt. Assn., Am. Mktg. Assn., Am. Bus. Communications Assn. (v.p. 1962-65, nat. fellow 1970), Internat. Soc. Bus. Edn. (pres. 1958-60), Internat. Fedn. Univ. Women (mem. internat. confs.), Am. Econ. Assn., World Affairs Council Phila., Phila. Mus. Art, Kappa Delta (province pres. 1948-50, 62-64, 70-72), Phi Delta Gamma, Pi Omega Pi, Am. Acctg. Assn. Republican. Episcopalian. Editor Am. Bus. Edn. Home: 1700 Benjamin Franklin Pkwy The Windsor Apt 1514 Philadelphia PA 19103

VEPRASKAS, NANCY MURPHY, corporate training executive; b. Pitts., Jan. 6, 1950; d. David Crockett and Margaret Ann (Weaver) Murphy; m. Marc Brian Vepraskas, June 19, 1976; children: David Marc, Thomas Ryan. BS, Fla. State U., 1972, MS, 1976; MBA, Mercer U., 1986. Tchr. Douglass Mid. Sch., Thomasville, Ga., 1972-76; circulation mgr. Bradenton (Fla.) Herald, 1976-77; asst. adminstr. Grady Hosp., Atlanta, 1978-86; mgr. corp. tng. Lithonia Lighting, Conyers, Ga., 1986—; pres. mgmt. club Lithonia Lighting, Conyers, 1988-89. Editor newsletter Mies Muse, 1986-89. Coord. cub scout troop, Lithonia, Ga., 1988-89; chmn. United Way, Grady Hosp., Atlanta, 1984-85. Mem. NAFE, Am. Soc. Tng. and Devel., Toastmasters (v.p. 1986-87, CTM award 1988). Democrat. Presbyterian. Office: Lithonia Lighting 1305 Industrial Blvd Conyers GA 30207

VERANI, DANIELA ELDA, family practice physician; b. Londonderry, N.H., May 30, 1955; d. Osvaldo and Patricia (Lewis) V.; m. Nick Schlangen, Apr. 7, 1990. BS magna cum laude, U. N.H., 1977; MD, Wright State U., Dayton, Ohio, 1983. Diplomate Am. Bd. Family Practice. Resident U. Mass. Family Practice, Fitchburg, 1986; physician Milby Med. Ctr., Zebulon, Ga., 1986-89; ptnr. Londonderry, N.H., 1989—. Mem. Am. Acad. Family Practice, Upson County Med. Soc., Poetry Soc. N.H., Phi Beta Kappa, Phi Rho Sigma. Republican. Roman Catholic. Home: 4 Weymouth Rd Rte 14 Londonderry NH 03053

VERCIGLIO, TINA MARIA, publishing executive, consultant; b. Birmingham, Ala., Sept. 20, 1955; d. Norman Frank and Katherine (Zaden) V. BS in Edn., U. Ala., 1977. Cert. elem. tchr.; lic. life ins. agt. Tchr. early childhood Pasco County Bd. Edn., Dade City, Fla., 1977-80; specialist child devel. Emma Pendleton Hosp., Providence, 1980-81; tchr. early childhood Jefferson County Bd. Edn., Birmingham, 1981-83; pub., editor Birmingham Bus. Jour., 1983—; pub. Ala. Health News, Birmingham, 1988—, Shoppers Guide and News, Birmingham, 1989—; pub. cons., Birmingham, 1988—. Bd. dirs. Magic City Art Connection, Birmingham, 1988—. Mem. Women's Network. Office: Birmingham Bus Jour 2101 Magnolia Ave S Ste 400 Birmingham AL 35205

VERDUIN, BERT M., real estate executive; b. Benton, Ark., Feb. 9, 1947; d. Elvis Lee and Helen Lee (McBride) Moses; m. Michael Hankins Verduin, May 23, 1970; children—Valerie Ann, Clinton Logan. A.A.S., Brookhaven Coll., 1982. Acct., Realty Devel. Corp., Dallas, 1970-77; owner, mgr. Tax Service, Dallas, 1977-83; sr. v.p., controller Realty Devel. Corp., Dallas, 1983-87; pres. Strobe Mgmt. Services, Inc., Dallas, 1987—. Republican. Mem. Ch. of Christ. Avocations: reading; crafts.

VERDUIN, CLAIRE LEONE, publishing company executive; b. Chgo., Mar. 23, 1932; d. David R. and Helen (Vande Velde) Ellman; m. J. Richard Verduin, Aug. 25, 1956 (Mar. 1979); children: Pamela A., Paul D., Beth L. Verduin Cain. BBA, U. Wis., 1954. Editorial asst. Brooks/Cole Pub. Co., Pacific Grove and Monterey, Calif., 1973-74, project devel. editor, 1974-85, editor, 1978-85, mng. editor, 1985—. Treas. Am. Field Service, Pacific Grove, 1978; mem. Pacific Grove Sch. Bd., 1983. Mem. Am. Assn. for Counseling and Devel., Nat. Assn. Human Service Educators, Acad. Criminal Justice Scis., Am. Soc. Criminology, Coun. Social Work Edn. Office: Brooks/Cole Pub Co 511 Forest Grove Pacific Grove CA 93950

VERED, RUTH, art gallery director; b. Tel Aviv, Sept. 26, 1940; d. Abraham and Helen (Psisuska) Rosenblum; m. Mark Kalb, Jan. 21, 1961 (div. Jan. 1970); children: Sharon, Oren. BA in Art Hisotry with honors, Bezalel U., Jerusalem, 1964. Freelance art cons., Israel and N.Y.C., 1965-75; dir. Vered Gallery, East Hampton, N.Y., 1977—. Sgt. paratroops Israeli Army, 1958-60. Home: 891 Park Ave New York NY 10021 Office: Vered Gallery East Hampton NY 11937

VERGERONT, SUSAN BOWERS, state legislator, public relations consultant; b. Milw., Nov. 30, 1945; d. Arthur William and Mary (Oberly) Bowers; m. David J. Vergeront, May 2, 1945; children: Margaret, John W., David E. BS, U. Wis., 1967. Research assoc. Wis. Legis. Council, Madison, 1967-70; exec. dir. Grafton (Wis.) C. of C., 1978-80; account exec. Vollrath & Assocs., Cedarburg, Wis., 1981-84; mem. Wis. Assembly, 1984—; dir. Rep. Assembly Campaign Com.; mem. Wis. State Bd. Am. Legis. Exchange Coun., Madison, 1985-87, Ozaukee Econ. Devel. Corp., 1989—. Bd. dirs. Women's Bus. Initiatives Corp., Milw., 1987—, Manitou Council Girl Scouts U.S.A., Manitowic, Wis., 1984-87, Ozaukee Council on Alcohol and Drug Abuse. Named One of Outstanding Young Women Am. Grafton Jaycettes, 1980, Outstanding Young Wisconsinite, Wis. Jaycees, 1981. Mem. Nat. Conf. State Legislators (nat. com.), Wis. Women's Coun. (chmn. 1988-89), U.S. Jaycees (life), Grafton C. of C. (v.p. 1980-81). Presbyterian. Office: Wis State Legislature PO Box 8953 Madison WI 53708

VERGONA, KATHLEEN DOBROSIELSKI, biology educator, researcher; b. Pitts., Dec. 6, 1948; d. Raymond Henry and Sophie Bernice (Rabazinski) Dobbs; m. Ronald Joseph Vergona, Sept. 1, 1973; 1 child, Raymond. BS, U. Pitts., 1970, PhD, 1976. Rsch. fellow Cancer Rsch. Ctr. Allegheny Gen. Hosp., Pitts., 1976; rsch. fellow dept. anatomy and cell biology Sch. Medicine U. Pitts., 1977-79, asst. prof. dept. anatomy and histology Sch. Dental Medicine, 1976-81, assoc. prof. dept. anatomy and histology, 1982—, rsch. asst. prof. dept. neurobiology, anatomy and cell sci. Sch. Dental Medicine, 1982—, acting chmn. dept. anatomy/histology Sch. Dental Medicine, 1990—; lectr. Carnegie Mus. of Natural History, Pitts., 1984-85; faculty fellow Geriatric Edn. Ctr., Pitts., 1986—. Editor: The Biology of Salivary Glands; contbr. articles to profl. jours. Judge Pa. Jr. Acad. of Sci., Pitts., 1976—, Am. Student Dental Assn., Pitts., 1978—. Recipient Rsch. Fellowship award Nat. Inst. on Aging, 1976, Achievement of Excellence award Geriatric Edn. Ctr. of Pa., 1987. Mem. Am. Soc. Cell Biology, Am. Assn. Oral Biologists (founder Pitts. chpt.), Am. Assn. Dental Rsch. (councilor Pitts. chpt. 1989—), Tissue Culture Assn., Salivary Rsch. Group, Beta Beta Beta, Sigma Xi. Democrat. Roman Catholic. Home: 1167 Brintell St Pittsburgh PA 15201 Office: U Pitts Sch Dental Medicine 615-2 Salk Hall Pittsburgh PA 15261

VERHOEK, SUSAN ELIZABETH, botany educator; b. Columbus, Ohio, 1942; m. S.E. Williams. Student, Carleton Coll., 1960-62; BA, Ohio Wesleyan U., 1964; MA, Ind. U., 1966; PhD, Cornell U., 1975. Herbarium supr. Mo. Bot. Garden, St. Louis, 1966-70; asst. prof. Lebanon Valley Coll., Annville, Pa., 1974-82, assoc. prof., 1982-85, prof., 1985—; vis. researcher Cornell U., Ithaca, N.Y., 1982-83; content cons. Merrill Pub. Co., 1987-89. Author: How to Know the Spring Flowers, 1982; contbr. articles to profl. jours., newspapers, and bulls. Bd. trustees Lebanon Valley Coll., Annville, 1979-82, 84-90. Named one of Outstanding Young Women of Am., 1976. Mem. Soc. for Econ. Botany (pres. 1985-86), Bot. Soc. Am., Am. Soc. Plant Taxonomists, Internat. Assn. Plant Taxonomists, Am. Assn. Bot. Gardens and Arboreta. Office: Lebanon Valley Coll Pa Annville PA 17003

VERLICH, JEAN ELAINE, writer, public relations executive; b. McKeesport, Pa., July 5, 1950; d. Matthew Louis and Irene (Tomko) V.; m. S(tanley) Wayne Wright, Sept. 29, 1979 (div. June 1988). Student, Bucknell U., 1968-69; BA, U. Pitts., 1971. Press sec. Com. to Re-elect President, S.W. Pa., 1972; adminstrv. asst. Pa. Rep. James B. Kelly III, 1972-73; reporter Beaver (Pa.) County Times, 1973-74; proofreader Ketchum, MacLeod & Grove, Pitts., 1975-76; community rels. specialist, PPG Industries, Pitts., 1976-77, editor PPG News, 1977-79, sr. staff writer, 1979-84, communications coord., 1984-85; pub. rels. assoc. Glass Group, 1986-87; mgr. pub. rels. Glass Group PPG Industries, 1987—. Mem. Internat. Assn. Bus. Communicators (bd. dir. Pitts. chpt. 1981, v.p. pub. rels. Pitts. chpt. 1982, v.p. programs Pitts. chpt. 1985, pres. Pitts. chpt. 1986), Aviation/Space Writers Assn., Phi Beta Kappa, Delta Zeta. Office: PPG Industries 1 PPG Pl 32 E Pittsburgh PA 15272

VERMEER, MAUREEN DOROTHY, sales executive; b. Bronxville, N.Y., Mar. 21, 1945; d. Albert Casey and Helen (Valentine Casey) Vermeer; m. John R. Fassnacht, Feb. 11, 1966 (div. 1975); m. George M. Dallas Peltz IV, Oct. 26, 1985. Grad., NYU Real Estate Inst., 1976. Lic. real estate broker, notary pub., N.Y. Personnel mgr. Douglas Elliman, N.Y.C., 1965-74, mgmt. supr., 1974-78, v.p., 1978-83; real estate broker Rachmani Corp., N.Y.C., 1983-84; v.p. sales and mktg. Carol Mgmt. Corp., N.Y.C., 1984-90, The Sunshine Group, N.Y.C., 1990—; bd. dirs. Woodrow Wilson Inc., N.Y.C., Alfred Condo Assn., N.Y.C.; speaker in field. Mem. Real Estate Bd. N.Y., Assn. Real Estate Women, Sales and Mktg. Coun. Republican. Presbyterian. Home: 206 County Rd Demarest NJ 07627 Office: The Sunshine Group 520 Madison Ave New York NY 10022

VERMEULE, EMILY TOWNSEND (MRS. CORNELIUS C. VERMEULE, III), classicist, educator; b. N.Y.C., Aug. 11, 1928; d. Clinton Blake and Eleanor (Meneely) Townsend; m. Cornelius C. Vermeule III, Feb. 2, 1957; children: Emily Dickinson Blake, Cornelius Adrian Comstock. A.B., Bryn Mawr Coll., 1950; student, Am. Sch. Classical Studies, Athens, 1950-51, St. Anne's Coll., Oxford U., 1953; M.A., Harvard, 1954; Ph.D., Bryn Mawr Coll., 1956; D. Litt., Douglass Coll., Rutgers U., 1968, Tufts U., 1980, U. Pitts., 1983, Bates Coll., 1983, U. Miami, Oxford, Ohio, 1986; LL.D., Regis Coll., 1971; D. Fine Arts, U. Mass, Amherst, 1971; D.Litt., Smith Coll., 1972, Wheaton Coll., 1973, Trinity Coll., 1974; L.H.D., Emmanuel Coll., 1980, Princeton U., 1989. Instr. Greek lang. Bryn Mawr Coll., 1956-57; instr. Wellesley (Mass.) Coll., 1957-58, prof. art and Greek, 1965-70, chmn. dept. art, 1966-67; asst. prof. classics Boston U., 1958-61, assoc. prof. classics, 1961-65; fellow for research Boston Mus. Fine Arts, 1965—; James C. Loeb vis. prof. classical philology Harvard, 1969; dir. univ. Cyprus expdn. Harvard U., 1971—, Samuel and Doris Zemurray Stone-Radcliffe prof., 1970—; Sather prof. U. Calif., Berkeley, 1975; Geddes-Harrower prof. Greek art and archaeology U. Aberdeen, 1980-81; Bernhard vis. prof. Williams Coll., 1986; mem. bd. gov's. U. Calif. Humanities Rsch. Inst., 1988, 90; excavations in Greece, Turkey, Libya, Cyprus. Author: Euripides V. Electra, 1959, Greece in the Bronze Age, 1964, The Trojan War in Greek Art, 1964, Götterkult, 1974, Toumba tou Skourou, The Mound of Darkness, 1975, Death in Early Greek Art and Poetry, 1978, (with V. Karageorghis) Mycenaean Pictorial Vase-Painting, 1982, Toumba tou Skourou, A Bronze Age Potters' Quarter on Morphon Bay in Cyprus, 1990; contbr. articles to profl. jours. Judge Nat. Book Award, 1977; bd. dirs. Humanities Rsch. Inst., U. Calif., 1988—. Recipient Gold medal for distinguished achievement Radcliffe Coll. Grad. Soc., 1968; Guggenheim fellow, 1964-65. Fellow Soc. Antiquaries, Brit. Acad. (corr.), German Archaeol. Inst. (corr.); mem. AAAS, Am. Inst. Archaeology, Am. Philos. Soc. (v.p. 1978-81), Am. Philol. Assn. (Charles J. Goodwin award of merit 1980), Classical Assn. New Eng., Smithsonian Council (bd. scholars 1983—), Hellenic Soc., Classical Assn., Library of Congress. Office: Harvard U Dept Classics 319 Boylston Hall Cambridge MA 02138

VERMIGLIO-SMITH, JANICE ANNA, foundation administrator, consultant; b. Boston, Aug. 6, 1948; d. Rocco Jerome and Hannie (Joseph) V.; m. David MacEachern, Dec. 3, 1968 (div.); m. Jeff Smith, Nov. 12, 1983; 1 child, Rachel. MSN, Ariz. State U., 1977. Asst. dir. Ariz. State Hosp., Phoenix, 1980-82; asst. adminstr. Scottsdale Camelback Hosp., Ariz., 1982-90; clin. dir. Anasazi Found., Mesa, Ariz., 1990—; cons. in field. Fellow Ortopsychiatric Assn.; mem. AGPA, CAC, ANA, Ariz. Nursing Assn. Democratic. Lutheran. Office: Anasazi Found 435 N Harris Mesa AZ 85203

VERNA, BARBARA, agricultural products executive; b. Camden, N.J., Sept. 6, 1942; d. Daniel Charles and Ida Harriet (Hornstein) Flemming; m. Albert Vittorio Verna, May 12, 1963; children; George W., Nicholas P. AS, Bucks Community Coll., 1990. With Gen. Accident Group, Phila., 1960-61; sec. Dow Chem. Co., Camden, 1961-63; office mgr. Vodges Real Estate, Maple Shade, N.J., 1963-65; mgr. Stockton Sta. Apts., Camden, 1965-67; gen. mgr. Great N.E. Lumber, Phila., 1985—. Sec. Armstrong PTA, Ben Salem, Pa., 1982-85; treas. Shaffer PTA, Ben Salem, 1984-88; pres. Belmont Hills PTG, Ben Salem, 1979-84. Mem. Lumbermen's Exch. (bd. dirs. Phila. chpt. 1990—). Democrat. Roman Catholic. Office: Great NE Lumber & Millwork 4929 Cottman Ave Philadelphia PA 19135

VERNERDER, GLORIA JEAN, librarian; b. Ft. Wayne, Ind., June 2, 1930; d. John Otto and Verge W. (Geiger) Krieg; m. Carl Penrod Vernerder, Dec. 25, 1952 (dec. Sept. 1984); children: Carla Jeanne Vernerder Kelly, Nina Marie Vernerder Anderson. Grad., Midway (Ky.) Coll.; student, Ind. U., Ft. Wayne, U. Ky. Br. libr. Pub. Libr. of Ft. Wayne and Allen County, 1950-52; children's libr. La Grange (Ill.) Pub. Libr., 1952-59; children's libr. Hinsdale (Ill.) Pub. Libr., 1961-68, head of youth svcs., 1969—. Contbr. articles to profl. jours.; editor: Sunlight and Shadows, 1983, 87, 90. Adminstrv. bd. First United Meth. Ch., LaGrange, 1986-88, Stephen Ministry, 1986—. Mem. ALA, Ill. Library Assn., Library Adminstrs. Conf. of No. Ill. (treas. 1969). Republican. Methodist. Home: 732 S 7th Ave La Grange IL 60525 Office: Hinsdale Pub Library 20 E Maple St Hinsdale IL 60521

VERNON, FAYE MARIE, textile company software technician; b. Leaksville, N.C., May 30, 1959; d. William Edgar Broadnax and Rosa Lee Vernon; children: Keith Dwayne Vernon, Marie Antonete Wilson. BA, Winston-Salem State U., 1981. Sales clk. Macks Dept. Store, Madison, N.C., 1976-77; data entry operator Hanes Corp., Winston-Salem, N.C., 1978-79; programmer trainee Hanes Hosiery, Winston-Salem, 1979-80, programmer analyst, 1980-82; systems analyst fed. systems Honeywell Inc., McLean, Va., 1982-83, sr. systems analyst fed. systems, 1983-85; sr. systems analyst Underwriters Labs., Rsch. Triangle Park, N.C., 1985-86; systems rep. Honeywell Bull, Charlotte, N.C., 1987-88, sr. systems rep., 1988-90; data processing coord. Qualitex, Inc., Charlotte, 1990—. Mem. NAFE, Assn. Info. Systems Profls. Democrat. Baptist. Office: Qualitex Inc 604 Pressley Rd Charlotte NC 28217

VERNON, JOYCE ANN, nurse; b. Dayton, Ohio, Jan. 4, 1947; d. John W. and Gladys (Luthman) Lammert; m. Carl W. Vernon, Sept. 6, 1969; children: William J., Mark C. BSN, Ohio State U., 1969. RN, Va., Pa. Staff nurse Nat. Orthopedic & Rehab., Arlington, Va., 1969-70; office nurse Dr. Kenneth Berger, Falls Church, Va., 1972-74, Drs. Rottscaeffer & Shetty, Murrysville, Va., 1979-84; assoc. nurse Vis. Nurse Assn. Western Pa., New Kensington, 1983-87; interviewer Upjohn Health Care, Pitts., 1988-89; mem. staff Vis. Nurse Assn. Allegheny County, Pitts., 1989—. Mem. com. Murrysville Rep., 1980-86. Mem. AAUW, Sigma Theta Tau.

VERNON, LILLIAN, mail order company executive; b. Leipzig, Germany; d. Herman and Erna Menasche; m. Sam Hochberg (div.); children: Fred, David; m. Robert Katz, Oct. 24, 1970 (div.). PhD (hon.), Mercy Coll., Dobbs Ferry, N.Y., 1984, Bryant Coll., Coll. New Rochelle, Baruch Coll. Chief exec. officer Lillian Vernon, Mt. Vernon, N.Y., 1951—. Contbr. articles to profl. jours. Bd. dirs. Westchester County Assn., N.Y.; mem. Com. of 200, Americas Bus. Conf. Recipient Entrepreneural award Women's Bus. Owners of N.Y., 1983. Mem. Women's Forum. Office: Lillian Vernon Corp 510 S Fulton Ave Mount Vernon NY 10550

VERPLANKE, ANNA LOUISE, nutritionist; b. Camden, Tenn., Mar. 22, 1935; d. Wiley Leonard and Rosa Belle (Clark) Noles; m. Edward Ely Verplanke, Jul. 19, 1953; children: Rose Anne & Mary Anne (twins), Julia Edwina. Student, U. Fla., 1976-77; B of Restaurant and Hotel Mgmt., Purdue U., 1983. Cert. Dietetic Food Service Mgmt. Chef., asst. mgr. Paducah (Ky.) Country Club, 1955-65, Drew (Miss.) Country Club, 1965-71; dir. food service Lexington House Inc., Crestwood, Ill., 1971-73; chef, asst. mgr. Burlington (Iowa) Country Club, 1973-76; dir. dietetics Rosewood Convalscent Ctr., Memphis, 1976-80; dir. food service Carolina Village Inc., Hendersonville, N.C., 1980—; cons. Dearfield Episcopal Home, Asheville, N.C., 1981; mem. organizing com. Satellite Food Program Elderly, Memphis, 1978. Vol. NRC, Paducah, 1961-65; troop leader Girl Scouts Am., Drew, 1968-71. Mem. Nat. Dietary Mgrs. Assn. (pres. 1984-86), Nat. Assn. Female Execs., bus. and Profl. Women's Club (Woman Day 1985). Democrat. Baptist. Home: 23 Appleblossom Ln Hendersonville NC 28739 Office: Carolina Village Inc 600 Carolina Village Rd Hendersonville NC 28739

VERSAGE, LINDA MARIE, development and construction executive; b. Cleve., June 17, 1956; d. Sylvester Colecchio and Carmel (Cicchino) Mancini; m. Paul Joseph Versage, Mar. 13, 1961; 1 child, M. Skylar. BEd, Ariz. State U., 1980. Tchr. Mesa (Ariz.) Schs., 1980-81, Scottsdale (Ariz.) Schs., 1982-83, Galloway Sch., Atlanta, 1983-84, Deer Valley Schs., Phoenix, 1984-89; law receptionist Harrison & Lerch, Phoenix, 1981-82; exec. Bricklind Cos., Inc., Phoenix, 1987—; cons. Southwest Equities, Phoenix, 1988—; bd. dirs. Molson Properties, Phoenix, 1988—. Mem. Ariz. Tchrs. Math., Ariz. Gen. Contractors, Ariz. C. of C. Republican. Office: Bricklind Cos Inc 14040 N Cave Creek Rd #308 Phoenix AZ 85022

VERSON, KAROL RUTH, educational gerontologist; b. Chgo., Apr. 12, 1939; d. Stanley David and Rae (Vetzner) Buckner; m. Ronald L. Verson, July 14, 1963 (div. 1986); children: Ranya, Marissa, Ilanna, Serena. BA, U. Mich., 1960; MA, Northeastern Ill. U., Chgo., 1978; grad. cert. in gerontology, U. Ill., 1988. Performer, dir. Imagination Theatre, Chgo., 1971-77; communications tchr. Oakton Community Coll., Des Plaines, Ill., 1977-86, dir. touring co., 1980-86; creative arts specialist, dir. Acting Up!, Des Plaines, Ill., 1978-86; mgr. Older Adult Inst. Coll. DuPage, Ill., 1986-88; mgr. mature adult svcs. Jewish Community Ctr., Chgo., 1988—, mgr. mature services, 1988--; cons. Life & Times Inst., Chgo. 1988--; workshops Reminiscence Libraries, Mt. Prospect Downers Grove 1988; travel advisor Lampert Tours, Chgo. 1988. Author: Acting Up!, 1986; editor Writing Down!, 1987. Women's adv. bd. Oakton Community Coll., Des Plaines, 1970-75; exec. bd. LWV, Morton Grove, Niles, Ill., 1970-85; Niles Arts Coun., 1988—. Mem. Gerontol. Soc. Am., Nat. Coun. on the Aging.

Democrat. Office: Horwich Kaplan Jewish Community Ctr 3003 W Touhy Ave Chicago IL 60645

VER STEEG, DONNA LORRAINE FRANK, nurse, sociologist, educator; b. Minot, N.D., Sept. 23, 1929; d. John Jonas and Pearl H. (Denlinger) Frank. B.S. in Nursing, Stanford, 1951; M.S. in Nursing, U. Calif. at San Francisco, 1967; M.A. in Sociology, UCLA, 1969, Ph.D. in Sociology, 1973; m. Richard W. Ver Steeg, Nov. 22, 1950; children: Juliana, Anne, Richard B. Clin. instr. U. N.D. Sch. Nursing, 1962-63; USPHS nurse rsch. fellow UCLA, 1969-72; spl. cons., adv. com. on physicians' assts. and nurse practitioner programs Calif. State Bd. Med. Examiners, 1972-73; asst. prof. UCLA Sch. Nursing, 1973-79, assoc. prof., 1979—, asst. dean, 1981-83, chmn. primary ambulatory care, 1976-87, assoc. dean, 1983-86; co-prin. investigator PRIMEX Project, Family Nurse Practitioners, UCLA Extension, 1974-76; assoc. cons. Calif. Postsecondary Edn. Commn., 1975-76; spl. cons. Calif. Dept. Consumer Affairs, 1978; accredited visitor Western Assn. Schs. and Colls., 1985—; mem. Calif. State Legis. Health Policy Forum, 1980-81. Contbr. articles to profl. jours. Recipient Leadership award Calif. Area Health Edn. Ctr. System, 1989; named Outstanding Faculty Mem. UCLA Sch. Nursing, 1982. Fellow Am. Acad. Nursing; mem. AAAS, Am. Pub. Health Assn., Am. Soc. Law and Medicine, Gerontol. Soc. Am., Nat League Nursing, Calif. League Nursing, N.Am. Nursing Diagnosis Assn., Am. Assn. History Nursing, Soc. Study Social Problems, Assn. Health Svcs. Rsch., Am. Nurse Assn., Calif. Nurse Assn. (pres. 1979-81), Am. Sociol. Assn., Stanford Nurses Club, Sigma Theta Tau, Sigma Xi. Home: 708 Swarthmore Ave Pacific Palisades CA 90272 Office: UCLA Sch Nursing 10833 LeConte Ave Los Angeles CA 90024-6919

VERTS, LITA JEANNE, university administrator; b. Jonesboro, Ark., Apr. 13, 1935; d. William Gus and Lolita Josephine (Peeler) Nash; m. B. J. Verts, Aug. 29, 1954 (div. 1975); 1 child, William Trigg. BA, Oreg. State U., 1973; MA in Lingustics, U. Oreg., 1974; postgrad., U. Hawaii, 1977. Librarian Forest Research Lab., Corvallis, Oreg., 1966-69; instr. English Lang. Inst., Corvallis, 1974-80; dir. spl. svcs. Oreg. State U., Corvallis, 1980—. Editor ann. book: Trio Achievers, 1986, 87, 88; contbr. articles to profl. jours. Precinct com. Republican Party, Corvallis, 1977-80; adminstrv. bd. First United Meth. Ch., Corvallis, 1987—, mem. fin. com., 1987—, tchr. Bible, 1978—. Mem. N.W. Assn. Spl. Progs. (pres. 1985-86), Nat. Council Ednl. Opportunities Assns. (bd. dirs. 1984-87), Nat. Gardening Assn. Republican. Methodist. Home: 530 SE Mayberry Corvallis OR 97333 Office: Spl Svcs Project Waldo 337 OSU Corvallis OR 97331

VERWYS, BONNIE, bed and breakfast owner; b. Lansing, Mich., June 3, 1934; d. Earle Clifton and Mary Leah (Krause) McVoy; children: Wendy Winslow Tomlinson-Westrate, Kimberly Knight Tomlinson-Westrate, Heather Lynn Tomlinson-Westrate, Brian Earle Westrate. Student, Grand Valley Coll., Allendale, Mich., Davenport Coll., Grand Rapids, Mich. Supr. activities workshop, program coord. Kandu Industries, Holland, Mich., 1970-81; owner The Parsonage 1908 Bed and Breakfast, Holland, 1984—; small bus. adv. Appeared on cover Rapids mag., 1988; holder 2 trademarks for Bed and Breakfast Flag, 1985 and 1986. Mem. NAFE, Alliance of Women Entrepreneurs, Inventors Coun. Mich., Profl. Women's Network. Episcopalian. Home and Office: 6 E 24th St Holland MI 49423

VESPERI, MARIA DAVOREN, anthropologist, educator, journalist, gerontology specialist; b. Worcester, Mass., June 24, 1951; d. Arthur Ernest and Mary Elizabeth (Davoren) V.; 1 child, Corinna Aline Calagione. BA, U. Mass., 1973; MA, Princeton U., 1975, PhD, 1978. Vis. asst. prof. anthropology, U. South Fla. Grad. Coll., Tampa, 1978-81, adj. asst. prof. anthropology, 1981—; vis. asst. prof. anthropology New Coll., Sarasota, 1985-86; cons., writer St. Petersburg Times (Fla.), 1980, staff writer, 1981-87, editorial dept. 1986—, editorial bd., 1988—; project dir. folk arts documentary supported by Nat. Endowment for Arts; cons. hist. photo exhibit Mus. Fla. History. Active Gray Panthers. Commonwealth scholar, U. Mass., 1969-73; Princeton U. fellow, 1973-75, NIH Pub. Health Service research fellow, 1976-78; doctoral dissertation grantee NSF, 1975-76, grantee Adminstrn. on Aging, 1975-76, Nat. Endowment for Arts, 1983. Mem. Am. Anthropol. Assn., Gerontol. Soc. Am., N.Y. Acad. Scis., Soc. Humanistic Anthropology (program chairperson 1987), Assn. for Anthropology and Gerontology (newsletter editor 1982-87, pres. 1988-89), Nat. Council on Aging, Fla. Press Club, Phi Beta Kappa, Alpha Lambda Delta. Author: City of Green Benches: Growing Old in a New Downtown, 1985. Contbr. articles to publs. in field. Home: 1209 Alcazar Way S Saint Petersburg FL 33705 Office: PO Box 1121 Saint Petersburg FL 33731

VESPO, JO ELLEN, psychology educator; b. Queens, N.Y., Dec. 12, 1956; d. Charles John and Josephine Marie (Mahoney) Hofmann; m. Joseph Jude Vespo, Nov. 22, 1980. BA, SUNY, Stony Brook, 1978, PhD, 1985; MA, U. Md., Baltimore County, 1980. Instr. SUNY, Stony Brook, 1983-84, vis. asst. prof., 1985-87; asst. prof. psychology and psychology-child life Utica (N.Y.) Coll. of Syracuse U., 1987—, sec. coll. coun., 1988-89; presenter Nat. Issues Forum: Daycare Dilemma, Utica, 1989; conf. presenter, 1983—. Contbr. articles to profl. jours., chpt. to book. Bd. dirs. Mid York Child Care Coordinating Coun., Utica, 1987—; chmn. children's health Herkimer-Oneida County Health Promotion Coalition, Utica, 1987—; mem. Herkimer-Oneida County Adv. Com. on Child Care, 1987-88; presenter State Tchr.'s Ctr. and Neighborhood Ctr., Utica, 1987-89. Grantee SUNY, Stony Brook, 1985, Utica Coll. of Syracuse U., 1989. Mem. Am. Psychol. Soc., Soc. for Rsch. in Child Devel., Internat. Network Analysis Soc., Assn. for Care of Children's Health, Child Life Coun., Cen. N.Y. Psychol. Assn., Iowa Network on Personal Relationships, Phi Beta Kappa, Sigma Xi (grantee 1982, 84). Office: Utica Coll of Syracuse U Burrstone Rd Utica NY 13502

VESSEY, JUDITH ANN, nursing educator; b. Phila., Aug. 19, 1951; d. Eric Wigston and Leora Dorothy (Lawson) V. BS in Nursing, Goshen Coll., 1973; Devel. Pediatric Nurse Practitioner, U. Miami, 1978; MS in Nursing, U. Pa., 1980, PhD, 1986. RN, Pa. Staff nurse pediatrics dept. Tri-County Hosp., Springfield, Pa., 1973-75; charge nurse Melmark Home and Sch., Berwyn, Pa., 1975-77; nurse cons. Sunrise Sch., Miami, Fla., 1977-78; health tng. specialist Temple U., Phila., 1978-80; instr. nursing U. Pa., Phila., 1981-86, asst. prof., 1986-88; Robert Wood Johnson clin. nurse scholar U. Calif., San Francisco, 1988-90; assoc. prof. U. Ark. for Med. Scis. Coll. Nursing, Little Rock, 1990—; rsch. facilitator Ark. Children's Hosp., Little Rock, 1990—; cons. U. Jordan, Amman, 1986, Head Start, Phila., 1987—. Assoc. editor Nursing Rsch., 1988—. Nurses' Ednl. Fund scholar, 1979. Mem. Nat. Assn. Pediatric Nurses and Practitioners (cert.), Am. Nurses Assn., Assn. for Care Children's Health, Soc. for Rsch. in Child Devel., Sigma Theta Tau. Office: U Ark for Med Scis Sch Nursing 4301 W Markham Slot 529 Little Rock AR 72205-0610

VEST, MARLYN MARIE, marketing professional, consultant; b. Pensacola, Fla., July 29, 1947; d. Arthur Frederick and Marlyn (Shaw) Farwell; m. Bill Robert Vest, Oct. 25, 1969; 1 child, Scott Brian. BS in Recreation Adminstrn., U. Fla., 1969; MS in Continuing and Vocat. Edn., U. Wis., 1976. Recreation supr. Beloit Recreation Dept., Wis., 1969-70; recreation therapist Mendota Mental Health Inst., Madison, Wis., 1970-75; acting unit chief Mendota Deaf Treatment Ctr., Madison, 1976; instr. U. Wis., Madison, 1977; dir. activity and rehab. therapy Mendota Mental Health Inst., Madison, 1976-87; cons. therapies Dept. Health and Social Svcs., Madison, 1976-87; mgr. mktg. Badger State Industries, Madison, 1987-89; dir. mktg. and sales N.E. region Correctional Products and Svcs., Inc., Westminster, Colo., 1987—; preceptor U. Wis., Madison, 1984-87; clin. asst. prof. U. Wis., Milw., 1983-87; dir. tourism and recreation adv. com. Madison Area Tech. Coll., 1982—; lectr. in field. Contbr. articles to profl. jours. Instr., advocate Tourette Syndrome Assn., Wis. chpt., 1981—. Recipient Gov.'s Merit award State Wis. Dept. Health and Social Service, Madison, 1982, Exceptional Performance award, 1981, 83, 86. Mem. Wis. Parks and Recreation Assn. Therapeutic Soc. (chmn. 1970, Outstanding Contbns. to Field award 1979), Wis. Parks and Recreation Assn. (service recognition award 1985), Dane County Recreation Coordinating Council (chmn. 1974), P. Lambda Theta Nat. Honor Assn. Methodist. Avocations: travel, cross-country skiing, wind surfing, gardening, canning. Office: Correctional Products and Svcs Inc 1491 W 124th Ave Westminster CO 80234

VEST, MARY ELIZABETH, transportation company official; b. Roanoke, Va., Nov. 19, 1954; d. Robert Ellsworth and Margaret (Taylor) V. Student, St. Andrew's Coll., Laurinburg, N.C., 1972-74, U. S.C., 1976. Mng. editor Richlands (Va.) News-Press, 1976-78, Delmarva News, Millsboro, Del., 1979-83; ops. mgr. Mer-Lou Transp. Inc., 1983—; part-time journalism tchr. Del. Tech. and Community Coll., 1981-83; profl. cons. sch. publs.; dir. Millsboro Hut, Inc. Recipient awards for spot news, series, and photo story, Va. Press Assn., 1977; award for layout, design, photo series, feature series, and editorials Md.-Del.-D.C. Press Assn., 1980, 81, 82. Mem. Sigma Delta Chi. Roman Catholic. Home: 41 C Blue Teal Rd Selbyville DE 19975 Office: Box 247 Millsboro DE 19966

VESTAL, JEANNE MARIE GOODSPEED, book publishing company executive; b. Ithaca, N.Y., Oct. 30, 1930; d. Alvin Francis and Margaret Josephine (Stoddart) Goodspeed; m. Fred Lowe Vestal, July 17, 1959. B.A., Nazareth Coll., 1952. Sec. G.P. Putman's Sons, N.Y.C., 1953-56; asst. editor Alfred A. Knopf, N.Y.C., 1956-60; editor-in-chief Dial Press, Inc., N.Y.C., 1960-63; v.p., editor-in-chief J.B. Lippincott, Inc., N.Y.C., 1963-73; sr. v.p., editorial dir. Franklin Watts, Inc., N.Y.C., 1975—. Mem. Children's Book Council (pres. 1966-67). Home: 1161 York Ave New York NY 10021 Office: Franklin Watts Inc 387 Park Ave S New York NY 10016

VETERE, COLLEEN MARIE, nurse; b. Washington, Sept. 10, 1957; d. Alphonse Louis and Margaret Hilda (Nolan) V. BA in Biology, U. Tex., 1980, BS in Nursing, 1982; postgrad., U. Tex., Houston, 1990—. RN, Tex. Nurse intensive care unit Brackenridge Hosp., Austin, Tex., 1983; nurse emergency room Brackenridge Hosp., Austin, 1984; quality rev. supr. Tex. Med. Found., Austin, 1985-86; asst. dir. Peer Rev. Orgn. Tex., Austin, 1986-87, asst. to exec. dir., 1987-88, dir. quality rev. statewide, 1988-90; nurse emergency rm. St. Luke's Hosp., Houston, 1990—. Med. support organizer Area 13 Tex. Spl. Olympics, Austin, 1985-89, vol. support Area 4, Houston, 1990—. 1st. lt. Nurse Corps, USAR, 1983—. Recipient Army Achievement medal USAR-ANC, 1986. Mem. NAFE, Tex. Nurses Assn. Democrat. Roman Catholic. Office: St Lukes Hosp Emergency Rm 6720 Bertner Houston TX 77030

VETRANO TIBERGE, J. BEA, marketing professional; b. Bronx, N.Y., May 17, 1956; d. Joseph J. and Rose Faith (Ventigli) V.; m. Raymond Tiberge, Feb. 14, 1988. BA in Mktg. and Mgmt., Rider Coll., 1980. Sales rep. Office Products div. IBM Corp., Lawrenceville, N.J., 1980-81; asst. product mgr. Hunt Mfg. Co., Phila., 1981-84; acct. exec. Mktg. Group, Ft. Washington, Pa., 1984-87; dir. mktg. Matrix Devel. Group, Cranbury, N.J., 1987—. Active Bus. Vols. for the Arts. Mem. Nat. Assn. Female Execs. Episcopalian. Home: 1 Austin Rd Yardley PA 19067 Office: Matrix Devel Group Forsgate Dr CN 4000 Cranbury NJ 08512

VETTER, EMILY DURSO, association executive; b. Washington, Aug. 28, 1950; d. Thomas Anthony and Frances (Davern) Durso. BA in History, Georgetown U., 1973. Owner, operator Francis Scott Key Book Shop, Washington, 1973-78; exec. asst. to pub. parking adminstr. D.C. Dept. Transp. 1978-79; legis. aide to mem. D.C. City Coun., 1979-80; asst. dir. D.C. Office of Bus. and Econ. Devel., 1980-83, dir. promotions, 1983-84; spl. asst. to dep. mayor for econ. devel., Washington, 1984-85; mktg. mgr. Techworld, Washington, 1985-87, v.p. mktg., 1987-89; exec. v.p. Hotel Assn. of Washington, 1990—; bd. dirs. Fed. City Nat. Bank, 1988—; mem. exec. bd. Washington Conv. and Visitors Assn., 1982-85, 90—; bd. dirs. Internat. Visitors' Info. Svc., Washington, 1983-88, Mayor's Design Commn., Com. to promote D.C., Dist. Curators; mem. adv. com., adv. bd. Northern Va. Community Coll., Washington, 1984; vice chair Washington Urban League; mem. Fed. City Coun. Home: 5126 Fulton St NW Washington DC 20016 Office: Hotel Assn of Washington 1201 New York Ave NW Washington DC 20005

VETTER, MARY MARGARET (PEGGY VETTER), investment manager financial consultant; b. Richmond, Va., June 7, 1945; d. Robert Joseph and Miriam Thomas V.; B.A., Cath. U. Am., 1967; M.B.A. with distinction, N.Y.U., 1978; m. Dimitri Yannacopoulos, May 24, 1980. Asst. to controller N.C. Trading Co., N.Y.C., 1972-74; asst. controller Shaheen Natural Resources Inc., N.Y.C., 1974-76; fin. coordinator mining div. Nat. Bulk Carriers, Inc., N.Y.C., 1976-77; corp. cons. mktg. and strategic planning Gen. Electric Co., Bridgeport, Conn., 1978-80; v.p., internat. mktg. strategy Bankers Trust Co., N.Y.C., 1980-83; fin. cons. Shearson Lehman/Am. Express, Stamford, Conn., 1984—. Bd. dirs. South Central Conn. Emergency Med. Services Council. Named Woman of Yr., N.Y.U. Alumnae Assn., 1978. Mem. Fin. Women's Assn. N.Y., Women in Mgmt., Beta Gamma Sigma. Republican. Roman Catholic. Home: 11 Don Bob Rd Stamford CT 06903 Office: 5 High Ridge Park Stamford CT 06905

VEZINA, MONIQUE, Canadian government official; b. Rimouski, Que., Canada, July 13, 1935; m. Jean-Yves Parent; 4 children. Mem. cabinet, minister external relations, mem. Parliament, Govt. of Canada, Ottawa, Ont., 1984-86, minister supply and services and receiver gen., 1986-87; minister of state for transport Govt. of Canada, 1987-88, minister of state for employment and immigration, minister of state for srs., 1988—. Chmn. parents com. Lower St. Lawrence Sch. Bd., 1964-67; bd. dirs., pres. Assoc. Family Orgns., Que., Can., 1974-81; nat. pres. Dames Helene de Champlain, 1976-79; pres. Fedn. des Caisses populaires Desjardins du Bas St-Laurent, 1976-84, Girardin-Vaillancourt Found., 1981-84; bd. dirs. Confedn. des Caisses populaires et d'economies Desjardins, 1977-84, Societe immobiliere du Que., 1984; mem. Conseil a superieur de l'education du Que., 1978-82, chmn. secondary sch. bd., 1978-82; dep. bd. chmn. Regie de l'assurance automobile du Que., 1978-81; chmn. bd. dirs. Institut cooperatif Desjardins, 1978-81. Office: House of Commons, Parliament Bldgs, Ottawa, ON Canada K1A 0A6

VIA, SARA STEPHENSON, marketing executive; b. Roanoke, Va., Feb. 22, 1942; d. Walter Greenland and Elizabeth Thomas (Wingfield) Stephenson Wood; m. John William Via Jr., June 17, 1961 (div. 1973); children: John W. III, Walter Stephenson, Henry Fleming. BA, George Washington U., 1978, MA, 1980. Mktg. sec. Dynatech, Alexandria, Va., 1981-83; customer service adminstr. Dynatech, Alexandria, 1983-85; adminstrv. asst. Dynatech, Chantilly, Va., 1985-86; mktg. adminstr. Dynatech, Chantilly; advt. adminstr. Dynatech Laboratories, Chantilly, 1986-87; advt., promotion adminstr. Dynatech Data Systems, Va., 1987-88; advt., promotion mgr. Dynatech Communications, Woodbridge, Va., 1988-89; mktg. coord. advt. and promotion Flow Labs., Inc., McLean, Va., 1989—. Republican. Episcopalian. Home: 3615 Oval Dr Alexandria VA 22305

VIA, SUSAN R., lawyer; b. Utica, N.Y., Aug. 5, 1951; d. Alfonso and Marie Bernice (Vitullo) V.; m. Harold J. Harrison Jr., May 8, 1982. AB, Syracuse U., 1972; student, U. Va., 1970-71; JD, Columbia U., 1976. Bar: Colo., Vt., Pa. and Mass. Trial atty. EEOC, Denver and Dallas, 1977-78; chief dep. state's atty. Chittenden County, Burlington, Vt., 1978-82; dep. commr. Vt. Dept. Health, Burlington, 1982-83; atty. Buchanan Ingersoll, P.C., Pitts., 1983-84; asst. U.S. atty. Dist. of Mass., Boston, 1985-90; asst. U.S. Atty. Dist. Virgin Islands, St. Thomas, 1990—; lectr. Atty. Gen. Adv. Inst., Washington, 1989—; cons. Nat. Dist. Atty.'s Assn., Washington, 1989—. Contbr. (monograph) Interviewing Child Victims, 1988. Vol. Italian Home for Children, Jamaica Plain, Mass., 1989-90, Parental Stress Ctr., Pitts., 1983-84. Recipient Spl. Recognition award Town of Essex, Vt., 1981, U.S. Customs Svc. award, 1987, Chief Postal Insp.'s award U.S. Postal Inspection Svc., 1988. Mem. ABA, Mass. Bar Assn., Vt. Bar Assn., Am. So. Profls. Working with Abused Children. Republican. Home: Charlotte Amalie Virgin Island Office: US Attys Office, PO Box 1440, 00801 Saint Thomas 1440, Virgin Islands

VIACAVA, LILLIAN D., librarian; b. Bklyn.; d. Frank and Camille (Raffetto) V. B.A., Coll. New Rochelle, 1951; M.S. in Library Service, Columbia U., 1954. Reference librarian Iona Coll., New Rochelle, 1954-59, asst. librarian, 1960-75, assoc. librarian, 1976—. Mem. ALA, AAUP, Cath. Library Assn. Westchester Library Assn. (chair coll. sect. 1978-79), Spl. Libraries Assn. Office: Iona Coll Ryan Library New Rochelle NY 10801

VIALLE, KAREN, mayor; b. Tacoma. B in Polit. Sci., U. Puget Sound; postgrad., Wash. State U. Prof. U. Puget Sound Sch. Bus. and Pub. Adminstrn.; adminstrv. asst. dept. city planning City of Tacoma, now mayor; program analyst, asst. dir. Office of Fin. Mgmt., Office of Dep. Commr. and Office of State Ins. Commr. Gov. of Wash. Office: City of Tacoma Office of Mayor 747 Market St Ste 1220 Tacoma WA 98402*

VIAT, MARIJANE, graphic artist; b. Chgo., Jan. 8, 1939; d. Arthur Lewis and Loretta Rose (Rehm) Clark; m. Gabriel Anthony Chopey, Feb. 4, 1961 (div. 1965); children: Natalie, Loretta; m. Wallace Donald Jones, July 25, 1968 (div. 1974); 1 child, Adam Bradford; m. Arthur Carl Viat, Jr., Oct. 7, 1978. BS in Apparel Design, UCLA, 1964. Asst. publicity dir. Rose Marie Reid Swimwear, L.A., 1960-62; field sales rep. Polaroid Camera, Inc., L.A., 1963-64, Sunbeam Appliance Co., L.A., San Francisco, 1964-74; v.p. mktg. LaDonna Cosmetics, Burlingame, Calif., 1974-75; ins. sales rep., then mgr. Forman & Forman, Inc., San Francisco, 1975-78; designer, sales rep. Sunkist Swimming Pools, Marin County, Calif., 1978-80; ins. sales mgr. Gish & Assocs., San Francisco, 1980—; prin., graphic designer Mj Design, Marin County, 1987—. Mem. fin. and speaking com. Reps. for Ronald Reagan, 1968-70; program editor Marin County Little League, 1978-81; local and area chmn. adv. and scholarship com. UCLA, 1978-86; officer, now pres. Bay Area Bruins Support Club, 1980—. Mem. Marin County Women's Bowling Assn. (bd. dirs. 1986—), Alpha Chi Omega. Roman Catholic. Home: 98 Trinidad Dr Tiburon Paradise Cay CA 94920 Office: Mj Design/Encore! Litho 63 Paul Dr San Rafael CA 94903

VICE, LAVONNA LEE, lawyer; b. Lexington, Ky., May 27, 1952; d. Keith Romould and Helen (Singer) V. BA summa cum laude, U. Balt., 1980, JD, 1983. Bar: Md. 1983, U.S. Ct. Appeals (4th cir.) 1987, U.S. Dist. Ct. Md. 1988, D.C. 1989, U.S. Supreme Ct. 1989. Trial atty. Ellin & Baker, Balt., 1983—; writer, researcher med., surg. and hosp. standards of care. Home: 2222 Tufton Ridge Rd Baltimore MD 21136 Office: Ellin & Baker 1101 St Paul St Baltimore MD 21202

VICENTE, TRACI ELIZABETH, special education teacher; b. Bklyn., Feb. 11, 1963; d. Thomas and Elaine (Katz) V. BA, St. Josephs Coll., 1986; MA in Liberal Studies, SUNY, Stony Brook, 1989. Cert. elem. and spl. edn. tchr., N.Y. Tchr. South Country Sch., Bellport, N.Y., 1987-88, Boces II, Patchogue, N.Y., 1988—. Mem. Coun. Exceptional Children. Roman Catholic. Home: 30 Mackay Dr Hauppauge NY 11788

VICK, JUDITH ANOLA, journalist; b. Spring Grove, Minn., Aug. 19, 1939; d. Alvin Manuel and Ruth Virginia (Quandahl) V. BS, Mankato State U., 1962; postgrad., N.Y. U., 1966; MA, U. Minn., 1977. Feature writer Mankato (Minn.) Free Press, 1960-62; reporter, columnist Mpls. Star Tribune, 1962-65; asst. commr. City of N.Y., 1966-67; tchr. Mpls. Pub. Schs., 1965-66; sr. pub. rels. rep. U. Minn., Mpls., 1967-80, teaching specialist, 1983—; prin. Minn., 1980—. Co-author: Our Story by George D. Dayton II, 1987; contbr. articles to profl. jours. Home and Office: 4201 Parklawn Ave Edina MN 55435

VICKERS, MONTEZ MOSER, public relations executive; b. North Miami, Fla., Oct. 12, 1953; d. William Thomas and Merrill Catherine (Small) Moser; m. Lewie Marks Vickers, Jan. 17, 1987; 1 stepson, Christopher. BA in Communications magna cum laude, U. Ala., 1981. Admissions clk. Bapt. Med. Ctr.-Montclair, Birmingham, Ala., 1971-72; bus. mgmt. technician U.S. Small Bus. Adminstrn., Birmingham, 1972-79; intern Totalcom, Inc., Tuscaloosa, Ala., 1980-81; writer Birmingham (Ala.) Mag., 1981-82; dir. pub. relations, copywriter Gillis, Townsend and Riley Adv., Birmingham, 1982-83; free-lance copywriter Birmingham, 1983-85; adminstrv. sec. U. Ala., Birmingham, 1983-85; dir. pub. relations Enterprise (Ala.) State Jr. Coll., 1985—. Contbr. numerous articles to various mags., 1981-85. Mem. Coffee County Humane Soc., 1985-86, Nat. Coun. for Mktg. and Pub. Rels., Coffee County Arts Alliance, 1987; bd. dirs. Nat. Spring Chicken Festival, Enterprise, 1986. Mem. Hunter-Jumper Assn. Ala. (3 state championships 1983), Am. Bus. Womens Assn. (enterprise chpt., sec. 1987, Woman of Yr. 1988), Ala. Edn. Assn., Ala. Coll. System Assn., Dixie Horse Show Assn., Ala. Coll. Pub. Rels. Assn., Silver Spurs Saddle Club. Baptist. Office: 600 Pla Dr Enterprise AL 36330

VICKERS, NAOMI R., real estate executive; b. Anderson, Ind., Mar. 25, 1917; d. Floyd Leroy and Gertrude Marie (Richards) Stamm; m. Robert Ross Vickers (dec.); children—Robert V. Vickers, Richard R. Vickers, Philip L. Vickers, Denise (Mrs. Jack L. Healey). Sec., treas. Vickers Fine Homes, Anderson, 1951—, Vickers Apts., 1956—; sec., treas. Comml. Bldgs., 1958—. Mem. Toy Collectors Am. (antique toy train collector). Mem. Order Eastern Star, White Shrine, Madison County Shrine. Home: 2003 E 7th St Anderson IN 46012 Office: 724 Alhambra Dr Anderson IN 46012

VICKERY, BYRDEAN EYVONNE HUGHES (MRS. CHARLES EVERETT VICKERY, JR.), library services administrator; b. Belleview, Mo., Apr. 18, 1928; d. Roy Franklin and Margaret Cordelia (Wood) Hughes; m. Charles Everett Vickery, Jr., Nov. 5, 1948; 1 child, Camille. Student, Flat River (Mo.) Jr. Coll., 1946-48; B.S. in Edn., S.E. Mo. State Coll., 1954; M.L.S., U. Wash., 1964; postgrad. Wash. State U., 1969-70. Tchr. Ironton (Mo.) Pub. Schs., 1948-56; elem. tchr. Pasco (Wash.) Sch. Dist. 1, 1956-61, jr. high sch. libr., 1961-68, coord. librs., 1968-69; asst. libr. Columbia Basin Community Coll., Pasco, 1969-70, head libr., dir. Instructional Resources Ctr., 1970-78, dir. libr. svcs., 1979-87, assoc. dean libr. svcs., 1987—; chmn. S.E. Wash. Libr. Svc. Area, 1977-78, 88-90. Bd. dirs. Pasco-Kennewick Community Concerts, 1977-88, pres., 1980-81, 87-88; bd. dirs. Mid-Columbia Symphony Orch., 1983-89; trustee Wash. Commn. Humanities, 1982-85. Author, editor: Library and Research Skills Curriculum Guides for the Pasco School District, 1967; author (with Jean Thompson), also editor Learning Resources Handbook for Teachers, 1969. Recipient Woman of Achievement award Pasco Bus. and Profl. Women's Club, 1976. Mem. ALA, AAUW (2d v.p. 1966-68, corr. sec. 1969), Wash. Dept. Audio-Visual Instrn., Wash. Libr. Assn., Am. Assn. Higher Edn., Wash. Assn. Higher Edn., Wash. State Assn. Sch. Librs. (state conf. chmn. 1971-72), Tri-Cities Librs. Assn., Wash. Libr. Media Assn. (community coll. levels chmn. 1986-87), Am. Assn. Rsch. Libr., Soroptimist Internat. Assn. (rec. sec. Pasco-Kennewick chpt. 1971-72, treas. 1973-74, pres. 1978-80, v.p. 1989-90), Columbia Basin Coll. Adminstrs. Assn. (sec.-treas. 1973-74), Pacific N.W. Assn. Ch. Libr., Women in Communications, Pasco Bus. and Profl. Women's Club, PEO, Beta Sigma Phi, Delta Kappa Gamma, Phi Delta Kappa (sec. 1981-82, Outstanding Educator award 1983). Home: 4016 W Park St Pasco WA 99301 Office: Columbia Basin Community Coll 2600 N 20th Ave Pasco WA 99301

VICKREY, HERTA MILLER, microbiologist; b. San Gregorio, Calif.; d. John George and Hertha Lucy (Mehrstedt) Miller; m. William David Vickrey; children: Ellean H., Carlene L. Smith, Corrine A. Pochop, Arlene A.; m. Robert James Fitzgibbon, Dec. 28, 1979. BA, San Jose State U., 1957; MA, U. Calif., Berkeley, 1963, PhD in Bacteriology and Immunology, 1970. Cert. immunologist, microbiologist. Pub. health microbiologist Viral & Rickettsial Diseases Lab., Calif. Dept. Pub. Health, Berkeley, 1958-60, 61-62; postgrad. rsch. bacteriologist dept. bacteriology U. Calif., Berkeley, 1963-64; bacteriologist Children's Hosp. Med. Ctr. No. Calif., Oakland, 1958-70; asst. prof. U. Victoria, B.C., Can., 1970-72; rsch. assoc. rsch. dept. Wayne County Gen. Hosp., Wayne, Mich., 1972-83; lab. supr. med. rsch. and edn. U. Mich., Ann Arbor, 1977-83; pub. health lab. dir. Shasta County Pub. Health Svcs., Redding, Calif., 1983-84; sr. pub. health microbiologist Tulare County Health Dept. Lab., Visalia, Calif., 1984—; vis. scientist MIT, Cambridge, 1982; organizer, lectr. mycology workshop Tulare County Health Dept. Lab., Visalia, 1988; USPHS trainee U. Calif., Berkeley, 1965, 66; rsch. fellow U. Calif., Berkeley, 1969-70. Author: Isolation and Identification of Mycotic Agents, 1987-88; contbr. articles to profl. jours. Fundraiser Battered Women's Shelter, Redding, 1983, Real Opportunities for Youth, Visalia, 1986, Open Gate Ministries, Dinuba, Visalia, 1987, 88, 89. NIH predoctoral fellow, 1966, 67, 68; faculty rsch. grantee U. Victoria, 1971, 71; med. rsch. grantee Med. Rsch. and Edn. and Med. Adminstrn., U. Mich., Wayne and Ann Arbor, 1973, 74, 75, 76, 77, 78, 79, 80, 81, 82, 83. Mem. N.Y. Acad. Scis., Delta Omega, Phi Kappa Phi, Phi Beta Kappa, Beta Beta Beta, Calif. Scholarship Soc. Home: 3505 Campus Ave Apt 5 Visalia CA 93277 Office: Tulare County Pub Health County Civic Ctr Visalia CA 93291

VICTOR, SHERRI BETH, school psychologist; b. Phila., May 8, 1959; d. Julius Harry and Sylvia Dorothy (Rothman) V. BS, Tufts U., 1981; MS in Edn., Queens Coll., 1983; postgrad., grad. sch. and U. of N.Y., 1988—. Lic. sch. psychologist, N.Y. Tchr., presch. unit Cambridge (Mass.)-Somerville

Mental Health Ctr., 1980-81; sch. psychology intern Camp Ave. Elem. Sch., Merrick, N.Y., 1981-82, Saulk Jr. High Sch. and MacArthur High Sch., Levittown, N.Y., 1981-82, Pub. Sch. 223, South Ozone Pk., N.Y., 1982-83, Queens Hosp. Ctr., Jamaica, N.Y., 1982-83; psychometrician Queens Coll., Flushing, N.Y., 1982-83; sch. psychologist Dist. 27, N.Y.C., South Ozone Pk., 1983-87, Dist. 30, N.Y.C., Long Island City, N.Y., 1987—; cons. Hewlett (N.Y.) High Sch., 1983, rschr. N.Y.C. Sch. Dist. 27, 1983, N.Y.C. Sch. Dist. 30, 1990; lecturer various N.Y.C. pub. schs., 1984—; supr. of sch. psychology interns, 1986—. Mem. Am. Psychological Assn., Nat. Assn. of Sch. Psychologists, Am. Ednl. Researchers Assn., Assn. for the Advancement of Behavioral Therapy, Psi Chi. Democrat. Jewish. Home: 44 E 12th St New York NY 10003 Office: New York City Bd of Edn 36-36 10th St Long Island City NY 11106

VICTORY-HANNISIAN, KATHLEEN MARY, editor; b. Lynn, Mass., Aug. 27, 1961; d. Peter Thomas and Cynthia Ann (Looker) Victory; m. Robert Hannisian, Oct. 15, 1988. BA, Boston Coll., 1983. Reporter, writer Donoghue Orgn., Holliston, Mass., 1983-84, editor, 1984-85; editor Bankers Pub. Co., Boston, 1986-89, Cambridge Corp., Ipswich, Mass., 1985-89; with Cutter Info. Corp., Arlington, Mass., 1989—; freelance writer, 1989—. Editor: The Merger Directory, 1989, 88. Vol. Boston Coll. Alumni Network, Chestnut Hill, Mass., 1987—. Mem. Freelance Editorial Assn., New Eng. Newsletter Assn. Office: Cutter Info Corp 37 Broadway Arlington MA 02174

VIDEAN, ANN NARCISIAN, public relations executive; b. Denver, July 4, 1959; d. Harry K. and Madge Carole (Evans) Narcisian; m. Robert A. Videan, Oct. 17, 1987. BA, Ariz. State U., 1981. Coord. pub. rels. Western Savs. and Loan, Phoenix, 1981-83; mgr. mktg. and pub. rels. Bapt. Health System, Phoenix, 1983-84; pub. rels. officer United Bank of Ariz., Phoenix, 1984-88; mgr. internal communications Citibank, Phoenix, 1988; pub. rels. account supr. Communications Ptnrs. Inc., Phoenix, 1988—. Chmn. media com. Phoenix Urban League, 1985; reader Sun Sounds, Phoenix, 1980-82; participant Corp. Mem. Campaign for Scottsdale Ctr. for the Arts, 1989. Recipient Cert. Excellence, Strathmore Graphics Gallery, 1984. Mem. Women in Communications Inc. (bd. dirs. 1983-88, pres. 1987-88, Award of Merit 1983, nat. mem. com. 1988-89), Pub. Rels. Soc. Am. (bd. dirs. 1984-87, 88—, pres. 1990), Ariz. Bankers Assn. (pub. rels. com. 1984-88). Republican. Office: Communication Ptnrs Inc 5150 N 16th St Ste C256 Phoenix AZ 85016

VIDOVIC, AGNES ANN, physical education educator; b. Chgo., Jan. 28, 1929; d. Joseph and Mary (Kirincic) Radich; m. Martin P. Vidovic, Sept. 14, 1957; children—Janice Geralyn, Christopher Martin. A.A., Wilson Jr. Coll., 1949; B.S., U. Ill.-Urbana, 1951; M.S., W.Va. U., 1952; postgrad. numerous univs. Instr., ARC, 1947-49, YMCA, Chgo., 1953-55, YWCA, Chgo., 1956-57, Chgo. Park Dist., 1951; waterfront dir. Clearwater Camp for Girls, Minocqua, Wis., 1955; instr. U. Chgo. Lab. Sch., 1952-54, Lindblom High Sch., Chgo., 1954-62; chair girls' dept. phys. edn. Hubbard High Sch., Chgo., 1962-63, Morgan Park Acad., Chgo., 1965-67; prof. phys. edn. Truman Coll., Chgo., 1967—, mem., chairperson phys. plant com., 1988—; judge/referee Ill. High Sch. Assn., 1969-74; ednl. film distbr. U.S. Gymnastics Fedn. Women's Com., 1969-72; timer/scorer Midwest Open Gymnastics Championship for Women, 1969-70; vol. lectr. Mayfair Coll. Adult Edn., 1968-74, cons. 1968-73; voting rep. Chgo. City Colls. Faculty Council, 1983-85; mem. Nat. Bd. Women Athletics, 1974-80. Bd. dirs. Mothers Assn. U. Ill., 1977-85, chair fall conf., 1983, 2d v.p., 1984-85; mem. choir Assumption Cath. Ch., Chgo., 1953-59, St. Monica Cath. Ch., Chgo., 1968-71; mem. 41st Ward Women's Democratic Orgn.; faculty rep. Truman Coll. Community Council, 1981-83. State of Ill. scholar, 1949-51; Oscar Mayer scholar, 1962; recipient 25-Yr. Service award ARC, 1984. Mem. AAHPERD and Dance (life; charter 500, Nat Intramural Sports Council 1967-71), Nat. Dance Assn. (higher edn. div.), Ill. Assn. Health, Phys. Edn., Recreation and Dance. Democrat. Club: St. Monica Women's (Chgo.). Office: Truman Coll 1145 W Wilson Ave Chicago IL 60656

VIELHAUER, MICHELLE RENEE, nurse; b. Cin., Jan. 22, 1964; d. Siegfried Gunther and Brigitte (Klobutowski) V. BSN, U. Cin., 1987, postgrad., 1989—. Student nurses asst. Our Lady of Mercy Hosp., Cin., 1985-87; RN Carnival Cruise Lines, Miami, Fla., 1989—, Am. Nursing Care, Cin., 1989—, U. Cin. Hosp., 1987—; diabetic resource nurse, U. Hosp., Cin., 1987—, clin. ladder commn., 1988-89. Mem. Am. Nurse Assn., Cin. Ski Club, U. Cin. Sailing Club. Republican. Roman Catholic. Home: 7239 Longfield Dr Cincinnati OH 45243

VIETS, KAREN JOYCE, electrical engineer; b. Albuquerque, Feb. 4, 1963; d. Kenneth Henry and Joyce Helen (Blacka) Miller; m. Thomas James Viets, May 25, 1963. BS in Elec. Engring., U. Va., Charlottesville, 1985. Mem. tech. staff MITRE Corp., McLean, Va., 1985—. Mem. IEEE, Raven Soc., Omicron Delta Kappa, Eta Kappa Nu, Tau Beta Pi.

VIGERSTAD, ALICE EMILY FROST, retired educator; b. Bklyn., Sept. 6, 1907; d. Vincent Morse and Alice (Randall) Frost; m. Josef Ewald Vigerstad, May 30, 1942; 1 child, Torgny Josef. AB cum laude, Radcliffe Coll., 1930; MA, Montclair State Coll., 1965. Cert. secondary sch. tchr., N.J. Substitute tchr. Essex County, N.J., 1930-31; clerk Mutual Benefit Life Ins. Co., Newark, N.J., 1931-35, Tchrs. Ins. Annuity Assn., N.Y.C., 1935-36, 1st Boston Corp., N.Y.C., 1936-43, Western Electric Co., N.Y.C., 1943-48; substitute tchr. Essex County high schs., N.J., 1956-66; math. tchr. Seton Hall U., South Orange, N.J., 1966-69, Fairleigh Dickinson U., Madison, N.J., 1969-73; substitute tchr., home instr. Essex County high schs., N.J., 1973-89; tutor East Orange, West Orange, South Orange, Maplewood, N.J., 1930—. Mem. Neighborhood Coalition, 1988—, campaign worker Elec. Bd. Edn., 1955—, West Orange High Sch. PTA. Recipient plaque for svc. to student athletes West Orange High Sch. Athletic Booster Club, 1979, plaque for 35-yr. PTA membership West Orange Bd. Edn., 1989. Mem. AAUW (treas. 1974-78), LWV (treas. 1983-87), N.J. Congress PTAs (life mem.), Triggue (sec. lodge #88 1984-87), Ind. Order Vikings (sec. 1980-89). Republican. Mem. Swedenborgian Ch. Home: 55 Riggs Pl West Orange NJ 07052

VIGIL-GIRON, REBECCA D., state official; b. Taos, N.Mex., Sept. 4, 1954. Grad., New Mex. Highlands Univ. Formerly with Public Service Co. of N.Mex., elected sec. of state of N.Mex., Santa Fe, 1986. Democrat. Office: Office of State Sec 491 Old Santa Fe Trail Lamy Bldg Santa Fe NM 87503

VIGLER, MILDRED SCEIFORD, retired chemist; b. North East, Pa., Sept. 6, 1914; d. William and May Elizabeth (Currie) Sceiford; m. Roland Elmer Vigler, Mar. 19, 1934 (div. May 1952). BA, Lake Erie Coll., Painesville, Ohio, 1935. Tchr. Ashtabula County Bd. Edn., Cork, Ohio, 1935-36, Geneva Twp., Ohio, 1936-38; chemist Interlake Iron Corp., Erie, Pa., 1942-45; analytical rsch. chemist Standard Oil Co. Ohio, Cleve., 1945-79, part-time researcher, 1981-84, ret., 1979. Contbr. articles to sci. jours. including SAS Jour., Analytical Chemistry, Applied Spectroscopy. Named Disting. Alumna, Lake Erie Coll., 1983. Mem. Am. Chem. Soc. (Ameritus award 1986), AAUW, Lake View Country Club. Episcopalian.

VIGLIANCO, MARSHA LOUISE, small business owner; b. Clarksburg, W. Va., June 28, 1956; d. Matt and Joan (Hart) V; 1 child, Allen Robert. Owner Chums Early Learning Day Care Ctr., Clarksburg, W. Va., 1985—, Fairmont, W.Va., 1989—, Wilsonburg, W.Va., 1990—; bd. dirs. North Central Community Action Head Start, Clarksburg. Mem. C. of C. (bd. dir.), Jr. Woman's Club. Republican. Home and Office: Chums Early Learning Day Ctr 212 Liberty Ave Clarksburg WV 26301

VIGNEAU, NANCÉ JEAN, architect; b. Hartford, Conn., May 25, 1952; d. Francis John and Jo Anne (Clark) Vigneau; m. Arthur Wynne Vaast, Oct. 4, 1987. BFA in Interior Design, Pratt Inst., 1982, BArch, 1983. Registered profl. architect, N.Y. Interior architect Lee Ltd., N.Y.C., 1983-85; architect Skidmore, Owings & Merrill, N.Y.C., 1985—; Docent Nat. Acad. Design, N.Y.C., 1989-90, acad. circle, 1990. Mem. AIA (women's caucus N.Y.C. chpt.), N.Y. Jr. League, Nat. Arts Club. Home: PO Box 912 Southport CT 06490

VIGNOCCHI, MADALENA JOAN, accountant; b. Lake Forest, Ill., July 2, 1952; d. Anthony and Juanita Dolly (Thompson) V.; m. Thomas Stanley Lawrence, Nov. 21, 1981; children: David, Michael. BS in Fin., U. Ill., 1973. CPA, Ill. Staff acct. Ernst & Whinney, Chgo., 1974-75, in-charge acct., 1975-76; semi-sr. internal auditor McGraw-Edison Co., Elgin, Ill., 1976-77, tax acct., 1977-79; sr. tax analyst Safety Kleen Corp., Elgin, 1980-84, acctg. supr., 1984-85, mgr. capital budget, property acct., 1985—. Mem. Am. Inst. CPA's, Women in Mgmt. (pres. No. Fox Valley chpt. 1984-86), Ill. CPA's. Roman Catholic.

VIGNOS, SUSAN LOUISE, municipal official; b. Canton, Ohio, June 9, 1958; d. Edward Henry and Helen (Paulus) Hawkins; m. Richard Charles Vignos, Sept. 9, 1978 (div. Oct. 1987), remarried Aug. 27, 1988; children: Andrea Lynn, Jacquelyn Marie. Student, Bowling Green (Ohio) State U., 1976-78, Kent (Ohio) State U., 1978-81, Walsh Coll., 1982—. Coord. admissions Valley View Nursing Home, Akron, Ohio, 1978-79; adminstrv. asst. Manor Care Nursing Home, Akron, 1979-81; corp. auditor city income tax dept. City of Canton, 1982, clk., investor treas.'s dept., 1982-83, chief dep. treas., 1983-85, city treas., 1985—. With USNR, 1989. Mem. Ohio Mcpl. Treas. Assn., Nat. Mcpl. Treas. Assn. U.S. and Can. (legis. com.), Mcpl. Fin. Officers Assn., NE Ohio Tax Adminstrs., Ohio Mcpl. League, Canton Jaycees, City Club Canton, Canton Exchange Club (sec.). Episcopalian. Home: 246 31st St NW Canton OH 44709 Office: City of Canton 218 Cleveland Ave Canton OH 44702

VIGREN, SUZANNE JO, educator; b. Rochester, N.Y., Feb. 6, 1965; d. David Lawerance and Carol Sue (Lechlitner) V. AS, Cazenovia Coll., 1985; BS, Nazareth Coll., Rochester, 1987. Cert. tchr., N.Y. Tchr. bus. Honeoye (N.Y.) Cen. Sch., 1987—; coach cheerleading (sect. VI championship title 1989), girls soccer Honeoye (N.Y.) Cen. Sch. Adviser, Richmond Recreation, Honeoye, 1989. Mem. Bus. Tchrs. Assn. N.Y. Republican. Episcopalian. Home: 983 Park Ave Rochester NY 14610 Office: Honeoye Cen Sch Main St Honeoye NY 14471

VIGUERA, LAUREL M., professional association executive; b. Washington, Apr. 25, 1961; d. Edward E. Viguera; m. Juan J. Vega, Dec. 2, 1988. BA cum laude, Smith Coll., 1983; postgrad., U. Cordoba, Spain, 1984, George Washington U. Cert. in mgmt. Dir. lang. program French Consulate, Cordoba; intercultural specialist Eurolingua, Cordoba; interpreter, translator NIBCO-ATCOSA, Inc., Cordoba; sr. rsch. assoc. Am. Coun. Life Ins., Washington; assoc. mgr. rsch. and info. Am. Soc. Assn. Execs., Washington. Mem. NAFE, Am. Mgmt. Assn., Nat. Archives Assn., Smith Club of Washington. Address: 4970 Battery Ln Apt 205 Bethesda MD 20814

VIKING, NANCY LEE, festival management consultant; b. St. Paul, Nov. 2, 1943; d. Clarence Lee and Helen Voila (Olson) Law; m. Don Stuart Johnson, Aug. 1, 1963 (div. 1967); 1 child, Eric Don; m. Robert Edward Viking, Dec. 31, 1985. Student, U. Minn., 1961-62. cert. Festival Exec. degree, Purdue, 1986. Adminstrv. asst. St. Paul Winter Carnival Assn., 1966-67, First Bank St. Paul, 1967-69; festival mgr. Mpls. Aquatennial Assn., 1969-86; adminstrv. coordinator Internat. Festivals Assn., Mpls., 1970-83; parade coordinator City of Santa Ana (Calif.) Community Events Ctr., 1986-87; pres. Times Orange County Holiday Parade, 1988—. Pub. relations dir. Minn. Little Gophers Baseball Team, Mpls., 1983-86. Mem. Internat. Festivals Assn. (bd. dirs. 1986-87), Minn. Press Club, Pub. Relations Soc. Am., Mpls. Chinese Am. Assn. of Minn., Exec. Women in Tourism, Mpls./Iberaki (Japan) Sister City Assn. Republican. Lutheran. Lodge: Zonta.

VILIM, NANCY CATHERINE, advertising executive; b. Quincy, Mass., Jan. 15, 1952; d. John Robert and Rosemary (Malpede) V.; m. Jesse J. Cajda, Sept. 13, 1980; children: Matthew Edward, Megan Catherine. Student, Miami U., Oxford, Ohio, 1970-72. Media asst. Draper Daniels, Inc., Chgo., 1972-74; asst. buyer Campbell Mithun, Chgo., 1974-75; buyer Tatham, Laird & Kudner, Chgo., 1975-77; media buyer Adcom, Inc. div. Quaker Oats Corp., Chgo., 1977-79; media supr. G.M. Feldman, Chgo., 1979-81; v.p. media dir. Media Mgmt., 1981-83; v.p. broadcast dir. Bozell, Jacobs, Kenyon & Eckhardt, Chgo., 1983-88; media mgr. McCann-Erickson, Inc., 1989—; judge 27th Internat. Broadcast Awards, Chgo., 1987. Mem. local PTA, Berwyn, Ill., 1988, Berwyn Parents Assn., Inc., Ill., 1988. Recipient Media All Star awards Sound Mgmt. Mag., N.Y.C., 1987. Mem. Broadcast Advt. Club Chgo., Mus. Broadcast Communications, NAFE. Office: McCann-Erickson Inc 625 N Michigan Ave Chicago IL 60611

VILLAGONZALO, AMPARO DE LA CERNA, management analyst; b. Cebu, Philippines, Oct. 30, 1939; came to U.S.A., 1970; d. Ignacio Carangue and Josefa (De La Cerna) V.; children: Victor, Emerald. AA, U. Visayas, 1956, LLB magna cum laude, 1960; postgrad., U. Philippines, 1966-67. Bar: Philippines, 1961. Atty. Villagonzalo Law Offices, Cebu City, Philippines, 1960-62; mgmt. analyst Presdl. Com. on Adminstrn. Performance Efficiency, Manila, Philippines, 1962-65; mgmt. analyst II Commn. on Elections, Manila, Philippines, 1965-70; spl. correspondent Bankers Life Ins. Co., Chgo.; from transit mgmt. analyst to assoc. mgmt. analyst N.Y.C. Transit Authority, 1974-80, mgr., materials mgmt. dept., 1980—. Scholar U. Visayas, 1954-60, U. Philippines, 1966-67. Roman Catholic. Home: 158 11 86th St Howard Beach NY 11414

VILLA-KOMAROFF, LYDIA, molecular biologist; b. Las Vegas, N.Mex., Aug. 7, 1947; d. John Dias and Druculla (Jaramillo) V.; m. Anthony Leader Komaroff, June 18, 1970. BA, Goucher Coll., 1970; PhD, MIT, 1975. Rsch. fellow Harvard U., Cambridge, 1975-78; asst. prof. dept. microbiology U. Mass. Med. Ctr., Worcester, 1978-81, assoc. prof. dept. molecular genetics micro, 1982-85; assoc. prof. dept. neurology Harvard Med. Sch., Boston, 1986—; sr. rsch. assoc. neurology Children's Hosp., Boston, 1985—, assoc. dir. mental retardation rsch. ctr., 1987—. Contbr. articles to profl. jours.; patentee in field. Helen Hay Whitney Found. fellow, 1975-78. Mem. NIH (rsch. grantee 1989—, mammalian genetics study sect 1982-84, reviers res. 1989, neurol. disorders program project rev. com. 1989—), Soc. for Advancement of Chicanos and Native Americans in Sci. (founding mem. 1972, bd. dirs. 1987—, v.p. 1990—), Am. Soc. for Microbiology, Assn. for Women in Sci., Soc. for Neurosci., Am. Soc. Cell Biology. Office: Children's Hosp Enders 2 300 Longwood Ave Boston MA 02115

VILLALON, DALISAY MANUEL, nurse; b. Angat, Bulacan, Philippines, Apr. 27, 1941; came to U.S., 1967; d. Federico Manuel and Librada (Garcia) Manuel; divorced; children: Ricky, May, Liberty, Derrick, Dolly Rose. BS in Nursing, Manila Cen. U., 1961; postgrad. in nursing, U. Ill., Chgo., 1972-74. RN, Ill. Instr. nursing Cen. Luzon Sch. Nursing, Philippines, 1966-67; staff nurse St. Alexis Hosp., Cleve., 1968-70, Augustana Hosp., Chgo., 1972-74; nurse mgr. Holy Child Med. Clinic, Chgo., 1976-80; nurse auditor 1st Health Care, Rosemont, Ill., 1982-83; dir. nurses North Shore Terr., Waukegan, Ill., 1983—. Columnist Philippine News. Bd. dirs. Filipino Am. Coun., Chgo., 1978-80, v.p., 1980-82; bd. dirs. Asian Human Svcs., Chgo.; pres. Am.-Filipino Profl. Civic Alliance, Chgo., 1984—; chmn. Philippine Week Com., 1979; v.p. Filipino Ams. Concerned for Elderly; trustee Rizal-MacArthur Found.; v.p. Filipino Svc. League, 1989—; exec. v.p. Asian Festival, Inc.; past chmn. various civic coms.; mem. Asian-Am. Adv. Coun. Mayor Daley, 1989—; coord. 48th ward Filipino Am. Polit. Assn.; mem. adv. com. to continuing edn. on nursing coll. Recipient Cert. Appreciation Rizal-MacArthur Found., 1977, Most Outstanding Filipino in Midwest award Cavite Assn. Am., 1980, Outstanding Community Svc. Appreciation award Filipino Am. Coun., 1981, 89, NGHIA Sinh Internat., Inc., 1989, Outstanding Svc. award Asian-Am. Coaliton, 1989, Outstanding Contrn. award Dirs. Nursing and Adminstrs. Conf., 1988. Mem. Ill. Nurses Assn. (senator dist. 16 1989-90, mem. human rights and ethics commn. 1990—, bd. dirs. 1990—, chmn. legis. com. 1990—), Philippine Med. Assn. Aux. (pres. 1980, Outstanding Leadership award 1981), Chgo. Med. Soc. Aux. (v.p. 1980), Chgo.-Philippine Lioness Club (pres. 1983-84, Outstanding Svc. award 1985), Ill. Orgn. Nurse Execs. Democrat. Roman Catholic. Home: 5901 Sheridan Rd Apt 7F Chicago IL 60660 Office: Northshore Terrace 2222 W 14th St Waukegan IL 60085

VILLALÓN, SILVIA DURÁN, real estate executive; b. La Havana, Cuba, Apr. 7, 1941; d. Mario Andrés and Ondina (Paredes) Durán; m. Jose R. Garrigó, Apr. 5, 1959 (div. Oct. 1983); children: Jose R., Silvia M., Jorge I.; m. Andrés Villalón, Aug. 17, 1984. BS, Instituto Del Vedado, La Havana, 1958; AA, Miami Dade Community Coll., 1984. Pres. Silvia Garrigo Interiors, Key Biscayne, Fla., 1974-89, Garrigo, Duran & Assocs., Realtors, Key Biscayne, 1976-87; v.p. The Royal Poinciana Group, Inc., Cape Coral, Fla., 1984-89; pres. Sailfish Co., Realtors, Cape Coral, 1986-87, Poinciana Realty of Cape Coral, Inc., Cape Coral, 1987-89, The Tile Wholesaler, Inc., Key Biscayne, Fla., 1987—; pvt. practice mortgage broker Key Biscayne, 1986, pvt. practice realtor, 1987—; sr. sales cons., internat. sales coord. The Gables, Coral Gables, Fla. Home: 600 Grapetree Dr 3C-S Key Biscayne FL 33149 Office: The Gables 10 Edgewater Dr Coral Gables FL 33133

VILLALPANDO, CATALINA VASQUEZ, treasurer of U.S.. Congl. liaison OEO; bus. specialist Dallas region U.S. Dept. Commerce, 1973-78; v.p. Mid-South Oil Co., Dallas; staff asst. White House Office Presdl. Pers., 1981—; sr. v.p. communications Internat., Inc.; special asst. for pub. liaison Pres. Reagan, 1983-85; treas. Govt. of U.S., 1989—; chmn. Rep. Nat. Hispanic Assembly, 1987-90. Bd. dirs. S.W. voter registration and edn. project S.W. Tex. State U. Found. Mem. Nat. Coun. Hispanic Women, Nat. Assn. Latino Elected and Appointed Ofcls., League United Latin Am. Citizens, Hispanic C. of C. of Va., Am. G.I. Forum. Office: Treas of the US 15th & Pennsylvania Ave NW Washington DC 20220*

VILLAVECCHIA, ROBERTA LEE GRIFFIN, controller; b. L.A., Oct. 25, 1938; d. John Martin and Eleanor (Long) Griffin; divorced; children: Candace, Robert, Kathy, Joan, Lisa, Barbara; married. Student, Trinity U., San Antonio, 1970; BA, Brooks Inst. at Santa Barbara, Calif., 1976. Systems engr. Bendix Corp., Cape Kennedy, Fla., 1964-71; asst. dir. Confederate Air Force Mus., Harlingen, Tex., 1976-84; systems engr. Calcutron Corp., Houston, 1984-86; gen. mgr. Jiffco Systems, Inc., Houston, 1986-87, v.p., 1987-89; major account rep. Western Union Corp., Houston, 1987-90; controller Nationwide Steel Svcs., Houston, 1990—; cons. Confederate Air Force Mus., Rio Computers, San Antonio, 1984—. Author: History of the Ghost Squadron, 1977; asst. editor CAF Dispatch, 1978-83; contbr. articles to Flypast Mag., Time-Life Series on WWII War in the Air, 1978; patentee lab. glassware for Project Apollo, 1966. Bd. dirs. Confederate Air Force Flying Mus., 1970. Recipient Merit awards Profl. Photographers Am., 1977, Gold Medal photography award Los Angeles County Fair, 1976. Mem. Houston Air Cargo Assn., Houston World Trade Assn. Republican. Roman Catholic. Home: 1100 Langwick #2109 Houston TX 77060 Office: Nationwide Steel Svcs 4740 W Little York #308 Houston TX 77091

VILLINES, DEBIANNE, health care consultant; b. Buffalo, Apr. 2, 1955; d. Louis David Lo Vallo and Virginia Iona (Tagg) Du Bois, m. John Clay Villines, Jan. 17, 1973 (div. Oct. 1984); 1 child, Coop Joshua. AS in Nursing, Ga. State U., 1976, BS in Nursing, 1981; M in Nursing., Emory U., 1984. Cert. in neonatal intensive care. Charge nurse Crawford Long Hosp., Atlanta, 1976-78; staff nurse specializing in Ob-Gyn Atlanta, 1978-79; staff nurse specializing in neonatal care Northside Hosp., Atlanta, 1979-80, asst. unit mgr. specializing in neonatal care, 1980-86; coord. intensive care units Scottish Rite Children's Hosp., Atlanta, 1986-89; asst. dir. spl. projects blood svcs. nursing ARC, Atlanta, 1990—; chmn. ethics com. Northside Hosp., 1983-86; profl. relations com. Scottish Rite Children's Hosp.; Ga. Nurses' Polit. Action Com.; Ga. rep. Mead Johnson Symposium Perinatal Med., 1982; lectr. in field, 1985-88. Named to Dean's List Mortar Bd. Ga. State U. Mem. Ga. Nurses' Assn., Ga. Nurses for Life, Ga. Perinatal Assn., Ga. Women's Health Adminstrn. Network, Nat. Assn. Neonatal Nurses, Nurses' Assn. Am. Coll. Obstetrics and Gynecologists, Masterpeace (Atlanta). Republican. Home: 2143 N Lake Park Dr Smyrna GA 30080 Office: ARC 2581 Piedmont Rd NE Ste C 1150 Atlanta GA 30324

VILLOCH, KELLY CARNEY, art director; b. Kyoto, Japan, July 22, 1950; d. William Riley and stepdaughter Hazel Fowler Carney; m. Joe D. Villoch, Aug. 9, 1969; children: Jonathan Christopher, Jennifer. Assoc. in Fine Arts, Dade Community Coll., Miami, Fla., 1971; student, Metro Fine Arts, 1973-74, Internat. U., 1985-88. Design asst. Lanvin, Miami, 1971—, Fieldcrest, Miami, 1974-77; art dir. Advercolor, Miami, 1977-78; art dir. copywriter ABC, Miami, 1978-89; art dir. writer Miami Write, 1979—; lectr. Miami Dade Community Coll, cons. ABC Studio Masters, North Miami, 1979-89. Principal works include mixed media, 1974 (Best of Show 1974), pen and ink drawing 1988 (Best Poster 1988); writer, dir. editor, producer (video film): Bif 1988. Mem. Am. Film Inst., Phi Beta Kappa.

VILLONE, MARYANN, hospital administrator; b. Clifton, N.J., Jan. 11, 1951; d. Edward J. and Joan C. (Strominski) Kraiger: m. Dennis Alan Villone, May 3, 1975; children: Dennis Edward, Richard Alan. AAS, County Coll. Morris, N.J., 1971. RN. ICU charge nurse Morristown (N.J.) Meml. Hosp., 1972-74, supr. hemodialysis units, 1974-77, cardiac nurse, 1978-79, adminstrv. dir. nursing div., 1987-88, adminstrv. dir., 1988—; with med. rev. bd. and quality assurance com. N.j. Renal Network Coun., 1979-87; renal cons., 1988—. Active Chester PTA, N.J., 1985—. Mem. NAFE, Am. Nephrology Nurses Assn., Orgn. Nurse Execs. N.J., Council Mid. Nurse Mgrs. Home: RD #5 Box 621C Chester NJ 07930 Office: Morristown Mem Hosp 100 Madison Ave Morristown NJ 07960

VINCELLI, SISTER MARY NICHOLAS, nurse; b. St. Paul, Feb. 2, 1927; d. Nicholas Mario and Mary Josephine (Sauro) V. BS in Nursing, Coll. St. Catherine, St. Paul, 1948; MA in Nursing, State U. Iowa, 1966. Joined Sisters St. Joseph of Carondelet, Roman Cath. Ch., 1950. Various nursing and teaching positions, 1948-66; instr. med.-surg. nursing Sisters St. Joseph Sch. Nursing N.D., Grand Forks, 1952-58, 66-67, State U. Iowa, Iowa City, 1966; evening supr. St. Michael's Hosp., Grand Forks, 1968-70; asst. prof. nursing Coll. St. Catherine, 1967-68; pub. health nurse Hidalgo County Dept. Health, Edinburg, Tex., 1970-79; dir. nurses Hidalgo County Dept. Health, Edinburg, 1979-86; program mgr. family health svcs. Tex. Dept. Health, Harlingen, 1986—; mem. N.D. Bd. Nurse Examiners, 1956-58; mem. adv. bd. Lower Rio Grande Sub-Area Coun. Health Systems Agy., 1980-82; mem. Tex. Sudden Infant Death Adv. Com., 1981-82, Coun. for Handicapped, 1982-84; mem. nursing adv. com. Pan. Am. U., 1982-83; bd. dirs. Rio Grande Health and Med. Svcs., Inc.; mem. Hidalgo County Day Care Adv. Com., 1985-86; mem. adv. com. Tex. Early Childhood Intervention Program, 1981—, chairwoman, 1985; mem. adv. com. Tex. Maternal and Infant Health Improvement Act, 1985-90. Mem. Foster Grandparents Adv. Com., 1984-86. Recipient Disting. Svc. award Tex. Pediatric Soc., 1987. Fellow Tex. Pub. Health Assn. (Outstanding Svc. award 1981, 86, grantee 1983-90); mem. Am. Nurses Assn., Am. Red Cross Nursing Svc., U.S. Mex. Border Health Assn. (Outstanding U.S. Mex. Border Health Profl. award 1987), Tex. Nurses Assn., Dist. Nurses Assn., Tex. Pub. Employees Assn., Sigma Theta Tau. Office: Tex Dept Health 601 W Sesame Dr Harlingen TX 78550

VINCENT-RODRIGUEZ, KELLI ANN, legal assistant, educator; b. Schenectady, N.Y., Feb. 20, 1961; d. Ronald Charles and Marlene Ann (Ille) Vincent; m. Vidal Rodriguez, Sept. 28, 1985. BA, Siena Coll., 1983; postgrad., George Washington U., 1989. Cert. legal asst. Legis. asst. N.Y. State Senators, Albany, 1983-85; legal asst. Sinkler & Boyd, Charleston, S.C., 1985-87, Dechert Price & Rhoads, Washington, 1987-89; instr. legal asst. program Ill. Cen. Coll., East Peoria, 1990—; bd. dirs. Entre Nous. Rep. Rep. Women of the Legis., Albany, 1983-85. Mem. Nat. Paralegal Assn. (bd. dirs.), Profl. Assn. Legal Assts. (rep. 1987), Childbirth and Parenting Edn. Assn. (bd. dirs. 1990—). Roman Catholic.

VINES, DEBORAH KAYE, nurse anesthetist; b. San Francisco, May 16, 1961; d. Donald Hoyt and Dolores Marie (Crosby) V.; m. James S. Lowe III, Dec. 16, 1989. BS, McNeese State U., Lake Charles, La., 1983; M.Health Sci., Tex. Wesleyan Coll., Ft. Worth, Tex., 1985. Nurse anesthetist self-employed Hurst, Tex., 1986—. Mem. Am. Assn. Nurse Anesthetists, Phi Kappa Phi.

VINES, PAMELA LYNN DYSON, hematology technician, educator; b. Chgo., Oct. 5, 1955; d. David Thomas and Edythe Louise (Dyson) V. AA, Kankakee Community Coll., 1976; AAS, Malcolm X Coll., Chgo., 1988; BA, Mundelein Coll., 1978; MLT, Cook County Hosp., Chgo., 1988; postgrad. in clin. lab. scis., U. Ill., 1989—. Tutor Retarded Citizens, Inc., Chgo., 1986-88; instr. med. lab. tech. Malcolm X Coll., 1987—; hematology technician Evanston (Ill.) Hosp., 1988—. Co-founder Profls. Volunteering Svcs.; mem. Health Aid for the Homeless; bd. advisors Am. Biog. Inst. Rsch. Mem. Am. Soc. Clin. Pathology (assoc., cert. med. lab. technician), Am. Soc. Med.

Technicians (assoc.), Internat. Platform Assn., Beta Beta Beta. Home: 5250 N Glenwood Ave Apt 3C Chicago IL 60640

VINOCUR, PATRICIA ANA, pediatrician; b. Mendoza, Argentina, July 11, 1961; came to U.S., 1970; d. Simeon Manuel and Maria Ester (Miyara) V. BS in Biology, Ind. U., Bloomington, 1982; MD, Ind. U., Indpls., 1986. Diplomate Am. Bd. Pediatrics. Intern Meth. Hosp., 1986-87, resident, 1987-89; resident in pediatrics Meth. Hosp., Indpls., 1986-89; pediatrician/capt. U.S. Army, Augusta, Ga., 1989—. Recipient Margaret Hatfield award Ind. U. Sch. Medicine, 1982, Sr. Latino award, Ind. U., 1982, student rsch. grantee, biology dept. Ind. U., 1981, Disting. Mil. Grad. award U.S. Army, Ind. U., 1980. Fellow Am. Acad. Pediatrics; mem. Phi Beta Kappa. Home: 3714 Ridgecrest Dr Augusta GA 30907 Office: Eisenhower Army Med Ctr Dept Pediatrics Fort Gordon GA 30905

VINOGRADOFF, ANNA PATRICIA, research chemist; b. Rochford, Essex, England; d. Alexander Nicholas and Mary (Moylan) V. BSc, UCLA, 1976, PhD, 1981. Sr. rsch. chemist Dow Chem. USA-Pharm. Process, Pitts., 1981-84; project leader Dowelanco Agrl. Products Group, Walnut Creek, Calif., 1984—. Contbr. articles to sci. publs.; patentee in field. Mem. Am. Chem. Soc. Office: Dowelanco 2800 Mitchell Dr Walnut Creek CA 94598

VINSON, LEILA TERRY WALKER, retired gerontological social worker; b. Lynchburg, Va., July 28, 1928; d. William Terry and Ada Allen (Moore) Walker; m. Hughes Nelson Vinson, Aug. 11, 1951; children: Hughes Nelson, William Terry. Student, Agnes Scott Coll., 1946-48; BA, U. Ala., Tuscaloosa, 1950; postgrad., U. Ala., Birmingham, 1980-81, U. Va., 1950-51. Cert. gerontol. social worker, Ala. Tchr. English and Latin Marion County Bd. Edn., Hamilton, Ala., 1959-72; social worker I Marion County Dept. Pensions and Security, 1963-72, gerontol. social worker II, 1972-85; ret., 1985. Bd. dirs. Marion County Dept. Human Resources, 1985—; speaker on gen. subjects. Recipient Ala. Woman Committed to Excellence award Tuscaloosa coun. Girl Scouts U.S., 1987; named Mrs. Marion County, PTA, Gwin, Ala., 1969, Woman of Yr. Town of Hamilton, 1980, New Retiree of Yr. Ala. Ret. State Employees Assn., 1988, Woman of Yr. Black Profl. Women, 1985; Gessener Harrison fellow U. Va., 1950-51. Mem. AAUW, DAR (flag chmn. Bedford chpt. 1988-90), UDC, Bus. and Profl. Women's Club (dist. dir. 1984-86, Outstanding Dir. award 1986), Ala. Fedn. Women's Club. Home: Rte 6 Box 296 Bedford VA 24523 also: Military Rd Hamilton AL 35570

VINSON, SANDRA TIPTON, sales executive; b. San Pedro, Calif., July 30, 1951; d. Densial Owen and Bonnie Rhea (Lloyd) Tipton; m. Gary Wayne Wood, June 26, 1970 (div. 1981); 1 child, Rebekah Dawn; m. George William Vinson, Apr. 10, 1982. Student, State Coll. Ark., 1969-70, U. Ark., Little Rock, 1970, 79-81. Co-owner, mgr. Wood Pharmacy, Cabot, Ark., 1976-81; asst. mgr. BP's, Little Rock, 1981-83; sales mgr. The Creative Circle, Little Rock, 1983-84, Littleton, Colo., 1984-85; sales mgr. The Creative Circle, Marietta, Ga., 1985-86, regional sales dir., 1986-89; sr. sales dir., image cons. BeautiControl Cosmetics, Marietta, 1989—. Troop leader Girl Scouts U.S., Calico Rock, Ark., 1972-75; judge Cobb County Jr. Miss Pageant, Marietta, 1988; vol. Am. Cancer Soc., Marietta, 1988. Mem. C. of C., Bus. and Profl. Women. Democrat. Baptist. Home: 2238 Oakrill Ct Marietta GA 30062

VINSON-NIEVES, ANNE HARTMAN, paralegal, human services advocate; b. Charleston, W.Va., Feb. 2, 1959; d. Kaye Ward and Sherrie Louise (Hartman) Vinson; m. Orlando Nieves, May 25, 1985. AA, Bucks County Community Coll., Newtown, Pa., 1979; postgrad., Rutgers U., Camden, N.J., 1979-81; paralegal cert., Widener U., 1982. Mental health worker Elmcrest Psychiat. Hosp., Portland, Conn., 1981-82; residential counselor Path, Inc., Phila., 1982-83; paralegal Community Health Law Project, Trenton, N.J., 1983—; co-founder Community Svc. Network, Trenton, 1987—. Mem. community adv. com. Hyacinth Found. Rutgers U. President's scholar, 1981. Mem. Nat. Paralegal Assn., Bucks County Community Coll. Alumni Assn., Phi Theta Kappa. Democrat. Unitarian. Office: Community Health Law 212 W State St Trenton NJ 08608

VIOLAND, CAROL ANN, sales executive; b. Canton, Ohio, Sept. 3, 1954; d. Dominick Anthony and Stella Ann (Grezewlski) DiRuscio; children: Matthew Alan, Carly Elizabeth. BA, U. Akron, 1976. Sales rep. NCR Corp., Dayton, Ohio, 1977-79, Am. Optical, Southbridge, Mass., 1979-82, Fisons Corp., Rochester, N.Y., 1985—. Tchr. religion St. Collette Cath. Ch., Brunswick, Ohio, 1988-89; room mother Chapman Elem., Strongsville, Ohio, 1987-89. Roman Catholic. Home and Office: 18023 Tresure Isle Strongsville OH 44136

VIOLETTE, DIANE MARIE, small business owner, consultant; b. Pontiac, Mich., Apr. 19, 1958; d. Bernard Desmond and Mary Virginia (Bartosh) V.; m. Glenn Martin Payette, Apr. 18, 1987. BA in Journalism, Mich. State U., 1980; cert. in govt. contracts and mgmt., UCLA, 1987; postgrad., Calif. State U., Northridge, 1987—. Contract adminstr. Def. Contract Adminstrn. Services Mgmt. Area, Van Nuys, Calif., 1980-84, adminstrv. contract officer, 1984-87; pres. govt. contracting Diane Violette & Assocs., Northridge, 1987—. Contbr. articles to profl. jours. Mem. Am. Businesswomen's Assn., Nat. Contract Mgmt. Assn., Kappa Tau Alpha, Phi Kappa Phi.

VIRGA, KAREN FAYE, physical therapist; b. San Jose, Calif., Apr. 14, 1951; d. Nicholas and Edna Faye (Bishop) Chimento; m. Richard Virga, June 22, 1975; children: Jason, Justin. BS, NYU, 1975; MA, Columbia U. Lic. phys. therapist, N.Y., Conn. Phys. therapist Burke Rehab. Ctr., White Plains, N.Y., 1975-79, Danbury (Conn.) Ortho. Assocs., 1980—; lab instr. neurobiology NYU, 1978-79; lectr. Danbury Orthopedic Assocs., 1983—; pvt. practice phys. therapy, N.Y. and Conn., 1975—; ptnr., officer Concepts in Total Health, Avon, Conn., 1986—; evaluation specialist Worklab, Inc., Danbury, 1988—; bd. dirs. Back Sch., Danbury Orthopedic Assocs., 1985—. Contbr. articles to profl. jours. Mem. Am. Phys. Therapy Assn., Arthritis Found., Paraplegic Found. Democrat. Home: 12 Kilian Dr Danbury CT 06811 Office: Danbury Orthopedic Assocs 73 Sandpit Rd Danbury CT 06811

VIRGILI, MARIANNE KATHLEEN, association executive; b. Cleve., Jan. 10, 1948; d. Orlando James and Mary Grace (Ruccella) Balotta; m. John A. Virgili, Oct. 2, 1971; children: Brian, Megan. BA, Kent State U., 1970. Dir. pub. rels. Cath. Charities, Cleve., 1970-72; asst. dir. pub. rels. Cleve. Orch., 1972-76; freelance writer various locations, 1976-82; dir. pub. rels. Ski Sunlight, Inc., Glenwood Springs, Colo., 1982-87; dir. spl. events Glenwood Springs C. of C., 1984-87; exec. dir. Glenwood Springs Chamber Resort Assn., 1987—; bd. dirs., Colo. Mountain Coll. Bus. Adv. Coun., Glenwood Springs, 1989. Garfield County Dem. committeeperson, Glenwood Springs, 1982. Mem. NAFE, Colo. C. of C. Execs. (bd. dirs. 1988—), Berea Jr. Women's Club, Casper Svc. League. Roman Catholic. Home: 1107 Parkwood Ln Glenwood Springs CO 81601 Office: Glenwood Springs Chamber 1102 Grand Ave Glenwood CO 81601

VIRGIN, CHERI LYN, small business owner; b. L.A., Feb. 27, 1959; d. Kenneth Larry and Kathleen (McLaughlin) V. BS in Phys. Edn., Brigham Young U., Provo, Utah, 1981. Coordinator/individual/dual sports Brigham Young U. Intramurals, Provo, 1978-79; sr. recreation leader Mission Viejo (Calif.) Recreation Ctrs., 1981-85; missionary Ch. of Jesus Christ of Latter Day Saints, Guatemala, 1983-84; tchr. Missionary Tng. Ctr., Provo, 1985; recreation leader City of San Juan Capistrano, Calif., 1985-86; recreation supr. Mission Viejo Recreation Ctrs., 1986-88; dir./owner Sports Link, San Juan Capistrano, 1988—; employee fitness coord. Capistrano Unified Sch. Dist., 1989—. Recipient Leone Holbrook Love of Sport award, Brigham Young U., 1980. Mem. Calif. Parks and Recreation Soc., Irvine C. of C., Nat. Recreation and Parks Assn., Am. Coll. Sports Medicine, Assn. Fitness in Bus. Republican. Mem. Ch. of Jesus Christ of Latter Day Saints. Office: Sports Link 31921 Camino Capistrano 109 San Juan Capistrano CA 92675

VIRGO, KATHERINE SUE, health services researcher; b. East Alton, Ill., Feb. 14, 1959; d. John William and Doris Ann (Spencer) Ulmrich; m. John Michael Virgo, Sept. 6, 1980. BSBA, So. Ill. U., 1981, MBA, 1983; postgrad. in Health Svcs. Rsch., St. Louis U., 1986—. Asst. coord. Atlantic Econ. Soc., Edwardsville, Ill., 1978-79, exec. asst., 1979-81, exec. adminstr., 1981-86; co-founder, exec. adminstr. Internat. Health Econs. and Mgmt. Inst., Edwardsville, Ill., 1983-87; rsch. asst. Vets. Adminstrn. Med. Ctr., St. Louis, 1986—; bd. dirs. Internat. Health Econs. and Mgmt. Inst., Edwardsville, 1983-87. Mem. Acad. Mgmt., Assn. for Health Svcs. Rsch., Am. Soc. for Assn. Execs., Health Econs. Rsch. Org., Soc. for Ambulatory Health Care Profls. Democrat. Roman Catholic. Home: 315 Edwards Dr Edwardsville IL 62025 Office: Vets Adminstrn Med Ctr 151JC 915 N Grand Saint Louis MO 63125

VIRTUE, JOYCE SWAIN, nutritionist; b. San Antonio, Apr. 13, 1936; d. Gladstone Benjamin and Delphine (Tafolla) Swain; m. Nick Virtue, Sept. 16, 1963; children: Eugene Michael, David Alexis, Paul Nicholas. Student, San Antonio Coll., 19652; BA, PhD, Internat. U. Nutrition Edn., 1979; postgrad., Internat. Coll. Applied Nutrit, 1981, Johns Hopkins U., 1984--. Cert. nutritional specialist Nat. Bd. Nutritional Examiners, 1986. Paralegal, adminstrv. sec. various attys. L.A., 1969-80; owner, operator beauty boutique Beverly Hills, Calif., 1976-80; nutritional supr. Optimum Health Labs., Encino, Calif., 1980; dir. nutrition and food sci. Ford-Kennedy Labs., Reseda, Calif., 1980-82; dir. nutritional therapeutics Nutritional Sci. Testing Labs., Sherman Oaks, Calif., 1982-85; adminstr., dir. nutritional therapeutics Silver Virtue Med. & Nutrition Group, L.A., 1985-87; health educator Med. Health Ctr., Indio, Calif., 1987—; cons. various physicians, med. ctrs. Author: (with Sally Struthers) The Natural Beauty Book, 1979, Your Appearance and Allergies, 1983, Pesticides, Insecticides and Allergens--Their Impact on the Human Body, 1987. Contbr. articles to profl. jours. Recipient Golden Eagle award Nosotros, 1980. Mem. Am. Coll. Nutrition (assoc.), Internat. Coll. Applied Nutrition, Internat. Acad. Med. Preventics, Am. Soc. for Parenteral and Enteral Nutrition. Roman Catholic. Office: Nat Health Cons 555 Tachevah Dr Ste 201E Palm Springs CA 92262

VISANESCU, JANET WINKLER, dentist; b. Charlottesville, Va., Oct. 21, 1952; d. Frank Odell and Isabelle Alea (Johnson) Winkler; m. Dan C. Visanescu, Aug. 14, 1976; 1 child, Katherine Brooke. BS in Nursing, U. Va., 1975; DMD, U. Louisville, 1984. Lic. dentist Ky., Fla., Va. RN U. Va. Hosp., Charlottesville, 1975-78, Jewish Hosp., Louisville, 1978-80; cosmetic dentist Lagrange, Ky., 1984—. Recipient sr. student award Am. Assn. Orthodontists, 1984. Mem. ADA, Ky. Dental Assn., Louisville Dental Soc., Am. Acad. Cosmetic Dentistry, Rotary, Phi Delta, Psi Omega. Office: 1025 Sanibel Way Ste H Lagrange KY 40031

VISCELLI, THERESE RAUTH, materials management consultant; b. Bitburg, Germany, Nov. 18, 1955; d. David William and Joyce (Kelly) Rauth; m. Eugene R. Viscelli, Feb. 4, 1978; children: Christopher, Kathryn, Matthew. BS, Ga. Inst. Tech., 1977; postgrad., So. Tech. Inst., 1977-78, Ga. State U., 1982-83. Mktg. engr. Hughes Aircraft Corp., Carlsbad, Calif., 1978-79; indsl. engr. Kearfott-Singer, San Marcos, Calif., 1979-80; product analyst Control Data Corp., Atlanta, 1981-84; dir. R&D Am. Software, Inc., Atlanta, 1984—. Mem. Right to Life, Atlanta, 1980—. Mem. Am. Prodn. and Inventory Control Soc. (program chmn. 1982-83, v.p. 1983-84). Republican. Roman Catholic. Office: Am Software Inc 470 E Paces Ferry Rd Atlanta GA 30305

VISCO, DENISE MARIE, research scientist; b. Winthrop, Mass., July 27, 1957; d. Joseph Anthony and Patricia Ann (Koeppe) V. BS, U. N.H., 1979; MS, U. Tenn., 1981; PhD, Purdue U., 1987. Rsch. assoc. Med. Ctr. anatomy dept. Ind. U., Indpls., 1988-89, postdoctoral fellow Med. Ctr. anatomy dept., 1989; scientist Miles Rsch. Ctr. Miles Rsch. Ctr. Inst. for Arthritis and Autoimmunity, West Haven, Conn., 1989—; vis. asst. prof. Med. Ctr., Ind. U., 1987-88. Contbr. articles to profl. jours. Grantee Canine Disease Rsch. Funds, 1984, USDA Formula Fund, 1984, NIH, 1988. Mem. Orthopaedic Rsch. Soc., Am. Coll. Sports Medicine, Sigma Xi (assoc.), Gamma Sigma Delta (assoc.). Roman Catholic. Office: Inst Arthritis & Autoimm Miles Rsch Ctr 400 Morgan Ln West Haven CT 06516

VISCO, SUSAN JOSEPHINE, psychologist, consultant; b. Boston, Aug. 15, 1938; d. Hugh and Rose Marion (Sacco) V. AA, Mass. Bay Community Col., Boston, 1965; BS, Suffolk U., 1967; MEd, Boston Coll., 1968, PhD, 1973. Lic. psychologist, Mass.; cert. tchr., Mass. Tchr. spl. edn. pre-sch. and grade sch. Wakefield, Mass., 1968-70; tchr. brain damaged children Brooline, Mass., 1969-71; asst. prof., dir. child devel. dept. Stonehill Coll., Easton, Mass., 1971-76; assoc. prof. edn. Suffolk U., Boston, 1976-78; psychologist, coord. pre-sch. evaluation program Medford (Mass.) Sch. System, 1978-77; dir. Psychoednl. Evaluation and Learning Ctr., Saugus, 1971—; dir. learning disabilities program Bradford (Mass.) Coll., 1980-82; cons. psychologist Tewksbury (Mass.) Sch. System, 1983—; cons. in field; vis. prof. Southeastern Mass. U., 1969, Salem State Coll., 1971-72; organizer, mgr. Lowell Mass. U., 1973-77; guest lectr. in field. Mem. Assn. Children with Learning Disabilities, Coun. on Exceptional Children, MAss. Assn. Children with Learning Disabilities. Home and Office: 438 Essex St Saugus MA 01906

VISCONTI, JANNA PEARL, lawyer, artist; b. N.Y.C., Dec. 17, 1952; d. Stanley Schwartz and Marion Sue (Wasserman) Goldstein; m. Richard D. Visconti, Dec. 31, 1985. B.F.A., Pratt Inst., 1975; J.D., St. John's U., 1979. Bar: N.Y. 1979, Ariz. 1982, Conn. 1987. Assoc. firm Rogers & Wells, N.Y.C., 1979-82, Snell & Wilmer, Phoenix, 1982-85, Cummings & Lockwood, Stamford, Conn., 1985—. Active Parent Ctr., chmn. libr. com., 1989. Mem. ABA (real property section), N.Y. State Bar Assn., State Bar Ariz. Episcopalian. Office: Cummings & Lockwood 10 Stamford Forum Stamford CT 06904

VISHNEVSKY, VALENTINA MICHAILOVNA, pianist, ballet consultant; b. Rostow, USSR; came to U.S., 1949; d. Michael and Vassa (Velikopolskaya) Cherednichenko; m. Vadim Vitali Vishnevsky, Mar. 9, 1952. Degree, Konservatorium, Heidelberg, Fed. Republic Germany, 1949. Prin. pianist Am. Ballet Theater Sch., N.Y.C., 1951-82; pianist Alvin Ailey Dance Sch., N.Y.C., 1983; ind. ballet cons. Vero Beach, Fla., 1984—; pianist 1st Internat. Ballet Competition, 1979. Pianist: (film) First Position, 1973, (album series) Ballet Class, 1963-79, (TV show) Today, 1972. Home and Office: 1991 Sandalwood Rd Vero Beach FL 32963

VISOCKI, NANCY GAYLE, infosystems manager; b. Dumont, N.J., May 13, 1952; d. Thomas and Gloria (Valle) V. BA in Maths., Manhattanville Coll., 1974; MS in Ops. Rsch. and Stats., Rensselaer Poly. Inst., 1977. Rsch. asst. Coll. Physicians and Surgeons Columbia U., N.Y.C., 1974-75; programmer analyst R. Shriver Assocs., Parsippany, N.J., 1977-79; sr. tech. rep. GE Info. Svcs. Co., East Orange, N.J., 1979-81; mgr. project office GE Info. Svcs. Co., Morristown, N.J., 1981-83, tech. dir., 1983-87, tech. mgr., 1988-89; area mgr. system devel., cons. GE Info. Svcs. Co., Parsippany, 1989—. Active Western Hills Christian Ch., Tranquility, N.J., 1986—; vol. Women's Ctr., Hackettstown, N.J., 1989—. Manhattanville Coll. grantee, Purchase, N.Y., 1970-71; tuition fellow Rensselaer Poly. Inst., Troy, N.Y., 1976-77. Mem. NAFE. Home: 23 Wood Duck Ct Hackettstown NJ 07840 Office: GE Info Svcs Co 20 Waterview Blvd Parsippany NJ 07054

VISSCHER, HELGA BJORNSON, reference librarian; b. Reykjavik, Iceland, June 16, 1946; came to U.S., 1946; d. K. Valdimar and Gudrun (Jonsdottir) Bjornson; m. Pieter Bernard Visscher, June 17, 1972; children: Kristina, Paul. BA cum laude, U. Minn., 1968; MLS, U. Calif., 1970; CAS, U. Ill., 1973. Librarian Chanhassen (Minn.) Elem. Sch., 1970-72, La Jolla (Calif.) Country Day Sch., 1973-75, McLure Edn. Library, U. Ala., Tuscaloosa, 1981-85, 86—; temporary librarian Los Alamos Nat. Rsch. Lab., 1986. Cons., vol. TomBigBee council Girl Scouts U.S., 1982-87. Mem. Capstone Women's Network, ALA (nat. com. 1988—), Assn. Library Svcs. for Children (internat. relations com. 1990), Assn. Coll. and Rsch. Libraries (library instrn./curriculum materials com. 1990—), Internat. Assn. Sch. Librarians, Ala. Library Assn. (chmn.-elect library instrn. roundtable 1990), Guild Profl. Writers for Children (sec.-treas. 1983-85), Delta Kappa Gamma, Beta Phi Mu. Republican. Lutheran. Home: 1-C Vestavia East Northport AL 35476 Office: U Ala Library 23 McLure Box 870266 Tuscaloosa AL 35487-0266

VITA, DIANA, aerobics instructor; b. N.Y.C., Aug. 22, 1955; d. Michael Joseph and Lillian Diana (Mandracchia) V. B.A., CUNY, 1978. Cert. aerobic instr. Instr. aerobics and slimnastics YMCA, Bklyn., 1981-83; owner, mgr. Dianaerobics Studio, Bklyn., 1983—. Instr. Sch. Settlement, Bklyn., 1982-83, 85, 89, Mut. of N.Y. (MONY), N.Y.C., 1983, ITT, N.Y.C., 1983-86, Pratt Inst., Bklyn., 1985—. Mem. Internat. Dance-Exercise Assn., Aerobics and Fitness Assn. Am. Office: Dianaerobics Studio 776A Manhattan Ave Brooklyn NY 11222

VITALE, ANNA M., construction company executive, real estate management executive; b. Newark, July 17, 1942; d. Andrew and Pearl (Chelak) Franchak; m. Frederick R. Vitale, May 7, 1961; children—F. Richard, J. Steven, J. Christipher. Student Trenton State Coll., 1967-68. Vice pres. Vitran, Inc., Allentown, N.J., 1972-80, pres., 1980—, also dir.; ptnr. Hampton Manor Ltd., Mt. Holly, N.J., 1983—, also dir.; mgr., owner LaChez Salon, Allentown, 1966-76, Colonial Manor Salon, Jacobstown, N.J., 1977-88. Mem. U.S. Trotting Assn., N.J. and Pa. Racing Commn., Am. Soc. Noteries, Internat. Platform Assn. Home: RD 1 Box 111-5 Wrightstown NJ 08562

VITALIANO, DOROTHY BRAUNECK, geologist, technical translator; b. N.Y.C., Feb. 10, 1916; d. William Daniel and Adele (Bernhard) Brauneck; m. Charles J. Vitaliano, Oct. 19, 1940; children: Judith E., Peter W. AB, Barnard Coll., 1936; AM, Columbia U., 1938, MPhil, 1973. Geologic field asst. U.S. Geol. Survey, Nev., 1942-43; geologist U.S. Geol. Survey, Bloomington, Ind., 1953-86; freelance geologist-translator Bloomington, 1986—; adj. prof. Ind. U., Bloomington, 1983-86; nat. lectr. Soc. Sigma Xi, 1981-83. Author: Legends of the Earth, 1973; co-author: Atlantis: Fact or Fiction, 1978; contbr. articles to profl. jours. Fellow AAAS, Geol. Soc. Am.; mem. LWV, Phi Beta Kappa, Sigma Xi. Democrat. Unitarian.

VITENAS, BIRUTE KAZLAUSKAS, systems engineer; b. Los Angeles, Feb. 12, 1949; d. Vincent and Valeria (Dambrauskaite) Kazlauskas; B.S. in Stats., Stanford U., 1970; M.S. in Ops. Research, Columbia U., 1972; postgrad. Rutgers U., 1976; m. Almis T. Vitenas, July 4, 1970; 1 son, Aleksas Joseph. Mem. of tech. staff-switching maintenance Bell Labs., Holmdel, N.J., 1970-71, mem. tech. staff PAR Radar Evaluation, Whippany, N.J., 1971-74, mem. tech. staff, operator services planning, Holmdel, 1974-77, supr. operator services planning, 1977-81, dept. head network project planning, 1981-83; asst. to v.p. customer systems AT&T Info. Systems, Lincroft, N.J., 1983-85; dir. tech. program analysis AT&T Bell Labs, 1985-86, exec. dir. resource planning, 1986-89, exec. dir. fin. Telecom, MIS, 1989—. Mem. Ops. Research Soc. Am., Am. Statis. Assn. Republican. Roman Catholic. Office: AT&T Bell Labs Holmdel NJ 07733

VITTADINI, ADRIENNE, fashion designer; b. Gyor, Hungary; came to U.S., 1957; d. Alexander and Aranka (Langhiel) Toth; m. Gian Luigi Maria Vittadini, 1972; 1 stepchild, Emanuele. Ed., Moore Coll. Art, Phila. Designer Rosanna-Warneco, N.Y.C., 1970-76; v.p. for design Kimberly Knitwear-Gen. Mills, N.Y.C., 1976-78; chmn. bd. Adrienne Vittadini Inc., N.Y.C., 1979—. Recipient Design award Retail Fashion Authorities Am., 1979, Outstanding Phila. Fashion Designer award Council for Labor and Industry, Phila., 1984, Coty Am. Fashion Critics award, 1984. Office: Adrienne Vittadini Inc 575 7th Ave New York NY 10018

VITTER, PATRICIA BUTLER, lawyer; b. Gainesville, Fla., Dec. 31, 1951; d. Robert Hardy and Charleton (Galloway) Butler; children: Robert S., Brittany C. B.S.Ed., Fla. State U., 1973, J.D., 1975. Bar: Fla. 1976. Jud. asst. 2d Dist. Ct. Apls., Lakeland, Fla., 1976-77; atty. Charles Mixon, Tampa, 1977-79; sole practice, Inverness, Fla., 1979-86; ptnr. Bradshaw, Mountjoy & Vitter, Inverness, 1986—. Bd. dirs. Withlacochee Area Legal Services, Ocala, Fla., 1980-82; trustee Central Fla. Community Coll., Ocala, 1984, vice chmn. bd. trustees, 1985-87, chmn. bd. trustees, 1987-89; mem. regional citizens adv. council Withlacochee Regional Planning Council, 1982-84, adv. bd. dirs. First Fla. Bank, N.A. of Inverness. Mem. Fla. Bar Assn., ABA, Citrus County Bar Assn., Tri County Bar Assn., Citrus County C. of C. (bd. dirs. 1985—, pres. 1988), Beta Sigma Phi, Rotary (bd. dirs. 1989). Democrat. Methodist. Club: Altrusa. Home: Henderson Trail Inverness Fl 32650 Office: 209 Courthouse Sq PO Box 881 Inverness FL 32651

VITTETOE, MARIE CLARE, educator; b. Keota, Iowa, May 19, 1927; d. Edward Daniel and Marcella Matilda (Peiffer) V. BS, Marycrest Coll., 1950; MS, W.Va. U., 1971, EdD, 1973. Staff technician St. Joseph Hosp., Ottumwa, Iowa, 1950-70; instr. Ottumwa Hosp. Sch. Med. Tech., 1957-70, St. Joseph Hosp. Sch. Nursing, Ottumwa, 1950-70; asst. prof. U. Ill., Champaign Urbana, Ill., 1973-78; prof. U. Ky., Lexington, 1978—. Contbr. articles to profl. jours. Mem. Am. Soc. Med. Tech. (chair 1986-89). Office: 122 Medical Ctr Annex 2 Lexington KY 40536-0080

VIVIAN, LINDA BRADT, sales and public relations executive; b. Elmira, N.Y., Nov. 22, 1945; d. Lorenz Claude and Muriel (Dolan) Bradt; m. Robert W. Vivian, Apr. 5, 1968 (div. Sept. 1977). Student, Andrews U., 1966. Adminstrv. asst. Star-Gazette, Elmira, 1966-68; editor Guide, staff writer Palm Springs (Calif.) Life mag., 1970-75; dir. sales and pub. rels. Palm Springs Aerial Tramway, 1975—; sec. Hospitality and Bus. Industry Coun. Palm Springs Desert Resorts, 1989—. Mem. Hotel Sales and Mktg. Assn. (allied nominating chmn. Palm Springs chpt. 1986-88), Am. Soc. Assn. Execs., Travel Industry Assn., Hospitality Industry and Bus. Coun. of Palm Springs Resorts (sec. 1989—), Nat. Tour Assn., Calif. Travel Industry Assn., Palm Springs C. of C. (bd. dirs. 1984-85), Navy League. Republican. Office: Palm Springs Aerial Tramway One Tramway Rd Palm Springs CA 92262

VIVION, DELLA MAIER, small business owner; b. Sheridan, Wyo., Dec. 16, 1925; d. Joseph August and Edna Sybil (Fauver) Maier; m. Vern Vivon, Mar. 8, 1947; children: Vari, Kirsten, Mary. BA, U. Wyo., 1947; postgrad., Inst. D'Allende, San Miguel, Mexico. Owner, mgr. Cedar Chest Galleries, Saratoga, Wyo.; bd. dirs. COVE. First woman mayor of Rawlins, Wyo.; bd. dirs. Landmark Commn., Econ. Devel. Commn., Kids Found. Bd. Named Woman of Yr. Mem. AAUW, LWV, C. of C., (president's award), Cen. Rawlins Assn., Soroptomists. Republican. Episcopalian. Home: Box 674 Rawlins WY 82301

VLAHOKOSTA, FRIDERIKI Y., health foundation executive; b. Trikala, Greece; d. Vissarion and Efthimia (Batagianni) V. Med. student, Aristotelion U., Thessaloniki, Greece, 1968. Chmn., chief exec. officer The Hippocrates Internat. Med. Found., Boston. Mem. AMA, Am. Diabetes Assn., Am. Med. Women Assn. Am. Fed. for Clin. Rsch., Mass. Med. Soc., N.Y. Acad. Sci., Diabetes Assn. of Ea. Mass., New Eng. Hellenic Med. Soc.

VLASTOS, CAROL JO, state legislator, educational/nursing consultant; b. Louisville, July 30, 1941; d. Willard Keith and Josephine (Preston) Sloan; m. Joseph Vlastos, Mar. 29, 1961; children: Emanuel Joseph, Keith Joseph, George Joseph. AA in Nursing, Casper (Wyo.) Coll., 1976; BA in Edn., U. Wyo., 1964; BS in Nursing, U. Wyo., Casper, 1981. RN; cert. tchr., Wyo. Elem. sch. tchr. Natrona County #1, Casper, 1966-68; staff nurse Natrona County Meml. Hosp., Casper, 1976-81; nurse, dir. Newcap Family Planning, Casper, 1982-88; ednl./nursing cons. State of Wyo., 1986-89, edn. coord. AIDS, 1987-89, mem. Ho. of Reps., 1989—; cons. health and AIDS edn. State Dept. Edn., Cheyenne, Wyo., 1988-89, cons. Wyo. Sch. Bds., 1987-89. Mem. sch. bd. Natrona County Sch. Dist., Casper, 1983-88. vice chmn., 1986, chmn. 1987, treas., 1988; mem. western conf. Coun. State Govt., 1989—, mem. nat. conf. com. transp. and communications State Legis., 1989—. Named Woman of Yr. Casper C. of C., 1988, Outstanding Sch. Vol. Wyo. Edn. Assn., 1988; recipient Exceptional Svc. award State of Wyo., 1988. Republican. Methodist. Home: 3411 S Coffman Casper WY 82604

VOCHT, MICHELLE ELISE, lawyer; b. Detroit, Sept. 27, 1956. BA with honors, U. Mich., 1978; JD, Wayne State U., 1981. Bar: Mich., U.S. Dist. Ct. (ea. and we. dist.) Mich., U.S. Ct. Appeals (6th cir.), 1981. V.p., sec. Roy, Shecter & Vocht PC, Birmingham, Mich., 1981—; mem. pro bono teaching faculty Detroit chpt. Fed. Bar Assn.; mediator Mediation Tribunal Wayne County Cir. Ct., 1989—; pre-sentencing probation officer 48th Dist. Ct., 1989—. Mem. com. for re-election of current Mich. Supreme Ct. Justice, 1986; exec. bd. Birmingham Women's Community Ctr., 1987-88; bd. dirs. Community Adv. Bd.-Arbor Clin. Group, Inc., 1989—; mem. drug and alcohol abuse spl. task force County of Oakland, 1989—. Mem. Assn. Trial Lawyers Am., Mich. Trial Lawyers Assn., Women Lawyers Assn. Mich., Oakland County Trial Lawyers Assn (exec. bd. dirs. 1982-84, 88—, sec. 1990—), State Bar Assn. Mich. (chmn. gen. practice section 1984-86, sec.

1982-83, vice-chmn. 1983-84, mem. civil procedure com. 1982-84, assoc. mem. lawyers and judges assistance com., 1988-89, hearing panelist atty. discipline bd., 1982—, labor and employment sect., domestic rels. sect.), Mich. Employment Law Assn., Am. Inn of Ct. (barrister 1984-87), Internat. Platform Assn., Indsl. Rels. Rsch. Assn. Roman Catholic. Home: 901 N Adams Birmingham MI 48008 Office: Roy Shecter & Vocht PC 877 S Adams Ste 302 Birmingham MI 48011

VOGEL, DIANE DOROTHY, copyediting and proofreading company executive; b. N.Y.C., Jan. 27, 1944; d. Maurice and Elaine (Doris) V. AAS, Mercer County Community Coll., 1984. Exec. sec. Riegel Textile Corp., N.Y.C., 1964-68; legal sec. Kaye Scholer, N.Y.C., 1968-72; editor, compositor Scarecrow Press, Metuchen, N.J., 1968-89; pres. Words Words Words, Cranbury, N.J., 1989—. Author: Rooms, 1989; contbr. articles to profl. jours. Mem. Hightstown br. AAUW, 1984. Mem. Recording for the Blind (vol.), Profl. Register. Office: Words Words Words 164 North II Princeton Arms Cranbury NJ 08512

VOGEL, IRENE SUSAN, psychologist; b. N.Y.C.; d. Alex and Nettie (Klein) Kuzminsky; m. Leonard Vogel (dec. 1987); children: Kenneth, Jason, Dianna. PhD, Am. U., 1972. Diplomate Am. Assn. Sex Educators and Therapists, Am. Assn. Profl. Psychotherapy. Staff psychologist Great Oaks Ctr., Silver Spring, Md., 1972; dir. drug rehab. program Prince George's County (Md.) Health Dept., 1972-73; dir. alcohol and drug abuse program Walter Reed Army Med. Ctr., Washington, 1973-75; pvt. practice Bethesda, Md., 1974—; dir. Hypnosis and Psychotherapy Ctr., Inc., Washington, 1983—, The Vogel Group, Washington, 1987—; adv. bd. Cancer Counseling Inst., Bethesda, 1988—; ptnr. Stress Mgmt. Inst., Md., 1982-84; dir. Positive Approaches to Success Skills program, Md., 1984-87; speaker in field. Fellow Am. Assn. Profl. Psychotherapy, Am. Assn. Sex Educators and Therapists; mem. Am. Psychol. Assn., Md. Psychol. Assn. (com. chmn. 1988-89), Assn. Practicing Psychologists Prince George's and Montgomery Counties (pres. 1981-82), Am. Assn. Profl. Psychotherapy. Office: The Vogel Group 7708 Greentree Rd Bethesda MD 20817

VOGEL, MALVINA GRAFF, video and infosystems specialist; b. N.Y.C., May 5, 1932; d. Daniel Louis and Rose Miriam (Kanarick) Graff; m. Seymour Vogel, Jan. 27, 1952 (div.); children: Howard Ferris, Hal Steven, Scott Leslie, David Michael, Lisa Gayle. AB, Hunter Coll., 1952, postgrad., 1953. Cert. tchr., N.Y., N.J. Tchr. Norwood (N.J.) Pub. Schs., 1952-53, Farmingdale (N.Y.) Pub. Schs., 1953-55; researcher, writer Sy Vogel Realty, Commack, N.Y., 1965-67; writer-editor E.D.L.-McGraw Hill, N.Y.C., 1967-73; writer ednl. programs Ednl. Concepts, Inc., Babylon, N.Y., 1973-75, Instructional Concepts, Inc., New Hyde Park, N.Y., 1973-75; editor-in-chief Waldman-Playmore Pub. Co., N.Y.C., 1976-83; v.p. creative services Kid Stuff/GameTek, Inc., North Miami Beach, Fla., 1983—. Author short stories, reading and social studies programs; adaptor lit. classics for children; editor over 200 books for children and adults, over 50 computer software and video cartridge programs for preschoolers, children, teens and adults. Pres. Old Bethpage Elem. Sch. PTA, 1967-71; founder, pres. women's aux. Plainview, N.Y. Little League, 1968; scholarship chair Plainview-Old Bethpage Scholarship Fund, 1972-73. Scholarship for children's writing, Hofstra U., 1975. Mem. Nat. Assn. Female Execs., Soc. Children's Book Writers, Women in Communications, Soc. Preservation of English Lang. and Lit. Home: 9225 NW 45th St Sunrise FL 33351 Office: GameTek Inc 2999 NE 191st St North Miami Beach FL 33180

VOGEL, MARY STALGAITIS, dentist, dental educator; b. Hazleton, Pa., Aug. 2, 1949; d. Joseph George and Sylvia (Nicholas) Stalgaitis. B.S., Pa. State. U., 1974; D.M.D., U. Pitts., 1974. Dental extern Home for Crippled Children, Pitts., 1973-75; pres. Mary Vogel, D.M.D., P.C., Pitts., 1976—; asst. clin. prof. Sch. Dental Medicine U. Pitts., 1974—; panel discussant on Women's Careers, Pa. Sect. Edn., Indiana U. Pa. Demonstrator dental procedures TV, 1981. Troop leader Girls Scouts U.S.A., Forrest Hills, P.A., 1983; active health fair booth Women's Task Force on Alcoholism, Pitts., 1982; keynote speaker Marian High., Tamaqua, Pa., 1981. Mem. Am. Assn. Women Dentists (v.p. Pitts. br. 1982-83), ADA, Pa. Dental Assn. (del. 1980), East End Pitts. Odontol. Soc. (pres. 1978-79), Acad. Oral Medicine, (Sr. Dental Student award 1974), U. Pitts. Dental Alumni (exec. com. 1977—), Nat. Assn. Women's Bus. Owners. Roman Catholic. Club: Equicess. Home and Office: Suite 340 Gateway Towers Pittsburgh PA 15222

VOGEL, WILLA HOPE, restaurateur; b. Valley Falls, Kans., Jan. 14, 1929; d. Henry Ray Tosh and Freda Alice (Brunton) Jackson; m. David L. Vogel, Dec. 25, 1943 (dec. 1987); children: Randall Daniel, Diana. Grad. high sch., Topeka, Kans. Owner, mgr. Drapery Shop, Topeka, 1956-68, Plantation Steak House, Topeka, 1962—, North Star Supper Club, Topeka, 1972—. Mem. Kans. Restaurant Assn., Topeka Restaurant Assn. (3rd v.p.), Greater Topeka C. of C. Office: Plantation Steak House 6646 N Topeka Blvd Topeka KS 66617

VOGELGESANG, SANDRA LOUISE, federal government official; b. Canton, Ohio, July 27, 1942; d. Glenn Wesley and Louise (Forry) Vogelgesang; m. Geoffrey Ernest Wolfe, July 4, 1982. BA, Cornell U., 1964; MA, Tufts U., 1965, MA in Law and Diplomacy, 1966, PhD, 1971. With Dept. State, Washington, 1975—, policy planner for sec. state and European Bur., 1975-80, dir. Econ Analysis Office, Orgn. Econ. Coop. and Devel., 1981-82, econ. minister U.S. Embassy, Ottawa, Can., 1982-86, dep. asst. sec. Internat. Orgn. Affairs Bur., 1986-89; dep. asst. adminstr. Office Internat. Activities Environ. Protection Agy., Washington, 1989—; bd. dirs. Edward R. Murrow Ctr. for Pub. Diplomacy, Fletcher Sch., Medford, Mass., 1978—; bd. advisors Am.'s Soc., N.Y.C., 1986—. Author: Long Dark Night of the Soul, The American Intellectual Left and the Vietnam War, 1974, American Dream-Global Nightmare: The Dilemma of U.S. Human Rights Policy, 1980. Recipient Meritorious Service awards, 1973, 74, 82, 83, 86, Disting. Honor award, 1976 Dept. State, Pres.' Disting. Service award, 1985. Mem. Council on Fgn. Relations. Home: 9009 Charred Oak Dr Bethesda MD 20817 Office: Environ Protection Agy 401 M St SW Washington DC 20460

VOGELSANG, JOHANNA, artist; b. Ft. Thomas, Ky., June 18, 1929; d. Randolph and Kathryn (Lull) Schmalhorst; m. Frederic Vogelsang, Sept. 19, 1929 (dec. 1981); children: Kirsten, Hana. BA, Rockford Coll., 1951; postgrad., N.Y. U., 1951-54. Self employed artist, 1963--, bus. owner and graphic artist, 1972--. Pol. mem. Women Strike for Peace, Washington, D.C., 1965-75. Home: 502 Boston Ave Takoma Park MD 20912

VOGLER, JODY LOUISE, nurse; b. Wichita, Kans., Sept. 5, 1960; d. Arnold Joe and E. Blanche (Kouba) Blecha; m. Robert Willis Vogler, June 16, 1984. Diploma, Wesley Sch. Nursing, Wichita, 1981. RN, Kans. Staff nurse med. intensive care Hosp. Corp. Am., Wichita, 1981—. Tchr. Sunday sch. Mem. Navigators. Republican. Mem. Bible Ch.

VOGT, MOLLY THOMAS, medical college official; b. Lyndhurst, Eng., Apr. 15, 1939; came to U.S., 1962; d. Gordon H.S. and Evelyn N. (Edwards) Thomas; m. William George Vogt, June 10, 1964 (div. Nov. 1980); children: William Brian, Keith Thomas. BSc, U. Bristol (Eng.), 1960; PhD, U. Pitts., 1967. Rsch. officer Med. Rsch. Coun., London, 1960-62; postdoctoral fellow U. Pitts., 1967-70, asst. prof., 1970-72, assoc. prof., 1973-77, prof., 1977-86, chmn. interdisciplinary programs, 1972-74, assoc. dean health related professions, 1977-83, dir. continuing med. edn. and testing svcs., 1984-86; assoc. dean curriculum and continuing med. edn. Med. Coll. Ohio, Toledo, 1986—; cons. Pa. Dept. Edn., 1976, Comm. on Accreditation, Pa. Med. Soc., 1986; mem. task force on environ. forces Alliance Continuing Med. Edn., 1986-87. Assoc. editor Jour. Allied Health, 1972-79; contbr. articles to profl. jours. Charter mem. Exec. Women's Coun., Pitts., 1975-86; treas. troop 49, Boy Scouts Am., Edgewood, Pa., 1979-81. Recipient Exemplar award, Ohio Acad. Sci., 1987. Fellow Am. Coun. on Edn., Am. Soc. Allied Health Professions (chmn. edn. com. 1979-82, task force on status of women 1980-81, President's award 1981, J. Warren Perry Disting. Author award 1983); mem. Ohio Continuing Higher Edn. Assn. (vice chmn. rsch. and data collection com. 1988—), AAUW, Sigma Xi (pres. U. Pitts. chpt. 1979-81). Office: Med Coll Ohio PO Box 10008 Toledo OH 43699-0008

VOIGHT, ELIZABETH ANNE, lawyer; b. Sapulpa, Okla., Aug. 6, 1944; d. Robert Guy and Garnetta Ruth (Bell) Voight; m. Bodo Barske, Feb. 22, 1985; children: Anne Katharine, Ruth Caroline. BA, U. Ark.-Fayetteville, 1967, MA, 1969; postgrad. U. Hamburg (W.Ger.), 1966-67; J.D., Georgetown U., 1978. Bar: N.Y. 1979. Lectr. German, Oral Roberts U., Tulsa, 1968-69; tchr. German, D.C. pub. schs., 1971-73; instr. German, Georgetown U., Washington, 1973-74, adminstrv. asst. to dean Sch. Fgn. Svc., 1974-77; law clk. Cole & Corette, Washington, 1977-78; atty. Walter, Conston, Alexander & Green, P.C., N.Y.C., 1978-88; sole practice, Munich, Fed. Republic Germany, 1988—. Translator articles for profl. jours. Chmn. regional screening Am. Field Svc., N.Y.C., 1981-86. German Acad. Exchange Program fellow, 1966-67. Mem. Assn. Bar City N.Y., ABA, Internat. Fiscal Assn., Phi Beta Kappa, Kappa Kappa Gamma.

VOIGT, CYNTHIA, author; b. Boston, Feb. 25, 1942; d. Frederick C. and Elise (Keeney) Irving; married, 1964 (div. 1972); m. 2d Walter Voigt, Aug. 30, 1974; children: Jessica, Peter. B.A., Smith Coll., 1963. High sch. tchr. English Glen Burnie, Md., 1965-67; tchr. English Key Sch., Annapolis, Md., 1968-69, 71-79, tchr., chmn., from 1981. Author: (children's books) Homecoming, 1981, Tell Me If Lovers Are Losers, 1982, Dicey's Song, 1982 (Newbery medal 1983), The Callendar Papers, 1983, A Solitary Blue, 1983, Building Blocks, 1984, Jackaroo, 1985, The Runner, 1985, Come a Stranger, 1986, Izzy, Willy Nilly, 1986, Stories About Rosie, 1986, Sons From Afar, 1987, Tree By Leaf, 1988, Seventeen Against the Dealer, 1989. *

VOIGT, JANE ELLEN, instructor; b. Sheboygan, Wis., Nov. 3, 1945; d. Milton Herman and Elfriede Fitger (Stoelting) Kuether; m. Robert Arthur Voigt, Feb. 3, 1968; children: Carolyn J., Jacqueline J. B in Music Edn., Alverno Coll., 1968. Pvt. practice piano instr. Kiel, Wis., 1969—; accompanist St. Peter's United Ch. Christ, Kiel, 1969—, Kiel High Sch., 1969—; sr. accompanist Sr. Citizens, Kiel, 1969—. Dep. clk. Kiel Area Sch. Dist. Bd. Edn., 1984-89; program dir. Manitou coun. Girl Scouts U.S.A., Manitowoc, Wis., 1981-89, bd. dirs., 1986—. Mem. AAUW (mem.-at-large Sheboygan chpt. 1970—), Michibago Wis. Music Tchrs. Assn. (v.p. 1988-89), Wis. State Music Tchrs. Assn. (asst. treas. 1986-89, sec. Chilton, Wis. chpt. 1986-88), Nat. Guild Musicians, Quit Qui Oc Women's Golf League. Home: 1001 2d St PO Box 127 Kiel WI 53042

VOIVODAS, GITA KEDAR, small business owner, research and editing consultant; b. Baroda, Gujarat, India, May 2, 1942; came to U.S., 1962; d. Kedarnath and Emily Nirmala (Lederer) Kulshreshtha; m. Constantin Voivodas, May 12, 1972 (dec. 1973). BS, Maharaja Sayajirao U., 1960; postgrad., Cornell U., 1962; MA, Stanford U., 1963; PhD, Columbia U., 1977. Teaching fellow Child Devel. Ctr., N.Y.C., 1964-67; research asst. Tchrs. Coll. Columbia U., N.Y.C., 1972-76; asst. prof. Fordham U., N.Y.C., 1977-84; cons. Liebling Assocs., N.Y.C., 1985—; dir. research Louis Harris and Assocs., N.Y.C., 1986-87; pres. Profl. Papers Assocs., N.Y.C., 1983—; cons. Child Trends Inc., Washington 1979, dir. numerous profl. confs., N.Y.C. 1977-83. Guest editor: Jour. Edn. Psychol., 1976-84; contbr. articles to profl. jours. Cons. Sex Discrimination Assistance Ctr., Columbia U. 1979, Women's Action Alliance, 1979, Project Right-to-Read, Fordham U. 1979-80, N.Y. State Nat. Abortion Action League, 1986—, mem. exec. bd. Early Childhood Edn. Council, 1977-84. Fellow U.S. Office Edn. 1972-76; grantee Fordham U. 1981. Mem. Am. Ednl. Research Assn., Soc. Research Child Devel., Nat. Soc. Study Edn., Am. Mktg. Assn., Nat. Assn. Female Execs. Office: Profl Papers Assocs 390 Riverside Dr #14B New York NY 10025

VOLK, PATRICIA GAY, fiction writer, essayist; b. N.Y.C., July 16, 1943; d. Cecil Sussman and Audrey Elaine (Morgen) Volk; m. Andrew Blitzer, Dec. 21, 1969 (div.); children—Peter Morgen, Polly Volk. BFA cum laude, Syracuse U., 1964; student, Sch. Visual Arts, N.Y.C., 1968, New Sch., N.Y.C., 1975, Columbia U., 1977-88. Art dir. Appelbaum & Curtis, N.Y.C., 1964-65, Seventeen Mag., Triangle Publs., N.Y.C., 1966-68; copywriter Doyle, Dane, Bernbach, Inc., N.Y.C., 1969-88, also sr. v.p., creative mgr., 1969-87, sr. v.p.- assoc. creative dir., 1987-88. Author: The Yellow Banana, 1985 (Word Beat Press Fiction Book award 1984), White Light, 1987, All it Takes; contbr. articles to N.Y. Times mag. and other mags.; contbr. short stories to popular and small press publs. Recipient Stephen E. Kelly award, 1983, various Andy, Clio, Effie and One Show awards, 1970-88; Yaddo fellow, 1983, MacDowell fellow, 1984. Mem. Author's Guild, PEN.

VOLKEMA, KAY SUMMERS, advertising executive; b. Idaho Falls, Idaho, Mar. 1, 1951; d. Thorland Price Summers and Bonnie Lou (Johnson) Summers Briggs; m. D. Ray Volkema, Aug. 1, 1981 (div. 1988); 1 child, Alexandra Marie. AA, Dodge City Community Coll., Kans., 1971; BS in Edn., Emporia State U., 1973, MA in English, 1976. Account exec. Competitve Edge Advt., Colorado Springs, Colo., 1978-79; account exec., producer Pelz, Griego & Ashida Advt., Colorado Springs, 1979-80, Channel 1 Prodns., Colorado Springs, 1980-81; copywriter ZCMI Dept. Stores, Salt Lake City, 1981-82; advt. copy chief May D&F Dept. Stores, Denver, 1982-84; advt. specialist II Gates Rubber Co., Denver, 1984-86, mgr. merchandising svcs., 1986-88, mgr. creative svcs., 1986-89, European advt. mgr., 1989; exec. v.p. The Exline Agy., 1990; mktg. dir. Charter Hosp. Aurora, Colo., 1990—. Copywriter, project mgr. brochure including Gates Poly Chain Belt, 1986 (Gold Addy award 1986, named Best of Show Bus. Profl. Advt. Assn. Colo. chpt. 1986). Mem. membership dr. com. Denver C. of C., 1987. Honoree Women of Achievement award Denver YWCA, 1988. Mem. Denver Advt. Fedn. (bd. dirs. 1990—, vice chmn. ad recognition 1990—, publicity chair 1988-89), Am. Advt. Fedn., Guys and Dolls Golf Club (sec. 1984-85, treas. 1987-88). Democrat. Presbyterian. Office: Charter Hosp of Aurora 14101 E Evans Aurora CO 80014

VOLKENING, DEBRA LYNN, disc-jockey; b. St. Louis, Feb. 13, 1962; d. Anton R. and Loretta (McCracken) V. BA in Communications, Maryville Coll., St. Louis, 1984. Reporter St. Louis & Jefferson County News, Fenton, Mo., 1984-85; writer, proofreader Maritz Travel Co., Fenton, 1986-87; mobile disc-jockey Travelin' Tunes, St. Louis, 1984—. Mem. Women in Communication (chpt. publicity chmn. 1985-86), Gateway Portacle Disc-Jockey Assn. (dir. pub. relations 1985-87).

VOLKERING, MARY JOE, special education educator; b. Covington, Ky., Mar. 13, 1936; d. Everett Thomas and Edna Mae (Bohmer) Foley; m. Jack Lawrence Volkering, Aug. 19, 1961 (dec. Jan. 11, 1989); 1 child, Tara. BA, Thomas More Coll, 1961; MEd, U. Cin., 1977. Cert. educator of mentally handicapped, Ohio, Ky. Asst. engr. AT&T Co., Cin., 1956-63; tchr. severe & profound Comprehensive Care, Covington, Ky., 1970-76; tchr. mentally retarded Riverside Good Counsel Sch., Ft. Mitchell, Ky., 1976-79; tchr. trainable handicapped Covington (Ky.) Ind. Sch., 1979—; bd. dirs. No. Ky. Assn. for Retarded, Covington, 1980—; adj. prof. No. Ky. U., Highland Heights, 1987-88. Leader Girl Scout Troop, Ft. Wright, Ky., 1973. Named John Bauer Spl. Edn. Tchr. of the Yr. North Ky. Assn. Retarded, 1979, Tchr. of the Yr. G.O. Swing Sch., Covington Ind. Schs., 1986, Golden Apple Nominee Tchr., Ky. Post and Jaycees, 1988. Mem. No. Ky. Assn. Retarded (treas. 1984-86, sec. 1980-82). Democrat. Roman Catholic.

VOLKMANN, FRANCES COOPER, psychologist, educator; b. Harlingen, Tex., May 4, 1935; d. Edward O. and Elizabeth (Bass) C.; m. John Volkmann, Nov. 1, 1958; children—Stephen Edward, Thomas Frederick. A.B. magna cum laude, Mt. Holyoke Coll., 1957; M.A., Brown U., 1959, Ph.D., 1961; DSci., Mt. Holyoke Coll., 1987. Research assoc. Mt. Holyoke Coll., South Hadley, Mass., 1964-65; lectr. U. Mass., Amherst, 1964-65, Smith Coll., Northampton, Mass., 1966-67; asst. prof. Smith Coll., 1967-72, assoc. prof., 1972-78, prof. psychology, 1978—, dean faculty, 1983-88; Harold E. Israel and Elsa M. Siipola prof. psychology, 1988—; vis. assoc. prof. Brown U., Providence, 1974, vis. prof., 1978-82; vis. scholar U. Wash., Seattle, summer 1977. Contbr. articles to profl. jours. Trustee Chatham Coll., 1987—. USPHS fellow, 1961-62; NSF grantee, 1974-78; Nat. Eye Inst. grantee, 1978-82. Fellow Am. Psychol. Assn., AAAS, Optical Soc. Am.; mem. Eastern Psychol. Assn., Soc. Neurosci., Psychonomic Soc., Assn. Research in Vision and Ophthalmology. Home: 11 McIntosh Dr Amherst MA 01002 Office: Smith Coll Northampton MA 01063

VOLLAND, CAROL TASCHER, financial services executive; b. Morris, Ill., Mar. 23, 1935; d. Murl Elvyn and Helen Marie (Lindquist) Tascher; m. George William Volland, Aug. 12, 1978. Student Monmouth Coll., 1953-55; B.S. in Interior Design, U. Ill., 1957; postgrad. Art Inst. Chgo. Evening Sch., 1959-62. Lic. real estate broker, ins. and securities broker, Colo., Ill. Archtl. and interior designer Peoples Gas Light & Coke Co., Chgo., 1957-65, consumer lectr., corp. architect and interior designer, 1965-70, dir. home planning bur., 1970-74; corp. fashion coord. Ozite Corp. div. Brunswick Corp., Libertyville, Ill., 1974-75, dir. pub. rels., 1975-77, contract sales mgr., 1977-78; pres. Volland & Assocs., Lakewood, Colo., 1982-88; pres. Asset Planning Svcs., Lakewood, 1989—; mem. corp. responsibilities bd. Brunswick Corp. Internat., 1976-77. Author: Creative Moneystretchers for the Home, 1973. Mem. Nat. Home Fashions League (exec. v.p. 1977-78), Am. Soc. Interior Designers, Women in Communications, LWV, Nat. Trust Hist. Preservation, Genesee Found. Republican. Methodist. Home: 1962 Montane Dr E Golden CO 80401 Office: Asset Planning Svcs 143 Union Blvd Ste 900 Lakewood CO 80228

VOLLMAN, RITA RAE, psychologist, administrator; b. Elgin, Ill., Feb. 6, 1942; d. Everett John and LaMar Ethelyn (Spiegler) V. BA magna cum laude, Lawrence U., 1963; PhD, UCLA, 1970. Lic. psychologist, Colo. Clin. psychologist Ft. Logan Mental Health Ctr., Denver, 1969-71; pvt. practice Denver, 1971; adult div. psychologist Ft. Logan Mental Health Ctr., Denver, 1972-80, 82—, geriatrics div. psychologist, 1980-82, clin. adminstr., 1990—; clin. affiliate Sch. Profl. Psychology, U. Denver, 1976-79; cons. Police Civil Svc. Commn., Denver, 1978-81; cons. in field; site visitor com. on accreditation Am. Psychol. Assn., 1972—; mem. profl. adv. com. Sch. Profl. Psychology, 1977-79; mem. mental health adv. bd. State of Colo., 1982-89; panelist, moderator profl. confs. Contbr. to profl. publs. Grantee NIMH, 1969-71. Mem. ACLU, NOW, Am. Psychol. Assn., Colo. Psychol. Assn. (chair pub. sector com. 1981-85), Colo. Women Psychologists (bd. dirs. 1985-89), Denver Mus. Natural History, Denver Art Mus. Home: 1555 S Columbine St Denver CO 80210 Office: Ft Logan Mental Health Ctr 3520 W Oxford St Denver CO 80236

VOLTZ, JEANNE APPLETON, magazine editor, writer, food consultant; b. Collinsville, Ala., Nov. 12, 1920; d. James Lamar and Marie (Sewell) Appleton; m. Luther Manship Voltz, July 31, 1943 (dec. Aug. 1977); children: Luther Manship, Jeanne Marie; m. Frank B. Macknight, Aug. 6, 1988. AB, U. Montevallo, Ala., 1942. Corr., The Birmingham (Ala.) News, 1939-42; reporter The Press-Register, Mobile, Ala., 1942-45; reporter, feature writer The Miami Herald, 1947-53, food editor, 1953-60; food editor Los Angeles Times, 1960-73, Woman's Day, N.Y.C., 1973-84; free-lance writer, food cons., N.Y.C., 1984-88, Chapel Hill, N.C., 1988—; instr. wine and food in civilization UCLA, 1972-73; expert witness Senate Com. on Nutrition and Health, Ft. Lauderdale, Fla., 1980; adj. prof. Home Econs. Hotel Mgmt. NYU, 1987—. Author: The California Cookbook, 1970 (Tastemaker award 1970); The Los Angeles Times Natural Foods Cookbook, 1974; The Flavor of the South, 1976 (Tastemaker award 1976), An Apple A Day, 1983; Barbecued Ribs and Other Great Feeds, 1985 (Tastemaker award 1985), Community Suppers, 1987. Mem. Met. Mus. Art, N.Y.C., 1975. Recipient Vesta award Am. Meat Inst., 1962-72; Alumni of Yr. award U. Montevallo, 1981. Mem. Les Dames d'Escoffier (dir. 1976, pres. 1985-86, internat. pres. 1986-87), Inst. Food Technologists, Soc. Nutrition Edn., Women in Communication, Soc. Women Geographers, Internat. Assn. Cooking Profls., N.Y. Acad. Scis., Phi Tau Sigma. Democrat. Methodist.

VON ARNAULD DE LA PERIÈRE, ANGÉLIQUE, company executive; b. Berlin, Germany, Sept. 21, 1940; d. Horst Herbert Albert Walter and Waltraut Magarete (Neuendorf) Von A.; m. Walter V. Di Masi, Aug. 11, 1962 (div. Apr. 1970); 1 child, Marcella Darlene; m. Mark Richard Lasslett; children: Heather E., Brianna C. V.p. Von Arnauld Corp., Franklin Lakes, N.J., 1958—. Mem. NAFE, N.J. Country Music Assn. Lutheran. Office: Von Arnauld Corp 509 Commerce St Franklin Lakes NJ 07417

VON BEHREN, RUTH LECHNER, adult day health care specialist; b. Dubuque, Iowa, Apr. 10, 1933; d. Adolph J. and Elva M. (Fedeler) Lechner; m. Donald D. Von Behren, Dec. 16, 1952 (div. 1965); children: Debi, Jerry, LuAnn. BS, Ill. State U., 1965, MA, 1968; PhD, U. Calif., Davis, 1972. Tchr. Centennial Sch., El Paso, Ill., 1962-65; grad. asst. Ill. State U., Normal, 1967-68; assoc. in History U. Calif., 1968-71; rsch. asst. Calif. Health and Welfare Agy., Sacramento, 1972-74; asst. prof. Sacramento State U., 1970-71, 78-79; analyst Calif. Dept. Health Svcs., Sacramento, 1974-75, sect. chief adult day health care, 1975-80; project dir. State Health and Welfare Agy., Sacramento, 1980-82; adult day health care specialist On Lok Sr. Health Svcs., San Francisco, 1982—; cons. adult day health care various orgns. Author: Adult Day Care in America, 1986, Adult Day Care: A Program for the Functionally Impaired, 1989, (with others) Planning and Managing Adult Day Care, 1989; contbr. articles to profl. jours. Sec. Yolo County Hist. Soc., Woodland, Calif., 1976-80; dir. Yolo County Mus. Assocs., Woodland, 1980-82. Recipient Adult Day Health Care Tech. Assistance award Kaiser Found., 1983-86, Rural Adult Day Care Model award Sierra Found., 1988-89. Mem. Nat. Coun. on Aging, Inc., Nat. Inst. on Adult Day Care (chair 1988-90), Phi Alpha Theta, Alpha Phi Gamma, Alpha Psi Omega, Kappa Delta Phi, Phi Kappa Phi. Office: On Lok Sr Health Svcs 1455 Bush San Francisco CA 94109

VON BRIESEN, DOROTHY ALICE, retired lawyer; b. Moline, Ill., Sept. 1, 1912; d. William P. and Eva (Pratt) Clark; m. Ralph E. von Briesen, June 10, 1939; children: Richard, Mary, Katherine Chilton, Ann Lewis. Student, Cornell U., 1930-31; BA, Northwestern U., 1935; LLB, U. Wis., 1937. Bar: Wis. 1937. Social worker Racine (Wis.) County Welfare Dept., 1937-39; atty. Legal Aid Soc., Milw., 1965-66; pub. defender Children's Ct. Milw. (Wis.) County, 1966; ret., 1982; vol. atty. Milw. Bar Assn., 1968-81; bd. dirs. Wis. Correctional Svcs., Internat. Inst. Wis. Bd. mem. Milw. YWCA, 1965 (outstanding achievement award, 1984), Milw. Psychiat. Svcs., 1966, Nat. Coun. for Internat. Visitors, Washington, 1980-82; Wis. rep. Am. Field Svc. Internat. Scholarships, N.Y.C., 1963; v.p. Milw. United Way, 1985 (leadership award, 1985); pres. Coll. Endowment Assn., Milw., 1985-87. Recipient Community Svc. award Theta Sigma Phi, Milw., 1963, Spl. Svc. award Met. Civic Alliance, Milw., 1979, Citation by Wis. State Legis., 1988; named Woman of Achievement, Quota Club Milw., 1970. Mem. AAUW (Svc. award 1989), Wis. Bar Assn., Milw. Bar Assn. (Pro Bono award for legal svc. to needy, 1983). Lutheran. Home: 3535 N Hackett Milwaukee WI 53211

VONDERHEIDE, HEIDI TAUSCHER, lawyer; b. Orlando, Fla., June 11, 1960; d. Don W. and Jeanne (Rogers) Tauscher; m. Paul Francis VonderHeide, Oct. 11, 1986. BA with high distinction and honors, Rollins Coll., 1982; JD, Wake Forest U., 1985. Bar: Fla. 1985. Assoc. Zimmerman, Shuffield, Kiser & Sutcliffe, P.A., Orlando, Fla., 1985-87, Winerweedle, Haines, Ward & Woodman, P.A., Winter Park, Fla., 1987-90; pvt. practice law Winter Park, 1990—. Asst. city atty. City of Winter Park, Fla., 1988-90; participant Orange County Guardian Ad Litem Program, 1988—. Recipient Algernon Sydney Sullivan medallion N.Y. So. Soc., 1982; Outstanding Scholar in Social Scis., Rollins Coll., 1982. Mem. Fla. Bar Assn. Orange County Bar Young Lawyers Assn. (sec. com. 1987-89), Orange County Bar Assn., Seminole County Bar Assn., Am. Inns. of Ct., Internat. Law Soc. (pres. 1984-85), Moot Ct. Republican. Roman Catholic. Office: Winderweedle Haines et al PO Box 880 S Park Ave Winter Park FL 32790-0880

VONDERHEIDE, SUSAN GWEN, psychologist; b. Haverhill, N.H., Sept. 28, 1957; d. Edwin Alfred and Barbara Jane (Allen) V.; m. Carl George Hindy, May 30, 1981; children: Nicholas Carl, Jacqueline A. BA, U. R.I., 1979; MA, U. Conn., 1981, PhD, 1985. Lic. psychologist, N.H. Intern in psychology Judge Baker Children's Ctr., Boston, 1981-82; psychologist Child Guidance Clinic, Jacksonville, Fla., 1984-86, Brookside Hosp., Nashua, N.H., 1986-87; pvt. practice Nashua, 1987—. Contbr. articles to profl. jours. Recipient Psychology award U. R.I., 1979. Mem. Am. Psychol. Assn. Democrat. Methodist. Office: Hindy & Vonderheide 3B Taggart Dr Nashua NH 03060

VON EYE, ROCHELLE KAY, mathematics educator; b. Parkston, S.D., Nov. 3, 1949; d. John Lawrence and Mary Ann (Mansheim) Thury; m. James Roger, Aug. 24, 1978; children: Denise Ann, Janae Lynn, Douglas James. Student, S.D Sch. of Mines, 1969; BA, S.D. State U., 1971, MA, 1984. Instr. math. Brookings (S.D.) Middle Sch., 1970-74, Lake Area Vocat. Sch., Watertown, S.D., 1974-76; engrs. aide Mo. Basin Power Plant, Wheatland, Wyo., 1976-77; carpenter, bookkeeper self-employed, Pine Ridge Indian Reservation, S.D., 1977-78; instr. math., bus. Wessington Springs

High Sch., S.D., 1978-80; instr. math., sci, bus. Plankinton (S.D.)High Sch., 1980-84; asst. prof. Dakota Wesleyan U., Mitchell, S.D., 1984—; tax cons., S.D., 1971—; hog and grain farmer, self-employed, S.D., 1978—; edn. cons., self-employed, S.D., 1978—; state dir. Presdl. awards, NSF, S.D., 1986—; owner, mgr. Proud Angler Bait and Tackle, Watertown, S.D., 1973-76. Author, presenter: Daily Use of Computers, Mathematics and Reading, Anamorphic Art, Questioning Techniques. word judge, Mitchell Sch. System Spelling Bee, S.D., 1987-88; NAIA faculty athletic rep. Dakota Wesleyan U., 1987—; rev. com. S.D. Dept. Edn., Pierre, 1988; tour co-leader, Koka U. Japan, 1989. W.K. Kelogg Nat. fellow; recipient Presdl. Award for Excellence, NSF, Washington, 1984. Fellow Woodrow Wilson Found.; mem. S.D. Coun. Tchr. Maths. (pres. 1988—), Nat. Coun. Tchrs. of Maths., AAUW (v.p., 1987-88), State Assn. Microcomputer Educators (pres. 1985-88), S.D. Pork Producers, Coun. of Presdl. Awardees in Math, Parent/Tchr. Club, Music Boosters. Roman Catholic. Office: Dakota Wesleyan U 1200 West U Ave Mitchell SD 57301-4398

VON FURSTENBERG, DIANE SIMONE MICHELLE, fashion designer; b. Brussels, Belgium, Dec. 31, 1946; came to U.S., 1969; d. Leon L. and Liliane L. (Nahmias) Halfin; m. Eduard Egon von Furstenberg, July 16, 1969 (div.); children: Alexandre, Tatiana. Student, U. Madrid, 1965-66, U. Geneva, 1966-68. Founder, pres. Diane von Furstenberg Studio, N.Y.C., 1970—; pres. Diane Von Furstenberg Ltd., N.Y.C. Office: Diane Von Furstenberg Studio 745 Fifth Ave 24th Fl New York NY 10151*

VON HERRMANN, DENISE KEEFER, educator; b. Atlanta, Sept. 24, 1962; d. Clyde Andrew and Dolores Jean (Mahanna) Keefer; m. Andrew Benjamin von Herrmann, Aug. 18, 1990. BA, Washington and Jefferson Coll., 1984; MA, Jacksonville State U., 1989; postgrad., U. Ala., 1990—. Pub. relations dir. Dalton Jr. Coll., Dalton, Ga., 1985; bus. writer Marietta Daily Jour., Marietta, Ga., 1985-86; freelancer Atlanta, 1986; box office mgr., promotions dir. Jacksonville State U. Drama, Jacskonville, Ala., 1987-89; promotions dir. Jacksonville State U. Summer Dinner Theatre, 1989-90; instr. DeKalb Coll., Atlanta, 1990—; instr. Job Tng. Partership Act Programs, Dalton, 1985; seminar leader Non-Profit Orgn. Assn., Morrow, Ga., 1986. Pub. relations asst. United Way Cobb County, Marietta, 1985-86; campaign staffer Browder for Congress campaign, Anniston, Ala., 1989; registrar The Civics Bee sponsored by Closeys Found., 3rd Congl. Dist., Ala., 1989. Mem. Kappa Kappa Gamma (charter mem. Washington, Pa. and alumnae clubs in Ga.). Democrat. Methodist.

VON HOLT, LAEL POWERS, psychotherapist, psychiatric social worker; b. Boston, Apr. 9, 1927; d. Merritt Adams and Rea Francisca (Hunt) Powers; m. Henry William Von Holt, Jr., Sept. 18, 1954; children: Gardner, Dudley, Edward. BA, U. Mass., 1950; MSW, U. Mo., 1972, postgrad., 1978; postgrad. Menninger Found., Topeka, 1977-85. Diplomate Bd. Clin. Social Work, Internat. Acad. of Behavioral Medicine Counseling and Psychotherapy. Psychiat. social worker N.Y. Dept. Mental Hygiene, Wingdale, 1950-51, Mass. Dept. Mental Health, Worcester, 1951-54; instr., social worker U. Oreg., Eugene, 1954-59; psychiat. social worker Mo. Dept. Mental Health, Fulton State Hosp., 1973-81, Columbia (Mo.) Regional Hosp. Psychiat. Services, Inc., 1977-82, Family Mental Health Ctr., Jefferson City, Mo., 1982—; field instr. U. Mo., Columbia, 1988. Bd. dirs. PTA, 1970-74, 77-78; mem. health com. Boone County Community Services Council, 1975-76; vol. Meals on Wheels, 1972-73, 76-79; den mother Boy Scouts Am., 1968-69, 71-72; mem. by-laws com. Springdale Neighborhood Assn., 1977. Named Social Worker of Yr. Cen. Mo., 1986. Mem. Nat. Assn. Social Workers, Acad. Cert. Social Workers, LWV (city council observor 1976-82, chmn. local action com. 1979-80, sec. 1974-77, chmn. Observer Corps 1981-83, chmn. com. mental health 1988—), Kappa Kappa Gamma. Republican. Methodist. Club: Stephens Coll. Faculty Wives (pres. 1979-80, 89-90). Home: 378 Crown Point Columbia MO 65203 Office: Family Mental Health Ctr 1905 Stadium Jefferson City MO 65101

VON RAFFLER-ENGEL, WALBURGA, linguist, educator, writer; b. Munich, Sept. 25, 1920; came to U.S., 1949, naturalized, 1955; d. Friedrich J. and Gertrud E. (Kiefer) von R.; m. A. Ferdinand Engel, June 2, 1957; children: Lea Maxine, Eric Robert von Raffler. DLitt, U. Turin, Italy, 1947; MS, Columbia U., 1951; PhD, Ind. U., 1953. Freelance journalist, 1949-58; mem. faculty Bennett Coll., Greensboro, N.C., 1953-55, Morris Harvey Coll., Charleston, W.Va., 1955-57, Adelphi U., CUNY, 1957-58, NYU, 1958-59, U. Florence, Italy, 1959-60, Istituto PostUniversitario Organizzazione Aziendale, Turin, 1960-61, Bologna Center of Johns Hopkins U., 1964, Vanderbilt U., Nashville, 1965—; prof. linguistics Vanderbilt U., 1977-85, prof. emerita, sr. rsch. assoc. Inst. Pub. Policy Studies, 1985—, dir. linguistics program, 1978-86; chmn. com. on linguistics Nashville U. Ctr., 1974-79; Italian NSF prof. Psychol. Inst. U. Florence, Italy, 1986-87; prof. NATO Advanced Study Inst., Cortona, Italy, 1988; pres. Kinesics Internat., 1988—; prof. linguistics Shanxi U., Peoples Republic China, 1985; vis. prof. U. Ottawa, Ont., Can., 1971-72, Inst. for Lang. Scis., Tokyo, 1976; grant evaluator NEH, NSF, Can. Council; manuscript reader Ind. U. Press, U. Ill. Press, Prentice-Hall; cons. Trinity U., Simon Frazer U. Author: Il prelinguaggio infantile, 1964, The Perception of Nonverbal Behavior in the Career Interview, 1983; co-author: Language Intervention Programs 1960-74, 1975; editor, co-editor 12 books; author film and videotape; contbr. over 300 scholarly articles, 200 gen. articles to profl. and popular publs. Recipient grants from Am. Council Learned Socs., grants from NSF, grants from Can. Council, grants from Ford Found., grants from Kenan Venture Fund, grants from Japanese Ministry Edn., grants from NATO, grants from Finnish Acad., grants from Meharry Med. Coll., grants from Internat. Sociol Assn., grants from Internat. Council Linguists, grants from Tex. A&M U., grants from Vanderbilt U., grants from others. Mem. AAUP, Internat. Linguistics Assn., Linguistic Soc. Am. (chmn. Golden Anniversary film com. 1974), Internat. Assn. for Applied Linguistics (com. on discourse analyses, sessions chmn. 1978), Lang. Origins Soc. (exec. com. 1985—, chmn. internat. congress, 1987), Internat. Sociol. Assn. (rsch. com. for sociolinguistics, session co-chmn. internat. conf. 1983, session chmn. profl. conf. 1983), Internat. Assn. for Study of Child Lang. (v.p. 1975-78, chmn. internat. conf. 1972), Inst. for Nonverbal Communication Research (workshop leader 1980-81), Tenn. Conf. on Linguistics (pres. 1976), Southeastern Conf. on Linguistics (hon. mem. 1985—), Semiotic Soc. Am. (organizing com. Internat. Semiotics Inst. 1981), Kinesics Internat. (pres. 1988—). Office: Vanderbilt U Box 26B Nashville TN 37235

VON ROEMER, BEATRICE, representative of international labor federation; b. Riga, Latvia, Feb. 23, 1929; came to the U.S., 1949; d. Theodore Erwin and Antonina (Bartsch) von Roemer. BA, Randolph Macon Women's Coll., 1951. Rep. Internat. Confedn. of Free Trade Unions to UN, N.Y.C., 1968—. Democrat. Roman Catholic. Office: Internat Confedn Free Trade Unions 104 E 40th St New York NY 10034

VON ROSENBERG, MARJORIE TAYLOR, author; b. Cambridge, Mass., Aug. 18, 1932; d. Alonzo and Margaret Isabel (York) Taylor; m. Dale Ursini von Rosenberg, June 12, 1953; children: Carol, Eugene, Byron, Clyde. BFA, Tulane U., 1970. Freelance artist Dallas, 1953—, freelance author and lectr., 1982—; travel author various civic groups, schs. and librs., 1985-90. Author: German Artists of Early Texas, 1982, Max and Martha, The Twins of Fredericksburg, 1986, Elisabet Ney, Sulptor of American Heroes, 1990. Mem. Park Cities Rep. Women's Club, Dallas, 1985-90, Dallas (Tex.) Symphony, 1990, Dallas (Tex.) Heritage Soc., 1980-90, Soc. Mayflower Descendents, Tex., 1980-90. Recipient purchase award Dallas (Tex.) Mus. of Fine Arts, 1957, La. Watercolor Soc., Baton Rouge, 1961, Montgomery (Ala.) Mus. of Fine Arts, 1965, Tulsa (Okla.) City-County Libr., 1978. Mem. Tex. Visual Arts Assn. (historian 1986, 87, second prize membership exhibit 1987), Colonial Dames of the 17th Century, Dallas Mus. Art, S.W. Watercolor Soc., Artist and Craftsmen Assn., Seekers Antique Club (recording sec., 1990). Republican. Presbyterian. Home: 6036 Del Norte Ln Dallas TX 75225

VON SELDENECK, JUDITH METCALFE, executive search firm executive; b. High Point, N.C., June 6, 1940; d. Frederick Maurice and Harriet (Curtis) Metcalfe; BA, U. N.C., 1962; postgrad. Am. U., 1963-64; m. George Clay von Seldeneck, Apr. 8, 1980; children: Rodman Clay, Kevin Clay. Senatorial asst., 1963-72; pres., chief exec. officer Diversified Search, Inc., Phila., 1972—, Diversified Health Search; bd. dirs. Meridian Corp., Keystone Life Ins. Co., Greater Phila. Partnership, Pvt. Industry Coun., Com. of 200; bd. dirs. Econ. Devel. Coalition Greater Phila., Boy Scouts Am., Zool. Soc. Mem. Forum Exec. Women (co-founder, bd. dir.), Com. 200, Assn. Exec. Search Cons. Democrat. Episcopalian. Clubs: Phila. Cricket, Sunneybrook Golf, Wharton Club of Phila. (bd. mem.). Home: 8124 Saint Martins Ln Philadelphia PA 19118

VON STADE, FREDERICA, mezzo-soprano; b. Somerville, N.J., June 1, 1945; m. Peter Elkus, 1973; children: Jennie, Lisa. Student, Mannes Coll. Music, N.Y.C., Ecole Mozart, Paris; DMus (hon.), Yale U., 1985. Former nanny, salesgirl; sec. Am. Shakespeare Festival. Debut in Die Zauberfloete with Met. Opera, 1970, later resident mem., Covent Garden debut, 1975; appeared with opera cos. including Paris Opera, San Francisco Opera, Salzburg Festival, London Royal Opera, Spoleto Festival, Boston Opera Co., Santa Fe Opera, Houston Grand Opera, La Scala; recital artist, soloist with symphony orchs.; appeared in operas The Marriage of Figaro, Faust, The Magic Flute, Don Giovanni, Tales of Hoffman, Rigoletto, Der Rosenkavalier, The Seagull, Werther, The Barber of Seville; albums Frederica Von Stade Sings Mozart-Rossini Opera Arias, French Opera Arias, Pelleas and Melisande, Idomeneo, La Sonnambula; created roles of Nina in the Seagull (Pastieri), 1974, Tina in the Aspern Papers (Arganto), 1988. Mem. Am. Guild Mus. Artists. Roman Catholic. Office: care Columbia Artists Mgmt 165 W 57 St New York NY 10019*

VON TAUBER, OLGA MARIA, psychiatrist; b. Vienna, Austria, Apr. 12, 1911; came to U.S., 1946; d. Edward H. and Annie (Fletcher) Beck; m. Robert Frank von Tauber, Dec. 14, 1934. MD, State Univ. Vienna, Vienna, Austria, 1936. Diplomate Am. Bd. Psychiatry, Am. Bd. Neurology. Asst. physician Boston State Hosp, Boston, 1943-45; supervising psychiatrist Kings Park Psychiatric Ctr., L.I., N.Y., 1950-60; dep. dir. Kings Park Psychiatric Ctr., L.I., 1960-68; women dir. Northeast Nassau Psychiatric Ctr., Kings Park, 1968-76; cons. Northshore Univ. Hosp., Manhasset, N.Y., 1970—, Nassau County Med. Ctr., East Meadow L.I., 1972—, Huntington Hosp., L.I., 1970—; assoc. prof. Health Sci. Ctr., Stonybrook, N.Y., 1968—. Fellow Am. Psychiat. Assn.; mem. AMA, Am. Med. Women's Assn., N.Y. State Med. Soc. Home and Office: 198 W Neck Rd Huntington NY 11743

VON UHLIT, RUTH RAEDER, retired teacher, fruit farmer; b. Ouray, Colo., Feb. 15, 1911; d. Irving Peter and Esther Vera (Davis) Raeder; m. George Henry von Uhlit, May 8, 1933 (dec.); children: Martha, Raeder, Greta, Charles. AB, U. Calif., Berkeley, 1931, gen. secondary credential, 1932. Substitute tchr. Napa Valley (Calif.) Unified Sch. Dist., 1932-61, secondary sch. tchr., 1961-67; tchr. citizenship Napa Valley Adult Sch., 1955-88; ret., 1988—; instr. water safety, First Aid Am. Red Cross, Napa, 1939-60. Pres. Citizens Coun. Napa Tomorrow, 1978; active in Citizens for Growth Mgmt., 1980. Named Citizen of Yr. Napa Elks Lodge, 1970, Outstanding Adult Tchr. of Yr., State of Calif., 1989; recipient Award of Merit Upper Napa Valley Assocs., St. Helena, Calif., 1981, honor medal DAR, Napa, 1984. Mem. AAUW (pres. 1970), Napa County Farm Bur. (bd. dirs. 1976—, Dir. of Yr. 1984), Calif. Fedn. Rep. Women (1st Americanism award 1988), Napa C. of C. Home and Office: von Uhlit Ranch 3011 Soscol Ave Napa CA 94558

VON WINCKLER, BEVERLY ANN PURNELL, personnel consultant; b. Joliet, Ill., Feb. 16, 1935; d. Edwin Dodd and Viola U. (Nelson) Purnell; m. David F. von Winckler, Sr., Oct. 26, 1957 (div. Aug. 1985); 1 child, David Franz. Student Joliet Jr. Coll., 1953-55, Brenau Coll., Ga., 1956-57. Sec. Office of Govt. P.R., Chgo., 1973-76; sales rep. Standard Register Co., Schiller Park, Ill., 1976-77; dir. devel. Irish Found., Chgo., 1978-79; pres. BEverly von Winckler & Assocs., Inc. div. Von Winckler Temporaries, Chgo., 1980—; lectr. Northwestern U. Program on Women, 1983—; prin. Hispanic-Am. Film Festival, Chgo., 1979; panelist Mundelein Coll., Chgo., 1985; lectr. Midwest Women's Ctr., 1988-90, Chgo. chpt. Am. Womens Bus. Assn., 1989; guest various local TV shows. Vol., Sta. WTTW-TV, 1966-72, Chgo. Internat. Film Festival, 1964-85; bd. dirs. Evanston (Ill.)-North Shore YWCA; pub. relations dir. Democratic mayoral campaign, Evanston, 1981; docent Evanston Hist. Soc., 1989; benefit chmn. YWCA, 1990. Recipient Service award Chgo. Internat. Film Festival, 1964. Mem. Evanston Jr. Women's Club, Alpha Delta Pi. Avocation: wood crafts. Home: 1018 Lee St Evanston IL 60202 Office: 105 W Madison St #1600 Chicago IL 60602

VON ZWEHL, JOANNE, real estate executive; b. Flushing, N.Y., Sept. 27, 1959; d. Joseph and Noreen (O'Gorman) Von Z. BBA, Ft. Lewis Coll., 1981. Lic. realtor, real estate broker. Loan cons. Verex Assurance, Inc., Jericho, N.Y., 1981-83; prin. various real estate corps., N.Y.C., 1982-84; pres. Holding Corp., Farmingdale, N.Y., 1984—, All Island Building Corp., Melville, N.Y., 1984—; pres., broker Cayman Realty, Melville, 1984-88; pres., constrn. supr. CMS Quality Devel. Corp., Melville, 1986—; pres. R.D.A. Enter of N.Y., Farmingdale, N.Y., 1987—; owner Varn Products Co., Ltd, Manchester, Eng., 1982—, Varn Products Co., GMBH, Dusseldorf Fed. Republic. Germany, 1982—; broker State of N.Y. Dept. Real Estate, 1983—. Fellow Nat. Assn. Female Execs.; mem. Animal Protection Inst. of Am., N.Y. State Assoc. Realtors, Inc., Multiple Listing Service of L.I., Inc., Am. Power Boat Assn. Republican. Roman Catholic. Home: 12 Cross St Port Washington NY 11050 Office: RDA Enter of NY 431 Conklin St Farmingdale NY 11735

VOORHEIS, MARION MARASCIO, educator; b. Red Bank, N.J., Dec. 14, 1946; d. Anthony William Marascio and Martha Edith Glenfield; m. Patrick Joseph Voorheis, Sept. 16, 1978; 1 child, Alexis Glenfield Mahood. AB, Regis Coll., Weston, 1968; MS, Georgetown U., 1970; Cert., Cleveland State, 1977. Tchr. Calvert County Bd. Edn., Prince Frederick, Md., 1969-71; counselor Patterdell Sch. for Girls, Phoenix, 1971-73; dept. chair Radio Immuno Assay Lab., nuclear med. technologist Elyria (Ohio) Mem. Hosp., 1973-77; tchr. Cleve. Bd. Edn., 1977-78, Sparta (Ill.) High Sch., 1978-79, South Burlington High Sch., 1979—; participating mem. com. for human rsch. Med. Ctr. Hosp. Vt., Burlington, 1984-87; chair curriculum com. South Burlington High Sch., 1985-87; in-svc. drug & alcohol dir. South Burlington High Sch., 1985-88. Co-mgr. Burlington String Tng. Orch., 1987-88; testified before Vt. Legislature drug and alcohol issues in schs., 1987; founder South Burlington High Sch. drug and alcohol free parties after prom and graduation, 1987; yearbook advisor South Burlington High Sch., 1984-90. Named Outstanding Biology Tchr. State of Vt. Nat. Assn. Biology Tchrs., 1990. Roman Catholic. Home: 24 Derby Circle South Burlington VT 05403 Office: S Burlington High Sch 550 Dorset St South Burlington VT 05403

VOORHESS, MARY LOUISE, pediatric endocrinologist; b. Livingston Manor, N.Y., June 2, 1926; d. Harry William and Helen Grace (Schwartz) V. BA in Zoology, U. Tex., 1952; MD, Baylor Coll., Houston, 1956. Diplomate Am. Bd. Pediatrics and Pediatric Endocrinology. Rotating intern Albany (N.Y.) Med. Ctr., 1956-57, asst. resident pediatrics, 1957-58, chief resident pediatrics, 1958-59; rsch. fellow pediatric endocrinology and genetics SUNY Health Sci. Ctr., Syracuse, 1959-61, asst. prof. pediatrics, 1961-65, assoc. prof. pediatrics, 1965-70, prof. pediatrics, 1970-76; prof. pediatrics SUNY Sch. Medicine and Biomed. Scis., Buffalo, 1976—; co-chief div. endocrinology Children's Hosp. Buffalo, 1976—; ad hoc reviewer Jour. Pediatrics, Pediatrics, Am. Jour. Diseases Children, other. Contbr. sci. articles to profl. jours., chpts. to books. Med. dir. Childrens Growth Found., Buffalo, 1976—; community advisor Assn. for Rsch. Childhood Cancer, Buffalo, 1990—. Recipient Rsch. Career Devel. award Nat. Career Inst., 1961-71. Fellow Am. Acad. Pediatrics, AAAS; mem. Soc. Pediatric Rsch., Am. Pediatric Soc., Endocrine Soc., Lawson Wilkins Pediatric Endocrine Soc., N.Y. Acad. Sci., Buffalo Pediatric Soc., Zonta Internat., Phi Beta Kappa, Alpha Omega Alpha. Presbyterian. Home: 325 Lincoln Pkwy Buffalo NY 14216 Office: Children Hosp 219 Bryant St Buffalo NY 14222

VOORHIES, ALICE JOYCE, guidance service company executive; b. New Iberia, La., Dec. 4, 1940; d. Richard P. and Joyce (Vedrines) V. BA, U. Southwestern La., 1961, MEd, 1969. lic. profl. couselor, speech pathologist, La. Counselor Magnolia Sch., Inc., New Orleans, 1961-64; speech pathologist Iberia Parish, New Iberia, La., 1964-67; asst. prof. spl. edn. U. Southwestern La., Lafayette, 1967-86; dir. Voorhies Guidance Svcs., Lafayette, 1987—; mem. adv. coun. RSVP, Lafayette, 1988—; mem. med.-profl. staff CDU Hosp., Lafayette 1988—. Named Spl. Person of Yr., Coun. for Exceptional Children, Lafayette, 1987. Mem. Am. Assn. for Counseling and Devel., Nat. Assn. Career Devel. Democrat. Roman Catholic. Office: 720 E Universtiy Ave Lafayette LA 70503

VOORHIES, BARBARA, anthropology educator. BS in Geology magna cum laude, Tufts U., 1961; PhD in Anthropology, Yale U., 1969. Lectr. So. Conn. State Coll., New Haven, 1969; asst. prof. San Diego State Coll., 1969-70; vis. prof. U. Calif., Santa Barbara, 1970-71, asst. prof., 1971-77, assoc. prof., 1977-82, prof., 1982—, chair dept. anthropology, 1985-87; field asst. U.S. Geol. Survey, 1961; research asst. Peabody Mus. Natural History, Yale U., 1963-65; with archeol. survey Caribbean Research Ctr., Guatemala; with excavations dept. anthropology Yale U., San Felipe, Guatemala, 1966-68; archeol. researcher NSF, Chiapas, Mex., 1973, 78-79, New World Archeol. Found., 1977, Nat. Geog. Soc., Chiapas, 1981, 83, 88. Author (with M. Kay Martin): La Mujer: Un Enfoque Antropológico, 1978; editor spl. issue Am. Antiquity, 1977. Fellow Am. Anthrop. Assn.; mem. Soc. for Am. Archaeology, Sociedad Mexicana Antropologia, Sigma Xi (pres. local chpt. 1981-82). Office: U Calif Santa Barbara Dept Anthropology Santa Barbara CA 93106*

VORE, MARY EDITH, pharmacology educator, researcher; b. Guatemala City, Guatemala, June 27, 1947; came to U.S., 1962; d. Charles Schrater and Sammye (Smith) V.; m. Edgar Tadasu Iwamoto, Dec. 27, 1976; children: Kenneth Edgar, Daniel Vore. BA, Asbury Coll., Wilmore, Ky., 1968; PhD, Vanderbilt U., Nashville, Tenn., 1972. Postdoctoral fellow Hoffman-LaRoche, Nutley, N.J., 1972-74; asst. prof. U. Calif., San Francisco, 1974-78; asst. prof. pharmacology U. Ky., Lexington, 1978-81, assoc. prof., 1981-86, prof., 1986—, vice chmn. dept., 1983—; cons. NIH, Bethesda, Md., 1983-87. Contbr. numerous articles to profl. jours., chpts. to books. USPHS grantee, 1979—. Mem. Soc. Toxicology, Am. Assn. Study of Liver Disease, Am. Soc. Pharmacology and Exptl. Therapeutics (sec.-treas. 1986-89). Office: U Ky Coll Medicine 800 Rose St Lexington KY 40536

VOSBEIN, ELEANOR EDNA, insurance company official; b. New Orleans, June 24, 1935; d. Max G. and Edna Camille (Gonzales) Frank; m. Ernest Edwin Vosbein, Oct. 31, 1954; children: Michael, Terry, Gary, Ken. Student, La. State U., 1952-53, DeKalb Coll., Decatur, Ga., 1978-80. Group svc. rep. Liberty Life Ins. Co., Atlanta, 1975-87, Protective Life Ins. Co., Tucker, Ga., 1987—. Mem. NAFE, Nat. Assn. Life Underwriters. Roman Catholic. Home: 3648 Oregon Trail Decatur GA 30032 Office: Protective Life Ins Co 3522 Habersham at Northlake Tucker GA 30084

VOSBURGH, VICTORIA LYNN, rehabilitation services executive; b. Putnam, Conn., Aug. 7, 1965; d. Douglas Warren Vosburgh and Margaret Jean (Grenier) Baggetta; m. Michael R. DeNardis, Aug. 7, 1988. Diploma, Westchester Sch., 1985. Adminstrv. asst. Hospitality House T.C., Inc., Albany, N.Y., 1985-87, human immunodeficiency virus issues coord., 1987—; HIV-related issues coord. Hospitality House T.C., Inc., 1989—. Mem. People for the Ethical Treatment of Animals. Mem. NAFE, Am. Mus. Natural History (assoc.), World Wildlife Fund, North Shore Animal League. Home: 49 N Pine Ave Albany NY 12203 Office: Hospitality House TC Inc 271 Central Ave Albany NY 12206

VOSEFSKI, EDITH KING, human resource development consultant; b. Joliet, Ill., Aug. 27, 1930; d. Victor Milton and Esther (Livingston) King; m. Joseph F. Vosefski, Nov. 1, 1952; children: Stephen John, Gregory Richard. BS, Northwestern U., Evanston, Ill., 1952; MA, Governor's State U., University Park, Ill., 1980. Tng. coordinator Operation ABLE, Chgo., 1981-84; from seminar designer, facilitator trainer to pub. aid coordinator Coll. of DuPage, Glen Ellyn, Ill., 1984-89; employee devel. specialist MIDCON Corp., Lombard, Ill., 1989; pres. People Unlimited, Downers Grove, Ill., 1989—; nat. trainer, Bus. and Profl. Women USA, Washington, D.C., 1987-88. Pres. Downers Grove B.P.W., 1987-88; sec. Assoc. to Advanced Ethnical Hypnosis Ill. Chpt. 2, 1987-88, 88-89. Episcopalian.

VOSO, DEBORAH ELIZABETH, financial planning executive; b. Camden, N.J., Mar. 29, 1950; d. H. David and Elizabeth Ann (Lesicko) Rau; m. Richard F. Voso, Oct. 2, 1971; children: Jennifer, Lisa. AA, Frederick Community Coll., 1979; BA, Shepherd Coll., 1983. Cert. fin. planner. Fin. planner Fin. Mgmt. Resources, Churchton, Md., 1983-84, Investment Mgmt. and Research, Greenbelt, Md., 1984-85, Capital Fin. Group, Silver Spring, Md., 1985-86; pres. Voso Assocs., Frederick, Md., 1986—; lectr. Frederick County Adult Edn., 1987—, Frederick Community Coll., 1987—; mktg. chair Pvt. Industry Coun., 1989—. Bd. dirs. Heartly House, Frederick, 1987—; chmn. Frederick County Women's Fair, Bus. Women's exhibits, 1986-88; treas. Frederick County Women's Ctr. Coun., 1986-88; mem. devel. coun., ann. support com. Frederick Meml. Hosp., 1988-90. Named Bus. Person of Yr., C. of C., 1989. Mem. Frederick Community Coll. Alumni Assn. (pres. 1988-89), Internat. Assn. Fin. Planners, Inst. Cert. Fin. Planners, Surburban Md. Life Underwriters Assn. (bd. dirs. 1986, chmn. pub. svc. com. 1986-87, chmn. pub. rels. 1987-88, pvt. industry coun. 1989—), Rotary (v.p. Fredericktowne club), Toastmasters (exec. v.p. Downtown Frederick 1989). Republican. Methodist. Home: 9005 Mountainberry Circle Frederick MD 21701 Office: Voso Assocs 220 W Patrick St Frederick MD 21701

VOSS, HELEN HARRIS, artist; b. Wichita Falls, Tex., Nov. 18, 1933; d. Evan Pinkney Harris and Elizabeth (Wood) Cudd; m. Ronald Eugene Voss, May 23, 1982; children: Susan Elizabeth Heimbach, Shelley Elaine Robertson. Student, Rice U., 1952-53; BA, U. Calif., Davis, 1989. Ordained deacon Presbyn. Ch. of U.S., 1972. Dir. legal edn. Houston Legal Found., 1964-69; dept. chairperson vol. svcs. U. Calif.-Davis Med. Ctr., Sacramento, 1976-80; mgr. Giselles Travel, Davis, 1981-85; program asst. acad. reentry program U. Calif. Davis, 1989. Art shows include Basement Gallery, 1985-89, Calgene juried show (annually), 1989, Pence Gallery Invitational, 1988, 89, Davis Art Ctr., 1989; artist (sculpture, painting) My God, 1989. Bd. dirs. Pvt. Industry Coun., JTPA, Yolo County, Calif., 1985-87, Pence Gallery, Davis, Episc. Community Svc. Diocese of No. Calif., 1983-84; joint bd. dirs. Diocese of San Francisco and No. Calif., Episc. Ch. Bishop Ranch; vol. svcs. U. Calif. Davis Med. Ctr., 1976-86, chmn. curriculum review 4-H Arts, U. Calif. Recipient Hansen Meml. award, 1989, Moseman award Moseman Corp., Calif., 1987; regents scholar U. Calif. Bd. Regents, 1987-89. Mem. Vol. Hosp. Assn. Am. (region pres. 1978-79), U. Calif. Davis Alumni, Faculty Wives Club (Davis, pres. 1975-76), Soroptimist Internat. (spl. projects 1987), Phi Beta Kappa, Phi Kappa Phi. Democrat. Episcopalian. Home and Office: 24530 County Rd 22 Lambs Valley Esparto CA 95627-9713

VOSS, KATHERINE EVELYN, management consultant; b. Cleve., Sept. 2, 1957; d. Wendell Grant and Ann Terry (Miller) Voss; m. James Everett Mathias, Oct. 6, 1984 (div. Dec. 1988). BS, Bowling Green State U., 1979, MBA, 1981. Sci. systems analyst Eli Lilly & Co., Indpls., 1981-83, systems tng. cons., 1983-84; customer liaison mgr. Ind. U., Bloomington, 1985; prodn. ops. mgr. Ind. U., Indpls., 1985-86; sr. systems cons. Wang Labs., Inc., Carmel, Ind., 1986—; cons. Ind. U., Bloomington, 1984-85. Contbr. (book) Introduction to Business, 1980, Introduction to Accounting, 1981, Computers and Data Processing, 1981. Presidental advisor Jr. Achievement, Indpls., 1982-83; pres. PEO Chpt. AM, Indpls., 1987-89. Mem. Beta Beta Beta. Republican. Presbyterian. Home: 9519 Maple Way Indianapolis IN 46268 Office: Wang Labs Inc 11350 N Meridian St Ste 600 Carmel IN 46032

VOSS, MARY LOUISE, city official; b. Seymour, Ind., Aug. 9, 1950; d. Ralph Gilbert and Audrey Verona (Speck) Colvin; m. Gary Wayne Voss, June 28, 1969; children: Christopher, Amy, Cheyne. Student, Purdue U., 1981, Syracuse U., 1988-89, Mich. State U., 1988. Operator Ind. Telephone Corp., Seymour, 1968-74; layout clk. Seymour Tribune, 1974-75; clk. Steltenpohls, Seymour, 1975-76; accts. payable supt. Union Camp Corp., Seymour, 1976-88; clk.-treas. City of Seymour, 1988—; workshop instr. Ind. U., Purdue U., Columbus, 1989. Player Womens Volleyball League, Seymour, 1979—, Co-ed Softball League and Volleyball League, Seymour, 1986—; coach, mgr. Youth Softball League, Seymour, 1982—; asst. Joyus Garde coun. Girl Scouts U.S.A., 1985. Mem. Seymour Bus. and Profl. Women (pres. 1986-88), Ind. Assn. Cities and Towns, Ind. League Mcpl. Clk. and Treas., Internat. Inst. Mcpl. Clks., Dem. Womens Club, Dau. Isabella (treas. 1987—), Epsilon Sigma Alpha (1st v.p. 1984-85). Democrat. Roman Catholic. Home: 605 E 15th St Seymour IN 47274 Office: City of Seymour 220 N Chestnut St Seymour IN 47274

VOSS-JONES, ROSEMARY, real estate executive; b. Milw., Feb. 10, 1946; d. William Bernard and Priscilla Eugenie (Pendleton) V.; m. Phillip Wendell Jones III, 1989. BS, U. Wis., Oshkosh, 1969; M, Calif. State U., Long Beach, 1975. Cert. real estate broker, Calif. Tchr. Long Beach Unified Sch. Dist., 1969-71, 72-76, U.S. Dept. Def., San Vito, Italy, 1971-72; salesperson Century 21 Sparrow, Long Beach, 1976-78; broker, owner Century 21 A Marketpl., Long Beach, 1978—; tchr. Long Beach City Coll., 1984—. Fund raiser Easter Seals, Long Beach, 1978—; bd. dir. fund raising Sarah Ctr., Long Beach, 1984—; mem. Innaugural Group, Leadership, Long Beach, 1990. Mem. Nat. Assn. Realtors, Nat. Million Dollar Round Table, Fedn. Internationale des Administrateurs de Biens Conseils Immobiliers, Sales and Mktg. Execs. Long Beach, Long Beach Bd. Realtors (1st v.p., 2d v.p.), Long Beach C. of C. (women's coun.), NAFE, Long Beach C. of C. (bd. dirs. 1990, 1st v.p. women's coun. 1990-93), Nat. Broker's Communication Coun. Office: Century 21 A Marketplace 1650 Ximeno Ave Ste 120 Long Beach CA 90804

VOTAVA, KATHRYN MCCABE, administrator visiting nurse service; b. Elmira, N.Y., June 9, 1954; d. Paul H. and Mary Patricia (Cain) McCabe; m. G. Joseph Votova, Aug. 13, 1976; children: Gerald J. III, Mary Pat. BSN, U. Georgetown, 1976; MS, U. Rochester, 1983. RN, N.Y. Coronary care staff nurse Good Samaritan Hosp., Dayton, Ohio; cardiopulmonary nurse Rochester (N.Y.) Vis. Nurses Assn., clin. specialist, geriatric med. nurse, dir. of clin. specialties and edn. Author: Quality Assurance Outcome Criteria for the Tracheostomy Patient in the Home. Recipient numerous awards. Mem. Am. Heart Assn., Gerontology Soc. Am.

VOTIK, BARBARA MEIER, cleaning and disaster restoration firm owner; b. Clearwater, Fla., Apr. 10, 1944; d. James O. and Ethel Constance White; m. J. Carl Votik Jr., Sept. 21, 1985; children: Harvey T. Meier, MaryEllen Meier. BS in Bus Edn., James Madison U., 1965; student, U. Va., 1978-79. Cert. bus. tchr. Tchr. Prince William (Va.) County Sch. Dist., Manassas, 1966-67, 75-80; bus. tchr. Temple Bus. Sch., Alexandria, Va., 1967-69, Greenville County (Va) Sch. Dist., Emporia, 1981-82; account rep. Weaver's Bus. Machines, Charlotte, N.C., 1983-84; market support rep. Brother Internat. Corp., Atlanta, 1984-85; sales devel. mgr. Brother Internat. Corp., Piscataway, N.J., 1985-86; dist. sales mgr. Brother Internat. Corp., Miami, Fla., 1986-90, Charlotte, N.C., 1990; ptnr. SERVPRO of North Mecklenburg, Charlotte, 1990—. Author: (book) Brother Dealer Guide, 1986, (tng. guides) Self-Paced Training, 1984, 85; editor: (book) Brother Training Guide, 1986. Mem. Bic President's Club. Home: 11501 Abernathy Rd Charlotte NC 28216

VOWELL, EVELENE C., real estate broker; b. Hickman, Ky., May 11, 1940; d. Haughty Chester and Lottie Bell (Williams) Craddock; m. Darrell Odine, Dec. 27, 1959; children: Amy Darlene, Kerry Don, Dal Keith. Student Memphis State U., 1976-85; cert. residential specialist, Realtors Inst., 1988, grad., 1988. Lic. real estate affiliate broker. County agrl. sec. Extension Svc., Hickman, Ky., 1957-59; payroll sec. Roper Pecan Co., Hickman, 1961-63; PR3 inspector Gen. Electric Co., Memphis, 1969-71; sec. Swift and Co., Memphis, 1971-73; affiliate broker John R. Thompson Realtors, Memphis, 1976-83, Crye Leike Realtors, Memphis, 1983—. Mem. Memphis Bd. Realtors, Ind. Order Foresters. Home: 2808 Charles Bryan Rd Memphis TN 38134

VOWELS, ELEANOR ELAINE, speech pathologist; b. Pitts., Mar. 10, 1937; d. Arnett Lloyd and Amanda (Anthony) Wooding; B.S. in Psychology, Howard U., 1962, PhD, 1988; M.A. in Speech Pathology and Audiology (Vocat. Rehab. fellow 1965-67), Catholic U. Am., 1967; postgrad. U. Md.; m. Aug. 27, 1960; 1 son, David Scott. Speech pathologist Prince George County (Md.) Diagnostic Teaching Center, 1967-70; speech pathologist Dept. Human Resources D.C., 1970-72, dir. speech pathology and audiology, 1972—; dir. speech pathology and audiology children and youth project D.C. Gen. Hosp., 1972—, dir. handicapped infant intervention project, 1977—, dir. tng. grant, 1980—; v.p. D.C. Consortium Handicapped Children's Programs, 1979, pres., 1980. Pres., D.C. Area chpt. Children Internat. Summer Villages, Inc., 1981, 82-83, mem. expansion com., trustee-at-large Nat. Children's Internat. Summer Villages, Inc. 1982—, also mem. long range planning com.; chmn. com. on handicapped Commn. Pub. Health, 1982, advisor to commr., 1986—; mem. Mayor's Com. on the Handicapped, 1986—, Devel. Disabilities Council, 1986—. HEW Bur. Edn. grantee, 1977—. Mem. Am. Speech and Hearing Assn. (cert. clin. competence), D.C. Assn. Retarded Citizens (dir. 1972—), D.C. Speech and Hearing Assn., Md. Speech and Hearing Assn., Nat. Assn. Retarded Citizens, Zeta Phi Beta. Democrat. Baptist. Producer audio visual slide presentations on handicapped children, 1962, 70. Home: 7718 Jaffrey Rd Fort Washington MD 20744 Office: Commn of Pub Health 1875 Conneticut Ave NW Washington DC 20009

VOYLE, KIM MARCIA KEMPTON, career planning administrator; b. Salem, N.J., Jan. 1, 1958; d. Ernest Leroy and Frances Elizabeth (Kinnear) Kempton; m. Robert John Voyle, Jan. 24, 1987. AA in Liberal Arts, Prince George's Community Coll., Largo, Md., 1977; BS in Psychology, Evangel Coll., 1979; MA in Human Resources, Azusa Pacific U., 1988. Personnel analyst II City of El Paso, Tex., 1981-85; sr. personnel analyst City of Santa Anna, Calif., 1988-89; County of Ventura, Calif., 1989—; sr. personnel analyst Ventura County, Ventura, Calif., 1985-87, mgr. career devel., 1989—; cons. various orgns., Ventura, 1987—. Mem. Personnel Testing Coun., Internat. Personnel Mgmt. Assn. Episcopalian. Home: 9608 Las Cruces Ventura CA 93004 Office: County of Ventura 800 South Victoria Ventura CA 93009

VRABEL, MARILYNN PATRICIA, health care agency administrator; b. Syracuse, N.Y., Jan. 20, 1948; d. William Ambrose and Jame (Kearney) Erwin; m. Peter Donald Vrabel, May 2, 1970; children: Gregory William, Sarah Jane, Peter Michael, Molly Meaghan. Student, Onondaga Community Coll., Syracuse, N.Y., 1982, SUNY at Oswego, Syracuse, 1982-83. owner, operator Regional Home Care Svc. Inc., Syracuse, 1988—, Regional Svcs. of N.Y., Inc., 1989—. Nurse staff St. Joseph's Hosp., Syracuse, 1969-70; clin. instr. Cen. Tech., Syracuse, 1979-84; owner, operator Extended Hosp. Svc., Syracuse, 1984—, Regional Home Care Svcs., Inc., Syracuse, 1988—. Chmn. Holy Family Lotto Program, Syracuse, 1985. Recipient Clairol Scholarship Avon Corp., 1982; named Nurse of Distinction nominee N.Y. Legislature, 1989. Mem. N.Y. State Dist. 4 Nurse Assn., Nat. League Nursing Coun. for Nursing Ctrs., Oncology Nursing Soc., NAFE, Nat. Home Care Assn., Empire State Med. Equipment Dealers Inc., Cen. N.Y. Assn. Health Care Providers. Democrat. Roman Catholic. Office: Regional Home Care Svcs 5424 W Genesee St Camillas NY 13031

VRADENBURG, BEATRICE WHITE, symphony orchestra executive; b. Manhattan, Kans., Nov. 1, 1922; d. Richard Peregrine and Marian (Tyler) White; m. George Albert Vradenburg, Jr., Sept. 10; 1 son, George Albert. Student Oberlin Coll., to 1944. Mgr. Colorado Springs (Colo.) Symphony Orch., 1954—. Active Colo. Coun. on the Arts, 1965-71; pres. Spring-spree. Recipient Gov.'s award for Excellence in the Arts, 1978, Mayor's award, Colorado Springs, 1979. Mem. Am. Symphony Orch. League (Louis Sudler award 1980, Bonfils award 1989), Nat. Endowment for the Arts (music panel 1979-82), El Paso Club, arden of the Gods. Republican. Episcopalian. Office: PO Box 1692 Colorado Springs CO 80901

VREDENBURG, JO ANN, advocate, consultant; b. Rome, N.Y., June 20, 1940; d. Lawrence J. Deeley and Anna (Haskins) Francisco; m. James D. Vredenburg, Dec. 14, 1962; children: Debora Sue Vredenburg Finnigan, Scott J. Student, Onondaga Community Coll., Syracuse, N.Y., 1973, Univ. Coll., 1979. From bookkeeper to office mgr. Am. Bapt. Chs. of N.Y. State, Syracuse, 1971-78; from bookkeeper to acct. N.Y. Conf. United Ch. of Christ, Syracuse, 1979-85, bus. and fin. cons., 1986-89; coord., dir. Religious Coalition for Abortion Rights N.Y. State, Syracuse, 1985—. Mem. polit. action com. Friends of Choice, Syracuse, 1989—; mem., spokesperson Concerned Rational Adults for Family Teaching, Baldwinsville, N.Y., 1988; organizer Coalition for Choice, Syracuse, 1989—. Democrat. Baptist. Office: Religious Coalition for Abortion Rights NY State Syracuse NY 13224

VROMAN, KAREN LYN, accountant; b. Lake Placid, N.Y., June 3, 1963; d. Paul Richard and Hilda June (Wells) V. AS, Paul Smith's Coll., 1983; BS, SUNY, Plattsburg, 1985. Bookeeper, mgr. on duty Butcher Block Restaurant, Raleigh, N.C., 1986-88; jr. acct. Enviroscis. Inc., Raleigh, 1986-88; acct. Urbach, Kahn and Werlin PC, Glens Falls, N.Y., 1988-89; fin. mgr. Warren County Health Svcs., Lake George, N.Y., 1989—. Mem. pub. health com. County of Warren; tchr. local ch. sch. First United Meth. Ch., Glens Falls. Recipient Adirondack Merit scholarship Paul Smith Coll., N.Y. Mem. NAFE. Home: 16 Charlotte St Glens Falls NY 12801 Office: Warren County Health Svcs Mcpl Ctr Lake George NY 12845

VUCANOVICH, BARBARA FARRELL, congresswoman; b. Camp Dix, N.J., June 22, 1921; d. Thomas F. and Ynez (White) Farrell; m. Ken Dillon, Mar. 8, 1950 (div. 1964); children: Patty Dillon Cafferata, Mike, Ken, Tom, Susan Dillon Stoddard; m. George Vucanovich, June 19, 1965. Student, Manhattanville Coll. of Sacred Heart, 1938-39. Owner, operator Welcome Aboard Travel, Reno, 1968-74; Nev. rep. for Senator Paul Laxalt, 1974-82; mem. 98th-102nd Congresses from 2d Nev. dist., 1983—; mem. coms. interior and insular affairs, house adminstrn. Pres. Nev. Fedn. Republican Women, Reno, 1955-56; former pres. St. Mary's Hosp. Guild, Lawyer's Wives. Roman Catholic. Club: Hidden Valley Country (Reno). Office: US Ho of Reps 206 Cannon House Office Bldg Washington DC 20515*

VUCKOVICH, CAROL YETSO (MRS. MICHAEL VUCKOVICH), librarian; b. East Liverpool, Ohio, Sept. 23, 1940; d. Stephen A. and Louise (Sever) Yetso; m. Michael Vuckovich, Sept. 24, 1970. BS, Geneva Coll., 1966; MLS, U. Pitts., 1968. Computation analyst Crucible Steel div. Colt Industries, Midland, Pa., 1958-62; library dir. Community Coll. Beaver County, Monaca, Pa., 1968—, instr. human anatomy and physiology, 1970—. Mem. Am. Library Assn., Pa. Library Assn., Spl. Libraries Assn., Am. Inst. Biol. Scis., Am. Anti-Vivisection Soc., Nat. Wildlife Fedn., Coll. and Research Libraries. Home: 21 Elm St Midland PA 15059

VUICH, ROSE ANN, state legislator; b. Cutler, Calif.; d. Obren and Stana V. Ed. Cen. Calif. Comml. Coll. Mem. Calif. Senate from 15th dist., 1976—. Mem. Nat. Soc. Pub. Accts., Beta Sigma Phi. Democrat. First woman elected to Calif. State Senate. Office: State Capitol Rm 5066 Sacramento CA 95814

VUILLEMOT, PATRICIA MARETTA, business executive; b. Chgo., Dec. 6, 1953; d. Patrick Clarence and Theresa Lucy (Fuoco) M.; m. Eric Harold Vuillemot, Oct. 4, 1986. With telemktg. dept. A.G. Becker, 1980-81; investment exec. Warburg Paribas Becker, 1981-83; instnl. sales exec. Chgo. Corp., 1983-85; investment exec. Tucker Anthony & R.L. Day, 1985-88; pres. F&M, Inc., Berwyn, Ill., 1988—, also bd. dirs. Mem. Brit. Home Planning Com., 1990. Named Miss Rotary, Rotary Internat., 1973. Mem. Berwyn Econ. Devel., First United Referrals Real Estate, Berwyn Profl. Women's Orgn. (fundraising co-chairperson 1983-84), Lions. Republican. Home: 634 S Stone LaGrange IL 60525 Office: F&M Inc 3208 S Grove Berwyn IL 60402

VUJOVICH, CHRISTINE M., engine manufacturing company executive; b. 1951. BS, U. Ill., 1974, MS, 1978. Asst. to hydrologist Ill. State Water Svc., 1977-78; environ. specialist Cummins Engine Co., Inc., Columbus, Ind., 1978-81, environ. mgr., 1981-83, dir. environ. and govtl. rels., 1983-85, chief application engr. customer accts. dept., then v.p., 1985—. Office: Cummins Engine Co Inc 500 Jackson St PO Box 3005 Columbus IN 47202*

VUKICH, SUSAN CLAYPOOL, hospital volunteer services executive; b. Newport, R.I., Oct. 3, 1926; d. James Vernon and Elizabeth (Sheldon) Claypool; m. Harry Flickinger Helm, Feb. 1, 1947 (div. 1967); children: Caroline Elizabeth (dec.), Susan Eleanor Spencer; m. Robert Vukich, Dec. 3, 1972. BS, Coll. of William and Mary, 1946. Tchr. Little People's Sch., Mt. Vernon, N.Y., 1946-47, Cascade Kindergarten, Yakima, Wash., 1952-55; dir. women's activities Nat. Found. March of Dimes, Wash., 1952-67; home dialysis cons. Univ. Hosp., Seattle, 1968-71; asst. in orthopedic rsch. Children's Hosp., Seattle, 1971-73; dir. vol. svcs. N.W. Hosp., Seattle, 1973—. Bd. dirs. N.W. Kidney Ctr., Seattle, 1984—; chmn. bd. dirs. Puget Sound Kidney Ctr., Everett, Wash., 1985-88; active Evergreen Rep. Women, South Snohomish County, Wash., 1989. Recipient Svc. to Youth award Atlantic St. Ctr., Seattle, 1968. Mem. AAUW (Wash. br., pres. 1978-79), Am. Soc. Dirs. of Vol. Svcs. (pres. 1987-88), Am. Hosp. Assn. (mem. coun. on vols. 1984-88), Wash. State Soc. Vol. Svcs. (chmn. 1979-80), Cen. Puget Sound Dirs. of Vol. Svcs. (pres. 1976-78), Coll. of William and Mary Soc. of Alumni (pres. Wash. state 1982-87), Lady Lions (pres. 1966-67). Methodist. Home: 528 Pine St #1 Edmonds WA 98020 Office: NW Hosp 1550 N 115th St Seattle WA 98133

VUKIN, GERRI PATRICIA, real estate relocation company executive; b. Sharon, Conn., Oct. 17, 1939; d. Edmond William and Nuala (Houston) Kearney; m. Richard L. Vukin, July 3, 1965 (div. June 1982); children: Greg, Nick. RN diploma, Hartford Hosp. Sch. Nursing, 1960; student, Columbia U., 1960-61; B.S.P.H.N., U. Mich., 1964; postgrad., County Coll. of Morris, Randolph, N.J., 1985-86. Pub. health nurse Wayne County Health Dept., Wayne, Mich., 1964-65; sch. nurse Houston Independent Sch. Dist., Houston, 1965-66; pres., communications cons. GNG Enterprises, Chatham, N.J., 1983-84; corp. account mgr. relocation dept. Burgdorff Realtors, Murray Hill, N.J., 1984—; mem. Employee Relocation Coun., 1985-89; speaker Am. Assn. Personnel Adminstrn., N.J., 1988; developer assertiveness tng. course, 1983-84. Vol. Alanon, N.J., 1980-89, United Way, Chatham, N.J., 1984; treas. N.J. Task Force-COA, N.J., 1982-84. Grantee Profl. Edn. Orgn. (PEO), N.J., 1985. Mem. Nat. Assn. for Female Execs., Real Estate Assn., Sales Exec. Club, U. Mich. Club N.J., Fairmount Country Club (chmn. pool-social 1980), Gamma Phi Beta. Republican. Roman Catholic. Office: Burgdorff Realtors 560 Central Ave Murray Hill NJ 07974

VUKOVICH, S(HERYL) JAN, telecommunications company executive; b. Medicine Lodge, Kans., Oct. 15, 1952; d. Maurice Martin and Jean (Smith) Cleveland; m. Darrell Lee Oldham, May 27, 1972 (div. May 1984); m. Alex Vukovich, May 12, 1985. BS in Edn., West Tex. State U., 1974; postgrad., U. Denver, 1988-89. Mgr. Southwestern Bell, Ft. Worth, 1974-77, St. Louis, 1977-79; dir. AT&T, Parsippany, N.J., 1980-84, U.S. West, Denver, 1984—; cons. Vukovich Enterprises, Denver, 1986—. Mem. community orchs. and jazz bands, 1970—; chmn. Rodeo Drive Archtl. Control Com., Denver, 1986-88; pres. Rodeo Drive Homeowners Assn., 1989-90; mem. adv. bd. Regis Coll., Denver, 1990-91. Recipient Young Career Woman of Yr. award St. Louis Bus. and Profl. Womens Assn., 1979, Woman of Achievement award Metro YWCA, Denver, 1989. Mem. Am. Mgmt. Assn., Human Resources Planning Assn., Aurora Athletic Club. Republican. Office: US West 6300 S Syracuse Ste 100S Englewood CO 80111

VUMBACO, BRENDA J., small business owner; b. Meriden, Conn., July 11, 1941; d. Frank and Mary (Zipoli) V. BA, Seton Hill Coll., 1963; MA, Trinity Coll., 1966. Cert. adminstrv. psychology. Assoc. editor Holt, Rinehart and Winston, Inc., N.Y.C.; mng. editor population reports George Washington U., Washington; mgr. publs. Nat. acad. Scis., Washington; prin. Bren Way Enterprises, Meriden. Acting exec. dir. Am. Silver Mus., Meriden. Recipient Community Svc. awards, numerous writing awards. Mem. Conn. Small Bus. Fedn., Greater Meriden C. of C. Republican. Roman Catholic. Office: Bren Way Enterprises 99 Colony St Ste 4 Meriden CT 06450

WAALEN, ANNMARIE, bar and restaurant owner, computer analyst; b. Brighton, Mass., Sept. 22, 1960; d. James Francis and Cecilia M. (McHugh) W. AS, Aquinas Jr. Coll., Newton, Mass., 1980; BS in Mgmt., U. Mass., 1982. Computer support analyst Harvard U. Med. Sch., Boston, 1978-88; proprietor Lincoln St. Grille, Brighton, 1989—; computer cons. T & A Assocs., Boston, 1988—. Democrat. Roman Catholic. Home: 15 N Beacon St # 802 Allston MA 02134 Office: Lincoln St Grille 8 Lincoln St Brighton MA 02135

WACHNER, LINDA JOY, apparel marketing and manufacturing executive; b. N.Y.C., Feb. 3, 1946; d. Herman and Shirley W.; m. Seymour Applebaum, Dec. 21, 1973 (dec., 1983). BS in Econs. and Bus., U. Buffalo, 1966. Buyer Foley's Federated Dept. Store, Houston, 1968-69; sr. buyer R.H. Macy's, N.Y.C., 1969-74; v.p. Warner div. Warnaco, Bridgeport, Conn., 1974-77; v.p. corp. mktg. Caron Internat., N.Y.C., 1977-79; chief exec. officer U.S. div. Max Factor & Co., Hollywood, Calif., 1979-82, pres., chief exec. officer, 1982-83; pres., chief exec. officer Max Factor & Co. Worldwide, 1983-84; mng. dir. Adler & Shaykin, N.Y.C., 1984-86; owner, pres., chief exec. officer Warnaco Inc., N.Y.C., 1986—; bd. dirs. Standard Brands Paints, Reebok Internat.; mem. Co-operation Ireland. Presdl. appointee Adv. Com. for Trade Negotiations, Commn. on Workforce Quality and Market Efficiency; trustee Martha Graham Ctr. Contemporary Dance, Inc.; mem. bd. trustees U. Buffalo Found. Recipient Silver Achievement award L.A. YWCA; named Outstanding Woman in Bus. Women's Equity Action League, 1980, Woman of Yr., MS. Mag., 1986, one of the Yr.'s Most Fascinating Bus. People, Fortune Mag., 1986, one of 10 Most Powerful Women in Corp. Am., Savvy Woman Mag., 1989. Mem. Young Pres.'s Orgn., Com. of 200, Am. Mgmt. Assn., Am. Apparel Mktg. Assn. (bd. dirs.). Republican. Jewish. Office: Warnaco Inc 90 Park Ave New York NY 10016 also: Warnaco Inc 11111 Santa Monica Blvd Los Angeles CA 90025

WACHNIAK, LANA JANE, sociology and criminal justice professor; b. Hamilton, Ont., Can., Sept. 28, 1952; d. William and Armande Bernadette (Sevigny) W.; m. William Hall Wallace Jr., Sept. 9, 1983. BS in Criminal Justice, Ga. So. Coll., 1972; MS in Criminology, Fla. State U., 1976; PhD in Sociology, U. Ga., 1987. Asst. prof. Ga. So. Coll., Statesboro, 1979-88; assoc. prof. Kennesaw State Coll., Marietta, Ga., 1988—. Contbr. articles to profl. jours. Vol. coord. Ga. Spl. Olympics, Statesboro, 1984-88; bd. dirs. Victim-Witness Program, Statesboro, 1987-88. Named Prof. of the Yr., Ga. So. Coll., 1988. Mem. Acad. Criminal Justice Scis., Ga. Sociol. Assn., AAUW (legis. chair Bulloch County, Ga. chpt. 1986-88), Ga. So. Coll. Alumni Assn. (bd. dirs. 1984—, Alumnus of Yr. in Edn. 1988). Democrat. Methodist. Office: Kennesaw State Coll PO Box 444 Marietta GA 30061

WACHOLTZ, MARY CATHERINE, internist, educator; b. Delta, Colo., Nov. 27, 1947; d. John Ernest and Martha Marie (Freeman) W. BS, Mich. State U., 1969; PhD, Harvard U., 1976; MD, U. Conn., 1981. Diplomate Am. Bd. Internal Medicine. Intern and resident in internal medicine Parkland Meml. Hosp., Dallas, 1982-85; fellow in rheumatology U. Tex. Southwestern Med. Ctr., Dallas, 1985-88, asst. prof. div. rheumatology, 1988—. Contbr. articles to med. jours. Nat. Merit scholar, 1965-69. Mem. Phi Beta Kappa, Phi Kappa Phi. Office: U Tex Southwestern Med Ctr 5323 Harry Hines Blvd Dallas TX 75235

WACHS, KATE MARY, psychologist; b. Chgo.; d. Charles Herbert and Rose Ann W. BA magna cum laude, Rosary Coll., 1974; MA, U. S.D., 1976, PhD, 1980. Licensed psychologist, Ill., Mich. Asst. clin. psychologist Lewis & Clark Mental Health Ctr., Yankton, S.D., 1977-78; intern clin. psychology Rush Presbyn. St. Luke's Med. Ctr., Chgo., 1978-79, house staff in psychology, 1979-80; psychologist Bay Med. Ctr., Bay City, Mich., 1980-83; pvt. practice psychology Mich., 1983-86, Chgo., 1983—; pres. IntiMate Introduction Service, Inc., Advanced Degrees Introductions, Inc.; columnist Chgo. Life Mag., 1984—, CampusUSA, 1989—, Midwest Men Mag., 1989—, Women In Mgmt. Newsletter, 1984-86, Amplifier, 1986-88; contbr. articles to local and nat. pubs.; guest on local and nat. radio and TV programs, 1982—. Mem. Assn. for Media Psychology (bd. dirs. 1985-87), Am. Psychol. Assn. (bd. dirs. Div. 46 1986—, sec. 1989-90, pres.-elect 1990, chmn. ethics/guidelines com. 1986-87, chmn. membership com. 1987—, liaison to Pub. Info. Com. 1987—, co-chair Div. 35 task force 1989—). Office: 875 N Dearborn Ste 400 Chicago IL 60610

WACHSMAN, KATHRYN MARY, lawyer; b. Providence, Oct. 27, 1949; d. Anthony and Mayme D'Agostino; m. Harvey F. Wachsman, Jan. 31, 1976; children: Dara Nicole, David Winston, Jacqueline Victoria, Lauren Elizabeth, Derek Charles. BA in Math., Avila Coll., 1971; JD, Washburn U., 1974. Bar: Conn., N.Y., Fla., D.C., Kans., U.S. Supreme Ct. Assoc. firm Pegalis & Wachsman, Great Neck, N.Y., 1978—. Mem. ABA, N.Y. State Bar, Conn. Bar, Fla. Bar, D.C. Bar, N.Y. State Trial Lawyers Assn., Kans. Bar, Am. Coll. Legal Medicine (assoc. in law), Assn. Trial Lawyers Am. Office: Pegalis & Wachsman PC 175 East Shore Rd Great Neck NY 11023

WACHSMAN, PHYLLIS GERI, advertising executive; b. N.Y.C., Feb. 2, 1947; d. Benjamin Gilbert and Leonora (Kleidman) Brown. BA, New Sch. for Social Research, N.Y., 1978; MHA, New Sch. for Social Research, 1980. RN, N.Y., N.J. Staff nurse Mt. Sinai Hosp., N.Y.C., 1968-70; supr. Hackensack (N.J.) Hosp., 1970-75; dir. of community psychology program Hackensack (N.J.) Hosp., Hackensack, 1975-80; sr. writer Kallir, Phillips, Ross Inc., N.Y.C., 1980-81, sr. v.p. assoc. creative dir., 1986—, copy supr., 1981-84, v.p. copy supr., 1984-85; v.p. copy supr. Smithouse, Torre & Ferrante, Rutherford, N.J., 1985-86; judge Clio awards, 1986, Triangle awards, 1987. Mem. Mental Health Assn. N.J. Recipient Jacob Javits award, 1980, Starch award MD. Mag., 1985, 86, Triangle awards Modern Medicine, 1984, 85. Mem. Am. Contract Bridge League. Office: Kallir Phillips Ross Inc 333 E 38th St New York NY 10016*

WACHTELL, ESTHER, music center executive; b. N.Y.C., June 30, 1935; m. Thomas Wachtell, Jan. 27, 1957; children: Roger Bruce, Wendy Anne, Peter James. BA, Conn. Coll., 1956; MA, Cornell U., 1957. Bd. dirs. Music Ctr. L.A. bd. govs., Music Ctr. Oper. Co., Music Ctr. Edn. Div., L.A. Visitors & Conv. Bur., L.A. Cen. City Assn., Mchts. and Mfrs. Assn., L.A. Ptnrship., Calif. Community Found., Am. Coun. Arts, Trusteeship for the Betterment of Women (bd. dirs.). Mem. Regency Club. Republican. Office: Music Ctr of LA 135 N Grand Ave Los Angeles CA 90012

WACKER, MARGARET MORRISSEY, communications executive; b. Washington, Dec. 12, 1951; d. Warren Ernest Clyde and Ann Romeyn (MacMillan) W. BA, Carnegie Mellon U., 1974. Promotion specialist Millipore Corp., Bedford, Mass., 1974-77, corp. communications mgr., 1982—, dir. communications Lab. Products div., 1981-82; dir. advt. IVAC div. Eli Lilly Co., San Diego, 1977-79, dist. sales mgr., L.A., 1979-80; bus. unit mgr. Sage div. Orion Rsch., Cambridge, Mass., 1980-81; counselor to handicapped individuals in bus. Mem. Internat. Assn. Bus. Communicators, Boston Computer Soc. Democrat. Episcopalian. Avocations: painting, sewing. Home: The Brook House Atrium 99 Pond Ave Unit 322D Brookline MA 02146 Office: Millipore Corp 80 Ashby Rd Bedford MA 01730

WADDELL, SANDRA SUE, media specialist, educator; b. Lebanon, Ind., Mar. 24, 1940; d. Roderick R. and Helen B. (Snyder) Witt; m. James D. Waddell, Sept. 1, 1962; children: James M., Jeffrey A., Jennifer R. BS, Ball State U., 1962; MS, U. Tenn., 1978. Head libr. Northwhite Sch. Corp., Monon, Ind., 1962-64, Columbus (Ind.) High Sch., 1964-65; libr. Riceville (Tenn.) Elem. Sch., 1967-69; head libr. E.G. Fisher Pub. Libr., Athens, Tenn., 1969-78; instr. Cleveland (Tenn.) State Community Coll., 1978-81; media specialist Trewhitt Jr. High Sch., Cleveland, 1978-81, Lakeview Mid. Sch., Greenville, S.C., 1981—; instr. Greenville Tech. Coll., 1982—; chmn. Middle Sch. Media Specialists, Greenville, 1983-84. Mem. edn. com. Buncombe St. Meth. Ch., Greenville, youth coordinator; past dist. pub. relations chmn. Cleveland United Meth. Ch. Mem. S.C. Edn. Assn., Greenville County Edn. Assn., S.C. Sch. Library Assn. Home: 8 Holgate Ct Greenville SC 29615 Office: Lakeview Mid Sch 3801 Old Buncombe Rd Greenville SC 29609

WADDINGTON, BETTE HOPE (ELIZABETH CROWDER), violinist, educator; b. San Francisco, July 27, 1921; d. John and Marguerite (Crowder) Waddington; BA in Music, U. Calif. at Berkeley, 1945, postgrad.; postgrad. (scholarship) Juilliard Sch. Music, 1950, San Jose State Coll., 1955; MA in Music, San Francisco State U., 1953; violin student of Joseph Fuchs, Melvin Ritter, Frank Gittelson, Felix Khuner, Daniel Bonsack, D.C. Dounis, Naoum Blinder, Eddy Brown; life cert. music and art Calif. Jr. Coll. Violinist Erie (Pa.) Symphony, 1950-51, Dallas Symphony, 1957-58, St. Louis Symphony, 1958—. Cert. gen. elem. and secondary tchr., Calif.; life cert. music and art for jr. coll.; cert. in librarianship from elem. sch. to jr. coll., Calif. Toured alone and with St. Louis Symphony U.S., Can., Middle East, Japan, China, Europe; concert master Pa. Symphony, Redwood City and San Mateo, Calif., Grove Music Soc., N.Y.C., St. Louis Symphony, 1958—; numerous recordings St. Louis Symphony, 1958—. Mem. Am. Musicians Union (St. Louis and San Francisco chpts.), U. Calif., San Francisco State Univ. Alumni Assn., Am. String Tchrs. Assn., San Jose State Univ. Alumni Assn., Sierra Club (life), Alpha Beta Alpha. Avocations: travel, art and archeology history, drawing, painting. Office: St Louis Symphony Orch Powell Hall Grand Ave and Delmar Blvd Saint Louis MO 63103

WADE, INGRID SLETTEN, advertising agency specialist; b. Janesville, Wis., May 4, 1954; d. Ivan Wayne and Grace Lorraine (Zastrow) Sletten; m. George Harry Wade, Dec. 29, 1986. BA, U. Mo., 1976; postgrad., Washington U., St. Louis, 1977. With Darcy MacManus Masius, St. Louis, 1979-89, rsch. analyst, 1981-82, sports media supr., 1983-89; media supr. various planning groups Darcy Masius Benton Bowles, St. Louis, 1989—. U. Mo. scholar, 1975-76, Washington U. scholar, 1976-77. Mem. Am. Mgmt. Assn., NAFE, Presenter's Anonymous, Bus. Writing Devel. Group (exec. bd. St. Louis chpt. 1988—), Media Tng. and Devel. Com. Office: Darcy Masius Benton Bowles 1 Memorial Dr Saint Louis MO 63102

WADE, MARY CARROLL, pyschologist, educator, government official; b. Rome, Ga., Sept. 1, 1909; d. Seaborn Rosa and Dollie Savannah (Hill) Carroll; student Maryville Coll., 1926-31, B.A., 1931; postgrad. U. of the South, summer, 1938; M.A., George Washington U., 1948; Ed.D., Am. U., 1970; lic. psychologist, Washington; m. Richard Rudolph Wade, Apr. 1, 1967 (dec.). Tchr., Hawkins County, Tenn., 1934-36, Pittman Center, Tenn., 1936-37, Meigs County, Tenn., 1937-38, Chattanooga, 1938-42; with War Dept., Washington, 1942-43; library asst. Library of Congress, Washington, 1943-44; planner, U.S. Govt. Printing Office, Washington, 1944-67, planner-in-charge, 1967-72, chief marginally punched continuous forms sect., Specifications Div., 1972-80, chmn. Fed. Women's Program, 1972-73; cons. psychologist Va. Vocational Rehab. Dept., 1954-57; lectr. Montgomery Coll., Rockville, Md., 1981-82; freelance writer and lectr., 1982—; lectr. Fed. Office Systems Expo, 1982, No. Va. Community Coll., 1984. Bd. dirs. United Cerebral Palsy, D.C., 1970-82; active ARC; hon. staff mem. Tenn. State Senator Annabelle Clement O'Brien, 1982. Recipient United Svc. Orgn. award, 1946, Superior Svc. award, U.S. Govt. Printing Office, 1963, 66, 67, 68, Spl. Achievement award, 1971-72, Luther Rice award George Washington U., 1989, Alumni Svc. award George Washington U., 1990; named Woman of the Yr. Fairfax County Bus. and Profl. Womens' Club, 1986, others. Mem. Am. Psychol. Assn., Va. Psychol. Assn., D.C. Psychol. Assn., Soc. for Personnel Adminstrn., Nat. Vocat. Guidance Assn., Am. Personnel and Guidance Assn., Pub. Personnel Assn., Franklin Tech. Soc., Bus. Forms Mgmt. Assn. (rec. sec. 1980-81), Am. U. Alumni Assn., George Washington U. Alumni Assn., Maryville Coll. Alumni Assn., Nat. Trust Historic Preservation, Poetry Soc. Va., Va., Nat. Mus. Women in the Arts, Nat. Assn. Ret. Fed. Employees (rec. sec. 1984-85), Am. Assn. Ret. Persons, Smithsonian Assocs., Kappa Delta Epsilon, Psi Chi, Phi Delta Gamma (nat. v.p. 1988-90, pres. Beta chpt., nat. coun. rep.). Presbyterian. Clubs: Toastmistress (sec.-treas., v.p. No. Va. chpt. 1986-87, pres., v.p. coun. 1985-86, internat. tng. in communications), Wash. of Printing House Craftsmen, Wash. Litho, George Washington Univ., Americana (pres., v.p.), Altrusa, (corr. sec. 1982-84, rec. sec. 1984-85, pres. 1986-87), Columbian Women, (corr. sec. 1984-85, pres. 1987-89), Interservice Club Coun. of Alexandria (rec.-sec. 1983), Fairfax County Bus. and Profl. Women's (recording sec. 1973-74, v.p. 1974-75, pres. 1975-76), Nat. Dem. Women's Club. Contbr. articles to profl. jours.

WADE, MERRY GAYLE, educational administrator; b. Salem, Ill., Nov. 30, 1937; d. Clinton Lee Annis and Marcella Claris (Clemins) Allen; children: Marvin, Angel Wade Loucks, Mark, Matt. BA, U. Colo., 1970, MA, 1973, EdS, 1976. Adminstrv. asst. U. Iowa, Iowa City, 1960-62; substitute tchr. Lebanon (Ind.) Sch., 1962-64; tchr. Foothills Elem. Sch., Lakewood, Colo., 1971-76; prin. Copeland (Kans.) Elem. Sch., 1976-83, Washington Elem. Sch., McPherson, Kans., 1983-87, McPherson Mid. Sch., 1987—; presenter in field. Leader 4-H Club, Copeland, 1976-83; mem. Copeland Recreation Commn., 1976-80; choir dir. Christian Ch., Copeland, 1976-78; dir. Copeland Community Theatre, 1980-83; participant Gov.'s Conf., 1989. Named Kans Outstanding Rural Sch. Adminstr. Kans. State U., 1981; recipient Exec. Educator 100 award, 1987, Sch. award kans. Focus, 1989. Mem. Kans. Assn. Elem. Sch. Prins. (pres. 1986-87, dist. IV Outstanding Adminstr. award 1987), Kans. Internat. Reading Assn. (sec. 1979-81), Western Kans. Reading Coun. (pres. 1978-79), United Sch. Adminstrs. (exec. bd. 1987-90, pres. 1990), Phi Delta Kappa (pres. Hutchinson chpt. 1990, v.p. Western Trails chpt. 1980-81), Reed scholar 1987, appreciation of svc. award 1987). Home: 201 Center St McPherson KS 67460 Office: McPherson Mid Sch 700 E Elizabeth St McPherson KS 67460

WADE, PATRICIA JOAN, educator; b. Lexington, Nebr., Mar. 21, 1949; d. Harold Brice and Mary (Balfany) Owens; m. Lowell Dennis Wade, Dec. 3, 1967 (div. 1975); 1 child, Lowell Chad. BA, Kearney (Nebr.) State Coll., 1980, MS, 1984; postgrad., U. S.D., 1990—. Assessor Dawson Co., Lexington, 1974-76; sec. Mut. of Omaha, 1976-77; bus. instr. Stratton (Nebr.) Pub. Schs., 1980-84; dir. secretarial sci. Inst. of Computer Sci., Omaha, 1984-85; word processing instr. Omaha Coll. of Health Careers, Omaha, 1985-86; instr. secretarial sci. N.E. Community Coll., Norfolk, Nebr., 1987—, instr. community edn. classes, 1987-89; evening instr. Met. Community Coll., Omaha, 1985-86; sec. Kelly Svcs., Omaha, summer 1984, 85. Sunday sch. tchr. 1st Christian Ch., Lexington, 1974-77; leader Dawson County 4-H Club, Lexington, 1975. Mem. Nat. Assn. Bus. Educators, Nebr. Bus. Edn. Assn., AAUW (program dir. 1989—), Univ. Women (program dir. Norfolk chpt. 1989—), Dawson County Exentsion Club (pres., v.p., sec. Lexington and Elwood, Nebr. chpt. 1968-77). Democrat. Home: 112 Little Caesar Norfolk NE 68701 Office: NE Community Coll 801 E Benjamin Ave Norfolk NE 68701

WADE, PATRICIA LYNNE, office administrator; b. Phoenix, Oct. 24, 1950; d. Buster and Tomi Tiny (Kishiyama) Collins; m. Howard William Wade III, Aug. 15, 1970 (div. July 1971); 1 child, Nicole Michelle. AAS, Maricopa Tech. Community Coll., 1985. Asst. dir. edn. Camelback Hosps., Inc., Phoenix, 1973-80; systems mgr. Laventhol & Horwath, CPA's, Phoenix, 1981-83; v.p. adminstrn. Total Info. Systems, Inc., Phoenix, 1983-87; adminstrv. dir., info. systems mgr. Spector Devel. Corp., Scottsdale, Ariz., 1987-88; mgr. ops. PSI World Seminars, Phoenix, 1988-89; office adminstr. East Valley Dental Svc., Mesa, Ariz., 1989—. Mem. Data Processing Mgmt. Assn. (edn. chair 1986-87), Nat. Computer Conf. (human resources com. 1984-85), JJP Booster Club (v.p. Tempe chpt. 1985-86, pres. 1987-88). Democrat.

WADE, SUSIE ANN, special projects manager; b. Columbus, Ga., Jan. 18, 1955; d. Clarence and Espnolia (Ellison) Holt; m. Arthur Lee Wade, Feb. 26, 1953; children: Shanntonnette Layioene, Kellie Maurise. Student, Philips Coll., 1975. Buyer Microbiological Assocs., Washington, 1976-78; adminstrv. asst. Am. Home Econs. Assocs., Washington, 1978-80, Electronic Industries Assn., Washington, 1980-82; day care provider At Home Day Care, Washington, 1982-86; adminstrv. asst. Electronic Industries Assn., Washington, 1986-87; spl. projects mgr. Consumer Electronics Shows, Washington, 1987—. Vol. Temple Hills (Md.) Community Ctr., 1987—. Mem. NAFE, Meeting Planners Am. Democrat. Pentecostal. Home: 6101 Harley Ln Temple Hills MD 20748 Office: Consumer Electronic Shows 2001 Eye St NW Washington DC 20006

WADE, SUZANNE, advisory system engineer; b. Chgo., Dec. 29, 1938; d. Edward Peter and Dorothy Rose Traxel; m. Robert Gerald Wade (div. Feb. 1980); children: Peter John, Robert Gerald Jr., Suzette Marie, Francesca Louise Felde, Elizabeth Rose Quigley. AA, Orange Coast Coll., 1980; BA, Calif. State U., Fullerton, 1985. Analyst data info. Motorola, Mesa, Ariz., 1972-75; planner prodn. Ford Aerospace, Newport Beach, Calif., 1975-79; supr. prodn. control Shiley, Inc., Irvine, Calif., 1979-81; mgr. bus. systems Hughes Aircraft Co., Fullerton, 1981-85; systems adminstr. Long Beach, Calif., 1985-89; adv. systems engr. IBM, Rockville, Md., 1989—; lectr. to clubs, classes Calif. State U., Fullerton, 1984-85; speaker in field. Author: (manual) Data Services, 1985; columnist, 1984-85. Mem. NAFE, Am. Prodn. and Inventory Control Soc., L.A. Aerospace and Def. Spl. Interest Group (dir. publicity 1987—, editor digest), Toastmasters (treas. Long Beach chpt. 1986). Episcopalian. Home: 7630 Coddle Harbor Ln Potomac MD 20854

WADE, VICKI LYNNE, medical center executive; b. Sanford, Fla., Jan. 22, 1953; d. Herbert Alvin Penley and Lois Jeannette (Rosier) Lee; m. Larry Dean Wade, July 16, 1976; children: Gregory, Eric, Tara Wade. AA, Seminole Community Coll., Sanford, 1983; BA, Rollins Coll., 1986; MS, Fla. Inst. Tech., 1986; assoc. in risk mgmt., Ins. Inst. Am., Malvern, Pa., 1988. Cert. healthcare risk mgr., Fla. Sales rep. Ramada Inns Inc., Clermont, Fla., 1977-78; officer Eustis (Fla.) Police Dept., 1978-82, asst. police chief, 1982-85; adminstrv. asst., risk mgr. Waterman Med. Ctr., Eustis, 1985, dir. med. staff, risk mgmt. and quality assurance, adminstr. for profl. svcs.; pres. Vicki L. Wade, doing bus. as Quality Assurance & Risk Mgmt. Cons., Inc., Eustis, 1988—. Contbr. articles to profl. publs. Vol. Rape Crisis Ctr., Eustis; seminar speaker on self-protection for women. Mem. Am. Soc. for Healthcare Risk Mgrs., Fla. Soc. for Health Care Risk Mgmt. (chmn. edn. 1987-88, pres.-elect 1989-90, bd. dirs. 1988-89). Republican. Home: 1407 Fahnstock Ave Eustis FL 32726 Office: Waterman Med Ctr 201 N Eustis St Eustis FL 32726

WADLEY, SUSAN SNOW, anthropologist; b. Baltimore, Nov. 18, 1943; d. Chester Page and Ellen Snow (Foster) W.; m. Bruce Woods Derr, Dec. 28, 1971 (div. July 1989); children: Shona Snow, Laura Woods. BA, Carleton Coll., Northfield, 1965; MA, U. Chgo., 1967, PhD, 1973. Instr. Syracuse U., 1970-73, asst. prof., 1973-76; dir. Fgn. and Comparative Studies Program, Syracuse, 1978-83; assoc. prof. Syracuse U., prof., 1982; dir. So. Asia Ctr. Syracuse U., 1985—; chair anthropology dept. Syracuse U., 1990—; Trustee Am. Inst. of Indian Studies, Chgo., 1984-89; mem. joint com. South Asia Social Sci. Rsch. Coun., 1982-89. Author: Shakti: Power in the Conceptual Structure of Karimpur Women, 1975, Women in India: Two Perspectives, 1978; editor: Powers of Tamil Women, 1980, Oral Epics in India, 1989. Pres. Edward Smith Parent Tchr. Orgn., Syracuse, 1988-89. Grantee Doctoral Diss. Research grant Nat. Sci. Found., Wash., 1967-69, Faculty Research grant U.S. Dept. Edn., 1983-84, Smithsonian Institute Research grant, 1983-84, Faculty Research grant Am. Inst. Indian Studies, 1989; Recipient Marc Perry Galler Prize for best doctoral dissertation in social scis. U. Chgo., 1974. Mem. Am. Anthropological Soc., Am. Folklore Soc., Soc. for Ethnomusicology, Assn. for Asian Studies. Office: Syracuse U 308 Bowne Hal Syracuse NY 13244

WADOWICZ, KAREN ANN, cosmetic company executive; b. New Haven, Conn., Apr. 9, 1964; d. Eugene Carroll and Loretta Ann (Motel) Wajdowicz. AA, U. Fla., 1984, BS, 1986. Cons. Clinique Cosmetics, West Palm Beach, Fla., 1986; counter mgr. Clinique Cosmetics, Boynton Beach, Fla., 1987; account coordinator for south Fla. Clinique Cosmetics, 1987-89, regional sales adminstr. for State of Fla., 1989—. Mem. com. Sunfest 90, West Palm Beach, 1990. Mem. Am. Mktg. Assn., Alpha Delta Pi Alumni Assn.

WAECHTER, ELEANOR HORWOOD MORRISON, not for profit corporation administrator; b. Yonkers, N.Y., Sept. 3, 1939; d. John Knox and Eleanor Wilfong (Horwood) Morrison; m. Robert Louis Waechter, Mar. 21, 1964; children: Elizabeth Anne, Robert Louis Jr. BS, SUNY, New Paltz, 1961, postgrad., 1963. Cert. tchr., N.Y. Tchr. English Yonkers Pub. Sch. System, 1961-65; dir. camp Taconic Girl Scout Coun., Inc., Katonah, N.Y., 1973-78, field exec., 1975-77, mgr. field svc., 1977-79; asst. exec. dir. Girl Scouts of Westchester-Putnam, Inc, Valhalla, N.Y., 1979-82; exec. dir. Girl Scouts of Westchester-Putnam, Inc, Pleasantville, N.Y., 1982—; mem. N.Y. Girl Scout Legis. Network, Albany, 1985—. Instr. ARC, Westchester, White Plains, N.Y., 1975-82; campaign vol. United Way of Westchester, White Plains, 1982—; bd. dirs. Vol. Svc. Bur., Westchester, 1989—. Mem. Westchester County Assn., Alpha Delta Kappa. Presbyterian. Office: Girl Scouts of Westchester-Putnam Inc 2 Great Oak Ln Pleasantville NY 10570

WAECHTER, JULIE MARIE, university publications director; b. Erie, Pa., Nov. 18, 1958; d. Russell E. and Winifred A. (Winter) W. BA in Profl. Writing, Gannon U., 1981, MA in Social Sciences, 1988. Dir. pub. info. WQLN Pub. Broadcasting of Northwest Pa., Erie, 1981-85; dir. pub. Gannon U., Erie, 1985—. Mem. Coun. for Advancement & Support of Edn. Office: Gannon University University Sq Erie PA 16541

WAELSCH, SALOME GLUECKSOHN, geneticist, educator; b. Danzig, Germany, Oct. 6, 1907; came to U.S., 1933, naturalized, 1938; d. Ilya and Nadia Gluecksohn; m. Heinrich B. Waelsch, Jan. 8, 1943; children—Naomi Barbara, Peter Benedict. Student, U. Konigsberg, Germany, U. Berlin, 1927-28; Ph.D., U. Freiburg, Germany, 1932. Rsch. assoc. in genetics Columbia U., 1936-55; assoc. prof. anatomy Albert Einstein Coll. Medicine, 1955-58, prof., 1958-63, prof. genetics, 1963—, chmn. dept. genetics, 1963-76; mem. study sects. NIH. Contbr. numerous articles on devel. genetics. Fellow AAAS, Am. Acad. Arts and Scis.; mem. NAS, N.Y. Acad. Scis. (hon. life), Am. Soc. Zoologists, Am. Assn. Anatomists, Genetics Soc., Soc. Devel. Biology, Am. Soc. Naturalists, Am. Soc. Human Genetics, Sigma Xi. Office: Albert Einstein Coll Med Dept Molecular Genetics 1300 Morris Park Ave Bronx NY 10461

WAELTY, BEATRYCE ANN, rubber and tire company executive; b. Mpls., Aug. 25, 1938; d. Paul Peter and Marion Ann (Hopkins) Heltemes Jerome; m. Thomas K. Hallcock, June 21, 1963 (div. 1977); m. Waldo G. Waelty, Apr. 7, 1979; children—Thomas J.P., Shawn M. (dec.), Kimberley A., Scott E. A.A., Stephens Coll., 1958; B.S., U. San Francisco, 1986. Mgr., Shasta Valley Realty, Weed, Calif., 1978-79; sec., account clk. Area Agy. on Aging, Weed, Calif., 1980-81; data reductionist Aerojet Tactical Co./Aerojet Strategic Propulsion Co., Sacramento, 1982-84; documentation coordinator, 1984, documentation supr., 1984-89, program adminstr., 1989—. Lodge: Order Eastern Star (worthy matron). Avocations: Gardening; needlepoint; carpentry. Home: 1806 Sheffield Way Roseville CA 95678 Office: Aerojet Strategic Propulsion Co Hwy 50 and Hazel Ave Sacramento CA 95813

WAGENER, MARGUERITE MARY, free lance writer, advertising sales consultant; b. North Kingston, R.I., Feb. 12, 1954; d. Richard V. and Lucille M. Wagener; B.A. in English and Communication Arts, St. Mary's Coll., Winona, Minn., 1975. Reporter, photographer, anchorperson Sta.-WKBT-TV, La Crosse, Wis., 1975-78; salesperson Anything Groes Corp., La Crosse, 1978-79; audio-visual scriptwriter Trane Co., La Crosse, 1979-81, mgr. dept. tech. lit., 1981-82; freelance writer, advt. sales, cons., 1982-83; asst. sales mgr. WISQ-FM, La Crosse, 1983-85; co-owner Peregrine Marine. Vice pres. alumni bd. dirs. St. Mary's Coll., 1980-86.

WAGENHEIM, LAURA ROBIN, management consultant; b. N.Y.C., July 7, 1965; d. Frances Adele (Dick) W. BA in Geology, Oberlin Coll., 1987; postgrad., Manhattan Coll. Dental asst. Comprehensive Dental Care Assocs., Riverdale, N.Y., 1982-83; computer cons. Oberlin (Ohio) Coll. Computing Ctr., 1984-87; PC programmer/analyst Bank of N.Y., N.Y.C., 1987-88; corp. fin. analyst Deloitte & Touche, Newark, 1988—. Recipient youth grant Explorer's Club, N.Y.C., 1982, award Sch. for Field Studies in Iceland, Cambridge, Mass., 1982, Sch. for Field Studies in Limnology Rsch., Cambridge, 1982. Mem. Manhattan Coll. Grad. Bus. Students Orgn. (co-founder 1990—). Home: 4901 HH Pkwy Apt 3M Riverdale NY 10471 Office: Deloitte & Touche 1 Gateway Ctr 11th Flr Newark NJ 07102-5311

WAGGONER, PAULETTE AMBURGEY, real estate appraiser; b. Mercedes, Tex., Oct. 1, 1945; d. L.S. Amburgey, Pauline (Shows) and Fred C. Gage; m. John Carlton Waggoner. AA, Stephens Coll., 1966; BS, La. State U., 1970. Real estate appraiser John C. Waggoner & Assoc., Odessa, 1987-88. Sec. Odessa Symphony Assn., 1985-86; sustainer Jr. League of Odessa, 1988; treas. Odessa Symphony Guild, 1988-89; worker Rep. Party, Odessa, 1988; com. chmn. Oil Baron Com., Am. Cancer Soc., Odessa, 1989-90, mem. bd. Mem. Odessa Art Assn., Kappa Gamma Alumnae Club (pres., treas., ref. chmn.). Presbyterian.

WAGNER, ALLISON JEAN, vocational nurse; b. Los Angeles, Calif., Dec. 14, 1960; d. Kurt Joseph and Barbara Jean (Wallace) Wagner. AA/BA, U. of the Pacific, 1979-83; LVN, Maric Coll., 1984-85. Lic. vocat. nurse. Editor/distbr. Winning Images, Beverly Hills, Calif., 1985-86; med. cons. Kurt J. Wagner, M.D., Inc. (formerly Ctr. for Spl. Surgery), Los Angeles, 1985—; publicist You're Becoming, Los Angeles, 1986. Mem. Calif. Theatre Council, Los Angeles, 1986; Phoenix Art Mus., 1987-88, The Woman's Bldg., 1986-89. Recipient Multiple Athletic awards, scholastic awards, The Buckley Sch. Mem. Nat. Assn. Female Execs., Alpha Chi Omega. Methodist. Club: Mary Duque Guild. Avocations: tennis; weight training; scuba diving; racquetball; golf. Office: Kurt J Wagner MD Inc 1125 S Beverly Dr Ste 500 Los Angeles CA 90035-1148

WAGNER, ANN KARLEN, infosystem specialist; b. Wadsworth, Ohio, Mar. 27, 1944; d. Robert Jerome and Audrey (Cartwright) Karlen; m. Gene Edward Wagner, Sept. 2, 1966 (div. 1977). BS in Math. Edn., U. Ill., 1966; MS in Math., No. Ill. U., 1968; MBA in Mktg., U. Chgo., 1984. Systems analyst Univac, Louisville, 1967-69; system analyst to data processing mgr. United Airlines, Elk Grove Village, Ill., 1969-81; quality assurance mgr., dir. applications programming Time, Inc., Chgo., 1982-87; quality assurance mgr. Citicorp Savs. Ill., Chgo., 1987-88; data processing cons. Glen Ellyn, Ill., 1988—. Mem. Chgo. Quality Assurance Assn. (bd. dirs. 1987—, treas. 1989—).

WAGNER, CAROL ANNE, lay worker; b. Louisville, Oct. 9, 1942; d. John Andrew and Helen Marguerite (Herzog) Hammond; m. John Philip Wagner, June 14,1969; children: John J., Timothy A. BA, St. Josephs Coll., 1964. Rschr. Nat. Security Adminstrn., Ft. Meade, Md., 1964-65; tchr. Balt. (Md.) City Sch. System, 1965-71; staff St. Thomas Aquinas Ch., College Sta., Tex., 1987—. Mem. Coll. Sta. (Tex.) Parent Teacher Orgn., City Coun., Parents Supporting Students Tchrs.; candidate Coll. Sta. Ind. Sch. Dist. Bd. Trustees. Recipient Leadership Brazos, Coll. Sta. C. of C., 1988-89. Mem. AAUW (various coms.), Tex. A&M Women's Social Club, Mothers Club, Bryan/Coll. Sta. Newcomers, C. of C., Supporters of Excellence Edn. Roman Catholic. Home: 203 Ember Glow Circle College Station TX 77840

WAGNER, CHARLENE BROOK, educator, consultant; b. L.A.; d. Edward J. and Eva (Anderson) Brook; m. Gordon Boswell Jr. (div.); children: Gordon, Brook, John. BS, Tex. Christian U., 1952; MEd, Sam Houston U., 1973; postgrad., U. Tex., Austin, 1975, Tex. A&M U., 1977. Sci. educator Spring Br. Ind. Sch. Dist., Houston, 1970—; cons. Scott Foresman Pub. Co., 1982-83; owner Scientific Instructional Systems Co., 1988—. Mem. Houston Symphony League, 1989; social chmn. Encore, 1988; mem. Houston Grand Opera Guild, 1989, Museum Fine Arts, 1989, Museum of Art of the Am. West, Houston, 1989,Women's Christian Home, Houston, 1989. Mem. Tex. State Tchrs. Assn., NEA, Spring Br. Edn. Assn., Watercolor Arts Soc. of Houston, Art League Houston, Clan anderson Soc. Republican. Episcopalian. Home: 2711 Teague TX 77080 Office: Spring Oaks Jr High Sch 2150 Shadowdale Houston TX 77043

WAGNER, CINDY LOUISE, artist, computer graphics designer, painter; b. Somerset, N.J., Aug. 6, 1962; d. Charles Frederick and Jean Hellen (Closter) W.; m. Irwin Jay Miller, Sept. 10, 1989. AA in Visual Communication, Art Inst. Pitts., 1982; student, Rutgers U., summer 1985, Art Students League, N.Y.C., 1985-86, 88. Trainee Genigraphics, Pitts., Fall 1982; genigraphic artist N.J. Bell, Newark, 1983-84; artist designer Berry Assocs., Chatham, N.J., 1984-85; sr. artist Bell Labs, Piscataway, N.J., 1984-85, Slidemakers, N.Y.C., N.J., 1985-87; artist, cons. N.Y.C., 1987-89; sr. computer graphics designer Citibank, N.A., N.Y.C., 1989—; cons., artist Media Design Group, Miami, Fla., 1988; designer, cons. Mobil Oil, N.Y.C., 1987-89. Painter oils; illustrator July cover Computer Graphics mag., 1990. Painter Mt. Bethel Fire Co., Warren, N.J., 1983-84; designer, artist Vietnam Vets. Leadership Program, Chatham, N.J., 1984-85. Mem. Allied Artists Am. (assoc.), NAFE, Farm Bur., Nat. Assn. Artists Orgn., Women in Arts, Art Students League N.Y. Home: 60 Ridgecrest Rd Lake Peekskill NY 10537 Office: Citibank NA 850 Third Ave New York NY 10043

WAGNER, CYNTHIA KAYE, business administration educator, consultant; b. Lincoln, Nebr., Jan. 29, 1957; d. Richard and Gloria Jean (Larsen) W. BS in Agronomy with honors, Ohio State U., 1979, MS in Agronomy, 1980; PhD in Bus. Adminstrn., U. Pa., 1986. Rsch. assoc. Physiology Lab., Ohio State U., Columbus, 1977-80; rsch. scientist Battelle Columbus Labs., 1980-82; rsch. asst. Mgmt. and Behavioral Sci. Ctr., Wharton Sch., U. Pa., Phila., 1983-85; cons. UN Devel. Program, N.Y.C., 1985-86; bus. mgr. Pioneer Hi-Bred Internat., Des Moines, 1987-90; asst. prof. bus. adminstrn. U. Pacific, Stockton, Calif., 1990—. Contbr. articles on tech. in agr. to profl. jours. Dean's fellow Wharton Sch., U. Pa., 1983-84. Mem. AAAS. Office: U Pacific Sch Bus-Pub Admin 3601 Pacific Ave Stockton CA 95211

WAGNER, DONNA MAE, health service manager; b. New Prague, Minn., Dec. 15, 1939; d. Otto L. and Lucy G. (Nytes) Karcewski; m. Gervase J. Wagner, June 10, 1961; children: Gregory S., Thomas A., Barbara A. RN grad., St. Mary's Sch. Nursing, Mpls., 1960; BA in Human Svcs., Met. State U., St. Paul, 1978; M. in Nursing Adminstrn., Pacific Western U., 1979; MBA, Calif. U., 1988. Mgr. St. Johns Hosp., St. Paul, 1976-78; cons. Found. for Health Care Evaluation, Mpls., 1978-79; adminstr. Prospect Park Health Ctr., Mpls., 1979-80; cons. J.D.W. Assocs., Apple Valley, Minn., 1978-84; adminstr. Wilder Found., St. Paul, 1980-82, Upjohn Health Care Svcs., Mpls., 1983-84; nat. mgr. quality assurance Upjohn Health Care Svcs., Kalamazoo, Mich., 1984-89; mgr. Cen. Okla. Med./Prudential, Oklahoma City, 1989-90; mgr. med. svcs. Prudential Health Plans, Oklahoma City, 1990—; pres. bd. Upjohn Community Nursing Home, Kalamazoo, 1988-89; bd. dirs. Heritage of Kalamazoo, Nat. Accreditation Coun., N.Y.C.; mem. adv. coun. S. Cen. Commn. on Aging, Kalamazoo, 1984-89. Author: Managing for Quality in Home Health Care, Effective Business Strategies, 1988; co-author: Quality Assurance in Home Care, 1988; contbr. articles to profl. jours. Community adv. coun. Sch. Dist. 196, Apple Valley, 1980-84, adv. bd. Dakota County Human Svcs., Rosemount, Minn., 1980-84; scout leader Troop 230, Apple Valley, 1978-83. Mem. Nat. Assn. Quality Assurance Profls. (program com. 1988), Am. Soc. for Quality Control, Nat. Assn. for Home Care (com. mem. 1986-89), Am. Nurses Assn., Nat. League for Nursing, Mich. League for Nursing, Women in Bus., Women's Network (com. mem. 1985-87). Home: 2405 SW 117th St Oklahoma City OK 73170 Office: Prudential Health Plans 3330 NW 56th St Ste 500 Oklahoma City OK 73112

WAGNER, DOROTHY MARIE, court reporting service executive; b. Milw., June 8, 1924; d. Theodore Anthony and Leona Helen (Ullrich) Wagner; grad. Milw. Bus. U., 1944; student Marquette U., U. Wis., Milw. Stenographer, legal sec., Milw., 1942-44; hearing reporter Wis. Workmen's Compensation Dept., 1944-48; ofcl. reporter to judge Circuit Ct., Milw., 1952-53; owner, operator ct. reporting service Dorothy M. Wagner & Assocs., Milw., 1948—; guest lectr. ct. reporting Madison Area Tech. Coll., 1981—. Recipient Gregg Diamond medal Gregg Pub. Co., 1950. Mem. Nat. (registered profl. reporter, certificate of proficiency), Wis. shorthand reporters assns., Am. Legion Aux., Met. Milw. Assn. Commerce. Roman Catholic. Home: 214 Williamsburg Dr Thiensville WI 53092 Office: 135 Wells St Ste 400 Milwaukee WI 53203

WAGNER, ELIZABETH ANN, manufacturing and financial consultant; b. Crowder, Okla., Nov. 21, 1934; d. William Robert and Lillian Edna (Scott) Bristow; m. Richard Arthur Wagner, June 25, 1955 (div. Sept. 1961); children: Kathleen Elizabeth, Richard Arthur Jr. Student, UCLA, 1961, Compton City Coll., 1963, 65. Controller Artistic Brass div. Norris Industries, Los Angeles, 1967-72; controller Classic Brass div. FamilianCorp., Carson, Calif., 1973; internal auditor Van Nuys, Calif., 1974; controller Dyna div. Compton, Calif., 1975; v.p. fin. Electronic Applications Co., El Monte, Calif., 1977-84; fin. cons. El Monte, Calif., 1984—, also bd. dirs.; contr. Amcor Industires, 1989—; owner Western Gen. Services, Diamond Bar, Calif., 1980—; pres. Calif. Transformers, El Monte, 1982-84, U.S. Relays, El Monte, 1982-84; pres. Pacific Wing and Rotor, Long Beach, Calif., 1982-83. Active Downey (Calif.) Community Theater, 1961-65. Mem. Nat. Assn. Relay Mfrs., People for the Am. Way, Greenpeace. Republican. Club: Quota (treas. 1967) (Downey). Home: 259 N Rock River Dr Diamond Bar CA 91765

WAGNER, FLORENCE SIGNAIGO, botanist; b. Birmingham, Mich., Feb. 18, 1919; d. Frank Edmund and Frances Gertrude (Kerr) Signaigo; m. Warren Herbert Wagner, Jr., July 16, 1948; children: Warren Charles, Margaret Frances. AB, U. Mich., 1941, MA, 1943; PhD, U. Calif., Berkeley, 1952. Herbarium asst. U. Calif., Berkeley, 1946-49; asst. in rsch. botany U. Mich., Ann Arbor, 1961-68, rsrch. assoc. in botany, sr. rsch. assoc. in botany, 1968-76, assoc. rsch. scientist in biology, 1976—, adj. lectr. biology, 1986; Univ. Ctr. adult edn. lectr. Wayne State U., Ann Arbor, 1971-77. Contbr. articles to profl. jours. James Sutton fellow, 1949-50; Investigatora Asociada ad hom. en Citologia, Museo Nacional de Costa Rica, 1978. Mem. Am. Fern Soc. (pres. 1986-88), Bot. Soc. Am. (chmn. pteridological sect. 1982-84), Brit. Pteridological Soc., Internat. Assn. Pteridologists, Am. Soc. Plant Taxonomists, Internat. Assn. Plant Taxonomists, Mich. Bot. Club (pres. chpt. 1966-67), Womens Rsch. Club U. Mich. (pres. 1970-71), Phi Beta Kappa. Office: U Mich Dept Biology Ann Arbor MI 48109-1048

WAGNER, JUDITH BUCK, investment firm executive; b. Altoona, Pa. Sept. 25, 1943; d. Harry Bud and Mary Elizabeth (Rhodes) B.; m. Joseph E. Wagner, Mar. 15, 1980; 1 child, Elizabeth. BA in History, U. Wash., 1965; grad. N.Y. Inst. Fin., 1968. Chartered fin. analyst; registered Am. Stock Exchange; registered N.Y. Stock Exchange; registered investment advisor. Security analyst Morgan, Olmstead, Kennedy & Gardner, L.A., 1968-71; rsch. cons., St. Louis, 1971-72; security analyst Boettcher & Co., Denver, 1972-75; pres. Wagner Investment Counsel, 1975-84; chmn. Wagner & Hamil, Inc., Denver, 1983—; chmn., bd. dirs. The Women's Bank, N.A., Denver, 1977—, organizational group pres., 1975-77; chmn. Equitable Bankshares Colo., Inc., Denver, 1980—; bd. dirs. Equitable Bank of Littleton, 1983-88, pres., 1985; bd. dirs. Colo. Growth Capital, 1979-82; lectr. Denver U., Metro State, 1975-80. Author: Woman and Money series Colo. Woman Mag., 1976; moderator 'Catch 2' Sta. KWGN-TV, 1978-79. Pres. Big Sisters Colo., Denver, 1977-82, bd. dirs., 1973—; bd. fellows U. Denver, 1985—; trustee Graland Sch.; bd. dirs. Red Cross, 1980, Assn. Children's Hosp., 1985, Colo. Health Facilities Authority, 1978-84, Jr. League Community Adv. Com., 1979—, Brother's Redevel., Inc., 1979-80; mem. Hist. Paramount Found., 1984, Denver Pub. Sch. Career Edn. Project, 1972; mem. investment com. YWCA, 1976-88; mem. adv. com. Girl Scouts U.S.; mem. agy. rels. com. Mile High United Way, 1978-81, chmn. United Way Venture Grant com., 1980-81; fin. chmn. Schoettler for State Treas., 1986; bd. dirs. Downtown Denver Inc., 1988—; bd. dirs., v.p., treas. The Women's Found. Colo., 1987—. Recipient Making It award Cosmopolitan Mag., 1977, Women on the Go award, Savvy mag., 1983, Minouri Yasoni award, 1986, Salute Spl. Honoree award, Big Sisters, 1987; named one of the Outstanding Young Women in Am., 1979; recipient Woman Who Makes A Difference award Internat. Women's Forum, 1987. Fellow Fin. Analysts Fedn.; mem. Women's Forum of Colo. (pres. 1979), Women's Found. Colo., Inc. (bd. dirs. 1986—), Denver Soc. Security Analysts (bd. dirs. 1976-83, v.p. 1980-81, pres. 1981-82), Rotary (treas. Denver chpt. found.), Leadership Denver (Outstanding Alumna award 1987), Pi Beta Phi (pres. U. Wash. chpt. 1964-65). Office: Wagner & Hamil Inc 410 17th St #840 Denver CO 80202

WAGNER, KAREN SHEILA, education educator; b. Bklyn., Dec. 6, 1946; d. Norman and Miriam (Miller) Fleischman; m. Michael Drew Wagner, July 24, 1971; children: Lesley Susan, Aaron Jordan. BSEd., Adelphi U., Garden City, N.Y., 1968; MEd., Georgia State U., Atlanta, 1970. Lic. Supervisor, N.Y., N.J. Tchr. Dekalb County Bd. Ed., Atlanta, 1968-70, Moorestown Bd. Ed., N.J., 1970-80, 1986-; pre-school cons. Jewish Community Ctr., Cherry Hill N.J., 1983-85; girl scout trainer Camden County, Cherry Hill N.J., 1985-87; pres. M'Kor Shalom Congregation PTA, Mt. Laurel N.J. 1988-. Bd. Mgrs. Jewish Community Ctr., Cherry Hill N.J. 1987; Bd. Trustees Congregation M'Kor Shalom,Mt. Laurel N.J. 1987; Chmn. Masada Division Allied Jewish Appeal, Cherry Hill N.J. 1987; Bd. Dirs. Golden Cradle, Cherry Hill N.J. 1989. Recipient Service award Congregation M'Kor Shalom 1987, Leadership award Jewish Fed. S. Jersey 1988, Mission to Israel award Jewish Fed. 1989; Named Vol. Yr. Jewish Community Ctr. 1988. Mem. Moorestown Edn. Assn., Burlington County Tchrs. Assn., N.J. Edn. Assn., Nat. Edn. Assn., Women's Am. Art. Democrat. Home: 24 Lake View Hollow Cherry Hill NJ 08003 Office: William Allen 3d Mid Sch Stanwick Rd Moorestown NJ 08057

WAGNER, KATHLEEN ANN, systems manager; b. Geneva, N.Y., Aug. 8, 1947; d. Lawrence R. and Margaret E. (Skinner) Goodman; m. Robert W. Wagner, Aug. 22, 1970 (div. Dec. 1981). BA, SUNY, Albany, 1969. Region billing coord. Xerox Corp., White Plains, N.Y., 1973-76; customer adminstr. Xerox Corp., Tarrytown, N.Y., 1976-80, customer svc. mgr., 1980-82, credit mgr., 1982-84; mgr. invoicing systems quality assurance Xerox Corp., Rochester, N.Y., 1984-89; mgr. application maintenance equipment billing Xerox Corp., Henrietta, N.Y., 1990—. Office: Xerox Corp 1350 Jefferson Rd Henrietta NY 14623-3106

WAGNER, KAYE MARIE, flutist, flute educator; b. Beaver Dam, Wis., Oct. 10, 1951; d. Frederick William and Ardella Ann (Sawyer) Kronenberg; m. David Jay Wagner, June 21, 1975. B of Mus. Edn., U. Wis., Stevens Point, 1973; MS in Continuing and Vocat. Edn., U. Wis., Madison, 1981. Prin. 2nd flute Cen. Wis. Symphony, Stevens Point, 1978-87; flute instr. Wausau (Wis.) Conservatory Music, 1981-87; flutist Fauxbordon Chamber Ensemble, Wausau, 1986-87; ind. flute instr. Colorado Springs, Colo., 1987—; prin. flutist Chamber Orch. of the Springs, Colorado Springs, 1988—; flutist Panache Chamber Ensemble, Colorado Springs, 1989—; adj. music instr. Univ. Wis.-Marathon County, Wausau, 1979-87, guest lectr., 1984; rsch. cons. North Cen. Tech. Inst., Wausau, 1983-87; panelist Wis. Music Educators Conf., Madison, 1982; dir. feasibility and curriculum devel. studies for founding Wausau Conservatory Music, mem. founding bd., 1981-82. Ward Brodt music scholar, U. Wis., Stevens Point, 1971, Susan Coleman Music award, 1973, concerto competition winner, 1973. Mem. Nat. Flute Assn., Internat. Suzuki Assn., Suzuki Assn. of the Ams., Am. Music Soc., Am. Fedn. Musicians.

WAGNER, LESLIE, lawyer; b. Houston, July 18, 1953; d. Jacob and Geraldine (Harris) W.; m. Stuart A. Kovar. BA cum laude, U. Tex., 1975; JD, U. Houston, 1980. Bar: Tex. 1980, U.S. Dist. Ct. (so. dist.) Tex. 1981. Trial atty. civil rights EEOC, Houston, 1981-84; pvt. practice Houston, 1984-85, 87-88; dir. law placement U. Houston Law Ctr., 1985-87; employee rels. atty., asst. mgr. The Meth. Hosp. System, Houston, 1988—; cons. EEOC, Houston, 1984—. Editor: U. Houston Law Rev., 1979, assoc. editor, 1980. Mem. health and edn. com. Jewish Community Ctr., Houston, 1983-85; polit. cons., Houston, 1984-85. Named Honors Day Honoree U. Tex., 1971; Arts and Sciences scholar U. Tex., 1971-74. Mem. ABA (com. employee and labor rels. 1983-85, employment rights com. gen. practice sect. 1986), Houston Bar Assn., Assn. Trial Lawyers Am., Tex. Young Lawyers Assn. (job fair com.), Tex. Hosp. Assn., Houston Personnel Assn., Nat. Assn. Law Placement (careers com. 1986-87, minority placement com. 1987), Am. Studies Assn., Houston Festival Dancers (treas. 1976-77), Eta Phi Sigma. Democrat. Home: 5407 Wigton Dr Houston TX 77096 Office: Meth Hosp Tex Med Ctr 2718 Magnolia Ct Stafford TX 77477

WAGNER, LOUISE HEMINGWAY BENTON, educational company executive; b. Chgo., July 29, 1937; d. William and Helen (Hemingway) Benton; student Skidmore Coll., 1955-57; B.A. in English, Finch Coll., 1960; m. Ralph C. Wagner, May 23, 1979. Pub. relations asst. Look mag., N.Y.C., 1960-62, Compton Ency., Chgo., 1962-63; mktg. services Ency. Brit. Press, Chgo., 1963-66; dir. exhibits Ency. Brit. Ednl. Corp., Chgo., 1966-70, v.p. mktg. services, 1970-83, chmn. bd. dirs., 1983-87, vice chmn. 1988—. Bd. dirs. Chgo. Lying-In Hosp., Cradle Soc., Evanston, Ill., Reading is Fundamental, Chgo.; mem. women's bd. U. Chgo.; governing mem. Orchestral Assn. Chgo., Art Inst. Chgo. Mem. Assn. for Edn. Communication Tech.; trustee Plimoth Plantation, Plymouth, Mass. Episcopalian. Clubs: Racquet, Mid-Am., Arts; Country of Fairfield (Conn.); Thorngate Country (Deerfield, Ill.); Paradise Valley Country (Paradise Valley, Ariz.). Office: Ency Brit Ednl Corp 310 S Michigan Ave Chicago IL 60604

WAGNER, MARY ANTHONY, student advisor; b. Miesvillle, Minn., Dec. 5, 1916; d. Anton M. and Marie (Wagner) W. BA, St. Louis U., 1945; MA, Cath. U. Am., 1948; PhD, St. Mary's Notre Dame, 1957. Joined Benedictine Sisters, Roman Cath. Ch., 1936. Elem. sch. tchr. various schs., Buckman, Minn., 1936-39, Famington, Minn., 1939-43; tchr. St. Benedict's High Sch., St. Joseph, Minn., 1945-48, high sch. prin., 1950-54; tchr. Coll. of St. Benedict, St. Joseph, 1948-1986; prof. emerita Coll. St. Benedict, St. Joseph, 1986—; dean grad. sch. and asst. dean St. John's U., Collegeville, Minn., 1957-78; editor The Liturgical Press, Sisters Today, Collegeville, 1979—; retreat dir. Religious women and priests in midwest; lecturer at various parishes for men, women, and youth groups, 1960—. Contbr. articles to profl. jours. Fellow Danforth Found. Democrat. Home: St Benedicts Convent Saint Joseph MN 56374 Office: College of St Benedict 37 S College Ave Saint Joseph MN 56374

WAGNER, MARY INNES, metal products company executive; b. Batavia, N.Y., Mar. 23, 1947; d. John Frederick and Madonna Beatrice (Lapp) Innes; m. Gary Frederick Wagner, Aug. 21, 1982. AAS in Bus. Adminstrn., Monroe Community Coll., Rochester, N.Y., 1984. Cert. profl. sec., credit adminstrn. Factory worker Allen Bailey Tag Co., Caledonia, N.Y., 1966-68; clk. Electro-Networks, Inc., Caledonia, 1968-70; sec. U. Rochester, N.Y., 1970-81; office mgr. Rabco Precision Products, Inc., Rochester, 1981-85; office mgr. J. Kozel & Son, Inc., Rochester, 1985-88, officer, 1988—. Friends coun. WXXI Pub. Broadcasting Station, Rochester, 1989-90, steering com. fund raiser, 1987—. Mem. Nat. Assn. Women in Constrn. (bd. dirs., chmn. scholarship award com. 1989—, treas. 1990), Profl. Secs. Internat. (publicity chmn. 1988—, past treas., exec. bd. mem. 1984-88), Soc. Mfg. Engrs. (exec. bd. 1983-85, 1st woman elected to bd. Rochester chpt.), TNT Toastmasters (pres. 1990—, membership chmn., asst. area gov. 1990—). Home: 160 Oakland St Rochester NY 14620

WAGNER, MARY KATHRYN, state legislator; b. Madison, S.D., June 19, 1932; d. Irving Macaulay and Mary Browning (Wines) Mumford; m. Robert Todd Wagner, June 23, 1954; children: Christopher John, Andrea Browning. BA, U. S.D., 1954; MEd, S.D. State U., 1974, PhD, 1978. Sec. R.A. Burleigh & Assocs., Evanston, Ill., 1954-57; dir. resource ctr. Watertown (S.D.) Sr. High Sch., 1969-71, Brookings (S.D.) High Sch., 1971-74; asst. dir. S.D. Com. on the Humanities, Brookings, 1976-90; asst. prof. rural sociology S.D. State U., 1990—; mem. S.D. Ho. of Reps., 1981-88, S.D. Senate, 1988—. Mem., pres. Brookings Sch. Bd., 1975-81; chairwoman fund dr. Brookings United Way, 1985; bd. dirs. Brookings Chamber Music Soc., 1981—. Named Woman of Yr., Bus. and Profl. Women, 1981, Legislator Conservationist of Yr., Nat. and S.D. Wildlife Fedn., 1988. Mem. Population Assn. Am., Midwest Sociol. Soc., Rural Sociol. Soc., Brookings C. of C. (mem. indsl. devel. com. 1988—), PEO, Rotary. Republican. Episcopalian. Home: 929 Harvey Dunn St Brookings SD 57006

WAGNER, NANCY ESTHER, product manager; b. Quantico, Va., Oct. 29, 1947; d. Herbert Pratt and Betty Jean (McCord) Mosca; m. John C. Wagner. BS in Fashion Design, Carnegie Mellon U., 1969. Pub. rels. membership coord. Pelican Bay County Club, Daytona Beach, Fla., 1984-85; community rels. coord. Adolescent Mental Health Unit Humana Hosp., Daytona Beach, 1985; exec. dir. Resort & Comml. Recreation Assn., Ormond Beach, Fla., 1985-88; edn. coord. Fla. Assn. Realtors, Orlando, 1988-90; product mgr. anesthesiology Customized Communications, Inc., Vero Beach, Fla., 1990—; cons. Orlando Internat. Aquatic Ctr., 1987—. Mem. Jr. League Daytona Beach, 1983--. Mem. Am. Soc. Assn. Exec. Republican. Home: 1550 56th Ct Vero Beach FL 32966 Office: Customized Communications Inc PO Box 3506 Vero Beach FL 32964

WAGNER, NANCY LYNN, ship pilot; b. Englewood, N.J., Mar. 3, 1955; d. Jules A. and Florence I. (Froeba) W. Student, Syracuse U., 1973-74, Ramapo Coll., 1974; BS, U.S. Merchant Marine Acad., 1978. Unltd. Master Lic., 1985. Ship officer Exxon Shipping Co., Houston, 1978-87; ship pilot San Francisco (Calif.) Bar Pilot, 1987—. Officer USNR, 1978—, lt. comdr., 1988—. First woman grad. of U.S. Marine Merchant Acad. to obtain Unltd. Master Lic., 1985; first woman ship pilot in U.S., 1990. Office: San Francisco Bar Pilots Pier 9 San Francisco CA 94111

WAGNER, PATRICIA A., medical nurse; b. Wilmington, Del., Apr. 25, 1947; d. Welden Earl and Dorothy Farrar (Coverdale) Curl; m. Charles G. Wagner; children: R. Tate Keene Garey II, Elizabeth J., Geoffrey C. BSN, Wesley Coll., 1987. RN, Del., Md.; cert. CPR instr. and diabetes educator. Nurse, cons., diabetes educator Milton (Del.) Med. Assocs., The Diabetes Connection; charge nurse CICU Nanticoke Meml. Hosp., Seaford, Del.; mem. faculty Del. Tech. and Community Coll., Georgetown; mem. med. staff Milford (Del.) Meml. Hosp.; co-owner med. practice; guest lectr. OMP program Eli Lilly Co. Mem. diabetes adv. coun. State of Del. Health Care Commn. Mem. ANA, Del. Nurses Assn. (legis. com.), Am. Diabetes Assn. (pres. bd. Del. chpt., past pres. and founder Sussex chpt., lectr. adminstr. profl. edn. workshops of nat. CEP faculty), Am. Assn. Diabetes Educators.

WAGNER, SARA BAILEY, educator, consultant; b. Connellsville, Pa., May 20, 1921; d. William Orel and Bertha (Hooper) Bailey; m. William Vernon Wagner, Jr., Mar. 24, 1945; children—Mary Louise, William Vernon, III. B.A., Pa. State U., 1942; M.A., Mich. State U., 1967; Ed.D., Wayne State U., 1972. Dir. research Nat. Council on Aging, Washington, 1972-75; sr. assoc. JWK Internat. Corp., Annandale, Va., 1975-78, v.p., 1978-86, ret. 1986; cons. 1986—; adj. prof. Wayne State U., Detroit, 1967-72, Marygrove Coll., Detroit, 1972—, George Mason U., Fairfax, Va., 1972-74. Contbr. reports to profl. publs. Mem. Am. Psychol. Assn., Nat. Council Measurement in Edn., Am. Assn. Univ. Women. Republican. Presbyterian. Avocations: photography, travel, growing roses.

WAGNER, SUE ELLEN, state official; b. Portland, Maine, Jan. 6, 1940; d. Raymond A. and Kathryn (Hooper) Pooler; m. Peter B. Wagner, 1964 (dec.); children: Kirk, Kristina. B.A. in Polit. Sci., U. Ariz., 1962; M.A. in History, Northwestern U., 1964. Asst. dean women Ohio State U., 1963-64; tchr. history and Am. govt. Catalina High Sch., Tucson, 1964-65; reporter Tucson Daily Citizen, 1965-68; mem. Nev. Assembly, 1975-83; mem. Nev. Senate from 3d dist.; elected lt. gov. of Nev., 1990. Author: Diary of a Candidate, On People and Things, 1974. Mem. Reno Mayor's Adv. Com., 1973-84; chmn. Blue Ribbon Task Force on Housing, 1974-75; mem. Washoe County Republican Central Com., 1974-84, Nev. State Rep. Central Com., 1975-84; mem. Nev. Legis. Commn., 1976-77; del. social service com. Council State Govts.; v.p. Am. Field Service, 1973, family liaison, 1974, mem.-at-large, 1975. Kappa Alpha Theta Nat. Grad. scholar, also Phelps-Dodge postgrad. fellow, 1962; named Outstanding Legislator, Nev. Young Republicans, 1976. Mem. AAUW (legis. chmn. 1974), Bus. and Profl. Women, Kappa Alpha Theta. Episcopalian. Home: 845 Tamarack Dr Reno NV 89509*

WAGNER, SUSAN JANE, communications executive; b. Englewood, N.J., Aug. 11; d. Jules A. and Florence I. (Froeba) W.; m. Mark E. McKenna, May 4, 1984. MusB with honors, Syracuse U., 1974; MPA with honors, Fairleigh Dickinson U., 1983. Dir. music, theater dependant sch. U.S. Dept. Def., Fed. Republic Germany, 1976-82; grad. asst. Fairleigh Dickinson U., Rutherford, N.J., 1982-83; account exec. Katz Radio/Katz Communications, Inc., N.Y.C., 1983-85; account mgr. network Katz Radio Group, N.Y.C., 1985-87, v.p., dir. mktg., 1987—. Mem. Am. Women in Radio and Television, Electronic Media Mktg. Assn., Am. Mktg. Assn., Gamma Phi Beta, Signa Alpha Iota. Office: Katz Radio/Communications Inc 1 Dag Hammarskjold Pla New York NY 10017-2289

WAGNER, SUZANNE ELIZABETH, property leasing manager; b. Macon, Ga., Apr. 16, 1958; d. Roy Sidney Wagner and Peggy Elizabeth (Champion) Young; m. Donald Ray Brown, Mar. 15, 1980 (div. July, 1981). AAS in Secondary Edn., Macon (Ga.) Jr. Coll., 1979; student, Mercer U., 1976, '81. Office mgr., adminstrv. asst. Voyager Group, Inc., Macon, Ga., 1980-83; sales asst. Interstate Securities Corp., Macon, 1983-84; dir. of premium acctg. and policy svc. Hermitage Health & Life Insur., Franklin, Tenn., 1984-87; bus. mgr. Cornel, Inc., Athens, Gainesville, Ga., 1987—. Chmn. publicity Singles Ministry, First Bapt. Ch., Gainesville, Ga., 1989; bd. dirs. Jr. Achievement of Gainesville/Hall County. Mem. NAFE, Am. Bus. Women's Assn., Gainesville C. of C. Democrat. Home: 1858 Thompson Bridge Rd #402 Gainesville GA 30501 Office: Spring Valley 1858 Thompson Bridge Rd Gainesville GA 30501

WAGNER, TERRI LEE, interior decorating company executive; b. Albuquerque, Mar. 8, 1953; d. William Herman and Patricia Warfield (Short) Shawley; m. Gaylord Edgar Wagner, Dec. 8, 1979. BA in Sociology, Colo. State U., 1975. Asst. buyer Neiman-Marcus, Dallas, 1976-77; coll. mktg. rep. McGraw-Hill Inc., Dallas, 1977-80; gift rep., Dallas, 1981-83; account rep. Waterford Crystal, Denver, 1983-84; account coord. Lancôme Cosmetics, San Francisco, 1985; regional tng. mgr. Lancôme Cosmetics, Foster City, Calif., 1986-87; dist. mgr. Decorating Den, Foster City, 1988-90, regional exec., 1990—; cons. Bay Area Playworks, San Mateo, Calif., 1988—. Fundraiser capt. Am. Cancer Soc., Foster City, 1987-90; spl. event coord., treas. Foster City Newcomers, 1988; mem. Pacific Light Opera Co. Mem. AAUW, Foster City C. of C., Leads Club (treas. 1989). Republican. Home and Office: Decorating Den 22 Dory Ln Foster City CA 94404

WAGNER DAHL, MARGARET GILMAN, director technology transfer licensing program; b. Evanston, Ill., Sept. 24, 1956; d. Mathrias John and Esther Eleanor (Buchen) Wagner; m. Eric Carl Dahl, Dec. 19, 1987. BA with honors, St. Patrick's Coll., Maynooth County, Kildare, Ireland, 1978. Sr. sales rep. Noctech Ltd., 1980-82; sales rep. Video Electronics, Dublin, Ireland, 1979-80; export sales and mktg. mgr. Tru-Life Ltd., Dublin and London, 1982-84; area mgr. Pharmacia (U.K.) Ltd./Noctech, Dublin, 1984-86; area sales supr. Orgawon Teknika, Seattle, 1986-87; mgr. tech. transfer div. U. Wash., Seattle, 1987-88, asst. dir., 1988-89, dir. licensing, 1989—. Support person Shanti Found., L.A., 1987. Mem. Wash. State Biotech. Assn. (co-chair 1989—), Assn. Univ. Tech. Mgrs., N.W. Biotech. Breakfast Com. (bd. dirs. 1989—). Democrat. Office: U Wash Tech Transfer 4225 Roosevelt Way NE Seattle WA 98105

WAGNER-MARMALUK, DIANA, English educator; b. Neenah, Wis., Oct. 2, 1965; d. Gerald Anthony and Elaine Mary (Safford) Wagner; m. Gregory Joseph Marmaluk, July 9, 1988. Student, Mount Senario, Ladysmith, Wis., 1984-86; BA, Alverno Coll., 1988. Copywriter Alverno Coll., Milw., 1987, resource asst., 1987-88; writer, editor Jobs with Peace, Milw., 1988; technician Pitman Theatre, Milw., 1986-88; drama dir. Lower Moreland Sch. Dist., Huntingdon Valley, Pa., 1988; editorial asst. Temple U. Press, Phila., 1989; tchr. English Archdiocese of Phila., 1989—. Liason Circle K. Internat., Milw., 1986-87; project tutor Project Lit. U.S., Milw., 1987; mem. Alverno Coll. Peace Network, Milw., 1987-88. Mem. AAUW, Internat. Fedn. Univ. Women, Alverno Coll. Nat. Alumnae Assn. Eastern Orthodox. Home: 703 Sterner Mill Rd Feasterville PA 19053

WAGNER-WESTBROOK, BONNIE JOAN, utilities company administrator, consultant; b. Watertown, N.Y., July 18, 1953; d. Elmer Ethan and Joan Eleanor (Niedermeier) Wagner; m. John Drewry Westbrook Jr., Aug. 21, 1982. BS, SUNY, Geneseo, 1975, MS, 1981; EdD, Rutgers U., 1989. Tchr. elem. Rochester (N.Y.) Sch. for the Deaf, 1975-80; instr. adult basic edn. Rochester City Sch. Dist., 1981-82; profl. interpreter Nat. Tech. Inst. for the Deaf, Rochester, 1981-83; instr., interpreter Henrietta (N.Y.) Cen. Sch. Dist., 1983-84; intern Middlesex County Vocat. Tech. Schs., New Brunswick, N.J., 1985; cons. on urban initiative for N.J. Dept. Edn., Rutgers U., New Brunswick, N.J., 1985-86; program specialist Rutgers U., New Brunswick, N.J., 1987-88, rsch. assoc. for N.J. Commn. on Employment and Tng., 1988-89; adminstr. Pub. Svc. Electric and Gas Co., Newark, 1990—; also senator Grad. Sch. Edn. Rutgers U., New Brunswick, N.J., 1985-87; cons. Rutgers U., 1985—, Pub. Svc. Electric & Gas Co., Newark, 1986-89. Vol. Rochester Sch. for the Deaf, 1977; mem. Rochester Oratorio Soc., 1978-81. Rutgers U. scholar, 1986; Rutgers U. fellow, 1987. Mem. Am. Ednl. Rsch. Assn., Am. Vocat. Assn., Am. Mgmt. Assn., Am. Soc. for Tng. and Devel., Nat. Registry Interpreters for Deaf, Rochester Amateur Radio Assn., Omicron Tau Theta. Republican. Home: 327 Becker St Highland Park NJ 08904 Office: Pub Svc Electric and Gas Co 80 Park Pla T-12A Newark NJ 07101

WAGSTAFF, JOAN KAY, marketing, sales, education executive; b. Shawnee, Okla., Nov. 14, 1951; d. Prentice Alton Wagstaff and Lorain (Cole) Markwell; m. James J. Smith, June 20, 1980; children: Jessica, Zachary, Veronica. BA Math., Physical Edn., William Jewell Coll., 1973; MEd., U. Okla., 1974. Systems cons. Southwestern Bell, Oklahoma City, 1974-76, account exec., 1976-79, tech. cons., 1979-80; systems mgr. Southwestern Bell - AT&T, Oklahoma City, 1980-84; dist. mgr. tech. edn. AT&T, South Plainfield, N.J., 1984-86, dist. mgr. sales devel. and edn., 1986-88; data br. mgr. AT&T, Dallas, 1988—; mktg. cons. Lorain's Tot's to Teens, Shawnee, 1979-81. Author: Systems Manager Skills, 1984. Mem. Adoptive Parents Com., L.I., N.Y., 1984—. Mem. NAFE, Am. Hosp. Assn., Symposium Healthcare Mktg., Zeta Tau Alpha. Republican. Presbyterian. Office: AT&T 5501 LBJ Frwy Dallas TX 75240

WAGSTAFF, SUZANNE, mortgage company executive; b. Galopolis, Ohio, May 24, 1941; d. Rex F. and Sue H. (Launius) Lineberry; m. Donald Wagstaff, June 21, 1981; children: Todd A., Kelly L. BA, U. Tex., Dallas, 1989. Mgr. mtg. loan svc. Allianz Investment Corp., Dallas; v.p. Tex. State Mtgs., Dallas. Mem. NAFE, Am. Bus. Women's Assn., Dallas Area Credit Mgrs., Downtown Network Career Women.

WAHL, JOAN CONSTANCE, technical writer, editor; b. Phila., Dec. 23, 1921; d. Frank L. and Sara E. (Timoney) O'Brien; B.A., Rosemont Coll., 1943; postgrad. U. Calif., Los Angeles, 1960-61; m. John Carl Wahl, Jr., Dec. 31, 1943 (div. 1959); children—John, Mark, David, Lawrence, Thomas, Jeanne, Madeleine Sophie, Eugene. Substitute tchr. Los Angeles City Bd. Edn., 1961; editor, proofreader Renner/Cal-Data Corp., Los Angeles, 1962-63; editor, tech. writer Volt Tech. Corp., 1964-66; sr. tech. editor, writer, project editor Aerospace Corp., El Segundo, Calif., 1966—. Sect. chmn. United Way, Los Angeles, 1963-64; mem. communications com. St. Paul the Apostle, Westwood, Calif., 1976-78. Recipient Outstanding Service award United Way, 1964. Mem. Soc. Tech. Communications (sr.), Aerospace Women's Com., Mental Health Assn. Los Angeles County, Kistler Honor Soc. Contbr. articles to profl. jours. Office: Aerospace Corp M3/377 2350 El Segundo Blvd El Segundo CA 90245

WAHL, JOAN LYDIA, magazine editor; b. N.Y.C., Oct. 18, 1935; d. Michael and Faye (Blaustein) W.; m. Sy M. Boorstein, Nov. 15, 1955; children: Lynne, Deborah, Holly. BA in Theatre Arts, U. Miami (Fla.), 1954, elem. sch. cert., 1961, secondary sch. cert., 1956. Tchr. Auburndale Elem. Sch., Miami, 1962-64; tchr. Conway Elem. Sch., Orlando, Fla., 1964-65, Park Ave. Elem. Sch., Winter Park, Fla., 1965-66, Mollie Ray Elem. Sch., Orlando, 1966-67, Lakemont Elem. Sch., Winter Park, 1967-68, Aloma Elem. Sch., Winter Park, 1968-75; author, writer Sunshine Artists Mag., Winter Park, 1971-75, editor, 1975-78; exec. editor Sunshine Artists Mag., Longwood, Fla., 1978—. Pres. Women's Artist Group, Longwood, 1989—, Writers/Playwrights Cen. Fla., Winter Park, 1978-84; exec. dir. Children's Theatre on Tour, Ltd., Winter Park, 1984-85; founder, pres. Cen. Fla. Puppet Guild, Longwood, 1987-89, Joan Wahl's Puppet Theatre Co., Longwood, 1984-89. Mem. Fla. Motion Picture/TV Assn., Puppeteers of Am., So. Theatre Conf., Fla. Theatre Conf., Fla. Mag. Assn. Office: Sunshine Artists USA 1700 Sunset Dr Longwood FL 32750-9697

WAHL, MARTHA STOESSEL, mathematics educator; b. Ottumwa, Iowa, Mar. 9, 1916; d. Theodore A. and Anna Theresa (Coday) Stoessel; m. John Schempp Wahl, Dec. 27, 1943 (dec. Aug. 1982); children: Elizabeth A. O'Connor, Rick, Patrick Theodore. Aa, Ottumwa Heights Coll., 1936, diploma; BA, U. Iowa, 1938; AM, Columbia U., 1942; diploma. Asst. prof. maths. Western Conn. State Coll., Danbury, 1959-78, assoc. prof. maths., 1978-85, prof. maths., 1985-86, ret., 1986; lectr., instr. NSF, Winona, Minn., summer 1963; lectr. discovery series Western Conn. State U., 1988.90. Author: I Can Count the Petals of a Flower, 1976, 2d edit., 1985 (Edn. Pres. award Picture Story 1977); contbr. articles to profl. jours. Participant meetings City of Ridgefield, Conn., 1955—; grantor John and Stacey Wahl scholar, 1982—; participant elder hostels U. Iowa, 1980—. Mem. Nat. Coun. Tchrs. Maths. (life), AAUW (life), AAUP, DAR, Phi Delta Kappa (exec. bd., Excellence in Teaching award 1985), Delta Kappa Gamma. Demcorat. Roman Catholic. Home: 1 Huckleberry Ln Ridgefield CT 06877

WAHL, ROSALIE E., state supreme court associate justice; b. Gordon, Kans., Aug. 27, 1924; children: Christopher Roswell, Sara Emilie, Timothy Eldon, Mark Patterson, Jenny Caroline. B.A., U. Kans., 1946; J.D., William Mitchell Coll. Law, 1967. Bar: Minn. 1967. Asst. state pub. defender Mpls., 1967-73; clin. prof. law William Mitchell Coll. Law, 1973-77; assoc. justice Minn. Supreme Ct., St. Paul, 1977—. Fellow Am. Bar Found; mem. ABA (legal edn. and bar admissions, sect. jud. adminstrn., criminal justice sect., individual rights and responsibility sect.), Minn. State Bar Assn. (com. legal assistance to disadvantaged), Am. Judicature Soc., Nat. Assn. Women Judges, Minn. Women Lawyers Assn., Am. Law Inst. Office: Minn Jud Ctr 25 Constitution Ave Saint Paul MN 55155

WAILAND, ADELE ROSEN, lawyer; b. N.Y.C., Feb. 16, 1949; d. Jack A. and Eleanor (Salomon) Rosen; m. George Wailand, Aug. 20, 1972; children: J. Zachary, William J. BA magna cum laude, Harvard U., 1970; JD cum laude, NYU, 1973. Bar: N.Y. 1973, U.S. Dist. Ct. (so. dist.) N.Y. 1974, U.S. Ct. Appeals (2d cir.) 1974. Assoc. Paul, Weiss, Rifkind, Wharton & Garrison, N.Y.C., 1973-74, 75-80; law sec. N.Y. Supreme Ct., N.Y.C., 1974-75; assoc. gen. counsel Colt Industries, Inc., N.Y.C., 1980-86; v.p., gen. counsel Case, Pomeroy & Co., Inc., N.Y.C., 1987—; bd. dirs. Essex Offshore, Inc., Houston; trustee Mt. Lebanon Shaker Village Mus., New Lebanon, N.Y., 1987—. Mem. ABA, Assn. of Bar of City of N.Y. Home: 1050 Park Ave New York NY 10128

WAINESS, MARCIA WATSON, legal administrator; b. Bklyn., Dec. 17, 1949; d. Stanley and Seena (Klein) Watson; m. Steven Richard Wainess, Aug. 7, 1975. Student, UCLA, 1967-71, 80-81, Grad. Sch. Mgmt. Exec. Program, 1987-88, grad. Grad. Sch. Mgmt. Exec. Program, 1988. Office mgr., paralegal Lewis, Marenstein & Kadar, L.A., 1977-81; office mgr. Rosenfeld, Meyer & Susman, Beverly Hills, Calif., 1981-83; adminstr. Rudin, Richman & Appel, Beverly Hills, 1983; dir. adminstrn. Kadison, Pfaelzer, L.A., 1983-87; exec. dir. Richards, Watson and Gershon, L.A., 1987—; faculty mem. UCLA Legal Mgmt. & Adminstrn. Program, 1983, U. So. Calif. Paralegal Program, L.A., 1985; mem. adv. bd. atty. asst. tng. program, UCLA, 1984-88. Mem. ABA (chmn. Displaywrite Users Group 1986, legal tech. adv. coun. litigation support working group 1986-87), State Bar Calif., L.A. County Bar Assn. (exec. com. law office mgmt. sect.), Assn. Profl. Law Firm Mgrs., Assn. Legal Adminstrs. (bd. dirs. 1990—), asst. regional v.p. Calif. 1987-88, regional v.p. 1988-89, pres. Beverly Hills chpt. 1985-86, membership chmn. 1984-85, chmn. new adminstrn. sect. 1982-84, mktg. mgmt. sect. com. 1989-90, internat. conf. com.), Internat. Platform Assn., Internat. Bd. Dirs. (dir. edn. 1990-92). Office: Richards Watson & Gershon 333 S Hope St 38th Fl Los Angeles CA 90071

WAINWRIGHT, CAROL ANN, healthcare consultant; b. Altadena, Calif., June 19, 1948; d. Bartholomew Nicholas and Dorothy Nell (Davis) Locanthi; m. Robin Wayne Wainwright, Aug. 30, 1969; children: Luke John (dec.), Mark Catlin, Karissa Rose. BA in Human Rels., Westmont Coll., Santa Barbara, Calif., 1970; MHA, Govs. State U., University Park, Ill., 1989. Adminstrv. asst. Williams & Lane, Inc., Berkeley, Calif., 1973-76, DeAvila, Duncan & Assocs., San Rafael, Calif., 1978-80; adminstrv. sec. Unity Med. Ctr., Fridley, Minn., 1981-85; exec. asst. Jubilee Found., Chgo., 1987-88; healthcare cons., Oak Forest, Ill., 1990—. Vol., camp cook Sea and Summit Expdns., Santa Barbara, 1969-71. Mem. Am. Coll. Healthcare Execs. (nominee), Women Health Execs. Network, Am. Hosp. Assn. Democrat.

WAINWRIGHT, HILDA ALEXANDER, small business owner; b. Teheran, Iran, June 18; came to U.S., 1946; naturalized 1947; d. Mamikon and Balasan (Carapetyan) Ohanian; m. Boris Alexander, May 27, 1945 (dec. Aug. 1961); children: Ronald Boris, Douglas Haig; m. Richard A. Wainwright, Feb. 18, 1977. Student, Ecole Jean D'Arc, Teheran, 1945, Brown Bus. Sch., 1947, Gemological Inst. Am., 1963, Banford Acad. Styling, 1950. Design stylist Elizabeth Arden, N.Y.C., 1949-52; owner, pres. Randough, N.Y.C., 1960; sales rep. Roux Labs., Jacksonville, Fla., N.Y.C., 1968-71, Mackey Internat. Airline, Ft. Lauderdale, Fla., 1971-73; owner, pres. CIR-Q-TEL Inc., Kensington, Md., 1980-89, exec. v.p., pres. 1982-84, treas., 1984—; owner franchises Hairperformers Hair Salons; pres. H.A.W. Enterprises. Pres. Armenian Gen. Benevolant Union, N.Y.C. and Fla., 1945—. Mem. Washington Speakers Club, Black Tie Club, Chevy Chase Women's Club, Columbia Country Club, Old Crows. Avocations: tennis, gardening, painting in oil and acrylic, bridge, languages. Home: 3333 University Blvd W #212 Kensington MD 20895 Office: CQT Electronics Inc 6600 Virginia Manor Rd Beltsville MD 20705

WAITE, ELLEN JANE, library director; b. Oshkosh, Wis., Feb. 17, 1951; d. Earl Vincent and Margaret (Luft) W.; m. Thomas H. Dollar, Aug. 19, 1977 (div. July 1984). BA, U. Wis., Oshkosh, 1973; MLS, U. Wis., Milw., 1977. Head of cataloging Marquette U., Milw., 1977-82; head catalog librarian U. Ariz., Tucson, 1983-85; assoc. dir. libraries Loyola U., Chgo., 1985-86, acting dir. libraries 1986-87, dir. libraries, 1987—; cons. Loyola U., Chgo., 1984, Boston Coll., 1986, U. San Francisco, 1989. Contbg. author: Research Libraries and Their Implementation of AACR2, 1985; author: (with others) Women in LC's Terms: A Thesaurus of Subject Headings Related to Women, 1988. Mem. ALA. Office: Loyola U Cudahy Library 6525 N Sheridan Rd Chicago IL 60626-5385

WAITES, CANDY YAGHJIAN, state official; b. N.Y.C., Feb. 21, 1943; d. Edmund Kirken and Dorothy Joanne (Candy) Yaghjian; m. Robert Geddings Waites, Sept. 4, 1965; children—Jennifer Lisa, Robin Shelley. B.A., Wheaton Coll., Mass., 1965. Elected county councilwoman Richland County, S.C., 1976-88, elected S.C. Ho., 1988—; vice chmn. Adv. Commn. on Intergovtl. Relations, S.C., 1977-87; bd. dirs. Interagy. Council on Pub. Transp., S.C., 1977—, Central Midlands Regional Planning Council, Columbia, S.C., 1977-84; dir. S.C. Nat. Bank. Vice pres. bd. dirs. United Way of Midlands, 1977-89; trustee Columbia Mus. Art, 1982-88; bd. dirs. Rape Crisis Network, 1984-87; chmn. County Coun. Coalition; mem. C. of C. Leadership Forum, S.C. Fedn. of the Blind; mem. adv. bd. U. S.C. Hunanities and Social Scis. Coll., Family Shelter, Nurturing Ctr.; pres Trinity Housing Corp. Named Outstanding Young Career Woman, Columbia YWCA, 1980; Outstanding Young Woman of Yr., Columbia Jaycees, 1975; Pub. Citizen of Yr. Nat. Assn. Social Workers. Mem. S.C. Women in Govt. (vice chmn. 1984-86), S.C. Assn. Counties (bd. dirs. 1982-88 , Pres's award 1983), Network Female Execs., LWV (pres. 1973-76). Democrat. Episcopalian. Club: Univ. Assocs. (Columbia). Avocations: exercising; drawing; walking. Home: 818 Gregg St Columbia SC 29201 Office: SC Ho 310B Blatt Bldg Columbia SC 29211

WAJDOWICZ, ELIZABETH KING, nursing educator; b. Florala, Ala.; d. Clary Monroe and Bertha (Cales) King; m. George Thomas Wajdowicz; 1 child, Ellen Janice Sackman. BS in Nursing, Fla. State U.; MA, U. South Fla.; PhD, U. Tex. Chairperson, instr. nursing program St. Petersburg (Fla.) Jr. Coll.; head nurse, various staff nursing positions W.T Edwards Hosp., Tallahassee; prof. nursing St. Petersburg (Fla.) Jr. Coll. Contbr. articles to profl. jours. Adv. com. southern regional edn. bd. ARC; mem. Commn. on Future Nursing, Fla. Mem. Fla. Nurses Assn. (fla. dist. coord., chairperson coun. on rsch. 1989-90, various positions), Nat. League for Nursing, Fla. League for Nursing (various coms., adv. com.), Southern Coun. Collegiate Edn. in Nursing (adv. bd.), Fed. Project Computers in Nursing Edn., U. Tex. at Austin Alumnae Assn. (life), U. South Fla. Alumnae Assn., Gamma Phi Beta, Sigma Theta Tau, Phi Kappa Phi. Presbyterian. Office: St Petersburg Jr Coll Health Edn Ctr PO Box 13489 Saint Petersburg FL 33733

WAKE, MARVALEE HENDRICKS, zoology educator; b. Orange, Calif., July 31, 1939; d. Marvin Carlton and Velvalee (Borter) H.; m. David B. Wake, June 23, 1962; 1 child, Thomas A. BA, U. So. Calif., 1961, MS, 1964, PhD, 1968. Teaching asst./instr. U. Ill., Chgo., 1964-68, asst. prof., 1968-69; lectr. U. Calif., Berkeley, 1969-73, asst. prof., 1973-76, assoc. prof., 1976-80, prof. zoology, 1980-89, chmn. dept. zoology, 1985-89, chmn. dept. integrative biology, 1989—, assoc. dean Coll. Letters and Sci., 1975-78, prof. integrative biology, 1989—. Editor, co-author: Hyman's Comparative Vertebrate Anatomy, 1979; co-author: Biology, 1978; contbr. articles to profl. jours. NSF grantee, 1978—; Guggenheim fellow, 1988-89. Fellow AAAS, Calif. Acad. Scis.; mem. Am. Soc. Ichthyology and Herpetology (pres. 1984, bd. govs. 1979—), Internat. Union Biol. Scis. (U.S. Nat. Com. 1986-92). Home: 999 Middlefield Rd Berkeley CA 94708 Office: U Calif Dept Integrative Biology Berkeley CA 94720

WAKELEE, ADAH MAE, microbiologist; b. Conneaut, Ohio, Apr. 6, 1935; d. Walter Ivan and Arleen Louise (Beach) Terrill; B.S. in Med. Tech., Wittenberg U., 1960; m. Robert L. Wakelee, Jr., May 23, 1963; children—Kieth Robert, Kent Walter. Staff technologist, Mercy Hosp. Lab., Springfield, Ohio, 1959-63, Grant Hosp. Lab. Columbus, Ohio, 1963-64, J. Mark Handley, M.D., Santa Maria, Calif., 1965-69; microbiologist Rome (N.Y.) City Hosp. Lab., 1972-79; chief technologist MDS Health Systems Inc. (formerly Lorkim Labs.), Rome, 1980-85; asst. lab. supr. Slocum Dickson Med. Group, 1985—; cons. in microbiology Rose Hosp., Rome, Slocum-Dickson Med. Group, Utica, N.Y. Mem. Oneida County Profl. Adv. Council, 1977, 78; trustee Rome Acad. Scis., 1978—, pres., 1979-81; mem. Rome Mayor's Water Com., 1983-85; Cert., registered Am. Soc. Clin. Pathologists; lic. clin. med. technologist, Calif. Mem. Am. Soc. Clin. Pathology, Am. Soc. Microbiology, N.Y. State Assn. Public Health Labs., Northeastern Assn. for Clin. Microbiology and Infectious Disease, Mohawk Valley Engrs. Exec. Council (chmn. 1981-82, sec. 1983-84), AAUW (pres. Rome br. 1980-82). Republican. Congregationalist. Clubs: Order Eastern Star, Daus. of the Nile. Determined causes of illnesses, Rome, 1975, Holland Patent (N.Y.) area, 1976; co-author article in field for profl. jour. Home: 123 Glen Road S Rome NY 13440

WAKEMAN, MARY LALLEY, lawyer; b. West Palm Beach, Fla., Aug. 21, 1955; d. John Peter and Jane (Warwick) W. BA, Fla. Atlantic U., 1984; JD cum laude, Stetson U., 1986. Bar: Fla. 1987. Clk. to presiding justice Fla. Supreme Ct., Tallahassee, 1987-89; assoc. McConnaughhay, Roland, Maida, Cherr and McCranie, P.A., Tallahassee, 1989—. Recipient Am. Legion Memorial Scholarship, West Palm Beach, 1985; named Dana Scholar, Stetson U., 1985-86. Mem. ABA, Fla. Bar Assn., Fla. Assn. for Women Lawyers, Tallahassee Bar Assn., Phi Alpha Delta (historian 1986). Home: 1445 Mitchell Ave Tallahassee FL 32303-5840 Office: PO Drawer 229 Tallahassee FL 32302-0229

WAKIN, FRANCES BATTIPAGLIA, psychologist; b. N.Y.C.; d. Daniel E. and Florence R. (Mercadante) Battipaglia; children: Eric Thomas, Lawrence Christopher. BA, Barnard Coll.; MA, New Sch. for Social Rsch., N.Y.C.; PhD, NYU. Lic. psychologist, N.Y., Fla. Chief psychologist Glen Cove (N.Y.) Community Mental Health Ctr.; psychol. dir. Lee Meml. Hosp., Ft. Myers, Fla.; lectr. Edison Coll., Ft. Myers, U. So. Fla., Ft. Myers; pres. Waystations, Ft. Myers; pvt. practice Fla. Author: Way Stations to Self Awareness, 1984, How to Wake Yourself Up from Being Unconscious, 1988. Mem. Forum, Am. Psychol. Assn., Southeastern Psychol. Assn.

WALBRIDGE, HAYDEE, management company executive; b. Cali, Colombia, July 3, 1936; came to U.S., 1964; d. Miguel and Cecilia Lora Lizarralde; m. John C. Walbridge, June 17, 1961; children: James Arthur, Yvonne, Adrienne. Student, U. Valle, Cali, 1958, Fla. Atlantic U., 1982. Dir. membership Arvida Corp., Boca Baton, Fla., 1983-84; dist. records mgr., 1984—; cons. in field, Dallas. Mem. Assn. Info. and Image Mgmt., Co., Boca Baton, Fla., 1983—; exec. adminstrv. asst. Arvida Corp., Boca Baton, Fla.; contr.'s sec. Boca Baton Hotel and Club. Mem. NAFE, CAI.

WALD, FRANCINE JOY WEINTRAUB (MRS. BERNARD J. WALD), physicist; b. Bklyn., Jan. 13, 1938; d. Irving and Minnie (Reisig) Weintraub; student Bklyn. Coll., 1955-57; B.E.E., CCNY, 1960; M.S., Poly. Inst. Bklyn., 1962, Ph.D., 1969; m. Bernard J. Wald, Feb. 2, 1964; children—David Evan, Kevin Mitchell. Engr., Remington Rand Univac div. Sperry Rand Corp., Phila., 1960; instr. Poly. Inst. Bklyn., 1962-64, adj. research assoc., 1969-70; lectr. N.Y. Community Coll., Bklyn., 1969, 70; instr. sci. Friends Sem., N.Y.C., 1975-76, chmn. dept. sci., 1976—. NDEA fellow, 1962-64. Mem. Am. Phys. Soc., Am. Assn. Physics Tchrs., Assn. Tchrs. in Ind. Schs., N.Y. Acad. Scis., Nat. Sci. Tchrs. Assn., AAAS, Sigma Xi, Tau Beta Pi, Eta Kappa Nu. Home: 520 LaGuardia Pl New York NY 10012

WALD, MARY S., risk management and personal finance educator; b. Baker, Oreg., June 17, 1943; d. Paul H. and Mary Elsie (Bartshe) Stoner; m. Lance Albert Wald, June 22, 1968. BA in English, Coll. of Idaho, Caldwell, 1966; MBA in Fin., Temple U., 1984. Tchr. Salt Lake City Bd. Edn., 1967-74; office mgr. Montgomery County Homemaker-Home Health Aide Svc., Inc., Blue Bell, Pa., 1975-82; adj. lectr. risk mgmt. and personal fin. Temple U., Phila., 1984—. Co-author: Controlling Your Money, Step By Step, 1987. Named Outstanding Tchr. of Yr., Salt Lake City Bd. Edn., 1973-74. Mem. Am. Risk and Ins. Assn., Gamma Iota Sigma. Republican. Office: Temple U Ambler Campus 580 Meetinghouse Rd Ambler PA 19002-3999

WALD, PATRICIA MCGOWAN, federal judge; b. Torrington, Conn., Sept. 16, 1928; d. Joseph F. and Margaret (O'Keefe) McGowan; m. Robert L. Wald, June 22, 1952; children—Sarah, Douglas, Johanna, Frederica, Thomas. BA, Conn. Coll., 1948; LLB, Yale U., 1951; HHD (hon.), Mt. Vernon Jr. Coll., 1980; LLD (hon.), George Washington Law Sch., 1983, CUNY, 1984, Notre Dame U., John Jay Sch. Criminal Justice, Mt. Holyoke Coll., 1985, Georgetown U., 1987, Villanova U. Law Sch., Amherst Coll., N.Y. Law Sch., 1988, Colgate U., 1989. Bar: D.C. 1952. Clk. to judge Jerome Frank U.S. Ct. Appeals, 1951-52; asso. firm Arnold, Fortas & Porter, Washington, 1952-53; mem. D.C. Crime Commn., 1964-65; atty. Office of Criminal Justice, 1967-68, Neighborhood Legal Service, D.C., 1968-70; codir. Ford Found. Project on Drug Abuse, 1970, Center for Law and Social Policy, 1971-72, Mental Health Law Project, 1972-77; asst. atty. gen. for legis. affairs U.S. Dept. Justice, Washington, 1977-79; judge U.S. Ct. Appeals (D.C. cir.), 1979-86; chief judge U.S. Ct. of Appeals, D.C. circuit, 1986—. Author: Law and Poverty, 1965; co-author: Bail in the United States, 1964, Dealing with Drug Abuse, 1973; contbr. articles on legal topics. Trustee Ford Found., 1972-77, Phillips Exeter Acad., 1975-77, Agnes Meyer Found., 1976-77, Conn. Coll., 1976-77; mem. Carnegie Council on Children, 1972-77. Mem. ABA (bd. editors ABA Jour. 1978-84), Am. Law Inst. (council 1979—, exec. com. 1985—, 2d v.p. 1988—), Inst. Medicine, Phi Beta Kappa. Office: US Ct Appeals US Courthouse 3rd & Constitution Ave NW Washington DC 20001

WALD, SYLVIA, artist; b. Phila., Oct. 30, 1915. Ed., Moore Inst. Art, Sci. and Industry. Exhibited one-woman shows, U. Louisville, 1945, 49, Kent State Coll., 1945, Nat. Serigraph Soc., 1946, Grand Central Moderns, N.Y.C., 1957, Devorah Sherman Gallery, Chgo., 1960, New Sch., 1967, Book Gallery, White Plains, N.Y., 1968, Benson Gallery, Bridgehampton, L.I., 1977, Knoll Internat., Munich, Germany, 1979, Amerika Havs, Munich, 1979, Aaron Berman Gallery, N.Y.C., 1981, group shows, Nat. Sculpture Soc., 1940, Sculpture Internat., Phila., 1940, Chgo. Art Inst., 1941, Bklyn. Mus., 1975, Library of Congress, 1943, 52, 58, Smithsonian Instn., 1954, Internat. Print Exhbn., Salzburg and Vienna, 1952, 2d Sao Paulo Biennial, 1953, N.Y. Cultural Center, 1973, Mus. Modern Art, N.Y.C., 1975, Benson Gallery, Bridgehampton, L.I., 1982, Dumon-Landis Gallery, New Brunswick, N.J., 1982-83, Suzuki Gallery, N.Y.C., 1982, Sid Deutch Gallery, N.Y.C., 1983, Aaron Berman Gallery, N.Y.C., 1983, Full House Gallery, Kingston, N.J., 1984, others; represented in permanent collections, Aetna Oil Co., Am. Assn. U. Women, Ball State Tchrs. Coll., Bibliotheque Nationale, Paris, Bklyn. Mus., Howard U., State U. Iowa, Library of Congress, U. Louisville, Nat. Gallery, Mus. Modern Art, Phila. Mus., N.C. Mus., Rose Mus. Art at Brandeis U., Whitney Mus., N.Y.C., Finch Coll. Mus., N.Y.C., U. Nebr., Ohio U., U. Okla., Princeton, Victoria and Albert Mus., Walker Gallery, Worcester (Mass.) Art Mus., Guggenheim Mus., N.Y.C., Grunewald Mus., U.Calif. Los Angeles, Rutgers Mus., N.J., Aschenbach Collection Mus., San Francisco, Grunewald Coll. Mus. UCLA; Contbr. to profl. publs. Address: 417 Lafayette St New York NY 10003

WALDAU, HELEN FRANCES, educator; b. Torrington, Conn., Mar. 21, 1925; d. Teofil and Michaelena (Plaga) Budney; B.A., U. Conn., 1953, 6th yr. certificate, 1968; M.A., U. Hartford; divorced; children—Geoffrey, Christopher, Peter, Sandra. Mem. faculty Hopewell Sch., Glastonbury, Conn., 1966—; tchr. academically talented, Glastonbury, 1982-85; dir. Apple Computer Project, 1984; supr. U. Conn. open edn. interns, 1971-75. Fellow U. Conn., 1967-68. Mem. NEA, Conn., Glastonbury edn. assns., Greater Conn. Council for Open Edn. (charter), Glastonbury Task Force for Gifted Edn., Conn. Tchrs. Center for Humanistic Edn., Psi Upsilon Omicron. Home: 1808 Main St Glastonbury CT 06033

WALDBAUM, JANE COHN, art history educator; b. N.Y.C., Jan. 28, 1940; d. Max Arthur and Sarah (Waldstein) Cohn. B.A., Brandeis U., 1962; M.A., Harvard U., 1964, Ph.D., 1968. Research fellow in classical archaeology Harvard U., Cambridge, Mass., 1968-70, 72-73; asst. prof. U. Wis.-Milw., 1973-78, assoc. prof., 1978-84, prof. art history, 1984—, chmn. dept., 1982-85, 86-89; Dorot rsch. prof. W.F. Albright Inst. Archeol. Rsch., Jerusalem, 1990—. Author: From Bronze to Iron, 1978; Metalwork from Sardis, 1983; author (with others), editor Sardis Report I, 1975. Contbr. numerous articles to profl. jours. Bd. dirs. Milw. Soc. of Archaeol. Inst., 1973—, pres., 1983-85. Woodrow Wilson Found. fellow, dissertation fellow, 1962-63, 65-66, NEH post-doctoral rsch., Jerusalem, 1989-90; grantee Am. Philos. Soc., 1972, NEH, summer 1975, U. Wis.-Milw. Found., 1983. Mem. Am. Schs. Oriental Research, Assn. for Field Archaeology, Soc. for Archaeol. Sci., Archaeol. Inst. Am. (exec. com. 1977-81, chmn. com. on membership programs 1977-81, nominating com. 1984, chmn. com. on lecture program 1985-87), Phi Beta Kappa. Office: Dept Art History U Wis-Milw PO Box 413 Milwaukee WI 53201

WALDECK, JACQUELINE ASHTON, author; b. Chgo.; d. John and Maria Teresa (Arneri) Ashton; m. William George Waldeck, Sept. 20, 1947 (div. June 1964). BA, U. Colo., 1948; postgrad. Tex. Agrl. & Mech. U., 1970. Staff and vol. writer Montrose Daily Press, Colo., 1949-66; feature editor Fiesta Mag., Boca Raton, Fla., 1971-76; free-lance writer, historian, pub., lectr., Boca Raton, 1971—. Author: Boca Raton from Pioneer Days, 1980, Boca Raton: A Romance, 1981, Boca Raton Pioneers and Addison Mizner, 1984; also numerous mag. articles. Sec. Tri-County Mental Health

Assn., Montrose, 1964-65; pub. rels. chmn. Montrose County chpt. ARC, 1950-63; bd. dirs. Friends Boca Raton Mus. Art, 1983-84; mem. Friends Boca Raton Libr., Friends Caldwell Play House, Boca Raton, 1983—. Mem. Nat. League Am. Pen Women (by v.p. 1984-88, Nat. Biennial award for non-fiction article 1984). Nat. Soc. Arts and Letters (chpt. bd. dirs. 1983-88, pub. rels. chmn. drama, music, dance, arts and letters contests 1984-88), Fla. Hist. Soc., Boca Raton Hist. Soc., Greater Boca Raton C. of C., Tex. A&M Federated Garden Club. Avocations: dancing, psychology, anthropology, internat. rels., history. Home: PO Box 5313 Bryan TX 77805-5313

WALDEMAR, SHIRLEY ELISE, professional association administrator; b. Kingston, Jamaica, W.I., Nov. 24, 1944; d. Lester Levy and Nancy Jane (Perkins) Shelley; (div. May 1988); 1 child, Anne Marie Brent. BSc, CUNY, 1981; MPA, NYU, 1986. Adminstrv. mgr. ob.-gyn. dept. Mt. Sinai Hosp., N.Y.C., 1977-88; exec. adminstr. for rsch. Am. Cancer Soc., Atlanta, 1988—. Mem. NAFE, NAACP. Democrat. Home: 772 Stone Breeze Ln Stone Mountain GA 30087 Office: Am Cancer Soc 1599 Clifton Rd NE Atlanta GA 30329

WALDEN, SUE COLE, records manager; b. Dallas, Dec. 12, 1947; d. Harry Roosevelt and Kathryn (Conibear) Cole. BS, Tex. Tech. U., 1970. Records analyst Tenneco Inc., Houston, 1971-75; contract adminstr. Pullman-Kellogg, Houston, 1975-81; micrographics coordinator Dallas County Community Coll. Dist., 1983-84, dist. records mgr., 1984—; cons. in field, Dallas. Mem. Willow Falls Restoration Com., Dallas, 1987. Mem. Assn. Records Mgrs and Adminstrs. (chair legisl. com., bd. dirs. 1986-87), Assn. of Info. and Image Mgmt., Inst. Cert. Records Mgrs., Tex. Jr. Coll. Tchrs. Assn., Bus. Forms Mgmt. Assn., Am. Philatelic Soc. Republican. Methodist. Office: Dallas County Community Coll Dist 4343 N Hwy 67 Mesquite TX 75150

WALDERA, KATHERINE ANN, librarian; b. Hankinson, N.D., Feb. 12, 1956; d. Clarence Joseph and Eileen Marie (Parrow) W. AS, N.D. State Sch. Sci., 1976; BA, Moorhead (Minn.) State U., 1978; MLS, U. Wash., 1985. Libr. clk. N.D. State U., Fargo, 1978-83; reference libr. Vets. Meml. Pub. Libr., Bismarck, N.D., 1985—. Mem. ALA, N.D. Libr. Assn. (sect. chmn. 1988-89, 90—), Bismarck-Mandan Libr. Assn. (pres. 1990—), AAUW (pres. Bismarck 1987-89, sec. 1989-90), Bismarck Jaycees. Democrat. Roman Catholic. Office: Vets Meml Pub Libr 515 N 5th St Bismarck ND 58501

WALDHAUSER, CATHY HOWARD, insurance company executive, actuary; b. St. Paul, Oct. 18, 1949; d. Jack Roger and Lois (Johnson) Howard; m. Stanley Jay Waldhauser, Feb. 3, 1973. BA in Math. and Econs., Gustavus Adolphus Coll., 1971. Various actuarial positions IDS Life Ins. Co., Mpls., 1971-81; v.p. IDS Life Ins. Co., 1981—. Mem. Golden Valley (Minn.) LWV, 1986—; sec.-treas. Calvary Luth. Ch. Golden Valley, 1988-89; allocations vol. United Way, Mpls., 1988—; mem. Gustavus Adolphus Alumni Bd., 1984-90. Fellow Soc. Actuaries (product devel. sect. coun. & rsch. com. 1985-88, edn. & exam. com. 1980-81, 83, panelist/lectr. 1980, 87-88), Am. Acad. Actuaries, Minn. Life & Health Guarantee Assn. (bd. dirs. 1984—), Life Office Mgmt. Assn. (mgmt. rsch. com. 1987—), Twin Cities Actuarial Club.

WALDHEIM, BETTY JEAN, psychologist; b. L.A., July 30, 1947; d. Charles Stuart and Marguerite Christine (Yunker) Meagher; m. William W. Waldheim (div. June 1984); children: Richard W., Steve Russell. AA, Santa Ana (Calif.) City Coll., 1981; BA, Chapman Coll., 1983; MA, Calif. Sch. Profl. Psychology, San Diego, 1985, PhD in Clin. Psychology, 1989. Lic. counselor. Psychology intern Calif. Psychol. Svcs., San Diego, 1983-84; predoctoral intern U. Calif. Dept. Psychiatry, San Diego, 1984-86; post-doctoral intern Vista Hill Found., San Diego, 1989-90, Charter Hosp., San Diego, 1989-90; therapist Pscyhiat. Ctrs., San Diego, 1990—; pre-doctoral psychol. testing supr. Vista Hill Found., San Diego, 1989-90; supr. MFCC interns Charter Hosp., San Diego, 1989-90. Mem. Am. Psychol. Assn., Calif. Assn. Marriage Therapist. Home: 4321 Caminito del Diamante San Diego CA 92121

WALDMAN, JUDITH L., clinical psychologist; b. N.Y.C., Aug. 28, 1942; d. Abraham and Adele Pauline (Wolitzer) W.B.S., SUNY-New Paltz, 1964; M.A., Hofstra U., 1975, M.A., 1980, Ph.D., 1983. Cert. tchr.; psychologist Tchr. North Babylon, N.Y., 1964-79; psychologist, Schwartz & Assocs., Brightwaters, N.Y., 1982—; N.Y. Mental Health Services, Bay Shore and Bethpage, N.Y., 1985—. Mem. Am. Acad. Psychotherapists, Am. Psychol. Assn., N.Y. State Psychol. Assn., Suffolk County Psychol. Assn. Home: 9 Hiawatha Rd Babylon NY 11702 Office: NY Mental Health Services 1322 5th Ave Bay Shore NY 11706

WALDOCH, DONNA MAE, computer aided design specialist; b. St. Paul, Oct. 23, 1951; d. Raymond and Shirley Marie (Dupre) W. BA in Art and Edn., Cardinal Stritch Coll., Milw., 1969-73; postgrad., Rock Valley Coll., Rockford, Ill., 1987, 89, So. Ill. U., 1983; cert. of tng., Computervision Tech. Ctr., Itasca, Ill., 1986, 88. Electric assembler Warner Electric Co., Marengo, Ill., 1973-75, machine hand, 1976-78, quality assurance lead insp., 1978-80, draftswoman, 1980-86, CAD-sr. draftswoman, 1986-87; tchr. art Stephen Mack Sch. Dist., Rockford, 1975, Harrison Sch. Dist., Wonder Lake, Ill., 1975-76; CAD specialist Greenlee Textron Inc., Rockford, 1988-89, resigned, 1989; asst. buyer Ingersoll Milling, Rockford, 1989-90; asst. office mgr. Shake-A-Leg Signs, Rockford, 1990—. Author: (with others) Treasured Poems of America, 1990. Mem. choir St. James Ch., Belvidere, Ill., 1985—. Recipient leadership award YWCA, Rockford, 1988. Mem. NAFE, Exptl. Aircraft Assn., Nat. Audubon and Wildlife Assn., Boone County Arts Coun. Roman Catholic. Office: 6935 11th St Rockford IL 61109

WALDRON, CAROL WATERS, microcomputer company executive; b. Washington, July 31, 1942; d. Odale Dabney and Lucile Elizabeth (McGehee) Waters; m. Robert L. Waldron, Dec. 6, 1966 (div. 1973); children: Elizabeth Lane, Carter Weir. Student, Walsingham Acad., 1960, U. Tokyo, 1962; BS, George Washington U., 1965. V.p. sales Entre Computer Ctr., Melbourne, Fla., 1983; pres. DOS Computer Ctr., Melbourne, 1985-89; v.p., bd. dirs. DOS Computer Ctrs. of Fla., Miami, Fla., 1987-89; gen. mgr. Inacomp Computer Ctr., Melbourne, 1989; bd. dirs. DOS Computer Ctrs, Inc., Miami. Advisor White House Consumer's Affairs Council, Washington, 1974. Mem. Nat. Contract Mgmt. Assn., Nat. Purchasing Mgmt. Assn., Navy League of U.S., Am. Bus. Women's Assn., Coast Club (Melbourne). Republican. Episcopalian. Home: 1260 Cedar Lane Indialantic FL 32903 Office: Inacomp Computer Ctr 1164 W New Haven Ave Melbourne FL 32904

WALDRON, DELORIS META, real estate appraiser; b. Detroit, May 22, 1949; d. Wesley Karl and Julia Deloris (Trusendi) Strehlau; m. Robert Jennings Waldron Jr., Aug. 28, 1971. BA, Mich. State U., 1971. Cert. sr. real estate analyst, sr. real property appraiser, sr. residential appraiser. Sr. appraiser Valuation Counselors, Century City, Calif., 1980-82; investment property appraiser Glendale (Calif.) Fed. Bank, 1975-80, investment property appraisal mgr., 1988—. Contbr. articles to profl. publs. Mem. Soc. Real Estate Appraisers (1st v.p. Long Beach 1981-82, pres. 1982-83, instr.), Am. Inst. Real Estate Appraisers. Home: PO Box 3l57 Manhattan Beach CA 90266 Office: Glendale Fed Bank 40l N Brand Blvd Glendale CA 91203

WALDRON, INGRID LORE, biology educator; b. Nyack, N.Y., Dec. 8, 1939; d. Paul Henry and Esther Hildegard (Sachs) W.; m. Joseph Eyer (div.); children: Jessie Eyer, Katie Rebecca Eyer. AB summa cum laude, Radcliffe Coll., 1961; PhD, U. Calif., Berkeley, 1967. Asst. prof. biology U. Pa., Phila., 1968-72, assoc. prof., 1972-90, prof., 1990—. Co-author: Population and Environment—Problems and Solutions, 1973; contbr. articles to various publs., 1964—. Organizer workshops Reevaluation Counsellors, Phila., 1988-90; vol. tchr. Upattinas Sch., Glenmoore, Pa., 1989-90. Mem. Population Assn. Am., Educators for Social Responsibility, Phi Beta Kappa. Office: Univ Pa Dept Biology Philadelphia PA 19104-6018

WALDRON, MARGARET ANN, food consultation director; b. Ft. Collins, Colo., July 14, 1927; d. Charles Gehlert and Katharine (Graham) Humphrey; m. David Waldron (div.); 1 child. Sara Waldron Stotts; m. Gene Tepper. BS, Cornell U., 1950; diploma, La Varenne, Paris, 1978. Assoc. food editor McCall's mag., N.Y.C., 1951-54; food cons. Paris, 1954-56; TV producer Gen. Foods, N.Y.C., 1956-58; with Calif. Foods Research Inst., San Francisco, 1960, Cunningham & Walsh Advt., San Francisco, 1960-63, J. Walter Thompson, San Francisco, 1964; prin. Maggie Waldron Assocs., San Francisco, 1965-73; with Ketchum Communications, San Francisco, 1973—; dir., sr. v.p. Ketchum Food Ctr., San Francisco. Author: Fire and Smoke, 1980. Mem. Am. Inst. Wine and Food (patron, bd. dirs. nat. chpt. 1984-86), San Francisco Profl. Food Soc. (founding mem.), Women's Forum. Democrat. Presbyterian. Home: Kappas Marina Gate 6 E Pier 29 Sausalito CA 94965 Office: Ketchum Communications 55 Union St San Francisco CA 94111

WALDSTEIN, SUSAN M., librarian; b. Rochester, N.Y., July 17, 1947; d. Howard A. and Elizabeth A. Walker; m. Arnold A. Waldstein; 1 child, Asa. BA in English, Ohio U., 1969; MLS, U. Wash., 1981. Libr. asst., annotator B.C. (Can.) Law Libr. Found., Vancouver, 1978-79; litigation freelancer Perkins, Coie, Stone, Olsen & Williams, Seattle, 1981-82; dir. libr. svcs. Moss Adams, Seattle, 1982-84; supr. info. resources Dataquest Inc., San Jose, Calif., 1984-86, corp. librarian, 1986—. Opportunities for Education Grants fellow U. Wash., Seattle, 1979. Mem. Spl. Librs. Assn., Soc. Competitor Intelligence Profs. Office: Dataquest Inc 1290 Ridder Park Dr San Jose CA 95131

WALGREN, BETTE JO WEBER, learning disabilities teacher; b. Staples, Minn., Sept. 10, 1942; d. Rupert and Josephine (Weber) Jones; m. Floyd B. Walgren, Mar. 11, 1961 (dec. Nov. 1982); children: Kristin, Kelda, Karlisle. BS in Edn. summa cum laude, Kent State U., 1975, MEd, 1977, PhD, 1986. Cert. in elem. edn., spl. edn.; cert. reading supr., learning disabilities supr. Tchr. learning disabled Bode Elem. Sch., Cuyahoga Falls, Ohio, 19975-77, Richardson Elem. Sch., Cuyahoga Falls, 1977-79; learning disabilities supr. Cuyahoga Falls City Schs., 1979-81; tchr. 1st grade Lincoln Elem. Sch., Cuyahoga Falls, 1981-83; tchr. learning disabled Price Elem. Sch., Cuyahoga Falls, 1983—; prof. Cleve. State U., summer 1981; sch. adminstr. learning disabilities summer sch. Kent State U., 1983. Home: 410 Kehner Suffield OH 44260 Office: Price Elem Sch 2610 Delmore St Cuyahoga Falls OH 44221

WALHOUT, JUSTINE SIMON, chemistry educator; b. Aberdeen, S.D., Dec. 11, 1930; d. Otto August and Mabel Ida (Tews) S.; m. Donald Walhout, Feb. 1, 1958; children: Mark, Timothy, Lynne, Peter. BS, Wheaton Coll., 1952; PhD, Northwestern U., 1956. Instr. Wright City Community Coll., Chgo., 1955-56; asst. prof. Rockford (Ill.) Coll., 1956-59, assoc. prof., 1959-66, 81-89, prof., 1989—; dept. chmn., 1987—; cons. Pierce Chem. Co., Rockford, 1968-69; bd. trustee Rockford Coll., 1987—. Contbr. articles profl. jours. Mem. Ill. State Bd. Edn., 1974-81. Mem. Am. Chem. Soc., AAUW (Ill. bd. mem. 1985-87), Rockford LWV (bd. dirs. 1983-85), Sigma Xi. Presbyterian. Home: 320 N Rockford Ave Rockford IL 61107 Office: Rockford Coll 5050 E State St Rockford IL 61108

WALKE, JEAN HOLLAND, software systems engineer, computer systems consultant; b. Detroit, May 16, 1950; d. Harold Ferguson and Anne (Kostrick) Holland; m. Le Verne Douglas Rizor, June 19, 1971 (div. Aug. 1977); 1 child, James Delbert; m. Sanford E. Walke, III, Aug. 23, 1980. Student U. Mich., 1968-71; B.B.A., Eastern Mich. U., 1980. Office mgr. Mich. Testing Engrs., Inc., Ann Arbor, 1972-75, Constrn., Testing & Inspection, Inc., Ann Arbor, 1977-78; pvt. practice word processor, Ann Arbor, 1978-81; systems analyst ADP Network Services, Dearborn and Ann Arbor, 1981-84; tech. mgr. ADP Dealer Services, Southfield, Mich., 1984-85; engring. supr. Applicon-Schlumberger, Ann Arbor, 1985-86; pvt. practice computer systems cons., 1986—; v.p., dir. Bay & Tool Rental, Inc., Ann Arbor, 1977-83; v.p., dir., cons. Am. Lender Services, Inc., Ann Arbor, 1984—. Named Steward of the Meet, Criterium du Quebec, 1977; recipient award of appreciation City of Grayling, Mich., 1978; 6th Overall Nat. Championship for Co-Drivers, Sports Car Club Am., 1979; named tech. cons. of yr. Mich. region ADP Network Services, Ann Arbor, 1982. Mem. Nat. Assn. Female Execs., Sports Car Club Ann Arbor (pres. 1973-74). Republican. Presbyterian. Club: Ralligators (treas. 1973-74) (Dearborn, Mich.). Avocations: contract bridge; sports car rallying. Home: 3509 Hillside Dr Ypsilanti MI 48197 Office: Am Lender Services Inc 2006 Hogback Rd Ste 7 Ann Arbor MI 48105

WALKER, ALICE MALSENIOR, author; b. Eatonton, Ga., Feb. 9, 1944; d. Willie Lee and Minnie (Grant) W.; m. Melvyn R. Leventhal, Mar. 17, 1967 (div. 1977); 1 dau., Rebecca Walker Leventhal. B.A., Sarah Lawrence Coll., 1966; Ph.D. (hon.), Russell Sage U., 1972; D.H.L. (hon.), U. Mass., 1983. Author: Once, 1968, The Third Life of Grange Copeland, 1970, In Love and Trouble, 1973, Langston Hughes, American Poet, 1973, Meridian, 1976, I Love Myself When I Am Laughing, 1979, You Can't Keep a Good Woman Down, 1981, The Color Purple, 1982, In Search of Our Mothers' Gardens, 1983, Good Night, Willie Lee, I'll See You in the Morning, 1979, Revolutionary Petunias, 1974, Horses Make a Landscape Look More Beautiful, 1984, Living By the Word: Selected Writings, 1988, The Temple of My Familiar, 1989. Recipient Lillian Smith award, 1979; recipient Rosenthal award Nat. Inst. Arts and Letters, 1973, Guggenheim Found. award, 1979, Am. Book award, 1983, Pulitzer prize, 1983. Address: care Washington Sq Press 1230 6th Ave New York NY 10020 also: care G K Hall 70 Lincoln St Boston MA 02111

WALKER, BERNADETTE MARIE, city official; b. Detroit, Apr. 2, 1960; d. Charles Legreair and Dorris Willedith Walker. BA, U. Detroit, 1982. Asst. pub. svc. attendant Detroit Zool. Park, 1979-85; clk. Dept. Pub. Works, City of Detroit, 1985-86, sr. clk., adminstrv. liaison complaint svc. reps., 1986-87, sr. clk./acting asst. supr., 1988-89, jr. govtl. analyst, 1989—. Mem. women's and young adult coms. NAACP, Detroit, 1986—; mem. SCLC; mem.-at-large Mus. African-Am. History; adminstrv. sec. Christian Edn. Ministry-New Prospect, 1982—; vol. Nursery Sch., New Prospect, 1982—; contbg. supporter Detroit Assn. Black Orgns.; mem. Founder's Soc.-DIA. Mem. Am. Mgmt. Assn., Assn. Mcpl. Profl. Women (assoc.). Democrat. Baptist. Home: 20040 Snowden Detroit MI 48235 Office: City of Detroit Dept Pub Works 2 Woodward Ave Rm 513 City County Bldg Detroit MI 48226

WALKER, BILLIE RAE, human services administrator, counselor; b. Clifton Springs, N.Y., Dec. 7, 1944; d. Raymond Arthur and Leone Martha (Knight) W. BA in Anthropology, SUNY, Oswego, 1967, postgrad., 1968, 74-76; postgrad., SUNY, Buffalo, 1967-68. Pub. welfare and family svcs. counselor Oswego County Dept. Social Svcs., Mexico, N.Y., 1968-73; fin. aides counselor SUNY, Oswego, 1973-74; child protective caseworker Oswego County Dept. Social Svcs., Mexico, 1974, staff devel. coord., 1974-83; dir. Wayne County Youth Bur., Lyons, N.Y., 1983—; Wayne County rep. Inter County Task Force on Missing Children, 1985—; mem. Wayne County bd. emergency food and shelter program Fed. Emergency Mgmt. Adminstrn., 1987—; past mem. bd. dirs. Homer's Kids, Ltd., Palmyra, N.Y. Vol. emergency mgmt. CD, Wayne and Oswego Counties, 1968—; mem. Wayne County Youth for Christ, Marion, 1987, Wayne County Crime Victims Task Forcce; mem. Wayne County Criminal Justice Coun., vice chmn., 1987-89. Recipient cert. of appreciation Family Counseling Svc. Finger Lakes, 1985, Wayne County Dept. Head Assn., 1986, vol. awards Project Head Start Wayne County, 1987, 89. Mem. Am. Assn. for Counseling and Devel., Am. Mental Health Counselors Assn., Assn. N.Y. State Youth Burs., N.Y. State Assn. for Counseling and Devel., Wayne County Chem. Dependency Svc. Providers Consortium, Wayne County Humane Soc., Wayne County Hist. Soc., Phi Gamma Mu. Baptist. Home: 620 E Main St Palmyra NY 14522 Office: Wayne County Youth Bur 9 Pearl St PO Box #287 Lyons NY 14489

WALKER, CAROL ANN, real estate broker, consultant; b. Zurich, Mont., July 25, 1937; d. Thomas Hugh and Iona (Williams) Murphy; m. Fred A. Shelton, Jan. 18, 1970 (div. May 1974); children: F. Kevin, Kelly Andrew; m. Gene Glen Walker, Feb. 17, 1977; children: Jesse Clayton, Dylan Buck, Kimberly Brooke. AA, Ricks Coll., 1958. Mgr. div. Am. Western Life Ins. Co., Salt Lake City, 1966-70; real estate broker Profl. Investment Cons., Salt Lake City, 1974-78; investment counselor Profl. Investment Cons., Idaho Falls, 1979—; owner Fin. Freedom Enterprises, Idaho Falls, 1987—; bd. dirs. Gen. Agts. and Mgrs. Assn., 1968-70; established Carol Walker Fin. Fitness Program, Inc., 1990. Author: How To Succeed In Business Without Being a Man, 1979; contbr. articles to various jours. Pres. Ensign Jr. High Sch. PTA, Salt Lake City 1977; chmn. Making Am. Confs., Idaho Falls

1986; mem. Bi-Centennial Constitution Commn., Idaho Falls, 1987; pres. Jr. Achievement, Idaho Falls 1987-89; bd. dirs. Utah Tech. Coll., 1972-77. Mem. Sales and Mktg. Exec. (Salesman Yr. 1978), Salt Lake City, Devel. Workshop Inc., Idaho Falls, Salt Lake Bd. Realtors, Nat. Assn. Securities Dealers. Republican. Mormon. Home: 7050 Val Verde Idaho Falls ID 83401 Office: Walker Investments 7050 Val Verde Idaho Falls ID 83401 also: Fin Freedom Enterprises 132 N Woodruff Idaho Falls ID 83401

WALKER, CAROL LEE, dentist, naval officer; b. Ashland, Ky., Mar. 23, 1957; d. James Hart and Nancy Annette (Gibson) W.; m. Ronald Ashley Hunter. DMD, U. Ky., 1983. Lic. dentist, Ky., Va. Commd. lt. Dental Corps USNR, 1986, advanced through grades to lt. comdr.; staff dentist Mary Breckinridge Hosp.-Frontier Nursing Sv., Hyden, Ky., 1983-86; with Marine Corps Combat Devel. Command, Quantico, Va., 1986-88; served on USS Holland, Charleston, S.C., 1988-90; asst. dental officer in operative Dentistry Dept. U.S. Naval Acad., Annapolis, Md., 1990—. Office: US Naval Acad Br Dental Clinic Annapolis MD 21402

WALKER, CAROLYN, state legislator; b. Yuma, Ariz.. Mktg., pub. rels. exec.; state rep. Ariz., 1983-86, now state senator from dist. 23. Democrat. Home: 2239 E Wier Phoenix AZ 85040*

WALKER, CAROLYN PEYTON, English educator; b. Charlottesville, Va., Sept. 15, 1942; d. Clay M. and Ruth (Newman) Peyton. BA in Am. History and Lit., Sweet Briar Coll., 1965; cert. in French, Alliance Francaise, Paris, 1966; EdM, Tufts U., 1970; MA in English and Am. Lit., Stanford U., 1974, PhD in English Edn., Stanford U., 1977. Tchr. Elem. and jr. high schs. in Switzerland, 1967-69; tchr. elem. grades Boston Sch. System, 1966-67,69-70; Newark (Calif.) Unified Sch. System, 1970-72; instr. div. humanities Canada Coll., Redwood City, Calif., 1973, 76-78; instr. Sch. Bus.. U. San Francisco, 1973-74; evaluation cons. Inst. Profl. Devel., San Jose Calif., 1975-76; asst. dir. Learning Assistance Ctr., Stanford U., Calif., 1972-77, dir., 1977-84, lectr. Sch. Edn., 1975-84, dept. English, 1977-84, supr. counselors, tutors and tchrs., 1972-84; assoc. prof. dept. English, San Jose State U., Calif., 1984—; bd. dir. English dept. Writing Ctr., 1986—, Steinbeck Rsch. Ctr., 1986-87; head cons. to pres. to evaluate coll.'s writing program, San Jose City Coll., 1985-87; cons. U. Tex., Dallas, 1984, Stanford U., 1984, 1977-78, CCNY, 1979, U. Wis., 1980—, numerous testing programs; pres. San Diego State U., 1982, Ednl. Testing Svc., 1985—, also to numerous univs. and colls.; pres. Waverley Assocs., ednl. cons., 1980—; condr. reading and writing workshops, 1972—; reviewer Random House Books, 1978—, Rsch. in the Teaching of English, 1983—; cons. Basic Skills Task Force, U.S. Office Edn., 1977-79, Right to Read, Calif. State Dept. Edn., 1977-82 , Program for Gifted and Talented, Fremont (Calif.) Unified Sch. Dist., 1981-82; bd. dirs. high tech. sci. ctr., San Jose, 1983-84. Recipient award ASPIRE (federally funded program), 1985, two awards Student Affirmative Action, 1986, award Western Coll. Reading & Learning Assn., 1984; numerous other awards and grants. Mem. MLA, Calif. Profs. of Reading, Western Coll. Reading Assn. (treas. 1982-84, bd. dirs. 1982-84), Nat. Coun. Tchrs. English, Nat. Coll. Reading Assn. (sec.-treas. 1976-78), Am. Assn. U. Profs., Jr. League Palo Alto (bd. dirs. 1977-78, 83-84); vol. fund-raiser, Peninsula Ctr. for the Blind, Palo Alto, Calif., 1982—; The Resource Ctr. for Women, Palo Alto, 1975-76. Author: (with Patricia Killen) Handbook for Teaching Assistants at Stanford University, 1977; How to Succeed As a New Teacher: A Handbook for Teaching Assistants, 1978; (with Karen Wilson) Tutor Handbook for the Writing Center at San Jose State University, 1989; (with others) Academic Tutoring at the Learning Assistance Center, 1980, Writing Conference Talk: Factors Associated with High and Low Rated Writing Conferences, 1987, Lifeline Mac: A Handbook for Instructors in the Macintosh Computer Classrooms, 1989,; contbr. articles to profl. jours, also chpts. to Black American Literature Forum, 1990. Home: 2350 Waverley St Palo Alto CA 94301 Office: San Jose State U English Dept San Jose CA 95192

WALKER, CEIL ANN, advertising executive; b. Charleston, W.Va., Dec. 28, 1952; d. Paul Stephen Thomas and Lois Ann Sowers Kraemer; m. V. Deloss Walker, Dec. 30, 1979; children: Deloss Thomas, Cecilia Lona. Student, Stephens Coll., Columbia, Mo., 1970-71, Bradley U., 1971-72; BA, U. South Fla., 1974. Dir. NFL properties & Pro Mag. NFL Properties & Pro Mag. Tampa Bay (Fla.) Buccaneers, Tampa, Fla., 1975-77; dir. mktg. Memphis Rogues, 1977-78; dir. pub. relations Racquet Club of Memphis, 1978-81; exec. v.p. Walker & Assocs., Memphis, 1985—, also bd. dirs. Chmn. Memphis Symphony Ball, 1984; Epicurean chmn. Memphis Symphony, 1985; bd. dirs. Memphis Devel. Found., 1987-89, Memphis Symphony League, 1983, 85, pres. 1988; mem. inaugural com. Gov. Ned McWherter, 1987; active LeBonheur Children's Hosp. Club. Mem. Pub. Relations Soc. Am., Memphis Advt. Fedn., Chickasaw Country Clu, Racquet Club Memphis, Summit Club, Petroleum Club, Kiwanis. Presbyterian. Clubs: Chickasaw Country, Cresent, Racquet of Memphis, Summit, Petroleum (Memphis). Home: 485 Ripplebrook Rd Memphis TN 38119 Office: Walker & Assocs 50 N Front St Memphis TN 38103

WALKER, CHARLOTTE GERALDINE, educator; b. Atlanta, Dec. 31, 1944; d. Frank William and Agnes Evelyn (Evans) Bundy; m. James Pickett Walker, Dec. 28, 1965; children: Clark, Michael. BS in Edn., Ga. So. Coll., 1966; MEd, Valdosta State Coll., 1972. Cert. tchr., Ga. Tchr. Tift County Pub. Schs., Tifton, Ga., 1966-69, 79-86; reading cons. Turner County Schs., Ashburn, Ga., 1972-73; program evaluator Flint Area Child Devel., Cordele, Ga., 1974-76; children's libr. Tift County Libr., Tifton, 1986-88; edn. coord. Arts Experiment Sta., Tifton, 1988—. Chair Kids' Advocacy Coalition, Tifton, 1988—; vice-chair Bd. Elections and Registration, Tifton, 1989—. Grantee Am. Assn. Univ. Women Edn. Found. Program, 1989, Save the Children, Atlanta, 1990; recipient community svc. award Tift County United Way, 1989. Mem. AAUW (program v.p. 1988—), Ga. Assn. Young Children (dist. rep. 1985-88, sec. 1988-90), Tift Area Children with Learning Disabilities (v.p. 1978, pres. 1979), Nat. Assn. Edn. Young Children. Democrat. Methodist.

WALKER, CONSTANCE MAXFIELD, management consultant; b. Washington, Mar. 16, 1949; d. Orville Eldred and Rose Mary (Stiarwalt) Maxfield; m. Robert Charles Kneip, III, Aug. 21, 1971 (div. Apr. 1981); 1 dau., Stephanie Alexandra; m. Richard Howard Cowles, May 16, 1981 (dec.); m. Phillip Walker, July 25, 1985. Clk.-typist HEW, Social Security Adminstrn., New Orleans, 1971-72, service rep., 1972-73; mgmt. analyst Office Comptroller of Currency, Treasury Dept., Washington, 1974-77; dir. mgmt. analysis div. U.S. Customs, New Orleans, 1978-80, mgmt. analyst, Houston, 1980-81, program analyst, 1981-82, chief data processing br., 1982-83, chief mgmt. analysis br., 1983-85; pres. Constance Walker Assocs., Inc., 1985—. Author: MBO Handbook, 1979, Professional Problem Solving, 1985, The Productivity Assault, 1987, Participative Problem Solving: A Guide for Work Teams, 1988; (with others) Program Management Handbook, 1983, Introduction to Employee Involvement, 1985; contbr. numerous articles to profl. jours. Mem. Friends of Stehlin Found., 1982-88, Friends of the Cabildo, 1978-80. Named Customs Woman of Yr., U.S. Customs, 1979, recipient Outstanding Performance award, 1979, 80, 81, 82, 83, 84, 85; named Fed. Exec. Bd. Woman of Yr., 1979; recipient Outstanding Service award Office of Sec. of Treasury, 1976; Cora Bell Wesley scholar, UDC, 1969. Mem. Assn. for Quality and Participation, Treasury Hist. Assn., DAR, Daus. Rep. of Tex., Daus. 1812, UDC, Va. Tech. Alumni Assn., Delta Zeta. Episcopalian. Home: 1711 Mission Springs Dr Katy TX 77450 Office: Constance Walker Assocs Inc 1711 Mission Springs Dr Katy TX 77450

WALKER, DARCY LYNN, banker; b. Chgo., June 29, 1949; d. Blake Mitchell and Dorothy Virginia (Schlickan) Walker. BA, Yale U., 1971; MBA, Wharton Sch., 1971, U. Pa., 1973. Lending officer Citibank N.Y., N.Y.C., 1973-75; lending officer Citibank Houston, N.Y.C., 1975-79; v.p., dir. corp. mtg. Citibank N.Y., N.Y.C., 1979-82; v.p., dir. Bankcard credit policy Citicorp Credit Services Inc., N.Y.C., 1982-84, v.p., dir. nat. collections, 1984-87; bus. mgt. trading markets Citicorp Securities Market, Inc., N.Y.C., 1987-89; dir. credit cards Citicorp Europe, Brussels, 1990—. Bd. advisor Girl Scout Council Greater N.Y., 1982-84. Mem. Fin. Women's Assn. Republican. Methodist. Clubs: Tuxedo (N.Y.); Jr. League, Yale (N.Y.). Office: Citibank, Ave de Terveren 249, 1150 Brussels Belgium

WALKER, DEBORAH COLLEEN ROSE, store owner; b. Dayton, Ohio, June 7, 1959; d. Woodrow Jefferson and Marjorie Colleen (Ogle) Rose; m. John Harris Walker, Dec. 6, 1986. BS in Bus. Adminstrn., Tenn. Tech. U.,

Cookeville, 1982. Sales clk. Cape Craft Inc.,, Pigeon Forge, Tenn., 1979-80; sec. Tenn. Tech U., 1980-82; mktg. asst. Family Inns, Pigeon Forge, 1982-83; store owner Chapman Mkt., Seymour, Tenn., 1983—. Mem. Nat. Assn. Female Execs., Delta Gamma. Republican. Baptist. Office: Chapman Market 12221 Chapman Hwy Seymour TN 37865

WALKER, DEBORAH LOU, economics educator; b. Cortez, Colo., Jan. 19, 1958; d. Thomas M. and Ruby L. (Terrell) W. BS, Ariz. State U., 1980, MBA, 1982; PhD, George Mason U., 1987. Asst. prof. Loyola U., New Orleans; instr. George Mason U., Fairfax, Va. Contbr. articles to profl. jours. Recipient Community Svc. award, 1989, Outstanding Teaching awards, 1989, 90; Earhart fellow, 1985-86, Bradley fellow, 1990. Mem. NAFE, Am. Econ. Assn., Southern Econ. Assn., Austrian Econs. Soc. Office: Loyola U 6363 St Charles Ave New Orleans LA 70118

WALKER, DEBRA MAY, retail marketing professional; b. Flint, Mich., May 11, 1956; d. Vern Luke and Rosemary (Deanhofer) W.; m. Stephen Robert Strong, Aug. 14, 1982; 1 child, Evan Walker Strong. BA in Advt., Mich. State U., 1978, MA in Advt., 1979. Sr. bus. analyst Goodyear Tire & Rubber Co., Akron, Ohio, 1979-81, mgr. advt. rsch., 1981-82, mgr. market planning systems, 1982-85; mktg. strategy mgr. Europe Goodyear Tire & Rubber Co., Brussels, 1985-89; mktg. strategy mgr. U.S. Goodyear Tire & Rubber Co., Akron, 1989-90, mktg. mgr. retail stores div., 1990—; speaker on mktg. and distbn. topics. Contbr. articles to various pubs. Vocalist St. Eugene's Cath. Ch., Munroe Falls, Ohio, 1989—. Mem. NAFE. Office: Goodyear Tire & Rubber Co 1144 E Market St Akron OH 44316

WALKER, ELAINE NOGAY, media executive; b. Ogden, Utah, Aug. 6, 1951; d. William Anthony and Mary Agnes (Sagan) Nogay; m. Charles Dorian Walker; children: Erin Michelle, Evan Todd. Student, U. Md., 1969-72. Legis. aid and press aid U.S. Congressman Bud Shuster, Washington, 1974-75; adminstrv. aide to pres. A.S. Nemir Assn., Washington, 1975-76; congl. liaison Can Mfrs. Inst., Washington, 1976-80; housing program mgr. Calif. Assn. Realtors, Los Angeles, 1980-82; press sec. Los Angeles Council Pres., 1982-85; dir. communications Pvt. Sector Systems, Los Angeles, 1985-86, Los Angeles West C. of C., 1986; pub. affairs and editorial mgr. Sta. KCAL-TV, Los Angeles, 1986—; producer pub. affairs talk show Sta. KCAL-TV, 1986—, Group W Cable TV Talk Show, Santa Monica, Calif., 1986; creator, producer, host Family Talk Show, Sta. KCAL-TV, 1987-89; instr. Atwater Elem. TV Class, L.A., 1986—. Author: Directions For Solving The Housing Crunch, 1981. Pres. adv. coun. Ret. Sr. Vol. Program; sec. Hollywood Little Red Schoolhouse PTA, 1988-89. Recipient Journalism award for excellence Best TV Editorials, 1989. Mem. Radio and TV News Assn., Women in Pub. Affairs (chair 1989). Club: Greater Los Angeles Press. Office: Sta KCAL-TV 5515 Melrose Ave Los Angeles CA 90038

WALKER, ELIZABETH ANNE, financial specialist and administrator; b. Albuquerque, Aug. 20, 1959; d. Richard Thomas an dGloria Louise (Jesuit) Baff; m. Patrick W. Ferron, Feb. 16, 1985 (div. Jan. 1989); m. Scott V. Walker, May 27, 1989. BBA, U. N.Mex., 1986. Payroll deduction clk. Los Alamos (N.Mex.) Credit Union, 1981; fin. specialist State Treas.'s Office, Santa Fe, N.Mex., 1982-85; fin. systems analyst Sci. & Engring. Assocs., Inc., Albuquerque, 1986-89; fin. adminstr. def. avionics systems div. Honeywell Inc., Albuquerque, 1989—; cons. Engring.-Applied Sci., Inc., Albuquerque, 1988—. Mem. U. N.Mex. Aderson Sch. Mgmt. Alumni Assn., N.Mex. Ballet Guild. Republican. Roman Catholic.

WALKER, ELIZABETH SUE, librarian; b. Somerset, Pa., Oct. 29, 1948; d. Guy E. and Betty (Egolf) W. BA, Hood Coll., 1970; MFA, Pa. State U., 1972; MLS, U. Pitts., 1974. Librarian music dept. Carnegie Library, Pitts., 1974-76; asst. librarian Curtis Inst. Music, Phila., 1977-80, head librarian, 1980—. Soloist Phila. Singers, 1979—, Opera Co. Phila., 1979—, West Jersey Chamber Music Soc., Moorestown, N.J., 1981—. Mem. Music Library Assn. (chmn. Pa. chpt. 1982-84), Am. Guild Mus. Artists (bd. govs. 1984—), AFTRA, Savoy Co., Mus. Fund Soc. Phila. Office: Curtis Inst Music 1726 Locust St Philadelphia PA 19103

WALKER, ELJANA M. DU VALL, civic worker; b. France, Jan. 18, 1924; came to U.S., 1948; naturalized, 1954; student Med. Inst., U. Paris, 1942-47; m. John S. Walker, Jr., Dec. 31, 1947; children—John, Peter, Barbara. Pres., Loyola Sch. PTA, 1958-59; bd. dirs. Santa Claus shop, 1959-73; treas. Archdiocese Denver Catholic Women, 1962-64; rep. Cath. Parent-Tchr League, 1962-65; pres. Aux. Denver Gen. Hosp., 1966-69; precinct committeewoman Arapahoe County Republican Women's Com., 1973-74; mem. re-election com. Arapahoe County Rep. Party, 1973-78, Reagan election com., 1980; block worker Arapahoe County March of Dimes, Heart Assn., Hemophilia Drive, Muscular Dystrophy and Multiple Sclerosis Drive, 1978-81; cen. city asst. Guild Debutante Charities, Inc. Recipient Distinguished Service award Am.-by-choice, 1966; named to Honor Roll, ARC, 1971. Mem. Cherry Hills Symphony, Lyric Opera Guild, Alliance Francaise (life mem.), ARC, Civic Ballet Guild (life mem.), Needlework Guild Am. (v.p. 1980-82), Kidney Found. (life), Denver Art and Mus., U. Denver Art and Conservation Assns. (chmn. 1980-82), U. Denver Women's Library Assn., Chancellors Soc, Passage Inc. Roman Catholic. Clubs: Union (Chgo.); Denver Athletic, 26 (Denver); Welcome to Colo. Internat. Address: 6185 S Columbine Way Littleton CO 80121

WALKER, EVELYN, retired educational TV executive; b. Birmingham, Ala.; d. Preston Lucas and Mattie (Williams) W.; AB, Huntingdon Coll., 1927; MA, U. Ala., 1963; LHD, Huntingdon Coll., 1974. Speech instr. Phillips High Sch., Birmingham, 1930-34; head speech dept. Ramsay High Sch., Birmingham, 1934-52; chmn. radio and TV, Birmingham Pub. Schs., 1944-75, head instructional TV programming svcs., 1969-75; Miss Ann, broadcaster children's daily radio program, Birmingham, 1946-57; producer Our Am. Heritage radio series, 1944-54; TV staff producer programs shown daily Ala. Pub. TV Network, 1954-75; past cons. Gov.'s Ednl. TV Legis. Study Com., 1953; summer faculty extension div. U. Va., 1965-67; nat. del. Asian-Am. Women Broadcasters Conf., 1966; past chmn. Creative TV-Radio Writing Competition; former regional cons. Ednl. TV Broadcasting. Mem. emerita Nat. Def. Adv. Com. on Women in Svcs.; past TV-radio co-chmn. Gov.'s Adv. Bd. Safety Com.; past TV chmn. Festival of Arts; past audiovisual chmn. Ala. Congress, also past mem. Birmingham coun. PTA; media chmn. Gov.'s Commn. on Yr. of the Child; bd. dirs. Women's Army Corps Found. Recipient Alumnae Achievement award Huntingdon Coll., 1958; Tops in Our Town award Birmingham News, 1957; Air Force Recruiting plaque, 1961; Spl. Bowl award for promoting arts through Ednl. TV. Birmingham Festival of Arts, 1962; citation 4th Army Corps., 1962; cert. of appreciation Ala. Multiple Sclerosis Soc., 1962; Freedoms Found. at Valley Forge Educator's medal award, 1963; Top TV award ARC, 1964; Ala. Woman of Achievement award, 1964; Bronze plaque Ala. Dist. Exch. Clubs, 1969; cert. of appreciation Birmingham Bd. Edn., 1975; Obelisk award Children's Theatre, 1976; 20-Yr. Svc. award Ala. Ednl. TV Commn.; key to city of Birmingham, 1966; named Woman of Yr., Birmingham, 1965; named Ala. Woman of Yr., Progressive Farmer mag., 1966; hon. col. Ala. Militia. Mem. Am. Assn. Ret. Persons, Ala. Assn. Ret. Tchrs., Huntingdon Coll. Alumnae Assn. (former internat. pres.), Former Am. Women in Radio and TV, Ala. Hist. Assn., Arlington Hist. Assn. (dir., pres. 1981-83), Magna Charta Dames (past state sec.-treas.), DAR (former pub. rels. com. Ala., TV chmn., state program chmn. 1979-85, state chmn. Seimes Microfilm com. 1985-88, state chmn. Motion Picture, Radio TV com. 1988—, tricom. chmn. 1988—), Colonial Dames 17th Century (chmn. pub. rels. com.), U.S. Daus. 1812 (past state TV chmn.), Daus. Am. Colonists (past 2d v.p. local chpt., past state TV and radio chmn.), Ams. Royal Descent, Royal Order Garter, Plantagenets Soc. Am., Salvation Army Women's Aux., Symphony Aux., Humane Soc. Aux., Eagle Forum, Nat. League Am. Pen Women, Women's Com. 100 for Birmingham (bd. dirs.), Royal Order Crown, Women in Communications (past local pres.; nat. headliner 1965), English Speaking Union, Birmingham-Jefferson Hist. Soc., Delta Delta Delta (mem. Golden Circle), Ladies Golf Assn., Birmingham Country Club, Downtown Club, The Club. Methodist. Home: 744 Euclid Ave Mountain Brook Birmingham AL 35213

WALKER, F. ANN, chemistry educator, researcher; b. Adena, Ohio, May 11, 1940; d. Robert Watson and Marian (Schuff) Walker; m. Frederick R. Jensen, Aug. 14, 1976 (dec. Feb. 1987). BA, Coll. of Wooster, 1962; PhD, Brown U., 1966. DuPont teaching fellow Brown U., Providence, 1965-66;

NIH postdoctoral fellow UCLA, 1966-67; asst. prof. chemistry Ithaca (N.Y.) Coll., 1967-70; asst. prof. chemistry San Francisco State U., 1970-72, assoc. prof. chemistry, 1972-76, prof. chemistry, 1976-90; prof. chemistry U. Ariz., Tucson, 1990—; mem. NIH Metallobiochemistry Study Sect., Washington, 1981-84; sci. advisor U.S. FDA, San Francisco, 1988-90; mem. adv. com. Rsch. Corp. Grants Program, Tucson, 1988-89. Contbr. articles to profl. jours. Mem. adult ministries com. Lafayette-Orinda Presbyn. Ch., 1989-90, chmn. current affairs forum com., 1989-90. NATO fellow 1974; Fulbright vis. schoarl 1977; NIH-Rsch. Career Devel. awardee, 1976-81. Fellow AAAS; mem. Am. Chem. Soc. (chmn. inorganic div., chmn. bioinorganic subdiv. 1990), Calif. Acad. Scis., Sierra Club, Sigma Xi. Office: U Ariz Dept Chemistry Tucson AZ 85721

WALKER, FRANCES OLA, environmental management executive, consultant; b. Phila., Jan. 20, 1939; d. Joseph Willie and Ola Mac (Jones) W.; children: Gregory, Michelle, Roslyn, Darlene; 1 adopted child, Patricia Williams. Student, Temple U., 1970, Phila. Community Coll., 1979. Congl. aide U.S. Rep. William H. Gray, Phila., 1979-89; v.p. govt. affairs Internat. Environ. Mgmt. Corp., Phila., 1989—. Exec. mem. West Branch NAACP, Phila., 1975; pres. Dunlap Community Citizens Coun., Phila., 1976; organizer William H. Gray III, Phila., 1976; co-founder Parents Against Drugs, Phila., 1987. Recipient Community Svc. award Chapel of Four Chaplins, 1985, 87, Community Svc. award Neighborhood Youth Achievement, 1985, Community Svc. award Lancaster Ave Bus. Assn., 1986. Democrat. Baptist. Home: 4906 Aspen St Philadelphia PA 19139 Office: Internat Environ Mgmt Corp 2133 Arch St 1st Fl Philadelphia PA 19103

WALKER, GAIL FLANAGAN, registered nurse; b. N.Y.C., Sept. 26, 1946; d. Matthew Garrett and Edith Alexandria (Russell) Flanagan; m. Bruce Lee Walker, Apr. 8, 1972; children: Erin Edria, Kendra Leigh. Diploma in nursing, Mt. Sinai Med. Ctr., N.Y.C., 1966; BS, Adelphi U., 1971; MS in Nursing Adminstrn., U. N.H., 1990. RN. Staff nurse neonatal dept. Mt. Sinai Med. Ctr., 1966-69, head nurse neonatal dept., 1969-71, head nurse pediatrics dept., 1971-72; instr. Cen. Maine Med. Ctr., Lewiston, 1972-78; instr. staff devel. St. Mary's Hosp., Lewiston, 1978-80; nurse recruiter Family Hosp., Milw., 1981-82; instr. staff devel. Waukesha (Wis.) Meml. Hosp., 1982-83, Holy Family Hosp., Methuen, Mass., 1984-86; dir. maternal-child health Cath. Med. Ctr., Manchester, N.H., 1986—; Mem. Mayor's Com. on Prenatal Care, N.H. State Task Force on Prenatal Care. Mem. Nat. Assn., Neonatal Nurses, Assn. for Care of Children's Health, Nurses Assn. Am. Coll. Obstetricians and Gynecologists. Home: 41 Gordon Dr Londonderry NH 03053 Office: Cath Med Ctr 100 McGregor St Manchester NH 03102

WALKER, GAIL JUANICE, electrologist; b. Bosque County, Tex., Sept. 3, 1937; d. Hiram Otis and Hazel Ruth (Carmichael) Gunter; cert. Shults Inst. Electrolysis, 1971; children—Lillian Ruth, Deborah Lynn. In quality control Johnson & Johnson, San Angelo, Tex., 1962-70; owner, pres., electrologist Ariz. Inst. Electrolysis, Scottsdale, 1979—; ednl. cons. Gail Walker's Internat. Sch. Electrolysis, Tokyo, 1980; area corr. Hair Route mag., 1981; participant continuing edn. program in electrology Shelby State Coll., 1981. Editor Electrolysis World. Cert., Pvt. Bus. and Tech. Schs., State of Ariz. Mem. Ariz. Assn. Electrologists (pres. 1980—), Am. Electrolysis Assn., Internat. Guild Profl. Electrologists, Nat. Fedn. Ind. Businessmen, Ariz. Assn. Electrologists (organizer 1980). Republican. Baptist. Club: Order of Eastern Star.

WALKER, GAYLE JEAN, civilian military employee; b. St. Joseph, Mo., Oct. 13, 1947; d. Harry Rolland Jr. and Betty Jean (Young) W.; divorced; children: Christopher James Ganoe, Michelle Diane Ganoe. Assoc. in Gen. Edn., Missouri Western Coll., 1967; BA in Sociology, U. Iowa, 1971; MBA, Fla. Inst. Tech., 1983. Cert. contract mgmt. Field advisor Girl Scouts U.S., Sioux City, Iowa, 1970-71; clk. typist Tng. and Doctrine Command, Ft. Leonard Wood, Mo., 1974-75, U.S. Army Armament Command, Rock Island, Ill., 1975-76; procurement employee U.S Army Missile Command, Huntsville, Ala., 1976—. Bd. dirs. publicity Huntsville Swim Assn., 1980-83; bd. dirs. property All Saints Luth. Ch., Huntsville, 1982-84; troop unit leader Girl Scouts of No. Ala., Huntsville, 1977-84; activities chmn. Singles Ministry Holy Spirit Cath. Ch., Huntsville, 1988. Democrat. Roman Catholic. Office: US Army Missile Command Attn: AMSMI-CM Redstone Arsenal AL 35898

WALKER, GERRI HENDRICKS, city administrator; b. Phila., July 14, 1944; d. Charles George and Ethel Viola (Lee) Hendricks; m. Reginald Edmond Walker, June 1, 1964; children: Rana, Tschaka. BA, U. Pitts., 1966; MEd, Temple U., 1975. Pre-sch. tchr. Sch. Dist. Phila., 1966-68, pers. trainee, 1969—, pers. examiner, 1971, ednl. adminstr., 1971-76; employment supr. Camden (N.J.) County Coll., 1978-79; pers. adminstr. Sch. Dist. Phila., 1980-82; dir. personnel U. Pa. Dental Sch., Phila., 1982-83; mgr. employment U. Pa., Phila., 1983-85; dir. innovation and staff devel. Community Coll. Phila., 1985-88; dir. commerce Mayor's Office Phila., 1988—; adj. faculty U. Pa., Antioch U., Phila. Ctr., 1982-88; pres. The Walker Group Mgmt. Cons., Phila., 1986—; bd. dirs. Greater Phila. Internat. Network, Interstate Land Mgmt. Corp. Bd. dirs. CHOICE, Phila. Orchestra, Phila. Dance Co., Greater Phila. Econ. Devel. Corp.; v.p. Met. YWCA, Phila., 1981-85; bd. dirs. Pa. Women's Campaign Fund, Harrisburg, Pa., 1986—; chair Phila. CARE's for Africa, 1987—; mem. Educators to Africa, 1970-72; coun. pres. Internat. Tng. in Communications, Inc.; pres. Penn's Landing Corp., 1989; exec. bd. Phila. Indsl. Devel. Corp.; exec. com. Phila. Convention and Visitors Bur. Mem. Am. Soc. Tng. and Devel., Assn. Black Women in Higher Edn., Phila. Human Resouces Planning Group, Internat. Platform Assn., Nat. Polit. Congress Black Women, Rainbow Club (Phila.) Delta Sigma Theta. Democrat. Office: 1660 Mcpl Services Bldg Philadelphia PA 19102-1684

WALKER, JANE BECK, civic worker; b. Monroe, Mich., May 25, 1933; d. Elmer William and Rose B. (Corner) Beck; m. Thomas J. Walker, May 2, 1959; children: Rose Ann, William Thomas. BA, Marietta (Ohio) Coll., 1955; MSc, U. Fla., 1957. Vol., Suwannee River coord. Fla. Defenders Environ.; mem. Alachua County Commn., 1982-86, chmn., 1985-86; chmn. North Cen. Fla. Regional Planning Coun., 1986-87. Recipient Community Svc. award Gainesville (Fla.) Sun, 1980, Woman of Yr. award Gainesville Area Women's Network, 1986. Mem. Gainesville Women's Forum, LWV (pres. Alachua County-Gainesville 1987-89, bd. dirs. Fla. 1989—). Democrat. Home: 10601 NW 23d Ave Gainesville FL 32606

WALKER, JUANITA FAY, university administrator; b. Weimar, Tex., Feb. 8, 1959; d. Daniel Clifton and Bernice Lillian (Ermis) Ulbricht; m. Rome Willard Walker, Aug. 22, 1981; 1 child, Meredith Danielle. BBA in Fin., Tex. A&M U., 1981. Auditor Tex. A&M U. System, College Station, 1981-83; EDP acctg. systems analyst Tex. A&M U., College Station, 1983-84, coord. micro support and spl. projects, 1984-88, coord. spl. projects, 1988-89, asst. dir. ops., 1989—.

WALKER, KAREN (KAREN ROBERTS), professional entertainer and justice of peace; b. Boston, Apr. 2, 1935; d. Robert Francis O'Donnell and Louise Eleanor Rogan; m. Richard M. Penta, June 14, 1968 (div. 1978); children: Robert Penta, Karyn Penta, Donna Penta Luther, James Penta; m. William Joseph Walker, July 1, 1979. Profl. entertainer, 1954-89; sales rep. Elizabeth Arden, Portsmouth, N.H., 1971-78. Singer and composer of recorded songs: My Wedding Day, 1987, Lady of the Night, 1987, America I Love You, 1988, Nashville, 1988, Sold on Country, 1988. Delegate Dem. Party N.H.,1983. Named Dover Woman of the Year, 1987, N.H. First Lady of Country Music, 1987; nominee Female Vocalist of the Year, Record of the Year, Mass. Entertainer of the Year, 1987, Outstanding Woman of Yr., 1990; nominee Mass. Country Music Female Entertainer, Female Vocalist, Single Record and Album of Yr., 1988-89, Mass. Country Music Female Entertainer of Yr., 1990, N.H. Female Entertainer and Vocalist of Yr., 1990. Mem. Mass. Country Music Assn., Am. Fedn. TV., Spotlighters Inc., N.H. Country Music Assn., Internat. Fan Club. Home: 69 Walden Pond Dr Nashua NH 03060

WALKER, KATHLEEN MAE, health facility administrator; b. Springfield, Ill., Sept. 23, 1947; d. Warren H. and Ruth E. (Berlin) Wille; m. Truman G. Walker, Jan. 29, 1972 (div. June 1988); 1 child, Janet Marie. BA in History, Valparaiso U., 1969. Registered respiratory therapist. Staff respiratory therapist Michael Reese Med. Ctr., Chgo., 1976; supr. respiratory care Community Meml. Gen. Hosp., LaGrange, Ill., 1976-81; mgr. cardiopulmonary svcs. Longmont (Colo.) United Hosp., 1981—. Vice chmn. accountability & accreditation com. St Vrain Valley Schs., 1989—; vol. Bruce Fischer Div. Class, Longmont, 1989, 90. Mem. Am. Assn. Respiratory Care, Colo. Soc. Respiratory Care (no. chpt. pres. 1985, chmn. respiratory dirs. 1984). Lutheran. Home: 651 Buchanan Ln Longmont CO 80501

WALKER, KIMBERLY LOUISE, personnel specialist; b. Atlanta, June 22, 1964; d. Larry Ernest and Marlene Mary (Brugger) W. BSBA in Mktg., Robert Morris Coll., Coraopolis, Pa., 1986. Territory mgr. Future Security Industries, Atlanta, 1987; membership sales rep. AAA Ga. Motor Club, Atlanta, 1987-88, with accounts payable/payroll, 1988-89; personnel asst. AAA Fla./Ga., Inc. motor club, Atlanta, 1989-90; office asst. Powers, Boland, Farmer, CPA, Atlanta, 1990—. Mem. NAFE. Roman Catholic.

WALKER, LOIS VIRGINIA, multi-media artist, poet, editor, educator; b. Wheaton, Ill., Oct. 23, 1929; d. Earl William and Gertrude Johanna (Wuster) W.; m. Nicolas N.K. Kittrie, Apr. 20, 1951 (div. 1957). Student, Coll. of Emporia, Kans., 1948-49; BA, U. Kans., 1951, BS, 1954; postgrad., Columbia U., N.Y.C., 1957-59. Cert. elem. edn. tchr., N.Y. Tchr. Dist. 17, Hicksville, N.Y., 1954-86; freelance poet, 1964—, freelance artist, 1974—; panelist decentralization panel N.Y. State Coun. of the Arts, 1989—; host radio shows Adelphi U., Garden City, N.Y., 1980—; treas. L.I. Poetry Collective, Huntington, N.Y., 1988—, chairperson, treas., 1980-87. Editor Xana Du and Process, 1979-86. Mem. Environ. Def. Fund, 1985—. Mem. AAUWPoetry Soc. Am., Nat. League Am. Pen Women, Suburban Art League, Huntington Township Art League, Friends of Poets and Writers, Inc., N.Y. State Ret. Tchrs. Assn. Inc. (life), Sierra. Home: 149 Harbor S Amityville NY 11701 Studio: 107 Kerrigan Rd Copiague NY 11726

WALKER, LORENE, retired educator; b. Clovis, N.Mex., July 27, 1911; d. Jessie H. and Tille Eula (Harlan) Black; m. Carl Westley Walker, June 9, 1934; children: Wesley, Charles. BS, N.Mex. State U., 1933; M Family Life, Cen. Wash. U., 1959, postgrad., 1956-74. Tchr. home econs. Floyd Sch., near Portales, N.Mex., 1933-34, Navajo Meth. Mission, Farmington, N.Mex., 1947-48; home agt. extension svc. Wash. State Coop. Extension Svc., Yakima, 1948-56; family life, counseling tchr. West Valley Sch., Yakima, 1956-71, spl. elem. reading tchr., 1971-75; tour organizer, leader Mission Tour, Yakima, 1966—; coord. 4-H camps, fairs and programs Wash. Coop. Extension Svc., Yakima, 1950-56. Chairperson Experiment for Internat. Living, Yakima Valley Rep. Women's Club, 1960-67; docent, tour leader Yakima Valley Mus., 1976—; trustee Found. Pacific Northwest United Meth. Ch., 1984—. Mem. AAUW (treas. 1962-66, bd. dirs., chair internat. rels. 1962-89; spl. honor award 1989), United Meth. Women (pres. 1987-89; spl. recognition 1989), Wesleyan Svc. Guild Meth. Women. (officer 1964-68), Alpha Delta Kappa (pres. 1967-69). Home: 101 N 48th Ave Apt 25A Yakima WA 98908

WALKER, LYNDA JEAN, educator; b. Abilene, Tex., Nov. 9, 1944; d. Noble Aubrey and Opal Imogene (Cooper) Finch; m. James Thomas Walker, Dec. 22, 1966; children: Meredith Michelle, Wade Thomas. BS, Tex. Christian U., 1967; MEd, Tex. Woman's U., 1981. Tchr. Dallas Ind. Sch. Dist., 1967, Richardson (Tex.) Ind. Sch. Dist., 1967-68, Lubbock (Tex.) Ind. Sch. Dist., 1968-69, Valdosta (Ga.) Ind. Sch. Dist., 1969-70; tchr. Plano (Tex.) Ind. Sch. Dist., 1977-80, PACE resource tchr., 1980—; coach Tex. Future Problem Solving Program, Austin, 1980—, evaluator, 1984—; evaluator Nat. Future Problem Solving Program, Laurinburg, N.C., 1987-88. Named Outstanding Coach, Tex. Future Problem Solving Program, Austin, 1986. Mem. Tex. Asns. Gifted and Talented, Assn. Supervision and Curriculum Devel. Republican. Baptist. Office: Plano Ind Sch Dist 1517 Ave H Plano TX 75074

WALKER, MARGARET ELIZABETH, chief executive officer; b. Rutherfordton, N.C., Sept. 16, 1955; d. William Decatur and Margaret Elizabeth (Wilkins) W. Diploma, Sch. Radiol. Technology, 1976. Staff radiol. technologist Rutherford Hosp., Rutherfordton, N.C., 1976-77; computed tomography technologist Century City Med. Plaza Radiology, Beverly Hills, Calif., 1977-78; sect. chief computed tomography dept. Presbyn. Hosp., Charlotte, N.C., 1978-82; applications specialist Picker Internat., Highland Heights, Ohio, 1982-83; computed tomography product sales specialist Picker Internat., Boston, 1983—; CT product sales specialist Picker Internat., Charlotte, 1986—; pres., chief exec. officer Treasures on the Lake, Inc., Sherrills Ford, N.C., 1988—, The Juke Box, Inc., Sherrills Ford, 1989—. Recipient Sales Specialist of the Year award REgion Mgmt., 1984, SAles Council awaard Nat. Sales Mgmt., 1987. Mem. NAFE, Am. Registry Radiol. Technologist. Democrat. Methodist. Home: 7930 Vista View Dr Sherrills Ford NC 18673

WALKER, MARY ANN, lawyer; b. Anderson, S.C., Aug. 21, 1953; d. Ernest McCreary and Virginia (Selman) Glymph; m. Thomas M. Walker, Aug. 28, 1976. BS, U. Va., 1975; JD, U. Richmond, 1979. Bar: Va. 1979, U.S. Dist. Ct. (ea. dist.) Va. 1980, U.S. Ct. Appeals (4th cir.) 1980, U.S. Ct. Appeals (5th and 7th cirs.) 1984, U.S. Ct. Appeals (D.C. cir.), 1984, U.S. Ct. Appeals (10th cir.) 1987, U.S. Supreme Ct. 1987, D.C. 1988. Assoc. Wickwire, Gavin & Gibbs, P.C., Washington and Vienna, Va., 1980-86; ptnr. Wickwire, Gavin & Gibbs, P.C., Washington, 1986-89, Pepper, Hamilton & Scheetz, Washington, 1989—; bus. mgr. Energy Law Jour., Washington, 1986-88; sec. Cogeneration Coalition Am. Inc., Washington, 1985-87. Contbr. articles to profl. jours. Named Outstanding Atty. in Va. Met. Women's Bar Assn., Va. Womens Attys. Assn., 1986. Mem. ABA, Va. Bar Assn., Fairfax Bar Assn., Fed. Bar Assn., Fed. Energy Bar Assn. (vice chmn. practice and procedures com. 1985-86, vice chmn. phsy. facilities com. 1987-88), Midwest Gas Assn. (exec. bd. legal affairs sect.), Va. Oil and Gas Assn. Presbyterian. Office: Pepper Hamilton & Scheetz 1300 19th St NW Washington DC 20036

WALKER, MARY CUNNINGHAM, lawyer; b. Cleve., Sept. 4, 1944; d. Geoffrey Everett and Katherine E. (Danforth) Cunningham; J.D., U. Tenn., 1975; B.A., Smith Coll., 1966; M.A.T. in French, Wesleyan U., 1967; m. John Albert Walker, Jr., Nov. 26, 1977; children—Christopher Danforth Swann, John Albert III, Katherine Goddard. Admitted to Tenn. bar, 1975; atty. fin. div. Office Procs., ICC, Washington, 1975-76, Office Gen. Counsel, 1976-77; atty. U.S. Dept. Energy, Oak Ridge, 1977-78; mem. firm Fowler & Rowntree, Knoxville, Tenn., 1979-83, Walker & Walker, P.C., Knoxville, 1983—. Bd. dirs. Children's Center, Inc., Knoxville, 1980—; chair alumnae admissions Smith Coll., 1989—; regional dir. Am. Field Service, N.Y.C., 1974—. Mem. Am. Bar Assn., Tenn. Bar Assn., Knoxville Bar Assn., Phi Delta Phi. Clubs: LeConte, Knoxville Symphony League. Home: 800 Blows Ferry Rd Knoxville TN 37919 Office: 715 1st American Ctr Knoxville TN 37902

WALKER, MARY L., lawyer; b. Dayton, Ohio, Dec. 1, 1948; d. William Willard and Lady D. Walker; 1 child, Winston. Student, U. Calif., Irvine, 1966-68; BA in Biology/Ecology, U. Calif., Berkeley, 1970; postgrad., UCLA, 1972-73; JD, Boston U., 1973. Bar: Calif. 1973, U.S. Supreme Ct. 1979. Atty. So. Pacific Co., San Francisco, 1973-76; from assoc. to ptnr. Richards, Watson, & Gershon, L.A., 1976-82; dep. asst. atty. gen. lands div. U.S. Dept. Justice, Washington, 1982-84; dep. solicitor U.S. Dept. Interior, Washington, 1984-85; asst. sec. of energy, environment, safety and health U.S. Dept. Energy, Washington, 1985-87; spl. cons. to chmn. bd. Law Engring., Atlanta, 1988-89; v.p., West Coast and the Pacific Law Environ., Inc., San Francisco, 1989; ptnr., head environ. law dept. Richards, Watson & Gershon, San Francisco, 1989—; U.S. Commr. InterAm. Tropical Tuna Commn., 1989—. Mem. Pacific Basin Econ. Coun.; U.S. commr. Inter-Am. Tropical Tuna Commn., 1988—. Mem. ABA, Calif. Bar Assn., San Francisco Bar Assn., Nat. Fedn. Rep. Women, World Affairs Council, Renaissance Women.

WALKER, MARY YVONNE, protective service official; b. Memphis, Tenn., Jan. 2, 1958; d. James and Rosie Lee (Matthews) W. Student, Memphis State U., 1980—. With Shelby County Sheriff's Dept., Memphis, 1974—; capt. Shelby County Sheriff's Dept., 1984—. Sunday sch. tchr. Castalia Bapt. Ch., 1988, fin. con., 1988, v.p. drama club, 1988. Mem. NAFE, Am. Correctional Assn., Am. Jail Assn. Democrat. Baptist. Home: 4973 Shelter Cove Memphis TN 38118 Office: 201 Poplar Ave Memphis TN 38103

WALKER, MOIRA KAYE, sales executive; b. Riverside, Calif., Aug. 2, 1940; d. Frank Leroy and Arline Rufina (Roach) Porter; m. Timothy P. Walker, Aug. 30, 1958 (div. 1964); children: Brian A., Benjamin D., Blair K., Beth E. Student, Riverside City Coll., 1973. With Bank of Am., Riverside, 1965-68, Abitibi Corp., Cucamonga, Calif., 1968-70; with Lily div. Owens-Illinois, Riverside, 1970-73; salesperson Lily div. Owens-Illinois, Houston, 1973-77; salesperson Kent H. Landsberg div. Sunclipse, Montebello, Calif., 1977-83, sales mgr., 1983-85; v.p., sales mgr. Kent H. Landsberg div. Sunclipse, Riverside, 1985—. Mem. Nat. Assn. Female Execs., Women in Paper (treas. 1978-84). Lutheran. Office: Kent H Landsberg Div Sunclipse 1180 Spring St Riverside CA 92507

WALKER, PATRICIA LILLIAN, editor; b. Chgo., Jan. 2, 1943; d. Robert Warren and Virginia Margaret Walker; B.A., U. Ill., 1965; M.S. in Communications, Mich. State U., 1967; m. Peter Klaus Jeziorski, Aug. 28, 1971; 1 son, Peter. Reporter, Chgo. Tribune, 1967-69, Metalworking News, Chgo., 1969-71; mng. editor Am. Metal Market and Metalworking News, N.Y.C., 1971-74, editor-in-chief, 1974-87; pres. Exec. Press Inc., 1981-84; dir. mags. Inst. of Electronics and Engring., 1989—; trustee Inst. Archeo-Metall. Studies; bd. dirs. Copper Club. Office: 7 E 12th St New York NY 10003

WALKER, PEGGY JEAN, social work agency administrator; b. Carbondale, Ill., Aug. 9, 1940; d. George William and Lola Almeda (Black) Robinson; children—Edith Nell and Keith Alan. B.A., So. Ill. U., 1962, Ph.D., 1986; M.S.W., Washington U., St. Louis, 1967. Caseworker, casework supr. Ill. Dept. Public Aid, 1964-71; child welfare adminstr. Ill. Dept. Children and Family Service, 1971-75; mem. faculty social work program So. Ill. U., 1975-79; exec. dir. Western div. Children's Home Soc. of Fla., Pensacola, 1979—; appointed to Ill. Juvenile Justice and Delinquency Prevention Adv. Council, 1978-79; adj. adv. bd. dept. social work U. West Fla., 1982—; appt. by Fla. Dept. Edn. to task force Edn. for Children of the Homeless, 1989—, Dept. of Health and Rehab. Svcs. Dist. Task Force on Child Abuse and Neglect Prevention, 1985—, chmn. 1988, 89. Bd. dirs. Hoyleton (Ill.) Children's Home, 1975-79, Pvt. Industry Coun., 1988—, N.W. chpt. March of Dimes, 1988—; mem. Leadership Fla., 1988—. Mem. Nat. Assn. Social Workers, Acad. Cert. Social Workers. Presbyterian. Club: Pensacola Yacht. Home: 613 Silverthorn Rd Gulf Breeze FL 32561 Office: 5375 N 9th Ave Pensacola FL 32504

WALKER, RENEE KELLEY, educational administrator; b. Macon, Ga., June 26, 1961; d. Joseph A. and Grace (Fountain) Kelley; m. Anthony Scott Walker, June 22, 1986; children: Brian David, Brendan Scott. A.S., Macon Jr. Coll., 1980; B.S., Ga. Coll., 1982, M.S., 1985. Dir., prin., Briarwood Acad., Macon, 1982—; tchr. annex program, 1985—; tchr. sci. Macon Youth Devel. Ctr., 1985—. Recipient Excellence award Bd. Dirs. Briarwood Acad., 1983. Mem. NEA, Correctional Edn. Assn., Nat. Council Social Studies, Ga. Correctional Assn. Office: Briarwood Acad 800 Lackey Dr Macon GA 31206

WALKER, RUTH ANN, journalist; b. Elmhurst, Ill., June 22, 1954; d. Robert F. and Jeanne (Carsman) W. AB, Oberlin (Ohio) Coll., 1976. Staff reporter Aiken (S.C.) Standard, 1977-78; various editing and writing positions Christian Sci. Monitor, Boston, 1978-83, bus. corr., 1983-85, editorial writer, 1985-88, asst. editor editorial page, 1988, asst. mng. editor, 1988-90, dep. editor, 1990—. Recipient Exceptional Merit Media award Nat. Women's Polit. Caucus, 1987. Christian Scientist. Home: 26 Waverly St #402 Brighton MA 02135

WALKER, RUTH FERGUSON, banker; b. Richmond, Ohio, Oct. 10, 1922; d. Edgar Lemoin and Gertrude Elizabeth (Harbourt) Wilson; m. Howard W. Ferguson, June 4, 1946 (dec. Oct. 1967); 1 child, Charlotte Ruth Ferguson Saunders; m. Maynard W. Walker, Mar. 17, 1969. Student, Asbury Coll. Teller Miners Mechs. Bank, Steubenville, Ohio, 1941-46; clk., mgr. data processing Jefferson County Treas., Steubenville, 1946-51; asst. bookkeeper Asbury Coll., Wilmore, Ky., 1952-59; office mgr. Arthur O. Hall, P.A., Columbus, Ohio, 1959-64; v.p. Diamond Savs. and Loan Co., 1964—, Diamond Savs. & Loan Co., Findlay, Ohio, 1984—; pres. Zonta Internat., 1988—. Mem. Columbus Symphony League, 1987—. Mem. Zonta (internat. pres. 1988-90). Republican. Methodist.

WALKER, SALLY BARBARA, retired glass company executive; b. Bellerose, N.Y., Nov. 21, 1921; d. Lambert Roger and Edith Demerest (Parkhouse) W. Diploma Cathedral Sch. St. Mary, 1939; AA, Finch Jr. Coll., 1941. Tchr. interior design Finch Coll., 1941-42; draftsman AT&T, 1942-43; with Steuben Glass Co., N.Y.C., 1943—, exec. v.p., 1959-62, exec. v.p. ops., 1962-78, exec. v.p. ops. and sales, 1978-83, exec. v.p., 1983-88, ret. 1988. Pres. E. 66th St. Corp. Mem. Fifth Ave. Assn. Republican. Episcopalian. Clubs: Rockaway Hunting, Lawrence Beach, U.S. Lawn Tennis, Colony, English-Speaking Union. Home: 116 E 66th St New York NY 10021

WALKER, SALLY WARDEN, state legislator; b. Wilmette, Ill., Feb. 5, 1929; d. Sydney C. and Florence (Collins) Warden; m. O.B. Walker, Dec. 28, 1948; children: Richard, Christine, Nancy, Catherine, Sara. Student, William Jewell Coll., 1947-48. Commr., chmn. Univ. Pl. Parks and Recreation Bd., Tacoma, 1979-85; mem. Wash. Ho. of Reps., 1985—, environ. affairs, edn., and commerce and labor coms., transp. com. Formerly vol. dir. Pierce County Rep. Party, del. Pierce County Conv., precint committeewoman 28th dist., 1978—; past bd. dirs. Town Hall Lecture Series; former dir. Christian Edn., mem. vestry St. Mary's Episc. Ch. Recipient Woman of Community award Inter-Chpt. Council Am. Bus. Women's Assn., 1986, Achievement award Puget Sound Inter-Chpt., Golden Acorn award PTA. Mem. Tacoma/Pierce County C. of C., Lakewood C. of C., LWV. Clubs: 28th Dist. Rep., Lakewood Rep. Women's. Home: 4617 Bellview St W Tacoma WA 98466 Office: House Office Bldg Olympia WA 98504

WALKER, SHIRLEY DAWN KINCAID, realtor; b. Kincaid, W.Va., May 3, 1935; d. Carlos Holt and Minnie Virginia (Burke) Kincaid; m. B.J. Walker, July 25, 1959 (div. Jan. 1990); children: Dawn R. Walker, Stephanie K. Walker Huss, Cheryl L. Walker Vatsaas. BA, W.Va. Wesleyan Coll., 1957; MA, W.Va. U., 1959. Cert. residential specialist. Secondary educator Miamisburg (Ohio) High Sch., 1957-58; asst. prof. W.Va. U., Morgantown, W.Va., 1958-59; secondary educator Mad River High Sch., Dayton, Ohio, 1959-60; exec. sec. Fort Bliss Army Base, El Paso, Tex., 1960-62; reporter Washington County Bulletin, Cottage Grove, Minn., 1970-71; tchr. So. Washington County Schs., Cottage Grove, 1966-79; realtor Edina Realty, Inc., Woodbury, Minn., 1979—; dir. St. Paul Area Assoc. of Realtors, 1986-89. Bd. edn. Com., SPAAR, St. Paul, 1986-89. Recipient Disting. Svc. award St. Paul Are Assoc. Realtors, 1988, 89, 90. Mem. Cert. Residential Specialists, Profl. Women in Real Estate, Woodbury C. of C., Woodbury Women's Club (past pres.), Woodbury Mrs. Jaycees (past pres.), Woodbury Fire Dept. Aux. (past pres.), LWV, Woodbury Heritage Soc., Woodbury Community Theatre Guild, Washington County Friends Libr. Methodist. Home: 1612 Wexford Way Woodbury MN 55125 Office: Edina Realty Parkwood Pl 7650 Currell Woodbury MN 55125

WALKER, SUE BRANNAN, English educator; b. Montgomery, Ala., Apr. 6, 1940; d. Louie and Katherine (King) Brannan; m. Ron Walker; children: Wesley, James, Jason. BS, U. Ala., 1961; MEd, Tulane U., 1967, MA, 1968, PhD, 1977. Prof. English U. So. Ala., Mobile. Author: Traveling My Shadow, 1981; editor Negative Capability lit. quarterly, 1981. Editor's grant, Coord. Coun. Lit. Mags., N.Y.C., 1982; writer's fellow, Ala. Coun. on Arts, 1987. Mem. Ala. State PoetrySoc. (pres. 1987-88), Nat. League Am. Pen Women (pres. Mobile chpt. 1987-88, Ala. chpt. v.p. 1987-88), MLA, Poetry Soc. Am., Gayfer's Career Club (Career Woman of Yr. 1985). Presbyterian. Home: 6116 Timberly Rd N Mobile AL 36609

WALKER, TERESA LEE, business consultant; b. L.A., Calif., July 10, 1943; d. Edward Macauley and Dorothy (Hill) Lee; m. David William Walker, June 13, 1970; children: Michele, Joshua. BA, Immaculate Heart Coll., 1968. Tchr. Calif. and Wash. Pvt. and Pub. Schs., 1963-84; dir. of devel. Marymount Sch., Santa Barbara, Calif., 1984-86; pvt. Terry Walker Cons. Svcs., Santa Barbara, 1986—. Orgn. cons. Jeanne Graffy Campaign for re-election, 1987. Mem. Santa Barbara C. of C. (com. mem. 1986—), AAUW, , Univ. Club of Santa Barbara, Santa Barbara Sch. Dist GATE (adv. mem. 1980—), South Coast Bus. Network, Leads (treas. 1984—).

Roman Catholic. Office: Terry Walker Cons Svcs 827 State St Santa Barbara CA 93101

WALKER, VANESSA JANE, writer, theatrical stagehand; b. Seattle, June 6, 1962; d. Judith Ann (Spack) Mucha; m. Howard Murphy Walker, May 18, 1988. BA, U. Pitts., Johnstown, Pa., 1984. Journalist Gateway Press, Pitts., 1986; touring theatrical stagehand, 1986-89; local stagehand Internat. Alliance of Theatrical and Stage Employees, 1985—; freelance writer, 1985—. Democrat. Office: PO Box 4180 Saint Simons Island GA 31522

WALKER, WENDY DIANA KNIGHT, insurance company specialist; b. Elizabeth, N.J., Nov. 11, 1961; d. William Henry Jr. and Catherine Lillian (Fulton) Knight; m. George Russell Walker, Jr., Oct. 25, 1986. Student, U. Warwick, Eng., 1981-82; BA, Duke U., 1983. Lic. real estate agent. Underwriter Chubb & Son, Inc., N.Y.C., 1983-86; sr. underwriter Atlantic Mut. Ins. Cos., N.Y.C., 1986-87, producer specialist, 1987-88, underwriting supr., 1988; asst. brokerage mgr. Continental Ins. Cos. div. Nat. Brokerage Svcs., N.Y.C., 1988-90; mgr. comml. property underwriting Gt. Am.-West, Inc., Salt Lake City, 1990—; tchr. internship program Howard U., N.Y.C., 1986; bus. advisor internship program Inroads, Inc. Active St. John's Choir. Mem. Nat. Assn. Realtors, Assn. Profl. Ins. Women, NAFE, Oranges/Maplewood Bd. Realtors, Am. Biog. Inst. (mem. rsch. bd. advisors). Democrat. Episcopalian. Home: 1962 E Falcon Hurst Ct Sandy UT 84092 Office: Gt Am-West Inc 60 E South Temple Ste 1500 Salt Lake City UT 84111

WALKER-HARRISON, ALICE M., financial executive; b. Beaver Dam, Wis., Jan. 13, 1962; d. Arnold Fernidan and Angie Janet (Dolgner) Bregi; m. Roger D. Harrison, May 5, 1989. AA, Madison (Wis.) Bus. Coll., 1982. Cert. in System 83 computer tng. Asst. auditor M&I Bank of Hilldale, Madison; br. mgr., sr. regional mgr. ITT Fin. Svcs., Milw.; spl. projects mgr. Norwest Fin., Littleton, Colo. Mem. NAFE, NOW. Home: 4931 W Rowland Ave Littleton CO 80123 Office: 8055 W Bowles Ave Littleton CO 80123

WALKER-NELSON, COLLEEN MAE, nurse; b. Seattle, Dec. 11, 1944; d. Chester Byron and Wilma Christina (Carlson) Walker; m. Steven John. AA, Shoreline City Coll., 1968; BS in Nursing, Seattle Pacific U., 1977. RN, Wash., Mont. Nurse U.S. Pub. Health Svc., Seattle, 1968-69; nurse instr. Tacoma Gen. Hosp., 1977-78; RN emergency Harborview Med. Ctr., Seattle, 1969-77; RN coord. Evergreen Gen. Hosp., Kirckland, Wash., 1979-81; dir. nursing Pondera Med. Ctr., Conrad, Mt., 1982-83, 85-87; RN Pondera Med. Ctr., Conrad, Mont., 1988-89, infection control coord. Polson unit, 1990—. Mem. Faith Luth. Ch., Ronan, Mont., 1989-90; pres. PTA, Ronan, 1990-91. Mem. Alpha Kappa Sigma. Home: 410 5th Ave SW Ronan MT 59864

WALKER-RATLIFF, JOAN CHARLENE, chemical engineer; b. Beaver, Okla., Oct. 21, 1957; d. Charles William and Bonnie Louise (Conley) W.; m. Ralph Edward Ratliff, May 24, 1980. BS in Chem. Engring., Okla. State U., 1981. Chem. engr. Conoco, Ponca City, Okla., 1980-83, process engr., 1983-85; staff engr. Conoco, Ponca City, 1985-88, sr. engr., 1988—, utility rate cons., 1986-90; mem. Okla. Engring. Tech. Guidance Coun., Oklahoma City, 1983-85, dir., 1986. Recipient Outstanding Achievement award DuPont Co., 1987. Mem. AAUW (v.p. 1986-87). Republican. Methodist. Home: 4 Skinner Ln Rt 2 Ponca City OK 74601 Office: Conoco Box 1267 Ponca City OK 74601

WALKER-SMITH, ANGELIQUE KETURAH, minister, religious organization administrator; b. Cleve., Aug. 18, 1958; d. Roosevelt Victoreold and Geneva (Willis) Walker; m. R. Drew Smith. BA, Kent State U., 1980; M in Div., Yale U., 1983. Prodn. asst. Sta. WFSB-TV, Hartford, Conn., 1980-81; assoc. min. Convent Ave. Bapt. Ch., N.Y.C., 1981-82, Horace Bushnell United Ch. Christ, Hartford, 1981, 83; overseas leader Operation Crossroads Africa, N.Y.C., 1983-86; assoc. pastor Cen. Bapt. Ch., Hartford, 1983-86; exec. dir. Trenton (N.J) Ecumenical Area Ministry, 1986-90; ecumenical liaison Nat. Bapt. Conv. USA, Inc., Bloomington, Ind., 1990—; co-mem. team seminars Princeton Sem. Continuing Edn., 1987—. Contbr. articles to profl. jours. Pub. rels. coordinator Urban League, Cleve., 1979-80, staff mem., 1979, 81-83; subcom. chmn. Mayor's Task Force on Hunger/Homelessness, Trenton, 1986—; mem., minister Hartford Action Plan on Infant Health, 1984-86; mem. NAACP, Hartford, 1981-85. Recipient Mercer County Recognition award Mercer County Exec., 1987. Mem. Ptnrs. in Ecumenism (officer for internat. affairs 1986—), Nat. Assn. Ecumenical Staff (sec. 1987—), Women in Communications, Minister Council-Am. Bapt. Chs. (v.p. Hartford 1984-86), Commn. on Local and Regional Ecumenism, Black Women in Ministry (founder, coordinator Hartford chpt. 1984-86), Nat. Bapt. Conv. U.S.A. Inc., Am. Bapt. Chs., Blue Key. Office: Nat Bapt Conv USA Inc PO Box 6295 Bloomington IN 47407

WALKUSH, MARGARET ANN, speech writer; b. Belle Vernon, Pa., Jan. 5, 1963; d. Joseph Francis and Adeline Angeline (Pierotti) W. BA, Ind. U. Pa., 1985. Staff writer Sci. Applications Internat. Corp., San Diego, 1985-86, video prodn. specialist, 1986-87; assoc. producer Sci. Applocations, San Diego, 1987; account exec. Primavera Video Prodns., Solana Beach, Calif.; speech writer Sci. Applications Internat. Corp., San Diego, 1988—; communications cons. Found. for Enterprise Devel., La Jolla, Calif., 1988—, editor newsletter, 1989. Producer, dir. Poised for the Future, 1987. Democrat. Roman Catholic. Office: SAIC 10260 Campus Point Dr MS 47 San Diego CA 92121

WALL, BETTY JANE, real estate consultant; b. Wichita Falls, Tex., Mar. 23, 1936; d. Albert Willis and Winnie Belle (Goodloe) Beard; m. Richard Lee Wall, Feb. 21, 1959; 1 child, Cynthia Lynn. BS, Vocat.Home Econs. Edn, U. Okla., 1958; MEd, Midwestern U., 1959. Lic. real estate salesperson, Tex. Tchr. San Diego County Schs., 1959-60, Long Beach (Calif.) City Schs., 1960-61, Norman (Okla.) Kindergarten Assn., 1960-65; nat. coun., nat. panhellenic del. Alpha Chi Omega Fraternity, 1978-83, 85—, nat. v.p. membership, 1985-88; real estate salesperson WestMark Realtors, Lubbock, Tex., 1984-85; now ind. real estate salesperson Lubbock; coll. panhellenic adviser Nat. Panhellenic Conf., Tex., 1979—; judge, youth beauty pageants, Tex., N.Mex., Okla., 1984—. Treas. Lubbock Symphony Guild, 1985-87, v.p. ways and means, 1987-88, chmn. ball, 1990. Mem. Tex. Real Estate Assn., Jr. League Lubbock (treas. 1976-78, sustaining adviser fin. com. 1979-83), Lubbock Women's Club, Women's C. of C., Alpha Chi Omega. Republican. Methodist. Home and Office: 3610 63d Dr Lubbock TX 79413

WALL, CAROLYN RAIMONDI, communications executive; b. Springfield, Mass., July 2, 1942; d. Amedio G. and Celestina F. (Penna) Raimondi; m. Peter M. Wall, Oct. 24, 1964 (div. 1972); children: Christina, Suzanne; m. Warren J. Keegan, June 17, 1984 (div. 1989). A.B., Trinity Coll., Washington. Advt dir. Beldoch Industries, N.Y.C., 1972-74; promotion dir. "W" Fairchild Pubs., N.Y.C., 1974-76; v.p., pub. Adweek, N.Y.C., 1976-83; assoc. pub. N.Y. Mag., N.Y.C., 1983-84, pub., 1984-85; exec. v.p. consumer div. Murdoch Mags., 1985-87; v.p., gen. mgr. Sta. WNYW, N.Y.C., 1987—; Mem. bus. adv. bd. Lubin Schs. Bus., Pace U., 1982-88; bd. dirs. N.Y. Urban League, Found. for Minority Interests in Media, MacDuffie Sch., Internat. Radio and TV Found. Mem. Internat. Radio and TV Soc., N.Y. TV Acad. Arts and Scis., Advt. Women N.Y. (bd. dirs., pres. 1981-83). Mem. Advt. Women of N.Y. (bd. dirs., pres. 1981-83). Democrat. Roman Catholic. Office: Sta WNYW 205 E 67th St New York NY 10021

WALL, DOROTHY CELESTE, office manager; b. Bowling Green, Ky., July 11, 1948; d. Walter Scott and Dorothy Jean (Sparks) Stone; children: Tracie Jo, James F., Joey Wallace. Student, Western Ky. U., Bowling Green; AA, North Tenn. Bible Inst., Clarksville, 1978, BA, 1979; MEd, Geneva Theol Coll., Merrillville, Ind., 1982; M of Bus. Studies, St. Martin's Coll., Milw., 1990. Cert. Nat. Acad. Counselors and Family Therapists. Clk., accounts receivable Cain-Sloan Dept. Store, Nashville; adminstr. Community Ch., Clarksville; registrar North Tenn. Bible Inst.; office mgr. William Corley and Assocs., Clarksville. Mem. Nat. Acad. Counselors and Family Therapists (sec.). Anglican. Home: 2094 Memorial Dr Clarksville TN 37043 Office: PO Box 762 Clarksville TN 37041-0762

WALL, ELEANOR ANN, construction company executive; b. Birmingham, Ala., Nov. 28, 1932; d. F.J. and Flossie Eleanor (Thompson) Shelton; m. Frank Gillis Wall, Jr., Aug. 23, 1953; children: Patti Ann, Frank Gillis III, Eleanor Lee. Grad. pub. high sch., Birmingham. Asst. mgr. Telco Credit Union, Birmingham, 1951-59; jobsite officer mgr. Marbury-Pattillo Constrn. Co., Birmingham, 1961-70; sec.-treas. W & P Constrn. Co., Leeds, Ala., 1971-74, Springhill Constrn. Co., Leeds, Ala. and McIntyre, Ga., 1974—; Attendant Computers in Constrn. Seminar, Atlanta, 1982, Ga. Unemployment Compensation Seminar, Savannah, 1986, Ga. Sales and Use Tax Seminar, Atlanta, 1986, Kirby Bldg. Seminars. Sponsor Little League Girsl and Boys Softball, Wilkinson County, Ga.; sponsor, donor McIntyre May Day, McIntyre Library, Wilkinson County 4H Clubs; mem. Friends of the Library, Irwinton, Ga.; bd. dirs. Oceans of Amelia Assn., 1987—, treas., 1988—; donor Toomsboro Nursing Ctr., Wilkinson County Tip-off Club, Wilkinson County Touchdown Club; co-chmn. Wilkinson County Zell Miller for Gov. campaign. Mem. Nat. Assn. Exec. Secs., Nat. Assn. Female Execs., Am. Inst. Profl. Bookkeepers, Am. Soc. Concrete Constrn., Ga. Mining Assn. Republican. Baptist. Club: Ga. Bulldog (Athens, Ga.). Lodge: Elks. Home: Springhill Farm Rt 1 Box 273 Irwinton GA 31042 Office: Springhill Constrn Co Hwy #57 McIntyre GA 31054

WALL, JEAN MARIE, lawyer; b. Jersey City, Apr. 16, 1936; d. Joseph Edward and Marie (Kilian) Destler; 1 child, Elizabeth Anne. BA cum laude, St. Lawrence U., 1957; MA, Middlebury Coll., 1962; JD, San Fernando Valley Coll. Law, 1977. Bar: Calif. 1977. Pvt. practice law, Glendale, Calif., 1977—; lectr. atty. assisted paralegal program UCLA. Mem. NAFE, Calif. Bar Assn., Glendale Bar Assn., South Coast Assn. Female Execs., Glendale C. of C. (membership com., bd. dirs.), Rotary (internat. svc. chmn., sec. 1989-90), Phi Beta Kappa, Pi Sigma Alpha. Avocations: gardening, travel, photography. Roman Catholic. Office: 517 E Wilson Ave Ste 101 Glendale CA 91206

WALL, SHELLEY MARIE, personnel consultant; b. Pasadena, Calif., May 22, 1949; d. Hubert William and Laurina Marie (Champeau) Sutton; m. Robert Patrick Wall, Nov. 13, 1976 (div. 1980); 1 child, Sean. AA, Pasadena City Coll., 1973. Legal sec., supr. O'Melveny & Myers, L.A., 1975-84; owner, mgr. S.M. Wall & Co., San Gabriel, Calif., 1985-88; legal sec. Jones, Day, Reavis & Pogue, L.A., 1987-89; pers. cons. Park Place Pers., Newport Beach, Calif., 1989—. Mem. NAFE, Calif. Assn. Pers. Cons., Le Tip Internat. (social chmn. 1990—). Republican. Roman Catholic. Home: 29713 Niguel Rd Apt C Laguna Niguel CA 92677 Office: Park Place Pers 1100 Quail Ste 200 Newport Beach CA 92660

WALL, SONJA ELOISE, nurse; b. Santa Cruz, Calif., Mar. 28, 1938; d. Ray Theothornton and Reva Mattie (Wingo) W.; m. Edward Gleason Holmes, Aug. 1959 (div. Jan. 1968); children: Deborah Lynn, Lance Edward; m. John Aspesi, Sept. 1969 (div. 1977); children: Sabrina Jean, Daniel John; m. Kenneth Talbot LaBoube, Nov. 1, 1978 (div. 1989); 1 child, Tiffany Amber. BA, San Jose Jr. Coll., 1959, BS, Madonna Coll., 1967; student, U. Mich., 1968-70. RN, Calif., Mich., Colo. Staff nurse Santa Clara Valley Med. Ctr., San Jose, Calif., 1959-67, U. Mich. Hosp., Ann Arbor, 1967-73, Porter and Swedish Med. Hosp., Denver, 1973-77, Laurel Grove Hosp., Castro Valley, Calif., 1977-79, Advent Hosp., Ukiah, Calif., 1984-86; motel owner LaBoube Enterprises, Fairfield, Point Arena, Willits, Calif., 1979—; staff nurse Northridge Hosp., L.A., 1986-87, Folsom State Prison, Calif., 1987; co-owner, mgr. nursing registry Around the Clock Nursing Svc., Ukiah, 1985—; RN Kaiser Permanente Hosp., Sacramento, 1986-89, hospice nurse, 1990—. Contbr. articles to various publs. Leader Coloma 4-H, 1987, 88, 89, 90. Mem. NAFE, Soc. Critical Care Medicine, Am. Heart Assn. (CPR trainer, recipient awards), AACCN, Calif. Bd. RNs, Calif. Nursing Rev., Calif. Critical Care Nurses, Soc. Critical Care Nurses, Am. Motel Assn., (beautification and remodeling award 1985), Soroptimist Internat. Calif., Am. Miniature Horse Assn. (winner nat. grand championship 1981-82, 83, 85, 89), DAR (Jobs Daus. hon. mem.), Cameron Park Country Club. Republican. Episcopalian. Home and Office: Around the Clock Nursing Svc PO Box 543 Coloma CA 95613

WALLACE, ANNETTE, field representative; b. Bath, Maine, Feb. 24, 1958; d. Althea Clinton Taylor and Ethel (Brown) White; m. William Edward Harley Wallace, June 19, 1981 (div. Sept. 1987); children: Raynard, Kenric, Demra, Jonathan. Student, Ohio State U., 1976-81, Franklin U., 1986-87, Inst. Med. and Dental Tech., 1986-87. Chief of communication, supr. of dispatch Enforcement Security Corp. of Jacksonville, Jacksonville, Fla., 1981-83; communication clk., dispatcher Charleston (S.C.) County Police Dept., 1983-83; direct care asst. Geriatric Svcs. Orgn., Columbus, Ohio, 1985-87; home health technologist Franklin County Bd. of Health, Columbus, 1985-87; dir. care asst. Hienzerling Found., Columbus, 1985-87; property mgr., rental agt. Sherrod Enterprises, Columbus, 1985-88; field rep., supr., coord. Med-Cor, Saratoga, Calif., 1988—; liaison Med-Cor, Columbus, 1988—. Vol. Urban League, Columbus, 1988—, Am. Diabetes Assn., Columbus, 1987; v.p. Piketon Dist. Missionary Assn., Columbus, 1987-88. Named Miss Congeniality Miss Charleston S.C. Beauty Pageant, 1975, outstanding coach Columbus (Ohio) Soccer Assn., 1985-88; recipient participation, achievement award State Rep. Ray Miller, Columbus, 1986. Mem. NAFE, Rep. Century Club (Columbus). Republican. Baptist. Home: 1563 Burley Dr Columbus OH 43207 Office: Med-Cor 4466 Darrow Rd Ste 8 Stow OH 44224

WALLACE, BARBARA FAITH, linguistics educator; b. N.Y.C., Dec. 15, 1952; d. Robert Earl and Faith Willi (Jones) Wallace Ringgold; m. Glenn Ronald Gadsden, Feb. 14, 1980 (div. 1982); 1 child, Faith Willi; m. Melvin Wilson Orr, June 8, 1984 (dec. 1989); children: Theodora-Michele Alexandria, Martha Xaviar Underwood. Diploma, U. London, 1977; MA, CUNY, 1981, M Philosophy, 1981. Tchr. linguistics Queens Coll., N.Y.C., 1979-80, John Jay Coll., N.Y.C., 1981-82, CCNY, 1981-84, N.Y.C. Bd. Edn., 1986—; lang. arts dir. Coll. New Rochelle/Harlem, N.Y.C., 1982-84; prison instr. LaGuardia Community Coll., 1984-85, Higher Edn. Devel. Fund, Bronx, 1984-85; tchr. computer literacy NYU, 1987; critic reader Scott, Foresman and Co., Glenview, Ill., 1989—; mem. NYU Ctr. for Latin Am. and Caribean Studies Summer Seminar, 1986. Critic reader math. textbooks Scott, Foresman and Co., 1989; exhibitor; contbr. articles to profl. jours. Bd. dirs., Nat. Women Artists of Color, 1989—, Coast-to-Coast Artists' Collaborative. Council Internat. Edn. Exchange grantee, 1974; Brit. Fedn. U. Women scholar, 1976; fellow CUNY, 1977-81. Mem. Linguistic Soc. Am. (travel grant 1978), MLA, Am. Dialect Soc., Nat. Council Tchrs. Eng., Internat. Apple Core Assn., Nat. Council Tchrs. Math. Jehovah's Witness. Home: W 135 St New York NY 10037-2625 Office: John B Russwurm Sch 2230 Fifth Ave New York NY 10037

WALLACE, BARBARA LIVINGSTONE, public relations executive; b. Edmore, Mich., Apr. 7, 1941; d. Nuel Nichols and Ruth Lucille (Purdon) Donley; m. James Louis Wallace; 1 child, Wendy Ruth Borden. B.A., Mich. State U., 1964; postgrad. Central Mich. U., 1975-76. Social worker, asst. to bd. Oesterlin Home for Children, Springfield, Ohio, 1967-70; office mgr. Farmers Ins. Group, Boulder, Colo., 1971-74; adminstrv. asst. to dean Ferris State U., Big Rapids, Mich., 1974-77; exec. dir. crime prevention grant 720 Lilac, Big Rapids, 1980; exec. dir. Mich. Coalition to Prevent Shoplifting, 1981; exec. dir. Mecosta County Area C. of C., Big Rapids, Mich., 1982-88; v.p. Livingstone Kay, Inc., 1978—, sr. pub. relations administrator, Amway Corp., Ada, Mich., 1989—. adv. bd. Mich. Consol. Gas Co., 1986-89; sec. West Mich. Crime Prevention Assn., Grand Rapids, Mich., 1980-85; state adv. bd. Distributive Edn. Clubs of Am., 1980-86; tech. asst. Nat. Coalition to Prevent Shoplifting, 1981; lectr. crime prevention, 1980—; various chairs Internat. Soc. Crime Prevention Practitioners, Alexandria, Va., 1984—; Author, editor newsletter: Ferris State Pharmacy Alumni, 1974-77, Mich. Coalition to Prevent Shoplifting, 1980, Mecosta County Area C. of C., 1982-88. Author mag.: Michigan Backroads, 1979. Mem., co-chmn. fundraising Mecosta County Gen. Hosp. Aux., Big Rapids, 1978; crime prevention com. Mich. Commn. on Criminal Justice, Lansing, 1979-83; trustee cemetary bd. City of Big Rapids, 1979-84; sec. Big Rapids Ind. Devel. Corp., 1982-88 ; mem. Republican Women's Task Force, Lansing, 1982-87 , Mecosta County Council for the Arts, Big Rapids, 1982—; bd. dirs. Mecosta County Council for the Humanities, Big Rapids, 1983-84; West Central Mich. Community Growth Alliance Task Force, 1984-89, Mich. Leadership Found. of Hugh O'Brien Youth Found., 1986—, Town/Gown Council, Big Rapids, 1985-89; pres. GFWC-MI Edn. Found., 1988—. Recipient Vol. of Yr. award Internat. Soc. of Crime Prevention Practitioners, 1982, Outstanding Leadership award Nat. Crime Prevention Coalition, 1980, Outstanding Service award Distributive Edn. Clubs Am., Mich. chpt., 1983; named Prevention Practitioner of Yr., West Mich. Crime Prevention Assn., 1988. Mem. Gen. Fedn. Women's Clubs (pres. Mich. chpt. 1984-86, bd. dirs. 1984-88, nat. pub. affairs dept. chmn. 1986—), W.Mich. Tourist Assn. (bd. dirs., 1985-88), Nat. Sheriff's Assn. Crime Prevention Com., Nat. Orgn. Victim Assistance (crime and the elderly com. 1989—), Omicron Delta Kappa. Office: 7575 Fulton St E Ada MI 49355

WALLACE, BETTY ANN WOOLARD, pediatrics nurse; b. Morehead City, N.C., Sept. 8, 1954; d. Thomas Virgil and Janie Kathleen (Woodson) Woolard; m. James Quimby Wallace III, July 9, 1979; children: James Q. IV, Mary Kathleen. BS in Nursing, East Carolina U., 1976; MS, U. N.C., 1983. PNP. Nurse pediatrics dept. Craven County Hosp., New Bern, N.C., 1976-79; PNP Harnett County Health Dept., Lillington, N.C., 1979-83; dir. nursing Harborview Nursing Ctr., Morehead City, 1983; cardiac rehab. program dir. Carteret Family Practice Ctr., Morehead City, 1983-84; coordinator New Ideals Nursing Svc., Morehead City, 1984-85; owner, exec. dir. Profl. Nursing Svcs., Inc., Morehead City, 1985—; owner Coastal Pediatric Care, Inc., Morehead City, 1985—; clin. instr. Craven Community Coll., New Bern, 1984-85; child abuse liaison Harnett County Health Dept., 1981-83. Mem. Dem. Women of Carteret County; adv. bd. Carteret Head Start Program, 1984-87. Ruth P. Council Research Found. grantee, 1983. Mem. Nat. Found. Pediatric Nurse Practitioners, Am. Nurses Assn., N.C. Nurses Assn. (legis. com. 1984-85), N.C. Pub. Health Assn., Nat. Assn. Pediatric Nurse Assocs. and Practitioners (state v.p. 1982-83, state pres. 1984-86), Sigma Theta Tau. Office: Profl Nursing Svcs Inc 112 Camp Glenn Dr 35th St Morehead City NC 28557

WALLACE, BETTY JEAN, educator; b. Denison, Tex., Dec. 5, 1927; d. Claude Herman and Pearl Victoria (Freels) Moore; m. Billy Dean McKneely, Sept. 2, 1950 (div. Nov. 1963); children: Rebecca Lynn, Paul King, David Freels, John Walker, Philip Andrew McKneely. BA, Baylor U., 1949; postgrad., Tulane U., 1947, U. Houston, 1949-50, 74, 81, U Colo., 1969-70, U. No. Colo., 1965, 68, 72; MEd, Houston Bapt. U., 1985. Cert. life profl. elem., high sch., life profl. reading specialist, Tex. Tchr. Galena Park (Tex.) Ind. Sch. Dist., 1949-50; tchr. Corpus Christi (Tex.) Independent Sch. Dist., 1950-51, Galena Park (Tex.) Independent Sch. Dist., 1952-53, Denver Pub. Schs., 1953-54, 63-72, Galena Park Independent Sch. Dist., 1972—. Author: The Holy Spirit Today, 1989. Mem. Rep. Senatorial Inner Circle, Washington, 1989-90, Round Table for Ronald Reagan, Washington, 1989-90; tchr. Kindergarten Ch., Denver, 1960-63; helper Feed the Poor, Houston, 1983-85; active Suicide Prevention, Houston, 1973-76, Literacy, Houston, 1976-81; rep. NEA, Denver, 1966-72; mem. Retirement Com., Denver, 1970-72. Grantee NSF, 1969-70. Mem. Tex. Classroom Tchrs. Assn. (officer rep., pres. Galena Park chpt. 1988-89), Delta Alpha Pi (pres. Waco, Tex. chpt. 1948-49), Alpha Epsilon Delta. Republican. Home: 14831 Anoka Dr Channelview TX 77530 Office: North Shore Elem 14310 Duncannon Dr Houston TX 77015

WALLACE, BONNIE ANN, biophysics educator, researcher; b. Greenwich, Conn., Aug. 10, 1951; d. Arthur Victor and Maryjane Ann W. B.S. in Chemistry, Rensselaer Poly. Inst., 1973; M. in Philosophy, Yale U., 1975, Ph.D. in Molecular Biophysics and Biochemistry, 1977. Postdoctoral rsch. fellow Harvard U., Boston, 1977-78; asst. prof. dept. biochemistry and molecular biophysics Columbia U., N.Y.C., 1979-86, assoc. prof. 1986 ; prof. dept. chemistry, dir. Ctr. for Biophysics Rensselaer Poly. Inst., 1987—; vis. scientist MRC Lab. Molecular Biology, Cambridge, Eng., 1978; Fogarty sr. fellow Birkbeck Coll., U. London, 1990. Contbr. numerous articles to profl. jours. and books. Jane Coffin Childs fellow, 1977-79; recipient Irma T. Hirschl award, 1980-84; Camille and Henry Dreyfus tchr.-scholar, 1986. Mem. N.Y. Acad. Scis. (chmn. biophysics sect. 1983-85, adv. bd. 1986), Aspen Ctr. for Physics Fellowship, 1986, Biophys. Soc. (nat. coun., Dayhoff award 1985), Am. Chem. Soc., Am. Crystallographic Assn., Sigma Xi, Phi Lamda Upsilon. Office: Rensselaer Poly Inst Dept Chemistry Troy NY 12180-3590

WALLACE, BRIDGET KELLY, accountant; b. Des Moines, Feb. 8, 1962; d. Leonard Joseph and Edith Mary Emily (Walsh) Wilson; m. Bryan Rollin. BS in Bus. Computer Metho, Calif. State U., Long Beach, 1984. Asst. contr. J. Hewitt Inc., Irvine, Calif., 198587; staff accountant Pre-Foam Inc., Anaheim, Calif., 1987-89; asst. contr. Tamarack Sci. Co., Inc., Anaheim, 1989—. Mem. Delta Gamma (sec. 1980-84). Republican. Roman Catholic. Home: 1261 Brian St Placentia CA 92670

WALLACE, ELIZABETH M., insurance company executive; b. Scranton, Pa., Oct. 8, 1954; d. William and Louise C. (Pruzinsky) W. BA, Johns Hopkins U., 1976, MHS, 1978; MBA, Wharton Sch., U. Pa., 1990. Assoc. Block, McGibony and Assocs., Silver Spring, Md., 1980-83; project dir. Psychiat. Inst. Am., Washington, 1983-85; pres. Mgmt. Strategies Devel., Falls Church, Va., 1985-88; ops. analyst Healthcare, Phila., 1988-90; dir. N.Y. Life Ins. Co., N.Y.C., 1990—. Mem. gov.'s adv. bd. on aging Commonwealth of Va., 1980-88. Home: 220 E 25th St Apt 5D New York NY 10010 Office: NY Life Ins Co 51 Madison Ave New York NY 10010

WALLACE, HELEN MARGARET, physician, educator; b. Hoosick Falls, N.Y., Feb. 18, 1913; d. Jonas and Ray (Schweizer) W. A.B., Wellesley Coll., 1933; M.D., Columbia U., 1937; M.P.H. cum laude, Harvard U., 1943. Diplomate: Am. Bd. Pediatrics, Am. Bd. Preventive Medicine. Intern Bellevue Hosp., N.Y.C., 1938-40; child hygiene physician Conn. Health Dept., 1941-42; successively jr. health officer, health officer, chief maternity and new born div., dir. bur. for handicapped children N.Y.C. Health Dept., 1943-55; prof., dir. dept. pub. health N.Y. Med. Coll., 1955-56; prof. maternal and child health U. Minn. Sch. Pub. Health, 1956-59; chief profl. tng. U.S. Children's Bur., 1959-60, chief child health studies, 1961-62; prof. maternal and child health U. Calif. Sch. Pub. Health, Berkeley, 1962-80; prof., head div. maternal and child health Sch. Pub. Health, San Diego State U., 1980—; Univ. Research lectr. San Diego State U., 1985—; cons. WHO, Uganda, 1961, Philippines, 1966, 68, 75, Turkey, 1968, India, Geneva, 1970, Iran, 1972, Burma, India, Thailand, Sri Lanka, 1975, East Africa, 1976, Australia, 1976, Burma, 1977, India, Indonesia, Thailand, Burma, 1978, 79, India, 1981, Burma, 1985, Peoples Republic of China, 1988; Cons. Ford Found., Colombia, 1971; Traveling fellow WHO, cons., 1989—; U.N. cons. to Health Bur., Beijing, China, 1987; WHO cons. to China, 1988; dir. Family Planning Project, Zimbabwe, 1984-87. Author 8 textbooks; contbr. numerous articles to profl. jours. Recipient Alumnae Achievement award Wellesley Coll., 1982, Outstanding Faculty award San Diego State U., 1983, Martha Eliot award Am. Pub. Health Assn., 1978, Job Smith award Am. Acad. Pediatrics, 1980, U. Minn. award, 1985, Ford Found. study grants 1986, 87, 88; Fulbright fellow, 1989—. Fellow Am. Acad. Pediatrics (Job Smith award 1980, award 1989), Am. Pub. Health Assn. (officer sect., Martha May Eliot award 1978); mem. AMA, Assn. Tchrs. Maternal and Child Health, Am. Acad. Cerebral Palsy, Ambulatory Pediatric Assn., Am. Sch. Preventive Medicine. Home: 850 State St San Diego CA 92101 Office: San Diego State U San Diego CA 92182

WALLACE, HOLLY SALOP, lawyer; b. N.Y.C., Sept. 27, 1956; d. Arnold Salop and Lynne (Gusikoff) Hawes; m. Michael J. Wallace; 1 child, Benjamin. BA, Colgate U., 1978; MA, NYU, 1982; JD, Syracuse (N.Y.) U., 1985. Bar: N.Y 1986, U.S. Dist. Ct. (no. dist.) N.Y. 1988. Assoc. Melvin & Melvin, Syracuse, 1990—. Mem. ABA, N.Y. State Bar Assn., Onondoga County Bar Assn. Democrat. Jewish. Office: Melvin & Melvin 220 S Warren St Syracuse NY 13202

WALLACE, JANE YOUNG (MRS. DONALD H. WALLACE), editor; b. Geneseo, Ill., Feb. 17, 1933; d. Worling R. and Margaret C. (McBroom) Young; m. Donald H. Wallace, Aug. 24, 1959; children: Robert, Julia. BS in Journalism, Northwestern U., 1955, MS in Journalism, 1956; LittD (hon.), Johnson and Wales U., 1990. Editor house organ Libby McNeill & Libby, Chgo., 1956-58; prodn. editor Instns. Mag., Chgo., 1958-61; food editor Instns. Mag., 1961-65, mng. editor, 1965-68, editor-in-chief, 1968-85; editor Restaurants and Instns., 1970-85, editorial dir., 1985-89, assoc. pub., 1985-89, pub., 1989—; pub. R & I Market Pl., 1989—; editorial dir. Hotels and Restaurants Internat. Mag., 1971-89, Foodservice Equipment Specialist Mag., 1975-89; v.p. Cahners Pub. Co. (Reed USA), 1982; cons. Nat. Restaurant Assn., dir., 1977-82; cons. Nat. Inst. for Foodservice Industry.; vis. lectr. Fla. Internat. U., 1980. Editor: The Professional Chef, 1962, The

Professional Chef's Book of Buffets, 1965, Culinary Olympics Cookbook, 1980, 3d edit., 1988, Academy of American Culinary Foundation Cookbook, 1985, American Dietetic Association Foundation Cookbook, 1986; contbr.: restaurant chpt. World Book Ency., 1975, Food Service Trends, American Quantity Cooking, 1976. Mem. com. investigation vocat. needs for food service tng. U.S. Dept. Edn., 1969; mem. Inst. Food Editors' Conf., 1959-88, pres., 1967; mem. hospitality industry edn. adv. bd. Ill. Dept. Edn., 1976, mem. adv. bd. Ill. sch. foodservice, 1978; mem. corp. adv. bd. Am. Dietetic Assn. Found., 1981—; trustee Presbyn. Ch., Barrington, Ill., 1983-85, Culinary Inst. Am., 1987—. Recipient Jesse H. Neal award for best bus. press editorial, 1969, 70, 73, 76, 77, 79, 82, 87; named Outstanding Woman Northwood Inst., 1983. Fellow Soc. for Advancement Foodservice Research (dir. 1975—, sec. 1980); mem. Internat. Foodservice Mfrs. Assn. (Spark Plug award 1979), Nat. Assn. Foodservice Equipment Mfrs., Am. Bus. Press Assn. (chmn. editorial com. 1978), Am. Inst. Interior Designers (asso.), Women in Communications (v.p. Chgo. 1957-58), Ivy Soc. Restauranteurs of Distinction (co-founder 1970—), Am. Dietetic Assn. (hon.), Roundtable for Women in Food Service (bd. dirs. 1980-84; Foodservice Woman of Yr. 1988), Les Dames d'Escoffier (charter mem.), Culinary Inst. of Am. (ambassador, trustee 1987), Brotherhood of Knights of Vine (Gentlelady award 1980, 81), Gamma Phi Beta, Kappa Tau Alpha. Home: 186 Signal Hill Rd Barrington IL 60010 Office: Restaurants & Instns 1350 E Touhy Ave Box 5080 Des Plaines IL 60018

WALLACE, JOAN S., international government administrator, social scientist; b. Chgo., Nov. 8, 1930; d. William Edouard and Esther (Fulks) Scott; m. John Wallace, June 12, 1954 (div. Mar. 1976); children—Mark, Eric, Victor; m. Maurice A. Dawkins, Oct. 14, 1979. A.B., Bradley U., 1952; M.S.W., Columbia U., 1954; postgrad., U. Chgo., 1965; Ph.D., Northwestern U., 1973; H.H.D. (hon.), U. Md., 1979; L.H.D. (hon.), Bowie State Coll., 1981; LLD (hon.), Ala. A&M U., 1990. Lic. social psychologist, social worker. From asst. prof. to assoc. prof. U. Ill.-Chgo., 1967-73; assoc. dean, prof. Howard U., Washington, 1973-76; v.p.-programs Nat. Urban League, N.Y.C., 1975-76; v.p. adminstrn. Morgan State U., Balt., 1976-77; asst. sec. adminstrn. USDA, Washington, 1977-81, adminstr. Office Internat. Cooperation and Devel., 1981-89; rep. to Trinidad and Tobago Inter Am. Inst. for Cooperation in Agr., USDA, 1989; speaker in field. Contbr. articles, chpts. to profl. publs. Chair Binat. Agrl. Research and Devel. Fund, 1987. Recipient Disting. Alumni award Bradley U., 1978, Meritorious award Delta Sigma Theta, 1978, award for leadership Lambda Kappa Mu, 1978, award for outstanding achievement and svc. to nation Capital Hill Kiwanis Club, 1978, Links Achievement award, 1979, Presdl. Rank for Meritorious Exec., 1980, NAFEO award, 1989, Community Svc. award Alpha Phi Alpha, 1987, Pres.' award for outstanding pub. svc. Fla. A&M U., 1990. Mem. Am. Psychol. Assn., Am. Consortium for Internat. Pub. Adminstrn. (exec. com., governing bd. 1987), Soc. Internat. Devel. (Washington chpt.), Sr. Exec. Assn., Soc. for Internat. Devel., AAAS, Soc. Internat. Devel., White House Com. on Internat. Sci., Engring. and Tech., Internat. Sci. and Edn. Coun. (chmn. 1981-89), Am. Evaluation Assn., Consortium Internat. Higher Edn. (adv. com.), Caribbean Studies Soc., Caribbean Assn. of Agriculture Economists, Assn. Polit. Psychologists, Pi Gamma Mu. Episcopalian. Home: 5 Poui Hill Rd, Lady Chancellor, Port of Spain Trinidad and Tobago Office: IICA in Trinidad/Tobago, Orange Grove Rd, Tacarigua Trinidad and Tobago

WALLACE, KATHLEEN DAWN, cosmetologist; b. Albany, N.Y., Jan. 18, 1963; d. George Thomas and Ruth Virginia (Coyle) Wallace. Cosmetologist, Boces, Lakeside, N.Y., 1981. Cosmetologist DeRoma Salon, Baldwinsville, N.Y., 1981-83, Baldwinsville, 1983—; cosmetologist/educator Kayser Design Team, Syracuse, N.Y., 1986—; assoc. John Paul Mitchell Systems, Calif., 1986-89, sr. assoc., 1989—, dist. coord., 1989—. Contbr. articles to profl. jours. Recipient numerous hair dressing awards. Mem. NAFE, NOW, Nat. Hairdresser Assn. (bd. dirs. 1983-84, rec. sec. 1986-87). Roman Catholic. Home and Office: 59 E Genesee St Baldwinsville NY 13027

WALLACE, KATHRYN L., accountant; b. Lubbock, Tex., Dec. 24, 1945; d. C.L. and Ione K. (Lyle) Strickland; m. Jerry A. Wallace, Sept. 5, 1965; children: Anthony, Marissa. Student, Odessa (Tex.) Coll. Cert. CPR; notary pub. Bookkeeper, sec. Carbery Fabrication Co., Inc., Odessa; v.p., treas. Customart Sign and Display Co., Odessa. Mem. NAFE, Nat. Notary Assn., Odessa Bus. and Profl. Women, Tex. Notary Pub. Assn. Office: 2512 Remington Rd Odessa TX

WALLACE, MARY ANN, development company executive; b. Reno County, Kans., Feb. 19, 1939; d. Ivan Lewis and Vina Sue (Smith) Newell; m. Alexander Wallace III, Feb. 17, 1968 (div. June 1982); 1 child, Alexander IV. BS, Wichita State U., 1961. Property mgr. 650 S. Grand Bldg. Co., Los Angeles, 1961-68; v.p. Milner Devel., Santa Monica, Calif., 1981-83; chief fin. officer Milner Devel., L.A., 1983—; cons. Kitty Prodns., L.A., 1978—; cons., v.p. Am. Mut. Prodns., Redlands, Calif., 1975—. V.p. Sister Servants of Mary Guild, L.A., 1970-77; treas. Hosp. of Good Samaritan Aux., L.A., 1969-75; pres sec. Orphanage Guild Jrs., L.A., 1974. Named Downtown Working Angel, Downtown Businessmen's Assn., Best Fund Raiser, Sister Servants of Mary Guild, 1974-76. Mem. L.A. World Affairs Coun., L.A. Women in Bus., Nat. Art Assn. Republican. Roman Catholic. Club: L.A. Country (Beverly Hills, Calif.). Office: Milner Investment Corp 439 N Bedford Dr Beverly Hills CA 90210 Office: 924 Bellevue Way NE Bellevue WA 98004

WALLACE, MARY ANN, volunteer; b. Little Rock, Mar. 24, 1944; d. William Elmer and Seawillo (Cunningham) Gosdin; m. John Riley Wallace, Oct. 4, 1969; children: John, David. BS in Psychology and Sociology, Ouachita Coll., 1962. Asst. libr. Children's Colony, Conway, Ark., 1966-69; mgr. customer svc. dept. Sears Roebuck & Co., Augusta, Ga., 1978-80; interim dir. Coffee County United Way, Enterprise, Ala., 1990—. Vol. sec. Boy Scouts Am., Enterprise, 1988-90; vol. crisis counselor Mental Health Assn., Enterprise, 1989-90, Coffee County Tng. Ctr., 1987—. Mem. AAUW (pres. 1989—), Officer's Wives Club (reservations chmn. 1987, 3d v.p. 1987-88, 1st v.p. 1988-89, pres. 1989). Republican. Methodist. Home: 200 E Silver Oak Dr Enterprise AL 36350-1572

WALLACE, PAULA KATHLEEN, microcomputer consultant; b. San Diego, June 3, 1951; d. Paul W. and Betty J. (Moore) W. Auditor Stinson Beach (Calif.) Water Dist., 1978-83; mgr. support and tng. McClure Mgmt. Systems, Larkspur, Calif., 1984-86; owner Wallace & Assocs., Novato, Calif., 1986—; instr. Calif. CPA Soc., Palo Alto, 1985-88. Mem. NAFE, Internat. Platform Assn., Commonwealth Club. Office: Wallace & Assocs 8 Los Cedros Dr Novato CA 94947

WALLACE, ROANNE, hosiery company executive; b. Greenwood, Miss., Dec. 18, 1949; d. Robert Carter and Lois Anne (Vick) W. BM, U. Tenn., 1971; MA, U. N.C., 1976; MBA, Wake Forest U., 1982. Exec. dir. Am. Bd. Clin. Chemistry, Winston-Salem, N.C., 1977-78; administrv. officer Winston-Salem/Forsyth County Office Emergency Mgmt., 1978-79, sr. asst. dir., 1979-82; with Sara Lee Hosiery, Winston-Salem, 1982—; product mgr. L'eggs Products, Inc., Winston-Salem, 1986-88; mktg. dir. Sara Lee Hosiery, Winston-Salem, 1988—. Mem. adv. coun. Winston-Salem/Forsyth County Office of Emergency Mgmt. Miss University of Tenn., 1970. Mem. Am. Mgmt. Assn., Winston-Salem Sales and Mktg. Execs. Home: 803 Devon Ct Winston-Salem NC 27104 Office: L'eggs Products Inc PO Box 2495 Winston-Salem NC 27102

WALLACE, SUSAN C., career consultant; b. Mercedes, Tex., Apr. 12, 1947; d. Frank Samuel and Jean Elizabeth (Stafford) C. BA in English, SUNY, 1971; MS in Social Work, Columbia U., 1977. Social worker N.Y. Svc. Program for Older People, Inc., N.Y.C., 1977-85, dir. mental health clinic, 1980-85; career cons. N.Y.C., 1985—; field instr. Hunter Coll. Sch. Social Work, N.Y.C., 1980-82. Mem. Columbia U. Alumni Assn. Republican. Home: 315 E 86th St #2LE New York NY 10028

WALLACH, ANNE JACKSON See JACKSON, ANNE

WALLACH, BETH KAKERBECK, freelance writer; b. Tarrytown, N.Y., June 15, 1934; d. John and Elizabeth (Lawson) Kakerbeck; m. Brian Wallach, Sept. 13, 1959; children: Jennifer Leigh Nolletti, Todd Brian. Cert., N.Y. Sch. of Design, 1955, Inst. Children's Lit., 1984. Adminstrv. asst. W&J Sloane, Inc., White Plains, N.Y., 1953-61; freelance writer White Plains, 1961—. Producer, host (TV show) This Blooming City; contbr. articles to profl. jours. Mem. White Plains Hist. Soc.; advisor Westchester Community Coll. Found. Adv. Coun., Valhalla, N.Y., 1984—; pres. White Plains Beautification Found., 1987-90; sr. warden Christ Episcopal Ch., Tarrytown, 1989—; bd. dirs. Music for a Sunday Afternoon, Tarrytown, N.Y. Mem. Nat. Writers Union. Home: 31 Park Circle White Plains NY 10603

WALLACH, MAGDALENA FALKENBERG (CARLA WALLACH), writer; b. Brussels; came to U.S., 1930; d. Carl Albert and Renee Antoinette (Meunier) Falkenberg; m. Philip Charles Wallach, Mar. 14, 1950. Student, Columbia U., Hunter Coll., New Sch. for Rsch. Ptnr., chief copywriter Williams-Falkenberg Advt. Assocs., Inc., N.Y.C., 1951-55. Author: Reluctant Weekend Gardener, 1971, Interior Decorating with Plants, 1976, Gardening in the City, 1976, Garden in a Teacup, 1978; contbr. articles to N.Y. Times, Glamour, Working Woman, others. Active in past ARC; active Bruce Mus., 1987—, chmn. spl. events, chmn. 75th Anniversary Gala, mem. Renaissance Ball benefit com., chmn. nominating com., bd. dirs., mem. joint Bruce Mus. Assocs. com., bd. trustees, long range planning com., other fundraising activities. Mem. Authors Guild Inc., Garden Writers Assn., Am., Nat. League Am. PEN Women (pres. Greenwich br. 1987—), English-speaking Union, Alliance Francaise, Nat. Inst. Social Scis. Roman Catholic. Home: 84 Lower Cross Rd Greenwich CT 06831

WALLACH, ROCHELLE LAMM, financial services executive, publisher, writer; b. Fargo, N.D., Apr. 16, 1948; d. Barney Eyles and Marion LaVerne (Peterson) Lamm; m. Alan Victor Wallach, Apr. 26, 1978. BA, Loretto Heights Coll., 1970; MBA, U. Denver, 1980. Cert. fin. planner. Inst. salesman Kraft Foods, Inc., Ft. Worth, 1973-75; dir. adminstrn. Coll. Fin. Planning, Denver, 1975-77; regional v.p. Oppenheimer Mgmt., N.Y.C., 1977-80; exec. v.p., nat. sales mgr. Integrated Resources, Inc., N.Y.C., 1980-86; pres. Lamm Wallach Communications Group, Inc., Denver, 1985-87, AAL Advisors, Inc./AAL Distbrs., Inc., Appleton, Wis., 1987—. Author, pub.: On the Road Again, How to Succeed in the Competitive World of Wholesaling, 1985; author: On the Road Again, A Success Guide for Business Women Who Travel, 1985; author, producer video: Nanny Comes to Your House, How to Take Care of Your Newborn, 1986. Named Disting. Alumna, U. Denver, 1985. Mem. Inst. Cert. Fin. Planners, Internat. Assn. Fin. Planning (speakers bur.). Avocations: traveling, writing, fishing, private pilot. Office: AAL Distbrs Inc 222 W College Ave Appleton WI 54914

WALLACK, RINA EVELYN, lawyer; b. Pitts.; d. Erwin Norman and Gloria A. (Schacher). AD in Nursing, Delta Coll., 1973; BS cum laude in Psychology, Eastern Mich. U., 1980; JD cum laude, Wayne State U., 1983. Registered nurse Mich.; bar: Calif. 1983. Psychiat. head nurse Ypsilanti State Hosp., Mich., 1973-77, instr., nursing educator, 1977-80; teaching asst. contracts Wayne State U., Detroit, 1981-83; legal asst. Wayne County Prosecutor's Office, 1982-83; atty. NLRB, L.A., 1983-86, dir. employee rels. legal svcs. Paramount Pictures Corp., L.A., 1986-89, v.p., 1989—. Contbr. articles to profl. jours. Instr., ARC, Mich., 1978-80. Recipient Am. Jurisprudence Book award, 1983; Order of Coif, 1983. Mem. ABA, Am. Trial Lawyers Assn., Mich., Calif. bar assns. Avocations: shooting, movies, dancing, reading, photography. Office: Paramount Pictures Corp 5555 Melrose Ave Los Angeles CA 90038

WALL-ANGELIDES, PHYLLIS, marketing professional; b. Boston, Sept. 29, 1957; d. Frederick Leonard and Alice (Keedy) Wall; children: Brendan Nathaniel, Michael John, Nicholas Harry. Student, U. Mass., 1978-80. Rep. customer svc. GTE Sprint (formerly So. Pacific Communications Corp.), Washington, 1982-83, sr. customer svc. rep., 1983-84; from specialist customer care to sr. sales rep. GTE Sprint, Boston, 1984, account rep., 1984-85, select account mgr., 1985; nat. account exec. Nynex Corp., Boston, 1985-86; dir. mktg. and corp. sales Stonington Inst., North Stonington, Conn., 1986-88; dir. sales adminstrn. Stonington Inst., North Stonington, 1988—. Complaint mediator Mass. Atty. Gen.'s Office, Boston, 1979-80; citizen rep. State Adv. Com. on Substance Abuse, Boston, 1979-81; mem. Concerned Citizens for Drug Abuse Prevention, Hanover, Mass., 1978-79; supporter Columbia (Conn.) Youth Recreation Council, 1986—, Slater Meml. Mus., Norwich, Conn., 1986—. Mem. Conn. Assn. Labor/Mgmt. Alcohol Counselors. Office: Stonington Inst Swantown Hill Rd North Stonington CT 06359-0216

WALLENBORN, JANICE RAE, elementary educator; b. Chgo., Jan. 22, 1938; d. Ramon Joseph and Anne Joan (Seaquist) W. BEd, Beloit Coll., 1960; MEd, The George Washington U., 1966; postgrad., George Mason U., 1987-88, U. Va., 1965-85; BE in Ministry, U. of the South, 1989. Cert. tchr. Va. Tchr. Quantico (Va.) Marine Base, 1960-62; elem. tchr. Pearl Harbor Elem. Sch., Honolulu, 1962-64, Quantico Dependents Sch. System, 1964—. Counselor Diet Ctr., Springfield, Va., 1979-89. Mem. Quantico Edn. Assn. (treas. 1968-72), Va. Edn. Assn., NEA (life), Pi Lambda Theta, Kappa Alpha Theta (treas. 1979-81, pres. North Va., 1981-85, alumni dist. pres. Va. 1989). Republican. Episcopalian. Home: 8576 Gwynedd Way Springfield VA 22153 Office: Quantico Dependents Schs WW Burrows Bldg 3308 Quantico VA 22134

WALLENS, LAURA BETH, lawyer; b. Boston, Nov. 3, 1953; d. Jack Gordon and Anne (Myerson) W. BA, Northeastern U., 1976; JD, Vanderbilt U., 1979. Bar: Ohio 1979, U.S. Dist. Ct. (so. dist.) Ohio 1983. Sr. trust officer Bank One, Dayton, Ohio, 1979-85; v.p. AmeriTrust Co., Cleve., 1985-87; assoc. Hahn Loeser & Parks, Cleve., 1987—. Jewish. Office: Hahn Loeser & Parks 1965 E 6th St Cleveland OH 44114

WALLENSTEIN, SANDRA L., education educator; b. Balt., Dec. 21, 1951; d. Leonard and Emily (Seidenman) Wallenstein. BA, U. Rochester, 1973, MEd, 1976, EdD, 1980. Part time prof. San Francisco State U., 1980-82, Antioch U., San Francisco, 1980-82; asst. mgr. computer ops. Wells Fargo Bank, San Francisco, 1983-85; chmn. dept. liberal studies John F. Kennedy U., Orinda, Calif., 1986-88; chmn. dept. edn. John F Kennedy U, Orinda, Calif., 1989—; cons. Earth Talk, Children as Peacemakers, San Francisco, 1988—. Mem. Am. Assn. Higher Edn. Jewish. Office: John F Kennedy U 12 Altarinda Rd Orinda CA 94563

WALLER, J. GARLAND, television producer; b. Charlottesville, Va., Apr. 17, 1950; d. John Suter Waller and Jane (Dreifus) St. Lawrence; m. Michael Aaron Avery, Feb. 10, 1990. BS in Edn., U. Va., 1972; MS in Broadcast Journalism, Boston U., 1981. Tchr. English Virginia Beach (Va.) Jr. High Sch., 1974-78; producer TV segments World of People, Washington, 1981-82; children's producer Sta. WBZ-TV, Boston, 1982, spl. projects producer, 1985—; part-time prof. Boston U., 1987-89. Recipient Bronze and Gold awards Internat. Film & TV of N.Y., 1985. Mem. Nat. Assn. TV, Arts and Scis. (bd. govs. Boston chpt. 1989-90), Women in Film. Democrat. Mem. Soc. of Friends. Office: Sta WBZ-TV 1170 Soldiers Field Rd Boston MA 02134

WALLER, PAMELA RAWN, medical manufacturing company executive; b. Chgo., Mar. 6, 1947; d. Melville Murray Rawn and Jean Louise (Eilenberger) Rowley; m. Robert Pendleton, Nov. 27, 1965 (div. 1972); children: Jennifer Lee, Elizabeth Jean; m. Harry Franklin Waller, Mar. 22, 1986. Student, Carroll Coll., 1964-66. Owner craft shop Little Women, Racine, Wis., 1973-79; owner, gen. mgr. Tennis Togs, Racine, 1973-80; customer svc. rep. Surgitek, Racine, 1980-82; sales rep. Surgitek, Houston, 1982-85; regional mgr. Surgitek, Charlotte, N.C., 1985—. Mem. Jr. League (bd. dirs. local chpt. 1979—), Medearis Women's Club (treas. 1989). Republican. Episcopalian. Home: 200 Medearis Dr Charlotte NC 28211 Office: Surgitek 3037 Mt Pleasant Racine WI 53404

WALLER, SANDRA KAY, educator; b. Crestline, Ohio, Jan. 6, 1943; d. Hoy Elwood and Evelyn Irene (Taylor) Ryan; m. Jeffrey William Waller (div. Aug. 1989); 1 child, Erin Jessica. BS, Bowling Brook State U., 1965; MA, Stony Brook U., Stony Brook, 1972; SUNY, Stony Brook. Tchr. English, Garfield Elem. Sch., Toledo, 1965-69, Cold Spring Harbor (N.Y.) High Sch., 1969—. Mem. AAUW. Home: 35 Terry Rd Northport NY 11768

WALLER, WILHELMINE KIRBY (MRS. THOMAS MERCER WALLER), civic worker, organization official; b. N.Y.C., Jan. 19, 1914; d. Gustavus Town and Wilhelmine (Claflin) Kirby; m. Thomas Mercer Waller, Apr. 7, 1942. Ed., Chapin Sch., N.Y.C. Conservation chmn. Garden Club Am., 1959-61, pres., 1965-68, chmn. nat. affairs, 1968-74, dir., 1969-71; mem. adv. com. N.Y. State Conservation Commn., 1959-70; mem. Nat. Adv. Com. Hwy. Beautification, 1965-68; trustee Mianus River Gorge Conservation Com. of Nature Conservancy, 1955—, Arthur W. Butler Meml. Sanctuary, 1955-79; mem. Rachel Carson council Nat. Audubon Soc., 1964—; v.p. Bedford (N.Y.) Farmers Club, 1954-74; dir. Westchester County Soil and Water Conservation Dist., 1967-74; adviser N.Y. Gov.'s Study Commn. Future of Adirondacks, 1968-70; adv. com. N.Y. State Parks and Recreation Commn., 1971-72; adv. com. to sec. state UN Conf. Human Environment, 1971-72; mem. Pres.'s Citizens Adv. Com. on Environ. Quality, 1974-78. Mem. planning bd., Bedford, 1953-57; mem. Conservation adv. coun., Bedford, N.Y., 1968-70, Westchester County Planning Bd., 1970-88; bd. govs. Nature Conservancy, 1970-78; Mem. Lyndhurst council Nat. Trust for Historic Preservation, 1965-74; bd. dirs. Scenic Hudson, Inc., 1985-88. Recipient Frances K. Hutchinson medal Garden Club Am., 1971, Holiday mag. award for beautiful Am., 1971, Conservation award Am. Motors Corp., 1975, Oak Leaf award Nature Conservancy, 1988. Mem. Nat. Soc. Colonial Dames, Huguenot Soc. Am., Daus. of Cincinnati. Address: Tanrackin Farm Bedford Hills NY 10507

WALLERSTEDT-WEHRLE, JOANNA KATHERINE, poet, writer, lyricist; b. Columbus, Ind., Sept. 14, 1944; m. Jason W. Wehrle, June 24, 1979; children: Christian J., Michelle L., Gina R. Student, Ind. U., Indpls., 1967-69. Former model, bookkeeper, employment counselor, exec. sec., 1936-86. 127 poems pub.; composer (with others) popular songs.

WALLIN, FANNY MAE, special education educator, writer; b. Mt. Vernon, Ky., Feb. 11, 1943; d. Bob and Rose (Jones) Jasper; m. Thomas Edward Wallin, Jan. 21, 1967; children: Regina Mae, Thomas Frederick (dec.), Tomina Nichole. BS, Ea. Ky. U., 1969, postgrad., 1970-74, 81-86. Cert. spl. edn. dir., elem. edn. tchr., educably mentally handicapped tchr., learning and behavioral disorders tchr., Ky. Tchr. educably mentally handicapped Owen County Bd. Edn., Owenton, Ky., 1966-67, Rockcastle County Bd. Edn., Mt. Vernon, 1968-74; tchr. elem. edn. Rockcastle County Bd. Edn., 1974-81, tchr. learning and behavior disorders, 1981—. Author several poems; songwriter It's Not What You Did To Me Dear. Mem. NAFE, NEA, Ky. Edn. Assn. Home: Rte 4 Box 164 Ferguson St Mount Vernon KY 40456

WALLIN, JUDITH KERSTIN, pediatrician, educator; b. Paris, Apr. 23, 1938; came to U.S., 1938; d. Theodore Bror and Ella Charlotte (Butler) Wallin. BS in Chemistry, Elizabethtown (Pa.) Coll., 1960; MD, Temple U., 1964. Diplomate Am. Bd. Pediatrics. Intern Bellevue Hosp., N.Y.C., 1964-65, resident specializing in pediatrics, 1965-67, attending pediatrician, 1967—; instr. pediatrics, NYU, 1967-71, asst. prof. clin. pediatrics, 1971-74, assoc. prof., 1974—. Trustee Elizabethtown Coll., 1988—. Recipient Educate for Service through Profl. Achievement award, O.F. Stambaugh Alumni award Elizabethtown Coll., 1978. Home: 300 E 33d St New York NY 10016 Office: Bellevue Hosp Dept Pediatrics 27th St and 1st Ave New York NY 10016

WALLING, GEORGIA, psychotherapist b. Cedarhurst, N.Y.; d. William English and Anna (Strunsky) W.; student U. Paris, 1931-32, Vassar Coll., 1932-34; BA, Rollins Coll., 1935; MA, Columbia U., 1937, MS in Social Work, 1947. Diplomate in clin. social work. Caseworker, Family Service Soc., Atlanta, 1948-49, Bklyn. Bur. Social Service, 1951-53, Inwood House, N.Y.C., 1954-58; sr. psychiat. casework therapist Childrens Village, Dobb's Ferry, N.Y., 1959-60; assoc. staff mem. Postgrad Center for Mental Health, N.Y.C., 1960-65; pvt. practice psychotherapy and psychoanalysis, N.Y.C. Mem. Nat. Assn. Social Workers, Acad. Cert. Social Workers, N.Y. State Soc. Clin. Social Work Psychotherapists, Postgrad. Psychoanalytic Soc., Nat. Assn. for the Advancement Psychoanalysis.

WALLING, SUSAN EILEEN FEMRITE, interior designer; b. Glenwood, Minn., Oct. 4, 1944; d. Sigvold Elmer and Sally Evangeline (Amundson) Femrite; B.S., U. Minn., 1966, cert. interior design, 1980; m. Greg Thomas Walling, Aug. 13, 1966; children—Christopher, Kari. Tchr., Roseville (Minn.) Public Schs., 1966-68, St. Louis Park (Minn.) Public Schs., 1968-73; interior designer Sue Walling Interiors, Edina, Minn., 1978-81; pres., interior designer SW Design, Inc., Mpls., 1981—. Pub. in Designer Mag., 1983, 84, 85, 89, Medical and Dental Space Planning For The 1990's. Active, Children's Health Center Aux., Friends of Mpls. Art Inst.; bd. life and growth Mt. Olivet Luth. Ch., PTSO bd. South View Jr. High, action teams Edina Pub. Schs. Mem. Am. Soc. Interior Designers (assoc.). Club: Edina Country (swim club bd.). Office: 925 Southgate Office Plaza 5001 W 80th St Minneapolis MN 55437

WALLINGTON, MARIA JOANNE, cardiologist; b. Saginaw, Mich., Feb. 9, 1946; d. Dale and Ailene F. (Pearce) W. AB, Stanford U., 1968; MD, U. Calif., San Francisco, 1972. Diplomate Am. Bd. Pediatrics. Pediatric intern Stanford (Calif.) Med. Ctr., 1972-73, resident in pediatrics, 1973-74, pediatric cardiology fellow, 1974-76; pvt. practice Pacific Med. Ctr., San Francisco, 1976-78, Anchorage, 1979—. Mem. Am. Acad. Pediatrics (sec., treas. Alaska chpt. 1988—), Alaska State Med. Soc. Mem. Unity Ch. Office: 3300 Providence Dr Ste 208 Anchorage AK 99508

WALLIS, ELIZABETH SUSAN, air traffic control specialist; b. Tulsa, Dec. 20, 1953; d. Ralph David and Margaret Ella (Nolen) W. Student, Drury Coll., 1972-73; BS, U. Ark., 1976. Resident asst. U. Ark., Fayetteville, 1974-76; placement interviewer Okla. Employment Service, Tulsa, 1977-78; air traffic control specialist FAA Houston, 1978-84, regional staff specialist, Los Angeles, 1984-85, plans and programs specialist, Olathe, Kans., 1985, supervisory air traffic control specialist, 1985-87; FAA quality assurance specialist FAA Cen. Region, 1987-89; NAS implementation specialist, 1989—. Bd. dirs. Westmont Homes Assn., 1987-89. Mem. Profl. Women Controllers (charter, cen. regional area dir. 1985-86, nat. sec. 1987-89), Air Traffic Control Assn., Women's Leadership Inst. Avocation: travel. Office: FAA Cen Region Hdqrs Air Traffic Div 601 W 12th Kansas City MO 64106

WALLIS, ELLEN MAE, health care consultant; b. Plainfield, N.J., May 25, 1953; d. Robert Elsworth and Ruth Elizabeth (Doris) W.; m. Richard Bayer, July 2, 1977 (div. Dec. 1980). BA/Psychology cum laude, Fairleigh Dickinson U., 1975, BS/Nursing cum laude, 1975, MBA in Mgmt., 1984; MS in Nursing, Ohio State U., 1976. Nurse various orgns., N.J., Ohio, 1975—; instr. Capital U., Columbus, Ohio, 1977, Ohio State U., Columbus, 1977-80; asst. prof. Seton Hall U., South Orange, N.J., 1980-81; adminstrv. dir. DRG Mgmt. Systems Robert Wood Johnson U. Hosp., New Brunswick, N.J., 1984-86; cons. Ohio State U. Hosps., Columbus, 1979; participant EFMI Working Conf. on DRG's, 1989, Brussels; speaker Internat. Symposium Computers, 1988; participant Internat. Conf. European Computer Group, 1989, Third Internat. Symposium on Nursing Use of Computers and Info. Sci., Dublin. Bd. advisors Fairleigh Dickinson U., Rutherford, N.J., 1982—, Hemophilia Assn., New Brunswick, 1984. Recipient grad. fellowship Fairleigh Dickinson U., 1982, master's fellowship Ohio State U., 1976. Mem. Internat. Soc. Quality Assurance, N.J. State Nurse's Assn., DRG com. 1987-88), Health Care Fin. Mgmt. Assn. (DRG com. 1987-88), Nat. Assn. Health Data Orgns., Psi Chi, Phi Omega Epsilon, Phi Zeta Kappa, Phi Kappa Phi, Sigma Theta Tau (com. chmn. 1978-80, nat. com. 1979-83). Roman Catholic.

WALLISON, FRIEDA K., lawyer; b. N.Y.C., Jan. 15, 1943; d. Ruvin H. and Edith (Landes) Koslow; m. Peter J. Wallison, Nov. 24, 1966; children—Ethan S., Jeremy L., Rebecca K. A.B., Smith Coll., 1963; LL.B., Harvard U., 1966. Bar: N.Y. 1967, DC 1982. Assoc. Carter, Ledyard & Milburn, N.Y.C., 1966-75; spl. counsel, div. market regulation Securities & Exchange Commn., Washington, 1975; exec. dir., gen. counsel Mcpl. Securities Rulemaking Bd., Washington, 1975-78; ptnr. Rogers & Wells, N.Y.C. and Washington, 1978-83, Jones, Day, Reavis & Pogue, Washington, 1983—; mem. Govtl. Acctg. Standards Adv. Council, Washington, Nat. Council on Pub. Works Improvement, Washington; mem. environ. fin. adv. bd. EPA. Fellow Am. Bar Found.; mem. Nat. Council Govtl. Acctg., Nat. Assn. Bond Lawyers, Fed. Bar Assn., ABA, N.Y.C. Bar Assn. Contbr. articles to profl.

jours. Office: Jones Day Reavis & Pogue Met Sq 1450 G St NW Ste 600 Washington DC 20005

WALLS, VICKI L., human resources executive; b. Cedar Rapids, Iowa, Nov. 4, 1946; d. Paul Richard and Nadene Ruth (Kinney). BS, Calif. State U., Fresno, 1970, postgrad. V.p. human resources Guarantee Fin. Corp., Fresno; group human resources dir. Foster Poultry Farms, Livingston, Calif.; chief exec. officer Comprehensive Youth Svcs., Inc., Fresno; owner, pres. Human Resource Mgmt. Assocs., Madera, Calif. Mem. Madera County Arts Coun. Mem. Health Plan of Am., Calif. Assn. Health Svcs. at Home. Address: 36599 Ave 12 Madera CA 93638

WALLSKOG, JOYCE MARIE, nursing educator, psychotherapist; b. Melrose Park, Ill., Apr. 20, 1942. BSN, Alverno Coll., 1977; MSN, U. Wis., Milw., 1982; postgrad., Marquette U. RN, Wis.; cert. psychotherapist, Wis. Staff nurse St. Mary's Hill Hosp., Milw., 1977-78; Staff nurse Waukesha (Wis.) Meml. Hosp., 1978-80, clin. nurse specialist, 1980-87; asst. prof. nursing Marquette U., Milw., 1986—; psychotherapist Psychiat. Assocs. Comprehensive Services, Ltd., Milw., 1982-85; nurse psychotherapist Counseling and Wellness Ctr., Waukesha, 1982—; cons. Alverno Coll., Milw., 1983-84, Health Care Cons., Sussex, Wis., 1985—; coordinator Waukesha Premenstral Syndrome Program, 1980—. Contbr. articles to profl. jours. Bd. dirs. Waukesha County Mental Health Assn., 1982; mem. Waukesha County Unified Services, 1984; advisor Resolve Through Sharing, 1986—, Women's Health Services, 1987—. Mem. Am. Nurses Assn. (council psychiat and mental health nursing), Wis. Nurses Assn. (rep. Wis. Coalition on Sexual Misconduct by Psychotherapists and Counselors 1988—), Forum for Death Edn. and Counseling, Sigma Theta Tau, Delta Upsilon Sigma. Office: Marquette Coll Nursing Milwaukee WI 53233

WALMSLEY, JUDITH ABRAMS, chemistry educator; b. Oak Park, Ill., Feb. 6, 1936; d. Kenneth Frederick and Edna Martha (Grau) Abrams; m. Frank Walmsley, Aug. 29, 1959; children: Katherine Ellen, Susan Jennifer. BA in Chemistry, Fla. State U., 1958; PhD in Chemistry, U.N.C., 1962. Rsch. scientist Owens-Ill., Inc., Toledo, 1963-66; rsch. assoc., instr. Mich. State U., East Lansing, 1979-80; sr. rsch. assoc. U. Toledo, 1974-87; asst. prof. U. Tex., San Antonio, 1987—; instr. U. Toledo, 1968-69, 75-77, 83-87. Patentee in field; author lab. manuals, 1985; contbr. articles to profl. jours. Recipient rsch. grants Rsch. Corp., U. Tex., 1988-90, NIH, 1990—, DeArce Biomed. Rsch., U. Toledo, 1984-87. Mem. Am. Chem. Soc., Assn. Women in Sci., AAAS, Sigma Xi, Phi Beta Kappa, Phi Kappa Phi, Delta Gamma. Presbyterian. Office: Div Earth/Phys Scis Univ Tex at San Antonio San Antonio TX 78285

WALSCH, NELLIE LEE, steel warehousing executive; b. Garrison, Ky., Mar. 18, 1920; d. Thomas Edgar and Essie Beatrice (Akers) Martin. Student public and pvt. schs., also various coll. courses; m. Herman W. Walsch, Nov. 19, 1949; 1 child, Daniel Lee. With United Iron & Metal Co., Inc., Balt., from 1946, office mgr., bookkeeper div. Curtis Steel products Co.; corp. sec., bookkeeper Marlen Trading Co., Inc., Balt., Chesapeake Internat. Corp., Balt.; corp. sec. LSL Assocs., Balt. Democrat. Methodist. Office: 4101 Curtis Ave Baltimore MD 21226

WALSH, ANNMARIE HAUCK, research firm executive; b. N.Y.C., May 5, 1938; d. James Smith and Ann-Marie (Kennedy) Hauck; m. John F. Walsh, Jr., Aug. 20, 1960; children: Peter Hauck, John David. B.A., Barnard Coll., 1961; M.A., Columbia U., 1969, Ph.D., 1971. Sr. staff mem. Inst. Pub. Adminstrn., N.Y.C., 1961-72, pres., 1982-89, Gulick scholar, 1989—; dir., assoc. prof. Ctr. for Urban and Policy Studies, CUNY Grad. Ctr., N.Y.C., 1972-79; dir. Govs.' Task Force on Regional Planning, N.Y., Conn., N.J., 1979-81; cons. pub. enterprise, civil svc., urban and regional mgmt. UN, China, Indonesia, Bangladesh, state and local govts., 1982—; cons. pub. enterprise and bond fin., 1978—, People's Republic of China, Republic of Indonesia, State of N.J., N.Y.C., 1989—. Author: Urban Government for Zagreb, Yugoslavia, 1968, Urban Government for Lagos, Nigeria, 1968, Urban Government for the Paris Region, 1968, The Urban Challenge to Government: An International Comparison of Thirteen Cities, 1969, The Public's Business: Politics and Practices of Government Corporations, 1978, 2d edit., 1980; editor: Agenda for a City, 1970. Project dir. 20th Century Fund, Pub. Enterprise, 1972-76, pub.-pvt. partnerships, 1989—; bd. dirs. Ralph Bunche Inst., UN, 1978-82, Regional Plan Assn., 1987—. Herbert Lehmann fellow, 1966-69. Fellow, Nat. Acad. Pub. Adminstrn. (ADP mgmt. deregulation in govt., civil svc. reform, NASA reorgn., nominating com.); mem. Regional Plan Assn., Phi Beta Kappa. Office: Inst Pub Admistrn 55 W 44th St New York NY 10036

WALSH, BEATRICE METCALFE PASSAGE, civic worker; b. Schenectady, N.Y., Mar. 6, 1917; d. William Riley and Jessamine (Littlefield) Passage; student Western Res. U., 1941-42, Cleve. Community Coll., 1980—; m. Thomas Joseph Walsh, July 12, 1941; 1 dau., Joan Beatrice (Mrs. Peter Michael Waltz). Vol. worker ARC, 1941-46, 47-53; leader council Cleve. Beachwood (Ohio) Girl Scouts, 1952-57; vol. worker Community Chest, 1947-50; mem. women's com. Cleve. Orch., 1962—; Am. Red Cross, 1963—; ladies program chmn. Am. Chem. Soc., 1960, Am. Inst. Chem. Engrs., 1961, ladies program conv. com., 1969; mem. Orange Community Arts Council, 1969—, Pepper Pike Civic League, 1966—; ladies program co-chmn. Nat. Heat Transfer Conf., 1964; mem. women's com. Chagrin Valley Little Theater; mem., corr. sec. exec. bd. Case Western Res. U. Mem. Nat. Huguenot Soc., Nat. Soc. Founders and Patriots, Nat. Soc. New Eng. Women (sec. Cleve. Colony 1980—), Shaker Heights LWV, Case Faculty Wives (pres. 1958-59), Western Res. Rep. Women's Club, DAR, (Shaker chpt., corr. sec. 1962-64, registrar 1964-69, publicity chmn. 1968-70, chaplain 1969-71, librarian 1972-73, vice regent 1973-74, regent 1974-76, dir. 1985—, del. state conv. 1963, 64, 66, 69, 73, 74, 75, chmn. reception, del. nat. conv. 1964, 73, 74, 75), Friends of Orange Community Library, Daus. Am. Colonists (regent Charter Oak chpt. 1977-79, parliamentarian 1981-86), Nat. Soc. Daus. of Founders and Patriots Am., Order Crown of Charlemagne, Soc. Magna Charta Dames, Nat. Soc. New Eng. Women, Colonial Dames 17th Century, (corr. sec. 1985—), Nat. Soc. Women Descs. of Ancient and Honorable Arty. Co., Nat. Soc. Daus. 1812, Early Settlers of the Western Res., Western Res. Hist. Soc., Garden Center Greater Cleve., Blackbrook Country Club, Landerhaven Golf Club, Moreland Hills Golf Club, Landerwood Swim Club, Suburban Garden Club, Green Valley Garden Club (club rep. 1972-73, corr. sec. 1976-77, pres. 1988—), Case-Western Res. U. Club (exec. bd. 1981—), Univ. Women's Club. Presyterian. Home: 32555 Creekside Dr Pepper Pike Cleveland OH 44124

WALSH, CATHERINE A., small business owner; b. N.Y.C., July 9, 1953; d. John Joseph and Mary Margaret C. Walsh; m. Gregory Wybern, Sept. 23, 1989. Grad., Kean Coll., Union, N.J. Cert. in early childhood edn., N.J. Mgr. Red Lobster, Phila.; gen. mgr. Peninsula House, Sea Bright, N.J.; mgr. Lopat Industries, Ocean, N.J.; entrepreneur, ptnr. in restaurant Hook Line and Sinker, Ramson, N.J. Mem. Rumson Profl. Assn. Address: 393 E Freehold Rd Freehold NJ 07730

WALSH, CHRISTINA LEE, public relations executive; b. Missoula, Mont., Jan. 24, 1961; d. Francis Eugene and Donna Lee (Sammons) W. BA in History and Journalism, St. Mary-of-the-Woods Coll., 1983. Editorial asst. Tex. Med. Assn., Austin, 1982-83; news monitor, analyst Teleclip, Inc., Austin, 1983-84; pub. rels. account exec. Fellers, Lacy & Gaddis, Austin, 1983-86; dir. communications Am. Heart Assn./Tex. Affiliate Inc., Austin, 1986-89; pub. rels. mgr. Walsh Pub. Rels. Rsch. & Counseling, Austin, 1989—, Leadership Tex., Class 1989, 1990—. Campaign vol. Ann Richards for Gov. campaign, Austin, 1989-90; mem. communications com. Travis County Adult Literacy Coun., Austin, 1989-90; active Leadership Tex., class of 1989. Mem. Women in Communications (pres. 1990). Democrat. Roman Catholic. Home: 7406 Sordello Dr Austin TX 78752-2150 Office: Walsh Pub Rels Rsch 3933 Steck Ave #B-107 Austin TX 78759

WALSH, DEBORAH QUINTMAN, advertising executive; b. N.J., June 6, 1959; d. Lawrence A. and Judith L. (Goldfarb) Quintman; m. David Donlon Walsh,. BA in Psychology, Douglas Coll., 1981; MBA in Mktg., Farleigh Dickinson U., 1986. Media dir. Naimark & Barba, Cedar Knolls, N.J., 1982-. Contbr. articles to profl. jours. Home: 51 Spruce St Cranford NJ 07016 Office: Naimark and Barba Inc 248 Columbia Turnpike Florham Park NJ 07932

WALSH, DIANE, pianist; b. Washington, Aug. 16, 1950; d. William Donald and Estelle Louise (Stokes) W.; m. Henry Forbes, 1969 (div. 1979); m. Richard Pollak, 1982. MusB, Juilliard Sch. Music, 1971, MusM, Mannes Coll., 1982. N.Y.C. debut Young Concert Artists Series, 1974; founder Mannes Trio, 1982; solo appearances include: Kennedy Ctr. for Performing Arts, Washington, 1976, Met. Mus., N.Y.C., 1976, Wigmore Hall, London, 1980; with Mannes Trio: Lincoln Ctr.'s Alice Tully Hall, Library of Congress, 1987; appeared with maj. orchs. worldwide, including St. Louis Symphony, Indpls. Symphony, San Francisco Symphony, Buffalo Philharm., Bavarian Radio Symphony of Munich, Berlin Radio Symphony, Radio Symphony Frankfurt, Radio Symphony Stuttgart; has toured Europe, N.Am., S.Am., Cen. Am., Soviet Union; recs. for Nonesuch Records, 1980, 82, Book-of-Month Records, 1985, Music and Arts, 1990, CRI, 1991; mem. piano and chamber music faculty Mannes Coll. Music. Recipient 3d prize Busoni Internat. Piano Competition, Italy, 1974, 2d prize Mozart Internat. Piano Competition, Salzburg, Austria, 1975, 1st prize Munich Internat. Piano Competition, 1975, Naumburg Chamber Music award, 1986; Nat. Endowment Arts. grantee, 1981.

WALSH, EILEEN FRANCES, college educator; b. Bronx, Apr. 25, 1943; d. Arthur and Yolanda (Bratti) W. BS, Nazareth Coll., Rochester, 1965; MS, Fordham U., Bronx, 1967, PhD, 1971. Prof. Westchester Community Coll., Valhalla, N.Y., 1969. Co-Author: Laboratory Studies in General Biology, 1978; contributor: Biology, 1982. Grantee Nat. Sci. Found., 1979; Recipient Chancellor's award for Excellence in Teaching, N.Y., State U., 1980, WCC Medallion award Westchester Community Coll. Found., 1987. Mem. Sigma Xi. Republican. Roman Catholic. Office: Westchester Community Coll 75 Grasslands Rd Valhalla NY 10595

WALSH, ELEANOR LUCILLE, real estate executive; b. Chgo., June 20, 1962; d. John Alexander and Ann Francis (Mangan) Carnes; m. Brian Michael Walsh, July, 11, 1987. Student, Northwestern U., 1980-84. Lic. real estate salesperson. Data rsch. asst. Baird and Warner Inc., Chgo., 1984-85; property mgr. Baird and Warner, Inc., Chgo., 1985-86; real estate mgr. Balcor Property Mgmt., Skokie, Ill., 1986-90, Coldwell Banker, Rosemont, Ill., 1990—. Mem. NAFE. Roman Catholic. Office: Coldwell Banker 6133 N River Rd Ste 502 Rosemont IL 60018

WALSH, EVA BARNETT, home health administrator; b. Highland County, Ohio, Dec. 21, 1929; d. Joseph F. and Anita S. (Huffenberger) Barnett; children: James, Suella, Jack. Diploma, Jewish Hosp. Sch. Nursing, Cin., 1950; BS in Nursing cum laude, Ohio U., 1978. Cert. diabetic educator; cert. in community health. Health handicap coord. Highland County Head Start, Hillsboro, Ohio; dir. med. svcs. Greenfield (Ohio) Area Med. Ctr., program planner in rehab., dir. home health; instr. community diabetic edn. classes. PTO pres. City of Hillsboro, 1976. Mem. Am. Pub. Health Assn. Democrat. Methodist. Home: 8325 State Rte 138 Hillsboro OH 45133 Office: 545 South St Greenfield OH 45123

WALSH, JANE ELLEN MCCANN, health care official; b. Uniontown, Pa., Jan. 16, 1941; d. Albert Benton and Dorothy Rose (Ruble) McCann; B.A., Hood Coll., 1963; postgrad. Northwestern U., 1964-65; M.A., Antioch Coll., 1978; m. John Daniel Walsh, June 8, 1973; stepchildren—Christopher, Mark, Jonathan, Jennifer. Research asst. Cert. Nat. Interviewers, Chgo., 1963-64; project dir. Assn. Am. Med. Colls., Evanston, Ill., 1965-68; systems analyst Research Found. Mental Hygiene, Inc., Orangeburg, N.Y., 1968-72; systems analyst Nat. Center Health Svcs. Research, Rockville, Md., 1972-73; research coord. U. Calif., Berkeley, 1973-75; coord. Pvt. Initiative in PSRO, San Francisco, 1975-76; cons., 1977-78; asso. dir. tech. svcs. Western Consortium for Health Professions, Inc., San Francisco, 1978—; cons. pub. health info. systems, health svcs. evaluation, mental health info systems, data sources. Recipient Martha Schaeffer Shaw award, 1960. Mem. Am. Public Health Assn., Assn. Health Svcs. Research, Common Cause, Mus. Soc. San Francisco, Smithsonian Instn. Democrat. Presbyterian. Club: Highlands Country. Author: Introduction to Standard Mumps, 1978; developer automated system for storage and retrieval of clin. psychiat. data, 1969; designed and assisted in implementation of state-wide mgmt. info. system for indigent care program; 1986-87; research on multi-splty. group practices delivering primary care, procedures for conducting concurrent quality assurance. Home: 50 Schooner Hill Oakland CA 94618 Office: 2001 Addison St Ste 200 Berkeley CA 94704

WALSH, JANET LAURENTIA, human resources executive, educator; b. Lowell, Mass., June 22, 1954; d. William P. and Ruth (Laird) W. BA in Econs., Bucknell U., 1976; MBA in Mgmt., Loyola Coll., Balt., 1982. Mgr. human resources P.H.H. Group Inc., Balt., 1982-84; mgr. employee rels. The Am. Sterilizer Co., Erie, Pa., 1984-86; mgr. U.S. pers. Soc. for Worldwide Interbank Fin. Telecommunications, Culpeper, Va., 1987—; instr. Gannon U., Erie, 1985-86, Howard Community Coll., Columbia, Md., 1979-84. Pres. adv. com. on Bus. and Econ. Affairs U. Md., 1978-79; bd. dirs. Dunbarton Concerts, Washington, 1989—. Mem. Am. Soc. Pers. Adminstrs., Employment Mgmt. Assn., Bucknell Alumni Club (pres. 1977-80), Alpha Lambda Delta, Alpha Sigma Nu. Office: Soc Worldwide Interbank Fin Telecommunications 2005 McDevitt Dr Culpeper VA 22701

WALSH, JEANNE See SINGER, JEANNE

WALSH, JULIA MONTGOMERY, investment banking executive; b. Akron, Ohio, Mar. 29, 1923; d. Edward A. and Catherine Skurkay Curry; m. John G. Montgomery, Apr. 7, 1948 (dec. 1957); children: John, Stephen, Michael, Mark; m. Thomas M. Walsh, May 18, 1963; 1 child, Margaret; stepchildren: Mary F., Patrick J., Kathleen Carr, Thomas D., Joan Cassedy, Daniel, Ann Walton; BBA magna cum laude, Kent State U., 1945, LLD, 1967; postgrad. Harvard U., 1962; LLD Smith Coll., 1983. Dir. Fulbright Program, Ankara, Turkey; personnel officer Am. Consulate Gen., Munich, Fed. Republic of Germany; sr. v.p., registered rep. Ferris & Co., 1955-74; vice chmn. Ferris & Co., Inc., 1974-77; chmn. Julia M. Walsh & Sons, Inc., Washington, 1977-83; mng. dir. Julia M. Walsh & Sons (div. Tucker Anthony & R.L. Day), Washington, 1983—; bd. dirs. Pitney Bowes, Stamford, Conn.; mem. Investment Banking Adv. Com. Am. Stock Exchange, former gov. and exchange ofcl.; trustee Dole Commn.; mem., dir. exec. com. Greater Washington Bd. of Trade, pres. 1985; panelist TV program Wall Street Week. Bd. dirs. Nat. Bd. of Shrine of Immaculate Conception, Neighborhood Econ. Devel. Corp. D.C.; trustee Kent State U. Found., Nat. Assn. Bank Women, Mount St. Mary's Coll., Emmitsburg, Md.; past trustee Georgetown U.; mem. adv. bd. First Am. Bank; former trustee Simmons Coll., Boston. Roman Catholic. Home: 5001 Millwood Ln Washington DC 20016 Office: Tucker Anthony Inc 1300 I St NW Ste 450E Washington DC 20005

WALSH, MARIE LECLERC, nurse; b. Providence, Sept. 11, 1928; d. Walter Normand and Anna Mary (Ryan) Leclerc; m. John Breffni Walsh, June 18, 1955; children: George Breffni, John Leclerc, Darina Louise. Grad., Waterbury Hosp. Sch. Nursing, Conn., 1951; BS, Columbia U., 1954, MA, 1955. Team leader Hartford (Conn.) Hosp., 1951-53; pvt. duty nurse St. Luke's Hosp., N.Y.C., 1953-57; sch. nurse tchr. Agnes Russel Ctr., Tchrs. Coll. Columbia U., N.Y.C., 1955-56; clin. nursing instr. St. Luke's Hosp., N.Y.C., 1957-58; chmn. disaster nursing ARC Fairfax County, Va., 1975; course coordinator occupational health nursing U. Va. Sch. Continuing Edn., Falls Church, 1975-77; mem. disaster steering com. No. Va. Community Coll., Annandale, 1976; adj. faculty U. Va. Sch. Continuing Edn., Falls Church, 1981; disaster nurse ARC Disaster Svcs., Wichita, Kans., 1985—; rsch. and statis. analyst U. Va. Sch. Continuing Edn. Nursing, Falls Church, 1975; rsch. libr. Olive Garvey Ctr. for Improvement Human Functioning, Inc., Wichita, 1985. Sec. Dem. party, Cresskill, N.J., 1964-66; county committeewoman, Bergen County, N.J., 1965-66; pres., v.p., Internat. Staff Wives, NATO, Brussels, Belgium, 1978-80; election officer, supr. Election Bd., Wichita, 1987, 88. Mem. AAAS, AAUW, N.Y. Acad. Sci., Wichita State U. Alumni and Faculty Club, Pi Lambda Theta, Sigma Theta Tau. Home: 13822 NE 37th Pl Bellevue WA 98005

WALSH, MARY D. FLEMING, civic worker; b. Whitewright, Tex., Oct. 29, 1913; d. William Fleming and Anna Maud (Lewis) Fleming; B.A., So. Meth. U., 1934; LL.D. (hon.), Tex. Christian U., 1979; m. F. Howard Walsh, Mar. 13, 1937; children—Richard, Howard, D'Ann Walsh Bonnell, Maudi Walsh Roe, William Lloyd. Pres. Fleming Found.; v.p. Walsh Found.; partner Walsh Co.; mem. Lloyd Shaw Found., Colorado Springs, Big Bros. Tarrant County; guarantor Fort Worth Arts Council, Scholar Cantorum, Fort Worth Opera, Fort Worth Ballet, Fort Worth Theatre, Tex. Boys Choir; hon. mem. bd. dirs. Van Cliburn Internat. Piano Competition; co-founder Am. Field Service in Ft. Worth; mem. Tex. Commn. for Arts and Humanities, 1968-72, mem. adv. council, 1972-84; bd. dirs. Wm. Edrington Scott Theatre, 1977-83, Colorado Springs Day Nursery, Colorado Springs Symphony, Ft. Worth Symphony, 1974-81; hon. chmn. Opera Ball, 1975, Opera Guild Internat. Conf., 1976; co-presenter (with husband) through Walsh Found., Tex. Boy's Choir and Dorothy Shaw Bell Choir ann. presentation of The Littlest Wiseman to City of Ft. Worth; granter with husband land and bldgs. to Tex. Boy's Choir for permanent home, 1971, Walsh-Wurlitzer organ to Casa Manana, 1972. Sem. Recipient numerous awards, including Altrusa Civic award as 1st Lady of Ft. Worth, 1968; (with husband) Disting. Service award So. Bapt. Radio and Television Commn., 1972; Opera award Girl Scouts, 1977-79; award Streams and Valleys, 1976-80; named (with husband) Patron of Arts in Ft. Worth, 1970, Edna Gladney Internat. Grandparents of 1972, (with husband) Sr. Citizens of Yr, 1985; Mary D. and Howard Walsh Meml. Organ dedicated by Bapt. Radio and TV Commn., 1967, tng. ctr. named for the Walshes, 1976; Mary D. and Howard Walsh Med. Bldg., Southwestern Bapt. Theol. Sem.; library at Tarrant County Jr. Coll. N.W. Campus dedicated to her and husband, 1978; Brotherhood citation Tarrant County chpt. NCCJ, 1978; Spl. Recognition award Ft. Worth Ballet Assn.; Royal Purple award Tex. Christian U., 1979; Friends of Tex. Boys Choir award, 1981; appreciation award Southwestern Bapt. Theol. Sem., 1981, B. H. Carroll Founders award, 1982; numerous other award for civic activities. Mem. Ft. Worth Boys Club, Ft. Worth Children's Hosp., Jewel Charity Ball, Ft. Worth Pan Hellenic (pres. 1940), Opera Guild, Fine Arts Found. Guild of Tex. Christian U., Girl's Service League (hon. life, hon. chmn. Fine Arts Guild Spring Ballet, 1985), AAUW, Goodwill Industries Aux., Child Study Center, Tarrant County Aux. of Edna Gladney Home, YWCA (life), Ft. Worth Art Assn., Ft. Worth Ballet Assn., Tex. Boys Choir Aux., Friends of Tex. Boys Choir, Round Table, Colorado Springs Fine Art Center, Am. Automobile Assn., Nat. Assn. Cowbelles, Ft. Worth Arts Council (hon. bd. mem.), Am. Guild Organists (hon., Ft. Worth chpt.), Rae Reimers Bible Study Class (pres. 1968), Tex. League Composers (hon. life), Chi Omega (pres. 1935-36, hon. chmn. 1986), others. Baptist. Clubs: The Woman's (Club Fidelite), Colorado Springs Country, Garden of Gods, Colonial Country, Ridglea Country, Shady Oaks Country, Chi Omega Mothers, Chi Omega Carousel, TCU Woman's. Home: 2425 Stadium Dr Fort Worth TX 76109 also: 1801 Culebra Ave Colorado Springs CO 80907

WALSH, MARY FRANCES, educator; b. Dallas; d. Edward Hampton and Letha Martha (Bruce) W. BS, East Tex. State U., 1951; postgrad., So. Meth. U., Sorbonne U., Paris; MS, North Tex. U., 1961. Cert. tchr. Tchr. Dallas Ind. Sch. Dist., 1951, Robert E. Lee Sch., Dallas, E H. De Golyer, Dallas, Herbert Marcus, Dallas, 1990—. Group chairperson AAUW, Dallas, 1958; mem. DAR, Dallas, 1990; mem. com. Dallas Art Museum, 1985; hon. life mem. Tex. PTA, Dallas, 1987. Mem. NEA, Tex. State Tchr.'s Assn. (life), Classroom Tchrs. of Dallas (dist. chairperson 1951—), Delta Kappa Gamma (various positions 1957-90), Alpha Delta Pi. Republican. Methodist. Home: 5502 Mercedes Dallas TX 75206

WALSH, MAUREEN MARIE, marketing and management consultant; b. Dubuque, Iowa, Apr. 16, 1949; d. Michael Eugene and Rosemary Veronica (Anthony) W. BA, U. Wis., 1972, MBA in Mktg., 1976. Gen. mgr. Phila. Theater Co., 1976-78; dir. mktg. Children's Theatre Co., Mpls., 1978-80, Bklyn. Acad. Music, 1980-81, Joffrey Ballet, N.Y.C., 1981-82; account exec. Ogilvy & Mather Dir., N.Y.C., 1982-83; pres. Walsh Ptnrs., N.Y.C. and Phila., 1983—; mem. faculty Temple U., Phila., 1976-78; asst. prof. Bklyn. Coll., 1982-84, Adelphi U., N.Y.C., 1980-84; cons. Minn. Arts Bd., 1978-80, Yellow Springs Inst., Phila., 1981—, Genesis New Age Ctr., Phila., 1988—, Collaborations, Inc., Phila., 1983—, Marilyn Grammar Cons. Svcs., N.Y.C., 1983—. Campaign mgr. for county freeholder, N.J., 1977; bd. dirs. 6 arts orgns., N.Y.C., 1983—. Home: 277 W 10th St Apt 7E New York NY 10014

WALSTON, LYNN MAURYNE, banker; b. Indpls., Mar. 20, 1956; d. Frank, Jr. and Lula Lenora (Adams) Jameson; m. Gregory D. Walston, July 2, 1977 (div. Mar. 1985); children—Tamara J., Stacey V. Assoc. degree Ind. U., 1978; bus. mgmt. degree Ind. U./Purdue U.-Indpls., 1987. With Mchts. Nat. Bank, Indpls., since 1976—, bus. devel. officer, since 1982—, br. mgr., since 1982—, asst. v.p., since 1985—. Troop leader local Girl Scouts U.S., 1983—; vol. Planned Parenthood, Indpls., 1985—; treas. Riverside Park United Meth. Ch., 1984—; bd. mem. Forest Manor Multiservice Ctr., 1988; com. mem. Community Ctrs. of Idpls., 1989. Recipient Vol. Service award Indpls. Humane Soc., 1983, Girl Scouts Just Friends Program, Indpls., 1985. Mem. Nat. Assn. Bank Women (scholar 1983, 85), Indpls. Urban Bankers (assoc. v.p. 1986, v.p. 1987), NAFE. Democrat. Avocations: aerobics, bowling, reading. Home: 3211 N Sharon Ave Indianapolis IN 46222 Office: Mchts Nat Bank 950 N Shadeland Ave Indianapolis IN 46219

WALT, MELANIE GAY MILLER, owner mortgage brokerage company; b. Amarillo, Tex., June 20, 1947; d. Fred Cruse Miller and Marzelle Hale; m. Lawrence Cecil Walt, Apr. 1, 1970; (div. 1982). BA, Tex. Tech U., Lubbock, 1969. Tchr. English Secondary Sch. System, Pensacola, Fla., 1971-72, Kailua, Hawaii, 1972-75; tax cons. Kailua, Hawaii, 1972-76; interior designer Mallory's, Jacksonville, N.C., 1976-78; instr. adult edn. Coastal Carolina Coll., Jacksonville, 1976-78; real estate sales mgr. Gallery of Homes, Jacksonville, 1978-82; asst. v.p. First Fed. Savs. and Loan, Amarillo, 1982-87; real estate broker Amarillo, 1984—; owner Athlan Mortgage Corp., Amarillo, 1987—. Mem. Amarillo Art Alliance, 1985—; vol. Big Bros./ Sisters Amarillo, 1988; patron Lone Star Ballet, Amarillo, 1985-90, bd. dirs. Mem. Nat. Assn. Realtors, Am. Soc. Interior Designers, Women's Nat. Sorority (treas. 1989-90), Amarillo Women's Network, Women's Coun. Realtors, Investment Club Amarillo (treas. 1985-88), Am. Contract Bridge League. Republican. Episcopalian. Office: Athlan Mortgage Corp 3505 Olsen Blvd Ste 214 Amarillo TX 79109

WALTER, ANITA R., elementary school teacher; b. Chambersburg, Pa., Feb. 5, 1949; d. Robert David and Ruth (Metz) W. BS in Elem. Edn., Shippensburg (Pa.) U., 1970, MS in Elem. Edn., 1973. 4th grade tchr. Guilford Hills Elem. Sch., Chambersburg, 1970—. Vol. Cystic Fibrosis Found. of Cen. Pa., 1983—, Am. Cancer Soc., Franklin County, Pa., 1984—, United Way, Chambersburg, 1986—, Cen. Pa. Synod Youth Ministry, Luth. Ch. in Am., Cen. Pa., 1982-86; mem. St. John Luth. Ch. and Coun. of Greenvillage, pres. 1984, v.p. 1983, sec. 1982; mem. St. Luke Luth. Ch.-Scotland. Mem. AAUW (Franklin County br. pres. 1988-90, v.p. for program 1977-79, sec. 1974-76), Chambersburg Area Edn. Assn. (bldg. rep. sec.), Delta Kappa Gamma (membership chmn. 1988-92).

WALTER, BEVERLY TONEY, cosmetic company executive; b. Comfort, W.Va., Mar. 27, 1946; d. Charles Leftridge Toney and Ruth Areta (Leadingham) Dail; divorced; children: Beth Yvonne Walter, Nathan Andrew Walter. Mgr. dist. Nutri-Metrics, 1974-76; regional mgr. Nutri-Metrics, Inc., 1976-78; sr. regional mgr. Nutri-Metrics, Inc., City of Industry, Calif., 1978-82, mgr. corp. sales, 1982-84, v.p. sales and mktg., 1985-87, exec. v.p., chief operating officer, 1987-89; exec. v.p., chief operating officer Walter, Southworth & Assocs., Diamond Bar, Calif., 1989—; owner, mgr. Here's To Your Health Store, Latrobe, Pa., 1977-82; pres. Beverly T. Walter Seminars Internat., Mission Hills and Pomona, Calif., 1978—; pres., owner Aries & Co., speaking orgn., Mission Hills, Calif., 1987—. Speaker Sen. Campbell Conv. on Women, Los Angeles, 1987-88. Mem. Internat. Platform Assn., L.A. Bus. and Profl. Women's Club. Metephysicist. Home: Santa Rita Carmel CA 93923 Office: 2801 Salinas Hwy Monterey CA 93940

WALTER, CHRYSANDRA LOU, national park superintendent; b. Toledo, Nov. 29, 1947; d. Richard Lambert Walter and Winifred May (Buckley) Moore. BA, San Jose State U., 1969. Park ranger Point Reyes (Calif.) Nat. Seashore, 1969-70; education specialist Pacific Northwest Region, Nat. Parks Service, Seattle, 1970-73; interpretive specialist Manhattan Sites unit N.Y.C. Nat. Parks), N.Y.C., 1973-76; chief of interpretation George Washington Meml. Pkwy., Washington, 1976-78; mgr. San Francisco Area Golden Gate Nat. Recreation area, 1978-82; park supt. Lyndon B. Johnson Nat. Hist. Park, Johnson City, Tex., 1982-84; dep. supt. Gateway Nat. Recreation Area, N.Y.C., 1984-85; park supt. Lowell (Mass.) Nat. Hist. Park, 1985—.

Bd. dirs. Merrimack Reperetory Theatre, Lowell, 1985—, Lowell Girls' Club, 1984—, Tully/Tsongas Found., Lowell, 1985—; chmn. bd. dirs. Women in the Wilderness, San Francisco, 1981-82. Mem. Lowell C. of C. (bd. dirs., sub-chairwoman Women's com., 1985—). Republican. Methodist. Club: Johnson City Women's (pres. 1984). Lodge: Rotary (Lowell). Office: Lowell Nat Park 171 Merrimack Lowell MA 01852

WALTER, DEVON SLOAN, hotel executive; b. Columbus, Ohio, Apr. 28, 1948; d. Dan Ryan and Patience Lou (Loving) Hixenbaugh; m. Philip Martin Walter, June 30, 1979. BA, Pa. State U., 1971. Dir. sales Holiday Inn, Belmont, Calif., 1976-77; corp. sales mgr. Holiday Inn, San Francisco, 1977-78; area dir. sales Holiday Inn, Seattle, 1979-81; assoc. dir. sales and mktg. Le Baron Hotel, San Jose, Calif., 1978-79; dir. sales Mayflower Park Hotel, Seattle, 1982-83; regional sales mgr. Seattle Sheraton Hotel and Towers, 1983-84, nat. sales mgr., 1984-86, sr. sales mgr., 1986-87, mgr. conv. svcs., 1987—; vis. lectr. Seattle U., 1986. Contbr. articles to various publs. Bd. dirs. Seattle's Table Food Program. Named Outstanding Conv. Svcs. Mgr., Successful Meetings mag., 1987, 88. Mem. Meeting Planners Internat. (bd. dirs. 1986-88), Wash. Soc. Assn. Execs. (bd. dirs. 1985-86, Rhinoceros award 1984), Am. Bus. Womens' Assn. (pres. San Francisco 1977-78, Woman of Yr. award 1978). Republican. Methodist. Office: Seattle Sheraton Hotel 1400 6th St Seattle WA 98101

WALTER, ELIZABETH THOMAS, protective services official; b. Glencove, N.Y., Jan. 30, 1958; d. Robert Wheaton and Patricia Marie (Ward); m. Stephen Barnhill, Feb. 12, 1983 (Mar. 1986). Postgrad., Carleton Coll., Northfield, 1976-77; student, U. Denver, 1977. Sherrif's cadet Arapahoe County Sheriff's Dept., Englewood, Colo., 1975-79; retail security Assorted Major Dry Goods, Denver, 1977-80, patrol officer, 1980-85; detective Denver Police Dept., 1985-88, sgt., 1988—; cadet advisor Denver Police Dept., 1981-83. Mem. NAFE, Denver Police Protective Assn., Colo. Police Protective Assn., Neightborhood Watch & Crime Prevention Assn. Republican. Episcopalian. Office: Denver Police Dept 3555 Colorado Blvd Denver CO 80205

WALTER, HELEN JOY, executive director, teacher; b. Bronx, May 22, 1938; d. David and Frieda (Halpern) Presby; m. Wolfgang Walter, Feb. 4, 1962; children: Cheryl, Rochelle, Laurie. BA, Yeshiva U., 1961; MEd, Northeastern U., Boston, 1979. Tchr. Maimonides Day Sch., Brookline, Mass., N.Y.C. Pub. Schs.; counselor Northeastern U.; exec. dir. Brookline C. of C., 1979—. Office: Brookline C of C 1330 Beacon St Brookline MA 02146

WALTER, LINDA JO, marketing and sales executive; b. Detroit, Dec. 18, 1959; d. Elmer James and June Louise (Schultze) Bozzi; m. Stephen Craig Walter, May 21, 1983. BA in Communications, Mich. State U., 1983; MA in Mgmt., Nazareth Coll., 1987. Asst. officer mgr. Pohoryles & Greenstein PC, Washington, 1983-84; employment counselor Olsten Svcs., Kalamazoo, 1985-86; rep. Upjohn HealthCare Svcs., Kalamazoo, 1986-87; program coord., cons. Ctr. Women's Svcs., Kalamazoo, 1987; dir. mktg. and sales Kinko's Copies, Las Vegas, 1988-89, gen. mgr., 1989—. Contbr. World Wildlife Fund, 1985—, Christian Children's Fund, 1986—; vol. Muscular Dystrophy Assn., Detroit, 1973—; vol., performer Theatre Guild of Livonia, Dearborn Civic Theatre, 1974-80. Mem. Nat. Assn. Profl. Saleswomen, Internat. Assn. Bus. Communicators (v.p. 1988-89), Las Vegas C. of C. (Women's Council, Women's Conv. Sales, Assn., Nazareth Coll. Grad. Student Assn. (pres. 1986-87). Office: Kinko's Copies 4440 S Maryland Parkway Las Vegas NV 89119

WALTER, MAY ELIZABETH, retail company executive; b. N.Y.C.; d. Peter J. and Elizabeth (Shaub) W.Co-founder, treas., exec. v.p., vice chmn. Mut. Buying Syndicate, Inc., 1931-65; pres. Retail Marketers Advt., Inc., N.Y.C., 1966-67, cons., adviser, 1968-71. Sec., trustee, mem. exec. com. Am. Crafts Council, N.Y.C., 1962-77, hon. trustee, 1977—; adv. council Snite Mus. Art, U. Notre Dame. Recipient Salute to Women award Republican Women in Bus. and Professions, 1962. Home: 923 Fifth Ave New York NY 10021

WALTER, MIRIAM GULLY, steel company executive; b. Newark, Ohio, Sept. 9, 1940; d. Berj Hrant and Lillian Mae (Boyajian) Guleserian; m. Clair E. Walter, Dec. 26, 1971 (div. 1981); 1 child, Maris Dawn. BS, No. Ill. U., 1965; postgrad., U. N.H., 1978-79. Tchr. DeKalb (Ill.) Community Unit Schs., 1965-69; tchr. Dept. of Def. Overseas Schs., Japan, 1969-70, Philippines, 1970-71; congressional rsch. service Library of Congress, Washington, 1980; asst. to regional dir. St. Jude Children's Rsch. Hosp., Washington, 1980-81; spl. asst. Dept. of Interior, Secretariat for Energy and Minerals, Washington, 1981-84; exec. dir. Nat. Strategic Materials and Minerals, Program Adv. Com., Washington, 1984-88; mgr. govt. affairs Tempel Steel Co., Chgo., 1988—; commr. Pres. Task Force on Women, Minorities and Handicapped in Sci. and Tech., Washington, 1987-88; mem. Interagy. Group on Space Policy, Washington, 1985-86; chmn. Math. Curriculum Com., DeKalb, Ill., 1968-69. Bd. mem. McCormick Boys and Girls Club, Chgo., 1988—; patron Lyric Opera Guild, Chgo., 1988—; hon. mem. Hadassah, Portsmouth, N.H., 1977; sec., v.p. Officers Wives Club, Pease AFB, N.H., 1972-78. Mem. NEA, NAFE, Assn. Women in Metals Industries, Women in Mining (program chmn. 1987-88), Nat. Strategy Forum, East Bank Club (Chgo.). Republican. Roman Catholic. Office: Tempel Steel Co 1940 W Balmoral Chicago IL 60640

WALTERS, ANNA LEE, writer, educational administrator; b. Pawnee, Okla., Sept. 9, 1946; d. Luther and Juanita Mae (Taylor) McGlaslin; children: Anthony, Daniel. BA Goddard Coll. Dir. Navajo Community Coll. Press, Tsaile (Navajo Nation), Ariz., 1982—; contbg. author: The Man to Send Rainclouds, 1974, Warriors of the Rainbow, 1975, Shantih, 1976, The Third Woman, 1979, The Remembered Earth, 1979, American Indians Today, Thought, Literature, Art, 1981; co-author textbook: The Sacred Ways of Knowledge, Sources of Life, 1977; author: The Otoe-Missiouria Tribe, Centennial Memoirs, 1881-1981, 1981; Earth Power Coming, 1983; The Sun is Not Merciful, 1985, Ghost Singer, 1988, The Spirit of Native America, 1989; contbr. articles to jours.; guest editor Frauen Offensive, 1978; also poet, feature writer. Recipient Am. Book award The Before Columbus Found., 1986, Virginia Scully McCormick Lit. award, 1986. Office: Navajo Community Coll Press Tsaile AZ 86556

WALTERS, BARBARA, television journalist; b. Sept. 25, 1931; d. Lou and Dena (Selett) W.; m. Merv Adelson, May 10, 1986; 1 child, Jacqueline. G-rad., Sarah Lawrence Coll., 1953; LHD (hon.), Ohio State U., Marymount Coll., Tarrytown, N.Y., 1975, Wheaton Coll., 1983. Former writer-producer WNBC-TV; then with sta. WPIX and CBS-TV; joined Today Show, 1961, regular panel mem., 1964-74, co-host, 1974-76; moderator syndicated program Not For Women Only, 1974-76; newscaster ABC Evening News (now ABC World News Tonight), 1976-78; host The Barbara Walters Spls., 1976—; co-host ABC TV news show 20/20, 1979—. Contbr. to ABC programs Issues and Answers. Author: How To Talk With Practically Anybody About Practically Anything, 1970; contbr. to Reader's Digest. Recipient award of yr. Nat. Assn. TV Program Execs., 1975, Emmy award Nat. Acad. TV Arts and Scis., 1975, Mass Media award Am. Jewish Com. Inst. Human Relations, 1975, Hubert H. Humphrey Freedom prize Anti-Defamation League-B'nai B'rith, 1978, Matrix award N.Y. Women in Communications, 1977, Barbara Walters' Coll. Scholarship in Broadcast Journalism established in her honor Ill. Broadcasters Assn., 1975, Pres.'s award Overseas Press Club, 1988, Lowell Thomas award Marist Coll., 1990; named to 100 Women Accomplishment Harper's Bazaar, 1967, 71, One of Am.'s 75 Most Important Women Ladies' Home Jour., 1970, One of 10 Women of Decade Ladies' Home Jour., 1979, One of Am.'s 100 Most Important Women Ladies' Home Jour., 1983, Woman of Year in Communications, 1974, Woman of Year Theta Sigma Phi, Broadcaster of Yr. Internat. Radio and TV Soc., 1975, One of 200 Leaders of Future Time Mag., 1974, One of Most Important Women of 1979 Roper Report, One of Women Most Admired by Am. People Gallup Poll, 1982, 84, to Hall of Fame Acad. TV Arts and Scis., 1990. Office: ABC News 7 W 66th St New York NY 10023

WALTERS, CAROL PRICE, educator, researcher; b. Lansing, Mich., Oct. 15, 1941; d. Gale Hubert and Ida Leona (Wood) Price; m. Merle Geoffrey Smith, June 15, 1963 (div. Mar. 1977); 1 child, Jennifer Jill; m. David Lloyd Walters, Apr. 4, 1988. AB, Albion (Mich.) Coll., 1963; PhD, U. Vt., 1972. With U. Vt., Burlington, 1963—, rsch. asst. prof., 1977-82, rsch. assoc. prof., 1982—; lab. technician U. Pitts., 1967-68; coord. Vt. Newborn Screening Program, Burlington, 1989—; dir. Vt. AFP Prenatal Screening Program, Burlington, 1980—. Mem. exec. bd. March of Dimes Birth Defects Found., Vt., 1984—. Mem. Am. Assn. Clin. Chemistry, Am. Assn. for Cancer Rsch., Sigma Xi (v.p. 1986, pres. 1987-89). Episcopalian. Office: U Vt Med Alumni Bldg Dept Pediatrics Burlington VT 05405

WALTERS, CELESTA SCOTT, retired educator and business executive; b. Oxford, Nebr., Jan. 2, 1906; d. George A. and Bertha May (Mullen) Scott; m. Charles Herbert Walters, Mar. 28, 1945. BS, U. Nebr., 1933; MS, U. So. Calif., 1938; postgrad., U. Oreg., U. Calif., Riverside. Mem. faculty U. Soc. Calif., L.A., U. Oreg., Eugene; airport exec. Ontario (Calif.) Airport, City of Ontario. Active in community orgns.; founder Sister Cities of Ontario. Recipient Community Svc. award, 1976; named Outstanding Woman of Yr. Mem. AAUW, Future Bus. Leaders Am. (pres. state clubs), Chaffey Tchrs. Assn. (pres.), Bus. and Profl. Women's Club, Kappa Kappa Iota (state pres.), Theta Alpha Delta, Delta Pi Epsilon, Delta Kappa Gamma, Alpha Eta Rho. Address: 18655 W Bernardo Dr Unit 445 San Diego CA 92127

WALTERS, DEBORAH, computer company executive; b. Columbia, S.C., Jan. 16, 1955; d. Beverly and Mollie (Wilson) W. BS, Boston U., 1976; MBA, Harvard U., 1979. Br. mgr. IBM Corp., N.Y.C.; pres. Expert Tech. Svcs., Altanta. Bd. dirs. UNICEF, 1989—; mng. dir. adminstrn. Atlanta Youth at Risk, 1990—. Mem. NAFE. Democrat. Baptist. Home: 5106 Pine Heights Dr Atlanta GA 30324

WALTERS, DEBORAH KAYE WRIGHT, vision scientist, educator; b. Balt., June 14, 1951; d. Donald Harold and Hazel (Allen) Wright; m. Christopher J. Percival, July 13, 1985; children: Thomas, Anna. Student, Swarthmore Coll., 1969-71; BA, BS, Guilford Coll., 1973; MS, U. Birmingham, Eng., 1977, PhD, 1980. Rsch. fellow U. Birmingham, 1979-81; vis. asst. prof. SUNY, Buffalo, 1981-83, asst. prof., 1983-89, assoc. prof., 1989—; cons. Nat. Security Assn., Washington, 1983, Calspan Corp., Buffalo, 1984, LTV Sicria Corp, Buffalo, 1988—. Contbr. articles to profl. jours. Judge Buffalo Sci. Congress, 1988-90. Recipient rsch. grant NSF, 1984-89, 87-90, E.D.S., 1985-86, Fourtes Meml. Trust fellowship NIH, 1984. Mem. IEEE, Internat. Neural Network Soc., Am. Assn. Artificial Intelligence, Assn. Computing Machinery (speaker 1989), Cognitive Sci. Soc., Optical Soc. Am., Asn. Rsch. Vision and Opthalmology. Home: 95 Mill St Williamsville NY 14271 Office: SUNY Dept Computer Sci 776 Bell Hall Buffalo NY 14260

WALTERS, JUDITH RICHMOND, neuropharmacologist; b. Concord, N.H., June 20, 1944; d. Samuel Smith and Hazel Albertina (Stewart) Richmond; m. James Wilson Walters, Aug. 23, 1969 (div. 1990); children: James Richmond, Gregory Stewart, Douglas Powers. BA, Mt. Holyoke Coll., 1966; PhD, Yale U., 1972. Postdoctoral fellow dept. psychiatry Yale U. Med. Sch., New Haven, rsch. assoc. dept. pharmacology, asst. prof. dept. psychiatry; unit chief physiol. neuropharmacology unit ETB, NINDS, Bethesda, Md., 1976-81; sect. chief, physiol. neuropharmacology sect. Exptl. Therapeutics br. Nat. Inst. Neurol. Disease & Stroke, Bethesda; sci. adv. bd. Hereditary Disease Found., L.A., 1977-80, 82-86. Contbr. over 80 articles on neuropharmacology and neurophysiology to profl. jours. Mem. Am. Soc. Pharmacology and Exptl. Therapeutics, Soc. for Neuroscience. Home: 3615 Littledale Rd Kensington MD 20895 Office: NIH Bethesda MD 20892

WALTERS, MARTHA BERNADINE, program control professional; b. Great Falls, Mont., Mar. 13, 1947; d. John Oliver and Loretta Bernadine (Coy) Gage; m. Robert Alexander Walters Jr., Aug. 28, 1987. BA in Psychology, Ea. Wash. U., 1971; postgrad., U. Denver, 1986—. Counselor Wash. State Job Svc., Spokane, 1975-78; system devel. specialist U.S. Dept. Labor, Washington, 1978-82; program control mgr. Sci. Applications Internat. Corp., McLean, Va., 1982-88; mgr. program mgmt. systems Planning Rsch. Corp., McLean, 1988-89; mgr. program control BDM Internat., Inc., McLean, 1989—; network cons. No. Va. Women's Ctr., Vienna, 1988—. Mem. Va. Assn. Female Execs. (pres. 1990—), Project Mgmt. Inst., Bus. and Profl. Women's Assn., Internat. Assn. Personnel in Employment Security (local chpt. officer 1976-81), Fairfax (Va.) County C. of C. Democrat. Roman Catholic. Home: 11552 Hemingway Dr Reston VA 22094

WALTERS, MARY COON, state supreme court justice; b. Baraga, Mich., Jan. 29, 1922; d. Marvin Leonard and Nancy Claire (Conway) Coon; m. Asa Lane Walters, July 9, 1952 (dec. June 1974); 1 child, Mark Richard. J.D., U. N.Mex., 1962. Bar: N.Mex. 1962, U.S. Supreme Ct., U.S. Ct. Appeals (4th and 10th cir.). Pvt. practice Albuquerque, 1962-71, 73-78; judge 2d Jud. Dist. N.Mex., Albuquerque, 1971-72; judge N.Mex. Ct. Appeals, Santa Fe, 1979-81, chief judge, 1981-83; justice N.Mex. Supreme Ct., Santa Fe, 1984-89; del. N.Mex. Constnl. Conv., 1969. Served with Women's Airforce Service Pilots, 1943-44, USAF, 1951-55. Named to N.Mex. Women's Hall of Fame, 1986. Mem. ABA, N.Mex. Bar Assn. (Disting. Jud. Svc. award 1988), Albuquerque Bar Assn., Santa Fe Bar Assn. Democrat. Roman Catholic.

WALTERS, NANCY ETHEL, trust company executive; b. Queens, N.Y., Feb. 21, 1953; d. Joseph E. and Ethel (McConville) W.; children: Nicole, Michael, Jason, Anthony. Student, Queens Coll. Office mgr., ops. asst., sec. Mfrs. Hanover Trust, N.Y.C., ops. cons., asst. mgr. Mem. Golden Key. Home: 155-07 71 Ave 3A Flushing NY 11367 Office: 450 W 33d St New York NY 11367

WALTERS, NANCY LU, medical services educator; b. Luverne, Minn., Sept. 25, 1938; d. H. Calvin and Bijou (Stockton) Knock; divorced; children: Mary Patricia, Anthony Thomas, Deborah Kay. AB, Lindenwood Coll., 1960. Med. technologist St. Joseph Hosp., Kirkwood, Mo., 1960-63, Good Samaritan Hosp., Vincennes, Ind., 1963-65; chief med. technologist Johnson County Meml. Hosp., Franklin, Ind., 1965-68; health occupations coord. Ind. Vocat. Tech. Coll., Tippewa Tech. Inst., Lafayette, Ind., 1968-70; head allied health dept. Cin. Tech. Coll., 1970-76, coord. med. assts., 1976—. Mem. profl. edn. com. Am. Cancer Soc., Cin., 1976-82; bd. dirs. ACLU, Cin., 1988—; pres. Cin. chpt. Ind. Voters of Ohio, 1975-77; active various coms. Hyde Park Community United Meth. Ch., Cin., 1986—, chairperson singles commn., 1982-83, chairperson stewardship commn., 1983-86, chairperson coun. on ministries, 1987-90. Recipient Drummer's award Cin. Conv. and Vis. Bur., 1978. Mem. Am. Soc. Allied Health Professions (bd. dirs. 1976-78), Ohio Soc. Allied Health Professions (pres. 1981-82), Ohio Soc. Med. Technology, Woman's City Club, Single Parent Ctr. Club (group leader), Ohio Soc. Med. Technologists (dist. 8 pres. 1977-78), Omicron Pi. Democrat. Home: 1317 Grace Ave Cincinnati OH 45208 Office: Cin Tech Coll 3520 Central Pkwy Cincinnati OH 45223

WALTERS, PATRICIA DIANE, television sales executive; b. Seattle, Sept. 20, 1961; d. Edward William and Carole Diane (Burrus) Taylor; m. Lawrence Clayton Walters, June 25, 1983. BS in Sociology, Lewis and Clark Coll., 1983. Local sales account exec., then nat. sales asst. Sta. KGWN-TV, Cheyenne, Wyo., 1984-86, nat. sales mgr., 1986-89; nat. sales mgr. Gt. Western Network, Cheyenne, 1989—. Office: KGWN TV 2923 E Lincolnway Cheyenne WY 82001

WALTERS, REBECCA RUSSELL YARBOROUGH, medical technologist; b. Lancaster, S.C., Mar. 9, 1951; d. William Peurifoy and Anna Beth (Cheatham) Yarborough; m. Thomas Edward Walters, Oct. 15, 1983; 1 child, Katherine Rebecca. BA, Winthrop Coll., 1972; postgrad. in med. tech., Bapt. Med. Ctr., Columbia, S.C., 1974; MA, Cen. Mich. U., 1978. Teaching asst. in biology Winthrop Coll., Rock Hill, S.C., 1972-73; microbiology technologist Bapt. Med. Ctr., 1974-76, night shift supr., 1976-77, asst. adminstrv. dir., 1977—, tchr. Sch. Med. Tech., 1974—; article reviewer Med. Lab. Observer; mem. Nat. Cert. Agy. for Med. Lab. Personnel. Hycel, Inc. scholar, 1976, 77. Mem. Am. Soc. for Med. Tech. (scholar 1977), S.C. Soc. Med. Tech. (pres. 1979-80, scholar 1976), Am. Soc. Clin. Pathologists (assoc.), Clin. Lab. Mgmt. Assn., Beta Beta Beta, Alpha Mu Tau (scholar 1977). Republican. Presbyterian. Home: 155 Shawn Rd Chapin SC 29036 Office: Bapt Med Ctr Taylor at Marion Columbia SC 29220

WALTERS, SHARON BEVERLY, small business owner; b. Winthrop, Mass., Oct. 17, 1948; d. Edward Maurice and Pearl Marion (Miles) Huyffer; m. Gerald Marshall Walters, Aug. 11, 1970; children: Renee Michelle, Kerry Lynn, Shoshana Nicole. Grad., Santa Monica City Coll., 1967; postgrad., Gemological Inst., Santa Monica, Calif., 1984. Customer svc. rep. AT&T, Culver City, Calif.; demonstrator J.C. Penney, Northridge, Calif.; asst. mgr., bridal cons. Schaffer and Sons Creative Jewelers, Northridge; pres., designer Sharon Paul Diamonds and Fine Jewelry, Northridge, also chmn. bd. Past rec. sec. young adults sect. B'nai B'rith; past pres. Young Reps. Mem. NAFE, NOW, Northridge C. of C., Women's Am. Orgn. for Rehab. Through Tng. Jewish.

WALTHER, ZERITA, paralegal; b. N.Y.C., Nov. 22, 1927; d. James Alexander and Sarah Rebecca (Esperance) Potter; m. George P. Walther II, Dec. 30, 1946; children: Joseph, Leona. BS in Edn., Met. Inst., London, 1973; cert. in labor studies, Cornell U., 1979; paralegal cert., Manhattanville Coll., 1984. Tchr. OEO, L.I. City, N.Y., 1966-69, Washington Bus. Inst., N.Y.C., 1969-70; editorial asst., feature writer N.Y. Times, N.Y.C., 1973-85; corp. legal asst. Kim Taylor Profls., White Plains, N.Y., 1988—; casting cons. Am. Model Agy., N.Y.C., 1961-62, casting cons., 1962-63; bd. dirs., cons. Rockingchair Press News Service, Elmsford, N.Y., 1978—. Sec. Women of Westchester, 1978-80; mem. Westchester Black Women's Polit. Caucus, 1989—; coord. Elmsford chpt. Women in Self Help, 1982—; mediator, vol. Better Bus. Bur., White Plains, 1983-85, Westchester Mediation Ctr., Yonkers, N.Y., 1988—; legis. asst. to 12th dist. Westchester County legislator, White Plains, 1984—. Lily Endowment Found. and Smithsonian Inst. scholar Sarah Lawrence Coll., summer 1979. Mem. Manhattan Paralegal Assn., Am. Soc. Notararies. Democrat. Roman Catholic.

WALTON, AMANDA LORETTA, educator; b. Millen, Ga., Sept. 16, 1941; d. Willie and Gussia (Wilson) Jones; m. Van L. Walton, July 3, 1966; children: Myshiel Alston, Van Lawrence Walton Jr. AA in Liberal Arts, Manhatten Community Coll., 1975; BA in Polit. Sci., York Coll., 1980; M, City Coll. of N.Y., 1983, postgrad., 1985. Teacher asst. Pub. Sch. 200, Manhatten, 1970-73; aux. trainer Pub. Sch. 132, N.Y.C., 1974-81; tchr. Pub. Sch. 274, Bklyn., 1981—; ednl. cons., Queens, N.Y., 1981—. Mem. legisl. adv. com., Albany, N.Y., 1981, Queens Village Bellrose Dems., Queens Village, 1983. Mem. NAFE, Internat. Reading Assn., Manhattan Reading Coun. Democrat. Roman Catholic. Home: 221-39 112 Ave New York NY 11429

WALTON, CARMELITA NOREEN, nurse; b. Chgo., Nov. 15, 1926; d. Elmo Augusta and Evelyn Mae (Terry) Desobrey; student St. Marys Coll., U. Notre Dame, 1943-45; grad. Cook County Sch. Nursing, 1949; student DePaul U., 1978-79; children from previous marriage—Michael Jerome. Head nurse, supr., nurse clinician Cook County Hosp., Chgo., 1951-71; supr. U. Chgo. Hosps./Clinics, 1963-68; dir. nursing Woodlawn Child Health Center, Chgo., 1968-69; dir. nursing prison health care Cermak Health Services, Cook County Jail, Chgo., 1973—; cons., surveyor Nat. Commn. on Correctional Health Care, speaker 13th ann. conv., 1989. Contbr. articles to profl. jours. Recipient Superior Pub. Service award City of Chgo., 1984. Mem. Am. Nurses Assn. (cert. in nursing adminstrn., mem. Council Nursing Adminstrn.), Ill. Nurses Assn., Nat. League Nursing, Am. Pub. Health Assn., Am. Correctional Health Services Assn. Democrat. Roman Catholic. Home: 5050 Lake Shore Dr S Apt 1608 Chicago IL 60615 Office: 2800 California Ave S Chicago IL 60608

WALTON, KAREN KAY, health science association managing director; b. Brownwood, Tex., Sept. 24, 1944; d. Samuel Emmett and Crystal (Fine) W. BA, U. Tex., 1966; MBA, San Jose State U., 1978. Unit dir. ARC, Korea, 1966-67; program supr. Seoul, Korea, 1968-69, asst. dir., 1969-70; div. rep. Hartford, Conn., 1970-71, asst. div. mgr., 1971-72, asst. to mgr., 1972-73; asst. nat. dir. Blood Services Donor Resources Devel., Washington, 1973-76; tng. cons. Washington, 1976; dir. personnel tng. and devel. Burlingame, Calif., 1978-79, asst. mgr. service to divs. and chpts., 1979-83, mng. dir., 1983—; personnel asst. Nauta-Line Houseboat Co., Nashville, 1967-68; tng. cons. Am. Red Cross, Washington, 1976; research project dir. Calif. High Sch. Bus. Edn. Depts. Evaluation, 1977; long range planning cons. Calif. Nurses Assn., San Francisco, 1980. Mem. Rep. presdl. task force, Washington, 1980-82; mem. LWV, San Jose, Calif., 1980-83; exec. com. Am. Cancer Soc., San Jose, 1980-83. Named an Outstanding Alumni. Mem. Beta Gama Sigma, Phi Mu. Club: Commonwealth of Calif. Office: ARC 1870 Ogden Dr Burlingame CA 94010

WALTON, LORRAINE HOPSON, educator, consultant; b. Donalsonville, Ga., Apr. 10, 1934; d. Benjamin Franklin and Lula (Wilcox) Hopson; m. Jesse Issac Walton, Dec. 18, 1956; children: Angela Deshae', Jesse Kipp. BS, Albany (Ga.) State Coll., 1955; MA, Atlanta U., 1967; EdS, 1978, EdD, 1981. Tchr., drama coach Seminole County Sch. System, Donalsonville, 1956-57; tchr., basketball coach Gwinnett County Sch. System, Lawrenceville, Ga., 1958-63; tchr., dept. chairperson Atlanta Pub. Schs., 1963-70; program coord. Atlanta Area Tech. Sch., 1970-83, asst. dir., 1983—; cons. program U. Ga., Athens, 1977; cons. allied health program Clark Coll., Atlanta, 1982-85; cons. leadership program Ga. State U., Atlanta, 1983—. Vice chmn. Gov.'s Sml. and Minority Bus. Commn., Atlanta, 1983—; sponsor Parents Anonymous, Atlanta, 1983-85; vol. hostess dir. Dem. Conv., Atlanta, 1988; chmn. bd. Friends of Atlanta Pub. Library, 1979-86. Recipient Outstanding Contbn. award Atlanta Urban League, 1977, Leadership award Top Ladies of Distinction, Inc., 1988, Bronze Woman of the Yr. Community Svc., 1988. Mem. Am. Vocat. Assn. (presenter Anaheim, Calif. chpt. 1983, MIND award 1983), United Negro Coll. Fund (chairperson com. 1977-79, Cert. 1977, 78), Atlanta Assn. Profls., Inc. (pres. 1983—), Nat. Assn. Black Educators, Atlanta LWV, Jewels (pres. Atlanta chpt. 1979-85), Pacesetters (pres. Atlanta chpt. 1977-84), Alpha Kappa Alpha (chmn. Founder's Day com. 1988—). Democrat. Home: 4621 Lanark Dr SW Atlanta GA 30331 Office: Atlanta Area Tech Sch 1560 Stewart Ave SW Atlanta GA 30310

WALTON, SANDRA STEVENSON, personnel executive; b. Richmond, Va., May 14, 1949; d. William Blake Jr. and Frances (Brock) Stevenson; divorced; 1 child, Evan. BSBA, Va. Commonwealth U., 1981. Office personnel employment mgr. Reynolds Metals Co., Richmond, 1977-78, mgmt. info. sci. personnel mgr., 1978-79, hdqrs. personnel mgr., 1981—. Mem. career devel. coun. J. Sargeant Reynolds Community Coll., 1980-81; mem. task force CETA Consortium, 1980-82; mem. bus. adv. coun. Va. Dept. Rehab. Svcs., 1982-85; arbitrator Better Bus. Bur., 1985—; mem. Richmond Childcare Coordinating Coun., 1988—. Recipient Cert. Appreciation and Recognition, Va. Dept. Rehab. Services, 1982, 83, Gov.'s Adv. Council, 1983. Baptist. Clubs: Westwood Racquet, Forest Heights Garden (pres. 1977-79). Office: Reynolds Metals Co 6601 W Broad St Richmond VA 23230

WALTON, VALLI YVONNE, financial services company executive; b. Bronx, N.Y., May 24, 1950; d. William Jackson Sr. and Addie Ruby (Scott) Foy; m. Haywood Walton Sr., May 23, 1981. BA magna cum laude, Barrington Coll., 1971; postgrad., New Sch. for Social Rsch., 1975; cert. small bus. mgmt., NYU, 1976; MA in Liberal Studies, SUNY, Stony Brook, 1980; postgrad., Rutgers U., 1980. Approver group health benefits Metro. Life Ins. Co., Hauppauge, N.Y., 1971-73; account analyst, sales agt., publs. specialist group benefits dept. Equitable Life Assurance Soc. of the U.S., N.Y.C., 1973-76, litigations specialist, 1980-82; supr. major med. and death benefits Program Planners Ins. Cons., N.Y.C., 1976-77; group health and disability benefits specialist Operating Engrs. Local 825 Welfare Fund, Newark, N.J., 1977-80; various positions to dir. legis. svcs. assn. ops. MONY Fin. Svcs., Purchase, 1982—; assoc. mem. Practising Law Inst., N.Y.C., 1985—; dep. gov. Am. Biog. Inst., 1989, rsch. bd. advisors, 1989. Mem. Nat. Com. to Preserve Social Security and Medicare, Rep. Nat. Com., Washington, 1986—; dir. Bklyn. Dist. Children, Christian Edn. Durham A.M.E. Zion Ch., 1972. With USAR and Nat. Guard, 1974-76. Recipient Cert. of Outstanding Profl. Performance, Community Leaders of Am., 1989. Mem. NAFE (certificate 1987), N.Y. Acad. Scis. (assoc.). Home: 1 Fordham Hill Oval Bronx NY 10468 Office: MONY Fin Svcs 4 Manhattanville Rd Purchase NY 10577

WALZ, MARY KATHRYN, lawyer; b. Buffalo, July 24, 1951; d. Richard Nicholas and Francis Marie (Koehmstedt) W.; m. Gerald John Vogt, Aug.

19, 1972; 1 child, Brian W. Vogt. BA in Chemistry, Clarke Coll., Dubuque, Iowa, 1972; student, U. Vienna, Austria, 1971; JD, Golden Gate U., 1975. Bar: Calif. 1975, Minn. 1976, N.Mex. 1977, U.S. Ct. Appeals (10th cir.). Patent atty. Alexander, Sell, Steldt & DelaHunt, St. Paul, 1976; sr. atty. Los Alamos (N.Mex.) Nat. Lab., 1981-85; ptnr. Herter, Walz & Marr, Santa Fe, 1985-87; sr. atty. Sutin, Thayer & Browne PA, Santa Fe, 1987-89; pvt. practice, Los Alamos, 1977-81, 89—; prof. U. N.Mex., Los Alamos, 1986-88, 89; lectr. U. Calif., Los Alamos, 1989-90; bd. dirs. Optomec Inc., Santa Fe; mem. adv. coun. on nuclear exposure data U.S. Dept. Energy, Washington, 1983—. Mem. Los Alamos Planning and Zoning Commmn., 1977; mem. Los Alamos County Coun., 1978, vice chmn., 1979; treas. Sundberg for State Rep., Los Alamos, 1986, 88. Mem. ABA, N.Mex. Bar Assn. (banking and probate com. 1989—), Calif. Bar Assn., Minn. Bar Assn., Los Alamos Bar Assn. (sec. 1988, 90). Republican. Roman Catholic. Office: PO Box 951 Los Alamos NM 87544

WALZ, MONA LANGGUTH, realtor, broker; b. Mpls., Sept. 1, 1931; d. Karl Hoffman and Ellen E.M. (Peterson) Langguth; m. Garry Richard Walz, Mar. 18, 1955; children: Ann Eileen, Eric Carl, Narda Christine. BA, U. Minn., 1952, BS, 1955, MA, 1956; M of Urban Planning, U. Mich., 1974. Counselor Hopkins (Minn.) Jr. High Sch., 1956-57, Edina (Minn.) Jr. High Sch., 1957-58; lectr. N.D. State U., Fargo, 1959-60, Moorhead (Minn.) State Coll., 1959-60; sch. diagostician Dearborn Heights (Mich.) Schs., 1963-64; dep. drain commr. Washtenaw County, Ann Arbor, Mich., 1976-78; dist. mgr. US Census Bur., Ann Arbor, 1980; market researcher Arbitron, Livonia, Mich., 1982-83; realtor, assoc. broker Edward Surovell Co., Ann Arbor, 1984—; bd. dirs. Community Residential Corp., Ypsilanti, Mich., Child Care Coordinating and Referral Svc., Ann Arbor. Bd. dirs. Washtenaw County Bd. Pub. Works, Ann Arbor, 1985—, Housing Bur. for Srs., Ann Arbor, 1984—. Mem. AAUW, LWV, Am. Planning Assn., Ann Arbor Area Bd. of Realtors, Urban Planning Alumni Assn. (bd. dirs.), Am. Psychol. Assn., Sara Brown Smith Club. Democrat. Home: 1718 Arbordale Ann Arbor MI 48103 Office: Ed Surovell Co 1886 W Stadium Ann Arbor MI 48103

WALZER, ANN ELAINE, environmental scientist; b. Rochester, N.Y., Mar. 16, 1957; d. Clyde Willard and Edith Grace (Crane) W. AAS, Monroe Community Coll., 1977; BS, Brockport Coll., 1979; MS, U. Rochester, 1987. Research asst. Brockport (N.Y.) Coll., 1979; scientist, mgr. Eastman Kodak Co., Rochester, N.Y., 1980-89; environ. rsch. scientist Oak Ridge (Tenn.) Nat. Labs., 1990—. Mem. AAAS, Audubon Soc., Nat. Wildlife Fedn., Am. Fisheries Soc. Office: Oak Ridge Nat Labs Environ Scis Div Oak Ridge TN 37831-6351

WALZOG, NANCY LEE, television producer; b. Balt., Feb. 12, 1963; d. William Richard and Barbara Jane (Lombardi) W. BFA, NYU, 1983; postgrad., Pace U. Dir. TV sales and mktg. Internat. Film Exch., N.Y.C., 1984-86; producer ABC Entertainment, N.Y.C., 1984; comml. producer Nancy Walzog Film and TV, Ltd., N.Y.C., 1982-84; v.p. Tapestry Internat., Ltd., N.Y.C., 1986—. Recipient Emmy award, Acad. TV Arts and Scis., N.Y.C., 1987, Emmy nominiation, 1990, ACE award, Nat. Acad. Cable TV Programming, Washington, 1987, Gold award San Francisco Internat. Film Festival, 1987, Hugo award Chgo. Internat. Film Festival, 1988. Office: Tapestry Internat 924 Broadway New York NY 10010

WAMBLES, LYNDA ENGLAND, academic administrator, consultant; b. Nashville, Dec. 30, 1937; d. Henry Russell and Doris Olivia (Stuart) England; m. Byron Adolph Wambles, Sept. 3, 1965; 1 child, Teri Leigh Moore Wambles Taylor. Student, U. Tenn., 1964-65, 73-74, Washington U., St. Louis, 1984-86. Cert. profl. sec. Exec. sec. Gen. Truck Sales, Knoxville, Tenn., 1972-74; asst. to dean Coll. Law U. Tenn., Knoxville, 1974-76; office mgr. Washington U. Sch. Bus., St. Louis, 1977-78, registrar, dir. info. systems, 1978-83, asst. dean for faculty and adminstrn. services, 1983-86; cons. in field St. Louis, 1978-86, Overland Park, Kans., 1986—; cons. in field, St. Louis, 1978—; lectr. div. continuing edn. Washington U., St. Louis, 1978-80. Author: (with others) Procedures Manual and Information for State Guaranty Associations, 1987. Active United Way of Greater Knoxville, 1973-74; leader lunch participant YWCA, St. Louis, 1981-83. Fellow Acad. Cert. Profl. Secs.; mem. Profl. Secs. Internat., Nat. Secs. Assn. (Tenn. div. Sec. of Yr. 1975), Assn. Info. Systems Profls. Republican. Presbyterian. Home and Office: 8425 W 113th St Overland Park KS 66210

WAMBOLD, KAREN J., registered nurse; b. Oakland, Calif., June 25, 1961; d. William Eldreidge and Liselotte (Gross) W. Diploma in Nursing, L.A. County Med. Ctr., 1984. Cert. advanced cardiac life support. RN L.A. County/U. So. Calif. Med. Ctr., L.A., 1983-86; firefighter/EMS coord. Sierra Madre Fire Dept., Sierra Madre, Calif., 1985-88; RN Beverly Hosp., Montebello, Calif., 1987—, Arcadia Meth. Hosp., Arcadia, Calif., 1989—; bd. dirs. Calif. Firefighter's Burn Relay, Monrovia; program developer continuing edn. program, 1988. Assoc. editor, contbr. (newsletter) Relay, 1989. Coord. for field office speaker's bur. Alisa Ann Ruch Calif. Burn Found., Canoga Park, 1988—. Recipient speaker's award Alisa Ann Ruch CAlif. Burn Found., 1988. Republican. Lutheran. Office: Ruch Calif Burn Found Monrovia Field Office Speakers Bur 525 S Myrtle Ste 102 Monrovia CA 91016

WAMPLER, BARBARA BEDFORD, entrepreneur; b. New Bedford, Mass., July 23, 1932; d. William and Mary (Fitzpatrick) Bedford; m. John H. Wampler, Oct. 21, 1950; children: John H. Jr., William C., James B., Robert T. AS, Tunxis Community Coll., 1975. Lic. real estate agt., Mass. Counselor Wampler Counseling Rehab. Services, Farmington, Conn., 1975-85; owner, mgr. Wampler Mktg., Farmington, 1980-84, Earth Campgrounds I and II, Otis, Mass., 1984—; pres., mgr. Earth Works (name now Earth Enterprises), Otis, Mass., 1984—; founder, pres. Advt. Matters, Otis, 1989—; v.p. Mastery Books, Otis, 1989—; mem., clk. ZBA, Otis, Mass., 1988; notary pub., 1988. Contbr. articles to profl. jours. Dir. music 1st Congl. Ch., Otis; mem., clk. Otis Zoning Bd. Appeals. Faculty scholar U. Hartford, 1976. Mem. Bus. Mgrs. Assn., Nat. Campground Owners Assn., Mass. Assn. of Campground Owners, Kiwanis. Home and Office: Earth Enterprises PO Box 690 Rte 8 Otis MA 01253

WANAT, NANCY ANNE, insurance company executive; b. New Haven, May 7, 1953; d. Edward John and Lena (Lobudek) W. AA in Nursing, Norwalk Community Coll., 1978; BS in Biology, So. Conn. State U., 1981; MPA, NYU, 1988. RN. Asst. head nurse Coronary Care Unit/Yale New Haven Hosp., 1982-84; health systems cons. The Travelers Health Network, Hartford, Conn., 1985-87; legis. dir. govt. affairs Travelers Ins. Co., Hartford, 1987-88; mgr. issues analysis customer cons. Altna Ins. Co., Middletown, Conn., 1988-89; asst. dir. product mgmt. Travelers Inc. Co., Hartford, 1989—. Campaign ops. Congressman Burce Morrison Re-ection Campaign, New Haven, 1989; scheduler Gloria Sandillo for Mayor Campaign, Hamden, 1985; field coord. Bruce Morrison for Gov. Campaign, New Haven, 1990. Scholarship NYU, 1986. Democrat. Home: 650 Quinnipiac Ave New Haven CT 06513 Office: The Travelers One Tower Sq 21 MS New Haven CT 06183

WANBERG, GENEVE CHRISTENSEN, office manager; b. Salt Lake City, July 13, 1952; d. Max Harry and Dorothy (Hill) Christensen; m. John Gerald Wanberg, Dec. 15, 1972; children: John, Stephanie, Emily, Jenny. BS, Utah State U., 1973; MBA, U. Phoenix, 1990. Cert. constrn. document technologist. In sales and new bus. devel. Alder's, Salt Lake City, 1982-84; in archtl. sales ASI Sign Systems, Salt Lake City, 1984; in contract sales I.S.E.C., Salt Lake City, 1984-85; owner Monitor S.W., Tempe, Ariz., 1986; br. mgr. Dow Diversified, Inc., Phoenix, 1987-88; in archtl. sales EMSER Tile, Phoenix, 1989; office mgr. Stephen Andros Specification Consultants, Phoenix, 1989—; cons. D.L. Withers Constrn., Phoenix, 1990. Mem. Constrn. Specifications Inst. (membership chmn. 1988-89, program chmn. 1989-90, bd. dirs. 1990—, Pres.'s award 1988, 89), NAFE. Mem. Latter Day Saints Ch. Home: 758 E Glade Mesa AZ 85204

WAND, MARILYN MAXINE, pharmacist; b. Detroit, July 7, 1951; d. Robert William and Mabel Maxine (Riley) Fruth; m. Harlan Francis Wand Jr., May 21, 1977; 1 child, Peter Robert. BS in Pharmacy, U. Ariz., 1974. Lic. pharmacist, Ariz., Calif. Pharmacist Phoenix Bapt. Hosp., 1974-76, MD Pharmacy, Phoenix, 1976-77, Med. Ctr. Pharmacy, Buckeye, Ariz., 1977—. Catechist St. Henry's Religious Edn., Buckeye, 1986—. Mem. Am. Soc. Hosp. Pharmacists. Roman Catholic. Home: 23003 W Watkins Buckeye AZ 85326 Office: Med Ctr Pharmacy 303-1/2 4th St Buckeye AZ 85326

WANDEL, LEE PALMER, educator; b. Detroit, Aug. 27, 1954; d. Kenneth Eugene and Mary Somerville (Palmer) W.; m. Laurence Hutchinson Winnie, Apr. 20, 1982; 1 child, Matthew McKay Winnie. BA with honors, U. Calif., Santa Cruz, 1976; AM, Brown U., 1977; PhD, U. Mich., 1985. Lectr. Stanford (Calif.) U., 1985-87; asst. prof. Yale U., New Haven, Conn., 1987—. Author: Always Among Us: Images of the Poor in Zwingli's Zurich, 1990; contbr. articles to profl. jours. Mem. coun. 16th Century Studies Conf. Mem. Am. Hist. Assn., Renaissance Soc. Am., Soc. Reformation Research,. Office: Yale U PO Box 1504A Yale Sta New Haven CT 06520-7425

WANG, AMY CHI-WEN, journalist; b. Hangchou, Tse Jiang, China, July 11, 1928; d. Sui Jen Liang and Jin Zhen (Wang) Liang; m. Chih Wong Wang, June 3, 1951 (dec. 1970); children: Lucille C., S. William, Edwin J. AB, Fu Dan U., Shanghai, Republic of China, 1950; postgrad., U. Mo., Columbia, 1951. News reporter Taiwan News Agy., Taipei, 1950-51; freelance journalist Boston, 1951—. Author: World Journal, 1977; contbr. articles to women's mags. Named Outstanding American, Ellis Island Restoration, 1989. Mem. Nat. Assn. Am. Pen Women, Purchase Country Club. Republican. Episcopalian. Office: MPO Box 39 Purchase NY 10577

WANG, PEARL YUN, computer science educator; b. Boston, Nov. 27, 1949; m. Thomas E. Gerasch, Aug. 9, 1980. AB, Wheaton Coll., Norton, Mass., 1971; MS, U. Wis., Milw., 1973, PhD, 1980. Asst. prof. U. Md.-Baltimore County, Catonsville, 1980-83; asst. prof. computer sci. George Mason U., Fairfax, Va., 1983-89, assoc. prof., 1989—; cons. Inst. for Def. Analyses, Falls Church, Va., 1985; organizer Frontiers of Massively Parallel Computation Conf., IEEE, Washington, 1988, 90; presenter in field. Coauthor: Assembly Language Programming in Compass, 1987; contbr. articles to profl. jours. Math. and computer sci. judge Va. State Sci. Fair, Loudoun, 1986, 87. Rsch. grantee Va. Ctr. for Innovative Tech., 1988. Mem. Ops. Rsch. Soc., Assn. for Computing Machinery. Office: George Mason U Computer Sci 4400 University Dr Fairfax VA 22030-4444

WANG, SUE HWA, jewelry wholesale executive; b. Taichung, Taiwan, China, May 5, 1948; came to U.S., 1968; d. Ting-Yi and Shiu-Ying (Hsu) Wang; m. Sam Kuo, Nov. 26, 1970; children: Roger Kuo. BA, Tamkang U., Taipei, China, 1968. Pres. Sue Trading Co., Inc., San Francisco, 1970—. Mem. Mfg. Jewelers and Silversmiths of Am., Jewelers Bd. Trade, Green Hill Country Club. Office: Sue Trading Co Inc 888 Brannan St #191 San Francisco CA 94103

WANGER, SHELLEY ANTONIA, magazine editor; b. Los Angeles, July 4, 1948; d. Walter and Joan (Bennett) W. Student, Vassar Coll., 1966-68; BA, Sarah Lawrence Coll., 1970. Asst. to editor N.Y. Rev. of Books, N.Y.C., 1975-82; articles editor House & Garden mag., N.Y.C., 1982-87; cons. editor Conde Nast's Traveler, 1987—. Editor-in-chief Interview mag., 1987-89.

WANLAND, RUBY EVELYN, educator; b. Orlando, Fla., July 30, 1937; d. Algot Waldemar and Lydia Albertina (Mattson) W. AA, Cottey Coll., 1957; BA, So. Ill. U., 1959; MA, Nova U., 1983. Cert. tchr. social studies secondary edn., Fla. Tchr. Howey-in-the-Hills (Fla.) Acad., 1959-63, North Miami (Fla.) Sr. High Sch., 1963-70, Northwestern Sr. High Sch., Miami, Fla., 1970—; tchr. rep. north Dade Area PTA bd., chairperson human relations council North Miami Sr. High Sch., 1968-70; sponsor Close-Up Northwestern Sr. High Sch., Washington, 1970-73, county Silver Knights, Miami, 1970—, chmn. 5-yr. evaluation So. Assn. Schs. and Colls., 1975, chmn. social studies dept., mem. curriculum council, mem. faculty council, 1975—, peer tchr., 1981-83, 85; adj. tchr. Dade Acad. Teaching Arts Miami (Fla.) Beach Sr. High, 1987. Author ednl. packages for schs. Active Dem. campaigns, North Miami, 1975-76, 80-87; vol. voter registration Northwestern Sr. High Sch., Miami, 1975—. Recipient recognition award Dade County Sch. Bd., 1971-72, award Northwestern Sr. High Sch. PTO, 1973-77, 86; named Tchr. of Yr., Northwestern Sr. High Sch., 1986; Dade Bar Assn. scholar, 1965. Mem. Nat. Social Studies Coun., Fla. Social Studies Coun., Dade County Social Studies Coun., United Tchrs. of Dade (rep. 1968, 74-79, human rels. coun. 1968-70, del. Fla. Edn. Assn. 1980, 83-84, tchr. rep., sabbatical leave com., professionalization of edn. task force 1986-87, award 1968, 73, del. nat. studies conf. 1989, Professionalization Recognition award 1988), AFL, Fla. Trails Assn., Appalachian Trail Conf. Presbyterian. Home: Miami Beach Sr High Acad 2031 Prairie Ave North Miami FL 33161

WANMAN, AGNES WHITE, state agency professional, dance educator, performer/entertainer; b. Statesville, N.C., May 1, 1945; d. Hugh Sylvanus and Margaret Elizabeth (Carrithers) White; m. Chris Arthur Wanman, 1978 (div.). BA, Radford (Va.) Coll., 1968; student, W.Va. Wesleyan Coll., 1963-66; postgrad., Va. Polytech. Inst. & State U., 1974-75. Community planner N.C. Dept. Econ. & Community Devel., Fayetteville, N.C., 1975—; regional corr. N.C. Downtown Devel. Assn., Wake Forest, 1990—. Bd. dirs. Arts Coun. Fayetteville/Cumberland County, 1986—, Universal Brotherhood, Inc., Durham, N.C., 1990—. Recipient Svc. award N.C. Dept. Natural Resources and Community Devel., 1986. Mem. Cumberland Photo Club (sec. 1980-82, v.p. 1983-84, pres. 1985-86, treas. 1987—), Zeta Tau Alpha. Home: 4804 Old Field Rd Fayetteville NC 28304 Office: NC Dept Econ & Community 714 Wachovia Bldg Fayetteville NC 28301

WANN, PATSY GORDON, lumber company executive; b. Aberdeen, Miss., June 8, 1952; d. Wilbur M. and Travis Elaine (Dill) Gordon; 1 child, Stacy Leigh. Student, Holmes Jr. Coll., 1970-71, Miss. Coll., 1980-81. Adminstrv. sec. U. Miss. Med. Ctr., Jackson, 1972-78; adminstrv. asst. Miss. Meth. Hosp. and Rehab. Ctr., Jackson, 1978—; pres. K&W Lumber Co., Jackson, 1987—; notary pub. Hinds County, State of Miss., Jackson, 1978—. Vol. VA, Jackson, 1977-78; mem. aux. Miss. Meth. Rehab. Ctr., Jackson, 1978-81; mem. Jackson Symphony League, 1986—; bd. dirs. Goodwill Industries, Jackson, 1988—. Mem. NAFE, Jackson Booster. Republican. Baptist. Home: 130 Cedars of Lebanon Rd Jackson MS 39206 Office: K&W Lumber Co 123 Lake Cavalier Rd Jackson MS 39216

WANTA, DEBRA ANN, accountant; b. Milw., Aug. 9, 1964; d. Ted H. and Joan A. (Welch) W. AA in Computer Programming, Moraine Park Tech. Coll., Fond du Lac, Wis., 1984; AA in Acctg., Moraine Park Tech. Coll., West Bend, Wis., 1985. Asst. acct. Eulert Acctg., West Bend, 1985; lead pricing coord. Sola/Barnes-Hind, San Diego, 1985-89; now shipping technician Sundstrand Power Systems, San Diego, 1989—. Home: PO Box 80223 San Diego CA 92138

WANTLAND, EVELYN KENDRICK, retired mathematics educator; b. Suffolk, Va., June 22, 1917; d. Marion Kelly and Mary Douglas (Causey) Kendrick; m. John Rankin Kinney, May 16, 1939 (div. Apr. 1949); 1 child, Lois Kinney Dimmitt; m. Wayne Warde Wantland, Apr. 19, 1964 (dec. Mar. 1971). BA in Math., U. Ill., 1948, MA in Math, 1949, PhD in Math, 1958. Prof. math. Ferrum (Va.) Jr. Coll. (now Ferrum Coll.), 1949-51; asst. prof. math. Ill. Wesleyan U., Bloomington, 1951-57, prof., head dept. math., 1964-76; assoc. prof. math. Kans. State Coll. (now Kans. State U.), Manhattan, 1957-62; prof. math. U. Miss., Oxford, 1962-64. Mem. Am. Math. Soc., Math. Assn. Am., Sigma Xi, Pi Mu Epsilon. Republican. Mem. Christian Ch. Home: 110 E Beecher St Bloomington IL 61701

WAPNER, PEGGY ANN, portfolio manager; b. Joliet, Ill., Sept. 8, 1950; d. Glenn Howard and Arlene (Janssen) Nissen; m. Frank Duane Adair, (div. 1976); m. Gary Lee Wapner, July 24, 1976; 1 child, Allison Ann. BS in Edn., Eastern Ill. U., 1972. Sec. T. Rowe Price Assn., Baltimore, 1974, trading desk asst., 1975, money market trader, 1976, money market portfolio mgr. Office: T Rowe Price Assoc Inc 100 E Pratt St Baltimore MD 21202

WARBRITTON, PATRICIA ANN, travel agency administrator; b. Glendale, W.Va., Jan. 27, 1949; d. Wilbert and Arlene Margaret (Nagel) Miner; m. David Scott Warbritton, July 6, 1974; children: Jeffrey Scott, Jason Patrick. BA, U. Fla., 1971. Exec. dir. Brandon (Fla.) Cultural Ctr., 1981-84; account mgr. Tampa (Fla.) Travel Service, Inc., 1986—. Mem. exec. com. Hillsboro County Reps., 1986-87; bd. dirs. Hillsboro County Bd. Children's Services, Tampa, 1986—, Bloomingdale Little League, Brandon, 1987—. Mem. Greater Brandon C. of C., Jr. Service League, Fla. Fedn. Women's Clubs (Judy M. Martin award 1985, vice dir. Jr. clubs 1986-88, dir. 1988—). Republican. Methodist. Home: 2821 Fairway View Dr Valrico FL 33594

WARD, BARBARA CONNER, risk management professional, consultant; b. Plainview, Tex., Apr. 13, 1940; d. William Elbert and Sarah Pauline (Lovell) Conner; m. Dalton L. Ward, Sept. 13, 1958; children: Dana Renyce, Lisa Suzaune. Student, Wharton (Tex.) Jr. Coll., 1978-82; BS, U. Houston, 1982. Office adminstr., cashier Interstate Securities, Odessa, Tex., 1964-65; dept. asst. supr. Ft. Bend Ind. Sch. Dist., Sugar Land, Tex., 1974-78; organ. cons. B.C. Ward Enterprises, Inc., Sugar Land, 1982-86; ins. sales, cons. Multi-Ins. Service Co., Houston, 1986-87; coordinator flexible benefits Tex. Sch. Services Found., 1987—; risk mgmt. cons., 1988—. Host paretn Am. Field Service, Houston, 1980; elder First Presbyn. Ch., Sugar Land, 1982-85; community liaison Ft. Bend Assn. Retarded Citizens, 1984-87, fundraiser, 1985-87, Vol. of Yr., 1985; bd. dirs. Youth Opportunities Unltd., Richmond, Tex., 1985. Recipient Service award Richmond State Sch., 1985-87. Mem. Tex. Investors Tng. Enterprises (sec. 1986-87), Houston Assn. Life Underwriters. Republican.

WARD, BETHEA, artist, small business owner; b. Montgomery, Ala., July 6, 1924; d. Charles E. and Lucy (Walter) W. BFA, Syracuse U., 1946; postgrad., Trinity U., San Antonio, 1965, 66, 68, San Antonio Art Inst., 1967, Houston Mus. Fine Arts Sch., 1973-75. Interior designer Davison-Paxon, Atlanta, 1946-47; assoc. prof. interior design U. Tex., Austin, 1947-51; interior designer Heminways-Bundrick, Shreveport, La., 1951-55; draftsman, supr. Ark. Fuel subs. Cities Service Co., Shreveport, 1955-60, Cities Svc. Co. Midland, San Antonio, 1961-82; visual artist, owner Tex. Notables Studio-Gallerie, Houston, 1983—. Juried shows include (watercolor paintings) Midland (Tex.) Art Fest. (2d place award, 1962), 35th Ann. Local Artist Exhbn., San Antonio (Wofford award 1965), Wichita, Kas. Centennial Nat. Exhbn. (inclusion award 1970), Cen. Tex. Hist. on Canvas Exhbn. (1st place award TFAA 1972), Houston Pub. Libr.; group exhibits include U. Houston, 1986; contbr. ink drawing to Southwestern Hist. Quarterly, 1977; commns. include drawing for Moody Found. of Galveston; one person shows include Star of the Republic Mus., Houston Pub. Libr., Harris County Heritage Soc., San Antonio Pub. Libr. Recipient Award of Distinction Juried Art Fair, Houston Internat. Festival, 1987, numerous awards for watercolor paintings. Mem. Hoover Watercolor Soc. (founding mem. 1952), Watercolor Art Soc. Houston (chmn bd. social chmn., sec., co-founder), Art League Houston, Columbus (Tex.) C. of C., Cultural Arts Council Houston, Coppini Acad. Fine Arts (life), Tex. Arts Alliance, Tex. Commn. on the Arts, Southwestern Watercolor Soc. (founding mem., pub. chmn.), Tex. State Hist. Assn., Tex. Hist. Found., Nat. Mus. of Women in the Arts, Cultural Arts Council of Houston. Republican. Presbyterian. Home and Studio: Tex Notables Studio-Gallerie 9614 Valverde St Houston TX 77063

WARD, CYNTHIA VAUNE, editor; b. Boston, May 9, 1958; d. John Peter and Joyce (Maunder) W. BA in Polit. Sci., Chinese, Wellesley Coll., 1981; postgrad., Yale U., 1988—. V.p. publs. Western Monetary Cons., Ft. Collins (Colo.) and Washington, 1984-88; sr. editor, columnist Conservative Digest, Washington, 1985-88; mng. editor Am. Press Internat., Washington, 1987-88. Office: Conservative Digest/ Am Press Internat 1210 National Press Bldg Washington DC 20045

WARD, DEVA JEAN, early childhood education educator; b. Fayetteville, N.C., Mar. 10, 1953; d. Bill and Sherrelle (Whitney) Matson; m. Dennis L. Ward, June 28, 1977; 1 child, Whitney. BS, Ea. Mont. Coll., 1975; MEd, Idaho State U., 1985; postgrad., Walden U., Mpls., 1989—. Cert. tchr., Idaho, Wyo., Wash. Tchr. Sch. Dist. No. 411, Twin Falls, Idaho; prof. Coll. So. Idaho, Twin Falls. Named one of Outstanding Young Women of Am., 1979, 84. Mem. Nat. Assn. Curriculum Devel. and Supervision, Delta Kappa Gamma. Home: 1304 Holly Dr Twin Falls ID 83301

WARD, DIANE KOROSY, lawyer; b. Cleve., Oct. 17, 1939; d. Theodore Louis and Edith (Bogar) Korosy; m. S. Mortimer Ward IV, July 2, 1960 (div. 1978); children: Christopher LaBruce, Samantha Martha; m. R. Michael Walters, June 30, 1979. AB, Heidelberg Coll., 1961; JD, U. San Diego, 1975. Bar: Calif. 1977, U.S. Dist. Ct. (so. dist.) Calif. 1977. Ptnr. Ward & Howell, San Diego, 1978-79, Walters, Ward & Howell, A.P.C., San Diego, 1979-81, 90—; mng. ptnr. Walters & Ward, A.P.C., San Diego, 1981-90; dir., v.p. Oak Broadcasting Systems, Inc., 1982-83; dir. Elisabeth Kubler-Ross Ctr., Inc., 1983-85; sheriff Ranchos del Norte Corral of Westerners, 1985-87; trustee San Diego Community Defenders, Inc., 1986-88. Pres. bd. dirs. Green Valley Civic Assn., 1979-80; dir. Poway Ctr. for the Performing Arts; trustee Palomar-Pomerado Hosp. Found., chmn. Deferred Giving Found., 1985-89; v.p. Endowment Devel., 1989—; bd. dirs. Clean Found.; trustee Episc. Diocese of San Diego. Mem. ABA, Rancho Bernardo Bar Assn. (chmn. 1982-83), Lawyers Club San Diego, Profl. and Exec. Women of the Ranch (founder, pres. 1982—), San Diego Golden Eagle Club, Soroptimist Internat. (pres. chpt. 1979-80), Phi Delta Phi. Republican. Episcopalian. Home: 16503 Avenida Florencia Poway CA 92064 Office: Walters Ward & Howell 11665 Avena Pl Ste 203 San Diego CA 92128

WARD, DORIS ELIZABETH, career counselor, biologist, educator; b. Charlotte, N.C., Jan. 11, 1935; d. James Hopkins and Florie Kathryn Cofield; m. Eddie Eugene Ward, Sept. 18, 1954; children: Eddie Eugene, Tanya Devonne, Tracia Lynnore, Tamara Elizabeth. BS, Howard U., 1966, postgrad., 1967-70; MEd in Guidance and Counseling, Bowie State U., 1985; EdS, George Washington U., 1987, EdD, 1990. Cert. sci. tchr. and guidance counselor, Md. Med. technician U.S. Dept. Agr., Washington, 1958-64; biol. lab. technician U.S. Dept. Agr., Bethesda, Md., 1964-65; histologic tech. lab. instr. Howard U., Washington, 1966-67; biologist (histopathology) NIH, Bethesda, 1969-71; tchr. Our Lady Queen of Peace Sch., Washington, 1972-74; program analyst/mgmt. analysis HHS, Washington, 1974-82; career counselor Prince Georges Community Coll., Largo, Md., 1985—; doctoral intern in counseling Career Devel. Ctr., U. Md., College Park, 1988-89. Hospice vol.; developer, facilitator bereavement support ministry St. Joseph's Ch., Landover, Md., 1984; cons./vol., career counselor for transition and spl. needs populations Cerebral Palsy Assn. Prince Georges County, 1986. Recipient Tchr. Appreciation award Our Lady Queen of Peace Sch., 1974. Mem. Am. Vocat. Assn., Am. Soc. Clin. Pathologists, Am. Assn. for Counseling and Devel., Nat. Career Devel. Assn., Chi Sigma Iota. Democrat. Roman Catholic. Home: 13003 Keverton Dr Upper Marlboro MD 20772

WARD, EMMA PAYNE, program analyst, government; b. Coffeeville, Ala., June 21, 1944; d. Claudia Barney; divorced; 1 child, Abiri Ward. BA, U. D.C., 1973; MA, U. Md., 1974. Secretary U.S. Govt., Washington, 1964-69; job counselor Dept. Employment Svcs., Washington, 1969-80; program analyst Dept. Agriculture, Alexandria, Va., 1980—. Area rep. Southwest Neighborhood Assembly, Washington, 1988. Recipient Fellowship Study in Africa, U. D.C., Accra, Ghana, 1974. Mem. Soc. Govt. Meeting Planners, Agriculture Communications in Edn., Bus. Club. Democrat. Baptist. Home: 1214 Carrollburg Pl Sw Washington DC 20024

WARD, HILARY MARGARET, college dean; b. Findlay, Ohio, July 1, 1957; d. Henry P.J. and Maryann (Griffin) W. BA, MA summa cum laude, Rosary Coll., River Forest, Ill., 1979; MA, Northwestern U., Evanston, Ill., 1980, PhD, 1989. Coord. specialized student svcs. Ctr. Disabled Student Svcs., Chgo. City-Wide Coll, 1981-83, coord. human resources, 1983-84; coord. student affairs and acad. progress Univ. Coll., Northwestern U., Chgo., 1984-86, asst. dean, 1986—; mem. Staff Adv. Coun. Northwestern U., Chgo., 1989—. Chmn. fund-raising com. Sheil Ctr., Evanston, Ill., 1986-87; presenter Alumni Career Day, Sacred Heart High Sch., Rolling Meadows, Ill., 1983—; mem. steering com. Rosary Coll. Alumni Network, River Forest, 1987—. Northwestern U. fellow, 1979-80. Mem. NAFE, Am. Coun. Edn./Nat. Identification Project, Ill. Assn. Collegiate Registrars and Admissions Officers, Ill. Assn. Fin. Aid Adminstrs., Assn. Northwestern Exempt Women, Book Club (coord. publicity 1986—), Lambda Iota Tau. Roman Catholic.

WARD, JANE ABERCROMBIE, property administration executive, consultant land systems; b. Phila., Oct. 5, 1930; d. Joseph Albert and Evelyn Holt (Harker) Abercrombie; m. Robert Dee Ward, Feb. 5, 1952 (div. 1972);

1 child, Lynda Susan. B.A., Ind. U., 1951. Sr. lease analyst Reynolds Mining Corp., Houston, 1954-62; landman Barnhart Co., Houston, 1973-77; adminstr. Pan Eastern Exploration Co., Houston, 1977-79; adminstrv. landman Kirby Exploration Co., Houston, 1980-86. Author: User's Manual-Lease/Contract Information for Input, on-line computer system, 1984, Manual System, 1986. Fund raiser Houston Grand Opera, 1973, 87, Houston Zool. Soc., 1986-89, Mus. Fine Arts, Houston, 1985-89; tutor Literacy Advance. Mem. Am. Assn. Petroleum Landmen, Houston Assn. Petroleum Landmen, West Houston Assn. Petroleum Landmen, Nat., Houston assns. division order analysts. Democrat. Episcopalian. Avocations: classical music; bridge; word puzzles and games; baseball; numismatics. Home: 1360 Winrock #2402 Houston TX 77057

WARD, JANE PAMELA, psychiatric social worker; b. Sioux City, Iowa, Feb. 10, 1948; d. Robert James and Alice Noreen (Gullickson) Ward. BA, Wartburg Coll., 1970; MSW, U. Iowa, 1975. Diplomate Clin. Social Work. Psychiat. therapist Community Mental Health Center of Scott County, Davenport, Iowa, 1975-76, coordinator of consultation and edn., 1976-77; dir. social work program Viterbo Coll., LaCrosse, Wis., 1977-79; asst. exec. dir., dir. social services Bremwood Luth. Children's Home, Waverly, Iowa, 1979-82; exec. dir. Three Crosses Ranch, Strawberry Point, Iowa, 1982-83; psychiat. pvt. practice and cons., 1983—; adj. prof. U. No. Iowa, Cedar Falls, 1983; asst. prof. U. Wis., Oshkosh, 1984—; mem. Gov.'s Commn. Planning Com. for Conf. on Children, Iowa, 1976; cons. South Cen. Community Justice Planning Commn., La Crosse, 1977, Viterbo Coll., 1979. Mem. Nat. Assn. Social Workers (dir. 1978-79), Bi-County Mental Health Assn. (dir. 1976), Acad. Cert. Social Workers (diplomate), Nat. Registry Clin. Social Workers (diplomate). Lutheran. Office: 324 Clow Faculty Dept Social Work U Wisconsin Oshkosh WI 54901

WARD, JEAN MARIE, government official; b. Washington, Sept. 14, 1954; d. John James Thomas and Genevieve Rita (Biferie) W.; m. G. Gregory Steven Uchrin, Mar. 10, 1984. BA, So. Meth. U., 1975. Stringer Today's Post, King of Prussia, Pa., 1976-77; intern Army Missile Command, Huntsville, Ala., 1977, Army Materiel Command, Alexandria, Va., 1978-80; pub. affairs specialist Maritime Adminstrn., Washington, 1980-82, Dept. Def., 1982—. Recipient Meritorious Civilian Svc. award Dept. Def., 1989. Mem. Mil. Classics Seminar. Office: OASD/PA Directorate Pub Communication The Pentagon Rm 2E777 Washington DC 20301-1400

WARD, JEANNE PATRICIA, family counselor, consultant; b. Bklyn., Mar. 23, 1945; d. James Joseph and Grace Frances (Brennan) Lawton; m. Robert L. Bucher, June 11, 1966 (div. Aug. 1977); children: Barbara Anne, Laura Jeanne; m. Charles F. Ward Jr., Aug. 19, 1983. BA in Edn., St. Catherine's Coll., St. Paul, 1966; MA in Counseling and Psychology, Coll. St. Thomas, St. Paul, 1972. Tchr. Mpls. Pub. Schs., 1966-70; tchr. spl. edn. Duval County Schs., Jacksonville, Fla., 1977-79, sch. counselor, 1979-83; instr. Fla. Jr. Coll., Jacksonville, 1977—; pvt. practice family counseling, Jacksonville, 1983—; adj. prof. U. North Fla., 1986—; cons. direct mktg. tng. design and devel. Am. Transtech, Jacksonville, 1985-87; cons. child care Community Coll. Jacksonville; founder, dir. Divorce Ministry Diocese of St. Augustine, Jacksonville, 1979-83; Fla. del. White House Conf. on Families, 1980; regular panelist Sta. WJXT, Jacksonville, 1982—. Author curriculum. Bd. dirs., chmn. pers. com. Child Guidance Clinic, Jacksonville, 1977—; bd. dirs. Girls Club of Jacksonville, 1981-83; chairperson Mayors Commn. on Status of Women, Jacksonville, 1985-87; bd. dir. tng. and staff devel. City of Jacksonville, 1986-87; chmn. task force Corp. Child Care, 1985—, founding dir., 1985—; cons. Fla. Community Coll., 1988—; bd. dirs. YWCA; mem. Literacy Coalition, Coalition for a Drug Free Jacksonville. Recipient Eve award for volunteerism Fla. Times Union. Mem. AAUW, NAFE, ASTD, Nat. Coun. of Family Rels., Phi Delta Kappa, N.E. Fla. Soc. Parents of Visually Impaired Children Club (program chmn. 1985—). Democrat. Roman Cathlic. Home: 3523 Park St Jacksonville FL 32205 Office: Fla Community Coll Jacksonville 101 W State St Jacksonville FL 32202

WARD, JEANNETTE POOLE, psychologist, educator; b. Honolulu, June 19, 1932; d. Russell Masterton and Bessie Naomi (Hammett) Poole; children: John Russell Ward, Lisa Joy Ward. BA, Birmingham (Ala.) So. Coll., 1963; PhD in Psychology, Vanderbilt U., 1969. NSF summer rsch. asst. U. Iowa, Iowa City, 1962; NSF summer rsch. asst. Vanderbilt U., Nashville, 1963, NASA fellow, 1963-66, NIH postdoctoral fellow, 1966-67; spl. rsch. fellow Duke U., Durham, N.C., 1970-71; asst. prof. psychology Memphis State U., 1967-72, assoc. prof. psychology, 1972-77, prof. psychology, 1977—. Editor: Current Research in Primate Laterality, 1990; contbr. chpts. to books and articles to profl. jours.; reviewer: Journal of Comparative Psychology, 1988—. Mem. Psychonomic Soc., Am. Psychol. Soc., Animal Behavior Soc., Am. Psychol. Assn., Am. Primatology Soc., Southeastern Psychol. Assn., Soc. for Neurosci., Internat. Soc. for Comparative Psychology (treas. 1989-90), Sigma Xi (pres. Memphis State U. chpt. 1989-90, rsch. award 1985). Democrat. Office: Memphis State U Dept Psychology Memphis TN 38152

WARD, JUDY KITCHEN, bank executive; b. Asheville, N.C., Jan. 19, 1940; d. Jesse Enrest and Mary Daisy (Pressley) Kitchen; m. Wayne Leigh; children: Robert Wayne, Shari Leigh, Rodney Victor; m. Jerry Ellsworth Ward; 1 child, Jerry E. Jr. Student, Thomas Nelson Community Coll., Hampton, Va., 1987. Bank teller 1st City Bank, Newport News, Va., 1977-82; adminstrv. asst. Va. Nat. Bank, Newport News, 1982-84; br. mgr. 1st Am. Bank Va., Newport News, 1984—. Treas. Alternatives/Drug Abuse, Newport News and Hampton, 1986-88, bd. dirs., 1986—; cabinet mem. United Way, Newport News, 1988; mem. ways and means com. Dem. Orgn., 1987—; sec. Denbigh Little League, 1974-76; pres. local PTA, 1972-73, Block Mother's Prevention Against Child Abuse, 1967-69. Recipient cert. United, 1984-88, Mar. of Dimes, 1982-88. Mem. Am. Inst. Banking (chief consul 1986, award 1987, v.p. 1990—), Exch. Club (pres. James River chpt. 1990—). Episcopalian. Home: 193 Compton Pl Newport News VA 23606 Office: 1st Am Bank Va 2901 Huntington Ave Newport News VA 23607

WARD, KATHY ANN, educator; b. Chattanooga, Oct. 17, 1956; d. Stanley James and Katherine Louise (Phillips) Farmer; m. William Ray Ward, Apr. 6, 1979 (div. Mar. 1989). BS, Middle Tenn. State U., Murfreesboro, 1977, MEd, 1978, EdS, 1980. Tchr. Hamilton County Dept. Edn., Chattanooga, 1977—, Queensland Dept. Edn., Brisbane, Queensland, Australia, summer 1989; group leader to Japan and Australia, Experiment in Internat. Living, Brattleboro, Vt., summers 1985-88. Vol. Am. Heart Assn., Chattanooga, 1989—. Ambassador scholar Experiment in Internat. Living, 1983; recipient Lyndhurst Tchr.'s award Lyndhurst Found., 1988. Mem. AAUW (bd. dirs. election found. 1987-88), Delta Kappa Gamma (chmn. rsch. com. 1983). Democrat. Methodist. Home: 2506 Allegheny Dr Chattanoog TN 37421-2032 Office: Ooltewah Middle Sch 5100 Ooltewah-Ringgold Rd Ooltewah TN 37363

WARD, LESLIE ALLYSON, journalist, editor; b. L.A., June 3, 1946; d. Harold Gordon and Marilyn Lucille (Dahlstead) W.; m. Robert L. Biggs, 1971 (div. 1977); m. Colman Robert Andrews, May 26, 1979 (div. 1988). AA, Coll. San Mateo, 1966; BA, UCLA, 1968, MJ, 1971. Reporter, researcher L.A. Bur. Life mag., 1971-72; reporter, news asst. L.A. bur. N.Y. Times, 1973-76; sr. editor New West mag., L.A., 1976-78, 79-80; L.A. bur. chief US mag., 1978-79; Sunday style editor L.A. Herald Examiner, 1981-82, editor-in-chief Sunday mags., 1982-83, Olympics editor, 1984, sports editor, 1985-86; sr. writer L.A. Times mag., 1986, sr. editor, 1988-90, travel editor, 1990—. Democrat. Office: LA Times Times-Mirror Sq Los Angeles CA 90053

WARD, LINDA ELAINE, state agency administrator; b. Wabash, Ind., Jan. 17, 1949; d. Tom G. and Veda G. (Juday) Pruitt; m. Jonathan L. Ward, Jan. 21, 1949; children: Johnny, Scotty, Chris. AS in Bus. Adminstrn., Lake City Community Coll., 1989. Cert. mgmt. supr., pub. mgr. Ptnr. Auto Emporium, Lake City, Fla.; dist. acct., dist. fin. adminstr. Fla. Dept. Transp., Lake City, cons. mgr. operation and mgmt. Active Smithsonian Assocs. Mem. NAFE, Am. Acad. Cert. Pub. Mgrs., Fla. Soc. Cert. Pub. Mgrs., Nat. Womens Transp. Orgn., Miami Womens Transp. Orgn., Fla. Govt. Acctg. Mgrs. Assn., Fla. Tax Watch, Lake City C. of C., Phi Theta Kappa. Office: PO Box 1089 Lake City FL 32056-1089

WARD, MARGARET ANNE (PEGGIE WARD), psychologist; b. N.Y.C., Apr. 28, 1944; d. Alan Leon and Alma Lucille (Goldberg) Rosenblum; m. William E. Ward, Apr. 29, 1967 (div. 1971); children: Whitney, Morgan; m. Michael Joseph Doran, July 11, 1982; 1 child, Jesse Alan. BA, Conn. Coll., 1966; MA in Psychology, Calif. State U., L.A., 1976; PhD in Clin. Psychology, U. S.D., 1980. Lic. psychologist, N.H., Mass. Presch. tchr., dir. NYU Nursery Sch., 1967-70; tchr., counselor High Sch. Redirection, Bklyn., 1972-74; grad. asst., lectr. in statistics Calif. State U., 1974-76; rsch. asst. div. allied health and Indian affairs U.S.D., Vermillion, 1976-77; psychol. cons. Gordon Chem. Dependency Ctr., Sioux City, Iowa, 1977-79; clin. intern Children's Hosp. Med. Ctr., Boston, 1979-80; psychologist family crisis program Tufts/New England Med. Ctr., 1980-82; staff psychologist Children's Hosp. Med. Ctr., 1980-84; psychologist, pres. Slatoff & Ward Psychol. Profl. Assn., Nashua, N.H., 1984—; lectr. in psychology Calif. State U., 1974-76; instr. in personality theory dept. psychology U. S.D., 1977; staff psychologist Siouxland Mental Health Ctr., St. Vincents Hosp., Sioux City, 1977-79; clin. fellow Harvard U. Med. Sch., 1979; instr. in psychiatry Tufts U. Med. Sch., 1981-82, Harvard U. Med. Sch., 1981-85; co-chmn. eating disorder awareness com. State of N.H., 1987—. Contbr. numerous articles to profl. jours. Chmn. Cable TV Com., Sudbury, Mass., 1983-86. Mem. Am. Psychol. Assn., Mass. Psychol. Assn., N.H. Psychol. Assn. Democrat. Jewish. Home: 60 Raymond Rd Sudbury MA 01776 Office: Slatoff & Ward Psychol 280 Main St Nashua NH 03060

WARD, MARIA FRANCES, community relations manager; b. Cleve., Aug. 14, 1949; d. Frank K. and Mary (Crawford) Ward. BA magna cum laude, U. Detroit, 1971, MA, 1974, postgrad. Sch. Law., 1971-72. Cert. tchr. Grants rsch. analyst City of Southfield, Mich., 1974-78, community devel. coordinator, 1978-80, dir. legis. svcs., 1980-87, asst. city adminstr., 1987-90; mgr. community rels., midwest, state and local govt. affairs Consol. Rail Corp., Dearborn, Mich., 1990—; instr. Henry Ford community Coll., 1977-80; researcher, labor union arbitrator, Warren, Mich., 1974. Author: Glossary of Terms, 1981; Southfield Auto Insurance Report, 1986; editor: Southfield 2001, 1983. Mem. Zoning Bd. of Appeal, City of Berkley, Mich., 1987—; charter mem. Hist. Commn., Berkley, 1977—. Mem. Mich. Community Devel. Dirs. Assn. (sec. 1978-81, pres. 1979-80), Am. Soc. for Pub. Adminstrn. (pres. 1986-88), Mich. City Mgmt. Assn., Women's Econ. Club, Rotary Internat., Alpha Sigma Nu. Roman Catholic. Home: 1838 Rosemont Rd Berkley MI 48072 Office: Consol Rail Corp 17301 Michigan Ave Dearborn MI 48126

WARD, MICHELLE ANNETTE, pharmacist; b. Ft. Worth, Tex., Aug. 2, 1961; d. John Clayton and Patricia Ann (Slaton) W. BS in Pharmacy, U. Colo., 1985. Registered pharmacist, Colo. Pharmacy intern Luth. Med. Ctr., Wheatridge, Colo., 1984-85; staff pharmacist St. Joseph Hosp., Denver, 1985—. Mem. Colo. Soc. Hosp. Pharmacists. Office: St Joseph Hosp 1835 Franklin St Denver CO 80218

WARD, NANCY ELIZABETH, production executive, print consultant; b. Lima, Ohio, July 28, 1942; d. Marion Delbert Staup and Virginia Louise (Conner) Staup Meyers; m. Terry David Crider, Sept. 20, 1960 (div. 1972); children—Cristina, Heather, Jay, Danielle Elizabeth; m. Kenneth Earl Ward, Dec. 20, 1980. Student in mktg., Edison State U., 1974-78; student in print mgmt., Cin. Tech. Coll., 1980-81. Prodn. dir. Lark Communications, Asheville, N.C., 1981-84, TMI Pub., Charlotte, N.C., 1984-85; prodn. mgr. print and advt. Uptons, Atlanta, 1985-86; sales mgr. Comdata Corp., 1987—; advisor graphics Western Carolina U., Culowhee, N.C., 1983. Prodn. dir. (book) Fiberarts Design Book 2, 1982, Quiltmakers Art, 1983. Republican. Methodist. Avocations: antique collector, furniture refinishing, piano, ballet. Home: 1018 Autumn Crest Ct Stone Mountain GA 30083

WARD, NANCY ELIZABETH, medical librarian; b. Detroit, Sept. 7, 1946; d. Connie Garret and Ruth (Babbitt) W. BS in Edn., Wayne State U., 1968, MS in LS, 1971. Cert. health scis. libr., Mich. Tchr. Lincoln Park (Mich.) Pub. Schs., 1968-69; libr. aide Southgate (Mich.) Pub. Libr., 1969-71; med. libr. Lafayette Clinic, Detroit, 1971—, chmn. action com. for women, 1989—. Reporter, feature writer various libr. orgns. newsletters. Vol. Dukakis Campaign, Dearborn, Mich., 1988. Mem. Spl. Librs. Assn. (mem. chmn. 1986-87, pub. rels. com. 1988—), Coun. State Agy. Librs. (bd. dirs. 1988-89, v.p./pres. elect 1990), Mich. Health Scis. Librs. Assn. (publ. com. 1986-88), NOW, Founders Soc. Detroit Inst. Arts, Mensa, Dearborn Cycling Saddlemen. Office: Lafayette Clinic Libr 951 E Lafayette Detroit MI 48207

WARD, PAULETTE CLEMMA, administrative assistant, academic program director; b. Va., Aug. 31, 1945; d. John and Elizabeth (Coleman) W.; children: Roxane Coleman, Kim Coleman. AAS, Am. Bus. Inst., Newark, 1986; postgrad., Upsala U. Sec., adminstrv. asst. Newark Normal Sch. and Day Care; data entry operator Blue Cross and Blue Shield, Newark; sec. Montclair (N.J.) State Coll.; with sales, mktg. and promotional dept. Stevens Mktg. Group, Upper Montclair, N.J., 1988—; bd. advisors ABI, Inc.; assoc. dir. bus. Montclair State Coll. Mem. Rep. Presdl. Task Force, 1982-83; mem. affirmative action and equal opportunity and treatment coms. Gov. Thomas H. Kean, 1988; mem. parents assn. Rutgers U., New Brunswick, N.J., 1987-89. Mem. NAFE, Internat. Profl. and Office Workers, Communication Workers Am., Montclair State Coll. Staff Assn., Nat. Assn. Exec. Secs.

WARD, PAULINE See MOUNT, WARD

WARD, RACHEL, actress; b. Eng., 1957; m. Bryan Brown; 1 dau. Former model; movie debut in Three Blind Mice; other movies include: Night School, 1981, Sharky's Machine, 1981, Dead Men Don't Wear Plaid, 1982, The Final Terror, 1984, Against All Odds, 1984, Fortress, 1985, How to Get Ahead in Advertising, 1989, After Dark My Sweet, 1990; TV miniseries: The Thorn Birds, 1983; other TV appearances include film Fortress, HBO, 1985. Office: Creative Artists Agy care David Schiff 1888 Century Park E Ste 1400 Los Angeles CA 90067*

WARD, SHARON LYNNE, registered nurse; b. Grand Rapids, Mich., July 19, 1942; d. Elwood and Margaret (Fitzsimmons) W. Student, Grand Rapids Jr. Coll., 1960-61; BSN, U. Mich., 1964. Staff nurse neuropsychiat. inst. U. Mich. Med. Ctr., Ann Arbor, 1964-68; asst. dir. nursing Kent Oaks Psychiat. Unit, Grand Rapids, 1968-69, dir. nursing, 1969-88; adminstrv. asst. for nursing Kent Community Hosp., Grand Rapids, 1988—; instr. adult edn. Kent Intermediate Sch. Dist., Grand Rapids; nursing adv. group West, Mich. Health Systems Agy., Grand Rapids; m. West Cen. Dist. Hosp. Coun., 1971-82, ad hoc com. for Mich. Mental Health Code, 1979, nursing adv. com. Grand Rapids Jr. Coll. Sch. Nursing, 1987—; past guest lectr. Butterworth Hosp. Sch. Nursing, Blodgett Meml. Med. Ctr. Sch. Nursing, Mercy Cen. Sch. Nursing, Grand Rapids Jr. Coll. Sch. Nursing; instr. in adult edn. Kent Intermediate Sch. Dist. Mem. Vallie Jones Guild Kent Oaks Psychiat. Unit, 1978—; sec., mem. nursing adv. com. Grand Rapids Jr. Coll., 1989-90. Republican. Office: Kent Community Hosp 750 Fuller Ave NE Grand Rapids MI 49503

WARD, SHEILA DANEEN, educator; b. Ottawa, Kans., Oct. 13, 1935; d. James Delridge and Halbur Gertrude (Bartlett) Dye; m. William Gordon Ward, Nov. 7, 1964 (dec. May 1984); 1 child, Dana Carolyn. AB in Home Econs. and Spanish, U. Kans., 1957; MS in Nutrition, U. Iowa, 1959; DMSc, Ind. U., 1978. Dietetic intern nutrition dept. U. Iowa Hosps. & Clinics, Iowa City, 1957-58; rsch. dietitian Med. Sch. Harvard U., Cambridge, Mass., 1959-62; rsch. dietitian, asst. prof. Sch. of Medicine Ind. U., Indpls., 1962-67; nutrition counselor, cons. Tavel, Lamkin & Gabovitch, MDs, Indpls., 1967-70; lectr. in nutrition Marian Coll., Indpls., 1974; sch. lunch dir. St. Luke's Cath. Sch., Indpls., 1973-76, postdoctoral fellow dept. med. genetics Sch. Medicine, 1978-79, dietetic internship dir., asst. prof., assoc. dir., 1979—. Mem. Pan-Hellenic Coun., Indpls., 1972-75; vol. United Way, Indpls., 1970-72, 87-89, Am. Heart Assn., Indpls., 1980—; precinct vice chair Marion County Reps., Indpls., 1966-67; bd. dirs. Ind. Arthritis Found., Indpls., 1972-80. Mem. Ind. Dietetic Assn. (invited speaker 1979), Ind. Nutrition Coun., Cen. Ind. Dietetic Assn. (pres. 1968-69), Am. Dietetic Assn. (coun. on edn. Chgo. chpt. 1985—, bd. dirs. Jour. Am. Dietetics 1980-88), Indpls. U. Alumni Assn., Alpha Omicron Pi (pres. 1970-72), Sigma Xi. Episcopalian. Home: 6902 Warwick Rd Indianapolis IN 46220 Office: U Hosp Dept Nutrition 926 W Michigan D-132 Indianapolis IN 46202

WARD, SUSAN MARIE, curator; b. Detroit, Jan. 29, 1954; d. Richard Guerin and Helen Marie (Stone) W. BA in Art History, Wayne State U., 1983; MA in Decorative Arts, Parsons Sch. Design, 1985. Intern Met. Mus. Art, N.Y.C., 1985; asst. curator Biltmore Estate, Asheville, N.C., 1985-86, curator, 1987—; sec. Biltmore Village Hist. Mus., Asheville, 1989—. Vol., adv. com. Big Bros. and Sisters, Asheville, 1988—; com. mem. Bele Cher, Asheville, 1989. Mem. Am. Assn. State and Local History (state membership chmn. 1989), N.C. Mus. Coun., S.E. Museums Conf. (chmn. intern staff devel. com.). Office: Biltmore Co 1 N Pack Square Asheville NC 28801

WARD, SUZANNE MARY, information specialist; b. Sydney, Australia, Apr. 28, 1956; came to U.S., 1958; d. John Robert and Cicely Marian (Kearns) W.; m. Kenneth J. Potts, Nov. 20, 1982. BA, UCLA, 1978; MLS, U. Mich., 1981; MA, Memphis State U., 1985. Archivist Ctr. So. Folklore, Memphis, 1981; reference librarian, then engrng. librarian Memphis State U., 1982-87; info. specialist Purdue U., West Lafayette, Ind., 1987—. Reader, West Tenn. Talking Library, Memphis, 1983-86. Mem. Spl. Libraries Assn. (pres. Mid-South chpt. 1985-86), ALA (group newsletter editor 1989—). Office: Purdue Univ Mgmt Library West Lafayette IN 47907

WARD, VIRGINIA LEE, consumer foods company executive; b. Grand Forks, N.D., Aug. 16, 1944; d. Vernol Lee Smith and Betty Louise (Scott) Perrin; m. William Edward Ward, Jr., July 23, 1977; children—Brian Scott Green, William E. Ward III, Andrew T. Ward, Wendy Helen Ward. B.S., U. N.D., 1966. Cert. tchr. Tchr. Ind. Sch. Dist. 279, Osseo, Minn., 1966-68; various mktg. mgmt. and human resource positions, IBM, 1973-81; dir. human resource planning The Pillsbury Co., Mpls., 1981-82, v.p. human resources, 1982-89; pres. Scott's Inc., Mpls., 1989— ; trustee Voyageur Outward Bound, Mpls., 1981—, v.p. 1989—; mem. human resource com. Nat. Food Processors, Washington, 1984—; bd. dirs. Secural Cos. (chair nominating com.). Mem. benefit com. Children's Cancer Research, Mpls., 1985; fund raiser United Arts Council, St. Paul, 1985; mem. exec. com. Pillsbury PAC, 1984-89 ; mem. Minn. Women's Polit. Campaign Fund, 1983—, bd. dirs., 1985—, chair, 1989—; mem. Women's Econ. Roundtable, 1986—. Recipient Leadership award Pillsbury Exec. Office, 1985, IBM Achievement award, 1981, Sioux Alumni award U. N.D., 1986. Mem. Am. Soc. for Personnel Adminstrn., Am. Mgmt. Assn., Human Resource Planning Soc. (pres. 1986-89, bd. dirs. 1982—, mem. exec. com., 1982—), Internat. Bus. Fellows, Internat. Women's Forum. Republican. Episcopalian. Clubs: Somerset (St. Paul); Mpls. Athletic. Avocations: backpacking, running, golfing, flyfishing, wildlife conservation. Home: 110 1st Ave NE #1703 Minneapolis MN 55413 Office: The Pillsbury Co 200 S 6th St Minneapolis MN 55402

WARDELL, VIRGINIA SIMONSON, elementary school educator; b. Camden, N.J., Mar. 14, 1943; d. Walter Joseph Simonson and Ethel (Derleth) Rinakamp; m. Roland Clifton Wardell, June 7, 1975; 1 child, Joseph Andrew. BA in Elem. Edn., Trenton State Coll., 1967, MA in Spl. Edn., 1971; EdD, Rutgers U., 1980. Tchr. Trenton (N.J.) Sch. Bd., 1967-69, demonstration tchr., 1969-72; demonstration tchr. Trenton State Coll., 1972-74; resource tchr. Trenton Sch. System, 1974-76; asst. dir. N.J. State Dept. Edn., Trenton, 1976-79; tchr., chpt. I Franklin County Schs., Rocky Mountain, Va., 1979-86, coord. gifted/talented, computer assisted instrn., 1986—; prin. Tappahannock (Va.) Elem. Sch., 1990—; chmn. Franklin County adv. bd. for gifted edn., 1988—, computer instrn. panel, 1987—. Author: (manual) Computer Assisted Instruction, 1989, Safety in the Elementary School, 1979. Pres. women's fellowship, Antioch Ch. of the Brethren, Rocky Mountain, 1990—; sponsor Health Club Mentorship, 1985. Grantee N.J. State Dept. Edn., 1970, 72, 74. Mem. Assn. Supervision and Curriculum, NEA, Va. Educators Assn., Franklin County Edn. Assn., Va. Assn. for Edn. of Gifted, Kappa Delta Phi, Delta Kappa Gamma (pres. 1984-86). Home: Rt 4 PO Box 615 Rocky Mountain VA 24151 Office: Essex County Pub Schs Tappahannock VA 22560

WARDLE, RHEA ROSE, educator, counselor; b. Springfield, Mass., Aug. 10, 1951; d. Morris Harry and Josephine Naomi (Kazeroid) Kalman; m. Steven Robert Wardle, Apr. 29, 1983. BS in Secondary Edn., U. Conn., 1973; MEd in Counseling, Springfield (Mass.) Coll., 1978. Tchr. Kiley Jr. High Sch., Springfield, 1973-77, Hazelwood High Schs., St. Louis, 1977—; counselor Hazelwood High Sch. Tchr. Never Too Old To Read, Springfield, 1974-77; organizer Adopt-A-Grandparent, St. Louis, 1979-81, Scholarship Run-Walk, St. Louis, 1988; counselor Drug Addiction Clinic, St. Louis, 1978-80. Fellow NEA, Nat. Coun. Tchrs. English, Greater St. Louis Tchrs. English, Assn. for Curriculum and Supervision, Mo. Counselors Assn. Home: 1535 Surfside Dr Saint Louis MO 63138 Office: Hazelwood East High Sch 11300 Dunn Rd Saint Louis MO 63138

WARD-MCLEMORE, ETHEL, research geophysicist, mathematician; b. Sylvarena, Miss., Jan. 22, 1908; d. William Robert and Frances Virginia (Douglas) Ward; m. Robert Henry McLemore, June 30, 1935; 1 child, Mary Frances. BA, Miss. Woman's Coll., 1928; MA, U. N.C., 1929; postgrad., U. Chgo., 1931, Colo. Sch. Mines, 1941-42, So. Meth. U., 1962-64. Head math. dept. Miss. Jr. Coll., 1929-30; instr. chemistry, math. Miss. State Coll. for Women, 1930-32; rsch. mathematician Humble Oil & Refining Co., Houston, 1933-36; ind. geophys. rsch., Tex. and Colo., 1936-42, Ft. Worth, 1946—; geophysicist United Geophys. Co., Pasadena, Cal., 1942-46; tchr. chemistry, physics, Hockaday Sch., Dallas, 1958-59, tchr. math., 1959-60; tchr. chemistry Ursuline Acad., Dallas, 1964-67, Hockaday Sch., 1968-69; geophys. cons., Dallas, 1957—; with Eugene McDermott Libr., U. Tex., rsch. geophysicist. Author: China, 1983, Bibliography of the Publications of the Texas Academy of Science, 1929-87, 1989, The Academies of Science of Texas (1880-1987), 1989, also annotated bibliographies of sedimentary basins, 1981; contbr. articles to profl. jours. Mem. AAAS, Am. Math. Soc., Acads. of Sci. Tex., Math. Assn. Am., Am. Geophys. Union (40 yr. Mem. Rsch. Silver Pin award 1988), Seismol. Soc. Am., Soc. Exploration Geophysicists (50 yr. Gold cert. 1986, Hon. Membership award 1989, hon. life), Soc. Indsl. and Applied Math., Am. Chem. Soc., Inst. Math. Statis., Tex Acad. Sci. (Appreciation cert. 1985), Dallas Geophys. Soc. (hon. life 1986, Disting. Svc. award 1988), Sigma Xi. Home: 8600 Skyline Dr # 1107 Dallas TX 75243 Office: U Tex Eugene McDermott Libr MC3-418 Box 830643 Richardson TX 75083

WARD-SHAW, SHEILA THERESA, nurse; b. N.Y.C., June 20, 1951; d. Arthur and Cynthia Melba (Mapp) Jenkins; m. Howard V. Ward, Nov. 1977 (div. 1981); m. Thomas N. Shaw, Sept. 1988. Student, Rockland Community Coll., 1973, U. Nev., 1984. Charge nurse Hillcrest (N.Y.) Nursing Home, 1973-74; infirmary nurse St. Agatha's Home for Children, Nanuet, N.Y., 1974-75; temp. bldg. charge nurse Letchworth Village, Thiells, N.Y., 1976; charge nurse New Paltz (N.Y.) Nursing Home, 1977; non secure detention, foster bdg. parent St. Agatha's Home for Children, Nanuet, 1977-79; asst. nursing supr., inservice coord., infection control nurse So. Nev. Menal Retardation, Las Vegas, 1979-84; mental nurse II evening duty officer Harbor View Devel. Ctr., Valdez, Ala., 1987-89; charge nurse North Star Hosp., Anchorage, 1989—. Campaign worker Nev. Gov. Bryan Dem. Candidate, Las Vegas, 1983-84, Pearson for County Commn. Race, Las Vegas, 1984; pres. Clark County Health Educators, 1983; mem. APIC., 1980-85. Mem. Assn. for Practioners of Infection Control. Roman Catholic. Home: 1441 Carolyn Circle Anchorage AK 99504 Office: North Star Hosp 1650 S Bragaw Anchorage AK 99508

WARE, JUDITH LEE, educator, consultant; b. Seattle, June 29, 1939; d. Elkan James and Georgia Lee (Nelson) Druxman; m. James Edman Ware, July 17, 1959; children: Bradford James, Heather Lee. BA, Calif. State U., L.A., 1961; MA, Boise State U., 1981; PhD, U. Oreg., 1987. Cert. tchr., Idaho. Tchr. Montebello (Calif.) Unified Sch. Dist., 1961-62; reading specialist Boise schs., 1980-85; instr. Boise (Idaho) State U., 1984-87, Coll. Idaho, Caldwell, 1985-89; cons. profl. devel. Ctr. for Profl. Devel. N.W. Nazarene Coll., Nampa, Idaho, 1989-90, prof. edn., 1989—; sch. evaluator State Dept. Edn., Idaho, 1984-85; tchr. evaluator Boise schs., 1983-85; cons. various internat. schs., 1983-89. Editor Idaho Reading Report, 1988-90; contbr. articles to profl. jours. V.p. Jr. League, Boise, 1979. Recipient Best New Tchr. award NEA, 1962; U. Oreg. fellow, 1985-86. Mem. Internat. Reading Assn. (sec. 1984-85), Nat. Coun. Tchrs. English, Assn. for Supervision and Curriculum Devel., Am. Soc. Tng. and Devel. (conf. chmn. 1989—, Outstanding Practitioner award 1989), Phi Delta Kappa (sec. 1984-85).

Republican. Home: 425 Hearthstone Boise ID 83702 Office: NW Nazarene Coll Nampa ID 83686

WARE, MARGARET ISABEL ROSE, personnel consultant; b. Fullerton, Nebr., Feb. 1, 1915; d. William Lawson and Edith Isabel (Ridell) Rose; m. Charles Albert Ware, Apr. 25, 1943 (dec. May, 1986). AA, Pomona Jr. Coll., Pomona, Calif., 1936; BA, U. Calif., Berkeley, 1938; MA, Claremont (Calif.) Coll., 1940. Intern Nat. Inst. Pub. Affairs, Washington, 1940-41; placement officer Office of Emergency Mgmt., Washington, 1941-42; asst. employment officer Office War Info., Washington, 1942-45; placement officer Dept. Army, L.A., 1946-48; personnel officer VA, Honolulu, 1949-61; adminstrv. asst. State Legislature, Honolulu, 1962-63; survey officer State Dept. of Personnel, Honolulu, 1963-64; personnel cons. pvt. practice Honolulu, 1964—. Adminstrv. asst. Thomas Gill Campaign Com. for Hawaii Gov., 1963. Mem. Soc. for Personnel Adminstrs. (seminar dir. 1959-61), League of Women Voters, Phi Beta Kappa. Democrat. Presbyterian. Home: 810-F N Kalaheo Ave Kailua HI 96734

WARE, MARY BLANTON, sales professional; b. Ashland, Ky., Nov. 3, 1964; d. Samuel Harder and Carolyn Varden (Collier) Ware. Student, U. Ky., 1985-89. Sales assoc. Dawahares, Lexington, Ky., 1984, Gadsby's, Ashland, 1985; sales assoc., cons. Talbots, Lexington, 1986-89; buyer, mgr. trainee McAlpins, Lexington, 1989—. Asst. chair coll. work, Episcopal Churchwomen, Lexington, 1988. Mem. Chi Omega. Republican.

WAREING, CAROL, dean graduate studies; b. Lawrence, Mass., Jan. 20, 1950; d. Angelo Antonio and Dora (D'Agostino) Giarrusso; m. Michael Allen Wareing, June 2, 1972. BS, Northeastern U., 1972; MST, Boston Coll., 1975, PhD, 1979. Tchr. Wilmington (Mass.) Pub. Schs., 1972-76; asst. prof. Tufts U., Medford, Mass., 1977-82; asst. supt. Plymouth (Mass.) Pub. Schs., 1982-83, supt., 1983-84; asst. supt. Stoughton (Mass.) Pub. Schs., 1984-86; assoc. prof. Claif. State U., Long Beach, Calif., 1986-88; dean Worcester (Mass.) State Coll., 1988-90; Univ. Assocs. cons., Tewksbury, Mass., 1978-86. Sch. bd. mem., 1980-86. Mem. Nat. Assn. Rsch. in Sci. Teaching, Assn. Educators for the Teaching of Sci., Nat. Sci. Tchrs. Assn., Am. Assn. Sch. Adminstrs., Nat. Assn. Women Deans, Adminstrs. and Counselors. Democrat. Roman Catholic.

WARFIELD, JANET SMITH, lawyer; b. Phila., Sept. 6, 1936; d. Norman Perry and Dorothy Imogene (Warfield) Smith; m. Alexander Stilwell Traub, III, Mar. 22, 1958 (div. May 1979); children—William Fairley, Stephen Alexander, Russell Perry. BA, Swarthmore Coll., 1958; JD with honors, Rutgers U.-Camden, 1980. Bar: N.J. 1980. Rsch. asst. Towers Perrin Forster & Crosby, Phila., 1959-61; rsch. asst. Cumberland Advisors, Vineland, N.J., 1973-78; assoc. Cooper Perskie, April Niedleman & Wagenheimand predecessors, Atlantic City, 1979-83; title examiner N.J. Realty Title Ins. Co., Toms River, 1984-86; v.p., in-house counsel, Chelsea Title and Guaranty Co., Northfield, 1986-88. Am. Field Svc. exch. student, 1953; mediator Community Justice Ctr. Mem. ABA, N.J. Bar Assn., Atlantic County Bar Assn., Community Justice Inst., Pi Sigma Alpha.

WARING, VIRGINIA, publisher, musician; b. Dinuba, Calif., Oct. 18, 1915; d. M. Rene and Elma (Merritt) Clotfelter; m. Livingston Hawley Gearhart, Feb. 28, 1940 (div. 1953); 1 child, Paul Alexander; m. Frederic Malcolm Waring, Dec. 2, 1954; 1 child, Malcolm Merritt. BA and MusB, Mills Coll., 1937; piano student of Robert Casadesus, Paris, 1937-39. Mem. 2-piano team Morley & Gearhart, 1940-53; owner Interior Design Assocs., East Stroudsburg, Pa., 1962-68; creative costume designer Fred Waring's Pennsylvanians, 1969-83, asst. condr. and mistress of ceremonies, 1980-83; chmn. bd. Fred Waring Enterprises, Delaware Water Gap; pres., owner Shawnee Press, Inc., Delaware Water Gap, Pa., 1983—; artistic dir. Fred Waring U.S. Chorus, Pa. State U., 1985. Rec. artist (Morley and Gearhart) 4 Two-Piano Record Albums (Columbia Records and Omni Sound). Founding bd. dirs. Child Help U.S.A., 1965—; pres. bd. trustees Joanna Hodges Piano Competition, Palm Desert, Calif., 1983, 84, 85; bd. dirs. Palm Valley Sch., Palm Springs, Calif., 1967, 68, 69; founding bd. dirs. Pocono Arts Ctr., Stroudsburg, Pa., 1965-75. Mills Coll. scholar, 1934, 35, 36, 37; Fleischman Trustee Fund scholar, 1937-39. Mem. Am. Soc. Interior Designers, Music Pubs., Ch. Music Pubs. Assn., ASCAP. Republican. Avocations: needlework, reading, tennis, golf. Home: The Gatehouse Shawnee-on-Delaware PA 18356 Office: Shawnee Press 1 Waring Dr Delaware Water Gap PA 18327

WARNATH, MAXINE AMMER, organizational psychologist, educator; b. N.Y.C., Dec. 3, 1928; d. Philip and Jeanette Ammer; m. Charles Frederick Warnath, Aug. 20, 1952; children: Stephen Charles, Cindy Ruth. B.A., Bklyn. Coll., 1949; M.A., Columbia U., 1951, Ed.D., 1982. Lic. psychologist, Oreg. Various profl. positions Hunter Coll., U. Minn., U. Nebr., U. Oreg., 1951-62; asst. prof. psychology Oreg. Coll. Edn., Monmouth, 1962-77; assoc. prof. psychology, chmn. dept. psychology and spl. edn. Western Oreg. St. Coll., Monmouth, 1978-83, prof. 1986—, dir. organizational psychology program 1983—; pres. Profl. Perspectives Internat., Salem, Oreg., 1987—; cons., dir. Orgn. Rsch. and Devel., Salem, Oreg., 1982—, seminar leader Endeavors for Excellence program. Author: Power Dynamism, 1987. Mem. Oreg. Psychol. Assn. (pres. 1980-81, pres.-elect 1979-80, legis. liaison 1977-78), Am. Psychol. Assn. (com. pre-coll. psychology 1970-74), Western Psychol. Assn. Office: Profl Perspectives Internat PO Box 2265 Salem OR 97308

WARNER, ANN MARIE, toxicology educator; b. Denver, Mar. 31, 1944; d. Oscar George and Evelyn Marie (Blaha) Bowman; m. Victor Duane Warner, June 1, 1968; 1 child, Eric Allen. BS, Marymount Coll., 1966; PhD, U. Kans., 1970; postgrad., Northeastern U., 1971-73. Assoc. lab. dir. Lahey Clinic Found., Boston, 1974-81; assoc. prof. U. P.R., San Juan, 1981-85; assoc. prof. U. Cin., 1986—, assoc. dir. div. toxicology, 1985—. Editor: Substance Abuse Testing: Meeting the Challenge for Laboratories-Employers, 1988; contbr. articles to profl. pubis. NIH fellow, 1971-73. Mem. Am. Assn. Clin. Chemistry (sec. therapeutic drug monitoring/clin. toxicology div. 1988—, chmn. elect 1991, award 1987), Assn. for Clin. Scientists, Am. Acad. Forensic Scis. Office: U Cin 234 Goodman St Cincinnati OH 45267-0714

WARNER, CAROL JOYCE, marketing professional; b. St. Louis, Apr. 4, 1959; d. John Mandiville Warner and Janice (Mullen) Cooke. BA, DePauw U., 1981. Mgr. mktg. communications Globe Glass and Mirror Co., Chgo. Mem. Am. Mktg. Assn., Am. Mgrs. Assn., Internat. Exhibitors Assn. Home: 605 W Fullerton Apt 3 Chicago IL 60614 Office: Globe Glass and Mirror Co 1880 W Fullerton AVe Chicago IL 60614

WARNER, CAROLYN, business and marketing consultant, lecturer; b. Ardmore, Okla., Aug. 2, 1930; d. Senator Uriah Thomas and Mary Wilma (Tullis) Rexroat; m. Ronald H. Warner, Dec. 28, 1950; children: Cathy Ann, Caron Suzanne, Steve Van, Constance Kay, Christopher John, Christi Mary. Student, U. Okla., 1948-50; BA, Stephens Coll. Radio work, 1946; children's dramatic program WKY, Oklahoma City, 1947; producer and host Coffee with Carolyn; producer and host Guest Room, The Best Years, Thru the Looking Glass Sta. WKY-TV, Oklahoma City, 1948; polit. speaker for Gov. Roy Turner, U.S. Senator Robert Kerr, U.S. Senator Elmer Thomas Okla., 1943-50; v.p., treas. Warners Furniture & Interiors, Phoenix, 1953—; supt. of Pub. Instrn. Ariz., 1974-86. Kappan editorial cons. Phi Delta Kappa edn. mag. Mem. Nat. Commn. Pub. Service; Dem. candidate U.S. Senate, Ariz., 1976, gov. of Ariz., 1986; Phoenix Union Dist. Bd. of Trustees, 1968-73, pres. com. Paperwork Reduction, bd. trustees; Gov.'s commn. on Ariz. Environ.; Ariz.-Mexico Commn.; Ariz. Bd. Regents, 1974-86; Ariz. Community Coll. Bd.; cons. Nat. Sch. Bds. Assn.; v.p. Ariz. Sch. Bds. Assn.; bd. dirs. Jobs for Am. Grads.; mem., Pres.'s commn. on Fin. Elementary and Secondary Edn., Council of Chief State Sch. Officers; founder, charter mem. Ariz. Ednl. Found.; chairperson Presdl. Classroom for Young Ams. bd. of advisors; mem. nat. commn. on Higher Edn., United Meth. Ch. Mem. Council of Chief State Sch. Officers, Western Correctional Assn. Clubs: Phoenix Execs. (pres.), Dem. Women's, LWV, Nat. Conf. of Christians and Jews, Nucleus, Phoenix Met. C. of C. Office: Carolyn Warner & Assocs 5245 N 21st St Phoenix AZ 85016

WARNER, JUDITH EBRIGHT, educator; b. Mussoorie, India, May 29, 1940; (parents Am. citizens); d. Donald Fossett and Elinor (Baker) Ebright; m. John R. Warner, Jr., July 22, 1960; children: Peter, Stephen, Jennifer. BA, Boston U., 1962; MA, W.Va. U., 1976. Cert. reading specialist, W.Va. Elem. tchr. Upshur County Bd. Edn., Buckhannon, W.Va., 1979—. Mem. Buckhannon Chamber Orch., 1984—. Mem. Internat. Reading Assn., W.Va. Profl. Educators, AAUW (sec. Buckhannon 1985-87). Democrat. Methodist. Home: 30 College Ave Buckhannon WV 26201

WARNER, LAVERNE, education educator; b. Huntsville, Tex., Aug. 14, 1941; d. Clifton Partney and Velma Oneta (Steely) W. BS, Sam Houston State U., 1962, EdM, 1969; PhD, East Tex. State U., 1977. Cert. elem. sch. tchr., Tex. First grade tchr. Port Arthur (Tex.) Ind. Sch. Dist., 1962-64; kindergarten tchr. Burlington (Vt.) Community Schs., 1964-66; first grade tchr. Aldine Sch. Dist., Houston, 1967-68; music tchr. Crawfordsville (Ind.) Community Schs., 1968-71; prof. Elem. Edn. Sam Houston State U., Huntsville, 1975—; chair faculty senate Sam Houston State U., 1990—, chair-elect, 1989-90. Author: (with P. Berry) Tunes for Tots, 1982, (with K. Craycraft) Fun With Familiar Tunes, 1987 (in press) Kids Communicating; contbg. editor for Good Apple, Inc., Carthage, Ill., 1986-88; contbr. over 50 articles to profl. jours. Mem. Huntsville City Parks Bd., 1986-90; bd. dirs. Huntsville Leadership Inst., 1986-88, chmn. adv. bd. 1987-88, chmn. 1987-88; Community Child Care Assn. Huntsville, 1988—. Mem. Tex. Assn. Coll. Tchrs. (life, past pres.), Nat. Assn. for Edn. Young Children (life), Tex. Elementary-Kindergarten-Nursery Educators (state pres. 1982-84), Tex. Assn. for Edn. Young Children (v.p. 1988-89), Huntsville Leadership Inst. Alumni Assn. (pres. 1988-89), Phi Delta Kappa (area 3H coordiantor 1986—), Sam Houston Assn. for Edn. Young Children (charter), Sam Houston Univ. Women (pres. 1985-86), Huntsville High Sch. Ex-Students Assn. (charter, pres. 1989—). Mem. Ch. of Christ. Office: Sam Houston State U Coll Edn and Applied Sci Huntsville TX 77341

WARNER, LOUISE OMAN, physician, researcher; b. Columbus, Ohio, Jan. 19, 1930; d. Galen Francis and Mary Caroline (Hills) Oman; m. E. Jackson Warner, Sept. 12, 1953; children: David O., Gale L. BSc, Ohio State U., Columbus, 1951; MD, Ohio State U., 1955. Diplomate Am. Bd. Anesthesiology. Staff anesthesiologist Children's Hosp., Columbus, 1960-85, dir. clin. anesthesia rsch., 1986—. Bd. dirs. Pickaway County YMCA, Circleville, Ohio, 1977—. sem. AMA, Ohio State Med. Assn., Pickaway County Med. Soc. (pres. 1976), Am. Women's Med. Assn. Home and Office: 5353 Williams Rd Ashville OH 43103

WARNER, SUSAN, lawyer; b. Phila., Dec. 23, 1940; d. Edward and Clara (Stein) Rosen; m. Larry T. Warner, Mar. 20, 1965; 1 child, Dana Lynn. BS Summa Cum Laude, Marywood Coll., 1982; JD, Temple U., 1986. Regional mgr. Profiles Internat., Phila., 1977-78; from personnel mgmt. specialist to employment mgr. Hahnemann U., Phila., 1978-84; corp. dir. of personnel Dechert Price and Rhoads, Phila., 1984-85; dir. of human resources Community Home Health Services of Phila.; sole practitioner Warner and Assocs., Phila., 1986-87; ptr. Mirin and Warner, 1987-88; assoc. Myerson and Kuhn, Phila., 1988-89; dir. human resources adminstrv. svcs. United Way S.E. Pa., 1989—; workshop presenter Am. Soc. Healthcare Human Resources, Nashville, Tenn., 1987, ASHHRA (Nat. Conf.) Denver, 1986. Mem. Indsl. Relations Assn. of Phila. (officer, bd. dirs.), Am. Soc. Pers. Adminstr. (v.p., bd. dirs.), ABA, Phila Bar Assn., Am. Trial Lawyers Assn., Phila. Trial Lawyers Assn., Am. Acad. Hosp. Attorneys, Delta Epsilon Sigma. Democrat. Office: United Way SE Pa 7 Ben Franklin Pkwy Philadelphia PA 19103

WARNER, VANESSA ANNE, telephone company official; b. Lewiston, Maine, Sept. 20, 1953; d. Gilbert Roy and Teresa Emily (Nedeau) Daigle; m. Winfield Larry Warner, Feb. 5, 1984; children: Brandon Tyler, Shianne Ruth. Student, Patricia Stevens Career Coll., Tampa, Fla., 1971-72; Grad. magna cum laude, Seminole Community Coll., 1980. Sales mgr. J.C. Penney Co., St. Petersburg, Fla., 1970-85; sales rep. Design Flooring Co., Orlando, Fla., 1985-86; corp. trainer Am. Pioneer Telephone Co., Orlando, 1986—. Mem. NAFE, Am. Soc. Tng. and Devel. Roman Catholic. Office: Am Pioneer Telephone Co 135 W Central Blvd Ste 1050 Orlando FL 32738

WARNER, WYANNETTE, municipal official; b. Rockwood, Tenn., Dec. 1, 1943; d. Wyatt and Marzella-Marie (Williams) Zornes; m. Victor Von Theumer, June 22, 1962 (div. 1975); m. Cecil Carl Warner, Feb. 7, 1976; children: Eric, Michael. Student, Citrus Coll., Glendora, Calif., 1974, Rio Hondo Coll., Whittier, Calif., 1978. Personnel sec. Ole's Home Ctrs., Pico Rivera, Calif., 1975-79; records clk. Glendora (Calif.) Police Dept., 1979-81, sgt., 1976-87; parking enforcement officer Covina (Calif.) Police Dept., 1982—. Recipient Service award, Meritorious award City of Glendora, 1988. Mem. Super C's Club (sec. 1988-90), Camping Club. Republican. Home: 703 E Ada Glendora CA 91740 Office: Covina Police Dept 444 N Citrus Ave Covina CA 91723

WARNKEN, VIRGINIA MURIEL THOMPSON, social worker; b. Anadarko, Okla., Aug. 13, 1927; d. Sam Monroe and Ruth L. (McAllister) Thompson; A.B., Okla. U., 1946; M.S.W., Washington U., 1949; m. Douglas Richard Warnken, Sept. 16, 1957; 1 son, William Monroe. Med. social cons. Crippled Children's Svcs., Little Rock, 1950-54; supr. VA Hosp., 1954-55; asst. prof. U. Tenn. Sch. Social Work, Nashville, 1955-57; dir. social svcs. N.Y. State Rehab. Hosp., Rockland County, 1957-58; asst. prof. U. Chgo. Sch. Social Svc. Adminstrn., 1958-59; free lance editor, 1960—; instr. evening div. Coll. of Notre Dame, Belmont, Calif., 1967-68; asso. Mills Hosp., San Mateo, Calif., 1978—; med. aux. Community Hosp., Pacific Grove, Calif., 1980—. Com. mem. C. of C. Miss Belmont Pageant, 1971-84, co-chmn., 1975-78; mem. Monterey Bay Aquarium, 1987—. U.S. Children's Bur. scholar, 1947-49. Mem. Assn. Crippled Children and Adults (dir. 1952-55), Assn. Mentally Retarded (dir. 1953-55), Am. Assn. Med. Social Workers (practice chmn. 1954-55), Nat. Assn. Social Workers (dir. 1962-66), Acad. Cert. Social Workers, Am. Assn. Med. Social Workers, Nat. Rehab. Assn., Am. Psychol. Assn., Am. Orthopsychiat. Assn., Coun. Social Work Edn. Democrat. Presbyterian. Clubs: Carmel Valley Golf and Country, Peninsula Golf and Country, Monterey Golf and Country (Palm Desert, Calif.). Author: Annotated Bibliography of Medical Information and Terminology, 1956. Address: 1399 Bel Aire Rd San Mateo CA 94402

WARR, SUSAN NAOMI, family counselor; b. Augres, Mich., Apr. 5, 1960; m. Joseph B. Warr, June 14, 1980; children: Joseph M., Margaret. BA, Mich. State U., 1982. Cert. Juvenile Ct. Probation Officer. Staff writer Valley Vangurard SVSU, Univ. Ctr., Mich., 1978-79; asst. juvenile officer Areanac Co. Probate Ct., Standish, Mich., 1982-83; family counselor Iosco County Probate Ct., Tawas City, Mich., 1986--; mem. Iosco Interagy. Coun., Tawas City, 1986-89, Task Force on Youth, Tawas City, 1988-89, Task Force on Santanism, Oscoda, Mich., 1988-89, Arenac Interagy. Coun., Standish, Mich., 1982-83. Author: Valley Vanguard, 1979. Leader Youth Group, St. Paul Luth. Ch., 1984—, 4-H Club Augres, Mich., 1982-83, 84; coach, dir. Mich. Interscholastic Forensics, Augres, 1986-87, 88, 89, 90; panelist Muscular Dystrophy Assn., Indpls., 1979; com. mem. St. Paul Luth. Ch., Augres, 1988-90. Democratic. Lutheran ELCA. Home: 420 N Main Augres MI 48703 Office: Iosco County Probate Ct PO Box 421 Tawas City MI 48764

WARREN, ADRIENNE ROCHELLE, state agency administrator; b. Balt., Nov. 24, 1957; d. Reginald C. and Margaret C. (DuBois) W. BS, Towson State U., 1978. Employment security specialist State of Md. Dept. Human Resources, Balt.; fin. agt.-in-charge Md. Dept. Health and Mental Hygiene, Owings Mills, Rosewood Hosp. Ctr.; mgr. quality assurance unit div. reimbursements Md. Dept. Health and Mental Hygiene, Balt. Adminstrv. asst. Hemingway Temple African Meth. Episcopal Ch., Balt. Named Outstanding Lay Person Connectional Lay Orgn. African Meth. Episcopal Ch., 1985. Mem. NAFE. Democrat. Home: 65 Straw Hat Rd Apt 2D Owings Mills MD 21117

WARREN, BARBARA KATHLEEN, wildlife biologist; b. Appleton, Wis., Oct. 3, 1943; d. Richard Grant and Beatrice Marie (Kath) Henika. Diploma, St. Luke's Sch. Nursing, San Francisco, 1965; AS in Forest Tech., Green River Community Coll., Auburn, Wash., 1976; BS in Wildlife Biology, U. Calif., Davis, 1990. RN, Calif. Nurse ICU, Ross (Calif.) Gen. Hosp., 1965-66; nurse emergency room CCU, St. Luke's Hosp., 1966-68; head nurse ICU and CCU, Valley Gen. Hosp., Auburn, 1971-76; forest technician Wash. Dept. Natural Resources, Husum, 1976-77; nurse emergency room ICU, Marshall Hosp., Placerville, Calif., 1977-78; forestry and wildlife biology technician U.S. Forest Svc., Pioneer, Calif., 1978-89, wildlife biologist, 1989—, trainer for critical incident stress, Region 5, 1987—, career advisor, 1990—. Chmn. outdoor program com. Girl Scouts U.S.A., Sacramento, 1981-85, master planning cons., 1984-86; vol. ARC, Sacramento, 1985—, vol. disaster nurse, 1986—. With Nurse Corps, U.S. Army, 1968-71. Recipient award for outstanding svc. Girl Scouts U.S.A., 1987, Role Model of Yr. award, 1989; Sustained Superior Performance and Host of Yr. award Eldorado Nat. Forest, 1988, Regional Affirmative Action award U.S. Forest Svc., 1990. Mem. Wildlife Soc. Democrat. Office: US Forest Svc 26820 Silver Dr Pioneer CA 95666

WARREN, BETH IMOGENE, academic administrator, consultant; b. Atlanta, Oct. 3, 1938; d. Gladstone Lewis and Erdie (Wade) Chandler; m. Theodore J. Warren Jr., Aug. 29, 1964; 1 child, Beth Angela. BA, Wheaton Coll., 1959; MSW, Simmons Coll., 1963. Asst. commr. for social svcs. Mass. Dept. Pub. Welfare, Boston, 1975-76; cons. to sec. Mass. Exec. Office Human Svcs., 1976-77; dir. Office EEO U. So. Maine, Portland, 1978-80, acting exec. asst. to the pres., 1980, exec. dir. human resources, 1980-89, assoc. v.p. human resources, exec. dir. Child & Family Inst., 1980—; speaker in field. Past bd. dirs. Community Conseling Ctr. Greater Portland, Big Sister Internat., Child Adv. Program, United Way Greater Portland; 2d v.p. YWCA of Greater Portland, mem. adv. bd.; trustee U. of Lowell, Mass.; pres. bd. Big Sister Assn. of Greater Boston; chair Maine Human Rights Commn., 1990—. Mem. Nat. Assn. Social Workers, So. Maine Handicapped Assn. Office: U So Maine 37 College Ave Gorham ME 04038

WARREN, DEBRA LYNN, social worker; b. Great Lakes, Ill., Sept. 22, 1960; d. Robert Ellis and Julia Marie (Brugioni) Warren; m. James Edward Schelinski, July 30, 1983. B.A. in Psychology, Lake Forest Coll., 1981, B.A. in Sociology and Anthropology, 1981; M.A., U. Chgo., 1983, postgrad. 1983—. Cert. social workers, Ill. Therapist/intake coordinator Bradley Counseling Ctr., Lake Villa, Ill., 1983-85; dir. North Suburban Counseling & Therapeutic Services, Lake Bluff, Ill., 1985—; cons. mem. Cons. Resource Assn., Lake Forest, 1985—; cons., pub. speaker various orgns. Author: The Highwood Centennial History Book, 1987; co-author: (with Virginia Smiley) screenplay, Robots, 1986. Sec. Regione Emilia Romagna del Nord Am. in the Chgo. Italian Consular Dist.; vol. coordinator Dem. Com. to Re-elect the Pres., Highland Park, 1980; religious edn. instr. St. James Ch., Highwood, Ill., 1979-86; vice chmn. Youth Service Network, Gurnee, Ill., 1985-86, chmn., 1986-87; bd. dirs. Lake County Domestic Violence Task Force, Waukegan, 1984—; chmn. centennial com. City of Highwood; mem. joint civic com. Italian Americans. Mem. Acad. Cert. Social Workers, Nat. Assn. Social Workers, Ill. Soc. Clin. Social Work, Nat. Assn. Female Execs., Nat. Registry of Health Care Providers in Clin. Social Work. Democrat. Roman Catholic. Office: North Suburban Counseling & Therapeutic Services 11 N Skokie Hwy Lake Bluff IL 60044

WARREN, DIANA LYNN, human relations consultant; b. Jeannette, Pa., May 23, 1946; d. Egnitis Joseph and Anna (Orange) Warziski; m. Myron L. Morey, Aug. 11, 1984. BS, Wayne State U., 1975, MA, 1977. Cert. fin. planner; cert. social worker Mich., cert. specialist in aging. With consumer affairs dept. City of Detroit, 1974-75; instr. Madonna Coll., Livonia, Mich., 1976-77; home support coord. Oakland-Livingston Human Svc. Agy., Pontiac, Mich., 1976-77; instr. Wayne State U., Detroit, 1977; dir. adult deaf project Madonna Coll., Livonia, Mich., 1977-78; dir. home health aides Vis. Nurse Assn. Met. Detroit, 1978-80; instr. Wayne County Community Coll., Detroit, 1980-81; rep. Mut. Svc. Corp., Detroit, 1980-88; pres., chief cons. The Strategic Planning Group and DLW Assocs. Inc., Troy, Mich., 1983—; mem. consumer com. Fed. Exec. Bd., Detroit, 1974-75, 84-85; trainer, speaker numerous Mich. corps. and businesses, 1987-89; speaker Mich. Women's Found., Lansing, 1988. Author: Financial Strategies for 80's, 1986; co-author: Life Directions, 1988. Founding ptnr. Women's Investment Network, Detroit, 1981-83; bd. dirs., fin. chmn. Caregivers, Detroit, 1987—. Adminstrn. on Aging fellow, Washington, 1976-77. Mem. Wayne State U. Alumni Assn. (pres., treas. 1984-86, bd. dirs. Women of Wayne 1979-83), Internat. Assn. Fin. Planning (newsletter editor 1986), Internat. Soc. Cert. Fin. Planners (bd. dirs. 1986-88), Internat. Soc. Pre-Retirement Planners (mem. pub. awareness Detroit chpt. 1983-87), Am. Soc. Tng. and Devel., Older Women's League, Am. Home Econs. Assn. (vice chmn. human svcs. sect. 1982-83), Mich. Home Econs. Assn. (bd. dirs. 1978-79), Detroit Women's Forum, Polish Geneal. Soc., Ukrainian Grads. (treas. 1982-83). Home: 866 S Bates Birmingham MI 48009 Office: Strategic Planning Group 335 E Big Beaver Rd Ste 115 Troy MI 48083

WARREN, HELEN BILLETT, educator; b. Elmhurst, Ill., Sept. 25, 1932; d. George Edwin and Helen (Hoskins) Billett; m. John Michael Warren Jr., Aug. 25, 1956 (div. 1979); children: Mary-Jane, Peter, Jeffrey. AB, Ripon Coll., 1954; MA, U. Oreg., 1956; EdD, Pa. State U., 1979. Research assc. Psychology Dept., Palo Alto, Calif., 1956-59; research assoc. Yerkes Labs. of Primate Biology, Orange Park, Fla., 1959-60, Animal Behavior Lab, Univ. Park, Pa., 1960-69; psychology instr. Pa. State U., Univ. Park, Pa.; planning analyst Office of Planning and Budget, Univ. Park, Pa., 1979-83; Assoc. dir. Summer Sessions, Pa. State, Pa., 1983--; dir. Palmer Museum of Art, Univ. Park, Pa. 1983, Culinary Inst. of Am., Hyde Park, N.Y., 1983-86. Editor: Frontal Cortex and Behavior, 1964; contbr. articles to profl. jours. Vol. Earthwatch, Belize, 1987-88, Ctr. Community Coll., State Coll., 1973-82, leader Girl Scout, 1967-71, dir. Jr. Museum of Cen. Pa., 1964-67. Mem. Assn. for Study of Higher Edn., Assn. for Inst. Research, Am. Assn. for Higher Edn., N. Am. Assn. of Summer Sessions, PEO, Archaeol Inst., Phi Beta Kappa, Sigma Xi. Episcopalian. Home: 222 Woodland Dr State College PA 16803 Office: Pa State U Office of Summer Sessions Spruce Cottage University Park PA 16802

WARREN, KATHERINE VIRGINIA, art gallery director; b. Balt., Aug. 10, 1948; d. Joseph Melvin and Hilda Virginia (Thiele) Heim; m. David Hardy Warren; 1 child, Gabriel Kristopher. BA, U. Calif., Riverside, 1976, MA, 1980. Asst. curator Calif. Mus. Photography, Riverside, 1979-80, acting dir., 1980-81, asst. dir., curator of edn., 1981-84; dir. univ. art gallery U. Calif., Riverside, 1980-84, 1980—. Bd. dirs. Riverside Arts Found., 1980-89, chmn. bd., 1986-88. Marius De Brabant fellow U. Calif., 1977-79. Mem. Am. Assn. Mus., Calif. Confederation of the Arts, Calif. Assn. Mus. Office: U Calif Art Gallery Riverside CA 92521

WARREN, MARY SIGMAN, technical editor; b. Tulsa, Nov. 21, 1961; d. Thomas Edward Jr. and Emma Margarette (Murphy) Sigman; m. Frank Waldrep Warren, Sept. 12, 1981 (div. Aug. 1990); children: Joshua Robert, Morgan Kerr. AB in Journalism, U. Ga., 1984. News editor The Colonnade, Milledgeville, Ga., 1979-80; contbg. editor Walking Jour., Athens, Ga., 1983, UGAzine, Athens, Ga., 1983; editorial specialist IPC Communications, Anderson, S.C., 1984-85; system adminstr. Communities mag., Atlanta, 1985-87; freelance typesetter So. Raised, Marietta, Ga., 1987-88; freelance writer Enterprise Communications, Marietta, 1987-88; freelance editor Armed Svcs. News, Marietta, 1987-88; tech. writing coord. Ohmeda Med. Engring., Norcross, Ga., 1988—. Recipient Best News Story of Yr. award. Mem. NAFE, Soc. for Tech. Communications, North Shore Animal League (Gold Club). Republican. Christian Scientist. Office: Ohmeda Med Engring 2775 Northwoods Pkwy Norcross GA 30071

WARREN, MINNIE MAE, union official; b. Dowagiac, Mich., Nov. 5, 1945; d. Wyndell and Mollie (Matthew) Macon; m. Willie Warren, May 16, 1964 (div. May 1988); children: Kelly, Willis, Chris. Student, Ind. U., South Bend, 1982, Mich. State U., 1983, George Meany Labor Inst., Silver Spring, Md., 1984, 88. Internat. rep. Internat. Union Electronic, Elec. Salaried Machine and Furniture Workers, Washington, 1984—; social action chmn. for Ind., Mich., Wis., and Ill. Internat. Union Electronic, Elec. Salaried Machine and Furniture Workers, 1988—, women's coun. chmn. Great Lakes dist. Ind., Ill., Mich., Wis. Corr. sec. 4th Congl. Dem. Com., 1988—; chmn. housing com. NAACP, Dowagiac, Mich., 1988—. Mem. NAFE, Coalition Labor Union Women (nat. exec. bd. 1983—). Pentecoastal. Office: 2136 E 52d St Indianapolis IN 46205

WARREN, RENEE ELAINE, journalist; b. Chesapeake, Va., Mar. 11, 1965; d. Lewis McCoy and Viola (Faltz) W. BS, Old Dominion U., 1987; postgrad., So. Ill. U., 1987. Assoc. producer Sta. WTKR-TV, Norfolk, Va.; reporter The Virginian Pilot, Norfolk; journalist Dow Jones and Co., Inc.,

N.Y.C., 1988-90; assoc. producer C-NBC, N.Y.C., 1990—. Contbr. numerous articles to newspapers and mags. Mem. Nat. Assn. Black Journalists, Nat. Assn. Press Women, Sigma Delta Chi, Alpha Kappa Alpha. Baptist. Home: 325 W 56th St New York NY 10019 Office: 2200 Fletcher Ave 6th Fl Fort Lee NJ 07024

WARREN, RITA SIMPSON, manufacturing company executive; b. Borger, Tex., Jan. 17, 1949; d. William D. and Bobbie J. (Hindman) S.; m. Harry E. Warren, Jr., June 10, 1978. BA in Sociology, U. Tex., 1977; MBA, North Tex. State U., 1982. V.p. communications Tetra Pak Inc., Dallas, 1977-85; v.p. mktg. Devex Inc., Dallas, 1986-87; v.p. Neotech Industries, Inc., Irving, Tex., 1987-88; regional sales mgr. Optek Tech., Inc., 1989—. Recipient various awards Dairy and Food Industries Supply Assn., 1979, 84, Soc. Visual Communication, 1979, Dallas Ad League TOPS, 1984. Mem. Pub. Relations Soc. Am., Internat. Assn. Bus. Communicators, Jaguar Owners Assn. S.W. (co-pres. 1979-83), Tex. chpt. Mktg. Communications Execs. Internat., The Women's Ctr. of Dallas (WISER project), YWCA of Dallas. Republican. Club: Tex. T Register (MG). Avocations: classic European automobiles, vintage car racing, gardening. Office: 1215 W Crosby Rd Carrollton TX 75006

WARREN, SALLY ANN, management consultant; b. Detroit, Nov. 22, 1943; d. Kenneth Wayne and Ann (Trimble) W. BA, Swarthmore (Pa.) Coll., 1965; MA, Stanford (Calif.) U., 1969. Analyst Aerospace Tech. Div. Library of Congress, Washington, 1965-67; mgmt. trainee Bank of Boston, 1969-72; internat. officer Bank of Boston, London, 1972-74; asst. v.p. Bank of Boston, Hong Kong, 1974-76; dep. mgr. 1st Nat. Boston (Hong Kong) Ltd., Hong Kong, 1974-76; v.p. Salomon Bros., N.Y.C., 1977-81; pvt. practice mgmt. cons. in internat. fin. svcs. N.Y.C., 1981—, exec. dir. conf. bd. chmn., 1985—; mem. alumni coun. Swarthmore Coll., 1979-87, acting dir. career planning and placement office, 1984-85. Chmn. beautification com. East 63d St. Block Assn., N.Y.C., 1981—; elected mem. N.Y.C. Dem. County Com., 1983; bd. dirs. N.Y. State Coun. Econ. Edn., 1983-88, exec. com., fin. com., chmn. nominating com.; bd. mgrs. Swarthmore Coll., 1988—, investment, property and governance coms., vice chmn. devel. com.; pres. class 1965 Swarthmore coll., 1980—. Mem. Fin. Women's Assn. N.Y., Bus. Execs. for Nat. Security, The Asia Soc. (vol. 1981—), Swarthmore Coll. Alumni Assn. (pres. 1985-87).

WARREN, TANJA EIKENBOOM, lawyer, artist; b. Madrid, Dec. 24, 1957; d. Robert and Alieta (Hilling) Eikenboom; m. Manning Gilbert Warren, Feb. 7, 1987; children: Saskia Elizabeth, William Marnix. LLD, Leiden U., The Netherlands, 1985. Cert. Lawyer. Legal advisor Dutch Red Cross, The Hague, The Netherlands, 1986-87; artist Louisville, 1990—; legal advisor Netherlands Delegation Internat. Conf. Red Cross, Geneva Switzerland 1986. Mem. ARC, 1987--.

WARREN, WENDY KAYE, English language educator, writing consultant; b. Woodbury, N.J., Jan. 6, 1957; d. John C. and Elinor M. (Kaye) Warren; 1 child, Nicholas Christopher. BA in Humanities, U. Houston, Victoria, Tex., 1985; MA in Rhetoric and Composition, Purdue U., 1988. Asst. editor Victoria Bus. Mag., 1985; copy editor Waco (Tex.) Tribune-Herald, 1985-86; teaching asst. Purdue U., West Lafayette, Ind., 1986-88; instr. English Edinboro U. of Pa., 1988—; freelance writing cons., 1987—. Vol., Hospitality House, Erie, Pa., 1987-88. Mem. Nat. Council Tchrs. English, Women in Communications Inc.

WARRICK, MILDRED LORINE, librarian, volunteer; b. Kellerton, Iowa, June 21, 1917; d. Webie Arthur and Bonnie Lorine (Hyatt) DeVries; m. Carl Wesley Warrick, Feb. 11, 1937; children: Carl Dwayne, Arthur Will. BS in Edn., Drake U., 1959; M of Librarianship, Kans. State Tchrs. Coll., 1970. Cert. tchr., libr., Iowa. Elem. tchr. Monroe Ctr. Rural Sch., Kellerton, Iowa, 1935-37, Denham Rural Sch., Grand River, Iowa, 1945-48, Grand River Ind. Sch., 1948-52, Woodmansee Rural Sch., Decatur, Iowa, 1952-55, Centennial Rural Sch., Decatur, 1955-56; elem. tchr., acting libr. Cen. Decatur Sch., Leon, Iowa, 1956-7l; media libr. jr. and sr. high sch., 1971-79; media libr. Jr. and Sr. High Sch. Decatur, 1971-79; libr. Northminster Presbyn. Ch., Tucson, 1985—; media resourse instr. Graceland Coll., Lamoni, Iowa, 1971-72; lit. dir. S.W. Iowa Assn. Classroom Tchrs., 1965-69. Editor (media packet) Mini History and Quilt Blocks, 1976, Grandma Lori's Nourishing Nuggets for Body and Soul, 1985, As I Recall (Loren Drake), 1989, Foland Family Supplement III, 1983; author: (with Quentin Oiler) Van Der Vlugt Family Record, 1976; contbr. articles to publs. Leader Grand River 4-H Club for Girls, 1945-48; sec. South Cen. Iowa Quarter Horse Assn., Chariton, 1967-68; chmn. Decatur County Dems., 1981-83, del., 1970-83; pianist Amphi League of Mercy, Salvation Army, Tucson, 1984—, Rhythm Noters, 1984—, pianist, leader, 1990—. Named Classroom Tchr. of Iowa Classroom Tchrs. Assn., 1962, Woman of Yr. Leon Bus. and Profl. Women, 1978; recipient grant for English and Reading Nat. Dept Edn., 1966. Mem. AAUW (creative writing chair Tucson br. 1986—), Pima County Ret. Tchrs. Assn. (pres. 1989-90), Tucson Bus. and Profl. Women, Cen. Community Tchrs.'s Assn. (pres. Clarke, Ringgold, Decatur chpts. 1967-68), Decatur County Retired Tchrs. Assn. (historian 1980-83), Leon Bus. and Profl. Women (pres. 1963-64), Internat. Reading Assn. (pres. Clarke chpt. 1967-68), Decatur County Edn. Assn. (pres. 1962-63), Iowa State Edn. Assn. (life), NEA (life), Delta Kappa Gamma (pres. Beta Xi chpt. 1974-76), Alpha Gamma (historian 1986—). Democrat. Presbyterian. Home: 2879 E Presidio Rd Tucson AZ 85716

WARRIOR, KATHRYN ANN, educator; b. Emerson, Iowa, Feb. 14, 1939; d. Robert E. Lee and Edna (Gillen) Grayson; m. Allan Ray Warrior, June 10, 1961; children: Allan Scott, Dawn Celeste, Kristin Noelle. BS Edn., U. Omaha, 1960; MEd., Oreg. State U., 1986. Cert. tchr., Oreg. Elem. tchr. Omaha Pub. Schs., 1960-62, Kennewick (Wash.) Pub. Schs., 1971-72, Klamath County Sch. Dist., Klamath Falls, Oreg., 1974-77, Lincoln County Sch. Dist., Newport, Oreg., 1977-82; equity resource tchr. Lincoln County Sch. Dist., 1982-83, elem. tchr., 1983-89, resource tchr. academically gifted program, 1989—; presented Nat. Coun. Tchr. English, Mo., 1988, N.W. Math. Conf., 1981-89, Oreg. Reading Assn. Conf., 1987. Named Tchr. of Yr., 1982, Tchr. of Yr.-West Area, 1987, Lincoln County Edn. Assn. Mem. Seacoast Reading Coun. (pres. 1987-88), Oreg. Reading Assn., Oreg. Coun. Tchrs. English, Nat. Coun. Tchrs. Math., Oreg. Coun. Tchrs. Math. (pres. 1989—), AAUW (pres. Newport branch 1980-81), Delta Kappa Gamma (pres. Alpha Eta chpt. 1982-84, scholar 1983, 84). Republican. Methodist. Home: 1332 NE 21st Ave Portland OR 97232 Office: Yaquina View Elem Sch 351 SE Harney Newport OR 97365

WARSHAW, EILEEN REILLY, real estate developer; b. Algona, Iowa, Mar. 20, 1948; d. Louis H. and Bernadette F. (Zook) Reilly; ; 1 child, Ann Christine Humphreys. BA, U. No. Ill., 1970; M., U. Denver, 1974; BS, Colo. State U., 1983; Dr. (hon.), Trinity Coll., 1980. Cert. property mgr. Restoration dir. Ballyhaise (Ireland) Agr. Coll., 1978-80; dir., mgr. Univ. Mall, Ft. Collins, Colo., 1980—. Recipient Abby Theater award, Dublin, Ireland, 1980. Mem. Rocky Mountain Shopping Ctr. Assn., Nat. Bd. Review Landmark Commn. Republican.

WARSHAWSKY, REBECCA JON, computer company executive; b. Oklahoma City, Dec. 24, 1952; d. John Warren Hall and Bobbie Nell (Griffin) Moore; m. Paul Brian McKay, Aug. 19, 1972 (div. Mar. 1979); children: Jason, John; m. Marc Stewart Warshawsky, Sept. 18, 1982; children: Sarah, Benjamin. BA in Edn., U. Wyo., 1979, MA in Gifted and Talented Edn., 1980; MEd in Film and Video, Harvard U., 1981. Rsch. asst. Harvard Ul, Cambridge, Mass., 1980-81; cons. in tng. and communications Polaroid Corp., Cambridge, 1981-83; mgr. media svcs. Wang Labs., Lowell, Mass., 1983-86; mgr. broadcast and media prodns. Digital Equipment Corp., Bedford, Mass., 1986—; bd. dirs. Bus. TV, Atlanta, Ga. Producer: (broadcast documentaries) The Hidden Poor, 1981, The Little Victims, 1981, (sales tng. film) Profile of a Retailer, 1982. Co-dir. Kids Interactive Telecommunications by Satellite Kites, Lowell, 1988—; com. mem. Waste Treatment Plan, Westford, Mass., 1989—, Sch. Improvement, Day Middle Sch., Westford; officer Parent Tchr. Assn., Belleville Sch., Newburyport, Mass., 1986-87. Mem. Internat. Teleconferencing Assn. (bd. dirs. 1989—), Soc. of Satellite Profls., Internat. Video Assn., Alumni Assn. of Harvard U. Republican. Home: 16 Reinsway Circle Westford MA 01886

WARWICK, DIONNE, singer; b. East Orange, N.J., Dec. 12, 1941; m. Bill Elliott (div. 1975); 2 sons. Ed., Hartt Coll. Music, Hartford, Conn. As teen-ager formed Gospelaires, then sang background for rec. studio, 1966; debut, Philharmonic Hall, N.Y. Lincoln Center, 1966; appearances include London Palladium, Olympia, Paris, Lincoln Ctr. Performing Arts, N.Y.C.; records include I'll Never Love This Way Again, That's What Friends are For; albums include Valley of the Dolls and Others, 1968, Promises, Promises, 1975, Dionne, 1979, Then Came You, Friends, 1986, Reservations for Two, 1987, Dionne Warwick Sings Cole Porter, 1990; TV appearances Sisters in the Name of Love, 1986; screen debut The Slaves, 1969, No Night, So Long, also, Hot! Live and Otherwise; co-host: TV show Solid Gold; host: TV show A Gift of Music, 1981; star: TV show Dionne Warwick Spl. Recipient Grammy awards, 1969, 70, 80. Address: care Arista Records Inc 6 W 57th St New York NY 10019*

WASCOU, ELLEN FERN, radio news and public service director; b. Lancaster, Pa., Jan. 12, 1950; d. Albert E. and Anne F. (Weil) W. AS in Fine Arts, Vernon Ct. Jr. Coll., 1969. With ad layouts Lancaster Newspapers, Inc., 1969-72; front office mgr. Host Resort Hotels, Lancaster, 1972-76; news broadcaster WLAN AM & FM Radio, Lancaster, 1976, WNOW AM & WQXA FM RDIO, York, Pa., 1977; news & pub. svc. dir. WLAN AM & FM Radio, Lancaster, 1977—. Dir., anchor: AP Outstanding Regularly Scheduled Newscast, 1982, 83, 86,88, AP Outstanding Pub. Affairs Program, 1983, Pa. Women in Communications-Hard News Coverage, 1988 (Best Regularly Scheduled Program News 1989). Bd. dirs. Crispus Attucks Community Ctr., Lancaster, Lancaster Dance Co.; com. mem. March of Dimes, Lancaster. Recipient Community Spirit award United Way Lancaster, 1978, Friend Edn. award Pa. State Edn. Assn., 1983, Patriotic Svc. award U.S. Dept. Treasury, 1984, Appreciation award NAACP Lancaster, 1986; named one of Outstanding Young Women of Am., 1979. Mem. Radio & Television News Dirs. Assn., Pa. AP Broadcasters Assn. (bd. dirs. 1980, pres. 1987—, 1st CommunitySvc. award 1982). Office: WLAN AM/FM Radio 252 N Queen St Lancaster PA 17603

WASH, MARILYN JOHNSON, purchasing manager, accountant; b. Jackson, Miss., Sept. 26, 1954; d. Tommie Johnson and Lucille (Anderson) W. BSBA, Jackson State U., 1976. Profl. pub. buyer. Acctg. clk. Am. Nat. Ins. Co., Jackson, 1976-78; acctg. clk. II Miss. Dept. Welfare, Jackson, 1978-79, acctg. clk. III, 1979-80; acct., supr. purchasing energy and transp. div. Miss. Dept. Econ. and Community Devel., Jackson, 1980—. Mem. Miss. Assn. Govtl. Purchasing Agts. (sec. 1986, 1st v.p. 1989, Pres.'s Citation 1986), Nat. Inst. Govtl. Purchasing (profl. pub. buyer cert.), NAFE. Roman Catholic. Office: Miss Dept Econ & Community Devel 510 George St Ste 101 Jackson MS 39202-3096

WASHBURN, MARY WILSON, sales executive; b. Sanford, N.C., May 20, 1957; d. Lorraine (Smith) Wilson; divorced; children: Amy Sue, John Morton, Jr. Student, LaSalle U., Chgo., 1977, Patrick Henry Coll., 1986, Averett Coll., 1987-88. Administrv. asst. Piedmont Trust Bank, Martinsville, Va., 1977-81; patient acct. rep. Mem. Hosp., Martinsville, 1981-84; gen. mgr. Charles Trent & Co. Inc., Martinsville, 1984-88; polyplank account mgr. Astro-Valcour, Inc., Glens Falls, N.Y., 1988—. Treas. Knights Pythias Sisters, Martinsville, 1987, guard, 1989. Recipient Acad. All-Am. award, U.S. Achievement Acad., Lexington, Ky., 1987. Mem. NAFE, Phi Beta Lambda, Phi Theta Kappa. Republican. Home and Office: 1506 Mulberry Rd #14 Martinsville VA 24112

WASHBURN, PATRICIA JANE, newspaper editor; b. Worcester, Mass., Apr. 1, 1965; d. Stewart Putnam and Josephine Fuller (Foster) W. BS in Journalism, Boston U., 1987. Copy editor New Bedford (Mass.) Standard Times, 1984-87, Middlesex News, Framingham, Mass., 1987-89, Portland (Maine) Press Herald, 1989—. Author: Come and Have a Bathe, 1989. Tutor Adult Basic Learning Exch., Portland, 1989—. Mem. Soc. Profl. Journalists, Newspaper Guild, NOW, Maine Writers and Pubrs. Assn. Home: 14 Stetson Ct Portland ME 04101 Office: Portland Press Herald 390 Congress St Portland ME 04104

WASHINGTON, ANGELA YVETTE, program director; b. Norfolk, Va., July 15, 1961; d. Benjamin Franklin and Evelyn Carol (Smalls) W. BS, Lander Coll., Greenwood, S.C., 1983. From athletic dir. to asst. dir. Beaufort (S.C.) County Recreation, 1983-86; program dir. Boys Club of Greater Beaufort (S.C.), 1986--. Com. mem. Boys Club Am. SW, Atlanta, 1987, chmn., 1988; active in Big Brothers Big Sisters, Beaufort, S.C., Boys & Girls Club of Greater Beaufort, Leadership Beaufort Class 1990. Mem. Alpha Kappa Alpha Sorority (historian 1988-89). Home: 2404 Walsh Ave Beaufort SC 29902 Office: Boys Club of Greater Beaufo PO Box 1482 Beaufort SC 29901

WASHINGTON, BARBARA JEAN WRIGHT, personnel administrator; b. Chgo., July 31, 1946; d. Jacob Henry and Barbara Mae (Pearson) Wright; m. Paul Joseph Washington Jr., Sept. 6, 1969; children: Paul Joseph, Barbara Jeanine, Nyree Jeanine. Student, Bethel Coll., 1964-66; Grad., Bus. Methods Inst., Chgo., 1967; cert. in real estate, Prince George Coll., 1976; student, U. Md., 1978-79, Germanna Community Coll., Orange, Va., 1985-86. Payroll clk. Carson Pirie Scott & Co., Chgo., 1965-67; underwriter Zurich Ins. Co., Chgo., 1967-68; receptionist, sec. Roosevelt U., Chgo., 1968-69; sales rep. Avon Co., Crofton, Md., 1973-75; dist. mgr. Avon Co., Washington, 1975-77; office mgr. Bailey, Banks & Biddle, Landover, Md., 1974-76; teller Md. Nat. Bank, Riverdale, 1977; subs. tchr. Prince Georges Sch. System, New Carrollton, Md., 1977-80; from dept. mgr. to mgr. personnel Montgomery Ward, Inc., Fredericksburg, Va., 1980-87; coll. recruit officer, pers. staffing specialist Dept. of Navy, Crystal City, Va., 1987—; diamond counselor Montgomery Ward, Inc., Fredericksburg, 1981-83; employer adv. mem. Va. Employment Commn., Fredericksburg, 1983-87; advisor bus. edn. Fredericksburg and Germanna Colls., 1983-87. Adv. counsel Germanna Community Coll., Orange, Va., 1986; chairperson Spotsylvania County Vocat. and High Sch., Fredericksburg, 1985; bd. dirs. Fredericksburg Area Food Clearing House; mem. Spotsylvania County Vocat. Adv. Council. Named Retail Pace Setter Rappahannock area United Way, 1986; recipient Meritorious Service in Bus. award AME Meth. Ch., 1985. Mem. Am. Soc. Personnel Administrs., Nat. Assn. Female Execs., Beta Kappa. Democrat. Home: 11181-G Salem Sta Blvd Fredericksburg VA 22401

WASHINGTON, BEVERLY DIANA, publishing executive; b. N.Y.C., Mar. 1, 1956; d. James Robert and JoAnn (Aycox) W. BA Secondary Edn.-Dance, U. Ill., 1978. Asst. buyer, dept. mgr. Marshall Field & Co., Chgo., 1981-85; territory sales rep. Advo Direct Mktg., Schaumburg, Ill., 1985-86; regional sales mgr. Earl Graves Pub. Co., Chgo., 1986—; pres., founder Image Factor. Pace vol. Cook County Jail, Chgo., 1986-88; deacon 4th Presbyn. Ch., Chgo., 1988—. Mem. NAFE, Targeted Advt. Profls., Chgo. Advt. Club. Democrat. Home: 211 E Ohio St Apt 1807 Chicago IL 60611 Office: Earl Graves Pub Co 625 N Michigan Ave Ste 1910 Chicago IL 60611

WASHINGTON, CATHERINE ELIZABETH MAHRT, bank marketing manager; b. Columbus, Ga., May 21, 1962; d. William Rudolf and Mary-Ellen (Hawken) Mahrt; m. Patrick John Washington, Aug. 29, 1986. BS in Mktg., Niagara U., 1984. Mktg. sales rep. Heany Industries, Inc., Scottsville, N.Y., 1985-87; mktg. coord. Verax Systems, Inc., Fairport, N.Y., 1987-88; mktg. mgr. Goldome Bank, Rochester, N.Y., 1988—. Coord. PaceSetter div. United Way, Rochester, 1989. Mem. Am. Mktg. Assn., Alpha Kappa Psi (sec. Niagara U. chpt. 1982-84). Republican. Roman Catholic. Home: 16 Semmel Rd Honeoye Falls NY 14472 Office: Goldome Bank 16 E Main St Rochester NY 14614

WASHINGTON, C.J., journalist; b. Camden, Ark., Nov. 27, 1957; d. William Carroll and Marie (Thompson) Renfro; 1 child, Amber Nichole Jones. AS, West Ark. Community Coll., 1986; BS in Journalism, Tex. Woman's U., 1990. Mng. editor Daily Lasso-Tex. Women's U., Denton, 1986-87; editor Daily Lasso-Twu, Denton, 1989-90, arts editor, 1990; anchor Channel 19 News-Tex. Women's U., Denton, 1987-89; court reporter Roswell (N.Mex.) Daily Record, 1990—. Editorial writer Daily Lasso, 1985-86 (5 Star All Am. award 1986). Recipient Press Club of Dallas Scholarship award, 1985, Ft. Worth Press Club Scholarship award, 1986, Tex. Press Women Scholarship award, 1987; named Person Most Likely to Win a Pulitzer, Caro Brown, 1988. Mem. Women in Communications, Soc. Profl. Journalists. Democrat. Home: 2901 E Mescalero Rd Roswell NM 88201

WASHINGTON, DAWN CARTER, food service professional; b. Harrisburg, Pa., Mar. 11, 1970; d. Edward Earl Sampson and Judith Ellen (Carter) Boampong; m. Bernard Antonio Washington, Aug. 18, 1988. Student, Georgetown U., 1987-88, Howard U., 1989—. Sales assoc. Garfinckels Dept. Store, Washington, 1988-89; supr. trainee Traditions Restaurant, Alexandria, Va., 1989—; founder, pres. Auroura Prodns., 1989—. Rep. Mayor's Youth Leadership Program, Washington, 1987; sr. advisor youth coun. NAACP, Alexandria, 1988. Mem. Nat. Assn. Female Execs. Democrat. Baptist. Home: 1500 Southview Dr Apt 306 Oxon Hill MD 20745 Office: Old Colony Inn 625 1st St Alexandria VA 22314

WASHINGTON, DEBORAH KAYE, personnel executive; b. Alton, Ill., Jan. 21, 1958; d. Clyde and Sue (Morgan) Henning; m. Ronald Washington, Aug. 30, 1980 (div. Oct. 1987); 1 child, Brandon Jeffrey. BSBA, Eastern Ill. U., 1981. Personnel clk. Calgon Corp., St. Louis, 1981-85; personnel analyst Citicorp Acceptance, St. Louis, 1985-86; personnel asst. Meml. Hosp. of Tampa, 1986; personnel coord. Citicorp Acceptance, St. Louis, 1986-89; personnel asst. St. Louis Pub. Libr., 1989, personnel mgr., 1989—. Mem. NAFE. Baptist. Home: 4008 Westminster Pl #F Saint Louis MO 63108

WASHINGTON, EVELYN BURRELL, educator; b. New Haven, Mar. 12, 1961; d. Samuel Abbott and Gertrude (Williams) Burrell; m. Gordon Allen Washington, Nov. 30, 1985. BA, Yale U., 1983; postgrad. bus. adminstn., Pace U., 1984—. Cert. social studies and history tchr., Conn. Tchr. social studies Greenwich (Conn.) Pub. Schs., 1983—, chmn. dept., 1986-89; mem. Conn. Social Studies Adv. Com., 1986—; writer nat. tchr. exam. test questions Ednl. Testing Svc., 1988. Mem. Greenwich Affirmative Action Com., 1983—. Recipient Disting. Tchr. award Greenwich Pub. Schs., 1986, Outstanding History Tchr. award, DAR, 1987, recognition, 1989. Mem. NEA, Conn. Edn. Assn., Conn. Assn. for Supervision and Curriculum Devel. Democrat. Congregationalist. Office: Western Jr High Sch 1 Western Junior Hwy Greenwich CT 06830

WASHINGTON, JEAN B., software engineer; b. Chgo., Apr. 22, 1926; d. George U. and Lillian R. (Rosenzweig) Birkenstein; m. Atlee D., May 1951 (div. May 1959); children: Glen Gordon Washington, Robin Birk Washington. BA in Fine Arts Music, Middleburg (Vt.) Coll., 1948; BA in Art, Art Inst. of Chgo., 1952; postgrad., IIT, Chgo., 1970-80. Computer sci. instr. Triton Coll., River Grove, Ill., 1982-83; software engr. Victor Bus., Chgo., 1981, A.B. Dick Corp., Skokie, Ill., 1981-82, Rocklan Corp., Arlington Heights, Ill., 1982-83; tel. engr. GTE, Northlake, Ill., 1978-81; instr. Malcom X Coll., Chgo., 1970-78, West Side Learning Ctr., Chgo., 1989—; pres. Jeanius, Inc., Chgo., 1985—. Artist with paintings in many exhibits, 1980-88; designer children's software program, 1989; author poetry. Officer Rain Forest Action Group, Chgo., 1989—, CORE, Chgo., 1960-63; civil rights activist, Chgo., 1954-64, others. Mem. AAAS, IEEE, Assn. Computing Machinery, NAACP (officer 1957-60). Jewish. Home: 2111 N Halsted Chicago IL 60614

WASHINGTON, LINDA LITTLE, nursing educator; b. Miami, Fla., Aug. 24, 1950; d. George Chatman and Ida Mae (Haynes) Little; m. Larry Redie Washington, Jan. 3, 1970; children: Sherry, Ramona, Bridget, Larechia, Larry Redie Jr., Moses. Assoc. Sci. Nursing, Miami Dade Community Coll., 1972; BS in Nursing, Fla. Internat. U., Miami, 1984; MS in Nursing, U. Miami, 1987, postgrad., 1987. Cert. trauma nurse/instr., adv. registered nurse practitioner. Pub. health nurse Dade County Health Dept., Miami, 1973-75; home health nurse, weekend coordinator Upjohn Health Care, Miami, 1975-82; instr. Dade County Sch. Bd., Miami, 1982-84; ctr. dir. Youth Crusade Ednl., Miami, 1978-86; instr. Miami Dade Community Coll., 1985—; mem. Affirmative Action, U. Miami, 1984-86; state chmn. edn. com. ENA; clin. educator/coord. quality assurance, Jackson Meml. Hosp., Emergency Care Ctr., 1989—. Treas. Crusade for Christ Sisterhood; active Urban League, Greater Miami chpt., 1984-86. Mem. Orgn. for Obstetrice, Gynecologic and Neonatal Nursing, Am. Nursing Assn., Fla. Nursing Assn., So. Fla. Assn. Children Under Six, Sigma Theta Tau. Democrat. Pentecostal. Home: 6283 NW 201 Terr Miami Lakes FL 33015 Office: Miami Dade Community Coll 950 NW 20th St Miami FL 33127

WASHINGTON, MARGARET, medical association administrator; b. Pitts., Oct. 31, 1935; d. Walter C. and Anna Mae (Harris); m. Charles E., Nov. 24, 1956; 1 child, Charles Michael. BA, Chatham Coll., Pitts., 1957; MSW, U. Pitts., 1970, M in Med. and Hosp. Admin, 1974. Interviewer Unemployment Compensation Claims, Pa., 1963-67; caseworker Allegheny County Bd. of Assistance, 1963-67; dir. of social svcs. and adult edn. Brushton Inner-City Project, Pitts., 1963-67; dir. Brushton Inner-City Encouragement Project; cons. Maurice Falk Med. Fund, 1967-80; dir. adult programs Mercy Hosp., 1968-70; dir. of training Homewood-Brushton Neighborhood Health Ctr., Pitts., 1968-70. Bd. dir. Urban League of Pitts., Health Edn. Ctr. Com., Nat. Kidney Found. of Western Pa., Inc., Rodman St. Missionary Baptist trustee. Named One of 25 Outstanding Black Wommen in Pitts., Talk Mag., 1876, United Way Vol. of Yr., 1989; recipient Harold B. Gardner Citizen award Allegheny County Med. Soc., 1975, Community Health award Nat. Council of Negro Women, Inc., 1977, Appreciation award Urban League of Pitts., 1982, Urban League Guild of Pitts., 1982. Office: Presbyn Univ Hosp De Soto & O'Hara Sts Pittsburgh PA 15213

WASHINGTON, VALORA, foundation administrator; b. Columbus, Ohio, Dec. 16, 1953; d. Timothy Washington and Elizabeth (Jackson) Barbour; 1 child, Omari. BA in Social Sci. with honors, Mich. State U., 1974; PhD, Ind. U., 1978. Assoc. instr. sch. edn. Ind. U., Bloomington, 1975-77; dir., cons. Urban League Ind., Indpls., 1977-78; substitute tchr. Indpl. Pub. Schs., 1978; dir. U. N.C., Chapel Hill, 1980-82; congrl. sci. fellow Soc. for Rsch. in Child Devel., Washington, 1981-82; prof. edn. U. N.C., Chapel Hill, 1978-83; asst. dean, assoc. prof. Howard U., Washington, 1983-86, Am. U., Washington, 1986-87; prof., v.p. Antioch Coll., Yellow Springs, Ohio, 1987—; cons. Ford Found., N.Y.C., 1990; project evaluator Carnegie Corp., N.Y.C., 1989-90, Ohio Bd. Regents, Columbus, 1990—. Author: (with others) Creating New Linkages for the Adoption of Black Children, 1984, Project Head Start: Past, Present and Future Trends in the Context of Family Needs, 1987, Black Children and American Institutions: An Ecological Review and Resource Guide, 1988, Affirmative Rhetoric, Negative Action: The Status of Black and Hispanic Faculty in Higher Education, 1989; contbr. articles to profl. jours; contbr. chapters to numerous books. Recipient Capital U. award, 1990, award Springfield Alliance Black Educators, 1989; named one of Ten Outstanding Young Women Am., 1980, Outstanding Young Woman N.C., 1980, one of 100 Young Women of Promise Good Housekeeping Mag., 1985. Mem. Nat. Coun. Negro Women (chmn. 1982-83), Am. Assn. for Higher Edn. (sec. black caucus 1989), Soc. for Rsch. in Child Devel. (pres. black caucus 1987-89), Nat. Assn. for the Edn. of Young Children (sec. of bd. dir. 1990—), Phi Delta Kappa, Delta Kappa Gamma.

WASHINGTON, VIVIAN EDWARDS, social worker, former government official; b. Claremont, N.H., Oct. 26, 1914; d. Valdemar and Irene (Quashie) Edwards; m. George Luther Washington, Dec. 22, 1950; 1 child, Valdemar Luther. AB, Howard U., 1938, MA, 1946, MSW, 1956. Tchr., guidance counselor, sch. social worker, asst. prin., prin. Edgar Allan Poe Sch. Program for Pregnant Girls, Balt., 1939-73; cons. Office Adolescent Pregnancy Programs, HEW, Washington, 1978-80, program devel. specialist, 1980-81; exec. dir. Balt. Coun. on Adolescent Pregnancy, Parenting and Pregnancy Prevention Inc., 1982-86, cons., 1986—; cons. to adolescent parents. Author: I Am Somebody, I Am Me, 1986; contbr. articles to profl. jours. Bd. dirs. Nat. Alliance Concerned with Sch.-Age Parents, 1970-76, pres., 1970-72; YWCA, Balt., 1966-69, United Way Central Md., 1971-80; bd. visitors U. Balt., 1978-80; adv. commn. on social services City of Balt., 1978-85, Govs. Coun. on Adolescent Pregnancy, 1986; chmn. Md. Gov.'s Commn. on Children and Youth, 1972-77, active 1987. Recipient Alumni award Howard U. Sch. Social Work, 1966, Clementine Peters award United Way, 1980, Sojourner Truth award Nat. Bus. and Profl. Women, 1979, Vashti Turley Murphy award Balt. chpt. Delta Sigma Theta, 1981, Balt.'s Best Blue and Silver award, 1983, Pvt. Sector Vol. Svc. award Pres. Reagan, 1984, United Way Community Svc. award, 1985, ; named to Balt. Women's Hall of Fame, 1989; Paul Harris fellow Balt. Rotary, 1985. Mem. Nat. Assn. Social Work, LWV, Nat. Coun. Negro Women (life), Balt. Urban League (Equal Opportunity award 1987), Balt. Mus. Art, Delta Sigma Theta (nat. treas. 1958-63,

Las Amigas Svc. award Balt. chpt. 1973), Pierians Club. Democrat. Episcopalian. Home: 3507 Ellamont Rd Baltimore MD 21215

WASHINGTON, WILMA J., company executive; b. Magnolia, Miss., Oct. 14, 1949; d. Melvin and Wilma Magee; m. Michael Washington, Dec. 18, 1971 (div. 1978); children: Charisse, Jay. Student, Ind. U., 1973-80. Adminstrv. asst. Fred Harvey, Inc., Chgo., 1970-72; office mgr. Model Cities Agy., Gary, Ind., 1972-76; adminstrv. mgr. Med. Ctr. of Gary, 1976-81; events coordinator Genesis Convention Ctr., Gary, 1981-83, exec. mgr., 1983-85; mgr. corp. devel. Dimensions Unltd., Inc., Chgo., 1985-87, v.p., 1987—. Mem. Chgo. Convention and Tourism Bur., 1986-87, Miller Citizen Orgn., 1976—; officer Wirt Band Boosters, 1987. Recipient appreciation cert. Northwest IN Black Expo, 1985. Mem. Gary C. of C. Baptist. Home: 7741 Oak Ave Gary IN 46403 Office: Dimensions Unltd Inc 1525 E 53d St Ste 907 Chicago IL 60615

WASHOW, PAULA BURNETTE, security company executive; b. Milw., Feb. 14, 1948; d. John W. and Darlene A. (Johnson) Hudson; m. William E. Toepfer, Jan. 1, 1988; children: Kimberly Anderson, Paul Washow. Cert. detective agy. owner, Wis.; in advanced criminal interrogations, audio surveillance and countermeasures. Owner Alpha Omega Security, Milw., 1976-90; owner, pres. Always Freight Inc., Franklin, 1980-85, Amrac Trucking, Franklin, Wis., 1985-90. Vol. Make-a-Wish Found. of Wis., 1989. Mem. Am. Soc. Indsl. Security, Nat. Assn. Chiefs of Police, Wis. Chiefs of Police Assn., Inter-County Assn. of Crime Prevention Practitioners, World Assn. Detectives. Office: 312 E Wisconsin Ave Ste 601 Milwaukee WI 53202

WASINGER, VIRGINIA LEE, quality engineer; b. Paris, Tex., Sept. 21, 1932; d. Theo Lee and Elizabeth Virginia (Cartter) White; B.B.A., Tarleton State U., 1978; children—Janet Wasinger Dickson, James, Richard, Lee Anne, Cynthia. Counselor, Nat. Bus. Con., Dallas, 1969; indsl. relations mgr. Voltaic Internat. Corp., 1969-71; property mgr. Sky-Harbour Lake Property, Granbury, Tex., 1974-75; owner Granbury Picture Framing, 1973-76; quality engr., documentation specialist Brown & Root Constrn., Glen Rose, Tex., 1979-83; quality assurance engr. UE&C, N.H., 1983—. Mem. Am. Assn. for Quality Control.

WASKO, CASSIE HORTON, newspaper editor; b. Raleigh, NC, Feb. 26, 1949; d. Harry Perryman and Doris (Goerch) Horton; m. Peter Jerry Wasko, June 21, 1967; children: Peter Jerry Jr., Carl Goerch. Student, Campbell Coll., 1967-68, Wilson Tech. Inst., 1968-69. Reporter The News-Jour., Raeford, N.C., 1977-79, The Sandhill Citizen, Southern Pines, N.C., 1979, The Chatham Record, Pittsboro, N.C., 1980-86; news editor The Chatham Record/ The Chatham News, Pittsboro, N.C., 1986—. Vice chmn. Pittsboro (N.C.) Bicentennial Com., 1986—; bd. dirs., sec. East Chatham Med. Ctr., Pittsboro; bd. dirs., chmn. com. Hospice Chatham County, Pittsboro, 1984-90; bd. dirs. Chatham County Home Health, Pittsboro, 1987-90; chmn. Chatham County Com. to Honor Vols., 1990—. Mem. N.C. Press Assn. (News Writing award 1982, 83, 89, Editorial Writing award 1987, Investigative Writing award 1989, Community Service Writing award 1989). Democrat. Methodist. Club: Pittsboro Bridge. Home: 400 Credle St Pittsboro NC 27312 Office: The Chatham Record Courthouse Sq Pittsboro NC 27312

WASKO, MELODY ANN, home builders association executive; b. Rochester, N.Y., Oct. 2, 1948; d. George W. and Matilda M. (Schickler) McCoy; m. Stephen P. Wasko, May 31, 1969 (div. Dec. 1989); children: Joseph W., Nicole A. BSBA, Rochester Inst. Tech., 1982. Notary pub., N.Y. Sec. Rochester Home Builders' Assn., 1967-72, office mgr., 1972-81, adminstrv. asst., 1981-85, asst. exec. dir., 1985-88, interim exec. dir., 1988-89, dir. ops., 1989—. Bd. dirs. Better Contractors Bur., Rochester, 1989—, Ct. Apptd. Spl. Advs., Rocheste,r 1988—; DePaul Mental Health Clinic, Rochester, 1989—. Mem. Am. Soc. Assn. Execs., Urban Land Inst., Monroe County Bldg. Ofcls. Assn., Finger Lakes Bldg. Ofcls. Assn., Rochester Profl. Sales Assn., NAFE, Rochester C. of C. (bd. dirs., exec. com. 1987—), Am. Legion Aux. Democrat. Roman Catholic. Home: 595 Stottle Rd Scottsville NY 14546 Office: Rochester Home Builders 2024 W Henrietta Rd Rochester NY 14623

WASKO-FLOOD, SANDRA JEAN, artist, educator; b. N.Y.C., Mar. 12, 1943; d. Peter Edmund and Margaret Dalores (Kubek) Wasko; m. Michael Timothy Flood, June 28, 1969. BA, UCLA, 1965, postgrad., 1968-69; postgrad., Calif. State U., Northridge, summer 1968; student, Otis Art Inst., L.A., 1969, Marie Kaufman, Rio de Janeiro, 1970-72, Museo de Arte Moderno, Rio de Janeiro, 1970-73, Foothill Coll., Los Altos, Calif., 1973-74, Claremont (Calif.) Coll., 1975, U. Wis., Janesville, 1977, Beloit (Wis.) Coll., 1977-78, U. Wis., 1977-78. Printmaking instr. Washington Women's Ctr., 1983; artist-in-residence U. Md., College Park, 1984; printmaking instr. Arlington (Va.) Arts Ctr., 1984-85; prof. St. Mary's (Md.) Coll., 1985; printmaking instr. Arlington (Va.) County Art, 1989; edn. coord. dept. Parks and Recreation and Community Resources Cultural Affairs div. Arlington (Va.) County, 1989—. One woman shows include Wisconsin Women in the Arts Gallery, Madison, 1977, Mbari Art, Washington, D.C., 1981, Miya Gallery, Washington, D.C., 1981, Slavin Gallery, Washington, D.C., 1982, Stuart Mott House, Washington, D.C., 1983, Washington Printmakers Gallery, 1986, 88, St. Peter's Ch., N.Y.C., 1989; mus. and internat. shows include Boston Printmakers: The 39th North Am. Print Exhbn., Framingham, Mass., Jan.-Mar., 1986, Internat. Graphic Arts Found. and Silvermine Guild Arts Ctr., New Canaan, Conn., Feb., 1988, prints: Washington, The Phillips Collection, Washington, D.C., Sept.-Oct., 1988, and numerous others; juried shows include Washington Women's Arts Ctr.: Printmakers VII show, 1985, Washington Womens Arts Ctr., 1981, 82, Seventh Ann. Faber Birren Color Show Nat. Juried Open Exhibit, Stamford, Conn., 1987, Acad. of the Arts 25th Ann. Juried Exhbn., 1989, and numerous others; invitational shows include Office of the Mayor, Mini Art Gallery, Washington, D.C., "Glimpses: Women Printmakers", 1981, Pyramid Paperworks, Balt., 1984, Gallery 10 "Nightmare Show": Washington, D.C., 1987, The Intaglio Process, The Benedicta Art Ctr. Gallery, St. Joseph, Minn., 1988 and numerous others; galleries: Slavin Gallery, Washington, D.C., 1981-83, Washington Printmakers Gallery, Washington, D.C., 1985-90, White Light Collaborative, Inc., N.Y.C., 1988-89, Montana Gallery, Alexandria, Va., 1989-90, and numerous others; collections include Nat. Mus. of Women in the Arts, Washington, D.C., Corcoran Gallery of Art, Washington, D.C., Am. Mus. of Art, Washington, D.C., Museo de Arte Moderno, Buenos Aires. Pres. Washington Area Printmakers, Washington, D.C., 1985-86; pub. rels. dir. Washington Women's Arts Ctr., 1980; bd. dirs. Washington Women's Arts Ctr., 1981-82. Grantee Friends of the Torpedo Factory Art Ctr., Alexandria, Va., 1989; recipient Award of Honorable Mention Nat. Gallery of Art, 1989. Mem. Nat. Print Orgn., Nat. Mus. Women, Pyramid Atlantic, Washington Photography Ctr., Women's Caucus for Art, Coalition Washington Artists. Home: 8106 Norwood Dr Alexandria VA 22309 Office: Lee Arts Ctr 5722 Lee Hwy Arlington VA 22207

WASMUND, SUZANNE, school system administrator; b. Chgo., Apr. 25, 1936; d. James Marvin and Eleanor (Spiker) W. BS, Ind. State U., 1959; MS, U. Ill., 1963. Cert. spl. edn. tchr. Tchr. spl. ed. East Chgo. (Ind.) Pub. Schs., 1959-68, Highland (Ind.) Pub. Schs., 1968-70; coordinator work-study N.W. Ind. Spl. Edn. Coop., Crown Point, 1970-73, supvr., 1973—; supr. student tchrs. Highland, East Chicago, 1966-70. Bd. dirs. United Way, Crown Point, 1984-90; leader spl. edn. Girl Scouts U.S.A., East Chicago, 1966-68. Mem. Ind. Coun. Adminstrs. Spl. Edn., Coun. Exceptional Children, Ind. Vocat. Assn., Ind. Vocat Assn. for Spl. Needs Personnel, LWV, MADD, AAUW, NOW, NRA, Humane Soc., Kappa Kappa Gamma. Republican. Methodist. Home: 249 Evergreen Ln Munster IN 46321

WASMUNDT, SUZANNE MARIE BAYER, neurology program administrator; b. Detroit, Oct. 5, 1950; d. Ernest Fred and May Dorothy (Butler) Bayer; divorced; children: Laura Marie, Mary Yvonne. AA, Macomb City Community Coll., 1973; BSBA, Wayne State U., 1975, postgrad., 1983-84. Dir. dept. neurology program Wayne State U., Detroit, 1976—; treas. Univ. Affiliated Neurologists, Detroit, 1987—. Mem. NAFE, Med. Group Mgmt. Assn., Am. Mgmt. Assn., Am. Fedn. of Musicians. Office: Wayne State U Dept Neurology 4201 St Antoine 6E Detroit MI 48201

WASS, HANNELORE LINA, educator; b. Heidelberg, Germany, Sept. 12, 1926; came to U.S., 1957, naturalized, 1963; d. Hermann and Mina (Lasch) Kraft; m. Irvin R. Wass, Nov. 24, 1959 (dec.); 1 child, Brian C.; m. Harry H. Hisler, Apr. 13, 1978. B.A., Tchrs. Coll., Heidelberg, 1951; M.A., U. Mich., 1960, Ph.D., 1968. Tchr. W. Ger. Univ. Lab. Schs., 1958-60; mem. faculty U. Mich., Ann Arbor, 1958-60, U. Chgo. Lab. Sch., 1960-61, U. Mich., 1963-64, Eastern Mich. U., 1965-69; prof. ednl. psychology U. Fla., Gainesville, 1969—; cons., lectr. in thanatology. Author: The Professional Education of Teachers, 1974; Dying-Facing the Facts, 2d edit., 1988; Death Education: An Annotated Resource Guide, 1980, vol. 2, 1984; Helping Children Cope With Death, 2d edit., 1984; Childhood and Death, 1984; founder, editor Death Studies, 1977—; cons. editor Ednl. Gerontology, 1977—, Death, Aging, and Health Care, Hemisphere Pub. Corp.; contbr. articles to profl. jours. Mem. Am. Psychol. Assn., Gerontol. Soc., Internat. Work Group Dying, Death and Bereavement (bd. dirs.), Assn. Death Edn. and Counseling (bd. dirs.). Home: 6014 NW 54 Way Gainesville FL 32606 Office: U Fla 1418 Norman Hall Gainesville FL 32611

WASSENBERG, EVELYN M., medical and surgical nurse, educator; b. Oct. 8, 1933; d. Patrick A. and Mary A. (Kieffer) L'Ecuyer; m. Maurice P. Wassenberg, Oct. 29, 1955; children: Sherry Ann Gaines, Laura Marie O'Neil. Diploma in nursing, Marymount Sch. Nursing, Salina, Kans., 1955; BS in Nursing, Marymount Coll. of Salina, 1982; MN, Wichita State U., 1987. Dir. nursing svc. Community Meml. Hosp. Inc., Marysville, Kans., 1962-79; house supr. Luth. Hosp., Beatrice, Nebr., 1980-82; primary nurse Beatrice Community Hosp.; instr., coord. Ft. Scott (Kans.) Community Coll., 1983—. Mem. Mary Queen of Angels Cath. Ch. Mem. Am. Nursing Assn., Kans. State Nursing Assn., Sigma Theta Tau. Address: 216 S Crawford Fort Scott KS 66701 Office: 2108 S Horton Fort Scott KS 66701

WASSERMAN, MARLIE P(ARKER), publisher; b. Chgo., Feb. 14, 1947; d. Theodore E. and Faye (Beller) Parker; m. Mark Wasserman, Nov. 24, 1968; children—Aaron David, Danielle Elizabeth. B.A., Duke U., 1969; M.A., Old Dominion U., 1970. Editor, U. Chgo. Press, 1970-78; sr. editor Rutgers U. Press, New Brunswick, N.J., 1978-83, asst. dir. and editor-in-chief, 1983-87, assoc. dir., editor-in-chief, 1987—. Office: Rutgers U Press 109 Church St New Brunswick NJ 08901

WASSERSTEIN, WENDY, playwright; b. Bklyn., Oct. 18, 1950; d. Morris and Lola W. B.A., Mt. Holyoke Coll.; M.A., CCNY, postgrad. Yale Drama Sch. Adapted John Cheever's The Sorrows of Gin for PBS TV series Great Performances; author: (plays) Any Woman Can't, Montpelier Pazazz, When Dinah Shore Ruled the Earth, Uncommon Women and Others, Isn't It Romantic, The Heidi Chronicles, (Recipient Pulitzer prize for drama, 1989, Outer Critics Circle award for best Broadway play, 1989, Antoinette Perry award, 1989, Susan Smith Blackburn prize, 1989), (screenplay, with Christopher Durang) The House of Husbands, (essays) Bachelor Girls, 1990. Office: ICM care Arlene Donovan 40 W 57th St New York NY 10019

WASSON, BARBARA HICKAM, music educator; b. Spencer, Ind., Feb. 12, 1918. Student, DePauw U., 1937-38; BA, Vassar Coll., 1939; MusM, Chgo. Mus. Coll., 1944; postgrad., Ind. U., 1962-63. Founder, co-dir. Wasson Piano Studios, Dayton, 1946—; instr. Cedarville (Ohio) Coll., Dayton, 1970-72; adj. prof. Wright State U., Dayton, 1973-78; asst. prof. U. Cin., 1982-87. Mem. Ohio Music Tchrs. Assn. (pres. 1980-82), Dayton Music Club (pres. 1989—), Mu Phi Epsilon (Dayton Alumnae chpt. pres. 1986-88). Home: 5797 Paddington Rd Dayton OH 45459

WASSON, CATHERINE CHURCH, program manager, consultant; b. Memphis, Jan. 11, 1948; d. Eugene Conner Sr. and Effie Mae (Harpole) Church; m. David George Wasson Sr., Nov. 4, 1966; children: David George Jr., Walter Eugene Harpole Wasson. BS, Miss. State U., Starkville, 1970; MEd, Delta State U., Cleveland, Miss., 1980. Cert. elem. and secondary edn. tchr., Miss. Tchr. Miss. Pub. Schs., Gulfport and Greenville, 1970-80; curriculum coord. Leland (Miss.) Pub. Schs., 1980-85; dir. migrant edn. project Cen. Delta Coop., Leland, 1983-85; instructional coord. Greenville Pub. Schs., 1985-89; program mgr. Sch. Exec. Mgmt. Inst. Miss. Dept. Edn., Jackson, 1989—; cons. Anguilla (Miss.) Sch. Dist., 1983-84; local coord. Program for Rsch. and Evaluation in Pub. Schs., Leland, 1983-85; trainer Miss. Dept. Edn., Jackson, 1987-89, lead project dir., 1989—. Mem. Presbyn. Women, Greenville, 1978-89, Washington Sch. PTA, Greenville, 1980-89, Washington Sch. Athletic Boosters, Greenville, 1980-89, Greenville Edn. Found., Greenville, 1988-89. Mem. Miss. Assn. Supervision and Curriculum Devel., AAUW (com. on women, auction chair 1987-89). Republican. Home: 1609 Lyncrest Jackson MS 39211 Office: Miss Dept Edn Sch Exec Inst PO Box 771 Jackson MS 39205

WASSON, ELEANOR WALSH, volunteer; b. Salt Lake City, Feb. 28, 1908; d. John William and Mary Ann (Dalrymple) Walsh; m. George F. Wasson; children: E. Dianne Wright, Joan Smith. Student, Nat. Park Seminary, Washington D.C., 1926-27, U. Utah, 1927-28, UCLA, 1929-30. Coordinator vol. services UCLA Ctr. for Health Sciences; founder, pres. Internat. Assn. for Vol. Effort, pres. Am. Soc. Dirs. Vol. Services, American Hosp. Assn. Co-producer Exhibit, Continuum, the Immortality Principle. Mem. Adv. com. mem. UCLA Med. Ctr. Aux., Com. on Status of Women, Community Advs. Jr. League of L.A., com. mem. Beyond War, bd. dirs. John Douglas French Found. for Alzheimer's Disease, Voters to End the Arms Race, Women for Internat. Understanding, chmn. planning com. Symposium-Our Common Future, Healing the Planet, 1989; bd. dirs. Santa Cruz Environ. Coun.; mem. EarthSave Found. Recipient Women's Achievement award, Los Angeles Times, 1975, Vol. Spirit award King, Drew Med. Ctr, Aux., 1980, Merit award by the Com. for Adv. Sci. Tng., 1974, Agy. Leadership award, L.A. Welfare Fedn., Disting. Svc. award, UCLA Alumni, award for Advancement Status of Women, award Physicians of Social Responsibility, 1989. Mem. Commonweatlh Club of Calif. Democrat. Episcopalian. Home: 660 Escalona Dr Santa Cruz CA 95060

WASSON, LILA ELIZABETH, educational consultant; b. Bradenton, Fla., Jan. 6, 1924; d. Lawyer and Margaret Jane (Moore) Jenkins; m. Robert Paul Wasson, June 14, 1951; children: Robert Paul Jr., Sandra Wasson Brown, Kathy Elaine. BS, Fla. A&M U., 1945, MS, 1968. Tchr. sci. Union Acad., Bartow, Fla., 1946; tchr. phys. edn. Rosenwald High Sch., Panama City, Fla., 1946-51; subs. tchr. Sun Flower and Wilson Village Schs., Anchorage, 1960-63; elem. tchr. Hanscom Primary Sch., Hanscom AFB, Mass., 1965-87; ednl. cons. J.B. Enterprises, Bedford, Mass., 1990—; master tchr. MA in Teaching program Harvard U., Cambridge, Mass., 1968-71. Author: Fundamentals of Effective Teaching, 1990. Mem. AAUW (rec. sec. 1990-91), LWV, Mass. Ret. Tchrs. Assn. Democrat. Baptist. Home: 26 Gould Rd Bedford MA 01730

WASSON, MARGARET, educator; b. Kaesong, Korea, Mar. 30, 1908; d. Alfred Washington and Mabel (Sutton) W. BA, So. Meth. U., 1930, MA, 1931; EdD, Columbia U., 1951. Cert. tchr., Tex. Dir. of instruction Highland Park Ind. Schs., Dallas, 1947-73; asst. dir. human rels. summer workshop NCCJ, Dallas, 1954-56, 58-59; leader UMW Schs. of Christian Mission, 1978-85. Mem. Univ. Park Master Plan, Dallas, 1988-89; essayist, local chair Goals for Dallas, 1966-67; bd. dirs. Park Cities Hist. Soc., Dallas, 1989—. Recipient Sch. Men's medal Freedoms Found., 1971. Mem. AAUW (pres. 1952-53), Dallas UN Assn., U.S.-China Peoples Friendship Assn., United Meth. Women (pres. 1977-78), Delta Kappa Gamma (pres. 1951-52, 84-86). Democrat. Home: 4831 W Lawther Dr #213 Dallas TX 75214

WASZKIEWICZ, JANICE LYNN VITALE, account representative food products company; b. Akron, Ohio, June 21, 1955; d. Eugene Blaze and Faye (Santacruse) Vitale; m. Stephen Paul Waszkiewicz, May 26, 1979. Student, Kent State U., 1974-76, Akron U., 1976-77. Office, flr. mgr. Eagle Lucky Stores, Houston, Tex., 1979-84; sales rep. N.Y. Life Insur., Houston, 1984-85, Beatrice, Hunt Wesson, Inc., Houston, 1985-87; account rep. Beatrice Hunt Wesson Inc., Houston, 1987—. Vol. actress, soloist Intrepid Troupers (charity perfomances) Houston, 1988, 89; vol. Child Abuse Network of Houston, 1989—; supporter Nat. Wildlife Fed., Greenpeace. Mem. NAFE, Am. Bus. Women's Assn., Theater Under Stars. Home: 2379 Briarwest Blvd #110 Houston TX 77077

WATANABE, JOANNE ELLEN STEEN, controller; b. Chgo., July 13, 1955; d. Henry Justin and Marilyn Eileen (Schulz) Steen; m. Robert T. Watanabe, Aug. 4, 1979; children: Carly Marie, Kelly Anne. BS in Biology cum laude, Calif. State Poly. U., 1977. Mgr. Majestic Party Sales, Temple City, Calif., 1977-80; contr. Be Slim Enterprise, Inc., Costa Mesa, Calif., 1980-89, gen. mgr., 1989—; cons. in field. Treas. Girl Scouts U.S., Fountain Valley, Calif., 1989. Mem. Huntington Beach Mothers Club (bd. dirs. 1985). Republican. Home: 10421 Amberwood Cir Fountain Valley CA 92708

WATANABE, RUTH TAIKO, music historian, library science educator; b. Los Angeles, May 12, 1916; d. Kohei and Iwa (Watanabe) W. B.Mus., U. So. Calif., 1937, A.B., 1939, A.M., 1941, M.Mus., 1942; postgrad., Eastman Sch. Music, Rochester, N.Y., 1942-46, Columbia U., 1947; Ph.D., U. Rochester, 1952. Dir. Sibley Music Library Eastman Sch. of Music, Rochester, N.Y., 1947-84; prof. music bibliography Eastman Sch. of Music, 1978-85, historian, archivist, 1984—; adj. prof. Sch. Library Sci. State U. Coll. at Geneseo, 1975-83; coordinator adult edn. program Rochester Civic Music Assn., 1963-75; mem. adv. com. Hochstein Music Sch.; lectr. on music, book reviewer, 1966—; program annotater Rochester Philharmonic Orch., 1959—. Author: Introduction to Music Research, 1967, Madrigali-II Verso, 1978; editor: Scribners New Music Library, vols. 2, 5, 8, 1973, Treasury of Four Hand Piano Music, 1979; contbr. articles to profl. jours., contbr. symphony orchs. of U.S., 1986, internat. music jours.; modern music librarianship, 1989; contbr. to Festschrift for Carleton Sprague Smith, 1989, DeMúsica Hispana et aliis, 1990. Mem. overseers vis. com. Baxter Sch. Library Sci., Case Western Res. U., 1979-85, Alderman Book Com., 1986-89. Mem. AAUW (Pa.-Del. fellowship. 1949-50, 1st v.p. Rochester 1964-65, mem. N.Y. state bd. 1965-66, mem. nat. com. on soc.'s reflection on arts 1967-69, nat. com. Am. fellowships awards 1969-74, br. pres. 1969-71, hon. co-chair Capital Fund Drive, 1986-88, Woman of Yr. award 1990), Internat. Assn. Music Libraries (2d v.p. commn. on conservatory libraries, commn. research libraries), Am. Musicol. Soc., Music Library Assn. (v.p. 1968-70, citation 1986, mem. editorial bd. 1967—, pres. 1979-81), ALA, Music Library Assn./Internat. Assn. Music Libraries (joint com., 1986-87), Civic Music Assn. Rochester, Riemenscheider Bach Inst. (hon.), Hanson Inst. Am. Music (bd. mem. 1981—), Phi Beta Kappa (pres. Iota chpt. of N.Y. 1969-71), Phi Kappa Phi, Mu Phi Epsilon (gen. chmn. nat. conv. 1956, nat. librarian 1958-60, recipient citation 1977, Ora Ashley Lambke award 1989), Pi Kappa Lambda (sec. 1978—, treas. 1980—), Delta Phi Alpha, Epsilon Phi, Delta Kappa Gamma (parliamentarian 1986-88). Club: Soroptimist (chmn. North Atlantic Conf. 1961, pres. 1964-66), Univ. (Rochester). Home: 111 East Ave Apt 610 Rochester NY 14604 Office: Eastman Sch Music Rochester NY 14604

WATERFORD, CHERI DENISE, naval officer; b. West Memphis, Ark., July 11, 1960; d. Lavaughn and Pearl Jean (Whitley) W. BA in Psychology magna cum laude, San Francisco State U., 1981; AA, Leeward Coll., Pearl City, Hawaii, 1979; MA in Edn., San Diego State U. Cert. ops. officer, communications officer. Commd. ensign USN, 1982, advanced through grades to lt., 1986; ops. and communications officer Naval Facility Pacific Beach, San Nicholas Island, 1982-83, Wash., 1983-86; dept. head navy officer prgms., comdg. officer Capt. S.N. Hallmark, San Diego, 1986-89; comdg. officer Navy ROTC Unit, San Diego, 1989—. Mem. Nat. Naval Officers Assn. (v.p. San Diego chpt., pres. San Diego chpt. 1990), Bus. and Profl. Women's Assn. (2d v.p. Southland chpt.), All Naval Svcs. Officers Profl. Assn. Home: 3175 Cauby St Apt 42 San Diego CA 92110

WATERHOUSE, MONA ELISABETH, artist; b. Grangesberg, Dalarna, Sweden, June 9, 1942; came to U.S., 1966; d. Rolf Folke and Gunborg Sofia (Skog) Johansson; m. John Fredric Waterhouse, Aug. 17, 1961; 1 child, Andrew John. Student, Coventry (Eng.) Coll. Art, 1961-63; BFA summa cum laude, U. Mass., 1975, MAT, 1978. Cert. art instr., Mass., Wis. Tchr. art Covington (Va.) High Sch., 1968-70; art and critic tchr. Clarke Sch. for Deaf, Northampton, Mass., 1976-78; tchr. art John F. Kennedy Jr. High Sch., Florence, Mass., 1978, Westfield (Mass.) State Coll., 1979; instr. art U. Mass., Amherst, 1978-81; tchr. art Hadley (Mass.) Elem. Schs., 1979-81; asst. adminstr. Appleton (Wis.) Gallery Arts, 1981-84; instr. art St. Thomas More Sch., Appleton, 1983-89; free-lance artist Peachtree City, Ga., 1989—; art cons. Dignity of Man Found., San Francisco, 1975-81; art judge various art events; mem. Diocesan Art Curriculum Com., Green Bay, Wis., 1987-89. Active Amnesty Interant., Save the Children. Mem. Nat. Art Edn. Assn., Internat. Assn. Paper Artists, Internat. Soc. Edn. through Art, Wis. Women in Arts, Friends Dard Hunter Paper Mus. Democrat. Home and Office: 102 Delbank Point Peachtree City GA 30269

WATERMAN, HELEN ANNE, engineer; b. Providence, Dec. 22, 1940; d. Frederick Lord and Dorothy Lillian (Dingee) Drowne, Jr.; m. James Alfred Waterman, June 16, 1958; children: James, Richard, John, Robert. Cert., Hall Inst., Pawtucket, R.I., 1980; BS magna cum laude, R.I. Coll., 1990. Designer Amperex Electronics, Smithfield, R.I., 1979-81; product design, field engr. Nat. Air Systems, Inc., Canton, Mass., 1981-83; designer Astro-Med Inc., West Warwick, R.I., 1983-84; tool engr. Stanley-Bostitch, East Greenwich, R.I., 1984—; instr. drafting Community Coll.(Warwick) R.I., mem. speakers bur. Equity in Career Options and Edn. Commr. Smithfield (R.I.) Conservation Comm., 1982-89. Named apprentice Epsilon Pi Tau, Providence, 1985. Mem. NAFE, Am. Design Drafting Assn., Soc. Mfg. Engrs. chpt. 53 (v. chmn. 1989—,Sigma Beta Frat. (treas. 1988—). Baptist. Home: 102 Blackamore Ave Cranston RI 02910

WATERS, BARBARA KRUMSIEG, divorce and family mediator, psychotherapist; b. Chgo., Mar. 5, 1942; d. Edwin C. and Dorothy M. (Taggart) Krumsieg; m. James H. Waters, June 19, 1965 (div. Oct. 1986); children: Susan Margaret, Eric David. AB, Smith Coll., Northampton, Mass., 1963; MAT, Yale U., 1965; MA, Antioch U., 1987. Bar: Vt. 1983. Phys. sci. aide U.S. Geol. Survey, Boston, 1963-64; sci. tchr. Winooski High Sch., Winooski, Vt., 1965-69; elem. tchr. Sheldon Cen. Sch., Sheldon, Vt., 1970-71; tchr., dir. Spring St. PreSchool, Swanton, Vt., 1972-76; law clk. Agel, Carroll & Sussman, Burlington, Vt., 1979-82, Carroll & Sussman, Burlington, 1982-83; divorce & family mediator, psychotherapist Burlington, 1987—; mediator Vt. Family Mediation Program, Worcester, 1987-89. Mem. Vt. Bar Assn. (family law com.), Vt. Mediators Assn. (standards com.), Vt. Psychol. Assn. (assoc. continuing edn. com.), Acad. Family Mediators. Office: 2 Church St Burlington VT 05401

WATERS, BETTY LOU, newspaper reporter, writer; b. Texarkana, Tex., June 13, 1943; d. Chester Hinton and Una Erby (Walls) W. AA, Texarkana Jr. Coll., 1963; BA, East Tex. State U., 1965. Gen. assignment reporter Galveston County Pub. Co., Galveston and Texas City, 1965-68; news and feature writer Ind. and Daily Mail, Anderson, S.C., 1968-69; reporter Citizen-Times newspaper, Asheville, N.C., 1969-74; edn. and med. reporter News Star World Pub. Co., Monroe, La., 1974-79; reporter, writer Delta Democrat Times, Greenville, Miss., 1980-89; staff writer Tyler (Tex.) Morning Telegraph, 1990—. Recipient 1st place award for articles La. Press Women's Contest, 1978, 1st place for interview, 1979; news media award N.C. Easter Seal Soc., 1973; 3d place award for feature writing Miss. Press Assn., 1984, for gen. news, 1983, for investigative reporting, 1988, 1st place for best series of articles, 1990; hon. mentions Tex. AP, 1966. Mem. Sigma Delta Chi.

WATERS, ELLEN MAUREEN, publishing executive, writer; b. Liberty, Ill., Aug. 19, 1938; d. Charles Francis and Virginia Elizabeth (Robinson) Linker; m. Gerald Louis Waters, Jan. 18, 1957 (div. 1990); children: Tamara, Gerri-Layne, Christina, Andrea. Student, Baker U., 1977-82, 88—; grad., Auila Coll., 1990. Typesetter, reporter Baldwin (Kans.) Ledger, 1967-73; editor Wellsville (Kans.) Globe, 1973-74; asst. registrar Baker U., Baldwin City, 1975-77, registrar, 1977-82; mng. editor mag. design and prodn. Southwind Pub. Co., Prairie Village, Kans., 1985—; freelance writer, Baldwin City, 1974—, Overland Park, 1984—; owner, operator Watermarks Editorial Svc., Overland Park; lectr. on mentoring. Editor, publ. Mentor newsletter. Mem. Nat. Writers Club (manuscript critic ghostwriter 1987—). Office: PO Box 4382 Overland Park KS 66204 also: Southwind Pub Co 8340 Mission Rd Ste 106 Prairie Village KS 66206

WATERS, MARTHA ELIZABETH, lawyer; b. Birmingham, Ala., Jan. 17, 1959; d. Daniel Howard and Martha Virginia (Canant) W. BSBA summa cum laude, U. Ala., 1981, JD with honors, 1984. Bar: Tex. 1984, U.S. Dist. Ct. (no. dist.) Tex. 1984, U.S. Dist. Ct. (ea. dist.) Tex. 1987, U.S. Dist. Ct. (so. and we. dists.) Tex. 1988, U.S. Claims Ct. 1987, U.S. Ct. Appeals (fed.

cir.) 1989. Assoc. Baker, Mills & Glast, Dallas, 1984-90; dir. Baker, Glast & Middleton, Dallas, 1990—. Fellow Tex. Bar Found.; mem. Dallas Assn. Young Lawyers (sec. 1989, treas. 1990—), Order of Coif, Beta Gamma Sigma. Home: 6142 Woodcrest Ln Dallas TX 75214 Office: Baker Glast & Middleton 2001 Ross Ave Ste 500 Dallas TX 75201

WATERS, MAXINE, congresswoman; b. St. Louis, Aug. 15, 1938; d. Remus and Velma (Moore) Carr; m. Sidney Williams, July 23, 1977; children by previous marriage: Edward, Karen. Grad. in sociology Calif. State U., Los Angeles; honorary doctorates, Spelman Coll., N.C. Agrl. & Tech. State U. Former tchr. Head Start; mem. Calif. Assembly from dist. 48, 1976-91, Dem. caucus chair, 1984; mem. 102nd Congress from Dist. 29, Calif., 1991—. Mem. Dem. Nat. Com.; del. Dem. Nat. Conv., 1972, 76, 80, 84, 88, mem. rules com. 1984; mem. Nat. Adv. Com. for Women, 1978—. Office: Calif State Assembly State Capitol Sacramento CA 95814*

WATERS, SHEILA MARIE, cultural organization administrator; b. Coshocton, Ohio, Dec. 29, 1961; d. William Harold and Shirley Sue (Bauer) W. BA, Denison U., 1984; MA, Ohio U., 1988. Asst. to dir. Zanesville (Ohio) Art Ctr., 1984-86; art instr. Zanesville Art Ctr., 1988; dir. Pomerene Fine Arts Ctr., Coshocton, 1988—. Exhibited photographs in one-woman shows and group exhbns., 1980, 84—. Bd. dirs., Big Bros./Big Sisters, Coshocton, 1989. Mem. Ohio Regional Assn. Concert and Lecture Enterprises, Rotary. Office: Pomerene Fine Arts Ctr 317 Mulberry St Coshocton OH 43812

WATERSTON, REBECCA LYNN, recycling company executive; b. Mpls., Oct. 15, 1950; d. Russell Carl Westberg and Betty Elizabeth (Tranberg) Kallstrom; m. Bruce Waterston, June, 1973 (div. 1976); 1 child, Nathaniel. BS, Mankato State U., 1973; postgrad., U. Minn. Lead tchr., spl. edn. Burnsville (Minn.) Schs., 1976-80; copywriter, acct. exec. Princeton Advt., St. Paul, 1980-81; owner, acct. exec. Waterston-Mazal & Mazal, Golden Valley, Minn., 1984-88; with Liberty Diversified Industries, Mpls., 1981-88; mgr. Diversified Recycling Systems, Mpls., 1988—; cons., speaker in field. Editor: Burnsville Tchr. Fedn. newspaper, 1978-80; contbr. articles, poems, stories to various publs.; patentee in recycling field. Del. Minn. Dem. Conv., 1985; fundraiser Minn. Assn. Retarded Citizens, 1983; tchr. Adult Retarded Social Group, Mpls., 1983-84; mem. Blue Ribbon Metro Bus. Commn. on Solid Waste. Recipient Hon. Mention award Star & Tribune Club News, 1988. Mem. Twin West C. of C., NAFE, St. Paul C. of C., Minn. Coalition Recyclers, Nat. Recycling Coalition, Bus. and Profl. Assn., Minn. Author's Guild (pres. 1978-79). Mem. Christian Missionary Alliance. Office: Diversified Recycling 5606 N Hwy 169 Minneapolis MN 55428

WATFORD, JAMIE DENISE (JAMIE DENISE JONES), mechanical engineer; b. Gadsden, Ala., Aug. 16, 1955; d. James A. and Jennie Ruth (Amberson) Jones; m. William Edward Reinecke, May 21, 1977 (div. Nov. 1981); 1 child, Jennifer Louise; m. Robert Michael Watford Jr., Aug. 14, 1982; 1 child, Robert James. Student, Jacksonville (Ala.) State U., 1975; BSME, U. Ala., 1977. With chem. div. PPG Industries, Lake Charles, La., 1976, summers 1977-79, mech. engr., 1979-80, design engr., mech., 1980-81, tech. asst. maintenance, 1981-85, design engr. mech., 1981-85; mech. engr. maintenance dept. Shawnee Fossil Plant TVA, West Paducah, Ky., 1986—. Seamstress Joan Crawford Sch. of Dance, Paducah, 1990—; pianist music Makers Choir, Reidland Bapt. Ch., Paducah, 1990—, asst. dir. adult handbell choir, 1990—, dir. youth handbell choir, 1988. Recipient one of Outstanding Young Women Am. award, 1979. Mem. NAFE, TVA Engrng. Assn., Capstone Engrng. Soc., U. Ala. Nat. Alumni Assn. Delta Gamma (Outstanding Pledge 1974), Pi Tau Sigma. Home: 1005 Tyree Rd Paducah KY 42003 Office: TVA Shawnee Fossil Plant PO Box 2000 West West Paducah KY 42086

WATFORD, PAULA SARGENT, recycling company executive; b. Atlanta, May 30, 1954; d. Paul Richardson and Mary Margaret Sybil (Bolton) Sargent; m. Victor L. Watford, Apr. 18, 1969 (div. 1972); children: Stephanie Marie, Michael Lee. With Sheraton Inn, Rome, Ga., 1978-80; night mgr. Crown Liquors, St. Petersburg, Fla., 1984-86; mgr. Ace Recycling, Inc., St. Petersburg, 1986—. Designer kennel advertisements. Mem. Nat. Beagle Club Am. (chmn. com. 1985), Owner Handler Assn. Home: 2767 52d Ave N Saint Petersburg FL 33714 Office: Ace Recycling 1963 4th Ave S Saint Petersburg FL 33712

WATKINS, DIANE MARGARET OTTO, polygraph examiner, army officer; b. Bklyn., Apr. 5, 1955; d. George Jacob and June Emily (Becker) W. AS, SUNY, Albany, 1979; BS, U. Md. European Div., West Germany, 1985; MS, Armstrong State Coll., Savannah, Ga., 1990; grad., Dept. Def. Polygraph Inst., 1988. Cert. U.S. Army polygraph examiner, criminal investigator. Commd. U.S. Army, 1973, advanced through grades; spl. agt. in charge Walter Reed Resident Agy., Washington, Mainz Resident Agy., Germany, Hunter Br. Office, Savannah; ops. officer Ft. Stewart (Ga.) dist. U.S. Army Criminal Investigation Command; polygraph examiner U.S. Army Criminal Investigation Command, Ft. Knox, Ky. Decorated three Meritorious Svc. medals, Army Commendation medal. Mem. Am. Polygraph Assn., Warrant Officer Assn., Fraternal Order Police, Golden Field Day (chmn. fund raising com. 1989-91). Address: Ft Knox Dist 3d Region USACIDC Fort Knox KY 40121

WATKINS, JULIA M., college dean; b. Pocatello, Idaho, Sept. 24, 1941; d. Emory J. and Elaine (Steele) Herndon; m. Dennis A. Watkins, Sept. 20, 1963; children: Matthew, Christopher, Andrew. BS, U. Utah, 1963, MSW, 1965, PhD, 1970. Chmn. dept. sociology and social work U. Maine, Orono, acting dean Coll. Arts and Scis., dean Coll. Social and Behavioral Scis. Author: Social Policy and the Rural Setting; contbr. articles to profl. jours. Grantee Adminstrn. on Aging, Am. Assn. Ret. Persons Andrus Found.; ACE fellow. Mem. Nat. Assn. Social Workers, Gerontol. Soc. Am., Am. Assn. Higher Edn., Phi Kappa Phi. Address: 122 Grant St Bangor ME 04401

WATKINS, PIA MARIE, mechanical engineer; b. Kingston, Jamaica, July 24, 1964; came to U.S., 1978; d. Edwin Horatio and Kathleen (Martin) W.; m. James Summerton, Aug. 27, 1988. BSME with honors, U. Miami, Coral Gables, Fla., 1985. Sr. analytical engr. Pratt and Whitney Corp., West Palm Beach, Fla., 1985—. Bd. dirs. Jupiter (Fla.) Homeowners Orgn. Mem. ASME (assoc., sec. 1984—), Soc. Women Engrs. (Service Award Fla. chpt. 1986). Home: 14732 N 69th Dr Palm Beach Gardens FL 33418 Office: Pratt and Whitney PO Box 2691 West Palm Beach FL 33402

WATKINS, ROSALIND JEANNETTE, owner, advertising executive; b. Many, La., Sept. 17, 1942; d. Hanson A. and Imogene (Alford) Teague; m. Jerry M. Watkins, Mar. 13, 1970 (dec. Aug. 1987). Student, Kilgore Jr. Coll., 1964, Hinds Jr. Coll., Raymond, Miss., 1988. Legal sec. Dist. Atty. Office, Longview, Tex., 1960-69; sec. Tom Wheatley, Ind. Oil. Operator, Denver, 1969-71; sales person Dixie Advt., Jackson, Miss., 1971-83; owner Rosalind Watkins & Assocs., Jackson, 1983—. Mem. Sales and Mktg. Execs. Jackson (pres. 1987-88), Willowwood Devel. Ctr. (bd. dirs. 1989—), Specialty Advt. Assn. Internat. (distbrs. com. 1988-90). Office: Rosalind Watkins Assocs Inc 5738 C Hwy 80 West Jackson MS 39209

WATKINS, SALLY MARIE, nursing administrator; b. Roswell, N.Mex., Aug. 17, 1954; d. William Chester and Pauline Ruth (Cumpsten) Allbright; divorced; 1 child, Avery Marie. BS in Nursing, U. Tex., Houston, 1976; MS, U. Utah, 1986. Staff nurse Univ. Hosp., Salt Lake City, 1976-77, 78-79, head nurse, 1980-84, dir. nursing, 1984-90; asst. head nurse St. Lukes Hosp., Boise, Idaho, 1977-78; assoc. adminstr. nursing Tacoma (Wash.) Gen. Hosp., 1990—; adj. asst. dir. parent-child div. coll. nursing U. Utah; lectr. in field. Mem. Healthy Mothers/Healthy Babies Coalition Utah, Salt Lake City, 1986-90; troop leader Girl Scouts U.S., Salt Lake City, 1987-90. Mem. Am. Orgn. Nursing Execs., Wash. Orgn. Nurse Execs., Nurses Assn. of Am. Coll. Ob-Gyn, Utah. Perinatal Assn. (sec. 1988-90), Utah Nurses Assn. (pres. dist. 1 1988-90), Sigma Theta Tau. Office: Tacoma Gen Hosp 315 S K St Tacoma WA 98405

WATLACK, LINDA ANN, director computer resource center; b. N.Y.C., Aug. 3, 1959; d. John Matthew and Nerida Jean (Perez) W. BA, Hampshire Coll., 1985; grad., Boston Coll., 1986; diploma, Suffolk U. Cert. instr. vocat. edn., Mass. Researcher Mayor's Office/Women's Affairs, Boston, 1985-86; instr. Am. Bus. Ins., Boston, 1986-88; dir. computer resource ctr. Suffolk U. Law Sch., Boston, 1988—; freelance tng. and system devel., non-profit ednl. inst., Boston, 1985—; video festival judge Internat. TV Assn., Boston, 1990; system operator, bulletin bd., Suffolk U. Law Sch., 1990. Producer, rsch: (video) Indian Burial Grounds, 1990; contbr. articles to profl. jours., newsletter. Counselor, sec. Help Phone, Mass., 1975-77; computer cons. various city and statewide polit. races, Boston, 1985-89. Mem. Assn. Computing Machinery, Network for Women in Politics and Govt., Computing Profls. for Social Responsibility, Soc. for Mgmt. of Profl. Computing, Inc., Mass. Women's Polit. Caucus. Democrat. Home: 199 Mass Ave Boston MA 02115 Office: Suffolk Univ Law Sch 41 Temple St Boston MA 02114

WATLEY, MARTHA JONES, health care executive; b. Jacksonville, Fla., July 18, 1936; d. Louis Kato and Annie Mae (Hartley) Jones; m. George Benjamin Watley, July 13, 1957 (dec. Aug. 1983); children: Cynthia, Harry II, Phyllis, Kevin, George IV, Baron, Sandee, Stacey. ADN, Cameron U., 1968; BA, U. Okla., 1975, MEd, 1976. RN; lic. profl. counselor; cert. drug and alcohol counselor; cert. chemotherapist; cert. grant writer and fundraiser. Emergency supr. Comanch County Meml. Hosp., Lawton, Okla., 1963-69; nursing instr. Great Plains Area Sch., Lawton, 1969-72; nurse counselor Reynolds Army Hosp., Ft. Sill, Okla., 1972-73; nurse-therapist, supr. VA Med. Ctr., Oklahoma City, 1975-78; staff psychologist Tri City Youth and Family Svc., Choctaw, Okla.; exec. dir. Arcadia Youth Family Multipurpose Assn., Arcadia, Okla., 1978-79; chief exec. officer Arcadia Youth & Family Life Ednl. Assn., 1979—; chief exec. officer Family Life Edn. Assocs., Oklahoma City, 1979—, program developer, 1981-86; program developer Family Life Ctrs., Irving, Tex., 1981-86, chief exec. officer, 1986—; staff psychologist, trainer Harbingers Women Alcohol Treatment, Oklahoma City, 1977-79; cons. spl. survey projects Tri City Youth & Family, Choctaw, 1978-79; cons. spl. project aging Am. Pers. and Guidance, Midwest City, Okla., 1981. Author: Family Life Education; Family Life Centers and Life Centers, 1979. Instr. ARC, Oklahoma City, 1975—; trainer of trainers Nat. Inst. Drug Abuse, Oklahoma City, 1978; trainer Gordon's Effectiveness P.E.T. Y.E.T. T.E.T., Tex, Oklahoma City, 1976, Evangelism Explosion Internat., Dallas, 1981. Named one of Top 20 Adminstrs. in Mental Health, NIMH, 1986. Mem. Am. Assn. Mental Health Counselors, Am. Assn. Counseling & Devel. (Nat. Disting. Svc. Registry 1989), Assn. Supervisors Curriculum Devel., Okla. Assn. Counseling & Devel., Okla. Assn. Mental health Counselors. Democrat. Baptist. Office: Family Life Edn Assn Family Life Ctrs PO Box 165065 Irving TX 75016

WATMAN, CAROLYN PRESCOTT, personnel executive; b. Altus, Okla., July 5, 1944; d. John Carl and Helen Loraine (Eikner) Prescott; B.B.A., U. Okla., 1966; postgrad. North Tex. State U.; M.A., U. N.Mex., 1985; m. Gerald S. Watman, July 31, 1975 (div. 1988); 1 dau., Carrie Michele. Personel mgr. Neiman-Marcus, Dallas, 1966-72; dir. records and research Hockaday Sch., Dallas, 1972; dir. personnel and payroll Herman Marcus, Inc., Dallas, 1972-75; pvt. personnel cons., 1973-75; v.p. dir. Santa Fe Merc. Co., Inc., 1975-81; instr. mktg. mgmt. No. N.Mex. Community Coll., Espanola, 1981-83; instr. mktg. Los Alamos High Sch., 1983-85; instr. bus. adminstrn. Santa Fe Community Coll., 1984-85; personnel rep. Dillard Dept. Stores, Inc., 1985-86; mgr. bus. Corrections Corp. Am., Santa Fe, 1986—; part time instr. bus. Santa Fe Community Coll., 1989—. Vol. Voter Registrar, Santa Fe County. Mem. Am. Soc. Personnel Adminstrs., Am. Correctional Assn., Am. Vocat. Assn., N.Mex. Vocat. Assn., N.Mex. Correctional Assn., No. N.Mex. Personnel Assn., N.Mex. C. of C. (edn. coun.), Pilot Club (area leader local chpt. edn. coun., v.p.). Episcopalian.

WATROUS, JOAN CHEEVERS, state government legislative administrator; b. Binghamton, N.Y.; d. Thomas Joseph and Antoinette Marie (Casella) Cheevers; divorced; children: Susan Marie, Stephen Richard. BA, SUNY, Binghamton, 1963; MS, Syracuse U., 1974. With guest relations dept. NBC Studios, N.Y.C.; host/producer talk show Stas. WCNY-TV and WNYS-TV, Syracuse, N.Y., 1971-73; dir. pub. relations N.Y. Urban Devel. Corp., Radisson, N.Y., 1973-75; mgr. mktg. Sta. WUNC, Chapel Hill, N.C., 1975-77; account exec. Sta. WPTF-TV, Raleigh, N.C., 1977-79; v.p. Broome County C. of C., Binghamton, 1980-84; dir. mktg. Pub. Broadcasting, Binghamton, 1984-86; dep. dir. N.Y. Senate Commerce Com., Albany, 1986-89; sr. policy analyst N.Y. Senate Rsch., Albany, 1989—; community ambassador to West Pakistan; mem. regional adv. bd. SBA, 1988—. Bd. dirs. Tri-Cities Opera Co., Binghamton, 1980—. Mem. Albany N.Y. Jr. League, SUNY-Binghamton Alumni Assn. (bd. dirs., past pres.), SUNY-Binghamton Found. Roman Catholic. Home: 2417 High Ave Vestal NY 13850 Office: NY Senate Rsch Senate Chamber Albany NY 12247

WATSON, ADA LOUISE MITCHELL, biotechnology company administrator, researcher; b. Gloucester, Mass., Dec. 8, 1951; d. William Low, Sr. and Leona (Locke) Mitchell; m. Donald R. Watson, Sr., July 3, 1971; chldren: Donald R., Jr., Thomas Locke. BA, Drew U., 1975. Rsch. asst., sec. Rockefeller U., N.Y.C., 1975-77; rsch. technician Dana-Farber Cancer Inst., Boston, 1977-80, immunogenetics lab. supr., 1980-85, assoc. in pathology, 1985—; immunogenetics supr. The Ctr. for Blood Rsch., Boston, 1983-86, rsch. assoc., 1986-88; assoc. in pathology Harvard Med. Sch., Boston, 1985—; mgr. adminstrn. Internat. Biotechnology Labs., Inc., Cambridge, Mass., 1988—; mem. lab. safety com. Dana-Farber Cancer Inst., Boston, 1986-88, mem. animal care and use com., 1988; mem. joint com. on status of women Harvard Med., Dental, and Pub. Health Schs., Boston, 1988; mem. internal biohazard com. Internat. Biotechnology Labs, Inc., Cambridge, 1988—. Contbr. articles to profl. jours. Mem. com. to study excellence in edn. sub-com. Gloucester Sch. Com., 1983; cons. N.E. Regional Red Cross Blood Program, Boston, 1983-84; bd. dirs. Am. Cancer Soc., Gloucester, 1977-78, Open Door/Food Pantry, Gloucester, 1986-87. Methodist. Home: 30 Gloucester Ave Gloucester MA 01930 Office: Internat Biotechnology Labs 67 Rogers St Cambridge MA 02142

WATSON, ANN MCWHINNEY, advertising executive; b. Denver, Feb. 22, 1925; d. Leroy and Alice Barse (Houston) McWhinney; m.Robert Warren Watson, Aug. 6, 1948 (dec. 1959); children: Christine, Robert, Barbara (dec.), Jeffrey, Candace. MA, Skidmore Coll., Saratoga Springs, N.Y., 1946; postgrad., U. Denver, 1947-48. Asst. statistician Opinion Rsch. Ctr., Denver, 1946-49; media asst. Rippey, Henderson, Bucknum, Denver, 1961-65; media dir. Frye, Sills & Bridges, Denver, 1966-68, Neuwirth-Koller, Inc., Denver, 1976-89; co-owner, mgr. Wrenn-Watson Media Rsch., Denver, 1969-74; owner, mgr. Watson Rsch., Denver, 1975-76, Watson Media Svc., Denver, 1989—; guest faculty Colo. State U., Ft. Collins, 1984-89; speaker in field. Pres. Women's Med. Aux., Cortez, Colo., 1958, treas., Denver, 1960-61; chair Montezuma County Rep. party, Cortez, 1957-58. Mem. Denver Advt. Fedn. (bd. dirs. 1966-68, v.p. 1968-69, chair rsch. for centennial 1989—). Episcopalian. Office: Watson Media Svc 550 E 12th Ave STe 907 Denver CO 80203

WATSON, BEVERLY ANN, nurse; b. Springfield, Mass., Aug. 31, 1948; d. Paul Michael and Ann Theresa (Wheeler) Urekew; m. Kenneth A. Watson Jr., Dec. 17, 1977. Diploma in Nursing, Framingham Union Hosp., 1970. RN; cert. nursing supr., Ga. Staff nurse Hartford (Conn.) Hosp.; charge nurse Ridgeview Nursing Home, Springfield, Vespers Nursing Home, Wilkesboro, N.C.; supr. North Macon Health Care, Macon, Ga. Mem. ANA, Ga. Nurses Assn., Assn. Practitioners in Infection Control. Address: PO Box 13144 Macon GA 31208

WATSON, CAROL, accountant; b. Nagoya, Japan, Apr. 10, 1957; (parents Am. citizens); d. Crestle and Annie Lee (Brown) W. Student, U. Md., 1975-77, Prince Georges Community Coll., 1979; BS, Bowie (Md.) State Coll., 1981; postgrad., Cen. Mich. U., 1989—. Operating acct. Maritime Adminstrn., Washington, 1981-85; supervisory cost acct. Dept. Transp., Office of Sec. of Transp., Washington, 1985-87; operating acct. spl. programs and analysis sect. U.S. Dept. Treasury, Washington, 1987, operating acct. U.S. Mint, 1987—; tax cons. H&R Block, Washington, 1982-84. tutor Hine Jr. High Sch., Washington, 1985-86; citizen ambassador All China Women's Fedn., Boise, 1987. Served with USAFR, 1985—. Named Outstanding Airman of Yr. 459th Mil. Airlift Wing, Andrews AFB, 1987. Mem. Nat. Assn. Female Execs., Assn. for Profl. And Exec. Women. Democrat. Home: 117 Panorama Dr Oxon Hill MD 20745 Office: Benchmark Communications Mgmt 2164 Wisconsin Ave NW Washington DC 20007

WATSON, CAROL ANN, hospital administrator; b. Des Moines, Apr. 20, 1948; d. John Francis Jr. and Phyllis Arlene (Epps) Mason; m. Douglas Dean Watson, Dec. 9, 1970; children: Michael Douglas, Kari Ann. BS in Nursing, U. Iowa, 1970, MA, 1973, PhD, 1979. RN, Iowa. Staff nurse U. Iowa Hosps., Iowa City, 1970-71; instr. U. Iowa, Iowa City, 1972-76, adminstrv. asst., 1976-77, asst. prof., 1979-81; asst. prof. Grand View Coll., Des Moines, 1977-80, assoc. prof., 1980-81; staff nurse Mercy Hosp. Med. Ctr., Des Moines, 1980-81; clin. dir. nursing U. Iowa Hosps., Des Moines, 1981-87; assoc. adminstr. Mercy Med. Ctr., Cedar Rapids, Iowa, 1987—; mem. Iowa Bd. Nursing Statewide Planning, Des Moines, 1987-91, Iowa Adv. Coun. on Head Injury, Des Moines, 1989-92; bd. dirs. Am. Bd. Neurosci. Nursing, N.Y.C., 1987-88, v.p., 1985-86, pres., 1986-87; investigator in field. Editorial bd. Series of Nursing Adminstrn., Redwood, Calif., 1988—, Applied Nursing Rsch., Phila., 1988—; co-author books; contbr. articles to profl. jours. Chair Iowa Head and Spinal Cord Injury Prevention Project, Waterloo, 1987—; mem. Nat. Head Injury Found., Boston, 1982. Nursing scholar Gamma chpt. Sigma Theta Tau, Iowa City, 1973, Zeta Chi chpt. Sigma Theta Tau, Iowa City, 1984. Mem. Am. Orgn. Nurse Execs., Iowa Orgn. Nurse Execs. (treas. 1990), Am. Nurses Assn., Iowa Nurses Assn., Am. Assn. Neurosci. Nurses, World Fedn. Neurosci. Nurses, Iowa Head Injury Assn. (bd. dirs. 1982—, editor newsletter 1984-86). Democrat. Home: 43 Lakeview Dr N Iowa City IA 52240 Office: Mercy Med Ctr 701 10th St SE Cedar Rapids IA 52403

WATSON, CATHERINE ELAINE, journalist; b. Mpls., Feb. 9, 1944; d. Richard Edward and LaVonne (Slater) W.; m. Al Sicherman; children: Joseph Sicherman, David Sicherman. B.A. in Journalism, U. Minn., 1967; M.A. in Teaching, Coll. of St. Thomas, 1971. Reporter Mpls. Star Tribune, 1966-72; editor Picture mag., 1972-78, Travel sect., 1978—. Author: Travel Basics, 1984. Contbr. articles to newspapers and travel mags. Newspaper Mag. Picture Editor's award Pictures of Year Competition, 1974, 75; awards writing and photography Soc. Am. Travel Writers, 1983, 84, 85, 86, 87, 88, 89. Mem. Am. Newspaper Guild, Soc. Am. Travel Writers, Minn. Exec. Women in Tourism, Phi Beta Kappa, Kappa Tau Alpha, Alpha Omicron Pi. Office: 425 Portland Ave Minneapolis MN 55488*

WATSON, CHARLOTTE ALLENE, social services administrator; b. Hobbs, N.Mex., Sept. 7, 1953; d. Charles Ernest Watson and Bennie Allene (Johnson) Huddleston. Student, Austin Coll., 1981. Cert. peace officer, Tex.; cert. indsl. firefighter, Tex. Technician quality control Tex. Instruments, Inc., Sherman, 1972-77, specialist tng. and devel., 1977-84, indsl. hygiene technician, 1984-86; exec. dir. My Sisters' Place, Yonkers (N.Y.) Women's Task Force, Inc., 1986—; co-founder Grayson County Women's Crisis Line, Inc., Sherman, also bd. dirs., pres.; bd. dirs. Women Care, Inc., 1988T, v.p. 1989—. Res. officer Sherman Police Dept., 1985-86; vol. Bella Abzug for Congress, 1986, Ann Richards for Tex. State Treas., 1980, Ronnie Eldridge for N.Y.C. Coun., 1989, Jeanine Ferris Pirro for Weschester County Ct. Judge, 1990; chair legis. com. Westchester Coalition Family Violence Agys., 1986; founding mem. Coalition for Responsible Govt. Funding N.Y., 1987—; mem. adv. bd. Women's Info. Network, 1988—; mem. com. Women's Equality Day and Take Back the Night events, Dallas, 1979-86; bd. dirs. Greater Westchester Human Rights Fund, 1987, Lebian/Gay Democrats Tex., 1980-86, Tex. Lesbian/Gay Rights Advs., 1980-86, N.Y. State Coalition Against Domestic Violence, 1986—, chairwoman membership com., 1988-89; co-founder Survivors Healing Collective. Mem. NOW (chpt. pres. 1978-81, chairwoman Domestic Abuse and Incest Task Force N.Y. State chpt. 1989—), Nat. Coalition Against Domestic Violence. Home: 247 E 235th St New York NY 10470 Office: My Sisters' Place Inc PO Box 1245 Yonkers NY 10702

WATSON, CHRISTINE DONNA, accounting manager, consultant; b. Carmel, Calif., Dec. 20, 1958; d. Thomas Harold and Barbara Glee (Leedom) W. BBA, Suffolk U., 1980, MBA, 1981. CPA. Office acct. Deloitte Haskins & Sells, Boston, 1979-81; staff auditor Wolf & Co. Mass., Boston, 1981-82; controller Capron Lighting & Sound Co., Needham, Mass., 1982-83, BFC Enterprises, Inc., Boston, 1983-84; mgr. acctg. Hersey Products Inc., Dedham, Mass., 1984-87; acct. mgr. The Pathfinder Fund, Watertown, Mass., 1988—; cons. Boston Waterfront Realty, 1979-80, Grinnell Fire Protection System, Cleve., N.C., 1987, Ctr. Design Industry Schedule, 1981, 82, Harvard U., 1981-83, Brigham and Women's Hosp., 1983-84. Commd. officer Army N.G., 1977—. Recipient Mass. Medal Merit, 1987; fellow Suffolk U. 1980. Mem. Nat. Assn. Accts., Nat. Assn. Women Accts., Mass. Soc. CPA's., Nat. Speleological Soc., Tech Sqs. Club, Boston Grotto Club.

WATSON, CLAIRE, sales professional; b. Selma, Ala., Aug. 21, 1936; d. Leslie Warren and Norma (Green) W.; children: Susan, Steven. BS, U. Ala., 1958; postgrad., Volusia Coll., 1970, Seminole Coll., 1978. Sec., treas. Watson Sales Co., Maitland, Fla., 1963-80; pres. Watson Sales Co., Altamonte Spring, Fla., 1980—; v.p., owner S&C Assocs., Altamonte Spring, 1984—; sec., bd. dirs. Fla. Bus. and Industry Recycling Program, 1987—. Pres. English Estates Civic Assn., Maitland, 1961; bd. dirs. Fla. Symphony, Orlando, 1960-70, PESO, Orlando, 1969-70. Named one of Outstanding Young Women Yr., Jr. League, 1968, Outstanding Young Women Am., 1970. Mem. Fla. Soft Drink Suppliers (pres. 1983-84), Ala. Soft Drink Suppliers (pres. 1984-85), Chi Omega Alumnae Assn. Presbyterian. Club: Citrus. Home: 108 Camphor Tree Ln Altamonte Springs FL 32714 Office: 224 W Center St Ste 1016 Altamonte Springs FL 32714

WATSON, CYNTHIA LOU, registered nurse; b. Greensburg, Pa., Nov. 12, 1952; d. Willis Ray and Ella Marie (Copper) W. Diploma in nursing, West Pa. Hosp., 1973; BS in Nursing, Pa. State U., 1982; MS, U. Pitts., 1989. RN, Pa. Nursing asst. Monsour Med. Ctr., Jeannette, Pa., 1971-73, staff nurse, 1973-75, supervisory nurse, 1975-79, dir. utilization review, 1979-84; dir. utilization review and quality assurance OPTIONS-Health Care Cost Containment, Pitts., 1984—; instr. McKain Edn. and Devel., Ford City, Pa., 1983-85. Mem. Am. Med. Peer Review Assn., Western Pa. Hosp. Nurses Alumni Assn., Pa. State Alumni Assn., Hosp. Assn. of Pa., Nat. Assn. of Quality Assurance Profls., Pa. Assn. of Quality Assurance Profls., Western Pa. Assn. Quality Assurance Profls. Democrat. Methodist. Home: 802 Gaskill Ave Jeannette PA 15644 Office: OPTIONS Health Care 400 Penn Ctr Blvd Pittsburgh PA 15235

WATSON, DIANE EDITH, state legislator; b. Los Angeles, Nov. 12, 1933; d. William Allen Louis and Dorothy Elizabeth (O'Neal) Watson. B.A., UCLA, 1956; M.S., Calif. State U., Los Angeles. Tchr., sch. psychologist Los Angeles Unified Sch. Dist., 1960-69, 73-74; assoc. prof. dept. guidance Calif. State U., Los Angeles, 1969-71; health occupations specialist Bur. Indsl. Edn., Calif. Dept. Edn., 1971-73; mem. Los Angeles City Bd. Edn., 1975-78; mem. Calif. Senate from dist. 28, 1978—, chairperson health and welfare com., Legis. Black Caucus, joint commn. pub. rights and commn. on tchr. equality. Author: Health Occupations Instructional Units-Secondary Schools, 1975; Planning Guide for Health Occupations, 1975; co-author; Introduction to Health Care, 1976. Del. Democratic Nat. Conv., 1980. Recipient Mary Church Terrell award, 1976, Brotherhood Crusade award, 1981, Black Woman of Achievement award NAACP Legal Def. Fund, 1988; named Alumnus of Yr., UCLA, 1980, 82, Senator of Yr., Calif. Trial Lawyers, 1982. Mem. Calif. Assn. Sch. Psychologists, Los Angeles Urban League, Calif. Tchrs. Assn., Calif. Commn. on Status Women. Roman Catholic. Office: State Capitol Rm 4040 Sacramento CA 95814*

WATSON, EVELYN EGNER, program director; b. Corbin, Ky., Dec. 15, 1928; d. Edgar Mattison and Bertha Mae (Mayfield) Egner; m. Earl Greene Watson, Nov. 10, 1953; children: Nancy Eileen, Philip Allen. Student, Lincoln Meml. U., 1947-48; BA, U. Ky., 1949; postgrad., U. Tenn., 1968; AA, Cumberland Coll., 1946. Math. and sci. tchr. Lynch (Ky.) High Sch., 1949-50; office mgr. Whitley County Sch. System, Williamsburg, Ky., 1950-53; sr. lab. tech. Radiopharm. Internal Dose Ctr. Oak Ridge (Tenn.) Assoc. Univs., 1961-71, scientist, 1971-79, program mgr., 1979-89, program dir., 1989—; lectr. in field; cons. USFDA, Rockville, Md., 1983-88. Assoc. editor Jour. Nuclear Medicine, 1981-86; editor newsletter Soc. Nuclear Medicine, 1988—; co-author: MIRD Primer, 1988; contbr. articles to profl., chpts. to books. Bd. dirs. Youth Haven, Oak Ridge, Tenn., 1970-74, Clinch River Home Health, Clinton, Tenn., 1988—. Recipient Excellence in Tech. Transfer award Fed. Lab. Consortium, 1985. Mem. Soc. Nuclear Medicine (med. internal radiation dose com. 1980—), Health Physics Soc. (Disting. Svc. award 1981, treas. 1976-77), Nat. Coun. on Radiation Protection and

Measurements (sci. com. 1986—), Sigma Xi. Mem. Ch. of Christ. Home: 206 Lakeview Ln Oak Ridge TN 37830 Office: Oak Ridge Assoc Univs Po Box 117 Oak Ridge TN 37831

WATSON, FELICIA, data processing executive; b. Flint, Mich., Aug. 19, 1962; d. Hugh and Priscilla Juanice (Gragg) W.; 1 child, Pierre Henri Fuller. Data processing cert., Genesee Area Skill Ctr., Flint, Mich., 1980; BS, U. Mich., 1986; postgrad., Cen. Mich. U., 1988—. Intern parts div. GM, Swartz Creek, Mich., 1979-83, asst. electronics mail adminstr. warehousing dept., 1983-85, asst. office automation adminstr. warehousing dept., 1983-85; computer programmer Electronic Data Systems, Swartz Creek, 1985-86; assoc. analyst Consumers Power Co., Jackson, Mich., 1987-88; programmer analyst Consumers Power Co., Jackson, 1988-89; system engr. Electronic Data System, Flint, Mich., 1989—. Mem. Toastmasters Internat. (ednl. v.p. 1988-89, Jackson, Mich. chpt.), U. Mich. Alumnus Soc., Delta Sigma Theta. Democrat. Baptist. Home: 6418 Karen Dr Flint MI 48504

WATSON, GEORGIA BROWN, author; b. Atlanta; d. George C. and Willie (Willingham) Watson; B.S., Ga. So. Coll., 1946; M.A., George Peabody Coll., Vanderbilt U., 1947, Ph.D., 1949. Tchr., Ga. pub. schs., 1931-42; prof. psychology Ga. So. Coll., Statesboro, from 1949, now emeritus prof., emeritus chmn. psychology dept.; postdoctoral research fellow Yale U., 1961-62. Served to maj. WAC, 1942-46. Mem. Internat. Platform Assn. Methodist. Author: How to Enjoy Retirement: Climb a Tree and Holler, 1979, Life in the Retirement Bed of Roses, 1982, Retirement Tracks: After Showing the Wisdom of Age, Leave in a Hurry, 1984, World War II in a Khaki Skirt, 1985, Doses of Humor to be Taken by Citizens of Mature Age, 1988; weekly columnist Georgian local newspaper. Home: 4 Preston Dr Statesboro GA 30458

WATSON, GEORGIANNA, librarian; b. Lock Haven, Pa., Feb. 18, 1949; d. George and Anna (Eisenhower) Rhine; children: Sharga Nicolle, George Winfield-Martin. BS in Edn., Lock Haven State U., 1971; MLS, Brigham Young U., 1978; M in Pub. Adminstrn., John Jay Coll. Criminal Justice, N.Y.C., 1986. Tchr. Mifflin County Sch. Dist., Lewistown, Pa., 1971-72; librarian Shiprock Boarding Sch. Bur. Indian Affairs, Shiprock, N.Mex., 1972-79, Ft. Sill Indian Sch. Bur. Indian Affairs, Lawton, Okla., 1979-80; librarian U.S. Mil. Acad., West Point, N.Y., 1980-83, head pub. services, library, 1983—; mem. N.Y. State adv. council for use of govt. documents. Mem. Southeastern N.Y. Library Resource Council (mem. continuing edn. com., chairperson govt. documents interest group), Southeastern N.Y. Reference Library Interest Group, Am. Soc. Equine Appraisers (cert.), Am. Quarter Horse Assn., Internat. Arabian Horse Assn., Pi Alpha Alpha. Republican. Home: 237C Plains Rd Walden NY 12586 Office: US Mil Acad Dept Army West Point NY 10996-1799

WATSON, JAN CAROLE, teacher; b. Aiken, S.C., Feb. 5, 1942; d. C.J. Watson and Mary Lee (Taylor) W. BS, Winthrop Coll., 1964; MA, Appalachian State U., 1967; EdD, U. N.C., Greensboro, 1980. Program dir. Camp Birchwood, Brandon, Vt., 1963-74; tchr., coach Newport News (Va.) City Schs., 1964-66, Appalachian State U., Boone, N.C., 1967—. Mem. Am. Alliance for Health, Phys. Edn., Recreation and Dance, So. Assn. For Physical Edn. Coll. Women, Nat. Assn. Physical Edn. in Higher Edn., U.S. Field Hockey Assn. (v.p. for fund devel. 1986—), Alpha Delta Kappa. Methodist. Office: Appalachian State U Dept Health Leisure & Exercise Scis Boone NC 28608

WATSON, JANET LEE COX, city clerk; b. Kokoma, Ind., Oct. 19, 1940; d. Donald Chester and Pearl Lavina (Lewis) Sweeney; m. Roscoe Franklin Cox, Oct. 25, 1958 (dec. Oct. 1983); children: Cynthia S. Nilson, Terry R., Karen A. Robinson, Scott L.; m. Rex Lee Watson, Sept. 20, 1986. Grad. high sch., Kokomo, Ind. 2nd dep. Howard County Recorders Office, Kokomo, 1971-76, Howard County Treas. Office, Kokomo, 1976-84; 1st dep. Howard County Auditor's Office, Kokomo, 1984-86; city clk. City of Kokomo, 1988—. Mem. Howard County Reps. Women Club (scholarship chairperson 1988), Kokomo, 1976—. Mem. Am. Bus. Women (pres. 1986-87, sec. 1990—), Ind. Assns. Cities and Towns, Ind. League Mcpl. Clks. and Treas., Kiwanis. Baptist. Home: 1314 W Sycamore St Kokomo IN 46901

WATSON, KATE J., real estate manager; b. New Bedford, Mass., Sept. 25, 1936; d. Maurice Franklin Sr. and Cathrine Muirhead (Knight) W. AAS in Mech. Engring., Erie County Tech. Inst., Buffalo, 1964; B in Engring. Tech., Northeastern U., 1976. Systems instr., systems engr., project engr. Foxboro (Mass.) Co., 1967-87; real estate salesman TI-Share Systems Corp., Dennisport, Mass., 1988—; time share resort mgr. Delray Beach Club, Dennisport, 1988—. Pub. affairs officer, flotilla sec. USCG Aux., 1990—. Mem. Coast Guard Aux., Mensa, Sigma Epsilon Rho. Home: PO Box 1398 Dennisport MA 02639 Office: PO Box 1247 188 Captain Chase Rd Dennisport MD 02639

WATSON, KATHARINE JOHNSON, art museum director, art historian; b. Providence, Nov. 11, 1942; d. William Randolph and Katharine Johnson (Badger) W.; m. Paul Luther Nyhus, Dec. 17, 1983. BA, Duke U., 1964; MA, U. Pa., 1967, PhD, 1973. Teaching asst. U. Pa., 1966-67; instr., curator exhbns. U. Pitts., 1969-70; curator of art before 1800 Allen Meml. Art Mus., Oberlin, Ohio, 1973-77; lectr. Oberlin Coll., 1973-77; dir. Peary-MacMillan Artic Mus. Bowdoin Coll., Brunswick, Maine, 1977-83, dir. Mus. of Art, 1977—; trustee Mus. Art of Ogunquit, 1977-89, Regional Art Conservation Lab., Williamstown, Surf Point Found., York, Maine, 1977-90. Author: Pietro Tacca, 1983; author text for exhbn. catalogues; co-editor: Allen Meml. Art Mus. Bull, 1974-77; contbr. articles to profl. jours. Mem. profl. adv. com. Victoria Soc. Maine; mem. adv. coun. Archives of Am. Art, 1982-90. Kress Found. fellow, Chester Dale Fellow, Am. Council Learned Socs. fellow, 1977-78, Villa I Tatti fellow, 1977-78. Mem. Assn. Art Mus. Dirs., Am. Assn. Mus., Coll. Art Assn., Smithsonian Coun. Office: Bowdoin Coll Mus Art Walker Art Bldg Brunswick ME 04011

WATSON, KITTIE WELLS, speech communication educator; b. Newburgh, N.Y., July 31, 1953; d. Cody Usry and Bettie Richards (Todd) Watson. AA, Gainesville Jr. Coll., 1973; BS, U. Ga., 1975; MA, Auburn U., 1977; PhD, La. State U., 1981. Cert. tchr., Ga. Grad. teaching asst. Auburn U. (Ala.), 1975-77, instr., 1977-79; instr. Tulane U., New Orleans, 1979-81, asst. prof. speech communication, 1981-85, assoc. prof., 1985—, also acting head dept. speech communication, 1981-83, chmn. dept., 1982-84, assoc. dir. Inst. for Study Intrapersonal Processes; staff writer and reviewer Prentice-Hall, Wm. C. Brown, Addison Wesley pub. cos.; exec. v.p. SPECTRA Communication Assocs.; pres. SPECTRA Creations; v.p., co-owner, treas. SPECTRA Inc.; treas. SPECTRA Inc. Pubs.; co-owner operator Rainbow River Studios. Author: Instructional Objectives and Evaluation, 1980, Effective Listening, 1983, Groups in Process, 3d edit., 1987; co-editor: Intrapersonal Communication Processes: Original Essays, 1989, Interpersonal and Relational Communication, 1990; mem. editorial bd. and contbr. numerous articles to scholarly jours.; creator audio and video tapes: Watson-Barker Listening Test; Willing Yourself to Listen. Mem. Am. Coun. for Career Women, task force nat. tchr. cert. examination Ednl. Testing Svc. Recipient Mortar Bd. Teaching Excellence award Tulane U., 1982, Achiever award Am. Coun. for Career Women, 1987; inducted Listening Hall of Fame 1988. Mem. Inst. Study of Intrapersonal Processes (assoc. dir., Ralph Nichols Rsch. award 1988, Program Design award 1989), Speech Communication Assn., Internat. Communication Assn., Am. Soc. Tng. and Devel. (v.p. profl. devel., Program Design award), So. Speech Communication Assn., Eastern Speech Assn., Internat. Listening Assn. (1st. v.p., pres., mem.-at-large, chmn. rsch. com., Rsch. award 1985, Delta Delta Delta. Home: 701 Jefferson Ave Metairie LA 70001 Office: Tulane U Dept Communications Newcomb Hall New Orleans LA 70118

WATSON, MARSHA JEAN, writer; b. Kansas City, Kans., July 18, 1957; d. John Stanley and Doris Jean (Elliott) W. Student, U. Mo., Kansas City and Columbia, 1977-85, U. Kans., Lawrence, 1989-90. Pres. Watson Writing Svcs., Bonner Springs, Kans., 1983—; writer Copilevitz, Bryant, Gray & Jennings, Kansas City, Mo., 1990—. Contbr. articles, fiction and poetry to mags. and jours. Vol. Human Rescue Inc., Kansas City, 1979-81. Mem. NAFE, Nat. Writers Club. Republican. Home: 231 Sheidley Ave Bonner Springs KS 66012

WATSON, MARY STONE, speech and drama educator; b. Marcellus, N.Y., May 24, 1909; d. James Horace and Ethel (Cowles) Stone; B in Oral English, Syracuse U., 1931; MA, U. Md., 1965; m. Harry P. Watson, June 27, 1936; children: Ruth Watson Lancaster, Robert S., Rollin J., Harry P., Douglas J., Donald M., Sara L. High sch. tchr. English, speech, drama, N.Y., Pa., Md., 1931-37, 62-64; prof. speech Essex Community Coll., Baltimore County, Md., 1965-89, part-time instr., 1970-89, former head speech and drama dept.; lectr., condr. workshops in communications and therapeutic communication, 1965—; producer, anchor person Cable TV show The Best Is Yet To Be, 1981-82. Vol. day care and summer camp YMCA; active 2d Presbyn. Ch., Balt. Home: 108 W 39th St Apt 8 Baltimore MD 21210

WATSON, MURIEL ANITA ELLIS, finance executive, consultant; b. Oklahoma City, Dec. 24, 1951; d. Hughes Van Sr. and Mable Vivian (Withers) Ellis; 1 child from previous marriage, Meyanna Kamilah. BS in Bus. Adminstrn., U. No. Colo., 1973; M of Urban Adminstrn. and Urban Affairs, U. Colo., Denver, 1978, postgrad., 1987. Extension agt. Colo. State U., Denver, 1974-75; grad. asst. U. of Colo., Denver, 1975-76, legis. intern, 1976; sec. Regional Transportation Dist., Denver, 1976-78; bus. planning specialist Colo. Econ. Devel. Assn., Denver, 1978; presdl. mgmt. intern Bur. of Reclamation, Dept. of Interior, Denver, 1978-80; chief program and budget staff Bureau of Land Mgmt., Dept. of Interior, Denver, 1980-83; cost analyst, comptroller US Air Force Acctg. and Fin. Ctr., Denver, 1983-84, budget analyst, comptroller, 1984—; vice chair, bd. dirs. Colo. State Bd. Social Work Examiners, Denver, pub. mem.-at-large, exec. com., 1989—; vice chair, bd. dirs. Am. Found. for Rsch. and Consumer Edn. in Social Work Regulation: cons., co-founder Women's Network and Resource Consortium of Colo., Denver, 1987—. Mem. parish coun., lector, eucharistic minister Cure d' Ars Cath. Ch., Denver, 1981—; sec., chmn. nominating com., bd. dirs. Urban League of Met. Denver, 1983—, past chairperson; mem. adv. bd. Montbello Rainbow Assn., Denver, 1983—; vol. Girl Scouts U.S., Denver, 1983—; sec., bd. dirs. Blessed Sacrament Sch. PTA, Denver, 1986—; vol. Western States Black Women in Bus., Denver, 1986; vol. United Negro Coll. Fund, Denver, 1986—; co-chairperson, co-founder Black-Jewish Young Leadership Alliance, Denver. Named Colo. fellow U. of Colo., 1976, Outstanding Young Woman of Am., 1986; recipient Outstanding Contbn. to the Minority Bus. Community award Colo. Econ. Devel. Assn., 1978, Kenneth J. Hansen Scholar award, 1972, Presdl. Mgmt. Intern award, 1978, Alpha Kappa Alpha Book award, 1970. Mem. NAFE, Am. Soc. Mil. Comptrollers, Presdl. Mgmt. Intern Alumni Group, Fed. Women's Program (subcom. mem. 1980-83), Black United Dedicated Govt. Employees, Am. Assn. State Social Work Bds. (exec. com. 1989—). Democrat. Roman Catholic. Clubs: Sippers N'Sliders; Nat. Brotherhood of Skiers. Office: USAF Acctg and Fin Ctr Bldg 444 CWBP Lowry AFB CO 80279

WATSON, NANCY LOUISE, editor; b. Mpls., Apr. 25, 1948; d. Roland S. and Kathleen M. (DeSpain) Roemer; m. Richard C. Watson, Sept. 2, 1981 (div.). PhB in Communications, Northwestern U., 1980; postgrad., Roosevelt U., 1983—. Exec. editor AMA, Chgo., 1970—. Freelance writer Pioneer Press, Evanston, Ill., 1978-80. Active Humane Soc. Am., Smithsonian Inst. Roman Catholic. Office: AMA 515 N State St Chicago IL 60610

WATSON, PATRICIA LEONARD, party production and convention service company executive; b. Sanford, Fla., June 29, 1945; d. William Thomas and Letitia Summerlyn (Hopkins) Leonard; m. Lawrence Ray Watson, Sept. 4, 1965 (div. Oct. 1977); children: William Kirk, Scott Bradley; m. Charles Richard Covert, Jr., July 15, 1978. BA, North Tex. State U., 1966. Tchr. Dallas Ind. Sch. Dist., 1966-68; real estate broker Larry Watson Realtors, Mesquite, Tex., 1970-72; founder, pres., chief exec. officer Magic by PTS, Inc., Dallas 1972—; chief exec. officer Conf. Mgmt. Assocs., Inc., Dallas, 1979—; mem. community service bd. Hotel Sales Mgrs. Assn., 1983. Featured in Good Housekeeping mag., 1986, Oprah Winfrey Show, 1986. Chmn. tours com. Republican Nat. Conv., Dallas, 1984; mem. women's bd. Northwood Inst. Recipient Disting. Sales award Sales and Mktg. Execs. Internat., 1983, Disting. Service award Meeting Planners Internat., 1979, Hero award Meeting Planners Internat., 1980. Mem. Conv. Service and Sightseeing Network (v.p. 1984—), Profl. Conv. Mgrs. Assn., Am. Soc. Assn. Execs., Assn. Women Entrepreneurs of Dallas, Nat. Assn. Catering Execs., Alpha Phi. Avocations: cooking; reading. Home: 1010 Allen #231 Dallas TX 75204 Office: Magic by PTS Inc 11106 Stemmons Fwy Dallas TX 75229

WATSON, PATTY JO, anthropology educator; b. Superior, Nebr., Apr. 26, 1932; d. Ralph Clifton and Elaine Elizabeth (Lance) Andersen; m. Richard Allan Watson, July 30, 1955; 1 child, Anna Melissa. M.A., U. Chgo., 1956, Ph.D. in Anthropology, 1959. Archaeologist-ethnographer Oriental Inst.-U. Chgo., 1959-60, research assoc., archaeologist, 1964-70; instr. anthropology U. So. Calif., Los Angeles, 1961, UCLA, 1961, Los Angeles State U., 1961; asst. prof. anthropology Washington U., St. Louis, 1969-70; assoc. prof. Washington U., 1970-73, prof., 1973—; mem. rev. panel NSF, Washington, 1974-76; fellow Ctr. Advanced Study in Behavioral Scis., Stanford, Calif., 1981-82. Author: The Prehistory of Salts Cave, Kentucky, 1969, Archaeological Ethnography in Western Iran, 1979; (with others) Man and Nature, 1969, Explanation in Archeology, 1971, Archeological Explanation, 1984; author, editor: Archeology of the Mammoth Cave Area, 1974, Prehistoric Archeology Along the Zagros Flanks, 1983. Grantee NSF, 1959-60, 68, 70, 72-74, 78-79, NEH, 1977-78, Nat. Geog. Soc., 1969-75. Fellow Am. Anthropol. Assn. (editor for archaeology 1973-77), AAAS (chair sect. H 1991—); mem. NAS, Soc. Am. Archaeology (exec. com. 1974-76, 82-84, editor Am. Antiquity 1984-87, Fryxell medal 1990), Cave Rsch. Found., Assn. Paleorient (sci. bd.), Nat. Speleological Soc. (hon. life, editorial bd. bull. 1979—). Office: Washington U Dept Anthropology Saint Louis MO 63130-4899

WATSON, ROBERTA CASPER, lawyer; b. Boise, Idaho, July 11, 1949; d. John Blaine and Joyce Lucile (Mercer) C.; m. Robert George Watson, July 22, 1972; 1 child, Rebecca Joyce. BA cum laude, U. Idaho, 1971; JD, Harvard U., 1974. Bar: Mass. 1974, U.S. Dist. Ct. Mass. 1975, U.S. Supreme Ct. 1979, U.S. Ct. Appeals (1st cir.) 1979, U.S. Tax Ct. 1979, Fla. 1985, U.S. Dist. Ct. (mid. dist.) Fla. 1985, U.S. Dist. Ct. (so. dist.) Fla. 1987. Assoc. Peabody & Brown, Boston, 1974-78, Mintz, Levin, Cohn, Ferris, Glovsky & Popeo, Boston, 1978-84; sr. dir. Wolper Ross & Co., Miami, 1983-85; assoc. Trenam, Simmons, Kemker, Scharf, Barkin, Frye & O'Neill P.A., Tampa, Fla., 1985-87, ptnr., 1988—. Contbr. articles to profl. jours.; co-author: A Physician's Guide to Professional Corporations. Pres. Performing Arts Ctr. of Greater Framingham, Mass., 1983; bd. dirs. Northside Community Mental Health Ctr.; mem. South Fla. Employee Benefits Coun.; trustee Unitarian Universalist Found., Clearwater, Fla. Mem. ABA (tax sect.), Hillsborough County Bar Assn., Fla. West Coast Employee Benefits Coun., Harvard Club (bd. dirs.west coast Fla. chpt.). Republican. Unitarian Universalist. Club: Tampa. Lodge: Order Eastern Star. Home: 124 Adalia Ave Tampa FL 33606 Office: Trenam Simmons Kemker Scharf Barkin Frye & O'Neill PA 2700 Barnett Pla Tampa FL 33602

WATSON, SANDRA STILES, special education educator; b. Eagle Pass, Tex., Feb. 7, 1944; d. Andrew Thomas and Linda D. (Davis) W. BA, Furman U., 1965; MEd, Memphis State U., 1970; ArtsD in Edn., George Mason U., 1988. Master tchr. U. Va., Charlottesville, 1976; univ. supr., lectr. George Mason U., Fairfax, Va., 1984-89; ednl. diagnostician, gifted & talented curriculum developer Alexandria (Va.) Pub. Schs., 1965—; cons. in field. Author: Computer Software Trading in Southeast Asia, 1988, Yourtown, 1986. Recipient Study Grant Anthropology NSF, 1975. Mem. NEA, AAUW, Edn. Assn. Alexandria (sec. 1971-74), Va. Edn. Assn., Am. Ednl. Rsch. Assn., Assn. Supervision & Curriculum Devel., Phi Delta Kappa. Home: 3039 S Abingdon St Arlington VA 22206 Office: Alexandria City Pub Schs 4800 W Braddock Rd Alexandria VA 22302

WATSON, SHAREE LEIGH, retail executive; b. Keosauqua, Iowa, Nov. 23, 1951; d. Hudson Vollie and Betty Jean (White) Turner; 1 child, Lena Anne. BA, Oral Roberts U., 1974; postgrad., U. Ctr. Tulsa. Mgr. Sunglass Hut of Am., Inc., Miami; co-owner Pip Printing, Houston; elem. tchr. Sapulpa (Okla.) Pub. Schs. Active Victory Christian Ctr., Tulsa. Recipient Mgr. of Month awards Woodland Hills Mall. Mem. NAFE. Democrat.

WATSON, SHARON GITIN, psychologist, association executive; b. N.Y.C., Oct. 21, 1943; d. Louis Leonard and Miriam (Myers) Gitin; m. Eric Watson, Oct. 31, 1969; 1 child, Carrie Dunbar. B.A. cum laude, Cornell U., 1965; M.A., U. Ill., 1968, Ph.D., 1971. Psychologist City N.Y. Prison Mental Health, Riker's Island, 1973-74; psychologist Youth Services Ctr., Los Angeles County Dept. Pub. Social Services, Los Angeles, 1975-77, dir. clin. services, 1978, dir. Youth Services Ctr., 1978-80; exec. dir. Crittenton Ctr. for Young Women and Infants, Los Angeles, 1980-89, Assn. Children's Svcs. Agys. of So. Calif., L.A., 1989—. Contbr. articles to profl. jours. Pres. Calif. Assn. Services for Children, 1986-87, chmn. nominating com., 1987-88, chmn. program com. 1985-86, chmn. mgmt. info. services com., 1984-85, sec., treas., chmn. budget and fin. com., chmn. membership com., 1983-84; mem. community adv. com. Div. of Adolescent Medicine, Children's Hosp. of Los Angeles; bd. dirs. Los Angeles Children's Roundtable, Adolescent Pregnancy Child Watch; co-chair Los Angeles Children's Services Planning Council, 1986-88; pres. Assn. Children's Services Agys. So. Calif., 1984-85, sec., 1981-83; mem. steering com. western region Child Welfare League of Am., 1985-87. Mem. Am. Psychol. Assn., Am. Mgmt. Assn., Town Hall Calif., Cornell Alumni Assn. So. Calif., So. Calif. Inter-Club Assn. (vice chmn.), Pasadena Figure Skating Club (pres.). Home: 4056 Camino Real Los Angeles CA 90065 Office: Assn Childrens Svcs Agys of So Calif 3910 Oakwood Ave Los Angeles CA 90004

WATSON, STELLA MARIE, business manager; b. El Paso, Tex., May 26, 1953; d. Ralph D. and Emma (Fornazierza) Mayfield; m. Jimmy H. Watson, Dec. 30, 1972; children: Courtney J., Brittany L. Student, N.Mex. Highlands U., 1989—. Exec. sec. 1st Nat. Bank in Tucumcari, N.Mex., 1972-76; dep. county clk. County of Quay, Tucumcari, 1976-80; fiscal officer Tucumcari Area Vocat. Sch., 1980-90, bus. mgr., 1990—. Mem. supervisory com. Tucumcari Schs. Fed. Credit Union; sec. Tucumcari Jr. PTO; pres. Quay County unit Am. Heart Assn., Tucumcari, 1988-90. Mem. NAFE, Pace N.Mex., Aware N.Mex., Nat. Assn. Accts., Soc. for Human Resource Mgmt. Methodist. Home: 714 Mesquite St Tucumcari NM 88401 Office: Tucumcari Area Vocat Sch 824 W Hines St Tucumcari NM 88401

WATSON, SUSAN ELIZABETH, insurance company executive; b. Rocky Mount, N.C., June 16, 1960; d. Norman Ray and Mary Elizabeth (Rowland) W. BA in Edn., U. N.C., 1982. Assoc. Claims; Cert. in Gen. Ins. Tchr. Greensville County Schs., Emporia, Va., 1982-84; sales & mktg. rep. Marshall Industries, Raleigh, N.C., 1984-86; claims rep. N.C. Farm Bureau Ins., Raleigh, 1986-88; tng. specialist Gay & Taylor, Inc., Winston-Salem, N.C., 1988-89, mktg. coord., 1989—; adv. bd. mem. Ins. Tech. Training Inst., Dallas; grad. asst. Dale Carnegie, Greensboro, N.C. Mem. Winston-Salem Jaycees, 1988—. Mem. Raleigh Claims Assn., Winston-Salem Claims Assn. (alt. state dir. 1988, v.p. 1989, pres. 1990—), Soc. Ins. Trainers and Educators, NAFE, Internat. Assn. Arson Investigators, N.C. Adj. Assn. (sec. 1989). Republican. Presbyterian. Office: Gay & Taylor Inc 3334 Healy Dr Winston-Salem NC 27104

WATSON-BRODNAX, SHIRLEY JEAN, industrial hygienist; b. Norfolk, Va.; d. John B. and Louise (Booker) Holloway; m. Jack Leon Brodnax, July 31, 1976; children: Melodie, Tracey, Maisha. AA, Contra Costa Coll., 1978; BS in Cell and Molecular Biology, San Francisco State U., 1985. Jr. accountant Philco Corp., Phila.; sec., supr. U.S. Govt., Phila. and San Francisco, 1968-76; research asst., microbiologist Kelly Tech. Services, Oakland, Calif., 1986; microbiologist Nabisco Brands, Inc., Oakland, 1986-89; indsl. hygienist Naval Hosp., NSC Med. Command, Oakland, Calif., 1989—. Kennedy King scholar Contra Costa Coll., 1978-80. Mem. AAAS, Internat. Platform Assn., Am. Microbiology Soc., Am. Chem. Soc., Inst. of Food Technologists, Am. Biog. Inst. Rsch. Assn. (dep. gov. bd. of govs. 1988—). Roman Catholic. Home: 1537 Hellings Ave Richmond CA 94801 Office: Naval Hosp San Francisco Bay Indsl Hygiene Div Bldg 590 Oakland Army Base Oakland CA 94630

WATSON-LEE, DEBRA ANN, accountant; b. Leland, Miss., May 17, 1956; d. Willie J. and Doris (Ferguson) W; m. Leadell Lee, June 25, 1941. BBA, Chgo. State U., 1975-81. Adminstrv. asst. Myriam Wilson Med. Ctr., Chgo., 1973-74; acct., EEO counselor Dept. of Justice, Fed. Bur. of Investigation, Chgo., 1974-88; agt. Dept. of Treasury, IRS, Laguna Niguel, Calif., 1988—; treas. FBI Recreation Assn., Chgo., 1983-84. Mem. NAFE, Nat. Assn. Black Accts., Assn Improvement Minorities, Am. Athletics & Fitness Assn.

WATT, JAIMIE JACOBS, accountant; b. Norman, Okla., Dec. 13, 1943; d. Herbert Charles and Ina Loretta (Wilkerson) Jacobs; m. Jimmy Albert Watt, Mar. 15, 1964 (div. Nov. 1985); children: Greggory Scott, James Christopher. BFA, U. Okla., 1978. Cert. in Managerial Finance. Sec., jr. acct. McNulty and Andrews CPA, Montrose, Col., 1965-66; sec., bookkeeper Norman (Okla.) C. of C., 1967,68,70; mgr. Ladies Health Center, Fort Rucker, Ala., 1971-72; exec.sec., acct. John Carroll High Sch., Ft. Pierce, Fla.; sec., therapist Dr. R. W. Elb, Norman, Okla., 1976-78; acctg. mgr. Town Services, Inc., Tex., 1978-81; exec. sec. Hubbell Incorp., Orange, Conn., 1981-83, staff acct., 1983-84; acctg. mgr. Hubbell Corp. Transp., Seymour, Conn., 1984--; assoc. mem. Am. Mgmt. Assn., 1985--. Mem. Sweet Adelines Inc., various chpts. Tulsa 1967--, asst. dir. Yankeemaid chpt., Norwalk 1982-87, asst. dir. Mtn. Laurel chpt., Hartford 1988--, Officers' Wives Orgns., US Army 1968-85. Mem. Sigma Alpha Iota, Zeta Tau Alpha (social chmn. 1963-64), Zeta Tau Alpha Alumnae (pres. 1977). Republican. Roman Catholic. Home: 4 Beacon Hill Terr Huntington CT 06484 Office: Corp Transp Ops 26 Progress Ave Seymour CT 06483

WATTERS, CYNTHIA ELLEN, preschool owner, operator; b. Milford, Mass., Feb. 1, 1944; d. John Donald Geake and Grace Virginia (Donahue) Barone; m. Mark Lynn Watters, Aug. 3, 1968 (div. Dec. 1981); children: Lynne Marie, Eric Robert. BA in Edn., U. Fla., 1966. Cert. secondary tchr. Tchr. Dade County Pub. Schs., Miami, Fla., 1966-68, Cen. Dauphin Sch. Dist., Harrisburg, Pa., 1968-69; tng. specialist Commonwealth of Pa., Harrisburg, 1969-70; direct distbr. Amway Corp., Harrisburg, 1970-72; office mgr. Doctor's Bldg., Miami, 1974-81; support svcs. supr. North Miami Found. for Sr. Citizens' Svcs., Inc., 1982-84, acting exec. dir., 1983; presch. owner, dir. 3 R.R.R.s Full Svc. Sch., Miramar, Fla., 1985—; pres., sec., treas. Cinderlyn, Inc., Miramar, 1985—; mem. numerous coms. Dade County Assn. Svc. Providers for the Aging, Miami, 1982-84, sec., 1983-84. Chmn. vol. svcs., mem. exec. bd. St. Stephen Sch. PTO, Miramar, 1986-88; team mother S.W. Broward Jr. Athletic Assn., Miramar, 1979-81; chmn. pub. relations com. St. Stephen Edn. Endowment Found., Miramar, 1987. Mem. AAUW, Fla. Assn. for Children Under Six, Broward County Assn. for Children Under Six, South Fla. Assn. Pvt. Schs., Broward County Kindergarten and Nursery Sch. Assn., Miramar-Pembroke C. of C. Democrat. Roman Catholic. Home: 11136 Long Boat Dr Cooper City FL 33026

WATTERS, LAURA LYNN, sales executive; b. Colby, Kans., June 22, 1961; d. Ronald Ray and Betty Jean (Schenk) W. BSBA, Emporia State U., 1983. Sales exec. Hallmark Cards Inc., Spokane, Wash., 1984-87, Kansas City, Mo., 1987-88; sales exec. Surgikos div. Johnson & Johnson Corp., Santa Barbara, Calif., 1989—. Vol. Spl. Olympics, 1979-85; cons. Miss Am. pageant, 1984—. Winner Miss Kans. pageant, 1983; winner talent award Miss Am. pageant, ATlantic City, 1983. Mem. Am. Assn. Female Execs., Reading Club (Denver), Chi Omega (pledge advisor 1988-89). Home: 1419 Olive St Santa Barbara CA 93101

WATTERS, PATRICIA ANNE, social work administrator, data processing consultant; b. Annapolis, Md., Feb. 13, 1948; d. Edward Charles and Mary Margaret (Cusack) W. BS in Zoology, U. Md., 1970, MSW, 1977, advanced profl. cert. in social work, 1974; postgrad., Washington Theol. Union, Silver Spring, Md., 1988—. Social worker Anne Arundel County Dept. Social Svc., Annapolis, Md., 1970-78, supr., 1978-82; protective svcs. specialist Social Svcs. Adminstrn., Balt., 1982-83; program adminstr. Dept. Human Resources and Info. Mgmt., Balt., 1983-87; adminstr. assessment ctr. Montgomery County Dept. Social Svcs., Rockville, Md., 1987-88, chief child welfare, 1988—; chmn. bd. Raft Houses, Inc., Annapolis, 1974-76. Scholar State of Md., 1975-76. Mem. Nat. Orgn. Social Workers (diplomate). Roman Catholic. Office: Montgomery County Dept Social Svcs 5600 Fishers Ln Rockville MD 20852

WATTERSON, JOAN COOK, English educator; b. Birmingham, Ala., Aug. 30, 1931; d. Phillip Mallory and Jesse Inez (Goodwin) Cook; m. Donald Hodges Watterson, Sept. 2, 1950; children: Susan Joan, Melanie Carol Dunn, Leisa Ellen DeVenny, Starla Dawn Weatherell. BA, Mobile Coll., 1970. Tchr. French Bishop Toolen High Sch., Mobile, Ala., 1969-70; tchr. English Robert E. Lee High Sch., Montgomery, Ala., 1971—. Youth leader First Bapt. Ch., Montgomery, 1980—. Mem. NEA, Nat. Tchrs. English, Ala. Edn. Assn., Ala. Bapt. Ministers Wives (pres. 1987-88), Alpha Delta Kappa (pres. 1985, 89), Zeta Tau Alpha. Democrat. Home: 3909 Croydon Rd Montgomery AL 36109 Office: Robert E Lee High Sch 225 Ann St Montgomery AL 36107

WATTLETON, FAYE, association executive; b. St. Louis, July 8, 1943; d. George and Ozie Wattleton; divorced; 1 child, Felicia. B in Nursing, Ohio State U., 1964; M in Maternal and Infant Health Care, Columbia U., 1967. Tchr. Miami Valley Hosp. Sch. Nursing, Dayton, Ohio, 1964-66; asst. dir. Montgomery County Combined Pub. Health Dist., Dayton, 1967-69; exec. dir. Planned Parenthood, Dayton, 1970-78; pres. Planned Parenthood Fedn. Am., Inc., N.Y.C., 1978—. Bd. dirs. U.S. com. UNICEF, Young Pres.'s Orgn.; mem. nat. adv. com. Tufts Sch. Pub. Svc. Recipient numerous humanitarian awards. Office: Planned Parenthood Fedn Am 810 7th Ave New York NY 10019*

WATTS, DORIS EARLENE, retired librarian; b. Palatka, Fla., Jan. 7, 1923; d. Charles Franklin and Elouise A.C. (Hagler) Foster; m. Fernand Cortez Watts, Aug. 30, 1950 (dec. 1955); children: Varick Steven, Franklin Cortez. A.B., Howard U., 1950; postgrad., Cath. U. Am., 1960-61, Cath. U. Am., 1965. Clk. War Dept., Washington, 1942-46, VA, Washington, 1949; editorial clk. Dept. Army, Washington, 1950-52; clk. Dept. Army, 1953-59, Dept. Commerce, Washington, 1959; with ICC, Washington, 1959—, librarian, to 1983. Recipient Spl. Achievement award ICC, 1983; recipient Spl. Achievement award, 1984. Mem. ALA, Delta Sigma Theta. Democrat. Methodist. Home: 2502 Perry St NE Washington DC 20018

WATTS, EMILY STIPES, educator; b. Urbana, Ill., Mar. 16, 1936; d. Royal Arthur and Virginia Louise (Schenck) Stipes; m. Robert Allan Watts, Aug. 30, 1958; children: Benjamin, Edward, Thomas. Student, Smith Coll., 1954-56; A.B., U. Ill., 1958, M.A. (Woodrow Wilson Nat. fellow), 1959, Ph.D., 1963. Instr. in English U. Ill.-Urbana, 1963-67, asst. prof. English, 1967-73, assoc. prof., 1973-77, prof., dir. grad. studies dept. English, 1977-79; bd. dirs. U. Ill. Athletic Assn., chmn., 1981-83; mem. faculty adv. com. Ill. Bd. Higher Edn., 1984—, vice chmn., 1986-87, chmn., 1987-88. Author: Ernest Hemingway and The Arts, 1971, The Poetry of American Women from 1632 to 1945, 1977, The Businessman in American Literature, 1982; contbr. articles on Jonathan Edwards, Anne Bradstreet to lit. jours. John Simon Guggenheim Meml. Found. fellow, 1973-74. Mem. Authors Guild, Ill. Writers Assn., Phi Beta Kappa, Phi Kappa Phi. Republican. Presbyterian. Home: 1009 W University Ave Champaign IL 61821 Office: U Ill 208 English Bldg Urbana IL 61801

WATTS, HEATHER, ballerina; b. Long Beach, Calif., Sept. 27, 1953; d. Keith Nevin and Sheelagh Maud (Woodhead) W. Student, Sch. Am. Ballet, N.Y.C. Mem. corps de ballet N.Y.C. Ballet Co., 1970-78, soloist, 1978-79, prin., 1979—; dir. N.Y. State Summer Sch. of Arts Sch. of Dance, Saratoga Springs, from 1982. Created roles in George Balanchine's Robert Schumann's Davidsbündlertänze, Peter Martin's Rossini Pas de Deux, Lille Suite, Suite from Histoire du Soldat, Calcium Light Night, Sonate di Scarlatti, Concerto for Two Solo Pianos, Tango, A Schubertiad, Song of the Auvergne, Ecstatic Orange, Jerome Robbins' Piano Pieces, Chamber Works, I'm Old Fashioned, & The Four Seasons; PBS-TV appearances include Bournonville Dances, The Magic Flute, A Choreographer's Notebook (all Dance in America series), and Lincoln Center Special: Balanchine Celebrates Stravinsky. Recipient Dance Mag. award, 1985; L'Oreal Shining Star award, 1985, Lions of the Performing Arts award N.Y. Pub. Library, 1986. Office: NYC Ballet Inc NY State Theater Lincoln Ctr Pla New York NY 10023 also: care Sharon Wagner Artists Service 150 West End Ave New York NY 10023*

WATTS, HELENA ROSELLE, military intelligence analyst; b. East Lynne, Mo., May 29, 1921; d. Elmer Wayne and Nellie Irene (Barrington) Long; m. Henry Millard Watts, June 14, 1940; children—Helena Roselle Watts Scott, Patricia Marie Watts Foble. B.A., Johns Hopkins U., 1952, postgrad., 1952-53. Assoc. engr., Westinghouse Corp., Balt., 1965-67; sr. analyst Merck, Sharp & Dohme, Westpoint, Pa., 1967-69; sr. engr. Bendix Radio div. Bendix Corp., Balt., 1970-72; sr. scientist Sci. Applications Internat. Corp., McLean, Va., 1975-84; mem. tech. staff The Mitre Corp., McLean, 1985—; adj. prof. Def. Intelligence Coll., Washington, 1984-85. Contbr. articles to tech. jours. Mem. IEEE, AAAS, Nat. Mil. Intelligence Assn., U.S. Naval Inst., Assn. Old Crows, Mensa, N.Y. Acad. Sci. Republican. Roman Catholic. Avocations: photography; gardening; reading. Home: 4302 Roberts Ave Annandale VA 22003 Office: The Mitre Corp W842 7525 Colshire Dr McLean VA 22102

WATTS, JOYCE LANNOM, university administrator; b. Los Angeles, June 1, 1942; d. Kenneth Loren and Elsie (Weston) Lannom; m. John Ransford Watts, Dec. 20, 1975. B.A. cum laude, Calif. State U.-Long Beach, 1976; MBA, Northwestern U., 1987. Exec. asst. to pres. Calif. State U.-Long Beach, 1964-75, exec. dir. alumni affairs, 1976-79; mem. staff vice chmn. U.S. Commn. Civil Rights, 1975-76; regional adminstr. Career Research, Chgo., 1979-81; 2d v.p. No. Trust Co., Chgo., 1981-84; asst. dean, dir. career devel. and placement Kellogg Grad. Sch. Mgmt., Northwestern U., Evanston, Ill., 1984-88; sr. v.p. Drake Beam Morin Inc., 1989—. Mem. Employment Mgmt. Assn., Women in Mgmt. (pres. 1989, Nat. Woman of Achievement award 1987), Dorothy L. Sayers Soc. Home: 614 Forest Ave Evanston IL 60202

WATTS, KATHERINE, investor, business owner; b. Roanoke, Va., July 12, 1949; d. William and Mary Elizabeth (Brown) W.; m. Dale Evans McIvor. BA summa cum laude, Washington U., St. Louis, 1971; MBA, NYU, 1975. Sr. security analyst Merrill Lynch, N.Y.C., 1971-74, assoc. investment banking dept., 1974-76; mgr. acquisitions and strategic planning Norton Simon, N.Y.C., 1976-81; prin. mergers and acquisitions div. L.F. Rothschild, N.Y.C., 1981-86; founding ptnr. Southport (Conn.) Ptnrs., 1986—. Mem. C.T. Venture Group, Pequot Yacht Club, West Side Tennis. Office: Southport Ptnrs 2425 Post Rd Southport CT 06490

WATTS, MARY ANN, retired educator; b. Harrisburg, Pa., Sept. 13, 1927; d. Major Allan and Ellana Susan (Robinson) Brown; m. Spencer R. Watts, June 23, 1951; children: Shelley Lynn, Allison Dee, Howard Allan. BS, Cheyney U., 1949; student, Temple U., 1965-67, Pa. State U., 1969-72. Tchr. Harrisburg Sch. Dist., 1949-51, 59-69, Balt. Sch. Dist., 1951-57, tchr. Reading (Pa.) Sch. Dist., 1969-89, mem. sch. dist. dress and discipline code com., 1977-79; corr. Hamburg Item. Mem. Bernville Borough Council, 1976—, v.p., 1988—; sec., treas. Berks County Boroughs Assn., 1977—. Mem. NAACP, LWV, Pa. Elected Women's Assn., Pa. Assn. Sch. Retirees, Berks County Assn. Sch. Retiress, Delta Sigma Theta. Democrat. Mem. United Ch. Christ. Clubs: Bernville Woman's (pres. 1978-80, 86-88, Woman of Yr. 1985, Grange Community Svc. award 1988), GNO of Harrisburg.

WATTS, PATSY JEANNE, management company executive; b. Portland, Oreg., Oct. 19, 1943; d. Eugene Estelle and Maxine (Muldoon) Nicks; m. James Lowell Watts, June 5, 1964 (div. Aug. 1974); 1 child, Douglas James. Hon. cert. in realty, Grossmont Coll., 1978; paralegal cert., U. San Diego, 1980. Realtor assoc. Schwab Realty, La Mesa, Calif., 1976-78; office mgr. Office of Dist. Atty., Fallon, Nev., 1978-81; cons., adminstr. Calif. and Fla., 1981-85; real estate and legal exec. adminstr. Keegan Mgmt. Co., San Jose, Calif., 1985—. Co-Author: Real Estate Marketing, 1977. Fund-raiser Citizens for Pete Wilson, San Diego, William Cleator for San Diego City Coun., 1981-82; staff reporter Citizens vs. Pub. Funds for Pvt. Contracting of San Diego Conv. Ctr., 1983. Named Miss Water Festival City of Portland, 1961. Mem. NAFE, San Francisco Assn. Legal Assts., Internat. Council Shopping Ctrs., Ams. For Legal Reform. Republican. Office: Keegan Mgmt Co 1798 Technology Dr San Jose CA 95110

WATTS, VALERIA KAY, revenue management executive; b. Pomeroy, Ohio, Feb. 6, 1929; d. Charles Milton and Virginia Pauline (Buck) Haley; m. Joseph Woodrow Watts, July 20, 1946; children: Kevin Lee, James Joseph, Charles Addison, Jeffrey Alan. Student, Ohio U. Br. Deputy dir. of revenue mgmt. Treas. of State of Ohio, Columbus; statewide labor coord. State Treas., Columbus; regional v.p. Federated Dem. Women of Ohio. Recipient Hat's Off award.

WATTS, VALERIE ROBBIN, accountant; b. Washington, Aug. 29, 1953. BS in Sociology, George Washington U., 1975; MA in Mgmt., Central Mich. U., 1976; MS in Pub. Acctg., U. Hartford, 1981. CPA, N.Y. Adminstr. Howard U. Hosp., 1977-79; auditor Deloitte, Haskins & Sells, 1981-83; sr. fin. analyst IBM, 1983-86; mgr. budget and fin. N.Y.C. Transit Authority, 1986-87; owner Watts & Assocs., Bklyn., 1987—; asst. prof. acctg. City Univ., Borough of Manhattan Community Coll., N.Y.C., 1989—; adj. prof. Touro Coll., 1985-86, CUNY, 1984-85. Mem. Queensboro Soc. for Prevention Cruelty to Children, 1989, Women's Polit. Caucus, 1989. Mem NAFE, AICPA, Nat. Assn. Accts., Am. Inst. CPA's, N.Y. Soc. CPA's. Democrat. Baptist. Office: Watts Cons Svcs 299 Broadway Ste 902 New York NY 10007

WAUCHOPE, DOROTHY THOMSON, freelance journalist; b. Clintondale, N.Y., Apr. 7, 1912; d. J. Wells and Nina (Hurd) Weaver; m. Sidney Thomson, July 3, 1937 (dec. 1943); 1 child, Jean Thomson Dalber; m. Capt. F. Wauchope, 1950 (dec. 1974); 1 child, Donald A. BLitt in Journalism, Rutgers U., 1933; BA in Anthropology, SUNY, New Paltz, 1984. Reporter, copy desk editor, features editor Eagle-News and New Yorker, Poughkeepsie, 1936-44; reporter New Orleans Times-Picayune, 1944-45, feature writer, 1956-58; info. officer Office War Info., USPHS, Washington, 1944-50; reporter WNS, women's nat. news svc., Washington and N.Y.C., 1946-47, 49; freelance journalist; freelance journalist New Orleans Times-Picayune, others, 1956-57, 1979—; tutor English composition SUNY, New Paltz, 1984-90. Bd. dirs. United Seamen's Svc., New Orleans, 1945, co-chmn. Washington Day Care Parents Com., 1945-48, Norfolk-Chesapeake Planned Parenthood, Norfolk, Va., 1964-74; v.p. Oakwood Sch. Bd., Poughkeepsie, 1987-89. Mem. Nat. Press Club. Democrat. Mem. Soc. of Friends. Home: 151 N Ohioville Rd New Paltz NY 12561

WAUGH, CAROL-LYNN RÖSSEL, writer, artist; b. Staten Island, N.Y., Jan. 5, 1947; d. Carl Frederick Leopold and Muriel Alice (Kiefer) Rössel; m. Charles Gordon Waugh, Nov. 11, 1967; children: Jenny-Lynn, Eric-Jon Rössel. BA in Humanities, SUNY-Binghamton, 1968; MA in Art History, Kent State U., 1979. Sewing instr. Singer Co., Augusta, Maine, 1971-72; instr. art history U. Maine, Augusta, 1977; art instr. Adult Edn., Winthrop, Maine, 1978; pvt. practice writer, artist, Winthrop, 1973—. Author: Petite Portraits, 1982; My Friend Bear, 1982; Octagon Houses of Maine, 1982; Teddy Bear Artists, 1984; (with Susanna Oroyan) Contemporary Artist Dolls, 1986, (with Kim Brewer) The Official Price Guide to Antique and Modern Teddy Bears, 1990; editor (with Isaac Asimov and Martin H. Greenberg) anthologies: The Twelve Crimes of Christmas, 1981, 2d edit. 1982, Japanese, Italian, Swedish edits.; Big Apple Mysteries, 1982, Japanese edit.; Show Business Is Murder, 1983, German edit.; Thirteen Horrors of Hallowe'en, 1983; Murder on the Menu, 1984; (with B. Pronzini and M.H. Greenberg) Manhattan Mysteries, 1987; (with M.H. Greenberg and Frank D. McSherry, Jr.) Murder and Mystery in Boston, 1987; (with H.H. Greenberg and Isaac Asimov) Hound Dunnit, 1987; (with M.H. Greenberg) The New Adventures of Sherlock Holmes, 1987, Brit., German, Japanese edits.; Murder and Mystery in Chgo., 1988, The Sport of Crime, Purr-fect Crime, 1989, Senior Sleuths, 1989; co-author short story (in anthology); contbr. chpts. to books on dolls; reviewer children's books, art books, books about bears for various mags. and Sunday Sun-Jour., Lewiston-Auburn, Maine; authority on teddy bears; contbr. articles on dolls, teddy bears, antiques to mags.; lectr. in fields; sculptor original artist dolls, 1973—; designer original teddy bears produced by House of Nisbet, Avon, Eng., 1987—, Effanbee Dolls, 1989—, Ashton-Drake Galleries, 1989—, collector's plates for Brimark, Ltd., 1986; exhibited watercolor paintings and photography. Justice of Peace, Kennebec County, Maine, 1972-78; mem. Kennebec County Democratic Com., Augusta, 1972-80, 88. Buttonwood scholar, N.Y. Stock Exchange, 1964-68, 70-71; recipient awards for original artist dolls, awards for color photography Nat. Fedn. Press Women, 1987. Mem. Soc. Children's Book Writers, Original Doll Artist Council Am., Mystery Writers Am. Home: 5 Morrill St Winthrop ME 04364

WAUGH, JENNIE SUITER, health facility administrator, nurse; b. Chesapeake, Ohio, Dec. 23, 1930; d. Orville Keith and Lola Mae (Rupe) Suiter; m. Jack A. Waugh, Sept. 14, 1952; children: Jeffrey Jay, Jeri Waugh Rector, John Andrew. Diploma in nursing, Holzer Hosp. Sch. Nursing, Gallipolis, Ohio, 1952; BA, W.Va. State Coll., 1981, MA in Counseling and Guidance, 1984. Cert. social worker; lic. counselor. Mem. faculty Holzer Hosp. Sch. Nursing; asst. dir. nursing Pleasant Valley Hosp., Point Pleasant, W.Va.; dir. nursing Jackson Gen. Hosp., Ripley, W.Va., 1974—; unit dir. Jackson Gen. Hosp. Treatment Ctr., Ripley, 1984—; mem., cons. allied health staff Jackson Gen. Hosp. Vice pres. W.Va. Bd. Examiners for Licensed Practical Nurses, Charleston, 1989-90. Mem. Am. Assn. Mental Health Counselors, Am. Assn. Nurse Execs., Am. Assn. for Counseling and Guidance, W.Va. Assn. Alcoholism and Drug Abuse Counselors, Am. Nurses Assn., W.Va. Nursing Assn. Home: 803 S Ritchie Ave Ravenswood WV 26164 Office: Jackson Gen Hosp Pinnell St Ripley WV 25271

WAX, NADINE VIRGINIA, banker; b. Van Horne, Iowa, Dec. 7, 1927; d. Laurel Lloyd and Viola Henrietta (Schrader) Bobzien; divorced; 1 child, Sharlyn K. Wax Munns. Student, U. Iowa, 1970-7l; student real estate fin., Ohio State U., 1980-8l. Jr. acct. McGladrey, Honsen, Dunn (name McGladrey-Pullen Co., CPAs), Cedar Rapids, Iowa, 1944-47; office mgr. Iowa Securities Co. (now Norwest Mortgage Co.), Cedar Rapids, 1954-55; asst. cashier Mchts. Nat. Bank, Cedar Rapids, 1956-75, asst. v.p., 1976-78, v.p., 1979—. Bd. dirs., v.p. Kirkwood Community Coll. Facilities Found., Cedar Rapids, 1970—; bd. dirs., treas. Kirkwood Community Coll., 1984—; trustee Indian Creek Nature Ctr., Cedar Rapids, 1974—; vol. St. Luke's Hosp. Aux., Cedar Rapids, 1981-85; mem. Linn County Regional Planning Commn., 1982—, Cedar Rapids-Marion Fine Arts Coun., 1984—, Bd. Suprs. Compensation Commn. for Condemnation, 1987—; bd. dirs. Am. Heart Assn., Cedar Rapids, 1983—; mem. Iowa Employment and Tng. Coun., Des Moines, 1982-83. Recipient Outstanding Woman award Cedar Rapids Tribute to Women and Industry, 1984. Mem. Nat. Assn. Bank Women (state edn. chmn. 1982-83), Am. Inst. Banking (bd. dirs. 1968-70), Soc. Real Estate Appraisers (treas. 1978-80), Linn County Bankers Assn. (pres. 1979-80), Cedar Rapids Bd. Realtors, Cedar Rapids C. of C. (bus.-edn. com. 1986—), Cedar Rapids Country Club. Republican. Lutheran. Home: l47 Ashcombe Dr SE Cedar Rapids IA 52403

WAXMAN, JOANNE, art librarian; b. Portland, Maine, Apr. 16, 1934; d. Samuel and Lillian (Rapoport) Silverman; m. Kenneth Eliot Waxman, Sept. 5, 1954; children: Rebecca, Jane, Paula. Student, Simmons Coll., 1952-54; BA, U. So. Maine, 1971; MLS, U. Maine, 1974. Libr. Portland Sch. Art, 1976—; mem. Maine Libr. Commn., Augusta, 1981—; chmn. So. Maine Libr. Dist., 1980-82. Bd. dirs. Skowhegan (Maine) Sch. Painting and Sculpture, 1973-75; mem. bldg. com. Portland Pub. Libr., 1976-79; del. White House Conf. on Librs., 1979. Mem. Art Librs. Soc. N.Am., Art Librs. Soc. New Eng., Coll. Art Assn., Maine Libr. Assn., Phi Kappa Phi. Democrat. Jewish. Home: 28 Westminster Terr Cape Elizabeth ME 04107 Office: Portland Sch Art Libr 619 Congress St Portland ME 04101

WAY, CAROL JANE, non-profit organization administrator; b. Providence, Jan. 24, 1940; d. Wilfred Bartholomew and Lillian Elizabeth (Tainsh) Martineau; m. Paul Howard Way, June 28, 1958 (div. 1986); children: Laura L. Way Jordahl, P. Craig, Victoria L. Way Hermansen, J. Brent. EdB, R.I. Coll., 1960; postgrad., U. R.I., 1960; MPA, Mankato (Minn.) State U., 1978; postgrad., Universidad Internacional, Mexico City, 1985. Cert. in secondary edn.; lic. in real estate. Tchr. pub. secondary schs. Scotia, N.Y., 1962-64, 67-68, Schenectady, N.Y., 1968-69; reporter, freelance writer The Long Islander newspaper, Huntington, N.Y., 1969-71; tchr. pub. secondary schs. Avon, Conn., 1971-72; asst. to dir. Ret. Sr. Vol. program, Hartford, Conn., 1972-73; dir. pub. info. Mankato Schs., 1974-78; tchr. pub. secondary schs. Fairfield, Conn., 1979-80; assoc. dir. YWCA of Greater Bridgeport, Conn., 1980-81; dir. alumni relations Sacred Heart U., Fairfield, 1982-84; exec. dir. Westport (Conn.) C. of C., 1986-88, West Hartford (Conn.) C. of C., 1988—; bd. dirs. Child Guidance Ctr. of Greater Bridgeport, 1986—; participant English Inst. SUNY chpt. N.Y. State Tchrs. Assn., 1964. Contbr. articles to mags. and newspapers. Lt. gov. R.I. Girls' State, Providence, 1955; mem. Housewives for Rockefeller and Schenectady Reps., 1964; registered lobbyist various non-partisan groups, Minn. and Washington, 1975-78; chairwoman Blue Earth County (Minn.) Reps., 1975-78; town com. Fairfield Reps., 1980-83; bd. dirs. YMCA of West Hartford. Mem. Nat. Assn. Bus. Economists, Nat. Assn. Female Execs., AAUW (life, bd. dirs. 1963-81, nat. legis. com. 1976-78, 80-83), Women in the Arts (charter), Fairfield Network Exec. Women, Women in Mgmt., Farmington Woods Country Club. Episcopalian. Lodge: Rotary. Home: 48 Gate Ridge Rd Fairfield CT 06432 Office: West Hartford C of C 948 Farmington Ave West Hartford CT 06107

WAYLOR, CHERYL WATSON, insurance services company owner, consultant; b. Montreal, Que., Can., Sept. 8, 1943; came to U.S., 1954; d. Alan Douglas and Jean Mary (Hughes) Watson; m. Joseph Robert Earl Waylor, Apr. 5, 1969 (div. Feb. 1979). BBA, Ga. State U., 1980, postgrad. Supr. div. Liberty Mut., Atlanta, 1969-76; instr. ins. DeKalb Community Coll., Clarkston, Ga., 1978-79; mgr. div. Kemper Group, 1979-85; owner, pres. h.m.s. Co. Ins. Svcs. (name changed to Ins. Support Svcs., Inc.), Overland Park, 1986—; lectr. in field; ins. cons. Fortune and Co. Risk Mgrs. Inc., 1987—. Contbr. articles to profl. jours. Vol. Leukemia Soc. Am., 1987; vol. explorer Boy Scouts Am., 1987; vol. Girl Scouts U.S.A. Leadership Devel., 1987—. Mem. Ins. Women of Greater Kansas City-Nat. Assn. Ins. Women (bd. dirs. 1985-86, v.p. 1987-88, pres.-elect 1988-89, pres. 1989—, Rookie of Yr. 1985, Best Speaker in Communicate with Confidence Speakoff, Kansas City, State Mo. 1987), Nat. Assn. Women Bus. Owners, Toastmasters Internat. (area gov. 1986-87, adminstrv. v.p. 1986, v.p. edn. 1987, pres. 1988, lt. gov. 1989—, best evaluator 1985). Republican. Avocations: sky diving, fencing, running, reading, traveling. Office: 6901 W 63d St Suite 121 Shawnee Mission KS 66202

WAYMOUTH, CHARITY, retired cell biologist, editor; b. Blackheath, Eng., Apr. 29, 1915; came to U.S., 1953; d. Charles Sydney Herbert and Ada Curror (Scott Dalgleish) W. BSc, Bedford Coll., U. London, 1936; PhD, U. Aberdeen, Scotland, 1944; DD (hon.), Gen. Theol. Sem., N.Y.C., 1979; ScD (hon.), Bowdoin Coll., 1982. Biochemist City of Manchester Hosps., Eng., 1937-44; head tissue culture dept. Chester Beatty Research Inst., London, 1947-52; staff scientist Jackson Lab., Bar Harbor, Maine, 1953-63, sr. staff scientist, 1963-81, assoc. dir., 1977-80, interim dir., 1980-81, sr. staff scientist emeritus, 1981—; Rose Morgan vis. prof. U. Kans., Lawrence, 1971; bd. dirs. W. Alton Jones Cell Sci. Ctr., Lake Placid, N.Y., 1980-82. Editor symposium proc. and research monographs. Contbr. articles to tech. jours., chpts. to books. Dep. triennial gen. convs. Episcopalian Ch., 1970—. Recipent achievement award AAUW, 1962, Deborah Morton award Westbrook Coll., 1981; fellow Beit Meml. Found., Copenhagen and London, 1944-46, Am. Cancer Soc., 1952-53. Fellow AAAS; mem. N.Y. Acad. Scis., Tissue Culture Assn. (pres. 1960-62, editor-in-chief 1968-75, editor Decennial Rev. Conf. 1984-87). Avocations: reading, gardening, bread making. Home: 16 Atlantic Ave Bar Harbor ME 04609

WAYNE, ELSIE ELEANORE, mayor; b. Shediac, N.B., Can., Apr. 20, 1932; d. Paxton Lee Fairweather and Ada (Catherine) Cook; m. Richard Seymour Wayne, July 4, 1968; children: Daniel Allan, Stephen Paxton. LLD (hon.), St. Thomas U., Fredericton, N.B., Can., 1988. Mem. St. John (N.B., Can.) Common Coun., 1977-83; mayor City of St. John, 1983—; mem. Econ. Devel. Adv. Bd.; bd. dirs. Market Sq. Corp. Chairwoman Red Shield Campaign Salvation Army, mem.; hon. chairwoman St. John Coun. Women, YMCA/YWCA Fund Raising Campaign, 1986, Big Bros./Big Sisters Campaign, 1987; hon. v.p. Canadian Red Cross; past mem. Exec. Com. Family Svcs, 2d Bn. Delancey's Brigade; past commr., ex-officio mem. St. John Transit Commn., planning adv. coun. City of St. John; mem. St. John Boys and Girls Club Endowment Fund; bd. dirs. St. John Non-Profit Housing, United Way Greater St. John, St. John Found., St. John Port and Devel. Commn., Youth Enterprise Ctr.; past bd. dirs. Gertrude Aarela Sheltered Workshop Physically Handicapped, Centracare Hosp.; bd. govs. U. N.B. Mem. Fedn. Canadian Mcpls. (nat. bd. dirs., mem. transp. com.), Cities of N.B. Assn. (past pres.), Carleton and York Regtl. Assn. (assoc., hon.), St. George's Soc. (hon.), Royal Canadian Legion (hon. local br.), Quota Club (hon. v.p.). Office: PO Box 1971, Saint John, NB Canada E2L 4L1

WAYNE, JUSTINE WASHINGTON, teacher; b. Darling, Miss., Mar. 8, 1945; d. Booker T. and Arneal (Johnson) Washington; m. James Wardell Wayne, Dec. 22, 1968. BA, Harris Tchrs. Coll., 1968; postgrad., San Diego State U., 1971-74; MS magna cum laude, Pepperdine U., 1977; postgrad., various univs. Cert. elem. tchr., Mo., Calif., tchr. effectiveness and assertiveness tng., instr. computers, ednl. specialist, neighborhood youth community counselor. Cashier, sales Jupiter Discount Ctr., St. Louis, 1963-65; clerk carrier U.S. Post Office, St. Louis, 1965-66; tchr., grade level chair San Diego Unified Sch. Dist., 1969—; cashier, sales Sears Roebuck, Long Beach, Calif., 1970; beauty, color cons. J. Wayne Enterprises, Spring Valley, Calif., 1985-88; part-time tchr. Solano Opportunity Coun., Vallejo, Calif., 1969; conductor workshops and mem. program com. Christian Women Seminar, 1981-88, chair, 1985. Contbr. articles to profl. jours. Alt. rep. San Diego Svc. Ctr. Coun., 1986, 87, 88-89. Mem. NAACP, NEA (del. to rep. 1986-89), NEA Polit. Action Com. 100 Club, Calif. Tchrs. Assn. (alt. del. to coun. 1983, 84), Assn. Supervision and Curriculum Div., San Diego Tchrs. Assn. (chmn. minority affairs com. 1986-89, named Sch. Site Tchr. of Yr. Rep. 1988), Assn. Black Educators, Nat. Found. for Improvement of Edn., Computer Using Educators, San Diego Coun. of Adminstrv. Women in Edn., Pepperdine Alumni Assn., Nat. Coun. Negro Women, San Diego Christian Found., Calif. State Sheriff's Assn. Office: San Diego Unified Sch Dist 4100 Normal St San Diego CA 92103

WAYNE, KYRA PETROVSKAYA, author; b. Crimea, USSR, Dec. 31, 1918; came to U.S., 1948, naturalized, 1951; d. Prince Vasily Sergeyevich and Baroness Zinaida Fedorovna (Fon-Haffenberg) Obolensky; m. George J. Wayne, Apr. 21, 1961; 1 child, Ronald George. B.A., Leningrad Inst. Theatre Arts, 1939, M.A., 1940. Actress, concert singer, USSR, 1939-46; actress, U.S., 1948-51; enrichment lectr. Royal Viking Line cruises, Alaska-Can., Greek Islands-Black Sea, Russia/Europe, 1978-79, 81-82, 83-84, 86-87, 88. Author: Kyra, 1959; Kyra's Secrets of Russian Cooking, 1960; The Quest for the Golden Fleece, 1962; Shurik, 1971; The Awakening, 1972; The Witches of Barguzin, 1975; Max, The Dog That Refused to Die, 1979 (Best Fiction award Dog Writers Assn. Am. 1980); Rekindle the Dreams, 1979, Quest for Empire, 1986, Li'l Ol' Charlie, 1989. Founder, pres. Clean Air Program, Los Angeles County, 1971-72; mem. women's council KCET-Ednl. TV. Served to lt. Russian Army, 1941-43. Decorated Red Star, numerous other decorations USSR; recipient award Crusade for Freedom, 1955-56; award Los Angeles County, 1972, Merit award Am. Lung Assn. L.A. County, 1988. Mem. Soc. Children's Book Writers, Authors Guild, P.E.N., UCLA Med. Faculty Wives (pres. 1970-71, dir. 1971-75) UCLA Affiliates (life), Los Angeles Lung Assn. (life), Friends of the Lung Assn. (pres. 1988), Idyllwild Sch. Music, Art and Theatre Assn. (trustee 1987), Los Angelenos Club (life). Home: 25031 Hidden Mesa Ct Monterey CA 93940

WEARY, MARLYS ELAINE, microbiologist; b. Chgo., Mar. 13, 1939; d. Harold Everett and Irene Edna Anna (Eichman) W. BA, Valparaiso U., 1960; MS, U. Ill., Chgo., 1962; MBA, Lake Forest Sch. Mgmt., 1981. Pharmacologist Baxter Labs. Inc., Morton Grove, Ill., 1962-66, lab supr., 1966-81; lab. mgr. Baxter Travenol Labs., Inc., Morton Grove, 1981-89; sr rsch. scientist Baxter Healthcare Corp., Round Lake, Ill., 1989—; tech. cons. Merit Consulting Svcs., Mt. Prospect, Ill., 1990; course instr. Inst. for Applied Pharmacology Scis., East Brunswick, N.J., 1981-82, 84-85. Co-inventor, patentee method for determining endotoxin concentration, 1980. Rsch. fellow U. Ill., 1960-61; recipient YWCA Leadership award, Chgo., 1983, 89, Women of Achievement award, Lake County, 1986, Baxter Applied Tech. Achievement award, 1989. Mem. Parenteral Drug Assn. (bacterial endotoxin test task force chmn., charter mem. Midwest chpt.), N.Y. Acad. Scis., Internat. Endotoxin Soc. Home: 513 S George St Mount Prospect IL 60056

WEATHERBEE, ELLEN GENE ELLIOTT, university administrator; b. Lansing, Mich., Sept. 16, 1939; d. Eugene Bradley and Wilma Alcott (Gardner) Elliott; m. Lee Weatherbee, Aug. 18, 1959; children: Anne Susan, Brent Robert, Julie Patricia. BA in Edn., U. Mich., 1960, postgrad., 1972-

77; MA in English Lit., Eastern Mich. U., 1962. Cert. tchr. Tchr. adult edn. Schoolcraft Coll., Livonia, Mich., 1983-85; tchr. adult edn. lifelong learning program U. Mich./Wayne State U., Ann Arbor and Detroit, 1973-84; tchr. adult edn. Leelanau Schs./Sleeping Bear Nat. Lakeshore, 1982—; tchr., nature trip leader adult edn. program Matthaei Bot. Gardens, U. Mich., Ann Arbor, 1984—, dir., founder adult edn. program, 1984—; founder, dir. Weatherbee's Bot. Expdns. and Excursions, 1990; poison control ctr. cons., plant and mushroom identification Mich. Hosps., 1978—; cons. botanist Matthaei Bot. Gardens, U. Mich., Ann Arbor, 1977—. Co-author: Edible Wild Plants, A Guide to Collecting and Cooking, 1982; mem. editorial bd. Mich. Botanist, 1978—; contbr. articles to profl. jours. Constable Dem. party,Ann Arbor Twp., Mich. Mem. Austrian Mountain Climbing Soc., British Canoe Union, Fedn. Ont. Naturalists, Great Lakes Sea Kayaking Club, Mich. Acad. Sci., Mich. Bot. Club, Nature Conservancy, N.Am. Mycological Assn., Pipsissewa Chamber Music Soc. Home: 11405 Patterson Lake Dr Pinckney MI 48169 Office: Matthaei Bot Gardens U Mich 1800 N Dixboro Rd Ann Arbor MI 48105

WEATHERBEE, LINDA, insurance executive; b. Decatur, Ill., July 20, 1956; d. Carl and V. Lucile (Westwood) W. BA magna cum laude, James Millikin U., 1977; postgrad., Ill. State U., 1981-82. CLU, chartered fin. cons. Fin. analyst State Farm Life Ins., Bloomington, Ill., 1979-82; supr. State Farm Life Ins., Austin, Tex., 1982-86; asst. supt. State Farm Life Ins., Salem, Oreg., 1986—. Cellist Decatur Civic Orch., 1973-75; ch. pianist, 1975-77, youth advisor Cen. Ill, 1979-81; Rep. vol., Bloomington, 1982; tutor adult edn. program Chemeketa Community Coll., Salem, 1986, 87; tchr. high sch. religion course, Salem, 1987—. Fellow Life Mgmt. Inst.; mem. Adminstrv. Mgmt. Soc., Life Office mgmt. Assn., Williamette Soc. CLU and Chrtered Fin. Cons. (bd. dirs. 1987—), Am. Horse Show Assn., N.W. Horse Council (Oreg.), Am. Bus. Women's Assn. (Townlake chpter Austin, Tex. 1984-86), Nat. Assn. Female Execs., Phi Kappa Phi. Mem. LDS Church. Office: State Farm Ins 4600 25th Ave NE Salem OR 97313

WEATHERBY, SUSAN MOORMANN, educator; b. Cin., Dec. 14, 1950; d. Ambrose Francis and Susan (Guckes) Moormann; 1 child, Shannon Rose Lydon Weatherby. BA, U. So. Fla., Tampa, 1974, MA, 1976, MEd, 1989. Cert. tchr., Fla. Tchr., reading coord. St. Cecelia Sch., Clearwater, Fla., 1974-81; tchr. Meadowlawn Middle Sch., St. Petersburg, Fla., 1981-82; vol. Pinellas County Schs., Clearwater, Fla., 1982-85; tchr. Ponce de Leon Elem., Clearwater, 1985-88; adj. instr. St. Petersburg Jr. Coll., Clearwater, 1987; reading specialist North Ward Elem., Clearwater, 1988—; rep. Tchr. Edn. Coun., Pinellas County, Fla., 1988—. Recipient Teach for Excellence award Edn. Found., Largo, Fla., 1987; Poynter Inst. Media Studies writers camp fellow, St. Petersburg, 1988. Mem. Assn. for Childhood Edn., Internat., Assn. for Supervision and Curriculum Devel., Internat. Reading Assn., Fla. Reading Assn., Pinellas Reading Coun., Phi Kappa Phi, Kappa Delta Pi, Phi Delta Kappa. Home: 13810 Kimberly Dr Largo FL 34644 Office: Pinellas County Sch 1960 Druid Rd Clearwater FL 34618

WEATHERUP, WENDY GAINES, insurance agent, writer; b. Glendale, Calif., Oct. 20, 1952; d. William Hughes and Janet Ruth (Neptune) Gaines; m. Roy Garfield Weatherup, Sept. 10, 1977; children—Jennifer, Christine. B.A., U. So. Calif., 1974; Lic. ins. agt. Ins. agt. Gaines Agy., Northridge, Calif., 1974—. Mem. Nat. Assn. Female Execs., U. So. Calif. Alumni Assn., Alpha Gamma Delta. Republican. Methodist. Avocations: photography; travel; writing novels; computers. Home: 17260 Rayen St Northridge CA 91325 Office: Gaines Agy 8448 Reseda Blvd Northridge CA 91324

WEAVER, AMANDA LOUISE, consultant, real estate executive; b. Waco, Tex., May 1, 1948; d. Thomas Marshall and Nancy Louise (Rhea) W.; m. James E. Beard, July 7, 1973 (div. 1979). BA in Sociology, Southwestern U., 1970; MBA, Ariz. State U., 1978. Residential dir. Job Corps, McKinney, Tex., 1970-71; dist. dir. Camp Fire Girls, Dallas, 1971-73; cons. Camp Fire Girls, Denver, 1973-74; mktg. dir. Lincoln Property Co., Des Plaines, Ill., 1974-76; cons. Med. Bus. Cons., Phoenix, 1979-81; dir. practice mgmt. J. Prekup & Assoc., Phoenix, 1981-82; v.p. Physician Mgmt. Consultants, Phoenix, 1982-83, Devenney Assoc. Ltd., Phoenix, 1983-86; pres. Weaver Enterprises, Phoenix, 1987—. Contbr. articles profl. jours. Bd. dirs., Artes Belles, Phoenix, 1980-88, pres., 1984-86; bd. dirs. City of Phoenix Solicitations, 1981-85, chmn., 1986; bd. dirs. Phoenix chpt. Nat. Council on Alcoholism, 1988—. Named Outstanding Young Women in Am. Mem. Women in Comml. Real Estate, Pres.' Club, Phoenix City Club. Democrat. Office: Weaver Enterprises 1661 E Camelback Rd Ste 250 Phoenix AZ 85016

WEAVER, BARBARA FRANCES, librarian; b. Boston, Aug. 29, 1927; d. Leo Francis and Nina Margaret (Durham) Weisse; m. George B. Weaver, June 6, 1951; 1 dau., Valerie S. Clark. B.A., Radcliffe Coll., 1949; M.L.S., U. R.I., 1968; Ed.M., Boston U., 1978. Head libr. Thompson (Conn.) Pub. Libr., 1961-69; dir. Conn. State Libr. Svc. Ctr., Willimantic, 1969-72; regional adminstr. Cen. Mass. Regional Libr. System, Worcester, 1972-78; asst. commr. of edn., state libr. State of N.J., Trenton, 1978—; lectr. Simmons Coll., Boston, 1976-78. Mem. ALA, N.J. Library Assn., Chief Officers State Library Agys. Office: NJ State Library Dept of Edn CN 520 Trenton NJ 08625-0520

WEAVER, CONNIE MARIE, foods and nutrition educator; b. LaGrande, Oreg., Oct. 29, 1950; d. Robert Chesley and Avevil Jean (Harris) Shelton; m. Lloyd Rollin Weaver, Dec. 22, 1971; children: Douglas, Mark, Richard. BS, Oreg. State U., 1972, MS, 1974; PhD, Fla. State U., 1978. Teaching asst. Oreg. State U., Corvallis, 1973-74; instr. Grossmont Coll., El Cajon, Calif., 1974-75; rsch. assoc. U. R.I., Kingston, 1975; teaching asst. Fla. State U., Tallahassee, 1975-78, mem. adj. faculty, 1977-78; asst. prof. foods and nutrition Purdue U., West Lafayette, Ind., 1978-84, assoc. prof., 1984-88, prof., 1988—; rsch. fellow Kraft, Inc., Glenview, Ill., 1988—; mem. rsch. adv. com. Nat. Livestock and Meat Bd., 1989. Contbr. articles to profl. jours. Recipient Mary L. Matthews Teaching award Purdue U., 1985; grantee AMOCO Found. Inc., 1986. Mem. Inst. Food Technologists (sci. lectr. 1988-91, program chmn. 1989-90, Outstanding Svc. and Recognition award Ind. sect. 1984), Am. Chem. Soc., Am. Inst. Nutrition (program chmn. 1989-90), Soc. for Exptl. Biology and Medicine, Sigma Xi, Gamma Sigma Delta (pres. Ind. sect. 1989-90). Office: Purdue U Foods-Nutrition Stone Hall West Lafayette IN 47907

WEAVER, DAWN LERENE, printing company executive; b. Lancaster, Pa., May 22, 1948; d. James Fisher and Sarah Helen (Hanna) W.; m. June 28, 1970 (div. 1980); children: James Russell Saurbaugh, Jennifer Saurbaugh Weaver. Student, St. Petersburg Jr. Coll., 1966-67, Millersville (Pa.) U., 1967-68. Prin. Dawn's House of Ceramics, Bird-in-Hand, Pa., 1969-79; paste-up artist Lancaster Newspapers, 1970-73; art dir. Wickersham Printing, Lancaster, 1974-76; customer svc. account mgr. Intelligencer Printing Co., Lancaster, 1976-81; salesperson Veitch Printing Corp., Lancaster, 1981-84, dist. mgr., 1984—; prin. Opus II, Lancaster, 1989—. Mem. NAFE. Republican. Lutheran. Home: 4 N School Ln Lancaster PA 17603 Office: Veitch Printing Corp 1740 Hempstead Rd Lancaster PA 17601

WEAVER, DONNA RAE, dean; b. Chgo., Oct. 15, 1945; d. Albert Louis and Gloria Elaine (Graffis) Florence; m. Clifford L. Weaver, Aug. 20, 1966; 1 child, Megan Rae. BS in Edn., No. Ill. U., 1966, EdD, 1977; MEd, De Paul U., 1974. Tchr. H.L. Richards High Sch., Oak Lawn, Ill., 1966-71, Sawyer Coll. Bus., Evanston, Ill., 1971-72; asst. prof. Oakton Community Coll., Morton Grove, Ill., 1972-75; vis. prof. U. Ill., Chgo., 1977-78; dir. devel. Mallinckrodt Coll., Wilmette, Ill., 1978-80, dean, 1980-83; campus dir. Nat.-Louis U., Chgo., 1983—, dean div. applied behavioral scis., 1985-89, dean Coll. of Mgmt. Scis. and Bus., 1989—; cons. Nancy Lovely and Associs., Wilmette, 1981-84, North Cen. Assn., Chgo., 1982—. Contbr. articles to Am. Vocat. Jour., Ill. Bus. Edn. Assn. Monograph, Nat. Coll. Edn.'s ABS Rev., Nat. Nat. View. Mem. Ill. Quality of Work Life Council, 1987—, New Trier Twp. Health and Human Services Adv. Bd., Winnetka, Ill., 1985-88; bd. dirs. Open Lands Project, 1985-87, Kenilworth Village House, 1986-87. Recipient Achievement award Women in Mgmt., 1981; Am. Bd. Master Educators charter disting. fellow, 1986. Mem. Nat. Bus. Edn. Assn., Delta Pi Epsilon (past pres.). Office: Nat-Louis U 18 S Michigan Ave Chicago IL 60603

WEAVER, ELISSA BARBARA, Italian literature and language educator; b. Springfield, Ill., Apr. 11, 1940; d. John Owen and Florina Marie (Rebuffoni) W.; m. John Chamberlain, Dec. 28, 1968 (div. 1973). BS in Math., U. Ill., 1961; MA in Italian, UCLA, 1965, PhD in Italian, 1975. Instr. Italian, Rutgers U., New Brunswick, N.J., 1968-72; asst. prof. Italian, U. Chgo., 1972-78, assoc. prof., 1978-89, prof., 1989—. Editor: Amor di Virtu (Beatrice del Seara), 1990; contbr. numerous articles on Renaissance Italian lit. to profl. jours. Recipient Burlington award U. Chgo., 1988; Fulbright fellow, Florence, Italy, 1965-66, AAUW fellow, Florence, 1983-84, Harvard U.-NEH I Tatti fellow, Florence, 1988-89. Mem. Am. Boccaccio Assn. (sec.-treas. 1978-80, v.p. 1980-81, pres. 1981-85, co-editor newsletter 1978-86), Renaissance Soc. Am., MLA, Am. Assn. Italian Studies, Renaissance Inst. Ferrara, Europa delle Corti. Office: U Chgo Dept Romance Langs 1050 E 59th St Chicago IL 60637

WEAVER, LINDA M., law enforcement professional; b. Johnstown, Pa., Aug. 7, 1946; d. William Stewart and Alma Louise (Rogalla) W. Student, Ind. U. Pa., 1969-72, Allentown Police Acad., 1972, U. Minn., 1974. With Johnstown Police Dept., 1969—, youth svc. officer, juvenile div. officer, 1972-86, chief of police, 1986—; Mem. Cambria County Policy Bd., 1986, Pa. Atty. Gen.'s Task Force on Family Violence, 1987. Bd. dirs., Johnstown YWCA, 1987, Johnstown United Way, 1988, Cambria County March of Dimes, 1988; pres., Women's Help Ctr., Johnstown, 1988. Mem. Chiefs of Police Assn., Rotary. Republican. Office: Johnstown Police Dept 401 Washington St Johnstown PA 15901

WEAVER, LINDA SUSAN, advertising executive; b. Shelby, N.C., Mar. 4, 1965; d. Jerry Stokes Weaver and Mary Ann (Lane) Holbrook. Student, Clemson U., 1983-84, Greenville (S.C.) Tech. Coll., 1984-86. Media buyer, office mgr. Florence Agy., Greenville, 1984-86; media dir., account exec. Himmelsbach, Wilson & Hearl, Myrtle Beach, S.C., 1986; media dir. Eison Goot Group, Greenville, 1987, account exec., 1987—; mem. adv. bd. Up Mag., Greenville, 1987—. Mem steering com. Vol. Connection for Greenville; com. mem. Met. Arts Coun. Supporters, Greenville. Mem. Advt. Fedn. Greenville (membership chmn. 1988—, bd. dirs. 1989—, Bronze Addy award 1988, 2 Gold Addy awards 1989). Republican. Baptist. Home: 18A Jones Ave Greenville SC 29601 Office: Eison Goot Group 105 E North St Ste 200 Greenville SC 29601

WEAVER, MARGUERITE MCKINNIE (PEGGY WEAVER), state legislator, plantation owner; b. Jackson, Tenn., June 7, 1925; d. Franklin Allen and Mary Alice (Caradine) McKinnie; children: Elizabeth Lynn, Thomas Jackson III, Franklin A. McKinnie. Student, U. Colo., 1943-45; student, Am. Acad. Dramatic Arts, 1945-46, S. Meisner's Profl. Classes, 1949, Oxford U., 1990. Actress, 1946-52; mem. staff Mus. Modern Art, N.Y.C., 1949-50; radio journalist radio sta. WTJS-AM-FM, Jackson, Tenn., 1952-55; editor, radio/TV Jackson Sun Newspaper, 1952-55; columnist Bolivar (Tenn.) Bulletin-Times, 1986—; chmn. Ho. of Reps. of Old Line Dist., Hardeman County, Tenn., 1985—. Founder Paris-Henry County (Tenn.) Arts Council, 1965; charter mem. adv. bd. Tenn. Arts Commn., Nashville, 1967-74, Tenn. Performing Arts Ctr., Nashville, 1972—; chmn. Tenn. Library Assn., Nashville, 1973-74; regional chmn. Opera Memphis, 1979—; mem. nat. coun. Met. Opera, N.Y.C., 1980—. Mem. Am. Women in Radio and TV, DAR, Jackson Golf and Country, English Speaking Union, Summit (Memphis), Crescent (Memphis). Methodist. Home: Heritage Hall Heritage Farms Hickory Valley TN 38042

WEAVER, MARTHA LOUISE, nurse; b. Auberndale, Fla., Oct. 11, 1926; d. Joseph and Grace Ann (Cooper) Van der Bush; m. Haralson Sinclair Weaver, Mar. 19, 1918; children: Richard Haralson, Thomas Joseph, Kenneth Carleton. RN, St. Luke Hosp., Denver, 1948. Staff nurse Southwest Meml. Hosp., Cortez, Colo., 1948-60, operating rm. supr., 1962-70, dir. nursing, 1970-72, operating rm. supr., 1973-79; pres. Montezuma County Hosp. Dist., Cortez, 1979—. Com. woman Dem. party, Montezuma County, Colo., 1976—; bd. dirs. We. Colo. Area Health Edn. Ctr., Grand Junciton, 1980-89. Recipient Svc. and Dedication award, We. Colo. Area Health Ctr., 1988. Mem. DAR, Order Eastern Star. Home: 8950 County Rd 41 Mancos CO 81328

WEAVER, MOLLIE LITTLE, lawyer; b. Alma, Ga., Mar. 11; d. Alfred Ross and Annis Mae (Bowles) Little; m. Jack Delano Nelson, Sept. 12, 1953 (div. May 1970); 1 dau., Cynthia Ann; m. 2d, Hobart Ayres Weaver, June 10, 1970. B.A. in History, U. Richmond, 1978; J.D., Wake Forest U., 1981. Bar; N.C. 1982, Fla. 1983; Cert. profl. sec.; cert. adminstrv. mgr. Supr., Western Electric Co., Richmond, Va., 1952-75; cons., owner Cert. Mgmt. Assocs., Richmond, 1975-76; sole practice, Ft. Lauderdale, Fla., 1982-86, Emerald Isle, N.C., 1986-89, Richmond, 1989—. Author: Secretary's Reference Manual, 1973. Mem. adv. council to Bus. and Office Edn., Greensboro, N.C., 1970-73, adv. com. to bus. edn. Va. Commonwealth U., Richmond, 1977. Recipient Key to City of Winston-Salem, N.C., 1963; Epps award for scholarship, 1978. Mem. ABA, N.C. Bar Assn., Fla. Bar Assn., Carteret County Bar Assn., Word Processing Assn. (v.p., founder Richmond 1973-75), Adminstrv. Mgmt. Soc. (com. chmn. Richmond, 1973-75), Phi Beta Kappa, Eta Sigma Phi, Phi Alpha Theta. Republican. Home: 12605 Wilde Lake Ct Richmond VA 23233

WEAVER, PAMELA ANN, marketing professional; b. Little Falls, N.Y., July 7, 1947; d. Floyd Aron Weaver and Norma May (Putnam) Hoyer; m. Ken Ward McCleary, Mar. 2, 1947; children: Brian Wilson, Blake McCleary, Ryan McCleary. AA, Fulton Montgomery Community Co, Amsterdam, NY, 1968; BA, SUNY, 1970; MA, U. S. Fla., 1973; PhD, Mich. State U., East Lansing, 1978. Mem. Mathematics Dept., Riviera Jr. High Sch., Miami, Fla., 1970-72; grad. asst. Office of Med., Edn. Research and Devel., Mich. State U., East Lansing, 1973-74, Dept. of Mktg., Mich. State U., East Lansing, 1974-75; instr. mktg. Mich. State U., East Lansing; asst. prof. mktg., hospitality svcs. administrn. Cen. Mich. State U.,, Mt. Pleasant, 1978-79, Cen. Mich. U., 1982-86; chair acad. senate Cen. Mich. U., Mt. Pleasant, 1985-86, prof. mktg., hospitality svcs. administrn., 1986-89; prof. Dept. Hotel, Restaurant and Instl. Mgmt. Va. Poly. Inst. and State U., Blacksburg, 1989—. Contbr. articles to profl. jours. Mem. Coun. on Hotel, Restaurant and Instln. Edn., Acad. Mktg. Sci., Am. Mktg. Assn., So. Mktg. Assn., Internat. Acad. Hospitality Rsch. Office: Va Poly Inst and State U Hillcrest Hall Blacksburg VA 24061-0429

WEAVER, RITA MARGARET, art association executive; b. N.Y.C., Oct. 28, 1925; d. Newcomb and Lucy Elizabeth (Roche) Gaylord; B.A., N.Y. U., 1945; postgrad Lady Margaret Hall, Oxford (Eng.) U., 1945-46; m. Robert A. Weaver (dec.); children—Richard L.N., Michael Cameron. Concert pianist, 1940; reporter Nuremberg trials, 1946-48; syndicated columnist Fashions from New York, Escort Publs., London, 1949-51; actress, Off Broadway productions and summer stock, 1952-56; pres. Empire State chpt. Nat. Soc. Arts and Letters, N.Y.C., 1978-80, chmn. ballet career awards conv., 1980, v.p. and chmn. lit. career awards dinner and music career awards dinner, 1980-82, ways and means chmn. nat. bd., 1982-84, credentials chmn., 1986-84, credentials chmn., 1986-88, v.p., career awards chmn.; chmn. liaison internat. consulates, 1982-84, v.p. chmn. by laws, 1984-86, nat. dance com., 1984-86; producer Off-Broadway Musical, 1980; bd. dirs. Eleanor Gay Lee Gallery Found., N.Y.C., 1977, membership chmn., 1978-80, chmn. benefit com., 1981-82.

WEAVER, SHARON TAMARGO, university educator, director; b. Jacksonville, Fla., May 27, 1947; d. Felix Anthony and Rose (Solomon) Tamarago; m. Charles Otis Weaver, May 5, 1968 (div. June 1977); children: Jason Felix, Dax Martin. AS, Loyola U. of the South, 1967; BS, U. North Fla., 1980, MS in Health, 1981; PhD, U. Fla., 1984; MEd in Counseling, U. North Fla., 1990. Cert. rehab. counselor, health edn. specialistl; lic. rehab. provider. Dental hygienist, office mgr. Dr. C.O. Weaver, Jacksonville Beach, Fla., 1971-77; dental hygienist Drs. P.J. Cakmis and A.J. Bauknecht, Jacksonville, 1978-81; instr., evaluator counselor N.E. Fla. Safety Coun., Jacksonville, 1981-83; rehab. counselor Internat. Rehab. Assocs., Jacksonville, 1981-83; vis. instr. U. North Fla., Jacksonville, 1983-84, asst. prof., 1984-89, dir. ctr. for alcohol and drug studies, 1984—, assoc. prof., 1989—; cons. St. Johns River Hosp., Jacksonville, 1988—, Pride, Inc., West Palm Beach, Fla., 1989—, CDM Group, Washington, 1988—; trainer, cons. S.E. Regional Ctr. for Drug Free Schs. and Communities, Atlanta, 1989—; chairperson spl. rev. com. Office of Substance Abuse Prevention, Washington, 1989—; clin. program cons. Greenfield Treatment Ctr., Jacksonville, 1989—; clin. cons. Duval County Pub. Sch. System, 1990—. Mem., prog. chmn. Leadership Jacksonville, 1988; bd. dirs., co-chairperson Duval County Pub. Sch. health Adv. Bd., Jacksonville, 1983—; vice chairperson Jacksonville Says No to Drugs Coalition, 1986—, Jacksonville Community Coun., Inc., 1985—; bd. dirs. Jr. League of Jacksonville, 1989—, Mental Health Assn., 1989—, N.E. Fla. Coun. on Alcoholism and Drug Abuse, 1984—, Fla. Sch. Addiction Studies, 1987-89; pres. Greater Jacksonville Families in Action, 1987-88; NE Fla. Safety Coun., 1985—. Named U. North Fla.'s First Outstanding Alumnus, 1989, Outstanding Tchr. of the Yr., 1987; recipient Outstanding Community Svcs. award Fla. Coun. on Crime and Delinquency Prevention & N.E. Fla. Coun. on Alcohol & Drugs & Greater Jacksonville Families-in-Action, 1988. Mem. Eta Sigma Gamma (chpt. pres. 1978-79), Internat. Network for High Risk Youth and Families (com. chair 1988—), Ribault Garden Club (chpt. pres. 1974-75), Selva Marina Country Club (tennis team pres. 1975—), Am. Assn. Counseling and Devel. (chairperson women's issue com.), Phi Kappa Phi, Phi Delta Kappa, Kappa Delta Pi. Democrat. Roman Catholic. Office: U North Fla 4567 St Johns Bluff Rd S Jacksonville FL 32216

WEAVER, SIGOURNEY (SUSAN WEAVER), actress; b. N.Y.C., 1949; d. Sylvester (Pat) Weaver and Elizabeth Inglish; m. James Simpson, 1984; 1 child, Charlotte. BA, Stanford U.; M in Drama, Yale U. First profl. theater appearance in The Constant Wife, 1974; other roles in Beyond Therapy, Hurlyburly, 1984, The Merchant of Venice, 1987; films include: Alien, 1979, Eyewitness, 1981, Deal of the Century, 1983, The Year of Living Dangerously, 1983, Ghostbusters, 1984, Aliens, 1986 (Acad. award nomination for best actress), Half Moon Street, 1986, One Woman or Two, 1987, Working Girl, 1988, Gorillas in the Mist, 1988, Ghostbusters II, 1989. Recipient Golden Globe award, 1989. Office: Internat Creative Mgmt care Sam Cohn 40 W 57th St New York NY 10012*

WEAVER, VICKY LYNN, business owner; b. Winamac, Ind., Apr. 14, 1950; d. Ralph Edward and Mary June (Davis) Moore; m. Marc Harmon Lindley, Dec. 21, 1974 (div. 1980); children: Heather, Holly; m. Johnnie McArthur Weaver, June 30, 1984. AS in Social Svcs., St. John's River Community Coll., 1985. Announcer Sta. WSUZ, Palatka, Fla., 1980; cashier Orange State Pipe & Supply Co., Palatka, 1981-82; asst. mgr. Diana Shop, Palatka, 1982; counselor Juvenile Alternative Svc. Program, Palatka and Starke, 1982-85; v.p. spl. projects S.E. Wood & Assocs., Palatka, 1985-86; pres., bd. dirs. Human Resources Devel. Svcs., Inc., Palatka, 1986—; Palatka Ct. Svcs. Am. Inc., Patalka, 1988; pres., bd. dirs. Ct. Svcs. Am. Inc., Palatka, 1988—; dir. Putnam County Probation Dept., Patalka; cons. N.E. Fla. Ednl. Consortium, Palatka, 1987-89. Vol. Community Arbitration Program, Palatka, 1983—; bd. dirs. Putnam County Alcohol and Drug Coun., 1983-88; mem. Project Freeway Task Force, 1984—, chmn. 1988—; mem. Vol. Support Network, Palatka, 1987—, pres., 1988—; sch. vol. Putnam County Schs., 1986—; mem. coun. dist. 3, Fla. Alcohol and Drug Mental Health Bd. Mem. Putnam C. of C., Pilot Club. Office: Human Resources Devel Svcs 200 N 3d St Palatka FL 32077

WEAVER, VIRGINIA DOVE, museum executive; b. Westerly, R.I.; d. Ronald Cross and Elva Gertrude (Burdick) Dove; m. Water Albert Weaver, Jr. (div. Apr. 1982); children—Marshall Gueringer, Claudia Cross, Leila Jane. B.A., Tulane U., 1973; M.A., 1977. Dir. vols.Hermann Grima Hist. House, New Orleans, 1976-77; adminstrv. analyst City Chief Adminstrv. Office, New Orleans, 1977-83; dir. pub. rels. New Orleans Mus. Art, 1983—. Coeditor: Letters From Young Audiences, 1971; contbr. articles to profl. jours. Bd. dirs. New Orleans chpt. Young Audiences, Inc., 1968-77; co-chmn. New Orleans Symphony Book Fair, 1973-74; mem. city coun. investigative panel SPCA, New Orleans, 1981-82; nat. pub. rels. chmn. Nat. Soc. Daus. of Founders and Patriots Am., 1985-88, publicity chmn. Spirit of 76 chpt., 1988—. Nat. Coun. Jewish Women grantee, 1977. Mem. Pub. Rels. Soc. Am. (So. Classics anvil award 1985, 87, So. Classics award Excellence 1986), La. Press Assn. (assoc.), La. Travel and Promotion Assn., Deep South Hotel/Motel Assn. Episcopalian. Bd. dirs. Symphony Womens Com., 1982-86; mem. steering com. Mayors Arts Task Force, New Orleans, 1978-79. Clubs: Orleans (fine arts com., current events com. 1990—); Le Petit Salon (chmn. publicity for 150th anniversary 1988, co-chmn. programs 1989, 90—). Avocation: Piano. Home: 7478 Hurst St New Orleans LA 70118 Office: New Orleans Mus Art PO Box 19123 New Orleans LA 70179

WEBB, DANA LUANNE, computer software company official; b. Borger, Tex., Sept. 2, 1952; d. Tommy Joe and Mary Frances (Wiseman) McCord; m. Douglas L. Hunter, Jan. 8, 1972 (div. Aug. 1986); children: Jared Lyle, Carly Lauren; m. James Austin Webb, July 4, 1987. AElective studies, Brazosport Coll., 1983, AS, 1985. Software technician Brazosview Sch., Freeport, Tex., 1984-85; mgr. software devel. Warren-Forthought, Inc., Angleton, Tex., 1985—; also sec., bd. dirs. Warren-Forthough, Inc., Angleton, Tex. Co-inventor graphical interactive software tng. system. Mem. NAFE. Republican. Office: Warren Forthought Inc 1212 N Velasco St Angleton TX 77515

WEBB, DONNA LOUISE, associate director of lifelong learning; b. Yakima, Wash., Aug. 12, 1929; d. Manuel Lawrence and Rena May (Sewell) Matson; (div.); children: Marlene Park, Ed Webb III. AA in Vocat. Edn., Portland (Oreg.) Community Coll., 1976; BA in Psychology, Warner Pacific Coll., 1980; MEd in Career and Vocat. Edn., Oreg. State U., Corvallis, 1980, EdD in Career and Vocat. Edn., 1983. Dir. placement Andrews U., Mich., 1969-74; dir. career edn. and coop. work experience Portland, 1976-78; coord. youth program Fed. Experiment/Chronically Unemployed Youth, Vancouver, Wash., 1979; dir. career counseling Clark Coll., Vancouver, 1979; tchr. coorp. edn. project Multnomah County ESD, Portland, 1981; pvt. practice counselor Portland, 1982-84; dir. career devel. Walla Walla (Wash.) Coll., 1984-87; assoc. dir. Ctr. for Lifelong Learning Loma Linda (Calif.) U., 1987—; home decorator Frederick & Nelson; payroll and computerized bookkeeper Hilo Care Ctr.; with pers. office Flour-Utah Minine; employment counselor Snelling & Snelling Employment Agy.; tchr. bus. edn. Portland Adventist Acad. Contbr. articles to profl. jours. Mem. ASTD, Assn. Pers. Adminstrs. (columnist San Bernardino Sun newspaper), Coun. for Adult and Exptl. Learning, Calif. Assn. for Counseling and Devel., Coop. Edn. Assn., Nat. Commn. for Coop. Edn., Phi Delta Kappa. Home: 112 Tamarisk St Redlands CA 92373 Office: Loma Linda U 4700 Pierce St Riverside CA 92515

WEBB, GLORIA O., mayor; b. Omaha, Apr. 4, 1931; m. Thomas H. Webb; children: Wendy, Tom IV, Patricia, Bob. BS in Social Work, U. Nebr.; postgrad. in Guidance Counseling, Old Dominion U. Former stewardess United Airlines; former recreation dir. Omaha Urban League; probation officer Douglas County Juvenile & Domestic Relations Ct., Omaha, until 1988; mayor City of Portsmouth (Va.), 1988—. Bd. dirs. Nat. Women's Polit. Caucus, Friends of Women's Studies Old Dominion U., Salvation Army, ARC; mem. community and econ. devel. Va. Mcpl. League; mem. Portsmouth Partnership Council, Auxs. of Medicine, Faculty Wives Eastern Va. Med. Sch., Portsmouth City Council, Colonial Coast Girl Scouts Council Adv. Bd., Established Concerned Parents for Quality Edn. Churchland Elem. Sch., Family Life Com. Tidewater Planning Council, COMPLAN Task Force; mem. steering com. med. symposium Second Ann. Citizens Trust Disting. Prof. Lectures; sec. Portsmouth Service League; v.p. Churchland Parks & Recreation Forum; elected to bd. dirs. Women in Local Govt. Nat. League of Cities; participant C. of C. Leadership Devel. Inst.; chmn. C. of C. Leadership Com.; chmn. hon. membership sect. PTA Council; campaign co-chmn. Spl. Gifts to Women United Way; former mem. Portsmouth Sch. Bd., 1972-80, chmn., 1978-80; former mem. Mental Health Assn.; vol. worker Girl Scouts, Portsmouth Girl's Club, Kirk Cone Ctr., Wesley Community Ctr. Kindergarten, Friends of Juvenile Ct., Drug Referral/Crisis Ctr., Churchland Elem. Sch. Recipient Portsmouth Woman of Yr. award Portsmouth Jaycettes for Outstanding Service to Community, 1981. Home: 310 North St Portsmouth VA 23704 Office: City of Portsmouth PO Box 820 Portsmouth VA 23705*

WEBB, HÉLÈNE B., graphic artist, designer; b. Johnson City, N.Y., May 27, 1951; d. Daniel Louis and Frederique (Gendron) W.; m. Ralph Wiley, June 12, 1972 (div. 1975). BFA, U. of South Fla., Tampa, 1972. Illustrator St. Petersburg Times Floridan Mag., 1972-73, Harpers, N.Y. Times, Ms. and others, N.Y.C., 1973-78; bookstore owner Three Lives and Co., Ltd., N.Y.C., 1978-84; graphic artist, illustrator, designer various mags., L.A., 1985-87; graphic artist Disney Channel Mag., Burbank, Calif., 1987-89;

graphic artist, designer Hollywood (Calif.) Reporter, 1989, L.A. Times, 1989—. One woman show, Beside Ourselves (hand colored photographs), Heliotrope Theatre, L.A., 1986. Art tchr. Family Assistance League, Hollywood, 1988-89. Mem. Women in Design, Graphic Artists Guilde (v.p. 1987-88). Democrat. Office: Los Angeles Times Times Mirror Sq Los Angeles CA 90053

WEBB, JILLA ROSE, small business owner; b. Detroit, July 26, 1923; d. Arthur Joseph and Rosaria (Mannino) Weber; div.; 1 child, Jilla Rosaria Robertson. Student pub. sch., Detroit. Dancer Jake Shubert, N.Y.C., 1941-42; singer Sonja Henie Ice Show, N.Y.C., 1943-45, MGM Record Co., N.Y.C., 1945-48, WMCA Radio, N.Y.C., 1948, Mercury Records, N.Y.C., 1948, Mario Lanzo Show, L.A., 1950, Tommy Dorsey Orchestra, N.Y.C., 1958, Jimmy Dorsey Orch., N.Y.C., 1958, Harry James, L.A., 1954-60; owner Jillas Sch. of Dance, Alpena, 1972—. Choreographer Jr. Miss Shows Awards in 1983, 84, 85, 88. Recipient Nat. award for best J.R. Home: Box 161 RR 3 Hillman MI 49746 Office: Jillas Sch of Dance 210 N 2nd Ave Alpena MI 49707

WEBB, KRISTI CHAMBERS, human resources director; b. Brockton, Mass., Dec. 8, 1946; d. Jonas Bud and Marjorie Marion (Young) Chambers; m. Stephen Lewis Webb, May 17, 1980 (div. Dec. 1989). BA, Wheaton Coll., 1968; MA, U. Fla., 1976. Personnel adminstr. Harvard Coop Soc., Cambridge, Mass., 1968-70; tchr. Chatham (Mass.) High Sch., 1970-72; mgr. Gator Country Restaurant, Gainesville, Fla., 1975; catering dir. Svc. Am. Corp., Gainesville, 1977-84; asst. program dir. U. Fla., Gainesville, 1985-86; ops. mgr. Svc. Am. Corp., Gainesville, 1986-88; foodsvc. dir. I Dept. Corrections, Lowell, Fla., 1988-89; dir. human resources Svc. Am. Corp., Gainesville, 1989—; intern coord. Food Sci. & Human Nutrition, Gainesville, 1989—. Bd. dirs. Job Svc. Employers' Com., Gainesville, 1990. Scholar Fla. Suprs. of Elections, 1974, 76; recipient 1st prize non-comml. Am. Egg Bd., 1989, 1st prize Food Mgmt. Mag., 1987, 3rd prize Food Mgmt. Mag., 1979, 81, 83, 1st runner-up Kitchen Bouquet, 1980, 81. Mem. Am. Soc. Trainers & Developers (v.p. for programs), NAFE, Am. Culinary Fedn., John Marshall Bar Assn. (hon.). Republican. Mem. Christian Ch. Home: 525 NW 19 Ln Gainesville FL 32609 Office: Svc Am Corp Rm 160 JWRU Gainesville FL 32611

WEBB, LISE MCCLENDON, writer; b. Carmel, Calif., Feb. 8, 1952; d. John Haddaway and Betty Virginia (Morgan) McC.; m. Kipp Bradley Webb, June 15, 1973. BA, U. Nebr., 1974; MA, U. Mo., 1981. Ednl. media prodocer Creighton U., Omaha, 1974-76; film critic, writer Bakerfield, Calif., 1977-78; instr. radio-TV Central Wyo. (Riverton) Coll., 1981-83; owner Mountain Media, Lander, Wyo., 1983-87; writer Billings, Mont., 1987—; cons. Lander C. of C., 1986, Lander Centennical Com., 1989. Author: Sharp Horns Rising, 1989; contbr. articles to profl. jours.; video producer documentary Basques of Kern County, 1977. Vol. Rimrock Elem. Sch., Billings, 1987-89, March of Dimes, Billings, 1988-89. Mem. Rim Writers, Kappa Tau Alpha (jounalism hon.), Alpha Epsilon Rho. Democrat. Home and Office: 2704 Virginia Ln Billings MT 59102

WEBB, LYNNE MCGOVERN, communication educator, consultant; b. Shamokin, Pa., Mar. 20, 1951; d. Charles Ralph and Ethel Elizabeth (Harris) McGovern; m. Ronald E. Webb, Sept. 28, 1978 (div. June 1981); m. Robert Blakely Moberly, Apr. 6, 1984; children: Laura Ellen, Richard Edward, Reed Jee Min Seo. BS, Pa. State U., 1972; MS, U. Oreg., 1975, PhD, 1980. Field rep. East Central Ill. Area Agy. on Aging, Campaign, Ill., 1972-74; grad. teaching asst. U. Oreg., Eugene, 1974-78; instr. Berea Coll., Berea, Ky., 1978-80; asst. prof. U. Fla., Gainesville, assoc. prof., 1986—; vis. assoc. prof. speech U. Hawaii, Honolulu, 1990—; cons. Am. Coll. Nursing Home Adminstrs., Miami, 1981, Fla. Farm Bur., Gainesville, 1981, Clay County Electric Coop., Keystone Heights, Fla., 1987, Retirement Rsch. Found., Chgo., 1988. Mem. Fla. Speech Communication Assn. (v.p. 1986-87), So. States Communication Assn. (chair applied communication div. 1989-90), Speech Communications Assn. (com. on communication and aging 1982-83). Democrat. Methodist. Office: U Fla 335 Dauer Hall Gainesville FL 32611

WEBB, MARGARET TAYLOR, small business owner; b. Akron, Colo., Jan. 14, 1928; d. Athel Ross and Marjorie Verle (Walters) Taylor; m. Hobert Hester Webb, Dec. 5, 1945 (dec. 1981); children: Diana Lynn Fausz, Paula Sheryl Graves; m. Carl Long, Sept. 5, 1987. Grad. high sch., Grand Junction, Colo., 1945. With sales dept. Aurora Realty, Denver, 1953-62; exec. sec. Western Electric, Denver, 1962-72; sales mgr. Crown, Better Homes and Gardens, Denver, 1983; owner, operator 1st Am. Properties, Denver, 1983-85, Coral Sands Mobile Home Estates, Phoenix, 1985—; exec. v.p. Sweeping Beauties, Inc., Phoenix. Active Richards-Hart Task Force Com., Wheatridge, Colo., 1981-89; bd. dirs. Wheatridge Sr. Ctr.; adv. com. 6th Congrl. Dist. Mem. Nat. Assn. Women Bus. Owners. Republican. Home: 1304 E Commodore Tempe AZ 85283 Office: Coral Sands Mobile Home 11425 W University Apache Junction AZ 85220

WEBB, MARTHA JEANNE, film producer; b. Grinnell, Iowa, Oct. 26, 1947; d. Frederick Winfield and Helen (Potter) W.; m. Bruce A. Clark; children: Marjorie, Paula, David. Student, St. Cloud State U., 1965-67, U. Minn., 1967-69, Coll. of St. Catherine, 1979-81. Personnel, pub. relations, drug abuse edn. NIH, 1967-77; account services Doremus & Co., Mpls., 1977-79; v.p. adminstrn. Webb Enterprises, Inc., Mpls., 1979-81; v.p. Russell-Manning Prodns., Mpls., 1981-88; pres. Clark Webb, Inc., Mpls., 1986—; pres. Minn. Film Bd., 1986-87, BCW Corp., 1988—; com. mem. Minn. Media Tech. Adv. Com., 1986. Commr. Minn. Commn. Bicentennial US Constitution, St. Paul, 1986-87; bd. dirs. Woods Acad., Maple Plain, Minn., 1987-88; mem. Minn. Super Bowl Task Force, St. Paul, Minn. Task Force on Research and Tech. Recipient numerous film awards including Silver award Interant. Film and TV Festival of N.Y., 1983, 84, 85, 86, 87, Golden Eagle award CINE Festival, 1985, Gold award Best in the West Fest, 1986, Gold award Telly Awards, 1987. Office: Clark Webb Inc 630 Kickernick Bldg 430 First Ave North Minneapolis MN 55401

WEBB, PEGGY SUE EZZELL, forecast inventory analyst; b. Denton, Tex., July 22, 1958; d. Jack Howard and Dorris Jean (Durham) Ezzell; m. Rickey Eugene Webb, June 30, 1978 (div. Dec. 1989); children: Matthew Wesley, Steven Wayne, Amanda Sue. Student, U. North Tex., 1976—; A.A.A.S. in Mid. Mgmt., Brookhaven Coll., 1987. Dancer Dance Dynamics, Dallas, 1977-79; customer svc. rep. Omega Optical, Dallas, 1979-80; forecast and inventory analyst Otis Engring. Corp., Dallas, 1981—; cons. Jr. Achievement, Dallas, 1982—; corp. treas. SBJ Corp., Lewisville, Tex., 1987—. Contbr. articles to profl. jours. and newspapers. Mem. Denton County Hist. Commn., 1978-86; mem. Congressman Armey's drug com., Lewisville, 1987—; active Leadership Metrocrest, Carrollton, Tex., 1990; pres. Lake Cities Hist. Soc.; bd. dirs. Women's Charity Orgn. Metrocrest, 1990. Named Co-Woman of Yr. Lake Cities C of C., Lake Dallas, Tex., 1979. Mem. Metrocrest Profl. Womens Assn., Am. Bus. Womens Assn., Am. Prodn. Inventory Control Soc. (local dir. 1981-84), Toastmasters (Able Toastmaster-Silver, lt. gov. dist. 25 north div. 1990), Metrocrest C. of C. (edn. com. 1989—), Rebekah Lodge. Methodist. Home: 3502 Meadowview Corinth TX 76205 Office: Otis Engring Corp 2601 Beltline Rd Carrollton TX 75006

WEBBER, DIANA L., career officer; b. Sacramento, May 12, 1960; d. Ralph and Mary P. (Chace) Van Tuyl. BS, Tex. A&M U., 1983; MCSM, Creighton U., 1987; student, Air Force Tech. Sch., 1979. Commd. 2d lt. USAF, advance through grades to capt., 1978—. Mem. NAFE, AIAA, Air Force Assn., Nebr. Soccer Assn. (coach 1987). Democrat. Home: 1244 E 3d St #103 Long Beach CA 90802

WEBBER, EDYTHE MARIE, business consultant; b. Detroit, Nov. 22, 1954; d. Austin Joseph and Ruby Lee (Ennis) McClendon; m. Steven Carl Webber, July 19, 1986; children: Kalese Marie, Steven Carl. AGS, Highland Park Community Coll., Mich., 1977, AS, 1982. Lic. respiratory therapist; registered money broker. Switchboard operator Finney High Sch., Detroit, 1970-73; dishwasher-clothwasher Grosspointe (Mich.) Country Club, 1973-74; med. asst. Detroit Med. and Surg. Ctr., 1976-79; nursing aide St. Anne Nursing Home, Detroit, 1977-80; med. asst. pediatric care Detroit Med. and Surg. Ctr., 1977-80; respiratory therapist Harper-Grace Hosp., Detroit, 1982-84, Binsons Med., Centerline, Mich., 1984-85; charge respiratory therapist intensive care St. Johns Hosp., Grosspointe, 1985-86; pres. K. S. Webber Corp., Southfield, Mich., 1990—; regional dir. The Hempell Group, Southfield, Mich., 1990—. Mem. NAACP, NAFE, The Kesseler Exchange (outstanding small bus. achievement award 1989), Am. Fin. Coords. Assn., Better Bus. Bur., Southfield C. of C. (membership com. person 1989). Office: KS Webber Corp 28440 Southfield Rd Ste 188 Lathrup Village MI 48076-2885

WEBBER, JANET DEE, medical administrator; b. Kansas City, Mo., Apr. 19, 1958; d. Walter O. and Dorothy L. (Begole) W. BS in Phys. Therapy, U. Mo., 1980. Lic. profl. phys. therapist. Staff phys. therapist Still Osteo. Hosp., Jefferson City, Mo., 1980-81, acting phys. therapy dir., 1981; staff phys. therapist Columbia (Mo.) Regional Hosp., 1981-83, chief phys. therapist, 1983-86, rehab. svcs. dir., 1987-89; med. adminstr. Columbia Spine Rehab. Ctr., 1988—, rehab. cons., 1988—; health occupations adv. bd. Columbia Voc. Tng. Ctr., Columbia, 1982-86; profl. adv. bd. Columbia Vis. Nurses' Assn., 1983-85; speaker in field. Author: (with others) Care of the Low Back: A Patient Guide. Exec. com. Multiple Sclerosis Soc., 1986—. Fellow Am. Back Soc.; mem. Am. Phys. Therapy Assn., Mo. Phys. Therapy Assn. Office: Columbia Spine Rehab Ctr 3501 Berrywood Dr Lower Level Columbia MO 65201

WEBBER, JANET ELLEN, nurse, healthcare consultant; b. Chgo., Mar. 23, 1963; d. Emil Frank and Mary (Strauel) Stuermer. BS in Nursing, Creighton U., 1985. RN, Ill., Tex., Minn. Pediatric ICU nurse Rush-Presbyn.-St. Luke's Med. Ctr., Chgo., 1985-87; health care mgr. Inst. for Latin Am. Concern, Dominican Republic, 1987; dir. nursing Nurse Finders, Inc., Chgo., 1987-88; regional nurse recruiter Nurse Am., Inc., Overland Park, Kans., 1988-89, healthcare cons., 1989—. Mem. Am. Assn. Critical Care Nurses, Ill. Nurses Assn., Chgo. Nurses Assn. (membership com.), NAFE.

WEBBER, LISA MARIE, financial analyst; b. L.A., Oct. 12, 1964; d. Michael Gibbons and Joanne Elfrieda (Schwedler) W. BS in Math., U. Portland, 1986; MBA in Fin., U. Chgo., 1988. Fin. analyst Air Products and Chems., Inc., Allentown, Pa., 1988—. Tchr. religion St. Ann's Ch., Emmaus, Pa., 1988—; sec. TOPS, Allentown, 1989—. Republican. Roman Catholic. Office: Air Products & Chems Inc 7201 Hamilton Blvd Allentown PA 18195

WEBBER, MILDRED, federal agency administrator; b. Bklyn., Feb. 28, 1956; d. Milton Clamp and Mildred Farrer (Jordan) W.; m. William Watson Pascoe III, Apr. 29, 1989. BA, U. N.C., 1978. Staff asst. steering com. U.S. Senate, Washington, 1979-81; projects editor Senate Rep. Conf., Washington, 1981-85; assoc. dir. The White House, Washington, 1986-88; dep. asst. sec. U.S. Dept. Transp., Washington, 1988-89; assoc. dep. undersec. HUD, Washington, 1989—; dir. legislation The Heritage Found., Washington, 1985-87. Active Jr. League of Wash., 1985—. Episcopalian. Home: 3492 Paul St Alexandria VA 22311 Office: HUD 451 7th St SW Rm 10140 Washington DC 20410

WEBER, BARBARA M., sales executive; b. Oneonta, N.Y., Apr. 27, 1945; d. Peter J. and Helen (Bettiol) Macaluso; m. Peter Biddle Weber, July 29, 1972 (div. July 1988). Student, SUNY, Cortland, 1963-67; AAS in Merchandising and Retail Mgmt., SUNY, Mohawk Valley. Service cons. N.Y. Telephone, Albany, N.Y., 1966-68; sr. service advisor N.Y. Telephone, Albany, 1970-73; data communications instr. AT & T, nationwide, 1968-70; equipment mgr. Rushmore & Weber, Albany, 1978-82; v.p. ops. Rushmore & Weber, 1983—, gen. mgr., v.p., 1987-88, pres., chief exec. officer, 1988, also bd. dirs. Republican. Roman Catholic. Club: Schuyler Meadows Country. Home: PO Box 236 Newtonville NY 12128 Office: Rushmore & Weber Inc 272 Wolf Rd PO Box 757 Latham NY 12110

WEBER, CAROL A., publishing company executive; b. Washington, May 3, 1940; d. Harry Lee and Rosa Lee (McCannon) Almond; m. Romann H. (John) Weber, Aug. 6, 1966; 1 son, Romann Matthew. B.A. in English, Madison Coll. (now James Madison U.), 1962. Gen. assigment reporter Roanoke Times (Va.), 1962-64; gen. assigment reporter The Miami Herald (Fla.), from 1964, successively edn. writer, investigative reporter, asst. city editor, Broward editor, to 1982, asst. mng. editor features, 1982-84, assoc. pub., 1985-89; dir. customer satisfaction and exec. asst. to chmn. and chief exec. officer, Knight-Ridder, Inc., Miami, 1989—. Bd. dirs. Com. of 100, Mus. Art, Broward Performing Arts Found., Inc., Vinnette Carroll Repertory Co., Broward Community Coll. Found., Salvation Army; bd. govs. Ft. Lauderdale C. of C. Recipient various state, nat. awards for writing; named Woman of Yr., Women in Communication, Broward County, Fla., 1981. Office: Knight-Ridder Inc 1 Herald Pla Miami FL 33101

WEBER, CHARLENE LYDIA, social worker; b. Phila., Mar. 2, 1943; d. Walter Gotlieb and Dorothy (Peart) W.; m. Billy Mack Carroll, Oct. 3, 1959 (div. Sept. 1974); children: Dorothy Patricia, Robert Walter, Lydia Baker, Billy Bob, Elizabeth Louise; m. John Edward Thomaston, Sept. 26, 1974 (div. July 1986). BSW with honors, Coll. Santa Fe, 1983; MSW, N.Mex. Highlands U., 1988. Client service agt. I Social Services div. Dept. Human Services, Albuquerque, 1975-78, client service agt. IV, 1978-83; social worker II Social Services div. Dept. Human Services, Bernalillo, N.Mex., 1983, social worker III, 1983—. Mem. Nat. Assn. Social Workers, N.Mex. Council on Crime and Deliquency, Albuquerque Retarded Assn., Child Welfare League. Democrat. Home: 72 Umber Ct Rio Rancho NM 87124 Office: Dept Human Svcs Div Social Svcs PO Box 820 Bernalillo NM 87004

WEBER, ENID W., executive secretary; came to U.S., 1961; d. Eric and Frances (Waterhouse) Williams; 1 child, Laura. Student, Wheaton Coll., 1963-65; BA, U. Calif., Berkeley, 1966; MA, U. Calif., San Francisco, 1970. Coord. Hispanic employment program Nat Labor Rels. Bd., Washington; rsch. economist Olympus Rsch., San Francisco; adminstrv. asst. San Francisco State Coll.; assoc. exec. sec. Nat. Labor Rels. Bd., Washington. Past bd. dirs. Va. chpt. IMAGE; vol. arbitrator County of Fairfax. Carnegie scholar, Mexico, 1963. Mem. NAFE, NOW, Indsl. Rels. Rsch. Assn. Home: 8609 Forest St Annandale VA 22003 Office: Nat Labor Rels Bd 1717 Pennsylvania Ave NW Washington DC 20570

WEBER, EVELYN JOYCE, biochemical consultant; b. Pana, Ill., Nov. 9, 1928; d. John Henry and Emma Caroline (Schoch) W. BS with highest honors, U. Ill., 1953; PhD, Iowa State U., 1961. Rsch. asst. U. Ill., Urbana, 1954-56, rsch. assoc., 1961-65, asst. prof., 1965-72, assoc. prof., 1972-82, prof., 1982-87, prof. emerita, 1987—; grad. asst. Iowa State U., Ames, 1956-61; rsch. chemist USDA, Urbana, 1965-87; freelance cons. Urbana, 1987—. Author several book chpts.; contbr. numerous articles to profl. jours. Predoctoral pub. health fellow, USPHS, 1960-61. Fellow Am. Inst. Chemists; mem. Am. Chem. Soc., Am. Oil Chemists' Soc., Am. Soc. Plant Physiologists, Alpha Lambda Delta, Sigma Xi, Gamma Sigma Delta, Iota Sigma Pi (pres. Iowa state chpt. 1960-61, U. Ill. chpt. 1962-63), Sigma Delta Epsilon (v.p. 1965-66), Phi Kappa Phi (sec. 1969-70). United Ch. of Christ. Home: 808 E Mumford Dr Urbana IL 61801

WEBER, JANET M., nurse; b. Lansdale, Pa., Mar. 12, 1936; d. Russell H. and Naomi (Moyer) W. Diploma in nursing, Washington County Hosp. Sch. Nursing, 1959; B.S. in Nursing, Grace Coll., 1960; M.Ed., Duquesne U., 1969. Staff nurse, supr. Murphy Med. Ctr., Warsaw, Ind., 1959-60; coll. nurse Grace Coll., Winona Lake, Ind., 1959-60; med. surg. nursing instr. Washington County Hosp. Sch. Nursing, Hagerstown, Md., 1961-64; pvt. duty nurse Washington County Hosp., Hagerstown, 1964; chmn. found. of nursing Presbyn. Univ. Hosp. Sch. Nursing; Pitts., 1964-72; curriculum coordinator Albert Einstein Med. Ctr. Sch. Nursing, Phila., 1972-73; assoc. dir. Albert Einstein Med. Ctr. Sch. Nursing, 1973-74, acting dir., 1974, dir., 1974-87; staff nurse ARC Penn-Jersey Blood Drive Donor Services, Phila., 1988—; cons. Md. Bd. Higher Edn., 1981-82. Author: The Faculty's Role in Policy Development, 1981, Assisting Students with Educational Deficiencies, 1975. Mem. Pa. League Nursing (pres. 1982-86, bd. dirs. Area I 1974-76), Washington County Hosp. Nurses Alumni Assn. (pres. 1962-64), Nat. League Nursing (bd. rev. 1980-84, chmn.-elect Council Diploma Programs 1985-87), Am. Hosp. Assn. Assembly Hosp. Schs., Hosp. Assn. Pa. (sec. council hosps. with schs. nursing 1979), Grace Coll. Alumni Assn., Duquesne U. Alumni Assn. Republican. Home: 5640 Arbor St Philadelphia PA 19120 Office: ARC Blood Donor Svcs 23d and Chestnut Sts Philadelphia PA 19103

WEBER, KARIN MICHELE, accountant; b. St. Louis, July 23, 1965; d. Walter Clarence and Melva Mabel (Huttegger). BBA, Tex. Christian U., 1987. CPA, Mo. Proctor tutor acctg. dept. Tex. Christian U., Ft. Worth, 1984-87; editor, proofreader Practitioners Pub. Co., Ft. Worth, 1986-87; acctg. clk. Robert D. Cocanower Jr., CPA, Ft. Worth, 1986-87; sr. staff acct. Bergman Schraier & Co., St. Louis, 1987—. Mem. AICPAs, NAFE, Mo. Soc. CPAs, St. Louis Soc. Women CPAs, Kappa Delta. Lutheran. Home: 59 Branford Dr Saint Louis MO 63132 Office: Bergman Schraier & Co 7777 Bonhomme Saint Louis MO 63105

WEBER, KATHLEEN SUSAN, sales engineer; b. Berwyn, Ill., Sept. 12, 1954; d. Richard Albert and Dolores B. (Kostecki) George; m. Richard Dale Weber, Dec. 29, 1979; children: Aimee, Travis. AS in Biology, Triton Coll., River Forest, Ill., 1973; BS in Biology, Loyola U., Chgo., 1975. Chemist Ill. Racing Bd. Lab., Chgo., 1976-78; sales rep. Wilkens-Anderson Co., Chgo., 1978-80, Rinchem Co., El Paso, Tex., 1982-85; supr. Shaklee Corp., Denver, 1980-82; account exec. U.S. Postal Svc., Coppell, Tex., 1985-87; sales engr. Leybold Inc., Carrollton, Tex., 1987—. Ill. State scholar, 1971. Mem. NAFE, Phi Theta Kappa. Republican. Roman Catholic. Office: Leybold Inc 1313 Valwood Pkwy Carrollton TX 75019

WEBER, LINDA FICKLIN, therapist; b. Columbia, Mo., Mar. 11, 1926; d. Nathan Clyde and Helen Othelia (Erickson) Ficklin; m. Joseph Ralph Weber, Sept. 29, 1946; children: Barry, Cynthia, Amy, Gwen. BA cum laude, Elmhurst Coll., 1968; MS, No. Ill. U., 1975; postgrad., Bethany Theol. Sem., Oakbrook, Ill., 1989—. Tchr. Dist. #45 Schs., Villa Park, Ill., 1968-74, counselor, 1974-84; counselor, therapist Linda Weber & Assocs., Villa Park, 1982-85; adminstrv. sec. Washington office Ch. of the Brethren, 1985-88; counselor Washington Pastoral Counseling Svc., 1988-89. Mem. nat. bd., mem. exec. com. Women for a Meaningful Summit, Washington, 1985—, chair, 1990—; mem. core group nat. bd., YWCA, Washington, 1985-89. Mem. AACD, Am. Assn. Pastoral Counselors, Women's Caucus, Alpha Xi Delta. Home: 19W010 13th St Lombard IL 60148

WEBER, MARGARET LAURA JANE, accountant; b. Fairview, Mo., Jan. 4, 1933; d. Mert James and Margaret Orr (Mortensen) Joel; m. James E. Jennings, Mar. 1953 (div.); children: James Edward Jennings, Janie Lea Franks, David Alan Jennings; m. Albert H. Weber, June 1956; children: Luhwanna Stonecipher, Margaret Anne Shadwick. AA, Crowder Coll., Mo., 1972; postgrad. Mo. So. Coll., 1988. Teller, First State Bank, Joplin, Mo., 1951-53; clk. Mo. Lic. Dept., Joplin, 1954-57, U. Mo. Ext. Dept., Neosho, 1967-68; cashier Crowder Coll., Neosho, Mo., 1968-83, acct., 1983—. Mem., Newton County Welfare Com., 1984—. Mem. Am. Bus. Women's Assn. (Woman of Yr. 1982, Bus. Assoc. of Yr. 1987), Nat. Assn. Female Execs., Mo. Assn. Community Jr. Colls. (bd. dirs. 1978-82). Republican. Baptist. Home: Rte 6 Box 197 Neosho MO 64850 Office: Crowder Coll 601 Laclede Ave Neosho MO 64850

WEBER, MARILYN ANN MINCH, travel executive, international consultant; b. Continental, Ohio, May 5, 1934; d. Paul John and Alma Margaretta (Hoffman) Minch; m. Eugene Thomas Weber, Aug. 31, 1957; children: Craig Weber, Susan Weber. Student, St. Mary's Coll., 1952-54; piano pedagogy, Nat. Piano Found., Chgo., 1974. With banking dept. City Loan & Savs. Co., Lima, Ohio, 1954-55; home economist Ohio Power Co., Lima, Ottawa, Ohio, 1955-58; T.V. program co-host Continental Cablevision, Findlay, Ohio, 1975-76; treas., v.p. sales Allen Bag Co., Kenton, Ohio, 1981-83; internat. cons. Cen. Travel, Findlay, 1985—, account exec., 1984—; Pub. relations, program speaker Cen. Travel, Findlay, 1984—. Originator (T.V. game show and graphic puzzle) TRAVELGRAM, 1988. Recipient Amigo do Brazil Ministry of Industry and Commerce, 1988. Mem. C. of C. (Hancock Co. Adv. Bd. Conv. and Visitors Bur.), Findlay Country Club (bridge co-chmn.), Orphan Annie Investments. Roman Catholic. Home: 1331 Brookside Dr Findlay OH 45840 Office: Central Travel 1800 Tiffin Ave Findlay OH 45840

WEBER, MOLLY SMITH, sales executive; b. Durham, N.C., Sept. 4, 1957; d. H. Ralph and Sally Ann (Simmons) Smith; m. Walter Charles Weber, July 13, 1985. BA in Psychology, Yale U., 1979; MA in Edn., Stanford U., 1980. Dir. aquatics SUNY, Purchase, 1980-81; sales rep. Prentice-Hall, Inc., Englewood Cliffs, N.J., 1981-83; sales rep. West Ednl. Pub., St. Paul, 1983-85, acquisitions editor, 1985-89; sales mgr. western region MacMillan Pub. Co., 1989—. Active Dem. Polit. Campaigns, 1987—; mem. Nat. Dem. Com. Mem. Am. Mgmt. Assn., NOW. Avocations: swimming, snow and water skiing, running, photography. Home: 28363 N Evergreen Ln Santa Clarita CA 91350 Office: MacMillan Pub Co PO Box 800058 Santa Clarita CA 91380-0058

WEBER, NANCI TRIVERS, travel agency owner; b. N.Y.C., Jan. 28, 1935; d. Samuel E. and Claire (Miller) Trivers; m. George J. Weber, Mar. 13, 1964 (div. May 1976); children: Carin Ann Carey, Christopher G. Weber (dec.). Student, SUNY, Albany, 1953-54. Ticket agt. Am. Airlines, N.Y.C., 1957-59; mgr. Travelcade Tours, N.Y.C., 1959-64; owner Poughkeepsie Travel Ctr., Poughkeepsie, N.Y., 1964—, Travel Tips Advt., Poughkeepsie, 1973—, Upscale Imports, Poughkeepsie, 1983—. Editor, columnist Travel Trade (N.Y.C.) Mag., 1967—. Bd. dirs. Hudson Valley Philharmonic Dutchess County Coun., 1984-88. Mem. Greater So. Dutchess C. of C. (bd. dirs. 1981—), Rotary (bd. dirs. 1987—, v.p. 1989—, Poughkeepsie South chpt. pres.-elect 1990, pres. 1990—), Zonta Internat., All Women in Bus. Home: 70 Ninham Ave Wappingers Falls NY 12590 Office: Poughkeepsie Travel Ctr 491 South Rd Poughkeepsie NY 12601

WEBER, NANCY DWORKIN, agency administrator; b. Bklyn., June 26, 1951; d. Lawrence Jewel and Ruth (Glauber) Dworkin; children: Lisa, Geordana. BS, Cornell U., Ithaca, 1973; MS in Social Work, Columbia U., N.Y., 1975; student, City U. Grad. Sch. & U. Ctr., N.Y., 1987. Social Worker. Supr. Vacations and Community Svcs. for the Blind, N.Y., 1975-79, asst. dir., 1979-83; social worker Met. Jewish Geriatric Ctr., Bklyn., 1983-85; dir. of community svcs. Queens Lighthouse, Queens, N.Y.; exec. dir. VISIONS Svcs. for the Blind and Visually Impaired, N.Y., 1987--; bd. dirs. Coun. Sr. Ctr. and Svcs. Mem. editorial bd. Jour. Gerontological Social Work; contbr. articles to profl. jours. Recipient Recognition award N. Bklyn. Coalition of Sr. Citizen Council's, 1982, Annual Recognition award Nat. Hispanic Council on Aging, N.Y., 1989. Mem. Nat. Assn. Social Workers (bd. dirs. 1987-90), Assn. for Edn. and Rehab. of Blind (bd. dirs. 1988-92, Meritorious Achievement award 1989), Disabled Elderly Advocates N.Y., Cornell U. Coll. Human Ecology Alumni Assn., Lions (club treas.). Democrat. Jewish. Office: VISIONS Svcs for the Blind 817 Broadway 11th Fl New York NY 10003

WEBER, PATRICIA FRANCES, psychometrist, psychotherapist. BA, U. South Ala., 1980; MS in Clinical Psychology, U. South Ala. Grad. Sch., 1985. Contractor Behavioral Ednl. Tng. Assn., Gulfport, Miss., 1985-87; psychometrist, psychotherapist Seacoast Psychol. Assn., Inc., Biloxi, Miss., 1987-89; psychometrist Rotary Rehab. Svc., Mobile, Ala., 1989; psychometrist, psychotherapist Singing River Mental Health, Pascagoula, Lucedale, Miss., 1989—. Joint Honor scholar, 1953; named Outstanding Girl in Sci. and Math., 1953. Mem. Mobile Opera Guild Aux., Psi Chi. Episcopalian. Home: 7053 Carrabelle Key Mobile AL 36695

WEBER, REBECCA CECILE, marketing professional; b. Port Arthur, Tex., Jan. 9, 1959; d. Edward Andrew Weber and Caroline Christine (Elmer) Sorrells; m. David Paul Holzknecht, Aug. 9, 1980 (div. 1989). Student, U. Tex., 1977-80, U. Thomas, 1989—. With N.Am. Mortgage Co., Houston, 1981-89; v.p. systems N.Am. Mortgage Co., 1985-87, v.p. nat. systems support, 1987-89; with indirect sales Svc. Automation, Houston, 1989—. Vol., Leukemia Soc., Cystic Fibrosis Assn., Houston,1 985—; mem. Concerned Parents and Tchrs. Meml. Sch. of Oaks, Houston, 1986—, Lifeline, Houston, 1988—; tchr., Pre-Sch. Ministry, Houston, 1989—. Mem. NAFE, Assn. Women in Computing, Mortgage Bankers Assn. Am., Psi Chi. Republican. Baptist. Home: 12580 Piping Rock Houston TX 77077 Office: Svc Automation 4801 Wood Way #450W Houston TX 77056

WEBER, SUSAN LEE, marketing consultant; b. Honolulu, Nov. 30, 1948; d. Kenneth Charles and Valerie (June) W. BBA, San Jose (Calif.) State U., 1970; postgrad., U. Calif., Berkeley, 1972-73, Pepperdine U., 1977-78; Cert.

in Mktg., Harvard U. Small bus. organizer VISTA, Roseville, N.C., 1970-72; cosmetics buyer USN Commissary Supply, Oakland, Calif., 1972-74; cosmetics product mgr. Shaklee Corp., San Francisco, 1974-76; mktg. mgr. Max Factor, Inc., Hollywood, Calif., 1976-81; v.p. electronic mktg. Bank of Am., San Francisco, 1981-83, v.p. bank card merchandising, 1983-85, v.p., upscale mktg., sales, 1985-88; mng. prin. Mktg. Fundamentals, San Francisco, 1988—. Mem. Am. Mktg. Assn., Bay Area Women's Network, NAFE, Fin. Insts. Mktg. Assn. Republican. Presbyterian. Office: Mktg Fundamentals 1 Hallidie Pla Ste 701 San Francisco CA 94102

WEBERLING, PATRICIA KAY, management executive; b. Elmhurst, Ill., Sept. 11, 1959. BS in Accountancy, Fin., No. Ill. U., 1981. CPA, Ill. Staff auditor Esmark, Chgo., 1981-82, sr. auditor, 1982-84; mgr. internat. acctg. Swift Adhesives, Downers Grove, Ill., 1984-86; mgr. div. reporting and planning Swift Adhesives, Downers Grove, 1987—. Republican. Office: Swift Adhesives 3100 Woodcreek Dr Downers Grove IL 60515

WEBER-RIES, SUSAN ANN, technologist; b. Hendricks, Minn., May 30, 1956; d. James Bernard and Gail Marlys (Kerr) Weber; m. Robert James Ries Jr., Aug. 10, 1984. Student, S.D. State U., 1974-76, Met. State U., 1985—. Quality control insp. 3M Co. Med. Products div., Brookings, S.D., 1976; quality control technician 3M Co. and Med. Products, Brookings, S.D., 1976-79; sr. quality assurance technician 3M Surg. Products, St. Paul, 1979-83, master quality assurance technician, 1983-85; technologist, standards system adminstr. 3M Med.-Surg. Div., St. Paul, 1985—. Com. chairperson for 3M Club Winter Carnival Coms., St. Paul, 1984-86; vol. 3M Meals on Wheels. Mem. 3M Downhill Ski Club (sec. 1980-81, v.p. 1981-83), 3M Women's Golf League, Bowling Leagues. Office: 3M Co 3M Ctr Bldg 270-5N-01 Saint Paul MN 55144

WEBSTER, HELEN KAY, design drafter; b. Statesville, N.C., Apr. 12, 1947; d. Felix H. Webster and Jacqueline (Jackson) Shafer; m. Lee E. Davis Jr. (div. 1985); children: Dale Lee, Dennis Harlan. Student, TCJC, Hurst, 1962-65. Tech. illustrator Pointer Internat., Ft. Worth, 1974-76, Vought Corp., Dallas, 1976-79; contract engr. Global Group, Ft. Worth, 1979-87; design drafter Gen. Dynamics Corp., Ft. Worth, 1987—; freelance illustrator Jim Marrs, Inc., Irving, Tex., 1975-76. Republican. Home: 2312 Shady Turf St Bedford TX 76022 Office: Gen Dynamics Fort Worth TX 76022

WEBSTER, LINDA MAE, human services planner; b. Homer, Mich., Sept. 16, 1941; d. Newman Isaac and Annabelle Mary (Denbrock) Enos; divorced; 1 child, Adam J. Locketz. BS, Western Mich. U., 1963; MS, U. Ariz., 1977. Health planner/analyst Manitoba Dept. Health, Winnipeg, Can., 1981-85; rsch. fellow Sch. Pub. Health U. Minn., Mpls., 1985-87, project coord. Sch. Medicine, 1987-89; policy analyst Minn. Dept. Human Svcs., St. Paul, 1989—. Editor: (newsletter) Prairie Star Women, 1989-90. Rep., Minn. Women's Consortium, St. Paul, 1988-90; vice chair Ramsey County Community Health Adv. Com., St. Paul, 1989-91. Mem. Nat. Assn. Govt. Communicators (jour. reviewer), Nat. Mus. Women in Arts (charter). Unitarian Universalist. Home: 821 Cleveland Ave S Saint Paul MN 55116 Office: Minn Dept Human Svcs 444 Lafayette Rd Saint Paul MN 55155-3853

WEBSTER, LOIS SHAND, association executive; b. Springfield, Ill., Sept. 25, 1929; d. Richings James and C. Odell (Gilbert) S.; m. Terrance Ellis Webster, Feb. 12, 1954 (dec. July 1985); children: Terrance Richings, Bruce Douglas, Andrew Michael. BA, Millikin U., 1951; cert. in library tech., Coll. Du Page County, Glen Ellyn, Ill., 1974; postgrad. library sci., No. Ill. U., 1977-82. Mgr. info. resources Am. Nuclear Soc., La Grange Park, Ill., 1973—. Contbr. articles and book chpts. to profl. publs. Field dir. Springfield council Girl Scouts U.S., 1951-54; library advisor Du Page County council Girl Scouts U.S., 1973-74. Recipient Octave J. Du Temple award Am. Nuclear Soc., 1989. Mem. Am. Soc. for Info. Sci., Spl. Librs. Assn. (chair div. 1985-86, chair by-laws com. 1987-89, bd. dirs. 1989—, sec. 1990—), ALA, Coun. Engring. and Sci. Soc. Execs., Met. Chgo. Libr. Assembly (bd. dirs. 1982-85). Republican. Home: 560 Dorset Ave Glen Ellyn IL 60137 Office: Am Nuclear Soc 555 N Kensington Ave La Grange Park IL 60525

WEBSTER, RUTH ANN, lawyer; b. New Ulm, Minn., Feb. 21, 1949; d. John E. and Mary Virginia (Milliman) W.; m. Philip Edward Meidl, June 8, 1979. BS, U. Minn., 1970, JD cum laude, 1980. Bar: Minn. 1980, U.S. Dist. Ct. Minn. 1982, U.S. Ct. Appeals (8th cir.) 1984. Ptnr. Gislason, Dosland, Hunter & Malecki, New Ulm, 1981—. Troop adviser, Boy Scouts Am., New Ulm, 1988-89. Mem. Minn. State Bar Assn., 9th Dist. Bar Assn. Democrat. Office: Gislason Dosland et al 1 S State St New Ulm MN 56073

WEBSTER, SHELLEY ROSE, entrepreneur; b. Trenton, N.J., July 11, 1952; d. Charles Dale and Ethel (Goulding) W. BA, Trenton State Coll., 1974; MBA, Rider Coll., 1979. Asst. mgr. McDonalds, Trenton, N.J., 1970-75; regional mgr. Rustler Steak House, Phila., 1975-85; area devel. mgr. Sizzler Restaurants Internat., Phila., 1985-87; pres., owner Webmor Enterprises, Inc. Home Testing Labs., Belle Mead, N.J., 1987—. Mem. Am. Assn. Radon Scientists and Technologists. Office: Webmor Enterprises Inc 609 County Rte 601 Belle Mead NJ 08502

WECHSLER, JESSICA See JOSELL, JESSICA

WECHSLER, MARLENE EDITH, educator; b. Bklyn., May 6, 1934; d. Julius and Muriel Gertrude (Bezviner) Bresalier; m. Arnold Wechsler, June 14, 1953 (dec. 1986); children: Jeffrey, Faith Fleischman, Stephen. BA, Queens Coll., 1973, MS, 1975, cert. in Adminstrn. and Supervision, 1982. Resource room cons., tchr. Merrick (N.Y.) Union Free Sch. Dist., 1973—; adj. lectr. Queens Coll., 1980-83, Adelphi U., 1980-81; dir. summer instrn. Merrick Schs., 1987—. Contbr. articles to profl. jours. Mem. Coun. Exceptional Children (regional rep. 1987-90, pres. local chpt. 1990-91), B'nai B'rith, Hadassah. Office: Merrick Union Free Sch Dist Chatterton Sch 108 N Merrick Ave North Merrick NY 11566

WECHTER, CLARI ANN, paint manufacturing company executive; b. Chgo., June 1, 1953; d. Norman Robert and Harriet Beverly (Golub) W.; m. Gordon Jay Siegel, Feb. 10, 1980; 1 child, Alix Jessica. BA, U. Ariz., 1975; BE, Loyola U., Chgo., 1977. Cert. tchr., Ill. Saleswoman Federated Paint Mfg. Co., Chgo., 1979-84, v.p. sales, 1984—. Republican. Jewish. Home: 25 E Cedar St Chicago IL 60611 Office: Federated Paint Mfg Co 1882 S Normal Chicago IL 60616

WECK, KRISTIN WILLA, savings and loan association executive; b. Elgin, Ill., Nov. 5, 1959; d. John Francis and Florence Elaine (Ebel) W. BBA, Augustana Coll., Rock Island, Ill., 1981. Lic. real estate broker, Ill. Intern with investment banking group First Chgo. Bank, London, 1980; intern Prudential-Bache Co., Ft. Lauderdale, Fla., 1981; residential appraiser Fox Valley Appraisal Counselors, Ltd., West Dundee, Ill., 1982-84; asst. real estate loan officer First Nat. Bank, Barrington, Ill., 1982-84; savs. and loan field examiner III Office of Thrift Supervision, Chgo., 1984-90; mng. agt. Resolution Trust Corp., Elk Grove Village, Ill., 1990—. V.p. Brandywine Condo Assn., Crystal Lake, Ill., 1983. Recipient Outstanding Achievement award Fed. Home Loan Bank Bd., 1985. Mem. Soc. Real Estate Appraisers (candidate). Republican. Lutheran. Home: 435A Brandy Dr Crystal Lake IL 60014 Office: Resolution Trust Corp 25 Northwest Point Ste 800 Elk Grove Village IL 60007

WECKERLE, KATHERINE ELIZABETH, clinical social worker, psychotherapist; b. Sanford, Fla., May 17, 1952; d. George Donald Jr. and Katherine Elizabeth (Gordon) Bishop; m. Joseph A. Weckerle III, Mar. 19, 1977 (div. Nov. 1989); 1 child, Katherine. Student, U. Fla., 1970; BS in Social Work summa cum laude, U. Cen. Fla., 1974; MSW, Fla. State U., Tallahassee, 1979. Lic. clin. social worker, Fla.; diplomate in clin. social work. Clin. social worker Community Mental Health Ctr. Orange Meml. Hosp., Orlando, Fla., 1975-84; coordinator outpatient svcs. Mental Health Ctr. Orlando Reg. Med. Ctr., 1984-87, adminstrv. dir. Ctr. for Life Mgmt., 1987-89; dir. eating disorder program Glenbeigh Hosp. of Orlando, 1989—; clin. social worker in pvt. practice Winter Park, Fla., 1980—; student supr. Fla. State U., 1986—, U. So. Fla., Tampa, 1988-89; nursing and edn. supr. U. Fla., 1987-89. Facilitator, organizer Project Cope: Families of Mentally Ill, 1981-88. Recipient 1st prize Fla. Poetry Contest, U. Cen. Fla., 1974. Mem. Nat. Assn. Social Workers, Mental Health Assn. Cen. Fla. (bd. dirs. 1982-88, Golden Bell fellowship award 1982), Internat. Assn. Eating Disorder Profls., Delta Tau Kappa. Democrat. Episcopalian. Office: 1065 W Morse Blvd Ste 202 Winter Park FL 32789

WEDDINGTON, PATRICIA DIANE, journalist, educator; b. Mooresville, N.C., July 7, 1950; d. Luther Monroe and Annie Rowena (Cox) W. BA, Duke U., 1972, MDiv, 1976; MA, U. Mo., 1977; postgrad., U. Calif., Berkeley. Librarian Grad. Theol. U. Library, Berkeley, 1982; dir. admissions dept. psychology New Coll. Calif., San Francisco, 1983; mgr. Calif. Planners, Berkeley, 1985; religion editor Contra Costa Times, Walnut Creek, Calif., 1986—. Author: (with others) Sexual Harassment, 1979, Media Ethics, 1983; contbr. articles to profl. jours. Active Child Abuse Prevention Council of Contra Costa, East Bay Elder Abuse Prevention Consortium. Recipient Troy Grove award East Bay Elder Abuse Prevention Consortium, Pub. Svc. award Child Abuse Prevention Coun. Contra Costa, 1987; Ralph Stoody fellow, 1976; Nat. Press Inst. fellow, 1988. Mem. Women in Communications, Am. Acad. Religion, Religion Newswriters Assn., Garden Writers Am., Soc. Profl. Journalists. Democrat. Episcopalian. Office: Contra Costa Times 2640 Shadelands Dr Walnut Creek CA 94596

WEDEMAN, SARA CAPEN, marketing professional, psychologist; b. Washington, May 24, 1956; d. Miles George and Martha (Hall) W.; m. Michael Allan Feagans, Oct. 26, 1985. BA, Swarthmore Coll., 1978; MSS, Bryn Mawr Coll., 1981; MS, U. Pa., 1982, PhD, 1985. Lic. psychologist, Pa. Doctoral intern U. Pa. Counseling Svc., Phila., 1982-84; mktg. mgr. First Pa. Bank, Phila., 1985-88, v.p. rsch., 1988-90; v.p. market rsch. Corestates First Pa. Bank, Phila., 1990—; adj. prof. Temple U. Sch. Bus., Phila., 1990—. Author: (with others) Educational Block Grants, 1984, (with others) Measuring & Monitoring Service Quality, 1988. Fellow Pa. Psychol. Assn.; mem. Am. Mktg. Assn. (bd. dirs. Phila. chpt.), Soc. Indsl./Organizational Psychology, Am. Psychol. Assn., Mid-Atlantic Andover-Abbot Alumni Assn. (coun.). Office: Corestates First Pa Bank 1500 Market St W Tower Philadelphia PA 19101-7558

WEDGE, DOROTHY ANN, education educator; b. Bridgeport, Conn., Aug. 19, 1935; d. William Walter and Anne (Guit) W. BS in Edn., Wagner Coll., N.Y.C., 1957; Masters, U. Bridgeport, 1961; PhD, The Ohio State U., 1974. Tchr. Bridgeport Conn. Schs., 1957-62; cons., weekly reader publ. Xerox Edn., Middletown, Conn., 1962-70; student Doctoral Student at OSU, Columbus, Ohio, 1970-1973; asst. prof. SUNY at Fredonia (N.Y.); prof. edn. Fairmont (Wv.) State Coll., 1977--. Mem. Leadership Marion II Class, 1983-84. Mem. Internat. Reading Assn., Nat. Council Social Studies, Nat. Council Tchrs. English, Assn. Childhood Edn. Internat., Assn. Supervision and Curriculum Devel. Democrat. Episcopalian. Office: Fairmont State Coll Locust Ave Fairmont WV 26554

WEDGWORTH, RUTH SPRINGER, fertilizer company executive; b. Eaton Rapids, Mich., May 10, 1903; d. Clarence P. and Minnie L. (Washburn) Springer; student Mich. State U., 1921-23; LL.D. (hon.), U. Fla., 1965; H.H.D. (hon.), Fla. So. Coll., 1976; m. Herman H. Wedgworth, June 23, 1923 (dec. Oct. 1938); children—Helen Jean, George H., Barbara Ann. Pres., Wedgworth Farms, Inc., Belle Glade, Fla., 1938-80, Wedgworth's Inc., Belle Glade, 1954—, pres. Wedgworth Produce, Inc., Belle Glade, 1955-65; sec. Seminole Life Ins. Co., West Palm Beach, Fla., 1955-65. Mem. Palm Beach County (Fla.) Bd. Edn., 1947-53; bd. dirs. Western Palm Beach County Hosp. Dist., 1940-47; chmn. Highlands Glades Drainage Dist., 1942-68; mem. Gov.'s Com. on Migrant Work, 1942-46; trustee Fla. So. Coll., 1970—; mem. migrant work com. Nat. Council Chs., 1948-56; leadership mem. Boy Scouts Am., 1979. Recipient Award of Merit, Gamma Sigma Delta, 1978; Council of Farmers Cooperatives award, 1979; named Woman of Yr. (Progressive Farmer, 1947), Belle Glade, Fla., 1975, Fla. Agr., 1986, Fla. Woman of Yr. in Agr., 1987; award for excellence in industry and bus. Palm Beach County Com. on Status of Women, 1978; Disting. Service award Fla. Farm Bur., 1979, Fla. Fruit and Vegetable Assn., 1958; Outstanding Service award for employment and community leadership Everglades Progressive Citizens, 1970; Achievement award, Lions, 1961; inducted to Fla. Agrl. Hall of Fame, 1988. Mem. Fla. Hort. Soc. (past pres.), Fla. Soils Sci. Soc., Beta Sigma Phi. Methodist. Clubs: Belle Glade Women's, PEO, Lions (internat. hon.). Office: 651 NW 9th St Belle Glade FL 33430

WEEBER, CLAIRE JOANNE, poet; b. Lansing, Mich., Mar. 5, 1936; d. Elmer Theodore and Dorothy May (Futrell) Gates.; m. Edward Curtis Nave, July 3, 1954 (div.); children: Patricia Lynn Nave Laug, James Edward Nave, Debra Ann Nave Stevens; m. John Lance Weeber, Aug. 27, 1977. BA, Grand Valley State U., 1971; MA, Western Mich. U., 1977. Cert. tchr., Mich. Tchr. Southkent Community Edn., Kentwood, Mich., 1977-80; program supr. Southkent Community Edn., 1980-81; tchr. Grand Rapids (Mich.) Jr. Coll., 1981-82, Detroit Coll. Bus., Grand Rapids, Mich., 1982-83. Author poems in Midwest Poetry Rev., 1985-86, Peninsula Poets, 1986-89, Muskegon Chronicle, 1988,, Glory Mag., 1974 (2nd prize). Mem. Poetry Soc. Mich., Nat. Fedn. State Poetry Socs. Republican.

WEEDEN, MARY ANN, management executive; b. Troy, N.Y., July 23, 1948; d. John James and Antionette Catherine (Carcasole) Foley; m. Paul Joseph Weeden, Aug. 31, 1968; 1 child, Eric Paul. BSBA, Russell Sage Coll., 1978; postgrad., Ariz. State U., 1990—. Exec. sec. to v.p. ops. State Bank Albany, N.Y., 1970-73; indsl. rels. rep. Albany Internat. Corp., 1973-74; asst. to comptroller First Albany Corp., 1975-76; spl. asst. State Govt. N.Y., Albany, 1976-78; sr. rep. Bell System, Albany, 1978-83; corp. rels .rep. Ariz. Pub. Svc., Phoenix, 1983-85, contract adminstr., 1985-88, sr. trainer mgmt. devel., 1988—; quality circle leader and facilitator Ariz. Nuclear Power Project, Phoenix, 1988—; internal cons. Ariz. Pub. Svc., Phoenix, 1988—; cons., trainer, Inroads of Phoenix, 1988—. Editor The Signature, 1973. Candidates' forum coord. LWV, Albany, 1975-80; coord. Project S.H.A.R.E., Phoenix, 1984-85; exec. advisor Jr. Achievement, Phoenix, 1985-87, Bus. Leader Advisor award 1986, 87; environ. issues coord. Maricopa County Dem. Platform, Phoenix, 1986-88. Recipient Community Action award Salvation Army, 1985. Mem. NAFE (chpt. dir. 1990), Am. Mgmt. Assn., Am. Soc. Tng. & Devel., Am. Bus. Women's Assn. (exec. bd. mem., edn. com. chmn. 1984-86). Democrat. Roman Catholic. Home: 4725 E Shangri La Rd Phoenix AZ 85028 Office: Ariz Pub Svc Co 400 N 5th St MS# 8328 Phoenix AZ 85072-3999

WEEKLEY, ANNE NICHOLS, controller; b. Chattanooga, Oct. 31, 1947; d. Gordon Lewis and Dorothy Millard (Shugart) Nichols; 1 child, David Bones. BA, U. Tex., Austin, 1969, MBA, 1980. C.P.A; C.D.P. Programmer analyst Tex. Instruments, Dallas, 1969-72; project analyst Frito-Lay, Inc., Dallas, 1972-75; systems analyst Mobil Oil Co., Dallas, 1975-76; sr. systems analyst Zale Corp., Dallas; mgmt. services cons. Arthur Young & Co., San Antonio, 1980-81; supr. fin. systems Ethyl Corp., 1981-83; mgr. fin. acctg. system Penn. Cen. Corp., Greenwich, Conn., 1983-87; dir. corp. acctg. Penn Cen Corp., Cin., 1987-89; asst. controller Penn Cen. Corp., Cin., 1989—. V.p., bd. dirs. Big Brothers/Big Sisters of Greater Cin., 1988-89; vol. Big Sister. Mem. Nat. Assn. Acct. Christian. Office: Penn Cen Corp 1 E Fourth St Cincinnati OH 45202

WEEKLEY, MARY E., veterinary diagnostics and therapeutics executive; b. Bartlesville, Okla., Aug. 19, 1956; d. Charles Harvey and Mary Jane (Kincaid) Whittington; children: Shannon Leigh, Ryan Brett. BS, U. Nev., 1978. Rsch. assoc. Scripps-Miles, Inc., La Jolla, Calif., 1980-82; supr. cell culture lab., sr. scientist Synbiotics Corp., San Diego, 1982-85; monoclonal coord., mgr. cell culture lab. Synbiotics Corp., San Diego, 1985-87; mgr. project adminstrn. Synbiotics Corp., 1987—. Author: Veterinary Immunology and Immuno Pathology. Mem. NAFE, Product Devel. and Mgmt. Assn., Project Mgmt. Inst. Office: Synbiotics Corp 11011 Via Frontera San Diego CA 92128

WEEKS, BRIGITTE, publishing executive; b. Whitchurch, Hants, Eng., Aug. 28, 1943; came to U.S., 1965; d. Jack and Margery May (Millett) W.; m. Edward A. Herscher, Sept. 6, 1969; children—Hilary, Charlotte, Daniel. Student, Univ. Coll. of North Wales, Bangor, 1962-65. Asst. editor Boston Mag., 1966-70; editor Kodansha Internat., Tokyo, 1969-72, Resources for the Future, 1973-74; asst. editor The Washington Post Book World, 1974-78, editor, 1978-88; editor in chief Book-of-the-Month Club, N.Y.C., 1988—; pres. Nat. Book Critics Circle, 1984-86. Office: Book-of-the-Month Club 485 Lexington Ave New York NY 10017

WEEKS, GWENDOLEN BRANNON, nursing educator; b. Durham, N.C., Aug. 23, 1943; d. Gus Travers and Valerie Dunster (Baker) B.; m. John Luther Weeks, May 28, 1983; step-children: Cynthia Weeks Kelly, John Luther Weeks Jr. BS in nursing, U. N.C., 1967; MS, Med. Coll. Va., 1971. Maternity staff nurse N.C. Meml. Hosp., Chapel Hill, 1967-68; obstetrics instr. Watts Hosp. Sch. Nursing, Durham, N.C., 1968-69; maternity instr. U. N.C., Greensboro, N.C., 1971-72; clin. specialist Petersburg (Va.) Gen. Hosp., 1972-77; assoc. prof. J. Sargeant Reynolds Community Coll., Richmond, Va., 1977—; clin. assoc., staff nurse St. Mary's Hosp., Richmond, 1969—. Bd. dirs. Jr. League of Richmond, 1969—; hospitality bd. dirs. chmn. Hist. Richmond Coun., 1987—. Named Outstanding Young Woman of Am., 1973. Mem. Nat. Assn. of Am. Coll. of Ob-Gyn. Nurses Assn. (cert. inpatient obstetric nursing 1987), Nurses Assn. Am. Coll. Ob-Gyn. (Richmond sect. chmn. 1972-74), Nat. Soc. of Colonial Dames, George Mason Meml. Soc., Sigma Theta Tau (sec. 1974-77). Home: 3803 Timber Ridge Rd Midlothian VA 23112 Office: J S Reynolds Community Coll 8th Jackson St Richmond VA 23232

WEEKS, JANET HEALY, judge; b. Quincy, Mass., Oct. 19, 1932; d. John Francis and Sheila Josephine (Jackson) Healy; m. George Weeks, Aug. 29, 1959; children: Susan, George. AB in Chemistry, Emmanuel Coll., Boston, 1954; JD, Boston Coll., 1958; LLD (hon.), U. Guam, 1984. Bar: Mass. 1958, Guam 1972. Trial atty. Dept. Justice, Washington, 1958-60, Trapp & Gayle, Agana, Guam, 1971-73; ptnr. Trapp, Gayle, Teker, Weeks & Freidman, Agana, 1973-75; judge Superior Ct. Guam, Agana, 1975—; chmn. task force cts., prosecution and def. Terr. Crime Commn., 1973-76; mem. Terr. Crime Commn. Bd., 1975-76, Guam Law Revision Commn., 1981—; rep. Nat. Conf. State Trial Judges, 1982. Mem. Cath. Sch. Bd. Guam, 1973. Mem. Nat. Assn. Women Judges (charter), Am. Judges Assn., ABA, Fed. Bar Assn. (chpt. sec. 1974), Guam Bar Assn. Club: Internat. (Guam). Office: Superior Ct Guam Judiciary Bldg Agana GU 96910

WEEKS, KARREN GENTLE, pharmacist, administrator; b. Huntsville, Ala., Oct. 3, 1951; d. Robert William Gentle and Rose Ivella (Sharp) Renfroe; m. Paul Richard Weeks; children: Paul Richard Jr., Brook Jamison. BS in Biology, U. Ala., 1973; BS in Pharmacy, Samford U., 1976. Lic. pharmacist, Ala. Pharmacy resident The Children's Hosp., Birmingham, Ala., 1976-77; clin. staff pharmacist U. Ala. Hosps., Birmingham, 1977-79; clin. staff pharmacist Huntsville (Ala.) Hosp., 1979-80, pharmacy supr., 1980-83, asst. dir. clin. svcs., 1983-85, dir. pharmacy, 1985—; adj. prof. Sch. of Pharmacy, Auburn (Ala.) U., 1983—. Mem. Am. Soc. Hosp. Pharmacists, Southeastern Soc. Hosp. Pharmacists, Ala. Soc. Hosp. Pharmacists (treas. 1983-85, pres. 1988-89), Ala. Commn. on Pharmacy (sec.-treas. 1988—), Dental Aux. Huntsville (pres. 1988-89), Beta Sigma Phi (sec. 1987-88). Democrat. Methodist. Office: Huntsville Hosp 101 Sivley Rd Huntsville AL 35801

WEEKS, MARTHA G., advertising executive; b. Jackson, Miss., Oct. 30, 1950; d. Charles Ford and Ruby Conn (Brock) W.; children: Tracy R. Schroeder, Kenneth, Sandra, Charles. Student, Montgomery Community Coll. Classified advt. mgr. The Gaithersburg (Md.) Gazette Newspaper Group; recruiter outside sales advt. The Gaithersburg (Md.) Gazette Newspapers; commission sales Montgomery Ward, Gaithersburg. Co-chair spl. needs Area 3 PTA, 1987; mem. PTA exec. bds. M.L. King Jr. High Sch., 1987-89, Seneca Valley High Sch., 1988-89, Washington Grove Elem. Sch., 1988-89; mem. job svc. employer com. Md. Job Svc., Montgomery County; rm. mother, vol. Summit Hall Elem. Sch., 1986-88, Washington Grove Elem. Sch., 1988-89, Ivymount Sch. for Exceptional Children, Potomac, Md., 1989—; asst. den mother Weleelos den #1, Cub Scouts. Mem. Gaithersburg-Upper Montgomery C. of C., Am. Press Inst., D.C. Md-Del Press Assn. Democrat. Home: 1010 Travis Ln Gaithersburg MD 20879 Office: PO Box Caller 6006 Gaithersburg MD 20884

WEEKS, PATSY ANN LANDRY, librarian, teacher; b. Luling, Tex., Mar. 3, 1930; d. Lee and Mattie Wood (Callihan) Landry; m. Arnett S. Weeks, Dec. 2, 1950; children: Patsy Kate, Nancy Ann, Janie Marie. B.S., Southwest Tex. State U., San Marcos, 1951; M.L.S., Tex. Woman's U., Denton, 1979. Tchr. art, reading, math. Grandview Ind. Sch. Dist., Tex., 1950-52; tchr. phys. edn. Beaumont Ind. Sch. Dist., Tex., 1953; tchr. art, coll. algebra Cisco Jr. Coll., Tex., 1957-58; tchr. remedial reading Taylor County Schs., Tuscola, Tex., 1965-66; tchr. remedial reading Anson Ind. Sch. Dist. Tex., 1971-73; librarian Bangs Ind. Sch. Dist., Tex., 1973-79, learning resources coord., 1979-90; dir. Heart of Tex. Ctr. for the Rev. and Examination of Children's and Young Adults' Lit., 1988—; adv. com. Edn. Svc. Ctr., 1978-83; coord. Reading is Fundmental Program, 1978-83, Heart of Tex. Ctr. for Rev. and Exam. of Children's and Young Adult's Lit. Bd. dirs. Anson Pub. Libr., Tex., 1971-72. Exhibitor oil paintings, pastels at Tex. fairs (1st prize 1952, 60). Mem. ALA, Assn. Libr. Svc. to Children (Caldecott award com. 1986, mem. Grosset and Dunlap Group award selection com. 1988, chair 1989-90, nominating com. 1989), Am. Assn. Sch. Librs., Intellectual Freedom Round Table, Tex. Libr. Assn. (mem. intellectual freedom and profl. responsibility com. 1979-81, mem. Tex. Bluebonnet award com. 1982-85, chair adv. com. 1987, chair children's round table 1987), Tex. Assn. Sch. Librs. (media prodns. award com. 1985-86), Tex. Assn. Improvement Reading, Teenage Libr. Assn. Tex. (chmn. audio-visual award com. 1984), Tex. Assn. Sch. Libr. Adminstrs., Tex. State Tchr. Assn. (life), Phi Delta Kappa, Kappa Pi, Alpha Chi, Beta Phi Mu, Delta Kappa Gamma. Baptist. Clubs: Bangs Progressive Women's (treas. 1974-76). Home: 110 Poco St Bangs TX 76823 Office: Howard Payne U Sta Walker Meml Libr Heart of Tex Ctr Brownwood TX 76801

WEEKS, VIRGINIA LYNN, research and development executive; b. March AFB, Calif., Feb. 6, 1952; d. John Edward and Azella Virginia (Morrill) Anderson; m. Calvin George Weeks, Feb. 14, 1980; children by previous marriage: Raymond Edward, Jerry Glenn Jr. Student, Sinclair Community Coll., 1981-83, U. Tex., San Antonio, 1980. Procur asst. specialized contracting USAF, Wright-Patterson AFB, Ohio, 1973-77; buyer logistics contracting USAF, Kelly AFB, Tex., 1977-81; contract specialist USAF, Wright-Patterson AFB, Ohio, 1981-84; spl. asst. Peace Log, Tehran, Iran, 1977; acting chief of contracts cruise missile program Gen. Dynamics/Convair, San Diego, 1984-86; contracts mgr. VERAC, Inc., San Diego, 1986—; cons. Gen. Dynamics, San Diego, 1985, Efratrom, 1986. Mem. Nat. Assn. Female Execs., Nat. Mgmt. Assn., Nat. Contract Mgmt. Assn. Republican. Office: VERAC Inc 9605 Scranton Rd Suite 500 San Diego CA 92121

WEEMS, CLARA C., educator, counselor, consultant; b. N.Y.C., June 15, 1933; d. Joseph and Itala (Nerone) Carbonara; m. Clarence Norwood Weems, Dec. 28, 1954; children: Nancy M., Clarence N. BA in Chemistry, Hunter Coll., 1954; postgrad. in law, NYU, 1954-55, Franklin Pierce Coll., 1969-72. Cert. med. lab. technologist. Chemistry lab. instr. Fairleigh Dickinson U., Rutherford, N.J., 1956-57; tchr., med. lab. techniques Mandl Sch., N.Y.C., 1962-64; sci. tchr., chmn. sci. dept. Holy Trinity High Sch., Westfield, N.J., 1973-76; med. lab. tchr. Advanced Career Tng., N.Y.C., 1976-78; med. lab. tchr., placement dir. Allen Sch. for Physicians Aides, Jamaica, N.Y., 1978—; dir., organizer Clara Barton Sch., Nutley, N.J., 1986-87. Mem. AAUW, Am. Assn. Med. Assts., Faculty Wives of Franklin Pierce Coll. (pres. 1970-72). Roman Catholic. Home: 14 Donna Ct Nutley NJ 07110 Office: Allen Sch Physician Aides 163-18 Jamaica Ave Jamaica NY 11432

WEERTMAN, JULIA RANDALL, materials science and engineering educator; b. Muskegon, Mich., Feb. 10, 1926. BS in Physics, Carnegie-Mellon U., 1946, MS in Physics, 1947, DSc in Physics, 1951. Physicist U.S. Naval Rsch. Lab., Washington, 1952-58; vis. asst. prof. Dept. Materials Sci. and Engring., Northwestern U., Evanston, Ill., 1972-73, assoc. prof., 1978-82, prof., 1982—, dept. chmn., 1987—, asst. to dean grad. studies and rsch. Tech. Inst., 1973-76. Co-author: Elementary Dislocation Theory, 1964, also pub. in French, Japanese and Polish; contbr. numerous articles to profl. jours. Mem. Evanston Environ. Control Bd., 1972-79. Recipient Creativity award NSF, 1981, 86; Guggenheim Found. fellow, 1986-87. Fellow Am. Soc. Metals Internat.; mem. ASTM, NAE, Minerals, Metals and Materials Soc., Am. Phys. Soc., Materials Rsch. Soc., Soc. Women Engrs. Home: 834

Lincoln St Evanston IL 60201 Office: Northwestern U Dept Materials Sci & Engring 2145 Sheridan Rd Evanston IL 60208

WEESE, CYNTHIA ROGERS, architect, educator; b. Des Moines, June 23, 1940; d. Gilbert Taylor and Catharine (Wingard) Rogers; m. Benjamin H. Weese, July 5, 1963; children: Daniel Peter, Catharine Mohr. B.S.A.S., Washington U., St. Louis, 1962; B.Arch., Washington U., 1965. Registered architect, Ill. Pvt. practice architecture Chgo., 1965-72, 74-77; draftsperson, designer Harry Weese & Assocs., Chgo., 1972-74; prin. Weese Hickey Weese Ltd., Chgo., 1977—; design critic Weese Langley Weese Ltd., Muncie, Ind., Miami U., Oxford, Ohio, 1979, U. Wis.-Milw., 1980, U. Ill.-Chgo., 1981, 85, Iowa State U., Ames, 1982, Washington U., St. Louis, 1985, U. Ill., Champaign, 1987-89; design critic U. Ill., Champaign, 1987-88, 89-90. Bd. regents Am. Architecture Found., 1990. Mem. AIA (bd. dirs. Chgo. chpt. 1980-83, v.p. 1983-85, 1st v.p. 1986-87, pres. 1987-88, regional dir. 1990—, Disting. Bldg. awards 1977, 81, 82, 83, 86, Interior Architecture award 1981, Disting. Svc. award 1978), AIA Found. (pres. Chgo. chpt. 1988-89), Am. Archtl. Found. (regent 1990—), Chgo. Women in Architecture (regional dir. 1990—), Chgo. Network, Nat. Inst. Archtl. Edn. (bd. dirs. 1988-90), Chgo. Archtl. Club (pres. 1988-89), Alpha Rho Chi, Lambda Alpha. Democrat. Clubs: Arts, Chgo. Archtl. Office: Weese Langley Weese Ltd 9 W Hubbard Chicago IL 60610

WEGHORST, MARGARET LYNN, telephone company official, educator; b. Pasadena, Calif., Jan. 3, 1948; d. Gerald Robert and Genevieve Marilyn (Scheffler) Eilers: m. Dwight Edward Weghorst, Aug. 20, 1978 (div. Dec. 1982). BS in Mgmt., No. Ill. U., 1970; MBA in Systems, De Paul U., 1984. Lic. real estate broker, Ill. Various managerial positions Ill. Bell Telephone, Chgo., 1970-87, mgr. computer ops., 1987—. Recipient Leadership in Bus. award YWCA, Chgo., 1984. Mem. Computer Ops. Mgmt. Assn. (v.p. 1987-88, pres. 1988-89), Bell Mgmt. Women (pres. Chgo. 1984-85). Roman Catholic. Home: 1105 W Hillgrove Ave La Grange IL 60525 Office: Ill Bell Telephone 3206 W 61st St Chicago IL 60629

WEGMANN, KAREN, bank executive; b. 1944. BA, Pa. Acad. Fine Arts, 1964. Formerly with Am. Cypress, Morgan Guaranty Trust; with Wells Fargo Bank NA, 1981—, v.p., sr. v.p., 1983-87, exec. v.p., 1987—. Office: Wells Fargo Bank NA 420 Montgomery St San Francisco CA 94163*

WEHE, DIANA JOYCELYN, company executive; b. Okla., Jan. 6, 1943; d. Hugh F. and Myra Kiku (Setsuda) Doss; m. Albert Gary Wehe, June 24, . Asst. to dean Coll. Cont. Edn. Am. U., Wash., 1969-73; typesetter Thor Assocs., Wash., 1974-75, Cybergraphic Typographers, Honolulu, 1976-77; typographer Pacific Phototype, Honolulu, 1977-78; head typesetter The Maui News, Kahului, Hawaii, 1978-82; computer cons. Maui, 1982-83; owner Creative Computing of Maui, Makawao, Hawaii, 1983-86; v.p., sec., treas. Creative Computing of Maui, Inc., Kahului, 1986-89, pres., 1989—. Bd. dirs. Mauians for Justice, 1979-82. Republican. Office: Creative Computing Maui Inc 255A Alamaha St Kahului HI 96732

WEHMAN, ADELE See BAYNE, ADELE WEHMAN

WEHRENBERG, KATHLEEN ANN, chiropractor, consultant; b. Lancaster, Wis., July 6, 1960; d. Robert Lewis Henry Frederick and Alda Pearl (Evenson) W. Student U. Wis., La Crosse, 1978-82; D of Chiropractic, Palmer Coll., 1985. Chiropractor Apache Chiropractic, Mesa, Ariz., 1986-88, Gavin Chiropractic, Baton Rouge, 1988-90, Wehrenberg Chiropractic, Phila., 1990—. Mem. NAFE, VFW Aux., Am. Bus. Assn., East Ascension Women's Club, Am. Legion Aux, Toastmasters. Republican. Lutheran. Home: 1511 Sean Ct Lakewood NJ 08701 Office: 2240 E Allegheny Ave Philadelphia PA 18760

WEHRHEIM, CAROL ANN, writer, editor; b. Red Bud, Ill., Dec. 18, 1940; d. Elbert Elles and Fern Agnes (Gregson) W.; m. Harrison Henry Bender, Dec. 28, 1969 (div. 1976); m. Charles Daniel Kuehner Sr., June 6, 1982. BA, So. Ill. U., 1962; MA in Religious Edn., McCormick Theol. Seminary, Chgo., 1964. Cert. ch. educator United Ch. of Christ. Dir. Christian edn. Woods Meml. Presby. Ch., Severna Park, Md., 1964-69, Hammond St. Congl. Ch., Bangor, Maine, 1971-72, St. John's United Ch. of Christ, Catonsville, Md., 1972-74; tchr. Union 90, Alton, Maine, 1970-71; dir. Woods Meml. Child Devel. Ctr., Severna Park, Md., 1974-76; sec. early childhood edn. United Ch. Bd. Homeland Ministries, N.Y.C., 1976-79; asst. dir. dr. ministry program McCormick Theol. Seminary, Chgo., 1979-82; writer, editor Princeton, N.J., 1982—. Author: Planning Your Educational Ministry, 1988, The Journey Ahead, 1990; editor: Caregiver's Guide for Bible Discovery, 1989—, Growing Together Series, 1989—. Mem. AAUW (Outstanding Young Women Am. 1968), Assn. United Ch. Educators, Assn. Presbyn. Ch. Educators, Religious Edn. Assn. Home and Office: 40 Mountain Ave Princeton NJ 08540

WEHRLE, MARTHA GAINES, former state legislator; b. Charleston, W.Va., Nov. 30, 1925; d. Ludwell Ebersole and Betty (Chilton) Gaines. AB, Vassar Coll., 1948; MA, Harvard U., 1954; m. Russell Schilling Wehrle, Oct. 16, 1954; children: Michael H., Ebersole Gaines, Katherine S., Philip N., Martha Chilton. Tchr., W.Va. schs., 1949-50, Belmont (Mass.) Day Sch., 1951-53; mem. W.Va. Ho. of Dels., 1974-84, vice chmn. edn. com., 1976, chmn. constl. revision com., 1977-84, mem. fin. com.; dir. United Nat. Bank, 1984-89; mem. W.Va. State Senate, 1989—; bd. dirs. McJunkin Corp. Bd. dirs. Arthur B. Hodges Ctr., Inc.; mem. adv. coun. W.Va. Woman's Commn.; mem. V.Wa. State Senate, 1989— Mem. LWV, Garden Club Am. (chmn. nat. affairs and legis. 1987-89), Kanawha Garden Club, Charleston Jr. League Club. Democrat. Episcopalian.

WEHRMAN, STEPHANIE ANN, physician; b. Lockwood, Mo., Oct. 8, 1959; d. Harlan Henry and Natalie Ann (Seboldt) W. AB in Biology with honors, Washington U., St. Louis, 1981; MD, U. Mo., Columbia, 1986. Diplomate Nat. Bd. Med. Examiners. Resident in psychiatry Washington U., St. Louis, 1986-90; physician Psychiat. Assocs., St. Louis, 1990—. Mem. AMA, So. Med. Assn., Mo. State Med. Assn., Am. Quilters Soc. Republican. Lutheran. Office: Psychiat Assocs 3009 N Ballas Ste 227 Saint Louis MO 63131

WEIDA, DONNA LEE, entrepreneur; b. Logansport, Ind., Oct. 29, 1939; d. Donald L. and Leila J. (Sweet) Kleckner; children from previous marriage: P. Mark, Traci L., Teri L. Weida Folsom; m. Robert G. Swigert, 1989. AA in Bus. Mgmt., Saddleback Coll. Sec., bookkeeper K.L.K. Mfg. Co., Logansport, 1957-60, 63-65; sec. Sch. Edn., Mich. State U., 1962-63; sec. Sch. Fine Arts, U. Calif., Irvine, 1966-69; co-founder Plaza Vet. Clinic, Upland, Calif., 1969-70; office mgr. Bob Bondurant Sch. High Performance Driving, Ontario (Calif.) Motor Speedway, 1970-73; mgr./pub. relations exec. Chuck Jones Racing, Costa Mesa, Calif., 1973; exec. sec. Dana Steel, Newport Beach, Calif., 1974; estimator/acct./corp. treas. Hardy & Harper, Tustin, Calif., 1975-76; contr. Gillen/Kloss Advt., Newport Beach, 1977-78; purchasing adminstr. Butler Housing, Irvine, 1979; contr. XMark Corp., Costa Mesa, 1980-81; adminstrv. mgr. Concept Devel., Costa Mesa, 1981; adminstrv. mgr. corp. sec./co-founder Persyst Inc., Irvine, Calif., 1981-83; founder/owner Numbers & Words, Irvine, 1982—; Donna Weida Agy., 1984-85; dir. administrn. Data Voice Solutions, New Port Beach, 1985; co-owner Fawnview Cabins, Fawnskin, Calif., 1985-89; contr. The Keith French Group, San Clemente, Calif., 1986-87; systems coord. analyst Controls Inc., Logansport, 1987-89; founder, prin. Numbers & Words, Inc., Logansport, 1989—, DLS Properties, Logansport, 1989—. Mem. Beta Sigma Phi. Republican. Methodist. Home: 206 Winding Brook Trail Logansport IN 46947 Office: Numbers & Words Inc 325 Court St Logansport IN 46947 Office: Data Voice Solutions 200 Sandpointe, 7th Fl Santa Ana CA 92704

WEIDEL, LYNNE CATHERINE, consulting firm executive; b. Ridley Park, Pa., Sept. 13, 1946; d. Daniel Gossard and Antoinette Marie (Maccinile) W. BA, U. Del., 1968; MHA, U. Minn., 1976. Dir. instl. planning Met. Hosps., Inc., Portland, Oreg., 1979-81, v.p., 1982-83; chief exec. officer Clackamas Health Care Consortium, Portland, 1982-83; prin. Weidel & Assocs., Portland, 1983-88; v.p. Dearing and Assocs., Spokane, Wash., 1988—; sports network coord. Inst. for Managerial and Profl. Women, Portland, 1980-81; mem. Multnomah sub-area council N.W. Oreg. Health Systems Agy., Portland, 1982-83; preceptor U. Minn., Mpls., 1982—. Co-author: Marketing Women's Health Care, 1987. Bd. dirs. Portland YWCA, 1983-84, Lake Grove Neighborhood Assn.; vol. Big Sister/Big Bro. program. Mem. Am. Coll. Hosp. Execs., Am. Soc. Hosp. Care Planning and Mktg., Oreg. Health Care Planning and Mktg. Assn. (steering com. 1984-86). Club: Bergfunde Ski (Portland). Avocations: white water rafting, hiking. Office: Dearing and Assocs S 1414 Bernard Spokane WA 99203

WEIDELL, CAROLYN L., delivery service executive; b. Long Beach, Calif., Apr. 24, 1955; d. Charles Manley and Jacqueline Dorothy (Nay) W. BA in Anthropology, Calif. State U., 1986; postgrad., Calif. Sch. Profl. Psychology, 1987; AA, El Camino Coll., 1977. Mgmt. devel. coord., courier Fed. Express Corp., L.A., San Francisco; sr. mgr. Fed. Express Corp., L.A.; sr. auditor The Southland Corp., Redondo Beach, Calif. Author: Student's Course Guide for Descriptive Statistics, Sexual Harassment in the Work Place. Office: Fed Express Corp 18115 S Main St Gardena CA 90248

WEIDEMANN, CELIA JEAN, social scientist, international development consultant; b. Denver, Dec. 6, 1942; d. John Clement and Hazel (Van Tuyl) Kirlin; m. Wesley Clark Weidemann, July 1, 1972; 1 child, Stephanie Jean. BS, Iowa State U., 1964; MS, U. Wis.-Madison, 1970, PhD, 1973; postgrad. U. So. Calif., 1983. Advisor, UN Food & Agr. Orgn., Ibadan, Nigeria, 1973-77; ind. researcher, Asia and Near East, 1977-78; program coord., asst. prof., rsch. assoc. U. Wis., Madison, 1979-81; chief institutional and human resources U.S. Agy. for Internat. Devel., Washington, 1982-85, team leader, cons., Sumatra, Indonesia, 1984; dir. fed. econs. program Midwest Rsch. Inst., Washington, 1985-86; pres. Weidemann Assocs., Arlington, Va., 1986—; cons. U.S. Congress, Aspen Inst., Ford Found., World Bank, Nigeria, Gambia, Pakistan, Indonesia, U.S. Agy. for Internat. Devel., Kenya, Jordan, Internat. Ctr. Rsch. on Women, Zaire, UN Food and Agriculture Orgn., Ghana, Internat. Statis. Inst., The Netherlands, Global Exchange, 1986-87. Author: Planning Home Economics Curriculum for Social and Economic Development, Agricultural Extension for Women Farmers in Africa, 1990; contbr. chpts. to books and articles to profl. jours. Am. Home Econs. Assn. fellow, 1969-73 (recipient research grant Ford Found. 1987-89). Mem. Soc. Internat. Devel., Am. Sociol. Assn., U.S. Dirs. of Internat. Agrl. Programs, Assn. for Women in Devel. (pres. 1989, founder, bd. dirs.), Internat. Devel. Conf. (bd. dirs., exec. com.), Am. Home Econs. Assn. (Wis. internat. chmn. 1980-81), Internat. Fedn. Home Econs., Internat. Platform Assn., Pi Lambda Theta, Omicron Nu. Roman Catholic. Avocations: mountain trekking, piano/pipe organ, canoeing, photography, poetry. Home and Office: 2607 N 24th St Arlington VA 22207

WEIDEMANN, JULIA CLARK, principal, professor; b. Batavia, N.Y., May 21, 1937; d. Edward Thomas and Grace Eloise (Kenna) Clark; m. Rudolph John Weidemann, July 9, 1960; 1 child, Michael John. BA in English, Daemen Coll., 1958; MS in Edn., SUNY, Buffalo, 1961, MEd in Reading Edn., 1973. Remedial reading tchr. West Seneca (N.Y.) Cen. Sch. Dist., 1972-79, coord. chpt. I reading program, 1974-79, reading coord., 1980-87; prin. Parkdale Elem. Sch./East Aurora (N.Y.) Union Free Sch., 1987—. Democrat. Roman Catholic. Home: 50 Boxwood Circle Hamburg NY 14075 Office: Parkdale Elem Sch 80 Parkdale Ave East Aurora NY 14052

WEIDENBRUCH, ANNA MAE, nurse; b. Owosso, Mich., July 26, 1926; d. Robert Harry and Della Jane (Gander) Thompson; m. Manley Lavern Nixon, Aug. 3, 1946 (div. 1961); children: Terry Lee, Douglas Kent, LaVerna Ann, Norma Jean; m. Donald F. Clewley, Aug. 27, 1961 (dec. 1973); m. Heinz Weidenbruch, 1984. Assocs. of Nursing, Lansing (Mich.) Community Coll., 1983. RN, Mich. Staff nurse Sparrow Hosp., Lansing, 1958-62, Ingham Med. Hosp., Lansing, 1962-64, Lansing Gen. Hosp., 1964-66, 77-88, Hazel I. Findlay Country Manor, St. Johns, Mich., 1987-89. Democrat. Home: 2123 Northwest Ave Lansing MI 48906

WEIDENFELD, SHEILA RABB, television producer, author; b. Cambridge, Mass., Sept. 7, 1943; d. Maxwell M. and Ruth (Cryden) Rabb; BA, Brandeis U., 1965; m. Edward L. Weidenfeld, Aug. 11, 1968; children: Nicholas Rabb, Daniel Rabb. Assoc. producer Metromedia, Inc., WNEW-TV, N.Y.C., 1965-68; talent coord. That Show with Joan Rivers, NBC, N.Y.C., 1968-71; coord. NBC network game programs, N.Y.C., 1968-71; producer Metromedia, WTTG-TV, Washington, 1971-73; creator/producer Take It From Here, NBC (WRC-TV), Washington, 1973-74; press sec. to first lady Betty Ford and spl. asst. to Pres. Gerald R. Ford 1974-77; mem. Pres.'s Adv. Commn. on Historic Preservation, 1977-81; TV producer, moderator On the Record, NBC-TV, WRC-TV, Washington, 1978-79; pres. D.C. Prodns., Ltd., 1978; producer, host Your Personal Decorator, 1987; mem. Sec. State's Adv. Commn. on Fgn. Service Inst., 1972-74. Author: First Lady's Lady, 1979. Mem. U.S. Holocaust Meml. Council, 1987—; corporator, Dana Hall Sch., Wellesley, Mass; bd. dirs. Wolf Trap Found., Women's Campaign Fund, 1978-79; bd. dirs. D.C. Contemporary Dance Theatre, 1986-88, D.C. Rep. Cen. Com., 1984—, D.C. Preservation League, 1987-90; chmn. C&O Canal Nat. Hist. Park Commn, 1988—; bd. dirs. Am. Univ. Rome, 1988—. Recipient awards for outstanding achievement in the media AAUW, 1973, 74, Silver Screen award A Campaign to Remember for the U.S. Holocaust Meml. Coun., 1989, Bronze medal Internat. Film and Video Festival N.Y., 1990; named hon. consul of Republic of San Marino to Washington; knighted by Order of St. Agatha, Republic of San Marino, 1986. Mem. NATAS (Emmy award 1972), Washington Press Club, Am. Newspaper Women's Club, Am. Women in Radio and TV, Cosmos Club, Sigma Delta Chi. Home and Office: 3059 Q St NW Washington DC 20007

WEIDENFELLER, GERALDINE CARNEY, speech and language pathologist; b. Kearny, N.J., Oct. 12, 1933; d. Joseph Gerald and Catherine Grace (Doyle) Carney; BS, Newark State U., 1954; postgrad. Northwestern U., summer 1956, U. Wis., summer 1960; MA, NYU, 1962; m. James Weidenfeller, Apr. 4, 1964; children: Anne, David. Lic speech/language pathologist, N.J. Speech pathologist Kearny (N.J.) Public Schs., 1954-61, North Brunswick (N.J.) Public Schs., 1961-65, Bridgewater (N.J.) Public Schs., 1969-72; speech therapist Somerset County Ednl. Commn., 1983-88; real estate agt., N.J., 1982-89; pvt. practice speech therapy, Somerville, N.J., 1980—; speech therapist no. br. Midland Sch., 1989, No. Plainfield, N.J., 1989-90. V.p. Rosary Soc., Hillsborough, N.J., 1986—; Rep. county com. woman, 1989-90. Mem. Am. Speech and Hearing Assn., N.J. Speech and Hearing Assn. Roman Catholic. Club: Toastmasters (winner dist. humorous speech contest 1984, sec. 1985, advanced Toastmaster 1986). Home: 3 Banor Dr Somerville NJ 08876

WEIGEL, BARBARA BROBACK, community activist; b. Orange, N.J., Nov. 26, 1935; m. Robert F. Weigel, June 3, 1961; children: Eric P., Dana E. BA in Art History, Wellesley Coll., 1957. With pub. rels. dept., exec. sec. NBC, N.Y.C., 1957-58; sec. to dir. pub. rels., compt. and curator Mus. Primitive Art, N.Y.C., 1958-62; teaching asst. libr. and spl. edn. Piscataway (N.J.) Bd. Edn., 1975-77; pvt. tutor spl. edn., reading, math., 1977; ind. sales rep. Avon, Piscataway, 1977-87. Mem. state and nat. congl. coms., 1980—; co-dir. New Market Residents Assn., 1986—; mem. Dist. Election Bd., Middlesex County, 1972-79; committeewoman Piscataway Rep. Orgn., 1986—, corr. sec., membership chair, 1988—; candidate Piscataway Twp. Coun., 1989; mem. environ. adv. com. Congressman Jim Courter for Gov. campaign, 1989; vol. Senator Dick Zimmel for Congress campaign, 1990; advisor Piscataway Rep. campaign, 1990. Mem. AAUW (bd. dirs. Plainfield chpt., chair pub. policy, mem. scholarship com., Outstanding Young Woman of Am. award 1971), LWV, Friends of Rutgers Ecol. Preserve, Piscataway Environ. Protection Orgns., N.J. Wellesley Club.

WEIGEL, ELSIE DIVEN, publishing executive, writer, editor; b. Phila., May 31, 1948; d. William Bleakley Diven and Elsie May (Betts) Darling; m. John C. Weigel, Dec. 19, 1970 (div. 1979); 1 Child, Kimberly Joy. BA, Am. U., 1970. Editorial asst. Water Pollution Control Fedn., Alexandria, Va., 1970-72; Asst dir. publs. Am. Speech, Hearing, and Lang. Assn., Rockville, Md., 1972-78; editor-in-chief Potato Chip/Snack Food Assn., Alexandria, 1978-79; dir. publs. Nat. Soc. Pub. Accts., Alexandria, 1979-80; editorial project dir. Energy Info. Adminstrn. U.S. Dept Energy, Washington, 1980—. Editor newsletter Rittenhouse Family Assn.; contbr. articles to profl. jours. Mem. Life Skills Ctr. (bd. dirs. 1987—) Washington. Mem. Nat. Assn. Govt. Communicators (Blue Pencil award), Nat. Assn Female Execs., Sigma Delta Chi. Home: 8303 Pondside Terr Alexandria VA 22309 Office: US Dept Energy 1000 Independence Ave Washington DC 20003

WEIGHTMAN, JUDY MAE, lawyer; b. New Eagle, Pa., May 22, 1941; d. Morris and Ruth (Gutstadt) Epstein; children: Wayne, Randall, Darrell. BS in English, California U. of Pa., 1970; MA in Am. Studies, U. Hawaii, 1975; JD, U. Hawaii, 1981. Bar: Hawaii 1981. Tchr. Fairfax County Sch. (Va.), 1968-72, Hawaii Pub. Schs., Honolulu, 1973-75; lectr. Kapiolani Community Coll., Honolulu, 1975-76; instr. Olympic Community Coll., Pearl Harbor, Hawaii, 1975-77; lectr. Hawaii Pacific Coll., Honolulu, 1977-78; law clk. to atty. gen. Hawaii & Case, Kay & Lynch, Davis & Levin, 1979-81, to chief judge Intermediate Ct. Appeals, Honolulu, 1981-82; dep. pub. defender Office of Pub. Defender, Honolulu, 1982-84; staff atty. Dept. Commerce & Consumer Affairs, State of Hawaii 1984-86; pres., bd. dir. Am. Beltwrap Corp., 1986—; asst. prof. law, dir. pre-admission program, asst. prof. Richardson Sch. Law, U. Hawaii, 1987—. Patentee in field; mem. Richardson Law Rev., 1979-81. Mem. neighborhood bd. No. 25 City and County Honolulu, 1976-77; vol. Legal Aid Soc., Honolulu, 1977-78; bd. dirs. Jewish Fedn., Protection and Advocacy Agy.; parent rep. Wheeler Intermediate Adv. Coun., Honolulu, 1975-77; Hawaii rep. Metropolis Studios; trustee Carl K. Mirikitani Meml. Scholarship Fund, Arts Coun. Hawaii; membership dir. ACLU, 1977-78, bd. dirs., Hawaii, 1988—, treas. Amicus; founder Hawaii Holocaust Project; trustee Jewish Fedn. Hawaii. Community scholar, Honolulu, 1980; grantee in internat. rels. Chaminade U., 1976. Mem. ABA, Afro-Am. Lawyers Assn. (bd. trustee), Hawaii Women Lawyers, Assn. Trial Lawyers Am., Hawaii State Bar Assn., Am. Judicature Soc., Richardson Sch. Law Alumni Assn. (alumni rep. 1981-82), Phi Delta Phi (v.p. 1980-81), Hadassah Club, Women's Guild Club. Democrat. Jewish. Office: U Hawaii William S Richardson Sch Law 2515 Oole St Honolulu HI 96822

WEIGLE, MARTA, folklorist, educator; b. Janesville, Wis.; d. Richard D. Weigle. Student, St. John's Coll., Annapolis, Md., 1961-62; AB cum laude in Social Relations, Harvard U., 1965; MA, U. Pa., 1968, PhD, 1971. Asst. prof. anthropology and English U. N.Mex., Albuquerque, 1972-77, assoc. prof., 1977-83, prof. anthropology, English and Am. studies, 1983-87, prof. Am. studies and anthropology, 1987—, chmn. dept. Am. studies, 1984—; mgr., co-owner Abacus Books, Inc., 1973-74; rev. panelist NEH; cons. Hispanic heritage wing Mus. Internat. Folk Art, Sante Fe, 1986—; lectr. in field. Author: Follow My Fancy: The Book of Jacks and Jack Games, 1970, The Penitentes of the Southwest, 1970, Spiders and Spinsters: Women and Mythology, 1982, (with David Johnson) Lightning and Labyrinth: An Introduction to Mythology, 1979, At the Beginning: American Creation Myths, 1980, (with Kyle Fiore) Santa Fe and Taos: The Writer's Era, 1982, (with Peter White) The Lore of New Mexico, 1988, Creation and Procreation: Feminist Reflections on Mythologies of Cosmogony and Parturition, 1989; editor: Echoes of the Flute, 1972, Hispanic Villages of Northern New Mexico, 1975, (with Charles L. Briggs) Hispano Folklife of New Mexico: The Lorin W. Brown Fed. Writers' Project Manuscripts, 1978, New Mexicans in Cameo and Camera, 1985, (with C. and S. Larcombe) Hispanic Arts and Ethnohistory in the Southwest, 1983, Two Guadalupes, 1987, Indian Tales from Picuris Pueblo, 1989; cons. editor: Chamisal and Penasco: The Farm Security Administration Photography of Russell Lee, 1985, Colonial Frontiers: Art and Life in Spanish New Mexico, 1982-83; assoc. editor Ancient City Press, 1972-74, ptnr., editor, 1981—; contbr. numerous articles to revs. and papers to profl. jours. Recipient award of honor Cultural Properties Rev. Com., State of N.Mex., 1976, Zia award N.Mex. Press Women, 1977, Twitchell award Hist. Soc. N.Mex., 1989; grantee Nat. Endowment for Humanities, 1979-81, Exxon Edn. Found., 1979. Bd. dirs. Santa Fe Hist. Soc., 1977-81, Spanish Colonial Arts Soc., 1979—; trustee Am. Folklife Ctr., 1987-89. Mem. N.Mex. Folklore Soc. (2d v.p. 1977-78, 1st v.p. 1978-79, pres. 1979-80, Roll of Honor 1978), Am. Folklore Soc. (editor Folklore Women's Communication 1977-79, editor publs., series, vols. 1-8, exec. bd. 1983-86, fellow 1987). Office: U N Mex Dept Am Studies Albuquerque NM 87131

WEIL, NANCY HECHT, psychologist, educator; b. Chgo., Apr. 15, 1936; d. Theodore R. and Jenice (Abrams) Hecht; children: Lynda Jo, Edward S. Student Cornell U., 1954-57; M.Ed., Nat. Coll. Edn., Ill., 1974; Ph.D., Northwestern U., 1976; postgrad. Chgo. Inst. Psychoanalysis, 1972-74; attending staff Michael Reese Hosp., 1978—; clin. asst. prof. U. Chgo. Pritzker Sch. of Medicine, 1985-90; adj. asst. prof. psychiatry Coll. Medicine, U. Ill. at Chgo., 1990; mental health cons.; vice-chair Ill. Mental Health Planning Bd., 1973-75; cons. Ill. Comprehensive Health/Planning Agency, 1974; bd. trustees Chgo Inst. for Psychoanalysis, 1973—, faculty continuing edn., 1976, 87; asst. prof. Northwestern U. Med. Sch., 1976-77, assoc. prof., 1977-79; lectr. U. Chgo. Pritzker Sch. Medicine, 1978-85; chmn. adv. council Ill. Dept. Mental Health 5-Yr. Plan, 1975-80. Bd. dirs. Chgo. Focus. Fellow Am. Orthospsychiat. Assn.; mem. Am. Psychol. Assn., Ill. Psychol. Assn., Nat. Health Register Assn., Chgo. Assn. Psychoanalytic Psychology, AAUP. Contbr. articles to profl. jours.; lectr. applied psychoanalysis. Home: 200 E Delaware Pl Unit 24 C Chicago IL 60611 Office: 180 N Michigan Ave Chicago IL 60601

WEIL, SUZANNE S. FERN, arts institution administrator; b. Mpls., June 22, 1933; d. Maurice and Esther (Sperling) Swiller; m. Fred Weil, Jr., Sept. 14, 1952 (dec. Apr. 1983); 1 dau., Peggy. Student, U. Minn.-Mpls. Coordinator performing arts Walker Art Center, Mpls., 1969-76; dir. dance program Nat. Endowment for Arts, Washington, 1968-78; sr. v.p., mng. dir. Pub. Broadcasting Service, Washington, 1980-81; sr. v.p. programming Pub. Broadcasting Service, 1981-90; exec. dir. The Sundance Inst., 1990—; mem. media adv. com. Am. Inst. Architects, Washington, 1983—; dir. Nat. Arts Adv. Bd., Action for Children's TV, Boston, 1978—; cons. editor Jour. Arts ad Mgmt. and Law, Washington, 1982—. Bd. dirs. Cunningham Dance Found., N.Y.C., 1982—; bd. dirs. Film in the Cities, St. Paul, 1976—, Guthrie Theater, Mpls., 1982—, Twyla Tharp Dance Found., N.Y.C., 1978—; trustee Dance USA, Washington, 1982-83; mem. panel Nat. Sci. Found., 1989—. Bush fellow Harvard U. Inst. for Arts Adminstrn., 1973. Mem. Nat. Acad. TV Arts and Scis. Club: Mpls. Home: RR3 Box B2 Sundance UT 84604 Office: RR3 Box 624B Sundance UT 84604

WEILBACKER, KRISTINE, urban planner; b. Englewood, N.J., Feb. 9, 1961; d. Howard Garrett and Dee (David) W. BA, George Washington U., 1983, M of Urban and Regional Planning, 1987. Project mgr. MUSCLE, Inc., Washington, 1985-88; loan underwriter Patrician Mortgage Co., Washington, 1988-89; urban planner DeLeuw, Cather & Co., Washington, 1990—; cons. Brotherhood 7th day Adventist, Washington. Mem. Planned Parenthood, Washington, 1989-90. Mem. LWV, Nat. Abortion Rights Action League, Nat. Assn. Housing and Rehab. Officers, Amnesty Internat.

WEILMINSTER, ANNE ELIZABETH, computer company executive; b. Bklyn., Aug. 12, 1948; d. Harold Norman and Bernadette Gertrude (Krapf) Mathisen; m. Richard Joseph Weilminster, Aug. 17, 1968; children: Richard Joseph, Eric Joseph, Mark Joseph. AS in Acctg., Williamsport Community Coll., 1980, AS in Bus. Mgmt., 1980. Bus. mgr. Ettinger's Landscape, Montoursville, Pa., 1977-80; acct. Williamsport (Pa.) Hosp., 1980-82; computer supr. Williamsport Area Community Coll., 1982-88, instr., 1985-88; instr. Lock Haven (Pa.) U., 1986-88; pres. Maxact, Inc., Williamsport, 1986—. Mem. Pa. Assn. Sch. Bd. Officials, Pa. Assn. Student Transp., Kiwanis Internat., Beta Sigma Phi. Democrat. Roman Catholic. Office: Maxact Inc 428 Market St Ste 104 Williamsport PA 17701

WEIN, CYNTHIA ELLEN, marketing executive; b. Takoma Park, Md., Dec. 24, 1957; d. Arthur Benjamin and Mary Louise (Barker) W. BS, Purdue U., 1979; M, Antioch Sch. Law, 1982-83. Mktg. researcher Sheraton, Washington, 1979-80; sales mgr. Sea Pines Plantation Co., Hilton Head Island, S.C., 1980-81; dir. sales Sheraton Potomac Hotel, Rockville, Md., 1981-82, Ritz Carlton Hotel, Washington, 1982-83; pres. Creative Planning Internat., Washington, 1983—; dir. membership Great Inns Am., Annapolis, 1987-89. Author: Getaway Inn Style, America's Fifty Best Inns, 1990; editor Travel Inn Style Newsletter, 1990—. Mem. Meetings Planners Internat., Washington Conv. and Visitors Assn., Greater Washington Soc. Assn. Execs., Found. for Internat. Meetings (bd. govs. 1985-86), Purdue Club (pres. 1982—). Clubs: Conservative, Purdue (pres. 1982—)(Washington). Office: Creative Planning Internat PO Box 2405 Kensington MD 20891

WEINBERG, LILA SHAFFER, author, editor; d. Sam and Blanche (Hyman) Shaffer; m. Arthur Weinberg, Jan. 25, 1953; children: Hedy Merrill Cornfield, Anita Michelle Miller, Wendy Clare Rothman. Editor Ziff-Davis

Pub. Co., 1944-53; assoc. chief manuscript editor jours. U. Chgo. Press, 1966-80, sr. manuscript editor books, 1980—; mem. faculty Sch. for New Learning DePaul U., Chgo., 1976—; vis. faculty continuing edn. programs U. Chgo., 1984—. Author: (with A. Weinberg) The Muckrakers, 1961 (selected for White House Library 1963), Verdicts Out of Court, 1963, Instead of Violence, 1963, Passport to Utopia, 1968, Some Dissenting Voices, 1970, Clarence Darrow: A Sentimental Rebel, 1980; contbr. articles and revs. to various publs. Recipient Friends of Lit. award Chgo. Found. Lit., 1980, Social Justice award Darrow Community Ctr., 1980, Disting. Body of Work award Friends of Midwest Authors, 1987. Mem. Soc. Midland Authors (dir. 1977-83, pres. 1983-85, Best Biography award 1980), ACLU, Pioneer Women, Clarence Darrow Commemorative Com., YIVO, Authors' League. Home: 5421 S Cornell Ave Chicago IL 60615

WEINBERG, SARAH KIBBEE, pediatrician; b. Boston, Sept. 18, 1940; d. Austin Staats Kibbee and Betty (Urban) McNeely; m. John Lee Weinberg, July 6, 1963; children: Ruth Kibbee Weinberg, Leo Edward. BA, Swarthmore (Pa.) Coll., 1961; postgrad., U. Rochester, N.Y., 1961-62; MS, U. Chgo., 1965; MD, U. Wash., Seattle, 1977. Med. dir. North End Community Health Care, Seattle, 1981-84; pvt. practice Pediatric Ctr. of Woodinville, Wash., 1984—; clin. asst. prof. dept. pediatrics U. Wash., Seattle, 1989—. Med. dir. U.S. Synchronized Swimming, Indpls., 1984-87. Mem. Am. Acad. Pediatrics, Am. Coll. Sports Medicine, Wash. State Med. Assn., King County Med. Soc. Office: Pediatric Ctr Woodinville 17330 135th Ave NE Woodinville WA 98072

WEINBERG, SYDNEY STAHL, historian; b. N.Y.C., Oct. 2, 1938; d. David Leslie and Berenice (Jarvis) Stahl; B.A., Barnard Coll., 1960; M.A., Columbia U., 1964; Ph.D., 1969; m. Michael Weinberg, Sept. 1, 1957; children: Deborah Sara, Elisa Rachel. Instr. history N.J. Inst. Tech., 1967-69, asst. prof., 1969-72; asso. prof. history Ramapo Coll. N.J., Mahwah, 1972-74, prof., 1974—; dir. Garden State Immigration History Consurtium, 1987—. Nat. Endowment for Humanities fellow, 1977-78. Mem. Inst. for Rsch. in History, CCWHP, Middle Atlantic Radical Historians Orgn., Am. Hist. Assn., Orgn. Am. Historians, Am. Studies Assn., Jewish Studies Assn. Author: The World of Our Mothers: The Lives of Jewish Immigrant Women, 1988; contbr. articles to profl. jours. Home: 80 LaSalle St New York NY 10027 Office: Ramapo Coll NJ Dept History Mahwah NJ 07430

WEINBERGER, DOREEN ANNE, optical sciences educator; b. Bethlehem, Pa., Jan. 27, 1954; d. Joseph C. and Irene (Farkas) W. BA in Physics and Astronomy, Mount Holyoke Coll., 1975; postgrad., MIT, 1975-78; PhD in Optical Sci., U. Ariz., 1984. Assoc. faculty instr. Dept. Physics Pima Community Coll., Tucson, 1980; asst. prof. U. Mich., Ann Arbor, 1984—. Contbr. articles to profl. jours. Recipient Presdl. Young Investigator award NSF, 1986. NSF grantee. Mem. AAAS, Assn. for Women in Sci., Optical Soc. Am. (Newport Rsch. award com. 1988—, chair 1990—), Phi Beta Kappa, Sigma Xi. Democrat. Office: U Mich Dept Elec Engring Computer Sci 1301 Beal Ave Ann Arbor MI 48109-2122

WEINER, ANNETTE B., anthropology educator; b. Phila., Feb. 14, 1933; d. Archibald W. and Phyllis M. (Stein-Goldman) Cohen; m. Martin Weiner, 1953 (div. 1973); children: Linda Matisse, Jonathan Weiner; m. Robert Palter, 1979 (div. 1982); m. William E. Mitchell, 1987. B.A., U. Pa., 1968; Ph.D., Bryn Mawr Coll., 1974. Vis. asst. prof. Franklin and Marshall Coll., Lancaster, Pa., 1973-74; asst. prof. anthropology U. Tex., Austin, 1974-80, assoc. prof., 1980-81; prof., chmn. dept. anthropology NYU, N.Y.C., 1981—; David B. Kriser prof. NYU, 1985—. Author: Women of Value: Men of Renown: New Perspectives in Trobriand Exchange, 1976, The Trobrianders of Papua New Guinea, 1989; editor: (with J. Schneider) Cloth and Human Experience, 1989; contbr. articles to profl. jours. Guggenheim fellow, 1980; grantee Wenner-Gren Found. Anthrop. Rsch., 1982, 85, 85, NEH, 1976, 85, Am. Council Learned Socs., 1976, NIMH, 1972-73. Fellow Am. Anthrop. Assn. (pres.-elect 1989—), Royal Anthrop. Inst. Gt. Britain and Ireland, Assn. Social Anthropology in Oceania, Soc. Cultural Anthropology (bd. dirs. 1985-87, pres. 1988-89); mem. Inst. Advanced Study, Cibola Anthrop. Assn. (pres. 1977-79), Commn. Visual Anthropology. Office: NYU Dept of Anthropology 25 Waverly Pl New York NY 10003

WEINER, CAROLYN JUDITH, journalist; b. N.Y.C., Apr. 24, 1932; d. Jacob and Rose (Kraus) Michaels; m. Stanley Weiner, Apr. 19, 1952; children: Jeffrey, Stephen. Student, Bklyn. Coll., 1949-51. Religion editor, staff writer The Herald Statesman, Yonkers, N.Y., 1969-75; editor, exec. dir. Jewish Coun. of Yonkers, Jewish Chronicle, Yonkers, 1975-88; asst. to mayor City of Yonkers, 1988-89; dir. Yonkers COMMIT, 1989—. Co-author: Catch A Falling House, 1976. Recipient Faith and Freedom award Religious Heritage of Am., 1974, Bicentennial award City of Yonkers, 1976. Mem. Women in Communications, Inc. (Clarion award 1989). Office: Yonkers COMMIT 733 Yonkers Ave Ste 502 Yonkers NY 10704

WEINER, CLAIRE MURIEL, freelance writer; b. Bronx, N.Y., Dec. 18, 1951; d. David and Norma (Berry) W. BA, U. Miami, Coral Gables, Fla., 1973; MA, U. Md., 1980. Pub. rels. specialist Hialeah Recreation Div., Hialeah, Fla., 1974-77; freelance writer North Miami Beach, 1977—, Germantown, Md., 1989—; govt. affairs liaison for new ednl. data base co. being formed, Montgomery County, 1982—. Contbr. articles to local newspapers; contbr. travel articles to profl. jours, mags. Active membership com., newsletter Greater Miami Jewish Fedn., Miami, Fla., 1974-77; charter mem. Women for Today chpt. B'nai B'rith Women, Washington, 1985—. Mem. Pub. Relations Soc. Am. Jewish. Home: 18828 Sky Blue Cir Germantown MD 20874

WEINER, KAREN LYNN (KAREN LYNN COLBY), psychologist, lawyer; b. Oak Park, Ill., Oct. 28, 1943; d. Leonard L. and Mildred Irene (Berman) Colby; m. J. Laevin Weiner, July 26, 1964; children: Joel Laevin, Doren Robin, Anthony Justin. BA, Mich. State U., East Lansing, 1964; JD, U. Detroit, 1977, MA, 1986, PhD, 1988. Bar: Mich. 1977, D.C. 1978. Speech therapist Oak Park Sch. Dist., 1965-68; law clk. justice G. Mennen Williams Mich. Supreme Ct., Lansing, 1977-79; assoc. Dickinson, Wright, Moon, Van Dusen & Freeman, Detroit, 1979-83; intern in psychology Detroit Psychiat. Inst., 1986-88; psychologist Northland Clinic, Southfield, Mich., 1987-88, Counseling Assocs., Southfield, 1988—; intern Wyandotte (Mich.) Hosp. and Health Ctr., 1988-90; hearing panelist Atty. Discipline Bd., Detroit, 1982—; hearing referee Mich. Civil Rights Commn., Detroit, 1983—. Contbr. articles to profl. jours. Chair Mich. Bar Spl. Com. for Expansion of Under Represented Groups in the Law, 1980-83. Mem. Mich. Psychol. Assn., Am. Psychol. Assn., Mich. Soc. for Psychoanalytic Psychology, Assn. for advancement of Psychoanalysis, Women Lawyers Assn. Mich. (pres. 1981-82, found. pres. 1982-83), Anti-Defamation League (mem. adv. bd. Mich. chpt. 1981-90). Democrat. Jewish. Home: 1718 Morningside Way Bloomfield Hills MI 48302 Office: Counseling Assocs 26699 W Twelve Mile Rd #100 Southfield MI 48034

WEINER, KATHERINE SHEPHARD, hospital planner; b. Stockton, Calif., Aug. 4, 1964; d. Thomas Joseph Sr. and Irene (Woodworth) Shephard; m. Jon Randolph Weiner, Aug. 27, 1988. BA in Psychology, U. Calif., Davis, 1986; M Health Svc. Adminstrn., U. Mich., 1988. Adminstrv. intern St. Joseph's Healthcare Corp., Stockton, Calif., 1986, Little Co. of Mary Hosp., Torrance, Calif., 1987; rsch. asst. hosp. adminstrn. program U. Mich., Ann Arbor, 1987-88; planner St. Mary's Regional Med. Ctr., Reno, 1988—. Project bus. cons., Jr. Achievement, Reno, 1989-90; vol. Internat. Winter Spl. Olympics, Reno, 1989; lector, eucharistic minister Little Flower Cath. Ch., Reno, 1989-90. Mem. Am. Hosp. Assn., Cal Aggie Alumni Marching Band. Democrat. Office: St Mary Regional Med Ctr 1155 W 4th St Reno NV 89503

WEINER, LYNN JOY, technical writer; b. Bklyn., Jan. 22, 1959; d. Herman and Shirley (Campi) W. AA, Nassau Community Coll., Garden City, N.Y., 1980; BA, L.I. U., 1982, MPA, 1983. Systems control asst. Standard Chartered Bank, N.Y.C., 1983-84, asst. adminstr. internat. cash mgmt., 1984-86, tech. documentation officer, 1986; officer's asst. for spl. projects Chem. Bank, N.Y.C., 1986-87; mgr. med. office Dr. Harvey H. Jay, N.Y.C., 1987-88; tech. writer Seaman Furniture Co., Inc., Uniondale, N.Y., 1988—; tech. cons. Kaplan Theatres, Bronx, N.Y., 1988. Co-editor: (newsletter) The Living Society. Vol. Syosset (N.Y.) Sr. Day Care Ctr., 1982-83. Recipient vol. award Syosset Sr. Day Care Ctr., 1982. Mem. Congregation and Brotherhood Monastir Inc. Home: 2941 Carlyle Rd Wantagh NY 11793 Office: Seaman Furniture Co Inc 70 Charles Lindbergh Blvd Uniondale NY 11553

WEINER, MARIAN MURPHY, insurance executive, consultant; b. N.Y.C., Mar. 20, 1954; d. Stephen Patrick and Evelyn (McTiernan) Murphy; m. Joseph Longo, Feb. 15, 1975 (div. May 1977); m. Ira Elliott Weiner, Sept. 23, 1983; children: Joshua Stephen, Samantha Beth. BA, William Paterson Coll., 1984. CPCU; cert. ins. counselor. Bookkeeper RJT, Inc. trading as The Turner Group, Pine Brook, N.J., 1973-75; ins. broker RJT, Inc. T-A The Turner Group, Pine Brook, N.J., 1975-80, office mgr., 1980-82, exec. v.p., 1982—. Bd. dirs. Homeowners Assn., Vernon, N.J., 1989. Mem. Profl. Ins. Agts. Democrat. Roman Catholic. Home: 99 Curtis Dr RD 4 Vernon NJ 07462 Office: The Turner Group 350 Main Rd Montville NJ 07045

WEINER, SUSAN BETH, consultant, writer; d. Robert Sherman and Rita Lena (Chimes) Weiner; m. Allan Clark Lewis. BA, Oberlin Coll., 1975; MA, Harvard U., 1977, PhD, 1984. Chartered fin. analyst. Rsch. scholar U. Tokyo, 1979-81; rsch. asst. Harvard Bus. Sch., Boston, 1984; mng. Japan desk Global Competitiveness, Boston, 1984-87; trustee Batterymarch Fin. Mgmt., Boston, 1987-89; cons., writer Newton, Mass., 1989—; Organizer Japan Young Profls., Boston, 1987—; tchr. Babson Coll., Wellesley, Mass., 1990, Boston Security Analysts Soc., 1989. Author articles on Asian business. Fulbright scholar, Tokyo, 1979-80; Japan Found. scholar, 1978-79. Mem. Japan Soc. Boston, Women in World Trade. Office: PO Box 381 Newtonville MA 02160-9998

WEINERT, FRITZIE JOHANNA, nurse administrator; b. N.Y.C., Dec. 27, 1933; d. William Gerders and Magda Agnes (Kalbhern) Strobach; m. Alfred C. Weinert, July 25, 1953 (div. 1979); children: Frederick Alexander, Suzanne Lorraine, Jeanette Christine. ASA, Orange County Community Coll., Middletown, N.Y., 1968. RN, N.Y. Mental hygiene therapy aide Middletown Psychiat. Ctr., 1957-68, staff nurse I, 1968-69, head nurse II, 1969-79, nurse adminstr., 1979—; nurse technician Horton Meml. Hosp., Middletown, 1968-69. Mem. ANA, N.Y. State Nurses Assn., Middletown Psychiat. Ctr. Nurses Assn., German Am. Club of Middletown. Republican. Lutheran. Home: Pine St and 1st Ave Wurtsboro NY 12790 Office: Middletown Psychiat Ctr Monhagen Ave Middletown NY 10940

WEINGARTEN, KATHY, clinical psychologist; b. Bklyn., Jan. 13, 1947; d. Victor and Violet (Brown) W.; m. Hilary Goddard Worthen, June 15, 1969; children: Benjamin, Miranda Eve. BA, Smith Coll., 1969; PhD in Arts and Sci., Harvard U., 1974. Pvt. practice Newton, Mass., 1974—; asst. prof. dept. psychology Wellesley (Mass.) Coll., 1975-78; rsch. assoc. Wellesley (Mass.) Coll. Ctr. for Rsch. on Women, 1975-79; founder, dir. family tng. program, Dept. Psychiatry Judge Baker Children's Ctr., Harvard Med. Sch., Boston, 1979-87, teaching assoc., cons. Dept. Psychiatry, 1979—; co-dir. Program in Systemic Therapies Family Inst. of Cambridge, Watertown, Mass., 1982—; presenter for psychol., med. and family therapy orgns. Co-author: Sooner or Later: The Timing of Parenthood in Adult Lives, 1982; contbr. articles to profl. jours. Fellow Mass. Psychol. Assn.; mem. Am. Assn. Marriage and Family Therapists, Am. Family Therapy Assn., Am. Psychol. Assn., Nat. Register Health Svc. Providers, Soc. for Family Therapy and Rsch. Office: Family Inst of Cambridge 51 Kondazian St Watertown MA 02172

WEINHEIM, DONNA L., creative director; b. N.Y.C., Mar. 4, 1951; d. Walter and Eva (Domingo) W. BFA, Rochester Inst. Tech., 1972. Asst. art dir. Ogilvy and Mather, N.Y.C., 1973-74; art dir. Rosser Reeves Inc., N.Y.C., 1974-79; creative dir. D.F.S. Dorland Worldwide Inc. (later Saatchi & Saatchi Advt.), N.Y.C., from 1979; now sr. v.p., creative dir. Cliff Freeman & Ptnrs., N.Y.C. Designer (book jacket) Math Anxiety, 1978. Recipient awards including Art Dirs., Andy, Clio, Cannes Film Festival. Home: 345 E 80th St New York NY 12022 Office: Cliff Freeman & Ptnrs 375 Hudson St New York NY 10014

WEINKAUF, MARY LOUISE STANLEY, educator; b. Eau Claire, Wis., Sept. 22, 1938; d. Joseph Michael and Marie Barbara (Holzinger) Stanley; m. Alan D. Weinkauf, Oct. 12, 1962; children: Stephen, Xanti. BA, Wis. State U., 1961; MA, U. Tenn., 1962, PhD, 1966; grad. studies, Luth. Sch. Theology, Chgo., 1989—. Grad. asst., instr. U. Tenn., 1961-66; asst. prof. English, Adrian Coll., 1966-69; prof., head dept. English, Dakota Wesleyan U., Mitchell, S.D., 1969-89. Mem. Mitchell Arts Council; bd. trustees, The Ednl. Found., 1986—. Mem. Nat. Council Tchrs. English, S.D. Council Tchrs. English, Sci. Fiction Research Assn., Popular Culture Assn., Milton Soc., AAUW (div. pres. 1978-80), S.D. State Poetry Soc. (pres. 1982-83), Delta Kappa Gamma (pres. local chpt., mem. state bd. 1972—, state v.p. 1979-83, state pres. 1983-85), Sigma Tau Delta, Pi Kappa Delta, Phi Kappa Phi. Republican. Lutheran.*

WEINMAN, CONNIE GERMANN, banker, lawyer; b. Celina, Ohio, Jan. 2, 1943; d. Elmer John and Berniece (Buck) Germann; m. George C. Weinman; children: Matthew, Jeffrey. BS, Capital U., 1965; JD, Hamline U., 1977. V.p. Nat. City Bank, Mpls., 1978—; bd. dirs. Fairview, Mpls., Wheatridge, Chgo., Overseas Edn. Fund, Washington. Mem. Minn. Women's Econ. Round Table. Republican. Lutheran. Office: National City Bank PO Box E1919 Minneapolis MN 55480

WEINSHIENK, ZITA LEESON, federal judge; b. St. Paul, Apr. 3, 1933; d. Louis and Ada (Dubov) Leeson; m. Hubert Troy Weinshienk, July 8, 1956 (dec. 1983); children: Edith Blair, Kay Anne, Darcy Jill; m. James N. Schaffner, Nov. 15, 1986. Student, U. Colo., 1952-53; BA magna cum laude, U. Ariz., 1955; JD cum laude, Harvard U., 1958; Fulbright grantee, U. Copenhagen, Denmark, 1959. Bar: Colo. 1959. Probation counselor, legal adviser, referee Denver Juvenile Ct., 1959-64; judge Denver County Ct., 1964-71; Denver dist. judge, 1972-79, U.S. dist. judge for dist. Colo., 1979—. Precinct committeewoman Denver Democratic Com., 1963-64; bd. dirs. Crime Stoppers. Named One of 100 Women in Touch with Our Time Harper's Bazaar Mag., 1971. Mem. ABA, Colo. Bar Assn., Denver Bar Assn., Nat. Conf. Fed. Trial Judges, Colo. Women's Bar Assn., Women's Forum of Colo., Harvard Law Sch. Assn., Denver League Women Voters, Order of Coif (hon. Colo. chpt.). Office: US Dist Ct US Courthouse Rm C-550 1929 Stout St Denver CO 80294

WEINSTEIN, DIANE GILBERT, lawyer; b. Rochester, N.Y., June 14, 1947; d. Myron Birne and Doris Isabelle (Robie) Gilbert; m. Allen Weinstein, June 14, 1969; children: Andrew, David. BA, Smith Coll., Northampton, Mass., 1969; postgrad., Stanford U., 1977-78, Georgetown U., 1978; JD, Boston U., 1979. Bar: D.C. 1979, Mass. 1979. Law clk. to sr. judge D.C. Ct. Appeals, Washington, 1979-80; assoc. Peabody, Lambert & Meyers, Washington, 1980-83; asst. gen. counsel Office of Mgmt. and Budget, Washington, 1983-86; dep. gen. counsel U.S. Dept. Edn., Washington, 1986-88, acting gen. counsel, 1988-89; counsel to Vice Pres. White House, Washington, 1989—; judge U.S. Claims Ct., Washington, 1990—. Recipient Young Lawyer's award Boston U. Law Sch., 1989. Mem. ABA, Federalist Soc. Republican. Home: 2022 Columbia Rd NW #601 Washington DC 20009

WEINSTEIN, JOYCE, artist; b. N.Y.C., June 7, 1931; d. Sidney and Rose (Bier) W.; student CCNY, 1948-50, Art Students League, 1948-52; m. Stanley Boxer, Nov. 28, 1952. Exhibited in one-women shows: Perdalma Gallery, N.Y.C., 1953-56, L.I. U., Bklyn., 1969, U. Calif.-Santa Cruz, 1969, T. Bortolazzo Gallery, Santa Barbara, Calif., 1972, Dorsky Gallery, N.Y.C., 1972, 74, Galerie Ariadne, N.Y.C., 1975, Gloria Cortella Gallery, N.Y.C., 1976, Meredith Long Contemporary Gallery, N.Y.C. 1978, 79, Martin Gerard Gallery, Edmonton, Alta., Can., 1981, 82, 84, Galerie Wentzel, Cologne, W.Ger., 1982, Haber Theodore Gallery, N.Y.C., 1983, 85, Cologne, W.Ger., 1987, Gallery One, Toronto, Ont., Can., 1983, Paul Kuhn Gallery, Calgery, 1985, Eva Cohn Gallery, Highland Park, Chgo, Ill., 1985, Galerie Wentzell, Cologne, 1987, Meredith Long & Co., Houston, 1988, Alena Adlung Gallery, N.Y.C., 1989, Meredith Long & Co., Houston, 1990; group shows: Marlborough Gallery, N.Y.C., 1968, Bula Mus. Art, Calcutta, India, 1970, Phoenix Gallery, N.Y.C., 1988, Pumpkin Gallery, Ancram, N.Y.C., 1988, Provident Nat. Bank, Phila., 1988, Alena Adlung Gallery, N.Y.C., 1989, 90, Edmonton Art Mus., 1989, Rose Fried Gallery, N.Y.C., 1970, Hudson River Mus., 1971, Dorsky Gallery, 1972, Suffolk Mus., Stony Brook, N.Y., 1972, New York Cultural Center, 1973, Stamford (Conn.) Mus., 1973, Landmark Gallery, N.Y.C., 1974, Women's Interart Center, N.Y.C., 1974, 75, 78, New Sch. Social Research, N.Y.C., 1975, Bklyn. Mus., 1975, Galerie Areadne, N.Y.C., 1975, Edmonton Art Gallery Mus., Alta., Can., 1989, Mus. of Modern Art N.Y.C., 1980, The Queens Mus. N.Y., 1984, The Centre de Creacio Contemporania, Barcelona, Spain, 1987, Fairleigh Dickinson U., Hackensack, N.J., 1976, Gloria Cortella, Inc., 1976, Edmonton Art Gallery Mus., 1977, 77, 83, Northeastern U., Boston, 1977, Lehigh (Pa.) U., 1977, Meredith Long Contemporary Gallery, 1977, 78, 79, 80, Mus. Modern Art, N.Y.C., 1981, Galerie Wentzel, Cologne, W.Ger., 1981-85, Martin Gerard Gallery, Edmonton, 1981, Gallery One, Toronto, 1983, 84, Martin Girard Gallery, 1981-84, Haber Theodore Gallery, 1982-85, Queens Mus., N.Y.C., 1984, Jerald Melberg Gallery, Charlotte, N.C., 1984, Edmonton Art Gallery Mus., 1985, Richard Green Gallery, N.Y.C., Centre de Creacio, Barcelona, Spain, 1987; also numerous univs. and colls.; represented in permanent collections: Pa. Acad. Fine Arts, N.J. State Mus., Ciba-Geigy Corp., New Sch. Social Research, Bula Mus. Art, U. Calif., Mus. Modern Art, N.Y.C., McMullen Gallery, Edmonton, Ga., De Spisset Mus., U. Santa Clara, Edmonton Art Gallery Mus., Edmonton, The Hines Collection, Boston, others; represented by Paul Kuhn Gallery, Calgary, Alta., Hokin Gallery, Palm Beach and Miami, Fla., Galerie Wentzel, Cologne, W. Ger., Meredith Long and Co., Houston, Alena Adlung Gallery, N.Y.C., The Shayne Gallery, Montreal; exec. coordinator Women in Arts Found., Inc., 1975-79, 81-82, coordinating bd., 1983-87. Recipient Lambert Fund award Pa. Acad. Fine Arts, 1955; Susan B. Anthony award NOW, 1983. Home and Studio: 37 E 18th St New York NY 10003

WEINSTEIN, NANCY ANNE, box manufacturing company executive; b. Richmond, Va., Oct. 21, 1925; d. Morris Hyman and Bertha (Batkins) W.; cert. commerce, U. Richmond, 1971. With C&O Ry., 1942-57; with Va. folding box div. WESTVACO, Richmond, 1957-86, supr. acctg. dept., 1971-86. Pres. Highland Springs Civic Assn., 1953-55, Highland Springs Jr. Women's Club, 1951-53; treas. Belmont Meth. Ch., Richmond, 1965-79; mem. budget and allocations com. United Way Greater Richmond, 1981—. Recipient Cert. of Recognition for Vol. Svcs. Women's Resource Ctr.-U. Richmond, 1987-88. Mem. Am. Soc. Women Accts. (pres. Richmond chpt. 1978-80, chmn. nat. subcom. 1981, trustee ednl. found.1982-84), Am. Women's Soc. CPA's (trustee ednl. found.). Republican. Club: Richmond Coin (past treas.). Home: 3556 Marquette Rd Richmond VA 23234

WEINSTOCK, ELEANOR, state legislator; b. N.Y.C., Jan. 25, 1929; m. Sander Weinstock; children: Jane, Charles, Ann. BS, Skidmore Coll., 1950. State rep., Fla., 1978-86, state senator., 1986—. Mem. LWV (pres. Fla. 1973-75). Democrat. Jewish. Office: 327 Datura St Ste 311 West Palm Beach FL 33401

WEINSTOCK, GRACE EVANGELINE, librarian, retired educator; b. Currie, Minn., Dec. 16, 1904; d. Charles Clementine and Lydia Hannah (Halland) O'Neill; m. Joseph Marshall Weinstock, Sept. 1, 1945 (dec. July 1973). BA, Hamline U., 1925; AAS in Libr. Sci. Tech., Coll. Lake County, 1988. High sch. tchr. Latin, history, phys. edn. Bd. Edn., Grafton, N.D., 1925-27; high sch. tchr. Latin, history, phys. edn. Bd. Edn., Norwood, Minn., 1928-32; high sch. tchr. Latin, English, libr. Bd. Edn., Wells, Minn., 1932-38; interviewer I Minn. State Employment Svc., Redwood Falls, Minn., 1938-45; interviewer II U.S. Employment Svc., Mpls., 1938-45; substitute tchr. English and bus. depts. North Chicago (Ill.) High Sch. Dist. 123, 1956-72; contractual employment instr. typing U.S. Dept. Army 5th U.S. Army Edn. Ctr., Ft. Sheridan, Ill., 1959-71; mil. personnel clk. Dept. Def., USN, Great Lakes, Ill., 1972-86; part-time libr. Outboard Marine Corp., Waukegan, Ill., 1988-90; part-time clerical worker Highland Park (Ill.) Hosp., 1990—. bd. dirs. Lake County Community Concert Orgn., Waukegan, 1990. Mem. AAUW (program chmn. Waukegan br. 1960), Navy League U.S., Phi Theta Kappa, Alpha Kappa Delta, Pi Gamma Mu. Home: 450 Pine Ct Lake Bluff IL 60044

WEINSTOCK, MARYA, psychologist, consultant; b. N.Y.C., Aug. 15, 1928; d. Morris and Rose (Hellenbrand) Shapiro; m. Jack K. Weinstock, 1947 (div. 1958). BA in Edn., Calif. State U., L.A., 1952, MA in Psychology, 1963; EdD, UCLA, 1974. Lic. psychologist, Calif. Counseling intern UCLA Counseling Ctrs., 1964-67; counseling psychologist U. Calif., Santa Barbara, 1967-89; pvt. practice psychologist Santa Barbara, 1981—; cons. in field. Bd. dirs. Santa Barbara Women's Polit. Com., 1989-90, Mid-Life Zest, Santa Barbara, 1989-90. Mem. Am. Psychol. Assn., Santa Barbara County Psychol. Assn. (pres. 1983-84), Nat. Women's Studies Assn. Democrat. Unitarian. Home and Office: 1009 Del Sol Ave Santa Barbara CA 93109

WEINTRAUB, AMY, nursing home executive; b. N.Y.C., June 3, 1951; d. Milton and Rosemary (Goodman) W.; divorced; 1 child, Marlana Ruth. BA summa cum laude, Boston U., 1973. Assoc. producer Sta. WNVT-TV, Annandale, Va., 1973-74; assoc. dir. Sta. WTAE-TV, Pitts., 1974-76; producer, dir. Sta. KDKA-TV, Pitts., 1976-78; producer, dir. Sta. WPXI-TV, Pitts., 1978-79, exec. producer, pub. affairs dir., 1979-81; free-lance writer Pitts., 1974-80; v.p. Catherine Manor, Inc., Newport, R.I., 1981-86, pres., 1987—. Author: (play) Tin Cans, 1990, Im' Okay, 1990; writer, producer (film documentary) Walking the Tightrope, 1975 (Golden Quill award 1976); producer, dir. (film documentary) Eyewitness Mag. (Matrix award 1979); author, photographer: Childcare—Where Are You?, 1974. Recipient Nat. Broadcast award Women at Work, 1979, Broadcast Media award U. San Francisco, 1979, Headliner award Pa. AP, 1980. Mem. Guest House Assn. (sec. 1983-85, v.p. 1986), Dramatists Guild, Internat. Women's Writing Guild, Newport Hospitality Assn. (bd. dirs.).

WEINTZ, CAROLINE GILES, advertising consultant, travel writer; b. Columbia, Tenn., Dec. 8, 1952; d. Raymond Clark Jr. and Caroline Higdon (Wagstaff) Giles; m. Walter Louis Weintz; children: Alexander Harwood, Elizabeth Pettus. AB, Princeton U., 1974; MA, U. London, 1976. Dir. advt. and promotion E.P. Dutton Pubs., N.Y.C., 1977-86; advt. cons. Assn. Jr. Leagues Internat., N.Y.C., 1986—. Author: The Discount Guide for Travelers over 55, 4th edit., 1988. Vol. Researcher St. Paul's Nat. Hist. Site and Bill of Rights Mus., Westchester, N.Y., 1986—; mem. Jr. League, Pelham, N.Y. Mem. Authors Guild, Nat. Soc. Colonial Dames, Huguenot Soc. Am., Daughters Cin. Episcopalian. Home: 444 Wolf's Ln Pelham Manor NY 10803

WEIR, GLORIA JANE (MRS. N. LYLE EVANS), pediatrician, educator, consultant; b. Baton Rouge, Jan. 18, 1921; d. Claude Arnold and Peggy (Downing) W.; student Sullins Coll., 1936-37; B.S., La. State U., 1940, M.D., 1943; m. N. Lyle Evans, July 26, 1952; children—Peggy Jane, David Lyle. Intern, Charity Hosp. La., New Orleans, 1944, resident in pediatrics, 1949-50, chief resident, 1950-51; pvt. practice medicine specializing in pediatrics, Baton Rouge, 1952-80; staff mem. Baton Rouge Gen. Med. Ctr., vice chief staff, 1965, vice chief pediatrics, 1969, chief pediatrics, 1970-71, now pediatric cons. Child Day Care Ctr.; mem. staff Our Lady of Lake Regional Med. Ctr., Baton Rouge, chief pediatrics, 1959-60, mem. instl. rev. bd.; mem. staff Women's Hosp., chief pediatrics, 1969-70; vis. staff Earl K. Long Meml. Hosp.; clin. asst. prof. pediatrics La. State U. Med. Sch.; chief med. cons. Disability Determination Services, Baton Rouge Area, State of La. Diplomate Am. Bd. Pediatrics. Fellow Am. Acad. Pediatrics (alt. state chmn. La. chpt. 1975-78); mem. AMA, La. State Med. Soc., East Baton Rouge Parish med. socs., Am. Med. Women's Assn., Baton Rouge Women in Medicine, Baton Rouge Assn. for Retarded Citizens (bd. dirs. 1978-79), La. Heart Assn., Baton Rouge Pediatric Socs., Cancer Soc. Baton Rouge (dir. 1963-67, 76-79), Sullins Alumnae Assn., La. State U. Med. Sch. Alumni Assn., Baton Rouge Symphony Aux. (benefactor), Delta Zeta (mem. house corp.), La. State U. Alumni Fedn. Episcopalian. Club: Harlequins. Home: 5885 Eastwood Dr Baton Rouge LA 70806 Office: 2730 Wooddale Blvd PO Box 66498 Baton Rouge LA 70896

WEIS, JUDITH SHULMAN, biologist, educator; b. N.Y.C., May 29, 1941; d. Saul B. and Pearl (Cooper) Shulman; m. Peddrick Weis; children: Jennifer, Eric. BA, Cornell U., 1962; MS, NYU, 1964, PhD, 1967. Lectr. CUNY, 1964-67; asst. prof. Rutgers U., Newark, 1967-71, assoc. prof., 1971-76, prof., 1976—; program dir. NSF, Washington, 1988-90; congl. sci. fellow U.S. Senate, Washington, 1983-84; mem. grant rev. panel NSF, Washington,

1976-82, EPA rev. panel, 1984—; NSF program dir., 1990—. Grantee NOAA, 1977—, N.J. EPA Rsch., 1978-79, 81-83, N.J. Marine Scis. Consortium Rsch., 1987—; NSF fellow, 1962-64. Mem. NOW (pres. Essex County chpt. 1972), Am. Inst. for Biol. Scis. (bd. dirs. 1986-88, 90—), Soc. Environ. Toxicology and Chemistry (bd. dirs. 1990—), Estuarine Rsch. Fedn., Ecol. Soc. Am., Sierra Club (bd. dirs. N.J. chpt. 1986-88). Office: Rutgers U Dept Biol Scis Newark NJ 07102

WEISBERG, RUTH, artist. Laurea in Painting and Printmaking, Acad. di Belle Arti, Perugia, Italy, 1962; BA, U. Mich., 1963, MA, 1965. lectr., demonstrator, juror, curator U. Mich., 1987, 88, U. Hawaii, Honolulu, 1988, Pa. Acad., Phila., 1987, Queens Coll., N.Y.C., 1987, CCNY, 1987, U. Iowa, 1978, 87, U. N.D., Grand Forks, 1987, Fresno (Calif.) Arts Ctr. and Mus., Carnegie Mellon U., Pitts., 1986, 87, U. Tenn., Knoxville, 1986, U. Calif., Santa Cruz, 1985, U. Washington, Seattle, U. Kans., Lawrence, Skirball Mus. Hebrew Union Coll., Los Angeles, Calif. Inst. Arts, Valencia, Otis Art Inst., Los Angeles, Mass. Coll. Art, Boston, Norwegian Graphic Artists' Assn., Oslo, Coll. Art Assn. Conf., Detroit, many others. Solo and two-person exhibitions include: Pollack Gallery, Toronto, 1969, 71, Richard Nash Gallery, Seattle, 1971, 72, 74, Seaberg-Isthmus Gallery, Chgo., 1972, Mcpl. Art Gallery, Oslo, 1972, Triad Gallery, Los Angeles, 1974, Norwegian Graphic Arts Assn., Oslo, 1976, Palos Verdes (Calif.) Art Gallery, 1976, El Camino Coll., Los Angeles. 1977, Oglethorpe U., Atlanta, 1978, Peppers Art Gallery, U. Redlands (Calif.), 1980, Kellas Gallery, Lawrence, Kans., 1979-81, M. Shore and Sons, Santa Barbara, Calif., 1981, U. Richmond, Va., 1985, U. Tenn., Knoxville, 1986, Sierra Nev. Mus. Arts Reno, 1987, The Alice Simsar Gallery, Ann Arbor, Mich., 1968, 69, 72, 74, 77, 88, Associated Am. Artists, N.Y.C., 1987, Jack Rutberg Fine Arts, Los Angeles, 1983, 85, 88; group exhibitions include: Chgo. Art Inst., 1978, E.B. Crocker Art Mus., 1978-80, Contemporary Arts Ctr., New Orleans, 1980, Pratt Graphic Ctr., N.Y.C., 1978-80, U. Art Mus., U. N.M., 1981, Loyola Marymount U., Los Angeles, 1982, Kenkeleba House, N.Y.C, 1984, The Design Ctr., Los Angeles, 1984, Palos Verdes Art Ctr., 1984, Gallery in the Plaza, Security Pacific Bank, Las Angeles, 1985, Thomas Ctr. Gallery, Gainesville, Fla., Associated Am. Artists, N.Y.C, 1987, many others; works published in The Survey Exhibition Catalogues, 1968-88; permanent collections include: The Achenback Found. for Graphic Arts, Fine Arts Mus., San Francisco, Ariz. State U. Mus., Tempe, The Art Inst. Chgo., The Dance Collection, Lincoln Ctr., N.Y.C., Detroit Inst. Arts, Grunwald Found. for Graphic Arts, U. Calif., Los Angeles, The Bibliotheque Nat. France, Paris, Los Angeles County Mus. Art, The Jewish Mus. N.Y.C, The Nat. Gallery, Washington, The Nat. Musl Women in the Arts, many others; contbr. articles to profl. jours. Mem. Coll. Art Assn. (co-chair studion sessions), Tamarind Inst. (mem. nat. adv. bd.), Los Angeles Artists Equity (mem. adv. bd.), Los Angeles Printmaking Soc. Home: 2421 3rd St Santa Monica CA 90405 Office: U So Calif Sch Fine Arts Los Angeles CA 90089-0292*

WEISBERG, RUTH MAXINE, radio reporter, television talk show host; b. Phila., Pa., May 31, 1956; d. William and Libby (Magness) W.; m. Peter Paul Kerch; 1 child, Julia Genevieve. BS with honors in Spl. Edn., Pa. State U., 1977. Traffic reporter Shadow Traffic Network, Phila., 1978-82; news dir., morning anchor Sta. WIFI-FM, Phila., 1982-83; features editor Sta. WPEN, Phila., 1983-85; arts and entertainment editor Sta. WSNI-FM, Phila., 1985-88; TV, radio talk show host CBS, Phila., 1988—; Contbg. editor Internat. TV Assn., Phila., 1982—; ind. filmmaker, voice over narrator. Contbg. editor monthly ITVA Newsletter. Recipient Miss Am. Pageant scholarship, 1980, Radio Features awards Phila. Press Assn., 1983, AP, 1983, Women in Communications, 1984. Mem. Internat. TV Assn, Narberth Community Theater. Home and Office: 37 Sabine Ave Narberth PA 19072

WEISBERGER, BARBARA, choreographer, artistic director, educator; b. Bklyn., Feb. 28, 1926; d. Herman and Sally (Goldstein) Linshes; m. Sol Spiller, Sept. 3, 1945 (div. 1948); m. Ernest Weisberger, Nov. 15, 1949; children: Wendy, Steven. B.S. in Edn., Psychology, Pa. State U., 1945; L.H.D. (hon.), Swarthmore Coll., 1970; D.F.A. (hon.), Temple U., 1973, Kings Coll., 1978, Villanova U., 1978. Founder, dir., tchr. Wilkes-Barre (Pa.) Ballet Theater, 1953-63; founder, dir. Pa. Ballet, Phila., 1962-82, Carlisle (Pa.) Project, 1984—; vice chmn. dance panel Nat. Endowment for the Arts, Washington, 1975-79. Performed with Met. Opera Ballet, N.Y.C., 1937, 38, Mary Binney Montgomery Co., Phila., 1940-42, ballet mistress, choreographer, Ballet Co. of Phila. Lyric Opera, 1961-62, ; choreographic works include Italian Concerto, Bach, Symphonic Variations, Franck; also operas for, Phila. Lyric Opera Co. Ford Found. grantee, 1963, 65, 68, 71, 84; Named Disting. Dau. of Pa., 1974, Disting. Alumna, Pa. State U., 1972; recipient 46th ann. Gimbel Phila. award, 1978. Mem. Psi Chi. Home: 571 Charles Ave Kingston PA 18704 Office: Carlisle Project 9 S Pitt St Carlisle PA 17013

WEISBURGER, ELIZABETH KREISER, retired chemist, editor; b. Greenlane, Pa., Apr. 9, 1924; d. Raymond Samuel and Amy Elizabeth (Snavely) Kreiser; m. John H. Weisburger, Apr. 7, 1947 (div. May 1974); children: William Raymond, Diane Susan, Andrew John. BS, Lebanon Valley Coll., Annville, Pa., 1944, DSc (hon.), 1989; PhD, U. Cin., 1947, DSc (hon.), 1981. Rsch. assoc. U. Cin., 1947-49; col. USPHS, 1951-89; postdoctoral fellow Nat. Cancer Inst., Bethesda, Md., 1949-51, chemist, 1951-73, chief carcinogen metabolism and toxicology br., 1972-75, chief Lab. Carcinogen Metabolism, 1975-81, asst. dir. chem. carcinogenesis, 1981-89, ret.; cons. in field; lectr. Found. for Advanced Edn. in Scis., Bethesda, 1980—; adj. prof. Am. U., Washington, 1982—. Asst. editor-in-chief Jour. Nat. Cancer Inst., 1971-87; contbr. articles to profl. jours. Trustee Lebanon Valley Coll., 1970—, pres. bd. trustees, 1985-89. Recipient Meritorious Service medal USPHS, 1973, Disting. Service medal, 1985; Hillebrand prize Chem. Soc. Washington, 1981. Fellow AAAS (nominating com. 1978-81); mem. Am. Chem. Soc. (Garvan medal 1981), Am. Assn. Cancer Research, Soc. Toxicology, Am. Soc. Biochem. and Molecular Biology, Royal Soc. Chemistry, Am. Conf. Govtl. Indsl. Hygienists, Grad. Women in Sci. (hon.), Iota Sigma Pi (hon.). Lutheran.

WEISE, JOAN CAROLYN, electronics company administrator; b. Libertyville, Ill., Feb. 3, 1939; d. James Gardner McDearmid and Anne Louise (Quist) Nehls; m. James Edward Weise, Aug. 15, 1959; children: Renee, James, Laura. Student, U. Ill., 1956-58; BA in Edn., Carthage Coll., 1973. Cert. tchr., Ill. Dir. nursery sch. Rosa Kahn Sch., Mundelein, Ill., 1971-73; tchr. Avon Sch., Round Lake, Ill., 1973-77; with customer service, contracts depts. AM Documentor, Santa Ana, Calif., 1978-81; mgr. customer service Plessey Semicondr., Irvine, Calif., 1981-84, mgr. ops. support, 1984-87; profl. beauty cons. Mary Kay Cosmetics, Irvine, 1987-89; sales office mgr. Newport Corp., Fountain Valley, Calif., 1989—. chmn. Library Friends, Millburn, Ill., 1969-73, Citizen Sch. Adv., Millburn, 1974-75; leader 4-H, Millburn, 1972-77; vol., tutor Laubach Literacy, 1988—. Mem. NAFE, Internat. Customer Svc. Assn.

WEISER, ELSIE LIEVENS, education educator; b. Nashua, N.H., Oct. 3, 1930; d. Edward and Alice Elfrida (Rundgust) Lievens; m. Harry Eugene Weiser,. BS, Skidmore Coll., 1952. Coach, tchr. Middlebury (Vt.) High Sch., 1952-54; tchr. physical edn. Alvirne High Sch., Hudson, N.H., 1955-56; physical edn. instr., coach River Coll., Nashua, 1955-66; coach, tchr., physical edn. N. Middlesex Regional Sch., Pepperell, Mass., 1961-63, Littleton (Mass.) High Sch., 1965; tchr. physical edn. Rochester (Vt.) Elem. Sch., 1968-69, Rockingham Elem. Sch., Saxton's Riv, Vt., 1970-71; coach, tchr. physical edn. Bellows Falls Middle Sch., 1971--. Leader Girl Scouts Swift Water Coun., N.H., 1950-70; Vt. Pub. Sch. Approval; vol. Reach to Recovery. Mem. Windham Northeast Edn. Assn., Vt. and Am. Assn. Health Phys. Edn. Recreation Dance, Vt. Edn. Assn., NEA, Delta Kappa Gamma Beta Chpt., AAUW, Southeast Vt. Bd. Realtors, First Congregational Ch. Republican. Home: Box 226 Main St Westminster VT 05158 Office: Bellows Falls Middle Sch School St Bellows Falls VT 05101

WEISHAAR, SANDRA J., export executive; b. Indpls., Aug. 14, 1947; d. Edward Ferguson and Marian Ann (Fehrman) Deeter; m. Donald E. Weishaar, July 15, 1972. Student, Ind. U., Inst. Children's Lit. Customer ops. mgr. Wavetek RF Products, Inc., Indpls., export compliance mgr. Vol. VISTA, 1965-66. Mem. World Trade Club of Ind. (bd. dirs.), Nat. Notary Assn., JA Project Bus. Cons., WE Fed. Credit Union (pres.).

WEISKEL, CATHERINE LACNY, orchestra administrator; b. DuBois, Pa., Sept. 3, 1950; d. John Francis and Lucie Ann (Anasti) Lacny. BA, Seton Hill Coll., 1972; MA, Villa Schifanoia, Florence, Italy, 1976. Adminstrv. asst. Yale Sch. Music, New Haven, 1977-79; mgr. concerts, asst. Yale Summer Sch. Music, Norfolk, Conn., 1979; orch. mgr. Hartford Symphony Orch., Conn., 1979-81; gen. mgr. New Haven Symphony Orch., 1981—. Mem. Am. Symphony Orch. League (panelist 1983—), Regional Orch. Mgrs. Assn. (pres. 1988, 89). Democrat. Roman Catholic. Avocations: knitting, furniture refinishing, cooking, reading. Home: 66 Main St West Haven CT 06516 Office: New Haven Symphony Orch 33 Whitney Ave New Haven CT 06510-1068

WEISMAN, BARBARA, lawyer; b. Jersey City, N.J., Jan. 19, 1954; d. Albert and Estelle (Platt) W. BA magna cum laude, Douglass Coll., New Brunswick, N.J., 1975; JD, Seton Hall Law Ctr., Newark, 1979. Bar: N.J. 1979, U.S. Dist. Ct. N.J. 1979, U.S. Supreme Ct. 1986, N.Y. 1989. Law clk. Lamb, Hutchinson, Chappell, Ryan & Hartung, Jersey City, 1977-79; asst. prosecutor Hudson County Prosecutor's Office, Jersey City, 1980-82; atty. N.J. Solicitor's Office Port Authority of N.Y. & N.J., 1982-88; assoc. DeGonge, Chappell, P.A., Belleville, 1988—. Mem. ABA, N.J. State Bar Assn. Home: 4 Bergen Ct Bayonne NJ 07002 Office: DeGonge Chappell PA 727 Joralemon St Belleville NJ 07109

WEISMAN, LESLIE HELEN, analyst; b. Allegany County, Md., Jan. 20, 1953; d. Martin Eric and Sarah Betty (Franklin). BA, Beaver Coll., 1976. Paralegal specialist U.S. Dept. Justice, Washington, 1977-78; mgmt. analyst U.S. Govt. Printing Office, Washington, 1978-80; with U.S. Dept. Edn., Washington, 1980—, mgmt. analyst, 1980—, Insp. Gen's liaison to Pres.'s Coun. on Integrity and Efficiency, 1987—. Mem. Am. Soc. Access Profls. (chairperson tng. com. 1985-86, treas. 1986, 88, v.p. 1989, pres. 1990—). Office: US Dept Edn 400 Maryland Ave SW Washington DC 20202-1510

WEISNER, LYNNETTE BRANT, family therapist, social worker; b. Meyersdale, Pa., Nov. 10, 1958; d. Rupple Devon and Gladys Orlena (Walker) Brant; m. Michael Joseph Weisner, Aug. 11, 1984. B in Social Work, W.Va. U., 1980, MSW, 1982. Lic. cert. social worker, Pa., W.Va. Clin. social worker social svc. dept. Geisinger Med. Ctr., Danville, Pa., 1982-85; dir. social svcs. home health care program So. W.Va. Regional Health Coun., Beckley, 1985-86; clin. social worker Community Health Systems, Beckley, 1986-88—; family therapist Northumberland Co. Counseling Svc., Sunbury, Pa., 1989—. Mem. Milton (Pa.) Hist. Soc., 1989—, Milton aux. Evang. Hosp., 1989—; bd. dirs., chairperson svc./rehab. com. Raleigh County, W.Va. unit Am. Cancer Soc., 1987-88; organist, mem. coun. St. Luke Luth. Ch., Beckley, 1986-88; mem. worship com. and music com., altar guild, Sunday sch. tchr. Trinity Luth. Ch., Milton, 1988—. Recipient cert. of merit W.Va. U. Grad. Sch., 1980. Mem. Nat. Assn. Social Workers (mem. registry of clin. social workers), Acad. Cert. Social Workers, Phi Kappa Phi, Phi Beta Phi (mem. various alumni coms.). Republican. Home: RD 1 Box 224 Milton PA 17847 Office: Northumberland Counseling Svc 370 Market St Sunbury PA 17801

WEISS, ANN, editor, writer, photographer, information specialist, consultant; b. Modena, Italy, July 17, 1949; came to U.S., 1951, naturalized, 1959; d. Leo and Athalie Weiss; children: Julia Emily, Rebecca Lauren. BA magna cum laude in English Lit. and Edn., U. Rochester, 1971; MA in Info. Sci. summa cum laude, Drexel U., 1973; postgrad. on the Holocaust and communication, U. Pa., 1989—. Editor, chief cons. monographs, articles, freelance photographer, 1974—; cataloguer Drexel U., Phila., 1971-73; libr. Akiba Lower Sch., Merion, Pa., 1973; head children's dept. Tredyffrin Pub. Libr., Strafford, Pa., 1973-79, co-head reference dept., 1979-87; cons. in edn. and librs. Gulf Arab States Edn. and Rsch. Ctr., UNESCO, 1977—; cons. Rabbi Zalman Schachter-Shalomi, P'nai Or Fellowship, 1987-88; photojournalist in Ea. Europe, mainly Poland and Czechoslovakia, 1987—. Dir. (video documentary and archive creation) oral history project Inst. Pa. Hosp.; producer, dir., writer: (video documentary with David Rosenberg) Lighting Six Candles, 1991—, (video documentary) Eyes From The Ashes, 1989-90; writer, producer narrator documentary Eyes From the Ashes, archival photographs from Auschwitz, 1989-90; co-author, lyricist (with Thaddeus Lorentz) (musical) Zosia Story, 1987-88; chief editorial cons. Puppetry and the Art of Story Creation, 1981, Puppetry in Early Childhood Education, 1982, Puppetry, Language and the Special Child: Discovering Alternative Language, 1984, Humanizing the Enemy... and Ourselves, 1986, Imagination, 1987, Celebrate! Holidays, Puppetry and Creative Dramatics, 1987. Active So. Poverty Law Ctr., Common Cause, advocacy and fundraising for Ethiopian Jews, promoting dialogue and understanding between Jews and Arabs, Jews and Poles; active Coun. for Soviet Jews, Internat. Network Children Holocaust Survivors; photographer Bob Edgar's Campaign U.S. Senate, 1985-86, David Landau's Congl. Campaign, 1986; active Ed Mezvinsky's Lt. Gov. campaign, 1990; project dir. Psychiatry Documentary Inst. of Pa. Hosp., 1989—. Mem. ACLU, Free Wallenberg Alliance, Union Concerned Scientists, SANE, Physicians for Social Responsibility, Amnesty Internat., Shalom Ctr., New Jewish Agenda, New Israel Fund, NOW. Home: 438 Barclay Rd Rosemont PA 19010

WEISS, BETTEJANE, educator; b. Bklyn., July 22, 1947; d. Sidney James and Florence (Kaye) Newman; m. Daniel Arthur Weiss, May 4, 1969; 1 child, Jennifer. BEd, U. Hawaii, 1981; M. Edn., Chaminade U., 1982. Cert. Montessori, elementary and adult educator. Teaching asst. The Little Sch. House, Fairfield, Calif., 1977-78; teaching asst. Montessori Community Sch., Honolulu, 1979-80, educator, 1980-82; educator Barrie Sch., Silver Spring, Md., 1982—; div. leader Barrie Mid. Sch., Silver Spring, 1986—; intern coord. Inst. for Advanced Montessori Studies, Silver Spring, 1988—. Mem. Friends of Kennedy Ctr., Washington, 1990—, Planned Parenthood, Washington, 1990—, Greenpeace, 1990—. mem. Am. Montessori Soc. (cons. 1989—), Temple Shalom (bd. trustees 1988—). Home: 3033 Mozart Dr Silver Spring MD 20904

WEISS, DEBRA S., construction company executive; b. Three Rivers, Mich., Dec. 4, 1953; d. Harold E. and Winifred (Dunn) W. Student Albion Coll., 1972-73, Lake Superior State Coll., 1974-76; cert. Industrialized Housing Inst., Wausau, Wis., 1975. Lic. builder and mech. contractor, Mich. Sales mgr. Weiss Constrn., Inc., Alanson, Mich., 1976-80; owner, chmn. bd. dirs. Weiss Constrn., St. Ignace, Mich., 1980—; corp. sec., supr. spl. projects Weiss Corp., St. Ignace, 1984—. Bd. dirs. Eastern Upper Peninsula Pvt. Industry Council, Sault Ste. Marie, Mich., 1984—, pres. 1987-89, Downtown Devel. Authority, Mackinaw City, Mich., 1985-87; mem. St. Ignace Zoning Bd., 1984—, St. Ignace City Council, 1985—; bd. dirs., pres. Eastern Upper Peninsula Pvt. Industry Council. Recipient Ruth Huston Whipple award, 1986, Garden City award, 1986. Mem. NOW, St. Ignace Bus. and Profl. Women (pres. 1980-81; Woman of Yr. 1980, Anna Howard Shaw award 1981, 82), Mich. Fedn. Bus. and Profl. Women. (mem. strategic long range planning com. 1985-87, chmn. issues mgmt. com., named Outstanding Young Career Woman 1982), Nat. Fedn. Bus. and Profl. Women (long range strategic planning comm., 1987-89), Silver Mountain Ski Assn. (bd. dirs. 1982-85), St. Ignace C. of C., St. Ignace Tourist Assn., Upper Peninsula Tourist and Recreation Assn., Silver Mountain Cross Country Club, Nat. Assn. Female Execs. Avocations: skiing, reading, rock repelling. Office: Weiss Constrn 99 Bertrand St Saint Ignace MI 49781

WEISS, ELAINE LANDSBERG, community development official; b. N.Y.C.; d. Louis and Sadie Blossum (Schoenfeld); divorced. BA in Philosophy and Polit. Sci., Bklyn. Coll., 1960; postgrad., NYU Law Sch., 1960-62; MA in Sociology, Hunter Coll., N.Y.C., 1969. Social investigator N.Y.C. Dept. Social Services, 1963-64; intern, fellow Eleanor Roosevelt Meml. Found., Nat. Assn. Intergroup Relations Ofcls., 1964-65; asst. dir. housing and asst. project dir. Operation Equality, Nat. Urban League, 1965-67; program assoc. housing div. ch. missions Am. Bapt. Home Mission Socs., 1967-70; pres. E.L. Weiss Assocs., 1970-76; exec. dir. Suffolk Community Devel. Corp., Coram, N.Y., 1976-89, E.L. Weiss Assocs., East Quaque, N.Y., 1990—; mem. citizens adv. com. N.Y.C. Dept. Housing Preservation and Devel.; exec. com. L.I. Community Devel. Orgn.; past 2d v.p. Suffolk Housing Task Force; chmn. Suffolk County Citizens Adv. Com., 1981-82. Recipient cert. of commendation L.I. Council Chs., 1981. Mem. Nat. Assn. Housing Ofcls., N.Y. State Assn. Housing and Redevel. Ofcls., Am. Contract Bridge League (life master). Home: PO Box 1532 East Quogue NY 11942

WEISS, JOAN R., sales executive; b. Montgomery, Ala., May 31, 1937; d. William W. and Ann (Frohlich) Rosenblum; m. Arnold M. Weiss, July 1, 1958; children: Cynthia Parr, Barbara Kimmel, Susan Lynn Orenstein. Student, U. Miami, Peabody Coll. Pres., bus. cons. Joan Weiss, Inc., Memphis; founder Personally Yours, Inc. Performer (ballroom dancing) with Memphis Symphony Orch., 1990; performed in dance exhbn. for Tenn. Bar Conv., 1988. Mem. Memphis Symphony Orch. Golden Circle, Symphony League Bd., guest artist liaison; bd. dirs. Temple Israel Sisterhood; active Cotton Carnival, Cancer Research of Am.; bd. dirs. Family Service of Memphis; appointed to bd. review Mayor of Memphis. First place winner all dances entered in Mid Am. Dance Championships in Louisville, first place winner ann. Ritz competitions, Memphis, 1988; recipient 6 first place trophies for all dances entered in Ritz competition, Fall 1989, numerous others. Mem. Nat. Coun. Jewish Women (bd. dirs.), Memphis Mental Health (bd. dirs.), Brandais (bd. dirs.), Tenn. Bar Assn. Aux. (pres.), Memphis and Shelby County Bar Assn. Aux. (charter, bd. dirs.), Am. Law Aux., U.S. Amateur Ballroom Dancers Assn.

WEISS, JUDITH KELNER, lawyer; b. Phila., May 29, 1950; d. Bernard G. and Esther (Levin) Kelner; m. Jeffrey C. Weiss, June 13, 1971; children: Jacob Ian, Rebecca Emily. BS, U. Pa., 1970; JD summa cum laude, Ohio State U., 1974. Bar: N.Y. 1974, Pa. 1975. Tchr. Phila. Pub. Schs., 1970-71; asst. Office of Counsel to the Chancellor N.Y.C. Pub. Schs., 1974; atty. N.Y.C. Dept. of Social Svcs., 1974-75; assoc. Schnader, Harrison, Segal & Lewis, Phila., 1975-88, sr. atty., 1988—. Mem. long range planning com. Bala Cynwyd (Pa.) Mid. Sch., 1988-89; counsel Big Sisters Phila., Inc. Mem. ABA, Pa. Bar Assn., Phila. Bar Assn., Lawyers for Alternative Work Schedules, Cosmopolitan Club, Pi Lambda Theta. Office: Schnader Harrison et al 1600 Market St Ste 3600 Philadelphia PA 19103

WEISS, LUCINDA, writer, editor; b. St. Louis, Jan. 13, 1950; d. Louis Clark and Mary Elizabeth (Rawls) Honig; m. Robert Alan Weiss, Aug. 18, 1972; children: Tracy Elizabeth, Noah Alan. BS, Northwestern U., 1972. Reporter Daily Hampshire Gazette, Northampton, Mass., 1973-75, Daily Sun, Texas City, Tex., 1976-77; market editor Footwear News Fairchild Publs., N.Y.C., 1977-80; writer publs. dept. U. Conn., Storrs, 1980-84; pub. info. officer Conn. Dept. Banking, Hartford, 1984-86; freelance writer/editor Storrs, 1986—; editor Mansfield (Conn.) Record, 1989—. Recipient Exceptional Achievement in Writing award Coun. for Advancement and Support of Edn., 1984. Mem. Women in Communications, LWV (co-chmn. Know Your Town Fair 1990). Congregationalist. Home: 128 Davis Rd Storrs CT 06268

WEISS, MABEL LOUISE, retired English language educator, civic worker; b. Santa Claus, Ind., Nov. 29, 1897; d. Samuel and Caroline S. (Winkelman) W. BA, Ill. Women's Coll. (name now MacMurray Coll.), Jacksonville, 1919; MS in Edn., Ind. U., 1943; postgrad., Evansville (Ind.) U. Cert. tchr., Ind. Tchr. English also critic tchr. several years Cen. High Sch., Evansville, 1920-62; with vol. svcs. Good Samaritan Nursing Home, Evansville, 1962—. Co-organizer high sch. English Bible study course 1946. Vol. tchr. Meth. Ch. Vacation Sch., South Chicago, Ill., 1919; active ch. and Sun. sch. United Ch. of Christ, Evansville, 1921—, tchr. Sun. sch. Bethel Ch. bible Sch., 1921-75; organizer, sponsor Cen. High Schs. World Neighbor Coun., 1947-62. Recipient highest rating, life lic. Ind. State Bd. Edn., 1928. Mem. AAUW (charter, life, bd. dirs. 1965, reviewer book rev. sect.), Ret. Tchrs. Assn., Aux. Good Samaritan Nursing Home, Mac Murray Coll. Alumna (rep. Class 19 1975-80). Republican.

WEISS, MARIA CRISTINA RODRIGUEZ, cardiovascular nurse; b. San Antonio, Tex., Dec. 4, 1949; d. Rodolfo and Gregoria (Gonzales) R.; m. Laurence Rosen, May 12, 1973 (div. Feb. 1980); m. Martin Weiss. Assoc. degree, San Antonio Coll., 1971; BS in Nursing, U. Tex., San Antonio, 1973, postgrad., 1977, 1980—. Lic. nurse, Tex., 1973. Charge nurse Bexar County Hosp., San Antonio, 1973-74; ground floor supr. Luth. Gen. Hosp., San Antonio, 1974; charge nurse Audie Murphy Vets. Adminstrn. Hosp., San Antonio, 1974-77; office mgr., cardiovascular nurse specialist Robert N. Schnitzler, M.D., San Antonio, 1977—; med. cons. City of San Antonio Papal Visit, 1987, Mayor's Task Force Earthquake Relief, 1985; freelance consulting office mgr., San Antonio, 1977—; freelance fundraiser cons., San Antonio, 1977—; lectr. in field, 1979-82. Treas. Yolanda Vera for City Councilwoman, San Antonio, 1986; del. Michael Dukakis for Pres., Bexar County, Tex., 1988; fundraising, phone coord. Judge Roy Barrera for Atty. Gen., 1986; bd. dirs. Arthritis Found., 1982-85, Target 90, San Antonio, 1985—, Cen. Bario Med. Clin., 1988; active San Antonio Drug Task Force, 1985-88; steering com. mem. Am. Diabetes Assn., 1986; speakers bur. mem. Am. Lung Assn. Smoking Coalition, 1986; community liaison St. Joseph's, St. Peter's Children's Homes, 1980-82; adv. bd. San Antonio Handicap Access, 1985. Named Outstanding Young Woman Fuller and Dees, 1977; recipient Outstanding Accomplishments in Nursing by a Nursing Cons. in Edn. and Health Svcs., 1990. Mem. Am. Heart Assn. (bd. dirs., cardiovascular nursing task force 1977-84, cardiopulmonary resuscitation task force 1980-82, community svc. task force 1980-82, legis. network 1986—, speakers bur. 1986—, active numerous fundraisers, Outstanding Achievement award 1990), Nat. Chicano Health Orgn., Am. Critical Care Nurses Assn., N.Am. Soc. Electrophysiology, San Antonio 100, Tex. Women's Alliance, Spanish Honor Soc., Sigma Theta Tau (Nurse Image Maker award Delta Alpha chpt. 1984).

WEISS, MARILYN MAGALIFF, artist; b. Bklyn., Sept. 4, 1932; d. Max and Anna (Haber) Ackerman; B.S. magna cum laude, N.Y. U., 1953; m. Howard Jerry Weiss, Nov. 24, 1972; children: Jodi Kim Magaliff Gittelman and Barry Todd Magaliff (twins). Exhibited one-woman shows: Alper-Goldberg Gallery, Cedarhurst, N.Y., 1977, Fred Leighton Madison Ltd., 1975, Port Washington (N.Y.) Libr., 1974, Adelphi U., 1974, Hewlett Woodmere Libr., 1972, Bodley Gallery, N.Y.C., 1983, Discovery Gallery, Glencove, N.Y., 1988, 90; exhibited in group shows Firehouse Gallery Nassau Community Coll., Garden City, 1971, Pallazzio Vechio, Florence, Italy, 1972, Palazzio Nat., Naples, Italy, 1972, Brockton (Mass.) Library, 1972, Roanoke (Va.) Fine Arts Ctr., 1972, Milliken U., 1972, U. Okla., 1973, Southeastern Ark. Art. and Sci. Ctr., 1973, Tuskegee Inst., 1974, Albrecht Gallery, 1974, Bergen Community Mus., 1974, 84, 85, Jesse Besser Mus., 1976, Cen. Wyo. Mus. Art, 1977, U. Wis., 1978, City Gallery, N.Y.C., 1981, Community Mus., 1974, Equitable Gallery, N.Y.C., 1979, Fed. Bldg., N.Y.C., 1979, 81-90, U.S. Painting Exhbn., 83-85, 85-88, Traveling Painting Exhbn. U.S.A., 1972-74, 88-90, Traveling Watermedia Exhbn. U.S.A., 1976-78, Oil and Watermedia Exhbn., 1978-80, Cayuga Mus. History and Art, Auburn, N.D., 1983, Stephanie Roper Gallery, 1985, Sarah Lawrence Coll., 1985, Lighthouse Gallery, Fla., 1986, McPherson Coll., 1986, Schenectady Mus., N.Y., 1987, Adelphi U., N.Y., 1987, Nabisco Art Gallery, N.J., 1987, Pace U. Art Gallery, N.Y., 1988, Maier Mus. Art, Va., 1988, Lever House, N.Y.C., 1988, Fine Arts Mus. Nassau County, 1988, Fine Arts Mus. L.I., 1988 (Bronze award 1988), Midge Karr Gallery L.I., 1989, Discovery Gallery, 1989, Cork Gallery, Lincoln Ctr., N.Y.C., 1989, Marbella Gallery, N.Y.C., 1989, Firehouse Gallery, Garden City, 1990, numerous others; author: Digby's The College Handbook, 1985. Recipient maj. prize Suburban Art League Ann. Show, 1968, 71, Elizabeth Morse Genius Found. prize for water media, 1983, Cecil Shapiro Meml. award, 1988, Spl. award Innovation Drawing Show, 1989. Mem. Hempstead Harbor Art Assn., Contemporary Artists Guild, Nat. Assn. Women Artists, Beta Gamma Sigma. Address: 1100 Park Ave New York NY 10128

WEISS, MARJORIE, social worker; b. N.Y.C., Apr. 2, 1954; d. Elias Louis and Ruth Weiss. BA, Bklyn. Coll., 1976; MSW, N.Y. U., 1980. Diplomate Am. Bd. Clinical Social Work. Social worker St. Vincents Svcs. Cath. Charities, Bklyn.; med. social worker Kingsbrook Jewish Med. Ctr., Bklyn. Mem. Nat. Assn. Social Workers.

WEISS, MARY ALICE, insurance economics educator; b. Cleve., June 12, 1957; d. Richard Alfred And Julianna (Scerbik) W.; m. J. David Cummins. BSBA, Quincy Coll., 1979; MS in Ins. Econs., U. Pa., 1982, PhD in Ins. Econs., 1984. Lectr. La Salle Coll., Phila., 1983; asst. prof. U. S.C., Columbia, 1984, Rider Coll., Lawrenceville, N.J., 1984-86, Temple U., Phila., 1986—; cons. IBM, N.Y., 1985-87; speaker nat. and internat. ins. confs. Reviewer Jour. Risk and Ins., 1985—, book rev. editor, 1986—; contbr. articles to profl. jours. Active Clean Water Action, Phila., 1986—; faculty advisor Gamma Iota Sigma, Phila., 1987—. Huebner fellow Huebner

Found., U. Pa., 1979-82; presdl. scholar Quincy Coll., 1975-79. Mem. Am. Risk & Ins. Assn. (coms., nat. & internat. conf. speaker), Western Econ. Assn., Penjerdel Employee Benefit Assn. Democrat. Home: 625 New Gulph Rd Bryn Mawr PA 19010 Office: Temple U Ritter Hall Annex Rm 479 Philadelphia PA 19122

WEISS, MYRNA GRACE, investment banker, consultant; b. N.Y.C., June 22, 1939; d. Herman and Blanche (Stiftel) Ziegler; m. Arthur H. Weiss; children: Debra Anne, Louise Esther. BA, Barnard Coll., 1958; MA, Hunter Coll., 1968; MPA, NYU, 1978; cert. in Mktg., U. Pa. Tchr. N.Y.C. and Vallejo, Calif., 1959-68; dir. admissions Columbia Prep. Sch., N.Y.C., 1969-72; dir. PREP counselling NYU, N.Y.C., 1973-74; dept. head Hewitt Sch., N.Y.C., 1974-79; mgr. Met. Ins. Co., N.Y.C., 1979-84; mktg. exec. Rothschild, Inc., N.Y.C., 1984-85; pres. First Mktg. Capital Group Ltd., N.Y.C., 1985—; ptnr. Lared Group, N.Y.C., 1987—; advisor Gov.'s Hwy. Safety Com., N.Y.C., 1985-88; pres. Fin. Women's Assn. N.Y., 1984-85. Bd. dirs. 92nd St. YWCA, N.Y.C., 1972-90, ARC, 1989—. Mem. Internat. Women's Forum (bd. dirs.), Econ. Club N.Y., Women's Econ. Roundtable (bd. dirs. 1988-90). Office: 1st Mktg Capital Group Ltd/Lared Group 1056 Fifth Ave New York NY 10128

WEISS, RITA S., traffic safety program analyst; b. Phila., May 24, 1935; d. Jack J. and Cecelia (Alper) Brown; m. Irvin J. Weiss, Oct. 29, 1955; children: Brett David, Judith Weiss Bohn. BS in Edn., Temple U., 1955; MA in Edn., U. Md., 1976. Cert. elem. tchr., Md. Ednl. cons. Am. Automobile Assn., Falls Church, Va.; dir. Har Shalom Nursery Sch., Potomac, Md.; tchr. Geneva Nursery Sch., Rockville, Md., Solis-Cohen Elem. Sch., Phila.; program analyst U.S. Dept. of Transp./NHTSA, Washington. Author numerous traffic safety pubs. Mem. bd. Georgetown Hill Elem. Sch., editor newsletter, 1966-71; den mother Cub Scouts, 1966-70, den coach, 1969-70. Mem. NHTSA Profl. Women's Assn. (recording sec., area rep. Administrator's award for Merit 1990, Outstanding Performance award 1989, Sp. Task Accomplishment award 1988, Superior Accomplishment award 1988, Performance award 1988), Nat. Safety Coun. (bd. dirs., chmn. edn. resources div., chmn. community agencies sect.), Md. Community Assn. for the Edn. of Young Children (pres., newsletter editor, historian), Childhood Edn. Internat. (assoc.), U. Md. Alumni Assn. Office: US Dot/NHTSA Office of Occupant Protection NTS-11 400 Seventh St SW Washington DC 20590

WEISS, SHIRLEY F., urban and regional planner, economist; b. N.Y.C., Feb. 26, 1921; d. Max and Vera (Hendel) Friedlander; m. Charles M. Weiss, June 7, 1942. BA, Rutgers U., 1942; postgrad., Johns Hopkins U., 1949-50; M in Regional Planning, U. N.C., 1958; PhD, Duke U., 1973. Assoc. research dir. Ctr. for Urban and Regional Studies U. N.C., Chapel Hill, 1957—, lectr. in planning, 1958-62, assoc. prof., 1962-73, prof., 1973—; research assoc. Inst. for Research in Social Sci., U. N.C., 1957-73, research prof., 1973—; acting dir. Women's Studies Program, Coll. Arts and Scis., U. N.C., 1985; faculty marshal U. N.C., 1988—; mem. tech. com. Water Resources Research Inst., 1976-79; mem. adv. com. on housing for 1980 census Dept. Commerce, 1976-81; cons. Urban Inst., Washington, 1977-80; mem. rev. panel Exptl. Housing Allowance Program, HUD, 1977-80; mem. adv. bd. on built environ. Nat. Acad. Scis.-NRC, 1981-83, mem. program coordinating com. fed. constrn. council of adv. bd. on built environ., 1982-83; mem. Planning Accreditation Bd., Site Visitation Pool, Am. Inst. Cert. Planners and Assn. Collegiate Schs. Planning, 1985—; mem. discipline screening com. Fulbright Scholar awards in Architecture and City Planning, Council for Internat. Exchange of Scholars, 1985-88. Author: The Central Business District in Transition: Methodological Approaches to CBD Analysis and Forecasting Future Space Requirements, 1957, New Town Development in the United States: Experiment in Private Entrepreneurship, 1973; co-author: A Probabilistic Model for Residential Growth, 1964, Residential Developer Decisions: A Focused View of the Urban Growth Process, 1966, New Communities U.S.A, 1976; co-author, co-editor: Urban Growth Dynamics in a Regional Cluster of Cities, 1962; co-editor: New Community Development: Planning Process, Implementation and Emerging Social Concerns, vols. 1, 2, 1971, City Centers in Transition, 1976, New Communities Research Series, 1976-77; mem. editorial bd.: Jour. Am. Inst. Planners, 1963-68, Rev. of Regional Studies, 1969-74, 82—, Internat. Regional Sci. Rev, 1975-81. Fellow Urban Land Inst. (sr., exec. Group Community Devel. Council 1978—); mem. Am. Inst. Planners (sec., treas. southeast chpt. 1957-59, v.p. 1960-61), Am. Inst. Cert. Planners, Am. Planning Assn., Am. Econ. Assn., So. Regional Sci. Assn. (pres. 1977-78), Regional Sci. Assn. (councillor 1971-74, v.p. 1976-77), Interamerican Planning Soc., Internat. Fedn. Housing and Planning, Town and Country Planning Assn. (Eng.), Econometric Soc., Econ. History Assn., Internat. New Towns Assn., History Econs. Soc., Am. Statis. Assn., Am. Real Estate and Urban Econs. Assn. (regional membership chmn. 1976-82, 84-85, dir. 1977-80), Royal Econ. Soc. (Eng.), AAUP (chpt. pres. 1976-77, pres. N.C. Conf. 1978-79, mem. nat. council 1983-86), Douglass Soc., Order of Valkyries, Phi Beta Kappa. Home: 155 Hamilton Rd PO Box 1368 Chapel Hill NC 27514 Office: Univ NC Dept City & Regional Planning CB #3140 New East Chapel Hill NC 27599-3140

WEISS, THERESA DOMINGUEZ, nurse practitioner; b. Los Angeles, Aug. 16, 1950; d. Richard Joseph and Norma (Romero) Dominguez; m. Fred Toby Weiss, Dec. 5, 1982; 1 stepchild, Rebecca. Grad. in Nursing, Rio Hondo Coll., Whittier, Calif., 1975. RN. Rehab. nurse pediatric and spinal cord Rancho Los Amigos Hosp., Downey, Calif., 1969-75; critical care nurse Beverly Hosp., Montebello, Calif., 1975-78; co-dir. Cardiac Rehab. Ctr., Whittier, 1978-79; jr. faculty medicine U. Calif., Irvine, 1982-84; med. cons., adminstr. Health Mgmt. Ctr., Orange, Calif., 1984-87, The Headache Inst., Newport Beach, Calif., 1987-89; v.p. Power Places Tours, 1989—; researcher in field; instr. pre-natal care Chope Community Hosp., San Mateo, Calif., 1982, Coastline Coll., Costa Mesa, Calif., 1985—. Mem. NAFE, Am. Nurses Assn., Calif. Nurses Assn., Calif. Coalition of Nurse Practitioners, Laguna Beach Art Mus.

WEISS, VICKEY EVELYN, registered nurse therapist; b. Stroud, Okla., Dec. 19, 1938; d. Robert Victor and Evelyn Eleanor (Fillman) Kutin; m. Gordon Stewart Weiss, Jan. 9, 1962; children: Sheldon Michael, Anthony Victor. RN, St. Anthonys Sch. Nursing, 1958; BA in Psychology, Chaminade U.; MA in Psychology, U. No. Colo. RN U.S. Army, El Paso, Tex., 1958-61, Heildelberg, Germany, 1961-62; RN Dept. Army, Ft. Huachuca, Denver, Ariz., 1963; civil service Dept. Army, Honolulu; RN VA Med. Ctr., Tucson, 1978—. V.p. Am. Fedn., Tucson, 1983-89. Lt. U.S. Army, 1958-62. Mem. Pi Theta Kappa.

WEISSENBERG, CATHERINE ANNE, college lecturer; b. Dayton, Ohio, Jan. 6, 1960; d. Joseph William Weissenberg and Oma Creda (Walton) Millsap. Student, So. Ill. U., 1981-85, Santa Barbara City Coll., 1985-86; BA with highest honors, U. Calif., Santa Barbara, 1988, postgrad., 1988—. Store mgr. Darrell's Glad Rags, Alton, Ill., 1978-79; rental mgr. Bert's Sales and Rentals, Granite City, Ill., 1980-85; tutor math. Santa Barbara City Coll., 1986; companion to aged Santa Barbara, 1987-88; teaching asst. in communication studies U. Calif., Santa Barbara, 1988-90; lectr. communication studies Santa Barbara City Coll., 1990—; cons. TMC, Santa Barbara, 1988. Co-author: Teaching Assistant Handbook, 1989. Named U. Calif. President's fellow, 1987; recipient award for Outstanding Acad. Achievement, U. Calif., Santa Barbara, 1988, Edwin Schoell Award for Excellence in Teaching, U. Calif., Santa Barbara, 1989. Mem. U. Calif.-Santa Barbara Alumni Assn., Golden Key. Democrat. Roman Catholic. Home: 584 Via Rueda Santa Barbara CA 93110 Office: Santa Barbara City Coll 721 Cliff Dr Santa Barbara CA 93109

WEISS GELINE, DEBORAH LYNN, publishing company executive; b. Huntington, W.Va., Jan. 17, 1951; d. Donald L. and Charlene (Thomas) Weiss; m. Robert J. Geline, July 30, 1989. BA, Denison U., 1973. Project editor Chelsea House Pubs., N.Y.C., 1973-76; editor Rutledge Books, N.Y.C., 1978-81; freelance editor, 1982-86; dir. copy editing William Morrow & Co., N.Y.C., 1986—. Author: Eye Care, 1986; editorial dir. Famous Brands Cookbook Library. Mem. Editorial Freelancer Assn. Home: 39 W 74th St New York NY 10023

WEISSMAN, CAROL SACKER, management consultant; b. Bklyn., July 12, 1944; d. Jacob and Mitzie (Seigel) Sacker; m. Seymour Weissman, Feb. 7, 1967 (div. Aug. 1987); 1 child, Jacqueline Lee. BA, Bklyn. Coll., 1966; MEd, U. Mass., 1970; EdD, Lehigh U., 1973; PhD, Adelphi U., 1985. Lic. psychologist, N.Y. Asst. prof. Lafayette Coll., Easton, Pa., 1973-74; program evaluator Edn. Devel. Ctr., Newton, Mass., 1974-76; dir. rsch. & devel. Welfare Rsch. Inc., N.Y.C., 1976-77; dir. rsch. Bank St. Coll., N.Y.C., 1977-80; ind. cons. Plainview, N.Y., 1980—; psychologist N.Y.C. Police Dept., Queens, N.Y., 1985-87; mgmt. cons. Chase Manhattan Bank N.A., N.Y.C., 1987—; psychotherapist, Great Neck, N.Y., 1989—. Mem. Assn. Internal Mgmt. Cons., Am. Psychol. Assn., Nat. Assn. Banking Woman, METRO-Applied Psychology.

WEISSMAN, RONEE FREEMAN, tour agency owner, speech pathologist; b. N.Y.C., Apr. 16, 1951; d. Jonas Herbert and Marion (Rosen) Freeman; B.A. magna cum laude, Queens Coll., 1973, M.A. in Speech Pathology, 1978; m. Eugene Weissman, Jan. 28, 1973; children—Ilana Nicole, Adam Scott. Tchr. high sch. speech, theatre and English, N.Y.C., 1973-75; speech pathologist Byram Hills (N.Y.) Sch. Dist., part-time, 1979-80, E. Ramapo Sch. Dist., Rockland, N.Y., 1981-82; speech pathologist Vis. Therapy Assocs., 1983-84; owner, v.p., dir. Weissman Teen Tours, Inc., Ardsley, N.Y., 1974—. Youth dir., Sunday sch. tchr. Temple Israel, New Rochelle. Speech and hearing handicapped cert., speech arts cert., N.Y.; lic. speech pathologist, N.Y. Mem. Am. Speech, Lang. and Hearing Assn. (cert. clin. competency), N.Y. State Speech, Lang. and Hearing Assn., Am. Camping Assn. (cert.), Westchester Assn. Women Bus. Owners, Sales and Mktg. Execs. of Westchester, Phi Beta Kappa, Kappa Delta Pi. Home and Office: 517 Almena Ave Ardsley NY 10502

WEISSMANN, HEIDI SEITELBLUM, radiologist, educator; b. N.Y.C., Feb. 4, 1951; d. Louis and June (Joseph) Seitel Bloom; m. Murray H. Weissmann, June 16, 1973; 1 dau., Lauren Erica. BS in Chemistry magna cum laude, Bklyn. Coll., CUNY, 1970; MD, Mt. Sinai Sch. Medicine, N.Y.C., 1974. Diplomate Nat. Bd. Med. Examiners. Intern Montefiore Med. Ctr. Bronx, N.Y., 1974-75, resident in diagnostic radiology, 1975-78; fellow in computerized transaxial tomography and ultrasonography N.Y. Hosp.-Cornell U. Med. Ctr., N.Y.C., N.Y., 1978-79; instr. in radiology and nuclear medicine Albert Einstein Coll. Medicine and Montefiore Med. Ctr., Bronx, N.Y., 1979-80, asst. prof. radiology and nuclear medicine, 1980-84, assoc. prof. nuclear medicine, 1984—, assoc. prof. radiology, 1986—; adj. attending physician Montefiore Med. Ctr., 1979-87; chmn. Nuclear Medicine Grand Rounds: Greater N.Y., 1980-87; physician coord. Nuclear Medicine Technologist In-Service Tng. Program, 1982-86; cons. NIH, 1984-86, NIH Diagnostic Radiology, 1985-86. Assoc. editor Nuclear Medicine Ann., 5 vols., 1979-84, editor, 5 vols., 1985—; contbr. chpts. to books, articles to jours.; reviewer Jour. of Radiology, 1981—, mem. editorial adv. bd., 1985-86, assoc. editor, 1986—; reviewer. Jour. of Nuclear Medicine, 1981—, Am. Jour. of Roentgenology, 1986—, Gastroenterology, 1986—, Western Jour. of Medicine, 1985—; contbr. audiovisual programs and films. Recipient Saul Horowitz, Jr., Meml. award (Disting. Alumnus award), Mt. Sinai Sch. Medicine, 1980, Pres.' award, Am. Roentgen Ray Soc., 1979, Berta Rubinstein, M.D., Resident award, 1978, others. Mem. Radiol. Soc. N.Am. (mem. subcom. for nuclear medicine of program com., 1981, 82, 83, chmn. 1984, 85, 86), Soc. Nuclear Medicine (trustee 1983-87, 88—, sec.-treas. Correlative Imaging Council 1979-82, exec. bd. 1982-84, pres. 1984-86, exec. bd. 1986—, mem. acad. council 1980—, task force on interrelationship between nuclear medicine and nuclear magnetic resonance 1983-85 , gov. Greater N.Y. chpt. 1983-85, treas., 1985-86, 86-87, 2d ann. Tetalman award of Edn. and Research Found. 1982, mem., vice chmn. coms. and subcoms.), Soc. Gastrointestinal Radiologists, Am. Inst. Ultrasound in Medicine, N.Y. Acad. Scis., Assoc. Alumni Mt. Sinai Med. Ctr., Nuclear Radiology Club (chmn. 1983—). Phi Beta Kappa.

WEISTROP, DONNA ETTA, astronomer; b. N.Y.C., June 10, 1944; d. Nathan and Charlotte Leah (Bagno) W.; m. David Bruce Shaffer, Aug. 12, 1979. BA, Wellesley Coll., 1965; PhD, Calif. Inst. Tech., 1971. Postdoctoral fellow Ohio State U., Columbus, 1973-74; asst. astronomer Kitt Peak Nat. Observatory, Tucson, 1974-77; rsch. fellow U. Arizona, Tucson, 1977-78; astrophysicist NASA/Goddard Space Flight, Greenbelt, Md., 1978-85; sr. scientist Applied Rsch. Corp., Landover, Md., 1985-90; assoc. prof. physics dept. U. Nev., Las Vegas, 1990—; vis. lectr. Tel Aviv Univ., 1971-73; participant astronomy/relativity NASA, Washington, 1981-84; vis. scientist U. Ariz., 1978-80. Contbr. articles to profl. jours. Mem. Am. Astron. Soc. (com. status women, 1983-87), Internat. Astron. Union, AAAS (nominating com. 1983-86, chmn. 1986). Office: U Nev Dept of Physics 4505 S Maryland Pkwy Las Vegas NV 89154

WEITH, JERRIE KAY, healthcare administrator; b. East St. Louis, Ill., Feb. 10, 1956; d. John T. Jr. and Ladonna Jeanette (Volluz) Hitch; m. Mel Ernest Weith, May 12, 1984. Cert., Am. Inst. Banking, 1979; BBA, So. Ill. U., 1983; MBA, St. Louis U., 1987. Bookkeeper Centerre Trust co., St. Louis, 1978-80; acct. May Ctrs., Inc., St. Louis, 1980-82; asst. to controller Labarge, Inc., St. Louis, 1982-83; dir. adminstrv. svcs. City of Fairview Heights (Ill.), 1983-85; bus. mgr. St. Louis U., 1985—. Fin. chmn. Belleville (Ill.) 175th Anniversary, Inc., 1988-90. Mem. Healthcare Fin. Mgmt. Assn. (editor 1990—), Ill. Jaycees (Keyman award 1988-89, Exec. Officer of Yr. 1988-89, Outstanding Local v.p. 1988-89, Outstanding Stae Chmn. 1988-89), Med. Group Mgmt. Assn., St. Clair NOW (treas. 1990—). Home: 205 Gilbert St Belleville IL 62220

WEITZEL, LORI LOUDERBACK, university administrator; b. Phila., July 11, 1960; d. Thomas Kendall and Lynn (Jones) Louderback; m. Bradley David Weitzel, July 22, 1983. BS in Edn., U. Ga., 1982; MEd, U. N. Fla. Asst. fitness dir. YMCA of Palm Beaches, West Palm Beach, Fla., 1984-85; phys. edn. tchr. Palm Beach County Sch. Bd., West Palm Beach, 1985-87; adapted phys. edn. tchr. Duval County Sch. Bd., Jacksonville, Fla., 1987; acad. advisor U. N. Fla., Jacksonville, 1987—. Instr. water safety ARC, Jacksonville, 1988-90. Mem. AAHPERD, Fla. Student Leaders Assn. of Tchr. Educators (faculty sponsor 1988—), Fla. Assn. Tchr. Educators, U. North Fla. Osprey Club, Southeastern Advising Assn., Palm Beach Runners, Jacksonville Track Club, Optimist. Methodist. Home: 2811 Hillsdale Harbor Way Jacksonville FL 32216 Office: U North Fla 4567 St Johns Bluff Rd S Jacksonville FL 32216

WEITZMAN, MARILYN, management analyst; b. Muncie, Ind., June 12, 1950; d. Richard D. and Jessie (Carpenter) Clair; m. Dan Edward Wilson, June 13, 1970 (div. May 1982); children: Jorja Rae, Jacob Vincent; m. Burton Charles Weitzman, July 30, 1988. Grad. high sch., Rushville, Ind. With Internat. Packings Corp., Morristown, Ind., 1978-82; sec., bookkeeper Dr. James L. Shoot, Indpls., 1982-85; budget asst. U.S. Mil. Acad., West Point, N.Y., 1985-87; mgmt. analyst FDA, Rockville, Md., 1987—. Mem. Regulatory Affairs Profl. Soc., Federally Employed Women, NAFE, Am. Mensa Soc. Home: 5 Lodge Ct Rockville MD 20850 Office: FDA 5600 Fishers Ln #HFD-50 Rockville MD 20857

WEIZNER, DENISE CECILE, fundraiser, public relations executive; b. N.Y.C., June 28, 1962; d. Oscar and Fern Denise (Dion) Weizner. BA in Communications cum laude, SUNY, Buffalo, 1985. Substitute tchr. Yonkers (N.Y.) Pub. Schs., 1985-86; coordinator coll. events Mercy Coll., Dobbs Ferry, N.Y., 1986-89; dir. spl. projects N.Y. Med. Coll., Valhalla, 1989-90; dir. devel. Am. Heart Assn., Port Chester, N.Y., 1990—. Vol., Am. Cancer Soc., Westchester, 1989. Mem. Women in Communications (bd. dirs., sec., v.p. membership 1989—), Assn. for Devel. Officers, NAFE. Republican. Home: 214 Etville Rd Yonkers NY 10701 Office: Am Heart Assn 3020 Westchester Ave Purchase NY 10577

WELBORN, ELSIE ELENDER JENKINS, nurse executive, nurse; b. Crandall, Miss., May 13, 1937; d. Perry Lamar and Esther Lou (Napp) Jenkins; m. Eldon Coy Welborn, Apr. 4, 1957; children: Link Von, Coy. Diploma in nursing, South Miss. Charity Hosp., 1963; BSN, U. Miss., 1971; MS, U. South Fla., 1976. Relief house supr., float nurse Hinds Gen. Hosp., Jackson, Miss., 1970-71; asst. dir. nursing svcs. Kings Daughters Hosp., Greenville, Miss., 1971-72; with VA Med. Ctr., 1972—; chief nursing svc. VA Med. Ctr., Boise, Idaho, 1982-84, Biloxi, Miss., 1984—; preceptor grad. nursing program U. So. Miss., Long Beach. Mem. Am. Nurses Assn., Miss. Nurses Assn., U. Miss. Sch. of Nursing Alumnae Assn., Daughters of the Nile, Sigma Theta Tau. Home: PO Box 6674 Gulfport MS 39506 Office: VA Med Ctr Biloxi MS 39531

WELBORN, SARAH, photographer, marketing consultant; b. Greenville, S.C., Aug. 19, 1943; d. William Ernest Welborn and Elsie Jocelyn (Bowen) Hemphill; m. Nabil M. Sbitani, June 18, 1958 (dec.); children: Omar N., Ameen N.; m. Christian Heurich, Jr., Apr. 28, 1970 (div. May 1971); m. James Edwin Carroll, Dec. 19, 1974 (div. Jan. 1986); children: Salina J.A. Longo-Carroll. Student, Am. U., 1969-71; cert. in Real Estate, Prince Frederick Community Coll., 1974; cert., Merrill Lynch Relocation Mgmt., 1977, Real Estate Tng. Ctr., 1979, Real Estate Prep., 1981, Moore Sch. of Real Estate, 1982, Nat. Real Estate Sch., 1986; student, DePaul U., 1989-90. From ad copy writer to head of pub. and govt. relations dept. Lewis, Dobrow and Lamb Advt. and Pub. Relations Co., Washington, 1961-68; broker, sales assoc. Various Real Estate Firms, Reston, Va. and Denver, 1974-84; owner, broker Welborn Properties Realtors and Mktg. Cons., Denver, 1984-86; mktg. mgr., trainer Realty World Western, Berwyn, Ill., 1987—; mktg. and pub. rels. cons., 1987-88; prin. Life Forms by Sarah, Cicero, Ill., 1988—; Chmn. pub. relations com. various realty bds., Reston, Lakewood, Colo., 1975-86; investment cons. J-B Assocs., Inc., Denver, 1984; pub. relations cons. Red River Inns, Rifle, Colo., 1985; telemktg. cons. Assocs. Nat. Mortgage Co., Dallas, 1986; pres. Women's Council Realtors, Jefferson County, Colo., 1985-86. Contbr. polit. and travel articles and poetry to profl. jours. Commr. Health and Welfare commn., Alexandria, 1966-68; vol. coordinator Presdl. campaign of George McGovern, 1971-73. Mem. Am. Mensa Soc., West Town Bd. Realtors (chmn. RPAC com. 1987—), Ill. Assn. Realtors, Nat. Assn. Realtors. Democrat. Home and Office: 5333 W 23d Pl Cicero IL 60650

WELCH, BETTY LEONORA, accountant; b. Missoula, Mont., July 18, 1961; d. George Oliver and Betty June (Dolton) W. BBA, U. Mont., 1983. CPA, Mont. Staff acct. Ellis & Assocs., Boise, Idaho, 1984; acct. Glacier Electric Coop., Cut Bank, Mont., 1984-86, office mgr., 1986—; income tax cons. Mem. AICPA, Beta Gamma Sigma. Democrat. Roman Catholic. Avocations: skiing, sewing, reading, hunting. Office: Glacier Electric Coop Inc 410 E Main St Cut Bank MT 59427

WELCH, CAROL MAE, lawyer; b. Rockford, Ill., Oct. 23, 1947; d. Leonard John and LaVerna Helen (Ang) Nyberg; m. Donald Peter Welch, Nov. 23, 1968 (dec. Sept. 1976). B.A. in Spanish, Wheaton Coll., 1968; J.D., U. Denver, 1976. Bar: Colo. 1977, U.S. Dist. Ct. Colo. 1977, U.S. Ct. Appeals (10th cir.) 1977, U.S. Supreme Ct. 1981. Tchr. State Hosp., Dixon, Ill., 1969, Polo Community Schs., Ill., 1969-70; registrar Sch. Nursing Hosp. of U. Pa., Phila., 1970; assoc. Hall & Evans, Denver, 1977-81, ptnr., 1981—; mem. Colo. Supreme Ct. Jury Inst., Denver, 1982—; vice chmn. com. on conduct U.S. Dist. Ct., Denver, 1982-83, chmn., 1983-84; lectr. in field; speaker Women and Bus. Conf., Denver, 1982. Pres. Family Tree, Inc. Named to Order St. Ives, U. Denver Coll. Law, 1977. Mem. ABA, Colo. Def. Lawyers Assn. (treas. 1982-83, v.p. 1983-84, pres. 1984-85), Denver Bar Assn., Colo. Bar Assn. (mem. litigation sect. coun. 1987—), Colo. Bar Found., Def. Rsch. Inst. (chmn. Colo. chpt. 1987—), William E. Doyle Inn. Republican. Office: Hall & Evans 1200 17th St Ste 1700 Denver CO 80202

WELCH, DAWN RENEE, legal assistant; b. Lincoln, Nebr., Jan. 21, 1965; d. David Eugene and Helen Bessie (Hypes) W. BA in Pre-Law, Hawaii Loa Coll., 1989. Dept. mgr. sales Jay Jacobs, Anchorage, 1982-83; paralegal asst. Atkinson, Conway & Gagnon, Anchorage, 1988, intern, 1988; contract paralegal Anchorage, 1989—; legal asst. Bogle & Gates, Anchorage, 1989, Bradbury, Bliss & Riordan, Anchorage, 1990—; legal asst. Bogle & Gates. Vol. Rep. Party of Alaska, 1987, State of Alaska Community Clean-Up, 1981-82, Concerned Citizens of Anchorage, 1981-82. Hawaii Loa Coll. grantee, 1987-88; named to Outstanding Young Women Am., 1987. Mem. NAFE, NOW, Nat. Fedn. Paralegal Assns., Alaska Assn. Legal Assts., Nat. Assn. Legal Assts. Home: 7040 Joseph St Anchorage AK 99518 Office: Bogle & Gates 1031 W 4th Ave Anchorage AK 99501

WELCH, ELIZABETH ANN, dermatologist; b. Buffalo, Feb. 26, 1950; d. Thomas Harris and Jane E. (Todd) W.; m. Stephen E. Glinick, June 5, 1976; 1 child, Emily B. BA, NYU, 1972; MD, Columbia Coll. Physicians and Surgeons, 1976. Med. intern then resident Roger Williams Gen. Hosp., Providence, 1976-78, resident in dermatology, 1978-81; owner Ocean State Dermatology Assocs., Providence, 1981—; clin. asst. prof. medicine Brown U., Providence, 1989—. Contbr. articles to profl. jours. Fellow Am. Acad. Dermatology; mem. Providence Med. Soc., R.I. Med. Soc. (del. ho. reps. 1984—), R.I. Am. Med. Women's Assn. (treas. 1983-88), R.I. Dermatologic Soc. Office: Ocean State Dermatology Assocs 100 Highland Ave Providence RI 02906

WELCH, JEANIE MAXINE, librarian; b. L.A., Jan. 22, 1946; d. Howard Carlton and Roberta Jean (Dunsmuir) W. BA, U. Denver, 1967, MA, 1968; M of Internat. Mgmt., Am. Grad. Sch. Internat. Mgmt., 1981. Asst. libr. Am. Grad. Sch. Internat. Mgmt., Glendale, Ariz., 1968-83; reference libr. Lamar U., Beaumont, Tex., 1983-85, head reference, 1985-87; reference unit head U. N.C., Charlotte, 1988—. Contbr. articles to profl. jours. Chpt. pres. NOW, Beaumont, 1985-87, state sec., Tex., 1986; exec. bd. Ariz. State Libr. Assn., 1976-80. Rsch. grantee Tex. Libr. Assn., 1986. Mem. AAUP, ALA, Metrolina Libr. Assn., N.C. Libr. Assn., Southeastern Libr. Assn., Spl. Librs. Assn. Democrat. Methodist. Office: U N.C. Atkins Libr Charlotte NC 28223

WELCH, J(OAN) KATHLEEN, dance studio executive; b. Pensacola, Fla., Jan. 28, 1950; d. Leslie Peter and Frances Louise (Hughes) Morales. Salesperson with Arthur Murray Dance Studio, Colo., Fla., Pa. and N.J., 1970-81; sales rep. Warner-Lambert Co., Morris Plains, N.J., 1981-83; supr., mgr. Dance Club Internat., Chatham, N.J., 1983—; judge Nat. Dance Coun. of Am., 1977—; dance coach, 1975—; choreographer, 1971—; competitor, 1972-81. Recipient awards Arthur Murray Studio, 1971-81, 1st place counselor award Arthur Murray All Star Tournament, 1977, 1st Place Supr. award Dance Club Internat., 1st Place Registrar award Dance Club Internat. in the Tournament of Champions, 1984. Mem. Imperial Soc. Tchrs. of Dancing (assoc. Ballroom br., Latin-Am. br), Am. Dance Tchrs. Assn. Inc. Mem. Unity Ch. Home: 117 E Westfield Ave Roselle Park NJ 07204 Office: Dance Club Internat 6 S Passaic Ave Chatham NJ 07928

WELCH, KATHY JANE, waste service company executive; b. San Antonio, Aug. 5, 1952; d. John Dee and Pauline Ann (Overstreet) W.; m. John Thomas Unger, Jan. 8, 1977. B.A.S. in Computer Sci., So. Meth. U., 1974; M.B.A. in Fin., U. Houston, 1978. Programmer, analyst Tex. Instruments, Houston, 1974-76, project leader, 1976-78, br. mgr., 1978-81; mgr. systems and programming Global Marine, Houston, 1981-84, mgr. office automation, 1984-85, mgr. user systems, 1985-88, dir. MIS, Advanced Tech. div. Browning-Ferris Industries, Houston, 1988—. Mem. Am. Mgmt. Assn., Fedn. Houton Profl. Women, Ops. Rsch. Soc. Am., Assn. Women in Computing (pres. Houston chpt. 1986-87), Mensa, Beta Gamma Sigma. Office: Browning-Ferris Industries PO Box 3151 Houston TX 77253

WELCH, LINDA OGDEN, sales executive; b. Wabash, Ind., Apr. 3, 1958; d. Russell Devon and Nancy Rebecca (Bright) O.; m. Albert Darius Welch III. Jan. 31, 1990. BS, Oral Roberts U., 1980. Sales coord. Sta. KIRO, Seattle, 1980-81; account exec. Sta. KRAV/KGTO, Tulsa, 1981-84, Sta. KOTV-TV, Tulsa, 1984-86, Sta. KHOU-TV, Houston, 1986-87, Sta. KTXA-TV, Dallas, 1987-89, Sta. KATZ-TV, Dallas, 1989-90, Petry TV, Dallas, 1990—. Vol. Children's Hosp., Tulsa, 1981-84. Mem. Am. Women in Radio and TV (soaring spirits com. 1988-89), Assn. Broadcast Execs. Tex., S.W. Broadcast Reps. Republican. Office: Petry TV 3811 Turtle Creek Blvd Ste 520 Dallas TX 75219

WELCH, MARY EDDISON, town official; b. N.Y.C., Nov. 17, 1917; d. William Barton and Mary Corbin Eddison; m. E. Sohier Welch, Dec. 27, 1940; children: Edward S., William B., Mary C., Anne E. Welch Lazor. BA, Bennington Coll., 1940. Adminstr., Mystic Valley Mental Health Ctr., Lexington, Mass., 1970-77; mem. Bd. Selectmen Town of Harvard, Mass., 1980-86; pres. Harvard LWV, 1986-88; bd. dirs. Girl Scouts U.S.A., N.Y.C., 1955-66; trustee Bennington Coll., Vt., 1964-71; bd. dirs. Minute Man Home Care Corp., Lexington, 1977-80, Dana McLean Greeley Found for Peace and Justice, Inc., 1988—. Democrat. Unitarian. Club: Chilton (Boston). Avocation: sailing.

WELCH, MARY FRANCES, registered nurse; b. Milw., July 13, 1938; d. Frank P. and Alberta C. (Carrigan) De Sio; m. Gary P. Welch, Oct. 11, 1969; 1 child, Lance E. BSN, Marquette U., 1959; MS in Nursing Adminstrn., Ariz. State U., 1979; PhD in Nursing Adminstrn., Columbia Pacific U., 1987. RN, Calif., Ariz., N.Mex., Okla., La.; cert. nursing adminstr., advanced. Staff, head nurse St. Mary's Hosp., Long Beach, Calif., 1959-65; staff, asst. head nurse St. Michael Hosp., Milw., 1965-67, St. Francis Hosp., Lynwood, Calif., 1967-69; staff nurse Cedars of Lebanon Hosp., Hollywood, Calif., 1969; staff, asst. head nurse Dominguez Valley Hosp., Compton, Calif., 1969-70; from head nurse to asst. dir. nursing Boswell Meml. Hosp., Sun City, Ariz., 1970-79; dir. nursing svcs. Lea Regional Hosp., Hobbs, N.Mex., 1980-82, Enid (Okla.) Meml. Hosp., 1982-89; dir. nursing for ancillary div. Lake Charles (La.) Meml. Hosp., 1989—. Mem. Am. Assn. Critical Care Nurses, Am. Orgn. Nurse Execs., La. Orgn. Nurse Execs., Am. Nurses Assn., La. Nurses Assn. Democrat. Roman Catholic. Office: Lake Charles Meml Hosp 1701 Oak Park Blvd Lake Charles LA 70601

WELCH, MARY-SCOTT (STEWART WELCH), writer; b. Chgo., Dec. 14 1919; d. William Scott and Myrtle (Ferrin) Stewart; A.B., U. Ill., 1940; m. Barrett Farley Welch (dec.); children: Farley, Laurie, Margaret, Mary Barrett. Newsstand promotion mgr. Esquire-Coronet, Chgo., 1940-42; West Coast editor Esquire, Hollywood, Calif., 1943-45; assoc. editor Pageant mag., N.Y.C., 1947-50; entertainment editor Look mag., N.Y.C., 1950-52; food editor Glamour mag., N.Y.C., 1953-55; columnist Seventeen, N.Y.C., 1960-63, Vogue mag., McCall's, 1974-76, Exec. Female, 1981-82; tchr. mag. writing Womanschool and Ethical Culture Soc., N.Y.C., 1975-77. Coord. rape prevention com. NOW, N.Y.C., 1972-74; mem. adv. bd. Inst. for Women and Work, Cornell U.; former mem. adv. bd. Working Women, Nat. Assn. Office Workers; mem. Nat. Abortion Rights Action League, Planned Parenthood, People For Environ. Orgns. With USNR, 1942-43. Mem. ACLU, NOW (bd. dir. 1973-75, adv. bd. 1982), Authors Guild, Authors League, Women in Communications (named one of 60 outstanding mems. 1984), Nat. Women's Polit. Caucus, CLU, Phi Beta Kappa, Kappa Kappa Gamma. Author: Networking: The Great New Way for Women to Get Ahead, 1980; The Family Wilderness Handbook, 1973; (with Ronnie Welch) Esquire Party Book, 1970; Seventeen Guide to Travel, 1970; Esquire Etiquette, 1958; What Every Young Man Should Know, 1970; Handbook for Hosts, 1950; Your First Hundred Meals, 1947, others; contbr. articles various mags. including Redbook, McCall's, Ladies Home Jour., Woman's Day, Working Woman, Mademoiselle, Ms., Seventeen, Modern Maturity, Glamour, Vogue, others. Home and Office: 30 Waterside Pla Apt 2K New York NY 10010

WELCH, MICHELLE LESLIE, lawyer; b. Bridgeport, Conn., Sept. 3, 1953; d. Russell Moreton and Patricia Aldona (Yasonis) Cory; m. Jeffrey S. Welch, May 24, 1978; 1 dau., Stephanie Cory. B.A. in Biol. Sci., U. Del., 1976; J.D., Del. Law Sch., Widener U., 1979. Bar: Del. 1979, Pa. 1980. Law clk. Schmittinger & Rodriguez, P.A., Wilmington, Del., 1977-79; jud. clk. Del. Ct. Chancery, Wilmington, 1980-81; assoc. legal counsel Bank of Del. and Bank of Del. Corp., Wilmington, 1981-84, gen. counsel, 1984—; mem. exec. com. bd. dirs. Industry Council for Tangible Assets, Washington, 1983-86; state rep. Conf. of State Bank Supervisors, 1986—. Elected bd. dirs. New Castle County Econ. Devel. Corp. Mem. ABA, Del. Bar Assn., Fin. Women Internat., Del. Valley Corp. Counsel Assn. (bd. dirs. 1986-89), Lawyers Forum, Del. Bankers Assn. (govt. affairs com.), Del. State C. of C. (elected dir. 1989). Republican. Roman Catholic. Home: 2618 Tonbridge Dr Wilmington DE 19810 Office: Bank of Del 222 Delaware Ave Wilmington DE 19899

WELCHER, STEPHANIE DENISE, public relations executive; b. Tulsa, Sept. 19, 1961; d. Richard Harvey and Judith Carol (Holtzinger) Welcher; m. Jeffery Lee Taylor, June 16, 1990. BS, Okla. State U., 1983; postgrad., U. Okla. Reporter The Daily O'collegian, Stillwater, Okla., 1980-83; news anchor KOSU-FM, Stillwater, 1981, KRXO-FM, Stillwater, 1982; asst. producer KTVY-TV, Oklahoma City, 1983-84; anchor/reporter KTEN, Ada, Okla., 1985-86; producer America's Shopping Channel, Oklahoma City, 1987; pub. rels. coordinator South Community Hosp., Oklahoma City, 1988-89; pub. rels. assoc. South Community Hosp., 1990—; cons. on brochure, Women to Woman, 1990. Mem. communications com. United Way, Oklahoma City, 1989-90; bd. dirs. Nat. Clown & Laughter Hall of Fame, 1989-90. Recipient Good Guy award, KTVY-TV, 1988, 89. Mem. Women in Communications (v.p. 1981-82), Am. Hosp. Assn., Okla. Hosp. Assn., Am. Soc. Hosp. Mktg. and Pub. Rels., Oklahoma City C. of C., South Oklahoma City C. of C. Democrat. Presbyterian. Office: South Community Hospital 1001 SW 44th St Oklahoma City OK 73109

WELD, TUESDAY KER (SUSAN KER WELD), actress; b. N.Y.C., Aug. 27, 1943; d. Lathrop Motley and Aileen (Ker) W.; m. Claude Harz, Oct., 1965 (div. 1971); 1 dau., Natasha; m. Dudley Moore, Sept. 20, 1975 (div.); 1 son, Patrick; m. Pinchas Zukerman, Oct. 18, 1985. Attended Hollywood (Calif.) Profl. Sch. Actress: (TV programs) including Cimarron Strip, Playhouse 90, Kraft Theatre, Alcoa Theatre, Climax, Ozzie and Harriet, The Many Loves of Dobie Gillis, 77 Sunset Strip, The Millionaire, Tab Hunter Show, Zane Grey Theatre, Follow the Sun, Bus Stop, Dick Powell Theatre, Adventures in Paradise, Naked City, Eleventh Hour, DuPont Show of the Month, The Greatest Show on Earth, Mr. Broadway, Fugitive, The Crucible, (films) including debut in Rock, Rock, Rock, 1956, Rally Round the Flag Boys, The Five Pennies, The Private Lives of Adam and Eve, Return to Peyton Place, Wild in the Country, Bachelor Flat, Lord Love A Duck, Pretty Poison, I Walk the Line, A Safe Place, Play It As It Lays, Because They're Young, High Time, Sex Kittens Go to College, The Cincinnati Kid, Soldier in the Rain, I'll Take Sweden, Who'll Stop the Rain, Looking for Mr. Goodbar, 1977, Serial, 1980, Thief, 1981, Author! Author!, 1982, Once Upon a Time in America, 1984, Heartbreak Hotel, 1988, (TV movies) including Reflections of Murder, 1974, F. Scott Fitzgerald in Hollywood, 1976, A Question of Guilt, 1978, Mother and Daughter: The Loving War, 1980, Madame X, 1981, The Rainmaker, 1982, The Winter of Discontent, 1983, Scorned and Swindled, 1984, Circle of Violence, 1986. *

WELDER, SISTER THOMAS, academic administrator; b. Linton, N.D., Apr. 27, 1940; d. Sebastian Welder and Mary Ann Kuhn. BA in Music, Coll. St. Scholastica, 1963; MusM, Northwestern U., 1968; cert., Harvard Inst. Ednl. Mgmt. Joined Annunciation Priory, Benedictine Community of Religious Women, 1961. Asst. prof. music Mary Coll, Univ. of Mary, Bismarck, N.D., 1963-76, dir. deferred giving and ch. relations, 1976-78; pres. U. Mary, Bismarck, 1978—; bd. dirs. Provident Life Ins. Co., Bismarck, MDU Resources Group Inc., Bismarck. V.p. bd. dirs. St. Alexius Med. Ctr., Bismarck, 1984—, Health Care United, Inc., Bismarck, 1986—; charter mem. Theodore Roosevelt Medora Found.; mem. N.D. 2000 Com. Bush Found. fellow, Mpls., 1987. Mem. Coun. Ind. Colls., Am. Coun. Edn. Nat. Identification Program, N. Cen. Assn. Colls. & Schs. (cons., evaluator, accreditation rev. coun. mem.). Office: U Mary 7500 University Dr Bismarck ND 58504

WELDON, DORIS MAY, former computer programmer; b. Lincoln, Nebr., May 18, 1925; d. Marcus Dunlap and Pauline Mayham (Bancroft) W. BA, U. Nebr., 1947; MS in Mgmt., Am. U., 1978. Clk., typist, stenographer various cos., Lincoln and Denver, 1944-52; clk., typist, stenographer U.S. Army, Japan, 1952-54, London and Heidelberg, Fed. Republic Germany, 1954-59; sec., stenographer U.S. Army, Arlington, Va., 1966-70; sec., stenographer, bilingual sec. Office of U.S. Army Attache, Am. Embassy, Australia and Republic of Panama, 1959-64; stenographer Conf. Am. Armies, 1964; computer programmer U.S. Pentagon, Arlington, Va., 1970-73; computer programmer CSC, Washington, 1973-78, ret., 1978. Mem. AAUW (editor bull.), AARP, Nat. Assn. Ret. Fed. Employees, Sun City Geneal. Soc., Sun City Photo Club and Workshop (sec.), Spanish Club, French Club. Home: 10741 Wedgewood Dr Sun City AZ 85351

WELDON, ELAINE JOYCE, psychologist; b. N.Y.C.. BS, Columbia U., N.Y.C., 1969, MS, 1970; PhD, Fordham U., 1977. Unit chief Payne Whitney Clinic Cornell U. Med. Ctr., N.Y.C., 1975-76; dir. psychiat. svcs. Cottage Hosp., Santa Barbara, Calif., 1977-79; pvt. practice Santa Barbara, 1979—. Contbr. articles to profl. jours. Mem. Am. Psychol. Assn.

WELDON, EUNICE BERTHA, government official; b. Westmoreland, Va., July 29, 1941; d. Jesse Arthur and Mary Nannie (Jones) W. Grad., Cortez Peters Bus. Coll.; student, George Washington U. With D.C. Govt., Washington, 1962—, audit verification specialist Dept. Human Services, 1979-80, acting acctg. tech. supr., 1980, acting staff asst., 1980-81, acting program analyst, 1981, audit verification payment specialist, 1981-83, program analyst, 1983-88, acting br. chief exec. dir., support sec., 1988—. Mem. Nat. Assn. Female Execs. Baptist. Office: DC Dept Human Services 801 N Capitol NE Washington DC 20001

WELDON, KARLA ELAINE HART, occupational therapist; b. Jacksonville, Ill., July 2, 1935; d. Arthur Charles and Charlotte Elizabeth (Engelbach) Hart; m. Robert William Weldon, Apr. 13, 1958; children: Deborah, Susan, Scott, Cynthia. BS in Occupational Therapy, Colo. State U., 1957. Registered and lic. occupational therapist. Staff therapist Lemuel Shattuck Hosp., Boston, 1958-59; sch. therapy cons. Woodford County, Eureka, Ill., 1980-81; occupational therapy cons. Abraham Lincoln Hosp., Lincoln, Ill., 1982-83, Bloomington (Ill.) Nursing and Rehab., 1983-85; registry/home health BroMenn Med. Ctr., Bloomington, 1988—; occupational therapy cons. Mackinaw Valley and Dist. 87 Spl.Svcs., Bloomington/Normal, 1989—; bd. dirs. First Nat. Bank, Arenzville, Ill. Regional leader CampFire, Mpls. and Normal, 1965-78; v.p., treas., bd. dirs. Sweet Adelines, Inc., Bloomington, 1976—; mem. Bloomington-Normal Symphony Guild, 1989—. Mem. Am. Occupational Therapy Assn., Nat. T.T.T. Soc., Nat. P.E.O. Soc. (guard), AAUW (bd. dirs. 1988-89), Delta Zeta. Home: 1305 Baugh Dr Normal IL 61761

WELDON, VIRGINIA V., corporate executive, physician; b. Toronto, Sept. 8, 1935; came to U.S., 1937; d. John Edward and Carolyn Edith (Swift) Verral; children: Ann Stuart, Susan Shaeffer. A.B. cum laude, Smith Coll., 1957; M.D., SUNY-Buffalo, 1962; L.H.D. (hon.), Rush U., 1985. Diplomate Am. Bd. Pediatrics in pediatric endocrinology and metabolism. Intern Johns Hopkins Hosp., Balt., 1962-63, resident in pediatrics, 1963-64; fellow pediatric endocrinology Johns Hopkins U., Balt., 1964-67, instr. pediatrics, 1967-68; instr. pediatrics Washington U., St. Louis, 1968-69, asst. prof., 1969-73, assoc. prof. pediatrics, 1973-79, prof. pediatrics, 1979-89, v.p. Med. Ctr., 1980-89, dep. vice chancellor med. affairs, 1983-89; v.p. sci. affairs Monsanto Co., St. Louis, 1989, v.p. pub. policy, 1989—; mem. gen. clin. rsch. ctrs. adv. com. NIH, Bethesda, Md., 1976-80, rsch. resources adv. coun., 1980-84; bd. dirs. Southwestern Bell Corp., Gen. Am. Life Ins. Co., G.D. Searle & Co., The NutraSweet Co., Wetterau Inc., Rsch./Am., Monsanto Co. (adv.). Contbr. articles to sci. jours. Commr. St. Louis Zool. Park, 1983—; bd. dirs. United Way Greater St. Louis, 1978-90, St. Louis Regional Health Care Corp. Fellow Am. Acad. Pediatrics, AAAS; mem. Inst. Medicine, Assn. Am. Med. Colls. (del., chmn. council acad. socs. 1984-85, chmn. assembly 1985-86), Am. Pediatric Soc., Nat. Bd. Med. Examiners (bd. dirs. 1987-89), Endocrine Soc., Soc. Pediatric Rsch., AAU (joint com. health policy), Nat. Assn. Biomed. Rsch. (bd. dirs. 1985-87, 89—), CORETECH (vice chmn.), Coun. on Competitiveness (tech. adv. com.), St. Louis Med. Soc., Sigma Xi, Alpha Omega Alpha. Roman Catholic. Home: 242 Carlyle Lake Dr Saint Louis MO 63141 Office: Monsanto Co DIA 800 N Lindbergh Blvd Saint Louis MO 63167

WELDY, NORMA JEAN, nursing educator; b. Bremen, Ind., Aug. 26, 1929; d. Eldon Joseph and Lucile L. (Martin) W. BS, Goshen Coll., 1954; diploma in Nursing, La Junta Mennonite Sch., 1954; postgrad., Ind. U., 1961; MS, U. Colo., 1962. RN, Ind. Asst. instr. La Junta (Colo.) Mennonite Sch. Nursing, 1954-56; staff nurse Cancer Inst., NIH, Bethesda, Md., 1956-57; asst. med. head nurse Elkhart (Ind.) Gen. Hosp., 1957-58, head surg. nurse, 1958-60, staff nurse, 1979-80; prof. nursing Goshen (Ind.) Coll., 1960—; staff nurse Cedars of Lebanon Hosp., L.A., 1971-72, St. Joseph's Med. Ctr., South Bend, Ind., 1989; nurse advisor Ostomy Club, Am. Cancer Soc., Elkhart, 1965—; mem. faculty continuing edn., Goshen, Elkhart, South Bend. Author: Body Fluids and Electrolytes: A Programmed Presentation, 1972, 5th edit., 1988. Mem., com. chmn. Am. Heart Assn., 1977—, past pres. Elkhart County unit. Named Nurse of Yr., Mennonite Nurses Assn., 1984, Woman of Yr., North Cen. Ind. div. Am. Heart Assn., 1985. Mem. Am. Nurses Assn. (bd. dirs., former v.p., com. mem. and chmn. Goshen chpt. 1954), Nat. League for Nursing, Am. Assn. Critical Care Nurses, Ind. Nurses Assn., Delta Kappa Gamma (sec. Alpha Iota chpt. 1980-82, chmn. rsch. com. 1982-84). Office: Goshen Coll 1700 S Main St Goshen IN 46526

WELLER, PENNY SUE, pharmaceutical executive; b. Grand Rapids, Mich., Nov. 27, 1948; d. Joseph P. and Emma (Bridge) W.; children: Bridget Elizabeth, Lawrence Joseph. BBA, Western Mich. U., 1975, MBA, 1977. Cert. mgmt. acct. Libr. Caledonia (Mich.) Community Schs., 1966-68; acctg. clk. Shakespeare Co., Kalamazoo, Mich., 1969-72; head Internat. Gen. Acctg., 1972-84; mgr. subs. gen. acctg. The Upjohn Co., Kalamazoo, 1984—. Mem. Nat. Acctg. Assn. Office: The Upjohn Co 7000 Portage Rd Kalamazoo MI 49002

WELLES, FERNE BINGHAM MALCOLM, retired archivist; b. Fayetteville, Ark., June 2, 1921; d. William Thomas and Nellie E. (Coffey) Bingham; m. Eugene G. Malcolm, Sept. 5, 1940 (dec. 1975); children: Rebecca Malcolm Schubert, Rachel Malcolm Woods, Eugene Glenn Jr.; m. Edward Randolph Welles II, Nov. 2, 1984. AA, Penn Valley Coll., Kansas City, Mo., 1977; BA in Am. Culture, U. Mo., Kansas City, 1981, MA in History, 1986. Archival intern Regional Br. Nat. Archives, Kansas City, Mo., 1976; historian, archivist, hist. writer St. Luke's Hosp. Kansas City, 1975-85; archivist, historiographer, researcher Episc. Diocese West Mo., Kansas City, 1974-85; historian, archivist, writer Grace and Holy Trinity Cathedral, Kansas City, 1972-79, 86-87; supr. grad students Emporia (Kans.) State U., 1983; presenter paper at history conf. Contbr. to numerous hist. publs. Pres. Kansas City Bus. and Profl. Women's Guild, 1982-83; mem. Women's C. of C., Kansas City, 1980-83; vestry mem. Grace and Holy Trinity Cathedral, 1982-84. Mem. AAUW (chmn. ednl. found. program 1989-91), Kansas City Area Archivists (edn. com.), Woman's City Club, Nat. Episc. Historians Assn., Phi Alpha Theta. Republican. Episcopalian. Home: 4545 Wernall Rd 1002 Kansas City MO 64111 also: HCR 33 Box 145 Manset ME 04656

WELLES, MARILYN TEETER, engineer, researcher; b. Chgo., Jan. 4, 1935; d. Milo Clare and Mary Cecelia (Hitchcock) Teeter; 1 child, Stephen Anderson. BA, Albright Coll., 1957; MS, George Wash. U., 1982, DSc, 1990. Programmer IBM Corp., N.Y., 1958-60; programmer analyst Bell Lab., Whippany, N.J., 1961-64; programmer, analyst Ohio State Univ., Columbus, 1965-70; cons. Cen. Computing, Inc., Wichita, Kans.; program mgr. NCR Corp., Wichita, 1973-75; project engr. Booz, Allen & Hamilton, Md., 1976-78; dir., bus. system div. Automated Sci. Group, Silver Spring, Md., 1979-81; research fellow Logistics Mgmt. Inst., Bethesda, 1982-84; systems engr. MITRE Corp.; adj. prof. Geogre Washington U., 1984—; lectr. Marymount U., Arlington, Va., 1986—; bd. trustees Wash. Ops. Res. Mgmt. Sci. Coun., 1986—; guest editor Jour. Wash. Acad. Sci., Wash., 1989. Pres. ACLU Nat. Capitol Area, Wash., 1978-80, WEAL Nat. Capitol Area, 1988—, Assn. D.C. Condominium bd., 1986-87. Mem. Soc. Info. Mgmt., Nat. Capitol Rsch., Mgmt. Sco. Coun., Assn. Computing Machinery. Democrat.

WELLES, MELINDA FASSETT, artist, educator; b. Palo Alto, Calif., Jan. 4, 1943; d. George Edward and Barbara Helena (Todd) W. Student, San Francisco Inst. Art, 1959-60, U. Oreg., 1960-62; BA in Fine Arts, UCLA, 1964, MA in Spl. Edn., 1971, PhD in Ednl. Psychology, 1976; student fine arts and illustration Art Ctr. Coll. Design, 1977-80. Cert. ednl. psychologist, Calif. Asst. prof. Calif. State U., Northridge, 1979-82, Pepperdine U., L.A., 1979-82; assoc. prof. curriculum, teaching and spl. edn. U. So. Calif., L.A., 1980-89; mem. acad. faculty Pasadena City Coll., 1973-79, Art Ctr. Coll. Design, 1978—, Otis Art Inst. of Parsons Sch. Design, L.A., 1986—, UCLA Extension, 1980-84, Coll. Devel. Studies, L.A., 1978-87, El Camino Community Coll., Redondo Beach, Calif., 1982-86; cons. spl. edn.; pub. adminstrn. analyst UCLA Spl. Edn. Rsch. Program, 1973-76; exec. dir. Atwater Park Ctr. Disabled Children, L.A., 1976-78; coord. Pacific Oaks Coll. in svc. programs for L.A. Unified Schs., Pasadena, 1978-81. Author: Calif. Dept. Edn. Tech. Reports, 1972-76; editor: Teaching Special Students in the Mainstream, 1981, Educating Special Learners, 1986, 88, Teaching Students with Learning Problems, 1988, Exceptional Children and Youth, 1989; group shows include: San Francisco Inst. Art, 1960, U. Hawaii, 1978, Barnsdall Gallery, L.A., 1979, 80; represented in various pvt. collections. HEW fellow, 1971-72; grantee Calif. Dept. Edn., 1975-76, Calif. Dept. Health, 1978. Mem. Calif. Assn. Neurologically Handicapped Children, Am. Council Learning Disabilities, Clearing House for Info. on Learning Disabilities, Calif. Scholarship Fedn. (life), Alpha Chi Omega. Office: 700 Levering Ave 1 Los Angeles CA 90024

WELLING, KATHRYN MARIE, editor; b. Ft. Wayne, Ind., Feb. 4, 1952; d. Arthur Russell Sr. and Genevieve (Disser) W.; m. Donald Robert Boyle, Oct. 21, 1978; 1 child, Brian Joseph. BS in Journalism, Northwestern U., 1974. Copy reader Dow Jones News Retrieval, N.Y.C., 1974-75; copy reader/reporter AP-Dow Jones, N.Y.C., 1975-76; copy editor Wall Street Jour., N.Y.C., 1976; assoc. editor Barron's, N.Y.C., 1976-81, asst. to editor, 1981, mng. editor, 1982—. Office: Barron's 200 Liberty St New York NY 10281

WELLINGTON-JOHNSON, SHARON L., registrar; b. Salisbury, N.C., Nov. 26, 1957; d. Willie Sr. and Nadine (Crump) Wellington; m. Carvin Allen Johnson, Aug. 5, 1988. BA, U. N.C., 1980; MS, Bank St. Coll. of Edn., 1990. Asst. registrar Columbia U., N.Y.C., 1983-85; registrar Bank St. Coll. of Edn., N.Y.C., 1985—. Cellist Philharmonia Orch. of N.Y., N.Y.C., 1985-88, Manhattan Opera Assn., N.Y.C., 1985-88, Bloomingdale Chamber Orch., N.Y.C., 1985-88. Mem. Am. Assn. Collegiate Registrars and Admissions Officers, N.Y. Assn. Collegiate Registars and Admissions Officers, N.J. Assn. Collegiate Registrars and Admissions Officers, Assn. Black Women in Higher Edn., NAFE. Home: 426 Fifth Ave New Rochelle NY 10801 Office: Bank St Coll of Edn 610 W 112th St New York NY 10025

WELLMAN, DAWN ELIZABETH, lawyer; b. Valparaiso, Ind., Aug. 14, 1949; d. Willard Frederick and Joan Elizabeth (Larsh) W. BA with distinction, Valparaiso U., 1971, JD with honors, 1976. Atty. Cohen and Thiros, Merrillville, Ind., 1976-87, ptnr., 1983; atty. Brand and Allen, Greenfield, Ind., 1987--; ptnr. Brand and Allen, Greenfield, Ind.,; faculty Nat. Inst. Trial Advocacy, Indpls. 1985--. Mem. Lake County Women's Bar Assn. (pres. 1979, bd. dirs. 1985-87, sec. treas. 1982), Hancock County Bar Assn. (pres. 1990—), Ind. Trial Lawyers Assn., Am. Trial Lawyers Assn. Democrat. Lutheran. Home: 4214 E State Rd 234 Greenfield IN 46140 Office: Brand and Allen 5 Courthouse Plaza PO Box 455 Greenfield IN 46140

WELLNITZ, BARBARA LOUISE, information systems specialist; b. Michigan City, Ind., Dec. 26, 1945; d. Harold P. and Helen A. (Schmock) Cashbaugh; 1 child, Brian A. BS, Ind. U., 1967. Legal sec. Sweeney, Dabagia, Donoghue & Thorne, Michigan City, 1975-86; adminstrv. sec. Holy Cross Health System Corp., South Bend, Ind., 1987-88; documentation specialist Holy Cross Health System Corp., South Bend, 1988-89, project control analyst, 1989—. Mem. AAUW (Mich. City br. sec. 1989-91, pres. 1981-83), NAFE, Soc. Tech. Communicators, Michiana Profl. Connection. Office: Holy Cross Health System 3606 E Jefferson Blvd South Bend IN 46615

WELLS, BERNADETTE NICKLE, pediatrician; b. Cleve., Sept. 26, 1951; d. Bernard Michael and Dorothy Theresa (Bright) Nickle; m. James Howard Wells, Oct. 15, 1977 (div. Dec. 1989). BA, Ind. U, 1974; MD, Ind. U., Sch. Medicine, Indpls., 1978. Diplomate Am. Bd. Pediatrics. From intern to resident N.C. Baptist Hosp./Bowman Gray Sch. Medicine, Winston-Salem, N.C., 1978-81; clin. pediatrician Guilford County Health Dept., Greensboro, N.C., 1981-82; pvt. practice Mt. Airy, N.C., 1982—. Fellow Am. Acad. Pediatrics; mem. N.C. Pediatric Soc. Office: Bernadette Wells, MD 933 Old Rockford St Mount Airy NC 27030

WELLS, BERRI ANN, sales executive; b. L.A., Aug. 30, 1963; d. Charles W. Peters and Thelma M. (Williams) Wells. BBA, Howard U., Washington, 1987. Libr. asst. Sch. Edn. Howard U., 1982-83; sales reservationist Delta Airlines, Rockville, Md., 1985; contraband analyst U.S. Secret Svc., Washington, 1984-86; with mktg. rsch. and devel. coop. Gen. Foods, White Plains, N.Y., 1986; fragrance model Calvin Klein Cosmetics, Washington, 1987-90; sales rep. Honeywell Inc., McLean, Va., 1988-90; sales mgr. Guest Quarters Hotel, Washington, 1990—; exec. dir. Cherry Blossom Acad. Tng. and Devel., Alexandria, Va., 1990—. Vol. Italian Embassy, Cultural Attache, Washington, 1982-83; tutor northstar Tutorial for Homeless Children, Washington, 1988-90; exch. student Am. Field Svc., Ancona, Italy, 1982. Mem. NAFE, Dynamic Interactions, Coalition of 100 Black Women. Home: PO Box 11013 Alexandria VA 22312

WELLS, BETTY RUTH, science consultant, farmer; b. Jefferson County, Ill., June 23, 1927; d. James Norris and Carrie (Shelton) Baker; m. J. Eugene M. Wells, Apr. 27, 1946; children: Catheryn Wells Stanford, Janice Wells Senftleber. BS in Edn. cum laude, So. Ill. U., 1960, MS in Supervision, 1964. Cert. tchr., adminstr., Ill. Tchr., prin. Mt. Vernon (Ill.) Pub. Schs., 1954-82; corp. sec. Mt. Vernon Meml. Gardens, 1963—, sales person, 1979—; co-owner, mgr. Tel Aviv Farms, Waltonville, Ill., 1960—; sci. edn. cons., Mt. Vernon, 1974—; presenter travel lectures to civic and ednl. groups; participant seminar Oxford U., Eng., 1989. Bd. dirs., Murdale Gardens of Memory, Murphysboro, Ill., 1974—; trustee, Rend Lake Conservancy Dist., Benton, Ill., 1984—; mem. Greater Egypt Regional Planning and Devel. Commn., 1984—. Mem. So. Ill. Assn. Mgmt. (bd. dirs. 1975—), Mt. Vernon Art Guild, Ill. Edn. Assn., NEA. Democrat. Home: Rte 1 Box 62 Waltonville IL 62894

WELLS, DEBORAH LUCILLE, legal administrative assistant; b. Kansas City, Kans., July 24, 1957; d. Robert Lee and Frances Lucille (Klasinski) W. AA, Kansas City Community Coll., 1987; student, U. Mo., Kansas City, 1988—. Legal sec. Bernard B. Levine, P.C., Kansas City, 1979-84; ptnr., office mgr. Citizens Against Crime, Kansas City, 1984-86; corp. legal asst., office mgr. Barbieri & Barbieri, Kansas City, 1986-90; legal adminstrv. asst. United Telephone Co., Overland Park, Kansas, 1990—. Bd. dirs., fund raiser, corp. mem. Linwood-Downtown YMCA, Kansas City; actress, fund raiser Kansas City Met. Bar Assn., 1988. Recipient fund raising awards Linwood-Downtown YMCA, 1987-89. Mem. NAFE, Nat. Assn. Legal Assts., Am. Bus. Women's Assn. Office: United Telephone Co 5454 W 110th St Overland Park KS 66211

WELLS, DONNA FRANCES, distribution company executive; b. Lima, Ohio, Dec. 19, 1948; d. Arthur Robert and Frances Lucille (Knudtson) W.; m. Darrell Donald Erickson, Nov. 26, 1980. Cert., Parks Bus. Sch., 1972; student, Sheridan Coll., 1984—. Dir. purchasing Wolff Distbg., Gillette, Wyo., 1973—. Mem. Nat. Assn. Purchasing Mgmt., Nat. Assn. of Female Execs., Gillette Racing Assn. (aux. v.p. 1986—), VFW Aux., Am. Legion Aux. Home: 105 Sequoia Gillette WY 82716

WELLS, DONNA JO, accountant; b. Waco, Tex., Jan. 2, 1966; d. Weldon Clay and Joann (Richards) W.; m. Roy Allen Upton, Sept. 26, 1984 (div. Aug. 1987); children: Michelle Anne, Michael Anthony. AAS, McLennan Community Coll., Waco, 1989; Student, Baylor U., 1989. Asst. office mgr. Ozark Leather Saddle King of Tex., Waco, 1983-84; mgr. TACO Villa, Amarillo, Tex., 1984, Domino's Pizza, Waco, 1986; mktg. mgr. Water Resources of Waco, 1986-87; health caregiver Adaptive Living Ctr., Waco, 1986-87; sales clk. Leon's Fashions, Waco, Tex., 1987-88; sec., receptionist, bookkeeper, office mgr. Lorena (Tex.) Therapeutic Ctr., 1988; tutor, clk. McLennon Community Coll., Waco, 1988-89; sec. Associated Ct. Reporters, Waco, 1988-89; credit clk. Sears & Roebuck, Waco, 1989; acctg. clk. Pattillo, Brown & Hill, CPAs, Waco, 1990—. Coun. mem. First Bapt. Woodway, 1988-89. Recipient Sonatina award Piano Guild U.S.A., 1980, Scholastic Honor award Midway High Sch., Hewitt, Tex., 1983, First Div. award Tex. Mktg. Distributive Edn. Area 5, 1983; named to Outstanding Performance Am. Biog. Inst., 1988—. Mem. Am. Assn. Community and Jr. Colls., Phi Theta Kappa (reporter 1988-89, student scholar, Outstanding Svc. award 1989). Avocations: piano playing, my children, racquet ball. Home: 458 Catalina Waco TX 76712

WELLS, ELAINE LOUISE, state legislator, health care administrator; b. Emporia, Kans., May 26, 1951; d. Walter Lawrence and Ruth Maxine (Mangold) Laue; m. Richard Dean Wells, Sept. 24, 1967; children: Dane Eric, Daric Ean. Student, Washburn U., 1978-85. Asst. activities dir. Brookside Manor, Overbrook, Kans., 1975-76, adminstr., 1976-86; adminstr. Rolling Hills Health Ctr., Fairlawn Heights, Topeka, 1987-89; life and health agt. Bankers Life & Casualty, 1989—; mem. Ho. of Reps., Topeka, 1987—.

Vice chair Osage County (Kans.) Dem. Com., 1982-86; bd. dirs. Osage County Farm Bur., 1986. Mem. Kans. Health Care Assn. (bd. dirs. 1985-87), Am. Bus. Women's Assn., Lyndon Bus. Profl. Women (vice chairperson 1989), Ins. Women of Topeka (legis. dir.). Home: Rte 1 Box 166 Carbondale KS 66414 Office: Kans State Capitol Rm 155E W Topeka KS 66612

WELLS, FAY GILLIS, writer, lecturer, broadcaster; b. Mpls., Oct. 15, 1908; d. Julius Howells and Minnie Irene (Shafer) Gillis; student Mich. State Coll., 1925-28; m. Linton Wells, Apr. 1, 1935 (dec. 1976); 1 son, Linton Wells, II. Free-lance corr. in USSR for N.Y. Herald Tribune and AP, 1930-34, aviation mags., 1930-36; fgn. corr. N.Y. Herald Tribune, 1935-36, spl. Hollywood corr., 1937-38, syndicated boating columnist, 1960-62; contbr. book revs. Saturday Review, 1939-42; dep. chief of mission for U.S. Comml. Co., Portuguese W. Africa, 1942-46; White House corr. Storer Broadcasting Co., 1964-77; aircraft pilot, 1929; designer yacht interiors Alta Grant Samuels, 1958-62; now co-chmn. Internat. Forest of Friendship; hon. co-chmn. Nat. Air Heritage Council; mem. com. to select 1st journalist in space, 1985—. Recipient Sherman Fairchild Internat. Air Safety Writing award, 1965, Amelia Earhart medal, 1967, Golden Age of Flight award Nat. Air and Space Mus.-Dept. Transp., 1984, award Internat. Conf. Women Engrs. and Scientists, 1984. Mem. 1967. Mem. Aviation/Space Writers Assn., Am. Women in Radio and TV (pres. Washington chpt. 1968-69, CBS Charlotte Friel award 1972), Radio-TV Corrs. Assn., White House Corrs. Assn., Aircraft Owners and Pilots Assn., The Ninety-Nines (charter mem.; Most Valuable Pilot, Washington chpt. 1975), OX5 Aviation Pioneers (Outstanding Woman of Year award 1972), Internat. Soc. Woman Geographers, Broadcast Pioneers, Zonta Internat., Nat. Bus. and Profl. Womens Clubs, Nat. League Am. Pen Women, Nat. Aero. Assn. (named elder statesman 1984). Clubs: Georgetown, Overseas Press (founding mem. 1939), Am. Newspaper Women's, Nat. Press, Internat. Forest Friendship (co-gen. chmn. 1976—). Home: 4211 Duvawn St Alexandria VA 22310-2024

WELLS, JANE FRANCES, computer science educator; b. Davenport, Iowa, Feb. 24, 1944; d. Justus Neff and Margie (Janssen) W.; m. Burt C. Ferrini, Oct. 30, 1981; 1 child, Katherine Claire. BA, Marycrest Coll., 1966; MS, U. Iowa, 1967, PhD, 1970; MS, U. Ill., 1990. Asst. prof. math. Purdue U., Ft. Wayne, Ind., 1970-74; prof. in computer sci. Gov.'s State U., University Park, Ill., 1974—; cons. U.S. EPA, Chgo., 1980-81, 82-83. Author: Using Minitab in Statistics for Decision Making, 1984; contbr. articles to profl. jours. Bd. dirs. Jane Addams Ctr. for Hull House, Chgo., 1974-83, pres., 1979-81. Mem. Computer Soc. of IEEE, Assn. for Computing Machinery, Math. Assn. Am., Am. Statis. Assn. (bd. dirs. Chgo. chpt. 1981-87, treas. 1985-87). Home: 3930 N Pine Grove #315 Chicago IL 60613 Office: Gov's State U University Park IL 60466

WELLS, KAREN KAY, medical librarian; b. Petaluma, Calif., Jan. 9, 1956; d. Albert Lee and Miyoko (Kay) W.; m. John Edward Guth, Aug. 4, 1979 (div. 1986). BS with honors, U. Colo., 1977; MEd with honors, U. Ill., 1980, MS with honors, 1982. Cert. tchr., Colo., Ill. Grad. asst. grad. libr. U. Ill., Urbana, 1981-82; asst. prof. med. libr. svcs. sch. medicine Mercer U., Macon, Ga., 1982-83; libr., head Presbyn.-St. Luke's Med. Ctr., Presbyn.-Denver Hosp., 1983-84; libr., dept. head AMI-St. Luke's Hosp. Health Scis. Libr., Denver, 1984-88, instr., cons. dialog pharm. database, 1985-87; head libr. Manville Health, Safety and Environ. Libr., Denver, 1988-89; info. cons. Wells Info. Svc., Denver, 1989—; sr. rsch. analyst EG & G, Golden, Colo., 1990—. Editor Infosource newsletter, 1983-88. Mem. ALA, Med. Libr. Assn., Colo. Coun. Med. Librs. (cons. med.-sci. databases 1984—), Denver Area Health Scis. Libr. Consortium, IBM PC XT Users Group, U. Colo. Alumni Assn., U. Ill. Alumni Assn., Beta Phi Mu, Kappa Delta Pi. Democrat. Presbyterian. Office: EG & G Rocky Flats PO Box 464 T130A Cub 88 Golden CO 80402

WELLS, KENDRA BUCKEL, educator; b. Balt., May 24, 1954; d. William Max and Blodwen Gwladyss (Jones) Buckel; m. John Howard Wells, Oct. 20, 1979; children: Kelsey Elizabeth, Ashley Jennifer. BS in Recreation, U. Md., 1976, MS in Extension Edn., 1982. Extension agt. 4H Md. Coop. Extension Svc., Derwood, 1976—. Chmn. Montgomery County Coun. on Adolescents, Rockville, 1986-87; youth com. mem. Am. Inst. Cooperation, Washington, 1988-89; mem. Montgomery County Youth Workers Tng. Com., Rockville, 1988—; mem./awds. chmn. Montgomery County Intergenerational Com., Rockville, 1986-89; mem. Montgomery County Employment Devel. Commn. 1979-81, Parkland Community Adv. Coun., 1987-89; chmn. presch. com. St. John's Luth. Ch., Rockville, 1986-88. Nat. Collaboration for Youth grantee, 1980; IBM grantee, 1984. Mem. Md. Assn. Extension 4-H Agts. (pres. 1984-85), Nat. Assn. Extension 4-H Agts. (Disting. Svc. award 1985), Md. Assn. Adult and Continuing Edn. (treas. 1979-80). Democrat. Lutheran. Officed: Montgomery County Coop Ext 18410 Muncaster Rd Derwood MD 20853

WELLS, L. ROSEMARY SIPLON, graphic artist; b. Charles City, Iowa, Dec. 12, 1930; d. Joseph Jason and Emma (Wogsland) Siplon; m. Warren Frey Wells, Nov. 23, 1950; children: Wendy Rose, Jeffrey Joe, Jerrold Patrick. BA, U. No. Iowa, 1951, MA, 1953; PhD, Northwestern U., 1973. Elem. tchr. English Clear Lake (Iowa) Pub. Schs., 1951-52; owner R.W. Typing & Editing Svc., Evanston, Ill., 1953-63; sr. high sch. tchr. English Roycemore Sch., Evanston, 1963-65; tchr. humanities and English Kendall Coll., Evanston, 1965-69; dir. program devel. Hallmark Edn. Systems, Chgo., 1969-70; asst. prof. English Northwestern U., Chgo., 1967-86; dir. communications Aparacor (Fashion House), Evanston, 1979-89; owner, operator Star-Desk Graphics, Deerfield, Ill., 1989—; speaker to various orgns. in field. Author: Colorful Meal Planning, 1970, With Heart & With Voice, 1984; co-author: English Writing Patterns, Books 11-12, 1968; contbr. articles to profl. jours. Personnel mgr. Evanston Symphony Orch., Evanston; sect. leader (2d violins) Evanston Symphony; mem., pres. North Shore Theater Co.; charter mem., past pres., life mem. Savoy-Aires; advisor rsch. bd. advisors Am. Biog. Isnt., 1988—. Mem. MLA, Coll. English Assn., Coll. Composition & Communication, Popular Culture Assn. Presbyterian. Home and Office: Star-Desk Graphics 1129 Cherry St Deerfield IL 60015

WELLS, MARY ELIZABETH THOMPSON, real estate official, model-actress; b. Dallas, Oct. 9, 1936; d. Owen Perry and Ruth Marie (Baker) Thompson; children: Tadd Whitney, Britony Ruth. BA in Sociology, Syracuse (N.Y.) U., 1958; MA in Child Devel., Tufts U., 1964, MEd in Counseling Psychology, 1974. Asst. dir. pub. relations Inst. for Crippled and Disabled, N.Y.C., 1958-59; head tchr. Eliot-Pearson Children's Sch., Tufts U., Medford, Mass., 1964-66; psychotherapist Mental Health Ctr. of Greater Cape Ann, Gloucester, Mass., 1974-89; realtor assoc. Plum Realty, Delray Beach, Fla., 1990—; freelance fashion model, 1989—. Mem. Am. Psychol. Assn., Am. Orthopsychiat. Assn., Delray Beach Bd. Realtors, Seagate Beach Club. Home: 924 Seagate Dr Delray Beach FL 33483 Office: Plum Realty Inc 101 SE 6th Ave Delray Beach FL 33483

WELLS, MARY LAYTON, lawyer; b. Nacogdoches, Tex., July 31, 1958; d. William Isaac and Eva James (Wade) Layton; m. Robert N. Wells, Jr., July 14, 1984; 1 child, Robert Layton Wells. BA, U. S.C., 1980, JD, 1983. Bar: S.C. 1983, U.S. Dist. Ct. S.C. 1985, U.S. Ct. Appeals (4th cir.) 1985. Law clk. to justice S.C. Supreme Ct., Florence, 1983-85; assoc. The Hyman Law Firm, Florence, 1985—. Mem. ABA, S.C. Bar Assn., Order of Coif. Methodist. Office: The Hyman Law Firm PO Box 1770 Florence SC 29503

WELLS, MARYANN MICHELLE, perioperative head nurse; b. Phila., Oct. 30, 1953; d. George Thomas Papanier and Carmella (LaPalomento) Di Primio; m. Charles Joseph Wells, Aug. 13, 1977; 1 child, Alexandra Anne. BA in Biology, Immaculata Coll., 1975; AD in Nursing, Hahnemann Coll., 1978; MS in Health Edn., St. Joseph's Coll., Phila., 1982; postgrad., U. Pa., 1984—. RN, Operating Rm. Cert. Nurse day surgery Hosp. U. Pa., Phila., 1978-79, charge nurse day surgery, 1979-80, head nurse, 1980—; preceptor Villanova Sch. Nursing, PHila., 1980-82, Delaware County Community Coll., Media, Pa., 1983-85; lectr. various groups, orgns., 1983—. Editor: (book) Decision Making in Perioperative Nursing, 1987; contbr. articles in profl. jours. Mem. Assn. Operating Room Nurses, Assn. Nurse Execs., ANA, Pa. Nurses Assn. Home: 411 Pritchard Pl Newton Square PA 19073 Office: Hosp of U Pa 3400 Spruce St Philadelphia PA 19104

WELLS, MELISSA FOELSCH, foreign service officer; b. Tallinn, Estonia, Nov. 18, 1932; emigrated to U.S., 1936, naturalized, 1941; d. Kuno Georg and Miliza (Korjus) Foelsch; m. Alfred Washburn Wells, 1960; children: Christopher, Gregory. BS in Fgn. Service, Georgetown U., 1956. Fgn. svc. officer Dept. State, Washington, 1958-61; consular officer Dept. State, Trinidad, 1961-64; econ. officer mission OECD, Paris, 1964-66; econ. officer London, 1966-71; internat. economist, 1971-73; dep. dir. maj. export projects Dept. Commerce, 1973-75; comml. counselor Brazil, 1975-76; amb. to Guinea-Bissau and Cape Verde Dept. of State, 1976-77; U.S. rep. ECOSOC, UN, N.Y.C., 1977-79; resident rep. UNDP, Kampala, Uganda, 1979-81; dir. IMPACT program UNDP, Geneva, 1982-86; amb. to Mozambique, 1987—. Mem. Am. Fgn. Service Assn. Office: Am Embassy, Ave Kaunda 193, PO Box 783, Maputo Mozambique

WELLS, PATRICIA BENNETT, business administration educator; b. Park River, N.D., Mar. 25, 1935; d. Benjamin Beekman Bennett and Alice Catherine (Peerboom) Bennett Breckinridge; AA, Allan Hancok Coll., Santa Maria, Calif., 1964; BS magna cum laude, Coll. Great Falls, 1966; MS, U. N.D., 1967, PhD, 1971; children: Bruce Bennett, Barbara Lea Ragland. Fiscal acct. USIA, Washington, 1954-56; pub. acct., Bremerton, Wash., 1956; statistician USN, Bremerton, 1957-59; med. svcs. accounts officer U.S. Air Force, Vandenberg AFB, Calif., 1962-64; instr. bus. adminstrn. Western New Eng. Coll., 1967-69; vis. prof. econs. Chapman Coll., 1970; vis. prof. U. So. Calif. systems Griffith AFB, N.Y., 1971-72; assoc. prof., dir. adminstrn. mgmt. program Va. State U., 1973-74; assoc. prof. bus. adminstrn. Oreg. State U., Corvallis, 1974-81, prof. mgmt., 1982-90, emeritus prof. mgmt., 1990—, univ. curriculum coord., 1984-86, dir. adminstrv. mgmt. program, 1974-81, pres. Faculty Senate, 1981, Interinstl. Faculty Senate, 1986-90, pres., 1989-90; cons. process tech. devel. Digital Equipment Corp., 1982. Pres., chmn. bd. dirs. Adminstrv. Orgnl. Svcs.,Inc., Corvallis, 1976-83, Dynamic Achievement, Inc., 1983—; bd. dirs. Oreg. State U. Bookstores, Inc., 1987—. Cert. adminstrv. mgr. Pres. TYEE Mobil Home Park, Inc. Fellow Assn. Bus. Communication (mem. internat. bd. 1980-83, v.p. Northwest 1981, 2d v.p. 1982-83, 1st v.p. 1983-84, pres. 1984-85); mem. Am. Bus. Women's Assn. (chpt. v.p. 1979, pres. 1980, named Top Businesswoman in Nation 1980, Bus. Assoc. Yr. 1986), Assn. Info. Systems Profls., Adminstrv. Mgmt. Soc., AAUP (chpt. sec. 1973, chpt. bd. dirs. 1982, 84-89, pres. Oreg. conf. 1983-85), Am. Vocat. Assn. (nominating com. 1976), Associated Oreg. Faculties, Nat. Bus. Edn. Assn., Nat. Assn. Tchr. Edn. for Bus. Office Edn. (pres. 1976-77, chmn. public relations com. 1978-81), Corvallis Area C. of C. (v.p. chamber devel. 1987-88, pres. 1988-89, chmn. bd. 1989-90, Pres.' award 1986), Sigma Kappa. Roman Catholic. Lodge: Rotary. Contbr. numerous articles to profl. jours. Office: Oreg State U Coll Bus 1855 NW Division Pl Corvallis OR 97330

WELLS, RONA LEE, consumer products company executive; b. Beaumont, Tex., Aug. 23, 1950; d. Ray Peveto and Frances (Manning) Reed; m. Harry Hankins Wells, Mar. 22, 1975. BS in Systems Engring, So. Meth. U., 1972. Registered profl. engr., Tex. With initial mgmt. devel. program Southwestern Bell Corp., Houston, 1972-73, engr. and inventory coord., 1973-74, sr. engr. supr., 1974-75, engring. project supr., 1975-77, dist. supr. maj. project, 1977-79, dist. supr. materials, 1979; mgr. field svcs. CNA Fin. Corp., Chgo., 1979-80, mgr., asst. to v.p., 1980, area mgr. support svcs., 1980-82, area mgr. acctg. svcs., 1982; dir. bldg. and office mgmt. Kimberly-Clark Corp., Neenah, Wis., 1982-85; ops. specialist Kimberly-Clark Corp., New Milford, Conn., 1985-86, acting supt., 1985, project leader, 1985-88, ops. mgr., 1988-89; mill mgr. Kimberly-Clark Corp., Neenah, 1990—. Mem. Nat. Def. Exec. Res., Washington, 1979—; bd. dirs. Faulkner County United Way, 1989-90. Named one of Outstanding Young Women of Am., 1978. Mem. Inst. Indsl. Engrs. (sr.), Soc. Women Engrs. (sr.), NSPE, NAFE, Sigma Tau.

WELLS, ROSALIND LEA, economist; b. N.Y.C., Dec. 31, 1936; d. Joseph A. and Goldie (Fader) Leifer; m. Martin I. Roth, June 24, 1956 (div. 1967); children: Andrew, Karen; m. Alfred Newburgh, Feb. 26, 1984. BA magna cum laude, Queens Coll., N.Y.C., 1958; MA, Columbia U., 1960. Econ. analyst Boni, Watkins, Jason, N.Y.C., 1958-61, Exxon, N.Y.C., 1965-67, Citibank, N.Y.C., 1967-68; economist Union Carbide Petroleum, N.Y.C., 1968-71; mgr. econs. Monsanto Textiles, N.Y.C., 1971-78; chief economist J.C. Penney, N.Y.C., 1978-88; pres. Wells & Assocs., N.Y.C., 1988—; chief economist Nat. Retail Mchts. Assn., N.Y.C., 1988—. Mem. Nat. Assn. Bus. Economists, Nat. Bus. Econs. Coun., Retail Mktg. Soc., Textile Analysts Group, Forecasters Club (sec. N.Y. chpt. 1987). Home: 67-34 Juno St Forest Hills NY 11375 Office: Wells & Assocs Inc 875 Ave of the Americas New York NY 10001

WELLS, SANDRA, financial planner; b. Greensboro, N.C., Oct. 12, 1948; d. Kenneth F. and Carolyn A. (Schwartz) Bevan; children: Erick Rodney, Brett Gardner, Sara Elizabeth, Bryan Hamilton, Deborah Grace. BA, NYU, 1971. Cert. fin. planner, practitioner ednl. kinesiology. Mgmt. cons. Virginia Sandlin Assocs., N.Y.C.; fin. cons. N.Y. Adv. Group, Inc., Middletown; faculty mem., instr. quantum profits and creating fin. aliveness Starfire Inst. Bd. dirs. Ednl. Kinesiology Found. Mem. NAFE, Internat. Assn. Fin. Planners. Home: 142A Cragston Highland Falls NY 10928 Office: NY Adv Group Inc 200 Midway Park Dr Middletown NY 10940

WELLS-OWENS, SARAH JEAN, federal agency administrator; b. Memphis, Feb. 9, 1951; d. Taft and Sarah (Cousette) Wells; m. Edward Labron Owens, Sept. 1978 (div. 1983); 1 child, Sterling DeShawn. Student, Tuskegee (Ala.) Inst., 1972; BA in Sociology with honors, LeMoyne-Owen Coll., Memphis, 1973; postgrad., Memphis State U., 1977. Taxpayer svc. rep. IRS, Chattanooga, 1973-74; claims rep. Social Security Adminstrn., Memphis, 1974—; trainer in field. Author nat. TV announcement; contbr. articles to profl. jours. Active in Snowden Sch. PTA, Memphis, 1985—; vol. Memphis Bot. Gardens. Mem. NAFE, Nat. Fedn. Fed. Employees, Am. Assn. Baby Boomers, Greenpeace. Democrat. Baptist. Office: Social Security Adminstrn 1255 Alynnfield Rd #295 Memphis TN 38119

WELNA, SHARON KAY, data processing and finance executive; b. Omaha, Nebr., July 28, 1951; d. Raymond Arthur and Blanche June (Stahlecker) Wahlstrom; m. Gary Hunter Welna, Mar. 23, 1974; children: Matthew Aaron, Michael Arthur. BA, U. Nebr., 1973. Govt. intern State of Nebr., Lincoln, 1972-73; programmer Con Agra, Omaha, 1973-77; systems analyst Cen. Telephone, Lincoln, 1977-79; mgr. data processing St. Joseph Hosp., Omaha, 1979-88, dir. data processing and fin., 1988—. Editor: (book) County Boards Handbook, 1974. Mem. Assn. Systems Mgmt., Data Processing Mgmt. Assn. (exec. forum), NAFE, Hosp. Info. and Mgmt. Systems Soc., Delta Zelta. Republican. Lutheran. Office: St Joseph Hosp 601 N 30th St Omaha NE 68131

WELS, MARGUERITE SAMET (MRS. RICHARD H. WELS), interior decorator; b. N.Y.C.; d. Max and Bertha (Levine) Samet; student N.Y. U., 1937, N.Y. Sch. Interior Design, 1938-41; m. Richard H. Wels, Dec. 12, 1954; children—Susan Rebecca, Amy Elizabeth. Interior decorator—Marguerite Samet, N.Y.C., 1946-60; interior decorator, head Marguerite Samet Assos., 1960—; co-ordinator U.S. Army Spl. Services, 1942-46; cons. United Bowling Centers, Inc., Interboro Gen. Hosp. Active in William Alanson White Inst. Psychiatry, Psychoanalysis and Psychology, Am. Jewish Com., Islands Research Found. Mem. Am. Inst. Interior Designers (exec. bd., v.p. N.Y. Met. chpt.), Democratic Women's Workshop. Jewish. Clubs: Women's City, Woman Pays. Home: 480 Park Ave New York NY 10021

WELSH, DIANNE H.B., management educator, researcher; b. Peoria, Ill., Aug. 3, 1956; d. Holden Edward Sr. and Helen Gertrude (Bowker) W.; 1 child, Shannon Dianne Welsh-Cole; m. Clay S. Bleck, Aug. 5, 1990. BA in English, U. Iowa, 1978; MS in Indsl. Psychology, Emporia (Kans.) State U., 1984; PhD in Bus. Adminstrn., U. Nebr., 1988. Personnel exec. collegiate assns. coun. U. Iowa, Iowa City, 1976-78; sales rep. Boyt Div., Iowa Falls, Iowa, 1970-78, George A. Hormel, Kansas City, Mo., 1978-82; analyst intern St. Mary's Hosp., Emporia, 1984; teaching asst. U. Nebr., Lincoln, 1985-87; asst. prof. mgmt. Eastern Wash. U., Cheney and Spokane, 1988—; rsch. asst. U. Nebr., 1985-87; cons. Burger King dba Cormack Enterprises, Inc., Lincoln, 1987-88, Internat. Ambassadors, Spokane, 1988-89. Contbg. author: Real Managers, 1988. Coord. rsch. luncheons Ea. Wash. U. Sch. Bus., Cheney, 1988-89; nat. del. Air Force Spl. Educators Tour, San Antonio, 1989; elem. tchr. St. Rose Cath. Ch., Cheney, 1988-89; mgmt. faculty rep. acad. senate Ea. Wash. U., 1988-89. Mem. Acad. Mgmt. (consortium rep. 1987), Indsl. Rels. Rsch. Assn., U. Nebr. Alumni Assn., U. Iowa Alumni Assn., Alpha Xi Delta, Psi Chi. Roman Catholic. Office: Ea Wash U Dept Mgmt MS46 Cheney WA 99004

WELSH, DONNA BARHAM, actuarial consulting executive; b. Aberdeen, Md., Aug. 16, 1956; d. John Ernest and Carol Marie (Preston) Barham; m. James Howard Welsh, Oct. 18, 1980; 1 child, Megan McKenzie. BS, U. Md., 1978. Qualified pension administr. Actuarial analyst S.M. Hyman Co., Balt., 1978-79; plan adminstr. The Stuart Hack Co., Balt., 1979-80, account mgr., 1980-81, account exec., 1981-83, mgr. plan adminstrn., 1983-84, dept. head plan design, 1984-85, owner, exec. v.p., 1985—. Mem. NAFE, Am. Soc. Pension Actuaries (assoc.), Md. State Bar Assn. (employee benefits subcom.), Alpha Xi Delta. Democrat. Roman Catholic. Home: 4238 Darleigh Rd Baltimore MD 21236 Office: The Stuart Hack Co 4623 Falls Rd Baltimore MD 21209

WELSH, J. ERICA, executive secretary; b. Livingstone, Zambia, Mar. 7, 1947; d. Eric Russell and Alice Henrietta (Keal) W. AA, Ala. Christian Coll., 1976; BA, Lubbock Christain U., 1978; postgrad., Abilene Christain U., 1990—. Sec. Joe Mabee Ranch and Classic Aero, Inc., Midland, Tex.; found. rsch. asst. to vice chancellor Abilene (Tex.) Christian U.; exec. asst., sec. J.E. and L.E. Mabee Found., Midland. Recipient Senator James Allen Leadership award; George Taylor scholar. Mem. NAFE, The Single Life Inst., Alpha Chi.

WELSH, JUDITH SCHENCK, educator; b. Patchogue, L.I., N.Y., Feb. 5, 1939; d. Frank W. and Muriel (Whitman) Schenck; B.Ed., U. Miami (Fla.), 1961, M.A. in English, 1968; m. Robert C. Welsh, Sept. 16, 1961; children: Derek Francis, Christopher Lord. Co-organizer Cataract Surg. Congress med. meetings, 1963-76; grad. asst. instr. Dale Carnegie Courses Internat., 1967; adminstr. Office Admissions, Bauder Fashion Coll., Miami, 1976-77, instr. communications, 1977—, also pub. coll. monthly paper; freelance writer regional and nat. publs.; guest speaker Optifair Internat., N.Y.C., 1980; guest speaker, mem. seminar faculty Optifair West, Anaheim, Calif., 1980, Optifair Midwest, St. Louis, 1980, Face to Face, Kansas City, Mo., 1981. Mem. NAFE, Fla. Freelance Writers Assn., Nat. Writers Club (award), Delta Gamma. Congregationalist. Clubs: Coral Reef Yacht, Riviera Country, Royal Palm Tennis. Co-editor: The New Report on Cataract Surgery, 1969, Second Report on Cataract Surgery, 1974; editor: Surgidev's Cataract Surgery N.O.W., 1982—; contbr. Miami Today, 1985—, Ft. Lauderdale Sun/Sentinel, 1986—, Prime Times, Club Life, Gainesville Sun, The Oklahoman, South Fla. mag. Home: 1600 Onaway Dr Miami FL 33133 Office: 1600 Onaway Dr Miami FL 33133

WELSH, RITA MAY, probation officer; b. San Mateo, Calif., Dec. 20, 1942; d. Albert Edward and May (Chan) Wong; m. David Joseph Welsh, July 3, 1982. AA, Foothill Jr. Coll., 1967; BA in Social Svcs., San Jose State U., 1969, MS, 1980. Cert. community coll. tchr., Calif. Bookkeeper Avco Thrift, Campbell, Calif., 1969-70; eligibility worker County of Santa Clara, San Jose, Calif., 1970-72; dep. probation officer, probation dept. County of Santa Clara, 1972—. Mem. altar guild, Trinity Episcopal Ch., San Jose, 1988—; vol., San Jose Mus. Art, 1988—. Mem. Calif. Probation and Parole Assn. (treas. 1983, sec. 1984). Republican.

WELSH, SACHIKO ANN, media specialist, librarian, language educator; b. Tokyo, Feb. 10, 1931; came to U.S., 1957; d. Makizo and Tama (Takino) Kasama; m. Kenneth A. Welsh, Apr. 26, 1956 (div. 1988); children: Kay Dianne, June Joanne, Kim Susanne Welsh Hajaistron. AA, Miami-Dade Community Coll., 1975; B Gen. Studies cum laude, U. Miami, Coral Gables, Fla., 1978; MLS, Fla. State U., 1981. Cert. tchr., sch. libr., Fla. Sec. CBS-TV, NBC-TV and UPS, Tokyo, 1950-53; adminstrv. asst. USIA, Tokyo, 1953-56; media clk. Dade County Pub. Schs., Miami, 1969-79, computer edn. tchr., 1981-85, fgn. lang. tchr., 1985—, media specialist, 1979—; freelance translator, Miami, 1977—. Contbr. articles to profl. jours. Fulbright scholar U.S. Dept. Edn., Japan, 1986. Mem. AAUW, Fla. Assn. Media in Edn., Japan-Am. Soc. South Fla., Fulbright Alumni Assn., Dade County Media Specialist Assn., Fla. state U. Alumni Assn., U. Miami Alumni Assn. Democrat. Home: 13703 SW 101st Ter Miami FL 33186 Office: Southwood Middle Sch 16301 SW 80th Ave Miami FL 33157

WELSH, SUZANNE P., treasurer; b. Phila., Mar. 20, 1953; d. David Lee and Harriet (Roberts) Painter; m. Robert E. Welsh Jr., Jan. 12, 1980; children: EMily, Elizabeth, Mary. BS in Acctg., U. Del., 1975, BA in Math., 1975; MBA, U. Pa., 1976. Fin. mgr. DuPont Co., Wilmington, Del., 1976-83; asst. treas. Swarthmore (Pa.) Coll., 1983—; treas. Swarthmore Coll., 1989—. Treas. Trinity Coop. Day Nursery, Swarthmore, 1984-88. Mem. Nat. Assn. Coll. and Univ. Bus. Officers. Home: 316 N Princeton Ave Swarthmore PA 19081 Office: Swarthmore Coll Swarthmore PA 19081

WELTER, VANESSA MARIE, public relations specialist; b. Ft. Worth, Dec. 31, 1959; d. Leo Richard and Mary Ellen (O'Connell) W. BS in Journalism, U. Wis.-Milw., 1986. Mgr. LaPlaya Marcus Corp., Milw., 1983, 84; pub. rels. specialist Vol. Ctr. Inc., Milw., 1987; communications specialist ARC, Greater Milw., 1987-89; pub. rels. writer Curative Rehab. Ctr., Wauwatosa, Wis., 1989—. Editor: mag. Crossties, 1988 (recipient Nat. Clarion Award for Excellence in Non-Profit Communication, Nat. Award ARC "Star Search", 1989). Mem. Women in Communications Inc., Internat. Assn. of Bus. Communicators, Health Care, Pub. Rels. and Mktg. Soc. Home: 4378 N Wilson Dr #2 Shorewood WI 53211 Office: Curative Rehab Ctr 1000 N 92d St Wauwatosa WI 53226

WELTON, LYNN, mechanical engineer; b. Ft. Worth, Dec. 21, 1960; d. Ralph E. and Francis Joyce (Casburn) W. BSME, Tex. Tech. U., 1984. Engr.-in-tng. Mech. engr. Fed. Aviation Adminstrn., Ft. Worth, 1984—. Mem. ASHRAE, NPSE, ASME, Tex. Tech Ex-Students Assn. Office: Fed Aviation Adminstrn DOT/FAA Fort Worth TX 76193-0441

WELTY, EUDORA, author; b. Jackson, Miss.; d. Christian Webb and Chestina (Andrews) W. Student, Miss. State Coll. for Women; B.A., U. Wis., 1929; postgrad., Columbia Sch. Advt., 1930-31. Author: A Curtain of Green, 1941, The Robber Bridegroom, 1942, The Wide Net, 1943, Delta Wedding, 1946, The Golden Apples, 1949, The Ponder Heart, 1954, The Bride of the Innisfallen, 1955, The Shoe Bird, 1964, Losing Battles, 1970, One Time, One Place, 1971, The Optimist's Daughter, 1972 (Pulitzer prize 1973), The Eye of the Story, 1978, The Collected Stories of Eudora Welty, 1980, One Writer's Beginnings, 1985; contbr.: New Yorker. Recipient creative arts medal for fiction Brandeis U., 1966, Nat. Inst. Arts and Letters Gold Medal, 1972, Nat. Medal for Lit., 1980, Presdl. Medal of Freedom, 1980, Commonwealth medal, 1984, Nat. Medal of Arts, 1987; Chevalier de l'Ordre des Arts et Lettres (France), 1987. Mem. Am. Acad. Arts and Letters. Home: 1119 Pinehurst St Jackson MS 39202

WEMPLE, DONNA WACHTER, obstetrician/gynecologist; b. Frederick, Md., Sept. 17, 1944; d. Elmer Elroy and Lois Katharyn (Shaw) Wachter; m. Christopher Yates Wemple, June 13, 1964 (div. Sept. 1989); children: Christopher Yates Wemple III, Jonathan Barent Wemple; m. Leonard Dean Turner, Oct. 14, 1989. BS, U. Md., 1973; MD, George Washington U., 1978. Attending physician Washington Adventist Hosp., Takoma Park, Md., 1983—; attending physician Holy Cross Hosp., Silver Spring, Md., 1984—. Fellow Am. Coll. Obstetrics and Gynecology; mem. AMA. Office: 12200 Tech Rd #340 Silver Spring MD 20904

WENC, KAREN MARIE, cell biologist, researcher; b. Springfield, Mass., May 2, 1954; d. Joseph John and Mildred Mary (Orzech) W. Student, Boston U., 1972-73; AB, Smith Coll., 1976. Research asst. Yale U. Sch. Medicine, New Haven, Conn., 1976-78, Mass. Gen. Hosp., Boston, 1978-80, Beth Israel Hosp., Boston, 1980-85; research assoc. St. Elizabeth's Hosp., Boston, 1985—. Mem. Brookline Town Meeting, Mass., 1985—; bd. dirs. treas. Mass. Jobs With Peace, Boston, 1986—; mem. Adv. Council Pub. Health, Brookline, 1986—. Democrat. Home: 439 Washington St Apt #1 Brookline MA 02146 Office: St Elizabeth's Hosp Biomed Research 736 Cambridge St Boston MA 02135

WEND, JOANNE LENORE, accountant; b. Detroit, Nov. 26, 1960; d. Joseph H. and Eleanor Marie (Hadock) Denys; m. Dennis James Wend, Oct. 8, 1982. BBA in Acctg., Detroit Inst. Tech., 1981. Bookkeeper Swick Bus.

Assocs., St. Clair Shores, Mich., 1978-80; cashier St. Joseph Hosp., Mt. Clemens, Mich., 1981-82, jr. acct., 1983-84; acct. Detroit Macomb Hosp. Corp., 1984-85; sr. budget analyst Pontiac (Mich.) Osteo. Hosp., 1986-88; contr. Annie's House Inc., Birmingham, Mich., 1989-90; owner Automated Fin. Svcs., East Detroit, 1989—. Vol. PIME Missionaires, Fraser, Mich., 1985—. Mem. Nat. Assn. Female Execs., Healthcare Fin. Mgmt. Assn. Roman Catholic. Home: 1546 S Barlett Rd Saint Clair MI 48079 Office: Automated Fin Svcs Saint Clair MI 48079

WENDEL, FAYE F., equipment manufacturing executive; b. Newark, Sept. 16, 1928; d. John Thomas and Sara Rose (Agliozzo) Fiorenza; m. Daniel C. Wendel, Nov. 26, 1949; children: Catherine C., Daniel C. III, Wayne J. Sec., P. Ballantine & Sons, Newark, 1946-49; head hostess, asst. to mgr. Bambergers-Carriage House Restaurant, 1971-74; sec. Peter Wendel & Sons, Inc., Irvington, N.J., 1961-78; sec. Wendel Industries, Inc., Union, N.J., 1978-80, pres., 1980—; pres. D.C. Wendel Corp., 1982—; mem. adv. bd. State Bank South Orange, N.J. Tchrs. aide St. Ann Sch.; asst. treas. Ladies Aux. St. Rose of Lima Ch., 1963. Mem. Short Hills Assn., Twig Group of Overlook Hosp., Rotary Assn., Am. Soc. Profl. and Exec. Women, Republican Club, Short Hills Racquet Club. Home: 33 Quaker Rd Short Hills NJ 07078 Office: 1012 Greeley Ave N Union NJ 07083

WENDEL, PAMELA L., auditor, banker; b. St. Albans, N.Y., Aug. 18, 1960; d. Henry H.H. and Lois H. (Paul) Plehn; m. William A. Wendel, June 28, 1980. Diploma, Am. Bankers Assn. Nat. Compliance Sch., Norman, Okla., 1983; diploma in audit mgmt., Sch. for Bank Adminstrn., Madison, Wis., 1989. Compliance officer Creditbank, Miami, Fla., 1983-86, internal auditor, 1983-87; internal auditor Megabank, Miami, 1987—. Mem. Fin. Women Internat. (pres. 1990-91, formerly Nat. Assn. Bank Women), Bank Adminstrn. Inst. (bd. dirs. South Fla. chpt. 1989—, Chuck Myers scholar 1987), South Dade Bankers Assn. (chmn. 1985-87), South Fla. Compliance Assn., NAFE, Inst. Internal Auditors (bd. govs., chmn. Speakers Bur. 1989-90), Fin. Women Internat. (pres. 1990-91). Office: Megabank 11430 N Kendall Dr Miami FL 33176

WENDELL, PATRICIA LYNN, human resources executive. BA, U. at Albany, 1974; MBA, Russell Sage Coll., 1987. Cert. employee benefits specialist. Sr. cons. Peat Marwick Main & Co., Albany, N.Y., 1974-81; pension svcs. adminstr. Nat. Savs. Bank, Albany, 1981; benefits mgr. Garden Way Inc., Troy, N.Y., 1982—. Mem. cert. employee benefits specialists adv. bd. Coll. of St. Rose, Albany, 1989—; mem. MBA adv. bd. Russell Sage Coll., Albany, 1989—; bd. dirs. Rensselaer County Chamber, Troy, 1986—; chair personnel com. Rensselaer County Arts Coun., Troy, 1988—. Mem. Internat. Soc. Cert. Employee Benefits Specialists. Office: Garden Way Inc 102nd St and 9th Ave Troy NY 12180

WENDLETON, TINA LYNNE, small business owner; b. Wichita, Kans., Nov. 17, 1961; d. James Emmett and Betty Louise (Somers) Martin; m. Ronald Roy Wendleton Jr., June 4, 1989. Grad. high sch., Candler, N.C. Asst. chef Biltmore Village Inn, Asheville, N.C., 1980-81; snack bar cook Pisgah Inn, Waynesville, N.C., 1981; sous chef Point Restaurant, Sheffield, Ala., 1984-85; cook, asst. to owner Court 9 Restaurant, Florence, Ala., 1985-86; cook Pizza Hut, Florence, 1986; owner Four Seasons Bistro, Florence, 1986-87; with food bar Bonanza Restaurant, Florence, 1988. Seventh Day Adventist. Home: 2630 Salem Joplin MO 64801

WENDLING, ELIZABETH LOUISE, electronics technician; b. Cleve., Aug. 13, 1949; d. Leroy A. and Annette Louise (Day) W. Student, Women's Tech. Inst., 1986, Women's Tech. Inst., 1988—, Total Tech. Inst., 1987. Constrn. clk. Ohio Bell Telephone, Cleve., 1972-81; inventory control Bobbie Brooks, Cleve., 1982-83; svc. order asst. New England Telephone, Boston, 1983-86; toner development tech. Delphax Systems, Randolph, Mass., 1986; cen. office tech. New England Telephone, Boston, 1987—; reviewer IEEE Computer Dictionary Project, Washington, 1986—. Table leader St. Basil Parish Renewal, Brecksville, 1979. Roman Catholic. Office: New England Telephone 41 Belvidere St 3rd Fl Boston MA 02115

WENDROW, SYLVIA DIANN, speech and language pathologist; b. Ann Arbor, Mich.; d. Barnaby Alex and Margaret (Myers) W. AB, U. Mich., 1959, MS, 1963. Speech pathologist Lenawee Intermediate Sch. Dist., Adrian, Mich., 1959—; critic tchr. U. Mich., Ann Arbor, Mich., 1966-69; guest lectr. Adrian Coll., 1984; speech cons. Adrian Community Nursery, 1969-70. Sec., bd. dirs., performer Lenawee Pops Orch., Adrian, 1970-74; bd. dirs. Lenawee Community Concert Assn., Adrian, 1969-78. Named Spl. Edn. Itinerant Tchr. of Yr., 1990. Mem. Mich. Speech-Lang.-Hearing Assn., Am. Speech-Lang.-Hearing Assn. (Continuing Edn. award 1990), Lenawee Intermediate Edn. Assn., Mich. Edn. Assn., NEA, AAUW (pres. 1966-68, bd. dirs.), LWV (bd. dirs. Lenawee chpt. 1974-78), Sigma Alpha Iota. Office: Lenawee Schs Spl Edn Ctr 2946 Sutton Rd Adrian MI 49221

WENGER, DOROTHY MAE, retired dietitian; b. Rozel, Kans., Jan. 20, 1917; d. John Edward and Irene Margaret (McElroy) Franz; m. Edward Lawrence Wenger (dec.); 1 child, Edward Lawrence III. Student, Iowa State Tchrs. Coll., Cedar Falls, 1937-39; BS, Lindenwood Coll. for Women, St. Charles, Mo., 1940; postgrad., U. W.Va., 1941, Columbia U., 1945, 47. Registered dietitian. Dietetic intern Mayo Clinic, Rochester, Minn., 1941, Western Pa. Hosp., Pitts., 1941-42; head dietitian, dir. dept. St. Luke's Hosp., Bluefield, W.Va., 1942-44, Monongalia Gen. Hosp., Morgantown, W.Va., 1944-49, Elyria (Ohio) Meml. Hosp., 1949-57; chief dietitian Lakewood Hosp., Cleve., 1957-58; dir. dietary dept. Beach Hosp., Ft. Lauderdale, Fla., 1959-61, North Broward Med. Ctr., Pompano Beach, Fla., 1961-75; chief dietitian North Broward Med. Ctr., Pompano Beach, 1975-89; ret., 1989; supr. clin. practicum program for student from various schs. including Atlantic Vocat. Sch., Broward Community Coll., Fla. Internat. Coll.; community nutrition lectr. North Broward County Hosp. Dist., 1985-89. Developer dietetic course programs for various levels. Guidance vol. children and adults with Dyslexia, 1965—; lector Episcopal Ch., 1986—, Episcopal Cursillista, 1990. Mem. Am. Dietetic Assn., Tri-county Clin. Mgrs., W.Va. Dietetic Assn. (state pres. 1942-44), Greater Miami Dietetic Assn. (adv. com. for dietetic tech. 1974-80), Cons. Dietitians for Long Term Facilities (Fla. state dietetic rep. 1978-79), Fla. Dietetic Assn. (chmn. dist. edn. com. 1975-77), Nat. Honor Soc. (Norfolk, Nebr.), Quota Club (Morgantown), Triangle Club (St. Charles).

WENGER, VICKI, interior designer; b. Indpls., Aug. 30, 1928. Ed., U. Nebr., Internat. Inst. Interior Design, Parsons in Paris. Pres. Vicki Wenger Interiors, Bethesda, Md., 1963-71, Washington, 1982—; pres. Beautiful Spaces Inc., Washington, 1982—; chief designer Creative Design, Capitol Heights, Md., 1969-84; lectr. Nat. Assn. Home Builders, 1983-88; mem. programs com. D.C. Assn. Home Builders, 1983-88. Author-host: (patented TV interior design show) Beautiful Spaces 1984; producer, host (cable TV show) Design Edition, 1988—. Designer Gourmet Gala, March of Dimes, Washington, 1986-88; designer and decorator showhouse Nat. Symphony Orch., Washington, 1983-88, Am. Cancer Soc., Washington, 1983, Alexandria Community YWCA, 1990. Mem. Am. Soc. Interior Designers (profl. mem. 1973—; mem. nat. bd. 1973-75, nat. examining com. 1977-78, pres. Md. chpt. 1976, bd. dirs. D.C. chpt., mem. president's barrier free com. 1980), Nat. Trust Hist. Preservation, Smithsonian Instn. (sponsor), Friends of Corcoran Mus. (sponsor), Friends of Kennedy Ctr., Friends of Vieilles Maisons Françaises, Pisces Club (Washington). Democrat. Presbyterian. Office: Vicki Wenger Interiors 2801 New Mexico NW Washington DC 20007

WENIG, MARY MOERS, law educator; b. N.Y.C.; d. Robert and Celia Lewis (Kauffman) Moers; m. Jerome Wenig, Dec. 19, 1946; children: Margaret Moers Wenig Rubenstein, Michael M. Wenig. BA, Vassar Coll., 1946; JD, Columbia U., 1951. Bar: N.Y. 1952, U.S. Ct. Appeals (2d cir.) 1954, U.S. Dist. Ct. (so. dist.) N.Y. 1956, Conn. 1977. Assoc. Cahill, Gordon, Reindel & Ohl, N.Y.C., 1951-57; assoc. Greenbaum, Wolff & Ernst, N.Y.C., 1957-60, Skadden, Arps, Slate, Meagher & Flom, N.Y.C., 1960-71; asst. prof. sch. law St. John's U., N.Y.C., 1971-75, assoc. prof. sch. law, 1975-78; rsch. affiliate Yale Law Sch., New Haven, 1978-79; prof. sch. law U. Bridgeport (Conn.), 1978-82, Charles A. Dana prof. law, 1982—; cons. The Merrill Anderson Co., Stratford, Conn., 1982—, Conn. Permanent Commn. on Status of Women, 1978-79; vis. prof. sch. law Pace U., White Plains, N.Y., 1979; bd. dirs. Tax Analysts/TAX NOTES, Fairfax, N.Y., 1980—; bd. dirs., pres. Conn. Women's Ednl. & Legal Fund, Inc., New Haven, 1973; commr. State of Conn. Permanent Commn. on Status of Women, 1987—; mem. Conn. Gen. Assembly's Adv. Commn. to Study the Uniform Marital Property's Act, 1985-86; lectr. in field. Editor: PLI Tax Handbooks, 1978-86; co-editor: Bittker, Fundamentals of Federal Income Taxation , 1983; co-author: (with Douthwaite) Unmarried Couples and the Law, 1979; contbr. tax, estate planning, trust and estates and marital property articles to profl. jours.; editorial adv. bd. Estate Planning for the Elderly & Disabled, 1987—, Community Property Jour., 1986-88, Estate Planning, 1975—, Estates, Gifts & Trusts Jour., 1976—. Mem. probate com. Conn. Law Revision Commn., 1985—, com. to study the probate system Conn. Probate Assembly, 1988—, task force on the legal rights of women in marriage NOW, 1987—; 2nd cir. rep. Fedn. of Women Lawyers Jud. Screening Panel, 1979; bd. govs. Radcliffe Club N.Y., 1975-77; mem. 1st selectman's com. on taxation relief for the elderly Town of Westport, 1974-75; pres. bd. dirs. Conn. Women's Ednl. and Legal Fund, Inc., 1975-79, bd. dirs., 1973-79. Named Salute to Women honoree Outstainding Women of Conn., Greater Bridgeport YWCA, 1990, Women in Leadership honoree New Haven YWCA, 1979, honoree U. Bridgeport Sch. Law Women's Law Assn., 1990; Harlan Fiske Stone scholar Columbia U. Sch. Law, 1949; recipient Award for Equality United Nations Assn.-USA of Conn., 1987; Summer Stipend grantee NEH, 1984, rsch. grantee Conn. Bar Found., 1980. Fellow Am. Coll. Trust & Estate Counsel (bd. regents 1985—); mem. ABA (adisor to NCCUSL 1980-84, sect. council mem. 1970-72), Internat. Acad. Estates & Trust Law (academician), Conn. Bar Assn. (sects.' exec. econs., Disting. Svc. commendation 1977), Assn. Am. Law Schs., Assn. of Bar of City of N.Y., Conn. Estate & Tax Planning Coun., N.Y. State Bar Assn., Am. Law Inst. (hon.), Am. Coll. Trust and Estate Counsel (hon.), Am. Coll. Tax Counsel (hon.), Internat. Acad. Estate & Trusts Law (hon.). Democrat. Jewish. Home: 5 Lamplight Ln Westport CT 06880 Office: U Bridgeport School of Law 303 University Ave Bridgeport CT 06601

WENIGER, NELL, school system administrator; b. Groom, Tex., July 20, 1931; d. George Richardson and Nelle Estelle (Hess) Baucum; m. Delbert Kenneth, May 23, 1954; 1 child, Andrew Alan. BS, Okla. Panhandle State U., Goodwell, 1953; MEd, Our Lady of the Lake U., San Antonio, 1965. Tchr. San Antonio Montessori Sch., 1962-64, head tchr., 1964-66; head mistress Children's House & Montessori Sch., San Antonio, 1967-78; vol. Mus., San Antonio; cons. Self-Employed, 1978-80; library dir. Comfort Pub. Library, Tex., 1980-88; exec. dir. Montessori Sch. of Raleigh, N.C., 1988; bd. dirs. Children's House & Montessori Sch., San Antonio, 1988; workshop presenter N. Am. Montessori Tchrs. Assn., 1975-80; art cons. Assn. Montessori Internat.. Author: Art Activities in Montessori, 1975. Vice-pres. Kendall County Hist. Com., 1982-88; Sesquicentennial Com. Comfort C. of C., 1985-86. Recipient Pres. award Comfort C. of C., 1986, Tex. Historical Commn., 1985-87. Mem. Montessori Adminstrs. Coun., N. Am. Montessori Tchrs. Assn. (life mem.), Am. Montessori Soc., Assn. Montessori Internat. (life mem.), Literary Social. United Methodist. Office: Montessori Sch of Raleigh 7005 Lead Mine Rd Raleigh NC 27615

WENNER, LETTIE MCSPADDEN, political science educator; b. Battle Creek, Mich., Apr. 9, 1937; d. John Dean and Isma Doolie (Sullivan) McSpadden; m. Manfred Wilhelm Wenner, Apr. 3, 1962; children: Eric Alexis, Adrian Edward. AB, U. Chgo., 1959; MA, U. Calif., Berkeley, 1962; PhD, U. Wis., 1972. Fgn. svc. officer Dept. State, Washington, 1961-63; rsch. assoc. Dept. HEW, Washington, 1965-67; asst. prof. polit. sci. U. Ill., Chgo., 1972-79, assoc. prof. polit. sci., 1979-88; prof. and chair dept. polit. sci. No. Ill. U., De Kalb, 1988—. Author: One Environment Under Law, 1976, The Environmental Decade in Court, 1982. Mem. LWV (natural resources chair), Am. Polit. Sci. Assn., Midwest Polit. Sci. Assn., Law and Soc., Pub. Policy Assn., Audubon Soc., Sierra Club. Democrat. Home: 440 Flock Ave Naperville IL 60565 Office: No Ill U Dept Polit Sci De Kalb IL 60115

WENNHOLD, ANN RUHMANN, psychiatrist, educator; b. N.Y.C., June 12, 1932; d. Warren Howard and Gertrude Ann (Oldis) Ruhmann; m. Phil Wennhold, Apr. 8, 1967; children: Kim, BJ. BA with honors, Seton Hill Coll., Greensburg, Pa., 1954; MD, SUNY, Bklyn., 1958. Diplomate Am. Bd. Psychiatry and Neurology. Resident in medicine U. Utah Hosps., Salt Lake City, 1959-60; USPHS rsch. fellow radiobiology lab. U. Utah, Salt Lake City, 1960-63; dir. RIA Lab. LDS Hosp., Salt Lake City, 1974-82; from instr. to assoc. prof. dept. anatomy and medicine U. Utah Coll. Medicine, 1965-82, chief resident psychiatry, 1984, asst. prof. psychiatry, 1984-89, assoc. prof., 1989—, asst. dean student affairs, 1990—; staff psychiatrist Salt Lake VA Med. Ctr., Salt Lake City, 1984—; mem. instl. rev. bd., dir. psychiatry clerkships U. Utah, 1988—. Contbr. articles to med. jours., chpts. to books. Fellow Tobacco Industries, SUNY, 1955, Josiah Macy Found., 1956, 58. Mem. Am. Fedn. Clin. Rsch., Utah Med. Soc., Salt Lake County Med. Soc., Western Soc. Clin. Investigation, Wasatch Mountain Club. Office: Salt Lake VA Med Ctr 500 Foothill Blvd Salt Lake City UT 84148

WENNLUND, DOLORES MARIE, health and rehabilitation services executive; b. Bronx, N.Y., May 17, 1922; d. John J. and Grace R. (Horgan) Neyland; m. Lester E. Wennlund, Apr. 6, 1946; children: Gerald, John. BS in Nursing cum laude, St. John's U., 1960, MS in Pub. Health, 1962. RN, N.Y. Cons. health and rehab. svcs. Dept. Health and Rehab. Svc., State Health Office, Tallahassee, 1970-74, dir. of nursing svcs., 1974-89; ret. adj. asst. prof. U. Fla, Gainesville; nursing cons. State Div. of Health, Jacksonville, Fla.; asst. prof. Adelphi U., Garden City, N.Y. Author: Preventive Health Services for the Elderly, 1987, Lay Midwifery, 1979, Public Health Nursing Services for School Children, 1977. 1st lt. U.S. Army Nurse Corps, 1943-46. Recipient Ruth B. Freeman award Am. Pub. Health Assn. Mem. Nat. League for Nursing, Am. Nurses Assn., Assn. of State and Territorial dirs. of Nursing (sec. and treas.), Sigma Theta Tau.

WENTLING, ROSE MARY, business educator, consultant, researcher; b. Trinidad, Colo., July 27, 1955; d. Cruz and Ruth (Sanchez) Cordova; m. Tim L. Wentling, Dec. 10, 1983; 1 child, Kimberly R. AA, Otero Jr. Coll., La Junta, Colo., 1975; BA, U. No. Colo., 1976, MA, 1977; PhD, U. Ill., Champaign, 1982; post doctorate, Inst. Edn. Leadership, Washington, 1983. Bus. tchr. Aims Community Coll., Greeley, Colo., 1977-78, Loveland (Colo.) High Sch., 1978-79; grad. rsch. assoc. U. No. Colo., Greeley, 1977-78; grad. rsch. assoc. U. Ill., Champaign, 1979-80, assoc. project dir., 1980-82, vis. asst. prof., 1981-83; field ops. coord. Evaluation Cons., Champaign, 1983-84; asst. prof. U. Wis., Madison, 1984-85; assoc. prof. Ill. State U., Normal, 1985-90, prof., 1990—; cons. Western Ill. U., Macomb, 1982-83, N.W. Ednl. Coop., Arlington Heights, Ill., 1982-84, Calif. State U., Northridge, 1984-85, Small Bus. Devel. Ctr., Madison, 1984-85. Contbr. articles to profl. jours. Recipient scholarship La Junta C. of C., 1973, Grad. Leadership Devel. fellowship U. Ill, 1979, Ednl. Policy fellowship Inst. Ednl. Leadership, Washington, 1982. Mem. Inter. Soc. Bus. Edn., Nat. Bus. Edn. Assn., Am. Ednl. Rsch. Assn., Omicron Tau Theta (sec. 1980), Delta Pi Epsilon (advisor- sponsor 1984—). Democrat. Baptist. Home: 1010 Hadley Dr Champaign IL 61821 Office: Ill State U Coll Bus Williams Hall 130 Normal IL 61761

WENTWORTH, MALINDA ANN NACHMAN, real estate, small business owner; b. Greenville, S.C.; d. Mordecai and Frances (Brown) Nachman; m. William A. Wentworth, June 22, 1964; children: William Allen Jr., Linda Ann. BBA, U. Miami, 1960. Registered rep. brokerage, real estate broker. Personnel Mgrs. Asst. Jordan March, Miami, 1960-61; stock broker Barron & Co., Inc., Greenville, 1961-64; real estate agt. Par Realty, Inc., Conyers, Ga., 1969-72; real estate broker Par Realty, Inc., Conyers, 1972-83; owner/ops. Rockdale Cablevision, Conyers, 1979-83; real estate broker Coldwell Banker, Conyers, 1983-85; owner/ops. Wentworth's Gym & Fitness Ctr., Conyers, 1981—; real estate broker First Realty, Conyers, 1981-89; ptnr. and dir. Santa Barbara (Calif.) Cellular Systems, Inc., 1986-89; v.p. Santa Barbara Cellular Systems, Inc., Atlanta, 1986-87. Producer and dir.: local sport events on cable to sta., 1979, '80, '81, '87. Founding dir., past pres. Porterdale PTO, 1972-79; mem. Nat. Cable TV Assn., 1979-83, pres. Unity Ch. of Rockdale, Conyers, 1984-85, dir., 1984-89. Named Lt. Col.--Aide-De-Camp, Gov. Staff, state of Ga., Gov. George Bushee, 1979, Appreciation Plaque award, Rockdale County High Sch. Football, 1987. Mem. Nat. Health & Strength Assn., Rockdale County Bd. of Realtors, Cellular Telephone Industry Assn., Rockdale County C. of C.

WENZEL, SALLY ELLEN, physician; b. Milw., July 12, 1956; d. Frederick Edward and Dorothy Louise (Recknagel) W. BS, U. Fla., 1978, MD, 1981. Diplomate Am. Bd. Internal Medicine. Intern N.C. Bapt. Hosp., Winston-Salem, 1981-82, resident, 1982-84; fellow Med. Coll. Va., Richmond, 1984-86, inst., 1986-87; inst. Nat. Jewish Ctr. for Immunology and Respiratory Medicine, Denver, 1987-88, asst. prof., 1988—. Contbr. articles to profl. jours. Vol. Stout St. Med. Clinic, Denver, 1988—. Mem. Am. Coll. Physicians, Am. Coll. Chest Physicians, Am. Thoracic Soc. Democrat. Lutheran. Office: Nat Jewish Ctr Immunology 1400 Jackson St Denver CO 80224

WERA, ANNE REGINA, elementary and secondary educator; b. Winona, Minn., June 1, 1936; d. Bernard Stanislaus and Alvina Anne (Konter) W. BA, Viterbo Coll., 1958; MusM, U. Minn., 1960; PhD, U. Iowa, 1969; MA in Edn. Administrn., Loras Coll., 1989. Cert. sch. supt., Wis., Ill., Iowa, Minn.; music educator, Iowa, Ill., Wis., Minn.; K-12 adminstr. Mid. sch. educator Logan Mid. Sch., LaCrosse, Wis., 1958-60; asst. to supr. music various schs., LaCrosse, 1960-64; acting head music U. Nev., Reno, 1965-66; asst. prof. U. Whitewater & River Falls, Wis., 1966-67; intern secondary adminstrn. Dubuque (Iowa) High Sch., 1973-74; regional supt. cons. Jo Davies County Sch. System, Galena, Ill., 1977-78; pers. head, asst. condr. Nat. Am. Youth Symphony & Chorus U.S.A., Duquaine U., Pitts., 1979-83; music specialist Dubuque (Iowa) Pub. Schs., 1968-87; tchr., long term substitute, music cons. West Salem and LaCross Schs., Lake Crescent, Wis., 1986—. Mem. Phi Delta Kappa, Am. Assn. Sch. Adminstrn., Nat. Assn. Secondary Sch. Principals, Assn. Supr. & Curriculum Devel., I./D./E./A., Wis. Sch. Music Assn. Home: 1008 LaCrosse St Onalaska WI 54650

WERBIL, JENNIFER LEE VINSON, publications director, educator; b. Anderson, Ind., Jan. 8, 1952; d. Theodore Fredrick and Eleanor Lee (Crecelius) Vinson; m. David Olin Werbil, May 22, 1976. BS in Journalism/Radio and TV, Ball State U., 1974, MA in Pub. Relations/Advt., 1975; postgrad., Ind. U., Indpls., 1987. Lic. secondary tchr. Sec. dept. journalism Ball State U., Muncie, Ind., 1972-74; sales and pub. relations Hoyt Wright Co., Anderson and Muncie, 1974-76; dir. publs. Indpls. Pub. Schs. at Arlington High Sch., 1977—; tchr. English and journalism, newspaper and yearbook adviser Indpls. Pub. Schs., 1977—. Mem. Women in Communications, NEA, Ind. State Tchrs. Assn., Indpls. Edn. Assn., Ind. High Sch. Press Assn., Quill and Scroll, English Tchrs. of Greater Indpls., Ball State U. Alumni Assn., Sigma Delta Chi, Kappa Alpha Theta. Republican. Methodist. Home: 7113 McIntosh Ln Indianapolis IN 46226 Office: Arlington High Sch 4825 N Arlington Ave Indianapolis IN 46226

WERFT, FRANCES MARIE, entrepreneur; b. Siguatepeque, Honduras, Nov. 1, 1956; d. Edward Oliver Seiford and Helen Marie (Bundy) Seiford; m. Gary Randall Werft. Nov. 2, 1982 (div. 1989). BA, Biola U., La Mirada, Calif., 1979. Buyer Biola U. Bookstore, La Mirada, Calif., 1976-80; asst. art dir. Earthy Endeavors, Inc., Santa Fe Springs, Calif., 1980-84; pres. Stampendous, Inc., Fullerton, Calif., 1982-89. Mem. Women Manfs. Network. Office: Stampendous Inc 1945 W Commonwealth #N Fullerton CA 92633

WERKMAN, ARLINE SUE LOUISE, administrative manager; b. Yonkers, N.Y., Feb. 28, 1945; d. Richard J. Kelly and Arline L. (Sloat) Kelly-Southard; m. Richard J. Hoffman, Sept. 14, 1963 (div. 1985); 1 child, Rachelle P.; m. Hendrik J. Werkman, Apr. 19, 1986. Student, Hudson Valley Community Coll., 1978. Sec. various offices, N.Y., 1965-81, Zenaida Q. Tana, M.D., Albany, N.Y., 1981-90; placement counselor The Vol. Ctr., Albany, 1984-87; bus. mgr. Dr. Gary L. Moscowitz, East Greenbush, N.Y., 1987—. Lead singer, mgr. music group Sue's Co. Leader Girl Scouts U.S., Delmar, N.Y., 1975-78. Named Health Care Profl., Palmer Assocs., 1988. Mem. NAFE, Am. Country Collection Bed and Breakfast. Republican. Home: 1183 Maple Hill Rd Castleton on Hudson NY 12033

WERLEY, CAROLYN CORRINE, economist; b. L.A., Dec. 5, 1957; d. M. Hardy and Ethel Corrine (Spence) W.; m. John B. Charles Jr., Dec. 20, 1986. BA, Northwestern U., 1979; MPA, Princeton, 1981; postgrad., U. Calif., 1985—. Summer assoc. FCC, Washington, 1979; researcher UN, N.Y.C., 1979-80; cons. USAID, Dakar, Senegal, 1980; asst. program officer CARE, N.Y.C., 1981-83; field rep. CARE, Chad and Bangladesh, 1983-85; teaching asst. U. Calif., Berkeley, 1985—, rsch. asst., 1987—; summer assoc. The World Bank, Washington, 1986; cons. Ford Found., N.Y.C. Mem. Sierra Club. Office: UC Berkeley Dept Econs Evans Hall Berkeley CA 94720

WERMUTH, LORA DUNNAM MORGAN, publishing executive; b. Flagstaff, Ariz., July 19, 1929; d. Cullen Grimes and Neal (Bryan) Dunnam; m. Charles Warren Morgan (div. 1983); children: John Stephen, Susan Lynn, James Cullen, Charles David, Russell Bryan; m. Anthony Lewis Wermuth. BA, U. Ariz., 1951; postgrad., U. So. Calif., L.A., 1952, U. N.Mex., 1953, L.A. State U., 1955. Cert. secondary sch. educator, Calif. High sch. English tchr. Anoakia Prep, Sierra Madre, Calif., 1952-53; tchr. English Foothill High Sch., Albuquerque, 1953-54, Covina (Calif.) High Sch., 1955-56; office mgr. Poly Chem. Corp., La Verne, Calif., 1957-61; tchr. Ghost Ranch Conf. Ctr., Abiquiu, N.Mex., 1975-78, Menucha (Oreg.) Ctr., 1979; columnist Palos Verdes News, Rolling Hills, Calif., 1973-80; pub. Morgan Press, Rolling Hills, 1975-83; pub., cons. Palos Verdes Books, Lomita, Calif., 1983—; cons. in field. Support mem. Save Our Coastline, Palos Verdes, 1971—; co-organizer AAUW Recycle Ctr., Palos Verdes, 1971—. Named Fellowship Honoree AAUW, 1973. Mem. AAUW (life), Ghost Ranch Found. (bd. dirs. 1977—), English Speaking Union, Univ. Club Winter Park. Presbyterian.

WERNER, DORIS THERESA, electrical engineer; b. St. Johnsburg, Vt., Oct. 24, 1948; d. Gaston Simon and Diana (Rapoza) Couture; m. Gerald Andrew Werner, Mar. 4, 1981; 1 child, Kimberly Anne. AS in Bus., Champlain Coll., 1970; BS in Elec. Engring. Tech., Milw. Sch. Engring., 1983. Lab technician State of Vt., Roxbury, 1969-71; with product control dept. Alloy Products, Waukesha, Wis., 1972-73; with internal sales dept. Husco, Waukesha, 1973-77; office mgr. Hartmann Controls, Hartland, Wis., 1977-78; insp. Donohue & Assocs., Waukesha, 1979-81, team leader, 1983-84; jr. engr. Gen. Electric Corp., Milw., 1984; elec. engr. Empire Generator, Germanton, Wis., 1984-85, Harley Davidson Inc, Milw., 1985—. Active Zool. Soc., Milw. County, 1985—. Mem. Harley Employee Recreation Orgn., Inst. Environ. Sci. (environ. stress screening electronic hardware Chgo. chpt. 1989). Roman Catholic. Home: 15755 Heather Hill Dr Brookfield WI 53005 Office: Harley Davidson 3700 W Juneau Ave Milwaukee WI 53208

WERNER, GLORIA S., librarian; b. Seattle, Dec. 12, 1940; d. Irving L. and Eva H. Stolzoff; m. Newton Davis Werner, June 30, 1963; 1 son, Adam Davis. BA, Oberlin Coll., 1961; ML, U. Wash., 1962; postgrad. UCLA, 1962-63. Reference librarian UCLA Biomed Library, 1963-64, asst. head pub. services dept., 1964-66, head pub. services dept., head reference div., 1966-72, asst. biomed. librarian public services, 1972-77, asso. biomed. librarian, 1977-78, biomed. librarian, assoc. univ. librarian, dir. Pacific S.W. regional Med. Library Service, 1979-83; asst. dean library services UCLA Sch. Medicine, 1980-83; assoc. univ. librarian for tech. services, 1983-89, dir. libraries, acting univ. librarian, 1989—; adj. lectr. UCLA Grad. Sch. Library and Info. Sci., 1977-83. Mem. ALA, Med. Library Assn., Assn. Acad. Health Sci. Library Dirs. (dir. 1981-83). Editor, Bull. Med. Library Assn., 1979-82, asso. editor, 1974-79; mem. editorial bd. Ann. Stats. Med. Sch. Libraries U.S. and Can., 1980-83; mem. accrediting commn. Western Assn. Schs. and Colls. Office: UCLA Research Library Library Adminstrv Office Los Angeles CA 90024

WERNER, JOANNE LUCILLE, financial executive; b. Midland, Mich., Jan. 20, 1940; d. Ewald George and Martha (Yuchlal) W. AAS, Ea. Nazarene Coll., Quincy, Mass., 1972; BAS, Boston U., 1977; MBA, Suffolk U., Boston, 1979. Prog. asst. Dept. Def., Washington, 1966-68, budget analyst, 1968-70; budget analyst Dept. of Navy, Washington, 1970-72; budget analyst GSA, Boston, 1972-77, sr. budget analyst, 1977-79; sr. fin. mgmt. specialist HUD, Boston, 1979-90; sales coord. Environ. Concepts Internat., Braintree, Mass., 1990—. Editor newsletter Baystatement, 1980-81. With USNR. Sioux Falls Coll. grantee, 1959; named Sailor of Yr. USNR, 1985. Mem. Am. Soc. Women Accts. (bd. dirs. 1986-88), Nat.

Safety Assocs. (dir. distbn. 1990—), South Shore C. of C. Home and Office: 1449 Quincy Shore Dr Quincy MA 02169

WERNER, JULIA STEWART, educator, historian; b. Washington, Iowa, Sept. 25, 1936; d. Arthur Donald and Ethel Janet (Griner) Stewart; m. Steven Erwin Werner, Apr. 3, 1972. AB, Grinnell (Iowa) Coll., 1958; MA, U. Wis., 1969, PhD, 1982. Tchr. Kemper Hall, Kenosha, Wis., 1962-68; teaching asst. U. Wis., Madison, 1969-71; tchr. Nicolet High Sch., Glendale, Wis., 1972—. Author: The Primitive Methodist Connexion: Its Background and Early History, 1984. NEH grantee, 1985, 87, 90—. Mem. Am. Hist. Assn. (teaching div. 1987-90), Orgn. History Tchrs. (exec. bd. 1987—), Soc. for History Edn. (bd. dirs. 1988—), Soc. for Ch. History, World History Assn. Democrat. Eastern Orthodox. Office: Nicolet High Sch 6701 N Jean Nicolet Rd Glendale WI 53217

WERNER, SUSAN M., food company executive; b. St. Marys, Pa., Apr. 1, 1947; d. Francis Joseph and Rose Mary (Sager) Kneidel; m. Anthony Werner, Sept. 6, 1969. BA in English, Villa Maria Coll., Erie, Pa., 1969. Ins. asst. Hardee's Food Sys., Inc., Rocky Mount, N.C., 1973-78; risk mgr. Hardee's Food Sys., Inc., 1978-82, dir. risk mgmt., 1982—; lectr. in field. Author column, Business Insurance, Ask A Risk Manager, 1988—. Lobbyist N.C. Project, Inc., Raleigh, 1986. Named Alumna of the Yr., Villa Maria Coll., 1988; named to Bus. Ins. Risk Mgmt. Honor Roll, 1987. Mem. Risk and Ins. Mgmt. Soc., Nat. Restaurant Assn. (safety officers group), Ea. Caroline Safety Council. Republican. Roman Catholic. Office: Hardees Food Systems Inc 1233 Hardees Blvd Rocky Mount NC 27802-1619

WERNER, VIVIENNE ELLEN, educator; b. Plainfield, N.J., July 14, 1948; d. William Edward and Vivienne Gertrude (Jennings) Herbst; m. Philip James Werner, Sept. 27, 1968; children: Edward James, Vivienne Lorraine. BS in Bus. Edn., Rider Coll., 1970. Cert. tchr. Tchr. William Annin Jr. High Sch., Basking Ridge, N.J., 1970-73; tchr. Netcong (N.J.) High Sch., 1973-74, Green Brook (N.J.) High Sch., 1974-90, Frederick (Md.) High Sch., 1990—. Advisor (yearbook) EPOCH, 1978-90 (Pica award 1989). Mem. Ladies Aux. #5479, Dunellen, N.J., 1965—; mem. First Presbyn. Ch., Dunellen, 1962—, Sunday sch. tchr., 1973—. Grantee for office simulation Vocat. Edn. Dept. N.J., 1985, 86, 87, 88, 89; recipient Gov.'s award N.J. Outstanding Tchr.; named Green Brook Tchr. of Yr., 1989-90. Mem. Internat. Thespian Soc. (N.J. dir. 1985-90, Earl W. Blank award 1987, 89), N.J. Bus. Edn. Tchrs. Assn. (nominee Tchr. of Yr. 1982). Republican. Home: 18928 Shooting Star Ct Germantown MD 20874 Office: Frederick High Sch 650 Carroll Pkwy Frederick MD 21701

WERNICK, SANDIE MARGOT, advertising and public relations executive; b. Tampa, Sept. 13, 1944; d. Nathan and Sylvia (Bienstock) Rothstein. BA in English, U. Fla., 1966. Tchr. English Miami Beach (Fla.) Sr. High Sch., 1967; adminstrv. asst. pub. rels. Bozell & Jacobs, Inc., N.Y.C., 1968-69; asst. to dir. pub. rels. Waldorf-Astoria, N.Y.C., 1969-70; dir. advt. and pub. rels. Hyatt on Union Square, San Francisco, 1974-82; pres. Wernick & Assocs., San Francisco, 1982—. Bd. mem. Nat. Kidney Assn., San Francisco, 1985-87; advisor Swords to Plowshares, San Francisco, 1988-89. Recipient Award of Merit, San Francisco Advt. and Cable Car Awards, 1979, Award of Excellence, San Francisco Art Dirs, 1978, awards Am. Hotel and Motel Assn., 1981, 82, awards of excellence San Francisco Publicity Club, 1990. Mem. Women in Communications (bd. mem. 1987-89), Am. Women in Radio and TV (bd. mem. 1989-90), Pub. Rels. Soc. Am., San Francisco Publicity Club (pres. 1989), Variety Club. Democrat. Jewish. Home: 1690 Broadway Apt 705 San Francisco CA 94109 Office: Wernick & Assocs 1690 Broadway Ste 704 San Francisco CA 94109

WERNIKOFF, NANCY KASDON, speech and language pathologist; b. Cleve., Apr. 6, 1938; d. Eli David and Doree (Sands) Kasdon; B.A., N.Y. U., 1962; M.S. in Edn., Queens Coll., 1969; m. Sergio Wernikoff, Oct. 26, 1958; children: Laura Sue, Daniel Mark. Speech pathologist Speech Rehab. Inst., N.Y.C., 1962-63, acting speech supr. speech therapy dept., 1963-65; speech-lang. cons. pre-sch. program Pascack Valley (N.J.) Council Spl. Edn., 1976-77; cons. speech-lang. pathologist Ramsey (N.J.) Public Schs., 1978—; pvt. practice, 1967—; cons. in field. Mem. exec. bd. Archer Nursery Sch., Allendale, N.J., 1973-74; active local Boy Scouts Am., Girl Scouts U.S.A., 1972-78; mem. exec. bd. sisterhood Temple Beth Or, Washington Twp., N.J., 1976-81, mem. exec. bd. Temple Beth Or, 1981—. Recipient Griffith Hughes Meml. prize Washington Sq. Coll. of Arts and Scis., N.Y. U., 1962. Mem. Am. Speech, Lang. and Hearing Assn. (cert.), N.J. Speech Language and Hearing Assn. (chair judiciary com.), Bergen County Speech and Hearing Assn. (co-founder), Speech and Hearing Study Group (co-founder). Home: 42 Somerset Dr Woodcliff Lake NJ 07675

WERNIMONT, CHERYL ANN, postal service administrator; b. Ottumwa, Iowa, May 24, 1944; d. Raymond Peter and Dorothy Grace (Grimes) Greiner; m. Raymond Thomas Wernimont (dec. Nov. 1974); children: Brian Thomas, Cindy Ann. Student, U. Iowa, 1963-65, 87—. Owner, operator Talleyrand Tavern/Cafe, Keota, Iowa, 1970-71; clk. U.S. Postal Service, North Liberty, Iowa, 1971-72; clk., operator letter sorting machine Cedar Rapids, Iowa, 1972-78, supr. mail processing, 1978-79; mgr. customer service Iowa City, Iowa, 1980-86; postmaster Marion, Iowa, 1986—; bd. dirs. U.S. Postal Service Women Program, Cedar Rapids, 1976-78, east Cen. Iowa Postal Customer Council, Cedar Rapids, 1980-87; mem. promotion bd. U.S. Postal Service Upward Mobility, Cedar Rapids; coord. 1990 census U.S Postal Svc., Cedar Rapids, 1988—. Loaned exec. United Way, Cedar Rapids, 1989. Mem. Am. Bus. Women's Assn. (pres. local chpt. 1981-82, 86-87, v.p. 1982-83, chmn. ways and means com. 1984-85, 87-88, Achievement award 1982, Boss of Yr. award 1983, Woman of Yr. award 1983, 89-90), Marion C. of C. (ambassador 1986—, sec. ambassadors 1989, exec. dir. 1987—, pres. 1989-90), Cedar Rapids Metro Pilot Club (charter pres. 1990—). Democrat. Roman Catholic. Club: Coralville Water Ski (sec. 1984-85). Lodge: Rotary (editor newsletter 1989). Office: US Postal Svc 1101 6th Ave Marion IA 52302-9998

WERTHEIM, AUDREY DARWIN, marketing, public relations consultant; b. N.Y.C., Mar. 14, 1933; d. Hippolyte Maurice and Esther (Darwin) Wertheim. Student Shipley Sch., Bryn Mawr, Pa., 1948-50, Lake Erie Coll., Painesville, Ohio, 1950-53. Sec. publicity dept. Columbia Pictures, N.Y.C., 1958-60; exec. sec., editorial asst. Cholly Knickbocker column N.Y. Jour. Am., 1961-63; publicity dir. Sheraton Corp. Am., N.Y.C., 1963-66; spl. events promotion dir. ABC-TV, N.Y.C., 1965-67; propr. Wertheim & Assocs., N.Y.C., 1967—; chief oper. officer, exec. v.p. SportsMark, Inc. and SportsMark Internat., N.Y.C. Recipient numerous letters of commendation, Nat. Myasthania Gravis Found., Outstanding Fundraising and Pub. Awareness awards, 1978. Republican. Episcopalian. Office: 227 E 57th St New York NY 10022

WERTHEIM, MARY CAROLE, advertising agency executive; b. Albuquerque, Dec. 25, 1939; d. Joseph and Stella (Mensio) May; m. Jerry Wertheim, Aug. 20, 1960; children—Jerry Todd, John Vincent. Student U. N.Mex., 1958-60, George Washington U., 1960-61. Treas. Wertho Ranch, N.Mex., 1972—; billing systems coordinator JGS&W, P.A., Santa Fe, 1973-74; founder, pres. Creative Images, LTD., Santa Fe, 1978—. Past mem. N.Mex. Com. Children and Youth, N.Mex. State Library Com. Recipient numerous awards for advt. prodn., 1978—. Mem. Santa Fe C. of C. (bd. dirs. 1983-88, treas. 1984-86), No. N.Mex. Advt. Fedn. (bd. dirs. 1981-82), Gen. Fedn. Women's Clubs (nat. bd. dirs. 1970-80), N.Mex. Fedn. Women's Clubs (state pres. 1976-78). Avocations: skiing; swimming; reading. Office: Creative Images Ltd 355 E Palace Ave Santa Fe NM 87501

WERTHEIM, SALLY HARRIS, dean, consultant, professor; b. Cleve., Nov. 1, 1931; d. Arthur I. and Anne (Manheim) Harris; m. Stanley E. Wertheim, Aug. 6, 1950; children: Kathryn, Susan B., Carole J. BS, Flora Stone Mather Coll., 1953; MA, Case Western Res. U., 1967, PhD, 1970. Cert. elem. and secondary edn. tchr., Ohio. Social worker U. Hosps., Cleve., 1953-54; tchr. Fairmont Temple Religious Sch., Cleve., 1957-72; with John Carroll U., Cleve., 1969—, prof., 1980—, dean grad. sch., rsch. coord., 1986—; cons. in field; cons. Jennings Found., Cleve.; chmn. sch. com. Cleve. Commn. on Higher Edn., 1987—. Contbr. articles to profl. jours. Sec. County Mental Health Bd., Cleve., 1978-82; pres. Jewish Family Svc. Assn., Cleve., 1974-77, Montefiore Home for Aged, Cleve., 1986—; bd. dirs. Mt. Sinai Med. Ctr., Cleve., 1984—. Named one of 100 Most Influential Women, Cleve. Mag., 1983; Jewish Community Fedn. award; Jennings Found. grantee, 1984-87, Cleve. and Gund Found. grantee, 1987—, Lilly Found. grantee, 1988. Mem. Am. Assn. Colls. for Tchrs. Edn. (bd. dirs. 1982-85), Ohio Assn. Colls. for Tchrs. Edn. (pres. 1981-83), Coun. of Grad. Schs. Office: John Carroll U Grad Sch Cleveland OH 44118

WERTZ, ALTA HAPP, artist, educator; b. Kennewick, Wash., Feb. 19, 1921; d. Henry Lewis and Annie Elizabeth (Yates) Leckliter; student Bakersfield Jr. Coll., 1939-40; m. Richard Clarence Smith (div. 1961); children: Robin (Mrs. Bernard Charles Danylchuk), Alan Montgomery, Shelley (Mrs. Thomas William Stoye); m. 2d. William Morris Happ, Jan. 19, 1967 (dec. 1980); m. 3d Harvey William Wertz, Feb. 26, 1984. Instr. oil painting, adult edn. Palomar Coll., San Marcos, Calif., 1958-62; pvt. tchr., lectr. in field, 1962—. One-woman shows The Atheneaum, La Jolla, Calif., 1959, Jeane's Gallery, La Jolla, 1961, Palomar Coll., 1959-61, The Little Galleries, Escondido, Calif., 1964, La Pina Ltd., La Jolla, 1965, 66, 67, Gray's Gallery, Escondido, 1973, Carlsbad Oceanside Art League Gallery, 1973; exhibited in group shows San Diego Mus. Art, San Diego Art Inst., Riverside Mus. Art, San Bernardino Mus. Art, So. Calif. Expn., Del Mar, also various galleries represented in permanent collections; lectr. on psychology and symbology of color in music and art. Active Palomar Hosp. aux., 1957-59; pres. Showcase of Arts, Escondido, 1961-62; rep. to San Diego Coun. of Visual Arts, 1966-67; mem. Escondido Cultural Arts Com., 1972-73; chmn. Mission Valley (Calif.) Expn. Art, 1967; bd. dirs. Philos. Religious Free Libr., 1970-74, Pala Mission Indian Sch., 1965-72. Huntington Hartford Found. fellow, Pacific Palisades, Calif., 1964. Recipient numerous other awards. Mem. San Diego Art Inst., San Diego Art Guild of Fine Arts Soc., San Diego Watercolor Soc., Nat. League of Am. Pen Women (pres. 1974-76), Watercolor West. Home: 11302 Moorpark St North Hollywood CA 91602

WERTZ, JANE KARR, broadcaster; b. Chgo., Aug. 16, 1934; d. Kenneth L. and Catharine C. (Carpenter) Karr; m. Edwin P. Neubauer, Aug. 10, 1956 (div. 1979); children—Kenneth Paul, Kathryn J., Keith E. (dec.); m. Charles W. Wertz, June 21, 1980. B.A., Beloit Coll., 1956. Tchr., Winnebago County Schs., Rockford, Ill., 1956-57; broadcaster Sta. WREX-TV, Rockford, 1964-80; pub. relations dir. Swedish Am. Hosp., Rockford, 1976-80; on-air talent Beloit Cable TV, Wis., 1970-80; broadcaster, program dir. Sta. KSTS-TV, San Jose, Calif., 1981-86; instr. advt. San Jose State U., 1984—. Bd. dirs. Peninsula Ctr. for Blind, Palo Alto, Calif., 1981-86. Mem. AFTRA, P.E.O. Sisterhood, Delta Gamma. Republican. Methodist. Home: 463 Los Rios Ct Pleasanton CA 94566 Office: San Jose State U Dept Journalism and Mass Communications One Washington Sq San Jose CA 95192-0055

WESCHLER, ANITA, sculptor, painter; b. N.Y.C.; d. J. Charles and Hulda Eva (Mayer) W.; married. Exhibited Met. Mus., Mus. Modern Art, Art Inst. Chgo., Phila. Mus. Internat., Am. Acad., Inst. Arts and Letters, Bklyn. Mus., Newark Mus., Hofstra Mus., Carnegie Inst. Internat., Whitney Mus. Annuals, museums and galleries, throughout U.S.; represented in permanent collections U. Pa., Met. Mus. Art, Syracuse U., Butler Art Inst., Whitney Mus., Norfolk Mus., Brandeis U., Amherst Coll., Yale U., Wichita State Mus., SUNY Binghamton, U. Iowa, U. Nebr., La Salle U., Pa. Acad. Fine Arts, Art Students League; 13 one-man shows in N.Y.C., 12 group traveling shows, 30 one-man shows nationwide, 1964—; one-man shows include Birmingham (Ala.) Mus. Art, Main Library, Winston-Salem, N.C., U. Wis., Milw., del., U.S. Com. of Internat. Assn. Art, Fine Arts Fedn. N.Y., creator, plastic resins and synthetic glazes as painting media; author: poetry book Nightshade, A Sculptors Summary. Recipient prizes Corcoran Gallery, San Francisco Mus., Am. Fedn. Arts Traveling Show, Montclair Art Mus.; fellow MacDowell Colony, Yaddo. Mem. Archtl. League, Sculptors Guild (past bd. dirs., treas.), Nat. Assn. Women Artists, Internat. Inst. Arts and Letters, Artist Craftsmen N.Y., Fedn. Modern Painters and Sculptors. Address: 136 Waverly Pl New York NY 10014

WESLEY, FERN D., program analysis specialist; b. Antioch, Calif., Aug. 4, 1938; m. T.J. Wesley, Oct. 27, 1962; Children: Michael, Timothy, James, Teri Marie. Steno sec. KWAT-FM, Douglas, Ariz., 1957, U.S. Army, Ft. Huachuca, Ariz., 1958-59; supervisory clk. USAF, Sacramento, 1960-62; mgmt. analyst USN, Point Mugu, Calif., 1962-67; sec. USN, Point Hueneme, Calif., 1984-85; resources officer USN, Point Mugu, 1985-89, program analysis officer, 1989—. Pres. Valle Lindo (Calif.) Elem. Sch. PTA, 1980-83; communicator Monte Vista Intermediate Sch. PTA, 1982-85; active Rio Mesa High Sch. PTA, 1983-85; chmn. bd. Christian edn. Pleasant Valley Bapt. Ch., 1973-75, clk., 1972, supr. pre-sch. depts., 1962-68. Recipient The Golden State award, 1989. Mem. Fed. Mgr. Assn., Fed. Women's Assn. Republican. Office: Pacific Missle Test Ctr Systems Instrumentation Div Point Mugu CA 93042-5000

WESLEY-HOSFORD, ZIA, cosmetics company executive, author, consultant; b. N.Y.C., Mar. 3, 1945; divorced; 1 child, Ariane Lee Heller. Student, Endicott Jr. Coll., 1964, Vidal Sassoon Acad., San Francisco, 1978. Lic. cosmetologist, Calif. Singer, dancer Broadway musicals, San Francisco and Los Angeles, 1969-77; owner, operator Zia Full Service Salon, Sausalito, Calif., 1979-83; pres. Zia Cosmetics, San Francisco, 1983—; instr. skincare, San Francisco, 1983-86; cons. Zia Image Consulting, San Francisco, 1980—. Author: Being Beautiful, 1983, Putting on Your Face, 1985 (Bestseller 1986), Face Value, 1986, Skincare for Men Only, 1987, The Beautiful Body Book: A Lifetime Guide to Healthy Younger-Looking Skin, 1989; (video) Great Face, 1987. Co-chmn. Mill Valley (Calif.) Film Festival Guild, 1983-86.

WESOLOWSKI, GERMAINE MARIE VELICER, educator; b. Kewaunee, Wis., June 17, 1941; d. George Matthew and Elsie (Cherney) Velicer; divorced; children: Katherine Wesolowski Brumm, James R. BS in Elem. Edn., Oshkosh State Coll., 1963; MS in Curriculum and Instrn., U. Wis., Milw., 1985. Kindergarten tchr. Pulaski (Wis.) Elem. Sch., 1967-87; elem. tchr. Sunnyside Sch., Sobieski, Wis., 1987—; mem. Early Childhood Outreach Team, Pulaski, 1987—. Named Tchr. of Yr., Pulaski Elem. Sch., 1981. Mem. NEA, Wis. Edn. Assn., Pulaski Edn. Assn. Roman Catholic. Home: 192 E Cedar St Pulaski WI 54162

WESSEL, JOAN STRAUSS, art consultant; b. N.Y.C., Oct. 24, 1929; d. Edgar L. and Hermine (Heidenheimer) Strauss; m. Milton Ralph Wessel, Jan. 29, 1953; children: Douglas C., Kenneth L., Michael R. BA, Manhattanville Coll., 1977. Curator Katonah (N.Y.) Mus. Art, 1977-84; dir. pub. rels. The Textile Mus., Washington, 1985-88; ind. design cons. Washington, 1988—; bd. dirs. Katonah (N.Y.) Mus. Art, 1979-84; bd. dirs., v.p. Pyramid Atlantic, Washington; bd. dirs., pres. Arlington (Va.) Arts Ctr.; bd. dirs. Renwick Alliance, Renwick Gallery, Smithsonian Instn., Washington. Author: American Design Classics, 1985. Pres. Am. Field Svc., White Plains, N.Y., 1972-74. Recipient Bronze Apple award Indsl. Designers Soc. Am., 1985. Democrat. Jewish. Home: 4410 Westover Pl NW Washington DC 20016

WESSLER, MARY HRAHA, marketing executive; b. Des Moines, Nov. 4, 1961; d. Francis M. and Shirley A. (Malone) Hraha; m. Stephen A. Wessler, May 21, 1988. BJ in Mass Communications, Iowa State U., 1984; postgrad., U. Denver, 1990. Dir. mktg. Real Estate Mgmt. Corp., Scottsdale, Ariz., 1984-87; asst. mktg. dir. Des Moines Ballet Co.; asst. press sec. Governor State of Iowa, Des Moines; v.p. mktg. Great West Mgmt. and Realty, Inc., Denver, 1987—. Mem. Apt. Assn. of Metro Denver (2nd v.p.), Women in Communications, Inc. Home: 11303 E Warren Ave Aurora CO 80014

WESSNER, DEBORAH MARIE, telecommunications executive, computer consultant; b. St. Louis, Aug. 15, 1950; d. John George and Mary Jane (Beetz) Eyerman; m. Brian Paul Wessner, Sept. 15, 1972; 1 child, Krystin. BA in Math. and Chemistry, St. Louis U., 1972; M Computer Info. Sci., U. New Haven, 1980. Statistician Armstrong Rubber Co., New Haven, 1972-74; programmer analyst Sikorsky div. United Techs., Stratford, Conn., 1974-77; project engr. GE, Bridgeport, Conn., 1977-79; software mgr. GE, Arlington, Va., 1979-81; mgr. software ops. Satellite Bus. Systems, McLean, Va., 1981-83; v.p. ops. DAMA Telecommunications, Rockville, Md., 1983-87; dir. network ops. and adminstrn. Data Gen. Network Svcs., Rockville, 1987—; assoc., cons. KDB Assocs., Columbia, Md., 1986—. Mem. Am. Bus. Women's Assn., NAFE. Office: Data Gen Network Svcs 2098 Gaither Rd Rockville MD 20850

WEST, CYNTHYA THOMAS, municipal agency administrator; b. Massillon, Ohio, Sept. 12, 1947; d. Anthony Frank and Beverly Elaine Thomas; m. William Alan West, Oct. 13 1985. BS, Kent (Ohio) State U., 1969. Purchasing agt. Masoneilan/Dresser, Houston, 1981-85; supervising buyer supply and commodity contracts Purchasing and Material Mgmt. Orange County Gen. Svcs. Agy., Santa Ana, Calif., 1985—. Assisted in restoration of the Hist. Orange County Courthouse, Santa Ana, 1985-87; negotiated contract for design and devel. of mus. exhibit gallery, 1988; assisted in preparing Rancho Del Rio, Calif. for visit from Pres. George Bush, 1989. Mem. Nat. Assn. Purchasing Mgmt., Purchasing Mgmt. Assn. of Houston (co-chmn. Houston pub. relations com. 1984-85), Purchasing Mgmt. Assn. Orange County (chmn. planning com. 1988—), Nat. Assn. for Female Execs., Calif. Assn. Pub. Purchasing Officers (chairperson conf. registration com. 1986), Friends of San Juan Capistrano Library, Friends of South Coast Repertory and Orange County Performing Arts Ctr. Office: Orange County Gen Svcs Agy Purchasing and Materiels Mgmt 1300 S Grand Bldg A Santa Ana CA 92705

WEST, DANA L., engineer; b. Price, Utah, June 21, 1944; d. George Louis and Lamarjorie (Jewkes) Curtis; 1 child, Wendy Ryan (dec.). AS, Coll. of Ea. Utah, 1964. With Mountain Bell, Salt Lake City, 1972-84; asst. mgr. Mountain Bell, Helena and Great Falls, Mont., 1983-84; detail engr. U.S. West Communications, Denver, 1983-89; project mgr. Bell Atlantic Internat., Madrid, 1989—; retirement chairperson Mountain Bell, 1966-86. Team capt. Jr. Achievement, Salt Lake City, 1982-85; chairperson Sub for Santa, Salt Lake City, 1985. Mem. U.S. West Women Relief Soc. Mormon. Home: 5890 S Lowell Way Apt 102 Littleton CO 80123

WEST, DEBRA LEE, veterinarian; b. Waupaca, Wis., Sept. 25, 1953; d. Roy Elwyn and Shirley Jean (Koski) W.; m.David Phillip Swenson, Oct. 2, 1982. AA, Vermilion Community Coll., Ely, Minn., 1973; BS, U. Minn., 1975, DVM, 1977. Staff veterinarian Waupaca (Wis.) Vet. Svc., 1977—. Mem. Am. Vet. Med. Assn., Am. Assn. Bovine Practitioners, Assn. Women Veterinarians, Wis. Vet. Med. Assn., Northeastern Wis. Vet. Med. Assn., Phi Theta Kappa. Republican. Lutheran. Home: E1062 Haase Rd Waupaca WI 54981 Office: Waupaca Vet Svc 780 Bowling Ln Waupaca WI 54981

WEST, KATHLEEN FISHER, director career services; b. Canton, Ohio, Nov. 17, 1960; d. Edward Koessler and Margaret Rose (Janson) Fisher; m. Donald Edward West, Oct. 15, 1988. BA, U. Akron, 1983; MS, Miami U., 1985. Dir., career planning and placement Ashland Coll., 1985-87; dir., career services Knox Coll., Galesburg, Ill., 1987--; chair employer recognition com. Midwest Coll. Placement Assn., 1988—, vice-chmn. liberal arts and scis. group, chair think tank com. Flutist Knox-Sandburg Community Symphony, Galesburg, 1987--. Mem. Coll. Placement Council, Midwest Coll. Placement Assn., Ill. Small Coll. Placement Assn., Liberal Arts Group, Small Bus. Com. Home: 66 W Carl Sandburg Dr Galesburg IL 61401

WEST, KATHRYN MARIE, pianist; b. Lansing, Mich., Apr. 15, 1935; d. Harry Allen and Mabel Agnes (Dyer) Strait; student Central Mich. U., 1952-55, Eastern Mich. U., 1979-81, Washtenaw Community Coll., 1988—; m. David Roche West, June 11, 1955 (div. 1989); children—Julie, Martha, Nancy, Jean, Mark. Profl. accompanist Ann Arbor Civic Theatre, U. Mich. Gilbert and Sullivan Soc., U. Mich. Summer Theater, 1965-72, Comic Opera Guild, 1983, 86-87; duo pianist with Naomi Donaldson, 1970-76, with Margaret Bond, 1972-85; sec. Office of Pres. U. Mich., Ann Arbor, 1976-77, exec. sec., 1978-83; sec. U. Mich. Law Sch., Ann Arbor, 1984—; concerts in Kansas City, Mo., Ohio, Mich. Organist, choir dir. 1st Congl. Ch., Chelsea, Mich., 1987—; keyboard player WCC Jazz Combo, 1989—. Mem. Friends of Four Hand Music, Amateur Chamber Music Players, Sigma Alpha Iota. Home: 1105 Granger Ann Arbor MI 48104

WEST, LOLA C., special events planner, consultant; b. Bklyn., Aug. 5, 1947; d. George William and Adele (Vaughn) W. BA, CUNY, Bklyn., 1970; M in Urban Planning, CUNY, N.Y.C., 1972. Field analyst Greenleigh Assocs., Inc., N.Y.C., 1971-73; counselor, instr. John Jay Coll. of Criminal Justice, N.Y.C., 1973-74; adminstrv. dir. Langston Hughes Headstart Program of N.Y., N.Y.C., 1975; bldg. adminstr. United Cerebral Palsy Assns. of N.Y. State, Inc., N.Y.C., 1977-79, unit-wide adminstr., 1979-80, dir. Warner community project, 1980-82, asst. regional dir., 1982-85, dir. community residences, 1986-88; pres., cons. spl. events, organizational devel. Lola C. West & Assocs., Bklyn., 1989—; cons. N.Y.C. Bd. of Edn., Bronx, 1974, 1989—, The Hawver Group, N.Y.C., 1984, 86, 87, assessor. Bd. dirs. N.Y. Women Against Rape, N.Y.C., 1985-86. Proclamation Lola C. West Day, N.Y.C., 1987. Democrat. Home and Office: 125 Willoughby Ave Brooklyn NY 11205-3726

WEST, LORETTA MARIE, underwriter; b. N.Y.C., Feb. 2, 1950; d. James L. and Alice (Richardson) W. AB, Washington Coll., Chestertown, Md., 1972. CPCU; cert. profl. ins. woman. Disbursements cashier Middlesex Ins. Co., Concord, Mass., 1972-76, tech. asst., 1976-78, comml. lines underwriter, 1978-83; sr. comml. lines underwriter Sentry Ins. Co., Concord, 1983-86, large acct. underwriter, 1986-88, sr. large account underwriter, 1988—. Mem. Framingham Rep. Town Com.; pres. Framingham Womens' Rep. Club, Nat. Fedn. Rep. Women, 1990—, Greater 12th Precinct Neighborhood Assn., 1990—; trustee Prescott Gardens Condos, 1984-88. Mem. Soc. CPCU, Nat. Assn. Ins. Women, Mass. Assn. Ins. Women (various coms. Middlesex and South Middlesex chpts., co-dir. South Middlesex chpt. 1986-88, bd. dir. South Middlesex chpt. 1988-90, treas. 1990—, Woman of Yr. award 1980), Women's Rep. Club Mass., Middlesex Club. Roman Catholic. Home: 6 Prescott St Framingham MA 01701 Office: Sentry Ins Rte 2 Concord MA 01742

WEST, MARILYN BESS, management consultant; b. San Angelo, Tex., Oct. 7, 1941; d. William David and Bessie B. (Perkins) Mauldin. BA, U. Tex., 1963. Coordinator Internat. Bus. Machines, Houston, 1966-72; mktg. rep. Service Bur. Co., Houston, 1972-78; headquarters staff U. Computing Corp., Dallas, 1978-79; dir. computing services Lloyd Bush & Assoc., Dallas, 1979-81; owner Info. Design Cons., Wilton, Conn., 1981-86; pres. Info. Cons., Lewisville, Tex., 1986--. Historian Poco Mas Theatre Guild, Lewisville, 1988. Mem. Nat. Assn. Female Execs. Republican. Methodist. Office: Info Concepts Inc 250 S Stemmons Ste 300 Lewisville TX 75057 Home: 1910 Sierra Lewisville TX 75067

WEST, MARJORIE EDITH, educator; b. Lawrence, Kans., Aug. 18, 1940; d. Merwin Hales and Helen Aletha (Fellows) Wilson Polzin; m. Hammond Dean Watkins, Feb. 17, 1968 (div. 1971); 1 child, Michele Dawn; m. Merlin Avery West, Apr. 2, 1975 (div. 1984). BA in Elem. Edn., U. No. Colo., 1962, MA in Reading, 1970; postgrad., La. State U./U. New Orleans, 1981-82. Cert. tchr., Colo. Tchr. Sch. Dist. 11, Colorado Springs, Colo., 1962-64, Nat. Def. Overseas Teaching Program, Wiesbaden, Fed. Republic Germany, 1964-65, Alaska On-Base Schs., Fairbanks, 1965-66, Great Bend (Kans.) Sch. Dist., 1966-67, Killeen (Tex.) Sch. Dist., 1967-68, Jefferson County Schs., Lakewood, Colo., 1969—. Recipient Alumni Trail Blazer award U. No. Colo., 1988. Mem. NAFE, AAUW, NEA, PTA (by-laws com. 1989-90, hon. life mem.), Colo. Edn. Assn. (del. to assembly 1985-90), Jefferson County Edn. Assn. (spl. svcs. com. 1989-90), Internat. Reading Assn., Phi Delta Kappa, Pi Lambda Theta, Epsilon Sigma Alpha (edn. chair 189-90, chair ways and means com. 1990-91). Democrat. Home: 10810 W Exposition Ave Lakewood CO 80226

WEST, MAXINE MARILYN, psychologist; b. St. Thomas, Ont., Can., Apr. 25, 1945; came to U.S., 1945; d. James and Selma Laura (Khoury) Toms; m. Gordon James West, Jan. 8, 1966 (div. Nov. 1978); children: Gregory, Laura, Amy, Nicholas. BA, Oakland U., 1966; postgrad., Mpls. Community Coll., 1978; MA, St. Mary's Coll., Winona, Minn., 1982. Lic. psychologist, Minn. Chem. dependency counselor Chrysalis-A Ctr. for Women, Mpls., 1979-82; chem. dependency counselor Mpls., 1982-88, pvt. practice psychologist, 1988—. Author: (monograph) Shame Based Family Systems: The Assault on the Esteem, 1980; co-author and producer: (video film) Shame: When it Happens to a Child, 1989. Mem. Am. Psychol. Assn. (assoc.). Office: 337 C H Oak Grove Minneapolis MN 55403

WEST, MICHELLE LYNNE, television personality; b. Cleve., July 20, 1961; d. Leonard Carlton and Anne (Braxton) W.; m. Michael Donell Scott,

Nov. 29, 1986; children: Michael Donell II, Brittany Anne Scott. BA in Journalism, Calif. State U., Northridge, 1983. Anchorwoman, reporter KIEM-TV, Eureka, Calif., 1984-85, KJEO-TV, Fresno, Calif., 1985—. Campaign worker Dukakis for Pres., Fresno, 1988. Mem. Nat. Assn. Black Journalists. Democrat. Office: KJEO-TV 4880 N 1st St Fresno CA 93726

WEST, SHARON ANNE, emergency physician, ophthalmologist; b. Gulfport, Miss., Dec. 12, 1944; d. Ben Marshall and Marjorie Dee (Hopkins) W.; div. 1970; children: Nusa Patricia Maal, Eduardo Maal, Pieter Maal. BS, Tulane U., 1971; MD, U. Miss. Med. Ctr., 1976. Pvt. practice gen. and emergency medicine, 1976-81; intern, resident in surgery and ophthalmology Tulane U. Med. Sch., 1981-86; emergency physician S.W. Miss. Regional Med. Ctr., McComb, 1986-87, DeLaRonde Hosp., Chalmette, La., 1987—, Chalmette Gen. Hosp., 1987-89, Elmwood Med. Ctr., Jefferson, La., 1989—. Major USAR Med. Corps. Mem. Am. Coll. Emergency Physicians, Am. Acad. Ophthalmology, So. Med. Assn., La. Med. Soc., St. Bernard Parish Med. Soc., Res. Officers Assn., Order Ea. Star. Republican. Office: Chalmette Med Ctrs 9001 Patricia St Chalmette LA 70043

WEST, ULLA CHRISTINA, ophthalmologist; b. Halsingborg, Sweden, Oct. 20, 1944; came to U.S., 1953; d. Niels Jespersen and Ulla Brigitta (Rappe) W.; m. William Booth Conerly, Nov. 29, 1985; children: Peter Ulysses, Thomas William. BA, U. Calif., Riverside, 1967; MD, U. So. Calif., 1971. Intern med. ctr. U. So. Calif., L.A., 1971-72; resident in ophthalmology med. ctr. U. So. Calif., 1973-76; fellow in cornea, external disease Proctor Found., San Francisco, 1978-80; ophthalmologist Ross-Loos Med. Group, L.A., 1976-78, N.W. Permanente, Portland, Oreg., 1981—; mem. adv. bd., Lions Eye Bank Oreg., Portland, 1982—. Office: Northwest Permanente 3414 W Kaiser Ctr Dr Portland OR 97227

WESTBERG, CHARLOTTE GENE, retired airline executive; b. Mpls.; d. Andrew Ludwig and Gail Eileen (Jeffers) W.; m. James J. Dunkerly, Sept. 5, 1942 (div. 1955). Student, Carleton Coll., 1936-37; BA, U. Minn., 1940. Cert. profl. sec. Various positions, 1940-42, 51-54; sec. to pres. North Cen. Airlines (name changed to Republic Airlines 1979), Mpls., 1954-55, staff asst. to pres., 1955-65; mgmt. staff coord. AID project for Bolivian Airline, Mpls., 1962-64; asst. corp. sec. North Cen. Airlines (name changed to Republic Airlines 1979), Mpls., 1962-74, staff asst. to chmn. and chief exec. officer, 1965-74, v.p. staff adminstrn., 1974-76, staff v.p., 1976-84, ret., 1984, cons., 1984-86. Bd. dirs. Community Settlement House, Corpus Christi, Tex., 1949-50; sec. adv. com. Normandale State Jr. Coll., Mpls., 1971-74. Mem. AAUW, U. Minn. Alumni Assn., Carleton Coll. Alumni Assn., Friends Assn. Symphony Orch., Delta Delta Delta. Republican. Mem. Christian Ch. (Disciples of Christ). Home: 2500 Wayside Dr Bryan TX 77802

WESTBROOK, KARLA RENEÉ, fashion designer, wholesale company executive; b. Hollywood, Fla., Nov. 26, 1964; d. William Fred and Maggie (Williams) W. BA in Fashion, Am. Coll. for Applied Arts, L.A., 1988; cert. merchandising, Bauder Fashion Coll., Atlanta, 1984. With retail sales Three Sisters, Ft. Lauderdale, Fla., 1981-82, Susie's Casuals, Hollywood, Fla., 1982-84; waitress numerous restaurants, Atlanta and Encino, 1985-88; v.p. asst., with sales Frank L. Robinson Co., L.A., 1988—; freelance designer Wild Textiles, L.A., 1989—. Home and Office: 6619 Leland Way #217 Hollywood CA 90028

WESTBROOK, LADAWN KAY, office services executive; b. Santa Cruz, Calif., Mar. 29, 1955; d. Edwina (Reynolds) Herman. Student, Kans. Wesleyan, 1973-75; BA in Biology, Colo. U., 1977. Owner, operator Desiree's Room & Groom, Golden, Colo., 1983-84; legal sec. O'Connor & Hannan, Mpls., 1984-85; legal sec./paralegal Sieben, Grose & VonHoltum, Mpls., 1985-87; pers. and mktg. mgr. Goodwin/Nelligan Temp. Svcs., Inc., Denver, 1987-88, v.p., gen. mgr., 1988—; advisor Denver Bus. Coll., 1989-90. Vol. Spl. Olympics, Denver, 1989; vol. tutoring program, Denver, 1990. Mem. Colo. Assn. Commerce and Industry, Denver C. of C. (coord. chief exec. officer group 1989-90), Sertoma (pres. Cherry Creek chpt. 1988—, chmn. ways and means com. 1988-90, Sertoman of Yr. 1988-89). Office: Goodwin/Nelligan Temp Svcs 1325 S Colorado Blvd #404 Denver CO 80222

WESTBROOK, MARIANNE MCINTIRE, psychologist; b. Cambridge, Mass., Oct. 2, 1948; d. Kenneth Sweetzer and Marian Esther (Muller) McIntire; ;m. Philip A. Pierce, Sept. 4, 1976 (div. 1987); m. J. Michael Westbrook, Aug. 8, 1987; 1 chld, Ashley Nicole. AS, Penn Hall Jr. Coll., Chambersburg, Pa., 1968; BGS, U. N.H., 1975; MS, Pacific Luth. U., Tacoma, Wash., 1978; PhD, U. Md., 1982. Lic. psychologist, N.Mex., profl. counselor, Tex.; diplomate Am. Bd. Med. Psychotherapists (fellow). Psychologist, clin. teach leader Guidance Ctr. Lea County, Hobbs, N.Mex., 1983-85; div. coord., asst. prof. Coll. Southwest, Hobbs, 1985-87; psychologist Zia Cons., Inc., Hobbs, 1985—, pres., 1990—; workshop leader N.Mex. Jr. Coll., Hobbs, 1984—; case cons., trainer OPTION, Hobbs, 1988—; presenter seminars Coll. Southwest, 1990—; presenter 9th Ann. Fall Conf. on Children and Youth, 1989. Contbr. articles to profl. jours. Mem. adv. bd. Parents Anonymous, Hobbs, 1987—; mem. steering com. Parents Anonymous Resource Ctr. N.Mex., 1989—. Mem. Am. Psychol. Assn., N.Mex. Psychol. Assn., Am. Assn. Counseling and Devel., Internat. Soc. Prevention Child Abuse and Neglect, Nat. Bd. Cert. Counselors (cert.). Office: Zia Cons Inc 215 W Broadway Ste 1 Hobbs NM 88240

WESTCOTT, SHIRLEY JOYCE, education educator; b. Erie, Pa., Oct. 12, 1926; d. James and Ruth Confrey (Harris) Dalglish; m. David Russell Westcott, Dec. 15, 1951 (div. 1978); children: Nora, Molly, David, Janet, James, Michael. AB, Grove City Coll., 1948. Tchr. Lawrence Park High Sch., Erie, 1963-66, Iroquois High Sch., Erie, 1966—; mem. faculty Nat. Endowment Humanities Allegheny Coll., 1985, participant Shakespeare N.E.H. Inst. Ind. U., 1987. Mem. Nat. Coun. Tchrs. English. Home: 607 Smithson Ave Erie PA 16511

WESTCOTT, THERESA COMMERTON, insurance executive, nurse; b. Queens, Oct. 20, 1954; d. George Mark and Norma Marie (Galvin) Commerton; m. Robert David Westcott, Aug. 20, 1983. AAS, S.I. Community Coll., 1974; BS, Lehman Coll. CUNY, 1981. RN, N.Y. Critical care nurse Peninsula Hosp. Ctr., Rockaway, N.Y., 1974-76; critical care and clin. rsch. nurse Mt. Sinai Med. Ctr., N.Y.C., 1976-80; mgmt. cons. Brooks Internat. Corp., Montvale, N.J., 1981-82; exec. recruiter Kenmore, N.Y.C., 1982-83; methods analyst, mgr. Empire Blue Cross Blue Shield, N.Y.C., 1983-87, dir. support svcs., 1987-88, asst. v.p. corp. support svcs., 1988—. Office: Empire Blue Cross Shield 622 Third Ave New York NY 10017

WESTER, BARBARA ANN, news reporter; b. Rock Island, Ill., Oct. 11, 1966; d. Charles John and Ann Marie (Shaffer) W. BA in Pub. Rels. and Journalism, U. No. Iowa, 1989. Mktg. asst. TeleDirect Internat. Inc., Davenport, Iowa, 1989-90; freelance writer Leader Newspaper, Davenport, 1989-90; news reporter Ottumwa (Iowa) Courier Newspaper, 1990—. Chair pub. rels. Am. Heart Assn., 1989-91; communications com. United Way of Am., 1989-90. Mem. AAUW, Pub. Rels. Soc. Am. (publicity com. 1989-90), Iowa Press Women. Democrat. Roman Catholic. Home: 2455 N Court #1 Ottumwa IA 52501 Office: 213 E 2d St Ottumwa IA 52501

WESTERHOLD, RUTH ELIZABETH, psychologist, educator; b. Youngstown, Ohio, Aug. 4, 1926; d. Samuel Gordon and Grace Elizabeth (Green) Meadows; BS, Youngstown U., 1946; postgrad. Ohio U., 1947, U. Ill., 1947-49; PhD, So. Ill. U., 1978; m. Walter Charles Westerhold, June 1, 1949; children: Marsha L., Carl E. Chief clin. psychologist Alton (Ill.) State Hosp., 1952-55; psychologist St. Louis (Mo.) County Spl. Sch. Dist., 1963-68; chief psychologist Kaskaskia Spl. Edn. Dist., Centralia, Ill., 1968-78; dir. learning communications E. Miss. Jr. Coll., Scooba, 1978-83, coordinator instnl. techniques, 1987—, coordinator devel. edn., 1987-88; consulting psychologist div. vocat. rehab. State of Ill., Alton, 1954-55. USPHS fellow, U. Ill., 1947-49. Cert. school psychologist, Mo., Ill. Mem. Am. Psychol. Assn., AAAS, Psi Chi Counselor, lectr., writer child-rearing, family, learning. Home: PO Box 135 Artesia MS 39736

WESTFALL, CAROL ANN, artist, educator; b. Everett, Pa., Sept. 7, 1938; d. Carroll Francis and Doris Lucille (Hawkins) Dooley; m. Jon David Westfall, Jan. 27, 1962 (div. Aug. 1976); children: Camille, Maigann. BFA, Rhode Island Sch. Design, 1960; MFA, Md. Inst., 1972. Instr. Md. Inst., Balt., 1968-72; asst. prof. fine arts Montclair State Coll., Upper Montclair, N.J., 1987, assoc. prof. fine arts, 1979-87, prof. fine arts, 1987—; residency Artpark, Lewiston, N.Y., 1989; assoc. prof. Columbia U. Tchrs. Coll., N.Y.C., 1976-86; artist-in-residence Memphis Coll. art, 1985, Am. Craft Mus., N.Y.C., 1987; mem. artists in schs. panel N.J. Coun. on Arts, Trenton, 1978-88; mem. disting. faculty selection com. Montclair State Coll., 1987, v.p. senate Sch. Fine and Performing Arts, 1987-89; study leader India tour Textile Mus., Washington, 1987. Co-author: Plaiting: Step by Step, 1976; exhibited at Lausanne Biennale, 1975, Am. Craft Mus., 1987, Kyoto (Japan) Internat. Textile Exhbn., 1989. Recipient purchase award N.J. State Mus., 1975; Indo-Am. fellow, 1980-81, fellow N.J. Coun. on Arts, 1987; rsch. grantee Montclair State Coll., 1987, 89. Mem. N.Y. Rug Soc. Office: Montclair State Coll Dept Fine Arts Upper Montclair NJ 07043

WESTFALL, HELEN NAOMI, microbiologist; b. Grafton, W. Va., June 23, 1933; d. Banks and Thelma Gertrude (Conwell) Roach; m. Andrew Robert Westfall, May 13, 1952; children: Steven Neal, Aleta June, Bryce Ruell. BS, Old Dominion U., 1971, MS, 1974; PhD, W. Va. U., 1980. From lab. tchrs. asst. to grad. tchr. asst. Old Dominion U., Norfolk, Va., 1969-74; tchr. Portsmouth (Va.) Cath. High Sch., 1974-75; instr. biology Alderson-Broaddus Coll., Philippi, W. Va., 1975-77; from postdoctoral res. assoc. to rsch. microbiologist Naval Med. Rsch. Inst., Bethesda, Md., 1980-85; from asst. prof. to assoc. prof. S.D. State U., Brookings, S.D., 1985—. Contbr. articles to profl. jours. Bd. dirs. S.D. Infection Control Coun. Recipient Claude Worthington Benedum Predoctoral fellowship W. Va. U., 1977-80, Outstanding Performance awd., Naval Med. Rsch. Inst., 1984, Sustained Superior Performance awd., Naval Med. Rsch. Inst., 1983, 1985; named Faculty Mem. of Yr., Student Microbiology Club., S.D. State U., 1987. Mem. Am. Soc. Microbiology, N. Cen. Br. Am. Soc. Microbiology, Am. Leptospirosis Rsch. Conf., Assn. Women in Sci., Old Dominion U. Alumni Assn., W. Va. U. Sch. Medicine Alumni Assn., Sigma Xi (pres. SDSU chpt. 1989-90, pres. elect 1988-89). Home: 1734 Orchard Dr Brookings SD 57006

WESTHEIMER, MARY HELEN, writer, consultant; b. Cin., Apr. 27, 1955; d. Charles Irvin and May (Orton) W.; m. Paul Alvin Vogel, Feb. 13, 1987. AAA in Journalism, Morehead (Ky.) State U., 1982. Asst. mgr. Litte Prof. Book Ctr., Cin., 1974-75, Moby Book Shop, Ft. Collins, Colo., 1976; owner, mgr. Dollar Bill's Gen. Store, Wellington, Colo., 1979-80; printer's devil Powell Printing & Pub., Frenchburg, Ky., 1981; writer Office of News Svcs. Morehead State U., 1981-82; mem. staff Appalachian News-Express, Pikeville, Ky., 1982; writer, asst. editor DIN Found., Phoenix, 1983; pres. PWS Writing-Editing, Phoenix, 1983—; exec. dir. Ariz. Authors Assn., Phoenix, 1987-89; instr. Pla. Three Acad., Phoenix, 1985; trainer AIM Seminars, Tempe, Ariz., 1989—. Editor: Quail in My Bed, 1989, Corporate Madness, 1989; contbr. articles to profl. jours.; contbg. editor: Am. West Airlines mag., 1989—. Mem. com. Phoenix Clean & Beautiful, 1986-87; petitioner Mecham Recall Com., Phoenix, 1987; vol. Camelot Therapeutic Horsemanship, Scottsdale, Ariz., 1987—; dep. registrar Maricopa County, Ariz., 1987—. Mem. Women in Communications (freedom of info. chair 1984), Ariz. Weather Watchers, Valley Epson Users Group (v.p. 1985), Nat. Assn. Women Bus. Owners (co-chair pub. rels. com. 1986, chair policy com. 1987), Ventura Users Group, Phoenix PC Users Group. Office: PWS Writing Editing 5831 N 46th Pl Phoenix AZ 85018-1236

WESTHEIMER, (KAROLA) RUTH SIEGEL, psychologist, television personality; b. Frankfurt, Fed. Republic Germany; came to U.S., 1956; m. Manfred Westheimer; children: Miriam, Joel. Grad. psychology, U. Paris Sorbonne; Master's degree, New Sch. for Social Research, N.Y.C., 1959; EdD, Columbia U., 1970. Research asst. Columbia U. Sch. Pub. Health, N.Y.C., 1967-70; assoc. prof. Lehman Coll., Bronx, N.Y., 1970-77; with Bklyn. Coll.; counsellor, radio talk show hostess Sexually Speaking Sta. WYNY-FM, N.Y.C., 1980—; hostess TV series Good Sex, Dr. Ruth Show, Ask Dr. Ruth, 1987—. Author: Dr. Ruth's Guide to Good Sex, 1983, First Love: A Young People's Guide to Sexual Information, 1985, Dr. Ruth's Guide for Married Lovers, 1986, autobiography All In a Lifetime, 1987; contbr. articles to mags.; appeared in film A Woman or Two, 1986. Office: King Features Syndicate Inc 235 E 45th St New York NY 10017*

WESTHEIMER, RUTH WELLING, management consultant; b. Detroit, May 17, 1922; d. Benjamin Dennis and Elsa (Friedenberg) Welling; m. Robert Irvin. BA, U. Wis., 1944. V.p., bd. dirs. Stepping Stones Ctr., Cin., 1976-85; chmn., developer Vol. Action Ctr., Cin., 1979-82; trustee United Way Community Chest, Cin., 1980-88; organizer Coopоrate Voluntarism Council, Cin., 1982-85; v.p., exec. com. United Way Community Chest, Cin., 1983-85; chmn. Evaluation Com. United Way, Cin., 1985-88; advisor YWCA Career Women Achievement, Cin., 1981--; bd. dirs. Cancer Family Care, Cin., 1986--; chmn. United Way Agy. Partnership Devel., Cin., 1988--; treas. Workum Scholarship Found., Cin., 1969-86; chmn. Fine Arts Fund,. Trustee Cin. Psychoanalytic Found., 1974-78, Ohio Citizens Council, Columbus, 1967-70. Mem. Woman's City Club, League of Women Voters (treas. 1959-68),. Home: 2525 Rookwood Pl Cincinnati OH 45208

WESTLUND, LOIS CHRISTOPHER, florist; b. Armstrong, Iowa, Aug. 18, 1933; d. Leslie Ben and Iva (Eastman) Christopher; m. Carl Daniel Westlund, May 21, 1955; children: Carl Christopher, Anne Elizabeth. Student, Mankato State Coll., 1953-55. Sec. GE, Richland, Wash., 1955-59; jr. fed. asst. Selective Service System, Pasco, Wash., 1974-75; rep., group sales leader Avon Products, Inc., Pasadena, Calif., 1977-84; owner, caterer Custom Catering, Richland, 1984-87; owner, florist Custom Floral, Richland, 1987—. Den mother Boy Scouts Am., Richland, 1968-71; leader Campfire Girls, Richland, 1974-76; reading tutor Wash. State Literacy Coun., Kennewick, Wash., 1987—; bd. dirs. Friends of Richland Library, 1988—. Mem. Richland C. of C., Allied Arts (crafts tchr., 1975-77). Methodist. Office: Custom Floral 2124 Davison Richland WA 99352

WESTMORELAND, BARBARA FENN, neurologist, electroencephalographer, educator; b. N.Y.C., July 22, 1940; d. Robert Edward and Wanda Helen (Zabawski) Westmoreland. BS in Chemistry, Mary Washington Coll., 1961; MD, U. Va., 1965. Diplomate Am. Bd. Psychiatry and Neurology. Intern Vanderbilt Hosp., Nashville, 1965-66; resident in neurology U. Va. Hosp., Charlottesville, 1966-70; fellow in electroencephalography Mayo Clinic, Rochester, Minn., 1970-71, assoc. cons. neurology, 1970-71; asst. prof. neurology Mayo Med. Sch., Rochester, 1973-78, assoc. prof., 1978-85, prof., 1985—. Co-author: Medical Neurosciences, 1978, rev. edit., 1986. Mem. Am. Epilepsy Soc. (treas. 1978-80, pres. 1987-88), Am. EEG Soc. (sec. 1985-87), Cen. Assn. Electroencephalographers (sec.-treas. 1976-78, pres. 1979-80), Mayo History of Medicine Soc. (pres. 1990—), Sigma Xi (pres. chpt. 1987-88).

WESTON, JANICE LEAH COLMER, librarian; b. Phila., Jan. 3, 1944; d. Robert Henry and Mildred Viola (Hale) Colmer; m. Stephen Paul Oksala, Aug. 21, 1965 (div. 1970); m. Leonard Charles Weston, Oct. 28, 1972. BA in History, U. Mich., 1966; MS in LS, Wayne State U., 1969; postgrad., Cath. U. Am., 1975, Brigham Young U., 1975. Cert. profl. libr., Va. Library clk. Edn. Libr., U. Mich., Ann Arbor, 1966-67; reference libr. John Tyler Community Coll., Chester, Va., 1969-70, Tech. Libr., Aberdeen Proving Ground, Md., 1971-72; br. libr. Chester Pub. Libr., 1969-70; libr. Gen. Equipment Test Activity, Ft. Lee, Va., 1970-71; chief libr. Army Ordnance Ctr. and Sch., Aberdeen Proving Groud, 1972—; mem. job analysis task force Dept. Army, Washington, 1976; chmn. Aberdeen Proving Ground Media Svcs. Com., 1978, 83, 88. Author: Operating Procedures, 1988. Mem. James Buchanan Found., Lancaster, Pa., 1977—, Fulton Opera House Found., Lancaster, 1985—, Friends Libr. So. Lancaster County, Quarryville, Pa., 1985—; Humane League Friends, Lancaster, 1988—. Recipient exceptional performance awards Ordnance Ctr. and Sch., 1978—. Mem. Spl. Librs. Assn., Fed. Libr. and Info. Network, Tng. and Doctrine Command Libr. and Info. Network, Allemande Dance Club (Lancaster). Episcopalian. Home: 25 Oakridge Dr Quarryville PA 17566 Office: USA Ordnance Ctr and Sch Libr Bldg 3071 Simpson Hall Aberdeen Proving Ground MD 21995-5201

WESTON, PHYLLIS J., art gallery director; b. Cleve.; d. Armin and Wilma H. (Wasserman) Hornstein; m. Leo F. Weston, Oct. 18, 1963; children: H. Todd Cobey, John Cobey. Ed., Yale U. Director, AB Closson Jr. Co. Art Gallery, Cin., 1964—; art cons. Proctor & Gamble Co., Cin., 1983—; cons., lectr. in art. Named Woman of the Yr. Cin. Enquirer, 1987; recipient Post Corbett award, 1989. Chmn., founder Enjoy the Arts; founder Cin. Commn. on the Arts, The Post Corbett awards; bd. dirs., mem. numerous arts and civic orgns. including Cin. Bicentennial Com., Friends of Cin. Parks, med. arts com. U. Cin. Sch. Medicine. Home: 4 Taft Rd Ln Cincinnati OH 45206 Office: 401 Race St Cincinnati OH 45202

WESTPHAL, MARY JOSEPHINE, public relations executive, consultant; b. Toledo, Dec. 5, 1956; d. John Joseph and Dorothy Helen (DeMet) Newton; m. Robert Gerald Westphal, June 11, 1988; 1 child, Glenn Robert. BS in Journalism, Bowling Green (Ohio) State U., 1978. Asst. dir. pub. rels. Toledo Hosp., 1979-82; dir. pub. rels. Flower Meml. Hosp., Sylvania, Ohio, 1982-85; sales and advt. rep. Thomas Regional, Dallas, 1985-86; dir. devel. and pub. rels. McAuley High Sch., Toledo, 1986-87; asst. v.p. pub. rels. Nat. Emergency Svcs., Toledo, 1987—; alumni cons. Bowling Green State U., 1985; cons. McAuley High Sch., 1987. Mem. mktg. com. Women Alive!, Toledo, 1987; mem. spl. events com. Toledo Festival, 1985; bd.d irs. Mobile Meals, Toledo, 1985. Mem. Women in Communications, Inc. (v.p. membership com. 1980, pres. elect 1981, pres. 1982), Pub. Rels. Soc. Am., Am. Soc. for Hosp. Mktg. and Pub. Rels., Jr. League. Republican. Roman Catholic. Office: Nat Emergency Svcs 5565 Airport Hwy Toledo OH 43615

WESTPHAL, RUTH LILLY, educational audiovisual company executive, author, publisher; b. Glendale, Calif., July 27, 1931; d. Glen R. and Margaret E. (John) Lilly; m. H. Frederick Westphal, June 25, 1953. B.A. in Edn., UCLA, 1953; M.A. in Instructional System Tech., Chapman Coll., 1966. Cert. tchr. Calif. Tchr. pub. schs., Los Angeles, Glendale, Whittier, Calif., 1953-65; instuctional systems analyst Litton Industries, Anaheim, Calif., 1965-67; dir. devel. Trainex Corp., Garden Grove, Calif., 1967-69; owner, pres. Concept Media, Inc., Irvine, Calif., 1969—, Westphal Pub., Irvine, 1980—. Co-founder Friends of City Library, LaHabra, Calif., 1960-65; mem. Los Angeles County Mus. Art, 1975—, Laguna Beach Mus. Art, 1979—, Nautical Heritage Soc. Dana Point, Calif. 1982—. Author, editor numerous ednl. filmstrip programs. Author: Plein Air Painters of California: The Southland, 1982 (Western Books award 1982), Plein Air Painters of California: The North, 1986 (Western Books award 1986). Recipient numerous awards Info. Film Producers Am., Internat. Film and TV Festival N.Y., Chgo. Film Festival, Am. Jour. Nursing Media Festival, Author Recognition award U. Calif., 1983. Mem. Nat. Audiovisual Assn., Assn. Media Producers. Avocations: Art history. Office: Concept Media Inc 2493 DuBridge Ave Irvine CA 92714

WESTROPE, MARTHA RANDOLPH, psychologist, consultant; b. Gaffney, S.C., May 19, 1922; d. Gordon Robert and Hannah (Brown) W.; 1 adopted child, Ashley Randolph. BS, Winthrop Coll., 1942; MA, U. N.C., 1944; PhD, State U. of Iowa, Iowa City, 1952. Lic. psychologist, S.C. Pvt. practice Greenville, S.C., 1960—, part-time pvt. practice, 1987—; part-time staff mem. Spartanburg (S.C.) Mental Health Clinic, 1971-73, Greenville Mental Health Ctr., 1974-85, Patrick B. Harris Psychiat. Hosp., Anderson, S.C., 1985-87; med. cons. S.C. Vocat. Rehab. Dept., Anderson, 1987—; cons. S.C. Parole Bd. for Psychol. Evaluation, S.C. Dept. Corrections, 1983-87. Mem. Am. Psychol. Assn., Southeastern Psychol. Assn., S.C. Psychol. Assn., Am. Assn. for Advancement of Psychology, AAAS, Greenville County Mental Health Assn., Am. Group Psychotherapy Assn., Coun. for the Nat. Register of Health Svc. Providers in Psychology. Democrat. Presbyterian. Home: 11 Darien Way Greenville SC 29615 Office: 506 Pettigru St Greenville SC 29601

WESTWICK, CARMEN ROSE, nursing educator, university dean, consultant; b. Holstein, Iowa, Feb. 2, 1936; d. J. Alfred and Hazel C. (Lage) Armiger; m. Richard A. Westwick, Dec. 28, 1957; children: Timothy, Ann. BS in Nursing, U. Iowa, 1958; MS, U. Colo., 1960; PhD, Denver U., 1972. RN, S.D., Iowa, Mass., N.H. Instr. Sch. Nursing West Suburban Hosp., Oak Park, Ill., 1958-59, 60-62; nurse Navajo Presch., Carson's Trading Post, N.Mex., 1967; lectr. then prof. U. Colo., Denver, 1968-69, 72-77; program dir. Western Coun. on Higher Edn. in Nursing, Boulder, Colo., 1976-77; prof. nursing, dean U. N.Mex, Albuquerque, 1977-81, Boston U., 1982-85, S.D. State U., Brookings, 1988—; exec. dir. N.H. Bd. Nursing, Concord, 1986-87; case reviewer Joint Underwriters Assn., Boston, 1983—; mem. pubs. and rsch. com. Aberdeen (S.D.) Area Indian Health Svc., 1988—; manuscript reviewer Midwest Alliance in Nursing, Indpls., 1989—; mem. adv. com. S.D. Office of Rural Health, Pierre, 1989—. Contbr. articles to profl. jours. Nurse trainee fellow Nursing div. Dept. Health and Human Svcs., 1959-60, Predoctoral fellow, 1969-72; Nat. Merit scholar, 1954-56. Fellow Am. Acad. Nursing; mem. Sigma Theta Tau (nat. 1st v.p. 1968), Phi Kappa Phi, Kappa Delta Phi. Lutheran. Office: SD State U Coll Nursing Box 2275 Brookings SD 57007

WESTWOOD, JEAN MILES, country club administrator; b. Price, Utah, Nov. 22, 1923; d. Francis Marion and Neltie (Patter) Miles; m. Richard Elwyn Westwood, Sept. 6, 1941; children: Richard Elwyn, Beth Davies. BA, Coll. Eastern Utah, Price. Legis. aide Congressman David King, Salt Lake City, 1964-66; lectr. Program Corp. Am., N.Y.C., 1973-80; prodn. controller Consolidated Vultee Aircraft, San Diego, 1942-45; co-chair western states dir. McGorm for Pres., Washington, 1971-72; chair Nat. Dem. Com., Washington, 1972; dir. Terry Samuel for Pres., Washington, 1975-76; co-chair Babbitt for Pres., Phoenix, 1986-88; gen. ptnr. Westwood Mink Farms, West Jordan, Utah, 1946-73, Westwood Investments, Phoenix, 1974—; pres., chief exec. officer Pinewood Country Club, Inc., Phoenix, 1986—; cons. state and local campaigns, Ariz., Utah, 1964—. Columnist Nat. Tax News, Denver, 1950-71; contbr. articles to profl. jours. Nat. committeeman Utah Dem. Nat. Com., 1964-76; chair, vice chair state and local Dem. parties, Ariz., Utah, 1960—; bd. mem. Ariz. State Dept. Commerce Adv. Bd., Phoenix, 1978-86; del. Dem. Nat. Convs., 1964-84; v.p. Americans for Dem. Action, Washington, 1977—; bd. mem. Ariz. Stae Commn. on Employment, PHoenix, 1989—; state advisor Nat. Women's Polit. Caucus, 1985—. Recipient Susa Yang Gates award Utah Women's Coun., Salt Lake City, 1974, Outstanding Svc. award Friends of the Family, Phoenix, 1985. Mem. Women in Communications, Ariz. State Hist. Soc., Utah State Hist. Soc., N.Mex. State Hist. Soc., Nat. Conservancy, Wilderness Soc., Mt. Shadows Country Club (v.p., sec., tournament chair), Pinewood Country Club (membership chair). Democrat. Mormon. Home: 5302 N 79th Pl Scottsdale AZ 85250

WETCHER, GOLDIE RAPPAPORT, psychotherapist, clinic administrator; b. Camden, N.J., July 12, 1939; d. Morris G. and Jean (Gordon) Cohen; m. Martin Paul Rappaport, June 7, 1959 (div. 1975); children: Karen Leah, Steven Aaron; m. Kenneth Wetcher, Apr. 11, 1976. B.A., Newcomb Coll., Tulane U., 1961, postgrad. Sch. Social Work, 1963; M.S.W., U. Houston, 1969-70; cert. employee assistance counselor. Psychotherapist Mental Health Mental Retardation, La Marque, Tex., 1970-72; psychotherapist Family Counseling Assoc. and Wetcher Clinic, Houston, 1972—. Organizer Crisis Mgmt. Svc., Houston, 1984; active Bay Area Med., Houston, Orgn. Rehab. Tng., Houston; trustee Congregation Shaar Hashalom, Houston, 1984-85. Fellow Nat. Assn. Social Workers, Acad. Cert. Social Workers; mem. Houston Group Psychotherapy Assn. (tng. faculty), Am. Assn. Marriage and Family Therapists (approved supr.), Am. Group Psychotherapy Assn., Phi Beta Kappa, Phi Kappa Phi. Republican. Avocations: water sports; nutrition. Home: 2010 Port Royal Houston TX 77058 Office: Wetcher Clinic 16902 El Camino Real Suite 2C Houston TX 77058

WETHERALD, MARGARET ELIZABETH, lawyer; b. Seattle, May 30, 1958; d. Stanley Morey and Dorothy (Denworth) W.; m. Leonard Bruce Barson, July 20, 1985. AB cum laude, Mount Holyoke Coll., 1980; JD, Cornell Law Sch., 1983. Bar: Wash. 1983. Vis. fellow Columbus Sch. Law The Cath. U. of Am., Washington, 1983-85; assoc. Betts, Patterson & Mines, P.S., Seattle, 1985—. Pres. bd. dirs. New Beginnings, 1989. Mem. ABA, Wash. State Bar Assn., Seattle-King County Bar Assn., Fed. Bar Assn., Assn. Am. Trial Lawyers, Phi Beta Kappa. Democrat.

WETHERALD, MICHELE WARHOLIC, lawyer; b. Lakewood, Ohio, June 17, 1954; d. Michael and Veronica (Walkuski) Warholic; m. Gary R. Wetherald, Nov. 26, 1987. AAB, Lorain County Community Coll., Elyria, Ohio, 1977; BA, Hiram Coll., 1980; JD, U. Akron, 1985. Bar: Ohio, 1986;

U.S. Dist. Ct. (no. dist.) Ohio, 1987. Sec., dispatcher State Highway Patrol Ohio Turnpike Commn., Berea, Ohio, 1973-77; pers. and employee benefits rep. Terex Div. Gen. Motors Corp., Hudson, Ohio, 1978-83; labor relations rep. Lordstown Assembly Div. Gen. Motors Corp., Warren, Ohio, 1984-86; supr. labor relations and hourly employment Inland Div. Gen. Motors Corp., Livonia, Mich., 1986-87; staff atty. Hyatt Legal Svcs., Niles, Ohio, 1987-89; mng. atty. Hyatt Legal Svcs., Boardman, Ohio, 1990; assoc. Newman, Olson & Kerr, Youngstown, Ohio, 1990—. Mem. Exec. Bd. Hiram (Ohio) Coll. Alumni, 1990-93. Mem. ABA, Ohio State Bar Assn., Trumbull County Bar Assn., Mahoning County Bar Assn. Roman Catholic. Home: 106 Diamond Way Cortland OH 44410 Office: Newman Olson & Kerr 1200 Metropolitan Tower Youngstown OH 44503

WETHERBEE, ROBERTA JANIS, drama therapist; b. N.Y.C., Oct. 13, 1948; d. Max H. and Sylvia (Freedenberg) Blumert; m. Roger Wetherbee, June 22, 1986. BA, L.I. U., Bklyn., 1969; MA, NYU, 1972, postgrad., 1981-. Drama therapist Kings Terrace Nursing Home, Bronx, 1983-84; supr. Empire State Coll., N.Y.C., 1984; drama therapist Postgrad. Ctr. for Mental Health, N.Y.C., 1985-86, Our Lady of Mercy Med. Ctr., Bronx, 1986-89; instr. ednl. theater NYU, 1986—; drama therapist Creative Arts Rehab. Ctr., N.Y.C., 1987—; dir. activities therapy St. Barnabas Hosp., Bronx, 1989—. Co-author: Play, For Everyone Who Knows a Woman, 1984. Mem. Nat. Assn. Drama Therapy (cert., pres. 1990—, chairperson conf. 1988), Am. Group Psychotherapy Assn., Ea. Group Psychotherapy Assn., Soc. for Self Psychology. Democrat. Office: St Barnabas Hosp 3rd Ave & 183rd St Bronx NY 10458

WETHERELL, CLAIRE, state legislator; b. Flandreau, S.D., Feb. 18, 1919; d. Thomas James and Margaret (Hefron) H.; m. Robert Miles Wotherell (dec. 1943); children: Michael Edward, Dennis Hart, Ellen Ann Hermann, Robert Thomas. Student, U. Calif., Berkeley, 1937-39; RN, Mercy Hosp. Sch. Nursing, 1942. City councilwoman Mountain Home, Idaho, 1971-78; mem. Idaho State Senate. Dem. committeewoman Elmore County, 1955—; vice chmn. Idaho State Dem. Party, 1962-72. Served as ensign, Navy Nurse Corps, 1942-43. Named Disting. Citizen Idaho Daily Statesman, Boise, 1978. Mem. Mountain Home Com. of Fifty, Bus. and Profl. Women (named Woman of Progress, S.W. Idaho, 1976), C. of C. (pres. 1971-72), Idaho Land Title Assn. (pres. 1977-78). Roman Catholic. Home: 360 E 15th N Mountain Home ID 83647*

WETLI, PEGGY MARIE, theater company executive; b. Green Bay, Wis., Oct. 10, 1949; d. Alois Bernard and Viola Marie (Frye) W.; m. Timothy Hugh McCloskey, 1990. Founder, exec. and artistic dir. CLIMB Theatre, St. Paul, 1975—; founding ptnr. BINGOPLUS; cons., lectr. U. Minn., St. Paul. Author 20 plays for children and adults. Bd. dirs. Minn. Alliance for Art in Edn., 1978-81. Roman Catholic. Office: CLIMB Theatre 500 N Robert Ste 200 Saint Paul MN 55101

WETMORE, KAREN E., accounting executive; b. Needham, Mass., Dec. 28, 1953; d. Harold Bostwick and Gladys Adeline (Hillman) W. BSBA, Babson Coll., 1976, MBA, 1988; AS, Bay Path Jr. Coll., 1974. V.p. acctg. Gen. Energy Devel. Corp., Quincy, Mass., 1976-85; chief acct. United Christian Evangelistic Assn., Brookline, Mass., 1985-88; owner, pres. Falcon Acctg. Svcs., Needham, Mass., 1988—. Mem. NAFE, New England Women Bus. Owners, Women West of Boston (adv.), Am. Inst. of Profl. Bookkeepers, United Meth. Women (treas.), Am. Soc. of Notaries.

WETSTONE, JANET MEYERSON, designer, journalist; b. Spartanburg, S.C.; d. Louis Alexander and Ella (Levinson) Meyerson; m. Richard J. Wetstone, Sept. 21, 1947 (div. Dec. 1973); children—John B., Gregory S., Linda Wetstone Sherman. Student U. Mo., 1945-47, Ga. State U., 1970, 80. Interior designer Jan's Interiors, Atlanta, 1965-68; pres. Wetstone Crafts Co., Atlanta, 1968—; instr. women in bus. Emory U., 1972; cons. Plaid Enterprises Inc. Author: Rags to Riches with Mod-Podge, 1969; Specially Yours Decorating With Sheets, 1977; Needle-Podge Book, 1976; Creative Frame Maker, 1972; patentee craft paint mod-podge, frame maker. Pres. edn. guild Ringling Mus., Sarasota, Fla., 1963-64, chairperson 1st creative art carnival, 1963-64; decorating chairperson Jimmy Carter Election Night, Atlanta, 1976; Democrat. nominee Fla. State Legis., 1988; dir. communications Carter Mondale 1980 Campaign, Atlanta, 1980; chmn. visual arts Sarasota Centennial, 1985-86. Mem. United Inventors and Scientists Am., Women in Film (v.p. 1982-83), Fla. Assn. Realtors, Million Dollar Club, Phi Sigma Sigma. Club: Jimmy Carter 1980 (Atlanta). Avocations: riding; painting; golf. Home: 3969 Glen Oaks Manor Dr Sarasota FL 33582

WETTERHAHN, KAREN ELIZABETH, chemistry educator; b. Plattsburgh, N.Y., Oct. 16, 1948; d. Gustave George and Mary Elizabeth (Thibault) W.; m. Leon H. Webb, June 19, 1982; children—Leon Ashley, Charlotte Elizabeth. B.S., St. Lawrence U., 1970; Ph.D., Columbia U., 1975. Chemist, Mearl Corp., Ossining, N.Y., 1970-71; research fellow Columbia U., N.Y.C., 1971-75, postdoctoral fellow, 1975-76; asst. prof. chemistry Dartmouth Coll., Hanover, N.H., 1976-82, assoc. prof., 1982-86, prof., 1986—. Contbr. articles to profl. jours., 1974—. A.P. Sloan fellow, 1981. Mem. Am. Chem. Soc., Am. Assn. Cancer Research, AAAS, N.Y. Acad. Scis. Office: Dartmouth Coll Dept Chemistry Hanover NH 03755

WETTHER, KAREN LEE, nurse, consultant; b. Atascadero, Calif., Sept. 2, 1948; d. Norman A. and Joyce E. (Reid) W. BSN, Biola Coll., 1971. RN, Calif. Staff nurse pediatric outpatient clinic U. Ill. Med. Ctr., Chgo., 1971-73; nurse Morrison Acad., Taichung, Taiwan, 1973-74; clin. nurse med.-surg. orthopedic unit Cen. DuPage Hosp., Winfield, Ill., 1974-76, discharge planning nurse, 1976-79; clin. nurse II newborn nursery U. Calif. Med. Ctr., San Diego, 1979-80; med. legal nurse cons. Wingert, Grebing, Anello & Brubaker, San Diego, 1983-89; exec. dir., owner Med. Legal Resources, San Diego, 1989—; cons., speaker, founder, exec. dir. Med. Legal Resources, San Diego, 1987—. Vol. Make-A-Wish Found., San Diego, 1985—. Recipient Best Workshop award Arthritis Health Professions Assn., 1987. Mem. Am. Assn. Legal Nurse Cons. (founding mem., chair chpt. liaison com., charter mem. San Diego chpt., sec. 1987), San Diego Trial Lawyers Assn. (assoc.), Nat. Nurses in Bus. Assn., Rsch. Coun. of Scripps Clinic (charter mem.), San Diego C. of C., Am. Women Entrepreneurs. Democrat. Methodist. Office: Med Legal Resources 6565 Riverdale St San Diego CA 92120 Also: 6565 Riverdale St San Diego CA 92120

WETTIG, PATRICIA, actress; b. Cin., Dec. 4; m. Ken Olin, 1982; children: Clifford, Roxanne. Student, Ohio Wesleyan U., U. Aberdeen, Scotland; grad. in drama, Temple U.; studies with Bill Esper, Neighborhood Playhouse, N.Y.C. Personal dresser to Shirley MacLaine; mem. Circle Repertory Co. Appeared in theater prodns. including The Woolgatherer, The Diviners, Talking With, TV series thirtysomething (Emmy award for best supporting actress in drama 1988, for best lead actress in drama 1990); guest appearances on L.A. Law, Hill Street Blues. Office: care Capital Cities/ABC Inc 1330 Ave of the Americas New York NY 10019*

WETZEL, KAREN J., nurse; b. Milw., Dec. 1, 1953; d. Carl William and Shirley Ann (McFarlane) Hoffman; m. David A. Wetzel, July 24, 1971; children: Michael David, Brian Lee, Terry Alan, Robyn Janel. Student, Good Samaritan Med Ctr. Sch., 1983, Graceland Coll. Clin. coord., oral surgery Marquette U., Milw.; nurse corinary ICU Sheboygan (Wis.) Meml. Med. Ctr.; head nurse Milw. Med. Clinic, Port Washington, Wis.; head nurse obstetrics/gynecology L&D/nursery St. Mary's Hosp., Ozaukee, Port Washington; instr. neonatal advanced life support, basic life support; lectr. nursing diagnosis, care plans, maternal and newborn assessment; researcher in self hypnosis, pain control and behavioral modification. Active ARC, instr. Neonatal Advanced Life Support, Basic Life Support; youth group counselor United Ch. of Christ; active ARC, community health awareness programs, civil and animal rights causes, politics. 2nd lt. U.S. Army, 1985-87. Home: 1390 Jay Rd Belgium WI 53004 Office: 743 N Montgomery Port Washington WI 53007

WEXLER, HELENE SHELLEY, sales executive; b. Queens, N.Y., Aug. 6, 1956; d. Eugene and Pearl (Barnett) W. BS in Acctg., U. Md., 1977, postgrad., 1990. Mktg. rep. Armstrong World Industries, Tampa, Fla., 1977-79; corp. mktg. salesperson Armstrong World Industries, Boston, 1979-80; account exec. WBCN-FM - Infinity Broadcasting, Boston, 1980-86; account exec. WQHT-FM - Emmis Broadcasting, N.Y.C., 1986-87, nat. sales mgr., 1988—. Office: WQHT 1372 Broadway 16th fl New York NY 10018

WEXLER, JACQUELINE GRENNAN (MRS. PAUL J. WEXLER), association executive, former college president; b. Sterling, Ill., Aug. 2, 1926; d. Edward W. and Florence (Dawson) Grennan; m. Paul J. Wexler, June 12, 1969; stepchildren: Wendy, Wayne. A.B., Webster Coll., 1948; M.A., U. Notre Dame, 1957; LL.D., Franklin and Marshall Coll., 1968, Phila. Coll. Textiles and Sci., 1987; D.H.L., Brandeis U., 1968; LL.D., Skidmore Coll., 1967, Smith Coll., 1975; HHD, U. Mich., 1967, U. Ohio, 1976; D.H.L., Carnegie Inst., 1966, Colo. Coll., 1967, U. Pa., 1979; HHD (hon.), U. Hartford, 1987. Tchr. English and math. Loretto Acad., El Paso, Tex., 1951-54; tchr. English and math. Nerinx Hall, St. Louis, 1954-59; tchr. English Webster Coll., 1959-60, asst. to pres., 1959, v.p. devel., 1960, exec. v.p., 1962-65, pres., 1965-69; v.p., dir. internat. univ. studies Acad. for Ednl. Devel., N.Y.C., 1969; pres. Hunter Coll., City U. N.Y., 1969-79, Acad. Cons. Assoc., N.Y.C., 1980-82; pres. NCCJ, 1982—; writer, commentator, cons.; mem. Am. Council on Edn., Commn. on Internat. Edn., 1967; mem. adv. com. to dir. NIH, 1978-80; mem. exec. panel chief naval ops. U.S. Navy, 1978-81; bd. examiners Fgn. Service, Dept. State, 1981-83; dir. Interpublic Group of Cos., Inc., United Techs. Corp.; mem. Pres.'s Adv. Panel on Research and Devel. in Edn., 1961-65; mem. Pres.'s Task Force on Urban Ednl. Opportunities, 1967. Author: Where I Am Going, 1968; contbr. articles to profl. jours. Trustee U. Pa. Recipient NYU Sch. Edn. Ann. award for creative leadership in edn., 1968, Elizabeth Cutter Morrow award YWCA, 1978, Abraham L. Sachar Silver medallion Brandeis U.'s Nat. Women's Com., 1988, The Albert Einstein award Am. Soc. Technion, 1989; named One of Six Outstanding Women of St. Louis Area St. Louis chpt. Theta Sigma Phi, 1963, Woman of Achievement in Edn. St. Louis Globe-Democrat, 1964, Woman of Accomplishment Harpers Bazaar, 1967, one of Am.'s Most Important 100 Women Ladies Home Jour., 1988; Kenyon lectr. Vassar Coll., 1967. Mem. Mo. Acad. Squires, NCCJ (pres. 1982—), Kappa Gamma Pi. Office: NCCJ 71 Fifth Ave New York NY 10003

WEY COOKE, SHARON KAY, educational association administrator; b. Terre Haute, Ind., June 7, 1954; d. Wilson Woodrow and Effie Nell (Rector) Wey; m. Joseph Craig Cooke, Aug. 21, 1982. BS in Sociology, Ind. State U., 1976. Pres. Jr. Achievement Danville, Ill. Inc., 1976—. Chairperson Bus. Community Rels. Com. Danville Sch. Dist., 1987-89; mem. Citizens Adv. Com. Danville Schs., 1985-86, Gannett Found. Scholarship Com., Danville, 1978-80; vol. Am. Heart Assn., Danville, 1984-85; bd. dirs. East Cen. Ill. Partnership for Excellence in Edn., 1988—. Mem. Exec. Club, Chi Omega. Office: Jr Achievement Danville 603 N Gilbert Danville IL 61832

WEYEN, WENDY LEE, marketing executive; b. Indpls., July 29, 1963; d. Harvey Lee and Louise Marie (Eberhart) W. BA in Journalism, Ind. U., 1985, MBA, 1986; cert. in Internat. Bus., Tilburg (The Netherlands) U., 1985. Assoc. instr. Ind. U., Bloomington, 1985-86; reporter, staff writer St. Petersburg (Fla.) Times, 1986-89, asst. to mktg. dir., 1989—. Bd. dirs. St. Petersburg Family YWCA,. Poynter scholar St. Petersburg Times, Ind. U., 1985. Mem. Ind. U. Alumni Assn. (Herman B. Wells award), Beta Gamma Sigma, Phi Beta Kappa. Lutheran.

WEYERS, SUSAN JOYCE, dentist; b. Ft. Collins, Colo., Feb. 6, 1958; d. Kenneth Dean and Joyce Louise (Visek) W. BS in Nursing, Mont. State U., 1980; DDS, U. Mo., 1986. RN, Mont., Mo. Staff nurse C.H. Steele MD, Great Falls, Mont., 1980-82, Landmark Med. Ctr., Kansas City, Mo., 1982-83, Nutri-Systems Weight Loss Clinic, Kansas City, 1984-85; phys. examiner Am. Svc. Bur., Bodimetric Profiles, Kansas City, 1984-87; pvt. practice dentistry Payson, Ariz., 1987—; instr. dept. oral surgery U. Mo.-Kansas City Sch. Dentistry, 1986-87; dentist dental screening Julia Raldall Elem. Sch., Payson, 1987, 88. Recipient Munksgaard award, 1986. Mem. Am. Dental Assn., Acad. Gen. Dentistry, NAFE, Alpha Tau Delta. Republican. Baptist. Home: 801 E Frontier #39 Payson AZ 85541 Office: 704 S Meadow Payson AZ 85541

WEYFORTH, MIMI See DAWSON, MIMI

WHALA, STACEY ANN, publishing professional, technical writer; b. Houston, Dec. 2, 1962; d. James Merrill and Ernestine (Johnson) W. BA, Okla. State U., 1985. Svc. document asst. Compaq Computer Corp., Houston, 1987-88, desktop pub. coord., 1988-90; publs. specialist community health cons. Welcon Software Tech, Houston, 1990—. Mem. Cultural Arts Coun. Houston, 1987—; advt. chmn. Walk Am., March of Dimes, Houston, 1988. Republican. Methodist. Office: Welcon Software Tech 15995 N Barkers Landing Houston TX 77079

WHALEN, ELIZABETH JOAN, fundraising professional; b. Yonkers, N.Y., July 15, 1956; d. Patrick John and Elizabeth Terese (Mahon) W. BFA magna cum laude, Coll. of New Rochelle, N.Y., 1978; MBA with honors, Iona Coll., 1983. Asst. dir. The River Gallery, Irvington, N.Y., 1979-86; assoc. campaign dir. Charles Webb Co., N.Y.C., 1986-88; dir. devel. Hudson Valley Philharm., Poughkeepsie, N.Y., 1988—. Reunion chmn. class of 1978, Coll. of New Rochelle, 1978-88; v.p. membership Sleep Hollow Concert Assn., Irvington, N.Y., 1984-86; v.p., dir. pub. rels. Ossining Choral Soc., Briarcliff Manor, N.Y., 1987-89. Mem. Coll. New Rochelle Alumni Assn. (bd. dirs), N.Y. State Arts and Cultural Coalition Advisory Com., Camerata Chorale. Roman Catholic. Office: Hudson Valley Philharmonic PO Box 191 Poughkeepsie NY 12602

WHALEN, LORETTA THERESA, educator; b. Bklyn., May 21, 1940; d. William Michael and Loretta Margaret (Malone) Whalen; children: Ann Force, Margaret Force. RN, St. Vincent's Hosp., N.Y.C., 1960; BSN, U. Pa., 1965; MA in Edn., Fordham U., 1971; cert. in sociology religion, Louvain U., Belgium, 1974; postgrad., Union Grad. Sch., 1990—. Staff nurse Holy Family Hosp., Atlanta, 1967-69; Latin Am. communication dir. Med. Mission Sisters, Maracaibo, Venezuela, 1969-71; intensive care nurse St. Vincent's Hosp., N.Y.C., 1971-72; mem. ministry team Med. Mission Sisters, various locations, 1972-74; dir. communications Med. Mission Sisters, Phila., 1974-77; asst. to exec. Interreligious Peace Colloquium, Washington, 1977; freelance writing, photography Ch. World Svc., N.Y.C., 1978-79; dir. Office Global Edn. Nat. Council Chs., N.Y.C., 1980—. Mem. editorial bd., rev. editor Connections Mag., 1984-87; contbr. articles to profl. jours. Mem. Peace and Justice Commn., Archdiocese of Balt., 1985-89. Mem. Amnesty Internat., Bread for the World, NOW, World Wildlife Fund, Greenpeace, Sigma Theta Tau. Democrat. Roman Catholic.

WHALEN, LUCILLE, academic administrator; b. Los Angeles, July 26, 1925; d. Edward Cleveland and Mary Lucille (Perrault) W. B.A. in English, Immaculate Heart Coll., Los Angeles, 1949; M.S.L.S., Catholic U. Am., 1955; D.L.S., Columbia U., 1965. Tchr. elem. and secondary parochial schs. Los Angeles, Long Beach, Calif., 1945-52; high sch. librarian Conaty Meml. High Sch., Los Angeles, 1950-52; reference/serials librarian, instr. in library sci. Immaculate Heart Coll., 1955-58; dean Immaculate Heart Coll. (Sch. Library Sch.), 1958-60, 65-70; assoc. dean, prof. SUNY, Albany, 1971-78, 84-87; prof. Sch. Info. Sci. and Policy Sch. Info. and Library Sci., SUNY, 1979-83; dean grad. programs, libr. Immaculate Heart Coll. Ctr., Los Angeles, 1987—; dir. U.S. Office Edn. Instn. Pub. Reference Services in Archives, 1986, Human Rights: A Reference Handbook, 1989. Mem. Spl. Libraries Assn. (chmn. com. research 1974-80, chmn. social and human services sect. 1983-84), ACLU, Common Cause, Amnesty Internat. Democrat. Roman Catholic. Home: 320 S Gramercy Pl Apt #101 Los Angeles CA 90020 Office: Immaculate Heart Coll Ctr 10951 Pico Blvd Los Angeles CA 90064

WHALEN, NANA LEE, diet counselor, writer; b. Mullens, W.Va., Nov. 12, 1937; d. Gerald Eugene and Hilda Belle (Fowls) Richards; m. John M. Whalen, Dec. 15, 1959; children: Timothy John, Maria Marye, Angela Sue. BS in Edn., Ohio State U., 1959. Free-lance columnist The Village Voice, Severna Park, Md., 1975-76, The Annapolis (Md.) Evening Capitol, 1977, The Baltimore Sun, 1978-82; counselor, owner Diet Ctr. of Severna Park, 1983—, Worthington (Ohio) Dietcenter, 1985—; mem. Diet Ctr. Nat. Profl. Adv. Bd., 1988—. Author: Whale of a Cookbook, 1978, Whale of a Cookbook II, 1979, Hooked on Seafood, 1982, Strawberries, 1983. Mem. Assn. Met. Washington Diet Ctr. Owners, Am. Bus. Women's Assn., Prospect Bay Country Club, Kappa Alpha Theta. Methodist. Home: 49 Prospect Bay Dr W Grasonville MD 21638 Office: Diet Ctr of Severna Pk 480C Ritchie Hwy Severna Park MD 21146

WHALEN, PATRICIA MAY (PATRICIA (RYAN) WHALEN), creative designer, painter; b. Greenfield, Mass., May 25, 1945; d. Dale Ryan and Doris M. (Nichols) Taylor; m. David F. Whalen, Sept., 1970 (div. 1973). Student, Boston Mus. Sch., 1964-65; grad. with honors, Art Inst. Boston, 1967; postgrad., Worcester (Mass.) Art Sch., 1969-71. Indsl. designer Boguss Assocs., Everett, Mass., 1968-70; art dir. L&Z Kamman Co., Gardner, Mass., 1970-73; creative dir., mgr. Artistic Carving Co., Gardner and Boston, 1973-76; creative designer Simplex Time Recorder Co., Gardner, 1979—; freelance designer, Gardner, 1967—; art tchr. Area Head Start Children, Gardner, 1974-76. Bd. dirs. Mass. Lottery Arts Coun., Gardner, 1988—; dep. sheriff, Worcester County, Mass., 1983—; coordinator recreation dept. City of Gardner, 1975-77; active City First Art Show, Gardner, 1972, Gardner Mus., 1988—. Recipient 1st Pl. Concord (Mass.) Art Assn., 1968, Copley Art Show, 1967, Templeon (Mass.) Businessmen Assn., 1968; numerous honorable mentions. Mem. Women in Arts, Women in Communications, Am. Inst. Graphic Arts, NAFE. Home: Off Airport Rd Box 860 Gardner MA 01440

WHALEN-CRUZ, WANDA JO, management analyst; b. Balt., June 16, 1958; d. Ervin David and Joyce Eileen (Hahn) Whalen; m. David Cruz, Apr. 4, 1987. Student, Catonsville Community Coll., 1979; tng. in pers. mgmt. program, Women's Exec. Leadership Program, 1990. Clk. typist Md. State Police, Pikesville, 1975-76; sec. State Hwy. Adminstrn., Balt., 1976-78; sec. U.S. Army C.E., Columbia, Md., 1978-80, Al Batin, Saudi Arabia, 1980-85, Balt., 1985; mgmt. asst. U.S. Army, Ft. Irwin, Calif., 1985, mgmt. analyst, 1985—; equal opportunity counselor U.S. Army, Ft. Irwin, 1986—. Mem. NAFE, NOW, Am. Soc. Mil. Compts., Federally Employed Women, Fed. Women's Program (pres. 1985—, mgr. 1988—), United Humane Soc., Doris Day Animal League. Home: 312 Forest Ave Barstow CA 92311

WHALEY, CHARLOTTE TOTEBUSCH, publisher, editor, writer; b. Pitts., June 21, 1925; d. Charles R. and Elizabeth G. (Dunn) Totebusch; m. Gould Whaley, Jr., Aug. 24, 1951; children: John Gould, Robert Dunn. BA, So. Meth. U., 1970, MA, 1976. Editorial asst. Southwest Rev., So. Meth. U., Dallas, 1971-72, asst. editor, 1972-74, assoc. editor, 1974-75, asst. to dir. So. Meth. U. Press, mng. editor Southwest Rev., 1975-81, editor Southwest Rev., 1981-83, asst. dir., editor So. Meth. U. Press, 1981-82, editor, 1982-83; editor/pub. Still Point Press, 1984—. Mem. Book Pubs. Tex. (treas. 1987-89, media awards chmn. 1989-90, sec. 1990-92), Book Club Calif., Book Club Tex., Southwestern Booksellers Assn. (chmn. lit. awards com. 1987-88), Phi Beta Kappa (asst. sec. So. Meth. U. chpt. 1979-82, pres. North Tex. chpt. 1982-84). Home and Office: 4222 Willow Grove Rd Dallas TX 75220

WHALEY, PEGGY ELAINE (ELLIS WHALEY), advertising executive; b. Cleveland, Tenn., Nov. 30, 1939; d. Edward Darrell and Pauline (Earley), E.; m. Leo J. Whaley, Mar. 29, 1957; children: Sherri, Angela, Traci. Student, Cleve. Coll., 1964-65, Dalton Coll., 1970-72. Office mgr., corp. officer So. Gen. Products Inc., Ringgold, Ga., 1967-73; office mgr. Joe Goodson CPA, Dalton, Ga., 1974-78; comptroller Profl. C&C, Inc., Dalton, 1980-83; editor, assoc. pub. S.E. Floor Covering mag., Dalton, 1983; prin. Whaley & Assocs., Dalton, 1983—; pub., editor Peggy Whaley News Report Internat., Dalton, 1982-85. Co-editor: Today and Tomorrow Became Yesterday, 1986; editor, columnist Am.'s Internat. Mag.; contbr. numerous articles to newspapers, mags. Sec., v.p. Whitfield County Reps., Dalton, 1968-80; pub. info. person, Am. Cancer Soc. Mem. World Trade Coun., Creative Arts Guild Writers Group, N.Y. Bus. Press Editors Inc., Nat. Assn. Accts., Nat. Assn. Women Cons., Inc., SBA Adv. Coun., Nat. Assn. Floor Covering Women (nat. dir. 1984—), Dalton C. of C., Dalton Regional Library Bd. (chmn. 1980-86), Dalton-Whitfield Regional Libr. Found. (bd. mem. 1986—), Pilot Club, LWV (publicity chmn. 1976-81), Toastmasters Internat. (v.p. 1982). Republican. Baptist. Home and Office: Whaley & Assocs PO Box 205 Dalton GA 30722

WHAM, DOROTHY STONECIPHER, state legislator; b. Centralia, Ill., Jan. 5, 1925; d. Ernest Jospeh and Vera Thelma (Shafer) Stonecipher; m. Robert S. Wham, Jan. 26, 1947; children: Nancy S. Wham Mitchell, Jeanne Wham Ryan, Robert S. II. BA, MacMurray Coll., 1946; MA, U. Ill., 1949. Counsellor Student Counselling Bur. U. Ill., Urbana, 1946-49; state dir. ACTION program, Colo./Wyo. U.S. Govt., Denver, 1972-82; mem. Colo. Ho. of Reps., 1986-87; mem. Colo. Senate, 1987—, chair jud. com., 1988—, vice-chair capital devel. com., health, environ., welfare and instns. Mem. LWV, Civil Rights Commn. Denver, 1972-80; bd. dirs. Denver Com. on Mental Health, 1985-88, Denver Symphony, 1985-88. Mem. Am. Psychol. Assn., Colo. Mental Health Assn. (bd. dirs. 1986-88), Colo. Hemophilia Soc. Republican. Methodist. Lodge: Civitan. Home: 2790 S High St Denver CO 80210 Office: State Capitol Rm 333 Denver CO 80203

WHARTON, SHIRLEY GRANGER, hospital administrator, nurse; b. Portsmouth, Va., Nov. 3, 1947; d. William Woodard and Norma Mae (White) Granger; m. Earin D. Wharton, May 3, 1969; 1 child, Ryan Granger. Diploma in Nursing, Norfolk Gen. Hosp. Sch., 1968. RN, Va. Staff nurse Sentara Norfolk (Va.) Gen. Hosp., 1968-73, head nurse, 1973-76, asst. dir. nursing, 1976-79, asst. adminstr. nursing, 1979-86, sr. v.p., 1986—. Active Keel Club-United Way Hampton Roads, Va., 1987-89, Green Run High Sch. PTA, 1987—, Salem High Sch. PTA, 1990, Lake James Homeowners Assn., Virginia Beach, Va., 1986—, Sentara Hosps. Aux., 1980—. Mem. Am. Orgn. Nurse Execs., Exec. Women Internat. (pres. Hampton Roads chpt. 1989—), Va. Orgn. Nurse Execs. (bd. dirs. 1987-89), Pilot Club of Virginia Beach, Inc. (pres. 1990). Baptist. Office: Sentara Norfolk Gen Hosp 600 Gresham Dr Norfolk VA 23507

WHATLEY, JACQUELINE BELTRAM, lawyer; b. West Orange, N.J., Sept. 26, 1944; d. Quirino and Eliane (Gruet) Beltram; m. John W. Whatley, June 25, 1966. BA, U. Tampa, 1966; JD, Stetson U., 1969. Bar: Fla. 1969, Alaska 1971. Assoc. Gibbons, Tucker, McEwen Smith & Cofer, Tampa, Fla., 1969-71; pvt. practice, Anchorage, 1971-73; ptnr. Gibbons, Tucker, Miller, Whatley & Stein, P.A., Tampa, 1973-81, pres., 1981—. Bd. dirs. Travelers Aid Soc.; trustee Humana Women's Hosp., Tampa, Keystone United Meth. Ch., 1986-89. Mem. ABA, Fla. Bar Assn., Alaska Bar Assn., Tenn. Walking Horse Breeders and Exhibitors Assn. (v.p. 1984-87, dir. for Fla. 1981-87), Fla. Walking and Racking Horse Assn. (bd. dirs. 1988-89, pres. 1980-82). Republican. Methodist. Club: Athena (Tampa). Home: PO Box 17595 Tampa FL 33682 Office: 101 E Kennedy Blvd Ste 1000 Tampa FL 33602

WHEATLEY, BRIANA MARIE, labor relations executive; b. North Tonawanda, N.Y., Jan. 4, 1942; d. Raymond George and Helen Dorothy (Arnts) Tessmer; m. Donald Paul Wheatley (div. Aug. 1978); children: Deborah, David. AAS in Retail and Promotion, Tobe Coburn Sch., 1963; BS in Personnel Mgmt. with honors, Purdue U., 1973; postgrad., Ind. U., Ft. Wayne, 1983-86. Asst. dir. personnel Ind.-Purdue U., Ft. Wayne, 1973-76; adminstrv. asst. dir. community devel. and planning City of Ft. Wayne, 1976-77; personnel coordinator govt. compliance GTE Ind., Ft. Wayne, 1977, personnel coordinator labor relations, 1977-79, div. mgr. personnel, 1979-82, mgr. compensation and staffing, 1982-83, mgr. labor relations, 1983-84; mgr. employee relations GTE North, Indpls., 1984-87, GTE Supply, Irving, Tex., 1987—; instr. Purdue U., Ft. Wayne, 1978-80. Mem. Pvt. Industry Council, Ft. Wayne, 1982-84, Hanicap Adv. Council, Ft. Wayne, 1977-84. Gov.'s Council on Mgmt. and Labor, Indpls., 1987. Mem. Am. Soc. for Personnel Adminstrs. (trea. 1980-82, bd. dirs. 1982-83), Nat. Assn. for Female Execs., Indsl. Relations Research Assn., Alpha Xi Delta. Republican. Presbyterian. Home: 2831 Timber Hill Dr Grapevine TX 76051 Office: GTE GTE Pl W Fuller Dr Airport TX 75261-9785

WHEATLEY, MARGARET BISSON (PEGI WHITE), small business owner, personnel consultant; b. Washington, Dec. 27, 1941; d. Robert Omer Bisson and Margaret (Dysart) Redfield; m. Richard Withington Wheatley, Jr., June 5, 1971. B.S. in Psychology, Philosophy, Ripon Coll., 1963. Cert. employment specialist. Dep. probation officer Orange County, Calif., 1964-71; personnel cons., office mgr. James Holder Placement, San Francisco, 1972-77; owner Margaret Bisson Wheatley Designs, Mill Valley, Calif., 1976—; pres., co-owner, personnel cons. McCall Personnel Services, Inc.,

San Francisco, 1978—; dir., co-owner MTS/McCall Temporary Service, Inc., San Francisco, 1982—; owner P&L Resources, San Francisco, 1983—; career advisor Alumni Resources, San Francisco, 1980—; active Options fro Women Over 40, 1989—; curriculum advisor City Coll. San Francisco, 1987—. Mem. Nat. Assn. Personnel Cons., Calif. Assn. Personnel Cons. Republican. Club: Commercial (San Francisco) (bd. dirs. 1986-88). Avocations: tennis, international travel. Office: McCall Personnel Services Inc 369 Pine St Suite 700 San Francisco CA 94104

WHEATON, CARLA ANN, computer information scientist; b. Mineral Wells, W.Va., Nov. 29, 1960; d.d Lewis Glenvile and Carol Ann (Stroehman) W. AS, Ohio Valley Coll., Parkersburg, W.Va., 1981; BS, David Lipscomb Coll., Nashville, 1983. Computer programmer Ohio Valley Data Control, Belpre, Ohio, 1983-84; sr. software specialist Digital Equipment Corp., Charleston, W.Va., 1984--; part-time tchr. Mountain State Coll., 1987-88. Vol. tutor Mountain State Coll., Parkersburg, 1987-88; tchr. Camden Ave. Ch. of Christ, Parkersburg, 1986-89. Named Software Profl. of Quarter, Perfect 10 Software Svcs., 1988, Excellence award Survey Digital Equipment Copr., 1989, Outstanding Sophomore Bandsman Ohio Valley Coll. Mem. Mid-Ohio Valley Christian Singles, Fellowship Bowling League (team capt.). Office: Digital Equipment Corp 1 Player's Club Dr Charleston WV 25311-1689

WHEELER, BETSY, human relations consultant; b. Schenectady, N.Y., May 11, 1939; d. James A. and Helen (Reedy) Forkas; children: William J., Susan R., James D. BS, Cortland State Coll., 1962; postgrad., Gannon Coll., 1990—. Dir., adminstrv. svcs. Schenectady County YMCA; tech. editor Gen. Electric, Schenectady; dir. ednl. svcs. Mohawk Pathways GS Coun., Schenectady; English tchr. Niskayuna (N.Y.) Pub. Schs.; cons., owner Wheeler Communications, Schenectady. Mem. N.Y. State Fedn. of Bus., Profl. Women Recording Sec., Bd. Dirs. of Schenectady BPW, NAFE. Home: 1465 Regent St Schenectady NY 12309

WHEELER, CAROL ESTELLE, educational administrator; b. Mobile, Ala., Sept. 9, 1936; d. Frederick G. and A. Estelle (Ryan) W. AB, Maryville Coll., St. Louis, 1958; MA in Philosophy, Georgetown U., 1971; MA in Edn., U. Chgo., 1976. Joined Sisters of Mercy, Roman Cath. Ch., 1959. Tchr. Mercy High Sch., Balt., 1961-68, asst. prin., 1971-72, advisor to beginning tchrs., 1976-77, pres., prin., 1977—; tchr. Bishop Toolen High Sch., Mobile, 1968-69; supr. student tchrs. U. Chgo., 1974-75, adminstrv. asst. MST program, 1975-76; mem. profl. standards and tchr. edn. adv. bd. Md. Dept. Edn., 1984-86. Trustee Loyola Coll., Balt., 1982-88, Mercy Med. Ctr., Balt., 1985—, Cathedral Found. Bd., Archdiocese Balt., 1983-88; del. provincial chpt. Sisters of Mercy, Balt., gen. chpt. Sisters of Mercy of the Union. Rsch. fellow Yale U. Sch. Divinity, 1988-89. Mem. Mercy Secondary Edn. Assn. (pres. 1983-87), Assocs. Research in Pvt. Edn., Assn. Supervision and Curriculum Devel., Nat. Assn. Secondary Sch. Prins., Nat. Cath. Edn. Assn.

WHEELER, CATHY JO, federal agency professional; b. Birmingham, Ala., Feb. 14, 1954; d. Charles Edwin and Hazel Josephine (Hollis) W. BA, U. Montevallo, Ala., 1975; postgrad., U. Ala., 1982-84. With Social Security Adminstrn., Birmingham, 1975—, sr. employment devel. specialist, 1983-85, mgr. tech. tng. dept., 1985—; v.p. Fed. Women's Program, Birmingham, 1984-85; treas., charter mem. Federally Employed Women, Birmingham, 1984-88. Mem. Am. Soc. Tng. Devel. (treas. 1987-88, pres. 1990—), Soc. Govt. Meeting Planners (chartered, v.p. 1989-90, sec. 1990—), Jaycees (v.p. mgmt. devel. Hoover, Ala. chpt. 1988-89), Chi Omega Alumni Assn. Home: 1108 Columbiana Rd Homewood AL 35209 Office: Southeastern Program Svc Ctr 2001 12th Ave N Birmingham AL 35285

WHEELER, DONNA MARIE, filmmaker; b. Tulsa, June 12, 1962; d. Clifford Keith and Elizabeth (Bonilla) W. BS with honors, U. Fla., 1985; MFA, Fla. State U., 1989—. Asst. dir. mktg. and media dept. Miami-Dade Community Coll., Miami, Fla., 1985-86; casting dir. Casting Dirs., Inc., North Miami, Fla., 1986-88; copywriter West & Co. Advt., Jacksonville and Tampa, Fla., 1988-89; acting instr. local colls., 1987. Writer, producer, dir. multi-media, video and film projects. Dupont scholar, 1983. Mem. Fla. Motion Picture and TV Assn., Internat. Thespian Soc., Women of Motion Picture Industry, Fla. Freelance Writers Assn., Nat. Assn. Female Execs., Kappa Tau Alpha. Home: 4554 SW 128th Pl Miami FL 33175

WHEELER, KATHERINE WELLS, state legislator; b. St. Louis, Feb. 8, 1940; d. Benjamin Harris and Katherine (Gladney) Wells; m. Douglas Lanphier Wheeler, June 13, 1964; children: Katherine Gladney, Lucille Lanphier. BA, Smith Coll., 1961; MA, Washington U., St. Louis, 1966. Founder auction N.H. Pub. TV, Durham, 1973-76; pub. mem. N.H. Pub. Broadcasting Council, Durham, 1975-80; founding mem. bd. govs. N.H. Pub. TV, 1980-88; mem. N.H. Ho. of Reps., Concord, 1988—; pres. adv. coun. Currier Gallery, Manchester, N.H., 1988—; coord. internat. visitors program N.H. Coun. World Affairs, 1981—; bd. dirs. Planned Parenthood No. New Eng., Gt. Bay Sch. and Tng. Ctr., Newington, N.H. Mem. exec. com. Stafford County, 1988, N.H., N.H. State Dem. Comm., 1988, Commn. on Health, Human Svcs. and Elderly Affairs N.H. Ho. of Reps., Concord, 1988; bd. mgrs. Dover Children's Home, 1990—. Named Woman of Yr. Union Leader Newspaper, 1984, Citizen of Yr. Homemakers of Strafford County, 1990; recipient Elizabeth Cambell Outstanding Pub. TV Vol. award Nat. Friends of Pub. Broadcasting, 1984. Mem. LWV, Order of Women Legis., N.H. Smith Coll. Club (v.p. 1974-76, pres. 1976-78), Durham/Great Bay Rotary. Democrat. United Ch. Christ. Home and Office: 27 Mill Rd Durham NH 03824

WHEELER, KYLE THORN, writer, technical; b. Cambridge, Mass., Apr. 5, 1952; d. Robert Nicol Thorn and Betty Lou (Vogel) Wilde; m. Michael Gary Wheeler, May 2, 1982; step children: Katherine, Eric. BS in Psychology, U. Utah, 1974. Sec., educator Planned Parenthood, Santa Barbara, 1976-78; writer, editor Los Alamos (N.M.) Nat. Lab., 1979--; county councilor Los Alamos (N.M.) County, 1989--. Writer, Division Annual Review and Operating Plan, 1987, 1988, 1989. Councilor Los Alamos County, 1989. Mem. Soc. for Tech. Communication, Los Alamos Ski Club. Democrat. Home: 2987 Woodland Rd Los Alamos NM 87544 Office: Computer Documentation Grp MS B253 Los Alamos NM 87545

WHEELER, M. CATHERINE, state official; b. Plainfield, N.J., May 31, 1942; d. William R. and Josephine S. (Ford) W. BA in Politics, Hollins Coll., 1964; MA in Theatre, U. Kans., 1966. Asst. mgr. South Shore Music Circus, Cohasset, Mass., 1967; pub. rels. asst. Trinity Square Repertory Co., Providence, 1967-68; co. mgr. Acad. Playhouse, Wilmette, Ill., 1968; adminstrv. asst. Am. U. Theatre, Washington, 1968-71; pub. rels. asst. Winterthur Mus. and Gardens, Wilmington, Del., 1972-76, dir. pub. rels., 1976-84; dir. Del. Tourism Office, Dover, 1984—; pub. rels. cons. Historic Deerfield (Mass.), 1983. Editor Winterthur Newsletter, 1972-84, Del.: Tourism News in Small Wonder State newsletter, 1988—. Mem. Del. Heritage Commn., 1984—, Discover Am. Task Force, 1990—. Mem. Nat. Coun. State Travel Dirs. (chmn. nominating com. 1987-89, chmn. edn. com. 1989—, bd. dirs. U.S. Travel Data Ctr. 1989—), Travel Industry Assn. Office: Del Tourism Office 99 Kings Hwy Box 1401 Dover DE 19903

WHEELER, MARILYN MILLER, school assistant principal; b. Valparaiso, Fla., Jan. 8, 1955; d. Ira Owen and Ruth Mae (Manning) Miller; m. Floyd Douglas Wheeler, July 1, 1978; 1 child, Jonathan Douglas. AA, Pensacola Jr. Coll., 1975; BS, U. North Fla., 1977, MS, 1983. Cert. tchr., adminstr., Fla. Tchr. Rufus Payne Sixth Grade Ctr., Jacksonville, Fla., 1977, Parkwood Heights Elem. Sch., Jacksonville, 1977-78, Mayport Elem. Sch., Jacksonville, 1978-88, Ft. Caroline Elem. Sch., Jacksonville, 1988-89; asst. prin. Long Branch Elem. Sch., Jacksonville, 1989—; tchr. gifted student programs, Jacksonville Pub. Schs., 1985, 87. Mem. Assn. Supervision and Curriculum Devel., Fla. Reading Coun., University Park Civic Assn., Phi Delta Kappa. Democrat. Baptist. Home: 5367 Coppedge Ave Jacksonville FL 32211 Office: Long Branch Elem Sch 3723 Franklin St Jacksonville FL 32206

WHEELER, NANCY ALICE, nurse; b. Kansas City, Mo., July 4, 1954; d. Sidney Kenyon and Elizabeth Ann (Biddle) W. BS in Nursing, Avila Coll., 1977. RN; CEN. Nurse surg.-trauma intensive care units U. Kans. Med. Ctr., Kansas City, Kans., 1976-79; nurse med. intensive care unit Bethany Med. Ctr., Kansas City, Kans., 1979—. Mem. Nat. Abortion Rights League, Washington, 1990, Greenpeace, 1990. Mem. Am. Assn. Critical Care Nurses. Democrat. Roman Catholic. Office: Bethany Med Ctr 51 N 12th St Kansas City KS 66102

WHEELER, PATRICIA HARRIETT ANN, communications professional; b. Washington, Dec. 29, 1950; d. Harry C. and Inez P. (Parks) W. BS, U. Md., 1973; MBA, Columbia U., 1981. Reporter WRVA-AM, Richmond, Va., 1973-74; producer, dir. KOAP-TV, Portland, Oreg., 1974-76; asst. community svcs. dir. Sta. WBAL-TV, Balt., 1976-79; bus. intern N.Y. Times, Washington, 1980; asst. dir. mktg. Time-Life Books, Alexandria, Va., 1981-84; lectr. mktg. Howard U., Washington, 1983-86; dir. mktg. Gannett New Media Svcs., Arlington, Va., 1984-86; dir. advt. and pub. rels. Gannett Outdoor, N.Y.C., 1987-88; dir. communications D.C. Dept. Corrections, Washington, 1988—; vice-chair corrections chiefs/pub. info. officers com. Coun. of Govts., Washington, 1989—; mem. Leadership Washington, D.C. Bd. Trade, 1989-90; participant humanities seminar for journalists, NEH, Berkeley, Calif., 1978. Producer TV film Freedom Frontier, 1976. Phillip Graham grantee Columbia U., 1979, N.W. Ayer grantee, 1980; named Outstanding Woman in D.C. Govt., D.C. Women's Program Mgrs. Com., Washington, 1989. Mem. NAACP, LWV (mem. edn. fund com. D.C. chpt.), Nat. Black MBA Assn. (com. mem. D.C. chpt.), Washington Women in Pub. Rels. (awards dinner com. 1989—, program chair 1990—), Nat. Assn. Blacks in Criminal Justice, Nat. Forum Black Pub. Adminstrs., Toastmasters, African-Am. Lit. Guild (founder), Am. Correctional Assn. Democrat. Roman Catholic. Office: DC Dept Corrections 1923 Vermont Ave NW Washington DC 20001

WHEELER, VIVIAN BARBARA, manuscript editor; b. N.Y.C., Oct. 20, 1927; d. Frank Joseph and Alma (Schutt) Wille; m. Colin Livingstone Wheeler, Oct. 12, 1957 (div. 1971); children: Kathryn Ann, Susan Leigh. BA, Wellesley Coll., Mass., 1948. Tech. asst. Bell Tel. Labs, N.Y.C., 1948-50; writer, editor Rockefeller Found., N.Y.C., 1950-54; project control officer U.S. Army Q.M.C., Natick, Mass., 1954-59; editor Harvard U. Press, Cambridge, Mass., 1971-81, sr. editor, 1981—; asst. mng. editor Harvard U. Press, 1988—. Editor numerous works, 1960—. Sec. Magnolia (Mass.) Hist. Soc., 1982-84; bd. dirs. Magnolia Neighborhood Assn., 1988—; Mem. Manchester (Mass.) Women's Chorus. Recipient sustained superior performance award U.S. Army Q.M.C., 1957, outstanding achievement award, 1957. Mem. Bookbuilders Boston, Wellesley Club Winchester and North Shore (pres. 1967-69), Winton Club (Winchester, Mass.). Home: 37 Shore Rd Magnolia MA 01930 Office: Harvard U Press 79 Garden St Cambridge MA 02138

WHEELER, WENDY ROBIN, computer company executive; b. Washington, Aug. 25, 1953; d. Malcolm Frederick and Aurora Dorothy (Anas) W.; m. Ian Stanley Reid, Aug. 16, 1986; 1 child, Emily Claire. B.A. in Modern Lang. and Lit., Trinity Coll., 1975. Mktg. rep. IBM, Waltham, Mass., 1975-80; product mgr. Prime Computer, Natick, Mass., 1980-82, asst. to pres., 1982-83, dir. product mktg., 1983-86, v.p. systems mktg., 1986, v.p. sales support, 1986-90; v.p. mktg. Xyvision Corp., Wakefield, Mass., 1990—; bd. dirs. Mass. Product Devel. Corp. Named 1984 Woman of Achievement in Bus. and Industry, Boston, YWCA, 1984. Mem. Profl. Council Boston (bd. dirs.), Women in Info. Processing. Office: Xyvision Inc 101 Edgewater Dr Wakefield MA 01880-1291

WHEELOCK, CAROLYN MINNETTE, developer, fundraiser; b. St. Louis, May 28, 1923; d. Charles William and Marion Elizabeth (Ross) McClellan; m. Ralph Hervey Wheelock, July 12, 1947; 1 child, Gary Ross. BA, Washington U., St. Louis, 1944; MA in U.S. History, Washington U., 1945. Cert. tchr. Tchr. pub. schs. Mo., R.I., 1945-48; tchr. Edgewood Jr. Coll., Barrington, R.I., 1947-48; substitute tchr. Cranston and Warwick, R.I., 1948-49, 56-59; nursery sch. tchr. Peter Piper Sch., Warwick, 1959; active various community and civic orgns., R.I., 1959—. Bd. dirs. St. Elizabeth Home, Providence, 1981—; active Am. Cancer Society, Warwick, Providence, 1951—, Meals on Wheels, Providence, 1968—; lay leader Asbury Meth. Ch., Warwick, 1981-85. Mem. AAUW, Eastern Star (Pawtuxet chpt.), Warwick Country Club, Alpha Xi Delta. Republican. Home: 37 Anderson Ave Warwick RI 02888

WHEELOCK, MARTHA ELLEN, film and video producer, director and distributor; b. Exeter, N.H., Sept. 24, 1941; d. Frederic M. and Dorothy (Rathbone) W. BA, Earlham Coll., 1963; MA, NYU, 1965, postgrad., 1967-78. Tchr. English Great Neck (N.Y.) Pub. Schs., 1966-84; mem. faculty, Eng. instr. Elizabeth Seton Coll., White Plains, N.Y., 1980-84; owner, pres. Ishtar Films, N.Y.C. and Hollywood, Calif., 1978—; participant Ind. Feature Project; mem. media task force Woman's Bldg., 1986-89. Producer, dir. films World of Light: A Portrait of May Sarton, 1978, Kate Chopin's Story of an Hour, 1982, One Fine Day, 1984, Take the Power, 1987, Madeleine L'Engle: Star-Gazer, 1989. Mem. Women in Film (bd. dirs. 1988—), Modern Lang. Assn., Nat. Women's Studies Assn., NOW (organizer 1970-85). Democrat. Office: Ishtar Films 6253 Hollywood Blvd Ste 623 Hollywood CA 90028

WHELAN, LAURA DOZIER, real estate broker; b. Augusta, Ga., Mar. 16, 1922; d. Edward Clouis and Laura (Murphy) Dozier; m. Thomas B. Whelan, Aug. 7, 1943 (dec. Nov. 1978); children: James, Thomas II. Assoc. broker WJD and Assocs., Alexandria, Va. Mem. aux. bd. Alexandria Hosp. Fellow: Va. Assn. Realtors, Md. Bd. Realtors; mem. Belle Haven Women's Club, Belle Haven Country Club, Grove Investment Club, Delta Delta Delta. Republican. Roman Catholic. Home: 6208 Foxcroft Rd Alexandria VA 22307

WHELAN, VIRGINIA, auto recycling center executive; b. Long Branch, N.J., Sept. 28, 1950; d. Salvatore and Ida (Russo) Parrino; m. David Charles Whelan, Aug. 1, 1970; children: Jade Ida, Kelly Ann. BA, Morningside Coll., 1972. Cert. tchr. N.J., Iowa. V.p., sec., treas. Parrino Auto Inc., Ocean, N.J., 1983—, Salida Inc., Ocean, 1983—; 2nd v.p. United N.J. Auto Salvage Assn., Morganville, N.J., 1986— (mem. conv. com. 1980, chmn. fin. com. 1989); regional dir. Auto Dismantlers & Recyclers Assn., Washington, 1988— (pub. rels. com., communications com.); writer Recycler Digest. Religious instr. St. Anselm Ch., Ocean, 1984—. Recipient cert. of commendation CNA Ins. Co., 1988. Mem. Greater Ocean Twp. C. of C. Home: 917 West Park Ave Ocean NJ 07712

WHELAN-COTA, MARIE ELAINE, writer researcher; b. Everett, Mass., Apr. 22, 1952; d. William Francis and Edna Claire (Gardner) Whelan; m. Joseph Ambrose Cota, Sept. 8, 1979; children: G. William Cota, Christopher J. Cota, Katherine C. Cota. With Millipore Corp., Bedford, Mass., 1975-81; freelance writer, researcher Tewksbury, 1981—; corr. The Lowell (Mass.) Sun, 1984-85; writer Merrimack Valley Advertiser, Tewksbury, Mass., 1985-87. Supporter various child abuse prevention programs and youth athletic programs; adv. for gifted children; founder Children with Spl. Promise. Mem. The Nat. Writer's Club, Soc. for Tech. Communication, Am. Med. Writers' Assn., Soc. of Children's Book Writers. Republican. Roman Catholic. Home: PO Box 508 Tewksbury MA 01876 Office: PO Box 648 Tewksbury MA 01876

WHELCHEL, LUCY BEASLEY, business owner, consultant in gerontology; b. Douglas, Ga., Dec. 27, 1942; d. Charles Ernest and Margaret Louise (Penn) Beasley; m. Robert Edward Whelchel Jr., Aug. 16, 1964; 1 child, Patrick Jones. BA, LaGrange Coll., 1964; MA, Ga. State U., 1981. Pub. health educator Hall County Health Dept., Gainesville, Ga., 1977-79; project dir. Atlanta Pub. Schs., 1974-76, Gainesville Coll., 1979-81, Sr. Opportunity Svcs., Gainesville, 1981-84; dir. devel. Lakeview Acad., Gainesville, 1985-86; bus. owner Whelchel and Assocs., Gainesville, 1984—, Nursing Care, Inc., Gainesville, 1984—; trainer in gerontology Gainesville Coll., 1984—; cons. Chicopee Mfg., 1988; presenter of programs in field to profl. groups. Chair Community Coun. on Aging, Gainesville, 1983-84; founder The Guest House Adult Day Rehab., 1984-85. Recipient Bd. award March of Dimes, 1984; Lucy Whelchel Rm. named in her honor The Guest House Community Coun. on Aging, 1985. Mem. LWV, NOW, Ga. Gerontology Soc., Commerce Club Gainesville, Gainesville C. of C., N.E. Georgians for Choice, Ga. State U. Gerontology Alumni Club. Democrat. Methodist. Office: Nursing Care 205 Boulevard St Gainesville GA 30501

WHELCHEL, SANDRA JANE, writer; b. Denver, May 31, 1944; d. Ralph Earl and Janette Isabelle (March) Everitt; m. Andrew Jackson Whelchel, June 27, 1965; children: Andrew Jackson, Anita Earlyn. BA in Elem. Edn., U. No. Colo., 1966; postgrad. Pepperdine Coll., 1971, UCLA, 1971. Elem. tchr. Douglas County Schs., Castle Rock, Colo., 1966-68, El Monte (Calif.) schs., 1968-72; br. librarian Douglas County Libraries, Parker, Colo., 1973-78; zone writer Denver Post, 1979-81; reporter The Express newspapers, Castle Rock, 1979-81; history columnist Parker Trail newspapers, 1985—; writing tchr. Aurora Parks and Recreation, 1985—; columnist Authorship mag.; contbr. short stories and articles to various publs. including: Ancestry Newsletter, Empire mag., Calif. Horse Rev., Host mag., Jack and Jill, Child Life, Children's Digest; author (non-fiction books): Your Air Force Academy, 1982, (coloring books): A Day at the Cave, 1985, A Day in Blue, 1984, Pro Rodeo Hall of Champions and Museum of the American Cowboy, 1985, Pikes Peak Country, 1986, Mile High Denver, 1987; co-author: The Register, 1989; lectr. on writing. Mem. Internat. Platform Assn., Nat. Writers Club (treas. Denver Metro chpt. 1985-86, v.p. membership 1987, sec. 1990), Parker Area Hist. Soc. (pres. 1987, 88, 89).

WHELEHAN, PATRICIA ELIZABETH, anthropology educator; b. Rochester, N.Y., Mar. 4, 1947; d. Charles Thomas and Betty F. (Freisner) W.; 1 child, Rachel Alexandra Scout Galgoul. BA, SUNY, Potsdam, 1969; MA, SUNY, Albany, 1973, PhD, 1979. Cert. sex therapist, AIDS instr./counselor; diplomate Am. Bd. Sexologists. Group home houseparent LaSalle Sch. for Boys, Albany, 1973-75; grad. asst. SUNY, Albany, 1976-78; adj. assoc. prof. Counseling Ctr. Potsdam (N.Y.) Coll., 1985—, assoc. prof. anthropology, 1978—; sex and relationship therapist referral North Country MDs, 1982—; campus AIDS coordinator, assoc. prof. Inst. for Advanced Study Human Sexuality, San Francisco, 1988—; cons. Polaris Inst., San Francisco, 1988—. Co-author: Human Sexuality Text, 1989; editor: Women and Health, 1988; cons. editor Jour. Sex Edn. and Therapy, 1987—; contbr. articles to profl. jours. Bd. dirs. Citizens Against Violent Acts, Syracuse, N.Y., 1986—, AIDS Task Force Cen. N.Y., Potsdam, 1988—, St. Lawrence County Coun. on AIDS, Potsdam, 1988—. SUNY travel grantee, 1987-88; Potsdam Coll. mini grantee, 1979, 88. Mem. Am. Anthropol. Assn., Am. Coll. Sexology, Soc. Sci. Study Sex, AAUW, NOW, NARAL, Phi Delta Kappa. Home: Rt 2 May Rd Box 95 Potsdam NY 13676 Office: SUNY Anthropology Dept 122 MacVicar Hall Potsdam NY 13676

WHIDDON, CAROL PRICE, writer, editor, consultant; b. Gadsden, Ala., Nov. 18, 1947; d. Curtis Ray and Vivian (Dooly) Price; m. John Earl Caulking, Jan. 18, 1969 (div. July 1987); m. Ronald Alton Whiddon, Apr. 13, 1988. BA in Applied Music, McNeese State U., 1968; BA in English, George Mason U., 1984. Flute instr. Lake Charles, La., 1966-68; flutist Lake Charles Civic Symphony, 1966-69, Beaumont (Tex.) Symphony, 1967-68; freelance editor The Washington Lit. Rev., 1983-84, ARC Hdqrs., Washington, 1984; writer, editor Jaycor, Vienna, Va., 1985-87, Albuquerque, 1987—; owner Whiddon Editing Svc., Albuquerque, 1989—. Contbr. various articles to Albuquerque Woman and mil. dependent pubs. in Fed. Rpublic Germany. Dep. mgr. Fed. Women's Program, Ansbach, Fed. Republic Germany, 1980-81; pres. Ansbach German-Am. Club, 1980-82; sec. Am. Women's Activities, Fed. Repubic Germany, 1980-81, chairwoman, 1981-82. Named Outstanding Young Women of Am., 1981; recipient cert. of appreciation Amb. Arthur T. Burns, Federal Republic Germany, 1982, medal of appreciation Comdr., 1st Armored div., Ansbach, 1982. Mem. NAFE, Women in Communications (newsletter editor 1989-90, v.p. 1990-91), Soc. Tech. Communication, Nat. Assn. Desktop Pubs., N.Mex. Cactus Soc. (historian 1989—, various show ribbons 1989, 90). Republican. Home: 1129 Turner Dr NE Albuquerque NM 87123

WHIGHAM, TERRI LEE, marketing executive; b. Riverside, Calif., May 8, 1953; d. Gordon Terrance and Virginia Lee (Warren) W. Student Merced Jr. Coll., 1979. Asst. to pres. BAC-Pritchard, Inc., Merced, Calif.; asst. to pres. Valley Sheet Metal, South San Francisco, Calif.; asst. to supt. Herman Christensen & Sons, San Carlos, Calif.; corp. treas. TransGlobal Mktg. Corp., San Francisco; v.p., sec./treas. D&B Buying Group; pres. Internat. Trading Resources, Internat. Almond Brokerage; exec. dir. Am. Sports Merchandising; dist. rep. Modern Woodman of Am.; owner, exec. dir. Nat. Retailers Coalition. Treas. Le Grand United Meth. Ch., chmn. fund raising com. Mem. Nat. Assn. Female Execs., Nat. Sporting Goods Assn., Far West Ski Assn. Democrat. Office: 557 W Main Ste 3E Merced CA 95340

WHIPPLE, JACQUELINE CONANT, writer, media specialist; b. Columbus, Ohio, Mar. 31, 1921; d. William Horace and Gertrude Virginia (Bryant) Conant; A.B. magna cum laude, Mt. Holyoke Coll., 1943; postgrad. Art. Inst. Boston, 1974-79; m. David Collins Whipple, Sept. 6, 1944; children: Nancy, Roger, Leah, Benjamin. Reporter, Scarsdale (N.Y.) Inquirer, summers, 1939-43; scriptwriter radio dept. J. Walter Thompson Co., N.Y., 1943-45; reporter Washington Daily News, 1945-47; broadcast journalist, chief editorial writer Sta. WCRB-AM-FM, Waltham, Mass. and Boston, 1960-67; with Sch. div. Houghton Mifflin Co., Boston, 1967-88; freelance all media; jury chmn. excellence in pub. writing/support of edn. Council for Advancement and Support of Edn., Washington, 1981. Chmn. "Know Your Town"-Waltham LWV, 1951, v.p., 1953; pres. Cohasset (Mass.) PTA, 1963. Recipient Tom Phillips award, UPI Broadcasters of Mass., 1963; cert. of merit Art Inst. Boston, 1976, Cohasset Yacht Club. Democrat. Unitarian. Contbr. articles to popular mags. Home and Office: 119 N Main St Cohasset MA 02025

WHISENTON, MILDRED JAMES, small business owner, consultant; b. Wewoka, Okla., May 4, 1937; d. Jessie Jim and Ethel (Reed) James; m. Wendell Waldo Whisenton, July 7, 1956; 1 child, Alvin Waldo. AA, Long Beach (Calif.) City Coll., 1958. With Procter & Gamble, Long Beach, 1959-79; owner Ms. Whis Inc., Long Beach, 1973—; pres. Ms. Whis Inc. Talent Search, Long Beach, 1980-89. Organizer Jr. League Football in Long Beach, 1965; mem. census com. Long Beach Mayor's Every One Counts, 1989; fin. sec. Pack 121 Boy Scouts Am., Long Beach, 1965; bd. dirs. West Long Beach Adv. Com., Long Beach, 1990—. Recipient Community Svc. award Recreation Area Adv. Couns., 1973, Poly Pop Warner award Long Beach Youth Football, 1975, Youth of Am. award Harbor Teen Post, 1985. Mem. Nat. Coun. Negro Women (life, fin. sec. 1965-69, Humanitarian award 1975), NAACP (life, Humanitarian award 1989), VFW (life), Garfield Bapt. Ch. Missionary Soc. (Humanitarian award 1980), Procter & Gamble Golf Club (Best Golfer 1975), Canyon Lake Country Club. Democrat. Home and Office: 2350 Easy Ave Long Beach CA 90810

WHISMAN, NANCY, automotive executive; b. Milah, Ind., Aug. 13, 1948; d. Paul L. and Manetta V. (Lewis) Rump; m. Harold F. Whisman, Mar. 10, 1972; 1 child, Angel. Cert. in acctg., Ivy Tech., 1980. Adminstrv. asst. Riverview Foods, Inc., Warsaw, Ky.; pres. Corvette Enterprises, Inc., Aurora, Ind. Mem. Ohio Horseman's Coun. (bd. trustees), Southwestern Ohio Appaloosa Assn. Home: PO Box 385 Aurora IN 47001

WHITACRE, DIANE LOUISE, communications executive; b. Cumberland, Md., July 16, 1953; d. Frank Terrence and Thelma (Martin) Delsignore; m. Terry W. Trout, May 25, 1974 (div. 1983); 1 child, Lindsay Ann; m. James E. Whitacre, Feb. 14, 1989. AA, Strayer Coll., Washington, 1973; BA with honors, Nat. Coll. Edn., McLean, Va., 1987. Mgmt. loan banker Fairfax, Va., 1982-85; Sales adminstr. Reston, Va., 1985-86; sales adminstr. Computers, Reston, Va., 1985-86; sales rep. Fairfax, Va., 1986-88; sr. acct. mgr. Telecomm., Fairfax, 1986-88, Telcom, Contel Corp., Chantilly, Va., 1988—. Pres. Cyrandall Valley Homeowner's Assn., Vienna, Va. 1982-83 (treas. 1981-82); mem. Contel-PAC Pol. Action Com. Telecommunications Washington, 1989. Mem. Nat. Assn. Female Execs., Va. Assn. Female Execs. Republican. Roman Catholic.

WHITAKER, EILEEN MONAGHAN, artist; b. Holyoke, Mass., Nov. 22, 1911; d. Thomas F. and Mary (Doona) Monaghan; m. Frederic Whitaker. Ed., Mass. Coll. Art, Boston. Annual exhibits in nat. and regional watercolor shows; represented in permanent collections, Charles and Emma Frye Mus., Seattle, NAD, U.S. Internat. U., San Diego. Hispanic Soc., N.Y.C., High Mus. Art, Atlanta, U. Mass., Norfolk (Va.) Mus., Springfield (Mass.) Mus. Art, Reading (Pa.) Art Mus., Nat. Acad. Design, U. Mass., Okla. Mus. Art, St. Lawrence U., Wichita State U., Retrospective show, Founders Gallery U. San Diego, 1988, invitational one-person show Charles and Emma Frye Art Mus., 1990; included in pvt. collections; featured in cover article of American Artist mag., Mar. 1987; author: Eileen Monaghan Whitaker Paints San Diego, 1986. Recipient numerous major awards, including; several awards Allied Artists Am.; Fist Prize Providence Water Color Club; several awards Am. Watercolor Soc.; Wong award Calif. Watercolor Soc.; De Young award Soc. Western Artists; Springville (Utah) Mus. First award; Ranger Fund purchase prize; Orbrig prize NAD; silver medal Am. Watercolor Soc.; Watercolor West. Fellow Huntington Hartford Found., 1964; Walter Biggs Meml. award Nat. Acad. Design, 1987. Academician NAD; mem. Am. Watercolor Soc., Watercolor West (hon.), San Diego Watercolor Soc. (hon.). Home: 1579 Alta La Jolla Dr La Jolla CA 92037 Office: care Riggs Galleries La Jolla CA

WHITAKER, ELIZABETH DIANE, medical records professional; b. Omaha, Apr. 10, 1945; d. Joseph Phillip and Elizabeth (Neil) Blank; div.; 1 child, Julie Diane. BS, Coll. St. Mary, Omaha, 1982; postgrad., Westark Community Coll., Ft. Smith, Ark., 1988—. Lead med. transcriptionist St. Joseph Hosp., Omaha, 1978-80; med. records dir., quality assurance coord. Myrtue Meml. Hosp., Harlan, Iowa, 1982-84; med. records dir. St. Edward Mercy Med. Ctr., Ft. Smith, 1984—. Campaign fund raiser United Way, Ft. Smith, 1986. Mem. Am. Med. Record Assn., Ark. Med. Record Assn. (pres. 1989—, chmn., editor reference manual 1988). Roman Catholic. Home: 3505 Fleming Pl Circle Fort Smith AR 72903 Office: Saint Edward Mercy Med Ctr PO Box 17000 Fort Smith AR 72917-7000

WHITAKER, MARY See MANNING, MARY

WHITAKER, PENELOPE ANN, company executive; b. New Albany, Ind., Jan. 10, 1941; d. Judd Arthur Byerley and Loweth Lynn (Beck) Lerner; m. Wil A. Whitaker, Nov. 9, 1963 (div. 1970); children: Shammi Lynne Pudsey, Jay Morgan Whitaker, Julie Starr Whitaker. Student, Ind. U., New Albany, 1959-61, 68, Ind. U., 1982-84, Louisville Sch. Art, 1959-60. With Commonwealth Life Ins., Louisville, 1959-63; copywriter John Ward & Assocs. Advt., Louisville, 1968-70; continuity and promotions dir. Sta. WAKY Radio, Louisville, 1970-79; continuity dir. Sta. WAVG Radio, Louisville, 1979-84; band battle mgr. Show Cars, Inc., Louisville, 1971-86; asst. to children's librarian Jeffersonville (Ind.) Twp. Pub. Library, 1974-81; asst. dir. spl. events Louisville C. of C., 1985-86; publicity asst. Solters/Roskin/Friedman & L.A. Area C. of C., 1987; exec. asst. and office mgr. Apollo Pictures, Inc., Culver City, Calif., 1987-89; exec. asst. Hollywood (Calif.) Entertainment Mus., 1989—. Active Clarksville Little Theatre, 1959-69, bd. dirs., 1966-69; actress Summer of Stock/Sheraton Hotels, Louisville, 1963-64; vol. St. Joseph Med. Ctr., Burbank, 1989—. Mem. Am. Women in Radio and TV, Beta Sigma Phi. Republican. Methodist. Office: Hollywood Entertainment Mus 5555 Melrose Ave Hollywood CA 90038

WHITAKER, SHIRLEY ANN, telecommunications company marketing executive; b. Asmara, Eritea, Ethiopia, Oct. 13, 1955; (parents Am. citizens); d. Calvin Randall and Ruth (Ganeles) Peck; m. John Marshall Whitaker, June 16, 1973; 1 child, Kathryn Ann. AA, Tacoma Community Coll., 1974; BA, Wash. State U., 1977, MBA, 1978. Planning adminstr. for econ. rsch. GTE NW, Everett, Wash., 1978-80; specialist in demand analysis western region GTE Svc. Corp., Los Gatos, Calif., 1980-81; fin. analyst GTE Svc. Corp., Stamford, Conn., 1981-83, staff specialist demand analysis and forecasting, 1983-84; group mgr. for rate devel. Nat. Exch. Carrier Assn., Whippany, N.J., 1984-87; mgr. pricing strategy and migration GTE Calif., Thousand Oaks, 1987-88; mgr. market forecasting GTE Telephone Ops. Hdqrs., Irving, Tex., 1989—. Mem. Am. Mktg. Assn. (membership com. 1984), Beta Gamma Sigma, Phi Kappa Phi. Office: GTE Telephone Ops Hdqrs 4500 Fuller Dr FO3A05 Irving TX 75038

WHITAKER, SUSANNE KANIS, veterinary medical librarian; b. Clinton, Mass., Sept. 10, 1947; d. Harry and Elizabeth P. (Cantwell) Kanis; m. Daniel Brown Whitaker, Jan. 1, 1977. A.B. in Biology, Clark U., 1969; M.S. in Library Sci., Case Western Res. U., 1970. Regional reference librarian Yale Med. Library, New Haven, 1970-72; med. librarian Hartford Hosp., Conn., 1972-77; asst. librarian Cornell U., Ithaca, N.Y., 1977-78; vet. med. librarian Coll. Vet. Medicine, Cornell U., 1978—; sec. SUNY Council Head Librarians, 1981-83. Mem. Med. Library Assn. (cert., sec.-treas. vet. med. libraries sect. 1983-84, chmn. 1984-85, directory editor 1984—), Med. Library Assn. (upstate N.Y. and Ont. chpt.). Home: 502 The Parkway Ithaca NY 14850 Office: Cornell U NY State Coll Vet Medicine Flower Vet Libr Ithaca NY 14853

WHITCOMB, MARION INEZ, company executive; b. Trenton, N.J., Feb. 6, 1927; d. Russell Owen Aring and Leila Inez (Dunlap-Mackey) Bowman; m. Mack Michel Perkins (div.); children: Randy Hall, Stephen Christopher; m. Thomas Nims Whitcomb (dec.); 1 child, Jan Whitcomb Bacallao. Student, Pace Inst., 1944-45, Washington Secretarial Sch., N.Y.C., 1944-45, Grace Inst., Manhasset, N.Y., 1950. Varitypist, chartist GM, N.Y.C., 1947-57; office mgr. Audio Equipment Div. Walter Kidde, Port Washington, N.Y., 1957-58; bookkeeper, acct. various acctg. firms, N.Y.C., 1959-76; bookkeeper S.S. Pennock Co., N.Y.C., 1976-80; controller Actioncraft Products, Inc., Port Washington, 1980-89, treas., 1989—. Singer GM Chorus, N.Y.C., 1948-57. Republican. Office: Actioncraft Products Inc 2 Manhasset Ave Port Washington NY 11050

WHITE, ALBERTA LAVERNE, retired elementary educator; b. Montrose, Colo., Feb. 12, 1913; d. Lawrence Morton and Rosa Lena (Harms) Fender; m. Homer Harrison White, June 12, 1938; children: Kenneth Lockwood, Bona Sue. BA, Western State Coll., Gunnison, Colo., 1951, MA, 1960; EdS in Guidance and Counseling, Western State Coll., 1966. Tchr. Ouray (Colo.) Sch. Dist., 1934-35, Riverside Rural Dist., Montrose, 1935-36, Montrose City Elem., 1937-38, 45-82; ret., 1982; endorsement counselor Colo. State Bd. Edn., Denver, 1966. Author numerous stories for children; contbr. numerous articles to profl. jours. Instr. Helpmobile-Colo. Edn. Assn., Denver, 1972-74; active Montrose Girl Scout Troop, 1938-40; vol. Montrose Pub. Libr., 1960. Mem. AAUW (chmn. Eleanor Roosevelt Loan Fund, Ednl. Found. 1989-91), Ret. Tchrs. Assn. (pres. Montrose chpt. 1987—), Colo. Ret. Tchrs. Employees Assn. (bd. dirs. 1987—), Uncompahgre Valley Tchrs. Assn. (sec.), Rep. Women, GFWC Woman's Club (pres. Montrose chpt. 1988—), Cliolian Club, Emblem Club (pres. local chpt. 1977-78, state pres. 1987-88), Elks, Eastern Star Lodge (worthy matron 1985-86, dist. instr. 1990-91), Beta Sigma Phi (pres. Laureate chpt. city coun. Montrose, 1987), Laureate Xi Internat. BSP (named Woman of Yr. 1986, 87, recipient Order of Rose 1986), Kappa Delta Pi Internat. Honor Soc. in Edn.

WHITE, ALICE VIRGINIA, administrative assistant; b. Wichita, Kans., June 30, 1946; d. Harry Houston White and Margaret V. (Milligan) Gabbert. BA, U. Kans., 1967; MS, Ft. Hays (Kans.) State U., 1973; postgrad., U. Tex., 1987—. Tchr. Russian and Spanish Ingalls (Kans.) Sch. Dist., 1969-72; with Dodge City (Kans.) Community Coll., 1972-73, asst. dir. Ctr. for Bus. & Industry, 1984-85, dir. community rels. and resource devel., 1985-87; treas. Breitenbach Farms, Inc., Dodge City, 1970-79, pres., co-founder, 1979-85; asst. dean for devel. Coll. Communication U. Tex., 1990—; asst. instr. in journalism U. Tex., Austin, 1988—; pub. rels. asst. U. Tex. Coll. Communication Placement, Austin, 1988—; judge Headliners' Found., Austin, 1989. Lifetime mem., donor Austin-Travis County Humane Soc., 1987—; active Leadership Austin, 1990—. U. Tex. fellow, 1987-89. Mem. Tex. Pub. Rels. Soc. (mentor Austin chpt. 1989—), Women in Communications (liaison to student chpt. 1989—), Tex. Exes Alumni Assn. (life), AAUW (Kans. pres. 1979-81), U. Kans. Alumni Assn. (nat. bd. dirs. 1977-82), Austin C. of C., U. Tex. Pres.'s Assocs., U. Kans. Chancellor's Club, Phi Beta Kappa, Phi Kappa Phi. Home: 7207 Winecup Austin TX 78750-8234 Office: U Tex at Austin Coll of Communication Austin TX 78712

WHITE, BEVERLY ANITA, television personality; b. Frankfurt, Fed. Republic of Germany, Aug. 4, 1960; d. Freeman and Modesta (Brown) W. BA in Journalism, U. Tex., 1981. Reporter, photographer, producer, editor KCEN-TV, Temple, Tex., 1981-84; anchor, reporter KENS-TV, San Antonio, 1984-85, WKRC-TV, Cin., 1985—. Guest speaker Cin. Pub. Schs., 1985—, keynote speaker United Way Cin., 1988—. Mem. AFTRA, Nat. Assn. Black Journalists, Greater Cin. Assn. Black Communicators (past co-pres. 1988-89). Democrat. Baptist. Office: WKRC TV 1906 Highland Ave Cincinnati OH 45219

WHITE, BEVERLY JEAN, state legislator, corrections technician; b. Salt Lake City, Sept. 28, 1928; d. Gustave R. and Helene (Sterzer) Larson; m. M. Floyd White, Apr. 8, 1947; children—Susan White Morris, Douglas Floyd, Robyn White Bauder, David Scott (dec.), Wendy Jo White McCleery. Mem. Utah Ho. of Reps., 1971—; mem. Gov.'s Commn. on Status of Women, 1986—. Chairwoman, bd. dirs. Tooele Valley Regional Hosp., 1987—; Sunday Sch. tchr. Ch. of Jesus Christ of Latter Day Saints. Recipient Legislator of Year award Utah Social Workers, 1982, Woman of Year award Beta Sigma Phi, 1982; named Dem. Legislator of 1987, Utah State Dem. Com. Mem. Nat. Order Women Legislators (past treas.), Utah Orgn. Women Legislators (treas.), Tooele Dem. Women's Orgn., Bus. and Profl. Women's Club, Tooele Women's Club (past pres.). 1st women in Utah to serve on State Bd. of Corrections.

WHITE, CAROL ELAINE, chemical company official; b. South Charleston, W.Va., Apr. 24, 1953; d. Lester Holly and Frances Evelyn (O'Dell) W. Student, Center Coll., Charleston, W.Va., 1971-72. Sales sec. Center Coll., 1972-74; stenographer Union Carbide Corp., Sistersville, W.Va., 1974-77, sec., 1977-82, expediter, 1977-82, buyer, 1982-88, advanced purchasing agt., 1988—. Office: Union Carbide Corp PO Box 180 Sistersville WV 26175

WHITE, CAROL MARTIN, administrative director; b. New London, Conn., Nov. 4, 1946; d. Lester Joseph and Lyda Emeline (Pratt) M.; married. BA, Smith Coll., 1968; MA, U. Wash., 1972. Pub. info. officer Dept. Health and Social Svcs., Juneau, Alaska, 1976-78, press sec., 1978-79; devel. dir. pub. rels. Sta. KMXT-FM, Kodiak, Alaska, 1979-80; adminstrv. asst. Sr. Citizens Kodiak, 1980-81; staff asst. U.S. Sen. Ted Stevens, Washington, 1981-83, exec. asst., 1983-86, adminstrv. dir., 1986—. Pres. Juneau chpt. NOW, 1978-79; bd. dirs. Alaska state league LWV, 1978-81, Mt. Vernon (Va.) Unitarian Ch., 1974-76. Mem. NAFE, Am. Mgmt. Assn., Smith Coll. Club of Washington, Capitol Hill Equestrian Soc. Home: 5170 Woodfield Dr Centreville VA 22020 Office: 522 Hart Senate Bldg Washington DC 20222

WHITE, CHRISTINE, educator; b. Taunton, Mass., Apr. 1, 1905; d. Peregrine Hastings and Sara (Lawrence) W. Cert., Boston Sch. Phys. Edn.; BS, Boston U., 1935, MEd, 1939. Instr. Winthrop Coll., Rock Hill, S.C., 1927-29; instr., asst. prof. The Woman's Coll. U. N.C., Greensboro, N.C., 1929-41; assoc. prof., head dept. physical edn. Meredith Coll., Raleigh, N.C., 1941-43; assoc. prof., prof. chair dept. physical edn. Wheaton Coll., Norton, Mass., 1943-70, prof. emerita, 1970—. co-editor Taunton Architecture: A Reflection of the City's History, 1981, 89. Mem. chair Historic Dist. Study Com., 1975-78, recreation Commn., 1972-81, sec. Historic Dist. Commn., 1979—, Park and Recreation Commn., 1981—. Fellow mem. Am. Assn. for Health Physical Edn. Recreation and Dance, AAUW, mem. AAUP, (Wheaton coll. chpt. pres. 1960-61), Eastern Assn. Physical Edn. for Coll. Women, (bd. dirs. 1950-52, 1961-62), Mass. Assn. for Health Physical Edn. Recreation and Dance, Nat. Assn. Physical Edn. for Coll. Women, League Women Voters, Pi Lamda Theta. Home: 40 Highland Terr Taunton MA 02780

WHITE, CLARA JO, graphoanalyst; b. County Cherokee, Tex., June 26, 1927; d. William and Elmira (Johnson) Walker; m. Jeff Davis White, May 5, 1950; children: Anita, Jackie, Mona Lisa, Jeris, Gina. Cert., Ft. Worth Bus. Coll., 1947; AA, Riverside City Coll., 1986; cert. mgmt. and supervisory devel., U. Calif., Riverside, 1986, cert. counseling skills, 1990. Cert. Graphoanalyst 1977; cert. master graphoanalyst 1979; cert. mus. docent tng., 1977. Owner, pres. White Handwriting Analysis Svc., Riverside, Calif., 1982—; lectr., cons. Graphoanalysis, Riverside, 1977—; instr. Internat. Congress and Resident Inst. sponsored by Internat. Graphoanalysis Soc., 1989, disuccion group leader, 1988; presenter in field. Asst. editor: (commemorative book) Reflections, 1986; author poem: The Many Facets of Love, 1987. Mem. YWCA, Riverside; mem. children's conf. planning com. Riverside Mental Health Assn., 1981—; mem. U.S. Olympic Com., 1984; v.p. Heritage House Mus., Riverside, 1981—, co-pres., 1985-86, pres. 1986-87; historian Riverside Juvenile Hall Aux., 1984—, pres., 1987—; vol. teacher's aide County of Riverside Juvenile Ct. Schs., 1979—; mem. Riverside Mus. Assocs., bd. dirs., 1985-87, vol. 1985-88, aux. historian 1984—, pres., 1987-88; mem. Met. Mus. Assocs., 1960—. Recipient Cert. of Appreciation vol. svcs. program Riverside County Probation Dept., 1986, County Riverside Suprs., 1988; award F.H. Butterfield Sch., 1980, Golden Poet award, 1987; named Vol. of Yr., recipient community svc. cert. Riverside City Coll., 1982; named to Hall of Fame, Riverside Juvenile Hall Aux., 1984; recipient Cert. of Appreciation, Riverside Mental Health Assn., 1990, Golden Poet award, 1990. Fellow Internat. Biog. Assn. Eng.; mem. Internat. Graphoanalysis Soc. (life, cert. master graphoanalyst; 2d and 1st v.p., pres. So. Calif. chpt., pres. excellence award 1982, 83, 84, cert. of merit 1981, pres. citation of merit 1988), Am. Biog. Inst. Rsch. Assn. (appt. dep. gov. 1988, bd. advisor 1988), U.S. Olympic Soc., Nat. Assn. Female Execs., Smithsonian Inst. (assoc.), Riverside C. of C., The Research Council of Scripps Clinic and Research Found. Club: Women's Networking (Riverside). Home and Office: 7965 Helena Ave Riverside CA 92504

WHITE, CRICKET GEISINGER, municipal public information officer; b. Richmond, Va., Apr. 18, 1950; d. Joseph Francis and Jackie Marion (Gordon) Geisinger; m. Ralph Rochefort White, Oct. 20, 1984. Student, Va. Commonwealth U., 1968-70, 86-90. Environ. educator City of Richmond, 1979-84, sr. graphics designer, 1984-88, communication specialist, 1988-89, pub. info. officer, asst. to dir. pub. info., 1989—. Bd. dirs. Maymont Found., Richmond, 1989—; steering com. Golden Olympics, 1979-81; publicity chair Rainbow Games, 1983-86. Mem. Richmond Pub. Rels. Assn., Va. Recreation and Parks Soc. (publicity co-chair 1985-86), Cen. Intercollegiate Athletic Assn. (steering com. 1990-93), Va. Mcpl. Leqague, Nat. Recreation and Parks Assn., Nat. Assn. Govt. Communicators, Richmond Audubon Soc. (edn. com. 1984), Va. Native Plants Soc. (edn. chair 1985), Sierra Cub (speakers bur. Falls of the James group 1987—). Democrat. Unitarian Universalist. Office: City of Richmond 900 E Broad St Richmond VA 23219

WHITE, CYNTHIA CAROL, sales executive; b. Ft. Worth, Oct. 16, 1943; d. Charlie Bounds and Bernice Vera (Nunley) Rhoads; m. Franklin Earl Owen, Oct. 20, 1961 (div. Jan. 1987); children: Jeffrey Wayne, Valeria Ann, Carol Darlena, Pamela Kay; m. John Edward White, Jan. 1, 1988. Cert. Keypuncher, Comml. Coll., 1963; student, Tarrant County Jr. Coll., 1974-77; BBA in Mgmt., U. Tex., Arlington, 1981. Keypunch operator Can-Tex. Industries, Mineral-Wells, 1966-67; sec. Electro-Midland Corp., Mineral-Wells, 1967-68; exec. sec. to v.p. sales Pangburn Co., Inc., Ft. Worth, 1972-78; bookkeeper, sec. CB Svc., Ft. Worth, 1978-82; sales coord. Square D Co., Ft. Worth, 1982—. Mem. NAFE. Baptist. Home: 121 Plaza Blvd #1034 Hurst TX 76053 Office: Square D Co 3301 W Airport Frwy Ste 212 Bedford TX 76021

WHITE, DANA RAE, healthcare facility program administrator; b. Johnstown, Pa., Dec. 26, 1963; d. Stan Ray and Linda Louise (Helsel) McQuaide; m. Michael Joseph White, Oct. 3, 1987. BA, Dickinson Coll., 1985; MHA, U. Pitts., 1988. Hosp. intern Harrisburg (Pa.) Hosp., 1985; adminstrv. intern Conemaugh Valley Meml. Hosp., Johnstown, 1986, adminstrv. resident, 1987-88, acting dir. social svcs., 1988; dir. outpatient svcs. program Rehab. Hosp. of Altoona, Pa., 1988—. Cheerleading coach St. Benedicts Jr. High Sch., Johnstown, 1987-88; tutor Adult Literacy Coun. Cambria County, Johnstown. Mem. NAFE, Am. Coll. Healthcare Execs. Home: Rte 1 Box 316T Sidman PA 15955 Office: Rehab Hosp Altoona 2005 Valley View Blvd Altoona PA 16602

WHITE, DENISE, computer consultant; b. Phila., Feb. 20, 1950; d. Gabriel Pont and Mary Louise Theresa Cecelia Zimmerman. AAS in Journalism, Community Coll. Phila.; cert. in mktg. rsch., Villanova U.; student, U. Houston, 1988—. Mktg. adminstrv. asst. Pa. Coll. Optometry Phila., 1981-82; dir. publ relations Northeast Med. Ctr. Hosp., Humble, Tex., 1982-85; v.p. ops. North Am. Cons., Houston, 1985-87; cons., slaeswomen Compurite Computer Ctr., Houston, 1987-88; computer cons. on desktop pub. Houston, 1988—. Fundraiser various orgns., 1972-79; committeewoman Phila. Democratic Com., 1978. Recipient various awards for fundraising activities; Delphian scholar, U. Houston, 1988—. Mem. NAFE, Student Nat. Soc. Advt. Execs., Delphian Soc., Phi Kappa Theta, Phi Beta Kappa (past pres., sec.). Home: 5237 Arboles Dr Unit N Houston TX 77035

WHITE, DORIS ANNE, artist; b. Eau Claire, Wis., July 27, 1924; d. William I. and Mary (Dietz) W. Grad., Art Inst. Chgo., 1950. One woman shows, IFA Galleries, Washington, Berestrum Art Center and Museum, Neenah, Wis., Bradley Gallery, Milw.; exhibited in group shows, Ill. Mus., Springfield, 1963, Art Alliance, Phila., 1963, Museum Modern Art, N.Y.C., 1967, Pa. Acad. Fine Arts, Phila., 1963, 64, 66, Art Inst. Chgo., 1963, Met. Museum, 1966, N.A.D., N.Y.C., 1962, 63, 64, 65, 67, Butler Inst. Am. Art, Youngtown, Ohio, 1960, 61, 63, 64, 65, Smithsonian Instn., Washington, 1960, Walker Art Center, Mpls., 1963, 64, Madison (Wis.) Salon Art, 1958-63, 64, Spanish Internat. Pavilion, St. Louis, 1969, Utah State U., Logan, 1969, 70, Cleve. Inst. Art, Miami (Fla.) U., Chautauqua (N.Y.) Art Assn., Soc. Four Arts, Palm Beach, Fla., Instituto de arte de Mexico, others; represented in permanent collection, Butler Inst. Am. Art, Walker Art Center, Milw. Art Center. Recipient Grand award, 1963, Grumbacker award, 1965, Paul Remmy award, 1964; all Am. Watercolor Soc.; Ranger Fund Purchase award; Obrig award both NAD; medal of honor Knickerbocker Artists, 1963; Four Arts award Soc. Four Arts, Palm Beach, 1963. Mem. NAD. Home: 2750 Church Rd Jackson WI 53037

WHITE, DOROTHY T., nursing educator; b. N.Y.C., Dec. 11, 1923; d. Joseph V. and Pearle E. (Salter) Raymond; diploma in nursing L.I. Coll. Hosp. Sch. Nursing, Bklyn.; B.S., M.A., Ed.D., Columbia U.; diploma, Inst. Ednl. Mgmt., Harvard U., 1982; m. G.M. White, Jan. 5, 1952. Prof. nursing Med. Coll. Ga., Augusta, 1971-77, dean Sch. Nursing, 1971-76; prof. Nova U., Ft. Lauderdale, Fla., 1977-78, dir. The Louise Mellen Inst. Nursing, 1977-78; prof. Calif. State U., Sacramento, 1978-79, chmn. div. nursing, 1978-79; prof. Hunter Coll.-City U. N.Y., Hunter-Bellevue Sch. Nursing, N.Y.C., 1979—, dean, 1979-82; cons. Office of Chancellor, City U. N.Y.; dir. Augusta Radiation Center, 1973-76; govtl. appointee Master Planning Com. for Nursing in Ga., 1971-75. Bd. dirs. Nurses House, Nurse Ednl. Fund (pres. 1986-88); trustee Mt. St. Mary Coll., 1960-61, assoc. trustee, 1961-65. Recipient citation Office of Sec. State of Ga., 1977; Cert. of Appreciation, U.S. Army Health Services Command, 1977. Mem. Group for Advancement in Nursing (founder), Am. Acad. Polit. and Social Scis., AAUW, Am. Assn. Women in Higher Edn., Am. Assn. Female Execs., Am. Assn. Higher Edn., AAUP, Am. Assn. Univ. Adminstrs., Nat. Assn. Women Deans, Adminstrs. and Counselors, N.Y. Acad. Scis. Author papers in field. Office: 440 E 26th St New York NY 10010

WHITE, ELIZABETH LOCZI, academic researcher, civil engineer; b. McKees Rock, Pa., Mar. 9, 1936; d. Victor and Elizabeth (Vezendy) Loczi; m. William Blaine White, Mar. 27, 1959; children: Nikki Elizabeth White McCurry, W. Brion (dec.). BS in Civil Engring., U. Pitts., 1958; MS in Civil Engring., Pa. State U., 1969, PhD in Civil Engring., 1975. Registered profl. engr., Pa. Civil engr. IV Pa. Dept. Hwys., Harrisburg, 1958-59; part-time rsch. asst. Pa. State U., University Park, 1964-74; Anna L. Rhodes Hawkes fellow AAUW, State College, Pa., 1974-75; rsch. assoc. Pa. State U., University Park, 1975-83, sr. rsch. assoc., 1983—; hydrologic cons., State College, Pa., 1975—. Fellow Nat. Speleological Soc. (editor caving pubs. 1961—); mem. Grad. Women in Sci. (life, treas.), Am. Soc. Civil Engrs., Nat. Soc. Profl. Engrs., AAUW, Sigma Sigma Sigma. Republican. Hungarian Reformed. Home: 542 Glenn Rd State College PA 16803 Office: Pa State U Dept Civil Engring 212 Sackett Bldg University Park PA 16802

WHITE, FRANKIE LEE, newspaper executive; b. Chgo., Sept. 17, 1945; d. Frank Milton and Florida (Smith) Hudson; m. John Charles White; 1 child, Anthony D. BA, U. Ill., Chgo. Intake specialist Ill. Dept. Pub. Aid, Chgo., 1968-79; account exec. The Chgo. Daily Defender, 1979-80; cons. Chgo. Bd. Edn., 1981; gen. advt. mgr. The Observer Newspaper, Chgo., 1980-81; exhibitor All Products Internat. Import & Export Co., 1982; demonstrator Sunbeam Corp., Chgo., 1981-82; media rep. Hyde Park Herald Newspaper, Near South Herald Newspaper, Chgo., 1982-86, classified advt. mgr., 1986—; columnist The Observer Newspaper, 1979-80, The Citizen Newspaper, 1980-83; asst. gen. mgr. Lena Horne's The Lady and Her Music, 1983, I Am Almost Famous, Apollo Theatre, Chgo., 1983. Pub. rels. chairperson Host Com. of U.S. Dept. Labor, Women's Bur, 1980-82, Howalton Sch., 1976-86; fundraising chairperson Washington Park YMCA Swim Team Parent Club, 1979-81; pres. Howalton Parent Coun., 1981-83; bd. dirs. Howalton Sch., 1981-86; bd. advisors Elam House, 1980. Recipient Cert. of Recognition, Washington Park YMCA, 1980, U.S. Dept. Labor Women's Bur., 1981, 82, Outstanding Achievement award for Promotion of Tourism to Africa, 1983; named Outstanding Mother of Yr., Howalton Sch., 1980, one of Outstanding Young Women of Am., 1980. Mem. Delta Sigma Theta (pub. rels. chairperson Chgo. alumane chpt. 1988-90). Home: 5050 S Lake Shore Dr 3606 Chicago IL 60615 Office: Hyde Park Herald Newspaper 5240 S Harper Chicago IL 60615

WHITE, GENEVA M., dentist; b. Bronx, Jan. 13, 1958; d. John and Julia (McKenzie) White. BA, Mt. Holyoke Coll., South Hadley, Mass., 1980; DMD, N.J. Dental Sch., Newark, 1984. Research assoc. Albert Einstein Coll. Medicine, Bronx, 1975, 78 summer; surgeon's aid Jacobi Hosp., Bronx, 1977 summer; lab tech. Western Mass. Hosp., Westfield, 1978 summer; dentist Peoples Dental Ctr., E. Orange, N.J., 1985-87, Dr. P. Freeman, Jersey City, 1984-88, Dr. P. White, Newark, 1984-85; assoc. Dr. S. Herman, Newark, 1988—. Mem. Am. Dental Assn., Acad. Dentistry for Children, Acad. Gen. Dentistry., Nat. Dental Assn. Democrat.

WHITE, GLORIA WATERS, university administrator; b. St. Louis County, Mo., May 16, 1934; d. James Thomas and Thelma Celestine (Brown) W.; B.A., Harris-Stowe Tchrs. Coll., 1956; M.A., Washington U., St. Louis, 1963, M. Juridical Studies, 1980; m. W. Glenn White, Jan. 1, 1955; 1 child, Terry Anita White. Tchr., St. Louis Bd. Edn., 1956-63, psychol. counselor, 1963-67; dir. office spl. projects Washington U., 1967-76, asst. to asso. vice chancellor personnel and affirmative action, 1975-88, vice chancellor for personnel, affirmative action officer, 1988—. Bd. dirs. Am. Assn. Affirmative Action, 1974-77; instl. chair Arts and Edn. Fund, 1975-88; mem. Eastern Dist. Mo. Desegregation and Adv. Com., 1981-82; bd. trustees, Blue Cross/Blue Shield of Mo., 1984—, The Caring Found., 1989—; adv. bd., Tchrs. Ins. Annuity Assn., 1988—; bd. dirs. ARC, 1990—. Accredited exec. in personnel; cert. life counselor, life tchr. Recipient citations Urban League, Pres.'s Council Youth Opportunities, Distinguished Alumni award Harris State Coll., 1987. Mem. Coll. and Univ. Personnel Assn. (bd. dirs. 1981-88, pres. 1986-87, 87-88, v.p. research and publs. 1981-85, pres.-elect 1985-86, immediate past pres. 1987-88, v.p., Creativity award 1981, Disting. Service award 1988, Kathryn G. Hansen Publs. award 1989), Am. Soc. Personnel Adminstrn., Pers. Accreditation Inst. (bd. dirs.), St. Louis Symphony Soc., Delta Sigma Theta (v.p. St. Louis Alumnae chpt. 1989—, nat. social action commr. 1988—). Roman Catholic. Home: 545 Del Price Ct Saint Louis MO 63124 Office: Box 1184 Saint Louis MO 63130

WHITE, JAN TUTTLE (MRS. BENJAMIN WINTHROP WHITE), computer company executive; b. Bridgeport, Conn., Nov. 5, 1943; d. Michael and Jennie Agnes (Leko) Soltis; m. David Dustin Tuttle, Oct. 7, 1972 (div. 1988); m. Benjamin Winthrop White, May 6, 1989. BS in Math., Bates Coll., 1965; MBA in Mktg. and Ops. Rsch., Columbia U., 1967. With corp. staff IBM Corp., Armonk, N.Y., 1966; systems engr. IBM Corp., N.Y.C., 1967-69; mktg. rep. to Harvard U. IBM Corp., Cambridge, Mass., 1969-72; asst. to dir. info. processing svcs. MIT, Cambridge, Mass., 1972-75; mng. dir. Tuttle Family Trust, Cambridge, Mass., 1975-81; VAX product mktg. mgr., then sr. product mgr. Digital Equipment Corp., Marlborough, Mass., 1981-86, artificial intelligence market conditioning mgr., 1986-87, fin. systems group market devel. mgr., 1987—, market devel. mgr. banking/investments group, 1990—; program mgr. MIT Internat. Fin. Svc. Rsch. Ctr.; Speaker in field. Appeared in Disney channel documentary film Silver Men, 1987. Chmn. Concord Coun. Boston Symphony Orch., assoc. assn. vols., supporter Tanglewood scholarship programs, capt. Centennial Major Gifts campaign; active guild bd. Opera Co. Boston, patron Fledrmaus Ball; life mem., chmn. Emerson Hosp. Aux.; bd. trustees mgmt. rev. com. Women's Ednl. and Indsl. Union; active ladies assn. bd. Concord Antiquarian Mus., bd. advisors Boston Mus. Sci., Sci. Mus. Exhibit Collaborative, Garden Club Concord; life mem. Nat. Trust for Scotland, Friends of Loch Lomond, Mus. Fine Arts, Boston; mem. fin. com. Trinitarian Congl. Ch.; trustee, life mem. Women's Ednl. and Indsl. Union; bd. dirs., life mem. Hannah Duston Garrison House Assn., Mus. Fine Arts, Boston; patron mem. Friends of Music at the Mus. Fellow Internat. Biog. Ctr. (life); mem. NAFE, Am. Assn. Artificial Intelligence, Am. Biog. Inst. Rsch. Assn. (dep. gov., hon. advisor, nat. rsch. bd.

advisors), Harwich Hist. Assn. (life), Stratford Hist. Soc. (life), Internat. Platform Assn., Bates Coll. Class 1965 (sec., treas., reunion chmn., com. chmn. 25th reunion major gifts), Columbia U. Grad. Sch. Bus. Alumni Assn. (nat. chmn. membership, bd. dirs.), Hurrican Island Outward Bound Sch. Invitational Alumni, Columbia Bus. Club Boston (founding dir., bd. dirs.), Columbia Club New Eng. (founding dir.), Columbia Club N.Y., Concord Country Club, Harvard Club, Stone Horse Yacht Club, Women's City Club (com. membership), Royal Scottish Automobile Club, Mass. Hort. Soc., So. Mass. Yacht Racing Assn. Republican. Home: 77 Francis Ave Cambridge MA 02138 Office: Digital Equipment Corp 397 Williams St Marlborough MA 01749

WHITE, JANET MURPHREE, educational administrator; b. Kansas City, Mo., Mar. 14, 1946; d. John Clarence and Ella Emma Mary (Waack) Murphree; m. Harold S. White, July 4, 1970; children: Julia Lee, Alan Edward. BA, William Woods Coll., 1968; MA, U. Mo., 1985; PhD, Kent State U., 1988. Asst. dean admissions William Woods Coll., Fulton, Mo., 1968-70; tchr. Fountain (Colo.)-Ft. Carson Schs., 1971-73, Boone Grove (Ind.) Schs., 1978-79; dir. fin. aid William Woods Coll., 1979-82, v.p. coll. svcs., 1982-85; v.p. instl. advancement Notre Dame Coll., Cleve., 1987—. Contbr. to edn. periodicals. Episcopalian. Office: Notre Dame Coll 4545 College Rd Cleveland OH 44121

WHITE, JEANNINE A., interior designer; b. Richwood, W.Va., Dec. 11, 1929; d. Alton Park and Dixie Aileen (Sparks) Bennett; m. Lehmon A. White, May 25, 1948; children: Gary, Michael. AA, Tampa U., 1979; postgrad., Tampa Art Inst. V.p. East Coast Printing, Charlotte, N.C.; regional promotional trainer Frances Denney Cosmetics, Tampa, Fla.; art dir. La Marick Beauty Systems, Charlotte; spl. promotions dir. Stone Brook Advt.; interior designer, owner Jeannine's Interiors, Tampa. Mem. Tampa Advt. Fedn., NAFE. Home: 8304 Oak Forest Ct Tampa FL 33615

WHITE, JOAN M., methods engineering executive; b. Albuquerque, Sept. 17, 1948; d. Leon Alexander Sr. and Vessie (Blackmon) Mitchell; 1 child, Valencia Sherise. BA in Polit. Sci., UCLA, 1975; MPA, Calif. State U., L.A., 1981; MBA, City U., Seattle, 1981; cert., U.S. Officer's Adminstrn. Sch., 1983. Cert. tchr., Calif. Methods analyst Safeco Corp., Seattle; systems analyst Boeing Corp., Seattle, Exec. Life Ins. Co., West Los Angeles; mgr. Tandy Corp., Sante Fe Springs, Calif.; methods enging. executive Boeing Mil. Airplane Co., Palmdale, Calif. Capt. USAR, 1981—. Howard Wood Johnson Found. grantee. Mem. Toastmasters (past. v.p. edn.). Home: 43124 30th St W #222 Lancaster CA 93536

WHITE, JOY MIEKO, communications executive; b. Yokohama, Japan, May 1, 1951; came to U.S., 1951; d. Frank Deforest and Wanda Mieko (Ishiwata) Mellen; m. George William, June 5, 1948; 1 child, Karen. BA in Communications, Calif. State U., Fullerton, 1974, teaching cert., 1977; cert. bus. mgmt., Orange Coast Coll., 1981. Cert. secondary tchr., Calif. Secondary tchr. Anaheim (Calif.) Union High Sch. Dist., 1977-80; tech. writer Pertec Computer Corp., Irvine, Calif., 1980-81; supr. large systems div. Burroughs, Mission Viejo, Calif., 1981-83; mgr. Lockheed div. CalComp, Anaheim, 1983-86; owner, pres. Communicator's Connection, Irvine, Calif., 1986—; pres. Info Team; lectr. UCLA, 1983—; adj. faculty, coord. tech. communication program Golden West Coll., Huntington Beach, Calif., 1987—; instr. U. Calif., Irvine, 1987—, Calif. State U., Fullerton, 1988—; condr. numerous workshops, profl. presentations, 1982—. Active Performing Arts, Costa Mesa, 1986—. Mem. NAFE, Soc. for Tech. Communication (sr., Mem. of Yr. Orange County chpt. 1987), Soc. Profl. Journalists, Women in Communications (pres. elect 1988-89, pres. Orange County Profl. chpt. 1989-90), Rembrandts Wine Club (Yorba Linda). Democrat. Home: 21651 Vintage Way El Toro CA 92630 Office: 13700 Alton Pkwy Ste #154 Irvine CA 92718

WHITE, JUDITH FOX, healthcare administrator; b. Newark, Dec. 25, 1943; d. Morris and Ida (Fidel) Fox; m. Robert M. Figi, Oct. 9, 1981 (dec. Dec. 1986). BA, Boston U., 1965; MA, Northwestern U., 1968. Editor Ency. Britannica, Chgo., 1971-72; contract compliance officer City of Syracuse, N.Y., 1972-75; sr. adminstrv. analyst UCLA Hosp., 1975-79; with Kaiser Permanente, 1979—; asst. adminstr. Kaiser Permanente, San Diego, 1983-85; adminstr. Kaiser Permanente, Anaheim, Calif., 1985—. Mem. Orange County Indsl. League, Irvine, Calif., 1989—. Mem. Med. Group Mgmt. Assn., Healthcare Execs. Assn., Healthcare Fin. Mgrs., Jewish Fedn. Health Industries Div. Democrat. Jewish. Office: Kaiser Permanente 411 Lakeview Ave Anaheim CA 92807

WHITE, JUDITH LOUISE, social worker; b. Lodi, Ohio, Feb. 27, 1939; d. Henry and Charlotte Virginia (Spahr) Schmelzer; m. Downer Dale White, Sept. 4, 1959; children: Mark, Kelly, Kristy, David. AA, Northland Pioneer Coll., Holbrook, Ariz., 1980; postgrad., No. Ariz. U., 1984—, Ariz. State U., 1985—. Tchr. White Mountain Apache Head Start Program, Whiteriver, Ariz., 1976-80, child services coord., 1980-87; cons. Nat. Indian Head Starts, 1980—; trainer Indian Child & Family Conf., Phoenix and Albuquerque, 1982-86, Fetal Alcohol Syndrome-Indian Health Services, Whiteriver, 1984—; cons. White Mountain Apache Head Start Resource Access Project, 1984—; assoc. tchr. Northland Pioneer Jr. Coll., Holbrook, Ariz., 1985—; trainer pilot parent program; coord. Whiteriver Pilot Parents. Mem. Coalition for Chronically Ill Children, Phoenix, 1985—. Mem. Council Exceptional Children, Nat. Assn. for Edn. Young Children, White Mt. Assn. for Edn. Young Children. Avocations: music, reading, spending time with grandchildren. Home: Box 707 Whiteriver AZ 85941 Office: Whiteriver Elem Sch PO Box 190 Whiteriver AZ 85941

WHITE, JULIA ZITA, nurse, health science administrator, consultant; b. Onslow county, N.C., Apr. 27, 1951; d. Henry Richard and Joan Eileen (Speilmann) W. BSN, D'Youville Coll., Buffalo, 1973; MS, Marshall U., 1983; MSN, W. Va. U., 1987. RN N.Y., Ky., W.Va. Staff nurse Appalachian Reg. Hosp., Williamson, Ky., 1973-83; nursing instr. So. W.Va. Community Coll., Williamson, W.Va., 1979-83; area program coord. W. Va. Dept. of Health, Charleston, W.Va., 1983-90; coord. sudden infant death syndrome program W.Va. Dept. Health, Charleston, W.Va., 1989-90; adminstr. Boone County Health Dept., Madison, W.Va., 1990—. Bd. advs. Tug Valley Recovery Shelter, Williamson, W.Va., 1985-89. Mem. AAUW (treas., bd. dirs. Mingo-Pike br. 1989—), W.Va. League for Nurses (treas. 1989-91), W.Va. Pub. Health Assn., Assn. of Sudden Infant Death Syndrome Program Profls., Sigma Thea Tau (Zeta Nu chpt.). Democrat. Roman Catholic. Home: 509 Maple Walk Williamson WV 25661 Office: Boone County Health Dept Box 209 Madison WV 25130

WHITE, KATE, editor-in-chief. Former editor-in-chief Child mag.; editor-in-chief Working Woman mag., N.Y.C., 1989—. Office: Working Woman 342 Madison Ave New York NY 10173*

WHITE, KATHERINE ELIZABETH, retired pediatrician; b. Syracuse, N.Y., Mar. 23, 1920; d. Rufus Macandie and Marguerite Mary (Eselin) W.; m. Nicholas V. Oddo, Feb. 27, 1947 (dec. 1966); 1 child, Sandra S. Qualls. BA, Syracuse U., 1941, MD, 1943. Intern Syracuse U. Med. Ctr., 1944-45; asst. resident Buffalo Children's Hosp., 1945-46, chief resident, 1946-47; instr. pediatrics L.A. Children's Hosp., 1947; pvt. practice Long Beach, Calif., 1947—; mem. med. staff Miller Children's Hosp., Long Beach, 1966—; mem. bd. trustees Miller Children's Hosp., 1970—. Bd. dirs. Children's Clinic, Long Beach, 1968-87. Recipient Meml. Med. Ctr. Found., 1984; Cert. of Recognition, Children's Clinic, 1987, Found. for Children's Health Care, 1987; Humanitarian award Kiwanis, 1990. Fellow Am. Acad. Pediatrics; mem. Calif. Med. Assn., L.A. County Med. Assn., Long Beach Med. Assn., Soroptimist (Woman of Distinction 1989, Hall of Fame award 1990), Phi Beta Kappa. Republican. Roman Catholic. Home: 6354 Riviera Circle Long Beach CA 90815

WHITE, KATHERINE PATRICIA, lawyer; b. N.Y.C., Feb. 1, 1948; d. Edward Christopher and Catherine Elizabeth (Walsh) W. BA in English, Molloy Coll., 1969; JD, St. John's U., 1971. Bar: N.Y. 1972, U.S. Dist. Ct. (ea. and so. dists.) N.Y., 1973, U.S. Supreme Ct. 1976. Atty. Western Electric Co., Inc., N.Y.C., 1971-79, AT&T Co., N.Y.C., 1979—; adj. prof. law N.Y. Law Sch., N.Y.C., 1987-88, Fordham U. Sch. of Law, 1988—. Vol. Sloan Kettering Inst., 1973, North Shore U. Hosp., 1975, various fed., state and local polit. campaigns; judge N.Y. State Bicentennial Writing Competition, N.Y.C., 1977-78; chmn. Com. to Elect Supreme Ct. Judge, N.Y.C., 1982. Mem. Am. Corp. Counsel Assn., N.Y. State Bar Assn. (bus. and banking law com. real estate law sect., corp. counsel sect.), Assn. of Bar of City of N.Y. (adminstrv. law com. 1982-85, young lawyers com. 1976-79, judge nat. moot ct. competition 1979—), Cath. Lawyers Guild for Diocese of Rockville Ctr. (pres. 1980-81), St. John's U. Sch. Law Alumni Assn. (pres. L.I. chpt. 1986-88), Women's Nat. Rep. Club (bd. govs. 1988—), Met. Club, Wharton Bus. Sch. Club. Home: 1035 Fifth Ave Apt 14D New York NY 10028 Office: AT&T Communications Inc 32 Ave of Americas New York NY 10013

WHITE, KATHLEEN MAE, social worker; b. Lamar, Colo., Feb. 12, 1941; d. Cornelius William and Lillian Mae (Oswald) Hogan; A.A., U. Md., 1969; M.S.W., Our Lady of Lake U., 1976; B.S. cum laude, Tex. A. and I. U., 1972; m. Larry F. White, Mar. 30, 1959; children—Thomas William, Richard Edward, Judy Lynn, Ramona Marie. With Vol. Services, ARC, Wright Patterson AFB, Ohio, 1964-65, Randolph AFB, Tex., 1965-66, Sembach AFB, Ger., 1966-69; tchr. St. Augustines Cath. Sch., Laredo, Tex., 1970-71; social worker Tex. Dept. Public Welfare, San Antonio, 1972-74; tchr. Edgewood Ind. Sch. Dist., San Antonio, 1976-78; coordinator teenage mother's sch. Harlandale Ind. Sch. Dist., San Antonio, 1978-83; pvt. practice mental health social work, 1976—. VA stipend, 1975-76. Mem. Acad. Cert. Social Workers, Am. Assn. Social Workers, Am. Bus. Women's Assn., Our Lady of Lake U. Alumni Assn. Republican. Roman Catholic. Home: Rt 3 Box 180 B Cibolo TX 78108 Office: 214 Rosewood Universal City TX 78148

WHITE, KATHY A., education educator; b. Indpls., Aug. 13, 1944; d. Paul Edwards and Anna Marie (Dziewas) W. BS, Ball State U., Muncie, Ind., 1966; MS, Ind. U., 1968. Substitute tchr. I.P.S., 1968; tchr. Washington Twp. North Cen. High Sch., Indpls., 1986—; mem. faculty Ind. U.-Purdue U., Indpls., 1970-76; tchr. Independent Study Faculty, Ind. U.; bus. edn. tchr. JEL Career Ctr., 1968—. Mem. adv. coun. Ind. Women's Prison, 1983—; mem. alumni adv. com. Ind. U.-Purdue U., Indpls., 1985-88; mem. ch. bd. Zions United Ch. of Christ, 1982-85, also member evangelism, membership care, pastoral rels., personnel coms. Named Outstanding Alumni Bus. Tchr., Ball State U., 1988. Mem. Adminstrv. Mgmt. Soc. (Educator of Yr. award 1986), Am. Vocat. Assn. (life, merit award 1987), Nat. Bus. Edn. Assn., Ind. Vocat. Assn. (life, sec. 1983-84, merit award 1982, svc. award 1986), Ind. Bus. Edn. Assn. (pres. 1983-84, Outstanding Classroom Tchr. award 1983), Ind. Bus. Edn. Coun. (pres. 1981-82), North-Cen. Bus. Edn. Assn. (Outstanding Secondary Svc. award 1986), Nat. Bus. Edn. Assn., Office Tech. Mgmt. Assn., Ind. Bus. Educators Club (v.p. 1984-85, sec.-treas. 1987), Profl. Secs. Internat., Delta Pi Epsilon, Phi Delta Kappa, others. Home: 25 E 40th St #5E Indianapolis IN 46205-0265 Office: JEL Career Ctr 1901 E 86th St Indianapolis IN 46240

WHITE, LANA JOYCE, English educator; b. Canyon, Tex.; d. Orva Odis and Leona Estelle (Dawdy) Henry; m. Billy Gene White, Feb. 19, 1960; 1 child, Denise. BA, West Tex. State U., 1960, MA, 1964; PhD, Tex. Christian U., 1983. Cert. tchr., Tex. Tchr. Kelton (Tex.) Ind. Schs., 1960-61, Gruver (Tex.) Ind. Schs., 1961-62, Farwell (Tex.) Ind. Schs., 1962-64, Amarillo (Tex.) Ind. Schs., 1964-81; assoc. prof. English West Tex. State U., Canyon, 1983—. Contbr. articles to profl. jours. Recipient accolade Amarillo Globe-News, 1972; fellow Tex. Christian U., 1981-83. Mem. MLA. Democrat. Presbyterian. Office: West Tex State U WT Sta Canyon TX 79016

WHITE, LAVARNE, social worker; b. Sherrill, Ark., Mar. 17, 1952; d. Edward and Earnestine (Smith) W. Student, U. Ark., 1973; MSW, U. Mich., 1981. Line supr. Saginaw Valley Rehab. Ctr., Saginaw, Mich., 1978-79; substitute tchr. Saginaw Bd. Edn., 1979-81; child care worker St. Vincent Home, Saginaw, 1980-81, social worker, 1981-84; instr. Delta Coll., Saginaw, 1984-86; clin. social worker White Pine Psychiat. Ctr., Saginaw, 1984-88; sch. social worker Saginaw Bd. Edn., 1988—. Mem. Nat. Assn. Social Workers, Mich. Assn. Sch. Social Workers, Zeta Phi Beta. Baptist.

WHITE, LIBBY KRAMER, librarian; b. Boston, Sept. 30, 1934; d. Samuel and Ida (Drucker) Kramer; m. Gerald Milton White, June 6, 1956; children: Charles, Andrew, Judith, Abigail White D'Costa. BS in Social Sci., Simmons Coll., Boston, 1956; MLS, SUNY, Albany, 1972. Librarian Temple Israel, Albany, N.Y., 1966-73; bookmobile librarian Schenectady County Pub. Library, 1973, br. librarian, 1973-76, ref./YA librarian, 1976-85, ref./ethnic culture librarian, 1985—; chmn. Nat. Library Wk., Schenectady, 1985. Book reviewer Sch. Libr. Jour., 1980—, Libr. Jour., 1989; cons. various encys., mags. Sec. bd. trustees Beth Israel Synagogue, Schenectady, 1986—, Jewish Community Ctr., 1979-88; resident advisor Summer Seminars in Judaic Studies, Skidmore Coll., Saratoga, N.Y., 1987—. Mem. ALA, N.Y. Library Assn., Hudson Mohawk Library Assn. (pres. 1989—). Jewish. Home: 1274 Hawthorn Rd Schenectady NY 12309 Office: 99 Clinton St Schenectady NY 12305-2083

WHITE, LINDA HARDY, marketing research executive; b. Albion, Okla., Nov. 25, 1946; d. Clayton H. and Ethel M. (Pettyjohn) Hardy; m. Wesley D. White, Mar. 18, 1978. BA, N.E. La. U., 1968, Ambassador Coll., 1973; postgrad., Murray State U., 1969, Ambassador Coll., 1975-76. Assoc. editor Ambassador Inst., Pasadena, Calif., 1971-81; dir. English Dynamics, Houston, 1981-83; industry analyst Future Computing/McGraw-Hill, Dallas, 1983-89; pres. Marketline, Carrollton, Tex., 1990—; cons. in field; industry analyst Leading Technologies Seminars, 1988-89. Editorial dir. IBM's PC Strategy: 1988 & Beyond, 1987; sr. analyst Director of Vendor Strategies, 1988-89; writer Office Products Dealers, 1984; editor Future Views, 1989-89, Event Horizon, 1989. Recipient Merit award Soc. Tech. Communications, 1988. Mem. Soc. Tech. Communications, Women in Communications. Republican. Home: 1537 Ranchview Ln Carrollton TX 75007

WHITE, LOIS M., editor; b. Detroit, Aug. 4, 1931; d. Arnold George and Cecyl Abbie (Pond) Barker; m. George White, Sept. 25, 1954; children: Susan, Karen, Michael. Grad. high sch., Detroit. Claim adjuster Detroit Ins. Agy., 1951-54; sec. U.S. Govt. Office, Newport News, Va., 1954-55, Ford Motor Co., Novi, Mich., 1956-58; tech. writer Bendix Rsch. Labs., Southfield, Mich., 1958-64; spl. writer Detroit News, 1977-80; mng. editor Audecibel Mag. div. Nat. Hearing Aid Society, Livonia, Mich., 1980—. Contbr. articles to profl. jours. Office: Nat Hearing Aid Soc 20361 Middle Belt Livonia MI 48152

WHITE, LOIS R., producer; b. Chgo.; d. Lewis Walton and Corinne Gwendolyn (Coleman) Cass. Student, Roosevelt U., So. Ill. U. Pres. Bus. Planning Svcs., Chgo.; exec. producer, writer Lovinus Prodns., Inc., Chgo. Author TV comedy series The Love Lottery. Chair communications com. Jane Addams Conf. Mem. Assn. Ind. Video Producers, Chgo. Assn. Commerce and Industry, Women in Films. Home: 1300 N Astor St #8A Chicago IL 60610

WHITE, MARGIT TRISKA, financial advisor; b. Greenport, N.Y., June 4, 1932; d. Joseph A. and Esther M. (Olstad) Triska; m. Robert Lamar Cannon (div. 1971); children: Catherine Margit, Sandra Leigh, Robert Milchrist II. BA, Duke U., 1954. Cert. fin. planner. Adminstr. Washington Opportunities for Women, 1971-80; account exec. Merrill Lynch, Bethesda, Md., 1980-82; assoc. v.p. investments, fin. planner Prudential Bache Securities, Washington, 1982—. Mem. Internat. Assn. Fin. Planning, Inst. Cert. Fin. Planners, Women in Housing and Fin., Zeta Tau Alpha. Presbyterian. Office: Prudential Bache Securities 1130 Connecticut Ave Washington DC 20036

WHITE, MARGITA EKLUND, television association executive; b. Linköping, Sweden, June 27, 1937; came to U.S., 1948; d. Eyvind O. and Ella Maria (Eriksson) Eklund; m. Stuart Crawford White, June 24, 1961 (div. 1987); children: Suzanne Margareta, Stuart Crawford Jr. B.A. magna cum laude in Govt, U. Redlands, 1959, LL.D. (hon.), 1977; M.A. in Polit. Sci. (Woodrow Wilson fellow), Rutgers U., 1960. Asst. to press sec. Richard M. Nixon Presdl. Campaign, Washington, 1960; adminstrv. asst. Whitaker & Baxter Advt. Agy., Honolulu, 1961-62; minority news sec. Hawaii Ho. of Reps., 1963; research asst. to Senator Barry Goldwater and Republican Nat. Com., 1963-64; research asst., writer Free Society Assn., 1965-66; research asst. to syndicated columnist Raymond Moley, 1967; asst. to Herbert G. Klein, White House dir. communications, 1969-73; asst. dir. USIA, 1973-75; asst. press sec. to Pres. Gerald R. Ford, 1975; asst. press sec. to Pres., dir. White House Office of Communications, Washington, 1975-76; commr. FCC, 1976-79; dir. Radio Free Europe-Radio Liberty Inc., 1979-82, vice chmn., 1982; dir. Taft Broadcasting Co., 1980-87, Armtek Corp., 1987-88; pres. Assn. Maximum Svc. Television; bd. dirs., ITT, Rayonier Forest Resources Co., Washington Mut. Investors Fund; U.S. del. Internat. Telecommunications Union Plenipotentiary Conf., Nairobi, 1982; coordinator TV Operators Caucus, Inc., 1985-88. Mem. George Foster Peabody Adv. Bd., 1979-86. Recipient Disting. Service award U. Redlands Alumni Assn., 1974; Superior Honor award USIA, 1975. Mem. Exec. Women in Govt. (founding mem., sec. 1975), Women's Forum of Washington. Home: 7238 Evans Mill Rd McLean VA 22101 Office: 1400 16th St Washington DC 20036

WHITE, MARIA B., marketing consultant; b. Havana, Cuba, Feb. 28, 1955; came to U.S. 1962; d. Manual Baez Hidalgo and Lidia Rosa (Hernandez) Feliz; m. H. Burke White, Jr.; children: Christian, Rebecca. BBA, Fla. Internat. U., Miami, 1985; student, Fla. State U., 1984-85; postgrad., Fla. Internat. U. Prin. Flower Girl, Homestead, Fla., 1979-82; travel writer, aide Dept. Tourism and Commerce, Tallahassee, 1983-84; profl. rel. coord. St. Francis Hosp., Miami Beach, Fla., 1987-88; dir. mktg. Coral Gables (Fla.) Hosp., 1988—; cons. Rep. Health Corp., Dallas, 1985. MIT grantee, 1986. Mem. Am. Mktg. Assn., Pub. Rel. Soc. Am., So. Fla. Hosp. Pub. Rel. and Mktg. Assn., Fla. Hosp. Assn., Phi Theta Kappa. Office: Coral Gables Hosp 3100 Douglas Rd Coral Gables FL 33134

WHITE, MARILYN ELAINE, elementary bilingual specialist; b. L.A., Oct. 17, 1944; d. Ela Nelson and Mary Laurenza Susan (Johnson) W.; m. Leon Leroy Milligan, Jan. 5, 1974 (annuled June 1975); 1 child, Leon Leroy, Jr. BS, Pepperdine U., 1967; MA, U. Calif. Dominguez, 1974. Cert. bilingual specialist. Athletic asst. Santa Monica (Calif.) Boys Club, 1964-66; recreation asst. L.A. Recreation and Parks, 1966-67; drama tchr. St. Alban's Sch. for Boys, D.C., 1967; phys. edn. tchr. D.C. Pub. Schs., 1967-68; phys. edn. tchr. L.A. Unified Sch. Dist., 1968-73, elem. edn. tchr., 1973-78, bilingual specialist, 1978—; master tng. tchr. L.A. Unified Sch. Dist., 1985-86. Designer Pictoral Geneal. Pedigree Chart, 1989. Pub. speaker Olympic Speakers Bur., L.A., 1983-84; del. Black Cath. Congress, D.C., 1987; vol. Internat. Spl. Olympics, L.A., 1978—, Jesse Owens Games, L.A., 1980—; mem. Interdenominational Gospel Choir (Pilgrim award 1981). Recipient Am. Record award Nat. Athletic Congress, Cleve., 1963, Gold, Bronze medals Pan. Am. Games, Sao Paulo, Brazil, Olympic Silver medal Internat. Olympic Com., Tokyo, 1964, ednl. grant Tchr. Initiative Grant Commn., L.A., 1987, commendation City of L.A., 1984; named Woman of Yr. L.A. Sentinel Newspaper, L.A., 1984, nat. anthem soloist L.A. Dodgers, 1983-84, Western Regional Masters Champion SO. Pacific Althetic Congress, The Athletic Congress-Amateur Athletic Union, 1984. Mem. Calif. African Geneal. Soc. (bd. dirs., recording sec. 1987—), Geneal. Rsch. Soc. New Orleans, Nat. Geneal. Soc., Educare (award 1984), Delta Kappa Gamma (1st v.p.), Alpha Kappa Alpha. Democrat. Roman Catholic. Home: 9605 Sixth Ave Inglewood CA 90305-3207

WHITE, MARY LOUISE, retail drug chain executive; b. N.Y.C., Aug. 8, 1933; d. Henry Fred and Martha (Meyer) Behrmann; m. Roger Stevenson White, July 15, 1953; children: Stevenson Rogers, William Henry. BBA, Hofstra Coll., 1954. Instr. Dept. Army, Poitiers, France, 1954-55; bus. office rep. N.Y. Telephone Co., Hempstead, N.Y., 1955-56; sec. admissions Duke U. Med. Sch., Durham, N.C., 1955-56; substitute tchr. St. Paul's Episcopal Sch., Clearwater, Fla., 1968-74; tutor Clearwater, 1974-77; adminstrv. asst. Arthur Rutenberg Homes, Clearwater, 1977-80, Castro Homes, Juno Beach, Fla., 1980-81; mgr. adminstrv. svcs. and purchaser of optometric equip. Eckerd Vision Group (Div. Jack Eckerd Corp.), Clearwater, 1982—; mgmt. cons., Clearwater, 1983—. Pres. South Ward Sch. PTA, Clearwater, 1966. Mem. AAUW, NAFE. Republican. Methodist. Home: 1565 Alexander Rd Belleair FL 34616 Office: Jack Eckerd Corp 8333 Bryan Dairy Rd Largo FL 34647

WHITE, MARY RUTH WATHEN, social services administrator; b. Athens, Tex., Dec. 27, 1927; d. Benedict Hudson and Sara Elizabeth (Evans) W.; m. Robert M. White, Nov. 10, 1946; children: Martha Elizabeth, Robert Miles, Jr., William Benedict, Mary Ruth, Jesse Wathen, Margaret Fay, Maureen Adele, Thomas Evan. BA, Stephen F. Austin State U., Nacogdoches, Tex., 1948. Chmn. Regional Drug Abuse Com., San Antonio, 1975-81, Met. Youth Council, San Antonio, 1976-78; state chmn. Citizens United for Rehab. Errants, San Antonio, 1978—; sec. Bexar County Detention Ministries, San Antonio, 1979-88; chmn. Bexar County (Tex.) Jail Commn., 1980-82; chmn. com. on role of family in reducing recidivism Tex. Dept. Criminal Justice, Austin, 1985—; chmn. Met. Community Corrections Com., San Antonio, 1986—; bd. dirs. Tex. Coalition for Juvenile Justice, 1975—, Target 90 Youth Coordinating Coun., San Antonio, 1986-89; local chmn. vol. adv. bd. Tex. Youth Commn., 1986-87. Pres. San Antonio City Coun. PTA, 1976-78, Rep. Bus. Women Bexar Coutny, San Antonio, 1984-86; legis. chmn. Archdiocese of San Antonio Coun. Cath. Women; pres. North Urban Deanery; regent St. Anthony's Cath. Ch.; mem. allocation com. United Way, San Antonio, 1986—. Named Today's Woman Honoree, San Antonio Light Newspaper, 1985, Outstanding Rep. Women, Rep. Bus. Women Bexar County, San Antonio, 1987. Mem. Am. Corrections Assn., Assn. Criminal Justice Planners, LWV (pres. San Antonio chpt. 1981), Fedn. Women (bd. dirs. 1984—), Conservation Soc., DAR (vice regent), Colonial Dames (pres.), Cath. Daus. Am. (regent Ct. of St. Anthony). Home: 701 E Sunshine Dr E San Antonio TX 78228 Office: 7461 Callaghan Rd #307 San Antonio TX 78229

WHITE, MICHELLE JO, economics educator; b. Washington, Dec. 3, 1945; d. Harry L. and Irene (Silverman) Rich; m. Roger Hall Gordon, July 25, 1982. AB, Harvard U., 1967; MSc in Econs., London Sch. Econs., 1968; PhD, Princeton U., 1973. Asst. prof. U. Pa., Phila., 1973-78; assoc. prof., prof. NYU, N.Y.C., 1978-83; prof. econs. U. Mich., Ann Arbor, 1984—; vis. asst. prof. Yale U., New Haven, 1978; vis. prof. People's U., Beijing, fall 1986; cons. Pension Benefit Guaranty Corp., Washington, 1987; chmn. adv. com. dept. econs. Princeton U., 1988-90. Editor: The Non-profit Sector in a Three Sector Economy, 1981; contbr. numerous articles to profl. jours. Fellow Resources for Future, 1972-73; grantee NSF, 1979, 82, 88, Sloan Found., 1984, Fund for Rsch. in Dispute Resolution, 1989. Mem. Am. Econ. Assn., Com. on Status Women in Econs. Profession (bd. dirs. 1984-86). Office: U Mich 611 Tappan St Ann Arbor MI 48109

WHITE, NANCY, fashion consultant; b. Bklyn., July 25, 1916; d. Thomas J. and Virginia (Gillette) W.; student pvt. schs.; m. Ralph Delahaye Paine, Jr., July 25, 1947 (div. Dec. 1977); m. Clarence J. Dauphinot; children—Gillette Dauphinot Piper, Katharine Delahaye Paine; m. George Keys Thompson, Nov. 1978. Fashion editor Pictorial Rev. mag., 1936-40; asst. fashion editor Good Housekeeping mag., 1940-47, fashion editor, 1947-57; asst. editor Harper's Bazaar, N.Y.C., 1957-58, editor-in-chief, 1958-71; fashion dir. Bergdorf Goodman, N.Y.C., 1972-74; dir. Gen. Mills; fashion cons., N.Y.C., 1974—; cons. fashion design Channel 13 Public TV; cons. spl. events Nat. Found. March of Dimes. Former mem. Nat. Council of Arts; mem. women's bd. Lighthouse for the Blind. Decorated knight Order Merit (Italy), Silver medal Merit (Spain); recipient N.Y. Designers award. Mem. Fashion Group (past pres.). Address: 3 E 77th St Apt 5C New York NY 10021

WHITE, NANCY A., insurance agency administrator; b. Teaneck, N.J., Aug. 17, 1959; d. Ernest and Iola Belle (Foote) Barlow; m. James E. White, July 25, 1987; children: Chris LaFever, Chad LaFever, Michele LaFever. Student, Niagara U. Owner, mgr. Ernest Barlow Ins. Agy., Ransomville, N.Y.; asst. mgr. Permanent Savs. Bank, Lockport, N.Y.; office mgr. Smith-March and Assoc., Inc., Newfane, N.Y. Mem. NAFE, Lock City Bus. and Profl. Women. Home: 3186 Lockport-Olcott Rd Newfane NY 14108

WHITE, NANCY ELAINE, reading teacher; b. Mason City, Iowa, Nov. 21, 1952; d. Ronald Tapager and Noreen Elaine (Vinge) Burdick; m. Gary Thomas White, Aug. 10, 1974. BA, U. No. Iowa, 1975, MA in Edn., 1980, EdS, 1989. Cert. tchr., Iowa. Tchr. Oak Grove Elem. Sch., Montrose, Colo., 1975-76; gen. equivalency diploma instr. Camp Sunnyside, Des

Moines, 1976; tchr. English Oelwein (Iowa) Jr. High Sch., 1977; reading tchr. Mid. Sch., Independence, Iowa, 1977—. Author booklets on ednl. topics. Bd. dirs. Wapsipinicon Golf Club, Independence, 1989—. Mem. NEA, AAUW (pres. Independence chpt. 1981-83, 86-87), Ea. Iowa Reading Coun. (pres. 1989-90), Iowa Author/Illustrator Com. (chair 1990-91), Iowa Reading Assn., Internat. Reading Assn., Iowa State Edn. Assn., Independence Tchrs. Assn. (sec. 1984-86), Alpha Upsilon Alpha. Democrat. Methodist. Home: 818 7th St NW Independence IA 50644 Office: Middle Sch 1301 1st St W Independence IA 50644

WHITE, NANCY HELEN, communications executive; b. Teaneck, N.J., Aug. 17, 1959; d. Joseph Patrick and Ruth Ann (Schultz) W. AA, Guilford Tech. Inst., Greensboro, N.C., 1979; postgrad., Guilford Coll., 1989. Various clerical positions Greensboro, 1976-87; project mgmt. specialist AT&T, Greensboro, 1987—. Vol. United Way, Greensboro, 1986-87. Dana Found. scholar, 1988. Mem. NAFE. Republican. Home: 6446 Old Burlington Rd Whitsett NC 27377

WHITE, NANCY-CECILE JEEP, federal agency official; b. Virginia, Minn., Jan. 23, 1955; d. Harold Earl and Helen Arlene (Steinberg) Adamson; m. Ray Alan White, June 25, 1989; 1 child, Jennifer Lee. BA, U. Minn., 1979. Helicopter instr., asst. chief pilot Hervert Aviation, Mpls., 1983-84; helicopter pilot, 1st officer Omniflight Helicopters, N.Y.C., 1984-85; simulator and ground instr. pilot Flight Safety, West Palm Beach, Fla., 1985; helicopter instr. pilot Golden State Aviation, El Cajon, Calif., 1986; pilot, law enforcement officer U.S. Customs, Riverside, Calif., 1987—; wildlife survey pilot James Wyatt Enterprises, Homestead, Fla., 1989-90; pipeline survey pilot J R Helicopters, St. Paul, 1990. Mem. Whirly Girls, Ninety-Nines. Home: 1405 Ivory Gull Ct Homestead FL 33035

WHITE, PAMELA JOYCE, music educator; b. Phila., Apr. 11, 1950; d. Johnnie Cleveland and Ann (Etheredge) W. BA in Edn., Jersey City State Coll., 1972. Cert. tchr., N.J. Music educator Old Bridge (N.J.) Bd. Edn., 1972—. Asst. choir dir. Simpson United Meth. Ch., Old Bridge, 1980—; mem. viola section Jersey City State Coll. Community Orchestra, 1972-77. Mem. NEA, N.J. Edn. Assn., Middlesex County Edn. Assn., Old Bridge Edn. Assn., Alpha Delta Kappa (sec. 1986-90). Methodist.

WHITE, PATRICIA ANN, management consultant; b. Newark, Oct. 23, 1942; d. Edgar Dennis and Anna Patricia (Simile) Savacool; m. Ronald Lee White, June 16, 1962; children: Lisa Anne, Christopher Lee. BS in Social Sci magna cum laude, Montclair State Coll., 1979; postgrad., Columbia U., 1979-80, New Sch. Social Rsch., N.Y.C., 1984; MA in Orgn. Devel., Norwich U., 1989. Tchr. elem. sch. Absecon (N.J.) Bd. of Edn., 1968-70; sales rep., trainer Savacool Real Estate, Bloomfield, N.J., 1971-73; utilization coord. Mountainside Hosp., Montclair, N.J., 1973-76; med. asst. Gastroent. Assocs., Montclair, 1976-77; exec. dir. Women Helping Women, Montclair, 1977-80; sr. mgmt. trainer Automatic Data Processing, Inc., Clifton, N.J., 1980-84; sr. mgmt. cons. The Equitable, N.Y.C., 1984-86; dir. mgmt. and orgnl. devel. Equicor, Nashville, 1986-88; pres. The Spectrum Group, Brentwood, Tenn., 1988—; chairperson Women's Bus. Resource Group, N.Y.C., 1986-87; prin. cons. D.R. & W. West Caldwell, N.J., 1985-87. Co-founder Career Women's Network, No. N.J., 1982; bd. dirs. YWCA, Montclair, 1979-81. Mem. Human Resource Planning Soc., Organizational Devel. Network, Am. Soc. of Tng. and Devel. Democrat. Home and Office: The Spectrum Group 1323 Robert E Lee Ln Brentwood TN 37027

WHITE, PATRICIA SMITH, community developer; b. Greenville, R.I., Dec. 13, 1928; d. Ernest Leslie and Ruth Althea (Leathers) Smith; m. Winfield Horace White III, June 21, 1949 (div. July 1969); children: Cynthia Ellen, Deborah Lynn (dec.), Brian Winfield. BS in Textiles, Clothing and Related Arts, U. R.I., 1950; MS in Family and Community Devel., U. Md., 1972, PhD in Human Devel. Edn., 1981. Statis. quality control technician Oscar Mayer Meat Packing Co., Chgo., 1954; textile research technician Gillette Research Inst., Rockville, Md., 1965-67; extension agt. home econs. U. Md. Coop. Extension Service, College Park, 1967-77, area extension agt. community resource devel., 1978—; supervising agt. expanded food and nutrition edn. program USDA, Prince George's County, Md., 1969-77, Balt., 1971-72; community nutritionist St. Mary's Assn. Retarded Citizens, Leonardtown, Md., 1983-89; agt. trainer U. Md. Coop. Extension Service, 1985. Author: (video) Parliamentary Procedure Instruction, 1987. Initiator, bd. dirs. Friends of Margaret Brent Garden, St. Mary's City, Md., 1983—; bd. dirs. Resource Conservation and Devel. Bd., La Plata, Md., 1986—. Fellow U. Md. Coop. Extension Svc., 1971-72; U. Md. grantee, 1977; recipient Tak Pride in Am. awards Dept. Natural Resources, USDA, 1988. Mem. LWV (pres. St. Mary's County br. 1987—, Woman of Yr. 1981), AAUW (pay equity com., rep. Md. women com., chair choices St. Mary's County chpt. 1986—, Woman of Yr. 1986, 87, 88), NOW (St. Mary's chpt.), Common Cause, Orgn. to Save Social Security, Md. Community Resource Devel. (charter, chmn. membership, past pres. 1978—), Community Devel. Soc. (publs. com., past chair low income com. 1978—), Am. Home Econs. Assn. (cert., grantee 1982), Am. Inst. Parliamentarians. Democrat. Mem. Unitarian Ch. Club: Toastmasters (Leonardtown) (initiator, ednl. v.p. 1983—). Home: Rt 2 Box 82-1 Leonardtown MD 20650 Office: U Md Coop Extension Svc Box 663 State Rt 245 Govtl Ctr Leonardtown MD 20650

WHITE, PEGI See WHEATLEY, MARGARET BISSON

WHITE, RHEA AMELIA, information scientist; b. Utica, N.Y., May 6, 1931; d. John Raymond and Rhea Jane (Parry) W. BA, Pa. State U., University Park, 1953; MLS, Pratt Inst. Libr. Sch., Bklyn., 1965; postgrad., SUNY, 1990—. Editor Jour. Am. Soc. Psychical Rsch., N.Y.C., 1959-62, 84—; libr. dept. psychiatry Maimonides Med. Ctr., Bklyn., 1965-67; dir. info. Am. Soc. Psychical Rsch., N.Y.C., 1965-80; reference libr. East Meadow (N.Y.) Pub. Libr., 1965—; founder, dir. Parapsychology Sources of Info. Ctr., Dix Hills, N.Y., 1981—; editor Rsch. in Parapsychology, Metuchen, N.J., 1981-85, Theta, Durham, N.C., 1981-86; founder, editor Parapsychology Abstracts Internat., Dix Hills, 1983—; founder, producer PsiLine Database, Dix Hills, 1983—; mng. editor Advanced in Parapsychol. Rsch., N.Y.C., 1977; rsch. fellow Menninger Found., Topeka, 1963-65; abstractor Psychol. Abstracts, Washington, 1967—; cons. Scarecrow Press, Metuchen, N.J., 1980-85; referee Jour. Parapsychology, Durham, 1981-85; sr. rsch. cons. Ctr. Sci. Anomalies Rsch., 1981—. Author: Parapsychology: Sources of Information, 1973, Surveys in Parapsychology, 1975 (with M. Murphy) The Psychic Side of Sports, 1978; editor: Research in Parapsychology, 1981, 82, 83, 84; parapsychology book reviewer Libr. Jour., N.Y.C., 1974-86; regional editor European Jour. Parapsychology, 1975—; mem. editorial bd. Advances in Parapsychology Rsch., 1980-85, Archaeus, 1985—; editor Parapsychology Abstracts Internat., 1983—; contbr. articles to profl. jours. Recipient Hans Peter Luhn award Am. Soc. Info. Sci., N.Y.C. chpt., 1965; Coll. Human Scis. hon. fellow Internat. Inst. Integral Human Scis. Mem. Parapsychol. Assn. (mem. coun. 1958, 62-63, 82—, pres. 1984, dir. 1986), Soc. Psychical. Rsch., Acad. Religion and Psychical Rsch. (mem. bd. 1982-84, publs. com. 1982—), Spiritual Frontiers Fellowship, Internat. Assn. Near-Death Studies, Soc. Sci. Study of Religion, Soc. Sci. Exploration, AAUW, Nassau County Libr. Assn., Internat. Assn. Religion and Parapsychology, Internat. Inst. Integral Human Scis., Inst. Noetic Scis. Home: 2 Plane Tree Ln Dix Hills NY 11746 Office: East Meadow Pub Libr Front St and E Meadow Ave East Meadow NY 11554

WHITE, RHEA ANDERSON, education educator; b. New Orleans, Oct. 27, 1947; d. Alvin Alfred and Lorena (Branch) Anderson; m. Robert Elery, Sept. 5, 1975; 1 child, Robyn Eunice. BS in Edn., Dillard U., 1969; MEd, U. New Orleans, 1973. Tchr. Special edn. tchr. New Orleans Pub. Schs., 1969-73; instr. edn. cons. U. New Orleans, 1973-80; ednl. evaluator New Orleans Pub. Schs., 1980-84, coordinator test & evaluators, ednl. cons., 1985-86, coordinator special edn. programs, 1986, reading tchr., 1986-87, third grade tchr., 1987-88, special edn. tchr., 1988-89.; owner Tutoring Svc., New Orleans, 1987—; awards chairperson Robert E. Lee Sch., New Orleans, 1987—, spl. edn. chairperson, 1989. Author: Child of the Promise. Asst. Troup Leader Girl Scouts of Am., New Orleans, 1987--. Mem. Coun. of Exceptional Children, Internat. Reading Assn., S.E. La. Coun. Ednl. Diagnosticians, Eighth Dimension Civic Club (v.p., pres.), Alpha Kappa Alpha. Democrat. Baptist. Office: Robert E Lee Sch 1607 S Carrollton Ave New Orleans LA 70118

WHITE, ROBERTA LOUISE (BOBBIE WHITE), artist, educator; b. Hollywood, Calif., Sept. 21, 1936; d. Robert Alden Cady and Thelma Louise Weller; m. Rolan L. White, Feb. 8, 1957; children: Peter D., Sam L., Shannon L. White Grant. Employment mgr. MGM Grand Hotel and Casino, Las Vegas, Nev., 1974-86, The Mirage Hotel and Casino, Las Vegas, Nev., 1988-89; artist, tchr. City of Las Vegas, 1986—. Exhibitor Nev. Fram and Gallery, Las Vegas, 1988—, Bill W. Dodge Gallery, Carmel, Calif., 1990—. Recipient numerous art awards, Las Vegas ARt Mus., others. Mem. Nat. League Am. Pen Women, Water Color West, Nev. Watercolor Soc. (v.p. 1987-88), Las Vegas Art Mus., Boulder City Art Guild, Nev. Hist. Mus. Home and Office: Paintings and Etc 1761 Linn Ln Las Vegas NV 89115

WHITE, SALLY REY, health science facility administrator; b. Oakland, Calif., Mar. 11, 1948; d. Harold Thomas and Patricia (Reynolds) W. AS, River Community Coll., 1988; postgrad., Calif. State, San Bernardino, 1988—. Spl. project coord. Riverside Community Hosp., 1982—.

WHITE, SANDRA LAVELLE, medical educator, immunologist; b. Columbia, S.C., Aug. 30, 1941; d. Christopher Other and Roseana Ellender (Benson) W.; m. Kenneth Olden, May 19, 1984; 1 child, Heather Alexis Benson Olden. BA, Hampton U., 1963; MS, U. Mich., 1971, PhD, 1974. Rsch. asst. Sloan Kettering Cancer Inst., N.Y.C., 1963-69; asst. prof. microbiology coll. medicine Howard U., Washington, 1974-76; staff fellow Nat. Cancer Inst., NIH, Bethesda, Md., 1976-79; asst. prof. coll. medicine Howard U., Washington, 1979-84, assoc. prof. coll. medicine, 1984—, mem. cancer ctr. coll. medicine, 1984—; mem. pathology B study sect. NIH, Bethesda, 1980-84, bd. sci. dirs., 1985-89; mem. microbiology test com. Nat. Bd. Med. Examiners, Phila., 1989-93. Co-author books; contbr. articles to profl. jours. Mem. Soc. for Leukocyte Biology, Am. Soc. for Cell Biology, Am. Soc. Microbiology, The Links Inc., Delta Sigma Theta (v.p. local chpt. 1988-90). Baptist. Office: Howard U Med Sch Cancer Ctr 2041 Georgia Ave NW Washington DC 20060

WHITE, SANDRA LEE, fund raising consultant; b. Cleve., Sept. 28, 1946; d. Alfred Edward and Pearl (Adell) Saltzman; m. Philip Stuart White Jr., Dec. 16, 1967; children: Matthew Ruben, Paul Jason, Zachary Bryan, Farrah Dawn. AA, Cleve. Inst. Art, 1968; student, U. Ill., 1964-65. Staff artist Bobbie Brooks Inc., Cleve., 1964-67, West Side Newspaper, Cleve., 1968, Sun Newspapers, Cleve., 1968-69; community activist, leader Hadassah/State of Israel Bonds, Cleve., 1969-89; dir. Ohio region Israel Histadrut and Histadrut of Greater Cleve., 1989—; mem. nat. maj. gifts task force Hadassah, N.Y.C., 1985-87, Israel task force and community relations com. Jewish Community Fedn. of Cleve., 1981—; nat. assoc. chmn. State of Israel Bonds, N.Y.C., 1986—; cons. Union Am. Hebrew Congregations Midwest Lakes Coun. Region. Editorial columnist Cleve. Plain Dealer newspaper, 1983-87. Dir. devel. Montefiore Home for the Aged, Cleve., 1986-87; trustee Footpath Dance Co., Cleve., 1985-87; cons. Cleve. Children's Mus., 1987-88; mem. Fedn. Community Planning, Cleve.; cons. for state polit. campaigns, fundraiser. Mem. Ohio Coun. Fundraising Execs. Democrat. Office: Histadrut of Greater Cleve 23611 Chagrin Blvd Ste 250 Cleveland OH 44122

WHITE, SHARON, elementary school educator; b. Nov. 25, 1959. BS, So. Ill. U., 1981, MS, 1984; AA, Rend Lake Jr. Coll., 1978. Cert. elem. tchr., spl. edn. tchr., Ill. Tchr. Bluford (Ill.) Grade Sch., 1981-85; adminstr. Wayne City (Ill.) Unit 100, 1985—, tchr.; coord. sch. and community alcohol and drug program. Bd. dirs. South Cen. Spl. Olympics; co-dir., acteens leader vacation bible sch. Wayne City First Bapt. Ch., 1989-90. Mem. NAFE, Delta Kappa Gamma, Pi Lambda Theta. Home: Rt 2 Box 53A Cisne IL 62823

WHITE, SUSIE MAE, school psychologist; b. Madison, Fla., Mar. 5, 1914; d. John Anderson and Lucy (Crawford) Williams; m. Daniel Elijah White, Oct. 20, 1958 (dec. Sept. 29, 1968). BS, Fla. Meml. Coll., St. Augustine, 1948; MEd, U. Md., 1953; postgrad., Mich. State U., 1955, Santa Fe Community Coll., 1988. Elem. tchr. Grove Park (Fla.) Elem. Sch., 1943; tchr. Douglas High Sch., High Springs, Fla., 1944-55; sch. psychologist Alachua County Sch. Bd., Gainesville, Fla., 1956-69; coord. social svcs. Alachua County Sch. Bd., Gainesville, 1970; owner, dir. Mother Dear's Child Care Ctr., Gainesville, 1989—. Del. Bapt. World Alliance, Bapt. Conv. Fla., Tokyo, 1970; state dir. leadership Fla. Bapt. Gen. Conv., 1971-85. Recipient Cert. of Appreciation Fla. State Dept. Edn., Tallahassee, 1971, Appreciation for Disting. Svc. award Fla. Gen. Bapt. Conv., Miami, 1979. Mem. Nat. Ret. Tchrs. Assn., Alachua County Tchrs. Assn., Fla. Meml. Coll. Nat. Alumni Assn., AAUW, Heroines of Jerico, Masons. Democrat. Office: Child Care Ctr 811 NW 4th Pl Gainesville FL 32601

WHITE, VERNA HESBY, girl scout professional executive; b. Arlington, S.D., Mar. 9, 1919; d. John Eivind and Sarah Emelia (Kalvig) Hesby; m. Michael Dean White, Dec. 29, 1962 (div. Dec., 1973). BA, Augustana Coll., Sioux Falls, S.D., 1940; Certificate, Harvard Mgmt. Seminar, 1979. Music tchr. Pub. Schs., Colton, S.D., 1940-45; exec. dir. Girl Scouts U.S., Grand Forks, N.D., 1946-49; dist. dir. Girl Scouts U.S., Seattle, 1949-53; coun. adv. Girl Scouts U.S., Kansas City, Mo., 1953-57; trainer, team coord. Girl Scouts U.S., N.Y.C., 1957-61, mgmt. cons., 1978-81; coun. cons. Girl Scouts U.S., Washington, 1961-73, dir. tng. sch., 1974-78; exec. dir. USA Girl Scouts in Europe, 1981-85. Co-editor: (tng. syllabus) Management in Girl Scouting, 1984. Dir. Norwegian Choral Group, Washington, 1986—; com. mem. Norwegian Am. Music Exchange Program, Washington, 1988—; vol. Smithsonian Inst., Washington, 1986—; pres. Nat. Women's Symphony, Washington, 1990—. Recipient Thanks Badge Girl Scouts U.S., Commendation, Dept. of Army, U.S., Heidelberg, Fed. German Rep., U.S. Air Force, Heidelberg, Fed. German Rep., 1985. Mem. AAUW (pres. Silver Springs, Md. chpt. 1988-90, program v.p. Md. div. 1990—). Republican. Lutheran. Home: 14614 Bauer Dr #4 Rockville MD 20853

WHITE, VIRGINIA LOU, township official; b. Barberton, Ohio, Oct. 23, 1932; d. Lucius F. and Edith M. (Carlton) Converse; m. Neil Mason White, Sept. 8, 1956; children:William Neil, David Converse, Holly Susanne. BA, Baldwin-Wallace Coll., 1954. Sec. to exec. sec. Adult Edn. Found. (now Inst. for Civic Edn.) U. Akron, 1954-55, office mgr., 1955-57; tchr. bus. edn. Kenmore High Sch., Akron, 1957-59, Elyria (Ohio) Pub. high Sch., 1959-60; charter twp. clk Meridian Twp., Okemos, Mich., 1972—; del., alt. Mich. Rep. Conv., 1972—; pres. Converse Press; v.p. Cen. Vending, Inc. Author: How To Write Your Election Procedure Manual, 1988. Mem. Mid-Mich. chpt. MADD; sec. Mich. Rep. Issues Com., 1979-80; vice chmn., 1981-87, corr. sec. 1987—; mem. Ingham County Rep. Exec. Com., 1972—; mem. exec. com. Rep 6th Congl. Dist., 1980—, state historian Mich. Assn. Clks., 1988-89, 3rd v.p. 1990—, co-chmn. Ingham County Reagan/Bush Com., 1980-84; active com. Ruppe for Senate, 1982; chmn. Com. to Support Police and Fire Mileage, Meridian Twp., 1982, Pub. Safety Bldgs. Com., 1988—; co-chmn. Friends of Capital Area Transp. Authority, 1983; chaplain Mid-Mich. Rep. Women's Club, 1988—. Recipient Mich. Twp. Clk. of Yr. Mich. State U. and Mich. Twp. Assn., 1989. Mem. Internat. Inst. Mcpl. Clks., Mich. Mcpl. Clks., Mich. Assn. Clks., Okemos Book Club, Zonta (local pres. 1981-83). Home: 1641 Birchwood Dr Okemos MI 48864 Office: 5151 Marsh Rd Okemos MI 48864

WHITE, WINIFRED V., broadcast executive; b. Indpls., Mar. 23, 1953; d. Walter H. and Winifred (Parlean) W. AB, Radcliffe Coll., 1974; MA in Edn., Lesley Coll. Mgr. Project Peacock NBC, 1981-82, with children's programs dept., 1982-84, dir. children's programs dept., 1984-85, v.p. family programs, 1985-89, dir. films for TV, 1989—. Bd. dirs. Planned Parenthood, 1986—. Mem. Acad. TV Arts and Scis. (bd. govs. 1986—), Harvard-Radcliffe Club (bd. dirs. 1983—). Office: NBC Entertainment Burbank CA 90064*

WHITED, MAUREEN R., financial analyst; b. Oak Park, Ill., Mar. 16, 1960; d. Peter C. and Mary A. (Allen) Goulding; m. James Whited, June 18, 1982; 1 child, Alissa. BS in Acctg., U. Ill., 1982; postgrad. in econs., DePaul U. CPA, Ill. Mgr. competitor analysis Household Internat., Prospect Heights, Ill., 1985—. Mem. NAFE. Home: 277 Colony Green Bloomingdale IL 60108

WHITEHEAD, ARDELLE COLEMAN, advertising and public relations executive; b. Carrollton, Ohio, May 13, 1917; d. James David and Gilsie Dale (Hendricks) Coleman. BS, Wittenberg U., 1938. Account exec. Steve Hannagan Assocs., N.Y.C., 1946-52; dir. publicity Fieldcrest Mills, Inc., N.Y.C., 1952-55; account and pub. rels. exec. Calkins & Holden, N.Y.C., 1956-59; creative dir. Leslie Advt. Agy., Greenville, S.C., 1960-62; dir. advt. Lanz Originals, Los Angeles, 1962-64; account exec., copywriter, consumer affairs specialist Jennings & Thompson, Phoenix, 1965-73; mgr. pub. communications Valley Nat. Bank, Phoenix, 1974-75; pres. The Whiteheads, Inc., Phoenix, 1976—. Author: (pamphlets) How to Be a Client, 1979, Advertising Isn't Everything, 1981; contbr. articles to various Phoenix and regional art mags. Mem. mktg. com. cen. Ariz. chpt. ARC, Phoenix, 1985-88. Recipient Lulu award Los Angeles Advt. Women, 1974; named Adperson of Yr. Ad II of Phoenix, 1978. Mem. Pub. Relations Soc. (Percy award 1985), Women in Communications (Woman of Achievement award for west region 1981), Phoenix Advt. Club (hon. life mem.). Office: The Whiteheads Inc 337 E Pierson Phoenix AZ 85012

WHITEHEAD, DOLLIE GLOVER, healthcare facility administrator; b. Bradenton, Fla., Oct. 4, 1936; d. William Henry and Odessa Glover; m. James Walter Whitehead, Mar. 30, 1958; children: James Walter II, Cynthia Anne, Wesley William; 1 stepchild, Donald. BA, Spellman Coll., 1957; MSW, Atlanta U., 1961; MPH, U. Calif., Berkeley, 1978. Social worker Children's Home Soc., Cin., 1961-62; social worker VA Med. Ctr., Miami, Fla., 1962-69, Lyons, N.J., 1969-70, Fresno, Calif., 1971-76; trainee hosp. adminstrn. VA Med. Ctr. San Francisco and Fresno Community Hosp., 1976-78, specialist hosp. adminstrn., 1978-81; specialist hosp. adminstrn. VA Med. Ctr., Fresno, Calif., 1981-85; assoc. dir. trainee VA Med. Ctr., Long Beach, Calif., 1985—; assoc. dir. VA Med. Ctr., Ft. Howard, Md., 1987-89; specialist hosp. adminstrn. VA Med. Ctr., Alexandria, La., 1989—; adj. prof., field work supr. Calif. State U., Fresno, 1972-76, Calif. Sch. Profl. Psychology, Fresno, 1974-75; teaching asst. U. Calif., Berkeley, 1978; presenter workshops, cons., therapist grief and bereavement, death and dying, time and stress mgmt., Fresno, San Francisco and Long Beach, 1971—. Mem. Jack and Jill of Am. Inc., 1985-86; sec. bd. dirs. Jack and Jill of Am. Found., Fresno, 1974—; mem. exec. com. United Negro Coll. Fund, Fresno, 1982-86; mem. allocation com. United Way, Fresno, 1985, bd. dirs. Mem. NAFE, Nat. Assn. Social Workers (cert.), Federally Employed Women, Am. Coll. Healthcare Execs., Links Club, Toastmasters (area gov.), Alpha Kappa Alpha. Home and Office: VA Med Ctr Alexandria LA 71301

WHITEHEAD, GAIL, laboratory administrator; b. N.Y.C., Feb. 9, 1942; d. Robert George and Margaret (Fauback) W.; children: Sonya Ann, Serina Ayn. Student, U. Ill., Mary Beth Modeling Sch. With Dawson Advt.; v.p. McCue Labs., Houston. Participant Leadership Am. Fellow Am. Biog. Inst. Rsch. Assn. (life, inner circle of achievement); mem. Laredo Bus. and Profl. Women's Assn., Texican Cattlewomen, Am. Soc. Profl. and Exec. Women, Leadership Am., Rotary. Home: 700 E Hildebrand #303 San Antonio TX 78212

WHITEHEAD, HELEN MAY, small business owner, marketing consultant; b. Harrisburg, Pa., Sept. 1, 1951; d. Warren Benjamin Engle and Priscilla Jean (Zinkan) Kohlhaas; 1 child, Gregory James. AA in Liberal Arts, U. Md.-European div. Germany, 1978; certificado de Suficiencia, U. Zaragoza, Spain, 1978; BS in Mktg., Northeastern U., 1982; BS in Bus. Adminstrn. with high honors, Auburn U., 1983; MBA, Simmons Coll., 1987. Mgr., sales rep. M&S Indian Jewelry, Griesheim, Fed. Republic Germany, 1978-79; message distbn. shift supr. U.S. Air Force, Scott AFB, Belleville, Ill., 1971-75, communications detachment controller U.S. Air Force Europe, Ramstein, Fed. Republic Germany, 1975-78; tng. dept. coordinator Aviation Simulation Tech., Inc., Bedford, Mass., 1982-84; regional sales mgr. Huang's Trading Co., Skokie, Ill, 1984-87; staff engr. CTA, Inc., 1989—; substitute tchr. Hanscom Primary Sch., Bedford, 1986-87, Quincy High Sch., 1987-89; pres., small bus. entrepreneur Uniques, Bedford, 1983-87; speaker in field. Scholarship chairperson Hanscom Officers' Wives Club, Bedford, 1982-84. Served with U.S. Air Force, 1971-78, ETO. Mem. NAFE, Alpha Sigma Lambda. Home: 14 Penobscot Rd Nashua NH 03062-1851

WHITEHEAD, LOUISE, postal service official; b. Mobile, Ala., Nov. 22, 1940; d. Jake and Rose (Green) Irby; children: Vincent, Kenneth, Jeffrey. Student, Queensborough Community Coll. Supr. Vantines, Inc., Flushing, N.Y., Meldisco Shoe Co., Bklyn.; mgr. U.S. Postal Svc., N.Y.C. Mem. Nat. Assn. Postal Suprs., NAFE. Home: 140-60 G R Brewer Blvd Springfield Gardens NY 11434

WHITEHEAD, SUSAN, sales executive; b. Acushnet, Mass., Aug. 18, 1945; d. Gordon L. and Anne C. (Yates) Baker; children: Scott, Nicole, Candace, Brandon. Student, U. R.I., 1987. Sales rep. Interstate Uniform Svcs., New Bedford, Mass., 1979-82; sales, mktg. rep. Alden Corrugated Co., New Bedford, 1982-84; sales, mktg. coord. Alden Corrugated Container Co., New Bedford, 1982-84, Set Point Paper Co., 1984-86, Nat. Packaging, 1986-88; sales rep., packaging engr. Mark C. Specialties, Tolland, Conn., 1988—. Bd. dirs. Am. Cancer Soc., NB Harbor Svcs.-Adult Retardates; mem. Gov.'s Coun. on Women's Issues. Recipient cert. for Outstanding Fund Raising, Am. Cancer Soc., 1989. Mem. NAFE, Am. Bus. Women's Assn. (founder, pres. Greater New Bedford chpt., del. to dist. conv.), Fall River Bus. and Profl. Women's Fedn., Fall River C. of C., New Bedford C. of C. (bd. dirs.), Tribute to Women in Industry 1986, del. to nat. convention). Republican. Roman Catholic. Home: 89 R Dr Westport MA 02790

WHITEHOUSE, ANN MALINIAK, clinical psychologist, researcher; b. West Chester, Pa., Jan. 14, 1959; d. John and Janet (Borchers) Maliniak; m. Wayne George Whitehouse, Nov. 17, 1984. BA, Franklin and Marshall Coll., 1981; MA, West Chester U., 1987. Rsch. asst. Franklin and Marshall Coll., Lancaster, Pa., 1979-80, teaching asst., 1980; rsch. asst. unit for exptl. psychiatry Inst. of Pa. Hosp., Phila., 1981-87; clin. psychology assoc. Bryn Mawr Rehab. Hosp., Malvern, Pa., 1987—; adminstrv. asst. Internat. Jour. Clin. and Exptl. Hypnosis, Phila., 1982-85; mental health technician Elwyn (Pa.) Insts., 1985-87; facilitator Brain Injury Family Support Group, Malvern, 1989—; presenter at profl. confs. Mem. Am. Psychol. Assn. (assoc.), Assn. for Behavior Analysis, Nat. Head Injury Found., Keystone State Head Injury Found., Pa. Psychol. Assn. (affiliate), Pa. Soc. Behavioral Medicine and Biofeedback, Phila. Neuropsychology Soc., Psi Chi. Home: 522 Fernwood Ave Folsom PA 19033

WHITEHOUSE, PAULA MARIE, operations research analyst; b. Wash., Feb. 26, 1953; d. Paul Edward and Dorothy (Lakata) McCaskill; m. Michael Lloyd Whitehouse, May 24, 1980; children: Heather Michelle, Ian Asmund. AA with high honors, Prince George's C.C., Largo, Md., 1973; BA, Lake Erie Coll., Painesville, Ohio, 1975; MSSM, U. S Calif., 1984. Adminstrv. asst. Prince George's Motor Inn, Hillcrest Heights, Md., 1975-78; EW/SIGINT non-communications interceptor/analyst US Army Electronics Proving Grounds, Ft. Huachuca, Ariz., 1978-80; EW/SIGINT non-communications analyst 207th MI Group, Stuttgart-Moehringen, Fed. Republic of Germany, 1980-84; math. analyst Pacific Sierra Research, White Sands Missile Range, N.Mex.; op. research analyst US Army TRADOC Analysis Command, White Sands Missile Range, Mex., 1987--. Sec. Pam American Region, Sports Car Club Am., 1986, treas., 1988, 89, v.p. Sunland Sports Car Club, El Paso, Tex., 1989. Sgt. US Army, 1978-83. Home: 3233 Stone Edge Dr El Paso TX 79904

WHITEHURST, BETTY CAMPBELL, educator; b. Merkel, Tex., Feb. 15, 1934; d. Floyd Tracy and Orpah Elizabeth (Patterson) Campbell; m. Walter Allen Whitehurst, June 16, 1961; children: David Allen, Bruce Tracy, Monica Mae. BA, McMurry Coll., 1956; MA, U. Va., 1974, PhD, 1978. Missionary United Meth. Ch., Chile, S.Am., 1966-71; instr. U. Va., Charlottesville, 1976-77; tchr. Rustburg (Va.) High Sch., 1978-79; gifted/talented coord. Bedford (Va.) County Pub. Schs., 1979-80; asst. prof. Hollins Coll., Roanoke, Va., 1980-82; adj. prof. J. Sargeant Reynolds Community Coll., Richmond, Va., 1982-84; tchr. West End Christian Sch., Hopewell, Va., 1984-85; asst. prof. Coll. of William and Mary, Williamsburg, Va., 1985-87, U. Richmond, 1987—. Del. United Meth. Gen. Conf., Balt., 1984, St. Louis, 1988, World Meth. Conf., Nairobi, Kenya, Africa, 1986; mem. United Meth. Gen. Bd. of Discipleship, Nashville, 1984—. Recipient Govs. fellowship Commonwealth of Va., 1975. Mem. Am. Assn. of Tchrs. of Spanish and Portuguese (Va. chpt. sec., treas. 1988—), Modern Lang. Assn., Twentieth

Century Spanish Assn. of Am., Am. Coun. of Tchrs. of Fgn. Langs., Mid-Atlantic Conf. on Latin Am. Studies., United Meth. Women (dist. v.p. 1989—). Democrat. Home: 7731 Turf Ln Richmond VA 23225 Office: U Richmond Dept Modern Fgn Langs Richmond VA 23173

WHITELAW, ELIZABETH ANN, educator; b. El Paso, Oct. 23, 1941; d. Malcolm Rivers and Erma Elizabeth (McCord) Smith; m. James Waite Whitelaw, Dec. 21, 1963; 1 child, Marilyn Elizabeth. BE, Tex. Western U., 1963; MEd, Ariz. State U., 1972, postgrad. Cert. elem. and secondary tchr., reading specialist. Elem. tchr. El Paso Pub. Schs., 1963-64; kindergarten tchr. All Seasons Sch., Scottsdale, Ariz., 1974-75; reading specialist Phoenix Union High Sch. Dist., 1976-77; reading specialist, English tchr. Tempe (Ariz.) Union High Sch. Dist., 1977—; vol. cons. Okemah Day Care Ctr., Phoenix, 1969-76. Bd. dirs. Phoenix Planned Parenthood Aux., Okemah Neighborhood Devel. Bd. Mem. Ocotillo Reading Coun. (v.p. 1987-88), Nation Reading Conf., Assn. Supervision and Curriculum Devel., Internat. Reading Assn., Phoenix Early Music Soc., Tempe Secondary Tchrs. Assn. (sr. del.), Pi Lambda Theta. Methodist. Home: 2930 S Country Club Way Tempe AZ 85282 Office: Tempe Union High Sch Dist 500 W Guadalupe Tempe AZ 85283

WHITESELL, NANCY JANE, veterinarian; b. Washington, Apr. 6, 1953; d. Arthur DeVere and Margaret Joanne (Rowland) Talkington; m. Oct. 31, 1982 (div. June 1987); children: Collin, Allison. BS summa cum laude, U. Vt., 1974; DVM, Purdue U., 1977. Lic. vet, N.Y., Ind. Relief vet various vet. hosps., 1977-78; mgr. Emergency Animal Clinic, Ft. Wayne, Ind., 1980; vet. St. Joe Ctr. Vet. Hosp., Ft. Wayne, 1978—. Mem. AVMA, Ind. Vet. Med. Assn., Northeast Ind. Vet. Med. Assn., Phi Zeta, Alpha Delta Pi. Office: Saint Joe Ctr Vet Hosp 5812 Maple Crest Fort Wayne IN 46835

WHITESIDE, CAROL GORDON, mayor; b. Chgo., Dec. 15, 1942; d. Paul George and Helen Louise (Barre) G.; m. John Gregory Whiteside, Aug. 15, 1964; children: Brian Paul, Derek James. BA, U. Calif., Davis, 1964. Pers. mgr. Emporium Capwell Co., Santa Rosa, 1964-67; pers. asst. Levi Strauss & Co., San Francisco, 1967-69; project leader Interdatum, San Francisco, 1983—; with City Coun. Modesto, 1983-87; mayor City of Modesto, 1987—. Trustee Modesto City Schs., 1979-83. Named Outstanding Woman of Yr. Women's Commn., Stanislaus County, Calif., 1988. Republican. Lutheran. Office: City of Modesto Office of Mayor PO Box 642 Modesto CA 95353

WHITESIDE, ELIZABETH AYRES, lawyer; b. Columbus, Ohio, Feb. 24, 1960; d. Alba Lea and Virginia (Ayres) W. Student, Ind. U., 1978-80; BFA, U. Wis., Milw., 1982; JD, Ohio State U., 1985. Bar: Ohio, 1985, D.C., 1986, N.Y., 1988, U.S. Dist. Ct. (no. and so. dists.) Ohio, 1986, U.S. Ct. Appeals (6th and D.C. cirs.), 1986, U.S. Tax Ct., 1986. Dep. clk. Franklin County Mcpl. Ct, Columbus, 1981; law clk. Chester, Hoffman & Willcox, Columbus, 1983-84, Porter, Wright, Morris & Arthur, Columbus, 1984; assoc. Squire, Sanders & Dempsey, Columbus, 1985-87, Shearman & Sterling, N.Y.C., 1987-89; dep. gen. counsel Geraghty & Miller, Inc., Dublin, Ohio, 1989—. Mng. editor Ohio State Law Jour., 1984-85. Mem. ABA, D.C. Bar, Ohio State Bar Assn., Assn. of Bar of the City of N.Y., N.Y. State Bar Assn., Columbus Bar Assn., Am. Judicature Soc., Phi Delta Phi. Republican. Methodist. Home: 46 S Remington Rd Bexley OH 43209 Office: Geraghty & Miller Inc 425 Metro Pl N #150 Dublin OH 43017

WHITESIDES, ELIZABETH IGLER (MRS. LAWSON EWING WHITESIDES), lawyer, club woman; b. Glendale, Ohio, Oct. 12, 1910; d. Herman Einhaus and Matilda (Voegtle) Igler; LL.B., U. Cin., 1932, J.D., 1967; m. Lawson Ewing Whitesides, June 29, 1935; children—Elizabeth Lawson (Mrs. David Garth Holdsworth), Lawson Ewing. Admitted to Ohio bar, 1932, U.S. Supreme Ct., 1968; pvt. practice law, Cincinnati, 1932—. Mem. Cin. Woman's Club; Town Club, Cin., mem. Glendale Lyceum; pres. Monday Class, Glendale, 1948-49, Glendale Village Gardeners, 1966-67. Mem. Cin. Council on World Affairs. Mem. Cin., Ky. hist. socs., Cin. Bar Assn., Order of Coif, Phi Delta Delta, Kappa Alpha Theta (pres. Cin. alumnae 1954-55). Episcopalian. Address: 840 Woodbine Ave Glendale Cincinnati OH 45246

WHITFIELD, LEIGH COSBY, commercial property manager; b. Dallas, Aug. 19, 1952; d. Fred H. and Oneita F. (Needham) C. BA, So. Meth. U., 1974. Lic. real estate broker, Tex.; cert. property mgr. Office mgr. Exec. Enterprises, Inc., Dallas, 1974-78; office mgr. Joe V. Hawn, Jr., Developer, Dallas, 1978-79; assoc. buyer Zale Corp., Dallas, 1979-81; property mgr., supr. Fults Mgmt. Co., Dallas, 1981-84; mgr. Plaza of the Americas, Wynne/Jackson Mgmt. Co., Dallas, 1984-86; v.p. mgmt. Folsom Investments, Inc., Dallas, 1986—. Mem., vol. Dallas Mus. of Art, 1981-89; mem. Children's Arts & Ideas Found., Dallas, 1985; mem. Dallas Ballet Women's Com. Mem. Inst. Real Estate Mgmt., Bldg. Owners & Mgrs. Assn., Comml. Real Estate Women, Greater Dallas Bd. Realtors. Republican. Mem. Unity Ch. Avocations: floral arranging; antique collections; music performances.

WHITING, LISA LORRAINE, video production educator, producer, director; b. Lansing, Mich., July 22, 1959; d. Lowell Stanton and Ruth Lorraine (Gregory) W. BS in Psychology, Mich. State U., 1981, BA in Telecommunication cum laude, 1984, MA in Telecommunication, 1988; AA in Dance cum laude, Lansing Community Coll., 1984. Instr. Nancie Bauer Dance Studio, Holt, Mich., 1984—; instr. video prodn. Mich. State U., East Lansing, 1984—. Producer, dir.: (TV show) The Outreach Mass, 1984—, (video series) Horticultural Training Series, 1985—; dir., cons. video: Mich. Jour., 1986; mgr. prodn.: (cable TV program) Soaps, Lucy, The Hill and You, 1986; producer, co-dir.: (TV program) Don't Throw a Good Thing...Recycle Michigan!, 1986—. Mem. Audio Engring. Soc. Home: 2004 Wood St Lansing MI 48912 Office: Mich State U 508 Communication Arts East Lansing MI 48824

WHITING, MARY ALEXANDRA, lawyer; b. N.Y.C., Aug. 18, 1952; d. Richard and Margaret W. BS in Geology, Queens Coll., 1974, MS in Geology, 1978; JD, Bklyn Law Sch., 1981. Atty. Natoli & Pocchia, N.Y.C., 1985—; paralegal coord. Bklyn Coll., 1986—; adminstrv. law judge Parking Violations Bur. City of N.Y., 1987—; assoc. dir. Nynex Corp., N.Y.C. Mem. Sigma Xi Sci. Rsch. Soc., N.Y. County Lawyers Assn., Women in Law Depts. Office: Natoli & Pocchia 325 Broadway Ste 302 New York NY 10007

WHITINGER, LEILA LEE, education educator; b. Charlotte, Mich., Mar. 3, 1941; d. Elwood Edward and Eunice May (Fladebo) W. BS, BA, Valley State Coll., 1963; MA, Mich. State U., 1976. Cert. educator. Tchr. Charlotte High Sch., 1963-64, Grayling (Mich.) High Sch., 1964-65, DeWitt (Mich.) Mid. Sch., 1965-87; field rep. Minn. Edn. Assn., Mankato, 1987—; Mem. MEA Human Relations Comm., E. Lansing, Mich., 1986-87. Writer editor: "Activist", 1983-87. Mem. MEA-PAC Council, E. Lansing, Mich., 1985-87; Mich. Dem., Detroit, 1979-87, Ingham County Dem., Lansing, 1985-87; Clinton County Dem., St. Johns, Mich., 1979-85. Mem. Profl. Staff Assn., Nat. Curriculum Assn., Minn. Hist. Soc., Nat. Audobon Soc. Home: 129 S 5th St Mankato MN 56001 Office: Minn Edn Assn 1600 Madison Ave Mankato MN 56001

WHITLEY, CAROLYN DAVIS, special education resource teacher; b. Memphis, Tenn., Nov. 8, 1933; d. Joe Hudgins and Sara Ruth (Hipps) Davis; m. Ross Irvin Evans, Jr.,Jan. 5, 1955 (div. June, 1958); m. William Talmadge Whitley Jr., May 22, 1959; children: Michael Talmadge, Charles Davis. Student, Southern Meth. U., 1951-53, Vanderbilt U., 1953-55; BA, U. Chattanooga, 1957; MEd, Memphis State U., 1970. Cert. tchr. history, spl. edn., Tenn. Employment counselor Tenn. Dept. of Employment Security, Memphis, 1958-59; tchr. Memphis City Schs., 1971—. Tchr. Labach Literacy Program, Memphis; mem. Duration Club, Memphis, 1962-65; pres. Goodwill Industries Jr. Aux., Memphis, 1963; vol. worker St. Mary's Episc. Cathedral, 1980—. Recipient Pub. Edn. Fund grants, Memphis, 1987, 88. Mem. AAUW, NEA, Tenn. Ednl. Assn., Memphis Ednl. Assn., English Speaking Union. Home: 322 Shady Woods Cove Memphis TN 38119 Office: Snowden Sch 1870 N Parkway Blvd Memphis TN 38112

WHITLEY, JUANA LYNN, advertising executive; b. LaGrange, Ga., Aug. 11, 1964; d. John Hamilton and Lena Pearl (Knight) W. BA in Math. and Bus. magna cum laude, LaGrange Coll., 1986. Gen. mgr. Unique Advt. Specialties, LaGrange. Meighborhood capt. Am. Cancer Soc.; mem. La Fayette Singers, 1st Bapt. Ch. Choir; mem. Rep. Presdl. Task Force. Ty Cobb scholar. Mem. NAFE, Omicron Delta Kappa, Alpha Omicron Pi (chair philanthropy com.). Home: 811 Wisteria Way LaGrange GA 30240 Office: Unique Advt Specialties 818 N Greenwood St La Grange GA 30240

WHITLEY, NANCY O'NEIL, radiologist; b. Winston-Salem, N.C., Feb. 21, 1932; d. Norris Lawrence and Thelma Mae (Hardy) O'Neil; m. J.E. Whitley, Dec. 20, 1958; children—John O'Neil, Catherine Anne. Student, Duke U., 1950-53; M.D., Bowman Gray Sch. Medicine, 1957. Fellow in cardiology Bowman Gray Sch. Medicine, Winston-Salem, 1958-60; intern Jefferson Davis Hosp., Houston, 1957-58; resident in radiology Bowman Gray Sch. Medicine, 1966-69, instr., 1969-70, asst. prof., 1970-74, assoc. prof., 1974-78; prof. radiology U. Md. Med. Sch., Balt., 1978—; prof. oncology U. Md. Cancer Ctr., Balt., 1988—. Author: (with J.E. Whitley) Angiopgraphy, Techniques and Procedures, 1971. Office: U Md Hosp Dept Radiology 22 S Greene St Baltimore MD 21201

WHITLOCK, DENISE LUCILLE, accountant, financial analyst; b. Marietta, Ga., July 5, 1959; d. J. Winston and Martha Josephine (Phillips) Whitlock. BS in Bus. Adminstrn., Auburn U., 1981. CPA, Ga. Audit profl. Peat Marick Main & Co., Dallas, 1982-85; with exec. office Peat Marick Main & Co., N.Y., 1985-86; audit mgr. Peat Marick Main & Co., Atlanta, 1986-87; fin. analyst Columbian Chem. Co. div. Phelps Dodge Corp., Atlanta, 1987-90; asst. v.p. accounting policy and rsch. C & S/Souvran Corp., Atlanta, 1990—; founder, Balance the Books, Atlanta, 1988-89; co-founder Bus. & Fin. Frameworks, Inc., Atlanta, 1989—. Treas., chmn. fundraising Atlanta Symphony Assn., 1987-89; bd. dirs., treas. Morningside Terrace Condominium Assn., Atlanta, 1987-90. Mem. AICPA (editorial advisor), Ga. Soc. CPA's (continuing profl. edn. com.), Auburn U. Alumni Assn., Atlanta Lawn Tennis Club (team capt.), Delta Gamma.

WHITLOCK, MARY ELLEN JENKINS (MRS. DOUGLAS WHITLOCK), social worker, travel consultant; b. Brownville, Nebr., Sept. 3, 1906; d. John Crisler and Mabel (Sapp) Jenkins; student Sullins Coll., 1923-24, Ferris Inst., 1924; A.B., Ind. U., 1927; m. Douglas Whitlock, June 18, 1929; children—Douglas Whitlock II, Marilyn Whitlock Long, Sandra (Mrs. Theodore G. Driscoll, Jr.). Case worker Children's Aid Soc., Detroit, 1927-28, head adoption dept., 1928-29; case supr. Asso. Charities Washington, 1929-32; co-owner Global Travel, Inc.; travel cons., 1973-87. Mem. Women's Inaugural Com., Washington, 1953, 57. Chmn. women's com. Devereux Found., Devon, Pa., 1959-61. Mem. League Rep. Women, Family Service Assn. of Am., Goodwill Industries Assn., Mental Health Assn., Vis. Nurse Assn.; trustee Family and Child Services, Washington, 1951-65, 1st v.p., 1962-65; v.p. Episcopal Ch. Women of Washington, 1963-69, pres., 1969-72. Recipient award Alpha Omicron Pi, 1963; award Episcopal Diocese Washington, 1972. Mem. Ind. Soc. of Washington (mem. exec. bd. 1932—, award 1962), Ind. U. Alumni Assn., Alpha Omicron Pi. Republican. Episcopalian (vestrywoman 1968-71, 74-79). Clubs: Little Garden (pres. 1938-40), Wednesday (pres. 1940-42) (Sandy Spring, Md.); Internat. Neighbors (1st pres. 1956-58)) (Washington); Women of St. Thomas (pres. 1960-62). Home: The Westchester Apt 504-B 4000 Cathedral Ave NW Washington DC 20016

WHITMAN, HELEN HERRICK, elementary educator; b. Brewer, Maine, Feb. 16, 1925; d. Carleton Sewall and Helen Frances (Petrie) Herrick; m. Dana Trask Jr., Oct. 25, 1946; children: Dana III, Christian, Matthew, Noel. BA, U. Maine, Orono, 1946, MA, 1949. Tchr. Tchr. teaching asst. in psychology U. Maine, Orono, 1946-47; tchr. Old Town (Maine) High Sch., 1948-49; rsch. assoc. U. Mich., Ann Arbor, 1949-52; dir. of pre-sch. YWCA, Newton, N.J., 1962-64; elem. tchr. Fredon (N.J.) Sch. System, 1964-68, Wethersfield (Conn.) Sch. System, 1968—. Mem. NEA, Profl. Devel. Com. Edn. Assn. Wethersfield. Home: 341 Pleasant Valley Rd Rocky Hill CT 06067

WHITMAN, MARINA VON NEUMANN, economist; b. N.Y.C., Mar. 6, 1935; d. John and Mariette (Kovesi) von Neumann; B.A. summa cum laude, Radcliffe Coll., 1956; M.A., Columbia U., 1959, Ph.D., 1962; L.H.D., Russell Sage Coll., 1972, U. Mass., 1975, N.Y. Poly Inst., 1975, Baruch Coll., 1980; LL.D., Cedar Crest Coll., 1973, Hobart and William Smith Coll., 1973, Coe Coll., 1975, Marietta Coll., 1976, Rollins Coll., 1976, Wilson Coll., 1977, Allegheny Coll., 1977, Amherst Coll., 1978, Ripon Coll., 1980, Mt. Holyoke Coll., 1980; Litt.D., WilliamsColl., 1980; m. Robert Freeman Whitman, June 23, 1956; children—Malcolm Russell, Laura Mariette. Mem. faculty U. Pitts., 1962-79, prof. econs., 1971-73, distinguished pub. service prof. econs., 1973-79; v.p., chief economist Gen. Motors Corp., N.Y.C., from 1979, now group exec. v.p. pub. affairs; sr. staff economist Council Econ. Advisers, 1970-71; mem. U.S. Price Commn., 1971-72; mem. Council Econ. Advisers, Exec. Office of Pres., 1972-73; dir. Mfrs. Hanover Trust Co., Procter & Gamble Co.; mem. President's Commn. for Nat. Agenda for Eighties; mem. Trilateral Commn.; mem. adv. com. on reform internat. monetary system Dept. Treasury, from 1977; mem. Consultative Group on Internat. Econs. and Monetary Affairs (Group of 30), from 1979; econ. adv. com. U.S. Dept. Commerce, from 1979. Bd. overseers Harvard Coll., 1972-78; trustee Princeton U., from 1979. Recipient Columbia medal for excellence, 1973; George Washington award Am. Hungarian Found., 1975; fellow Earhart Found., 1959-60, AAUW, 1960-61, NSF, 1968-70, also Social Sci. Research Council. Mem. Am. Econ. Assn. (exec. com. 1977-80), Commn. on Critical Choices for Ams., Atlantic Council (dir.), Council Fgn. Relations (dir. 1977—), Am. Fin. Assn. (dir. from 1979), Phi Beta Kappa. Author: Government Risk-Sharing in Foreign Investment, 1965; International and Interregional Payments Adjustment, 1967; Economic Goals and Policy Instruments, 1970; Reflections of Interdependence: Issues for Economic Theory and U.S. Policy; also articles; bd. editors Am. Econ. Rev., 1974-77; mem. editorial bd. Fgn. Policy. Office: GM 3044 W Grand Blvd Detroit MI 48202*

WHITMAN, SIGRID TAILLÕN, public relations executive, writer; b. Quirigua, Guatemala, Feb. 12, 1932; came to U.S., 1943; d. William Lloyd and Hilda Gudrun (Halldorson) Taillõn; m. Edmund Spurr Whitman, Dec. 23, 1961 (dec. Nov. 1987); children: William Spurr, Wright Prescott. BA, Smith Coll., 1953; postgrad., Columbia U., 1954, 55, U. de San Carlos, Guatemala City, 1955. Reporter Time Inc. and Life Internat., N.Y.C., 1956-66; dir. Viviane Woodard Corp., Phoenix, 1972-75, Lady Finelle Corp., Phoenix, 1975-76; community info. dir. Phoenix Elem Sch. Dist., 1976-83; community rels. dir. Oklahoma City Pub. Schs., 1983-84; publ rels. cons Phoenix, 1984-85; pub. rels. dir. Sunnyside Unified Sch. Dist., Tucson, 1985—; cons., Phoenix, 1977—. Contbr. articles to popular mags., 1956—. Vol. Bellevue Hosp., N.Y.C., 1956-66; edn. campaign chairperson United Way and Am. Heart Assn., Oklahoma City, 1983-84; bd. dirs. N.Y.C. Ballet and Ballet Theatre Guild, 1956-66, Toby House Guild, Phoenix, 1970-76, Phoenix Children's Theatre, 1984-85. Recipient award for reorganizing Guatemala Ballet Sch. and Co. Pres. of Guatemala, 1956, award for reporting on Mexican Revolution Pres. of Mex., 1960, award for reporting on Guatemalan Archaeology Pres. of Guatemala, 1960. Mem. Nat. Sch. Pub. Rels Assn. (v.p. S.W. region 1989—, excellence awards 1978, 1980), Caribbean Conservation Corp., Ariz. Sch. Pub. Rels. Assn. (exec. bd. dirs. 1977-83, 86—, Outstanding Program in Pub. Rels. 1988, 89), Hispanic Adminstrs. Assn., Sunnyside Adminstrs. Assn., Smith Coll. Club (v.p. and sec. Phoenix club 1966, 70). Episcopalian.

WHITMER, RUTH C., education educator; b. Safford, Ariz., June 29, 1919; d. David Wimmer and Lydia Pearl (Montierth) Cheney; m. James Benjamin Whitmer, Jan. 1, 1942; children: James Benjamin Jr., Cordell Webb. BA, Ariz. State U., 1957, MA, 1965. Tchr. Safford Ind. U., 1957-59. Missionary LDS Ch., 1940-41; corr. Ariz. Retired J. Assn., Safford, Ariz., 1981—. Recipient Music award 1937, 1987. Mem. Ariz. State and Nat. Music Tchrs. Assn., Women State and Nat. Club, Ariz. Ret. Tchr.'s Assn., Graham County Hist. Soc. Democrat.

WHITMIRE, KATHRYN JEAN, mayor; b. Houston, Aug. 15, 1946; m. James Whitmire (dec.). B.B.A. with honors, U. Houston, 1968, M.S. in Acctg., 1970. C.P.A., Tex. Audit mgr. Coopers & Lybrand, Houston, 1971-76; controller City of Houston, 1977-81, mayor, 1982—; mem. faculty bus. mgmt. U. Houston, 1976-77, mem. adv. com. Coll. Bus. Adminstrn., 1978-80; chmn. standing com. on arts U.S. Conf. Mayors, 1984—, pres., 1989; past chmn. steering com. on fin., adminstrn. and intergovtl. rels. Nat. League Cities. Mem. adminstrv. bd. St. Paul's United Meth. Ch., Houston, 1972-75; bd. dirs., treas. Juvenile Diabetes Found., Houston, 1977; adv. bd. Houston YWCA, 1979-81, Houston Area Women's Ctr., 1978-79. Recipient Disting. Alumna award U. Houston, 1982, Pub. Svc. award Am. Soc. Women CPA's, 1982, Internat. Bus. award Houston World Trade Assn., 1985, Michael A. DiNunzio award U.S. Conf. Mayors, 1985, Mayor's award, 1988; recipient Inst. Human Rels. award Am Jewish Com., 1986, Humanitarian award Internat. New Thought Alliance, 1986, Disting. Sales award Sales and Marketing Exec. Soc. Houston, 1987, We're Changing Women's Lives award Houston Area Women's Ctr., 1987; named Woman of Yr. Tex. Women's Polit. Caucus, 1982, Disting. Profl. Woman Com. on Status of Women U. Tex. Health Sci. Ctr., 1986; named to All-Pro Mgmt. Team City and State Mag. 1988. Mem. Am. Soc. Women Accts. (bd. dirs. 1972-73), Tex. Soc. C.P.A.s (chpt. bd. dirs. 1973-75), Tex. Mcpl. League (pres.), Greater Houston Ptnrship. (bd. dirs.). Office: 901 Bagby 3d fl Houston TX 77002*

WHITMORE, BEATRICE EILEEN, labor association administrator; b. Harrisonburg, Va., Mar. 15, 1935; d. Everett Dulaney and Beatrice M. (Shorts) Ott; m. William Eugene Taylor, Sept. 30, 1955 (div. Mar. 1965); children: John David, Mark Wayne; m. Dale Wilford Whitmore, May 3, 1967; 1 child, Theresa Ann. High sch. grad., Harrisonburg. Clk. typist USAF Civil Service, Eglin AFB, Fla., 1956-58, Clark AFB, Phillipines, 1958-60; sec. USAF Civil Service, Wright-Patterson AFB, Ohio, 1960-75, fire insp., 1975-85, sec.-treas. local F-88, 1977-83, pres. local F-88, 1983-85, pres. emeritus, 1985—; fed. staff rep. Internat. Assn. Fire Fighters, Washington, 1985-89; assn. sec. Nat. Coffee Svc. Assn., Fairfax, Va., 1989-90; sec. Nat. Assn. Rehab. Facilities, 1990—; cons. Q&D Cons. Svc., Inc., 1989—. Leader, organizer Little Sparkies, Wright-Patterson AFB, 1976-79; den mother Boy Scouts Am., New Carlisle, Ohio, 1963-65; mem. Staff Reps. Union. Served with USAF, 1953-55. Mem. NAFE, Staff Reps. Union, Internat. Platform Assn., Job's Daus. Lodge: Job's Daughters. Home: 2311 Glade Bank Way Reston VA 22091 also: Q&D Cons Svc Inc 2311 Glade Bank Way Reston VA 22091

WHITMORE, MENANDRA M., librarian; b. Ancash, Peru; d. Rafael and Jacinta (Moreno) Mosquera; m. Jacob L. Whitmore III, Jan. 7, 1965; children: Jacqueline Grace, Michelle Jacinta. Degree in social work, U. Catolica del Peru, 1967; MLS, U. P.R., 1974, Catholic U. Am., 1984. Social worker Cornell U., Vicos, Peru, 1960-62, Servicio de Extension Agricola del Peru, 1962-63, Am. Friends Svc. Com., Mex. and Peru, 1963-65; libr. Colegio Maria Auxiliadora, P.R., 1971, Country Day Sch., San Jose, Costa Rica, 1975-76, Colegio San Ignacio, P.R., 1976-77; dir. libs. Am. Coll. P.R., 1977-80; libr. Lib. Gov. Printing Office, 1981-84; chief acquisitions sect., mgr. Hispanic employment program Pentagon Lib., Washington, 1984—. Author: (all books pub. under name Menandra Mosquera) Bibliografia Sobre los Manglares de Puerto Rico, 1973, Bibliography on Hypsipyla, 1976, Bibliography of Forestry of Puerto Rico, 1984, Useful Trees of Tropical North America, 1988. Recipient commendation Dept. Def., 1987, 88, 89. Mem. ALA, Soc. for Acquisition Latin Am. Libr. Materials, Reforma (treas. Washington chpt. 1988, current pres.). Home: 3904 Ridge Rd Annandale VA 22003

WHITNER, LILLIAN MADDOX (LILLIE WITNER), interior designer, consultant; b. Birmingham, Ala.; d. Milton udoxious and Harriette (Newell Coleman) Maddox; m. James Harrison Whitner II, Feb. 27, 1923 (div. 1942); children—Harriette, James Harrison III, Lillian II. Sweet Briar Coll., Owner, operator Mary Lewis Dress Shop, Charlotte, N.C., 1939-42; researcher Fortune mag., Charlotte, 1942-45, Nat. Research Ctr., Denver, 1942-45; artist's rep., Charlotte, 1946-48; prin. Lillian Whitner's Interiors, Charlotte, 1948—. Exhibited at Mint Mus. Art, Charlotte, 1955; decorator Queen's Sorority House, Charlotte, 1958; Davidson Coll. frat. (N.C.), 1958; asst. decorator Gov's home, Charlotte, 1958. Pres. Alumnae Orgn. Sweet Briar Coll., Charlotte, 1932; asst. Handicraft Div. Regional Art, Mint Mus. Art, 1938-39; radio worker Community Chest, Charlotte, 1939-40. Mem. Am. Soc. Interior Designers (cert.), Mint Mus. Art. Presbyterian. Clubs: Charlotte Country, Jr. League Charlotte (soc. editor 1929-30, corr. sec. 1931-32, chmn. ways and means com. 1933-34, editor-in-chief 1935-36, chmn. local advt. 1940-41), Jr. League U.S.

WHITNEY, CONSTANCE CLEIN, psychologist, educator, consultant; b. Seattle; BA, Stanford U.; MA; PhD, Washington U., St. Louis; children: Mark Wittcoff, Caroline Wittcoff. instr. U. Mo., St. Louis, 1976-78; rsch. assoc., Wash. U. Med. Sch., 1977-78; dir. Motivation Rsch. Inst. U. Wash., 1979-83; post doctoral fellow Grad. Sch. Bus. and Pub. Adminstrn. Wash. U., 1983-86; dir., exec. edn. Town Hall Calif., 1989—. Bd. dirs. UCLA Arts Coun., Club 100 Music Ctr., Stanford Alumni So. Calif., Nat. Commn. for UN Conv. to eliminate discrimination; mem. Pres.' Circle L.A. County Mus. Art; mem. Edn. Commn. L.A. C. of C. Mem. Robinson Garden, Friends of French Art, Bus. Profl. Women, Am. Psychol. Assn., Calif. Psychol. Assn., AAUP, ASTD, Acad. Mgmt., Orgn. Behavior and Teaching Soc. Author, producer, dir.: (film) Women and Money: Myths and Realities. Home: 10601 Wilshire Blvd Los Angeles CA 90024

WHITNEY, PHYLLIS AYAME, author; b. Yokohama, Japan, Sept. 9, 1903; d. Charles J. and Lillian (Mandeville) W.; m. George A. Garner, July 2, 1925; m. Lovell F. Jahnke, 1950 (dec. 1973). Grad., McKinley High Sch., Chgo., 1924. Instr. dancing San Antonio, 1 yr; tchr. juvenile fiction writing Northwestern U., 1945; children's book editor Chgo. Sun, 1942-46, Phila. Inquirer, 1947, 48; instr. juvenile fiction writing N.Y.U., 1947-58; leader juvenile fiction workshop Writers Conf., U. Colo., 1952, 54, 56. Author: A Place for Ann, 1941, A Star for Ginny, 1942; (vocat. fiction for teenage girls) A Window for Julie, 1943; Red Is for Murder (mystery novel for adults), 1943, The Silver Inkwell, 1945, Willow Hill, 1947, Writing Juvenile Fiction, 1947, Ever After, 1948, Mystery of the Gulls, 1949, Linda's Homecoming, 1950, The Island of Dark Woods, 1951, Love Me, Love Me Not, 1952, Step to the Music, 1953, A Long Time Coming, 1954, Mystery of the Black Diamonds, 1954, The Quicksilver Pool, 1955, Mystery on the Isle of Skye, 1955, The Fire and The Gold (Jr. Lit. Guild), 1956, The Highest Dream (Jr. Lit. Guild), The Trembling Hills (Peoples Book Club), 1956, Skye Cameron, 1957, Mystery of the Green Cat, (Jr. Lit. Guild), 1957, Secret of the Samurai Sword (Jr. Lit. Guild), 1958, The Moonflower, 1958, Creole Holiday, 1959, Thunder Heights, 1960, Blue Fire, 1961, Mystery of the Haunted Pool, 1961 (Edgar award Mystery Writers Am.), Secret of the Tiger's Eye, 1961, Window on the Square, 1962, Mystery of the Golden Horn, 1962, Seven Tears for Apollo, 1963, Mystery of the Hidden Hand, 1963 (Edgar award Mystery Writers Am. 1964), Black Amber, 1964, Secret of the Emerald Star, 1964, Sea Jade, 1965, Mystery of the Angry Idol, 1965, Columbella, 1966, Secret of the Spotted Shell, 1967, Mystery of the Strange Traveler, 1967, Silverhill, 1967, Hunter's Green, 1968, Secret of Goblin Glen, 1968, Mystery of the Crimson Ghost, 1969, Winter People, 1969, Secret of the Missing Footprint, 1970, Lost Island, 1970, The Vanishing Scarecrow, 1971, Listen for the Whisperer, 1971, Nobody Likes Trina, 1972, Snowfire, 1973, Mystery of the Scowling Boy, 1973, The Turquoise Mask, 1974, Spindrift, 1975, Secret of Haunted Mesa, 1975, The Golden Unicorn, 1976, Secret of the Stone Face, 1977, The Stone Bull, 1977, The Glass Flame, 1978, Domino, 1979, Poinciana, 1980, Vermilion, 1981, Guide to Fiction Writing, 1982, Emerald, 1983, Rainsong, 1984, Dream of Orchids, 1985, Flaming Tree, 1986, Silversword, 1987, Feather on the Moon, 1988, Rainbow in the Mist, 1989, The Singing Stones, 1990; sold first story to Chgo. Daily News; later wrote for pulp mags., became specialist in juvenile writing, now writing entirely in adult field. Pres. Authors Round Table, 1943, 44; pres. exec. bd. Fifth Annual Writers Conf., Northwestern U., 1944; spent first 15 years of life in Japan, China and P.I. (father in shipping and hotel bus.). Recipient Friends of Lit. award contbrs. children's lit., 1943; Reynal and Hitchcock prize ($3000) in Youth Today contest for book Willow Hill; Recipient Today's Woman award Coun. Cerebral Palsy Auxs., 1983, Agatha award Malice Domestic, 1990, Rita award Romance Writers Am., 1990. Mem. Mystery Writers Am. (pres. 1975, Grandmaster award for lifetime achievement 1988).

WHITNEY, PHYLLIS BURRILL, dietician; b. Bangor, Maine, Nov. 12, 1928; d. Clifford Loring and Marion (Davis) Burrill; m. Lester Frank Whitney, July 29, 1950; children: Marcia L., Mark L., Scott B., Dean W., David C., John L., Steven T. BS, U. Mass., 1972, MS in Nutrition, 1975. registered dietician. Cons. dietician Chapel Hill Nursing Home, Holyoke,

Mass., 1976—; cons. dietician Cozy Corner Nursing Home, Sunderland, Mass., Hillside Nursing Home, South Deerfield, Mass. Mem. Am. Dietetic Assn., Western Mass. Dietetic Assn., Mayflower Soc. (life), Phi Kappa Phi. Republican. Congregationalist. Home: 48 Jeffrey Ln Amherst MA 01002

WHITNEY, RUTH REINKE, magazine editor; b. Oshkosh, Wis., July 23, 1928; d. Leonard G. and Helen (Diestler) Reinke; BA, Northwestern U., 1949; m. Daniel A. Whitney, Nov. 19, 1949; 1 son, Philip. Copywriter edn. dept. circulation div. Time, Inc., 1949-53; editor-in-chief Better Living mag., 1953-56; assoc. editor Seventeen magazine, 1956-62, exec. editor, 1962-67; editor-in-chief Glamour mag., N.Y.C., 1967—. Mem. Fashion Group, Am. Soc. Mag. Editors (pres. 1975-77, exec. com. 1989—), Women in Communication, Matrix award 1980), Women in Media, U.S. Info. Agy. (mag. and print com. 1989—), Alpha Chi Omega. Home: Riverview Rd Irvington-on-Hudson NY 10533 Office: Glamour Condé Nast Bldg 350 Madison Ave New York NY 10017

WHITSON, BARBARA LEE, psychologist, consultant; b. Marietta, Ohio, Aug. 15, 1943; d. Richard Howard and Jean Elizabeth (Fox) Sullivan; m. Lish Whitson, Sept. 16, 1965; children: Lish Richard, Kimberly Shawn. BA, Swarthmore (Pa.) Coll., 1965; MEd, U. Wash., Seattle, 1971, PhD, 1981. Part time teaching asst. U. Wash., Seattle, 1971-74; sch. psychologist Seattle Pub. Sch., Mercer Island, Wash., 1973-75; instr. Seattle Pacific U., 1974, 81, 82, Seattle U., 1975, 77, U. Wash., Seattle, 1976; program specialist gifted and talented U.S. Office Edn., Seattle, 1976-77; program specialist gifted Edmonds Sch. Dist., Lynnwood, Wash., 1977-79; sch. psychologist, program specialist Shoreline Sch. Dist., Seattle, 1984—. Mem. title IV adv. coun. Wash. Spt. Pub. Instrn., Olympia, 1979-82. U.S. Office of Edn. fellow, 1976-77. Mem. Wash. Assn. Sch. Psychologists, Nat. Assn. Sch. Psychologists, N.W. Gifted Child Assn., Wash. Assn. Educators of Talented and Gifted, New Horizons for Learning, Assn. for Supervision and Curriculum Devel., Wash. Athletic Club, Womens Univ. Club. Office: Shoreline Pub Schs 18560 1st NE Seattle WA 98155

WHITSON, BETTY JO, broker; b. Miami Beach, Fla., Nov. 7, 1945; d. Jack Adrian and Josephine Elizabeth (Armstrong) Phillips; m. Warren Brian Whitson, Aug. 31, 1968; children: Elizabeth Kelly, Brian Carlton. BS in Nursing, U. S.C., 1968, postgrad.; postgrad., Med. Coll. Ga.; M in Nursing, U. Fla., 1969; cert. sex educator, Am. Assn. Sex Educators, Counselors & Therapists. Chair nursing div. U. S.C., Aiken, 1980-86, prof. in nursing, 1982-87; pres. Kay-Bee Properties, Aiken, 1985-90; pres., chief exec. officer Lilly Devel. Corp., Aiken, 1986-89; exec. broker Am. Gold Eagle, Inc., 1990—; owner Golden Opportunities; researcher in field. Co-author: Contemporary Pediatric Nursing, The Pediatric Nursing Skills Manual, I Don't Know What to Feed Alligators; contbr. articles to profl. publs. Active community svc. orgns.; del. leader 2d U.S. Nursing Del. People's Republic China. Named Disting. Tchr. of Yr. USCA, 1985. Mem. NAFE, Am. Nurses Assn., S.C. Nurses Assn., S.C. Deans and Dirs. Nursing Edn. (chair), Greater Aiken C. of C. Republican. Home: 1632 Huckleberry Dr Aiken SC 29801

WHITSON, LAURA ANN, superintendent of schools; b. Wellington, Tex., Jan. 30, 1952; d. Al Stanley and Olas Lois (Williams) W. BS in Edn., Abilene Christian U., 1973, MEd, 1975; postgrad., U. Tex., 1985-87. Cert. supt., mid-mgmt. supr., supr., counselor, elem. tchr., spl. edn. tchr., Tex. Tchr. Eula Ind. Sch. Dist., Clyde, Tex., 1973-81, elem. prin., 1981-82; tech. asst. Edn. Svc. Ctr. XIV, Abilene, Tex., 1982-85, Liberty Hill (Tex.) Ind. Sch. Dist., 1985-87; supt. Meyersville (Tex.) Ind. Sch. Dist., 1987—. Mem. Assn. Suprs. and Curriculum Dirs., Tex. Assn. Sch. Adminstrs. (pres. region III, 1989—), Delta Kappa Gamma, Phi Delta Kappa. Home: 604 W Thomas St Cuero TX 77954 Office: Meyersville Ind Sch Dist 1000 School Rd Meyersville TX 77974

WHITSON, SUSAN JEAN, library director; b. Hot Springs, S.D., June 20, 1951; d. Charles Krieg and Jean Marilyn (Barta) Failing; m. Stephen Stone Whitson, Jan. 11, 1987; 1 child, Shane Stephen. BA in English with distinction, Mont. State U., 1973; MA in Libr./Info. Sci., U. Wis., 1984. Libr. asst. Mont. State U. Libr., Bozeman, 1976-79, 82-83; rsch. asst. dept. of plant/soil sci. Mont. State U., Bozeman, 1980-82; owner, info. specialist, copy editor The Word Merchant, Bozeman, 1980-83; grad. student asst. U. Wis. Librs., Madison, 1984; reference libr. USAF Acad. Librs., Colorado Springs, Colo., 1985-88; base libr. USAF, Hurlburt Field, Fla., 1988—. H.W. Wilson fellow, 1983. Mem. AAUW, Spl. Librs. Assn., Phi Kappa Phi, Phi Beta Mu. Home: 109-B Birch Circle Eglin AFB FL 32542 Office: FL 4417 Base Libr Hurlburt Field FL 32544

WHITT, BARBARA SANDRA, finance administrator; b. San Diego, Aug. 9, 1943; d. William Charles and Laura Cecelia (Janczak) Tarditi; m. William Wesley Whitt, Dec. 1, 1962; children: Kristina Ann, Robert Earl, Kimberly Sue. Grad. high sch., Escondido, Calif. Office mgr. Washington-Idaho Concrete, Post Falls, Idaho, 1981-84, Step Into Your Future, Spokane, Wash., 1984-85; receptionist, sec. Anderson & Lutz, CPAs, Spokane, 1985-86; dir. adminstrn., personnel and fin. Econ. Devel. Alliance for Wash., Seattle, 1986—. Office: Econ Devel Alliance for Wash 917 Pacific Ave Ste 407 Tacoma WA 98402

WHITT, MARY F., reading specialist, educator; b. Montgomery, Ala.. BS, Ala. State U., 1958; MEd, U. Ariz., 1971; EdD, U. Ala., 1980; postgrad., various colls. ongoing. Camp counselor N.Y.C. Mission Soc., Port Jervis, summer 1956; recreation counselor Dayton (Ohio) Parks and Recreation Dept., summer 1963; adminstrv. asst. Wiley Coll./NDEA Inst., Marshall, Tex., summer 1965; tchr. Montgomery (Ala.) County Schs., 1958-62; coordinator sci. and math. Dayton (Ohio) pub. schs., 1962-67; reading and spl. edn. tchr. Vacaville (Calif.) Unified Sch. Dist., 1967-70; coordinator reading Dallas pub. schs., 1971-72; prof. reading Ala. State U., Montgomery, 1972—. Contbr. articles to profl. jurs. U.S. Office Edn. fellow, 1970, 76, 77, NSF fellow, 1961, 64, 66. Mem. Internat. Reading Assn., Capstone Coll. of Edn. Soc., AAUW, Phi Delta Kappa, Kappa Delta Pi. Home: 717 Genetta Ct Montgomery AL 36104

WHITTAKER, PATRICIA DIMAGGIO, media manager; b. Rochester, Pa., Feb. 28, 1952; d. Harry S. Eichler and Grace Louise (Jones) Kay; m. Robert Michael, Dec. 7, 1970 (div. Nov. 1980); m. William R. Whittaker, Oct. 29, 1988. Student, Duquesne U., 1965-68, Clarion U., 1970-71, Bluefield State U., 1984. Comml. teller 1st Nat. Bank Bluefield, W.Va., 1973-75; talk show host Sta. WHIS-TV, Bluefield, 1975-77; account mgr. Sta. WHIS-AM-FM, Bluefield, 1977-80; sales mgr. Sta. WHIS, Bluefield, 1980-83; nat. sales mgr. Adventure Communications, Inc., Bluefield, 1983-85; station mgr. Adventure Communications, Inc. Sta. WHIS/WHAJ, Bluefield, 1985-88; gen. mgr. Adventure Communication, Inc., Bluefield, 1988—; asst. instr. Dale Carnegie Courses, Bluefield, 1985-87; Nat. Telethon Host March of Dimes Found., Charleston, 1985-86. Mem. budget rev. bd. Greater Bluefield United Way, 1986-89; lay minister Luth. Mountain Ministries, Wytheville, Va., 1987—; mem. reading com., actress Summit Theatre, 1974—; vol. advisor W.Va. March of Dimes, Charleston, 1982-85. Mem. Communicators Roundtable of the Virginias (bd. dirs. 1986—), Bluefield Sales Execs. Club (bd. dirs. 1986-87, v.p. 1987-88, pres. 1988-89), W. Va. Broadcaster's Assn. (bd. dirs. 1987-89), Greater Bluefield C. of C., Nat. Assn. Broadcasters (mem. regulatory rev. bd. 1988—, mem. radio allocations com. 1990). Club: Quota (bd. dirs. 1984-86). Home: Rte 3 Box 300D Princeton WV 24740

WHITTAKER, SHEELAGH DILLON, broadcast executive; b. Ottawa, Ont., Can., Apr. 9, 1947; d. John Dean and E.M. Theresa (Tessie) (Sadlier-Brown) W.; m. Michael James Van Dusen; children: Meghan, Matthew, Daniel John. BSc, U. Alta., Can., 1967; BA, U. Toronto, 1970; MBA, York U., 1975. Sessional lectr. U. Alta., Edmonton, Can., 1967-68; asst. to the provost U. Guelph, Can., 1971-73; economist Ministryof Natural Resources Govt. of Quebec, Can., 1974-75; commerce officer dept. consumer and corporate affairs Govt. of Quebec, Ottawa, 1975-79; dir., mgmt. cons. The Can. Cons. Group, Inc., Toronto, 1979-85; v.p. planning and corp. affairs Can. Broadcasting Corp., Ottawa, Ont., Can., 1985-88; pres., chief exec. officer Can. Satellite Communications, Inc., Mississauga, Ont., Can., 1988—; dir. The Can. Cons. Group, Inc., Toronto, 1983, Sterling Trust, Toronto, 1987, Can. Advt. Found., Toronto, 1987. Gulf Oil scholar, 1967, Nat. Research Council scholar, 1968; Govt. of Ontario Exchange fellow, 1974. Office: Can Satellite Communications, 50 Burnhamthorpe Rd W 10 Fl, Mississauga, ON Canada L5B 3C2*

WHITTEMORE, DOROTHY JANE, librarian; b. San Jose, Calif., Nov. 9, 1920; d. Glen James and Jane Dorothy (Katz) Gordon; m. Robert Clifton Whittemore, June 15, 1959; children by previous marriage: Stanley Allen Lawton, Shirley Anne (Mrs. Anthony Kopcych). AB, San Jose State Coll., 1941, cert. librarianship, 1942, postgrad., 1952-53. Sch. library supr. Piedmont (Calif.) Sch. Dist., 1942-43; asst. post librarian Presidio of San Francisco, 1943-49; jr. librarian San Jose (Calif.) State Coll., 1951-53; reference librarian Tulane U. Library, New Orleans, 1953-76, acting dir., 1976-78, asst. dir. public service, 1978-80, dir. Norman Mayer Bus. Library, 1980-86, dir. Turchin Library, A.B. Freeman Sch. of Bus., 1986—; cons. Valley Software, 1985—. New Orleans chpt. LWV, 1964-66, dir. La. chpt., 1967-69, 73—; mem. citizens adv. com. City Planning Commn. of New Orleans, 1965-67; sec. New Orleans chpt. La. Consumers League, 1972-74; active Public Affairs Research Council; mem. adv. council La. State Bd. Nursing, 1977—. Council on Library Resources research grantee, 1972. Mem. Spl. Libraries Assn. (pres. La. chpt. 1975-77, sec.-treas. social welfare sect. 1977-79), La. Library Assn. (chmn. coll. and reference sect. 1968-69, exec. bd. 1973-74), New Orleans Library Club (past pres.), Am. Soc. Info. Sci., Nat. Microfilm Assn. Author: (with others) Citizen's Guide to Louisiana Government, 1969. Home: 7521 Dominican St New Orleans LA 70118 Office: Tulane U AB Freeman Sch Bus Turchin Library New Orleans LA 70118

WHITTEMORE, MARJORIE MAAS, economic developer, social worker; b. Detroit, Sept. 2, 1947; d. Albert Whitmore and Jeanne (Visel) Maas; m. Allan Pendleton Whittemore, Mar. 15, 1986. BA, Mich. State U., 1969; MSW, U. Ill., 1973. Tchr. Cleve. Pub. Schs., 1969-71; urban lending officer Hyde Pk. Bank & Trust, Chgo., 1973-75; project devel. officer BILD Corp., Lansing, Mich., 1975-77; asst. to exec. dir. Downriver Community Conf., Southgate, Mich., 1977-85, dep. dir., 1985-87; investment officer MBW Mgmt., Ann Arbor, Mich., 1985; dep. dir. Bus. Devel. Div. Wayne County, Detroit, 1987—; exec. dir. Bus. Devel. Team of Wayne County, Detroit, 1988—, Met. Growth & Devel. Corp., Detroit, 1988—. 1st v.p. Out Wayne County Human Svcs., Livonia, Mich., 1984; bd. dirs. Out Wayne County Youth Svcs., Inkster, Mich., 1979-84, Hyde Pk. Kenwood Community Conf., Chgo., 1975, N.W. Guidance Clinic, Garden City, Mich., 1988—. U. Ill. fellow, 1972. Mem. Mich. Indsl. Developers Assn., Women's Econ. Club. Presbyterian. Office: Dept Jobs & Econ Devel 600 Randolph Detroit MI 48226

WHITTIER, SARAJANE, social studies educator; b. North Manchester, Ind., Dec. 17, 1912; d. Charles and Ethel Clo (Free) Leckrone; m. C. Taylor Whittier, June 18, 1934; children: Chip, Tim, Cece, Penny. BA, U. Chgo., 1934, MA, 1946. Rsch. sec. Oriental Inst., Chgo., 1935-39; tchr. pub. schs., Flossmoor, Ill., 1939-41, Sta. WSUN-TV, St. Petersburg, Fla., 1955-56, Sta. GWETA-TV, Washington, 1961-62; substitute tchr. pub. schs., Fla. and Md., 1962-89; tchr. music Gretna United Meth. Pre-sch., 1989—. Co-author: Pasture Trails, 1941; asst. monthly newsletter Supt.'s Digest, 1983-85. Pres., PTA, St. Petersburg, 1960's; Kans. chmn. Friends of J.F.K. Ctr., Topeka, 1969-75, Tex. chmn., San Antonio, 1975-82; teaching music in pre-scholl, 1989—; guardian Camp Fire Girls, Chgo., 1936-41, bd. dirs. Camp Fire Kans., Tex., La. Gaithersburg, Md., 1958-64; Sunday sch. tchr. Christian Ch., Chgo., 1926-34, chmn. Westbank Forum Ch. Women United. St. Petersburg, 1950-57, pianist, San Antonio, 1975-82. U. Chgo. scholar, 1933-34. Mem. AAUW (past pres., life mem., pres. Algiers/Westbank). Republican. Club: Capital Speakers (Washington). Avocations: acting, music, directing little theatres, photography, world traveling. Home: 756 Fairlawn Dr Gretna LA 70056

WHITWORTH, KATHRYNNE ANN, professional golfer; b. Monahans, Tex., Sept. 27, 1939; d. Morris Clark and Dama Ann (Robinson) W. Student, Odessa (Tex.) Jr. Coll., 1958. Joined tour, 1959 and; Ladies Profl. Golf Assn.; mem. adv. staff Walter Hagen Golf Co., Wilson Sporting Goods Co.; winner 88 ofcl. tournaments; 8 times leading money winner; 7 times lowest scoring average; 7 times Player of Yr.; 2 times AP Woman Athlete of Year. Named to Hall of Fame Ladies Profl. Golf Assn., Tex. Sports Hall of Fame, Tex. Golf Hall of Fame, World Golf Hall of Fame. Mem. Ladies Profl. Golf Assn. (sec. 1962-63, v.p. 1965, 73, pres. 1967, 68, 71, 1st mem. to win over $1,000,000.00). Office: care Ladies Profl Golf Assn 4675 Sweetwater Blvd Sugar Land TX 77478

WIACZEK, PAMELA PAXTON, sales representative; b. Greenville, S.C., Oct. 27, 1961; d. John Henry and Margaret Elizabeth (Andrews) Paxton. BS in Ceramic Engring., Clemson U., 1983. Intern GE, Greenville, 1980-82; resident asst. Clemson U., 1982-83; assoc. process engr. Owens-Corning Fiberglas Corp., Aiken, S.C., 1983-84; intermediate process engr. Owens-Corning Fiberglas Corp., Aiken, 1984-86; sales rep. Owens-Corning Fiberglas Corp., L.A., 1986-87; advanced sales rep. Owens-Corning Fiberglas Corp., Santa Ana, Calif., 1987—. Mem. Soc. Advancement Mat. Process Engring., Composites Group Soc. Mech. Engrs., Soc. Plastics Industry. Republican. Home: 6600 Warner Ave #168 Huntington Beach CA 92647 Office: Owens-Corning Fiberglas Corp Four Hutton Centre Dr Ste 100 Santa Ana CA 92707

WICHER, DONNA CHRISTINE, assistant to president, educator; b. Portland, Oreg., Feb. 17, 1951; d. Donald Willard and Mary Frances (Jarocki) W. AB cum laude, Cornell U., 1974; MA, U. Ky., 1979; PhD, 1983. Lic. psychologist, Oreg. Family therapist Edgefield Lodge, Troutdale, Oreg., 1980-81; med. psychologist N.W. Pain Ctr., Portland, 1981-88; pvt. practice clin. psychologist Portland, 1985—; clin. cons. Commn. on Accreditation Rehab. Facilities, Tucson, 1986-90, N.W. Pain Ctr. Assocs., Portland, 1988-89. Cornell U. scholar, 1969, 71, 72, 73; NIMH grantee, 1975-76, U. Ky. grantee, 1977. Mem. Am. Psychol. Assn., Oreg. Psychol. Assn., Nat. Register Health Svc. Providers in Psychology, Portland Acad. Hypnosis. Office: 1618 SW First Ave Ste 318 Portland OR 97201

WICK, SISTER MARGARET, college president; b. Sibley, Iowa, June 30, 1942. BA in Sociology, Briar Cliff Coll., 1965; MA in Sociology, Loyola U., Chgo., 1971; PhD in Higher Edn., U. Denver, 1976. Instr. sociology Briar Cliff Coll., Sioux City, Iowa, 1966-71, dir. academic advising, 1971-72, v.p., acad. dean, 1972-74, 76-84, pres., 1987—; pres. Colls. of Mid-Am., 1985-87; bd. dirs. 1st Interstate Bank Sioux City. Bd. dirs. Mary J. Treglia Community House, 1976-84, Marian Health Ctr., 1987—, Iowa Pub. TV, 1987. Mem. North Cen. Edn. Assn. (cons.-evaluator for accrediting teams 1980-84, 89—), Sioux City C. of C. (bd. dirs.), Quota Internat., Rotary. Home: 4216 Perry Way Sioux City IA 51104 Office: Briar Cliff Coll 3303 Rebecca Sioux City IA 51104

WICKER, ELIZABETH ANN, community relations director; b. Paducah, Ky., Oct. 26, 1946; d. Harold Leslie and Sunshine Elizabeth (Jones) Phelps; m. Morris Dale Wicker, May 30, 1970 (div. Feb. 1978); 1 child, Leslie Dale. BS in Elem. Edn., Murray (Ky.) State U., 1968, MA in Sch. Social Work, 1972. U.S. II missionary Meth. Ch., Baldwin, La., 1968-69; tchr. Paducah (Ky.) Pub. Schs., 1969-72, Ballard Bd. of Edn., La Center, Ky., 1973-75; juvenile officer McCracken County Juvenile Dept., Paducah, 1975-80; instr. Ky. Alcoholism Coun., Lexington, 1982-83; dir. aftercare program Goodman Hill Hosp., Paudcah, 1983-86; dir. community rels. Koala Ctr., Bushnell, Fla., 1986—; instr. Attitude and Self Esteem, Paducah, 1980-82, Koala, Bushnell, 1986—, Alcohol and Drug Co-Dependency, Bushnell, 1986—. Mem. Lyman High Sch. P.T.A., 1986—; vol. work with AIDS patients Centaur, Orlando, Fla., 1987—. Mem. Mental Health Assn., FAADA, Chem. Dependency Network. Democrat. Roman Catholic. Office: Lifeworks Ctrs 1016 S North Lake Blvd Altamonte Springs FL 32714

WICKER, KRISTIN LEE, educator, musician; b. Ft. Dodge, Iowa, Nov. 7, 1953; d. Winford Lee and Helen Caroline (Brown) Egli; m. Kirk Michael Wicker, Jan. 1, 1982 (dec. June 1982). AA, Iowa Cen. Coll., 1974; B in Music Edn., Morningside Coll., 1976; M in Mus., U. S.D., 1983. Cert. tchr., Iowa. Tchr. instrumental music Garrigan Affiliated Schs., Algona, Iowa, 1976-77, Sioux City (Iowa) Community Schs., 1977—. asst. prin. bassist Sioux City Symphony, 1974—; freelance bassist, Sioux City, 1976—. Named Tchr. of Yr. Sioux City Community Schs., 1988-89. Mem. NEA, Iowa Edn. Assn., Sioux city Edn. Assn., Iowa Bandmasters Assn., Sioux City Musicians Assn., Zeta Sigma, Mu Phi Epsilon. Republican. Lutheran. Office: Woodrow Wilson Mid Sch 1010 Iowa St Sioux City IA 51105

WICKER, VERONICA DICARLO, federal judge; d. Vincent James and Rose Margaret DiCarlo; m. Thomas Carey Wicker Jr.; children: Thomas Carey III, Catherine Wicker. B.F.A., Syracuse U., 1952; J.D., Loyola U. of the South, 1966. Bar: La. 1966, U.S Dist. Ct. (ea. dist.) 1968. U.S. magistrate New Orleans, 1977-79; judge U.S. Dist. Ct. (ea. dist.) La., New Orleans, 1979—. Mem. vis. com. Loyola U. Law Sch. Mem. ABA, Fed. Bar. Assn., La. Bar Assn., New Orleans Bar Assn., Jefferson Parish Bar Aux., Fed. Dist. Judges Assn., Assn. Women Judges, Maritime Law Assn., Assn. Women Attys., Justinian Soc. Jurists, Rotary (bd. dirs. New Orleans club 1989—), Phi Alpha Delta, Alpha Xi Alpha, Phi Mu. Office: US Dist Ct C-406 US Courthouse 500 Camp St New Orleans LA 70130

WICKEY, BETH MARGARET, lawyer; b. Roslyn, N.Y., Dec. 9, 1951; d. Richard August and Margaret Jane (Rhind) W. BA, Hofstra U., 1974, JD, 1977. Bar: N.Y. Staff atty. Nassau County Hispanic Found., Hempstead, N.Y., 1977-78, Housing Options Made Equal, Inc., Hempstead, N.Y., 1978-84; sr. staff atty. Nassau/Suffolk Law Svcs. Com., Inc., Riverhead, N.Y., 1984—; chmn. Ea. Suffolk Housing Alliance, Hampton Bays, N.Y., 1989—; mem. Town of Southampton supr.'s adv. com. on affordable housing, 1987-89, Village of Westbury (N.Y.), bd. zoning appeals, 1976-79. Bd. dirs. Suffolk Housing Svcs., L.I., 1988—, Suffolk Community Devel. Corp., Coram, N.Y., 1986-88, Legal Aid Soc. of Nassau County, Inc., Mineola, N.Y., 1982-84; mem. East End Planning Initiatives, Sag Harbor, N.Y., 1989—, Town of Southampton Dem. Com., 1987—. Mem. Suffolk County Bar Assn., Amnesty Internat., Christian Children's Fund, Nature Conservancy, Phi Beta Kappa. Methodist. Office: Nassau/Suffolk Law Svcs Inc 425 W Main st Riverhead NY 11901

WICKHAM, PATRICIA MARIA-CLAIRE, automotive executive; b. Battle Creek, Mich., May 29, 1951; d. James and Maria (Meertens) Powell; 1 child, Richard James Wickham. BS in Fin., LaSalle U., 1979. Supr. Retail Grocers Inventory Specialists, El Paso, Tex., 1977-79; with GTE Communications, El Paso, 1979-83; master scheduler GTE Network, El Paso, 1983-84; customer service mgr. Consolidated Diesel Co., Rocky Mount, N.C., 1984-86, new products mgr., 1986-87; materials mgr. Europe Johnson Controls, Ann Arbor, Mich., 1988—. Fundraiser sickle cell anemia, El Paso, 1978-82, multiple sclerosis, El Paso, 1980-83; advisor Jr. Achievement, El Paso, 1982-84, Rocky Mount, 1984-87. Mem. Am. Prodn. and Inv. Control Soc. (pres. 1984-86), Atlantic Coast Symposium, Nat. Assn. Female Execs. (dir. 1981-82). Democrat. Roman Catholic. Home: 23A Marentak, 2232 1S Gravenwezel Belgium Office: Johnson Controls, Automotive NV, Bell Telephonelaan 2, 2440 Geel Belgium also: 10361 Mackinaw El Paso TX 79924

WICKIZER, CINDY LOUISE, teacher; b. Pitts., Dec. 12, 1946; d. Charles Sr. and Gloria Geraldine (Cassidy) Zimmerman; m. Leon Leonard Wickizer, Mar. 21, 1971; 1 child, Charlyn Michelle. BS, Oreg. State U., 1968. Tchr. Enumclaw (Wash.) Sch. Dist., 1968—. Mem. NEA, Wash. Edn. Assn., Enumclaw Edn. Assn., Enumclaw Ednl. Coun., Buckley Ednl. Agrl. Coun., Buckley C. of C., Washington Contract Loggers Assn., Am. Rabbit Breeders Assn. (judge, chmn. scholarship found. 1986-87, Disting. Svc. award 1987, pres. 1988—), Wash. State Rabbit Breeders Assn. (life, Pres.' award 1983), Vancouver Island Rabbit Breeders Assn. (life), Fla. White Rabbit Breeders Assn. (pres. 1984-88), Wash. State Evergreen Rabbit (sec., v.p., pres.), Alpha Gamma Delta. Home: 26513 112th St E Buckley WA 98321

WICKS, MARIE MAVIS, administrator intermediate care facility; b. Gaylord, Minn., Apr. 4, 1952; d. Edwin F. and Mavis Marie (Hildebrandt) Niebuhr; m. Larry G. Wicks, Oct. 18, 1975; children: Ryan, Kristal. BS in Spl. Edn., St Cloud State U., 1974. Student intern St. Cloud (Minn.) Pub. Schs., 1973-74; learning disabilities tchr. Fairview Elem. Sch., Mora, Minn., 1974-75; spl. edn. tchr Melrose (Minn.) Pub. Schs., 1975-79, Owatonna (Minn.) Pub. Schs., 1980-83; program coord. Rainbow Residence, Inc., Owatonna, Minn., 1983—; ABEIGED instr. Waseca Consortium, Owatonna, Minn., 1988—. Mem. Spl. Advocates for Devel. Disabilities Adult Park and Recreation com., Owatonna, 1985—, Recreation Task Force, 1990—; Laubach reading tutor, Literacy Coun., Owatonna, 1975—; mem. Willow Creek Parent Adv. Group, Owatonna, 1990. Mem. AAUW (named recipient Eleanor Roosvelt Fellowship, pres. 1988-90, nominating com. 1990-91), Grad. Women Investors, Craft Group, Welcome Wagon, Parents for Accelerated Learners. Lutheran. Home: 670 Lynwood St Owatonna MN 55060

WICKSTEN, MARY KATHERINE, marine biologist, educator; b. San Francisco, Mar. 17, 1948; d. Layton Hubert and Helen Scannel (Gordon) W. BA, Humboldt State Coll., 1970, MA, 1972; PhD, U. So. Calif., 1977. Lectr. Calif. State U., L.A., 1978-79, Northridge, 1979-80; asst. prof. Tex. A&M U., College Station, 1980-87, assoc. prof., 1987—; asst. marine scientist U.S. Bur. Land Mgmt., L.A., 1975-78. Contbr. sci. articles to profl. publs. Mem. Am. Soc. Zoologists, Crustacean Soc., Biol. Soc. Washington, So. Calif. Acad. Scis., Pacific Sci. Assn., Western Soc. Naturalists, Sigma Xi. Democrat. Roman Catholic. Home: 2300 Broadmoor #11 Bryan TX 77802 Office: Tex A&M U Dept Biology College Station TX 77843

WICKWIRE, PATRICIA JOANNE NELLOR, psychologist, educator; b. Sioux City, Iowa; d. William McKinley and Clara Rose (Pautsch) Nellor; BA cum laude, U. No. Iowa, 1951; MA, U. Iowa, 1959; PhD, U. Tex., Austin, 1971; postgrad. U. So. Calif., UCLA, Calif. State U., Long Beach, 1951-66; m. Robert James Wickwire, Sept. 7, 1957; 1 son, William James. Tchr., Ricketts Ind. Schs., Iowa, 1946-48; tchr., counselor Waverly-Shell Rock Ind. Schs., Iowa, 1951-55; reading cons., head dormitory counselor U. Iowa, Iowa City, 1955-57; tchr., sch. psychologist, adminstr. S. Bay Union High Sch. Dist., Redondo Beach, Calif., 1962—, dir. student svcs. and spl. edn.; cons. mgmt. and edn.; mem. exec. bd. Calif. Interagency Mental Health Coun., 1968-72, Beach Cities Symphony Assn., 1970-82; chmn. Friends of Dominguez Hills (Calif.), 1981-85. Lic. ednl. psychologist, marriage, family and child counselor, Calif. Mem. AAUW (exec. bd., chpt. pres. 1962-72), L.A. County Dirs. Pupil Svcs. (chmn. 1974-79), L.A. County Personnel and Guidance Assn. (pres. 1977-78), Assn. Calif. Sch. Adminstrs. (dir. 1977-81), L.A. County SW Bd. Dist. Adminstrs. for Spl. Edn. (chmn. 1976-81), Calif. Assn. Sch. Psychologist (dir. 1981—), Am. Psychol. Assn., Am. Assn. Sch. Adminstrs., Calif. Assn. for Measurement and Evaluation in Guidance (dir. 1981, pres. 1984-85), Am. Assn. Counseling and Devel. (chmn. Coun. Newsletter Editors 1989-90, mem. com. on women 1989-90), Assn. Measurement and Eval. in Guidance (Western regional editor 1987—, conv. chair 1986), Calif. Assn. Counseling and Devel. (exec. bd. 1984—, pres. 1988—), Internat. Career Assn. Network (chair 1985—), Am. Assn. Career Edn. (exec. bd. 1987—), Pi Lambda Theta, Alpha Phi Gamma, Psi Chi, Kappa Delta Pi, Sigma Alpha Iota. Contbr. articles in field to profl. jours. Home and Office: 2900 Amby Pl Hermosa Beach CA 90254

WIDENER, PERI ANN, public relations manager; b. Wichita, Kans., May 1, 1956; d. Wayne Robert and LuAnne (Harris) W. B.S., Wichita State U., 1978; postgrad. Ala. A&M U., 1981. Advt. intern Associated Advt., Wichita, 1978; pub. relations asst. Fourth Nat. Bank, Wichita, 1978-79; mktg. communications rep. Boeing Co., Wichita, 1979-83, pub. relations rep., Huntsville, Ala., 1983-85, pub. relations mgr., 1985—. Participant United Way. Preston Huston scholar, Wichita State U., 1978; recipient Best Electronic Ad award Def. Electronics mag., 1982, Best Total Pub. Relations Program award Huntsville Press Club, 1985, Huntsville Media awards, 1986, 87, 88, 89, Huntsville Advt. Fedn. Addys, 1988; named one of Outstanding Young Women of Am., 1986. Mem. Women in Communications, Pub. Relations Council Ala. (bd. dirs. 1985—, State bd. 1988, officer Huntsville chpt. 1984—, Excellence award 1986, Achievement award 1986, Pres.'s award Huntsville chpt. 1986, Practitioner of Yr. 1989, PRCA Medallion award excellence, total PR program 1986, long term PR program 1988), Internat. Assn. Bus. Communicators (D2 Silver Quills award 1985). Mem. Pub. Relations Soc. Am. (accredited 1989—), Huntsville-Madison County C. of C. (pub. rels. adv. com. 1987), Sigma Delta Chi. Club: Huntsville Press (bd. dirs. 1989—). Methodist. Office: The Boeing Co PO Box 1470 Huntsville AL 35807

WIDGERY, JEANNE-ANNA (JAN WIDGERY), retired educator; b. Upland, Pa., May 18, 1920; d. Eugene Edmond and Carol Cooke (Meeser) Ayres; m. Rolande Carpenter Widgery ; children: Carolyn Gail, Catherine Darcy, Claudia Joan. BA, Chatham Coll., Pitts., 1941; AM, Radcliffe Coll., 1946. Instr. Chatham Coll., Pitts., 1946-50; dir. of drama Ellis Sch., Pitts., 1956-60; chmn. english dept. Winchester-Thurston Sch., Pitts., 1960-75; lectr. U. Houston, 1976-77; tchr. Duchesne Acad., Houston, 1977-85; ret., 1985; mem. adv. bd. Internat. Poetry Forum, Pitts., 1970-74; dir. creative writing workshops Carnegie Libr., Pitts., 1970-72; staff mem. Southwest Writers Conf., Houston, 1976. Author: The Adversary, 1966, Trumpet at the Gates, 1970. Vol. Family Outreach Ctr., Houston, 1989-; bible moderator Meml. Dr. Presbyn. Ch., Houston, 1988-. Mem. AAUW (program v.p. 1980-81), Houston Harpsichord Soc. (pres. 1981-82, trea. 1988-89), Austin Writers League, Assn. for Authors, Mystery Writers Am., Poets and Writers Assn.

WIDING, CAROL SCHARFE, lawyer; b. South Orange, N.J., Dec. 18, 1941; d. Howard Carman and Marjorie (McConaghy) Scharfe; m. C. Jon Widing, July 2, 1966; 1 child, Daniel McClure. BA, Wellesley Coll., 1964; MEd, Harvard U., 1965; JD, Widener U., 1980. Bar: Del. 1981, Pa. 1981, U.S. Dist. Ct. Del. 1981, U.S. Ct. Appeals (3d. cir.) 1983, Conn. 1984. Tchr. elem. schs. Lexington, Mass. and Bryn Mawr, Pa., 1964-68; pvt. tutor Ibadan, Nigeria, 1965; tchr. Phila. Adult Basic Edn. Acad., 1970-72; dep. atty. gen. child protection services Del. Dept. Justice, Wilmington, 1981-83; staff atty. UAW Legal Services, Newark, Del., 1983; assoc. Hebb & Gitlin, P.C., Hartford, Conn., 1985-86, Steinberg & Louden, Hartford, 1986-87, Law Offices of Bruce Louden, Hartford, 1987-89, Louden and Forzani, Hartford, 1989—. V.p. program AAUW, Middletown, Del. 1974; chmn. pub. relations and fundraising Lower New Castle County Med. Ctr., Middletown, 1980; bd. dirs. Epis. Community Services, Phila., 1970-72, UN Children's Fund, 1970-72. Mem. ABA, Pa. Bar Assn., Del. Bar Assn., Conn. Bar Assn., Hartford County Bar Assn., Hartford Assn. Women Attys., Jr. League (program chmn. 1970), Phila. Homemakers' Assn. (bd. dirs. 1970-72),. Home: 14 Briar Hill Avon CT 06001

WIDLUS, HANNAH BEVERLY, lawyer; b. Montreal, Quebec, Can., Jan. 23, 1955; d. William Jayson and Martha (Klein) Widlus; m. Moses W. Gaynor, Dec. 20, 1986. BSBA cum laude, Miami U., Oxford, Ohio, 1976; JD with honors, George Washington U., 1979. Bar: Tex. 1979, N.Y. 1984, Ill. 1988, D.C. 1990. Assoc. Johnson & Gibbs (formerly Johnson, Swanson & Barbee), Dallas, 1979-82, Proskauer Rose Goetz & Mendelsohn, N.Y.C., 1982-83, Patterson, Belknap, Webb & Tyler, N.Y.C., 1983-86; assoc. Kirkland & Ellis, Chgo., 1987-88, ptnr., 1988—; lectr. on pension and profit sharing plans, 1988-90, seminar on employment regulations in Ill., 1987-90, seminar on basic employee benefits, 1988-90, NYU 45th Ann. Inst. on Fed. Taxation, 1986, inst. for paralegal studies NYU Sch. Continuing Edn., 1984-86, tax seminar Dallas Gen. Agts. and Mgrs. Assn., 1980, 81, Corpus Christi chpt. Tex. Soc. CPAs, 1981, sect. taxation Dallas Bar Assn., 1980. Contbr. articles to profl. jours. Mem. ABA (sect. taxation), State Bar Tex., Ill. State Bar Assn. Jewish.

WIDMANN, NANCY C., broadcast executive. Pres. radio div. CBS, N.Y.C. Office: CBS Radio Div 51 W 52nd St New York NY 10019*

WIDMAYER, PATRICIA, management consultant; b. Buffalo, Jan. 21, 1943; d. C. Lane and Elizabeth M. (Gillgus) Ramsdell; m. Lawrence C. Widmayer, June 15, 1963; children: Carole Lane, Christopher Almon. BA, Mich. State U., 1966, MA, 1969, PhD, 1971. Instr. Oakland U., Rochester, Mich., 1971-72; rsch. assoc. Office of the Speaker, Lansing, Mich., 1973-75; dist. staff dir. Congressman Bob Carr, Washington, 1975-77; dir. legis. Mich. Dept. Edn., Lansing, 1977-82; dir. policy Office of Gov., Lansing, 1982-83; exec. dir. Gov.'s Commn. on Higher Edn., Lansing, 1983-85; pres. Widmayer and Assocs., Chgo., 1985—; trainer Nat. Women's Edn. Fund, Washington, 1982-89; spl. project dir. colo. Commn. on Higher Edn., Denver, 1985-89; cons. Borg-Warner Found., Chgo., 1985-89, MacAuthur Found. 1987, Sears Found. 1987, Donors Forum Chgo., 1986, Associated Colls. Ill., 1986—, Colo. Dept. Edn., 1986—, Nat. Assn. Bank Women, 1987—, DePaul U., 1986-87, Dept. of Agri., 1986—, Mich. Community Coll. Assn., 1987-88, Nebr. Legis. Coun., 1989-90. Author numerous govt. papers, reports, 1977—; editor report: Putting our minds together, 1984. Vol. cons. to local, state and nat. campaigns and issue coalitions; coord. Nat. Women's Polit. Caucus of Mich., 1975-80, Mich. Women's Assembly, 1976-84; bd. dirs. Econ. Devel. Corp., East Lansing, Mich., 1979-85. Inst. for Ednl. Leadership fellow George Washington U., Washington, 1978-79. Mem. Am. Assn. Higher Edn., Execs.' Club of Chgo., Delta Delta Delta (officer 1968-85). Home: 420 Church St Evanston IL 60201 Office: Widmayer and Assocs 500 N Michigan #1400 Chicago IL 60611

WIDMER, RUTH LYNN, respiratory therapist; b. Detroit, June 13, 1955; d. Arthur Frederick and Helen Louise (Turner) Holland; m. Walter Roberts Widmer, Jan. 14, 1978; 1 child, Loren Rae. AS, Forest Park Community Coll., 1976; BA, Webster U., 1987. Registered respiratory therapist, Mo. Day shift leader respiratory care St. Mary's Health Ctr., St. Louis, 1975-76, chief respiratory therapist, 1977-80, assoc. dept. head respiratory therapy, 1980—; clin. coord. respiratory therapy Forst Park Community Coll., St. Louis, 1976-77; bd. adv. dirs. home health St. Mary's Health Ctr., St. Louis, 1987-90. Contbr. articles to profl. jours. Mem. Am. Soc. Respiratory Care, Mo. Soc. Respiratory Care (dist. I pres. 1983-85, chairperson legal credentialing 1989-90, del. 1988-90), Nat. Bd. Respiratory Care. Democrat. Roman Catholic. Home: 451 Lee Ave Saint Louis MO 63119

WIDNALL, SHEILA EVANS, aeronautics educator; b. Tacoma, Wash., July 13, 1938; d. Rolland John and Genievieve Alice (Krause) Evans; m. William Soule Widnall, June 11, 1960; children: William, Ann. BS, MIT, 1960, MS, 1961, PhD, 1964; PhD (hon.), New Eng. Coll., 1975, Lawrence U., 1987, Cedar Crest Coll., 1988. Asst. prof. MIT, Cambridge, 1964-70, assoc. prof., 1970-74, prof. aeronautics, 1974—; dir. univ. research U.S. Dept. Transp., Washington, 1974-75; dir. Chemfab Inc., Bennington, Vt., Aerospace Corp., Los Angeles, Draper Labs., Cambridge, Mass., ANSER, Arlington, Va.; bd. trustees Carnegie Corp., 1984—. Contbr. articles to profl. jours.; patentee in field; assoc. editor AIAA Jour. Aircraft, 1972-75, Physics of Fluids, 1981-88, Jour. Applied Mechanics, 1983-87; mem. editorial bd. Sci., 1984-86. Chmn. faculty MIT, Cambridge, 1970-81, com. on undergrad. admission and fin. aid, 1982-84; bd. visitors U.S. Air Force Acad., Colorado Springs, Colo., 1978-83. Fellow AAAS (bd. dirs. 1982-89, pres. elect 1986-87, pres. 1987-88, chmn. 1988-89), Am. Phys. Soc. (fellow, exec. com. 1979-82), AIAA (bd. dirs. 1975-77, Lawrence Spery award 1972), Boston Mus. Sci. (trustee 1989—, Washburn award 1988); mem. ASME, Am. Acad. Arts and Scis., Soc. Women Engrs. (Outstanding Achievement award 1975), Nat. Acad. Engring. Club: Seattle Mountaineers. Office: MIT 77 Massachusetts Ave Rm 33-218 Cambridge MA 02139

WIDULSKI, LAURA JEAN, accountant; b. New Rochelle, N.Y., Sept. 5, 1961; d. William Paul and Rosemarie Claire (Biscoglio) W. AS in Acctg., Westchester Community Coll., 1980; BBA in Acctg., Iona Coll., 1982; postgrad. bus. adminstrn. Pace U., 1985—. CPA, N.Y., realtor, 1987. CPA, N.Y.; lic. real estate salesperson. Staff acct. Litton Fin. Services, Stamford, Conn., 1982-83; asst. to controller, acct. Simon & Schuster Pub. Co., N.Y.C., 1983-85; auditor, staff acct. Lombardi & Palazzolo, CPA's, Yonkers, N.Y., 1985-86; owner, pres. Sun N Ski Tours, Inc., Scarsdale, N.Y., 1986—; acct. Prizzi and Melagraro, CPA's, 1986—; realtor N. Am. Group, 1987-88. Mem. Nat. Assn. Female Execs., Fin. Club Pace U. Republican. Roman Catholic. Avocations: skiing, tennis, running, dancing, singing. Home: Sentry Pl Scarsdale NY 10583 Office: Sun N Ski Tours Inc PO Box 592 Scarsdale NY 10583

WIDZER, HELEN MAGUN, obstetrician and gynecologist, educator; b. N.Y.C., July 5, 1950; d. Jack and Loraine (Gordon) Magun; m. Steven Joel Widzer, June 19, 1971; children: Joshua, Rebecca and Noah (twins). BA in Biology, Northwestern U., 1972; MS in Microbiology, U. Ill., Chgo., 1974; MD, Med. Coll. Pa., 1978. Diplomate Am. Bd. Ob-Gyn. Intern, resident ob-gyn. Med. Coll. Pa. Hosp., 1978-82; pvt. practice, Norristown, Pa., 1982—; Flourtown, Pa., 1982—; staff physician Chestnut Hill Hosp., Phila., 1982—, mem. obstet. task force, 1988—. Mem. Planned Parenthood. Fellow Am. Coll. Ob-Gyn.; mem. Am. Med. Womens Assn, NOW, Phila. Obstet. Soc. Office: 919 E Germantown Pike Norristown PA 19401 also: 1107 Bethlehem Pike Flourtown PA 19031

WIEBUSCH, JANICE MARIE, real estate broker; b. Broken Bow, Nebr., Apr. 20, 1946; d. George William and Corinna Jane (Beal) W. B in Music Edn., U. Nebr., 1968, MusM, 1970. Tchr. music Lincoln (Nebr.) Pub. Schs., 1970-71, Gibbon (Nebr.) Pub. Schs., 1971-73; real estate salesperson Gateway Realty, Kearney, Nebr., 1976-79; real estate broker, owner CBS Real Estate, Kearney, 1979-83; real estate owner Midland Ptnrs., Kearney, 1983—. Mem. Downtown Revitalization Task Force, Kearney, 1980—; chmn. fund drive Kearney Community Theater, 1989-90; co-chmn. fund drive Kearney State Coll. Found., 1986; bd. dirs. Community Concert Assn., Kearney, 1980—. Mem. Women's Coun. of Realtors, Nebr. Realtors Assn. (chmn. econ. devel. com. LIncoln chpt. 1988-90), Kearney Tomorrow Forum, Kearney Area C. of C. (2d vice chmn. 1990—). Republican. Episcopalian. Home: 3120 9th Ave Kearney NE 68847

WIEDEMANN, ANITA MELISSA, computer engineer; b. Knoxville, Tenn., Dec. 21, 1960; d. Tom Stanberry and Patricia Ann (Cox) Collier; adopted d. Samuel A. Collier; m. Jack Hunt Wiedemann, June 11, 1983. BA in Computer Sci., U. Tenn., 1984; MS, U. Cen. Fla., 1988. Computer engineer Martin Marietta Aerospace, Orlando, Fla., 1984—. Mem. Internat. Soc. Optical Engring., Am. Assn. Artificial Intelligence. Home: 6400 Lakeville Rd Orlando FL 32818

WIEDEN, MARION ANNA, microbiologist; b. Cleve., Oct. 16, 1937; d. Joseph Frank and Anna Barbara (Bohac) Rusnak; B.S., U. Ariz., 1959; m. Walter Carl Wieden, Aug. 8, 1959; children—Mark David, Jill Ann, Matthew Joe. MS, PhD Columbia Pacific U., 1987. Microbiologist, St. Mary's Hosp., Tucson, 1961-63, chief microbiologist, 1963-68; chief microbiology sect. VA Hosp., Tucson, 1968—; adj. asst prof. med. tech. U. Ariz., 1986—; chmn. Tucson Inter-hosp. Infections Control Com., 1974-77; mem. clin. lab. adv. bd. Ariz. State Dept. Health Services, 1983—. Registered microbiologist and clin. lab. specialist Nat. Registry, Am. Acad. Microbiology. Mem. Am. Soc. Med. Tech. (liaison officer for VA in Ariz.), Ariz. State Soc. Med. Tech. (Cert. of Merit 1975, 78, 79, 80, 83, 85, 89, Cert. of Achievement 1980; Outstanding Contbns. to Microbiology award 1981, 85, 87, 89. Mem. of Yr. award 1981, state dir. 1976-79, 80-81, 88—, program chmn. 1981, 89 conv., gen. chmn. 1983, 85, pres. Tucson chpt. 1980-81), Am. Soc. Microbiology (cert. specialist, chair microbiology sci. assembly 1986-87, 88-89), Ariz. Soc. Microbiology (program chmn. Tucson br. 1979-81), Am. Pub. Health Assn., Assn. Practitioners in Infection Control, Internat. Soc. for Human and Animal Mycology, Am. Soc. Clin. Pathologists (various coms.), Smithsonian Instn., U. Ariz. Alumni Assn., Coccidioidomycosis Study Group, Med. Mycol. Soc. of Ams., Beta Beta Beta, Alpha Delta Pi. Roman Catholic. Contbr. articles to profl. jours. Address: 7180 N Cathedral Rock Pl Tucson AZ 85718

WIEDL, MARYANN, mathematics educator; b. Danbury, Conn., Sept. 26, 1945; d. William Andrew and Mary Jane (Chowanec) W; 1 child, Craig. BA, Albertus Magnus Coll., New Haven, 1967; MEd, Bridgewater State Coll., Mass., 1976. Tchr. math. Danbury (Conn.) Jr. High Sch., 1967-68, Middleborough High Sch., Middleboro, Mass., 1968—; coord./newsletter editor Nat. Mensa Math Tchrs. Forum, 1987—. Treas. West Point Parents Club of Mass., 1987-89. Mem. Nat. Coun. Tchrs. Math., Assn. Tchrs. Math. in Mass., Mensa. Republican. Home: 103 Wall St Middleboro MA 02346

WIEDL, SHEILA COLLEEN, biologist; b. Buffalo, Feb. 19, 1950; d. Frank George and Corinne Ruth (Nuskay) W.; B.S., Daemen Coll., 1972; M.S., U. Notre Dame, 1974; Ph.D., SUNY-Buffalo, 1986. Instr., Holy Cross Jr. Coll., South Bend, Ind., 1973-74; research technician SUNY, Buffalo, 1975-78; entomol. asst. N.Y. State Health Dept., 1979-80; entomol. intern Ohio Dept. Health, 1981; prof. natural scis. Trocaire Coll., Buffalo, 1974-85; postdoctoral scientist Am. Cyanamid, Lederle Labs., Pearl River, N.Y., 1985-86, clin. research assoc., 1986-89; assoc. mgr. CIBA Consumer Pharmaceuticals, Edison, N.J., 1989—; adj. prof. Ramapo Coll. of N.J., 1988—, Rockland Community Coll., 1989—. Mem. N.Y. State Assn. Two-Year Colls., Assn. Gnotobiotics, N.Y. State Archeol. Assn. Roman Catholic. Club: Notre Dame Alumni. Contbr. articles to profl. jours. Home: 298 Country Club Ln Pomona NY 10970-2501 Office: CIBA Consumer Pharmaceuticals Raritan Pla III Edison NJ 08837

WIEDRICH, JOYCE LORRAINE, nurse; b. Rochester, N.Y., June 21, 1952; d. Ernest Lee Wiedrich and Lorraine Maxine (Barth) Mason. Diploma, Highland Sch. of Nursing, 1973; AAS, Monroe Community Coll., 1973; BS in Nursing, U. Rochester, 1978; MS in Nursing, Family Health, U. Rochester, 1981. Cert. nurse practitioner. Staff nurse U. Rochester (N.Y.), 1973-80; nurse practitioner Highland Hosp., Rochester, 1980-85; asst. prof. nursing Monroe Community Coll., Rochester, 1985-86; nurse practitioner Rochester Cardiothoracic Assocs., 1986-87, Dr. Richard H. Feins, Rochester, 1987—; clin. assoc. U. Rochester, 1983—; cons. in nursing Monroe Community Coll., Rochester, 1987. Served with capt. USAR, 1983—. Mem. N.Y. State Nurse Practitioner Coalition (local rep. 1987—), Reserve Officers' Assn., Sigma Theta Tau. Republican. Methodist. Home: 63 Lochnavar Pkwy Pittsford NY 14534 Office: Dr Richard Feins 601 Elmwood Ave Box Surgery Rochester NY 14642

WIEGAND, SYLVIA MARGARET, mathematician, educator; b. Cape Town, South Africa, Mar. 8, 1949; came to U.S., 1949; d. Laurence Chisholm and Joan Elizabeth (Dunnett) Young; m. Roger Allan Wiegand, Aug. 27, 1966; children: David Chisholm, Andrea Elizabeth. AB, Bryn Mawr Coll., 1966; MA, U. Wash., 1967; PhD, U. Wis., Madison, 1972. Mem. faculty U. Nebr., Lincoln, 1967—, now prof. math.; vis. assoc. prof. U. Conn., Storrs, 1978-79, U. Wis., Madison, 1985-86. Editor Communications in Algebra jour., 1990; contbr. rsch. articles to profl. publs. Troop leader Lincoln area Girl Scouts U.S., 1988-90. Grantee NSF, 1985-88, 90-93. Mem. AAUP, Am. Math. Soc., Assn. Women in Math., London Math. Soc., Math. Assn. Am. Office: Dept Math and Stats Univ Nebr Lincoln NE 68588-0323

WIEGNER, ELIZABETH ANN, computer consultant, educator; b. Montville, N.J., Mar. 13, 1949; d. Clifford Raymond and Delta Eva (Balliet) W.; m. Fred Kitterle, Mar. 18, 1967 (div. 1973). BA in Chemistry and Psychology, Fla. Atlantic U., 1980; postgrad., Oral Roberts U., 1980-81, Calif. State U., Bakersfield, 1988, Fla. Atlantic U., 1988-89. Freelance tech. writer, translator, San Francisco, 1981-82; scientist Bechtel Labs., San Francisco, 1983-86; tech. writer Wilson-Zublin, Inc., Bakersfield, Calif., 1986-87; instr. computer studies Bakersfield Coll., 1987-88; air quality technician Arco Oil & Gas Co., Bakersfield, 1987-88; chemist BC Labs. Inc., Bakersfield, 1987; instr. computer applications Palm Beach Community Coll., Boca Raton, Fla., 1988-89, Camden County Coll., Blackwood, N.J., 1989—. Mem. Am. Chem. Soc., Am. Running and Fitness Assn. Republican. Episcopalian. Home: 77 E 2d St Moorestown NJ 08057

WIEL, CAROL LEE, sales and marketing executive; b. Washington, Mar. 11, 1943; d. John Myron and Alice Shelton (Trollinger) Ehrmantraut; m. Thomas Theodore, Sept. 5, 1964; children: Jeffrey Scott, Gregory Todd. BA, U. Md., 1964; student Nashville Sch. Art. Tchr. St. Mary's County, Lexington Park, Md., 1965-72; owner, gen. mgr. Standard Sales Co., Nashville, 1977-82; mgr. Aladdin Industries, Nashville, 1982-88; dir. Ingram Video Inc., 1988-89, v.p. advt and market devel., 1990—. Bd. dirs. Nat. Assn. for Sight Conservation and Aid to Blind, Nashville, 1982; para-profl. counselor Crisis Intervention Ctr.; mem Franklin Rd. Acad. Athletic Boosters, Nashville Sch. Art; dept. chmn. United Way; mem. outreach com. Woodmont Christian Ch. Mem. Am. Telemktg. Assn., Nat. Assn. Female Execs., Nat. Housewares Mfrs. Assn., Video Dealers Assn., Nashville Warehouse Investors, Incentive Mfrs. Reps. Assn., Nat. Wildlife Fedn. (assoc.), Delta Gamma Alumnae Assn. Republican. Club: Md. Farms Racquet. Avocations: art and design, poetry, tennis. Home: 6043 Wellesley Way Brentwood TN 37027 Office: Ingram Video Inc 1123 Heil Quaker Blvd La Vergne TN 37086

WIEMER-SUMNER, ANNE-MARIE, psychotherapist, educational administrator; b. Ger., Mar. 3, 1938; came to U.S., 1949, naturalized, 1956; d. Franz and Margaret (Neubacher) Wiemer; BA, Hunter Coll., 1963; MA, N.Y. U., 1965; PhD Union Inst., 1989; cert. Psychoanalytic Individual and Group Therapy, Washington Square Inst. Psychotherapy, 1975, 76; m. Eric Eden Sumner, May 24, 1974; children: Erika, Trevor. Adminstrv. asst. counselor, asst. chmn. admissions N.Y. U., N.Y.C., 1956-69; asst. dean student Hunter Coll., N.Y.C., 1969-71; asso. dean students Cooper Union Advancement Art and Sci., N.Y.C., 1971—; supr. Washington Sq. Inst. for Psychotherapy, N.Y.C., 1977-81; pvt. practice psychotherapy, N.Y.C. Trustee Grace Ch. Sch., 1985—; pres. Washington Sq. Assn., 1987—. Mem. Coun. Psychoanalytic Psychotherapists, Am. Psychol. Assn., Am. Group Psychotherapy Assn., Am. Orthopsychiat. Assn., Internat. Assn. Group Psychotherapy, Nat. Accreditation Assn. and Am. Exam. Bd. Psychoanalysis, N.Y. State Assn. Practicing Psychotherapists, Coll. Placement Council, Eastern Coll. Personnel Officers. Home: 7-13 Washington Sq N New York NY 10003 Office: Cooper Union Cooper Sq New York NY 10003

WIENER, ANNABELLE, United Nations official; b. N.Y.C., Aug. 2, 1922; d. Philip and Bertha (Wrubel) Kalbfeld; ed. Hunter Coll.; married, Jan. 1, 1941; children: Marilyn Grunewald, Marjorie Petit, Mark. Chmn. UN Dept. Pub. Info., Nongovtl. Orgns. Exec. Com., spl. adviser to sec. gen. Internat. Women's Year Conf.; mem. exec. bd. Nongovtl. Orgns. Com. on Disarmament UN, UN Dept. Pub. Info's NGO Exec. Com.; bd. dirs. World Fedn. UN Assns., also founder, dir. art and philatelic program; bd. dirs. N.Y. chpt. UN Assn.-USA; bd. dirs., chmn. UN Day Programme, So. N.Y. State Div., v.p. North Shore chpt.; mem. UN Dept. Pub. Info.'s Non-Govtl. Orgn. Exec. Com.; mem., bd. dir. Non-Govtl. Orgn. for UNICEF at UN Hdqrs. Recipient Diplomatic World Bull. award for Distinction in politics and diplomacy and svc. to high edeals of UN, 1989. Mem. Am. Fedn. Arts, Mus. Modern Art, Musee Nat. Message Biblique Marc Chagall, Am. Philatelic Soc., UNO Philatelie (Fed. Republic Germany), UN Philatelic Soc., UN Assn. U.S., UNO Philatelie, Fed. Republic Germany. Address: UN Hdqrs New York NY 10017

WIENER, ELIZABETH MARGARET, writer; b. White Plains, N.Y., July 26, 1948; d. Lawrence Arthur Wiener and Barbara Jane (Dorf) Miltenburger. BA cum laude, Barnard Coll., 1971; MS in Journalism, Columbia U., 1975. Reporter Roll Call Newspaper, Washington, 1973; publicity dir. Nat. Consumer's League, Washington, 1974; reporter Montgomery County Sentinel, Washington, 1975-78, States News Service, Washington, 1978-81, 83; asst. dir. communications Nat. Com. for Responsive Philanthropy, Washington, 1986-87; freelance writer Washington, 1988—. Contbr. articles to profl. jours. Vol. VISTA, Washington, 1967-68; mem. Potomac River Albacore Fleet, Washington, 1987-88. Recipient 1st prize in News Story Weeklies Md.-Del.-D.C. Press Assn., 1975. Democrat. Jewish. Home and Office: 3509 Rodman St NW Washington DC 20008

WIENER, GABRIELE KATHRYN, bar association executive director; b. Berlin, Germany, May 7, 1938; came to U.S., 1939; d. Frank Samuel and Susie Ruth (Guttfeld) Heimberg; m. Herbert M. Wiener, June 24, 1960 (div. 1981); children: Jill Ann Koenig, Andrew Nelson, Jane Diane. BA, Queens Coll., 1959; MPA, NYU, 1979, cert. in grants mgmt., 1978; cert. mcpl. clk., Internat. Inst. Mcpl. Clks., 1983. Speech therapist Union Free Sch. Dist. #5, Levittown, N.Y., 1959-61; trustee/dep. mayor Village of Great Neck (N.Y.) Estates, 1974-79; clk.-treas. Village of Atlantic Beach, N.Y., 1979-84; exec. dir. Suffolk County Bar Assn., Commack, N.Y., 1984—; chmn. assn. execs. com. N.Y. State Bar, 1989—; mem. exec. coun. N.Y. Conf. of Bar Leaders, Albany, 1987—. Co-chairperson Great Neck Peninsula Planning Coun., 1975-79; active Nassau County Multi Mcpl. Task Force, Mineola, N.Y., 1977-79, Suffolk County Emergency Med. Svcs. Task Force, Hauppauge, N.Y., 1987-88; trustee, sponsor L.I. Mid-Suffolk Bus. Action, Ronkonkoma, N.Y., 1984—. Mem. Nat. Assn. Bar Execs. (mem. program com. 1988—), Bus. and Profl. Women (mem. L.I. del. 1986-89), Kiwanis (2nd v.p. Long Beach, N.Y. chpt. 1988-89). Home: 25 Neptune Blvd 1A Long Beach NY 11561 Office: Suffolk County Bar Assn 340 Veterans Meml Hwy Commack NY 11725

WIENER, ROBIN KIM, environmental consultant, chemical engineer; b. N.Y.C., Oct. 9, 1963; d. Donald Stuart and Wilma Rose (Katz) W. BSE in Chem. Engring., U. Pa., 1985; postgrad. in environ. engring., George Washington U. Rsch. asst. Uniroyal, Inc., Middlebury, Conn., 1984; assoc., lead chem. engr. ICF Inc., Fairfax, Va., 1985-89; compliance coordinator Inst. Scrap Recycling Industries, Washington, 1989—; presenter in field. Vol. tutor Phila. Sch. Dist., 1984-85, D.C. Sch. Dist., 1986-87; vol. Holiday Project, Washington, 1986-88. Mem. Am. Inst. Chem. Engrs., Woman's Transp. Seminar, Phi Lambda Upsilon. Office: Inst Scrap Recycling Inds 1627 K St NW Ste 700 Washington DC 20006

WIENER, VALERIE, consultant media relations, government affairs; b. Las Vegas, Nev., Oct. 30, 1948; d. Louis Isaac and Tui Ava (Knight) W. BJ, U. Mo., 1971, MA, 1972; MA, Sangamon State U., 1974; postgrad., McGeorge Sch. Law, 1976-79. Producer TV show "Checkpoint" Sta. KOMU-TV, Columbia, Mo., 1972-73; v.p., owner Broadcast Assocs., Inc., Las Vegas, 1972-86; pub. affairs dir. First Ill. Cable TV, Springfield, 1973-74; editor Ill. State Register, Springfield, 1973-74; producer and talent "Nevada Realities" Sta. KLVX-TV, Las Vegas, 1974-75; account exec. Sta. KBMI (now KFMS), Las Vegas, 1975-79; nat. traffic dir. six radio stas., Las Vegas, Albuquerque and El Paso, Tex., 1979-80; exec. v.p., gen. mgr. Stas. KXKS and KKJY, Albuquerque, 1980-81; exec. adminstr. Stas. KSET AM/FM, KVEG, KFMS and KKJY, 1981-83; press sec. U.S. Congressman Harry Reid, Washington, 1983-86; adminstrv. asst Friends for Harry Reid, Nev., 1986; press sec. U.S. Senator Harry Reid, Washington, 1987-88; owner Valerie Wiener Enterprises, 1988—. Sponsor Futures for Children, Las Vegas, Albuquerque and El Paso, 1979-83; mem. Exec. Women's Coun., El Paso, 1981-83; mem. VIP bd. Easter Seals, El Paso, 1982; appointee, media chair Gov.'s Coun. Small Bus., 1989-90, Clark Coun. Sch. Dist. and Bus. Community PAYBAC Speakers and Ptnrship. Programs; media dir. 1990 conf. on women Gov. of Nev.; media chair Congl. Awards Coun.; media chair, nat. rep. Nat. Assn. Women Bus. Owners, So. Nev.; alumni bd. Leadership Las Vegas. Named one of Outstanding Young Women of Am., 1982, Outstanding Vol. United Way, El Paso, 1983; recipient 4 1st pl. Nev. Press Women Media awards, 1990; 2 2d pl. nat. communications awards Nat. Fedn. Press Women, 1990. Mem. NAFE, Nat. Mgmt. Assn., Nat. Speakers Assn., Dem. Press Secs. Assn., El Paso Assn. Radio Stas., U.S. Senate Staff Club, Nat. Assn. Women Bus. Owners, Las Vegas C. of C., Nev. State Press Assn., Allied Arts Coun., Soc. Profl. Journalists, Internat. Platform Assn. Democrat. Christian Scientist. Office: 1500 Foremaster Ln Ste 2 Las Vegas NV 89101-1103

WIENS, DEBORAH (ANNE JAMES), features editor, producer; b. Van Nuys, Calif., Mar. 23, 1956; d. George Allen and Barbara Jane (Asdell) W. Diploma, Ron Bailie Sch. of Broadcast, San Jose, Calif., 1979. Cert. radiotelephone, FCC. News reporter Sta. KEEN/KBAY, San Jose, 1978-79; copywriter Sta. KYGN, Glendive, Mont., 1979-80; features editor, copywriter Sta. KSEN, Shelby, 1980—; freelance copywriter, Shelby, 1984—. Co-writer, co-producer (radio program) Inside Sports, 1984— (Program of the Yr 1984), 1984-87; producer KSEN/H-H Speech Contest, 1984— (Program of the Yr. 1985), 1982-87; producer, writer: What's Cookin' (Program of the Yr. 1986), Agriculture Today (Program of Yr. 1988); co-editor, advt. dir. (mag.) Shelby Showcase, 1985—. Photographer, producer Shelby Cert. Com., 1987, mem. Shelby Beautification, Inc., 1986—. Recipient Disting. Service Toole Co. 4-H Com., Shelby, 1986, Outstanding Achievement in Beef Edn. Am. Nat. Cattlewomen and Tri-County Cowbelles, Shelby, 1986. Mem. Shelby Bus. and Profl. Women (young careerist award 1982, pres. 1985-86), Soc. Profl. Journalists. Lutheran. Home: 215 6th Ave S Shelby MT 59474

WIENS, GLORIA JEAN, mechanical engineering educator; b. Meade, Kans., Oct. 7, 1958; d. Raymond Roy and O. Vernelle (Davidson) W. BSME, Kans. State U., 1980, MSME, 1982; PhDME, U. Mich., 1986. Asst. prof. SUNY, Binghamton, 1986-87, Auburn (Ala.) U., 1987—; summer faculty mem. Fed. Systems div. IBM, Owego, N.Y., 1986. Author various tech. papers. Exxon teaching fellow, 1982-85, NASA/ASEE summer faculty fellow NASA-Marshall Space Flight Ctr., 1989-90; recipient Nat. Sci. Found., Dept. Edn., Soc. Mfg. Engrs. grants. Mem. ASME, IEEE, Soc. Mfg. Engrs., Soc. Women Engrs., Sigma Xi (Outstanding Rsch. award 1982). Office: Auburn U Mech Engring Dept Auburn AL 36849-5341

WIER, PATRICIA ANN, publishing executive; b. Coal Hill, Ark., Nov. 10, 1937; d. Horace L. and Bridget B. (McMahon) Norton; m. Richard A. Wier, Feb. 24, 1962; 1 dau., Rebecca Ann. B.A., U. Mo., Kansas City, 1964;

M.B.A., U. Chgo., 1978. Computer programmer AT&T, 1960-62; lead programmer City of Kansas City, Mo., 1963-65; with Playboy Enterprises, Chgo., 1965-71; mgr. systems and programming Playboy Enterprises, 1971; with Ency. Brit., Inc., Chgo., 1971—; v.p. mgmt. services Ency. Brit. USA, 1975-83, exec. v.p. adminstrn., 1983-84; v.p. planning and devel. Ency. Brit., Inc., 1985, pres. Compton's Learning Co. div., 1985; pres. Ency. Brit. (USA), 1986—; exec. v.p. Ency. Brit., Inc., 1986—; mem. council U. Chgo. Grad. Sch. Bus., Northwestern U. Assocs.; chmn. Compton's Learning Co., 1987—; bd. dirs. NICOR, 1990. Mem. fin. Coun. Archdiocese of Chgo., Coun. of Grad. Sch. of Bus. U. of Chgo. Mem. Direct Selling Assn. (bd. dirs. 1984—, chmn. 1987—), Women's Council U. Mo. Kansas City (hon. life), Com. 200, The Chgo. Network. Roman Catholic. Office: Ency Brit Inc 310 S Michigan Ave Chicago IL 60604

WIERSMA, PEGGY ANN, nurse; b. Tacoma, Sept. 22, 1956; d. Ted and Winnie May (Kelbaugh) W.; 1 child, Anthony Cornelis. BS in Nursing, Pacific Luth. U., 1982. RN, Wash. Staff nurse Am. Lake VA Hosp., Tacoma, 1982—. Baptist.

WIESE, DOROTHY JEAN, business educator; b. Chgo., Sept. 20, 1940; d. Charles Ennis Chapman and Evelyn Catherine Flizikowski; m. Wallace Jon Wiese, Oct. 10, 1959; children: Elizabeth Jean Wiese Christensen, Jonathan Charles. BS in Edn., No. Ill. U., 1970, MS in Edn., 1976, postgrad. Bus. tchr. Hampshire High Sch., Hampshire, Ill., 1970-78; instr. bus. Elgin Community Coll., Elgin, Ill., 1978—; cons. Gould, Inc., Rolling Meadows, Ill., 1984; vocat. instr. practicum McDonald's Hamburger U., Ofcl. Airline Guides, Oak Brook, Ill., 1986; intern SBA/SCORE, Chgo., 1987; speaker SIEC, Sweden and Austria, 1987-88; facilitator small group Internat. Congress Mng. Human Capacity in the 21st Century, U. Helsinki, Lahti, Finland, 1990; speaker, presenter, moderator in field. Mem., sec. Northwest Kane Airport Authority, Ill., 1987—; host family Am. Intercultural Student Exch., 1988-90. Mem. Societe International pour l'Ensignement Commercial, Internat. Soc. Bus. Edn. (N. Cen. Bus. Edn. Assn. rep. 1989—), Nat. Bus. Edn. Assn., Ill. Bus. Edn. Assn., Ill. Vocat. Assn., Delta Pi Epsilon (historian Alpha Phi chpt.), Kappa Delta Pi. Lutheran. Office: Elgin Community Coll 1700 Spartan Dr Elgin IL 60123

WIESEMAN, MARY FOLLIARD, government official, lawyer; b. Washington, Sept. 14, 1942; d. Robert Joseph and Catherine Cecelia (Molloy) Folliard; m. J. Theodore Wieseman, June 27, 1970; children—Theodore M., Moira G., Joseph H. A.B., Catholic U. Am., 1964, LL.B., 1967. Bar: D.C. 1968, Md. 1975. Atty., Dept. Justice, Washington, 1967-68; asst. U.S. atty. U.S. Atty.'s Office, Washington, 1968-71; legal counsel St. Elizabeth's Hosp., Washington, 1971-72; cons. Law Enforcement Assistance Adminstrn., Washington, 1974; atty. HEW, Washington, 1975-76; ptnr. Wieseman & Wieseman, Rockville, Md., 1975-83; acting gen. counsel Legal Services Corp., Washington, 1982-83; insp. gen. SBA, Washington, 1983-86; spl. counsel of Merit Systems Protection Bd., Washington, 1986—. Editorial bd. Cath. U. Law Rev., 1967. Mem. ABA, D.C. Bar, Bar State Md. Republican. Roman Catholic. Office: Office Spl Counsel 1120 Vermont Ave N W Washington DC 20005

WIESEN, ANNE RHODA, association volunteer; b. Medford, N.J., Nov. 27, 1926; d. George William and Mary Rebecca (Hattman) W. BS, U. N.H., 1948; MRE, Andover Newton Theol. Sch., 1950. Cert. community coll. instr., Calif. Dir. Christian edn. Bapt. chs., Mass., R.I., 1950-54; tchr., recreator World Coun. Chs., France, 1955; dir. Christian edn. Bapt. chs., Norristown, Wayne, Pa., 1956-62; recreation worker U.S. mil. hosps. ARC, 1962-64, recreation supr. U.S. mil. hosps. and bases, 1964-1976; field dir. ARC, Wright Patterson AFB, Ohio, 1976-79; sta. dir. ARC, Osan AFB, Republic of Korea, 1979-80; asst. dist. dir. ARC, Camp Zama, Japan, 1981-83, March AFB, Calif., 1983-84; sta. mgr. ARC, Camp Pendleton, Calif., 1985-86; vol. resource assoc. ARC, Stuttgart, Fed. Republic Germany, 1986-88; sec. European Recreation Soc., Heidelberg, Fed. Republic Germany, 1973-74. Author: Children Around the World, 1960. Recipient medal for civilian svcs. in Vietnam, U.S. Govt., 1968. Mem. AAUW (cultural chair 1988—), Tiger Bay Club. Democrat. Baptist.

WIESENBERG, JACQUELINE LEONARDI, lecturer; b. West Haven, Conn., May 4, 1928; d. Curzio and Filmenia Olga (Turriziana) Leonardi; m. Russel John Wiesenberg, Nov. 23; children: James Wynne, Deborann Donna. BA, SUNY, Buffalo, 1970, postgrad., 1970-73, 80—. Interviewer, examiner Dept. Labor, New Haven, 1948-52; sec. W.I. Clark Co., Hamden, Conn., 1952-55; acct. VA Hosp., West Haven, 1956-60; acct.-commissary U.S. Air Force Missle Site, Niagara Falls, N.Y., 1961-62; tchr. Buffalo City Schs., 1970-73, 79; acct. Erie County Social Services, Buffalo, 1971-73; lectr., 1973—. Contbr. articles to CAP, U.S. Air Force mag., 1954—. Capt., Nat. Found. March of Dimes, 1969—, com. mem. telethon, 1983-86; den mother Boy Scouts Am., 1961-68; chmn. Meals on Wheels, Town of Amherst, 1975-76; leader, travel chmn. Girl Scouts Am., 1968-77; mem. Nat. Congress Parents and Tchrs., 1957—; heart fund vol. Heart Assn., 1960-86. Mem. NAFE, Internat. Platform Assn., Am. Astrol. Assn., Western N.Y. Conf. Aging, Nat. Geographic Soc., Epsilon Delta Chi, Alpha Iota. Home: 14 Norman Pl Amherst NY 14226

WIESENFELD, BESS GAZEVITZ, business executive, real estate developer; b. Elizabeth, N.J., May 6, 1915; d. Morris and Rebecca (Sokolov) Gazevitz; m. Benjamin Wiesenfeld, Oct. 23, 1938 (dec.); children: Myra Judith Wiesenfeld Lewis, Elaine Phyllis Wiesenfeld Livingston, Ira Bertram (dec.), Sarah Ann Wiesenfeld Wasserman. BFA, N.Y. Sch. Design, N.Y.C., 1982. Pres. Anasarca Corp., 1958—; real estate devel. Colonia, N.J., 1961—; interior designer, 1961—; chair Bess & Co., Phila., 1982—; pres. Carolier Lns., Inc., 1986—. Mem. Nat. Trust for Hist. Preservation, (assoc.) Am. Soc. Interior Designers, Met. Mus. Art., Mus. Modern Art, Smithsonian Inst., Victorian Soc. of Met. Opera Guild, Preservation, N.J., Inc. Republican. Jewish. Home: 374 New Dover Rd Colonia NJ 07067 also: 2600 Old South Ocean Blvd Palm Beach FL 33480

WIESER, JOAN ELIZABETH, university official, employee development programs consultant; b. Fall River, Mass., Mar. 14, 1948; d. James Edward and Theresa (O'Gara) Lenaghan; m. Paul B. Wieser, Sept. 7, 1968. Student Triton Coll., River Grove, Ill., 1969-71, Brown U., 1973; M.B.A., U. Miami-Coral Gables, 1982. Cost acct. Sylvaniz Electric, Fall River, Mass., 1967-68; support staff mem. Alberto-Culver, Melrose Park, Ill., 1968-70; exec. sec. Profl. Marketers, Inc., Broadview, Ill., 1970-75; asst. mgr. East Providence Credit Union, R.I., 1975-84; asst. personnel dir. U. Miami, Coral Gables, 1984—, personnel dir. Med. Campus, Miami, 1984—; mem. credit com. U. Miami Credit Union, 1979—; cons. devel. employment skills John S. Koubek Ctr., Miami, 1981—; condr. workshops and seminars in field. Named Outstanding Young Women in Am., Sales & Mktg. Execs. of Ft. Lauderdale, Inc., 1983, Woman of Year Am. Bus. Women's Assn., 1984. Mem. NAFE, U. Miami Women's Commn., Am. Bus. Women's Assn., Am. Mgmt. Assn., Am. Soc. Personnel Adminstrn., Am. Soc. Tng. and Devel., Med. Group Mgmt. Assn., Fla. Hosp. Assn., Pers. Adv. Bd., Toastmasters Internat. (Coral Gables). Office: Univ of Miami Med Campus 1800 NW 10th Ave Miami FL 33101

WIESLER-WUYTACK, EVELYN LYDIA, market analyst; b. Queens, N.Y., Sept. 21, 1959; d. Otto Franz and Lieselotte Elfriede (Prepens) Wiesler; m. Claude S. Wuytack, June 4, 1989. BBA, Pace U., 1983, postgrad. Legal sec. Morton A. Luchs Esq., N.Y.C., 1977-78, Mendes and Mount, N.Y.C., 1978; sr. communications analyst N.Y. Stock Exch., N.Y.C., 1978-88, enforcement investigator, 1988-89, sr. market analyst, 1989—. Mem. Empire Wit, Phi Chi Theta. Lutheran. Home: 61-14 69th Ln Flushing NY 11379 Office: NY Stock Exchange 11 Wall St New York NY 10005

WIESNER, JOAN RUTH, state senator; b. Passaic, N.J., Feb. 25, 1950; d. Harry James and Ruth Dorothy (Elander) Winslow; m. Albert Frederick Wiesner, III, June 12, 1971; 1 child, Albert Frederick, IV. B.A. in English, U. R.I., 1972. Research asst. Eastern Color and Chem. Co., Providence, R.I., 1972-73; personnel supr. Wiesner Mfg. Co., Providence, 1972-77; mem. R.I. Senate, 1983—; mem. exec. council USDA Research and Conservation and Devel. Council, 1978—. Chmn., Burrillville Republican Town Com., R.I., 1980-83; bd. dirs. Northwest Health and Community Nursing Com., 1984—, No. R.I. Mental Health Assn., Woonsocket, 1984—; mem. exec. com. R.I. Rep. State Central Com., Providence, 1984—. Mem. N. Providence Bus. and Profl. Women's Club. Baptist. Avocations: tennis; skiing; singing. Home: 60 Sherman Farm Rd Harrisville RI 02830 Office: R I State Senate Providence RI 02903*

WIESNER, SHARON MARIE, investment banker, oil production executive; b. Omaha, July 16, 1938; d. Ralph Remmington and Evelyn Adeline (Morris) Von Bremer; m. Virgil James Wiesner, Apr. 4, 1959 (div. 1982); children: Scott James, Lydia Marie, Michelle Elizabeth. B.A., Creighton U., 1959; M.A., U. Nebr.-Omaha, 1964, postgrad., 1979-82. Owner, v.p. Wiesner Distbg. Co. Inc., Lincoln, Nebr., 1966-72, Wiesner Tire Co. Inc., Omaha, 1972-75; v.p. Fin. Inc., Omaha, 1975-82; with fin., sales oil Am. Internat. Sales Corp., Dallas, 1982-83; pres. Joint Capital Resources, Dallas, 1983—;del. Richland Coll. Oil Industry Seminar, 1987, Dresser-Atlas Oil Logging Seminar. Editor: Born Rich: A Historical Book of Omaha, 1978. Author: Slanting News, 1959, Critical Study of Iago's Motivation, 1964. V.p. Assistance League Omaha, 1973-78; fund raiser Opera Omaha; v.p. women's bd. Omaha Community Playhouse; v.p. Lincoln Symphony Guild, 1966-71; bd. dirs. Omaha Jr. Theatre, 1975-79. Named Outstanding Young Woman Jr. C. of C., Norfolk, Nebr., 1964; recipient Valuable Svc. awards Lincoln Gen. Hosp., Omaha Community Playhouse. Mem. AAUW, Omaha Writers Group, The Quill, Landmarks Inc., Nat. Beer Wholesalers, Logging and Geol. Inst., Omaha Symphony Guild (v.p. 1973-78), Omaha C. of C., Lincoln C. of C., Brownville Hist. Soc., Internat. Platform Assn., Brownville Fine Arts Assn., Nebr. Kennel Club, Dalmatian Club Am., Minn.-St. Paul Dalmatian Club, Blue Ribbon Dog Breeders, Beta Sigma Phi, Omicron Delta Kappa, Phi Delta Gamma, Theta Phi Alpha (pres. 1958-59). Club: Womens (v.p. 1966-70). Avocations: painting, music, art, writing. Office: Joint Capital Resources 6036 Birchbrook #229 Dallas TX 75206

WIEST, DIANNE, actress; b. Kansas City, Mo., Mar. 28, 1948. Student, U. Md. Appeared in numerous plays including Ashes (off-Broadway), 1976, Leave It to Beaver is Dead, The Art of Dining (Theatre World award 1983), Bonjour La Bonjour, Three Sisters, Serenading Louie, Othello, After the Fall, Heartbreak House, Our Town, and Hunting Cockroaches, 1987; appeared in films including It's My Turn, 1980, I'm Dancing as Fast as I Can, 1982, Independence Day, 1982, Footloose, 1984, Falling in Love, 1984, The Purple Rose of Cairo, 1985, Hannah and Her Sisters, 1986 (Acad. award 1987), Radio Days, 1987, Lost Boys, 1987, September, 1987, Bright Lights, Big City, 1988, Parenthood, 1989, Cookie, 1989; TV appearances include The Wall, 1982, The Face of Rage, 1983. Office: care Sam Cohn Internat Creative Mgmt 40 W 57th St New York NY 10019*

WIESTER, LINDA MARIE, company executive; b. Boston, July 5, 1946; d. Lester and Marion (Ellsworth) Chisholm; m. Thomas Charles Wiester, June 23, 1972; children: Debra Marie, Thomas Charles Jr. Grad. high sch. Svc. mgr. Flower Drum Inn Restaurant, Randallstown, Md., 1976-86; pres. Cleany Boppers, Inc., Randallstown, 1986—. Active Liberty Community Devel. Corp., Randallstowns, 1988-89; conf. com. Md. Sml. Bus. Advocates, 1988—. Mem. Nat. Assn. Women Bus. Owners (exec. forum 1988—, v.p. 1989-90, pres. 1990—), Bldg. Svc. Contrs. Assn. Internat. Republican. Baptist. Home: 9319 Samoset Rd Randallstown MD 21133

WIEWEL, BETTY C., social services administrator; b. Adams City, Ill.; d. Fred T. and M. Olive (Quintemeyer) Schwartz; m. Gerald A. Wiewel, May 22, 1948; children: L. Tishia Suk, Bradford G., Mark A. BA, Quincy Coll.; diploma in nursing, St. Mary's Hosp. Sch. Nursing. RN, Ill. Asst. to pastor St. Francis Ch., Quincy, Ill.; coord., adminstr. special care div. Good Samaritan Home, Quincy; exec. dir. Young Women's Christian Assoc., Quincy. Mem. polit. candidate campaign for County Circuit Clerk, Adams City, Ill.; past pres. St. John's and Cath. Boys Sch., Boy Scouts, ARC; active Quincy Community Little Theatre, Teens Encounter Christ, Currsillo Orgn., Western Cath. Union, Quincy Ch. Women United Unit, St. Francis Ch., Gardner Mu. Architecture and Design, Quincy Art Ctr., Quincy Community Little Theatre; bd. dirs. Ch. Women United. Mem. NAFE, Nat. Assn. YWCA Exec. Dirs. (charter), Quincy Soc. Fine Arts (bd. dirs.), Quincy Coll. and St. Mary's Hosp. Alumni Assns., Sch. Sisters Notre Dame Assocs., Hist. Soc. Quincy and Adams County, Ladies of t. Francis, Altrusa Club, Women's City Club, Newcomer's Club, Bell Collectors Club. Republican. Roman Catholic. Office: YWCA 421 Jersey St Quincy IL 62301

WIGAND, PATRICIA ANN, corporate training, human resource executive; b. W. Hempstead, N.Y., Mar. 6, 1953; d. Gilbert and Helen Marie (Golden) Klein; m. Kenneth William Wigand, Aug. 10, 1979; 1 child, Kellyn Marie. BA, St. John's U., Queens, N.Y., 1975, MS, 1980. Jr. mgmt. position credit card customer svc. Citicorp, Melville, N.Y., 1978-80; ops. mgr. credit cards Citicorp, 1980-81; project mgr. credit card mktg. Citicorp, N.Y.C., 1981-82; dir. customer svc. (all bank products) European Am. Bank, Garden City, N.Y., 1982-83; product mgr. mktg. European Am. Bank, 1984-85; dir. svc. quality Citicorp, Melville, 1985-87; dir. corp. tng., human resource devel. & quality assurance Dreyfus Corp., Garden City, 1987—.

WIGGERS, CHARLOTTE SUZANNE WARD, magazine editor; b. Cleve., Dec. 14, 1943; d. Raymond Paul and Irene Mary (Knapp) W.; m. John Houston Black, Feb. 1975 (div. 1980). AB, Smith Coll., 1966. Asst. editor The Hudson Rev., N.Y.C., 1966-76; assoc. editor The Print Collector's Newsletter, N.Y.C., 1977-79; copy editor Electronics mag., McGraw-Hill, N.Y.C., 1979-81; sr. copy editor Spectrum mag., N.Y.C., 1981-85; mng. editor Essence mag., N.Y.C., 1985—. Home: 50 W 85th St Apt 5 New York NY 10024 Office: Essence Magazine 1500 Broadway New York NY 10036

WIGGERT, BARBARA NORENE, biochemist; b. Cleve., Jan. 7, 1938; d. Eugene Richard and Violetta Louise (Trask) Orchard; m. D. Jimitri Wiggert, June 19, 1958; children: Lara J., Thea C., Heidi E., Kristian E. BA in Chemistry, U. Wis., 1959; PhD in Biochemistry, Harvard U., 1963. Postdoctoral fellow Med. Sch. U. Wis., Madison, 1963-65; postdoctoral fellow Lab. of Vision Rsch. NIH, Bethesda, Md., 1975-76, staff fellow Lab. of Vision Rsch., 1976-78, rsch. chemist Lab. of Vision Rsch., 1978-86, sect. chief Lab. of Retinal Cell and Molecular Biology, 1986—. Contbr. numerous articles to profl. jours. Andelot predoctoral fellow Harvard U., 1959-60. Mem. Am. Chem. Soc., Am. Soc. for Biochemistry and Molecular Biology, AAAS, Assn. for Rsch. in Vision and Ophthalmology, Sigma Delta Epsilon. Home: 12405 Eastbourne Dr Silver Spring MD 20897 Office: NIH Bldg 6 Rm 218 Rockville Pike Bethesda MD 20892

WIGGINS, FRANCES KNOTTS, neurolinguistic programming trainer; b. Palmetto, Fla., Mar. 15, 1926; d. Leon Owen and Nettie Ruth (Whittemore) Knotts; m. Joe W. Wiggins, Aug. 16, 1950; children: Lesley, Steven, Judith, Sarah, Anne, Joseph. AA, Mars Hill Coll., 1946; BA, U. North Fla., 1975, MA, 1977. RN. Employee assistance program coordinator Johnson & Johnson's Vistakon, Jacksonville, 1982-85; trainer NLP Internat., Fla., 1985—, So. Inst. NLP, Indian Rock Beach, 1987—. Author: Changing Perspectives, 1985, Teaching Stress Mgmt. Skills, 1986, Learning Stress Mgmt. Skills, 1986, Matching Metaphors, 1988. Contbr. articles to profl. jours. Fellow: Nat. Assn. Neurolinguistic Programming; mem. NLP Internat. (bd. dirs., sec., 1986-88), Am. Assn. Counseling & Devel. Episcopalian. Home: PO Box 40 Welaka FL 32193

WIGGINS, IDA SILVER, teacher; b. Bklyn., Apr. 23; d. Joseph C. and Alice V. (Carter) Silver; m. G. Franklin Wiggins, Dec. 27, 1955; children: Bryan Franklin, Sharon-Amy. BS, NYU, 1955, MA, 1966; D Christian Letters (hon.), Shaw Divinity Sch., Raleigh, N.C., 1988. Cert. tchr., N.Y. Tchr. Durham (N.C.) County Pub. Sch., 1955-56, Johnston County Pub. Sch., Clayton, N.C., 1956-60; ednl. cons. Child Care Ctr., N.Y., 1960-61; tchr. Lakeland Cen. Schs., Shrub Oak, N.Y., 1961—; tchr. adv. panel Silver Burdett Pub. Co., Morristown, N.J., 1987-88; mem. lang. arts task force, elem. math com., social studies curriculum com. Lakeland Cen Schs., 1989—; bd. dirs. Tutorial Program, Peekskill, 1986—. Writer: (choral reading) Martin Luther King, Jr., 1970. Life mem. Peekskill Hosp. Aux., 1980; former bd. mem. Peekskill YMCA, 1982, Peekskill Mus., 1988; life mem. NAACP, Peekskill, 1989. Mem. AAUW, Am. Fedn. Tchrs., N.Y. State United Tchrs., Assn Math. Tchrs. in N.Y. State, Delta Kappa Gamma, Alpha Kappa Alpha. Baptist. Home: 1282 Maple Ave Peekskill NY 10566

WIGGINS, NANCY BOWEN, real estate broker, appraiser, market research consultant; b. Richmond, Va., Oct. 9, 1948; d. William Roy and Mary Virginia (Colson) Bowen; m. Samuel Spence Saunders, Aug. 16, 1969 (div. 1977); m. Edwin Lindsey Wiggins, Jr., Apr. 16, 1983; children: Neal Bowen, Mark Edwin. AA, St. Mary's Coll., Raleigh, N.C., 1968; postgrad., Trinity U., 1968-69; BA, U.S. Internat. U., San Diego, 1970; MA, U. Tex., Arlington, 1975; postgrad., Tulane U., 1976-77. Bank teller Bank of Am., San Diego, 1971-72; lectr. U. Tex., Arlington, 1974-76; instr. Johnson C. Smith U., Charlotte, N.C., 1977-78; human svcs. planner Centralina Coun. of Govt., Charlotte, 1978-80; mktg. rsch. analyst First Union Nat. Bank, Charlotte, 1980-81; mktg. rep. Burroughs Corp., Charlotte, 1981-83; ptnr., mktg. researcher George Selden & Assocs., Charlotte, 1983-84; pres., broker, appraiser Bowen Wiggins Co., Charlotte, 1984—; instr. U. N.C., Charlotte, 1984-85, 87—; bd. dirs. Roy Bowen, Inc., Frogmore, S.C. Contbr. articles to profl. jours. Vice chmn. United Cerebral Palsy Coun., Charlotte, 1984; chmn. bd. dirs. Carriage House Condominium Assn., Charlotte, 1980-82; mem. Mayor's Budget Adv. Com., Charlotte, 1980-81, Mecklenburg Dem. Women's Club, sec., 1989, pres., 1990, Charlotte Women's Polit. Caucus, YMCA. Mem. N.C. Assn. Appraisers (bd. dirs., pres. 1989-90), Charlotte Apt. Assn., Charlotte Sales Execs. Club, Internat. Platform Assn., Am. Bankruptcy Inst., Market Rsch. Assn., Tournament Players Club of Piper Glen, Pi Sigma Alpha. Democrat. Episcopalian. Home and Office: 6425 Felton Ct Charlotte NC 28277 Office: 2915 Providence Rd Charlotte NC 28211

WIGGINS, PENNY KAY, financial analyst; b. Dallas, Nov. 9, 1948; d. Frank LaRue and Merriam Thelma (Roebuck) W. BS, Centenary Coll., 1970; MBA, Corpus Christi (Tex.) State U., 1980. Tchr. algebra Parkway High Sch., Bossier City, La., 1970-73; geophys. technician Western Geophys. Co., Houston, 1974-78; economist Texoma Prodn. Co., Houston, 1980-83; econ. analyst Pelto Oil Co., Houston, 1983-89; planning coord. Energy Devel. Corp., Houston, 1989—. Vol. Ctr. for the Retarded, Houston, 1987—, Rep. Party of Harris County, Houston, 1988, Literacy Advance, Houston, 1989—. Mem. Houston Heights Exch. Club. Republican. Methodist. Home: 1397 Arlington Houston TX 77008 Office: Energy Devel Corp 1000 Louisiana Houston TX 77002

WIGGINS, WANDA, mortgage company executive; b. Chattanooga, Sept. 11, 1945; d. Thomas A. and Foye (Davis) Hamrick; m. Dennis Wiggins; children: Kimberly, Mark. Student, U. Tenn., FCCJ. Br. mgr., loan officer Ameri-First Mortgage, Jacksonville, Fla.; real estate broker Century 21 Paul Turner Realty, Memphis; mgr. Suntrust Mortgage, Inc., Jacksonville, Fla., 1987-90; asst. v.p., mortgage loan officer Point Vedra (Fla.) Nat. Bank, 1990—. Bd. dirs. FLARE, 1982-84; v.p. Civitan, 1985-87. Mem. Sales and Mktg. Coun., Jacksonville Assn. of Realtors, Mortgage Bankers of Am., Women's Coun. of Realtors, Civitan Internat. Republican. Baptist. Office: Ponte Vedra Nat Bank 100 Sawgrass Corners Dr Ponte Vedra FL 32082

WIGHT, DARLENE, retired speech educator; b. Andover, Kans., Jan. 5, 1926; d. Everett John and Claudia (Jennings) Van Biber; m. Lester Delin, Jan. 21, 1950; children: Lester Delin II, Claudia Leigh. AA, Graceland Coll., 1945; BA, U. Kans., 1948, MA, 1952. Permanent profl. cert., Iowa; life tchr.'s cert., Mo. Instr. U. Kans., Lawrence, 1949-50; instr. overseas program U. Md., Munich, 1954; speech pathologist Independence Pub. Sch. Dist., Independence, Mo., 1958-61; assoc. prof. Graceland Coll., Lamoni, Iowa, 1961-87; cons. Quad-County Sch. Dist., Leon, Iowa, 1966-67, Mt. Ayr, Iowa Community Sch. Dist., 1967-70, Head Start Program, SCIAP, Leon, 1972-75, Head Start Program, MATURA, Bedford, Iowa, 1973-75. Co-author: Speech Communication Handbook, 1979. Mem. Common Cause, 1989, Friends of Art, Des Moines, 1968—. Recipient Award of Merit U. Kans., 1982, Award of Distinction U. Kans., 1947-48. Mem. Am. Speech, Lang., and Hearing Assn. (speech pathology clin. competency), Coun. Exceptional Children, As You Like It Club, Entre Nous Club. Democrat. Mem. Reorganized Latter Day Saints Ch. Office: Graceland Coll Lamoni IA 50140

WIGREN, BARBARA LOUISE, artist; b. Oakland, Calif., May 19, 1932; d. Alvin Russell and Bertha Louise (Mallen) Kyte; m. Arthur A. Wigren, May 26, 1956. BA, U. Calif., 1954. Pres. Eastbay Watercolor Soc., Walnut Creek, Calif., 1980-82; also bd. dirs.; pres. Oakland Art Assn., 1985-87; v.p. San Francisco Women Artists, 1988-89; pres., 1989-90. contbr. article to profl. jour. Judge San Francisco Film Festival, 1981-84. Mem. San Francisco Women Artists, Eastbay Watercolor Soc., Oakland Art Assn. Republican. Home: 904 Hastings Dr Concord CA 94518

WIIG, ELISABETH HEMMERSAM, audiologist, educator; b. Esbjert, Denmark, May 22, 1935; came to U.S., 1957, naturalized, 1967; d. Svend Frederick and Ingeborg (Hemmersam) Nielsen; m. Karl Martin Wiig, June 10, 1958; children—Charlotte E., Erik D. B.A., Statsseminariet Emdrupborg, 1956; M.A., Western Res. U., 1960; Ph.D., Case Western Res. U., 1967; postgrad., U. Mich., 1967-68. Clin. audiologist Cleve. Hearing and Speech Center, 1959-60; instr. dept. phonetics Bergen (Norway) U., 1960-64; asst. prof., dir. aphasia rehab. program U. Mich., 1968-70; asst. prof. Boston U., 1970-73, asso. prof., chmn. dept., 1973-77, prof. dept. communication disorders, 1977-87, prof. emerita, 1987—. Author: Language Disabilities in Children and Adolescents, 1976, Language Assessment and Intervention for the Learning Disabled, 1980, 84, CELF Screening Tests: Elementary and Secondary Levels, 1980, Clinical Evaluation of Language Fundamentals, revised, 1987, Test of Language Competence, 1985, expanded edit., 1989; editor: Human Communication Disorders: An Introduction, 1981, 85; contbr. articles to profl. jours. Recipient Metcalf Cup and Prize for excellence in teaching Boston U., 1967. Fellow Am. Speech and Hearing Assn. (cert. clin. competence in speech pathology and audiology); mem. Coun. for Learning Disabilities, Coun. Exceptional Children, Internat. Neuropsychology Soc. Address: 7101 Lake Powell Dr Arlington TX 76016

WIJNEN, ADELINE FRANCES, French, Italian and reading educator; b. Bklyn., Sept. 20, 1933; d. Domenic and Francesca (Ferraro) Adamo; m. Joseph Wijnen, Nov. 18, 1967; children: Renee, Dirk. Student, U. Florence, summer 1957; BA in Humanities, Hunter Coll., 1963, postgrad., 1968-72. Actuarial asst. Morss & Seal, N.Y.C. and New Haven, 1954-60; dept. sec., asst. to pres. Hunter Coll., N.Y.C., 1961-63; market rsch. asst. Italian Econ. Corp. of BNL, N.Y.C., 1963-66; freelance interpreter and translator N.Y. and N.J., 1964-87; French/English adminstrv. asst. Edn. Internat., Algiers, Algeria, 1983-84; adminstrv. asst. Popsicle, Inc., Englewood, N.J., 1985-86; substitute tchr. Hackensack, Teaneck, Westwood (N.J.) System, 1986-90; tchr. reading IS 164, N.Y.C., 1990—; prof. Italian and French St. Peter's Coll., Englewood Cliffs, N.J., evenings 1988—. Pres., Council Parents and Tchrs., Teaneck, 1987-89, PTA of Lowell Sch., Washington Irving Sch., Teaneck High Sch.; trustee Community Scholarship, Teaneck, 1989—; mem. Curriculum Adv. Council, Teaneck, 1988—. Home: 608 Wyndham Rd Teaneck NJ 07666

WIKE, D. ELAINE, business executive; b. Ridgecrest, Calif., Sept. 26, 1954; d. Robert G. and Jimmie Mae (Sallee) Field; student U. Houston, 1975-77; m. Mike Wike, Oct. 14, 1978; children—Mike II, Angelina Elaine, William V., Danielle Elizabeth, Edward Lawrence. Legal sec. Morgan, Lewis & Bockius, Washington, 1977-78; legal asst. Alfred C. Schlosser & Co., Houston, 1972-77, 78-81, Jerry Sadler, atty., Houston, 1982-83; founder, owner DEW Profl. & Bus. Services, Houston, 1979—; office mgr. Law Offices Mike Wike, Houston, 1983—. Treas., Wilhelm Schole Parents Orgn., 1981-82; mem. Free, Inc.; vol. campaign worker, (Ron Paul for Congress and Reagan for Pres.), 1975, 76. Mem. Young Ams. for Freedom, Nat. Notary Assn., Nat. Assn. Female Execs., Am. Soc. Notaries, Nat. Paralegal Assn. Republican. Mem. Christian Ch. Office: 2421 S Wayside Dr Houston TX 77023

WIKE, DEJUANA DENIECE, executive secretary, business owner; b. Tyler, Tex., Nov. 4, 1960; d. Robert Burris Clay and DeJuana Jean (Wallace) Tackett; m. Stephen Jon Wike, Feb. 21, 1987. B in Music Edn., Lambuth Coll., 1981. Adminstrv. specialist comml. div., customer svc. rep. Union Planters Nat. Bank, Memphis, 1981-84; jr. programmer, analyst Union Planters Investment Bankers Corp., Memphis, 1984-88; dist. sec. Abbott Labs., North Chicago, Ill., 1988-89; loan adminstr. Enterprise Nat. Bank, 1989—; owner The Write Type, Memphis, 1988—. Recipient Good Citizens award DAR, 1978. Mem. NAFE, Memphis C. of C., Sigma Kappa (treas. Jackson, Tenn. chpt. 1980-81), Gamma Beta Phi (sec. Jackson, Tenn. chpt.

1980-81). Home: 1628 Whitewater Rd Memphis TN 38117 Office: The Write Type 1628 Whitewater Rd Memphis TN 38117

WIKER, NANCY EILEEN, educator, consultant; b. Lancaster, Pa., Dec. 29, 1949; d. Milton Brumbaugh and Anna Mae (Harnish) W.; (div. July 1987); children: Kristin Alanna Kellerman, Karolyn Andrea Kellerman. BS, Millersville (Pa.) U., 1971; MA, Trenton State Coll., 1974. Cert. elem. edn. Tchr. various grades and gifted/talented Bensalem (Pa.) Twp. Schs., 1971—; ednl. researcher Bensalem, 1989—; assoc. cons. Susan Kovalik Assocs., Village of Oak Creek, Ariz., 1989—; cons. Valley Profl. Tchrs. Assn., Bensalem, 1988—; ednl. cons. Nat. Pest Control Assn., 1989-90, Bensalem Acad., 1990; mgr., vocal instr. M.R. Prodns. Active variety club charities/camp. Mem. NEA, Pa. State Edn. Assn., Nat. Coun. Tchrs. Math., Nat. Coun. Tchrs. Sci., Assn. Supervision and Curriculum Devel., Am. Geol. Inst., Phi Delta Kappa. Democrat. Jewish. Home: 5107 Lighthouse Ln Bensalem PA 19020 Office: Bensalem Twp Schs 3100 Donallen Dr Bensalem PA 19020

WIKSTROM, LORETTA WERMERSKIRCHEN, artist; b. Willow River, Minn., Mar. 2, 1938; d. Jacob Joseph and Anna Bertha (Doege) Wermerskirchen; m. Donovan Carl Wikstrom, Aug. 16, 1958; children: Bradley Donovan, Kendra Kay, Brock Karl. Student, St. Paul Sch. of Art, 1956-57, U. Minn., 1957-58, Honolulu Acad. of Art, 1963-66, Dayton Art Inst., 1985-87. Exhibited in group shows Sinclair Coll., 1985, Arts Venture, 1985; one woman shows Beavercreek Library, 1986, City of Englewood, 1986. Vol. artist Boy Scouts Am., Charleston, S.C. and Minn., 1967-74; vol. artist, tchr. Girl Scouts Am., O'Fallon, Ill., 1975-76; vol. art judge pub. elem., jr. and sr. high schs., Charleston and Mascoutah, Ill., 1969-78, Ill. State Hist. Library, Belleville, Ill., 1979, Belbrook (Ohio) High Sch., 1988, 89. Recipient 2d place and hon. mention Nat. Nature and Wildfowl Show, 1987, hon. mention Wyoming (Ohio) Pub. Arts Commn. show, 1987. Mem. Guild S.C. Artists, Charleston Artists Guild, Minn. Artists Assn., Gateway East Artists Guild, St. Louis Artists Guild, Beavercreek Creative Artists Assn. (sec. 1987—, v.p. 1988-90), Dayton Soc. Painters and Sculptors. Home: 45 Hawthorne Glen Trail Beavercreek OH 45440

WILBUR, GEORGIA DELORES See WOODRUFF, GEORGIA DELORES

WILBUR, PATRICIA LYNN, entrepreneur; b. Paterson, N.J., Feb. 28, 1962; d. David Bailey and Marlene (Clark) W. Student, Trinity Coll., 1980; AS, Manchester Community Coll., 1986; BS, Charter Oak Coll., 1988. Enrolled agt. Alan W. Gates & Co., Inc., Manchester, Conn., 1986—; temporary acct. Accountemps, Hartford, Conn., 1986, 1989; freelance enrolled agt. Manchester, 1989—. Editor lit. mag. Calliope, 1976-78. comm. mem. Manchester Community Coll. - Bus. Careers Div., 1987; vol. speaker Conn. Guild of Craftsmen, 1988; mem. Nat. Rifle Assn. Recipient: Tiffany award, Manpower Inc., Hartford, 1986. Mem. NAFE, Nat. Assn. of Enrolled Agents, Conn. Soc. of Enrolled Agents, Nat. Assn. of Tax Practitioners, Conn. Computer Soc., Alpha Beta Gamma. Home: 70 Weaver Rd Manchester CT 06040

WILBURN, MARY NELSON, lawyer, writer; b. Balt., Feb. 18, 1932; d. David Alfred and Phoebe Blanche (Novotny) Nelson; m. Adolph Yarbrough Wilburn, Mar. 5, 1957; children: Adolph II, Jason David. AB cum laude, Howard U., 1952; MA, U. Wis., 1955, JD, 1975n: Adolph II, Jason David. Bar: Wis. 1975, U.S. Supreme Ct 1981. Lectr. U. Wis. Law Sch., 1975-77, 83, 84, 85; atty. adv. Bur. Prisons, Dept. Justice, 1977-82; chmn. Wis. State Parole Bd., Madison, 1986-87; gen. counsel D.C. Bd. Parole, 1987-89; commr. The Commn. to Restructure the Interstate Compact, 1988-89; consulting site mgr. Bethune Mus.-Archives, Inc., 1990—; mem. Wis. Sentencing Commn., 1986-87. Mem. Madison Met. Sch. Dist. Bd. Edn., 1975-77; assoc. mem. Schutz Am. Sch. Bd., Alexandria, Egypt, 1983-85; commr. Nat. Coun. of Negro Women Commn. on Edn., 1986—. Mem Internat. Assn. Paroling Authorities (exec. v.p. 1987-89), Nat. Assn. Black Women Attorneys (pres. Rolark chpt. 1989—), Howard U. Alumni Assn., Alpha Kappa Alpha. Club: Nat. Lawyers (Washington). Contbr. to Cairo Today, 1983-84. Office: Bethune Mum Archives Inc 1318 Vermont Ave NW Washington DC 20005

WILCHER, SHIRLEY J., lawyer; b. Erie, Pa., July 28, 1951; d. James S. Wilcher and Jeanne (Evans) Cheatham. AB cum laude, Mt. Holyoke Coll., 1973; MA, New Sch. Social Research, 1976; JD, Harvard U., 1979. Bar: N.Y. 1980. Assoc. Proskauer Rose Goetz and Mendelsohn, N.Y.C., 1979-80; staff atty. Nat. Women's Law Ctr., Washington, 1980-85; assoc. counsel Com. on Edn. and Labor U.S. Ho. Reps., Washington, 1985-90; dir. state rels., counsel Nat. Assn. Ind. Colls. and Univs., Washington, 1990—. Editor Harvard U. Civil Rights/Civil Liberties Law Rev., 1978-79; contbr. articles to profl. jours. Nat. bd. dirs. Nat. Polit. Congress of Black Women, Washington, 1985-87; convenor Black Women's Roundtable on Voter Participation, Washington, 1984-85. Mem. ABA, Nat. Bar Assn., Nat. Conf. Black Lawyers (local bd. dirs. 1980-87, nat. bd. dirs. 1986-87). Democrat. Buddhist. Office: Nat Assn Ind Colls and Univs 122 C St NW Washington DC 20001

WILCOX, COLLEEN BRIDGET, special education administrator; b. Rock Island, Ill., July 24, 1949; d. Wayne Eugene and Virginia Mae (Dewrose) W. BS, U. Iowa, 1971; MS, U. Ariz., 1974; PhD U. So. Calif., 1986; ednl. adminstrn. credential U. So. Calif. Asst. dir. parks and recreation City of Moline (Ill.), 1969-74; dir. speech pathology Instn. Guatemalteca Sequiridad, Peace Corps., Guatemala City, 1971-72; speech and lang. specialist Tucson Sch. Dist., 1974-75; aphasia tchr. specialist, itinerant specialist L.A. County Schs., 1975-77; program specialist in severe lang. disorder/aphasia L.A. County Supt. Schs., 1977-79, program adminstr./communication disorders, 1979-83, mem. budget standards com. 1979-82; mem. credential adv. bd., communications dept. Calif. State U., L.A., 1978, asst. prof., 1977-83, chmn. sabbatical rev. com.; dir. spl. edn. Tucson Unified Sch. Dist., 1983-88; supt. No. Suburban Spl. Edn. Dist., Highland Park, Ill., 1988—; art dir. the Great Stampede, 1981-83; Bd. dirs. dept. developmental disabilities Assn. Retarded Citizens; bd. dirs. Tuscon Chpt. Diabetes Assn., 1988—, Pima Coun. on Developmental Disabilities; chmn. spl. edn. adv. coun. Pima Coll. Spl. Edn.; co-chair Mayor's Com. Constitution Celebration, 1986. Recipient Harriett Rutherford Johnstown award Pi Beta Phi, 1971; Barnes Drill award U. Iowa, 1971; lic. speech pathologist, cert. tchr. speech and hearing therapy, severely handicapped credential, learning handicapped credential, Calif.; cert. speech and lang. therapist, Ariz. Mem. Calif. Speech and Hearing Assn. (exec. coun. 1986—), Am. Speech and Hearing Assn. (cert. clin. competence in speech pathology, conv. com. 1979, com. on manpower 1982-83, Ariz. legis. councilor 1986—), Jr. League of Evanston (bd. dirs. 1988-90), Coun. Exceptional Children (legis. com.), Pi Beta Phi Alumnae, Phi Delta Kappa. Co-author, illustrator: Let's Share, 1983, Super Soup, 1986, Understanding and Preventing AIDS, 1987.

WILCOX, GAIL PATRICIA WATERS, military officer; b. Antigo, Wis., Nov. 27, 1957; d. Joe Edward and Joan Eva (Carpenter) Waters; m. Jack Franklyn Wilcox Jr., Jan. 6, 1990. BBA, U. Montevallo, 1980; postgrad., U. Okla., 1986—. Commd. 2d lt. USAF, 1980, advanced through grades to capt., 1984; chief mgmt. engring. br. RAF Upper Heyford, Eng., 1980-81, comdr., 1981-82; organl. action officer Hdqtrs. Strategic Air Commd., Offult AFB, Nebr., 1982-83, chief manpower programmer, 1984-86; edn. industry student Honeywell Inc., USAF Inst. Tech., Clearwater, Fla., 1986-87; comdr. Mgmt. Engring. Squadron, Goodfellow AFB, Tex., 1987-89; chief Support Br., Lowry AFB, Colo., 1989—. Vol. Spl. Olympics, Omaha, 1984-86, Pinellas County Vol. Assn., Clearwater, 1987, Pub. Schs. San Angelo, Tex., 1988. Mem. NAFE, Inst. Indsl. Engrs., Air Force Assn., Co. Grade Officer's Assn. (rep. 1982—), Am. Soc. Mil. Comptrollers, Jaycees (dir. 1989). Republican. Baptist.

WILCOX, JEAN MARIE, accountant; b. Morristown, N.J., Sept. 10, 1958; d. Earl F. and Patricia A. (O'Brien) W. AA in Acctg., County Coll. of Morris, 1978; BSBA, Coll. of St. Elizabeth, Convent Station, N.J., 1986. Sec. to payroll supr. Monroe Calculator, Morris Plains, N.J., 1979-80; clk. typist Stewart Title, Morris Plains, 1980-81; with BASF Corp., Parsippany, N.J., 1981—; credit rep. chems. div. BASF Corp., Parsippany, 1986-88, sr. property acct. chems. div., 1988—. Co-leader folk group Sacred Heart Ch., Dover, N.J., 1981, adult leader youth group, 1982, eucharistic minister, 1986; spl. dep. registrar Boro Mountain Lakes, N.J., 1976. Named one of Outstanding Young Women in Am., U.S. Jaycees, 1985. Mem. Cath. Daughters Am. (treas. Dover chpt. 1987-89, regent 1989—). Republican. Home: 169 Oram Dr Dover NJ 07801 Office: BASF Corp 100 Cherry Hill Rd Parsippany NJ 07054

WILCOX, JEANNE BURDEN, publishing executive; b. Lancaster, Calif., Jan. 23, 1948; d. Lewis Arthur and Roma (Mintun) Burden; m. Peter Gavin Wilcox, Oct. 4, 1979; 1 child, Leslie Denise. BA, Calif. State U., 1971. Pub. relations asst. N.Y. Heart Assn., N.Y.C., 1973-75; editor Marcel Dekker, Inc., N.Y.C., 1975-77; publs. specialist N.Y. Assn. for the Blind (Lighthouse), N.Y.C., 1977-79; mgr. editorial svcs. Boys Clubs of Am., N.Y.C., 1979-81, editor Connections Mag., 1979-85; pres. Jeanne Wilcox Assocs., N.Y.C., 1981-89; sr. editor Prodigy Svcs., Inc., White Plains, N.Y., 1989—; proposal writer Statue of Liberty-Ellis Island Found., N.Y.C., 1985-86, Nat. Soc. Prevent Blindness, N.Y.C., 1986, U.S. com. for UNICEF, 1988; legal def. and ednl. fund NAACP, 1987-88; corp. history writer Girl Scouts of U.S., N.Y.C., 1986; presentations writer March of Dimes Birth Defects Found., White Plains, 1986-87; asst. adj. prof. CUNY, Bronx, 1987-88. Editor Prodigy Services Co., White Plains, N.Y., 1988. Chmn., co-founder W 26th St. Block Assn., N.Y.C., 1986—. Mem. N.Y. Women in Communications (membership com. 1983-85). Home: 130 W 26th St New York NY 10001 Office: Prodigy Svcs Inc 445 Hamilton Ave White Plains NY 10601

WILCOX, LYNN E., psychology educator; b. Huntsville, Ala., Sept. 4, 1935; d. William Francis and Anna Mae (Linthicum) Esslinger; 1 child, Gregory C. Haun. BS cum laude, Southwest Mo. State U., 1959; MEd, U. Mo., 1961, PhD, 1968; postgrad., U. Catolica, Quito, Ecuador, 1976-78, MTO Shahmagnsoudi, Foster City. Calif., 1984—. Cert. sch. counselor and sch. psychologist, Calif.; lic. marriage, family and child counselor, Calif. Tchr. high sch. Springfield, Mo., 1958-60; grad., rsch. asst. U. Mo., Columbia, 1960-64; counselor Pub. Schs., Smyrna, Ga., 1965-67; asst. prof. Ga. State U., Atlanta, 1968-69; prof. edn., dept. chmn., coord. Calif. State U., Sacramento, 1969—, dept. chair, 1973-75, counselor, edn. coord., 1986-88, mem. women's studies bd., 1972; pvt. practice Sacramento, 1970—; cons. Wayfinders, Inc., Sacramento, 1986—. Pres. Wayfinders Inc., Sacramento, 1986—; chmn. Am. Personnel & Guidance Assn. Com. for Women, 1972-74; bd. dirs. Community Interaction Program, Sacramento, 1982; prof. adv. com. Suicide Prevention Service, Sacramento, 1970-72; rep. Sacramento Community Commn. for Women, 1971-73. Fellow Gregory 1962, Danforth 1975; recipient Profl. Promise award Calif. State U., Sacramento, 1986, Meritorious Performance award, 1988. Mem. Am. Psychol. Assn., Am. Assn. for Counseling and Devel., Faculty Women's Assn. (v.p. 1971-73, pres. 1973-74), Western Psychol. Assn., Assn. for Counselor Edn. and Supervision, Middle Eastern Studies Assn., Western Assn. for Counselor Edn. and Supervision. Republican. Muslim. Office: Calif State U Dept Counselor Edn 6000 J St Sacramento CA 95819 Office: Wayfinders Inc 455 University Ave Ste 100 Sacramento CA 95825

WILCOX, MAUD, editor; b. N.Y.C., Feb. 14, 1923; d. Thor Fredrik and Gerda (Ysberg) Eckert; m. Edward T. Wilcox, Feb. 9, 1944; children: Thor (dec.), Bruce, Eric, Karen. A.B. summa cum laude, Smith Coll., 1944; A.M., Harvard U., 1945. Teaching fellow Harvard U., 1945-46, 48-51; instr. English Smith Coll., Northampton, Mass., 1947-48, Wellesley Coll., Mass., 1951-52; exec. editor Harvard U. Press, 1958-66, humanities editor, 1966-73, editor-in-chief, 1973-89, ret.; freelance editorial cons. Cambridge, 1989—; cons., panelist NEH, Washington, 1974-76, 82-84. Mem. Assn. Am. Univ. Presses (chmn. com. admissions and standards 1976-77, v.p. 1978-79), MLA (com. scholarly edits. 1982-86), Phi Beta Kappa. Home and Office: 63 Francis Ave Cambridge MA 02138

WILCOXEN, JOAN HEEREN, fitness company executive; b. Flushing, N.Y., May 30, 1948; d. Paul Arnold and Helena Catherina (Laskowski) Heeren; m. Eddie Dean Wilcoxen, Dec. 31, 1981. BA, Long Island U., 1971. Cert. referee. Real estate broker Heeren Agy., Riverhead, N.Y., 1970-72; 2d v.p. Levitt House, Inc., Medford, N.Y., 1972-78; radio broadcaster Sta. KWHW Radio, Altus, Okla., 1979-84; exec. dir. Ironworks Family Gym, Altus, 1984—; lectr. martial arts; lectr. Shortgrass Arts and Humanities Coun., Altus, 1988—. Vol. United Way of Jackson County, Altus, 1989-90; fundraiser Muscular Dystrophy Assn., Wichita Falls, Tex., 1987—; mem. Shortgrass Arts and Humanities Coun., 1988-89, Nat. Bd. Realtors, 1978-79; state coord., co-chair Sooner State Games Karate, Oklahoma City, 1989. Named for civic leadership Okla. State U. Coop. Extension Svc., Altus, 1988, S.W. Bell Tel. Co., Altus, 1989, Rotary Club and March of Dimes, Altus, 1989, Jackson County Free Fair, Altus, 1988, 89; Okla. State AAU karate champion, 1990, black belt. Mem. Altus C. of. C. (ambassador 1989-90), Am. Bus. Women's Assn., Biz-Tips Women's Assn. (v.p. 1989, 90), AAUW (v.p. Altus chpt. 1990), Am. Independent Karate Instrs. Assn. (instr. Christiansburg, Va. chpt. 1985—). Home: 712 E Walker Altus OK 73521 Office: Ironworks Family Gym 711 E Sutherland Altus OK 73521

WILCOXEN, SHIRLEY, association executive; b. Springfield, Ill., Jan. 12, 1937; d. Charles Raymond Sr. and Ada Blanche (Wadkins) Register; m. Harry T. Wilcoxen, Aug. 18, 1979; children: Debi, Dane, Kelly, Krystie. Student, Lincoln Land Community Coll. Exec. dir. S/M Contractors Assn., Springfield; exec. dir. w. cen. Ill. Plumbing and Pipe Contractors Assn., Springfield; exec. dir, Ill. SMACNA, Springfield. Mem. IAPHCC, NAPHCC, ISAE (past com. chmn.). Home: PO Box 2007 Springfield IL 62705

WILD, HEIDI KARIN, oil company executive; b. Detroit, July 28, 1948; d. Lauren Daggett and Eleanor Stephanie (Churchman) Wild; m. Francis Michael Robinson, Oct. 2, 1982. BS, Western Mich. U., 1971; MBA, U. Hawaii, 1985. Tchr. secondary edn. St. Clair Sch. System, St. Clair Shores, Mich., 1971-74; personnel asst. Union Camp Corp., Kalamazoo, 1974-76; receptionist, typist Pacific Resources Inc., Honolulu, 1976-77, sec., 1977-78, adminstrv. asst., 1978, mktg. and supply analyst, 1978-80, coord. light product supply and exch., 1980-81, mgr. product supply, 1981-83, dir. product supply, 1983-85, gen. mgr. light products, 1985, gen. mgr. supply and distbn. 1985-86, mgr. petroleum coordination, 1986-87, acting v.p. supply and distbn., 1987-88, regional mgr. Hawaii supply, 1988—; bd. dirs. PRI Fed. Credit Union. Mem. adv. bd. Coll. Bus. U. Hawaii. Mem. U. Hawaii MBA Alumni Group (pres. bd. dirs. 1988—), Hawaii Soc. Corp. Planners, Navy League, U. Hawaii Alumni Assn. (1st v.p., bd. dirs. 1988—), Western Mich. U. Alumni Assn., Sierra Club, Beta Gamma Sigma. Clubs: Plaza, PRI Golf. Avocations: golf, traveling. Office: Pacific Resources Inc 733 Bishop St Honolulu HI 96813

WILDE, PATRICIA, artistic director; b. Ottawa, Ont., Can., July 16, 1928; m. George Bardyguine; children: Anya, Youri. Dancer Am. Concert Ballet, Marquis de Cuevas Ballet Internat., 1944-45, Ballet Russe de Monte Carlo, 1945-49, Roland Petit's Ballet Paris, Met. Ballet Britain, 1949-50; prin. ballerina N.Y.C. Ballet, 1950-65; dir. Harkness Sch. Ballet, 1965-67; ballet mistress, tchr. Am. Ballet Theatre, 1969-77; dir. Am. Ballet Theatre Sch., 1977-82; artistic dir. Pitts. Ballet Theatre, 1982—; tchr. Am. Ballet Theatre, 1950-65; tchr. Joffrey scholarship program N.Y.C. Ballet, 1968-69; established Sch. of Grand Theatre of Geneva, 1968-69; adjudicator Regional Ballet in Am. S.E. and S.W., 1969-82; guest tchr. various ballet cos. and colls.; trustee Dance U.S.A.; panelist Nat. Choreographic Project. Office: Pitts Ballet Theatre 2900 Liberty Ave Pittsburgh PA 15201

WILDER, ELEANOR MARIE (NORA ROBERTS WILDER), writer; b. Washington, Oct. 10, 1950; d. Bernard Edward Robertson and Eleanor Margaret Harris; m. Ronald Eugene Aufdem-Brinke, Aug. 17, 1968 (div. 1985); children: Daniel, Jason; m. Bruce Allen Wilder, July 6, 1985. Grad. high sch., Silver Spring, Md. Legal sec. Wheeler & Korpec, Silver Spring, 1966-68; sec. R&R Lighting, Silver Spring, 1972-75; writer, 1979—. Author: The Heart's Victory, 1982, Golden Medallion, 1982-89, This Magic Moment, 1983, Untamed, 1983, A Matter of Choice, 1984, MacGregor Clan Series, 1985, Hot Ice, 1987, Brazen Virtue, 1988, O'Hurley Series, 1988, Sweet Revenge, 1989. First inductee Romance Writers of Am. Hall of Fame, 1986; recipient Waldenbooks award, 1985, 86, 88. Mem. Washington Romance Writers, Romance Writers Am., Writers' Guild. Democrat. Roman Catholic. Avocations: dancing, reading, films.

WILDER, MELISSA ANN, dental hygienist; b. Middlesboro, Ky., Aug. 24, 1963; d. James Edward and Virginia Louise (England) Evans; m. James Anthony Wilder, June 12, 1982; children: Lindsey Marie, Amanda Hope. AB in Applied Sci., U. Ky., Hazard, 1983. Cert. dental hygienist, Ky., Tenn. Dental hygienist Dr. C. Mark Russell, Harrogate, Tenn., 1987—; cons. in field. Named Female Alumni of Yr. Middlesboro High Sch., 1989. Mem. Southeast Ky. Dental Hygienist Assn. (pres. 1984-86). Republican. Baptist. Home: 204 Greenwood Rd PO Box 2267 Middlesboro KY 40965 Office: Dr C Mark Russell DDS Beech St Harrogate TN 37752

WILDER, NORA ROBERTS See WILDER, ELEANOR MARIE

WILDERMUTH, JO VOISARD, publishing company executive; b. Eng., Oct. 17, 1951; came to U.S., 1953; d. James Laverne and Thelma Isobel Joyce (Bradfield) Voisard; m. Rickey Lynn Wildermuth, Aug. 16, 1975; children: Stephanie, Alicia, Richard. AS, Edison State Coll., 1982. Cert. prodn. and inventory mgr. Machinist Copeland Corp., Sidney, Ohio, 1974-78; timekeeper Baumfolder Corp., Sidney, 1978-80; engring. clk. Hartzell Fan Co., Piqua, Ohio, 1980-84; cost acct. Broadway Cos., Inc., Dayton, Ohio, 1984-86; sr. indsl. cons. Antioch Pub. Co., Yellow Springs, Ohio, 1986—; instr. Edison State Coll., Piqua, 1987—; cons. Galsco Inc., Springfield, Ohio, 1987-88. Active Ohio United Way. Mem. NAFE, Internat. Platform Assn., Am. Bus. Women's Assn. (pres. Dayton chpt. 1987-88, Woman of Yr. 1988), Am. Prodn. and Inventory Control Soc. (adminstrv. asst. 1987—). Republican. Home: PO Box 661 Sidney OH 45365 Office: Cincom Systems Inc 2850 Presidential Dr Fairborn OH 45324

WILDING, DIANE, marketing and financial executive, computer systems engineer; b. Chicago Heights, Ill., Nov. 7, 1942; d. Michael Edward and Katherine Surian; m. Manfred Georg Wilding, May 7, 1975 (div. 1980). BSBA in Acctg. magna cum laude, No. Ill. U., 1963; postgrad., U. Chgo., 1972-74; Cert. German Lang., Goethe Inst., Rothenburg, Fed. Republic Germany, 1984. Lic. cosmetologist. Systems engr. IBM Corp., Chgo., 1963-68; data processing mgr. Am. Res. Corp., Chgo., 1969-72; system rsch. and devel. project mgr. Continental Bank, Chgo., 1972-75; fin. industry mktg. rep. IBM Can., Ltd., Toronto, Ont., 1976-79; regional telecommunications mktg. exec. Control Data Corp., Atlanta, 1980-84; v.p. fin. The Plant Plant, Atlanta, 1985—; pioneer installer on-line Automatic Teller Machines, Pos Equipment. Author: The Canadian Payment System: An International Perspective, 1977. Mem. Chgo. Coun. on Fgn. Rels.; bd. dirs. Easter House Adoption Agy., Chgo., 1974-76. Mem. Internat. Brass Soc., Goethe Inst., Mensa. Clubs: Ponte Verde (Fla.); Royal Ont. Yacht, Libertyville Racquet. Home: PO Box 95189 Atlanta GA 30347

WILE, JOAN, composer, lyricist, singer; b. Rochester, N.Y., July 17, 1931; d. Louis and Janet Louise (Wile) Meltzer; children: Ron Wasserman, Diana Wasserman McCloskey. BA, U. Chgo., 1952. Freelance composer, lyricist, musical book writer. Rec. artist Vanguard Records, 1954; singer Storyville, 1954, The Crystal Palace, 1957; mem. vocal-revue act The Neighbors performances include The Village Vanguard, Le Ruban Bleu, The Bon Soir and The Living Room ; singer, lyricist feature film The Happy Hooker, 1974; singer radio and TV jingles, movie sound tracks, supper clubs, hotels, TV music spls. and variety shows; lyricist, composer mus. Tobacco Road, 1974, Seven Ages of Woman, 1987 (named most promising new musical); writer, producer When They Turned on the Tap at the Watergate, The Truth Come Pourin' Out; lyricist songs for Romper Room, 1983; lyricist, composer, writer People is People, 1983; lyricist, composer script for children's albums for Golden and Peter Pan Records, others; lyricist, composer material in Julius Monk's Upstairs at the Downstairs, 1958; lyricist, composer, performer Nancy's Economic Plann, 1980; lyricist, composer Mothers and Daughters, 1984; lyricist, composer, author The Symposium, 1987; lyricist, composer From There to Here, 1987; writer Rhyme, Women and Song. Organizer Women in Def. Eleanor Roosevelt, N.Y.C., 1989—. Runner-up Am. Song Festival, 1976. Mem. Dramatists Guild, SAG, Theatre Artists Workshop, AFTRA, ASCAP (Popular award 1970-88). Home and Office: 484 W 43 Apt 22B New York NY 10036

WILEN, JUDITH BETH, psychologist, researcher, educator; b. Balt., Mar. 31, 1954; d. Stanley Herbert and Lillian (Scheinker) W.; m. Steven Roy Schloss, May 24, 1987; 1 child, Molly Janine. BA with honors, Emory U., 1976; MA, U. Chgo., 1979, PhD, 1986. Lic. psychologist, Ill. Rsch. asst. family life study U. Chgo., 1977-79; rsch. asst. early adolescence project Michael Reese Hosp., Chgo., 1979-86; psychologist adolescent program Northwestern Meml. Hosp., Chgo., 1983-87, psychologist Inst. of Psychiatry, 1987—, instr. in clin. psychiatry and behavioral scis., 1986—; pvt. practice Chgo., 1987—; coord. postdoctoral clin. rsch. tng. program in adolescence Northwestern Meml. Hosp., Chgo.; rsch. assoc. lab. for the study of adolescence Michael Reese Hosp., 1982-84, cons. Ctr. for Stress Edn., Evanston, Ill., 1986-88. NIH grantee U. Chgo., 1977-78, scholar, 1978-79; Michael Reese Hosp. fellow, 1980-83. Mem. Am. Psychol. Assn., Ill. Psychol. Assn., Chgo. Assn. Psychoanalytic Psychotherapy, Phi Beta Kappa, Pi Delta Epsilon, Psi Chi. Home: 2454 N Burling St Chicago IL 60614 Office: 333 E Ontario St Ste 305-B Chicago IL 60611

WILENSKY, GAIL ROGGIN, economist; b. Detroit, June 14, 1943; d. Albert Alan and Sophia (Blitz) Roggin; AB with honors, U. Mich., 1964, MA in Econs., 1965, PhD in Econs., 1968; m. Robert Joel Wilensky, Aug. 4, 1963; children: Peter Benjamin, Sara Elizabeth. Economist, President's Commn. on Income Maintenance Programs, exec. dir. Md. Council of Econ. Advs., 1969-71; sr. researcher Urban Inst., Washington, 1971-73; assoc. research scientist, public policy and public health U. Mich., Ann Arbor 1973-75, vis. asst. prof. econs., 1973-75; sr. research mgr. Nat. Center for Health Services Research, Hyattsville, Md., 1975-83; v.p. div. health affairs Project HOPE, Millwood, Va., 1983-90; adminstr. Health Care Fin. Adminstrn., Washington, 1990—; assoc. profl. lectr. George Washington U., 1976-78. Vol. Am. Heart Assn., 1980-85; commr. Physician Payment Rev. Commn., 1989-90; mem. health adv. com. Compt. Gen. of U.S., 1987-90. Flinn Found. disting. scholar, 1985; recipient Dean Conley award Am. Coll. Healthcare Execs, 1989. Mem. Am. Econ. Assn. (women's com. 1982-84), Fedn. Orgns. of Profl. Women (chmn. econ. task force 1981-83), Am. Statis. Assn., Nat. Tax Assn., Washington Women Economists, Assn. Health Svcs. Rsch. (dir. 1984-87), Found. Health Svcs. Rsch. (bd. dirs. 1987-90), Inst. Medicine, NAS, U. Mich. Alumnae Coun. Contbr. articles in field to profl. jours.; mem. internat. adv. bd. policy scis., 1978-84. Home: 2807 Battery Pl NW Washington DC 20016

WILEY, BONNIE JEAN, journalism educator; b. Portland, Oreg.; d. Myron Eugene and Bonnie Jean (Galliher) W. BA, U. Wash., 1948; MS, Columbia U., 1957; PhD, So. Ill. U., 1965. Mng. editor Yakima (Wash.) Morning Herald; reporter, photographer Portland Oregonian; feature writer Seattle Times; war correspondent PTO AP; western feature editor AP, San Francisco; reporter Yakima Daily Republic; journalism tchr. U. Wash., Seattle, Cen. Wash. U., Ellensburg, U. Hawaii, Honolulu; Adminstr. Am. Samoa Coll., Pago Pago; news features advisor Xinhua News Agy., Beijing. Mem. Women in Communications (Hawaii Headliner award 1985, Nat. Headliner award 1990), Theta Sigma Phi. Home: 2003 Kalia Rd 4-I Honolulu HI 96815

WILEY, HANNAH CHRISTINE, dance educator, choreographer; b. Spokane, Wash., Aug. 21, 1950; d. Owen and Martha M. (Spille) W. BA, U. Wash., 1973; MA, NYU, 1981. Instr. in dance Cornish Inst. Allied Arts, Seattle, 1973-75; dancer, tchr. ballet Folk Co., Moscow, Idaho, 1975-76; choreographer Empty Space Theatre, Seattle, 1975-77; asst. prof. dance Mt. Holyoke Coll., South Hadley, Mass., 1977-82, assoc. prof., 1982—; vis. prof. dance U. Wash., Seattle, summers 1980-86, assoc. prof., 1982-87, prof., chair of dance, 1987—; artist in resident U. Idaho, Moscow, 1975-76; chairperson Five Coll. Dance Dept., Western Mass., 1982-87; coordinator New Eng. Coll. dance Festival, Amherst, Mass., 1983-84. Choreographer numerous original ballets, 1977—; manuscript reviewer Schirmer Books, N.Y.C., 1983. Mem. Council on Arts and Humanities, South Hadley, 1981-83. Recipient Research Materials award Capezio Ballet Markers and Ballet Internat., 1982; faculty grantee Mt. Holyoke Coll., 1978, 82, 85, faculty fellow, 1980; bd. dirs. Allegro! Performance Support Svcs. Mem. Am. Coll. Dance Festival Assn. (dir. 1983-84), Congress on Research in Dance. Democrat. Unitarian. Office: U Wash Meany Hall AB-10 Seattle WA 98195

WILEY, MARQUITA TRENIER, mortgage company executive; b. Mobile, Ala., Dec. 8, 1950; d. Mark Jack and Jacqueline (Alexander) Trenier; m.

Gerald Edward Wiley, June 13, 1981; children: Raymond, Johanna. BS in Math., Marygrove Coll., Detroit, 1972; MBA, Washington U., St. Louis, 1975. Programmmer, analyst GM, Detroit, 1972-74; systems engr. IBM, St. Louis, 1974-76, mktg. rep., 1976-79; mgr. systems devel. Citicorp, St. Louis, 1979-84; staff v.p. Citicorp Person To Person, Inc., St. Louis, 1984-87; v.p. Citicorp Mortgage, Inc., St. Louis, 1987—; pres. Trenier Co., Belleville, Ill., 1988—. Mem. St. Louis Arts and Humanities Commn., 1978-83; bd. dirs. YWCA Met. St. Louis, 1978-83, Jack and Jill Am. Found., Chattanooga, 1989—; regional dir. cen. region Jack and Jill Am., Inc., 1989—. Democrat. Home: 13 Town Hall Estates Ln Belleville IL 62223 Office: Citicorp Mortgage Inc 15851 Clayton Rd Ballwin MO 63011

WILEY, ROBIN GAIL, association executive; b. Glendale, Calif., Jan. 20, 1963; d. Robert Shade and Bennita June (Russell) S. BA, Goucher Coll., 1985; MPA, Syracuse U., 1987. Presdl. mgmt. intern U.S. Dept. Health and Human Svcs., Washington, 1987-89; govt. rels. exec. Nat. Elec. Mfrs. Assn., Washington, 1988—. Editor Diagnostic Imaging and Therapy Systems Report, 1989. Mem. Women in Govt. Rels. Democrat. Methodist. Office: Nat Elec Mfrs Assn 2101 L St NW Ste 300 Washington DC 20037

WILGENBUSCH, NANCY, college administrator. B magna cum laude, Cath. U.; M, Tex. Women's U.; PhD in Edn., U. Nebr. Dean adult and continuing education then v.p. mktg. and pub. relations Coll. of St. Mary, Omaha, 1975-84; pres. Marylhurst (Oreg.) Coll., 1984—; bd. dirs. PacifiCorp, Portland, Oreg., Mutual of Omaha Fund Mgmt. Co. Commr. Port of Portland; gov's adv. com. on info. systems; bd. dirs. Portland Jr. Achievement. Fellow Am. Leadership forum (founder Oreg. chpt., exec. bd.); mem. Oreg. Ind. Colls. Assn. (pres.), Portland C. of C. (bd. dirs.). Office: Marylhurst Coll Lifelong Learing Marylhurst OR 97036-0261*

WILGOCKI, THERESA ANN, human resource executive; b. Chgo., Aug. 27, 1965; d. Ronald Walter and Marilyn Ruth (Krase) W. BS, San Diego State U., 1989. Pers. adminstr. Guild Mortgage Co., San Diego. Vol. Easter Seals Soc. San Diego, 1988—, Am. Heart Assn., 1989—, Zool. Soc. San Diego, 1986—; coord. (ETC) mgmt. employee transp. San Diego Traffic Demand, 1989—. Mem. Pers. Mgmt. Assn. Roman Catholic. Office: Guild Mortgage Co 4180 Ruffin Rd San Diego CA 92123

WILGUS, JOAN ELIZABETH, retail company executive; b. N.Y.C., May 27, 1947; d. Alfonso Granada and Charlotte Fitzsimmons Cunningham; m. Gerald W. Wilgus, Dec. 1, 1989. BBA, Thomas Edison U., 1980. Ind. cons. in computers Washington, 1977-80; v.p. sales Ross Systems, N.Y.C., 1980-83; ind. cons. in computers N.Y.C., 1983-85; owner Nature's Touch, Bethany Beach and Lewes, Del., 1985—; bd. dirs. Del. Nat. Bank, Ocean View. Fashion writer Beachcomber mag. of Del. Mem. C. of C. (bd. dirs. 1987, 88). Home and Office: PO Box 80 Bethany Beach DE 19930

WILHELM, BRENDA LEA, financial executive; b. Tyrone, N.Y., Feb. 5, 1960; d. Richard Claud and Marjorie Ruth (Thomason) W. Student, Corning Community Coll., 1978-79; postgrad., Elmira Coll., 1988--. Sec. Cornell U., Ithaca, 1979; office mgr. County Highway Dept., Watkins Glen, N.Y., 1979-88; acct. Seneca Lodge, Inc., Watkins Glen, 1976--; tax cons. Murph's Bus. Services, Watkins Glen; ins., fin. planner David Ryan Agy., Watkins Glen, 1988-89; fin. planner Thomas A. Ketrick Inc., Elmira Heights, N.Y., 1989—. Tutor Literacy Vol. Am., Watkins Glen, 1988--. Mem. Bus. and Profl. Women (chmn. 1988), Nat. Assn. Female Execs., Ins. Women of the Fingerlakes, Eastern Star. Episcopalian. Office: Thomas A Ketrick Inc 130 College Ave Elmira Heights NY 14903

WILHELM, KATE (KATY GERTRUDE), author; b. Toledo, June 8, 1928; d. Jesse Thomas and Ann (McDowell) Meredith; m. Joseph B. Wilhelm, May 24, 1947 (div. 1962); children: Douglas, Richard; m. Damon Knight, Feb. 23, 1963; 1 child, Jonathan. Writer, 1956—; co-dir. Milford Sci. Fiction Writers Conf., 1963-76; lectr. Clarion Fantasy Workshop, Mich. State U., from 1968. Author: (novels) More Bitter Than Death, 1962, (with Theodore L. Thomas) The Clone, 1965, The Nevermore Affair, 1966, The Killer Thing, 1967, Let the Fire Fall, 1969, (with Theodore L. Thomas) The Year of the Cloud, 1970, Abyss: Two Novellas, 1971, Margaret and I, 1971, City of Cain, 1971, The Clewiston Test, 1976, Where Late the Sweet Birds Sang, 1976, Fault Lines, 1976, Somerset Dreams and Other Fictions, 1978, Jupiter Time, 1979, (with Damon Knight) Better Than One, 1980, A Sense of Shadow, 1981, Listen, Listen, 1981, Oh! Susannah, 1982, Welcome Chaos, 1983, Huysman's Pets, 1986, The Hamlet Trap, 1987, Crazy Time, 1988, Dark Door, 1988, Smart House, 1989, (multimedia space fantasy) Axoltl, U. Oreg. Art Mus., 1979, (radio play) The Hindenburg Effect, 1985; editor: Nebula Award Stories #9, 1974, Clarion SF, 1976; contbr. short stories to anthologies and periodicals. Mem. PEN, Sci. Fiction Writers Am., Authors Guild. Address: 1645 Horn Ln Eugene OR 97404*

WILKE MONTEMAYOR, JOANNE MARIE, patient care executive; b. Jerome, Ark., Sept. 10, 1941; d. Karl Nickolas and Anna Linda (Worgt) Wilke; m. Casimiro L. Montemayor, Oct. 8, 1978. BS in Nursing, U. Colo., 1965; M in Nursing, U. Washington, 1974. Patient care coord. Vesper Hospice, San Leandro, Calif., 1989—. With USNR, 1959-79. Mem. Am. Nurses Assn. Democrat. Methodist.

WILKENING, LAUREL LYNN, university official, planetary scientist; b. Richland, Wash., Nov. 23, 1944; d. Marvin Hubert and Ruby Alma (Barks) W.; m. Godfrey Theodore Sill, May 18, 1974. BA, Reed Coll., 1966; PhD, U. Calif., San Diego, 1970. Asst. prof. to assoc. prof. U. Ariz., Tucson, 1973-80, dir. Lunar and Planetary Lab., head planetary scis., 1981-83, vice provost, prof. planetary scis., 1983-85, v.p. rsch., dean Grad. Coll., 1985-88; div. scientist NASA Hdqrs., Washington, 1980; prof. geol scis., adj. prof. astronomy, provost U. Washington, Seattle, 1988—; vice chmn. Nat. Commn. on Space, Washington, 1984-86, Adv. Com. on the Future of U.S. Space programs, 1990—; co-chmn. primitive bodies mission study team NASA/European Space Agy., 1984-85; chmn. com. rendezvous sci. working group NASA, 1983-85; mem. panel on internat. cooperation and competition in space Congl. Office Tech. Assessment, 1982-83. Author: (monograph) Particle Track Studies and the Origin of Gas-Rich Meteorites, 1971; editor: Comets, 1982. U. Calif. Regents fellow, 1966-67; NASA trainee, 1967-70. Fellow Meteoritical Soc. (councilor 1976-80); mem. Am. Astron. Soc. (chmn. div. planetary scis. 1984-85), Am. Geophys. Union, AAAS, Internat. Astron. Union (orgn. com. 1979-82), Phi Beta Kappa. Democrat. Office: U Wash Office of Provost AH-20 Seattle WA 98195

WILKENS, JANE RAE, physician; b. Northfield, Minn., Dec. 9, 1952; d. Kenneth Gerhardt and Aurelia Marie (Zahn) W. BA, St. Olaf Coll., 1975; MD, U. Minn., 1979. Resident in family practice St. Paul Ramsey Med. Ctr., 1979-82; Staff St. Croix Valley Clinic, Stillwater, Minn., 1983—. Mem. Am. Acad. Family Physicians, Minn. Med. Assn. Office: St Croix Valley Clinic 921 S Greeley St Stillwater MN 55082

WILKERSON, JANICE SHIPP, secretary; b. Chattanooga, July 30, 1935; d. Alvin Campbell Shipp and Dorothy Lorraine (Wilbur) Duncan; m. Charles H. Wilkerson Jr., June 19, 1954 (div. Sept. 1978); children: Charles H. III, Sandra Wilkerson Osbourn, Richard Thomas. AS in Secretarial Procedures, Brevard Community Coll., Cocoa, Fla., 1981; BS in Profl. Mgmt., Nova U., 1986, postgrad., 1989—. Substitute tchr. Brevard County Bd. Pub. Instrn., Titusville, Fla., 1973-75; bookkeeper, teller 1st Nat. Bank of Merritt Island, Fla., 1975-77; typist Pan-Am. World Airways, Cape Canaveral, Fla., 1977; with Computer Scis. Corp., Kennedy Space Ctr., Fla., 1977-78, br. sec., 1978-82, dept. sec., 1982-83; sec. grade B Grumman Tech. Svcs., Kennedy Space Ctr., 1983-86, sec. grade A, 1986-88, adminstrv. assoc., 1988—; beauty cons. Mary Kay Cosmetics, Merritt Island, 1985-89. Mem. Nat. Mgmt. Assn. (sec. 1986-88, 90—, pres. 1988-89), AAUW, Brevard County Alumni Assn., Beta Sigma Phi. Republican. Episcopalian. Office: Grumman Tech Svcs 1250 Grumman Pl Titusville FL 32780

WILKERSON, LYNDA HAYES, social worker; b. Greensburg, Ky., Dec. 8, 1956; d. James Arthur and Alice (Coomer) Hayes; m. Ken M. Wilkerson II, Nov. 10, 1974; 1 child, Robin Reeves. AA, Lindsey Wilson Coll., Columbia, Ky., 1978; BSW, Spalding U., 1982; MSSW, U. Louisville, 1982; postgrad., Columbia Pacific U. Cert. clin. social worker, Ky. Adult activity instr. Lake Cumberland Clin. Svcs., Columbia, 1976-78, children's specialist, 1978-79, coord. consultation and edn., 1979-85, clinic dir., 1985%; cons. Aaron Med. Ctr., Columbia, 1985—, Jane Todd Hosp., Columbia, 1988; mem. Ky. Chem. Dependency Cert. Bd., 1986—. Author: Weight No More, 1984, Health Care, 1985. Chmn. Adair County Inter Agy. Coun., Columbia, 1979-86; founder, advisor Adair County Teens Who Care, 1980-82. Recipient Outstanding Adair Woman of Yr. award Columbia Jaycees, 1982, Martha Davis award Ky. Assn. Social Workers, 1985. Mem. AAUW (corr. sec. 1988-89). Democrat. Baptist. Office: Lake Cumberland Clin Svcs 808C Jamestown St Columbia KY 42728

WILKERSON, MARJORIE JOANN MADAR, insurance company executive; b. Spokane, Wash., Dec. 2, 1930; d. Joseph Robert and Margaret Muriel (McKee) Madar; m. Billy E. Wilkerson, Jan. 9, 1953; 1 child, Wesley James McEarl. Student U. Puget Sound, 1948; B.A., UCLA, 1949; postgrad. So. Meth. U., 1958. Mgmt. to agt. Travelers Ins. Cos., Houston and Dallas, 1952-63; sr. account agt. Allstate Ins. Cos., Tacoma, 1966—; cons in field; lectr. various colls. and univs. Author: Sex and Society, 1976. Editor publ. Chiropractic Edn., also newsletter. Pres., co-founder Pierce County Women's Polit. Caucus, Tacoma; editor: (newsletter) Millionaire Life Ins. Agts., Caucus State of Wash., Seattle; lobbiest Caucus and prior for ERA, Olympia, Wash.; citizen lobbiest Worker Right to Know, Olympia, 1984-85; spokesperson Community effort to protect zoning, Gig Harbor, Wash., 1980-84; bd. dirs., sec. Beaumont Art Mus., Tex., 1954-57; pres. Walnut Hill League, N. Dallas, 1957-65; established first Girl Scout Program in Beaumont Girl Scouts U.S., 1955; mem. citizen lobby on indoor air quality and toxic exposures, 1984—. Grantee activist to study women's new role in soc. Washington Commn. for Humanities, 1974-75. Office: 15 Oregon Ste 304 Tacoma WA 98409

WILKES, LAURIE K., manager of employment and employee relations; b. Kansas City, Mo., Jan. 5, 1955; d. John P., Jr. and Ann Sue (Taylor) Downs; m. Thomas G. Wilkes, July, 30, 1977; children: Thomas R., Zachary J. BSBA, Emporia (Kans.) State U., 1977. Employment clk. Trinity Luth. Hosp., Kansas City, 1977-79, public rels. asst., 1979-80; employment rep. St. Joseph's Hosp., Kansas City, 1980-81, compensation mgr., 1981-82; employment adminstr. Rose Med. Ctr., Denver, 1983-86; pers. dir. Humana Hosp. Mount View, Thornton, Colo., 1986-88; human rels. dir. Charter Hosp. of Aurora, Colo., 1988-90; human resources mgr. St. Anthony Healthcare Systems, Denver, 1990—. Mem. Colo. Hosp. Assn. for Human Resources Mgmt. (sec. 1987-89, pres. 1990), Denver Area Health Care Recruiters Assn. (sec. 1983-86, pres. 1990). Office: St Anthony Healthcare Systems 4231 W 16th Ave Denver CO 80204

WILKES, SHAR (JOAN CHARLENE WILKES), educator; b. Chgo., July 15, 1951; d. Marcus and hattie (Ehrich) Wexman; 1 child, McKinnon. Student, U. Okla., 1973, U. Wyo., 1975—. Rsch. dirs., exhibit designer Nicolaysen Art Mus.-Children's Ctr., Casper, Wyo., 1984-85; tchr. Natrona County Sch. Dist. 1, Casper, Wyo., 1974—. Author: Fantastic Phonies Food Factory. Democrat candidate, Wyo. State Legisl., 1986, 88; edn. chair United Way, Casper, 1988; chair person Very Spl. Arts Festival, 1988, March of Dimes, 1989; grants person Casper Symphony, 1990. Mem. NEA, Nat. Coun. Edn. Assn., Wyo. Edn. Assn., Natrona County Sch. Dist. #1 (pub. rels.), League Women Voters, Soroptimist (charter), Phi Delta Kappa (exec. bd. 1988-90), Delta Kappa Gamma. Home: 4313 Coffman Ct Casper WY 82604 Office: Natrona County Sch Dist #1 Paradise Valley Casper WY 82604

WILKEY, YVONNE WILLIAMS, travel agency owner, consultant; b. Waynesville, N.C., Aug. 26, 1950; d. Ebb Columbus and Ruby Lee (Cooper) Williams; m. Rick Conway, July 20, 1968; children: Richard Everette, Kimberly Caroline, Sarah Angela. Student, Tenn. Tech. U., 1973; grad., Inst. Cert. Travel Agts., Wellesly, Mass., 1987. Travel cons. Vacation Travel, Easley, S.C., 1980-82, Exec. Travel, Greenville, S.C., 1982-83; mgr. Daniel Travel, Anderson, S.C., 1983-84; v.p. Greer (S.C.) World Travel, 1984-85; pres. New Horizons Travel, Clemson, S.C., 1985—; instr. travel agt. program Tri-County Tech. Coll., 1988—; cons. and lectr. in field; owner Horizon Hill Hunter Jumper Horse Farm, 1988—; co-owner Wilkey Engring.; instr. travel and tourism Tri-County Tech. Coll., Pendleton, S.C. Mem. Profl. Women in Travel (pres. 1985-88), Am. Soc. Travel Agts., Assn. Retail Travel Agts., Cruise Lines Internat. Assn., Travel Agts. of the Carolinas, Clemson C. of C. (welcome back com. 1987), Assn. of Women Profls. (Clemson). Home: 302 Rock Creek Dr Clemson SC 29631 Office: New Horizons Travel 1103 Tiger Blvd Clemson SC 29631

WILKINS, ARLENE, social worker; b. Balt., Oct. 20, 1936; d. Joseph Martin and Alice Gertrude (Mickey) Martin Patterson; m. E.J. Wilkins, Jan. 15, 1963; children—Del, Deirdre, Justin, Patrick. B.A., Wilkes Coll., 1959; M.A., U. Pa., 1962. Social worker Children's Service Inc., Phila., 1960-62, Western Psychiat. Inst. and Clinic, Pitts., 1966-67, Bethesda United Presbyterian Ch., Pitts., 1967-70; clin. social worker Allegheny Gen. Hosp., Northview Heights Health Ctr., Pitts., 1967-86. Program chmn. St. Andrew United Presbyn. Ch., Sewickley, Pa., 1981-83. Mem. Nat. Assn. Social Workers, Clin. Social Workers. Republican. Home: 416 College Park Dr Corapolis PA 15108 Office: Allegheny Gen Hosp Social Service Dept 320 E North Ave Pittsburgh PA 15212

WILKINS, CAROLINE HANKE, consumer agency administrator, political worker; b. Corpus Christi, Tex., May 12, 1937; d. Louis Allen and Jean Guckian Hanke; m. B. Hughel Wilkins, 1957; 1 child, Brian Hughel. Student, Tex. Coll. Arts and Industries, 1956-57, Tex. Tech. U., 1957-58; BA, U. Tex., 1961; MA magna cum laude, U. Ams., 1964. Instr. history Oreg. State U., 1967-68; adminstr. Consumer Services Div., State of Oreg., 1977-80, Wilkins Assoc., 1980—; mem. PFMC Salmon Adv. subpanel, 1982-86. Author: (with B. H. Wilkins) Implications of the U.S.-Mexican Water Treaty for Interregional Water Transfer, 1968. Dem. precinct committeewoman, Benton County, Oreg., 1964-90; publicity chmn. Benton County Gen. Election, 1964; chmn. Get-Out-the-Vote Com., Benton County, 1966; vice chmn. Benton County Dem. Cen. Com., 1966-70; vice chmn. 1st Congl. Dist., Oreg., 1966-68, chmn. 1968; vice chmn. Dem. Party Oreg., 1968-69, chmn. 1969-74; mem. exec. com. Western States Dem. Conf., 1970-72; vice chmn. Dem. Nat. Com., 1972-77, mem. arrangements com., 1972, 76, mem. Dem. charter commn., 1973-74; mem. Dem. Nat. Com., 1972-77, 85-89, mem. size and composition com., 1987-89, rules com. 1988; mem. Oreg. Govt. Ethics Commn., 1974-76; del., mem. rules com. Dem. Nat. Conv., 1988. Mem. AAUW, Nat. Assn. Consumer Agy. Adminstrs., Soc. Consumer Affairs Profs., Nat. Fedn. Dem. Women (1st v.p. 1983-85, pres. 1985-87), Oreg. State U. Folk Club (pres. faculty wives 1989-90). Lodge: Zonta Internat. Office: 3311 NW Roosevelt Corvallis OR 97330

WILKINS, JANET ROSEMARY, public relations executive; b. N.Y.C., Oct. 30, 1917; d. Harvey and Jeanette Margaret (Symes) W. BS magna cum laude, NYU, 1939, postgrad., 1946; postgrad. in Art History and Music, Manhattanville Coll. Indsl. rel. rsch. Nat. Ind. Conf. Bd., N.Y.C., 1940; mktg. rsch. N.Y. Daily News, N.Y.C., 1940-42; security analyst Mfrs. Hanover Bank, N.Y.C., 1942-51; rsch. economist Am. Can Co., N.Y.C., 1951-54; producer audio visual programs Nat. Assn. Mfg., N.Y.C., 1954-63; writer City Bank, 1963-64; recruitment specialist Girl Scouts Am., N.Y.C., 1964-66; mgr. econ. analysis & long range planning MacManus, John & Adams, N.Y.C., 1966-67; dir. Nat. League for Nursing, N.Y.C., 1967-80; freelance photographer, lectr., writer, 1980—; bd. dirs. Com. on Internat. Non-Theatrical Events, Wash., 1961-65, Nat. Visual Presentation Assn., N.Y.C., 1968-64. Contbr. articles to profl. jours. Chmn. bd. dirs. St. Paul's Nat. Historic Site & Bill of Rights Mus., 1983—; chmn. Bronxville Village Christmas Pagaent, 1984-90; bd. dirs. Bronxville LWV, 1987—, Pub. Health Nursing Orgn., Tuckahoe, 1975-81, Bronxville Women's Club, 1984—; trustee Westchester County Hist. Soc., 1971-88. Mem. AAUW, Photographic Soc. Am. (recipient APSA award), Bronxville Camera Club, Bronxville Field Club, Beta Gamma Sigma, Sphix, Mu Gamma Tau. Republican. Home and Office: 3 Alden Pl Bronxville NY 10708

WILKINS, RITA DENISE, real estate consultant, researcher, manager; b. Detroit, June 21, 1951; d. William H. and Alice L. (Hayes) Smith. Student, Geo. Peabody Coll., Cleveland (Tenn.) State Community Coll., George Peabody Coll. Mgmt. coord., legal coord. Arlen Realty and Devel. Corp., Chattanooga, Tenn., 1973-76; asst. v.p., office mgr. Newburger Andes & Co., Atlanta, 1976-78; asst. v.p., project mgr. Newberger Andes & Co., Atlanta, 1978-79; project mgr. Robinson-Humphrey, Atlanta, 1979-80; dept. head Office Properties Group Merrill Lynch Realty Comml. Svcs., Atlanta, 1980-83; acquisition devel. mgmt. rep. Cardinal Industries, Inc., Atlanta, 1983-86; pres., sr. cons. Comml. Property Cons., Charleston, S.C., 1986—. Contbr. articles to profl. jours. Mem. Indsl. Devel. Rsch. Found. (devel. and edn. coms.), S.C. Real Estate Brokers Assn., S.C. Econ. Developers Assn., Am. Real Estate Soc., Comml. Real Estate Women of Ga. (founder), Charleston World Trade Ctr. (steering com., growth strategy sub-com., facility sub-com.). Office: CPC/Foresite 2070 Northbrook Blvd B22 North Charleston SC 29418

WILKINS, SUSAN LINDA, paper company official; b. Reading, Pa., Apr. 20, 1950; d. James Francis and Yvonne Thuvia (Kuser) Hess; m. Donald Kenneth Wilkins, July 20, 1974. Student, Kutztown (Pa.) State Coll., 1968-71, Marywood Coll., Scranton, Pa., 1987—. Sec. Riddle Meml. Hosp., Media, Pa., 1971-73; order processing clk., sr. order processing clk. Scott Paper Co., Phila., 1973-74, asst. shift supr., 1974-79, shift supr., 1979-83, data base coord., 1983-85, rsch. analyst, 1985-88, planning and analysis specialist, 1988-89, mgr. rates and audit, 1989—. Office: Scott Paper Co Scott Pla Philadelphia PA 19113

WILKINSON, ANN MARIE, nurse, psychiatric clinical specialist; b. Yonkers, N.Y., Aug. 15, 1947; d. Michele and Marguerite Mary (Stanger) DeGiorgio; m. George L. Wilkinson III, Jan. 28, 1942; children: Lauren Ann, Ashley Michelle, Meredith Lloyd. BS, Syracuse U., 1969; MS in Nursing, U. Calif., San Francisco, 1976. Cert. specialist psychiat. mental health nursing. Staff nurse psychiatry Albert Einstein Coll. Hosp., N.Y.C., 1969, Payne Whitney Clinic N.Y. Hosp., N.Y.C., 1970; staff nurse, day treatment program San Mateo County Mental Health, Redwood City, Calif., 1970-74; pvt. practice specializing in psychotherapy Redwood City, Calif.; clin. faculty San Mateo County Psychiat. Residency Program, Redwood City, Calif., 1988—. Co-Author: Psychiatric Nursing, 1976. Vice pres. bd. dirs. Child Care Coordinating Coun., San Mateo, 1988—. Mem. Am. Nurses Assn. Office: Ann M Wilkinson MS RN CS 133 Arch St Redwood City CA 94062

WILKINSON, DORIS YVONNE, medical sociology educator; b. Lexington, Ky., June 13, 1936; d. Howard Thomas and Regina (Cowherd) W. BA, U. Ky., 1958; MA, Case Western Res. U., 1960, PhD, 1968; MPH, Johns Hopkins U., 1985. Asst. prof. U. Ky., Lexington, 1968-70; assoc. prof., then prof. Macalester Coll., St. Paul, 1970-77; exec. assoc. Am. Sociol. Assn., Washington, 1977-80; prof. med. sociology Howard U., Washington, 1980-84; vis. prof. U. Va., 1984-85; prof. sociology U. Ky., Lexington, 1985—; chmn. panel women in sci. program NSF, Washington, 1976; panelist pub. program div. NEH, Washington, 1976; rev. panelist Nat. Inst. Drug Abuse, Washington, 1978-79; mem. bd. sci. counselors Nat. Cancer Inst., Bethesda, Md., 1980-84. Author: Workbook for Introductory Sociology, 1968; co-editor: The Black Male in America, 1977, Alternative Health Maintenance and Healing Systems, 1987; contbr. articles to profl. jours. Bd. overseers Case Western Res. U., Cleve., 1982-87. Fellow Woodrow Wilson, 1959-61, Ford Found., vis. scholar DuBois Inst. Harvard U., 1989-90, Ford Harvard U., 1990; Social Sci. Rsch. Coun. grantee, 1975, Nat. Inst. Edn. grantee, 1978-80, Nat. Cancer Inst. grantee, 1986-88, Ky. Humanities Coun. grantee, 1988, Am. Coun. Learned Socs grantee, 1989-90; recipient Disting. Alumni award U. Ky., 1989; inducted Hall of Disting. Alumni U. Ky., 1989. Fellow Am. Orthopsychiatric Assn.; mem. D.C. Sociol. Soc. (pres. 1982-83), Soc. for Study of Social Problems (v.p. 1984-85, pres. 1987-88), Eastern Sociol. Soc. (v.p. 1983-84, I. Peter Gellman award 1987), Am. Sociol. Assn. (exec. office and budget com., 1985-88, Dubois-Johnson-Frazier award, 1988., v.p. 1990), N.Y. Acad. Scis., Phi Beta Kappa, Alpha Kappa Delta (outstanding grad. student 1964). Unitarian. Office: U Ky Dept Sociology Lexington KY 40506

WILKINSON, GLOVINIA PHIPPS, nurse, former educator; b. N.Y.C.; d. William Arthur and Amabel (Paris) Phipps; m. Chester G. Wilkinson, June 30, 1950 (dec.); children: Jean, Lenore. Diploma, Lincoln Sch. for Nurses, Bronx, N.Y., 1944; BS, Hunter Coll., 1949, MA, 1951; MA, Pace U., 1974. RN, N.Y.; cert. tchr. physically handicapped, supr., adminstr., N.Y. Tchr. N.Y.C. Bd. Edn., 1945-80, supr. spl. edn., 1980-82; cons. nurse Day Care Ctr., N.Y.C. Dept. Health, 1984—. Contbr. articles to profl. jours. Pres. Lakeview Dem. Club, West Hempstead, N.Y., Met. N.Y. chpt. Aux. Luth. Theol. Sem. at Phila.; leader Nassau County coun. Girl Scouts U.S.A., 1968-81, now life mem. Recipient Nat. Sojourner Truth Meritorious Svc. award Nat. Assn. Negro Bus. and Profl. Women, 1971. Mem. ANA, Ret. Sch. Suprs. and Adminstrs. Assn., Alumnae Assn. Lincoln Sch. for Nurses (pres. 1986-89), Chi Eta Phi (epistoleus NE region 1985-88, Community Svc. award Kappa Eta chpt. 1990). Home: 454 Rose Ave West Hempstead NY 11552

WILKINSON, JANE INSALACO, hospital executive; b. New Britain, Conn., Dec. 29, 1939; m. Lawson A. Wilkinson; children: L. Alan, Mary E. BS, Coll. of N.H., 1978; MBA, U. New Haven, 1982. Clin. dir. Yale New Haven Hosp., 1961-63; exec. dir. Hosp. Home Health Care of Conn., New Haven, 1984-86; assoc. dir. nursing The Park City Hosp., Bridgeport, Conn., 1983-84, v.p. patient svcs., 1986—. Mem. Conn. Nursing Assn. (pres. 1989—), Am. Coll. Healthcare Execs., Conn. Women in Health Care Mgmt., Sigma Theta Tau, Delta Mu. Office: Park City Hosp 695 Park Ave Bridgeport CT 06604

WILKINSON, JANET WORMAN, advertising and marketing consultant; b. Mpls., July 18, 1944; d. James Russell and Virginia Hale (Murty) Worman; m. Benjamin Delos Wilkinson, Jan. 7, 1967; children—David Delos, Steven Edward, John Douglas. B.A., Wells Coll., 1966. With Met. Life Ins. Co., N.Y.C., 1966-67; elem. tchr. pub. schs., Parkersburg, W.Va. and Orange, Tex., 1968-69; on-air prin. WTAV-TV, Parkersburg, 1969-70; corp. communications educator Delmarva Power Co., Wilmington, Del., 1979-83; market mgr. W.L. Gore & Assocs., Inc., Elkton, Md., 1983-85; advt. coordinator, promotion mgr. Views Mag., Chadds Ford, Pa., 1985-86; cons. mktg. communications, 1986—; mem. Bus.-Industry Ednl. Consortium, Wilmington, 1981-83; chmn. steering com. NE Utilities Educators, 1981-83. Contbg. editor Lattice News, 1984-85; editor Retailer newsletter, 1984-85. Chmn. publicity Wilmington Flower Market, 1984-85, Wells Coll. Capital Campaign Fund, Wilmington, 1983-84, Wilmington Christmas Shop, 1973-81; loaned exec. United Way, Wilmington, 1985; bd. dirs. Girls Clubs Del., 1983-84; founder, developer Help Stop the Hurt child abuse awareness program, 1983; dir. Christian edn. Trinity Ch., Wilmington, 1982-88. Republican. Episcopalian. Avocations: sketching, watercolor, writing. Home and Office: 1001 Westover Rd Wilmington DE 19807

WILKINSON, JESSIE LENORE, data processing executive; b. Balt., Mar. 12, 1957; d. Robert Warren Wilkinson and Eleanor Lambeth (Rankin) Brewster. Programmer, project leader Satbel, Ltd., Johannesburg, Republic of South Africa, 1976-77; sr. programmer Ned Equity, Ltd., Johannesburg, 1977-78; systems analyst, project leader Barlow Rand Computer Services, Johannesburg, 1978-82; sr. systems cons. Viable Info. Processing Systems, Hunt Valley, Md., 1983-89, Abacus Svcs. & Systems Group, Hunt Valley, Md., 1989-90; sr. cons. Disc, Inc., Balt., 1990—. Newsletter editor Md. Assn. Anorexia Nervosa and Bulimia, Balt., 1986, bd. dirs., 1987; mem. Black Sash, Johannesburg, 1980—. Mem. Data Processing Mgmt. Assn., Balti. Coun. Fng. Affairs. Republican. Methodist.

WILKINSON, LINDA CORNELIA PAINTON, retired city official; b. Painton, Mo., Aug. 21, 1927; d. Herbert James and Bess Carmen (Cobb) Painton; m. A. Scott Wilkinson, July 20, 1957; children: Jean Mary Wilkinson Martinis, Ann Elizabeth. BS in Edn., S.E. Mo. State U., 1951; postgrad., U. N.Mex., 1961, 67. Cert. tchr., Mo. Tchr. pub. schs., Mo., 1945-53; adminstrv. asst. real estate dept. Gulf Oil Corp., N.Y.C., 1953-56; sec., adminstrv. asst. Bklyn. Law Sch., 1956-58; co-owner, mgr. Music Mart, Albuquerque, 1961-68; owner, mgr. rental properties, Albuquerque, 1968-86; chief dep. county clk. Valencia County, Los Lunas, N.Mex., 1986-89; adminstr. Harvey House Civic Ctr., City of Belen (N.Mex.), 1989-90. Mem. Valencia County Citizens Adv. Bd., 1985—; sec., bd. dirs. Valencia County Hist. Soc., Belen, 1986—; bd. dirs. Keep N.Mex. Beautiful, 1986—, Shelter for Victims Domestic Violence, Valencia County, 1988—; Rep. candidate for county clk., 1988. Mem. AAUW, Civitan Club (pres. Belen 1989-90), Tierra del Sol County Club. Presbyterian. Home: 08 Meadow Lake Ln Los Lunas NM 87031

WILKINSON, MARY ELLEN, state institution administrator, social worker; b. Provo, Utah, Sept. 25, 1947; d. Ray Leland and Margaret (Guercio) W. BSW cum laude, Utah State U., 1969; MSW cum laude, U. Utah, 1971. Diplomate Am. Bd. Clinical Social Workers; cert. health care adminstr., drug and alcohol counselor, therapeutic recreation specialist, Utah. Social work cons. Vali Convalescent & Care Inc., Salt Lake City and Orem, Utah, 1975-76; adminstr. nursing home Vali Convalescent & Care Inc., Salt Lake City, 1976-81; forensic social worker Utah State Hosp., Provo, 1983-84, adminstrv. dir. adult unit, 1984-89; clin. social worker Utah State Tng. Sch., American Fork, 1971-75; owner, mgr. Choice Life Mgmt. Systems, Orem, 1986—; cons. Region III Youth Corrections, Springville, Utah, 1986—, instr. state div., Salt Lake City, 1987—; clin. instr. Brigham Young U. Grad. Sch. Social Work, Provo, 1986—; mgmt. cons. to various pvt. cos., Salt Lake City and Orem, 1987—. Author text materials. Del. Utah Dem. Conv., 1982; mem. gov. task force MADDm 1990; lobbyist various animal rights orgns.; presenter, panelist various pub. forums. NIMH scholar, 1969-71. Mem. Nat. Assn. Social Workers, Utah Drug and Alcohol Counselors, NAFE, Am. Coll. Health Care Adminstrs., C Bar C Equestrians, Elks, Phi Beta Kappa, Kappa Delta. Democrat. Home: 284 South 800 West Orem UT 84058 Office: Choice Life Mgmt Systems 555 S State PO Box 698 Orem UT 84057

WILKINSON, RACHEL ELIZABETH DIGGS, academic administrator, retired; b. Winston-Salem, N.C., Mar. 30, 1913; d. James Thackeray and Mabel (Kennedy) Diggs; m. William Henry Heberton Wilkinson, June 10, 1950 (dec.). BS, Winston-Salem State U., 1933; MA, Columbia U., 1937; PhD, N.Y. U., 1952; grad. cert., Radcliffe Coll., 1946. Tchr. pub. schs. Winston-Salem, 1933-40; alumni exec. sec., dean of women Winston-Salem State U., 1940-53; instr. CUNY, 1953-59; asst. prof. Yeshiva U., N.Y.C., 1959-62; assoc. prof., coord. coll. discovery, dir. fin. aid Bronx Community Coll., CUNY, 1962-66; assoc. prof., dir. student counseling ctr. CUNY, 1966-68, full prof., dir. community rels. seek program, 1968-70, coord. evaluation and rsch., 1970-72; newspaper reporter Winston-Salem Jour. and Sentinel, 1939-49; guest prof. grad. sch. Fla. A&M U., 1954; lectr. Brooklyn Coll., 1955; supr. student tchrs. Mills Coll. Edn., 1958-59; vis. prof. grad. sch. edn. NYU, 1962, Yeshiva U., 1963. Editor: (magazine) National Alumni Association, 1945-55; contbr. articles to profl. jours. V.p. Soroptimist, Bronx, N.Y., 1966-68; mem. Common Cause, Washington, 1979—, NAACP, Balt., 1950—, Planned Parenthood, Washington, 1980—; bd. mgrs. High Point I Condominium, Hartsdale, N.Y., 1989—. Recipient scholarship Bennett Coll., 1929, Citation of Achievement Wilson Coll., 1969, Disting. Alumnus award Winston-Salem State U., 1985; fellow Radcliffe Coll., 1945-46, Nat. Coun. Episcopal Ch., 1946. Mem. AAUP, AAUW (grantee N.Y.C. br. 1969), Am. Assn. for Counseling and Devel., Virginia Gildersleeve Internat. Fund for Univ. Women. Democrat. Episcopalian. Home: 200B High Point Dr #203 Hartsdale NY 10530

WILKIRSON, DEANNA JEAN, consulting company executive; b. Lexington, Ky., Mar. 6, 1948; d. Julian Stuart and Pearlie Mae (Maybrier) W. BBA in Acctg., Eastern Ky. U., 1970; MBA, Ind. U., 1985. Tchr. Spencerian Coll., Louisville, 1970-71; cost acct. Sq. D Co., Lexington, Ky., 1971-74; acctg. mgr. Parker Hannifin Co., Lexington, 1974-79; mgr. fin. planning Essex div. United Technologies Corp., Georgetown, Ky., 1979-81; dir. fin. planning Essex group United Technologies Corp., Fort Wayne, Ind., 1981-86; mgr. investor rels. United Technologies Corp., Hartford, Conn., 1986-89, dir. human resource, analysis and devel., 1989-90; pres., owner Planning For Success Cons., Ft. Wayne, Ind., 1990—. Bd. dirs., treas. Big Sisters, Lexington, 1978; officer, bd. dirs. Nat. Assn. of Accts., Lexington, 1975-81, pres. elect, 1980-81. Republican.

WILL, JERRIE ANN, psychologist; b. Hazleton, Pa., Apr. 6, 1950; d. Gordon John and Doris Griffiths (Brown) W.; m. Gene G. Kuehneman, June 26, 1982 (div. Oct. 1984). BA, Bucknell U., 1971; MA, W.Va. U., 1974, PhD, 1977. Lic. psychologist, Maine. Teaching fellow W.Va. U., Morgantown, 1974-76; clin. psychology intern U. Md. Hosp., Balt., 1976-77; sr. child psychologist Michael Reese Hosp., Chgo., 1977-82; cons. psychologist Ridgeway Psychiat. Hosp., Chgo., 1982-83, Sanford Sch. Dept., Maine, 1983—; pvt. practice Sanford and Wells, Maine, 1984—; team/child psychologist York County Counseling Svcs., Sanford, 1983-85; pvt. practice psychology, Chgo., Kennebunk and Wells, Maine, Sanford, 1982—; owner/mgr. Sanford Psychol. Assocs., 1987—; panelist/reviewer NSF, 1976. Contbr. articles to profl. jours. NIMH Grantee, 1972-75. Mem. Am. Psychol. Assn., Maine Psychol. Assn., Nat. Assn. Sch. Psychologists. Democrat. Home: 210 Webhannet Dr Wells ME 04090 Office: Sanford Psychol Assocs 100 Main St Sanford ME 04073

WILL, JESSIE GERMAN, handwriting expert, document examiner; b. Muskogee, Okla., Oct. 8, 1912; d. William Paxton Zacheus and Mabel Gussie (Ward) German; student Ward Belmont Coll., 1929-30, Drake U., 1930-32; B.S., Okla. U., 1933; cert. Internat. Graphoanalysis Soc., 1968, master cert., 1973; m. Edward Ray Will, Sept. 29, 1934; children—Henry German, Margaret Ann Will Cornell. Handwriting expert, document examiner, Tulsa, 1970—; lectr. Oklahoma City U., 1972-76, Tri-County Tech. Sch., Bartlesville, Okla., 1977-81. Pres. local PTA, 1948-49, 55-58; bd. dirs. Tulsa WYWCA, 1963, Tulsa Philharmonic, 1964; mem. nat. panel advisers Nat. Forensic Ctr., 1983-86. Mem. PEO (chpt. pres. 1962-63), Internat. Graphoanalysis Soc., Ind. Assn. Questioned Document Examiners (corr. sec. 1976-77, bd. dirs. 1978-87, rec. sec. 1989—), Tulsa Boys Home Women's Assn. (v.p. 1978-79), Internat. Assn. Forensic Scis., Kappa Alpha Theta (pres. alumni assn. 1961, coll. dist. pres. 1961-63), Mu Phi Epsilon. Republican. Mem. Disciples of Christ Ch. Expert witness in fed. cts., Okla., dist. cts. Okla., Kans., Mo., and Ark. Home and Office: 1727 E 31st St Tulsa OK 74105

WILL, ROSALYN NELL, writer, researcher; b. Coraopolis, Pa., Aug. 14, 1933; d. Arthur Dayton and Syvila May (Hyatt) Bailey; m. David Edwin Will, Dec. 31, 1955; children: Lindsay Patricia, Julie Anne, Eric David, Scott Andrew. Grad. high sch. Advt. copywriter Pitts. Mercantile Co., 1952-55; catalog copywriter Montgomery Ward, N.Y.C., 1955-57; salesperson Gimbels East Dept. Store, N.Y.C., 1972-83; pub. info. assoc. Council on Econ. Priorities, N.Y.C., 1983-87, project dir., 1988—. Contbr. articles to profl. jours.; project mgr. first edit. (consumer guide) Shopping for a Better World. Bd. dirs. Unitarian Ch. of All Souls, N.Y.C., 1984-86. Democrat. Unitarian. Office: Council on Econ Priorities 30 Irving Pl New York NY 10003

WILL, SUSAN JEAN, nursing educator; b. Toledo, Feb. 26, 1949; d. Edward E. and Vivien R. (Long) Ziemke. BS in Nursing summa cum laude, Capital U., 1971; MS summa cum laude, Ohio State U., 1972; postgrad., Portland State U. Nurse pub. health Columbus (Ohio) Pub. Health Nursing, 1971-72; clin. specialist Mushingum County Mental Health, Zanesville, Ohio, 1972; cons., evaluator Ohio Dept. Mental Health, Columbus, 1972-73; cons. staff devel. Bethesda Hosp., Zanesville, Ohio, 1972-73; cons. Alaska Psychiat. Inst., Anchorage, 1973-77; instr. Anchorage Community Coll., 1974-77; assoc. prof. Oreg. Health Scis. U., Portland, 1977-81, 1984-88; administr. Community Mental Health Svcs. Alaska Dept. Mental Health, Juneau, 1981-84; cons. Province Ala., Edmonton, Can. 1985-87, Dept Family Nursing 1984-85, Dept Mental Health Nursing 1986-88, Oreg. Health Scis. Commr. Planning Commn. Lake Oswego, Oreg. 1982-83. Mem. Am. Nurses Assn., Council Psychiat. Mental Health Nursing, Oreg. Nurses Assn., Sigma Theta Tau. Democrat. Home: 5205 SW 153rd Ave Beaverton OR 97007 OFFICE: 16055 SW Boones Ferry Rd Lake Oswego OR 97034

WILLADSEN, KAY A., marketing representative; b. Saginaw, Mich., May 11, 1947; d. W. Franklin and Elaine (Simkins) Brooks; m. Michael C. Willadsen, Dec. 5, 1964; children: Michael C., Erik J. AA, McComb Coll., 1973; student Eastern Mich. U., 1977-78, U. Ill., 1979; BBA, Bowling Green State U., 1982; postgrad. Ind. U., 1983-85. Mktg. rep. Credit Bur. of Hancock County, Inc., Findlay, Ohio, 1983-87; account exec. TRW Info. Services, 1987—; treas. Northwest Ohio Consumer Credit Assn., 1988-89. Choreographer dance Flowers and Confusion, 1974. Precinct del. Livingston County Republicans, Hamburg, Mich., 1976, state conv. del., 1976; treas. Hillcrest Gasline Project, Findlay, Ohio, 1984; membership chmn. Am. Bus. Women's Assn. Mem. Nat. Assn. Female Execs., Am. Business Women's Assn. (recording sec. 1986—), Ohio Mortgage Bankers Assn., Findlay Downtown Area Assn. (bd. dirs.), Bowling Green Alumni Assn., Credit Grantors Assn. (dir. 1983-86). Methodist. Club: Women's Lions (dir. 1974-75). Avocations: dance, reading, investments. Home: 3210 Byrnwyck Dr Findlay OH 45840 Office: TRW Info Svcs 5577 Airport Hwy Ste 205 Toledo OH 43615

WILLARD, BETTY RINER, telecommunications industry professional; b. Bristol, Va., June 9, 1948; d. Leon Edward and Bonnie Blue (Almaroad) Riner; m. Elmer Lynn Willard, Sept. 18, 1971. BS in Computer Sci., East Tenn. State U., 1987. With United Inter-Mountain Telephone Co., Bristol, 1967—; dial office adminstrn. analyst Inter-Mountain Telephone Co., Bristol, 1979-80, programmer analyst I, 1980-83, programmer analyst III, 1983-87, network separations mgr., 1987—. Mem. NAFE, East Tenn. State U. Nat. Alumni Assn. Office: United Inter-Mountain Telephone Co 112 6th St Bristol TN 37620

WILLARD, CORINNE WADHAMS, agricultural products executive; b. Hartford, Conn., May 25, 1920; d. Dwight Benedict and Ruth Adelaide (Strong) Wadhams; m. Richard Griswold Willard, Aug. 9, 1947; children: Jeanne, Richard Jr., Douglas, Anne. BS, U. Conn., 1942; MSc, Ohio State U., 1946. Mgr. orchid range Traendly and Schenck, Rowayton, Conn.; pres. Comstock, Ferre and Co., Wethersfield, Conn. Contbr. articles to popular mags. Named Bus. Person of Yr. award Wethersfield C. of C. Mem. Garden Writers Assn. of Am. (past pres.), All Am. Selections (pres., judge), Am. Seed Trade Assn. (pres. Home Garden div.), Conn. Agrl. Info. Coun. (Alumni award), U. Conn. Hort. Club, Gamma Sigma Delta.

WILLARD, NANCY MARGARET, writer, educator; b. Ann Arbor, Mich.; d. Hobart Hurd and Margaret (Sheppard) W.; m. Eric Lindbloom, Aug. 15, 1964; 1 child, James Anatole. B.A., U. Mich., 1958, Ph.D., 1963; M.A., Stanford U., 1960. Lectr. English Vassar Coll., Poughkeepsie, N.Y., 1965—. Author: poems In His Country: Poems, 1966; Skin of Grace, 1967; A New Herball: Poems, 1968, Testimony of the Invisible Man: William Carlos Williams, Francis Ponge, Rainer Maria Rilke, Pablo Neruda, 1970, Nineteen Masks for the Naked Poet: Poems, 1971, Childhood for the Magician, 1973, The Carpenter of the Sun: Poems, 1974, A Visit to William Blake's Inn: Poems for Innocent and Experienced Travelers, 1981 (Newberry Medal 1982), Household Tales of Moon and Water, 1983, Water Walker, 1989, The Ballad of Biddy Early, 1989; (short stories) The Lively Anatomy of God, 1968; (juveniles) Sailing to Cythera and Other Anatole Stories, 1974, All on a May Morning, 1975, The Snow Rabbit, 1975, Shoes Without Leather, 1976, The Well-Mannered Balloon, 1976, Night Story, 1986, Simple Pictures are Best, 1977, Stranger's Bread, 1977, The Highest Hit, 1978, Papa's Panda, 1979, The Island of the Grass King, 1979, The Marzipan Moon 1981, Uncle Terrible, 1982, Angel in the Parlor: Five Stories and Eight Essays, 1983, The Nightgown of the Sullen Moon, 1983, Night Story, 1986, The Voyage of Ludgate Hill, 1987, The Mountains of Quilt, 1987, Firebrat, 1988; (novel) Things Invisible To See, 1984; (play) East of the Sun, West of the Moon, 1989; illustrator: The Letter of John to James and Another Letter of John to James, 1982, The Ballad of Biddy Early, The Octopus Who Wanted to Juggle (Robert Pack). Recipient Hopwood award, 1958, Devins Meml. award, 1967; Woodrow Wilson fellow, 1960; NEA grantee, 1987. Mem. Children's Literature Assn., The Lewis Carroll Soc., The George MacDonald Soc. Office: Vassar Coll Dept English Raymond Ave Poughkeepsie NY 12601

WILLARD, PATRICIA RAE, personnel executive; b. Springfield, Mo., June 12, 1949; d. Conrad Raymond and LenaMae (Hicks) W. BA, Stephens Coll., 1971; MS in Counseling Psychology, U. Mo., 1973; PhD in Counselor Edn., U. Mo., Kansas City, 1982. Coord. edn. and counseling dept. Planned Parenthood of Cen. Mo., Columbia, 1972-74; coord. teenage obstetrics progam Kansas City Gen. Hosp. and Med. Ctr., 1974-76; program developer/counselor Planned Parenthood of Western Mo., Kansas City, 1976-78; v.p. Devel. Systems, Inc., Kansas City, 1978-83; mgr. PED Arthur Andersen & Co., St. Charles, Ill., 1983-85; human resource cons. Tektronix Inc., Portland, Oreg., 1985-88; mgr., dir. personal devel. Arthur Andersen & Co., S.C., Chgo., 1988—. Author: Counseling Teenage Clients in Family Planning Programs: A Training Manual, 1982, Orientation to Family Planning: A Self-Learning Module, 1982. Bd. dirs. Planned Parenthood, Chgo., 1991. Mme. Am. Psychol. Assn., Human Resource Planning Soc. Office: Arthur Andersen & Co 33 W Monroe Rm 1246 Chicago IL 60603

WILLARD-GALLO, KAREN ELIZABETH, molecular biologist; b. Oak Ridge, July 8, 1953; d. Harvey Bradford and Isabella Victoria (Rallis) Willard; student in microbiology U. Reading, Eng., 1973-74; A.B. in Biology, Randolph-Macon Woman's Coll., 1975; M.S. in Immunology, Va. Poly. Inst., 1978, Ph.D. in Molecular Biology, 1981; m. James Paul Gallo, July 31, 1982. Grad. teaching asst. Va. Poly. Inst., 1976-78; fellow Research Inst. in Cell Biology, Argonne Nat. Lab., Ill., 1977, lab. resident student assoc., 1978-81, postdoctoral fellow, 1981-82; research assoc. Ludwig Inst. for Cancer Research, Brussels, 1982-85; research scientist Internat. Inst. Cellular and Molecular Pathology, Brussels, Belgium, 1986—; advisor on Immunology WHO, 1987—; cons. in field. Recipient award for teaching excellence Va. Poly. Inst., 1977, 78. Mem. Am. Soc. Cell Biology, Electrophoresis Soc., Internat. Coordinating Com. Human Lymphocyte Protein Database, 1987—. Contbr. chpts., articles to profl. pubs.; patentee method for early detection infectious mononucleosis. Home: Ave Chevalier Jehan 117, 1300 Wavre Belgium Office: Internat Inst Cellular and, Molecular Pathology Dept Biochem, UCL 7539 Ave Hippocrate, 75 1200 Brussels Belgium

WILLARDSON, KIMBERLY ANN CAREY, editor, writer; b. Akron, Ohio, May 8, 1959; d. James David and Concetta Marie (Bonanno) Carey; m. Roger Michael Willardson, Oct. 4, 1980. Student, Kent State U., 1978-79, Akron U., 1979-80; BA in English, Wright State U., 1983, MA in English, 1987. Teaching asst. Wright State U., Dayton, Ohio, 1983-84; assoc. editor Nexus Lit. Mag., Dayton, Ohio, 1982, editor, 1982-83; features editor The Daily Guardian Newspaper, Dayton, 1983; editorial asst. communications Wright State U., Dayton, 1985-88; freelance editor Dayton, 1986-88; editor The Vincent Bros. Rev. Mag., Fairborn, Ohio, 1988—; pub. Vincent Bros. Desktop Pub., Fairborn, Ohio, 1988—; mgr., cons. Kinetic Imagineering Vincent Bros. Desktop Pub., Dayton, 1989—; adj. staff mem. Antioch Writers' Workshop, Yellow Springs, Ohio, 1990. Author: (poem) Overcast at the Cat Dance Cafe, 1989, The Missy May Hopnoodle Saga (2d place Creative Writing award Cof. Cin. Women, 1990); mem. bd. editors Fountain of Youth Literary Anthology, 1983-84. Regional organizer March of Dimes, Cuyahoga Falls, Ohio, 1977; canvasser Am. Heart Assn., Fairborn, 1989—. Wright State U. scholar, 1982-85; Ohio Arts Coun. grantee, 1989, Publs. Support grantee, 1990—. Mem. NAFE. Roman Catholic.

WILLBANKS, SUE SUTTON, investor, writer, artist; b. Luling, Tex., Sept. 24, 1935; d. William Herbert and Melba Ophelia (Ward) Sutton; m. Charles Walter Willbanks, Nov. 21, 1953 (dec. Feb. 1979); children—Jill Ann, Brenda Kay. B.S., Tex. Tech. U., 1955; M.A., U. Tex. Permian Basin, 1980. Cert. secondary, vocat. and elem. tchr., Tex. Tchr., Big Spring Ind. Sch. Dist., Tex., 1964-68, 1972-79, dept. chmn., 1980-82; owner, pres. Sutwill Co., Tucson, Ariz., 1981—; pvt. practice psychotherapy, Tex., Hawaii, Ariz., 1979—. Author short stories and poems. Contbr. articles to profl. jours. Organizer Silver Heels Vol. Fire Dept., Howard County, Tex., 1970-71; bd. dirs. Permian Basin Planned Parenthood Assn., Odessa, Tex., 1980-82; organist Immaculate Heart of Mary Ch., Big Spring, Tex., 1975-78. Methodist. Avocations: interior decorating, acting. Home: 6644 N Amahl Pl Tucson AZ 85704

WILLE, LOIS JEAN, newspaper editor; b. Chgo., Sept. 19, 1932; d. Walter and Adele S. (Taege) Kroeber; m. Wayne M. Wille, June 6, 1954. B.S., Northwestern U., 1953, M.S., 1954, Litt.D. (hon.), 1990; Litt.D. (hon.), Columbia Coll., Chgo., 1980, Rosary Coll., 1990. Reporter Chgo. Daily News, 1958-74, nat. corr., 1975-76, assoc. editor charge editorial page, 1977; assoc. editor charge editorial and opinion pages Chgo. Sun-Times, 1978-83; assoc. editorial page editor Chgo. Tribune, 1984-87, editorial page editor, 1987—. Author: Forever Open, Clear and Free: the Historic Struggle for Chicago's Lakefront, 1972. Recipient Pulitzer prize for public service, 1963, Pulitzer prize for editorial writing, 1989, William Allen White Found. award for excellence in editorial writing, 1978, numerous awards Chgo. Newspaper Guild, numerous awards Chgo. Headline Club, numerous awards Nat. Assn. Edn. Writers, numerous awards Ill. AP, numerous awards Ill. UPI. Mem. Chgo. Women's Network, Am. Soc. Newspaper Editors, Soc. Profl. Journalists, Chgo. Econ. Club. Home: 902 S Laflin St Chicago IL 60607 Office: Chgo Tribune Co 435 N Michigan Ave Chicago IL 60611

WILLENS, TINA KIRKWOOD, advertising executive; b. Bound Brook, N.J., June 11, 1962; d. John C. and Gloria (DePaolo) Kirkwood; m. Kevin Willens, Aug. 9, 1987. BA, Rutgers Coll., 1984; MBA, N.Y. U. Stern Sch. of Bus., 1989. Asst. account exec. Merling Marx and Seidman Advt., Inc., N.Y.C., 1984-85; project dir. Cunningham & Walsh, N.Y.C., 1985-86; rsch. account exec. N.W. Ayer, N.Y.C., 1986-88; rsch. supr. Lintas: USA, N.Y.C., 1988-89. Mem. Advt. Rsch. Found., Qualitative Rsch. Coun. Home: 26 Glenwood Dr Short Hills NJ 07078

WILLENZ, JUNE ADELE, writer, public affairs executive, playwright, screenwriter. BS, U. Mich., MA; ABD in Philosophy, New Sch. for Social Rsch. instr. English Montgomery Coll., Md.; conf. organizer Women in and After War, Bellagio, Italy; lectr. U.S. Info. Agy.; speaker conv. NAACP; radio and TV guest appearances; honored guest Internat. Vets. Assn. Author: Women Veterans: America's Forgotten Heroines, 1983; editor, author: Dialogue on the Draft, 1967, Human Rights of the Man in Uniform, 1969; editor: AVC Bull.; presenter Am. Hist. Assn., Am. Polit. Sci. Assn.; contbr. articles to profl. publs. on vets., mil., women's and internat. issues; columnist Stars and Stripes. Mem. VA Adv. Com. on Women Vets.; mem. UN Decade for Women com., head of working group on refugee women; spl. rep. to UN; pub. mem. 19th Fgn. Officer Selection Bd., U.S. Info. Agy.; chmn. Task Force on Veterans and Mil. Affairs for Leadership Con. on Civil Rights; speaker Nat. Urban League, Ctr. for Policy Rsch., Nat. League of Cities Vets. Program, advisor; mem. Nat. Civil Liberties Clearing House; bd. trustees Internat. Devel. Conf.; co-chmn. Coordinating Com. on Voluntary Nat. Svc., organized nat. conf. Dialogue on Nat. Svc., 1989; del. White House Conf. on Youth; exec. dir. Am. Vets. Com., 1965—; chairperson Standing Com. Women, World Vets. Fedn.; mem. Pres. Com. Employment of Persons with Disabilities, Inter-Univ. Seminar Armed Forces & Soc.; humanitarian. Mem. Authors Guild, Dramatists Guild, Nat. Press Club. Home: 6309 Bannockburn Dr Bethesda MD 20817

WILLENZ, NICOLE VALLI, management consultant; b. Washington, May 21, 1958; d. Eric and June Adele (Friedenberg) W. BA in Econs., Boston U., 1980. Legis. aide U.S. Ho. of Reps., Washington, 1980-81; asst. to dir. of communications World Council of Credit Unions, Washington, 1981-82; dir. program services, dir. computer and systems devel. Nat. Industrial Transp. League, Washington, 1982-86; dir. electronic data info. products and services Comtrac/First Nat. Bank Chgo., Chgo., 1987; mgr. Price Waterhouse, Chgo., 1988-89, sr. mgr., 1989—. Coordinator seminar series on electronic data info.; contbr. articles to mags. Chair spl. events Folger Shakespeare Theater, Washington, 1980-82; vol. Dollars for Dems., Bethesda, Md., 1980, Holloway for Ho. of Reps. Campaign, Bethesda, 1986, Young Leadership Jewish United Fund, Chgo., 1988; Chgo. Coun. Fgn. Rels. Mem. Am. Nat. Standards Inst. (UN del. 1986—, chmn. ASCX12 internat. project team 1988-89, chmn. transp. project team 1986, chmn. N.Am. EDIFACT bd. 1988-89, N.Am.rapporteur United Nations Econ. Commn. for Europe, 1988—), Nat. Indsl. Transp. League, Data Interchange Standards Assn., Lincoln Pk. West Civic Assn. Democrat. Jewish. Club: Traffic Chgo. Office: Price Waterhouse 200 E Randolph Dr Chicago IL 60601

WILLERT, SISTER ST. JOAN, health care corporation executive; b. Wheeling, W.Va., June 13, 1924; d. Arthur Edgar and Viola (Fitzsimmons) W. BA, Mt. St. Mary's Coll., 1946; human relations cert., Loyola U., L.A., 1951; MS, Mt. St. Mary's Coll., 1953; health care adminstrn., St. Louis U., 1975. Cert. health care adminstrn., elem. sch. adminstrn., secondary sch. adminstrn. Elem. sch. tchr. Diocese of San Francisco, L.A., and Fresno, 1945-54; elem. sch. prin. several cities, 1954-65; secondary sch. prin. Queen of the Valley Acad., Fresno, Calif., 1965-67, Salpointe Catholic High Sch., Tucson, 1967-70; regional superior Sisters of St. Joseph, L.A., 1970-74, Washington, Idaho, 1974-77; with health care adminstrn. Daniel Freeman Hosp., Inglewood, Calif., 1977-79; pres., chief exec. officer Health Care Corp. Ariz., Tucson, 1979—; bd. dirs. Freeman Health Ventures, St. John of God, L.A.; bd. sec. Downtown Devel. Corp., Tucson, 1986—; bd. pres. Our Lady of Lourdes Health Ctr., Pasco, Wash., 1975-81, 85—; bd. chairperson Health Care Corp., St. Louis, 1986—. Contbr. articles to MSMC, 1966, Health Progress, 1982. Chairperson state campaign Arizonans to Protect Quality Health Svc., Phoenix, Tucson, 1984-85. Named for Outstanding Svc. to Community Una Noche Plateada, Tucson, 1982; honoree Tucson Diocesan Found. Mem. Ariz. Hosp. Assn. (bd. dirs. 1979—, sec. 1988, chairperson-elect 1989-90, Salisbury Leadership award 1985), Cath. Health Assn. (bylaws com. 1985-86, nominating com. 1984-85), Health Care Corp. Sisters of St. Joseph (chairperson 1985—). Democrat. Roman Catholic. Office: Carondelet Health Care Corp 1601 W St Marys Rd Tucson AZ 85745

WILLHITE-WRIGHT, JEANNE ELMORE, biologist, researcher, teacher; b. Brownsville, Ky., Apr. 25, 1946; d. Parker and Crystal (Johnson) Elmore; m. Raymond Willhite, July 30, 1966 (div. 1970); 1 child, Raymond Parker; m. Clifford William Wright, May 21, 1984. Student, Jefferson Community Coll., 1974-76; BS in Edn., Ind. U. S.E., 1979; postgrad., U. Louisville, 1980-83. Rsch. technician U. Louisville, 1979-83, sr. med. technologist, 1983-87; sr. med. technologist BioTrax Internat., Fairlawn, N.J., 1987—; cons. Quail Run Dioxin Study, Mo. Dept. Social Svcs., Jefferson City, 1984-85; project coord. rsch. project VA Hosp., Louisville, 1985-86. Recipient Community award Ind. U., 1978. Mem. Am. Assn. Electrodiagnostic Technologists, Am. Diabetes Assn., Juvenile Diabetes Assn. (bd. dirs. 1987-88), Phi Eta Sigma. Republican. Baptist. Home: 1611 Dawn Dr Louisville KY 40258 Office: BioTrax Internat 22-08 Rte 208 Fairlawn NJ 07410

WILLIAMS, ANGELA, account executive; b. Savannah, Ga., Sept. 2, 1966; d. Dwight Reid and Jane (Harris) W. BBA in Mktg., Augusta (Ga.) Coll., 1988; postgrad., Winthrop Coll., 1990—. Asst. fin. cons. Robinson Humphrey Co., Augusta, 1985-88; account exec. AT&T, Columbia, S.C., 1988—. Mem., supporter Greenpeace; active drive com. United Way, 1988, 90. Mem. Palmetto Leadership Coun. (com. 1989-90), Columbia C. of C. (drive com. 1988). Republican. Methodist. Office: AT&T 1201 Main St 22d Fl Columbia SC 29201

WILLIAMS, ANGELA CAROL, legal assistant; b. Thomasville, N.C., Jan. 28, 1970; d. Thomas Clayton Williams and Judy Carolyn (Gerald) Spivey. Cert. paralegal specialist. Crew chief, customer svc. specialist Carabo, Inc. (Bo Jangles), Conway, S.C., 1985-88; receptionist Bates Buie, Lindsey, Evans & Rabon, CPAs, Myrtle Beach, S.C., 1988; file clk. Grand Strand Gen. Hosp., Myrtle Beach, 1988; legal sec., legal asst. Thompson, Henry, Gwin, Brittain & Stevens, P.A., Conway, 1988—. Dir.'s scholar Aynor/Conway Career Ctr., 1988, Rita Heape scholar Aynor/Conway Career Ctr., 1988. Home: 75 Pinehurst Ln Myrtle Beach SC 29575 Office: Thompson Henry Gwin et al 1318 3rd Ave Conway SC 29526

WILLIAMS, ANN C., federal judge; b. 1949; m. David J. Stewart. BS, Wayne State U., 1970; MA, U. Mich., 1972; JD, U. Notre Dame, 1975. Asst. U.S. atty. U.S. Dist. Ct. (no. dist.) Ill., Chgo., 1976-85, judge, 1985—; adj. prof., lectr. Northwestern U. Law Sch., Chgo., 1979—. Mem. Fed. Bar Assn., Fed. Judges Assn., League of Black Women, Women's Bar Assn. of Ill. Office: US Dist Ct 219 S Dearborn St Chicago IL 60604*

WILLIAMS, ANN HOUSTON, zoology educator; b. Red Bank, N.J., Dec. 18, 1943; d. Malcolm David and Juana Maria (Dreyfors) Houston; m. Delbert Erman Williams, July 31, 1976. BS, U. S.C., 1965; MA in Teaching, Duke U., 1972; PhD, U. N.C., 1977. Tchr. high sch. biology A.C. Flora High Sch., Columbia, S.C., 1966-73; teaching asst. U. N.C., Chapel Hill, 1973-77; asst. prof. Southwestern at Memphis (name now Rhodes Coll.), 1978-80; asst. prof. Auburn (Ala.) U., 1980-85, assoc. prof., 1985-90; program adminstr. Sigma Xi, The Sci. Rsch. Soc., Research Triangle Park, N.C., 1990—; cons. Normandeau Assocs., Mass., 1978; bd. dirs. Fed. Credit Union Auburn U.; vis. prof. Dauphin Island (Ala.) Sea Lab, 1981, 82, 84, 85. Author: Report to EPA, 1983; contbr. articles to profl. jours. Wilson fellow U. N.C., 1974-75; grantee NSF, 1975-77, 86-88. Mem. AAAS (EPA rsch. fellow 1983), LWV (bd. dirs. 1983-86), Ecol. Soc. Am., Ala. Acad. Sci. (sec. 1985-90), Mid-South Biology Tchrs. Assn. (pres. 1979-80), Marine Environ. Scis. Consortium (sec. program com. 1985-86, vice chair 1986-87, chair 1987-88), Orgn. for Tropical Studies (bd. dirs. 1986-90), Sigma Xi (chpt. pres.

elect 1988-89), Zeta Tau Alpha (gen. advisor 1981-87). Democrat. Home: 7110 Pine Hill Rd Durham NC 27707 Office: Sigma Xi 99 Alexander Dr Research Triangle Park NC 27709

WILLIAMS, ANN MEAGHER, hospital administrator; b. Hull, Mass., May 28, 1929; d. James Francis Meagher and Dorothy Frances (Antone) Mullins; m. Joseph Arthur Williams, May 15, 1954; children: James G., Mara A., A. Scott (dec.), Gordon M., Mark J., Antoinette M., Andrea M. BS, Chestnut Hill Coll., 1950; MS, Boston Coll., 1952. Radioisotope biologist Air Force Cambridge Rsch. Ctr., Bedford, Mass., 1952-55; asst. mgr. Roxbury Businessmen's Exch., Boston, 1956-66; owner, operator Chatterlane, Osterville, Mass., 1961-66; realtor James E. Murphy Inc., Hyannis, Mass., 1968-77; dir. community affairs Cape Cod Hosp., Hyannis, 1977—. Bd. dirs. Community Coun., Mid Cape, Mass., 1977-88, Cape Cod Mental Health Assn., 1977-82, Ctr. for Individual and Family Svcs., Mid Cape, 1982-87, Am. Cancer Soc., Mid Cape, 1981—; mem. sch. com. Cape Cod Regional Tech. High Sch., 1978—, United Way of Cape Cod, 1988-89; chmn. fin. com. City of Barnstable, Mass., 1969-77. Named Woman of Yr. Bus./Profl. Women's Club, 1982; recipient Cert. Appreciation Am. Cancer Soc., 1983, 88, Pres. Recognition award United Way Cape Cod, 1989. Mem. Am. Soc. Hosp. Mktg. and Pub. Rels., New Eng. Hosp. Pub. Rels. Mktg. Assn., Southeastern Mass. Hosp. Pub. Rels. Assn., Nat. Assn. Hosp. Devel., Chestnut Hill Coll. Alumnae Assn., Rotary. Roman Catholic. Home: 8 E Bay Rd Osterville MA 02655 Office: Cape Cod Hosp 27 Park St Hyannis MA 02601

WILLIAMS, ANNA FAY, economist, writer; b. Newark, July 23, 1935; d. Haney Fay and Mary Lillian Rodgers; children: Paul C. Friedlander, Mark T. Friedlander. B.S. in Journalism cum laude, U. Minn., 1957; M.A. in Broadcast Film Arts, So. Meth. U., 1968, M.A. in Econs., 1975. Editor Richardson (Tex.) News, 1960; asst. editor Sun News, Sun Oil, Dallas, 1960-69; field rsch. dir. Corp. for Pub. Broadcasting, Dallas-Ft. Worth, 1972-75; pres. Multi-Media, Inc., Dallas, 1968-70; instr. econs. So. Meth. U., Dallas, 1973-74, Richland Coll., Dallas, 1975-78, Northlake Coll., Irving, Tex., 1978-80; exec. and founding editor Solar Engring. Mag., Dallas, 1975-81; staff economist Keplinger Cos., energy cons., Houston, 1982-85; v.p. Tex. Commerce Bancshares, 1985-86; presenter profl. paper 18th Intersoc. Energy Conversion Engring. Conf., 1983, 19th, 1984. Author: The Shared Time Strategy, 1966, Dallas Food Finds, 1974, Handbook of Photovoltaic Applications, 1985, Wheeling: A Survey of State Activities, 1989; co-author: New Opportunities to Purchase Natural Gas, 1988; co-editor: Open Protocols, 1989. Mem. Am. Solar Energy Soc. (gen. chmn. ann. meeting 1982), Tex. Solar Energy Soc. (founder, bd. dir. 1978-80), Center for Renewable Resources (officer, bd. dir. 1978-80). Office: 3621 Wake Forest Houston TX 77098-5500

WILLIAMS, ANNIE JOHN, educator; b. Reidsville, N.C., Aug. 26, 1913; d. John Wesley and Martha Anne (Walker) W. AB, Greensboro Coll., 1933; MA, U. N.C., Chapel Hill, 1939; postgrad., Appalachian State U., summer 1944, Duke U., summer 1936, Cornell U., summer 1961. Tchr. math. Blackstone (Va.) Coll., 1934-35; tchr. Hoke High Sch., Raeford, N.C., 1935-37, Massey Hill High Sch., Fayetteville, N.C., 1937-42, Alexander Graham Jr. High Sch., Fayetteville, 1942-43, Carr Jr. High Sch., Durham, N.C., 1943-53; supr. math. N.C. Dept. Pub. Instrn., Raleigh, 1959-62; tchr. math. Durham High Sch., 1953-59, 62-78, ret., 1978; vol. in math. N.C. Sch. Sci. and Math., Durham, 1980—; adj. asst. prof. dept. math. and sci. edn. N.C. State U., Raleigh, 1966-73; mem. 16th Internat. Congress on Arts and Communications, Washington, 1989. Author: (with Brown and Montgomery) Algebra, First Course, 1963, Algebra, Second Course, 1963. Recipient cert. of recognition Dept. Math. and Sci. Edn. N.C. State U., 1979, Gov.'s award for outstanding vol. service, 1986, Disting. Alumni award Greensboro Coll., 1989; named Vol. of Yr., Key Vol. Program co-sponsored by Vol. Svcs. Bur. and Durham Morning Herald, 1986. Mem. Nat. Coun. Tchrs. Math. (life, bd. dirs. 1957-60), Math. Assn. Am. (life), N.C. Council Tchrs. Math. (hon. life, W.W. Rankin Meml. award 1975), Internat. Platform Assn., DAR (N.C. chpt. chair Am. History Month 1980-82, corr. sec. 1982-84, chaplain 1984-86, Gen. Davie chpt.), Pierian Lit. Club (sec. 1979-80, pres. 1980-81), Durham Woman's Club (co-chmn. internat. affairs dept. 1985-87, chmn. 1989—), Delta Kappa Gamma, Mu Alpha Theta (hon.). Methodist. Home and Office: 2021 Sprunt Ave Durham NC 27705

WILLIAMS, BARBARA ANNE, college president; b. Camden, N.J., Oct. 14, 1938; d. Frank and Laura Dorothy (Szweda) W. BA cum laude, Georgian Court Coll., 1963; MLS, Rutgers U., 1965; MA, Manhattan Coll., 1973; postgrad., NYU, 1976—. Cert. English tchr., N.J.; joined Sisters of Mercy, 1957. Sec. Camden Cath. High Sch., 1956-57; registrar Georgian Ct. Coll., Lakewood, N.J., 1960-66, dir. libr. svcs., 1966-74, dean acad. affairs, 1974-80, pres., 1980—; bd. dirs. Ind. Coll. Fund of N.J., N.J. Natural Gas Co., N.J. Woman mag. Bd. dirs. ednl. adv. coun. Diocese of Trenton, N.J., 1983-90; mem. adv. bd. Ocean County Ctr. for Arts, Lakewood, N.J., 1983—; mem. Ocean County Pvt. Industry Coun., 1983—; bd. dirs. Mounmouth/Ocean Devel. Coun., 1981-84. Named Outstanding Woman N.J. Assn. Women Bus. Owners, 1983; recipient Humanitarian award Monmouth/Ocean Devel. Coun., 1985, Salute to the Policymakers award Exec. Women N.J., 1986, Woman in Leadership award Monmouth Coun. Girl Scouts, 1987. Mem. Assn. of Mercy Colls. (pres. 1981-83), Mercy Higher Edn. Colloquium (mem. exec. com. 1980-87), Ocean County Bus. Assn. (trustee 1982-84), Nat. Assn. Ind. Colls. and Univs. (secretariat 1981-83, 87—). Home and Office: Georgian Ct Coll Office of Pres Lakewood NJ 08701

WILLIAMS, BARBARA IVORY, educational researcher; b. Detroit, Apr. 28, 1936; d. Henry Oliver and Willa Mae (Frazier) I.; m. Alney Elliott Whitener, Jan. 1, 1987. BS, Wayne State U., 1957, MEd, 1960; PhD, U. Washington, 1973. Tchr. Detroit Pub. Schs., 1957-68; program assoc. Mich.-Ohio Regional Lab., Detroit, 1968-70; lectr. predoctoral U. Wash., Seattle, 1970-73; sr. program assoc. Far West Lab. for Ednl. Research and Devel., San Francisco, 1973-76; sr. cons. E.H. White & Co., San Francisco, 1976-77; sr. program assoc. Northwest Regional Lab., Portland, Oreg., 1977-84; area coord. Ednl. Testing Service, Washington, 1984-85; edn. group dir. Research and Evaluation Assocs., Washington, 1985-87; ind. cons. Washington, 1987-89; sr. rsch. assoc. Westat, Rockville, Md., 1989—. Mem. Am. Ednl. Research Assn., Am. Psychol. Assn., Nat. Assn. Black Sch. Educators, Phi Delta Kappa, Alpha Kappa Alpha (pres. Portland chpt. 1980-84). Democrat. Baptist. Home: 408 Critenden St NW Washington DC 20011

WILLIAMS, BARBARA JEAN, insurance company executive; b. Binghamton, N.Y., Oct. 4, 1948; d. Walter William and Georgia E. (Bentley) Williams; m. Matthew J. Williams. Grad. high sch., Clyde, N.Y. Sec. Allstate Ins. Co., Rochester, N.Y., 1966-69, telephone adjuster, 1969-73, field auto and home adjuster, 1973-75, initial unit mgr., 1975-78; home office trainer Tech-Cor, Wheeling, Ill., 1978-79; security analyst Rochester, 1979-80; unit claim mgr., 1980, dist. claim mgr., 1980-86; property claim mgr. Rochester, 1987-88, Binghamton, 1988—. Mem. Nat. Assn. Female Execs. Republican. Methodist.

WILLIAMS, BARBARA LOU, library director; b. Seattle, Aug. 20, 1927; d. Lawrence Earl and LouElla Barbara (Eubank) W.; children: Chrstine Mikel, Patricia Hannum, Kathryn McLane, Douglas Alan Hannum. BA, U. Colo., 1948; MEd, U. Ariz., 1963, ednl. specialist, 1976; MLS, U. Okla., 1975. Tchr. Indian Oasis High Sch., Sells, Ariz., 1959-61, Sahuarita Sch., Tucson, 1961-62; elem. libr. Tucson Sch. Dist., 1963-65, high sch. libr., 1965-77; dir. libr. Western Coll., Yuma, 1977-82, Tarrant County Jr. Coll. Dist., Ft. Worth, 1982—. Co-author: History of Sheridan, Wyoming, 1956; editor: Directory of Libraries in Southern Arizona, 1972; contbr. to Nobel Prize Winners, 1987. Mem. ALA, Assn. Ednl. Communication and Tech., Tex. Libr. Assn., Tex. Assn. Ednl. Tech., Tex. Jr. Coll. Tchrs. Assn., Librs. Tarrant County (pres. 1990-91), Trinity Valley Quilters Guild, Ft. Worth Opera Guild. Home: 3003 Marigold Ave Fort Worth TX 76111 Office: Tarrant County Jr Coll 4801 Marine Creek Pkwy Fort Worth TX 76179

WILLIAMS, BETSY LYNN, sales executive; b. Covington, Ky., Aug. 15, 1950; d. John Orwin and Eleanor Margretta (Readle) W.; m. Jeffrey Lynn Goode, May 16, 1977; children: Joshua Langston, Brittany Green. BA, U. Ky., 1972. Tech. writer spl. machine dir. Cin. Milacron Mktg. Co., 1974-76, sales trainee machine tool div., 1977-80; sales engr., plastics machinery div. Cin. Milacron Mktg. Co., Batavia, Ohio, 1980-85, sales/mktg. coord., 1985-87, field sales engr., Cin., 1987-89, sales project eng., 1989—. Schmidd Lapp Found. scholar, Cin., 1968-72. Men. Cin. Area Profl. Saleswomen, Soc. Plastics Engrs. Presbyterian. Home: 6339 Coffey St Cincinnati OH 45230 Office: Cin Milacron Mktg Co 4701 Marburg Ave Cincinnati OH 45209

WILLIAMS, BRENDA JOAN, medical technologist, consultant; b. Clarinda, Iowa, June 9, 1965; d. Donald Lee and Brenda Joyce (Miller) W. BS, N.W. Mo. State U., 1988, MBA; AA, Iowa Western Community Coll., 1985. Registered med. technologist, 1988, lab. scientist, 1988. Product mgmt. technician The Blood Ctr. of Cen. Iowa, Des Moines, 1987-88; med. technologist Heartland Health Systems, St. Joseph, Mo., 1988—; med. technologist, installation cons. Cerner Corp., Kansas City, Mo., 1990—. Recipient Bus. and Profl. Women award and scholarship, 1985. Mem. NAFE, Am. Soc. Med. Technologists. Republican. Baptist. Office: Cerner Corp 2800 Rockcreek Pkwy Kansas City MO 64117 Mailing: RR 4 Box 163 Clarinda IA 51632

WILLIAMS, CAROL JORGENSEN, social work educator; b. New Brunswick, N.J., Aug. 12, 1944; d. Einar Arthur and Mildred Estelle (Clayton) Jorgensen; m. Oneal Alexander Williams, July 4, 1980. BA, Douglass Coll., 1966; MS in Computer Sci., Stevens Inst. Tech., 1986; MSW, Rutgers U., 1971, PhD in Social Policy, 1981. Child welfare worker Bur. Children's Svcs., Jersey City, 1966-67, Outagamie County Dept. Social Svcs., Appleton, Wis., 1967-69; supr. WIN N.J. Div. Youth and Family Svcs., New Brunswick, 1969-70; coord. Outreach Plainfield (N.J.) Pub. Libr., 1972-76; rsch. project dir. County and Mcpl. Govt. Study Commn., N.J. State Legislature, 1976-79; assoc. prof. social work Kean Coll. of N.J., Union, 1979—, assessment liaison social work program, 1987—; cons. NJ. Div. Youth and Family Svcs., 1979—, Assn. for Children N.J., 1985-88; cons., evaluator Thomas A. Edison Coll., 1977—, mem. acad. council, others. Mem. NAFE, NOW, Council on Social Work Edn., Nat. Assn. Social Workers, Assn. for Computing Machinery, Am. Evaluators' Assn., Kean Coll. Fedn. Tchrs. Democrat. Clubs: Good Sam (Agoura, Calif.); Outdoor World (Bushkill, Pa.). Home: 32 Halstead Rd New Brunswick NJ 08901 Office: Social Work Program Kean Coll of NJ Morris Ave Union NJ 07083

WILLIAMS, CAROLYN ANTONIDES, nursing educator; b. Louisville, Oct. 27, 1939; d. John Dwight and Dorothy Ida Marie (Hoffman) Antonides; m. Frank Canon Williams, Dec. 26, 1961. BS with honors in Nursing, Tex. Woman's U., 1961; MS in Pub. Health Nursing Edn., U. N.C., 1965, PhD in Epidemiology, 1969. Asst. prof. nursing Emory U., Atlanta, 1968, assoc. prof., 1969, prof., dir. grad. programs and rsch., 1969-81; assoc. prof. nursing, asst. prof. epidemiology U. N.C., Chapel Hill, 1971-81, assoc. prof. nursing, rsch. assoc. Health Svcs. Rsch. Ctr., from 1971, assoc. prof. epidemiology, from 1981; dean sch. nursing U. Ky., Lexington, 1984—; mem. Pres.'s Commn. Study of Ethical Problems in Medicine and Biomed. and Behavioral Rsch., 1980-82; chair rsch. adv. com. Am. Nurses Found., 1979-81; mem. planning com. study of nursing and nursing edn. Inst. Medicine of NAS, 1980; cons. WHO in S.Am. Editorial bd. Family and Community Health, 1977—, Advances in Nursing Sci., 1979—, Internat. Jour. Nursing Studies, 1981—; contbr. articles to profl. jours. and chpts. in books. USPHS fellow U. N.C., 1969. Fellow APHA (publs. bd., Young Practitioner award 1973), Am. Acad. Nursing (pres., governing coun.); mem. ANA (chair commn. nursing rsch. 1980-82), Coun. Nurse Researchers, Soc. Epidemiol. Rsch., Delta Omega, Sigma Theta Tau. Democrat. Baptist. Office: U Ky Sch Nursing 760 Rose St Lexington KY 40506*

WILLIAMS, CAROLYN ELIZABETH, manufacturing executive; b. Los Angeles, Jan. 24, 1943; d. George Kissam and Mary Eloise (Chamberlain) W.; m. Richard Terrill White, Apr. 9, 1972; children: Sarah Anne, William Daniel. BS, Ga. Inst. Tech., 1969; MM, Northwestern U., 1988. Saleswoman Ea. Airlines, Atlanta, Montreal (Can.) and Seattle, 1964-69; job analyst Allied Products Corp., Atlanta, 1969-70; mgr. Allied Products Corp., Frankfort, Mich., 1970-71; planning analyst, sr. planning analyst Allied Products Corp., Chgo., 1972-74, dir. planning, 1974-76, staff v.p. planning, 1976-79, v.p. planning and bus. research, 1979-86, v.p. corp. devel., chief planning officer, 1986—. Leader Girl Scouts U.S., Highland Park, Ill.; Sunday sch. tchr. Highland Park Presbyn. Ch. Office: Allied Products Corp 10 S Riverside Plaza Chicago IL 60606

WILLIAMS, CAROLYN KNIGHT, assistant principal; b. Malvern, Ark., Feb. 7, 0745; d. Clifford and Louella (Nix) Knight; m. william Hale Williams (div.); children; Christen, Cliff. BS, U. Arkansas, 1967; M of Adminstrn., Sam Houston State U., 1985. Tchr. Westwood Elem., Springdale, Ark., 1967-69, Hollibrook Elem., Houston, Tex., 1970-72; tchr. Roark Elem., Willis, Tex., 1972-81, instructional asst., tchrs. helper, 1984-85; asst. prin. Willis Elem., 1985—; Treas. Arrowhead Property Owners Assn., Willis, 1983—. Bd. dirs. Willis Youth Athletic Assn., 1987—, Am. Heart Assn., Montgomery County, Tex., 1988—; pres. elect Willis Community Edn. Bd., 1990, pres., 1990—. Mem. Am. Bus. Womens Assn. (Willis chpt. v.p. 1985-87, pres. 1987-88, chmn. Willis Community Scholarship, Woman of Yr. 1989), Assn. for Suprs. Curriculum Devel., Tex. Elem. Prins. and Suprs. Assn., Galveston Overall Econ. Devel. Com., Montgomery County Fair Assn. Republican. Episcopalian. Home: 2811 Arrowhead Bend Willis TX 77378 Office: Willis Ind Sch Dist 600 N Campbell Willis TX 77378

WILLIAMS, CAROLYN RUTH ARMSTRONG, educational administrator; b. Birmingham, Ala., Feb. 17, 1944; d. Lonnie and Lois Adel America (Merriweather) Armstrong; m. James Alvin Williams Jr., Nov. 9, 1942. BS, Tenn. State U., 1966; cert., Hawaii U., 1970; MA, Northwestern U., 1972; PhD, Cornell U., 1978. Special project asst. US Senator Paul Tsongas, Boston, Mass., 1983; asst. v. chancellor North Carolina Central Univ., Durham, N.C., 1983-87; asst. dean, assoc. prof. Vanderbilt Univ. Engr. Sch., Nashville, Tenn., 1987—; assoc. dir. Cornell U. Career Ctr., Ithaca N.Y., 1976-82, edn. cons. Youth Data, Ithaca, 1981-, Le Moyne Coll. Higher Edn. Preparation Program, 1977-83; cons. U.S. Dept. Edn. Rev. Bd. Contbr. several articles to prof. jours. Bd. mem. Southern Policies Educational Bd., 1983-87, Clean Comm. System of Durham Bd., 1983-87. Recipient Women of Achievement and Recognition award, YWCA. 1984-87, Black Engineer Leadership award, Natl. Soc. of Black Engr., 1988. Mem. Nat. Assn. Women Deans Adminstrv. Counselors (exec. bd. mem. 1981-), Cornell Women Studies Program (exec. bd. mem. 1981-), Nat. Soc. Black Engrs. (adv. bd., Charles E. Tunstall award for outstanding minority engring. program in U.S. 1990), Soc. Women Engrs. (tech. coord. 1988-, coord. tech. paper comptetition), Nat. Assn. Minority Engrs. Program Adminstrs. (sec., pres.-elect region B 1990—) , Assn. Women in Sci. (bd. dirs. 2 yr. term). Home: 305 Summit Ridge Cir Nashville TN 37235 Home: 36 Morningside Dr Cortland NY 13045 Office: Vanderbilt U Sch Engring PO Box 6006 Station B Nashville TN 37235

WILLIAMS, CHARLOTTE BELL (BUNNY WILLIAMS), sales and marketing executive; b. Houston, Mar. 29, 1944; d. Curtis Blucher and Annie Mae (Jacobs) Bell; m. Edward Arthur Williams, Oct. 24, 1980. Student, Tex. Christian U., 1962-63; BA, U. Tex., Dallas, 1977. Realtor James M. Brown Realtors, Tex., 1978-79; realtor, broker Hank Dickerson Realtors, Dallas, 1978-79, Merrill Lynch Realty, Plano, 1981-84; dir. mktg. KPT, Inc., Dallas, 1984-88; pres. Re:Source, Inc., Dallas, 1988-89; pres., chief exec. officer The Direct Source, Dallas, 1989—; bd. dirs. VRMC, Dallas; lectr. in field. Contbr. articles to profl. and popular jours. Patron Dallas Women's Found., 1986—, Susan G. Komen Found., Dallas, 1987—; sponsor 500 Inc., Dallas, 1987—; mem. Dallas Hist. Soc., 1989—, guild Week-end to Wipe-Out Cancer, Dallas, 1990—; active Women's Found., Dallas, 1986—; mem. Internat. Craniofacial Found. Inc., Dallas, 1990—; co-chmn. Rolex/Corrigan's Cup Polo Ball, Dallas, 1989—. Recipient Disting. Sales award Sales and Mktg. Execs., 1986, 87. Mem. Am. Soc. Profl. and Exec. Women, Doberman Pinscher Club Am. (del., chmn. nat. conv. 1980). Republican. Methodist. Home: 6509 Southpoint Dr Dallas TX 75248 Office: 6509 Southpoint Dr Dallas TX 75248 Office: The Direct Source Inc 2019 McKenzie Ste 150 Carrollton TX 75006

WILLIAMS, CHARLOTTE EVELYN FORRESTER, civic worker; b. Kansas City, Mo., Aug. 7, 1905; d. John Dougal and Georgia (Lowerre) Forrester; student Kans. U., 1924-25; m. Walker Alonzo Williams, Sept. 25, 1926; children: Walker Forrester, John Haviland. Trustee, Detroit Grand Opera Assn., 1960-87 , dir., 1955-60; chmn. Grinnell Opera Scholarship, 1958-66; founder, dir., chmn. adv. bd. Cranbrook Music Guild, Inc., 1952-59, life mem., 1952—; bd. dirs. St. Peter's Home for Boys, Detroit, 1951-53, Detroit Opera Theater, 1959-61, Severo Ballet, 1959-61; Detroit dist. chmn. Met. Opera Regional Auditions, 1958-66; patron-mem. Met. Opera Nat. Council; mem. Central Opera Service, Met. Opera Guild; mem. Friends of Children's Mus. at Singing Pines, Boca Raton Hist. Soc., Greater Miami Opera Guild, Fla. Atlantic U. Found.; past pres. Friends of Caldwell Playhouse, Boca Raton. Mem. Debbie-Rand Meml. Service League (life), DAR, English-Speaking Union, Vol. League Fla. Atlantic U., PEO, Order Eastern Star. Home: 2679 S Ocean Blvd 5C Boca Raton FL 33432

WILLIAMS, CINDY LEE, management consultant; b. Oakland, Calif., Nov. 30, 1958; d. Jess Willard and Betty Joan (Blair) W. A in Bus. Adminstrn., De Anza Coll., 1981; BSBA, San Francisco State U., 1983. Bus. mgr. Brown Matarazzi, San Francisco, 1983-84; adminstrv. asst. D.E.S., Inc., Redwood City, Calif., 1984-85; bus. mgr. Fitschen, Sambucetti, San Francisco, 1982-85, CSS Assocs. Architects, Palo Alto, Calif., 1985; owner, pres. Comprehensive Bus. Svcs., Mt. View, Calif., 1989—. Mem. Soc. Mktg. Profession Services, Soc. Arch. Adminstrs. Democrat. Presbyterian. Office: Comprehensive Bus Services 291 Escuela Ave Ste C Mountain View CA 94040

WILLIAMS, DEBRA ANN, medical technologist, laboratory supervisor; b. Dodge City, Kans., Feb. 28, 1954; d. Melvin Wayne and Marion Alene (Forrest) Marcy; m. Wade Alan Williams, Dec. 29, 1973; children: Renee Allison, Chad Thomas. Student, Colby (Kans.) Community Coll., 1972-73, Northwestern State U., Alva, Okla., 1974; BS in Med. Tech., Wichita State U., 1977, postgrad., 1987—. Cert. Med. Technologist Am. Soc. of Clin. Pathologist. Bench technician Hosp. Dist. 1 Sumner County, Caldwell, Kans., 1977-82; lab. supr. Hosp. Dist. 1 Sumner County, Caldwell, 1982—; co-chmn. First Annual Hosp. Dist. #1 Health Fair, 1987, Second Ann. Hosp. Dist. #1 Health Fair, 1988. Trustee United Presbyn. Ch., Caldwell, 1984-86; chmn. Annual Arts and Craft Fair, Caldwell, 1987. Scholastic scholar Colby Community Coll., 1972, Leoti (Kans.) Rough Riders Saddle Club, 1972, Kans. Soc. of Med. Technologists, Wichita, 1976. Mem. Town and Country Extention Homemakers Unit (pres. 1987, sec. 1986). Democrat. Presbyterian. Home: 119 W Central Caldwell KS 67022 Office: Hosp Dist #1 Sumner County 601 Osage Caldwell KS 67022

WILLIAMS, DENIECE, vocalist; b. 1951; m. Brad Westering; children by previous marriage: Ken, Kevin. Student, Purdue U. Debut album This is Niecey; other albums include Hot on the Trail, I'm So Proud, Let's Hear It for the Boy, My Melody, Niecey, Special Love, Water Under the Bridge, 1987, As Good As It Gets, 1989. Recipient Grammy award for female soul gospel vocal, 1986, group gospel performance (with Sandi Patti), 1986, female gospel performance, 1987. Office: care Gen Talent Internat 1700 Broadway 10th Fl New York NY 10019*

WILLIAMS, DIANE LYNN, food products executive; b. Burgaw, N.C., Aug. 28, 1951; d. James Clayton and Mary Urilla (Ruddell) W. Student, U. N.C., Charlotte, 1969-72, U. Cin., 1980-81. From salesperson to office mgr. Christian Foods Inc., Wilmington, N.C., 1972-75; sec. Swift Agrl. Chems. Co., Wilmington, 1975-76, Biggers Bros. Inc., Charlotte, N.C., 1976-78; sec. Internat. Salt Co., Charlotte, 1978-79, salesperson sodium sulfate, 1979, ter. mgr., 1979-81; mgr. nat. accounts Internat. Salt Co., Clarks Summit, Pa., 1981-88; sr. mgr. nat. accounts AK20 Salt, Inc., Clarks Summit, 1988—. Chair campaign Internat. Salt Co. United Way, 1984, loaned exec. Lackawanna chpt., Scranton, Pa., 1985; bd. dirs. United Cerebral Palsy N.E. Pa., Scranton, 1985—, chair pers. com. 1986—, mem. long range planning com., 1986-88; class participant Leadership Lackawanna, 1986-87; mem. long range planning com. Jr. League of Scranton, 1986-87, treas., 1987-88, bd. dirs., 1987-88, nominating com., 1989-90; advisor youth Clarks Green United Meth. Ch., 1984-85; chairperson Santa's Holiday World, 1988, nominating com. 1988—; bd. dirs. YWCA, 1988-89; co-chair Waverly Antique Show, Waverly, Pa., 1989, chmn. 1990—; mem. Jr. League of Scranton, 1984—, 1988-89, nominating bd., 1988-89, treas., 1987-88, bd. dirs. 1987-88; mem. Tripp House Renovation, 1989-90, Community Rsch., 1987-88, chairperson Santa's Holiday World, 1988. Mem. Am. Mgmt. Assn., Alpha Delta Pi. Republican. Presbyterian. Home: 214 Stoney Creek Rd Clarks Summit PA 18411

WILLIAMS, DIANE WRAY, legislator, teacher; b. Freemont, Ohio, Jan. 23, 1938; d. Daniel H. and Caroline Ruth (Woodward) Charles; m. James G. Wray, divorced; children: Caroline, Cynthia, Amanda; m. Thomas D. Williams, Dec. 11. BA, Syracuse U., 1959. Legislator State of Minn., St. Paul. Presbyterian. Home: 514 S 19th St Moorhead MN 56560-3138 Office: Ho of Reps 567 State Office Bldg Saint Paul MN 55155

WILLIAMS, DOLORES LOUISE, telecommunications executive; b. Rockford, Ill., Apr. 20, 1937; d. Arthur F. and Erma Lee (Johnson) Warner; divorced; 1 child, Leona Marie Williams Pierce. BE, Ottawa (Kans.) U., 1959. Cert. tchr., Kans., Tenn. Tchr., acting principal Navajo Indian Reservation, N.Mex. and Ariz., 1959-62; service rep. Ill. Bell., Rockford, 1972-74; sr. service rep. Michigan Bell, Jackson, 1964-67; sr. service rep. South Central Bell, Memphis, 1967-70, unit supr. bus. office, 1974-81; asst. sales mgr. AT&T and South Central Bell, Nashville and Memphis, 1981—; asst. dir. HWPC Child Care Tng. Program, Memphis, 1970-71; dir. Shelby County Headstart, Memphis, 1971-73. Recipient Outstanding Svc. award Warren Headstart Ctr., Memphis, 1973, Bell System Eagle award, 1981, Ops. Mgrs.' Coun. Excellence award, 1986, 87, Disting. Leadership award Outstanding Svc. in Communications Industry, 1989, White House Communication Cert. of Appreciation, 1988, 89. Mem. Am. Mgmt. Assn., NAACP, NSV Urban League, Robertson Assn. Home: 500 Michele Dr Antioch TN 37013

WILLIAMS, (EDITH) DOREEN, travel agency manager; b. Charlotte, N.C., Aug. 15, 1949; d. Leonard Augustus and Frances Edith (Long) W. AA, Wingate Coll., 1969; BA in Edn., U. N.C., 1971; MA in Edn., U. N.C., Charlotte, 1975. Tchr. Charlotte-Mecklenburg Pub. Schs., 1971-78; travel cons. All Seasons Travel, Charlotte, 1979-80, Trexler World Travel Svc., Charlotte, 1980-82; bus. travel mgr. New Horizons Travel, Charlotte, 1982-83; travel cons., then mgr. Profl. Travel Svcs., Charlotte, 1983-87; travel cons. Sea Gate Travel, Charlotte, 1987-89; gen. mgr. Domer Reeves Travel, Inc., Charlotte, 1989—. Mem. Charlotte Profl. Women in Travel, Earthwatch. Democrat. Home: 1834 Mimosa Ave Charlotte NC 28205 Office: Domer Reeves Travel Inc 2907 Freedom Dr Charlotte NC 28208

WILLIAMS, DOROTHEA WEBB, nursing educator; b. Nashville, June 7, 1948; m. Levy Williams; 1 child, Dorothea Emma Webb. BS in Nursing, Vanderbilt U., 1971; MS in Nursing, U. Mich., 1974, PhD, 1976. Asst. prof. U. Mich., Detroit, 1977-78; assoc. prof. Sch. Nursing, Howard U., Washington, 1978-79; clin. dir. nursing adminstrn. Provident Hosp., Balt., 1979-81; dean, prog. Coppin State Coll., Balt., 1979-81; dir. nursing Brook Lane Psychiatric Ctr., Hagerstown, Md., 1981-82; prof. William Patterson Coll. N.J., Wayne, 1982-84; mem. faculty of medicine Sch. Nursing, Columbia U., N.Y.C., 1985-86; clin. coordinator VA Med. Ctr., East Orange, N.J., 1983-86; dean, prof. Coll. Nursing, Prairie View A&M U., Houston, 1986—; nurse cons. VA, Houston, 1987-88, Harris County Psychiatric Hosp., Houston, 1987-88. Contbr. articles to mags. Bd. dirs. Mar. Dimes Birth Defects, 1987-88; mem. ARC. Mem. Am. Diabetes Assn., Am. Nurses Assn., Nat. League Nursing. Republican. Baptist. Home: 2213 S Braeswood Blvd Ste 13H Houston TX 77030

WILLIAMS, DOROTHY WASHINGTON, pharmacist; b. McCalla, Ala., Jan. 21, 1946; d. Obie and Eldonia (Davis) Washington; m. Vincent T.C. Williams, July 13, 1985. Student, Clark Coll., 1964-66; BS in Pharmacy, Mercer U., 1969. Staff pharmacist Crawford Long Hosp., Atlanta, 1969-75, pharmacy supr., 1975-80, asst. dir. pharmacy, 1980-82, dir. pharmacy, 1982—; adj. prof. Mercer U. Sch. Pharmacy, Atlanta, 1982—. Pfiffer Found. scholar, 1966-69; named to Outstanding Young Women Am., 1975, 76; recipient Community Svc. award Am. Bus. Women Assn., 1986. Mem. Am. Soc. Hosp. Pharmacists, Ga. Soc. Hosp. Pharmacists (dist. bd. dirs. 1985-87), Assn. Black Hosp. Pharmacists (Outstanding Svc. award 1984, arrangement chmn. 1983—), Southeastern Soc. Hosp. Pharmacists, Atlanta Acad. Instnl. Pharmacists. Democrat. Methodist.

WILLIAMS, EDA DUNSTAN, civic worker; m. Ichabod Thomas Williams, June 25, 1930 (dec. Aug. 1987); children: Thomas, Samuel Dunstan, Resolvert Waldron. AB, Vassar Coll., 1929; postgrad., Columbia U., 1957-58. Past chmn., bd. dirs. Far Rockaway (N.Y.) Mother's Health Ctr., Planned Parenthood Greater N.Y., N.Y.C., Peninsula Child Guidance Ctr., Woodmere, N.Y.; past. bd. dirs. Family Svcs. Five Towns, Cedarhurst, N.Y.; past mem. conservation com. Garden Club Am.; bd. dirs., officer Garden Club Lawrence (N.Y.), Clermont Hist. Site, Tivoli, N.Y.; former vol. Bok Tower Gardens, Lake Wales, Fla. Mem. Nat. Soc. Colonial Dames in N.Y. (past v.p., chmn. hist. activities), Pen and Brush Club (pub. poet). Democrat. Home: Mountain Lake Lake Wales FL 33859-0832

WILLIAMS, EDDIE RUTH, elementary educator; b. Shreveport, La., Dec. 23, 1947; d. Spencer Lee Gilliard and Carrie V. (Hollins) Cheese; m. Gerald Maurice Williams; children: Alycia, Tara. BS, Grambling U., 1969; MA, Ea. U., Ypsilanti, Mich., 1982. Cert. elem. tchr., Mich. Elem. tchr. Albion, Mich., 1969—; tchr. Calhoun and Mich. Reading Coun., Albion, 1979—; sch. rep. Sch. Wellness, Albion, 1989; cons. health and wellness class for disadvantaged girls, 1989; reading cons. Crowell Elem. Sch., Albion, 1989. Active Big Sisters/Big Bros., Albion, 1970-78; bd. dirs. Johnson Child Care, Albion, REACH, Inc., Albion; chief usher, v.p. local ch. Named Tchr. of Yr. Negro Bus. and Profl. Women, Albion, 1979; recipient Excellence award 4-H Club, Calhoun County, 1986, Cert. Appreciation REACH, Inc., 1983, United Way, 1986. Mem. Mich. Reading Assn., AAUW, Youth Mental Health Coun., Gifted and Talented Adv. Coun., NAACP, Albion Social Club (historian 1986—), Delta Kappa Gamma. Democrat. Baptist. Home: 704 Orchard Dr Albion MI 49224 Office: Albion Pub Sch 1418 Cooper Albion MI 49224

WILLIAMS, EDNA ALETA THEADORA JOHNSTON, journalist; b. Halifax, N.S., Can., Sept. 19, 1923; d. Clarence Harvey and Edna May (Lewis) Johnston; m. Albert Murray Williams, Apr. 16, 1949 (dec.); children: Murleta, Norma, Martin, Charla, Kerrick, Renwick, Julia. Student, Maritime Bus. Coll., 1943. Typist Dept. Treasury (Navy), Halifax, 1944-49; with Bedford (N.S.) Mag., Halifax br., 1954-55, Presbyn. Office, New Glasgow, N.S., 1965-67, Thompson and Sutherland, New Glasgow, 1967-69; family editor, columnist and reporter New Glasgow Evening News, 1969—. Bapt. rep. Pictou County Coun. of Chs., 1978-82, sec., 1980-82; pres. ch. aux. 2d United Bapt. Ch., 1979-83, organist, 1970—, chorus dir. Men's Choir, 1980—; organist St. James Anglican Ch., 1983-85; provincial pres. Women's Inst. of African United Bapt. Assn., 1983-86; mem. coun. Halifax YWCA; founding mem. Pictou County YM-YWCA, 1966—, bd. dirs., 1967-77, corr. sec., v.p., 1975-77, 1974-75; past pres., past provincial dir. Home and Sch.; provincial sec. African United Bapt. Assn. of Nova Scotia, 1988—; sec. area IV Altantic United Bapt. Conv., 1989—; past officer local interracial com.; bd. dirs. Big Bros./ Big Sisters, 1984-86, Pictou County United Way, 1983—, Pallative Care Aberdeen Hosp., 1985—, Black United Front. Mem. Can. Press Assn. Home: 230 Reservoir St, New Glasgow, NS Canada B2H 4K4 Office: Evening News, 352 East River Rd, Glasgow, NS Canada B2H 5E2

WILLIAMS, ELAINE, publishing executive; b. Cleve., Nov. 6, 1953; d. William S. and Frances M. (Tomsic) Selers; m. David E. Williams, Sept. 1, 1984. BS, DePaul U., 1975. Methods and procedures analyst Walgreen Co., Deerfield, Ill.; mgr. of work measurement Montgomery Wards, Chgo.; mgr. of electronic pub. AMA, Chgo.; dept. dir. of editorial svcs. Journal of the AMA, Chgo. Mem. ASAE (Distinguished Paper award), NAFE. Office: 515 N State Chicago IL 60610

WILLIAMS, ELEANOR JOYCE, government air traffic control specialist; b. College Station, Tex., Dec. 21, 1936; d. Robert Ira and Viola (Ford) Toliver; m. Tollie Williams, Dec. 30, 1955 (div. July 1978); children: Rodrick, Viola Williams Smith, Darryl, Eric, Dana Williams Jones, Sheila Williams Watkins, Kenneth. Student Prairie View A&M Coll., 1955-56, Anchorage Community Coll., 1964-65, U. Alaska-Anchorage, 1976. Clk./ stenographer FAA, Anchorage, 1965-66, adminstrv. clk., 1966-67, pers. staffing asst., 1967-68, air traffic control specialist, 1968-79, air traffic contr. supr., San Juan, P.R., 1979-80, Anchorage, 1983-85, airspace specialist, Atlanta, 1980-83, Washington, 1985—; with FAA, Washington, 1985-87; area mgr. Kansas City Air Rt. Traffic Control Ctr., Olathe, Kans., 1987-89, asst. mgr. quality Assurance, 1989—. Sec. Fairview Neighborhood Coun., Anchorage, 1967-69; mem. Anchorage Bicentennial Commn., 1975-76; bd. dirs. Mt. Patmos Youth Dept., Decatur, Ga., 1981-82; mem. NAACP; del. to USSR Women in Mgmt., 1990; activie Citizens Soviet Union; mem. ambassador program People to People Internat. Recipient Mary K. Goddard award Anchorage Fed. Exec. Assn. and Fed. Women's Program, 1985, Sec.'s award Dept. transp., 1985, Pres. VIP award, 1988. Mem. Nat. Coun. Negro Women, Bus. and Profl. Women U.S.A., Inc., Bus. and Profl. Women U.S.A., Inc.(North to the Future club, charter pres. 1975-76), Blacks In Govt., Nat. Black Coalition of Fed. Aviation Employees (pres. cen. region chpt. 1987—, recipient Over Achievers award, 1987, Disting. Svc. award 1988), Profl. Women Contrs. Orgn., Air Traffic Contrs. Assn., Internat. Platform Assn., Gamma Phi Delta. Democrat. Baptist. Avocations: singing; sewing. Home: 1049 Huntington Circle Olathe KS 66061 Office: FAA 201 S Clairborne Olathe KS 66062 other: PO Box 2728 Olathe KS 66062

WILLIAMS, ELISABETH GREEN, retired educator; b. Ocala, Fla., Mar. 13, 1915; d. Louen Newton and Edna (Sims) Green; m. Walter Arthur Williams, Nov. 13, 1948 (dec.); 1 child, Roberta Sims Williams. BS in Edn., Fla. State U., 1936; postgrad. various colls. Tchr. various schs.; English instr. Edgewater High Sch., Orlando, Fla., 1948-80, ret., 1980. First v.p., Fla. Symphony Guild, parliamentarian, historian; state historian United Daugs. of the Confederacy; lay leader First United Meth. Ch., Orlando; pres. United Meth. Women, Orlando, mem. Customer Adv. Bd., 1985-88, Cen. Fla. Coun. for Fla. House, Washington; pres. Winter Park Woman's Club, 1990—; trustee Fla. House, Washington, 1988; corresponding sec. Thousand Plus for Am. Cancer Soc.; publicity chmn. U. Club of Winter Park, 1988-90. Mem. AAUW (pres. Fla. div., 1968-72), United Nations Assn. (pres., recording sec. state bd.), Huguenot Soc., Retired Tchrs. Assn., DAR (regent Orlando chpt., mem. bd. dirs.), Magna Carta Dames, Delta Kappa Gamma (pres., chmn. coordinating coun., state membership chmn.). Democrat. Home: 1849 Oak Ln Orlando FL 32803

WILLIAMS, ELIZABETH, financial planner; b. San Francisco, Jan. 16, 1948; d. John and Myrtle Mary (Thierry) W.; children: Brian, Jonathan. Cert. in bus., U. Calif., 1979; student, Mike Russ Sch., 1988. Manpower coord., fed. programs U.S. Govt., San Francisco; patient svc. rep. Health Care Svc., Oakland, Calif.; ins. and real estate cons. Al Williams, Inc., Emeryville, Calif.; v.p. Investments Unlimited, Oakland, Calif. Recipient Pub. Speaking award; European Investment fellow. Mem. AAUW, NAFE, NAACP, Nat. Real Estate Owners Assn., Toastmasters Club. Office: 548 40th St Oakland CA 94609

WILLIAMS, ELIZABETH GERTNER, educator, department head; b. Tampa, Fla., Sept. 3, 1927; d. Ernest Richard and Mamie Eloise (Nolan) Gertner; m. Caley Vassar Williams, 1950; children: Michael David, Mark Alan. BA summa cum laude, Wake Forest U., 1949; MA, Columbia U., 1950. Cert. secondary tchr., Fla. Part-time instr. in English Fla. Inst. Tech., Melbourne, 1960-64, 65-67; English tchr. Melbourne High Sch., 1964-65, 67—. Pres. Friends of Melbourne Libr., 1967-68, Gt. Books leader. Mem. AAUW (pres. Melbourne br. 1965-67), Nat. Coun. Tchrs. English, Fla. Coun. Tchrs. English, Brevard Coun. Tchrs. English, Phi Beta Kappa, Phi Delta Kappa. Democrat. Baptist.

WILLIAMS, ELIZABETH GUNDLACH, controller; b. Richmond, Va., Feb. 15, 1944; d. Herman Charles and Dorothy Mary (Hardy) Gundlach; m. Matthew Thomas Williams, July 2, 1966; 1 child, Anne Cary. BA in Psychology, Boston Coll., 1966; MS in Fin., Va. Commonwealth U., 1987. Cert. tchr., Va. Elem. tchr. Charlottesville (Va.) Schs., 1966-67; elem. tchr., coord. St. Mary's Sch., Richmond, 1968-71; tchr. English lang., coord. Chesterfield (Va.) County Schs., 1971-79; acct. H.C. Gundlach Co., Richmond, 1979-80, office mgr., 1980-81, treas., mgr., 1981-85; contr. Sands Anderson Marks Miller, Richmond, 1985-86; cons. fin. and strategic planning svcs. Richmond, 1986-88; contr. Advanced Bus. and Computer Supplies and Svcs., Inc., Alexandria, Va., 1988—; chmn. Textbook Adoption Com., Chesterfield, Va., 1974-75. Sponsor Ameurop Cultural Exchange, Richmond, 1983-84, Fulbright Found., 1985; rep. Richmond Cath. Diocese on Exec. Com. for Ednl. TV, Channel 23, 1968-70; fir. Mid.-Atlantic Chamber Orchestra. Mem. NAFE, Nat. Assn. Accts. (bd. dirs., pub. relations dir. 1986-88), Am. Bus. Women's Assn. (v.p. 1983-84, rec. sec. 1983). Home: 1515 Jefferson Davis Hwy #1302 Arlington VA 22202

WILLIAMS, ELYNOR ALBERTA, public affairs specialist; b. Baton Rouge, Oct. 27, 1946; d. Albert Berry and Naomi Theresa (Douglas) W.; BS, Spelman Coll., 1966; MS, Cornell U., 1973. Home econs. tchr. Eugene Butler Jr.-Sr. High Sch., Jacksonville, Fla., 1966-68; publicist, pkg. editor, copy editor Gen. Foods Corp., White Plains, N.Y., 1968-71; writer, researcher Expended Nutrition Edn. program Cornell U., summer 1972, tutor, com. on spl. edn. projects, 1972-73; communication specialist N.C. Agrl. Ext. Service, N.C. A & T State U., Greensboro and N.C. State U., Raleigh, 1973-77; sr. pub. rels. specialist Western Electric, Greensboro, 1977-83; dir. corp. affairs Hanes Group, Winston-Salem, N.C., 1983-86; dir. pub. affairs, Sara Lee Corp., Chicago, Ill., 1985—. Bd. dirs. Greensboro Drug Action Coun., 1977-83, v.p., 1983; mem. Carolina Theatre Commn., 1977-81; mem. steering com. Guilford County Women's Coalition, 1978; agy. bd. mem. solicitor United Way Campaign, 1977-82; issues chmn. Triad council Girls Scouts Am., 1979-82; mem. Mayor's Energy Conservation Commn., 1977-78; vice-chmn. adv. com. dept. communication arts Cornell U., 1978-79; bd. dirs. Leadership Greensboro Alumni Assn., 1980-81, Women's Aid, 1980, Guilford Tech. Coll., 1981-84; pres. Guilford County Women's Polit. Caucus, 1980-81, Friends of Greensboro Coll. Adv. Com., 1980-82, Greensboro Symphony's Audience Devel. Adv. Com., 1980-82; candidate N.C. Ho. of Reps., 1980; mem. adv. bd. Greensboro Daily News Summer Journalism Inst., 1981; vice chmn. 6th Congressional Black Leadership Caucus, 1980-81; mem. pub. rels. adv. bd. YWCA, 1980-81; trustee U. N.C., Greensboro, 1981—; mem. steering com. N.C. 2000, 1982; mem. Nat. Women's Polit. Caucus; mem. policy coun. N.C. Women's Polit. Caucus, 1982; chmn. Employment Task Force, Gov.'s Assembly on Women and the Economy, 1981; deacon Chgo. United Ch., 1986—; bd. dirs. Hayes-Taylor YMCA, 1983-84, YWCA, Winston-Salem/Forsyth County, 1984-86; mem. adv. council Office of Women in Econ. Devel., N.C. Dept. Commerce, 1985; mem. exec. com. Nat. Women's Econ. Alliance, 1985—; mem. nat. tech. adv. com. OICs of Am., Inc., 1985—; mem. Greensboro Dialogue Task Force, 1983. Recipient Outstanding Svc. award Nat. Coun. Negro Women, 1988, Black and Hispanic Achievers Industry award, 1989; named to Black Women's Hall of Fame, 1988; named one of 10 Top Black Women in Corp. Am., Essence mag., 1989, one of 15 Women Who Make a Difference Minorities and Women in Bus. mag., 1989, one of Am.'s Top 100 Black Bus. and Profl. Women Dollars ans Sense mag., 1988; United Negro Coll. Fund scholar, 1962-66; Cornell U. Grad. Sch. fellow, 1972-73; regional finalist White House fellowship program, 1981-82. Mem. Exec. Leadership Council (founder, bd. dirs. 1986), Internat. Assn. Bus. Communicators, NAACP (Unsung Heroine award 1989), Pub. Rels. Soc. Am., LWV, NOW (mem. corp. adv. bd. legal def. and edn. fund), Cosmopolitan C. of C. (bd. dirs. 1988—), Alpha Kappa Alpha. Democrat. Methodist. Home: 2334 N Commonwealth Chicago IL 60614 Office: Sara Lee Corp 3 1st Nat Pla 46th Fl Chicago IL 60602

WILLIAMS, ERMA BROOKS, academic administrator; b. Lexington, Miss., May 25, 1957; d. Thomas and Rachel (Scott) Brooks; m. Paul L. Williams, Aug. 1, 1981; 1 child, Courtney Rachel. AA, Lincoln Land Community Coll., Springfield, Ill., 1977; BS, Sangamon State U., 1979; MPA, Roosevelt U., 1984. Supr. pages Ill. State Senate, Springfield, 1977-79; rsch. analyst Office of Compt., State of Ill., Springfield, 1977-79; budget analyst Ill. Ho. Reps., Springfield, 1980-81; spl. asst. Congressman Harold Washington, Chgo., 1981-83, Congressman Charles Hayes, Chgo., 1983-87; acting dir. coop. edn. U. Ill., Chgo., 1989-90, asst. to vice chancellor acad. affairs, 1986—. Mem. NAFE, Coun. for Coll. Attendance, Ill. Commn. on Black Concerns in Higher Edn., Ill. Minorities in Higher Edn. Office: Univ Ill 601 S Morgan St Box 4348 M/C 105 Chicago IL 60680

WILLIAMS, ETHEL FRANCES (CHINA WILLIAMS), minister, radio personality; b. Shanghai, Republic of China, Sept. 16, 1928; (parents Am. citizens); d. James M. Smith and Mary Edith (Steinwachs) Smith; m. Robert Gayle Williams, Dec. 2, 1950; children: Susan Marie, Joan Diane. BE, U. Hawaii, 1950; DD (hon.), Am. Fellowship, Monterey, Calif., 1981, Coll. D Metaphysics, Glendora, Calif., 1990. Cert. secondary tchr., Calif.; ordained to ministry Am. Fellowship, 1981, College Divine Metaphysics, 1989; grad., lic. tchr., counselor Unity Sch. of Practical Christianity. Tchr. Ontario (Calif.) Sch. Dist., 1956-61, La Mesa-Spring Valley (Calif.) Sch Dist., 1962-83; founding min., pres. Ch. Living Christianity, Spring Valley, 1983—. Bd. dirs. women's com. Rep. Women's Cub, 1983-84, exec. bd. dirs., 1989; bd. dirs. San Diego Youth Symphony, 1981; mem. bd. Spring Valley Youth and Family Svc.; chairperson Communications Com. INTA, 1990. Recipient Outstanding Svc. award La Mesa Tchrs. Assn., 1983, Outstanding Am. Svc. award Le Mesa C. of C., Bi-Centennial, Outstanding Spanish Rels. award Community Spanish Club, San Diego, 1984; named Spark Plug Toastmasters, La Mesa, 1981. Mem. NEA, AAUW, Calif. Retired Tchrs. Assn., Internat. New Thought Alliance (speaker 1989), Internat. Clergy Assn., Assn. Unity Chs., La Mesa Concert Assn. (sec., bd. dirs. 1975-77), Network of San Diego, Nat. Assn. TV Arts and Scis., Heartland Creative Community Assn., Murdock Cultural Found. Office: Ch of Living Christianity 10435 Campo Rd Spring Valley CA 92077

WILLIAMS, FLORA LEONA, economics educator; b. Talahassee, Jan. 21, 1937; d. Noble J. and Dorothy (Rohrer) Rouch; m. Leiw K. Williams, June 26, 1960; children: Chadwick, Lora Lu, Matthew. BS, Manchester Coll., 1959; MS, Purdue U., 1964, PhD, 1969. Tchr., Mishawaka, Ind., 1959-64, West Lafayette, Ind., 1964-68; research asst. Purdue U., West Lafayette, 1968-69, asst. prof., 1969-75, assoc. prof. home econs., 1975—; vis. prof. U. Calif., Davis, 1976; cons. in field. Author: The Family Economy, 1973, Guidelines to Financial Counseling, 1980; contbr. articles to profl. jours. HEW grantee. Mem. Assn. Consumer Research, Am. Econs. Assn., Am. Home Econs. Assn., Am. Council on Consumer Interest, Family and Consumer Research. Home: 3815 Gate Rd Lafayette IN 47905 Office: Purdue U MTHW Hall CSR Dept West Lafayette IN 47907

WILLIAMS, GAIL ANN, humorist, writer, actor, theater administrator; b. Berkeley, Calif., May 1, 1953; d. Larry C. and Lauretta W. BS, U. Calif., Berkeley, 1978. Founding adminstrv. dir. Plutonium Players, Inc., Berkeley, 1977—; co-founder Ladies Against Women, Berkeley, 1980—; mktg. dir. A Traveling Jewish Theatre, San Francisco, 1988—; artistic cons. Com. to Intervene Anywhere, Teaneck, N.J., 1987, Sara Felder's One Woman Show, San Francisco, 1989-90, One Other Side Project, Berkeley, 1989—; touring-booking cons. Tanya Shaffer's Miss America's Daughters, U.S. tour, 1988-89; jury mem. Nat. Women's Theatre Project Sexist Critic Awards, San Francisco, 1989-90. Co-author, performer: (play) Ladies Against Women, 1982, Women Who Think Too Much, 1989; author: (play) The Clinic, 1989; contbr. articles and cartoons to various publs.; creator Virginia Cholesterol, 1980; author or co-author over 20 produced humorous plays or monologues. Mem. Theatre Bay Area, Alliance for Cultural Democracy, Arts Dem. Club of San Francisco. Recipient Bernie award San Francisco Chronicle, 1983. Mem. NOW (honoree San Francisco chpt. 1987). Office: Ladies Against Women Tour Mgmt 4800 Shattuck Sq Ste 70 Berkeley CA 94704

WILLIAMS, GERTIE BOOTHE, retired home school coordinator; b. Smithfield, Va.; d. Claiborne Benton and Elnora Mae (Brown) Boothe; m. Jesse Cary Williams Sr., June 14, 1949; children: Linda, Jesse Cary Jr., Sharon. BS, Va. State Coll., 1945; postgrad., U. Va., 1971; MS, Va. State Coll., 1980. Technician Norfolk (Va.) Naval Base, 1942-43; filing clk. IRS, Bronx, N.Y., 1945-46; tchr. Sussex County, Waverly, Va., 1946-57; supervising tchr. Va. State U., Petersburg, 1957-59; tchr. Petersburg Pub. Schs., 1957-75, coordinator home sch., 1976-86. Mem. Women for Robb, Gov. of Va., Petersburg, 1979, Am. Heart Assn., MADD. Recipient vol. svc. award Cystic Fibrosis Found., 1979, cert. appreciation Mental Health Project Cen. State Hosp., 1980, Alumnus of Yr. award Petersburg chpt. Va. State U., 1978, Dir.'s award Va. State U., 1978. Mem. NEA, Va. Edn. Assn., Va. State U. Nat. Assn. (v.p. 1984), Am. Heart Assn., Wives Beaux-Twenty (reporter 1985-87), Jack and Jill Am. Ptnrs. (journalist 1957), Nat. Coun. Negro Women (local chmn. 1975), Internat. Platform Assn., Historic Petersburg Found. Inc., Petersburg Symphony Orchestra (women's com.), Mothers Against Drunk Driving, Order Easter Star (worth matron 1949-50), Links (pres. 1977-79, coord. 'Just Say No' 1986-87), Phi Delta Kappa (treas., historian 1978), Kappa Delta Pi (v.p., historian 1981-84), Delta Sigma Theta (pres. 1968-70, initiated "self help" teen program 1970-75). Democrat. Baptist. Home: 920 Shields St Petersburg VA 23803

WILLIAMS, HARRIET CLARKE, retired academic administrator, artist; b. Bklyn., Sept. 5, 1922; d. Herbert Edward and Emma Clarke (Gibbs) W. AA, Bklyn. Coll., 1958; student, Art Career Sch., N.Y.C., 1960; cert., Hunter Coll., 1965, CPU Inst. Data Processing, 1967; student, Chineses Cultural Ctr., N.Y.C., 1973. Adminstr. Baruch Coll., N.Y.C., 1959-85; mktg. researcher 1st Presbyn. Arts and Crafts Shop, Jamaica, N.Y., 1986—; tutor in art St. John's U., Jamaica, 1986—. Exhibited in group shows at Union Carbide Art Exhibit, N.Y.C., 1975, Queens Day Exhibition, N.Y.C., 1980, 1st Presbyn. Arts and Crafts Shop, N.Y.C., 1986, others. Vol. reading tchr. Mabel Dean Vocat. High Sch., N.Y.C., 1965-67; mem. polit. action com. dist. council 37, N.Y.C., 1973-77; mem. negotiating team adminstrv. contracts, N.Y.C., 1975-78; mem. Com. To Save CCNY, 1976-77, Statue Liberty Ellis Island Found., Woodrow Wilson Internat. Ctr. Scholars, Wilson Ctr. Assocs., Washington, St. Labre Indian Sch., Ashland, Mont. Appreciation award Dist. Council 37, 1979. Mem. Artist Equity Assn. N.Y., NAFE, Lakota Devel. Council, Am. Film Inst., Bklyn. Coll. Alumni, Nat. Geog. Soc., Nat. Mus. Woman in the Arts (Washington), Statue of Liberty Ellis Island Found. Inc., Am. Mus. Natural History, Internat. Ctr. for Scholars-Wilson Ctr. Assocs., Arrow Club-St. Labre Indian Sch. Mont. Roman Catholic. Office: Baruch Coll 17 Lexington Ave New York NY 10010

WILLIAMS, HARRIET ELIZABETH, educator; b. Greenville, S.C., July 13, 1918; d. Clairmont Allen and Lida Lee (Logan) Williams; m. Joshua Marcus Williams, May 27, 1989. BA, Spelman Coll., 1939; MA, Atlanta U., 1946; MEd, S.C. State U., Orangeburg, 1967; postgrad., Columbia U., 1962. Cert. maths. and secondary edn. tchr., S.C. Tchr. Gower St. Elem. Sch., Greenville, 1939-42; chair math. dept. Sterling High Sch., Greenville, 1942-61; tchr. math. S.C. State Coll., summers 1944-46; dir. guidance svcs. Washington High Sch., Greenville, 1961-71; guidance counselor Wade Hampton High Sch., Greenville, 1971-79, ret., 1979. Author: Some Applications of Vector Methods to Plane Geometry & Plane Trigonometry, 1946. Vol. Dem. Party of Greenville County, 1959—; mem. pub. arts com. City of Greenville, 1985—. Nat. Def. Edn. Act fellow, 1962-69. Mem. AAUW, Greenville chpt. Links, Inc. (charter). Baptist. Home: 215 Webster Rd Greenville SC 29607

WILLIAMS, HEATHER NILES, jewelry designer; b. Worchester, Mass., May 8, 1962; d. Norman Briscoe and Cynthia (Fulton) W. BFA, Phila. Coll. of Art, 1984. Jewerly designer Trifari, Krussman & Fishel, N.Y.C., 1984—. Mem. Cooper Hewitt Mus. Mem. U. of Arts Alumni Assn., U.S. Yacht Racing Union. Republican.

WILLIAMS, HELEN MARGARET, accountant; b. Fresno, Calif., Mar. 16, 1947; d. James Ray Jr. and Barbara (LaRue) Franklin; m. Phillip Dean Bangs, Apr. 16, 1977; children: Aluvia, Adevia, Rodney. AA in Home Economics, Sacramento City Coll., 1969, AA in Acctg., 1971; BS in Acctg. and Fin. cum laude, Calif. State U., Sacramento, 1988. Acct. Calif. Coun. on Criminal Justice; acct. I, revenue rn. controller Sacramento Regional Transit Dist., acct. II, editor employee newsletter, 1986-90. Past mother and worthy adv. Rainbow for Girls; past host parent Am. Field Svc. Mem. NAFE, Am. Soc. Women Accts., Calif. State U.-Sacramento Alumni Assn., Order of Ea. Star. Office: PO Box 2110 Sacramento CA 95812

WILLIAMS, JANELLE EVON, foundation official; b. Billings, Mont., July 20, 1959; d. John F. Williams and N. Karen (Young) Musgrave; m. Douglas L. Corbridge, Dec. 17, 1976 (div. June 1980); 1 child, Jason. Student, Ea. Mont. Coll., 1987—. Asst. mgr. Size 5.7.9 Shop, Billings, 1977-78; retail mgr. Satin Garter, Billings, 1978-79; night mgr. lounge Dos Machas, Billings, 1979-81; sales rep. US West Communications, Billings, 1981-90; program devel. coord. EMC Found., Billings, 1990—. Mem. telethon com. Arthritis Found., Billings, 1986-87; sec. bd. dirs. Billings Citizens Advocacy, 1987—; dir. spl. events summer games Mont. Spl. Olympics, Billings, 1987-88; mem. Spl. Olympics outreach program, 1988-90; mem. 1977 reunion com. Billings West High Sch., 1986-90. Mem. NAFE, U.S. West Women, Mont. Devel. Officers Assn. Republican. Methodist. Home: 2918 Silverwood St Billings MT 59102 Office: EMC Found 2615 Virginia Ln Billings MT 59101

WILLIAMS, JANET FAYE, education educator; b. Osage, Iowa, Oct. 17, 1934; d. Millard John and Vida Ann (Larson) Hovelson; m. Richard Edward Williams. AA, Mason City (Iowa) Jr. Coll., 1955; BS, Winona State U., 1970, MS in Edn., 1975. Tchr. Huxley (Iowa) Consol. Sch. Dist., 1955-56, Mason City Pub. Sch., 1956-57, Olmsted County, Rochester, Minn., 1969; resource tchr. Dist. #531, Byron, Minn., 1970—; spl. edn., reading dir. Ind. Sch. Dist 531, Byron, 1988-89; spl. learning disability resource tchr. Anclote Elem. Sch., Elfers, Fla., 1990—; cons. spl. edn. Winona (Minn.) State U., 1970-77. Inventor 100 Math Games, permanent exhibit at Winona State U. 1976. Vol. Good Samaritan Nursing Home, St. Ansgar, Iowa, 1985—. Mem. NEA, Minn. Edn. Assn., Byron Edn. Assn. (Tchr. of Yr. 1980). Lutheran. Home: 8251 Brent St #915 Port Richey FL 34668 Office: Anclote Elem Sch 4000 Madison S Elfers FL 34653

WILLIAMS, JANICE DENISE, physician; b. N.Y.C., Apr. 19, 1951; d. Ausborn John and Estelle (Mims) Williams. B.S., Fordham U., 1973. M.D., SUNY-Buffalo, 1977. Diplomate Am. Bd. Medicine and Surgery. Tchr. aide Bd. Edn. N.Y.C., Queens, 1973; extern surgery Harlem Hosp. Ctr., N.Y.C., 1974; resident ob-gyn Nassau County Med. Ctr., East Meadow, N.Y., 1977-81; attending phys. ob-gyn USPHS, Mt. Vernon, N.Y., 1981-84; attending phys. ob-gyn Mt. Vernon Neighborhood Health Ctr., 1981-86; attending physician ob-gyn Chenango Bridge Med. Group, 1986-89; attending gynecologist Nat. Health Service Corp. USPHS, 1981-83; attending obstetrician-gynecologist Mt. Vernon Hosp., 1981-86, United Health Services Wilson Meml. Hosp., Binghamton Gen. Hosp., Our Lady of Lourdes Hospital, 1986—; assoc. Camacho & Prosuad, Johnson City, 1990—; clin. instr. Mt. Vernon Hosp., 1981-83, Sch. Medicine SUNY, Binghamton, 1986-90, part-time physician Univ. Health Svc, 1989—; cons. Broome County Psychol. Ctr., 1989—. Active Leader Girl Scouts Am., N.Y.C., 1970-73; mem. NAACP, Jamaica, N.Y., 1982-83; bd. dirs. URBAN League Broone County div. Fellow N.Y. State Med. Soc., Broome County Med. Socl.; mem. Student Nat. Med. Assn. (scholar 1974), AMA, Am. Women's Med. Assn., Am. Coll. Ob-Gyn, Susan Smith McKinney Steward Med. Soc., Nat. Residents Assn., Chenango Forks Sch. Dist. Health Com., Am. Cancer Soc.

WILLIAMS, JEAN MYERS, research associate, consultant; b. McDowell County, W.Va., Nov. 2, 1948; d. Charles Henry and Ruby Virginia (Terry) Myrs; m. David Ramsay Williams, Aug. 22, 1970; children: Katherine Kelly Williams Small, Jonathan David. BA in Early Childhood Edn., U. N.C., Greensboro, 1970, MEd in Ednl. Rsch. and Evaluation, U. N.C., 1986. Cert. tchr. Tchr. Orange County Schs., Orlando, Fla., 1972, Seminole County Schs., Winter Park, Fla., 1972-77, High Point (N.C.) Pub. Schs., 1977-80, Henry County Pub. Schs., Martinsville, Va., 1980-85; grad. asst. U. N.C., Greensboro, 1985-86; coordinator institutional rsch., planning and edn. Patrick Henry Community Coll., Martinsville, 1986-89; rsch. assoc. Region B Tech. Assistance Ctr., Indpls., 1989—; cons. E.H. Turkle & Assocs., Hyde Park, Vt., 1988-89. Author reports and articles. Mem. Am. Ednl Rsch. Assn. Republican. Lutheran. Home: 648 E St Clair St Indianapolis IN 46202 Office: Tech Inc One Decatur Sq Ste 150 150 E Ponce de Leon Ave Decatur GA 30030

WILLIAMS, JEANNE FREEMAN, retired statistics educator; b. Providence, Feb. 9, 1924; d. Albert Moore and Helen (Bishop) Freeman; m. John Howard Williams, May 28, 1947; children: Deborah, John Bradford, Ross Freeman. BS, U. R.I., 1944; MS, N.C. State U., 1946; postgrad., U. N.C., Greensboro, 1958, 69, U. N.C., Chapel Hill, 1976. Instr. math. U. Conn., New London, 1947-48; assoc. prof. stats. Elon Coll., N.C., 1957-82, chmn. dept. acctg., econs. and bus., 1961-71; rsch. instr. N.C. State U., Raleigh, 1944-46; biometrician USDA, Washington, 1946-47; statis. cons. Mental Health Ctr., Burlington, N.C., 1972-76. Editor: Alamance County Health Services Directory, 1972. Former leader, officer Girl Scouts U.S.A.; chmn. Alamance Health Planning Coun., Burlington, 1973-76; mem. Community Coun. Alamance, 1988-90; vol. tutor Burlington Pub. Schs., 1989-90; vol. with elderly; mem. Almance Arts Coun., 1978—. Reynolds grantee

Elon Coll., 1975-76, rsch. grantee, 1978-79. Mem. AAUW (pres. N.C. div. 1969-70), Pi Gamma Mu. Mem. United Ch. of Christ. Home: 2209 Walker Ave Burlington NC 27215

WILLIAMS, JOY RHONDA, publishing company executive; b. Ipswich, Australia, May 30, 1945; came to U.S., 1954; d. Francis Leon and Ailsa Mary (Bailey) W.; m. Raymond Joel Bennett, Feb. 12, 1962 (div. 1974); 1 child, Melissa Anne Howell. AA in Psychology, DeAnza Coll., Cupertino, Calif., 1974. Exec. sec. Cobilt div. Computervision, Sunnyvale, Calif., 1972-74; tracking system analyst Memorex, Inc., Santa Clara, Calif., 1974-77; computer operator LCS Inc., Sunnyvale, 1977-78; project libr. Logisticon Inc., Sunnyvale, 1978-79, programmer-analyst, 1979-82; sr. programmer-analyst Microvertics, Inc., Mountain View, Calif., 1982-83; sr. systems analyst Data Architects, Inc., San Francisco, 1983-84; tech. editor Sci. Applications Internat. Inc., Los Altos, Calif., 1985-86; owner, pres. Artist Publs. Inc., Cupertino, 1984-89; west coast corr. MTV Music News, 1989; v.p. Williams-Feely Entertainment, Hollywood, Calif., 1990; owner, pres. Entertainment Svcs. Internat., Hollywood, 1990—; U.S. corr. Gosteleradio USSR, 1990—, Komsomolskaya Pravda, Moscow, 1990—; staff writer Rock Hard mag., Fed. Republic of Germany, 1990—, Jazz Forum Internat., 1988—. Contbg. editor Thrash Metal mag., 1989—, Metal mag., 1989—; writer BAM mag., 1990—; news corr. MTV Music, N.Y. Office: Entertainment Svcs Internat 7080 Hollywood Blvd Hollywood CA 90028

WILLIAMS, JOYCE ANN, educator; b. Kirksville, Mo., June 22, 1944; d. Hillis Edward and Betty Joyce (Graham) Ewing; m. Robert Dean William, May 22, 1965; children: Christian Ewing, Todd Evans. BS in Edn., Northeastern Mo. State U., 1965, MA, 1968; postgrad., U. Mo., 1974, Drake U., 1981, U. Iowa, Iowa State U. Cert. tchr., Mo., Kans., Iowa. High sch. tchr. LaPlata (Mo.) Pub. Schs., 1965-66, Kirksville Pub. Schs., 1966-68, Kansas City (Kans.) Pub. Schs., 1974-75; jr. high tchr., counselor Ottumwa (Iowa) Community Sch., 1968-74, dir. spl. edn., 1986—; spl. edn. cons. So. Prairie AEA, Ottumwa, 1975-85, supr. instructional svcs., 1985-86; mem. undergrad. faculty Buena Vista Coll., Ottumwa, 1983—; presenter to confs. in field. Program chmn. P.E.O., Ottumwa. Mem. AAUW, Coun. for Exceptional Children (past officer), Delta Kappa Gamma, Phi Delta Kappa. Office: Ottumwa Community Schs 426 McCarroll Dr Ottumwa IA 52501

WILLIAMS, JUDITH ANN, small business owner; b. Lancaster, Calif., Aug. 10, 1954; d. Robert Melvin Williams and Cora Lee (Clemow) Williams Campbell. AA, Ventura Coll., 1979; BA in Communications, U. Wash., 1982. Editor Nat. Oceanic & Atmospheric Adminstrn., Seattle, 1982; liaison asst. Navl Ship Weapon Systems, Washington, 1983; program mgr. Tech. Applications, Inc., Alexandria, Va., 1984-86; logistics analyst Value Systems Engring. Corp., Alexandria, 1986-87; tng. analyst Designers & Planners, Inc., Arlington, Va., 1987; prin. Ind. Profl. Writers & Assoc., Alexandria, 1987-88; sr. logistician Support Mgmt. Svcs., Inc., Oxnard, Calif., 1989—. Author newsletter articles, 1988; mng. editor USN newsletter, 1986. Mem. Soc. Naval Architects and Marine Engrs. (assoc., dir. 1987-88), Navy League of U.S. (dir. pub. affairs 1986-87), Nat. Assn. Female Execs.

WILLIAMS, JULIE BELLE, psychiatric social worker; b. Algona, Iowa, July 29, 1950; d. George Howard and Leta Maribelle (Durschmidt) W.; BA, U. Iowa, 1972, MSW, 1973. Lic. psychologist, ind. clin. social worker, marriage and family therapist, Minn., social worker, Iowa. Social worker Psychopathic Hosp., Iowa City, 1971-72; OEO counselor YOUR, Webster City, Iowa, 1972; social worker Child Devel. Clinic, Iowa City, 1973; therapist Mid-Eastern Iowa Community Mental Health Ctr., Iowa City, 1973; psychiat. social worker Mental Health Ctr. N. Iowa, Mason City, 1974-79, chief psychiat. social worker, 1979-80; asst. dir. Community Counseling Ctr., White Bear Lake, Minn., 1980-85, dir., 1985—; lectr., cons. in field. NIMH grantee, 1972-73. Mem. Nat. Assn. Social Workers (cert., pres. local chpt.), NOW, Am. Orthopsychiat. Assn., Am. Assn. Sex Educators, Counselors and Therapists, Minn. Women Psychologists, Minn. Lic. Psychologists, Phi Beta Kappa. Democrat. Office: 1280 Birch Lake Blvd N White Bear Lake MN 55110

WILLIAMS, KAREN B., advertising executive; b. Pittsburgh, Apr. 24, 1956; d. Robert Duane and Jean Carol (Niblett) B.; m. Lawrence Warner. BA in Fgn. Languages, No. Ill. U., DeKalb, 1978. Media research asst. Leo Burnett, Chgo., 1978-81, media research specialist, 1981-83, media research analyst, 1983-85; v.p., dir. media rsch. and systems Lewis Gilman & Kynett, Phila., 1985-89; mgr. computer svcs. Long, Haymes & Carr, Winston-Salem, N.C., 1989—. Republican. Presbyterian. Office: Long Haymes & Carr 150 Charlois Blvd Winston-Salem NC 27103

WILLIAMS, LA RONNIA VERNON DOBSON, retired educator; b. Kansas City, Mo., July 28, 1934; d. Arthur Burkes and Mary (Briscoe) Vernon; adopted parents: William Augustus and Gladys (Martin) Dobson; m. Elmo Green Jr., July 1956 (div. June 1970); children: Ruth Annette Sims, Patricia Griffin, Gladys Faye Haile, Elmo Green III; m. Franklin Don Williams, Mar. 24, 1973. BA, Spelman Coll., 1955; MA, Atlanta U., 1960; postgrad., U. Md., Annapolis, 1974-76; MA, Valdosta State coll., 1980. Tchr. Telfair County Bd. Edn., Lumber City, Ga., 1955-65; tch. spl. edn. Telfair County Bd. Edn., McRae, Ga., 1965-70, Atlanta City Schs. Bd. Edn., 1970-73; tchr. learning disabilities, dept. head Anne Arundel County Bd. Edn., Ft. Meade, Md., 1973-77; tchr. learning disabilities Valdosta (Ga.) City Schs. Bd. Edn., 1977-90; co-owner, dir. Valdosta Reading Clinic., Valdosta, Lowndes, Ga., 1986-88; workshop dir., presenter Valdosta City Schs. and Valdosta State Coll., 1985—; dept. head Valdosta Jr. High Sch., 1978-81. Weekly columnist, corr. Valdosta Daily Times, 1989—. Vol. instr. Camp Relitso Community Learning Ctr., Valdosta, 1979—; bd. dirs., treas., charter mem. Adoption Svcs.-Children With Spl. Needs, South Ga., 1988—; choir pres., clk., Bible sch. dir. St. James Missionary Bapt. Ch., Valdosta, 1981—; coord., com. mem. Census Edn. Project 1990, Valdosta, 1990; pres., charter mem. Ladies of Profession, Telfair County and Atlanta, 1955-74; troop leader Girl Scouts U.S., Telfair County; mem. Lowndes/Valdosta Polit. Action Com. Recipient Congl. Citation/Civic Svc., U.S. Ga. Congressman, 1983; named Tchr. of Yr., Telfair County Tchrs. and Edn. Assn., 1971, to Ga. Tchr. Hall of Fame in State Capitol, Ga. Assn. Educators, 1987, Educator of Yr., Black Hist. Action Soc., 1989, Woman of Achievement southeast dist. Bus. and Profl. Women, 1990, Mother of Yr., Community Bapt. Ch., 1976, Progressive Citizen of Yr., Citizens in Action, 1983, Citations-Outstanding Svc., Vols. for Pub. Schs., 1981-89; recipient Proclamation from Mayor of Valdosta, 1983. Mem. NEA, AAUW (br. v.p. 1987-89, br. pres. 1989—, state div. chairperson-elections 1988-89, regional leadership trainer 1988—, nat. diversity trainer 1989—), Telfair County Tchr.'s Assn. (sec., v.p., pres. 1955-72), Valdosta Assn. of Educators' (v.p., pres., chairperson 1982-86), Ga. Assn. Educators (chairperson women's concerns 1988-90, lobbyist and moderator for legis. forums 1979—), South Ga. Coun. Exceptional Children (sec.-treas. 1983, v.p., pres. 1989-90), Ga. Coun. Exceptional Children (named direct svc. tchr. of year 1987), Internat. Reading Assn., Delta Sigma Theta (Black action com.). Democrat. Home: 505 E New Hudson St Valdosta GA 31601 Office: Valdosta City Schs 1204 Williams St Valdosta GA 31603-5407

WILLIAMS, LILLIE B., systems analyst; b. Seguin, Tex., June 5, 1945; d. Anderson Jr. and Dovie V. (Pettit) Johnson; m. James Clint Williams, May 26, 1984; 1 child, Lisa. AA, St. Philip's Coll., 1965; BA, St. Mary's U., 1976; postgrad., U. Tex. Instr. St. Philip's Coll., San Antonio; systems analyst, tng. coord. City Pub. Svc., San Antonio. Mem. allocation panel United Way, 1987—. Named Miss St. Philip's, 1965. Mem. NAFE, ASTD, Hospices of San Antonio (bd. dirs.). Methodist. Office: City Pub Svc PO Box 1771 San Antonio TX 78298-1771

WILLIAMS, LINDA MANGHAM, corporate executive; b. Atlanta, Feb. 23, 1945; d. Harvey R. and Bernice (O'Kelley) Mangham; m. Jimmy L. Smith, Dec. 21, 1963 (dec. Jan. 1964); 1 child, Kellie Smith Williams Stein; m. Maryon J. Williams, Jr., June 9, 1968; 1 child, Claire Elaine. Student, Augusta Coll., 1972; student, U. Pa., 1989; BSBA, Thomas Edison Coll., 1989. Exec. sec. Firestone Tire & Rubber Co., Atlanta, 1966-68; Exec. asst. P & I Co., New Brunswick, N.J., 1968-72; vol. Med. Coll. Ga. Faculty Wives, Augusta, Ga., 1972-77; owner Freelance Editorial Svc., Princton Junction, N.J., 1977-79; recording sec. West Windsor Twp., Princton Junction, 1979-81; acting office mgr. Fellows Read & Assocs., Princeton, N.J., 1980-81; dir. corp. communications The Hillier Group, Princeton, 1981-86; dir. pub. affairs N.J. Dept. Commerce, Energy & Econ. Devel., Trenton, 1986—; pres. Entertainment Inc., Princeton Junction, 1989—; mem. Employer Support of Guard & Reserve, Trenton, 1985—; mem. econ. com. N.J. Bus. & Industry Assn., Trenton, 1985-87; chair meetings & conv. com. N.J. Alliance for Action, Edison, N.J., 1985-86; sr. assoc. Dunwoodie Communications, Inc. 1989—. Contbr. articles to profl. jours. Past mem. Grover's Mill Pond Restoration Com., Princeton Junction; mem. Faculty Wives Club, Med. Coll. Ga., Augusta, 1972-77; scout master Girl Scouts U.S., Piscataway, N.J., 1970-71, asst. scout master, Augusta, 1972-74. Named one of Outstanding Women in Govt., Gov. of N.J., 1987. Mem. Pub. Relations Soc. Am., N.J. Bus. and Industry Assn., Princeton Area C. of C. Office: Entertainment Inc 21 Quaker Rd Princeton Junction NJ 08550

WILLIAMS, LINDA TURNER, social services organization administrator; b. St. Louis, Oct. 28, 1941; d. Lucius Don IV and Louise Patton (Richardson) Turner; m. John Howard Williams, Aug. 17, 1963; children: Don Sheldon, John Rolland. AB, U. Ill., 1963; MA, Santa Clara U., 1976. Lic. marriage, family and child counselor, Calif. Tchr. Community Sch. Music and Art, Mountain View, Calif., 1972-77; therapist intern North County Mental Health, Palo Alto, Calif., 1975-77; dir. social svcs. Palo Alto chpt. ARC, 1977-80, exec. dir., 1982-89; exec. dir. Planned Parenthood Santa Clara County, San Jose, Calif., 1989—; project dir. Bus. Info. Analysis Corp., Haverford, Pa., 1980-82, mgmt. cons. Western chpts., 1987-89; vice chmn. Pvt. Industry Coun., Sunnyvale, Calif., 1987—; bd. dirs. Vol. Exch., San Jose, Calif., Planned Parenthood Affiliates of Calif., Sacramento, Woodside (Calif.) Consulting Group. Vol. Santa Clara (Calif.) United Way, 1983—. Mem. Assn. United Way Agys. (mem. exec. com., past pres. Santa Clara chpt.), Neighbors Abroad, Nat. Women's Polit. Caucus, Rotary, Phi Beta Kappa, Kappa Kappa Gamma. Republican. Office: Planned Parenthood 1691 The Alameda San Jose CA 95126

WILLIAMS, LORELLE (LOLLY WILLIAMS), automobile sales administrator; b. Seattle, June 24, 1945; d. Maximillian Herzig Best and May Best Tompkins; m. Don Armstrong Williams, Apr. 20, 1974. Student, Pasadena City Coll., 1962-64, North Bay Coll., 1968, No. Va. Community Coll., 1969-70. Lic. real estate agt., Va. Mgr. personnel City of Los Angeles, 1963-69; sales rep. Bellaire, Inc., Washington, 1969-72; sales mgr., rep. Brown's Volvo and Subaru, Alexandria, Va., 1972—; cons. Herzig and Assocs., Alexandria, 1985—; distbr. Nu-Skin Internat. Mem. Assn. for Research and Enlightenment.

WILLIAMS, LORETTA WALTON, geriatrics services professional; b. Pittsylvania County, Va., Jan. 20, 1938; d. Alfred L. and Ruth (Tarpley) Walton; m. Lee Conrad Williams, Sept. 25, 1965; 1 child, Rolanda Ruth. Student, St. Paul's Coll., Rutgers U., 1967. Mgr., buyer Garwood Mills Shopping Cen., Atlantic City, N.J.; charge office clerk Hombergers Dept. Store, Atlantic City; pharmacist asst. Lynn Drugs, East Orange, N.J.; sr. svcs. project dir. Pittsylvania County Community Action, Inc., Chatham, Va. Vol. Va. Sr. Olympics, 1989-90; asst. youth bible study tchr., 1989, 90; mem. NAACP, 1990. Recipient Cert. of Appreciation New Life Jaycees. Mem. NAFE. Baptist. Home: Rt 6 Box 168B Chatham VA 24531

WILLIAMS, LULA AGNES, retired writer, retired educator; b. Bentonville, Ark., May 11, 1904; d. Thomas Andrew and Nellie Louella (Mason) Nichols; m. Esmond Leonidas Williams, June 12, 1927 (dec. Jan. 1961). BA, U. Ark., 1956. Cert. secondary tchr., cert. to teach English and social studies. Stenographer Benton County Hardware Co., Bentonville, Ark., 1922-25; tchr. country sch. Cross Lanes, Bentonville, 1925-26; stenographer-sec. Skelly Oil Co., El Dorado, Kans., 1926-27; asst. adminstr. Benton County Home, Bentonville, 1935-40; acting postmaster U.S. Post Office, Bentonville, 1944-45; tchr. Bentonville Schs., 1956-70; acting postmaster U.S. Post Office, Bentonville, 1961-62; writer Bentonville, 1985-88. Author, pub.: Hills Are for Climbing, 1988. Pres. Bates Meml. Hosp. Aux., 1972, Qui Vive, Gen. Fedn. Women's Clubs, Bentonville, 1973; worthy matron Order of Eastern Star, Bentonville, 1936. Named Woman of Yr., Bus. and Profl. Women's Club, Bentonville, 1981-82; recipient Svc. award AAUW, Bentonville, 1981. Mem. Nat. Retired Tchrs. Assn. (life), Ark. Retired Tchrs. Assn. (life), U. Ark. Alumni Assn. (life). Democrat. Mem. Christian Ch. (Disciples of Christ). Home: 306 NW 6th Bentonville AR 72712

WILLIAMS, LULA MAE, nurse; b. Columbus, Ga., Aug. 12, 1947; d. Roosevelt and Lula Belle (Bridges) W. BS in Nursing, Tuskegee Inst., 1970; M of Nursing, Emory U., 1973. Staff nurse VA Med. Ctr., Tuskegee, Ala., 1971-72, clin. specialist, 1974-77; head nurse VA Med. Ctr., Nashville, 1977-81; asst. chief nurse VA Med. Ctr., Poplar Bluff, Mo., 1981-84; assoc. chief nurse VA Med. Ctr., Perry Point, Md., 1984-85, quality assurance coordinator, 1985—. Contbr. articles to profl. jours. Served to 2d lt. U.S. Army, 1967-70, lt. col. Res. Mem. NAFE, Nat. Assn. Quality Assurance Profls., Md. Assn. Quality Assurance Profls., Soroptimist Internat., Harve de Grace, Res. Officers Assn., Delta Sigma Theta (Harford County v.p. 1987, treas. 1988). Democrat. Mem. Church of Christ. Office: VA Med Ctr Bldg 5H Perry Point MD 21902

WILLIAMS, LYDIA FRANCES, telecommunications company official; b. New Orleans, Aug. 28, 1949; d. Edgar Joseph and Muriel (Bartholomew) W. BS in Math., Xavier U., New Orleans, 1971. Cert. info. systems auditor. Programmer Mountain Bell Telephone Co., Denver, 1973-74, sr. programmer, 1974-77, staff mgr., 1977-81, audit mgr., 1981-87; acctg. mgr. U S West Communications, Denver, 1987-89; mgr. internal controls U S West Communications, 1989—; cons. Bartholomew Enterprises, Denver, 1986—. Mem. U.S. West Women, Friends of Denver Pub. Library. Mem. NAACP, Black Career Women Inc., EDP Auditors Assn. (past CISA coord.), Inst. Internal Auditors, Project Mgmt. Inst., Soc. Info. Mgmt., Data Processing Mgmt. Assn., Nat. Brotherhood Skiers (Nordic activities dir. 1986—, editor newsletter 1986—, Pioneer award 1988, Pres.'s award 1987, Rocky Mountain Region award 1989), Soc Profl. and Exec. Females, Black Employees Assn. (editor newsletter 1979-84), Nat. Assn. Female Execs., U.S. Ski Assn., Am. Assn. Artificial Intelligence, USSA, Martin Luther King Club, Flyers Running Club (historian 1985-87), Martin Luther King Jr. Flyers Running Club, Zeta Phi Beta (editor newsletter 1982-84), Kappa Gamma Pi. Democrat. Roman Catholic. Office: U S W Communications 930 15th St Rm 750 Denver CO 80202

WILLIAMS, LYNDA ELAINE, small business owner; b. Topeka, Aug. 30, 1951; d. James David and Doris Darleen (Davis) Leek; m. Ronald O. Williams, July 10, 1977 (div. Jan. 1987); children: Rebecca Laura, Ryan Christopher. Student, Foothill Jr. Coll., 1969-70, Deanza Jr. Coll., 1971. Designer trainee Douglas Haylock Total Graphics, San Jose, Calif., 1971-78; architect, engr. ARAMCO, Dhahran, Saudi Arabia, 1978-79, creative dir. Material Supply, 1979-83, graphic designer, 1980-84, lectr., 1981-83; owner, designer Creative Designs, Napa, Calif., 1984—; cons. U. Petroleum and Minerals, Dhahran 1982-84, Nat. Paper Products Co., Dammam, Saudi Arabia 1981-84. Artist, designer Saudi Arabian Met/Ocean, 1979. Mem. Nat. Assn. Female Exec., Napa C. of C. Baptist. Club: Toastmaster Internat., (pres. 1982-83, treas. 1981-82).

WILLIAMS, M. JANE, marketing and sales executive; b. Salem, Ohio, Aug. 17, 1955; d. Robert Angus and Mary Elizabeth (Riddle) W.; 1 child, Landon Matthew Betsworth. BSBA, Youngstown State U., 1984. Cert. real estate agt. N.C. Corp. acct. Westminster Co., Greensboro, N.C., 1984-86; market analyst Zaremba Coms. N.C., Inc., 1986; sales mgr. Stonehaven Zaremba, Winston-Salem, N.C., 1987; sales and mktg. mgr. Laurel Brook at Adams Farm and Windsor Park R&D Homes, Inc., Greensboro, 1987-88, Westminster Co., Greensboro, 1988—. Mem. Profl. Women's Consortium (bd. dirs., pres. elect 1987, pres. 1988—, chmn. 1989—), Nat. Assn. Homebuilders (chmn. sales and mktg. coun. 1989—), Ambassadors Club-Greensboro C. of C. Unitarian Universalist. Home: PO Box 10224 Greensboro NC 27404

WILLIAMS, M. SUZANNE, computer programmer and analyst; b. Savannah, Ga., July 19, 1963; m. Jeffrey Allen Williams, Oct. 1, 1988. B. Applied Sci., Fla. Atlantic U., 1987. Jr. programmer IBM, San Jose, Calif., 1985-86; sr. programmer/analyst Siemens Credit Corp., Boca Raton, Fla., 1986—. Mem. AAUW.

WILLIAMS, MARGARET HELEN, education educator; b. Ft. Lauderdale, July 18, 1926; d. Robert Walter and Alice Estella (Pease) Williams. BS, Ga. State Coll.for Women, 1949; MEd, Coll. of William and Mary, Va., 1969. Tchr. Lowerly (Ga. High Sch., 1946-47; dietitian Battey State Hosp., Rome, Ga., 1948-50; tchr. Norfolk City (Va.) Pub. Schs., 1956—; freelance photographer. Past pres., past internat. bd. dirs. Tidewater Radio EMergency Communications Team, 1975-77; pilot CAP. Col. USAF, 1950-52, with Res. 1952-85, ret. Named Vol. of Yr. Tidewater, 1979. Mem. NEA (life), Am. Radio Relay League, Internat. Freelance, Coxswain and Pilot U.S. Coast Guard Auxiliary. Republican.

WILLIAMS, MARGARET KAY, editor; b. Washington Court House, Ohio, Dec. 7, 1946; d. John W. and Mildred A. (Kinzer) W. BA in Missions and Bible, Cin. Bible Sem., 1968. Missionary African Christian Mission, Zaire, Africa, 1968-78; med. sec. Jewish Hosp., Cin., 1978-80; editor R-A-D-A-R Standard Pub., Cin., 1980—. Dir. children's workshop Loveland (Ohio) Ch. of Christ. Home: 9321 Comstock Dr Cincinnati OH 45231

WILLIAMS, MARGARET LU WERTHA HIETT, nurse; b. Midland, Tex., Aug. 30, 1938; d. Cotter Craven and Mollie Jo (Tarter) Hiett; m. James Troy Lary, Nov. 16, 1960 (div. Jan. 1963); 1 child, James Cotter; m. Tuck Williams, Aug. 11, 1985. BS, Tex. Woman's U., 1960; MA, Tchrs. Coll., N.Y.C., 1964, EdM, 1974, doctoral studies, 1981. Cert. psychiat. mental health nurse practitioner. Nurse Midland Meml. Hosp., 1960-63; instr. Odessa (Tex.) Coll., 1963-67; dir. ADNP Laredo (Tex.) Jr. Coll., 1967-70; asst. prof. Pan Am. U., Edinburgh, Tex., 1970-72; nursing practitioner St. Luke's Hosp., N.Y.C., 1972-79; sgt. Burns Security, Midland, 1979-81; safety compliance officer Area Builders, Odessa, 1981-83; field supr. We Care Home Health Agy., Midland, 1983-87; pres. Nursing Rsch. and Consultation, Stanton, Tex., 1982—; night supr. Glenwood, A Psychiat. Hosp., Midland, 1987—; co-owner, operator MTW Elec. Contractors, Stanton, Tex.; adj. prof. Pace U., N.Y.C. Mem. exploration task force summer youth health careers West Tex. Rural Health Edn. Project, 1987, 88, 89, 90; active Girl Scouts U.S., Midland, 1962-72. Recipient Isabelle Hampton-Robb award Nat. League for Nursing, 1976, Achievement award Community Leaders of Am., 1989, Ladies 1st of Midland, 1974. Mem. NAFE, Tex. Nurses Assn. (pres. dist. 21 1962-65, dist. 32 1970-72), Am. Nurses Assn. (cert., del. 1966-72), Tex. Nurses Assn., Am. Psychiat. Nurses Assn. (cert.), Parkland Meml. Hosp. Nurses Alumnae Assn., Tex. Women's U. Alumnae Assn., Midland High Sch. Exes, Old Soreheads Community Band (keyboard player), Mensa. Democrat. Presbyterian. Office: PO Box 1218 Stanton TX 79782

WILLIAMS, MARI MELANIE, sales executive; b. Hayti, Mo., June 23, 1965; d. G. Robert and Annette (Phillips) W. BS in Journalism, Ark. State U., 1987. Asst. buyer, merchandise specialist Federated Dept. Stores, Memphis, 1987-88; acct. mgr. Eastman Kodak/Qualex, Jackson, Miss., 1988-90; profl. sales rep. Bristol Myers Squibb, Princeton, N.J. Mem. Miss. Coalition for Choice, Jackson; mem. allocation com. United Way, Jackson, vol. chmn. Federated Dept. Stores campaign, Memphis. Named to Outstanding Women Am., 1987. Mem. NAFE, Alpha Omicron Pi (v.p, 1987, Rose award 1987, various coms.), Kappa Tau Alpha, Gamma Beta Phi. Methodist. Home: 484 Kingston #260 Rochester Hills MI 48307 Office: Bristol Myers Squibb PO Box 4500 Princeton NJ 08543

WILLIAMS, MARILYN, health care organization executive; b. Ashland, Ky., July 28, 1950; d. Charley Thurman and Wilma Margaret (Burke) W. BS, Queens Coll., 1971; MS, U. Ala., Birmingham, 1977. Asst. biochemist So. Research Inst., Birmingham, 1972-75; asst. exec. dir. Jefferson County Med. Soc., Birmingham, 1977-78; dir. project rev. Birmingham Regional Health Systems Agy., 1978-80; v.p. planning and regulation Miss. Hosp. Assn., Jackson, 1980-82; v.p. planning, regulation and data Miss. Hosp. Assn., 1982-85; chief oper. officer Commn. on Profl. and Hosp. Activities, Ann Arbor, Mich., 1986—. Contbr. articles to profl. jours. Mem. allocations com. United Way, Jackson, 1985; bd. dirs. Modern Dance Collective, Jackson, 1985. Richards Co. scholar, 1970; named an Outstanding Young Women of Am., 1974, Woman of Yr. Jackson Bus. and Profl. Women's Club, 1984; recipient Commendation award VA, 1977. Mem. Am. Coll. Healthcare Execs., Am. Hosp. Assn. Soc. Hosp. Planning and Mktg., U. Ala. Alumni Assn. Grad. Program in Hosp. and Health Adminstrn. Democrat. Home: 1116 W Washington Ann Arbor MI 48103 Office: Commn Profl and Hosp Activities 1968 Green Rd PO Box 304 Ann Arbor MI 48106

WILLIAMS, MARION ELIZABETH, teacher, educational consultant; b. New Haven, Dec. 30, 1941; d. Taylor Leroy and Viola (Byrd) Lee; m. Paul Edward Williams; children: James L. Walker Jr., Coiln Lamonte Walker. AS, S.C.C.C, New Haven, 1977; BS, New Hampshire Coll., 1986; student, S.C.S. U., 1980. Tchr. New Haven Day Care Program, 1977-83; tchr. The Early Learning Ctr., New Haven, 1983--, cons. for workshops, 1983--; tchr. First Ch. of Christ Ch. Sch., New Haven; workshop presenter South Central Community Coll., New Haven, 1984--; teen coordinator Farnam Neighborhood House, New Haven, 1987-88. Mem. Assn. for Childhood Ednl. Internat., Nat. Head Start Assn., AAUP, Assn. for Supervision and Curriculum Development. Democrat. Home: PO Box 639 New Haven CT 06510 Office: The Early Learning Ctr SCCC 60 Sargent Dr New Haven CT 06510

WILLIAMS, MARLYS J., retired educator; b. Madison, Wis., Jan. 15, 1932; d. Raymond Shoults and Elizabeth Iva (Weghorn) Mallow; m. Dean G., July 15, 1972. BA, Milton Coll., 1953; MA, U. Wis., Madison, 1957. Tchr. Durand High Sch., Durand, Ill., 1953-54, Reedsburg (Wis.) High Sch., 1954-57, Viroqua High Sch., Viroqua, Wis., 1958-59; prof. U. Wis., Platteville, Wis. Mem. AAUW, MMLA, NCTEC. Methodist. Home: 845 Jewett St Platteville WI 53818

WILLIAMS, MARTHA ETHELYN, information science educator; b. Chgo., Sept. 21, 1934; d. Harold Milton and Alice Rosemond (Fox) W. B.A., Barat Coll., 1955; M.A., Loyola U., 1957. With IIT Rsch.Inst., Chgo., 1957-72, mgr. info. scis., 1962-72, mgr. computer search ctr., 1968-72; adj. assoc. prof. sci. info. Ill. Inst. Tech., Chgo., 1965-73, lectr. chemistry dept., 1968-70, rsch. prof. info. sci., coordinated sci. lab. Coll. engring.; also dir. info. retrieval research lab. U. Ill., Urbana, 1972—, affiliate, computer sci. dept., 1979—; chmn. large data base conf. Nat. Acad. Sci./NRC, 1974, mem. ad hoc panel on info. storage and retrieval, 1977, numerical data adv. bd., 1979-82, computer sci. and tech. bd., nat. rsch. network rev. com., 1987-88, chmn. utility subcom., 1987-88; mem. task force on sci. info. activities NSF, 1977; U.S. rep. review com. for project on broad system of ordering, UNESCO, Hague, Netherlands, 1974; vice chmn. Gordon Rshc. Conf. on Sci. Info. Problems in Rsch., 1978, chmn., 1980; mem. panel on intellectual property rights in age of electronics and info. U.S. Congress, Office of Tech. Assessment; program chmn. Nat. Online Meeting, 1980—; cons. to numerous cos., govt. agys. and rsch. founds. Editor-in-chief: Computer-Readable Databases—A Directory and Data Sourcebook, 1976-89, founding editor, 1989—; editor Ann. Rev. Info. Sci. and Tech., 1976—, Online Rev., 1979—; contbg. editor: column on Databases to Bull. Am. Soc. Info. Sci., 1974-78; editorial adv. bd. Database, 1978-88; editorial bd. Info. Processing and Mgmt., 1982-89; contbr. numerous articles to profl. jours. Trustee Engring. Info., Inc., 1974-87, bd. dirs., 1976—, chmn. bd. dirs., 1982-89, v.p., 1978-79, pres., 1980-81; regent Nat. Library Medicine, 1978-82, chmn. bd. regents, 1981; mem. task force on sci. info. activities NSF, 1977-78; mem. nat. adv. com. ACCESS ERIC, 1989-91. Recipient best paper of year award H. W. Wilson Co., 1975; NSF travel grantee Luxembourg, 1972; NSF travel grantee Honolulu, 1973; NSF travel grantee Tokyo, 1973; NSF travel grantee Mexico City, 1975; NSF travel grantee Scotland, 1976. Fellow AAAS (elected, computers, info. and communication mem.-at-large 1978-81, nominating com. 1983, 85); hon. fellow Inst. Info. Sci., 1985; mem. Am. Chem. Soc., Am. Soc. Info. Sci. (councilor 1971-72, 87-89, chmn. networks com. 1973-74, chmn. spl. interest group on SDI 1974-75, pres. elect 1986-87, pres. 1987-88, past pres. planning com. 1988-89, chmn. 1989, nominations com. 1989, chmn. budget and fin. com. 1987-89, Award of Merit 1984, Pioneer Info. Sci. 1987), Assn. for Computing Machinery (pub. bd. 1972-76), Assn. Sci. Info. Dissemination Ctrs. (v.p. 1971-73, pres. 1975-77), Nat. Acad. Sci. (joint com. with NRC on chem. info. 1971-73), U.S. Nat. Com. for Internat. Fedn. for Documentation. Home: RR1 Monticello IL 61856 Office: U Ill CSL 2-262 1101 W Springfield Ave Urbana IL 61801

WILLIAMS, MARY ALICE, journalist; b. Mpls.; m. Mark Haefeli; 1 child, Alice Ann. BA in English and Mass Communications, Creighton U. Reporter, news producer Sta. KSTP-TV, Mpls.; exec. producer, news mgr. Sta. WPIX-TV, N.Y.C.; reporter, anchor Sta. WNBC-TV, N.Y.C., from 1974; with Cable News Network, 1979-89, prime-time anchor, v.p., 1982-89; with NBC News, N.Y.C., 1989—, co-anchor Yesterday, Today and Tomorrow, 1989, co-anchor Sunday Today, 1990—. Recipient By Line award N.Y. Press Club, 1977, Headliner award, 1986; named Woman of Yr., Women in Cable, 1988. Office: NBC News 30 Rockefeller Pla New York NY 10112*

WILLIAMS, MARY BETH, technical writer, publisher; b. Kingsport, Tenn., Aug. 5, 1956; d. James Edwin and Sylvia Ann (Hamilton) Williams; m. Joel David Canon, Aug. 30, 1980; 1 child, Benjamin Franklin. BA in Philosophy, U. Tenn., 1977; MPA, Tenn. State U., 1984. Environ. planner I Tenn. Div. Air Pollution Control, Nashville, 1978-79, environ. planner II, 1979-83, environ. planner III, 1983-84; sr. staff writer Softlink, Bloomington, Ill., 1986-87; ptnr. Info. Mgmt. Assocs., Bloomington, 1987-90, owner, 1990—. Mem. AAUW (newsletter editor 1987-90), Soc. Tech. Communication, Women in Communications (v.p. 1990), Rotary (scholastic bowl com. chmn. 1989-90). Office: Information Mgmt Assocs 1101 Hollyridge Cir Bloomington IL 61704

WILLIAMS, MARY ELMORE, English and history educator, educational administrator; b. San Angelo, Tex., Sept. 19, 1931; d. Taylor and Florrine (Gee) Elmore; m. Mark B. Williams, Sept. 6, 1951; children: John Mark, Mary Jean. AA, San Angelo Coll., 1950; BS, Tex. Christian U., 1951; MS, Corpus Christi State U., 1983; postgrad. U. Chgo., 1954, Princeton U., 1961, Mansfield Coll., Oxford U., 1966. Tchr. 1st grade First Methodist Ch., Dallas, 1951-52; tchr. 8th grade Pleasant Grove Jr. High, Dallas, 1952-54; tchr. history Hamlin Jr. High Sch., Corpus Christi, 1958; tchr. 6th grade St. Christopher's Episcopal Sch., Lubbock, Tex., 1968; tchr. English and history Hamlin Jr. High, Corpus Christi, 1974—, asst. prin., 1989—; coord. Adopt-a-School Program, 1983—; organizer of Vet.'s Day Patriotic Rally; cons. KEDT-TV Tex. History series The Lone Star, Corpus Christi, 1984-85; cons. textbook com. Corpus Christi Ind. Sch. Dist., 1983, 86; mem. curriculum writing team Corpus Christi Ind. Sch. Dist., 1985-86. Mem. Animal Control Bd.; campaign coord. Ruth Gill for Mayor, Corpus Christi, 1979; del. Gov.'s Commn. for Women, San Antonio, 1985; mem. Corpus Christi Coun. for Women; chmn. Tchr. Task Force on Edn. for state rep. Ted Roberts, 1986-88, chmn. tchr. com. Better Sch. Program, 1987, chmn. tchr. task force for excellence in edn. for State Rep. Todd Hunter, 1988—. Named Outstanding Tchr., Am. History-Tex., DAR, 1986; recipient Robert A. Taft accolade for Excellence in Tchng. Govt. and Politics, 1986; named Tchr. of Yr. Corpus Christi Ind. Sch. Dist., 1990-91. Mem. Assn. Curriculum and Devel., Corpus Christi Council Social Studies (v.p. 1981-83), Nat. Coun. Social Studies, Tex. Council Social Studies (conv. chmn. 1988), Corpus Christi C. of C. (events chmn. 1983), PTA (life), YWCA (v.p., chmn. bldg. com. 1983—), AAUW (v.p. 1983-85, pres. 1986-88), Phi Delta Kappa, Delta Kappa Gamma. Avocations: tennis, reading. Home: 601 Barracuda Pl Corpus Christi TX 78411 Office: Hamlin Middle Sch 3900 Hamlin Dr Corpus Christi TX 78411

WILLIAMS, MARY IRENE, college administrator; b. Hugo, Okla., June 30, 1944; d. Primer and Hyler B. (Tarkington) Jackson; m. Lee A. Williams (div. June 1981); 1 child, Monica Ariane. BS in Bus. Edn., Langston U., 1967; MS in Bus., Emporia (Kans.) State U., 1973; EdS, U. Nev., Las Vegas, 1977; postgrad., U.S. Internat. U., 1987—. Instr. Spokane (Wash.) Community Coll., 1967-70; tchr. bus. Topeka Pub. Schs., 1970-73; instr. Clark County Community Coll., Las Vegas, 1973—, adminstr., 1978—. Named Educator of Yr. Nucleus Plaza Assn., 1985, New Visions, Inc., 1986. Mem. Internat. Assn. Bus. Communicators, Nat. Bus. Edn. Assn., Internat. Assn. Female Execs., Nev. Dist. Export Coun., Nev. World Trade Coun., Nat. Coun. on Black Affairs, Am. Assn. Community and Jr. Coll. Office: 3200 E Cheyenne Ave North Las Vegas NV 89030

WILLIAMS, MAXINE ELEANOR, reading educator; b. Birmingham, Ala., Nov. 8, 1940; d. Ocie and Annie Bell (McCants) Easter; m. Ardre Dell Williams, Aug. 3, 1968 (div. 1988); children: Andrea Babett, Roxanne Denise, John Ashley. BS, Tuskegee Inst., 1963; MA, Mich. State U., 1970. Elem. tchr. Chester A. Moore Elem. Sch., Ft. Pierce, Fla., 1963-64, R.J. Wallis Elem. Sch., Kincheloe AFB, Mich., 1964-66, Alexander Elem. Sch., Grand Rapids, Mich., 1966-67, Brown St. Elem. Sch., Milw., 1967-68, Jefferson T.P.L.L., Milw., 1968-78; team leader Twenty First Sch., Milw., 1978-80; reading tchr. Bryant & Parkview Sch., Milw., 1980-81; reading resource tchr. Morse Mid. Sch., Milw., 1981—. Census ctr. vol. Morse Mid. Sch., 1990. Recipient Excellence Pin Milw. Pub. Schs., 1983. Mem. NAACP, Milw. Tchrs. Edn. Assn., Wis. State Reading Assn. Democrat. Meth. Home: 11706 N Silver Ave Mequon WI 53092

WILLIAMS, MELVA JEAN, oil and gas company executive; b. Burke, S.D., June 11, 1935; d. Wayne and Mildred Eva (Graham) Mulholland; grad. Roberta's Finishing Sch., Miami, Fla., 1950, Charron-Williams Comml. Coll., 1954; m. J.B. Williams, Apr. 29, 1977; children—Mark, Doris, Robin, Jeannie. With Southeastern Resources Corp., Ft. Worth and Rising Star, Tex., 1968—, pres., 1979-83, vice chmn. bd., 1983—, also dir.; with Delta Gas Co., Inc., Tchula, Miss., 1973-81, sec., treas., 1974-81, also dir.; with SERPCO, Inc., Fort Worth, 1977-88 , v.p., 1980-84, pres., 1984-88 , also dir.; sec., treas. J J & L Drilling Co., Inc., Ft. Worth and Cisco, Tex., 1979-82, also dir.; with Rising Star Processing Corporation, Fort Worth, sec. treas. 1981—, also dir.; with Brownwood Pipeline Corporation, Fort Worth, sec. treas. 1981-88 , also dir.; gen. partner B & W Real Estate Investments, Nashville, 1980-90, F & W Real Estate Investments, Fort Worth, 1981-90, Westward Properties, Ft. Worth; bd. dirs. Aero Modifications Internat., Inc., Ft. Worth and Waco, Tex., GeoDyne Inc., Ft. Worth. Mem. adv. bd. Ctr. for Study of Addiction Tex. Tech U., Lubbock. Republican. Home: 6150 Indigo Ct Fort Worth TX 76112 Office: 2201 Scott Ave Fort Worth TX 76103

WILLIAMS, MELVA MAUREEN, medical technologist; b. New Orleans, Sept. 8, 1958; d. Everett Joseph and Melva Dier (Borris) W. BS, Loyola U., New Orleans, 1982; MT, Touro Infirmary Hosp., 1983. Non-registered lab. technician Alton Ochsner Med. Found., New Orleans, 1981-82, registered med. technologist, 1983-86, med. tech. supr., 1986-90; tech. dir. Ochsner Med. Found., New Orleans, 1990—. Mem. Am. Soc. Clin. Pathologists (registered med. technologist), Nat. Assn. Female Execs., La. Soc. Prevention of Cruelty to Animals, Humane Soc. of the U.S., Alton Ochsner Med. Found. Soc. Avocations: cooking, reading, stitching, writing, swimming, animals. Home: 1730 Constantinople St New Orleans LA 70115 Office: Alton Ochsner Med Found 1516 Jefferson Hwy New Orleans LA 70121

WILLIAMS, MELVENIA COREAN, college administrator; b. Norway, S.C., Nov. 11, 1945; d. Abe and Rosa Lee (Tyler) W. BS, S.C. State Coll., 1987. With Bright Hope Bapt. Ch., Phila., 1965-66; exec. sec. to pres. Voorhees Coll., Denmark, S.C., 1971-77; sec. to pres. Claflin Coll., Orangeburg, S.C., 1977-84; adminstrv. asst. to pres. Claflin Coll., Orangeburg, 1984—. Recipient cert. of honor for Outstanding Service, Claflin Coll., 1983, Presdl. Disting. Svc. award Voorhees Coll. 1974. Mem. Nat. Assn. Female Execs. AAUW, Zeta Phi Beta, Alpha Kappa Mu. Democrat. Baptist. Lodge: Order of Eastern Star. Home: 897 Magnolia St Orangeburg SC 29115

WILLIAMS, MEREDITH JANE, philosophy educator; b. Anniston, Ala., July 29, 1947; d. Wilbur Eric and Martha Jane (Felgar) Swenson; m. Michael James Williams, Apr. 21, 1974; 1 son, Paul Hereward. Student Coll. William and Mary, 1965-67; B.A., NYU, 1969, Ph.D., 1974; M.A., U. Chgo., 1970. Asst. prof. philosophy Wesleyan U., Middletown, Conn., 1974-79, assoc. prof., 1979-85, chairperson dept. philosophy, 1983-84; assoc. prof. Northwestern U., Evanston, Ill., 1985—; vis. assoc. prof. U. Mich., Ann Arbor, spring 1983. Contbr. articles to profl. jours., 1976—. Mem. Am. Philos. Assn., Soc. for Philosophy and Psychology. Office: Northwestern U Dept Philosophy Evanston IL 60201*

WILLIAMS, MICHELE OLGA, education educator; b. Indiana, Pa., Jan. 14, 1949; d. Michael and Olga (Dovensky) Smandra; m. Arthur E. Williams, Jr. BS, Ind. U., 1970, MEd, 1976, postgrad., 1989. Tchr. reading Conemaugh Twp. Sch., Davidsville, 1970-71; elem. tchr. Homer-Ctr. Sch., Homer City, Pa., 1972-82; reading specialist Homer Ctr. Sch., 1982-87, 89—; teaching assoc. Indiana U. of Pa., 1987-89. Fundraiser, chmn. Am. Assn. Univ. Women Ind., 1987-88; sec. Ind. Reading Coun., 1988-89. Mem. Nat. Edn. Assn., Pa. State Edn. Assn., Internat. Reading Assn., Keystone State Reading Assn. Home: 157 Mazza St Homer City PA 15748

WILLIAMS, MIKKI TERRY, speaker, trainer, consultant; b. Bronx, N.Y., July 4, 1943; d. Louis Schwartzbaum and Bette (Rubinstein) Rawson. m. Gabriel Michael Durishin, June 25, 1966 (dec. Feb. 1973); 1 child, Jason Todd; m. Anthony John Williams, June 4, 1977. BS in Phys. Edn., Ithaca Coll., 1965; MBA in Hotel Mgmt., U. New Haven, 1987. Instr. various high schs., N.Y., Conn., 1965-70; choreographer, performer various theaters, univs., N.Y., Conn., 1970-76; owner gourmet catering service The Happy Cooker, N.Y., Conn., 1973-79; owner A Dance Class, Westport, Conn., 1976-87, The Body Firm, Fairfield, Conn., 1980-87, Kisses Boutique, Westport, 1982-84; founder The Mikki Williams Dancers, Westport, 1977-87; sales and mktg. dir. Sportsplex, Embassy Hall, Belgie Imports, 1989—; dir. dance div. Univ. Bridgeport (Conn.), 1977-78; seminar speaker, cons. Mikki Williams Unltd., 1984—; program mktg. mgr. Conn. Pub. Broadcasting System; state rep. Internat. Dance Exercise Assn., Conn., 1985—; adv. bd. mem. Reebok, New Eng., 1986—. Artistic dir. Young Americans Dance Fest. (first place award, 1987). Governing bd. Levitt Pavilion Performing Arts, Westport, 1978—; ; mistress of ceremonies Leukemia Soc., March of Dimes, Westport, Stamford, 1980—; chmn. Town of Westport 150th Birthday Celebration, 1985. Recipient Am. regional cuisine award Culinary Inst. Am., 1986, showmanship and originality award Young Ams. Invitational, 1987, Presdl. Sports award, 1987, Eli Whitney Entrepreneurial award, 1987, community commitment award and bus. person of Westport, 1989, Outstanding Conn. Woman of Decade award UN, 1987, Internat. Fitness Bus. Person of Yr. award IDEA, 1989. Mem. Am. Soc. Assn. Execs. (convention mgmt. 1987), Nat. Assn. Female Execs., Nat. Speaker's Assn., Am. Coll. Sports Medicine, Entrepreneurial Women's Network (pres. 1987—), Am. Woman's Econ. Devel. Corp., Westport C. of C., SACIA. Democrat. Jewish. Home and Office: 40 Hermit Ln Westport CT 06880

WILLIAMS, MILDRED JANE, librarian; b. Charlotte, N.C. Nov. 9, 1944; d. Leonard Augustus and Frances Edith (Long) W.; m. George E. J. Singleton. BA, Pfeiffer Coll., Misenheimer, N.C., 1966; MS in Lib. Sci., U. N.C., 1968. Reference libr. Pub. Libr. Charlotte and Mecklenburg County (N.C.), 1967-70, assoc. dir., 1974-77; head dept. documents and serials Libr. of Davidson Coll. (N.C.), 1970-73; acting asst. dir. U. N.C.-Charlotte Libr., 1977-78; pub. libr. cons. N.C. State Libr., Raleigh, 1979-80, asst. state libr., 1980-85, state libr., 1986-89; rsch. assoc. U.S. Nat. Commn. on Librs. and Info. Sci., Washington, 1990—. Mem. N.C. Libr. Assn. (2d v.p. 1983-85), Southeastern Libr. Assn., ALA. Democrat. Baptist.

WILLIAMS, N. JANE, information systems specialist; b. Spartanburg, S.C., Aug. 24, 1955; d. John Evans and Frances Mae (Miller) West; m. John G. Williams, Dec. 21, 1974; 1 child, Jason Grant. Bs, U. S.C., 1976, MPA, 1980. Mktg. coord., systems analyst Wilbur Smith and Assocs., Columbia, S.C.; assoc. dir. Inst. of Info. Mgmt., Columbia; sr. assoc. The Fontaine Co., Inc., Columbia. Contbr. articles to profl. jours. Mem. bus. mgmt. adv. com. Midlands Tech. Coll. Mem. NAFE. Office: The Fontaine Co Inc PO Box 11665 Columbia SC 29211

WILLIAMS, NANCY ELLEN-WEBB, social services administrator; b. Quincy, Ill., Aug. 1; d. Charles and Garnet Naomi (Davis) Webb; m. Jesse B. Williams, Apr. 11, 1959; children: Cynthia L. Williams Clay, Troy Andrea Williams Redic, Bernard Peter. BA, Quincy Coll., 1957; postgrad., Tenn. A&I U., 1961; M Pub. Adminstrn., U. Nev., Las Vegas, 1977; LHD (hon.), U. Humanistic Studies, 1986. Cert. peace officer, Nev. (chmn. Standards and Tng. Com., 1978-81); cert. social worker. Tchr. Shelby County Tng. Sch., Memphis, 1957-61; dep. probation officer Clark County Juvenile Ct., Las Vegas, 1961-66, supervising probation officer, 1966-74, dir. probation services, 1974-80, dir. intake admissions, 1980-81, dir. Child Haven, 1989—; mem. Nev. Crime Commn., 1970-81. Author: When We Were Colored, 1986, Dinah's Pain and Other Poems of the Black Life Experience, 1988, Them Gospel Songs, 1989; contbr. poetry to various mags. Mem. exec. com. Clark County Econ. Opportunity Bd., Las Vegas, 1963-71; chmn. So. Nev. Task Force on Corrections, 1974-81; mem. Gov.'s Com. on Justice Standards and Goals, 1979-81; bd. dirs. U. Humanistic Studies, Las Vegas, 1984—. Recipient Friend of the Golden Gloves award Golden Gloves Regional Bd., 1981, Tribute to Black Women award U. Nev., Las Vegas, 1984. Fellow Am. Acad. Neurol. and Orthopedic Surgeons (assoc.); mem. AAUW, Nat. Council Juvenile Ct. Judges, Nat. Writers Assn. Democrat. Office: Child Protective Svcs 3401 E Bonanza Rd Las Vegas NV 89101

WILLIAMS, NOREEN, biochemistry professor; b. Brunswick, Maine, June 21, 1955; d. Franklin Sanford and Selina Ella (Malm) W.; m. Peter Lynn Pedersen, July 3, 1982; 1 child, Alicia Williams. BS, U. Maine, 1977; PhD, NYU, 1981. Teaching asst. U. Maine, Orono, Maine, 1975-77, NYU, N.Y., 1978-81; from postdoctoral fellow to resident assoc. Johns Hopkins Sch. Medicine, Balt., 1981-87; asst. prof. USUHS, Herbert Sch. Medicine, Bethesda, Md., 1987—; adj. lectr. Baruch Coll., N.Y. 1978-81. Contbr. articles to profl. jours. Recipient Nat. Rsch. Svc. awd. NIH, 1984-86. Mem. Am. Soc. Microbiology, Am. Soc. Biochemistry Molecular Biology, Biophysical Soc., NY Acad. Sci. Office: USUHS Dept Biochemistry 4301 Jones Bridge Rd Bethesda MD 20814

WILLIAMS, PAMELA BERNICE, psychiatric nurse; b. Pitts., Sept. 28, 1948; d. Edward and Eleanor (Paisley) Nappi; 1 child, Thomas Dameron. AA, Indian River Community Coll., Ft. Pierce, Fla., 1973, AS in Nursing, 1974; MS in Human Resource Mgmt., Nova U., 1981; BSN, Fla. Internat. U., 1978. Cert. clin. nurse specialist in adult psychiat. mental health ANA. Psychiat. nurse specialist forensic South Fla. State Hosp., Hollywood, 1978-81; psychiat. RN II Broward County Mental Health, Hollywood, 1981-86; nursing instr., psychiat. nurse Va. Med. Ctr., Northampton, Mass., 1987-89, head nurse 7 lower, 1989. Mem. Clin. Nurse Specialist Group, Sigma Theta Tau. Republican. Home: 716 Ryan Rd Northampton MA 01060

WILLIAMS, PATRICIA ANN, insurance company executive; b. Dalton, Ga., July 17, 1950; d. John E. and Cecile (Caylor) W.; m. Perry L. Kiker, May 30, 1970 (div. June 1975). Grad. Dalton High Sch., 1968. CLU. Exec. sec. DOM, Inc., Dalton, 1969-77, Dorsett Carpet, Dalton, 1977-79; sales agt. Allstate Ins. Co., Chattanooga, 1979-83, asst. market sales mgr., Jackson, Miss., 1983-84, market sales mgr., Memphis, 1984—. Mem. Life Underwriters Tng. Council, Gen. Agts. and Mgrs. Assn. (bd. dirs.), NAFE. Republican. Baptist. Club: Memphis Exchange. Avocations: travel; reading. Home: 2992 New London Dr Memphis TN 38115 Office: Allstate Ins Co Inc 1255 Lynnfield Ste 140 Memphis TN 38119

WILLIAMS, PATRICIA ANN, child development consultant; b. Bklyn., July 31, 1951; d. George Albert Graham and Catherine (Sommers) Murphy; m. George Williams; children: Amara Catherine, Baraka George. Student, St. Agnes Seminary, 1969. Counselor Camp Friendship, Bklyn., 1980-81; former counselor Planned Parenthood & Parent's Anonymous, N.Y.C.; singer Urban Arts Corp., N.Y.C., 1981-82; supr. St. Josephs Cath. Charities, Bklyn., 1982-83; tchr., cons. Bo Beep, Mont. and Ala., 1983-84; sec. US Peace Councel, N.Y.C., 1984; tchr. Bklyn., 1984-86; health benefit field rep. Day Care Council Local Welfare Fund, N.Y.C., 1987-88; child care cons. Bklyn., 1988—; day care tchr. Strong Pl., Washington, 1985-87. Author numerous poems, short stories. Health operator. Mem. Nat. Assn. Female Execs. Home and Office: 351-13 St Brooklyn NY 11215

WILLIAMS, PENNY, state legislator; b. N.Y.C., May 6, 1937; d. Peter and Polly Sheffield Potter Baldwin; children: Joseph Hill Jr., Peter Baldwin, James Chestnut. Student, Sarah Lawrence Coll., U. Tulsa. Mem. Okla. Ho. of Reps., 1981-89, Okla. State Senate, 1989—. Trustee St. Gregory's Coll.; mem. Tulsa Com. on Fgn. Rels. Mem. LWV, Tulsa C. of C. Democrat. Episcopalian. Home: 1366 E 25th St Tulsa OK 74114*

WILLIAMS, PETRA SCHATZ, antiquarian; b. Poughkeepsie, N.Y., Sept. 2, 1913; d. Grover Henry and Mayme Nickerson (Bullock) Schatz; m. J. Calvert Williams, Nov. 26, 1946; children: Miranda, Frederica, Valerie. AB, Skidmore Coll., 1936; JD, Fordham U., 1940. Founder Fountain House, Phoenix, 1953, Fountain House East, Jeffersontown, Ky., 1966. Author: Flow Blue China, An Aid to Identification, 1971, Flow Blue China II, 1973, Flow Blue China and Mulberry Ware, 1975, Staffordshire Romantic Transfer Patterns, 1979, Staffordshire II Romantic Transfer Patterns, 1986. Past pres. Meml. Hosp. Aux., Phoenix, Heard Mus. Guild, Phoenix; bd. dirs. Ky. Humane Soc. Mem. Nat. Soc. Interior Designers (nat. dir. for Ariz. 1957-58, Ky. 1968, pres. Ky. 1967-68), DAR, Ky. Hist. Soc., Flow Blue Internat. Collectors Club (hon.). Mem. Soc. of Friends. Club: Filson. Address: 4906 Chenoweth Run Rd Jeffersontown KY 40299

WILLIAMS, PHYLLIS CUTFORTH, retired state legislator; b. Moreland, Idaho, June 6, 1917; d. William Claude and Kathleen Jessie (Jenkins) Cutforth; m. Joseph Marsden Williams, Jan. 21, 1938 (dec. 1986); children: Joseph Marlis, Bonnie Lou, Nancy Kay, Marjorie, Douglas Claude, Thomas Marsden, Wendy Kathleen, Shannon Irene. Grad., Ricks Coll., 1935. Lics. real estate salesperson, Idaho. 1st grade tchr. Grace (Idaho) Elem. Sch., 1935-38; realtor Williams Realty, Idaho Falls, Idaho, 1972-77; senator Idaho State Legislature, Boise, 1977; with MicroFilm Ctr. Latter Day Saints Ch. Mission, 1989-90. Author: Cookin' Together, 1981. Block chmn. Easter Seals Soc.; v.p. Idaho State Legis. Ladies Club, 1982-84. Republican. Latter Day Saints Ch. Home: 1950 Carmel Dr Idaho Falls ID 83402

WILLIAMS, PHYLLIS ELEANOR, retired educator; b. Serene, Colo., Sept. 11, 1920; d. Thomas James and Rebecca Cecilia (Bruce) W. Diploma, Occupational Therapy Sch. U. Pa., 1948; BS in Occupational Therapy with honors, San Jose (Calif.) State U., 1959, MS in Sociology, 1963. RN, 1942. Dir. occupational therapy for cerebral palsied children St. Christopher's Hosp., Phila., 1948-50; occupational therapist Phila Easter Seal Soc., 1951-55; therapist Chandler Tripp Sch., San Jose, 1955-59; probation officer Santa Clara County Juvenile Probation Dept., San Jose, 1959-63; asst. supt. Juvenile Hall, San Jose, 1963-65; instr. sociology W. Valley Community Coll. Dist., Saratoga, Calif., 1965-78, chair dept. sociology, 1972-73, dir. human svcs., 1974-75, pres. acad. senate, 1975-76; provost Inst. Human Affairs West Valley and Mission Community Coll. Dists., Santa Clara, 1978-83; ret. West Valley and Mission Community Coll. Dists., Saratoga, 1983—; trustee West Valley and Mission Community Coll. Dists., 1985—; lectr. in field. lectr. in field; trustee West Valley Mission Community Coll. Dist., 1985—; pres. Saratoga Adult Day Care Ctr. Bd., Sr. Info. & Reference Svcs. Bd.; bd. mem. Pub. Access TV, Women's Fund Adv. Bd. With Nurse Corps, USN, 1942-46, 50-51. Mem. U. Calif. Alumni Assn., Faculty Assn. of Calif. Community Colls., LWV, AAUW. Democrat. Roman Catholic. Home: 15881 Ravine Rd Los Gatos CA 95030

WILLIAMS, RHONA LORAINE, public relations executive; b. Salina, Kans., Dec. 2, 1953; d. Joseph Henry and Constance Loraine (Hill) W. BA, U. Minn., 1975. News reporter, pub. affairs show host Sta. WEYI-TV, Saginaw, Mich., 1975; news anchor, reporter Sta. WOTV-TV, Grand Rapids, Mich., 1975-79; news anchor, reporter, pub. affairs show host Sta. WHAS-TV, Louisville, 1979-81; news anchor, reporter Sta. KCNC-TV, Denver, 1981-84; pub. rels. mgr., mktg. asst. Adolph Coors Co., Golden, Colo., 1984-87; dir. pub. affairs Blue Cross/Blue Shield of Colo., Denver, 1987-88, U. Nebr. Med. Ctr., Omaha, 1988—; mem. Nebr. Organ and Tissue Donor Task Force, 1988. Vis. prof. black exec. exchange program Urban League N.Y.C.; mem. Urban League Nebr.; bd. dirs. Urban League Denver, 1988, Minority Enterprises Inc., 1988, Omaha YWCA, 1989, Campfire Metro Denver, 1986; mem. com. Denver Dist. Attys. Com. on Crime, 1982-88, Denver Victim's Svc. Ctr., 1988; co-chmn. Dem. Precinct Caucus, Denver, 1988, alt. del., 1988; mem. Colo. Black Women for Polit. Action, Denver, 1981—; bd. dirs. Campire Metro Denver, 1986; mem. Omaha chpt. ARC, Omaha Girls Club; mem. exec.; mem. exec. bd. Mid Am. coun. Boy Scouts Am., 1989. Recipient Kizzy award Black Women's Hall of Fame, Chgo., 1985; CBS News fellow, 1979-81. Mem. NAFE, Pub. Rels. Soc. Am., Nat. Soc. Hosp. Mktg. and Pub. Rels., Coun. for Advancement and Support Edn., Assn. Am. Med. Colls. (pub. affairs group), U. Minn. Alumni Assn., Omaha Press Club. Office: U Nebr Med Ctr Omaha NE 68198

WILLIAMS, ROBIN JOY, chemical scientist; b. Berkeley, Calif., Jan. 7, 1964; d. Bernard and Yolanda Williams. BS in Microbiology, San Francisco State U., 1987. Temp. lab. technician Genentech, South San Francisco, Calif., 1987; lab. technician Brown and Caldwell Analytical Labs., Emeryville, Calif., 1987-88, scientist, chem. analyst, 1988—. Mem. NAFE, Phi Sigma Sigma.

WILLIAMS, ROBIN-MARIE, advertising executive; b. Scarsdale, N.Y., June 3, 1960; d. Richard Edward and Marie Anne (Rossi) W. BA in Poly-Sci., George Washington U., 1984; MA in Bus., John's Hopkins U., 1989. Gold account mgr. Revlon, Inc., Phila., 1984-86; key account mgr. Norcliff Thayer, Inc., 1986-88; v.p., mgmt. supr. RSI Mktg., Inc., N.Y.C., 1988—. Vol. Carter campaign, Washington, 1976; office mgr. Anderson campaign, Balt., 1980. Mem. NOW, NARAL. Home: 10 E Lee St #8045 Baltimore MD 21131 Office: RSI Mktg Inc 171 Madison Ave New York NY 10016

WILLIAMS, ROSANA FRISCHE, manufacturing executive; b. Waxahachie, Tex., Feb. 2, 1937; d. John Louis and Ruth (Liggette) Frische; children: Bradley J., John Keith. AA, El Centro Coll., Dallas, 1975; student, U. Tex., Arlington, 1976-78. Inventory control supr. Larkin Co., Waxahachie, 1961-81; sr. software implementation coordinator, cons. FMC Corp., Chgo., 1981-86; project mgr. Nelmor div. AEC Corp., North Uxbridge, Mass., 1986-88; prodn. and inventory control mgr. flow control div. Cooper Industries Inc., Waxahachie, 1988-89; materials mgr. Larkin Products, Inc., Waxahachie, 1989—. Bd. dirs. Ellis County Nature Soc. Mem. Am. Prodn. and Inventory Control Soc. (cert. prodn. and inventory mgr.). Office: Larkin Products Waxahachie TX 75165

WILLIAMS, RUTH ANN, telephone company supervisor; b. Gholson, Miss., Sept. 6, 1958; d. Elisha Junior and Elsie Mae (Cotton) McDaniel; m. Patrick Kevin Williams, Apr. 11, 1980; children: Jason Alexander, Jaanai Alexis. Applied Sci. in Physics, Ky. State U., 1979; BS, U. Nebr., Omaha, 1985. Elec. engr. intern Whirlpool Corp., Benton Harbor, Mich., 1979; wellness coord. Bergan Mercy Health Promotions, Omaha, 1985-86; grad. asst. U. Nebr., Omaha, 1987-88; staff supr., technician U.S. West Communications, Omaha, 1987—; coord., supr., counselor Bergan Mercy Health Svcs., Omaha, 1985-86; mgmt. supr. U.S. West Communications, Omaha, 1987—. Co-author (play) Foxxi Brown & Soulfur Dwarfs, 1985, producer, dir., 1987. Mem. Ideas Unlimited, Nat. Assn. Female Execs., Alpha Kappa Alpha (treas. 1978-79, Home-coming Queen rep. 1979). Seventh-day Adventist. Home: 3356 Camden Ave Omaha NE 68111

WILLIAMS, RUTH EVELYN, hospital executive; b. Wadley, Ga., Mar. 15, 1952; d. Talmadge and Nerisee (Spence) Kelly; m. Kenneth Brinkley; children: Bruce A., Aisha D. BS, DePaul U., 1981, MS, 1984. Staff nurse Michael Reese Hosp. and Med. Ctr., Chgo., 1975-78; head nurse Univ. Chgo. Hosps. and Clinic, 1978-79; asst. exec. dir. St. Anne's Hosp., Chgo., 1979-87; v.p. DePaul Health Ctr., Bridgeton, Mo., 1987—. Honoree, YWCA, St. Louis, 1988; mem. Modern Healthcare's "Up and Comers", 1989. Mem. Am. Nurses Assn., Am. Orgn. Nurse Execs., Am. Coll. Healthcare Execs. Office: DePaul Health Ctr 12303 DePaul Dr Bridgeton MO 63044

WILLIAMS, RUTH H., management consultant; b. Bklyn., Mar. 15, 1938; d. Oscar and Lillian (Steinberg) Forster; student schs., Los Angeles; children: Steven, Richard, Michael. Asst. studio mgr. Columbia Records, Los Angeles, 1966-71; West Coast adminstr. Custom div. RCA Records, Los Angeles, 1972-75; studio mgr. Motown Records, Los Angeles, 1975-80; central scheduling supr. Golden West TV/KTLA, 1980-85; ops. mgr. West Hollywood Paper, 1985-86.; ind. cons. mgmt., Los Angeles, 1987-88; pers. dir. Mag. Pub. Co., Beverly Hills, Calif., 1988—. Mem. Nat. Womens Political Caucus, Mcpl. Elections Com. Los Angeles, Polit. Advocacy com., West Hollywood Neighborhood Council, NOW; del. County Cen. Dem. Com.; alt. 45th Assembly Dist. Los Angeles Dem. Party; past commr. Rent Stabilization Bd. City of West Hollywood; founder, chair Citizens for Srs. Home and Office: 7548 Lexington Ave West Hollywood CA 90046

WILLIAMS, SALLY MAE, marketing professional; b. Oxford, Miss., July 13, 1954; d. Ned and Mary Elizabeth (Boykin) W. MusB, U. Miss., 1976;

MBA, U. Ill., 1981. Vocal music tchr. Clay City (Ill.) Unit Sch. Dist. 10, 1976-78; sales rep. Aluminum Co. Am., Pitts., 1981-84; with Frito-Lay, Inc., Dallas, 1984-87, product mgr. zone mktg., 1986-87; product mgr. new ventures Ralston Purina-Continental Baking Co., St. Louis, 1987-88, product mgr. new products, 1988-89, group product mgr. new products, 1989—. Mem. allocations panel United Way of Greater St. Louis, 1989—; vol. mentor Community in Partnership Family Ctr., St. Louis County, Mo., 1989—. Mem. Jr. League St. Louis (community rsch. and planning coordinationg com., vice chmn. 1990-91, leadership tng. track 1990-91), Nat. Abortion Rights Action League, Kappa Kappa Gamma (adv. bd. Washington U. chpt. 1990-91), Sigma Alpha Iota (pres. U. Miss. chpt. 1974-75). Methodist. Home: 7529 Cromwell Dr Clayton MO 63105 Office: Ralston-Purina Continental Baking Div Checkerboard Sq 5CBC Saint Louis MO 63164

WILLIAMS, SANDRA KELLER, postal service executive; b. Bethesda, Md., Oct. 3, 1944; d. Park Dudley and Julia Mildred (Hunter) Keller; m. Tommy Allen Williams, Dec. 24, 1970; children: Chris Allen, Wakenna, Barbara. BA, U. Colo., 1966; MBA, U. Mo., Kansas City, 1971; MS, Ga. Inst. Tech., 1973. Mathematician Colo. State U., Ft. Collins, 1966; sr. scientist Booz-Allen Applied Rsch., Kansas City, Mo., 1967-68; computer sci. instr. Mo. Western Coll., St. Joseph, 1968-71; systems planning analyst Decatur (Ga.) Fed. Savs. and Loan Assn., 1972-73; planning analyst Fed. Res. Bank, Atlanta, 1974-75; indsl. engr. so. region hdqrs. U.S. Postal Svc., Memphis, 1975-79; nat. mgr. quality control U.S. Postal Svc., Washington, 1979-86; dir. city ops. so. Md. div. U.S. Postal Svc., Capital Heights, 1986-87, dir., oper. supt. so. Md. div., 1987-88; postmaster U.S. Postal Svc., Reading, Pa., 1988—; cons. Personal Bus., St. Joseph, 1968-69; grad. teaching asst. Ga. Inst. Tech., Atlanta, 1971-73; adj. faculty Dekalb Community Coll., Clarkston, Ga., 1973-75, Memphis State U., 1976-78. Chmn. Combined Fed. Campaign, Reading, 1988-89, U.S. Postal Svc.-Berks County Savs. Bond Program, 1988-89, United Way's Govt. div., 1989; bd. dirs. YWCA, Reading and Berks County. Mem. NAFE, Nat. League Postmasters (legis. officer 1988—), Berks County Women's Network. Republican. Home: 1514 Hill Rd Reading PA 19602

WILLIAMS, SANDRA WHEELER, commercial artist; b. Glenns Falls, N.Y., Apr. 2, 1957; d. John Wheeler and Phyllis Yoder (Reihl) W.; m. Allen James Gencarelle, Sept. 18, 1980. BA, U. So. Fla., 1981. Mgr. prodn. Skydiving mag., DeLand, Fla., 1982-86; pres. AVOT Industries Inc., Orange City, Fla., 1987—; judge U.S. Parachute Assn., Alexandria, Va., 1982—; pres. Misty Blues All-Woman Skydiving Team Inc., Orange City, 1987—; participated in world record for 1st coed. 100-way free-fall formation, 1986; organized women's world record 60-way free-fall formation Federale Internat. Aeronautique, Paris, 1986, 79-way free-fall record, 1989. Home and Office: 549 Daley St Orange City FL 32763

WILLIAMS, SUE DARDEN, library director; b. Miami, Fla., Aug. 13, 1943; d. Archie Yelverton and Bobbie (Jones) Eagles; m. Richard Williams, Sept. 30, 1989. B.A., Atlantic Christian Coll., Wilson, N.C., 1965; M.L.S., U. Tex., Austin, 1970. Cert. librarian, N.C., Va. Instr. Chowan Coll., Murfreesboro, N.C., 1966-68; librarian's asst. Albemarle Regional Library, Winston, N.C., 1968-69; br. librarian Multnomah County Pub. Library, Portland, Oreg., 1971-72; asst. dir. Stanly County Pub. Library, Albemarle, N.C., 1973-76; dir. Stanly County Pub. Library, 1976-80; asst. dir. Norfolk (Va.) Pub. Libr., Va, 1980-83; dir. Norfolk (Va.) Pub. Libr., 1983—. Mem. ALA, Libr. Adminstrv. and Mgmt. Assn. (pub. rels. sec. 1985-87, Va. councillor 1988—), Southeastern Libr. Assn. (staff devel. com. 1986-88, Rothrock award com. 1984-86, sec. pub. libr. sect. 1982-84), Va. Libr. Assn. (coun. 1984, 88—, ad hoc conf. guidlines com. 1985-86, chmn. conf. program 1984, awards and recognition com. 1983, conf. program 1982), Pub. Libr. Assn. (bd. dirs.-at-large Met. area 1986-89, conf. exhibits com.), Va. State Libr. (coop. continuing edn. com. 1988-89). Home: 3534 Brest Ave Norfolk VA 23509 Office: Norfolk Pub Libr 301 E City Hall Ave Norfolk VA 23510-1776

WILLIAMS, SUSAN EILEEN, urban planner; b. Chgo., Dec. 13, 1952; d. Joseph Andrew and Alice (Regnier) W.; 1 child, Ryan Joseph. AA in Polit. Sci., Coll. of Desert, Palm Desert, Calif., 1971; BA in Polit. Sci., U. Calif., Riverside, 1973; M of Pub. Adminstrn., Consortium Calif. State Colls. and Univs., 1982. Planning trainee City of Indio, Calif., 1975-79, assoc. planner, 1979-80, prin. planner, 1980-90, prin. planner redevel. agy., 1983-90; supervising planner J.F. Davidson Assocs., Inc., Palm Desert, Calif., 1990—. Mem. Am. Planning Assn., Assn. Environ Profls., Ill. Geneal. Soc., Geneal. Club Am. Roman Catholic. Office: J F Davidson Assocs Inc 75-150 Sheryl Dr PO Box 12817 Palm Desert CA 92255

WILLIAMS, SUSAN M., association executive; b. Wilmington, Del., July 20, 1961; d. Alfred J. Williams Jr. and Arleen (Futty) Higgins; m. Paul A. Fioravanti Jr., Aug. 15, 1981 (div. 1986); children: Gina Marie, Paul A. III. Student, U. Del., 1979-87. News anchor, editor sta. WILM-AM, Wilmington, 1979-84, WNS-TV, New Castle, Del., 1984-85; spl. projects coord. Office of Lt. Gov., Wilmington and Dover, Del., 1985; asst. press sec. Office of Gov., Wilmington and Dover, 1986-90; asst. dir. programs Women Execs. in State Govt., Washington, 1990—; ind. media rels. cons., Washington and Del. Press liaison Com. to Elect Dale Wolf, Wilmington, 1988; asst. press sec. Pete duPont for Pres., Wilmington, 1988; trustee Grand Opera House Del., Wilmington, 1989—; bd. dirs. Ronald McDonald House Del., Wilmington, 1988-90. Recipient award for best documentary short, UPI, 1984. Mem. Wilmington Women in Bus., Nat. Assn. Govt. Communicators, Internat. Assn. Bus. Communicators. Republican. Methodist. Office: Women Execs in State Govt 200 M St Ste 730 Washington DC 20036

WILLIAMS, SYLVIA HILL, museum director; b. Lincoln University, Pa., Feb. 10, 1936; m. Charlton E. Williams. AB, Oberlin Coll., 1957; Cert. de Francais Parle, Ecole Pract. de l'Alliance Francaise, Paris, 1963; MA in Primitive Art, NYU Inst. of Fine Arts, 1975; LHD honoris causa, Amherst Coll., 1989. Program cons. Nat. Assembly for Social Policy and Devel., N.Y.C., 1963-68; account exec. Harry L. Oram, Inc., N.Y.C., 1968-71; Mellon research fellow The Bklyn. Mus., 1971-73, asst. curator, 1973-76, assoc. curator, 1976-78, curator, 1978-83; dir. Nat. Museum of African Art, Smithsonian Inst., Washington, 1983—; lectr. African art New Sch. for Social Rsch., N.Y.C., 1979-80; adj. asst. prof. NYU, 1980; mem. vis. com. Allen Meml. Art Mus. Oberlin Coll. Author: Black South Africa, Contemporary Graphics, 1976; contbg. author: African Art as Philosophy, 1974. Contbr. articles to Apollo Mag., African Arts, others. Curator, organizer major exbhns. Bklyn. Mus., Nat. Mus. African Art. Nat. Mus. Act grantee (Paris, Tervuren, London), 1974. Mem. African Am. Museums Assn., Assn. Art Mus. Dirs. (trustee), Assn. Primitive and Pre-Columbian Art (dept. art history and archeology Columbia U.), Am. Assn. of Mus., Am. Fedn. Arts (exhbn. adv. com.), Inst. Mus. Svcs. (panel). Office: Nat Mus-African Art Smithsonian Inst 950 Independence Ave SW Washington DC 20560

WILLIAMS, TONDA, entrepreneur, consultant; b. N.Y.C., Nov. 21, 1949; d. William and Juanita (Rainey) W.; 1 child, Tywana. Student, Collegiate Inst., N.Y.C., 1975-78, C.W. Post Coll., 1981-83; BA in Bus. Mgmt., Am. Nat. U., Phoenix, 1983. Notary pub. N.Y. Asst. controller Acad. Ednl. Devel., N.Y.C., 1971-81; mgr. office Chapman-Apex Constrn. Co., Bayshore, N.Y., 1982-84; specialist computer RGM Liquid Waste Removal, Deerpark, N.Y., 1985-87; cons. acctg. LaMar Lighting Co., Freeport, N.Y., 1987—; owner, pres. Omni-Star, Bklyn., 1981—. Author: Tonda's Songs in Poetry, 1978; co-author: Computer Management of Liquid Waste Industry, 1986. Recipient Golden Poet award World of Poetry, 1988. Mem. Am. Mus. Natural History, Am. Soc. Notary Pubs. Home: 74 Cedar Dr Bay Shore NY 11706

WILLIAMS, VALENA MARIE, corporate human resources administrator; b. Cleve., Dec. 22, 1948; d. John Bentley and Valena (Minor) W.; 1 child, Mosi Adesina Williams-Morrison. BS, San Jose State U., 1972, Calif. State Life Teaching Credential, 1973; MS, Ill. State U., 1978. Sr. tng. writer Allstate Ins. Co., Northbrook, Ill., 1978-82; performance cons. RIZULTS, 1979—; program mgr. Bank Adminstrn. Inst., Schaumburg, Ill., 1982-83; corp. tng. projects supr. Motorola, Inc., Schaumburg, 1984-85; dir. tng. and edn. corp. offices Merritt Peralta Med. Ctr., Oakland, Calif., 1985-86; personnel project analyst County of San Mateo, Belmont, Calif., 1986-89; sr. tng. cons. Bank of Am., Oakland, 1989-90; speaker, guest lectr. various assns., univs. and radios stas. Bd. dirs. Cen. Pl., Oakland, 1985-88, YMCA, Oakland, 1986—. Mem. Am. Soc. Tng. and Devel., Bay Area Orgn. Devel. Network, No. Calif. Human Resource Coun., Chgo. Orgn. Devel. Assn. (pres. 1980-82), Oakland Athletic Club. Home: 6505 Lucas Ave Oakland CA 94611

WILLIAMS, VERONICA ANN, management information systems marketing manager; b. Washington, Feb. 8, 1956; d. Vernon and Shirley Ann (Felton) W. BA, Brandeis U., 1977; MBA, Northwestern U., 1979. Systems mktg. rep. Control Data Corp., Chgo., 1979-81, mktg. rep., 1981-82; staff mgr. AT&T, Basking Ridge, N.J., 1982-84; nat. account exec. AT&T, N.Y.C., 1984-86; mgr. bus. planning AT&T, Berkeley Heights, N.J., 1986-87; product mgr. AT&T, Morristown, N.J., 1987-88; dist. mgr. Unisoft Corp., N.Y.C., 1988-89; acct. mgr. Lotus Devel. Corp., N.Y.C., 1989-90; sr. regional mgr. Software Corp. of Am., Stamford, Conn., 1990—; pres. Absolute Computer Techs., Inc., N.Y.C, 1989—; dir. mfg. Software Corp. Am., Stanford, Conn., 1990—. Mem. South Orange Planning Bd., 1985-87, South Orange Citizens Budget Adv. Com., 1983—. Mem. Nat. Black MBA Assn. (fin. chmn. Chgo. br. 1979-81, Performance award 1981). Home: 541 Scotland Rd South Orange NJ 07079 Office: Absolute Computer Techs 213 Valley St Ste 318 South Orange NJ 07079

WILLIAMS, VERONICA MYRES, psychiatric social worker; b. Shreveport, La., May 11, 1947; d. McEura and Margie Virginia (Reagan) Myres; B.A., La. Tech. U., Ruston, 1969; M.S.W., U. Mich., Ann Arbor, 1977; m. John L. Williams, Jr., Nov. 30, 1969; children—Nicole Leann, Jennifer Lyn, Erica Maria. Probation counselor Citizens Probation Authority, Flint, Mich., 1970-72; unit dir., therapist Services to Overcome Drug Abuse Among Teenagers, Flint, 1972-74; psychiat. therapist Psycho-Therapeutic Treatment Clin., P.C., Flint, 1974-77; psychiat. social worker Hurley Med. Center, Flint, 1977-79; field instr. Sch. Soc. Work, U. Mich., Ann Arbor, 1978-79, 86—; psychiat. social worker Inst. Mental Health, Flint, 1979-81, Psychotherapeutic Treatment Clinic, 1981-83; clin. social worker Flint Bd. Edn., 1979-83; pupil apprasial spl. edn. Caddo Parish Sch. Bd., Shreveport, La., 1983-85; developer dropout prevention program Flint Bd. Edn., 1986—; psychiat. therapist Mott Children's Health Ctr., 1986—. Cert. social worker, Mich. Mem. Nat. Assn. Social Workers, Acad. Cert. Social Workers, Mich. Edn. Assn., NEA. Democrat. Office: Pierson Sch 300 E Mott Flint MI 48505

WILLIAMS, VIVIAN LEWIE, college counselor; b. Columbia, S.C., Jan. 23, 1923; d. Lemuel Arthur Sr. and Ophelia V. (McDaniel) Lewie; m. Charles Warren Williams, Apr. 4, 1947 (div. Dec. 1967); children: Pamela Ann Williams-Coote, Charles Warren Jr. BA, Allen U., 1942; MA, U. Mich., 1946; MS, U. So. Calif., 1971, postgrad., 1971-72. Cert. marriage, family, child counselor, community coll. counselor. Asst. prof. psychology Tenn. State Agrl. and Indsl. U., Nashville, 1946-47; asst. prof. edn. Winston-Salem (N.C.) State U., 1947-50; asst. prof. edn., dir. tchr. edn. Allen U., Columbia, S.C., 1951-53; specialist reading, coord. lang. arts Charlotte (N.C.) Mecklenburg Schs., 1963-67; cons. for CSIP Charlotte (N.C.) Mecklenburg Schs., 1967-69; asst. prof. edn., psychology Johnson C. Smith U., Charlotte, 1967-69; counselor, team leader Centennial, U. So. Calif. Tchr. Corps, L.A., 1970-73; counselor Compton (Calif.) Community Coll., 1973—, adv. fgn. student, 1975-85. Pres. bd. dirs. Charlotte Day Nursery, 1956-59; bd. dirs. Taylor St. USO, Columbia, S.C., 1951-53; sec. southwest region Nat. Alliance Family Life, 1973-74; sec. bd. dirs. NCCJ, Charlotte, 1959-62. Recipient Faculty Audit Program award Ford/Carnegie Found., Harvard U., Boston, 1968, Pub. Svc. Achievement award WSOC Broadcasting Co.; fellow U. Mich., 1946. Mem. AAUW (life mem.), NEA (life mem.), Nat. Acad. Counselors and Family Therapists (life, clin. mem. pres. S.W. region 1989), Community Coll. Counselors Assn., The Links, Inc. (historian 1985-87), Jack and Jill Am. (charter mem., organizer Charlotte chpt., pres. 1954-56), Women on Target, Calif. Tchrs. Assn., Delta Sigma Theta, Alpha Gamma Sigma (Golden Apple award 1981). Democrat. Methodist. Home: 6621 E Caro St Paramount CA 90723 Office: Compton Community Coll 1111 E Artesia Blvd Compton CA 90221

WILLIAMS-BREESE, MARILYN OLIVE, financial consultant; b. Panama City, Panama, May 5, 1942; d. William Josiah and Millicent Margaret (Vierela) Whinnen; m. William Donald Breese, Dec. 28, 1985; children by previous marriage: Thomas Michael, Timothy Scott, Stacey Suellen. BS in Edn., Ball State U., 1965; MS in Gifted Edn., U. Bridgeport, 1975; postgrad., U. Buffalo, 1975-76. Cert. fin. planner. Tchr. elem. Pub. Schs., Ft. Rucher, Ala., 1967, Enterprise, Ala., 1968; tchr. elem. Project Explore, Stamford, Conn., 1974-75; coordinator gifted and talented programs Pub. Schs., Irvington, N.Y., 1976-82; bd. dirs. Programs for Gifted Bd. Cooperative Ednl. Services, South Westchester, N.Y., 1977-80; adj. prof. gifted program Manhattanville Coll., Harrison, N.Y., 1978-80; sales assoc. Nat. Pension Services Inc., White Plains, N.Y., 1981-85; pension planner Wimbry Fin. Services, North Salem, N.Y., 1985-88; owner, pres. The Heritage Group Ltd., New Milford, Conn., 1988—; cons. Dept. Edn. Gifted & Talented Devel. Ctr., 1980—. Mem. Am. Soc. Pension Actuaries, Nat. Assn. Life Underwriters, Inst. Cert. Fin. Planners (chpt. chmn. program and continuing edn.), Phi Delta Kappa. Home: 19 Maple Dr Vail's Grove Peach Lake NY 10509 Office: Heritage Group 221 Danbury Rd New Milford CT 06776

WILLIAMSON, ALYCE L., sales executive; b. Ft. Laramie, Wyo., May 3, 1935; d. William Alexander and Daisy Mildred (Hendrickson) Latta; m. Ralph Ward Blackhall, May 29, 1955 (div. Oct. 1971); children: Robert Ward Blackhall, Leigh Anne Blackhall Peltier; m. Michael Morton Williamson, Sept. 11, 1976 (dec. July 1988). PhD, Kans. State U., 1978. Substitute tchr. Wichita (Kans.) Pub. Schs., 1961-75; instr. Wichita Vocat. System, 1971-75; asst. dir. personnel svcs. Kans. State U., Manhattan, 1975-79; with vocat. svcs. Kans. State Dept. Edn., Topeka, 1979-81; account exec. J.J.B. Hilliard, W.L. Lyons, Terre Haute, Ind., 1981—; tchr. classes and workshops in investing Ind. State U., Terre Haute, 1981—; pub.speaker, Terre Haute, 1981—; rep. J.J.B. Hilliard, W.L. Lyons to Securities Industry Inst., Phila., 1986-90. Mem. pers. com. YWCA, Terre Haute, 1983—, bd. dirs., 1983-86; bd. dirs. Wabash Valley chpt. United Way, Terre Haute, 1982-86, Terre Haute Symphony Orch., 1988, pres.; co-chair ways and means Heart Assn., Terre Haute, 1982-84; bd. dirs., membership chairperson Leadership Terre Haute, 1983-85. Home: 2224 Ohio Blvd Terre Haute IN 47803 Office: JJB Hilliard WL Lyons Inc 22 N 5th St Terre Haute IN 47803

WILLIAMSON, BARBARA DIANE, lawyer; b. Riverside, N.J., July 24, 1950; d. Frederick Raymond and Dorothy (Jessup) Ott; m. Luis Williamson, May 4, 1973. BFA, William Paterson Coll., 1972; lic. vocat. nurse, Yakima Valley Community Coll., 1981; BS in Nursing with honors, Seattle U., 1983; MS in Community Health Nursing with honors, U. Wash., 1984; JD, U. Puget Sound, 1988. Bar: N.J. 1988; cert. hazardous control mgr. Art tchr. Delran (N.J.) Twp. Schs., 1972-78; recreational coord. Delran (N.J.) Twp. Summer Schs., 1973-76; nurse Yakima (Wash.) Valley Meml. Hosp., 1980-85; occupational health cons., researcher Evergreen Legal Svcs., Granger, Wash., 1986; environ. analyst Westinghouse Hanford Co., Richland, Wash., 1987; atty. Westinghouse Co., Richland, 1988—; cons. Occupational and Envirn. Cons. Svcs., 1988; occupational health and safety mgmt. researcher U. Hosp., Seattle, 1983-84; pesticide educator Evergreen Legal Svcs., Granger, Wash., 1986; smoking policy cons. U. Puget Sound Law Sch., Tacoma, 1986-87; researcher, legal assoc. Dept. of Ecology Wash. State Atty. Gen., Lacey, 1987. Grantee U. Puget Sound, 1986, Alaskan-Northwest Synod of Presbyn. Chs., 1986. Mem. ABA, Wash. Assn. Occupational Health Nurses, Wash. State Pub. Health Assn. (legis. com. 1984), N.W. Occupational Health Nurses Assn. (mem. nominating com. 1984), Am. Pub. Health Assn., Am. Assn. of Occupational Health Nurses, Phi Delta Phi, Alpha Sigma Nu, Sigma Theta Tau. Home: 1900 Stevens Dr Box 626 Richland WA 99352 Office: Westinghouse Hanford Co B315 1100 Jadwin Ave 1100 Jadwin Ave Richland WA 99352

WILLIAMSON, BARBARA JANE, mortgage loan originator; b. Prentiss, Miss., Mar. 24, 1963; d. Edwin Louis and Barbara Ann (Greene) Bass; m. James Keith Williamson, Jan. 22, 1983; 1 child, Amy Michelle Williamson. Student, U. So. Miss., 1981-82. Head cashier R & M Foods, Inc., Hattiesburg, Miss., 1979-83; mortgage loan originator Magnolia Fed. Bank for Savs., Hattiesburg, 1983--. Mem. Hattiesburg Bd. Realtors. Home: 159 Rogers Rd Hattiesburg MS 39401 Office: Magnolia Fed Bank 130 W Front St Hattiesburg MS 39401

WILLIAMSON, BARBARA WILLIAMS, educator; b. Tallahassee, Fla., Dec. 25, 1945; d. James Troy and Barbara Elizabeth (Symon) Williams; divorced; children: Paul N. Jr., Elizabeth Cecile. BS in Elem. Edn., Fla. State U., 1967, MS in Early Childhood Edn., 1987. Tchr. sci., phys. edn. Rickards High Sch., Tallahassee, 1967-68; tchr. Jupiter (Fla.) Elem. Sch., 1968-72; coord., tchr., asst. dir. Early Child Care Ednl. Ctr., Tallahassee, 1972-80; tchr. Gilchrist Elem. Sch., Tallahassee, 1980-87; vis. asst. prof. Fla. State U., Panama City, 1987—; with program devel. and analysis K-12 Fla. Edn. Ctr., Tallahassee, 1990—; educator Holy Comforter Episcopal Day Sch., Tallahassee,; supr. internat. student childhood edn. grad. program Fla. State U., London, 1987; cons. Fla. Edn. Standards Commn., 1989; parenting educator Leon County Adult and Community Edn., 1987—. bd. presch. Faith Presbyn. Ch., Tallahassee, 1986—; educator, cons. March of Dimes, Leon County Adult Edn. Dept., Tallahassee, 1987—; sustaining advisor, bd. dirs. Tallahassee Jr. League, 1973—, chmn. task force pub. affairs, 1978; active Citizens for Better Schs., Tallahassee, 1987; press attache Fla. Ho. Reps., Tallahassee, 1967; chmn. market days Tallahassee Jr. Mus., 1978; organizational com. Springtime Tallahassee, 1968; bd. dirs. Fla. State U. Coll. Edn. Alumni Bd., 1988—. Mem. NEA, Leon County Tchr. Assn., Alpha Delta Kappa. Democrat. Clubs: Pansy Garden (Tallahassee) (chmn. 1977-78); Jr. Woman's (Jupiter, v.p. 1969-70, projects chmn. 1968). Office: Fla Edn Ctr Program Devel Program Devel and Analysis K-12 Ste 401 Tallahassee FL 32399

WILLIAMSON, JANET A., nursing educator; b. Scranton, Pa., Sept. 5, 1934. Grad., Geisinger Med. Ctr., 1955; MA, NYU, 1966; PhD, Pa. State U., 1972. Former asst. prof. Baylor U., Fla. State U.; assoc. prof. Pa. State U., now dir. sch. nursing. Contbr. articles to profl. jours. Office: Penn State U 201 Health & Human Devel E University Park PA 17901*

WILLIAMSON, JEWEL, marketing company executive; b. Keokuk, Iowa, Feb. 7, 1965; d. Billy James and Jeanette (Smith) W. BA in Econs., Loras Coll., Dubuque, Iowa, 1987. Account mgr. Applied Communications, Inc., Omaha, 1987-89, ASTech mktg. specialist, spokesperson, 1989-90, regional mgr., 1990—. Mem. NAFE. Presbyterian. Home: 11640 Camden Ave Omaha NE 68164 Office: Applied Communications Inc 330 S 108 Ave Omaha NE 68154

WILLIAMSON, JUANITA V., English educator; b. Shelby, Miss.; d. John M. and Alice E. (McAllister) W. BA, LeMoyne-Owen Coll., 1938; MA, Atlanta U., 1940; PhD, U. Mich., 1961. Asst. prof. English LeMoyne-Owen Coll., Memphis, 1947-56, prof., 1956—, Disting. Svc. prof., 1980; adj. prof. Memphis State U., 1975—, linguist, summer 1969, 73, 75; vis. prof. Ball State U., Muncie, Ind., 1963-64, U. Tenn., Knoxville, summer 1975; vis. prof. U. Wis., Milw., summer 73, linguist, summer 1966-67; linguist French Inst. Atlanta U., summer 1963, Hampton (Va.) Inst., summer 1964, U. Ark., Pine Bluff, summer 1981; chmn. English faculty, LeMoyne-Owen Coll., Memphis, 1987—. Editor: A Various Language, 1971; contbr. articles to profl. jours. Mem. exec. com. United Way, Memphis, 1953-56; cons. Girl Scouts U.S., Memphis, 1956; bd. dirs. Integration Svc., Memphis, 1952-58; mem. exec. com. hist. council United Ch. Christ, 1976. Recipient citation for excellence in edn. Memphis City Council, 1973; fellow Rockefeller Found., 1949-51, Ford Found., 1954; HEW grantee, 1964-68. Mem. MLA (program com., minority affairs com.), Nat. Council Tchrs. English (coll. sect. exec. com. 1976-79), Am. Dialect Soc. (exec. com. 1979-82), Conf. on Coll. Composition and Communication (exec. com. 1969-71), Delta Sigma Theta. Home: 1217 Cannon St Memphis TN 38106 Office: LeMoyne-Owen Coll 807 Walker Ave Memphis TN 38126

WILLIAMSON, MARGERY PAYSINGER, teacher; b. Newberry, S.C., Mar. 7, 1927; d. Strother Culbreath and Frances Marion (Daniel) Paysinger; m. Nathan Kibler Williamson, Aug. 12, 1947 (dec. Mar. 1975); children: Ellen Williamson Kanervo, Frances Williamson Williams. BA, Randolph-Macon Woman's Coll., 1944-48; postgrad., Coll. of Charleston, 1947, U. S.C., 1975, Newberry Coll., 1971. Substitute tchr. Charleston City Schs., 1949; tchr. Newberry (S.C.) High Sch., 1955-85; officer Newberry County Edn. Assn.. Bd. mem. Newberry County Forestry Assn., 1985—, vice chmn. Newberry County Rep. Party, 1986—, coun. chmn. Luth. Ch. of the Redeemer, 1986, assisting minister, 1989. pres. elect Newberry Coll. Women's League, 1988—. Mem. AAUW (treas. 1986-87), Bus. and Profl. Women's Club (treas. 1986-87), S.C. Retired Educator's Assn. (treas. 1987—), Newberry County Am. Heart Assn. (residential chmn. 1987), Alpha Delta Kappa (Fidelis Delta Chpt. pres. 1986-88), S.C. Ednl. Assn., NEA, Nat. Council Tchrs. English. Home: 1734 Boundary St Newberry SC 29108

WILLIAMSON, MIRIAM BEDINGER, retired medical librarian; b. Asheville, N.C., Nov. 18, 1919; d. Robert Dabney and Mary Julia (Smith) Bedinger; m. Robert Lewis Williamson Sr., June 9, 1944 (div. June 1969); children: Robert Lewis Jr., John Bedinger, Ellen Richmond, Thomas Reid. BA, Agnes Scott Coll., 1941; MS, Presbyn. Sch. Christian Edn., 1943; postgrad., U. Tenn., 1969. Ch. social worker, kindergarten tchr. N.E. Community Ctr., Italian Presbyn. Mission, Kansas City, Mo., 1943-44; med. librarian Blount Meml. Hosp., Maryville, Tenn., 1972-89, ret. 1989; tchr. vocat. edn. programs, adult reading program Alcoa, Blount County, Maryville sch. systems. Mem. Blount County unit Bread for the World. Grantee Library Medicine, HEW, 1973, HHS, 1981, Blount County unit Am. Cancer Soc., 1982, Blount Meml. Hosp. Aux., 1986-87; recipient Outstanding Service award Vocat. Edn. Dept., 1983, 85. Democrat. Home: 103 Hopi Dr Maryville TN 37801

WILLIAMSON, MYRNA HENNRICH, lecturer, consultant, retired army officer; b. Gregory, S.D., Jan. 27, 1937; d. Walter Ferdinand and Alma Lillian (Rajewich) H. BS with highest honors, S.D. State U., 1960; MA, U. Okla., 1973; grad., U.S. Army Command and Gen. Staff Coll., 1977, Nat. War Coll., 1980. Commd. 2d lt. U.S. Army, 1960, advanced through grades to brig. gen., 1985; bn. comdr. Mil. Police Sch. U.S. Army, Fort McClellan, Ala., 1977-79; chief plans policy and service div. Jl 8th Army U.S. Army, Korea, 1980-81; chief mgmt. support Office Dep. Chief Staff for Research, Devel. and Acquisition U.S. Army, Washington, 1981-82; brigade comdr. U.S. Army, Fort Benjamin Harrison, Ind., 1983-84; comdg. gen. 3d ROTC Region U.S. Army, Fort Riley, Kans., 1984-87; dep. dir. mil. personnel mgmt. U.S. Army, Washington, 1987-89, ret., 1989; U.S. del. com. on women in NATO Forces, 1986-89. Pres. S.D. State U. Found. Recipient Disting. Alumnus award S.D. State U., 1984. Mem. Nat. Speakers Assn., Internat. Platform Assn., Assn. U.S. Army, Nat. Assn. Uniformed Svcs. (bd. dirs.), United Svcs. Automobile Assn. (bd. dirs.), Women In Meml. Svc. to Am. Found. (bd. dirs.), Phi Kappa Phi.

WILLIAMSON, NANCY DANOWITZ, psychiatric and mental health nurse and counselor; b. Ford Ord, Calif., Mar. 25, 1950; d. Edward Francis and Mary Ann (Kellenyi) Danowitz; m. Luin Daniel Wood, June 19, 1971 (div. Dec. 1975); m. Albert Williamson, Aug. 19, 1978; children: Andrea Kristine, Alexandra Lynn. BA in Social Scis., Rollins Coll., 1983; MS in Clin. Psychology, U. Cen. Fla., 1985; RN, DePaul Hosp. Sch. Nursing, Norfolk, Va., 1971. Lic. mental health counselor; RN, Va., Fla.; cert. psychiat. and mental health nurse. Pediatric staff RN Childrens' Hosp. of Kings Daugs., Norfolk, 1971-73, Winter Park (Fla.) Meml. Hosp., 1973-76; office nurse Jay M. Hughes, MD, Winter Park, 1976-78; standby pediatric office RN Luis Spinelli, MD, Winter Park, 1976-85; resident counselor, nurse La Amistad Found., Winter Park, 1978-82; clin. psychology intern Orlando (Fla.) Regional Med. Ctr., 1984-85; obstetrical and neonatal staff nurse Winter Park (Fla.) Meml. Hosp., 1978-88; M.S. mental health counselor Orlando (Fla.) Regional Med. Ctr., 1985; mental health counselor, psychiat. nurse Jose Quinones, MD, Winter Park, 1985—; cons. nurse to nursing adminstrn. Winter Park Meml. Hosp. Bereavement Team, 1985-88; cons. nurse Headache Treatment Ctr., 1985. Bd. dirs. La Amistad Found., Winter Park, 1978-84. Mem. Am. Psychol. Assn., Southeast Psychol. Assn., Rollins Coll. Alumnae Assn., U. Cen. Fla. Alumnae Assn., DePaul Hosp. Sch. Nursing Alumnae Assn. Democrat. Roman Catholic. Home: 1937 Heathwood St Winter Park FL 32792 Office: Jose E Quinones MD PA 111 N Lakemont Ave Ste 1B Winter Park FL 32792

WILLIAMSON, SHERRI REDIES, county official; b. Charlotte, N.C., Oct. 3, 1953; d. Robert F. and Sara F. (Riley) R.; m. Joe Linwood Williamson, Aug. 21, 1976. BS in Geography, East Carolina U., 1976. Trainee, Mecklenburg County, Charlotte, 1978-80; zoning insp. Charlotte-

Mecklenburg County, Charlotte, 1980—. Vice-pres. local Homeowners Assn., 1981-84. Mem. N.C. Assn. Zoning Ofcls. (charter), Charlotte Cath. High Sch. Alumni Assn. (charter, chmn. alumni bd.), Kerns Family (sec.-treas.). Democrat. Roman Catholic. Club: Women's. Avocations: gourmet cooking; aerobics; gardening; camping; crafts. Office: PO Box 31097 Charlotte NC 28231

WILLIAMSON, VIKKI LYN, finance executive; b. Huntington, W.Va., June 30, 1956; d. Ernest E. and Wanda C. (Cole) W. BA in Secondary Edn., English, Temple U., 1978; postgrad. in Acctg. and Fin., U. Cin., 1984—. CPA, Ohio; cert. tchr., Tenn., Ohio. Tchr. Springfield Christian Acad., Tenn., 1978-79; acctg. asst. Children's Hosp. Med. Ctr., Cin., 1979-84; asst. dir. fin. svcs. U. Cin. Med. Ctr., 1984-85, dir. fin. svcs., 1985-88, dir. fin. and adminstrn., 1988—; instr. Miami U., Oxford, Ohio, 1984—; bd. dirs. Contemporary Dance Theatre, 1987—. Mem. Healthcare Fin. Mgmt. Assn., Am. Assn. Blood Banks, Ohio Assn. Blood Banks (fin. com. mem. 1986—), Assn. Women Adminstrs. (fin. com. mem. 1987—), U. Cin. Assn. Mid-Level Adminstrs. (bd. dirs. 1987—), Am. Inst. CPA's, Alpha Epsilon Theta, Beta Gamma Sigma, Delta Mu Delta. Office: U Cin Med Ctr Hoxworth Blood Ctr 3231 Burnet Ave ML #55 Cincinnati OH 45267

WILLIAMS-SÁNCHEZ, TONI ADELLA, computer programmer analyst, mathematics, science and computer educator; b. N.Y.C., Sept. 4, 1952; d. Wesley Roger and Martha (Shuler) Williams; m. Enrique Everett Sánchez, Oct 22, 1951; children: Roger Bejamin, Marta Laura. BS, Claflin Coll., 1972; MA, Columbia U., 1976. Instr. Fla. State U., Canal Zone, Republic of Panama, 1977-79; coordinator educator St. Mary's Sch., Balboa, Republic of Panama, 1977-80; instr. Canal Zone Coll., Republic of Panama, 1979; edn. officer USN in Cen. and So. Am., Republic of Panama, 1980-81; adminstr. incentives awards U.S. Army 193rd Brigade, Republic of Panama, 1981-82; instr. Panama Canal Coll., 1981-83; educator Balboa High Sch., 1982-86, 87-90; computer programmer analyst 1109th Signal Brigade, Panama, 1990—; cons. Systems Edn. Enrichment, Republic of Panama, 1982-88, N.Y.C. Bd. Edn., 1976. Author: ADP Master Plan for the Directorate of Engineering, 1986; contbr. articles to profl. jours.; contbr. poems to jours. Bd. dirs. Yuma Red Cross, 1986-87; vice chmn., bd. sec. Sch. Installation Adv. Com., 1987-88; rep. Border Conf. Mex./U.S. Red Cross, El Paso, Tex., 1987; active Yuma Reading Coun., 1986-87; vice chairperson Overseas Del. Nat. Coun. Girl Scouts US., 1990; chair Girl Scouts U.S., Panama, 1990. Recipient Nat. Federally Employed Women award, 1982; Henry Krumb fellow, Columbia U., 1976, Domestic Mining, Mineral and Mineral Fuel Conservation fellow, Columbia U., 1976; Fielding Inst. scholar, 1988-89. Mem. Soc. Mil. Comptrs., Soroptomist Internat., Phi Delta Kappa (v.p. 1985-86, 88-89), Zeta Phi Beta. African Methodist Episcopalian. Clubs: Toastmasters Internat. (pres. 1981-82). Home: PSC 211 FPO Miami FL 34061 Office: Sistemas de Enriquecimiento Academico S.A., Apartado 6-3132, El Dorado Republic of Panama

WILLIAMS-STEINWENDER, KARIN MAE, artist; b. Santa Monica, Calif., Oct. 14, 1948; d. Marion Glen and Margaret Grace (Long) Williams; m. Helmut Adolf Ludwig Steinwender, Aug. 17, 1985. BA, Calif. State U., Carson, 1983. Cert. tchr. art-dance, Calif. Chmn. bd. South Bay (Calif.) Ballet Co., 1976-77, choreographer, 1977-79; gallery coord. F.O.T.A., Hermosa Beach, Calif., 1978-79; ballet instr. Act III Acad., Redondo Beach, Calif., 1972-86; self-employed ballet instr. Redondo Beach, 1972-86; artist, painter Syracuse, N.Y., 1972—. Author: Technique in Balance and Turning, 1985; artist more than 75 paintings and drawings; choreographer: (ballets) Woodcutter's Daughter, 1977, Power Plays, 1978. Vol. Republican Party, Syracuse, 1988-89, Park Assn., Syracuse, 1990, to keep Headstart from being cut out, early 1970's, F.O.T.A., 1978; mem. World Wildlife Fund. Recipient honor for one-man exhbn. Crackerjack TV Prodns., Redondo Beach, 1983. Mem. Rodale Inst., Nature Conservancy, Nat. Wildlife Fedn., Green Peace, Arbor Day Found., Coop Am., Rosicrucians.

WILLIAN, SUZANNE SPILLER, marketing professional; b. Austin, Tex., Oct. 29, 1962; d. Roger Wayne and Ann (Gault) Spiller; m. John Stuart Willian, June 17, 1989. BSCE, Purdue U., 1985. Systems engr. IBM, Oak Brook, Ill., 1985-86, mktg. rep., 1986-88; mktg. rep. Comdisco, Inc., Rosemont, Ill., 1988—. Mem. Bus. Resumption Planners Assn., Chgo. Area Runners Assn., Purdue Club Chgo., Jr. League Chgo., Tau Beta Pi. Office: Comdisco Inc 6111 N River Rd Rosemont IL 60018

WILLINGER, RHONDA ZWERN, optometrist; b. Bklyn., Apr. 26, 1962; d. Jerome Max and Jeanette (Zwern) Willinger; m. Wayne Ken Chan, Aug. 26, 1990. BS, U. Miami, 1983; OD with honors, New Eng. Coll. Optometry, 1987. Resident in optometry VA Med. Ctr., Bedford, Mass., 1987-88; pvt. practice, Burlington, Mass., 1988-89, Framingham, Mass., 1989—. Scholar New Coll., U. South Fla., 1979-81, U. Miami, 1981-83. Mem. Am. Optometric Assn. (contact lens sect.), Mass. Soc. Optometrists. Home: 1731 Beacon St Apt 706 Brookline MA 02146 Office: 150 Worcester Rd Framingham MA 01701

WILLINGHAM, JEANNE MAGGART, dance educator, ballet company executive; b. Fresno, Calif., May 8, 1923; d. Harold F. and Gladys (Ellis) Maggart. student Tex. Woman's U., 1942; student profl. dancing schs., worldwide. dance tchr. Beaux Arts Dance Studio, Pampa, Tex., 1948—; artistic dir. Pampa Civic Ballet, 1972—. Mem. Tex. Arts and Humanities, Tex. Arts Alliance, Pampa C. of C. (fine arts com.), Pampa Fine Arts Assn. Office: Pampa Civic Ballet Beaux Arts Dance Studio 315 N Nelson Pampa TX 79065

WILLINGHAM, MARY MAXINE, fashion retailer; b. Childress, Tex., Sept. 12, 1928; d. Charles Bryan and Mary (Bohannon) McCollum; m. Welborn Kiefer Willingham, Aug. 14, 1950; children—Sharon, Douglas, Sheila. BA, Tex. Tech U., 1949. Interviewer Univ. Placement Service, Tex. Tech U., Lubbock, 1964-69; owner, mgr., buyer Maxine's Accent, Lubbock, 1969—; speaker in field. Leader Campfire Girls, Lubbock, 1964-65; sec. Community Theatre, Lubbock, 1962-64. Named Outstanding Mcht., Fashion Retailor mag., 1971, Outstanding Retailer; recipient Golden Sun award Dallas Market, May 1985. Mem. Lubbock Symphony Guild, Ranch and Heritage Ctr. Club: Faculty Women's. Office: 10 Briercroft Ctr Lubbock TX 79412

WILLINGHAM, SUSAN ELIZABETH G., accountant, consultant; b. Lafayette, Ala., Dec. 2, 1957; d. Bryant Kennon and Marion Elizabeth (Garrett) Goggans; m. Randell Byrd Willingham, July 5, 1986; 1 child, Wendy Dawn. BS in Acctg., Auburn U., 1980. CPA, Va. Sr. acct. West Point (Ga.) Pepperell, 1980-86, Va. Tech. State U., Blacksburg, 1987-88; cons., acctg. svc. provider Greenville, S.C., 1988—; acctg. mgr. Advanced Composite Materials Corp., Greer, S.C., 1989—; cons., J.P. Stevens, Greenville, 1988-89. Baptist. Home: 20 Cross Ridge Greenville SC 29607

WILLIS, BARBARA CUMMINGS, secondary school educator; b. Atlanta, Sept. 30, 1949; d. Mayo and Mary Frances (Dickey) Cummings; m. John Richard Willis, Apr. 20, 1974; l child, Joel Richard. BS cum laude, Ga. State U., 1989. Acct., bookkeeper Oglethorpe U., Atlanta, 1968; exec. sec. Liller Neal Battle & Lindsey, Atlanta, 1968-70; mgr. computer systems Alston Miller & Gaines, Atlanta, 1970-8l, Hurt Richardson Garner Todd et al, Atlanta, 198l-84; adminstrv. asst. Ga.-Cumberland Conf., Calhoun, Ga., l984-86; tchr. bus. edn. Ga.-Cumberland Acad., Calhoun, 1986—. Vol. Jr. Achievement, Atlanta, 1988; mem. Gordon County Battered Women's Shelter, Calhoun, 1988—. Mem. Nat. Bus. Educators Assn., Assn. Supervision and Curriculum Devel., 7th Day Adventist Educators Assn., Exptl. Aircraft Assn., Quota Club (pres. Marietta, Ga. chpt. 1977-81), Met. Atlanta Ladies Amateur Radio Club, Golden Key Club, Mortar Bd., Kappa Delta Pi. Republican. Home: PO Box 1695 Calhoun GA 30703 Office: Ga-Cumberland Acad 397 Academy Dr SW Calhoun GA 30701

WILLIS, CATHERINE-ELIZABETH, construction executive; b. Kansas City, Mo., Dec. 19, 1960; d. Howard Melvin Willis and Patricia Ann (Pendleton) Engle. BA, Mo. Western State Coll., 1981. Adminstrv. asst. Mid-Western Constrn. Co., Raytown, Mo., 1980-83; asst. controller Guest Quarters Hotel, Tampa, Fla., 1983-84; asst. mktg., adminstrn. McCarthy Bros., Kansas City, 1984-88; estimator Musselman & Hall Contractors, Kansas City, 1988-89; projects administr. Oppenheimer Design/Build, Inc., Kansas City, 1989—. Kansas City coord. Webster for Atty. Gen., Grisham for Lt. Gov. campaigns State of Mo., 1988; active in campaigns various Rep. candidates, Young Friends of Arts (mem. coms. 1989); vol. Peter Marshall Golf Tournament Ronald McDonald Home, 1980-84. Mem. NAFE, Bacchus Found. (fundraising com. 1989), Mo. Fedn. Young Reps. (recording sec. 1988-89), Kansas City Young Reps. (treas. 1988-89). Presbyterian. Home: 8001 Jefferson Kansas City MO 64114 Office: Oppenheimer DesignBuild Inc 1617 Baltimore Kansas City MO 64108

WILLIS, DAWN LOUISE, paralegal, legal administrator; b. Johnstown, Pa., Sept. 11, 1959; d. Kenneth William and Dawn Louise (Joseph) Hagins; m. Marc Anthony Ross, Nov. 30, 1984 (div.); m. Jerry Wayne Willis, Dec. 16, 1989. Grad. high sch., Sacramento, Calif. Legal sec. Wilcoxen & Callahan, Sacramento, 1979-87, paralegal asst., 1987-88; legal adminstr. Law Office of Jack Vetter, Sacramento, 1989—. Vol. ARC, 1985. Mem. NAFE, Assn. Legal Adminstrs., Calif. Trial Lawyers Assn., Sacramento Legal Secs. Assn. Republican. Lutheran. Office: Law Office Jack Vetter 928 2d St Ste 300 Sacramento CA 95814

WILLIS, DEBORAH BLEDSOE, coordinator mobile mammography program; b. Birmingham, Ala., Nov. 12, 1956; d. William Joseph and Deborah Anne (Smith) Bledsoe; m. David Gordon Willis, Mar. 7, 1980. Student, Birmingham Southern Coll., 1973-74; BS in Allied Health, U. Ala., Birmingham, 1990, postgrad., 1990—. Radiologic technologist Carraway Meth. Hosp., 1979, Bessemer Carraway Med. Ctr., Ala., 1979-80, St. Vincent's Hosp., Birmingham, 1980-83; mammography technologist Life Diagnostics, Birmingham, 1984-86; sales rep. Integrated Med. Systems, Birmingham, 1987-88; mobile mammography program coord. U. Ala., Birmingham, 1988; radiologic technologist Lakeview Internal Medicine Group, Birmingham, 1988. Coordinator comml. ad Mammography X-Ray Unit, 1985. Participant Vietnam Vets United, Lakewood, Calif., 1985—, Jeffrey MacDonald Def. Team, 1984—; vol. Ala. Rep. Party, 1983. Mem. NAFE, Am. Registry of Radiologic Technologists, Lions Club. Presbyterian. Home: 5232 Old Mill Cir Helena AL 35080 Office: Lakeview Internal Medicine Group 2700 10th Ave 2700 10th Ave S Ste 406 Birmingham AL 35205

WILLIS, DIANA MAY, teacher; b. Tampa, Fla., May 4, 1943; d. Clarence Leslie and Sarah DeMain (Williams) Karr; m. James Russel Willis, Apr. 13, 1968 (div. Sept. 1974); children: James Leslie, Russel Lee Roy, Cleveland DeMain. BA in Elem. Edn., U. South Fla., 1965; MS in Elem. Computer Edn., Nova U., 1987, postgrad. Tchr. Hillsborough County Sch. Bd., Tampa, 1965-66, Pinellas County Sch. Bd., St. Petersburg, Fla., 1966-67, Bahamas Agrl. Industries, Ltd., Andros, 1967-69; tutor Fla. Sheriffs Boys Ranch, Live Oak, Fla., 1985—; tchr. Suwannee County Sch. Bd., Live Oak, 1970—; cons. Suwanee County Schs., Live Oak, 1988-89; reader, reviewer Nat. Ednl. Computing Conf., 1989, 90, presider, 1990; presenter Fla. Instructional Computing Conf., Orlando, 1987, presider, 1989. Mem. NAFE, Nat. Coun. Tchrs. Math., Assn. for Supervision and Curriculum Devel., Internat. Soc. for Tech. in Edn., Spl. Interest Group for Computer Coords., Internat. Reading Assn., AAUW. Home: Rte 10 Box 395 Live Oak FL 32060 Office: Suwannee Elem E Sch 1625 Walker St SW Live Oak FL 32060

WILLIS, ELEANOR LAWSON, university development director; b. Nashville, Sept. 15, 1936; d. Harry Alfred Jr. and Helen Russell (Howse) Lawson; m. Alvis Rux Rochelle, Aug. 25, 1956 (div. Mar. 1961); 1 child, Alfred Russell Willis; m. William Reese Willis Jr., Mar. 7, 1964; children: William Reese III, Brent Lawson. BA cum laude, Vanderbilt U., 1957. Host children's syndicated TV show Sta. WSIX-TV, Nashville, 1961-64; tchr. head start program Metro Pub. Sch., Nashville, 1965-67; co-investigator cognitive edn. curriculum project Peabody Coll., Nashville, 1979-81; dir., founder Heads Up Child Devel. Ctr., Inc., Nashville, 1973-87; dir. Tenn. Vols. for Gore for Pres. Campaign, Nashville, 1987-88; dir. devel. Vanderbilt Inst. Pub. Policy Studies, Vanderbilt U., Nashville, 1988—; mem. task force on child abuse Dept. Human Svcs., Nashville, 1976; mem. mental health ctr. adv. bd. Vanderbilt U., 1978-80, bd. dirs. Vanderbilt Child Devel. Ctr.; mem. instrumental enrichment adv. bd. Peabody/Vanderbilt U., 1981-82. Author: (with others) I Really Like Myself, 1973, I Wonder Where I Came From, 1973. Pres. Nashville Bar Aux., 1967-68, Nashville Symphony Guild, 1984-85, W.O. Smith Nashville Community Music Sch., 1987-89; founder, active in Rochelle Ctr., Nashville, 1968-90; vice chmn. Century III Com., Nashville, 1978-80; chmn. so. region Am. Symphony Orch. League Vol. Coun., Washington, 1984-86, Homecoming 1986 Steering Com., Nashville, 1985-86; mem. Cheekwood Fine Arts Ctr., Nashville City Ballet, Nashville Symphony Assn., Dem. Women of Davidson County. Recipient Leadership Nashville award, 1982; Seven Leading Ladies award Nashville Mag., 1984; Eleanor Willis Day proclaimed by City of Nashville, 1987. Mem. Nashville C. of C., Tenn. Conservation League, Vanderbilt Alumni Assn.. Presbyterian. Office: Vanderbilt U Inst Pub Policy Studies 1208 18th Ave S Nashville TN 37212

WILLIS, ELIZABETH, lawyer; b. Takoma Park, Md., June 3, 1936; d. Ira Farnum Sr. and Mary Frances (Lewis) Willard; div.; children: Mary Catherine Raymond, John Donald, Elizabeth Ann Tedio, Daniel Paul. BA, Jacksonville U., 1972; JD, Fla. State U., 1987. Bar: Fla. News editor Fla. Pub. Broadcasting, Tallahassee, 1973-75; cabinet aide Fla. Dept. State, Tallahassee, 1975-76; div. dir. Fla. Dept. Bus. Regulation, Tallahassee, 1976-81; ind. lobbyist, polit. cons. Tallahassee, 1981-88, pvt. practice, 1988—; treas. Legal Aid Bd., Tallahassee, 1990—. Mem. Mayor's Housing Coun., Tallahassee, 1969, Gov.'s Commn. on Migrant Workers, Tallahassee, 1978-80; campaign mgr. Sen. Patrick Neal, 1982. Named Outstanding Vol., Fla. Times Union, 1973, Outstanding Newsperson, Fla. Young Dems., 1974. Mem. Fla. Bar, Tallahassee Bar, Fla. League Profl. Lobbyists (sec. 1989—), Fla. Econs. Club (v.p. 1978-80). Roman Catholic. Home: 3160 Blairstone Ct Tallahassee FL 32301 Office: Fla Pub Employee Rels Commn 2586 Seagate Dr Ste 100 Tallahassee FL 32301

WILLIS, EMILY PISPEKY, librarian; b. Richmond, Va., Apr. 3, 1955; d. Frank John and Emily Adelaide (Green) Pispeky; m. John Morris Willis Jr., July 26, 1980. BA cum laude, Longwood Coll., Farmville, Va., 1976. Cert. secondary tchr., Va. Tchr. Culpeper County (Va.) High Sch., 1976-77; asst. libr. Culpeper County Jr. High Sch., 1977-81, libr. and dept. chair, 1981--. Mem. Va. Educational Media Assn., Culpeper County Edn. Assn. (treas. 1981-82), Va. Edn. Assn., NEA. Episcopalian. Office: Culpeper County Jr High 500 Achievement Dr Culpeper VA 22701

WILLIS, IDA DENNIE, retired educator; b. Kansas City, Mo., Mar. 6, 1929; d. Alfred Stanley and Ruth (Morris) Dennis; m. Robert Tyrone Willis Jr., Dec. 21, 1952; children: Robert Tyrone III, William Alan. BA, Morris Brown Coll., Atlanta, 1951; MA, U. Chgo., 1955. Tchr. Ind. Sch. Dist. 1, Tulsa, 1951-53, 57-60, 62-64, 65-84; master tchr. Chgo. Bd. Edn., 1955-57; interviewer Tulsa Urban Renewal Authority, 1961; coord. United Negro Coll. Fund, 1986; substitute tchr. Ind. Sch. Dist. 1, Tulsa, 1985—; rep. Freedom's Found., Valley Forge, Pa., 1978, Tulsa U. Career Fair, 1982, Northeastern State U. Econ. Seminar, Tahlequah, Okla., 1978. Bd. dirs. Tulsa Urban League, 1958-60, vi. Gilcrease Mus. Aux.; bd. dirs. heritage found. Greenwood Cultural Ctr., 1990—. Mem. AAUW, NEA, Nat. Assn. Miniature Enthusiasists, Womens Aux. Okla., Podiatry Assn., Morris Brown Coll. Nat. Alumni Assn. (southwestern regional dir.), Okla. Ret. Educators Assn., Madam Alexander Doll Club, Elite Ladies Club, Inc., Delta Sigma Theta Sorority, Inc. Democrat. African Meth. Episcopalian.

WILLIS, JANE MARLOW, writer; b. Brandenburg, Ky., Mar. 8, 1942; d. James Mercer and Thelma (Marlow) W.; BA, So. Meth. U., 1964; postgrad. (Mark Ethridge fellow), U. N.C., 1966, MS Eastern Ky. U., 1985; mem. staff Meade County Messenger, Brandenburg, 1964—, editor, 1966—, pub., 1978-83; owner Jane Marlow Willis, Wordsmith; tech. writer Rust Engring., Oak Ridge, Tenn., 1986—. With Peace Corps, Solomon Islands, 1986-88. Former den mother local Cub Scouts; mem. drive com. Patton Museum Fund, 1965; mem. local com. Ky. Bicentennial, 1973; patron Pioneer Playhouse, Danville, Ky., 1972; mem. Brandenburg Vol. Fire Dept., 1975-86, chmn. firemen's ball, 1977, chmn. Brandenburg Fire Sch., 1977, cert. fire fighter; group coordinator Brandenburg Unity Festival, 1975-76; participant 1977 inaugural parade, 1977 part-time instr. fire sci. Ky. Dept. Vocat. Edn. Recipient Beyond War award, 1987, Solomon Islands Nat. Achievement award, 1988, Shriver Peace Worker award, 1988. Mem. Ky. Press Assn., Western Ky. (pres. 1971) Press Assn., Nat. Newspaper Assn., Internat. Assn. Fire Svc. Instrs. (charter mem. Ky. chpt.), Dixie Firemen's Assn. (sch. com.), DAR, Mensa, Sigma Delta Chi. Democrat. Methodist. Editor: Since April Third, 1975; Meade County Messenger Happy Holidays Cookbook, 1975; Summertime and The Cookin' Is Easy, 1977. Co-author slide presentation, Does A Water Curtain Really Work?. Home and Office: 321 Main St Brandenburg KY 40108

WILLIS, LAURA SMITH, real estate sales professional; b. Greenville, Ala., Nov. 18, 1934; d. Benjamin Rogers and Mildred Frances (Plant) Smith ;m. Roy Arthur Willis, Oct. 16, 1957 (dec. Sept. 1981); children: Roy Arthur Jr., Nancy, Laura Ann. Student, Jefferson State U., 1977. Real estate salesperson Dixieland Real Estate, Alabaster, Ala., 1977-79, First Real Estate, Pelham, Ala., 1979-81, Realty House, Pelham, 1981-85, Liz Bishop Relaty, Pelham, 1985-87, Don Murphy Real Estate, Pelham, 1987—. Mem. Pelham Indsl. Devel. Bd., 1982—; trustee Shelby Med. Ctr., Alabaster, 1984. Mem. Birmingham Bd. Realtors, Million Dollar Club, Pelham Area C. of C. Republican. Presbyterian. Office: Don Murphy Real Estate 3135 Helena Rd PO Box 1015 Pelham AL 35124

WILLIS, LISA HART, public relations and media specialist, business owner; b. Dallas, Oct. 1, 1958; d. James Hart Jr. and Terry (Armstrong) W. BA, Rice U., 1981; student, Sorbonne, Paris. Account exec. Beacon and Assocs. Pub. Rels., Dallas, 1984-85; dir. pub. rels., account exec. Avrea/Pugliese Advt. and Pub. Rels., Dallas, 1985-88; owner Willis Pub. Rels., Dallas, 1988—. Recipient Shepherd Music award, 1977, Cardinal Mindzenty Freedom award, 1990; named one of Outstanding Young Women of Am., 1987. Mem. NAFE, UN Assn., Dallas Coun. on World Affairs, Internat. Soc. Young Reps., Dallas C. of C., Press Club Dallas. Home and Office: 5909 Luther Ln Ste 902 Dallas TX 75225

WILLIS, LUCILLE REED, teacher; b. Greenwood, Miss., Jan. 7, 1939; d. Samuel and Virginia (Southerland) Reed; m. Robert Henry Willis; 1 stepchild, Robert Henry Jr. BS, LeMoyne-Owen Coll., Memphis, 1959; MEd, Memphis State U., 1973. Cert. career level III tchr. Tchr. Memphis City Schs., 1960—. Author poems, stories, religious plays. Mem. Status of Women Com., Memphis, 1981-83, leader trainer, 1983-84. Recipient Silver Poet award World of Poetry, 1986, Golden Poet award, 1987. Mem. NEA, Tenn. Ednl. Assn., Memphis Ednl. Assn. (assn. rep. mem.), Women in Edn. Democrat. Mem. African Methodist Episcopal Church. Home: 8708 Pine Needle Dr Germantown TN 38138

WILLIS, MAXINE FRASURE, paralegal; b. Norman, Okla., Aug. 15, 1933; d. Claude Caswell and Edna Lee (Thomason) Gower; m. Eugene Frasure, Mar. 6, 1954 (div. 1980); children: Steven, James, Cheryl; m. James Emerson Willis, Sept. 7, 1985. Student, U. Okla., 1951-52. Lic. real estate agt., Calif. Legal sec. Peter F. Matranga Esq., El Monte, Calif., 1957-71; supr., bank officer Security Pacific Nat. Bank, Los Angeles, 1971-74; probate paralegal J. Robert Kotchick Inc., El Monte, 1974-76; paralegal, trust adminstr. Security Pacific Nat. Bank, L.A., 1976-79, Hawking Realtors, Temple City, 1979-80; paralegal, office mgr. Anderson, McPharlin & Conners, Los Angeles, 1980—. Mem. Assn. Legal Adminstrs., Los Angeles County Bar Assn. (probate and trust sect.). Republican. Baptist. Home: 1552 Belmont Park Rd Oceanside CA 92056 Office: Anderson McPharlin & Conners 624 S Grand St 19th Floor Los Angeles CA 90017

WILLIS, MERYLL MEACHUM, director of operations; b. Lewisburg, Pa., June 1, 1948; d. James Clair and Leila Pearl (Mobley) Meachum; m. Stanton P. Ryther, May 14, 1971 (div. 1974); 1 child, Katharine Elizabeth; m. George Henry Willis, Aug. 10, 1975; 1 child, Bennett James. BS, SUNY, Oswego, 1970. Mgr. Little Giant, Fayetteville, N.C., 1973-75; asst. mgr. Eckerds Drug Stores, Gadsden, Ala., 1976-78; mem. credit, collections staff Gordons Jewelers, Harrisburg, Pa., 1978-83; office mgr. ReMax I Real Estate, Harrisburg, 1985-86; exec. asst. to pres. Girsch-Turner Advt., Harrisburg, 1986-87; dir. ops. Infomax, Inc., Harrisburg, 1987—. Chair, Chem. People of Perry County, Blain, Pa., 1984-86; publicity chair, Chem. People Coun. Cen. Pa., Harrisburg, 1985-87. Mem. NAFE, Am. Mgmt. Assn., Jetsetters (publicity chair 1987), Golden Sabers of Harrisburg (publicity chair 1988-89), Patriots Cheerleaders (field mgr. 1987-89). Republican. Roman Catholic. Office: Infomax Inc 3540 N Progress Ave Harrisburg PA 17110

WILLIS, SHIRLEY ANN, retired educator; b. Findlay, Ohio, July 20, 1938; d. Mark H. and Annabelle D. (Cunningham) Donaldson; m. Gilbert Wayne Willis, July 20, 1963. BE, Bowling Green (Ohio) U., 1961; MA, Xavier U., 1977. Tchr. Middletown (Ohio) City Schs., 1961-90. Active Ohio Educators Polit. Action Com., Columbus, 1977-79; precinct chair Dem. Cen. Com., Trenton, Ohio, 1986; chair Educators Polit. Action Com., Middletown, 1962-90; candidate Ohio Ho. of Reps. Mem. Middletown Bus. and Profl. Women (pres. 1983-84), AAUW (treas. Ohio chpt. 1989—), White Shrine of Jerusalem (worthy high priestress 1983), Middletown Tchrs. Assn. (pres. 1986-89), Ohio Edn. Assn. (bd. dirs. Columbus 1975-89), NEA (steering com. women's caucus Washington 1987). Methodist.

WILLIS, YVONNE FRANCIS, business owner, researcher; b. Washington, May 22, 1940; d. Pleasant and Maria (Bolden) Morrow; m. Marvin P. Willis Jr. (div. 1967). BA, Fed. City Coll., 1971; postgrad., Am. U., 1971-72, Howard U., 1989. Rsch. fundraiser Student Non-Violent Coordinating Com., Washington, 1966-69; coord. So. Christian Leadership Conf., Washington, 1966-69; fiscal analyst HEW, Washington, 1967-68; co-dir. project inform Fed. City Coll., Washington, 1968-71; researcher Am. U., Washington, 1971-72; exec. dir. Am. Minority Enterprise, Washington, 1978-84, pres., owner, 1989—. Republican. Roman Catholic. Home: 4530 Ft Totten Dr NE #209 Washington DC 20011 Office: Am Minority Enterprise 4530 St Totten Dr NE #209 Washington DC 20011

WILLISCROFT, BEVERLY RUTH, lawyer; b. Conrad, Mont., Feb. 24, 1945; d. Paul A. and Gladys L. (Buck) W.; m. Kent J. Barcus, Oct. 1984. BA in Music, So. Calif. Coll., 1967; JD, John F. Kennedy U., 1977. Bar: Calif., 1977. Elem. tchr., Sunnyvale, Calif., 1968-72; legal sec., legal asst. various law firms, Bay Area, 1972-77. Assoc. Neil D. Reid, Inc., San Francisco, 1977-79; sole practice, Concord, Calif., 1979—; exam. grader Calif. Bar, 1979—; real estate broker, 1980-88; tchr. real estate King Coll., Concord, 1979-80; lectr. in field; judge pro-tem Mcpl. Ct., 1981—. Bd dirs. Contra Costa Musical Theatre, Inc., 1978-82, v.p. adminstrn., 1980-81, v.p. prodn., 1981-82; mem. community devel. adv. com. City of Concord, 1981-83, vice chmn., 1982-83, mem. status of women com., 1980-81, mem. redevel. adv. com., 1984-86, planning commnr. 1986—; co-chmn. Longshore Morning Forum, Concord, 1980-84; mem. exec. bd. Mt. Diablo council Boy Scouts Am., 1981-85. Named Woman of Achievement, Todos Santos Bus. and Profl. Women, Clayton, Calif., 1980, 81; recipient award of merit, Bus. and Profl. Women, Bay Valley Dist., 1981. Mem. Concord C. of C. (bd. dir., chmn. govt. affairs com. 1981-83, v.p. 1985-87, pres. 1988-89, Bus. Person of Yr. 1986), Calif. Women Lawyers, Calif. State Bar, Contra Costa County Bar Assn., Contra Costa Barristers. Clubs: Todos Santos Bus. and Profl. Women (co-founder, pres. 1983-84, pub. relations chmn. 1982-83), Soroptimists (fin. sec. 1980-81). Office: 3018 Willow Pass Rd Ste 201 Concord CA 94519

WILLS, AUDREY ELIZABETH, bank executive; b. Phila., Mar. 28, 1930; d. Theodore A. and Mary C. (Dixon) W. AA, Villanova, 1966. Operations officer First Pa. Bank, Phila., 1961-66, asst. v.p., div. head, 1966-74, v.p., 1974-85, divisional v.p., 1985—; bd. dirs. Del. Valley Bank Methods Assn., Phila.; cons. Fraud Control Bureau, PHila., 1970—, Hurst Assocs., Springfield, Pa., 1986—, L & L Custom Catering Inc., Frederick, Pa., 1980—. Author: Loss Prevention Awareness, 1979; author and exec. producer of film: Tell it to the Judge, 1986; contbr. articles to various publications; editor: Prevention Awareness newsletter. Mem. Phila. Art

Mus. Assn., 1975—; mem. New Hanover Civic Assn. (twp. Pa.), 1975-81; mem. Greater Phila. Cultural Alliance, 1976—; mem. Smithsonian Assocs., Washington, 1980—; mem. Paradise (environmental) Watchdogs, Frederick, Pa., 1987; mem. Phila. Clearing House Fraud Commn. (past chmn.); chmn. Women's Achievement Forum Phila. YWCA, 1988-90, trustee 1989, bd. dirs. 1990. Recipient Cert. of Appreciation Dept. Defense USAF Guard and Reserve, 1985, Cert. achievement Women's Forum YWCA of Phila., 1987. Mem. Pa. Bankers Assn., Am. Mgt. Assn., Am. Inst. of Banking, Bank Adminstrn. Inst., Del. Valley Fin. and Security Officer's Assn. Club: Cen. Perklomen Bus. and Profl. Women. Home: Renninger Rd Frederick PA 19435 Office: First Pa Bank 3020 Market Philadelphia PA 19101

WILLS, DONNA M., information systems specialist; b. Boston, Mar. 18, 1946; d. Ronald L. and Bernice M. (Hamm) Ballou; m. William F. Dean, July 24, 1965 (div. 1977); 1 child, Dawna A.; m. Travers H. Wills, Apr. 3, 1982 (div. 1987). BS in Math., U. Mass., 1969. Systems engr. Aetna Life and Casualty, Hartford, Conn., 1969-76; asst. dir. systems life div., group div. Cigna Corp., Hartford, 1977-81, dir. human resources life div., group div., 1982-85, asst. v.p. systems investment div., 1985-87, v.p. systems investment div., group div., 1988-89; v.p. systems John Alden Life Ins. Co., Miami, Fla., 1989—; investment systems LOMA, Atlanta, 1987-89; mgmt. forum Cigna Corp., Phila., 1988-89; mgmt. devel. task force Conn. Gen., Hartford, 1978-80; systems architecture com. Cigna Systems, Phila., 1989. Bd. dirs. Childrens Home Cromwell, Conn., 1989; vol. Nat. Ski Patrol-Magic Mountain, Londonderry, Vt., 1975-84; leader Girl Scouts Am., Cromwell, 1976-78; coach Girls Little League Softball Cromwell, 1975-78. Congregationalist. Home: 1265 Fairfax Ct Fort Lauderdale FL 33326 Office: John Alden Life Ins Co 7300 Corporate Center Dr Miami FL 33126

WILLS, KATHERINE VASILIOS, retail business owner; b. St. Louis, Sept. 30, 1957; d. Vasilios and Kalliope (Stratos) Tsiopos. BA, Washington U., 1979; MA, Ind. U., 1990. Rsch. dir. U. Chgo. (Ill.) Gynecology, 1980-82, Northwestern U., Chgo., 1982-86; pres. Port of Nashville (Ind.) Inc., retailer of nautical items and antiques, 1986—; Pub. reader various orgns. Contbr. articles and poetry to jours. Vol. Women's Writers' Conf., Chgo.; fundraiser Am. Bar Assn.; greeter World Congress on Equality and Freedom, St. Louis; student worker on dig for Am. Indian artifacts Tenn. River Archeol. Project; debutant Am. Hellenic Progressgive and Ednl. Assn. Recipient essay award Scholastic Mag., Inc., 1973, award for acad. excellence and community svc. Am. Hellenic Progessvie and Ednl. Assn., A poetry award Wednesday Club of St. Louis, Mo., 1977, Roger Conant Hatch hon. mention for writing, Washington U., 1977. Mem. NAFE, Nat. Histotechnologie Soc., MLA, Assn. Writers and Poets, Conf. on Coll. Composition and Communication, Midwest Regional Conf., Nat. Coun. Tchrs. English Poets and Writers Inc. Greek Orthodox. Home: RR2 Box 378 C Nashville IN 47448 Office: P O Box 806 Nashville IN 47448

WILLS, NANCY KAY, physiology educator; b. Wytheville, Va., Aug. 27, 1949; d. Henry Eugene and Norma Agnes (Umberger) W.; m. Simon A. Lewis, Dec. 6, 1975. BS, Ohio State U., 1971; MA, U. Va., 1974, PhD, 1977. Postdoctoral fellow U. Tex. Med. Br., Galveston, 1977; postdoctoral fellow Yale U., New Haven, 1978-80, assoc. rsch. scientist, 1980-84; vis. assoc. prof. SUNY, Stony Brook, 1984-85; rsch. scientist, lectr. Yale U. Sch. Medicine, New Haven, 1985-86; assoc. prof. dept. physiology and biophysics U. Tex. Med. Br., Galveston, 1987—. Mem. editorial bd. Am. Jour. Physiology: Gastrointestinal Physiology, 1986—, Am. Journ. Physiology: Cell Physiology, 1990—; contbr. chpts. to books, articles to jours. NDEA fellow U. Va., 1971-74; NIH USPH fellow Yale U., 1978-80; grantee NIH, 1981-84, 84-88, 88-93. Mem. Am. Physiol. Soc. (councilor, steering com. cell and gen. physiology sect.), Biophys. Soc., Soc. Gen. Physiologists, Assn. Rsch. in Vision and Ophthalmology, Am. Soc. Nephrology. Office: Dept Physiology/ Biophysics Univ Tex Med Br Galveston TX 77551

WILLS, SYLVIA LUCY, event coordinator, investor; b. Brussels, Belgium, Sept. 9, 1964; d. George Robert and Ludmilla-Boronen (Forani) W. AB, Occidental, L.A., 1988. Intern Entertainment Tonight, L.A., 1985-87; asst. to the editor The Occidental Mag., L.A., 1986; columnist Sierra Madre News, L.A., 1987; casting dir. L'Image Talent, L.A., 1988; events coord. Classic Affairs, Pasadena, Calif., 1988—; program dir. Le Tip Internat., Pasadena, 1989; event coord. Pasadena Pops, 1989. Mem. Spl. Events and Wedding Industry Network, NAFE, Pasadena C. of C., Beverly Hills C. of C., Beverly Hills Women's Network, Jaycees. Home and Office: 262 S Bonita Ave Pasadena CA 91107

WILLSON, JULIE, financial planner; b. Stockton, Calif., Jan. 30, 1958. BA, U. Calif., Irvine, 1979. Supr. tng. dept., br. investment officer Am. Savs. and Loan Assn., Whittier, Calif., 1979-83; fin. cons. Shearson Am. Express, Orange, Calif., 1983-84; investment svcs. officer Discount Investments Am. (now Griffin Fin. Svcs.), Long Beach, Calif., 1984-86; account exec. Morgan, Olmstead, Kennedy and Gardner, Newport Beach, Calif., 1986; fin. planner Christopher Weil and Co., Inc., Newport Beach, 1986-88; fin. cons. Empire Nat. Securities Inc., Irvine and Laguna Hills, Calif., 1988-89, Felton-Collins, Woodhouse and Assocs., Costa Mesa, Calif., 1989—; presenter seminars, Long Beach, Newport Beach, 1984—. Contbr. articles on personal fin. to local newspapers. Recipient Young Careerist award Bus. and Profl. Women, 1988. Mem. NAFE, Inst. Cert. Fin. Planners (cert.). Office: Felton Collins Woodhouse & Assocs 3070 Bristol #400 Costa Mesa CA 92626

WILLSON, LAURA FAULK, education consultant; b. San Antonio, Aug. 20, 1937; d. David Reynolds and Alma Laura (Reveley) Faulk; m. Robert Edward Willson, May 31, 1958 (div. 1983); children: Ryan Faulk, Brannan Faulk. BBA, U. Tex., Austin, 1958; MBA in Mktg., U. Houston, 1963; PhD in Psychology, U. Calif., Berkeley, 1973. Cert. tchr., adminstr., Tex. Tchr. San Antonio Ind. Sch. Dist., 1958-60; rsch. assoc. to pvt. practice consulting economist Houston, 1960-61; market analyst Cleco Tools, Houston, 1961-62; instr. San Jacinto Coll., Houston, 1962-63; teaching fellow U. Houston, 1964-65; assoc. dir. rsch. D'Arcy Advt. Agy., San Francisco, 1965-66; v.p., dean, prof. Marin Community Colls., Kentfield, Calif., 1966-86; vice chancellor academic affairs Calif. Community Colls., Sacramento, 1986-87; ind. cons. higher edn. Tiburon, Calif., 1974—; team mem., chair accrediting commn., Western Assn. Schs. and Colls., 1976-87. Treas., bd. dirs. Planned Parenthood of Marin, San Rafael, Calif., 1985; resource coord. area vols. Reach to Recovery, Marin County, 1987—; mem. Redwood High Parents Assn., Larkspur, Calif., 1987—; trustee Calif. Sch. of Profl. Psychology, 1990—. Mem. Assn. Calif. Community Coll. Adminstrs., Beta Gamma Sigma, Omicron Delta Epsilon. Office: 41 Greenwood Bay Tiburon CA 94920

WILLSON, MARY F., ecology researcher, educator; b. Madison, Wis., July 28, 1938; d. Gordon L. and Sarah (Loomans) W.; m. R.A. von Neumann, May 29, 1972 (dec.). B.A. with honors, Grinnell Coll., 1960; Ph.D., U. Wash., 1964. Asst. prof. U. Ill., Urbana, 1965-71, assoc. prof., 1971-76, prof. ecology, 1976-90; rsch. ecologist Forestry Scis. Lab., Juneau, Alaska, 1989—; adj. prof. zoology and botany Wash. State U., Pullman; prin. rsch. assoc. Inst. Arctic Biology U. Alaska, Fairbanks. Author: Plant Reproductive Ecology, 1983, Vertebrate Natural History, 1984; co-author: Mate Choice in Plants, 1983. Fellow Am. Ornithologists Union; mem. Soc. for Study Evolution, Am. Soc. Naturalists, Ecol. Soc. Am., Brit. Ecol. Soc. Office: Forestry Scis Lab PO Box 20909 Juneau AK 99802

WILLSON, SUSAN, midwife, nurse; b. West Palm Beach, Fla., Oct. 9, 1952; d. Jack Sloane and Mary Louise (Griffin) W. BA, Emory U., 1974, BSN, 1981; MS in Nursing, Yale U., 1984. Nurse-midwife USPHS, Chinle, Ariz., 1984-87; faculty coord. Omega Inst. for Holistic Studies, Rhinebeck, N.Y., 1983-86; clin. instr. Navajo Community Coll., Tsaile, Ariz., 1984-87; midwife-nurse Va. Mason Med. Ctr., Seattle, 1987--. Mem. Am. Coll. Nurse Midwives, Pre and Perinatal Psychology Assn., Sigma Theta Tau. Home: 1210 20th Ave E Seattle WA 98112 Office: Va Mason Midwifery 1201 Terry Ave Seattle WA 98101

WILMER, CHARLOTTE M., government relations specialist; b. Huntington, W. Va., Oct. 2, 1946; d. H.F. and Faye D. (Campbell) W. BA, Marshall U., Huntington, 1968. Adminstrv. asst. to U.S. Senator John Breaux Washington, 1972-76; regional coord. Carter-Mondale Campaign, Atlanta, 1976; dir., polit. coord. Dem. Nat. Com, Washington, 1977-78; legis. rep. Nat. Rural Electric Coop. Assn., Washington, 1979-87; dir. fed. affairs Nat. Solid Wastes Mgmt. Assn., Washington, 1987-88; v.p. R. Duffy Wall & Assocs., Washington, 1989—. Bd. dirs. Woolly-Mammoth Theatre Co., Washington, 1988, Internat. Eye Found., 1989. Mem. Women in Govt. Relations, Am. League Lobbyists. Democrat. Methodist. Office: R Duffy Wall & Assocs 1317 F St NW Washington DC 20004

WILMER, MARY CHARLES, artist; b. Atlanta, Aug. 25, 1930; d. William Knox and Harriott Creighton (Thomas) Fitzpatrick; student Wellesley Coll., 1948-50; AB, Agnes-Scott Coll., 1970; BFA, Coll. of Art, 1974; m. John Grant Wilmer, Dec. 28, 1950; children: John Grant, Knox Randolph, Charles Inman, Mary Catherine; m. Olin Grigsby Shivers, May 18, 1982. One-woman shows: Image South Gallery, 1974, Aronson Gallery, 1977, 79, Heath Gallery, 1982, Coach House Gallery, 1983, 89; exhibited in group show: Colony Sq., 1975; portrait painter, 1974—. Bd. dirs. Hillside Cottages, 1963-65, Atlanta Child Svcs., 1965-68, Atlanta Coll. Art, 1965-85, Atlanta Puppetry Arts, 1982-87; co-chmn. Ga. Commn. Nat. Mus. of Women in the Arts, 1985-87. Mem. Piedmont Driving Club, Jr. League, Piedmont Garden Club. Episcopalian. Address: 1 Vernon Rd Atlanta GA 30305

WILMERING, KATHY, social worker, nurse; b. St. Louis, Sept. 17, 1958; d. Thomas H. and Jean (Dahm) W. BS in Nursing, St. Louis U., 1981, MSW, 1988; cert. in family therapy, Montlake Inst., Seattle, 1990. Cert. mental health counselor, Wash. Nurse Cardinal Glennon Meml. Hosp., St. Louis, 1980-82; lead therapist, nurse Comprehensive Mental Health Ctr., Tacoma, Wash., 1982-86; counsellor Youth Emergency Svcs., St. Louis, 1986-87; clin. social work intern St. Louis County Child Mental Health Ctr., 1987-88; nurse practitioner Harborview Med. Ctr., Seattle, 1987—; therapist, community organizer Family Svcs., Seattle, 1987-89; implementer clin. svcs. of Family Devel. Program Harbor View Mental Health Ctr., Seattle, 1989—; pvt. practice therapist Seattle. Mem. Homeless Network Bd., St. Louis, 1986-88; mem. Ford Community Group, St. Louis, 1987-88; mem. task force on housing and homelessness Ch. Coun. Greater Seattle, 1988—; co-chmn. High Point Svc. Coalition, Seattle, 1989; chmn. pairing project Tacoma Speaker's Bur., 1984-85; vol. nurse Neighborhood Clinic, Tacoma, 1983, Family Care Ctr., St. Louis, 1982. Mem. Nat. Assn. Social Workers, Profl. Mental Health Practitioners Assn., Toastmasters, Sierra Club, Sigma Theta Tau, Psi Chi, Alpha Sigma Nu. Office: Harborview Mental Health Ctr 326 9th ZA-31 Seattle WA 98104

WILMOWSKI, WENDY ANN, television producer and director; b. Elmhurst, Ill., Dec. 10, 1962; d. Edward Joseph and Mary Ann (Dalyk) W. BA in Theology magna cum laude, Franciscan U. Steubenville, 1984, BA in Communications magna cum laude, 1984. Comml. dir., videogragher Community Video Svcs., Dallas, summer 1983, 84; dir. statewide communications Ariz. Dept. Corrections, Phoenix, 1985-86; producer, dir., writer LUMEN 2000, Dallas, 1986-88; owner, exec. producer InnerVision Prodns. Internat., Tempe, Ariz., 1988—; internat. cons., bd. dirs. LUMEN 2000-Brazil, Sao Paulo, 1988-89; internat. producer, bd. dirs., cons. LOGO Media-The Netherlands, Hilversum, 1989—; cons. South Am., Innervision Prodns. Internat., the Netherlands, 1988—. Producer, dir. (TV documentary) Evangelization 2000, 1987, (TV series) LUMEN 2000, 1989; producer, dir., writer (TV documentary) The Church in India, 1990; photographer The Manna Mag., 1990. Mem. Evangelization 2000. Republican. Roman Catholic. Office: LOCO Media InnerVisions, Prodns Emmastraat 51C, 1213AK Hilversum The Netherlands

WILNER, LOIS ANNETTE, speech pathologist; b. Newark, Jan. 15, 1935; d. Benjamin and Ida (Schwam) Friedman; m. Sherman Wilner, July 6, 1957; children: Bonnie Joy, Robert Steven. BS, Newark State Tchrs. Coll., 1953-57; MA, Newark State Coll., Union, 1969-73. 5th grade tchr. Maplewood, S. Orange Bd. Edn., South Orange, N.J., 1957-58; permanent subst. Parsippany- Troy Hills Bd. Edn., Parisppany, N.J., 1967-68; speech pathlogist Parsippany - Troy Hills. Bd. Edn., Parsippany, 1968—; cons., speech and lang. pathologist Ctr. for Communication Disorders, Livingston, N.J., 1987-89. Mem. NEA, N.J. Edn. Assn., Morris County Edn. Assn., N.J. Speech-Hearing Assn., Morris County Speech-Hearing Assn. (librarian 1987-90), B'nai B'rith Women (Roseland and Suburban Essex chpt. pres. 1985-88), AAUW, Alpha Delta Kappa (pres. Mu chpt. 1990—). Home: 9 Riker Hill Rd Livingston NJ 07039 Office: Parsippany Troy Hills Bd Brooklawn Mid Sch Beachwood Rd Parsippany NJ 07054

WILNER, LYNNE ANN, banker; b. Park Ridge, Ill., July 17, 1962; d. Alvin Gustuv and Lois Ann (Oehler) W. BA in English, St. Olaf Coll., 1984; postgrad., Cambridge (Eng.) U., Cambridge, England, 1984. Sales trainee Deluxe Check Printers, Bensenville, Ill., 1984-85; writing instr. Triton Coll., River Grove, Ill., 1985-86; prospecting banker Harris Trust and Savs. Bank, Chgo., 1986-87; asst. v.p. Harris Bank Winnetka, Winnetka, Ill., 1987—; bus. communication instr. Am. Inst. Banking, Chgo., 1989—; career advisor St. Olaf Coll. Career Ctr., Northfield, Minn., 1988—; speaker Svc. Corps Retired Execs., SBA, 1989. Counseling asst. Hines (Ill.) VA Hosp., 1985; fundraiser United Way, Chgo., 1987, 89. Recipient Nat. Fedn. Contribution award Nat. Fedn. Bus. and Profl. Women's Clubs, 1989. Mem. North Michigan Avenue Bus. and Profl. Women's Network (charter, found. chmn. 1988-89, editor newsletter 1988—, v.p., program planning chmn. 1989—), NAFE, Women's Exchange Club, Equal to Challenge Club. Republican. Lutheran. Home: 259 Scottswood Rd Riverside IL 60546 Office: Harris Bank Winnetka 520 Green Bay Rd Winnetka IL 60093

WILROY, HIABURNIA GAINES, title insurance company executive; b. DeSoto County, Miss., Apr. 22, 1929; d. Hubert Cornelius Gaines and Mattie Mae (Chamberlin) Gaines Troy; m. Leslie Lee Crawford, June 1, 1947 (div. June 1969); children—Leslie Lee, Jr., Richard Marvin; m. William Edwards Wilroy, Oct. 15, 1970 (div. Dec. 1985). B.B.A., U. Miss., 1979. Cert. profl. sec., 1975. Exec. sec. to county agt., Hernando, Miss., 1948-49; legal sec. W.E. Wilroy, Hernando, 1950-51, 53-57; chief clk. DeSoto County Agrl. Stblzn. and Conservation Service, Hernando, 1957-58; legal sec. Wilroy, Wilroy & Hagan, Hernando, 1958-69; corp. officer, asst. v.p. Mid-South Title Ins. Corp., Memphis, 1969—. Docent Ramesses The Great Exhibition. Mem. Profl. Secs. Internat. (treas. Memphis chpt. 1981-82, bd. dirs. 1984-85), Women's Soc. Christian Service (circle chmn. Hernando). Methodist. Club: Garden Study (sec.) (Hernando). Avocations: bridge, reading, needlepoint, knitting. Home: 96 Robinson St E PO Box 63 Hernando MS 38632 Office: Mid-South Title Ins Corp 1200 One Commerce Sq Memphis TN 38103

WILSON, ALICE BLAND, real estate consultant; b. Rainelle, W.Va., Apr. 1, 1938; d. Brady Floyd and Mildred Martha (George) Bland; m. Louis William Groves, Jr., Apr. 20, 1957 (div. 1981); children: Martha Rachel, Leonora Jayne; m. Glen Parten Wilson, Dec. 11, 1982. AB, W.Va. U., 1959, postgrad. in microbiology, 1975-78. Contract adminstr. Washington Plate Glass Co., Washington, 1979-80; mem. acctg. staff Forbes Co., Washington, 1981; customer relations rep. Stern's Co., Washington, 1982; real estate assoc. Prudential Preferred Properties, Washington, 1985—. Contbr. articles to Jour. Parasitology, Vol. coordinator John Glenn for Pres. campaign, Washington, 1983-84; co-chmn. hospitality com. Women's Nat. Democratic Club, Washington, 1985—; mem. internat. adv. council ARC, Washington, 1985—. Mem. Washington Assn. Realtors (mem. residential sales com. 1985—), Leading Edge Soc. Avocations: flying, aerobatics, nature study. Club: Million Dollar. Home: 433 New Jersey Ave SE Washington DC 20003 Office: Prudential Preferred Properties 2305 Calvert St NW Washington DC 20008

WILSON, ALMA D., state supreme court justice; b. Pauls Valley, Okla., May 25, 1917; d. William R. and Anna L. (Schuppert) Bell; m. William A. Wilson, May 30, 1948; 1 child, Lee Anne. AB, U. Okla., 1939, JD, 1941. Bar: Okla. 1941. Sole practice Muskegee, Okla., 1941-43; sole practice Oklahoma City, 1943-47, Pauls Valley, 1948-69; judge Pauls Valley Mcpl. Ct., 1967-68; apptd. spl. judge Dist. Ct. 21, Norman, Okla., 1969-75, dist. judge, 1975-79; assoc. justice Okla. Supreme Ct., Oklahoma City, 1982—. Mem. bd. visitors U. Okla., mem. alumni bd. dirs.; mem. Assistance League; trustee Okla. Meml. Union. Recipient Guy Brown award, 1974, Woman of Yr. award Norman Bus. and Profl. Women, 1975, Okla. Women's Hall of Fame award, 1983, Pioneer Woman award, 1985, Disting. Svc. Citation U. Okla., 1985. Mem. AAUW, Garvin County Bar Assn. (past pres.), Okla. Bar Assn. (co-chmn. law and citizenship edn. com.), Okla. Trial Lawyers Assn. (Appellate Judge of Yr. 1986, 89), Altrusa, Am. Legion Aux. Office: Okla Supreme Ct State Capitol Rm 247 Oklahoma City OK 73105*

WILSON, ANN D., singer, recording artist; b. 1950; d. John and Lou Wilson. Ed., Cornish Allied Inst. Fine Arts, Seattle. Lead singer rock group Heart, 1975—. Albums include: Dreamboat Annie, 1975, Magazine, 1975, Little Queen, 1977, Dog and Butterfly, 1978, Bebe le Strange, 1980, Heart Live-Gr, Private Audition, 1982, Passionworks, 1983, Heart, 1985, Bad Animals, 1987, Brigade, 1990; single recs. include: Magic Man, 1976, Barracuda, 1977, Crazy on You, 1976, Straight On, 1978, Even It Up, 1980, Sweet Darlin', 1980, Tell It Like It Is, 1981, Unchained Melody, 1981, This Man is Mine, 1982, City's Burning, 1982, Bright Light Girl, 1982, How Can I Refuse, 1983, Sleep Alone, 1983, Almost Paradise, 1984, The Heat, 1984, What About Love, 1985, Never, 1985, These Dreams, 1986, Nothin' at All, 1986, Alone, 1987, Who Will Run to You, 1987, There's The Girl, 1987, I Want You So Bad, 1988, Surrender to Me, 1988, All I Wanna Do Is Make Love To You, 1990, I Did'nt Want to Need You, 1990, Stranded, 1990. Office: 219 1st Ave N Ste 333 Seattle WA 98109

WILSON, BARBARA ANN, educator, speech-language pathologist; b. New Hartford, N.Y., July 3, 1962; d. Albro Carl Jr. and Doris Jean (Heinz) W. AS, Monroe Community Coll., Rochester, N.Y., 1983; BS, SUNY, Geneseo, 1985; MEd, U. Va., 1987. Lic. speech-lang. pathology, N.Y.; permanent cert. speech and hearing handicapped. Speech aide Empire State and Hearing Clinic, Inc., Elmira, N.Y., 1985; speech-lang. pathologist infant program Bd. Cooperative Ednl. Svcs., Spencerport, N.Y., 1987; adj. faculty speech-lang. dept. Nat. Tech. Inst. for the Deaf, Rochester Inst. Tech., 1987-88, cons. speech-lang. dept., 1988; speech tchr. Rochester Sch. for the Deaf, 1988—. Mem. Ch. of the Transfiguration Choir, Pittsford, N.Y., 1989; tchr., coord. confirmation classes Ch. of the Transfiguration, Pittsford, 1989, dir. jr. high youth group, 1989. Mem. Alexander Braham Bell Assn. for Deaf, Am. Speech-Lang.-Hearing Assn. (cert. in clin. competence), Conv. Am. Instr. of Deaf, N.Y. State Assn. Educators of Deaf. Roman Catholic. Home: 120 I Windsorshire Dr Rochester NY 14629 Office: Rochester Sch for the Deaf 1545 Saint Paul St Rochester NY 14621

WILSON, BARBARA HELEN, controller; b. Oklahoma City, Oct. 21, 1959; d. Robert H. and Alice Charlene (Bogle) Reynolds; children: Shauna, Erin, John. Student, Blackwood Bus. Coll. Mgr. acctg. Mana Exploration Co., Oklahoma City; acct. Gulf Oil, Oklahoma City, 1979-83; mgr. acctg. and land Joy Petroleum Co., Oklahoma City, 1983-87; contr., land mgr., corp. sec. Yellowstone Resources, Inc., Denver, 1987—; contr., corp. sec., asst. treas. Water Resources Assocs., Inc., Phoenix, 1990—; treas. Tower Exploration, Denver, 1990—. Mem. Assn. Mining Fin. Profls., Assn. Div. Order Analysts, Desk & Derrick Club Denver.

WILSON, BARBARA JOYCE, sales executive; b. Dalton, Ga., Oct. 12, 1947; d. Luther Frank Bivens and Helen Virginia (Crider) Goswick; m. Steve Dean Wilson, Dec. 24, 1965; children: Macy Helen, Sherry Lynette, Steve Dean Jr. Radio announcer, sales exec. Sta. WBLJ, Dalton, 1966—; gospel music dir. Sta. WBLJ, 1980-90. With pub. rels. com. Spl. Olympics Assn., Dalton, 1978-80; den leader Boy Scouts Am., Dalton, 1984, 85, 86; active pub. rels. com. Am. Cancer Soc., Dalton, 1983-85, Cen. Ch. of Christ, Dalton, 1987-90; bd. dirs. Harvest Outreach Ministries, Dalton, 1990—. Mem. Concerned Women of Am., MADD. Democrat. Home: 6005 Cedarwood Ln Dalton GA 30721 Office: Sta WBLJ 945 Riverbend Rd Dalton GA 30720

WILSON, BARBARA LOUISE, communications executive; b. Bremerton, Wash., Aug. 3, 1952; d. Algernon Frances and Dorothy Virginia (Martin) W.; m. Ashby A. Riley III, Feb. 7, 1979 (div. Dec. 1983). BA in Fin. and Econs., U. Puget Sound, 1974; MBA, U. Wash., Seattle, 1985. With Pacific N.W. Bell, Seattle and Portland, Oreg., 1974-86, dir. pub. communications, 1983-85, dir. number svcs. mktg., 1985-86; v.p. implementation planning US West, Inc., Englewood, Colo., 1986-87; pres. US West Info. Systems, Englewood, 1987-89; v.p. bus. div. US West Communications, Englewood, 1989; v.p. human resources U.S. West Communications, Denver, 1989—; bd. dirs. U.S. West New Vector Group, Bellevue, Wash., 1988-90; chair nat. adv. com. Telephone Pioneers Am., N.Y.C., 1989; mem. sr. adv. bd. Am. Soc. Tng. and Devel., Denver, 1989. Bd. dirs., exec. com. Wash. Coun. for Econ. Edn., Seattle, 1985-86; team capt. major gifts com. Boys and Girls Club, Seattle, 1986; chairperson co. campaign United Way, Seattle, 1985; bd. dirs. Denver Arts Ctr. Found., 1989—. Republican. Roman Catholic. Office: US West Communications 1801 California St Ste 5200 Denver CO 80202

WILSON, BERTHA, Canadian justice; b. Kirkcaldy, Scotland, Sept. 18, 1923; d. Archibald Wernham and Christina Noble; m. John. Wilson, 1945. MA, Aberdeen (Scotland) U., 1944; parchment, Tng. Coll. Tchrs., Aberdeen, 1945; LLB, Dalhousie U., Halifax, N.S., 1957, LLD (hon.), 1980; LLD (hon.), Queen's U., Kingston, 1983, U. Calgary, 1983, U. Toronto, 1984, U. Alta., 1985, York U., 1986, U. B.C., 1988, U. Aberdeen, 1989; LHD (hon.), Mt. St. Vincent U., Halifax, 1984; D. Hum. L., Mt. St. Vincent U., Halifax, N.S., 1984; DCL (hon.), U. Windsor, 1985; DCL, U. Western Ont., 1985. Bar: N.S. 1957, Ont. 1959. Assoc. Osler, Hoskin & Harcourt, Toronto, 1958-68, ptnr., 1968-75; created Queen's Council Can., 1973; judge Can. Ct. Appeals, Ont., 1975-82, Supreme Ct. of Can., Ottawa, Ont., 1982—, Can. Permanent Ct. Arbitration, 1984—. Trustee Clarke Inst. of Psychiatry, 1972-75; trustee Toronto Sch. Theol., 1975-81, mem. exec. com., 1977-81; chmn. Rhodes Scholarship Selection Com., Ont., 1980-84; bd. govs. Carleton U., 1983-85; bd. dirs. Can. Ctr. for Philanthropy, 1981—; mem. jud. com. United Ch. Can., 1985—. Mem. Can. Bar Assn. (mem. nat. council, mem. Ont. council 1970-73). Mem. United Ch. Can. Office: Supreme Ct, Wellington St, Ottawa, ON Canada K1A 0J1

WILSON, BERTINA IOLIA, educator, musician; b. Southampton, Va., Aug. 17, 1938; d. Purcell Lee and Clarine Branch; m. Aug. 25, 1963 (div. May 1977); children: Brian Keith, Linda Elizabeth. BA, Newark State Coll., 1960; MA, Kean Coll., 1981. Cert. elem. edn. tchr., N.J. Tchr. Newark Bd. of Edn., 1960-77, project coord., 1977—; ch. organist, choir dir. Zion Hill Bapt. Ch., Newark, 1974—. Mem. Newark Tchrs. Union, Project Coords. Assn. (exec. bd. Newark chpt. 1981—), Order of Eastern Star (Outstanding Ch. Musician 1986), Phi Delta Kappa (pub. rels. dir. 1987-89). Democrat. Home: 120 Washington St Apt 14 East Orange NJ 07017

WILSON, BETTY MAY, finance company executive; b. Moberly, Mo., Mar. 13, 1947; d. Arthur Bunyon and Martha Elizabeth (Denham) Stephens; m. Ralph Felix Martin, Aug. 22, 1970 (div. May 1982); m. Gerald Robert Wilson Sr., Mar. 3, 1984; stepchildren: Gerald Robert Jr., Heather Lynn, Jeffrey Michael. BS in Acctg. and Bus. Adminstrn., Colo. State U., 1969. CPA, Mo. Tax mgr. Arthur Andersen and Co., St. Louis, 1969-75; v.p., asst. sec., dir. taxes ITT Fin. Corp., St. Louis, 1975—; sr. v.p., bd. dirs. Lyndon Ins. Co., St. Louis, 1977—, ITT Lyndon Life Ins. Co., ITT Lyndon Property Ins. Co., St. Louis, 1977—. Mem. AICPA, Mo. Soc. CPA's, Am. Fin. Services Assn. (chmn. tax com. 1987-88), Tax Execs. Inst. Inc. (bd. dirs. St. Louis chpt., past sec., past. pres.), Mo. Girls Racing Assn. (pres. 1977-82). Baptist. Office: ITT Fin Corp 12555 Manchester Rd Saint Louis MO 63131

WILSON, BLENDA JACQUELINE, university chancellor; b. Woodbridge, N.J., Jan. 28, 1941; d. Horace and Margaret (Brogsdale) Wilson; m. Louis Fair Jr. AB, Cedar Crest Coll., 1962; AM, Seton Hall U., 1965; PhD, Boston Coll., 1979; DHL (hon.), Cedar Crest Coll., 1987, Loretto Heights Coll., 1988, U. Detroit, 1989; LLD (hon.), Rutgers U., 1989. Tchr. Woodbridge Twp. Pub. Schs., 1962-66; exec. dir. Middlesex County Econ. Opportunity Corp., New Brunswick, N.J., 1966-69; exec. asst. to pres. Rutgers U., New Brunswick, N.J., 1969-72; sr. assoc. dean Grad. Sch. Edn. Harvard U., Cambridge, Mass., 1972-82; v.p. effective sector mgmt. Ind. Sector, Washington, 1982-84; exec. dir. Colo. Commn. Higher Edn., Denver, 1984-88; chancellor U. Mich., Dearborn, 1988—; trustee Boston Coll., Children's TV Workshop. Mem. Nat. Coalition 100 Black Women, Detroit; mem. exec. bd. Detroit area coun. Boy Scouts Am.; bd. dirs. The Found. for Ctr., Commonwealth Fund, Henry Ford Hosp.-Fairlane Ctr., Met. Ctr. for High Tech. Mem. Assn. Governing Bds. (adv. coun. of pres.'s), Edn. Commn. of the States (student minority task force), Am. Assn. Higher Edn. Women Execs. State Govt., Internat. Women's Forum, Mich. Women's Forum, Women's

Econ. Club of Detroit, Econ. Club, Rotary. Office: U Mich Office of Chancellor 4901 Evergreen Dearborn MI 48128-1491

WILSON, CAROLYN TAYLOR, librarian; b. Cookeville, Tenn., June 10, 1936; d. Herman Wilson and Flo (Donaldson) Taylor; m. Larry Kittrell Wilson, June 14, 1957 (dec.); children: Jennifer Wilson Rust, Elissa Anne Wilson. BA, David Lipscomb Coll., 1957; MLS, George Peabody Coll., 1976. Tchr. of English Fulton County Sch. System, Atlanta, 1957-59; serials cataloger Vanderbilt U. Libr., Nashville, 1974-77; asst. libr. United Meth. Pub. House, Nashville, 1978-80; acquisition libr. David Lipscomb U., Nashville, 1980—; cons. and researcher in field. Rsch. asst. Handbook of Tennessee Labor History, 1987-89. Adv. bd. So. Festival of Books, Nashville, 1988-89, 90—, vol. coord., 1989. Recipient Nat. Honor Soc. award Phi Alpha Theta, 1956, Internat. Honor Soc. award Beta Phi Mu, 1980. Mem. ALA, Tenn. Hist. Soc., Tenn. Libr. Assn., Southeastern Libr. Assn., Women's Nat. Book Assn. (pres., v.p., treas., awards chair, 1980—). Democrat. Office: Crisman Meml Libr David Lipscomb U Nashville TN 37204

WILSON, CATHERINE COOPER (KITTY), communications executive, writer; b. Dallas, Sept. 17, 1955; d. William Edward and Suzanne (Blessington) Cooper; m. James Alan Wilson, Oct. 17, 1981; 1 child, Nicholas James. BA in Journalism, Tex. Tech U., 1977. Pub. rels. asst. Dallas Market Ctr., 1972-75, 77; pub. rels. coord. Herman Blum Engrs., Dallas, 1977-80, coord. new bus. devel., 1980; acct. exec. Helen Holmes & Assoc., Dallas, 1980; mktg. and pub. rels. coord. EDI Architects, Dallas, 1980-82; pres. Catherine Wilson Communications, Dallas, 1982—; owner, v.p. Wilson Creative, Inc., Dallas, 1988—. Contbr. articles to trade mags. Mem. membership com. North Tex. Commn., Dallas, 1979-81; mem. pub. rels. com., bldg. com. St. Rita Cath. Ch., Dallas, 1984-87. Mem. Women in Communications (programs co-chair 1989-90, Matrix finalist 1990), Greater Dallas Writers Assn. Roman Catholic. Home and Office: 6435 Sudbury Ln Dallas TX 75214

WILSON, CATHERINE MARY, small business owner; b. Chgo., May 7, 1957; d. Joseph Edward and Elizabeth Julia (Duda) Luckow; m. Leland Hugh Wilson, Nov. 18, 1979; children: Jynette Elizabeth, Cynthia Michelle, Richard Hugh. Student, Mueller Beauty Culture Sch., Waukegan, Ill., 1974-75, Foothill Coll., 1983-84, Cabrillo Coll., 1988, U. Calif., Santa Cruz, 1989—. Diet aid Condell Hosp., Libertyville, Ill., 1973-75; legal sec. to Rep. Donald E. Deuster and Hannigan, Jones & Deuster, Mundelein, Ill., 1975-76; administrv. asst. BNR Inc., Mountain View, Calif., 1977-85; administr. Apollo Computer, Santa Clara, Calif., 1985-87; bus. owner Finger Prints, La Selva Beach, Calif., 1987—, Trans Print, Santa Cruz, 1990—. Block Capt. Neighborhood Watch, La Selva Beach 1987—; mem. La Selva Beach Improvement Assn., 1987—; Brownie leader Girl Scouts Am., 1988—. Mem. C. of C., The Barter Connection, Nat. Notary Assn. Democrat. Roman Catholic. Home: PO Box 643 Aptos CA 95001

WILSON, CHARLENE WILLA, industrial sales specialist; b. Jim Thoppe, Pa., Feb. 13, 1943; d. Charles Byron and Jennie Larue (Levis) Frehulfer; m. Arthur David Wilson, Oct. 13, 1962 (div. Dec. 1982); 1 child, Edward; m. Arthur David Wilson, Dec. 23, 1987. Student, E. Stroudsburg State Coll., Pa., 1961-62. Tchr. part-time Lourdesmont Sch., Clarks Green, Pa., 1973-81; seamstress Barbini Bridals, Scranton, Pa., 1981-82; credit corr. Tose Fowler, Inc., Scranton, 1982-84; sales rep. Challenge Industries, Inc., Sparta, N.J., 1984-85, asst. dist. mgr., 1985-86, product specialist, 1986-87, dist. sales mgr. for Pa. and N.Y., 1987-90; corp. liaison Challenge Industries, Inc., Sparta, 5, 1990—. Author poems. Mem. Chinchilla (Pa.) Fire Co. Women's Aux., 1963-83. Mem. NAFE, VFW (women's aux. Clarks Summit, Pa. chpt. 1977—), Abington Players (bd. dirs. Waverly, Pa. chpt. 1975-81), Keynotes (sec. Clarks Summit chpt. 1969-77), Pa. Interscholastic Athletic Assn. (track official, swimming official Lackawanna, Pa. chpt. 1975—). Republican. Episcopalian. Home: 1206 Lackawanna Trail Clarks Summit PA 18411 Office: Challenge Industries Inc Rt 15 PO Box 965 Sparta NJ 07871

WILSON, CONSTANCE KRAMER, bank officer; b. Dayton, Ohio, Aug. 9, 1959; d. Michael Carl and Mona Louise (Miller) Kramer; m. Thomas Singleton Wilson, July 27, 1985; stepchildren: Thomas Douglas, Kirsten Lea, Heather Elizabeth, Ashley Paige. BS in Finance, Ind. U., 1981. Sr. credit analyst NCNB Nat. Bank, Charlotte, 1982-83, commercial loan officer, 1983-86, stockbroker, 1987-88, trust officer, 1988—; investment advisor Planned Mgmt. Co., Charlotte, 1986-87. Del. Rep. Pary County Dist. State, 1988-89; vice-chmn. Mecklenburg Young Reps., Charlotte, 1989; exec. com. Rep. County and State, 1989. N.C. Inst. fellow, Wilmington, 1989. Republican. Home: 726 Lansdowne Rd Charlotte NC 28255 Office: NCNB Nat Bank One NCNB Pla TO9-1 Charlotte NC 28255

WILSON, CYNTHIA MARIE, quality manager, engineer; b. Greensburg, Ind., Nov. 30, 1954; d. Daniel and Antoinette J. (Buening) Schwering; m. Frederick C. Wilson, Aug. 16, 1975; children: Edward C., Brock S. AA, Ind. Vocational Tech., 1981; B in Gen. Studies, Ind. U., 1987. Cert. quality engr. From inspection to quality control engr. Bohn Engring. and Foundry, Greensburg, Ind., 1977-87; quality assurance engr. Sheller Ryobi Corp., Shelbyville, Ind., 1987-89; quality mgr. Blackstone Corp., Greensburg. Mem. Am. Soc. for Quality Control, Soc. Die Cast Engr., Soc. of Mech. Engr., Soc. Automation Engrs., Nat. Assn. Female Executive, Beta Sigma Phi. Roman Catholic.

WILSON, DORIS FANUZZI, state agency administrator; b. N.Y.C., Oct. 17, 1935; d. Vitoantonio and Rose (Colavito) Panzarino; children: James Douglas Fanuzzi, Robert Alan Fanuzzi; m. Richard Gerard Wilson, Aug. 21, 1977 (div. 1987). BA cum laude, Hunter Coll., 1956; MA, Montclair State Coll., 1978. With Tri-County Ednl. Vocat. High Sch., Totowa, N.J., 1979-80; learning disabilities tchr., cons. Fairlawn (N.J.) Bd. Edn., 1980-82, Somerville (N.J.) Bd. Edn., 1982-83, Regional Child Study Team, Franklin, N.J., 1983-84; cons. curriculum and instrn. div. devel. disabilities N.J. Dept. Human Svcs., Trenton, 1984—. Active Rep. Women of 90s, Nat. Women's Polit. Caucus, N.J. Women's Polit. Caucus, Mercer County Women's Polit. Caucus, Rep. Task Force; mem. Friends of the N.J. State Mus. Mem. NAFE, AAUW, N.J. Assn. Learning Cons., Am. Assn. on Mental Retardation, Assn. Learning Disabilities, Internat. Platform Assn., Trenton Hist. Soc., Friends of N.J. State Mus. Home: 333 W State St Apt 10G Trenton NJ 08618 Office: Dept Human Svcs Div Devel Disabilities 2-98 E State St Capital Ctr Trenton NJ 08625

WILSON, DORIS FAYE BLACKWELL, plant rental and maintenance company executive; b. Campobello, S.C., Oct. 15, 1937; d. Marion McLain and Mazie Mae (Hutchins) Blackwell; m. Larry Leroy Wilson, May 4, 1957; 1 child, Larry Marc. Student, Inst. Fin. Edn., Chgo., 1974. Personnel mgr. 1st Fed. Savs. & Loan, Spartanburg, S.C., 1957-77; owner, mgr. Plant Mcht., Campobello, 1984—. Republican. Baptist. Home and Office: 65 Wilson Dr Campobello SC 29322

WILSON, ELIZABETH DOLAN NOLAN, investment company executive; b. Joplin, Mo., Mar. 9, 1909; d. John Lewis and Elizabeth (Hale) Dolan; m. Ralph Lauder Nolan, Oct. 17, 1929 (dec. Aug. 1971); children—Thomas Connor, John Keith; m. Alan Shepherd Wilson, Jr., Jan. 18, 1978 (dec. Oct. 12, 1987). Student Drury Coll., 1927, 28, Kans. State Tchrs. Coll., 1927, 28. Famouse Artists Sch. Illustration and Design, 1960-63, Famous Artists Writers Sch., 1968, Inst. Children's Lit., 1975. Pres. Connor Investment Co., Joplin, 1971-79, also dir. Illustrator: Tales About Joplin, Short and Tall, 1962, 2d edit., 1968, 3d edit., 1988; contbr. poetry, hist. articles and sports columns to profl. jours. Emeritus mem. women's aux. to bd. dirs. Drury Coll. Women's Aux., Springfield, Mo., 1961—, Joplin Hist. Soc. Dorothea B. Hoover Mus., Joplin; committeewoman Republican party, Joplin, 1964; bd. dirs. Spiva Art Ctr., 1956-60, 70-73. Mem. Pi Beta Phi. Republican. Presbyterian. Clubs: Century (Joplin), Twin Hills Golf and Country (Joplin). Avocations: golf; bridge. Home: 1240 Crest Dr Joplin MO 64801 Office: Connor Investment Co Joplin MO 64801

WILSON, EVALYN LEONARD, nurse, consultant; b. Fontana, Calif., June 30, 1951; d. William Robert and Wilda M. (Pirl) L.; m. Steven L. Wilson, Nov. 7, 1987; 1 child, Katrina Elaine. Diploma, St. Francis Sch. Nursing, 1975; BS in Interior Design, Kans. State U., 1984. RN. Staff nurse St. Francis Regional Med. Ctr., Wichita, Kans., 1973-81; rsch. nurse U. Kans. Sch. Medicine, 1981-82; staff nurse Sierra Vista Hosp., San Luis Obispo, Calif., 1981, Meml. Hosp., Manhattan, Kans., 1981-84, The St. Mary Hosp., Manhattan, 1982-84; med. planner Widom, Wein, Cohen, L.A., 1984-85; facility programmer Am. Med. Internat., Inc., Beverly Hills, Calif., 1985-86; pres. Lyn Leonard & Assoc., Fairway, Kans., 1986—. Mem. Inst. Bus. Designers (affiliate), Forum Healthcare Planning. Republican. Roman Catholic. Home and Office: 6033 Alhambra Fairway KS 66205

WILSON, FRANCES HELEN, occupational therapist; b. Pitts., Oct. 17, 1929; d. J. Vernon and Margaret Hassler (Prugh) Wilson; B.A., Conn. Coll., 1951; advanced standing certificate Columbia Sch. Occupational Therapy, 1953. Therapist, Washington County Soc. Crippled Children and Adults, Washington, Pa., 1953-54; staff therapist Oakland VA Hosp., U. Pitts., 1955-66; supr. Occupational Therapy Clinic, Aspinwall VA Hosp., Pitts., 1966-74, 81-85; supr. Occupational Therapy Clinic, Oakland VA Hosp., Pitts., 1974-80. Active Jr. League Pitts., Inc. Mem. Western Pa. (treas. 1967-69), Am. occupational therapy assns., Presbyterian Univ. Hosp. Pitts. Vol. Assn., 1986—. Republican. Presbyterian. Clubs: Conn. Coll. (treas. 1971—), Twentieth Century (Pitts.). Home: 14 Devon Ln Ben Avon Heights Pittsburgh PA 15202

WILSON, HELEN MARIE, real estate executive; b. San Francisco, Jan. 27, 1930; d. Ross Holcomb Rich and Helen Catherine (Squire) Thomas; m. Dale L. Wilson, Sept. 1, 1951 (dec.); children: Dale P., Paul C., Cynthia M. BS, U. Calif., Berkeley, 1952. Med. lab. technician various hosps., Calif., Minn., 1952-60; buyer-mgr. Fine Jewelry, Sacramento, Calif., 1975-80; realtor assoc. Lyon Real Estate, Sacramento, 1982—. Mem. Sacramento Assn. of Realtors Masters Club (life), Comstock Club, Phi Mu. Republican. Presbyterian. Home: PO Box 255763 Sacramento CA 95865 Office: Lyon & Assocs 2580 Fair Oaks Blvd Sacramento CA 95825

WILSON, IRA LEE, middle school educator; b. Taylor, La., Dec. 20, 1927; d. Henry and Sadie Mae (Milbon) Parker; m. Odie D. Wilson, Jr., May 11, 1946; children: Ervin Charles, Annie Jo, Carrido Michelle. BS, Grambling State U., 1954; postgrad., Pepperdine U., 1974, Pepperdine U., 1976; MEd, La Verne Coll., 1976. Tchr. Willowbrook Sch. Dist., Los Angeles, 1955-68, Compton (Calif.) Unified Sch. Dist., 1968—; grade level chairperson Roosevelt Middle Sch. P.T.A., Compton, 1988—; correspondence sec. Roosevelt Middle Sch. P.T.A., Compton, 1988—. Asst. sec. Los Angeles Police Dept. Sweethearts Area Club, Los Angeles, 1988—; mem. planning activities com. L.A. Football Classic Found., 1989. Recipient Perfect Attendance award Compton Unified Sch. Dist., 1987-88, S.W. Area Sweethearts for Outstanding Svcs. Los Angeles Police Dept., 1988, Disting. Svc. award Compton Edn. Assn., 1987-88, 83, Cert. of Achievement Roosevelt Jr. High Sch., 1984-85, Perfect Attendance award Roosevelt Middle Sch., 1984, Cert. of Achievement Mayo Elem. Sch., 1973-74, Roosevelt Mid. Sch., 1989, Disting. Svc. award Compton Edn. Assn., 1987-88, Key of Success award Am. Biog. Inst., Inc., 1990. Mem. NEA, Calif. Tchr. Assn., Grambling Alumni Assn. (life, asst. activity chairperson 1987—), Block Club. Democrat. Baptist. Home: 828 W 126 St Los Angeles CA 90044

WILSON, JANET SUE, travel company executive; b. Clarksburg, W.Va., Oct. 28, 1934; d. Glenn Everett and Edna Marie Shaver; m. Alwin D. Wilson, Sept. 21, 1957 (div. Aug. 1959); 1 child, Virginia Marie. Student Davis & Elkins Coll., 1952-54, U. S. Fla., 1981. Travel mgr. Central W.Va. Auto Club, Clarksburg, 1954-57, Peninsula Motor Club, Sarasota, Fla., 1958-63; travel dir. Boyce Travel Agy., Sarasota, 1963-72; pres. Janet Wilson Travel Inc., Sarasota, 1972—; sec. First Step of Sarasota, 1978-79, pres., 1981-85; mem. nominating com. Southeast Fla. Am. Soc. Travel Agts., 1988—. Chmn. Com. for an Elected Sheriff, Sarasota, 1985; bd. dirs. Crimewatch, Sarasota, 1985—; instr. Sarasota Voct. Sch. for Literacy Vols. of Am.; bd. dirs. Floyd Manor Retirement Ctr., Sarasota, Suncoast Travel Assn.; mem. Dem. exec. com. Recipient various awards from airlines and transp. cos. Mem. Internat. Platform Assn., Am. Soc. Travel Agts. (mem. nominating com. North Cen. Fla. chpt, Crest award 1983), Kiwanis, Phi Mu. Democrat. Presbyterian. Club: Altrusa (Sarasota) (treas. 1980-81). Avocations: needlepoint, professional sports, books. Home: 6449 Kahana Way Sarasota FL 34231 Office: 2136 Gulf Gate Dr Sarasota FL 33581

WILSON, JANICE DARLENE, computer programmer analyst; b. Audubon, N.J., May 18, 1955; d. Ernest George and Dorothy Antoinette (Miller) Wilson Farrow. BA, Am. U., 1977; MPA, Temple U., 1985. Personnel support specialist Fidelity Bank, Phila., 1981-83, programmer, 1983-86, programmer analyst, 1986-87, sr. programmer analyst, 1987-89, adv. programmer analyst, project leader, 1989—. Vol. adviros, tutor Literacy Vols. Am., Camden, N.J., 1985. Recipient Service award Camden County 4-H, 1986; Joseph E. Seagram's scholar. Mem. Black Data Processing Profls. Phila., Phila. Writers, Green Peace, Amnesty Internat., Nat. Coun. Negro Women Inc. Democrat. Episcopalian. Office: First Fidelity Bancorp Broad and Walnut Sts Philadelphia PA 19109

WILSON, JEAN L., state legislator; b. Phila., June 13, 1928; d. Horace and Catherine (Lennox) Terry; widowed; children: Sheryl J. Gordon, Denise T. Munn. BS in Edn., Pa. State U., 1949. Tchr. Columbia Inst., Phila., 1950-53, Wilkes Coll., Wilkes Barre, Pa.; office mgr., exec. sec. Camden Fibre MIlls, Warminster, Pa., 1968-80; mem. Pa. Ho. of Reps., 1988—. Active Bucks County Coun. Rep. Women, North Pa. Coun. Rep. Women, Warminster Rep. Club, Pennridge Rep. Club. Home: 12 Farview Rd Chalfont PA 18914 Office: 300 W Street Rd Warminster PA 18974

WILSON, JEAN MARIE HALEY, civic worker; b. Dallas, Oct. 16, 1921; d. William Eldred and Helen Marie (Littlepage) Haley; B.A., So. Meth. U., 1943; m. Edward Lewis Wilson, Jr., Mar. 19, 1943; children—Edward Lewis III, William Haley, Sarah. Bd. dirs. Dallas Symphony Orch. League, 1963-89, sec., 1964-68, 1st v.p., 1968-72, vice-chmn. spl. projects, 1977-78, rec. sec., 1984-85, 7th v.p., 1985-86, trustee, 1976-88, showhouse chmn., 1987, corresponding sec., 1987-88; v.p. activities Allegro Dallas, Inc., 1986-90, bd. dirs., 1990—; precinct chmn. Democratic Party, 1952-62; mem. Dallas County Dem. Exec. Com., 1952-62; bd. dirs. TACA (Com. for Fund Raising of the Arts), 1975-88; mem. Southwestern hospitality bd. Met. Opera; charter mem., bd. dirs., North Tex. Herb Club, 1974-78. Mem. Women in Communications, Am. Symphony Orch. Leagues, Herb Soc. Am. (life), Am. Hort. Soc., Pewter Collectors Club Am., Internat. Platform Assn., Le Cercle Francaise of Dallas (hon. chmn. 1985—), Les Femme du Monde, Herb Soc. of Old City Park, Kappa Alpha Theta. Methodist. Home: 3501 Lexington Ave Dallas TX 75205 Office: 2909 Maple Ave Dallas TX 75201

WILSON, JEANNETTE SOLOMON, retired elementary teacher; b. Columbus, Ga., Sept. 5, 1915; d. John C. and Mary L. (Parham) Solomon (adoptive parents, aunt and uncle); m. Harvie L. Wilson, Aug. 9, 1952; 1 child, Katrina M. Deese Turner. BS, Ft. Valley (Ga.) Coll., 1947; MS, Tuskegee (Ala.) Inst., 1951; postgrad., Syracuse U., 1961, U. Alaska, 1967. cert. elem. tchr. Elem. tchr. Muscogee County Sch. Dist., Columbus, 1939-53, 1954-60, 1969-71, home/hosp. tchr., 1971-75; elem. tchr. Am. Dependent Schs., Heilbronn, Fed. Republic Germany, 1953-54; ret., 1975; cons. in field. Active Girls Scouts Columbus chpt. Named one of Women of Achievement Girl Scouts, Inc., 1989; recipient Outstanding Svc. award Am. Cancer Soc., 1983-84. Mem. AAUW, The Links Club (founder Columbus, Ga. chpt. 1964), Urban League, Nat. Coun. Negro Women, Tuskegee Alumni Assn., Mr. and Mrs. Club (sec. 1960-64), Matrons Club (Gracious Lady of Ga. 1988), Alpha Kappa Alpha.

WILSON, JOYCE LYNN, broadcast company administrator; b. Brookhaven, Miss., July 28, 1961; d. R.W. and Elois (Sutton) W. AS, Utica Jr. Coll., 1981; BS, Jackson State U., 1983. Audio-visual asst. Memphis Cablevision, 1983-84, comml. insertion supr., 1984—; switcher, dir. N.Y. Times-WREG-TV, Memphis, 1985—. Mem. Alpha Epsilon Rho, Phi Kappa Phi. Democrat. Baptist. Home: 3823 Hickory Farm Dr Memphis TN 38115

WILSON, JUNE TAYLOR, computer software analyst; b. Carrizozo, N.Mex., Oct. 7, 1959; d. George Newton and Haruko (Shinohara) Taylor; m. Walter Bob Wilson, June 12, 1982. BS in Nursing, U. Ala., Huntsville, 1982; BS in Computer Sci., U. Ala., Birmingham, 1986, postgrad., 1987-88. Staff nurse Med. Ctr. Hosp., Huntsville, 1981-83; examiner Kimberly Nurses Meditest, Huntsville, 1983-84; researcher U. Ala., Birmingham, 1984-87; programmer South Cen. Bell Co., Birmingham, 1987-88; computer software analyst Colsa, Inc., Huntsville, 1988—; beauty cons. Mary Kay Cosmetics, Inc. Mem. AAUW (treas. 1990—), Assn. Women in Computing, Unix Users Group, Assn. Computing Machinery, East Jefferson Jaycees (v.p. 1986), Women's Network (v.p. 1990-91), Omicron Delta Kappa, Kappa Delta (pres. 1980-82). Methodist. Home: 3101 Knollwood Circle NW Huntsville AL 35810 Office: Colsa Inc 6726 Odyssey Dr Huntsville AL 35806

WILSON, KATHERINE SCHMITKONS, biologist; b. Lorain, Ohio, Jan. 22, 1913; d. H. William and Katherine (Bauman) Schmitkons; AB, Oberlin Coll., 1933; MS, Northwestern U., 1935; PhD, Yale U., 1944; m. George E. Woodin, Nov. 23, 1961. Instr. biology Muskingum Coll., New Concord, Ohio, 1935-40; bot. researcher Yale U., 1941-44, Sessel fellow in biology, 1948-49, instr. biology, 1953-56; biologist div. research grants NIH, Bethesda, Md., 1956-58, scientist adminstr. genetics, 1958-77; ret., 1977; cons., lectr. genetics, 1978—. Recipient High Quality Service award HEW, NIH, 1966. Fellow AAAS, N.Y. Acad. Sci.; mem. Am. Soc. Human Genetics (spl. citation 1973), Genetics Soc. Am. (Service citation 1979), Environ. Mutagen Soc., Am. Inst. Biol. Scis., Am. Genetic Assn., Sigma Xi. Congregationalist. Club: PEO. Author: Botany—Principles and Problems, 6th ed., 1963; contbr. articles to profl. jours. Home: 77 235 Indiana Ave Palm Desert CA 92260

WILSON, KATHLEEN JANE, insurance executive; b. N.Y.C., July 10, 1951; d. Joseph James Reilly and Mildred J. (Mariutto) Jensen; m. Jere Wayne Wilson, May 27, 1988; 1 child, Elizabeth Frances. AAS, Orange County Community Coll., 1970. Spl. chemist E.A. Horton Hosp., Middletown, N.Y., 1970-75; regulatory affairs specialist Union Carbide Corp., Sterling Forest, N.Y., 1975-77, Amersham Corp., Arlington Heights, Ill., 1977-78; v.p. spl. programs Orion Group, Inc., Farmington, Conn., 1978—. Mem. campaign com. Orion's United Way, Farmington, 1984—, chairperson campaign, 1986. Democrat. Office: Orion Group Inc 9 Farm Springs Rd Farmington CT 06032

WILSON, KATHY SHORES, developmental psychologist; b. New Orleans, Apr. 14, 1955; d. Murray Dawson and Margery Louise (Bauer) Shores; m. Frank Carl Wilson. BS in Psychology, Southern Meth. U., Dallas, 1976; MS, U. Tex., Dallas, 1979, PhD, 1987. Research asst. Psychology and Human Devel., U. Tex., Dallas, 1977-79, appointed research asst., 1982-86; substitute tchr. Callier Daycare Ctr. Callier Ctr. for Communication Disorders, Dallas, 1978-79; research technician Dept. Psychology and Human Devel., U. Tex., Dallas; vol. ch. counselor First United Meth. Ch., Richardson, Tex., 1983-85; coordinator child follow-up project Timberlawn Psychiatric Research Found., 1988--. Mem. Am. Psychol. Assn., Soc. for Research in Child Devel., Southwestern Soc. for Research in Human Devel., Internat. Conf. on Infant Studies, Tex. Assn. for Infant Mental Health, Hist. Preservation League, Wildlife Fedn. Democrat. Methodist. Office: Timberlawn Psychiat Rsch Found 2750 Grove Hill Rd PO BOx 270789 Dallas TX 75227

WILSON, LANA YVONNE, gallery art director, artist; b. Chattanooga, Tenn., Nov. 14, 1969; d. Walter Scott and Phyllis Jean (Burkhart) W. Student, Hunter Museum of Art, Chattanooga, Tenn., 1987. Gallery art dir. Gallery East, Chattanooga, 1986—; art coordinator Gallery east, Chattanooga, 1986—. Mem. Tenn. Watercolor Soc. Office: Gallery East Fine Arts 8800 E Brainerd Rd Chattanooga TN 37421

WILSON, LEVANNA MILDRED, principal; b. Little Rock, Feb. 15, 1940; d. Levi Stephen and Mildred Rosie Lee (Smith) Overall; m. Joe Aron Wilson, June 21, 1960 (div. 1980); children: Viveca, Gary, Tammy, Steven. BA, Ark. Bapt. Coll., Little Rock, 1970; MS, Henderson St. U., Arkadelphia, 1972. Tchr. Model Cities LRSD, Little Rock, 1970-73, Little Rock Sch. Dist., Little Rock, 1973-83, 1983-85; prin. Little Rock Sch. Dist., Little Rock.; bd. dir. LRCTA Little Rock, 1978-83, Peace Links Little Rock, 1988--; soc. function chair Prin. Roundtable Little Rock. Developer: Curriculum Source Multi Cult. Tchr. 1979; Asst. Research: History of Ark. Tea Assn., 1981; Trained Facility: Disc. Approach Least (NEA), 1984, Classroom Mgmt. (NEA), 1984. Recipient Challenge Grant Ark. Power & Light Co., Little Rock, 1987-88, Winthrop Rockefella Gr. Rockeffella Found. Little Rock, 1988. Mem. Nat. Assn. Elem. Sch. Prin., Ark. Assn. Elem. Sch. Prin., Prin. Roundtable, Cen. Ark. reading council, Aslah Little Rock Ark. Sec. Dem. African Methodist Episcopal. Home: 1818 S Jackson Little Rock AR 72204

WILSON, LINDA ANN, nurse; b. Johnson City, Tenn., Feb. 22, 1947; d. Andrew Jackson and Dorothy (Pate) Robertson; m. William Eugene Wilson, Feb. 17, 1968. Student, U. Tenn., 1969. Cert. nephrology nurse. Head nurse renal dialysis Johnson City (Tenn.) Med. Ctr. Hosp., with. Mem. Am. Nephrology Nurses Assn.

WILSON, LINDA CHERYL, accountant; b. Godfrey, Ill., Mar. 30, 1963; d. Robert Walter and Madie (Riley) W. BS in Acctg., Ill. State U., 1985; MBA, U. N.C., Charlotte, 1990. CPA, Ill., N.C. Sr. acct. Arthur Young & Co., Chgo., 1985-89; sr. internal auditor Springs Industries, Inc., Lancaster, S.C., 1989—. Mem. AICPA, N.C. Assn. CPA's, NAFE, Assn. MBA Execs. Office: Springs Industries Inc Hwy 9 at Grace Ave PO Box 111 Lancaster SC 29720

WILSON, LINDA LEE, finance company executive; b. Lakewood, Ohio, Nov. 9, 1943; d. John E. and Virginia L. (Weaver) Brown; m. Curtis Wilson, July 30, 1983; children: Catherine, Laura. BA in English, UCLA, 1970. Lic. securities. Pres. Americorp Fin. Group, Inc., Bellevue, Wash., 1984—. Co-founder panel discussion Women in Transition. Mem. AAUW (bd. dirs.), Internat. Assn. Fin. Planners (bd. dirs. Wash. chpt.), Soroptimist Internat.

WILSON, LINDA SMITH, university administrator; b. Washington, Nov. 10, 1936; d. Fred M. and Virginia D. (Thompson) Smith; m. Paul A. Wilson, Jan. 22, 1970; 1 dau. by previous marriage: Helen K. Whatley, a stepdau., Beth A. Wilson. B.A., Newcomb Coll., Tulane U., 1957; Ph.D., U. Wis., 1962. Postdoctoral rsch. assoc. U. Md., College Park, 1962-64, rsch. asst. prof., 1964-67; vis. asst. prof. U. Mo.-St. Louis, 1967-68; asst. to vice chancellor for rsch., asst. vice chancellor for rsch., assoc. vice chancellor for rsch. Washington U., St. Louis, 1968-75; assoc. vice chancellor for rsch. U. Ill., Urbana, 1975-85; assoc. dean Grad. Coll., U. Ill., Urbana, 1978-85; v.p. for research U. Mich., Ann Arbor, 1985-89; pres. Radcliffe Coll., Cambridge, Mass., 1989—; mem. dir.'s adv. coun. NSF, Washington, 1980-89, adv. com. sci. edn., 1990—; mem. Nat. Commn. on Research, Washington, 1978-80; mem. com. on govt.-univ. relationships NAS, 1981-83, mem. coun. for govt.-univ.-industry rsch.roundtable, 1984-89; mem. rsch. resources adv. coun. NIH, Bethesda, Md., 1978-82, energy rsch. adv. bd. DOE, 1987-90; chmn. adv. com. office sci. and engring. pers. NRC, 1990—. Author book chpts.; contbr. articles to profl. jours. Bd. govs. YMCA, Champaign-Urbana, Ill., 1980-83; mem. adv. bd. Nat. Coalition for Sci. and Tech., Washington, 1983-87. Recipient Centennial award Newcomb Coll., 1986; named One of 100 Emerging Leaders Am. Coun. Edn. and Change, 1978. Fellow AAAS (bd. dirs. 1984-88); mem. Am. Chem. Soc. (bd. council com. on chemistry and pub. affairs 1978-80), Soc. Research Adminstrs. (Disting. Contbn. to Rsch. Adminstrn. award 1984), Nat. Council Univ. Research Adminstrs., Assn. for Biomed. Research (bd. dirs. 1983-86), Inst. Medicine (mem. coun. 1986-89), Phi Beta Kappa, Sigma Xi, Alpha Lambda Delta, Phi Delta Kappa, Phi Kappa Phi. Home: 2524 Blueberry Ln Ann Arbor MI 48103 Office: Radcliffe Coll Office of Pres Fay House 10 Garden St Cambridge MA 02138

WILSON, LISA ANN, accountant; b. Kansas City, Mo., June 10, 1957; d. Eugene Edmond and Ruth Pearl (Rhodes) Pasewark; m. Chris Lee Wilson, June 17, 1978; children: Chase Tyler, Benjamin Andrew. BBA in Acctg., Abilene Christian U., 1980. Acct., Houston Natural Gas, 1981-83; oil and gas revenue acct. Earlsboro Energies, Oklahoma City, Okla., 1983-84; owner, acct. Bittersweet Memories, 1984-86; acct., adminstrv. asst. Deaconess Hosp., 1988—. Republican. Mem. Christian Ch. Club: Sigma Theta Chi. Avocations: sewing, racquetball, swimming, horse-back riding. Home: 4009 NW 32d St Oklahoma City OK 73112

WILSON, LORI LYNN, lawyer; b. Hastings, Nebr., June 7, 1954; d. Hal Chambliss and Margery Mae (Galley) Smith; m. Edmund George Wilson, Apr. 17, 1976. BS, Nebr. Wesleyan U., 1975; JD, U. Nebr., 1979. Bar: Nebr. 1979. Page Nebr. Unicameral, Lincoln, 1973-75; staff atty. Western Nebr. Legal Svcs., Grand Island, 1979-81; legis. aide to Senator Pat Morehead, Lincoln, 1982-83; mng. atty. Legal Svcs. S.E. Nebr., Beatrice, 1983-86; ptnr. Buhrmann, Johnson & Wilson, Crete, Nebr., 1986-88, Johnson & Wilson, Crete, 1989—. V.p. Grand Island Task Force on Domestic Violence, 1980-81, Nebr. Domestic Violence Coalition, Lincoln, 1986-88; Active Saline County Child Abuse/Neglect Network, Crete, 1986—, sec., 1989; bd. dirs. YWCA, Beatrice, 1981-83, Blue Valley Community Action, Fairbury, Nebr., 1986-89, Nebr. Tennis Assn., Omaha, 1987-89. Mem. Nebr. State Bar Assn. (chairperson poverty law sect. 1987-88, mem. ethics com. 1988—), 7th Jud. Dist. Bar Assn. (pres. 1989—), Rotary (pres. Crete club 1989—). Democrat. Mem. United Ch. of Christ. Office: Johnson & Wilson 334 E 13th St NE Crete NE 68333

WILSON, LOUITA DODSON, retired petroleum geologist, anthropologist; b. Dallas, Apr. 3, 1917; d. John Lester and Meda (Garner) Dodson; m. Thomas Carroll Wilson, Aug. 7, 1948 (dec. July 1969); children: Thomas Texas, Alison Carroll, Katherine. BA in Geology, U. Tex., 1940; MA in Anthropology, U. Colo., 1961. Soil conservationist West Tex. Range Improvement Co., Midland, 1940-43; geophysicist Geophys. Svc., Inc., Dallas, 1943-45; micropaleontologist Sun Oil Co., Dallas, 1945-46, Atlantic Refining Co., Caracas, Venezuela, 1946-48; tchr. anthropology Randell Sch., Denver, 1963-64; anthropology researcher U. Queensland, Brisbane, Australia, 1965-66. Author: Making The Most of Every Move, 1958. Membership chmn. Bexar County Women's Polit. Caucus, San Antonio, 1988-90; co-founder Doté Found., 1989. Grantee U. Tex., 1967-69. Mem. NOW, Monte Vista Hist. Soc., AAUW (various offices including pres. 1944-85), Am. Assn. Petroleum Geologists, Am. Anthrop. Assn. Democrat. Home: 121 W Woodlawn San Antonio TX 78212

WILSON, MALICIA HOWARD, human resources specialist; b. Macon, Ga., Jan. 23, 1960; d. Edward and Reba (Crumley) Howard; m. Jeffrey Doty Wilson, Feb. 20, 1988. AS in Bus. Adminstrn., Macon Coll., 1988; student, Ga. Coll., 1988—. Sec. advt. dept. Aquaquip Distbrs., Macon, 1980-82; personnel coord. Hosp. Corp. Am. Coliseum Med. Ctr., Macon, 1982-86; dir. human resources HCA Coliseum Psychiat. Hosp., Macon, 1986—. Adv. bd., Northeast High Diplomats, Macon, 1988-89; evangelish chair, 1st Christian Ch./Disciples of Christ, Macon, 1988, 89. Mem. Ga. Soc. Healthcare Human Resource Adminstrn. (bd. dirs. 1987-88), Am. Soc. Personnel Adminstrs., Middle Ga. Personnel Assn. Office: HCA Coliseum Psychiat Hosp 340 Hospital Dr Macon GA 31201

WILSON, MARILY SHARRONN, accountant; b. Seattle, May 27, 1942; d. Jack Edward Murphy and Cora Phyllis Toby; m. Ronald Duncan Nelson, May 5, 1961 (dec. 1966); children: Sharon Louise, Zeatra Corinne, Ronald Stanley; m. Lawrence William Wilson, Feb. 14, 1981. BA, Griffin Murphy Bus. Sch., 1968. Audit clk. Pay'n' Save Corp., Seattle, 1967; bookkeeper Chromium Co. Inc., Seattle, 1967-70, Sunderland's Wholesale Jewelry, Seattle, 1970-73; staff acct. Helwig, Bulter and Assocs., CPAs, Seattle, 1973-78, Otto R. Enger, Seattle, 1978-85; acct., controller, adminstr. Majiq, Inc., Redmond, Wash., 1985—; acct., owner Paradise Book-keeping and Tax Service, Mt. Vernon, Wash., 1985—; treas. Wilson Maintenance and Constrn., Inc., 1987—. Mem. NAFE, Ind. Bus. Assn. Home: 1869 Peter Burns Rd Mount Vernon WA 98273 Office: Majiq Inc 8343-154th Ave NE Redmond WA 98052

WILSON, MARJORIE PRICE, physician, medical commission executive; b. Pitts.; m. Lynn Minford Wilson, Sept. 15, 1951; children: Lynn Deyo, Liza Price. Student, Bryn Mawr Coll., 1942-45; M.D., U. Pitts., 1949. Intern U. Pitts. Med. Center Hosps., 1949-50; resident Children's Hosp. U. Pitts., 1950-51, Jackson Meml. Hosp., U. Miami Sch. Medicine, 1954-56; chief residency and internship div. edn. service Office of Research and Edn., VA, Washington, 1956; chief profl. tng. div. Office of Research and Edn., VA, 1956-60, asst. dir. edn. service, 1960; chief tng. br. Nat. Inst. Arthritis and Metabolic Disease, NIH, 1960-63; asst. to assoc. dir. for tng. Office of Dir. NIH, 1963-64; asso. dir. extramural programs Nat. Library Medicine, 1964-67; asso. dir. program planning and evaluation NIH, 1969-70; dir. dept. instl. devel. Assn. Am. Med. Colls., Washington, 1970-81; sr. assoc. dean U. Md. Sch. Medicine, Balt., 1981-86; vice dean U. Md. Sch. Medicine, 1986-88; pres., chief exec. officer Edl. Commn. Fgn. Med. Grads., Phila., 1988—; mem. Inst. Medicine, Nat. Acad. Scis., 1974—; bd. visitors U. Pitts. Sch. Medicine, 1974—; mem. Nat. Bd. Med. Examiners, 1980-87, 89—. Contbr. articles to profl. jours. Mem. adv. bd. Robert Wood Johnson Health Policy Fellowships, 1975-87; trustee Analytic Services, Inc., Falls Church, Va., 1976—. Fellow Am. Coll. Physician Execs., AAAS; mem. Assn. Am. Med. Colls., Am. Fedn. Clin. Research, IEEE. Office: Ednl Commn Fgn Med Grads 3624 Market St Philadelphia PA 19104-2685

WILSON, MARY ELIZABETH, physician; b. Indpls., Nov. 19, 1942; d. Ralph Richard and Catheryn Rebecca (Kurtz) Lausch; m. Harvey Vernon Fineberg, May 16, 1975. AB, Ind. U., 1963; MD, U. Wis., 1971. Diplomate Am. Bd. Internal Medicine, Am. Bd. Infectious Diseases. Tchr. of French and English Marquette Sch., Madison, Wis., 1963-66; intern in medicine Beth Israel Hosp., Boston, 1971-72, resident in medicine, 1972-73, fellow in infectious diseases, 1973-75; physician Albert Schweitzer Hosp., Deschapelles, Haiti, 1974-75, Harvard Health Svcs., Cambridge, Mass., 1974-75; asst. physician Cambridge Hosp., 1975-78; hosp. epidemiologist Mt. Auburn Hosp., Cambridge, 1975-79, chief of infectious diseases, 1978—; adv. com. immunization practices Ctrs. for Disease Control, Atlanta, 1988—, acad. adv. com. Nat. Inst. Pub. Health, Mexico, 1989—; cons. Ford Found., 1988; instr. in medicine, Harvard Med. Sch., Boston, 1975—. Author: A World Guide to Infections: Diseases, Distribution, Diagnosis; contbr. articles to profl. jours. Mem. Cambridge Task Force on AIDS, 1987—, Earthwatch, Watertown, Mass., Cultural Survival, Inc., Cambridge; bd. dirs. Horizon Communications, West Cornwall, Conn., 1990. Recipient Lewis E. and Edith Phillips award U. Wis. Med. Sch., 1969, Cora M. and Edward Van Liere award, 1971, Sr. Med. Residents' Teaching award, Mt. Auburn Hosp., 1983, 87, 89. Fellow Infectious Diseases Soc. Am., Royal Soc. Tropical Medicine and Hygiene; mem. Am. Soc. Microbiology, N.Y. Acad. Scis., Am. Soc. Tropical Medicine and Hygiene, Mass. Infectious Diseases Soc. (founding mem.), Mass. Med. Soc., Peabody Soc., Alpha Omega Alpha. Office: Mount Auburn Hosp 330 Mount Auburn St Cambridge MA 02238

WILSON, MARY ELLEN, educator, researcher; b. Eastman, Ga., Aug. 18, 1953; d. Perry Wade and Eva (Rowland) Tripp; m. James Richard Wilson, Sept. 5, 1986. AS, Mid. Ga. Coll., 1972; AB, Mercer U., 1974; MA, Fla. State U., 1975, PhD, 1983. Tchr. Chester (Ga.) Elem., 1975-76; teaching asst. Fla. State U., Tallahassee, 1978-79; prof. Tift Coll., Forsyth, Ga., 1980-81, Mid. Ga. Coll., Cochran, 1983—. Recipient Excellent Tchr. award Gamma Beta Phi, 1986-87. Mem. So. Hist. Assn., Ga. Assn. Historians, Ga. Hist. Soc., Delta Kappa Gamma. Democrat. Baptist. Home: Rte 5 Box 220 Cochran GA 31014 Office: Mid Ga Coll Sarah St Cochran GA 31014

WILSON, MELANIE ANN, clinical psychologist; b. Greenville, Miss., July 13, 1952; d. Charles Marshall and Beverly Ann (Plunkett) W. BA, Lebanon Valley Coll., 1974; MS, Millersville U., 1975; D of Clin. Psychology, Hahnemann U., 1987. Lic. psychologist; cert. sch. psychologist. Sch. psychologist Berks County Intermediate Unit, Reading, Pa., 1976-82; cons. psychologist Family Service of Phila., 1984—; pvt. practice clin. psychology Phila., 1984—; mem. clin. psychology staff Bryn Mawr (Pa.) Hosp. Youth and Family Ctr., 1987—; cons. psychologist Bryn Mawr Hosp. Inpatient Psychiat. Unit, 1987—, Northwestern Inst., Ft. Washington, 1988—. John Frederick Steinman fellow, Lancaster, Pa., 1983-84. Mem. Am. Psychol. Assn., Pa. Psychol. Assn., Phila. Soc. Psychoanalytic Psychology, Phila. Soc. Clin. Psychologists. Democrat. Presbyterian. Home: 1334 Montgomery Ave H-4 Narberth PA 19072 Office: Bryn Mawr Hosp Youth Family Ctr Old Lancaster Rd Summit Grove Ave Bryn Mawr PA 19010

WILSON, MIRIAM GEISENDORFER, physician, educator; b. Yakima, Wash., Dec. 3, 1922; d. Emil and Frances Geisendorfer; m. Howard G. Wilson, June 21, 1947; children—Claire, Paula, Geoffrey, Nicola, Marla. B.S., U. Wash., Seattle, 1944, M.S., 1945; M.D., U. Calif., San Francisco, 1950. Mem. faculty U. So. Calif. Sch. Medicine, L.A., 1965—, prof. pediatrics, 1969—. Office: U So Calif Med Ctr 1129 N State St Los Angeles CA 90033

WILSON, MOLLIE CROSS HALEY, investment counselor; b. Charlotte, N.C., May 5, 1942; d. Shaffer and Mollie Flournoy (Cross) Haley; m. Jack E. Grober. BSBA with honors, U. Ark., Fayetteville, 1963, MBA, 1972, PhD in Fin., 1979. Grad. asst. U. Ark., Fayetteville, 1971-73, instr., 1974-79; assoc. Robert E. Kennedy, Inc., Fayetteville, 1971-85; v.p. investment div. Mchts. Nat. Bank, Ft. Smith, Ark., 1979-83; pres. October Money Mgmt., 1983—; fin. cons. for pub. cos.; faculty mem. Webster U., St. Louis, 1989—. Contbr. articles to profl. publs. Bd. dirs. Ark. Community Found., 1979-83, Ft. Smith Heritage Found., 1979-83, Ft. Smith Salvation Army, 1982—, vice chmn., 1986-87, chmn. 1987-88, Comprehensive Juvenile Svcs., 1984-89. Mem. Inst. Chartered Fin. Planners, Internat. Assn. Registered Fin. Planners, Ark. Soc. Fin. Mgrs. (bd. dirs., 1972—), Dallas Soc. Investment Analysts, Fin. Analysts Fedn., Western Ark. Estate Planning Coun., Beta Gamma Sigma. Home: PO Box 5096 Fort Smith AR 72903 Office: 2220 S Waldron Rd Fort Smith AR 72903

WILSON, NANCY KEELER, research chemist; b. Walton, N.Y., Apr. 20, 1937; d. Donald Sargent and Leona Miriam (Siver) Keeler; m. James Frank Wilson, Jan. 24, 1959; children: David, John, Leslie. BS in Chemistry, U. Rochester, 1959; MS in Chemistry, Carnegie-Mellon U., 1962, PhD in Chemistry, 1966. Cert. profl. chemist. Instr. chemistry Point Park Jr. Coll., Pitts., 1962-63; lectr. math. Carnegie-Mellon U., Pitts., 1963-64; rsch. assoc. chemistry Ohio State U., Columbus, 1966-67; lectr. chemistry and physics Coll. St. Mary of the Springs, Columbus, 1966-67; rsch. assoc., lectr. chemistry U. N.C., Chapel Hill, 1967-69; sr. staff fellow Nat. Inst. Environ. Health Scis., Research Triangle Park, N.C., 1970-74; faculty affiliate chemistry Colo. State U., Ft. Collins, 1976-77; from rsch. chemist to chief chem. characterization sect. EPA, Research Triangle Park, 1974-81; rsch. chemist advanced analysis techniques br. EPA, 1981-84, chief analytical methods rsch. sect., 1984—. Author: NMR of Aromatic Compounds, 1982; contbr. articles to profl. jours. Regents scholar N.Y. State Bd. Regents, 1955-59, Genesee scholar U. Rochester, 1955-59; inst. fellow in spectroscopy Carnegie-Mellon U., 1959-66. Fellow Am. Inst. Chemists (nat. councillor 1990—), N.C. Inst. Chemists (pres. elect 1985-87, pres. 1987-89); mem. Am. Chem. Soc., Am. Fedn. Musicians, Delta Phi Alpha, Sigma Xi. Home: 1109 Archdale Dr Durham NC 27707 Office: US EPA MD 44 Research Triangle Park NC 27711

WILSON, NANCY L., college official; b. July 7; m. David N. Wilson. BA, U. Nebr., 1967; MS in Edn., Drake U., 1988. Assoc. ctr. dir. Buena Vista Coll., Marshalltown, Iowa, 1983-90, ctr. dir., 1990—. Treas. Mashalltown Assistance League; active Iowa Valley Leadership. Mem. AAUW (v.p.), Assn. for Supervision and Curriculum Devel., Iowa Assn. for Life-Long Learning, Marshalltown C. of C., P.E.O., Rotary, 20th Century Club.

WILSON, NANCY PARSONS, teacher; b. Ripley, W.Va., Feb. 4, 1941; d. W. King and Madaline (Casto) Parsons; children: Debra, Scott, Stacy Wilson. BA, Marshall U., 1962; MA, U. W.Va., 1985. Tchr. Jackson County Schs., Ravenswood, W.Va., 1976-85; mgr. K & M Co., Inc., Ripley, W.Va., 1972-76; coord. Gifted, Advanced Placement program Ripley High Sch., 1987-89, vice prin., 1989—. Chmn. Jackson County Libr. Commn., 1988—; mem. Jackson County Improvement Coun., Ravenswood Park Recreation Commn. Mem. AAUW (pres. Ravenswood br., v.p. state div.), Jackson County Tchr's. Assn., W.Va. Edn. Assn., Delta Kappa Gamma. Home: 415 Hillcrest Dr Ravenswood WV 26164

WILSON, PATRICIA BOYD, journalist; b. Everett, Wash., Oct. 22, 1911; d. John and Addie Alberta (Foss) Boyd; m. Robert Wilson, Jan. 18, 1952. BS, NYU, 1943; MS, Columbia U., 1944; LHD, Mobile (Ala.) Coll., 1989. Dean of edn. Fine Arts Mus. of South, Mobile, 1962-69; art columnist Christian Sci. Monitor, Boston, 1962—; disting. lectr. in art Mobile Coll., 1987—; lectr. Fine Arts Mus. South, 1989—; art appraiser Internat. Soc. Fine Arts Appraisers, Ltd. Cons. pilot project M.W. Smith Found., Mobile. Mem. Intertel, Nat. Trust Hist. Preservation, Humane Soc. U.S., Animal Rescue League, Nature Conservancy, Nat. League Am. Penwomen, Friends of Library. Home: 2769 Chadwick Dr N Mobile AL 36606 Office: PO Box 8426 Mobile AL 36689

WILSON, PATRICIA JANE, educator, educational and library consultant; b. Jennings, La., May 3, 1946; d. Ralph Harold and Wilda Ruth (Smith) Potter; m. Wendell Merlin Wilson, Aug. 24, 1968. BS, La. State U., 1967; MS, U. Houston-Clear Lake, 1979; EdD, U. Houston, 1985. Cert. tchr., learning resources specialist (librarian), Tex. Tchr., England AFB (La.) Elem. Sch., 1967-68, Edward White Elem. Sch., Clear Creek Ind. Schs., Seabrook, Tex., 1972-77; librarian C.D. Landolt Elem. Sch., Friendswood, Tex., 1979-81; instr./lectr. children's lit. U. Houston 1983-86; with U. Houston/Clear Lake, 1984-87, asst. prof. learning resources, 1988—; cons. Hermann Hosp., Baywood Hosp., 1986-87, Bedford Meadows Hosp., 1989-90, Wetcher Clinic, 1989. Trustee, Freeman Meml. Library, Houston, 1982-87, v.p., 1985-86, pres., 1986-87; mem. Armand Bayou Nature Ctr., Houston, 1980—, bd. dirs. 1989—; bd. dirs. Sta. KUHT-TV, 1984-87; mem. Bay Area Symphony League. Editor A Rev. Sampler, 1985-86, 89-90; dir. Learning Resources Book Rev. Ctr. Author: HAPPENINGS: Developing Successful Programs for School Libraries, 1987; contbg. editor Tex. Library Jour., 1988—; contbr. articles to profl. jours. Mem. ALA, Am. Assn. Sch. Librarians, Internat. Reading Assn., Nat. Council Tchrs. English, (Books for You com. 1985-88), Tex. Joint Council Tchrs. English, Antarctican Soc., Kappa Delta Pi, Phi Delta Kappa. Methodist. Club: Lakewood Yacht (Seabrook). Home: 1118 Appleford Dr Seabrook TX 77586 Office: U Houston Clear Lake 2700 Bay Area Blvd Houston TX 77027

WILSON, PATRICIA POPLAR, electrical manufacturing company executive; b. Chgo., Sept. 20, 1931; d. George and Leona (O'Brien) Poplar; BS U. Wash., 1966, MA 1967, PhD 1980; m. Chester Goodwin Wilson, Jan. 30, 1960; children: Susan Spadafora, Chester Wilson. Instr., U. Wash., Seattle, 1967-74; women's editor Nor'westing Mag., Seattle, 1969—; pres. Wilson & Assos. N.W. Inc., Seattle, 1974—; v.p. N.W. Mfg. & Supply, Inc., 1977-87, pres., 1987—; pres. Trydor Sales Alberta Ltd., Can. Mem. Electric League, N.W. Mfg. & Supply. Episcopalian. Club: Seattle Yacht. Author: Household Equipment, Guide to Surplus Equipment. Contbr. articles to profl. jours. Office: 4045 7th Ave S Seattle WA 98108

WILSON, PHYLLIS A., psychologist; b. Beckley, W.Va., June 12, 1941; d. Philip Hart Wilson and Barbara (Hoke) Braden; m. James E. Cook, Dec. 1974 (div. 1982); 1 child, Philip. BA in Psychology, U. Charleston, 1972; MS in Psychology, Radford (Va.) U., 1973, postgrad., 1974; postgrad., W.Va. U., 1978-79. Nat. cert. sch. psychologist; lic. psychol. assoc., N.C; cert. life sch. psychologist, W.Va. Sch. psychologist Raleigh County Schs., Beckley, 1974-75, Fayette County Schs., Fayetteville, W.Va., 1979-80, N.C. Dept. Corrections, Rocky Mt., 1980-81; asst. prof. psychology Bluefield (W.Va.) State Coll., 1977-79; pvt. practice, Tarboro, N.C., 1981—; co-dir. Rocky Mt. Assn. Children with Learning Disabilities Summer Sch., 1989. Committeewoman Raleigh County Rep. Exec. Com., 1963-72; mem. child welfare com. N.C. Inst. for Child Advocacy, Raleigh, 1983-88. Mem. Am. Psychol. Assn. (assoc.), Nat. Assn. Sch. Psychologists, Nat. Rehab. Assn., N.C. Rehab. Assn., AAUW, Phi Kappa Phi. Episcopalian. Home and Office: 807 St David St Tarboro NC 27886

WILSON, RITA ANN, office administrator; b. Chgo., Feb. 17, 1947; d. Arnold Joseph and Loraine Loretta (Radtke) Butkiewicz; O.G. Koske, Feb. 10, 1968 (div. 1978); m. Lawrence G. Wilson, Apr. 7, 1979. AA, NCTI, Wausau, Wis., 1967. Sec. Waukesha (Wis.) Engine Div., 1970-76, LaCross Holiday Inn, Wis., 1976-79; exec. sec. Eagle Family Discount Stores, Opalocka, Fla., 1979-80; adminstrv. asst. Jefferson Ward, Miami, Fla., 1980-85; corp. adminstr. Internat. Med. Ctrs., Miami, 1985-86, Yokogawa Corp. Am., Newnan, Ga., 1986—. Team mem. YCA March of Dimes walk-a-thon, Peachtree City, Ga., 1989. Mem. NAFE, Am. Bus. Women's Assn., West Ga. Archery League (sec. 1988-89), Tomo Chi Chi Archery League (sec. 1989), Phi Beta Lambda. Republican. Roman Catholic. Office: Yokogawa Corp of Am 2 Dart Rd Newnan GA 30265

WILSON, ROBERTA MAY, utility company financial executive; b. Essington, Pa., June 14, 1943; d. William Marshal and Jafreena Marie (Leon) Patton; m. Bruce Byer Wilson, May 20, 1967. BA, U. Pa., 1965; MBA, U. Colo., 1975. Caseworker Phila. Dept. Welfare, 1965-67; supr. Sears, Roebuck & Co., Denver, 1971-73; planner Denver Water Dept., 1975-76, analyst, 1976-79, mgr., 1979-85, chief fin. officer, 1985—; tchr., Colo. Woman's Coll., Denver, 1980; speaker in field; arbitrator, Mcpl. Securities Rulemaking Bd., Denver, 1984—; mem. Denver Investment Adv.Com., 1986—; bd. dirs., Blue Chip Value Fund, Denver. Contbg. author, editor, tng. manuals; contbr. revs. to various publs. Mgr. Ft. Hamilton Thrift Shop, Bklyn., 1967-71; mem., past chmn. Englewood (Colo.) Schs. Districtwide Com., 1977—; v.p. Englewood Bd. Edn., 1983-85, pres., 1985-87; mem. loan com. Englewood Housing Authority; v.p. Englewood Edn. Found., 1989, pres., 1990. Mem. Govt. Fin. Officers Assn. (exec. bd.), Am. Water Works Assn., Denver Security Analysts, Fin. Analysts Fedn., The Ranch Club, Met. Club, Beta Gamma Sigma. Democrat. Office: Denver Water Dept 1600 W 12th Ave Denver CO 80254

WILSON, SARAH J., nursing educator; b. Erie, Pa., Nov. 25, 1942; d. Russell R. and A. Glendine (Link) Leo; m. William R. Wilson, Dec. 14, 1963; children: Russell William, Michael David. BS, Gannon U., 1988, postgrad.; grad., Hamot Hosp. Sch. Nursing, Erie, 1963. RN, Pa. Instr. nursing Warren (Pa.) State Hosp., head charge nurse. Mem. Am. Nurses Assn. (cert. psychiat. mental health), Pa. Nurses Assn.

WILSON, SELMA PIERCE, anesthesiologist; b. Sidney, Nebr., July 21, 1956; d. Robert Elroy and Francis Marie (Humphrey) Pierce; m. Joseph Nathan Wilson, Dec. 27, 1977; children: Nathan Tate, Christina Rae, Joshua Alan. BS, N.Mex. State U., 1977; MS, U. N.Mex., 1980, MD, 1985. Diplomate Am. Bd. Anesthesiology. Intern St. Joseph's Hosp., Denver, 1985-86; resident in anesthesiology U. Colo. Health Scis. Ctr., Denver, 1986-88; fellow in anesthesia Harvard Med. Sch./Brigham and Women's Hosp., Boston, 1988-89, clin. asst., 1989—. Mem. Am. Soc. Anesthesiology, Mass. Med. Soc., Colo. Med. Soc., Alpha Omega Alpha, Phi Kappa Phi. Office: Brigham and Women's Hosp Dept Anesthesiology 75 Francis St Boston MA 02115

WILSON, SHARONN, automobile rental service executive; b. Bristol, Conn., Oct. 9, 1951; d. Blakeley and Betty-Claire (Botting) W. BA in Fine Arts, Dickinson Coll., 1973; MLS, SUNY, Albany, 1977. Mgmt. trainee Enterprise Rent-A-Car/Leasing, San Bruno, Calif., 1981; asst. mgr. Enterprise Rent-A-Car/Leasing, Berkeley, Calif., 1982; mgr. Enterprise Rent-A-Car/Leasing, San Leandro, Calif., 1982; mgr. Enterprise Rent-A-Car/Leasing, San Francisco, 1983, asst. area mgr., 1984-85, area mgr., 1985-89, human resources dir., 1989—. Mem. council Silver Bay (N.Y.) Assn., 1978—. Mem. Sierra Club. Home: 835 Vista Montara Circle Pacifica CA 94044 Office: Enterprise Rent-A-Car/Leasing 1133 Van Ness Ave San Francisco CA 94109

WILSON, SHERRIE DARLENE, mortgage banker; b. Jacksonville, Fla., Dec. 17, 1950; d. Joseph Frank and Marguerite Faye (Ponce) Dietz. Student, Fla. Jr. Coll., U. North Fla. Lic. mortgage broker, Fla. Credit investigator Credit Bur. Jacksonville (Fla.), 1968-70; loan processor Tucker Bros., Inc., Jacksonville, 1970-72, Collateral Investment, Jacksonville, 1972-73; personnel officer Barnett Mortgage Co., Jacksonville, 1973-82, v.p., mgr. loan inventory, 1982—. Bd. dirs. Mental Health Assn. Jacksonville, 1982—; vol. counselor Drug Abuse Program, Jacksonville, 1978-80; cons., women's com. rep. Am. Inst. Banking, 1974-81; advisor Community Bd. Bank, 1978; vol. Spl. Olympics, 1979-82. Mem. Young Mortgage Bankers Assn. (pres. 1978-79), Mortgage Bankers Assn. Fla. (bd. govs. 1985-87), Mortgage Bankers Assn. Jacksonville (pres. 1983-84, regional gov. of state assn. 1983-84), Am. Soc. Personnel Adminstrs. (dir. 1979-81). Democrat. Roman Catholic. Office: Barnett Mortgage Co 9000 Southside Blvd Bldg 700 Jacksonville FL 32256

WILSON, SKEETER J.H., hotel marketing executive; b. Pineville, La., Aug. 25, 1952; d. Gary Lee and Patricia Eleanor (Smart) Thomsen; m. Patrick Bing Renquist, Mar., 1971 (div. 1976); 1 child, Moon Ivy; m. Michael James Wilson, Feb. 12, 1977; 1 child, Shannon Michelle. Grad. high sch., Holdrege, Neb., 1970. Office mgr. So. New Eng. Eggs, Ledyard, Conn., 1970-73; asst. mgr. Topps & Trowsers, Denver, 1974-76; head teller Boeing Credit Union, Seattle, 1976-78; accounts clk. Stanley Structures, Denver, 1981-84; sales mgr. Sheraton Graystone Castle, Denver, 1985-87; dir. sales Ramada Hotel Denver/Boulder, 1987—; mem. Adams County (Colo.) Pvt. Industry Coun., 1988—. Tchr. Jr. Achievement, Denver, 1989—, Northglenn (Colo.) High Sch., 1989—; chair Metro N. Polit. Action Com., Denver, 1989; chair Com. to Re-elect Mayor Carpenter, Thornton, 1988; mem. zoning bd. appeals City of Thornton, 1990—. Mem. Rocky Mountain Bus. Travelers Assn., Colo. Ramada Mgrs. Assn. (sec. 1989—), Metro C. of C. (amb., chair, 1988—, Leadership award 1985-86, Bus. Woman of Yr. award 1988-89), Moose. Office: Ramada Hotel Denver/Boulder 8773 Yates Dr Westminster CO 80030

WILSON, TEDDY, finance and tax consultant; b. Kansas City, Mo., Oct. 20, 1938; d. Lonnie R. and Eva M. (Rice) W.; m. Michael D. Matsik, Dec. 28, 1969 (div. 1981); children: Cynthia, Mary. Student, UCLA, 1956-60, Calif. State U., Los Angeles, 1961-65. V.p., gen. mgr. Stanley S. Adler, Inc., Tarzana, Calif., 1967-83; pvt. practice in fin. and tax cons. Encino, Calif., 1983—; cons. Automac Parking, Inc., Long Beach, 1983—, Protocall, Inc., Signal Hill, Calif., 1982-88. Mem. Beta Alpha Psi. Republican. Presbyterian. Office: 16161 Ventura Blvd 216 Encino CA 91436

WILSON, VERNA JEAN, realtor; b. Hanover, Mich., Feb. 27, 1937; d. Claude Hill and Dorothy Verna (Service) Van Riper; m. Ramon Paul Lantz, Oct. 20, 1954 (dec. 1973); children: Lori Lantz Quinn, Jeff, Mitch; m. Joel James Wilson, Nov. 1, 1975; stepchildren: Cindy, Vicki, Tracey, Doug, Andy. Student, North Lake Coll., 1983—. Lic. realtor, Tex. Owner Ray Lantz Music, Jackson, Mich., 1960-75; interior decorator Horton House, Jackson, 1975-77; personnel counselor State of Mich., Jackson, 1977-81, Snelling & Snelling, Irving, Tex., 1982-83; mgr. Suzanne's Clothing, Dallas, 1981-82; realtor RE/MAX D/FW Assocs., Irving, 1983—; publicity chmn. RE/MAX D/FW Assocs., 1989—. Designer dress pattern. Vol., ARC, Jackson, Mich., 1966-81; fund raiser, speaker Juvenile Diabetes Found., 1974-75; vol. Rep. Nat. Convention, Dallas, 1984; campaign chair person County Sheriff, Jackson, 1980; Hospice vol. Visiting Nurses Assn., Dallas, 1983-87. Mem. Nat. Assn. REaltors, Tex. Assn. Realtors, Dallas Bd. Realtors, Irving Bd. Realtors (com. mem. 1984-85), Women's Coun. Realtors (membership chair person 1984-85), Make Am. better (women's coun. 1985-86), Kawanis (hon.). Republican. Home: 1529 Highcrest Ct Irving TX 75061

WILSON, WANDA LEE, entertainment promotions professional; b. Pitts., May 15, 1950; d. James A. Davis Jr. and Dorothy (Love) Anselmi; m. Kirby L. Wilson Sr., Apr. 23, 1976 (div. July 1984); children: Le Chon Kirb, Lia Shawnyea. Student, Connelly Tech. Sch., Pitts., 1968-71, Allegheny Community Coll., Pitts., 1968-71, U. Pitts., 1984, 86. Stand-in co-host The Together Show Sta. KDKA-TV, CBS, Pitts., 1971; adminstrv. sec. GE, Pitts., 1971-78; sec., notary public Sta. WPCB-TV, Wall, Pa., 1979-80; producer, host The Wanda Wilson Show Am. Cablevision Co., Monroeville, Pa., 1981-84, Warner Cable Co. and Pitts. Telecommunications, Inc., 1984-87; mktg. mgr. The Informer newspaper Homewood Brushton Revitalization and Devel., Pitts., 1984-87; pres. local, nat. internat. pub. rels. W-W Prodns./Wanda Wilson Enterprises, Pitts., 1984—; sr. clk./chemical monitor Gencorp Aerojet Tech. Systems, Rancho Cordova, Calif., 1987—; publicist, cons. Easy Internat., Pitts., 1990—; occasional writer, copywriter, announcer local radio shows, Pitts., 1972-85; radio show co-host, announcer Internat. People's Radio and TV, Sacramento, 1987. Author: (poetry) Love Traces on My Mind, 1972, (songs lyrics) The First Time I Saw You, 1982; performer poetry recitals, Pitts., 1973. Organizer civic and community events Energy Conservation, 1984-87. Mem. NAFE, AFTRA, Pitts. Model's Assn., Pitts. Media Fedn. Democrat. Home: 10814 Fair Oaks Blvd #5 Fair Oaks CA 95628 Office: Easy Internat and Metagram Am Inc 500 Holiday Dr Foster Pla 4 Pittsburgh PA 15220

WILSON, WILMA RUTH, utility company executive; b. East Chicago, Ind., June 20, 1950; d. William Vernon and Barbara Ann (Carson) Coward; m. Clyde Matthew Wilson, July 30, 1966; children: Dawn, Tracy. BS in Bus.

Adminstr., Ind. U., 1980; postgrad. Purdue U., 1984-84. Engring. record clk. No. Ind. Pub. Service Co., Hammond, 1970-72, application credit clk., Gary, 1972-76, asst. to chief clk., 1976-78, personnel rep., 1978-84, system cons., Hammond, 1984—; loaned exec. United Way, 1988; mem. speakers bur., 1983-84; dir. No. Ind. Fed. Credit Union, Merrillville; edn. cons. Gary Vocat. Office Edn. Program, 1985—. Multimedia instr. ARC, Hammond, 1982—; loaned exec. Lake Area United Way, 1984-88. Mem. Ind. U. Alumni Assn., Inst. Indsl. Engrs. Democrat. Baptist. Clubs: Xinos Beams, La Belle Femmes (Gary)(sec. 1983-84). Avocations: traveling, reading. Home: 3828 W 15th Ave Gary IN 46404 Office: No Ind Pub Service Co 5265 Hohman Ave Hammond IN 46320

WILSON-BUTLER, JOYCE ANN, service executive; b. Frankford, W.Va., Oct. 2, 1944; d. Dennis Rupert Yates and Gertrude Jean (Dunn-Yates) Parker; (div. 1981); children: Dennis R., William H., Mellissia M. Student, Broward County Bus. Coll., 1961. Owner Grade-A Dairy Farm, Milltown, Ky., 1968-81; with tng. and tech. Y-12 Plant, Oak Ridge, Tenn., 1981-82; exeditor Exxon; rep. Gulf States Inspection Svc., Inc., Houston, 1982; sec. Milburn's Custom Paint, Pasadena, Tex., 1982-84; sec. patrol div. City of Pasadena Police Dept., 1984-88; pres., owner T H E A Ins. Co., 1988—. Office: PO Box 4487 Pasadena TX 77502

WILSON-HOPKINS, DEBORAH DANA, laboratory assistant; b. Portsmouth, Va., Aug. 16, 1955; d. Bernice Audrey (Copeland) Wilson; m. Frederick Sherman Hopkins III, Dec. 29, 1986. BS, Iowa State U., 1978, MS, 1980; postgrad., Lancaster (Pa.) Theol. Sem., 1986-87, Howard U., 1988. Cert. food technologist, Md. Research asst. USDA Nat. Animal Disease, Ames, Iowa, 1980-81; agrl. cons. U.S. Peace Corps, Wash., 1981-83; premium prayer counselor Christian Broadcasting Network, Va. Beach, 1984-85; repairperson, mdse. asst. Stewart Sandwiches Internat., Norfolk, Va., 1985-87; cashier Roy Rogers-Marriott, Annapolis, Md., 1987; sales assoc. Home Port Property, Md., 1988; field aide Md. Dept. Agr., Annapolis, 1988; asst. Md. Fuels Testing Lab., Jessup, 1989—; chairperson Broadneck Muscular Dystrophy; former sec. canister coin campaign Broadneck Peninsula Jaycees, Annapolis, 1988-89. Textiles artisan: Storm at Sea, 1988 (award of Merit). Hugger Md. Spl. Olympics, Towson 1988; Christmas Food Basket/ Toy Distbr. Broadneck Peninsula Jaycees, Annapolis Md., 1988. Recipient Award of Merit. Mem. U.S. Jaycees, Inst. Food Technol., Md. Section IFT, Anne Arundel County Bd. Realtors, MIT Enterprise Forum of Tex. Home: 1385 Cape St Claire Rd Annapolis MD 21401

WILSON-HUREY, CAROLYN ANN, community program specialist; b. Hickman, Ky., Apr. 24, 1956; d. Annie M. Wilson; m. Ivan V. Hurey, Feb. 27, 1987; 1 child, Jorrie. BSBA, Bowling Green State U., 1979; student, Kennedy-King Coll., Chgo. computer systems analyst HHS, Chgo., 1986-88, computer systems analyst, pub. awareness specialist, 1987-88, community programs specialist, 1988—. Recipient Asst. Commrs. Cert. Appreciation award Office Human Devel. Svcs., 1990. Mem. NAFE (Spl. Act award 1989).

WILSON-SIMPSON, DOROTHY ANDREA, healthcare facility executive; b. Bremerton, Wash., July 27, 1945; d. Merritt Hampden Wilson and Eva Jane (Quaring) Daniell; m. Marion Ray Simpson, Mar. 11,1983; children: Kimberly Simpson Walter, Chad Mitchell. BA cum laude, La. Coll., 1967; MS, La. State U., 1970. Instl. counselor, social svcs. dept. Cen. La. State Hosp., Pineville, 1967-68, 70-74; psychiat. social worker dept. child psychiatry Western Mo. Mental Health Ctr., Kansas City, 1974-76; dir. child care, then dir. treatment The Spofford Home, Kansas City, 1976-82; interim exec. dir. The Spofford Home, 1983, pres., chief exec. officer, 1983—; subcom. chair, Gov.'s Com. on Children and Youth, Mo., 1980-81; mem. Western Mo. Psychiat. Adv. Coun., 1986; treas. children, youth and family section, United Meth. Assn. Health and Welfare Ministries, Dayton, Ohio, 1988-90. Contbr. to various publs. Community adviser, Kansas City Jr. League, 1988. Mem. Child Welfare League Am., Greater Kansas City Assn. United Way Agys., Mo. Child Care Assn. (sec. 1982-85, treas. 1985-87, pres.-elect 1987-89, pres. 1989-90, bd. dirs. 1982—), Nat. Fellowship Child Care Execs., Rotary, Kansas City South Club, Alpha Chi, Phi Kappa Phi. Democrat. Baptist. Office: Spofford Home 9700 Grandview Rd Kansas City MO 64134

WILUSZ, MELISSE DEBRA, environmentalist; b. South Amboy, N.J., Jan. 1, 1955; d. Canio James and Myrtle (Schulman) Carasia; m. Daniel Andrew Wilusz, Aug. 1, 1981. BS, Rutgers U., 1977. From lab technician to sr. technician Bio-Dynamics, Inc., East Millstone, N.J., 1977-79, technician-in-charge, 1979-80; with N.J. Dept. Environ. Protection, Trenton, 1980—, prin. environ. specialist div. water resources, 1985-88, supervising environ. specialist, 1988—. Cons. Franklin Citizens for Organized Planning, Franklin Twp., N.J., 1979-80. Mem. Audubon Soc., Sierra. Democrat. Office: NJ Dept Environ Protection 401 E State St Trenton NJ 08625

WILZACK, ADELE, state health official; Student Loyola Coll., R.N. diploma Mercy Hosp. Sch. Nursing, Balt., 1957; B.S. in Nursing, Mt. St. Agnes coll., 1959; M.S. in Nursing, U. Md., 1960; postgrad. in pub. adminstrn. U. So. Calif., 1976. Staff nurse Mercy Hosp., Balt., 1957-60, supr. non-profl. personnel, 1961-63, asst. dir. nursing services, 1963-65; project nurse operation REASON, Community Action Agy., Health and Welfare Council, Balt., 1965-67; asst. dir. bur. spl. home services Balt. City Health Dept., 1967-72, dir. bur. spl. home services, 1972-74, dir. health services for aging, 1974-76, asst. commr. health services for aging and med. care, 1976-79; asst. sec. for med. care programs Md. Dept. Health and Mental Hygiene, Balt., 1979-83, sec. dept., 1983—; mem. Gov.'s Drug and Alcohol Commn., chairperson, treatment subcom. Children and Youth Subcabinet; assoc. faculty mem. U. Md. Sch. Nursing; vis. faculty mem. U. Mich. Inst. Gerontology, Ann Arbor; past mem. Md. Gov.'s Task Force on Med. Malpractice Ins., Md. Gov.'s Task Force on Health Care Cost Containment; mem. Gov.'s Commn. on Black and Minority Health, Gov.'s Council on Adolescent Pregnancy, Gov.'s Adv. Bd. for Justice Assistance; past com. mem. and chmn. Central Md. Health Systems Agy.; past com. mem., past subcom. chmn. Md. Med. Assistance Adv. Com.; past chmn. Balt. City Sub-Area Adv. Council; past mem. regional adv. task force Johns Hopkins Hosp., task force on aging U. Md. Recipient award for outstanding contbns. to inter-group relations and dedicated humanitarian service to citizens of Balt. City, Balt. Community Relations Commn., 1978, Alumna of Yr. award Loyola Coll., 1978, Woman Mgr. of Yr., Conf. for Women in State Service, 1981; Merit scholar U. Md. Sch. Nursing. Mem. Md. Pub. Health Assn. (past mem. exec. com.), Am. Pub. Health Assn. (past mem. governing council state affiliate), Balt. City Med. Soc. (past mem. long-term care com.), Sigma Phi Sigma, Sigma Theta Tau. Office: Md Dept Health and Mental Hygiene 201 W Preston St Baltimore MD 21201

WIMBERLY, BEADIE RENEAU (LEIGH WIMBERLY), financial services executive; b. Fouke, Ark., Apr. 18, 1937; d. Woodrow Wilson and Grace B. (Winkley) Reneau; m. Benjamin Leon Price, 1954 (div. 1955); m. Elbert William Wimberly, Dec. 16, 1956; children: Stephanie Elaine Wimberly Davis, Jeffrey Scott, Lael Wimberly Carter Alston. Student William & Mary Coll., 1964-65, U. Md.-Ludwigsburg/Stuttgart, 1966-68, Northwestern State U. La., 1973-75, Cornell U., 1979, Leonard Sch., 1983. Cert. ins. agt.; registered gen. securities rep. SEC, registered investment adviser SEC. Internat. trainer of trainers North Atlantic coun. Girl Scouts U.S., Fed. Republic Germany, 1965-69, 76-78; inventory master The Myers Co., Inc., El Paso, Tex., 1970; abstract asst. Vernon Abstract Co., Inc., Leesville, La., 1970-71; sec. to chief utilities and pollution control Dept. Army, U.S. Civil Svc., Ft. Polk, La., 1971-72, asst. to post safety officer, 1972-73, adminstr. tech. Adj. Gen.'s Office, 1973-75, sr. library technician post libraries, 1975, pers. staffing specialist, Stuttgart, Fed. Republic Germany, 1976-79, voucher examiner Fin. and Acctg. Office, Ft. Polk, 1980-81; chief exec. officer Fin. Strategies, Inc., Leesville, La., 1981—, stockbroker, corp. exec., 1983—, mktg. exec., 1983—; labor cons. AFL/CIO, Ft. Polk, 1981—; br. office mgr. Anchor Nat. Fin. Svcs. Inc.; dir., treas. Wimberly Enterprises, Inc. Bd. dirs. Calcasieu Parish coun. Boy Scouts Am., 1982-83, active, 1988—; treas. Vernon Parish Hist./Geneal. Soc., 1986—; pres. Vernon Parish Helpline/Lifeline, 1985; charter mem. Nat. Mus. of Women in the Arts; mem. Vernon Parish Arts Coun.; mem. La. Supreme Ct. Task Force on Women in the Cts. of La. Mem. Pilot Internat., Internat. Assn. Fin. Planners, Nat. Assn. Govt. Employees (v.p. Ft. Polk chpt. 1980-81), Internat. Platform Assn., C. of C., Assn. U.S. Army, Am. Assn. Fin. Profls., Nat. Women's Polit. Caucus, Am. Soc. Mil. Comptrs., LWV (state bd. dirs. 1986-87, treas. Leesville chpt. 1982-87, La. chpt.), NOW (Ruston-Grambling chpt.), Hist./ Geneal. Soc. Republican. Club: Toastmasters (named Competent Toastmaster, 1979). Lodge: Rotary (bd. mem.-at-large Leesville club 1988—). Office: Fin Strategies Inc 302 N 5th St Leesville LA 71446

WIMMER, BILLIE KOPS, association executive; b. Detroit, Feb. 9, 1956; d. Herman Joseph and Stella (Goodrich) Kops; m. Joseph Charles Wimmer III, July 10, 1976; children: William Joseph, Daniel James. BA, Mich. State U., 1980. Exec. dir. Mich. Assn. of Non-Pub. Schs., Lansing, 1981—; exec. sec. Mich. Nonpublic Sch. Accrediting Assn., 1985—; mem. nat. adv. panel Ctr. for the Learning and Teaching of Elem. Subjects, E. Lansing, 1988—; mem. state adv. co . Leadership in Edn. Adminstn. Grant Project, Lansing, Mich., 1987; bd. dirs. Coun. Am. Pvt. Edn., 1989—, state affiliate coord., 1989—. Field rep. Com. to Re-elect U.S. Senator Griffin, Detroit, 1987; mem. ways and means com. Kent County Rep., Grand Rapids, Mich, 1984; mem. St. Marys Sch. Parent Club. Mem. Mich. Soc. of Assn. Exec. Roman Catholic. Office: Mich Assn of Non-Pub Schs 505 N Capitol Lansing MI 48933

WINANS, BARBARA ANN, media director; b. Moberly, Md., Oct. 15, 1939; d. Carl R. and Daisy (Blackwell) W. AA, Columbia Coll., 1959; BE, U. Mo., 1961; MEd, U. Mo., 1966. Cert. elem. tchr., Mo. History tchr. Fulton (Mo.) High Sch., 1961-64; libr. instr. U. Mo. Lab Sch., Columbia, 1965-67; libr. West Jr. High, Columbia, 1967-68; media specialist Hickman High Sch., Columbia, 1968-73; media dir. Rock Bridge High Sch., Columbia, 1973—; adv. coun. Grad. Sch. Libr. Information Sci., U. Mo., Columbia, 1977—; group discussion leader Mo. White House Govs. Conf. on Librarians, 1990. Bd. dirs. Boone County Tchrs. Credit Union, Columbia, 1989—; v.p. FA Chpt. PEO, Columbia, 1990—; mem. Parent Club West Highlant White Terrier Club Am., 1981. Recipient Alumnae Cert. Merit Zeta Tau Alpha, 1975, Sch. Manpower Project award Am. Assn. Sch. Librarians. Mem. Columbia Community Tchrs. Assn. (pres. 1965-66), Mo. State Tchrs. Assn., Mo. Assn. Sch. Librs. (pres. 1969-70, Spl. Svc. award 1973, Sch. Manpower Project award, 1973), Phi Delta Kappa, Delta Kappa Gamma (pres. 1974), Pi Lambda Theta. Democrat. Baptist. Home: 2019 Ridgemont Columbia MO 65203

WINCE-SMITH, DEBORAH L., federal agency administrator; m. Michael B. Smith; 2 children. Grad. magna cum laude, Vassar Coll., 1972; Master's, Cambridge (Eng.) U., 1974. Former program mgr. internat. programs NSF; asst. dir. internat. affairs and global competitiveness Office of Sci. and Tech. Policy The White House, 1984-89; asst. sec. tech. policy Dept. Commerce, Washington, 1989—. Office: Dept Commerce Tech Policy 15th & Constitution Ave NW Washington DC 20230*

WINCHELL, MARGARET WEBSTER ST. CLAIR, realtor; b. Clinton, Tenn., Jan. 26, 1923; d. Robert Love and Mayme Jane (Warwick) Webster; student Denison U., 1940, Miami U., Oxford (Ohio), 1947, 48; m. Charles M. Winchell, June 7, 1941; children—David Alan (dec.), Margaret Winchell Boyle; m. 2d, Robert George Sterrett, July 15, 1977 (dec. 1985). Saleswoman Fred K.A. Schmidt & Shirmer real estate, Cin., 1960-66, Cline Realtors, Cin., 1966-70; owner, broker Winchell's Showplace Realtors, Cin., 1972—; ins. agt. United Liberty Life Ins. Co., 1966—, dist. mgr., 1967-70, 77-82, regional mgr., 1982—; stockbroker Waddell & Reed, Columbus, Ohio, 1972—, Security Counselors; ins. broker, 1984, gen. agent; dir. Fin. Consultants, 1984, 85, 86, 87, owner; instr. evening coll. Treas., v.p. Parents without Partners, 1969, sec., 1968; pres. PTA; dir. Children's Bible Fellowship Ohio, 1953-76; dir. Child Evangelism Cin.; nat. speaker Child Evangelism Fellowship and Nat. Sunday Sch. Convs., 1955-57; pres. Christian Solos, 1974, Hamilton Fairfield Singles; chaplain Bethesda N. Hosp.; leader singles groups Hyde Park Community United Meth. Ch. Mem. Nat. Assn. Real Estate Bds. West Shell Realtors (v.p.), Womens Council Real Estate Bd. (treas.). Clubs: Alfonta, Travel go go, Guys and Gals Singles (founder, 1st pres.), Hamilton Singles (pres.). Home and Office: 8221 Margaret Ln Cincinnati OH 45242

WINCHESTER, JACQUELINE CANTON, county government official; b. Jacksonville, Fla., Feb. 7, 1930; d. Arthur Norman and Eleanor (Lummus) Canton; children: James Jr., Jon C., Sterling R., Melissa P. BA, U. Fla., 1961. Cert. tchr., Fla. Tchr. Palm Beach County Sch. System, Belle Glade, Fla., 1966-68; supr. elections Palm Beach County, West Palm Beach, Fla., 1973—. Bd. dirs. Forum Club Palm Beaches, 1975—, Fla. Women's Alliance, Tampa, 1985—; bd. dirs. Palm Beach Regional Vis. Nurse Assn. Mem. Am. Soc. Pub. Adminstrs., Fla. State Assn. Suprs. of Elections, Internat. Assn. Clks. and Recorders, Soroptimist (pres. West Palm Beach chpt. 1979-81), LWV (voter svc. chair 1973). Democrat. Episcopalian. Office: Palm Beach County Rm 105 301 N Olive Ave West Palm Beach FL 33401

WINCHESTER, JEANETTE M., financial service executive; b. Council Bluffs, Iowa, June 27, 1953; children: Jennifer, Jeffery. Cert. credit exec. Supr. region AVCO Fin. Svcs., Terre Haute, Ind. Recipient Gabriel award, 1984. Mem. Credit Women (past pres.), Internat. Credit Assn. (bd. dirs.).

WINCHESTER-VEGA, MICHELE RENEE, clinical social worker, educator; b. Hartselle, Ala., Mar. 27, 1960; d. Shannon Raven Winchester and Sally (Rocco) Donner, Darwin D. Donner (step-father); m. Felix E. Vega, June 19, 1982. AA, SUNY, Orange County, 1980; BA, SUNY, New Paltz, 1982; MSW, Columbia U., 1984, postgrad., 1988—. Cert. social worker, alcoholism counselor, N.Y. Family therapist Family Counseling Service, Newburgh, N.Y., 1984-86; pvt. practice New Windsor, N.Y., 1986—; clinic supr. Pius XII Cocaine Clinic, Goshen, N.Y., 1986-88; program supr. Pius XII Alcohol Program, Monroe, 1988—; instr. Orange County Community Coll., Middletown, N.Y., 1985—; adj. instr. SUNY at New Paltz Coll., 1986; adj. asst. prof. Wurzweiter Sch. Social Work, Yeshiva U., N.Y.C., 1989—; cons. psychiatric ctrs. and ctr., 1989—. Vice-pres. Orange County Youth Bur., Goshen, N.Y., 1989—. Named Miss Citizenship of Va., 1976; acad. full scholar Ortega Found., 1989—. Mem. Nat. Assn. Social Workers, Orange County Alumni Assn. (bd. mem.). Democrat. Baptist. Home: 2 Park Pl 32-36 Newburgh NY 12550 Office: 339 Blooming Grove Turnpike New Windsor NY 12550

WINDELS, CAROL ELIZABETH, plant pathology researcher; b. Long Prairie, Minn., July 12, 1948; d. Jerome Joseph and Genevieve Anna Maria (Clasemann) Schrenk; m. Mark Bernard Windels, Apr. 4, 1970. BA in Biology, St. Cloud State Coll., 1970; MS in Plant Pathology, U. Minn., 1972, PhD in Plant Pathology, 1980. Mem. sci. staff dept. plant pathology U. Minn., St. Paul, 1973-84; asst. prof. plant pathology N.W. Exptl. Sta. U. Minn., Crookstown, 1984-89, assoc. prof. plant pathology N.W. Exptl. Sta., 1989—; presenter papers at nat. and internat. meetings; organizer, instr. Fusarium identification workshops, other symposia and nat. meetings. Assoc. editor Phytopathology, 1986-88, Can. Jour. Plant Pathology, 1989—, Jour. Sugar Beet Rsch., 1989—; sr. editor symposium procs., 1984; contbr. rsch. papers to peer-rev. jours., chpts. to books. Mem. Am. Phytopathol. Soc. (sec.-treas. N. Cen. div. 1987-90, adv. com. Plant Disease jour. 1990—, councilor-at-large 1990—), Am. Soc. Sugar Beet Technologists, Can. Phytopathol. Soc., Internat. Soc. Plant Pathology (chair internat. com. on Fusarium 1989—), Mycol. Soc. Am. Office: Northwest Exptl Sta Univ Minn 211 Agr Rsch Ctr Crookston MN 56716

WINDSOR, NATALIE PRECKER, broadcast journalist; b. N.Y.C.; d. Bernard and Ruth (Paster) Precker. BFA, Kent State U., 1974. Radio news anchor various stas., Cleve., Rochester, N.Y., Chgo. and Phoenix, 1974-84; news anchor Sta. KPWR-FM, Los Angeles, 1987—. Para-counselor Los Angeles Free Clinic Helpline, 1984—; para-chaplain Los Angeles Bd. Rabbis, 1986—. Mem. NAFE, B'nai B'rith, Am. Internat. Reiki Assn., Sigma Delta Chi. Home: 1800 N Winona Blvd Los Angeles CA 90027

WINE-BANKS, JILL SUSAN, lawyer; b. Chgo., May 5, 1943; d. Bert S. and Sylvia Dawn (Simon) Wine; m. Ian David Volner, Aug. 21, 1965; m. Michael A. Banks, Jan. 12, 1980. BS, U. Ill.-Champaign-Urbana, 1964; JD, Columbia U., 1968. Bar: N.Y. 1969, U.S. Ct. Appeals (4th cir.) 1969, U.S. Ct. Appeals (6th and 9th cirs.) 1973, U.S. Supreme Ct. 1974, D.C. 1976, Ill. 1980. Asst. press. and pub. rels. dir. Assembly of Captive European Nations, N.Y.C., 1965-66; trial atty. criminal div. organized crime and racketeering sect. and labor racketeering sect. U.S. Dept. Justice, 1969-73; asst. spl. prosecutor Watergate Spl. Prosecutor's Office, 1973-75; lectr. law seminar on trial practice Columbia U. Sch. Law, N.Y.C., 1975-77; assoc. Fried, Frank, Harris, Shriver & Kampelman, Washington, 1975-77; gen. counsel Dept. Army, Pentagon, Washington, 1977-79; ptnr. Jenner & Block, Chgo., 1980-84; solicitor gen. State of Ill. Office of Atty. Gen., 1984-86, dep. atty. gen., 1986-87; exec. v.p., chief oper. officer, Am. Bar Assn., Chgo., 1987—. Bd. dirs. Northwestern U. Ctr. Urban Affairs, Internat. Women's Forum, The Chgo. Network; chmn. fund raising com. U. Ill. Coll. Communications; mem. Orgn. for Rehab. through Tng. Hon. Com.; bd. overseers Kent-IIT Sch. Law. Recipient Spl. Achievement award U.S. Dept. Justice, 1972, Meritorious award, 1973, Cert. Outstanding Service, 1975; decoration for Disting. Civilian Service, Dept. Army, 1979. Fellow Am. Bar Found.; mem. ABA (council sect. litigation 1979-80, chmn. ann. meeting 1982, Pres.'s club Fund for justice and edn.), Ill. Bar Assn., Womens Bar Assn. Ill., Chgo. Bar Assn., Chgo. Council Lawyers. Clubs: Economic, Legal. Office: ABA 750 N Lake Shore Dr Chicago IL 60611

WINEGRAD, DILYS VERONICA, university administrator; b. Grantham, Eng., Sept. 8, 1937; came to U.S., 1963; d. Geoffrey David and Ellen Rachel (Stringer) Pegler; m. Saul Winegrad, Apr. 24, 1963; children: Naomi Shireen, Gwyneth Natahsa. BA with honors, U. Oxford (Eng.), 1958, MA, 1962; PhD, U. Pa., 1970. Interpreter BASF, Ludwigshafen, Fed. Republic Germany, 1958-61; adminstr. London County Coun., 1962-63; teaching fellow U. Pa., Phila., 1963-66; lectr. in French Bryn Mawr Coll., 1970-71; asst. prof. French Haverford, 1972-73; asst. to pres. U. Pa., 1975—; producer WUHY, Phila., 1974-79; advisor, evaluator Pub. Com. for Humanities, Pa., 1980-81. Author: Gladly Learn and Gladly Teach, 1978; editor: The Intellectual Word of Benjamin Franklin, 1990; contbr. articles to profl. publs. Bd. dirs. Phila. Arts League, 1986—; mem. com. Rhodes Scholarships, Pa., 1978-81. Mem. AAUW (instnl. del. 1987—), Royal Heritage Soc. (bd. dirs. 1987—), Oxford and Cambridge Soc. Phila., AM. Poetry Soc. (adv. coun. 1989—), Greater Phila. Philosophy Consortium (adv. bd. 1989—). Office: U Pa 100 College Hall Philadelphia PA 19104

WINEKOFF, CONNIE J., accountant; b. Garden City, Mich., Oct. 26, 1962; d. CHarles Richard and Charlotte Ruth (Schroeder) W. A in Commerce, Henry Ford Community Coll., 1986. Office asst. Meyers Jewelers, Westland, Mich., 1979-80; bookkeeper Bank of the Common Wealth, Detroit, 1980-81, Mich. Nat. Bank, Livonia, 1981-82; mgr. acctg. div. Alexsis Risk Mgmt., Livonia, 1982—. Office: 19790 Haggerty Rd Livonia MI 48152

WINFIELD, MARY BETH, data processing consultant; b. Bridgeport, Conn., Nov. 28, 1957; d. Thomas Ward and Mary Frances (Durica) W.; m. Michael Alan Bailey, Apr. 21, 1984; children: Sarah, John. Student, U. Hartford, 1975-78; computer cert., Northeastern U., 1981. Prodn. analyst Epsilon Data Mgmt., Burlington, Mass., 1980-82; software systems programmer Aetna Life & Casualty Co., Windsor, Conn., 1982-83; data base adminstr. Martin Marietta Data Systems, Orlando, Fla., 1983-85, sr. systems programmer, 1985-87; data processing cons. Philip Morris Internat., 1987; data processing cons. IBM, Atlanta, 1987, Raleigh, N.C., 1988-89, Hartford, Conn., 1989—; owner Winfield Assocs., Stratford, Conn., 1989—; speaker on computer software Cambridge Systems Co., San Jose, Calif., 1986. Mem. Nat. Systems Programmers Assn. (charter, communications dir. N.C. chpt. 1989—), Computer Measurement Group, Am. Bus. Women's Assn. (edn. com. Raleigh 1988-89), NAFE. Democrat. Byzantine Catholic. Home: 4502 Mill Village Rd Raleigh NC 27612 Office: Winfield Assocs 80 Valley View Rd Stratford CT 06497

WINFREY, LAPEARL LOGAN, psychologist; b. Goochland, Va., Mar. 7, 1952; d. Gilbert Armstice Logan and Blanche (Britt) Logan-Parrish; m. Carl Marden Winfrey, Mar. 27, 1973; 1 child, Anedra LaPearl. AB, Oberlin (Ohio) Coll., 1973; MA, Roosevelt U., Chgo., 1977; PhD, SUNY, Stony Brook, 1988. Lic. clin. psychologist, Ill. From clin. therapist to clin. supr. Jackson Park Hosp., Chgo., 1976-79; intern VA Med. Ctr., Hines, Ill., 1982-83; psychologist I Bobby E. Wright CCMHC, Chgo., 1983-84; coord. testing Marsha Bennett & Assoc., Chgo.,, 1984-88; mgr. Mile Sq. Mental Health Ctr., Chgo., 1988-89; pvt. practice Chgo., 1988—; coord. Family Care Network Evang. Health Systems, Oak Lawn, Ill., 1989-90; allied profl. staff South Chgo. Community Hosp., 1990—; mental health cons. Westinghouse-Head Start Project, Chgo., 1979-82; cons. Abraham Lincoln Day Treatment Ctr., Chgo., 1989—; core faculty Chgo. Sch. Profl. Psychology, 1990—. Chairperson prin. evaluation Philip Neri Sch. Bd., Chgo., 1985, 86. Mem. Assn. Black Psychologists, Am. Psychol. Assn. (Minority fellow 1979-82), Ill. Psychol. Assn., Soc. Psychotherapy Rsch. Mem. United Ch. of Christ. Office: Chgo Sch Profl Psychology 806 S Plymouth Ct Chicago IL 60605

WINFREY, OPRAH, television talk-show hostess, actress, producer; b. Kosciusko, Miss., Jan. 29, 1954; d. Vernon and Vernita Lee. BA in Speech and Drama, Tenn. State U. News reporter Sta. WVOL Radio, Nashville, 1971-72; reporter, news anchorperson Sta. WTVF-TV, Nashville, 1973-76; news anchorperson Sta. WJZ-TV, Balt., 1976-77, hostess morning talk show People Are Talking, 1977-83; hostess talk show A.M. Chgo. Sta. WLS-TV, 1984; hostess The Oprah Winfrey Show, Chgo., 1985—, Harpo Prodns., Inc., Chgo., 1986—; launched into nat. syndication, 1986—; owner, producer Harpo Prodns., 1986—. Appeared in films The Color Purple, 1985 (nominated Acad. award), Native Son, 1986; producer, actress: ABC TV mini-series, The Women of Brewster Place, 1989, series Brewster Place, 1990—. Recipient Woman of Achievement award NOW, 1986, Emmy Award for Best Daytime Talk Show Host, 1987; named Broadcaster of Yr. Internat. Radio and Television Soc., 1988. Office: Harpo Prodns 110 N Carpenter St Chicago IL 60607

WINFREY, SHIRLEY MAUREEN, trucking company executive; b. Richwood, W.Va., Feb. 18, 1956; d. Barger Basil and Helen Kathlyn (Salisburg) Meadows; m. Richard Allen Winfrey, May 21, 1983; children: Christopher Allen, Matthew Aaron. Lic. Practical Nurse, Summers County Sch. Nursing, 1976; student, Greenbrier Community Coll.Ctr., Lewisburg, W.Va., 1986-87. Staff nurse Circle Terr. Hosp., Alexandria, Va., 1976-77, DePaul Hosp., Norfolk, Va., 1977-80, Summers County Hosp., Hinton, W.Va., 1980-81, Humana Hosp. GV Hosp., Fairlea, W.Va., 1981-86; v.p., sec., treas. Winfrey Trucking Co., Inc., Williamsburg, W.Va., 1984—. Mem. Williamsburg Jr. Women's Club (sec. 1988-90, term v.p. 1990—). Republican. Baptist. Home: Box 96 Pembrook Rd Williamsburg WV 24991 Office: Winfrey Trucking Co Box 96 Pembrook Rd Williamsburg WV 24991

WING, ELIZABETH SCHWARZ, museum curator, educator; b. Cambridge, Mass., Mar. 5, 1932; d. Henry F. and Maria Lisa (Gutherz) Schwarz; m. James E. Wing, Apr. 18, 1957; children: Mary Elizabeth Wing-Berman, Stephen R. BA, Mt. Holyoke Coll., 1955; MS, U. Fla., 1957, PhD, 1962. Interim asst. curator Fla. Mus. Natural History, U. Fla., Gainesville, 1961-69, asst. curator, 1969-73, assoc. curator, 1973-78, curator and chmn. dept. anthropology, 1978—; U.S. rep. Internat. Congress Archaeozoology, 1981—. Author: (with A.B. Brown) Paleonutrition, 1979; editor (with J.C. Wheeler) Economic Prehistory of the Central Andes, 1988; contbr. articles to profl. jours. NSF grantee, 1961-64, 68-70, 70-73, 79-80, 84-85, 89-91. Mem. Soc. Ethnobiology (pres. 1989-91). Office: U Fla Fla Mus Natural History Museum Rd Gainesville FL 32611

WING, JANET ELEANOR SWEEDYK BENDT, nuclear scientist; b. Detroit, Oct. 12, 1925; d. Jack and Florence C. (Springman) Sweedyk; m. Philip J. Bendt, Sept. 4, 1948 (div. Jan. 1972); children: Karen Ann Bendt Sox, Paul Philip, Barbara Jean Bendt Medlin, Linda Sue; m. G. Milton Wing, Aug. 26, 1972 (div. Jan. 1987). BSEE with distinction, Wayne State U., 1947; MA in Physics, Columbia U., 1950; postgrad., U. Oreg., 1966-67, U. N.Mex., 1968-71. Research engr. Gen. Motors Corp., Detroit, 1944-48; physicist, mathematician Manhattan Project Columbia U., N.Y.C., 1950-51; mem. research staff Los Alamos (N.Mex.) Nat. Lab, 1951-57, 68—, project leader, 1976-81, asst. group leader, 1980-84, assoc. group leader, 1985—. Bd. dirs., treas. Esperanza Shelter, Santa Fe, N. Mex., 1984—. Mem. Am. Nuclear Soc., AAAS, Women in Sci. and Engring., Los Alamos Women in Sci., Sigma Xi, Tau Beta Pi. Office: Los Alamos Nat Lab Los Alamos NM 87545

WING, KYLENE SCARBOROUGH (MRS. ROBERT L. WING), columnist; b. Charlotte, N.C.; d. Kyle and Tomi (Riggs) Scarborough; grad.

Stevens Schs. for Models, 1946-47, Ben Bard Acad. Theatre, Hollywood, Calif., 1952, Nat. Acad. Broadcasting Washington, 1957, UCLA Extension, 1965, Free U. Berlin Otto-Suhrz Inst. Extension, 1966. m. Robert L. Wing, Jan. 16, 1943; children—Susan, Jayme. Columnist, Kylene's Kalifornia Kapers, Inverness, Fla., 1965-66, Kylene's Kontinental Kapers, Berlin, Germany, 1966-68; publicity chmn. Am. Women's Club. Founder, patron Huntington Hartford Theatre; mem. Concerned Friend Nat. League Families POW-MIA, U.S. Congl. Adv. Bd. Recipient letter of Appreciation USAF, 1973. Mem. Planetary Soc., Hollywood C. of C., Freedom Found. at Valley Forge, Los Angeles World Affairs Council. Presbyn. Clubs: German American Women's, American Women's, American Yacht (all Berlin); Los Angeles Riding and Polo; Air Force Officers Wives; Bel-Air Republican Women's. Address: 3405 Blair Dr Hollywood CA 90068

WING, RENA RIMSKY, psychiatry educator; b. N.Y.C., Oct. 31, 1945; d. Robert and Jeanne (Meyers) Rimsky; m. Edward Joseph Wing. PhD, Harvard U., 1967. Instr. dept. psychiatry U. Pitts., 1973-74; lectr. dept. psychology Stanford (Calif.) U., 1975-77; instr. dept. psychiatry U. Pitts., 1977-79, assist. prof. dept. psychiatry, 1979-86, assoc. prof. dept. psychiatry, 1986—. Contbr. over 100 articles on obesity and weight control to profl. jours. Bd. dirs. Am. Diabetes Assn., 1987-90, Soc. Behavioral Medicine, 1988-91. Woodrow Wilson fellow, 1967, NSF fellow, 1967-71. Fellow Acad. Behavioral Medicine Rsch., Am. Psychol. Assn., Soc. Behavioral Medicine. Home: 1240 Murdoch Rd Pittsburgh PA 15217 Office: WPIC 3811 OHara St Pittsburgh PA 15213

WINGATE, BARBARA ANN, advertising executive; b. London, Nov. 26, 1955; came to U.S., 1988; d. Edward Arthur and Rose Maria (Smith) W. BS in Psychology first class, Bedford Coll. London U., 1978; PhD in Psychophysiology, Wolfson Coll. Oxford U., 1981. Planner Young and Rubicam, London, 1981-83, Zetland Advt., London, 1983-86; assoc. dir. J. Walter Thompson, London, 1986-88; v.p., planning dir. Livingston and Co., San Francisco, 1988—. Office: Livington and Co 250 Sutter St San Francisco CA 94108

WINGATE, TESSA ELIZABETH, medical management consultant; b. Houston, July 24, 1947; d. Albert William and Gilberta Renska (Coghill) W.; 1 child, Grant William Ayo. BS in Nursing, Tex. Women's U., 1973; postgrad., U. Nevada, 1978-79, U. Tex., Arlington, 1979-80, U. Houston, 1980-83. RN, Tex. Staff nurse Tex. Children's Hosp., Houston, 1973-74; staff nurse, office mgr. James Friedman, MD, Houston, 1974-77; adminstr. Drs. Adels, Friedman, Haufrect and Law, Houston, 1977-83; practice mgmt. cons. Am. Physician Svcs., Houston, 1983-87; mgmt. cons. Conomikes Assocs., Inc., L.A., 1987-88; prin., mgmt. cons. Wingate Cons. Group, Houston, 1988—. Co-author chpt.: Ambulatory Care Organization and Management, 1989. Active Braesplace Civic Club, Houston, 1982—; chmn. Neighborhood Esplanade Com., Houston, 1983. Mem. Am. Assn. Bus. and Profl. Women, Am. Assn. Female Execs., Med. Group Mgmt. Assn. (mem. cons. svc. 1988—, mem. capital devel. fund com. 1987—), Med. Adminstrs. of Tex., Houston Health Care Alliance. Office: Wingate Cons Group 3847 Aberdeen Way Houston TX 77025

WINGER, DEBRA, actress; b. Cleve., 1955; d. Robert and Ruth W.; m. Timothy Hutton, March 16, 1986; 1 child, Emmanuel Noah. Student, Calif. State U., Northridge. Made 1st profl. appearance in Wonder Woman TV series, 1976-77; appeared TV film Spl. Olympics, 1977; appeared in films Thank God It's Friday, 1978, French Postcards, 1979, Urban Cowboy, 1980, Cannery Row, 1982, An Officer and a Gentleman, 1982, Terms of Endearment, 1983, Mike's Murder, 1984, Legal Eagles, 1986, Black Widow, 1987, Made in Heaven, 1987, Betrayed, 1988, Everybody Wins, 1990, The Barber of Siberia, The Sheltering Sky. Served with Israeli Army, 1972. Office: care John West PMK Pub Rels Inc 8436 W Third St Ste 650 Los Angeles CA 90048*

WINIKOFF, BEVERLY, physician; b. N.Y.C., Aug. 26, 1945; d. Harry and Blanche (Tepper) W.; m. Michael Charles Alpert, July 15, 1973; children: Hilary Winikoff A., Lindsay Winikoff A. AB magna cum laude, Harvard U., 1966; MD, NYU, 1971; MPH, Harvard U., 1973, rsch. fellow Sch. Pub. Health, 1973-74. Diplomate Nat. Bd. Med. Examiners. Tchr. history, social studies Escola Americana do Rio de Janeiro, 1966-67; intern in mixed medicine Gen. Rose Meml. Hosp., Denver, 1971-72; physician East Side Neighborhood Health Ctr. Denver Dept. Health, 1972, Boston Evening Clinic, 1973-74; med. writer ambulatory care project Beth Israel Hosp., Boston, 1973-74; asst. dir. health scis. Rockefeller Found., N.Y.C., 1974-78; med. assoc. The Population Coun., N.Y.C., 1978-82, sr. med assoc., 1982—; cons. Congl. Office Tech. Assessment, 1976-77, 78, Senate Select Com. Nutrition and Human Needs, 1976-77, Internat. Vitamin A Consultative Group, 1977, Internat. Nutritional Anemia Consultative Group, 1978—, Nat. Inst. Aging Consultancy, 1977-78, NAS, 1978, 78-79, Rockefeller Found., 1978; lectr. to numerous profl. groups. Co-author, editor Nutrition and National Policy, 1978; guest editor spl. issue Social Sci. and Medicine, June 1980; editor spl. issue Studies in Family Planning, April 11 1981, mem. editorial bd., 1978—; contbr. chpts. to books, articles to profl. jours. Mem. White House Spl. Task Force on Internat. Health, 1977, Mayor's Emergency Med. Svcs. Adv. Com., 1978—, Steering Com. to Promote Breastfeeding in N.Y.C. Office Pub. Health, N.Y. State Health Dept., 1982—. Recipient scholarships Radcliffe Coll., 1962-66, GM, NYU, 1967; fellowship USPHS, 1970. Mem. Harvard Sch. Pub. Health Alumni Assn. (councillor 1983-85, pres. 1989—). Office: Population Coun 1 Dag Hammarskjold Pla New York NY 10017

WINKELHAKE, JEAN KATHRYN, educator; b. Nebr., Ind., Jan. 2, 1937; d. Leo W. and Hazel Kathryn (Iverson) Thimgan; m. Kenneth E.A. Winkelhake, Apr. 7, 1957 (div. 1973); children: Cathy Lynne, Karen Lea. BS in Elem. Edn., U. Nebr., Omaha, 1975, MS in Spl. Edn., 1977; postgrad. in edn., Vanderbilt U., 1981—. Learning disabilities tchr. Norfolk (Nebr.) Pub. Schs., 1976-77, Gretna (Nebr.) Pub. Schs., 1977-80; cons. of visually impaired Loess Hills Area Edn. Agy. 13, Council Bluffs, Iowa, 1980—. Vol. Am. Cancer Soc., Omaha, 1986, Omaha Workshop Theatre, 1988-89; vol. reader Radio Talking Book, Inc., Omaha, 1987. State of Iowa grantee, 1988-89. Mem. Assn. for Edn. and Rehab. Visually Impaired, Phi Alpha Theta, Kappa Delta Pi, Phi Delta Gamma, Kappa Kappa Iota. Democrat. Presbyterian. Office: Loess Hills Area Edn Agy 13 PO Box 1708 Council Bluffs IA 68131

WINKLER, AGNIESZKA M., advertising agency executive; b. Rome, Italy, Feb. 22, 1946; came to U.S., 1953, naturalized, 1959; d. Wojciech A. and Halina Z. (Owsiany) W.; children from previous marriage: children: Renata G. Sworakowski, Dana C Sworakowski.; m. Arthur K. Lund. BA, Coll. Holy Name, 1967; MA, San Jose State U., 1972; MBA, U. Santa Clara, 1981. Teaching asst., San Jose State U., 1968-70; cons. to ea. European bus., Palo Alto, Calif., 1970-72; pres./founder Commart Communications, Palo Alto, 1973-84; pres./founder, chmn. bd. Winkler McManus, Santa Clara, Calif., 1984—; bd. dirs. Lefcourt Group, Inc., 1984—, Living Bus. Press, 1987—. Trustee Santa Clara U., 1990—, O'Connor Found., 1987—, mem. exec. com., 1988—, mem. Capital Campaign steering com., 1989; project dir. Poland Free Enterprise Plan, 1989—; mem. adv. bd. Normandy France Bus. Devel., 1989—; mem. bd. regents Holy Names Coll., 1987—; mem. adv. bd. Nat. Assn Bus. Deans Jesuit Insts.; chair emeritus, mem. adv. bd. Leavey Sch. Bus. and Adminstrn. Univ. Santa Clara, 1989—; bd. dirs. San Jose Mus. Art, 1987; mem. San Jose Symphony, Gold Baton, 1986. Recipient CLIO award in Advt. and numerous others. Mem. Family Svc. Assn. (trustee 1980-82), Am. Assn. Advt. Agys., Bus. Profl. Advt. Assn., Polish Am. Congress, San Jose Advt. Club, San Francisco Ad Club, Beta Gamma Sigma (hon.), Pi Gamma Mu, Pi Delta Phi (Lester-Tinneman award 1966, Bill Raskob Found. grantee 1965). Office: Winkler McManus 150 Spear St16th Fl San Francisco CA 94105 also: 710 Lakeway Dr Ste 110 Santa Clara CA 94060 also: 1901 Ave of the Stars Ste 1774 Los Angeles CA 90067

WINKLER, AMELIA BLEICHER, writer; b. N.Y.C., Sept. 2, 1933; d. Max and Fannie (Klieger) Bleicher; m. Marvin Howard Winkler, Oct. 19, 1953 (div. 1976); children: Barbara Ruth, Joshua Seth, Sarah Ellen. BA, Barnard Coll., 1955; MA, Manhattanville Coll., 1977. Cert. tchr. English, N.Y., Mass. English tchr. Buffalo (N.Y.) Seminary, 1955-58, Needham (Mass.) High Sch., 1958-61; cons. Mcpl. Bond Investors Assurance Corp., Armonk, N.Y., 1987—. Contbr. articles to newspapers and mags., 1988-90. Mem. Greenwich (Conn.) Choral Soc., 1978-88; tutor Time-to-Read, Armonk, 1989. Mem. Pub. Rels. Soc. Am., Women in Communications, Inc., Nat. Writers Union (bd. dirs. 1989—, editor newsletter 1989—). Democrat. Jewish.

WINKLER, ANNE ELIZABETH, real estate developer; b. Dallas, June 2, 1957; d. Lowell Graves and Ruth Lenore (Lind) W. BBA in Fin. with honors, Emory U., 1979; MBA in Acctg. and Fin., U. Tex., 1983; MS in Real Estate Devel., MIT, 1988. Mgmt. trainee Citizens & So. Nat. Bank, Atlanta, 1979-81; banking assoc. Continental Ill. Nat. Bank, Chgo. and Dallas, 1983-85; asst. v.p., devel. assoc. Trammell Crow Residential, Dallas, 1985-87, Seattle, 1988—. Charles Harritt Jr. Presdl. scholar U. Tex., 1982, Alexander Grant scholar, 1982. Mem. Jr. League of Seattle, MIT Ctr. for Real Estate Devel. Alumni Assn., Alpha Epsilon Upsilon. Methodist.

WINKLER, LAURA, travel agency executive; b. Wichita, Kans., Oct. 10, 1948; d. Stuart and Myra (Warren) Richardson, m. David Winkler, May 12, 1975; children: Serena, Clarissa. BA, U. Kans., 1970, MA in Communications, 1972. Sales rep. Ft. Wayne (Ind.) C. of C., 1973-76, agt. incentive travel, 1976-78; agt. incentive travel Creative Group, Wheeling, Ill., 1978-88, sr. account rep., 1988—. Active Big Brother/Big Sister, Ft. Wayne, 1975-76. Mem. NAFE. Democrat. Roman Catholic. Home: 3008 W Phelps Rd Phoenix AZ 85023

WINKLER, NANCY ANN, bank executive; b. N.Y.C., Feb. 11, 1952; d. Andrew Melvin and Madeline Virginia (Mellon) Nordback; m. Herman Michael Winkler, Oct. 15, 1972; 1 child, Herman Andrew. B.B.A. in Acctg. and EDP, Pace U., 1972, M.B.A. in Acctg., 1976. CPA, Ill. With auditing dept. Bankers Trust Co., N.Y.C., 1972-82, v.p., 1979-82; v.p., unit head First Nat. Bank Chgo., 1982—, unit head ALCO audit, 1982-83, sect. head ALCO and svc. products audit, 1983-84, ALCO and staff depts. audit, 1984-86, mgr. fin. acctg. systems and ops., control dept., 1987—; adj. instr. acctg. Pace U., 1977-82; instr. various audit rev. courses, 1980-81; speaker industry confs. Chartered bank auditor. Vestry mem. St. John's Episcopal Ch. Mem. NAFE, Mem. Bank Adminstrn. Inst. (chartered bank auditor study group task force 1978-81, exam. com. 1982-87), Inst. Internal. Auditors (Chgo. chpt.), Bus. and Profl. Womens Assn. of NW Suburbs. Office: First Nat Bank of Chgo One First Nat Pla Ste 0319 Chicago IL 60670

WINLAND, DENISE LYNN, physician; b. Elizabeth, N.J., Aug. 9, 1951; d. James Edward and Audrey Anna (Hansen) W.; m. Charles F. Francke III, May 30, 1982; children: Shannon W. Franke, Eric W. Francke. BS with honors, Rutgers U., 1973; M in Phys. Therapy (hons.), U. Louisville, 1975; MD, Baylor U., Waco, Tex., 1982. Phys. therapist Vis. Nurse Assn., Louisville, 1977; resident in psychiatry U. Louisville, 1982-83, 90—, staff physician student health svc., 1983-89; resident Frazier Rehab. Ctr., Louisville, 1989-90; emergency room physician North Clark Community Hosp., Charlestown, Ind., 1983-87; physician Immediate Care Ctrs., Louisville, 1983-86. Capt. U.S. Army, 1974-77, mem. Res., 1977—. Teagle Found. scholar, 1978-82; named Outstanding Young Women Am., 1983, 84. Mem. Ky. Med. Soc., Jefferson County Med. Assn., Res. Officers Assn., Am. Med. Women's Assn. Democrat. Presbyterian. Home: 1103 Holly Springs Dr Louisville KY 40242 Office: U Louisville Dept of Psychiatry Louisville KY 40292

WINN, EWA, communications executive; b. Borislov, Poland, Sept. 11, 1938; came to U.S., 1953; d. Miroslav and Sofie (Krause) Winogrodski. Student, Columbia U., 1956-59. Exec. sec. Materials Rsch. Corp., Orangeburg, N.Y., 1980-82, APA Transport Corp., North Bergen, N.J., 1982-84, Castrol Inc., Hackensack, N.J., 1971-87; sec. to pres. Castrol Inc., Hackensack, 1983-84, exec. asst., 1984-86; communications mgr. Castrol Inc., Hackensack, N.J., 1986-87, Wayne, N.J., 1987—. Mem. Internat. Assn. Bus. Communicators, Wayne (N.J.) C. of C. (bd. dirs. 1988—). Office: Castrol Inc 1500 Valley Rd Wayne NJ 07470

WINN, JANE KAUFMAN, law educator; b. Pasadena, Calif., Apr. 30, 1957; d. John David Kaufman and Helen Clare (Shopbell) Lavin; m. Peter A. Winn, July 27, 1985. BS in Econs. with 1st class honours, U. London, 1980; JD cum laude, Harvard U., 1987. Bar: N.Y. 1988. Assoc. Shearman & Sterling, N.Y.C., 1987-89; asst. prof. law So. Meth. U., Dallas, 1989—.

WINN, JILL KANAGA KLINE, management executive; b. Oakland, Calif., Jan. 20, 1944; d. Lawrence Wesley and Virginia Louise (Honold) Kanaga; m. Donald Gene Kline, May 30, 1964 (div. 1979); children: Christian Lawrence, Kirsten Michael. Student, Northwestern U., 1961-63, Stella Adler Theater Studio, N.Y.C., 1963-64, Columbia Coll., Chgo., 1970-71. Comml. actress N.Y.C., 1964-77; v.p. Mid-Continent Agys., Inc., Glenview, Ill., 1980—; mgr. accouts receivable portfolio program Mid-Continent Agys., Inc., Glenview, 1983—, cons., 1985—, v.p. ednl. svcs., 1987—; dir. seminars, 1987—. Recipient CLIO award Am. TV Comml. Festival, 1966. Mem. NAFE, Nat. Assn. Women in Careers, Am. Soc. Profl. and Exec. Women, Kappa Kappa Gamma (v.p. Westport, Conn. chpt. 1966). Democrat. Home: 2050 Valencia Northbrook IL 60062

WINN, JUDITH KATZ, college administrator; b. Phila., May 19, 1938; d. Philip William and Audrey J. (Greenbarg) Katz; m. Carl Kodroff, Dec. 20, 1959 (div. 1976); children: Margo Elizabeth, Kurt Stuart; m. Harold Winn, Sept. 1, 1985. BS, Temple U., 1959, MEd, 1971, PhD, 1973. Assoc. prof. Community Coll. Phila., 1973-78, dept. head, 1976-78, div. dir., 1978-82; v.p. Burlington County Coll., Pemberton, N.J., 1982—. Mem. Am. Assn. Univ. Adminstrs., Am. Assn. Women in Community and Jr. Colls., Phi Delta Kappa. Office: Burlington County Coll Pemberton Browns-Mills Rd Pemberton NJ 08068

WINNER, ELLEN PLUCKNETT, lawyer; b. Long Beach, Calif., June 7, 1943; d. William Kennedy and Evaline (West) Plucknett; m. Robert Solomon Denberg, June 5, 1964 (div. 1970); children: Thomas David, William Aaron; m. Evans Hawthorne II Winner, Dec. 21, 1970 (div. 1989); children: Evans Hawthorne III, Keridwen Morgan. BA, Blake Coll., 1963; JD with honors, U. Denver, 1981. Bar; colo. 1981, U.S. Ct. Appeals (fed. cir.) 1977. Patent agent Sheridan, Ross & McIntosh, Denver, 1977-81; patent lawyer Sheridan, Ross & McIntosh, 1981-86, Agrigenetics Corp., Boulder, Colo., 1986-87, Greenlee & Assoc., Boulder, 1987—; Adv. bd. Inst. Shamanistic Studies, Santa Barbara, Calif., 1988—. Articles editor Denver jour. Internat. Law & Policy, 1980-81; contbr. articles to profl. jours. Mem. Am. Intellectual Property Law Assn. (biotech. com. 1982—), Colo. Bar Assn. (Patent, Trademark and Copyright sect. sec.-treas. 1985-86, v.p. 1986-87, pres. 1987-88), Denver Shamanic Assn. (founder 1985), Phi Alpha Delta. Office: Greenlee & Assoc 5370 Manhattan Cir Boulder CO 80303

WINNER, NATHALIE, media publishing consultant; b. Flushing, N.Y.; d. Isidore and Anna (Marks) Baratz; BBA, CCNY. Advt. mgr. of wine and liquor Commentary Mag., N.Y.C., 1968-82, Viva Mag., 1975-76, Ambiance Mag., 1977-78; v.p. Aronson and Jontry Co., pubs. reps., 1983—; wine and spirits advt. mgr. Dynasty Media Pub. Corp., 1984—; wine and liquor print advt. rep. for various trade publs. Mem. Metro. Package Store Assn. of N.Y. (dir. pub. rels., lobbyist, chmn. legis. com.), N.Y. Fedn. Package Stores (sec.), Women of the Alcoholic Beverage Industry (pub. rels. chmn., recipient Outstanding Achievement award), Internat. Platform Assn. Columnist various jours. including N.Y. Beverage Media, Ill. Beverage Jour., Conn. Beverage Jour., Beverage Market, Minn. Beverage Jour., N.D. Beverage Jour., S.D. Beverage Jour., R.I. Beverage Jour. Home: 888 Grand Concourse Bronx NY 10451

WINOGRAD, AUDREY LESSER, advertising executive; b. N.Y.C., Oct. 6, 1933; d. Jack J. and Theresa Lorraine (Elkind) Lesser; m. Melvin H. Winograd, Apr. 29, 1956; 1 child, Hope Elise. Student, U. Conn., 1950-53. Asst. advt. mgr. T. Baumritter Co., Inc., N.Y.C., 1953-54; asst. dir. pub. relations and creative merchandising Kirby, Block & Co., Inc., N.Y.C., 1954-56; div. mdse. mgr., dir. advt. and sales promotion Winograd's Dept. Store, Inc., Point Pleasant, N.J., 1956-73, v.p., 1960-73, exec. v.p., 1973-86; pres. AMW Assocs., Ocean Twp., N.J., 1976—. Editor bus. newsletters. Bd. dirs. Temple Beth Am, Lakewood, N.J., 1970-72. Mem. Jersey Pub. Rels. and Advt. Assn. (pres. 1982-83, bd. dirs. 1979-82, 84-85), Retail Advt. and Mktg. Assn. Internat., Monmouth Ocean Devel. Coun., Monmouth County Bus. Assn. (pres. 1988—, bd. dirs. 1985—), N.J. Assn. Women Bus. Owners, Am. Soc. Advt. and Promotion, Ocean C. of C., Soc. for Prevention of Cruelty to Animals, Humane Soc., United Animal Nation U.S., Internat. Fund for Animal Welfare, World Wildlife Fund, Friends of Animals, Animal Protection Inst., Retail Advt. Conf. Office: AMW Assocs 10 Pine Ln Ocean NJ 07712

WINSLOW, ANNE BRANAN, artist; b. Waynesboro, Ga., July 28, 1920; d. Walter Augustus and Rubie (Griffin) Branan; m. James Addison Winslow Jr., May 8, 1943; children: Lu Anne, Jan Renee. BS in Fine Art, Queens Coll., Charlotte, N.C., 1941; postgrad., U. South Fla., 1974-75. One-woman shows include The Brandon (Fla.) Cultural Ctr., 1980, Dunedin (Fla.) Art Ctr., 1980, Tampa (Fla.) Originals Gallery, 1982, Pub. Libr., St. Petersburg, Fla., 1982, Lee Scarfone Gallery, 1983, 84, Studio 1212, Clearwater, Fla., 1983, 87, 90, Gallery 600, Largo, Fla., 1986, Gallery of State Capitol, Tallahassee, 1987, Berghoff Gallery, Clearwater, 1988, Anderson-Marsh Gallery, St. Petersburg, 1989, Loveland (COlo.) Mus., 1990, Gallery at City Hall of Tampa, 1990; painting, oil painting, Fla. Series II, Images II, 1980, Amagedon, 1974, Eastern Series III, 1984, original handpulled serigraphs, 1989. Mem. Studio 1212, Inc., Fla. Artist Group, Inc., Artist Alliance, The Museum of Women in Arts, Fla. Printmakers Soc. Republican. Home and Studio: 5224 Neptune Way Tampa FL 33609

WINSLOW, FRANCES EDWARDS, city official; b. Phila., Sept. 12, 1948; d. Harry Donaldson and Anna Louise (McColgan) E.; m. David Allen Winslow, June 6, 1970; children: Frances Lavinia, David Allen Jr. BA, Drew U., 1969, MA, 1971; M Urban Planning, NYU, 1974, PhD, 1978. Adminstrv. asst. Borough of Florham Park, N.J., 1970-73; instr. Kean Coll., Union, N.J., 1973-75; adminstrv. asst. Irvine (Calif.) Police Dept., 1984-86; coord. emergency svcs. City of Irvine, 1986—. Contbr. articles to profl. publs., chpt. in book. Vice-pres. San Diego Chaplains Wives, 1976-79; treas. Girl Scouts U.S., Yokohama, Japan, 1980-81; vice-chmn. for curriculum Red Cross Disaster Acad., 1989-90. Recipient Vol. Svc. award Navy Relief Soc., Camp Pendleton, Calif., 1984; Lasker Found. fellow, 1972. Mem. Assn. Police Planning and Res. Officers (sec. Orange County 1984-85, v.p. 1985-86), Am. Soc. for Pub. Adminstrn. (program chmn. Orange County 1987-88, chmn. criminal justice sect. award 1989-90, 90-91, com. 1988-89), Am. Planning Assn. (Orange County regional conf. planning com. 1989-90), Acad. Criminal Justice Sci. (pub. com. 1987-89), Internat. City Mgrs. Assn. (assoc.), Creekers Club (Irvine, pres. 1986), Officer Wives Club (Camp Pendleton, pres. 1983-84, treas. 1982-83), others. Republican. Methodist. Home: 19 Soaring Hawk Irvine CA 92714 Office: City of Irvine 1 Civic Ctr Dr Irvine CA 92714

WINSOR, BARBARA ANN, graphic designer; b. Bar Harbor, Maine, July 4, 1943; d. Gordon Dow and Ruth Mary (Bennett) W. BA, Mass. Coll. Art, Brookline, 1965. Graphic designer Colorpicture, Inc., Boston, 1965-66, Associated Designers, Cambridge, Mass., 1966-67; art dir. Polaroid Corp., Cambridge, 1967-78; sr. artist Walt Disney Prodns., W.E.D. Enterprises, Lake Buena Vista, Fla., 1978-85; sr. graphic designer LMI Advt. Agy., Boston, 1985-87; freelance graphic designer, wildlife illustrator Concord, N.H., 1987—. Recipient 1st place award N.Y. Times Insert competition, N.E. Coun./Boston Ad Club, 1969, 1st place Paperback Booksmith Nat. Logo Design competition, 1969, N.Y. Type Dirs. Show award, 1971; winner Parsons Paper/Boston Ad Club design competition, 1978; also various other awards Boston Ad Club, 1967-78. Home and Studio: 169 Portsmouth St #C-82 Concord NH 03301

WINSTEAD, TERRI LEE, vocational rehabilitation counselor; b. Marysville, Calif., July 25, 1953; d. Lloyd Leslie and Arlene Marie (Dihel) Newham; m. Neil A. Winstead, May 5, 1979 (div. Feb. 1990); 1 child, Courtney Marie. BA in Psychology, Biola Coll., 1975. Cert. rehab. counselor, cert. ins. rehab. specialist. Claims adjuster, vocat. rehab. coord. State of Calif. Compensation Ins. Fund, Redding, 1978-83; vocat. rehab. counselor Stinson & Isom, Assocs., Chico, Calif., 1983—. Mem. Calif. Assn. Rehab. Profls., Rotary Club (charter mem. Red Bluff Sunrise chpt., bd. dirs., editor Rotary Ruminations, 1989—). Office: Stinson & Isom Assocs 1040 Washington St Red Bluff CA 96080

WINSTON, CHRISS HURST, communications professional; b. Sioux City, Iowa, Nov. 24, 1948; d. Robert Jacob and Margaret Ann (O'Brien) Hurst; m. David Howard Winston, July 14, 1984; 1 child, Ian O'Brien. BA, U. Iowa, 1971. News and rsch. dir. Rep. State Cen. Com., Des Moines, 1973-75; spl. asst. Rep. Nat. Com., Washington, 1975-76; press sec. U.S. Rep. Jim Leach, Washington, 1976-79; v.p. Campaign Planning, Inc., Washington, 1979-80; dep. dir. incumbent campaigns Nat. Rep. Congress Campaign, Washington, 1981-85; spl. asst. press and pub. rels. Occupational Safety and Health Adminstrn. U.S. Dept. Labor, Washington, 1985-86, dep. asst. sec. labor pub. and govtl. affairs, 1986-88; dep. dir. communications Bush-Quayle '88, Washington, 1988; dep. dir. pub. affairs Office Presdl. Transition, Washington, 1988-89; dep. asst. to Pres. of U.S. for communications, dir. speechwriting The White House, Washington, 1989—. Office: The White House Exec Office of Pres 1600 Pennsylvania Ave NW Washington DC 20500

WINSTON, JANE ELLEN, non-profit business consulting service executive; b. Milw., June 21, 1944; d. James Noel and Jane Ellen (Cantwell) Johnson; m. John Brooks Winston, Oct. 3, 1964 (div. Sept. 1986); children: Caroline, Elizabeth, Philip; m. Glen Scott Gustafson, June 18, 1988. Student, U. Wis., 1962-64; BA, Met. State U., St. Paul, 1985; cert., U. Minn. Mgmt. Inst., 1990. Tng. and program coord. Met. Econ. Devel. Assn., Mpls., 1984-85, pub. rels. dir., 1986-87, vol. program dir., 1987-88, bus. cons., 1988-89, dir. bus. devel., 1989—; exec. dir. Minn. Minority Purchasing Coun. Founding mem., bd. dirs. Children's Mus. Minn., St. Paul, 1982-84; participant Hubert H. Humphrey Inst. Pub. Affairs-Women in Leadership, 1987; bd. dirs. Jr. League Mpls., 1980-81, 83-84, Met. State U. Alumni Bd., 1986—. Bush Found. summer fellow, 1989. Mem. Greater Mpls. C. of C. (trade expo com. 1985-89), Women In Communication Inc. Office: Met Econ Devel Assn 2021 E Hennepin Ave Ste 370 Minneapolis MN 55413

WINSTON, JANET MARGARET, real estate professional, civic volunteer; b. Binghamton, N.Y., Sept. 30, 1937; d. Cornelius Adrian and Vera Helene (Strohman) Salie; m. Edmund Joseph Winston, Nov. 29, 1958 (dec. July 1981); children: Mark Edmund, Deborah Ann. Student, SUNY, 1955-57, Bliss Coll., 1978. Sales assoc. HER Realtors, Worthington, Ohio, 1979—. Dist. chairperson women's div. Community Chest ARC, Kalamazoo, Mich., 1970; docent Indpls. Mus. Art, 1975, Columbus (Ohio) Mus. Art, 1976—, beaux art mem., 1978-87, docent Chinese Son of Heaven Exhibit, 1989, mus. fund drive, 1980-87, 89; trustee Worthington Resource Ctr., 1979-84, v.p. 1984, chairperson youth employment svcs., 1980-83; trustee, sec. Worthington Hills Civic Assn., 1986-89. Mem. Columbus Bd. Realtors (pub. relations com. 1980, 82, 86, 88, sales adv. com. 1987, mem. svcs. task force, 1989), Nat. Assn. Realtors, Ohio Assn. Realtors, Worthington C. of C., Worthington Hills Country Club, Worthington Hills Women's Club, Worthington Hills Garden Club (bd. dirs. 1989), Columbus Ptnrs. Club (sec. 1989). Republican. Episcopalian. Home: 8036 Golfview Ct Worthington OH 43085 Office: HER Realtors 6902 N High St Worthington OH 43085

WINSTON, JUDITH ANN, lawyer; b. Atlantic City, Nov. 23, 1943; d. Edward Carlton and Margaret Ann (Goodman) Marianno; B.A. magna cum laude, Howard U., Washington, 1966; J.D., Georgetown U., 1977; m. Michael Russell Winston, Aug. 10, 1963; children—Lisa Marie, Cynthia Eileen. Dir. EEO Project, Council Great City Schs., Washington, 1971-74; legal asst. Lawyers Com. for Civil Rights Under Law, Washington, 1975-77; admitted to D.C. bar, 1977, U.S. Supreme Ct. bar; spl. asst. to dir. Office for Civil Rights, HEW, Washington, 1977-79; exec. asst., legal counsel to chair U.S. EEO Commn., Washington, 1979-80; asst. gen. counsel U.S. Dept. Edn., 1980-86; dep. dir. Lawyers Com. for Civil Rights Under Law, 1986-88; dep. dir. pub. policy Women's Legal Def. Fund, Washington, 1988—, chair employment discrimination com., 1979—; ednl. cons., 1974-77; guest lectr. Washington Coll. Law of Am. U. Active NAACP Legal Def. and Ednl. Fund, 1968-79 ; bd. dirs. Higher Achievement Program. Mem. ACLU (Nat. Capital Area), D.C. Bar Assn., Washington Council Lawyers, Washington Bar Assn., Nat. Bar Assn., Fed. Bar Assn., Links Inc., Alpha Kappa Alpha, Phi Beta Kappa, Delta Theta Phi. Democrat. Episcopalian. Author: Desegregating Schools in the Great Cities: Philadelphia, 1970; Chronicle of a Decade 1961-1970, 1970; Desegregating Urban Schools: Educational Equality/Quality, 1970. Home: 1371 Kalmia Rd NW Washington DC 20012

Office: Lawyer's Com for Civil Rights Under Law 1400 Eye St NW Washington DC 20005

WINTER, BARBARA ANN, psychologist; b. N.Y.C., Oct. 9, 1957; d. Benjamin Bernard and Judith Belle (Abrams) Winter. BA, Hofstra U., 1979; PhD in Clin. Psychology, Nova U., 1987. Lic. psychologist, Fla. Psychologist Clin. Psychology Inst., Ft. Lauderdale, Fla., 1986-88; pvt. practice Boca Raton, 1988—; instr. psychology Broward Community Coll., Ft. Lauderdale, 1987-88, Nova U., Ft. Lauderdale, 1987; ct. psychologist family and juv. div. Palm Beach County (Fla.) 1988-89; staff psychologist Anon Anew at Boca Raton, 1989—; presenter profl. confs.; chmn. pub. rels. and media com. Internat. Eating Disorders Awareness Week, 1987. Mem. Am. Psychol. Assn., Assn. for Advancement Behavior Therapy, Fla. Psychol. Assn.

WINTER, JOAN ELIZABETH, psychotherapist; b. Aiken, S.C., Feb. 24, 1947; d. John S. and Mary Elizabeth (Caldwell) Winter. BS, Ariz. State U., 1970; MSW, Va. Commonwealth U., 1977; EdS, Coll. William and Mary, 1989. Lic. clin. social worker, bd. approved supr., clin. group worker. Va. Counselor Child Psychiatry Hosp., Phoenix, 1969-70, Ariz. Job Coll., Casa Grande, 1970-71; dir. Halfway House, Richmond, Va., 1971-73; state supr. resdl. treatment, Richmond, 1973-75; psycotherapist Med. Coll. Va., Richmond, 1975-76, Va. Commonwealth U., 1976-77; exec. dir. Family Rsch. Project, Richmond, Va., 1979-81; dir. Family Inst. Va., Richmond, 1980—; examiner, approved supr. Bd. Behavioral Scis., Commonwealth of Va., 1982-86; mem. Avanta Network, Exec. Coun. and Faculty, Nat. Inst. of Drug Abuse, Rsch. Adv. Com. Author: The Phenomenon of Incest, 1977, The Use of Self in Therapy: The Person and Practice of the Therapist, 1987, Family Life of Psychotherapists, 1987 Enhancing the Marital Relationship: Virginia Satir's Parts Party, 1990; contbr. articles to profl. jours. Diplomate Nat. Assn. Social Workers; mem. Am. Soc. Cert. Social Workers, Am. Family Therapy Assn., Am. Assn. Marriage and Family Therapy (approved supr.), Avanta Network Faculty. Address: 2910 Monument Ave Richmond VA 23221

WINTERS, ALICE GRAHAM BUTLER (MRS. CARL S. WINTERS), civic worker; b. Linton, Ind., July 5, 1907; d. William Austin and Mary (Inman) Butler; A.B., Franklin Coll., 1932; spl. student U. Rochester, 1929-30, Colgate-Rochester Div. Sch., 1929-30; m. Carl S. Winters, May 23, 1925; children—Barbara (Mrs. Robert Kane), Janet (Mrs. Ralph Kuzmic), Linda (Mrs. Allen F. Jones). Minister junior ch., Jackson, Mich., 1931-39, 1st Bapt. Ch. Oak Park, Ill., 1939-59; lectr. Adult Edn. Council Chgo.; also freelance writer. Organizer, pres. Jackson (Mich.) Peace Council, 1933-35; pres. Jackson County LWV, 1935, Chgo. Drama League, 1948-50, Chgo. Mission Union, 1956-60; treas. Art Assocs. Oak Park, 1961-64; pres. Infant Welfare Soc., 1960-62; mem. Com. of 100, Nat. Council of Chs., 1963—; bd. dirs. Woman's Bd. Salvation Army, Chgo., 1960—, pres. bd., 1969—; bd. dirs. Women's Bd. Mental Health Assn., Chgo.; bd. dirs. Maywood (Ill.) Home and Hosp., 1940-62, v.p. bd., 1958-62; mem. woman's bd. Christian U. of Tokyo, 1963—. Recipient Outstanding Woman award Chgo. Assn. Commerce and Industry, 1976; citation for outstanding contbns. to humanity Franklin Coll., 1978; Disting. Service award Salvation Army Internat., 1980; Cert. of Recognition for outstanding service Comprehensive Community Services of Chgo., 1980; citation for achievement and influence Chautauqua Instn., 1982, Alice and Carl Winters Park named in their honor, 1985. Mem. Delta Zeta, Beta Sigma Phi, Kappa Delta. Clubs: Conference Club Presidents (bd. dirs. 1962—, chmn. pub. relations, sec.); 19th Century Woman's; Garden; Chautauqua (N.Y.) Women's; Oak Park Country; Zonta. Home: 404 N East Ave Oak Park IL 60602 Other: Packard Manor Chautauqua NY 14722

WINTERS, BARBARA JO, musician; b. Salt Lake City; d. Louis McClain and Gwendolyn (Bradley) W. AB cum laude, UCLA, 1960, postgrad., 1961; postgrad., Yale, 1960. Mem. oboe sect. L.A. Philharm., 1961—, now prin. oboist.; clinician oboe, English horn, Oboe d'amore. Recs. movie, TV sound tracks. Home: 3529 Coldwater Canyon Studio City CA 91604 Office: 135 N Grand Ave Los Angeles CA 90012

WINTERS, CHRISTINA MARGARET, sales executive; b. Cleve., Aug. 18, 1947; d. John and Mary Veronica (Barbalics) Sparenga; m. Michael Adrian Winters, Sept. 9, 1967 (div. Jan. 1970); m. Matthew Francis Wardell West, Dec. 18, 1981 (div. Apr. 1986). Grad. high sch., Garfield Heights, Ohio. Sec. various cos. Cleve., 1966-78; ins. salesperson Vets. Assn., L.A., 1979-81; fin. svcs. advisor United Resources, L.A., 1981-85, dist. mgr., 1985-87; v.p. United Resources, Irving, Tex., 1987-89; pres. Christina M. Winters Unltd., Irving, Tex., 1990—; cons. Classroom Tchrs. Dallas, 1988-89, Mo. NEA, St. Louis, 1988-89. Author: For the Sake of You, 1989. Bd. dirs. Children's Found., Dallas, 1989, Ch. Religious Sci., Glendale, Calif., 1987; mem. Dallas/Fort Worth Hosp. Coun., 1988-89; Dallas Mus. Art. Mem. NAFE, Nat. Assn. Women Bus. Owners, NOW, Nat. Speakers Assn., Dallas/Ft. Worth Hosp. Coun. Republican. Home: 3716 Santiago Ct Irving TX 75062 Office: 600 E Las Colinas Blvd Las Colinas TX 75039

WINTERS, MARY ANN, sister; b. Paterson, N.J., Nov. 15, 1937; d. Russell Lewis and Nellie Marie (Cramer) W. BA, Seton Hill Coll., 1967; PhD, U. Pitts., 1972. Tchr. various cath. schs., Pa., Ariz., 1957-67; from instr. to chmn. chemistry dept. Seton Hill Coll., Greensburg, Pa., 1967-68, 72-81; councilor Sisters of Charity Seton Hill, Greensburg, Pa., 1981-85, major superior, 1985—; mem. task force Leadership Conf. Women Religious, Silver Springs, Md. 1986-88; retreat dir. Sisters of Charity Seton Hill, Greensburg, Pa., 1977-81. Trustee Seton Hill Coll., Greensburg, Pa., Jeannette Dist. Meml. Hosp., Jeannette, Pa., DePaul Inst., Pitts.; mem. Ethics Task Force Forbes Regional, Pitts. Named Teacher of Yr., Seton Hill Coll., Greensburg, Pa., 1981. Mem. Am. Chem. Soc., Tri-Diocesan Sisters' Leadership Coun. (pres. 1988—), Fedn. Daus. Elizabeth Seton (exec. com. 1989—). Office: Sisters Charity Seton Hill De Paul Ctr Mt Thor Rd Greensburg PA 15601

WINTERS, MARY-FRANCES, small business owner; b. Buffalo, Mar. 13, 1951; d. Lawrence A. and Gladys M. (Molock) S.; m. Joseph R. Winters, June 2, 1973; children: Joseph, Mareisha. BA, U. Rochester, 1973, MBA, 1982. Pers. specialist Eastman Kodak Corp., Rochester, N.Y., 1973-79; mgr. Eastman Kodak Corp., Rochester, 1979-81, sr. market analyst, 1981-84; pres. Winters Group, Rochester, 1984—; bd. dirs. Eltrex Industries, Rochester. Trustee U. Rochester, 1986—; bd. dirs. Black Bus. Assn., Rochester, 1986—, United Way Greater Rochester, 1984—, Girl Scouts U.S., N.Y.C., 1987—; pres. bd. dirs. Genesee Valley Girl Scouts U.S., 1984-87. Named Bus. Women of Yr. Negro Bus. and Profl. Women's Orgn., Rochester, 1987. Mem. Am. Mktg. Assn., Alpha Kappa Alpha. Methodist. Home: 12 Port Meadow Trail Fairport NY 14450 Office: The Winters Group Inc 14 Franklin St Rochester NY 14604

WINTERS, MICHELLE G., insurance company executive; b. Cleve., Sept. 16, 1953; d. Alex Gill and Joan Genevieve (Corrigan) Gill; m. Gerald L. Winters, Aug. 20, 1988. Student, Cuyahoga Community Coll. CLU. Asst. v.p., mktg. agy. coord. Protective Life Ins. Co., Birmingham, Ala.; dir. internal ops. Empire Gen. Life, Cleve. Fellow Life Mgmt. Inst.; mem. Am. Soc. CLU and Chartered Fin. Cons. (Birmingham chpt.).

WINTERS, PHYLLIS JEAN, banker; b. Phoenix, Mar. 25, 1945; d. James S. and Jean (Hudson) Hull; m. David H. Reid, June 12, 1967 (div. June 1977); 1 child, Jennifer D.; m. Barry A. Winters, Oct. 11, 1980. BA, U. Oreg., 1967. With br. ops. 1st Interstate Bank of Ariz., Phoenix, 1969-77, trainer, 1977-79; tng. dir. Great Western Bank, Phoenix, 1979-82; mgmt. trainer Greyhound Corp., Phoenix, 1983-86; v.p., mgr. tng. Citibank Ariz. (formerly United Bank of Ariz.), Phoenix, 1986—; instr. Am. Inst. Banking, Phoenix, 1980—. Coord. family sect. AFS Exch. Program, Phoenix, 1988-89. Mem. ASTD (v.p. 1984-86, Merit award 1979), Phi Beta Kappa. Episcopalian. Office: Citibank Ariz 4041 N Central Ave Phoenix AZ 85012

WINTERS, SHELLEY (SHIRLEY SCHRIFT), actress; b. St. Louis, Aug. 18, 1922; m. Vittorio Gassman (div.); 1 child, Vittoria; m. Anthony Franciosa, 1957 (div. Nov. 1960). Student, Wayne U. Began acting career in vaudeville, later played roles on legitimate stage; motion pictures include The Diary of Anne Frank, 1958 (Acad. award best supporting actress), Odds Against Tomorrow, Let No Man Write My Epitaph, Matter of Convictions, Lolita, 1962, Wives and Lovers, 1963, The Balcony, 1964, A House Is Not a Home, 1964, Patch of Blue, 1966 (Acad. award best supporting actress), Time of Indifference, 1965, Alfie, 1965, The Moving Target, 1965, Harper, 1966, Enter Laughing, 1967, The Scalp Hunters, 1968, Buona Sera Mrs. Campbell, 1968, Wild in the Streets, 1968, The Mad Room, 1969, How Do I Love Thee, 1971, What's the Matter with Helen, 1971, The Poseidon Adventure, 1972, Blume in Love, 1973, Cleopatra Jones, 1973, Something to Hide, 1973, Diamonds, 1975, Next Stop Greenwich Village, 1976, The Tenant, 1976, An Average Man, 1977, Tentacles, 1977, Pete's Dragon, 1977, King of the Gypsies, 1978, The Visitor, 1980, Looping, 1981, S.O.B., 1981, My Mother, My Daughter, 1981, Over the Brooklyn Bridge, Ellie, Deja Vu, 1985, The Delta Force, 1986, Marilyn Monroe: Beyond the Legend, 1987, Purple People Eater, 1988; appeared in: TV films Revenge!, 1971, The Devil's Daughter, 1973, Double Indemnity, 1974, The Sex Symbol, 1974, Elvis, 1978; plays A Hatfull of Rain, 1955, Girls of Summer, 1957, Night of the Iguana, Cages, Who's Afraid of Virginia Wolf?, Minnie's Boys; TV miniseries The French Atlantic Affair, 1979; Author: play One Night Stands of a Noisy Passenger, 1971; autobiography Shelley: Also Known As Shirley, 1980, Shelley II: The Middle of My Century, 1989. Recipient Emmy award Best Actress, 1964, Monte Carlo Golden Nymph award, 1964, Internat. TV award as best actress Cannes Festival, 1965. Office: care Internat Creative Mgmt 8899 Beverly Blvd Los Angeles CA 90048*

WINTER-SWITZ, CHERYL DONNA, travel company executive; b. Jacksonville, Fla., Dec. 6, 1947; d. Jacqueline Marie (Carroll) Winter; m. Frank C. Snedaker, June 24, 1974 (div. May 1976); m. Robert William Switz, July 1, 1981. AA, City Coll. of San Francisco, 1986; BS, Golden Gate U., 1990. Bookkeeper, agt. McQuade Tours, Ft. Lauderdale, Fla., 1967-69; mgr. Boca Raton (Fla.) Travel, 1969-76; owner, mgr. Ocean Travel, Boca Raton, 1976-79; ind. contractor Far Horizons Travel, Boca Raton, 1979-80; mgr. Tara/BPF Travel, San Francisco, 1981-84; mgr. travel. dept. Ernst & Whinney/Lifeco Travel, San Francisco, 1984-86; ptnr. Travelmain Ltd., Walnut Creek, Calif., 1986—; travel cons. Siemer & Hand Travel, San Francisco, 1989—; instr. Golden Gate U., 1986—, U. San Francisco. Mem. Amateur Trapshooting Assn., Hotel and Restaurant Mgmt. Club. Republican. Episcopalian. Home: 642 Brussels San Francisco CA 94134 Office: Siemer & Hand Travel 101 California St Ste 1050 San Francisco CA 94111

WINTOUR, ANNA, editor; b. Eng., Nov. 3, 1949; came to U.S., 1976; d. Charles and Elinor W.; m. David Shaffer, Sept. 1984; children: Charles, Kate. Student, Queens Coll., 1963-67. Deputy fashion editor Harper's and Queen Mag., London, 1970-76; fashion editor Harper's Bazaar, New York, 1976-77; fashion and beauty editor Viva Mag., New York, 1977-78; contbg. editor fashion and style Savvy Mag., New York, 1980-81; sr. editor N.Y. Mag., 1981-83; creative dir. U.S. Vogue, N.Y., 1983-86; editor in chief British Vogue, London, 1986-87, House and Garden, N.Y., 1987-88, Vogue, N.Y., 1988—. Office: Vogue Mag Conde Nast Bldg 350 Madison Ave New York NY 10017*

WINZELL, DEBRA KAY, housing administrator; b. Cairo, Ill., Sept. 28, 1951; d. Arthur Ernest and Mary Elizabeth (Mason) Ellis; m. Terry Wayne Winzell, Aug. 9, 1975; 1 child, Douglas James. Assoc. Sci., Shawnee Coll., 1971. Exec. sec. Dravo-Groves-Newberg, Paducah, Ky., 1972-75; bookkeeper Sigman Buick, Griffin, Ga., 1975-76; payroll clk. So. Clay, Olmsted, Ill., 1976-77; sec., asst. mgr., adminstr. Jackson House, Paducah, Ill., 1977—; adminstr. W.B. Sanders Retirement Ctr., Paducah, 1982—; cons. in field. Mem. Dem. Women, Paducah, 1983. Named Ky. Col., State of Ky., 1974, Duchess of Paducah, Mayor of Paducah, 1983; recipient Woman of Achievement award, Bus. and Profl. Women, 1983, Outstanding Performance award, HUD, 1985. Mem. NAFE, Am. Assn. Homes for Aging (House of Dels.), Ky. Assn. Homes for Aging, Nat. Coun. Sr. Citizens, Am. Assn. Retired Persons. Home and Office: 301 S 9th St Paducah KY 42001

WIRICK, ELIZABETH ELLEN, financial analyst; b. Wauseon, Ohio, Dec. 16, 1940; d. Allen Keith and Georgetta Marie (Day) Callender; m. Clinton D. Wirick, Dec. 22, 1961, (div. Aug. 1987); children: Todd, Lisa. BS, Bowling Green State, 1962; MS, Mercer U., Atlanta, 1980. Registered rep. Tchr. Chattanooga Sch. System, 1967-73, DeKalb County Sch. System, Atlanta, 1973-83; agt., fin. advisor CM Alliance, Toledo, 1983—; chmn. dept. of bus. Davis Coll., Toledo; nursery dir. Vine St. Children's Home, Chattanooga, 1967-68; bd. dirs. Presch. Speech and Hearing Clinic, Chattanooga; assoc. The Interconnection, Toledo, 1986—; tchr. Jr. Achievement, Toledo, 1988. Sponsor Bonny Oaks Orphanage, Chattanooga, 1967-72; sec., v.p. local PTA, Chatttanooga, 1970-74; vol. Rainbow Ctr., Toledo, 1986-89. Recipient Tenn. Scrapbook award, 1970-73, Industry Leaders award, 1985-1987, Nat. Quality award, 1987, Agy. Investment award, 1988, Interconnection Scholarship award, 1988; named Outstanding Young Woman of Am., 1974. Mem. Nat. Assn. Life Underwriters, Ohio Assn. Life Underwriters, Toledo Assn. Life Underwriters, Beta Sigma Phi, Alpha Delta Pi. Republican. Methodist. Office: CM Alliance 5800 Monroe Bldg C Sylvania OH 43560

WIRTENBERG, THELMA JEAN (JEANA WIRTENBERG), research psychologist, marketing executive; b. N.Y.C., Jan. 28, 1950; d. Harold and Pearl Cecile (Hershberg) W. BS in Math. magna cum laude, CUNY, 1971; MA in Psychology, UCLA, 1972, PhD in Psychology, 1979. Social sci. analyst U.S. Commn. on Civil Rights, Washington, 1975-79; rsch. mgr. Nat. Inst. Edn., Washington, 1979-83; market rsch. mgr. AT&T Techs., Parsippany, N.J., 1983-85; market mgr. AT&T Info. Systems, Parsippany, N.J., 1985-88; human resources mgr., employee surveys AT&T, Morristown, N.J., 1988-90; mgr. mgmt. employment coll. rels. AT&T, 1990—; cons. Orbit Prodns., Inc., Washington, 1986—; cons. psychology of women div. Am. Psycol. Assn., Washington, 1976-83; Washington area mgr. Inst. Pub. Svc., 1982-83. Co-editor: Sex-Role Rsch.: Measuring Social Change, 1983; co-editor Psychology of Women Quar. spl. issue, 1981. Chancellors intern fellow UCLA, 1972-75. Mem. Soc. for Psychol. Study Social Issues (spl. issues dissertation award 1979), Phi Beta Kappa. Democrat. Jewish. Office: AT&T 100 Southgate Pkwy Morristown NJ 07960

WIRTH, WINIFRED PROZELLER, writer, educator, plangonologist, bacteriologist; b. Olean, N.Y., Sept. 10, 1916; d. Edwin Adam and Clara Eve (Bucher) Prozeller; m. Frederick Edward, June 22, 1937 (dec. Aug. 1979); children: Michael Edwin (dec.), Christine Elizabeth, Frederick Edward, David Noel, Richard Peter, Winifred Catherine, Constance Marianne. BS in Maths., St. Bonaventure U., 1938, MS in Biology and Physics, 1942; MA in Edn., Columbia Pacific U., 1985, PhD, 1985. Prof. Coll. St. Mary, Omaha, 1939-40; tchr. Duchesne Acad. Sacred Heart, Omaha, 1940-41, Bd. Edn., Allegany, N.Y., 1941-42, Brookfield (N.Y.) Cen., 1942-43, Manasquan (N.J.) Pub. Schs., 1943-44, Calvert Sch., Kans., 1945-55, Withamsville Tobasco Sch., Withamsville, Ohio, 1955-57, Goshen (Ohio) Rural Sch., 1957-58, St. Bridget's Sch., Xenia, Ohio, 1958-1959, St. Albert's the Gt. Sch., Kettering, Ohio, 1959-60; tchr. J.E. Prass Sch., Kettering, 1960-79, ret., 1979; cancer researcher Institutum Divi Thomae, Cinn., 1979-83; traveler to various countries for ednl. material and collecting dolls, 1962—. Contbr. articles to profl. jours.; 26 copyrights including Les Trois Ours et Chrysocome, La Famille de Chrysocome et Petit Ourson, Child's Dental Reader, Alaska for Children, Twice Each Year, Classroom Control, Teen-Age Writings of a Kansan Lad, Ohio's Red Fox, The Teeth That Cried. Contbr. fin. aid for 2 scholarships U. Dayton, Ohio, 1986—; specialist Alaska for children; endower Dr. Frederick Wirth scholarship St. Bonaventure U., Allegany, Allegany Pub. Libr.; organizer YMCA Met. Club, 1960, Camp Fire Girls, 1962-63; mem. PTA, Nat. Arbor Day Found., Nat. Wildlife Fedn., The Cleve. Clinic Found., Statue of Liberty-Ellis Island Found., UNICEF, Bradford Exch., Smithsonian Instn., S.C. Wildlife Preservation. Mem. UNESCO, NEA, Am. Assn. Ret. Persons, Ohio Edn. Assn., Ohio State Tchrs. Retirement Assn., Nat. Geographic Soc., U.S. Hist. Soc., Dept. Actively Retired Tchrs., Sci. and Cultural Orgn., Soc. Preservation Birds of Prey, Nat. Trust for Hist. Preservation, Greenpeace, St. Thomas Acad. Mothers Club (Minn.), St. Joan of Arc Womens Club. Democrat. Roman Catholic. Home: 4026 Home Rd Powell OH 43065

WIRTZ, DIANNE DEMPSEY, educator, consultant; b. Pittsfield, Mass., Feb. 7, 1945; d. William Stephen and Eleanor (Shandoff) Dempsey; m. Harold George Wirtz, May 7, 1970; children: David Anthony, Andrew Jacob, Brian Dempsey. BS, U. Vt., 1967, MEd, 1987. Cert. tchr., Vt. Asst. dir. dietary dept. Mary Hitchcock Meml. Hosp., Hanover, N.H., 1968-70; adminstrv. asst. Svc. Ctr. Camp Zama, Japan, 1970; pvt. practice dietitian, 1972—; tchr. South Royalton Sch. Dist., Royalton, Vt., 1984-87, Randolph (Vt.) Sch. Dist., 1987—; cons. dietitian Birchwood Nursing Home, Burlington, 1971-76k, Rowan Ct. Nursing Home, Barre, Vt., 1972-78, Mayo Nursing Home, Northfield, Va., 1972-90, ICF, Randolph, 1989-90. Author: Egg/Wheat Free Diets, 1968, Math Mission Impossible, 1989. Worker, donor ARC, Zama and Randolph, 1970, 72-90; officer, mem. AAUW, Randolph, 1980-89; chairperson Randolph Sports Booster, 1987-90, chairperson project grad., 1990—. State of Vt. grantee, 1985. Mem. Am. Dietetic Assn., Vt. Dietetic Assn., Student Health and Phys. Edn., Delta Delta Delta. Home: Box D Randolph Center VT 05061 Office: Randolph Sch 28 N Main St Randolph VT 05060

WIRUM, MARY LOU, real estate developer, investor; b. Oklahoma City, Dec. 7, 1937; d. Herman A. and Grace I. (Smith) Payne; m. C. Harold, Feb. 16, 1963; children: Andrea A., Jay Rhys, John Mitchell. Real estate broker pvt. practice, Anchorage, 1971; bd. dirs. Enstar Natural Gas Co. Bd. dirs. Anchorage Parking Authority, Anchorage Family Resource Ctr. Mem. Anchorage Bd. Realtors. Republican. Presbyterian. Home: 1240 S Street Anchorage AK 99501 Office: Wirum Comml/Investment Real Estate 500 L St Ste 100 Anchorage AK 99501

WISCH, MARILYN JOAN, pension design firm executive; b. Bklyn., Oct. 13, 1942; d. Irving Elmer and Sylvia (Manzar) Chezar; m. Steven Charles Wisch, Sept. 19, 1965 (div. Nov. 1981); 1 child, Beth Allyson. BS, NYU, 1964; MEd, Adelphi U., 1976, paralegal employee benefits program, 1982. Art dir. Doyle Dane & Bernbach, N.Y.C., 1964-69; tchr. Baldwin Sch. Dist., N.Y., 1977; real estate saleswoman Village Homes, Rockville Centre, N.Y., 1978-82; cons., v.p., ptnr., owner Accu-Plan Adminstrs., Inc., Rockville Centre, 1983-87; pres./owner Accrued Benefits Planning Ltd., Rockville Centre, 1987—; paralegal instr. Adelphi U., Garden City, N.Y., 1983—. Poll insp., Baldwin, 1977-78; v.p. Plaza PTA, Baldwin, 1978-79; v.p. Sisterhood, pres. Couples Club, Central Synagogue, Rockville Centre, 1978-81; vol. South Nassau Communities Hosp., Oceanside, N.Y., 1979-81. Mem. Nat. Assn. Female Execs. (network dir. 1985), Am. Soc. Pension Actuaries (coordinator for testing Rockville Centre 1986), Nat. Inst. Pension Adminstrs., Rockville Centre C. of C. (bd. trustees). Democrat. Jewish. Avocations: gardening, reading, seminars, public speaking. Home: 1276 Surrey Ln Rockville Centre NY 11570 Office: Accrued Benefits Planning Ltd 1276 Surrey Ln Rockville Centre NY 11570

WISDOM, GUYRENA KNIGHT, psychologist, educator; b. St. Louis, July 27, 1923; d. Gladys Margaret (Hankins) McCullin. AB, Stowe Tchrs. Coll., 1945; AM, U. Ill., 1951; postgrad. St. Louis U., 1952-53, 58, 62; Washington U., St. Louis, 1959-61; U. Chgo., 1966-67; Drury Coll., 1968; U. Mo., 1971-72; Fontbonne Coll., 1973; Harris-Stowe State Coll., 1974, 81-82. Tchr. elem. sch. St. Louis Pub. Sch. System, 1945-63, psychol. examiner, 1963-68, sch. psychologist, 1968-74, cons. spl. edn., 1974-77, supr. spl. edn. dept., 1977-79, coord. staff devel. div., 1979-81; pvt. tutor, 1971-72; sch. psychologist, 1984-85; pvt. practice psychologist, St. Louis, 1985-88; ednl. assessment specialist St. Louis Regional Ctr. for the Developmentally Disabled, 1988-89; pvt. practice, 1989—; instr. Harris Tchrs. Coll., St. Louis, 1973-74, Harris-Stowe Coll., 1979. Contbr. articles to profl. jours. Mem. Nat. Assn. Sch. Psychologists, Mo. Assn. Children With Learning Disabilities, Coun. for Exceptional Children, Assn. Supervision and Curriculum Devel., Pi Lambda Theta, Kappa Delta Pi. Roman Catholic. Home: 5046 Wabada St Saint Louis MO 63113

WISE, BLANCHE ANN, food service administrator, educator; b. Sanborn, Iowa, July 1, 1929; d. Francis William and Edna Viola (Allen) Irons; m. Gregory P. Wise, Sept. 10, 1960 (dec. Feb. 1983); 1 child, Matthew William. BS, U. N.D.; MS, U. Wis., 1960; PhD, Purdue U., 1974. Various positions Adrian and Marquette, Mich. and Madison, Wis., 1959-69; assoc. prof., chmn. dept. home econs. Albion (Mich.) Coll., 1969-73; assoc. prof., chm. dept. home econs. No. Mich. U., Marquette, 1973-78; assoc. prof., dir. coordinated undergrad. dietetics program U. Wis., Stevens Point, 1979-81; assoc. prof. Marywood Coll., Scranton, Pa., 1981-85; dietititian cons. Mental Health Dept. N.Y., Albany, 1986; chief adminstrv. dietetics sect. VA Hosp. Med. Ctr., Bklyn., 1987-88; community dietitian United Cerebral Palsy State of N.Y., 1988-89; food dir. Hudson Guild Cafe Coop., N.Y.C., 1989—. Contbr. articles to profl. jours. Delta Kappa Gamma scholar. Mem. Am. Dietetic Assn. (Mead Johnson award for grad. edn.), N.Y. Dietetic Assn., Am. Home Econs. Assn., N.Y. Home Econs. Assn. (Leader of Yr. 1988), Soc. for Nutrition Edn., Am. Diabetes Assn. (Outstanding Nonphysician Educator 1985), Am. Mgmt. Assn., Omicron Nu, Phi Upsilon Omicron, Kappa Omicron Phi, Delta Kappa Gamma, Sigma Delta Epsilon. Home: 249 7th St Brooklyn NY 11215 Office: Hudson Guild 119 9th Ave New York NY 10011

WISE, CINDY SUE, educator; b. Berea, Ohio, Sept. 8, 1955; d. Seth Brokaw and Beatrice Juanita (Starrett) W. BEd cum laude, Miami U., Oxford, Ohio, 1977; MEd, Wright State U., 1982. Cert. elem. tchr., in learning disabilities and behavior disorders, multihandicapped, Ohio. Learning disabilities tchr. Northmont City Schs., Englewood, Ohio, 1977—. Deacon Westminster Presbyn. Ch., Dayton, Ohio, 1980—, advisor jr. high sch. fellowship, 1989-90; vol. Dayton Art Inst., 1987—. Grantee Northmont City Schs., 1986-87, Montgomery County, 1986-87. Mem. Assn. for Children with Learning Disabilities, Found. for Exceptional Children, Ohio Edn. Assn., Northmont Edn. Assn., LWV, Phi Kappa Phi, Kappa Delta Pi. Democrat. Office: Northwood Elem Sch 6200 Noranda Dr Dayton OH 45415

WISE, CYNTHIA, management and trade consultant; b. N.Y.C., Oct. 26, 1944; d. Ralph Earle and Jane (Camp) W.; m. Amadou Moctar Diagne, May 5, 1988. BA, Conn. Coll. for Women, 1966; MA, Northwestern U., Evanston, Ill., 1968. Program dir. The African-Am. Inst., N.Y.C., 1968-83; chief human resources The Agy. for Internat. Devel., Mauritania, West Africa, 1984-86; v.p. Overseas Cons. Svcs., Inc., Mt. Pleasant, Iowa, 1986—; pres. Gold Star Internat. Inc., Wilmington, Del., 1989—; human resource devel. specialist Ronco Consulting Corp., Washington, 1984—. Inspector Bd. of Elections, N.Y.C., 1987—. Mem. Nat. Assn. for Female Execs., Am. Mgmt. Assn. Democrat.

WISE, DARLENE FAYE, director; b. Buena Vista, Iowa, June 17, 1931; d. Owen David and Edith Marie (Libby) Hughes; m. Leroy Wise, Nov. 19, 1950 (div. 1963); children: Dennis, Dwain, Emmett, Lorene, Denise, Randy, James, Mickey. Student, Bueno Vista Coll., 1949-50. Head start tchr. aide Upper Des Moines Opp Inc., Graettinger, Iowa, 1968-74; head start tchr. Upper Des Moines Opp. Inc., Graettinger, 1974-78; outreach dir. Buena Vista County, Graettinger, 1978-79, 8 County, 1989—. City Council, City of Linn Grove, Iowa, 1982—. Home: Box 14 Linn Grove IA 51033 Office: Upper Des Moine Opp Inc 101 Robbins Graettinger IA 51342

WISE, JANET EUGENIA WHERRY, social welfare agency administrator; b. New Brighton, Pa., Oct. 22, 1942; d. Robert Floyd and Ruth Eugenia (Miller) Wherry; m. Wilbert Henry Wise, III, July 11, 1964; 1 child, Greg Robert. BA, Geneva Coll., Beaver Falls, Pa., 1964. Caseworker Dept. Welfare, Rochester, Pa., 1966-72, casework supr., 1972-86, income maintenance mgr., 1986—; mem. Children's Task Force of Beaver County, 1989—; liaison Social Svc. Agys. in Beaver County, 1986—. Tchr. ch. sch. Methodist Ch. of New Brighton, 1965—; sec. New Brighton Band Parents, 1989-90; mem. Human Svc. Forum Beaver County, treas., 1970-71; pres. Meth. Guild Class, 1970s. Mem. Women's Club New Brighton, AAUW, New Brighton Hist. Soc., Merrick Art Gallery Assn., United Meth. Women (sec. 1966-70), Eastern Star. Republican. Home: 1632 2d St New Brighton PA 15066 Office: Dept of Welfare Jefferson St & Rhode Island Rochester PA 15074

WISE, JANIE DENISE, communications consulting company executive; b. Frankfort, Ky., Dec. 15, 1945; d. Joseph William and Kathryn (Smither) W.; B.A. in Edn. and Psychology, U. Ky., 1971; postgrad. U. Louisville, 1971-72. Tchr., Taylorsville (Ky.) High Sch., 1970-72; mental health specialist mental health-retardation bd. Gardiner Lane Center, Louisville, 1972-73; alcohol counselor W.T. Edwards Hosp., Tampa, Fla., 1973-74; community edn. coordinator, counselor First Step, Inc., Sarasota, Fla., 1974-75; dir. DWI Counter Attack Sch., 1975; pvt. practice; communications cons., coord. Tri-County Alcoholism Svcs., Inc., Winter Haven, Fla., 1975-78; communications specialist, select account, area sales rep. Visual Products div. 3/M, St. Paul, 1978-80; owner, pres. Effective Communications Group, Tampa, Fla., 1980-86, exec. com. mem., 1986-87; pres., owner ExecuCom Inc., Tampa, 1986—. Bd. dirs. Entrepreneurship Inst. Tampa Bay, YMCA, Lakeland., Tampa Bay Corp. Resource Coun. Mem. NAFE, Fla. Pub. Rels. Assn., Fla. Fedn. Safety Orgns., Nat. Task Force Women & Alcohol (bd. dirs.) Nat. Assn. Bus. & Indsl. Saleswomen (rep. Fla. office on women and alcohol Washington), Tampa C. of C., Small Bus. Council, U. Ky. Alumni Assn., AAUW, Aircraft Owners and Pilots Assn. Club: Porsche Club of Am. Home: 633 Prado Pl Lakeland FL 33803 Office: PO Box 16623 Temple Terrace FL 33687

WISE, MAUREEN KAMEN, public relations executive, editor; b. Los Angeles, Mar. 26, 1946; d. Murray Morton and Rosalyn Estelle (Horowitz) Kamen; m. Murray Jay Wise, Aug. 7, 1966; children: Stephanie Lauren, Tracey Meredith. BS, Elmira (N.Y.) Coll., 1966. Cert. elem. tchr., N.Y. Tchr. elem Horseheads (N.Y.) Cen. Sch. Dist., 1966-67, East Ramapo Sch. Dist., Spring Valley, N.Y., 1967-69; pub. relations dir. United Jewish Appeal of Rockland, Spring Valley, N.Y., 1971-86; publicity coordinator recreation dept. Town of Ramapo, Suffern, N.Y., 1973; community resources dir. Planned Parenthood of Rockland, West Nyack, N.Y., 1979-82; owner, pres. Wise Promotions, Spring Valley, 1981—; pub. relations dir. Women's League for Conservative Judaism, N.Y.C., 1985—; bd. dirs. United Jewish Community of Rockland, Rockland City, N.Y., 1976—; mem. chancellor's com. Jewish Theol. Sem., N.Y.C., 1987; founding mem., v.p. Rockland County Tourism Bd., Suffern, 1983-85. Mng. editor Women's League Outlook mag., 1985—; producer, dir. multimedia presentations, theatrical prodns. Mem. citizens adv. com. Rockland County, 1984. Recipient Woman of Achievement award, J.T. Sem. Torah Fund Campaign, 1986, Disting. Service award Rockland County, 1984. Mem. Pomona Jewish Ctr. (v.p.), Rockland Women's Network (In Celebration of Women award for Achievement in Bus., 1984), Westchester-Rockland Women's League (past pub. relations chmn.), Elmwood Playhouse Club, Hadassah. Democrat. Home: 24 Fairway Oval Spring Valley NY 10977 Office: Women's League for Conservative Judaism 48 E 74th St New York NY 10021

WISE, SUSAN TAMSBERG, management consultant; b. Memphis, Nov. 16, 1945; d. Joseph Lane and Mable Rosa (Koth) Tamsberg; m. Roy Thomas Wise, June 29, 1968; children: Kristin Rebecca, Mary Catherine. BA in Math., Columbia (S.C.) Coll., 1967; M in Edn., Ga. State U., Atlanta, 1986. Tchr. high sch. math. various pub. schs., N.C., S.C., and Ga., 1967-73; instr. Cen. Piedmont Community Coll., Charlotte, N.C., 1979; devel. dir. Classique, Inc., Kannapolis, N.C., 1979-81; asst. v.p. First Nat. Bank of Atlanta, 1981-87; Ga. dir. The Exec. Speaker, Inc., Atlanta, 1987-90; pres. TrimTime, Inc., Atlanta, 1988-90, Wise Cons., Atlanta, 1990—; speaker Girl Scouts USA, Jr. League, numerous med. assns., Atlanta and S.E. area, 1985—. Tng. cons. Jr. League of Atlanta, 1988-89; bd. mem. Incarnation Luth. Ch., Atlanta, 1984. Mem. Am. Soc. Tng. and Devel. (v.p., bd. dirs., Leadership award 1987), Nat. Speakers Assn., Ga. Speakers Assn., Atlanta C. of Co., Kappa Delta Pi. Republican. Lutheran.

WISE, SYBIL ZULALIAN, educator; b. Malden, Mass., Apr. 15, 1935; d. Badrig Barsam and Elmon (Jivelekian) Zulalian; m. Kenneth Kelly Wise, Aug. 15, 1959; children: Jocelyn Anne, Adam Kelly, Lydia Louise. BS in Early Childhood Edn, Wheelock Coll., Boston, 1957. Tchr. The Pike Sch., Andover, Mass., 1980—. Office: The Pike Sch Sunset Rock Rd Andover MA 01810

WISEHART, MARY RUTH, educator; b. Myrtle, Mo., Nov. 2, 1932; d. William Henry and Ora (Harbison) W. BA, Free Will Baptist Bible Coll., 1955; BA, George Peabody Coll. Tchrs., 1959, MA, 1960, PhD, 1976. Tchr. Free Will Bapt. Bible Coll., Nashville, 1956-60, chmn. English dept., 1961-85; exec. sec.-treas. Free Will Bapt. Woman's Nat. Aux. Conv., 1985—. Author: Sparks Into Flame, 1985; contbr. poetry to jours. Mem. Nat. Council Tchrs. English, Christian Ministries Mgmt. Assn., Religious Conf. Mgmt. Assn., Christian Mgrs. Assn., Scribbler's Club. Avocations: photography, music, drama. Office: Woman's Nat Aux Conv Free Will Bapt PO Box 1088 Nashville TN 37202

WISEMAN, SHIRLEY MCVAY, association executive; b. Gassville, Ark., June 17, 1937; d. Lloyd Ray and M. Maye (Powell) Byrd; m. Louis McVay (div. 1970); children—Larry, Sherri; m. I. Lynwood Wiseman, Dec. 5, 1977 (div. 1988). Student, Am. U., 1 yr. Homebuilder Wiseman Homes Inc., Lexington, Ky., 1964-82; dep. asst. sec. HUD, Washington, 1982-85; sr. officer Nat. Assn. Home Builders, 1986—; mem. com. Ednl. Testing Svc., Princeton, N.J., 1984-85; bd. dirs. Home Owners Warranty Corp., U.S. Home Corp., Fannie Mae. Del. Rep. Nat. Conv., 1972; mem. adv. bd. SBA, Washington, 1981-82, Social Security Task Force, Washington, 1982; mem. adv. bd. Rural Housing Coalition. Mem. Nat. Assn. Homebuilders (v.p. chpt., bd. dirs., pres. 1989), Fed. Nat. Mktg. Assn. (bd. dirs., adv. bd. 1990—). Lodge: Order Eastern Star. Office: Nat Assn Home Builders US 132 Carolwood Blvd Fern Park FL 32730

WISHART, JOYCE, marketing professional; b. Cin., Mar. 21, 1942; d. Robert H. and Thelma (Haar) K. Student, Ohio State U., 1983-87, Old Dominican Coll., Columbus, Ohio, 1987—. Mem. mktg., advt. staff ChemLawn Corp., Columbus, 1980-84, corp. communications coord., 1984-87, residential mktg. and sales coord., 1987-88, mktg. mgr., 1988-89; mktg. mgr. CheckFree Corp., Westerville, Ohio, 1989-90; owner Carousel Mktg. Svcs., Columbus, Ohio, 1990—. Recipient Echo award Direct Mktg. Assn., N.Y.C., 1987-88, 88-89. Mem. NAFE, Am. Mktg. Assn., Am. Mgmt. Assn., Mid-Ohio Direct Mktg. Assn. Home: 5065 Shadycrest Rd Columbus OH 43229

WISHERT, JO ANN CHAPPELL, choral director; b. Carroll County, Va., July 10, 1951; d. Joseph Lenox and Helen Alata (Wagoner) Chappell; m. Clarence Hinnant Wishert, Jr., June 10, 1987; 1 child, Kelly Marie Greco. BA, Oral Roberts U., 1974; MS, Radford U., 1977; Degree in Advanced Postgrad Studies, Va. Poly. Inst. and State U., 1981; postgrad., U. S.C., Spartanburg, 1990. Cert. elem. music supr., Va., elem. and secondary music tchr., S.C., music tchr., ednl. specialist, N.C. Head start tchr. Rooftop of Va., Galax, 1975; elem. music tchr. Carroll County Pub. Schs., Hillsville, 1975-78; grad. asst., supr., course advisor Coll. Edn., Va. Poly. Inst. and State U., Blacksburg, 1975-81, pregrad. interviewer placement svcs., 1981-83; music dir. Heritage Acad., Charlotte, N.C., 1984-85, fine arts specialist, 1985-86; choral dir. Chester County Schs., Chester, S.C., 1986—; guest condr. workshop Patrick County Schs., Stuart, Va., 1980. Soloist PTL TV Network, Charlotte, 1984-85. Guest speaker on battered women and marital abuse to chs. and workshops; entertainer; mem. Arts Coun. Chester County, 1988—; mem. S.C. Arts Alliance and Arts Advocacy. Named Tchr. of Yr., Chester Sr. High Sch., 1989. Mem. Music Educators Nat. Conf., S.C. Music Educators Assn., S.C. Edn. Assn., Am. Ednl. Rsch. Assn., Assn. for Supervision and Curriculum Devel., Am. Assn. Choral Dirs., Chester County Edn. Assn., Nat. Assn. Secondary Music Edn. (team evaluator div. tchr. edn. cert. 1989), AAUW (by-laws com. Chester 1987—, sec. 1988-89), All USA Chorus Student Group (alumni), 4-H Club (life). Republican. Methodist. Home: 1122 Virginia Dare Dr Rock Hill SC 29730

WISHNICK, MARCIA MARGOLIS, pediatrician, geneticist; b. N.Y.C., Oct. 10, 1938; d. Hyman and Tillie (Stoller) Margolis; m. Stanley Wishnick, June 12, 1960; 1 child, Elizabeth Anne. BA, Barnard Coll., 1960; PhD, NYU, 1970, MD, 1974. Diplomate Am. Bd. Pediatrics. Rsch. technician Lederle Labs./Am. Cyanamid, Pearl River, N.Y., 1960-66; postdoctoral fellow N.Y. Pub. Health Lab., N.Y.C., 1970-71; resident in pediatrics Bellevue Med. Ctr. NYU, N.Y.C., 1974-77, asst. prof. pediatrics Bellevue Med. Ctr., 1977-82, clin. assoc. prof. pediatrics Bellevue Med. Ctr., 1982-87, clin. prof. pediatrics Bellevue Med. Ctr., 1987—; pvt. practice N.Y.C., 1977—. Contbr. articles to profl. jours. Fellow Nat. Bd. Med. Examiners, Am. Acad. Pediatrics; mem. N.Y. Pediatric Soc., N.Y. Med. Soc., N.Y. Women's Med. Assn., AMA, Am. Soc. Human Genetics. Office: 51 E 73d St New York NY 10021

WISNER, LINDA ANN, advertising agency executive, publishing company executive, interior designer; b. Sidney, N.Y., Apr. 28, 1951; d. Herbert and Ruth (Usher) W. B.A. in Theatre and Art, Macalester Coll., 1973, postgrad. in journalism, 1974; postgrad. in graphic design Mpls. Coll. Art and Design, 1973-74; postgrad. in advtg. and mktg. U. Minn., 1974. Designer, publs. asst. Macalester Coll., St. Paul, 1973-76; designer Stretch & Sew Inc., Eugene, Oreg., 1976-78; free-lance designer, Eugene, 1978-79; owner, creative dir. Wisner Assocs., Eugene, 1979-87, Portland, 1987—, Interludes, Eugene, 1981—; ptnr. Instant Interiors, Eugene, 1979-88; mktg. dir. Palmer/Pletsch Assocs., 1988—; chmn. Bus. Images Exhibit, Eugene, 1983. Author: Creative Serging for the Home; designer, editor booklet series: Instant Interiors, 1979-83 (Woodie award 1980-83); designer, illustrator: Palmer/Pletsch Sewing Books, 1981—. Ambassador, City of Eugene, 1985-87 ; bd. dirs. Maude Kerns Art Ctr., Eugene, 1984-85, Oreg. Repertory Theatre, 1986-87, Oreg. Sales and Mktg. Exec., 1986, Portland Culinary Alliance, 1989—. Nat. Merit scholar Macalester Coll., 1969. Mem. Designers' Forum (pres. 1983-84, Designer of Yr. 1983), Sales and Mktg. Execs., Graphic Artists Guild, Exec. Bus. Women (pres. 1983-84), Mid Oreg. Ad Club (numerous certs. and trophy 1980-85), Portlandia-Eugene C. of C. (M.V.P. Leadership Program award 1986). Avocations: design, illustration, soft sculpture, event planning, catering.

WISNESKI, MARY JO ELIZABETH, educator; b. Saginaw, Mich., Dec. 18, 1938; d. Walter Frank and Hedwig Josephine (Borowicz) W. BS, Cen. Mich. U., 1961; MS, So. Ill. U., 1969; EdD, U. No. Colo., 1979; postdoctoral, U. Calif., Berkeley, Calif., 1980-81. Cert. elem. educator, elem. adminstr., reading specialist, Calif. Elem. educator various schs., various cities, 1960-75; coll. instr. U. No. Colo., Greeley, 1976-78, 79; reading specialist Vacaville (Calif.) Unified Sch. Dist., 1980—; lectr. San Francisco State U., 1983-86; prof. Chapman Coll., Travis AFB, Calif., 1986-90, retired, 1990; cons. in field. Author: Clifford Books Teacher Manual, 1981. Vol. Am. Red Cross, Travis Air Museum, Travis AFB; bd. dirs. Polish Arts & Culture Found., San Francisco, 1988—, Vistula Dancers. Recipient Tchr. in Space Certificate NASA, 1986, Outstanding Tchr. Commendation Dept. of Defense, 1973. Mem. Internat. Reading Assn., Phi Delta Kappa, Calif. Edn. Assn. Home: 314 Creekview Ct Vacaville CA 95688

WISNIEWSKI, JUDITH LEE, manufacturing company executive; b. Milw., July 16, 1941; d. Harry J. and Margaret L. (Schlass) W. BA, Alverno Coll., 1963. Owner, founder Pelican Industries, Inc., Milw., 1974—; apprenticeship advisor Waukesha County (Wis.) Tech. Coll., 1980—. Mem. Soc. Plastic Engrs. Office: Pelican Industries Inc 2225 S 38th St Milwaukee WI 53215

WISOCKI, PATRICIA A., psychologist, educator; b. Detroit, Jan. 12, 1943; d. Peter Edward and Anne Elizabeth (Necelis) Wisocki; m. John Lester Tierney, Dec. 28, 1972. BA, Marygrove Coll., Detroit, 1965; MA, Boston Coll., 1967, PhD, 1971. Lic. psychologist, Mass. Rsch. asst. Cushing Hosp., Framingham, Mass., 1968-69; psychologist Medfield (Mass.) State Hosp., 1969-70; asst. prof. R.I. Community Coll., Providence, 1970-72; prof. psychology, dir. clin. tng. U. Mass., Amherst, 1972—; cons. VA Hosp., Northampton, Mass., 1972-76, Groden Devel. Ctr., Providence, 1978—, State of R.I. Mental Health Svcs., Providence, 1986-89. Editor: Handbook of Clinical Behavior Therapy for Elderly, 1990; contbr. numerous articles to profl. jours. and chpts. to books. Fellow Am. Psychol. Assn. (chmn. site visit team 1983—), Soc. for Behavior Rsch. and Therapy; mem. Assn. for Advancement Behavior Therapy (bd. profl. affairs 1987—). Deomcrat. Roman Catholic. Office: U Mass Tobin Hall Amherst MA 01003

WISS, TERI FRANCINE, occupational therapist, consultant; b. Dallas, Mar. 31, 1958; d. Marvin Jack Wiss and Harriet (Harris) Light; m. Rex Bentham Miller, June 30, 1977 (div. 1980); m. Gary William Hartz, June 8, 1985. BS, Tex. Women's U., 1982; MA, U. So. Calif., 1989. Registered occupational therapist. Occupational therapist Austin (Tex.) Devel. and Therapy Clinic, 1982-83, Austin (Tex.) Ind. Sch. Dist., 1983-86; adminstrv. asst., occupational trainee U. Affiliated Program, Children's Hosp. of L.A., 1986-87; ind. contractor, occupational therapist, rsch. assoc. Ayres Clinic, Torrance, Calif., 1987-89; ind. contractor, occupational therapist Therapy West, Culver City, Calif., 1987-89; occupational therapist, consultant Sunnyvale, Calif., 1989—; cons. Sensory Intergration Internat., Torrance, 1989—. Contbr. articles to profl. jours. Vol. coord. U.S. Senatorial Campaign, Austin, 1983; sec. First United Ch. Social Action Com., Austin, 1985-86. Mem. Am. Occupational Therapy Assn., Occupational Therapy Assn. Calif. (chair pub. relations Santa Clara County chpt.), Autism Soc. Am., Sensory Integration Internat., Children with Attention Deficit Disorder, Sierra Club. Democrat. Office: Box 2807 Sunnyvale CA 94087

WISSLER-THOMAS, CARRIE, professional society administrator, artist; b. Ephrata, Pa., Nov. 2, 1946; d. Robert Uibel and Grace Urbane (Nicholas) Wissler; m. James Richard Gamber, June 12, 1968 (div. 1972); m. Scott Kerry Thomas, Mar. 3, 1972; 1 child, Dylan Crayton Llewellyn. BA, Hood Coll., 1968; MS, Temple U., 1986. Copywriter WGSA Radio, Ephrata, Pa., 1970-71, William Assocs., Harrisburg, Pa., 1977; correspondent "Art Matters" of Phila., Harrisburg, 1984-86; art columnist "Pennsylvania Beacon", Harrisburg, 1983-85; writer "Strictly Business", Harrisburg, 1985-86; painting instr. Art Assn. of Harrisburg, 1980-86; artist freelance, Harrisburg, 1968—; exec. dir. Art Assn. of Harrisburg, 1986—; mem. exhbn. panel Harrisburg City Govt. Ctr., 1983—; mem. art adv. panel Harrisburg Area Community Coll., 1985—; mem. gallery com. Univ. Ctr. at Harrisburg, 1988—; chmn. Easter Seals Art Show by Disabled Artists, Harrisburg, 1983-86. Prin. work includes "Broadway Babies" oil painting, 1982 (Grumbacher Gold Medallion 1982); over 30 solo exhibitions. Mem. Hist. Soc. Cocalico Valley, Ephrata, 1982—, Dauphin County Hist. Soc., Harrisburg, 1986—; minority inspector Paxtang Election Bd., Harrisburg, 1977-79; mem. ACLU, Pa., 1988—. Mem. Nat. Mus. Women in Arts, Doshi Ctr. for Contemporary Art, Pa. Soc. Assn. Execs., Am. Coun. on Arts, Art Assn. Harrisburg (pres. 1980-84), Rotary. Democrat. Lutheran. Home: 3252 Ridgeway Rd Harrisburg PA 17109 Office: Art Assn of Harrisburg 21 N Front St Harrisburg PA 17101

WISSMANN, CAROL RENEÉ, sales executive; b. Berkeley, Calif., July 9, 1946; d. Conrad Clayton and Carol Elizabeth (Ward) W. BA, Whittier Coll., 1968; Diploma, Coll. Notre Dame, Belmont, 1970. Dist. mgr. U.S. C. of C., Washington; assoc. Robert Jameson Assn., Newport Bch., Calif.; sales person Abigail Abbott Personnel, Tustin, Calif.; sales rep. Nat. Write Your Congressman; div. mgr. Classified Yellow Pages Inc., Cookeville, Tenn., 1986; ind. contractor MacDonald Geary, Renton, Wa., 1986-88; pres. The BelleMann Corp., Redmond, Wa., 1988—. Mem. Nat. Assn. Female Execs., Women Bus. Owners. Republican. Home: 5109 Point Fosdick Dr NW Ste E-305 Gig Harbor WA 98335 Office: The Limited Addition of the Yellow Pages 16541 Redmond Wy Ste 220C Redmond WA 98052

WISSORE, EILEEN FRANCES, television station official; b. St. Louis, June 14, 1944; d. Roy I. and Doreen Ellen (Ashton) Maxey; m. Thornton William Wissore III, Sept. 2, 1967; children: David, Kimberly, Lisa. BS in Edn., SE Mo. State U., 1966. Sec. to men's dir. Bapt. World Alliance, Ft. Worth, 1983-84; traffic and promotion coord. Acts TV Network, Ft. Worth, 1984-87; nat. continuity dir. Sta. KXAS-TV, NBC, Ft. Worth, 1987—; co-instr. stage and video makeup local cable co., St. Louis, 1982. Contbr. stories and poems to various publs. Advisor, judge youth oratory contest St. Louis Bapt. Assn., 1982; former officer PTA, St. Louis; former leader Boy Scouts Am., Girl Scouts U.S.A., Camp Fire, Mo., Tex.; mem. Ft.Worth Youth Orch. Aux., High Sch. Band Boosters, High Sch. Athletic Boosters, Ft. Worth. Recipient award of appreciation Fgn. Mission Bd., So. Bapt. Ch., 1984, 89, Crowley High Sch. Band, 1989, 90. Mem. Mo. Hist. Soc., Madison County Geneal. Soc., Moniteau County Geneal. Soc. Home: 1320 Marlborough Dr Fort Worth TX 76134

WISWELL, EMILY MARY HULL, real estate broker; b. Port Angeles, Wash., Sept. 21, 1918; d. Jay Tenneyson and Emily Anne (Edwards) H.; m. Andrew M. Wiswell, Oct. 24, 1947; children: Andrew M. Jr., Harry Stevens II, Hank Fenderson. Student, U. Wash., 1935-37, El Capitan Coll. of Theatre, L.A., 1937-39, Aiken Tech. Coll., 1980, 81, 87, 88; AB, U. S.C., Aiken, 1988; MS, Realtors Inst., 1983. Cert. real estate broker and real estate appraiser. With Buchanan & Co. Advt. Agy., L.A., 1938-42, Davis & Bevin, L.A., 1942-44, Dancer Fitzgerald & Sample, N.Y.C., 1944-47; rep. fashion sales and costumes Doncaster, Aiken and Bronxville, N.Y., 1967-71, 73-76; owner, broker-in-charge Mary Wiswell GRI Properties, Ltd., Aiken, 1984—; dealer Lincoln Home Logs. Actress (stage): Sleep No More, 1945, Soldier's Wife, 1946, Find the Woman, 1946; (film) Swamp Woman, 1942; (radio) Dorothy Dix Series, 1945-47, Judy Jill and Johnny Musical, 1946-47; lead actress age 15 The Little Princess. Tchr. Sunday sch., Reformed Ch., Bronxville, 1951-71, chair Royal Crown Ball, 1953, chair bridge party for blind children's fund, 1954; chair, founder Lawrence Hosp. Women's Aux. Patients Svc., Bronxville, 1958; asst. town meetings, Westchester County, N.Y., 1958; den mother, scout leader Boy Scouts Am., 1959-67; sec. Rose Hill Art Ctr., Aiken, 1975-76; chair harness race Am. Cancer Soc., Aiken, 1976—; mem. Aiken Art Coun., 1984—. Recipient Univ. Scouting award, 1962; named Eagle Scout Mother Boy Scouts Am., Bronxville, 1970. Mem. Nat. Assn. Realtors, S.C. Bd. Realtors, Aiken Bd. Realtors, Augusta/North Augusta Bd. Realtors, Panhellenic Assn., Internat. Orgn. Real Estate Appraisers, Wykagl C. of C., Siwanoy C. of C., Aiken Tennis Club, Pinnacle Club of Augusta, Green Boundary Club of Aiken, Alpha Chi Omega. Republican. Episcopalian. Home: 40 Lundee Ct Aiken SC 29801 Office: 327 Park Ave SW Aiken SC 29801

WITH, DAPHNE MARINA, management information analyst; b. St. John's, Can., Dec. 4, 1939; d. Arthur and Evelyn Mary (Kearley) Tuck; m. K. Ritchie D. With, Oct. 26, 1968; 1 child, K.A. Gregory. RN, Toronto (Ont.) East Gen. Hosp., Can., 1960. Various nursing positions Midland, Ont., Toronto, 1960-70; temp. staff Polysar Ltd., Sarnia, Ont., 1977-84, risk mgmt. info. analyst, 1984—. Mem. Progressive Party. Anglican. Office: Polysar Ltd, Vidal St S, Sarnia, ON Canada N7T 7M2

WITHAEGER, ROSEMARY ANN, civic volunteer, flight attendant; b. Chgo., Oct. 2, 1949; d. Edwin Louis and Marjorie Louise (Montgomery) W. Degree in nursing, Cook County Hosp., 1973. RN, Ill. Staff nurse Cook County Hosp., Chgo., 1973-76; charge nurse, staff nurse Northwest Community Hosp., Arlington Heights, Ill., 1976-80; flight attendant Northwest Airlines, Mpls., 1980—; model and product spokesperson, Chgo., 1980—. Vol., chmn. transitional living programs Ctr. for Abused Children, Chgo., 1986—; vol. Columbus-Maryville Children's Ctr., Chgo., Cabrini Alive Rehab., Chgo. Recipient Vol. award Transitional Living Programs, 1988. Mem. Chgo. Health and Tennis Club. Presbyterian. Home: 663 W Barry Apt K Chicago IL 60657 Office: Northwest Airlines 2700 Lone Oak Pkwy Eagan MN 55111

WITHERBEE-OLSON, VICKIE DIANNE, product manager; b. Chanute AFB, Ill., Sept. 25, 1953; d. Norman James and Margarette M. (Knapp) Witherbee; m. Stepen Edward Olson, Mar. 5, 1988. Student, George Fox Coll., Newberg, Oreg., 1977-79, SUNY New Paltz, 1979, Coll. Legal Arts, Portland, Oreg., 1989-90, Lewis & Clarke Coll., 1990—. From tech. clk. to project documentation librarian Intel Corp., Hillsboro, Oreg., 1980-82; ops. mgr., product mgr. Infosphere, Inc., Portland, Oreg., 1982-87; bus. systems analyst Cen. Point Software, Portland, Oreg., 1987-88; legal asst. Lane, Powell, Spears, Lubersky, Portland, 1990—. Author, editor, Sphere Programmer's Manual, 1982-83, Macserve, Laser Serve, 1984-87. Sgt. USAF, 1973-76. Mem. American Legion Women's Aux., American Legion, Nat. Assn. Female Execs. Home: 3132 SW Bvtn Hilsdale Portland OR 97201

WITHERS, BARBARA ANN, editor; b. Wichita, Kans., June 23, 1939; d. Robert R. and Mary (Stryker) W. BA, Whitman Coll., Walla Walla, Wash., 1961; MRE, Union Theol. Sem., N.Y.C., 1964; EdD, Columbia U., 1975. Dir. children's wk. Winnetka (Ill.) Congl. Ch., 1964-66; dir. middle sch. Riverside Ch., N.Y.C., 1966-72; interim dir. Christian edn., 1973; freelance ednl. cons. N.Y.C., 1973-75; editor ednl. resources Presbyn. Ch. U.S.A., N.Y.C., 1975-89; freelance editor and writer, 1989--. Editor: The Pilgrim Press, 1990—; editor/writer: Language about God in Liturgy and Scripture: A Study Guide, 1980, Language and the Church: Articles and Designs for Workshops, 1984, others; contbr. articles to profl. jours. Mem. Religious Edn. Assn., Assn. United Ch. Educators, NAFE, Orgn. for Study of Communication, Lang. and Gender. Home: 380 Riverside Dr Apt 7E New York NY 10025

WITHERS, LINDA CAROL, health care center administrator; b. St. Louis, Sept. 20, 1948; d. Richard Earl and Irene Maxine (Pearce) Withers. AB, U. Mo., 1970; MSW, Washington U., St. Louis, 1979; cert. in gerontology, St. Louis U., 1979. Cert. Am. Acad. Cert. Social Workers. Educator Hazelwood (Mo.) Sch. Dist., 1972-73; recreational therapist Jewish Ctr. for Aged, St. Louis, 1973-74, dir. recreational therapy, 1974, social svc. dir., 1974-81, asst. dir., 1981-85, assoc. dir., 1985-88; adminstr. McGuffey Health Care Ctr., Gadsden, Ala., 1988—, also bd. dirs., 1988—; part-time faculty mem. George Warren Brown Sch. Social Work, Washington U., 190-85, Lindenwood Coll., St. Louis, 1987-88. Sec., Etowah County Coun. Aging, Gadsden, 1988—; pres. Mo. Assn. Prevention of Adult Abuse, 1984-86. Recipient award United Way Greater St. Louis, 1987, St. Louis Area Agy. on Aging, 1987. Fellow Am. Coll. Health Care Adminstrs. (cert., pres. 1990), Gerontol. Assn., Nat. Assn. Social Work, Ala. Nursing Home Assn., Lions. Home: 209 Westminster Dr Gadsden AL 35901 Office: MdGuffey Health Care Ctr 2301 Rainbow Dr Gadsden AL 35901

WITHERSPOON, AUDREY GOODWIN, educational administrator; b. Greenwood, S.C., Aug. 19, 1949; d. Hudson and Essie Lue (Chenault) Goodwin; m. Lavern Witherspoon, Nov. 25, 1983; children: Jacintha Dyan, Andre LaVern. BA, Lander Coll., Greenwood, S.C., 1971; MEd, Clemson U., 1975; postgrad., Vanderbilt U., 1982-83. Cert. elem. tchr., S.C. Elem. tchr. McCormick (S.C.) Sch. Dist., 1971-72; social worker Greenwood, Laurens, Edgefield, Abbeville, Anderson, McCormick and Saluda (GLEAAMS) Head Start, Greenwood, 1972-73, parent coord., 1973-74, edn. dir., 1974-75; child devel. dir. GLEAAMS Human Resource Commn., Greenwood, 1975-90; region coord. Gov.'s Task Force for Citizen Participation, Columbia, S.C., 1979-82; mem. Gov.'s Ednl. Transition Team, Columbia, 1983-84; mem. State Adv. Com. on Regulation of Day Care Facilities, Columbia, 1987-89, S.C. Pub. Pvt. Child Care Coun., 1990. Trustee, Greenwood Sch. Dist. #50, 1977-90. Named to Outstanding Young Women Am., 1974, 82. Mem. Nat. Assn. for Edn. of Young Children, S.C. Assn. Child Devel. Providers (pres. 1987-88), NAACP (sec.-treas. local br. 1974-88, svc. award 1988). Home: 131 Valley Rd Greenwood SC 29646 Office: GLEAAMS Human Resource Comm PO Box 1326 Greenwood SC 29648

WITHERSPOON, FREDDA LILLY, educator; b. Houston; d. Fred D. and Vanita E. (Meredith) Lilly; AB, Bishop Coll.; MSW, Washington U., St. Louis, MA in Guidance and Counseling, MA in Ednl. Psychology, PhD, St. Louis U., 1965; m. Robert L. Witherspoon; children: Robert L., Vanita. Social worker, supr. St. Louis City Welfare Office, Homer G. Phillips Hosp.; tchr. English, guidance counselor St. Louis Pub. Schs.; prof. student personnel services Forest Park Community Coll., St. Louis, 1965—; cons. Ednl. Testing Service, Princeton, N.J., Head Start program, 1965-68; counseling cons. St. Louis Job Corps Center for Women, 1966-68. V.p. St. Louis chpt. NAACP, 1969-83, pres. Mo. Conf., 1973-84, also organizer Forest Park young adult coun., also bd. dirs.; mem. Challenge of 70's Crime Commn., 1970-75; mem. adv. coun., Central Inst. for Deaf, 1970-78; mem. exec. bd. Mayor's St. Louis Ambassadors; mem. Mayor's Coun. Youth, 1970-75; dir. teens fund drive March of Dimes, 1960-72, Lily Day drive for Crippled Children, 1966-72; mem. speakers bur. United Way, 1969-82; bd. dirs. children's services City of St. Louis; exec. bd. Mo. Heart Assn.; bd. dirs. United Negro Coll. Fund; bd. dirs. Social Health Assn., Conservatory Assn. Schs. for Arts, St. Louis Heart Assn., Girl Scouts; pres. St. Louis Met. YWCA, 1978-79, bd. dirs. St. Louis Urban League, vice chmn., 1977-81; organizer Jr. Annie Malone Service Guild; active St. Louis Ambassadors, Jr. League Community Adv. Bd., St. Louis, Salvation Army Adv. Coun. Named Woman of Year, Greyhound Bus Corp., 1967, St. Louis Argus, 1968, Nat. Outstanding Woman, Iota Phi Lambda, 1970; named Outstanding Woman of Achievement, Globe Dem., 1970, Outstanding Educator of Am., 1971, Nat. Top Lady Distinction, 1974; recipient Negro History award, 1971; George Washington Carver award, 1976; Health and Welfare Council award, 1975; Vol. of Yr. award United Negro Coll. Fund.; Continental Socs. award, 1984. Mem. NAACP (life; Nat. Outstanding Youth Adv. 1977, numerous awards 1977-88), Am. Assn. for Counseling and Devel., AAUP (pres. 1975-81), AAUW, Am. Vocational Guidance Assn., Assn. Measurement and Evaluation in Guidance, Nat. Assn. Jr. Colls., Nat. Faculty Assn. Jr. Colls., LWV, Nat. Coun. Negro Women (life), Mo. Assn. Social Welfare, Jack and Jill, Nat. Bar Assn., Mound City Bar Aux. (founder, pres. 1946-49), Nat. Assn. Women Lawyers, Nat. Assn. Bench and

Bar Spouses (founder, pres.), Top Ladies of Distinction (organizer Met. St. Louis chpt. founder), Metro St. Louis Inter-Alumni Coun. of UNCF, Continental Socs. (founder Met. St. Louis chpt.), The Links, Inc. (Gateway chpt.), Urban League Guild, Kappa Delta Pi, Iota Phi Lambda (nat. pres. 1977-81), Sigma Gamma Rho, Pi Lambda Theta, Phi Delta Kappa, Kappa Delta Pi. Office: St Louis Community Coll 20 Lewis Pl Saint Louis MO 63113

WITHROW, LUCILLE MONNOT, nursing home administrator; b. Alliance, Ohio, July 28, 1923; d. Charles Edward Monnot and Freda Aldine (Guy) Monnot Cameron; m. Alvin Robert Withrow, June 6, 1945 (dec. 1984); children: Cindi Withrow Hargrave, Nancy Withrow Townley, Sharon Withrow Hodgkins, Wendel Alvin. AA in Health Adminstrn., Eastfield Coll., 1976. Lic. nursing home adminstr., Tex. Held various clerical positions Dallas, 1950-72; office mgr., asst. adminstr. Christian Care Ctr. Nursing Home, Mesquite, Tex., 1972-76; head adminstr. Christian Care Ctr. Nursing Home and Retirement Complex, Mesquite, 1976—; mem. com. on geriatric curriculum devel., Eastfield Coll., Mesquite, 1979, 87. Recipient Volunteerism award, Tex. Atty. Gen., 1987. Mem. Tex. Assn. Homes for Aging, Am. Assn. Homes for Aging, White Rock Kiwanis. Republican. Mem. Ch. of Christ. Home: 11344 Lippitt Ave Dallas TX 75218 Office: Christian Care Ctr 1000 Wiggins Pkwy Mesquite TX 75150

WITHROW, LYDIA BRIZICKY, nurse; b. New Haven, Sept. 5, 1958; d. George Konstantine and Anna Nicholievna (Sobolewski) Brizicky; m. John Clarence Withrow, Oct. 7, 1989. BS in Psychology, BA in Anthropology, U. Mass., Boston, 1980; BS in Nursing, U. Mass., 1986. RN. Rsch. asst. psychology dept. U. Mass., Boston, 1977-80; retail mgr. Lee Jay Inc., dba Bed & Bath, Norwood, Mass., 1981-84; admitting emergency clk. Somerville (Mass.) Hosp., 1984-86; med./surg. nurse VA Med. Ctr., Boston, 1986-87, Nantucket (Mass.) Cottage Hosp., 1987; intensive care nurse Mt. Auburn Hosp., Cambridge, Mass., 1987-89; surg. intensive care nurse VA Med. Ctr., Lexington, Ky., 1989—. Participating photographer show of Venetian photography, 1990. Mem. Am. Assn. Critical Care Nurses, Ky. Assn. Critical Care Nurses. Russian Orthodox. Home: 2200 Richmond Rd 418 Lexington KY 40502

WITHROW, MARY ELLEN, state treasurer; b. Marion, Ohio, Oct. 2, 1930; d. Clyde Welsh and Mildred (Stump) Hinamon; m. Norman David Withrow, Sept. 4, 1948; children: Linda Rizzo, Leslie Legge, Norma, Rebecca. Mem. Elgin Local Bd. Edn., Marion, Ohio, 1969-72, pres., 1972; safety programs dir. ARC, Marion, 1968-72; dep. registrar State of Ohio, Marion, 1972-75; dep. county auditor Marion County, Ohio, 1975-77, county treas., 1977-83; treas. State of Ohio, Columbus, 1983—; chmn. Ohio State Bd. Deposits, from 1983. Mem. exec. com., resolutions com., co-chair farm crisis task force Dem. Nat. Com., Anthony Commn. on Pub. Fin.; mem. Met. Women's Ctr., Nat. Women's Polit. Caucus; pres. Marion County Dem. Club, 1976; participant Harvard U. Strategic Leadership '90 Conf. Inducted Ohio Women's Hall of Fame, 1986; named Outstanding Elected Dem. Woman Holding Pub. Office, Nat. Fedn. Dem. Women, 1987, Advocate of Yr. U.S. Small Bus. Adminstrn., 1988; fellow Women Execs. in State Govt., Harvard U., 1987; recipient Most Valuable State Pub. Ofcl. award City and State Newspaper, 1990. Mem. LWV, State Assn. County Treas. (legis. chmn. 1979-83, treas. 1982), Nat. Assn. State Treas. (v.p. midwest region 1983, sr. v.p.), Nat. Assn. State Auditors Compts. and Treas. (pres.), Coun. of State Govts. (exec. com., budget com.), Women Execs. in State Govt. (membership com.), Women Entrepreneurs, Inc., Altrusa (hon.), Delta Kappa Gamma (hon. Ohio mem.), Delta Sigma Pi (hon.). Club: Bus. and Profl. Women's. Office: State of Ohio Treasury Dept 30 E Broad St 9th Fl Columbus OH 43215

WITHROW-GALLANTER, SHERRIE ANNE, construction and audio company executive; b. Sacramento, Mar. 10, 1960; d. Jim and Ilene (James) Withrow; m. Michael Paul Gallanter, Jan. 7, 1990. Student, Diablo Valley Community Coll., Pleasant Hill, Calif., 1977, Tarrant County Jr. Coll., Ft. Worth, 1982-83, Coll. of Marin, Kentfield, Calif., 1988; AA in Bus. Adminstrn. and Mgmt., St. Louis Community Coll., Florissant, Mo., 1981. Internal cashier AAA Automobile Club Mo., St. Louis, 1977-79; receiving clk. Dayton-Hudson Target Stores, Florissant and Ft. Worth, 1979-81; supr. credit and collection World Svc. Life Ins. Co., Ft. Worth, 1982-83; bank br. balancer, data processing div. Tex. Am. Bank Svcs., Inc., Ft. Worth, 1984-85; asst. to contr. Positive Video-Post Prodn., Orinda, Calif., 1985-87; with contractor's desk Shell Oil Co., Martinezz, Calif., 1987-88; asst. to chief fin. officer J.T. Thorpe & Son, Inc., Richmond, Calif., 1988-89; gen. ptnr. HomeVisions, Oakland, Calif., 1989—; project fin. cons. various constrn. cos., Oakland and San Francisco, 1988—; founder, gen. ptnr. AudioVisions, Oakland, Calif., 1990—. Fundraiser Sr. Citizen Subsidized Housing Complex, Martinez, 1987, 88. Mem. NAFE, Phi Theta Kappa. Democrat. Office: HomeVisions PO Box 20918 Oakland CA 94620-0918

WITKIN, EVELYN MAISEL, geneticist; b. N.Y.C., Mar. 9, 1921; d. Joseph and Mary (Levin) Maisel; m. Herman A. Witkin, July 9, 1943 (dec. July 1979); children—Joseph, Andrew. A.B., N.Y. U., 1941; M.A., Columbia U., 1943, Ph.D., 1947; D.Sc. honoris causa, N.Y. Med. Coll., 1978. Mem. staff genetics dept. Carnegie Inst., Washington, 1950-55; mem. faculty State U. N.Y. Downstate Med. Center, Bklyn., 1955-71; prof. medicine State U. N.Y. Downstate Med. Center, 1968-71; prof. biol. scis. Douglass Coll., Rutgers U., 1971-79, Barbara McClintock prof. genetics, 1979—. Author articles; mem. editorial bds. profl. jours. Postdoctoral fellow Am. Cancer Soc., 1947-49; fellow Carnegie Instn., 1957; Selman A. Waksman lectr., 1960; Phi Beta Kappa vis. scholar, 1980-81; grantee NIH, 1956-89; recipient Prix Charles Leopold Mayer French Acad. Scis., 1977, Lindback award, 1979. Fellow AAAS; mem. Nat. Acad. Scis., Am. Acad. Arts and Scis., Environ. Mutagen Soc., Am. Genetics Soc., Am. Soc. Microbiology, Radiation Research Soc. Home: 88 Balcort Dr Princeton NJ 08540 Office: Rutgers U Waksman Inst Microbiology Piscataway NJ 08854

WITKIN, MILDRED HOPE FISHER, psychotherapist, educator; b. N.Y.C.; d. Samuel and Sadie (Goldschmidt) Fisher; AB, Hunter Coll., MA, Columbia U., 1968; PhD, NYU, 1973; children: Georgia Hope, Roy Thomas, Laurie Phillips; m. Jorge Radovic, Aug. 26, 1983. Diplomate Am. Bd. Sexology. Head counselor Camp White Lake, Camp Emanuel, Long Beach, N.J.; tchr. econs., polit. sci. Hunter Coll. High Sch.; dir., group leader follow-up program Jewish Vacation Assn., N.Y.C.; investigator N.Y.C. Housing Authority; psychol. counselor Montclair State Coll., Upper Montclair, N.J., 1967-68; mem., lectr. Creative Problem-Solving Inst., U. Buffalo, 1968; psychol. counselor Fairleigh Dickinson U., Teaneck, N.J., 1968, dir. Counseling Center, 1969-74; pvt. practice psychotherapy, N.Y.C., also Westport, Conn.; sr. faculty supr., family therapist and psychotherapist Payne Whitney Psychiat. Clinic, N.Y. Hosp., 1973—; clin. asst. prof. dept. psychiatry Cornell U. Med. Coll., 1974—; assoc. dir. sex therapy and edn. program Cornell-N.Y. Hosp. Med. Ctr., 1974—; sr. cons. Kaplan Inst. for Evaluation and Treatment of Sexual Disorders, 1981—; supr. master's and doctoral candidates, NYU, 1975-82; pvt. practice psychotherapy and sex therapy, N.Y.C., also Westport, Conn.; cons. counselor edn. tng. programs N.Y.C. Bd. Edn., 1971-75; cons. Health Info. Systems, 1972-79; vis. prof. numerous colls. and univs.; chmn. sci. com. 1st Internat. Symposium on Female Sexuality, Buenos Aires, 1984; exhibited in group shows at Scarsdale (N.Y.) Art Show, 1959, Red Shutter Art Studio, Long Beach, 1968. Edn. legislation chmn. PTA, Yonkers, 1955; publicity chmn. United Jewish Appeal, Scarsdale, 1959-65; Scarsdale chmn. mothers com. Boy Scouts Am., 1961-64; mem. Morrow Assn. on Correction N.J., 1969—. Recipient Bronze medal for services Hunter Coll.; United Jewish Appeal plaque, 1962; Founders Day award N.Y. U., 1973; diplomate Am. Coll. sexologists. Fellow Internat. Council Sex Edn. and Parenthood of Am. U.; mem. Am. Psychol. Assn., AAUW, Women's Med. Assn. N.Y.C., Am. Coll. Personnel Assn. (nat. mem. commn. II 1973-76), Nat. Assn. Women Deans and Counselors, Am. Assn. Sex Educators, Counselors and Therapists (regional bd., nat. accreditation bd., cert. internat. supr.), Soc. for Sci. Study Sex Therapy and Rsch., Eastern Assn. Sex Therapists, Am. Assn. Marriage and Family Counselors, N.J. Assn. Marriage and Family Counselors, Ackerman Family Inst., Am. Personnel and Guidance Assn., Am., N.Y., N.J. psychol. assns., Creative Edn. Found., Am. Assn. Higher Edn., Assn. Counselor Supervision and Edn., Profl. Women's Caucus, LWV, Am. Women's Med. Assn., Nat. Council on Women in Medicine, Argentine Soc. Human Sexuality (hon.), Am. Assn. Sexology (diplomate), Pi Lambda Theta, Kappa Delta Pi, Alpha Chi Alpha. Author: 45-And Single Again, 1985. Contbr. articles to profl. jours. and textbooks; lectr. internat. workshops, radio and TV. Home and Office: 9 Sturges Commons Westport CT 06880

WITKIN-LANOIL, GEORGIA HOPE, psychologist, lecturer, author. Student Wellesley Coll., 1961-63; B.A. in Sociology, Barnard Coll., 1965; postgrad. in elem. edn. Hunter Coll., 1967-69; M.A. in Psychology, New Sch. for Social Research, 1970, Ph.D. in Psychology, 1977. Lic. clin. psychologist, N.Y. State. Asst. producer Grey Advt., N.Y.C., 1966-68; teaching asst. New Sch. for Social Research, 1968-69; adj. lectr. Lehman Coll., CUNY, 1971-72; assoc. prof. dept. social and behavioral sci. SUNY-Valhalla, 1972—, mem. vis. faculty criminal justice dept., 1972—; supr. residency program human sexuality program Mt. Sinai Sch. Medicine, N.Y.C., 1982—; former mem. vis. faculty U. Conn., NYU Coll. Dentistry, also others; assoc. prof. psychology Westchester Community Coll., Valhalla; presenter at profl. confs., also papers; pvt. practice clin. psychology, Scarsdale, N.Y. and N.Y.C.; appeared on various TV shows including Donahue, Today Show, Hour Mag. Author: The Female Stress Syndrome, 1984 (also Dutch, Japan, German, English, Spanish and Australian edits.); Coping with Stress; Human Sexuality; The Male Stress Syndrome, 1986. columnist Your Emotional Best, Health Mag., also mem. editorial adv. bd.; mem. editorial adv. bd. Jour. Preventive Psychiatry. Contbr. articles to profl. publs., mags. and newspapers. Mem. steering com. Westchester Community Coll. Found., 1973-75. Mem. AAAS, Soc. for Sex Therapy and Research, Westchester County Psychol. Assn., N.Y. Acad. Scis., Am. Assn. Sex Educators, Counselors and Therapists (cert. sex educator; mem. regional bd., exec. com.), Am. Assn. for Profl. Law Enforcement, Mensa, Criminal Justice Educators Assn. N.Y. State, Am. Soc. Criminology, World Future Soc., N.Y. State United Tchrs., Eastern Psychol. Assn., Am. Med. Writers Assn. Home: 8 E 83d St Apt 3A New York NY 10028-0418 Office: Mt Sinai Med Coll Dept Psychiat New York NY 10053

WITNAUER, ERICKA, advertising agency executive; b. Phila.. Student, U. Del., U. Rochester. Former sr. v.p., now exec. v.p. Saatchi & Saatchi Advt., N.Y.C. Office: Saatchi & Saatchi Advt 375 Hudson St New York NY 10014*

WITSIL, ELIZABETH SMITH ALISON (MRS. WALTER EARLE WITSIL), former social worker; b. Wilmington, Del., Sept. 13, 1909; d. Alexander and Katharine Anna (Smith) Alison; A.B., Wilson Coll., 1931; postgrad. Columbia U., 1934-36; m. Walter Earle Witsil, Aug. 27, 1938 (dec. Feb. 1964); 1 child, Adah Elizabeth Witsil Unger; step-children: Walter Earle, Sarah Virginia Witsil Lloyd. Accounting clk. Remington Rand, Inc., Bridgeport, Conn., 1932-33; social case-worker Bridgeport Br.-New Eng. Home for Little Wanderers, 1933-36; social case worker Conn. Children's Aid Soc., Danbury, 1936-38; dir. membership, pub. relations and publicity YWCA, Bridgeport, 1964-75; dir. cultural tours and vols. Bridgeport Mus. Arts, Sci. and Industry, 1975-83. Mem. Bd. Fin. Fairfield (Conn.), 1955-79; mem. Fairfield Rep. Town Meeting, 1947-55; pres. bd. mgrs. Woodfield Maternity Home and Adoption Service, Bridgeport, 1954-57, mem. corp.; bd. dirs. Vis. Nurse Assn. Bridgeport, United Fund Council Eastern Fairfield County, Bridgeport Council Ch. Women, Child Guidance Center of Bridgeport, Conn. Conf. Social Work, Mountain Grove Cemetery Assn., Bridgeport; v.p. Fairfield Community Services; trustee Greater Bridgeport Symphony Soc., 1978—; mem. Sr. Citizens Tax Relief Com., Fairfield, 1980-85, Sr. Citizens Life Center Study and Bldg. Com., 1981-84; bd. assos. U. Bridgeport; mem. Republican Women's Assn. Fairfield. Mem. AAUW, LWV, DAR, Inst. for Ret. Profls., Bridgeport Hosp. Aux. (pres. 1961-63), Delta Kappa Gamma (hon.). Presbyterian (trustee, elder). Clubs: Contemporary (sec. 1957-64, pres. 1976), Wilson Coll. Home: 235 Millard St Apt C3 Fairfield CT 06430

WITSMAN, STARLA DIANNE, municipal official; b. Carbondale, Ill., Apr. 1, 1952; d. James Erwin and Beverly Ann (Cawvey) Harris; m. Sonny Witsman, Aug. 8, 1970; children: Amy Leigh, Tina Renee, Kristi Lyn, Clinton Matthew. Student, Bob Jones U., 1969-70. Cert. occupancy specialist. Salesperson, cashier Boston Store, Watseka, Ill., 1969-70; asst. dir. Grace Baptist Day Care, Kankakee, Ill., 1976-78; sec. First Baptist Ch., Pecatonica, Ill., 1978-84; clk. typist Altoona (Pa.) Housing Authority, 1988-89, tenant selection supr., 1989—; cert. occupancy specialist Nat. Ctr. Housing Mgmt., Washington, 1989—. Pres. Victory Assn. Women's Fellowship, Ill., 1983-85; tchr., leader Children's Ch./Awana, Ill. and Pa., 1987—. Mem. NAFE. Office: Altoona Housing Authority 1100 11th St PO Box 671 Altoona PA 16603

WITT, CATHLEEN M., health facility administrator; b. Dover, Del., Feb. 17, 1964; d. Charles Leroy and Cynthia (Keen) Witt. BA, York Coll. Pa., 1985; student, Wilmington Grad. Ctr. Cert. paramedic, Pa. Paramedic supr. Sacred Heart Med. Ctr., Chester, Pa., staff paramedic; staff paramedic Meml. Hosp., York, Pa.; asst. mgr. Household Fin. Co., York, Pa.; assoc. instr. Del. State Fire Sch. Mem. Del. County Paramedic Assn., Am. Heart Assn. Del., Speaker's Bur. Home: 604 Orchard Dr Wilmington DE 19803

WITT, DORLEEN EMMA, retired home economist; b. Monona, Iowa, Mar. 26, 1923; d. Emil Frederick and Amelia Dorothea (Schultz) Aulerich; m. Donald Charles Witt, Aug. 7, 1946 (dec. Feb. 1971); children: William George, Carol Sue, Donna Jean. BS in Home Econs., Iowa State U., 1944; postgrad., U. No. Iowa, 1972. Cert. tchr., Iowa. Tchr. home econs. high sch. Durant, Iowa, 1944-45; tchr. home econs. high sch. Elkader, Iowa, 1945-47, substitute tchr., 1964-72; substitute tchr. St. Louis Pub. Schs., 1947-48; consumer rep. Interstate Power Co., Oelwein, Iowa, 1974-88, ret., 1988. Pres. Oelwein Area Coun. Chs., 1987-90; dir. info. Alliance for Mentally Ill.; vol. United Way, other community and ch. orgns. Mem. Iowa Home Econs. Assn., Ret. Tchrs. Assn., Iowa Button Collectors Club, P.E.O. (officer chpt.), T.T.T. (historian 1985-90, chpt. D.E.). Methodist.

WITT, GEORGIA STRONG, poet, writer; b. Balt., Oct. 23, 1923; d. Theodore and Tasie (Shaak) Strong; m. William Wallace Witt, June 18, 1945; (div. 1967); 1 child, Anne Lord. BS, Trenton (N.J.) State Coll., 1945. Part-time tech. Princeton (N.J.) U.; editor-in-chief, The Chatham Chatter Literary Mag., Chatham, N.J.,1940-41, The Seal, Coll. Year book, Trenton State Coll, Trenton, N.J., 1944-45, The Open Book, Newsletter, Unitarian Ch. Princeton, N.J., 1960-63, Bits from the Chowder Bowl, Princeton U., N.J., 1986. Recipient 1st prize 1st All-Coll. Poetry Contest, 1944, 1st prize Nat. Am. Scene Poetry Contest Poetry Soc. Colo., 1947. Republican.

WITT, HELEN MERCER, government official, lawyer; b. Atlantic City, July 13, 1933; m. Edward A. Witt; 5 children. B.A., Dickinson Coll., 1955; J.D., U. Pitts., 1969. Mem. law firms Cleland, Hurtt & Witt, and Witt & Witt, 1970-74; asst. to chmn. U.S. Steel Corp./United Steelworkers Am. Bd. Arbitration, 1975-82, mem. Nat. Mediation Bd., 1983-88, chmn., 1984, 87; chmn. Iron Ore Industry Bd. Arbitration, 1989—; pvt. practice artibration, 1989—. Office: 108 Hawthorne Ave Pittsburgh PA 15205

WITT, KATHRYN LISA, project control specialist, real estate owner; b. Aurora, Colo., June 8, 1963; d. Arvid Vilas and Barbara Jean (Cassetty) W. BS, Colo. State U., Ft. Collins., 1985; MBA, U. Denver, Denver, 1988--. Coordinator title dept. Security Title Guaranty Co., Denver, 1985-86; project control specialist real estate Security Pacific Mortgage, Real Estate Svc., Inc., Denver, 1986-88; commercial loan analyst Rothschild Fin. Corp., Denver, 1988-89; project control specialist, real estate owned United Banks Colo., Inc., Denver., 1989—. Underwriting chair KRMA-TV auction com., Denver, 1988—, big money run chair, 1987, mktg. chair wine tasting party com., 1988-89. Mem. Comml. Real Estate Women, Alpha Phi Alumni. Office: United Banks Colo 1700 Lincoln St Denver CO 80274-0122

WITT, SALLY ELEANOR, psychologist, professor; b. Indpls.; d. Boyd and Eleanor (Huffman) Gurley; m. Donald W. Witt (dec. 1987); children: Leslie, Alison, Donald. BA, Calif. State U., Fullerton, 1965; MEd, Nat. Coll. Edn., 1974; PhD, Northwestern U., 1985. Dir. Deerfield (Ill.) Community Nursery Sch., 1966-69; instructional specialist Northbrook (Ill.) Sch. Dist., 1969-70; prof. Oakton Community Coll., Des Plaines, Ill., 1980—; pvt. practice Wheeling, Ill., 1985—; Bd. dirs. Chgo. Psychol. Assn., 1990. Producer (audiotapes) Counseling Psychology Self Hypnosis Tapes, 1989. Mem. Am. Psychol. Assn., Am. Soc. Clin. Hypnosis, Assn. For Humanistic Psychology. Office: Oakton Community Coll 1600 E Golf Rd Des Plaines IL 60016

WITT, SANDRA SMITH, federal agency official; b. Rockwood, Tenn., Aug. 27, 1944; d. William Perry and Imogene C. Smith; children: Whitney, Christian. Student, U. Chattanooga, 1966-67; AS in Nuclear Technology, Chattanooga State Tech. Coll., 1976; BS in Physics, U. Tenn., 1978; MS in Engring. Sci., U. Tenn. Space Inst., 1982. Cert. nuclear equipment qualification engr., Ala. Tech. writer, editor Tenn. Blue Cross-Blue Shield, Chattanooga, 1966-68; supr. editing dept. Copr. Law Firm, Chattanooga, 1968-77; asst. physics lab. U. Tenn., Chattanooga, 1977-78; oil field engr. Schlumberger Co., Houston, 1978; research assoc. U. Tenn. Space Inst., Tullahoma, Tenn., 1979-81; sr. project engr. Wyle Labs., Huntsville, Ala., 1981-82; sr. engr., br. chief U.S. Dept. Energy, Aiken, S.C., 1983—. Recipient spl. svc. award Dept. Energy, 1986, 87, 90, career award Nat. Bus. and Profl. Women, 1977; Diuguid fellow, 1976. Mem. NAFE, Am. Nuclear Soc., Fed. Womens' Program Adv. Coun., Phi Theta Kappa (past v.p.), Sigma Pi Sigma.

WITTENBERNS, MICHELLE-MAY, health club chain executive; b. Port Huron, Mich., Apr. 9, 1960; d. Wilson Joseph and Ethel Rose may; m. Joseph Roger Wittenberns, Feb. 18, 1956. AA, Northwood Inst., Midland, Mich., 1980. Asst. mgr. Winkelmans, Port Huron, 1980-81; coord. modeling sch. and fashion show, mdse. mgr. Ron Lendzions, Port Huron, 1981-83; self-employed clothing designer, Port Huron, 1983-84; v.p. Tex. Lady-Texan Spas, Houston, 1985-89, Lady of Am. Fitness Franchises, Woodland, Tex., 1989—. Mem. Nat. Assn. Female Execs., Alpha Sigma Tau. (dist. pres. beta chpt. 1982). Republican. Roman Catholic. Office: Tex Lady Texan Spas/Lady of Am 25231 Grogans Mill #308 The Woodlands TX 77380

WITTER, DIANA GONSER, public relations professional; b. Omaha, June 5, 1930; d. Bruce Winfred and Helen Marie (Vincent) Gonser; m. Richard P. DeVere, Aug. 30, 1952 (div. 1975); children: Scott Page DeVere, Denise DeVere Bauer, Don William DeVere II; m. Richard S. Witter, June 14, 1986. BS, Ohio State U., 1952. Housing asst. Ohio State U., Columbus, 1952-53; personnel asst. First Community Village, Columbus, 1970-72, adminstrv. asst. to adminstr., 1972-78, pub. relations dir., 1978—. Pres. Jazz Arts Group of Columbus, 1981-83, bd. dirs. N.W. Kiwanis scholar, 1948. Mem. Mirrors, Chimes and Mortar Bd., Childhood League, Pi Beta Phi. Home: 1235 Lake Shore Dr Columbus OH 43204 Office: First Community Village 1800 Riverside Dr Columbus OH 43212

WITTHUHN, KAY LYNN, securities brokerage executive; b. Flint, Mich., June 26, 1957; d. Marion Melvin Witthuhn and Phyllis Kay (Krueger) Allen. Student in interior dsgn., Ray-Vogue Sch., Chgo., 1978. Cons. Merl Norman Cosmetics, Chgo., 1978-79; mgr. Charleston Corp., Chgo., 1979-80; legal sec. Heinke, Burke & Healy, Chgo., 1980; new accts. clk. Heinold Commodities Inc., Chgo., 1980-82; customer svc. mgr. Heinold Securities, Inc., Chgo., 1982-87; ops. mgr. Index Securities Inc., Chgo., 1987—. Mem. NAFE. Democrat. Lutheran. Office: Index Securities 200 W Adams St Chicago IL 60606

WITTLER, JANET MARIE, poet, editor, writer; b. Warrens, Wis., Jan. 30, 1947; d. Leo Harold and Ruby LaVonne (Nienast) W.; m. Thomas Chambers Wayne Roberts, May 18, 1985. BS, U. Wis., Madison, 1970, MA, MS, 1974. Editorial asst. AMA, Chgo., 1970; spl. asst. to senator State Capitol, 1973-74; assoc. editor Law Alumni mag.; editor Norton Critical Edit. U. Wis., 1973-74; asst. to editor-in-chief Doubleday & Co., Inc.; assoc. editor Vintage mag., N.Y.C., 1974; legal asst. law firm, N.Y.C., 1975-77; gifted ednl. cons. N.Y. State, poet, tchr. Poets in Schs., 1978-80; pres. Campaign Coords., Green Bay, 1974; writer Bur. Nat. Affairs, Washington, 1978—; poetry contbr. Bennington (Vt.) Workshops, 1978; contbr Fiction Internat., Lake Saranac, N.Y., 1978; coord. gifted pilot program Bergen County, N.J., 1979; resource cons. Internat. Women's Yr. Com. UN, 1976; rsch. cons. Mcpl. Arts Soc.; supr. gifted cons.'s N.J. Dept. Edn., 1979; assoc., cons. Hanson, Silver & Assocs., N.Y.C., 1980—; chmn. English Speaking Union Bd. Oxford Nat. Campaign Com.; editorial dir. MacMillan, N.Y.C., 1983-84; program coord. Cooper Hewitt Mus., 1983-84; project mgr. Classic Chmn. Ctr. McGraw Hill, N.Y.C., 1984-85; asst. prof. writing Fordham U., N.Y.C., 1984-85, fgn. expert USCPFA, 1986-87; asst. prof. LaSalle U., Phila., 1987; asst. prof. English, coord. Lit. Ctr. Temple U., Phila., 1989-90; lectr. English and EFL U. Penn., 1989—; instr. The Hotch Kiss Sch., 1985-86. U. Wis. fellow, 1972-73, NJACA fellow, 1981-82; rsch. assoc. French dept., 1973; Seefurth Found. fellow, 1971, NDEA fellow, 1972-73, Nat. Edn. Policy fellow, 1979-80; Breadloaf Poetry contbr., 1972-74; Aspen Arts Poetry contbr., 1978-79, fellow, 1985, 87; recipient commendation Nat. Commn. Mental Health, 1977. Mem. Nat. Hist. Trust Guide, Poets and Writers, MLA, AAUW (state de., 1st pl. poetry award), U. Wis. Young Alumni (adv. bd. to bd. dirs., alumni bd. Phila. 1989-90). Unitarian. Office: 16 Stony Brook Ln Princeton NJ 08540

WITTMAN, CONNIE SUSAN, nurse; b. Hays, Kansas, June 30, 1956; d. Vernon M. and Armella M. (Herl) Wittman. BSN, Fort Hays State U., Hays, Kans., 1978; MN, The U. Kans., Kans. City, 1984. Staff nurse, charge nurse St. Anthony Hosp., Hays, Kans., 1978-81, oncology clinical nurse specialist, 1983--; adjunct prof. nursing Fort Hays State U., Hays Kans. 1986--. Pres. Cancer Council Ellis County, Hays Kans. 1986--. Recipient Heart of Gold award Edward D. Jones Co., Hays Kans. 1987, Alumni award Fort Hays State U., Hays Kans., 1988. Mem. ANA Council of Clin. Nurse Specialists, Internat. Soc. Nurses in Cancer Care. Home: 414 West 27th St Hays KS 67601

WITZMAN, AUDREY LORAINE, educator; b. Galva, Ill., July 22, 1937; d. Clarence Gilbert and Gladys Bernice (Westlin) Peterson; m. Thomas A. Witzman, Aug. 10, 1958; children: Johanna Marie, Jocelyn Anne. BA, Eureka Coll., 1958; MEd, Nat. Coll. Edn., 1962; PhD, Northwestern U., 1976. Pub. sch. tchr., Ill., 1958-67; asst. prof. early childhood edn. Northeastern Ill. U., Chgo., 1968-71; developer, owner/dir. Country Woods Nursery Sch. and Day Camp, Valparaiso, Ind., 1971—; prof. early childhood edn. Governors State U., University Park, Ill., 1979-87; edn. cons. Ill. State Bd. Edn., 1987—. Chmn., Porter County (Ind.) Child Protection Team, 1980, 86; bd. dirs. Family House, Valparaiso, 1981-87. Mem. Nat. Assn. for Edn. Young Children, Midwest Assn. Edn. Young Children (co-coordinator conf. Indpls. 1982, Ind. rep. to bd. 1981-83), Ind. Assn. for Edn. Young Children. Republican. Methodist. Home: 450 East 725 North Valparaiso IN 46383 Office: Ill State Bd Edn 100 N First St Springfield IL 62777

WIZMUR, JUDITH H., federal judge; b. 1949. BA, Rutgers U., 1971, JD, 1974. Law clk. Camden County Ct., 1974-75; mcpl. prosecutor Twp. of Berlin, N.J., 1976-78; atty. Lewis Katz, P.A., Cherry Hill, N.J., 1976-78; asst. dir. N.J. Div. Motor Vehicles, 1978-81; adminstrv. law judge State of N.J., 1982-85, worker's compensation judge, 1985; bankruptcy judge U.S. Dist. Ct. N.J., Camden, 1985—. Mem. ABA, N.J. Bar Assn., Camden County Bar Assn., Burlington County Bar Assn., Nat. Assn. Women Judges, Nat. Conf. Bankruptcy Judges, Tri-State Women Lawyers Assn. Office: US Dist Ct 15 N 7th St Camden NJ 08101*

WOCHINGER, MARILYNN TURNBULL, retired educator, church official; b. Oneida, N.Y., Oct. 1, 1923; d. George Elliot and Flossie (Harrington) Turnbull; m. Frank Wochinger, Mar. 30, 1947; children: Anne Wochinger Zimmerman, Nancy Wochinger Hayes, Mark, Carol, Alison Wochinger Siragusa. BEd cum laude, SUNY, Cortland, 1945; MS in Edn., Queens Coll., CUNY, 1971. Tchr. Malverne (N.Y.) Sch. Dist., 1945-49, 65-70, Lawrence (N.Y.) Pub. Sch., 1970-86; ret., 1986; adminstrv. asst. United Meth. Ctr., Far Rockaway, N.Y., 1987—; chmn. arts-in-edn. Lawrence (N.Y.) Pub. Schs., 1983-86. Vice pres. Lynbrook (N.Y.) Philharm. Orch., 1959-60; pres. United Meth. Women, Rockville Centre, N.Y., 1986-88. Mem. AAUW, N.Y. State Ret. Tchrs. Assn., Lawrence PTA (life), Fortnightly Club Rockville Centre (pres. 1989-91), Kappa Delta Pi. Home: 14 Spencer Ave Lynbrook NY 11563 Office: United Meth Ctr 1649 Smith St Far Rockaway NY 11691

WOFFORD, PATRICIA ANN MADONNA, marketing professional; b. Irvington, N.J., Feb. 26, 1961; d. Vincent C. and Mary Louise (Hickey) Madonna; m. russell W. Wofford, Sept. 11, 1982 (div. Apr. 1987); children:

Leslie Ann, Pamila Suzanne. Student, Thompson Inst., 1981. Facilities cost estimator U.S. Navy Exchange, San Diego, 1985-86; data processing mgr. Pine Shirt Co., Pottsville, Pa., 1986; account exec. Jetson Direct Mail Service, St. Clair, Pa.; asst. dir. mktg. Madonna Materials & Handling, Inc., Ashland, Pa., 1988--; cost estimator Grafika Comml. Printing, Pa., 1989—; pres., owner Atlantic Coast Mailers, Inc.; owner Madonna Direct Mail Svcs., Ashland Pa., 1989—. Sponsor, Save the Children, 1989. Mem. NAFE, Ashland Kiwanias, Cen. Susquehanna Valley C. of C. Republican. Roman Catholic. Office: Atlantic Coast Mailers Inc 752 E Main St Hegins PA 17938

WOFFORD, SANDRA SMITH (SANDI SMITH WOFFORD), legislator; b. Pautuxant River, Md., Jan. 26, 1952; d. Clarence A. and Helen (Owens) Smith; m. Thompson C. Wofford, Jr., Oct. 21, 1972; children: Tommy, Cindy. Student, Trident Tech. Coll., Charleston, 1970-71. Svc. rep. So. Bell. Tel. Co., Charleston, 1971-82; mem. S.C. Ho. of Reps., Columbia, 1988—. Pres. Tall Pines Civic League, Ladson, S.C. 1982; co-founder Citizens Against Violent Crimes, 1984, bd. dirs. 1984—, v.p. Charleston chpt., 1984-87; active sponsor, co-founder clubs Just Say No Sangaree Elem. Sch., 1986, Coll. Park Middle Sch., Sangaree Intermediate Sch.; sec. Coll. Park Elem. Sch. P.T.O.; active mem. Sangaree Civic Assn., Summerville, S.C., 1986; bd. dirs. S.C. Crime Victims Assistance Network, Columbia, 1988-89, active legis. coun.; bd. dirs. Victims Compensation Bd., Columbia, 1988-89; active Ladson Youth Orgn.; pres. Berkeley County Rep. Womens' Club; del. Nat. Rep. Womens' Conv., 1986; rep. candidate State Ho. Reps. for Berkeley adn Dorchester Counties.; sec. Rep. Party st Congl. Dist., 1986-88; apptd. by Gov. Campbell to State Crime Victims Compensation Bd. Named Woman of Yr. Beta Beta Sigma, Charleston, 1986; recipient Order of the Palmett Gov. S.C., Columbia, 1988. Mem. Bus. and Profl. Women (past legis. chmn., past nat. com. mem.). Baptist. Home: PO Box 384 Ladson SC 29456 Office: SC Ho of Reps 306-D Blatt Bldg Columbia SC 29211

WOHL, LISA GAY, ophthalmologist; b. Rochester, N.Y., Nov. 22, 1953; d. Milton and Blossom Lorraine (Gombiner) W. BA, U. Mich., 1975; MD, Tufts U., 1979. Diplomate Am. Bd. Ophthalmology. Intern Northwestern Meml. Hosp., Chgo., 1979-80, resident in ophthalmology, 1981-84; fellow in cataract and intraocular surgery under Dr. Oram Kline, Woodbury, N.J., 1984-85; pvt. practice Elmhurst, Ill., 1985—; fellow in glaucoma U. Ill., Chgo., 1990. Contbr. numerous articles to med. jours. Fellow Am. Acad. Ophthalmology; mem. AMA, DuPage County Med. Soc., Ill. Assn. Ophthalmology, Chgo. Ophthal. Assn., Women in Ophthalmology. Office: Elmhurst Clinic 172 Schiller St Elmhurst IL 60126

WOHLERS, DEBRA LOUISE, information systems consultant; b. Tampa, Fla., Aug. 23, 1955; d. Donald James Wohlers and Shirley Louise (Rimes) Lightfoot. BS in Engring. Sci., U. South Fla., 1977; MBA, Fla. Inst. Tech., 1986. Programmer, group systems mgr. Exchange Bank & Trust Co., Tampa, 1976-81; systems and programming mgr. Telecredit Inc., Tampa, 1981-83; systems devel. mgr. Seminole Electric Coop., Inc., Tampa, 1983-86; dir. utilities TTI Techs., Inc., Tampa, 1986-90; sr. mgr. Ernst & Young, 1990—; performance evaluator Abilities, Inc., Clearwater, Fla., 1985-86. Mem. Data Processing Mgmt. Assn. Democrat. Baptist. Home: 15157 Nighthawk Dr Tampa FL 33625

WOHLHETER, SUSAN HAZEL, accountant; b. Buffalo, Sept. 14, 1948; d. George S. and June E. (Miles) W. BBA in Fin., Aquinas Coll., Grand Rapids, Mich., 1980. Computer operator First Nat. Bank, Richmond, Ind., 1967-72, Old Kent Bank, Grand Rapids, 1970-71; payroll clk. Baker, Knapp & Tubbs, Inc., Grand Rapids, 1972-73, cost acct., 1973-77, supr. acctg., 1977-81, mfg. controller, 1981-88, dir. corp. acctg., 1988—. Lutheran. Club: Toastmasters (Grand Rapids) (pres. 1981-85). Home: 4501 Valleyridge SW Wyoming MI 49509 Office: Baker Knapp & Tubbs Inc 1661 Monroe Ave NW Grand Rapids MI 49505

WOHLTMANN, HULDA JUSTINE, pediatric endocrinologist, diabetologist; b. Charleston, S.C., Apr. 10, 1923; d. John Diedrich and Emma Lucia (Mohrmann) W. B.S., Coll. Charleston, 1944; M.D., Med. U. S.C., 1949. Diplomate Am. Bd. Pediatrics. Intern Louisville Gen. Hosp., 1949-50; resident in pediatrics St. Louis Children's Hosp., 1950-53; mem. faculty Washington U. Sch. Medicine, St. Louis, 1953-65, instr., 1953-58, asst. prof., 1958-65, postdoctoral fellow biochemistry, 1961-63; assoc. prof. pediatrics, head pediatric endocrinology Med. U. S.C., Charleston, 1965-70, prof., 1970—. Bd. dirs. Franke Home, Charleston, 1975—, treas., 1989-90; adv. com. for Ethics Ctr., Newberry (S.C.) Coll., 1989-90. Mem. Am. Pediatric Soc., Ambulatory Pediatric Assn., Endocrine Soc., Am. Diabetes Assn., Am. Acad. Pediatrics, Am. Fedn. Clin. Rsch., Midwest Soc. Pediatric Rsch., So. Soc. Pediatric Rsch., S.C. Diabetes Assn. (bd. dirs. 1970-86, pres. 1970-73, 84-85, v.p., 1982-83, Profl Svc. award 1977), Lawson Wilkins Endocrine Soc., Sugar Club. Lutheran. Contbr. articles to sci. jours. Home: 280 N Hobcaw Dr Mount Pleasant SC 29464 Office: Med U SC 171 Ashley Ave Charleston SC 29425

WOJAHN, R. LORRAINE, state legislator; b. Tacoma, Wash. M. Gilbert Wojahn; 2 children. Mem. Wash. State Ho. of Reps., 1969-76; mem. Wash. State Senate from dist. 27, 1977—, mem. commerce and labor, rules, fin. instrns., ways and means coms. Democrat. Office: State Senate Olympia WA 98504 Other: 3592 E K St Tacoma WA 98404*

WOJTACH, MARY ANN, telecommunications executive; b. Passaic, N.J., Jan. 13, 1954. EdB, Felician Coll., 1979, postgrad. Tchr. Most Sacred Heart Sch., Wallington, N.J., 1979-80; customer service rep. D. Klein & Sons, Lodi, N.J., 1980-82; supr. telecommunications PVM Oil Assocs., Inc., Ft. Lee, N.J., 1982—. Democrat. Roman Catholic. Home: 35 Dick St Clifton NJ 07013

WOLANIN, BARBARA ANN BOESE, art curator, art historian; b. Dayton, Ohio, Dec. 12, 1943; d. William Carl and Elisabeth Cassell (Barnard) Boese; m. Thomas R. Wolanin, June 11, 1966 (div. 1980); children: Peter Michael, Andrew Thomas. AB, Oberlin Coll., 1966, AM, 1969; MAT, Harvard U., 1967; PhD, U. Wis., 1981. Dir. children's art classes Allen Art Mus., Oberlin, Ohio, 1967-68; art tchr. Lorain (Ohio) Pub. Schs., 1968-69, Newton (Mass.) Pub. Schs., 1969-71; teaching asst. U. Wis., Madison, 1972-74; asst. prof. art. Trinity Coll., Washington, 1978-83; asst. prof. art James Madison U., Harrisonburg, Va., 1983-85; curator Architect of the Capitol, Washington, 1985—; guest curator Pa. Acad. of Fine Arts, Phila, 1980-83. Contbr. articles to profl. jours. Bd. dirs. Janney Extended Day, Washington, 1979-83; hon. bd. mem. Ft. Harrison, Dayton, Va., 1986. Woodrow Wilson fellow, 1967, Kress fellow U. Wis., 1974, Smithsonian fellow, 1976; recipient Faculty Devel. award James Madison U., 1985. Mem. S.E. Coll. Art Assn., Women's Caucus for Art., Am. Assn. Mus., Coll. Art Assn., Phi Beta Kappa (pres. Trinity Coll. 1982-83). Democrat. Episcopalian. Home: 4347 Brandywine St NW Washington DC 20016 Office: US Capitol Office Architect Capitol Washington DC 20515*

WOLANIN, SOPHIE MAE, civic worker; b. Alton, Ill., June 11, 1915; d. Stephen and Mary (Fijalka) W. Student Pa. State Coll., 1943-44; cert. secretarial sci. U. S.C., 1946, BSBA cum laude, 1948; PhD (hon.), Colo. State Christian Coll., 1972. Clk., stenographer, sec. Mercer County (Pa.) Tax Collector's Office, Sharon, 1932-34; receptionist, social sec., nurse-technician to doctor, N.Y.C., 1934-37; coil winder, assembler Westinghouse Electric Corp., Sharon, 1937-39, duplicator operator, typist, stenographer, 1939-44, confidential sec., Pitts., 1949-54; exec. sec., charter mem. Westinghouse Credit Corp., Pitts., 1954-72, hdqrs. sr. sec., 1972-80, reporter WCC News, 1967-68, asst. editor, 1968-71, asso. editor, 1971-76; student office sec. to dean U. S.C. Sch. Commerce, 1944-46, instr. math., bus. adminstrn., secretarial sci., 1946-48. Publicity and pub. relations chmn., corr. sec. South Oakland Rehab. Council, 1967-69; U. S.C. official del. Univ. Pitts. 200th Anniversary Bicentennial Convocation, 1986; mem. nat. adv. bd. Am. Security Council; mem. Friends Winston Churchill Meml. and Library, Westminster Coll., Fulton, Mo.; active U. S.C. Ednl. Found. Fellow; charter mem. Rep. Presdl. Task Force, trustee; sustaining mem. Rep. Nat. Com.; permanent mem. Nat. Rep. Senatorial Com.; patron Inst. Community Service (life), U. S.C. Alumni Assn. (Pa. state fund chmn. 1967-68, pres. council 1972-76, ofcl. del. rep. inauguration Bethany Coll. pres. 1973); mem. Allegheny County Scholarship Assn. (life), Allegheny County League Women voters, AAUW (life), Internat. Fedn. U. Women, N.E. Historic Geneal. Soc. (life), Hypatian Lit. Soc. (hon.), Acad. Polit. Sci. (Columbia) (life), Bus. and Profl. Women's Club Pitts. (bd. dirs. 1963-80, editor Bull. 1963-65, treas. 1965-66, historian 1969-70, pub. relations 1971-76, Woman of Year 1972), Met. Opera Guild, Nat. Arbor Day Found., Kosciuszko Found. (assoc.), World Literary Acad., Missionary Assn. Mary Immaculate Nat. Shrine of Our Lady of Snows; charter mem. Nat. Mus. Women in Arts, Statue Liberty Ellis Island Found. Inc., Shenago Conservancy (life); supporting mem. Nat. Woman's Hall of Fame; recipient numerous prizes Allegheny County Fair, 1951-56; citation Congl. Record, 1969; medal of Merit, Pres. Reagan, 1982; others. Fellow Internat. Inst. Community Service (founder), Internat. Biog. Assn., mem. World Inst. Achievement (rep.), Am. Biog. Inst. Rsch. Assn. (life patron, nat. advisor), Liturgical Conf. N. Am. (life), Westinghouse Vet. Employees Assn., Nat. Soc. Lit. and Arts, Early Am. Soc., Am. Acad. Social and Polit. Sci., Societe Commemorative de Femmes Celebres, Nat. Trust Historic Preservation, Am. Counselors Soc. (life), Am. Mus. Natural History (asso.), Nat. Hist. Soc. (founding mem.), Anglo-Am. Hist. Soc. (charter), Nat. Assn. Exec. Secs., Internat. Platform Assn., Smithsonian Assos., Asso. Nat. Archives, Nat., Pa., Fed. bus. and profl. women's clubs, Mercer County Hist. Soc. (life), Am. Bible Soc., Polish Am. Numismatic Assn., Polonus Philatelic Soc., UN Assn. U.S., Polish Inst. Arts and Scis. Am. Inc. (assoc.), N.Y. Acad. Scis. (assoc.), Am. Council Polish Cultural Clubs Inc. Roman Catholic (mem. St. Paul Cathedral Altar Soc., patron organ recitals). Clubs: Jonathan Maxcy of U. S.C. (charter); Univ. Catholic of Pitts.; Key of Pa., Fedn. Bus. and Profl. Women (hon.); Coll. (hon.) (Sharon). Contbr. articles to newspapers. Home: 5223 Smith-Stewart Rd SE Girard OH 44420

WOLCHANSKY, DOROTHY LOUISE LAVES, commercial real estate broker; b. Tyler, Tex., Feb. 24, 1942; d. Abe and Grace (Luskey) Laves; m. Lee M. Wolchansky, Aug. 23, 1964 (dec. June 1986); children: Michelle Lynn, Sandi Ilene, Howard Nathan. BJ, BA, U. Tex., 1963. Cert. secondary tchr. Nat. office mgr., interim exec. sec. Women in Communications, Inc., 1964-66; freelance writer Dallas, 1966-71; sec., researcher Goals for Dallas, 1967; editor Roderunner/Innside Rodeway Rodeway Inns of Am., Dallas, 1971-75; editor, publicist The Underground Pages, SusAnn Publs., Dallas, 1976-78; program dir. La Carte, Inc., Dallas, 1978; with sales/advt. Royal Park, Inc., Dallas, 1979-80; account coord. Dykeman Assocs., Inc., Dallas, 1981; comml. real estate broker William M. Paris & Assocs., Dallas, 1982—. Del. to state conv. Dallas precinct 1138 Dem. Party, 1990; pres. Starlight chpt. B'nai B'rith Women, 1973-74; youth bd. chmn. Congregation Shearith Israel, Dallas, 1987-89. Mem. Women in Communications (nat. office mgr., interim exec. sec.), Nat. Assn. Parliamentarians. Democrat. Jewish. Home: 3252 Galahad Dr Dallas TX 75229 Office: William M Paris & Assocs PO Box 810212 Dallas TX 75381

WOLD, NANA BEHA, social services administrator; b. N.Y.C., Nov. 4, 1943; d. William John and Margaret (Robinson) Beha. BA, Tex. Women's U., 1965; M in Social Welfare, U. Calif., Berkeley, 1967. Lic. clin. social worker. Psychiat. social worker Mendocino State Hosp., Talmage, Calif., 1967-70, Calif. State Dept. Mental Health, San Diego, 1972-74; supervising psychiat. social worker Calif. State Dept. Health, San Diego, 1974-81; assoc. chief, case mgmt. services San Diego Regional Ctr. Devel. Disabled, 1981—; instr. social work Chapman Coll., San Diego, 1972; mem. adv. com. Community Living Project, San Diego, 1973-76, Sr. Citizens Day Care Ctr., San Diego, 1976-77; mem. Assembly Woman Bentley adv. com. on devel. disabilities, San Diego, 1984—; co-chair Com. Community Care for Devel. Disabled, San Diego, 1978—. Co-author: Sex Education for the Mentally Retarded, 1975, (pamphlet) Happiness is a Good Home, 1977. Vol. Army Community Services, Ft. Wolters, Tex., 1968-69. Mem. Nat. Assn. Social Workers (diplomate in clin. social work), Am. Assn. Mental Deficiency. Republican. Roman Catholic. Office: San Diego Regional Ctr Devel Disabled 4355 Ruffin Rd #306 San Diego CA 92123

WOLESLAGLE, MILDRED MARIE, executive secretary; b. Aden, Va., July 8, 1937; d. Leonard Reading and Margaret Virginia (Rexrode) Weeks; m. Russell Albert Woleslagle, July 15, 1955 (dec. Oct. 1984); children: Michael Jay, Ronald Allen. Grad. high sch., Nokesville, Va., 1955. Sec. Dept. of the Navy, Washington, 1955-61, Prince William County Sch. Bd., Manassas, Va., 1973-77, Prince William County Govt., Manassas, 1978-86; exec. sec. Kenneth H. Michael Cos., Inc., College Park, Md., 1986-89; exec. sec. to pres. Am. Assn. State Colls. and Univs., Washington, 1990—. Mem. Prof. Secs. Internat. (sec. 1981-82, pres. 82-83, 83-84, treas. 84-85, 85-86, 88-89, 89-90). Republican. Home: 1805 Crystal Dr Unit 1113-S Arlington VA 22202 Office: Am Assn State Colls & Univs 1 Dupont Circle Ste 700 Washington DC 20036

WOLF, BERNICE FIX, vice mayor, educator; b. Cin.; d. Arthur Howard and Lillian (Kursban) Fix; m. Raymond Bernard Wolf, 1948; children: Randall K., Bradley, Leslie, Rae. BA, U. Cin., 1949, BEd, 1950. Tchr. Walnut Hills High Sch., Cin., 1950-52, Dearborn County (Ind.) High Sch., 1962-65, Whitewater (Ind.) Twp.; vice mayor City of Coffeyville, Kans., 1989—. Mem. Nat. League of Cities, Kans. Mcpls. League, S.E. Kans. Cities Coalition, AAUW, Cofffeyville Country Club. Home: 602 Overlook Coffeyville KS 67337

WOLF, CAROL EUWEMA, computer science educator; b. New Castle, Pa., June 11, 1936; d. Ben and Catherine (Michmerhuizen) Euwema; m. Edward Lincoln Wolf, June 15, 1958. BA, Swarthmore (Pa.) Coll., 1958; MA, Cornell U., 1962, PhD, 1964. Asst. prof. SUNY, Brockport, 1968-75; adj. asst. prof. Iowa State U., Ames, 1975-86; assoc. prof. Pace U., N.Y.C., 1986—, chmn. computer sci., 1988—. Mem. Assn. for Computing Machinery, IEEE Computer Soc., N.Y. Acad. Scis., Math. Assn. Am., Assn. for Women in Math., Upsilon Pi Epsilon. Home: 34 Plaza St #607 Brooklyn NY 11238 Office: Pace U Computer Sci Dept Pace Pla New York NY 10038

WOLF, CHERYL JEANE, surgical nurse; b. Palmerton, Pa., Jan. 2, 1951; d. Daniel and Helen (Bruszo) Torretta; 1 child, Christopher. BS, St. Joseph's Coll., 1989; diploma, Christ Hosp. Sch. Nursing, 1972. RN, N.J. Dir. nursing surgical svcs. St. Clares/Riverside Med. Ctr., Denville, N.J.; staff nurse Columbus Hosp., Newark, N.J.; charge nurse St. Vincents Hosp., Montclair, N.J.; supr. opr. rm. Riverside Hosp., Boonton, N.J. Mem. Assn. Opr. Rm. Nurses, Orgn. Nurse Execs. (legisl. com.).

WOLF, CLAIRE RUTH MARIE, writer; b. Elizabeth, N.J., Sept. 13, 1930; d. Charles Michael O'Brien and Susan Marie (Lanagan) Van Dever; m. Richard A. Wolf Sr., July 29, 1950; children: Richard A. Jr., Gerald J., Stephen R., Thomas C. Cert., Cittone Bus. Coll., Iselin, N.J., 1974. Office mgr. Planifield Country Club, Edison, N.J., 1974-79; receptionist AT&T, Piscataway, N.J., 1980-81, clk. typist, 1981-84; specialist writer Bell Communications Rsch., Piscataway, 1984-86, asst. mgr., writer cons., 1986—. Author: Stockroom, 1984, Distbn. Stor. Center, 1985, Shipping & Receiving, 1985, Corporate Purchasing, 1987, Traffen Software, 1988. Sec. Bd. of Adjustment, Dunellen, 1971-73; tutor Lit. Vols. Assn., Bound Brook, 1989. Roman Catholic. Home: 240 Walnut St Dunellen NJ 08812 Office: Bell Communications Rsch 8 Corporate Pl Piscataway NJ 08854

WOLF, ISABEL DRANE, food scientist, government official, consultant; b. Boston, Nov. 21, 1933; d. Louis Andrew and Anna (Whalen) Drane; m. Richard V. Lechowich, Jan. 21, 1983; children: Isabel, August L., Erika M. Wolf. BS, Simmons Coll., 1955; MS, U. Minn., 1971. Instr. dept. food sci. and nutrition U. Minn. 1972-79, asst. prof., 1979-81, assoc. prof., 1981—, extension food and nutrition specialist, 1972—; dir. Office of Consumer Advisor U.S. Dept. Agr., 1982-83, adminstr. Human Nutrition Info. Service, 1983-85; dir. communications and mktg. Nat. Ctr. for Food Safety and Tech., Ill. Inst. Tech., Summit Argo, Ill., 1989—; pvt. cons., 1985—; dir. mktg., ABC Research Corp., Gainesville, Fla., 1987—. Fellow Inst. Food Technologists; mem. Am. Assn. Cereal Chemists. Author: (with N.W. Jerome, J.G. McCleery) Help Yourself - Choices in Food and Nutrition, 1981; contbr. articles to profl. jours. Office: Nat Ctr for Food Safety 6502 S Archer Ave Summit Argo IL 60501

WOLF, JOAN SILVERMAN, special education educator; b. Boston, Aug. 28, 1936; d. Isaac and Rose (Berman) Silverman; m. Harold H. Wolf, Aug. 11, 1957; children: Gary, David. BS, U. Utah, 1960; MA, Ohio State U., 1970, PhD, 1976. Nat. cert. sch. psychologist; cert. tchr. in regular and spl. edn. Grad. rsch. assoc. Ohio State U., Columbus, 1974-76; clin. asst. prof. dept. spl. edn. U. Utah, Salt Lake City, 1976-82, asst. prof. dept. spl. edn., 1982-87, assoc. prof. dept. spl. edn., 1987—; cons. for sch. dists. on issues related to gifted edn., tng. of tchrs. and parents; coord. gifted program U. Utah, Salt Lake City, 1978. Contbr. articles on gifted edn. and the learning disabled to profl. jours.; co-author books. Mem. Am. Psychol. Assn., Nat. Assn. Sch. Psychologists, Utah Psychol. Assn., Western Psychol. Assn., Coun. for Exceptional Children, Nat. Assn. for Gifted Children. Office: U Utah Dept Spl Edn Salt Lake City UT 84112

WOLF, KATHLEEN ELLEN, medical supply company official, nurse; b. Rochester, N.Y., June 10, 1945; d. Frederick Henry and Eloise Marie (Albrecht) W.; m. John Robert Scoville Jr., Oct. 22, 1966; children: John Robert III, David William. Nursing diploma, Highland Hosp., Rochester, 1966. RN, N.Y. Staff nurse Highland Hosp., 1966, relief charge nurse, 1970-72; asst. head nurse St. Francis Hosp., Wichita, Kans., 1966-69; office nurse Dr. John States, Rochester, 1969-70; sales rep. Coppercraft Guild, Taunton, Mass., 1973-76; float nurse Med. Personnel Pool, Rochester, 1976-79; product mgr., sec., ptnr., bd. dirs. SPS Med. Supply Corp., Rochester, 1988—. Mem. A.C.O.R.N. (pres. 1986-88). Office: SPS Med Supply Corp 1250 Scottsville Rd Rochester NY 14624

WOLF, MARY, management and organization development specialist; b. Camden, N.J., July 7, 1938; d. Harry S. and Reba (Braun) Elkins; BS in Edn., Temple U., 1960; MA in Human Devel., Fairleigh Dickinson U., 1979; children: Alan Eric, Lisa Caryl, Marla Beth. Tchr., Camden High Sch., 1960-61, W. Phila. High Sch., 1961-64; instr. World-Wide Ednl. Svcs., Newark, 1979; pres. Dynamic Lifestyles, Inc., Belmar, N.J., 1979-85; tng. specialist Ocean County Coll., Toms River, N.J., 1979-81; tng. specialist Ocean County Employment and Tng. Adminstrn., Toms River, N.J., 1981-82; mgr. RCA, Eatontown, N.J., 1982-85; mgr. tng. and orgn. devel. GE Astro Space Div., Princeton, N.J., 1985—; cons. in field. Mem. Am. Pers. and Guidance Assn., Am. Soc. Tng. and Devel., Nat. Soc. Performance and Instrn., Nat. Assn. Female Execs., Assn. Humanistic Psychology. Office: GE Astro Space Div PO Box 800 Princeton NJ 08543

WOLF, MONICA THERESIA, procedures analyst; b. Germany, Apr. 26, 1943; came to U.S., 1953, naturalized, 1959; d. Otto and Hildegard Maria (Heim) Bellemann; children: Clinton, Danielle. BBA, U. Albuquerque, 1986. Developer Word Processing Ctr., Pub. Service of N.Mex., Albuquerque, 1971-74, word processing supr., 1974-78, budget coordinator, 1978-80, lead procedures analyst, 1980-88; owner Monica's Woodworks, 1988—; mem. adv. bd., student trainer APS Career Enrichment Ctr. Instr. firearm safety and pistol marksmanship. Mem. bd. dirs PACA Animal Shelter. Mem. Internat. Word Processing Assn. (founder N.Mex. chpt.), Nat. Assn. Female Execs., Nat. Rifle Assn., N.Mex. Shooting Sports Assn. Democrat. Club: Sandia Gun (adv. bd., coach). Home and Office: 305 Alamosa Rd NW Albuquerque NM 87107

WOLF, NANCY SCHOENHOLZ, physician; b. N.Y.C., Nov. 2, 1954; d. Daniel and Alice Marilyn (Onners) S.; m. Lawrence Wolf, Sept. 4, 1981. Diploma, Nice Conservatoire, Cimiez, France, 1976; BA magna cum laude, Barnard Coll., 1976; MusM, Yale U., 1978; MD, Mt. Sinai Sch. Medicine, 1989. Flutist Nat. Assn. Orchestra, N.Y.C., 1972, Somerset Symphony, N.J., 1979-82, Sterling Artists Internat., N.Y.C., 1980; dean of students N.Y. State Music Camp, Oneonta, 1973-81; prof. flute Queens Coll. L.I. U., N.Y.C., 1979-82; resident in psychiatry UCLA Neuropsychiat. Inst., 1989—; flutist Philharmonia Virtuosi, N.Y.C., 1979, 80, N.Y. Retrospective Ensemble, N.Y.C., 1980; soloist Cancer Care, Lincoln Ctr. Internat., 1981-82; med. researcher Mt. Sinai Dept. Psychiatry, N.Y.C., 1985-89. Author: (screenplay) Young Blood, 1980, Baldy, 1989, Biological Psychiatry, 1990. Vol. Bellevue Psychiat. Nursery, N.Y.C., 1982-84; foster parent Christian Children's Fund, 1981-85; musician benefit concerts, Cerebral Palsy, Cancer Care, 1970-85. Rock Sleyster scholar AMA, 1988-89; NIH fellow, 1986, 87; recipient Kaufman award in psychiatry Mt. Sinai Sch. Medicine, 1989, Honors award Columbia U., 1976, Dolan Prize for Instrumentalists, 1974. Democrat.

WOLF, RUTH ROCHELLE, marketing executive; b. N.Y.C., Apr. 10, 1937; d. Harry and Sally (Kleiner) Plesser; m. Allen E. Wolf, June 25, 1955; children: Risa Wolf Tepper, Janice Wolf Katz, Stuart. Grad. high sch., Kansas City, Mo. Telephone sales rep. Gracious Lady Svc., Park Forest, Ill., 1967-69; trainer, supr. Gracious Lady Svc., Homewood, Ill., 1969-75, regional supr., 1975-80; v.p., part owner Progressive Mktg. Svcs., Inc., Hazel Crest, Ill., 1981-84, exec. v.p., co-owner, 1984-88; pres. Pro Tel Mktg., Inc., Lansing, Ill., 1988—. Bd. dirs. March of Dimes, Chgo., 1985; planning bd. Jewish Community Ctr., Homewood-Flossmoor, 1988, 89. Office: Pro Tel Mktg Inc 2200 E 170th St Lansing IL 60438

WOLF, TERRY, art advisor; b. N.Y.C., Mar. 14, 1947; d. John and Edith (Stein) W. BA, Hunter Coll., 1973, MA, 1978. Writer ABC TV, N.Y.C., 1976-77; lectr. art history John Jay Coll., CUNY, 1977-78; art cons., N.Y.C., 1978-81; pres. Art Avenues, Inc., N.Y.C., 1981—. Arts and crafts vol. Hebrew Home for Aged. Mem. NAFE, Writers Guild Am. East. Office: Art Avenues Inc 240 West End Ave New York NY 10023

WOLFE, BRENDA L., psychologist; b. Montreal, Can., Oct. 5, 1956; came to U.S., 1980.; d. Joseph and Mania (Tisch) Lichtenstein; m. Kenneth E. Wolfe; children: Alissa Jennifer, Emily Jeanne. BA, McGill U., 1980; MA, U. Calif., Santa Barbara, 1982, PhD, 1985. Teaching assoc. U. Calif., Santa Barbara, 1980-85; mgr. project and curriculum prodn. Edn. Systems Corp., San Diego, 1985-86; sr. project mgr. Jostens Learning Corp., San Diego, 1986-89; dir. rsch. Jenny Craig, Inc., San Diego, 1989—. Contbr. numerous articles to profl. jours. Scholar Western Psychol. Assn., 1982, 83, McGill U., 1989, U. Scholar, 1979; First Class Honors, 1980. Mem. NAFE, Assn. Advancement Behavior Therapy, Western Psychol. Assn., Sci. Rsch. Soc., Sigma Xi.

WOLFE, CAROLINE MARGARET, nurse; b. Toledo, Dec. 9, 1943; d. Russet John and Angela Frances (Kelly) DuMont; m. Warren Dwight Wolfe, Dec. 29, 1973; children—Mark Russet, Jeremy Dean, Jason Kelly. Diploma in nursing St. Vincent Hosp., Toledo, 1964; B.S. in Nursing, Mary Manse Coll., Toledo, 1966. RN, Ohio; cert. clin. transplant coord., nephrology nurse. Staff nurse, asst. head nurse ICU, Maumee Valley Hosp., Toledo, 1964-69; asst. head nurse hemodialysis Med. Coll. of Ohio, Toledo, 1969-71, head nurse hemodialysis, 1971-73, head nurse renal unit, 1973-75, staff nurse renal unit, 1978-81, transplant nurse coordinator, 1981—. Co-author: (with others) An Instrument to Identify Stressors in Renal Transplant Recipients. Mem. Am. Nephrology Nurses Assn., N.Am. Transplant Coordinators Orgn., Kidney Found. Northwestern Ohio (pres. 1970-72, sec. 1973-74). Democrat. Avocations: skiing, reading, bowling. Home: 5617 Dianne Ct Toledo OH 43623 Office: Med Coll of Ohio PO Box 10008 Toledo OH 43699-0008

WOLFE, CORINNE HOWELL, retired social worker; b. El Paso, Tex., Dec. 15, 1912; d. David Emerson and Clara (Schultz) Howell; B.A., U. Tex., El Paso, 1933; M.S.W., Tulane U., 1944; LL.D. (hon.), N.Mex. State U., 1983; m. Howard Clark Wolfe, Jr., Feb. 29, 1936. Social worker Tex. Dept. Pub. Welfare, 1933-45, Family Svc. Assn., Ft. Worth, 1945-46, VA, Dallas, 1946-48; dir. staff devel. and tng. Social and Rehab. Svc., HEW, Washington, 1948-72; prof. social work N.Mex. Highlands U., Las Vegas, 1972-82, ret., 1982; cons. social svcs., social work edn. Mem. adv. panel N.Mex. Community Corrections; bd. dirs Gov's. Childrens Trust Fund. Recipient Disting. Svc. award HEW, 1973, N.Mex. Circle of Excellence, 1989, Outstanding Alumni award Tulane U., 1975, Father Reynolds Rivera Humanitarian award Bar Assn., 1987, N.Mex. Disting. Svc. award AAUW, 1990, Gov.'s award Outstanding N.Mex. Woman, 1990; named N.Mex. Vol. of Yr., 1983. Mem. Nat. Assn. Social Workers (Nat. Social Worker Yr. 1986), Coun. Social Work Edn. (Disting. Svc. award 1972), N.Mex. Alliance Mentally Ill, Northern N.Mex. Civil Liberties Union (chair), N.Mex. Human Svcs. Coalition (co-chair), Coun. Social Work Edn., Am. Pub. Welfare Assn., Nat. and Internat. Conf. on Social Welfare, Santa Fe Living Treasure. Democrat. Methodist. Contbr. articles to profl. jours. Home: 2509 Avenida de Isidro Santa Fe NM 87505

WOLFE, DEBORAH CANNON PATRIDGE, government education consultant; b. Cranford, N.J.; d. David Wadsworth and Gertrude (Moody) Cannon; 1 son, Roy. BS, N.J. State Coll.; MA, EdD, Tchrs. Coll., Columbia U.; postgrad., Vassar Coll., U. Pa., Union Theol. Sem., Jewish Sem. Am.; hon. doctorates, Seton Hall U., 1963, Coll. New Rochelle, 1963, Morris Brown U., 1964, Bloomfield Cooll., 1988, Monmouth Coll, 1988, William Paterson Coll., 1988; LLD (hon.), Kean Coll., 1981; LHD (hon.), Stockton State Coll.; LLD (hon.), Centenary Coll., William Paterson Coll., 1989, Tuskegee U., 1989, Glassboro State Coll., Tuskegee U., 1989, Jersey City State Coll., St. Peter's Coll., Georgian Court Coll., Rider Coll. Former prin., tchr. pub. schs. Cranford, also Tuskegee, Ala.; faculty Tuskegee Inst., Grambling Coll., NYU, Fordham U., U. Mich., Tex. Coll., Columbia U.; supervision and adminstrn. curriculum devel., social studies U. Ill., summers; prof. edn., affirmative action officer Queens Coll.; prof. edn. and children's lit. Wayne State U., summer; now edn. chief U.S. Ho. of Reps. Com. on Edn. and Labor, 1962—; vis. scholar Princeton Theol. Sem., 1989—; Fulbright prof. Am. lit. NYU; U.S. rep. 1st World Conf. on Women in Politics; chair non-govtl. reps. to UN (NGO/DPI exec. com.), 1983—; editorial cons. Macmillan Pub. Co.; cons. Ency. Brit.; adv. bd. Ednl. Testing Service; asso. minister First Bapt. Ch., Cranford, N.J.; mem. State Bd. Edn., 1964—; chairperson N.J. Bd. Higher Edn., 1967—; mem. nat. adv. panel on vocat. edn. HEW; mem. citizen's adv. com. to Bd. Edn., Cranford; mem. Citizen's Adv. Com. on Youth Fitness, Pres.'s Adv. Com. on Youth Fitness, White House Conf. Children and Youth, 1950, 60, White House Conf. Edn., 1955, White House Conf. Aging, 1960, White House Conf. Civil Rights, 1966, White House Conf. on Children, 1970, Adv. Council for Innovations in Edn.; v.p. Nat. Alliance for Safer Cities; cons. Vista Corps, OEO; vis. scholar Princeton Theol. Sem., 1989—. Contbr. articles to ednl. publs. Bd. dirs. Cranford Welfare Assn., Community Center, 1st Bapt. Ch., Cranford, Community Center Migratory Laborers, Hurlock, Md.; trustee Sci. Service, Seton Hall U.; mem. Public Broadcasting Authority.; bd. regents Seton Hall U.; sec. Kappa Delta Pi Ednl. Found.; mem. adv. com. Elizabeth and Arthur Schlesinger Library, Radcliffe Coll.; trustee Edn. Devel. Center. Recipient Nat. Achievement award Nat. Assn. Negro Bus. and Profl. Women's Clubs, 1958; Woman of Year award Delta Beta Zeta; Woman of Year award Morgan State Coll.; Achievement award Atlantic region Zeta Phi Beta. Mem. Council Nat. Orgns. Children and Youth, Am. Council Human Rights (v.p.), NCCJ, Nat. Panhellenic Council (dir.), Nat. Assn. Negro Bus. and Profl. Women (chmn. speakers bur.), Nat. Assn. Black Educators (pres.), NEA (life), LWV, N.Y. Tchrs. Assn., Am. Tchrs. Assn., Fellowship So. Churchmen, AAUW (nat. edn. chmn.), AAUP, Internat. Reading Assn., Comparative Edn. Soc., Am. Acad. Polit. and Social Sci., Internat. Assn. Childhood Edn., Nat. Soc. Study Edn., Am. Council Edn. (commn. fed. relations), Assn. Supervision and Curriculum Devel. (rev. council), AAAS (chmn. tchr. edn. com.), Nat. Alliance Black Educators (pres.), NAACP, Internat. Platform Assn., Ch. Women United (UN rep., mem. exec. com.), UN Assn.-U.S.A. (exec. com.), Delta Kappa Gamma Edn. Soc. (chmn. world fellowship com.), Kappa Delta Pi (chmn. ritual com.), Pi Lambda Theta, Zeta Phi Beta (internat. pres. 1954, chmn. edn. found. 1974—). Home: 62 S Union Ave Cranford NJ 07016 Office: NJ State Bd Higher Edn 20 W State St Trenton NJ 08625

WOLFE, JEAN ELIZABETH, medical illustrator; b. Newark, Oct. 3, 1925; d. Arthur Howard and Ethel (Harper) Wolfe; B.S., Russell Sage Coll., 1947; student Pratt Inst., 1949-50; diploma U. Rochester Sch. Medicine and Dentistry, 1955; postgrad. (W.B. Saunders fellow), U. Pa., 1955-56, U. Pa., 1980; M.F.A., U. Pa., 1973, M.A. (hon.), 1973. Exhibitor, Pratt Inst. Galleries, Bklyn., 1958, N.Y. Med. Coll., 1958, Assn. Med. Illustrators, 1961-86, AMA, N.Y.C., 1965, Phila., 1965, A.C.S., Atlantic City, 1965, Rsch. Study Club L.A., 1966, Phila. Art Alliance, 1967, 73, U. Pa. Ophthal. Soc., 1967-68, N.J. Med. Soc., 1968, Cayuga Mus. History and Art, 1968, Pensacola Art Ctr., 1969, FAA Aero. Center, Oklahoma City, 1970, Scheie Eye Inst., 1972-75, Assn. Med. Illustrators Traveling Salon, 1978, Moore Coll. Art, 1985, Mus. of Am. Illustration Soc. of Illustrators, 1986; represented in permanent collections Archives of Med. Visual Resources, Francis A. Countway-Harvard Med. Library, Boston, Mutter Mus., Phila. Coll. Physicians, comprehensive collection of major work donated by Scheie Eye Inst.; contbg. illustrator Adler's Textbook Ophthalmology, 8th edit., 1969. Illustrations in med. books, jours., pharm. house pubs.; instr. Pembroke Coll. Brown U., 1947-49; mem. faculty Kimberley Sch., Upper Montclair, N.J., 1950-52; free lance med. illustration Studio N.Y. Med. Coll., 1956-60; instr. Pratt Inst., 1958-59; asso. in med. illustration U. Pa. Sch. Medicine, 1960-72, research asst. prof. med. art in ophthalmology, 1972-85; free lance med. and sci. illustration, 1985—; guest lectr. Johns Hopkins Med. Sch., 1973, NIH; guest artist USAF, Air Force Acad. and NORAD, 1971. Recipient Merit certificate AMA; Appreciation certificate ACS; 1st prize Pensacola Art Center, Am. Heart Assn., 1969, Gold medal Graphic Arts Soc. of Del. Valley, 1973. Fellow Assn. Med. Illustrators; mem. Phila. Art Alliance, Assn. Med. Illustrators (Ralph Sweet, Tom Jones awards, gov. 1970—, chmn. nominating com. 1972-73, vice chmn. bd. govs. 1973-74, chmn. bd. 1974-75), Soc. Illustrators (cert. merit 1986), Graphic Artists Guild, AAUP, Women's Caucus for Art.

WOLFE, JUDITH ANN, constuction supply company executive; b. Austin, Minn., Mar. 11, 1946; d. Harold Lloyd and Lola Jean Lysne; m. Michael Dennis Wolfe; children: Anthony, Troy, Kimberly, Kelly. Cert. in credit adminstrn., Inst. Credit, Phoenix, 1986, cert. in advanced credit adminstrn., 1987. Credit mgr. Turf Irrigation, Phoenix, 1978—; corp. officer Turf Irrigation, 1978—. Author various wage and edn. surveys, 1987; reporter legis. updates newsletter, 1987. Mem. Nat. Assn. Credit Mgrs. (bd. dirs. 1987—, mem. ednl. group), Nat. Assn. Female Execs., Nat. Assn. Women in Constrn. Republican. Office: Turf Irrigation & Waterworks 3622 S 30th St Phoenix AZ 85040

WOLFE, LAURA CARNES, internatinal credit analyst; b. Jefferson, S.C., Aug 13, 1936; d. John Howard and Lottie Lula (Killough) Carnes; m. John Beasley Benton (dec. 1970); m. Elton Edwin Wolfe Jr., Apr. 2, 1972 (div. 1976); children: Deborah Elizabeth, Benton Parker. Student, U. S.C., 1955-56. Clk., Sears Roebuck, Florence, S.C., 1954-55; receptionist Am. Textile Mfrs. Inst., Charlotte, N.C., 1961-67, Pilot Life, Charlotte, 1958-60; sec. Chas. T. Main Inc, Charlotte, 1961-67; treas., mgr. Chipper Service, Lancaster, S.C., 1967-68; credit mgr. Buensod Div. Aeronca Inc., Pineville, N.C., 1968-72; export internat. credit analyst Scovill Inc., Monroe, N.C., 1972-87; bus. specialist broker, CPI Assocs., Lancaster, 1987-88; internat. credit analyst Homelite-Textron Corp., Charlotte, 1989—. Pres. Lancaster County Heart Assn., 1981. Mem. Internat. Assn. Execs. in Fin., Credit and Internat. Bus., Nat. Assn. Credit Mgmt., Am. Legion Aux. Democrat. Baptist. Club: Evening Garden, (pres. 1981-83) (Lancaster). Avocations: reading, gardening, travel, swimming. Home: 419 Churchill Dr Lancaster SC 29720

WOLFE, LINDA PRESS, food product executive; b. Rockville Centre, N.Y., Nov. 19, 1953; d. James W. and Virginia (Oxenchuk) P. Student Nassau Community Coll., SUNY-Farmingdale, C.W. Post Coll. Gen. mgr. Controlled Sheet Music Service Inc., Copiague, N.Y., 1974-80; sales adminstr. Modern Main Food Products, Garden City, N.Y., 1980-83; mktg. mgr. DCA, N.Y.C., 1983; v.p. Richheimer Coffee subs. Wechsler Coffee Co., Moonachie, N.J., 1984-88; ter. mgr. Bunge Foods Group, Kankakee, Ill., 1989—; corr. sec. Queens Women's Ctr., 1989-90; bd. dirs. Music Jobbers Assn., 1979-80. Mem. NAFE, The Exec. Network, Networking Exec. Women. Avocations: skiing, bicycling.

WOLFE, LISA ANN, electronic date processing auditor; b. New Kensington, Pa., Sept. 29, 1962; d. Otis Lawrence and Lois Ann (Smouse) Wolfe. BS, Ind. U. Pa., 1983; postgrad., Duquesne U., 1989—. Sr. internal auditor EDP Allegheny Power Svc. Corp., Greensburg, Pa., 1984—. Vol. Am. Cancer Soc. Mem. Zeta Tau Alpha (v.p. Ind. U. Pa. chpt. 1982-83). Republican. Home: 420 Spring Run Dr Monroeville PA 15146 Office: Allegheny Power Svc Corp 800 Cabin Hill Dr Greensburg PA 15601

WOLFE, MARGARET RIPLEY, historian, educator, consultant; b. Kingsport, Tenn., Feb. 3, 1947; d. Clarence Estill and Gertrude Blessing Ripley; B.S. magna cum laude, East Tenn. State U., 1967, M.A., 1969; Ph.D. (Haggin fellow), U. Ky., 1974; m. David Early Wolfe, Dec. 17, 1966; 1 dau., Stephanie Ripley. Instr. history East Tenn. State U., 1969-73, asst. prof., 1973-77, assoc. prof., 1977-80, prof., 1980—. Mem. Tenn. Com. for the Humanities, 1983-85 (exec. council 1984-85). Author: Lucius Polk Brown and Progressive Food and Drug Control, Tennessee and New York City, 1908-1920, 1978, An Industrial History of Hawkins County, Tennessee, 1983, Kingsport, Tennessee: A Planned American City, 1987; contbr. articles to profl. jours. Mem. coord. com. for women in the hist. profession. Recipient Disting. Faculty award East Tenn. State U., 1977; East Tenn. State U. Found. rsch. award, 1979, Alumni cert. merit, 1984. Mem. Am. Hist. Assn., Orgn. Am. Historians, So. Assn. Women Historians (pres. 1983-84, exec. com. 1984-86), So. Hist. Assn. (com. on the status of women 1987, program com. 1988), Smithsonian Assocs., ACLU, NOW, Tenn. Hist. Soc. Office: E Tenn State U Kingsport Ctr Kingsport TN 37660 also: E Tenn State U Dept History Johnson City TN 37614

WOLFE, NORMA LEE, construction company executive; b. Seneca, Mo., Mar. 12, 1932; d. Lawrence L. and Stella Mae Arehart; m. R. E. Wolfe, Mar. 7, 1957; children: Alan E., Deborah L. Student pub. schs., Seneca. Corp. sec. Ming of Am., Inc., Prairie Village, Kans., 1969-79, gen. mgr., 1969-75, dir., 1969—; sec.-treas. Alan E. wolfe Equipment & Constrn. Co., Kansas City, Mo., 1973—; commn. officer Joplin (Mo.) Police Dept., supr., 1953-57. Mem. ch. council, treas. Prince of Peace Luth. Ch., Grandview, Mo., 1970-75; mem. Luth. Ch. Women. Democrat. Office: 3001 E 83d St Kansas City MO 64132

WOLFE, TRACEY DIANNE, distributing company executive; b. Dallas, June 13, 1951; d. George F. Wolfe and Helen Ruth Cline Lemons; children: Bronson Alan, Travis Aaron; m. Johnny Wayne Murray. BS in Edn. and Social Sci., East Tex. State U., Commerce, 1973, MS in Elem. Edn., 1976. Asst. to dir. student devel. East Tex. State U., 1973-74; corp. sec., v.p. Wolfe Distbg. Co., beer distbrs., Terrell, Tex., 1974—. Mem. Pilot Club Internat., Kappa Delta (alumnae v.p. 1978-79, alumnae treas. 1979-81, province pres. 1980-82). Republican. Methodist. Club: Pilot (bd. dirs). Home: 3316 Lakeside Dr Rockwall TX 75087 Office: 100 Metro Dr Terrell TX 75160

WOLFENDEN, TERRY LYN, school system administrator; b. Dunkirk, N.Y., Oct. 5, d. Elton George Wolfenden and Evelyn (Brown) Baker. BA in Social Studies, State U. coll., 1966, MS, 1978; cert. of advanced study, State U. Coll., 1979. Social studies tchr. Westfield Academy and Central Sch., N.Y., 1966-68; social studies tchr. Dunkirk City Sch. Dist., N.Y., 1968-79, middle sch. prin., 1979-85, supt. of schs. bd. dirs. Salvation Army, Dunkirk, 1987-. Mem. Chautauqua County Coun. of Sch. Spt. (pres. 1989—), N.Y. State Coun. of Sch. Supt., Sch. Adminstr. Assn. N.Y. State, Am. Assn. Sch. Adminstrs., Am. Assn. for Supervision & Curriculum Devel., No. C. of C., Phi Delta Kappa (pres. 1984-85). Methodist. Office: Dunkirk Public Schools 201 Lake Shore Dr E Dunkirk NY 14048

WOLFERT, KAREN BARRETT, lawyer; b. Griffin, Ga., Dec. 2, 1959; d. Thomas Joseph and Barbara Anne (Davis) B. BA, Wake Forest U., 1981; JD, U. Ga., 1984. Bar: Tex. 1984, Ga. 1984. Assoc. Winstead, McGuire, Sechrest and Minick, Dallas, 1984—. Mem. Nat. Assn. Bank Women (chmn. com. 1987-88), Dallas Assn. Young Lawyers, Ga. Bar Assn., Tex. Bar Assn. Methodist. Home: 6618 Sunnyland Dallas TX 75214 Office: Winstead McGuire et al 1201 Elm St Ste 5400 Dallas TX 75270

WOLFERT, RUTH, gestalt therapist; b. N.Y.C., Nov. 10, 1933; d. Ira and Helen (Herschdorfer) W. BS summa cum laude, Columbia U., 1967, postgrad., 1966-68. Pvt. practice therapist N.Y.C., 1972—; dir. Action Groups, N.Y.C., 1974-76, Gestalt Groups, N.Y.C., 1976—; faculty, coordinating bd. Women's Interart Ctr., N.Y.C., 1971-75, bd. dirs., 1981—; faculty Inst. for Experiential Learning & Devel., 1988—, Woodstock U., 1989—, Gestalt Inst. of Atlanta, 1989—; presenter Stockton (N.J.) State Coll., 1974-75; presenter in field. Contbr. booklet A Consumer's Guide to Non-Sexist Therapy, 1978. Mem. Assn. Humanistic Psychology (bd. dirs. ea. regional network 1981-87, pres. 1985-87), N.Y. Inst. Gestalt Therapy (trainer 1979—, chair workshops program 1979-83, co-chair conf. 1983-85, internat. exec. com. 1988—), Assn. Transpersonal Psychology (co-chair N.Y. discussion group 1983-85), N.Y. Acad. Scis. Office: Gestalt Groups 161 E 91st St New York NY 10128

WOLFF, LINDA M., personnel executive; b. Chgo., June 30, 1953; d. Calvin and Marian Wolff. BA in Psychology and Speech Communications, Northeastern Ill. U., 1976. Recruiter Trans Union Corp., Chgo., 1977-78; compensation adminstr. Am. Res. Corp., Chgo., 1978-79; sr. compensation specialist Bankers Life and Casualty Co., Chgo., 1979-80; dir. human resources and devel. IDC Services, Inc., Chgo., 1980-84; v.p. regional dir. human resources Burson-Marsteller, pub. rels., Chgo., 1984-87; div. dir. human resources Hitachi Data Systems, 1988—. Mem. Am. Compensation Assn., Soc. Human Resources Mgmt., Soc. Human Resources Profls., Internat. Assn. Personnel Women, Am. Mgmt. Assn.

WOLFF, MILLIE BENDER, journalist; b. Mt. Pleasant, Pa.; d. Ben and Ruth (Murstein) Bender; children: Mack B. Shaw, Henry Shaw, Alvin Wolff Jr. BA in Communications, Webster U. Columnist St. Louis; dir. spl. events, pub. rels. Arts and Edn. Coun. Webster U., St. Louis; art editor, feature writer Palm Beach (Fla.) Daily, 1975-89; contributing editor Solo Mag., Boca Raton, Fla., 1990—. Active United Way, Palm Beach, 1990. Recipient numerous awards from Mo. Press Women, Fla. Press Women orgns. Mem. Women in Communications, Fla. Press Women. Nat. Fedn. Press Women. Home: 1200 S Flagler West Palm Beach FL 33401

WOLFF, SIDNEY CARNE, astronomer, observatory administrator; b. Sioux City, Iowa, June 6, 1941; d. George Albert and Ethel (Smith) Carne; m. Richard J. Wolff, Aug. 29, 1962. BA, Carleton Coll., 1962, DSc (hon.), 1985; PhD, U. Calif., Berkeley, 1966. Postgrad. research fellow Lick Obs, Santa Cruz, Calif., 1969; asst. astronomer U. Hawaii, Honolulu, 1967-71, assoc. astronomer, 1971-76; astronomer, assoc. dir. Inst. Astronomy, Honolulu, 1976-83, acting dir., 1983-84; dir. Kitt Peak Nat. Obs., Tucson, 1984-87, Nat. Optical Astronomy Observatories, 1987—. Author: The A-Type Stars--Problems and Perspectives, 1983, (with others) Exploration of the Universe, 1987, Realm of the Universe, 1988, Frontiers of Astronomy, 1990; contbr. articles to profl. jours. Trustee Carleton Coll., 1989—. Research fellow Lick Obs. Santa Cruz, Calif., 1967. Mem. Astron. Soc. Pacific (pres. 1984-86, bd. dirs. 1979-85), Am. Astron. Soc. (council 1983-86), Internat. Astron. Union. Office: Kitt Peak Nat Obs 950 N Cherry Ave PO Box 26732 Tucson AZ 85726

WOLFF, SUSAN (JOEY WOLFF), new products marketing executive; b. N.Y.C., Apr. 11, 1944; d. Seymour Barnett and Julia (Weiner) Joseph; m. Ivan Lawrence Wolff, June 18, 1967; 1 child, Adam Gregory. BS with honors, Cornell U., 1966; MS with honors, NYU, 1968. Mgr. mktg. research Mattel, Inc., Hawthorne, Calif., 1968-74; mgr. new product research Gillette Co., Boston, 1975-76; mktg. mgr. new products AT&T Consumer Products, Basking Ridge, N.J., 1977-81, dir. mktg. Advanced Mobile Phone Service, Inc. subs., Basking Ridge, 1981-83; pres. Wolff Assocs. Inc., Mountain Lakes, N.J., 1983—; mng. dir. Solomon-Wolff Assocs. Inc., Mountain Lakes, N.J., 1984-86, pres., 1981-86. NDEA fellow NYU, 1966-68. Mem. Cornell U. Alumni Assn. (pres. 1981-86), Am. Mktg. Assn. Office: Wolff Assocs Inc 165 Laurel Hill Rd Mountain Lakes NJ 07046

WOLFINGER, BARBARA KAYE, film company executive; b. N.Y.C.; d. Louis and Margaret (Goodman) Klatzkie; m. Raymond E. Wolfinger, Aug. 7, 1960; 1 child, Nicholas Holm. AB, U. Mich., 1951. Dir. design rsch. McCann-Erickson Advt., N.Y.C., 1954-58; research assoc. Calif. Dept. Pub. Health, Berkeley, 1961-64, Stanford (Calif.) U., 1968-70, Inst. Research in Social Behavior, Berkeley, 1971-73; producer Berkeley Stage Co., 1973-78; pres. Berkeley Prodns., Inc., 1978—. Producer: (ednl. films) Black Girl, Sister of the Bride, Poetry Playhouse, Chile Pequin, Nine Months, Almost Home, Your Move, 1980-87. Dir. Planned Parenthood, San Francisco, 1985—, v.p., 1988-89. Recipient Noble Hancock Found. award, 1973, NEH award, 1975, Golden Eagle award Coun. Internat. Nontheatrical Events, 1978, Creative Excellence award U.S. Industry Film Festival, 1979, Essa award U.S. Dept. Edn., 1979, 80, 81, 82, red ribbon Am. Film Festival, 1983, Learning award Nat. Coun. Human Rels., 1983, 84. Democrat. Jewish. Office: Berkeley Prodns 2288 Fulton Berkeley CA 94704

WOLFMAN, BRUNETTA REID, education administrator, educator; b. Clarksdale, Miss., Sept. 4, 1931; d. Willie Orlando and Belle Victoria (Allen) Reid Griffin; m. Burton Wolfman, Oct. 4, 1952; children: Andrea, Jeffery. BA, U. Calif., Berkeley, 1957, MA, 1968, PhD, 1971; DHL (hon.), Boston U., 1983; DP (hon.), Northeastern U., 1983; DL (hon.), Regis Coll., 1984, Stonehill Coll., 1985; DHL, Suffolk U., 1985; DET (hon.), Wentworth Inst., 1987; AA (hon.), Roxbury Community Coll., 1988. Asst. dean faculty Dartmouth Coll., Hanover, N.H., 1972-74; asst. v.p. acad. affairs U. Mass., Boston, 1974-76; acad. dean Wheelock Coll., Boston, 1976-78; cons. Arthur D. Little, Cambridge, Mass., 1978; dir. policy planning Dept. Edn., Boston, 1978-82; pres. Roxbury Community Coll., Boston, 1983-88, ACE sr. fellow, 1988-89; assoc. v.p. acad. affairs George Washington U., Washington, 1989—; bd. dirs. Am. Coun. Edn., Harvard Community Health Plan. Author: Roles, 1983. Bd. overseers Wellesley (Mass.) Coll., 1981; bd. dirs. Boston-Fenway Program, 1977, Freedom House, Boston, 1983. Boston Pvt. Industry Coun., 1983; bd. dirs. NCCJ, Boston, 1983, co-chair; bd. overseers Boston Symphony Orch.; trustee Mus. Fine Arts, Boston; councilor Coun. on Edn. for Pub. Health; mem. Black Women for Policy Action, 1976. Recipient Freedom award NAACP No. Calif., 1971; Amelia Earhart award Women's Edn. and Indsl. Union, Boston, 1983. Mem. AAUW, Adult Edn. Assn. U.S.A., Am. Sociol. Assn., Am. Ednl. Rsch. Assn., Greater Boston, C. of C. (edn. com. 1982), Pi Lambda Theta, Alpha Kappa Alpha (Humanitarian award 1984). Home: 2022 Columbia Rd NW Washington DC 20009 Office: George Washington U 2121 I St NW Washington DC 20052

WOLFORD, ELIZABETH JULE JOHNSON, cardiovascular specialist, ultrasound technologist; b. Breckenridge, Minn., Mar. 3, 1960; d. Clifford Eugene and Diana Mae (Strubel) Johnson; m. Scot Clinton Wolford, Aug. 6, 1983; children: Stephanie Elizabeth, Kirsten Diane. Student, U. N.D., 1978-81; BS in Radio Tech.-Ultrasound, U. Okla., 1983. Registered diagnostic med. sonographer. Sr. sonographer Oklahoma City Clinic, 1983-85; chief cardiovascular technologist Advanced Cardiovascular Tech., Albuquerque, 1985-87; sr. sonographer Diagnostic Mobile Ultrasound, Inc., 1987—. Mem. Okla. Sonographers Soc., Soc. Diagnostic Med. Sonographers, Am. Registry Diagnostic Med. Sonographers (cert.), Am. Inst. Ultrasound Medicine, Registry Vascular Technologist. Republican. Methodist. Home: 717 Westview Dr Yukon OK 73099 Office: Diagnostic Mobile Ultrasound Inc 902 S Bryant Edmond OK 73034

WOLFROM, JOAN MARGARET, educator; b. Rhinelander, Wis., Aug. 30, 1930; d. Louis Jr. and Jenny Laura Elizabeth (Ingberg) W. BA magna cum laude, Northland Coll., 1954; M Music Edn., U. Ariz., 1964; postgrad., Ariz. State U., 1965-82, Glendale Community Coll., 1979. Cert. tchr., Wis., Ariz. Tchr. choral music Winter (Wis.) High Sch., 1953-54; tchr. vocal music Racine (Wis.) Pub. Schs., 1954-55; dir. vocal music Neillsville (Wis.) Pub. Schs., 1955-58; tchr. music Glendale (Ariz.) Elem. Schs., 1958-70, tchr., 1970-87, part-time tchr., 1987—, sec. dist. negotiation com., 1974-75; head women counselors U. Wis. Music Clinic, Madison, 1957-58; head counselor Ariz. State U. Music Camp, Tempe, 1960; del. Ariz. Sch. Music Tchrs. Conf., 1965; with registration dept. Phoenix Community Coll., 1987—. Vol. St. Joseph's Hosp. and Med. Ctr., Phoenix, 1974—; sec. ladies aid Grace Luth. Ch., Glendale, 1976-78; dist. leader fund drive Am. Heart Assn., Phoenix, 1978; sec. Grand Caynon Cir., Luth. Women's Missionary Soc., 1988—; bd. dirs. Ariz. State U. Lyric Opera Theater Guild, 1989—. U. Wis. scholar, 1948, Julia R. Gilman scholar, 1952, Myrtle C. Beckman scholar, 1953; recipient Golden Poet award World of Poetry, 1990. Mem. Westside Ret. Tchrs. Assn., Phoenix Art Mus. League, Heard Mus. Guild. Republican. Home: 5008 N 13th Ave Phoenix AZ 85013 Office: Glendale Elem Schs 5734 W Glendale Ave Glendale AZ 85301

WOLICKI, NANCY FRIEDA, lawyer; b. Chgo., Sept. 8, 1953; d. Samuel and Ingrid (Rappel) W.; B.A. in Journalism and Sociology, U. Ariz., 1974, J.D., 1977. Bar: Ariz., 1977; law clk. Ariz. Ct. Appeals, 1977-78; legis. asst. fgn. policy and armed svcs. health, staff atty. Billy Carter investigation to U.S. Sen. Dennis DeConcini, 1979-81; staff dir. Senate Subcom. on Alcoholism and Drug Abuse, Washington, 1981-84; mem. staff Senator Gordon J. Humphrey, Washington, 1984-87; coord. adv. com. Voluntary Fgn. U.S. Aid, 1987; sr. analyst legal and congressional affairs President's Commn. on the HIV Epidemic, 1987-88; sr. policy analyst Commn. Exec. Legis. Jud. Salaries, 1988-89; counselor Sec. Energy, 1989—. Recipient William Spaid Meml. award U. Ariz. Coll. Law, 1977, Senate commendation for Billy Carter investigation, 1980. Mem. ABA, Ariz. Bar Assn., Phi Kappa Phi. Jewish. Office: Office of Sec US Dept Energy Washington DC 20585

WOLK, JOAN MARCIA, technical writer, consultant; b. Pitts., Dec. 2, 1947; d. Samuel David and Rhoda (Levy) Kopelman; m. Stephen Selis Wolk, Oct. 25, 1970 (div. Sept. 1977); 1 child, Jason. BA in English, Ohio U., 1969; postgrad. in linguistics, Ohio State U., 1970; MA in Linguistics, U. Mass., 1970. Tchr. English, chmn. dept. English Prince George County Bd. Edn., Upper Marlboro, Md., 1970-73; editor, 1977-81; sr. tech. writer Boeing Computer Services, Vienna, Va., 1981-85, systems analyst electronic pub., 1985-87; mgr. tech. writing VM Software, Inc., Reston, Va., 1987-88; mgr., cons. tech. writing Comsys Tech. Svcs., Rockville, Md., 1988—. Democrat. Jewish. Avocations: parapsychology/metaphysics, concerts, theater, opera, walking. Home and Office: 13 Story Dr Gaithersburg MD 20878

WOLLE, JUNE ROSE BUSH, counselor, educator, publishing executive, poet; b. N.Y.C., Feb. 13, 1941; d. Edward William and Marguerite Virginia (Kessler) Rose; m. Evan Morgan Bush, May 15, 1965 (div.) 1 child, Derek Morgan Bush; m. John Frederick Wolle, Dec. 8, 1984. AA, Packer Collegiate Inst., Bklyn., 1960; BA, NYU, 1962; MA, L.I. U., 1969. Rsch. asst. Downstate Med. Ctr., Bklyn., 1962-66; cons. and designer support group Learning to Be, Canastota, N.Y., 1982-90; founder, dir. Positive Ways of Living Ctr., Chittenango, N.Y., 1984—; founder, pub. Prosperity Pub. Co., Chittenango, 1988—; guest lectr. Herbert Lehman Coll., N.Y.C., So. Conn. State Coll., New Haven; lectr. Oneida Adult and Edn. Ctr., 1983-86, U. Coll., Syracuse U., 1987—, Westhill Adult Edn. Ctr., Onondaga Cortland Madison Adult Edn. Author (book of poetry) Treasury of Reflections, 1989; contbr. poetry to mags., newspapers and anthologies; co-author, editor (newsletter) Focus on Prosperity, 1988—; creator, presenter radio program Positive Ways of Living, Sta. WMCR, Oneida, N.Y., 1986-88; local personality on various radio shows; subject nat. TV interviews. Bd. dirs. Internat. Ctr. Syracuse, 1989—; membership co-chair mem.'s coun. Everson Mus., Syracuse, 1990; mem. Corinthian Found. Inc.; treas. Cumberland Hosp. Social Svc. Aux. Recipient Vol. medals United Hosp. Fund, Bklyn., 1966-69, 1st Place award for poem Sonnet, N.Y. State Fedn. Women's Clubs, 1990, hon. poetry mention Oneida Writer's League; fellowship endowment named in her honor AAUW, Mt. Kisco, N.Y., 1978. Mem. AAWU (pres.), Syracuse Fedn. Women's Clubs (corr. sec. 1988—), Nat. League Am. Pen Women, Inc., N.Y. State Preservation Assn., Syracuse Stage Guild (bd. dirs. 1989—), Landmark Theatre Guild, Syracuse Symphony Assn., English Speaking Union Club (bd. dirs. Syracuse chpt. 1990), Syracuse Libr. Assn., Packer Collegiate Inst. Alumnae Assn. (pres.), Harbor Club, Corinthian Club (bd. dirs. 1988—), Danforth Shakespeare Club, Zonta, Delta Kappa Gamma. Home and Office: 125 W Genesee St Chittenango NY 13037

WOLLENBERG, LYNN A., optometrist; b. Penn Yan, N.Y., Jan. 23, 1964; d. Allen R. and Judith A. (Melberg) W. Student, Westminster Coll., New Wilmington, Pa., 1982-85, SUNY, Morrisville, 1981-82; BS, Pa. Coll. Optometry, 1986, OD, 1989. Optometrist John C. Lee, M.D., S.C., Decatur, Ill., 1989—. Mem. Am. Optometric Assn., Ill. Optometric Assn., Profl. Women's Network, Decatur Jr. C. of C. Presbyterian. Office: John C Lee MD SC 1 Memorial Dr Ste 216 Decatur IL 62526

WOLLERSHEIM, JANET PUCCINELLI, psychology educator; b. Anaconda, Mont., July 24, 1936; d. Nello J. and Inez Marie (Ungaretti) Puccinelli; m. David E. Wollersheim, Aug. 1, 1959 (div. June 1972); children: Danette Marie, Tod Neil; m. Daniel J. Smith, July 17, 1976. AB, Gonzaga U., 1958; MA, St. Louis U., 1960; PhD, U. Ill., 1968. Lic. psychologist, Mont. Asst. prof. psychology, asst. dir. testing and counseling ctr. U. Mo., 1968-71; prof. psychology U. Mont., Missoula, 1971—, dir. chin. psychology, 1980-87; chair Mont. Bd. Psychologists, 1977-78; cons. Mont. State Prison, 1971-85, Trapper Creek Job Corps, 1973—; pvt. practice, Missoula, 1971—. Author numerous rsch. articles. Bd. dirs. Crisis Ctr., Missoula, 1972-73; mem. profl. adv. bd. Head Start, Missoula, 1972-79. Am. Psychol. Assn. fellow, 1980. Mem. Rocky Mountain Psychol. Assn. (pres. 1983-84), Nat. Council Univ. Dirs. Clin. Psychology (bd. dirs., 1982-88).

Roman Catholic. Home: 105 Greenwood Missoula MT 59803-2401 Office: U Mont Dept Psychology Missoula MT 59812

WOLLIN, LUCY ANN, Librarian; b. N.Y.C., Sept. 13, 1939; d. Maurice and Helen Sylvia (Garfinkel) Wollin. BA, Antioch Coll., 1961; MLS, Pratt Inst., 1966; MA, Middlebury Coll., 1982, MLitt, 1988. Librarian Lafayette High Sch., Girls High Sch., Bklyn., 1962-66; librarian in charge I.S. 70, N.Y.C., 1966-85; high sch. librarian Park West High Sch., N.Y.C., 1985-89; librarian in charge Fiorello LaGuardia High Sch. Music/Art and Performing Arts, N.Y.C., 1989—. Mem. MLA. Office: Fiorello LaGuardia High Sch 100 Amsterdam Ave New York NY 10023

WOLLSCHLAEGER, GERTRAUD, radiologist; b. Munich, Fed. Republic of Germany, Feb. 28, 1924; came to U.S., 1957; d. Joseph and Krescentia (Sicker) Hahn; m. Paul Bernhard Wollschlaeger, July 29, 1948 (wid. Mar. 1981); children: Ursula, Daria, Peter. MD, Ludwig-Maximillian U., Munich, 1957, PhD, 1957; BEd, U. Berlin, 1951. Intern St. Vincent Charity Hosp., Cleve., 1957-58; resident in radiology St. Luke's Hosp., Cleve., 1958-61; instr., fellow neuroradiology NIH/Albert Einstein Coll. Medicine, N.Y.C., 1961-64; asst. prof. radiology U. Mo., Columbia, 1964-67, assoc. prof. radiology, 1967-70, prof. radiology, 1970-71; prof. radiology Wayne State U., Detroit, 1973—; assoc. dir. neuroradiology William Beaumont Hosp., Royal Oak, Mich., 1971-73; dir. spl. programs in radiology, Detroit Gen. Hosp., 1973-85, dir. emergency radiology, Detroit Receiving Hosp., 1981—. Contbr. articles to profl. jours. Recipient fellowship NIH, 1967-70, Wayne State U., 1978-81. Mem. Oakland County Mid-Med. Soc./AMA (chmn. grad. fgn. med. sch. section 1984—), Neuroradiol. Soc. Am., European Neuroradiol. Soc., German Neuroradiol., Am. Roentger Ray Soc., Radiol. Soc. N. Am., Assn. Univ. Radiologists. Home: 5885 Wing Lake Birmingham MI 48010

WOLMAN, TARA SOPHIA, editor-in-chief; b. N.Y.C., Oct. 6, 1948; d. Martin and Sylvia (Baer) Levine; m. Steven Aaron Wolman, Dec. 4, 1944; children: Laini Michelle, Samantha Leigh. BA, Bklyn. Coll., 1970; M. Urban Affairs, Boston U., 1972. Cert. early childhood and elem. teaching, Mass., Conn., N.Y. Head tchr. Learning Pond Head Start, Bklyn., 1970; Title I modern math. tchr. Christopher Gibson Sch., Boston, 1971-72; host, creator The Childsplay Report, Sta.-WSPR radio, West Springfield, Mass., 1987-89; editor-in-chief Childsplay Mag., Springfield, Mass., 1984—; advocacy chairperson bd. dirs. Office for Children, Springfield, 1987—; mem. health adv. com. Holyoke (Mass.)/Chicopee Head Start, 1987—; mem. Pre-Sch. Adv. Com., Holyoke, 1987-88; mem. the Childsplay festival Childsplay Mag., Springfield, 1986-88. Contbr. numerous articles Childsplay Mag., 1984—. Mem. Valley Press Club, Valley Dist. Dental Women (pres. 1980-81, advisor 1988—), Longmeadow Book Club (pres. 1985-87). Jewish. Home: 292 Pinewood Dr Longmeadow MA 01106 Office: Childsplay 401 Dickinson St Springfield MA 01108

WOLOSZYK, HOLLY ARLENE, microbiologist; b. Chgo., Jan. 19, 1960; d. Leonard Benedict and Dorothy Elaine (Wegehenkel) W. BS, U. Ill., 1982. Quality control technician G.D. Searle Pharm., Mount Prospect, Ill., 1982-83, Am. Hosp. Supply, McGaw Park, Ill., 1983-84; sr. technician rsch. and devel. G.D. Searle, Skokie, Ill., 1984-86, microbiologist rsch. and devel., 1986-87, supr. microbiology svcs. rsch. and devel., 1987-89; microbiologist Intermedics, Inc., Freeport, Tex., 1989—. Mem. Am. Soc. Microbiology. Home: 110 Lake Rd #902 Lake Jackson TX 77566 Office: Intermedics Inc 240 West Second St Freeport TX 77541

WOLOTKIEWICZ, MARIAN M., college programs director; b. Camden, N.J., Apr. 22, 1954; d. Edward J. and Rita J. W.; m. Paul J. Sagan, Mar. 31, 1984. AB in Polit. Sci., Mount Holyoke Coll., 1976; JD, Suffolk U., 1979. Manuscript editor Little, Brown & Co., Boston, 1979-84; freelance editor, 1984-88; freelance writer Camp Dresser & McKee Inc., 1985-87; dir. pub. info. Regis Coll., Weston, Mass., 1988-90; assoc. dir. planned giving Clark U., Worcester, Mass., 1990—; various writing, editing and communications activities for Mass. Bar Assn., 1978-83, Womens Bar Assn., 1979-83; freelance editor for publishers including Little, Brown & Co., Artech Ho., Ballinger, Butterworth, 1984-88. Chmn. adv. com. Stow (Mass.) Cable TV, 1983—; active fundraising Mass. Assn. Womens Lawyers charity auction, 1984, Mt. Holyoke Coll., 1986—; notary pub. State of Mass. Mem. Coun. for Advancement and Support of Edn., Phi Delta Phi. Office: Clark U 950 Main St Worcester MA 01610

WOLPERT, SISTER JULIE, hospital executive; b. Alliance, Ohio, Aug. 3, 1950; d. Quentin Joseph and Bernice Mary (Davis) W. AA, Lourdes Coll., 1971; BS, Ohio State U., 1976; MSA, U. Notre Dame, 1984. Co-dir. phys. therapy St. Joseph Hosp., Bryan, Tex., 1976-81, adminstrv. asst., 1981-82, asst. adminstr., 1982-85; v.p. Holy Cross Hosp., Detroit, 1985—. Trustee St. Joseph Hosp., 1976-88, Good Samaritan Pregnancy Svc., Bryan, 1982-83, Brazos Valley Kidney Disease Fund, Bryan, 1982-85. Mem. Mich. Cath. Health Assn. (trustee 1988-89), Mich. Hosp. Assn. (coun. on cath. healthcare 1989-90). Roman Catholic. Office: St John Med Ctr Saint John Heights OH 43947

WOLTERING, MARGARET MAE, education educator; b. Trenton, Ohio, July 24, 1913; d. David Lindy and Nellie Stevenson; m. Elmer Charles Woltering, Apr. 9, 1938; 1 child, Eugene Anthony. Student, Mercy Sch. Nursing, Hamilton, Ohio, 1931-34; BS, Miami U., 1962, MEd, 1968, post-grad., 1975. RN; cert curriculum specialist educator. Pub. health nurse Ohio State Dept. Health, Butler County, 1936-49; supr. Swedish Hosp., Seattle, 1944-45; various high sch. teaching positions Cin., 1968-78; ednl. cons. Ohio, 1971-90; ednl. cons. specializing in curriculum devel., 1980-89. Author spelling book, 1981. Chmn. Hosp. Svc. for Children, Hamilton, 1981—; lectr. Sr. Citizens Ctr., 1981-89, ednl. cons., 1989—; active Friends of Libr. Book Reviewer, 1990—, Fine Arts Coun., 1990—. Mem. AAUW, Toastmasters. Democrat. Roman Catholic. Home and Office: 333 Columbia Rd Hamilton OH 45013

WOLTZ, MARY LYNN MONACO, management consultant; b. Columbus, Ohio, Mar. 11, 1951; d. Frank Guy and Mary Catherine (Montenaro) Monaco; m. James David Woltz, June 19, 1971; children: Joseph David, Bethany Anne. Student, Ohio State U. Tchr. Career Acad., Columbus, Ohio, 1971-72; supr., mgmt. Battelle Meml. Inst., Columbus, Ohio, 1973—; pub. speaker schs., bus., clubs and profl. orgns., Ohio, 1981. Amb. Assn. of World Affairs, Columbus, 1968; co-chmn. United Way, Columbus, 1976; committeewoman Ohio Crime Prevention Assn., Columbus, 1988; founding bd. mem. Ohio Crime Prevention Found., 1989—; founding mem., pres. Parents Support Group, 1990—; cons. Lao Mai Assn., Columbus, 1981-85. Named Ohio Crime Practitioner of the Yr., 1988; recipient Nat. Crime Prevention award Nat. Crime Prevention Coalition, Washington, 1988. Mem. Am. Soc. Indsl. Security. Roman Catholic. Office: Battelle Meml Inst 505 King Ave Columbus OH 43201

WOLVERTON, LINDA MAY, healthcare company executive; b. Abington, Pa., Apr. 9, 1943; d. James Charles and Gladys Elizabeth (McCarraher) Costello. Student, Pasco Hernando Coll., 1974-77, U. Ala., 1979-80, St. Petersburg Jr. Coll., 1981-82. Diplomate Am. Bd. Quality Assurance and Utilization Rev.; cert. med. staff coordinator. Med. records dir. Community Meml. Hosp., Hamilton, N.Y., 1963-76, Riverside Hosp., New Port Richey, Fla., 1976-77; quality assurance coordinator Shelby Meml. Hosp., Alabaster, Ala., 1977-80; clin. instr. quality assurance U. Ala., Birmingham, 1978-79; quality assurance coordinator Profl. Found. Healthcare, Tampa, Fla., 1980-81; mgr. quality assurance/utilization mgmt. Tampa Gen. Hosp., 1981-82; mgr. health info. Palms of Pasadena Hosp., St. Petersburg, Fla., 1982-84; quality assurance coordinator Seton Med. Ctr., Daly City, Calif., 1984-85; healthcare cons. Coopers & Lybrand, San Francisco, 1985-86; corp. dir. managed care services Parcelsus Healthcare Corp., Pasadena, Calif., 1986—. Pres. Mountain Meadows Homeowners Assn., Pomona, Calif., 1987—. Mem. Nat. Assn. Quality Assurance Profls. (cert., Calif. del. 1986-89, region III rep. nat. bd. 1983-84), Am. Med. Records Assn. (accredited), Calif. Assn. Quality Assurance Profls. (nominating com. 1987). Republican. Home: 1715 Calle De Oro Pomona CA 91768 Office: 155 N Lake Ave Ste 1100 Pasadena CA 91768

WOMACK, BOBBI HACKETT, teacher; b. Bakersfield, Calif., June 15, 1951; d. Robert Hunter and Jean (Osowski) Hackett; m. James Keith Womack, Aug. 4, 1985. AA, Bakersfield City Coll., Calif., 1971; BA, CSU, Bakersfield, 1973, MA, 1976. Tchr. Fairfax Sch. Dist., Bakersfield, Calif., 1973-89, 1986--, yearbook advisor, 1973-; dist. curriculum com. chair Fairfax Sch. Dist., Bakersfield Calif. Editor: Dist. Community Newsletter, Community Link 1988-89, Dist. Staff. Bd. Mem. Beautiful Bakersfield Com., Calif., 1988--. Named Tchr. Yr., Fairfax Sch. Dist. Bakersfield Calif. 1988, Outstanding. Mem. Tchr. Edn. and Computer Ctr., Kern County and Los Angeles Curriculum Lab. Assn. Home: 612 Holtby Rd Bakersfield CA 93304

WOMACK, PAMELA, state official; m. Ronald L. Womack, 1966; children: Hillary Tripp, Christine Downs. Student U. Calif. Legis. aide to mems. Va. Ho. of Dels.; campaign scheduler transition office Baliles for Gov., 1985-86; dir. Va. Dept. Volunteerism, 1986-89; exec. dir. Dem. Party Va., 1989-90; sec. Commonwealth of Va., 1990—; chmn. Chesterfield Dem. Com., 1985-89. Office: Sec of the Commonwealth PO Box 1-D Richmond VA 23201*

WOMACK, SHARON GENNELLE, librarian; b. Flora, Ill. Dir. Ariz. Libr., Archives and Pub. Records Dept., Phoenix, 1979—. Office: Libr Archives & Pub Records Ariz State Capitol 1700 W Washington Phoenix AZ 85007

WOMMACK, BARBARA KAY, educator; b. Strafford, Mo., Mar. 4, 1946; d. DeWayne Orin and Wilma June Womack. BS in Edn., S.W. Mo. State U., Springfield, 1968; MS in Edn., S.W. Mo. State U., 1973, postgrad., 1975—. Cert. tchr. Instr. bus. Aurora (Mo.) High Sch., 1968—; instr. night adult edn., Aurora, 1982—. Mem. Nat. Bus. Edn. Assn., Mo. State Tchrs. Assn., Mo. Vocat. Assn., Mo. Bus. Edn. Assn. (state audit com. 1976), S.W. Mo. Bus. Edn. Assn. (pres. 1985), Aurora Edn. Assn. (pres. 1973), AAUW (treas. 1987), S.W. Mo. State U. Alumni Assn., Delta Kappa Gamma (pres. 1988-90). Republican. Baptist. Home: 610 S Harrison Aurora MO 65605-1712 Office: Aurora High Sch West Locust Aurora MO 65605

WONG, ELAINE DANG, foundation executive; b. Canton, China, June 3, 1936 (parents Am. citizens); d. Robert G. and Fung Heong (Woo) Dang; A.A. (Rotary scholar), Coalinga Coll., 1956; B.S. (AAUW scholar, Grad. Resident scholar), U. Calif., Berkeley, 1958, teaching credential, 1959; m. Philip Wong, Nov. 8, 1959; children—Elizabeth, Russell, Roger, Edith, Valerie. Tchr. acctg. San Mateo (Calif.) High Sch., 1959-60; acct., 1960-75; substitute tchr. Richmond County Schs., Augusta, Ga., 1975-77; comptroller Central Savannah River Area, United Way, Augusta, 1977-82; asst. controller Hammermill Hardwoods div. Hammermill Paper Co., Augusta, 1982-84; controller SFN Communications of Augusta, Inc. (WJBF-TV), 1984-85; acct. Med. Coll. Ga. Found., Inc., 1986-88, Nat. Sci Ctr. Found., Inc., 1988—; cons. small bus.; pvt. tutor acctg. Mem. adv. bd. Richmond County Bd. Edn., 1985-87; bd. dirs. Cen. Savannah River chpt. Girl Scouts US, 1986—. Panel judge Jr. Achievement Treas. award, 1980, 81; treas. Chinese Lang. Sch., 1973-75, Merry Neighborhood Sch., 1974-75. Recipient Achievement award Bank of Am., 1954. Mem. Nat. Assn. Accts. (dir. 1978-85, treas. 1982-84), Chinese Assn. Republican. Presbyterian.

WONG, HELEN KA-NING, pharmacist; b. Kowloon, Hong Kong, Aug. 30, 1963; came to the U.S., 1981.; d. Hoi and Tsang (Wen) W. BS Summa Cum Laude, SUNY, Buffalo, 1986; MBA, NYU, 1990. Lic. pharmacist, Ct., Calif. Adminstv. pharmacy resident Montefiore Hosp., Bronx., N.Y., 1986-87; pharmacist The Stamford (Conn.) Hosp., 1987-89; part-time pharmacist Ridgeway Ctr. Pharmacy, Stamford, Conn., 1988-89. Author: Drug Use Review on I.V. Gamma Globulin, 1987, co-author Productivity Measurement, 1987. Mem. Dorot Vol. Svcs. for Sr. Citizens, N.Y., 1988—. Mem. N.Y. State Coun. of Hosp. Pharmacy, Am. Pharm. Assn., Am. Mgmt. Assn., NAFE, NAAAP, Rho Chi, Phi Eta Sigma.

WONG, PENELOPE LYNN, marketing consultant, writer; b. Salinas, Calif., May 22, 1945; d. Gung Jue and Nellie Sue (Lee) W. AB in English, U. Calif., Berkeley, 1967. Editor Stolen Paper Edits., San Francisco, 1967-71; co-founder The Innerspace Project, Mill Valley, Calif., 1969-72; publ. dir. Interaction Assocs., San Francisco, 1971-74; pres. Penelope Wong & Assocs., Berkeley, Calif., 1974-78; copy chief The Franklin Mint, Wawa, Pa., 1978-79; mng. dir. Jennifer Wong Ltd., N.Y.C., 1979-81; sr. v.p. Ogilvy & mather Direct, San Francisco, 1981-87; pres. Penelope Wong & Assocs., San Francisco, 1987—; lectr. U. Calif., Berkeley, Stanford U., faculty mem. pub. course. Author: Lift for Life, 1978; contbg. editor AsiAm mag. Bd. dirs. Oakland (Calif.) East Bay Symphony, 1989. Recipient Echo Silver award Direct Mktg. Assn., 1986, Pioneer Awards Direct Mktg. Creative Guild, 1983-87. Mem. Direct Mktg. Creative Guild, The City Club. Democrat. Roman Catholic. Office: 333 Broadway San Francisco CA 94133

WONG, RAYLICE YUK KWON, teacher, minister; b. Honolulu, Mar. 14, 1943; d. Raymond K.C. and Alice K.K. (Ching) W. BEd, U. Hawaii, 1965. Cert. secondary edn. tchr., Hawaii. Tchr. State of Hawaii-Kalakaua Intermediate, Honolulu, 1966—; tchr. adult edn. Farrington Community Sch. for Adults, Honolulu, 1967-84; tchr. lay ministry Templs Sch.-Reorganized Ch. of Jesus Christ Latter-day Saints Ch., Honolulu, 1986—; freshman adviser Kalakaua Intermediate Sch., Honolulu, 1988-89. Bd. dirs., sec. Alea Lani Estates; temple day elder Reorganized Ch. of Jesus Christ of Latter Day Saints, Honolulu, 1989—. Mem. Am. Assn. Tchrs. Spanish and Portuguese (treas. Honolulu chpt. 1984—), Kalakaua Mah Jong Club (pres. 1978—).

WONG, SUZANNE CRAWBUCK, librarian; b. Englewood, N.J., July 13, 1957; d. George Austin and Marion Elizabeth (Fournier) Crawbuck; m. Thomas Kay Wong, June 7, 1986; 1 child, Jeremy Richard. BA in Humanities, St. Peter's Coll., Englewood Cliffs, N.J., 1980. Resources control clk. Ernst & Young (merged with Ernst & Whinney), N.Y.C., 1982-85, libr. asst., 1985—. Mem. Amateur Press Assns. (contbr. assn. jour. 1979-86), Cesarean Prevention Movement. Democrat.

WOO, FRANCES MEI SOO, lawyer; b. San Francisco, Feb. 23, 1949; d. On Lung and Lai Shou (Wong) W.; m. Gary Duane Hoppe, May 3, 1986. BA, Wash. State U., 1971; JD, U. Wash., 1975; LLM in Tax, NYU, 1977. Bar: Wash. 1975, U.S. Dist. Ct. (we. dist.) Wash. 1975, U.S. Tax Ct. 1977, N.Y. 1978, U.S. Dist. Ct. (so. and ea. dist.) N.Y. 1978, U.S. Supreme Ct. 1982. Assoc. Brown & Wood, N.Y.C., 1977-80; tax counsel Westvaco Corp., N.Y.C., 1980-83, SCM Corp., N.Y.C., 1983-87; cons. Mercer Meidinger Hansen, Inc., 1987-88; tax counsel CBS Records, Inc., N.Y.C., 1988—; bd. dirs. Gramont Owners Corp. Contbr. articles to profl. jours. Mem. ABA, Wash. State Bar Assn., N.Y. State Bar Assn., Assn. Bar City N.Y. (employee benefits com.), Tax Execs. Inst. Home: 215 W 98th St Apt 10D New York NY 10025 Office: CBS Records Inc 666 Fifth Ave New York NY 10103

WOOD, BARBARA, author; b. Eng., Jan. 30, 1947; d. Alfons and Ruth (Pemberton) Lewandowski; m. George Wood, June 25, 1966. Student, U. Calif., Santa Barbara, 1964-66. Surg. technician Santa Monica (Calif.) Hosp., 1973-77. Author: The Magdalene Scrolls, 1978, Hounds and Jackals, 1978, Curse This House, 1978, Yesterday's Child, 1979, (with Gareth Wootton) Night Trains, 1979, The Watchgods, 1980, Childsong, 1981, Domina, 1983, Vital Signs, 1985, Soul Flame, 1987, Green City in the Sun, 1988, (as Kathryn Harvey) Butterfly, 1988. Office: care Harvey Klinger Inc 301 W 53d St New York NY 10019*

WOOD, BARBARA LOUISE CHAMPION, state legislator; b. Swampscott, Mass., Jan. 10, 1924; d. John Duncan and Eva Louise (Moore) Champion; m. Newall Arthur Wood, June 12, 1948; children: Gary Duncan, Craig Newall, Brian Scott, Dennis Michael, Joan Wood Unger. Diploma in Nursing, Mary Hitchcock Meml. Hosp. Sch. Nursing, Hanover, N.H., 1945; student, Simmons Coll., 1947-48. RN. Rep., mem. ho. edn. com. Vt. Gen. Assembly, Montpelier, 1981—, vice chmn. edn. com., 1983-87; trustee Vt. State Colls., Waterbury, 1986-90, Gifford Meml. Hosp., Randolph, Vt., 1986—; commr., Vt. rep. Edn. Commn. of the States, Denver, 1981-86. Sch. dir. Bethel Sch. Bd., Vt., 1963-85; mem.-at-large Vt. Sch. Bds. Assn., Montpelier, 1982-85. Served to 2d lt. U.S. Army, 1945-46. Mem. Am. Legion. Republican. Congregationalist. Clubs: Bethel Woman's (pres. 1976-78); Vt. Fedn. Women's Clubs (dist. pres. 1978-80). Home: Woodland Rd Bethel VT 05032 Office: Vt House of Reps State House Montpelier VT 05602

WOOD, BETTY A., utilities executive; b. Atlanta, May 22, 1943; d. William Robert and Ethleen (Beard) W. BS, U. Ga., 1965. Home economist Ga. Power Co., Lawrenceville, 1965-75; sr. home economist Ga. Power Co., Athens, Ga., 1975-77, customer edn. rep., 1977-79, residential rep., 1979-81, sr. residential rep., 1981-85, field mktg. rep., 1985—; coordinator div. speaker's bur. Ga. Power Co, 1985—, Adopt-A Sch. chmn., 1987. Chmn. pub. edn. Clarke-Oconee unit Am. Cancer Soc., 1986—; mem. Women of Ga. Power. Recipient Woman of Achievement award Athens Bus. and Profl. Women's Club, 1977. Mem. Nat. Assn. Women in Constrn., U. Ga. Alumni Soc., Am. Home Econ. Assn., Ga. Home Econ. Assn., Mountain Energy Consortium. Democrat. Home: 100 Woodhaven Circle Athens GA 30606-1951 Office: Ga Power Co 1001 Prince Ave PO Box 1312 Athens GA 30613-1899

WOOD, CAROLE DEE, county official; b. Haskell, Okla., May 18, 1939; d. Ermon Dee and Mary Ola (Shue) Standridge; m. Roy Lee Wood, June 15, 1963; 1 child, Kirk Lee Wood. BS, N.E. State U., Tahlequah, Okla., 1961; MS, Okla. State U., 1985. Asst. home demonstration agt. Tahlequah, 1961, Seminole County, Okla., Wewoka, 1961-68; extension home economist, Indian program various county areas, Holdenville, Okla., 1968-75; extension home economist Seminole County, Wewoka, 1975-89, extension home economist/county extension dir., 1989--; dist. dir. Okla. Assn. of Extension Home Economists, 1986-87; historian Okla. Assn. of Extension Home Economists, 1984-85. Recipient Norma Brumbaugh scholar Okla. Extension Homemakers Coun., 1981. Mem. Okla. Home Econs. Assn., Am. Home Econs. Assn. AAUW (pres. Wewoka chpt. 1973-75), Epsilon Sigma Phi, Delta Zeta, Wewoka Garden Club, Rainbow. Democrat. Baptist. Home: 1018 Sunnymeade Wewoka OK 74884 Office: Extension Courthouse PO Box 520 Wewoka OK 74884

WOOD, CHRISTIE ANN, marketing professional; b. Texas City, Tex., Dec. 6, 1955; d. Clarence Jefferson and Mary Ellen (Standley) W. BME, U. North Tex., 1978. Asst. ops. mgr. North Tex. State U. Computer Ctr., Denton, 1980-81, programmer, 1981; computer sci. tchr. La. Sch. Professions, Shreveport, 1981-82; computer analyst Bossier Parrish Sch. Bd., Bossier City, La., 1982-84; sr. mktg. support Unisys Corp., Dallas, 1984-87; mktg. mgr. Unisys Corp. WHQ, Blue Bell, Pa., 1987—; awards chmn. Data Processing Mgmt. Assn., Dallas, 1985. Illustrator: Startrek Fanzines, 1982—; editor: The LINC Systems Approach, 1989. Flutist Shreveport Symphony Orch., 1981-84; dir. Canterbury Chambre Consort. Recipient Exemplary Action award Burroughs Corp., 1985. Democrat. Office: Unisys Corp CSG/4GL PO Box 500 Mail Stop B260 Blue Bell PA 19424-0001

WOOD, DARLENE SPRINKLE, insurance executive; b. Arlington, Va., Jan. 17, 1954; d. Clovis Randolph Sprinkle and Othella Francis (Mills) Marlowe; m. James Kenneth Wood, Aug. 6, 1977; children: Lauren Gabrielle, Amber Danielle. BA, U. Va., 1976. Trainee The Gap, Springfield, Va., 1976-77; asst. mgr. The Gap, Pitts., 1977, store mgr., 1977-78; sr. staff casualty specialist Allstate, Pitts., 1978—. Mem. AAUW, DAR, Ins. Women Pitts., Ins. Club Pitts. Presbyterian. Home: 414 Morrison Dr Pittsburgh PA 15216

WOOD, DEE J., realtor; b. Blue Island, Ill., Sept. 3, 1929; d. Lloyd Eugene and Irma Louise (Thoeming) W.; m. Maurice Alston Laws, Apr. 30, 1952 (div. 1964); children: Wendy Allison, Christopher Scott. AA, Compton (Calif.) Jr. Coll., 1950; BA, SUNY, New Paltz, 1971; MA, Montclair (N.J.) State U., 1975. Cert., N.Y., Calif. Interior decorator, 1961-63; tchr. Nanuet (N.Y.) Pub. Schs., 1971, Palisades Schs., Palisades Park, 1972-74; owner A Different Drummer, Nyack, N.Y., 1974-75; tchr. Palm Springs (Calif.) Schs., 1978-81; instr. Coll. of the Desert, Palm Desert, Calif., 1979-82; realtor Merrill-Harris & Assocs., Desert Hot Springs, Calif., 1979—; edn. rep. Desert Hot Springs Bd. Realtors, 1989. Singer TV series, commls., records, and albums including Ed Sullivan Show, Perry Como, Patti Page, Gary Moore, Pat Boone, and Jimmy Dean, N.Y., 1951-70. Appointee Redevel. Adv. Group, Desert Hot Springs, 1986-88; pres. Mchts. Assn., Desert Hot Springs, 1985-87, Desert Hot Springs C. of C., 1988-89. Mem. Soc. of Singers (pres.). Home: 9840 Oakmount Blvd MLCC Desert Hot Springs CA 92240 Office: Merrill-Harris & Assoc 66435 Pierson Blvd Desert Hot Springs CA 92240

WOOD, EVELYN NIELSEN, reading dynamics business executive; b. Logan, Utah, Jan. 8, 1909; d. Elias and Rose (Stirland) Nielsen; m. Myron Douglas Wood, June 12, 1929 (dec. May 1987); 1 child, Carolyn Wood Evans. BA, U. Utah, 1929, MA, 1947; postgrad., Columbia U., 1956-57. Tchr. Weber Coll., Ogden, Utah, 1931-32; girls counselor Jordan High Sch., Sandy, Utah, 1948-57, tchr. jr. and sr. high schs., 1948-59; instr. U. Utah, 1957-59; founder, originator Evelyn Wood Reading Dynamics, 1959—; tchr. rapid reading U. Del., 1961; guest lectr. NEA, 1961, Internat. Reading Assn., Tex. Christian U., 1962; faculty Brigham Young U., research specialist for reading, 1973-74. Author, conductor radio programs, 1947; author: (With Marjory Barrows) Reading Skills, 1958, A Breakthrough in Reading, 1961, A New Approach to Speed Reading, 1962, Speed Reading for Comprehension, 1962, also articles. Home: 6024 E Wendrew Ln Tucson AZ 85711

WOOD, FAY S., marketing executive; b. Phila., Aug. 22; d. Paul and Dorothy (Berkowitz) Wiener; children: Deborah, Esther, Tiffany. BA in English, Pa. State U.; postgrad. RCA Corp. Real estate sales rep., 1968-70; cons. Hearing Ctrs., Inc., 1970-72; dist. sales mgr. Beltone Hearing Aid Ctrs., Inc., 1972-76; v.p. PhD Hearing Ctrs., Inc.; with RCA Svcs. Co., 1976-79, sales mgr., 1977-79, regional sales mgr., N.Y. dist., 1979; v.p. sales and mktg. Full Line Repair Ctrs., Inc., 1979-81; v.p. sales and mktg. Quantech Electronics Corp., Freeport, N.Y., 1981-85; v.p., gen. mgr. Elite Group, Inc., Torrance, Calif., 1985-87, exec. v.p., 1987-88; pres. Prestige Resources, Inc., Palos Verdes, Calif., 1987-88; pres., chief exec. officer Key Prestige, Inc., Cypress, Calif., 1988—; mgr. Keyprocessors, Inc., 1988. Mem. adv. bd. Dept. Consumer Affairs, mem. N.Y.C. Commn. on Status of Women. Recipient audiology cert. Dahlberg Electronics, Master Cons. award Beltone Electronics; 1st degree Black Belt in Tae Kwon Do Karate. Mem. AAUW, LWV, NAFE, Nat. Fedn. Bus. and Profl. Women, B'nai Brith, Fedn. Bus. and Profl. Women Club. Home: 14445 Baker St Westminister CA 92683 Office: Key Prestige Inc 6101 Ball Rd Ste 209 Cypress CA 90630

WOOD, JACALYN KAY, educational consultant, university administrator; b. Columbus, Ohio, May 25, 1949; d. Carleston John and Grace Anna (Schumacher) W. B.A., Georgetown Coll., 1971; M.S., Ohio State U., 1976; Ph.D., Miami U., 1981. Elem. tchr. Bethel-Tate Schs., Ohio, 1971-73, Columbus (Ohio) Christian Sch., 1973-74, Franklin (Ohio) Schs., 1974-79; teaching fellow Miami U., Oxford, Ohio, 1979-81; cons. intermediate grades Erie County Schs., Sandusky, Ohio, 1981-89, presenter, tchr. insvc. tng. Mem. council Sta. WVIZ-TV, 1981-88; assoc. prof. Ashland U., Elyria, Ohio, 1989, dir. elem. edn., 1989—; mem. exec. com. Perkins Community Schs., 1981-85; mem. community adv. bd. Sandusky Vols. Am., 1985-89, Sandusky Soc. Bank, 1987-88, vol. Firelands Community Hosp., 1986-87. Mem. Am. Businesswomen's Assn. (local pres. 1985), Assn. Supervision and Curriculum Devel., Internat. Reading Assn., Ohio Sch. Suprs. Assn. (regional pres. 1986, state pres. 1986-87), Phi Delta Kappa (local sec. 1985, 86), Phi Kappa Phi. Baptist. Home: 2425 W River Rd #18 Elyria OH 44035 Office: Ashland U at LCCC 1005 N Abbe Rd Elyria OH 44035

WOOD, JACKIE C., executive secretary, small business owner; b. Cin., Mar. 11, 1963; d. Jackie Lee and Jo Ann (Hendricks) White; m. Ronald J. Wood, Sept. 11, 1982; children: Jason Jerome, Maria Ann. Cert. exec. sec., Scarlet Oaks JVSD, cert. in mgmt. skills devel. Co-owner Apex Janitorial Svcs., Cin.; sec. purchasing McSwain Mfg. Co., Cin.; owner Apex Advt., Cin., Apex Enterprises, Cin. Mem. NAFE, Cin. C. of C., No. Ky. Women's Network Coun. Home: 6262 Stewart Rd Cincinnati OH 45227 Office: Scudder Stevens & Clark 600 Vine St Ste 2000 Cincinnati Commerce Ctr Cincinnati OH 45202

WOOD, JANE SEMPLE, editor, writer; b. Easton, Pa., June 23, 1940; d. Royer Daniel and Wilhelmina Annette (Weichel) Semple; m. James MacPherson Wood, Sept. 8, 1961; children: James MacPherson Jr., Robert Semple. BA in Journalism, U. Calif., Berkeley, 1961. Reporter San Jose (Calif.) Mercury News, 1962; asst. dir. pub. rels. Nat. Symphony Orch., Washington, 1963-65; free-lance writer and editor Adoption Listing Svc. of Ohio, Cleve., 1976, AIA, Cleve., 1977, City of Bedford Heights, Ohio, 1980-81; free-lance writer and editor City of Shaker Heights, Ohio, 1979-80, pub. info. officer, dir. publs., 1980-85; founding editor Shaker Mag., Shaker Heights, Ohio, 1983—; free-lance writer Exec. Living, Cleve., 1990—; pub. rels. cons. Cable TV Com., Shaker Heights, 1978-85, Oak Park Exch. Congress, Shaker Heights, 1981. freelance writer Exec. Living, 1990—. Vol. editor, columnist Friends of Shaker Sq., Cleve., 1979-82; vol. pub. rels. com. Cleve. Ballet, 1980, Cleve. Orch., 1983; vol. contbg. editor Univ. Hosps., Cleve., 1990—. Recipient Grand award City Hall Digest, 1983, 85, 87, Excellence in Journalism award Soc. Profl. Journalists, 1988. Mem. Press Club of Cleve., Cleve. Internat. Vol. Orgn., U. Calif. Alumni Assn. (permanent class sec. 1961). Office: Shaker Mag 3400 Lee Rd Shaker Heights OH 44120

WOOD, JEAN KATHLEEN, small business owner; b. Mpls., Nov. 28, 1940; d. Bruno Richard and Jenny Margaret (Laurilla) Ulku; m. Robert L. Wood; children: Peter Allen, Jenny Rebecca, R. Nathan. B degree, U. Minn., 1962; MA, Drake U., 1989. Trainee Lintex, Mpls., 1962-63; designer Farnham's, Mpls., 1963-65; design dir. Koch Brothers, Des Moines, 1965-69; owner Interior Planning, Des Moines, 1969-89; owner, pres. Creative Enterprises, Des Moines, 1984—; asst. prof. Iowa State U. 1985-86. Chmn. Iowa, U.S.- Stavropol, USSR, Sister States, 1988-90. Mem. AAUW (nat. bd. dirs.), Nat. Assn. Women Bus. Owners (organizer Des Moines 1984-86), Planned Parenthood Fedn. Am. (nat. bd. dirs. 1987-88), Nat. Peace Inst. Found. (nat. bd. dirs., chmn. Midwest sect.), Iowa Peace Inst. (bd. dirs.). Home and Office: 636 42d St Des Moines IA 50312

WOOD, JEANNETTE GRIFFIN, director; b. Houston, Tex., Dec. 17, 1928; d. James Conley and Annie (Marshall) Weaver; m. H. Frank Griffin, Sept. 26, 1954 (div. 1967); 1 child, Frances G. Allinsmith; m. Jack Wood (dec. 1977). Student, U. Houston, 1963. Cert. Color Analyst. Exec. sec. Mobil Exploration Co., Houston, Tex., 1963-84; cons., color analyst Mary Kay Cosmetics, Houston, Tex., 1979-84, dir., 1984--; conducted seminars Vocat. Guidance Sch., Houston, 1987-88, Meml. Jr. High Sch., 1989, guest night workshop Mary Kay Cosmetics, Bullhead City, Ariz., 1989. Mem. Houston West C. of C., Desk and Derrick Club of Bellaire (pres. 1979), Am. Bus. Women's Assn. Republican. Roman Catholic. Address: 2336 Triway Ln Houston TX 77043

WOOD, JEANNETTE SUZON, real estate investor, writer; b. Albuquerque, Jan. 26, 1967; d. Thurmon Burlon and Hettie Ruth (Tippin) Wood. B in U. Studies, U. N.Mex., 1989. Real estate investor Albuquerque, 1987—. Contbr. poetry to anthologies. Vol. Nat. Religious Coalition of Women for Choice, Albuquerque, 1985, March of Dimes, 1986, Dem. Party Presdl. Campaign, 1984. Recipient 2d place for editorial writing N.Mex. Press Women's Assn., 1985; 1st class/mark of distinction for writing and graphic arts Nat. Scholastic Press Assn., 1985. Mem. Nat. Assn. Female Execs., Quill and Scroll, Golden Key. Roman Catholic. Home and office: 8505 Hilton Ave NE Albuquerque NM 87111

WOOD, KIMBA M., judge; b. Port Townsend, Wash., Jan. 2, 1944; d. H. Glen and Nora (Brown) W. BA cum laude, Conn. Coll., 1965; MS in Econs., London Sch. Econs., 1966; JD, Harvard U., 1969. Bar: U.S. Dist. Ct. D.C. 1969, U.S. Ct. Appeals D.C. 1969, N.Y. 1972, U.S. Dist. Ct. (ea. and so. dists.) N.Y. 1974, U.S. Ct. Appeals (2d cir.) 1975, U.S. Supreme Ct. 1980, U.S. Dist. Ct. (we. dist.) N.Y. 1981. Assoc. Steptoe & Johnson, Washington, 1969-70; with Office Spl. Counsel, OEO Legal Services, Washington, 1970-71; assoc., then ptnr. LeBoeuf, Lamb, Leiby & MacRae, N.Y.C., 1971-88; judge, U.S. Dist. Ct. (so. dist.) N.Y., N.Y.C., 1988—. Mem. ABA (chmn. civil practice, procedure com. 1982-85, mem. Council 1985—), N.Y. State Bar Assn. (chmn. antitrust sect. 1983-84), Fed. Bar Council (trustee from 1978, v.p., 1984-85), Am. Law Inst. Office: US Dist Ct US Courthouse Foley Sq New York NY 10007*

WOOD, LARRY (MARY LAIRD), journalist, author, university educator, public relations executive, environmental consultant; b. Sandpoint, Idaho; d. Edward Hayes and Alice (McNeel) Small; children: Mary, Marcia, Barry. BA magna cum laude, U. Wash., 1939, MA with highest honors, 1940; postgrad., Stanford U., 1941-42; postgrad. teaching fellowship, 1940-43; postgrad., U. Calif., Berkeley, 1946-47, cert. in photography, 1971; postgrad. journalism, U. Wis., 1971-72, U. Minn., 1971-72, U. Ga., 1972-73; postgrad. in art, architecture and marine biology, U. Calif., Santa Cruz, 1974-76, Stanford Hopkins Marine Sta., Santa Cruz, 1977-80. Feature writer and columnist Oakland, Calif., 1939—; pub. rels. dir. 12-county East Bay Regional Park Dist., No. Calif., 1948-68; pres. Larry Wood Pub. Rels., 1946—; dir. pub. rels. 12 County East Bay Regional Park Dist., Calif., 1948-68; dir. pub. rels. East Bay Regional Pk. Dist., Calif., 1948-68; prof. pub. rels., journalism and investigative reporting, San Diego State U., 1974, 75; Disting. vis. prof. journalism San Jose State U., 1976; assoc. prof. journalism Calif. State U., Hayward, 1978; prof. sci. and environ. journalism U. Calif. Berkeley Extension grad. div., 1979—; press del. nat. convs. Am. Geophys. Union Internat. Conf., 1986, 87, 88, 89, AAAS, 1989, 90, Yellowstone after the fire, 1989, Nat. Assn. Sci. Writers, 1989, George Washington U./Am. Assn. Neurol. Surgeons Sci. Writers Conf., 1990, Am. Inst. Biol. Scis. Conf., 1990; expert witness on edn., affirmative action, pub. rels., journalism and copyright; cons. sci. writers interne project, Stanford U., 1989—; spl. media guest Sigma Xi, 1990; mem. numerous spl. press corps. Contbr. over 5,000 articles on real estate, architecture, edn., oceanography, science, environ., health, medicine, sports, recreation, bus. and travel for newspapers, nat. mags., popular sci. mags., nat. and internat. newspaper syndicates, inflight mags., city mags., travel and architecture mags. including L.A. Times, Washington Post, Phila. Inquirer, Chgo. Tribune, Miami Herald, Oakland Tribune, Seattle Times, San Francisco Chronicle, Parade, San Jose Mercury News (Nat. Headliner award), Christian Sci. Monitor, MonitoRadio, Sports Illus., Mechanix Illus., Popular Mechanics, Parents, House Beautiful, Am. Home (awards 1988, 89), Oceans, Sea Frontiers, PSA Mag., Off-Duty mag., AAA Westways, AAA Motorland, Hawaiian Airlines in Paradise, Linguapress, Travel & Leisure, Travelin' Family Handyman, Chevron USA, others. Significant works include home and garden columnist and editor, 5-part series Pacific Coast Ports, 5-part series Railroads of the West, San Francisco Cultural Scene, Portland (Oreg.), Idaho Panhandle, High-Tech Cattle Rustling, Spotted Owl Controversy, Yellowstone, S.F. Chinatown, World Earthquakes, California's Water Wars, Calif. Earthquake '89, Calif. Textbooks' Scandal, Missing Children Smithsonian/Computer-world Award, New Nipomo Dunes Preserve, Reclassifying Big Horn Sheep and Mt. Lion as Big Game, Calif. Sea Otter Relocation, Endangered Species Series, Megamouth New Species of Shark, Columbia Alaska's Receding Glacier (selected as top sci. article in U.S., 1987), Calif. Underwater Parks, Ebey's Landing Nat. Hist. Preserve, Los Angeles Youth Gangs, Hist. Carousels; author: Wonderful U.S.A.: A State-by-State Guide to Its Natural Resources, 1989; co-author over 20 books including: McGraw-Hill English for Social Living, 1944, Fawcett Boating Books, 1956-66, Fodor's San Francisco, Fodor's California, 1982-89, Charles Merrill Focus on Life Science, Focus on Physical Science, 1983, 87, Focus on Earth Science; 8 works selected for use by Woltors-Nordoff-Longman English Language Texts, 1988; author: (with others) anthology West Winds, 1989; reviewer fo Charles Merrill texts, 1983-84; book reviewer for Profl. Communicator, 1987—; selected writings in permanent collections Oakland Pub. Libr., U. Wash. Main Libr.; contest winning contbr., author Journalism Quar. Nat. chmn. travel writing st for U.S. univ. journalism students Assn. for Edn. in Journalism/Soc. Am. Travel Writers, 1979-83; judge writing contest for Nat. Assn. Real Estate Editors, 1982—; mem. of press selected to cover Gorbechev's Visit to Stanford U., 1990; V.I.P. press del. Expo '86, Vancouver, B.C., Rsch. Trips to Costa Rica, Jamaica and Mex.; V.I.P. press mem. L.A. Times-sponsored trip to Hong Kong, 1990. Numerous awards, honors, citations, speaking engagements including induction into Broadway Hall of Fame U. Wash., Seattle, 1984, citations for environ. writing from Nat. Park Service, U.S. Forest Service, Bur. Land Mgmt., Oakland Mus. Assn., Oakland C. of C., USN plague and citation, Best Mag. Articles citation Calif. Pubs. Assn., 1984; co-recipient Nat. Headliner award for Best Sunday Newspaper Mag.; co-recipient citation Oakland Mus. for archtl. features, 1983; honoree Nat. Mortar Bd. for Achievements in Journalism, 1988, 89; selected as one of ten V.I.P. press for Yellowstone Nat. Park field trip on "Let Burn" rsch., 1989; named one of Calif.'s top 40 contemporary authors for 1989; invited V.I.P. press, spl. press guest numerous events worldwide. Mem. San Francisco Press Club, Nat. Press Club, Pub. Rels. Soc. Am. (charter mem. travel, tourism and edn. div.), Nat. Sch. Pub. Rels. Assn., Environ. Cons. N.Am., Am. Assn. Edn. in Journalism and Communications (exec. bd. nat. mag. div. 1978, panel chmn. 1979, 80, book reviewer Journalism Quar. jour.), Women in Communications (nat. bd. officer 1975-77), Soc. Profl. Journalists (nat. bd. for hist. sites 1980—), Nat. Press Photographers Assn. (cons. Bay Area interne project 1989—), Bay Area Advt. and Mktg. Assn., Nat. Assn. Sci. Writers, Calif. Writers Club (state bd., Berkely bd. 1989—), Am. Assn. Med. Writers, Internat. Assn. Bus. Communicators, Am. Film Inst., Am. Heritage Found. (citation 1986, 87, 88), Soc. Am. Travel Writers, Internat. Oceanographic Found., Oceanic Soc., Calif. Acad. Environ. News Writers, Seattle Advt. and Sales Club (former officer), Nature Conservancy, Calif. Acad. Scis., Smithsonian Audubon Soc., Nat. Wildlife Fedn., Fine Arts Mus., San Francisco, Seattle Jr. Advt. Club (charter), U. Wash. Alumni (life, charter mem. ocean scis. alumni, Disting. Alumni 1987), U. Calif., Berkeley Alumni (life, v.p., scholarship chmn. 1975-81), Stanford Alumni (life), Mortar Board Alumnae Assn. (life, honoree 1988, 89), Am. Mgmt. Assn., Nat. Soc. Environ. Journalists (charter), Phi Beta Kappa (v.p., bd. dirs. Calif. Alumni Assn., statewide chmn. scholarship awards 1975-81), Pi Lambda Theta, Theta Sigma Phi. Home: 6161 Castle Dr Oakland CA 94611

WOOD, LESLIE ANN, retail administrator; b. Chgo., Apr. 9, 1957; d. Howard Arnold and Anita Eleanor (Andler) W. AA, Harper Coll., 1977; BS in Communication Scis., Ill. State U., 1979. Advt. asst. Harry Alter Co., Chgo., 1979-80; clk. typist Career Guild, Evanston, Ill., 1980-81; reporter Aparacor, Evanston, Ill., 1981-82; sales mgmt. trainee Prudential Ins. Co. Am., Millburn, N.J., 1983-84; fin. cons. Summit Fin. Resources, Livingston, N.J., 1984; mgr. Chgo. area Renault Inc. div. AMC/Jeep/Renault, Elk Grove Village, Ill., 1985-87; customer relations specialist Chrysler Motors, Lisle, Ill., 1987-88, Chrysler dist. svc. and parts mgr.; dist. parts mgr. Subaru Am., Addison, Ill., 1989—. Home: 6822 Northwest Hwy Chicago IL 60631

WOOD, LINDA DORIS, manufacturing company executive; b. Westfield, Mass., Dec. 17, 1953; d. Arthur James Wood and Catherine Margaret (Stinehour) Clark. AB in Biochem., Brown U., 1976; postgrad., Lowell U., 1978-81. Chemist Gen. Electric Co., Wilmington, Mass., 1976-79; program adminstr./program analyst Gen. Electric Co., Wilmington, 1979-81, program mgr., 1981-85; program mgr. Northrop Corp., Norwood, Mass., 1985-87; sr. program mgr. Northrop Corp., Norwood, 1987—. Patentee in field. Mem. Northrop Mgmt. Orgn. (officer). Home: 2 Birch Ln Norton MA 02766 Office: Northrop Corp 100 Morse St Norwood MA 02062

WOOD, LINDA GAYE, real estate development company executive; b. South Haven, Mich., May 12, 1959; d. Gene A. and Beatrice (McKamey) W.; m. Terry M. Shaw, July 20, 1980 (div. 1982). Corr. student broker registration U. San Francisco, 1985. Sr. loan processor Shearson Am Express Mktg., San Diego, 1977-80; office mgr. Lomas & Nettleton Mfg. Co., San Diego, 1980-81; escrow coordinator Barratt Developers, San Diego, 1981-83, Tara Escrow Inc., 1983-84; sales mgr. real estate devel. Watt Industries Inc., Rancho Sante Fe, Calif, 1984-85; asst. v.p., dir. sales and mktg. The Buie Corp., Laguna Niguel, Calif., 1985—. Mem. Orange County Sales and Mktg. Coun. (bd. dirs. 1985-88, 90—, mem. exec. bd. 1988, Pres.'s Achievement award 1989), Assn. Profl. Mktg. Women (rec. sec. 1984-85), NAFE, Niguel Beach Terr. Homeowners Assn. Republican. Avocations: Swimming, walking, hiking, travel, cycling.

WOOD, LINDA MAY, librarian; b. Fort Dodge, Iowa, Nov. 6, 1942; d. John Albert and Beth Ida (Riggs) Wiley; m. C. James Wood, Sept. 15, 1964 (div. 1984). BA, Portland State U., 1964; M in Librarianship, U. Wash., 1965. Reference libr. Libr. Assn. Portland (Oreg.), 1965-67, br. libr., 1967-72, adminstrv. asst. to libr., 1972-73, asst. libr., 1973-77; asst. city libr. L.A. Pub. Libr., 1977-80; library dir. Riverside (Calif.) City and County Pub. Libr., 1980—. Chmn. bd. dirs. Inland Libr. System, 1983-84; League of Calif. Cities Community Svcs. Com., 1985-89; mem. users coun. Online Computer Libr. Ctr., 1986-89. Mem. AAUW, ALA, Pub. Libr. Assn., Libr. Adminstrn. and Mgmt. Assn., Calif. Libr. Assn. (pres. 1985), Calif. County Librs. Assn., LWV. Democrat. Office: Riverside City & County Pub Libr 3851 7th St PO Box 468 Riverside CA 92502-0468

WOOD, MARGARET GRAY, dermatologist, educator; b. Jamaica, N.Y., May 23, 1918; d. C.W. Bromley and B. Eleanor (Niblack) Gray; m. Alfred Conard Wood, Mar. 24, 1950; children: Margaret Diana, M. Deirdre Harper, Moira Dorothy. BA, U. ALa., Tuscaloosa, 1941; MD, Med. Coll. Pa., 1948, DMS, 1989. Diplomate Am. Bd. Dermatology, Am. Bd. Dermatopathology. Intern Phila. Gen. Hosp., 1948-50; resident U. Pa. Hosp., 1950-53; instr. dept. dermatology U. Pa. Sch. Medicine, Phila., 1952-53, assoc., 1953-67, asst. prof., 1967-71, assoc. prof., 1971-75, clin. prof., 1975-80, prof. and chmn. dept. dermatology, 1980-82, prof., 1982-88, prof. emeritus, 1988—; assoc. prof. grad. sch. medicine U. Pa., Phila., 1957-71, cons. sch. dental medicine, sch. vet. medicine; asst. prof. Med. Coll. Pa., Phila., 1957—, vice chmn., bd. dirs. 1984—; mem. exec. com. Am. Med. Women's Hosp. Svc. Com., Washington, 1970—; dir. Alleghany Health System, Pitts., 1987—. Author (with others) 4 books; contbr. numerous articles to med. jours. Recipient Rose Hershfeld award Women's Dermatology Soc., 1989. Mem. AMA, Internat. Dermatology Assn., Internat. Dermatopathology Assn., Phila. Dermatology Soc. (pres. 1978-79), Alpha Omega Alpha. Republican. Episcopalian.

WOOD, MARILYN SUSAN, music educator; b. Tulsa, Jan. 14, 1950; d. William Dale and Zola F. (Gore) Cabe; m. Robert Stuart Wood, Jr., June 3, 1972. BME magna cum laude, Okla. Bapt. U., 1972; MME, U. North Tex., 1977. Children's choir coord. First United Meth. Ch., Denton, Tex., 1973-76; coll. music educator Okla. Bapt. U., Shawnee, Okla., 1976-79, 1985—, Seminole (Okla.) Jr. Coll., 1979-80; pub. sch. educator Shawnee (Okla.) Pub. Schs., 1980-85; clinician various state and nat. music orgns., 1972-90. Composer: (children's cantata) What is Easter?, 1973; arranger several children's choral music pieces, 1980-90. Vol. music tchr. Kindergarten Ctr., Shawnee, 1987-90. Recipient acad. and music scholarships Okla. Bapt. U., 1968-72; finalist for educator of yr. C. of C., Shawnee, 1984. Mem. AAUW, Okla. Music Educators (v.p. 1985-87), Okla. Choral Dirs. (sec., treas. 1983-85, elem. rep. 1989-90), Am. Orff-Schulwerk (Okla. chpt. bd. mem. 1989-90), Mus. Edn. Nat. Conf., Am. Choral Dirs., Okla. Music Tchrs. Assn., Nat. Music Tchrs. Assn., (presenter Nat. Music Conv. 1990), Okla. Kodaly Educators, Nat. Kodaly Educators, Pi Kappa Lambda. Home: 595 Hicks Rd 5A Nashville TN 37221 Office: Ensworth Sch 211 Ensworth Ave Nashville TN 37205

WOOD, MARTHA SWAIN, mayor; b. Sept. 14, 1943; m. Frank B. Wood, June 1965; children: Helen Maria, Wesley Swain, Daniel Hardison. BA, Wake Forest U., 1965. Tchr. English and French city high schs., Henderson, N.C., 1965-66; buyer, v.p., sec., treas. Swain's, Inc., Fayetteville, N.C., 1972-83; mgr. Swain Investments, Fayetteville, 1984—; mayor City of Winston-Salem, N.C. Named Woman of Yr., Winston-Salem Chronicle, 1987. Mem. Greater Winston-Salem C. of C., Kiwanis. Baptist. Office: 101 N Main St Winston-Salem NC 27101*

WOOD, NANCY ELIZABETH, psychologist, educator; d. Donald Sterret and Orne Louise (Erwin) W. B.S., Ohio U., 1943, M.A., 1947; Ph.D., Northwestern U., Evanston, Ill., 1952. Prof. Case-Western Res. U., Cleve., 1952-60; specialist, expert Dept. HEW, Washington, 1960-62; chief of research Pub. Health, Washington, 1962-64; prof. U. So. Calif., Los Angeles, 1965—; learning disabilities cons., 1960-70; assoc. dir. Cleve. Hearing and Speech Ctr., 1952-60; dir. licensing program Brit. Nat. Trust, London. Author: Language Disorders, 1964, Language Development, 1970, Verbal Learning, 1975 (monograph) Auditory Disorders, 1978, Levity, 1980, Stoneskipping, 1989. Pres. faculty senate U. So. Calif., 1987-88. Recipient Outstanding Faculty award Trojan Fourth Estate, 1982. Fellow Am. Speech and Hearing Assn. (elected, legis. council 1965-68), Am. Psychol. Assn. (cert.), AAAS; mem. Internat. Assn. of Scientists. Republican. Methodist. Office: U So Calif University Park Los Angeles CA 90089

WOOD, NANCY K., public relations consultant; b. Mobile, Ala., Sept. 20, 1955; d. Morris Boykin and Velma Eulyn (Kearley) Wood. BA, U. Ala., 1977, MA, 1981. Advt. and sales coordinator Sheraton Inn, Mobile, 1977-78; nat. advt. coordinator Mobile Press Register, 1978-79; grad. teaching asst. U. Ala., Tuscaloosa, 1979-80; office mgr. U. Ala. Office Rsch. and Svc., Tuscaloosa, 1980-81; pub. info. coordinator Oglethorpe Power Corp., Atlanta, 1981-85; adj. prof. Ga. State U., Atlanta, 1984-89; media communications mgr. St. Joseph's Hosp., Atlanta, 1986-88; owner, prin. Communications Consultants, Atlanta, 1988—&. Vol., March of Dimes, Atlanta, 1990. Mem. Pub. Relations Soc. Am. (accredited; mem. Ga. accreditation com. 1987, chmn. awards com. 1990), U. Ala. Alumni Assn., U. Ala. Sch. Communications Alumni Assn., Kappa Alpha Theta Alumni. Office: Communications Consultants 94 Adrian Pl NW Atlanta GA 30327

WOOD, PATRICIA ANN, research scientist, physician; b. Mpls., July 17, 1953; d. Lawrence Edward and Helen Gertrude (Canfield) W.; m. William J.M. Hrushesky, June 28, 1985; children: Cassandra Marie Nicole. BS, U. Minn., 1976, MD, 1980, PhD, 1989. Diplomate Am. Bd. Internal Medicine. Intern, resident physician U. Minn., Mpls., 1984-87, med. fellow, 1987-89; med. fellow Albany (N.Y.) Med. Coll., 1989-90; asst. prof. medicine Albany Med. Coll., VA Med. Ctr., Albany, 1990—. Recipient Career Devel. award Am. Cancer Soc., 1990. Mem. Am. Assn. Cancer Rsch.

WOOD, REBA MAXINE, educator; b. McCracken, Kans., Nov. 1, 1919; d. Ernest Carl and Clorah Mabel (Pipes) Langdon; m. Homer George Teeter, June 3, 1940 (div. 1952); children: Sharon, Glen Harl, Darien B., E. Kevin; m. Robert L. Wood, Dec. 10, 1952; children: Robert Lee, Alisa, Kelsey. BS in Elem. Edn., NE Mo. State U., 1967, MA, 1971. Elem. tchr. pub. schs., Linn County, Mo., 1940-42, Brookfield, Mo., 1945-46; primary tchr. pub. schs., Plains, Mont., 1946-47; with advt. dept. Teeter Pub. Co., Plains, 1947-51; saleswoman, trainer Oneida Prestige Silver, Newark, Mo., 1953-55; with advt. make-up dept. Walsworth Pub. Co., Marceline, 1954-55; office worker Mo. Pub. Svc. Dept., Brookfield andMarceline, 1957-58; office worker, receptionist Dr. R.L. Ryals, Brookfield, 1958-59; elem. tchr. Brookfield Rural 3 Sch., 1967-90; ret., 1990. Mem. Mo. Tchrs. Assn., Community Tchrs. Assn. (sec. 1969-70), AAUW (past legis. chmn., edn. chmn., sec., 1st. v.p., pres. Brookfield br., Woman of Yr. award 1980), Mo. Saddle Club Assn., Brookfield Saddle Club (past sec.-treas.). Democrat. Home: Rte 1 Brookfield MO 64628

WOOD, ROBERTA SUSAN, foreign service officer; b. Clarksdale, Miss., Oct. 4, 1948; d. Robert Larkin and Dorothy Eloise (Shelton) Wood; B.A. with distinction, Southwestern U., Memphis, 1970; postgrad. Nat. U. Cuyo, Mendoza, Argentina, 1970-71; M.P.A., Harvard U., 1980. Joined U.S. Fgn. Service, 1972; service in Manila, Naples and Turin, Italy and Port-au-Prince, Haiti; mgmt. analyst Dept. State, Washington, 1980-84; U.S. consul gen., Jakarta, Indonesia, 1984-87, NATO Def. Coll., Rome, 1987-88; U.S. Consul Gen. Marseilles, France, 1988—. Fulbright scholar, 1970-71. Mem. Am. Fgn. Service Assn., Consular Officers Assn., Friends of Nat. Zoo, Friends of Kennedy Center, Planned Parenthood Washington, Phi Beta Kappa. Home and Office: Marseille American Embassy APO New York NY 09777

WOOD, RUTH LUNDGREN WILLIAMSON See LUNDGREN, RUTH WILLIAMSON WOOD

WOOD, SHARON, mountaineer; b. Halifax, N.S., Can., May 18, 1957; d. Stan and Peggy Wood. LLD (hon.), U. Calgary, 1987. Climbed peaks Mt. McKinley (Alaska), Mt. Logan (Can.), Mt. Aconcagua (Argentina), Mt. Makalu (Himalayas), Mt. Everest (Himalayas, 1st N.Am. woman to climb); Can. Light Everest Expedition, 1986; lectr. in field. Recipient Tenzing Norgay Trophy, 1987. Address: Canmore, AB Canada T0L 0M0

WOOD, VIRGINIA MARGARET, nurse; b. N.Y.C., Jan. 1, 1936; d. Ivan Smyrna and Louise Catherine (Straub) W.; adopted children—Margaret Theresa, Christine Louise. Diploma Capital City Sch. Nursing, 1957; B.S. in Nursing, U. Nev., 1970; M.Ed. in Allied Health, U. Fla., 1979; Ph.D. in Nursing Adminstrn., Columbia Pacific U., 1983. Staff nurse D.C. Gen. Hosp., Washington, 1957-58, USPHS Indian Health Service, Whiteriver and Phoenix, Ariz., 1958-61, U.S. Air Force, Nellis AFB, Las Vegas, Nev., 1961-63; staff nurse, supr. VA Hosp., Phoenix, 1970-72; nurse instr. VA Hosp., Columbia, Mo. and Gainesville, Fla., 1972-79; nurse educator USPHS Indian Health Service, Whiteriver, 1979-80, dir. nurses, San Carlos, Ariz., 1980-89, area nurse cons., quality assurance, 1989—. Served to capt. USAF, 1963-68; maj. U.S. Army, 1975-79. Recipient Supr. of Yr. award USPHS Indian Health Service, 1983. Mem. Am. Nurses Assn., Nat. League Nursing, Ariz. Soc. Ariz. Nursing Service Adminstrs. (nominating com. 1983-84), Phi Kappa Phi, Pi Lambda Theta. Republican. Roman Catholic. Avocations: reading; sewing; walking. Home: 3744 E Emerald Mesa AZ 85206 Office: USPHS Indian Health Svc Phoenix Area Office 3738 N 16th St Ste A Phoenix AZ 85016-5981

WOOD, VIRGINIA RILEY, artist; b. Columbia, S.C., Jan. 24, 1938; d. Joseph Ivey and Nell Virginia (Riley) McCabe; m. Stephen Ashley Anderson, May 26, 1962 (div. 1967); 1 child, Stephen Ashley; m. John Calvin Wood, Dec. 2, 1967 (div. 1970). Student, U. S.C., 1956-59, Art Students League, N.Y.C., 1959-62, Bradley U., Peoria, Ill., 1964. art instr. Rocky Mt. Sch. Art & Design, Denver, 1980-83; tchr., conductor workshops in field. Represented by Reiss Gallery, Parker Blake, McGrath & Braun, Denver; works in corporate and pvt. art collections. Recipient Art in Pub. Places Purchase award Reg. Transp. Dist., Denver, 1984. Mem. Front Range Women in the Visual Arts. Office: Fine Arts Associates 2810 Wilderness Pl #E Boulder CO 80301

WOOD, VIVIAN POATES, mezzo soprano, educator, author; b. Washington, Aug. 19, 1923; d. Harold Poates and Mildred Georgette (Patterson) W.; studies with Walter Anderson, Antioch Coll., 1953-55, Denise Restout, Saint-Leu-La-Fôret, France and Lakeville, Conn., 1960-62, 64-70, Paul A. Pisk, 1968-71, Paul Ulanowsky, N.Y.C., 1958-68, Elemer Nagy, 1965-68, Vyautas Marijosius, 1967-68; MusB Hartt Coll. Music, 1968; postgrad. (fellow) Yale U., 1968; MusM (fellow), Washington U., St. Louis, 1971, PhD (fellow), 1973. Debut in recital series Internat. Jeunesse Musicals Arts Festival, 1953, solo fellowship Boston Symphony Orch., Berkshire Music Ctr., Tanglewood, 1964, St. Louis Symphony Orch., 1969, Washington Orch., 1949, Bach Cantata Series Berkshire Chamber Orch., 1964, Yale Symphony Orch., 1968; appearances in U.S. and European recitals, oratorios, operas, radio and TV, 1953-68; appeared as soloist in Internat. Harpsichord Festival, Westminister Choir Coll., Princeton, N.J., 1973; appeared as soloist in meml. concert, Landowska Ctr., Lakeville, 1969; prof. voice U. So. Miss., Hattiesburg, 1971—, asst. dean Coll. Fine Arts, 1974-76, acting dean, 1976-77; guest prof. Hochschule für Musik, Munich, 1978-79; prof. Italian Internat. Studies Program, Rome, 1986; Miss. coord. Alliance for Arts Edn., Kennedy Ctr. Performing Arts, 1974—; mem. Miss. Gov.'s Adv. Panel for Gifted and Talented Children, 1974—; mem. 1st Miss. Gov.'s Conf. on the Arts, 1974—; bd. dirs. Miss. Opera Assn. Author: Polenc's Songs: An Analysis of Style, 1971. Recipient Young Am. Artists Concert award N.Y.C., 1955; Wanda Landowska fellow, 1968-72. Mem. Nat. Assn. Tchrs. of Singing, Music Tchrs. Nat. Assn., Am. Musicolog. Soc., Golden Key, Mu Phi Epsilon, Delta Kappa Gamma, Tau Beta Kappa (hon.), Pi Kappa Lambda. Democrat. Episcopalian. Avocation: sailing. Office: U So Miss Sch Music South Sta Box 8264 Hattiesburg MS 39401

WOOD, YVONNE ROBERTA, clinical psychologist; b. Tacoma, Sept. 3, 1951; d. Robert James Wood and Genevieve (Neuman) Brown; m. David Oliver Antonuccio, May 28, 1983. AB in Psychology magna cum laude, Occidental Coll., 1973; MA, U. Hawaii, 1975, PhD, 1981. Prof. psychology U. Nev., Reno, 1981-86, dir. Psychol. Svcs. Ctr., 1983-86; pvt. practice, Reno, 1986—. Guest reviewer Jour. Cons. and Clin. Psychology, 1989—; contbr. articles to profl. jours., chpt. to book. Speaker to civic orgns.; trustee Meadows Hosp., Reno; mem. adv. bd. Women's Ctr., St. Mary's Hosp., Reno, 1987-90. Mem. APA, Assn. for Advancement Behavior Therapy, Am. Soc. Clin. Hypnosis, No. Nev. Assn. Lic. Psychologists (treas. 1987-89), Phi Beta Kappa. Democrat. Office: 1105 Terminal Way Ste 202 Reno NV 89502

WOODALL, CHARLOTTE DEE, county official; b. St. Louis, Feb. 10, 1945; d. Chandler Decatur and Lucille (Stauffer) Davis; m. Thomas G. Woodall, June 18, 1967 (div. Sept. 1978); 1 child, Robin Anne. BA, U. Ky., 1966; MS in Mgmt., Aquinas Coll., Grand Rapids, Mich., 1986. Cert. purchasing mgr., pub. purchasing officer. Asst. buyer Woodward & Lothrop, Washington, 1967-69; procurement officer fed. supply svc. GSA, Arlington, Va., 1969-73, career devel. officer, 1973-75; buyer Kent County, Grand Rapids, Mich., 1979-81, asst. dir. purchasing, 1981—. Bd. dirs., sec. Camp Henry, Grand Rapids, 1981-83; mem., sec., v.p. St. Andrew's Bd. Edn., Grand Rapids, 1983-86; trustee, treas. Westminster Ch., Grand Rapids, 1983-86, elder, 1987—, also ch. sch. tchr., dir. adult edn. program. Mem. Mich. Pub. Purchasing Officers Assn. (program chmn. winter conf. 1983, 90), Grand Rapids Area Purchasing Mgmt. Assn. Democrat. Home: 265 Alger St SE Grand Rapids MI 49507 Office: Kent County 300 Monroe St NW Grand Rapids MI 49503

WOODARD, ALFRE, actress; b. Tulsa, Sept. 8, 1953. Student, Boston U. Appeared in films Cross Creek, 1983, Extremities, 1986, Scrooged, 1988, TV series St. Elsewhere, Hill Street Blues (Emmy award for guest appearance in drama series 1984), L.A. Law (Emmy award for guest appearance in drama series 1987), TV films The Killing Floor, Unnatural Causes, plays For Colored Girls Who Have Considered Suicide, When the Rainbow is Enuf, Mark Taper Forum, L.A., off-Broadway play A Map of the World, 1985. Recipient Emmy awards for guest appearance in drama series. Office: care STE Representation Ltd 9301 Wilshire Blvd Ste 312 Beverly Hills CA 90210*

WOODARD, ANNE TAYLOR, librarian, insurance agent; b. Rocky Mount, N.C., Jan. 27, 1953; d. Sam Pierce and Doris (Satterwhite) Taylor; m. Calvin Staton Woodard Jr., June 4, 1972 (div. Nov. 1981). BS in Libr. Sci., East Carolina U., 1974; MS in Libr. and Info. Sci., Cath. U. Am., 1981. Media specialist G.R. Whitfield Elem. Sch., Grimesland, N.C., 1974-76; libr. asst. Tidewater Community Coll., Virginia Beach, Va., 1976-82; libr. Louise Obici Meml. Hosp., Suffolk, Va., 1982-83; librarian U.S. Geol. Survey, Reston, Va., 1983—; Pekingese dog breeder, Reston and Virginia Beach, 1977—; ins. agt. various cos., 1986—; realtor Long and Foster Realtors, Virginia Beach, 1990—. Mem. Alpha Beta Alpha (pres. 1973-74), Potomac Valley Pekingese (bd. dirs. Adelphi, Md. 1986—, Championship Plaque 1986, 88, 89), Greater Pitts. Pekingese, Pekingese Club of Am. (N.Y.C.). Methodist. Home: 2400 London Bridge Rd Virginia Beach VA 23456

WOODARD, CAROL JANE, education educator; b. Buffalo, Jan. 19, 1929; d. Harold August and Violet Maybelle (Landsittel) Young; m. Ralph Arthur Woodard, Aug. 19, 1950; children—Camaron Jane, Carsen Jane, Cooper Ralph. BA, Hartwick Coll., 1950; MA, Syracuse U., 1952; PhD, SUNY, Buffalo, 1972; postgrad., Bank St. Coll., Harvard U. Cert. tchr., N.Y. State. Tchr. Orchard Park, N.Y., 1950-51, Danville, Ind., 1951-52, Akron, N.Y., 1952-54; dir. Garden Nursery Sch., Williamsville, N.Y., 1955-65; tchr. Amherst (N.Y.) Coop. Nursery Sch., 1967-69; asst. prof. early childhood edn. SUNY Coll., Buffalo, 1969-72; lab. demonstration tchr. and student teaching supr. SUNY Coll., 1969-76, assoc. prof., 1972-79, prof., 1979-88, prof. emeritus, 1988—; co-dir. Consultants in Early Childhood, 1989—; cons. Lutheran Ch. Am., Villa Maria Coll., Buffalo Pub. Schs., Buffalo Mus. Sci., Headstart Tng. Programs, Erie Community Coll., N.Y. State Dept. Edn., numerous workshops.; cons. sch. systems, indsl. firms, pubs., civic orgns. in child devel.; vis. prof. The Netherlands and East China Univ., Shanghai, People's Republic of China, 1986. Author 7 books for young children, 2 textbooks in field; co-author Physical Science in Early Childhood, 1987; co-author nat. curriculum for ch. sch. for 3-yr.-olds; author: booklet You Can Help Your Baby Learn; author/coordinator TAKE CARE child protection project, 1987; contbr. chpt. to When Children Play, 1985; contbr. numerous articles in field to profl. jours. Bd. trustees Hartwick Coll., Oneonta, N.Y., 1978-87. Mem. Nat. Assn. Edn. Young Children, Early Childhood Edn. Council Western N.Y., Assn. Childhood Edn. Internat., Phi Delta Kappa, Pi Lambda Theta. Home: 1776 Sweet Rd East Aurora NY 14052

WOODARD, DOROTHY MARIE, insurance broker; b. Houston, Feb. 7, 1932; d. Gerald Edgar and Bessie Katherine (Crain) Floeck; student N.Mex. State U., 1950; m. Jack W. Woodard; June 19, 1950 (dec.); m. Norman W. Libby, July 19, 1982. Ptnr. Western Oil Co., Tucumcari, N.Mex., 1950—; owner, mgr. Woodard & Co., Las Cruces, N.Mex., 1959-67; agt., dist. mgr. United Nations Ins. Co., Denver, 1968-74; agt. Western Nat. Life Ins. Co., Amarillo, Tex., 1976—. Exec. dir. Tucumcari Indsl. Commn., 1979—; dir. Bravo Dome Study Com., 1979—; owner Libby Cattle Co., Libby Ranch Co.; regional bd. dirs. N.Mex., Eastern Plains Council Govts., 1979—. Mem. NAFE, Tucumcari C. of C., Mesa Country Club. Home: PO Box 823 Tucumcari NM 88401

WOODARD, KATHRYN DELORIS, social services administrator; b. Kearney, Nebr., Jan. 10, 1951; d. Bernard Brunson and Deloris Mae Hiner; stepfather, Eddie Hiner; m. Ronnie Duwayne Adams, Dec. 23, 1966 (div. June 1968); 1 child, Kevin Glenn; m. Douglas Walls, Aug. 1975 (div. 1979); m. Otis David Woodard, Feb. 19, 1983; 1 child, Otis Le Andrew; stepchildren: Otis Le' Analdo, Otis Le Antoni, Otis Le' Andre. Student, Kearney State Coll.; AA in Bus. Adminstrn., Cen. Community Coll. Community devel. dir. City of Harvard, Nebr., 1977-79; dir. food stamp ctr. H.D.C., Kansas City, 1981-83; grant cons. Luth. Family and Children's Services, St. Louis, 1984-85; dir. Contact Helpline, St. Louis, 1984—; v.p. Luth. North St. Louis Outreach, 1987—; founding mem. Nebr. State Task Force on Domestic Violence Intervention, 1976-78; founder, facilitator Clay County (Nebr.) Domestic Violence Intervention Project, 1978-79; asst. coord. Clay County Domestic Violence Project, 1978-79. Active Freedom Inc. Black Polit. Orgn., Kansas City, 1980-83; bd. dirs. So. Christian Leadership Conf., Kansas City, 1980-83. Mem. NOW (pres. Kearny chpt. 1972-75, sec. Hastings, Nebr. chpt. 1977-79), Phi Beta Lambda (2d place Nebr. Ms. Bus. Exec. 1977). Democrat. Lutheran. Home: 2023 Bissell Saint Louis MO 63107 Office: Luth North St Louis Outreach 2023 Bissell Saint Louis MO 63107

WOODARD, MELISSA JOY, banker; b. Yaeger, W.Va., Dec. 26, 1952; d. Roscoe and Jerusha (Robinette) Muncy; m. Craig Woodard, Oct. 15, 1978 (div. June 1984). Student in bus., psychology and English, Spokane (Wash.) Community Coll., 1978-80; student in human relations and communications, Diablo Valley Community Coll., Pleasant Hill, Calif., 1980; student, San Francisco U., 1981-82, U. Md., 1982-83; BBA, Nat. U., L.A., 1989, postgrad., 1989—. Retail and photography specialist U.S. Army and USAF Exchange, Spokane, 1970-76; fin. adminstr. Wash. Mut. Savs., Spokane, 1976-78; br. svc. mgr. Great Western Savs., Walnut Creek, Calif., 1978-81; rels. specialist U.S. Govt., Bremerhaven, Fed. Republic of Germany, 1982-83; br. v.p. Great Western Bank, Venice, Calif., 1983-89; br. mgr., v.p. Wells Fargo Bank, 1989—; mgr. Fed. Women's Program, Bremerhaven, 1982-83; trainer fed. employees, Bremerhaven, 1982-83; motivational speaker Toastmasters, Walnut Creek, 1981-82, Venice Skills Ctr., 1985—. Adminstrv. asst. Oakland (Calif.) Spl. Olympics, 1980-82. Century City Congrl. scholar, 1987. Mem. Venice C. of C. (bd. dirs. 1984—). Office: Great Western Bank 1415 Lincoln Blvd Venice CA 90291

WOODARD, NINA ELIZABETH, banker; b. L.A., Apr. 3, 1947; d. Alexander Rhodes and Harriette Jane (Power) Mathews; m. John David Woodard, Mar. 17, 1966; children: Regina M., James D. Grad. Pacific Coast Banking Sch., 1987. Dental asst. Donald R. Shire DDS, L.A., 1965-66; with Security Pacific Nat. Bank, Marina Del Rey, Calif., 1968-69; with First Interstate Bank, Casper, Wyo., 1971—, adminstr. asst. personnel, 1975-78, asst. v.p., asst. mgr. pers., 1978-82, v.p., dir. mktg. and pers., 1982-84, v.p., mgr. human resources, 1984-88; v.p., mgr. employee rels. First Interstate Bank Ltd., L.A., 1988—; instr. mktg. Am. Inst. Banking, 1983, Casper Coll., 1982. Mem. Civil Svc. Commn., City of Casper, 1983-88; bd. dirs. YMCA, 1984-87, Downtown Devel. Assn.; pres. Downtown Casper Assn. Named Bus. Woman of Yr., Bus. and Profl. Women, 1982, Young Career Woman, 1975. Mem. Nat. Assn. Bank Women, Bus. and Profl. Women (dist. dir.), Am. Soc. Pers. Adminstrn. (regional v.p., accredited sr. profl. in human resources, state coun. Wyo. 1987-89), Pers. and Indsl. Rels. Assn. (chmn. govt. affairs com. 1989—), Soc. Human Resources Mgmt. (Calif. state coun. 1989—), Cen. Wyo. Soroptimist, Order Eastern Star. Republican. Roman Catholic.

WOODARD, SUE CAROL, public relations professional; b. Cleve., Dec. 9, 1946; d. Herschel Payne and Dorothy Mae (Holsapple) Chapman; m. Eddie Ray Woodard, Apr. 18, 1969; children: Deborah Sue Lownsbery, Stacie Rae Herig. Student, Albion (Mich.) Coll., 1964-66, Western Mich. U., 1989—. Sec. State Farm Fire Ins., Holt, Mich., 1968-69; pub. rels. specialist VFW Nat. Home, Eaton Rapids, Mich., 1978-85, adminstrv. coord., 1985-89, pub. rels. mgr., 1989—. Exec. producer (video tape) Caring For Our Own, 1988. Mem. Nat. Soc. Fundraising Execs., Women in Communication, Inc., Bus. and Profl. Women Assn., Ladies Aux. to VFW (sec., treas. 1985—). Methodist. Office: VFW Nat Home 3573 Waverly Rd S Eaton Rapids MI 48827-9799

WOODBRIDGE, ANNIE SMITH, emerita librarian, foreign language educator; b. Wingo, Ky., July 7, 1915; d. Ernest Herbert and Flora Susan (Parrish) Smith; B.A., Murray State Coll., 1935; M.A., Peabody Coll., 1936; postgrad. U. Wis., Tex. State Coll. for Women, U. Ky., Sorbonne, Universidad Interamericana; m. Hensley C. Woodbridge, Aug. 28, 1953; 1 dau., Ruby Susan Woodbridge Jung. Tchr. Cadiz High Sch., 1936-37, David Lipscomb Coll., 1937-43, Bethel Coll., 1943-46, Murray State Coll., 1946-54, 59-65; instr. So. Ill. U., Carbondale, 1966-74, researcher Morris Library, 1974-85. Mem. NOW, Midwest Latin Am. Studies Assn., Ellen Glasgow Soc., Soc. Study of Midwestern Lit. Democrat. Mem. Ch. of Christ. Editor: (with others) Collected Short Stories of Mary Johnston; contbr. articles jours. and newsletters. Home: 1804 W Freeman St Carbondale IL 62901

WOODBURY, MARGARET CLAYTOR, physician, university administrator; b. Roanoke, Va., Oct. 30, 1937; d. John Bunyan and Roberta Morris (Woodfin) Claytor; m. Lawrence DeWitt Young, 1959 (div.); children: Laura Ruth, Lawrence DeWitt Jr.; m. 2d, David Henry Woodbury, Jr., Nov. 30, 1968; 1 child, David Henry III. A.B. cum laude, Mt. Holyoke Coll., 1958; postgrad. Albany Med. Coll., 1958-60; M.D., Meharry Med. Coll., 1962. Diplomate Am. Bd. Internal Medicine, Nat. Bd. Med. Examiners. Asst. chief medicine-endocrinology USPHS, S.I., N.Y., 1967-68; chief out-patient clinic USPHS Hosp., Detroit, 1968-69; med. officer-in-charge USPHS Out-patient Clinic, Detroit, 1969-71; instr. internal medicine-endocrinology U. Mich., Ann Arbor, 1969-80, asst. prof. internal medicine-endocrinology and metabolism, 1980—, asst. dean student and minority affairs, 1983—; project dir. Health Careers Opportunity Program/Assistance to Increase Matriculation and Earn Degrees, 1984—; cons. Bryant Neighborhood Clinic, Ann Arbor, 1978; vis. lectr. Morehouse Med. Coll., Atlanta, 1980-82; minority recruitment officer Admissions U. Mich. Med. Sch., Ann Arbor, 1975-83; mem. Adv. Com. on Affirmative Actions Program, 1982-85, chair, 1984-85. Contbr. chpts. to books, articles to profl. jours. Vol. Democratic Party, Ann Arbor, 1972—, co-chair precinct, 1973; parent rep. Engring. Indsl. Support Program, Ann Arbor, 1978-82; vol. Nat. Council Negro Women, Ann Arbor, 1974-76; mentor Ann Arbor Alliance for Achievement in Acads. and the Arts, sec., 1982-83; trustee Mt. Holyoke Coll., 1985—; mem. State of Mich. Dr. Martin Luther King, Jr. Holiday Commn., 1985—; mem. Health Braintrust, Congl. Black Caucus, 1985—. Recipient Biochemistry award Albany Med. Coll. (N.Y.), 1958-60; pediatrics prize Meharry Med. Coll., Nashville, 1960-62; Mount Holyoke Alumnae Med. Honor, 1983; fellow Bryn Mawr/HERS Summer Inst. for Women in Higher Edn. Adminstrn., 1987. Mem. Nat. Med. Assn., Am. Med. Women's Assn., Nat. Minority Health Assn. (charter), Alpha Omega Alpha, Sigma Gamma Rho. Presbyterian. Club: Mt. Holyoke (press rep. 1973-76, pres. 1976-80). Office: U Mich Furstenberg Ctr PO Box 0611 Ann Arbor MI 48109

WOODEN, JANET ILENE, savings and loan executive; b. St. Joseph, Mo., Dec. 6, 1962; d. E.B. and Winnie Leah (Byrd) Ross; m. Billy Joe Wooden, May 6, 1983. Student, Mo. Western State Coll., 1981-83, 88-90. Teller First Fed. Savs. and Loan, St. Joseph, 1981-83; br. mgr., asst. v.p. N.Am. Savs. Bank, St. Joseph, 1983—. Mem. Rotary. Office: North Am Savs Bank 920 North Belt Hwy Saint Joseph MO 64506

WOODEN, RUTH A., public service advertising executive; b. Madison, Wis., Aug. 4, 1946. BA, U. Minn., 1968, postgrad. Project dir. Lee Creative Rsch., St. Louis, 1970-72; project mgr. Ralston Purina, St. Louis, 1972-78; sr. v.p., account dir. N.W. Ayer, N.Y.C., 1978-88; pres. The Advt. Coun., Inc., N.Y.C., 1988—. Bd. dirs. CARE Inc., N.Y.C., 1980—, Talbot-Perkins Children's Svcs. Inc., N.Y.C., 1986-88. Office: The Advt Coun Inc 261 Madison Ave New York NY 10016

WOODFIN, BEULAH M., biochemist; b. Chgo., June 22, 1936; d. Rice Jacobs and Alma Antoinette (Curiel) W. BA, Vanderbilt U., 1958; MS, U. Ill., 1960, PhD, 1963. Rsch. assoc. Dept. Biological Chemistry U. Mich., Ann Arbor, 1963-66, instr., 1966-67; instr. Dept. Biochemistry U. N.Mex., Albuquerque, 1967-68, asst. prof., 1968-86, assoc. prof., 1986—. Mem. AAAS, Am. Soc. for Biochemistry and Molecular Biology, Protein Soc., N.Mex. Acad. Scis., Am. Chem. Soc., Assn. for Women in Sci., Internat. Assn. Women Bioscientists, Sigma Xi. Office: Dept Biochemistry Univ NMex Sch Medicine Albuquerque NM 87131

WOODFORK, NANCY ANN, telephone company executive; b. Boston, Jan. 16, 1948; d. Nelson Carter and Millicent Iona (Beckford) W. BA, U. Mass., 1970; MSW, Boston Coll., 1976. Social worker Adoption Placement Unit Dept. Social Svcs. Dept. Pub. Welfare, Boston, 1970-73, sr. social worker, 1973-76, supt. social services, 1976-79; market adminstr. New England Telephone Co., Boston, 1979-80, account exec., 1980-83; account exec. Nynex, Boston, 1983-84; cons. network New England Telephone Co., Boston, 1984-88; area ops. mgr. New England Telephone Co., 1988—; interviewer Child Welfare League Am., N.Y.C., 1974-76; trainer, supr. Rainbow Distrs. Inc., Waltham, Mass., 1976-77; interviewer Community Devel. Corp., Roxbury, Mass., 1977; chmn. Black Recruitment Com. Adoption and Foster Care Inc., Boston, 1983-84. Coordinator Com. to Elect Jimmy Carter Pres., Boston, 1976; bd. dirs. Cooper Community Ctr., 1978-82. Mem. Nat. Assn. Black Social Workers, Mass. Adoption Resource Exchange (bd. dirs.). Democrat. Episcopalian. Home: 12 Schuyler St Dorchester MA 02121 Office: New England Telephone Co 1089 Washington St West Newton MA 02165

WOODHAM, JEAN, sculptor; b. Midland City, Ala., Aug. 16, 1925; d. Marcus Morton and Alma (Clements) W.; m. James Lee Caraway, Nov. 18, 1949 (div. 1968); children: Susan Melissa, Elizabeth Leigh; m. Harold L. Friedman, July 13, 1986. BA, Auburn U., 1946; postgrad., Sculpture Ctr., N.Y.C., 1946-49. vis. lectr. Ga. Inst. Tech, Atlanta, 1971; vis. assoc. prof. Auburn U., 1971, assoc. prof. 1974-75; vis. critic Cornell U., Ithaca, N.Y., 1980; artist-in-residence Djerassi Found., Woodside, Calif., 1983. Commd. sculpture Internat. Bank, Washington, 1964, Flintkote Corp., White Plains, N.Y., 1968-69, Gen. Electric Credit Corp., Stamford, Conn., 1971-72, G.T.E. Corp. hdqrs., Stamford, 1973, Tex. Eastern Transmission, Houston, 1974-75, N.Y.C. Bd. Edn. Truman High Sch., 1975-76, Cooper Meml. Libr. and Art Ctr., Opelika, Ala., 1977, Auburn (Ala.) U., 1978-79, Norwalk (Conn.) Pub. Libr., 1980-81, Temple Beth Or, Montgomery, Ala., 1982, Westport (Conn.) Town Hall, 1982, Cen. Conn. State U., New Britain, 1986-87, Conn. State Art Commn., Farmington, 1988-89; one woman shows include Cen. Conn. State U., New Britain, 1987, Fairfield (Conn.) Libr. Gallery, 1989-90; exhibited group shows at Guild First Bi-Coastal Exhbn., San Francisco, Shidoni Sculputre Garden, Tesuque, N.Mex., Ann. Exhbn., N.Y.C., Ala. State Commn. on the Arts, 1989, The Gallery, Fairfield, Conn., 1989-90, Sculptors Guild Gallery, N.Y.C.; subject TV film Arts: Themes & Variations, 1984 acquired by Smithsonian Inst., pub. TV film Conn. Profiles, 1979, Jean Woodham Sculptor Extraordinare, 1989; cable TV Jean Woodham: Sculptor Extraordinarem 1989; curator in field; work featured in Sculpture. Technique. Form. Mem. Westport Symbolic Heritage Preservation Com., 1983-88; pres.' com. Auburn Generations Fund, 1983-85; chmn. visual arts Westport Arts Ctr., 1981, bd. dirs. 1982-86; charter mem. Coll. Liberal Arts Adv. Coun., Fine Arts Coun. Auburn U., Ala., 1987—, mem. adv. com. and coun., 1990. Name one of Outstanding Women of Conn., UN, 1987; recipient 37 awards including Finch award Art of Northeast U.S.A., New Canaan, Conn., 1985, Citation for Contbn. to Arts Gen. Assembly, Hartford, Conn., 1986, Outstanding Profl. and Community Achievements award YWCA Greater Bridgeport: Salute to Women, 1986, Citation Gov. Conn., 1987, Citation Gov. Ala., 1989. Mem. Sculptors Guild (exec. bd. 1966-86, 88-89, 90, v.p. membership 1983, 84, treas. 1962-67, sec. 1971-73, curator, pres. 1990), Silvermine Guild Artists (bd. trustees 1982-84, chmn. admissions 1983). Studio: 26 Pin Oak Ln Westport CT 06880

WOODHULL, NANCY JANE, newspaper publishing executive; b. Perth Amboy, N.J., Mar. 1, 1945; d. Harold and May (Post) Cromwell; m. William Douglass Watson, Sept. 24, 1976; 1 child, Tennie Jane. Student, Trenton State Tchrs. Coll., 1963-64. Dept. editor News Tribune, Woodbridge, N.J., 1964-73; reporter Detroit Free Press, 1973-75; mng. editor Times-Union, Rochester, N.Y., 1975-80, Democrat & Chronicle, Rochester, 1980-82; mng. editor USA Today, Arlington, Va., 1982-85, sr. editor, 1985-87; pres. Gannett News Media, Washington, 1986-90, Gannett News Svc., Washington, 1988-90; v.p. news svcs. Gannett Co., Inc., Washington, 1987-88; exec. v.p., editor-in-chief So. Progress Corp., Birmingham, Ala., 1990—. Home: 2021 Rhode Island Ave McLean VA 22101 Office: So Progress Corp PO Box 2581 Birmingham AL 35202

WOODIN, MARGARET CONBOY, bank officer; b. N.Y.C., Sept. 14, 1932; d. William Francis and Helen (Moore) Conboy; m. William B. Woodin, June 26, 1954; children: William B. Jr., Joann Margaret Lawrence. BS summa cum laude, Coll. Misericordia, Dallas, Pa., 1954; cert. banking, Williams Coll., Williamstown, Mass., 1982. Banking officer Conn. Nat. Bank subs. Shawmut Nat. Corp., Torrington, 1964—; bd. dirs., treas. Salvation Army, Torrington, 1982-85; pres., incorporator Litchfield County Women's Network, Torrington, 1980-82. Mem. quatro millenium com. City of Torrington, 1989—; mem. Torrington Rep. Women's Club, 1987—; campaign worker com. to re-elect Delia Donne Mayor, 1985, 87, 89; bd. dirs. March of Dimes, 1989—. Mem. Am. Inst. Banking, Altrusa Internat., Nat. Honor Soc. Cath. Women, Kappa Gamma Pi. Home: 193 Lincoln Ave Torrington CT 06790 Office: Conn Nat Bank 236 Prospect St Torrington CT 06790

WOODMAN, ELLEN ARMSTRONG, director nursing department; b. Chardon, Ohio, Sept. 17, 1937; d. John Jacob and Martha (Armstrong) Kulp; children: John Warren, Andrew James. BSN, U. Cin., 1959; MS, U. Mich., 1966, doctoral studies, 1990—. Staff nurse Cin. Gen. Hosp., 1959-60, Cleve. Met. Hosp., 1960-61; staff nurse U. Mich. Hosp., Ann Arbor, 1961-62, supr. adminstrv. nursing, 1962-63; instr. U. Mich. Sch. Nursing, Ann Arbor, 1963-64; sr. nurse clinician Wm. Beaumont Hosp., Royal Oak, Mich., 1966-68; asst. prof. U. Mich. Sch. Nursing, Ann Arbor, 1969-70; asst. dir. Mansfield (Ohio) Gen. Hosp., Mansfield, 1971-76; asst. prof. and dir. U. Mich., Flint, 1976—; chmn. Genesee County Community Mental Health Svc. Bd., Flint, Mich., 1988—, cons. nursing and legal matters, 1987—. Contbr. articles to profl. jours. Mem. Am. Nurses Assn., Mich. Nurses Assn., Flint Dist. Nursing Assn. (bd. dirs. 1987—, Profl. Nurse of the Year), Mich. Statewide Coord. Coun. (advisory bd. to dept. of pub. health. Home: 8254 Creekwood Dr Grand Blanc MI 48435 Office: U Mich 101 Laper Annex Flint MI 48502

WOODRING, CAROLE LYN, writer, consultant; b. State College, Pa., Nov. 7, 1945; d. Charles Elmer and Helen Pauline W.; m. Eric Marvin Berg, May 30, 1970; children: Nicole Leslie Woodring, Adam Trevor Woodring, Jessica Lynne Woodring. BA Pa. State U., 1967; MA Columbia U., 1969. Foster caseworker Dauphin County Child Care Agy., Harrisburg, Pa., 1967-68; pers. asst. dir. Conf. Bd., Inc., N.Y.C., 1969-70; mgr. tng. design and validation Chem. Bank N.Y. Trust Inc., N.Y.C., 1970-73; tng. cons. 1st Union Corp., Charlotte, N.C., 1978-79; adj. prof. Sacred Heart Coll., Belmont, N.C., 1978-80; dir., officer Fortune Cons., 1977-84; pvt. cons., Matthews, N.C., 1979-86; officer J.N. Adams & Assocs., 1982—; freelance writer. Trustee Charlotte Montessori Sch., 1980-83, pres., 1981-83; mem. parent coun. bd. Charlotte Latin Sch., 1984-85; bd. dirs. PTO Rodeo Park Sch., 1987—. Mem. Assn. for Psychol. Type, AAUW (past bd. dir.), Am. Psychol. Assn. (assoc.), Sigma Sigma Sigma (past chpt. pres.). Presbyterian. Home: 2528 Sleepy Hollow Dr State College PA 16803 Office: 315 S Allen St Ste 222 State College PA 16801

WOODRUFF, CORDELIA ELIZABETH, executive; b. Winston-Salem, N.C., Nov. 6, 1952; d. Edward L. and Betty (Amos) Simpson; m. Robert H. Woodruff, Mar. 20, 1976; children: Patrice Rochell, Robert Jr. BA, Winston-Salem State U., 1975. Lic. ins. agt. Field exec. Tarheel Trial coun. Girl Scouts U.S., Colfax, N.C., 1976-80; ops. mgr. Wachovia Svs., Inc., Winston-Salem, 1980-83; engr. coord. Jepson-Burns Corp., Winston-Salem, 1984—. Trainer Girl Scouts U.S., Colfax, 1986-88; v.p. Kimberly Park Elem. PTA, Winston-Salem, 1987-88, pres., 1989-90; chmn. YMCA Preschool Parents Orgn., Winston-Salem, 1988-90; mem. Nat. Women of Achievement, Kernesville, 1990. Mem. NAFE, A&T Alumni Asssn. (sec. 1985), Am. Assn. Girl Scout Execs Staff. Democrat. Home: 715 Swanson Ct Winston-Salem NC 27105 Office: Jepson Burns Corp 1455 Fairchild Rd Winston-Salem NC 27105

WOODRUFF, EDYTHE WILMA PARKER, retired mathematics educator; b. Bellwood, Ill., Jan. 15, 1928; d. Thomas Mack and Goldie Ellen (Brooks) Parker; m. Robert Wilson Woodruff, June 24, 1950; children: Andrew Wilson, Jeanne Karen. BA, U. Rochester, 1948, MS, 1952; MS, Rutgers U., 1964; PhD, SUNY, Binghamton, 1971. Instr. maths. Douglass Coll., Rutgers U., New Brunswick, N.J., 1970-71; asst. prof. Trenton (N.J.) State Coll., 1971-80, assoc. prof., 1980-90; ret. 1990; visitor Inst. for Advanced Study, Princeton, N.J., 1979-80. Contbr. articles on physics and topology to profl. jours. Scholarship winner Nat. Sci. Talent Search, Washington, 1945. Mem. Am. Math. Soc., Maths. Assn. Am., Assn. Women in Maths., Phi Kappa Phi, Phi Beta Kappa. Mem. Unitarian Ch. Home: 11 Fairview Ave East Brunswick NJ 08816

WOODRUFF, GEORGIA DELORES (GEORGIA DELORES WILBUR), nursing education administrator; b. Port Arthur, Tex., Mar. 31, 1926; d. Clarence Nelson and Gertrude Alice (Sewell) Wilbur; diploma St. Mary's Hosp. Sch. Nursing, 1948; A.A., Lamar Coll., 1947; m. James Calvin Woodruff, Sept. 27, 1957. Staff nurse various hosps. in Tex. and Ariz., 1948-61; nurse, Park Place Hosp., Port Arthur, Tex., 1961-65; dir. of nurses Newton County (Tex.) Hosp., 1966-67; dir. Home Health Assistance, Inc., Kirbyville, Tex., 1967-71; dir. Home Health-Home Care, Newton, Tex., 1972-76; inservice edn. dir. Mary E. Dickerson Hosp., Jasper, Tex., 1976-89, dir. nurses, 1989—. Mem. Am., Tex. nurses assns., Nat. League Nurses. Democrat. Home: 511 Mays St Jasper TX 75951 Office: Mary Dickerson Hospital 1001 Dickerson Dr Jasper TX 75951

WOODRUFF, HEIDI WAGNER, optometrist; b. Mansfield, Ohio, Oct. 9, 1961; d. Leslie Kermit and Betty May (Thompson) Wagner; m. Christopher Edwin Woodruff, Sept. 6, 1986. Student, Oxford U., 1981, U. Vienna, 1983; BS, Ohio State U., 1984, OD, 1986. Pvt. practice Mansfield, 1986—; ind. contractor John Kirkpatrick, Loudonville, Ohio, 1986-87; clin. instr. Ohio State U. Coll. Optometry, Columbus, 1988—. Sec. bd. dirs. YWCA, Mansfield, 1988, pres., 1989. Mem. Am. Optometric Assn., Ohio Optometric Assn., Optometric Extension Program, Coll. Vision Devel., AAUW, Bus. and Profl. Women. Democrat. Home: 52 Mayfair Rd Lexington OH 44904

WOODRUFF, JANET NORRIS, marketing and management professional; b. Des Moines, Apr. 8, 1950; d. Ora Earl and Norman Alice (Nunamaker) Norris; m. Dennis Duane Woodruff, Feb. 28, 1970 (div. 1985); children: Ryan, Kendra. Student, Des Moines Community Coll., 1969, LaSalle Extension U., Chgo., 1977, Iowa State U., 1972-74; BS in Mgmt. and Mktg., Upper Iowa U., 1990. Cert. dental asst., lic. life and health ins. agt., real estate broker. Coord., instr. Marshalltown (Iowa) Community Coll., 1972-74; mgr. Broadlawns Dental Clinic, Des Moines, 1976-78; owner, mgr. Decorating Den, Carlisle, Iowa, 1978-84; sr. account mgr. Total Health Network, Des Moines, 1984-88; adminstr., dir. Des Moines Hearing & Speech Ctr., 1990—; cons. Am. Mgmt. Resources, Des Moines, 1988—. Core group Multiple Sclerosis Soc., Des Moines, 1986; vol. Hospice Cen. Iowa, Des Moines, 1984—, Greater Des Moines Leadership Inst., 1990. Mem. NAFE, Am. Dental Assts. Assn. (dental examiners bd. 1987-88), Am. Bus. Womens Assn., Mid Iowa Soccer Officials Assn., Urbandale Soccer Club. Republican. Methodist. Home: 7109 Plum Dr Urbandale IA 50322

WOODRUFF, JUDITH MARIE, college official; b. East St. Louis, Ill., Jan. 18, 1953; d. Clarence John and Dolores Marie (Berry) Blase; m. Michael Ernest Woodruff, Apr. 6, 1974. MusB, So. Ill. U., Edwardsville, 1977; postgrad., Webster U. Dist. mgr. Coppercraft Guild, Taunton, Mass., 1976-83; account exec. Belleville (Ill.) News-Democrat, 1983-84; owner, mgr. Imperial Ice Cream & Confections, Belleville, 1984-88; promotions coord. Belleville Econ. Progress, Inc., 1986-87; exec. dir. YWCA of St. Clair County,

Belleville, 1987-88; assoc. dir. devel. McKendree Coll., Lebanon, Ill., 1988—. Chmn. Fountain Fest Auction, Belleville, 1985; co-chmn. ann. house tour St. Clair County Hist. Soc., 1987-88; bd. dirs. Belleville's 175th Anniversary Com., 1986-89; exec. v.p Masterworks Chorale, 1990-92. Mem. Nat. Parks and Conservation Assn., Nat. Hist. Soc., Nat. Wildlife Fedn., Belleville C. of C. (civic design com. 1985-87), Optimists, Nat. Honor Soc., Pi Kappa Lambda. Methodist. Office: McKendree Coll 701 College Rd Lebanon IL 62254

WOODRUFF, KATHRYN ELAINE, English educator; b. Ft. Stockton, Tex., Oct. 12, 1940; d. James Arthur and Catherine H. (Stevens) Borron; m. Thomas Charles Woodruff, May 18, 1969; children: Robert Borron, David Borron. BA, Our Lady of the Lake U., San Antonio, 1963; MFA, U. Alaska, 1969; PhD, U. Denver, 1987. Cert. tchr., Tex. English and journalism tchr. Owensboro (Ky.) Cath. High Sch., 1963-64, Grand Junction (Colo.) Dist. 12, 1964-66; English tchr. Monroe High Sch., Fairbanks, Alaska, 1966-67; teaching asst. U. Alaska, Fairbanks, 1967-69, instr., 1969-70; instr. U. Colo., Boulder, 1979, Denver, 1988-89; instr. Regis Coll., Denver, 1987-89; asst. prof. Econs. Inst., Boulder, 1990—; instr. Upward Bound, Fairbanks, 1968; instr. ethnic and women writers course U. Colo., Denver, 1988-89. Friend Chautauqua Music Festival, Boulder, 1985—; dir. 12th Annual Arts Festival, Fairbanks, 1969. Named one of Outstanding Young Women Am., 1966. Mem. AAUW, MLA, TESOL, COTESOL, Associated Writers Press, Sigma Tau Delta. Democrat. Mem. Christian Ch. Office: Econs Inst 909 14th St Boulder CO 80302

WOODRUFF, VIRGINIA, television and radio host, producer; b. Morrisville, Pa.; d. Edwin Nichols and Louise (Meredith) W.; m. Raymond F. Beagle Jr. (div.); m. Albert Plaut II (div.); 1 child, Elise Meredith. Past student, Rutgers U. News corr. Sta. WNEW-TV Metromedia, N.Y.C., 1967; nat., internat. critic-at-large Mut. Broadcasting System, 1968-75; lectr. circ. Leigh Bur., 1969-71; byline columnist N.Y. Daily Mirror, N.Y.C., 1971; first Arts critic Teleprompter and Group W Cable TV, 1977-84; host/producer The First Nighter N.Y. Times Primetime Cable Highlight program, 1977-84; pres., chief exec. officer Starpower, Inc., 1984—; affiliate news corr. ABC Radio Network, N.Y.C., 1984-86; perennial critic Off-Off Broadway Short Play Festival, N.Y.C., 1984—; was 1st Woman on 10 O'Clock News, WNEW-TV, 1967. Contbg. feature writer UAL Internat. Vis à Vis mag., 1988—. Mem. celebrity panel Arthritis Telethon, N.Y.C., 1976. Selected episodes First Nighter program in archives N.Y. Pub. Libr., Billy Rose Theatre Collection, Rodgers and Hammerstein Collection, Performing Arts Rsch.Ctr. Mem. Drama Desk. Presbyterian. Office: Starpower Inc 35 E 10th St New York NY 10003

WOODRUM, PATRICIA ANN, librarian; b. Hutchinson, Kans., Oct. 11, 1941; d. Donald Jewell and Ruby Pauline (Shuman) Hoffman; m. Clayton Eugene Woodrum, Mar. 31, 1962; 1 child, Clayton Eugene, II. BA, Kans. State Coll., Pittsburg, 1963; MLS, U. Okla., 1966. Br. libr. Tulsa City-County Libr. System, 1964-65, head brs., 1965-66, head reference dept., 1966-67, chief extension, chief pub. svc., 1967-73, asst., 1973-76, exec. dir., 1976—; bd. dirs. Local Am. Bank Tulsa. Mem. editorial bd. Jour. of Library Administration. Mem. bd. Downtown Tulsa Unltd.; mem. Friends of Tulsa Libr.; mem. Leadership Tulsa Alumni; mem. bd. Tulsa Area Libr. Coop; mem. community svc. coun. bd.; trustee Univ. Ctr. at Tulsa Trust Authority. Recipient Disting. Libr. award Okla. Libr. Assn., 1982, Leadership Tulsa Paragon award, 1987, Women in Communications Newsmaker award, 1989, Outstanding Alumnus award U. Okla. Sch. Libr. Info. Studies, 1989; inducted into Tulsa City-County Libr. Hall of Fame, 1989. Mem. ALA, Okla. Libr. Assn. (pres. 1978-79, C of C. Republican. Episcopalian. Office: Tulsa City-County Libr 400 Civic Ctr Tulsa OK 74103

WOODS, DIANE, chemicals executive; b. Chgo., Apr. 18, 1958; d. Thaddeus George and Helen Pricilla (Niemiec) Godfryt; m. Harold Woods, Oct. 24, 1985. BS in Chemistry, U. Ill., Chgo., 1980. Lab. technologist Nalco Chem. Co., Naperville, Ill., 1980-85, chemist, 1986-89, product specialist, 1989—. Mem. NAFE, Toastmasters (sec., treas. Nalco club 1988-89, adminstrv. v.p 1989-90, pres. 1990—). Office: Nalco Chem Co One Nalco Ctr Naperville IL 60563-1198

WOODS, DIANE HOLLIS, university official; b. Altadena, Calif., Apr. 17, 1956; d. Richard Owen and Barbara (Hoffman) Hollis; m. Michael Gage Woods, Aug. 16, 1980; children: Thomas Michael, Kathryn Elizabeth. BA, Ottawa U., 1978; postgrad., U. So. Calif., 1984—. Exec. sec. Fuller Theol. Sem., Pasadena, Calif., 1979-80; corp. legal sec. Barger & Wolen, L.A., 1980-81; employment counselor Lynn Carol Employment Agy., Pasadena, 1981-82; asst. to dean Annenberg Sch. Communications, U. So. Calif., L.A., 1982-85, asst. dir. continuing legal edn. programs Law Ctr., 1985-87, dir. insts. and confs., 1987—. Sec-treas. sanctuary choir Pasadena Covenant Ch., 1984—, editor newsletter, 1987—, chairperson, 1990—. Author: What It Means To Be An American Baptist Today, 1976. Named one of Outstanding Young Women of Am. Mem. NAFE, Am. Mgmt. Assns., Internat. Platform Assn., Assn. Continuing Legal Edn. Adminstrs., Women in Mgmt. Democrat. Avocations: writing, photography, travel. Office: U So Calif Law Ctr Office Insts and Confs Law 105-D University Park Los Angeles CA 90089-0071

WOODS, ELLEN, psychotherapist; b. Flushing, N.Y., May 25, 1953; d. Albert and Frieda (Mandel) Cohen; m. Gary Stephen Woods, July 1, 1951. BA, Goddard Coll., Plainfield, Vt., 1974; MA, John F. Kennedy U., Orinda, Calif., 1982. Lic. marriage and family therapist. Artist-in-residence Orange Elem. Sch., Vt., 1975; owner, mgr. Woven Thread Wks., San Francisco, 1977-80; artist-in-residence Phoenix Progs., Concord, Calif., 1982-84; art instr. Creative Growth, Oakland, Calif.; children's prog. dir. City of Oakland, 1985-87; marriage and family counselor Oakland, 1982-87; instr. Colo. Mt. Coll., Aspen, Basalt, Carbondale, 1987—; psychotherapist in pvt. practice Carbondale, 1988—; cons. Grand River Hospice, Glenwood Springs, Colo., 1988—, U. Without Walls, Denver, 1988—. Art work exhibited at Aspen Chapel Gallery, 1989, Bay Currents: New Artists, 1987, Contra Costa Competitive, 1984, Boston Archtl. Ctr., 1975, others. Acad. Art grantee, 1985. Mem. Colo. Fedn. Arts, Colo. Artists Register, Am. Assn. Artist-Therapists, Artitracts Gallery, Carbondale Council on the Arts. Office: 289 Main St Carbondale CO 81623

WOODS, EVELYN LOCKETT, information systems specialist; b. Lafayette, La., Nov. 3, 1949; d. Bethel and Evelyn Rose (Jones) Lockett; m. Gregory Frazier, Nov. 30, 1974 (div.); children: Keli Brooke, Kendra Evelyn; m. Richard C. Woods, Oct. 12, 1985. BA, U. Houston, 1972; M in Mgmt., Northwestern U., 1989. Cert. tchr., Tex. Math. tchr. Houston Ind. Sch. Dist., 1972-74; computer programmer Ill. Bell Telephone Co., Chgo., 1974-78, systems analyst, 1978-80, edp auditor, 1980-82, mgr., 1982-85, dist. mgr., 1985-88; sr. dir. Ameritech Applied Techs., Chgo., 1988—; adv. bd. SRA, Chgo., 1989—. Recognized Chicago's Up and Coming Business and Professional Women Black Enterprise mag., 1985. Mem. Black Data Processing Assocs. (adv. bd 1989—), Bell Mgmt. Women, Nat. Black MBA Assocs., Nat. Tech. Assocs., Delta Sigma Theta. Democrat. Roman Catholic. Office: Ameritech Applied Techs 500 W Madison Ste 2700 Chicago IL 60606

WOODS, HARRIETT RUTH, state official; b. Cleve., June 2, 1927; d. Armin and Ruth (Wise) Friedman; student U. Chgo., 1945; B.A.. U. Mich., 1949; m. James B. Woods, Jan. 2, 1953; children—Christopher, Peter, Andrew. Reporter, Chgo. Herald-Am., 1948, St. Louis Globe-Democrat, 1949-51; producer Star. KPLR-TV, St. Louis, 1964-74; moderator, writer Sta. KETC-TV, St. Louis, 1962-64; council mem. University City, Mo., 1967-74; mem. Mo. Hwy. Commn., 1974, Mo. Transp. Commn., 1974-76; mem. Mo. Senate, 1976-84, lt. gov. State of Mo., 1985-89; pres. Inst. for Policy Leadership, U. Mo., St. Louis. Bd. dirs. LWV of Mo., 1963, Nat. League of Cities, 1972-74; Democratic nominee for U.S. Senate, 1982, 86. Jewish. Office: 7952 Natural Bridge Rd Saint Louis MO 63121

WOODS, LAURIE, lawyer; b. N.Y.C., Nov. 18, 1947; d. William M. and Sylvia Leona (Bottsein) W.; m. John W. Corwin, June 1, 1968; children—Raquel Woods-Corwin, James Woods-Corwin. B.A., New Sch., N.Y.C., 1969; J.D., Boston U., 1973. Bar: N.Y. 1974. Staff atty. MFY Legal Services, N.Y.C., 1973-79; exec. dir. Nat. Ctr. on Women and Family Law, N.Y.C., 1979—; bd. dirs. N.Y. Women Against Rape, 1982—, Feminist Legal Strategies Project, Washington, 1983—. Contbr. articles in field to

publs. Bd. dirs. Gingerbread Day Care Ctr., N.Y.C., 1982-83. Mem. ABA, N.Y. State Bar Assn., Assn. Bar City N.Y., N.Y. Women's Bar Assn. Office: Nat Ctr on Women & Family Law 799 Broadway Room 402 New York NY 10003

WOODS, LINDSAY ELIZABETH, marketing executive; b. Pontiac, Mich., Aug. 2, 1948; d. George Edward Woods and Beth Yvonne (Tucker) Segula. Student, U. Mich., 1966-68; BA in Edn., Lang., Queens Coll., 1970; postgrad., Oakland U., 1975; student, Long Island U., 1981. French, German instr. Union Free Sch. Dist. #1, Mamaroneck, N.Y., 1970-75; dir. sales Nassau Gold Coast News, Suffolk, N.Y., 1976; exec. v.p. LIN-Z Stables, LTD., Old Westbury, N.Y., 1978-82; chief exec. officer, pres., founder Tyler-Woods, Ltd., Locust Valley, N.Y., 1982—; cons. Murray Electronics, Balt., 1982-83, cons., v.p. bd. dirs. Am. Vet. Products, Ft. Collins, Colo., 1988-90; dir. animal health div. Luitpold Pharms., Inc., Shirley, N.Y. Mem. Standardbred Owners Assn., U.S. Trotting Assn., Old Westbury Horsemans Assn. (v.p 1980, trustee 1981—), N.Y. State Tchrs. Assn., Nat. Assn. Female Execs. Address: 1044 2nd Cunningham Dr #2 Fort Collins CO 80526

WOODS, MERILYN BARON, psychologist, consultant; b. Bklyn., July 8, 1927; d. David Theodore and Helen (Mintz) Baron; m. John Galloway Woods, Sept. 15, 1948; children: Anne Helen, Elizabeth Ruth. BS, Cornell U., 1948; MEd, Temple U., 1957; PhD, Bryn Mawr Coll., 1968. Lic. psychologist, Pa. Rsch. asst. psychiatry Temple U., Phila., 1958-59, instr., counselor students, 1960-64; clin. psychologist Gloucester County Guidance Ctr., Woodbury, N.J., 1959-60; seminar coord. Bryn Mawr Coll., 1966-67, lectr., 1968-70, asst. prof., 1977-73; dir. Ctr. for Pers. and Profl. Devel. Pa. Coll. Optometry, Phila., 1983—; pvt. practice psychologist Phila., 1983—. Mem., pres. bd. mgrs. Sr. Employment and Edn. Svc., Phila., 1985—; chmn. Environ. Edn. Com., Phila., 1989—; bd. dirs. Awbury Arboretum Assn. 1986—. Mem. APA, Phila. Soc. Clin. Psychologists (bd. dirs. 1980—), Cornell Alumni Club of Phila. (co-pres. 1989—). Office: 5928 Devon Pl Philadelphia PA 19138

WOODS, ROBIN FUNNELL, doll manufacturing company executive; b. Lubbock, Tex., Mar. 29, 1943; d. Russell J. and Lois (Bledsoe) Funnell; m. Kent Hill, Aug. 22, 1964 (div. 1971); children: Leah, Andrea; m. Stephen Boyce Woods, June 7, 1972; 1 child, Mary Margaret; stepchildren: Jennifer, David, Drew. BA, Tex. Tech U., 1965, MA, 1968; PhD, U. Pitts., 1976. Asst. prof. English Mansfield State Coll., Mansfield, Pa., 1968-70; dir. pub. relations Mansfield State Coll., 1969-70; dir. day care Tioga County, Wellsboro, Pa., 1970-72; dir. Dravosburg Nursery Sch., Dravosburg Meth., Dravosburg, Pa., 1973-74; cons. Pitts. Ist born program U. Pitts., 1974-75, asst. prof. grad. sch. pub. health, 1976-80; dir. consultation and edn. St. Francis Hosp., Pitts., 1980-81; dir. children's mental health Penn Group Health Plan, Pitts., 1981-83; chief exec. officer Robin Woods, Inc. Mfg., Pitts., 1983—; cons. Mich. State Dept. Mental Health, 1976-80, Pa. State Dept. Pub. Welfare, 1970-80, Allegheny County Orphans Ct., Pitts., 1976-83, Neighborhood Legal Svcs., Pitts., 1976-83; dir. Appalachian regional commn. tng. project U. Pitts., 1977-80. Mem. Carnegie Inst., Pitts., 1986—. Recipient Parents Choice Gold award, Boston, 1988, Award of Excellence. DOLLS Mag., 1987, 88; named nominee Entrepreneur of Yr., VENTURE Mag., Arthur Young, 1987, for Doll of Yr., DOLL Reader Mag., 1986, 87, 88, 89. Mem. United Fedn. Doll Clubs, Smaller Mfr.'s Coun., E. Liberty C. of C. (Pitts.). Episcopalian. Home: 639 Hastings St Pittsburgh PA 15206 Office: Robin Woods Inc 6592 Hamilton Ave Pittsburgh PA 15206

WOODS, SANDRA KAY, real estate executive; b. Loveland, Colo., Oct. 11, 1944; d. Ivan H. and Florence L. (Betz) Harris; m. Gary A. Woods, June 11, 1967; children: Stephanie Michelle, Michael Harris. BA, U. Colo., 1966, MA, 1967. Personnel mgmt. specialist CSC, Denver, 1967; asst. to regional dir. HEW, Denver, 1968-69; urban renewal rep. HUD, Denver, 1970-73, dir. program analysis, 1974-75, asst. regional dir. community planning and devel., 1976-77, regional dir. fair housing, 1978-79; mgr. ea. facility project Adolph Coors Co., Golden Colo., 1980, dir. real estate, 1981, v.p. corp. real estate, 1982—; pres. Industries for Jefferson County (Colo.), 1985. Mem. Exec. Exchange, The White House, 1980; bd. dirs. Golden Local Devel. Corp. (Colo.), 1981-82; fundraising dir. Coll. Arts and Scis., U. Colo., Boulder, 1982-89, U. Colo. Found.; mem. exec. bd. NCCJ, Denver, 1982-89; v.p. Women in Bus., Inc., Denver, 1982-83; mem. steering com. 1984 Yr. for All Denver Women, 1983-84; mem. 10th dist. Denver br. Fed. Reserve Bd., 1990. Named one of Outstanding Young Women Am., U.S. Jaycees, 1974, 78, Fifty Women to Watch, Businessweek, 1987, Woman of Achievement YWCA, 1988. Mem. Indsl. Devel. Resources Council (bd. dirs. 1986-89), Am. Mgmt. Assn., Denver C. of C. (bd. dirs. 1988—, Disting. Young Exec. award 1974, mem. Leadership Denver, 1976-77), Colo. Women's Forum, Nat. Assn. Office and Indsl. Park Developers (sec. 1988, treas. 1989), Phi Beta Kappa, Pi Alpha Alpha. Republican. Presbyterian. Club: PEO (Loveland, Colo.). Office: Adolph Coors Co Real Estate 807 Golden CO 80401

WOODS, SUSANNE, university dean; b. Honolulu, May 12, 1943; d. Samuel Ernest and Gertrude (Cullom) W. BA in Polit. Sci., UCLA, 1964, MA in English, 1965; PhD in English and Comparative Lit., Columbia U., 1970; MA (hon.), Brown U., 1978. Staff Senator Daniel K. Inouye, 1963; asst. editor Rand Corp., Calif., 1963-65; instr. Ventura Coll., Calif., 1965-66; lectr. CUNY, 1967-69; asst. prof. U. Hawaii, 1969-72; asst. prof. English Brown U., Providence, 1972-77, assoc. prof., 1977-83, prof., 1983—; dir. grad. studies, 1986-88, assoc. dean faculty, 1987-90; vis. assoc. prof. U. Calif., 1981-82; dir. NEH-Brown Women Writers Project, 1988—. Author: Natural Emphasis, 1984; contbr. numerous articles to profl. jours. and scholarly books; reviewer for various profl. jours., including Renaissance Quar., Jour. of English and Germanic Philology; reader for PMLA Jour., SEL Jour., also others; editorial bd. Huntington Libr. Quar., 1987-90. Active various polit. campaigns, 1960-64, 68-76, 84. Bronson fellow, 1976, Huntington Library, 1979-80, 81, Clark Library, 1981, Huntington-NEH, 1984-85, Woodrow Wilson Found., 1968-70. Mem. Am. Council Edn. (R.I. women's council. 1988-90), MLA (chmn. div. 17th Century English lit. 1982), N.E. MLA (chmn. English Renaissance sect. 1978, Milton sect. 1983), Am. Assn. Higher Edn., Nat. Women's Studies Assn., Renaissance Soc. Am., Milton Soc. (exec. com. 1987-89), Lyrica Soc. (pres. 1987-90), Alpha Gamma Delta. Democrat. Episcopalian. Home: 179 University Ave Providence RI 02906 Office: Brown U PO Box 1852 Providence RI 02912

WOODS, WILLIE G., English and education educator; b. Yazoo City, Miss.; d. John Wesley and Jessie Willie Mae W. B.A., Shaw U., Raleigh, N.C., 1965; M.Ed., Duke U., 1968; postgrad., Temple U., Pa. State U., U. N.H., NYU. Tchr. schs. in N.C. and Md., 1965-69; mem. faculty Harrisburg (Pa.) Area Community Coll., 1969—, assoc. prof. English and edn., 1976-82, prof., 1982—; supr. Writing Ctr., 1975-78, coord. Act 101/Basic Studies Program, 1978-83, dir. Acad. Found. program 1983-87, asst. dean academ. affairs Acad. Found. and Basic Edn. Div., 1987-89, asst. dean acad. affairs, chmn. social sci., pub. svcs. and basic edn. div., 1989—, chmn. dirs. coun., 1981-82; chmn. Community Resources Inst., 1975—; moderator workshops, cons. in field. Asst. editor Black Conf. Higher Edn. Jour., 1980. Sec., exec. com. People for Progress, 1971-73; bd. mgrs., exec. com. Camp Curtin br. YMCA, 1971-79; bd. dirs. Alternative Rehab. Communities, 1978—; bd. mgrs. Youth Urban Svcs., Harrisburg Area YMCA, 1981—; bd. dirs. Dauphin Residences, Inc., 1981—. Recipient cert. of merit for community svcs. City of Harrisburg, 1971, Youth Urban Svcs. Vol. of Yr. award, 1983, Black Student Union award Harrisburg Area Community Coll., 1984. Mem. Pa. Assn. Devel. Educators (chmn. conf. 1980, sec. 1981-82, v.p 1986-87, pres. 1987-88), Pa. Black Conf. Higher Edn. (Outstanding Svc. award 1980, Central Region award 1982), Nat. Coun. Tchrs. English, Pa. Edn. Assn., Am. Assn. Community and Jr. Colls., Nat. Coun. on Black Am. (instl. rep. 1983—), AAUP, Alpha Kappa Alpha (Outstanding Svc. award 1983, Basileus award 1984), Alpha Kappa Mu. Baptist. Home: 1712 Fort Patton Dr Harrisburg PA 17112 Office: 3300 Cameron St Rd Harrisburg PA 17110

WOODSIDE, LISA NICOLE, college dean; b. Portland, Oreg., Sept. 7, 1944; d. Lee and Emma (Wenstrom) W. Student Reed Coll., 1962-65; M.A., U. Chgo., 1968; Ph.D., Bryn Mawr Coll., 1972; cert. Harvard U. Inst. for Ednl. Mgmt., 1979; postgrad. West Chester U., 1988—. Mem. dean's staff Bryn Mawr Coll., 1970-72; asst. prof. Widener U., Chester, Pa., 1972-77, asso. prof. humanities, 1978-83, asst. dean student services, 1972-76, asso. dean, 1976-79, dean, 1979-83; acad. dean, prof. of humanities Holy Family

Coll., Phila., 1983—; accreditor Commn. on Higher Edn., Middle States Assn., 1979-83. City commr. for community rels. Chester, 1980-83; mem. Adult Edn. Council Phila. Am. Assn. Papyrology grantee Bryn Mawr Coll.; S. Maude Kaemmerling fellow Bryn Mawr Coll. Mem. Am. Assn. Higher Edn., Council Ind. Colls. Eastern Assn. Coll. Deans, Pa. Assn. Colls. and Tchr. Educators, AAUW (univ. rep. 1975-83), Nat. Assn. Women in C. of C. Phi Eta Sigma, Alpha Sigma Lambda. Episcopalian. Club: Am. Fox Terrier. Home: 27 Wallingford Rd A-6 Wallingford PA 19086 Office: Holy Family Coll Torresdale Philadelphia PA 19114

WOODSON, CHERYL ANNE, psychology educator; b. Bristol, Pa., Jan. 16, 1959; d. Benjamin Franklin Woodson and Lucille (Weeks) Woodson-Lewis; m. Keith Byron Coleman, Nov. 7, 1977 (div. Feb. 1980). BS, Nova U., 1981, MS, 1983; PhD, Fla. Inst. Tech., 1987. Lic. psychologist, Fla. Vocat. counselor Minority Builders Coalition, Ft. Lauderdale, Fla., 1980; out-reach counselor Ft. Lauderdale Housing Authority, 1980-82, community svc. specialist, 1982-83; devel. coord. Neighborhood Reinvestment Corp., Ft. Lauderdale and Washington, 1983-84; doctoral psychology intern Nova U. Mental Health Clinic, Ft. Lauderdale, 1986-87; program evaluation coord. Dade County Pub. Schs., Miami, Fla., 1987-88; asst. prof. psychology Southeastern U. Health Scis., Miami, 1988—; cons. Concerned Orgn. Parents to Educate, Melbourne, Fla. 1985-86, Coun. of Minority Women, Melbourne, 1985-86, Family Life Inst. for Counseling, Ft. Lauderdale, 1987-89, The Starting Pl., Ft. Lauderdale, 1987-88. Guest lectr., educator Delta Sigma Theta Sorority, Melbourne, 1985, lectr., 1989; guest panelist Cablevision of Cen. Fla., Melbourne, 1985; guest speaker Alpha Kappa Alpha Sorority, Ft. Lauderdale, 1988; panelist Sta. WRBD-1470 Radio, Ft. Lauderdale, 1988-89; lectr. Sta. WLRN Channel 17 Focus on Health, Miami, 1988-89. Mem. APA, Am. Ednl. Rsch. Assn., Soc. Tchrs. of Family Medicine. Office: Southeastern U Health Scis 1750 NE 168th St North Miami FL 33162

WOODSON-HOWARD, MARLENE ERDLEY, state legislator; b. Ford City, Pa., Mar. 8, 1937; d. James and Susie (Lettrich) Erdley; m. Francis M. Howard; children: George Woodson, Bert Woodson, Robert Woodson, Daniel Woodson, David Woodson. BS, Ind. U. of Pa., 1958; MA, U. South Fla., 1968; EdD, Nova U., 1981. Prof. math. Manatee Community Coll. 1970-82, dir., Inst. Advancement, 1982-86; exec. dir. Manatee Community Coll. Foundation, 1982-86; pres. Pegasus Enterprises, Inc., 1986—; state senator Fla., 1986-90. Gubernatorial candidate, 1990; bd. dirs. Sarasota Opera, West Coast Symphony, Child Devel. Ctr. Mem. Nat. Assn. Women Bus. Owners, Women Owners Network, Manatee Symphony (past pres.), Manatee C. of C., Sarasota Tiger Bay Club. Republican. Roman Catholic. Home: Box 468 Bradenton FL 34206

WOODSUM, GAYLE M., social services administrator; b. Cambridge, Mass., Apr. 21, 1956; d. George Albert and Phyllis Marie (Tolman) W.; 1 child, Tristan P. (dec.). Grad. high sch., Kents Hills, Maine, 1973. Editor Northeast Horseman Mag., Hampden, Maine, 1980-82; exec. dir., co-founder "Looking Up", Augusta, Maine, 1983—; founder, facilitator support group for parents of terminally ill children. Lewiston, Maine, 1982; editor "Looking Up" Times mag., 1985—. Contbr. articles on incest-related topics to ednl. publs., 1985—. Democrat. Office: Looking Up PO Box K Augusta ME 04330

WOODSWORTH, ANNE, librarian, university official; b. Fredericia, Denmark, Feb. 10, 1941; d. Thorvald Ernst and Roma Yrsa (Jensen) Lindner; 1 child, Yrsa Anne. BFA, U. Man., Can., 1962; BLS, U. Toronto, Ont., Can., 1964, MLS, 1969; PhD, U. Pitts., 1987. Edn. libr. U. Man., 1964-65; reference libr. Winnipeg Pub. Library, 1965-67; reference libr. sci. and medicine dept. U. Toronto, 1967-68; med. librarian Toronto Western Hosp., 1969-70; research asst. to chief librarian U. Toronto, 1970-71, head reference dept., 1971-74; personnel dir. Toronto Pub. Library, 1975-78; dir. librs. York U., Toronto, 1978-83; assoc. provost for librs. U. Pitts., 1983-88, assoc. prof., 1988—; pres. Anne Lindner Ltd., 1974-83; bd. dirs. Population Rsch. Found., Toronto, 1980-83, Ctr. for Rsch. Libraries, 1987-88; mem. rsch. libraries adv. coun. OCLC, 1984-87. Author: The Alternative Press in Canada, 1972, Leadership for Research Libraries, 1988, Patterns and Options for Managing Information Technology on Campus, 1990. Can. Coun. grantee, 1974, Ont. Arts Coun. grantee, 1974, Coun. on Library Resources grantee, 1986, 88; UCLA sr. fellow, 1985. Mem. ALA, Can. Assn. Rsch. Libr. (pres. 1981-83), Assn. Rsch. Librs. (bd. dirs. 1981-84, v.p. 1984-85, pres. 1985-86), Pa. Libr. Assn., Am. Soc. Info. Sci. Scholarly Pub. Office: U Pitts Univ Libr 626 Librar Info Sci Bldg Pittsburgh PA 15260

WOODWARD, ANITA BARRETT, health care facility professional; b. Youngstown, Ohio, Feb. 10, 1950; d. John Paul and Lois (Handel) Barrett; m. James S. Woodward, June 11, 1977; children: Jennifer, Bernadette Miller. BA in Communication summa cum laude, Cleve. State U., 1988. Employment coms. Champion Personnel, Cleve., 1976-81; employment specialist MetroHealth Med. Ctr., Cleve., 1981-83, mgr. customer svcs., 1983—, dir. customer svcs., 1990—. Bd. trustees Ohio City Redevel. Assn., Cleve., 1985—, v.p., 1989-90. Recipient Pres.'s award Cleve. State U., 1989. Mem. Ohio Soc. Patient Reps. (pres. elect, treas., bd. dirs. Columbus, Ohio chpt. 1986-90, pres. 1990—), Nat. Soc. Patient Reps (profl. devel. com. Chgo. chpt. 1990—). Home: 1820 W 44th Cleveland OH 44113

WOODWARD, FAE BLANCHE, journalist; b. Santa Ana, Calif., Nov. 15, 1925; d. Louis George and Rhoda Miranda (Morris) Willits; m. Billy J. Woodward, Nov. 24, 1947; children—Billy, Bobby, Tonni, Clarissa, Kevin, Woodra. Cub reporter, society editor Progress Bull., Pomona, Calif., 1944-48; society editor Telegram Tribune, San Luis Obispo, Calif., 1948-49; Corcoran corr. Fresno Bee (Calif.), 1953-54; corr. Ukiah (Calif.) Daily Jour. 1956-58, 61-64, teletypesetter, 1960, 71, lifestyles editor, 1971—. Tenderfoot leader, mem. tng. com. Sonoma-Mendocino council Boy Scouts Am., 1967—, roundtable staff Yokayo Dist. Boy Scouts 1981—; mem. young women's program Ch. of Jesus Christ of Latter-day Saints, Ukiah, 1981-85; mem. sch. adv. com. compensatory edn. Ukiah Unified Sch. Dist., 1974-77, also adv. com. photography, 1979-85, Ukiah Com. Ctr. Bd., 1985-86. Recipient Golden Rule award Calif. Assn. for Retarded, 1980; Disting. Achievement Pub. Info. award North Coast Coordinating Council Devel. Disabilities, 1980, Silver Beaver award Boy Scouts Am., 1988. Mem. Calif. Press Women's Assn. Republican. Home: 6785 W Hwy 20 Star Route 2 Ukiah CA 95482 Office: Ukiah Daily Jour 590 S School St Ukiah CA 95482

WOODWARD, GRETA CHARMAINE, construction company executive, rental and investment property manager; b. Congress, Ohio, Oct. 28, 1930; d. Richard Thomas and Grace Lucetta (Palmer) Duffey; m. John Jay Woodward, Oct. 29, 1949; children: Kirk Jay, Brad Ewing, Clay William. Bookkeeper Kaufman's Texaco, Wooster, Ohio, 1948-49; office mgr. Holland Furnace Co., Wooster, 1948-49; acctg. clk. Columbus and So. Ohio Electric, 1949-50; interviewer, clk. State Ohio Bur. Employment Services, Columbus, 1950-51; clk. Def. Constrn. Supply Ctr. (U.S. Govt.) (formerly Columbus Gen. Depot), 1951-52; treas. Woodward Co., Inc., Reynoldsburg, Ohio, 1963—. Newspaper columnist Briarcliff News, 1960-63. Active Reynoldsburg PTA, 1960-67; Reynoldsburg United Meth. Ch.; mem. women's service bd. Grant Hosp. Avocations: bike riding, crocheting, writing poetry, stock market, financial mags. Office: Woodward Excavating Co Inc 7320 Tussing Rd Reynoldsburg OH 43068

WOODWARD, ISABEL AVILA, writer; b. Key West, Fla., Mar. 14, 1906; d. Alfredo and Isabel (Lopez) Avila; student Fla. State Coll. for Women, 1925, A.B. in Edn., 1938; cert. in teaching Spanish, U. Miami 1961; summer study U. Fla., Eckerd Coll.; postgrad. St. Lawrence U., U. Miami; m. Clyde B. Woodward, June 6, 1944 (dec.); children—Joy Avis Ball, Greer Isabel Woodward Sucke. Tchr., Key West, 1927-42, remedial reading cons., 1941-42; reading tchr., asst. reading lab. and clinic St. Lawrence U., summer 1941; Spanish translator U.S. Office of Censorship, Miami, 1943; tchr. Central Beach Elem. Sch., Miami Beach, Fla. 1943-44, Silver Bluff Elem. Sch., 1943-50, Henry West Lab. Sch., Coral Gables, Fla., 1955-57, Dade Demonstration Sch., Miami, 1957-61; author 125 sch. radio lessons for teaching Spanish, Dade County Elem. Schs., 1961; tchr. Spanish Workshop for Fla.; speaker poetry and short story writing, 1977; guest lectr. on writing the short story Fla. Inst. Tech., Jensen Beach, 1981; freelance writer; contbr. to Listen Mag., Sunshine Mag., Lookout Mag., Christian Sci. Monitor, Miami Herald, Three/Four, Child Life, Wee Wisdom, Fla. Wildlife, Young World; sponsor

Port St. Lucie Jr. Woman's Club, 1983. Recipient Honoris Causa award Alpha Delta Kappa, 1972-74, award Contra Costa Times, Calif., 1985; named one of 5 Outstanding Fla. Tchrs., 1972-74. Mem. Nat. League Am. Pen Women (1st v.p. Greater Miami br. 1974-76, historian 1978—; librarian 1978—), awards for writing 1973, 74, 77, 1st and 3d place state writing awards for adult and juvenile fiction 1983, state 1st prize short story 1985), AAUW, Alpha Delta Kappa, Psi Psi Psi. Address: 1950 Palm City Rd Apt 6-301 Stuart FL 34994

WOODWARD, JOANNE GIGNILLIAT, actress; b. Thomasville, Ga., Feb. 27, 1930; d. Wade and Elinor (Trimmier) W.; m. Paul Newman, Jan. 29, 1958; children: Elinor Terese, Melissa Stewart, Clea Olivia. Student, La. State U., 1947-49; grad., Neighborhood Playhouse Dramatic Sch., N.Y.C. First TV appearance in Penny, Robert Montgomery Presents, 1952; understudy broadway play Picnic, 1953; appeared in plays Baby Want a Kiss, 1964, Candida, 1982, The Glass Menagerie, Williamstown Theatre Festival, 1985, Sweet Bird of Youth, Toronto, 1988; motion pictures include Three Faces of Eve, 1957 (Acad. award Best Actress, Nat. Bd. Rev. award, Fgn. Press award), Count Three and Pray, 1955, Long Hot Summer, 1958, No Down Payment, 1957, Sound and the Fury, 1959, A Kiss Before Dying, 1956, Rally Round the Flag Boys, 1958, The Fugitive Kind, 1960, Paris Blues, 1961, The Stripper, 1963, A New Kind of Love, 1963, A Big Hand for the Little Lady, 1965, A Fine Madness, 1965, Rachel, Rachel, 1968, Winning, 1969, WUSA, 1970, They Might Be Giants, 1971, The Effect of Gamma Rays on Man-in-the-Moon Marigolds, 1972 (Cannes Film Festival award), Summer Wishes, Winter Dreams, 1973 (N.Y. Film Critics award), The Drowning Pool, 1975, The End, 1978, Harry and Son, 1984, Glass Menagerie, 1987, Mr. & Mrs. Bridge, 1990; TV appearances include All the Way Home; TV-film appearances in Sybil, 1976, Come Back, Little Sheba, 1977, See How She Runs, 1978 (Emmy award), Streets of L.A., 1979, The Shadow Box, 1980, Crisis at Central High, 1981, Do You Remember Love?, 1985 (Emmy award); narrator film documentary Angel Dust, TV documentary on Group Theatre, 1989. Democrat. Episcopalian. Office: William Morris Agy care Toni Howard 151 El Camino Beverly Hills CA 90212

WOODWARD, LINDA L., legal administrator; b. Cleve., Oct. 6, 1946; d. Henry J. and Margaret (Lindenmayer) W.; m. William G. Span, Jan. 6, 1968 (div. Sept. 1986); children: Juliann, Barbie Ann, David. BA, San Jose State U., 1989. Plant administr. Span Industries, Cleve., 1979-84; legal administr. Jerome & Smith, Cleve., 1984-86, Heller, Ehrman, White and McAuliffe, Palo Alto, Calif., 1986—; speaker Bar Assn. Ednl. Seminars, Santa Clara, 1989. Co-adminstr. Hospice Breavement Program Hillcrest Hosp., Cleve., 1984-85. Mem. ABA (law practice mgmt. com. 1987-90), Santa Clara County Bar Assn. (co-chmn. law practice mgmt. sect. 1988-89), Assn. Legal Adminstrs. (bar liaison 1988-90, com. chmn.), Decathlon Club. Home: 927 Bluebell Way Sunnyvale CA 94086 Office: Heller Ehrman White et al 525 University Ave Palo Alto CA 94301

WOODWARD, SUSAN ELLEN, economist, federal official; b. Loma Linda, Calif., June 14, 1949; d. Frank Colwin and Dollie Dorothy (O'Kane) W.; 1 child, Sonja Charlene Woodward Stenger. BA in Econs., UCLA, 1970, PhD in Mgmt./Fin., 1978. Instr. U. Wash., Seattle, 1975, U. Toronto, 1975-77, UCLA, 1976-83, 84-85, U. Calif., Santa Barbara, 1977-79, U. Rochester (N.Y.), 1983-84; sr. staff economist Coun. Econ. Advisers, Washington, 1985-87; dep. asst. sec., chief economist HUD, Washington, 1987—. Mem. Am. Econ. Assn. (editor 1983-87), Am. Fin. Assn. Home: 2129 Florida Ave NW No 304 Washington DC 20008 Office: HUD Econ Affairs 451 7th St SW Washington DC 20410

WOODWELL, MARGOT BELL, broadcasting executive; b. Pitts., Mar. 5, 1936; d. Davitt Stranahan and Marian (Whieldon) Bell; m. William Herron Woodwell, June 24, 1960; children: Davitt Bell, William Herron, James Ross. A.B., Vassar Coll., 1957. Dir. community support Sta. WQED, Pitts., 1978-84, v.p., sta. mgr., from 1984, now v.p., gen. mgr. Pres. bd. trustees St. Edmunds Acad., Pitts., 1972-75; pres. bd. trustees Episcopal Diocese Pitts., 1975-78; bd. dirs. Union Nat. Bank of Pitts., Cen. Blood Bank, County Bd. of Health, Lemington Home for Aged, Greater Pitts. Literacy Coun., Pitts. Literacy Initiative; mem. standing coms., 1982—; chmn. Episcopal Diocese Renewal Fund, Pitts., 1980—; trustee Vassar Coll., Poughkeepsie, N.Y., 1982—, chmn. devel. com.; mem. Allegheny County Bd. of Health, Health Edn. Ctr. adv. com., steering com. co-chmn. program com. Leadership Pitts., The Mayor's Commn. on Families, women's com. Mus. of Art of the Carnegie, community adv. bd. Jr. League of Pitts., adv. bd. Pa. State Coalition for Literacy, adv. coun. Pa. Dept. Edn. Workplace; bd. dirs. Greater Pitts. Literacy Coun., Pitts. Salvation Army; mktg. com. United Way of Allegheny County. Recipient A Celebration of Excellence award for Media Mgmt. Triangle Corner Ltd., 1986, Outstanding Svc. award Pa. Assn. Adult and Continuing Edn., 1987; named YWCA Woman of Yr. in Communications, 1988, Bishop's award Episcopal Diocese of Pitts., 1988. Office: Sta WQED 4802 5th Ave Pittsburgh PA 15217

WOODWORTH, LYNNE MARIE, construction equipment company executive; b. Rochester, N.Y., Sept. 16, 1953; d. Kenneth E. and Dolores (Russi) Bianchi; m. John F. Woodworth, Oct. 5, 1974 (div. 1981); children: Willow, Wade. AS, Rochester Inst. Tech., 1984. Exec. sec. to prin. Honeoye (N.Y.) Cen. Sch., 1973-77; exec. sec. mktg. div. Stone Constrn. Equipment, Inc., Honeoye, 1981-83, adminstrv. asst. to pres., 1983-87, asst. to pres. and chief exec. officer, 1987-89, dir. corp. communications, 1989—; bd. dirs. Nat. Ctr. Employee Ownership, Oakland, Calif.; mem. adv. com. participation and communication Employee Stock Ownership Plan Assn., Washington, 1989—. Mem. Soc. for Tech. Communication (editor newsletter 1990), Coun. for Communication Mgrs. Democrat. Roman Catholic. Office: Stone Constrn Equipment Inc 32 E Main St Honeoye NY 14471

WOODY, A-YOUNG MOON, biochemist; b. Pyungyang, Korea, Mar. 7, 1934; came to U.S., 1956; d. John M. Moon and Soon-Hae Choi; m. Robert Wayne Woody, Jan. 30, 1965; children: Michael Robert and David Matthew. BS, U. Calif., Berkeley, 1959; PhD, Cornell U., 1964. Rsch. assoc. in chemistry Cornell U., Ithaca, N.Y., 1964-65; rsch. assoc. in microbiology U. Ill., Urbana, 1965; rsch. assoc. in biochemistry U. Ill., Urbana, Ill., 1967-70; faculty rsch. assoc in zoology Ariz. State U., Tempe, 1972-75; rsch. assoc. in biochemistry Colo. State U., Ft. Collins, 1976-88, rsch. scientist in biochemistry, 1988 —. Office: Colo State U Dept Biochemistry Fort Collins CO 80523

WOODY, CAROL CLAYMAN, data processing executive; b. Bristol, Va., May 20, 1949; d. George Neal and Ida Mae (Nelms) Clayman; B.S. in Math., Coll. William and Mary, Williamsburg, Va., 1971; M.B.A. with distinction (IBM Corp. fellow 1978, Stephen Bufton Meml. Ednl. Found. grantee, 1978-79; Babcock Sch., Wake Forest U., 1979; m. Robert William Woody, Aug. 19, 1972. Programmer trainee GSA, 1972; Programmer/ analyst-tng. coordinator Blue Bell, Inc., Greensboro, N.C., 1975-79; supr. programming and tech. services J.E. Baker Co., York, Pa., 1979-82, fin. design supr. bus. systems Lycoming div. AVCO, Stratford, Conn., 1982-83; project mgr. Yale U., 1984—; co-owner Sign of the Sycamore, antiques; mem. Data Processing Standards Bd., 1977, CICS/VS Adv. Council, 1975; speaker Nat. Fuse Conf., 1989. Mem. Am. Bus. Woman's Assn. (chpt. v.p. 1978-79; Merit award 1978), Nat. Assn. Female Execs., Assn. for System Mgmt., Delta Omicron (alumni pres. 1973-75, regional chmn. 1979-82). Republican. Presbyterian. Author various manuals. Home: PO Box 1450 Guilford CT 06437 Office: 155 Whitney Ave New Haven CT 06510

WOODY, CATHERINE EVELYN, oceanographer; b. San Diego, Apr. 19, 1943; d. William Orland and Elsie (Drogan) W.; m. Kenneth Lee Warsh, Sept. 19, 1970 (div. Feb. 1979). BA in Math., Old Dominion U., 1965; MS in Oceanography, Fla. State U., 1971. Math tchr. Virginia Beach (Va.) City Schs., 1965-66; rsch. asst. Duke U., Beaufort, N.C., 1966-67; math. and oceanography tchr. Virginia Beach (Va.) City Schs., 1967-68; sci. tchr. Leon County Schs., Tallahassee, Fla., 1970-71; lab tech. Fla. State U., Tallahassee, 1971-72; environ. specialist Dept. Pollution Control, Tallahassee, 1973; contractor, oceanographer NOAA, Washington, 1974; oceanographer NOAA Dept. Commerce, Rockville, Md., 1974—; lectr. math. Montgomery Coll., Rockville, Md., 1988—; oceanographic lectr. Royal Viking Lines, Bahamas, 1988—, Marine Sci. Program for Jr. and Sr. High Schs., Washington, 1989; environ. lectr. Gillette Co., Balt., 1989, EPA, Phila., 1988-89; part-time instr.

Montgomery Coll., Rockville, Md., 1988—. Author: West Coast Physical Environments Section Data Atlas; contbr. articles to profl. jours. Office: NOAA N/OMA31 6001 Executive Blvd Rockville MD 20852

WOODY, JACQUELYN KAY, personnel director, medical services director, executive recruiter; b. Loup City, Nebr., Nov. 20, 1955; d. Don Lee and Elizabeth Marie (Elm) W. Student, U. Nebr., 1974-78. Researcher U. Nebr., Lincoln, 1974-76; cen. svcs. technician Bryan Meml. Hosp., Lincoln, 1976-80; cardiology technologist Creighton U., Omaha, 1980-83; med. svcs. dir. Pers. Search, Omaha, 1983—; judge Nebr. Distributive Edn. Clubs of Am., Lincoln, 1988—. Campaigner Dem. Party, Omaha, 1982-88. Disthg. Edn. Clubs of Am. scholar, 1974. Mem. Nebr. Pers. Assn. (sec. 1986-88), Nat. Pers. Assn. (program chairperson 1989—), Am. Hosp. Assn. Roman Catholic. Home: 1825 Happy Hollow #19 Omaha NE 68104 Office: Personnel Search 8744 Frederick St Omaha NE 61824

WOODY, JULIE See WYATT, JULIE

WOODY, KATHLEEN JOANNA, lawyer; b. Honolulu, May 3, 1949; d. Edward Franklin and Norma Lee (Harris) W.; m. Martin G. Baker, 1984; children: Mark G., Luke F. A.B. magna cum laude, U. Miami, 1973, BA in Russian and Econs. magna cum laude. J.D., 1976; LL.M., Columbia U., 1981, postgrad. Bar: Fla. 1976, D.C. 1977, U.S. Tax Ct. 1977, U.S. Supreme Ct. 1980, Md. 1989. V.p., tax cons. Franklin Tax Svc., Inc., Silver Spring, Md., 1967-76; real estate agt., sales mgr. Pershing Real Estate Co., Silver Spring, 1972-76; atty. U.S. Office Compt. of Currency, Washington, 1976-78, regional atty. N.Y.C., 1979-80; mem. faculty New Sch. for Social Rsch., N.Y.C., 1980; teaching fellow, dir. reg. internat. tax program Law Sch. Harvard U., 1981-82; mem. faculty Inst. Comparative Law in Paris, France for U. San Diego, 1982; teach. Oxford U., 1982; ptnr. Woody & Woody, 1983—; adj. prof. Law Sch. Georgetown U., 1983—. Author: Soviet Finance, International Banking and Finance, Legal Ethics in Law School Education, Medical Ethics of Informed Consent to Human Research; Legal Ethics and Informed Consent for Medical Research; contbr. articles to profl. jours. Mem. ABA, Internat. Bar Assn., D.C. Bar Assn., Fed. Bar Assn., Assn. Bar City N.Y. Baptist. Home: 9131 Sligo Creek Pkwy Silver Spring MD 20901

WOODYARD, CYNTHIA LEE, advertising executive; b. Grafton, W.Va., July 23, 1960; d. H. William and Jo Ann (Leach) W. BA in Mass Communications, Bethany Coll., 1982. Grad. asst. W. Va. U. Sch. Journalism, 1983-84; asst. account exec. Peter McMahon & Cygan, 1985; sales coord. telemarketing supr. NYNEX Mobile Communications, Pearl River, N.Y., 1985-87, asst. advt. mgr., 1987-89, mgr. advt.-pub. rels., 1990—. Recipient President's award Assn. Nat. Advts., 1989. Home: 4l Berwynn Rd Arden Forest Harriman NY 10926 Office: NYNEX Mobile Communications One Blue Hill Plaza Pearl River NY 10965

WOOLARD, DEBORAH JEAN, pediatrician; b. New Bern, N.C., Dec. 2, 1953; d. Hardy Gray and Mary Virginia (Hodges) W. BS with honors, Raldolph-Macon Coll., 1976; MD, Med. Coll. Va., 1982. Diplomate Am. Bd. Pediatrics. Intern and resident in pediatrics William Beaumont Army Med. Ctr., El Paso, Tex., 1982-85; instr. pediatrics Vanderbilt U. Med. Sch., Nashville, 1989-90; fellow in pediatric emergency medicine SUNY Health Sci. Ctr., Syracuse, 1990—. Maj. M.C., U.S. Army, 1982-89. Fellow Am. Acad. Pediatrics; mem. Phi Beta Kappa, Omicron Delta Kappa. Office: SUNY Health Sci Ctr Dept Critical Care-Emergency Med 750 E Adams St Syracuse NY 13210

WOOLDRIDGE, (MARY) JANE, writer; b. Raleigh, N.C., Apr. 3, 1958; d. Oscar Bailey Wooldridge Jr. and Martha Jane (Clarke) Wooldridge Jordan. AB in History, Duke U., 1980; summer study New Coll., Oxford, England, 1979. Gen. reporter, intern News & Observer, Raleigh, 1979-80; fashion writer N.Y. Times Mag., N.Y.C., 1980-81; freelance writer N.Y.C., 1981-82; asst. Eliot Janeway, Economist, N.Y.C., 1982-83; fashion and social writer, photo stylist Miami (Fla.) Herald, 1983—. Author (with others) Best Publications, 1982, also articles. Recipient Atrium award 1986, Fla. Med. Assn. award, 1987. Mem. N.C. Youth Adv. Bd., Raleigh, 1975-76; chmn. N.C. State Youth Couns., 1975-76. Angier B. Duke scholar Duke U., 1978-80. Democrat. Mem. Interdenominational Ch. Avocations: photography, traveling. Office: Miami Herald 1 Herald Pla Miami FL 33101

WOOLEVER, NAOMI LOUISE, retired editor; b. Williamsport, Pa., Sept. 17, 1922; d. Samuel Bruce and Kathryn Elizabeth (Schmidt) W. B.S., Pa. State U., 1944, M.A., 1966, postgrad., 1974-76. Reporter, women's editor Gazette & Bulletin, Williamsport, 1944-53; women's editor Sun-Gazette, Williamsport, 1953-72, assoc. city editor, 1972-74; prof. journalism Williamsport Area Community Coll., 1974-76; nat. editor, mng. editor Grit Pub. Co., Williamsport, 1976-81, editor in chief, 1981-88; career cons. high sch. and coll. journalism classes, Pa. Contbr. articles to profl. jours. Named Woman of Yr., Williamsport Univ. Women, 1967. Mem. Pa. Women's Press Assn. (pres. 1960-62, Pa. Newswoman of Yr. award 1958), Nat. Fedn. Press Women (dir. 1960-62), Soroptimist Club (pres. Williamsport chpt. 1958-60), Univ. Women Club (pres. 1961-63), Friends of Libr. Club (bd. dirs.), Williamsport Country Club, Lycoming County Hist. Soc., Clio Club (bd. dirs.), Phi Kappa Phi, Kappa Tau Alpha, Zeta Tau Alpha. Republican. Mem. United Methodist Ch. Home: 326 Montour St Montoursville PA 17754

WOOLLEY, BARBARA ELLEN, hospital administrator; b. Phila., Aug. 8, 1951; d. Melvin Edvin and Mary Margaret (McMenamin) Huntzinger; m. Stephen Michael Woolley, Aug. 24, 1974; children: Stephen Bradley, Jeffery Prescott, Jonathan Tyler. BA in History, Ursinus Coll., 1973; BS in Med. Records Adminstrn., SUNY, Bklyn., 1975; MBA, Rutgers U., Newark, 1989. Asst. dir. med. records St. Barnabas Med. Ctr., Livingston, N.J., 1975-77; designer med. records system Slate Belt Med. Ctr., Bangor, Pa., 1981; dir. med. records, utilization review Easton (Pa.) Hosp., 1977-83; dir. med. records Med. Ctr. Princeton, N.J., 1983—. Mem. Am. Med. Records Assn., Med. Records Assn. N.J. DRG Mgmt. Assn. (data com., various coms.), Pa. Med. Record Assn. (publ. com., legal com.), Lehigh Valley Med. Records Assn. (pres., chmn., various com.). Home: 35 Cheston Ct Belle Mead NJ 08502 Office: Med Ctr Princeton 253 Witherspoon St Princeton NJ 08540

WOOLLEY, CATHERINE (JANE THAYER), author; b. Chgo., Aug. 11, 1904; d. Edward Mott and Anna L. (Thayer) W. AB, UCLA, 1927. Advt. copywriter Am. Radiator Co., N.Y.C., 1927-31; freelance writer, 1931-33; copywriter, editor house organ Am. Radiator & Standard San. Corp., N.Y.C., 1933-40; desk editor Archtl. Record, 1940-42; prodn. editor SAE Jour., N.Y.C., 1942-43; pub. relations writer NAM, N.Y.C., 1943-47; condr. workshop in juvenile writing Truro Center for Arts, 1977, 78, Cape Cod Writers Conf., 1990; instr. juvenile writing Cape Cod Writers Conf., 1965, 66. Author: juvenile books (under name Catherine Woolley) I Like Trains, 1944, rev., 1965, Two Hundred Pennies, 1947, Ginnie and Geneva, 1948, paperback edit., 1988, David's Railroad, 1949, Schoolroom Zoo, 1950, Railroad Cowboy, 1951, Ginnie Joins In, 1951, David's Hundred Dollars, 1952, Lunch for Lennie, 1952 (pub. as L'Incontenabile Gigi in Italy), The Little Car That Wanted a Garage, 1952, The Animal Train and Other Stories, 1953, Holiday on Wheels, 1953, Ginnie and the New Girl, 1954, Ellie's Problem Dog, 1955, A Room for Cathy, 1956, Ginnie and the Mystery House, 1957, Miss Cathy Leonard, 1958, David's Campaign Buttons, 1959, Ginnie and the Mystery Doll, 1960, Cathy Leonard Calling, 1961, paperback edit., 1988, Look Alive, Libby!, 1962, Ginnie and Her Juniors, 1963, Cathy's Little Sister, 1964, paperback edit., 1988, Libby Looks for a Spy, 1965, The Shiny Red Rubber Boots, 1965, Ginnie and the Cooking Contest, 1966, paperback 1979, Ginnie and the Wedding Bells, 1967, Chris in Trouble, 1968, Ginnie and the Mystery Cat, 1969, Libby's Uninvited Guest, 1970, Cathy and the Beautiful People, 1971, Cathy Uncovers a Secret, 1972, Ginnie and the Mystery Light, 1973, Libby Shadows a Lady, 1974, Ginnie and Geneva Cookbook, 1975, adult book Writing for Children, 1990; (under name Jane Thayer) The Horse with the Easter Bonnet, 1953, The Popcorn Dragon, 1953, rev. edit. 1989, Where's Andy?, 1954, Mrs. Perrywinkle's Pets, 1955, Sandy and the Seventeen Balloons, 1955, The Chicken in the Tunnel, 1956, The Outside Cat, 1957, English edit., 1958, 83, Charley and the New Car, 1957, Funny Stories To Read Aloud, 1958, Andy Wouldn't Talk, 1958, The Puppy Who Wanted a Boy, 1958, rev., 1986, paperback edition, 1988, The Second-Story Giraffe, 1959, Little Monkey, 1959, Andy and His Fine Friends, 1960, The Pussy Who Went To the Moon,

1960, English edit., 1961, A Little Dog Called Kitty, 1961, English edit., 1962, 75, The Blueberry Pie Elf, 1961, English edit., 1962, Andy's Square Blue Animal, 1962, Gus Was a Friendly Ghost, 1962, English edit., 1971, Japanese edit., 1982, A Drink for Little Red Diker, 1963, Andy and the Runaway Horse, 1963, A House for Mrs. Hopper; the Cat that Wanted to Go Home, 1963, Quiet on Account of Dinosaur, 1964, English edit., 1965, 74, paperback edit., 1988, Emerald Enjoyed the Moonlight, 1964, English edit., 1965, The Bunny in the Honeysuckle Patch, 1965, English edit., 1966, Part-Time Dog, 1965, English edit. 1966, The Light Hearted Wolf, 1966, What's a Ghost Going to Do?, 1966, English edit. 1972, Japanese edit., 1982, The Cat that Joined the Club, 1967, English edit. 1968, Rockets Don't Go To Chicago, Andy, 1967, A Contrary Little Quail, 1968, Little Mr. Greenthumb, 1968, English edit., 1969, Andy and Mr. Cunningham, 1969, Curious, Furious Chipmunk, 1969, I'm Not a Cat, Said Emerald, 1970, English edit. 1971, Gus Was A Christmas Ghost, 1970, English edit. 1973, Japanese edit., 1982, Mr. Turtle's Magic Glasses, 1971, Timothy And Madam Mouse, 1971, English edit., 1972, Gus And The Baby Ghost, 1972, English edit. 1973, Japanese edit., 1982, The Little House, 1972, Andy and the Wild Worm, 1973, Gus Was a Mexican Ghost, 1974, English edit. 1975, Japanese edit., 1982, I Don't Believe in Elves, 1975, The Mouse on the Fourteenth Floor, 1977, Gus Was a Gorgeous Ghost, 1978, English edit., 1979, Where Is Squirrel?, 1979, Try Your Hand, 1980, Applebaums Have a Robot, 1980, Clever Raccoon, 1981, Gus Was a Real Dumb Ghost, 1982, Gus Loved His Happy Home, 1989; contbr. stories to juvenile anthologies, sch. readers, juvenile mags. Trustee Truro Pub. Libraries, 1974-84; Mem. Passaic (N.J.) Bd. Edn., 1953-56, Passaic Redevel. Agy., 1952-53; pres. Passaic LWV, 1949-52. Named mem. N.J. Literary Hall of Fame, 1987. Mem. Authors League Am., Friends of Truro Libraries, Truro Hist. Soc., Amnesty Internat. U.S.A., Kenilworth Soc. Democrat. Home: Higgins Hollow Rd Truro MA 02666

WOOLLEY, MARGARET ANNE (MARGOT WOOLLEY), architect; b. Bangor, Maine, Feb. 4, 1946; d. George Walter and Anne Geneva (Collins) W.; m. Gerard F. Vasisko, June 22, 1985. BA, Vassar Coll., 1969; MArch, Columbia U., 1974. Registered architect, N.Y. Urban designer Mayor's Office Lower Manhattan Devel., 1974-76, Mayor's Office Devel., N.Y.C., 1976-78; project mgr. Office Econ. Devel., N.Y.C., 1978-81, dep. dir. design and engring., 1981-83; dep. dir. design N.Y.C. Pub. Devel. Corp., 1983-85, asst. v.p. design, 1985-86, v.p. planning and design, 1986—. Mem. assoc. bd. regents L.I. Coll. Hosp., Bklyn., 1982—, mem. planning and devel. com., 1983—; pres. assoc. bd. regents, 1988-89. William Kinne Fellows scholar, 1973. Mem. AIA (bd. dirs. N.Y.C. chpt. 1988-90), N.Y. State Assn. Architects (bd. dirs. 1989—), Alliance Women in Architecture, Heights Casino Club, Vassar Club, Jr. League. Home: 135 Willow St Brooklyn NY 11201 Office: NYC Public Devel Corp 161 William St New York NY 10038

WOOLPERT, LAURA DIANE, marketing professional; b. North Hollywood, Calif., May 19, 1960; d. Gene Edward Woolpert and Louise Diane Moss; m. Charles Michael Slotnick, Sept. 24, 1988. BA, U. Conn., 1982. Adminstrv. asst. Yacht Racing/Cruising Mag., Darien, Conn., 1976-82; communications asst. Interrad Corp., Stamford, 1982-83; communications mgr. Interrad Corp., Fairfield, Conn., 1983-84; communications specialist Blue Cross & Blue Shield Conn., North Haven, 1984-85; dir. mktg. Palmer & Dodge, Boston, 1985-88, Hinckley, Allen, Snyder & Comen, Boston and Providence, 1988—; speaker Northeastern U. Sch. Law, Boston, 1988, Mass. Bar Assn., 1988, 90, ABA, 1989, 90. Mem. Am. Mktg. Assn. (speaker, bd. dris. Profl. Svcs. Mktg. div. Conf.), Nat. Law Firm Mktg. Adminstrs. Assn. (speaker, chmn. memberships com. 1988, 89), P.E.O. Sisterhood, Internat. Assn. Bus. Communication. Office: Hinckley Allen Snyder & Comen 1500 Fleet Ctr Providence RI 02903 also: One Fin Ctr Boston MA 02111-2625

WOOLSTON, EVELYN DORIS, arts administrator; b. Boston, Nov. 8, 1925; d. Paul Hermann and Louise Martha (Gesch) Franz; m. John Woolston, Apr. 7, 1945; (div. 1967); 1 son, Peter Christopher; m. 2d Robert Franklin May, Feb. 1, 1984. B.A., Emerson Coll., 1947. Asst. merchandising mgr. Sta. WCSC-TV-AM, Charleston, S.C., 1954-57; mgr. promotions and merchandising, Knight Broadcasting, Inc., Portsmouth, N.H., 1957-61; asst. advt. dir. Hahn Shoes, Landover, Md., 1961-70; advt. dir. W & J Sloane, Inc., Washington, 1970-76; exec. dir. Capitol Ballet, Inc., Washington, 1977-80; freelance arts adminstr., Washington, 1980—. Exec. dir. Off the Circle Theatre Co., Washington, 1982-84; gen. mgr. Interact Theatre Co., 1987—; chmn., coordinator fund-raising project League of Washington Theatres, 1984-85; bd. dirs. D.C. Contemporary Dance Theatre, 1985—, Washington Stage Guild, 1986—. League Washington Theatres, Helen Hayes Awards, co-chmn. Washington Theatre Fortnight, 1986 ; fund raiser various arts orgns., Washington, 1961—. Mem. Spanish Dance Soc., Emerson Coll. Alumni Assn. (mem. exec. bd. 1984-86). Republican. Club: ARTS Club of Washington (chmn. drama 1982-83, chmn. outreach 1985—). Avocations: theatre; travel; reading; Japanese literature; swimming. Home and Office: 2734 34th Pl NW Washington DC 20007

WOOTTON, BROOKII E., teacher; b. Uvalde, Tex., Mar. 4, 1965; d. Charles K. and Leona Agnus (Farley) W. BS, SW Tex. State U., 1988. Operator test floor Motorola, Austin, Tex.; stockbroker's asst. Shearson Lehman Hutton, Austin; instr. office adminstrn. Devine (Tex.) Ind. Sch. Dist. Active community and charitable orgns.; sponsor cheerleading and twirling. Mem. NAFE, NEA, Bus. Profls. Am. Club (sponsor), Tex. State Tchr's. Assn., Devine Educators Assn. (v.p.), Tex. Bus. Educators Assn., Alpha Phi. Home: 901 W Hondo Ave Devine TX 78016

WORCESTER, PATRICE HERZIG, hotel manager; b. Winchester, Mass., Apr. 28, 1960; d. John Duncan and Margaret (Herzig) W. BS in Hotel Adminstrn., Cornell U., 1984. Asst. hotel mgr. Harrah's Lake Tahoe Hotel/ Casino, Stateline, Nev., 1986, hotel mgr., 1986-88; gen. mgr. Embassy Suites Hotel, Irvine, Calif., 1988—. Vol. Planned Parenthood of No. Nev., Stateline, 1986-88; cons. Project Bus./Jr. Achievement, Reno, 1984-85. Mem. Nev. Hotel/Motel Assn., Calif. Hotel/Motel Assn., Cornell Soc. Hotelmen, Nat. Assn. Female Execs., Assn. Rep. Women. Office: Embassy Suites Hotel 2120 Main St Irvine CA 92714

WORDEN, KATHARINE COLE, sculptor; b. N.Y.C., May 4, 1925; d. Philip Gillette and Katharine (Pyle) Cole; m. Frederic G. Worden, Jan. 8, 1944; children: Rick, Dwight, Philip, Barbara, Katharine. Student Potters Sch., Tucson, 1940-42, Sarah Lawrence Coll., 1942-44. Sculptor; works exhibited Royce Galleries, Galerie Francoise Besnard (Paris), Cooling Gallery (London), Galerie Schumacher (Munich), Selected Artists Gallery, N.Y.C., Art Inst. Boston, Reid Gallery, Nashville, Weiner Gallery, N.Y.C., Boston Athanaeum, House of Humor and Satire, Gabrovo, Bulgaria, 1983, Newport Bay Club, 1984; pvt. collections Grand Palais (Paris), Dakar and Bathurst, Africa; dir. Stride Rite Corp., 1980-85; occupational therapist psychopathic ward Los Angeles County Gen. Hosp., 1953-57; Headstart vol., Watts, Calif., 1965-67; tchr. sculpture Watts Towers Art Center, 1967-69; participant White House Women Doers Luncheon meeting, 1968; dir. Cambridgeport Problem Center, Cambridge, Mass., 1969-71; mem. Jud. Nominating Commn., 1976-79; bd. overseers Boston Mus. Fine Arts, 1980-83; bd. govs. Newport Seamens Ch. Inst., 1989—; trustee Communication Research Inst., Miami, Fla., 1966-69, chmn. bd. 1966-69; trustee Newport Art Mus., 1984-86, Newport Health Found. 1986—, Hawthorne Sea Fund, 1990—; bd. dirs. Boston Center for Arts. 1976-80, Child and Family Svcs. of Newport County, 1983-90. Mem. Common Cause (Mass. adv. bd. 1971-72, dir. 1974-75), Mass. Civil Liberties Union (exec. bd. 1973-74, dir. 1976-77). Home: 24 Ft Wetherill Rd Jamestown RI 02835

WORDEN, ROXANE F., manufacturing executive; b. Wausau, Wis., Aug. 9, 1954; d. Ardell H. and Ila J. (Janisch) Goetsch; m. Loren L. Worden, Jan. 28, 1978; children: Ryan M., Randy J. Finished goods adminstr., supr. Marathon Electric, Wausau; mgr. prodn. and inventory control, systems and materials Cen. Fabricators, Schofield, Wis. Mem. NAFE, Am. Prodn. and Inventory Control Soc. (cert. prodn. and inventory mgmt.), exec. v.p. cen. Wis. chpt.). Home: 1507 Shorey Ave Rothschild WI 54474

WORK, JANE MAGRUDER, professional society administrator; b. Owensboro, Ky., Mar. 30, 1927; d. Orion Noel and Willie May (Stallings) Magruder; m. William Work, Nov. 26, 1960; children: Paul MacGregor, Jeffrey William. BA, Furman U., 1947; MA, U. Wis., 1948; PhD, Ohio State U., 1959. Dir. radio U. South Miss., Hattisburg, 1948-51; pub. rela-

Belleville, 1987-88; assoc. dir. devel. McKendree Coll., Lebanon, Ill., 1988—. Chmn. Fountain Fest Auction, Belleville, Belleville, 1985; co-chmn. ann. house tour St. Clair County Hist. Soc., 1987-88; bd. dirs Belleville's 175th Anniversary Com., 1986-89; exec. v.p. Masterworks Chorale, 1990-92. Mem. Nat. Parks and Conservation assn., Nat. Hist. Soc., Nat. Wildlife Fedn., Belleville C. of C. (civic design com. 1985-87), Optimists, Nat. Honor Soc., Pi Kappa Lambda. Methodist. Office: McKendree Coll 701 College Rd Lebanon IL 62254

WOODRUFF, KATHRYN ELAINE, English educator; b. Ft. Stockton, Tex., Oct. 12, 1940; d. James Arthur and Catherine H. (Stevens) Borron; m. Thomas Charles Woodruff, May 18, 1969; children: Robert Borron, David Borron. BA, Our Lady of the Lake U., San Antonio, 1963; MFA, U. Alaska, 1969; PhD, U. Denver, 1987. Cert. tchr., Tex. English and journalism tchr. Owensboro (Ky.) Cath. High Sch., 1963-64, Grand Junction (Colo.) Dist. 12, 1964-66; English tchr. Monroe High Sch., Fairbanks, Alaska, 1966-67; teaching asst. U. Alaska, Fairbanks, 1967-69, instr., 1969-70; instr. U. Colo., Boulder, 1979, Denver, 1988-89; instr. Regis Coll., Denver, 1987-89; asst. prof. Econs. Inst., Boulder, 1990—; tchr. Upward Bound, Fairbanks, 1968; instr. ethnic and women writers course U. Colo., Denver, 1988-89. Friend Chautauqua Music Festival, Boulder, 1985—; dir. 12th Annual Arts Festival, Fairbanks, 1969. Named one of Outstanding Young Women Am., 1966. Mem. AAUW, MLA, TESOL, COTESOL, Associated Writers Press, Sigma Tau Delta. Democrat. Mem. Christian Ch. Office: Econs Inst 909 14th St Boulder CO 80302

WOODRUFF, VIRGINIA, television and radio host, producer; b. Morrisville, Pa.; d. Edwin Nichols and Louise (Meredith) W.; m. Raymond F. Beagle Jr. (div.); m. Albert Plaut II (div.); 1 child, Elise Meredith. Past student, Rutgers U. News corr. Sta. WNEW-TV Metromedia, 1967-96; nat., internat. critic-at-large Mut. Broadcasting System, 1968-75; lectr. circ. Leigh Bur., 1969-71; byline columnist N.Y. Daily Mirror, N.Y.C., 1971; first Arts critic Teleprompter and Group W Cable TV, 1977-84; host/producer The First Nighter N.Y. Times Primetime Cable Highlight program, 1977-84; pres., chief exec. officer Starpower, Inc., 1984—; affiliate news corr. ABC Radio Network, N.Y.C., 1984-86; perennial critic Off-Off Broadway Short Play Festival, N.Y.C., 1984—; was 1st Woman on 10 O'Clock News, WNEW-TV, 1967. Contbg. feature writer UAL Internat. Vis à Vis mag., 1988—. Mem. celebrity panel Arthritis Telethon, N.Y.C., 1976. Selected episodes First Nighter program in archives N.Y. Pub. Libr., Billy Rose Theatre Collection, Rodgers and Hammerstein Collection, Performing Arts Rsch.Ctr. Mem. Drama Desk. Presbyterian. Office: Starpower Inc 35 E 10th St New York NY 10003

WOODRUM, PATRICIA ANN, librarian; b. Hutchinson, Kans., Oct. 11, 1941; d. Donald Jewell and Ruby Pauline (Shuman) Hoffman; m. Clayton Eugene Woodrum, Mar. 31, 1962; 1 child, Clayton Eugene, II. BA, Kans. State Coll., Pittsburg, 1963; MLS, U. Okla., 1966. Br. libr. Tulsa City-County Libr. System, 1964-65, head brs., 1965-66, head reference dept. 1966-67, chief extension, chief pub. svc., 1967-73, asst. dir., 1973-76, exec. dir., 1976—; bd. dirs. Local Am. Bank Tulsa. Mem. editorial bd. Jour. of Library Administration. Mem. bd. Downtown Tulsa Unltd.; mem. Friends of Tulsa Libr.; mem. Leadership Tulsa Alumni; mem. bd. Tulsa Area Libr. Coop; mem. community svc. coun. bd.; trustee Univ. Ctr. at Tulsa Trust Authority. Recipient Disting. Libr. award Okla. Libr. Assn., 1982, Leadership Tulsa Paragon award, 1987, Women in Communications Newsmaker award, 1989, Outstanding Alumnus award U. Okla. Sch. Libr. Info. Studies, 1989; inducted into Tulsa City-County Libr. Hall of Fame, 1989. Mem. ALA, Okla. Libr. Assn. (pres. 1978-79, C. of C.). Republican. Episcopalian. Office: Tulsa City-County Libr 400 Civic Ctr Tulsa OK 74103

WOODS, DIANE, chemicals executive; b. Chgo., Apr. 18, 1958; d. Thaddeus George and Helen Pricilla (Niemiec) Godfryt; m. Harold Woods, Oct. 24, 1985. BS in Chemistry, U. Ill., Chgo., 1980. Lab. technologist Nalco Chem. Co., Naperville, Ill., 1980-85, chemist, 1986-89, product specialist, 1989—. Mem. NAFE, Toastmasters (sec., treas. Nalco club 1988-89, adminstrv. v.p. 1989-90, pres. 1990—). Office: Nalco Chem Co One Nalco Ctr Naperville IL 60563-1198

WOODS, DIANE HOLLIS, university official; b. Altadena, Calif., Apr. 17, 1956; d. Richard Owen and Barbara (Hoffman) Hollis; m. Michael Gage Woods, Aug. 16, 1980; children: Thomas Michael, Kathryn Elizabeth. BA, Ottawa U., 1978; postgrad., U. So. Calif., 1984—. Exec. sec. Fuller Theol. Sem., Pasadena, Calif., 1979-80; corp. legal sec. Barger & Wolen, L.A., 1980-81; employment counselor Lynn Carol Employment Agy., Pasadena, 1981-82; asst. to dean Annenberg Sch. Communications, U. So. Calif., L.A., 1982-85, asst. dir. continuing legal edn. programs Law Ctr., 1985-87, dir. insts. and confs., 1987—. Sec.-treas. sanctuary choir Pasadena Covenant Ch., 1984—, editor newsletter, 1987—, chairperson, 1990—. Author: What It Means To Be An American Baptist Today, 1976. Named one of Outstanding Young Women of Am. Mem. NAFE, Am. Mgmt. Assn., Internat. Platform Assn., Am. Continuing Legal Edn. Adminstrs., Women in Mgmt. Democrat. Avocations: writing, photography, travel. Office: U So Calif Law Ctr Office Insts and Confs Law 105-D University Park Los Angeles CA 90089-0071

WOODS, ELLEN, psychotherapist; b. Flushing, N.Y., May 25, 1953; d. Albert and Frieda (Mandel) Cohen; m. Gary Stephen Woods, July 1, 1951. BA, Goddard Coll., Plainfield, Vt., 1974; MA, John F. Kennedy U., Orinda, Calif., 1982. Lic. marriage and family therapist. Artist-in-residence Orange Elem. Sch., Vt., 1975; owner, mgr. Woven Thread Wks., San Francisco, 1977-80; artist-in-residence Phoenix Rising, Concord, Calif., 1982-84; art instr. Creative Growth, Oakland, Calif., 1984; children's prog. dir. City of Oakland, 1985-87; marriage and family counselor Oakland, 1982-87; instr. Colo. Mt. Coll., Aspen, Basalt, Carbondale, 1987—; psychotherapist in pvt. practice Carbondale, 1988—; cons. Grand River Hospice, Glenwood Springs, Colo., 1988—, U. Without Walls, Denver, 1988—. Art work exhibited at Aspen Chapel Gallery, 1989, Bay Currents: New Artists, 1987, Contra Costa Competitive, 1984, Boston Archtl. Ctr., 1975, others. Acad. Art grantee, 1985. Mem. Colo. Fedn. Arts, Colo. Artists Register, Am. Assn. Artist-Therapists, Artitracts Gallery, Carbondale Council on the Arts. Office: 289 Main St Carbondale CO 81623

WOODS, EVELYN LOCKETT, information systems specialist; b. Lafayette, La., Nov. 3, 1949; d. Bethel and Evelyn Rose (Jones) Lockett; m. Gregory Frazier, Nov. 30, 1974 (div.); children: Keli Brooke, Kendra Evelyn; m. Richard C. Woods, Oct. 12, 1985. BA, U. Houston, 1972; M in Mgmt., Northwestern U., 1989. Cert. tchr., Tex. Math. tchr. Houston Ind. Sch. Dist., 1972-74; computer programmer Ill. Bell Telephone Co., Chgo., 1974-78, systems analyst, 1978-80, edp auditor, 1980-82, mgr., 1982-85, dist. mgr., 1985-88; sr. dir. Ameritech Applied Techs., Chgo., 1988—; adv. bd. SRA, Chgo., 1989—. Recognized Chicago's Up and Coming Business and Professional Women Black Enterprise mag., 1985. Mem. Black Data Processing Assocs. (adv. bd. 1989—), Bell Mgmt. Women, Nat. Black MBA Assocs., Nat. Tech. Assocs., Delta Sigma Theta. Democrat. Roman Catholic. Office: Ameritech Applied Techs 500 W Madison Ste 2700 Chicago IL 60606

WOODS, HARRIETT RUTH, state official; b. Cleve., June 2, 1927; d. Armin and Ruth (Wise) Friedman; student U. Chgo., 1945; B.A., U. Mich., 1949; m. James B. Woods, Jan. 2, 1953; children—Christopher, Peter, Andrew. Reporter, Chgo. Herald-Am., 1948, St. Louis Globe-Democrat, 1949-51; producer Star. KPLR-TV, St. Louis, 1964-74; moderator, writer Sta. KETC-TV, St. Louis, 1962-64; council mem. University City, Mo., 1967-74; mem. Mo. Hwy. Commn., 1974, Mo. Transp. Commn., 1974-76; mem. Mo. Senate, 1976-84, lt. gov. State of Mo., 1985-89; pres. Inst. for Policy Leadership, U. Mo., St. Louis. Bd. dirs. LWV of Mo., 1963, Nat. League of Cities, 1972-74; Democratic nominee for U.S. Senate, 1982, 86. Jewish. Office: 7952 Natural Bridge Rd Saint Louis MO 63121

WOODS, LAURIE, lawyer; b. N.Y.C., Nov. 18, 1947; d. William M. and Sylvia Leona (Bottsten) W.; m. John W. Corwin, June 1, 1968; children—Robert Woods-Corwin, James Woods-Corwin. B.A., New Sch., N.Y.C., 1969; J.D., Boston U., 1973. Bar: N.Y., 1974. Staff atty. MFY Legal Services, N.Y.C., 1973-79; exec. dir. Nat. Ctr. on Women and Family Law, N.Y.C., 1979—; bd. dirs. N.Y. Women Against Rape, 1982—, Feminist Legal Strategies Project, Washington, 1983—. Contbr. articles in field to

publs. Bd. dirs. Gingerbread Day Care Ctr., N.Y.C., 1982-83. Mem. ABA, N.Y. State Bar Assn., Assn. Bar City N.Y., N.Y. Women's Bar Assn. Office: Nat Ctr on Women & Family Law 799 Broadway Room 402 New York NY 10003

WOODS, LINDSAY ELIZABETH, marketing executive; b. Pontiac, Mich., Aug. 2, 1948; d. George Edward Woods and Beth Yvonne (Tucker) Segula. Student, U. Mich., 1966-68; BA in Edn., Lang., Queens Coll., 1970; postgrad., Oakland U., 1975; student, Long Island U., 1981. French, German instr. Union Free Sch. Dist. #1, Mamaroneck, N.Y., 1970-75; dir. sales Nassau Gold Coast News, Suffolk, N.Y., 1976; exec. v.p. LIN-Z Stables, LTD., Old Westbury, N.Y., 1978-82; chief exec. officer, pres., founder Tyler-Woods, Ltd., Locust Valley, N.Y., 1982—; cons. Murray Electronics, Balt., 1982-83, cons., v.p., bd. dirs. Am. Vet. Products, Ft. Collins, Colo., 1988-90; dir. animal health div. Luitpold Pharms., Inc., Shirley, N.Y. Mem. Standardbred Owners Assn., U.S. Trotting Assn., Old Westbury Horsemans Assn. (v.p. 1980, trustee 1981—), N.Y. State Tchrs. Assn., Nat. Assn. Female Execs. Address: 1044 2nd Cunningham Dr #2 Fort Collins CO 80526

WOODS, MERILYN BARON, psychologist, consultant; b. Bklyn., July 8, 1927; d. David Theodore and Helen (Mintz) Baron; m. John Galloway Woods, Sept. 15, 1948; children: Anne Helen, Elizabeth Ruth. BS, Cornell U., 1948; MEd, Temple U., 1957; PhD, Bryn Mawr Coll., 1968. Lic. psychologist, Pa. Rsch. asst. psychiatry Temple U., Phila., 1958-59, instr., counselor students, 1960-64; clin. psychologist Gloucester County Guidance Ctr., Woodbury, N.J., 1959-60; seminar coord. Bryn Mawr Coll., 1966-67, lectr., 1968-70, asst. prof., 1977-73; dir. Ctr. for Pers. and Profl. Devel. Pa. Coll. Optometry, Phila., 1983—; pvt. practice psychologist Phila., 1983—. Mem., pres. bd. mgrs. Sr. Employment and Ednl. Svc., Phila., 1985—; chmn. Environ. Edn. Com., Phila., 1989—; bd. dirs. Awbury Arboretum Assn. 1986—. Mem. APA, Phila. Soc. Clin. Psychologists (bd. dirs. 1980—), Cornell Alumni Club of Phila. (co-pres. 1989—). Office: 5928 Devon Pl Philadelphia PA 19138

WOODS, ROBIN FUNNELL, doll manufacturing company executive; b. Lubbock, Tex., Mar. 29, 1943; d. Russell J. and Lois (Bledsoe) Funnell; m. Kent Hill, Aug. 22, 1964 (div. 1971); children: Leah, Andrea; m. Stephen Boyce Woods, June 7, 1972; 1 child, Mary Margaret; stepchildren: Jennifer, David, Drew. BA, Tex. Tech U., 1965, MA, 1968; PhD, U. Pitts., 1976. Asst. prof. English Mansfield State Coll., Mansfield, Pa., 1968-70; dir. pub. relations Mansfield State Coll., 1969-70; dir. day care Tioga County, Wellsboro, Pa., 1970-72; dir. Dravosburg Nursery Sch., Dravosburg Meth., Dravosburg, Pa., 1973-74; cons. Pitts. 1st born program U. Pitts., 1974-75, asst. prof. grad. sch. pub. health, 1976-80; dir. consultation and edn. St. Francis Hosp., Pitts., 1980-81; dir. children's mental health Penn Group Health Plan, Pitts., 1981-83; chief exec. officer Robin Woods, Inc. Mfg., Pitts., 1983—; cons. Mich. State Dept. Mental Health, 1976-80, Pa. State Dept. Pub. Welfare, 1976-80, Allegheny County Orphans Ct., Pitts., 1976-83, Neighborhood Legal Svcs., Pitts., 1976-83; dir. Appalachian regional commn. tng. project U. Pitts., 1977-80. Mem. Carnegie Inst., Pitts., 1986—. Recipient Parents Choice Gold award, Boston, 1988, Award of Excellence, DOLLS Mag., 1987, 88; named nominee Entrepreneur of Yr., VENTURE Mag., Arthur Young, 1987, for Doll of Yr., DOLL Reader Mag., 1986, 87, 88, 89. Mem. United Fedn. Doll Clubs, Smaller Mfr.'s Coun., E. Liberty C. of C. (Pitts.). Episcopalian. Home: 639 Hastings St Pittsburgh PA 15206 Office: Robin Woods Inc 6592 Hamilton Ave Pittsburgh PA 15206

WOODS, SANDRA KAY, real estate executive; b. Loveland, Colo., Oct. 11, 1944; d. Ivan H. and Florence L. (Betz) Harris; m. Mark A. Woods, June 11, 1967; children: Stephanie Michelle, Michael Harris. BA, U. Colo., 1966, MA, 1967. Personnel mgmt. specialist CSC, Denver, 1967; asst. to regional dir. HEW, Denver, 1968-69; urban renewal rep. HUD, Denver, 1970-73, dir. program analysis, 1974-75, asst. regional dir. community planning and devel., 1976-77, regional dir. fair housing, 1978-79; mgr. ea. facility project Adolph Coors Co., Golden Colo., 1980, dir. real estate, 1981, v.p. corp. real estate, 1982—; pres. Industries for Jefferson County (Colo.), 1985. Mem. Exec. Exchange, The White House, 1980; bd. dirs. Golden Local Devel. Corp. (Colo.), 1981-82; fundraising dir. Coll. Arts and Scis., U. Colo., Boulder, 1982-89, U. Colo. Found.; mem. exec. bd. NCCJ, Denver, 1982-89; v.p. Women in Bus., Inc., Denver, 1982-83; mem. steering com. 1984 Yr. for All Denver Women, 1983-84; mem. 10th dist. Denver br. Fed. Reserve Bd., 1990. Named one of Outstanding Young Women Am., 1974; U.S. Jaycees, 1974, 78, Fifty Women to Watch, Businessweek, 1987, Woman of Achievement YWCA, 1988. Mem. Indsl. Devel. Resources Council (bd. dirs 1986-89), Am. Mgmt. Assn., Denver C. of C. (bd. dirs. 1988—), Disting. Young Exec. award 1974, mem. Leadership Denver, 1976-77), Colo. Women's Forum, Nat. Assn. Office and Indsl. Park Developers (sec. 1988, treas. 1989), Phi Beta Kappa, Pi Alpha Alpha. Republican. Presbyterian. Club: PEO (Loveland, Colo.). Office: Adolph Coors Co Real Estate 807 Golden CO 80401

WOODS, SUSANNE, university dean; b. Honolulu, May 12, 1943; d. Samuel Ernest and Gertrude (Cullom) W. BA in Polit. Sci., UCLA, 1964, MA in English, 1965; PhD in English and Comparative Lit., Columbia U., 1970; MA (hon.), Brown U., 1978. Staff Senator Daniel K. Inouye, 1963; asst. editor Rand Corp., Calif., 1963-65; instr. Ventura Coll., Calif., 1965-66; lectr. CUNY, 1967-69; asst. prof. U. Hawaii, 1969-72; asst. prof. English Brown U., Providence, 1972-77, assoc. prof., 1977-83, prof., 1983—, dir. grad. studies, 1986-88, assoc. dean faculty, 1987-90; vis. assoc. prof. U. Calif., 1981-82; dir. NEH-Brown Women Writers Project, 1988—. Author: Natural Emphasis, 1984; contbr. numerous articles to profl. jours. and scholarly books; reviewer for various profl. jours., including Renaissance Quar., Jour. of English and Germanic Philology; reader for PMLA Jour., SEL Jour., also others; editorial bd. Huntington Libr. Quar., 1987-90. Active various polit. campaigns, 1960-64, 68-76, 84. Bronson fellow, 1976, Huntington Library, 1979-80, 81, Clark Library, 1981, Huntington-NEH, 1984-85, Woodrow Wilson Found., 1968-70. Mem. Am. Council Edn. (R.I. women's coord. 1988-90), MLA (chmn. div. 17th Century English lit. 1982), N.E. MLA (chmn. English Renaissance sect. 1978, Milton sect. 1983), Am. Assn. Higher Edn., Nat. Women's Studies Assn., Renaissance Soc. Am., Milton Soc. (exec. com. 1987-89), Lyrica Soc. (pres. 1987-90), Alpha Gamma Delta. Democrat. Episcopalian. Home: 19 University Ave Providence RI 02906 Office: Brown U PO Box 1852 Providence RI 02912

WOODS, WILLIE G., English and education educator; b. Yazoo City, Miss.; d. John Wesley and Jessie Willie Mae W. B.A., Shaw U., Raleigh, N.C., 1965; M.Ed., Duke U., 1968; postgrad., Temple U., Pa. State U., U. N.H., NYU. Tchr. schs. in N.C. and Md., 1965-69; mem. faculty Harrisburg (Pa.) Area Community Coll., 1969—, assoc. prof. English and edn., 1976-82, prof., 1982—; supr. Writing Ctr., 1975-78, coord. Act 101/Basic Studies Program, 1978-83, dir. Acad. Founds. program 1983-87, asst. dean academ. affairs Acad. Found. and Basic Edn. Div., 1987-89, asst. dean acad. affairs, chmn. social sci., pub. svcs. and basic edn. div., 1989—, chmn. dirs. coun., 1981-82; tchr. Community Resources Inst., 1975—; moderator workshops, cons. in field. Asst. editor Black Conf. Higher Edn. Jour., 1980. Sec., exec. com. People for Progress, 1971-73; bd. mgrs., exec. com. Camp Curtin br. YMCA, 1971-79; bd. dirs. Alternative Rehab. Communities, 1978—; bd. mgrs. Youth Urban Svcs., Harrisburg Area YMCA, 1981—; bd. dirs. Dauphin Residences, Inc., 1981—. Recipient cert. of merit for community svcs. City of Harrisburg, 1971, Youth Urban Svcs. Vol. of Yr. award, 1983, Black Student Union award Harrisburg Area Community Coll., 1984. Mem. Pa. Assn. Devel. Educators (chmn. conf. 1980, sec. 1981-82, v.p. 1986-87, pres. 1987-88), Pa. Black Conf. Higher Edn. (Outstanding Svc. award 1980, Central Region award 1982), Nat. Coun. Tchrs. English, Pa. Edn. Assn., Am. Assn. Community and Jr. Colls., Nat. Coun. on Black Am. (instl. rep. 1983—), AAUP, Alpha Kappa Alpha (Outstanding Svc. award 1983, Basileus award 1984), Alpha Kappa Mu. Baptist. Home: 1712 Fort Patton Dr Harrisburg PA 17112 Office: 3300 Cameron St Rd Harrisburg PA 17110

WOODSIDE, LISA NICOLE, college dean; b. Portland, Oreg., Sept. 7, 1944; d. Lee and Emma (Wenstrom) W. Student Reed Coll., 1962-65; M.A., U. Chgo., 1968; Ph.D., Bryn Mawr Coll., 1972; cert. Harvard U. Inst. for Ednl. Mgmt., 1979; postgrad. West Chester U., 1988—. Mem. dean's staff Bryn Mawr Coll., 1970-72; asst. prof. humanities, 1978-83, asst. dean student services, 1972-76, asso. dean, 1976-79, dean, 1979-83; acad. dean, prof. of humanities Holy Family

Coll., Phila., 1983—; accreditor Commn. on Higher Edn., Middle States Assn., 1979-83. City commr. for community rels. Chester, 1980-83; mem. Adult Edn. Council Phila. Am. Assn. Papyrology grantee Bryn Mawr Coll.; S. Maude Kaemmerling fellow Bryn Mawr Coll. Mem. Am. Assn. Higher Edn., Council Ind. Colls., Eastern Assn. Coll. Deans, Pa. Assn. Colls. and Tchr. Educators, AAUW (univ. rep. 1975-83), Nat. Assn. Women in C. of C. Phi Eta Sigma, Alpha Sigma Lambda. Episcopalian. Club: Am. Fox Terrier. Home: 27 Wallingford Rd A-6 Wallingford PA 19086 Office: Holy Family Coll Torresdale Philadelphia PA 19114

WOODSON, CHERYL ANNE, psychology educator; b. Bristol, Pa., Jan. 16, 1959; d. Benjamin Franklin Woodson and Lucille (Weeks) Woodson-Lewis; m. Keith Byron Coleman, Nov. 7, 1977 (div. Feb. 1980). BS, Nova U., 1981, MS, 1983; PhD, Fla. Inst. Tech., 1987. Lic. psychologist, Fla. Vocat. counselor Minority Builders Coalition, Ft. Lauderdale, Fla., 1980; out-reach counselor Ft. Lauderdale Housing Authority, 1980-82, community svc. specialist, 1982-83; devel. coord. Neighborhood Reinvestment Corp., Ft. Lauderdale and Washington, 1983-84; doctoral psychology intern Nova U. Mental Health Clinic, Ft. Lauderdale, 1986-87; program evaluation coord. Dade County Pub. Schs., Miami, Fla., 1987-88; asst. prof. psychology Southeastern U. Health Scis., Miami, 1988—; cons. Concerned Orgn. Parents to Educate, Melbourne, Fla., 1985-86, Coun. of Minority Women, Melbourne, 1985-86, Family Life Inst. for Counseling, Ft. Lauderdale, 1987-89, The Starting Pl., Ft. Lauderdale, 1987-88. Guest lectr., educator Delta Sigma Theta Sorority, Melbourne, 1985, lectr., 1989; guest panelist Cablevision of Cen. Fla., Melbourne, 1985; guest speaker Alpha Kappa Alpha Sorority, Ft. Lauderdale, 1988; panelist Sta. WRBD-1470 Radio, Ft. Lauderdale, 1988-89; lectr. Sta. WLRN Channel 17 Focus on Health, Miami, 1988-89. Mem. APA, Am. Ednl. Rsch. Assn., Soc. Tchrs. of Family Medicine. Office: Southeastern U Health Scis 1750 NE 168th St North Miami FL 33162

WOODSON-HOWARD, MARLENE ERDLEY, state legislator; b. Ford City, Pa., Mar. 8, 1937; d. James and Susie (Lettrich) Erdley; m. Francis M. Howard; children: George Woodson, Bert Woodson, Robert Woodson, Daniel Woodson, David Woodson. BS, Ind. U. of Pa., 1958; MA, U. South Fla., 1968; EdD, Nova U., 1981. Prof. math. Manatee Community Coll. 1970-82, dir., Inst. Advancement, 1982-86; exec. dir. Manatee Community Coll. Foundation, 1982-86; pres. Pegasus Enterprises, Inc., 1986—; state senator Fla., 1986-90. Gubernatorial candidate, 1990; bd. dirs Sarasota Opera, West Coast Symphony, Child Devel. Ctr. Mem. Nat. Assn. Women Bus. Owners, Women Owners Network, Manatee Symphony (past pres.), Manatee C. of C., Sarasota Tiger Bay Club. Republican. Roman Catholic. Home: Box 468 Bradenton FL 34206

WOODSUM, GAYLE M., social services administrator; b. Cambridge, Mass., Apr. 21, 1956; d. George Albert and Phyllis Marie (Tolman) W.; 1 child, Tristan P. (dec.). Grad. high sch., Kents Hills, Maine, 1973. Editor Northeast Horseman Mag., Hamden, Maine, 1980-82; exec. dir., co-founder "Looking Up", Augusta, Maine, 1983—; founder, facilitator support group for parents of terminally ill children, Lewiston, Maine, 1982; editor "Looking Up" Times mag., 1985—. Contbr. articles on incest-related topics to ednl. publs., 1985—. Democrat. Office: Looking Up PO Box K Augusta ME 04330

WOODSWORTH, ANNE, librarian, university official; b. Fredericia, Denmark, Feb. 10, 1941; d. Thorvald Ernst and Roma Yrsa (Jensen) Lindner; 1 child, Yrsa Anne. BFA, U. Man., Can., 1962; BLS, U. Toronto, Ont., Can., 1964, MLS, 1969; PhD, U. Pitts., 1987. Edn. libr. U. Man., 1964-65; reference libr. Winnipeg Pub. Library, 1965-67; reference libr. sci. and medicine dept. U. Toronto, 1967-68; med. librarian Toronto Western Hosp., 1969-70; research asst. to chief librarian U. Toronto, 1970-71, head reference dept., 1971-74; personnel dir. Toronto Pub. Library, 1975-78; dir. librs. York U., Toronto, 1978-83; assoc. provost for librs. U. Pitts., 1983-88, assoc. prof., 1988—; pres. Anne Lindner Ltd., 1974-83; bd. dirs. Population Rsch. Found., Toronto, 1980-83, Ctr. for Rsch. Libraries, 1987-88; mem. rsch. libraries adv. coun. OCLC, 1984-87. Author: The Alternative Press in Canada, 1972, Leadership for Research Libraries, 1988, Patterns and Options for Managing Information Technology on Campus, 1990. Can. Coun. grantee, 1974, Ont. Arts Coun. grantee, 1974, Coun. on Library Resources grantee, 1986, 88; UCLA sr. fellow, 1985. Mem. ALA, Can. Assn. Rsch. Librs. (pres. 1981-83), Assn. Rsch. Librs. (bd. dirs. 1981-84, v.p. 1984-85, pres. 1985-86), Pa. Libr. Assn., Am. Soc. Info. Sci., Soc. Scholarly Pub. Office: U Pitts Univ Librs 626 Librar Info Sci Bldg Pittsburgh PA 15260

WOODWARD, ANITA BARRETT, health care facility professional; b. Youngstown, Ohio, Feb. 10, 1950; d. John Paul and Lois (Handel) Barrett; m. James S. Woodward, June 11, 1977; children: Jennifer, Bernadette Miller. BA in Communication summa cum laude, Cleve. State U., 1988. Employment cons. Champion Personnel, Cleve., 1976-81; employment specialist MetroHealth Med. Ctr., Cleve., 1981-83, mgr. customer svcs., 1983—, dir. customer svcs., 1990—. Bd. trustees Ohio City Redevel. Assn., Cleve., 1985—, v.p., 1989-90. Recipient Pres.'s award Cleve. State U., 1989. Mem. Ohio Soc. Patient Reps. (pres. elect, treas., bd. dirs. Columbus, Ohio chpt. 1986-90, pres. 1990—). Nat. Soc. Patient Reps. (profl. devel. com. Chgo. chpt. 1990—). Home: 1820 W 44th Cleveland OH 44113

WOODWARD, FAE BLANCHE, journalist; b. Santa Ana, Calif., Nov. 15, 1925; d. Louis George and Rhoda Miranda (Morris) Willits; m. Billy J. Woodward, Nov. 24, 1947; children—Billy, Bobby, Tonni, Clarissa, Kevin, Woodra. Cub reporter, society editor Progress Bull., Pomona, Calif., 1944-48; society editor Telegram Tribune, San Luis Obispo, Calif., 1948-49; Corcoran corr. Fresno Bee (Calif.), 1953-54; corr. Ukiah (Calif.) Daily Jour., 1956-58, 61-64, teletypesetter, 1960, 71, lifestyles editor, 1971—. Tenderfoot leader, mem. tng. com. Sonoma-Mendocino council Boy Scouts Am., 1967—, roundtable staff Yokayo Dist. Boy Scouts 1981—; mem. young women's program Ch. of Jesus Christ of Latter-day Saints, Ukiah, 1981-85; mem. sch. adv. com. compensatory edn. Ukiah Unified Sch. Dist., 1974-77, also adv. com. photography, 1979-85, Ukiah Com. Ctr. Bd., 1985-86. Recipient Golden Rule award Calif. Assn. for Retarded, 1980; Disting. Achievement Pub. Info. award North Coast Coordinating Council Devel. Disabilities, 1980, Silver Beaver award Boy Scouts Am., 1983. Mem. Calif. Press Women's Assn. Republican. Home: 6785 W Hwy 20 Star Route 2 Ukiah CA 95482 Office: Ukiah Daily Jour 590 S School St Ukiah CA 95482

WOODWARD, GRETA CHARMAINE, construction company executive, rental and investment property manager; b. Congress, Ohio, Sept. 28, 1930; d. Richard Thomas and Grace Lucetta (Palmer) Duffey; m. John Jay Woodward, Oct. 29, 1949; children: Kirk Jay, Brad Ewing, Clay William. Bookkeeper Kaufman's Texaco, Wooster, Ohio, 1948-49; office mgr. Holland Furnace Co., Wooster, 1948-49; acctg. clk. Columbus and So. Ohio Electric, 1949-50; interviewer, clk. State Ohio Bur. Employment Services, Columbus, 1950-51; clk. Def. Constrn. Supply Ctr. (U.S. Govt.) (formerly Columbus Gen. Depot), 1951-52; treas. Woodward Co., Inc., Reynoldsburg, Ohio, 1963—. Newspaper columnist Briarcliff News, 1960-63. Active Reynoldsburg PTA, 1960-67; Reynoldsburg United Meth. Ch.; mem. women's service bd. Grant Hosp. Avocations: bike riding, crocheting, writing poetry, stock market, financial mags. Office: Woodward Excavating Co Inc 7320 Tussing Rd Reynoldsburg OH 43068

WOODWARD, ISABEL AVILA, writer; b. Key West, Fla., Mar. 14, 1906; d. Alfredo and Isabel (Lopez) Avila; student Fla. State Coll. for Women, 1925, A.B. in Edn., 1938; cert. in teaching Spanish, U. Miami, 1961; summer study U. Fla., Eckerd Coll.; postgrad. St. Lawrence U., U. Miami; m. Clyde B. Woodward, June 6, 1944 (dec.); children—Joy Avis Ball, Greer Isabel Woodward Sucke. Tchr., Key West, 1927-42, remedial reading cons., 1941-42; reading tchr., asst. reading lab. and clinic St. Lawrence U., summer 1941; Spanish translator U.S. Office of Censorship, Miami, 1943; tchr. Central Beach Elem. Sch., Miami Beach, Fla., 1943-44, Silver Bluff Elem. Sch., 1943-50, Henry West Lab. Sch., Coral Gables, Fla., 1955-57, Dade Demonstration Sch., Miami, 1957-61; author 125 sch. radio lessons for teaching Spanish, Dade County Elem. Schs., 1961; tchr. Spanish Workshop for Fla.; speaker poetry and short story writing, 1977; guest lectr. on writing the short story Fla. Inst. Tech., Jensen Beach, 1981; freelance writer; contbr. to Listen Mag., Sunshine Mag., Lookout Mag., Christian Sci. Monitor, Miami Herald, Three/Four, Child Life, Wee Wisdom, Fla. Wildlife, Young World; sponsor

Port St. Lucie Jr. Woman's Club, 1983. Recipient Honoris Causa award Alpha Delta Kappa, 1972-74, award Contra Costa Times, Calif., 1985; named one of 5 Outstanding Fla. Tchrs., 1972-74. Mem. Nat. League Am. Pen Women (1st v.p. Greater Miami br. 1974-76, historian 1978—, librarian 1978—, awards for writing 1973, 74, 77, 1st and 3d place state writing awards for adult and juvenile fiction 1983, state 1st prize short story 1985), AAUW, Alpha Delta Kappa, Psi Psi Psi. Address: 1950 Palm City Rd Apt 6-301 Stuart FL 34994

WOODWARD, JOANNE GIGNILLIAT, actress; b. Thomasville, Ga., Feb. 27, 1930; d. Wade and Elinor (Trimmier) W.; m. Paul Newman, Jan. 29, 1958; children: Elinor Terese, Melissa Stewart, Clea Olivia. Student, La. State U., 1947-49; grad., Neighborhood Playhouse Dramatic Sch., N.Y.C. First TV appearance in Penny, Robert Montgomery Presents, 1952; understudy broadway play Picnic, 1953; appeared in plays Baby Want a Kiss, 1964, Candida, 1982, The Glass Menagerie, Williamstown Theatré Festival, 1985, Sweet Bird of Youth, Toronto, 1988; motion pictures include Three Faces of Eve, 1957 (Acad. award Best Actress, Nat. Bd. Rev. award, Fgn. Press award), Count Three and Pray, 1955, Long Hot Summer, 1958, No Down Payment, 1957, Sound and the Fury, 1959, A Kiss Before Dying, 1956, Rally Round the Flag Boys, 1958, The Fugitive Kind, 1960, Paris Blues, 1961, The Stripper, 1963, A New Kind of Love, 1963, A Big Hand for the Little Lady, 1966, A Fine Madness, 1965, Rachel, Rachel, 1968, Winning, 1969, WUSA, 1970, They Might Be Giants, 1971, The Effect of Gamma Rays on Man-in-the-Moon Marigolds, 1972 (Cannes Film Festival award), Summer Wishes, Winter Dreams, 1973 (N.Y. Film Critics award), The Drowning Pool, 1975, The End, 1978, Harry and Son, 1984, Glass Menagerie, 1987, Mr. & Mrs. Bridge, 1990; TV appearances include All the Way Home; TV-film appearances in Sybil, 1976, Come Back, Little Sheba, 1977, See How She Runs, 1978 (Emmy award), Streets of L.A., 1979, The Shadow Box, 1980, Crisis at Central High, 1981, Do You Remember Love?, 1985 (Emmy award); narrator film documentary Angel Dust, TV documentary on Group Theatre, 1989. Democrat. Episcopalian. Office: William Morris Agy care Toni Howard 151 El Camino Beverly Hills CA 90212

WOODWARD, LINDA L., legal administrator; b. Cleve., Oct. 6, 1946; d. Henry J. and Margaret (Lindenmayer) W.; m. William G. Span, Jan. 6, 1968 (div. Sept. 1986); children: Juliann, Barbie Ann, David. B.A, San Jose State U., 1989. Plant administr. Span Industries, Cleve., 1979-84; legal administr. Jerome & Smith, Cleve., 1984-86, Heller, Ehrman, White and McAuliffe, Palo Alto, Calif., 1986—; speaker Bar Assn. Ednl. Seminars, Santa Clara, 1989. Co-adminstr. Hospice Breavement Program Hillcrest Hosp., Cleve., 1984-85. Mem. ABA (law practice mgmt. com. 1987-90), Santa Clara County Bar Assn. (co-chmn. law practice mgmt. sect. 1988-89), Legal Adminstrs. (bar liaison 1988-90, com. chmn.), Decathlon Club. Home: 927 Bluebell Way Sunnyvale CA 94086 Office: Heller Ehrman White et al 525 University Ave Palo Alto CA 94301

WOODWARD, SUSAN ELLEN, economist, federal official; b. Loma Linda, Calif., June 14, 1949; d. Frank Colwin and Dollie Dorothy (O'Kane) W.; 1 child, Sonja Charlene Woodward Stenger. BA in Econs., UCLA, 1970, PhD in Mgmt./Fin., 1978. Instr. U. Wash, Seattle, 1975, U. Toronto, 1975-77, UCLA, 1976-83, 84-85, U. Calif., Santa Barbara, 1977-79, U. Rochester (N.Y.), 1983-84; sr. staff economist Coun. Econ. Advisers, Washington, 1985-87; dep. asst. sec., chief economist HUD, Washington, 1987—. Mem. Am. Econ. Assn. (editor 1983-87), Am. Fin. Assn. Home: 2129 Florida Ave NW No 304 Washington DC 20008 Office: HUD Econ Affairs 451 7th St SW Washington DC 20410

WOODWELL, MARGOT BELL, broadcasting executive; b. Pitts., Mar. 5, 1936; d. Davitt Stranahan and Marian (Whieldon) Bell; m. William Herron Woodwell, June 24, 1960; children: Davitt Bell, William Herron, James Ross. A.B., Vassar Coll., 1957. Dir. community support Sta. WQED, Pitts., 1978-84, v.p., sta. mgr., from 1984, now v.p., gen. mgr. Pres. bd. trustees St. Edmunds Acad., Pitts., 1972-75; pres. bd. trustees Episcopal Diocese Pitts., 1975-78; bd. dirs. Union Nat. Bank of Pitts., Cen. Blood Bank, County Bd. of Health, Lemington Home for Aged, Greater Pitts. Literacy Coun. Pitts. Literacy Initiative; mem. standing com., 1982—; chmn. Episcopal Diocese Renewal Fund, Pitts., 1980—; trustee Vassar Coll., Poughkeepsie, N.Y., 1982—, chmn. devel. com.; mem. Allegheny County Bd. of Health, Health Edn. Ctr. adv. com., steering com. co-chmn. program com. Leadership Pitts., The Mayor's Commn. on Families, women's com. Mus. of Art of the Carnegie, community adv. bd. Jr. League of Pitts., adv. bd. Pa. State Coalition for Literacy, adv. coun. Pa. Dept. Edn. Workplace; bd. dirs. Greater Pitts. Literacy Coun., Pitts. Salvation Army; mktg. com. United Way of Allegheny County. Recipient A Celebration of Excellence award for Media Mgmt. Triangle Corner Ltd., 1986, Outstanding Svc. award Pa. Assn. Adult and Continuing Edn., 1987; named YWCA Woman of Yr. in Communications, 1988, Bishop's award Episcopal Diocese of Pitts., 1988. Office: Sta WQED 4802 5th Ave Pittsburgh PA 15217

WOODWORTH, LYNNE MARIE, construction equipment company executive; b. Rochester, N.Y., Sept. 16, 1953; d. Kenneth E. and Dolores (Russi) Bianchi; m. John F. Woodworth, Oct. 5, 1974 (div. 1981); children: Willow, Wade. AS, Rochester Inst. Tech., 1984. Exec. sec. to prin. Honeoye (N.Y.) Cen. Sch., 1973-77; exec. sec. mktg. div. Stone Constrn. Equipment, Inc., Honeoye, 1981-83, adminstrv. asst. to pres., 1983-87, asst. to pres. and chief exec. officer, 1987-89, dir. corp. communications, 1989—; bd. dirs. Nat. Ctr. Employee Ownership, Oakland, Calif.; mem. adv. com. participation and communication Employee Stock Ownership Plan Assn., Washington, 1989—. Mem. Soc. for Tech. Communication (editor newsletter 1990), Coun. for Communication Mgrs. Democrat. Roman Catholic. Office: Stone Constrn Equipment Inc 32 E Main St Honeoye NY 14471

WOODY, A-YOUNG MOON, biochemist; b. Pyungyang, Korea, Mar. 7, 1934; came to U.S., 1955; d. John M. Moon and Soon-Hae Choi; m. Robert Wayne Woody, Jan. 30, 1965; children: Michael Robert and David Matthew. BS, U. Calif., Berkeley, 1959; PhD, Cornell U., 1964. Rsch. assoc. in chemistry Cornell U., Ithaca, N.Y., 1964-65; rsch. assoc. in microbiology U. Ill., Urbana, 1965; rsch. assoc. in biochemistry U. Ill., Urbana, Ill., 1967-70; faculty rsch. assoc in zoology Ariz. State U., Tempe, 1972-75; rsch. assoc. in biochemistry Colo. State U., Ft. Collins, 1976-88, rsch. scientist in biochemistry, 1988 --. Office: Colo State U Dept Biochemistry Fort Collins CO 80523

WOODY, CAROL CLAYMAN, data processing executive; b. Bristol, Va., May 20, 1949; d. George Neal and Ida Mae (Nelms) Clayman; BS in Math., Coll. William and Mary, Williamsburg, Va., 1971; M.B.A. with distinction (IBM Corp. fellow 1978, Stephen Bufton Meml. Ednl. Found. grantee, 1978-79), Babcock Sch., Wake Forest U., 1979; m. Robert William Woody, Aug. 19, 1972. Programmer trainee GSA, 1971-72; systems engr. Citizens Fidelity Bank & Trust Co., Louisville, 1972-75; programmer/ analyst-tng. coordinator Blue Bell, Inc., Greensboro, N.C., 1975-79; supr. programming and tech. services J.E. Baker Co., York, Pa., 1979-82, fin. design supr. bus. systems Lycoming div. AVCO, Stratford, Conn., 1982-83; project mgr. Yale U., 1984—; co-owner Sign of the Sycamore, antiques; mem. Data Processing Standards Bd., 1977, CICS/VS Adv. Council, 1975; speaker Nat. Fuse Conf., 1989. Mem. Am. Bus. Woman's Assn. (chpt. v.p. 1978-79; Merit award 1978), Nat. Assn. Female Execs., Assn. for System Mgmt., Delta Omicron (alumni pres. 1973-75, regional chmn. 1979-82). Republican. Presbyterian. Author various manuals. Home: PO Box 1450 Guilford CT 06437 Office: 155 Whitney Ave New Haven CT 06510

WOODY, CATHERINE EVELYN, oceanographer; b. San Diego, Apr. 19, 1943; d. William Orland and Elsie (Drogan) W.; m. Kenneth Lee Warsh, Sept. 19, 1970 (div. Feb. 1979). BA in Math., Old Dominion U., 1965; MS in Oceanography, Fla. State U., 1971. Math tchr. Virginia Beach (Va.) City Schs., 1965-66; rsch. asst. Duke U., Beaufort, N.C., 1966-67; math. and oceanography tchr. Virginia Beach (Va.) City Schs., 1967-68; sci. tchr. Leon County Schs., Tallahassee, Fla., 1970-71; lab tech. Fla. State U., Tallahassee, 1971-72; environ. specialist Dept. Pollution Control, Tallahassee, 1973; contractor, oceanographer NOAA, Washington, 1974; oceanographer NOAA Dept. Commerce, Rockville, Md., 1974—; lectr. math. Montgomery Coll., Rockville, Md., 1988—; oceanographic lectr. Royal Viking Lines, Bahamas, 1988—, Marine Sci. Program for Jr. and Sr. High Schs., Washington, 1989; environ. lectr. Gillette Co., Balt., 1989, EPA, Phila., 1988-89; part-time instr.

Montgomery Coll., Rockville, Md., 1988—. Author: West Coast Physical Environments Section Data Atlas; contbr. articles to profl. jours. Office: NOAA N/OMA31 6001 Executive Blvd Rockville MD 20852

WOODY, JACQUELYN KAY, personnel director, medical services director, executive recruiter; b. Loup City, Nebr., Nov. 20, 1955; d. Don Lee and Elizabeth Marie (John) W. Student, U. Nebr., 1974-78. Researcher U. Nebr., Lincoln, 1974-76; cen. svcs. technician Bryan Meml. Hosp., Lincoln, 1976-80; cardiology technologist Creighton U., Omaha, 1980-83; med. svcs. dir. Pers. Search, Omaha, 1983—; judge Nebr. Distributive Edn. Clubs of Am., Lincoln, 1988—. Campaigner Dem. Party, Omaha, 1982-88. Disthg. Edn. Clubs of Am. scholar, 1974. Mem. Nebr. Pers. Assn. (sec. 1986-88), Nat. Pers. Assn. (program chairperson 1989—), Am. Hosp. Assn. Roman Catholic. Home: 1825 Happy Hollow #19 Omaha NE 68104 Office: Personnel Search 8744 Frederick St Omaha NE 61824

WOODY, JULIE See **WYATT, JULIE**

WOODY, KATHLEEN JOANNA, lawyer; b. Honolulu, May 3, 1949; d. Edward Franklin and Norma Lee (Harris) W.; m. Martin G. Baker, 1984; children: Mark G., Luke F. A.B. magna cum laude, U. Miami, 1973, BA in Russian and Econs. magna cum laude. J.D., 1976; LL.M., Columbia U., 1981, postgrad. Bar: Fla. 1976, D.C. 1977, U.S. Tax Ct. 1977, U.S. Supreme Ct. 1980, Md. 1989. V.p., tax cons. Franklin Tax Svc., Inc., Silver Spring, Md., 1967-76; real estate agt., sales mgr. Pershing Real Estate Co., Silver Spring, 1972-76; atty. U.S. Office Compt. of Currency, Washington, 1976-78, regional atty. N.Y.C., 1979-80; mem. faculty New Sch. for Social Rsch., N.Y.C., 1980; teaching fellow, dir. tng. internat. tax program Law Sch. Harvard U., 1981-82; mem. faculty Inst. Comparative Law in Paris, France for U. San Diego, 1982; ind. rsch. Oxford U., 1982; ptnr. Woody & Woody, 1983—; adj. prof. Law Sch. Georgetown U., 1983—. Author: Soviet Finance, International Banking and Finance, Legal Ethics in Law School Education, Medical Ethics of Informed Consent to Human Research; Legal Ethics and Informed Consent for Medical Research; contbr. articles to profl. jours. Mem. ABA, Internat. Bar Assn., D.C. Bar Assn., Fed. Bar Assn., Assn. Bar City N.Y. Baptist. Home: 9131 Sligo Creek Pkwy Silver Spring MD 20901

WOODYARD, CYNTHIA LEE, advertising executive; b. Grafton, W.Va., July 23, 1960; d. H. William and Jo Ann (Leach) W. BA in Mass Communications, Bethany Coll., 1982. Grad. asst. W. Va. U. Sch. Journalism, 1983-84; asst. account exec. Peter McMahon & Cygan, 1985; sales coord. telemarketing supr. NYNEX Mobile Communications, Pearl River, N.Y., 1985-87, asst. advt. mgr., 1987-89, mgt. advt.-pub. rels., 1990—. Recipient President's award Assn. Nat. Advts., 1989. Home: 4l Berwynn Rd Arden Forest Harriman NY 10926 Office: NYNEX Mobile Communications One Blue Hill Plaza Pearl River NY 10965

WOOLARD, DEBORAH JEAN, pediatrician; b. New Bern, N.C., Dec. 2, 1953; d. Hardy Gray and Mary Virginia (Hodges) W. BS with honors, Raldolph-Macon Coll., 1976; MD, Med. Coll. Va., 1982. Diplomate Am. Bd. Pediatrics. Intern and resident in pediatrics William Beaumont Army Med. Ctr., El Paso, Tex., 1982-85; instr. pediatrics Vanderbilt U. Med. Sch., Nashville, 1989-90; fellow in pediatric emergency medicine SUNY Health Sci. Ctr., Syracuse, 1990—. Maj. M.C., U.S. Army, 1982-89. Fellow Am. Acad. Pediatrics; mem. Phi Beta Kappa, Omicron Delta Kappa. Office: SUNY Health Sci Ctr Dept Critical Care-Emergency Med 750 E Adams St Syracuse NY 13210

WOOLDRIDGE, (MARY) JANE, writer; b. Raleigh, N.C., Apr. 3, 1958; d. Oscar Bailey Wooldridge Jr. and Martha Jane (Carew) Wooldridge Jordan. AB in History, Duke U., 1980; summer study New Coll., Oxford, England, 1979. Gen. reporter, intern News & Observer, Raleigh, 1979-80; fashion writer N.Y. Times Mag., N.Y.C., 1980-81; freelance writer N.Y.C., 1981-82; asst. Eliot Janeway, Economist, N.Y.C., 1982-83; fashion and social writer, photo stylist Miami (Fla.) Herald, 1983—. Author (with others) Best Publications, 1982, also articles. Recipient Atrium award 1986, Fla. Med. Assn. award, 1987. Mem. N.C. Youth Adv. Bd., Raleigh, 1975-76; chmn. N.C. State Youth Couns., 1975-76. Angier B. Duke scholar Duke U., 1978-80. Democrat. Mem. Interdenominational Ch. Avocations: photography, traveling. Office: Miami Herald 1 Herald Pla Miami FL 33101

WOOLEVER, NAOMI LOUISE, retired editor; b. Williamsport, Pa., Sept. 17, 1922; d. Samuel Bruce and Kathryn Elizabeth (Schmidt) W. B.S., Pa. State U., 1944, M.A., 1966, postgrad.; 1974-76. Reporter, women's editor Gazette & Bulletin, Williamsport, 1944-53; women's editor Sun-Gazette, Williamsport, 1953-72, assoc. city editor, 1972-74; prof. journalism Williamsport Area Community Coll., 1974-76; nat. editor, mng. editor Grit Pub. Co., Williamsport, 1976-81, editor in chief, 1981-88; career cons. high sch. and coll. journalism classes, Pa. Contbr. articles to profl. jours. Named Woman of Yr., Williamsport Univ. Women, 1967. Mem. Pa. Women's Press Assn. (pres. 1960-62, Pa. Newswoman of Yr. award 1958), Nat. Fedn. Press Women (dir. 1960-62), Soroptimist Club (pres. Williamsport chpt. 1958-60), Univ. Women Club (pres. 1961-63), Friends of Libr. Club (bd. dirs.), Wiliamsport Country Club, Lycoming County Hist. Soc., Clio Club (bd. dirs.), Phi Kappa Phi, Kappa Tau Alpha, Zeta Tau Alpha. Republican. Mem. United Methodist Ch. Home: 326 Montour St Montoursville PA 17754

WOOLLEY, BARBARA ELLEN, hospital administrator; b. Phila., Aug. 8, 1951; d. Melvin Edvin and Mary Margaret (McMenamin) Huntzinger; m. Stephen Michael Woolley, Aug. 24, 1974; children: Stephen Bradley, Jeffery Prescott, Jonathan Tyler. BA in History, Ursinus Coll., 1973; BS in Med. Records Adminstrn., SUNY, Bklyn., 1975; MBA, Rutgers U., Newark, 1989. Asst. dir. med. records St. Barnabas Med. Ctr., Livingston, N.J., 1975-77; designer med. records system State Belt Med. Ctr., Bangor, Pa., 1981; dir. med. records, utilization review Easton (Pa.) Hosp., 1977-83; dir. med. records Med. Ctr. Princeton, N.J., 1983—. Mem. Am. Med. Records Assn., Med. Records Assn. N.J. DRG Mgmt. Assn. (data com., various com.), Pa. Med. Record Assn. (pub. com., legal com.), Lehigh Valley Med. Records Assn. (pres., chmn., various com.). Home: 35 Cheston Ct Belle Mead NJ 08502 Office: Med Ctr Princeton 253 Witherspoon St Princeton NJ 08540

WOOLLEY, CATHERINE (JANE THAYER), author; b. Chgo., Aug. 11, 1904; d. Edward Mott and Anna L. (Thayer) W. AB, UCLA, 1927. Advt. copywriter Am. Radiator Co., N.Y.C., 1927-31; freelance writer, 1931-33; copywriter, editor house organ Am. Radiator & Standard San. Corp., N.Y.C., 1933-40; desk editor Archtl. Record, 1940-42; prodn. editor SAE Jour., N.Y.C., 1942-43; pub. relations writer NAM, N.Y.C., 1943-47; contr. workshop in juvenile writing Truro Center for Arts, 1977, 78, Cape Cod Writers Conf., 1990; instr. juvenile writing Cape Cod Writers Conf., 1965, 66. Author: juvenile books (under name Catherine Woolley) I Like Trains, 1944, rev., 1965, Two Hundred Pennies, 1947, Ginnie and Geneva, 1948, paperback edit., 1988, David's Railroad, 1949, Schoolroom Zoo, 1950, Railroad Cowboy, 1951, Ginnie Joins In, 1951, David's Hundred Dollars, 1952, Lunch for Lennie, 1952 (pub. as L'Incantedile Gigi in Italy), The Little Car That Wanted a Garage, 1952, The Animal Train and Other Stories, 1953, Holiday on Wheels, 1953, Ginnie and the New Girl, 1954, Ellie's Problem Dog, 1955, A Room for Cathy, 1956, Ginnie and the Mystery House, 1957, Miss Cathy Leonard, 1958, David's Campaign Buttons, 1959, Ginnie and the Mystery Doll, 1960, Cathy Leonard Calling, 1961, paperback edit., 1988, Look Alive, Libby!, 1962, Ginnie and Her Juniors, 1963, Cathy's Little Sister, 1964, paperback edit., 1988, Libby Looks for a Spy, 1965, The Shiny Red Rubber Boots, 1965, Ginnie and the Cooking Contest, 1966, paperback 1979, Ginnie and the Wedding Bells, 1967, Chris in Trouble, 1968, Ginnie and the Mystery Cat, 1969, Libby's Uninvited Guest, 1970, Cathy and the Beautiful People, 1971, Cathy Uncovers a Secret, 1972, Ginnie and the Mystery Light, 1973, Libby Shadows a Lady, 1974, Ginnie and Geneva Cookbook, 1975, adult book Writing for Children, 1990; (under name Jane Thayer) The Horse with the Easter Bonnet, 1953, The Popcorn Dragon, 1953, rev. edit. 1989, Where's Andy?, 1954, Mrs. Perrywinkle's Pets, 1955, Sandy and the Seventeen Balloons, 1956, The Chicken in the Tunnel, 1956, The Outside Cat, 1957, English edit., 1958, 83, Charley and the New Car, 1957, Funny Stories To Read Aloud, 1958, Andy Wouldn't Talk, 1958, The Puppy Who Wanted a Boy, 1958, rev., 1986, paperback edition, 1988, The Second-Story Giraffe, 1959, Little Monkey, 1959, Andy and His Fine Friends, 1960, The Pussy Who Went To the Moon,

1960, English edit., 1961, A Little Dog Called Kitty, 1961, English edit., 1962, 75, The Blueberry Pie Elf, 1961, English edit., 1962, Andy's Square Blue Animal, 1962, Gus Was a Friendly Ghost, 1962, English edit., 1971, Japanese edit., 1982, A Drink for Little Red Diker, 1963, Andy and the Runaway Horse, 1963, A House for Mrs. Hopper; the Cat that Wanted to Go Home, 1963, Quiet on Account of Dinosaur, 1964, English edit., 1965, 74, paperback edit., 1988, Emerald Enjoyed the Moonlight, 1964, English edit., 1966, The Bunny in the Honeysuckle Patch, 1965, English edit., 1966, Part-Time Dog, 1965, English edit. 1966, The Light Hearted Wolf, 1966, What's a Ghost Going to Do?, 1966, English edit. 1972, Japanese edit., 1982, The Cat that Joined the Club, 1967, English edit. 1968, Rockets Don't Go To Chicago, Andy, 1967, A Contrary Little Quail, 1968, Little Mr. Greenthumb, 1968, English edit., 1969, Andy and Mr. Cunningham, 1969, Curious, Furious Chipmunk, 1969, I'm Not a Cat, Said Emerald, 1970, English edit. 1971, Gus Was A Christmas Ghost, 1970, English edit. 1973, Japanese edit., 1982, Mr. Turtle's Magic Glasses, 1971, Timothy And Madam Mouse, 1971, English edit., 1972, Gus And The Baby Ghost, 1972, English edit. 1973, Japanese edit., 1982, The Little House, 1972, Andy and the Wild Worm, 1973, Gus Was a Mexican Ghost, 1974, English edit. 1975, Japanese edit., 1982, I Don't Believe in Elves, 1975, The Mouse on the Fourteenth Floor, 1977, Gus Was a Gorgeous Ghost, 1978, English edit. 1979, Where Is Squirrel?, 1979, Try Your Hand, 1980, Applebaums Have a Robot, 1980, Clever Raccoon, 1981, Gus Was a Real Dumb Ghost, 1982, Gus Loved His Happy Home, 1989; contbr. stories to juvenile anthologies, sch. readers, juvenile mags. Trustee Truro Pub. Libraries, 1974-84; Mem. Passaic (N.J.) Bd. Edn., 1953-56, Passaic Redevel. Agy., 1952-53; pres. Passaic LWV, 1949-52. Named mem. N.J. Literary Hall of Fame, 1987. Mem. Authors League Am., Friends of Truro Libraries, Truro Hist. Soc., Amnesty Internat. U.S.A., Kenilworth Soc. Democrat. Home: Higgins Hollow Rd Truro MA 02666

WOOLLEY, MARGARET ANNE (MARGOT WOOLLEY), architect; b. Bangor, Maine, Feb. 4, 1946; d. George Walter and Anne Geneva (Collins) W.; m. Gerard F. Vasisko, June 22, 1985. BA, Vassar Coll., 1969; MArch, Columbia U., 1974. Registered architect, N.Y. Urban designer Mayor's Office Lower Manhattan Devel., 1974-76, Mayor's Office Devel., N.Y.C., 1976-78; project mgr. Office Econ. Devel., N.Y.C., 1978-81, dep. dir. design and engring., 1981-83; dep. dir. design N.Y.C. Pub. Devel. Corp., 1983-85, asst. v.p. design, 1985-86, v.p. planning and design, 1986—. Mem. assoc. bd. regents L.I. Coll. Hosp., Bklyn., 1982—, mem. planning and devel. com., 1983—; pres. assoc. bd. regents, 1988-89. William Kinne Fellows scholar, 1973. Mem. AIA (bd. dirs. N.Y.C. chpt. 1988-90), N.Y. State Assn. Architects (bd. dirs. 1989—), Alliance Women in Architecture, Heights Casino Club, Vassar Club, Jr. League. Home: 135 Willow St Brooklyn NY 11201 Office: NYC Public Devel Corp 161 William St New York NY 10038

WOOLPERT, LAURA DIANE, marketing professional; b. North Hollywood, Calif., May 19, 1960; d. Gene Edward Woolpert and Louise Diane Moss; m. Charles Michael Slotnick, Sept. 24, 1988. BA, U. Conn., 1982. Adminstrv. asst. Yacht Racing/Cruising Mag., Darien, Conn., 1976-82; communications asst. Interrad Corp., Stamford, 1982-83; communications mgr. Interrad Corp., Fairfield, Conn., 1983-84; communications specialist Blue Cross & Blue Shield Conn., North Haven, 1984-85; dir. mktg. Palmer & Dodge, Boston, 1985-88, Hinckley, Allen, Snyder & Comen, Boston and Providence, 1988—; speaker Northeastern U. Sch. Law, Boston, 1988, Mass. Bar Assn., 1988, 90, ABA, 1989, 90. Mem. Am. Mktg. Assn. (speaker, bd. dirs. Profl. Svcs. Mktg. div. Conf.), Nat. Law Firm Mktg. Adminstrs. Assn. (speaker, chmn. memberships com. 1988, 89), P.E.O. Sisterhood, Internat. Assn. Bus. Communication. Office: Hinckley Allen Snyder & Comen 1500 Fleet Ctr Providence RI 02903 also: One Fin Ctr Boston MA 02111-2625

WOOLSTON, EVELYN DORIS, arts administrator; b. Boston, Nov. 8, 1925; d. Paul Hermann and Louise Martha (Gesch) Franz; m. John Woolston, Apr. 7, 1945; (div. 1967); 1 son, Peter Christopher; m. 2d Robert Franklin May, Feb. 1, 1984. B.A., Emerson Coll., 1947. Asst. merchandising mgr. Sta. WCSC-TV-AM, Charleston, S.C., 1954-57; mgr. promotions and merchandising, Knight Broadcasting, Inc., Portsmouth, N.H., 1957-61; asst. advt. dir. Hahn Shoes, Landover, Md., 1961-70; advt. dir. W & J Sloane, Inc., Washington, 1970-76; exec. dir. Capitol Ballet, Inc., Washington, 1977-80; freelance arts adminstr., Washington, 1980—. Exec. dir. Off the Circle Theatre Co., Washington, 1982-84; gen. mgr. Interact Theatre Co., 1987—; chmn., coordinator fund-raising project League of Washington Theatres, 1984-85; bd. dirs. D.C. Contemporary Dance Theatre, 1985—, Washington Stage Guild, 1986—. League Washington Theatres, Helen Hayes Awards, co-chmn. Washington Theatre Fortnight, 1986 ; fund raiser various arts orgns., Washington, 1961— Mem. Spanish Dance Soc., Emerson Coll. Alumni Assn. (mem. exec. bd. 1984-86). Republican. Club: ARTS Club of Washington (chmn. drama 1982-83, chmn. outreach 1985—). Avocations: theatre; travel; reading: Japanese literature; swimming. Home and Office: 2734 34th Pl NW Washington DC 20007

WOOTTON, BROOKII E., teacher; b. Uvalde, Tex., Mar. 4, 1965; d. Charles K. and Leona Agnus (Farley) W. BS, SW Tex. State U., 1988. Operator test floor Motorola, Austin, Tex.; stockbroker's asst. Shearson Lehman Hutton, Austin; instr. office adminstrn. Devine (Tex.) Ind. Sch. Dist. Active community and charitable orgns.; sponsor cheerleading and twirling. Mem. NAFE, NEA, Bus. Profls. Am. Club (sponsor), Tex. State Tchr's. Assn., Devine Educators Assn. (v.p.), Tex. Bus. Educators Assn., Alpha Phi. Home: 901 W Hondo Ave Devine TX 78016

WORCESTER, PATRICE HERZIG, hotel manager; b. Winchester, Mass., Apr. 28, 1960; d. John Duncan and Margaret (Herzig) W. BS in Hotel Adminstrn., Cornell U., 1984. Asst. hotel mgr. Harrah's Lake Tahoe Hotel/ Casino, Stateline, Nev., 1986, hotel mgr., 1986-88; gen. mgr. Embassy Suites Hotel, Irvine, Calif., 1988—. Vol. Planned Parenthood of No. Nev., Stateline, 1986-88; cons. Project Bus./Jr. Achievement, Reno, 1984-85. Mem. Nev. Hotel/Motel Assn., Calif. Hotel/Motel Assn., Cornell Soc. Hotelmen, Nat. Assn. Female Execs., Assn. Rep. Women. Office: Embassy Suites Hotel 2120 Main St Irvine CA 92714

WORDEN, KATHARINE COLE, sculptor; b. N.Y.C., May 4, 1925; d. Philip Gillette and Katharine (Pyle) Cole; m. Frederic G. Worden, Jan. 8, 1944; children: Rick, Dwight, Philip, Barbara, Katharine. Student Potters Sch., Tucson, 1940-42, Sarah Lawrence Coll., 1942-44. Sculptor; works exhibited Royce Galleries, Galerie Francoise Besnard (Paris), Cooling Gallery (London), Galerie Schumacher (Munich), Selected Artists Gallery, N.Y.C., Art Inst. Boston, Reid Gallery, Nashville, Weiner Gallery, N.Y.C., Boston Athanaeum, House of Humor and Satire, Gabrovo, Bulgaria, 1983, Newport Bay Club, 1984; pvt. collections Grand Palais (Paris), Dakar and Bathurst, Africa; dir. Stride Rite Corp., 1980-85; occupational therapist psychopathic ward Los Angeles County Gen. Hosp., 1953-57; Headstart vol., Watts, Calif., 1965-67; tchr. sculpture Watts Towers Art Center, 1967-69; participant White House Women Doers Luncheon meeting, 1968; dir. Cambridgeport Problem Center, Cambridge, Mass., 1969-71; mem. Jud. Nominating Commn., 1976-79; bd. overseers Boston Mus. Fine Arts, 1980-83; bd. govs. Newport Seamens Ch. Inst., 1989—; trustee Communication Research Inst., Miami, Fla., 1960-69, chmn. bd., 1966-69; trustee Newport Art Mus., 1984-86, Newport Health Found., 1986—, Hawthorne Sea Fund, 1990—; bd. dirs. Boston Center for Arts, 1976-80, Child and Family Svcs. of Newport County, 1983-90. Mem. Common Cause (Mass. adv. bd. 1971-72, dir. 1974-75), Mass. Civil Liberties Union (exec. bd. 1973-74, dir. 1976-77). Home: 24 Ft Wetherill Rd Jamestown RI 02835

WORDEN, ROXANE F., manufacturing executive; b. Wausau, Wis., Aug. 9, 1954; d. Ardell H. and Ila J. (Janisch) Goetsch; m. Loren L. Worden, Jan. 28, 1978; children: Ryan M., Randy J. Finished goods adminstr., supr. Marathon Electric, Wausau; mgr. prodn. and inventory control, systems and materials Cen. Fabricators, Schofield, Wis. Mem. NAFE, Am. Prodn. and Inventory Control Soc. (cert. prodn. and inventory mgmt., exec. v.p. cen. Wis. chpt.). Home: 1507 Shorey Ave Rothschild WI 54474

WORK, JANE MAGRUDER, professional society administrator; b. Owensboro, Ky., Mar. 30, 1927; d. Orion Noel and Willie May (Stallings) Magruder; m. William Work, Nov. 26, 1960; children: Paul MacGregor, Jeffrey William. BA, Furman U., 1947; MA, U. Wis., 1948; PhD, Ohio State U., 1959. Dir. radio U. South Miss., Hattisburg, 1948-51; pub. rela-

K7H 3C3 Office: Venmar Lisi Inc, PO Box 861, 2 Air Care Dr, Smith Falls, ON Canada K7A 4W7

WRIGHT, KATIE HARPER, educational administrator, journalist; b. Crawfordsville, Ark., Oct. 5, 1923; d. James Hale and Connie Mary (Locke) Harper; B.A., U. Ill., 1944; M.Ed., 1959; Ed.D., St. Louis U., 1979; m. Marvin Wright, Mar. 21, 1952; 1 dau., Virginia K. Jordan. Elem. and spl. edn. tchr. East St. Louis (Ill.) Pub. Schs., 1944-65, dir. Dist. 189 Instructional Materials Program, 1965-71, dir. spl. edn. Dists. 188, 189, 1971-77, asst. supt. programs, 1977-79; adj. faculty Harris/Stowe State Coll., 1980; mem. staff St. Louis U., 1989—; cons. to numerous workshops, seminars in field; mem. study tour People's Republic of China, 1984. Mem. Ill. Commn. on Children, 1973-85, East St. Louis Bd. Election Commrs.; pres. bd. dirs. St. Clair County Mental Health Center, 1970-72, 87—; bd. dirs. River Bluff council Girl Scouts, 1979—, nat. bd. dirs., 1981-84; bd. dirs. United Way, 1979—, Urban League, 1979—; pres. bd. trustees East St. Louis Pub. Library, 1972-77; pres., bd. dirs. St. Clair County Mental Health Ctrs., 1987; adv. bd. Landmark Bank; charter mem. Coalition of 100 Black Women; mem. coordinating council ethnic affairs Synod of Mid-Am., Presbyn. Ch. U.S.A; charter mem. Metro East Links Group; charter mem. Gateway chpt. The Links, Inc. Recipient Lamp of Learning award East St. Louis Jr. Wednesday Club, 1965, Spelman Coll. Alumni award, 1990, A World of Difference award, 1990, Journalist award Sigma Gamma Rho, 1986; named woman of the yr. in edn. St. Clair County YWCA, 1987; Nat. Top Lady of the Yr., 1988; Outstanding Working Woman award Downtown St. Louis, Inc., 1967; Ill. State citation for ednl. document Love is Not Enough, 1974; Delta Sigma Theta citation for document Good Works, 1979; award Nat. Council Negro Women, 1983; Girl Scout Thanks badge, 1982; Community Service award Met. East Bar Assn., 1983; named Woman of Achievement, St. Louis Globe Democrat, 1974, Outstanding Adminstr. So. region Ill. Office Edn., 1975, Woman of Yr. in Edn. St. Clair County YWCA, 1987; named to Vashon High Sch. Hall of Fame, 1989. Mem. Am. Libraries Trustees Assn. (regional v.p. 1978-79, nat. sec. 1979-80), Ill. Commn. on Children, Mensa, Council for Exceptional Children, Top Ladies of Distinction (pres. 1987—), Delta Sigma Theta (chpt. pres. 1960-62), Kappa Delta Pi (pres. So. Ill. U. chpt. 1973-74), Phi Delta Kappa (Service Key award 1984, chpt. pres. 1984-85), Iota Phi Lambda, Pi Lambda Theta (chpt. pres. 1985—). Republican. Presbyterian. Club: East St. Louis Women's (pres. 1973-75). Contbr. articles to profl. jours.; feature writer St. Louis Argus Newspaper, 1979—. Home: 733 N 40th St East Saint Louis IL 62205

WRIGHT, KAY MORROW, computer educator; b. Baytown, Tex., Sept. 28, 1942; d. Morris Robinson and Martha (Whiteman) Morrow; m. Terry Frank Wright, June 4, 1966; children—Stephanie Lynn, Stacie Cole. BA in Math., U. Tex., 1964. Programmer, Bankers Life, Des Moines, 1966-68; programmer analyst Enjay Fibers and Laminates Co., Odenton, Md., 1968-69; dir. data processing Mercy Hosp. Med. Ctr., 1975-78, planning coordinator, 1978-79, computer planning coordinator, 1979-81, systems cons., 1981-82; mktg. assoc. XL-DP, Inc., Des Moines, 1982-84; instr. Coll. Bus. Adminstrn., Drake U., Des Moines, 1984—. Bd. dirs. Iowa Soc. To Prevent Blindness, 1977-83, Mercy Hosp. Credit Union, 1978-80; benefit chmn. Flip for Sight, 1977-81. Mem. Data Processing Mgmt. Assn., Iowa Health Computer Assn. (founding pres. 1978-79), Electronic Computing Health Oriented, Province Alumnae Iowa, Wis. (bd. dirs. 1979-84), League Attys. Wives, Delta Zeta (nat. networking chmn. 1984-86), Delta Sigma Pi (faculty advisor 1987—, Prof. of Yr. 1985-86). Democrat. Methodist. Office: Drake U 351 Aliber Hall Des Moines IA 50311

WRIGHT, LAURALI R. (BUNNY WRIGHT), writer; b. Saskatoon, Sask., Can., June 5, 1939; d. Sidney Victor and Evelyn Jane (Barber) Appleby; m. John Herbert, Jan. 6, 1962 (separated 1985); children: Victoria Kathleen, Johnna Margaret. Student, U. B.C., Carleton U., Banff Sch. Fine Arts, U. Calgary. Journalist The Calgary Herald, 1968-77; freelance writer Calgary, 1977—. Author: (novels) Neighbors, 1979 (Alta. Novelist award 1978), The Favorite, 1982, Among Friends, 1984, The Suspect, 1985 (Edgar Allan Poe Best Novel award Mystery Writers of Am. 1986), Sleep While I Sing, 1986, Love in the Temperate Zone, 1987, A Chill Rain in January, 1990. Mem. Writers Union Can., Authors' Guild of U.S., Internat. P.E.N., Mystery Writers of Am. Office: care Viking Penguin Inc 40 W 23rd St New York NY 10010*

WRIGHT, LILYAN BOYD, educator; b. Upland, Pa., May 11, 1920; d. Albert Verlenden and Mabel (Warburton) Boyd; B.S., Temple U., 1942, M.Ed., 1946; Ed.D., Rutgers U., 1972; m. Richard P. Wright, Oct. 23, 1942; 1 child, Nicki Wright Vanek. Tchr. health and phys. edn. Woodbury (N.J.) High Sch., 1942-43, Glen-Nor High Sch., Glenolden, Pa., 1944-46, Chester (Pa.) High Sch., 1946-54; chmn. women's dept. health and phys. edn. Union (N.J.) High Sch., 1954-61; with Trenton State Coll., 1961-90, head women's program health and phys. edn., 1967-77, chmn. dept. health, phys. edn. and recreation, 1977-86; mem. N.J. State Com. Div. Girls and Women's Sports, 1958-80; chmn. New Atlantic Field Hockey Sectional Umpiring, 1981-85; chmn. New Atlantic Field Hockey Assn., 1985-90. Active Chester United Fund; water safety, first aid instr. ARC Scholarship in her honor N.J. Athletic Assn. Girls, 1971; named to Hall of Fame, Temple U., 1976. Recipient U.S. Field Hockey Assn. award, 1989, named Nat. Honorary Field Hockey Umpire. Mem. AAUP, AAHPER (chmn. Eastern Dist. Assn. Div. Girls and Women's Sports, sec. to council for services Eastern dist. 1979-80, chmn. 1980-81, N.J. rep. to council for convs. 1984-85, Honor Fellow award 1986), N.J. AHPER (pres. 1974-75, past pres. 1975-76, v.p. phys. edn. div., Disting. Service and Leadership award 1969, Honor Fellow award 1977), N.J. Women's Lacrosse Assn. (umpiring chmn. 1972-76), Nat. Assn. Phys. Edn. in Higher Edn., Eastern Assn. Phys. Edn. Coll. Women, North Jersey, Central Jersey bds. women's ofcls., Am., Pa. (v.p. 1953-54), Chester (pres. 1949-54) fedns. tchrs., U.S. (exec. com.), North Jersey (past pres.) field hockey assns., Kappa Delta Epsilon, Delta Psi Kappa (past pres. Phila. alumni chpt.), Kappa Delta Pi. Episcopalian (vestry St. Luke's Episc. Ch. 1988—). Home: 260 Green Valley Rd Langhorne PA 19047

WRIGHT, LINDA DIANE, stockbroker; b. Toledo, May 6, 1948; d. Horace Osband and Peggy Joanne (Perkins) Loomis; m. Sammy Ross Dewyer, Feb. 24, 1968 (div. Apr. 1976); children: Jayme, Jeremy; m. C. Thomas Wright, July 30, 1977; 1 child, Christopher. Student, Bowling Green State U., 1966-67, Kent State U., 1971; grad., Investment Tng. Inst., Atlanta, 1979. Teller Mid-Am. Bank & Trust Co., Bowling Green, Ohio, 1966-71; br. mgr., loan officer Huntington Bank Inc., Bowling Green, 1971-78; rep. Ohio Co., Clearwater, Fla., 1979-82, Raymond, James & Assocs., St. Petersburg, Fla., 1982-84; fin. cons. Cert. Fin. Services, Tampa, Fla., 1984-86; investment exec. Pamco Securities and Ins. Services, St. Petersburg, 1986-88; sr. fin. cons. Integrated Resources Equity Corp., Clearwater, 1988—. Mem. adv. bd. Women's Ctr. of Morton Plant Hosp., Clearwater, 1987. Mem. Nat. Assn. for Profl. Saleswomen, Am. Bus. Women's Assn. Republican. Club: Stock and Bond (St. Petersburg). Home: 3860 Anglers Ln Largo FL 34644 Office: Integrated Resources Equity Corp 2900 US 19 N Suite #102 Clearwater FL 34623

WRIGHT, LINDA JEAN, banker; b. Chgo., Dec. 14, 1949; d. Eugene P. and Rosemary Margaret (Kiley) Kemph; student Loretto Heights Coll., 1967-69, U. Ill.-Urbana, 1970-71; m. Kelly W. Wright, Jr., Feb. 1979 (div. 1984); m. Samuel Neuwirth Klewans, Aug. 28, 1986. Asst. to v.p. Busey 1st Nat. Bank, Urbana, 1969-72; spa mgr., supr. sales tng. Venus and Apollo Health Club, San Antonio, 1973-76; owner Plant Shop, San Antonio, 1976-77; with Enterprise Bank, Falls Church, Va., 1977-84, comml. lending officer, 1976-84, sr. v.p., 1979-84, corp. sec. of bd. dirs., 1980-84; pres., chief exec. officer Fairfax Savs. Bank, 1984-87; pres., chief exec. officer Bankstar, N.A. (formerly Bank 2000 of Reston, N.A.), 1988—. Apptd. pub. official, chmn. Va. Small Bus. Fin. Authority, Richmond, 1984-88; mem. exec. com. Fairfax-Falls Ch. United Way, United Way Capital Area, Washington, 1984-85; Fairfax County Spl. Task Force, 1986; mem. Fairfax Com. of 100, 1987; mem., bd. dirs. Hospice No. Va., Arlington, 1985-86, chmn. No. Va. Local Devel. Corp., 1986; mem. operating bd. Fairfax Hosp., 1987—; pres. No. Va. Transp. Alliance, 1987—; bd. dirs. Va. Corp. for Analysis, Rsch. and Edn., Inc. Mem. Fairfax County C. of C. (dir., v.p., pres. 1987-88), Nat. Assn. Bank Women (chmn. No. Va. group 1980-81). Roman Catholic. Club: Fairfax Hunt. Avocations: aviation, fox hunting.

WRIGHT, LISA MARLENE, family practice physician; b. Bklyn., Jan. 6, 1954; d. Joseph and Joan Audrey (Kowohl) Roschko; m. James Kendel Wright, June 24, 1979; children: Joshua, Gabriel. BA in Biology, NYU, 1975; MD, Ea. Va. Med. Sch., 1978. Diplomate Am. Bd. Family Practice. Intern, then resident Middlesex Meml. Hosp., Middletown, Conn., 1978-81; Gen. med. officer Sacaton Indian Hosp., Sacaton, Ariz., 1981-83; family practitioner Thomas-Davis Med. Ctr., Tempe, Ariz., 1983—. Fellow Am. Acad. Family Physicians; mem. AMA (Physician's Recognition award), Am. Med. Women's Assn., La Leche League (med. cons.), Am. Soc. Psychoprophylaxis in Obstetrics/Lamaze, Maricopa County Med. Soc. Office: Thomas Davis Med Ctr 6301 S McClintock Tempe AZ 85283

WRIGHT, MARGARET TAYLOR, marketing consultant; b. Wilmington, N.C., Nov. 8, 1949; d. Thomas Henry and Margaret (Taylor) W. BA, U. N.C., 1972; MBA, Wake Forest U., 1978. Child advocacy specialist Child Advocacy Council Dept. Human Resources, Raleigh, N.C., 1973-74; region dir. N.C. Office for Children Dept. Human Resources, Winston-Salem, 1974-76; product mgr. food div. Am. Home Products, N.Y.C., 1978-80; account exec. Ted Bates Advt., N.Y.C., 1981; product mgr. C.F. Mueller div. McKesson, Inc., Jersey City, 1981-83; mgr. new products Popsicle div. Sara Lee Corp., Englewood, N.J., 1983-86; pres. Wright Mktg. Blueprint, N.Y.C., 1987—. Co-author: (pamphlets) Children--Helping Them Grow, 1973. Youth coord. Jim Holshouser Gubernatorial Campaign, New Hanover County, N.C., 1972; mem. Jr. League, N.Y. and N.C., 1972-84. Mem. Am. Mktg. Assn. (exec.). Episcopalian. Office: Wright Mktg Blueprint 400 E 54th Ste 2-D New York NY 10022

WRIGHT, MARIE ANNE, management information systems educator; b. Albany, N.Y., Oct. 21, 1953; d. Arthur Irving and Ethel (Knickerbocker) W. BS, U. Mass., Boston, 1981; MBA, Clarkson U., 1984; PhD, U. Mass., 1989. Systems analyst St. Lawrence U., Canton, N.Y., 1983-84; instr. Bentley Coll., Waltham, Mass., 1984-85; computer cons. Amherst (Mass.) Police Dept., 1986-88; asst. prof. Elms Coll., Chicopee, 1986-89; assoc. prof. Western Conn. State U., Danbury, 1990—; cons. Ctr. for Human Devel., Springfield, Mass., 1986-87, Early Childhood Ctr., 1986-87. Contbr. articles to mags. Recipient Teaching Assistantship, U. Mass., 1985, Rsch. Assistantship, 1986; Grad. Assistantship, Clarkson U., Potsdam, N.y., 1982, MIS award U. Mass., 1981. Mem. Assn. for Computing Machinery, Communications Security Assn., Info. Systems Security Assn. (contbr. articles to newsletter), Assn. Women in Math., Inst. of Elec. and Electronics Engr., Boston Computer Soc., Math. Assn. of Am., Beta Gamma Sigma. Democrat. Office: Western Conn State U MIS Dept Danbury CT 06810

WRIGHT, MARY BETH, math educator; b. Madison, Wis., Jan. 3, 1952; d. Harry Wesley and Rita Cecelia (Schreier) W. AA, U. Wis., LaCrosse, 1972; BA, U. South Fla., 1980, MA, 1982. Subsitute tchr. Hillsborogh Pasco County Schs., Tampa and Land O'Lakes, Fla., 1980-81; tchr. sci. learning disabilities Lutz (Fla.) Elem., 1981-86; tchr. specific learning disabilities, soccer coach Thomas Jefferson High Sch., Tampa, 1986-87; head tchr. Downtown Alt., Tampa, 1987-88; math tchr. Brandon (Fla.) Alt., 1988—; tutor Hillsborough County Schs., 1981—; cons. Hillsborough Community Coll., Tampa, 1984—; aerobics instr. Shapes Health Fitness, Tampa, 1985—. Scout leader Girl Scouts U.S.A., Tampa, 1981. Mem. Fla. ASsn. for Children with Learning Disabilities, Fla. Assn. Alt. Sch. Educators, NAFE, Hillsborogh Classroom Tchrs. Assn., Corpus Christi Youth (Temple Terr.). Republican. Roman Catholic. Home: 11822 Wildflower Pl Tampa FL 33617 Office: Brandon Alt 421 Wilbur St Brandon FL 33511

WRIGHT, MARY L., biology educator; b. Milford, Mass., Dec. 4, 1934; d. Herbert Edgar and Carmella Grace (Consoletti) W. BS, Coll. of Our Lady of the Elms, 1957; MS, U. Detroit, 1966; PhD, U. Mass., 1972. Elem. sch. tchr. Cathedral Grammar Sch., Springfield, Mass., 1957-58; biology tchr. Coll. of Our Lady of the Elms, Chicopee, Mass., 1958 --; grant reviewer NSF, Washington, D.C., 1974-84, cons., 1981-84. Contbr. articles to profl. jours. NSF Coll. Tchr. grantee, 1966; NIH predoctoral fellow, 1967-69; Rsch. Corp. grantee, 1976-87; NSF Rsch. Equipment grantee, 1980-82; NIH Rsch. grantee, 1988-91. Mem. Internat. Soc. Chronobiology, Am. Soc. Zoologists, AAUP, AAAS, Tissue Culture Assn., Cell Kinetics Soc., Soc. Rsch. on Biological Rhythms, Sigma Xi. Democrat. Roman Catholic. Office: Coll of OUr Lady of the Elm 291 Springgfield St Chicopee MA 01013

WRIGHT, MARY MCKENZIE, publishing executive; b. Ft. Benning, Ga., May 10, 1945; d. Erle Thomas and Mary Ruth (Smith) McKenzie; m. Wayne Lamar Wright, Sept. 3, 1966 (div. 1977); children: David Brian, Jeffrey Benjamin. Student in Mktg. and Bus., Ga. State U., 1963-67; student in sec. sci., DeKalb Coll., 1964. Sec., Ga. corr. Macmillan Pub. Co., Norcross, Ga., 1976-78; sec. to regional mgr. McGraw-Hill Book Co., Norcross, 1978-79, office supr., pvt. sch. specialist, 1979-82, adminstrv. mktg. asst., 1982-83; corp. sec., owner Action MultiSvcs. Atlanta, Inc., 1983-84; adminstrv. asst. Computer Curriculum Corp., Marietta, Ga., 1984-89, office mgr., 1989—. Mem. Profl. and Exec. Women. Methodist.

WRIGHT, MARY RUTH (MRS. WILLIAM KEMP WRIGHT), psychologist; b. St. Louis, Apr. 2, 1922; d. Leon Carl and Gwendolyn (Travis) Brown; R.N., Washington U., St. Louis, 1944; B.S., U. Houston, 1966, M.A., 1967; Ph.D., Union Grad. Sch., 1978; m. William Kemp Wright, Feb. 10, 1945; children—Gwendolyn, Veronica, Victoria, Jennifer. Instr. surgery Washington U. Sch. Nursing, 1944-45, U.S. Cadet Nurse Corps, USPHS, 1944; instr. pediatrics Children's Meml. Hosp., Chgo., 1945-46; teaching fellow U. Houston, 1965-66; instr. S. Tex. Jr. Coll., Houston, 1967-70; mental health cons. St. Joseph Mental Hosp., Houston, 1966-67; staff psychol. services Almeda Clinic, Houston, 1966-70; pvt. practice marriage and family counselor, Houston, 1970—; med.-psychol. researcher and writer, 1970—; psychologist Vasectomy Clinic, Houston Dept. Health, 1971-80; clin. asst. prof. psychology, dept. otorhinolaryngology and communicative scis. Baylor Coll. Medicine, Houston, 1979—. Recipient spl. award Security Agy., 1945. Mem. Am. Psychol. Assn., Am. Assn. Marriage and Family Counselors, Am. Assn. Sex Educators and Counselors, Internat. Council Psychologists, Nat. Council Family Relations, Nat. Assn. Social Workers, Mental Health Assn. Houston and Harris County (dir.). Contbr. articles to profl. jours. Home: 3671 Del Monte St Houston TX 77019 Office: 4200 Westheimer Suite 160 Houston TX 77027

WRIGHT, MARY VAN LEAR, municipal bond analyst; b. Chgo., Aug. 4, 1956; d. Robert V.L. and Sara Helen (Beeler) W.; m. Thomas G. Benner, Aug. 7, 1987; 1 child, Sara Eleanor. BA, Conn. Coll., 1979; MBA, Columbia U., 1983. Rsch. assoc. Acad. for Contemporary Problems, Washington, 1979-81; rating specialist Standard & Poor's, N.Y.C., 1983-84; asst. adminstr. Twp. of Princeton, N.J., 1984-86; v.p. Fin. Guaranty Ins. Co., N.Y.C., 1986—. Mem. Public Works Forum (bd. dirs. 1986-88). Methodist. Home: 33 Sommer Ave Maplewood NJ 07040 Office: Fin Guaranty Ins Co 175 Water St New York NY 10038

WRIGHT, NANCY DIANE, food products executive; b. Chgo., Nov. 19, 1947; d. Everett Charles and June Elizabeth (Stiff) W. Student, U. Ill., Chgo., 1966-67, Northwestern U., 1970-71. Mgr. Glen Lake Manor, Empire, Mich., summers 1968-79; customer svc. rep. McKesson Chem. Co., Chgo., 1978-83, with telemarketing dept., 1980-83; customer svc. mgr., telemarketing mgr., industry mgr. Kraft Chem., Melrose Pk., Ill., 1983—. Mem. Inst. Food Technologists (co-chmn. hospitality com., mem. gen. arrangements com.), Am. Assn. Candy Technologists, Am. Cereal Chemists, Am. Assn. Female Execs., Order of Ea. Star (pres. bd. dirs. 1980, Grand Ruth 1977, Worthy Grand Matron 1986). Republican. Home: 9000 Forest Dr Hickory Hills IL 60457

WRIGHT, NANCY HOWELL, interior designer; b. Detroit, Sept. 6, 1932; d. David Austin and Catherine (Bradley) Howell; BFA Ohio Wesleyan U.; student Parsons Sch. Design, 1977; m. Hastings Kemper Wright, June 19, 1954; children: Mark, Kenneth, Barbara, Donald. Interior decorator Country Manor of Branford (Conn.), 1971-75, design mgr., 1976—. Sec. Branford Art League, 1977; chmn. Harrison House Hist. House, Branford, Conn., 1983-84; mem. Rep. Town Com., Branford, 1990—. Allied mem. Am. Soc. Interior Designers (award for best Conn. retail store design, 1980); mem. Delta Phi Delta. Republican. Episcopalian. Home: 35 Wood Rd Branford CT 06405 Office: 312 E Main St Branford CT 06405

WRIGHT, NANNIE BELL, educator; b. Laing, W.Va., May 7, 1934; d. Samuel Thomas and Edna (Irving) W. BS in Edn., W.Va. State Coll., 1956; MA, U. Chgo., 1960; postgrad., NYU, 1966, L.I. U., 1990. English tchr. Wiley H. Bates Jr. High Sch., Annapolis, Md., 1956-63, Copiague (N.Y.) Jr. High Sch., 1963—; resource tchr. Copiague Jr. High Sch., 1970-75. Chmn. edn. com. AAUW, Annapolis, 1960; pres. women's aux. Crownsville Hosp., 1960-61; mem. NAACP, Friends of Libr. Amityville, N.Y., Friends of Pub. Libr. N.Y.C. Mem. Copiague Tchr.'s Assn., Nat. Coun. English Tchrs., U. Chgo. Alumni Assn., Noetic Scis., Delta Sigma Theta (v.p. Annapolis alumnae chpt. 1961), Pi Lambda Theta, Alpha Kappa Mu. Republican. Roman Catholic. Home: 27 Wellington Pl Amityville NY 11701

WRIGHT, PATRICIA, state legislator; b. South Bend, Ind., Feb. 28, 1931; m. Paul J. Wright, 1951; children: Timothy, Patrick M. Mem. Ariz. State Senate. Republican. Home: 5818 W Northern Ave Glendale AZ 85302 Office: Office of State Senate State Capitol Phoenix AZ 85007*

WRIGHT, PAULA CHRISTINE, educator; b. Cleve., Jan. 2, 1955; d. Paul R. and Gertrude R. (Christman) W. A.B. in French, John Carroll U., 1978, postgrad in edn., 1980—; postgrad. Cleve. Music Sch. Settlement. French and Spanish tchr. Glen Oak Sch. for Girls, Gates Mills, Ohio, 1978-79, Upward Bound Project, Case Western Res. U., Cleve., 1980—, Kirk Middle Sch., East Cleveland, Ohio, 1980-81, Shaw High Sch., East Cleve., 1981-84, Shaker Heights High Sch., Ohio, 1984—; Midwest del. Fgn. Lang. Tchrs. Inst., NEH, Purdue U., summer 1985; contralto Duffy Liturgical Dance Ensemble, 1985-87; owner Booties by Paula, 1987—. Recipient excellence in teaching award Case Western Res. U., 1983; named Tchr. of Yr., Univ. Project Upward Bound, 1984. Treas., v.p. St. Dominic Choir, 1984-85, publicist, 1983-84, investiture chair, 1982-83, person, libr., 1990—, asst. libr., 1989-90. Democrat. Roman Catholic. Club: Fortuna Investment II (treas 1976-83) (Cleve.). Avocations: reading, needlework, singing. Office: 15911 Aldersyde Rd Shaker Heights OH 44120

WRIGHT, PEGGY ANN, pharmacist; b. Sealy, Tex., Oct. 7, 1935; d. Charles Michael and Lottie Mae (Phillips) Keer; m. Joe Baker Wright, June 3, 1959; children: Mayanne, Charlotte Marie. BS, U. Tex., 1958; postgrad., Tulane U., 1962-63, Orange Coast Coll., Costa Mesa, Calif., 1973-76, U. So. Miss., 1981-83. Staff pharmacist Bapt. Hosp. of S.E. Tex., Beaumont, 1958-59; asst. chief pharmacist Athens (Ga.) Gen. Hosp., 1959-60; staff pharmacist Bapt. Hosp., New Orleans, 1960-61, Browne McHardy Clinic, New Orleans, 1961-63, Newport Gen. Hosp., Newport, R.I., 1967-68, Seton Med. Ctr., Austin, Tex., 1982-83; floating pharmacist Innovative Pharmacy Svcs., Austin, 1983-86; dir. pharmacy Burleson County Hosp., Caldwell, Tex., 1986-88; cen. office pharmacy specialist Tex. Dept. Health, Health Facility Licensure and Certification Div., Austin, 1988—. Author cookbook: Sea-Trash Gourmet; co-editor cookbook: Naval Officers' Wives Favorite Recipes, 1980. Mem. Am. Soc. Hosp. Pharmacists, Tex. Soc. Hosp. Pharmacists, Austin Area Soc. Hosp. Pharmacists, Nat. Mil. Family Assn., Naval Officers Wives Club, Rho Chi. Democrat. Unity Ch. Home: 2100 Wright St Austin TX 78704 Office: Tex Dept Health 1100 W 49th St Austin TX 78756

WRIGHT, ROSALIE MULLER, newspaper and magazine editor; b. Newark, June 20, 1942; d. Charles and Angela (Fortunata) Muller; m. Lynn Wright, Jan. 13, 1962; children: James Anthony Meador, Geoffrey Shepard. B.A. in English, Temple U., 1965. Mng. editor Suburban Life mag., Orange, N.J., 1960-62; assoc. editor Phila. mag., 1962-64, mng. editor, 1969-73; founding editor Womensports mag., San Mateo, Calif., 1973-75; editor scene sect. San Francisco Examiner, 1975-77; exec. editor New West mag., San Francisco and Beverly Hills, Calif., 1977-81; features and Sunday editor San Francisco Chronicle, 1981-87, asst. mng. editor features, 1987—; tchr. mag. writing U. Calif.-Berkeley, 1975-76; participant pub. procedure's course Stanford U., 1977-79; chmn. mag. judges Council Advancement and Support Edn. Conf., 1980, judge, 1984. Editor: Cornerstone for Growth: How Minorities are Vital for the Future of Newspapers, 1989; contbr. numerous mag. articles, critiques, revs., Compton's Ency. Mem. Am. Assn. Sunday and Feature Editors (treas. 1984, sec. 1985, 1st v.p. 1986, pres. 1987), Am. Newspaper Pub. Assn. (pub. task force on minorities in the newspaper bus. 1988-89, Chronicle minority recruiter 1987—, editor Cornerstone for Growth: How Minorities are Vital to the Future of Newspapers). Office: Chronicle Pub Co 901 Mission St San Francisco CA 94119

WRIGHT, SARAH BIRD, educator, writer; b. Wilmington, N.C., Nov. 25, 1933; d. Richard Oscar and Elise (Martin) Grant; AB, Bryn Mawr (Pa.) Coll., 1955; MA, Duke U., Durham, N.C., 1958; m. R.L. Wright, Sept. 7, 1963; 1 child, Alexander Grant. Tchr. English composition and lit. Boston U., 1959-60; rsch. asst. linguistics Harvard Computation Lab., 1960-62; copy editor Beacon Press and Allyn & Bacon, Boston, 1963-70; tchr. English U. Richmond (Va.), 1981—; Author: Ferries of America: A Guide to Adventurous Travel, 1987, Islands of the South and Southeastern United States, 1988, Islands of the Northeastern United States and Eastern Canada, 1990; contbr. to newspapers and mags. including Christian Sci. Monitor, Accent on Living, Newsday, Toronto Globe & Mail, N.Y. Times, Americana, Travel/Holiday, Chgo. Tribune, N.Z. Herald, Jour. Modern Lit. Dist. councillor Bryn Mawr Coll. Alumnae Assn., 1975-78; vol. Va. Mus., 1980-81. Mem. Authors Guild N.Y., MLA. Episcopalian. Club: Richmond Woman's. Home: 3505 Old Gun Rd Midlothian VA 23113 Office: U Richmond English Dept Ryland Hall Rm 322 Richmond VA 23227

WRIGHT, SUSAN LYNNE, communications company administrator; b. St. Louis, Dec. 31, 1964; d. John C. and Lynda R. (Langhi) Wright. BA in Telecommunications, Mich. State U., 1987; postgrad., U. Mo., St. Louis, 1987; St. Louis U., $D. Prodn. coordinator Maritz Communications Co., St. Louis, 1988—. Mem. Sunset Country Club. Roman Catholic.

WRIGHT, SUSAN WEBBER, law educator; b. Texarkana, Ark., Aug. 22, 1948; d. Thomas Edward and Betty Jane (Gary) Webber; m. Robert Ross Wright, III, May 21, 1983; 1 child, Robin Elizabeth. BA, Randolph-Macon Woman's Coll., 1970; MPA, U. Ark., 1972, JD with high honors, 1975. Bar: Ark. 1975. Law clk. U.S. Ct. Appeals 8th Circuit, 1975-76; asst. prof. law U. Ark.-Little Rock, 1976-78, assoc. prof., 1978-83, prof., 1983—, asst. dean, 1976-78; vis. assoc. prof. Ohio State U., Columbus, 1981, La. State U., Baton Rouge, 1982-83; mem. adv. com. U.S. Ct. Appeals 8th Circuit, St. Louis, 1983-88. Author: (with R. Wright) Land Use in a Nutshell, 1978, 2d edit., 1985; editor-in-chief Ark. Law Rev., 1975; contbr. articles to profl. jours. Mem. Ark. Bar Assn., Pulaski County Bar Assn., Ark. Assn. Women Lawyers (v.p. 1977-78). Episcopalian. Office: US Courthouse 600 W Capitol Ave Little Rock AR 72201

WRIGHT, TAMELA JEAN (T.J.), disc jockey, entertainer; b. Webb City, Mo., Jan. 20, 1962; d. Eugene I. and Fay Marie (Regenold) W. Student, Lindenwood Coll., 1980-82. With radio Sta. KSHE, St. Louis, 1982, Sta. KMJM, St. Louis, 1982-83, Sta. KHTR, Sta. KWK, St. Louis, 1985; with radio Sta. WKSS, Hartford, Conn., 1986, San Jose, Calif., 1986-87; with radio Sta. WPGC, Washington, 1987-88, Sta. WAVA, Washington, 1988, Sta. WDJY-FM, Washington, 1988-89, Sta. KHTK, St. Louis, 1989—; interviewee Nightwatch, CBS, All Things Considered, Nat. Pub. Radio, Washington, Dec., 1987. Narrator local fashion shows, Vandalia, Mo., San Jose, 1983-86; appearances include nat. syndicated show Party Am., 1986-87, Music Machine Video Sta. WFTY-TV, Washington, 1988, Nightwatch CBS and All Things Considered Nat. Pub. Radio, Washington, 1987; announcer radio commls., St. Louis, 1989—; contbr. Student Voice newspaper, 1989—; subject articles in various publs. Telethon vol. Easter Seals, Washington, 1989, Muscular Dystrophy Assn., St. Louis, 1989. Mem. AFTRA, Am. Women in Radio & TV, Friends of Kennedy Ctr. (assoc.). Home: 115 Reeb Ln #3 Saint Louis MO 63031 Office: Sta KHTK 7777 Bonhomme Saint Louis MO 63105

WRIGHT, YVONNE GIBSON, educator, reading specialist; b. Clinton, Ind., Aug. 8, 1921; d. William James and Reva (Fielden) Gibson; m. Kenneth L. Wright, Aug. 14, 1943; children: Ann Kathryn Haight, Kenneth L. Jr., Thomas G., Douglas S. BA, Kalamazoo Coll., 1943; MA in Teaching, Rollins Coll., 1968. Tchr. Satellite High Sch., Satellite Beach, Fla., 1965-70; reading specialist Vero Beach (Fla.) High Sch., 1970-84. Vol. Indian River County Libr., Vero Beach, 1984—. Mem. AAUW, Delta Kappa Gamma

(sec. 1980). Republican. Presbyterian. Home: 655 Bougainvillea Ln Vero Beach FL 32963

WRIGLEY, ELIZABETH SPRINGER (MRS. OLIVER K. WRIGLEY), foundation executive; b. Pitts., Oct. 4, 1915; d. Charles Woodward and Sarah Maria (Roberts) Springer; BA U. Pitts., 1935; BS, Carnegie Inst. Tech., 1936; m. Oliver Kenneth Wrigley, June 16, 1936 (dec. July 1978). Procedure analyst U.S. Steel Corp., Pitts., 1941-43; rsch. asst. The Francis Bacon Found., Inc., Los Angeles, 1944, exec., 1945-50, trustee, 1950—, dir. rsch., 1951-53, pres., 1954—, dir. Francis Bacon Libr.; mem. adv. coun. Shakespeare Authorship Roundtable, Santa Monica, Calif.; mem. regional Fine Arts adv. coun. Calif. State Poly. U., Pomona. Mem. ALA, Calif. Libr. Assn., Renaissance Soc. Am., Modern Humanities Rsch. Assn., Cryptogram Assn., Alpha Delta Pi. Presbyn. Mem. Order Eastern Star, Damascus Shrine. Editor: The Skeleton Text of the Shakespeare Folio L.A. (by W.C. Arensberg), 1952. Compiler: Short Title Catalogue Numbers in the Library of the Francis Bacon Foundation, 1958; Wing Numbers in the Library of the Francis Bacon Foundation, 1959; Supplement To Francis Bacon Library Holdings in the STC of English Books, 1967; (with David W. Davies) A Concordance to the Essays of Francis Bacon, 1973. Home: 4805 N Pal Mal Ave Temple City CA 91780 Office: Francis Bacon Libr 655 N Dartmouth Ave Claremont CA 91711

WRISTON, KATHRYN DINEEN, lawyer, business executive; b. Syracuse, N.Y.; d. Robert Emmet and Carolyn (Bareham) Dineen; m. Walter B. Wriston, Mar. 14, 1968; 1 stepchild. Student, U. Geneva, 1958-59; BA cum laude, Smith Coll., 1960; LLB, U. Mich., 1963. Bar: N.Y.1964, U.S. Ct. Appeals (2nd cir.) 1964, U.S. Supreme Ct. 1968. Assoc. Shearman & Sterling, N.Y.C., 1963-68; bd. dirs. Warner Computer Systems, Inc., Santa Fe Pacific Corp., Chgo., Santa Fe Energy Resources, Inc., Houston; Northwestern Mut. Life Ins. Co., Milw., AICPA, 1986—, Am. Arbitration Assn., 1982—, Ctrs. for Pub. Resources, 1989—. Chmn. President's com. White House Fellows, 1982-83; mem. vis. com. U. Mich. Law Sch., 1973—; bd. overseers Rand Inst. for Civil Justice, 1985—; vice chmn. Fordham U., Bronx, N.Y., 1980-81. Fellow Am. Bar Found.; mem. ABA, Nat. Assn. Accts., Fin. Women's Assn. N.Y., New York County Lawwyers Assn. (legal aid com. 1972-76), N.Y. State Bar Assn., Assn. of Bar of City of N.Y., Practicing Law Inst. (trustee 1975—, v.p. 1985—, bd. dirs.).

WROBBEL, PATRICIA ANN, registered nurse; b. Syracuse, N.Y., Oct. 9, 1959; d. Edward Clarence and Elizabeth Ann (Miller) W. BS in Nursing, Niagara U., 1981; MA in Nursing Edn., NYU, 1984. RN, N.Y., N.J.; cert. instr. basic cardiac life support. Staff nurse Columbia-Presbyn. Med. Ctr., N.Y.C., 1981-82, asst. head nurse Neurol. Inst., 1982-83, nursing care clinician Neurol. Inst., 1983-84, evening nurse coord. Neurol. Inst., 1983-84, neurosci. nursing instr. dept. edn., rsch. and devel., 1984-88, sr. mgr. dept. edn., rsch. and devel., 1988-90, dir. nursing, 1990—. Grant Dept. Health, Edn. and Welfare, 1983-84; scholarship Rosamond Gifford Found., 1977-81. Mem. ANA, Am. Assn. of Neurosci. Nurses (pres. greater N.Y. chpt. 1989-91), Nat. League for Nursing, Am. Coun. for Transplantation, Sigma Theta Tau. Roman Catholic. Home: 89 Teaneck Rd #A-1 Ridgefield Park NJ 07660 Office: Presbyn Hosp 622 W 168th St Cen Nursing Office HP-Main New York NY 10032

WROBLESKI, JEANNE PAULINE, lawyer; b. Phila., Feb. 14, 1942; d. Edward Joseph and Pauline (Popelak) Wrobleski; m. Robert J. Klein, Dec. 3, 1979. B.A., Immaculata Coll., 1964; M.A., U. Pa., 1966; J.D., Temple U., 1975. Bar: Pa. 1975. Pvt. practice law, Phila., 1975—. Mem. Commn. on Women and the Legal Profession, 1986-89; v.p. Center City Residents' Assn. Eisenhower citizen ambassador del. to Soviet Union. Rhea Liebman scholar, 1974; bd. dirs. South St. Dance Co. Mem. AAUW, ABA, Phila. Bar Assn. (chmn. women's rights com. 1986, com. on jud. selection and reform 1986-87), Pa. Acad. Fine Arts, Nat. Mus. Women in the Arts, Pa. Bar Assn., Am. Judicature Soc., Jagiellonian Law Soc., Alpha Psi Omega, Lambda Iota Tau. Democrat. Clubs: Lawyers, Founders, Peale. Office: Kohn Savett Klein & Graf PC 2400 One Reading Ctr 1101 Market St Philadelphia PA 19107

WROBLOWA, HALINA STEFANIA, electrochemist; b. Gdansk, Poland, July 5, 1925; came to U.S., 1960, naturalized, 1970; M.Sc., U. Lodz (Poland), 1949; Ph.D., Warsaw Inst. Tech., 1958; 1 dau., Krystyna Wrobel-Knight. Chmn. dept. prep. studies U. Lodz, 1950-53; adj. Inst. for Phys. Chemistry, Acad. Scis., Warsaw, 1958-60; dep. dir. electrochemistry lab. Energy Inst., U. Pa., Phila., 1960-67, dir. electrochemistry lab., 1968-75; prin. research scientist Ford Motor Co., Dearborn, Mich., 1978—. Served with Polish Underground Army, 1943-45. Decorated Silver Cross of Merit with Swords. Mem. Electrochem. Soc., Internat. Electrochem. Soc., Mensa, Sigma Xi. Contbr. chpts. to books, articles to profl. jours., patent lit. Office: Ford Motor Co SRL S-2079 PO Box 2053 Dearborn MI 48322

WU, ALLISON META, sales executive; b. Cin., Ohio, Apr. 24, 1958; d. William C. L. and Louise P. Y. (Lu) Wu. BS in Engring., U. Rochester, 1980. Devel. engr. foams packaging Mobil Chem. Co., Canandaigua, N.Y., 1980-84; group leader foams packaging Mobil Chem. Co., Canandaigua, 1985-86; sr. devel. engr. packaging div. Mobil Chem. Co., Pittsford, N.Y., 1986-87; end user sales rep., films div. Mobil Chem. Co., Owings Mills, Md., 1988-89; converter sales rep. films div. Mobil Chem. Co., Fairport, N.Y., 1989—. Mem. NAFE. Baptist. Office: PO Box 35 Fairport NY 14450

WU, ANNA FANG, physician, medical administrator; b. Chengtu, China, Mar. 25, 1940; d. Tsun Chun and Chi Chu Fang; m. Tai Te Wu, 1966; children—Richard Gee-Fang. B.A., Cornell U., 1962; Ph.D., MIT, 1967; M.D., U. Chgo., 1974. Diplomate Am. Bd. Internal Medicine. Research assoc. Muscle Inst., N.Y.C., 1967-68, Coll. Physicians and Surgeons Columbia U., N.Y.C., 1968-70; resident in internal medicine Northwestern U. Med. Sc., Chgo., 1974-77, instr., 1977-80, asst. prof. medicine, 1980—; med. dir. employee health service Northwestern Meml. Hosp., Chgo., 1979—. Mem. ACP, Am. Occupational Medicine Assn. Club: Med. Dirs. (Chgo.). Avocation: travel. Office: Northwestern Med Faculty Found 222 E Superior St Chicago IL 60611

WU, LILIAN SHIAO-YEN, mathematician, researcher, consultant; b. Beijing, July 6, 1947; came to U.S., 1964; d. Wen-Hui and Betty (Chiang) W.; m. Frank Wang, June 14, 1973 (div. 1975). BS, U. Md., 1968; MS, Cornell U., 1972, PhD, 1974. Mem. rsch. staff IBM T.J. Watson Rsch. Ctr., Yorktown Heights, N.Y., 1973—; vis. scientist Marine Biol. Lab., Woods Hole, lMass., 1975-78; adj. prof. NYU Grad. Sch. Bus., N.Y.C., 1988. Author: Proceedings of the 14th Symposium on the Interface of Computer Science & Statistics, 1982; (software program) The Wineglass, 1989; contbr. articles to profl. jours. Vol. Katonah (N.Y.) Gallery, 1984—, Met. Mus. Art, N.Y.C., 1987. Mem. Internat. Inst. Forecasters, Am. Statis. Assn. Office: IBM T J Watson Rsch Ctr Box 218 Yorktown Heights NY 10598

WU, NAN FAION, pediatrician; b. Malaysia, July 13, 1943; came to U.S., 1969; m. Chia F. Wu, June 22, 1969; children: Edwin, Karen. MD, Nat. Taiwan U., 1969. Diplomate Am. Bd. Pediatrics. Intern Atlantic City Med. Ctr., 1969-70; resident in pediatrics Maryland Hosp. CMDNJ, N.J. Med. Sch., Newark, 1970-73; pvt. practice pediatrics West Orange, N.J. Fellow Am. Acad. Pediatrics. Office: 35 Park Ave West Orange NJ 07052

WU, YING CHU LIN SUSAN, engineering research company executive, engineer; b. Beijing, June 23, 1932; came to U.S., 1957; d. Chi-yu and K.C. (Kung) Lin; m. Jain-Ming Wu, June 13, 1959; children: Ernest H., Albert H., Karen H. BSME, Nat. Taiwan U., 1955; MS in Aero. Engring., Ohio State U., 1959; PhD in Aeros., Calif. Inst. Tech., 1963. Sr. engr. Elecro-Optical Systems, Inc., Pasadena, Calif., 1963-65; asst. prof. aero. engring. U. Tenn. Space Inst., Tullahoma, 1965-67, assoc. prof., 1967-73, prof., 1973-88; adminstr. Energy Conversion R&D Programs, Tullahoma, 1981-88; pres., chief exec. officer ERC, Inc., Tullahoma, 1987—. Contbr. over 90 articles to profl. jours. Mem. Better Sch. Task Force, Tullahoma, 1985-86; founding mem. Tullahoma Edn. Found. for Excellence, 1988—. Recipient Chancellor's Rsch. award U. Tenn., 1978, Woman Achievement award, 1983. Fellow ASME, AIAA (assoc., chmn. Tenn. sect., H.H. Arnold award 1984); mem. Soc. Women Engrs. (life, achievement award 1985), Sigma Xi (chmn. U. Tenn. Space Inst. club). Home: 111 Lakewood Dr Tullahoma TN 37388 Office: ERC Inc PO Box 417 Tullahoma TN 37388

WUETIG, JOYCE LINDA, realtor; b. Little Rock, Feb. 11, 1938; d. John Clifford and Viva Emily (Summerhill) Dilbeck; m. James Russell McKinney, Aug. 30, 1958 (div. Sept. 1981); children: Melissa Ellen, James Blake; m. Frederick Lewis Wuetig, June 1, 1985. BA, Hendrix Coll., 1959; postgrad., Incarnate Word Coll., 1970-072. Cert. residential specialist; lic. real estate broker, Tex., Ark. Tchr. Little Rock Sch. Dist., 1959-62; fashion cons. Doncaster, Inc., San Antonio, 1975-83; tchr. Edgewood Ind. Sch. Dist., San Antonio, 1982-83; sales assoc. Dijon Plaza Realtors, San Antonio, 1978-83; relocation specialist HEB Grocery Co., San Antonio, 1981-82; asst. v.p. Independence Fed. Bank, Little Rock, 1984-85; sales assoc. Agar Realtors, Little Rock, 1986-89; sales assoc., cert. residential specialist McRay & Co. Residential Realtors, Little Rock, 1989—. Mem. com. Southwest Found. Forum, San Antonio, 1975-81; chmn. San Antonio Kitchen Tour, 1977-80; host mother, area activities chmn. Am. Field Svc., San Antonio, 1975-76, 77-78; life mem. Tex. PTA. Mem. Nat. Assn. Realtors, Ark. Realtors Assn., Little Rock Bd. Realtors, AAUW, Cert. Residential Specialists, DAR. Methodist. Home: 20 Inverness Circle Little Rock AR 72212

WUJCIAK, SANDRA CRISCUOLO, personnel executive; b. Newark, Nov. 26, 1949; d. Salvatore Michael Criscuolo and Maria (Agliata) Ventura; m. Alfred J. Wujciak Jr., Oct. 11, 1969; children: Kimberly, Joseph. Student, Morris County Coll., 1979-81. Parental cons. Lake Dr. Sch. Hearing Impaired, Mountain Lakes, N.J., 1975-83; mktg. rep. Accts. On Call, Livingston, N.J., 1981-84, Edison, N.J., 1984-85; br. mgr. Accts. On Call, Edison, 1985-87; area mgr. Accts. On Call, Edison, Princeton, N.J., Mpls., 1987-88; area v.p. Accts. On Call, Edison, Princeton, Atlanta, Cin., Miami, Fla., Mpls., 1988—. Pres. ad hoc com. Dodge Tract, Parsippany, N.J., 1979-80. Mem. N.J. Assn. Pers. Cons., Edison C. of C., Rockaway River Country Club (Denville, N.J.). Republican. Roman Catholic.

WUJEK, MARIANNE FELTZ, information systems scientist; b. Balt., Mar. 23, 1959; d. Michael Richard and Clara (Zamenski) Feltz; m. Harry Joseph Wujek,. Student, Essex Community Coll.; BS, Towson State U. Systems specialist Alex. Brown & Sons, Balt., 1982-85; info. ctr. cons. Black & Decker Corp., Balt., 1985-86; mgr. Rowles & Co., Balt., 1986; systems analyst CSX Tech., Balt., 1986-88; asst. mgr. CSX Transp., Balt., 1988—. Mem. Am. Compensation Assn., Human Resource Systems Profls. Office: CSX Transp 100 N Charles St Baltimore MD 21201

WULF, SHARON ANN, financial planner; b. New Bedford, Mass., Aug 23, 1954; d. Daniel Thomas and Norma Dorothy (McCabe) Vieira; m. Stanley A. Wulf, 1983. BS in Acctg. cum laude, Providence Coll., 1976; MBA, Northeastern U., 1977; PhD, Columbia Pacific U., 1984. Staff acct., intern Laventhol & Horwath, Providence, 1977; jr. fin. analyst Polaroid Corp., Waltham, Mass., 1977-78, fin. analyst, Freetown, Mass., 1978-79, Cambridge, 1979-81; sr. fin. cons., mktg. strategic planner Digital Equipment Corp., Stow, Mass., 1981-82, Maynard, Mass., 1982-83, mgr. fin. devel. program, 1983-84, strategic fin. cons. engring. div., 1984-86, group mgr. planning and strategic ops., Hudson, Mass., 1986-87, group mgr. strategic bus. planning, 1987-89, mktg. planning mgr. Digital Equipment Corp., Marlboro, 1989—; lectr. in fin. acctg. Southeastern Mass. U., 1979-81; adj. prof. acctg., mgmt. and fin., Northeastern U., Boston, 1980—; exec. com. enterprise forum MIT, 1987—; cons. in field. Chairperson pub. support and fund raising ARC, New Bedford, Mass., 1974-84. Mem. NAFE (bd. dirs. 1978-81), Univ. Coll. Faculty Soc., Phi Sigma Tau. Home: 902 Salem End Rd Framingham MA 01701 Office: Digital Equipment Corp 4 Results Way Marlboro MA 01752

WULFF, GERALDINE SCHEPKER, museum services company executive; b. Jefferson City, Mo., Jan. 30, 1947. Claims examiner, fraud investigator Dept. Employment Svcs., Washington, 1970—, fed. coord., supr. unemployment compensation, 1971—; v.p. Mus. Svcs. Internat., Washington, 1983—, also bd. dirs. Mem. Wash. Literacy Coun., 1988—; donor D.C. Chpt. ARC. Mem. English Speaking Union, Am. Fedn. Gov. Employees, Internat. Assn. of Pers. in Employment Security. Democrat. Home: 1716 17th St NW Washington DC 20009

WUNCH, KAREN ELIZABETH, assistant nursing director; b. Pasadena, Calif., Aug. 7, 1953; d. William Stuart and Joanne Shirley (Berger) W. BSN, U. Calif., San Francisco, 1975; MS in Nursing, Boston U., 1976. RN, Wis., Calif. Mem. nursing staff Univ. Hosp., Boston, 1976; rehab. clin. nurse specialist Sacred Heart Rehab. Hosp., Milw., 1976-81; coor. nursing care Northridge (Calif.) Hosp. Med. Ctr., 1982-88; dir. clin. nursing rehab. Rancho Los Amigos Med. Ctr., Downey, Calif., 1988—; mem. adj. clin. faculty Sch. Nursing U. So. Calif., L.A., 1989—. Mem. Nat. League for Nursing, Org. Nurse Execs., Am. Congress Rehab. Med., Assn. Rehab. Nurses (pres. Wis. chpt. 1979), Sigma Theta Tau. Home: 19729 Stagg St Canoga Park CA 91306

WUNDER, HAROLDENE FOWLER, accounting educator; b. Greenville, S.C., Nov. 16, 1944; d. Harold Eugene Fowler and Sarah Ann (Chaffin) Crooks. BS, U. Md., 1971; M Acctg., U. S.C., 1975, PhD, 1978. Vis. asst. prof. U. S.C., Columbia, 1977-78; asst. prof. U. Pa., Phila., 1978-81; vis. asst. prof. U. N.C., Chapel Hill, 1981-82; asst. prof. U. Mass., Boston, 1982-86; vis. assoc. prof. Suffolk U., Boston, 1986-87; assoc. prof. U. Toledo, 1987—. Contbr. articles to acad. and profl. publs. George Olson fellow, 1975; named to Outstanding Young Women Am., 1979. Mem. Am. Acctg. Assn., Am. Taxation Assn., Nat. Tax Assn.-Tax Inst. Am., NAFE, Beta Gamma Sigma. Office: U Toledo 2801 W Bancroft St Toledo OH 43606

WUNDER, JEAN BAKER, social services administrator; b. Bklyn., Oct. 1, 1934; d. William Michael and Lillian Jane (Trill) B.; m. Theodore Henry Wunder, Sept. 28, 1957 (div. July 1971); children: Susan Baker Armstrong, William Henry, Robert Theodore. Grad. high sch., Bklyn., 1952. Founder, exec. dir. The SOURCE-Family Support Group, Inc., Glen Rock, N.J., 1983—; lectr. Bergen County Dept. Health Service, Paramus, N.J., 1973—, Bergen County Respiratory Soc., Paramus, 1973—; community liaison Future Health Systems, 1986-87. Paramus, 1986—; chairperson Human Resource Coordinating Council, Ridgewood, N.J., 1986-88. Leader Cub Scouts Am., Glen Rock, 1972-74; founder, dir. Glen Rock Toughlove, 1981; lectr. substance abuse ministry Archdiocese N.Y.C., 1983—; mem. Bergen County Com. on Youth Substance Abuse, Paramus, 1985—, United Parents Ridgewood, N.J., 1985—; founder, dir. Bergen County Coalition Against Drug Abuse, Glen Rock, 1986, Bergen County Legal Svcs., 1989—. Recipient Jefferson award Pub. Inst., 1983, Gov.'s Vol. award State of N.J, 1987, Outstanding Woman award League of Women Voters, 1990; named Vol. of Yr. Suburban Newspapers, 1984; Bergen County Freeholders grantee, 1986. Mem. Nat. Fedn. for Drug Free Youth, N.J. Fedn. Parents for Drug Free Communities. Home: 178 Harding Rd Glen Rock NJ 07452 Office: Family Support Group Inc The SOURCE West Pla Glen Rock NJ 07452

WUNDERLE, ANN KATHRYN, personnel director; b. Canton, Ohio, Apr. 27, 1953; d. Paul Ellsworth and Kathleen May (Ramsburg) W. BA, Malone Coll., 1975; MS, U. Ill., 1985; postgrad., Keller Grad. Sch. of Mgmt., Deerfield, Ill., 1988. Lic. clin. social worker. Dir. special programs Northwestern U., Evanston, 1978-85; pvt. practice, social work Highland Park, Ill., 1985-86; human resources dir. Oneac Corp., Libertyville, Ill., 1987—; steering com. mem. Positive Alt. Svcs. for Students, Grayslake, Ill., 1988—; cons. Corp. Strategies, Inc., Bannockburn, Ill., 1986—. Mem. Am. Psychol. Assn., Am. Soc. Personnel Adminstr., Nat. Assn. Social Workers, Ill. Mgmt. Assn., No. Ill. Indsl. Assn., Electronics Personnel Assn. Republican.

WUNNICKE, BROOKE, lawyer; b. Dallas, May 9, 1918; d. Rudolph von Falkenstein and Lulu Lenore Brooke; m. James M. Wunnicke, Apr. 11, 1940; (dec. 1977); 1 child, Diane B. BA, Stanford U., 1939; JD, U. Colo., 1945. Bar: Wy. 1946, U.S. Dist Ct. Wy. 1947, Colo. 1971, U.S. Supreme Ct. 1958. Pvt. practice law, 1946-56; ptnr. Williams & Wunnicke, Cheyenne, Wyo., 1956-69; of counsel Calkins, Kramer, Grimshaw & Harring, Denver, 1969-73; chief appellate dep. atty. Dist. Atty's Office, Denver, 1973-86; of counsel Hall & Evans, Denver, 1986—; adj. profl law U. Denver, 1978—; lectr. Internat. Practicum Inst. Denver, 1978—. Author: Ethics Compliance for Business Lawyers, 1987; co-author: Standby Letters of Credit, 1989. Pres. Laramie County Bar Assn., Cheyenne, Wy., 1967-68; Dir. Cheyenne C. of C., Cheyenne, Wy., 1965-68. Recipient awards for Outstanding Svc., Colo. Dist. Attys. Coun., 1979, 82, 86, Disting. Alumni award U. Colo. Sch. of Law, 1986. Fellow Colo. Bar Found.; mem. ABA, Wyo. State Bar, Denver Bar Assn. (bd. trustees 1977-80), Colo. Bar Assn., Order of Coif, Phi Beta Kappa. Republican. Episcopalian. Office: Hall & Evans 1200 17th St Denver CO 80202

WUNSCH, KATHRYN SUTHERLAND, lawyer; b. Tipton, Mo., Jan. 30, 1935; d. Lewis Benjamin and Norene Marie (Wolf) Sutherland; m. Charles Martin Wunsch, Dec. 22, 1956 (div. May 1988); children: Debra Kay, Laura Ellen. AB, Ind. U., 1958, JD summa cum laude, 1977; postgrad., Stanford (Calif.) U., 1977. Bar: Calif. 1977, U.S. Dist. Ct. (we. dist.) Calif. 1977. Assoc. Hunt and Hunt, San Francisco, 1977-89; ptnr. Wunsch and George, San Francisco, 1989—. Articles editor Ind. U. Law Rev., 1975-76. Sec., treas. Internat. Visitors Com., Palo Alto, Calif., 1987—; bd. dirs. Neighbors Abroad, Palo Alto, 1988—. Mem. ABA, Calif. Bar Assn., Bar Assn. of San Francisco, Nat. Assn. Women Bus. Owners, Phi Beta Kappa, Psi Chi. Republican. Office: Wunsch and George 100 Pine St 21s Fl San Francisco CA 94111

WURTMAN, JUDITH JOY, research scientist; b. Bklyn., Aug. 4, 1937; d. Alexander Mordecai and Jeanette Teicher Hirschhorn; m. Richard Jay Wurtman; children: Rachael, David. BA, Wellesely (Mass.) Coll., 1959; M in Biology Edn., Harvard U., 1960; PhD, George Washington U., 1973. Tchr. Malden Sch. System, 1959-60; rsch. asst. Microbiol. Assocs., Bethesda, Md., 1962-67; exhibit researcher Boston Mus. Sci., 1973-74; asst. prof. Newton (Mass.) Coll., 1974-76; postdoctoral fellow dept. nutrition MIT, Cambridge, 1976-78, rsch. scientist dept. nutrition, dept. brain and cognitive sci., 1987—; mem. scientific adv. bd. NutriSystem, Phila., 1988—, Interneuron Pharms., Boston, 1989—. Author: Eating Your Way Through Life, 1979, The Carbohydrate Craver's Diet, 1983, The Carbohydrate Craver's Diet Cookbook, 1984, Managing Your Mind and Mood Through Food, 1987; editor: Nutrition and the Brain (8 vols.), 1983—. Mem. Am. Inst. Nutrition, Am. Dietitic Assn., Am. Soc. for Clin. Nutrition, Boston Soc. Psychiatry and Neurology, Soc. for Light Treatment and Biol. Rhythms, Sigma Xi (MIT chpt.). Office: MIT Dept of Brain and Cognitive Scis E25-604 Cambridge MA 02139

WURTZ, MERRYROSE, insurance executive; b. Potlatch, Idaho, Feb. 2, 1936; d. Van and Gladys Anna (Nygaard) Richardson; m. Francis R. Wurtz, Sept. 15, 1953 (div. Dec. 1985); children: Linda, Diane, Laura, Brian. AA in Bus., City Coll. Chgo., 1980. CPCU; assoc. in risk mgmt. Ins. clk. Victor Comptometer Corp., Chgo., 1967-71, ins. adminstr., 1971-75, asst. ins. dir., 1975-77; ins. analyst Allied Products Corp., Chgo., 1977-79, mgr. ins., 1979-82, dir. ins., 1982-87, staff v.p. risk mgmt., 1987—. Mem. Risk and Ins. Mgmt. Soc. (assoc.), Soc. CPCU's. Office: Allied Products Corp 10 S Riverside Pla Chicago IL 60606

WURZBACHER, TERRIE, military officer, osteopath; b. Rockeville Center, N.Y., Oct. 22, 1948; d. Frederick Marshall and Winona Marion (Oatley) W. BA, U. Vt., 1970; DO, Coll. Osteo. Medicine, 1975. Diplomate Am. Bd. Emergency Medicine. Commd. ensign USN, 1972, advanced through grades to capt.; head emergency medicine Phila. Naval Hosp.; asst. dir. combat casualty care course San Antonio; head emergency dept. Portsmouth Naval Hosp., Va., Great Lakes Naval Hosp., Waukegan, Ill.; dir. med. svcs. NMCL Quantico, Va. Fellow Am. Coll. Emergency Physicians. Home: 7237 Chancellor Rd Fredericksburg VA 22401 Office: NMCL Quantico Quantico VA 22401

WURZBERGER, SUZANNE ALICE WELLS, shop owner; b. Bridgeport, Conn., June 7, 1938; d. Daniel Marcus and Sarah Evelyn (French) Wells; m. Albert George Wurzberger, May 2, 1959; children—Carolsue, Albert John. A.S., Vt. Coll., 1958; diploma Internat. Corr. Sch., 1979. Owner, operator Norton House, Wilmington, Vt., 1966—; gen. mgr. The New Eng. Plantation, Inc., Wilmington. Author Living History Assn. Jour., 1982. Pres. Parent Tchrs. Club, Wilmington, Vt., 1974-75; troop leader brownies Girl Scouts U.S.A., Wilmington, 1967. Mem. Women Bus. Owners of Vt., Nat. Assn. Female Execs., Am./Internat. Quilt Assn. Republican. Congregationalist. Clubs: Ch. Guild (pres.), Green Mt. Quilters Guild. Avocations: sewing; snowshoeing. Home: Stowe Hill Rd RFD 1 Box 105 Wilmington VT 05363 Office: Norton House 1836 Country Store Village Wilmington VT 05363

WUSSLER, MARILYN THERESA, psychological therapist; b. St. Charles, Mo., Jan. 16, 1938; d. Edgar John and Bertha Catherine (Mueller) W. BA, Notre Dame Coll., St. Louis, 1959; MS, St. Louis U., 1967. Lic. psychologist, Wash. Tchr. various secondary schs., St. Louis, 1957-69; secondary tchr. Althoff Cath. High Sch., Belleville, Ill., 1969-72, St. Mary of Pines, Chatawa, Miss., 1972-73; assoc. prof. Notre Dame Coll., 1973-76; psychologist Living Resource Ctr., Belleville, 1976-83; coord. Spiritual Devel. Coun., St. Louis, 1983-86; therapist Personal Growth Ctr., Spokane, Wash., 1986—; coord. Team for Personal-Communal Life, St. Louis, 1983-86. Mem. Am. Psychol. Assn., Assn. for Psychol. Type (conf. speaker 1989), Internat. Group Psychotherapy Assn. Democrat. Roman Catholic. Office: Personal Growth Ctr N 1016 Superior St Spokane WA 99202

WYAND, ANNE LEWIS, management consultant, educator; b. Mobile, Ala., Jan. 5, 1943; d. Vernon Henry Lewis and Edna (Eastep) Bullington; m. Gerald Douglas Robinson, Sept. 10, 1960 (div. Dec. 1988); children: Richard D., John Michael, James Brennan; m. Robert Rice Wyand II, Mar. 9, 1989. Student, Ga. Inst. Tech., 1977, Ga. State U., 1983. Systems engr. Grady Hosp., Atlanta, 1977-80; mgr. cons. svcs. Sunhealth, Inc., Atlanta, 1980-84; prin. Kurt Salmon Assocs., Atlanta, 1984-90; sr. ptnr. Affiliated Dynamics, Inc., Atlanta, 1990—; adj. prof. Coll. of St. Francis, Joliet, Ill., 1987—. Coord. vols. Dukakis campaign, 1988. Mem. Am. Coll. Healthcare Execs., Hosp. Info. Mgmt. Systems Soc. (charter), Ga. State Exec MBA Alumni Group (bd. dirs.).

WYATT, EDITH ELIZABETH, educator; b. San Diego, Aug. 13, 1914; d. Jesse Wellington and Elizabeth (Fultz) Carne; m. Lee Ora Wyatt, Mar. 30, 1947 (dec. Jan. 1966); children: Glenn Stanley (dec.), David Allen. BA, San Diego State Coll., 1936. Elem. tchr. Nat. Sch. Dist., National City, Calif., 1938-76. Sec. San Diego County Parks Soc., 1986—; librarian Congl. Ch. Women's Fellowship, Chula Vista, Calif., 1980—; active Boy Scouts Am. Recipient Who award San Diego County Tchrs. Assn., 1968, Silver Fawn award Boy Scouts Am. Mem. AAUW (sec. 1978-80, pub. rels. 1985—), Calif. Retired Tchrs. Assn. (scholarhsip com. 1985-90), Starlite Hiking Club (sec.-treas. 1979—). Home: 165 E Millan St Chula Vista CA 92010

WYATT, FARICITA HALL, social services employment coordinator, consultant; b. Bakersfield, Calif., Oct. 29, 1912; d. William Mason Hall and Susie Sylindia Pinkney; m. Thomas Edward Wyatt, Oct. 20, 1953 (dec. 1954). BA in Speech, San Jose State U., 1935. Cert. tchr. (life). Employment officer State of Calif., Berkeley, 1946-58; exec. sec. Congressman Jeffrey Cohelan, Washington, 1959-61; tchr. English Skyline High Sch., Oakland, Calif., 1962-68; tchr., chmn. English dept. Skyline High Sch., Oakland, 1969-75; employment officer U. Calif., Berkeley, 1968-69; employment rep. retirees' employment program U. Calif., San Francisco, 1979—; founder, dir. Impact Assocs., San Francisco, 1976—; conductor workshops, consultant in field. Author (poetry) The River Must Flow, 1965, By The Banks of the River, 1974, TRIAD-ICAR, 1986—. Bd. suprs. Internat. Soc. Pre-retirement Planners, San Francisco, 1987; bd. dirs. Am. Soc. Aging, San Francisco, 1983—, Ret. Sr. Vol. Program, San Francisco, 1984—, San Francisco Sr. Ctr., 1984—. Capt. WAC, 1943-46. Mem. Internat. Interactive Communictions Soc. (San Francisco Bay Area chpt. 1988—). Democrat. Home: 1200 Lakeshore Ave Apt 6C Oakland CA 94606 Office: U Calif 1350 7th Ave San Francisco CA 94143

WYATT, JEANINE MOESSER, marketing executive; b. Salt Lake City. Student, Brigham Young U., 1969-72. Dir. ops. Salt Lake Valley Conv. and Visitors Bur., Salt Lake City, 1972-79; asst. gen. mgr. Ramada Inn, Salt Lake City, 1980-83; dir. sales Excelsior Hotel, Provo, Utah, 1983-88; dir. mktg. Seven Peaks Resort, Provo, 1988—; pres., chmn. Women in Mgmt. Coun., 1985-89; bd. dirs., past pres. Utah County Travel Coun., Provo. Active Little League Baseball Assn., Ute Conf. Football; past pres. Springhill Condominium Assn. Recipient Athena award Provo-Orem C. of C., 1989. Mem. Nat. Tour Assn., Am. Bus Assn., Hotel Sales Mgmt. Assn., Ski Utah Assn., Utah County Hotel Motel Assn. (pres. 1987—), Utah Hotel Motel

Assn. (bd. dirs.). Office: Seven Peaks Resort 101 W 100 North Provo UT 84601

WYATT, JENTA RAE, home economist; b. Chrisman, Ill., July 25, 1935; d. Edwin Boone and Maerene (Mason) Kendall; children: Kerry R., Charissa W. Leintz, Elizabeth R. BS, Rutgers U., 1967, MEd, 1973. Home econs. tchr. South Brunswick High Sch., Monmouth Junction, N.J., 1970-74; vocat. instr. VOTEC, Danville, Ill., 1974-78; extension home econs. agt. Fla. Coop. Extension Services, Wauchula, Fla., 1978-82, Ocala, Fla., 1982—; bd. dirs., chmn. bd. Consumer Credit Counseling Svc., Ocala, 1986-88. Pres. Village North Homeowners Assn., Ocala, 1986-87. Mem. Nat. Assn. Extension Home Economists (editor The Reporter 1989-91), Fla. Assn. Extension Home Economists (treas. 1983-84, bd. dirs. 1984-85, 2d v.p. 1985-86, pres.-elect 1987-88, pres. 1988-89), Fla. Home Econs. Assn., Pilot Club (pres.-elect Ocala chpt. 1987-88, pres. 1988-89, bd. dirs. 1986-90), Epsilon Sigma Phi. Home: 3823 NE 19th Circle Ocala FL 32670

WYATT, JOAN PORTIS, management consultant; b. Pasadena, Tex., Dec. 18, 1931; d. Ross Judson and Ermine Opal (Brammer) Portis; m. Gordon Beal Wyatt, Dec. 20, 1950; children: Michael Gordon, Judson Chandler. BS summa cum laude, Sam Houston U., 1985, MA, 1987. Teaching asst. Sam Houston U., Huntsville, Tex., 1985-86; cons. for social and cultural devel. City of Cleveland, Cleveland, Tex., 1987-88; cons. Birkman & Assocs. Inc., Houston, 1988—; tchr. North Harris County Coll., Kingwood, Tex., 1989—; pvt. practice mgmt. cons. Cleveland, 1988—; Chaplain Charter Regional Med. Ctr., Cleveland, 1988-90; outreach dir. St. Luke's Presbyn. Ch., Cleveland, 1988—. Bd. dirs., v.p. Kirbywood Country Club, Cleveland, 1985-86; bd. dirs. Cleveland (Tex.) Ednl. Found., 1987-89; precinct chair Rep. Party, Liberty County, Tex., 1986-88; pres. Tennis Assn., Cleveland, 1989. Mem. Am. Psychol. Assn. (assoc.), Greater Cleveland C. of C., Phi Sigam Tau, Psi Chi, Cleveland Golf Club. Republican. Presbyterian. Home: Route 1 Box 83 Cleveland TX 77327 Office: 111 West Crockett Cleveland TX 77327

WYATT, JUANITA GRAHAM, high school administrator; b. Jacksonville, Fla., July 9, 1929; d. Samuel and Elsie (Linton) Graham; m. Ernest Rudolph Wyatt, Nov. 26, 1955 (dec.); children: Cheryl Denise Wyatt Santos, Ernest Rudolph II. BA, Fla. A&M U., 1947; MA, Columbia U., 1951. Tchr. Davis St. Jr. High Sch., Jacksonville, 1948-52, James Weldon Johnson Jr. High Sch., Jacksonville, 1952-53; dean girls New Stanton Sr. High Sch., Jacksonville, 1953-59, A.L. Lewis Elem., Jr. High Sch., Jacksonville, 1960-61; asst. prin. student svcs. Northwestern Jr.-Sr. High Sch., Jacksonville, 1961—; part-time tchr. Fla. Jr. Coll., 1967-69, 83-86; guidance counselor Adult Vocat. Pilot Program Duval County Bd. Pub. Instrn., Jacksonville, 1973-75; cons., chmn. guidance com. Sanford (Fla.) High Sch., 1975-77. Cons. Human Rels. Better Living Clin., Jacksonville, bd. Christian Edn. Inst., Birmingham, Ala.; dir. counselors Nat. Christian Meth. Episcopal Ch. Youth, Young Adult Conf., Louisville, Ky., 1980, New Orleans, 1984; editor newsletter Christian Meth. Epsicopal Ch., Jacksonville, tchr. ch. leadership tng. sch. (Woman of Yr. 1984); contact person United Way, 1989-90, Negro Coll. Fund, 1987-88. Recipient hon. mention Outstanding Substance Abuse Program, Jacksonville, 1987, 88, State's Program of Excellence award Fla., 1989-90. Mem. NEA, Fla. Edn. Assn., Duval County Assn. Secondary Schs., Student Code Conduct Revision Com., Les Fleurs Social Club (past sec.), Delta Sigma Theta (sec. 1945-47). Democrat. Methodist. Home: 5218 Vernon Rd Jacksonville FL 32209 Office: Northwestern Jr High Sch 2100 W 45th St Jacksonville FL 32209

WYATT, JULIE (JULIE WOODY), interior designer; b. Washington, Okla., Dec. 2, 1939; d. Henry Edward and Nora Lee (Blalock) Woody; m. Kenneth Lynn Wyatt, June 23, 1961; children: Robert Adam, Nora Lynn. BA in Interior Design, U. Okla., 1963. Interior designer N. Ray Interiors, Norman, Okla., 1961-64, Slosky's, Oklahoma City, Okla., 1965, Stewart's, Oklahoma City, 1966-70, Pendergraft's, Inc., Oklahoma City, 1970-76; prin. J. Wyatt Interiors, Oklahoma City, 1976—; bd. visitors U. Okla. Coll. Architecture, Norman, 1987—. Mem. Am. Soc. Interior Designers (pres. 1986, nat. bd. dirs. 1987—, regional v.p. 1989—, judge design competition Houston chpt. 1989, 90, Pres. citation 1976, 1st Pl. Community Svc. project 1987, Medalist award 1989). Home: 7511 N Country Club Oklahoma City OK 73116 Office: Wyatt Interiors 2638 NW 50th St Oklahoma City OK 73112

WYATT, KATHLEEN ANN, publishing executive; b. Nelsonville, Ohio, June 23, 1951; d. Charles Edward and Ella Mae (Johnston) Covelle; m. Larry Gene Wyatt, May 12, 1972; children: Joel Andrew, Christopher Neal. Student, Ea. Ky. U., 1969-72; BS, U. Cin., 1975; MBA, Xavier U., 1987. Dir. subscription services Anderson Pub. Co., Cin., 1972—, also mem. employee recognition com., 1985—. Elected mem. community affairs com. St. Mary's Ch. of Hyde Park, Cin., 1985—; den leader St. Mary's Cub Scouts Am., Cin., 1987—. Mem. Nat. Assn. Female Execs., Xavier MBA Alumni Assn. (trustee 1987—), Alpha Phi Si. Republican. Clubs: Turpin Swim (Cin.); Xavier Blue Chips Investment (founder, pres. 1987—). Lodge: United Order True Sisters. Home: 2943 Erie Ave Cincinnati OH 45208 Office: Anderson Pub Co 2035 Reading Rd Cincinnati OH 45202

WYATT, KATHRYN ELIZABETH BENTON, psychologist, educator; b. Danville, Va., May 11, 1928; d. Joseph Nelson and Margaret (Davis) Benton; B.A., Randolph Macon Woman's Coll., Lynchburg, Va., 1949; M.Ed., U. Va., 1952; M.A., U. N.C., Greensboro, 1974, Ph.D., 1977; m. Landon Russell Wyatt, Aug. 30, 1952; children—Margaret Wyatt Scott, Landon Russell, III, Elizabeth Wyatt Ashe. Instr., then asst. prof. psychology Stratford Coll., Danville, 1949-74, chmn. dept., 1963-74; prof. psychology Danville Community Coll., 1977—. Mem. Danville Sch. Bd.; deacon, tchr. 1st Bapt. Ch., Danville; pres. so. region Va. Sch. Bds. Assn. Mem. Am. Psychol. Assn., Soc. Research Child Devel., Southeastern Psychol. Assn., Va. Psychol. Assn., Va. Acad. Sci. Clubs: Friends Danville Pub. Library (pres.), The Wednesday Club (pres.), Gabriella, Wayside Garden, Shakespeare. Author articles in field. Home: 301 Magnolia St Danville VA 24541 Office: Danville Community Coll Danville VA 24541

WYATT, MARSHA KAPNICKY, sales representative; b. Morgantown, W.Va., Oct. 7, 1956; d. Paul Nicholas and Iris Kathleen (Kelly) Kapnicky; m. Royce J. Watts, II, July 29, 1978 (div. Sept. 1981); m. A. James Wyatt, Jr., Jan. 7, 1984. BS in Journalism, W.Va. U., 1978. Sales rep., R.L. Polk Co., Richmond and Atlanta, 1978-79; sales rep. Designers Color, Inc., Atlanta, 1979-84; sr. sales rep. Techtron Imaging Network, Chgo. and Atlanta, 1984—. Mem. Atlanta Print Prodn. Assn., Nat. Assn. Female Execs., Atlanta Advt. Club (bd. dirs.), W.Va. U. Alumni Assn. Home: 3355 Floral Ct Suwanee GA 30174 Office: Techtron/Imaging Network 550 Bishop St Bldg E Atlanta GA 30318

WYATT, MARY CATHERINE, public relations executive; b. Taunton, Mass., Mar. 30, 1958; d. Frederick Joseph and Hilda (Nunes) W.; m. Frederick William Conery, Sept. 11, 1982. BA, U. Mass., 1980; postgrad bus. adminstrn., U. R.I., 1986—. Account coord. Leonard Monahan Saabye, Providence, 1980-82; account exec. LMS/Barrett, Providence, 1982-83; rep. Fleet Nat. Bank, Providence, 1983; sr. rep. Fleet Nat. Bank, 1984, officer, 1985-88, asst. v.p., 1989; v.p. Chaffee Bedard, Providence, 1989—. Editor, Keep Providence Beautiful, 1983-87. Bd. dirs. Nat. Com. for Prevention Child Abuse, Pawtucket, R.I., 1985—. Named Bell Ringer, Publicity Club Boston, 1981-2, 89, Young Career Woman, no. Providence chpt. Bus. and Profl. Women, 1985. Mem. Pub. Relations Soc. Am. (editor 1981-83), Internat. Assn. Bus. Communicators (pres. R.I. chpt. 1986, recipient Gold Quill, 1986), Southeastern New Eng. Pub. Relations Soc. (charter mem.), R.I. Bankers Assn. (chair pub. relations com. 1986-88). Republican. Roman Catholic. Office: Chaffee Bedard Inc 10 Davol Sq Providence RI 02903

WYATT, PHILLIPA KATHLEEN, marketing professional; b. Anderson, Ind.; d. Harold H. and Hilda W. (Keen) W. BS, Ind. U. TV and radio dir. Wm. H. Block Co., Indpls., 1952-55; writer, producer Sta. WFBM-TV, WFBM-AM Radio, Indpls., 1955-56; v.p. Jacobs Advt. Agy., Indpls., 1956-57; prin. Wyatt Advt. Agy., Indpls., 1957-71; pres. Wyatt Advt., Inc., Indpls., 1971-84; prin. Wyatt Mktg., Indpls., 1984—; cons. Personal Fin. Co., Olympia Fields, Ill., 1985—, Better Mobility Products, Indpls., 1988—, Yorktown Health Care Ctr., 1985—, Indpls. Retirement Home, 1987—, Havan Heritage House Children's Ctr., Shelbyville, Ind., 1987—, Sunbrite Homes, Indpls., 1986—; bd. dirs. Adv. Club Indpls., 1958-66, Sales and Mktg. Execs. Internat., 1971-72. Bd. dirs. Leukemia Soc. Am., Indpls., 1980-82; active Mayor's Downtown Improvement Com., Indpls., 1975; cons. NBA Ind. Pacers Inaugural Season, Indpls., 1976-77. Named Woman of Yr. Advt. Club Indpls., 1960; recipient 1st place award in direct mail Am. Industry Bankers, 1964, Merit award Fin. World, 1971, 1st place award TV Bur. Advt., 1977, Addy award, 1977. Mem. Ind. Healthcare Assn., Ind. Sch. Bus. Alumnae, Columbia Club, Highland Golf and Country Club. Republican. Lutheran. Office: Wyatt Mktg 9240 N Meridian St Indianapolis IN 46260

WYCKOFF, LINDA S., lawyer; b. Longview, Wash., Jan. 9, 1948; d. Leonard R. and Rae (Wisdom) Wilmot; m. Richard A. Wyckoff, June 14, 1987; 1 child, Michelle S. Wilson; stepchildren: Anna E., Dana E. BS, U. Pitts., 1971, JD, 1974. V.p., gen. counsel, sec. Action Industries, Inc., Cheswick, Pa., 1974—. Mem. Am. Bar Assn., Pa. Bar Assn., Allegheny County Bar Assn. Democratic. Office: Action Industries Inc Allegheny Industrial Pk Cheswick PA 15024

WYCKOFF, MARGO GAIL, psychologist; b. Omaha, Jan. 30, 1941; d. Winfield Jennings and Gail Claudia (Leach) Hartland; m. Tom Lawrence Wyckoff, Mar. 17, 1971; children: Ted, Elizabeth. BA, U. Wash., 1973, MSW, 1975; PhD, Union Grad. Sch., Seattle, 1978; cer. Licensed psychologist. Clin. lectr. U. Wash. Med. Sch., Seattle, 1976-78, asst. prof. univ. Pain Ctr., 1980-87; assoc. dir. pain ctr. Swedish Med. Ctr., Seattle, 1979-83, dir. behavioral svcs., 1979-83; pvt. practice Seattle, 1983—; psychology cons. Providence Med. Ctr., Seattle, 1979-87. Contbr. articles to jours., chpts. to books. Mem. Wash. Psychol. Assn. (bd. dirs. 1986-87), Nat. Orgn. Soc. Workers, Internat. Assn. for the Study of Pain, Psychoanalytic Assn. (bd. dirs. 1982-84), Wash. Environ. Council. Democrat. Office: Springbrook Psychol Group 4540 Sand Point Way NE Seattle WA 98105

WYCKOFF, SUSAN, astronomy researcher; b. Santa Cruz, Calif., Mar. 18, 1941; d. Stephen and Jean (Taft) W.; m. Peter Augustus Wehinger, July 29, 1967. BA in Astronomy, Mount Holyoke, 1962; postgrad., Swarthmore Coll., 1962-63; PhD in Astronomy, Case Inst. Technology, 1967. Postdoctoral fellow U. Mich., Ann Arbor, 1967-68; asst. prof. Albion (Mich.) Coll., 1968-70; rsch. assoc. U. Kans., Lawrence, 1970-72; sr. lectr. Tel-Aviv U., Israel, 1972-75; prin. rsch. fellow Royal Greenwich Observatory, Sussex, Eng., 1975-78; vis. prof. Ohio State U., Columbus, 1978-79; assoc. prof. Ariz. State U., Tempe, 1979-82, prof., 1982—; adj. prof. Sussex U., 1975-77, U. Heidelberg Theoretical Astrophysics Inst., 1980, U. Ariz., Tucson, 1984—; vis. astronomer Royal Grennwich Observatory, Sussex, Eng., 1983, Mt. Stromlo Observatory, Australian Nat. U., Canberra, 1987, Smith Coll., 1985; Shapley lectr., 1985-86; vis. com. Aura, Inc., Tucson, 1985-88; mem. Internat. Astron. Union Working Group High Resolution Spectra Comets, 1982—, space telescope working group key projects Extragalactic Astronomy, 1984-85. Contbr. articles profl. jours. Mem. Gov.'s Disease Control Commn., Phoenix, 1985-87. Named Woman of Achievement Yr. Phoenix Jr. League, 1983. Fellow Royal Astronomical Soc. (Eng.); mem. NSF adv. com. 1983—, Nat. Acad. Sci. space sci. bd. 1984—, Ariz. State U. Faculty Women's Assn. (pres. 1983-84, exec. bd. 1983—), Am. Astron. Soc. Coun. (A.J. Cannon award comm. 1982-87), Internat. Astron. Union, Mt. Graham Internat. Observatory (citizen's coun.), Am. Astronomical Soc. (mem. coun. 1985-88), Sigma Xi. Home: 2135 E Loma Vista Dr Tempe AZ 85282 Office: Ariz State U Physics/Astronomy Dept Tempe AZ 85287-1504

WYLIE, CATHY LYNN, training specialist; b. Sandusky, Ohio, May 4, 1964; d. Walter Mason and Nella Faye (Bussell) W. AS, Terra Tech. Coll., 1984; BS Che., Tech., Bowling Green State U., 1987. Chem. lab. asst. Terra Tech. Coll., Fremont, Ohio, 1983-84; nuclear tech. Toledo Edison Co. Davis Besse, Oak Harbor, Ohio, 1984-86; act. stn. corrective Davis Besse Nuclear, Oak Harbor, 1986-87; action coordinator Powerstation, Oak Horbor; training specialist Davis Besse Nuclear Power Stn., Oak Horbor, 1987-89; instr. assoc. skills Bayshore Generating Sta., 1989—; tech. instr. Terra Tech. Coll., Ohio, 1985—; pres. Northeasten Ohio Tech. Enterprises, Oak Harbor, 1989--. Mem. Natl. Soc. of Performance and Instruction, Nuclear Power Tech. Advisory Bd. Republican. Baptist. Home: 402 Mulberry St Clyde OH 43410

WYLIE, GRACE SCOTT, languages educator; b. Greenfield, Mass., July 25, 1925; d. Wolfe William and Jennie Yacabeth (Bramson) Cotton; children from previous marriage: Brandon Jay Scott, Trafford Guy Scott; m. Donald Ames Wylie, Dec. 18, 1975. BA in Edn., U. Conn., 1947; MA in Intercultural Edn., U. of the Americas, Mexico City, 1975. Cert. secondary sch. tchr., Conn. Tchr. Spanish and English Bristol (Conn.) Sr. High Sch., 1947-52; tchr. English as fgn. lang. Instituto Mexicano-Norteamericano de Relaciones Culturales, 1952-76; instr. English as fgn. lang. Universidad Iberoamericana, Mex., 1971-72; instr. U. Ams., Mex., 1974-76; instr. ESL George Washington U., Washington, 1976; dir. courses Eng. as fgn. lang. Centre Culturel Americain du Chad, Africa, 1977-78; instr. U. du Tchad, Chad, 1977-78, Jiao-Tong U., Shanghai, China, 1982; instr. Fla. Inst. Tech., Melbourne, 1978-80, asst. prof. applied linguistics, fgn. langs., 1980—; with U.S. info. svc. U. Poznan, Poland, 1989; cons. Eng. as fgn. lang. U.S. Info. Svc., Mexico, 1967-75; participant seminar Fla. Colombia ptnrs., U.S. Info. Svc., Colombia, 1985. Contbr. articles to jours., 1975-89. Bd. dirs. Space Coast Internat. Visitors Coun., Melbourne, 1987; judge fgn. lang. Young Floridian Award program, Melbourne, Spanish lang. Brevard County Schs., Melbourne, 1989; active on com. edn. and culture Fla.-Columbia Ptnr., Melbourne. Mem. AAUW, Tchrs. of English to Speakers of Other Langs., Gulf Area Tchrs. of English to Speakers of Other Langs. (bd. dirs. 1987, coord. promotions 1986—, Tchr. of Yr. award 1989), Fla. Fgn. Lang. Assn., Circulo Cultural Hispano (pres. 1986-88). Home: 1961 Port Malabar Blvd NE Palm Bay FL 32905 Office: Fla Inst Tech Lang Inst 150 W University Blvd Melbourne FL 32901

WYMAN, JANE (SARAH JANE FULKS), actress; b. St. Joseph, Mo., Jan. 4, 1914; d. R. D. and Emme (Reise) Fulks; m. Myron Futterman, 1937; m. Ronald Reagan, 1940 (div. 1948); children: Maureen Reagan Revell, Michael; m. Fred Karger (div.). Student, U. Mo., 1935. Formerly radio singer, chorus girl in movie musicals, actress. Chorus girl: Gold Diggers of 1937; actress: (featured roles) films My Man Godfrey, 1936, Brother Rat, 1938, Lost Weekend, 1945 (Acad. award nomination), The Yearling, 1946 (Acad. award nomination), Johnny Belinda, 1948 (Acad. award winner), Stage Fright, 1950, The Glass Menagerie, 1950, The Blue Veil, 1951 (Acad. award nomination), Magnificient Obsession, 1954 (Acad. award nomination), All That Heaven Allows, 1956, Miracle in the Rain, 1956, Holiday for Lovers, 1959, Pollyanna, 1960, Bon Voyage, 1962, How to Commit Marriage, 1969; TV shows Fireside Theater, 1955, Jane Wyman Theater, Falcon Crest, 1981—. Address: care Lorimar Prodns 3970 Overland Ave Culver City CA 90230*

WYMAN, LOTTE ANN NOVAK, civic worker; b. Vienna, Austria, Aug. 15, 1925; d. Josef and Hertha (Wallnstorfer) Novak; B.A., Barnard Coll., 1947; 1 dau., Leslie Andrea. Grey Lady, ARC, 1947-55; treas. Women's Assn. First Presbyn. Ch., Greenwich, Conn., 1963-65, chmn. mission interpretation program, 1975-77; bd. dirs. Friends of Sunny Hill Sch. for Phys. and Emotionally Handicapped Children, Greenwich, 1960-78 ; bd. dirs. YWCA, Greenwich, 1963-78, 81-87, chmn. world fellowship, 1965, mem. bldg. com., 1965-70, pres., 1967-70; bd. dirs. Drug Liberation Program of Greater Stamford, 1970-74, Community Chest, Greenwich, 1967-70, Community Forum, Greenwich, 1970—; bd. dirs. Turtle Bay Music Sch., N.Y.C., 1970-80; bd. dirs. Greenwich Arts Council, 1974-79, pres., 1976-79; bd. dirs. Neuberger Mus., SUNY, 1979-85 , M.I.T. Council for the Arts, 1980—, World Service Council YWCA, 1983—; mem. Met. Opera Assn., 1980—, adv. dir., 1982—; mem. Purchase Coll. Found., 1983—; cons. Nat. Exec. Service Corps, 1984—; elder 1st Presbyn. Ch. Greenwich, 1986-88; mem. Bd. Parks and Recreation, Greenwich, 1986—; vice chmn. bd. trustees, Bruce Mus, Greenwich, 1986—. Mem. N.Y. Zool. Soc., Ch. Women United (v.p. 1971-72), Stratton Mountain C. of C. Republican. Presbyterian. Clubs: Greenwich Country; Stratton Mountain (Vt.) Country. Home: Baldwin Farms North Greenwich CT 06830

WYNCOTT, APRIL FRANCES, health administrator; b. Berwyn, Ill., Aug. 29, 1958. BA, U. Ill., Chgo., 1980; MPH, U. Minn., 1982. Asst. adminstr. Hennepin County Mental Health Ctr., Mpls., 1980-82, mktg. mgr. vocat. svcs. program, 1982-86; asst. dir., ops. MetroCare, Chgo., 1986-87; mgr. programs Hegira Programs, Inc., Inkster, Mich., 1987—. Mem. Mich. Mental Health Assn., LWV, Mich. Masters Swimming Assn., The Athletic Congress, YMCA Masters Swimming Assn. (champion, All American), bd. dirs. U. Ill. Alumni Assn.

WYNN, PATRICIA W., accountant; b. San Diego, Aug. 9, 1947; d. Wayne O. and Agnes R. (Harkins) Wood; m. Troy L. Wynn, Dec. 24, 1968; children: Paul, Jennifer, Wayne. BBA, U. N. Tex., 1989, MBA, 1989; student, U. Colo. CPA, Tex. V.p. sales Panel Fold Doors, Inc., Miami, Fla.; exec., contr. Thor Corp., Coral Gables, Fla.; tax preparer, bookkeeper Moeller, Mayberry, Osborne & Gomolski, CPAs, Colorado Springs, Colo.; supr., gen. acct. Truswal Systems Corp., Arlington, Tex. Mem. NAFE, Assn. MBA Execs. Inc., Nat. Assn. Accts., Tex. Soc. CPAs, Mems. in Govt. and Industry Coun., Golden Key, Alpha Chi, Beta Gamma Sigma. Home: 7917 Miles Dr Watauga TX 76148 Office: Truswal Systems Corp 1101 N Great Southwest Pkwy Arlington TX 76011

WYNNE, JOAN, English language educator, painter; b. N.Y.C., July 4, 1932; d. Horace Ney and Mildred Lucile (Wynne) Broyles; m. Joseph H. Sullivan; childen: Patricia, Susan, Michael, Kathleen, Allison, Robert; m. Burton R. Pollack; m. Philip R. Carlin, Dec. 17, 1985. BA in Linguistics with honors, SUNY, Stony Brook, 1982, MA in Linguistics/TESOL. Instr. English as 2d lang. Instituto Allende, San Miguel de Allende, Mex., 1979-80; curriculum planner, instr. English as 2d lang. Interidiomas Lang. Sch., San Miguel de Allende, 1981-82; instr. English as 2d lang. advanced reading and composition SUNY, Stony Brook, 1980-83; instr. Commack (N.Y.) Pub. Schs., 1983; adj. prof. English as 2d lang. Union Coll., Elizabeth, N.J., 1984-85, Upsala Coll., Orange, N.J., 1985; adminstrv. asst., instr. English as 2d lang. Fairleigh Dickinson U., Rutherford, N.J., 1985-86; adj. prof. Hudson County Community Coll., West New York, N.J., 1986, Jersey City State Coll., 1987—. Artist, sculptor; works in collection at Newark Mus. Mem. N.J. Tchrs. English to Speakers of Other Langs., AAUW, N.J. Fedn. Bus. and Profl. Women (chmn. award scholarship com.), Ladies Assn. Llewellyn Park, Kappa Alpha Theta. Home: Llewellyn Park West Orange NJ 07052 Office: Jersey City State Coll Kennedy Blvd Jersey City NJ 07305

WYNNE, SUSAN WINCHESTER, school counselor; b. Nashville, Oct. 14, 1943; d. George William and Ollie Nell (Jennings) W. BS, Memphis State U., 1967, MEd in Counseling, 1971; postgrad., various univs. Lic. profl. counselor, Mo. Tchr. Memphis City Schs., 1967-73; counselor Webster Groves Schs., St. Louis, 1979-82; faculty, cooking instr. St. Louis Community Coll., 1983-87; counseor St. Louis City Schs., Marquette Visual Performing Arts, 1985—; adj. faculty Harris-Stowe State Coll., St. Louis, 1984, Webster U., 1988—, Maryville Coll., 1990; dir. teen latch key program YWCA, 1984-85; psychotherapist Adolescent Assocs., 1979—, pres. Met. St. Louis Middle Sch. Assn., 1969-84; counselor supr. Reproductive Health Svcs. Author (booklet) A Survival Manual For Parents of Adolescents, 1986. Pres. U. Heights Neighborhood Assn., St. Louis, 1976, bd. dirs. 1976-80. Mem. Mo. Assn. Counseling and Devel., Am. Assn. Counseling & Devel., St. Louis Psychol. Assn. (bd. dirs.), Network of Women Psychologists (bd. dirs. "Kids in the Middle", newsletter editor 1987—), St. Louis Counselor Assn. (v.p., pres.-elect 1986—). Democrat. Home: 736 Harvard Ave University City MO 63130

WYNSTRA, NANCY ANN, lawyer; b. Seattle, June 25, 1941; d. Walter S. and Gaile E. (Cogley) W. BA cum laude, Whitman Coll., 1963; LLB cum laude, Columbia U., 1966. Bar: Wash. 1966, D.C. 1969, Ill. 1979, Pa. 1984. With appellate sect., civil div. U.S. Dept. Justice, Washington, 1966-67; TV corr.-legal news Stas. WRC, NBC and Stas. WTOP, CBS, Washington, 1967-68; spl. asst. Corp. Counsel, Washington, 1968-70; dir. planning and rsch. D.C. Superior Ct., Washington, 1970-78; spl. advisor White House Spl. Action Office for Drug Abuse Prevention, Washington, 1973-74; fellow Drug Abuse Coun., 1974-75; gen. counsel Michael Reese Hosp. and Med. Ctr., Chgo., 1978-83; exec. v.p., gen. counsel Allegheny Health Svcs., Inc., Pitts., 1983—; pres., chief exec. officer Allegheny Health Svcs. Provider's Ins. Co., 1989—; adj. prof. Sch. of Urban and Pub. Affairs Carnegie Mellon U., 1985—; cons. to various drug abuse programs, 1971-78. Mem. ABA, Nat. Health Lawyers Assn. (bd. dirs. 1985—, chair publs. com. 1989—), Am. Soc. Hosp. Attys., others. Presbyterian. Contbr. articles to profl. jours. Office: Allegheny Gen Hosp 320 E North Ave Pittsburgh PA 15208

WYRICK, CHERYL RENEE, university educator; b. Dallas, July 24, 1960; d. Edward Warren Savage and Carole Auvonne Porter; m. Paul Robert Wyrick, Sept. 19, 1987. BA, UCLA, 1981; MA, Fisk U., 1983; doctoral studies, Calif. Sch. Profl. Psychology, 1990—. Mgmt. cons. So. Calif. Edison, Montebello, Calif.; rsch. cons. Pasadena Mental Health Ctr.; lectr. Calif. State U., Pomona, Calif., 1985--; pres., owner CRS Assoc., Huntington Beach, Calif., 1985--. Reviewer: Intro. to Mgmt., 1988. Recipient Clin. Traineeship NIMH, 1981-83. Mem. Assn. Black Psychologists, Am. Psychol. Assn. NAFE, Pers. and Indsl. Rels. Assn., Am. Mgmt. Assn. Office: Calif State Poly U 3801 W Temple Ave Pomona CA 91768

WYRICK, PRISCILLA BLAKENEY, microbiologist; b. Greensboro, N.C., Apr. 28, 1940; d. Carnie Lee and Prestine (Blakeney) W. BS in Med. Tech., U. N.C., Chapel Hill, 1962; MS in Bacteriology, U. N.C., 1967, PhD in Bacteriology, 1971. Technologist Clin. Microbiology Lab., N.C. Meml. Hosp., Chapel Hill, 1962-64; asst. supr. Clin. Microbiology Lab., N.C. Meml. Hosp., 1964-65, supr., 1965-66; sci. staff fellow Nat. Inst. Med. Rsch., Mill Hill, London, 1971-73; asst. prof. dept. microbiology U. N.C. Sch. Medicine, Chapel Hill, 1973-79; assoc. prof. U. N.C. Sch. Medicine, 1979-88, prof., 1988—. Grantee, NIH. Mem. Am. Acad. Microbiology, Am. Soc. Microbiology (pres. N.C. br. 1981-82, chmn. div. gen. med. microbiology 1981-82), AAAS, Soc. Infectious Diseases, Sigma Xi. Office: U NC Sch Medicine CB 7290 816 FLOB Chapel Hill NC 27599

WYSE, BONITA W(ENSINK), nutrition educator, researcher; b. Lorain, Ohio, Oct. 2, 1945; d. Norbert B. and Ruth B.(DeChant) Wensink. BS, Notre Dame of Ohio, 1967; MS, Mich. State U., 1970; PhD, Colo. State U., 1977. Registered dietitian. Clin. dietitian St. Lawrence Hosp., Lansing, Mich., 1968-69; instr. nutrition Utah State U., Logan, 1970-73, asst. prof., 1973-77, assoc. prof., dir. coordinated undergrad. med. dietetics program, 1977-81, prof., 1981—, acting dean Coll. Family Life, 1984-86, dean, 1986—; bd. dirs. Gerber Products Co., Fremont, Mich.; cons. Met. Life Found., N.Y.C., 1983-86; mem. adv. bd. Heart, Blood, Lung Inst., NIH, Bethesda, Md., 1984-87. Author: Nutritional Quality Index of Foods, 1979; contbr. articles to profl. jours. Bd. dirs. Citizens Against Phys. and Sexual Abuse, Logan, 1984. Recipient Outstanding Alumna award Dept. Food Sci. and Nutrition, Mich. State U., 1982. Mem. Am. Dietetic Assn. (council on research 1982-87, bd. dirs. 1984-87, Frances E. Fischer Meml. Nutrition Lectr., 1984), Utah Dietetic Assn. (pres. 1976-77), Am. Inst. Nutrition, Am. Home Econs. Assn. (Borden award for research 1981). Republican. Roman Catholic. Office: Utah State Univ Dean's Office Family Life Logan UT 84322-2900

WYSE, GERALDINE C., community health nurse; b. Boston, Aug. 22, 1947; d. John and Madeline (O'Brien) W. Diploma, Boston City Hosp. Sch. Nursing, 1968; BA, U. Mass., 1978. RN, Mass. Office nurse William J. Mulligan, MD, Brookline, Mass.; head nurse inpatient and gynecology depts. Boston City Hosp.; employee health nurse Dept. Health and Hosps., Boston. Contbr. monthly column to profl. publs. Mem. Mass. Pub. Health Assn., Nurses Assn. Am. Coll. Ob-Gyn., Profl. Women's Club Boston. Home: 509 E 6th St South Boston MA 02127

WYSE, LOIS, advertising executive, author; b. Cleve.; d. Roy B. Wohlgemuth and Rose (Swartz) Weisman; m. Marc Wyse (div. 1980); m. Lee Guber (dec. 1988); m. Harvey M Meyerhoff, 1990. Pres. Wyse Advt. Inc., N.Y.C., 1951—; bd. dirs. Consol. Natural Gas, Pitts., Catalyst, N.Y.C. Author 48 books. Trustee Beth Israel Med. Ctr., N.Y.C., Balt. Symphony Orch. Mem. Woman's Forum, Com. 200, PEN. Office: Wyse Advt Inc 1 Madison Ave New York NY 10010

WYSE, SHEILA RUTH, insurance company executive; b. N.Y.C., Feb. 4, 1950; d. Benjamin and Rhoda Wyse. BA, Bklyn. Coll., 1971. Underwriting asst. Beneficial Nat. Life Ins. Co., N.Y.C., 1973-75; mgr. Beneficial Nat. Life Ins. Co., 1975, asst. v.p., 1979; v.p. Nat. Benefit Life (formerly Beneficial Nat. Ins. Co.), N.Y.C., 1982; sr. v.p. Nat. Benefit Life, 1984—. Named to Acad. of Women Achievers YWCA of N.Y., 1985. Office: Nat Benefit Life Co 2 Park Ave New York NY 10016

WYSHAK, GEORGETTE TAFFY, management and motivation consultant; b. Boston, Dec. 6, 1953; d. Taffy and Georgette (Markè) W. Student, Boston Coll., 1987, Harvard U., 1988, Suffolk U., 1990. Mgr. SLAK-SHAK Co., various locations, Mass., 1970-73; distbn. mgr. You & You/Levis Stores, Medford, Mass., 1973-74; mgr., gen. mgr. Designs by Levi, Chestnut Hill, Mass., 1975; mgr. plants Growth Industries, Chestnut Hill, Mass., 1975-76; gen. mgr. Raxton Corp., Norwood, Mass., 1976-77, Geneses Salons, Boston and Newton, Mass., 1978-85; gen. mgr., edn. dir., mktg. dir. Geneses Internat., Boston, 1985-90; owner, pres. Creative Motivation Unlimited, Belmont, Mass., 1990—, Creative Hair Concepts, Boston, 1990—; founder, owner Life Enhancement Products, Inc., Belmont, 1990—; presenter seminars, lectr. in field. Contbr. articles on motivation and mgmt. to various publs. Bd. dirs. Young People's Assn., Boston, 1971-75. Mem. NAFE, Am. Mgmt. Assn. (bd. dirs. Boston chpt. 1987-88, 89), Boston C. of C., Nat. Cosmetology Assn., Internat. Franchise Assn., The Pres. Club Sandler Sales Inst. Syrian Orthodox. Home: 57 Trapelo Rd Belmont MA 02178 Office: Geneses Internat Faneiul Hall Market Pl 150 S Market St Boston MA 02109

WYSS, DIANNE DUNLOP, coal fuel company executive; b. Kingsport, Tenn., May 1, 1950; d. Donald D. and Maxine (Hooker) Dunlop; m. John Benedict Wyss, Aug. 12, 1978; children: John Christian, Kirsten Dunlop. BS in Phys. Therapy, U. Okla., 1973; MBA in Finance, Va. Poly. and State U., 1980. Chief fin. and adminstrv. officer Slurrytech Inc., Miami, Fla., 1980-83; pres. Fuels Mgmt. subs. Slurrytech Inc., Miami, Fla., 1982-83; v.p. Fuels Mgmt. Inc., Miami, 1983—; natural resources advisor Nat. Congress Am. Indians. Mem. fair share fundraising com. Sidwell Friends Sch., Washington, 1986-87; bd. dirs. Native Am. Model Resource Edn. Program. Mem. Vis. Nurse Assn. (profl. adv. com. 1979—), D.C. LWV (treas. 1980-81, v.p. 1982-83, 86-87). Democrat. Mem. Soc. Friends. Club: Washington Coal. Office: FMI/Slurrytech 7027 SW 148 Terr Miami FL 33158

WYSS, NORMA ROSE TOPPING, educator, writer; b. Wautoma, Wis., Jan. 7, 1919; d. Eugene Leonard Topping and Sylvia Maude (Attoe-Dumond) Topping Schubert; m. Werner Oscar Wyss; children: Werner Oscar II, Christine Camille (dec.). Diploma, 1939; BA in Elem. Edn., Fla. State U., 1949, MS, 1960; postgrad., U. Md., 1964; PhD, Walden U., 1986. Cert. employment counselor and supr. Tchr. Hoeft Sch., Berlin, Wis., 1939-40, Escambia County Sch. Bd., Pensacola, Fla., 1946-66; area I counselor supr. Fla. State Dept. of Labor, Pensacola, 1966-79; writer Vantage Press, N.Y.C., 1986-90; field interviewer Arbitron, Laurel, Md., 1985-88. Author: Core Counseling: The Christian Faith and the Helping Relationship: A Paradigm of Social Change, 1990. Mem. Nat. Assn. Ret. Tchrs., Escambia educators (life), Fla. Ret. Educators (life), DAR (treas. Pensacola chpt. 1988-90), Alpha Delta Kappa (1st pres. Fla. Alpha chpt.). Republican. Lutheran. Office: PO Box 3971 Pensacola FL 32516-3971

WYSZOMIRSKI, MARGARET JANE, political science educator; b. Amsterdam, N.Y., Mar. 2, 1949; d. Frank Gregory and Dorothea (Dybas) W. BA, Harpur Coll., Binghamton, N.Y., 1970; MA, SUNY, Binghamton, 1973; PhD, Cornell U., 1979. Instr. Dickinson Coll., Carlisle, Pa., 1976-78; asst. prof. Rutgers U., New Brunswick, N.J., 1978-84; adj. assoc. prof. Cornell in Washington Program, 1984-87; dir. grad. pub. policy program Georgetown U., Washington, 1985-88; mem. sr. faculty Fed. Exec. Inst., U.S. Office Pers. Mgmt., Washington, 1988—; guest scholar Brookings Instn., Washington, 1988; steering com. Presidency Rsch. Group, 1981-86, 89—; program co-chmn. Conf. on Social Theory, Politics and Arts, 1983-84. Book rev. editor: Governance Jour., 1987—; (with others) Art, Ideology and Politics, 1985, Congress and the Arts, 1987, The Cost of Culture, 1989, Executive Leadership and Executive Establishment, 1990; contbr. articles to profl. jours. Staff dir. Ind. Commn. on Nat. Endowment of Arts, 1990. Kellogg Found. grantee, 1987—, Nat. Endowment for Arts fellow, 1979. Mem. Am. Polit. Sci. Assn., Am. Coun. for Arts (rsch. adv. com. 1985—), Ctr. for Study of Presidency. Roman Catholic. Home: 1545 18th St NW Apt 620 Washington DC 20036 Office: Fed Exec Inst DC US Office Pers Mgmt PO Box 164 Washington DC 20044

YACH, CARLA JEAN, nursing home administrator, nurse; b. Kansas City, Mo., Dec. 2, 1954; d. Carl Eugene and Audrey Marceal (Summers) Y. Student, Cen. Mo. State U., 1974-78, Longview Community Coll., Kansas City, 1978-81, Longview Community Coll., Kansas City, 1983-86. Nurse Lakeside Hosp., Kansas City, 1973-76; asst. dir. nursing dept. Arkhaven Nursing Home, Kansas City, 1976-78; office and sales mgr. Jobst Inst., Kansas City, 1978-80; charge nurse St. Luke's Hosp., Kansas City, 1980-83; evening supr. Lee Summitt Care Ctr., Kansas City, 1983-84; adminstr Chippendale Nursing Home, Kansas City, 1984-85, dir. nursing to adminstr., 1985-86; adminstr. Colonial Nursing Home, Kansas City, 1986-87; corp. office ops. mgr. Comfort Care Inns, Kansas City, 1987-88; adminstr. Tutera Group/Oakwood Manor Nursing Home, Kansas City, 1988—; mem. adv. bd. Kansas City Med. Guide mag., 1988—, Home Health Depot and Drug Dept., Kansas City, 1989—. Lakeside Hosp. scholar, 1974. Mem. Mo. Health CAre Assn. (dist. 1 pres. 1989—, exhibit conv. chmn. 1989, edn. com. 1987—, Cert. of Recognition 1987, 88, Dist. 1 mem. of the yrf. 1988), Am. Health Care Assn., South Kansas City C. of C., Theta Alpha Phi. Democrat. Roman Catholic. Home: 109 W 132d St Kansas City MO 64145 Office: Oakwood Manor 11515 Troost Ave Kansas City MO 64131

YACOBIAN, SONIA SIMONE, metals company executive; b. Cairo, Egypt, Feb. 13, 1943; came to U.S., 1966, naturalized, 1971; d. Simon and Lucy (Guendimian) Samsonian; divorced; children: Tatiana, Richard. BS, Lycee of Cairo, 1962; BBA, U. Cairo, Egypt, 1965; student Pace U., 1978-80. Asst. mgr. new accounts Lincoln Savs. & Loan, Los Angeles, 1973-77; sr. acct. U.S. Industries, N.Y.C., 1977-81; dep. mgr. French C. of C., N.Y.C., 1981-82; mgr. mktg. Samancor Metals, New Rochelle, N.Y., 1982-84; pres. NIDDAM Inc., Dix Hills, N.Y., 1984—. Mem. Assn. Profl. Women in Metal. Republican. Orthodox Christian. Home: 37 Wintergreen Dr Dix Hills Long Island NY 11746 Office: NIDDAM Inc PO Box 877 Melville NY 11747

YACONETTI, DIANNE MARY, business executive; b. Chgo., Dec. 16, 1946; d. Anthony and Dora Marie (Mazzoni) Pontillo. Paralegal student, Mallinckrodt Coll., 1984-85. Various positions Brunswick Corp., Skokie, Ill., 1964-80, mgr. legal support services, 1980-83, asst. sec., 1984-86, corp. sec., 1986-88, v.p. adminstrn., corp. sec., 1988—. Mem. Am. Soc. Corp. Secs. Roman Catholic. Office: Brunswick Corp One Brunswick Plaza Skokie IL 60077

YACOVONE, ELLEN ELAINE, banker; b. Ithaca, N.Y., Aug. 4, 1951; d. Wilfred Elliott and Charlotte Frances (Fox) Drew; m. Richard Daniel Yacovone, June 2, 1979; stepchildren: Christopher Daniel, Kimberly Marie. Student Broome Community Coll., 1973-80; cert. Inst. Fin. Edn., Chgo., 1974. Sec. to exec. v.p. Ithaca Savs., N.Y., summer 1968; mortgage clk. Citizens Savs. Bank, 1968-69; with Lincoln Bank, Van Nuys, Calif., 1970-71; asst. bookkeeper Henry's Jewelers, Binghamton, N.Y., 1971-74; teller, br. supt., br. mgr. First Fed. Savs., Binghamton, N.Y., 1974-82, v.p., cen. regional sales mgr., 1982-86, dist. sales mgr., 1986-88; br. mgr. Great Western Bank, Pensacola, Fla., 1988-89, v.p., regional mgr. south region San Diego, 1989—. Mem. Gov.'s Commn. on Domestic Violence, Albany, N.Y., 1983-87; bd. dirs. S.O.S. Shelter, Inc., Endicott, N.Y., 1979-88, pres., 1982-83, treas., 1985-86; vol. United Way of Broome County, Binghamton, 1976-88, Sta. WSKG Pub. TV, Conklin, N.Y., 1974-88; mem. Found. State U. Ctr. at Binghamton. Named Woman of Achievement, Broome County Status of Women Coun., 1981. Mem. Triple Cities Bus. and Profl. Women (pres. 1979-81, young careerist award 1977), Sales and Mktg. Execs., Broome County C. of C., Broome County Bankers Assn. (bd. dirs. 1979-88, pres. 1983-84), Inst. Fin. Edn. (bd. dirs. 1976-88, pres. 1984-85, winner N.Y. State speech contest 1984). Republican. Methodist. Avocations: exercise, camping, wood working, gardening, needlecrafts. Home: 602 Myra Ave Chula Vista CA 92010 Office: Great Western Bank 707 Broadway Ste 1400 San Diego CA 92101

YACURA, SANDRA LEIGH, lobbyist; b. Elizabeth, Pa., Dec. 11, 1964; d. John M. and Sherry (Shelton) Y. BS in Polit. Sci., Ariz. State U., 1986; AA in Journalism, Community Coll. Allegheny Co., West Mifflin, Pa., 1984. Legis. affairs asst. to Senator Arlen Specter, U.S. Senate, Washington, 1985; legis. affairs asst. to Congressman and Senator John McCain Mesa, Ariz., 1986; staff asst. to Senator John Heinz U.S. Senate, Washington, 1987; legis. asst. Sporting Goods Mfrs. Assn., Washington, 1988—. Asst. editor Washington Update newsletter, 1988-89. Republican. Office: Sporting Goods Mfg Assn 1625 K St NW Ste 900 Washington DC 10006

YAEGER, BILLIE PATRICIA, advertising sales executive; b. Boston, Mar. 17, 1949; d. Harold Stern and Marie Frances (Levenson) Y. Student, Logos Bible Coll. Office mgr., NE rep. Ticketron, Inc., Boston, 1968-73; owner, mgr. Performance King, Natick, Mass., 1973-74, House of Portraits, Lakeland, Fla., 1974-75; employment counselor Snelling & Snelling, Lakeland, 1975-77; advt. sales account exec. The Ledger/N.Y. Times, Lakeland, 1977—. Commendation award Fla. Dept. Law Enforcement, 1986. Mem. Nat. Assn. Female Execs. Republican. Avocations: photography, writing, waterskiing.

YAGER, ANN MARIE, graphic design and marketing company executive; b. Shirley, Mass., Sept. 9, 1945; d. John William and Marie Agnes (Houde) Y. Student, U. Md., 1963, 64, Golden Gate U., 1986, 89. Lic. real estate broker. Corp. sec., office adminstr. Capital Engring., Honolulu, 1965-67; real estate salesman Island Homes, Honolulu, 1967-69; corp. treas., gen. mgr. Sandy's Ltd., Honolulu, 1969-75; account coord. Corp. Graphics, San Francisco, 1975-77; fin. dir. Greenpeace, San Francisco, 1977-79; account exec. Way Out West, San Francisco, 1979-86; owner Yager & Yager, San Francisco, 1986—; cons. Jr. Achievement, San Francisco, 1989. Pres. Dist. Area Reps., Honolulu, 1967-69. Recipient award Peninsula Women in Advt., Palo Alto, Calif., 1981. Mem. San Francisco Art Dirs., San Francisco Advt. Club, San Francisco Tennis Club. Home: 254 Cleveland Ave Mill Valley CA 94941 Office: Yager & Yager 480 Green St San Francisco CA 94133

YAKEL, LOUELLA MARIE, early childhood educator/program coordinator; b. Vandalia, Ill., Oct. 15, 1956; d. Charles and Marilyn R. (Miller) Y. BA in Sociology, Greenville Coll., 1974-78; MS in Edn., Southern Ill. U., Edwardsville, Ill., 1989. Aide, admissions Greenville (Ill.) Coll., 1976-78; assoc. dir. Kiddie Kompany, Inc., Vandalia, Ill., 1979-81; bookkeeper Gene's Red Fox, Brownstown, Ill., 1980-87; sec. Fayette Co. Coop. Ext., Vandalia, Ill., 1981-82; bookkeeper, sec., receptionist Mark Ervin, D.D.D., Vandalia, Ill., 1982-84; self-employed C & M Yakel Bookkeeping Service, Ill., 1978-89; office mgr. Michael K. Fulton, D.D.S., Vandalia, Ill., 1984-89; program coord. Birth-To-Three Svcs., Vandalia, Ill., 1989—; mem. Brownstown Schs. Occupation Edn. Adv. Com., Brownstown, Ill, 1974-75, Vandalia Schs. Vocational Edn. Adv. Com., 1988. Adult leader Vandalia Vikings 4-H Club, 1981-82, mem. 1983-87, pres. TRS-80 Users Group of Mid-Cent., Effingham, Ill., 1984-85. Mem. TAWL Whole Language Group, Kappa Delta Pi, Phi Kappa Phi.

YAKER, LYNDA E., marketing executive, data processor; b. El Paso, Tex., June 12, 1945; d. Hyman Louis and Sophie (Moscow) Y. BS, U. Houston, 1966. Engr. TRW Systems Group-NASA, Houston, 1966-69; systems engr. IBM, El Paso, 1969-72; market support rep. IBM, L.A., 1972-74; mgr. systems engring. IBM, Dallas, 1974-76, mgr. support ctr., 1976-77; mktg. mgr. IBM, St. Louis, 1977-80; adminstr. IBM, Dallas, 1980-83; br. market support mgr. IBM, Balt., 1983—. Author, editor: Houston Operations Predicter Estimator, 1968. Mem. Intrepid Investment Club (sr. fin. officer 1987—). Home: 1055 Trails End Pasadena MD 21122

YAKEY, PAULA SUE, banking executive; b. Ocala, Fla., Dec. 23, 1953; d. JOhn David and Dorothy Jennette (Fore) Y.; divorced, Feb. 1983; children: Weyman Herbert Maxey III, Heather Melinda Maxey. Assoc. in Bus., Dekalb Community Coll., Clarkston, Ga., 1983; cert. pvt. investigator, Dekalb Tech., Clarkston, 1989. With C&S Nat. Bank, Tucker, Ga., 1972-81; with The Abby & Mansion restaurant, Atlanta, 1981-83, Bromberg & Cohen CPAs, Atlanta, 1983-85, Heritage Bank, Atlanta, 1985-87, Metro Brokers, Tucker, 1987-89; fin. sales exec. Home Fed. Savs. Bank, Sandy Springs, Ga., 1989—; cons. Home Fed./Forgery Recovery, Sandy Springs, 1989—. Mem. NAFE, Sandy Springs C. of C., Sandy Springs Optimist Club. Baptist. Home: 5164 LaVista Rd Tucker GA 30084 Office: Home Fed Savs Bank 6010 Sandy Springs Circle Atlanta GA 30324

YAKIMOWSKI-ZUMWALT, JOSEPHINE ROSE, dance leader; b. Weymouth, Mass., June 13, 1953; d. Walter Stanley and Genevieve Helena (Ignatiwicz) Y.; m. Dale Lee Zumwalt, Aug. 26, 1989. BS, Boston State U., 1978. Adminstrv. asst. to sr. corp. v.p. United Liquors, West Roxbury, Mass., 1977-83; salesperson Fed. Distillers, Cambridge, Mass., 1983-84; receptionist Needham (Mass.) Chiropractic Assoc., 1988-89; with import dept. Carolina Wine, West Roxbury, 1989-90; adminstrv. asst. Vintage Am., 1990—; round dance leader Dedham, Mass., 1974—. Chmn. adv. bd. Square Dance Found. New Eng., Weymouth, 1983-85. Mem. VFW, ROUNDLAB (classics chmn. 1986-90), Universal Round Dance Coun., Southeastern Mass. Coordinating Assn. (sec. 1984-86, treas. 1986-90), Am. Legion Auxiliary. Democrat. Roman Catholic. Home: 177 Washington St Dedham MA 02026

YALKUT, ARLEN SPENCER, lawyer; b. N.Y.C., Apr. 10, 1945; d. Benjamin and Mollie Emma (Rowe) Yalkut; children: Michael, Brent. BS in Chemistry, CCNY, 1967; JD, NYU, 1971, LLM in Criminology, 1972. Assoc. Lenefsky, Gallina, Mass, Berne & Hoffman, Esqs., N.Y.C., 1971-72; law asst. N.Y.C. Criminal Ct., 1972-73; law sec. to presiding judge U.S. Ct. Claims, N.Y.C., 1973-75; pvt. practice N.Y.C., 1975-76, 78-87, White Plains, N.Y., 1987—; ptnr. Bleifer & Yalkut, P.C., N.Y.C., 1976-78. V.p. Thomas Jefferson Dem. Club, N.Y.C., 1966-68; pres. Eleanor Roosevelt Dem. Club, N.Y.C., 1968-71; v.p. Young Israel Spring Valley, N.Y., 1980—. Criminal law edn. and rsch. fellow Ford Found., 1971. Mem. N.Y. State Bar Assn., Bronx Bar Assn. Office: 175 Main St White Plains NY 10601

YALMAN, ANN, lawyer; b. Boston, June 9, 1948; d. Richard George and Joan (Osterman) Y. BA, Antioch Coll., 1970; JD, NYU, 1973. Trial atty. Fla. Rural Legal Svcs., Immokalee, Fla., 1973-74; staff atty. EEO, Atlanta, 1974-76; pvt. practice Santa Fe, N.Mex., 1976—; part time U.S. Magistrate, N.Mex., 1988—. Commr. Met. Water Bd., Santa Fe, 1986-88. Mem. N.Mex. Bar Assn. (commr. Santa Fe chpt. 1983-86). Home: 441 Calle La Paz Santa Fe NM 87501 Office: 304 Catron St Santa Fe NM 87501

YALOW, ROSALYN SUSSMAN, medical physicist; b. N.Y.C., July 19, 1921; d. Simon and Clara (Zipper) Sussman; m. A. Aaron Yalow, June 6, 1943; children: Benjamin, Elanna. A.B., Hunter Coll., 1941; M.S., U. Ill., Urbana, 1942, Ph.D., 1945; D.Sc. (hon.), U. Ill., Chgo., 1974, Phila. Coll. Pharmacy and Sci., 1976, N.Y. Med. Coll., 1976, Med. Coll. Wis., Milw., 1977, Yeshiva U., 1977, Southampton (N.Y.) Coll., 1978, Bucknell U., 1978, Princeton U., 1978, Jersey City State Coll., 1979, Med. Coll. Pa., 1979, Manhattan Coll., 1979, U. Vt., 1980, U. Hartford, 1980, Rutgers U., 1980, Rensselaer Poly. Inst., 1980, Colgate U., 1981, U. So. Calif., 1981, Clarkson Coll., 1982, U. Miami, 1983, Washington U., St. Louis, 1983, Adelphi U., 1983, U. Alta. (Can.), 1983, Columbia U., 1984, SUNY, 1984, Tel Aviv U., 1985, Claremont (Calif.) U., 1986, Mills Coll., Oakland, Calif., 1986, Cedar Crest Coll., Allentown, Pa., 1988, Drew U., Madison, N.J., 1988, Lehigh U., 1988; L.H.D. (hon.), Hunter Coll., 1978; DSc. (hon.), San Francisco State U., 1989, Technion-Israel Inst. Tech., Haifa, 1989; L.H.D. (hon.), Sacred Heart U., Conn., 1978, St. Michael's Coll., Winooski Park, Vt., 1979, Johns Hopkins U., 1979, Coll. St. Rose, 1988, Spertus Coll. Judaica, Chgo., 1988; D. honoris causa, U. Rosario, Argentina, 1980, U. Ghent, Belgium, 1984; D. Humanities and Letters (hon.), Columbia U., 1984; D.Phil. honoris causa, Bar-Ilan U., Israel, 1987; LHD (hon.), Coll. of St. Rose, Albany, N.Y., 1988. Diplomate: Am. Bd. Scis. Lectr., asst. prof. physics Hunter Coll., 1946-50; physicist, asst. chief radioisotope service VA Hosp., Bronx, N.Y., 1950-70, chief nuclear medicine, 1970-80, acting chief radioisotope service, 1968-70; research prof. Mt. Sinai Sch. Medicine, CUNY, 1968-74, Disting. Service prof., 1974-79, Solomon A. Berson Disting. prof.-at-large, 1986—; Disting. prof.-at-large Albert Einstein Coll. Medicine, Yeshiva U., 1979-85, prof. emeritus, 1986—; chmn. dept. clin. scis. Montefiore Med. Ctr., Bronx, 1980-85; cons. Lenox Hill Hosp., N.Y.C., 1956-62, WHO, Bombay, 1978; sec. U.S. Nat. Com. on Med. Physics, 1963-67; mem. nat. com. Radiation Protection, Subcom. 13, 1957; mem. Pres.'s Study Group on Careers for Women, 1966-72; sr. med. investigator VA, 1972—; dir. Solomon A. Berson Research Lab., VA Hosp., Bronx, N.Y., 1973—. Co-editor: Hormone and Metabolic Research, 1973-79; editorial adv. council: Acta Diabetologica Latina, 1975-77, Ency. Universalis, 1978—; editorial bd.: Mt. Sinai Jour. Medicine, 1976-79, Diabetes, 1976, Endocrinology, 1967-72; contbr. numerous articles to profl. jours. Bd. dirs. N.Y. Diabetes Assn., 1974. Recipient VA William S. Middleton Med. Research award, 1960; Eli Lilly award Am. Diabetes Assn., 1961; Van Slyke award N.Y. met. sect. Am. Assn. Clin. Chemists, 1968; award A.C.P., 1971; Dickson prize U. Pitts., 1971; Howard Taylor Ricketts award U. Chgo., 1971; Gairdner Found. Internat. award, 1971; Commemorative medallion Am. Diabetes Assn., 1972; Bernstein award Med. Soc. State N.Y., 1974; Boehringer-Mannheim Corp. award Am. Assn. Clin. Chemists, 1975; Sci. Achievement award AMA, 1975; Exceptional Service award VA, 1975; A. Cressy Morrison award N.Y. Acad. Scis., 1975; sustaining membership award Assn. Mil. Surgeons, 1975; Distinguished Achievement award Modern Medicine, 1976; Albert Lasker Basic Med. Research award, 1976; La Madonnina Internat. prize Milan, 1977; Golden Plate award Am. Acad. Achievement, 1977; Nobel prize for physiology medicine, 1977; citation of esteem St. John's U., 1979; G. von Hevesy medal, 1978; Rosalyn S. Yalow Research and Devel. award established Am. Diabetes Assn., 1978; Banting medal, 1978; Torch of Learning award Am. Friends Hebrew U., 1978; Virchow gold medal Virchow-Pirquet Med. Soc., 1978; Gratum Genus Humanum gold medal World Fedn. Nuclear Medicine or Biology, 1978; Jacobi medallion Asso. Alumni Mt. Sinai Sch. Medicine, 1978; Jubilee medal Coll. of New Rochelle, 1978; VA Exceptional Service award, 1978; Fed. Woman's award, 1961; Harvey lectr., 1966; Am. Gastroenterol. Assn. Meml. lectr., 1972; Joslin lectr. New Eng. Diabetes Assn., 1972; Franklin I. Harris Meml. lectr., 1973; 1st Hagedorn Meml. lectr. Acta Endocrinologica Congress, 1973; Sarasota Med. award for achievement and excellence, 1979; gold medal Phi Lambda Kappa, 1980; Achievement in Life award Ency. Brit., 1980; Theobald Smith award, 1982; Pres.'s Cabinet award U. Detroit, 1982; John and Samuel Bard award in medicine and sci. Bard Coll., 1982; Disting. Research award Dallas Assn. Retarded Citizens, 1982, Nat. Medal Sci., 1988; Abram L. Sachar Silver Medallion Brandeis U., Waltham, Mass., 1989, Disting. Scientist of Yr. award ARCS, N.Y.C., 1989, Golden Scroll award The Jewish Advocate, Boston, 1989, spl. award Clin. Ligand Assay Soc., Washington, 1988, numerous others. Fellow N.Y. Acad. Scis. (chmn. biophysics div. 1964-65), Am. Coll. Radiology (asso. in physics), Clin. Soc. N.Y. Diabetes Assn.; mem. Nat. Acad. Scis., Am. Acad. Arts and Scis., Am. Phys. Soc., Radiation Research Soc., Am. Assn. Physicists in Medicine, Biophys. Soc., Soc. Nuclear Medicine, Endocrine Soc. (Koch award 1972, pres. 1978), Am. Physiol. Soc., (hon.) Harvey Soc., (hon.) Med. Assn. Argentina, (hon.) Diabetes Soc. Argentina, (hon.) Am. Coll. Nuclear Physicians, (hon.) The N.Y. Acad. Medicine, (hon.) Am. Gastroent. Assn., (hon.) N.Y. Roentgen Soc., (hon.) Soc. Nuclear Medicine, Phi Beta Kappa, Sigma Xi, Sigma Pi Sigma, Pi Mu Epsilon, Sigma Delta Epsilon. Office: VA Med Ctr 130 W Kingsbridge Rd Bronx NY 10468

YAMADA, AYAKO, bank officer; b. Kobe, Japan, Sept. 18, 1963; came to U.S., 1989; d. Yoshitaka and Nakako (Kakio) Yamada. LLB, Waseda U., Tokyo, 1986. With Nippon Credit Bank Ltd., Tokyo, 1986-89; assoc. in corp. fin. Nippon Credit Bank Ltd., N.Y.C., 1989—. Office: Nippon Credit Bank Ltd 245 Park Ave 30th Fl New York NY 10167

YAMAKOSHI, LOIS, mathematics educator; b. Reedley, Calif., May 9, 1954; d. Frank Kazuo and Helen Shigeko (Kuwada) Y. BS, Pepperdine U., 1976; MA, Calif. State U., Northridge, 1980; postgrad., Calif. State U., Hayward, 1983-88, UCLA, 1977-81. Math. tchr. Malibu Park Jr. High Sch., Malibu, Calif., 1976-80, Southgate Lower Sch., London, 1980; math. instr. Los Medanos Coll., Pittsburg, Calif., 1981—; tax preparation instr. H&R Block Co., Walnut Creek, Calif., 1984; speaker Calif. Gt. Tchrs. Seminar, 1989; faculty designee for tutoring, 1988, 89; student com. mem. acad. senate Calif. Community Colls.; reader for selection of joint projects of English and maths., 1989; curriculum cons. Antioch High Sch., 1989. Contbr. articles to profl. pubs. Pres. Acad. Senate Los Medanos Coll., student rep.; project dir. Calif. Chancellor's Office, Sacramento, 1988. Recipient Most Valuable Player award, 1988; Elks Nat. Found. scholar, 1972. Mem. Nat. Coun. Tchrs. Math. (presider 1985), Math. Assn. Am., Calif. Math. Coun. Community Colls. (rep. at large 1989-91), United Faculty, Alameda Contra Costa County Math. Educators (sec. 1982—), Kappa Delta Pi, Kappa Kappa. Democrat. Buddhist. Club: Asians on Campus (Pittsburg). Office: Los Medanos Coll 2700 E Leland Rd Box 107 Pittsburg CA 94565

YAMANI, ELAINE REIKO, computer-peripheral company executive; b. Ogden, Utah, Apr. 2, 1945; d. Joe and Chieko (Kato) Yamani; m. Victor G. Sugihara, Aug. 10, 1970 (div. June 1973); 1 dau., Jo Ann Renae. B.S. in English and Psychology, Weber State U., 1965, A.A., 1967; M in Human Resource Mgmt., U. Utah, 1975-79. Personnel generalist Weber State U., Odgen, Utah, 1973-78; personnel specialist Cutter Lab., Ogden, 1978-81; human resource mgr. Iomega, Ogden, 1981-83, compensation and benefits mgr., 1983-85; dir. human resources Cericor Inc., 1983; personnel mgr., Hewlett-Packard, 1983—. Mem. Utah Personnel Assn. (pres. 1988), No. Utah Personnel Assn. (pres. 1980-81).

YAMASHIRO, JANE MIEKO, college administrator; b. Volcano, Hawaii, Mar. 29, 1939; d. Jay Jiro and Misayo (Goya) Y.; divorced; children: Michael, Kenneth Bates. BA, U. Wash., 1960; MA, U. Alaska, 1973; postgrad, U. Hawaii, 1989—. Cert. sch. adminstr. Dir. North Pacific Rim, Anchorage, Alaska, 1972-74; sr. assoc. Ctr. Equality of Opportunity in Schooling, Anchorage, 1974-78; research assoc. U. Alaska Inst. Social and Econ. Research, Anchorage, 1978-80; dir. Upward Bound U. Hawaii, Hilo, 1980-82; coordinator programs U. Hawaii Ctr. Continuing Edn. and Community Service, Hilo, 1982-86; program analyst U. Hawaii Community Coll., Honolulu, 1986-88, coord. community affairs and spl. project, 1988-90; asst. to dean Coll. Tropical Agr. and Human Resources, Honolulu, 1990—; participant Am. Assn. Women of Community and Jr. Colls. leadership program. Sec., organizer Hawaii Agrl. Leadership Found., Honolulu, 1980—; commr. Equal Rights Commn., Anchorage, 1976-80; chmn. Commn. on Status of Women, Anchorage, 1977-80, State del. Internat. Women's Yr., 1975; facilitator Kona Coffee Council, Kealakekua, Hawaii, 1984-85; mem. Family Peace Ctr., 1990. Recipient Nat. Alumni award 4-H Clubs, 1985. Mem. Big Island Ocean Recreation Tourism Assn. (organizer, sec. 1982-84). Democrat. Buddhist. Club: Hui Laulima (Honolulu). Home: 1455 Hunakai St Apt #2 Honolulu HI 96816

YAMASHITA, TOYOKO S., genetic epidemiologist, educator, consultant; b. Nara, Japan, Feb. 1, 1944; came to U.S., 1963; d. Jinshin Mori and Toshiko Yamashita. BS, U. Oreg., 1970; MS, U Hawaii, 1971, PhD, 1976. Rsch. specialist U. Hawaii, Honolulu, 1971-72, grad. rsch. asst., 1972-76; biostatisticlan Loyola U. Med. Ctr., Chgo., 1976-78; asst. prof. epidemiology and biodstats. Case Western Res. U., Cleve., 1979-89, asst. prof. pediatrics, 1982-89, assoc. prof. pediatrics, epidemiology and biostats., 1989—; cons. in field; dir. dept. pediatrics ctr. for med. informatics and stats. Rainbow Babies and Children's Hosp., Cleve., 1984—; stats. genetist Case Western Res. U., 1974—. Author: Immunology of HLA, 1988; contbr. articles to profl. jours. Grantee Diabetic Assn. Greater Cleve., 1980, 83, Case Western Res. U., 1982, NIH Arthritis Ctr., 1986-87; Case Western Res. U. fellow, 1978-79. Mem. AAAS, Am. Assn. Human Genetics, The Biometric Soc., Am. Stats. Assn., Soc. Clin. Data Mgmt. Systems, Am. Assn. Med. System and Informatics, Am. Assn. for Artificial Intelligence, Biometric Soc. Home: 19101 Aken Blvd Cleveland OH 44122 Office: Case Western Reserve Univ Dept Pediatrics 2101 Adelbert Rd Cleveland OH 44106

YANAGITANI, ELIZABETH, optometrist; b. Ogden, Utah, Nov. 24, 1953; d. Katsuyoshi and Yaeko (Watanabe) Y. AS, Weber State Coll., Ogden, Utah, 1974; BA magna cum laude, U. Utah, 1976; OD, Pacific U., Forest Grove, Oreg., 1980. Staff optometrist Gen. Med., San Diego, 1984-89, San Ysidro Health Ctr., Calif., 1985-87, Logan Heights Family Health Ctr., San Diego, 1989—; pvt. practice optometry Chula Vista, Calif., 1982—; asst. instr. Am. Bus. Coll., San Diego, 1982. Acad. scholar Weber State Coll., 1972, 73, scholar U. Utah, 1975; externship Tripler AMC/Schofield Barracks, Hawaii, 1979; recipient Henry M. Cohn award, Pacific U., 1980, Gates Meml. award, 1980. Mem. San Diego County Optometric Soc. (v.p. 1985),

Calif. Optometric Soc. (del. to leadership conf. 1985), Achievement Through Vision/COVO (pres. 1990), Beta Sigma Kappa, Beta Kappa Phi.

YANDELL, DONNETTA KAY, construction executive; b. Ft. Smith, Ark., Sept. 14, 1953; d. Merrill Harvey and Betty Louise (Hutson) Y.; m. Vernon Gober Davis Jr., Dec. 2, 1972 (div. Apr. 1975). Student, Memphis State U., 1971-72, 75-77, West Ark. Community Coll., Ft. Smith, 1984. Mgr./buyer Just Jeans, Memphis, 1973-75; night mgr., cook Fabian's Restaurant, Memphis, 1976-77; photographer Auto Trader, Miami, Fla., 1977-78; carpenter apprentice Carpenters Local Union, Nashville, 1978-79, Memphis, 1979-81; carpenter Fixture and Drywall Co. of Okla., Tulsa, 1984-86; carpenter apprentice Okla. Fixture Co., Tulsa, 1981-82, carpenter, 1982-84, field constrn. supt., 1986—. Mem. Carpenters Local Union #690. Democrat. Baptist.

YANDOW, VALERY WORTH, psychiatrist, educator; b. Plainfield, N.J., May 5, 1930; d. Robert Carlton and Edith (Sidon) Worth; separated; children: Tyler, Gwynn, Chris, Karen, Timothy. BA, U. Vt., 1951, MD, 1956. Asst. unit chief N.Y. Hosp. Westchester Div., White Plains, N.Y., 1979-83; asst. prof. psychiatry Cornell U. Med. Coll., N.Y.C., 1981-83; asst. prof. clin. psychiatry Dartmouth Med. Sch., Hanover, N.H., 1983—; dir. Div. of Addictions Brattleboro (Vt.) Retreat, 1983—; faculty mem. Nat. Coun. on Alcoholism, White Plains, 1979; mem. Vt. State Bd. of Med. Practice, 1989—. Contbr. articles to profl. jours. Sec. Community Chorus, Brattleboro, 1988—; mem. spl. events com. Brattleboro Music Ctr., 1987—. Fellow Am. Psychia. Assn., mem. Am. Soc. of Addiction Medicine, AMA, Am. Med. Womens Assn. Office: Brattleboro Retreat 75 Linden St Box 803 Brattleboro VT 05301

YANG, VIVIAN, ophthalmologist, educator; b. N.Y.C., May 25, 1937; d. Forman M. and Phoebe (Pong) Chen; m. Stephen H. Yang, Oct. 28, 1961; children: Preston Harvey, Kenneth Edward. BA cum laude, NYU, 1958, MD, 1962. Diplomate Am. Bd. Ophthalmology. Intern Kings County Hosp. Med. Ctr., Bklyn., 1962-63; resident in ophthalmology N.Y. Med. Coll.-Met. Hosp., N.Y.C., 1963-66; ophthalmologist Hunterdon Med. Ctr., Flemington, N.J., 1966-67; pvt. practice, East Brunswick, N.J., 1967—; instr. ophthmology Robert Wood Johnson Univ. Hosp., U. Med. and Dentistry N.J., New Brunswick, 1973—. Fellow ACS; mem. Med. Soc. N.J., Middlesex County Med. Soc., N.J. Acad. Ophthalmolgoy, Phi Beta Kappa. Office: Colonial Oaks Med Arts Ctr C-5 Cornwall Ct East Brunswick NJ 08816

YANOK, LINDA NAYLOR, sales professional; b. Euclid, Ohio, Feb. 5, 1953; d. Doulgas Falconer and Eleanor Ruth (Pavlik) Naylor; m. Joseph Edward Yanok Sr., Aug. 11, 1979; children: Joseph Edward Jr., Allyson Naylor, Emily Anna. BS in Chem. Biology, U. Pitts., 1976; AD in Allied Health, Jefferson Tech. Coll., 1978. Office and sales mgr. Barium and Chems., Inc., Steubenville, Ohio, 1970—; lab. asst., sec. Presbyn. Hosp., Pitts., summer 1976; med. lab. technologist Wheeling (W.Va.) Hosp., 1978-79; med. technologist, asst. supr. St. John Med. Ctr., Steubenville, Ohio, part-time, 1979—; bd. dirs. Jefferson County Children Svcs., Steubenville. Mem., tchr. christian edn. St. Paul's Episcopal, Steubenville, 1981—; mem., poll worker Steubenville Reps., 1988—; mem. Friends of ALIVE, Steubenville, 1988—. Mem. Am. Soc. Clin. Pathologists, Jefferson Tech. Coll. Alumni Assn. (pres. 1986-88), Jefferson County Alumni Assn. (bd. dirs. Steubenville chpt. 1985—), AAUW, U. Pitts. Alumni Assn., Steubenville High Sch. Boosters. Home: 1716 Norton Pl Steubenville OH 43952 Office: Barium and Chems Inc County Rd #44 PO Box 218 Steubenville OH 43952-5218

YANOSKI, EDITH M., financial services executive; b. Europe, May 15, 1944; came to U.S., 1948; m. Richard E. Heitzwebel. Student, ATES Tech. Inst., Youngstown State U. Mgr. cen. pruchasing office ITT Fin. Svcs., Bedford, Ohio, 1988—. Office: 22129 Rockside Rd Bedford OH 44146

YANSHA, BEVERLY ANN, hospital research director; b. McKeesport, Pa., Jan. 9, 1947; d. Frank and Julia (Kovey) Y. Grad. high sch., Pleasant Hills, Pa., 1964. Cert. asst. lab. animal technician, lab. animal techinician. Sales clk. Angus Pet Shop, Pleasant Hills, Pa., 1964-65; mgr. Angus Pet Shop, Pitts., 1965-71, Pet World, Pitts., 1971-74; animal care taker U. Pitts., 1974-75, asst. supr., 1975-77, supr., 1977-80; mgr. Montefiore Hosp., Pitts., 1980-90, Children's Hosp. Rangos Rsch. Ctr., Pitts., 1990—; cons. Allegheny Gen. Hosp., Pitts., 1986, 89. Mem. Am. Assn. for Lab. Animal Sci. (br. and nat. mem., cert. 1976, 78). Democrat. Roman Catholic. Office: Childrens Hosp Rangos Rsch Ctr 3705 Fifth Ave at Desoto St Pittsburgh PA 15213

YAO, CLARA SAI-HSI, computer scientist; b. Feng, Kiang-Su, People's Republic China, July 24, 1938; came to U.S., 1962; d. Hung-hao and Su-chen Li; m. Dick K. Yao, Aug. 6, 1965; children: Joyce, Andrew. BS, Chung-Hsin U., Tai-Chung, Republic of China, 1961; MS, DePauw U., Greencastle, Ind., 1964. Lab. asst. DePauw U., Greencastle, Ind., 1962-64; med. technologist St. Michael Med. Ctr., Newark, 1964-67; scientist A. Sandoz, Inc., East Hanover, N.J., 1967-71, scientist B, 1971-77, sr. scientist, 1977-82, system leader, 1983-88; system mgr. Sandoz Pharms. Corp., East Hanover, 1988—. Bd. dirs. No. Jersey Chinese Assn., Morristown, 1981-83; com. mem. U.S. China Found., Hackettstown, N.J., 1988, bd. dirs., 1989—. Mem. Drug Info. Assn., Pharm. Mfrs. Assn., SAS User's Group. Office: Sandoz Pharms Corp Rte 10 East Hanover NJ 07936

YAO, LILY KING, banker; b. Shanghai, Republic of China, July 14, 1943; came to U.S., 1966; d. J.L. and Y.Z. (Lok) King; m. James Yao, June 29, 1966. BBA, U. Hawaii, 1977. Teller-cashier Hwa-Nan Comml. Bank, Taipei, Republic of China, 1958-62; flight attendant Civil Air Transport, Taipei, 1962-66; teller Crocker Nat. Bank, San Francisco, 1967; from teller to exec. v.p. Pioneer Fed. Savs. Bank, Honolulu, 1968-84, pres., chief exec. officer, 1984—, also bd. dirs.; chmn., pres., chief exec. officer Pioneer Properties, Inc., Honolulu, 1985—, Pioneer Insurance, Inc., Honolulu, 1985—, Pioneer Real Estate, Honolulu, 1985—; chmn. Hawaii League of Savs. Instns., Honolulu, 1985-86; nat. dir. Inst. Fin. Edn., Chgo., 1987-88; bd. dirs. Fed. Home Loan Bank Seattle, 1990—. Mem. Gov.'s Congress on Hawaii's Internat. Role, 1988; bd. govs. Center for Internat. Comml. Dispute Resolution, Honolulu, 1987—; 2d vice-chmn. ARC, Honolulu, 1987—; bd. dirs. Aloha United Way, 1988, Oahu Pvt. Industry Council, 1986-89. Recipient Outstanding Achievement in Bus. award Honolulu YWCA, 1985, Cert. Appreciation ARC, 1988, Gov. Hawaii, 1985, Lt. Gov. Hawaii, 1984. Mem. U.S. League Savs. Instns. (nat. bd. dirs. 1987-88), Chinese C. of C. (bd. dirs. 1982—), Hawaii C. of C. (bd. dirs. 1987—), Grad. Sch. of Savs. and Loan Alumni Assn. (nat. pres. 1987-88), Pioneer Plaza Club. Office: Pioneer Fed Savs Bank 900 Fort Street Mall Honolulu HI 96813

YARBOROUGH, JUDITH ANN, bookstore executive, librarian; b. Williamsport, Pa., Aug. 26, 1949; d. Fred Arlington and Ethel Mary (Parker) Bingaman; m. John Henry Yarborough, Aug. 24, 1972; 1 child, Wendy Renee. BA in English, U. Tex., Arlington, 1970; MLS, U. North Tex., 1973. Tchr. Parker Found., Dallas, 1971-72; saleswoman Sanger-Harris, Dallas, 1972; mgr. br. libr. Irving (Tex.) Pub. Libr. N.W., 1974-78; libr. cons. Vaughn & Yarborough Libr. Cons., Irving, 1980-81; owner, mgr. Young Ideas, Irving, 1981—; speaker various orgns., 1974—. Bd. dirs. Brandenburg Elem. Sch. PTA, Irving, 1983-85, Irving Arts Reach Com., 1988; vol. coord. travelling exhbn. Smithsonian Instn., Irving, 1988. Mem. Am. Bookseller's Assn., Assn. Booksellers for Children (charter), AAUW (life, chmn. Ednl. Found. Irving br. 1987-88, v.p. programming 1988-89), Grad. Sch. Students Assn. (life, chmn. nominating com. 1987), Belles-Lettres Book Discussion Club (pres. 1987-88). Democrat. Methodist. Office: Young Ideas 389 Plymouth Park SC Irving TX 75061

YARBOROUGH, N. PATRICIA, human resources executive; b. Beckville, Tex., Dec. 7, 1936; d. James Lamar and Del (Davis) Y. BMus, North Tex. State U., 1958, EdD, 1969; MEd, U. Md., 1963. Edn. cons. Prentice-Hall, Inc., Englewood Cliffs, N.J., 1963-65; tchr. Dallas Ind. Sch. Dist., 1965-67, supr. music, 1968-69, coordinator staff devel., 1969-70; dean instrn. Mountain View Coll. of Dallas County Community Coll. Dist., 1976-77, chmn. div. humanities, 1970-73, dean instrn. and student devel., 1973-76; v.p. instrn. Brookhaven Coll. of Dallas County Community Coll. Dist., 1977-80; pres. Mattatuck Community Coll., Waterbury, Conn., 1980-82; v.p. human resources and corp. rels, Scovill Inc., Scovill World Hdqrs., Waterbury, Conn., 1982-86; pres. Teikyo Post U., Waterbury, 1986—; also trustee; proposal evaluator NEH, 1981; corporator The Banking Ctr. Bd. dirs. St. Mary's Hosp., Waterbury, 1981—, Conn. Pub. Broadcasting, Mahatuck Mus.; pub. mem. Conn. Humanities Council, NEH, 1982-84; bd. dirs. ARC, Waterbury chpt., 1982-85. U.S. Office Edn. grantee, N. Tex. State U., 1967. Mem. Sigma Alpha Iota, Alpha Chi, Phi Kappa Lambda. Office: Teikyo Post U 800 Country Club Rd Waterbury CT 06723-2540

YARBOROUGH, VALERIE LOUISE, internal auditor, consultant; b. San Antonio, Aug. 24, 1928; d. Wilbur G. and Grace Helen (Davis) Y.; m. Richard L. Storey (div. Nov. 1971); children: Christopher L., Dianna L., Paula L. Student, Colo. Woman's Coll., Santa Clarita Coll.; BA, Calif. State U., 1973. Mgr. Adams & Assocs., Seattle, 1973-76; staff acct. Helwig & Buttler, 1976-77, George Branley, CPA, Seattle, 1977-78; corp. acct. Westin Hotel Co., Seattle, 1978-79, staff auditor, 1979-85, sr. internal auditor, 1985—; bd. dirs. Christopher & Assocs., Seattle. Mem. Nat. Fedn. Womens Clubs (pres. Seville, Spain chpt. 1967), NOW, League Women Voters, Am. Soc. Women Accts., Nat. Mgmt. Accts. Home: 10019 Densmore N Seattle WA 98133 Office: Westin Bldg 20001 6th Ave Seattle WA 98121

YARBROUGH, AMELIA HERGYSTINE BURGESS, patent examiner; b. Coatsville, Pa., Feb. 27, 1939; d. Roberta E. Burgess; B.A., Eastern Coll., 1961; M.S., Howard U., 1964; Ph.D., George Washington U., 1985; 1 son, Antonio. Chemist, NIH, Bethesda, Md., 1963-74; patent examiner U.S. Patent and Trademark Office, Arlington, Va., 1974—. Mem. ch. choirs, dir. youth activities, trustee New Bethel Baptist Ch., Washington. Mem. Am. Chem. Soc., Sigma Xi.

YARBROUGH, DENA COX, special education educator; b. Gorman, Tex., June 20, 1933; d. William Thomas and Imogene (Dunlap) Cox; m. James Edgar Yarbrough, June 20, 1950. BA, Nicholls State U., 1964, MEd, 1971, postgrad., 1978. Supr. profl. pers., prin. schs., elem. tchr. Terrebonne Parish Sch. Bd., Houma, La., 1964-79, dir. spl. edn. svcs., 1980—. Bd. dirs. Terrebonne Literacy Coun., United Way of Houma-Terrebonne. Mem. La. Spl. Edn. Suprs. Assn. (past sec.), Coun. for Exceptional Children, La. Autism Soc., Mental Health Assn., La. Assn. Supervisors of Edn., Phi Delta Kappa. Democrat. Methodist. Home: 303 Westview Dr Houma LA 70364 Office: 711 Grinage St Houma LA 70360

YARBROUGH, DESIREE SIMONE, computer scientist, analyst; b. Pasadena, Calif., Feb. 16, 1964; d. Delano and Samella (Thomas) Y.; m. Daryl LaRon Irby. BS in Computer Sci., Tuskegee U., 1988. With Jet Propulsion Lab., Pasadena, 1982—; system engr. Jet Propulsion Lab., 1988-90; co-owner, mgr., Shopping Mates, Pasadena. Tutor, Alpha Mentor program, Pasadena, 1988-89, Met. Bapt. Ch., 1988-90. Mem. Assn. Computing Machinery, Alpha Kappa Alpha. Democrat. Baptist. Home: 5401 Rampart Houston TX 77081 Office: 1322 Space Park Dr Houston TX 77058

YARBROUGH, JOYCE LENORE, management consultant; b. Bowling Green, Ky., Oct. 7, 1948; d. William S. Yarbrough and Hortense Lenore (Bullock) Jackson; B.A., Fisk U., 1970; M.B.A., Golden Gate U., 1977. Spl. projects coordinator Econ. Opportunity Council, San Francisco, 1971-77; sales/statistician Macy's of Calif., San Francisco, 1971—; mgmt. cons. C.J. & Assos. Enterprises Inc., San Francisco, 1977-78; pres. Le Nore Co., Inc., 1978—; adminstrv. ops. supr. Bur. Census, U.S. Dept. Commerce, 1980; market researcher Western Pacific Industries, 1981-85; dist. sales rep. Calif. State Lottery, 1985—. Co-founder Scott-Wada Youth Fund; bd. dirs. Urban League San Francisco, 1973-79, Mental Assn. San Francisco, 1972-79; panelist United Way of Bay Area, 1971-76; treas. Westside Community Mental Health Center, 1976-79; sec. Cath. Youth Orgn., 1977-78; sec. Black Agenda Council San Francisco, 1984—. Mem. Mortar Bd. Home: 100 Font Blvd Apt 1K San Francisco CA 94132 Office: PO Box 15117 San Francisco CA 94115

YARBROUGH, MARTHA CORNELIA, music educator; b. Waycross, Ga., Feb. 8, 1940; d. Henry Elliott and Jessie (Sirmans) Y.; B.M.E., Stetson U., 1962; M.M.E., Fla. State U., 1968, Ph.D., 1973. Choral dir. Ware County High Sch., Waycross, Ga., 1962-64, Glynn Acad., Brunswick, Ga., 1964-70; asst. choral dir. Fla. State U., 1970-72; cons. in music Muscogee County Sch. Dist., Columbus, Ga., 1972-73; cons. in tchr. edn. Psycho-Edno. Cons., Inc., Tallahassee, 1972-73; asst. prof. music edn., dir. univs. choruses and oratorio soc. Syracuse U., 1973-76, assoc. prof. music edn., 1976-83, prof., 1983-86, acting asst. dean Coll. Visual and Performing Arts, 1980-82, acting dir. Sch. Music, 1980-82, chmn. music edn., 1982-86; prof. music La. State U., Baton Rouge, 1986—, coordinator music, edn., 1986—; artist in residence Sch. Music U. Ala., Tuscaloosa, 1989—. Mem. Music Educators Nat. Conf., N.Y. State Sch. Music Assn., Am. Ednl. Research Assn., Soc. Research Music Edn. (mem. exec. com. 1988—, AAUP, Pi Kappa Lambda, Phi Beta, Kappa Delta Pi. Co-author: Competency-Based Music Education, 1980; mem. editorial com. Jour. Research in Music Edn.; contbr. articles to profl. jours., chpts. in books. Office: La State U Sch Music Baton Rouge LA 70803

YARBROUGH, SONJA DIANNE, marketing and public relations professional; b. Trenton, Fla., June 6, 1948; d. George Charlie and Dorothy Mae (Carver) Y. BA in English, U. Fla., 1971; MS in Pub. Rels., Boston U., 1980. Pub. rels. asst. Digital Equipment Corp., Maynard, Mass., 1979; interim editor, rsch. asst. Rehab. Rsch. Inst., Gainesville, Fla., 1980-81; bus. mgr. Dental Specialty Practice, Atlanta, 1982-84; asst. account exec. Grizzard Advt., Atlanta, 1984-86; pub. rels. mktg. cons. Atlanta, 1987-88; account exec. Northlake Typography, Atlanta, 1988-89, TypoGraphics Atlanta, 1989-90; mktg./pub. rels. asst. Future Aviation Profls., Atlanta, 1990—. Mem. Dems. for Choice, Atlanta, 1990. Scholarship in Communications Boston U., 1979. Mem. Women in Communications, Inc. (co-chairperson ACE Competition, 1989-90, publicity guide 1989-90, v.p. programs 1990), Boston U. Alumni Sch. Com. Democrat. Home: 603 Cameron St SE Atlanta GA 30312 Office: Future Aviation Profls Am 4959 Massachusetts Blvd Atlanta GA 30337

YARD, MOLLY, social activist; d. James Maxon and Mabelle Merriam (Hickcox) Y.; m. Sylvester Garrett; 3 children. AB, Swarthmore Coll., 1933. Chmn. Am. Student Union; active in Dem. party politics, Pa. and Calif., 1940s and 50s; active in civil rights movement, Pa., 1960s and 70s; staff mem. VISTA, 1960s; active NOW, from 1970s, polit. dir., 1985-87, pres., 1987—. Office: NOW 1000 16th St NW Ste 700 Washington DC 20036*

YARDIS-VIGNOLA, PAMELA HINTZ, computer consulting company executive; b. N.Y.C., Sept. 23, 1944; d. Edward F. and Isabella (Sawers) Hintz; m. J.A. Yardis, Apr. 2, 1966 (div. July 1980); children: Bradley, Brent, Tricia, Todd, Ryan, Kara, Melissa; m. L. Vignola, Aug. 11, 1990. BA, Bethany Coll., 1966; MA, Columbia U., 1983, MEd, 1983. Tchr. Yonkers (N.Y.) Pub. Schs., 1966-68; cons. PHY, Inc., Stamford, Conn., 1978-83; account exec. Mgmt. Systems, Stamford, 1982-84; sr. account exec., cons. Mgmt. Dynamics, Yonkers, 1984-86; v.p. GMW Assn., Inc., N.Y.C., 1986-87; pres. Chestnut Hill Cons. Group, Inc., Stamford, 1987—. Chmn. Mayor's Commn. Prevention Youth Drug and Alcohol Abuse, Stamford, 1986—; mem. Dem. Com., Stamford, 1984—; bd. dirs. Alcohol and Drug Coun., Inc., Conn. Communities for Drug Free Youth, Childcare, Inc. Recipient Gov.'s Community Svc. award, 1988, Golden Rule award J.C. Penney. Mem. Women in Mgmt. (v.p. 1986-88, Ann. Recognition award), Data Processing Mgmt. Assn., Advt. Rsch. Found., Inst. Mgmt. Cons. (pres. Fairfield Westchester chpt. 1990—). Presbyterian. Home: 125 Chestnut Hill Rd Stamford CT 06903 Office: Chestnut Hill Cons Group PO Box 15755 Stamford CT 06901

YARDLEY, ANDREA, health facility administrator; b. N.J., June 10, 1955; d. Charles and Eva (Pawik) Tiazkun; m. Paul F. Yardley, Oct. 27, 1984. BS, Bloomfield Coll., 1979; MBA, U. Phoenix, 1985. Mgmt. resident Samaritan Health Svcs., Phoenix; mgr. cardiovascular diagnostics St. Joseph's Hosp. and Med. Ctr., Phoenix; systems analyst Mayo Clinic, Rochester, Minn.; asst. adminstr. Mayo Clinic Scottsdale (Ariz.). Mem. Med. Group Mgmt. Assn. Office: 13400 E Shea Blvd Scottsdale AZ 85259

YARDLEY, ROSEMARY ROBERTS, journalist, columnist; b. Albertville, Ala., Apr. 1, 1938; d. James Bailey Jr. and Mildred (Smith) Roberts; m. Jonathan Yardley, June 14, 1961 (div. 1975); children: James B., William W. II; m. Donald Arthur Boulton, Apr. 30, 1988. BA, U. N.C., 1960, MA, 1978. Staff writer The Charlotte (N.C.) Observer, 1960-61; editorial asst. The N.Y. Times, N.Y.C., 1962-64; staff writer The Greensboro (N.C.) News and Record, 1974-78, editorial writer, 1978-88, editorial columnist, 1988—. Contbr. articles, book revs. to various publs. Bd. dirs. Weatherspoon Art Mus. U. N.C., Greensboro, 1986—, U. N.C. Journalism Found., 1985—, Weatherspoon Art Found., 1989—, Friends U. Libr., Greensboro, 1988-90, Ea. Music. Festival., Greensboro, 1984-88. Recipient 2d prize N.C. Press Assn., 1976, 1st prize 1987; John S. Knight fellow Stanford U., 1980-81; Bosch Found. travel fellow, 1990, Atlantik Bruke Found. travel fellow, 1988. Democrat. Presbyterian. Home: 223 Elmwood Dr Greensboro NC 27408 Office: The Greensboro News and Record 200 E Market St Greensboro NC 27420

YARLETTS, CAROL LYNNE, nurse; b. New Castle, Pa., Nov. 10, 1959; d. Charles Lester and Carol Joan (Cox) Y. BSN, W.Va. Wesleyan Coll., 1983; MS, Ohio State U., 1989. RN, Ohio. Staff charge nurse Ohio State U. Hosp., Columbus, 1983-87; AIDS home care adminstr. Ohio Dept. Human Svcs., Columbus, 1987-89; AIDS nursing care specialist Columbus Health Dept., 1989—; pvt. practice AIDS educator, cons., 1984—; educator Ohio State U. Coll. Nursing, Columbus, 1984—; edn. cons. Columbus AIDS Task Force, 1985—; mem. adv. bd. Joshua Found. (AIDS housing) Columbus, 1987-88. AIDS educator various community orgns., Columbus, 1984—; vol. Columbus AIDS Task Force, 1985—. Mem. Am. Nurses Assn., Mid-Ohio Dist. Nurses Assn., Ohio Nurses Assn., Ohio Pub. Health Assn. Democrat. Methodist. Home: 1735 Worthington Run Rd Worthington OH 43235 Office: Columbus Health Dept 181 Washington Blvd Columbus OH 43215

YARNOLD, BARBARA MARIA, political science educator, lawyer; b. Sierra Vista, Ariz., Mar. 31, 1961; d. James Knapps and Helen (Suszko) Y. BA, U. Chgo., 1981; JD, DePaul U., 1984; PhD Pub. Policy Analysis, U. Ill., Chgo., 1988. Bar: Ill. 1984. Corp. counsel Midpack Corp., Chgo., 1986-87; law clk. Cir. Ct. Cook County, Chgo., 1987-88; assoc. Holstein, Mack & Dupree, Chgo., 1987; asst. prof. dept. polit. sci. Saginaw (Mich.) Valley State U., 1988-90; asst. prof. dept. pub. adminstrn. Fla. Internat. U., North Miami, 1990—; presenter in field. Author: Refugees Without Refuge, International Fugitives; contbr. articles, book revs. to profl. publs. Pullman scholar, 1976-80; U. Ill. fellow, 1986-88. Mem. Am. Polit. Sci. Assn., Am. Judicature Soc., Midwest Polit. Sci. Assn., Mich. Acad. Sci., Arts and Letters, Golden Key, Phi Kappa Phi. Home: 700 Bittersweet Chicago IL 60613 Office: Florida Internat Univ North Miami Campus North Miami FL 33181

YARRIGLE, CHARLENE SANDRA SHUEY, realtor, investment counselor; b. Redlands, Calif., July 25, 1940; d. Troy Frank and Anna (Miskew) Shuey; m. Robert Charles Yarrigle, Oct. 16, 1965 (div. July 1985); children: Stephanie Ann, Steven Charles. AA, San Bernardino (Calif.) Coll., 1965; student, Ariz. State U., 1965-66; BS, Northern Mich. U., 1976, postgrad., 1976-77. Clk. Bungalow Grocery, Redlands, 1957-59; operator Pacific Telephone Co., San Bernardino, 1958-61; service rep. So. Calif. Gas, San Bernardino, 1961-66; tchr. bus. Gwinn (Mich.) High Sch., 1976-78; realtor, investment counselor Century 21 Curragh Downs, Fair Oaks, Calif., 1978—; broker, 1990—; tchr. Project 100,000, Sheppard AFB, Wichita Falls, Tex., 1966-70. Mem. steering com., adv. bd. Sacramento (Calif.) Bd. Realtors, 1981—; vol. Easter Seal Soc., ARC San Bernardino, 1968-72. Mem. NAFE, Nat. Assn. Realtors (lic.), Calif. Assn. Realtors, Sierra Club, Eagles. Republican. Office: Century 21 Curragh Downs 4401 Hazel Ave Ste 115 Fair Oaks CA 95628

YASUDA, CATHY TOMI, television producer, consultant; b. Tokyo, May 2, 1957; d. Takeshi and Teruko (Saito) Y. BA, UCLA, 1979, MBA, 1983. Corp. banking officer 1st Interstate Bank, Ltd., Los Angeles, 1983-85; asst. sec. Mfrs. Hanover Trust Co., N.Y.C., 1985-86; asst. v.p. L.F. Rothschild & Co., N.Y.C., 1986-87; assoc. Morgan Stanley Internat., London, 1987-88; chief investment officer Takao Bldg. Devel. Co., Ltd., N.Y.C., 1988-89; pres., founder CTY Internat. Inc., N.Y.C., 1989—. Mem. NAFE. Am. Women's Econ. Devel. Coun. Republican. Home and Office: 2025 Broadway #10A New York NY 10023

YATES, ELLA GAINES, librarian, state official; b. Atlanta, June 14, 1927; d. Fred Douglas and Laura (Moore) Gaines; m. Joseph L. Sydnor (dec.); 1 child, Jerri Gaines Sydnor Lee; m. Clayton R. Yates (dec.). A.B., Spelman Coll., Atlanta, 1949; M.S. in L.S, Atlanta U., 1951; J.D., Atlanta Law Sch., 1979. Asst. br. librarian Bklyn. Pub. Library, 1951-54; head children's dept. Orange (N.J.) Pub. Library, 1956-59; br. librarian E. Orange (N.J.) Pub. Library, 1960-69; med. librarian Orange Meml. Hosp., 1967-69; asst. dir. Montclair (N.J.) Pub. Library, 1970-72; asst. dir. Atlanta-Fulton Pub. Library, 1972-76, dir., 1976-81; dir. learning resource ctr. S/OIC, Seattle, 1982-84; asst. dir. adminstrn. Friendship Force, Atlanta, 1984-86; state librarian Commonwealth of Va., 1986—; adv. bd. Library of Congress Center for the Book, 1977-85; cons. in field; vis. lectr. U. Wash., Seattle, 1981-83; mem. Va. Records Avd. Bd., 1986—; mem. Nagara Exec. Bd., 1987—. Contbr. to profl. jours. Vice chmn. N.J. Women's Coun. on Human Rels., 1957-59; chmn. Friends Fulton County Jail, 1973-81; bd. dirs. United Cerebral Palsy Greater Atlanta, Inc., 1979-81, Coalition Against Censorship, Washington, 1981-84, YMCA Met. Atlanta, 1979-81, Exec. Women's Network, 1979-82, Freedom To Read Found., 1979-85, Va. Black History Mus. Bd., 1990—; sec., exec. dir. Va. Libr. Found. Bd., 1986—. Named Profl. Woman of Yr, N.J. chpt. Nat. Assn. Negro Bus. and Profl. Women's Clubs, 1964, Profl. Woman of Yr., NAAACP, N.J., 1972, Outstanding Chum of Yr., 1976, Outstanding Alumni, Spelman Coll., 1977; recipient meritorious award Atlanta U., 1977, Phoenix award City of Atlanta, 1980, SERWA award Nat. Coalition 100 Black Women, 1989. Mem. ALA (exec. bd. 1977-83, commn. freedom and access to info., Black Caucus award 1989), NAACP, Va. Bd. Cert. Librs., Va. Libr. Assn., Southeastern Libr. Assn., Chief Officers of State Libr. Agys., Nat. Assn. Govt. Archives and Records Adminstrs., Delta Theta Phi, Delta Sigma Theta. Baptist. Home: 5216 Beddington Rd Richmond VA 23234 Office: State Libr and Archives Libr Bldg Richmond VA 23219

YATES, GAYLE GRAHAM, American and women's studies educator, writer; b. Wayne County, Miss., May 6, 1940; d. Robert C. and Gleta (Jones) Graham; m. Herschel Wilson Yates, Jr., July 21, 1961; children: Natasha, Stiles. BA, Millsaps Coll., 1961; MAT, Vanderbilt U., 1962; PhD, U. Minn., 1973. Mem. Faculty English dept. Boston U., 1964-67; vis. scholar Cambridge U., 1973-74, 78; chmn. women's studies U. Minn., Mpls., 1976-81, assoc. prof. women's studies and Am. studies, 1981—; vis. prof. Amerika-Institut der Universität München, 1989; founding mem. Big Ten panel on women's studies. Author: What Women Want: The Ideas of the Movement, 1975, Mississippi Mind: A Personal Cultural History of an American State, 1990; editor: Harriet Martineau on Women, 1984. Mem. Minn. Gov.'s Adv. Com. on Families, 1980-82. Mem. Am. Studies Assn. (chmn. women's com. 1981-83), Women Historians of Midwest, Nat. Women's Studies Assn. Democrat. Methodist. Home: 4105 Vincent Ave S Minneapolis MN 55410 Office: U Minn Am Studies 104 Scott Hall 72 Pleasant Ave SE Minneapolis MN 55455

YATES, JESSIE WARD, banker; b. Statesville, N.C., Feb. 21, 1929; d. Clarence Vernon and Alice Rebecca (Myers) Ward; children: Micah E. Rickard, Eric D. Rickard, Kimberly R. Sanders. Student, Ashmore Bus. Coll., Thomasville, N.C. Teller, teller supr., loan officer, corp. sec. Peoples Fed. Savs. & Loan, Thomasville, 1954-70; adminstrv. asst., loan officer Northwestern/First Union Bank, Thomasville, 1974-87; city exec. Lexington State Bank, Thomasville, 1987—. Bd. mem. United Way, Thomasville area, 1987—; bd. mem., treas. Habitat for Humanity, Thomasville, 1987—; bd. mem. Davidson County Cancer Soc., Thomasville, 1987—; mem. adminstrv. bd. Pine Wood United Meth. Ch., Thomasville; bd. mem. Thomasville Zoning Bd. Ajustments. Mem. Am. Bus. Womens Assn., Thomasville Area C. of C. (bd. mem. 1987—). Republican. Methodist. Home: 700 Nance Dr Thomasville NC 27360 Office: Lexington State Bank 941 Randolph St Thomasville NC 27360

YATES, JO ANN RUTH, communications educator; b. Chgo., Jan. 7, 1931; m. William R. Yates; children: James William, Douglas Andrew. BA in Speech, U. Ill., 1952; MA in Audiology, Hunter Coll., 1962; PhD in Communications Disorders, U. So. Calif., 1971. Cert. lang. pathologist, Calif.

Fellow Nat. Inst. Sensory and Neurol. Diseases U. So. Calif., L.A., 1964-66; founder, supr. Pre-sch. Lang. Devel. Clinic Calif. State U., Long Beach, 1968—, assoc. prof. communication disorders, 1968-78, prof., 1978-87, dept. chair, dir. speech and hearing, 1982-85. Adv. bd. Head Start, 1977—. Recipient Grad. Rehab. Lit. award, 1964, Phi Kappa Phi Faculty award 1975, Outstanding Prof. award Calif. State U. Long Beach, 1981-82. Fellow Am. Speech and Hearing Assn. (legis. coun. 1975-85); mem. Calif. Speech and Hearing Assn. (regional v.p. 1972-74, pres. elect 1981-83, pres. 1983-85, Honors of Assn. 1986), Coun. of Exceptional Children (Outstanding Achievement award 1985), Assn. State Coll. and Univ. Profs. (pres. Calif. State U. Long Beach chpt. 1986). Office: Calif State U-Long Beach Dept Communicative Disorders 1250 Bellflower Blvd Long Beach CA 90840

YATES, LENORE EASLEY, cosmetic company executive; b. Madisonville, Ky., Sept. 22, 1945; d. Howard Leon and Marguerite Melvin (Wicker) Easley; m. Kenneth Yates, Nov. 24, 1967. BS, Austin Peay State U., 1967; MS, Memphis State U., 1968; postgrad., Murray State U., 1975. Tchr., counselor Pine Breeze Ctr. Emotionally Disturbed Teenagers, Chattanooga, 1968-69, 70-72; instr. Guam Elem. Sch. and High Sch., 1969-70, Caldwell County Elem. Schs., Princeton, Ky., 1972—; founder, now pres., instr. Le'Colour Cosmetics Ltd., Fredonia, Ky., 1985—; park technician, U.S. Army Corps Engrs., Grand Rivers, Ky.; cons., Beauti Control Cosmetics, Dallas, 1984-86; pvt. image cons.; speaker in field. Fundraiser, Ky. div. Am. Heart Assn., 1983—. Mem. NAFE, NEA, Ky. Edn. Assn., Ky. Assn. Health, Phys. Edn., Recreation and Dance, Women's Missionary Union, Delta Kappa Gamma (Chi chpt.). Democrat. Baptist. Home: Rte 2 Box 21A Fredonia KY 42411 Office: Le Colour Cosmetics Ltd Rte 2 Box 21A Fredonia KY 42411

YAUS, HOLLY NILL, public relations consultant; b. Dayton, Ohio, May 4, 1964; d. Donald Arthur and Anne (Steele) Nill; m. Christopher Alan Yaus, June 13, 1987. BBA, U. Cin., 1986. Mktg. and sales mgr. Qmax Technology Group, Dayton, Ohio, 1986-88; exec. acctg. mgr. LeSome Labs., Dayton, 1988-89; ptnr. Wolf, Yaus & Assoc., Inc., Dayton, 1989—. Republican. Home: 2 Madden Pl Kettering OH 45420 Office: Wolf Yaus & Assoc Inc 2106 University Pl Dayton OH 45406

YAWKEY, JEAN R., baseball club executive; b. Bklyn., 1909; m. Tom Yawkey, 1944 (dec. 1976). Fashion model N.Y.C., 1934-44; former pres. Boston Red Sox, Am. League, from 1976, now majority owner, chairwoman bd. dirs. Trustee Yawkey Found.; past chmn. bd. and trustee Jimmy Fund Sidney Farber Cancer Inst. Office: Boston Red Sox 24 Yawkey Way Boston MA 02215*

YEAGER, BERNICE WHITTAKER, educator; b. Bethany, W.Va., June 26, 1915; d. Robert Helsabeck and Louise (McGraw) Whittaker; m. Roy Harold Yeager (dec. 1967). AB, Concord Coll., W.Va., 1934; MS, U. Tenn., 1937. Tchr./prin. Mercer County Schs., Princeton, W.Va., 1934-45; supr. instrn. Mercer County Schs., 1945-47; asst. prof., supervising tchr. Winthrop Tng. Sch.-Winthrop Coll., Rock Hill, S.C., 1948-64; coordinator reading Lancaster (S.C.) City Schs., 1964-70, Lancaster County Schs., 1970-75; tchr. Catawba Acad., Rock Hill, S.C., 1975-82; substitute tchr. Charlotte-Mecklenburg Schs., Charlotte, N.C., 1983—; cons. in field. Chmn. youth activities ARC, Rock Hill, 1970-75. Named Woman of the Yr., Rock Hill Bus. and Profl. Women, 1977, others. Mem. NEA, S.C. Edn. Assn., AAUW, S.C. Ret. Tchrs. Assn., Phi Kappa Phi, Delta Kappa Gamma. Lutheran. Address: 862 Mary Knoll Ct Rock Hill SC 29730

YEAGER, PAMELA CROWL, business executive; b. Danville, Pa., Feb. 12, 1949; d. Kenneth Summerfield and Helene Jeanette (Billig) Crowl; m. Theodore Thomas Yeager, July 10, 1982. Degree in secondary edn., Bloomsburg (Pa.) U., 1971. Substitute tchr. Danville Area Sch. Dist., 1972-76, Bloomsburg Area Sch. Dist., 1972-76; office mgr. Kenneth Crowl, Inc., Elysburg, Pa., 1972—; ballet instr., Elysburg, Pa., 1976-90. Coord., sec. Ralpho Twp. All Home Days Commn., Elysburg, 1986-90, trustee, 1986-89; trustee Hall of Fame, Shamokin, Pa., 1986-90; Sunday sch. tchr. United Meth. Chs., 1976—, v.p. adminstrv. bd. 1987-88, mem. fin. com., 1987—, mem. stewardship com., 1987—; co-chair of ecumenical Community Spirit, 1990—. Named Citizen of the Yr., All Home Days Assn., 1989. Mem. AAUW (v.p. membership 1989—, mem. social com. 1987—), Ea. Pa. Conf. United Meth. Ch. (mem. family and adult ministries 1990—). Democrat. Home: 44 W Center St Elysburg PA 17824

YEARGIN-ALLSOPP, MARSHALYN, medical epidemiologist, pediatrician; b. Greenville, S.C., May 17, 1948; d. Grady Andrew and Willie Mae (Blocker) Yeargin; m. Ralph Norman Allsopp, Apr. 5, 1975; children: Timothy Chandler, Whitney Marisha. Student Bennett Coll., 1964-66; BA, Sweet Briar Coll., 1968; MD, Emory U., 1972. Diplomate Am. Bd. Pediatrics. Intern Montefiore Hosp., Bronx, N.Y., 1972-73, resident, 1973-75; instr. pediatrics Albert Einstein Coll. Medicine, Bronx, 1975-77, asst. prof. pediatrics, 1977-78, 80-81; pediatrician Montefiore-Morrisania Comprehensive Health Care Ctr., Bronx, 1975-78, Louise Wise Adoption Agy., N.Y.C., 1975-80, Children's Evaluation and Rehab. Ctr., Rose F. Kennedy Ctr., Bronx, 1980-81; officer USPHS, 1981—, comdr., 1983—; epidemiologic intelligence surveillance officer birth defects br. Ctrs. for Disease Control, Atlanta, 1981-83, preventive medicine resident, 1982-84, med. epidemiologist, 1984—; pediatric cons. Clayton County Early Intervention Program, Jonesboro, Ga., 1983—; med. dir. Easter Seal Presch. Program, Atlanta, 1981-83; physician Com. on Handicapped, N.Y.C., 1979-81, United Cerebral Palsy Program, Bronx, 1980-81. Bd. overseers Sweet Briar Coll., 1981-89; bd. dirs. Neighborhood Arts Ctr., Atlanta, 1984-87; mem. prevention edn. com. Retarded Citizens, Atlanta, 1984—; mem. fundraising campaign Greater Atlanta YWCA, 1985; bd. trustees Pace Acad., 1986—; co-chmn. Minority Atlanta Families in Ind. Schs., Inc., 1986—; chair, Bd. dirs. profl. adv. com. Cerebral Palsey Ctr., Reach, Inc., Atlanta, 1988—; mem. State of Ga. Interagy. Coun. for Edn. of the Handicapped Act., 1988—. Fellow Am. Acad. Pediatrics, Am. Acad. Cerebral Palsy and Devel. Medicine; mem. AMA, Atlanta Med. Assn., Jack and Jill of Am., Phi Beta Kappa, Delta Sigma Theta. Home: 3783 Paces Ferry W Atlanta GA 30339 Office: Ctrs for Disease Control 1600 Clifton Rd Atlanta GA 30333

YEARLING, LOWETA LEE, community agency executive; b. Lawrence, Kans., Jan. 1, 1939; d. Leslie Clarence and Minnie Lee (Clayborne) Kimball; children: Debra Veola, Denise Kay. BA, Colo. Women's Coll., 1982. With U. No. Colo., Greeley, 1959-62, Compensation Ins. Fund, Denver, 1962-67, Colo. Dept. Pub. Health, 1967-77, Colo. Med. Ctr., Denver, 1977-81; dir. office svcs. Mile Hi coun. Girl Scouts U.S., Denver, 1981—; instr. Denver Auraria Community Coll. Bd. dirs. Community Colls. Denver; active NAACP, YMCA, Dem. Party; sch. supt., clk. AME Ch. Recipient recognition awards for civic vol. work. Mem. Colo. Pub. Health Assn. (pres.), Colo. Assn. Pub. Employees, Delta Sigma Theta. Office: Girl Scouts US Mile High Coun Denver CO

YEAZELL, RUTH BERNARD, educator; b. N.Y.C., Apr. 4, 1947; d. Walter and Annabelle (Reich) Bernard; m. Stephen C. Yeazell, Aug. 14, 1969 (div. 1980). BA with high honors, Swarthmore Coll., 1967; MPhil (Woodrow Wilson fellow), Yale U., 1970, PhD, 1971. Asst. prof. English Boston U., 1971-74, UCLA, 1975-77, assoc. prof., 1977-80, prof., 1980—. Author: Language and Knowledge in the Late Novels of Henry James, 1976; Death and Letters of Alice James, 1981; assoc. editor Nineteenth-Century Fiction, 1977-80; editor: Sex, Politics, and Science in the 19th Century Novel, 1986. Woodrow Wilson fellow, 1967-68, Guggenheim fellow, 1979-80, NEH fellow, 1988-89, Pres.'s Rsch. fellow U. Calif., 1988-89. Mem. MLA (exec. coun. 1985-88), English Inst. (supervising com. 1983-86). Office: UCLA Dept English Los Angeles CA 90024

YEE, DARLENE, health educator; b. N.Y.C., Sept. 19, 1958; d. Jimmy Tow and Yuen Hing (Chin) Y. BA in Biology, Barnard Coll., 1980; MS in Gerontology, Coll. New Rochelle, 1981; MS in Health Edn., Columbia U., 1984, EdD in Health Edn., 1985. Asst. lab dir. biology Barnard Coll., N.Y.C., 1980-83; rsch. asst., safety rsch. and edn. project Tchrs. Coll., N.Y.C., 1983-85; asst. prof. health and phys. edn. York Coll., N.Y.C., 1985-88; cons. Transp. Rsch. Bd., Washington, 1987, N.Y. State Dept. Edn., Albany, 1987; assoc. prof. clin. gerontology, health edn. and promotion U. Tex. Med. Br., Galveston, 1988-90; assoc. prof. health edn. San Francisco State U., 1990—. Contbr. articles to profl. jours. Mem. Am. Pub. Health Assn., Gerontol. Soc. Am., Am. Soc. on Aging, Assn. for Advancement of Health Edn., Nat. Coun. on Aging, Tex. Soc. Allied Health Profls., Soc. Health Educators. Home: 40 Meadow Park Circle Belmont CA 94002 Office: San Francisco State U Dept Health Edn San Francisco CA 94132

YEE, SUSAN G., social services administrator; b. Mpls., May 29, 1948; d. Amber Charles and Dayle (Walker) Gruetzmacher; m. George K. Yee, June 26, 1971 (div. Oct. 1987). BA, North Park Coll., Chgo., 1971. Claims examiner Blue Cross, Blue Shield Ill., 1971-73; service rep. Scheer Fin. Corp., Chgo., 1973-75; claims rep. CNA Ins. Cos, Chgo., 1975-80; sr. service rep. First Chgo. Corp., human resource officer, 1987--. Mem. ParkRidge Gilbert & Sullivan Soc. (pres. 1988-89). Republican. Evangelical. Office: First Chgo Corp 1 First National Pla Chicago IL 60670

YEH, CHARLOTTE SHAWING, physician; b. Ames, Iowa, Feb. 14, 1952; d. Charles Chia Ching and Sally Shing Shing (Liu) Y.; m. Frederick Murray Gale; children: Julianne Yulan Gale, Jessalyn Yulien Gale. BS, Northwestern U., Evanston, Ill., 1973; MD, Northwestern U., Chgo., 1975. Diplomate Am. Bd. Emergency Medicine. Surg. intern U. Wash., Seattle, 1975-76; surg. resident UCLA, L.A., 1976-77, emergency medicine resident, 1978-79; staff physician emergency dept. Newton Wellesley Hosp., Mass., 1980-86, chief emergency dept., 1986—. Recipient Elliot Strom Meml. award Am. Coll. Emergency Physcians (Mass. chpt.), 1985, Outstanding Mem. of Yr. award, 1986, Emergency Med. Svcs. award Commonwealth of Mass., 1987, Individual of Yr. award for Outstanding Achievement in Field of Occupant Protection for Citizens of Mass., 1986; named Outstanding Resident II of Yr. UCLA, 1977. Fellow Am. Coll. Emergency Physicians (bd. dirs. 1988—); mem. Alpha Lambda Delta, Alpha Omega Alpha. Office: Newton Wellesley Hosp Chief Emergency Dept Newton MA 02162

YEISER, DORIS BEVERLY, administrative assistant, secretary; b. Owensboro, Ky., July 31, 1920; d. George Stout and Mary Beatrice (O'Flynn) Y. Student, Campbellsville Coll., 1952; LLD (hon.), Georgetown Coll., 1989. Factory, radio tubes Ken-Rad, Owensboro, Ky., 1939-47; ch. sec. First Bapt. Ch., Owensboro, 1947-51; office sec. Ky. Bapt. Conv., Louisville, 1951-67, adminstrv. sec., 1967-76, adminstrv. asst., 1976-86, archivist, cons., 1986—; workshop leader Assn. Clks., Louisville, 1964-86. Mem. Ky. Bus. & Profl. Women (pres. 1975-76), Nat. Bus. & Profl. Women (com. mem. 1976-79), Coun. Women Pres. (pres. 1972-73), St. Matthews Bus. & Profl. Women (pres. 1972-73), Women's C. of C., Ky. (pres. 1984-86), Women's C. of C. Metro Louisville, Nat. Conf. Women in C. of C. (pres. 1989-90). Democrat. Baptist. Home: 246 Salisbury Sq #101 Louisville KY 40207

YELENICK, MARY THERESE, lawyer; b. Denver, May 17, 1954; d. John Andrew and Maesel Joyce (Reed) Y. B.A. magna cum laude, Colo. Coll., 1976; J.D. cum laude, Georgetown U., 1979. Bar: D.C. 1979, U.S. Dist. Ct. D.C. 1980, U.S. Ct. Appeals (D.C. cir.) 1981, N.Y. 1982, U.S. Dist. Ct. (so. and ea. dists.) N.Y. 1982. Law clk. to presiding justices Superior Ct. D.C., 1979-81; assoc. Chadbourne & Parke, N.Y.C., 1981—. Editor Jour. of Law and Policy Internat. Bus., 1978-79. Mem. Phi Beta Kappa. Democrat. Roman Catholic. Home: 310 E 46th St New York NY 10017 Office: Chadbourne & Parke 30 Rockefeller Plaza New York NY 10112

YELLEN, LINDA BEVERLY, film director, writer, producer; b. Forest Hills, N.Y., July 13, 1949; d. Seymour and Bernice (Mittelman) Y. BA magna cum laude, Barnard Coll., 1969; MFA in Film, Columbia U., 1971, PhD in Lang., Lit. and Communications, 1975. Mem. film faculty Columbia U., N.Y.C., 1971-73, Barnard Coll., 1971-73, Yale U., 1970-71, CUNY, 1974; prin. Chrysalis-Yellen Prodns., Inc., N.Y.C., 1982—; pres. The Linda Yellen Co., N.Y.C., 1988—. Producer, dir.: (films) Prospera, 1969; Come Out, Come Out, 1971; Looking Up, 1978; exec. producer (film) Everybody Wins, 1989; producer, dir., co-writer (film) Prisoner Without a Name, Cell Without A Number, NBC-TV, 1983 (Peabody award, Writers Guild nominee for best screenplay); exec. producer, producer (CBS network spls.): Hard Hat and Legs, 1980; Mayflower: The Pilgrims Adventure, 1979; Playing For Time, 1980 (Emmy award for best dramatic spl., Peabody award, Christopher award); exec. producer, producer, co-writer (CBS network spl.) The Royal Romance of Charles and Diana, 1982; exec. producer, producer (TV movies): Second Serve: The Renee Richards Story, CBS-TV, 1986 (Luminous award), Liberace, CBS-TV, 1988; exec. producer Hunt for Stolen War Treasures, syndicated TV, 1989, Sweet Bird of Youth, NBC-TV, 1989; contbr. articles to N.Y. Times, Village Voice, Interview, Hollywood Reporter. Mem. Dirs. Guild Am. (exec. council), Writers Guild Am., Acad. TV Arts and Scis. Address: Worldvision 660 Madison Ave 3rd Fl New York NY 10021

YERKES, SUSAN GAMBLE, columnist; b. Evanston, Ill., Sept. 5, 1951; d. Charles Anthony Yerkes and Darthea (Campbell) Higgins. BA, U. Tex., 1974; MA, Wichita State U., 1976. Anchor radio newsperson Sta. KAKE, Wichita, Kans., 1976; writer, anchor TV newsperson Sta. KAKE-TV, Wichita, 1976-80, dir. pub. affairs, 1977-81; freelance writer internat. and U.S. newspapers and mags., 1981-86; columnist San Antonio Light, 1986—; co-owner Y&S Communications, San Antonio, San Diego, 1987—; instr. communication arts Incarnate Word Coll., San Antonio, 1989—; contbg. writer Tex. Monthly, Austin, Tex., 1989—. Dir. Tex. Pub. Radio, San Antonio, 1986—, San Antonio's Opera Guild, 1986—, Bexar County Women's Ctr., San Antonio, 1989—. Fellow Amundsen Inst. for U.S./Mexico Studies; mem. Nat. Press Women (1st place nat. column award 1987), Pub. Rel. Soc. Am., Internat. Women's Forum, Phi Beta Kappa (San Antonio chpt. bd. dirs.). Episcopalian. Home: 7711 Broadway 25C San Antonio TX 78209 Office: San Antonio Light 420 Broadway San Antonio TX 78205

YICK, PAULINA Y., computer programmer; b. Kowloon, Hong Kong, Sept. 28, 1961; came to U.S., 1982; d. King Chiu and Oi (Chung) Y. BS, N.J. Inst. Tech., 1987. Mgmt. trainee AT&T Info. Svcs., Parsippany, N.J., 1986; analyst Exxon Cen. Svcs., Florham Pk., N.J., 1987-88; computer programmer The Fed. Res. Bank of N.Y., N.Y.C., 1989—. Radio broadcaster Overseas Chinese Mission, N.Y.C., 1986; peer counselor N.J. Inst. Tech., Newark, 1984-86. Mem. Omicron Delta Kappa, Upsilon Pi Epsilon, Sigma Epsilon Mu.

YIH, MAE DUNN, state legislator; b. Shanghai, China, May 24, 1928; d. Chung Woo and Fung Wen (Feng) Dunn; m. Stephen W.H. Yih, 1953; children—Donald, Daniel. B.A., Barnard Coll., 1951; postgrad. Columbia U., 1951-52. Asst. to bursar Barnard Coll., N.Y.C., 1952-54; mem. Oreg. Ho. of Reps. from 36th dist., 1977-83, Oreg. Senate from 19th dist., 1983—. State Democratic precinct woman; mem. Clover Ridge Elem. Sch. Bd., Albany, Oreg., from 1969-78, Albany Union High Sch. Bd., from 1975-79. Mem. AAUW, LWV, Linn County Citizens for Retarded, Linn County Mental Health Assn. Episcopalian. Office: Oreg State Senate Salem OR 97310 Home: 34465 Yih Ln NE Albany OR 97321

YIM, MARY ANCILLA, school principal, library director, educator; b. Honolulu, Feb. 17, 1927; d. Ernest K. and Wai Shan (Ching) Y.; student St. Francis Normal Sch., Maria Regina Coll., 1948-52; B.S. in Edn., U. Dayton, 1957; M.S. in L.S., Cath. U. Am., 1962; postgrad. U. Hawaii, Honolulu, 1961-69; cert. advanced studies in instructional adminstrn. SUNY, Oswego, 1975. Joined Third Order of St. Francis, 1948; sec., receptionist, real estate, ins. and law office, Honolulu, 1944-48; tchr. St. Paul's Ch., Whitesboro, N.Y., 1950-52; tchr.-librarian St. Joseph's High Sch., Hilo, Hawaii, 1952-65, prin., 1965-71; asst. prin. Oswego (N.Y.) Cath. High Sch., 1971-75; dir. libr. Maria Regina Coll., Syracuse, N.Y., 1975-88, instr., 1976-79, asst. prof., 1979-82, assoc. prof., 1982-88; prin. St. Daniel Sch., Syracuse, 1988—. NDEA grantee in English, U. Hawaii, 1964. Mem. ALA, (pres. Cath. chpt. 1980-82; facilitator continuing edn. program 1982—), Assn. Supervision & Curriculum Devel., N.Y. Libr. Assns., Assn. Coll. & Rsch. Librs., Nat. Cath. Edn. Assn. Office: 611 S Roxford Rd Syracuse NY 13208

YINGLING, ADRIENNE E(LIZABETH), auditor; b. Hershey, Pa., June 10, 1959; d. Richard Terry Yingling and Dolores Jean (Ott) Brown. BA in acctg. summa cum laude, N.C. State U., 1989. Lic. real estate assoc., N.C. Asst. mgr. Fast Fare, Raleigh, 1979-80; statis. analyst S.P.A.R., Elmsford, N.Y., 1980-81; relocation dir., sales assoc. Realty World, Cary, N.C., 1981-83; product mgr. Southeastern Electronics, Raleigh, 1983-84; results acct. No. Telecom, Research Triangle Park, N.C., 1984-88; auditor Deloitte and Touche, CPA's, 1989—. Vol. Larnivore Preservation Trust. Mem. NAFE, Nat. Assn. Accts., N.C. State U. Acctg. Soc., Ayn Rand Inst., Phi Kappa Phi, Omicron Delta Epsilon. Avocations: photography, painting, reading, aerobics, dance. Home: 6019 Dixon Dr Raleigh NC 27609 Office: Deloitte and Touche 2000 Ctr Pla Bldg Raleigh NC 27602

YINGLING, JULIE MARGARET, education educator; b. Washington D.C., Feb. 19, 1948; d. Howard Leo and Eileen Mildred (Lambert) Y. BA, U. R.I., 1970; MA, U. Denver, 1979, PhD, 1981. Teaching fellow U. Denver, 1978-81; from lectr. to asst. prof. U. Wisc., Milw., 1981-85; asst. prof. to assoc. prof. U. North Colo., Greeley, 1985-88; visiting lectr. Humboldt State U., Arcata, Calif. Contbr. articles to profl. jours. Bd. mem. YWCA, Denver, 1979-81. Mem. Colo. Speech Communication Assn., (v.p. 1987-88, pres. 1988-89), Orgn. for Rsch. in Women and Communication (instl. sec., assoc. editor 1986—). Office: Humboldt State U Dept Speech Communication Arcata CA 95521

YINGST, BEVERLY ANN, corporate professional; b. Effingham, Ill., Mar. 6, 1955; d. William Eugene and Lois Eileen (Gloyd) Myers; 1 child, Ramona. Grad. high sch., Effingham. With Dixie Truckers Home, Effingham, 1973-74; nurses aid Rolling Hills Nursing Home, Effingham, 1974; with Crossroads Press, Effingham, 1974-81; leadperson handmailing Vern-Wood Press, Mt. Vernon, Ill., 1981—. Baptist. Lodge: Women of the Moose (charter). Home: RR 7 Box 216 Mount Vernon IL 62864 Office: Vern-Wood Press PO Box 1628 #1 Vern-wood Dr Mount Vernon IL 62864

YINGST, DIANE MARIE, computer programmer; b. L.A., July 19, 1961; d. Charles Edward and Nancy Jane (Adams) Y. BSBA, Calif. State U., Northridge, 1983. Bus. programmer Litton Data Command Systems, Agora, Calif., 1983-84; project leader Nat. Med. Enterprises, Santa Monica, Calif., 1984—. Fund raiser Cystic Fibrosis, L.A., 1984. Recipient Leadership award YWCA, L.A., 1990. Mem. Pilot EIS Users Group, Mgmt. Sci. Assn. (sec. 1983), Golden Key Soc., Beta Gamma Sigma.

YLVISAKER, JANE PENELOPE MITCHELL, decorative accessories and furniture importing company executive; b. Lymnynge, Kent, Eng., June 22, 1946; came to U.S., 1971; d. James Alastair and Mary Frances (Wayland) Mitchell; m. William Townsend Ylvisaker, May 11, 1972; 1 child, Jon A. Student, Inst. Videmanette, Rougemont, Switzerland, 1962-64. Rsch. asst. Bowater Scott, London, 1965-66, Benton & Bowles Advt., London, 1966; office mgr. Hans Schleger & Assocs., London, 1966-68; owner, mgr. Plain Jane Discotheque, London, 1966-68; saleswoman, photojournalist, sec., model various hotels, offices, TV, Cape Town, Johannesburg, South Africa, Harare, Rhodesia, Nairobi, Kenya, Beirut, Tokyo, Hong Kong, Singapore, 1968-71; owner, mgr. Jane Ylvisaker Imports, Barrington, Ill., 1989—. Mem. Chgo.-No. Ill. bd. Multiple Sclerosis; governing mem. Art Inst. Chgo.; mem. woman's bd. Boys and Girls Club Chgo., ball chmn., 1983; mem. woman's bd. Chgo. Symphony Orch. Republican Episcopalian. Office: Rte 7 122 W County Line Rd Barrington IL 60010

YÑIGUEZ, LINDA ELLEN, psychologist; b. Whittier, Calif., Oct. 4, 1960; d. Richard Joseph and Carol Ann (Federlee) Y. BA, Whittier Coll., 1982; MA, Calif. Sch. Profl. Psychology, L.A., 1985, PhD, 1988. Registered psychol. asst., Calif. Intern psychology Alcoholism Ctr. for Women, L.A., 1983-84; counseling intern. Youth Svc. Program, Anaheim, Calif., 1984-85; psychol. asst. Brainard Psychol. Assn., Pasadena, Calif., 1986-87; psychol. asst. Affiliated Psychiatric Med. Group, Rosemead, Calif., 1987-89, Rosemead, 1987-89; prin. Village Psychol. Assocs., Whittier, Calif., 1989—; asst. clin. prof. Sch. Medicine U. Southern Calif., Whittier, 1988—, health educator Family Practice Residency, 1988—; med. and legal cons. Barrington Psychiatric Ctr., West L.A., 1988. Organizing mem. Hispanic Outreach Task Force, Whittier, 1990; juv. diversion counselor Community Svc. Program, Costa Mesa, Calif., 1984. Mem. Am. Psychol. Assn., L.A. County Psychol. Assn., Hispanic Women's Coun., Inc., Soc. Tchrs. of Family Medicine, Soroptomist.

YNTEMA, MARY KATHERINE, mathematics educator; b. Urbana, Ill., Jan. 20, 1928; d. Leonard Francis and M. Jean (Busey) Y. BA in Math., Swarthmore Coll., 1950; MA in Math., U. Ill., 1961, PhD in Math., 1965. Tchr., secondary math. Am. Coll. for Girls, Istanbul, Turkey, 1950-54, Columbus (Ohio) Sch. for Girls, 1954-57; computer programmer MIT Lincoln Lab., Lexington, Mass., 1957-58; tchr., secondary math Roundup (Mont.) High Sch., 1959-60; asst. prof. math U. Ill., Chgo., 1965-67; asst. prof. computer sci. Pa. State U., University Park, 1967-71; assoc. prof. to prof. math. Sangamon State U., Springfield, Ill., 1971—. Mem. Math. Assn. Am., Am. Math. Soc., Assn. for Computing Machinery, Am. Assn. U. Profs., Sigma Xi. Office: Sangamon State U Springfield IL 62794-9243

YOCHELSON, KATHRYN MERSEY, art researcher; b. N.Y.C., Oct. 22, 1910; d. Nathan and Esther Mary Mersey; m. Samuel Yochelson, June 21, 1930 (dec. Nov. 1976); children: John Norman, Bonnie Ellen. BA in Art Edn., New Haven Tchrs. Coll., 1930; postgrad., Yale U., Columbia U., Albright Art Sch., Am. U., U. Md. Art tchr. New Haven Sch. System, 1930-39. Researcher on artistic roots of Jewish people, 1940—. Organized permanent art collection at Buffalo Jewish Ctr., 1952; chmn. Seven Painters of Israel exhibition, Albright-Knox Art Gallery, 1953, 20 Artists for Israel, George Washington U., Washington, 1968, Personal Vision: Yochelson Collection of Israeli Art, George Washington U., 1987; author: Israeli Art: Golden Threads; lectr. and contbr. articles in field; reviewed books in field. Vol. edn. dept. Albright-Knox Art Gallery, Buffalo, 1940-60; internat. bd. govs. Tel Aviv Mus. Art, 1977; established Dr. Samuel and Kathryn Yochelson meml. lectr. Yale U. Sch. Psychiatry, 1980. Mem. Sunday Scholar Series Com., Albright-Knox Art Gallery (life), Brandeis Women's Com. (life), Washington Watercolor Soc. (sec. 1971-72), Nat. Am. Pen Women. Home: 4201 Cathedral Ave Apt 824 East Washington DC 20016

YOCHEM, BARBARA JUNE, sales executive, shooting coach, lecturer; b. Knox, Ind., Aug. 22, 1945; d. Harley Albert and Rosie (King) Runyan; m. Donald A. Yochem (div. 1979); 1 child, Morgan Lee; m. Don Heard, Dec. 12, 1987. Grad. high school, Knox, Ind., 1963. Sales rep. Hunter Woodworks, Carson, Calif., 1979-84, sales mgr., 1984-87; sales rep. Comml. Lumber and Pallet, Industry, Calif., 1987—; owner By By Prodns., Glendora, Calif., 1976—. Author: Barbara Yochem's Inner Shooting; contbr. articles to profl. jours. Head coach NRA Jr. Olympic Shooting Camp, 1990. Recipient U.S. Bronze medal U.S. Olympic Com., 1976, World Bronze Medal U.S. Olympic Com., 1980. Address: By By Prodns PO Box 1676 Glendora CA 91740

YOCHIM, MARIE HIRST, retired association executive; b. Washington; d. Herbert Nelson and Ellen (Mankin) Hirst; m. Eldred Martin Yochim, Dec. 24, 1942. Student, Strayer Coll., 1939-40. Exec. officer Jesse Johnson, Inc., Lakewood Builders & Glenbrook Corp., Arlington, Va., 1940-56; regent DAR Falls Ch. (Va.) Chpt., 1956-62; dir. dist. V Va. DAR, 1962-65, state regent, 1977-80, mem. fin. com. bd. trustees, 1987—; chief of Corresponding Gen.'s Office Nat. Soc. DAR, Washington, 1962-77, organizing sec. gen., 1980-83, 1st v.p. gen., 1983-86, 1983-86, pres. gen., 1989—. Recipient bronze medal Chapel of Four Chaplains, 1980, Medal of Appreciation Va. Chtp. SAR, 1980, Va. Honor Pin Children of Revolution Va. Chpt., 1981. Lutheran. Clubs: Jamestown Soc., U.S. Daus. of 1812, Colonial Dames of XVII Century, Order of Eastern Star. Home: 7314 Hughes Ct Falls Church VA 22046 Office: 1776 D St NW Washington DC 20006

YODER, ANNA A., educator; b. Beach City, Ohio, Sept. 5, 1934; d. Abram J. and Barbara D. (Miller) Y. BS, Ea. Mennonite Coll., 1966; MEd, Frostburg State Coll., 1974. Cert. elem. tchr., Ohio, recreational leader. Tchr. Garrett County Schs., Oakland, Md., 1966-70; prin. elem. sch. Garrett County Schs., 1970-74; tchr. E. Holmes Local Schs., Berlin, Ohio, 1974—; chairperson edn. com. German Culture Mus., Berlin, Ohio, 1987—; cons. bilingual edn. E. Holmes Local Schs., Berlin, Ohio, 1982—. Supporting mem. German Culture Mus., Berlin, Ohio, 1983—; mem. Killbuck (Ohio) Valley mus., 1988—, Holmes County Hist. Soc., Millersburg, Ohio, 1989—; life mem. Mennonite Info. Ctr., Berlin, Ohio, 1985—; sustaining mem. The Wilderness Ctr., Wilmot, Ohio, 1974—. Jennings scholar Martha Holden Jennings Found., 1983-84; Silver Poet award World of Poetry, 1986. Mem.

AAUW, Creative Arts (sec.-treas. 1987-89), Delta Kappa Gamma (sec. Beta Iota chpt. 1987-90, pres. 1990—). Mennonite. Home: 6583 SR Millersburg OH 44654

YODER, CAROLYN PATRICIA, editor; b. Greenwich, Conn., July 2, 1953; d. Rufus Wayne and Kathryn Louise (Mulhollen) Y. B.A., Washington U., St. Louis, 1975; M.A., U. Iowa-Iowa City, 1979. Editorial asst. D.C. Heath & Co., Lexington, 1979-81; publs. asst. Internat. Human Resources Devel. Corp., Boston, 1981-82, prodn. editor, 1982-83; asst. editor Cobblestone, Cobblestone Pub., Inc., Peterborough, N.H., 1983, editor, 1983-84, editor-in-chief, 1984—, editor-in-chief Faces, 1984—, Classical Calliope, 1984—. Contbr. illustrations to Sojourner, Women, Lake Hope, Off Our Backs. Mem. Bookbuilders of Boston (prodn. coordinator winning book and cover New England Book Show 1983), Assn. Earth Sci. Editors, Greater Boston Rights and Permissions Group, Soc. Scholarly Pub., Ednl. Press Assn. Am. Democrat. Office: Cobblestone Publishing Inc 30 Grove St Peterborough NH 03458

YODER, PATRICIA DOHERTY, public relations executive; b. Pitts., Oct. 30, 1939; d. John Addison and Camella Grace (Conti) Doherty; children: Shari Lynn, Wendy Ann. BA, Duquesne U., 1961. Press sec. U.S. Ho. of Reps., 1965-69; dir. office of pub. info. City of Ft. Wayne, 1973-76; asst. mgr. pub. and corp. communications Mellon Bank N.A., Pitts., 1977-79; v.p. pub. affairs Am. Waterways Operators Inc., Washington, 1980-83; sr. v.p., gen. mgr. Hill and Knowlton Inc., Pitts., 1983-86, exec. v.p., dir. internat. banking, 1989—; sr. v.p. corp. and pub. affairs, PNC Fin. Corp, Pitts., 1987-89. Trustee The Ellis Sch., Pitts., Shadyside Hosp., Pitts., Human Resources Rsch. Orgn., Arlington, Va.; bd. dirs. Children's Mus., Pitts.; bd. dirs., exec. com., Civic Light Opera. Mem. Pitts. Field Club, Duquesne Club, Pitts. Athletic Assn., Rivers Club. Roman Catholic. Home: 6112 Kentucky Ave Pittsburgh PA 15206 Office: 600 Grant St 47th Fl Pittsburgh PA 15219

YODER, SHARON KATHLEEN, education educator; b. Wooster, Ohio, Sept. 16, 1942; d. John Thompson and Margaret Evelyn (Flanagan) Yoder; m. Theodore Cooley Burrowes, Aug. 7, 1965 (div. Apr. 1988); children: David, Bethanne, Scott, Bonnie; m. David G. Moursund, Oct. 19, 1989. BA, Coll Wooster, 1964; MAT, Oberlin Coll., 1965; PhD, U. Akron, 1983. Maths. tchr. Battle Creek (Mich.) Pub. Schs., 1965-66; Maths., Computer Sci., tchr., computer coord. Wooster City Schs., 1976-87; edn. specialist Logo Computer Systems Inc., N.Y., 1987—; editor, Logo Exchange Logo Exch. Internat. Soc. for Tech. in Edn., Eugene, 1987-; prof. computer edn. Univ. Oreg., Eugene, 1988-; cons. Ednl. Computers Consortium Ohio, 1985-86. Author: Introduction to Logo Programming Using Logowriter, 1988, Introduction to Logo Programming Using Logo Plus, 1988; columnist The Computing Teacher, 1988—. Mem. Nat. Com. for Computer competency, Nat. Assessment of Ednl. Mem. Internat. Soc. for Tech. in Edn., N.W. Coun. Computers in Edn. Presbyterian. Office: U Oregon 1787 Agate St 21787 Agate St Eugene OR 97403

YODER WISE, PATRICIA SNYDER, nurse educator; b. Wadsworth, Ohio, July 2, 1941; d. Belford Grant and Leona Cora (Mohler) Snyder; m. Robert Thomas Wise, Feb. 17, 1973; children: Doreen Ellen, Deborah Ann. BS in Nursing, Ohio State U., 1963; MS in Nursing, Wayne State U., 1968; EdD, Tex. Tech. U., 1984. Cert. gerontol. nurse and nursing administr., RN, Tex., Ohio. Rsch. asst. Wayne State U., Detroit, 1968; ednl. dir. Ohio Nurses' Assn., Columbus, 1968-72; asst. dir. nursing Mt. Clemens (Mich.) Gen. Hosp., 1972-73; assoc. prof., head of nursing Ferris State Coll., Big Rapids, Mich., 1975-77; assoc. prof., dir. continuing edn. U. Colo., Denver, 1977-79; assoc. dean, assoc. prof. Sch. Nursing Tex. Tech. U. Health Scis. Ctr., Lubbock, 1979-86, assoc. dean, prof. Sch. Nursing, 1986-87, interim assoc. dean grad. program, 1988-89, exec. assoc. dean, prof. nursing, 1987—; prin. p.t. Wylan Assocs., Lubbock, 1989—; mem. acad. adv. panel nursing Hosp. Satellite Network, 1983—, Nurses Coalition Acad. adv. panel, nursing, 1902—, bd. dirs. RN Polit. Action Com., 1989—. Editor Jour. Continuing Edn. in Nursing, 1986—. Mem. Am. Nurses Assn. (site visitor continuing edn. 1982—), Tex. Nurses Assn. (bd. mem. 1989—, pres. dist. 18 1987-89), Coun. Continuing Edn., Tex. Nurses Found. (bd. dirs.), Century Club. Home: 3713 95th St Lubbock TX 79423

YOGEV, SARA, psychologist; b. Tel Aviv, May 23, 1946; came to U.S.A., Israel 1975; d. Israel and Cila (Fink) Frankel; m. Ram Yogev, Oct. 2, 1967; children: Eldad, Shelly, Tomer. BA, Hebrew U., 1965-69, MA, 1970-73; PhD, Northwestern U., Evanston, Ill., 1976-79. Reg. Psychologist, Ill., 1981. Clin. experience dist. sch. psychologist Office Edn. and Culture, Jerusalem, Israel, 1968-71; intern. Beer Yaakov Psychiatric Hosp., Israel, 1971-72; asst. dir. Dept. Psychology, Hebrew U., Jerusalem, Israel, 1972-73; psychotherapist Mental Health Ctr., Hebrew U., Jerusalem, Israel; clin. psychologist Inst. Psychoanalysis, Jerusalem, Israel, 1973-75; psychotherapist, supr. Youth and Family Services, Ill., 1977-80; reg. psychologist pvt. practice Skokie, Chgo., 1981-; academic experience instr. counseling psychology, 1977-79, asst. prof., Northwestern U., 1979-82, research psychologist at the rank asst. prof., 1983-86, visiting scholar, Ctr. Urban Affairs and Policy Research, 1987. Contbr. articles to profl. jours. and books. Mem. American Assn. for Marriage and Family Therapy, American Psyhological Assn., Nat. Register Health Service. Jewish. Office: 5225 Old Orchard Rd #32 Skokie IL 60077

YOHALEM, RONA A., advertising executive; b. N.Y.C., May 7, 1946; d. Al and Sue Aronson; children: Matthew David, Beth. BA, Queens Coll., 1965; MA, NYU, 1972, PhD, 1979. Dir. rsch. Manhattan Children's Psychiat. Ctr., Wards Island, N.Y., 1979-80; with rsch. dept. Dancer-Fitzgerald-Sample, N.Y.C., 1980-81, D'Arcy Macmaus & Masius, N.Y.C., 1981-82; sr. v.p., dir. strategic planning Geer DuBois Advt., N.Y.C., 1982—; adj. prof. NYU, 1979-82. Named one of 100 Best and Brightest Women in Advt., Advertising Age, 1988. Mem. Am. Mktg. Assn. (exec.), Am. Psychol. Assn., Advt. Women N.Y. Home: 340 W 87th St New York NY 10024 Office: Geer DuBois Inc 114 Fifth Ave New York NY 10011

YOHANN, MONICA JEAN, psychic consultant; b. Milw., Jan. 26, 1953; d. Eugene K. and Ruth Marion (Oleniczak) Drew; m. Peter William Yohann, June 3, 1955. Cert. data processing, Milw. Bus. and Tech. Inst., 1980. Nursing asst., lab. asst. Milw. County Med. Complex, 1971-76; pvt. practice Milw., 1976—; lectr. in field; needlework cons. Twixter's, Milw., 1980—; founder United New Age Ch., Milw., 1984—. Author, editor: newsletter Lunar Letter, 1977-80. Mem. NAFE, Twixter's of Milw. (record planner 1985). Democrat. Home and Office: 2008 S 31st Milwaukee WI 53215

YOHN, SHARON A., manufacturing executive; b. Altoona, Pa., Mar. 2, 1952. AS in Retail, Harcum Jr. Coll. (Pa.), 1972; BSBA, Villanova U., 1976. Dir. overseas ops. Europe airwalk div. Items Internat. Inc., Altoona, Pa. and Carlsbad, Calif., 1987—. Republican. Office: Items Internat/Airwalk 2042 Corte del Nogal Carlsbad CA 92009

YONUSAITIS, LINDA SUSAN, special education and elementary educator, environmentalist; b. Bklyn., Dec. 23, 1954; d. Edward Joseph and Dorothy Virginia (Brestlin) Y. Student, Nassau Community Coll., 1973-75; BA Child Study, Spl. Edn., St. Joseph's Coll., Brentwood, L.I., N.Y., 1977; MS in Deaf Edn. and Speech Pathology/Audiology, Adelphi U., 1986. Cert. elem., spl. edn., multihandicapped, deaf/hearing impaired tchr., State of N.Y., elem. and multihamdicapped deaf/hearing impaired Coun. on Edn. of Deaf, Washington. Direct care resident counselor, instr. EPIC House Epilepsy Found. Nassau County, Garden City, Hicksville, L.I., N.Y., 1981-87; naturalist, instr. outdoor and environ. edn. Caumsett State Park and various ctrs. L.I., N.Y. Nassau Bd. Coop. Ednl. Svcs., 1978-84, subs. tchr. spl. edn., multihandicapped, Rosemary Kennedy Ctr., 1979-80, 87-90; tutor/cons. elem., secondary study skills, spl. edn., deaf and hearing impaired, Wantagh, 1978, 81, 84-86, 88—; home instrn., spl. edn. biol. and earth sci, tutor, Creative Tutoring Inc., L.I., 1989; subs. tchr. deaf edn. early intervention and programs for hearing impaired Nassau Bd. Coop. Ednl. Svcs., Wantagh, Merrick and North Merrick, L.I., 1985-90; tchr. various extended year summer programs for multihandicapped, physically disabled, and mentally handicapped, deaf and hearing impaired, L.I., 1983, 87—. Author: College Study Guide in Anatomy and Physiology Questions and Answers, Methods Guide to Young Adult Meetings in Special Education: A Series of Applied Christian Living Skills, 1980-90; contbg. author studies of The Office of Mental Retardation and Devel. Disabilities, Horticulture Therapy Organic Gardening, 1983; founder Good Guys newsletter Let's Communicate, 1988; contbr. articles to mags., directories and newsletters. Vol. fund raiser United Cerebral Palsy Assn. Nassau County, 1969-79, Forest City Community Assn., Wantagh, 1973-80; tutor Elem. Remedial Reading Club Parochial Sch., Deer Pk., 1976; spl. edn. tchr. St. Frances de Chantal Religious Edn. Program, Wantagh, 1979-82; dir. and spl. edn. instr. Young Adult Evening Meetings, The Good Guys-Spl. Guides, Wantagh, Diocese of Rockville Ctr., L.I., 1982—; horticulture and organic gardening program developer Community Based Intermediate Care Facility, EPIC House, 1982-86; participant various antinuclear rallies, Shoreham, L.I., N.Y.C., 1979. Recipient rsch. assistantship Dept. Speech Arts & Communicative Disorders, Adelphi U., 1984-85, scholarship Grad. Sch. Arts & Scis., 1984, Honorable Mention Interdisciplinary Team Excellence Nat. Epilepsy Assn. Am. to EPIC House, 1982. Mem. AAUW, MADD, Am. Assn. on Mental Retardation, Bicultural Exch., Talking Over and Understanding Children with Handicaps, Endometriosis Assn., Nat. Coun. Therapy and Rehab. Through Horticulture, Sierra Club, Nature Conservancy, Women's Sports Found., Am. Hort. Therapy Assn.

YOPP, JOHANNA FUTCHS, management consultant; b. Wilmington, N.C., Sept. 6, 1938; d. Richard and Louise (Friedman) Futchs; m. James D. Yopp Jr., Dec. 26, 1959; children: Beverly, Lynn, James III, Sara Katherine. BA, U. N.C., Greensboro, 1960. Tchr. New Hanover County Schs., Wilmington, N.C., 1960-62, Winston-Salem (N.C.) Forsyth County Schs., 1962-68; mgr. James D. Yopp Jr. MD, Winston-Salem, 1971—. Vol. Winston-Salem/Forsyth County Schs., Winston-Salem Optimist Soccer Club, 1970-73; leader Girl Scouts U.S., Winston-Salem, 1970-73; pres. Mt. Tabor High Sch. PTA, Winston-Salem, 1986-87, 87-88; mem. Forsyth-Stokes Med. Aux., Bowman Gray Med. Ctr. Aux., Winston-Salem, U. N.C. Centennial Planning Bd. Mem. NAFE, Am. Mgmt. Assn. Republican. Lutheran. Home: 3410 Thoresby Ct Winston-Salem NC 27104 Office: 602 Forsyth Med Pk Winston-Salem NC 27103

YOPP, SUZANNE ANDERSON, commercial revitalization planner; b. Pitts., Nov. 17, 1948; d. Charles Pederick and Margaret (Hoch) Sheldon; m. Thomas Walter Anderson, Aug. 26, 1972(div. July 1976); m. Jesse Lawrence Yopp, Nov. 21, 1984; stepchildren: Marguerite Jane, Laura Beth. AS, Temple U., 1970; BS, U. Mass., 1972; M in City Planning, U. Va., 1977. Planning aide Cape May (N.J.) County Planning Commn., 1970-72; land planner Pharmer Engring., Holyoke, Mass., 1972-75; program asst. HUD, Washington, 1976-77; sr. planner City of Yonkers (N.Y.) Planning Bur., 1977-80; planning mgr. Montgomery County Comml. Revitalization Program, Rockville, Md., 1980—; promotions mgr. Silver Spring (Md.) Urban Dist., 1987—, Bethesda (Md.) Urban Dist., 1989—. Mem. Econ. and Bus. Devel. Corp., Rockville, 1983-86, Flower-Piney br. Local Devel. Corp., Silver Spring, 1980-86. Four Year Coll. Scholar Ocean City Tabernacle Assn., 1967-71, Grad. Scholar U. Va., 1975-77. Mem. Internat. Downtown Assn., Internat. Coun. of Shopping Ctrs. Republican. Lutheran. Office: Montgomery County Maryland 51 Monroe St Ste 1001 Rockville MD 20850

YORBURG, BETTY (MRS. LEON YORBURG), educator; b. Chgo., Aug. 27, 1926; d. Max and Hannah (Bernstein) Gitelman; Ph.B., U. Chgo., 1945, M.A., 1948; Ph.D., New Sch. Social Research, 1968; m. Leon Yorburg, June 23, 1946; children—Harriet, Robert. Instr., Coll. New Rochelle, 1966-67; lectr. City Coll. and Grad. Center, City U. N.Y., 1967-69, asst. prof., 1969-73, asso. prof. sociology dept., 1973-77, prof., 1978—; research asst. Prof. Clifford Shaw, Chgo. Area Project, 1946-47. Mem. Am., Eastern sociol. assns., Am. Council Family Relations, AAAS, N.Y. Acad. of Scis. Author: Utopia and Reality, 1969; The Changing Family, 1973; Sexual Identity: Sex Roles and Social Change, 1974; The New Women, 1976; Introduction to Sociology, 1982; Families and Societies, 1983. Home: 20 Earley St City Island NY 10464 Office: CCNY Sociology Dept 138th & Convent Ave New York NY 10031

YORIO, JUDITH MARY, physical education educator; b. Troy, N.Y., Sept. 12, 1952; d. Joseph Anthony and Sylvia Mary (Bonomo) Yorio. BS, Springfield Coll., 1974; MS, So. Conn. Coll., 1980; EdD, U. Ga., 1989. Jr.-sr. high sch. phys. educator, coach Somers (Conn.) High Sch., 1974-80; phys. edn. educator, adminstr. Dickinson Coll., Carlisle, Pa., 1980—. Contbr. articles to profl. jours. Named one of top 5 coaches in state State of Conn., 1975, 76; Nat. Student Lit. award Am. Assn. Leisure and Recreation, 1988; M.E. Soule award U. Ga., 1988. Mem. AAHPER, Am. Coll. Sports Medicine, Carlisle Running Club. Office: Dickinson Coll Kline Ctr Carlisle PA 17013

YORK, ANNE HALSTEAD, public relations executive; b. N.Y.C., Feb. 18, 1945; d. William Storm and Leslie (Munro) Halstead; m. Richard F. York, Jan. 29, 1966; 1 child, Halstead Winship Guthridge York. Grad. high sch., N.Y.C. Asst. mktg. coord. Vasserete, Inc., N.Y.C., 1970-71; fashion coord. Lyntex Co., N.Y.C., 1971-72; account exec. The Merchandising Group, N.Y.C., 1973; sr. account exec. McGrath, Power Assoc., N.Y.C.; pres. York Co., N.Y.C., 1978-84; bur. chief Calif. Apparel News, N.Y.C., 1984; pub. rels. couns. Combe, Incorp., N.Y., 1985; adj. tchr. Fashion Inst. Tech., Marist Coll. Communications, 1982, 84; bd. dirs. OPUS, High Falls, N.Y. Author: Family Circle, 1980. Mem. Jr. League of Bklyn., 1977-79. Mem. NAFE, Men's Fashion Assn. Democrat.

YORK, BERYL ROXANNE, management consultant; b. N.Y.C., Apr. 22, 1938; d. Joseph and Jean (Goldman) Y.; m. Donald Malawsky, Aug. 23, 1960; 1 child, Douglas. BS, U. Wis., 1960; MS, U. Denver, 1966; PhD, Union Grad Sch., 1976. Fellow U. Denver, 1966-68; instr. Colo. Woman's Coll., Denver, 1968-69; prof. CUNY, 1969-78; assoc. Human Systems Inc., Morristown, N.J., 1978-81; pres. York Assocs., Upper Montclair, N.J., 1981—. Author: Changing Role of Personnel Assistant, 1985, Role of Personnel Assistant, 1986, Assertiveness Training for Women In Business, 1987, Changing Role of Executive Secretary; contbr. articles to profl. jours. Mem. Nat. Assn. Female Execs., Am. Mgmt. Assn., Am. Soc. Tng. Devel., Phi Beta Kappa. Club: Princeton (N.Y.C.). Office: York Assocs 214 Little Falls Rd Fairfield NJ 07004

YORK, ELIZABETH JANE, innkeeper; b. Camden, N.J., July 27, 1934; d. Charles Evans and Christine (Taggart) Yorke; m. Anthony Neil Gaeta, April 2, 1960 (div. Jan. 1986); children: Greg, Anthony, Anne. BA, Wheaton (Ill.) Coll., Ill., 1957; postgrad., U. N.C., 1957-58. Owner Designing Woman, Minot, Mass., 1976-81; broker Vin Doyle Real Estate, Scituate, Mass., 1978-81; owner, innkeeper The Four Chimneys, Nantucket Island, Mass., 1981-90. Group dir. Scituate Newcomers Club, 1976-81; vol. Hosp. Thrift Shop, Nantucket, 1982—, Second Shop, Nantucket, 1982—; mem. Nantucket Conservation Found. Mem. Nantucket C. of C., Cape Cod C. of C., Nantucket Hist. Soc., Nantucket Lodging Assn. Republican. Episcopalian. Club: Cliffside Beach. Home: 22 Madaket Rd Nantucket Island MA 02554

YORK, JANET BREWSTER, nurse, family and sex therapist, sculptor; b. N.Y.C., Mar. 5, 1941; d. Edward Cox and Janet Stone Brewster; AA with honors, Briarcliff Coll., 1961; RN with highest honors, U. Iowa, 1965; BA summa cum laude, Marymount Manhattan Coll., 1975; MA with honors, N.Y. U., 1978; m. Albert Thompson York, Mar. 31, 1962 (dec.); children: Clifton Gaston, Torrance Brewster; 1 adopted child, Justin Brigham. Nurse, Manhattan Eye, Ear and Throat Hosp., N.Y.C., 1966-74; nurse, counselor Washington Free Clinic, 1969-71; family therapist Ackerman Family Inst., N.Y.C., 1976-80; sex therapist N.Y. Med. Coll., Flower Fifth Ave Hosp., N.Y.C., 1976-80; individual practice family and sex therapy, N.Y.C., 1978—; supervisory staff grad. edn. program in human sexuality N.Y.U. Med. Ctr., 1982—; sculpter, 1988—. Bd. dirs. Spence/Chapin Adoption Agy., Manhattan Eye, Ear and Throat Hosp. Fellow Internat. Coun. of Sex Edn. and Parenthood, Am. U., 1981; recipient Evelyn Monte Sculpture award, 1988. Mem. Am. Soc. for Sex Therapy and Research, Am. Assn. Sex Edn., Counseling and Therapy, Soc. for Sci. Study Sex, Sex Info. and Edn. Council U.S., Am. Assn. Marriage and Family Therapists. Clubs: Lawrence Beach, Rockaway Hunting, N.Y.U, Millbrook. Represented in permanent collection The Dog Mus. of Am., St. Louis; contbr. articles to profl. jours.; also videotape Death as a Part of Life. Home: 155 E 72d St New York NY 10021

YORK, JUDITH ANN, rehabilitation technology consultant; b. Johnson City, N.Y., Dec. 30, 1955; d. Edward R. and Helen Patricia (Tomasek) York. BS in Edn., SUNY, Geneseo, 1977; MS in Indsl. Relations, U. New Haven, 1989. Placement counselor The Kennedy Ctr., Bridgeport, Conn., 1977-78; placement specialist Easter Seal of Greater Waterbury, Conn., 1978-79; job seeking skills specialist Constructive Workshops, Inc., New Britain, Conn., 1979-80; prog. mgr. NEABIR, New Haven, 1980-86; v.p. progs. NEABIR, 1986-88; cons. Rehab. Engring. Assocs., Madison, Conn., 1988—. Mem. Nat. Rehab. Assn., N.E. Rehab. Assn. (nat. rep. 1986-88), Conn. Rehab. Assn. (pres. 1983-84). Home: 314 Chapman Mill Pond #10 Westbrook CT 06498 Office: Rehab Engring Assocs PO Box 1129 Madison CT 06443

YORK, LINDA KAYE, dental hygienist; b. Connersville, Ind., Feb. 28, 1948; d. Clyde Wayne and Camille Grace (Stewart) L.; m. Gary William York, Sept. 28, 1968; children: David Craig Hewitt, Stacy Lynn; (div. 1979). AS, Ind. U., Indpls., 1979; BA, Purdue U., 1983. Administrv. asst. Nichols Fin. Corp., Indpls., 1969-76; engr. York Equipment, Indpls., 1976-79; sales rep. Dynaforce, N.Y.C., 1979-82; cons., dental hygienist Dr. George E. Kirtley, Indpls., 1979—; realtor Mclane Reality, Indpls., 1986—. Author poems, 1981; contbg. editor Registrar, Voting Poll, 1976; contbr. articles to pubs. Registrar, Voting Poll, Indianapolis, 1976, Geriatric Screening, Oral. Mem., Am. Dental Hygenists Assn., Real Estate Commission.

YORK, NANCY ANN, educator; b. San Antonio, Sept. 2, 1947; d. James Malcolm and Jeannette Imogene (Collins) Graham; m. Victor Allen York, Dec. 19, 1969; children: Travis Allen, Sarah Jane. Student, San Antonio Coll., 1965-66; BA, U. Tex., 1968; MEd, S.W. Tex. State U., 1972; postgrad., U. Tex., San Antonio, 1974-76. Lic. profl. counselor. Tchr. San Antonio Ind. Sch. Dist., 1969-72, sch. counselor, 1972-90, asst. prin., 1990—; mem. fin. aid and scholarship task force U. Tex., San Antonio, 1987-88, standing com. on tchr. edn., 1982-84, grad. ednl. prog. curriculum com., 1988. Co-author: Guidance and Counseling Handbook for San Antonio District, 1975-76. Named Outstanding Young Woman of Am., 1980. Mem. South Tex. Assn. for Counseling and Devel., Assn. Tex. Profl. Educators, Tex. Assn. for Counseling and Devel., Nat. Assn. for Secondary Sch. Prins., Tex. Assn. for Secondary Sch. Prins., San Antonio Area Women Deans, Adminstrs. and Counselors, Assn. Profls. in Positions of Leadership in Edn., U. Tex. at Austin Ex-students Assn., U. Tex. at San Antonio Alumni Assn. (pres. 1981-83), U. Tex. San Antonio Roadrunner Club, San Antonio Execs. for Tex. (town co-capt. 1990), Kappa Delta Pi, Phi Delta Kappa (found. rep. 1982-83), Alpha Delta Kappa (treas. 1988-90, scholarship chair Beta Psi chpt. 1990—). Roman Catholic. Office: San Antonio Ind Sch Dist 141 Lavaca St San Antonio TX 78210

YORKE, MARIANNE, lawyer; b. Ridley Park, Pa., Nov. 4, 1948; d. Joseph George and Catherine Veronica (Friel) Y. BA, West Chester U., 1970; JD, Temple U., 1980; MS, U. Pa., 1987. Bar: Pa. 1981. Real estate mgr. CIGNA Service Co., Phila., 1981-85, asst. dir., Phila., 1985-89; v.p. real estate resources Chase Manhattan Bank, N.Y.C., 1989—; cons., 1981-82; real estate atty. Garfinkel & Volpicelli, Phila., 1980-81; prin., mng. ptnr. Yorke/Eisenman, Real Estate, Phila., 1976-88, prin., mng. ptnr. Yorke/Mac Lachlin Real Estate, Phila, 1989—; lectr. Women in the Arts, 1982—; guest speaker Wharton Sch. Bus. Class of 1989, U. Pa. Contbr. articles to profl. jours. Solicitor Pa. Ballet, Phila., 1983—, United Way, Phila., 1983—; mem. steering com. U. Pa., 1986—, dir. alumni assn., 1987—; mem. adv. com. for econ. devel. Luth. Settlement House Adv.; bd. dirs. Hamilton Townhouse Assn., 1989, chmn. ins. com., 1989-90. Mem. ABA (forum on constrn.), Pa. Bar Assn. (condominium and zoning coms.), Phila. Bar Assn., Phila. Women Real Estate Attys., Nat. Assn. Corp. Real Estate Execs. (internat. coun., comml. coun.), Internat. Atty's Roundtable, Women's Law Caucus, German Soc., Phi Alpha Delta. Republican. Roman Catholic. Office: Chase Manhattan Bank Real Estate Resources 1 New York Pla Ste 13 New York NY 10081

YOSHII, RIKA, computer science researcher; b. Osaka, Japan, Jan. 6, 1959; came to U.S., 1971; d. Tad George and Hiroko (Tatsumi) Y. BS summa cum laude, U. Calif., Irvine, 1981, MS, 1983, PhD, 1986. Mem. rsch. staff Northrop Rsch. & Tech. Ctr., Palos Verdes, Calif., 1987-89; lectr., rsch. assoc. U. Calif., Irvine, 1989—; reviewer NSF, Washington, 1988-89; participant Indsl. Initiative for Sci. and Math. Edn., L.A., 1988. Contbr. articles to profl. publs. Mem. Assn. Computational Linguistics, Assn. Computing Machinery, Assn. Artificial Intelligence, Computer Assisted Lang. Learning and Instrn. Consortium, Phi Beta Kappa. Republican. Office: ICS Dept U Calif Irvine Irvine CA 92717

YOSHIKAWA, VIVECA RUTH, library automation specialist; b. Lund, Sweden, Nov. 12, 1944; came to U.S., 1965; d. Walther Sigfried Gustav and Ruth Kerstin (Nilsson) Edenheim; m. Tetsuo Yoshikawa, Dec. 18, 1965; children: Miko Ingrid, Makoto Daniel, Akiko Kristina. AA in Latin, Malmö (Sweden) Latinskola, 1964; AS in Computer Sci., Hillsborough Community Coll., Tampa, Fla., 1988. Libr., cataloger Libr. Congress, Washington, 1968-72; libr. technician Hillsborough Community Coll., 1982-86, project leader libr. automation, 1986-88, libr. automation specialist, 1988—. Republican. Presbyterian. Home: 311 E Windhorst Rd Brandon FL 33510 Office: Hillsborough Community Coll 1502 E 9th Ave Tampa FL 33605

YOST, BERNICE, special agent Internal Revenue Service; b. Houston; d. Kenneth Wayne and Georgia (Sampson) Cox; m. Matthew Yost. Student, Los Angeles Trade Tech, 1968-70, Compton Coll., 1974-76, Ariz. State U., 1983-85. Staff acct. Moultrie, Liggens, Terrel CPA's, Los Angeles, 1969-72; spl. agt. IRS, Los Angeles, 1972-79; supervisory spl. agt. IRS, Phoenix, 1979--. Mem. Nat. Orgn. of Black Law Enforcement Execs. Democrat. Baptist. Home: 4901 Calle Los Cerros Tempe AZ 85282 Office: Internal Revenue Svc 2120 N Central Phoenix AZ 85004

YOST, ELLEN GINSBERG, lawyer; b. Buffalo, May 30, 1945; d. Irwin Arthur and Sylvia Ruth Ginsberg; children: Elizabeth Anne, Peter Andrew, Benjamin Lewis. AB, Mt. Holyoke Coll., 1966; JD, SUNY, Buffalo, 1983. Bar: N.Y., U.S. Dist. Ct. (we. dist.) N.Y. 1984. Assoc. Jaeckle, Fleischmann & Mugel, Buffalo, 1983-89, Saperston & Day, P.C., Buffalo, 1989—. Pres. Buffalo Coun. on World Affairs, 1987-89; bd. dirs. Buffalo World Trade Assn., 1988-90, Legal Svcs. for Elderly, Disabled, Disadvantaged, 1984—; mem. Erie County Can. Commerce Task Force, 1988. Mem ABA (co-chmn. Can. law com., internat. law and practice sect., 1990—), N.Y. State Bar Assn. (chmn. U.S. Can. law com. 1987-89, mem. exec. com. internat. law and practice sect. 1987-89, sec. commn. on internat. trade and transactions., 1984-87). Jewish. Office: Saperston & Day PC 1 Fountain Pla Buffalo NY 14203

YOST, MARLENE J., marketing and public relations professional; b. Williams County, Ohio, Apr. 6, 1934; d. Walter B. Beaverson and Ruth E. (Russell) Beaverson McQuillin; m. Gaylord C. Yost, May 5, 1952; children: Charles, Elizabeth. Student, U. Wis., Milw., 1984-85. Bus. mgr. Fayette (Ohio) Rev., 1958-62; exec. asst. St. John's Home Milw., 1978-87, dir. devel., mktg. and pub. rels., 1987—, curator Uihlein-Peters Gallery, 1988—. Mem. Wis. Women in Arts (bd. dirs. 1988—), Nat. Soc. Fund Raising Execs. Democrat. Office: St Johns Home Milw 1840 N Prospect Ave Milwaukee WI 53202

YOST, NANCY RUNYON, artist, wearable art designer, art educator; b. Eaton, Ohio, July 16, 1933; d. Stanley Everett and Treva (Geeting) Runyon; m. Kenneth John Yost, Aug. 17, 1952 (div. Dec. 1962); 1 child, Debra Colleen Yost Mews. BS in Art Edn., Miami U., Oxford, Ohio, 1966, MEd in Art, 1970. Cert. profl. permanent tchr., Ohio. Sec. N.Am. Aircraft, Columbus, Ohio, 1957; sec. Miami U., Oxford, 1957-61, textile instr., 1978; textile instr. Living Arts Ctr., Dayton, Ohio, 1972-73; coord. art, music and phys. edn. Stewart Jr. High Sch., Oxford, 1981-86; art instr. Talawanda Sch. System, Oxford, 1965—, dist. coord., 1986—; owner, creator Allegro Wearable Art Bus., 1988—; postgrad. Sem. Charles Jeffrey, Cleve. Inst. Art, Miami U., 1973, David Van Dommelen Penn State at U. Tenn., 1975, Bill Helwig, N.Y., 1975, Nik Krevitsky, N.Y., 1976, Tom Shafer, Columbus, Ohio, 1982; mem. Talawanda Sch. Dist. Curriculum Coun., 1982—; rep. Amway Corp., 1980-81, World Book Co., Chgo., 1986-88; lectr. Miami U., 1986. Contbg. artist: Wall Hangings, 1971, Knotting, 1973; One-woman exhibit at Creative Fibers Studio, Buffalo, 1974; exhibited in 4 woman show Dayton Art Inst., Invitational Fiber Artists Am., Ball State U., 1974; designer Oxford Bicentennial Calender, 1976; guest jewelry designer Saks 5th

Avenue. supr. Community Artworks, 1986. Mem. Southwestern Art Edn. Assn., Ohio Art Edn. Assn., Ohio Edn. Assn., Talawanda Edn. Assn., Ohio Designer Craftsmen, Ohio Arts and Crafts Guild, Oxford Arts Club, Kappa Delta Pi. Home and Office: 6674 Fairfield Rd Oxford OH 45056

YOTSUUYE, ELSIE LEILANI See TANIGUCHI, ELSIE LEILANI

YOUELL, MARY LOUISE, copywriter, consultant; b. Spencer, Iowa, Aug. 12, 1957; d. Eugene Wallace Jr. and Jane Belle (Hammett) Y. BA in French, Spanish, Wheaton Coll., 1979; AAS in Advt., Communications., Fashion Inst. Tech., N.Y.C, 1985. Auditor Bank Shares, Inc., Mpls., 1980-82; asst. to mktg. dir. Good Food Mag. (Triangle Communications Inc.), N.Y.C, 1985-87; copywriter PaineWebber Inc., N.Y.C, 1987-90; pvt. practice cons. N.Y.C, 1990—; chief fin. officer, pres. Bank Svc. Dept. Inc., Manson, Iowa, 1975—. Office: PaineWebber Inc 1200 Harbor Blvd Weehawken NJ 07087

YOUMAN, LILLIAN HOBSON LINCOLN, building services contractor; b. Powhatan, Va., May 12, 1940; d. Willie David and Arnetha (Hobson) Hobson; children: Darnetha LaRoi, Tasha Renee'. BA, Howard U., 1966; MBA, Harvard U., 1969. Account exec. Ferris & Co., 1972-76; exec. v.p. Unified, 1973-76; pres. Centennial One, Lanham, Md., 1976—. Bd. dirs. Citizens Bank of Md. Named Small Bus. Person of Yr., State of Md., 1981, Female Minority Contractor of Yr., Dept. of Commerce, 1984, Nat. Minority Entrepreneur of Yr., 1988; finalist Arthur Young/Inc. Entrepreneur of Yr., 1989. Mem. Bldg. Svc. Contractors Assn. (bd. dirs., treas.), Capitol Assn. Bldg. Svc. Contractors (dir.), Prince George C. of C. (dir. 1984). Republican. Baptist. Avocations: reading, traveling, golfing. Home: 1305 Lavall Dr Davidsonville MD 21035 Office: Centennial One Inc 9600 Martin Luther King Jr Hwy Suite E Lanham MD 20706

YOUNG, ANN ELIZABETH O'QUINN, historian, educator; b. Waycross, Ga.; d. James Foster and Pearl Elizabeth (Sasser) O'Quinn; student Shorter Coll.; B.A., M.A., U. Ga., Ph.D., 1965; m. Robert William Young, Aug. 18, 1968; children—Abigail Ann, Leslie Lynn. Asst. prof. history Kearney (Nebr.) State Coll., 1965-69, assoc. prof., 1969-72, prof., 1972—; participant Inst. on Islam, Middle East and World Politics, U. Mich., summer 1984. Mem. Am. Hist. Assn., NEA, PEO, World History Assn., Phi Alpha Theta, Delta Kappa Gamma (chpt. pres. 1978-79), Phi Mu. Republican. Presbyterian. Contbg. author Dictionary of Georgia Biography; contbr. articles to profl. revs. Office: Kearney State Coll Dept History Kearney NE 68849

YOUNG, BARBARA ALDIE, materials engineer; b. Sacramento, Nov. 2, 1964; d. John Chancellor Young and Nancy Marie Nolte. BS Materials Sci. Engring, UCLA, 1987, postgrad., 1990. Quality assurance liaison engring. intern Xerox Corp., Fremont, Calif., 1984; materials engr.-scientist intern McDonnell Douglas Corp., Long Beach, Calif., 1986; mem. tech. staff Rocketdyne Co., Canoga Park, Calif., 1987-88, 89—; mem. indsl. staff Los Alamos (N.Mex.) Nat. Lab., 1988-89; mem. nat. beryllium safety team, Nat. Aerospace Plane Joint Program Office, Westlake, Calif., 1989. Mem. Am. Soc. Metals, The Metals Soc., Rocketdyne Speakers Bur. Office: Rocketdyne AB 33 6633 Canoga Ave Canoga Park CA 91303

YOUNG, BARBARA PISARO, interior designer; b. Chgo., Apr. 14, 1939; d. Leon Jerome and Carolyn Ritchie (Rice) Johnson; m. Robert G. Pisaro, Sept. 3, 1960 (div. Nov. 1975); children: Michael James, Mark Jerome, Deborah Lynn; m. John V. Young, Feb. 5, 1977 (div. July 1985). BFA with distinction, U. Ariz., 1961. Interior designer Brady Wyte Furniture, Lombard, Ill., 1974-80; pres. Young Markovitz Interiors, Ltd., Clarendon Hils, Ill., 1980—; cons. Svc. Systems Corp., Buffalo, 1978-85, ARA Svcs., Detroit, 1983, Marriott Corp., Washington, 1985—. Contbr. articles to profl. publs. Pres. C. of C., 1983-87. Mem. Interior Design Soc. Republican. Home: 860 N Lake Shore Dr Chicago IL 60611 Office: Young Markovitz Interiors 30 S Prospect Clarendon Hills IL 60514

YOUNG, CAROL ANN, teacher; b. Phila., May 25, 1933; d. H. Allen and Ethlebird (Andrews) Wrigley; m. Robert N. Young, July 25, 1959; children: R. Neil Young Jr., Elizabeth Grace Zimmermann, Edward Allen. BS, Beaver Coll., 1954; MEd, Temple U., 1990. Tchr. Abington Twp. (Pa.), 1954-60; substitute tchr. Upper Dublin Twp. (Pa.), 1971--; pvt. tutor, 1960--. Stephen min. Presbyn. Ch. of Chestnut Hill, Phila., 1989—, trustee, 1982—; mem., guide Women for Greater Phila., 1987—; charter mem. Nat. Mus. for Women in the Arts, Washington, 1988—; host, dir. Swedish-Am. Student Exch., Dresher, Pa., 1981-86; leader, chmn. com. Cub Scout, Phila., 1974-78. Mem. Am. Soc. Tng. and Devel., Am. Vocat. Assn., AAUW (pres. Whitemarsh br. 1989--),. Republican. Presbyterian. Home: 1546 Cooper Dr Ambler PA 19002

YOUNG, CAROLE J., communications executive; b. Mattoon, Ill., Apr. 24, 1950; d. Kenneth and Floretta Thomas (Henkle) Clark; m. Emmett N. Young Jr., May 4, 1968; children: Kenneth, Craig, Christopher. Cert. in strategic mgmt., Lake Land Coll., 1988. Asst. engr.-network engr., communications analyst Ill. Console Telephone Co., Mattoon; centrex adminstr. Citizen's Utilities, Kingman, Ariz. Past pres. Ill. Area PTA Coun. Mem. NAFE, Am. Mgmt. Assn., Am. Bus. Women's Assn. (past pres.), Project Mgmt. Inst., DMS Centrex Users Group, CHOICE (bd. dirs.). Home: 2112 Golf #24 Kingman AZ 86401

YOUNG, CHRISTINE BROOKS, real estate development executive; b. Suffolk, Va., July 13, 1944; d. Waverly Earl and Martha Cavana (Parker) Brooks; m. Hubert Howell Young Jr., Dec. 31, 1964; 1 child, Hubert Howell III. Student, Mary Washington Coll. Owner Young Propertiesand related corps., Suffolk, 1979—. Contbr. articles to profl. jours., mags. Mem. United Ch. Christ. Mem. Cedar Point Club, Town Point Club. Del. Rep. Nat. Conv., 1984. Home: PO Box 3020 Suffolk VA 23434 Office: 444 N Main St Suffolk VA 23434

YOUNG, DARLENE LYNELLE, programmer analyst; b. Port Arthur, Tex., Dec. 31, 1963; d. Haywood Lewis and Verdine Altha (Jones) Y. BBA, U. Houston, 1986. Accounting clk. II Continental Airlines, Inc., Houston, 1986-87, acars analyst, 1987, systems stats. programmer, 1987-88, programmer, analyst, 1988—. Home: 12249 Thicket Green Houston TX 77035 Office: Continental Airlines, Inc. 2929 Allen Pkwy #1363 Houston TX 77019

YOUNG, DONA DAVIS GAGLIANO, lawyer, insurance executive; b. Bklyn., Jan. 8, 1954; d. Vincent Joseph and Shirley Elizabeth (Davis) Gagliano; m. Roland F. Young III, Aug. 18, 1979; children: Meghan Davis, Wesley Davis, Taylor Davis. BA and MA in Polit. Sci., Drew U., 1976; JD, U. Conn., 1980. Bar: Conn. 1980, U.S. Dist. Ct. Conn. 1980. With Phoenix Mut. Life Ins. Co., Hartford, Conn., 1980—, ast. v.p. reinsurance adminstrn., 1983-85, 2d v.p., ins. counsel, 1985-87, v.p. and asst. gen. counsel, 1987-89; sr. v.p. and gen. counsel Phoenix Mut. Life Ins. Co., Hartford, 1989—. Mem. legal assistance program adv. com. Hartford Coll. for Women, 1987-89, Family Devel. Resource Ctr., St. Joseph's Coll., West Hartford, Conn., 1987-89. Mem. ABA, Am. Coun. of Life Ins. (com. on risk classification 1985-88), Am. Corp. Counsel Assn. (bd. dirs. Hartford chpt.), Hartford County Bar Assn., Conn. Bar Assn., Am. Coun. Life Ins. (legis. com. 1989—). Republican. Congregationalist. Office: Phoenix Mut Life Ins Co 1 American Row Hartford CT 06115

YOUNG, ERNESTINA MUNOZ, insurance sales representative; b. Manila, July 6, 1954; came to U.S., 1978, naturalized 1985; d. Ireneo A. and Marcelina (Catabas) Munoz; m. Carl E. Young, Jr., July 30, 1980; children: Carl E. III, Alyssa M.R. BA in Econs., U. Santo Tomas, Manila, 1975, MBA, 1977. Lic. life and disability agt., fire and casualty agent, real estate agent, fire and casualty broker. Sales rep. Prudential Life Ins. Co., Los Angeles, 1982-84, Mut. of Omaha, Los Angeles, 1984-85, Met. Life Ins. Co., Los Angeles, 1985—. Roman Catholic. Office: Met Life Ins Co 100 W Broadway #1070 Glendale CA 91205

YOUNG, HOLLY PEACOCK, lawyer; b. Indpls., Sept. 21, 1949; d. John Edward and Sylvia (Griffith) Peacock; m. Gregory Glenn Young, Sept. 2, 1972; children: Reagan Wheelock, Trevor Griffith. Student Dartmouth Coll., 1969-70; B.A., Conn. Coll., 1971; M.A., U. Tex., 1973; J.D., So. Meth. U., 1982. Bar: Tex. 1983; state water program mgr. EPA, Dallas, 1973-75, 75-77; asst. mgr. Menlo Sport, Menlo Park, Calif., 1977-79; dir. Hindostan Co., Indpls.; with Jour. Air Law and Commerce, 1980-82. Bd. dirs. Montessori Sch. of Park Cities, 1983-87; bd. advisors Cottonwood Gulch Found., 1982—. Recipient Bronze medal EPA, 1974. Mem. ABA, Tex. Bar Assn., Dallas Bar Assn. Episcopalian. Home: 4711 Cherokee Trail Dallas TX 75209

YOUNG, JANET CHERYL, electrical engineer; b. Roanoke, Va., Oct. 3, 1960; d. Don Gordon and Barbara Hill (Mumpower) Y. BS in Physics, U. Tenn., Chattanooga, 1982; postgrad., Va. Tech. Inst., 1986—. Engr. Sci. Applications Internat. Corp., Springfield, Va., 1982—. Active in World Peace Mission Foundry United Meth. Ch., Washington, 1984, Community Band, Vienna, Va., 1985. Mem. IEEE (mem. Electromagnetic Compatibility Soc. 1987—). Methodist. Home: 7515 Woodside Ln #12 Lorton VA 22079 Office: Carl T Jones Corp Sci Applications Internat 7901 Yarnwood Ct Springfield VA 22153

YOUNG, JOAN CRAWFORD, advertising executive; b. Hobbs, N.Mex., July 30, 1931; d. William Bill and Ora Maydelle (Boone) Crawford; m. Herchelle B. Young, Nov. 23, 1971 (div.). B.A., Hardin Simmons U., 1952; postgrad. Tex. Tech. U., 1953-54. Reporter, Lubbock (Tex.) Avalanche-Jour., 1952-54; promotion dir. KCBD-TV, Lubbock, 1954-62; account exec. Ward Hicks Advt., Albuquerque, 1962-70; v.p. Mellekas & Assocs., Advt., Albuquerque, 1970-78; pres. J. Young Advt., Albuquerque, 1978—. Bd. dirs. N.Mex. Symphony Orch., 1970-73, United Way of Greater Albuquerque, 1985-89. Recipient Silver medal N.Mex. Advt. Fedn., 1977. Mem. N.Mex. Advt. Fedn. (dir. 1975-76), Am. Advt. Fedn., Greater Albuquerque C. of C. (dir. 1984). Republican. Author: (with Louise Allen and Audre Lipscomb) Radio and TV Continuity Writing, 1962. Home: 3425 Avenida Charada NW Albuquerque NM 87107 also: 303 Roma NW Albuquerque NM 87102

YOUNG, JUNE MAGNA, guidance counselor; b. Chippewa Falls, Wis., Feb. 12, 1936; d. Allen Hans and Hazel Cleone (LaRonge) Y. BS, Macalester Coll., 1959; MEd, U. Minn., 1967, specialist degree, 1978; MA, Coll. of St. Thomas, St. Paul, 1971. Cert. in phys. edn., coaching, secondary and vocat. guidance and counseling, Minn.; cert. nat. counselor. Tchr. Mpls. Pub. Schs., 1959-60; tchr. St. Paul Pub. Schs., 1960-65, 68-72, guidance counselor, 1972—; teaching assoc. U. Minn., Mpls., 1965-67; inst. U. N.Mex., Albuquerque, 1967-68. Mem. edn. com., elder Cen. Presbyn. Ch., St. Paul, 1984-85. Wis. Leadership scholar, 1954-55, Wis. Dept. Rehab. scholar, 1955-56. Mem. Nat. Cert. Counselors Assn., Am. Fedn. Tchrs., Minn. Sch. Counselors Assn., St. Paul Counselors Assn. (bd. dirs. 1978-79, 82-83). Republican. Office: Humboldt Sr High Sch 30 E Baker St Saint Paul MN 55107

YOUNG, LEIANNA MARY, public relations consultant; b. St. Louis, Jan. 24, 1944; d. Leo William and Sarah Ann (Cowgill) Rasche; m. Lawrence Martin Young, Nov. 25, 1967 (div. May 1986); children: Peter Leigh, Nathan Michael. BS in Geography, St. Louis U., 1966; postgrad., U. New Orleans, 1973, Inst. Politics Loyola U., New Orleans, 1980-81. Urban planner City of Columbia, Mo., 1966-68; planning geographer Mo. Hwy. Dept., Jefferson City, 1968-69; pvt. practice pub. rels. cons. New Orleans, 1980-85; realtor assoc. Coldwell Banker, New Orleans, 1982-87; dir. pub. info. Office of Civil Sheriff, New Orleans, 1983—; radio commentator Sta. WGSO, New Orleans, 1978-81; vice chmn. New Orleans Mayor's Adv. Com. on Coastal Zone Mgmt., 1979-81; coord. Pub. Libr. Free U., New Orleans, 1980-83. V.P. Alliance for Good Govt., New Orleans, 1981-82; bd. dirs. Friends of Pub. Libr., New Orleans, New Orleans Coalition, 1987-88; pres. Rosenwald Middle Sch. PTO, New Orleans, 1983-85; former den mother Boy Scouts Am.; bd. dirs., editor newsletter Bocage Civic Assn.; mem. Met. Area Com. Ad Hoc Com. on Edn.; mem. State Law Assn. (La. Supreme Ct. appointee). Fellow Loyola U., 1980-81. Mem. Jefferson Bd. Realtors, New Orleans Bd. Realtors, LWV (pres. New Orleans, 1989—). Democrat. Roman Catholic. Home: 3661 Rue Mignon New Orleans LA 70131 Office: Office Civil Sheriff 421 Loyola St Rm 403 New Orleans LA 70112

YOUNG, LISA SPERBER, lawyer; b. NYC, June 4, 1952; m. Sanford F. Young, Oct. 12, 1975; children: Michelle, Ashley. BA cum laude, NYU, 1973; JD cum laude, Syracuse U., 1976. Admitted N.Y. Bar, 1977. Ptnr. Young and Young, Attorneys-at-Law, NYC, 1978--. Mem. NY County Lawyers Assn., NY State Bar Assn. Office: Young and Young 225 Broadway New York NY 10007

YOUNG, LOIS ANNE, hospital administrator; b. Kingsport, Tenn., Sept. 7, 1936; d. Emmett Charles and Beulah (Dennison) Patrick; m. William David Young III, July 5, 1958 (dec. 1986); children: Leigh Anne, Elizabeth Suzanne. BS in Med. Tech., Va. Commonwealth U., 1958. Cert. med. technologist. Chemistry dept. head Holston Valley Hosp., Kingsport, Tenn., 1962-74; adminstrv. dir. of labs Holston Valley Hosp., Kingsport, 1974-87, asst. adminstr., 1987—; instr. and cons. in field. Bd. dirs. Health Occupations Adv. Group, Kingsport, 1977-81, Kingsport Symphony Orch., 1977-83, Valley Regional Blood Ctr., Knoxville, Tenn., 1985-87. Named Lion of the Year, 1988. Mem. Am. Soc. for Med. Technologists, Tenn. Soc. for Med. Technologists (pres. 1960-61), Am. Soc. for Clin. Pathologists, Am. Assn. Blood Banks, Clin. Lab. Mgmt. Assn., Lions Club (Kingsport, v.p. 1988). Democrat. Methodist. Home: 2224 Sheffield St Kingsport TN 37660 Office: Holston Valley Hosp W Ravine Rd Kingsport TN 37660

YOUNG, LOIS CATHERINE, public administrator, consultant; b. Wakeman, Ohio, Mar. 10, 1930; d. William McKinley and Leona Catherine (Woods) Williams; m. William Walton Young; children: Ralph, Catherine, William. BS, NYU, 1957; MS, Hofstra U., 1962, profl. diploma, 1967, EdD, 1981; M Pub. Adminstrn., Fla. Internat. U., 1988. Cert. tchr., sch. supr., N.Y., pub. mgmt., Fla. Tchr. Copiaque (N.Y.) Schs., 1957-59; research assoc. Columbia and Hofstra Univs., Hempstead, N.Y., 1964-69; tchr. Half Hollow Hills Pub. Schs., Dix Hills, N.Y., 1970-72; instr. Conn. Coll., New London, 1972-73; tchr., supr., reading coordinator Hempstead (N.Y.) Pub. Schs., 1975-85; cons. South African project Agy. Internat. Devel. Fla. Meml. Coll., Miami, Fla., 1987—; clinician Hofstra U., Hempstead, 1962-64; tchr. trainer Amityville (N.Y.) Pub. Schs., 1965, Hofstra Univ., 1982; key speaker Internat. Reading Assn., N.Y., Calif., Caribbean Islands, 1982-86. Author numerous poems. Sec. Jack and Jill of Am. Chpt., Nassau County, N.Y., 1960-62; pres. PTA, Uniondale, N.Y., 1962-68; active Boy Scouts Am., Uniondale, 1963-65; bd. dirs. United Nations Assn. Miami chpt., 1987—, 1st v.p., 1989—; contbr. Proceedings South Africa Project, 1987, multi-lateral project UN Greater Miami chpt., 1987, 88, 89. Recipient research grant N.Y. State Fed. Programs, 1978, Laurel Wreath award Doctoral Assn. of N.Y. Educators, 1982, Cert. of Award UN Assn., 1987, 88; fellow Fla. Internat. U., 1987. Mem. Am. Soc. Pub. Adminstrn., Fla. Internat. U. Alumni Assn., NYU Alumni Assn. (bd. dirs. 1983—, 2d v.p. 1986-87), Tuskegee Airmen, Inc., Phi Delta Kappa, Alpha Kappa Alpha, Kappa Delta Phi, Theta Iota Omega (global affairs com. 1984-86). Home: 14320 SW 105 Terr Miami FL 33186

YOUNG, LORETTA, actress; b. Salt Lake City, Jan. 6, 1913; M. Thomas Lewis (div.). Grad., Ramona Convent, Alhambra, Calif.; student, Immaculate Heart Coll., Hollywood, Calif. Motion picture appearances include Laugh Clown Laugh, 1928, Loose Ankles, 1929, The Squall, 1930, Kismet, 1930, The Devil to Pay, 1930, I Like Your Nerve, 1931, Platinum Blonde, 1932, The Hatchet Man, 1932, Big Business Girl, 1932, Life Begins, 1932, Zoo in Budapest, 1933, Man's Castle, 1933, The House of Rothschild, 1934, Midnight Mary, 1935, The Crusaders, 1935, Clive of India, 1935, Call of the Wild, 1935, Shanghai, 1936, Ramona, 1936, Ladies in Love, 1937, Wife, Doctor and Nurse, 1937, Second Honeymoon, 1938, Four Men and a Prayer, 1938, Suez, 1938, Kentucky, 1938, Three Blind Mice, 1938, The Story of Alexander Graham Bell, 1939, The Doctor Takes a Wife, 1939, He Stayed for Breakfast, 1940, Lady from Cheyenne, 1941, The Men in Her Life, 1941, A Night to Remember, 1942, China, 1943, Ladies Courageous, 1944, And Now Tomorrow, 1944, The Stranger, 1945, Along Came Jones, 1946, The Perfect Marriage, 1946, The Farmer's Daughter, 1947 (Acad. award 1947), The Bishop's Wife, 1948, Rachel and the Stranger, 1948, Come to the Stable, 1949, Cause for Alarm, 1951, Half Angel, 1951, Paula, 1952, Because of You, 1952, It Happens Every Thursday, 1953, others; appeared in TV series Loretta Young Show (Emmy awards 1954, 56, 59, Acad. Television Arts & Scis.), 1953-61, in TV films Christmas Eve (Golden Globe Award for best actress in a TV movie), 1986, Lady in a Corner, 1989. Roman Catholic. Office: care Lewis 1705 Ambassador Ave Beverly Hills CA 90210*

YOUNG, LORETTA A., organization administrator; b. Reading, Pa., Dec. 2, 1962; d. Milton and Delois Jean (Ridley) Young. BS, Towson State U., 1985. Auditor Irving Burton Assocs., Inc., Washington; tax technician Gen. Bus. Svcs., Germantown, Md.; auditor Montgomery County Govt., Rockville, Md.; dir. membership devel. Nat. Forum for Black Pub. Adminstrs., Washington. Mem. NAFE, Mid Atlantic Notary Assn. Home: 763 Quince Orchard Blvd #24 Gaithersburg MD 20878

YOUNG, LOUISE DILLON GRAY, molecular spectroscopist; b. Los Angeles, Oct. 4, 1935; d. Frank Elliot and Ruth Alice (Davis) Dillon; m. Bruce Everett Gray, Nov. 1953 (div. 1959); children: Gregory Edward, Elizabeth Marie; m. Andrew Tipton Young, Dec. 14, 1968. BS in Engring., UCLA, 1958, MS in Engring., 1959; PhD in Engring. Sci., Caltech, Pasadena, Calif., 1963. Sr. scientist Space Sciences Div., Jet Propulsion Lab., Los Angeles, 1963-65; mem. tech. staff Space Sci. Div., Jet Propulsion Lab., Pasadena, Calif., 1966-73; asst. prof. engring. dept. UCLA, Los Angeles, 1965-66; research assoc. Physics, Dept., Tex. A&M U., College Sta., 1972-80; adjunct assoc. prof. astronomy dept. San Diego State U., 1980—; cons. Gen. Dynamics Convair, San Diego, 1962, Douglas Aircraft, Santa Monica, Calif., 1963. Author: Radiation and Reentry, 1966; contbr. scientific articles to jours. Fellow Optical Soc. Am., mem. Am. Met. Soc., Am. Astron. Soc., Internat. Astron. Union, Div. of Planetary Scis., Mercedes Benz (sec., treas. Houston 1975-79). Home: 4906 63rd St San Diego CA 92115 Office: San Diego State U Astronomy Dept San Diego CA 92182

YOUNG, LUCY CLEAVER, physician; b. Wheeling, W.Va., Aug. 8, 1943. B.S. in Chemistry, Wheaton Coll. (Ill.), 1965; M.D., Ohio State U., 1969. Diplomate Am. Bd. Family Practice, Bd. of Ins. Medicine. Rotating intern Riverside Meth. Hosp., Columbus, Ohio, 1969-70; resident Trumbull Meml. Hosp., Warren, Ohio, 1970-71; practice medicine specializing in family practice, West Chicago, Ill., 1971-73, Paw Paw and Mendota, Ill., 1973-78; cofounder and med. dir. Wholistic Health Ctr. of Mendota, 1976-78; asst. med. dir. Met. Life Ins. Co., Gt. Lakes Head Office, Aurora, Ill., 1979-80; med. dir. Commonwealth Life Ins. Co., Louisville, 1980-85; assoc. prof. U. Ill. Abraham Lincoln Sch. Medicine, 1976-79; faculty monitor MacNeal Meml. Hosp. Family Practice Ctr. (Ill.), 1979-80; faculty preceptor U. Louisville Family Practice Dept., 1981-85; Locum Tenens Family Practice for Kron Med. Corp. of Chapel Hill, N.C., 1986-89; physician Red Bird Mission & Med. Ctr., Beverly, Ky., 1989—; mem. staffs Central DuPage Hosp., Winfield, Ill., 1971-73, Mendota Community Hosp., 1973-80. Fellow Am. Acad. Family Practice; mem. Am. Med. Women's Assn., Christian Med. Soc. Home: PO Box 1300 Chalmette LA 70044

YOUNG, MARGARET ALETHA MCMULLEN (MRS. HERBERT WILSON YOUNG), social worker; b. Vossburg, Miss., June 13, 1916; d. Grady Garland and Virgie Aletha (Moore) McMullen; BA cum laude, Columbia Bible Coll., 1949; grad. Massey Bus. Coll., 1958; MSW, Fla. State U., 1965; postgrad. Jacksonville U., 1961-62, Tulane U., 1967; m. Herbert Wilson Young, Aug. 19, 1959. Dir. Christian edn. Eau Claire Presbyn. Ch., Columbia, S.C., 1946-51; tchr. Massey Bus. Coll., Jacksonville, Fla., 1954-57, office mgr., 1957-59; social worker, unit supr. Fla. div. Family Svcs., St. Petersburg, 1960-66, dist. casework supr., 1966-71; social worker, project supr., program supr. Project Playpen, Inc., 1971-81, pres. bd., 1982-83, cons., 1986-89; pvt. practice family counselor, 1982—; mem. coun. Child Devel. Ctr., 1983-89; mem. transitional housing com., Religious Community Svcs., 1984-90. Mem. Acad. Cert. Social Workers, Nat. Assn. Social Workers (pres. Tampa Bay chpt. 1973-74), Fla. Assn. for Health and Social Services (pres. chpt. 1971), Nature Conservancy. Democrat. Presbyn. Rotary Ann (pres. 1970-71). Home: 6530 Bishop Ave Lot 2 Columbia SC 29203

YOUNG, MARGARET BUCKNER, civic worker, author; b. Campbellsville, Ky.; d. Frank W. and Eva (Carter) Buckner; m. Whitney M. Young, Jr., Jan. 2, 1944 (dec. Mar. 1971); children: Marcia Elaine, Lauren Lee. BA, Ky. State Coll., 1942, MA, U. Minn., 1946. Instr. Ky. State Coll., 1942-44; instr. edn. and psychology Spelman Coll., Atlanta, 1957-60; dir. Philip Morris, Inc., N.Y. Life Ins. Co. Alt. del. UN Gen. Assembly, 1973. Mem. pub. policy com. Advt. Coun. Trustee Lincoln Ctr. for Performing Arts; chmn. Whitney M. Young, Jr. Meml. Found.; trustee Met. Mus. Art; bd. govs. UN Assn., 1975-82; bd. visitors U.S. Mil. Acad., 1978-80. Author: The First Book of American Negroes, 1966, The Picture Life of Martin Luther King, Jr., 1968, The Picture Life of Ralph J. Bunche, 1968, Black American Leaders-Watts, 1969, The Picture Life of Thurgood Marshall, 1970, pub. affairs phamphlet. Home: 330 Oxford Rd New Rochelle NY 10804 Office: 100 Park Ave New York NY 10017

YOUNG, MARGARET HAYS, actress; b. N.Y.C., Sept. 25, 1954; d. Llewellyn Powers and Jean Eleanor (Johnson) Y.; m. Ashley Trimble Cole, III, Oct. 9, 1976. BA in English Lit., Bryn Mawr Coll., 1975; postgrad., NYU, Paris, 1977; Grad., Am. Acad. of Dramatic Arts, 1982. Sr. investigator Barclay's Bank Internat., N.Y.C., 1975-79; corr. banker Societe Generale, N.Y.C., 1979-80; dept. head Banque Francaise du Commerce Exterieur, N.Y.C., 1980-83; asst. head of mktg. Pechiney Group, N.Y.C. Mem. World Wildlife Fund, League of Conservation Voters, Greenpeace, Nat. Resources Def. Coun., N.Y. Acad. TV Arts and Scis., Actors Equity Assn., SAG, AFTRA, Sierra Club, Mus. Natural History, Audubon Soc., Nature Conservancy. Democrat. Home and Office: 703 President St Brooklyn NY 11215

YOUNG, MARGARET RUTH, decision sciences educator; b. Danville, Pa., Dec. 1, 1953; d. Donald Barr and Elsie Lehman (Wilson) Y.; m. Michael Charles Fries, June 2, 1952. BS, Bates Coll., 1975; MS, Vanderbilt U., 1982; PhD, Pa. State U., State College, 1986. Account analyst Western Electric, Chgo., 1977-79; market analyst TRW Vidar, Mountain View, Calif., 1979; market planner TRW Project Telecom, Campbell, Calif., 1979-81; planning analyst TRW IPG, Cleve., 1981-82; prof. decision scis. George Mason U., Fairfax, Va., 1985—; pvt. cons. forecasting, 1985—. Mem. Internat. Inst. Forecasting, Decision Scis. Inst., Am. Statis. Assn. Office: George Mason U 4400 University Dr Dept Decision Scis Fairfax VA 22030

YOUNG, MARJORIE H., state agency administrator; b. Bartow, Fla., Sept. 1, 1946; d. Alex and Nellie (Taylor) Harris; m. Francis Holmes Young, Jan. 10, 1970; 1 child, Franka Helaine. BA in Psychology, Morris Brown Coll., 1969; MEd. in Rehab. Counseling, Ga. State U., 1972, MPA, 1979. Faculty specialist rehab. counseling DHR Rehab. Svcs. Div., Atlanta, 1972-78; program coord. DHR Rehab. Svcs. Div., 1978-79, dist. dir., 1979-81; div. dir. DHR Human Devel. Div., Atlanta, 1981-83, DHR Youth Svcs. Div., Atlanta, 1983—; bd. dirs., committee chairperson Atlanta U. Criminal Justice Inst., Atlanta, 1984—; presenter, cons. Southeastern Regional Conf. on Juvenile Delinquency in the Black Community, U. S.C., 1984; presenter nat. conf. in criminal justice Nat. Assn. Blacks, Houston, 1985; com. mem., planner, conf. presenter Southeastern Network Runaways, Youth and Family Svcs., Inc., Atlanta, 1985. Contbr. articles to profl. jours. Mem. YMCA, Atlanta, 1980-81, 78—, membership drive com., 1981—; chairperson adv. bd. Ga. Legis. Black Caucus, 1986—; bd. dirs. Ga. Commn. on Accreditation for Corrections, 1987—; mem. Gov.'s Criminal Justice Coordinating Coun., 1983—, steering com. Gov.'s Juvenile Justice Coordinating Coun., 1987—. Recipient Book of Appreciation for Workshop Presentation Govt. Trinidad, 1985, certification of Appreciation Workshop, Gov. of St. Croix, U.S. V.I., 1984, Appreciation Plaque for Orgizing and Producing the Ms. Dogwood Sr. Pageant, Atlanta Women's C. of C., 1983, Stem-Y Ders award YMCA, 1981, Leadership award Ga. Legis. Black Caucus, 1988, Vol. of Yr. award, 1989. Mem. Nat. Assn. Juvenile Correctional Agys. (v.p. 1988—, chmn. adminstr. coun. 1988—), Coun. State Juvenile Correctional Agencies Adminstrs. (chmn. 1988—), Nat. Assn. Blacks in Criminal Justice, Am. Correctional Assn. (Balt. chpt. 1989, panel mem. town meeting 1989, presenter nat. juvenile corrections), Ga. Juvenile Svcs. Assn., Nat. Juvenile Detention Assn., So. State Correctional Assn., Morris Brown Coll. Alumni Assn. (treas. Atlanta chpt. 1984-86), Alpha Kappa Alpha. Baptist. Home: 2806 Spain Dr East Point GA 30344 Office: Div of Youth Svcs 878 Peachtree St NE Atlanta GA 30309

YOUNG, MARLENE ANNETTE, lawyer; b. Portland, Oreg., Mar. 3, 1946; d. Hardy Shelby and Eunice Jean (Gregory) Y.; m. Abdullah Samir Rifai,

June 3, 1973 (div. May 1981); m. John Hollister Stein, Jan. 1, 1986. BS, Portland State U., 1967; PhD, Georgetown U., 1973; JD, Willamette U., 1975. Bar: Oreg. 1975. Dir. research Multnomah County Sheriff's Office, Portland, 1975-77; sole practice Wilsonville, Oreg., 1975-81; exec. dir. Applied Systems Research & Data, Wilsonville, 1976-81, Nat. Orgn. Victim Assistance, Washington, 1981—; instr. Essex Community Coll., 1971-73, U. Utah, 1976-78, Portland State U., 1979; cons. U. Research Corp., Washington, 1979-83, ABT Assocs., Boston, 1984—. Author: Victim Service System, 1983; (manuals) Patrol Officers and Crime Victims, 1984, Prosecutors: Attorneys for the People, Advocates for the Victims, 1984; editor: Justice and Older Americans, 1977; contbr. articles to profl. jours. Mem. Ways and Means Com., Wilsonville City, 1977-79, planning commn., 1979-81; Bd. visitors Willamette Coll. Law, Salem, Oreg., 1981-83; bd. dirs. Chemeketa Community Coll., Salem, 1979. Recipient Presdl. award Nat. Orgn. Victim Assistance, Washington, 1981, Pub. Policy award World Fedn. Mental Health, Washington, 1983, Found. for Improvement of Justice award, 1988. Mem. ABA (criminal justice sect., adv. bd. 1981—), Am. Profl. Soc. Abuse of Children (bd. dirs. 1986—), Soc. Traumatic Stress Studies (bd. dirs. 1985—), World Soc. Victimology (adv. bd. 1979—, exec. com. 1988—, Hans Von Hentig award 1985). Democrat. Methodist. Office: Nat Orgn Victim Assistance 1757 Park Rd NW Washington DC 20010

YOUNG, MARY ELIZABETH, educator; b. Utica, N.Y., Dec. 16, 1929; d. Clarence Whitford and Mary Tippit Y. B.A., Oberlin Coll., 1950; Ph.D. (Robert Shalkenbach Found. grantee, Ezra Cornell fellow), Cornell U., 1955. Instr. dept. history Ohio State U., Columbus, 1955-58; asst. prof. Ohio State U., 1958-63, assoc. prof., 1963-69, prof., 1969-73; prof. history U. Rochester, N.Y., 1973—; cons. in field. Author: Redskins, Ruffleshirts, and Rednecks: Indian Allotments in Alabama and Mississippi, 1830-1860, 1961; co-editor, contbr.: The Frontier in Americal Development: Essays in Honor of Paul Wallace Gates, 1969. Recipient Pelzer award Miss. Valley Hist. Assn., 1955, Award Am. Studies Assn., 1982, Ray A. Billington award, 1982; Social Sci. Research Council grantee, 1968-69. Mem. Am. Hist. Assn., Orgn. Am. Historians, Am. Studies Assn., Am. Soc. Ethnic History, Soc. for Historians of the Early Am. Republic, Am. Antiquarian Soc. Home: 2230 Clover St Rochester NY 14618 Office: U Rochester Dept History Rochester NY 14627

YOUNG, MELANIE SUE, therapist; b. Presque Isle, Maine, Aug. 17, 1961; d. George Thomas and Cynthia Marcella (Smith) Y. BS in Edn., U. Tenn., Martin, 1983; MS in Edn., U. Tenn., 1987. Cert. tchr. Tchr. spl. edn. Benton County Sch. System, Camden, Tenn., 1983-84; grad. asst. Happy House Child Care, U. Tenn., Martin, 1984-86; tchr. spl. edn. Weakley County Sch. System, Dresden, Tenn., 1986-87; clin. therapist, crisis clinician N.W. Counseling Ctr., Martin, 1987—. Vol. ARC Weakley County. Mem. Am. Asns. Partial Hospilization, Choral Soc. (treas. 1987-89), Philharmonic Music Guild, Phi Delta Kappa. Republican. Baptist. Home: 239B Brooks Dr Martin TN 38237 Office: NW Counseling Ctr 457 Hannings Ln Martin TN 38237

YOUNG, MEREDITH ANNE, marketing professional; b. Newark, Apr. 12, 1952; d. W. Edward and Lois E. (Velthoven) Y. BA, Caldwell Coll., 1974. Advt., pub. rels. asst. Congoleum Corp., Lawrenceville, N.J., 1974-77; account mgr. Saatchi & Saatchi Compton, N.Y.C., 1977-82; dir. advt., sales promotion Singer Sewing Co., Edison, N.J., 1982-86, dir. product mktg., 1986-88; sr. mktg. rep. Walt Disney World Co., Lake Buena Vista, Fla., 1990—. Vol. North Brunswick Dem. Orgn., 1985-87; pub. rels. mgr. Cultural Arts Com., North Brunswick, 1986-87; props chair Adult Drama Group, North Brunswick, 1986-87. Mem. Mensa. Democrat. Home: 4405 S Kirkman Rd Apt 103 Orlando FL 32811 Office: Walt Disney World Co PO Box 10000 Lake Buena Vista FL 32830-1000

YOUNG, NANCY, lawyer; b. Washington, Dec. 3, 1954; d. John Young and Byounghye Chang; m. Paul Brendan Ford Jr., May 28, 1983; children: Paul Brendan Ford III, Ian Ford. BA, Yale U., 1975, MA, 1976; JD, Columbia U., 1979. Bar: N.Y. 1981. Assoc. Simpson Thacher & Bartlett, N.Y.C., 1979-82, Richards O'Neil & Allegaert, N.Y.C., 1982-86; ptnr. Richards & O'Neil, N.Y.C., 1986—. Contbr. articles to legal publs. Mem. ABA, Assn. of Bar of City of N.Y., Internat. Bar Assn., Am. Fgn. Law Assn., Internat. Lawyers Club, Coun. on Fgn. Rels. (bd. govs.), Yale Alumni Assn. Met. N.Y (bd. dirs., sec.), Columbia Law Sch. Alumnae/Alumni Assn. (bd. dirs.). Home: 945 Fifth Ave New York NY 10021 Office: Richards & O'Neil 885 3d Ave New York NY 10022-4802

YOUNG, PAMELA THORPE, lawyer; b. East Lansing, Mich., Dec. 6, 1959; d. Marion D. and Lula G. (Glenn) Thorpe; m. Reuben Franklin Young, Aug. 31, 1986. BA, U. N.C., Chapel Hill, 1980; JD, N.C. Cen. U., Durham, 1985. Legal staff Tex. State Property Tax Bd., Austin, Tex., 1985-87; legal clk. Travis County Atty.'s Office, Austin, 1987-88, atty., 1988-90; asst. dist. atty. Travis County Dist. Atty.'s Office, Austin, 1990—; bd. dirs. LAZI-FM Community Radio. Recipient Pre-Profl. Health Soc. U. N.C. Chapel Hill, 1980, Dean's List U. N.C. Chapel Hill, 1979-80. Mem. Tex. Bar Assn., Links Inc., Delta Sigma Theta Sorority, Tex. Young Lawyers Assn., Austin Black Lawyers Assn., Tex. Dist. and County Atty. Assn., Travis County Bar Assn., Austin Young Lawyers Assn. Home: 12015 Shady Springs Rd Austin TX 78758 Office: Travis County Distr Attys Office 314 W 11th St Austin TX 78727

YOUNG, REBECCA MARY CONRAD, state legislator; b. Clairton, Pa., Feb. 28, 1934; d. Walter Emerson and Harriet Averill (Colcord) Conrad; m. Merwin Crawford Young, Aug. 17, 1957; children: Eve, Louise, Estelle, Emily. BA, U. Mich., 1955; MA in Teaching, Harvard U., 1963; JD, U. Wis., 1983. Bar: Wis. 1983. Commr. State Hwy. Commn., Madison, Wis., 1974-76; dep. sec. Wis. Dept. of Adminstrn., Madison, 1976-77; assoc. Wadsack, Julian & Lawton, Madison, 1983-84; elected rep. Wis. State Assembly, Madison, 1985—. Translator: Katanga Secession, 1965. Supr. Dane County Bd., Madison, 1970-74; mem. Madison Sch. Bd., 1979-85. Recipient Pub. Interest award Ctr. for Pub. Representation, 1980, Woman of Distinction award YWCA, 1981, Clean 16 Environ. award WI Environ. Decade, Inc., 1985-88, Outstanding Contbns. in Supporting Women Nat. Women's Polit. Caucus Wis., 1985, Exemplary Work award Congress for Working Am., 1986, Wis. Pro-Choice Community award, 1987, Community Bldg. award Wis. Coalition for Advocacy, 1988, Legis. Leadership award Maternal & Child Health Coalition, 1988, 89, WISCAP Gaylord Nelson Human Svc. award, 1989, Outstanding Contbn. in Supporting Women's Right to Choice, Nat. Women's Polit. Caucus Wis., 1989, Support Network award Transitional Employment Program, 1989, Outstanding Community Svc. Recognition, Rainbow Project and Fmaily Mental Health Clinic, 1989. Mem. ABA. Democrat. Home: 639 Crandall St Madison WI 53711 Office: State Legislature-Assembly PO Box 8953 Madison WI 53708

YOUNG, SANDRA BETTY, management executive; b. Chgo., Nov. 30, 1940; d. Jack and Bernice (Berkowitz) Getzug; m. Michael H. Bloxberg, June 3, 1962 (div.); m. Howard L. Young, Sept. 4, 1989. Student, L.A. Pierce Coll., UCLA, Calif. State U., Northridge. Project supr. Michael H. Bloxberg, Encino, Calif., 1975-80; tax coord. Block, Good & Gagerman, Sherman Oaks, Calif., 1984-86, Block, Plant & Eglin, Encino, 1986-87; office mgr. Pomerantz, Kavinoky & Co., Woodland Hills, Calif., 1987-88, Lucky Drivers Ins. Svcs. Inc., Oxnard, Calif., 1988—. Mem. Calif. Soc. Enrolled Agts., Nat. Assn. Tax Prepares, Kiwanis Club. Office: Lucky Drivers Ins Svcs Inc PO Box 5307 Oxnard CA 93031

YOUNG, SANDRA COOPER, librarian; b. Schenectady, N.Y., Jan. 18, 1939; d. John Remington and Esther May (Carl) Cooper; m. Charles William Young Jr., July 26, 1959; children: Charles W. III, Kimberly Anderson, Kathryn Whalen, Karen. BA in Anthropology, Syracuse U., 1961; MSLS, U. Ky., 1980. Info. resources asst. Council of State Govts., Lexington, Ky., 1981-82; sr. tech. info. research analyst Ashland Oil Co., Lexington, Ky., 1983—. Chmn. libr. com., LWV, Lexington, 1985, bd. dirs., 1990—; chmn. libr. com. Philharm. Women's Guild, Lexington, 1987, 88; vol. KET Telefund, 1990. Named to Hon. Order of Ky. Cols., 1979. Mem. AAUW (pres. 1980-82), ALA, Spl. Librs. Assn. (pres. Ky. chpt. 1987), Cen.Ky. Online User's Group, Ky. Libr. Assn., Evergreen Garden Club (pres. 1989—), Kappa Kappa Gamma. Democrat. Roman Catholic. Home: 2031 Hart Rd Lexington KY 40502

YOUNG, SANDRA KAY, software engineer; b. L.A., Jan. 16, 1961; d. Jamie Ray and Tennessee (Taylor) Y.; m. Carl Travis Fields, Aug. 31, 1984 (div. Dec. 1987); 1 child, Devin Christopher. BS in Computer Engring., UCLA, 1983. With Hughes Aircraft Co., El Segundo, Calif., 1989—; tech. programmer Singer Librascope, Glendale, Calif., 1983-85; engr. II, Northrop Aircraft Co., Hawthorne, Calif., 1985-89, mem. tech. staff, 1989—. Mem. Youth Motivation Task Force, 1989—. Mem. Hughes Black Profl. Forum, Hughes Intergroup Women's Forum, L.A. Coun. Black Profl. Engrs. (tchr. Excell program 1988-90), UCLA Alumni Assn. (career network program, adv. and scholarship program). Democrat. Baptist. Home: 19403 Pricetown Ave Carson CA 90746 Office: Hughes Aircraft EDSG PO Box 902 El Segundo CA 90245

YOUNG, SHARON ANN, educator; b. Alamogordo, N.Mex., Oct. 10, 1959; d. James Leonard and Jeanne Pearl (Danley) Sanders; m. Clifford Craig Young, Aug. 23, 1980; children: Elizabeth Diane, Abigail Leigh. BS, N.Mex. State U., 1981. Tchr. Alamogordo Pub. Schs., 1982—. Grantee Alamogordo Ctr. for Exceptional Students, 1988. Mem. NEA. Democrat. Baptist. Home: 1506 Utah Alamogordo NM 88310 Office: Alamogordo Pub Schs Alamogordo NM 88310

YOUNG, SHARON LEE, pharmacy educator, consultant; b. L.A., July 20, 1955; d. Donald Clark and Betty Francis (Sidebotham) Y. BS in Biology, Calif. Polytech. U., 1978; PharmD, U. of the Pacific, 1982. Lic. pharmacist, Calif., Pa., N.J. Horse trainer Rocking RT Ranch, Pomona and Chino, Calif., 1973-78; pharmacy intern LMG Pharmacy, Inc., Stockton, Calif., 1981-82; resident in pharmacology U. Calif., San Diego, 1982-83; resident in pediatrics U. Ill. Med. Ctr., Chgo., 1983-84; asst. prof. clin. pharmacy Phila. Coll. of Pharmacy & Sci., 1984—; clin. pharmacist Children's Hosp. Phila., 1984—; poison info. specialist Del. Valley Regional Poison Control Ctr., Phila., 1985—. Author: chpt. Pediatric Nutrition, 1988; contbr. articles to profl. jours. Camp counselor McDonald's Oncology Summer Camp, Pocono Mountains, Pa., 1987-88, planner McDonald's Oncology Camp Planning, Phila., 1988—. Recipient Achievement award UpJohn Co., 1982, Achievement award Eli Lilly Co., 1982. Mem. Am. Soc. Hosp. Pharmacists, Pa. Soc. Hosp. Pharmacists. Republican. Office: Phila Coll Pharmacy & Sci Woodland Ave at 43d St Philadelphia PA 19104

YOUNG, SHIRLEY, automotive industry executive, strategic marketing consultant; b. Shanghai, China, May 25, 1935; d. Clarence and Juliana (Koo) Y.; divorced; children: David W., William C., Douglas H.L. Hsieh. B.A. in Econs., Wellesley Coll., 1955; postgrad., NYU, 1956-57; Dr. Letters (hon.), Russell Sage Coll., 1982. Research assoc. Alfred Politz Research, N.Y.C., 1955-57; research mgr. Hudson Paper Corp., N.Y.C., 1957-59; research assoc. Grey Advt. Inc., N.Y.C., 1959-69, dir. mktg. and research, 1969-71, exec. v.p., mem. agy. policy com., 1971—, exec. v.p. mktg., planning and strategy devel., 1980-83; pres. Grey Strategic Mktg. Inc., N.Y.C., 1983-88, chmn., from 1988; v.p. consumer market devel. Gen. Motors, Detroit, 1988—; bd. dirs. Holiday Corp., Bell Atlantic, Phila.; vice chmn. nominating com. N.Y. Stock Exch., 1980-81; cons., bd. dirs. dayton Hudson Corp., 1987—. Bd. dirs. United Way of Tri-State, N.Y.C., 1981, Catalyst, 1980—, Am. Pub. Radio; trustee Fonders Soc. of Detroit Inst. Art, Wellesley Coll.; mem. corp. adv. bd. NOW Legal Def. and Edn. Fund; mem. Com. of 200; bd. dirs. Assocs. Harvard Bus. Sch. Named Advt. Woman of Yr., Am. Advt. Fedn., 1974, Woman of Achievement, Am. Parkinson Disease Assn., 1980, Outstanding Corp. Dir., Catalyst, 1981; recipient WEAL Award in Advt., 1982, Alumna Achievement award Wellesley Coll., 1986, Alumna of Yr. award Chinese Am. Planning Coun., 1987. Mem. Advt. Research Found., Am. Assn. Advt. Agencies, Am. Mktg. Assn., Phi Beta Kappa. Office: GM Corp 3044 W Grand Blvd Detroit MI 48202*

YOUNG, SHIRLEY JEAN, small business owner; b. Galveston, Tex., Mar. 18, 1944; d. Rufus H. and Ena I. (Carter) Y. Diploma in computers, basic programming, Halix Inst., 1988. Histologic technician, med. sec. St. Mary's Hosp., Galveston, 1963-66; clk.-typist Am. Oil Co., Texas City, 1967-68, Am. Nat. Ins. Co., Galveston, 1969-75; med. sec. U. Tex. Med. Br., Galveston, 1975-83; owner WORDS ETC (Software Designer), Galveston, 1983—; cons. Art From The Heart, Livingston, Tex., 1984—. Author: Winning Words, 1987, T-A-C Telephone Area Codes, 1989, STAT-ECG, 1988; contbr. articles to bus. publs. Mem. Nat. Fedn. for Decency, 1984—. Mem. NAFE, Am. Soc. Profl. and Exec. Women, Computer Entrepreneur Assn. Am., Am. Soc. Clin. Pathologists (assoc.), 700 Club, 1000 Club. Baptist. Home: 8020 Stewart Rd Galveston TX 77551 Office: WORDS ETC 2705 61st St #308 Ste B Galveston TX 77551

YOUNG, SHIRLEY JUNE, insurance executive; b. Harrison, Ark., Nov. 26, 1937; d. Paul Loy and Mildred L. (Taylor) Turney; m. Sam A. Young, Feb. 4, 1956; children: Linda Young-Shumate, Susan A. Young Thomas, Lori Beth Young Griggs, Sammye Lynne. Grad., Longman R & R Newkirk, 1990. Cert. fraternal ins. counselor. Bookkeeper Harrison Grocer Co., Harrison, 1955-57; traffic mgr. Sta. KHOZ Radio, Harrison, 1957-59; co-owner, mgr. The Young Store, Pyatt, Ark., 1963-86; owner, mgr. Ozarks Satelite Systems, Pyatt, 1984-86; field rep. Woodmen of World Life Ins. Soc., Omaha, Nebr., 1986-88; area mgr. Woodmen of World Life Ins. Co., Yellville, Ark., 1988—. Author poems. Mem. Marion County Indsl. Devel., Yellville, 1983-88; tchr. Sunday sch., Pyatt, 1970-89; organist Pyatt First Bapt. Ch. Mem. Bus. and Profl. Women Found., Nat. Assn. Life Underwriters, Ark. Fraternal Ins. Counselors, Bapt. Women, Nat. Guild Piano Players, Marion County C. of C., Woodman of the World (pres. cabinet 1987, 88, pres. club 1989-90, sec. WOW lodge #1399 1986-90). Home: 1 Foster Pyatt AR 72672 Office: Woodmen of World Life Ins Soc PO Box 1237 Yellville AR 72687

YOUNG, SHIRLEY LOU, executive, administrative assistant, secretary; b. Frankfort, Ohio, Sept. 21, 1944; d. Owen W. and Charlotte E. (Vest) Hill; m. Alton Lee Click, Oct. 2, 1965 (div. 1973); 1 child, Kimberly; m. Jerry William Young, Dec. 26, 1985. Student, Columbus (Ohio) Bus. Coll., 1962-63. Clk., typist Ohio State U., Columbus, 1963-64; receptionist Ohio Rd. Improvement Co., Columbus, 1964-70; v.p., office mgr. Robert Hohl Cos., Inc., Columbus, 1972—. Mem. NAFE. Office: Robert Hohl Companies Inc 6161 Busch Blvd Columbus OH 43229

YOUNG, STEPHANIE DEE, director management program; b. Vallejo, Calif., Oct. 18, 1948; d. William Allen and Betty Lenore (Steele) Y. BA, U. Calif., 1969; MA, San Francisco State U., 1977; MFA, Lindenwood Coll., 1982. Cert. secondary tchr., Calif. Tchr. Petaluma (Calif.) High School, 1971-73; instr./designer Santa Rosa (Calif.) Jr. Coll., 1975-79; instr./resident designer Lindenwood Coll., St. Charles, Mo., 1979-81; asst. prof. U. N.C., Wilmington, N.C., 1981-85; dir. mgmt. program Calif. Inst. Arts, Santa Clarita, 1985-90; lectr. Calif. State U., Hayward, 1975; prodn. mgr. Summer Repertory Theatre, Santa Rosa, Calif., 1975, 1978, 1981-89, Colo. Shakespeare Festival, Boulder, 1986-90; participant Conv. panels, U.S. Inst. Theatre Tech., 1988-90. Grantee Calif. Inst. Arts, Santa Clarita, 1986-89. Bd. dirs. AAUW, U.S. Inst. Theatre Tech. (conv. treas. 1988, conf. mgr. 1985), N.Y. Democrat. Office: Calif Inst Arts 24700 McBean Pkwy Santa Clarita CA 91355

YOUNG, SUSAN ELIZABETH, writer; b. Akron, Ohio, July 23, 1946; d. Thaddeus John and Ruth Elizabeth (Lynch) Y. BA, Kent State U., 1968. Asst. editor, mng. editor Babcox Automotive Publs., Akron, 1968-74; mktg. mgr., mng. editor Penton/IPC Publs., Cleve., 1974-78; copyeditor J.H. Maish Advt. Co., Marion, Ohio, 1978-79; office mgr., copyeditor Alside, Inc., Cuyahoga Falls, Ohio, 1979-80; copywriter, supr. communications, support profl. bus. group The O.M. Scott & Sons Co., Marysville, Ohio, 1980—. Editor: Proturf Mag., 1986 (Bronze Quill 1986); photographer (book) A Day in the Life of Corporate America, 1990. Mem. NAFE, Internat. Assn. Bus. Communicators, Advt. Fedn. Am., Women in Communications, Inc. Roman Catholic. Office: The OM Scott & Sons Co 14111 Scottslawn Rd Marysville OH 43041

YOUNG, SUSAN FRANCES, financial representative; b. Rochelle, Ill.; d. Robert Ellison and Frances Louise (Naylor) Y. BS, Western Ill. U., 1976. Asst. mgmt. trainee Associated Milk Producers, Inc., Chgo., 1977-78, health care asst. adminstr., 1978-80; health care assoc. adminstr. Associated Milk Producers, Inc., Fond Du Lac, Wis., 1980-82; health care adminstr. Associated Milk Producers, Inc., Schaumburg, Ill., 1982-86; registered rep. Waddell & Reed, Inc., Sterling, Ill., 1987—; supr., interviewer Pub. Opinion Lab. No. Ill. U., DeKalb, 1988—; cons. credit mgmt. program Chgo. Midwest Credit Mgmt. Assn., Park Ridge, Ill., 1977-79, 83, health care basic tng. sch. Arthur Andersen & Co., Dallas, Tex., 1984, Women in Mgmt. program, office politics program Harper Coll., Palatine, Ill., 1984. Mem. Nat. Wildlife Fedn. (assoc.), Am. Mus. Nat. History (assoc.); charter mem. Rep. Task Force, Statue Liberty Ellis Island Found; apptd. sec. Adv. Bd. Health, Rochelle, 1987—. Mem. Nat. Assn. Female Execs., Am. Mus. Natural History (assoc.), Nat. Wildlife Fedn. (assoc.), Nat. Rifle Assn., Western Ill. U. Alumni Club., Audubon Soc. Home: 1030 Parkview Dr Rochelle IL 61068

YOUNG, TOMMIE MORTON, social psychology educator; b. Nashville. B.A. cum laude, Tenn. State U., 1951; M.L.S., George Peabody Coll. for Tchrs., 1955; Ph.D., Duke U., 1977; postgrad. U. Okla., 1967, U. Nebr., 1968. Coordinator, Young Adult Program, Lucy Thurman br. YWCA, 1951-52; instr. edn. Tenn. State U., Nashville, 1956-59; instr., coordinator media program Prairie View Coll. (Tex.), 1959-61; asst. prof. edn., assoc. prof. English, dir. IMC Ctr., U. Ark.-Pine Bluff, 1965-69; asst. prof. English and edn., dir. learning lab., N.C. Central U., Durhan, 1969-74; prof., dir./chairperson library media services and dept. ednl. media, dir. Afro-Am. Family Project, N.C. Agrl. and Tech. State U., Greensboro, 1975—; dir. workshops, grants. Contbr. research papers, articles to profl. jours. Nat. chmn. Com. to Re-Elect the Pres.; past sec. Fedn. Colored Women's Clubs; bd. dirs. southwestern div. ARC, dir. Volun-Teens; chairperson learning resources com. Task Force Durham Day Care Assn.; bd. dirs., chairperson schs. div. Durham County Unit Am. Cancer Soc.; past mem. adv. bd., bd. dirs. YMCA, Atlanta; 1st v.p. Durham br. NAACP; mem. Gilford County Commn. on Needs of Children; bd. dirs. NIH, N.C. Council of the Arts; mem. Guilford County Involvement Council; chmn. N.C. adv. com. U.S. Civil Rights Com.; N.C. chmn. Civil Rights Commn.; pres. Women Organized for Self-Realization and Leadership Devel.; mem. exec. planning com. Greensboro. Recipient awards ARC, 1968, 73, NAACP, 1973, HEW, 1978, U.S. Commn. on Civil Rights, 1982. Mem. Assn. Childhood Ednl. Internat., Comparative and Internat. Edn. Assn., Archives Assoc., ALA (past pres.), N.C. Assn. Coll. and Research Librarians, Internat. Platform Assn., Nat. Hist. Soc., NEA, AAUW (honor award 1983, pres. Greensboro br., chairperson internat. relations com.), Zeta Phi Beta (chairperson polit. action com. eastern region, nat. grammateus, Polit. and Civic Service award 1974, Outstanding Social-Polit. Service award 1982, Woman of Yr. 1977). Author: Afro-American Genealogy Sourcebook, 1987. Home: 4303 King Arthur Pl Greensboro NC 27405

YOUNG, VERA LEE HALL, educational administrator, association executive; b. Natchitoches, La., Jan. 9, 1944; d. Sidney and Gertrude (Bell) H.; m. Willie L. Young, Aug. 21, 1965 (div. June 1971). BA, Grambling State U., 1967; MA, Bank St. Coll., 1977; EdD, Century U., Beverly Hills, Calif., 1985. Cert. tchr., La., N.J., N.Y. Ednl. dir. Leslie Freeman Daycare Ctr., Bklyn., 1973-74; tchr. West N.Y. Bd. of Edn., 1978—; dir., founder Operation Super Inst., Ft. Lee, N.J., 1986—; speaker in field. Author: A Day Care Solution in America: The Learning Center, 1985; contbr. articles to field. Dept. Labor grantee, Jerusalem, 1982-83. Mem. NEA, N.J. Edn. Assn., Internat. Platform Assn., Internat. Reading Assn., Minority & Women Owned Business N.Y. Mem. Dutch Reform Ch. Office: Operation Super 229 Main St PO Box 1834 Fort Lee NJ 07024

YOUNGBERG, CHARLOTTE ANNE, education specialist; b. Hampton, Iowa, May 8, 1937; d. Sebo and Marion Bradford (Boutin-Clock) Reysack; B.A., U. No. Iowa, 1958; M.Ed., DePaul U. (Chgo.), 1966; postgrad. No. Ill. U.; m. Paul Gordon Neal, Mar. 29, 1969 (div. Jan. 1984); children—Rachel Elizabeth, Kory Bradford; m. Lyle Edwin Youngberg, June 30, 1990—. Tchr., 4th grade, Des Moines Ind. Sch. Dist., 1958-59; tchr., 3d grade Glenview (Ill.) Pub. Schs., 1959-61, tchr. 3d grade, psychol. ednl. diagnostic Schaumburg Dist. Schs., Hoffman Estates, Ill., 1961-69; supr. learning disabilities and behavior disorders Springfield (Ill.) Pub. Schs., 1969-73; psychoednl. diagnostician Barrington (Ill.) Sch. Dist. 220, 1973-77; ednl. strategist Area Edn. Agy. 7, Cedar Falls, Iowa, 1978-90; tchr. L.D. resource Verona (Mo.) R7 Sch. Dist., 1990—; ednl. cons. Spl. Edn. Dist. Lake County, Gurnee, Ill., summer, 1968. Certified K-14 teaching and supervising in guidance, counseling, elementary supervisory K-9, elementary K-9 teaching, spl. K-12 learning disabilities. Mem. NEA, Iowa Edn. Assn., Phi Delta Kappa. Home: PO Box 147 Verona MO 65769 Office: Verona R7 Sch Dist Box 28 Verona MO 65769

YOUNGBLOOD, MICHELLE KAREN WOLSTEIN, lawyer; b. Killeen, Tex., Jan. 14, 1958. BBA, Tex. A&M U., 1980; JD, Baylor U., 1983. Bar: Tex. 1983, U.S. Ct. Appeals (5th, 11th cirs.) 1986, U.S. Supreme Ct., 1986. Asst. city atty. City of Dallas, 1983-85; atty. advisor HUD, Ft. Worth, 1985-87; adminstrv. judge EEOC, Dallas, 1987—; adj. prof. Tarrant County Jr. Coll., Ft. Worth, 1988—; mcpl. judge pro-tem City of Ft. Worth, 1986—; instr. Dallas Community Coll., 1987—; pub. speaker various community orgns. and events, 1983—. Contbr. articles to prof. jours. V.p. Ft. Worth metro chapter Sweet Adelines Internat., 1985—; arbitrator BBB, Ft. Worth, 1986—. Named Woman of the Yr. Meadowbrook Bus. and Prof. Women, Ft. Worth, 1987, one of Outstanding Young Women of Am., 1988. Mem. Coll. State Bar Tex., Fed. Bar Assn. (pres. Ft. Worth chpt. 1987-88, sec. nat. young lawyers div. 1988—, nat. coun. 1988—) Tarrant County Young Lawyers Assn. (bd. dir. 1986-87), Tarrant County Women's Bar Assn. (bd. dir. 1986-88), Tarrant County Bar Assn., Tex. Young Lawyers Assn. (Cert. of Spl. Achievement), Bus. and Profl. Women (Young Career Woman of Yr. dist. 11 1987-88, Woman of Yr. Meadowbrook-Ft. Worth chpt. 1987). Home: PO Box 265 Forth Worth TX 76101 Office: EEOC 8303 Elm Brook Dallas TX 75247

YOUNGDAHL, PATRICIA LUCY, psychologist, educator; b. Cape Girardeau, Mo., Sept. 8, 1927; d. George B. and Alta Mae (Crites) Lucy; m. James E. Youngdahl, June 13, 1948 (div. Apr. 1974); children: Jay, Kristi, Lincoln, Sara. AA, Stephens Coll., 1946; BA, Washington U. (Mo.), 1948, MA, 1950; PhD, Fla. Inst. Tech., 1985. Lic. psychologist, Ark. Assoc. exec. dir. Social Planning Coun., St. Louis, 1950-52; instr. psychology U. Ark., Fayetteville, 1958-59, psychol. examiner Med. Ctr., Little Rock, 1961-64, asst. prof. Med. Scis. Campus, Little Rock, 1975—. Author: (with others) How to Use Transactional Analysis in the Public Schools, 1974. Mem. exec. com. Pulaski County Dem. Com., Little Rock, 1972—, State Dem. Party, 1980—; chmn. Ark. for Kennedy, 1979-80; del. Nat. Dem. Conv. 1976, 80, 84; chmn. Ark. Women's Polit. Caucus, 1973-83. Named to 100 Ark. Women of Achievement Ark. Press Women's Assn., 1980. Mem. Ark. Psychol. Assn., Am. Psychol. Assn. (assoc.). Unitarian-Universalist Ch. Home: 7108 Rockwood Rd Little Rock AR 72207 Office: Childrens Hosp 800 Marshall Little Rock AR 72202

YOUNGER, JUDITH TESS, lawyer, educator; b. N.Y.C., Dec. 20, 1933; d. Sidney and Kate (Greenbaum) Weintraub; m. Irving Younger, Jan. 21, 1955; children: Rebecca, Abigail M. B.S., Cornell U., 1954; J.D., NYU, 1958; LL.D. (hon.), Hofstra U., 1974. Bar: N.Y. 1958, U.S. Supreme Ct 1962, D.C. 1983, Minn. 1985. Law clk. to judge U.S. Dist. Ct., 1958-60; asso. firm Chadbourne, Parke, Whiteside & Wolff, N.Y.C., 1960-62; mem. firm Younger and Younger, and (successors), 1962-67; adj. asst. prof. N.Y. U. Sch. Law, 1967-69; asst. atty. gen. State of N.Y., 1969-70; assoc. prof. Hofstra U. Sch. Law, 1970-72, prof., assoc. dean, 1972-74; dean, prof. Syracuse Coll. Law, 1974-75; dep. dean, prof. law Cornell Law Sch., 1975-78, prof. law, 1978-85; vis. prof. U. Minn. Law Sch., Mpls., 1984-85; prof. law U. Minn. Law Sch., 1985—; of counsel Popham, Haik, Schnobrich & Kaufman, Ltd., Mpls., 1989—; Trustee CORNELL U., 1974-78; cons. NOW, 1972-74, Suffolk County for Revision of Its Real Property Tax Act, 1972-73; mem. Gov. Rockefeller's Panel to Screen Candidates of Ct. of Claims Judges, 1973-74. Contbr. articles to profl. jours. Mem. ABA (council legal edn. 1975-79), Am. Law Inst. (adv. restatement property 1982-84), AAUP (v.p. Cornell U. chpt. 1978-79), N.Y. State Bar Assn., Assn. of Bar of City of N.Y., Minn. Bar Assn. Home: 3520 W Calhoun Pkwy Minneapolis MN 55416 Office: U Minn Law Sch Minneapolis MN 55455

YOUNGER, MARY SUE, statistics educator, consultant, researcher; b. Roanoke, Va., Aug. 28, 1944; d. Douglas Lynch and Sue Menefee (Compton) Y. BA in Math., Hollins Coll., 1966; MS in Stats., Va. Polytech. Inst., 1969, PhD in Stats., 1972. Instr. Va. Polytech. Inst., Blacksburg, 1969-

72, asst. prof., 1972-74; asst. prof. U. Tenn., Knoxville, 1974-76, assoc. prof., 1976—, asst. dean for grad. bus. programs, 1985-86; statis. cons. St. Mary's Hosp., Knoxville, 1982, ELCON, Washington, 1981-82. Author: A Handbook for Linear Regression, 1979; A First Course in Linear Regression, 1985. Manuscript reviewer coll. textbook pubs. Contbr. articles to profl. jours. Mem. Am. Statis. Assn. (v.p. E. Tenn. chpt. 1985-88), SE Region Am. Inst. for Decision Scis. (pres. 1982). Methodist. Avocations: horse trials, equestrian events, foxhunting, dressage. Office: U Tenn Dept Statistics Knoxville TN 37996-0532

YOUNGHANS, CAROL LOU, educational staff developer; b. Denver, May 23, 1943; d. Sidney Lionel and Ruth Lee (Hayutin) Berger; divorced; 1 child, David. BS, U. Colo., 1965. Tchr., reading specialist Denver Pub. Schs., 1965-80; tchr. Adams County Sch. Dist. #12, Northglenn, Colo., 1980-85, staff developer, reading specialist, 1985—; facilitator site-based mgmt. and sch. improvement program Skyview Elem. Sch., Adams County Sch. Dist. #12, Thornton, Colo., 1986—, coord. student tchrs., 1987—; staff devel. cons. Colo. Dept. Edn., Thornton, 1988; cons. Nation Paideia Ctr., U. N.C.-Chapel Hill. U.S. Chpt. II novice tchrs. support grantee, Colo., 1987; Gov. Sch. Creativity grantee, 1989. Mem. Nat. Coun. for Study of Edn., Nat. Staff Devel. Coun., Internat. Reading Assn., Nat. Partnership for Ednl. Renewal, Colo. Partnership for Ednl. Renewal, Inst. for Devel. of Ednl. Activities, Inc. (disting. educator award 1987). Democrat. Jewish. Home: 12083 E Harvard Ave #103 Aurora CO 80014

YOUNG LIVELY, SANDRA LEE, nurse; b. Rockport, Ind., Dec. 31, 1943; d. William Cody and Flora Juanita (Carver) Thorpe; m. Kenneth Leon Doom, May 4, 1962 (div. 1975); children: Patricia, Anita, Elizabeth. AS, Vincennes U., 1979, student, U. So. Ind., 1987—. Nursing aide, nurse Forest Del Nursing Home, Princeton, Ind., 1975-80; charge nurse Welborn Bapt. Hosp., Evansville, Ind., 1979-80, 82-83; staff nurse Longview Regional Hosp., Tex., 1980-82; dir. home health Roy H. Laird Meml. Hosp., Kilgore, Tex., 1984-86; med. post-coronary nurse Mercy Hosp., Owensboro, Ky., 1987, Dept. of Corrections charge nurse, Branchville Trg. Ctr., Tell City, Ind, 1987—; staff nurse, asst. dir. Leisure Lodge Home Health, Overton, Tex., 1983-84. Grantee Roy H. Laird Meml. Hosp., 1986. Mem. NAFE, Menniger Found., Vincennes U. Alumni Assn., Ind. Correctional Nurses Assn., Internat. Platform Assn. Avocations: writing, research, cake decorating, house plants. Home: 1152 Diamond Pl Evansville IN 47710 Office: Branchville Tng Ctr Dept Corrections PO Box 500 Tell City IN 47586

YOUNGS, JOYCE ANN, metal processing executive; b. Watertown, N.Y., July 4, 1938; d. Clyde Bernard and Eleanor Ann (Jewett) Miller; m. Philip Levi Youngs, Oct. 17, 1963; children: Terry, Mark, Richard. Lic. practical nurse, Watertown Sch. Nursing, 1956; AAS magna cum laude, Corning Community Coll., 1972; BS, Elmira Coll., 1982. RN, N.Y. Nurse's aid House of Good Samaritan, Watertown, 1061-63; lic. practical nurse Watertown Sch. Practical Nursing, 1963-72; RN St. Joseph's Hosp., Elmira, N.Y., 1972-78; oncology nurse specialist Roswell Cancer Hosp., Buffalo, N.Y., 1978-80; clin. nurse specialist St. Joseph's Hosp., Elmira, 1982-84; v.p. Elmira Heat Treating, Inc., 1984-86, pres., 1986—. Contbr. articles to profl. jours. Coord. Elmira Downtown Devel., 1985—, Miss N.Y. State, Elmira, 1988-89; pres. St. Patricks Women Soc., Elmira, 1986-88; mem. Rep. Nat. Com., Washington, 1987—. Mem. NAFE, Am. Nurse's Assn., Metals Treating Inst., Am. Soc. Metals, Elmira Country Club (social dir. 1987—), Kiwanis, Elks. Roman Catholic. Home: 334 Beckwith Rd Pine City NY 14871 Office: Elmira Heat Treating Inc 407 S Kinyon St Elmira NY 14904

YOUNGS, SHIRLEY CEAN, artist; b. Watertown, N.Y., Apr. 7, 1939; d. Leonard Herbert and Thelma Eleanor (Schwalm) Cean; m. Frank Leslie Youngs; children: Leann Marchelle, Stacy Jon. Grad. with top honors, Famous Artists Sch., Westport, Conn., 1965; student, Robert Brackman Sch. Fine Arts, 1969, Daniel Greene Studio and Sch., N.Y.C., 1971. Instr. Leyard (Conn.) Community Ctr. for Arts, Lyman Allyn Art Mus., New London, Conn., Lyman Meml. High Sch., Lebanon, Conn., New London Art Students League, Nutmeg Nursing Home, New London, 1989-90; pvt. instr., Bozrah, Conn.; condr. workshops, demonstrator, lectr. Exhibited in numerous group shows including Nat. Arts Club, N.Y.C., Hudson Valley Art Assn., White Plains, N.Y., Lever House Gallery, N.Y.C., Conn. Coll., New London, Slater Meml. Mus., Norwich, Conn., William Benton Mus., Storrs, Conn., Cavalier Gallery, Stamford, Conn., Lyman Allyn Art Mus., GWS (Greenwich Workshop Southport, Conn.) Galleries; represented in permanent collections Embry-Riddle Aero. U., Daytona Beach, Fla., Nat. Mus. Women in Arts, Washington, also pvt. and co. collections. Mem. Pastel Soc. Am., Lyme Art Assn. (Mem.'s award 1987), Mystic Art Assn. (2d award for pastel 1989), Nat. Mus. Women in Arts, Internat. Soc. Artists. Office: C&C Impressions PO Box 63 Bozrah CT 06334

YOUNGSTER, ARDITHE, sales and service executive, independent contractor; b. Summit, N.J., Jan. 25, 1947; d. William Andrew and Mildred (Kutik) Y. BS in Biolog. Sci., Colo. State U., 1968; postgrad., Calif. State U., Long Beach, 1970. Cert. clin. lab. technologist. Clin. lab. technologist, sect. head St. John's Hosp. and Health Ctr., Santa Monica, Calif., 1970-75; product info. supr. Ortho Pharm. Corp., Raritan, N.J., 1975-76; client svcs. chemist Nichols Inst., San Pedro, Calif., 1976; dept. supr. Morton Maxwell Lab., L.A., 1977-79; sales rep. Metpath Labs., Inc., Teterboro, N.J., 1979-81; sales and customer svc. mgr. L.A., 1981—; coord. ednl. programs QualiMedTech, Inc., Long Beach, Calif., 1982-83; quality assurance analyst Pacific S.W. Airlines, San Diego, 1985-88; clin. lab. tng. mgr. Electro-Nucleonics, Inc., Fairfield, N.J., 1987—. Vol. Health Fair Expo, L.A., 1980-84. Mem. Colo. State U. Alumni Assn. (alumni ambassador 1984—), Nat. Notary Assn., Pacific Palisades C. of C., AAUW, Am. Assn. Clin. Chemists, Ninety Nines, Gamma Phi Beta, Alpha Mu Gamma. Republican. Presbyterian. Office: 845 Via de la Paz Suite 8 Pacific Palisades CA 90272

YOUNKER, PAMELA GODFREY, business owner, consultant, accountant; b. Copperhill, Tenn., Apr. 5, 1955; d. Thomas Marvin and Betty Jean (Thomas) Godfrey; m. Ronald Joseph Younker, Nov. 18, 1978; children: David, John. AS, Young Harris Jr. Coll., 1975; BBA in Acctg., U. Ga., 1977. Mgmt. trainee Oxford Industries, Inc., Atlanta, 1977-78, divisional acct., 1978-79, sr. internal auditor, 1979-81; sr. internal auditor Lockheed Corp., Marietta, Ga., 1981-85; acctg. mgr. med. benefits dept. Lockheed Aero. Systems Co., Marietta, 1985-88; owner, cons. Pam Younker Acctg. & Tax Svc., Marietta, 1988—; advisor U. Ga. Sch. Acctg., Athens, 1986—; med. benefits cons. Lockheed Aero. Systems Co., 1988—. Vol. battered women program YWCA, Marietta, 1979-87; mem. Atlanta Hist. Soc., 1988—; treas. Our House, Atlanta Area Hosp. House, 1988—; pres., state conv. chmn. Women of Ga. Power, Canton, 1986—. Mem. Inst. Internal Auditors (pres. so. region 1984), Young Harris Coll. Alumni Assn. (coord. 1984—), Alpha Chi Omega (province chmn. Tenn. 1988—, pres. Atlanta chpt. 1985-87, Nat. Coun. award 1985, Continuing Excellence award 1986). Home: 1001 Gentry Ln Marietta GA 30064

YOUNT, FLORENCE JANE, lawyer; b. Enid, Okla., Dec. 13, 1926; d. William Edward and Florence Evelyn (McCully) Y. B.A., State U. Iowa, 1948; J.D., S. Tex. Coll. Law, 1958; certificate, Parker Sch. Fgn. and Comparative Law, Columbia U., 1976. Bar: Tex. bar 1958. Atty. Ginther, Warren & Co., Houston, 1959-70; supr. internat. contracts Ea. Hemisphere div. CONOCO, Inc., N.Y.C., Stamford, Conn., 1970-75; sr. atty. Cities Service Co., Houston, 1975-83; contracts supr. Marathon, Houston, 1984—; adviser to Internat. Law Socs. of three Houston law schs.; bd. dirs. South Tex. Law Jour., Inc., 1959-88, v.p., 1969, 77, 84-87, pres., 1970, 78, 79. Contbr. articles to law jours. Bd. dirs. Park Ave. Christian Ch., N.Y.C., 1971-73, First Christian Ch., Houston, 1977-78; active Vols. of Shelter, N.Y.C., 1973-75; precinct chmn., asso. legal counsel, chmn. rules com. Harris County (Tex.) Republican Com., 1958-68. Recipient Distinguished Alumnus award South Tex. Coll. Law, 1976, Houston Matrix award, 1978, award Bus. and Profl. Women's Club Houston, 1976; named One of 100 Top Corporate Women Bus. Week, 1976. Mem. ABA, Tex. Bar Assn. (contbg. editor Internat. Law Newsletter), Houston Bar Assn., S. Tex. Coll. Law Alumni Assn. (dir. 1977-80), Zool. Soc. Houston. Mem. Christian Ch. Address: 701 Bering Dr 2003 Houston TX 77057

YOUNTS, PATTY LOU, interior design executive, researcher; b. Lexington, N.C., Feb. 20, 1950; d. Wayne Lohr and Rosetta Mae (Myers) Y. BS, U. N.C.-Greensboro, 1972; postgrad., Wake Forest U., Winston-Salem, N.C., 1976. Apprentice draftsman and interior designer Paul T. Briggs, AIA, Lexington, 1971, in-house designer, specifer, 1972-74; part-time interior designer Watkins Office Interiors, Winston-Salem, 1972-74; ptnr. IN-Ex Designs, Inc., 1974-75, corp. officer, head, 1975-81, pres., owner, 1981—; pres. decorative panel Koncepts, Inc., 1986—; sec./treas. J.P. Walls, Inc., 1989—; bd. dir. Industry Gen. Tire, GF Bus. Systems, Armstrong Industries, Mid-State Tile; guest speaker univs. Adv. bd. Lexington Meml Hosp., 1984— , Western Carolina U., 1983—. Recipient N.C. AIA awards for Sch. Planning, 1977, 79. Sperry and Hutchinson scholar, 1968-72, hon. scholar U. N.C.-Greensboro, 1971-72. Mem. Inst. Bus. Designers (mem., chmn. various coms., pres. Carolinas chpt. 1977-80, 82-84), Am. Soc. Interior Designers, Color Mktg. Group (chairholder 1985). Lexington C. of C. (com. chmn. 1980, bd. dirs. 1981-84, pres. 1990—). Democrat. Mem. United Ch. of Christ. Avocations: water skiing, golf. Office: Design Cons 302 W Center St Lexington NC 27292

YOUSHOCK, EVA LYNN, dermatologist; b. Jacksonville, Fla., Nov. 11, 1955; d. Joseph and Ann (Muraika) Y.; m. David Klionsky, June 22, 1980; 1 child, Rachel Lauren. BA, Smith Coll., 1977; MD, Northwestern U., Chgo., 1981. Diplomate Am. Bd. Dermatology, Nat. Bd. Med. Examiners. Staff dermatologist USAF Med. Ctr., Dayton, Ohio, 1985-89; sr. staff physician Henry Ford Hosp., Troy and Sterling Heights, Mich., 1989—; asst. clin. prof. Wright State U., Dayton; cons. VA Med. Ctr., Dayton. Maj. USAFR, 1977-89. Mem. Am. Med. Women's Assn., Women's Dematologic Soc., Am. Acad. of Dematology. Office: Henry Ford Hosp 2825 Livernois Troy MI 48083

YOVANOVICH, DEBORAH THERESA, management consultant; b. Metuchen, N.J., Apr. 27, 1953; d. Daniel and Theresa Mary (Chiera) Y.; m. Donald Bean, Dec. 5, 1982; (div. Dec. 13, 1985). Exec. asst. degree, Taylor Bus. Inst., Plainfield, N.J., 1972. Exec. sec. fin. div. Johnson & Johnson, New Brunswick, N.J., 1972-75, exec. sec. nat. purchasing dept., 1975-80; exec. asst. to chief exec. officer Bantam Books, Inc., N.Y.C., 1980-82; rsch. cons. Chase Manhattan Bank AG, Frankfurt, Fed. Republic Germany, 1982-84; mgr. mktg. svcs. Internat. Mktg. Network, N.Y.C., 1984-86; cons. Universal Trading Exch., 1986-87; dir., adminstr. Handy Assocs., N.Y.C., 1987—. Mem. Internat. Facilities Mgmt. Assn. Republican. Roman Catholic. Office: Handy Assocs 250 Park Ave New York NY 10177

YSTUETA, MARY CAROLINE, computer hardware engineer; b. Staten Island, N.Y., Feb. 4, 1964; d. William Francis and Janice Theodore (Smith) Y. SBEE, MIT, 1986. Software engr. Wang Labs., Inc., Lowell, Mass., 1986-88, product planner, 1988-89, hardware engr., 1989—. Vol. Boston Mus. Sci., Cambridge, Mass., 1989. Mem. IEEE, Soc. Women Engrs. (v.p. 1984-85), MIT Alumni Assn. (class treas. 1985, bd. dirs. 1990). Roman Catholic. Home: 29 Gordon St #103 Waltham MA 02154 Office: Wang Labs Inc 1 Industrial Ave MS 012 26A Lowell MA 01851

YU, JULIE HUNG-HSUA, marketing educator; b. Taipei, Republic of China, Nov. 22, 1954; came to U.S., 1959; d. Wei-Wen and Yueh-Hsin (Wang) Y.; m. Holger Gossmann, Feb. 1989. BA in Biol. Sci., U. Mo., 1975, MEE in Biomed. Engring., 1977, MBA in Mktg., 1981, PhD in Mktg., 1983. Rsch. asst. U. Mo., Columbia, 1975-81, grad. instr., 1981-82; asst. prof. mktg. Wake Forest U., Winston-Salem, N.C., 1983-84, Hofstra U., Hempstead, N.Y., 1984-86, U. Hawaii at Manoa, Honolulu, 1986-88, Chinese U. Hong Kong, 1988—; rsch. cons. Mktg. Metrics, N.J., 1985-86. reviewer Jour. Acad. Mktg. Sci., Internat. Jour. Rsch. in Mktg. Mem. Am. Mktg. Assn. (doctoral consortium fellow 1982), Acad. Internat. Bus., Am. Statis Assn., Mu Kappa Tau. Office: Chinese U Hong Kong, Dept Mktg Shatin, New Territories Hong Kong

YU, LINDA, newswoman, television anchorwoman; b. Xian, China, Dec. 1, 1946; m. Richard K. Baer, June 1982. BA in Journalism, U. So. Calif., 1968. With Sta. KTLA-TV, Los Angeles, Sta. KABC-TV, Los Angeles; news anchor, reporter Sta. KATU-TV, Portland, Oreg.; gen. assignment reporter Sta. KGO-TV, San Francisco; with Sta. WMAQ-TV, Chgo., 1979-84, gen. assignment reporter, weekend anchor, 1979-80, co-anchor Monday-Friday edit. NEWSCENTER5, 4:30 PM, 1980-81, co-anchor NEWSCENTER5, 10:00 PM, 1981-84; co-anchor Eyewitness News, WLS-TV, Chgo., 1984—; spl.: Linda Yu in China, 1980; anchor WLS-TV, Chgo., 1984—. Recipient Chgo. Emmy award, 1981, 82, 87. Office: Sta WLS-TV 190 N State St Chicago IL 60601

YU HUSSEIN, PATTIE, public relations agency executive; b. Washington, Nov. 15, 1956; d. Michael Yung-An and Maria (Chang) Yu; m. Sharif R. Hussein, June 21, 1980. BS in Journalism, U. Md., 1977, MA in Communications, 1982; cert. in journalism, NYU, 1977. Editorial intern Redbook Mag., 1977; editorial asst. Washington Star Newspaper, 1977-79; media coordinator U. Md. Univ. Relations, College Park, 1979-82; communications freelancer IBM, Bethesda, Md., 1981-82; assoc. Porter/Novelli Omnicom Pub. Relations Network, Washington, 1983-84, sr. assoc., 1984-86, v.p., 1987—; judge United Way corp. campaigns, Alexandria, Va., 1986, World Inst. for Black Communications, 1986; guest lectr. U. Md., Howard U., George Washington U., 1986-87. Freelance editorial writer Mt. Vernon Coll. Alumnae mag., 1982; contbr. articles to profl. jours. Co-chair devel. and pub. relations Regina High Sch., Hyattsville, Md., 1987; pub. relations advisor Beautiful Babies campaign March of Dimes, Washington, 1987; alumni adviser The M Space, U. Md. Journalism Alumni mag., 1981. Recipient awards of excellence Communications Excellence to Black Audiences, 1983, 84, 87, Gold Screen award Nat. Assn. Govt. Communicators, 1984, Addy Cert. of Excellence Washington Advt. Club, 1985, 87. Mem. Pub. Relations Soc. Am. (Nat. capitol chpt., Thoth award), Washington Women in Pub. Relations (bd. dirs.), U. Md. Journalism Alumni Chpt., U. Md. Alumni Assn. Internat., Sigma Delta Chi, Soc. Profl. Journalists. Democrat. Roman Catholic. Clubs: BCC Toastmaster's (Bethesda); Silver Spring Bus. and Profl. Women (com. chmn. 1981). Office: Porter/Novelli 1001 30th St NW Washington DC 20007

YUKL, TRUDY ANN, psychologist, medical social worker; b. Portsmouth, N.H., Feb. 5, 1947; d. Francis Joseph and Dorothy Helen (Pluff) Y. BA in psychology, U. Ky., 1969; MS in Counseling, Suffolk U., 1984; postgrad. in counseling psychology, Harvard U., 1984-85; EdD in Counseling Psychology, Boston U., 1985-89. Med. social worker Mass. Gen. Hosp., Boston, 1969-86, clin. fellow in psychology, 1986-87 clin. internship VA Outpatient clinic, Honolulu, 1987-88; psychologist crisis team North Essex Mental Health Ctr., Havenhill, Mass., 1988-89; co-founder, dir. Indian Clinic, 1973-86; cons. Boston Indian Council, 1973-86; lectr. in field. Contbr. articles to profl. jours. Health adv. bd. Tecumseh House, Boston, 1980-86; active Homeless Coalition, Boston, 1984-85, community service activities, Lunalilo Home, Kalaupapa Moloka'i, Leahi Hosp., Office Hawaiian Affairs; mental health cons. Hi. State Dept. Health, Communicable Disease div, bd. dirs., sec., Hui Hoa Aloha. Recipient Outstanding Profl. Human Services award, 1974-75, Disting. Leadership award, 1987-88, Acad. All-Am. Achievement award, 1988; nominated Disting. Alumni, U. Ky., 1985. Mem. Internat. Platform Soc. (Winnettca, Ill.), Nat. Assn. Social Workers, Am. Psychol. Assn., Mass. Psychol. Assn., Phi Delta Kappa. Avocations: travel; photography; music; native American culture; dancing; swimming. Office: 3627 Kilavea Ave Rm #401 Honolulu HI 96815

YUNG-FATAH, ELLEN MEEFONG, nurse consultant; b. Hong Kong, Jan. 15, 1953; d. James Yorkshing and Kwaifun (Chan) Young; m. Ali Ahmed Fatah, June 4, 1983. BS in Nursing, SUNY, 1980; MPH, Johns Hopkins U., 1983. Asst. educator health Chinatown Health Clinic, N.Y.C., 1978-80; clin. nurse Luth. Med. Ctr., Bklyn., 1980-81, Johns Hopkins Hosp., Balt., 1981-83; cons. nurse D.C. Dept. Consumer & Regulatory Affairs, 1983—; instr. Cath. U. Am. Grad. Sch. Nursing, Washington, 1988—; pub. health nurse Balt. City Health Dept., 1981; mem. task force, steering com. for health care regulations D.C., Washington, 1984—; advisor D.C. Health Planning & Devel. Agy., Washington, 1985—; resource person Senate Spl. Com. Aging, House Select Com. Aging, Am. Assn. Retired Persons, others; mem. profl. adv. com. Home Health Agy. Study Georgetown U., 1985-86; mem. Nat. Task Force for Hemodialysis User Edn., 1984—. Contbr. articles to profl. jours. Mem. task force on minority access to hospice care Nat. Hospice Orgn., 1987-88, mem. nat. com. on minority access to hospice care, 1989—. Mem. Am. Pub. Health Assn., Johns Hopkins U. Alumni Soc., Orgn. of Chinese Ams., NAFE. Democrat. Moslem. Office: Dept Consumer & Regulatory Affairs 614 H St NW Washington DC 20001

YUSK, JANICE WOODS, dermatologist, medical educator; b. Knoxville, Tenn., Feb. 27, 1942; d. Raymond Floyd and Inalee (Brooks) Woods; m. John F. Yusk, May 8, 1965; children: John David, Lisa Ashley. BS, U. Tenn., 1963, MD, 1966. Lic. dermatologist Am. Acad. Dermatology, Ky. Pvt. practice Drs. Davidson, Yusk & Faurest, Louisville, 1972--; assoc. prof. pediatrics Sch. Medicine U. Louisville, 1979--; assoc. prof. dermatology Sch. Medicine Sch. Medicine U. Louisville, 1978; chief pediatric dermatology Kosair-Children's Hosp., Louisville, 1979--. Fellow: Am. Acad. Dermatology. Office: 6400 Dutchmans Pkwyn The Springs Med Pla Ste 345 Louisville KY 40205

YUTHASASTRKOSOL, CHARIN, real estate corporation officer, family business owner; b. Bangkok, Dec. 30, 1930; came to U.S., 1954; d. Luang Prasertwithirut and Jaruke (Boontham) B.; m. Prapakorn Yuthasastrkosol, Feb. 23, 1953. A, Strayer Coll., 1959. Sr. v.p. Twining Corp., Balt., 1979—; chmn. bd., chief exec. officer Yuthasart-Kosol, Inc., Havertown, Pa. Performer of dances for charity. Recipient over 200 ballroom dancing awards, 1978—; named 2000 Notable Women in Am. Mem. Temple U. Assn. Ret. Profls. (faculty), Phila.-Del. Valley Restaurant Assn. (dir.), Bus, and Profl. Women Assn. Bangkok Thailand (life). Office: Twining Corp 4004 Greenway Baltimore MD 21218

ZABACK, CAROL FAY, food company executive; b. Dillon, Mont., June 12, 1942; d. George H. and Fay (Ellis) Whittaker; m. Edward T. Zaback, Dec. 6, 1963; children: Jodi Ann, Lori Lin, Tedi Jo. Student, Idaho State U., 1960-62; BA, U. Mont., 1963. Lic. real estate salesperson, N.Y. Sales rep. retail food group Kraft, Inc., Hillside, N.J., 1976-78; account rep. Kraft, Inc., Edison, N.J., 1978-79, sr. account exec., 1979-81, sales supr., 1981-89, tng. specialist parent co., 1983-89, sales category mgr. for produce enhancements and viscous products, metro N.Y.-Phila. markets, 1989—. Mem. Am. Mgmt. Assn., Am. Humane Soc., Animal Protection Inst. Am., Nat. Assn. Female Execs., Audobon Soc. Home: Rt 2 Box 780 Campbell Hall NY 10916 Office: Kraft Inc 4 Mayfield Ave Edison NJ 08837

ZABEL, FERN I. ROOKSTOOL, teacher; b. Seattle, July 18, 1945; d. Everett Wilson and Fern Gertrude (Ritscher) Rookstool; m. Ronald Clay. BA, U. Wash., 1967; MA, U. Denver, 1971, Fuller Theol. Sem., Pasadena, Calif., 1986. Elem. tchr. Alexandria (Va.) City Pub. Schs., 1967-69, The Internat. Sch. Bangkok, Thailand, 1969-70, Fairfax County Pub. Schs., Springfield, Va., 1972-73, Rosemead (Calif.) Sch. Dist., 1986; jr. high tchr. Los Angeles Unified Sch. DIst., 1985-86, Archdiocese of Los Angeles, 1989—; high sch. resource specialist Barstow (Calif.) Unified Sch. Dist., 1987. Recipient Ednl. Honorary for Scholarship award Phi Delta Kappa U., Denver 1970. Mem. U. Wash. Alumni Assn., U. Denver Alumni Assn., Phi Beta Kappa. Republican. Presbyterian. Home: 1891 Windsor Rd San Marino CA 91108 Office: Fern I Zabel MA PO Box 80073 San Marino CA 91118

ZABLE, MARIAN MAGDELEN, physician assistant, consultant; b. Beaver Dam, Wis., Oct. 13, 1933; d. John Joseph and Agatha Mary (Eschlie) Fernbach; m. Jerome Edward Zable, July 30, 1960 (div. 1970); children: Terrence, Andrea, Michael. BS, U. Wis., 1964; Physician Asst., U. Fla., 1975. Tchr. Brown Deer (Wis.) Sch. System, 1964, Orange County (Fla.) Schs., 1965-70; curriculum devel., adminstr. So. Coll., Orlando, Fla., 1970-72; physician asst., asst. dir. Longevity Ctr., Orlando, 1977; physician asst. Pritikin Longevity Ctr., Miami, Fla., 1978-83, Cardiovascular Assocs., Kissimmee, Fla., 1984—; pres., physician asst., cons. Physician's Svcs., Inc., Orlando, 1986—. Mem. Am. Acad. Physician Assts., Fla. Acad. Physician Assts. Home: 3407 Trentwood Blvd Orlando FL 32812 Office: Cardivascular Assocs 801 Oak St Kissimmee FL 32471

ZABUKOVEC, JAMIE JO, clinical psychologist; b. Waukegan, Ill., Oct. 27, 1954; d. John Joseph and Jennie Josephine (Zalaznik) Z. BA in Psychology and Maths., Ea. Ill. U., 1976, MS, 1977; PsyD, Ill. Sch. Profl. Psychology, Chgo., 1988. Lic. psychologist, Ill. Family counselor Warren Twp. Youth Svcs., Gurnee, Ill., 1977-84; staff psychologist Stress Disorder Treatment Unit, VA Med. Ctr., North Chicago, Ill., 1988—; mem. adj. faculty Columbia Coll., Ft. Sheridan, Ill., 1989—, Ill. Sch. Profl. Psychology, 1990. Mem. Lake County Sexual Abuse Task Force, Waukegan, 1984, Com. to Incorporate Beach Park, Ill., 1987. Recipient Liaison award Gurnee Police Dept., 1984. Mem. Am. Psychol. Assn. Office: VA Med Ctr Psychology Svc Greenbay & Rte 137 North Chicago IL 60064

ZACARIAS, REBECCA ANNE, business control analyst; b. Corpus Christi, Tex., July 8, 1961; d. Miguel Lara and Candelaria (Villa) Acuna; m. Martin Xavier Zacarias, May 20, 1989. BBA, North Tex. State U., 1983. Acct. adminstr. IBM Corp., Dallas, 1983-86; adminstrv. ops. mgr. IBM Corp., El Paso, Tex., 1987-89; bus. control analyst IBM Corp., Dallas, 1989—. Vol. Casa de Amigos, Dallas, 1984, Family Place, Dallas, 1985, Cary Jr. High Sch., Dallas, 1986; tchr. Holy Trinity Bible Sch., Dallas, 1985-86; tchr. Jr. Achievement Project Bus., El Paso, 1988. Recipient North Tex. 40 award Office of the Pres., 1982; leadership scholar Southwestern Life Ins., 1982. Mem. Exec. Women Internat., Chi Omega (v.p. 1981-82), Delta Sigma Pi, Order of Omega. Office: IBM 4191 N Mesa El Paso TX 79902

ZACCONE, SUZANNE MARIA, sales executive; b. Chgo., Oct. 23, 1957; d. Dominic Robert and Lorretta F. (Urban) Z. Grad. high sch., Downers Grove, Ill. Sales sec. Brookeridge Realty, Downers Grove, 1975-76; sales cons. Kafka Estates Inc., Downers Grove, 1975-76; adminstrv. asst. Chem. Dist., Inc., Oak Brook, Ill., 1976-77; sales rep., mgr. Anographics Corp., Burr Ridge, Ill., 1977-85; pres., owner Graphic Solutions, Inc., Burr Ridge, 1985—. Recipient Supplier Mem. award Internat. Bottled Water Assn., 1987-88, Supplier award for excellence, 1990; named Supplier of Yr. Gen. Binding Corp., 1988. Mem. NAFE, Women in Mgmt., Sales and Mktg. Execs. of Chgo., Women Entrepreneurs of DuPage County (sec.). Avocations: reading, sailing, cooking, needlepoint, scuba diving. Office: Graphic Solutions Inc 150 Shore Dr Burr Ridge IL 60521

ZACH, MIRIAM SUSAN, music literature educator; b. Muscatine, Iowa, Oct. 2, 1954; d. Herbert William and Margaret Emily (Munster) Z.; m. Mikesch Muecke. BS, Northwestern U., Evanston, Ill., 1976; MA, U. Chgo., 1980. Tchr. pvt. schs. Fed. Republic of Germany, 1981-85; music literature educator U. Fla., Gainesville, 1987—. Organist recital 20th-Century Organ Literature, Gainesville, Fla. and Lemgo, West Germany, 1988, Recital of Vocally, Gainesville, Fla., 1989, La Nativite du Seignerur, Gainesville, 1989; pianist The Birds Concert, Gainesville; produced opera Edgar and Emily, U. Fla., 1990. Valedictorican, North Chgo. Community High Sch. Mem. Am. Guild Organists (treas. Gainesville 1988-90), Coll. Music Soc., Am. Musicological Soc., Music Educators and Concert Artists (Fed. Republic of Germany), Phi Kappa Phi, Phi Kappa Lambda, Phi Beta Delta. Office: Univ Fla Dept Music Gainesville FL 32611

ZACHARY, ANDREA ANNE, geneticist; b. Cleve., Sept. 25, 1946; d. Anthony A. and Audrey J. (Klaus) Z. BS, Ohio State U., 1967, MS, 1969; PhD, Case Western Res. U., 1982. Research asst. Ohio State U., Columbus, 1969-70; technologist Cleve. Clinic Found., 1970-74, supr. lab., 1974-81, project scientist, 1981-82, staff, 82-84, assoc. lab. dir., 1984-86, co-dir. lab., 1986—; faculty histocompatibility specialist course South-Eastern Organ Procurement Found., 1983, 84, 86, 88; ad hoc cons. NIH, 1985-86. Co-editor: AACHT Lab. Manual, 1981; author audio-visual program on immunogenetics, 1983. Contbr. articles to profl. jours. and chpts. to scholarly tests. Grantee Kidney Found. of Ohio, 1984, 88, Cleve. Clinic Found., 1985-87. Mem. United Network for Organ Sharing (bd. govs. 1987-88, histocompatibility com. 1986-89, transp. com. 1988-89, ethics com. 1989—), Am. Soc. for Histocompatibility and Immunogenetics (councillor 1977-78, 83-86, edn. program faculty 1971-83, 85, 88, invited speaker sci. symposium 1988, chairperson tech. affairs com. 1982-84, chairperson accreditation com. 1986-88, editor Lab. Manual 1988, v.p. 1988-89, pres.-elect 1989-90), Am. Soc. Human Genetics, Am. Soc. Transplant Physicians (invited speaker 1988), Transplant Soc. of N.E. Ohio (mem. editorial bd. Transplantation jour.), Am. Bd. Transplant Coords. (expert adv. com. 1988—), Audubon Soc., Nat. Wildlife Fedn., N.Y. Acad. Scis., Sierra Club. Avocations: nature photography, cross-country skiing, music, leather carving. Office: Cleve Clinic Found 9500 Euclid Ave Cleveland OH 44106

ZACHARY, DOMNA, nurse, computer consultant; b. Elmhurst, N.Y., Sept. 30, 1957; d. Spyro and Stavroula (Halkiotis) Z. AAS, Suffolk County Community Coll., 1977; BSHA, St. Joseph's Coll., 1985; MPA, L.I. U., 1988. RN, N.Y. Asst. dir. nurses Sunrest Health Facilities, Port Jefferson, N.Y., 1982-86; pvt. duty nurse Alert Med. Personnel, East Setauket, N.Y., 1985-89; nurse cons. Hosp. Assn. N.Y. State, Albany, 1988; systems cons. Baxter Healthcare Corp., Hauppauge, N.Y., 1988-89; project leader clin. systems St. Vincent's Hosp. & Med. Ctr. N.Y., N.Y.C., 1989—. Sec. N.Y. State dist. Daughters of Penelope, 1989—. Lt. (j.g.) Med. Svc. Corps., USNR, 1990—. Mem. Nat. League Nursing, Am. Coll. Healthcare Execs., Nassau/Suffolk Health Systems Agy., Pi Alpha Alpha, Sigma Phi Omega. Greek Orthodox.

ZACHERL, ANITA MARIE, market specialist; b. Brookville, Pa., Sept. 13, 1946; d. Francis Augustine and Hilda Clara (Schill) Z. Diploma in Nursing, St. Vincent Hosp. Sch. of Nursing, 1967. Staff nurse NYU Med. Ctr., N.Y.C., 1967-71, Aspen (Colo.) Valley Hosp., 1971-79; dir. nursing services Med. Personnel Pool, Dallas, 1979-80; clin. specialist Datamedix, Inc., Dallas, 1981-82; nurse cons. Xanar, Inc., Dallas, 1982-87; clin. instr. Coherent Med. Group, 1987-89, regional edn. mgr., 1989, market specialist, 1990—; speaker nursing, physician seminars, 1984, 85, 86, 87, 88, 89. Assoc. editor Laser Nursing mag.; contbr. articles on lasers. Mem. NAFE, Assn. of Operating Rm. Nurses. Roman Catholic.

ZACHERT, VIRGINIA, psychologist, educator; b. Jacksonville, Ala., Mar. 1, 1920; d. R.E. and Cora H. (Massee) Z. Student, Norman Jr. Coll., 1937; A.B., Ga. State Woman's Coll., 1940; M.A., Emory U., 1947; Ph.D., Purdue U., 1949. Diplomate: Am. Bd. Profl. Psychologists. Statistician Davison-Paxon Co., Atlanta, 1941-44; research psychologist Mil. Contracts, Auburn Research Found., Ala. Poly. Inst.; indsl. and research psychologist Sturm & [illegible] engrs.), 1958-59; research project dir. Western Design, Biloxi, [illegible] psychologist Norman Park, Ga., 1961- [illegible] med. edn. Med. Coll. Ga., [illegible]-84, rsch. prof. [illegible] Baptist. [illegible] Ave Augusta GA 30904-4628 Office: Med Coll Ga Dept Ob-Gyn Augusta GA 30912

ZACKERY, BENNIE LEE, education educator; b. Chidester, Ark., Aug. 24, 1946; d. Benny Box and Mabel Tatum; m. Ulysses Zackery, Oct. 26, 1968; children: Katrinka, Marlon, Ulysses III, Marcus, Edna. AA, Shorter Jr. Coll., North Little Rock, Ark., 1968; BS, Philander Smith, Little Rock, Ark., 1969; postgrad., U. Minn., 1975. Spl. edn. tchr. Mpls. Pub. Schs., 1974-77, 82—, St. Paul Pub. Schs., 1978-82; cons. non-pub. special edn. Mpls., 1982—; tutor homebound program Mpls. Pub. Schs., 1988; active local PTOs. Mentor Cath. Charities Orgn., Mpls., 1987—; Dem. del., Mpls., 1988. Mem. Women's Network, Minn. Black Educators, Head Injury Assn., Women in Edn. Democrat. Methodist.

ZACKY, DOLORES, advertising executive; b. Mexico City, Sept. 22, 1947; came to U.S., 1976; d. German and Dolores (Menendez) Valdes; m. Ralf George Zacky, July 15, 1978; children: Lorena, Denise, Daphne. BA in Spanish and Latin Am. Studies, U. of the Ams., Mexico City, 1970; postgrad., Inst. Latin Am. Studies, London, 1970-71; MA in Spanish with distinction, UCLA, 1978. Producer McCann Erickson, Mexico City, 1971-72; copywriter Manin Display Internat., Mexico City, 1972-74; prof. lit. Colegio Columbia, Mexico City, 1974-76; account exec. Latmark Advt., Los Angeles, 1980-81; assoc. creative dir. Bermudez and Assocs., Los Angeles, 1981-82; v.p., creative dir. J. Walter Thompson/Hispania, Los Angeles, 1982-87; pres., creative dir. Valdes Zacky Assocs., Inc., Los Angeles, 1987—. Creative dir. (TV comml.s) Nature, 1987 (Don Belding award), Te Quiero Mucho, 1987 (Don Belding award 1987). Named one of 4 top women in advt. Adweek mag., 1986. Republican. Roman Catholic. Office: Valdes Zacky Assocs Inc. 1925 Century Park E 19th Fl Los Angeles CA 90067*

ZADEH, STELLA, talent agent; b. N.Y.C., July 27, 1947; d. Lotfi alisker and Fay (Sand) Z.; m. David Lewis Gersh, July 30, 1988. BA, Harvard U., 1969; MJ, UCLA, 1971. Reporter, editor AP, L.A., 1976-78; asst. met. editor L.A. Herald Examiner, 1978-79, city editor, 1979-80; news planning mgr. Sta. KCBS-TV, L.A., 1980; mng. editor CBS Teletext Project, L.A., 1980-84; owner Stella Zadeh & Assoc., L.A., 1985—; mgr. cable franchise effort CBS, Alameda, Calif., 1983; asst. city editor, edn. reports, ct. reports and travel editor Santa Monica (Calif.) Outlook, 1971-76. Mem. Acad. TV, Art and Scis., Hollywood Radio and TV Soc., Harvard Club. Office: 11759 Iowa Ave Los Angeles CA 90025 Home: 4660 Encino Ave Encino CA 91316

ZADYLAK, CONNIE LORRAINE, educator; b. Sewickley, Pa., Aug. 13, 1947; d. Roy Campbell and Anna Mae (Mountain) Smith; m. Andrew John Zadylak, June 6, 1970. BS, Edinboro (Pa.) U., 1970, MEd, 1976; elem. cert., Geneva Coll., Beaver Falls, Pa., 1978. Tchr. art Rochester (Pa.) Area Sch. Dist., 1970—, chmn. dept. spl. subjects, 1989—. Illustrator: The Squirrel that Found the Golden Egg, 1989. Vol. Aliquippa (Pa.) Hosp. Aux., 1979. Mem. NEA, Pa. State Edn. Assn., Rochester Edn. Assn. (exec. bd. 1989-90), Nat. Art Edn. Assn., Western Pa. Assn. for Primary Educators, Edinboro Alumni Assn., Rochester PTA (Kidcare award 1989), Alpha Gamma Delta. Democrat. Home: 2404 Marion St Aliquippa PA 15001 Office: Rochester Area Sch Dist 540 Reno St Rochester PA 15074

ZAEHRINGER, MARY VERONICA, retired home economics educator; b. Phila., May 27, 1911; d. Paul J. and Mary (Bolton) Z. BS, Temple U., 1946; MS, Cornell U., 1948, PhD, 1953. Asst. foods rsch. Cornell U., Ithaca, N.Y., 1951-53; instr. home econs. rsch. Mont. State Coll., Bozeman, 1948-49, asst. prof. econs. rsch., 1949-50; rsch. prof., head dept. home econs. rsch. U. Idaho, Moscow, 1953-72, rsch. prof. home econs. rsch., 1972-76; rsch. fellow Inst. Storage and Processing of Agrl. Produce, Wageningen, the Netherlands, 1967-68. Contbr. articles to profl. jours. Mem. Inst. Food Technologists, Am. Assn. Cereal Chemistry, Potato Assn. Am., Sigma Xi, Omicron Nu, Pi Lambda Sigma, Kappa Delta Epsilon. Home: 614 Ash St Moscow ID 83843

ZAFFIRINI, JUDITH, state senator; b. Laredo, Tex., Feb. 13, 1946; d. George and Nieves Pappas; m. Carlos Zaffirini, 1965; 1 child, Carlos Jr. BS, U. Tex., 1967, MA, 1970, PhD, 1978. Committeewoman Tex. State Dem. Exec. Com., 1978-84; mem. Tex. State Senate, 1987—; del. Dem. Nat. Conv., 1980, 84. Bd. dirs., dir. pub. relations Laredo Civic Music Assn., 1968—. Recipient Medal of Excellence Nat. League United Latin Am. Citizens, 1987, Jose Maria Morelos y Pavon Medal of Merit for leadership in strengthening U.S.-Mex. rels., 1987, George Washington Medal of Excellence for Individual Achievement Freedoms Found. at Valley Forge, 1988; named to Nat. Hispanic Hall of Fame, 1987; named Woman of Achievement Tex. Press Women. Democrat. Roman Catholic. Home: PO Box 750 Laredo TX 78042 Office: 1407 Washington St Laredo TX 78040

ZAGAME, SUSAN KOERBER, government administrator, lawyer; b. Newton, N.C., July 9, 1951; d. Carl August and Esther (Schmidt) Koerber; m. Dec. 14, 1974. B.A., Maxwell Sch., Syracuse U., 1973; LL.D., Syracuse Coll. Law, 1976. Bar: N.Y. 1977, U.S. Dist. Ct. N.Y. 1977, U.S. Supreme Ct. 1981. Assoc. Carroll, Caroll & Butz, Esquires, Syracuse, N.Y., 1977; ptnr. Klinger & Zagame, Esquires, Oswego, N.Y., 1977-81; atty. City Sch. Dist. Oswego, N.Y., 1980-81; spl. asst. SBA, Washington, 1981-83; dep. gen. counsel, legal counsel HHS, Washington, 1981—; sr. govt. mgr. HUD, Washington, 1983-89; v.p. Reagan Dep. Asst. Secs. group. Pres. crusade Am. Cancer Soc., Oswego, 1978-80; treas., vol. Citizens for Zagame Campaign Com., Oswego, N.Y., 1974, 76; campaign mgr. Cahill for Mayor Campaign Com., Oswego, 1979, Zagame for Congress Com., Oswego, 1980. Office: Dept HUD Fed Housing Adminstrn 451 7th St SW Washington DC 20410

ZAGARE, ISABELLA MARIA, accountant; b. N.Y.C., Nov. 1, 1955; d. Cosmo and Maria V. (Narvaez) Z. AB in Econs. and Music, Smith Coll., 1977; MBA, U. Calif., Berkeley, 1983. CPA, Calif. Researcher Met. Opera, N.Y.C., 1977-81; acct. Arthur Young Internat., San Francisco, 1983-84; mgr. Multiple Shared Svcs., Oakland, Calif., 1984-85; acctg. mgr. Sybex, Inc., Alameda, Calif., 1985-88; acct. Boydstun & Klingner, CPA's, San Francisco, 1988—. Mem. San Francisco Symphony Chorus, Oakland Symphony Chorus, Cantare Con Vivo. Citibank scholar, 1974. Mem. AICPA, Calif. Soc. CPA's, East Bay Smith Club (co-chmn. alumnae admissions 1987—). Office: Boydstun & Klingner CPAs 185 Berry St San Francisco CA 94107

ZAGORZYCKI, MARIA TERESA, physician; b. Trenton, N.J., Dec. 18, 1953; d. John M. and Janina Zofia (Jaworski) Z. BA in Biochemistry with distinction in all subjects, Cornell U., 1975; MD, George Washington U., 1979. Diplomate Am. Bd. Ob-Gyn. Intern UCLA Hosp., 1979-80, resident in ob-gyn., 1980-82, chief resident in ob-gyn., 1982-83, asst. clin. prof. ob-gyn, 1983—. Fellow Am. Coll. Ob-Gyn, Inter-Am. Coll. Physicians and Surgeons; mem. Am. Fertility Soc., Am. Med. Women's Assn., Am. Assn. Gynecologic Laproscopists, Los Angeles County Obstetrical and Gynecol. Soc., Phi Delta Epsilon. Club: Cornell of So. Calif. Office: 16500 Ventura Blvd Ste 414 Encino CA 91436

ZAHLER, MARY LYNNE QUINNAN, health educator, exercise physiologist; b. Detroit, Feb. 24, 1960; d. Brian Robert and Constance Marie (Smith) Quinnan; m. Gary Thomas Zahler, May 28, 1988. BA, Miami U., Oxford, Ohio, 1981, MA, 1986; postgrad., Xavier U., Cin., 1986—. Tchr. The Pre-Sch. Sch., Monroe, Ohio, 1981; activities coord. Carlisle (Ohio) Manor Health Care Ctr., 1982; psychology intern Longview State Mental Hosp., Cin., 1983-84; head recreation therapist, behavior mgr. Camelot Lake, Inc., Fairfield, Ohio, 1982-85; wellness program intern Miami U., Oxford, 1985-86; health promotion specialist, corp. wellness coord. Bethesda Hosp., Cin., 1986-88; dir. health promotion and cardiac rehab. Union Hosp., Dover, Ohio, 1988-89; pub. health educator, exercise physiologist Stark County [illegible] Canton, Ohio, 1989—; exercise physiologist Optifast of [illegible] 1990; adv. bd. Drage High Sch., Glen [illegible] Playhouse Spotlight on [illegible] Coalition, [illegible] Stark Inter-Agy. Health [illegible] 1989—, pres. 1990—), Animal Protection Guild, Greenpeace, World Wildlife Fund, Psi Chi (chpt. sec. 1983-84), Delta Psi Kappa. Roman Catholic. Home: 1252 Fulton Rd NW Apt 3 Canton OH 44703 Office: Stark County Health Dept 209 W Tuscarawas St Canton OH 44702

ZAHNER, SALLY LOVETT, communications executive; b. Neodesha, Kans., Apr. 1, 1953; d. Carl Glenn and Sybil Ione (Sheldon) L.; m. Steve Alan Zahner, Dec. 12, 1981. BS in Journalism, U. Kans., 1975. Dir. promotion Kans. City Regional Council for Higher Edn., Leawood, 1983-87; dir. program devel. Mental Health Assn. of Johnson County, Lenexa, Kans., 1987-88; community edn. coordinator Cedar Ridge Treatment Ctr., Shawnee, Kans., 1988–. Publicist The Future is Now, Kansas City, 1988. Mem. Women in Communications Inc.

ZAHNISER, JILL DIANE, program developer, editor, publisher; b. Pitts., Jan. 1, 1951; d. Frank Wright and Emma Jean (Hay) Z. BS in Speech and Theater, St. Cloud State Coll., 1971; MA in Am. Studies, U. Md., 1980; PhD in Women's Studies, U. Iowa, 1985. High sch. tchr. Chatfield (Minn.) Schs., 1971-72, Mpls. Area Schs., 1973-78; instr. St. Cloud (Minn.) State U., 1984; program devel. specialist N.J. Div. on Women, Trenton, 1985-86; project specialist N.J. Dept. Human Svcs., Trenton, 1987; dir. N.W. N.J. Women's Ctr., Hackettstown, 1987—; sec., bd. dirs. Northwest N.J. Community Action prog., 1987—; pres. Alice Paul Centennial Found., Moorestown, N.J., 1985—. Editor and pub. Caillech Press, Port Murray, N.J., 1989—; author, compiler: And Then She Said: Quotations by Women for Every Occasion, 1989. Com. mem. Domestic Abuse and Rape Crisis Ctr. Shelter Drive Campaign, Warren County, N.J., 1987—; mem. Women's Network Sen. Bill Bradley, N.J., 1989—, Women's Agenda of N.J., 1988—, Amnesty Internat., 1989—; vol. NORWESCAP, Alice Paul Found. Recipient Katharine Orne Meml. scholarship, U. Iowa, Iowa City, 1983. Mem. NOW, Nat. Women's Studies Assn., Nat. Women's Health Network, N.J. Women's Resource Consortium (co-chmn. 1986-88). Home: Box 246 Oxford NJ 07863 Office: NW NJ Womens Ctr Centenary Coll Hackettstown NJ 07840

ZAHOS, EFROSINE, computer system specialist; b. Rochester, N.Y., Aug. 2, 1961; d. Stavros M. and RoseAnn (Sculli) Z. BS, St. John Fisher Coll., 1983. Sr. systems cons. Sci. Calculations, Fishers, N.Y.; technician systems support and photoplotting Metro Circuits, Rochester. Mem. NAFE. Home: 15 North Ave Hilton NY 14468

ZAIK, CAROL FORD, museum director, art historian, educator; b. Springfield, Mass., Aug. 11, 1955; d. Edward William and Margaret (Ford) Z. BA, U. Mass., 1978; MA in Art Edn., Springfield Coll., 1979; PhD, NYU, 1984. Docent, adminstr. Currier Mus., Manchester, N.H., 1984—; actor Mt. Tom Playhouse, Holyoke, Mass., 1965-68. Restored one-man sch. house into a fine arts mus., West Ossipee, N.H. Active Smithsonian Assn., 1965-87, Acad. Polit. Sci., 1983-90, Audibon Soc., 1986-90. Mem. Nat. Art Ednl. Assn. (chair mus. div. 1987-90), Mass. Art Ednl. Assn., Internat. Soc. Ednl. Assn., Nat. Mus. Women in Arts, Amherst Fine Arts Assn., U.S. Soc. Edn. Through Art. Democrat. Roman Catholic. Home: 1062 Worthington St Springfield MA 01109-4021

ZAISER, SALLY SOLEMMA VANN, retail book company executive; b. Birmingham, Ala., Jan. 18, 1917; d. Carl Waldo and Einnan (Herndon) Vann; student Birmingham-So. Coll., 1933-36, Akron Coll. Bus., 1937; m. Foster E. Zaiser, Nov. 11, 1939. Acct., A. Simionato, San Francisco, 1958-65; head acctg. dept. Richard T. Clarke Co., San Francisco, 1966; acct. John Howell-Books, San Francisco, 1967-72, sec., treas., 1972-83, 84-85, dir., 1982-85; sec. Great Eastern Mines, Inc., Albuquerque, 1969-81, dir., 1980-85. Braille transcriber for ARC, Kansas City, Mo. 1941-45; vol. worker ARC Hosp. Program, São Paulo, Brazil, 1952. Mem. Book Club Calif., Calif. Hist. Soc., Soc. Lit. and Arts, Gleeson Library Assocs. (dir. 1984-87, editor GLA newsletter 1984-87), Nat. Notary Assn., Capital Hill Club, Theta Upsilon. Republican. Episcopalian. Home: 355 Serrano Dr Apt 4-C San Francisco CA 94132

ZAITZ, JOAN SALWEN, lawyer; b. N.Y.C., June 29, 1951; d. Sidney and Ruth (Starr) Salwen; m. Alan S. Zaitz, Oct. 18, 1980; children: Jacob Salwen, Jessica Sidney. AB cum laude, Syracuse U., 1973; JD, U. Pa., 1976. Bar: N.Y. 1977. Assoc. Louis E. Cherico, White Plains, N.Y., 1977-80, Joel Martin Aurnou, White Plains, 1980-82; sole practice, Hartsdale, N.Y., 1983-84, Scarsdale, N.Y., 1984—. Mem. N.Y. State Bar Assn., White Plains Bar Assn. (bd. dirs. 1982—, sec. 1988-89, treas. 1989-90), Westchester County Bar Assn. (bd. dirs. lawyer referral svc. 1983-84), Pi Sigma Alpha. Home and Office: 2 Crawford Ln Scarsdale NY 10583

ZAJAC, BARBARA ANN, pharmaceutical company executive; b. Fountain Springs, Pa., Mar. 15, 1937; d. Russell Alphonso and Mary (Dyszel) Procuda; m. Thor Zajac, 1957; 1 child, Andraej. BA, U. Pa., 1958, PhD, 1967; MD, Med. Coll. Pa., 1979. Diplomate Am. Bd. Internal Medicine/Subspeciality of Infectious Disease. Assoc. virology U. Pa., Phila., 1969-70; asst. prof. microbiology Med. Coll. Pa., Phila., 1970-75; assoc. prof. microbiology Med. Coll. Pa., 1975-76; resident in internal medicine Abington (Pa.) Meml. Hosp., 1979-82; fellow infectious diseases Hosp. U. Pa., Phila., 1982-84; dir. clin. rsch. Merck Sharp & Dohme Rsch. Labs., West Point, Pa., 1985-88; group dir. infectious disease/immunology E.I. DuPont de Nemours & Co., Wilmington, Del., 1988—; affiliate staff physician Abington Meml. Hosp., 1986—. Contbr. articles to profl. jours. Nat. Cancer Inst. fellow, 1973-76, Damon-Runyon-Waller Winchell Cancer Inst. fellow, 1973-76; Brown Hazen Rsch. Corp. grantee, 1972, Merck Sharp & Dohme grantee, 1971. Mem. ACP, Infectious Disease Soc. Am., AMA, Am. Med. Women's Assn. Office: EI DuPont De Nemours & Co Barley Mill Plaza Wilmington DE 19898

ZAJIC, DONNA JEAN, municipal official; b. Friend, Nebr., July 9, 1951; d. Charles and Anna (Svec) Z.; m. James Michael Mitchell, Aug. 11, 1944. BS, U. Nebr., Lincoln, 1973; MPA, U. Nebr., Omaha, 1986. Supr. Miller & Paine Dept. Store, Lincoln, 1973-74; clk. City of Lincoln, 1974-77, acct. clk., 1977-86, office ops. specialist, 1986—. Recipient 2d Place award No. Regional Camera Clubs, 1988. Mem. Am. Bus. Women's Assn. (com. liaison 1987-88, pres. 1988—, Woman of Yr. 1987), Am. Soc. Pub. Adminstrn., Cornhusker Ski Club (sec. 1985-86), Lincoln Camera Club (editor newsletter 1987-88). Democrat. Unitarian. Home: 1400 Meadow Dale Dr Lincoln NE 68505 Office: City of Lincoln Dept Parks and Recreation 2740 A St Lincoln NE 68502

ZAJICEK, IVA MARIE, educator; b. Hastings, Nebr., June 19, 1925; d. Harold Loper and Laura Jean (Evans) Foreman; m. Jerome Robert Zajicek, Sept. 10, 1944; children: James Craig, Ashley Marie. BSc, U. Nebr., 1959, ME, 1960, EdD, 1978. Tchr. pub. schs. York, Nebr., 1956-57, Ceresco, Nebr., 1957-58; art/libr. pub. schs. Los Alamos, N.Mex., 1960-64; edn. advisor, Advance Tchrs. Coll. Ohio U./U.S.A.I.D./Nigeria Project, Kano, 1964-68; elem. edn. advisor Washington County Elem. Schs., Title III, Marietta, Ohio, 1968-70; prin. Fort Frye Schs., Beverly, Ohio, 1970-71; prof. Marietta (Ohio) Coll., 1971-81; edn. advisor Botswana U. Ohio U./U.S.A.I.D., Gaborone, Botswana, 1981-85; edn. advisor U. Swaziland/Ohio U., Mbabane, Swaziland, 1985-87; cons. in field. Mem. DAR, PEO. Republican. Methodist. Home: 5580 E Binghampton Dr Tucson AZ 85712

ZAJICEK, LYNN ENGELBRECHT, educational administrator; b. Newport News, Va., Mar. 25, 1950; d. Herbert Charles and Lois (Kohler) Engelbrecht; m. Jon M. Zajicek, June 6, 1970; children: Carlye Lynn, Kate Elizabeth. BA, Kearney State Coll., 1971; MEd, U. Nebr., 1973, EdS, 1988. Cert. profl. adminstr./supr., Nebr. Tchr. Lincoln (Nebr.) Pub. Schs., 1971-73; instr. U.S. Army PREP Program, Crailsheim, Fed. Republic of Germany, 1974-76; subs. tchr. Grand Island (Nebr.) Pub. Schs., 1976-77; mgr., owner rental property Grand Island, 1978—; asst. on survey project U. Nebr., Lincoln, [illegible]-88; adminstr. ednl. diagnostician Nebr. Ctr. for Evaluation of Devel. and Learning, Inc., Grand Island, 1988—; bd. dirs. Reorganized Mark V Mortgage Corp. Bd. mem. PTA, Grand Island, 1980—; supt. Bible Sch. St. Stephen's Ch., Grand Island, 1984-85; mem. Christian edn. com. St. Stephen's, 1985—, subcom. for adult and continuing edn. of strategic planning com. Grand Island Pub. Schs., 1987, coach Odyssey of the Mind Grand Island Pub. Schs., 1986—; active in heart and cancer funds in Grand Island; bd. dirs. Episc. Ch. Women; candidate cmpaign mgr. Rep. Women, 1978; bd. dirs., exec. com. Marque of Nebr., 1989—. Recipient Gen. Arnold scholarship USAF, 1967. Mem. AAUW, Assn. Supervision and Curriculum Devel., Nat. Assn. Secondary Sch. Prins., Nebr. Coun. Sch. Adminstrs., Nebr. Assn. Elem. Sch. Prins., Nebr. Dental Assn. Aux. (numerous offices including pres. 1981-82), Hall County Dental Aux. (sec., treas. 1976—), St. Francis Med. Aux., Nebr. Assn. for Children and Adults with Learning Disabilities, Phi Delta Kappa, Pi Delta Phi, Alpha Mu Gamma, Sigma Tau Delta, Xi Phi. Home: 1618 S Harrison St Grand Island NE 68803 Office: Nebr Ctr for Evaluation of Devel and Learning Inc 2121 N Webb Rd Ste 305 Grand Island NE 68803

ZAK, CHERYL MARIE, marketing professional; b. Oak Park, Ill., June 18, 1952; d. Donald Arden adn Marilyn Francès (Kobart) Wing; m. Alan Charles Zak, Sept. 21, 1974. BBA in Mgmt. summa cum laude, Ga. So. U., 1981. Bus. analyst Digital Equipment Corp., Atlanta, 1982-85; mktg. rep. IBM, Southfield, Mich., 1985—. Legis. asst. to rep. Ill. Ho. of Reps., Elmhurst, 1976-77. Mem. AAUW (scholarship chair 1982-83), Phi Kappa Phi, Beta Gamma Sigma. Mem. United Ch. of Christ. Home: 3220 Caircross Dr Oakland MI 48363

ZAK, DOROTHY ZERYKIER, psychologist; b. Katowice, Poland, Jan. 11, 1950; came to U.S., 1969; d. Mieczystaw and Helena (Stahl) Zerykier; m. Jesse Cooper Brake (dec.); m. Sheldon Jerry Zak, July 6, 1986. BA, Queens Coll., 1973; MA, New Sch. Social Research, 1975. Clin. intern Bergen Pines Hosp., Paramus, N.J., 1976-77; psychologist State Sch. Mentally Retarded, Kinston, N.C., 1977-78, Dorothea Dix Hosp., Raleigh, N.C., 1978-83; pvt. practice cons. N.Y.C., 1983-84; psychologist Fed. Employment and Guidance Services, N.Y.C., 1984-85; vocat. counselor N.Y. Assn. for New Ams. Inc., N.Y.C., 1985-88; ednl. counselor B'nai Brith Career and Counseling Services, N.Y.C., 1988—; part-time cons. St. John's Hosp.-Cath. Med. Ctr. Bklyn. and Queens Weight Loss Program, 1987—. Mem. Am. Psychol. Assn., Polish Inst. Arts and Scis., Am. Assn. for Counseling and Devel., N.Y. Acad. Scis. Office: B'nai Brith 823 UN Pla New York NY 10017

ZAKHEIM, BARBARA JANE, international business company consulting executive; b. London, Jan. 31, 1953; d. David Sloma and Sarah Frances (Leifer) Portnoi; m. Dov Solomon Zakheim, Aug. 20, 1972 (div. 1990); children: Keith Samuel, Roger Israel, Scott Elisha. BA, Oxford U., Eng., 1974, MA, 1978. Economist Maxima Corp., Silver Spring, Md., 1979, U.S. Dept. Energy, Washington, 1979-80; sr. project analyst Applied Mgmt. Scis., Silver Spring, 1980-83, staff assoc., 1983-85; prin. analyst NUS Corp., Gaithersburg, Md., 1985-87, cons. analyst, 1987-89; pres. Keith R. Scott Assocs., Inc., 1989—, African Treasures, Inc., 1990—; U.S. rep. Coll. Petroleum Studies, Oxford, 1984—; N. Am. rep. Twirltrade Ltd., London, 1985—. Contbr. articles to profl. jours. Bd. dirs. SE Hebrew Congregation, Silver Spring, 1977-78. Mem. NAFE, World Affairs Coun., Soc. Govt. Economists, Nat. Assn. Environ. Profls. Republican. Home and Office: 911 Kenbrook Dr Silver Spring MD 20902

ZAKS, PAULA KAY S., artist; b. Detroit, Dec. 23, 1949; d. Eugene and Sylvia (Pikin) Steinberger; m. Michael I. Zaks, Mar. 31, 1974 (dec. July 1983); 1 child, David Philip Martin Zaks; m. Saul Silverstein, June 28, 1987. BFA, Eastern Mich. U., 1973, MFA, 1976. Exhibited in group shows at Troy (Mich.) Art Gallery, 1985, 87, 89, Mich. Water Color Soc., Krasl Art Ctr., St. Joseph, 1986, Olin Fine Arts Ctr. of Battle Creek, Mich., 1986, Met. Detroit Jewish Community Ctr., West Bloomfield, Mich., 1987, Eastern Mich. U., 1988, U. of Arts Printmaking Gallery, Phila., 1989; represented in permanent collections Battle Creek Art Ctr., Mich. Bell Telephone, U. Mich., also pvt. collections. Mem. Art Exchange, Mich. Water Color Soc. (1st place award 1976, honorable mention 1978, purchase prize, 1981, Grumbacher Silver Medallion award 1982). Home: 33000 Covington Club Dr #67 Farmington Hills MI 48018

ZALESKI, JEAN, artist; b. Birkirkara, Malta; d. John M. and Carolina (Micallef) Busuttil; children: Jeffrey, Philip, Susan Jean. Student, Art Students League, N.Y.C., 1955-58, New Sch., N.Y.C., 1967-69, Moore Coll. Art, Phila., 1970-71, Parsons Sch. Design, N.Y.C., 1974-75, Pratt Inst., N.Y.C., 1976-77. Dir. Art Studio 733, Great Neck, N.Y., 1963-67; sr. art instr. Hussian Coll. Art, Phila., 1970-71; dir. Naples (Italy) Art Studio, 1972-74; corp. sec. Women in The Arts, N.Y.C., 1974-75, exec. coord., 1976-78; adj. lectr. Bklyn. Coll., 1974-75, Hofstra U., 1977-82, Cooper Union, 1986—. One-woman shows include: Galleria Stuciv, Florence, Italy, 1973, Adelphi U., 1975, Women in Arts Gallery, N.Y.C., 1975, Il Gabbiano Gallery, Naples, 1973, Wallnuts Gallery, Phila., 1971, Neikrug Gallery, N.Y.C., 1970, Alonzo Gallery, N.Y.C., 1979, 80, Va. Ctr. for Creative Arts, Sweet Briar, 1981, Hodgell Galleries, Sarasota, Fla., 1982, 83, Elaine Starkman Gallery, N.Y.C., 1986, Romano Gallery, Barnegat Light, N.J., 1987, 88, Citicorp Ctr., N.Y.C., 1988-89; group exhbns. include Art U.S.A., N.Y.C., 1969, Internat. Art Exhbn., Cannes, France, 1969, Frick Mus., Pitts., 1970, NAD, N.Y.C., 1970-71, Phila. Mus. Art, 1971, Am. Women Artists, Palazzo Vecchio, Florence, 1972, Internat. Women's Arts Festival, Milan, Italy, 1973 (Gold medal), Bklyn. Mus., 1975, Sweet Briar Coll., 1977, CUNY, 1978, Va. Ctr., 1988, Mus. Hudson Highlands, 1982, Pace U. Gallery, N.Y.C., 1982, Bayly Mus., Charlottesville, Va., 1986, Allbright Knox Mus., Buffalo, 1986, E. Starkman Gallery, N.Y.C., 1987, Nabisco, 1989; co-author COW/LINES, 1983; represented in permanent collections Easter Seal Human Resource Ctr., N.Y., N.Y. Pub. Library, Met. Mus. Art, Va. Ctr. for Creative Arts, Nat. Mus. Women in Arts, Mus. of City of N.Y.; vis. artist, critic various colls. and univs., 1976—. Recipient Susan B. Anthony award NOW,

N.Y.C., 1986; Artists Space grantee, 1988, Book grantee Nat. Endowment for Arts, 1982; MacDowell fellow, 1970—, Ragdale fellow, Va. Ctr. for Creative Arts. Mem. Artists Equity, Women in The Arts, Women's Caucus for Art, Manhattan Pl. Health Club. Democrat. Roman Catholic. Home and Studio: 55 Bethune St New York NY 10014

ZALKA, LORI MARLENE, county official; b. Miami, Fla., Oct. 10, 1955; d. Saul and Eleanor (Rich) Z. BA in Sociology, U. Fla., 1977, MPA, 1979. From budget mgmt. analyst I to budget mgmt. analyst IV Broward County Office Budget and Mgmt. Policy, Ft. Lauderdale, Fla., 1979-85; dir. Collier County Office Mgmt. and Budget, Naples, Fla., 1985-89; fin. coord. Oakland County, Pontiac, Mich., 1989—. Mem. Fla. Govt. Fin. Officers Assn. (legis. com. 1988), U. Fla. Inst. Govt. (steering com. 1987). Office: Oakland County 1025 N Telegraph Rd Pontiac MI 48053

ZALUTSKY, AUDREY ENGLEBARDT, medical social worker; b. Schenectady, N.Y., Apr. 9, 1935; d. Samuel and Augusta (Gewirtzman) Englebardt; m. Morton H. Zalutsky, June 16, 1957; children: Jane R., Diane L., Samuel J. BA in Sociology, Skidmore Coll., 1957; MSW, Portland State U., 1975. Cert. social worker, Oreg. Med. social worker Good Samaritan Hosp., Portland, Oreg. Chair Community Conf. on Health, 1986; mem. Portland com. Am. Friends Hebrew U. Mem. NASW. Office: Good Samaritan Hosp 1015 NW 22d Portland OR 97201

ZAMBOUKOS, CYNTHIA SOTERIA, administrative assistant, travel consultant; b. San Francisco, June 17, 1957; d. James Neal and Nafsika Vasiliki (Katsoulos) Z. BA in French and Italian, San Francisco State U., 1980. Asst. sec.-treas. Pacific Am. Group, Inc., San Francisco, 1980-84; freelance travel cons. and legal asst., San Francisco, 1984-86, adminstrv. asst. Wells Fargo Bank, 1986—. Mem. Alliance Francaise, Hellenic Am. Profl. Soc. Democrat. Greek Orthodox.

ZAMECNIK, SUSAN MARIE, registered professional nurse; b. Buffalo, Feb. 16, 1960; d. Edward Michael and Barbara Jean (Denz) Griffin; m. Paul Arthur Zamecnik, June 19, 1987; 1 child, Julia Lynn. BS, State U., Buffalo, 1982; MS, Case Western Res. U., Cleveland, 1989. Licensed as RN. Staff nurse Millard Fillmore Hosp., Buffalo, 1982-83, St. Joseph's Hosp., Syracuse, 1983-85, Mass. Gen. Hosp., Boston, 1986-87; diabetes educator, staff nurse Hillcrest Hosp., Mayfield Heights, Ohio. Mem. Am. Assn. Diabetes Educators Internat., Sigma Theta Tau. Roman Catholic. Home: 6515 Longridge Rd Mayfield Heights OH 44124

ZAMORA, MARJORIE DIXON, political scientist; b. Farm Randolph, N.Y., Nov. 8, 1933; d. Wendell Hadley and Jessie (Mercer) Dixon; m. Cornelio Raul Zamora, Dec. 20, 1969; 1 child, Daniel Cornelio. BA, Earlham Coll., 1956; MA, U. Ill., 1968; postgrad., U. Ill., Chgo., 1989—. Tchr. Ridge, Sch., Godsman Sch., Stenson Sch., various cities, 1956-62; with U.S. Peace Corps, tchr. Palmares High Sch., Costa Rica, 1963-64; reporter Lerner Newspaper, Chgo., 1965; dormitory counselor, researcher Univ. Ill., Urbana, 1966-68, 86; instr. Chgo. City Coll., 1968-69; prof. Moraine Valley Community Coll., Palos Hills, Ill., 1969—; researcher, Univ. Ill., Chgo., 1985-88. Contbr. articles on Costa Rican polit. economy, land reform to various publs. in U.S., Cen. Am. Campaign dir. Polit. State Legis., 1974-76. Mem. AAUW, Moraine Valley Community Coll. Faculty Assn., Am. Polit. Sci. Assn. (chair profl. and community coms.). Home: 3820 Lawn Ave Western Springs IL 60558 Office: Moraine Valley Community Coll 10900 S 88th St Palos Hills IL 60465

ZAMORE, ELLEN RUBINSON, speech and language pathologist; b. Bklyn., Feb. 11, 1938; d. Albert and Martha (Rosenberg) Rubinson; m. Leonard Zamore, July 5, 1959 (dec. 1985); children: Phillip David, Mary Ida. BA, Skidmore Coll., 1959; MA, Columbia U., 1961. Lic. speech and lang. pathologist, N.Y. Tchr. psychology Brookland-Cayce High Sch., West Columbia, S.C., 1959-60; speech therapist Elmont (N.Y.) Pub. Schs., 1961-63; clin. supr. in speech Hofstra U., Hempstead, N.Y., 1963-73; prof. Nassau Community Coll., Garden City, N.Y., 1973—; prof. pub. speaking, Webb Inst. of Naval Architecture, Glen Cove, N.Y., 1975-85; clin. speech dept. Martin de Porres Sch., Springfield Gardens, N.Y., 1985—; clin. supr. and lectr. Adelphi U., 1976-80. Named Brookdale fellow in geriatrics, fellowship in speech pathology, Adelphi U., 1976-80; recipient Community Fund Vol. award, Garden City, 1987. Mem. L.I. Speech and Hearing Assn., Am. Speech and Hearing Assn., N.Y. State Speech and Hearing Assn., AAUW. Democrat. Jewish. Home and Office: 7 Laurel St Garden City NY 11530

ZAMPA, ROBBIE C., manufacturing company executive; b. Columbus, Ohio, Dec. 1, 1947; d. Robert M. and Beryl (Cain) May; m. Ronald A. Zampa, June 10, 1975; 1 child, Anthony J. AA in Bus., Foothills Jr. Coll., 1968; cert. in mfg. mgmt., Stanford U. R and D technician Fairchild Semiconductor, Mountain View, Calif.; prodn. mgr., prodn. supr., mgr. mfg. ops. Andros Analyzers, Berkeley, Calif. Mem. NAFE.

ZANDE, SUSAN ELAINE, newspaper editor; b. Bradford, Pa., Oct. 15, 1959; d. Robert Lewis and Margaret Mary (Sapko) Z.; m. David John Geary, Sept. 1987. BA, Penn State U., State Coll., 1981. News reporter Olean Times Herald, Olean, N.Y., 1980-84; news editor Wolfe Publication, Inc., Rochester, N.Y., 1984—; pres. Irondequoit Council of the Greater Rochester Metro C. of C., 1987. Editor: Irondequoit Press weekly newspaper, 1987—. Cons. Irondequoit Vol. Ambulance Capital Fund Planning Com., 1988; bd. dirs. Maplewood YMCA, Rochester, 1988. Recipient Past Pres. award Irondequoit Council of the Greater Rochester Metro C. of C., 1987. Mem. Irondequoit Council Rochester C. of C. (v.p. 1989). Democrat. Roman Catholic.

ZANDI, AVA SONYA NELSON, environmental planner; b. Daytona Beach, Fla., Sept. 30, 1954; d. William and Ann (Sherman) Nelson; m. Mark Manssur Zandi, Dec. 30, 1984. Student, Tulane U., 1972-74; BA in Environ. Studies, U. Pa., 1976; postgrad., London Sch. Econs., 1978-79; PhD in City and Regional Planning, U. Pa., 1983; UN grad. program in energy, Geneva, 1980. Rsch. asst. U.S. Dept. Agr., Agrl. Rsch. Svc., Beltsville, Md., 1975; coord. Internat. Symposium on Freight Pipelines U. Pa. and U.S. Dept. Transp., Phila., 1976; rsch. asst. dept. civil and urban engring. U. Pa., Phila., 1977-78; cons. Pipeline Ednl. Svcs. Ctr., Phila., 1983; analyst econs. and policy div. coordinating and planning dept. Conoco, Inc., E.I. duPont & Co., Wilmington, Del., 1983-87; environ. scientist, sr. staff U.S. EPA, Region III, Phila., 1987—; panel participant U. Pa. Seminar on Environ. Risk and Pub. Policy, Phila., 1988—; del. Energy Policy and Planning Symposium, London, 1979. Chmn., founder Environ. Action Com., Tulane U., New Orleans, 1973-74, bd. mem. Community Action Coun., 1973-74; active Jr. League Phila., 1988—. Recipient Ednl. award Rotary Internat., 1978-79, Spl. Achievement award U.S. EPA, Region III, Phila., 1989. Mem. Women in Sci. and Engring. (cert. of appreciation 1987), Soc. Risk Analysis, Am. Friends of London Sch. Econs., Phi Beta Kappa. Democrat. Jewish. Home: 1004 Wharton Ct Newtown Square PA 19073 Office: US EPA Region III 841 Chestnut St Philadelphia PA 19107

ZANGARI, ROSE MARIE, retired educator; b. New Haven, Nov. 29, 1917; d. Francesco and Maria Catherine Luca; m. James Anello Zangari, June 22, 1939 (dec. 1967); children: Joseph Carl, Janet Elissa Carbetta. BS cum laude, Cen. Conn. U., 1970, MS, 1975. Clk.-sec. Internat. Silver Co., Meriden, Conn., 1935-39, 52-53; clk.-typist United Aircraft, Meriden, 1953-62, Southington, Conn., 1962-65; tchr. English Platt High Sch., Meriden, Conn., 1970-83; ret. Illustrator: Folk Tales of Conn., Vol. I, 1977, Vol. II, 1981; poetry pub. in weekly poetry column. Mem. Meriden Poetry Soc. (pres., treas.), Meriden Women's Club (recording sec.), Meriden Arts and Crafts Assn., Meriden Coun. Cath. Women. Democrat. Roman Catholic. Home: 369 Coe Ave #188 Meriden CT 06450

ZANKOFSKI, DEBORAH ANN, military officer, oceanographer; b. Cleve., Apr. 16, 1955. BS in Math., John Carroll U., 1977; MS in Math., Ohio State U., 1979; MS in Meterology and Oceanography, Naval Postgrad. Sch., Monterey, Calif., 1985. Teaching assoc. Ohio State U., Columbus, 1977-79; tchr. Bishop Watterson High Sch., Columbus, 1979; instr., Naval Nuclear and Power Sch. USN, Orlando, Fla., 1979-83; meteorologist, USS Lexington USN, Pensacola, Fla., 1985-87; regional officer, Naval Western Oceanography Ctr. USN, Pearl Harbor, Hawaii, 1987—. Mem. MADD, Pearl Harbor, 1987. Mem. Am. Meteorological Assn., Surface Warfare Assn. Roman Catholic. Home: 92-1268 Kikiha St #56 Makakilo HI 96707 Office: NWOC Box 113 Pearl Harbor HI 96860-5050

ZANNIERI, NINA, museum director; b. Summit, N.J., Feb. 1, 1955; d. Angelo Joseph and Louise Mary (Brumm) Z. BA, Boston Coll., 1977; postgrad., Coll. of William & Mary, 1977-78; MA, Brown U., 1980. Curatorial asst. R.I. Hist. Soc., Providence, 1980-81, asst. curator, 1981-83, curator, 1983-86; dir. Paul Revere Meml. Assn., Boston, 1986—; bd. dirs. Freedom Trial Found., Boston. Gen. editor: (exhbn. catalog) Paul Revere: The Man Behind the Myth, 1988; collaborator: (house guide) A Most Magnificent Mansion; project dir.: (exhbn. catalog) Let Virtue Be A Guide To Thee, 1983. Mem. Am. Assn. Mus.'s, New Eng. Mus. Assn. (curators com. 1984-86, bd. dirs. 1988—), Am. Assn. State and Local History, Phi Beta Kappa. Office: Paul Revere Meml Assn 19 North Sq Boston MA 02113

ZANOTTI, MARIE LOUISE, hospital admininstrator; b. Pitts., May 3, 1954; d. Louis Charles and Josephine Rose (Antoniella) Z. BS, U. Pitts., 1976; M of Pub. Health, Yale U., 1980. Adminstrv. asst. Presbyn.-Univ. Hosp., Pitts., 1980-82; dir. Meml. Hosp. Burlington County, Mt. Holly, N.J., 1982-85; asst. dir./adminstr. The Milton S. Hershey Med. Ctr.-Univ. Hosp., Hershey, Pa., 1985—; workshop presenter Healthcare Fin. Mgmt. Assn., 1988-89. Active Hershey Bus. Assn., 1988—. Mem. Am. Coll. Healthcare Execs., Healthcare Adminstrs. Group (pres. 1987—), Hosp. Assn. of Pa., Pa. Assn. Rehab. Facilities, Yale U. Hosp. Adminstrn. Alumni Assn. Home: 1411 Cambridge Ct Palmyra PA 17078 Office: Univ Hosp PO Box 850 Hershey PA 17033

ZANOW, LOIS A., tour planner; b. Sioux Falls, S.D., Mar. 3, 1933; d. David Henry and Myrtle Geneva (Ruble) Miller; m. Markus William Zanow, Aug. 27, 1960; children: Paula Elizabeth, Yuri Markus. BA, U. Minn., 1960. Project asst., editor Dept. Indian Studies U. Wis., Madison, [illegible] writer Suburban-Life Newspaper, Downers Grove, Ill., [illegible] laney Adult Ctr., Towson, Md., 1984—; tour [illegible] 1983—. Contbr. articles to profl. [illegible] Com. of 100, Hinsdale, Ill. [illegible] Balt. Symphony [illegible] Towson Aug. 16, 1925; d. Philip and Lena (Zapolsky) U.; m. Louis Zansky, N.Y.C., Mar. 28, 1944; (wid. 1978); children: Michael, Shelley; m. Eugene Gluck, June 22, 1983. BA, Brooklyn U., N.Y.C., 1944; MA, Columbia Coll., N.Y.C, 1947. Asst. prin. JHS N.Y.C. Bd. of Edn., N.Y.C., 1944-89; prof. of English Bronx Community Coll., N.Y.C., 1957—. Mem., Am. Assn. of U. Women; Exec. Bd., Brandeis U. Nat'l Womens Assn.; Mem., Hadassah of New City, Rockland. Dem. Hebrew.

ZAPATA, ELSSY-FEDORA, international developer; b. Bogota, Colombia, Nov. 17, 1950; came to U.S., 1973; d. Nelson Zapata-Fergusson and Ines Gonzalez-Crossway. BSBA in Internat. Bus., The Am. U., 1985. Staff on spl. assignment Inter-Am. Devel. Bank, Washington, 1975-80; research asst. Ctr. for Strategic and Internat. Studies, Washington, 1983-85; sr. credit analyst Mfrs. Hanover Trust Co., N.Y.C., 1986-87; mgmt. assoc. Internat. Sci. and Tech. Inst. Inc., Washington, 1989—; chief Latin-Am. and Caribbean unit UN Devel. Fund for Women, N.Y., 1990—. Vol. Children's Hosp., Washington, 1979. Recipient scholarships League of United Latin Am. Citizens, 1981, 85, Charlotte Newcombe Foundation, 1982, Hurst and Marion Anderson scholar, 1982, 83, Am. U. Gen. 1984, 85; named one of Outstanding Young Women Am., 1985. Mem. Nat. Assn. Female Execs.

ZAPPONE, MARY SLAGLE, financial analyst; b. Palo Alto, Calif., July 15, 1964; d. James Robert and Frances Jeanne (Galassi) Slagle; m. John Anthony Zappone, Sept. 5, 1987. BS in Chem. Engring., Johns Hopkins U., 1986; MBA, Columbia U., 1988. Researcher biotech. Johns Hopkins U., Balt., 1984-86; researcher abrasives 3M Co., St. Paul, 1985; bus. planning intern Am. Cyanamid, Wayne, N.J., 1987; facilitator, quality cons. downstream acctg. Exxon, Houston, 1988-89, quality cons. ops. acctg., 1989-90; bus. analyst Exxon, Baytown, Tex., 1990—. Big sister Big Bros./Big Sisters, N.Y.C., 1986—; tutor Johns Hopkins Tutorial Program, Balt., 1985; vol. Houston Sports Found., 1989—; active Johns Hopkins U. Mentoring Program, 1988—, Alumni Ambassadors Columbia U., 1988—. MEm. MENSA, Johns Hopkin's U. Alumni Assn., Columbia Club of Houston. Roman Catholic. Office: Exxon Co USA 2800 Decker Dr Baytown TX 77520

ZAR, CAROL B., association administrator; b. Chgo., Nov. 21, 1945; d. Herbert and Margarette (Wertheim) Bachenheimer; m. Jerrold H. Zar, Jan. 15, 1967; children: David, Adam. BA, U. of Ill., 1966; MPA, No. Ill. U., Dekalb, 1981. Housing officer HUD, Chgo., 1966-67; program coord. No. Ill. U., Dekalb, 1980-84; dir. program for improvement pub. mgmt. Ctr. for Govt. Studies, No. Ill. U., DeKalb, 1986—; exec. dir. Ill. City Mgmt. Assn., Dekalb, 1984—. Mem. DeKalb Zoning Bd. Appeals, 1987-88. Mem. Internat. City Mgmt. Assn., Am. Soc. for Pub. Adminstrn., LWV (pres. Dekalb County 1977-79). Jewish. Office: No Ill U Ctr for Govt Studies De Kalb IL 60115

ZARALEYA-HARARI, SARAH, psychologist, psychotherapist; b. Bklyn., Dec. 30, 1926; d. Phillip and Goldie (Simon) Kurzweil; m. Lawrence H. Strear, Aug. 24, 1947 (div. Sept. 1969); children: Peter M., Marcy, K. Jody, Marcus; m. Carmi Harari, Dec. 31, 1979; stepchildren: Karen Tarnofsky, Michelle Chino. BA, Bklyn. Coll., 1948; MS, CUNY, 1961; EdD, Yeshiva U., 1969. Lic. psychologist, sch. psychologist; nat. cert. sch. psychologist; registered health svc. provider in psychology. Psychologist Wyandanch (N.Y.) Pub. Schs., 1961-63, Uniondale (N.Y.) Pub. Schs., 1963-69; pvt. practice N.Y.C., 1969—; asst. prof. CUNY, 1970-75; mem. field faculty grad. program Goddard Coll., N.Y.C., 1977-78; cons. psychologist Greek-Woodycrest Children's Svcs., Pomona, N.Y., 1980-82; psychologist East Ramapo Cen. Sch. Dist., Spring Valley, N.Y., 1982—; lectr. Nassau Community Coll., Garden City, N.Y., 1967-69, Coll. of New Rochelle, N.Y., 1977-78, Rockland Community Coll., Suffern, N.Y., 1977-80; lectr. speaker's bur. Rockland County Mental Health Assn., Pomona, 1977—; cons. drug rehab. Topic House, L.I., N.Y., 1965-69; clin. dir. homosexual walk-in ctr. Identity House, N.Y.C., 1972-76; bd. dirs. women's issues div. Humanistic Psychology Ctr., N.Y.C. Contbr. chpts. to books; creator Zaraleya psychoenergetic technique, 1972. Editor yearbook Bklyn. Coll., 1946-47; parent seminar leader New City (N.Y.) Libr., spring 1981; conf. presenter E. Ramapo Cen. Sch. Dist., 1982, 84, 87; newsletter editor Rocklan Ctr. for the Arts, W. Nyack, N.Y., 1986-88. Recipient Gold Key award Bklyn. Coll., 1947. Mem. Am. Psychol. Assn. (exec. bd. div. humanistic psychology, newsletter editor 1977-79, svc. award 1977), Nat. Assn. Sch. Psychologists, N.Y. Soc. Clin. Psychologists, Rockland County Psychol. Soc. (chmn. clin. com., svc. award 1981, 82), Nassau and Suffolk County Psychol. Assn., AAUW. Home and Office: 10 Wyndham Ln New City NY 10956 Office: 473 West End Ave New York NY 10024

ZARATE, LENORE BEATRICE, non-profit administrator; b. N.Y.C., Sept. 21, 1937; d. Saul and Ida Sarah (Friedman) Trushin; m. Alvan O'Neil Zarate, Aug. 31, 1958 (div. Aug. 1971); children: Steven A., Jeffrey T., Jason R. BS with distinction, U. Conn., 1958; postgrad., U. Tex., 1965-66; MA, Cen. Mich. U., Mt. Pleasant, 1981. Adminstrv. asst. U. Conn., Storrs, 1959-60; research asst. U. R.I., Kingston, 1960-61, U. Tex., Austin, 1965-66, 66-67, Dept. of Mental Health and Mental Retardation, Austin, 1966; adminstrv. asst. Am. Social Health Assn., Columbus, Ohio, 1971-75, dir. midwest region, 1976-82, dir. no. region, 1982-87, dir. so. region, 1987, dir. United Way activities, 1988-89; exec. dir. Actors' Summer Theatre Co., Columbus, Ohio, 1989—. Author curriculum guide VD: Getting the Right Answers, 1976. Steering com. Venereal Disease Action Coalition, Detroit, 1978—; bd. dirs. Columbus VD Hotline, 1976-86. Mem. Am. Pub. Health Assn., Am. Venereal Disease Assn., Nat. Soc. Fund Raising Execs. Democrat. Jewish. Office: Actors Summer Theatre Co 1000 City Park Columbus OH 43206

ZAREMBA, CAROLYN WEIS, health facilities administrator; b. Toledo, Mar. 17, 1953; d. David Lyle and Emma Lou (Rubloff) Weis; m. Michael Dennis Zaremba, May 24, 1975; 1 child, Rachel Elizabeth. BS, Bowling Green State U., 1974; MA, U. Akron, 1977, MBA, 1984. Cert. profl. counselor, Ohio, tchr., Ohio. Teen counselor Cleve. Metro Gen. Hosp., 1974-78, family planning coordinator, 1978-82, edn. and info. coordinator, 1982; adminstrv. dir. maternity and infant health care MetroHealth Med. Ctr., Cleve., 1982—; instr. Cuyahoga Community Coll. West, Parma, Ohio, 1980-82; family planning adv. bd. Fedn. for Community Planning, Cleve., 1988; family planning tng. adv. bd. Ohio Dept. Health, Columbus, 1983-88; perinatal standards subcom. Cleve. Health Care Alternative, 1985; early intervention planner Multiple Agy. Consortium, Cleve., 1989; planner Child and Family Health Services Consortium, Cleve., 1984—; speaker and workshop leader in field. Youth religious instr. St. Barnabus Cath. Ch., Northfield, Ohio, 1976-78; program evaluator State Vocat. Family Life Edn. Study, Brecksville, Ohio, 1974-80; adv. bd. Greater Cleve. Sexuality Network, 1981-82, peer approach counseling by teens program YWCA, Cleve., 1982. Named Area E-1 Outstanding Comdr. Regional Angel Flight/Arnold Air Soc., Detroit, 1974. Mem. Health Care Adminstrv. Assn. Northeast Ohio, Am. Pub. Health Assn. (caucus program chmn. 1988—), Am. Assn. Sex Educators, Counselors and Therapists, Beta Gamma Sigma, Sigma Iota Epsilon, Kappa Delta Phi. Democrat. Home: 1094 Woodhaven Blvd Akron OH 44313 Office: MetroHealth Med Ctr Maternity and Infant Care 3395 Scranton Rd Cleveland OH 44109

ZAREMBA, KAREN ANN, nail technician; b. Berwyn, Ill., Nov. [illegible] d. Theodore John Zaremba and Margaret [illegible] Newman. Student, Alma Coll., 1972-76. Licensed [illegible] owner The Painted Lady, Redondo [illegible] Redondo Beach, 1984-88; [illegible] 1988-89, The Marg[illegible] Bay Ctr [illegible] 1966—; program mgr. South Huntington Mentor Program, Huntington Station, 1987—; dir. South Huntington Tchr. Ctr., Huntington Station, 1986—; pub. cons., McGraw Hill-Webster div., N.Y.C., 1979-80; TV cons., On The Air, N.Y.C., 1981-85; cons. Hudson River Regional Tchr. Ctr., Peekskill, N.Y., 1988, Suffolk County Orgn. for Promotion of Edn., Smithtown, N.Y., 1988, Tchr. Ctr. Levittown, N.Y., 1989; coord. L.I. Network Mentor Tchr. Internship programs. Author tng. manuals, tchr. guides; editor study guides; editor history text: From Sea to Shining Sea, 1979. Chmn. Citizens Com. to Save Roslyn Harbor, North Hempstead, N.Y., 1985-87, Steering Com. Environ. Orgns., North Hempstead, 1985-87. Grantee, State of N.Y., 1986—, Woman's Action Alliance, 1989. Mem. N.Y. State Assn. Supervision and Curriculum Devel. (conf. coord. 1989-90), Nat. Staff Devel. Coun. Office: South Huntington Tchr Ctr Weston St Huntington Station NY 11746

ZARKY, KAREN JANE, newspaper editor; b. St. Louis, Jan. 20, 1948; d. Herbert Lee Lawrence and Alice Ruth (Harrison) Lawrence Robison; m. Robert Gerald McCoy, Feb. 15, 1964 (div. Feb. 1982); 1 child, Karen; m. A.A. Zarky, Aug. 29, 1986. BA, Maryville Coll., St. Louis, 1988. Asst. to dir. fin. Clayton Mark Corp., Chgo., 1966-68; office mgr. A.R. Musical Enterprises, Columbus, Ind., 1969-75; owner, pres. Antique Galleries Inc., Louisville, 1975-81; sales mgr. Rainbow Graphics and Displays, St. Louis, 1981-87; editor, pres. Senior Circuit, Inc., St. Louis, 1987—; tchr. St. Louis Community Coll., 1987-89. Bd. dirs. Greeley Community Ctr., St. Louis, 1988—; mem. reorgn. com. United Way, St. Louis, 1988—. Mem. Nat. Assn.Women Bus. Owners, Women in Communication, Internat. Assn. Bus. Communicators.

ZARRETT, LINDA PAULINE, childbirth educator; b. Minot, N.D., Apr. 6, 1956; d. James Eugene and Inez Dolores (Koch) Tillema; m. Robert Warren Zarrett, Sept. 2, 1983 (div. Aug. 1990); children: Diana Christine, David Andrew. Diploma, St. Luke's Sch. of Nursing, Fargo, N.D., 1980; BS in Nursing, Moorhead State U., 1985. Cert. childbirth educator, N.D. Nurse St. Luke's Hosps., Fargo, 1980-82, 85—, Trinity Med. Ctr., Minot, 1982-83; nurse women's unit Dakota Hosp., Fargo, 1990; instr. infant massage, Fargo, 1987—; lactation cons. Breast Feeding Support, Fargo, 1988—, Med. Ctr. One, Bismarck, N.D.; asst. to membership chmn. Internat. Lactation Cons.'s Assn. Contbr. articles to profl. jours. Mem. YMCA. Mem. Internat. Childbirth Edn. Assn. (state coord. 1985-87, 89—), Internat. Assn. Infant Massage Instrs. (med. editor Tender Loving Care newsletter), N.D. Nurses Assn. (dir. membership and mktg.), Assn. Psychoprophylaxis in Obstetrics, Gate City Nurses Assn. (bd. dirs. 1986-88), Nurses Assn. of Am. Coll. Ob-Gyn (vice chmn. sect. 1989—). Democrat. Lutheran. Home: 431 W Century Ave #3 Bismarck ND 58501

ZARRETT, MARY ANN, counselor; b. Big Clifty, Ky., July 8, 1949; d. Julius Forest and Gladys Mae (Hawkins) Duvall; m. Robert Warren Zarrett, Dec. 27, 1969 (div. Aug. 1983); children: Rob Warren, Elizabeth Duvall. BS in Nursing, U. Ky., 1971; MS in Counseling, Cen. Mo. State U., 1977. RN, N.D., Minn.; lic. counselor, N.D. Rsch., cataloging and circulation asst. U. Ky. Med. Ctr. Library, Lexington, 1969-71; nurse aide Taylor Manor Nursing Home, Versailles, Ky., 1970; self-employed Burlington, Vermont, 1971-74; counselor, asst. prof. Moorhead State U., 1985—, dir. tng. Moorhead State U. Counseling Ctr., 1987-90, outreach coord., 1989—; nurse psychiat. ward St. Luke's Hosp., Fargo, N.D., 1988—; cons. Minn. Army Nat. Guard through Met. State U., 1987; presenter Expanding Your Horizons, 1988—. Adv. bd. mem. Compassionate Friends Fargo, N.D., 1986—; chmn. music Plymouth Congregational Ch., Fargo, 1986-88; chmn. Fargo Clinic Art Gallery, 1982-84. Mem. Am. Assn. Counseling and Devel., Minn. Assn. Specialist in Group Work, Am. Mental Health Counselors Assn., Nat. Bd. for Cert. Counselors, Phi Kappa Phi. Republican. Congregationalist. Office: Moorhead State U Counseling Ctr Moorhead MN 56560

ZARRO, JANICE ANNE, lawyer; b. Newark, June 30, 1947; d. Samuel James and Elma Dora (Monaco) Z.; m. Bobby C. Wood, Nov. 7,1977. BA, Rutgers U., 1969; JD, Ill. Inst. Tech., 1973. Bar: Pa. 1974. Counsel jud. com. U.S. Ho. Reps., Washington, 1973-77; profl. staff mem. labor and human resources com. U.S. Senate, Washington, 1977-80; dir. Avon Products, Inc., N.Y.C., 1980-81; dir. Avon Products, Inc., Washington, 1982-86, v.p., 1986—; gen. counsel Nat. Italian-Am. Found., 1989—; mem. Bus.-Govt. Rels. Coun., Washington, 1987—. Bd. dirs. YMCA Met. Washington, 1978-80, Nat. Multiple Sclerosis Soc., 1988—; chmn. women in bus. com. Overseas Edn. Found., Internat., Washington, 1986—. Recipient Leadership Recognition award Nat. Women's Econ. Alliance, 1984. Mem. ABA, Pa. Bar Assn., Internat. Club (bd. dirs. 1988—). Office: Fox Bennett & Turner 750 17th St NW Washington DC 20006

ZARZYCKI-BERG, DONNA, paralegal; b. Villach, Austria, Feb. 5, 1948; came to U.S., 1950; m. Donald Leon Berg, Sept. 5, 1986; children: Pamela Aguirre, Tamara Estes, Patty Berg. Student, Durham Bus. Coll., Beaumont, Tex., 1973; B in Applied Arts and Sci., Lamar U., Beaumont, 1990, paralegal cert., 1988. Sec. Champion Internat., Silsbee, Tex., 1973-77, Tex. Home Health, Inc., Silsbee, 1977-78, Kirby Forest Industries, Silsbee, 1978-87; legal intern Atty. Gen.'s Office, Beaumont, 1989—; Vol. gov.'s campaign com., Jasper, Tex., 1990. Mem. SE Tex. Assn. Legal Assts., Tex. Quarter Horse Assn., Omega Theta Alpha, Beta Sigma Phi. Republican. Roman Catholic. Home: Rte 5 737 Dogwood St Jasper TX 75951 Office: Kirby Forest Industries 5550 Eastex Fwy Beaumont TX 77708

ZASLOVE, PHOEBE, investment company executive. Pres. London & Bishopsgate Internat. Inc., N.Y.C. Office: London & Bishopsgate Internat 866 3rd Ave 28th Fl New York NY 10022*

ZAVADA, MARY ROBERTA, public relations executive; b. Passaic, N.J., Jan. 11, 1936; d. John Michael and Sophie (Majewicz) Z. BA magna cum laude, Coll. St. Elizabeth, 1957; MA in Creative Writing, DePaul U., Chgo., 1959; postgrad., London U., 1962-64. Feature writer UP Internat., London, 1964; tech. writer Honeywell, Inc., Newton Highs, Mass., 1966-67; editor Sylvania Electronic Systems, Waltham, Mass., 1968-69; account exec. Anderson Assocs., Boston, 1969-70; sr. editor Ednl. Testing Svc., Princeton, N.J., 1971-74, mng. editor, 1974-82; dir. press rels. Ins. Info. Inst., N.Y.C., 1982-86, v.p. publs., 1986—. Contbr. articles to profl. jours. and gen. interest pubs. Recipient First prize Vogue mag. Prix de Paris competition, 1957. Mem. N.Y. Women in Communications (named one of sixty Outstanding Women in Communications 1984). Roman Catholic. Home: 6040 Blvd E West New York NJ 07093 Office: Ins Info Inst 110 William St New York NY 10038

ZAVORSKI, LISA MARIE, hospital administrator; b. Phila., Nov. 30, 1960; d. Vincent Francis and Elizabeth (Miller) Salvino; m. Michael Paul Zavorski. BS in Health Records Adm, Temple U., Phila., 1984. Reg. records adinstr. Quality assurance staff asst. Hosp. of U. Pa., Phila., 1984-85; asst. dir. med. records Hosp. of U. Pa., 1985-88; dir. med. records St. Agnes Med. Ctr., Phila., 1988—. Mem. Am. Med. Records Assn., Pa. Med. Records Assn. Office: St Agnes Med Ctrr 1900 S Broad St Philadelphia PA 19145

ZAYACHEK, MARY KATHERINE, hospital administrator, nurse; b. Jersey City, Aug. 18, 1943; d. Chester Charles and Olga Pauline (Miko) Fabian; m. Jon Martin Zayachek, Sept. 24, 1966; children: Lea, Keith, Joel. BS, Russell Sage Coll., 1965; M in Mgmt., Southwestern U., 1985. RN, N.J. Charge nurse St. Barnabas Med. Ctr., Livingston, N.J., 1965-66; nurse critical care Spohn Hosp., Corpus Christi, Tex., 1966-67, Overlook Hosp., Summit, N.J., 1968-74; clin. instr. Passaic County Community Coll., Paterson, N.J., 1975-76, Clara Maass Sch. Nursing, Belleville, N.J., 1975; asst. adminstr. Mountainside Hosp., Montclair, N.J., 1976-80, utilization supr. quality assurance, 1980-85, asst. adminstr., 1985-86, asst. v.p., 1986—; sr. cons. Med. Rsch Cons., Inc., 1988—; guest lectr. William Paterson Coll., Wayne, N.J., 1978. Guest cons. nursing mag. Bd. dirs. Health Adv. Bd., Montclair, 1981-83; sec. PTA Council, Montclair; v.p. PTA, Grove St. Sch., Montclair; trustee The Hospice, Inc., chmn. nominating com., 1988—, mem. adv. bd. Haven Alcohol Rehab. Ctr., Montclair. Mem. Nat. Assn. Quality Assurance Profls. (cert., mem. nominating com.), N.J. Assn. Quality Assurance Profls. (north region rep., chmn. nominating com., treas. 1983-85, nominating com. 1985—, v.p.). Roman Catholic. Avocations: sailing, jogging, aerobic dance. Office: Mountainside Hosp Bay and Highland Ave Montclair NJ 07042

ZAYDON, JEMILLE ANN, educator; b. Peckville, Pa., Feb. 21, 1940; d. Joseph and Catherine Ann (Hazzouri) Z.; student Barry Coll. for Women, 1957-59; B.S., Marywood Coll., 1963; M.S. in Edn., Wilkes Coll., 1978; doctoral candidate Temple U. Tchr. St. Hugh Elementary Sch., Coconut Grove, Fla., 1963-64; Allapattah Elementary Sch., Miami, 1964-65, Columbus Elementary Sch., Westfield, N.J., 1965-66; communications instr. Keystone Job Corps, Drums, Pa., 1966-73; vol. instr. Keystone Rehab. Ctr., Scranton, Pa., 1970-71; curriculum cons. for mentally retarded, Vienna, Austria, 1974; prof. English and reading Lackawanna Jr. Coll., Scranton, 1974—, head dept. English, speech and reading, 1976—, chmn. dept. arts, humanities and social studies, 1977—; adj. prof. English, U. Scranton, 1980—; communications instr. Lackawanna County Vocat. Tech. Sch., 1974—. Supr. recreation program, Hazleton, Pa., summer 1968; founder, adviser Keystone Kourier, 1967-69. Sec. Fedn. Youth, William W. Scranton, 1963; coord. annual Christmas for Mentally Retarded Keystone City Residence, Scranton, 1975—; supr. students Heart Fund campaign, 1968-71; developer program mentally retarded Allied Svcs. for Handicapped Scranton, 1973; Class rep. Marywood Coll. Fund Dr., 1978; gen., 1980—; active ARC, March of Dimes, Heart Fund, Leukemia and United Fund drives, also Sickle Cell Anemia Found. Bd. dirs. Michael F. Harrity Meml. Fund., 1969-73; mem. exec. bd. Northeastern Pa. Environ. Council, also co-chmn. public edn. and funding. Recipient Staff Mem. of Year award, Job Corps, 1969, Humanitarian award, 1980; Educators award Dade County, 1973, 75; named Tchr. of Yr., 1973; Service scholar, Barry Coll., 1958; Mem. Nat., Pa. State edn. assns., Beta Lambda Tau, Sigma Tau Delta, Theta Chi Beta (charter pres. 1961-63), Lambda Iota Tau (life). Democrat. Roman Catholic (instr. Confraternity Christian Doctrine 1956-71). Editor Lebanese Am. Jour., 1957-63. Home: 608 N Main Ave Scranton PA 18504

ZBUZEK, VLASTA KMENTOVA, biologist; b. Velka Losenice, Czechoslovakia, Sept. 6, 1933; came to U.S., 1969; d. Karel Kment and Anezka (Novotna) Kmentova; m. Vratislav Zbuzek, Oct. 23, 1965. MS, Charles U., Prague, Czechoslovakia, 1963, PhD cum laude, Dr. Rerum Naturalis, 1969, Candidate of Sci., 1969. Rsch. fellow Population Coun. Rockefeller U., N.Y.C., 1969-71; rsch. scientist NYU, 1971-78; rsch. physiologist VA Med. Ctr., N.Y.C., 1978-79; asst. prof. U. N.J. Med Sch., Newark, 1979-85, assoc. prof., 1985—. Author: Gonado-Thyroidal Relationship in the Rat, 1969; author, co-author numerous scientific papers in field. Grantee NIH, Bethesda, Md., 1982-85, Smokeless Tobacco Rsch. Coun., N.Y.C., 1987-90. Mem. Endocrine Soc., Gerontol. Soc., N.Y. Acad. Scis., Internat. Soc. Neuroendocrinology. Home: 100 Manhattan Ave #1314 Union City NJ 07087

ZEARES, MELINDA ANN, educator; b. N.Y.C., June 7, 1947; d. Olen Jessie and Alma Arlene (Steinruck) Watts; m. William Dennis Zeares, May 28, 1966 (div. July 1981); children: Michael Dennis, Jennifer Marie. BS in Edn. with honors, Bloomsburg U., 1972; MS in Edn. with honors, East Tex. State U., 1982; postgrad., Tex. Wesleyan Coll., 1986. Cert. elem. tchr., Tex., Pa. Tchr. math. Clinton P. Russell Elem. Sch., Dallas Ind. Sch. Dist., 1972-76, N.W. Harllee Elem. Sch., 1980—; tchr. remedial math. and Title I, Seneca Highlands Intermediate Unit 9, Smethport, Pa., 1976-77; substitute tchr. spl. edn. Lincoln Intermediate Unit 12, Gettysburg, Pa., 1978-80; cons., workshop presenter Lincoln Intermediate Unit 12, 1985—; cons. Harcourt, Brace, Jovanovich, Dallas, 1986-87; curriculum writer, Dallas Ind. Sch. Dist., 1984—. Treas. N.W. Harllee Sch. PTA, 1988—. Named Subdist. II Tchr. of Yr, Dallas Ind. Sch. Dist., 1984, Tchr. of Yr, 1988; recipient Prin.'s award N.W. Harllee Sch., 1986, 87, Golden Apple award Cabell's Dairy, 1988. Mem. NEA, Tex. Edn. Assn. Republican. Methodist. Home: 6048 Village Glen Apt 4145 Dallas TX 75206 Office: NW Harllee Elem Sch 1216 E 8th St Dallas TX 75203

ZEBRASKI, KATHLEEN, accountant, educator; b. Ridley Park, Pa., Aug. 16, 1950; d. Joseph John and Doris (Mathews) Kaminski; m. Samuel D. Bogden, Nov. 29, 1969 (div. Feb. 1980); 1 child, Cynthia Eve; m. James Zebraski, Mar. 25, 1988. BS, West Chester U., 1978; MBA, Widener U., 1985. Acct. West Chester (Pa.) Area Sch. Dist., 1978-83; mgr. acctg. Tredyffrin-Easttown Sch. Dist., Berwyn, Pa., 1983—; instr. acctg. Immaculata (Pa.) Coll., 1988—, Unisys, Paoli, Pa., 1988—. Mem. Am. Assn. Sch. Bus. Ofcls., Pa. Assn. Sch. Bus. Offcls. (registered), Delaware Valley Assn. Sch. Bus. Ofcls. (sec. 1987-89). Home: 36 Harrison Rd W West Chester PA 19380-6762 Office: Tredyffrin-Easttown Schs 738 lst Ave Berwyn PA 19312-1779

ZEBROWSKI, MARILYN FRANCES, psychologist; b. Perth Amboy, N.J., Nov. 14; d. Stephan Charles and Louise Mary (Kowalski) Dobranski; m. Leonard T. Zebrowski, Jan. 28, 1951; children: Diane, Leonard S. Degree in Oral Hygiene, Temple U., 1951, BA in Psychology, 1980; MEd, Antioch U., 1983; PhD, Union Grad Sch., Cin., 1990. Nat. cert. counselor; cert. gambling counselor, hypnotherapist, dental hygienist. Tchr. bus. Drake Coll., Perth Amboy, 1942-46; tchr., counselor Pub. Sch. 9, Perth Amboy, 1947-49; dental hygienist Dr. Leonard T. Zebrowski, Camden, N.J., 1951-74; editor, writer for syndicated columnist Blair, 1974—; counselor, tchr., hypnotherapist Haddonfield, N.J., 1979—; psychology intern Camden County Health Svcs., Blackwood, N.J., 1981-83, 88-89; psychologist Haddonfield, 1983—. Bd. dirs. Maryville Inc., Glassboro, N.J., 1984-89. Recipient svc. award Maryville Inc., 1987. Mem. Am. Psychol. Assn., Alcohol Counselors Assn., N.J. Compulsive Gambling Assn., Nat. Assn. Compulsive Gamblers, Dental Hygiene Assn., Colwick Women's Club (Cherry Hill, N.J., treas. 1968-72), Zonta, Cherry Hill Gourmet Club. Roman Catholic.

ZECHELLO, ANNI L., image consultant; b. Gross Damen, Germany, July 9, 1943; came to U.S., 1952; d. Immanuel and Olga Natalia (Reinke) Reder; m. James Francis Zechello, July 21, 1962; children: Anne-Marie Gooley, James Vito, Ronald Matthew. Student cosmetology, LaBaron Acad.; cert. in cosmetology, SMU. Hair stylist Turning Point Salon, Canton, Mass.; sales assoc. Petite Sophisticate, Braintree, Mass.; pres. Image Coords., Stoughton, Mass. Mem. NEWBO, Assn. Fashion and Image Cons., Women's Success Network, Am. Sewing Guild, Greater Boston Women Network (membership com), Stoughton C. of C., Altrusa Club. Lutheran. Home: 284 Bay Rd Stoughton MA 02072 Office: 710 Turnpike Rd Stoughton MA 02072

ZEEMAN, JOAN JAVITS, writer, inventor; b. N.Y.C., Aug. 17, 1928; d. Benjamin Abraham and Lily (Braxton) Javits; m. John Huibert Zeeman III, Mar. 20, 1954; children: Jonathan, Andrea Zeeman Deane, Eloise Zeeman Scharff, Phoebe Zeemon Fitch, Merrily Margaret. BA, Vassar Coll., 1949; MEd, U. Vt., 1976. Pub. relations exec. Benjamin Sonnenberg, N.Y.C., 1949-51; freelance writer, 1952—. Trustee TheatreWorks(formerly Performing Arts Repertory Theatre), N.Y.C., 1953-83, Profl. Childrens Sch., N.Y.C., 1980-89. Author: The Compleat Child, 1964. Lyricist musical plays: Young Abe Lincoln, 1961; Hotel Passionato, 1965; song lyricist: Santa Baby, 1953. Patentee Alphocube. Mem. ASCAP, Dramatists Guild, Gilbert and Sullivan Soc., Vassar Club (sec. 1978-84, v.p. 1984-86) (Westchester, N.Y.). Home: 230 Palmo Way Palm Beach FL 33480 Office: 520 Hommocks Rd Larchmont NY 10538

ZEFF, SUSAN LEAH, advertising executive; b. Modesto, Calif., Mar. 22, 1945; d. Alvin and Eleanor Frances (Baker) Zeff. AA, Modesto Jr. Coll., 1964; student, San Francisco State U., 1964-65. Sec. Modesto High Sch., 1965-66; bishop's sec. San Francisco, 1969-71; legal sec. Modesto, 1971-73, 76-84; paralegal T.W. Salter, Inc., Modesto, 1984-87; TV advt. account exec. Post Newsweek Cable, Modesto, 1987—. Bd. dirs. Am. Cancer Soc., Modesto, 1969-84, Stanislaus Rape Crisis, Modesto, 1987—, Women's Ctr. of Stanislaus, Modesto, 1984—; mem. adv. bd. Cen. Cath. High Sch., Modesto, 1987—, Soc. for Handicapped, 1988—; mem. Stanislaus Edn. Coun., 1989—. Recipient Nat. Sales Achievement grand prize CAB Conf., N.Y.C., 1989; Nat. Telly award for excellence regional and local TV commls., 1990. Mem. Orchid Soc. Jewish. Home: 1925A Edgebrook Dr Modesto CA 95354 Office: Post Newsweek Cable 1639 Princeton Ave Modesto CA 95350

ZEGIOB-DEVEREAUX, LESLIE ELAINE, clinical psychologist; b. Cleve., Oct. 17, 1948; d. Charles G. and Elinore Lois (Jones) Zegiob; m. James Michael Devereaux, July 11, 1981. Student Allegheny Coll., 1966-68; BA, Am. U., 1971; MS, U. Ga., 1974, PhD, 1976. Lic. psychologist, Ariz., Ind. Asst. prof. dept. psychology Ariz. State U., Tempe, 1976-78, dir. psychology clinic, 1977-78; dir. childrens svcs. Dogwood Village, Memphis, 1978; adj. prof. dept. psychology Notre Dame (Ind.) U., 1979-80; clin. psychologist dept. psychology and psychiatry The Med. Group, Michigan City, Ind., 1978—; cons. child protective svcs. LaPorte County Dept. Pub. Welfare, Headstart program, 1979-84, Michigan City schs., 1979-84; mem. adv. bd. Headstart, 1979-84. Contbr. articles to profl. jours. Ariz. State U. faculty grantee, 1978. Mem. Am. Psychol. Assn., Assn. for Advancement Behavior Therapy, Southeastern Psychol. Assn., Sierra Club, Animal Protection Inst., Wilderness Soc., Ind. Cat Soc. Phi Kappa Phi, Phi Beta Kappa. Democrat. Office: 1225 E Coolspring Ave Michigan City IN 46360

ZEHRING, KAREN, publishing executive; b. Washington, Dec. 5, 1945; d. Robert William Zehring and Gretchen (Lorenz) Proos; m. George Lang, 1970 (div. 1979); m. Peter Frank Davis, June 10, 1979; children: Timothy, Nicholas, Jesse, Antonia. BA, U. Denver, 1967; postgrad., Yale U., 1967-68. Assoc. pub. mktg. and sales Instl. Investor Systems, Inc., N.Y.C., 1968-74; owner, pub. The Corp. Fin. Letter, N.Y.C., 1976-78; group dir. planning and devel. Bus. Week mag., N.Y.C., 1977-78; owner, pub., exec. editor The Zehring Co., N.Y.C., 1979-84; chmn., pres., pub., editor-in-chief Corp. Fin. mag., N.Y.C., 1986—. Mem. The Women's Forum, Am. Soc. Mag. Editors, Overseas Press Club. Unitarian. Office: Corp Fin Mag 810 Seventh Ave 18th Fl New York NY 10019

ZEILIG, NANCY MEEKS, magazine editor; b. Nashville, Apr. 28, 1943; d. Edward Harvey and Nancy Evelyn (Self) Meeks; m. Lanny Kenneth Fielder, Aug. 20, 1964 (div. Dec. 1970); m. Charles Elliot Zeilig, Jan. 6, 1974 (div. Dec. 1989); 1 child, Sasha Rebecca. BA, Birmingham-So. Coll., 1964; postgrad., Vanderbilt U., 1971-73. Editorial asst. Reuben H. Donnelley, N.Y.C., 1969-70; asst. editor Vanderbilt U., Nashville, 1970-74; editor U. Minn., St. Paul, 1975; asst. editor McGraw-Hill Inc., Mpls., 1975-76; mng. editor Denver mag., 1976-80; editor Jour. Am. Water Works Assn., Denver, 1981—. Editor, co-pub.: WomanSource, 1982, rev. edit. 1984; editor: 100 Years, 1975; contbr. articles to consumer mags. Office: Jour Am Water Works Assn 6666 W Quincy Denver CO 80235

ZEINER, ANN ORESKI, bank teller, administrator; b. Bridgeport, Conn., Jan. 16, 1939; d. John Victor and Mary Margaret (Kwik) Oreski; m. Robert Allen Zeiner, Sept. 16, 1961; children: Allen Robert, Loraine Doris, David Michael. Grad., Am. Inst. Banking, Bridgeport, 1985. Head teller Peoples Bank, Bridgeport, 1975-80; teller supr. Peoples Bank, Bridgeport and Milford, Conn., 1980—. Mem. Monroe (Conn.) Bd. Edn., 1973-79; sec. Monroe Fedn. Dem. Women, 1981-89; sec. Dem. Town Com., Monroe, 1983-89; commr., treas. Monroe Housing Authority, 1987-91; clk. Monroe Congl. Ch., 1989-91. Home: 78 Twin Brook Ter Monroe CT 06468 Office: Peoples Bank 190 Broad St Milford CT 06460

ZEIT, RUTH MAE, foundation administrator; b. N.Y.C., May 13, 1945; d. Albert Joseph and Gertrude (Goldberg) Janover; m. Robert Martin Zeit, Dec. 28, 1969; children: Rachael Miriam, Rebecca Madeleine. BA, U. Pa., 1967, postgrad., 1969-70; postgrad., Temple U., 1967-69. Teaching fellow Temple U., Phila., 1967-69, U. Pa., Phila., 1969-70; dir. piano music studio Phila., 1969—; pres. Lupus Found. of Del. Valley, Ardmore, Pa., 1983—; Mem. Winner's Ball com. Lupus Found. of Del. Valley, Ardmore, 1986-87, presiding officer, bd. dirs., med. adv. bd., 1983—, prin. organizer Ednl. Symposia, 1983—, prin. organizer patient support groups, 1983—; lectr. Prin. coordinator Lupus Found. of Del. Valley Newsletter, 1983—. Liaison with Mayor W. Wilson Goode; liaison between Julius Erving and Children's Hosp. of Phila.; coord. Julius Erving Lupus Rsch. Fund; target chairperson Undergraduate Admissions, U. Pa.. Mem. Am. Coll. of Musicians, Sigma Delta Gamma, Music Tchrs. Nat. Assn., Pa. Music Tchrs. Assn. Democrat. Jewish. Home: 1610 Gerson Dr Narberth PA 19072 Office: Lupus Found Delaware Valley 44 W Lancaster Ave Ardmore PA 19003

ZEITLAN, MARILYN LABB, lawyer; b. N.Y.C., Sept. 17, 1938; d. Charles and Florence (Geller) Labb; m. Barrett M. Zeitlan, Apr. 14, 1957; children: Adam Scott, Daniel Craig. BA, Queens Coll., 1958, MS, 1970; JD, Hofstra U., 1978. Bar: N.Y. 1979. Tchr. N.Y.C., 1958-61; pvt. practice law, Roslyn, N.Y., 1983—. Mem. Law Rev., Hofstra U., 1976-78. Contbr. articles to profl. jours. Commr. East Hills Environ. Commn., 1971-75; co-founder Roslyn Environ. Assn., 1970; v.p. Roslyn LWV, 1974-75. Hofstra Law Sch. fellow, 1976. Mem. ABA, Nassau County Bar Assn., N.Y. State Bar Assn., Nassau-Suffolk Women's Bar Assn., Phi Beta Kappa. Avocation: horseback riding. Office: 1025 Northern Blvd Ste 201 Roslyn NY 11576

ZEITLER, DEBORAH LEILA, oral/maxillofacial surgeon; b. Sioux City, Iowa, Jan. 26, 1952; d. John William and Dorothy Pauline (McDermott) Parris; m. Rodney Ray Zeitler, Aug. 16, 1975; children: William Andrew, Elizabeth Leila, Joseph Dean. BA, U. Iowa, 1974, DDS, 1978, MS, 1982. Cert. Am. Assn. Oral and Maxillofacial Surgeons. From resident to assoc. prof. oral.maxillofacial surgery U. Iowa Hosps. & Clins., Iowa City, 1978—; cons. Commn. on Dental Edn., 1987—. Author 30 abstracts; contbr. chpts. to books and articles to profl. jours. Named Outstanding Young Women in Am., 1983; Sleichter scholar, 1977; AAUW fellow, 1977-78. Mem. Am. Assn. Oral and Maxillofacial Surgeons, Am. Assn. Women Dentists (dist. x chair 1982), Am. Cleft Palate Assn., Am. Bd. Oral/Maxillofacial Surgery, Am. Assn. Dental Schs., ADA, Internat. Assn. Dental Rsch., Iowa Assn. Oral/Maxillofacial Surgeons, Iowa Dental Assn., Johnson County Dental Assn., Univ. Dist. Dental Assn. Office: Univ Iowa Hosps Dept Hospital Dentistry Iowa City IA 52242

ZEITLIN, EUGENIA PAWLIK, retired college administrator, educator, librarian; b. N.Y.C., Jan. 29; d. Charles and Pauline Pawlik; m. Herbert Zakary Zeitlin, July 3, 1949; children: Mark Clyde, Joyce Therese Zeitlin Harris, Ann Victoria, Clare Katherine. MA in Libr. Sci., Bklyn. Coll., 1951; MA, NYU, N.Y.C., 1951; MS, Rosary Coll., 1968. Teaching credential N.Y., Ariz., Calif., Ill. English tchr. Sea Cliff, L.I., N.Y., 1945-47; English, math. tchr. Merrick (N.Y.) Sch. Dist., 1948-49; English tchr. Wilson Sch. Dist., Phoenix, 1949-50; counselor West Phoenix (Ariz.) High Sch., 1953-56; English instr. Antelope Valley Coll., Lancaster, Calif., 1961-62, Grossmont Community Coll., El Cajon, Calif., 1962-64; asst. prof. English Wright Coll., Chgo., 1965-67; asst. prof. English, asst. to v.p. curriculum and instrn. Oakton Community Coll., Des Plaines, Ill., 1975-76; rsch. assoc. Triton Cons., Woodland Hills, Calif., 1977—; libr. City of L.A., Northridge, Calif., 1984—. Contbr. articles to profl. jours. Chairperson fund raiser Tierra Del Sol Sch., 1989; dir. Shut In Program, L.A., 1985 (Northridge Employee of Yr. 1958-59). Named Northridge City Employee of Yr., 1986. Mem. AAUW (br. pres. Lancaster, Calif. 1959-60), The Thoreau Soc. (life), Polish Am. Orgn., Beta Phi Mu. Roman Catholic. Home: 20124 Phaeton Dr Woodland Hills CA 91364

ZEKIND, DIANE MARIE, management executive; b. Detroit, Mar. 18, 1961; d. Charles Frederick and Bernice Louise (Woskoski) Z. BS in Indsl. Engring., Gen. Motors Inst., 1984; postgrad., Gen. Motors Engring. Mgmt. GMI coop student Chevrolet/Cen. Foundry, Saginaw, Mich., 1979-84; project engr., melting Cen. Foundry, GMC, Saginaw, Mich., 1984, indsl. engr., 1984-85, process engr., 1985-86, sr. project engr., 1986-88, staff engr., 1988; mgr. product planning CMI Tech. Ctr., Ferndale, Mich., 1988—. Recipient scholarship Material Handling Inst., 1982-83, Indsl. Engring. Thesis Award of Excellence Am. Inst. Indsl. Engrs. Chpt., Saginaw, 1984, Thesis of Distinction GMI, Flint, Mich., 1984, Tau Beta Pi, Alpha Pi Mu (past-pres. GMI chpt.). Mem. Am. Foundryman's Soc. (bd. dirs. 1985-88, edn. chmn. 1985-88), Soc. Automotive Engrs., Am. Soc. Quality Control, Am. Mgmt. Soc. Roman Catholic. Home: 27674 Westcott Crescent Cir Farmington Hills MI 48018 Office: CMI Tech Ctr 1600 W 8 Mile Rd Ferndale MI 48220

ZEKMAN, TERRI MARGARET, graphic designer; b. Chgo., Sept. 13, 1950; d. Theodore Nathan and Lois (Bernstein) Z.; m. Alan Daniels, Apr. 12, 1980; 1 child, Jesse Logan. BFA, Washington U., St. Louis, 1971; postgrad, Art Inst. Chgo., 1974-75. Graphic designer (on retainer) greeting cards and related products Recycled Paper Products Co., Chgo., 1970—; apprenticed graphic designer Helmuth, Obata & Kassabaum, St. Louis, 1970-71; graphic designer Container Corp., Chgo., 1971; graphic designer, art dir., photographer Cuerden Advt. Design, Denver, 1971-74; art dir. D'Arcy, McManus & Masius Advt., Chgo., 1975-76; freelance graphic designer Chgo., 1976-77; art dir. Garfield Linn Advt., Chgo., 1977-78; graphic designer Keiser Design Group, Van Noy & Co., Los Angeles, 1978-79; owner and operator graphic design studio Los Angeles, 1979—. Recipient cert. of merit St. Louis Outdoor Poster Contest, 1970, Denver Art Dirs. Club, 1973.

ZELBY, RACHEL, realtor; b. Sosnowiec, Poland, May 6, 1930; came to U.S., 1955; d. Herschel Kupfermintz and Sarah Rosenblatt; m. Leon W. Zelby, Dec. 28, 1954; children: Laurie Susan, Andrew Stephen. Student, U. Pa., 1955, Realtors' Inst., Norman, Okla., 1974; grad., Realtors Inst., Oklahoma City, 1978. Lic. realtor, broker, Okla.; cert. residential specialist, Okla. Realtor, broker, ptnr. Realty World Norman Heritage, 1973-81; realtor, broker Century 21 Parker Real Estate, Norman, 1981—, residential specialist, 1986—. Mem. Jr. Svc. League, Norman, 1980—; charter mem. Assistance League Norman, 1970—; bd. dirs. Juvenile Svcs., Inc., Norman, 1975-76. Mem. Nat. Assn. Realtors, Norman Bd. Realtors, Women's Coun. Realtors (treas. 1985), U. Okla. Women's Assn. (past pres.), Norman C. of C., LWV. Home: 1009 Whispering Pines Norman OK 73072 Office: Century 21 Parker Real Est 319 W Main St Norman OK 73069

ZELENY, MARJORIE PFEIFFER (MRS. CHARLES ELLINGTON ZELENY), psychologist; b. Balt., Mar. 31, 1924; d. Lloyd Armitage and Mable (Willian) Pfeiffer; B.A., U. Md., 1947; M.S., U. Ill., 1949, postgrad., 1951-54; m. Charles Ellingson Zeleny, Dec. 11, 1950 (dec.); children—Ann Douglas, Charles Timberlake. Vocational counseling psychologist VA, Balt., 1947-48; asst. U. Ill. at Urbana, 1948-50, research asso. Bur. Research, 1952-53; chief psychologist dept. neurology and psychiatry Ohio State U. Coll. Medicine, Columbus, 1950-51; research psychologist, cons., Tucson, Washington, 1954—. Mem. Am., D.C. psychol. assns., AAAS, Southeastern Psychol Assn., DAR, Mortar Bd., Delta Delta Delta, Sigma Delta Epsilon, Psi Chi, Sigma Tau Epsilon. Roman Catholic. Home: 6825 Wemberly Way McLean VA 22101

ZELITZKY, GAIL P., management executive; b. Chgo., Dec. 5, 1941; d. Irving and Sylvia (Robbin) Robins; m. Harvey J. Olsher, June 18, 1961 (div. Oct. 1976); m. Alvin Zelitzky, Aug. 10, 1980; children: Cindy, Scott, Steve. B Ed., Nat. Coll., 1963. Spl. projects dir. Foremost Sales Promotions, Inc., Chgo., 1977-79, exec. v.p., 1979-81, pres., 1981—. Mem. Ill. Retail Mchts. Assn., Ill. Liquor Stores Assn., Beverage and Food Jewish United Fund, Women's Alliance Alcohol Beverage Ind. Office: Foremost Sales Promotion 5252 N Broadway Chicago IL 60640

ZELLEN, CAROL ANN, teacher; b. Kenosha, Wis., July 1, 1947; d. Clarence John and Mary Susan (Aceto) Z.; m. Leonard August Prorok, Aug. 16, 1986. BA, Edgewood Coll., 1969; MS in Edn., U. Ill., 1982. Tchr. Sts. Peter & Paul Sch., Tulsa, 1969-73, St. Thomas More Sch., Chgo., 1971-73, Sch. Dist. 140, Tinley Pk., Ill., 1973—; speech coach Sch. Dist. 140, 1973-86, dist. spelling coord., 1973-88, drama coach, 1977-83, aviation club sponsor, 1983-88. Past v.p., bd. dirs. Crisis Ctr. for S. Suburbia, Palos Hills, Ill.; bd. dirs. Ill. Women's Agenda, Chgo., 1982-84. Named one of Outstanding Young Women in Am., 1980. Mem. Am. Fedn. Tchrs., Ill. Fedn. Tchrs., AAUW (life, pres. 1979-81), Ninety-Nines, Inc., Investment Club (Orland Park chpt. 1980-83). Democrat. Roman Catholic. Office: Virgil I Grisson Jr High 17000 S 80th Ave Tinley Park IL 60477

ZELLER, BARBARA ANN, nun, healthcare facility administrator; b. Evansville, Ind., Aug. 18, 1945; d. Wilbert John and Dorothy Elizabeth (Tremor) Z. BA in Edn., St. Mary-of-the-Woods Coll., 1968; MA Studies in Aging, North Tex. State U., 1971. Dir. gerontology Sisters of Providence, St. Mary-of-the-Woods, Ind., 1971-76, 78-81; adminstrv. asst. archdiocesan social ministries Cath. Charities Archdiocese of Indpls., 1976-78; exec. dir. Maryvale, Inc., S. Mary-of-the-Woods, 1978-81; dir. social svcs. Pfister and Co., Inc., Terre Haute, Ind., 1981-82; exec. dir. Providence Retirement Home, Inc., New Albany, Ind., 1982—; cons., Poor Handmaids of Jesus Christ, Donaldson, Ind., Little Company of Mary Sisters, Evergreen Park, Ill., Sisters of St. Francis, Joliet, Ill., numerous other orders and ednl. instns. in Ind., Ill., Ohio and Ky.; presenter courses, seminars and workshops on aging and retirement; speaker in field. Author materials and problem solving kits in field. Recipient George E. Davis award, Interfaith Fellowship on Religion and Aging,1985; named Ky. Col., 1988, Sagamore of the Wabash, Gov. of Ind., 1988, Disting. Hoosier Gov. of Ind., 1988. Mem. Ind. Assn. of Homes for Aging, Internat. Soc. Pre-Retirement Planners. Democrat.

ZELLER, BRENDA LYNN, airline pilot; b. River Falls, Wis., Nov. 21, 1964; d. James Edward and Elena Louise (Fleck) Z. BSBA, Ariz. State U., 1986. Cert. flight instr., comml. pilot, flight engr. FAA. Flight instr. SAS Exec., Mesa, Ariz., 1986-87, Panorama Flight Svc., White Plains, N.Y., 1988-89; 2d officer, pilot United Airlines, Chgo., 1989—. Cast mem. Up with People, Tucson, 1987; vol. Big Bros.-Big Sisters, N.Y.C., 1988—. Regents acad. scholar Ariz. State U., 1986. Mem. Internat. Soc. Women Airline Pilots. Home: 108 E 38th St Apt 1902 New York NY 10016

ZELLI, MARY DIANE, orthodontist; b. Buffalo, N.Y., Nov. 6, 1957; d. Frank Joseph and Mary Josephine (Schneider) Z. BS in Dentistry, Case Western Reserve, 1979, DDS, 1981; cert. in Orthodontics, Eastman Dental Ctr., 1984. Orthodontist Orthodontic Assocs. of Cen. N.Y., Oneida, 1984-86, Drs. Baker, Lieberman and Filios, Ithaca, N.Y., 1986-87, Gary D. Husion, DDS, P.C., Fredericksburg, Va., 1987 --; staff mem. Mary Washington Hosp., Fredericksburg, 1989 --. Mem. ADA, Am. Assn. Orthodontists, Va. Dental Assn., Va. Orthodontic Soc., Southern Assn. Orthodontists, Richmond Dental Soc., Rappahannock Valley Dental Soc. (treas., 1989-90). Republican. Roman Catholic. Home: 807 College Ave Fredericksburg VA

22401 Office: Drs Hussion and Zelli 312 Butler Rd Fredericksburg VA 22405

ZELMAN, PATRICIA GRACE, history educator; b. Cin., Jan. 15, 1944; d. Louis George and Althea (Moyer) Grace; m. Donald Lewis Zelman, Apr. 29, 1940; 1 child, Julie Grace. BA, U. N.C., 1966; MA, Ohio State U., 1967, PhD, 1980. Instr. Tarleton State U., Stephenville, Tex., 1979-81; asst. prof. history Tarleton State U., 1981-88, assoc. prof. history, 1988—. Author: Women, Work and National Policy: The Kennedy-Johnson Years, 1981. Election judge Erath County Precinct 3, 1981-85, precinct chmn. Dem. Party, 1982-86. Named Erath County Woman of the Yr., Erath County Womens Clubs, 1985. Mem. So. Hist. Assn., Tex. Assn. Coll. Tchrs., Tex. Assn. for Advancement of History, Tex. Hist. Assn., Tarleton Faculty Womens Forum (pres. 1987-88), Erath County Womens Polit. Caucus. Democrat. Office: Tarleton State Univ Dept Social Sciences Stephenville TX 76402

ZEMAN, PAULA REDD, dean of faculty/college; b. N.Y.C., Jan. 23, 1956; d. M. Paul and Orial A. (Banks) Redd; m. Jiri J. Zeman, June 28, 1986. MusB, Ind. U., 1978, MusM, 1980. Mgr.office svcs. YWCA of White Plains (N.Y.) Cen. Westchester, 1981-82, office svcs. supr., 1982-84; office svcs cons. Inst. of Audio Rsch., N.Y.C., 1984-85, pers. mgr., 1985-86, dean of adminstrn., 1986-88, dean, 1988—; advt. dir. Westchester County Press, White O Plains, 1986-88, sec., treas., 1986—. Mem. Port Chester/Rye Br. NAACP, 1970—, West Coalition for Legal Abortion, White Plains, 1981—; exec. com. Young Dem. of Westchester, White Plain, 1983—. Mem. NAFE, Nat. Assn. Pers. Adminstrn., Nat. Assn. Tng. Devel., NOW. Democrat. Presbyterian. Home: 2 Ashdown Ct Peekskill NY 10566 Office: Inst of Audio Rsch 64 University Pl New York NY 10003

ZEMBA, DOROTHY IRENE, oil and mining company executive; b. Cuyahoga Falls, Ohio, Nov. 20, 1928; d. Raymond Clarence and Anna Frances (Knapp) Dorner; m. John Zemba, Mar. 10, 1951 (dec. Nov. 1978); children: John Raymond, Joel Dennis. Student pub. schs., Akron, Ohio. Sec. Akron Bd. Edn., 1946-47; with printing office Ohio Match Co., Wadsworth, 1947-48; payroll clk. Akron Parcel Co., 1948-50; payroll clk. Ace Rubber Co., Akron, 1950-53, acct., 1953-77; exec. v.p. Gasoil Energy, Inc., Canton, Ohio, 1977-82; corp. sec. Davage Oil & Gas Co., Phoenix, 1982—, bd. dir., Profile Mgmt., Inc., Canton; bd. dirs., sec. Davage Tech. Inc., Chandler, Ariz., 1987—; cons. Sq. Circle Devel. Corp., Phoenix, 1985; sec. bd. dir. Paragon Steel Structures, Inc., Chandler, Ariz., 1986—; real estate agt. Roy H. Long Realty Co., Tucson. Mem. NAFE, Am. Soc. Profl. and Exec. Women, Precious Moments Club, Goebel Collectors, Riker-Bartlett Club (Ft. Collins, Colo.). Republican. Lutheran. Avocations: collecting antiques, art and limited editions of pewter, glass and porcelain. Home: 8660 N Hollybrook Ave Tucson AZ 85741

ZENDT, ESTHER VIRGINIA, teacher; b. Indpls., May 20, 1914; d. Guy Israel and Virginia (Dillinger) Hoover; m. Frederick Eugene Zendt, Sept. 9, 1939; children: Stephen Hoover, Virginia Swift Zendt Lomax, Mary Eugenia (dec.). BA, Butler U., 1936; MA, U. N.Mex., 1962. Tchr. Garfield Jr. High Sch., Albuquerque, 1958-61; English and reading tchr. Hermosa Jr. High Sch., Farmington, N.Mex., 1961-64, Don Julio Jr. High Sch., North Highlands, Calif., 1965-72; ret. Don Julio Jr. High Sch., 1972. Author poetry. Mem. NEA, Calif. Edn. Assn. (life), AAUW, Kappa Alpha Theta. Democrat. Presbyterian. Home: 3432 A Ardendale Ln Sacramento CA 95825

ZENI, JANE ELIZABETH, English educator; b. N.Y., Oct. 4, 1945; d. Rudolph R. and Doris (Auclair) Z.; m. Frank K. Flinn, Aug. 20, 1966 (div. 1986); children: Adam Pablo, Mark Hosteen. BA in English, Harvard U., Cambridge, 1968; MA in English, U. Pa., Phila., 1969; MEd, Ontario Inst. for Studies in Edn., 1977; EdD, U. Mo., 1985. Tchr. English, urban studies Community Camp Sch., Phila., 1969-70; resource tchr. No. Pueblos Schs, Bur. of Indian Affairs, N.Mex., 1970-72; sec. English tchr. St. Michael's High Sch., Santa Fe, N.Mex., 1973-75; freelance writer, editor, translator Toronto, 1975-77; lectr. English and edn. U. Mo., St. Louis, 1977-86, asst. prof., 1986—; dir. Gateway Writing Project UM-St. Louis, 1981—; cons. various schs. Writing Process, Computers, Writing Assessment, 1984—; co-chmn. Acad. Teleconference on Composition and Design Computers, 1985-87. Editor: Reflections on Writing, 1981; co-editor: New Routes to Writing, 1984; Author: Role of Instruction in Revising with Computers, 1986; contbr. articles to profl. jours. Mem. Greater St. Louis English Tchrs. Assn., Nat. Council of Tchrs of English, Conf. on Coll. Composition & Communication, Ethnography in Edn. Research Forum, Nat. Writing Project, Fund for Improvement of Postsecondary Edn. (tech. study group, grantee 1984-87), Harvard Club (St. Louis), Phi Beta Kappa. Office: Univ Mo St Louis English Dept 8001 Natural Bridge Rd Saint Louis MO 63121

ZENKOVSKY, BETTY JEAN, modern languages educator; b. Mankato, Minn., Mar. 6, 1927; d. William and Sarah Carroll (Cloyd) Bubbers; m. Serge A. Zenkovsky, May 10, 1952. AB, U. Mich., 1950; AM, Ind. U., 1954. Instr. in modern langs. Stetson U., DeLand, Fla., 1958-60, asst. prof., 1962-65; instr. in fgn. langs. U. Colo., Boulder, 1960-62; vis. lectr. Vanderbilt U., Nashville, 1967-68; rsch. assoc., translator NEH, DeLand, 1978-82. Co-translator: The Nikonian Chronicle, (5 vols.), 1984, 86, 88, 89. Mem. AAUW (pres. Deland chpt. 1982-84, sec. Daytona Beach, Fla. chpt. 1984-86), Am. Assn. for Advancement of Slavic Studies, Am. Assn. Tchrs. Slavic and Ea. European Langs., DAR (chpt. James Ormond br., vice regent 1988-89), UN Assn. Democrat. Greek Orthodox. Home: 1224 S Peninsula Dr #507 Daytona Beach FL 32118

ZENO, JO ANN, sales executive; b. Akron, Ohio, Sept. 25, 1952; d. Ross and Mary Francis (Gerbec) Z. BA in French and Edn., BS in Spanish, U. Akron, 1975. Tchr. French, Spanish S.E. Local, Ravenna, Ohio, 1975-77, Akron Pub. Schs., 1977-80; sales rep. Xerox Corp., Akron, Cleve., 1980-83; cert. stapling technician U.S. Surg. Corp., Norwalk, Conn., 1983-88; rep. cardiovascular surg. products Medtronic Inc., 1988—. Home: 272 Somerset Rd Akron OH 44313

ZENOR, CATHRYN LENORA, financial executive; b. Opp, Ala., Dec. 30, 1955; d. Donald Franklin and Betty Jean (Huff) Colquett; m. Mark David Gray, Aug. 1978 (div. Oct. 1979); m. Phillip Lee Zenor, Apr. 4, 1980; 1 child, Jessica Florance. BA in Psychology, Auburn U., 1977; MBA in Fin., Calif. State U., San Bernadino, 1983. Instr. math and fin. Auburn (Ala.) U., Ala.; mgr. Johnson Sterling Paul & Co., Auburn, 1985—; bd. dirs. Formal Systems Design & Devel., Inc., Auburn, 1986—. Recipient Student Achievement award Wall St. Jour., 1983. Republican. Office: Johnson Sterling Paul & Co 223 E Magnolia Ave Auburn AL 36830

ZEOLLA, CONNIE, marketing consultant; b. Decorata, Beneviento, Italy; d. Pietro Paulo and Caterina (Piacquadio) Z.; m. Daniel Mark Levine, Nov. 24, 1989. BA, NYU; MBA, Pace U. Account exec. Ketchum, N.Y.C., 1983-87; freelance mktg. cons. N.Y.C. and, Italy, 1988—. Mem. Advt. Women of N.Y.

ZERA, CAROL JOYCE, management consultant; b. Pitts., Oct. 18, 1943; d. James K. and Kathleen (Lantz) Carpenter; m. Ronald Joseph Zera, Jan. 28, 1981. BA, Westminster Coll., New Wilmington, Pa., 1965; MA, U. Pitts., 1968. Tchr. State Coll. (Pa.) High Sch., 1968-69; staff asst. Carnegie Mellow U., Pitts., 1970-74; asst. prof., lectr. U. Pitts., 1974-86; dir. Writing Cons. Assoc., Pitts.; cons. Westinghouse Electric Co., 1980-, Pitts., Electric Power Research Inst., Palo Alto, Calif., 1983--. Contbr. articles to profl. jours. Com. woman Democratic Group, Wilkinsburg, Pa. Mem. Nat. Assn. Women Bus. Owners, Soc. Tech. Communication, Assn. Profl. Writing Cons., Assn. for Bus. Communication. Home: Writing Cons Assn 917 S Braddock Ave Pittsburgh PA 15221

ZERBA, JANET ANN, home health care company administrator; b. Lansing, Mich., Sept. 29, 1941; d. Clare Jay and Thelma Marie (Hollenbeck) Reynolds; m. Jimmy A. Zerba, Mar. 21, 1959; divorced; remarried, Feb. 3, 1979; children: Michael, Russell, Jeffrey (dec.), Melinda (dec.); m. Winton Erwin Walker, Nov. 27, 1975 (dec. Nov. 1976). LPN, Lansing Community Coll., 1970, AS in Nursing, 1976. RN, charge nurse Hayes Green Beach Hosp., Charlotte, Mich., 1976-78; RN, nursing supr. Kelly Health Care, Lansing, 1978-84; adminstr. Comprehensive Med. Home Care, Lansing, 1984-86; v.p. home care services Medair Equipment Supply, Lansing, 1986-87; dir. clin. services Americor Home Health Services, Lansing, 1987-88; adminstr. UpJohn Health-Care Services, Lansing, 1988; regional mgr. Allen Health Care, Cass City, Mich., 1988-89; adminstr. Shoreline Healthcare Svcs., Lansing, 1989—; profl. adv. and clin. record rev. bds., Americor Home Health Services, Lansing, 1984—; cons. Home Health Services of Mid-Mich., Midland, 1986. Mem. Assn. Career Women (bd. dirs. 1983-84), Capitol Area Discharge Planners (co-chmn. 1980-81, 84-85). Home: 4914 Hudson Dimondale MI 48821

ZERBE, PAMELA LYNN, human resources executive, director; b. Harrisburg, Pa., Dec. 9, 1959; d. Harvey Charles and Goria Mae (Harris) Z. BA in Labor Rels., Pa. State U., 1981. Labor rels. and tng. specialist Office of Atty. Gen. Commonwealth of Pa., Harrisburg, 1981-85; employee rels. rep. Diversified Printing, Atglen, Pa., 1985-87; supr. human resources Computer Scis. Corp., Dayton, Ohio, 1987-88; mgr. human resources Computer Scis. Corp., Fairfax, Va., 1988-89; dir. human resources Presearch Inc., Fairfax, 1989—. Mem. Smithsonian Inst., Washington, 1987—, Mothers Against Drunk Driving, 1989—. Mem. Assn. for Part Time Profls., Soc. for Human Resources Mgmt., NAFE, Willow Club, Pa. State Alumni Assn., Nat. Mus. of Women in the Arts. Republican. Lutheran. Office: Presearch Inc 8500 Executive Park Ave Fairfax VA 22031

ZERBO, RITA MICHAELLE, small business owner; b. Indpls., Aug. 13, 1946; d. Robert Cherry Day and Rose Mary Margaret (Anderson) Philabaum; m. Joseph Nels Zerbo, Feb. 11, 1966 (div. Feb. 1979); children: Phillip Brian, Andrea Michaelle. Student, Howard Community Coll., 1978-82. Clk. Blue Cross/Blue Shield, Indpls., 1964-66; advt. rep. The Post Register, Idaho Falls, 1969-71; real estate sales rep. Grempler Real Estate, Columbia, Md., 1977—; advt. coordinator real estate mag. Stromberg Pubs., Elliott City, Md., 1977-79; advt. sales rep. Army Times Publ. Co., Washington, 1979-80, The News Am., Balt., 1980; owner, pres. Classy Maids Inc., Elliott City, 1980—. Founder, pub. Sagebrush News, Idaho Falls, 1969-71. co-dir. exposition Nat. Housing Mgmt., Washington, 1977. Episcopalian. Club: Navy Wives (Idaho Falls) (pres. 1969-70). Office: Classy Maids Inc 10744 Frederick Rd Ellicott City MD 21043

ZERBY, JUDY ANN, journalist, consultant; b. Neenah, Wis., Mar. 5, 1941; d. Frank B. and Virginia M. (Huss) De Bruin; m. Michael Zerby (div.); children: M. Scott, Christopher M., Laura K.; m. Charles C. Classen, Dec. 31, 1988. B. Elected Studies, U. Minn., 1978. Assoc. news producer Sta. KMSP/TV, Mpls., 1977-78; producer Sta. WCCO/TV, Mpls., 1978-80; author, pub. Mijaz, Inc., Mpls., 1980-84; dir. pub. rels. Vinland Nat. Ctr., Loretto, Minn., 1984; v.p. Barron and Zerby, Inc., St. Paul, 1985-86; pres., freelance writer Cygnet Communications, Ltd., Lindenhurst, Ill., 1987—. Author: Wisconsin Travel Companion, 1983; editor: Minnesota Travel Companion, 1982. Mem. Fridley (Minn.) High Sch. Bd., 1984-87, vice chmn., 1986. Mem. Women in Communications, Ninety-Nines, U. Minn. Alumni Assn. (pres. Mpls. chpt. 1985-86). Democrat. Office: Cygnet Communications Ltd 151 Dittmer Ln #2D Lindenhurst IL 60046

ZERFOSS, LINDA LOUISE, ruminant nutritionist; b. Rochester, Minn., Jan. 22, 1953; d. Ivan Stewart and Iona Louise (Wilker) Behnken; m. John Frederick Zerfoss, Dec. 20, 1974; children: Jeremy, Jessey, Leah. BS in Animal Sci., Utah State U., 1977; MS in Ruminant Nutrition, U. Minn., 1981. Lic. artificial inseminator - bovine and equine. Assoc. grad. U. Minn., St. Paul, 1977-81; research beef tech. U. Nebr., North Platte, 1981-84; office mgr. computers Sharie Swenson CPA, Boulder City, Nev., 1986-89; substitute Clark County Sch. Dist., Las Vegas, Nev., 1986—. Contbr. articles to Jour. of Animal Sci., 1984, 86-88. Daycamp dir. Boy Scouts Am., Boulder City, 1987-89; recreation coach Boulder City Pks. and Recreation, 1984-89; mem., chmn. Boulder City Community Health Bd., 1986-89; pres. PTA, Boulder City, 1986-88; mem. Parenting Resource Com., Boulder City, 1987-89. Recipient Golden Rose award Lambda, 1988, Scouter award Boy Scouts Am., 1989, Boy Scout Religious award. Mem. Am. Soc. Animal Sci., AAUW (pres. 1988-90), U. Minn. Alumni Assn. Democrat. Lutheran. Home: 704 Ave A Boulder City NV 89005 Office: 533 Nevada Hwy Boulder City NV 89005

ZETTLER, VALLORIE RAYE, investment company executive; b. Ft. Worth, Feb. 21, 1961; d. Cecil Ray Vossler and Vivian Leigh (Schoeppey) Bransford; m. Stephen Dale Zettler, Apr. 12, 1980; children: Lauren Michelle, Jennifer Shannon. Registered gen. securities rep. Investment advisor A.G. Edwards & Sons, Inc., Ft. Worth, 1982—. Vol. United Way, Ft. Worth, 1988, Mayfest, Ft. Worth, 1986, Campfire, Ft. Worth, 1990. Recipient Cert. of Appreciation Tex. Edn. Agy., 1990. Fellow Exec. Women Internat. (sgt.-at-arms 1987), Securities Dealers. Republican. Lutheran. Office: A G Edwards & Sons Inc 1701 River Run Ste 100 Fort Worth TX 76107

ZEVON, SUSAN JANE, editor; b. N.Y.C., July 23, 1944; d. Louis and Rhea (Alter) Z. BA, Smith Coll., 1966. Asst. editor trends and environments House & Garden, N.Y.C., 1970-80; account supr. Jessica Dee Communications, N.Y.C., 1981-84; editor architecture House Beautiful, N.Y.C., 1985—. Author: (with others) Decorating On The Cheap, 1984. Mem. Archtl. League N.Y., Smith Coll. N.Y. Club (v.p. 1987-88, pres. 1988-89). Office: House Beautiful 1700 Broadway New York NY 10019

ZEZZA, MARGARET ANN, publishing executive; b. Pitts., May 17, 1962; d. Louis and Regina (Rossetti) Z. BA, Point Park Coll., Pitts., 1984. Prodn. designer Pitts. Cath., 1984-87, circulation mgr., 1987—. Asst. St. Maurice Parish Newsletter, Pitts., 1990; CCD tchr. St. Maurice Parish, 1989. Mem. Women in Communications, Cath. Press Assn. Home: 29 Fairview Rd Pittsburgh PA 15221 Office: Pittsburgh Catholic 100 Wood St #500 Pittsburgh PA 15222

ZICCARDI, KAREN M. MYERS, interior designer; b. Jersey City; d. Harold Charles Myers and Margaret Elizabeth (Moore) Natelli; m. Raymond John Ziccardi; 1 child, Brooke Lillian. BA in Art Edn., Jersey State Coll., 1968; student, U. Copenhagen, 1967; MA in Environ. Design, UCLA, 1970, MFA in Environ. Design, 1971. Cert. tchr., Calif. Teaching asst. UCLA, Westwood, 1968-71; art instr. El Camino Coll., Torrance, Calif., 1971; pres. Interior Design Devel., Inc., Costa Mesa, Calif., 1971—; speaker, Calif. State U., Long Beach; adv. bd., Bus. to Bus. mag. Contbr. articles to profl. publs. Mem. Am. Soc. Interior Designers (Celebrity Suites award), Bldg. Industry Assn., Newport Harbor Art Mus., Orange County Performing Arts Ctr., Chancellor's Club U. Calif. Irvine, UCLA Alumni Assn. Episcopalian. Office: Interior Design Devel Inc D 3188 Airway Ave Costa Mesa CA 92626

ZICH, SUE SCHAAB, nursing administrator, consultant; b. Buffalo, Oct. 18, 1946; d. Milan Harvey and Mary Margaret (Olmsted) Schaab; B.S. in Nursing, Villa Maria Coll., 1968; m. Timothy John Zich, Nov. 25, 1976; children—John Paul Trottman, Scott Francis Trottman. Staff nurse, charge nurse, team leader Children's Hosp., Buffalo, 1968-71; staff nurse plasmapheresis unit Roswell Park Meml. Inst., Buffalo, 1971-72, 73-75; staff devel. coordinator Episcopal Ch. Home, Buffalo, 1975-77; pediatric unit charge nurse Loudoun Meml. Hosp., Leesburg, Va., 1977; nursing instr. No. Va. Mental Health Inst., Falls Church, 1977-78; dir. nursing service Barcroft Inst., Falls Church, Va., 1978—; cons. nursing home design and remodeling systems, 1986—. Troop com. mem. Troop 884, 1978—, den leader, 1980-85, den leader coach Pack 1182, 1983-88, dist. mem. Prince William Dist. Boy Scouts Am., day camp dir. Cub Scout Camp Tomahawk, 1983-87, asst. cub roundtable commr., 1986—, Prince William Dist. tng. team, 1981-87, co-chmn., 1988—, vice chmn. membership, 1988; mem. Buckhall Fire Dept. Aux. Recipient Key Leader award Prince William dist. Boy Scouts Am., 1982, Den Leader Tng. award Boy Scouts Am., 1982, Dist. Merit award Boy Scouts Am., 1985, Den Leader Coach Tng. award Boy Scouts Am., 1986, Scouter's Tng. award Boy Scouts Am., 1986. Mem. Dir. Nurses Group No. Va. (sec.-treas. 1980-81, v.p. 1981-87), Va. Dirs. Nursing Assn., Nat. Campers and Hikers Assn., Friends of Nat. Zoo, Smithsonian Assocs., Met. Washington Soccer Referees Assn., Va. High Sch. League Ofcl., Commonwealth Indoor/Outdoor Soccer Ofcls. Assn., D.C./Nova Soccer Referees Assn., Piedmont Soccer Referees Assn., NIFOA, Villa Maria Coll. Alumnae Assn. (life, past. pres. Buffalo chpt.), Mt. St. Mary Alumnae Assn. (life), St. Edmund's Ladies Guild (pres. 1972-73, advisor 1973-74). Roman Catholic. Home: 9709 Evans Ford Rd Manassas VA 22111 Office: 2960 Sleepy Hollow Rd Falls Church VA 22044

ZICK, JANICE LEE, financial executive; b. Litchfield, Ill., Nov. 11, 1958; d. Harold Gene and Donna Lee (Duelm) Knoche; m. Stanton Jerome Zick, Jan. 9, 1982; 1 child, Lacie Dawn. BS in Bus., Eastern Ill. U., 1980. Tax technician Horace Mann Co., Springfield, Ill., 1980, planning analyst, 1980-82, mgr. corp. tax compliance, 1982-87, dir. corp. budget and fin. planning, 1987%. Bible sch. tchr. Zion Luth. Ch., Bunker Hill, Ill., 1972; Sunday sch. tchr. Immanuel Luth. Ch., Riverton, Ill., 1989. Fellow Life Office Mgmt. Assn. Republican. Office: Horace Mann 1 Horace Mann Pla Springfield IL 62715

ZIDE-BOOTH, ROCHELLE DEENA, dance educator; b. Boston, Apr. 21, 1938; d. David Sewell and Ruthe (Sawyer) Zide; m. Robert Elliot Booth, Aug. 2, 1964; children: Jeremy Scott, James Israel, Elissa Anne. BA, Adelphi U., 1990. Soloist Ballet Russe de Monte Carlo, 1954-58; prin. dancer Robert Joffrey Ballet, 1958-62; prima ballerina N.Y.C. Opera Ballet, 1962-65; ballet mistress Joffrey Ballet, 1965-67; artistic dir. Netherlands Dance Theatre, The Hague, 1973-75; prof. dance Adelphi U., Garden City, N.Y., 1975—; head ballet dept. Jacob's Pillow Dance Festival, Lee, Mass., 1975-79; adjudicator Nat. Assn. Regional Ballet, N.Y.C., 1973, 77, 80, 82, 84, 88, 90, 1st Nat. Regional Dance Festival, 1990; mem. faculty Alvin Ailey Am. Dance Ctr., 1989—. Choreographer: (ballets) Psalms, 1979, As Quiet As..., 1982, Russian Suite, 1982, Folksing, 1983, Freeplay, 1984, Screen Scenes, 1984, Glory Songs, 1985, Silent Woods, 1986, Rococo Variations, 1986, Gershwin!, 1987, A Midsummer Night's Dream, 1987, The Sisters of My Sister, 1988, Mujerio, 1989, Bagatelle, 1989, ; lectr., co-chmn. Yom-Hashoah Com., Merrick-Bellmore, N.Y., 1984; cert. reconstructor Dance Notation Bur., N.Y.C.; contbr. articles to profl. jours. Mem. Am. Guild Mus. Artists (bd. govs. 1959-65), Am. Coll. Dance Festival (adjudicator 1989, 90). Democrat. Jewish. Avocations: theater, classical music concerts, reading, traveling, baseball. Home: 170-16 Henley Rd Jamaica Estates NY 11432 Office: Adelphi U Woodruff Hall Garden City NY 11530

ZIEFF, LEAH ROSE, counselor, instructor; b. Newton, Mass., Mar. 8, 1941; d. Israel and Lillian (Aronson) Kahalas; (div. 1974); children: Eric, Jonathan, Julie. BA, Boston U., 1963; MEd, U. Maine, 1974. Cert. secondary edn. tchr., Mass. Substitute tchr. Newton Pub. Schs., 1975-77; adminstrv. asst. Phys. Measurements, 1977-78; trainer, workshop leader Nevest, Waltham, Mass., 1977-78; employment counselor/interviewer Mass. Div. Employment Security, Waltham, 1978-88; workshop instr. Needham (Mass.) Pub. Schs., 1980-88; vocat. counselor Guinobin, Wellesley, Mass., 1981-85; guidance counselor Blue Hills Regional Tech. Sch., Canton, Mass., 1985—; career counselor, 1979—. Home: 15 Birch St Needham MA 02194

ZIEGEL, BARI ANN, marketing professional; b. N.Y.C., Nov. 25, 1959; d. Leonard and Norma (Nemeth) Z.; m. Steven M. Rosman, Sept. 8, 1984; 1 child, Michal Sima Ziegel Rosman. BBA, Hofstra U., 1980. Ops., sales rep. Unitours, Inc., N.Y.C., 1980-82; adminstrv. asst. Bozell and Jacobs, Inc., N.Y.C., 1982-83, Parfums Stern, Inc., N.Y.C., 1983-85; mgmt. assoc. Citicorp Indsl. Credit, Inc., Harrison, N.Y., 1985-87; mktg. officer Citicorp Indsl. Credit, Inc., Rye, N.Y., 1987-88; mgr. area AT&T Credit Corp., Valhalla, N.Y., 1988—. Mem. NAFE, Women in Equipment Leasing. Jewish. Office: AT&T Credit Corp 100 Summit Lake Dr 2d Fl Valhalla NY 10595

ZIEGLER, BEVERLY ANN, advocate; b. Los Angeles, Nov. 7, 1934; d. Francis Raymond and Fern Alberta (Price) McGerty; m. Edward Nile, Apr. 27, 1956, (dec. Nov., 1983). Registered legis. advocate. Political cons. Ziegler Assocs., L.A., 1964—; adminstrv. dir. Calif. Electric Sign Assn., 1973-76; adminstrv. mgr. Calif. Apt. Assn., 1976-80, Apt. Assn. L.A., 1980-82; owner Beverly Ziegler & Assocs., L.A., 1982—; bd. dirs. L.A. Water & Power Assocs.; pres. Griffith Park Hills CRA, L.A., 1985—; polit. cons. rental housing industry; rep. community rels. Kawada Co. Am., Ltd. Past Pres. Women's Div., Los Angeles Greater Area C. of C., 1975-76, So. Calif. Rep. Women; Sr. V.p. So. Calif. Rep. Women; active L.A. City Atty. Housing Task Force, Women's Crusade for a Common Sense Economy, Los Fiesteros, Cultural Heritage Found., Griffith Park Hills CRA, Calif. Fedn. Rep. Women, Los Angeles County Cen. Com.; mem. Atty. Gen's. Task Force on Womens Rights. Recipient Meritorious Community Svc. Cert., Los Angeles, Los Angeles Human Relations Commn., Los Angeles Neighborhood Youth Corp., Bd. of Edn.; Cert. of Appreciation Bulgarian Am. Reps. Mem. Citizens Legal Defense League. Republican. Roman Catholic. Home and Office: 200 N Mariposa Ave Los Angeles CA 90004

ZIEGLER, DHYANA, broadcasting educator; b. N.Y.C., May 5, 1949; d. Ernest and Alberta Allie (Guy) Z. BS cum laude, CUNY, 1981; MA in Radio and TV, So. Ill. U., 1983, PhD in Higher Edn., 1985. Freelance researcher Essence Mag., N.Y.C., 1972-75; copywriter, radio producer Rosenfeld, Sirowitz & Lawson Advt. Agy., N.Y.C., 1974-75; exec. v.p. Patten & Guest Prodns., N.Y.C., 1976-79; prodn. intern Sta. WNEW TV, N.Y.C., 1979-80; upward bound counselor Seton Hall U., South Orange, N.Y., 1979-81; prodn. intern Sta. WCBS TV, N.Y.C., 1980-81; asst. prof. Jackson (Miss.) State U., 1984-85; assoc. prof. U. Tenn., Knoxville, 1985—; bd. dirs. Knoxville Women's Ctr., 1989-92; bd. trustees East Tenn. Discovery Ctr., Knoxville, 1989-92; adv. bd. Bethel Love Kitchen, Knoxville, 1990-93. Contbr. articles to profl. jours.; producer, dir. (video documentary) Single Parenting, 1988 (second place award Nat. Fedn. Press Women), Rape is a Reality, 1982 (UPI award outstanding achievement 1982). Chair communications Knoxville chpt. NAACP, 1990—, chpt. advisor U. Tenn. student chpt., 1989—; chair social action com. Delta Sigma Theta, Knoxville, 1986-89; bd. dirs. E. Tenn. reg. The Am. Herat Assn., 1990—; mem. athletics bd. U. Tenn., 1990—; reg. devel. edn. coordinator Delta Rsch. and Ednl. Found. Grantee, FIPSE, U.S. Dept. Edn., 1989—, Delta Rsch. & Ednl. Found., 1987, 90. Mem. Women in Communications (pres. Knoxville chpt. 1990—), Broadcast Edn. Assn. (chair minority div. 1989—), Radio & TV News Dirs. Assn., Speech Communications Assn., Kappa Tau Alpha, Phi Delta Kappa, Sigma Delta Chi. Office: U Tenn 295 Communications Bldg Knoxville TN 37996

ZIEGLER, JAN, science writer; b. Hartford, Conn., Oct. 18, 1953; d. Richard T. and Margaret (Whinnem) Z. BA, U. Conn., 1975. Reporter, photographer, features editor The Norwich (Conn.) Bulletin, 1975-78; reporter UPI, Hartford, Conn., 1978-79; sci. writer, broadcast writer, New England weekend editor UPI, Boston, 1979-82; editor fgn. desk UPI, N.Y.C., 1982-83; sci. writer UPI, Washington, 1983-87, sci. editor, 1987-88; free-lance writer, media cons. Washington, 1989—. Contbr. Omni, National Geographic, The Scientist. Bd. dirs. Cleve. Park hist. Soc., Washington, 1986-87; cons. nat. vaccine program USPHS. Mem. Women in Communications, Inc. Home and Office: 3726 Connecticut Ave NW 508 Washington DC 20008

ZIEGLER, JANET CASSARO, nurse; b. Bklyn., Oct. 26, 1946; d. Dominic Michael and Rose (Locascio) Cassaro; m. Paul Dennis Ziegler, Nov. 1, 1970; children: Paul Dennis, Daniel Peter, Michael Tyson. BS in Nursing, D'Youville Coll., 1968; M in Nursing, U. Pitts., 1975. Instr. Norfolk (Va.) State Coll., 1970-72; pvt. practice in childbirth edn. Va., 1971-72, Pitts., 1972-81; clin. nurse specialist Vis. Nurse Assn. Allegheny County, Pitts., 1975-83; nurse-healer Therapeutic Rehab. Services, Pitts., 1982—; educator, cons. Am. Soc. Psychoprophylatis in Obstetrics, Pitts., 1971-81; practitioner, educator Clin. Hypnosis, Pitts., 1982—, Biofeedback Inst. Am., Wheat Ridge, Colo., 1983—; practitioner, cons., educator Therapeutic Touch, Pitts., 1981—. Served to lt. USN, 1968-70. Mem. Am. Holistic Nurses Assn., Nurse Healer's Profl. Assocs., Biofeedback and Behavioral Medicine Assn. of Western Pa., Assn. Clin. Nurse Specialists, Aloha Internat., People's Med. Soc., Inst. Noetic Scis. Republican. Roman Catholic. Home: 4566 Dogwood Dr Allison Park PA 15101

ZIEGLER, LYNDA K., nurse; b. Columbus, Ind., Feb. 21, 1964; d. Donald J. and Dorothy Jean (Harris) Burton; m. John E. Ziegler, Jan. 30, 1988. BS in Nursing, U. Indpls., 1987. RN, Ind. Dist. nurse Vis. Nurse Assn. Louisville; head nurse Columbus (Ind.) Convalescent Ctr., asst. dir. nursing.

ZIEGLER, SANDRA KAY, editor; b. Chalmers, Ind., May 25, 1938; d. Hanley Jay and Geneva Margaret (Wilson) Summers; m. Neil C. Ziegler, Nov. 16, 1968 (dec. Jan. 1988). B in Christian Edn., Minn. Bible Coll. 1962. Product editor Standard Pub., Cin., 1962-66; new products mng. editor David C. Cook Pub. Co., Elgin, Ill., 1966-73; freelance writer, editor Corpus Christi, Tex., 1973-78; bus. form designer Moore Paper Forms of the Valley, Harlingen, Tex., 1978-79; freeland writer, editor Richland, Wash., 1979-83; children's book editor The Child's World, Inc., Elgin, 1983—; speaker 15th Annual Ill. Young Author's Conf., Normal, Ill., 1989; pres. Christian Women's Fellowship, Elgin, 1989-90. Pub. books including A Visit to the Airport, 1988, A Visit to the Post Office, 1989, A Visit to the Natural History Museum, 1989; contbr. articles to jours. Bd. dir. Elgin (Ill.) Community Theatre (publicity chmn. 1972, 73). Mem. Chgo. Women in Pub., Children's Reading Round Table. Republican. Mem. Church of Christ. Home: 1162 Manchester Ct South Elgin IL 60177-1410 Office: The Childs World Inc 1750 Grandstand Pl Elgin IL 60123

ZIEGLER, SHEILA GERBER, systems consultant, sales executive; b. Bklyn., July 14, 1949; d. Irving and Anne (Wolf) Gerber; m. Ivan Donald Ziegler, June 14, 1970; children: Craig Howard, Alison Jaye. BA in Elem. Edn., Bklyn. Coll., 1970; MS in Reading and Edn., Queens Coll., 1973. Cert. tchr. N.Y. Tchr. N.Y.C. Bd. Edn., 1970-75; office mgr. C and D Bus. Products, Inc., Hicksville, N.Y., 1982-86; forms cons., sales rep. Standard Forms, Inc., Westbury, N.Y., 1986—. Pres. Newcomers Club, Plainview, N.Y., 1977; v.p. edn. Temple Beth Torah, Westbury, 1988-90; pres. Young Couples Club-Bethpage (N.Y.) Jewish Community Ctr., 1979, Young Couples Club, Temple Beth Torah, 1980; v.p. Women's Am. Orgn. for Rehab. Through Tng., Plainview, 1978. Mem. NAFE. Republican. Jewish. Office: Standard Forms Inc 6800 Jericho Turnpike Jericho NY 11753

ZIEGRA, ALICE STEVENSON, state legislator; b. Boston, Feb. 26, 1927; d. Thomas Milton and Ruth Elinor (Tisdale) Stevenson; m. Louis Richard Ziegra, May 23, 1953 (dec. June 1985); children: James Cornwell, Ames Folger. BS in Nursing, Skidmore Coll., 1949. RN, N.H., Conn. Staff nurse Boston Vis. Nurse Assn., 1950-52, State Dept. Health, Hartford, Conn., 1952-55, Rural Dist. Health Coun., Farmington, N.H., 1975—; legislator N.H Gen. Ct. (Ho. of Reps.), Concord, 1988—. Mem. Am. Nurses Assn., Nat. Nurses Assn. Republican. Home: RFD 1 Box 165 Alton NH 03809

ZIELECK, KARIN LAURA LEE, marketing executive; b. Houston, Dec. 2, 1948; d. Thomas Leland and Margie Mae (Winsman) Mangum; m. Rock Lawrence Zieleck. BA, U. Houston, 1976; postgrad., U. Tex., Houston, 1989. Fin. coord. western hemisphere Martin Decker div. Cooper Industries, Houston, 1979-82; cons. spl. projects Clear Lake sports Medicine Profl. Leisure Seminars, Houston, 1982-86, The Penmark Group, League City, Tex., 1986—; pres. KRZ Enterprises, Inc., Bellaire, Tex., 1982—. Mem. Nat. Soc. Performance and Instrn., Am. Med. Writers Assn., Clear Lake Area C. of C. (pub. rels. co-chmn. 1988, 89). Democrat. Episcopalian. Office: KRZ Enterprises Inc 4905 Welford Bellaire TX 77401

ZIELSKI, GLENDA JOYCE, health administrator; b. Beaver Dam, Wis., Nov. 26, 1952; d. Herman and June Beatrice (Douma) Westra; m. Dennis James, June 2, 1973; children: Michael D., Kristen A. BS, UW, River Falls, 1974. Social svc. dir. River Falls Care Ctr., River Falls, Wis., 1974-76; asst. nursing home adminstra. River Falls Care Ctr., 1976-78, nursing home adminstra., 1978—; bd. dirs. Wis. Assn. Nursing Home, Madison, Pierce-St. Croix Employer Com., Hudson, Long Term Support Com., Hudson. Bd. dirs. United Way of River Falls, River Falls, 1987. Fellow: Am. Coll. of Health Care Adminstra. Office: River Falls Care Center 640 N Main Street River Falls WI 54022

ZIERCHER, JULIA ANN, managing editor; b. St. Louis, June 28, 1937; d. Herbert William and Elizabeth Ziercher. B.A., Washington U., St. Louis, 1959; M.S. in English Lit., U. Wis.-Madison, 1962. Jr. high sch. English tchr. Huntington, N.Y., 1960-63, Ladue, Mo., 1963-65; copy editor Surgery jour., C.V. Mosby Co., St. Louis, 1965-66; sr. editing supr. McGraw-Hill Book Co., St. Louis and N.Y.C., 1966-72; sales rep. Alex Taylor & Co. Inc., N.Y.C., 1972-74; copy editing supr. Harper & Row, N.Y.C., 1974-77; mng. editor children's books, Dutton Children's Books, N.Y.C., 1977-89, The Trumpet Club, 1989—. Office: The Trumpet Club 35th Fl 666 Fifth Ave New York NY 10103

ZIGMOND, SALLY HOUSEHOLDER, biology educator; b. Kalamazoo, Mich., Feb. 5, 1944; d. Frank and Elizabeth (Gardner) Householder; m. Richard Zigmond, Aug. 1969 (div. 1976); m. Peter Sterling, Aug. 16, 1986. BA, Wellesley Coll., 1966; PhD, Ruckefeller U., 1972; MA (hon.), U. Pa., Phila., 1977. Prof. biology U. Pa., Phila., 1976, chair cell biology Med. Sch., 1987-90, chair biology dept., 1990—. Mem. Am. Soc. Cell Biology (mem. coun. 1988-91, asst. editor jour. Cell Biology 1986-89).

ZIGUN, SYLVIA HELENE, psychotherapist, health educator; b. N.Y.C., July 28, 1934; d. David J. and Anna (Felenstein) Moscovitz; m. Charles Zigun, June 9, 1957; children: Jeffrey, Benjamin. BA, Brown U., 1954; MN, Yale U., 1957; MS, U. Bridgeport, 1980; PhD, The Union Inst., 1989. R.N., Conn. Psychotherapist Psychotherapy Assocs. Fairfield, Conn., 1979—; cons. State of Conn. div. ARC health nursing programs, 1974-79; chmn. nursing svcs. Southeastern Fairfield chpt. ARC, 1974-76, childbirth educator, 1974-76. Mem. ANA, Internat. Acad. Nutrition and Preventive Medicine, N.Y. Acad. Scis., Conn. Nurses Assn., Sigma Xi, Phi Beta Kappa. Home and Office: Psychotherapy Assocs Fairfield 400 Post Rd Fairfield CT 06430

ZIKMUND, BARBARA BROWN, minister, seminary president, church history educator; b. Ann Arbor, Mich., Oct. 16, 1939; d. Henry Daniels and Helen (Langworthy) Brown; m. Joseph Zikmund II, Aug. 26, 1961; 1 child, Brian Joseph. BA, Beloit Coll., 1961; BDiv, Duke U., 1964, PhD, 1969; D in Div (hon.), Doane Coll., 1984, Chgo. Theol. Sem., 1985, Ursinus Coll., 1989. Ordained to ministry United Ch. of Christ, 1964. Instr. Albright Coll., Reading, Pa., 1966-67, Temple U., Phila., 1967-68, Ursinus Coll., Collegeville, Pa., 1968-69; asst. prof. religion studies Albion Coll., Mich., 1970-75; asst. prof. ch. history, div. studies Chgo. Theol. Sem., 1975-80; dean and assoc. prof. ch. history Pacific Sch. Religion, Berkeley, Calif., 1981-85, dean and prof. ch. history, 1985-90; pres. Hartford (Conn.) Sem., 1990—; chmn. United Ch. of Christ Hist. Coun., 1983-85, mem. coun. for ecumenism 1983-89; mem. Nat. Coun. Chs. Commn. on Faith and Order, 1979-87, World Coun. of Chs. Programme Theol. Edn., 1984—. Author: Discovering the Church, 1983. Editor: Hidden Histories in the UCC, 1984, vol. 2, 1987; (with Manschreck) American Religious Experiment, 1976; editorial bd. Jour. Ecumenical Studies, 1987—; contbr. articles to profl. jours. Mem. City Coun., Albion, Mich., 1972-75. Woodrow Wilson fellow, 1964-66; NEH grantee, 1974-75; vis. scholar Schlesinger Libr. Women's History, Radcliffe Coll., 1988-89. Mem. Assn. Theol. Schs. (v.p. 1984-86, pres. 1986-88, issues implementation grantee 1983-84), Am. Soc. Ch. History (council 1983-85), Internat. Assn. Women Ministers (v.p. 1977-79), AAUW (v.p. 1973-75). Democrat. Office: Hartford Sem 77 Sherman St Hartford CT 06105

ZIMMER, NANCY CHILD, educator; b. N.Y.C., May 8, 1932; d. Andrew Roe Child and Nellie (Rossman) Smith; m. Layton Parkhurst Zimmer, June 13, 1953 (dec. 1975); children: Sally Paine Zimmer Knight, Layton Austin. BA in English, Coll. of William & Mary, Williamsburg, Va., 1953; MLS, Conn. Wesleyan U., 1987. Sec. Conn. Mental Health Assn., Hartford, Conn., 1973-74; sec. edn. studies program Conn. Wesleyan U., Middletown, 1974-75; dir. community rels. Elmcrest Psychiat. Inst., Portland, Conn., 1975-82; program cons. Stonington Inst., North Stonington, Conn., 1982-84; ind. trainer Portland, 1982—; mem. faculty elder hostel Episcopal Camp & Conf. Ctr., Ivoryton, Conn., 1985—; trainer Phys. Mgmt. Tng. Inc., Middletown, 1988-90. Corporator Middlesex Meml. Hosp., 1977—; bd. dirs Middlesex Community Coll., Middletown 1978—, YMCA, Middletown, 1978-90, YMCA Women's Bd., Middletown, 1990—, Greater Middletown Preservation Trust, 1990—; mem. regional mktg. com. United Way, Middletown, 1990—; pres. First Congl. Ch. of Portland, 1978-80, 84-86. Mem. Conn. Conf.-Middletown Assn. (ch. and ministry com.). Republican. Com. Personality Types, No. Middlesex C. of C. Republican. Home: 496 Main St Portland CT 06480 Office: RFP Assocs 141 Durham Rd Madison CT 06443

ZIMMERMAN, ALISA JEANNE, historic facility director; b. Lebanon, Pa., Jan. 15, 1959; d. Norman William and Ruth Anne (Brown) Z. Student, Ill. Wesleyan U., 1977-79; BA in Music, Am. U., 1981, MA in Performing Arts Mgmt., 1985. Cons. Homespun, Inc., Washington, 1981; pub. rels. asst. Cultural Alliance, Washington, 1981; group sales rep. SUNY, Purchase, 1982, mktg. coord., 1983; info. specialist Am. U., Washington, 1982-83, adminstrv. coord., 1983-85, asst. dir., 1985-87; cons. Women's City Club, Boston, 1987; dir. Meml. Hall-Harvard Real Estate, Cambridge, Mass., 1987—; bd. dirs. Very Spl. Arts of Mass., Boston; mem. facilities com. Harvard Mgrs. Exch., Cambridge, 1988—. Recipient direct mail merit award Admissions Mktg. Report, 1986, 1st place direct mail award Nat. Univ. Continuing Edn. Assn., 1986. Mem. Am. Coun. for the Arts (assoc.). Democrat. Methodist. Office: Harvard Real Estate 21 Pearson Ave Cambridge MA 02138

ZIMMERMAN, AMY J., auditor general, accountant; b. Royal Oak, Mich., July 19, 1967; d. Robert Louis and Marilyn Joy (Bostater) Z. AS in Bus., Baker Coll., Flint, Mich., 1987, BBA, 1989. Acct. Charles B. Kelly & Assocs., Flint, 1987-88; asst. auditor gen. Office of Auditor Gen. State of Mich., Lansing, 1989—; mem. adv. bd. gen. edn. div. Baker Coll., 1988—. Mem. Nat. Assn. Accts., State Assn. Accts., Auditors and Bus. Adminstrs.

ZIMMERMAN, BETTY JANET, civic volunteer; b. Lincoln, Ill., Oct. 17, 1918; d. Carey and Rosa Jane (Allen) Behrends; m. Dwight Frederick Zimmerman; children: Janis J. Zimmerman Watson, Arlis Dwight, Arlene Clara Zimmerman Bruhn. BS, U. Ill., 1940. Cert. home econs. tchr., Ill. High sch. instr. Crescent City, Ill., 1940-41; ptnr. Cream Ridge and Valley Farms, San Jose, Ill., 1941-76; vol. various orgns., Lincoln, 1976—; substitute tchr. various high schs., 1964-76; mgr., owner Wax Lane Farms, Easton, Ill., 1979—. Contbr. articles to periodicals and local newspapers. V.p. U. Ill. Mothers Assn., 1966-67, 73-75, Logan County chair; mem. U. Ill. Parent Liaison Com., 1973-75; trustee, sec. Abraham Lincoln Meml. Hosp., Lincoln, 1983-85, trustee, 1982-85, chmn. hospice adv. coun., 1984—; treas. Abraham Lincoln Healthcare System, Lincoln, 1985-88, chairperson, 1990—; legis. chmn. Ill. Hosp. Assn. (region 3A); vol. coordinator St. Clara's Manor, Lincoln, 1977-87; sec. adv. coun. local sch. dist., 1987; trustee Meth. Ch., 1988—. Named Citizen of Month Lincoln Courier Daily, 1983; recipient Leadership award Ill. Hosp. Assn. Coun. on Vols. Div., 1980. Mem. AAUW (legis. chmn. 1986—), League Women Voters (bd. dirs 1977-88), Ill. Farm Bur. Republican. Methodist.

ZIMMERMAN, CAROL JEAN, geophysicist; b. Pitts., Aug. 21, 1951; d. John and Olga (Clista) Jigliotti; m. Michael Henry Zimmerman, Jan. 15, 1983; children: Michelle Anne, Jason Michael. BS, Rensselaer Poly. Inst., 1973; MS, U. Wis., 1976, PhD, 1980. Rsch. asst. dept. geophysics U. Wis., Madison, 1973-80; rsch. geophysicist Exxon Prodn. Rsch., Houston, 1980-81, sr. rsch. geophysicist, 1982-83, rsch. specialist, 1983—. Patentee in field. Mem. Soc. Exploration Geophysicists, Geophys. Soc. Houston. Republican. Roman Catholic. Office: Exxon Prodn Co PO Box 2189 ST594 Houston TX 77001

ZIMMERMAN, DIANE LEENHEER, law educator, lawyer; b. Newton, N.J., Apr. 16, 1941; d. Adrian and Mildred Eleanor (Booth) Leenheer; m. Earl A. Zimmerman, Sept. 24, 1960 (div. Aug. 1982); m. 2d, Cavin P. Leeman, Feb. 18, 1984. B.A., Beaver Coll., Glenside, Pa., 1963; J.D., Columbia U., 1976. Bar: N.Y. 1977, U.S. Supreme Ct. 1983. Reporter, Newsweek mag., N.Y.C., 1963-71; spl. features writer N.Y. Daily News, N.Y.C., 1971-73; law clk. U.S. Dist. Ct. (ea. dist.) N.Y., Bklyn., 1976-77; asst. prof. law NYU, N.Y.C., 1977-80, assoc. prof., 1980-82, prof., 1982—; mem. faculty Practicing Law Inst., N.Y.C., 1979, 84; mem. subcom. on cts.' environment 2d Cir. Adv. Planning Com., N.Y.C., 1979-80. Articles and book rev. editor Columbia Law Rev., 1975-76. Recipient citation of merit Columbia U. Sch. Journalism, 1972; Kent scholar and Stone scholar, 1973-76. Mem. ABA (vice chmn. tort liability study com. tort and ins. sect. 1986-87), Am. Law Inst., Assn. Bar City N.Y. (chairperson com. civil rights 1981-83), Fed. Bar Council (asst. sec. 1982-84), Met. Women Law Tchrs. Assn. (pres. 1979-83), Soc. Am. Law Tchrs., ACLU, Women's Polit. Caucus. Office: NYU Sch Law 40 Washington Sq S New York NY 10012*

ZIMMERMAN, DIANE MARIE, nurse midwife; b. Lorain, Ohio, Aug. 25, 1957; d. Joseph C. and Mary (Vulcas) Z.; m. Bill G. Wall, Aug. 4, 1984; 1 child, Luka. BSN, Alfred U., 1987; MSN, Yale U., 1989; BA, Alfred U., 1987. Cert. nurse midwife, Mass. Staff nurse Yale New Haven (Conn.) Hosp., 1987-89; nurse midwife Baystate Med. Ctr., Springfield, Mass., 1989—. Mem. Am. Coll. Nurse Midwives, Sigma Theta Tau. Home: 78 River Lodge Rd South Hadley MA 01075 Office: Baystate Med Ctr 759 Chestnut Springfield MA 01199

ZIMMERMAN, ELAINE, policy analyst, community organizer, psychotherapist; b. Rockville Ctr., N.Y., June 9, 1950; d. Hal and Cecelia (Sachs) Z.; 1 child, Hannah Lynn. Student, Tufts U., 1968-70; BA, U. Calif., Berkeley, 1972; MSW, U. Calif., 1976. Lic. marriage, family, and child counselor; lic. clin. social worker. Psychotherapist Berkeley, Calif., 1976-86; sr. cons. Assembly Human Svcs. Com. Calif. Legislature, Sacramento, 1985-87; sr. cons. Joint Select Task Force on Changing Family Calif. Legislature, 1987-89; project dir. Conn. Commn. Children, Hartford, 1989—; program coordinator Inst. Labor and Mental Health, Oakland, Calif., 1978-81; mem. staff Psychotherapy Inst., Berkeley, 1977-78; cons. and speaker in field. Contbr. articles to profl. jours. Calif. regional dir. Women U.S.A., 1982; founder, dir. Women's Econ. Agenda Project, 1983-85, Berkeley Women's Ctr., 1973-75, Demeter House, Berkeley, Calif., 1975-77; bd. dirs. Calif. Project, San Francisco, 1983-84. Named Speaker of Yr., People Speaking, 1985. Democrat. Jewish. Home: 800 Mount Carmel Dr North Haven CT 06473 Office: Commn on Children 450 Broad St Hartford CT 06106

ZIMMERMAN, EVELYN NELLIE, municipal and county official; b. Pittsville, Wis., Jan. 8, 1922; d. Herman John and Margaret Johanna (Cook) Christensen; m. George Glen Zimmerman, Mar. 26, 1938 (dec. Apr. 1976); children: Nancy Zimmerman Wyman, Dorene Zimmerman Russell, Kathleen Zimmerman Chansley, George Herman; m. Don. C. Peterson, Apr. 9, 1988; stepchildren: Dorothy Gorich, Franklynn. Student Mid-State Tech., Wisconsin Rapids, 1977-78, 85-86, U. Wis.-Stevens Point, 1978-79. Pvt. practice sewing and designing, Wisconsin Rapids, 1962-81; mem. Wood County Bd. Supervision, Wisconsin Rapids, 1978-90; Welfare Fraud Coalition, 1978-90, Wis. Pub. Health Affiliate, 1986-90; clk. Family Natural Foods, Wisconsin Rapids, 1981-85, election bd. Wood County, 1949-62, 73-80; chmn. child support and veterans svcs. Bd. Social Svcs., Wisconsin Rapids, 1978-90, Area Comprehensive Health, Wood County, 1979-83, Community Options Program, 1978-90; sec. Wood County Health Com., 1978-88, vice-chair, 1988-90. Transp. Com., 1980-82; chmn. Community Options Program, 1978-90; trustee Moravian Ch., Wisconsin Rapids, 1976-83; pres., bd. dirs. Wis. Human Svcs. Assn., 1986-90. Recipient Presdl. Recognition award Wis. Human Svc. Bd. Mems. and Dirs. Assn., 1988 Mem. Wis. Social Svcs. Assn. (county bd. mem. Recognition award 1988), Wisconsin Rapids Bus. & Profl. Women's Club (treas. 1973-75, 2d vice chmn. 1975-77, 1st vice chmn. 1977-79, bd. dirs. 1979-82, Woman of Yr. Achievement award 1986), North Cen. Dist. Social Svcs. Assn. (pres. 1985-90), Wisconsin Rapids C. of C. (rep. govt. affairs 1988-90), Wis. Child Support Enforcement Assn. Democrat. Avocations: creative writing, sewing, reading, swimming. Home: 2330 6th St S Wisconsin Rapids WI 54494

ZIMMERMAN, FAITH, architect; b. Denville, N.J., Apr. 1, 1960; d. Alan Philip and Ruth Elizabeth (Morgan) Z. BArch, N.J. Inst. of Tech., 1986. Draftperson Theodore Weiss Assoc., Livingston, N.J., 1984; architect Cybul and Cybul Architects, Edgewater, N.J., 1986-88, Houghton, Quary, Warr, Architects, Newton, N.J., 1988—; team mem., Forest Hills Historic Sites Survey Team, 1984. Democrat. Home: 235 Chincopee Ave Hopatcong NJ 07843

ZIMMERMAN, FLORENCE ARLINE, nurse; b. New Holland, Pa., Dec. 2, 1924; d. Milton Burkhart and Florence Marie (Jackson) Z. BSN, Goshen Coll., 1954; MS, U. Pa., 1962; EdD, Temple U., 1980. Nurse advisor Pusan Children Charity Hosp., Korea, 1957-62; with WHO, SEARO, Project India, 1963-64; instr. Lankenau Sch of Nursing, Phila., 1964-65; nurse Sch. Dist. of Phila., 1965-66; asst. prof. Goshen (Ind.) Coll., Goshen (Ind.) Coll., Ea.

Mennonite Sch. Nursing, Harrisonburg, Va., 1967-68; nursing supr. Sch. Dist of Phila., 1968-88; v.p. Rambo Com Sight for Blind, Media, Pa., 1980—; advisor Diamond St. Health Ctr., Phila. 1985-86, Primary Health Care Nurse Role, Mungeli India, 1981-87. Author: Pediatric Nurse Manual-India, 1964, Relationship Between Health Factors and Academic Performance, 1979, School Nurse Manual, 1982. Sch. nurse Child Abuse Task Force Hall Mercer, Phila., 1976-80; mem. Presdl. Task Force, Washington, 1987-88; sch. nurse cons. Strawberry Mansion Task Force, Phila. 1986-87. Mem. Mennonite Nurses Assn., Mennonite Health Assn., Nat Coun. Internat. Health, Am. Nurses Assn., Phila. Assn. Sch. Adminstrs. Home: 108 Hill Rd New Holland PA 17557 Office: Rambo Com Sight for Curable Blind 411 Old Forge Rd Media PA 19063

ZIMMERMAN, HELENE LORETTA, business educator; b. Rochester, N.Y., Feb. 26, 1933; d. Henry Charles and Loretta Catherine (Hobert) Z. BS, SUNY, Albany, 1953, MS, 1959; PhD, U. N.D. 1969. Cert. records mgr. Bus. tchr., chmn. bus. dept. Williamson (N.Y.) Cen. Sch., 1953-69; asst. prof. U. Ky., Lexington, 1969-70; assoc. prof. bus. Cen. Mich. U., Mt. Pleasant, 1970-74, prof., 1974—. Author General Business, 1977; contbg. author to records mgmt. text book, 1987. Sec. Isabella County Christmas Outreach, Mt. Pleasant, 1983-87. Mem. Assn. Records Mgrs. and Adminstrn., Inst. Cert. Records Mgrs. (sec. 1985—),Internat. Soc. Bus. Edn. (internat. v.p. Eng. speaking nations 1986—), Nat. Bus. Edn. Assn., Mich. Bus. Edn. Assn. (bd. dirs. 1985—, pres. 1988-89), AAUW (pres. 1984-86), Delta Kappa Gamma (state pres. 1987-89). Office: Cen Mich U Grawn 337 Mount Pleasant MI 48859

ZIMMERMAN, JANICE MARIE, savings and loan executive; b. Chgo., June 27, 1958; d. Edward Chester and Frances (Baranowski) Pawlowski; m. Michael Scott Daniel, May 13, 1980 (div. Oct. 1983); m. Daniel Victor Zimmerman, Sept. 7. 1985. B.S. in Fin., Eastern Ill. U., 1980; M.S. in Fin., St. Louis U., 1987. Asst. examiner Fed. Res. Bank, Chgo., 1980-82; fin. analyst Fed. Res. Bank St. Louis, 1982-84; v.p., treas. Illini Fed., Fairview Heights, Ill., 1984-87; asst. v.p. Community Fed., St. Louis, 1987—. Mem. Fin. Mgrs. Soc., Nat. Assn. Female Execs., Internat. Platform Assn. Republican. Jewish. Club: Creve Coeur Racquet (Mo.). Avocation: reading. Office: Community Fed One Community Ctr Saint Louis MO 63131

ZIMMERMAN, JEAN, lawyer; b. Berkeley, Calif., Dec. 3, 1947; d. Donald Scheel Zimmerman and Phebe Jean (Reed) Doan; m. Gilson Berryman Gray III, Nov. 25, 1982; children: Charles Donald Buffum, Catherine Elisabeth Phebe (twins); stepchildren: Alison Travis, Laura Rebecca, Gilson Berryman. BSBA, U. Mo., 1970; JD, Emory U., 1975. Bar: Ga. 1975, D.C. 1976, N.Y. 1980. Asst. mgr. investments FNMA, Washington, D.C., 1970-73; assoc. counsel Fuqua Industries Inc., Atlanta, 1976-79; assoc. Sage Gray Todd & Sims, N.Y.C., 1979-84; assoc. counsel J. Henry Schroder Bank & Trust Co., N.Y.C., 1984-85, asst. gen. counsel, 1985-86; assoc. gen. counsel, 1987, assoc. gen. counsel, IBJ Schroder Bank & Trust Co., N.Y.C., 1987—; asst. sec., 1988—; founder, officer ERA Ga., Atlanta, 1977-79; bd. dirs. Ct. Apptd. Spl. Advs., 1988—. Mem. ABA, N.Y. State Bar Assn., Ga. Assn. Women Lawyers (bd. dirs. 1977-79), LWV, DAR, Democrat. Office: IBJ Schroder Bank & Trust Co 1 State St New York NY 10004

ZIMMERMAN, JO ANN, lieutenant governor, nurse; b. Van Buren County, Iowa, Dec. 24, 1936; d. Russell and Hazel (Ward) McIntosh; m. A. Tom Zimmerman, Aug. 26, 1956; children: Andrew, Lisa, Don and Ron (twins), Beth. Diploma in Nursing, Broadlawns Sch. of Nursing, Des Moines, 1958; BA with honors, Drake U., 1973; postgrad., Iowa State U., 1973-75. RN, Iowa. Asst. head nurse maternity dept. Broadlawns Med. Ctr., Des Moines, 1958-59, weekend supr. nursing services, 1960-61, supr. maternity dept., 1966-68; instr. maternity nursing Broadlawns Sch. Nursing, Des Moines, 1968-71; health planner, community relations assoc. Iowa Health Systems Agy., Des Moines, 1978-82; mem. Iowa Ho. Reps., 1982-86; lt. gov. State of Iowa, 1986—. Contbr. articles to profl. jours. Mem. advanced registered nurse practitioner task force on cert. nurse mid-wives Iowa Bd. Nursing, 1980-81, Waukee, Polk County, Iowa Health Edn. Coordinating Coun., Iowa Women's Polit. Caucus, Dallas County Women's Polit. Caucus; chmn. Des Moines Area Maternity Nursing Conf. Group, 1969-70, task force on sch. health svcs. Iowa Dept. Health, 1982, task force health edn. Iowa Dept. Pub. Instruction, 1979, adv. com. health edn. assessment tool, 1980-81, Nat. Lt. Govs. Conf. on Agrl. and Rural Devel., mem. exec. com., 1989; Dallas County Dem. Cen. Com., 1979-84; bd. dirs Iowa PTA, 1979-83, Waukee Community Sch. Bd., 1976-79, pres., 1978-79; chairperson Health Com., 1980-84. Mem. Am. Nursing Assn., Iowa Nurses Assn., Iowa League for Nursing (bd. dirs. 1979-83), Family Centered Childbirth Edn. Assn. (childbirth instr., advisor), LWV, Met. Des Moines LWV (health chmn.), Iowa Cattlemen's Assn., Am. Lung Assn. Iowa (bd. dirs. 1988—). Mem. Christian Ch. Office: Office of Lt Gov State Capitol Bldg Des Moines IA 50319

ZIMMERMAN, KATHLEEN MARIE, artist; b. Floral Park, N.Y., Apr. 24, 1923; d. Harold G. and Evelyn M. (Andrade) Z.; m. Ralph S. Iwamoto, Nov. 23, 1964. Student, Art Students League, N.Y., 1942-44, Nat. Acad. Sch. Fine Arts, N.Y.C., 1944-47, 50-54. tchr. drawing and painting Midtown Sch. Art, N.Y.C., 1947-52. Illustrator: (with Ralph S. Iwamoto) Diet for a Small Planet, 1971; one woman shows include Westbeth Gallery, N.Y.C., 1973, 74; exhibited in group shows at Woodstock Art Gallery, N.Y., 1945, Nat. Arts Club, N.Y.C., 1948-56, 84, Emily Lowe Award Show, 1951, Contemporary Arts Gallery, N.Y.C., 1952, 60, Allied Artists Ann., N.Y.C. 1956, 78, 80-89, Art USA, 1958, Village Art Ctr., 1956-61, ACA Gallery, 1958, 59, Studio Gallery, 1957-60, City Center Gallery, 1960, Janet Nessler Gallery, N.Y.C., 1961, Silvermine Guild, Conn., 1962, Pioneer Gallery, Cooperstown, N.Y., 1962, 63, Audubon Artists Anns., N.Y.C., (various shows) 1963-90, NAD, (11 shows) 1969-90, Nat. Assn. Women Artists Anns., N.Y.C., 1957-85, 87-90, Women Artists Award Winners Show, N.Y.C., 1974, Am. Watercolor Soc. N.Y.C., 1975-78, 80, Cheyenne (Wyo.) Western Galleries, 1975, 76, 77, Edward-Dean Mus., Cherry Valley, Calif., 1975, 76, 77, Frye Mus., Seattle, 1975, 76, 77, Boise Gallery Art, 1975, Central Wyo. Mus. Art, 1975, 76, Willamette U., 1975, Yellowstone Art Ctr., Billings, Mont., 1975, Utah State U., 1975, Applewood Art Gallery, Colo., 1976, Charleston Art Gallery, W.va., 1976, Kent State U., 1976, Cin. Art Club, 1976, Marble Mus., Key West, Fla., 1976, Buecker Gallery, N.Y.C., 1976, Anchorage Fine Arts Mus., 1976, Davis and Long Gallery, N.Y.C., 1977, Butler Inst. Am. Art, 1978, Washington Square Rast Gallery, NYU, 1979, Internat. Festival Women Artists, Copenhagen, 1980, City Gallery, N.Y.C., 1981, Bergen Community Mus., Paramus, N.J., 1983, Kenkeleba Gallery, N.Y.C., 1985, Adelphi Univ., Garden City, N.J., 1987, Lotos Club, N.Y.C., 1987, Temperance Hall Gallery, Bellport, N.Y., 1987, Monmouth Mus., Lincroft, N.J., 1987, Marbella Gallery, N.Y.C., 1989; represented in permanent collections, Butler Inst. Am. Art, Youngstown, Ohio, Sheldon Swope Art Gallery, Terre Haute, Ind., Lauren Rogers Mus. Art, Laurel, Miss., U. Wyo. Art Mus., Laramie, U. Miami Lowe Art Mus., Coral Gables, Fla., N.C. Mus. Art, Raleigh, Swarthmore Coll., Pa., Erie Art Ctr. (Pa.) bibliography James Mellow, N.Y. Times Art Review, 1973, Hilton Kramer, N.Y. Times Review, 1977; contbr. bibliography to Gerald F. Brommer's The Art of Collage, 1978, Christopher Schink's Mastering Color & Design in Watercolor, 1981, John and Joan Digby's The Collage Handbook, 1985; contbr. art revs. to publs. John. F. and Anna Lee Stacey scholar, 1951; recipient Barse Miller Meml. award Am. Watercolor Soc., 1976, Henry Ward Ranger Fund purchase NAD, 1976, 82, John Wenger Meml. award Audubon Artists, 1978, cert. of merit NAD, 1980, Ralph Fabri medal Audubon Artists, 1981, Dr. Maury Leibovitz award N.Y. Artists Equity, 1985, J.&E. Liskin Meml. award Audubon Artists, 1987, L.G. Sawyer prize Nat. Acad. Design, 1988. Mem. Audubon Artists, Am. Watercolor Soc., Nat. Assn. Women Artists (12 prizes 1957-89), Allied Artists Am. (silver medal 1981, Jane Peterson award 1985, Creative Watercolor prize 1989), N.Y. Artists Equity Assn. Home: 463 West St A1110 New York NY 10014

ZIMMERMAN, LENORE STENZEL, educator; b. Marion, Kans., June 17, 1919; d. Frederick George and Lydia (Vogel) Stenzel; m. John Richman Zimmerman, Jr., Dec. 19, 1942; children: John Preston, Kathryn Annette, Tamara Lea. Cert., Wichita Bus. Coll., 1937; BS in Edn., AB, Kans. State Tchrs. Coll., 1941. Tchr. Washington (Kans.) High Sch. 1941-42; sec. Kans. State Tchrs. Coll. Emporia, 1942-43, ARC, Washington, D.C., 1943-45, Ohio High Sch. Athletic Assn., Columbus, Ohio, 1947-49; sec., tchr. Upper

Arlington High Sch., Columbus, 1945-47; substitute tchr. Dallas Ind. Sch. Dist., 1961-69, Commerce (Tex.) Ind. Sch. Dist., 1981—. Pres., officer various PTA's, Dallas, 1955-69; troop leader Girl Scouts U.S.A., Carbondale, Ill., 1969-75; mem., chmn. Hunt County Appraisal Rev. Bd., Greenville, Tex., 1982-89; chmn. LWV, Dallas, 1955-61. Mem. AAUW (past pres. Commerce), Dallas City Coun. PTA's (life, pres. 1962-63), M.B. Henderson Sch. PTA (life), Delphian Club (pres. 1988—), Coterie Culture club (pres. 1981-83), Kappa Delta Pi, Kappa Mu Epsilon. Baptist. Home: 2609 Sterling Hart Dr Commerce TX 75428

ZIMMERMAN, LINDA FRAN, periodical publisher, writer; b. Chgo., Sept. 30, 1946; d. Louis Joseph and Sydell Muriel (Lakowitz) Z. Student, Roosevelt U., 1963-65, Santa Monica Coll., 1981-83. Prodn. asst. films, asst. video editor various features, 1970-81; freelance photographer, 1979-86, freelance writer, 1983—; editor, pub. The Food Yellow Pages, L.A., 1987—; contbg. editor Food Arts Mag., L.A.; creative svcs. dir. El Cholo Restaurants, L.A.; instr. food journalism UCLA and various colls.; speaker radio and TV; specialist food and restaurants L.A. Author: Puddings, Custards and Flans, 1990; contbr. articles to mags. and newspapers. Mem. Women's Culinary Alliance (bd. dirs. 1988—), So. Calif. Culinary Guild (bd. dirs.). Home: 135 S Harper Ave Los Angeles CA 90048 Office: The Food Yellow Pages PO Box 461449 Los Angeles CA 90046

ZIMMERMAN, MARI SPERRY, real estate professional, interior designer; b. Saginaw, Mich., Apr. 27, 1942; d. John McClain and Monica Agnes (Wisk) Sperry; m. Jon Clifford Zimmerman, Sept. 14, 1963 (div. 1988); children: Sperry Lee, Jon, Margaret. BA, Mich. State U., 1964, MA, 1970; grad., Realtors Inst., 1989. Cert. tchr., Mich. Tchr. Saginaw Twp. Schs., 1965-66; tchr., chmn. art dept. Swan Valley Schs., Saginaw, 1971-78; space planner, designer Consultation & Design, Saginaw, 1976—; real estate sales assoc. Coldwell Banker, Saginaw, 1984—, relocation specialist, 1987—; space planner, designer, Custom Office Furnishings, Iona, Mich., 1985—. Sec. Saginaw Arts Coun., 1976-77; vol. art tchr. Hemmeter Sch., Saginaw, 1983-86; tchr. Sunday sch. 2d Presbyn. Ch., Saginaw, 1985-86. Mem. AAUW (bd. dirs. 1979), Saginaw Panhellenic Soc. (pres. 1980), Saginaw Bd. Realtors (program chmn. 1989, edn. chmn. 1990, Realtor Assoc. of Yr. 1988-89), Delta Zeta Alumnae of Saginaw (pres. 1977), Mich. Assn. Realtors. Home: 420 Stoneham St Saginaw MI 48603 Office: Coldwell Banker Ste 2 4855 State St Saginaw MI 48603

ZIMMERMAN, MARTHA ROSENBERGER, home economist; b. Mt. Vernon, Ill., Aug. 6, 1937; d. Stanley and Vaneta (Walker) Rosenberger; m. Donald D. Zimmerman, Dec. 27, 1959; children: John William, Christopher Keiser. BS, U. Ill., 1958, MEd, 1960. Home econ. tchr. Taylorville (Ill.) High Sch., 1958-78; home economist Zimmerman Farms Inc., Harvel, Ill., 1978—; bd. mem. Ill. Home Econ. Assn., 1960-70, Ill. Voc. Home Econ. Tchrs., 1962-72, chmn., adv. bd., Ill. Future Homemakers, 1968. Editor: Centennial History, 1973. Pres. Gen. Colonial Daus. 17th Century, 1985-88; reg. 3A chmn. Ill. Hosp. Assn., 1988-89; pres. St. Vincent's Hosp. Aux., Taylorville. Mem. Am. Home Econs. Assn., Home Economists in Bus., U. Ill. Alumni Assn., Alpha Gamma Delta, Nat. Soc. DAR (registrar gen. 1986-89), Delta Kappa Gamma, Ill. U.S. Daughter 1812 (pres.), Phi Upsilon Omicron, PEO Sisterhood. Methodist. Home: Harvel IL 62538 Office: Zimmerman Farms Harvel IL 62538

ZIMMERMAN, MURIEL ELAINE, educational administrator; b. Harper, Iowa, Sept. 26, 1942; d. Merlin Edwin and Lois Elizabeth (Jasper) Gibson; m. Jerome L. Zimmerman, June 11, 1966 (div. Nov. 1985); children: Angela Beth, Gregory Allen. BS, McPherson Coll., 1964; MS, Kans. State U., 1969; postgrad., U. Mo., 1980-82, N.W. Mo. State U., 1980-87. County extension home economist Kans. State U., Eureka, 1964-67; dir. homemaker svc. demonstration project Kans. State U., Manhattan, 1968-70; instr. home econs. N.W. Mo. State U., Maryville, 1978-85; coord. adult and community edn. Maryville Region II Schs., 1984—; instr., coord. workshops U. Mo., Maryville, 1981-85; presenter in field. Mem. Maryville Community Wellness Coun., 1986—; mem. Parents as First Tchrs. Adv. Com., 1987—; participant Leadership Maryville, 1988—; coord. retail tng. Maryville C of C., 1988—. Recipient vol. leadership award U. Mo. Extension Svc., 1983. Mem. Am. Home Econs. Assn. (cert.), Am. Vocat. Assn., Nat. Coun. Vocat. Adminstrs., Mo. Tchrs. Assn., Mo. Assn. Adult Continuing and Community Edn. (bd. dirs. 1986—, conf. chmn. 1988, Newcomer's award 1989), Mo. Home Econs. Assn. (v.p., pres., treas. 1982—), Missouri Valley Edn. Assn., Mo. Coun. Vocat. Adminstrs. (program chmn. 1987—), AAUW. Home: 1809 Village O Dr Maryville MO 64468 Office: NW Mo Area Tech Sch 1515 S Munn St Maryville MO 64468

ZIMMERMAN, SARAH E., immunologist; b. Indpls., Oct. 29, 1937; d. Abraham and Mary (Caplan) Zimmerman. AB, Ind. U., 1959, MA, 1961; PhD, Wayne State U., 1969. Postdoctoral rsch. assoc. dept. chemistry Ind. U., Bloomington, 1969-71; postdoctoral rsch. assoc. dept. microbiology sch. medicine Ind. U., Indpls., 1971-73, rsch. immunologist dept. pathology sch. medicine, 1973—. Contbr. articles to profl. jours. Vol. leader 4-H Clubs, Indpls., 1971—, mem. Washington Twp. adv. bd., 1984-89. Mem. Am. Assn. Immunologists, Am. Chem. Soc., Am. Soc. for Microbiology, Ind. Arabian Horse Club, Indpls. Wine Soc., Les Amis du Vin, Sigma Xi, Sigma Delta Epsilon, Iota Sigma Pi. Office: Ind U Sch Medicine Dept Pathology Riley Hosp A-20 702 Barnhill Dr Indianapolis IN 46202-5200

ZIMMERMAN, SUSAN G., sales executive; b. Lincoln, Nebr., Aug. 3, 1952; d. Robert Loyal and Marion Lucille (Brown) Mueller; m. Steven D. Zimmerman, Jan., 1988; children: Kathryn, Jamison, Sari, Desiree. BS, U. Minn., 1974. Traffic coordinator Barrickman Red Barron Advt., Mpls., 1974-75; high sch. tchr. Robbinsdale, Osseo and Blaine Schs., Mpls., 1974-83; adult edn. instr. Osseo, Robbinsdale Sch. Dist., Mpls., 1983; conf. coordinator Lakewood Pub./Tng. Mag., Mpls., 1983-84; from project mgr. to dir. sales Cardinal Health Systems, Mpls., 1984-87, exec. dir. sales, 1987-88; registered rep./trainer Equitable Fin. Cos., St. Paul, 1987—; pres. Mgmt. Edn. Cons. Corp. of Am., Mpls., 1984—. Free-lance writer Mpls. Star & Tribune, 1982-83. Mem. Nat. Assn. Female Execs., Nat. Assn. Profl. Saleswomen (pres. local chpt., chmn. women's leads exch.), Minn. Alumni Assn., Am. Soc. Tng. and Devel., Community Edn. Assn., Am. Mgmt. Assn. Presbyterian. Club: Flagship (Eden Prairie, Minn.). Home: 7142 Upper 139th St W Apple Valley MN 55124 Office: Zimmerman Fin Group 325 Cedar Ste 300 Saint Paul MN 55101-3636

ZIMMERMAN, ZELMA LUCILLE, music educator, music and drama director; b. Belle Plaine, Kans.; d. Theodore Janson and Josephine Loretta (Robinson) Z. AB in Music, BE, Kans. State Tchrs. Coll., Emporia, 1940; MA, EdD, Columbia U., 1948, profl. diploma, 1959; postgrad. in music, U. Houston, UCLA. Tchr. Kans. Bd. Edn., Sumner County, 1925-36; tchr. music Kans. Bd. Edn., Wichita, 1937-52, prin. elem. sch., 1952-65, cons. vocal music, 1965-75; pvt. practice Wichita, 1975—; dir. mus. plays and programs, Wichita, 1975—. Author: An Enchiridion for Music Teachers, 1985, An Anthology of Literature for Children, 1980, Doorways to Healthier Living, 1988. Mem. NEA, Kans. Edn. Assn., Wichita City Tchrs. Assn., Wichita Hist. Mus., Wichita Symphony Soc., Roger Wagner Chorals, Kappa Delta Pi.

ZIMOWSKI, JOYCE ANN, service executive; b. Pitts., Oct. 25, 1955; d. Stanley and Vera Jean (Baker) Z. BBA, St. Bonaventure U., 1977. Auditor Arthur Andersen & Co., Rochester, N.Y., 1977-81; controller Park Ridge Hosp., Rochester, 1981-84, asst. v.p., 1984-87, v.p., 1987—; adv. bd. Roberts Weslyan Coll., Rochester, 1986—. Bd. dirs. Vis. Nurse Svc. Rochester, 1988—. Home: Healthcare Fin. Mgmt. Assn. (treas. v.p. to pres. 1986—). Office: Park Ridge Hosp 1555 Long Pond Rd Rochester NY 14626

ZINAMAN, HELAINE MADELEINE, teacher; b. N.Y.C., Sept. 11, 1951; d. Harold Joseph and Charlotte (Orenstein) Z. BA, Am. U., 1973; MEd, U. Md., 1979. Spl. edn. resource tchr. John Eager Howard Elem. Sch., Capitol Heights, Md., 1973-85; coord. talented and gifted program Glenarden Woods TAG Magnet, Lanham, Md., 1985—; pvt. tutor, Washington, 1983-85; tchr. overview course GED, Bladensburg, Md., 1983; tchr. creative thinking Prince George's Community Coll., Largo, Md., 1983, 85; tchr. Thinktank, U. Md., College Park, 1989—. Asst. editor Sci. Bowl, 1990—. Judge Md. State Odyssey of the Mind Competition. Mem. Nat. Assn. for Gifted Children, Assn. for Supervision and Curriculum Devel., Md. State

---

Tchrs. Assn., Nat. Educators Assn., Prince Georges County Educators Assn. Democrat. Jewish. Home: 4434 Indigo Ln Harwood MD 20776 Office: Glenarden Woods Elem Glenarden Pkwy and Echols Lanham MD 20706

ZINGALE, MARY GENEVIEVE, social services administrative supervisor; b. Bklyn., Oct. 14, 1928; d. Salvatore and Mary (Fornito) Z. Vocat. edn. cert., SUNY, Albany, 1961; BA in Social Studies, Coll. St. Rose, Albany, 1966; MSW, Adelphi U., 1977; Cert., Suffolk County Inst. for Psychoanalytic Psychotherapy, 1986; cert., Adelphi U., 1989. Entered Congregation of Religious of Good Shepherd of Angels, 1946; child care worker Euphrasian Residence, N.Y.C., 1950-51; child care worker St. Anne Inst., Albany, 1951-72, trade sewing tchr., 1952-61, tchr. social studies and religion, 1963-72, children's clothing buyer, purchasing agt., adminstr. campus shop, 1951-72, tchr. bus., case aide, 1972-76, social worker, 1976-81, purchasing agt., 1976—, casework supr., 1981-90, co-dir., 1990—; field instr. Adelphi U., 1983—. Mem. Nat. Assn. Social Workers, N.Y. State Soc. Clin. Social Work Psychotherapists Inc. (cert. 1986). Roman Catholic. Office: 151 Burrs Ln Dix Hills NY 11746

ZINGALE, ROXANNE, feature film editor; b. Cleve., July 11, 1961; d. Joseph Thomas and Mary Jo (Erbland) Z. Student, U. Ariz., 1979-81, Loyola U. Rome Ctr., Rome, Italy, 1983; BA, Loyola Marymount U. L.A. 1984. Pvt. practice feature film editor L.A., 1984—. Asst. editor: (films) The Ladies Club, Wired to Kill, Aloha Summer, That's Life, 1984; editor: (films) Vicious Lips, 1985, Journey to the Center of the Earth, 1986-87, Cyborg, 1988, Deceptions, 1989; dir. editor: (short film) Electricity, 1984 Jack Haley award, Samuel Arkoff award, 1984. Democrat. Roman Catholic.

ZINSER, ELISABETH ANN, university president; b. Meadville, Pa., Feb. 20, 1940; d. Merle and Fae Zinser. BS, Stanford U., 1964; MS, U. Calif., San Francisco, 1966, MIT, 1982; PhD, U. Calif., Berkeley, 1972. Nurse VA Hosp., Palo Alto, Calif., 1964-65, San Francisco, 1969-70; instr. Sch. Nursing U. Calif., San Francisco, 1966-69; pre-doctoral fellow Nat. Inst. Health, Edn. and Welfare, 1971-72; adminstr. Sch. Medicine U. Wash., Seattle, 1972-75, Coun. Higher Edn., State of Ky., 1975-77; prof., dean. Coll. Nursing U. N.D., Grand Forks, 1977-83; vice chancellor acad. affairs U. N.C., Greensboro, 1983-89; pres. Gallaudet U., Washington, 1988, U. Idaho, Moscow, 1989—; cons. Ctr. Leadership Devel. Am. Coun. Edn., Washington, Boeing Aircraft Co., Seattle, Nat. Workshop Acad. Deans, Higher Edn. Exec. Assocs., Denver, Bush Found., St. Paul. Author: (with others) Contemporary Issues in Higher Education, 1985, Higher Education Research, 1988; co-author: Nurse: A Changing World in a Changing World, 1982. Bd. dirs. Humana Hosp., Greensboro, 1986-88; v.p., bd. dirs. Ea. Music Festival, Greensboro, 1987-89; trustee N.C. Coun. Econ. Edn., 1985-89, Greensboro Day Sch., 1987-89. Leadership fellow Bush Found., 1981-82. Mem. Am. Assn. Higher Edn., Assn. Am. Colls. (Coun. Liberal Learning), Am. Assn. Univ. Adminstrs., AAUP, AAUW, Rotary, Pi Lambda Theta, Sigma Theta Tau. Home: 1026 Nez Perce Dr Moscow ID 83843 Office: U Idaho Office of Pres Moscow ID 83843

ZION, LEELA CLARICE, educator; b. San Francisco, Nov. 4, 1929; d. Edwin Ray and Clarice Leela (Davis) Z. AA, San Mateo Jr. Coll., 1948; BA, Chico State Coll., 1950; MA, Stanford U., 1951; postgrad., UCLA, 1958. Tchr. San Juan Union High Sch., Fair Oaks, Calif., 1951-53, Cen. Washington Coll., Ellensburg, 1953-55; service club dir. U.S. Govt., Laon, France, 1955-58; lectr. Mills Coll., 1958-59; prof. Humboldt State U. Arcata, Calif., 1959—. Co-author The Physical Side of Thinking, 1986; producer film Love All, 1970. Mem. Am. Soc. for the Prevention of Cruelty to Animals, Ethical Treatment of Animals, Greenpeace. Mem. Am. Alliance for Health, Physical Edn., Recreation, and Dance, Internat. Soc. for Gen. Semantics, Am. Badminton Assn., Human Psychology Assn. Democrat. Home: 1747 Blakeslee Ave Arcata CA 95521 Office: Humboldt State U Arcata CA 95521

ZIPPERER, LAURA LOVE, society rights director; b. Savannah, Ga., June 6, 1959; d. Edward Helmey and Nina Dorris (Arnold) Z. BA, Converse Coll., 1981. Mgmt. trainee Milliken & Co., Spartanburg, S.C., 1981-82; admissions counselor Converse Coll., Spartanburg, 1982-83; rsch. asst. Ga. Inst. Tech., Atlanta, 1984-86; dir. devel. Ga. Inst. Tech., 1986-87, assoc. dir. devel., 1987-89; dir. major gifts Am. Cancer Soc., Atlanta, 1989—; cons. to various colls. and univs., 1986—. Chair Atlanta coun. Converse Coll. Alumnae Assn., 1986-89. Recipient Outstanding Profl. Achievement award Ga. Tech. Found., 1988. Mem. Coun. for the Advancement & Support Edn., Am. Prospect Rsch. Assn., Mortar Bd. Alumni Club. Democrat. Lutheran. Home: 1913 Pair Rd Marietta GA 30060 Office: Am Cancer Soc 1599 Clifton Rd Atlanta GA 30329

ZIPPRODI-ZONKA, CONSTANCE, educational organization administrator; b. Evanston, Ill.; d. Herbert Edward and Agnes Irene (Turpin) Zipprodt; m. Robert F. Zonka, Aug. 5, 1970; children: Heidi Zapanta, Milo Matthew. BA, U. Fla., 1958; postgrad., U. Chgo., 1960. Account exec. Daniel J. Edelman, Inc., Chgo., 1964-68; pres. Connie Zonka Assocs., Chgo., 1974-89; dir. coll. rels. Columbia Coll., Chgo., 1970-89; sr. dir. univ. rels. Roosevelt U., Chgo., 1990—. Mem. NAFE, Pub. Rels. Soc. Am., Publicity Club Chgo., Nat. Assn. Women Bus. Owners, Friends of WFMT (sec. 1989—), Friends of Downtown, Friends of the Parks. Democrat. Home: 901 S Plymouth Ct Apt 1205 Chicago IL 60605

ZIPPRODT, PATRICIA, costume designer. B.A., Wellesley Coll.; student, Art Inst. Chgo., Art Students League N.Y., Fashion Inst. Tech. Asst. to various theatre designers; designer Broadway musicals including Fiddler on the Roof, 1964; Cabaret, 1966, 87, Zorba, 1968, 1776, 1969, Pippin, 1972, Mack and Mable, 1974, Chicago, 1975, King of Hearts, 1978, Alice in Wonderland, 1982, Smile, 1983, The Accidental Death of an Anarchist, 1984, Sweet Charity, 1985, Big Deal, 1986; designer Broadway plays including: A Period of Adjustment, 1962, Little Foxes, 1967, Plaza Suite, 1968, Scratch, 1971, All God's Chillun' Got Wings, 1975, Poor Murderer, 1976, Kingdoms, 1981, Fools, 1981, Brighton Beach Memoirs, 1983, The Glass Menagerie, 1983; MacBeth, 1988; designer Broadway plays including: Cat on a Hot Tin Roof, 1989, Shogun, 1990; designer Off Broadway plays including: Our Town, 1960, The Balcony, 1960, Camino Real, 1961, Oh Dad Poor Dad etc., 1962, A Man's A Man, 1963, The Blacks, 1962; designer regional theatre including: Waiting for Godot, Guthrie theatre, Mpls., 1973, Don Juan, Guthrie Theatre, Mpls., 1982; The Bacchae, Guthrie Theatre, 1987; designer operas including: Madam Butterfly, Boston Opera Co., 1962, Hippolyte E Aricie, Boston Opera Co., 1966, Katerina Ismailova, N.Y.C. Opera, 1967, The Flaming Angel, N.Y.C. Opera, 1968, The Rise and Fall of the city of Mahagonny, Boston Opera Co., 1972, The Mother of us All, Guggenheim Mus., N.Y.C., 1972, Lord Byron, Juilliard Opera, N.Y.C., 1973, Tannhäuser Met. Opera, N.Y.C., 1977, Naughty Marietta, N.Y.C. Opera, 1978, The Barber of Seville, Met. Opera, 1982, The Fall of The House of Usher, Am. Repertory Theatre, Cambridge, Mass., 1988; designer ballets Les Noces, Am. Ballet Theatre, 1969, Watermill, N.Y.C. Ballet, 1972, Dybbuk Variations, N.Y.C. Ballet, 1974, The Leaves Are Fading, Am. Ballet Theatre, 1975, Estuary, Am. Ballet Theatre, 1982, Helgi Tommasen, Houston Ballet Co., 1985, Cada Noche Tango Jnez de Castro Tres Cantos, Ballet Hispanico, 1988; designer feature films including The Graduate, 1967; designer TV spls. Anne Brancroft spl., CBS, 1970, June Moon, WNET, 1973, The Glass Menagerie ABC, 1973, Alice in Wonderland, WNET, 1983; lectr., condr. master classes various univs., Yale U. Sch. Drama, Harvard Coll.; vis. lectr. theatre arts NYU; vis. lectr. Yivsig Siskind prof. theatre arts Brandeis U., 1985-88. Exhibitor design sketches Wright-Hepburn, London, 1966, Capicorn Galley, N.Y.C., 1968, Mus. City N.Y., 1972, U. Calif.-San Diego, 1974, Toneelmuseum, Amsterdam, Netherlands, 1975, U.S. Internat. Theatre Inst. traveling exhibit, 1974-78, Am. Ballet Theatre traveling exhibit, 1976-78. Recipient Antoinette Perry award Fiddler On The Roof, 1964, for Cabaret, 1966, for Sweet Charity; Drama Desk award for Zorba, 1968, for 1776, 1969, for 1986, for Pippin, 1973; Joseph P. Maharam award for 1776, 1970, for Alice in Wonderland, 1983, for Don Juan, 1983; award for Spl. costumes Nat. Acad. TV Arts and Scis., 1970; Alumnae Achievement award Wellesley Coll., 1971; Spl. award New Eng. Conf., 1973; Ritter award Fashion Inst. Tech., 1977; Disting. Career award S.E. Theatre Conf., 1985. Mem. United Scenic Artists, Costume Designers Guild, Nat. Acad. Arts and Scis. Address: 29 King St New York NY 10014

ZIPSER, JANET ROSE, information manager; b. Hartford, Conn., May 6, 1952; d. David Bernard (dec.) and Ruby (Carroll) Z. BA, U. N.C., 1974; MSLS, Cath. U. Am., 1986. Computer systems analyst Dept. of State, Washington, 1978-85; libr. Nat. Libr. Medicine, Bethesda, 1987—; treas. Cath. U. Sch. Libr. and Info. Sci. Alumni Bd., Washington, 1989—. Mem. Beta Phi Mu. Home: 2028 N Vermont St #12 Arlington VA 22207 Office: MEDLARS Mgmt Sect Nat Libr Medicine 8600 Rockville Pike Bethesda MD 28904

ZIRUK, CAROLYN J., bank marketing professional; b. Worcester, Mass., Dec. 28, 1948; d. Armand and Eileen (Bedard) Laurence; m. W. Matthew Ziruk, May 19, 1971; children: Jennifer, Phaedra. BS, Cen. Conn. State U., 1971; cert., Am. Inst. Banking, 1979, 80. Asst. dept. head mktg. Conn. Nat. Bank, Bridgeport; v.p., contr. fin. instns. group Conn. Nat. Bank, Hartford. Mem. Nat. Assn. Bank Women.

ZITELLO, MARY CATHERINE, free-lance editor; b. Youngstown, Ohio, Mar. 31, 1954; m. Joseph M. McGuire, Apr. 11, 1981; children: Garrett, Connor. BS in Journalism, Bowling Green State U., 1976. Dir. publs. Nat. Assn. Bus. and Ednl. Radio, Washington, 1976-80; communications assoc. United Way Nat. Capitol Area, Washington, 1980-81; dir. communications Nat. Soc. Pub. Accts., Alexandria, Va., 1981-86; editorial supr. Aspen Systems Corp., Rockville, Md., 1986-90; freelance editor Washington, 1990—. Editor numerous articles. Vol. Com. To Re-elect Gerald Ford, Washington, 1976, Edward Kennedy Campaign, Washington, 1980. Mem. Women in Communications, Lafayette Home and Sch. Assn. Democrat. Roman Catholic. Home and Office: 6622 31st St NW Washington DC 20015

ZITRIN, CHARLOTTE MARKER, psychiatrist, educator, researcher; b. N.Y.C., Sept. 30, 1918; d. Abraham and Regina (Adler) Marker; m. Arthur Zitrin, Oct. 4, 1942; children: Richard Alan, Elizabeth Ann. BA cum laude, NYU, 1939, MD, 1943. Diplomate Am. Bd. Med. Examiners. Intern Kings County Hosp., 1943-44; resident in pediatrics Bellevue Hosp., 1944-45; asst. in pediatrics NYU Bellevue Med. Ctr., 1945-46, from rsch. fellow to asst. prof. pediatrics, 1948-58; attending physician pediatrics L.I. Jewish Hosp., 1958-60; resident in psychiatry Hillside Hosp., 1960-63, clin. asst., 1964-65; supervising psychiatrist Hillside Hosp. Div. L.I. Jewish Med. Ctr., Glen Oaks, N.Y., 1965—, dir. Behavior Therapy Clinic, 1970—, dir. Phobia Clinic, 1972—; asst. clin. prof. pediatrics NYU Bellevue Med. Ctr., 1958-60; asst. prof. clin. psychiatry Dept. Psychiatry and Behavioral Scis. Ctr. Stony Brook, 1973-81, clin. assoc. prof. psychiatry, 1982—; lectr. in field. Contbr. articles to med. jours. Fellow Am. Psychiat. Assn., Am. Psychopathological Assn.; mem. AAAS, Assn. Advancement Behavior Therapy, Nassau County Acad. Medicine, Nassau County Med. Soc., Nassau County Psychiat. Soc., N.Y. Acad. Scis., N.Y. State Med. Soc., Psi Chi. Office: Hillside Hosp Div L I Jewish Med Ctr PO Box 38 Glen Oaks NY 11004

ŽIVKOVIC, MARINA, meteorology researcher; b. Belgrade, Yugoslavia, June 21, 1953; came to U.S., 1979; d. Tomislav and Olga Bozhak Z.; m. Dušan Nesic (div. 1980); 1 child, Mladen. BS, U. Belgrade, 1976; PhD, U. Md., 1986. Meteorologist Fed. Hydro-Meteorol. Inst., Belgrade, 1976; faculty teaching asst. U. Belgrade, 1976-79; rsch. asst. U. Md., College Park, 1979-83, faculty rsch. asst., 1983-86; post-doctoral rsch. assoc. Purdue U., West Lafayette, Ind., 1986-89; sr. rsch. assoc. Atmospheric and Environ. Rsch., Inc., Cambridge, Mass., 1989—. Recipient Borivoje Dolorilovic World Meteorol. Org., Geneva, Switzerland, 1975. Mem. Am. Meteorol. Soc., Am. Geophys. Union, Am. Inst. Physics. Office: Atmospheric and Environ Rsch Inc 840 Memorial Dr Cambridge MA 02139

ZIVLEY, GLORIA JUNE, auditor; b. Cameron, Tex., Feb. 24, 1949; d. Benette Ransom and Dorothy Grace (Simmons) B.; m. Lane Alton Zivley, Nov. 1, 1966; children: Benette Lamar, Rebecca Grace. Student, Austin Community Coll., 1967-68. Clk. III Tex. R.R. Commn., Austin, 1967-68; acctg. clk. II Dept. Mental Health and Retardation, Austin, 1968-72; acct. I Austin-Travis County Mental Health Mental Retardation, 1972-74; sr. tax supr. Comptroller of Pub. Accts., Austin, 1974—. Mem. Employees Polit. Action Council, Austin, 1985—. Mem. Tex. Pub. Employees Assn. (state pres. 1987—, bd. dirs. 1983, 88). Democrat. Anglican. Clubs: Hyde Park Booster, Williamson County Pop Warner (bd. dirs.). Home: 19 Martin Ln Pflugerville TX 78660 Office: Tex Pub Employees Assn PO Box 12217 Austin TX 78711

ZMITROVICH, ANN CARROLL, behavioral neuroscientist; b. N.Y.C., Nov. 11, 1961; d. Peter and Mary Gail (Bonsall) Z.; m. Peter Mark Goldstone, Oct. 8, 1989. BA, U. Pa., 1983; postgrad., CUNY, 1989. Research assoc. Dept. Physiology and Anatomy U. Calif., Berkeley, 1983-84; research technician Dept. Devel. Psychobiology N.Y. State Psychiat. Inst., 1985—; tchr., grad. asst. Hunter Coll., N.Y.C., 1985-87. Grantee NIMH, 1989; recipient fellowship CUNY, 1985-87. Mem. Internat. Soc. Devel. Psychobiology, Am. Psychol. Assn. Home: 180 Cabrini Blvd #23 New York NY 10033 Office: NY State Psychiat Inst Dept Devel Psychobiology 722 W 168th St Box 40 New York NY 10032

ZMUDA, SHARON LOUISE, construction executive; b. Chgo., May 31, 1942; d. Theodore Edward and Virginia (Fleig) Z. Student, Sch. Art Inst. Chgo., 1961-62; BA, Mundelein Coll., Chgo., 1964. In student services dept. La Salle Extension U., Chgo., 1965-69; sales coordinator S.K. Smith Co., Chgo., 1969-71; customer service specialist Am. Express Co., Chgo., 1971-73; office mgr. North Shore Cement, Inc., Chgo., 1975-84; pres. Abacor Rd. Constrn., Inc., Chgo., 1984—; broadcaster Bus. Desk CRIS radio, 1983—. Fundraiser Sch. Art Inst. of Chgo., 1987—. Mem. Women's Bus. Devel. Ctr., Nat. Assn. Women in Constrn. Roman Catholic. Home and Office: Abacor Rd Constrn Inc 4858 W Berteau Ave Chicago IL 60641

ZOBEL, RYA W., federal judge; b. Germany, Dec. 18, 1931. A.B., Radcliffe Coll., 1953; LL.B., Harvard U., 1956. Bar: Mass. 1956, U.S. Dist. Ct., Mass., 1956, U.S. Ct. Appeals (1st cir.) 1967. Mem. Hill & Barlow, Boston, 1967-73; mem. Goodwin, Procter & Hoar, Boston, 1973-79; U.S. dist. judge of Mass. Boston, 1979—. Mem. ABA, Boston Bar Assn., Am. Bar Found., Mass. Bar Assn., Am. Law Inst. Office: US Dist Ct McCormack PO & Courthouse Rm 1802 Boston MA 02109*

ZOBLE, ADRIENNE KAPLAN, advertising agency executive; b. Newark, July 11, 1940; d. Herman Israel and Ada (Goodglass) Kaplan; m. Jacob Manus Zoble, Aug. 23, 1962; children: Allison Leigh, Jennifer Hope. BA, Rutgers U., Newark, 1963. Sec. media dept., broadcast estimator J. Walter Thompson Co., N.Y.C., 1961-64; asst. buyer Maxon, Inc., N.Y.C., 1964; media dir. Bruce Friedlich & Co., N.Y.C., 1965-66; media dir. Keyes, Martin & Co., Springfield, N.J., 1966-76; pres. Adrienne Zoble Advt., Green Brook, N.J., 1977—; mem. Active Corps Execs., U.S. SBA, 1977—. Mem. LINK (founder, past pres.), N.J. Assn. Women Bus. Owners (founder, past pres. Cen. N.J. chpt.), U.S. C of C. (coun. small bus.), Middlesex County Regional C. of C. (trustee, chmn. small bus. coun.), Bus. Forum (founder, pres.). Office: Adrienne Zoble Advt Inc 933 Washington Ave Green Brook NJ 08812

ZOELLICK, PAULINE ANGIONE, computer consultant; b. Rochester, N.Y., Sept. 19, 1944; d. Charles Francis and Genevieve Rita (McCarthy); m. Roy E. Smillie, Aug. 5, 1983 (dec. Apr. 1984); m. Bill N. Zoellick, Feb. 17, 1990. BS, Nazareth Coll., Rochester, 1966; MA, U. Chgo., 1968. Med. Librarian Rsch. assoc., lectr. U. Chgo., 1968-72; asst. prof. Rosary Coll. Grad. Libr. Sch., River Forest, Ill., 1972-79; sales customer svc. mgr. SDC, Santa Monica, Calif., 1979-81; new product mgr. SDC, Santa Monica; dir., software products ISI, Phila., 1984-85; mgr. distributed databases UMI, 1986-88; cons. Ann Arbor, Mich., 1988-90; computer cons. Boulder, Colo., 1990—. Editor: Euphausiacia Bibliography, 1979. Fellow Nat. Library of Medicine. Mem. Med. Library Assn., Special Library Assn., Am. Soc. for Info. Sci. Home and Office: 924 Kelly Rd W Boulder CO 80302-9638

ZOELLNER, SANDRA ANN, accountant; b. Fond du Lac, Wis., Aug. 25, 1964; d. Daniel Lee and Marguerite Frances (Wildenberg) Z. BS, Okla. State U., 1986. Revenue agt. IRS, Dallas, 1987; credit analyst Mercury Marine, Dallas, 1988-89; asst. controller Leather Ctr., Dallas, 1989—. Mem. NAFE, All Saints Singles Club, Alpha Kappa Psi. Republican. Roman

Catholic. Home: 11333 Amanda Ln Apt 732 Dallas TX 75238 Office: Leather Ctr 1100 Venture Ct Carrollton TX 75006

ZOLBER, KATHLEEN KEEN, nutrition educator; b. Walla Walla, Wash., Dec. 9, 1916; d. Wildie H. and Alice (Johnson) Keen; m. Melvin L. Zolber, Sept. 19, 1937. BS in Foods and Nutrition, Walla Walla Coll., 1941; MA, Wash. State U., 1961; PhD, U. Wis., 1968. Registered dietitian. Dir. food service Walla Walla Coll., 1941-50, mgr. coll. store, 1951-59, asst. prof. food and nutrition, 1959-62, assoc. prof., 1962-64; assoc. prof. nutrition Loma Linda (Calif.) U., 1964-72, prof. nutrition, 1973—, dir. dietetic edn., 1967-84, dir. dietetics Med. Ctr., 1972-84, dir. nutrition program, 1984—. Mead Johnson grantee, 1965-67; recipient Alumna of Yr. award Walla Walla Coll., 1977; Delores Nyhus award Calif. Dietetic Assn., 1978. Mem. Am. Dietetic Assn. (pres. 1982-83), Am. Pub. Health Assn., Am. Home Econs. Assn., Am. Mgmt. Assn., AAUP, Soc. Food Service Research, Soc. Personnel Adminstrn., Grad. Faculties in Programs Pub. Health Nutrition Assn. (pres. 1990—), Omicron Nu, Delta Omega. Office: Loma Linda U Sch Pub Health Dept Nutrition Loma Linda CA 93350

ZOLOTOW, CHARLOTTE SHAPIRO, author, editor; b. Norfolk, Va., June 26, 1915; d. Louis J. and Ella F. (Bernstein) Shapiro; m. Maurice Zolotow, Apr. 14, 1938 (div. 1969); children: Stephen, Ellen. Student, U. Wis., 1933-36. Editor children's book dept. Harper & Row, N.Y.C., 1938-44; sr. editor Harper & Row, 1962-70; v.p., asso. pub. Harper Jr. Books, 1976-81; editorial cons., editorial dir. Charlotte Zolotow Books, 1982-90; pub. emerita Harper Collins Children's Books, 1991—; tchr. U. Colo. Writers Conf. on Children's Books, U. Ind. Writers Conf.; also lectr. children's books. Author: The Park Book, 1944, Big Brother, 1960, The Sky Was Blue, 1963, The Magic Words, 1952, Indian Indian, 1952, The Bunny Who Found Easter, 1959, In My Garden, 1960, But Not Billy, 1947, 2d edit, 1983, Not a Little Monkey, 1957, 2d edit., 1989, The Man With The Purple Eyes, 1961, Mr. Rabbit and the Lovely Present, 1962, The White Marble, 1963, A Rose, A Bridge and A Wild Black Horse, 1964, 2d edit., 1987, Someday, 1965, When I Have a Little Girl, 1965, If It Weren't for You, 1966, 2d edit., 1987, Big Sister, Little Sister, 1966, All That Sunlight, 1967, When I Have A Son, 1967, My Friend John, 1968, Summer Is, 1968, Some Things Go Together, 1969, The Hating Book, 1969, The New Friend, 1969, River Winding, 1970, 79, Lateef and His World, 1970, Yani and His World, 1970, You and Me, 1971, Wake Up and Goodnight, 1971, William's Doll, 1972, Hold My Hand, 1972, 2d edit., 1987, The Beautiful Christmas Tree, 1972, Janie, 1973, My Grandson Lew, 1974, The Summer Night, 1974, 2d edit. 1987, The Unfriendly Book, 1975, It's Not Fair, 1976, 2d edit., 1987, Someone New, 1978, Say It, 1980, If You Listen, 1980, 2d edit. 1987, The New Friend, 1981, One Step, Two ..., 1981, The Song, 1982, I Know a Lady, 1984, Timothy Too!, 1986, Everything Glistens, Everything Sings, 1987, I Like to be Little, 1987, The Poodle Who Barked at the Wind, 1987, The Quiet Mother and the Noisy Little Boy, 1988, others; compiler An Overpraised Season, Early Sorrow. Mem. PEN, Authors League. Home: 29 Elm Pl Hastings-on-Hudson NY 10706 Office: 10 E 53d St New York NY 10022

ZONNEBELT-SMEENGE, SUSAN JEAN, clinical psychologist; b. Holland, Mich., July 27, 1948; d. William G. and Norma J. (Albers) Zonnebelt; m. D. Richard Smeenge, June 5, 1970; 1 child, Sarah J. Diploma with distinction, Mercy Cen. Sch. Nursing, Grand Rapids, Mich., 1969; BA magna cum laude, Aquinas Coll., 1974; MA in Counseling with honors, We. Mich. U., 1979, EdD with honors, 1988. RN, Mich. Charge nurse Holland Community Hosp., 1970-71; surgical nurse Burnham City Hosp., Champaign, Ill., 1971-72; instr. med. surgical nursing, coord. Mercy Cen. Sch. Nursing, 1972-75; instr., lectr. Butterworth Hosp. Sch. Nursing, Grand Rapids, 1975-76; med. social worker Holland Community Hosp., 1982-85; predoctorial psychology intern West Mich. Guidance Ctr., Grand Rapids, 1985-87, psychologist, 1987-88; clin. psychologist out-patient svcs. Pine Rest Christian Hosp., Grand Rapids, 1988—; began staff counseling svcs. Pine Rest-Butterworth Women's Health Connection Counseling Svcs., Grand Rapids, 1989—; cons. Blodgett Meml. Hosp. EAP program, Grand Rapids, 1988—. Vol. projects Jr. League, Grand Rapids, 1976-84, facilitator groups Scan project, 1983-84. Mem. Am. Psychol. Assn., Mich. Psychol. Assn. Office: Pine Rest Christian Hosp 300 68th St SE Grand Rapids MI 49508-6999

ZOOK, MARTHA FRANCES HARRIS, retired nursing administrator; b. Topeka, Nov. 15, 1921; d. Dwight Thacher and Helen Muriel (Houston) Harris; m. Paul Warren Zook, July 2, 1948; children: Mark Warren, Mary Elizabeth Zook Hughey. RN, Meriden (Conn.) Hosp. Sch. Nursing, 1947; student U. Kans., 1948-49, Kans. State U., 1960-61, Barton County Community Coll., 1970-73; BA, Stephens Coll., 1977; postgrad. Ft. Hays State U., 1978-79. Staff nurse Stormont Hosp., Topeka, 1947-48; staff nurse Watkins Meml. Hosp., Lawrence, Kans., 1948-49; nursing supr. Larned State Hosp., 1949-53, sect. supr., 1956-57, dir. nursing, 1958-61, 83-86; sect. nurse Sedgewick Sect., 1961-76, clin. instr. nursing edn., 1976-77, dir. nursing edn., 1977-83; clinic nurse for podiatrist; sect. supr. Dillon Bldg., Larned, 1957-58; Vol. Am. Cancer Soc. Mem. AAUW. Republican. Roman Catholic. Home: 1109 Johnson St Larned KS 67550

ZOPFI, ANNE KATHERINE, advertising executive; b. Manchester, N.H., June 30, 1945; d. William and Anna Elsa (Baer) Z.; m. Emery J. Stephans, Jan. 1, 1981. BA, Wheaton Coll., 1967; MS in Organic Chemistry, N.Y. U., 1969; MBA, Columbia U., 1971. Teaching fellow N.Y. U., N.Y.C., 1968-69; acct. exec. J. Walter Thompson, N.Y.C., 1971-76; acct. exec. Young & Rubicam, N.Y.C., 1976-78, acct. supr., 1978-82, mgmt. supr., 1982-87, sr. v.p., group dir., 1987—; bd. dirs. Hanover Fund., N.Y.C. Democrat. Office: Young & Rubicam Inc 285 Madison Ave New York NY 10017*

ZOTTOLA, CARLA JEAN, insurance executive; b. Pitts., Oct. 21, 1959; d. Henry and Sheila Naomi (Cataldo) Z. AAS in Mktg. and Retailing Sales, Cen. Piedmont Community Coll. Lic. broker, N.C. Rep. sales Western-So. Ins., Charlotte, N.C., 1981-87; owner, proprietor 'Z' Best Ins. Svcs., Charlotte, 1986—; fin. cons. H.B. Fin. Resources, Ltd., Charlotte, 1989, asst. v.p. Mem. NAFE, Optimist Club. Methodist.

ZOYHOFSKI, SHARRON ANNE, automotive company executive; b. Minot, N.D., Feb. 22, 1961; d. Eugene Arthur and Patricia Louise (Burke) Z. BS in Trade Technical Edn., Ferris State U., Big Rapids, Mich., 1983, AAS in Automotive Svc., 1981. Svc. tech. adviser Chevrolet Motor Div., Warren, Mich., 1983-85, 87-88; svc. engr., tech. assistance system Gen. Motors Corp., Detroit, 1985-87; staff specialist customer assistance Chevrolet Motor Div., Tampa, Fla., 1988, svc. tng. instr., 1988—. Mem. Chevrolet Dealership Orgn., Ferris State U. Alumni Assn. Office: Chevrolet Motor Div 3030 N Rocky Point Dr West Tampa FL 33607

ZSENYUK, AILEEN MURPHY, medical office administrator; b. Detroit, Aug. 7, 1936; d. George H. and Ethel D. Murphy; m. William P. Zsenyuk, Aug. 28, 1954; children: Michael W., Annette M., Maureen C. Student, Wayne State U. Pub. Melting Pot Press, Manchester, Mich.; bus. mgr. Jackson (Mich.) Radiology Cons. Mem. Med. Group Mgmt. Assn., Radiology Bus. Mgrs. Assn. (pres.). Office: 600 S Brown St Jackson MI 49203

ZUBER, NORMA KEEN, career counselor, educator; b. Iuka, Miss., Sept. 27, 1934; d. William Harrington and Mary (Hebert) Keen; m. William Frederick Zuber, Sept. 14, 1958; children: William Frederick Jr., Michael, Kimberly, Karen. BS in Nursing, U. Southwestern La., 1956; MS in Counselling, Calif. Luth. U., 1984. Nat. cert. counselor, nat. cert. career counselor. Intensive care nurse Ochsner Found. Hosp., New Orleans, 1956-59; career devel. counselor BFC Counseling Ctr., Ventura, Calif., 1984-87; owner, mgr., counselor Career and Life Planning-Norma Zuber and Assocs., Ventura, 1987—; instr. adult continuing edn. Ventura Community Coll., 1987—; instr. Calif. State U., Northridge, 1988-89; mem. adv. coun. on tchr. edn. Calif. Luth. U., Thousand Oaks, 1984-88. Chmn. bd. dirs. women's ministries Missionary Ch., Ventura, 1987-89; chairperson Legis. Task Force, 1987-89; bd. dirs. Calif. Registry Profl. Counselors and Paraprofls. Recipient profl. contbn. award H.B. McDaniel Found.-Stanford U. Sch. Edn., 1988; named to Nat. Disting. Svc. Registry for Counseling and Devel., 1990. Mem. Am. Assn. for Counseling and Devel. (Govt. Rels. Com. cert.), Nat. Career Devel. Assn. (western regional govt. rels. rep.), Calif. Assn. for Counseling and Devel. (chmn. legis. task force 1987-89, Jim Saum Govt. Rels. award 1989, bd. dirs. 1985—), Calif. Career Devel. Assn. (bd. dirs. 1985—, Leadership and Professionalism award 1988, 89, founder and chairperson area coun. Ventura and Santa Barbara counties and San Fernando Valley 1986-89, coord. so. Calif. area couns. 1990), Ventura County Profl. Women's Network (dir. membership 1990—), NAFE. Republican. Home: 927 Sentinel Circle Ventura CA 93003 Office: Career and Life Planning 3585 Maple St Ste 237 Ventura CA 93003

ZUCK, WYNONA COLLEEN, editor; b. Kansas City, Mo., Sept. 30, 1939; d. Earl Albert and Bertha (Drake) Howell; m. James Daniel Bardwell (div. 1967); 1 child, John Albert; m. Willard Alonzo Zuck; step-children: Cathy, Dawn, Sherrie, Linda. Student, Longview Community Coll. Paste-up artist Western Auto, Kansas City, Mo., 1957-60; keyline artist Trainor, Christianson & Barclay, Kansas City, 1960-61, Art, Inc., Kansas City, 1961-62, Nat. Bellas Hess, N. Kansas City, Mo., 1965-69, Unity Sch. Christianity, 1969-72; assoc. editor Wee Wisdom, Unity Village, Mo., 1972, editor, 1977-85; assoc. editor Daily Word, Unity Village, 1985, editor, 1985—; mem. editorial adv. com. Unity Sch., Unity Village, 1986—. Mem. Phi Theta Kappa. Office: Daily Word Unity School of Christianity Unity Village MO 64065

ZUCKER, JEAN MAXSON, nurse; b. Dunmore, Pa., Aug. 9, 1925; d. Earl L. and Florence M. (Cromwell) Maxson; R.N., Kings County Hosp. Center, 1948; cert. gerontol. nurse; children—Lawrence F., Pamela J., Diane K. Pvt. duty nurse various locations, N.Y., N.J., 1959-64; indsl. nurse Bendix Corp., Eatontown, N.J., 1955; asst. head nurse Point Pleasant Hosp., N.J., 1964-66; head nurse intensive and coronary care unit VA Hosp., Ft. Howard, Md., 1974-78; clin. nurse USPHS Hosp., Balt., 1978-81; nursing supr. VA Hosp. Center, Ft. Howard, 1981—; tchr. in field. Mem. Am., Md. nurses assns., Am. Assn. Critical Care Nurses. Democrat. Methodist. Address: 2013 Barry Rd Baltimore MD 21222

ZUCKER, MARJORIE BASS, medical researcher, hematologist; b. N.Y.C., June 10, 1919; d. Murray H. and Agnes (Naumburg) Bass; m. Howard D. Zucker, June 25, 1938; children: Andrew A., Ellen Zucker Harrison, Joan, Barbara Zucker-Pinchoff. AB, Vassar Coll., 1939; postgrad., Columbia Coll. Medicine, 1943-45; PhD, Columbia U., 1944. Rsch. asst. Coll. Physicians and Surgeons Columbia U., 1944-49; asst. to assoc. prof. physiology Coll. of Dentistry NYU, 1949-54; assoc. mem. Sloan Kettering Inst., N.Y.C., 1955-63; asst. rsch. dir. Am. Red Cross Rsch. Lab NYU Med. Ctr., N.Y.C., 1963-70, assoc. prof. pathology, 1963-71, prof. pathology, 1971—; mem. various rev. coms. NIH, Bethesda, Md., 1971-85. Co-author: The Physiology of Blood Platelets, 1965; co-patentee composition containing platelet factor 4, 1988; contbr. numerous articles to prof. jours. Recipient award N.Y. Met. chpt. Am. Women in Sci., 1986. Mem. Internat. Soc. Thrombosis, (mem. coun., recipient Marian Barnhart Lecture award 1989), Soc. for Exptl. Biology and Medicine (pres. 1983-85), Nat. Coun. on Death and Dying (dir., v.p. 1990). Democrat. Home: 333 Central Park West New York NY 10025 Office: NYU Med Ctr 550 First Ave New York NY 10016

ZUCKER-FRANKLIN, DOROTHEA, health facility administrator, researcher; b. Berlin, Aug. 9, 1929; came to U.S., 1949; d. Julian and Gertrude (Feige) Zucker; m. Edward C. Franklin, May 15, 1956 (dec. 1982); 1 child, Deborah Julie. BA, NYU, 1952, MD, 1956. Diplomate Am. Bd. Internal Medicine. Intern Phila. Gen. Hosp., 1956-57; resident in internal medicine Montefiore Hosp., N.Y.C., 1957-59, postdoctoral fellow in hematology, 1959-61; with Med. Sch. NYU, N.Y.C., 1962—, prof. Med. Sch., 1974—, dir. lab., 1966—; asst. attending physician Montefiore Hosp., 1961-65; assoc. attending physician Univ. Hosp., 1968-74, attending physician, 1974—; assoc. attending physician Bellevue Hosp., 1968-74, attending physician, 1974—; cons. physician Manhattan (N.Y.) VA Hosp., 1970—; sci. adv. bd., rev. panel Israel Cancer Rsch Fund, 1982—; mem. U.S.-Israel Binat. Sci. Found., 1980—; bd. dirs. Henry M. and Lillian Stratton Found., Inc., 1987—. Mem. editorial bd. Blood, 1973-76, 80-86, Jour. Reticuloendothelial Soc., 1964-74, 80—, Am. Jour. Pathology, 1979—, Blood Cells, 1980—, Ultrastructural Pathology, 1979, Am. Jour. Medicine, 1981—, Hematology Oncology, 1982—, Jour. Immunology, 1986—; author: (with others) The Physiology and Pathology of Leukocytes, 1962, Atlas of Blood Cells, Funciton and Pathology, 1st edit. 1981, 2d edit. 1989. Recipient Career Devel. award NIH, 1965-70; NIH Rsch. grantee, 1970—. Fellow N.Y. Acad. Scis.; mem. Am. Fedn. Clin. Rsch., Am. Soc. Clin. Investigation, Am. Assn. Physicians, Am. Soc. Hematology (chairperson subcom on leukocyte physiology 1977, chairperosn subcom. on immunohematology 1984, exec. coun. 1985—), Soc. Exptl. Biology and Medicine, Am. Soc. Exptl. Biology, Am. Soc. Immunologists, Am. Soc. Cell Biology, Reticuloendothelial Soc. (pres. program and nominatingcoms. 1984-85), N.Y. Soc. Electron Microscopists (pres. 1962, 84-85), N.Y. Soc. for Study Blood. Office: NYU Med Ctr 550 First Ave New York NY 10016

ZUKOWSKI, VIRGINIA A., naval officer; b. Rochester, N.Y., Dec. 5, 1950; d. John Rueben and Dolleen Margaret (Edelblute) Rhoades; m. Walter C. Zukowski, Aug. 27, 1988; children: Mellissa, Christopher, Jeremy, Rebecca. BPA, Nat. U., 1982, MS, 1983. Enlisted USN, 1975, advanced through grades to sr. chief petty officer; phys. security specialist in anti- and counter-terrorism. USN, San Diego. V.p. Chief Petty Officer Assn., 1989—; sec. Sundance PTA, 1988-89. Baptist. Office: Comdr Amphibious Group 3 Naval Station PO Box 201 San Diego CA 92136

ZUMALT, JOANNA MAUDIE, hospital association administrator; b. Red Bluff, Calif., Apr. 1, 1942; d. Charles Williams and Margery Mae (Haller) Martin; m. Michael Dearl Zumalt, Sept. 1, 1963; children: Aaron Albert, Beth Marie. AA, Shasta Jr. Coll., Redding, Calif., 1962; BSBA, Calif. State U., 1984; postgrad., U. San Francisco, 1990—. Adminstrv. mgr. Pain Ctr. of Sacramento, Calif., 1984-85; adminstrv. asst. II U. Calif., Davis Med. Ctr., 1978-86; dir. membership svcs. Calif. Assn. of Hosp. and Health Systems, Sacramento, 1987-88; asst. regional dir., region 9 Am. Hosp. Assn., Sacramento, 1988—; assoc., legis. advocate Willie Hausey and Assoc., Inc., 1984-87. Mem. NAFE, Healthcare Forum, Sacramento Soc. of Assn. Execs., Am. Soc. of Assn. Execs., Am. Mktg. Assn., Sacramento Pathology Soc. (bd. dirs.). Home: 3501 Condor Ct Carmichael CA 95608

ZUMO, BILLIE THOMAS, biologist; b. Cheyenne, Wy., Sept. 25, 1936; d. Thomas Elias and Katherine A. (Pappas); m. Charles Vincent, Aug. 21, 1959; 1 child, Dr. Thomas J. BA, U. Wyoming, Laramie, 1958; MA, U. N. Colo., Greeley, 1963; student, U. Wyoming, 1964, U. N. Colo., 1964. Cert. Educator. Tchr. Carey Jr. High Sch., Cheyene, Wy., 1958-61; English tchr. McCormick Jr. High, Cheyenne, 1961; tchr. Carey Jr. High Sch., Cheyenne, 1961-63; freshman biology Laramie Co. Community Coll., Cheyenne; tchr. Central High Sch., Cheyenne, 1963; exec. bd. Sch. Dist. curriculum adv., 1982-85; Cen. High Sch. Sci. Dept. chmn., 1988-. Author: Genetics Accepted by Sch. Dist. Football Statistician Central Football Team, Cheyenne, 1976; Lay Mem. Research Com. of The Pharmacy Therapetics Com., 1985; Judge Sch. Dist. Sci. Fair, Cheyenne, 1987-88; Choir Dir. Ch. Choir, Cheyenne. Named Wyoming Biology Tchr. of the Year Nat. Assn. of Biology Tchrs., 1976; Recipient Distinguished Service award Sts. Constantineo Helen Orthodox Ch., Cheyenne, 1979, Distinguished Service award as Choir Dir. Archbishop Iakovas, N.Y., 1988. Mem. Nat. Assn. Biology Tchrs., NEA, Cheyenne Tchrs. Edn. Assn., Wyo. Edn. Assn., Nat. Forum of Greek Orthodox Musicians, Ladies Philoptochos Soc. of Denver Diocese (treas., 1989--), AAUW, Phi Delta Kappa. Democrat. Eastern Greek Orthodox. Home: 900 Ranger Dr Cheyenne WY 82009 Office: Cen High Sch 5500 Education Dr Cheyenne WY 82009

ZUMPE, DORIS, ethologist, psychiatry educator; b. Berlin, May 18, 1940; came to U.S., 1972; d. Herman Frank and Eva (Wagner) Z. BSc, U. London, 1961, PhD, 1970. Asst. to K.Z. Lorenz, Max-Planck-Inst. für Verhaltensphysiologie, Seewiesen, Fed. Republic Germany, 1961-64; rsch. asst. and assoc., lectr. Inst. Psychiatry, U. London, 1965-72; rsch. assoc. Emory U. Sch. Medicine, Atlanta, 1972-74, asst. prof. psychiatry (ethology), 1974-77, assoc. prof., 1977-87, prof., 1987—; reviewer NSF, 5 sci. jours. Contbr. over 100 articles to profl. jours., chpts. to books. Grantee NIMH, 1971-91. Mem. AAAS, Internat. Soc. Psychoneuroendocrinology, Internat. Primatological Soc., Internat. Soc. for Human Ethology, Am. Soc. Primatologists, N.Y. Acad. Scis., Earl Music Am., Viola da Gamba Soc. Am. Office: Emory U Sch Medicine Dept Psychiatry Atlanta GA 30322

ZUNDEL, CAROLYN STEIDLEY, printing company executive; b. Albuquerque, May 13, 1940; d. Howard Benjamin and Dorothy (House) Steidley; m. William Zundel, Nov. 22, 1961; children: William David, Tamera Ann, Michael Edward. Degree, Ea. Wash. U., 1980. Co-owner, v.p. A1 and Artcraft Printing, Inc., Spokane, Wash., 1971—; owner, mgr. Twisted Pine Art Shop, 1987—. Mem. NAFE, Spokane C. of C., Ind. Bus. Assn. Office: A1 and Artcraft Printing W 331 Main St Spokane WA 99201

ZUNKER, SHARON JIENELL, commercial expediters company executive; b. Charleston, W.Va., July 28, 1943; d. Clifford W. and Iva A. (Neeley) Kenneway; m. Anthony F. Zunker, Sept. 19, 1980; children: Tibor Kreiter, James A. Kreiter, Melissa J. Diploma, Sprayberry High Sch., 1963. Various clerical positions N.Y. and Ga.; mgr. Winn Dixie, Ft. Lauderdale, Fla., 1973-76; owner, operator Union 76 Svc. Sta., Manistee, Mich., 1980-82; pres., owner Am. Commercial Expediters, Pompano Beach, Fla., 1988—; sec.-treas. Atlanta Envelope Co., 1962-64. Mem. Am. Legion, Odd Fellows, Rosecrucions. Republican. Home: 6250 SW 6th St Margate FL 33068 Office: Am Comml Expediters 1791 Blount Rd Ste 303, 312 Pompano Beach FL 33069

ZUPKO, KAREN ANNE, medical consulting company executive; b. Chgo., Jan. 10, 1950; d. George and Marie (Lausen) Z. BS, U. Kans., 1972. Program dir. AMA, Chgo., 1973-79, dir. dept. practice mgmt., 1978-85; pres. Karen Zupko & Assocs., Chgo., 1985—. Editor: Starting Your Plastic Surgery Practice; contbr. articles to profl. jours.; author, producer 5 tapes, 1985-90. Bd. trustees Grant Hosp., Chgo., 1989—; bd. dirs. Gastrointestinal Rsch. Found., Chgo., 1988—, counseling ctr. 4th Presbyn. Ch., Chgo., 1987—. Mem. Am. Hosp. Assn., Soc. for Healthcare Mktg. & Planning (at-large rep. Chgo. 1990—), Soc. Profl. Bus. Consultants, Women in Communications, Am. Mktg. Assn., Woman's Athletic Club Chgo. Office: Karen Zupko & Assocs 980 Michigan Ave Ste 1360 Chicago IL 60611

ZUPON, KAREN ELIZABETH, state official; b. Salinas, Calif., Jan. 17, 1944; d. Charles Edward and Muriel Scott (Barber) Kneib. B.A., U. Calif., Davis, 1972, also postgrad. Courtroom artist, writer KMGH-TV, Denver, 1978-79; news reporter, anchor, producer, courtroom artist KCRL-TV, Reno, Nev., 1979-81; news reporter, anchor, producer KGUN-TV, Tucson, 1981-83, KTVN-TV, Reno, 1983-84, KOLO-TV, Reno, 1984-85; exec. aide, press sec. Office of Gov. Nev., Carson City, 1985-89, chief dep. sec. state, 1989—. Mem. Nev. State Press Assn. Democrat. Office: Office of Sec State Capitol Complex Carson City NV 89710

ZUR, JANICE MAE, relocation company executive; b. N.Y.C., July 11, 1942; d. Charles and Roslyn (Zemon) Epand; m. Harvey Namm, Jan. 21, 1961 (div. 1980); children: Frederick Michael, Audra Aileen; m. Eitan Zur, Mar. 14, 1985. Degree in Interior Design, Wilsey Inst., 1966. Lic. real estate broker and gen. contractor. Comptroller Island Floor Installers, L.I., N.Y., 1970-79; pres. Distinctive Concepts, Inc., N.Y.C., 1979-84, Distinctive Concepts West, Los Angeles, 1985—. Mem. Nat. Assn. Realtors, Los Angeles Bd. Realtors, Nat. Assn. Contractors, Century City Bus. Group, Los Angeles C. of C., Westchester County (N.Y.) C. of C., Swiss Am. Bus. Assn., German-Am. C. of C., Australian-Am. C. of C., Brit.-Am. C. of C., French-Am. C. of C. Republican. Jewish. Clubs: Braemar (Reseda, Calif.); Monterey (Palm Desert, Calif.). Office: Distinctive Concepts West 1888 Century Park East Suite #1208 Los Angeles CA 90067

ZURAW, KATHLEEN ANN, special education educator; b. Bay City, Mich., Sept. 29, 1960; d. John Luke and Clara Josephine (Kilian) Z. AA with high honors, Delta Community Coll., 1980; BS with high honors, Mich. State U., 1984, MA, 1987. Cert. spl. edn., mentally impaired phys. edn. grade K-12, adaptive phys. edn. tchr., Mich. Summer water safety instr. Camp Midicha, Columbia, Mich., 1982, Bay Cliff Health Camp, Big Bay, Mich., 1983; summer spl. edn. tchr. Jefferson Orthopedic Sch., Honolulu, 1984, 85, 86, Ingham Intermediate Sch. Dist., Mason, Mich., 1987; spl. edn. tchr. Bay Arenac Intermediate Sch. Dist., Bay City, 1985-87, Berrien County Intermediate Sch. Dist., Berrien Springs, Mich., 1987—. Area 17 coach Mich. Spl. Olympics, Berrien Springs, 1987—; mem. YMCA, St. Joseph, Mich., 1987—, Y-Ptnrs., 1989, Coun. Exceptional Children. Mem. Am. Alliance Health, Phys. Edn., Recreation and Dance, Phi Theta Kappa, Phi Kappa Phi, Phi Delta Kappa. Roman Catholic. Home: 7306 W S Saginaw Rd Bay City MI 48706

ZURKAMMER, LAVETA FAYE, civic worker; b. Franklin, Ill., Dec. 3, 1916; d. George Adam and Eva Mae (Jeffers) Baker; divorced; children: Phyliss Jean Zurkammer White, Thomas Dale. Student, Lincoln (Ill.) Coll., 1936-37. Activity therapist Lincoln Devel. Ctr., 1963-85. Dir. bowling, Lincoln Women's City Assn., 1960-66, 83—, treas., 1966-82; bd. dirs., vice-chmn. Foster Grandparents Adv. Bd., Lincoln Devel. Ctr., 1985—; pres., Participants' Coun. Sr. Citizen's Ctr., Lincoln, 1986—; dir. local AARP; leader Fun-O-Leers Band; singer Sr. Singers; vol. homebound srs.; meml. gifts com. Neighborhood Watch Program, block capt., 1987—; mem. I Live Alone Program, 1989—. Mem. Lincoln Coll. Alumni Assn. (sec.-treas. exec. bd.1985—), Amvets Aux. (chaplain 1953-55, Nat. Coun. Therapeutic Recreation, Chester Women's Club (past treas., v.p.), Eagles. Republican. Methodist. Home: 1 Latham Pl Apt 5 Lincoln IL 62656

ZUSSY, NANCY LOUISE, librarian; b. Tampa, Fla., Mar. 4, 1947; d. John David and Patsy Ruth (Stone) Roche; m. R. Mark Allen, Dec. 20, 1986. BA in Edn., U. Fla., 1969; MLS, U. So. Fla., 1977, MS in Pub. Mgmt., 1980. Cert. librarian, Wash. Ednl. evaluator State of Ga., Atlanta, 1969-70; media specialist DeKalb County Schs., Decatur, Ga., 1970-71; researcher Ga. State Libr., Atlanta, 1971; asst. to dir. reference Clearwater (Fla.) Pub. Libr., 1972-78, dir. librs., 1978-81; dep. state libr. Wash. State Libr., Olympia, 1981-86; state libr. Wash. State Library, Olympia, 1986—; chmn. Consortium Automated Librs., Olympia, 1982—; cons. various pub. librs., Wash., 1981—; exec. officer Wash. Libr. Network, 1986—. Contbr. articles to profl. jours. Treas. Thurston-Mason Community Mental Health Bd., Olympia, 1983-85, bd. dir., 1982-85; mem. race com. Seafair Hydroplane Race, Seattle, 1986—. Mem. ALA (Assn. Specialized and Coop. Libr. Agys. legis. com. 1983-86, chmn. legis. com. 1985-87, vice chmn. state libr. agys. sect. 1985-86, chmn. state libr. agys. sect. 1986-87, chmn. govt. affairs com. Libr. Adminstrn. and Mgmt. Assn. 1986-87), Freedom to Read Found. (bd. dirs. 1987—), Chief Officers of State Libr. Agys. (dir.-at-large 1987—), Wash. Libr. Assn. (co-founder legis. planning com. 1982—, fed. rels. coord. 1984—), Fla. Libr. Assn. (legis. and planning com. 1978-81), Pacific N.W. Libr. Assn., Rotary, Phi Kappa Phi, Phi Beta Mu. Home: 904 E Bay Dr #B-404 Olympia WA 98506 Office: Wash State Libr MS AJ-11 Olympia WA 98504-0111

ZWAAN, GARNETTA SUE, secretary; b. Sulphur, Okla., Dec. 10, 1951; d. Floyd Albert and Vera Enid (Keeran) Graves; m. Louis Jimenez, Sept. 29, 1973 (div. July 1978); 1 child, Michael Louis (Jimenez) Zwaan; m. Robert Stephen Zwaan, Aug. 5, 1979; 1 child, Casey Stephen Zwaan. Student, Cameron U., 1976. Tchr. Lawton (Okla.) Pub. Schs., 1977-87; tchr. for gifted students Lawton Pub. Schs., 1984-86; team coord. Country Club Heights Sch., Lawton, 1986-87; newspaper in edn. week chmn. Lawton Area Reading Coun., 1986-87. Pres. Beta Alpha chpt. Kappa Kappa Iota, Lawton, 1986-87. Mem. Lawton Shakespeare Club (treas. 1989-90). Democrat. Methodist. Home: 3303 Atlanta Lawton OK 73505 Office: The HiFi Shop 1314 W Gore Blvd Lawton OK 73501

ZWEIGENTHAL, GAIL, magazine editor; b. N.Y.C., Feb. 27, 1944; d. Joseph and Bessie (Lang) Z. B.A., Tufts U., 1965. Editorial asst. Gourmet mag., N.Y.C., then assoc. editor, sr. editor, mng. editor, now exec. editor. Office: Gourmet Mag 560 Lexington Ave New York NY 10022*

ZWEIMAN, BEVERLY HEAFITZ, lawyer; b. Springfield, Mass., June 17, 1944; d. Israel and Sylvia Heafitz; m. Franklin G. Zweiman, June 1968; children: Ari, Jayna. BA, Brown U., 1966; MA in Edn., Stanford U., 1967; JD, Suffolk U., 1980. Bar: Mass. 1981, U.S. Dist. Ct. Mass. 1981, U.S. Ct. Appeals (1st cir.) 1989. Tchr. Fremont Union High Sch. Dist., Sunnyvale, Calif., 1967-68, Cupertino, Calif., 1968-70; Tchr. Wayland (Mass.) High Sch., 1967-68; pvt. practice Boston, 1981—; in-house counsel Heafitz & Co., Inc., Boston, 1984—; lectr. in field. Mem. ABA, Mass. Bar Assn., Mass. Conveyancers Assn., LWV (bd. dirs. Newton, Mass. chpt. 1973-76). Office: care Heafitz & Co 40 Rowes Wharf PO Box 1742 Boston MA 02110

ZWICKE, DIANNE LYNN, internist, cardiologist, educator; b. Marshfield, Wis., Oct. 27, 1952; d. Edward Raymond and Donna Mae (Erickson) Z. Diploma in nursing, St. Joseph's Hosp., Marshfield, 1973; BS in Nursing, Marquette U., 1975; postgrad. in nursing, U. N.C., 1977-79, MD, 1982. RN, Wis.; diplomate Am. Bd. Internal Medicine. Staff nurse St. Luke's Hosp., Milw., 1973-75; supr. emergency nursing St. Sinai Med. Ctr., Milw., 1975-77; resident in internal medicine U. Wis.-Marshfield Clinic-St. Joseph's Hosp., 1982-84, chief resident, 1984-85; fellow in cardiology U. Wis. Clin. Campus-Sinai Samaritan Med. Ctr., Milw., 1985-87, asst. prof. medicine, 1987—; mem. active staff in cardiology and emergency medicine U. Wis. Clin. Campus-Sinai Samaritan Med. Ctr., Milw., 1987—; clin. instr. surgery emergency-trauma svcs. Med. Coll. Wis., Milw.; mem. attending and assoc. staff St. Luke's Hosp., Milw.; active staff in cardiology St. Francis Hosp., St. Michael's Hosp., West Allis Meml. Hosp.; presenter in field. Contbr. articles and abstracts to med. jours. Recipient attending teaching award Sinai Samaritan Med. Ctr., 1988. Mem. Am. Coll. Cardiology, Am. Coll. Chest Physicians, Am. Soc. Internal Medicine, AMA, ACP, Am. Heart Assn., Soc. Critical Care Medicine, Wis. Med. Soc. (commn. on continuing med. edn. 1987), Milwaukee County Med. Soc., Sigma Theta Tau. Democrat. Lutheran. Office: U Wis Clin Campus 950 N 12th St Milwaukee WI 53233

ZWILICH, ELLEN TAAFFE, composer; b. Miami, Fla., Apr. 30, 1939; d. Edward Porter and Ruth (Howard) Taaffe; m. Joseph Zwilich, June 22, 1969 (dec. June 1979). MusB, Fla. State U., 1960, MusM, 1962; D Mus. Arts, Juilliard Sch., 1975; studies with Roger Sessions and Elliott Carter; MusD (hon.), Oberlin Coll., 1987. composer in residence Santa Fe Chamber Music Festival, 1990, Am. Acad., Rome, 1990. Premier Symposium for Orch., Pierre Boulez, N.Y.C., 1975, Chamber Symphony and Passages, Boston Musica Viva, 1979, 82. Symphony 1. Gunther Schuller. Am. Composers Orch., 1982; violinist Am. Symphony, N.Y.C., 1965-73; composer: Sonata in Three Movements, 1973-74; String Quartet, 1974; Clarino Quartet, 1977; Chamber Symphony, 1979; Passages (for Soprano and Chamber Ensemble), 1981; String Trio, 1982; Symphony 1:3 Movements for Orch., 1982 (Grammy nomination New World Records, 1987); Divertimento, 1983; Einsame Nacht, 1971; Emlekezet, 1978; Im Nebel, 1972; Passages for Soprano and Orch., 1982; Trompeten, 1974; Fantasy for Harpsichord, 1983; Intrada, 1983; Prologue and Variations, 1983; Double Quartet for Strings, Chamber Music Soc.

of Lincoln Ctr., 1984; Celebration for Orch., Indpls. Symphony, John Nelson, 1984; Symphony #2 (Cello Symphony) San Francisco Symphony, Edo De Waart, 1985; Concerto Grosso 1985, Handel Festival Orch., Steven Simon, 1986; Concerto for Piano and Orch., Detroit Symphony, Gunther Herbig, Marc-André Hamelin, 1986; Images for 2 Pianos and Orch., Nat. Symphony Orch., F. Machetti, 1987; Tanzspiel, Peter Martins N.Y.C. Ballet, 1987; Praeludium Boston chpt. AGO, 1987; Trio for piano, violin and cello; Piano Trio, Kalichstein, Laredo and Robinson trio; 1987; Symbolon, Zubin Mehta and the N.Y. Philharm., Leningrad and Moscow (USSR), N.Y.C., 1988; concerto for trombone and orch. J. Friedman, Sir Georg Solti, Chgo. Symphony, 1989, concerto for flute and orch. D.A. Dwyer, Seija Ozawa, Boston Symphony, 1990, quintet for clarinet and strings David Schiffrin, Chamber Music N.W., 1990; New World Records: Music By Ellen Taaffe Zwilich; N.Y. Philharm. conducted by Zubin Mehta. Recipient Elizabeth Sprague Coolidge Chamber Music prize, 1974, Gold medal G.B. Viotti, Vercelli, Italy, 1975, citation Ernst von Dohnani, 1981, Pulitizer prize, 1983, Nat. Inst. Arts and Letters award, 1984, Composers award Lancaster Symphony Orch., Arturo Toscanini Music Critics award, 1987; Martha Baird Rockefeller Fund rec. grantee, 1977, 79, 82, Guggenheim fellow, 1981. Mem. Am. Fedn. Musicians (hon. life). Am. Music Ctr. (bd. dirs., v.p. 1982-84), Internat. League Women Composers, Am. Composers Orch. (bd. dirs.). Home: 600 W 246th St Riverdale NY 10471 Office: care Music Assocs Am 224 King St Englewood NJ 07631

ZWILLING, JANE RIEGELHAUPT, psychologist; b. Bklyn., July 10, 1957; d. Jack and Eileen (Pullman) Riegelhaupt; m. Howard Zwilling, July 26, 1980; 1 child, Amanda. BS, CUNY, 1978, MS, cert. in sch. psychology, 1980; D of Psychology, Pace U., 1983. Lic. psychologist, N.Y. Intern in clin. psychology The Children's Village, Dobbs Ferry, N.Y., 1982-83; psychologist Blythedale Children's Hosp., Valhalla, N.Y., 1983-84; sch. psychologist Half Hollow Hills Sch. Dist., Dix Hills, N.Y., 1984—; pvt. practice psychologist Woodbury and Plainview, N.Y., 1984-88. Author: (with others) Advances In Therapies for Children, 1986. Mem. Am. Psychol. Assn., Suffolk County Psychol. Assn., Nassau County Psychol. Assn., Assn. Play Therapy (editor newsletter 1982-83, 83-84, v.p. 1982-83, 83-84), Assn. Sch. Psychology (pres. Bklyn. Coll. chpt. 1979-80). Office: 1117 Old Country Rd Plainview NY 11803

ZYKAN, MARY SUSAN, solid waste disposal company owner; b. St. Louis, Oct. 7, 1946; d. Edward Patrick and Edna Elenora (Showalter) Schneider; m. Robert Walter Zykan, Mar. 27, 1965; children—Robert, Ronald, Steven, Karen. Grad. high sch., Overland, Mo. Sec. Greater St. Louis Foster Parent Assn., 1975-78; owner R & Z Hauling Service, St. Ann, Mo., 1965—; waste industry advisor Bi-State Devel. Agy., St. Louis, 1977-78; com. mem. St. Louis County Solid Waste Adv. Com., 1977-78; waste industry advisor Mo. Dept. Natural Resources Task Force, 1982-83. Editor newsletter Greater St. Louis Foster Parent Assn., 1970-76. Vol. Emergency Foster Home, St. Louis County Welfare Agy., Mo., 1972-74; planner, guest speaker Forest Park Community Coll. Waste Conf., 1980. Recipient Service awards St. Louis County Juvenile Ct., 1973, 78, Community Service award St. Charles County Solid Waste Task Force, 1986-87. Mem. Nat. Solid Waste Mgmt. Assn. (pres. Mo. chpt. 1981-82, legis. sec. 1985, chmn. solid waste legis. com. 1984-85), Met. San. Haulers Assn. (pres. 1985, bd. dirs. 1974-85, service award 1979), Nat. Fedn. Ind. Bus., Mo. Waste Coalition (conf. exhibit com. 1982, Achievement award 1985). Lutheran. Club: Am. Bdll. Avocations: bowling; swimming; bell colleclting; writing. Home: 10319 Millwood St Saint Ann MO 63074 Office: R & Z Hauling Service 10319 Millwood St Saint Ann MO 63074

ZYROFF, ELLEN SLOTOROFF, information scientist; b. Atlantic City, N.J., Aug. 1, 1946; d. Joseph George and Sylvia Beverly (Roth) Slotoroff; m. Jack Zyroff, June 21, 1970; children: Dena Rachel, David Aaron. AB, Barnard Coll., 1968; MA, The Johns Hopkins U., 1969, PhD, 1971; MS, Columbia U., 1973. Instr. The Johns Hopkins U., Balt., 1970-71, Yeshiva U., N.Y.C., 1971-72, Bklyn Coll., 1971-72; libr. U. Calif., 1979, 81; libr., instr. San Diego State U., 1981-85; instr. San Diego Mesa Coll., 1981—; dir. The Reference Desk Rsch. Svcs., La Jolla, 1983—; prin. libr. San Diego County Libr., 1985—; v.p. Archeol. Soc. Am., Balt., 1970-71; chairperson div. coms., Am. Library Assn., 1981—. Author: The Author's Apostrophe in Epic from Homer Through Lucan, 1971, Cooperative Library Instruction for Maximum Benefit, 1989. Pres. Women's Am. ORT, San Diego, 1979-81. Mem. ALA, Am. Philological Assn., Calif. Libr. Assn., Am. Soc. Info. Sci., Am. Classical League, Beta Phi Mu. Office: San Diego County Libr 5555 Overland Ave Bldg 15 San Diego CA 92123